The

EUROPA WORLD OF LEARNING

2012

62nd Edition

D1503128

VOLUME I

INTRODUCTORY ESSAYS
INTERNATIONAL ORGANIZATIONS
AFGHANISTAN–MYANMAR

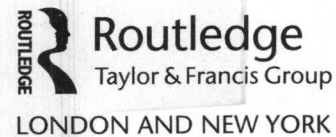

Routledge
Taylor & Francis Group

LONDON AND NEW YORK

First published 1947
Sixty-second Edition 2011
© **Routledge 2011**

2–4 Park Square, Milton Park, Abingdon, Oxfordshire, OX14 4RN, United Kingdom
(Routledge is an imprint of the Taylor & Francis Group, an Informa business)

All rights reserved. No part of this
publication may be photocopied, recorded,
or otherwise reproduced, stored in a retrieval
system or transmitted in any form or by any
electronic or mechanical means without the
prior permission of the copyright owner.

ISBN13: 978-1-85743-620-4 (The Set)
ISBN13: 978-1-85743-621-1 (Vol. I)

ISSN 0084-2117

Library of Congress Catalog Card Number 47-30172

Senior Editor: Anthony Gladman

Team Leader: Joan Rita O'Brien

Senior Researcher: Sabiya Ashraf

Researchers: Neha Attre, Nilanjana Bose, Sandeep Kaur, Aastha Manocha, Shveta Sharma

Editorial Assistant: Eleanor Jones

Associate Editor, Directory Research: James Middleton

Editorial Director: Paul Kelly

Typeset in New Century Schoolbook

FSC
www.fsc.org
MIX
Paper from
responsible sources
FSC® C006021

Typeset by Data Standards Limited, Frome, Somerset
Printed and bound in Great Britain by Polestar Wheatons, Exeter

FOREWORD

It gives us great pleasure to introduce the 2012 edition of THE EUROPA WORLD OF LEARNING. First published in 1947, it has since become established as an authoritative reference work on academic institutions all over the world.

THE EUROPA WORLD OF LEARNING is unique in offering information over the entire spectrum of academic activity. Our listings cover not just universities and colleges, but also research institutes, libraries and archives, museums and galleries and learned societies. Further to this, regulatory and representative bodies are covered in a section which also has details of relevant ministries, accrediting bodies and funding organizations. Each chapter has an introductory survey outlining the country's higher education system.

Each year we invite entrants to review and update their entries. Entrants may do so online at updates.worldoflearning.com, or by sending an email to wol@informa.com. We are, as ever, grateful to those who help bring our information up to date with their prompt replies. Continuous research on the internet and in the world's press, as well as contact with official sources worldwide, supplements this method of revision.

In addition to the regular updating of our entries, this edition has expanded coverage of institutions in Western Europe. Chapters covering Austria, Belgium, Denmark, Finland, France, Germany, Iceland, Ireland, Italy, Liechtenstein, Luxembourg, Malta, Monaco, Netherlands, Norway, Portugal, San Marino, Spain, Sweden, Switzerland and the United Kingdom all have specially expanded chapters.

THE EUROPA WORLD OF LEARNING also contains a collection of essays on themes pertinent to international higher education. In this edition subjects covered include the higher education sector's use of social media, academic integrity in the digital age, changes to higher education funding and a global move towards the privatization of higher education, whether education is getting lost in university mergers, and the scholarship of teaching and learning in higher education. For details of the authors contributing to this edition see page ix.

In the sections on Universities and Colleges, our classification follows the practice of the country concerned. This in no way implies any official evaluation on our part. Readers who are interested in the matter of the equivalence of institutions, degrees or diplomas should correspond directly with the institutions concerned, or with the national or international bodies set up for this purpose. Further information on these can be found in the Regulatory and Representative Bodies section of each chapter under the subheading Accreditation.

The online version of THE EUROPA WORLD OF LEARNING offers quarterly updates of content and an unprecedented level of access to institutions of higher education and learning worldwide, and to the people who work within them. See page vi or visit www.worldoflearning.com for further details.

August 2011

The Europa World of Learning
www.worldoflearning.com

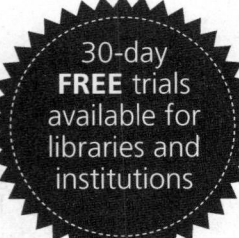

30-day **FREE** trials available for libraries and institutions

The Europa World of Learning Online

The online version of *The Europa World of Learning* builds on the success of the printed version by providing a full range of sophisticated search and browse functions, and regular updates of content.

Key Features:

- fully searchable by country, institution name, type, professorial subject specialization, and many more options
- contains around 40,000 clickable links to institutional sites and email addresses
- fully networkable to allow multi-user access.

> **"I can't imagine why any library would not opt to give its users greater, enhanced access to valuable information via the web-based product. Highly recommended."** – *Reference Reviews*

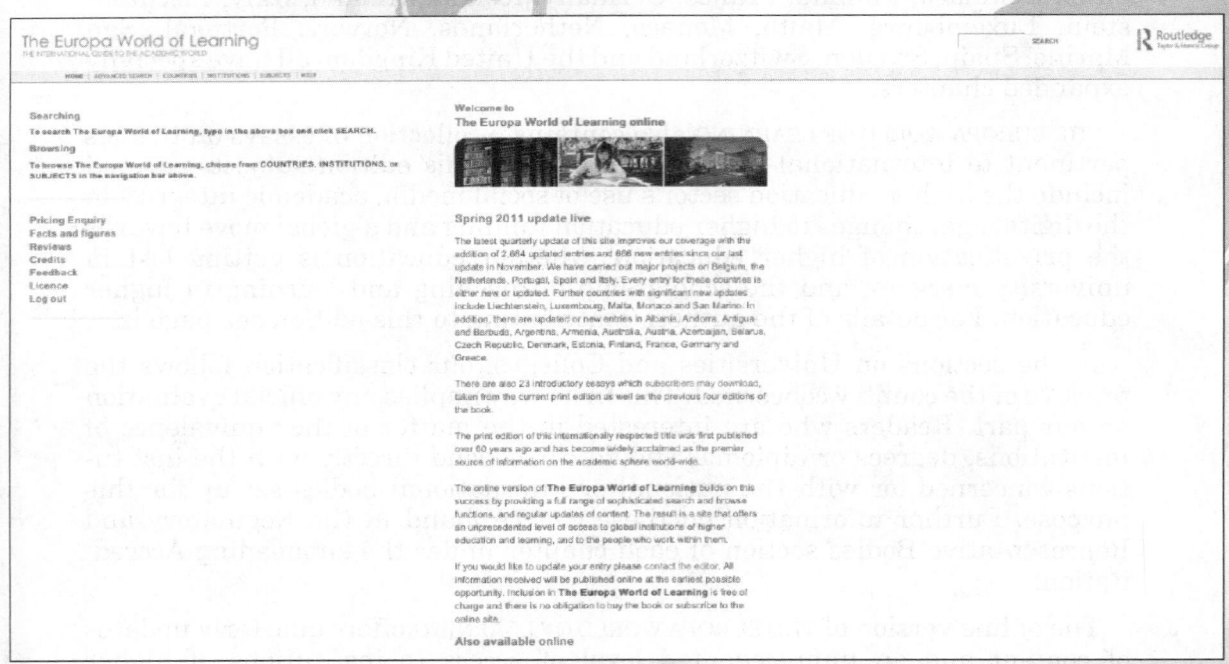

30-DAY FREE TRIALS AVAILABLE   30-DAY FREE TRIALS AVAILABLE   30-DAY FREE TRIALS AVAILABLE

Alternatively, to register for your free 30-day trial or for more information please contact your sales representative:

UK and Rest of World customers:
Tel: +44 (0)20 701 76062
Fax: +44 (0)20 701 76699
Email: **online.sales@tandf.co.uk**

US, Canadian and South American customers:
Tel: 1-888-318-2367
Fax: 212-244-1563
Email: **e-reference@taylorandfrancis.com**

Taylor & Francis
Taylor & Francis Group

CONTENTS

CONTENTS

• An Index of Institutions is to be found at the end of Volume II

THE CONTRIBUTORS

Helena Aittola is a Senior Researcher at the Finnish Institute of Educational Research, University of Jyväskylä, Finland. Her research interests are graduate schools, the supervision of doctoral students, and the assessment of doctoral theses.

Denise Chalmers is Winthrop Professor at the University of Western Australia, and Director of the Centre for Advancement of Teaching and Learning (incorporating WebCT and Lectopia). She is currently leading a national AUTC project on rewarding and recognising quality teaching and learning through developing teaching and learning performance indicators in Australian universities. She is responsible for supporting the enhancement of teaching and learning in higher education through professional development of academic staff, assessment and academic standards, curriculum development, evaluation of teaching and e-learning across the University. She is President of the Council of Australian Directors for Academic Development.

Teddi Fishman became the Director of the the International Center for Academic Integrity after five years of teaching and research as a faculty member in Clemson University's Masters of Professional Communication Program in the college of Architecture, Arts, and Humanities. Her interest in ethics and writing integrity dates back to her pre-academic career in law enforcement which inspired her master's thesis on the rhetoric of police writing. She investigates, speaks, and writes about communication practices in contexts ranging from the emergency communications of first responders to students writing in traditional academic settings. Her work also includes analyses of online communication and the evolving mores of virtual communities.

Dr Charles Henderson is an Associate Professor of Physics at the University of Michigan, where he holds a joint appointment in the Physics Department and the Mallinson Institute for Science Education. His current work is focused on the development of theories and strategies for promoting change in the teaching of STEM subjects. This includes issues related to the diffusion and adoption of research-based instructional strategies. Dr Henerson is the editor of Physics Education Research Section of the American Journal of Physics and former chair of the American Association of Physics Teachers (AAPT) Committee on Research in Physics Education. During 2010 he conducted research and worked with graduate students at the University of Jyväskylä in Finland.

Neil Selwyn is a social scientist working at the Institute of Education, University of London, UK. His research and writing focuses on a number of issues, including digital exclusion, education technology policymaking and the student experience of technology-based learning. Recent books include 'Schools and Schooling in the Digital Age' (2011, Routledge), 'Education & Technology: Key Issues and Debates' (2011, Continuum) and 'Adult Learning in the Digital Age' (2005, Routledge).

Jani Ursin is a Senior Researcher at the Finnish Institute of Educational Research, University of Jyväskylä, Finland. His research interests include the assessment of higher education learning outcomes, quality assurance in higher education, and mergers of universities.

Jussi Välimaa is a professor at the Finnish Institute of Educational Research, University of Jyväskylä, Finland. He heads the Institutes research area for education and social change and its research group on higher education.

Dr Gill Wyness is a Research Officer at the Centre for Economic Performance within the London School of Economics. She specialises in researching Higher Education Finance in the UK, and has published research on the impact of tuition fees on university participation, the financial impact of the UK's tuition fee reforms on the taxpayer, universities and graduates, and tuition fee reforms in Scotland. She has also given evidence at the UK's recent Independent Review of Higher Education Finance, chaired by Lord Browne.

ABBREVIATIONS

AB	Alberta	Corpn	Corporation	HQ	Headquarters
Abog.	Abogado (lawyer)	Corresp.	Correspondent; Corresponding	HRH	His (Her) Royal Highness
Acad.	Academician; Academy	CP	Caixa postal; Case postale;		
ACT	Australian Capital Territory		Casella postale (Post Box)	IA	Iowa
Admin.	Administration; Administrative	Cr	Contador	ID	Idaho
AIDS	acquired immunodeficiency	CRC	Cooperative Research Centre	IL	Illinois
	syndrome	CT	Connecticut	ILO	International Labour
AK	Alaska	Cttee	Committee		Organization
AL	Alabama	cu	cubic	IN	Indiana
Apdo	Apartado (Post Box)			Inc.	Incorporated
appr	approximately	DC	District of Colombia	incl.	include; includes; including
AR	Arkansas	DE	Delaware	Ind.	Independent
Arq	Arquitecto (Spanish); Arquiteto	Del.	Delegate; Delegation	Ing.	Ingénieur (Engineer)
	(Portuguese)	Dept	Department	Instn	Institution
Asⁿ	Association	Deptl	Departmental	Int.	International
Aoc.	Associate	devt	development	Ir	Insinyur (Engineer)
t	Assistant	DF	Distrito Federal	irreg.	irregular
ty	Attorney	Dipl.	Diploma		
vda	Avenida	Dir	Director	Jl	Jalan (street)
ve	Avenue	Dist.	District	Jr	Junior
Avv.	Avvocato (Advocate)	Div.	Division	JSC	Joint Stock Company
AZ	Arizona	Divs	Divisions	jt	joint
		Doc.	Docent	jtly	jointly
BA	Bachelor of Arts	Dott.	Dottore		
BC	British Columbia	Dott.ssa	Dottoressa	küç.	küçasi (street)
Bd	Boulevard	Doz.	Dozent (lecturer)	km	kilometre(s)
Bdul	Bulevardul	Dr	Doctor	KS	Kansas
BEng	Bachelor of Engineering	Dr Hab.	Doktor Habilitowany (Assistant	kv.	kvartal (apartment block);
Bld	Boulevard		Professor)		kvartira (apartment)
Bldg	Building	Dr.	Drive	KY	Kentucky
Blv	Boulevard	Dra	Doctora		
Blvd	Boulevard	Drs	Doctorandus (Dutch or	LA	Louisiana
Blvr	Bulevar		Indonesian higher degree)	Lic.	Licenciado
BP	Boîte postale	DVD	digital versatile disc	Licda	Licenciada
Br.	Branch			Lt	Lieutenant
BRGM	Bureau de Recherches	E	East; Eastern	Ltd	Limited
	Géologiques et Minières	e.g.	exempli gratia		
Brig.	Brigadier	Edif.	Edificio (Building)	m	metre(s)
Bro.	Brother	edn	edition	m.	million
Brs	Branches	Eng.	Engineer	MA	Massachusetts; Master of Arts
BSc	Bachelor of Science	EngD	Doctor of Engineering	Mag.	Magister (Masters degree)
Bul.	Bulvar (boulevard)	esp.	especially	Man.	Manager; Managing
bulv.	bulvarÿs (boulevard)	Est.	Established	MB	Manitoba
		etc.	et cetera	MBA	Master of Business
c.	circa (approximately)	EU	European Union		Administration
c/o	care of	Exec.	Executive	MD	Maryland
CA	California			ME	Maine
CAR	Central African Republic	f.	founded	Mem.	Member
Ccl	Council	F.t.e.	Full-time equivalent	Mems	Members
CD-ROM	compact disc read-only memory	FAO	Food and Agriculture	MEng	Master of Engineering
CEA	Commissariat à l'Energie		Organization	Mgr	Monseigneur; Monsignor
	Atomique	Fed.	Federal; Federation	MI	Michigan
CEO	Chief Executive Officer	FL	Florida	Min.	Minister; Ministry
Chair.	Chairman; Chairperson;	fmr	former	misc.	miscellaneous
	Chairwoman	fmrly	formerly	mm	millimetre(s)
CIRAD	Centre de Coopération	Fr	Father	MN	Minnesota
	Internationale en Recherche	ft	feet	MO	Missouri
	Agronomique pour le			MRC	Medical Research Council
	Développement	GA	Georgia	MS	Mississippi
Cmdr	Commander	Gdns	Gardens	MSc	Master of Science
CNR	Consiglio Nazionale delle	Gen.	General	MSS	Manuscripts
	Ricerche	Gov.	Governor	MT	Montana
cnr	corner	Govt	Government		
CNRS	Centre National de la	GPOB	Government Post Office Box	N	North; Northern
	Recherche Scientifique			nám	náměstí (square)
CO	Colorado	HE	His (Her) Excellency; His	NASA	National Aeronautics and
Co	Company; County		Eminence		Space Administration
Col	Colonel	HEI	Higher Education Institution	Nat.	National
Col.	Colonia (District)	HI	Hawaii	NB	New Brunswick
colln	Collection	HIV	human immunodeficiency virus	NC	North Carolina
Comm.	Commission	HM	His (Her) Majesty	ND	North Dakota
Commr	Commissioner	HND	Higher National Diploma	NE	Nebraska; Northeast;
Conf.	Conference	Hon.	Honorary; Honourable		Northeastern

NGO	Non-Governmental Organization	QC	Québec	Treas.	Treasurer
NH	New Hampshire	q.v.	quod vide (to which refer)	TRNC	Turkish Republic of Northern Cyprus
NJ	New Jersey	rd	road	TX	Texas
NL	Newfoundland and Labrador	Rep.	Representative		
NM	New Mexico	retd	retired	u.	utca (street)
NS	Nova Scotia	Rev.	Reverend	UK	United Kingdom
NSW	New South Wales	RI	Rhode Island	ul.	ulica; ulitsa (street)
NT	Northwest Territories	RP	Révérend Père	UN	United Nations
NU	Nunavut Territory	Rr.	Rruga	UNESCO	United Nations Educational, Scientific and Cultural Organization
NV	Nevada	Rt Hon.	Right Honourable		
NW	Northwest; Northwestern	Rt Rev.	Right Reverend		
NY	New York			Univ.	Universidad; Universidade; Università; Università; Université; Universitas; Universitat; Universitata; Universiteit; Universitet; Universiteti; Universiti; University; Univerza; Univerzita; Univerzitet; Uniwersytet
NZ	New Zealand	S	South; Southern		
		s/n	sin número (without number)		
obl.	oblast	SA	South Africa(n); South Australia		
Of.	Oficina				
OH	Ohio	SAR	Special Administrative Region		
OK	Oklahoma	SC	South Carolina		
ON	Ontario	SD	South Dakota		
OR	Oregon	SDI	Selective Dissemination of Information	USA	United States of America
Org.	Organization			UT	Utah
		SE	Southeast; Southeastern		
PA	Pennsylvania	Sec.	Secretary		
PE	Prince Edward Island	Sis.	Sister	VA	Virginia
PEN	Poets, Playwrights, Essayists, Editors and Novelists (Club)	SK	Saskatchewan	Vols	Volumes
		Soc.	Society	VT	Vermont
PhD	Doctor of Philosophy	spec.	special	vul.	vulitsa; vulytsa (sreet)
pl.	place; platz; ploshchad (square)	Sq.	Square		
PMB	Private Mail Bag	Sr	Senior	W	West; Western
POB	Post Office Box	St	Saint; Sint; Street	WA	Washington (State); Western Australia
pr.	prospekt (avenue)	Sta	Santa		
Pres.	President	Ste	Sainte	WI	Wisconsin
Prin.	Principal	str.	stradă; strada; Strasse (street)	WV	West Virginia
Prof.	Professor	SW	Southwest; Southwestern	WY	Wyoming
Profa	Professora				
Publ.	Publication	tel.	telephone		
Publs	Publications	TN	Tennessee	YT	Yukon Territory

INTERNATIONAL TELEPHONE CODES

To make international calls to telephone and fax numbers listed in *The Europa World of Learning*, dial the international code of the country from which you are calling, followed by the appropriate country code for the institution you wish to call (listed below), followed by the area code (if applicable) and telephone or fax number listed in the entry.

	Country code	+ or − GMT*		Country code	+ or − GMT*
Afghanistan	93	+4½	Djibouti	253	+3
Albania	355	+1	Dominica	1 767	−4
Algeria	213	+1	Dominican Republic	1 809	−4
Andorra	376	+1	Ecuador	593	−5
Angola	244	+1	Egypt	20	+2
Antigua and Barbuda	1 268	−4	El Salvador	503	−6
Argentina	54	−3	Equatorial Guinea	240	+1
Armenia	374	+4	Eritrea	291	+3
Australia	61	+8 to +10	Estonia	372	+2
Austria	43	+1	Ethiopia	251	+3
Azerbaijan	994	+5	Fiji	679	+12
Bahamas	1 242	−5	Finland	358	+2
Bahrain	973	+3	Åland Islands	358	+2
Bangladesh	880	+6	France	33	+1
Barbados	1 246	−4	French Guiana	594	−3
Belarus	375	+2	French Polynesia	689	−9 to −10
Belgium	32	+1	Guadeloupe	590	−4
Belize	501	−6	Martinique	596	−4
Benin	229	+1	New Caledonia	687	+11
Bhutan	975	+6	Réunion	262	+4
Bolivia	591	−4	Gabon	241	+1
Bosnia and Herzegovina	387	+1	Gambia	220	0
Botswana	267	+2	Georgia	995	+4
Brazil	55	−3 to −4	Germany	49	+1
Brunei	673	+8	Ghana	233	0
Bulgaria	359	+2	Greece	30	+2
Burkina Faso	226	0	Grenada	1 473	−4
Burundi	257	+2	Guatemala	502	−6
Cambodia	855	+7	Guinea	224	0
Cameroon	237	+1	Guinea-Bissau	245	0
Canada	1	−3 to −8	Guyana	592	−4
Cape Verde	238	−1	Haiti	509	−5
Central African Republic	236	+1	Honduras	504	−6
Chad	235	+1	Hungary	36	+1
Chile	56	−4	Iceland	354	0
China, People's Republic	86	+8	India	91	+5½
Hong Kong	852	+8	Indonesia	62	+7 to +9
Macao	853	+8	Iran	98	+3½
China (Taiwan)	886	+8	Iraq	964	+3
Colombia	57	−5	Ireland	353	0
Comoros	269	+3	Israel	972	+2
Congo, Democratic Republic	243	+1	Italy	39	+1
Congo, Republic	242	+1	Jamaica	1 876	−5
Costa Rica	506	−6	Japan	81	+9
Côte d'Ivoire	225	0	Jordan	962	+2
Croatia	385	+1	Kazakhstan	7	+6
Cuba	53	−5	Kenya	254	+3
Cyprus	357	+2	Kiribati	686	+12 to +13
'Turkish Republic of Northern Cyprus'90	392	+2	Korea, Democratic People's Republic (North Korea)	850	+9
Czech Republic	420	+1	Korea, Republic (South Korea)	82	+9
Denmark	45	+1	Kosovo	381†	+3
Faroe Islands	298	0	Kuwait	965	+3
Greenland	299	−1 to −4			

	Country code	+ or – GMT*
Kyrgyzstan	996	+5
Laos	856	+7
Latvia	371	+2
Lebanon	961	+2
Lesotho	266	+2
Liberia	231	0
Libya	218	+1
Liechtenstein	423	+1
Lithuania	370	+2
Luxembourg	352	+1
Macedonia, former Yugoslav republic	389	+1
Madagascar	261	+3
Malawi	265	+2
Malaysia	60	+8
Maldives	960	+5
Mali	223	0
Malta	356	+1
Marshall Islands	692	+12
Mauritania	222	0
Mauritius	230	+4
Mexico	52	–6 to –7
Micronesia, Federated States	691	+10 to +11
Moldova	373	+2
Monaco	377	+1
Mongolia	976	+7 to +9
Montenegro	382	+1
Morocco	212	0
Mozambique	258	+2
Myanmar	95	+6½
Namibia	264	+2
Nauru	674	+12
Nepal	977	+5¾
Netherlands	31	+1
Aruba	297	–4
Netherlands Antilles	599	–4
New Zealand	64	+12
Nicaragua	505	–6
Niger	227	+1
Nigeria	234	+1
Norway	47	+1
Oman	968	+4
Pakistan	92	+5
Palau	680	+9
Palestinian Autonomous Areas	970 or 972	+2
Panama	507	–5
Papua New Guinea	675	+10
Paraguay	595	–4
Peru	51	–5
Philippines	63	+8
Poland	48	+1
Portugal	351	0
Qatar	974	+3
Romania	40	+2
Russian Federation	7	+2 to +12
Rwanda	250	+2
Saint Christopher and Nevis	1 869	–4
Saint Lucia	1 758	–4
Saint Vincent and the Grenadines	1 784	–4
Samoa	685	–11
San Marino	378	+1
São Tomé and Príncipe	239	0
Saudi Arabia	966	+3
Senegal	221	0

	Country code	+ or – GMT*
Serbia	381	+1
Seychelles	248	+4
Sierra Leone	232	0
Singapore	65	0
Slovakia	421	+1
Slovenia	386	+1
Solomon Islands	677	+11
Somalia	252	+3
South Africa	27	+2
Spain	34	+1
Sri Lanka	94	5½
Sudan	249	+2
Suriname	597	–3
Swaziland	268	+2
Sweden	46	+1
Switzerland	41	+1
Syria	963	+2
Tajikistan	992	+5
Tanzania	255	+3
Thailand	66	+7
Timor-Leste	670	+9
Togo	228	0
Tonga	676	+13
Trinidad and Tobago	1 868	–4
Tunisia	216	+1
Turkey	90	+2
Turkmenistan	993	+5
Tuvalu	688	+12
Uganda	256	+3
Ukraine	380	+2
United Arab Emirates	971	+4
United Kingdom	44	0
Northern Ireland	44	0
Bermuda	1 441	–4
Gibraltar	350	+1
Guernsey	44	0
Isle of Man	44	0
Jersey	44	0
United States of America	1	–5 to –10
Guam	1 671	+10
Puerto Rico	1 787	–4
United States Virgin Islands	1 340	–4
Uruguay	598	–3
Uzbekistan	998	+5
Vanuatu	678	+11
Vatican City	39	+1
Venezuela	58	–4
Viet Nam	84	+7
Yemen	967	+3
Zambia	260	+2
Zimbabwe	263	+2

* Time difference in hours + or – Greenwich Mean Time (GMT). The times listed compare the standard (winter) times. Some countries adopt Summer (Daylight Saving) Time — i.e. +1 hour — for part of the year.

† Mobile telephone numbers for Kosovo use either the country code for Monaco (377) or the country code for Slovenia (386).

Note: Telephone and fax numbers using the Inmarsat ocean region code 870 are listed in full. No country or area code is required, but it is necessary to precede the number with the international access code of the country from which the call is made.

PART ONE

Introductory Essays

SOCIAL MEDIA IN HIGHER EDUCATION

NEIL SELWYN

INTRODUCTION

Few people will have failed to notice the recent emergence of social media—especially much-publicized applications such as Facebook, Twitter, YouTube and Wikipedia. Even the most casual of internet users will now be aware of the notion of social network sites and blogs, maybe even wikis and virtual worlds. Since being declared *Time Magazine*'s 'Person of the Year' at the end of 2006, social media have come to dominate the ways in which digital technology is now used around the world. Of course, there are distinct geographical and cultural variations within this global adoption—whereas people in the USA may log on to Facebook and Twitter, Chinese users are more likely to access Renren and NetEase. Yet in all these guises, the general principles of social media remain the same. These are internet applications that rely on openly shared digital content that is authored, critiqued and re-configured by a mass of users. Social media applications therefore allow users to converse and interact with each other; to create, edit and share new forms of textual, visual and audio content; and to categorize, label and recommend existing forms of content. Perhaps the key characteristic of all these social media practices is that of 'mass socialization'—i.e. harnessing the power of the collective actions of online user communities rather than individual users (see Shirky, 2008).

The growth of social media over the past five years has transformed the ways in which the internet is experienced by most end users. Now the internet is no longer a one-way broadcast delivery system where the individual user downloads data, information and other resources produced by a relatively small number of content providers. Instead, the internet is now driven by (and to some extent determined through) the activities of its ordinary users—what has been described as many-to-many rather than one-to-many connectivity. The social web is therefore seen to be arranged along substantially different lines than the cyberspace-era internet of the 1990s and 2000s. This sense of internet use now being a participatory and collective activity is reflected in the language used to describe social media applications. Social media use is often described in terms of collaboration, conviviality and creativity. Social media applications are seen to be open rather than closed, bottom-up rather than top-down. Social media users go online to share and rate, mash-up and remix, friend and trend. The ways in which the internet is imagined in 2012 is certainly very different to that of 10 years earlier—hence the coining of the label web 2.0.

Amidst these technological developments, many higher education institutions (and educators) now find themselves expected to catch up with this world of social media applications and social media users. Of course, accusations of a technological lag between higher education and the rest of society can be traced back to the introduction of film and radio during the first decades of the 20th century. Indeed, as with most of these previous waves of new technology, social media remain an area of considerable expectation, exaggeration and hyperbole. It is essential, therefore, that the higher educators are able to approach social media in a considered and objective manner. The issues addressed in the rest of this chapter are necessarily straightforward. What are the key features of social media and just what is their significance to contemporary higher education? How are social media applications currently being used in higher education settings? What changes does higher education need to make in order to remain relevant in the apparently fast-changing digital age?

UNDERSTANDING THE SIGNIFICANCE OF SOCIAL MEDIA FOR HIGHER EDUCATION

As computer scientists are quick to point out, most of the apparently new characteristics of social media existed long before the advent of Facebook. Since the early 1970s, internet applications have allowed users to exchange messages with each other, maintain personal profiles, curate lists of 'friends' and write blog-like journal entries. It is therefore important to remember from the outset that 'the web has always been social' (Halpin and Tuffield, 2010). Yet while the technical necessity of re-branding and re-versioning the web '2.0' may be challenged, the current generation of social media applications are undeniably distinct from the earlier internet in terms of scale of use. Unlike the web tools of even 10 years ago, contemporary social media are used by hundreds of millions of users (in the case of Facebook a figure that surpasses 500m.). As such, the social media of the 2010s now boast a sufficient critical mass of users *and* applications to be of genuine collective benefit and social significance. As Christakis and Fowler (2009: 30) conclude, 'as part of a social network, we transcend ourselves for good or ill, and become a part of something much larger'.

So what, then, is the social significance of social media in terms of higher education? Despite most discussions of social media tending to focus either on the very prosaic *or* the very profound (e.g. the role of social media in perpetrating individual narcissism *or* supporting popular revolts in Iran and Egypt), growing numbers of educationalists are beginning to consider the possible significance and likely implications of social media for education practice and provision—especially in terms of higher education. These issues can be described along at least three different lines.

Social media and new types of learners?

Social media constitute an increasingly important context wherein individuals live their everyday lives. Indeed, some commentators talk of the 'networked self'—acknowledging the importance of social media as a key site of sociality and identity performance in many people's lives (Papacharissi, 2010). As such, the most immediate significance of social media for higher education is the apparently changing nature of the students who are entering university. In a practical sense, the highly connected, collective and creative qualities of social media applications are seen to reflect (and to some extent drive) more flexible, fluid and accelerated ways of being. Social media are therefore associated with an increased tendency for young people to multitask, to rely on a 'digital juggling' of daily activities and commitments (Subrahmanyam and Smahel, 2011). More subtly, these technologies are also associated with an enhanced social autonomy—with young people now used to having increased control over the nature and form of what they do, as well as where, when and how they do it. Indeed, social media users are described as having an enhanced capacity to self-organize and provide for themselves. As Tapscott and Williams (2007: 52) continue, these young people 'are not content to be passive consumers, and increasingly satisfy their desire for choice, convenience, customization, and control by designing, producing, and distributing products themselves'.

While these descriptions could be said to apply to users of all ages, often the changes associated with social media are seen in distinct generational terms. Commentators point to incoming cohorts of students who know nothing other than a life with the internet, having been 'born into a world woven from cabled, wired or wireless connectivity' (Bauman, 2010: 7). For many educators, therefore, the increased presence of social media in higher education settings is essential if universities are to (re)connect with these students. For example, social networking sites are now being used by universities as alternative spaces wherein students can adapt to the university lifestyle through interacting online with peers and faculty (Yu et al., 2010). Indeed, many universities now maintain profiles and groups on social networking sites such as Facebook, where students and faculty can interact, share resources and express 'learner voice'. As Mason and Rennie (2007: 199) reason, 'shared community spaces and inter-group communications are a massive part of what excites young people and therefore should contribute to [their] persistence and motivation to learn'.

Of course, it could be argued that the top-down, mass institution of 'the university' is poorly placed to be a meaningful part of students' hyper-individualized social media use. Some critics point towards an ever-growing digital disconnect between students and their education institutions. Here it is argued that even the best-intentioned universities are able only to offer their students an artificially regulated and constrained engagement with social media. Thus, alongside other institutions such as schools, libraries and museums, universities are seen to face distrust and a growing loss of faith amongst younger generations (Downes, 2010). This clash is particularly evident in terms of the linear and hierarchical ways in which universities set out to structure communication, learning and access to knowledge. As Ulbrich et al. (2011) contend:

> Members of the net generation use the web differently, they network differently, and they learn differently. When they start at university, traditional values on how to develop knowledge collide with their values. Many of the teaching techniques that have worked for decades do not work anymore because new students learn differently too. The net generation is used to networking; its members work collaboratively, they execute several tasks simultaneously, and they use the web to acquire knowledge.

Social media and new types of learning?

As this last quotation implies, a major educational implication of social media is the apparently changing nature of learners' relationships with information and knowledge. Indeed, it could be argued that social media support forms of knowledge consumption and knowledge construction that are very different to the epistemological principles of formal education and individualized instruction. These changes are encapsulated in Douglas Thomas and John Seely-Brown's (2011) description of a technology-enhanced 'new culture of learning'—i.e. learning that is based around principles of collective exploration, play and innovation rather than individualized instruction. As well as chiming with currently fashionable constructivist and socio-cultural learning theories, some educationalists have been led to completely reassess the nature of learning in light of changing relationships that social media users seemingly have with information. These ideas are reflected most explicitly in the notion of connectivism—the idea that learning in a social media age now rests upon the ability to access and use distributed information on a 'just-in-time' basis. From this perspective, learning can be seen as an individual's ability to connect to specialized information nodes and sources as and when required. Thus being knowledgeable can be seen as the ability to nurture and maintain these connections (see Chatti et al., 2010). As George Siemens (2004) puts it, learning can therefore be conceived in terms of the 'capacity to know more' via social media rather than a reliance on the individual accumulation of prior knowledge in terms of 'what is currently known'.

Of course, these arguments are by no means new. Samuel Johnson was arguing in the 1700s that 'knowledge is of two kinds. We know a subject ourselves, or we know where we can find information upon it'. However, descriptions such as connectivism reflect a growing belief amongst educationalists that the fundamental skills of learning in an age infused with social media are changing. As such, the emphasis placed by higher education institutions on supporting learners to passively retain information is perhaps less important than supporting the skills to access and actively augment information stored elsewhere when required. In this respect current forms of higher education are seen to be at odds with notions such as technology-based collective or fluid intelligence and the 'produsage' (production/use) of knowledge—i.e. 'where knowledge remains always in the process of development, and where information remains always unfinished, extensible, and evolving' (Bruns, 2008: 6).

This is not to say that higher education is unable to adapt to and benefit from these changes. Indeed, many educationalists believe that universities are in a good position to utilize social media practices to support the collective creation of knowledge amongst students and the wider community (Moskaliuk et al., 2009). Many universities are now striving to develop ways of using social media to support these new forms of learning (see Conole and Alevizou, 2010). Yet whereas these changes can be seen in a wholly beneficial light, some commentators remain sceptical—especially in terms of potential diminishment of students' intellectual abilities and scholarship. Well-publicized concerns continue to be raised over an intellectual dumbing-down and de-skilling associated with using social media to access information and knowledge. Nicolas Carr, for example, contends that social media users 'are evolving from cultivators of personal knowledge into hunters and gatherers in the electronic data forest. In the process, we seem fated to sacrifice much of what makes our minds so interesting' (Carr, 2010). Similar issues have been raised by critics such as Andrew Keen (2007: 23), bemoaning the 'younger generation of intellectual kleptomaniacs'. Although rarely based on robust research evidence, such arguments have proved to be remarkably popular—even amongst students themselves.

Social media and new forms of higher education provision

For better or worse, then, it is clear that social media tools and applications present a challenge to the concept of the formal educational establishment as it currently exists. In this sense, social media are also significant in terms of their implications for the nature and form of higher education provision. Social media in any form sit uncomfortably with some of the central tenets of the formal provision of education. The use of social media implies, for example, that learners should be 'active co-producers' of knowledge rather than 'passive consumers' of content, and that learning should be a 'participatory, social process' supporting personal life goals and needs (Lee and McLoughlin, 2010). In this sense, tensions remain between those who believe that social media can be used to strengthen and improve the higher education institution in its current form, and those who believe that social media exist to disrupt (and ultimately replace) the university altogether.

From the former perspective, many educators maintain that social media can be used successfully to support the provision of what Goodyear and Ellis (2008) term 'serious student-centred learning'. Of course, even the most structured implementation of social media in university settings implies a degree of 'user-driven' education—that is, allowing learners to take more active roles in what they learn as well as how and when they learn it. Nevertheless, many higher educators believe that universities are capable of accommodating (and benefiting from) these shifts in emphases. Some commentators have therefore begun to talk of the need to develop a 'pedagogy 2.0'—i.e. 'innovative pedagogies that leverage these affordances to support learner choice and autonomy' (Lee and McLoughlin, 2010: 1).

Yet for others, the very essence of social media is seen to negate the need for institutionally provided learning altogether. At present, some of the more significant trends in social-media supported learning are positioned outside—as opposed to within—the formal higher education system. Much has been made, for example, of the growth of social media platforms from which universities can distribute learning content and courseware such as YouTube EDU, iTunes U and Academic Earth. At present, many of these spaces are, at best, analogous to more formal modes of higher education provision. A further instance of these open, communal approaches to higher education provision can be found in the International University of the People—a not-for-profit volunteer 'university' that offers online courses, largely free of charge and that have been designed deliberately around altruistic, social networking principles. Here, groups of students participate in weekly discussion forums in which they can access lecture transcripts and associated reading material prepared by volunteer professors (often moonlighting from their official, paid university positions elsewhere). Students are expected to contribute to discussions and comment on their peers' ideas, with community-wide forums of all the university's teaching faculty and students supporting broader discussions and further learning.

Examples such as Academic Earth, YouTube EDU and the International University of the People therefore pose a serious challenge to the very concept of the traditional university institution. Perhaps then—as some critics are arguing—the campus university is nothing more than an anachronistic relic of the industrial age that is now rendered obsolete by contemporary digital technology (Suoranta and Vadén, 2010).

MAKING BETTER SENSE OF THE REALITIES OF SOCIAL MEDIA AND HIGHER EDUCATION

The continued growth of social media presents a set of clear challenges to the future nature of higher education provision and practice. Yet as with many previous new technologies, academic discussion and debate remains largely speculative rather than well-informed and certain. Of course, there is an emerging literature of small-scale, 'empirical' studies that confidently reports all manner of specific learning gains and benefits from social media. We have been recently told, for example, about the positive effect of Twitter use on college student engagement and grades (Junco et al., 2011), and the ability of social networking sites to engender 'favourable feelings regarding learning experiences' (Hung and Yuen, 2010: 703). Yet, rather than being a wholly good (or wholly bad) thing for higher education, social media are perhaps best understood in more ambiguous terms. This is especially the case when one considers the complex and often compromised realities of students' *actual* uses of social media within educational contexts and in their wider everyday lives.

Indeed, when examined in more detail, there are a number of contradictions in the actual nature of social media use that raise some significant limitations to the exaggerated claims and counter-claims discussed previously. First and foremost, discussions of social media assume a level of ubiquity of internet access and use that simply does not exist in many people's lives. According to survey data across the world, people's engagement with social media tools (as well as computers and the internet in general) has remained significantly differentiated over time—even in high-tech regions such as North America and Europe. These digital inequalities are especially pronounced in terms of socio-economic status, social class, race, gender, geography, age and educational background—divisions that hold as true for younger generations of university students as they do for older generations of university staff (Jones and Fox, 2009; Helsper and Eynon, 2009). While no longer a popular term, the spectre of the digital divide looms large over any discussion of the potential benefits of social media in higher education.

There is also growing evidence that social media use is not the equitable and democratic activity that it is often portrayed to be. Even when able to access the technology, the types of social media tools that an individual uses, the ways in which they are used and the outcomes that accrue are all compromised by a set of second-order digital divides. For instance, recent studies suggest that students' preferences for particular social media applications over others follow class-based patterns of taste and distinction. In terms of social networking, for example, Hargittai (2008) reports that US college students' preferences for an application such as Facebook as opposed to MySpace appear to be patterned consistently along lines of social class and educational background. Clear socio-economic differences also exist in individuals' predilection to produce (rather than consume) online content, be it posting to blogs, sharing resources or creating profiles (see Schradie, 2009). Other US college studies report that social media environments are no more socially integrated than offline contexts. For example, race has been found to remain the overriding predictor of whether college students are Facebook 'friends' or not (Mayer and Puller, 2008). Similarly, social media do not necessarily overcome issues of offline disabilities but instead often exacerbate the boundaries of disability (Lewthwaite,

2011). All in all, it is unhelpfully idealistic to imagine social media as providing a level playing field for all.

Many of the current discussions and debates over social media are also (deliberately) unclear as to what aspects of social media use actually relate to education, learning and knowledge. One study of United Kingdom students' use of Facebook suggested that the vast majority (around 95%) of students' interactions were completely unrelated to their university studies (Selwyn, 2009). Thus while social media may well have the potential to support communal learning and knowledge generation, this is by no means guaranteed. In this sense, Hosein et al. (2010) make the useful distinction between living technologies (i.e. technologies that students choose for their everyday social lives and for leisure purposes) and learning technologies (i.e. technologies that students use primarily for study purposes). As this distinction suggests, while there may be some overlap between the two, we should not mistakenly presume all of the everyday life aspects of social media use to be of educational significance.

Indeed, the majority of social media uses are perhaps most accurately described as constituting 'the ordinary stuff of life' (Shirky, 2008: 86), rather than avowedly creative, communal and convivial activities. There is currently little evidence that social media applications are being used by the majority of users in especially innovative, participatory, interactive or even sociable ways (see Jones et al., 2009). Recent empirical studies of student social media use highlight a lack of what could be considered authentic or even useful participative learning activity. Indeed, a number of recent studies report a surprising lack of sophisticated or advanced use of social media applications amongst university students (Waycott et al., 2010; Lee and McLoughlin, 2010; Nicholas et al., 2009). At best, many students' engagement can be said to lead to what Crook (2008) terms a 'low bandwidth exchange' of information and knowledge.

These findings certainly challenge the vision of a 'produsage generation' of students learning through creating and sharing their own knowledge. Instead, it would seem that social media applications—despite their undoubted potential for communal activity—are most often appropriated for the one-way passive consumption of content. This is readily apparent in the ways in which the majority of users of social media applications such as YouTube and Wikipedia prefer to passively take pre-existing content rather than actively make their own. Wikipedia continues to depend heavily on a small core of a few thousand highly active participants who write and edit the entries that are then consumed by an audience of millions of users (Leadbeater, 2008). At best, most social media users are responsible merely for the creation and sharing of their profiles and other personal ephemeralia. In terms of any more substantive creation of content, it would appear that the open philosophy that lies at the heart of the social media ethos encourages most people to choose to free-ride on the efforts of a minority—a situation that economists term the 'logic of collective action'.

Finally, it may also be a mistake to presume that students are necessarily enthused and motivated by the use of social media. For example, Hargittai's (2008) study of US college students found that a significant proportion made little use of social media applications, with students as likely to be dabblers or outright dissenters as they were to be social media omnivores (see also Hargittai and Hsieh, 2010). In this sense, it is unwise to assume that the interest, motivation or affinity of all students will be enhanced by the inclusion of social media technologies in any educational context. Indeed, a number of commentators warn against attempts to motivate and engage students simply through the introduction of consciously trendy forms of social media technology use into educational processes and practices. As Tapscott and Williams (2007: 54) conclude with regard to the (mis)application of social media tools in the workplace, young people's 'appetite for authenticity means that they are resistant to ill-considered attempts by older generations to "speak their lingo"'.

SOCIAL MEDIA AND HIGHER EDUCATION—WHERE NEXT?

That there are clear disparities between the educational rhetoric and educational realities of social media use should come as little surprise. There has been a long-standing tendency in education for digital technologies to eventually fall short of the exaggerated expectations that initially surrounded them—what can be described as a cycle of 'hype, hope and disappointment' (Gouseti, 2010). In this sense, perhaps the most pressing challenge for the higher education community at present is to engage in considered and realistic debates over how best to utilize social media in appropriate ways that hopefully reduce this eventual disappointment.

Of course, clear lines need to be drawn between the immediate practical tasks of developing forms of social media use that better fit within the current 'grammar' of formal higher education systems, and addressing the rather more difficult longer-term issues of system-wide reform and redesign. In terms of this latter point, there is a clear need to thoroughly consider and discuss what higher education is, and what forms it should take in a 21st-century digital age. Indeed, many of the controversies and tensions concerning the use of social media in higher education have little to do with the technology itself. Instead, these are issues that are driven by personal belief and opinion about 'the essentially ethical question [of] what counts' as worthwhile learning and worthwhile education (Standish, 2008: 351). In this sense, social media are socially disruptive technologies that prompt a range of deeply ideological (rather than purely technical) questions about the nature of institutionalized education.

Yet these wider debates notwithstanding, higher educators also face the immediate task of integrating social media into their current provision and practice. As such, universities clearly need to continue to consider, for example, the practical challenges of how to assess students' collaboratively authored work or how best to design blended curricula (see Gray et al., 2010; Buckley et al., 2010). Further thought certainly needs to be given to how best to support staff and students alike in making sustained and meaningful use of these internet technologies. In these ways, universities need to play an important role in supporting students' supposedly self-directed activities—providing students with a good core and governance in 'arranging the furniture' of technology-based learning (Crook, 2008).

All these issues will certainly became clearer as the 2010s progress, and as society's expectations and general understanding of social media become less exaggerated and more realistic and objective. Indeed, many technological commentators have now moved on to enthuse about the next set of 'next big things' within the world of digital technology—such as the semantic web, cloud computing and the internet of things. In this sense, there is now room for the higher education community itself to assume a greater role in shaping the development of social media on the ground in higher education settings. After all, social media technology is something that is supposed to be created by its users—higher education institutions and educators included.

BIBLIOGRAPHICAL REFERENCES

Bauman, Z. *Forty-four letters from the liquid modern world*. Cambridge, Polity, 2010.

Bruns, A. *Blogs, Wikipedia, Second Life and beyond*. New York, Peter Lang, 2008.

Buckley, C., Pitt, E., Norton, B. and Owens, T. 'Students' approaches to study', in *Active Learning in Higher Education*, 11, 1, pp. 55–65, 2010.

Carr, N. 'The web shatters focus, rewires brains', in *Wired*, June 2010.

Chatti, M., Amine, J. and Quix, C. 'Connectivism', in *International Journal of Learning Technology*, 5, 1, pp. 80–99, 2010.

Christakis, N. and Fowler, J. *Connected*. New York, Little Brown, 2009.

Conole, G. and Alevizou, P. *A literature review of the use of web 2.0 tools in higher education*. Higher Education Academy, 2010.

Crook, C. 'Theories of formal and informal learning in the world of web 2.0', in Livingstone, S. (ed.). *Theorising the benefits of new technology for youth*. Oxford, Oxford University Press, 2008.

Downes, S. 'Deinstitutionalizing education', in *Huffington Post*, 2 November 2010, www.huffingtonpost.com/stephen-downes/deinstitutionalizing-educ_b_777132.html.

Goodyear, P. and Ellis, R. 'University students' approaches to learning', in *Distance Education*, 29, 2, pp. 141–52, 2008.

Gouseti, A. 'Web 2.0 and education', in *Learning, Media and Technology*, 35, 3, pp. 351–56, 2010.

Gray, K., Thompson, C., Sheard, J., Clerehan, R. and Hamilton, M. 'Students as web 2.0 authors', in *Australasian Journal of Educational Technology*, 26, 1, pp. 105–22, 2010.

Halpin, H. and Tuffield, M. *Social Web XG Wiki*. World Wide Web Consortium (W3C), 2010.

Hargittai. E. 'Whose space?', in *Journal of Computer-Mediated Communication*, 13, 1, pp. 276–297, 2008.

Hargittai, E. and Hsieh, Y. 'From dabblers to omnivores', in Papacharissi, Z. (ed.). *A networked self*. London, Routledge, 2010.

Helsper, E. and Eynon, R. 'Digital natives: where is the evidence?', in *British Educational Research Journal*, 36, 3, pp. 503–20, 2009.

Hosein, A., Ramanau, R. and Jones, C. 'Learning and living technologies', in *Learning, Media and Technology*, 35, 4, pp. 403–18, 2010.

Hung, H. and Yuen, S. 'Educational use of social networking technology in higher education', in *Teaching in Higher Education*, 15, 6, pp. 703–14, 2010.

Jones, S. and Fox, S. *Generations online in 2009*. Washington, DC, Pew Internet and American Life Project, 2009.

Jones, S., Johnson-Yale, C., Millermaier, S. and Seoane Perez, F. 'US college students' internet use', in *Journal of Computer-Mediated Communication*, 14, pp. 244–64, 2009.

Junco, R., Heiberger, G. and Loken, E. 'The effect of Twitter on college student engagement and grades', in *Journal of Computer Assisted Learning*, 27, 2, pp. 119–32, 2011.

Keen, A. *The cult of the amateur*. London, Nicholas Brealey, 2007.

Leadbeater, C. *We-think*. London, Profile, 2008.

Lee, M. and McLoughlin, C. *Web 2.0-based e-learning*. Hershey PA, Information Science Reference, 2010.

Lewthwaite, S. 'Student experiences of social networking and disability in higher education', unpublished PhD thesis, University of Nottingham, 2011.

Mason, R. and Rennie, F. 'Using web 2.0 for learning in the community', in *Internet and Higher Education*, 10, pp. 196–203, 2007.

Mayer, A. and Puller, S. 'The old boy (and girl) network', in *Journal of Public Economics,* 92, 1–2, pp. 329–47, 2008.

Moskaliuk, J. Kimmerle, J. and Cress, U. 'Wiki-supported learning and knowledge building', in *Journal of Computer Assisted Learning*, 25, 6, pp. 549–61, 2009.

Nicholas, D., Gunter, B. and Rowlands, I. *The Google generation*. Oxford, Chandos, 2009.

Papacharissi, Z. *A networked self*. London, Routledge, 2010.

Schradie, J. 'The digital production gap', paper presented to the *American Sociological Research Association* conference, San Francisco, August 2009.

Selwyn, N. 'Faceworking: exploring students' education-related use of Facebook', in *Learning, Media and Technology*, 34, 2, pp. 157–74, 2009.

Shirky, C. *Here comes everybody*. London, Allen Lane, 2008.

Siemens, G. 'Connectivism: a learning theory for the digital age', 2004, www.elearnspace.org/Articles/connectivism.htm.

Standish, P. 'Preface', in *Journal eophy of Education*, 42, 3–4, pp. 349–53, 2008.

Subrahmanyam, K. and Šmahel *gital youth*. Berlin, Springer, 2011.

Suoranta, J. and Vadén, T. *Wikiu*ondon, Pluto Press, 2010.

Tapscott, D. and Williams, A. *Wiki* New York, Atlantic, 2007.

Thomas, D. and Seely-Brown, J. *culture of learning*. Charleston, SC, Createspace, 201

Ulbrich, F., Jahnke, I. and Mårtensson, P. 'Special Issue on knowledge development and the net generation', in *International Journal of Sociotechnology and Knowledge Development*, 2011.

Waycott, J., Bennett, S., Kennedy, G., Dalgarno, B. and Gray, K. 'Digital divides?', in *Computers and Education*, 54, 4, pp. 1202–11, 2010.

Yu, A., Tian, S., Vogel, D. and Kwok, R. 'Embedded social learning in online social networking', in *ICIS 2010 Proceedings*, 2010, aisel.aisnet.org/icis2010_submissions/100.

PAYING FOR HIGHER EDUCATION: THE GLOBAL SHIFT TOWARDS PRIVATISATION

GILL WYNESS

INTRODUCTION

The issue of how to finance higher education (HE), a question constantly debated by policy-makers around the world, is once again high on the agenda. Increases in university participation, demographic change and the financial crisis in the West—as well as unwillingness or inability of governments to foot the growing bill for higher education (often as a result of the above)—have led to worldwide financial instability in public institutions.

In response to this, many institutions that are traditionally reliant on governments for their core funding have begun to look for private sources of income. In their quest to move towards a more privatized model, institutions in many countries have looked to the USA as an example. Privatization is well-established in the US HE sector. Of the 4,352 degree-granting colleges and universities in the USA, the majority (2,667) are private institutions. Free from federal control and without the layers of state bureaucracy, these institutions can make important efficiencies, expand as they see fit and set tuition fees at market-clearing levels, subsidizing low-income students with the fees of those students able and willing to pay more for their degrees.

However, it is by no means certain that the US-style privatization model is a solution to the financial problems experienced in other countries. There are important cultural and political differences between the USA and other developed and developing countries which may make the model harder to implement. Furthermore, even with these well-established alternative sources of funding, private-sector institutions in the USA must be increasingly inventive in finding ways to meet costs which tend to increase annually, at a rate well above inflation or average household earnings growth. In response to these increasing costs, private-sector universities have, like their publicly run counterparts, increased tuition fees and fundraising from other sources to compensate. Their efforts have been effective for a number of years, but the costs of HE show no signs of abating. Indeed, recent history shows a pattern of constantly increasing costs—published tuition fees in the private sector in the USA have increased at an average annual rate of 3% above inflation over the past 30–40 years (Johnstone, 2009). This implies that private-sector sources of funding—while highly useful in the short run—will also become exhausted without decisive action to increase sector-wide efficiency.

GOVERNMENT INTERVENTION IN HIGHER EDUCATION

In many countries in Western Europe, e.g. France, Spain and Germany, HE has traditionally been considered the fiscal responsibility of the government, so the role of the private sector is limited. In these institutions, the academic staff are civil servants and the government controls student admission numbers. They are mainly reliant on a core of government funding, while tuition is free or kept at a minimum. For example, in Germany the private HE sector consists of 70 institutions, mainly universities of applied science and theological colleges, whilst there are almost 400 public-sector institutions. In France, while there are a large number of privately run institutions, these are small and specialized; the university sector, which educates over 2.2m. students, consists of 84 public universities and only 19 private.

The predominance of publicly owned institutions in Western Europe is an historical tradition and typically centres on issues of externalities and equity. First, education in these countries is seen as a positive externality. That is, individuals do not take account of the benefits to society associated with a more educated population when deciding whether or not to partici-pate. For example, research has identified positive effects of HE in the form of crime rates, increased productivity, economic growth, international competitiveness through a more educated workforce, and improving the nation's health (Dolton et al., 19...). Since private education tends to be expensive, it may be in the interests of the government to offer free or low-cost education, even at a high cost to the taxpayer, to assure that its population participates in HE. Second, governments may want offer free education for equity reasons—e.g. if they believe certain groups of people may under-consume HE because they are unable to afford to pay for it, or lack information about benefits of higher education. Since such individuals tend to be from poorer backgrounds (Goodman and Kaplan, 2003), they may therefore be under-represented in HE. Consequently, in the countries such as Germany, France and Spain, the governments may wish to maintain control of the university sector by levying only minimal or no tuition fees. Nevertheless, while universities in these countries are predominantly reliant on government finance, they do derive a significant proportion of their funding from private sources, in the form of tuition fees, endowments and research contracts.

REASONS FOR PRIVATIZATION IN HIGHER EDUCATION

While somewhat less prevalent in the West, private-sector institutions have emerged quite rapidly in other parts of the globe, particularly in the countries with emerging economies. Growth of private institutions has been rapid in Latin America, Asia and Africa—in some cases—e.g. the Philippines, Bangladesh and the Republic of Korea (South Korea)—the majority of students being educated in private institutions. In the People's Republic China, which has the largest higher education system in the world, the private sector grew rapidly after the adoption of a socialist market system in the 1990s and now accounts for 10% of tertiary enrolment.

Unlike their publicly funded counterparts, private institutions do not rely on government teaching funds, but instead derive their income exclusively from tuition fees paid by private individuals, endowments and charitable donations, and research contracts.

In a third type of model, present in the United Kingdom, Australia and Hungary among other countries, public and private institutions have merged; publicly owned institutions still make up the majority of HE institutions, but they derive an increasing proportion of their finance from private-sector sources, usually through tuition fees.

There are a number of factors that make either full or partial privatization in the HE sector appealing to both governments and institutions.

1. Lack of government funds

There may be insufficient public-sector funds available to finance a country's HE institutions. This may be particularly true when university enrolment rises rapidly and the government is unable to increase spending at the same pace. The massification of higher education is a relatively recent phenomenon in many Western countries, and has occurred intermittently and for varying reasons. Participation in the United Kingdom, which remained the privilege of the elite for many years, rose dramatically during the 1990s as the British Government expanded the sector both by building new institutions and by converting technical colleges to universities. This, coupled with rising demand and large increases in school staying-on rates driven by introduction of the General Certificate of Secondary Education (GCSE) exam, resulted in the proportion of 18–30-years attending university rising from 10% to almost 40% between 1995 and 2006.

A similar phenomenon occurred in Australia over the past 20 years, with enrolment rising from 24% in 1975 to 72% in 1995. Enrolment in Hungary quadrupled between 1989 and 2005, with over 400,000 students enrolled in an institution in 2005, driven in part by demand for practical training-based courses. Meanwhile, rapid growth in participation occurred in China in the 1980s and in India at around the same time. In each case, increases in participation were not matched with proportionate increases in state funding.

The developing world has also seen a rise in participation for different reasons—mainly as a result of increases in educational attainment at lower levels, resulting in growing numbers of university-ready students, such as in Uganda and Ethiopia.

In each case, without access to non-governmental funding of some sort, either standards would drop as funding per student decreased, or the government would have to tightly control capacity. Such capacity constraints are increasingly common in the United Kingdom, where the government still tightly controls the capacity of its universities, placing strict limits on the number of students that can enter each year. Thus, demand for places has, to date, far outstripped supply. Meanwhile, in the USA private institutions can be used to mop up excess demand, allowing students with no university place, but willing to pay high fees, to take up places.

2. Publicly financed HE systems are regressive
Economic theory suggests that the provision of free tuition fees and grants to students is regressive in economic terms, since the costs of HE must be paid for by all taxpayers regardless of whether or not they actually participate, while the benefits are largely private. Graduates derive a high private return from going to university (estimated to be 25%–27% for women and 18%–21% for men—see OECD, 2010), so many economists (e.g. Goodman and Kaplan, 2003; Greenaway and Haynes, 2003) argue that they should contribute to at least some of the cost of their tuition and maintenance, rather than enjoy large subsidies from low-income taxpayers who are unlikely to go to university and therefore reap the benefits enjoyed by graduates.

3. Marketization and efficiency
The process of privatization of the HE system may lead to the creation of a market system, generating important efficiencies.

For example, private universities are able to set their own levels of tuition fees, responding to supply and demand in a way that those without tuition fees, or with tuition fees set at government or state level cannot. Private institutions such as Harvard and Princeton can increase their quality and competitive edge through access to a lucrative source of funds from students (and their parents) who are willing and able to pay.

Efficiencies can also be generated through varying fees by subject. For example, universities could charge more for subjects that are more expensive to teach, such as medicine, making incomes more relevant. Despite the high demand for engineering and mathematics degrees, in the United Kingdom students must currently pay the same tuition fee for both, even though engineering subjects are far more costly to teach; meanwhile, the Australian Higher Education Contribution Scheme (HECS), for example, has different charges for different bands of subjects. Similarly, in China and Russia fees also vary by subject and institution.

Private institutions may even be better placed to draw revenue from students and graduates in the form of tuition fees—the predominance of private institutions in the USA has somewhat aided its ability to bring in tuition fee revenues. Unregulated by the government, such institutions have been able to increase their fees substantially, and often use such revenues to offer scholarships to those unable to pay—effectively cross-subsidizing poorer students with richer ones. This culture has meant that individuals—particularly those from better-off families—have got used to a culture of fee increases and are more willing to pay.

All across the Organisation for Economic Co-operation and Development (OECD) countries, the proportion of HE finance coming from the private sector has been increasing. Table 1 depicts the trend towards the privatization of the cost of HE

among a selection of OECD countries. It shows the proportion of expenditure on tertiary institutions coming from non-governmental sources between 1995 and 2007. For example, in Australia the proportion of expenditure coming from non-public sources has increased from 35% in 1995, to over 50% in 2007. Similarly, in the United Kingdom the private sector now accounts for almost 65% of expenditure on tertiary institutions, compared with just 20% in 1995. Even the USA has seen expansion of the share of expenditure from the private sector, though the increase has been less dramatic, rising from 63% in 1995 to 68% in 2007.

Table 1: Share of expenditure on tertiary institutions from non-public sources, %

	1995	2000	2002	2004	2006	2007
Australia	35.4	50.4	n.a.	n.a.	n.a.	55.7
Denmark	0.6	2.4	2.1	3.3	3.6	3.5
Finland	2.2	2.8	3.7	3.7	4.5	4.3
France	14.7	15.6	16.2	16.2	16.3	15.5
Germany	10.8	11.8	n.a.	n.a.	n.a.	n.a.
Hungary	19.7	23.3	21.3	21.0	22.1	100.0
Italy	17.1	22.5	21.4	27.4	27.8	30.1
Japan	64.9	61.5	64.7	63.4	67.8	67.5
Korea (Republic)	n.a.	76.7	85.1	79.0	76.9	79.3
New Zealand	n.a.	n.a.	37.5	39.2	37.0	34.3
United Kingdom	20.0	32.3	28.0	30.4	35.2	64.2
USA	62.6	68.9	60.5	64.6	66.0	68.4
OECD Average	22.7	24.3	25.1	25.9	31.2	31.1

Note: The author's calculations, derived from OECD, 2010, table B3.3.

PRESSURES ON THE UNIVERSITY FUNDING MODEL
While private institutions have no reliance on the public-sector teaching money on which public institutions count, both types of institutions face the same issues of rising costs in the sector. Moreover, both types of institutions share the same sources of private-sector funds, with public-sector institutions increasingly drawing on such funds to maintain finance as government coffers run dry.

The pattern of continuously rising costs in the HE sector is driven by a number of phenomena, often unique to the sector. Unlike many other industries, the HE sector is predominantly labour-intensive. A university's main functions are to teach their students and to carry out research. Both of these functions are dependent on highly skilled staff. Staff have traditionally experienced, and therefore expect, their real incomes to rise with time as their skill levels increase. In addition, the sector has become increasingly competitive, with universities competing directly with each other to attract the best students and the most lucrative research contracts. This means rising building and maintenance costs as universities attempt to seduce high-performing students with impressive facilities and campuses, and growing wage bills as universities compete for the highest ranking professors. Competition has been exacerbated by the increased use of rankings and market share data, which in turn drive universities to seek out the most prestigious—and most expensive—staff, and build the best amenities, to improve their rankings.

Globalization has forced many universities to compete with institutions overseas as students are more and more willing to leave their own country to study. For many years students around the world have travelled to universities in English-speaking countries, largely due to the predominance of published research in the English language. This has traditionally boosted the university coffers of the elite institutions of the USA and the United Kingdom, but more recently other English-speaking countries such as Australia, New Zealand and Singapore have entered the field, meaning that universities in all these countries are now in direct competition for lucrative overseas students. Competition for overseas students will inevitably grow as other institutions start to offer courses in the English language. Again, this is likely to result in increased costs to universities as they race to become the most prestigious.

Thus, when labour costs are a majority of costs, and when the cost of skilled labour rises faster than that of unskilled, the default is a highly expensive system with annual increases in costs. A possible exception to this rule can be found in the US community college model, a teaching-based rather than research-intensive model. There are some 4,000 community colleges in the USA charging relatively low tuition fees in comparison with the high rates charged by Ivy League schools (since their staff command lower salaries), but which offer good quality teaching and, in many cases, a springboard towards a degree at a major university. Tuition fees at these colleges are less than half of those at major institutions (see National Center for Education Statistics, 2008), suggesting that a teaching-based model may be an effective way to create a lower-cost, more efficient system. That said, fees at community colleges have, albeit from a smaller base, increased at a rate similar to those in private institutions between 1976/77 and 2006/07, with an average tuition fee increase of 105% over that period (compared with 133% in private institutions and 165% at public institutions over the same period).

Naturally, those institutions, incentivized by lower public funding, have made efforts to cut costs and improve their productivity. Lecture halls in the West have increased in occupancy as the ratio of students to staff increases, and many students are taught in part by graduate teaching assistants who command lower salaries than lecturers or professors. Moreover, technology, such as internet and computer-assisted learning, is frequently used to assist in instruction, cutting down on printing and paper and making it possible to reach a wider range of students, as well as facilitating rapid improvements in research output.

However, such improvements are minor compared with other industries and the university sector has been largely unsuccessful in substituting capital for labour to the extent that other industries have. Nevertheless, the model could be radically changed with technology. Major institutions could, for example, license video lectures by top professors to institutions not in direct competition. Universities made up of video lectures, with a teaching element largely staffed by low-paid graduate teaching assistants, could potentially be run at a far lower cost and still maintain quality teaching. Massachusetts Institute of Technology (MIT), for example, through its 'Open-CourseWare' scheme (see ocw.mit.edu/index.htm), makes course materials used in MIT courses freely and openly available to others for non-commercial educational purposes.

Without such major changes to the university model, unit costs in higher education may be set to continue to increase for the foreseeable future, somewhat calling into question the sustainability of private sources of income.

THE SUSTAINABILITY OF THE PRIVATE MODEL
As Table 1 showed, the world is shifting away from using public sources of finance in HE. Given the cost pressures described above, however, can a privatized model be sustainable in the long term? The principal sources of finance in the privatized model are students themselves, their parents, endowments and other sources of revenue, particularly research contracts. In many countries, these sources of finance are already under pressure.

1. Students and graduates
In the majority of countries that adopt some kind of privatization, a principal source of funds comes from students themselves, either at the point of entry via up-front tuition fees or, more commonly, in the form of deferred tuition fees, payable after graduation.

The move towards such 'cost-sharing' happened in each country quite soon after massification, with China introducing student loans in 1986, Australia in 1989, New Zealand in 1992, India in 2000 and Hungary in 2001. In these countries, students can borrow the full amount for their tuition fees and also borrow money for living costs from the government, and then repay their loans after graduation.

In a number of these countries, fee levels have risen many times since their introduction, putting increased pressure on students and graduates as a source of finance. For example, tuition fees in the United Kingdom were originally set at £1,300 per student per year, but were subsequently increased

to £3,300 per year in 2006. Universities lobbied for such fees to be increased even further, resulting in the government lifting the fee-cap to £9,000 per year, starting in 2012. These increases were met with mass student protests and will almost certainly result in falling participation as students refuse to take out loans of such magnitude. Costs to students have also risen consistently since the introduction of contributions in 1988, rising in 2003, 2005, 2006 and 2007. Fees have also risen a number of times since their inception in Australia and New Zealand.

In the USA, which is one of the most competitive HE markets in the world, tuition fees continue to rise in both the public and private sectors, suggesting that marketization has failed to control prices.

> After three decades of increases at more than double the rate of inflation, the cost of attending an American private university has reached a politically unpalatable new height. This autumn, one year of tuition, room and board and mandatory fees will surpass the US annual median household income of $48,023 (£25,800). (Times Higher Education Supplement, 28th August 2008)

A further, less obvious limit to fee increases arises in these countries due to the subsidized nature of fee-loans. While increases in tuition fees result in a larger proportion of university teaching money coming from students and graduates, the state must also make a large contribution to the cost of HE through subsidizing these student loans. Often the cost of financing such loans is high—students in the United Kingdom do not repay their loans until they earn above £15,000 (at 2010 prices), and then pay 9% of such earnings. In Hungary repayment is at 6%–8% of minimum wage, while in Australia repayment varies by income, between 4% and 8% of graduate earnings. This means that many graduates do not repay the full, or indeed, any amount of their fee-loan, meaning that the expense falls on the government. Further costs to the public sector come from interest subsidies—for example, under the United Kingdom's current system interest rates on loans are covered by the government at considerable expense. This is also the case for certain students in New Zealand.

The cost to the government of providing loans to students effectively limits the amount of money that can come from this source of income, since governments must limit their lending to students (or indeed, as has been the case in the United Kingdom, increase their lending to students but offset the cost with pound-for-pound cuts to university funding). Unless students can borrow effectively from the private sector, it is unlikely that future rises in tuition fees will be met by students and graduates, making this particular source of revenue unsustainable in the long term.

2. Parents
Aside from students and graduates, an alternative source of revenue from the private sector, largely untapped in the United Kingdom, Australia, Sweden and New Zealand, is that of the parents of students.

In Germany, parents are a key source of revenue and are legally obliged, depending on their financial means, to support their children's living costs and books. Indeed, children in Germany have the right to sue their parents for this money, should they be unwilling to pay it. However, German tuition fees are still minimal at less than US $500 per year in 2007, so it is unclear how German parents would react to a substantial increase in fees.

In the USA contribution to the costs of university in the form of tuition fees and the living costs of students is considered to be a parental responsibility, and so US parents are among the biggest contributors to HE in the world. While grants and student loans are in place in the USA, these are predominantly means-tested (as opposed to being partially means-tested in the United Kingdom, with no enforcement for parental contribution, or with no means-testing at all, as in Hungary), with the expectation that parents who are able to meet the cost of their child's education will do so. Such a strategy has been highly effective in the USA, with parents used to bearing the cost of their children's degrees and traditionally planning for many years ahead to bear their share of the cost.

This strategy has distinct funding advantages: in many countries, parents are a potentially substantial source of wealth. Many middle- and upper-class parents see HE as a hugely valuable asset, and are hence willing and able to meet the cost of their child's university education.

While this strategy has been effective in managing the rising cost of HE in the USA, again it is questionable that US parents can continue to be effective. This is particularly a concern for families in the middle and lower classes, who may already be struggling to meet their expected share and who are unlikely to be able to increase their contributions.

Furthermore, it is hard to envisage the effectiveness of using parents as an additional revenue source in such countries as the United Kingdom, Australia and New Zealand. In these countries and others, particularly in Scandinavia, the age at which an individual is considered to be independent of his or her parents—and instead a young adult—is considerably younger than in the USA, resulting in less emphasis on the parental contribution to university. Indeed, in many countries this may be culturally unacceptable. Furthermore, as countries have moved away from up-front fees, often paid for by parents, towards a culture of graduate responsibility, it will be extremely difficult to reverse this decision and place a responsibility on both parents and graduates.

3. Endowments

Another largely untapped source of revenue outside of the USA is that of charitable giving. The USA sees many billions of dollars donated and several institutions receive endowments in excess of US $1,000m. This extraordinary source of institutional revenue is somewhat unique to the USA, however—the majority of other countries do not have such a culture of charitable giving to HE. Such a culture can be encouraged through tax laws (e.g. in the United Kingdom a recent reform allows estates a 10% reduction in inheritance tax if 10% of the estate is donated to charity), but it may require many years of effort to develop such a culture in other countries unused to such giving—particularly given the long-established culture of HE being the fiscal responsibility of the government or, more recently, students themselves.

4. Revenues from other activities

A final source of revenues for both public and private institutions comes from research grants and contracts. These sources account for considerable money in richer countries, particularly for the most prestigious 'research-intensive' universities. While research grants are an extremely lucrative source of finance, the provision of these services is similarly labour intensive. Again, the increasingly competitive system of research contracts requires universities to recruit and pay the most prestigious staff members in order to win the contracts.

THE FUTURE OF HIGHER EDUCATION FINANCE

Despite some serious questions over the sustainability of the university model, with increasing strain on private sources of funding as costs in HE rise, it is likely that privatization in HE will continue for the foreseeable future, and is likely to spread to institutions in countries still largely controlled by the public sector. While costs remain low in countries such as Ethiopia and Uganda, their enrolment levels remain low and are likely to increase. Increasing unit costs and competition through globalization will further exacerbate the need for private sources of income.

A case in point is Scotland. In 1998, as part of the United Kingdom, tuition fees were introduced in Scotland. However, in 1999 Scotland was granted devolution and the devolved government abolished the fees, citing its belief that its citizens had the right to a free education. In 2011 the Scottish Government, under increased pressure from the global financial crisis as well as steadily rising enrolment, looked set to reverse this decision. A particular factor is increased competition, both globally and particularly from England. Scotland's universities have been traditionally very well funded and among the best in the world. While the recent financial crisis has put pressure on both England and Scotland, in terms of university funding English universities have been able to derive additional funds from students in the form of tuition fees, while Scotland has been unable to do so and, as a result, funding per head in Scotland has fallen behind that of England for the first time.

As a result of this, a Scottish White Paper, released in February 2011, discussed the possibility of introducing a deferred fee for at least some students studying in Scotland (Scottish Executive, 2010). The decision to reverse its position on tuition fees seems inevitable, and it seems that those other countries that rely on public funding will inevitably follow suit and begin to move towards a privatized system. For some countries, such as France and Germany, HE is something of a captive market, with the majority of students coming from their own country, indicating that perhaps they can continue to rely on public money without the risk of quality sliding and students being tempted away to higher-quality institutions. Scotland, however, with one of the most captive HE markets in the world (over 80% of Scottish students study in Scotland), provides a clear illustration of the difficulties faced by those institutions without access to private finance.

CONCLUDING REMARKS

All around the globe, higher education institutions are increasingly adopting the privatization model pioneered in the USA. In some cases—particularly in Latin America and Asia—this has taken the form of rapid increases in private institutions, but in the majority of countries, particularly in Western Europe where public institutions are still the norm, institutions are increasingly seeking revenue from private sources.

Private-sector sources of HE finance are not unlimited, however. While the US example has shown that graduates, students and their parents are willing to pay tens of thousands of pounds for their degrees, for the average family a private higher education costs about two and a half times as much (as a percentage of family income) today as it did three decades ago. Such increases in costs may be unsustainable over the long term, and are likely to be met with growing concern by the public and policy-makers concerned about accessibility. Further, the practice of charitable giving, enjoyed traditionally by private-sector institutions in the USA but now spreading to public institutions, is not easily emulated in countries without a culture of charitable giving to HE.

Therefore, while drawing revenue from private sources may be a short-term solution to the economic problems faced by institutions throughout the world, in the long term more radical solutions may need to be found. The US community college model may be one such solution, in general offering good-quality tuition at less than half the cost of major institutions. Prioritizing teaching over research keeps the wage bill lower and students are able to move onto a four-year degree if they show sufficient promise. Furthermore, economies of scale through use of the internet, new technology and remote learning could lead to major efficiencies, with 'universities' consisting of licensed video-lecture content, staffed by graduate teaching assistants, potentially offering a reduced-cost alternative to the current model.

In the absence of such radical ideas, privatization is unlikely to be a sufficient panacea to the rising costs experienced by HE institutions throughout the world.

BIBLIOGRAPHICAL REFERENCES

Dolton, P., Greenaway, D. and Vignoles, A. 'Whither Higher Education? An Economic Perspective from the Dearing Committee of Inquiry', in *The Economic Journal*, 107, 710–26, 1997.

Goodman, A. and Kaplan, G. 'Study Now, Pay Later or HE for free? An assessment of alternative proposals for HE finance', in *IFS Commentaries*. Institute for Fiscal Studies, 2003.

Greenaway, D. and Haynes, M. 'Funding Higher Education in the UK: The Role of Fees and Loans', in *Economic Journal*, 113, F150–F166, 2003.

The International Comparative Higher Education Project. *Higher Education and Finance Country Profiles*. gse.buffalo.edu/org/inthigheredfinance/project_profiles.html.

Johnstone, D. Bruce. 'An International Perspective on the Financial Fragility of Higher Education Institutions and Systems', in Martin, J., Samuels, J. E. and Associates (eds). *Turnaround: Leading Stressed Colleges and Universities to Excellence*. Baltimore, The Johns Hopkins University Press, 2009, pp. 31–48.

National Center for Education Statistics. *Community Colleges: Special Supplement to the Condition of Education*. US Department of Education, 2008.

OECD. *Education at a Glance 2010: OECD Indicators*. OECD Publications, 2010, www.oecd.org/dataoecd/46/24/45925258.pdf.

Scottish Executive. *Building a Smarter Future: Towards a Sustainable Scottish Solution for the Future of Higher Education*. Scottish Green Paper, 2010 (online only: www.scotland.gov.uk/Publications/2010/12/15125728/0).

ACADEMIC INTEGRITY IN THE DIGITAL AGE: ARE STANDARDS CHANGING, OR ON THE DECLINE?

TEDDI FISHMAN

INTRODUCTION

Concern about integrity in scholarly and intellectual work is not a new phenomenon. As far back as the first century AD, Pliny the Elder expressed concern about what contemporary educators would term 'academic dishonesty' in the form of plagiarism. Pliny took pride in identifying and crediting over 400 sources upon which his work was based, and criticized his peers who neglected to do so (Pliny, Natural History: 22, 23). In Pliny's day, however, academic misconduct was limited to the relative few who had access to scholarly texts and could write. Today, the internet puts millions of documents within reach of anyone with a computer, and the ease of 'copying and pasting' makes it possible to 'write' without composing a single original sentence. The facility with which it is possible to cobble together a text or even download one, ready-made, from the web has prompted some to declare that we are in the midst of a 'plagiarism plague' ('The Plagiarism Plague') or 'epidemic' (Howard, 2003).

Many factors have been put forth as possible causes of the current unacceptably high rates of academic dishonesty. Teachers report that their students are under-prepared, unmotivated, or simply do not understand how to do the work that is required, and thus resort to cheating. Students report that they are unsure of the rules, that they see no point in many of their assignments, or simply that they were too busy to do an adequate job and felt that their best option was to take a chance by cheating. Other factors are rarely mentioned by students, but seem likely to have an effect, such as increasingly drastic shifts toward simplistic, objective evaluation methods that focus attention exclusively on marks and scores rather than cumulative, distributed, or interconnected knowledge acquisition. In order to be successful, students are likely to have internalized the unintended message that marks, scores and grades are the goals of education, rather than providing a 'snapshot' indicator of how they are doing at a particular time. At the point at which the score or mark becomes more important than the learning experience, the impulse to cheat is likely to become more compelling than struggling to complete the activity itself.

Increasing competition for a limited number of places at competitive universities and graduate schools also probably contributes to the high rates of cheating, particularly when coupled with the perception that 'everyone else is doing it'. Students typically overestimate the numbers of their classmates who are cheating and express concern that they are disadvantaged by it. Some students who do cheat justify their behaviour by saying that because so many others are cheating, they can't be competitive unless they cheat as well. Perhaps most troubling are the students who admit cheating but say that cheating is acceptable in 'the real world'. Regardless of the accuracy of this assertion, if the students believe it is true, it is likely that it factors into their decisions about whether or not to cheat.

Don McCabe, researcher and founding president of the International Center for Academic Integrity, has conducted a 20-year longitudinal survey of undergraduates that asks about the cheating behaviours they have engaged in during the past year. These are his results as reported to the American Association of Colleges and Universities, October 2009:

	Undergraduate (report having engaged in)	Graduate (report having engaged in)	Faculty (report having observed)
Test Cheating	21%	10%	55%
Written Cheating	48%	31%	86%

Numbers responding to survey: 75,000 undergraduates, 12,500 graduate students, 15,800 faculty members.
USA only; Undergraduates.
Excludes first year students.

Although these numbers have remained relatively static throughout the years of the survey, they can in no way be seen as reassuring when nearly half of undergraduates admit to engaging in written cheating and one in 10 graduate students admits to cheating in tests. These numbers, perhaps more than any high-profile story about a particular school, are an indication that we need to look more carefully at the messages we send our students about the processes of education and the reasons to engage in it.

Plagiarism and test cheating are only two aspects of the broader issue of maintaining a healthy ethical climate in academic institutions. Since the 1960s, critics have suggested that attention be paid to the 'ethical health' of educational institutions, and, moreover, that academic integrity should be addressed as a legitimate and necessary concern (Bertram Gallant & Goodchild, 2011). While the degree to which educational institutions have responded to this charge has been mixed, media accounts of widespread cheating have become increasingly frequent, inspiring books and websites decrying the 'cheating culture' (Callahan, 2004). The British Broadcasting Corporation (BBC) describes academic dishonesty as 'easy to get away with' ('Students Using the Net to Cheat') and plagiarism as 'a natural part of undergraduate life'. Sadly, however, academic misconduct is not limited to undergraduates nor even to students. Recent news stories of misconduct in academic settings have included sports recruiting scandals, falsification of research, admissions corruption, fraud and falsification of faculty credentials. It seems that no aspect of the educational system is immune. If media accounts are to be believed, we are witnessing a crisis of integrity in academia, fuelled by technology which, while perhaps not directly responsible for the prevalence of cheating, at least serves as a catalyst. In addition to cheating and plagiarism, fabrication and falsification are also serious academic integrity concerns. They are distinct from each other in that fabrication involves making up data or evidence where it did not exist, while falsification involves the manipulation of data or evidence so as to alter or affect the implications or results.

EVOLUTION OF THE ACADEMIC INTEGRITY MOVEMENT

The impetus for the development of the modern academic integrity movement arose from increased awareness of student cheating. Early researchers, including Don McCabe and others, began looking at the numbers of students who reported that they themselves had engaged in cheating behaviour: the researchers were shocked by the results. Whether or not cheating had actually became more common, or just more apparent, is subject to some debate, but two things are clear: first, modern assessment mechanisms, e.g. standardized objective tests and essays in electronic form, made it a relatively simple matter to detect many instances of scholarly misdeeds; and second, the rates of cheating were (and are) unacceptably high. Interested individuals, primarily faculty members and researchers, formed groups to address the problem, including the International Center for Academic Integrity (ICAI) in the USA, the Asia Pacific Forum on Educational Integrity (APFEI), based in Australia, and others around the world, each of which set about responding to the troubling findings.

Given the genesis of the problem, it is no surprise that early academic integrity efforts focused primarily on student behaviour, specifically detecting, correcting, and punishing the 'cheaters'. The hallmark of the initial efforts is the tendency to look at cheating as an individual character flaw or mistake, rather than as a systemic issue. The focus for improvement was primarily on identifying those students who needed guidance or correction. One key element in the student-centred approach to academic integrity is increasing students' understanding and appreciation of the significance of integrity in scholarly work. Drawing explicit linkages, for instance, between pre-professional preparation and the work an engineer does can make the point that we all have a vested interest in the integrity of their education. Likewise for doctors, pilots, teachers, etc.

Another key is to help develop the capacity to make well-reasoned, defensible decisions, even when competing interests must be weighed against one another. Having a framework, particularly when one has practised using it, helps prepare the student for tough ethical choices they may face when under pressure. A third, typical element of the student-centred approach is to put into place a penalty for those who, after learning why integrity is important and how to make ethical decisions, still choose to cheat. This element turns out to be important not only for those tempted to break the rules, but also for those inclined to follow them. As mentioned above, when students believe that other students are cheating and getting away with it, they themselves are often more tempted to cheat so as not to be adversely affected themselves. Conversely, when students know that the institution and its representatives value integrity, they are more likely to conform to that expectation. All three elements, understanding why integrity is important, learning to make good ethical decisions, and visible institutional support, are critical to success with the student-centred approach.

Examples of student-centred approaches to academic integrity include:

Explaining your expectations regarding academic integrity, and the penalty students face if conditions are not met.

Listening to students; soliciting and answering questions.

Addressing breaches of integrity 'head on'.

The second stage of the academic integrity movement came about with the growing realization that students were only one part of the academic integrity equation, and that, to be successful, the effort should also focus on teachers. Gradually, integrity efforts broadened to include more pedagogical approaches as instructors began to explore ways to promote integrity in their classrooms through teaching innovation. Teachers were encouraged to create unique, situational, assignments and incorporate more authentic inquiry (and less rote memorization) into their curricula, as well as doing obvious things like creating new tests rather than 'recycling' the old. Key features of the pedagogical approach included focusing on processes rather than solely on work products. For instance, instead of requiring a 25-page paper, an instructor might instead ask for two drafts of a 15-page paper, plus 'prewriting' work that might include an outline, peer revision and commentary, and a reflection at the end. The hope was that by guiding students through the writing process, they would have less need or desire to cheat, not to mention the fact that it would be nearly as much trouble to manufacture all of the 'accessory' writings as to write the paper oneself. The pedagogical approach improved upon the fully student-centred approach, but still did not fully address the breadth of the issue.

Pedagogical tactics to discourage cheating include:

Using applied, interconnected assignments that serve to illustrate the usefulness of the activities and the ways in which the acquisition of the knowledge helps contribute to the students' ongoing development.

Using reflection as a way to explore ethical issues as well as to encourage students to consider problems from multiple perspectives.

Assigning value (points) to process pieces as well as final 'products'.

The shift to the third (and current) wave in academic integrity practice was marked by the inclusion of institutional and/or contextually based approaches. Based on the premise that part of the enculturation process that students undergo when they enter an educational institution has to do with becoming acclimatized to the ethical norms of the prevailing culture, this approach looks at ways to promote the values of academic integrity throughout the educational environment, rather than focusing solely on individual teachers and learners. The institutional approach resonates with educators, who have long recognized that students are often inclined to adapt the habits of their peers, but thought there was little that could be done to affect those habits. Optimally, this approach includes support from the institution as well as an active role for students, which might converge in the establishment of a student-led, university-endorsed honour code and/or pledge-signing ceremony, or the establishment of a student-led honour board to adjudicate academic integrity hearings. When successful, this approach has the critical advantage of promoting student 'buy-in' which, in most cases, is essential for success.

The institutional approach has several strengths. One is that it encourages cooperation among different elements of the institution, all of whom have a stake in maintaining its reputation and, by extension, the value of the diplomas or degrees that it grants. Students who may not have been persuaded not to cheat when they believed that the only harm that would come from it would be failure to acquire knowledge might see things differently when they consider the possibility that potential employers would be put off by the notion of hiring a graduate of a school with a reputation for cheating. Likewise, a professor who hadn't considered cheating to be a top priority might reconsider after contemplating the potential harm to her reputation, should a cheating scandal occur at her school. Another advantage to this approach is that it changes the nature of the relationship between students and instructors, vis à vis academic integrity. With the other two approaches, the teacher bears primary responsibility for making and enforcing academic integrity standards, whereas the institutional approach calls for a far more collaborative relationship, with both constituencies working towards a mutually shared goal. Additionally, when students take ownership of and responsibility for establishing and maintaining high standards of integrity on campus, the effect of the peer to peer communication is often far greater than when that same message is delivered from faculty to student.

Institutional tactics for promoting academic integrity include:

Institutional leaders giving voice to the idea that all members of the institutional community have a stake in protecting its reputation (and that the value of students' diplomas are tied to the ethos of the school).

Faculty members across the institution engaging students in ongoing dialogues about shared values and ideals.

Making explicit the connection between educational integrity, professional integrity, and sustainable, thriving societies.

TECHNOLOGY AND CHEATING

Certainly, technology plays a role in academic integrity issues. Students take advantage of the ease with which online information can be accessed and integrated nearly seamlessly into their own compositions, often without proper attribution. Online test banks have replaced fraternity and sorority files as the place to access test questions, often without the knowledge of their originator. The ubiquity of mobile telephones makes them a favourite means of tapping into unauthorized assistance during exams, and online videos provide lessons on topics like 'how to cheat with an iPod'. Even technologies like word-processing programs that are so seemingly innocuous that we scarcely consider them technologies at all can be used to cheat. The 'auto summarize' function, for instance, can be used to scramble a summary just enough to escape detection as having been lifted from an unattributed source. Likewise, online translation programs like Google Translator or Babylon.com can be used in a similar way, to alter text enough that it cannot be identified.

Technology is also used to deter and detect cheating. Laborious library searches to identify and track down plagiarized source material have been replaced by quick, easy search engine queries and optimized text matching applications. Even images can be checked for originality using programs like TinEye. Specialized plagiarism detection software like eTBLAST, Viper and TurnItIn can be used by students checking their own work for potential problems, or by instructors checking their students' work for originality. Educators must take time, however, to familiarize themselves with the various strengths and weaknesses of these programs. They do a good job finding bits of identical text, but cannot discriminate between a source that has been properly documented and one that's been lifted and used without acknowledgement. Although faculty members may have high hopes that using these programs will relieve them from having to pore over their students' work, in reality they will still have to follow up on any suspicious text that is flagged. Each technological 'fix', moreover, seems to inspire yet another advance in deception, with the unhappy result being a technical 'arms race' between students and instructors, as each vies for the upper hand. It is also important to note that using technological means to prevent or discourage students from cheating precludes the development of the necessary skills to make sound ethical choices in the future.

Strategies for Addressing Technology Assisted Cheating:

Engage students in a dialogue about technology and cheating. Let them know you know it's a temptation but that you expect them to resist.

Keep abreast of current technologies. Know what is out there.

Set clear boundaries. Encourage appropriate use of new technologies, but be prepared to address inappropriate uses.

It is important to recognize that although the term 'academic integrity' is most often associated with issues concerning students, by its very nature it is correctly applied not only to the university but also to the environment in which the university functions. It is useful to consider 'integrity' as a structural property that relies on the sum of its parts and which cannot endure if its support or infrastructure are compromised.

ONLINE COURSES

Technology also plays a significant role in the many increasingly popular online and hybrid courses, which have the additional challenge of establishing the identity of the students doing the work in the course. Webcams, fingerprint readers, biometric scanners and keystroke algorithm programs have all been utilized to establish that the student enrolled in (and receiving credit for) the course is who he or she purports to be. Though it is necessary to authenticate the identities of students in an online class, once their identity has been established there are a number of ways to help online instructors 'know' their students. Best practices, both for identity and academic integrity purposes, include using a variety of different kinds of assessments, in 'real time' as well as asynchronously, to allow the instructor to become familiar with the vocabulary and communication style of the students in a variety of contexts, rather than only via formal writing assignments. Also, including a number of low- as well as high-stakes evaluation methods, such as blog posts, reflections, and smaller themes throughout the semester, instead of relying on one or two larger papers, can serve both to help the student develop his or her ideas and writing skills and to allow the teacher a greater degree of familiarity. Process-based assignments are also useful, both because they provide an opportunity for the instructor to intervene in cases where a student needs additional help or resources, and because they provide the scaffolding that helps all students succeed without tempting them to resort to availing themselves of unauthorized assistance.

HONOUR CODES AND CLIMATES OF INTEGRITY

One of the ways that many institutions promote integrity is through the development, publication, and promotion of honour codes. At some institutions, the honour codes are nearly as old as the school, and students regard them as esteemed components of the school heritage. Other schools have more recently developed codes, some of which were adopted in response to academic integrity issues or scandals. Although there are considerable variations, typically the codes prohibit lying, cheating, and stealing. Often they include an edict stating that students will not tolerate anyone else engaging in the practices either. Though the codes themselves serve an important function, perhaps the most important thing they do is to raise the profile of academic integrity issues as a topic of conversation. It appears that those conversations, rather than the codes themselves, are the critical thing in terms of having a positive effect.

FUNDAMENTAL VALUES

Some schools identify a set of core values or principles, either in addition to their honour code or in lieu of one. Typical values include qualities like honesty, respect, truth, responsibility, fairness, and courage, though this list is in no way exhaustive or inclusive. Lists of values and principles serve a different function from that of honour codes, since they identify values rather than proscribing behaviour, but in terms of their effect, their value is quite similar in that, when successful, they raise awareness of academic integrity issues and start conversations which can significantly improve the climate of integrity on campus.

When students first arrive at an institution of higher learning, they often struggle to 'decode' the tacit rules that will be key to thriving in the new environment. While avoiding lying, cheating, and stealing might seem like a straightforward enough set of instructions, in practice it is often more complicated than it seems, and it is often students' peers who will guide them as they attempt to make sense of the rules. For this reason, whether or not an institution develops and promotes an honour code, it is essential that all students receive a clear and consistent message from their peers, their instructors, and the administration. Each of these groups should be clear that academic integrity is an important concern for all and that they are all responsible for safeguarding it.

BIBLIOGRAPHIC REFERENCES

Bertram Gallant, T. and Goodchild, L. *Creating the Ethical Academy* (Introduction). New York and London, Routledge, 2011.

Callahan, D. *The cheating culture: why more Americans are doing wrong to get ahead*. Harcourt, Orlando, 2004. Accessed at http://www.loc.gov/catdir/toc/ecip046/2003015529.html.

Howard, R. M.. *The Search for a Cure: Understanding the 'Plagiarism Epidemic.'* McGraw-Hill, November 2003. Accessed at http://www.mhhe.com/socscience/english/tc/howard/HowardModule03.htm.

'The Plagiarism Plague'. BBC News, World Edition, 7 February 2003. Accessed at http://news.bbc.co.uk/2/hi/uk_news/2736575.stm.

Pliny. *Natural History*: English translation by H. Rackham. London, Heinemann; Cambridge, Mass., Harvard University Press, 1938.

'Students Using the Net to Cheat'. BBC News, Education, 13 November 2003. Accessed at http://news.bbc.co.uk/2/hi/uk_news/education/3265143.stm.

IS EDUCATION GETTING LOST IN UNIVERSITY MERGERS?*

JANI URSIN, HELENA AITTOLA, CHARLES HENDERSON and JUSSI VÄLIMAA

Mergers are common phenomena in higher education institutions. Improving educational quality is typically one of the stated goals of university mergers. Yet, little information exists about how merging institutions approach this goal. This paper presents results from a study of planning documents created prior to four mergers in the Finnish higher education system. These documents show that there was little concrete attention given to the educational issues related to the mergers. Most attention was placed on administrative issues and issues related to research. When educational issues were mentioned, it was almost always in the form of vague goals with few details provided about how the goals were to be reached. We conclude that this lack of attention to the educational aspect of mergers is a significant weakness of the planning process in these mergers.

INTRODUCTION

Mergers are common phenomena in higher education institutions. Although one of the stated goals of most university mergers is to improve educational quality in the merged university, there is little information in the literature on the impact of mergers on educational quality. Most literature, instead, focuses on issues such as organisational structures and various outcome measures (often in comparison with pre-merger measures) such as numbers of students, diversity of course offerings, and level of external funding (e.g. Mao, Du, & Liu, 2009). This is very similar to the literature on mergers in industry that focus primarily on organisational structures and outcome measures such as stock prices and profitability (e.g. Andrade, Mitchell, & Stafford, 2001).

Since educating students is one of the primary university functions and improving educational quality is a commonly stated goal of the mergers, the lack of information related to changes in educational quality during mergers in higher education is an area in need of significant work. This paper will address one aspect of this void in the literature by examining written planning documents related to the goals and methods of four recent mergers in the Finnish higher education system. The purpose of this paper is to describe how educational issues were framed in planning documents used in four Finnish university mergers. The planning phase of a merger is particularly important in that the documents and discourse created in this phase are designed to shape the merger process.

BACKGROUND AND RESEARCH CONTEXT

Social pressures to change the structures of Finnish higher education and its legislative basis originate in two main sources. On the one hand, there are significant internal pressures due to administrative and management structures which are overloaded by new personnel categories (e.g. project researchers). In addition, expanding social and societal expectations, expressed as needs to increase the 'third mission', of higher education institutions have resulted in an explosion of project management problems. The problems related to decreasing public funding and the increasing numbers of fixed-term academic staff have also drawn public attention to the problems of universities. On the other hand, the pressures to change Finnish higher education are caused by and related to changes in Finnish society and the Finnish national economy. These problems have been seen increasingly in the context of a competitive globalised economy and higher education because the production of knowledge has been defined as crucial for the effectiveness and competitiveness of the Finnish national economy—like in other parts of the globe.

There are two main national strategies to respond to these pressures. The first one is to change the legal framework for universities. This was carried out by introducing the new Universities Act (558/2009) in 2009. It aims to increase the institutional autonomy of universities (see Välimaa, in press). The second main strategy applied by the Ministry of Education and Culture is to force—or to encourage—universities to merge with other universities. According to the Ministry of Education and Culture, the purpose of the reorganisation of the Finnish higher education system is to generate (inter)-nationally a more competitive network of higher education institutions, enhance the quality of research and education, as well as identify and recognise strategic areas in research and education (Opetusministeriö, 2008).

The Finnish higher education system is a dual one consisting of universities and polytechnics (universities of applied sciences). At the time that the data for this study were collected (year 2008), there were 46 higher education institutions (20 universities, 26 polytechnics) in Finland. The goal is to reduce the number of higher education institutions to 33 (15 universities, 18 polytechnics) by the year 2020 and to make these institutions bigger in terms of student numbers: there should be at least 3,000 full-time students in each university and for polytechnics the corresponding figure is 2,500 (Opetusministeriö, 2008). This trend of increasing the size of higher education institutions typically calls for changes in the internal organisation of universities towards larger units and faculties (Taylor, 2006). To move towards this goal, in 2008 the Finnish Ministry of Education and Culture funded several merger projects with the aim of establishing three new universities to open in January 2010. Funding for each merger project was negotiated annually between the Finnish Ministry of Education and each merging university. However, the amounts of this funding were not revealed in all cases. The information was available for the University Consortium of Turku (2008–2010, 7.5 million Euros) and the University of Eastern Finland (2008–2010, 7.5 million Euros; see Tulossopimus, 2008a, 2008b). Exact sums were not available in the case of the University Alliance or Aalto University. However, Aalto University was guaranteed to have a much higher level of governmental support than the other mergers as it is expected to be a world-class university (Virtanen, T., 2008).

Finland is not alone in its desire to consolidate its higher education system. Various global, European, and national developments have prompted mergers within many higher education systems in Europe during the last decade (see Kyvik, 2004; Liefner, Schätzl, & Schröder, 2004; Musselin, 2007; Teichler, 2006). Previous studies on university mergers show that the consolidation of organisational and institutional cultures (Kezar & Eckel, 2002) and management styles (Locke, 2007) of the merging universities plays a crucial role. Furthermore, a merger is dependent on the interaction of governmental macro-politics and institutional micro-politics (Sehoole, 2005) as well as geographical distance (Dahl Norgård & Skodvin, 2002), which thus create a specific merger context. Therefore, it is important to recognise that each merger is organisationally, culturally, and territorially unique.

Planning is perhaps the most important phase of the entire merger process. A successful merger requires the development of new structures and ways to work as well as an adaptation of novel ways of thinking from the whole academic community (Kezar & Eckel, 2002). The management of the university plays a crucial role in executing a merger and creating a new organisational culture (Eckel & Kezar, 2003; Kyvik, 2002; Locke, 2007; Sehoole, 2005). Institutional leadership must create a vision of the merged institution that retains the

*This essay first appeared in *Tertiary Education and Management*, Vol. 16, No. 4, December 2010, pp. 327–340. See http://dx.doi.org/ 10.1080/13583883.2010.533379.

strengths of the merging universities but at the same time is responsive to external constraints. This visioning and communication process begins in the planning phase, well before the actual merger takes place.

For academic staff, a merger can have both positive and negative consequences. It can, for example, enhance professional identity by providing better academic career prospects. As a consequence of reallocation of academic positions, a merger may also create tensions between staff members (Becker et al., 2004). Hence, one of the main missions of a university's management during the planning process is to reduce uncertainty by communicating openly on the aims and progress of a merger to staff and students (Cerych & Sabatier, 1986; Sehoole, 2005), and providing opportunities for academic staff to participate in decision-making (Becker et al., 2004).

RESEARCH QUESTIONS, DATA, AND METHODS

The purpose of this paper is to analyse and describe how educational issues were described in planning documents used in four Finnish university mergers. The main research question is: How are issues related to teaching and learning addressed during the planning of university mergers?

The target group consists of the following university mergers (the names of universities involved are in brackets): Aalto University (Helsinki School of Economics, Helsinki University of Technology, University of Art and Design Helsinki), University of Eastern Finland (University of Joensuu, University of Kuopio), University Consortium of Turku (Turku School of Economics, University of Turku), and University Alliance Finland (Tampere University of Technology, University of Jyväskylä, University of Tampere).

Institutional mergers in higher education have various forms, ranging from informal collaborations to affiliation agreements to full amalgamations (see e.g. Harman & Harman, 2003). In our data, we have three full mergers (Aalto University, University of Eastern Finland, and University Consortium of Turku) and one affiliation (University Alliance Finland).

Aalto University has approximately 16,400 students and 4,300 staff members in three campuses which are located close to each other in the Helsinki Metropolitan area. The University of Eastern Finland has approximately 13,000 students and 3,000 staff members. It is spread into three campuses (Joensuu, Kuopio and Savonlinna) at great geographical distances. University Consortium of Turku, located on the southwest coast of Finland, has approximately 21,000 students and 3,000 staff members. It is located in one campus. These three new universities officially started their activities on 1 January 2010. University Alliance Finland is an exception, however, as the three universities that form the alliance will not have a full merger but rather will enhance their cooperation by making affiliation agreements. The universities involved in the alliance have more than 40,000 students and 6,000 staff members. University of Jyväskylä is located about 150 km from the other two universities, which are situated in Tampere.

The data used for this study consist of planning documents (reports, strategies, official records, memoranda, and other relevant documents) from all four of the above-mentioned mergers (Table 1). Documents were obtained in two ways. University web sites were searched for relevant documents. In addition, the coordinators of the merging process in administrative offices from each university were contacted to obtain documents which were not officially available from the university web sites. These coordinators were all willing to support the study and supplied documents that, although not seen as confidential or secret, were not publicly available. The quantity and volume of documents varied according to the actual phase of the merging process and the communication practices of universities. Some of the documents were formulated for the need of the Ministry of Education and Culture and central administration; some others were more general and directed at informing university staff and students about the planning process. The data were collected in 2008, thus representing the starting point for the mergers.

Table 1. Summary of documents analyzed in this study

Type of Document	Merged Institution			
	Aalto	Eastern FI	Turku	Alliance
Reports	2 (152)	1 (38)	1 (66)	3 (72)
Strategies	—	1 (3)	2 (49)	—
Memoranda	5 (17)	9 (35)	2 (8)	5 (15)
Newsletters	13 (41)	—	2 (8)	—
Agreements	1 (7)	—	—	1 (6)
Total	21 (217)	11 (76)	7 (131)	9 (93)

Note. Table reports number of documents and, in parentheses, approximate number of pages in each category.

The analysis was completed in three phases. In the first phase, all relevant documents were reviewed in order to form a general understanding of the merger processes and contexts as well as the available data for analysis. As we expected based on the literature cited earlier, these documents suggest that the planning process at these four institutions is similar to planning for other university mergers in that the focus is mainly on administrative issues. Nonetheless, many of the documents did address educational issues. The second phase of analysis began by extracting all of the text discussing education and teaching. The analysis was conducted using content analysis so that, first, similar notions were coded under preliminary categories and then these categories were modified and combined until a final set of categories was reached. The third phase involved combining the individual analyses. Categories that were similar to all four mergers were combined and further elaborated based on the four data sets as well as on available theory. This process resulted in five main themes that were common for all four mergers.

RESULTS

Here, we present and briefly discuss the five main education-related themes that were common for all four mergers:

Justifying the merger

Synergies between merging institutions

The role of working groups and allocation of resources

Professional development of lecturers

Possible obstacles and challenges

Justifying the merger

One of the main emphases in the documents was to justify why the merger is important. From the perspective of education, the main arguments were related to the enhanced quality of university training, improved competitiveness in educational markets, and internationality. For example, in the final report of the planning group of the University Alliance Finland, it is said that:

> The University Alliance Finland is a cooperation process between the University of Jyväskylä, Tampere University of Technology, and the University of Tampere that aims at self-governed development. The purpose is to strengthen the educational and scientific quality, competitiveness and regenerative ability of the independent member universities. (Yliopistoallianssi, 2007, p. 4)

Hence, it was expected that by uniting education and teaching resources, a merged university could better compete for the best teachers, researchers, and students.

Being more competitive internationally was a common way of justifying the mergers. In order to be an international actor, a merging university needs to define its profiles and find its strengths in relation to other actors in the same (global) field. However, little was written about practical measures on how to make an internationally attractive university. One example can be drawn from a draft of a teaching strategy for the University of Eastern Finland:

The University of Eastern Finland is nationally and internationally well-known for high-quality, strongly research-based instruction. [...] The University of Eastern Finland is both nationally and internationally an attractive place for learning. (Itä-Suomen yliopisto, 2008, p. 1)

This type of writing was common in the planning documents. Notice that this is essentially a goal statement rather than an action plan. It is also a very non-controversial goal—having high quality instruction and being an attractive place for learning. The only actual concrete part of this statement is the emphasis on research-based instruction. This could be indicative of an action plan, but without more details about what is meant by 'research-based instruction' (which were not found anywhere in this document nor in the other documents from this institution) it is far too vague to significantly inform action.

In some cases a more detailed description of how to succeed in international competition was given, as an example from Aalto University shows:

Succeeding in competition calls for the possibility to use the same kinds of reward, generally speaking clearly higher wages and better resources for forming own research teams. However, because of the use of tenures the Finnish recruitment practice is legalistic and often unbearably slow, and universities do not have sufficient resources to hire top researchers and to create a favourable research environment to support their work. (Opetusministeriö, 2007b, p. 53)

Getting rid of regulation concerning the titles establishment, filling, duties and salaries of academic teaching and research posts makes it possible to create a new, internationally more competitive personnel policy system. (Opetusministeriö, 2007b, p. 70)

In this case, though, it is a justification based on improved administrative processes. Although there is some mention of hiring academic teachers, the most important improvements mentioned in this citation refer to hiring researchers and improving the research environment. As mentioned previously, this focus on research over teaching was common in the planning documents.

Synergies between merging institutions

The mergers were expected to build on existing educational strengths so that the most competent and knowledgeable teachers would be available for the courses and the flexibility of study programmes would be increased to better meet the students' and working life's needs. Although discussion of synergies between merging institutions was partially used to justify the mergers, these discussions appeared to be aimed primarily at heralding the unique strengths of each of the merging institutions and assuring stakeholders that these strengths would be maintained and even magnified. There was not discussion about redundancies between the merging institutions that might result in the elimination of positions in the merged institution. A descriptive example can be found from the University Consortium of Turku:

The two unifying universities are very different in terms of size. Hence, there are relatively few overlapping activities as well. The diverse and internationally successful academic foundation of the University of Turku will now be linked to the business expertise of Turku School of Economics by creating such study programmes and interdisciplinary teams and projects for research and instruction that genuinely respond to modern challenges. (Virtanen, K., 2008)

Various concrete forms of building on these educational synergies were discussed in the documents. University Consortium of Turku, for example, bases its educational cooperation on already existing collaboration between merging universities, especially in business studies and in a multidisciplinary study programme on sustainable development. In Aalto University, there are three 'New Expertise Workshops' which bring academic projects and companies together. These workshops, named Design Factory, Media Factory, and Service Factory, provide interactive environments for learning, teaching, research, and co-operation. For example the Design Factory is described as follows:

The Design Factory is an attempt to speed up the change of teaching and work cultures and also to create an inspiring model for the future projects of the innovation university. The ways and practices support interdisciplinary problem- and project-specific learning and research. In the Factory people also learn multiculturalism, managerial skills, collaboration skills, as well as about the views of the economic life and researchers alike, communication skills as well as holistic perception. Higher expertise and increased self-confidence, which are intended outcomes of the projects, are characteristic of Factory-based activities. (Inno News, 2008, p. 3)

University Alliance Finland, in turn, will finance joint educational initiatives between universities, especially those which include new educational openings and innovations and those that belong to strength areas of the Alliance. These strength areas are formed so that they:

[...] will tie together strengths displayed in the universities' own profiles and strategies in the research areas of culture, nature, technology, health, and society. (Yliopistoallianssi, 2007, p. 29)

The forms of educational cooperation vary. Typically merging universities have started to plan joint courses and study programmes. University of Eastern Finland, for instance, focuses on how to shift more resources to Master and Doctoral education. This means that there will be joint Bachelor courses but separate Master studies based on the profiles of merging universities:

For studies at the undergraduate stage, a so-called y-model will be introduced, including a Bachelor degree in common to different subject areas, but to be followed by a differentiated Master stage. The objective is to save in costs and transfer thus created new resources from the basic studies to the Master's and doctoral studies and also to research. (Opetusministeriö, 2007a, p. 24)

The University Alliance Finland [Sisä-Suomen yliopistoallianssi] highlights that increased cooperation between the three universities involved in the alliance can strengthen the position and status of small fields of study so that: 'the diversity of smaller fields can be maintained within the alliance' (Sisä-Suomen yliopistoallianssi, 2007, p. 2). Thus, the planning process for these mergers suggests that the mergers will likely have the concrete educational impact of increasing the diversity of course and programme offerings available to students. However, few concrete details were found in the planning documents to describe how this might occur.

The role of working groups and allocation of resources

It was typical that working groups were established in order to promote educational cooperation. Working groups were typically either thematic (e.g. information and communication technology [ICT] in education) or discipline specific and consisted of stakeholders from each of the merging universities, including students. According to the documents, the engagement of all staff members and students was seen as important in the success of a merger. The main task for working groups was to concretise general aims related to educational cooperation: what does collaboration mean from the perspective of staff and students; what kinds of resources are needed; what is the schedule for cooperation, and so forth. A typical example of this can be found in the University of Eastern Finland:

> Three field-specific working groups were set up: for economics, natural sciences, and social sciences. The working groups were to pay special attention to research and teaching co-operation in their respective fields. Besides the objectives and forms of such cooperation, the working groups were expected to evaluate possible shared activity structures and outline a schedule for the development of co-operation. (Opetusministeriö, 2007a, p. 11)

The role of working groups, however, often changed during a merger process. In Aalto University, for example, the ad hoc-based working groups established at the beginning of the merger were changed into a more systematic transformation organisation with team leaders and clear roles and responsibilities: This happened in Aalto University after The Aalto University Foundation Board started work in August 2008:

> From each higher education institute people have been sought for to join in the transformation teams of Aalto University. The transformation teams include the active key persons, who are oriented towards the future and considering new things. The aim is that these teams will assist the Rector and the Board of Directors in preparing for the new university. The teams operate in accordance with the Board's decisions and report to it. The agenda includes, e.g. change management, planning for the new organisation, rules and task descriptions, as well as for the mission and vision. (Aalto News, 2008, p. 1)

The resources required to promote educational amalgamations and cooperation were also discussed in the documents. Typically merger projects direct resources to those educational initiatives associated with the evolving strength areas of a merging university. This was also one way of promoting a clear profile of a new university. At the first stage, staff members' teaching expertise will be utilised so that lecturers from each of the merging universities will teach courses belonging to their own expertise. Later on, it is planned that joint teaching positions will be established. It was stressed in the documents that at the beginning the reorganisation of teaching activities will require a lot of resources but in the long run it was expected to bring gains in the form of more rationalised teaching arrangements. As with other educational aspects, the exact meaning of 'rationalised teaching arrangements' was not explicated in greater detail.

Professional development of lecturers

Pedagogical models and goals were presented in the documents to some extent. Special focus was put on the development of university teachers' and researchers' pedagogical know-how and expertise. Typically, merging universities planned to organise either short- or long-term personnel training to achieve this goal. The pedagogical competence of university lecturers was highlighted in the University of Eastern Finland in the following way:

> The teaching provided at the University of Eastern Finland is based on scientific research. The student is seen as an active party in the teaching process. Teaching processes are based on interaction with regard to the development of teaching methods, curricula, and feedback systems. The University invests in the pedagogical quality of teaching, and diverse teaching methods are applied in instruction. The study places at our university are in great demand and competed for. (Itä-Suomen yliopisto, 2008, p. 1)

In order to achieve this goal, University of Eastern Finland will organise a basic course of pedagogical competence for university teachers as well as a study programme for pedagogical qualifications for lecturers. Furthermore, a quality assurance system of educational activities is expected to enhance teaching and learning. In the University of Turku, the aim is to utilise already existing cooperation between the two merging universities so that the development of teaching, already existing in the University of Turku and the Turku School of Economics, is based on common practices. Thereby the educational and technological capabilities of teaching staff can be developed in a more systematic way.

In Aalto University, a pedagogical centre will be established in order to promote lecturers' teaching competences:

> Aalto University will get a pedagogical centre, which will support all teachers. The centre will operate close to the teachers. By means of the centre the university will make use, more broadly than before, of the pedagogic and didactic expertise regarding various existing teaching methods. Teachers will be introduced to the use of these methods. The development of teaching will also be accompanied by peer tutoring. The methods will be successfully disseminated across the whole university. Also skills related to the planning of teaching will be further improved by concentrating on course and module planning and also on study programme design. The pedagogical choices will be based on research findings on learning. (Oppimisen tilat, 2008)

Each university is proposing to increase their emphasis on professional development of teachers—and has plans to use 'best practices' and 'research-based models'. This was one of the most concrete goals and examples that the documents proposed in terms of improving educational activities as a consequence of a merger. Partly, this relates to the fact that the new Universities Act which came into being on 1 January 2010 allowed universities to put more formal emphasis on the teaching qualifications of university lecturers than during the time when each university employee was also a civil servant. Without additional details, it is difficult to judge how likely it is that these plans to focus on teaching will be successful. Using quality assurance measures and professional development, however, is known to be very difficult to implement in a way that is highly effective (e.g. Patriquin et al., 2003; Sheldon, Golub, Langevin, St. Ours, & Swartzlander, 2008).

Possible obstacles and challenges

Possible obstacles and challenges to educational cooperation were also considered in the documents. Especially, continuation and sufficiency of funding during a merger process raised concerns—a matter that the Ministry of Education and Culture was expected to take good notice of. In the background report of the University Consortium of Turku, it is mentioned that:

> The reinforcement of the basic activities of the University, especially for profiling the areas of strength, teaching and research, that the universities have defined in their strategies as well as the implementation of essential development schemes (e.g. a researcher collegium and advancing business expertise) call for more funding. (Opetusministeriö, 2007c, p. 63)

It was also stressed in the documents that mergers and increased cooperation between higher education institutions do not abolish competition. On the contrary, in the future, universities are expected to contend for the best researchers and teachers harder than ever before. Furthermore, a demand for more international competition raised a concern on how to deal with national missions. For example, in Aalto University the importance of international students was highly valued, but at the same time it was regarded as crucial to give teaching in Finnish and Swedish (official languages in Finland) in order to maintain cultural heritage:

The university would aim to compete for the best students at the international level. At the same time, however, we must keep in mind the need for teaching provided in domestic languages. It is significant not only for the Finnish culture but also for the efficiency and quality of learning. (Opetusministeriö, 2007b, p. 53)

The geographical distance between merging universities was especially a concern in the University of Eastern Finland and University Alliance Finland. Partly, this reflects the concerns that small campuses have, as the overall goal of the Ministry of Education and Culture is to reduce the fragmentation of the higher education network by expecting universities to reconsider their need for various campuses and branches (Opetusministeriö, 2008). However, in the documents, rather than closing down campuses, ICT and well-considered teaching arrangements were seen as the main solutions for the problems caused by the geographical distance of different campuses that emerged as a consequence of a merger:

For example, geographical distance poses a challenge to the collaboration between the Universities of Jyväskylä and Tampere, but it can be solved through ICT arrangements and well thought-out mobility of students and teachers. (Yliopistoallianssi, 2007, p. 13)

Furthermore, different cultures and value orientations as well as ways of doing things between merging universities may raise challenges. This was highlighted by the comment made by student unions of the merging universities in Aalto University:

Co-operation must be developed based on values. Our primary aim must be to promote science, arts, education and culture—not the economic life, enterprises and competitiveness suggested in the now published proposal. The student unions underline that the harmful aspect of the suggestion does not come from the notion of co-operation as such but from the ways and the set of values on the basis of which the merger is proposed. (Taideyliopilaskunnat, 2007)

However, it was hoped that these would be prevented from developing into problems by engaging the whole academic community in a merger process.

CONCLUSIONS AND DISCUSSION

The purpose of this document analysis was to understand how educational issues were treated in the planning phases of these four university mergers. The majority of the planning documents focused on administrative and research issues. The overall finding is that educational issues received relatively little attention in the merger documents and that the attention they did receive was largely in the form of non-controversial goals. There was little description of concrete goals or plans and little description of the possible negative aspects of the mergers. The most concrete educational aspects discussed in the planning documents had to do with the synergies between the programme offerings of the merging institutions. Thus, these mergers will likely have the concrete educational impact of increasing the diversity of course and programme offerings available to students. This is consistent with the results of other research (Kyvik, 2002; Skodvin, 1999). There were also pledges to develop more robust professional development activities for academic staff. However, it was not clear in the planning documents how these pledges would be transformed into functional and useful professional development activities.

For example, one might expect that, to achieve the goal of becoming a world-class institution, the merger documents would point to specific innovations in teaching and learning that would be used. Similarly, when merging two institutions, in addition to a discussion about synergies and new opportun-

ities, a realistic planning document would also be expected to discuss redundancies and the need to eliminate certain overlapping operations (see Kyvik, 2002). Yet, these sorts of issues were rare in the planning documents.

We present two tentative explanations for the lack of focus on educational issues during mergers. The first is that the merger documents collected were largely written by those who have been charged with implementing the mergers. The optimistic tone of most documents suggests that one of the underlying goals of the documents is to sell the merger to members of the merging institutions. Thus, the documents tend to present only the upsides of mergers and avoid any aspects of the merger that are potentially threatening to faculty or staff. It is relatively easy to talk about efficiencies and synergies in administration and research. In teaching, though, it is difficult to talk about efficiencies and synergies without discussing the elimination of teaching positions or academic programmes (compare Dahl Norgård & Skodvin, 2002). Thus, the specifics related to teaching are not discussed much during merger planning. When specifics are discussed, the emphasis is placed on planning to capitalise on the synergistic differences between the institutions and not on planning to reduce redundant offerings. While this is a useful strategy to build support for the merger among academic staff, avoiding careful planning and not discussing possible negative aspects is likely to lead to problems once the merger occurs.

The second, complementary, explanation is that the people who initiate and manage the merger process are usually not experts in the area of teaching and learning. They also do not typically have any good ways to measure the degree of teaching excellence and, thus, focus their energies on areas where clear outcome measures exist and where they know they will be held accountable. This issue of the difficulty of assessing educational quality is an ongoing problem for higher education. Based on this study, however, a merger does not seem to provide a solution to this problem—not in the short run at least.

The results presented here suggest that the lack of emphasis on educational issues during mergers is likely an important problem. There are only a few other studies that have sought to specifically examine the emphasis on educational issues during mergers (see e.g. Kyvik, 2002). Clearly, this is an area where more research is needed. It seems reasonable to expect that not planning carefully for educational excellence during mergers is a significant problem which results in many missed opportunities for educational improvement. However, it is not clear exactly what effective planning would look like and how much of an emphasis on education is possible given the other demands that a merger presents. Until more research is conducted, though, institutions undergoing mergers should be reminded not to lose sight of one of their main missions—that of providing high quality education to their students.

REFERENCES

Aalto News. *Innovaatioyliopisto: Uutiskirje 8* [Innovation university: Newsletters 8/2008]. Aalto University, 2008 (unpublished).

Andrade, G., Mitchell, M., and Stafford, E. 'New evidence and perspectives on mergers', in *Journal of Economic Perspectives*, Vol. 15 No. 2, pp. 103–120, 2001.

Becker, L. R., Beukes, L. D., Botha, A., Botha, A. C., Botha, J. J., Botha, M., et al. 'The impact of university incorporation on college lecturers', in *Higher Education*, Vol. 48 No. 2, pp. 153–172, 2004.

Cerych, L., and Sabatier, P. *Great expectations and mixed performance: The implementation of higher education reforms in Europe.* Stoke-on-Trent, Trentham Books, 1986.

Dahl Norgård, J., and Skodvin, O.-J. 'The importance of geography and culture in mergers: A Norwegian institutional case-study', in *Higher Education*, Vol. 44 No. 1, pp. 73–90, 2002.

Eckel, P., and Kezar, A. 'Key strategies for making new institutional sense: Ingredients to higher education transformation', in *Higher Education Policy*, Vol. 16 No. 1, pp. 39–53, 2003.

Harman, G., and Harman, K. 'Institutional mergers in higher education: Lessons from international experience', in *Tertiary Education and Management*, Vol. 9 No. 1, pp. 29–44, 2003.

Inno News. *Innovaatioyliopisto: Uutiskirje 2* [Innovation university: Innonews 2/2008]. Aalto University, 2008 (unpublished).

Itä-Suomen yliopisto. *Itä-Suomen yliopiston opetuksen strategialuonnos* [A draft of teaching strategy of University of Eastern Finland]. Joensuu, 2008.

Kezar, A., and Eckel, P. D. 'The effect of institutional culture on change strategies in higher education: Universal principles or culturally responsive concepts', in *Journal of Higher Education*, Vol. 73 No. 4, pp. 435–460, 2002.

Kyvik, S. 'The merger of non-university colleges in Norway', in *Higher Education*, Vol. 44 No. 1, pp. 53–72, 2002.

'Structural changes in higher education systems in Western Europe', in *Higher Education in Europe*, Vol. 29 No. 3, pp. 393–409, 2004.

Liefner, I., Schätzl, L., and Schröder, T. 'Reforms in German higher education: Implementing and adapting Anglo-American organizational and management structures at German universities', in *Higher Education Policy*, Vol. 17 No. 1, pp. 23–38, 2004.

Locke, W. 'Higher education mergers: Integrating organizational cultures and developing appropriate management styles', in *Higher Education Quarterly*, Vol. 61 No. 1, pp. 83–102, 2007.

Mao, Y., Du, Y., and Liu, J. 'The effects of university mergers in China since 1990s: From the perspective of knowledge production', in *International Journal of Educational Management*, Vol. 23 No. 1, pp. 19–33, 2009.

Musselin, C. 'The transformation of academic work: Facts and analysis', in M. Kogan and U. Teichler (Eds), *Key challenges to the academic profession* (pp. 175–189). Werkstattberichte 65, INCHER-Kassel, Paris: UNESCO Forum on Higher Education Research and Knowledge, 2007.

Opetusministeriö. *Itä-Suomen yliopisto—tulevaisuuden yliopisto ajassa. Opetusministeriön työryhmämuistiota ja selvityksiä 2007:15* [The University of Eastern Finland—The future university today. Reports of the Ministry of Education, Finland 2007:15]. Helsinki, 2007a.

Teknillisen korkeakoulun, Helsingin kauppakorkeakoulun ja Taideteollisen korkeakoulun yhdistyminen uudeksi yliopistoksi. Opetusministeriön työryhmämuistiota ja selvityksiä 2007:16 [New university in the field of technology, business studies and art and design. Reports of the Ministry of Education, Finland 2007:16]. Helsinki, 2007b.

Turusta tieteen huippukeskittymä. Opetusministeriön työryhmämuistiota ja selvityksiä 2007:14 [Towards research excellence in Turku. Reports of the Ministry of Education, Finland 2007:14]. Helsinki, 2007c.

Korkeakoulujen rakenteellisen kehittämisen suuntaviivat vuosille 2008–2011 [Guidelines for the structural development of higher education institutions for the years 2008–2011]. Helsinki, 2008.

Oppimisen tilat. *Aalto-yliopiston opetuksen teemaryhmä* [A thematic group for teaching in Aalto University]. Helsinki, 2008.

Patriquin, L., Bensimon, E. M., Polkinghorne, D. E., Bauman, G., Bleza, M. G., and Oliverez, P. M. 'Posttenure review: The disparity between intent and implementation', in *Review of Higher Education*, Vol. 26 No. 3, pp. 275–297, 2003.

Sehoole, M. T. C. 'The politics of mergers in higher education in South Africa', in *Higher Education*, Vol. 50 No. 1, pp. 159–179, 2005.

Sheldon, M. R., Golub, A. J., Langevin, J. R., St. Ours, P. A., and Swartzlander, B. J. 'Improving institutional effectiveness: Description and application of an implementation model', in *Planning for Higher Education*, Vol. 36 No. 2, pp. 17–26, 2008.

Sisä-Suomen yliopistoallianssi. *Visio ja tavoitteet vuoteen 2015* [Vision and goals by the year 2015]. 2007 (unpublished).

Skodvin, O. J. 'Mergers in higher education: Success or failure?' in *Tertiary Education and Management,* Vol. 5 No. 1, pp. 65–80, 1999.

Taideylioppilaskunnat. *Yliopistojärjestelmää kehitettävä arvopohjaisesti: Kannanotto 6.3.2007* [University system must be developed from its values: A statement 6.3.2007]. Helsinki, 2007.

Taylor, J. '"Big is beautiful": Organisational change in universities in the United Kingdom—new models of institutional management and the changing role of academic staff', in *Higher Education in Europe*, Vol. 31 No. 3, pp. 251–273, 2006.

Teichler, U. 'Changing structures of the higher education systems: The increasing complexity of underlying forces', in *Higher Education Policy*, Vol. 19 No. 4, pp. 447–461. 2006.

Tulossopimus. *Opetusministeriön ja Kuopion yliopiston välinen tulossopimus kaudelle 2007–2009 ja voimavarat vuodelle 2008* [Performance agreement between Ministry of Education and University of Kuopio for 2007–2009 and resources for 2008]. 2008a (unpublished).

Opetusministeriön ja Turun yliopiston välinen tulossopimus kaudelle 2007–2009 ja voimavarat vuodelle 2008 [Performance agreement between Ministry of Education and University of Turku for 2007–2009 and resources for 2008]. 2008b (unpublished).

Välimaa, J. 'Uusi yliopistolaki ja kansallisen yliopistolaitoksen yhtiöittäminen' [New Universities Act and the incorporation of national university institution], in J. Lasonen and J. Ursin (Eds), *Koulutus yhteiskunnan muutoksissa: Jatkuvuuksia ja katkoksia* [Education in the transformations of society: Continuity and disassociation]. (In press.)

Virtanen, K. *Tieteidenvälisyys ja uusi suomalainen yliopisto: Rehtori Keijo Virtasen puhe Turun yliopiston lukuvuoden avajaisissa 4.9.2008* [Interdisciplinarity and a new Finnish university: Speech of Rector Keijo Virtanen in the opening ceremony of academic year 4.9.2008]. Retrieved from http://www.utu.fi/faktat/hallinto/rehtorin_puheet/avajaispuhe2008.html, 2008.

Virtanen, T. 'Merging and privatising to reach for the top: A new Finnish University of Technology, Business and Art and Design', in T. Aarrevaara and F. Maruyama (Eds), *University reform in Finland and Japan* (pp. 53–76). Tampere, Tampere University Press, 2008.

Yliopistoallianssi. *Suunnitteluryhmän loppuraportti: Julkaisematon* [A final report of the planning group of University Alliance Finland]. 2007 (unpublished).

PROGRESS AND CHALLENGES TO THE RECOGNITION AND REWARD OF THE SCHOLARSHIP OF TEACHING IN HIGHER EDUCATION*

DENISE CHALMERS

For more than 20 years there have been growing and widely expressed concerns that teaching is not sufficiently rewarded and recognized in universities, particularly in comparison to research. Individuals, institutions and governments have each responded in different ways to promote changes in institutional systems and practices. Two of the major initiatives to raise the status of teaching have been the Scholarship of Teaching and Learning and Teaching Quality movements. These share similar goals and many concepts, but began with a different impetus. This paper reviews initiatives to increase the status of teaching through better recognition and reward of teaching in universities. Current practices and evidence of change are reviewed. The paper concludes that while there has been significant progress made to date, the ultimate symbols of recognition and reward—promotion and tenure—are proving to be elusive but not unattainable for those who focus on the Scholarship of Teaching.

INITIATIVES TO REDRESS THE IMBALANCE OF STATUS AND RECOGNITION AND REWARD BETWEEN RESEARCH AND TEACHING

During much of the twentieth century, promotion and career progression were contingent on achieving success in disciplinary research in universities. Academics choosing to pursue research into teaching and learning and directing their attention to the learning of their students risked career progression and access to tenure and promotion (Diamond, 1993; Huber, 2004). It was widely acknowledged that the reward and recognition systems of academic work were out of balance and that in order to redress this imbalance, teaching needed to be better recognized and rewarded.

There were two largely independent movements to improve the status of teaching taking place on opposite sides of the world in the 1990s: Scholarship of Teaching in North America and Teaching Quality in the UK and Australia. Initiatives were also taking place in Europe but for the sake of brevity, the major focus in this paper will be limited to North America, the UK and Australia.

Scholarship of Teaching movement

There was a significant grass roots movement to better recognize the importance and value of teaching in universities, primarily in North America, captured in Ernest Boyer's (1990) seminal paper, *Scholarship reconsidered*. In his 'call to arms', Boyer argued that universities should recognize the richness of academic work and reward contributions in what he proposed were four different forms of scholarship—teaching, integration, application of knowledge and discovery. He also argued that academic reward systems should stress the forms of scholarship most closely aligned with the university mission. Boyer asserted that if formal changes were made to reward systems to encourage not only discovery *but also* teaching, integration and application of knowledge, there would be greater acceptance and appreciation of these multiple forms of scholarship by academic staff and administrators and greater alignment between academic staff rewards and institutional mission (O'Meara, 2006). This argument was readily accepted, with administrators and academics agreeing that the criteria used for tenure and promotion were inappropriately skewed towards disciplinary research (Diamond, 1993, 2002). Significant funding was provided to support the development of statements that described the work of the academic

in disciplines and in the broader university context by the Carnegie Academy for the Scholarship of Teaching and Learning (Hutchings, 2000).

By the end of the twentieth century, many universities were committed to improving their tenure and promotion systems to expand the definition of academic work that acknowledged the Scholarship of Teaching. Universities progressively changed their language, criteria, processes and structures for appointment, tenure and promotion to more fully recognize the broader work of the academic (Glassick, Huber, & Maeroff, 1997; O'Meara, 2005; Paulsen & Feldman, 2006).

Teaching Quality movement

The teaching quality movement in Australia and the UK was driven by national governments and their agencies in response to many of the same issues that had been identified by Boyer. For example, the highly influential Dearing report in the UK stated that teaching was of low status in relation to research, promotion was awarded for disciplinary research performance, that little or no funding was available for research and development projects in learning and teaching and that there was no national policy on the quality of teaching (Department for Education and Skills, 2003; Gosling, 2004). A number of national initiatives, with significant funding, have attempted to redress the imbalance between teaching and research and to focus university leaders' attention on the quality of teaching and learning and the underlying systems and processes that support it. A brief overview of the teaching quality movement in Australia and the UK is outlined below. For a comprehensive review of teaching quality models in use across 17 countries see Chalmers, Lee and Walker (2008).

The Australian government's teaching quality initiatives have been primarily targeted at the institutional level. For example, from the mid-1990s the national government established national student surveys, reporting of student progression and institutional quality audits with a strong focus on teaching quality and processes. The Learning and Teaching Performance Fund (LTPF) scheme, established in 2003, was a controversial initiative designed to differentially reward the higher education providers that best demonstrate excellence in learning and teaching based on a limited number of quantitative indicators. The rationale for the fund was to promote teaching quality within the sector and to place excellence in learning and teaching alongside research excellence.

The Australian Learning and Teaching Council (ALTC) was established in 2004 to provide a national focus to enhance learning and teaching in Australian higher education institutions. The ALTC was preceded by a number of limited-term committees to promote and support teaching and learning in higher education, with the first established in 1990. These provided funding for competitive grants and projects, for example, funding for professional development, using technology to enhance teaching and learning, student learning, research and discipline-based projects (Chalmers, 2007). The focus for these initiatives were individuals and teams within and across universities to provide them with access to competitive funding to parallel research funding models, encourage academics to engage in teaching and learning issues in scholarly ways and to enhance the overall quality of teaching and learning in universities.

Another teaching quality initiative was the Australian Awards for University Teaching, established in 1997 to celebrate and reward excellence in university teaching. These national teaching awards have been expanded over the years to include teams, disciplines and institutional programmes. While the criteria for these awards have primarily sought

* This essay first appeared in *Higher Education Research & Development*, Vol 30. No. 1, February 2011, pp. 25–38. See http://dx.doi.org/10.1080/07294360.2011.536970.

evidence of excellent teaching, they were revised in 2006 to explicitly include a criterion of demonstrating scholarship in teaching.

The UK governments and agencies have taken an explicit enhancement approach to teaching quality. For example, the Higher Education Funding Council for England (HEFCE) distributed significant funding for initiatives designed to enhance the quality of teaching in universities and colleges. The most substantial of these has been the Teaching Quality Enhancement Fund (TQEF), established in 1995. This multi-year, multi-level initiative had three major strands: the subject strand, which established the Learning and Teaching Support Network and the Fund for the Development of Teaching and Learning, the institutional strand, where universities received funding for developing and implementing a Learning and Teaching Strategy, and the individual strand, which allowed each institution to nominate one candidate as part of the National Teaching Fellowship Scheme (Gosling, 2004). In 2004, the Higher Education Academy (HEA) was established to support activities that contribute to improvement in student learning, professional development and recognition of scholarly practices and teaching. More recently, HEFCE's largest single enhancement initiative funded 74 Centres of Excellence for Teaching and Learning to reward excellent teaching practice and to further invest in those practices that deliver substantial benefits to students, teachers and institutions. The TQEF has now been superseded by the Teaching Enhancement and Student Success (TESS) fund (HEFCE, 2009).

The teaching quality initiatives in Australia and the UK were designed in large part to address the perceived lack of change by institutions to recognize and reward teaching and to enhance the status of teaching relative to research. By establishing incentives, the governments wished to prompt universities to pay attention to the quality of their teaching and learning and to implement reward and recognition processes and practices that were comparable or equivalent to those in research.

Together, the Scholarship of Teaching and Teaching Quality movements have been highly influential in focusing universities' attention on the status of teaching and the ways it is recognized and rewarded. Universities have done this through utilizing a number of common mechanisms.

COMMON MECHANISMS TO RECOGNISE AND REWARD TEACHING

The 1996 *Campus trends* (El-Khawas, 1996) report on US universities identified that the primary mechanisms for recognising and rewarding teaching were: (1) annual awards for good teaching, (2) offering programmes (professional development and grants) to improve teaching and (3) giving teaching more importance among the criteria for evaluating staff for performance review and promotion. These mechanisms were widely adopted, regardless of the type of university. For example, 86% of US universities gave awards for outstanding teachers, 76% periodically evaluated the performance of their tenured academics (though the criteria were not specified), 56% had instituted formal programmes to foster teaching improvement, 25% had revised their promotion and tenure criteria to give greater importance to good teaching and 33% had increased the importance of good teaching in their appointment practices (El-Khawas, 1996). A decade later, the same three mechanisms remain the most common.

1. Awards and fellowships for excellent teaching

Awards for teaching predominate as the most obvious form of recognizing and rewarding teachers and teaching within universities. National awards programmes have been introduced more recently. For example, in the UK and Australia, national awards schemes have been credited with prompting universities that previously had no teaching awards schemes to establish them (Gosling, 2004). Chalmers and Thomson (2008), in their review of Australian universities' teaching and learning indicators, identified that all had established institutional-level awards for university teaching, with the majority adopting the criteria used by the national awards. While a number of these universities had well established

teaching awards prior to the first national awards in 1997, the significant prize money, prestige and marketing potential prompted the remaining universities to establish their own. The UK national teaching fellowships were established in 2000 (Gosling, 2004). Many North American universities have long-established teaching awards (El-Khawas, 1996), with national teaching awards and fellowships conferred by organisations such as the Carnegie Foundation and professional associations.

Awards for teaching were largely introduced to recognize and reward excellent teachers and teaching to signal that teaching was valued (Jackson, 2006; Skelton, 2004). It is only relatively recently that awards applications also require evidence of Scholarship of Teaching. Some have argued that these distinctions may be unnecessary, for 'excellence is not accidental, it requires engagement with pedagogy, a reflection on practice and a responsive institutional context' (Allen, 2003, as cited in Palmer & Collins, 2006, p. 198). Others disagree, asserting that 'scholarship of teaching is *not* synonymous with excellent teaching' (Hutchings & Shulman, 1999, p. 13).

Although awards and fellowships for teaching are the predominant form of reward and recognition of teaching, the extent to which they serve this purpose is challenged (Frame, Johnson, & Rosie, 2006; Menges, 1996; Skelton, 2004; Young, 2006). Criticisms include:

The awards may not be perceived as highly valuable by many academic staff. There is evidence of active resistance against those who engage in Scholarship of Teaching from colleagues and disciplines where 'pedagogical knowledge' is perceived as generic and low level by fellow academics and administrators (Hardre & Cox, 2008; Henkel, 1997, 2005).

The criteria and processes used for deciding awards are not always explicit or arrived at in a methodologically sound manner (Badri & Abdulla, 2004). This can lead to scepticism that the process and decisions are not rigorous and defensible.

It is not clear what is being recognized—excellent practice or scholarship or combinations of both. For many, they have become conflated.

Awards privilege the contributions of individuals rather than teams (Benjamin, 2000).

Awards are perceived to require a great deal of effort for questionable value—how much effort must be expended and how likely is it to be successful. Would comparable effort produce more valuable results in the form of publication and research applications (Frame et al., 2006; Menges, 1996)?

Award winners who are nationally recognized are often relatively isolated from the ethos of their department and disciplinary colleagues and may not be celebrated or acknowledged by their institution (Frame et al., 2006; Gosling, 2004; Huber, 2004).

Awards, on the whole, remain a 'special' reward, a prize in the form of a single payment that can be spent on 'approved' activities such as professional development, conference attendance and computer equipment (Jackson, 2006). Rarely are awards a personal payment, to be spent at an individual's discretion. Promotion and tenure, on the other hand, are a 'continuing' reward, with salary and increments that continue throughout the career of the academic. For awards to be taken more seriously by the academic community, providing the award in the form of an ongoing salary increment is more likely to be seen as an institutional commitment to more appropriately recognising and rewarding teaching. This view is supported by Menges (1996), who questioned the value of awards for teaching that stand 'alone and apart' from institutional systems of reward and recognition (p. 8). For academic staff, reward and recognition is understood as promotion and tenure (Hardre & Cox, 2008; Higher Education Academy, 2009; O'Meara, 2005; Young, 2006).

While teaching awards have been established with the best of intentions, there is little evidence that these have contributed to any substantial change in the culture and substance of rewarding and recognizing the status of teaching relative to research (Frame et al., 2006; HEA, 2009; Huber, 2004).

2. Grants and professional development

There has been a significant investment at the national level to fund grants for teaching and learning initiatives and projects. Centres of teaching excellence have also been established in the UK and will soon be established in Sweden (Swedish National Agency for Higher Education, 2008).

Success in winning a teaching grant or centre is achieved through highly competitive application processes. The applications are subject to extensive peer review and selection processes. Centres of teaching excellence in the UK are funded to a similar level and duration as research centres. There has been significant national and institutional funding allocated to teaching grants in an attempt to establish structures and processes that replicate those in research so that teaching can be regarded as having the same scholarly opportunities and status as research.

The role of professional development in contributing to the understanding and practice of scholarship in teaching is well recognized (Healey & Jenkins, 2003; Kreber, 2006). The UK universities have established professional development programmes, with introductory teaching programmes accredited by the HEA and assessed against the Professional Standards Framework. These programmes have introduced university academics to the Scholarship of Teaching and scholarly practice with over 20,000 new staff having completed an accredited programme (Ramsden, 2008). There are currently no requirements for ongoing professional development to maintain accreditation.

In Australia, there is more variation of participation in professional development though most universities offer introductory teaching programmes (Preparing Academics to Teach in Higher Education, 2009). More recently, some universities now require that all new academic staff complete a Graduate Certificate in Tertiary Teaching to be eligible for a tenured position. This move to promote formal qualifications and professional development programmes is in the context of an international trend to professionalise teaching in universities (Ramsden, 2008; Ryan, Fraser, & Dearn, 2005). Strong evidence exists that sustained and extensive pedagogical teaching programmes are effective in encouraging teachers to adopt a reflective, learning-focused approach to teaching and subsequent improvement of students' learning outcomes (Postereff, Lindblom-Ylanne, & Nevgi, 2007; Prosser, Ramsden, Trigwell, & Martin, 2003), all outcomes of Scholarship of Teaching envisaged by Boyer (Diamond, 2002).

The provision of and access to professional development is regarded as a measure of an institution's commitment to the profession of teaching and an aid to assessing teaching quality (HEA, 2009). However, access to these programmes can be limited for part-time and casual teachers (Anderson, 2007). While universities rarely exclude their part-time and limited-term staff from professional development programmes, few pay their additional salary costs to ensure their attendance. With increasing numbers of academic staff in part-time and limited-term positions, this presents a serious challenge to universities to ensure that their staff are adequately prepared and supported to carry out their teaching effectively.

While professional development is recognized as a valuable way to assist staff to understand the complex facets of teaching and to better equip them for this part of their university role, it is not widely considered to be a reward or recognition of teaching. Rather, academic staff and their supervisors tend to consider professional development to be a hurdle that is undertaken on top of other competing demands on their time. Despite these reservations, professional development programmes offer the greatest promise in changing attitudes and values towards the Scholarship of Teaching (Elton, 2009).

3. Revised teaching criteria for evaluating and rewarding staff

Throughout the 1990s and 2000s, there has been a major shift in universities' commitment to improve tenure and promotion systems and to redefine and expand the definition of university work to more fully recognize the multiple forms of scholarship, in particular the Scholarship of Teaching (Braxton, Luckey, & Helland, 2006; Diamond, 2002; Glassick et al., 1997; O'Meara, 2005, 2006; Paulsen & Feldman, 2006). The extent to which universities have changed their mission statements and teaching evaluation criteria, developed institutional teaching strategies, provided incentive grants and developed flexible workloads to encourage a broader definition of scholarship has been well documented (Gibbs, 2001; O'Meara, 2005, 2006).

The three mechanisms for recognising and rewarding teaching have become more refined and embedded in university policy and practice over the past two decades. All three mechanisms now require evidence of Scholarship of Teaching in their criteria and practice, representing significant changes in the way that teaching is understood. However, the extent to which the status of teaching has changed relative to research, as was intended, has yet to be demonstrated.

IMPROVING THE STATUS OF TEACHING—ARE WE THERE YET?

A recent UK study of academic staff perceptions of whether the status, and hence reward and recognition of university teaching, is appropriate relative to research was a resounding 'no' (HEA, 2009). The participants uniformly agreed that research should be recognised as important and that it is recognized in promotions. However, they also agreed that teaching should be important but that it is not recognised in promotions. These findings and conclusions vary little from an earlier study carried out in Australia (Ramsden & Martin, 1996). The conclusion that 'teaching in UK higher education is still perceived to be valued and rewarded too little, both in formal personnel processes and in the dominant culture of institutions' (HEA, 2009, p. 53) is disappointing, given the initiatives that have been implemented over the previous 20 years to redress this imbalance.

It could be argued that academic staff may perceive that little has changed even though significant progress has been made. The university leaders in both studies did not think that the gap between the extent that teaching should be and is recognized is as great as their staff perceive (HEA, 2009; Ramsden & Martin, 1996). Has the situation actually changed with academic staff bound by a persistent misconception or myth that pervades academic work (Fairweather, 2002)?

A study of the review, promotion and tenure standards, processes and documents of 62 departments in 23 research universities in 13 states in the USA found that there had been significant broadening of the criteria and guidelines for tenure and promotion to encompass the Scholarship of Teaching (Hardre & Cox, 2008). The study also found that while there was greater clarity on the sources of evidence and documentation required, there existed a great deal of variation in judgments of academic performance with different conclusions being drawn on suitability for promotion or tenure on the same evidence. The judgments were highly influenced by the values of the discipline, department and institution. Despite this variability, these departments overwhelmingly continued to place research as primary, with teaching comparable or secondary and service last. It could be argued that this is an appropriate response from research universities. However, O'Meara (2005, 2006) also drew similar conclusions. Drawing on responses from almost 730 chief academic officers from universities in the USA she found that research universities, and those with research aspirations, were least likely to agree that aspects of teaching might be defined as scholarship on their campuses. She also noted the resistance of disciplines and academic staff to recognising different forms of scholarship, the variations within institutions, and the lack of clarity and agreement on what constitutes scholarship.

While these findings are disappointing, there are some examples where change has successfully taken place. For example, a regional comprehensive US university successfully established a system to recognise and reward the Scholarship of Teaching and Learning (Cruz, Ellern, Ford, Moss, & White, 2009). With strong leadership and commitment to realize its institutional mission, it is argued that the Scholarship of Teaching can be rewarded through tenure and promotion.

Fairweather (2005) investigated the relative value of teaching and research as evidenced by academic salary and whether this value changed during the late-1990s when the Boyer scholarships were gaining momentum. Using number of hours spent in teaching and number of publications as measures, Fairweather found that regardless of type of institution, time spent teaching was negatively reflected in salary, while publishing was positively reflected in salary. The lowest salaries were reserved for those who spent more time teaching, with this trend worsening in universities with a central mission of teaching and those who spent more hours teaching undergraduate students being the lowest paid of all. Fairweather argued that unless the value of teaching is reflected in salaries, universities will fail to convince their staff that their teaching work is valued. Fairweather's study does not attempt to determine the quality of the teaching or the quality of publications, using just the simple measures of hours in the classroom and number of publications related to salary. It should not be surprising that academic staff continue to perceive that they should devote more time to research and publications than to teaching.

The evidence suggests that on measures of perception, promotion, tenure and salary, teaching continues to be relegated to a lower status with promotion, tenure and higher salary directed to those who do disciplinary research and publish. With so many initiatives to promote the status of teaching at institutional and national levels over two decades, why has such limited success been achieved? Four tensions are proposed as contributing to the lack of progress.

1. Lack of a common agreement on the meaning and criteria for Scholarship of Teaching

There has been a significant body of scholarly work that has focused on developing, defining and clarifying what Scholarship of Teaching encompasses (Braxton et al., 2006; Kreber, 2002, 2005; Trigwell & Shale, 2004) and identifying ways in which it might be assessed (Braxton & Del-Favero, 2002; Glassick et al., 1997). The Carnegie Foundation with others have dedicated significant resources to promoting the Scholarship of Teaching through publications, journals, conferences, scholars, projects, discipline and institutional initiatives.

Despite this attention, the concept of the Scholarship of Teaching remains elusive and highly contested (Badley, 2003; Boshier, 2009; Kreber, 2002, 2005; Nicholls, 2004; Richlin, 2001; Skelton, 2004). Conceptual papers tease out distinctions between scholarship *of* teaching, scholarship *in* teaching and scholarship of *learning*, they highlight the growing tendency to link the term scholarship to the activities of teaching, such as teaching *as* scholarship, improvement of teaching, excellent teaching as evidence of scholarship and teaching professional development programmes as engaging in scholarship. While the overall intent continues to be focused on raising the status of teaching and highlighting the complexity of teaching, the result is confusion and contested understandings. Questions of quality, distinctions between practice, excellence and scholarship and developing shared meanings across disciplines, institutions and the sector are hurdles still to be overcome.

2. Research assessment, status and funding

The ways in which research is afforded higher status and is rewarded differentially from teaching was brought into sharp relief through the Research Assessment Exercise (RAE) in the UK. Disciplinary research has carried considerable status and financial benefits for many years (Gordon, D'Andrea, Gosling, & Stefani, 2003; Hardre & Cox, 2008; Young, 2006). As a consequence, many teaching-focused universities have diverted effort and resources from teaching to maximize their RAE scores. The RAE process also highlighted that not all research was considered to be of equal value in the eyes of those determining the quality of research. For example, in early RAE assessments, pedagogical research was not eligible for entry or funding (Trowler, Fanghanel, & Wareham, 2005). While pedagogical research in higher education can now be considered, it remains marginal in university and disciplinary practice. Some disciplines 'allow' pedagogical research, while others have actively discouraged or excluded it from the assessment exercise (Witman & Richlin, 2007; Young, 2006). The message from the disciplinary communities that determine what counts and what does not, is that pedagogical research is not 'real' or 'equal' to disciplinary research.

Funding is a key message that reinforces the status of research. Research assessment exercises carry considerable funding and confer status on the universities that do best. In contrast, funding for teaching is primarily formula driven, based on numbers of students or types of courses taught. Assessment of teaching quality carried out through the quality audit agencies confers no funding and status.

The general consensus is that the RAE has had a negative impact on teaching (Powney et al., 2003) and has been instrumental in the gradual structural separation of research and teaching at all levels of the university (Gordon et al., 2003). With this comes segmentation of the academic roles with increasing numbers of teaching-only and research-only positions and new categories of educational workers (Trowler et al., 2005). The language used in workload policy and associated guidelines highlights this role separation, with universities 'freeing up' the time of researchers by allocating more teaching to the 'non-research' staff. Hardre and Cox (2008) found that academic staff identified as being insufficiently research productive were assigned increased teaching loads, while those who were sufficiently productive were 'spared' increased teaching loads (p. 19). The very clear and consistent message such practices send is that successful academics do disciplinary research and less successful academics teach. This is concerning as Australia prepares to begin its research assessment exercise.

Worldwide, universities that occupy the top tiers of status are research intensive. Their academic staff are afforded the highest salaries, autonomy and scholarly esteem. US universities aspire to move 'up' the Carnegie classifications. The research intensive universities such as the Russell Group in the UK and the Group of Eight in Australia enjoy the highest status. Research universities are ranked the highest in almost all ranking systems.

3. Changing employment practices

Significant changes have been taking place in university workplace and employment practices in response to the increasing numbers of students entering higher education, the decreasing level of government funding and the segmentation of academic work. Part-time, limited-term, teaching-only, research-only and non-tenured positions have been created in greater numbers, with a decreasing proportion of tenured academic positions (Fairweather, 2005; Stromquist et al., 2007). This is considered to be a positive trend by governments and university management as a way to provide greater flexibility and efficiency to universities, a trend that has been mirrored in many other higher education systems (Stromquist et al., 2007). Staff in these positions are often excluded from opportunities to attain tenure and promotion and have little access to research or grant funding, collegial engagement, mentoring, disciplinary communities or professional development (Anderson, 2007; Powney et al., 2003). The discussion about rewarding and recognizing teaching in universities needs to be contextualised in an environment where there are decreasing numbers of full-time and tenured academics and increasing numbers of disempowered, disenfranchised, casual and short-term contract academics.

4. Difficulty of changing attitudes, particularly within disciplines

Identity is shaped and formed by strong and stable communities and the social processes generated within them (Henkel, 2005). For academics, the discipline is at the core of their academic identity and is reinforced by entrenched reward systems and interests, values and deeply ingrained ways of understanding research and inquiry (Henkel, 2005). For many academics, the concepts and practices of the Scholarship of Teaching are far removed from their disciplinary ways of understanding research and so are less valued or appreciated. Braxton et al. (2006) found that academics value the scholarship of discovery higher than all other forms of scholarship.

Concern that raising the status of teaching might lower the status of disciplinary research may lie at the heart of many academic's resistance to changing the status quo.

CONCLUSION

Universities have traditionally conferred more status and rewards on research achievements. Teaching has been acknowledged to have a lower status and therefore less access to rewards and recognition in comparison. A number of initiatives have attempted to redress the balance through defining the Scholarship of Teaching, revising university performance criteria, systems and processes, providing funding to establish equivalent structures to research such as centres of excellence, grants and awards. Many of the initiatives have been driven from outside the universities by governments and foundations, accompanied by a degree of grass roots support for reform from within the universities. At the same time, there has been an increase in the segmentation of academic work. The status and rewards associated with research continue to increase, with universities aspiring to achieve higher status and funding through research.

There have been a number of positive changes that have taken place in universities with significant shifts in policy (Gibbs, 2001; Gordon et al., 2003) but their articulation with funding models and human resource practices and systems remains variable at the university level and more variable at the department level (Hardre & Cox, 2008; O'Meara, 2005; Young, 2006). Awards, grants and professional development remain the primary mechanisms for recognising and rewarding teaching, whether it is for excellence in teaching or Scholarship of Teaching. Promotion and tenure continues to remain less certain for those whose academic work is focused on teaching and the learning of students.

Many of the initiatives to better recognize teaching have been driven from outside the university by state and national bodies strongly signalling to universities that they are serious about changing the current state of affairs (Gibbs, 2001; Gosling, 2004). However, many of the initiatives, such as the RAE, are at cross-purposes and demonstrate a lack of 'joined up thinking', which creates tensions that are not easily resolved (Trowler et al., 2005). Governments themselves will need to take some responsibility for contributing to the lack of progress made by universities. Universities, too, will need to examine the culture and values of their institutions and be clear in the signals they are sending to their staff. There are some promising university initiatives that are committed to rewarding and recognising the Scholarship of Teaching. For example, Lund University in Sweden has established a pedagogical academy that rewards those admitted with an award and salary increase and also rewards the department in which they are based (Andresson & Roxa, 2004). The University of Sydney introduced a Scholarship Index as one of a number of strategies to re-emphasise teaching as a scholarly activity (Asmar, 2002) and Western Carolina University successfully established promotion criteria and processes that recognize the Scholarship of Teaching (Cruz et al., 2009).

Leadership would appear to be the distinction between the universities that have made systematic and deep changes to recognizing and rewarding all four of the Boyer scholarships (O'Meara, 2005, 2006). There is evidence of changing attitudes by leaders and, with emerging leaders who have participated in professional development programmes or received grants or awards for teaching now moving up the promotion ranks, there is optimism that real change is possible. Ensuring that promotion committees include a senior member to champion Scholarship of Teaching would be a useful step to reinforce this message. However, if we are to separate out the perceptions, rhetoric and passions about what changes are and are not taking place, we will require comprehensive, systematic institutional research (Dooris, 2002), such as that carried out in the University of Illinois (McKinney et al., 2007). We need to proclaim and celebrate those who have been promoted on the basis of their teaching quality and scholarship. Not doing so will only perpetuate perceptions that teaching remains under recognized and unrewarded.

It is clear that many challenges remain to be addressed before we can claim that the Scholarship of Teaching is appropriately recognized and rewarded through tenure and promotion. However, the picture is not bleak, as the current mechanisms do provide significant opportunities for university staff to gain recognition. While the reward and recognition of Scholarship of Teaching must include tenure and promotion, it can and should be understood as broader than this. In a relatively short time, in university terms, there has been consistent and substantial progress. While some frustration may be expressed that more progress has not been made, few would suggest that we should not persist.

REFERENCES

Anderson, V. 'Contingent and marginalized: Academic development and part-time teachers' in *International Journal for Academic Development*, 2007, Vol. 12 No. 2, pp. 111–121.

Andresson, P. and Roxa, T. 'The pedagogical academy: A way to encourage and reward scholarly teaching' in *European Journal of Engineering Education*, 2004, Vol. 29 No. 4, pp. 559–569.

Asmar, C. 'Strategies to enhance learning and teaching in a research-extensive university' in *Journal for Academic Development*, 2002, Vol. 7 No. 1, pp. 18–30.

Badley, B. 'Improving the Scholarship of Teaching and Learning' in *Innovations in Education and Teaching International*, 2003, Vol. 40 No. 3, pp. 303–309.

Badri, M. A. and Abdulla, M. H. 'Awards of excellence in institutions of higher education: An AHP approach' in *International Journal of Educational Management*, 2004, Vol. 18 No. 4/5, pp. 224–242.

Benjamin, J. 'The Scholarship of Teaching in teams: What does it look like in practice?' in *Higher Education Research and Development*, 2000, Vol. 19 No. 2, pp. 191–204.

Boshier, R. 'Why is the Scholarship of Teaching and Learning such a hard sell?' in *Higher Education Research and Development*, 2009, Vol. 28 No. 1, pp. 1–15.

Boyer, E. *Scholarship reconsidered: Priorities of the professoriate.* Jossey-Bass, San Francisco, 1990.

Braxton, J. M. and Del Favero, M. 'Evaluating scholarship performance: Traditional and emergent assessment templates' in *New Direction in Institutional Research*, 2002, Vol. 114, Summer, pp. 19–31.

Braxton, J. M., Luckey, T. M. and Helland, P. A. 'Ideal and actual value patterns towards domains of scholarship in three types of colleges and universities' in *New Direction in Institutional Research*, 2006, Vol. 129, Spring, pp. 67–76.

Chalmers, D. *A review of Australian and international quality systems and indicators of learning and teaching*, 2007, V1.2, from www.catl.uwa.edu.au/projects/tqi. retrieved 3 August 2009.

Chalmers, D. and Thomson, K. *Snapshot of teaching and learning practice in Australian universities*, 2008, from www.catl.uwa.edu.au/projects/tqi retrieved 3 August 2009.

Chalmers, D., Lee, K. and Walker, B. *International and national quality teaching and learning performance models currently in use*, 2008, from www.catl.uwa.edu.au/projects/tqi. retrieved 3 August 2009.

Cruz, L., Ellern, J., Ford, G., Moss, H. and White, B. 'Recognition and reward: SOTL and the tenure process at a regional comprehensive university' in *MountainRise: The International Journal of the Scholarship of Teaching and Learning*, 2009, Summer, pp. 1–27.

Department for Education and Skills (DfES). *The future of higher education.* Department for Education and Skills, London, 2003.

Diamond, R. M. 'Changing priorities and the faculty reward system' in *New Directions in Higher Education.* Jossey-Bass, San Francisco, 1993, 81.

Diamond, R. M. 'Defining scholarship for the twenty-first century' in *New Directions for Teaching and Learning*, 2002, Vol. 90, Summer, pp. 73–79.

Dooris, M. J. 'Institutional research to enhance faculty performance' in *New Directions for Institutional Research*, 2002, Vol. 114, Summer, pp. 85–95.

El-Khawas, E. *Campus trends: Adjusting to new realities*. Higher Education Panel Report No. 86. American Council on Education, Washington, DC, 1996.

Elton, L. 'Continuing professional development in higher education: The role of Scholarship and Teaching and Learning' in *International Journal for the Scholarship of Teaching and Learning*, 2009, Vol. 3 No. 1, pp. 1–10.

Fairweather, J. 'The ultimate faculty evaluation: Promotion and tenure decisions' in *New Directions for Institutional Research*, 2002, Vol. 114, Summer, pp. 97–108.

Fairweather, J. 'Beyond the rhetoric: Trends in the relative value of teaching and research in faculty salaries' in *Journal of Higher Education*, 2005, Vol. 76 No. 4, pp. 401–422.

Frame, P., Johnson, M. and Rosie, A. 'Reward or award? Reflections on the initial experiences of winners of a National Teaching Fellowship' in *Innovations in Education and Teaching International*, 2006, Vol. 43 No. 4, pp. 409–419.

Gibbs, G. *Analysis of strategies for learning and teaching: Research report*, 2001, HEFCE 01/37a.

Glassick, C. E., Huber, M. T. and Maeroff, G. I. *Scholarship and the purpose of the university*. Jossey-Bass, San Francisco, 1997.

Gordon, G., D'Andrea, V., Gosling, D. and Stefani, L. *Building capacity for change: Research on the Scholarship of Teaching*. Report to HEFCE, 2003.

Gosling, D. 'The impact of a national policy to enhance teaching quality and the status, England, the United Kingdom' in *Quality Assurance in Education*, 2004, Vol. 12 No. 3, pp. 136–149.

Hardre, P. and Cox, M. 'Evaluating faculty work: Expectations and standards of faculty performance in research universities' in *Research Papers in Education*, 2008, Vol. 24 No. 4, pp. 383–419.

Healy, M. and Jenkins, A. 'Educational development through the disciplines' in Macdonald, R. and Eggins, H. (Eds), *The scholarship of academic development*. Open University Press and SRHE, Buckingham, 2003.

Henkel, M. 'Academic values and the university as a corporate enterprise' in *Higher Education Quarterly*, 1997, Vol. 51 No. 2, pp. 134–143.

Henkel, M. 'Academic identity and autonomy in a changing policy environment' in *Higher Education*, 2005, Vol. 49, pp. 155–176.

Higher Education Academy (HEA). *Reward and recognition of teaching in higher education*. Interim Report. Higher Education Academy and GENIE Centre for Excellence in Teaching and Learning, University of Leicester, Leicester, UK, 2009.

Higher Education Funding Council for England (HEFCE). *Enhancement, learning and teaching*, 2009, from www.hefce.ac.uk/learning/. retrieved 3 August 2009.

Huber, M. T. *Balancing acts: The Scholarship of Teaching and Learning in academic careers*. American Association for Higher Education and the Carnegie Foundation for the Advancement of Teaching, Washington, DC, 2004.

Hutchings, P. and Shulman, L. S. 'The Scholarship of Teaching: New elaborations, new developments' in *Change*, 1999, Vol. 31 No. 5, pp. 11–15.

Hutchings, P. *Approaching the Scholarship of Teaching and Learning*. The Carnegie Foundation for the Advancement of Teaching, Menlo Park, CA, 2000.

Jackson, M. 'Great classroom teaching and more: Awards for outstanding teaching evaluated' in *International Journal of Educational Management*, 2006, Vol. 20 No. 4, pp. 261–278.

Kreber, C. 'Controversy and consensus on the scholarship of university teaching movement' in *Studies in Higher Education*, 2002, Vol. 27 No. 2, pp. 151–167.

Kreber, C. 'Charting a critical course on the scholarship of university teaching movement' in *Studies in Higher Education*, 2005, Vol. 30 No. 4, pp. 389–405.

Kreber, C. 'Promoting inquiry-based learning through educational development units' in *New Directions for Teaching and Learning*, 2006, Vol. 107, Fall, pp. 79–88.

McKinney, K., Jarvis, P., Klass, T., et al. *The status of SoTL at Illinois State University*, 2007, from www.sotl.ilstu.edu/downloads/pdf/sotlQuant2007.pdf, retrieved 1 October 2009.

Menges, R. J. 'Awards to individuals: In honoring exemplary teaching' in *New Directions for Teaching and Learning*, 1996, Vol. 65, Spring, pp. 3–10.

Nicholls, G. 'Scholarship in teaching as a core professional value: What does this mean to the academic?' in *Teaching in Higher Education*, 2004, Vol. 9 No. 1, pp. 27–42.

O'Meara, K. A. 'Encouraging multiple forms of scholarship in faculty reward systems: Does it make a difference?' in *Research in Higher Education*, 2005, Vol. 46 No. 5, pp. 479–510.

O'Meara, K. A. 'Encouraging multiple forms of scholarship in faculty reward systems: Have academic cultures really changed?' in *New Directions in Institutional Research*, 2006, Vol. 129, Spring, pp. 77–95.

Palmer, A. and Collins, R. 'Perceptions of rewarding excellence: Motivation and the Scholarship of Teaching' in *Journal of Further and Higher Education*, 2006, Vol. 30 No. 2, pp. 193–205.

Paulsen, M. B. and Feldman, K. A. 'Exploring the dimensions of the Scholarship of Teaching and Learning: Analytics for an emerging literature' in *New Directions in Institutional Research*, 2006, Vol. 129, Spring, pp. 21–36.

Postereff, L., Lindblom-Ylanne, S. and Nevgi, A. 'The effect of pedagogical training on teacher education' in *Teacher and Teaching Education*, 2007, Vol. 23 No. 5, pp. 557–571.

Powney, J., Hamilton, S., Wilson, V., Kirk, S., Edward, S., Proctor, J., et al. *Appointment, retention and promotion of academic staff in higher education institutions*. Report to HEFCE by the Scottish Council for reaching in Education. University of Glasgow and Nottingham Trent University, 2003.

Preparing Academics to Teach in Higher Education (PATHE), 2009, from www.flinders.edu.au/teach/foundations/pathe.html, retrieved 1 November 2009

Prosser, M., Ramsden, P., Trigwell, K. and Martin, E. 'Dissonance in experience of teaching and its relation to the quality of student learning' in *Studies in Higher Education*, 2003, Vol. 28 No. 1, pp. 37–48.

Ramsden, P. *The future of higher education teaching and the student experience*, 2008, from www.dius.gov.uk/higher_education/shape_and_structure/he_debate/~/media/publications/T/teaching_and_student_experience_131008, retrieved 3 August 2009.

Ramsden, P. and Martin, E. 'Recognition of good university teaching: Policies from an Australian study' in *Studies in Higher Education*, 1996, Vol. 21 No. 3, pp. 299–315.

Richlin, L. 'Scholarly teaching and the Scholarship of Teaching' in *New Directions for Teaching and Learning*, 2001, Vol. 86, Summer, pp. 57–68.

Ryan, Y., Fraser, K. and Dearn, J. 'Towards a profession of tertiary teaching: Academic attitudes in Australia' in Fraser, K. (Ed.), *Educational development and leadership in higher education*. RoutledgeFalmer, London, 2005.

Skelton, A. 'Understanding "teaching excellence" in higher education: A critical evaluation of the National Teaching Fellowships Scheme' in *Studies in Higher Education*, 2004, Vol. 29 No. 4, pp. 451–468.

Stromquist, N. P., Gil-Anton, M., Colatrella, C., Mabokela, R. O., Smolentseva, A. and Balbachevsky, E. 'The contemporary professoriate: Towards a diversified or segmented profession' in *Higher Education Quarterly*, 2007, Vol. 61 No. 2, pp. 114–135.

Swedish National Agency for Higher Education. *National quality assurance for the period 2007–2012*, 2008, Report 2008,4.R, from www.hsv.se/download/18.4103c723118f5a4ec8f8000350/0804R.pdf, retrieved 1 October 2009.

Trigwell, K. and Shale, S. 'Student learning and the scholarship of university teaching' in *Studies in Higher Education*, 2004, Vol. 29 No. 4, pp. 523–536.

Trowler, P., Fanghanel, J. and Wareham, T. 'Freeing the chi of change: The Higher Education Academy and enhancing teaching and learning in higher education' in *Studies in Higher Education*, 2005, Vol. 30 No. 4, pp. 427–444.

Witman, P. D. and Richlin, L. 'The status of the Scholarship of Teaching and Learning in the disciplines' in *International Journal for the Scholarship of Teaching and Learning*, 2007, Vol. 1 No. 1, pp. 1–16.

Young, P. 'Out of balance: Lecturers' perceptions of differential status and rewards in relation to teaching and research' in *Teaching in Higher Education*, 2006, Vol. 11 No. 2, pp. 191–202.

PART TWO
International Organizations

INTERNATIONAL ORGANIZATIONS

UNITED NATIONS EDUCATIONAL, SCIENTIFIC AND CULTURAL ORGANIZATION (UNESCO)

7 place de Fontenoy, 75352 Paris 07 SP, France

Telephone: 1-45-68-10-00
Fax: 1-45-67-16-90
E-mail: bpi@unesco.org
Internet: www.unesco.org

Founded UNESCO was established in 1946 'for the purpose of advancing, through the educational, scientific and cultural relations of the peoples of the world, the objectives of international peace and the common welfare of mankind'.

Functions

UNESCO's activities are funded through a budget provided by member states and also through other sources, particularly the UNDP.

International Intellectual Cooperation

UNESCO assists the interchange of experience, knowledge and ideas through a world network of specialists. Apart from the work of its professional staff, UNESCO cooperates regularly with the national associations and international federations of scientists, artists, writers and educators, some of which it helped to establish.

UNESCO convenes conferences and meetings, and coordinates international scientific efforts; it helps to standardize procedures of documentation and provides clearing house services; it offers fellowships; and it publishes a wide range of specialized works, including source books and works of reference.

UNESCO promotes various international agreements, including the Universal Copyright Convention and the World Cultural and Natural Heritage Convention, which member states are invited to accept.

Operational Assistance

UNESCO has established missions that advise governments, particularly in the developing member countries, in the planning of projects; and it appoints experts to assist in carrying them out. The projects are concerned with the teaching of functional literacy to workers in development undertakings; teacher training; establishing of libraries and documentation centres; provision of training for journalists, radio, television and film workers; improvement of scientific and technical education; training of planners in cultural development; and the international exchange of persons and information.

Promotion of Peace

UNESCO organizes various research efforts on racial problems, and is particularly concerned with prevention of discrimination in education, and improving access for women to education. It also promotes studies and research on conflicts and peace, violence and obstacles to disarmament, and the role of international law and organizations in building peace. It is stressed that human rights, peace and disarmament cannot be dealt with separately, as the observance of human rights is a prerequisite to peace and not vice versa.

Member States

(July 2011)

Afghanistan
Albania
Algeria
Andorra
Angola
Antigua and Barbuda
Argentina
Armenia
Aruba (Associate Member)
Australia
Austria
Azerbaijan
Bahamas
Bahrain
Bangladesh
Barbados
Belarus
Belgium
Belize
Benin
Bhutan
Bolivia
Bosnia and Herzegovina
Botswana
Brazil
British Virgin Islands (Associate Member)
Brunei
Bulgaria
Burkina Faso
Burundi
Cambodia
Cameroon
Canada
Cape Verde
Cayman Islands (Associate Member)
Central African Republic
Chad
Chile
China, People's Republic
Colombia
Comoros
Congo, Democratic Republic
Congo, Republic
Cook Islands
Costa Rica
Côte d'Ivoire
Croatia
Cuba
Cyprus
Czech Republic
Denmark
Djibouti
Dominica
Dominican Republic
Ecuador
Egypt
El Salvador
Equatorial Guinea
Eritrea
Estonia
Ethiopia
Fiji
Finland
France
Gabon
Gambia
Georgia
Germany
Ghana
Greece
Grenada
Guatemala
Guinea
Guinea-Bissau
Guyana
Haiti
Honduras
Hungary
Iceland
India
Indonesia
Iran
Iraq
Ireland
Israel
Italy
Jamaica
Japan
Jordan
Kazakhstan
Kenya
Kiribati
Korea, Democratic People's Republic
Korea, Republic
Kuwait
Kyrgyzstan
Laos
Latvia
Lebanon
Lesotho
Liberia
Libya
Lithuania
Luxembourg
Macao (Associate Member)
Macedonia, former Yugoslav republic
Madagascar
Malawi
Malaysia
Maldives
Mali
Malta
Marshall Islands
Mauritania
Mauritius
Mexico
Micronesia, Federated States
Moldova
Monaco
Mongolia
Montenegro
Morocco
Mozambique
Myanmar
Namibia
Nauru
Nepal
Netherlands
Netherlands Antilles (Associate Member)

New Zealand
Nicaragua
Niger
Nigeria
Niue
Norway
Oman
Pakistan
Palau
Panama
Papua New Guinea
Paraguay
Peru
Philippines
Poland
Portugal
Qatar
Romania
Russia
Rwanda
St Christopher and Nevis
St Lucia
St Vincent and the Grenadines
Samoa
San Marino
São Tomé e Príncipe
Saudi Arabia
Senegal
Serbia
Seychelles
Sierra Leone
Slovakia
Slovenia
Solomon Islands
Somalia
South Africa
Spain
Sri Lanka
Sudan
Suriname
Swaziland
Sweden
Switzerland
Syria
Tajikistan
Tanzania
Thailand
Timor-Leste
Togo
Tokelau (Associate Member)
Tonga
Trinidad and Tobago
Tunisia
Turkey
Turkmenistan
Tuvalu
Uganda
Ukraine
United Arab Emirates
United Kingdom
United States of America
Uruguay
Uzbekistan
Vanuatu
Venezuela
Viet Nam
Yemen
Zambia
Zimbabwe

Organization

GENERAL CONFERENCE

The supreme governing body of the Organization. Meets in ordinary session once in two years and is composed of representatives of the member states and associate members.

EXECUTIVE BOARD

Consists of 58 members with a four-year term of office. Prepares the programme to be submitted to the Conference and supervises its execution. Meets twice or three times a year.

SECRETARIAT

Director-General KOÏCHIRO MATSUURA.

The Director-General has an international staff of some 2,500 civil servants. Of the professional staff (specialists in various disciplines and administrators), about two-thirds are on technical assistance missions in member states.

COOPERATING BODIES

In accordance with UNESCO's constitution, national commissions have been set up in most member states. These help to integrate work within the member states and the work of UNESCO.

UNESCO LIAISON OFFICES

UNESCO Liaison Office New York: Suite 900, 2 United Nations Plaza, New York, NY 10017, USA; tel. (212) 963-5995; fax (212) 963-8014; e-mail newyork@unesco.org; Dir HELENE-MARIE GOSSELIN.

UNESCO Liaison Office Geneva: Villa 'Les Feuillantines', Palais des Nations, 1211 Geneva, Switzerland; tel. 229173381; fax 229170064; e-mail geneva@unesco.org; Dir INGEBORG BREINES.

UNESCO FIELD OFFICES

(See also under relevant country)

Africa: Bujumbura (Burundi), Yaoundé (Cameroon), Kinshasa (Democratic Republic of Congo), Brazzaville (Republic of Congo), Addis Ababa (Ethiopia), Libreville (Gabon), Accra (Ghana), Nairobi (Kenya), Bamako (Mali), Maputo (Mozambique), Windhoek (Namibia), Abuja (Nigeria), Dakar (Senegal), Dar es Salaam (Tanzania), Harare (Zimbabwe).

Arab States: Cairo (Egypt), Amman (Jordan), Beirut (Lebanon), Rabat (Morocco), Ramallah (Palestinian Authority), Doha (Qatar).

Asia and the Pacific: Kabul (Afghanistan), Dhaka (Bangladesh), Phnom Penh (Cambodia), Beijing (People's Republic of China), New Delhi (India), Jakarta (Indonesia), Tehran (Iran), Almaty (Kazakhstan), Kathmandu (Nepal), Islamabad (Pakistan), Apia (Samoa), Bangkok (Thailand), Tashkent (Uzbekistan), Hanoi (Viet Nam).

Europe and North America: Venice (Italy), Bucharest (Romania), Moscow (Russia).

Latin America and the Caribbean: Santiago (Chile), San José (Costa Rica), Havana (Cuba), Guatemala (Guatemala), Port-au-Prince (Haiti), Kingston (Jamaica), México (Mexico), Lima (Peru), Montevideo (Uruguay).

Activities

EDUCATION

UNESCO has an overall policy of regarding education as a lifelong process. As an example, one implication is the increasing priority given to basic education for all, including early childhood care and development, primary education and adult education. This approach has been the guideline for many of the projects recently planned.

Each year, expert missions are sent to member states on request to advise on all matters concerning education. They also help with programmes for training abroad, and UNESCO provides study fellowships; in these forms of assistance, priority is given to the rural regions of developing member countries. The issues and problems involved in human resources development have been at the forefront of UNESCO's education

programme since the Organization's foundation. Objectives include the eradication of illiteracy, universal primary education, secondary education reform, technical and vocational education, higher education, adult, non-formal and permanent education, population education, and education of women and girls. 1990 was 'International Literacy Year', in the course of which a world conference on 'Education for All' was held in Thailand. In addition to its regular programme budget, UNESCO's extra-budgetary sources include the UN Development Programme (UNDP), the UN Children's Fund (UNICEF), the UN Population Fund (UNFPA) and the World Bank.

NATURAL SCIENCES

UNESCO's activities under the programme 'The Sciences in the Service of Development' aim to support and foster its member states' endeavours in higher education, advanced training and research in the natural sciences as well as in the application of these sciences to development, while at the same time attaching great importance to integrated and transdisciplinary approaches in its programmes. Activities in the natural sciences focus on the advancement, sharing and transfer of scientific and technological knowledge. At the same time, UNESCO continues to enhance human resources development and capacity-building through fellowships, grants, workshops, and seminars, and has produced a number of training tools. At national level, upon request, UNESCO also assists member states in policy-making and planning in the field of science and technology generally, and by organizing training programmes in these fields.

At the international level, UNESCO has over the years set up various forms of intergovernmental cooperation concerned with the environmental sciences and research on natural resources.

The Man and Biosphere Programme (MAB) gives emphasis to the reinforcement of the World Network of Biosphere Reserves, which aims to reconcile the conservation of biodiversity, the quest for social and economic development, and the maintenance of associated cultural values. The MAB also promotes an interdisciplinary approach to solving land-use problems through research and training, covering topics such as arid-land crops, sacred sites, coastal regions, the Sahel-Sahara observatories, and the biology and fertility of tropical soils.

The International Geological Correlation Programme, networking in more than 150 countries, contributes to comparative studies in earth sciences, including the history of the earth and its geological heritage. Geoscientific programmes have resulted in the production of thematic geological maps, postgraduate training, the application of remote sensing and geodata handling, and studies on climate change and industrial pollution. Guidelines and other awareness-building material on disaster prevention, preparedness and mitigation are also prepared.

The International Hydrological Programme deals with the scientific aspects of water resources assessment and management; and the Intergovernmental Oceanographic Commission (*q.v.*) promotes scientific investigation into the nature and resources of the oceans through the concerted action of its member states.

UNESCO provides the secretariat for the World Solar Programme (instituted in 1996) and has been designated lead agency for the Global Renewable Energy Education and Training Programme.

Major disciplinary programmes are promoted in the fields of physics (including support to the Abdus Salam Centre for Theoretical Physics), the chemical sciences, life sciences, including applied microbiology, mathematics, informatics, engineering sciences and new sources of energy.

SOCIAL AND HUMAN SCIENCES

UNESCO promotes teaching and research in the field of social and human sciences and encourages their application to a number of priority issues relating to education, development, urbanization, migration, youth, human rights, democracy and peace. The social sciences constitute a link between the Organization's two main functions: international intellectual cooperation leading to reflection on major problems, and action to solve these problems.

Among the Organization's subjects of research are: the complex relations between demographic changes and socio-cultural transformation on a global scale; the ways in which societies react to global climatic and environmental change; and changes affecting women and families.

UNESCO's programme gives high priority to the problems of young people, who are the first victims of unemployment, economic and social inequalities, and the widening gap between developing and industrialized countries. Under the mobilizing project 'Youth shaping the Future', an International Youth Clearing House and Information Service was to be established in order to increase awareness among public and private decision-makers of the needs, aspirations and potential of young people.

The struggle against all forms of discrimination is a central part of the Organization's programme. It disseminates scientific information aimed at combating racial prejudice, works to improve the status of women and their access to education, and promotes equality between men and women.

CULTURE

In the field of cultural heritage, the programme concentrates on three major lines of action: activities designed to foster the worldwide application of three international conventions aiming at protecting and preserving cultural property and inserting it into the life of contemporary societies; operational activities such as international safeguarding campaigns designed to help member states to conserve and restore monuments and sites; activities designed to improve the quality of museum management, to train specialists, to disseminate information, such as the most up-to-date conservation methods and techniques, and to promote greater public awareness of the value of cultural heritage.

In addition to a new edition of the *History of the Scientific and Cultural Development of Mankind,* work is continuing on histories of Africa, Latin America, the Caribbean and the civilizations of Central Asia, as well as on a six-volume publication on the various aspects of Islamic culture. A 10-year programme for the collection and safeguarding of the non-physical heritage (oral traditions, traditional music, dance, medicine, etc.) was launched in 1988.

With respect to the cultural dimension of development, the programme includes continuing assistance to member states in the preparation and evaluation of cultural development policies, plans and projects and in the training of cultural development personnel. Proclaimed by the UN General Assembly in December 1986, the World Decade for Cultural Development was launched in January 1988 and ended in 1997. The principal objectives of the Decade were: acknowledging the cultural dimension in development; asserting and enhancing cultural identities; broadening participation in cultural life; and promoting international cultural cooperation.

Following the approval by the General Conference of the Recommendation Concerning the Status of the Artist, efforts are being made to encourage its systematic application in the member states. Particular attention is given to the promotion of music, dance, theatre, architecture, fine arts, design, and arts and crafts, as well as the organization of interdisciplinary workshops and other experimental workshops related to the use of new technologies in artistic creation. To contribute to the mutual appreciation of cultures, UNESCO fosters, in the framework of the UNESCO Collection of Representative Works, translation and publication of literary masterpieces, publishes art albums, and produces and disseminates records, cassettes, audiovisual programmes and travelling art exhibitions.

UNESCO's programme for the promotion of books and reading includes activities for the development of book publishing, production and distribution infrastructures as well as for the training of personnel in all the book fields (including editing, layout and design, ad hoc management courses and courses at university level). A major thrust of the programme is aimed at reinforcing the development of reading at all levels of society (and especially that of children) through promotional activities, reading animation programmes, book weeks and book years.

COPYRIGHT

UNESCO's programme in the field of copyright consists of the following types of activities: (i) those aimed at heightening member states' awareness of the role played by copyright as a stimulant to intellectual creativity; (ii) the preparation of international instruments, the implementation of which is assured by the Secretariat (among these instruments should be cited the Universal Copyright Convention, which, guaranteeing the minimal protection of authors, facilitates the circulation of intellectual and cultural materials); (iii) activities intended to ensure the adequacy of traditional laws vis-à-vis the means of reproduction and of successive diffusion made possible by the latest technological revolutions in the field of reprography, satellites, computers, cable television, cassettes and magnetic discs; (iv) the organization of individual or group training courses intended mainly for the nationals of developing countries; (v) activities to promote access to protected works; (vi) publications and a database on legislation for copyright specialists; (vii) production of a video to increase public awareness of the importance of copyright.

COMMUNICATION, INFORMATION AND INFORMATICS

UNESCO's Communication, Information and Informatics Programme is designed to encourage the free flow of ideas and to help reinforce communication, information and informatics capacities in developing countries. Its major innovation is the extension of the 'free flow' principle to all forms of information contributing to the progress of societies, coupled with a comprehensive approach to challenges posed by the converging communication, information and informatics technologies.

Priorities in the area of communication include support for press freedom and the independence and pluralism of the media, reflection on their educational and cultural dimensions, and efforts to reduce violence on the screen. A series of regional seminars on independence and pluralism of the media has resulted in the declarations and plans of action adopted by those fora being implemented in collaboration with professional media organizations. Furthermore, World Press Freedom Day, initiated by UNESCO in commemoration of the Windhoek Declaration, is celebrated every year on 3 May. UNESCO supports the International Freedom of Expression Exchange network, which counts some 260 subscribers committed to protecting press freedom and the safety of journalists. The network of UNESCO Chairs in Communication (ORBICOM), which counts 16 chairs in all regions of the world, provides an enlarged framework for cooperation among media practitioners, researchers and industries. UNESCO also supports the Global Network of Journalism Training and the International Network of Women in the Media. The main operational arm of UNESCO's communication strategy, and a major funding channel, is the International Programme for the Development of Communication (IPDC), which focuses on strengthening news agencies, media training, community media and endogenous audiovisual production in developing countries. Since 1992, the IPDC has given priority to projects in favour of independent and pluralist media. The Programme is governed by a Council of 39 member states.

The General Information Programme (PGI) pursues its efforts to promote international cooperation in the fields of libraries, archives and documentation, with emphasis on appropriate policies, in particular for the widest possible access to information in the public domain, and for methodologies and tools for information management. Among recent initiatives is the launching of the UNESCO Network of Associated Libraries (UNAL), which already includes some 300 members. The Memory of the World Programme aims at safeguarding the recorded memory of humanity, with a number of pilot projects under way in different countries. Furthermore, UNESCO organizes international aid campaigns in this field, such as the programme for the restoration of the National and University Library of Bosnia and Herzegovina. PGI's enlarged mandate covers trends and societal impacts of information technologies. The International Congress on Ethical, Legal and Societal Aspects of Digital Information, held for the first time in Monte Carlo, Monaco in March 1997, provided a forum for reflection and debate in this field.

UNESCO also supports the development of computer networking and the training of informatics specialists, through its Intergovernmental Informatics Programme (IIP). UNESCO-sponsored regional informatics networks—RINAF (Africa), RINAS (Arab States), RINSCA and RINSEAP (Asia/Pacific) and RINEE (Eastern Europe)—serve as test grounds for effective networking options, including links to the Internet.

PUBLICATIONS

(Mostly in English, French and Spanish editions; Arabic, Chinese and Russian versions are also available in many cases.)

Atlas of the World's Languages in Danger of Disappearing (online).

Copyright Bulletin (4 a year).

Encyclopedia of Life Support Systems (online).
International Review of Education (4 a year).
International Social Science Journal (4 a year).
Museum International (4 a year).
Nature and Resources (4 a year).
The New Courier (4 a year).
Prospects (quarterly review on education).
UNESCO Sources (12 a year).
UNESCO Statistical Yearbook.
World Communication Report.
World Educational Report (every 2 years).
World Heritage Review (4 a year).
World Information Report.
World Science Report (every 2 years).

INTERNATIONAL BUREAU OF EDUCATION (IBE)

CP 199, 1211 Geneva 20, Switzerland
Telephone: 229177800
Fax: 229177801
E-mail: doc.centre@ibe.unesco.org
Internet: www.ibe.unesco.org
Founded 1925, the IBE became an intergovernmental org. in July 1929 and was incorporated into UNESCO in January 1969 as an int. centre of comparative education.

COUNCIL

The Council of the IBE is composed of representatives of 28 member states designated by the General Conference of UNESCO.
Dir: PIERRE LUISONI (Switzerland).

FUNCTIONS

International Conference on Education (irregular).
International Education Library: 120,000 vols; c. 1,000 journals received regularly; 500,000 research reports on microfiche.

BUDGET

Financed from the budget of UNESCO.

PUBLICATIONS

Educational Innovation and Information (4 a year, newsletter).
Prospects, international comparative education review (4 a year).

INTERNATIONAL INSTITUTE FOR EDUCATIONAL PLANNING (IIEP)

7–9 rue Eugène Delacroix, 75116 Paris, France
Telephone: 1-45-03-77-00
Fax: 1-40-72-83-66
E-mail: information@iiep.unesco.org
Internet: www.unesco.org/iiep

(Regional office: IIEP–Buenos Aires, Aguero 2071, 1425 Buenos Aires, Argentina; tel. (114) 806-9366; fax (114) 806-9458; e-mail webmaster@iipe-buenosaires.org.ar)
Founded 1963 to serve as a world centre for advanced training and research in educational planning. Its purpose is to help all member states of UNESCO in their social and economic development efforts, by enlarging the fund of knowledge about educational planning and the supply of competent experts in this field.
Legally and administratively a part of UNESCO, the Institute enjoys intellectual autonomy, and its policies and programme are controlled by its own Governing Board, under special statutes voted by the General Conference of UNESCO.
Chair. of Governing Board: Dato' ASIAH BT ABU SAMAH (Malaysia)
Dir: Dr GUDMUND HERNES (Norway)
Publication: A catalogue of publications, listing 440 titles, is available on request.

UNITED NATIONS UNIVERSITY (UNU)

53–70, Jingumae 5-chome, Shibuya-ku, Tokyo 150-8925, Japan
Telephone: (3) 3499-2811
Fax: (3) 3499-2828
E-mail: mbox@hq.unu.edu
Internet: www.unu.edu
(Office in Europe: c/o UNESCO, 1 rue Miollis, 75732 Paris Cedex 15, France; tel. 1-45-68-30-08; fax 1-40-65-91-86)
(Office in North America: Room DC2-1462-70, United Nations, New York, NY 10017, USA; tel. (212) 963-6387; fax (212) 371-9454)
The University is an autonomous institution within the UN framework and is sponsored jointly by the UN and UNESCO. It is guaranteed academic freedom by a charter approved by the General Assembly in 1973. Its work began in September 1975. The UNU is governed by a 24-mem. Council who are appointed by the Sec.-Gen. of the UN and the Dir-Gen. of UNESCO to serve for six years. They come from various regions of the world and have diverse academic backgrounds.

The UNU is funded by voluntary contributions from the govts of many countries, bilateral and multilateral development assistance agencies, foundations, and other public and private sources. The UNU receives no funds from the budget of the UN; contributions are made to the UNU Endowment Fund, which yields investment income, and to its operating funds, as well as to specific programmes and projects.

The UNU undertakes problem-oriented, multidisciplinary research on the problems of human survival, development and welfare that are the concern of the UN and its agencies, and works to strengthen research and training capabilities in developing countries. The programme covers the areas of peace and governance, development, environment, and science and technology. Although the UNU has no students or degree courses, it conducts various training activities in association with its programme and provides fellowships for postgraduate scientists and scholars from developing countries.

The research, training and dissemination activities of the UNU are carried out mainly through networks of collaborating institutions and individual scientists and scholars. These include associated institutions, which are universities and research institutes linked with the University under general agreements of cooperation. The programme is coordinated by the University Centre in Tokyo, Japan, and by research and training centres and programmes that are being established by the UNU to deal with long-term problems and needs. The UNU's research and training centres and programmes include: the UNU World Institute for Development Economics Research in Helsinki, Finland; the UNU Institute for New Technologies in Maastricht, Netherlands; the UNU International Institute for Software Technology in Macao; the UNU Institute for Natural Resources in Africa in Accra, Ghana, with a mineral resources unit in Lusaka, Zambia; the UNU Institute of Advanced Studies in Tokyo, Japan; the UNU Programme for Biotechnology in Latin America and the Caribbean in Caracas, Venezuela; the UNU International Leadership Academy in Amman, Jordan; the UNU International Network on Water, Environment and Health in Ontario, Canada; the UNU Programme on Comparative Regional Integration Studies in Bruges, Belgium; the UNU Food and Nutrition Programme for Human and Social Development, based at Cornell University, USA; the UNU Geothermal Training Programme and UNU fisheries Training Programme, both based in Iceland; and the initiative on Conflict Resolution and Ethnicity, jointly managed by the UNU and the University of Ulster, UK.
Rector: Prof. HANS J. A. VAN GINKEL
Sr Vice-Rector for Environment and Sustainable Development Programme: Prof. ITARU YASUI
Sr Vice-Rector for Peace and Governance Programme: Prof. RAMESH THAKUR

UNIVERSITY FOR PEACE

Apdo postal 138, Ciudad Colón, Costa Rica
Telephone: 2-49-10-72
Fax: 2-49-19-29
E-mail: info@upeace.org
Internet: www.upeace.org
Founded 1980 by the UN but financially independent; conducts academic research on all aspects of peace, including disarmament, conflict resolution and mediation, the relation between peace and development, and the effects on peace of migration and refugees; various international and governmental institutions are collaborating with the University; initiated a programme of extensive reforms and expansion in 1999; World Centre for Research and Training in Conflict Resolution established in Bogotá, Colombia, in 2001.
Library of 8,000 vols
First students were admitted in 1985.
Chancellor: Dr GRAÇA MACHEL (Mozambique)
Rector: JULIA MARTON-LEFÈVRE (France)
Number of teachers: 16
Number of students: 130
Publication: *Peace and Conflict Monitor* (12 a year, in English).

INTERNATIONAL COUNCIL OF SCIENTIFIC UNIONS

International Council of Scientific Unions (ICSU)/Conseil International des Unions Scientifiques: 5 rue Auguste Vacquerie, 75116 Paris, France; tel. 1-45-25-03-29; fax 1-42-88-94-31; e-mail secretariat@icsu.org; internet www.icsu.org; f. 1931; succeeded the Int. Research Council (f. 1919), to coordinate int. efforts in the different brs of science and its applications; to initiate the formation of int. asscns or unions deemed to be useful to the progress of science; to enter into relations with the govts of the countries adhering to the Council in order to promote investigations falling within the competence of the Council; adhering orgs represent 103 countries and 27 int. unions; in December 1946 an agreement was signed between UNESCO and ICSU recognizing the latter as the coordinating and representative body of int. scientific unions; Pres. JANE LUBCHENKO; Sec.-Gen. ANA MARIA CETTO (Mexico); Treas. ROGER ELLIOTT (UK).

UNIONS FEDERATED TO THE ICSU

International Astronomical Union/Union Astronomique Internationale: 98 bis blvd Arago, 75014 Paris, France; tel. (1) 43-25-83-58; fax (1) 43-25-26-16; e-mail iau@iap.fr; internet www.iau.org; f. 1919 to facilitate cooperation between astronomers internationally and to advance the study of astronomy in all aspects; 66 affiliated countries, 9,000 individual mems; Pres. RONALD D. EKERS (Australia); Gen. Sec. ODDBJØRN ENGVOLD (Norway); publs *Transactions of the International Astronomical Union Symposia organized by the International Astronomical Union*, *Highlights of Astronomy* (every 3 years).

International Geographical Union/Union Géographique Internationale: c/o Prof. Ronald F. Abler, 2246 North Pollard St, Arlington, VA 22207-3805, USA; tel. (202) 431-6271; fax (703) 527-3227; e-mail igu@aag.org; internet www.igu-net.org; f. 1922 to encourage the study of problems relating to geography, to promote and coordinate research requiring int. cooperation, and to organize int. congresses and commissions; 83 mem. countries; Pres. Prof. ADALBERTO VALLEGA; Sec.-Gen. and Treas. Prof. RONALD F. ABLER; publ. *Bulletin* (1 a year).

International Mathematical Union: c/o Phillip A. Griffiths, Institute for Advanced Study, Einstein Dr., Princeton, NJ 08540, USA; fax (609) 683-7605; internet www.mathunion.org; f. 1950 to promote int. cooperation in mathematics; to support the Int. Congress of Mathematicians and other int. scientific meetings or conferences; to encourage and support other int. mathematical activities that contribute to the devt of mathematical science—pure, applied or educational; 52 mem. countries; 2 commissions: Int. Comm. on Mathematical Instruction, Comm. for Devt and Exchange; Jt Int. Comm. on the History of Mathematics, with the Int. Comm. on the History of Mathematics; Pres. JOHN M. BALL (UK); Sec. PHILLIP A. GRIFFITHS (USA).

International Union for Physical and Engineering Sciences in Medicine: c/o Prof. Heikki Terio, Biomedical Eng., MTA C2:44, Karolinska, Univ. Hospital, Huddinge, Stockholm 14186, Sweden; tel. (8) 585-808-52; fax (8) 585-862-90; e-mail heikki.terio@karolinska.se; internet www.iupesm.org; f. 1982; organizes and coordinates the triennial World Congress for Medical Physics and Biomedical Engineering; organizes and/or coordinates int. meetings or conferences for constituent orgs; represents the interests of members in the Int. Council for Science; disseminates, promotes and/or develops standards of practice in the fields of medical physics and biomedical engineering to enhance the quality of health care worldwide; 40,000 mems; Pres. Prof. BARRY ALLEN (Australia); Sec.-Gen. Prof. HEIKKI TERIO (Sweden).

International Union for Pure and Applied Biophysics: c/o Institute of Physics, 76 Portland Garching, Germany; tel. (20) 74704937; fax (20) 74704804; e-mail admin.iupap@iop.org; internet www.iupab.org; f. 1961 to organize int. cooperation in biophysics and promote communication between biophysics and allied subjects, to encourage nat. cooperation between biophysical socs, and to contribute to the advancement of biophysical knowledge; 59 affiliated mems, 19 int. commissions, 4 int. assoc. commissions; Pres. Prof. S. USHIODA (Japan); Sec.-Gen. Prof. Dr ROBERT KIRBY HARRIS (UK); publ. *Quarterly Reviews of Biophysics*.

International Union of Biochemistry and Molecular Biology: c/o Prof. Michael P. Walsh, Dept. of Biochemistry & Molecular Biology, Univ. of Calgary, 3330 Hospital Drive N.W., T2N 4N1 Calgary Canada; tel. 3-90-24-18-32; fax 3-90-24-19-21; e-mail walsh@ucalgary.ca; internet www.iubmb.org; f. 1955 to encourage the continuance of a series of Int. Congresses and Conferences of Biochemistry and Molecular Biology; to promote int. coordination of research, discussion and publication; to organize permanent cooperation between the socs representing biochemistry and molecular biology in the adherent countries; to contribute to the advancement of biochemistry and molecular biology in all its int. aspects; mems: 49 adhering bodies, 24 assoc. adhering bodies, 7 assoc. orgs; Pres. Prof. ANGELO AZZI (USA); Sec.-Gen. Prof. MICHAEL WALSH (Canada); Treas. Prof. JOAN GUINOVART (Spain); publs *Biochemistry and Molecular Biology Education* (12 a year), *Biofactors* (4 a year), *Biotechnology and Applied Biochemistry* (6 a year), *IUBMB Life* (12 a year), *Molecular Aspects of Medicine* (6 a year), *Trends in Biochemical Sciences* (12 a year).

International Union of Biological Sciences/Union Internationale des Sciences Biologiques: Bâtiment 442, Université Paris-Sud 11, 91405 Orsay, France; tel. 1-69-15-50-27; fax 1-69-15-79-47; e-mail secretariat@iubs.org; internet www.iubs.org; f. 1919; mems: 41 countries and 83 int. scientific orgs; promotes int. cooperation in biological research and studies; IUBS programmes on biological diversity, integrative biology, bioethics, biological education, ageing, bio-energy, integrative climate change biology; organizes int. congresses on biological sciences; Pres. GIORGIO BERNARDI (Italy); Exec. Dir NATHALIE FOMPROIX (France); publ. *Biology International* (2 a year).

International Union of Crystallography/Union Internationale de Cristallographie: c/o M. H. Dacombe, 2 Abbey Sq., Chester, CH1 2HU, UK; tel. (1244) 345431; fax (1244) 344843; e-mail execsec@iucr.org; internet www.iucr.org; f. 1947 to promote int. cooperation in crystallography; to contribute to the advancement of crystallography in all its aspects, including related topics concerning the non-crystalline states; to facilitate int. standardization of methods, of units, of nomenclature and of symbols used in crystallography; and to form a focus for the relations of crystallography to other sciences; 20 commissions; 40 mem. countries; Pres. Prof. S. LARSEN (Denmark); Gen. Sec. and Treas. Prof. S. LIDIN (Sweden); Exec. Sec. M. H. DACOMBE; publs *Acta Crystallographica* (Sections A and B, 6 a year; Sections C, D, E and F, 12 a year), *Journal of Applied Crystallography* (6 a year), *Journal of Synchrotron Radiation* (6 a year).

International Union of Food Science and Technology: POB 61021, No. 19, 511 Maple Grove Drive, Oakville, ON L6J 6X0, Canada; tel. (905) 815-1926; fax (905) 815-1574; e-mail secretariat@iufost.org; internet www.iufost.org; f. 1970; encourages int. cooperation and exchange of scientific and technical information among scientists, food technologists and specialists of mem. nations; supporting int. progress in both theoretical and applied areas of food science; advances technology in the processing, manufacturing, preservation, storage and distribution of food products; encourages appropriate education and training in food science and technology; fostering professionalism and professional organization among food scientists and technologists; nat. representatives in 65 mem. countries; Pres. GEOFFREY CAMPBELL-PLATT (UK); Sec.-Gen. and Treas. JUDITH MEECH (Canada); publs *Food Science and Technology* (6 a year), *The International Review of Food Science and Technology* (1 a year), *The World of Food Science* (online, jtly with Institute of Food Technologists), *Trends in Food Science and Technology* (12 a year).

International Union of Geodesy and Geophysics/Union Géodésique et Géophysique Internationale: ; tel. (721) 60844494; fax (721) 71173; e-mail secretariat@iugg.org; internet www.iugg.org; f. 1919 to promote the study of problems relating to the form and physics of the earth; to initiate, facilitate and coordinate research into those problems of geodesy and geophysics that require int. cooperation; federation of 8 asscns representing Cryospheric Sciences, Geodesy, Geomagnetism and Aeronomy, Hydrological Sciences, Meteorology and Atmospheric Physics, Physical Sciences of the Oceans, Seismology and Physics of the Earth's Interior, and Volcanology and Chemistry of the Earth's Interior, which meet at the Gen. Assemblies of the Union; jt cttees of the various asscns either among themselves or with other unions; organizes scientific meetings and sponsors various permanent services, the object of which is to collect, analyse and publish geophysical data; 69 mem. countries; Pres. TOM BEER (Australia); Vice-Pres. HARSH GUPTA (India); Sec.-Gen. ALIK ISMAIL-ZADEH (Germany); publs *IUGG E-Journal*, *IUGG Yearbook*, *Proceedings of Assemblies*.

International Union of Geological Sciences/Union Internationale des Sciences Géologiques: IUGS Secretariat, MS-917, US Geological Survey, Reston, VA USA; tel. (703) 648-6050; fax (703) 648-4227; e-mail iugs@usgs.gov; internet www.iugs.org; f. 1961 from the International Geological Congress; 120 mem. countries; Pres. Prof. ALBERTO C. RICCARDI (Argentina); Vice-Pres. Prof. JACQUES CHARVET (France), Prof. OCHIR GEREL (Mongolia); Sec.-Gen. Dr PETER T. BOBROWSKY (Canada); Treas. Prof. WILLIAM CAVAZZA (Italy); publs *Episodes*, *International Geoscience Newsmagazine* (4 a Year), Reviews or annotated bibliographies on geological topics of current interest (irregular).

International Union of Immunological Societies/Union Internationale des Sociétés d'Immunologie: c/o Gerlinde Jahn, Vienna Academy of Postgraduate Medical Education and Research, Alser Str. 4, 1090 Vienna, Austria; tel. (1) 405138318; fax (1) 4078274; e-mail iuis-central-office@medacad .org; internet www.iuisonline.org; f. 1971; 65 nat. and regional socs; Pres. STEFEN E. H. KAUFFMANN (Germany); Sec.-Gen. Prof. SEPPO MERI (Finland).

International Union of Microbiological Societies/Union Internationale des Sociétés de Microbiologie: c/o Dr Robert Samson, Head of Applied and Industrial Mycology, Centraalbureau voor Schimmelcultures, Utrecht, 3508 AD, The Netherlands; tel. (30) 2122600; fax (30) 2512097; e-mail samson@cbs.knaw.nl; internet www .iums.org; f. 1930; mems: 90 nat. socs; Pres. KARL-HEINZ SCHLEIFER (Germany); Sec.-Gen. Dr ROBERT SAMSON (Australia); publs *Archives of Virology* (12 a year), *Biological* (4 a year), *International Journal of Food Microbiology* (26 a year), *International Journal of Systematic and Evolutionary Microbiology* (12 a year).

International Union of Nutritional Sciences/Union Internationale des Sciences de la Nutrition: c/o Dr Osman Galal, UCLA School of Public Health, Community Health Sciences, 36-081 CHS, POB 951772, Los Angeles, CA 90095-1772, USA; tel. (310) 206-9639; fax (310) 794-1805; e-mail info@iuns.org; internet www.iuns .org; f. 1946 to study the science of nutrition and its applications; 80 adhering bodies; Pres. Dr RICARDO UAUY (Chile); Sec.-Gen. Dr OSMAN GALAL (USA).

International Union of Pharmacology/ Union Internationale de Pharmacologie: c/o Lindsay Hart, Dept of Pharmacology, College of Medicine, University of California, Irvine, CA 92697, USA; tel. (949) 824-1178; fax (949) 824-4855; internet www.iuphar.org; f. 1959 as section of Int. Union of Physiological Sciences, independent 1966; promotes international coordination of research, discussion, symposia, and publication in the field of pharmacology; cooperates with WHO in matters concerning drugs and drug research, and with related int. unions; four-yearly int. congresses; 52 national and 3 regional mem. socs; integral Division of Clinical Pharmacology and sections of Toxicology, Drug Metabolism and Gastro-intestinal Pharmacology, which also arrange int. meetings; Pres. Prof. PAUL M. VANHOUTTE (People's Republic of China); Sec.-Gen. Dr SUE PIPER DUCKLES (USA).

International Union of Physiological Sciences/Union Internationale des Sciences Physiologiques: c/o Susan Orsoni, LGN, Bâtiment CERVI, Hôpital de la Pitié Salpêtrière, 83 blvd de l'Hôpital, 75013 Paris, France; tel. 1-42-17-75-37; fax 1-42-17-75-3; e-mail orsoni@chups.jussieu.fr; internet www.iups.org; f. 1953 for the advancement of physiological sciences, to facilitate the dissemination of knowledge in the field of physiology, to promote the Int. Congresses of Physiology and such other meetings as may be useful for the advancement of physiological sciences; 54 mem. countries; Pres. Prof. AKIMICHI KANEKO (Japan); Sec.-Gen. Prof. OLE PETERSEN (UK); publ. *Physiology* (4 a year).

International Union of Psychological Science/Union Internationale de Psychologie Scientifique: c/o Pierre Ritchie, Ecole de Psychologie, Université d'Ottawa, 145 Jean-Jacques Lussier, CP 450, Succur-

sale A, Ottawa, ON K1N 6N5, Canada; tel. (613) 562-5800 ext. 4827; fax (613) 562-5169; e-mail pritchie@uottawa.ca; internet www .iupsys.org; f. 1951 at the 13th Int. Congress of Psychology; Int. Congress of Psychology held every 4 years; WHO spec. consultative status; mem. of UN Economic and Social Council, Int. Council for Science, Int. Social Science Council; 70 nat. mems; Pres. BRUCE OVERMIER (USA); Sec.-Gen. PIERRE RITCHIE (Canada); publs *International Journal of Psychology* (6 a year), *Psychology Resource CD-ROM* (1 a year).

International Union of Pure and Applied Chemistry/Union internationale de chimie pure et appliquée: POB 13757, Research Triangle Park, NC 27709-3757, USA; tel. (919) 485-8700; fax (919) 485-8706; e-mail secretariat@iupac.org; internet www.iupac.org; f. 1919 to promote cooperation among chemists of the mem. countries; to study topics of int. importance that require regulation, standardization or codification; to cooperate with other int. orgs that deal with topics of a chemical nature; to contribute to the advancement of pure and applied chemistry in all its aspects; 49 mem. countries; Pres. Prof. BRYAN R. HENRY (Canada); Exec. Dir Dr JOHN W. JOST (USA); Sec.-Gen. Prof. DAVID ST C. BLACK (Australia); publs *Chemistry International* (6 a year), *Pure and Applied Chemistry* (12 a year).

International Union of Pure and Applied Physics/Union internationale de physique pure et appliquée: c/o Institute of Physics, 76 Portland Pl., London, W1B 1NT, UK; tel. (20) 7470-4849; fax (20) 7470-4861; e-mail admin.iupap@iop.org; internet www.iupap.org; f. 1922; promotes and encourages int. cooperation in physics and facilitate worldwide devt of science; 53 mem. countries; Pres. SUKATSU USHIODA (Japan); Sec.-Gen. ROBERT KIRBY-HARRIS (UK); publ. *IUPAP News Bulletin* (5 or 6 a year).

International Union of the History and Philosophy of Science: c/o Prof. Juan José Saldaña, National University of Mexico, Apdo Postal 21-388, 04000 Mexico, DF, Mexico; tel. (55) 5622-1864; fax (55) 5544-6316; e-mail dhs@servidor.unam.mx; f. 1956; divisions of History of Science and of Logic, Methodology and Philosophy of Science; Sec.-Gen. Prof. JUAN JOSÉ SALDAÑA.

International Union of Theoretical and Applied Mechanics/Union Internationale de Mécanique Théorique et Appliquée: c/o Prof. Dick H. van Campen, Dept of Mechanical Eng., Technische Universiteit Eindhoven, Den Dolech 2, POB 513, 5600 MB Eindhoven, The Netherlands; fax (40) 2461418; e-mail sg@iutam.net; internet www .iutam.net; f. 1946; provides a forum for persons and orgs engaged in scientific work (theoretical or experimental) in mechanics and related sciences; organizes int. meetings for subjects in this field; and engages in other activities to promote the devt of mechanics as a science; the Union is directed by its Gen. Assembly, which is composed of representatives of the orgs affiliated to the Union and of elected mems; 51 mem. countries; Pres. Prof. BEN FREUND (USA); Sec.-Gen. Prof. DICK H. VAN CAMPEN (Netherlands); publs *Proceedings of IUTAM Symposia* (irregular), *Proceedings of IUTAM World Congress* (every 4 years).

International Union of Toxicology: 1821 Michael Faraday Drive, Suite 300, Reston, VA 20190, USA; tel. (703) 438-3103; fax (703) 438-3113; e-mail iutoxhq@iutox.org; internet www.iutox.org; f. 1980; fosters int. scientific cooperation among toxicologists and pro-

motes global acquisition, dissemination and use of knowledge in the science of toxicology; ensures continued training and devt of toxicologists worldwide; International Congress on Toxicology every 3 years; sponsors Congresses on Toxicology in Developing Countries every 3 years; affiliated to WHO; 55 nat. and regional mems representing c. 20,000 toxicologists; Pres. Dr DANIEL ACOSTA (USA); Sec.-Gen. Prof. Dr ELAINE FAUSTMAN (USA).

International Union of Radio Science/ Union Radio-Scientifique Internationale: c/o INTEC, Ghent Univ., Sint-Pietersnieuwstraat 41, 9000 Ghent, Belgium; tel. (9) 264-33-20; fax (9) 264-42-88; e-mail info@ursi .org; internet www.ursi.org; f. 1919; encourages and coordinates research in the field of radio, telecommunication and electronic sciences, and facilitates the establishment of common radio measurement techniques and standards; 44 mem. cttees; Pres. Prof. FRANÇOIS LEFEUVRE (France); Sec.-Gen. Prof. PAUL LAGASSE (Belgium); Exec. Sec. INGE HELEU (Belgium); Admin. Sec. INGE LIEVENS (Belgium); publs *Records of General Assemblies* (every 3 years), *The Radio Science Bulletin* (4 a year).

COMMITTEES

Tasks that fall within the sphere of activities of two or more Unions have been undertaken by the following Scientific or Special Committees set up by the ICSU:

Committee on Capacity Building in Science: c/o Dr Shirley Malcom, AAAS, 1200 New York Ave, Washington, DC 20005, USA; tel. (202) 326-6720; f. 1993; promotes to the public and to policy-makers an understanding and appreciation of the role of science in modern society and provides science education information to primary school teachers worldwide; Chair. Dr SHIRLEY MALCOM.

Committee on Data for Science and Technology: c/o Kathleen Cass, 5 rue Auguste Vacquerie, 75016 Paris, France; tel. (1) 45-25-04-96; fax (1) 42-88-14-66; e-mail codata@dial.oleane.com; internet www.codata.org; f. 1966; promotes improvement in quality, reliability and accessibility of scientific data, incl. quantitative information on the properties and behaviour of matter, and other experimental and observational data; 19 nat. and 15 scientific union mems; Pres. Prof. HUADONG GUO (China); Exec. Dir KATHLEEN CASS (France); Sec.-Gen. Dr ROBERT CHEN (USA); publs *International Compendium of Numerical Data Projects*, *International Conference Proceedings*.

Committee on Space Research: c/o CNES, 2 pl. Maurice Quentin, 75039 Paris Cedex 01, France; tel. 1-44-76-75-10; fax 1-44-76-74-37; e-mail cospar@cosparhq.cnes.fr; internet cosparhq.cnes.fr; f. 1958 to promote scientific research in space on an int. level, with an emphasis on the exchange of results, information and opinions; promotes the use of space science for the benefit of mankind and for its adoption by developing countries and new space-faring nations; organizes scientific assemblies every 2 years; advises the UN and other int. orgs on space research matters and on the assessment of scientific issues in which space can play a role; prepares scientific and technical standards related to space research; mems: 44 countries and 13 int. scientific unions; Pres. Prof. R.-M. BONNET (France); Exec. Dir Dr J.-L. FELLOUS; Assoc. Dir A. JANOFSKY; publs *Advances in Space Research*, *Space Research Today*.

Scientific Committee on Antarctic Research: SCAR Secretariat, Scott Polar Research Institute, Lensfield Rd, Cambridge, CB2 1ER, UK; tel. (1223) 336-550; fax (1223) 336-549; e-mail info@scar.org; internet www .scar.org; f. 1958 by ICSU to continue the promotion of int. cooperation in scientific research in the Antarctic; holds biennial conference; organizes meetings, workshops and symposia; establishes and coordinates int. programmes to address major scientific questions in Antarctica; 31 full mems (nat. acads of science and scientific unions), 9 union mems, 5 assoc. mems; Pres. Prof. MAHLON C. KENNICUTT (USA); Exec. Dir Dr MIKE D. SPARROW; Exec. Officer Dr RENUKA BADHE; publs *SCAR Bulletin* (4 a year), *SCAR Report* (irregular).

Scientific Committee on Oceanic Research: Robinson Hall, College of Earth, Ocean, and Environment, Univ. of Delaware, Newark, DE 19716, USA; tel. (302) 831-7011; fax (302) 831-7012; e-mail secretariat@ scor-int.org; internet www.scor-int.org; f. 1957 to advance int. scientific activity in all brs of oceanic research; c. 20 active working Groups, Cttees and Panels investigate a broad range of oceanographic problems; library of 300 vols; mems: nominated mems by Cttees for Oceanic Research in 38 countries; rep. mems of affiliated orgs; invited mems by the exec. cttee; Pres. Prof. Dr WOLFGANG FENNEL (Germany); Sec. Dr JORMA KUPARINEN (Finland); Exec. Dir Dr EDWARD R. URBAN, Jr (USA); publ. *SCOR Proceedings* (1 a year).

Scientific Committee on Problems of the Environment: c/o UNESCO, Bât. VII, Room 3.16, 1 rue Miollis, 75116 Paris, France; tel. 1-45-68-45-71; e-mail secretariat@icsu-scope .org; internet www.icsu-scope.org; f. 1969; identifies and provides scientific analyses of emerging environmental challenges and opportunities caused by or impacting on humans and environment; reviews current understanding of environmental issues; interacts with policy and devt needs to inform options and recommendations for environmentally sound policy and management strategies; mems: 40 Nat. Cttees and 22 International Unions; Pres. Prof. YONGLONG LU (China); Sec.-Gen. Prof. MARY C. SCHOLES (South Africa); publs *SCOPE Reports*, *UNESCO-SCOPE-UNEP Policy Briefs Series*.

Scientific Committee on Solar-Terrestrial Physics: HAO/NCAR, 3080 Center Green Drive, Boulder, CO 80301, USA; tel. (303) 497-1591; fax (303) 497-1580; e-mail ganglu@ucar.edu; internet www.scostep.ucar .edu; f. 1966 as an Inter-Union Commission by ICSU and became a Scientific Cttee in 1978 to promote and coordinate int. interdisciplinary programmes in solar-terrestrial physics and to work with other ICSU bodies in the coordination of symposia in the field of solar-terrestrial physics; 400 mems; Pres. M. A. GELLER (USA); Scientific Sec. Dr GANG LU (USA).

SERVICES AND INTER-UNION COMMISSIONS

Federation of Astronomical and Geophysical Data Analysis Services: c/o Dr Niels Andersen, Kort and Matrikelstyrelsen, Rentemestervej 8, 2400 Copenhagen NV, Denmark; fax 35-87-50-57; e-mail fags@kms .dk; internet www.kms.dk/fags/index.html; f. 1956; federates the following Permanent Services: International Earth Rotation Service, Bureau Gravimetrique International, International GPS Service for Geodynamics, International Center for Earth Tides, Permanent Service for Mean Sea Level, International Service of Geomagnetic Indices, Quarterly Bulletin of Solar Activity, International Space Environment Service, World Glacier Monitoring Service, Centre des Données Stellaires, Sunspot Index Data Center; Pres. D. PUGH (UK); Sec. N. ANDERSEN (Denmark).

Scientific Committee on Frequency Allocations for Radio Astronomy and Space Science/Comité scientifique pour l'allocation des fréquences à la radio astronomie et la recherche spatiale: c/o Observatoire de Paris, 5 place Jules Janssen, 92195 Meudon, France; tel. 1-45-07-77-31; fax 1-45-07-77-09; e-mail iucafchair@iucaf .org; internet www.iucaf.org; f. 1960 under auspices of URSI with representatives of URSI, IAU and COSPAR, to study the requirements for frequency bands and radio frequency protection for research in the fields of radio astronomy, earth exploration and space science; and to make their requirements known to the appropriate frequency-allocation authorities; 10 mems; Chair. WIM VAN DRIEL (France).

INTERNATIONAL COUNCIL FOR PHILOSOPHY AND HUMANISTIC STUDIES

International Council for Philosophy and Humanistic Studies (ICPHS)/Conseil International de la Philosophie et des Sciences Humaines: Secretariat Maison de l'UNESCO, 1 rue Miollis, 75732 Paris Cedex 15, France; tel. 1-45-68-48-85; fax 1-40-65-94-80; e-mail cipsh@unesco.org; internet www.unesco.org/cipsh; f. 1949 under the auspices of UNESCO to encourage respect for cultural autonomy by the comparative study of civilization, to contribute towards int. understanding through a better knowledge of man, to develop int. cooperation in philosophy, humanistic and related studies, to encourage the setting up of int. orgs, to promote the dissemination of information in these fields, to sponsor works of learning, etc.; the Council is composed of 13 int. NGOs; these orgs represent 145 countries; in 1951 an agreement was signed between UNESCO and ICPHS recognizing the latter as the coordinating and representative body of orgs in the field of philosophy and humanistic studies; Pres. CHA IN-SUK (Korea); Sec.-Gen. MAURICE AYMARD (France); publs *Bulletin of Information* (every 2 years), *Diogenes* (4 a year).

UNIONS FEDERATED TO THE ICPHS

International Association for the History of Religions/Association Internationale pour l'Histoire des Religions: c/o Prof. Tim Jensen, IFPR, Univ. of Southern Denmark, Campusvej 55, 5230 Odense M, Denmark; tel. 6550-3315; fax 3887-5095; e-mail t.jensen@ifpr.sdu.dk; internet www .iahr.dk; f. 1950 by the 7th Int. Congress for the Study of the History of Religions to promote the study of the history of religions through the int. collaboration of scholars who research the subject, to organize congresses and to encourage the production of publs; annual spec. or regional conferences, and Quinquennial World Congresses; 37 mem. countries, 5 regional assoc. mems; Pres. Prof. ROSALIND HACKETT (USA); Gen. Sec. Prof. TIM JENSEN (Denmark); publ. *Numen* (4 a year).

International Committee of Historical Sciences/Comité International des Sciences Historiques: c/o Prof. Jean-Claude Robert, Dépt d'Histoire, Université du Québec à Montréal, CP 8888, Succursale Centre ville, Montréal, QC H3C 3P8, Canada; tel. (514) 987-30-00; fax (514) 987-78-13; e-mail cish@uqam.ca; internet www.cish.org; f. 1926; int. congresses since 1900 to work for the advancement of historical sciences by means of int. coordination (every 5 years); mems in 54 countries; gen. assembly every 2–3 years; Pres. Prof. JOSÉ LUIS PESET (Spain); Sec.-Gen. Prof. JEAN-CLAUDE ROBERT (Canada); publs *Bibliographie Internationale des Sciences Historiques*, *Bulletin d'Information*.

International Committee for the History of Art/Comité international d'histoire de l'art: c/o Philippe Sénéchal, Institut national d'histoire de l'art, 2 rue Vivienne, 75084 Paris, France; tel. 1-47-03-79-25; fax 1-47-03-86-36; internet www.esteticas.unam .mx/ciha; f. 1930 by the 12th Int. Congress on the History of Art for collaboration in the scientific study of the history of art; mems in 31 countries; int. congress every 4 years; int. colloquium every year; Pres. Prof. STEPHEN BANN (UK); Scientific Sec. PHILIPPE SÉNÉCHAL (France); Treas. and Admin. Sec. Prof. Dr OSKAR BÄTSCHMANN (Switzerland); publ. *Bibliography of the History of Art* (CD-ROM, quarterly).

International Federation for Modern Languages and Literatures/Fédération Internationale des Langues et Littératures Modernes: c/o Anders Pettersson, Umeå Univ., 901 87 Umeå, Sweden; tel. (90) 786-5797; e-mail anders.pettersson@ littvet.umu.se; internet www.fillm.ulg.ac.be; f. 1928 as the Int. Cttee on Modern Literary History; present name and status 1951; aims to establish permanent contact between historians of literature, to develop or perfect facilities for their work and to promote the study of the history of modern literature; 18 mem. asscns, with mems in 92 countries; Pres. Prof. THEO D'HAEN (Belgium); Sec.-Gen. Prof. ANDERS PETTERSSON (Sweden); publ. *Acts of the Triennial Congresses*.

International Federation of Philosophical Societies/Fédération Internationale des Sociétés de Philosophie: c/o Ioanna Kuçuradi, Human Rights Centre, Maltepe Univ., Maltepe, 34857 Istanbul, Turkey; tel. (216) 626432; fax (216) 626425; e-mail ioanna@fisp.org.tr; internet www.fisp.org.tr; f. 1948 under the auspices of UNESCO to encourage int. cooperation in the field of philosophy, and to promote congresses, symposia and publs; 114 mem. socs from 52 countries and 27 int. mem. socs; Pres. WILLIAM MCBRIDE (USA); Sec.-Gen. LUCA SCARANTINO (Italy); publs under the auspices of FISP, *Proceedings of the International Congresses of Philosophy*.

International Federation of the Societies of Classical Studies/Fédération Internationale des Associations d'Etudes Classiques: c/o Prof. Paul Schubert, 7 rue des Beaux-Arts, 2000 Neuchâtel, Switzerland; e-mail paul.schubert@unige.ch; internet www.fiecnet.org; f. 1948 under the auspices of UNESCO to encourage research on the ancient civilizations of Greece and Rome; to group the main nat. asscns of this field; to ensure collaboration with relevant int. orgs; affiliated bodies incl. the Int. Soc. for Classical Bibliography, Int. Soc. for Classical Archaeology, Int. Soc. for Byzantine Studies, Int. Asscn for Greek and Latin Epigraphy, Int. Asscn of Papyrologists, Unione internazionale degli Istituti di Archaeologia, Storia e Storia dell'Arte in Roma, Société d'histoire des droits de l'antiquité, Comité int. des Etudes mycéniennes, Asscn int. des Etudes patristiques, etc.; 79 mem. socs in 44 countries; Pres. Prof. AVERIL CAMERON (UK); Sec.-Gen. Prof. PAUL SCHUBERT (Switzerland); publ. *L'Année Philologique* (bibliography, 1 a year).

International Musicological Society/Société Internationale de Musicologie: Nadelstr. 60, 8706 Feldmeilen, Switzerland; tel. (44) 9231022; fax (44) 9231027; e-mail dorothea.baumann@ims-online.ch; internet www.ims-online.ch; f. 1927; promotes musicological research, encourages study in the field and coordinates the work of musicologists worldwide; int. congress every 5 years, intercongressional symposia, int. study groups; 49 mem. countries, 1,000 individual mems; Pres. Prof. Dr TILMAN SEEBASS (Austria); Sec.-Gen. Dr DOROTHEA BAUMANN (Switzerland); Vice-Pres. Prof. Dr MALENA KUSS; Vice-Pres. Dir CATHERINE MASSIP; publs *Acta Musicologica* (2 a year, online), *Catalogus Musicus* (irregular), *Documenta Musicologica* (irregular), *International Inventory of Musical Sources* (RISM, online and print), *International Repertory of Musical Iconography* (RIDIM, online databases), *International Repertory of Music Literature* (RILM, annual, online), *Répertoire International de la Presse Musicale* (RIPM, online and print).

International Union of Academies/Union Académique Internationale: Palais des Académies, 1 rue Ducale, 1000 Brussels, Belgium; tel. 550-22-00; fax 550-22-05; e-mail info@uai-iua.org; internet www.uai-iua.org; f. 1919; promotes int. cooperation through collective research in philology, archaeology, history, social sciences and humanities in general; affiliated countries: Argentina, Australia, Austria, Belgium, Bosnia and Herzegovina, Bulgaria, Canada, Chile, China, Costa Rica, Croatia, Czech Republic, Denmark, Egypt, Estonia, Finland, France, Georgia, Germany, Ghana, Greece, Hungary, India, Iran, Ireland, Israel, Italy, Japan, Republic of Korea, Latvia, Luxembourg, former Yugoslav republic of Macedonia, Madagascar, Mexico, Moldova, Montenegro, Morocco, Netherlands, Norway, Paraguay, Peru, Poland, Portugal, Romania, Russia, Serbia, Slovakia, Slovenia, South Africa, Spain, Sweden, Switzerland, Tunisia, Turkey, Ukraine, UK, USA, Uruguay, Vatican City, Viet Nam; members: International Academy of History of Science, African Academy of Languages, World Islamic Academy of Sciences; Pres. JANUSZ KOZLOWSKI (Poland); Vice-Pres. ANTONIO DIAS FARIWHA (Portugal), NICHOLAS SIMS-WILLIAMS (UK); Admin. Sec.

HERVE HASQUIN JEAN-LUC DE PAEPE (Belgium); publs *Archivum Latinitatis Medii Aevi* (every 2 years), *Compte rendu (de la session annuelle) du Comité* (1 a year), *Novum Glossarium*.

International Union of Anthropological and Ethnological Sciences (IUAES)/Union Internationale des Sciences Anthropologiques et Ethnologiques: see under ISSC.

International Union of Prehistoric and Protohistoric Sciences/Union Internationale des Sciences Préhistoriques et Protohistoriques: Prof. Luiz Oosterbeek, Instituto Politécnico de Tomar, Av. Dr Cândido Madureira 13, 2300-531 Tomar, Portugal; tel. (249) 34-63-63; fax (249) 34-63-66; e-mail loost@ipt.pt; internet www.uispp.pt.vu; f. 1931 to promote congresses and scientific work in the fields of pre- and protohistory; 120 mem. countries; 40,000 mems; Pres. Prof. IGNACIO SCHMIDT (Brazil); Sec.-Gen. Prof. LUIZ OOSTERBEEK (Portugal); publs *Archaeologia urbium*, *Inventaria archaeologica*, *Proceedings of the XV world Congress, Lisbon*.

Permanent International Committee of Linguists/Comité International Permanent des Linguistes: c/o Prof. P. G. J. van Sterkenburg, IPOB 3023 2301 DA Leiden, The Netherlands; tel. (71) 522-77-37; e-mail cipl.secretary-general@planet.nl; internet www.ciplnet.com; f. 1928 to work for the advancement of linguistics worldwide and to encourage int. cooperation in this field; 33 mem. countries and 2 int. orgs; Pres. Prof. F. KIEFER (Hungary); Sec.-Gen. Prof. P. G. J. VAN STERKENBURG; publ. *Linguistic Bibliography* (1 a year).

INTERNATIONAL SOCIAL SCIENCE COUNCIL

International Social Science Council (ISSC)/Conseil International des Sciences Sociales: Maison de l'UNESCO, 1 rue Miollis, 75732 Paris Cedex 15, France; tel. 1-45-68-48-60; fax 1-45-66-76-03; e-mail issc@unesco.org; internet www.unesco.org/ngo/issc; f. 1952; advancement of the social sciences worldwide and their application to the major problems of the world and cooperation at an int. level between specialists in the social sciences; Standing Cttees on Int. Human Dimensions of Global Environmental Change Program (IHDP, co-sponsored by ICSU), Comparative Research Programme on Poverty (CROP) and Globalization, Gender and Democratization (GGD), Int. Global Social Change Programme, Research on Ethnic Conflicts and Approaches to Peace (RECAP); 13 mem. assocs, 22 mem. orgs, 18 assoc. mems; Pres. Prof. LOURDES ARIZPE (Mexico); Sec.-Gen. Dr ALI KAZANCIGIL (France); publ. *e-bulletin*.

ASSOCIATIONS FEDERATED TO THE ISSC

International Association of Legal Sciences/Association Internationale des Sciences Juridiques: c/o ISSC, UNESCO, 1 rue Miollis, 75015 Paris, France; tel. (1) 45-68-25-58; fax (1) 43-06-87-98; e-mail leker

.meir@libertysurf.fr; f. 1950 to promote the mutual knowledge and understanding of nations and the increase of learning by encouraging worldwide the study of foreign legal systems and the use of the comparative method in legal science; governed by a President and an executive bureau of 10 members known as the International Committee of Comparative Law; national cttees in 46 countries; Pres. Prof. KONSTANTINOS KERAMEUS (Greece); Sec.-Gen. MEIR M. LEKER; Dir of Scientific Research Prof. P. SARCEVIĆ (Croatia).

International Economic Association/Association Internationale des Sciences Economiques: 23 rue Campagne-Première, 75014 Paris, France; tel. 1-43-27-91-44; fax 1-42-79-92-16; e-mail iea@iea-world.org; internet www.iea-world.org; f. 1949 to promote int. collaboration for the advancement of economic knowledge, to develop personal contacts between economists, and to encourage provision of means for the dissemination of economic knowledge; mem. associations in 57 countries; Pres. JANOS KORNAI (Hungary); Sec.-Gen. JEAN-PAUL FITOUSSI (France).

International Federation of Social Science Organizations/Fédération Internationale des Organisations de Science Sociale: 245/69 Baromtrilokanart Rd, Muang District, 65000 Phitsanulok, Thailand; tel. (55) 244-240; e-mail contact@ifsso.org; internet www.ifsso.org; f. 1979 to succeed the Conference of Nat. Social Science Councils and Analogous Bodies (f. 1975) to encourage int. cooperation in the social sciences, to advance the devt of the social sciences, especially in the developing world, to advance the exchange of information, ideas and experiences among its mems, to promote a more effective organization of research and teaching and the building of instns in the social sciences; 22 mems; Pres. Prof. Dr CARMENCITA T. AGUILAR (Philippines); Sec.-Gen. Prof. J. BLAHOZ (Czech Republic); publ. *International Directory of Social Science Organizations*.

International Geographical Union/Union Géographique Internationale: see under ICSU.

International Institute of Administrative Sciences/Institut International des Sciences Administratives: 1 rue Defacqz, Bte 11, 1000 Brussels, Belgium; tel. (2) 536-08-80; fax (2) 537-97-02; e-mail info@iias-iisa.org; internet www.iias-iisa.org; f. 1930 for the comparative examination of admin. experience in mem. countries; research and programmes for improving admin. law and practices and for technical assistance; consultative status with ECOSOC, ILO and UNESCO; int. congresses; considers impact of new technologies on admin., management of multicultural societies, admin. in transitional economies, admin. aspects of political transition, women in public admin., new regulations and new modes of control, implications of globalization and internationalization for nat. and local admin., interaction between NGOs and public admin., public admin. and the social sectors, innovations in int. admin.; 36 mem. states, 30 nat. sections, 3 int. govt orgs, 38 corporate and individual mems, 6 individuals; Pres. Prof. Dr PAN SUK KIM (Republic of Korea); Dir-Gen. ROLET LORETAN (Belgium/Switzerland); publ. *International Review of Administrative Sciences/ Revue internationale des sciences administratives* (4 a year).

International Law Association/Association de Droit International: Charles Clore House, 17 Russell Sq., London, WC1B 5DR, UK; tel. (20) 7323-2978; fax (20) 7323-3580; e-mail info@ila-hq.org; internet www.ila-hq.org; f. 1873 for the study and advancement of int. law, public and private, and the promotion of int. understanding and goodwill; 50 regional brs worldwide; 4,200 mems; 25 int. cttees; Pres. Prof. KARL-HEINZ BOCKSTIEGEL; Chair. Exec. Council Lord SLYNN OF HADLEY (UK); Sec.-Gen. DAVID J. C. WYLD.

International Peace Research Association/Association Internationale de Recherche pour la Paix: c/o Luc Reychler, University of Leuven, Van Evenstraat 2B, Leuven, Belgium; tel. (16) 323241; fax (16) 323088; e-mail luc.reychler@soc.kuleuven.ac.be; internet www.human.mie-u.ac.jp/~peace/about-ipra; f. 1964 to encourage the development of interdisciplinary research into the conditions of peace and the causes of war; mems in 93 countries: 1,050 individuals, 400 corporate, 10 nat. and regional asscns; Sec.-Gen. LUC REYCHLER (Belgium).

International Political Science Association (IPSA)/Association Internationale de Science Politique: 1590 ave Docteur-Penfield, Bureau 331, Montreal, QC H3G 1C5, Canada; tel. (514) 848-8717; fax (514) 848-4095; internet www.ipsa.org; f. 1949; promotes internationally planned research and scholarly collaboration, organizes int. conferences, symposia, triennial world congresses, and provides documentary and reference services; nat. asscns in 50 countries:

97 assoc. mems, 3,100 individual mems; Pres. Dr LOURDES SOLA (Brazil); Sec.-Gen. Prof. GUY LACHAPELLE (Canada); publs *International Political Science Abstracts* (6 a year), *International Political Science Review* (4 a year).

International Sociological Association/ Association Internationale de Sociologie: Facultad CC. Políticas y Sociología, Universidad Complutense, 28223 Madrid, Spain; tel. 91-352-76-50; fax 91-352-49-45; e-mail isa@isa-sociology.org; internet www.isa-sociology.org; f. 1949; promotes sociological research, develops personal contacts among the sociologists of all countries and ensures the exchange of sociological information; 53 research cttees on a wide variety of sociological topics; holds World Congresses every 4 years; ISA Forum every 4 years; 5,000 individual mems, 150 collective mems; Pres. Prof. MICHAEL BURAWOY (USA); Exec. Sec. Dr IZABELA BARLINSKA (Poland); publs *Current Sociology/Sociologie Contemporaine* (6 a year), *e-Bulletin* (3 a year), *International Sociology* (6 a year).

International Studies Association: 324 Social Sciences Bldg, University of Arizona, Tucson, AZ 85721, USA; tel. (520) 621-7715; fax (520) 621-5780; e-mail isa@u.arizona.edu; internet www.isanet.org; f. 1959; promotes research and cooperation into international studies; 3,000 mems in 80 countries; Pres. JACEK KUGLER (USA); Exec. Dir THOMAS J. VOLGY (USA); publs *International Studies Notes, International Studies Quarterly*.

International Union of Anthropological and Ethnological Sciences (IUAES)/ Union Internationale des Sciences Anthropologiques et Ethnologiques: c/o Prof. Peter Nas, University of Leiden, Institute of Cultural and Social Studies, POB 9555, 2300 RB Leiden, Netherlands; tel. (71) 5273992; fax (71) 5273619; e-mail nas@fsw.leidenuniv.nl; internet www.leidenuniv.nl/fsw/iuaes; f. 1948 under the auspices of UNESCO to promote research and cooperation among anthropological and ethnological institutions; mems: 20 national, 80 institutional and over 200 individuals worldwide; also federated to ICPHS, ISSC and ICSU; Pres. Prof. LUIS ALBERTO VARGAS (Mexico); Sec.-Gen. Prof. Dr PETER NAS (Netherlands).

International Union of Psychological Science (IUPsyS)/Union International des Sciences Psychologiques: see under ICSU.

International Union for the Scientific Study of Population/Union Internationale pour l'etude Scientifique de la Population: 3–5 rue Nicolas, 75980, Paris Cedex 20, France; tel. 1-56-06-21-73; fax 1-56-06-22-04; e-mail iussp@iussp.org; internet www.iussp.org; f. 1928, reconstituted 1947, to advance the progress of quantitative and qualitative demography as a science; promotes science of demography; organizes scientific meetings and training activities; 2,247 mems, 779 student assocs from 142 countries; Pres. JACQUES VALLIN (France); Exec. Dir ERIK KLIJZING (Netherlands); Sec.-Gen. MARY KRITZ (USA); publs *IUSSP papers, Proceedings* (conferences and seminars).

World Association for Public Opinion Research: c/o UNL Gallup Research Center, Univ. of Nebraska, 201 N 13th St, Lincoln, NE 68588-0242, USA; tel. (402) 472-7720; fax (402) 472-7727; e-mail renae@wapor.org; internet wapor.unl.edu; f. 1947; to establish and promote contacts between persons in the field of survey research on opinions, attitudes and behaviour of people worldwide, and to advance the use of scientific survey research in nat. and int. affairs; 485 individual mems in over 60 countries; Pres. Dr TOM W. SMITH (USA); Gen. Sec. Prof. Dr ALLAN L. MCCUTCHEON (USA); publ. *International Journal of Public Opinion Research* (4 a year).

World Federation for Mental Health/ Fédération Mondiale pour la Santé Mentale: 12114 Winona Drive, Woodbridge, VA 22192, USA; tel. (703) 494-6515; fax (703) 519-7648; e-mail info@wfmh.com; internet www.wfmh.org; f. 1948; promotes among all people and nations highest possible standard of mental health in broadest biological, medical, educational, and social aspects; works with ECOSOC, UNESCO, WHO and other agencies of the UN, to promote mental health; to help other voluntary asscns in the improvement of mental health services; 1,000 individual mems, 65 voting orgs, 30 affiliated orgs; Pres. DEBORAH WAN (Hong Kong); Sec.-Gen. Dr VIJAY GANJU (USA).

INTERNATIONAL ASSOCIATION OF UNIVERSITIES (IAU)

1 rue Miollis, 75732 Paris Cedex 15, France; tel. 1-45-68-48-00; fax 1-47-34-76-05; e-mail iau@iau-aiu.net; internet www.iau-aiu.net; f. 1950 to provide a centre of cooperation at int. level among univs and similar instns of higher education of all countries; 650 univs and instns of higher education in 150 countries; 12 assoc. mems (int. and nat. univ. orgs)

Organization

GENERAL CONFERENCE

Composed of the full and assoc. mems. Meets every 5 years. Discusses topics of importance for the future of univ. education, determines gen. policy and elects the Pres. and mems of the Admin. Board. Twelfth Gen. Conference was held in São Paulo, Brazil, in 2004.

ADMINISTRATIVE BOARD

Chaired by the Pres. of the IAU, and composed of 20 eminent univ. leaders and scholars and a maximum of 20 deputy mems from all continents. Meets annually, ensures that decisions of the Gen. Conference are implemented and guides the work of the Int. Univs Bureau.

Pres.: JUAN RAMÓN DE LA FUENTE (Former Rector, National Autonomous University of Mexico).

Sec.-Gen. and Exec. Dir EVA EGRON-POLAK

INTERNATIONAL UNIVERSITIES BUREAU (IUB)

The IUB, created in 1949, provides the Permanent Secretariat for the IAU. It is the principal instrument for the execution of the activities of the IAU. Its main tasks include facilitating and promoting the exchange of information, experience and ideas, of students, teachers, researchers and administrators, and of publications and material for teaching and research.

Exec. Dir (Ex-Officio) EVA EGRON-POLAK.

Principal Activities

Information

Under a formal Agreement with UNESCO, the IAU operates a joint IAU/UNESCO Information Centre on Higher Education at its Int. Univs Bureau. The Centre holds 40,000 vols and a large colln of unpublished materials; it has subscriptions to 300 current specialized periodicals and maintains a colln of 4,000 prospectuses of higher education instns, as well as conference reports, occasional papers, CD-ROMs, etc. The Centre was fully computerized in 1989, and all holdings were subsequently catalogued in the Centre's own database (IAUDOC). All references can be found in the int. bibliographical database (HEDBIB), accessible via the IAU website. The database links to nat. and int. information centres and data networks. The IAU acts as the coordinating agency for the World Academic Database (WAD).

Studies, Research and Meetings
The IAU coordinates and carries out studies and research on issues of higher education and higher education policies that are either common to instns and systems worldwide, or where a comparative analysis between different situations and approaches is of par-

ticular benefit to higher education instns. Conferences, symposia, colloquia, seminars, round tables and workshops provide an int. forum for the discussion of topics of common concern to higher education leaders and specialists.

Cooperation
The IAU provides an important clearing-house function to its mems for academic exchange and cooperation. The IAU has adopted the *Kyoto Declaration and Agenda for Sustainable Development 1993*, to promote and support univ. cooperation; the *Durban Declaration on Internationalization 2000* to ensure that higher education instns seize the initiative in the process of internationalization rather than reacting to the forces of globalization and the market; and the *São Paolo Declaration on Information and Communication Technologies (ICTs)*

2004, to act as a platform for information-sharing in regard to the use of ICTs in higher education.

SELECTED PUBLICATIONS
Guide to Higher Education in Africa (irregular).
Higher Education Policy (4 a year, English).
International Handbook of Universities (every 2 years, English).
Issues in Higher Education (3 or 4 a year, English).
World Academic Database (WAD)(CD-ROM; 1 a year, English and French).
World Higher Education Database (CD-ROM; 1 a year, English).
World List of Universities and Other Institutions of Higher Education (every 2 years, English and French).

OTHER INTERNATIONAL ORGANIZATIONS

General

Academia Europaea: 4th Fl., 21 Albemarle St, London, W1S 4HS, UK; tel. 7495-3717; e-mail admin@acadeuro.org; internet www.acadeuro.org; f. 1988; a free asscn of individual scholars working in Europe in all disciplines; aims to encourage European activities in scholarship and the undertaking of ind. studies on matters of European importance; holds meetings, symposia, study groups, etc.; 2,300 mems; Pres. Prof. LARS WALLOE (Norway); Exec. Sec. Dr DAVID COATES; publ. *European Review* (4 a year).

Academia Scientiarum et Artium Europaea (European Academy of Sciences and Arts): St Peter-Bezirk 10, 5020 Salzburg, Austria; tel. (662) 84-13-45; fax (662) 84-13-43; e-mail office@euro-acad.at; internet www.euro-acad.at; f. 1990; promotes an overall view of the sciences and arts on a European level; 1,400 mems; Pres. Prof. Dr FELIX UNGER; Vice-Pres. Prof. Dr NIKOLAUS LOBKOWICZ.

Islamic World Academy of Sciences (IAS): POB 830036, Amman 11183, Jordan; tel. (6) 5522104; fax (6) 5511803; e-mail ias@go.com.jo; internet www.ias-worldwide.org; f. 1986, present name 2005; int., ind., non-political NGO of scientists and technologists, working to promote science, technology and devt in the Islamic and developing worlds; organizes confs and seminars; supervises training workshops; comms research; acts as the scientific adviser to the OIC (Org. of the Islamic Conf.) and developing countries; collaborates with other nat., regional and int. academies of science, UNESCO, COMSTECH; 107 fellows and 13 hon. fellows from 40 countries; Dir-Gen. Dr MONEEF R. ZOU'BI; publs *Islamic Thought and Scientific Creativity* (4 a year), *Medical Journal* (4 a year), *Proceedings* (1 a year).

Agriculture and Veterinary Science

Food and Agriculture Organization of the United Nations/Organisation des Nations Unies pour l'Alimentation et l'Agriculture: Viale delle Terme di Caracalla, 00153 Rome, Italy; tel. 06-57051; fax 06-57053152; e-mail fao-hq@fao.org; internet www.fao.org; f. 1945; raises level of nutrition and living standards, improves production and distribution of food and agricultural products, and improves the conditions of rural populations; improving production in all areas of agriculture, forestry and fisheries; promoting the conservation and management of plant and animal genetic resources; increasing investment in agriculture through irrigation, fertilizer, seed and other rural devt schemes; collecting, analysing and disseminating information needed by govts and int. bodies; making available technical data through the FAO-coordinated AGRIS, CARIS and FAOSTAT computer-based int. information systems; working towards greater world food security by ensuring production of adequate food supplies, maximizing stability in the flow of supplies, and securing access to available supplies for those who need them; and by promoting rural devt schemes; the interpretation and dissemination of information obtained from satellites to predict crop failure is an illustration of FAO's GIEWS and ARTEMIS systems to monitor the world food situation; library: FAO David Lubin Memorial Library (fao.org/library) holds 1m. vols and 13,000 journals, 1,450 electronic journals; 192 mem. nations and 1 org. mem. (EU); Dir-Gen. Dr JACQUES DIOUF (Senegal); publs *Animal Health and Fertilizers*, *Commodity Review and Outlook*, *FAO Quarterly Bulletin of Statistics*, *Food and Agricultural Legislation* (2 a year), *Forestry and Fisheries*, *Plant Protection Bulletin*, *Rural Development* (1 a year), *The State of Food and Agriculture* (1 a year), *State of Food Insecurity in the World*, *Unasylva* (4 a year), *World Animal Review* (4 a year), *Yearbooks of Trade and Production in Agriculture*.

OTHER ORGANIZATIONS

CAB International (CABI): Nosworthy Way, Wallingford, Oxon, OX10 8DE, UK; tel. (1491) 832111; fax (1491) 833508; e-mail corporate@cabi.org; internet www.cabi.org; f. 1929; global non-profit organization specializing in sustainable solutions for agricultural and environmental problems; CAB International offices in Wallingford (UK), New Delhi (India); CABI Bioscience: centres in Ascot and Egham (UK), Rawalpindi (Pakistan), Delémont (Switzerland); CABI regional centres for Africa (Nairobi, Kenya), Caribbean and Latin America (Curepe, Trinidad), South-East Asia (Serdang, Malaysia), China (Beijing); CABI Publishing: offices in Wallingford (UK) and Cambridge, MA (USA); CABI Trust in Wallingford (UK); CEO TREVOR NICHOLS; publs *Animal Health Research Reviews* (2 a year), *Aquatic Resources, Culture and Development* (4 a year), *British Journal of Nutrition* (12 a year), *Bulletin of Entomological Research* (6 a year), *Chinese Journal of Agricultural Biotechnology* (3 a year), *Equine and Comparative Exercise Physiology* (4 a year), *Forestry Abstracts* (12 a year), *Horticultural Science Abstracts* (12 a year), *International Journal of Tropical Insect Science* (4 a year), *Journal of Helmintology* (4 a year), *Leisure, Recreation and Tourism Abstracts* (4 a year), *Pig News and Information* (4 a year), *Plant Breeding Abstracts* (12 a year), *Plant Genetics Resources* (3 a year), *Renewable Agriculture and Food Systems* (4 a year), *Rural Development Abstracts* (4 a year), *Seed Science Research* (4 a year), *Soils Use and Management* (4 a year), *World Poultry Science* (4 a year).

Commonwealth Forestry Association: The Crib, Dinchope, Craven Arms, Shropshire, SY7 9JJ, UK; tel. (1588) 672868; fax (870) 011-6645; e-mail cfa@cfa-international.org; internet www.cfa-international.org; f. 1921; 1,500 mems; Pres. J. BALL; Chair. J. INNES; publ. *International Forestry Review* (4 a year).

Consultative Group on International Agricultural Research (CGIAR): 1818 H St, NW, MSN G6-601, Washington, DC

20433, USA; tel. (202) 473-8951; fax (202) 473-8110; e-mail cgiar@cgiar.org; internet www.cgiar.org; f. 1971; co-sponsors: World Bank, FAO, IFAD and UNDP; 58 mems incl. govts, int. orgs and private foundations; Dir FRANCISCO J. B. REIFSCHNEIDER.

Institutions Supported by CGIAR:

Africa Rice Centre (WARDA)/Centre du Riz pour l'Afrique (ADRAO): 01 BP 2031, Cotonou 01, Benin; tel. 35-01-18; fax 35-05-56; e-mail warda@cgiar.org; internet www.warda.cgiar.org; f. 1970; 17 West and Central African mem. states; funds provided through CGIAR by mem. states, donor nations and orgs, and various foundations; library of 16,442 monographs, 1,523 periodicals; Dir-Gen. Dr KANAYO F. NWANZE; publs *Participatory Rice Improvement and Gender/user Analysis Proceedings* (workshop papers, 1 a year), *Program Report* (1 a year), *Rice Interspecific Hybridization Project Research Highlights* (1 a year), *WARDA Current Contents* (12 a year), *West Africa Rice Research Brief* (irregular, in French and English).

Bioversity International: Via dei Tre Denari 472A, 00057 Maccarese, Rome, Italy; tel. 06-61181; fax 06-61979661; e-mail bioversity@cgiar.org; internet www.cgiar.org; f. 1974 to advance the collection, conservation and use of crop genetic resources worldwide and to encourage research; Dir-Gen. Dr EMILE A. FRISON; publ. *Geneflow*.

Centre for International Forestry Research (CIFOR): POB 6596 JKPWB, Jakarta 10065, Indonesia; Jl. CIFOR, Situ Gede, Sindangbarang, Bogor Barat 16680, Indonesia; tel. (251) 622622; fax (251) 622100; e-mail cifor@cgiar.org; internet www.cifor.cgiar.org; seeks the balanced management of forests and forest lands through collaborative strategic and applied research and related activities; regional offices in Brazil, Cameroon and Zimbabwe; Dir-Gen. DAVID KAIMOWITZ.

International Centre for Agricultural Research in the Dry Areas (ICARDA): POB 5466, Aleppo, Syria; tel. (21) 2213433; fax (21) 2213490; e-mail icarda@cgiar.org; internet www.icarda.cgiar.org; f. 1977; serves the entire developing world for the improvement of lentil, barley and faba bean production; all dry-area developing countries for the improvement of on-farm water-use efficiency, rangeland and small-ruminant production; and West and Central Asia and North Africa for the improvement of bread, durum wheat and chickpea production, and farming systems; promotes sustainable natural-resource management practices; library of 16,129 vols, 958 periodicals; Dir-Gen. Dr MAHMOUD SOLH; publ. *ICARDA Caravan* (2 a year).

International Centre for Tropical Agriculture/Centro Internacional de Agricultura Tropical: Apdo aéreo 6713, Cali, Colombia; tel. (2) 4450000; fax (2) 4450073; internet www.ciat.cgiar.org; f. 1967; research on cultivation of beans, cassava, rice, tropical fruit and fodder, combined with applied social sciences; library of 100,000 records and documents; 1,300 mems; Dir-Gen. JOACHIM VOSS; publ. *Pasturas Tropicales* (3 a year).

International Crops Research Institute for the Semi-Arid Tropics (ICRISAT): Patancheru, Andhra Pradesh 502 324, India; tel. (40) 23296161; fax (40) 23296180; e-mail icrisat@cgnet.com; internet www.icrisat.org; f. 1972 as world centre for genetic improvement of sorghum, millets, pigeonpea, chickpea and groundnut production, and for research on the management of resources in the world's semi-arid tropics; research covers all physical and socio-economic aspects of improving farming systems on un-irrigated land; Dir-Gen. WILLIAM D. DAR (India); publs *International Arachis Newsletter* (1 a year), *International Chickpea and Pigeonpea Newsletter* (1 a year), *International Sorghum and Millet Newsletter* (1 a year), *Research and Information Bulletins*, *Workshop Proceedings*.

International Food Policy Research Institute: 2033 K St NW, Washington, DC 20006, USA; tel. (202) 862-5600; fax (202) 467-4439; e-mail ifpri@cgiar.org; internet www.ifpri.org; f. 1975 to identify and analyse alternative nat. and int. strategies for improving the food situation of the low-income countries; 6 divs: Environment and Production Technology (EPT), Food Consumption and Nutrition (FCN), Markets, Trade and Institutions (MTI), Int. Service for Nat. Agricultural Research (ISNAR), Devt Strategy and Governance (DSG), Communications and 2020 Vision Initiative; library of 4,200 research reports, 3,000 monographs, 175 periodicals; Dir-Gen. JOACHIM VON BRAUN; publs abstracts, research reports, working papers, etc.

International Institute of Tropical Agriculture: c/o Lambourn (UK) Ltd, Carolyn House, 26 Dingwall Rd, Croydon, CR9 3EE, UK; field office: Oyo Rd, PMB 5320, Ibadan, Oyo State, Nigeria; tel. (2) 241-2626; fax (2) 241-2221; e-mail iita@cgiar.org; internet www.iita.org; f. 1967; projects incl. preserving and enhancing germplasm and agrobiodiversity; developing biological control options; impact, policy and systems analysis; starchy and grain staples in eastern and southern Africa; diverse agricultural systems in the Humid Zone of West and Central Africa; improving and intensifying cereal-legume systems in the moist and dry savannahs of West and Central Africa; library of 76,500 vols and in-house database of 105,500 records; Dir-Gen. PETER HARTMANN.

International Livestock Research Institute: POB 30709, Nairobi 00100, Kenya; tel. (20) 422-3000; fax (20) 422-3001POB 5689, Addis Ababa, Ethiopia; tel. (1) 463-215; fax (1) 463-252; internet www.ilri.cgiar.org; f. 1995 as an interdisciplinary research, training and information centre to promote and improve livestock production worldwide; principal research units in Kenya and Ethiopia and field programmes in Ethiopia, Kenya, Niger and Nigeria; library of 37,500 vols, 32,000 microfiches, 1,800 periodicals; Dir-Gen. Dr CARLOS SERÉ; publs *Bulletin*, *Systems Studies Monographs*, progress and research reports, manuals, bibliographies.

International Maize and Wheat Improvement Centre/Centro Internacional de Mejoramiento de Maíz y Trigo: Apdo 6-641, 06600 México, DF, Mexico; tel. (55) 5804-2004; fax (55) 5804-7558; e-mail cimmyt@cgiar.org; internet www.cimmyt.org; f. 1966; supported by Mexican Min. of Agriculture, various int. agencies, govts and private foundations; aims to help impoverished people in developing countries by improving maize and wheat productivity and promoting environmentally sound farming practices; regional offices in Africa, Asia and South and Central America; Dir-Gen. Dr MASA IWANAGA.

International Potato Centre/Centro Internacional de la Papa: POB 1558, Lima 12, Peru; tel. (1) 349-6017; fax (1) 317-5326; e-mail cip@cgiar.org; internet www.cipotato.org; f. 1971; non-profit instn dedicated to the increased and more sustainable use of potato, sweet potato and other roots and tubers in developing countries, and to the improved management of agricultural resources in mountain areas; regional offices in Lima, Nairobi, Bogor and New Delhi; library of 13,000 vols, 131 online journals, 16,000 reprints, 65,000 references; Dir-Gen. Dr PAMELA K. ANDERSON; publ. *Program Report* (every 2 years).

International Rice Research Institute: DAPO Box 7777, Metro Manila, Philippines; tel. (2) 580-5600; fax (2) 580-5699; e-mail irri@cgiar.org; internet www.irri.org; f. 1960; research on rice and rice-based cropping systems; library of 158,000 vols; Dir-Gen. Dr ROBERT S. ZEIGLER (acting); Deputy Dir-Gen. Dr WILLIAM G. PADOLINA; publs *Facts about Cooperation* (1 a year), *IRRI Hotline* (4 a year), *International Rice Research Notes* (2 a year), *Rice Literature Update* (2 a year), *Rice Today Magazine* (1 a year).

International Water Management Institute (IWMI): POB 2075, Colombo, Sri Lanka; 127 Sunil Mawatha, Pelawatte, Battaramulla, Sri Lanka; tel. (11) 288-0000; fax (11) 278-6854; e-mail iwmi@cgiar.org; internet www.iwmi.cgiar.org; non-profit org. for sustainable management of water and land resources for food, livelihood and nature; national and international partners across Africa and Asia; Dir-Gen. Dr COLIN CHARTRES.

World Agroforestry Centre: United Nations Ave, Gigiri, POB 30677, 00100 Nairobi, Kenya; tel. (20) 7224000; fax (20) 7224001; e-mail icraf@cgiar.org; internet www.worldagroforestry.org; f. 1977; conducts collaborative research on sustainable forestry and its impact on farming, to alleviate poverty and protect the environment; research sites in 23 tropical countries; Dir-Gen. DENNIS PHILIP.

WorldFish Centre: POB 500, GPO 10670 Penang, Malaysia; Jl. Batu Maung, Batu Maung, 11960 Bayan Lepas, Penang, Malaysia; tel. (4) 6261606; fax (4) 6265530; e-mail worldfishcenter@cgiar.org; internet www.worldfishcenter.org; f. 1977; non-profit org. involved in collaborative research in developing countries to promote the sustainable use of living aquatic resources based on environmentally sound management; library of 16,000 books, monographs and reprints, 1,376 periodicals; Dir-Gen. Dr STEPHEN HALL; publ. *NAGA—WorldFish Centre Quarterly*.

Inter-American Institute for Cooperation on Agriculture/Instituto Interamericano de Cooperación para la Agricultura: Apdo 55, 2200 Coronado, San José, Costa Rica; tel. (506) 216-02-22; fax (506) 216-02-33; e-mail iicahq@iica.int; internet www.iica.int; f. 1942; a specialized agency of the inter-American system; aims to encourage, promote and support the efforts of the mem. states to achieve agricultural devt and rural well-being; offices in 29 of its 33 countries; Dir-Gen. CHELSTON W. D. BRATHWAITE (Barbados); publ. *Turrialba* (4 a year).

International Association of Agricultural Economists/Conférence Internationale des Economistes Agricoles: 555 E Wells St, Suite 1100, Milwaukee, WI 53202, USA; tel. (414) 918-3199; fax (414) 276-3349; e-mail iaae@execinc.com; internet www.iaae-agecon.org; f. 1929 to foster the application of the science of agricultural economics to the improvement of the economic and social conditions of rural communities; to advance knowledge of agricultural processes and the economic organization of agriculture; and to facilitate communication and exchange of information among those concerned with rural welfare worldwide; 1,700 mems in 95 countries; Pres. KEIJIRO OTSUKA (Japan); Sec.-Treas. WALTER J. ARMBRUSTER (USA); publ. *Agricultural Economics: the Journal of the International Association of Agricultural Economists* (incl. Proceedings of Conferences).

International Association of Horticultural Producers/Association Internationale des Producteurs de l'Horticulture: Pasteurlaan 6, POB 280, 2700 AG Zoetermeer, Netherlands; tel. (79) 347-07-07; fax (79) 347-04-05; internet www .aiph.org; f. 1948 to represent through its professional mem. orgs the common interests of commercial horticultural producers by means of frequent meetings, regular publs, press notices, resolutions and addresses to govts and int. authorities; mems: Australia, Austria, Belgium, Canada, China, Colombia, Czech Republic, Denmark, Finland, Luxembourg, Netherlands, Norway, Poland, Spain, Sweden, Switzerland, UK, USA; Pres. Dr DOEKE FABER; Sec.-Gen. SJAAK LANGESLAG.

International Centre for Advanced Mediterranean Agronomic Studies/Centre International de Hautes Etudes Agronomiques Méditerranéennes: Secretariat 11 rue Newton, 75116 Paris, France; tel. 1-53-23-91-00; fax 1-53-23-91-01; internet www.ciheam.org; f. 1962 to provide a supplementary technical, economic and social education for graduates of the higher schools and faculties of agriculture in Mediterranean countries at a postgraduate level; to examine the int. problems posed by rural devt and regional planning; to develop methods of investigation in ecological topics; to contribute to the devt of int. cooperation among agronomists and economists in Mediterranean countries; scholarships may be granted by the governing body; mems: Albania, Algeria, Egypt, France, Greece, Italy, Lebanon, Malta, Montenegro, Morocco, Portugal, Serbia, Spain, Tunisia, Turkey; Chair. MOUÏN HAMZÉ (Lebanon); Sec.-Gen. BERNARD HERVIEU (France); publ. *Options Méditerranéennes*.

Component Institutes:

Mediterranean Agronomic Institute of Bari: c/o Cosimo Lacirignola, Via Ceglie 9, 70010 Valenzano, Bari, Italy; tel. 080-4606204; fax 080-4606206; internet netserver.iamb.it; courses on irrigation and drainage, soil conservation, pathology of Mediterranean fruit tree species; Dir COSIMO LACIRIGNOLA.

Mediterranean Agronomic Institute of Chania: c/o Alkinoos Nikolaidis, Alsyllio Agrokepiou, POB 85, Chania 73100, Makedonias 1, Alsyllio Agrokepio, Crete, Greece; tel. 28-21035002; fax 28-21035001; e-mail info@maich.gr; internet www.maich.gr; f. 1985; courses on business economics and management; food quality and chemistry of natural products; geoinformation in environmental management; horticultural genetics and biotechnology; sustainable agriculture; Dir ALKINOOS NIKOLAIDIS.

Mediterranean Agronomic Institute of Montpellier: c/o Vincent Dollé, 3191 route de Mende, 34093 Montpellier Cedex 5, France; tel. 4-67-04-60-00; fax 4-67-54-25-27; internet www.iamm.fr; courses on economics and politics of the agricultural sector and food supplies, economics and agricultural policies, rural devt and popularization; Dir VINCENT DOLLÉ.

Mediterranean Agronomic Institute of Zaragoza: c/o Luis Estruelas, Av. Monta-

ñana, 1005, 50059 Zaragoza, Spain; tel. (976) 716 000; fax (976) 716 001; e-mail iamz@iamz.ciheam.org; internet www .iamz.ciheam.org; postgraduate courses on animal production, animal nutrition, animal genetics and reproduction, rural development, environment, plant breeding and genetics, agricultural systems, agricultural technologies, agricultural and food products, agro-food marketing, pisciculture, fisheries; Dir LUIS ESTERUELAS

International Commission for Food Industries/Commission internationale des industries agricoles et alimentaires: 42 rue Scheffer, 75116 Paris, France; tel. 1-43-31-30-36; fax 1-43-31-32-02; e-mail ciia@ wanadoo.fr; internet www.ciia-c.com; f. 1934 to develop international cooperation in promoting agricultural and food industries; to organize int. congresses, annual study sessions and advanced training courses for executives and high-level technicians of agricultural and food industries in the scientific, technical, management and economic fields; Sec.-Gen. MICHEL FOUCAULT (France); publs *Industries Alimentaires et Agricoles*, Proceedings of Congresses, Symposia and Seminars.

International Commission of Agricultural Engineering: see under Engineering

International Committee on Veterinary Gross Anatomical Nomenclature (ICVGAN)/Commission Internationale de la Nomenclature Macroanatomique Vétérinaire: Dept of Veterinary Anatomy, Bischofsholer Damm 15, 30173 Hanover, Germany; tel. (511) 856-7211; fax (511) 856-7683; f. 1957; language of instruction English; 40 mems; Chair. Prof. HELMUT WAIBL (Germany); Sec. Prof. HAGEN GASSE (Germany); publ. *Nomina Anatomica Veterinaria*.

International Congress on Animal Reproduction/Congrès Internationale de Physiologie et Pathologie de la Reproduction Animale: Faculty of Veterinary Science, University of Sydney, Sydney, NSW 2006, Australia; tel. (2) 9351-3363; fax (2) 9351-3957; e-mail gareth.evans@sydney .edu.au; internet www.vetsci.usyd.edu.au/ icar; f. 1948 following the first congress in Milan, Italy; Pres. Prof. HENK BERTSCHINGER (USA); Sec.-Gen. Prof. G. EVANS (Australia); publ. *ICAR Proceedings* (every 4 years).

International Dairy Federation/Fédération Internationale de Laiterie: Diamant Bldg, Blvd Auguste Reyers 80, 1030 Brussels, Belgium; tel. (2) 733-98-88; fax (2) 733-0413; e-mail info@fil-idf.org; internet www.fil-idf.org; f. 1903 to link all dairy asscns in order to encourage the solution of scientific, technical and economic problems affecting the dairy industry; mems: nat. cttees in 35 countries; Pres. RICHARD DOYLE; Dir-Gen. CHRISTIAN ROBERT; publs *Bulletin* (online), *International Standards* (online).

International Federation of Agricultural Producers/Fédération International des Producteurs Agricoles: 60 rue Saint-Lazare, 75009 Paris, France; tel. 1 45-26-05-53; fax 1-48-74-72-12; e-mail ifap@ ifap.org; internet www.ifap.org; f. 1946 to represent, in the int. field, the interests of agricultural producers, by laying the coordinated views of the nat. member orgs before any appropriate int. body; to act as a forum in which leaders of nat. farmers' orgs can meet to exchange information, experiences and ideas, and bring farmers' concerns to the attention of int. meetings of govts and other bodies; 114 mem. farmers' orgs in 82 countries; Pres. JACK WILKINSON (Canada); Sec.-Gen. DAVID KING; publ. *General Conference Reports* (every 2 years).

International Organization for Biological Control of Noxious Animals and Plants (IOBC)/Organisation Internationale de Lutte Biologique Contre les Animaux et les Plantes Nuisibles: c/o Prof. Dr Joop van Lenteren, Laboratory of Entomology, Wageningen University, POB 8031, 6700 EH Wageningen, Netherlands; tel. (317) 482327; fax (317) 484821; e-mail joop.vanlenteren@wur.nl; internet www .iobc-global.org; f. 1956 to promote and coordinate research on biological and integrated control of pests and weeds; comprises regional sections based on biogeographical zones; mems: public or private from over 50 countries; Pres. Prof. Dr JACQUES BRODEUR (Canada); Sec. Gen. Prof. Dr JOOP C. VAN LENTEREN (Netherlands); publs *BioControl*, *Entomophaga* (4 a year).

International Seed Testing Association: Zuerichstr. 50, 8303 Bassersdorf, Switzerland; tel. 448386000; fax 448386001; e-mail ista.office@ista.ch; internet www.seedtest .org; f. 1924; promotes uniformity in seed quality evaluation, through research and by organizing triennial congresses, annual ordinary meetings and periodic training courses; produces internationally agreed rules for seed sampling and testing; accredits laboratories; promotes research; provides int. seed analysis certificates and training; disseminates knowledge in seed science and technology; 76 mem. countries, 201 mem. laboratories (120 accredited); Pres. Dr JOËL LÉCHAPPÉ (France); Sec.-Gen. Dr MICHAEL MUSCHICK (Switzerland); publs *ISTA International Rules for Seed Testing* (1 a year), *Seed Science and Technology* (3 a year), *Seed Testing International (ISTA News Bulletin)* (2 a year).

International Society for Horticultural Science/Société Internationale de la Science Horticole: POB 500, 3001 Leuven 1, Belgium; located at: Decroylaan 42 (01.21), 3001 Leuven, Belgium; tel. (16) 22-94-27; fax (16) 22-94-50; e-mail info@ishs.org; internet www.ishs.org; f. 1959 to promote and to encourage research in all branches of horticulture and to facilitate cooperation of scientific activities and knowledge transfer on a global scale by means of its publs, events and scientific structure; 6,500 mems in 150 countries; Pres. Dr NORMAN E. LOONEY (Canada); Exec. Dir JOZEF VAN ASSCHE; publs *Acta Horticulturae* (about 35 a year), *Chronica Horticulturae* (4 a year).

International Society for Tropical Crop Research and Development (ISTCRAD): c/o Prof. N. K. Nayar (Associate Director of Research (Planning)), Kerala Agricultural University, Thrissur 680656, Kerala, India; tel. (487) 370497; fax (487) 370019; e-mail dr@kau.in; f. 1990; provides a forum for interaction among scientists, progressive farmers and entrepreneurs; Dir Dr D. ALEXANDER; publs *News Bulletin* (4 a year), *Scientific Journal* (4 a year).

International Society for Tropical Root Crops (ISTRC): c/o I.S.H.S., Englaan 1, 6703 ET Wageningen, Netherlands; tel. (8370) 21747; fax (8370) 21586; internet www.istrc.org; f. 1964; 300 mems; Pres. Dr S. K. HAHN; Sec. Ir H. H. VAN DER BORG.

International Union of Forest Research Organizations/Union Internationale des Instituts de Recherches Forestières/Internationaler Verband Forstlicher Forschungsanstalten: Hauptstr. 7, 1140 Vienna–Hadersdorf, Austria; tel. (1) 877-01-51-0; fax (1) 877-01-51-50; e-mail office@iufro .org; internet www.iufro.org; f. 1892; int. cooperation in the various branches of forest research and related fields; 600 mem. orgs in 100 countries; Pres. Prof. NIELS ELERS KOCH

(Denmark); Exec. Dir ALEXANDER BUCK (Austria); publs *Congress Proceedings*, *IUFRO News* (10 a year, online), *IUFRO World Series*, scientific papers.

International Union of Soil Science (IUSS)/Association Internationale de la Science du Sol/Internationale Bodenkundliche Gesellschaft: c/o Prof. Stephen Nortcliff, Dept of Soil Science, Univ. of Reading, POB 233, Reading, RG6 6DW, UK; tel. (118) 378-6559; fax (118) 378-6666; e-mail iuss@rdg.ac.uk; internet www.iuss .org; f. 1924 to promote soil science and its applications; federated to ICSU; 45,000 mems in 70 countries; Pres. Prof. R. SWIFT; Sec.-Gen. Prof. STEPHEN NORTCLIFF; publ. *Bulletin* (2 a year).

World Association for Animal Production: Via Tomassetti 3-1/A, 00161 Rome, Italy; tel. 06-44202639; fax 06-86329263; e-mail waap@waap.it; internet www.waap .it; f. 1965; organizes a conference every 5 years; regional discussions; mems: 17 societies (nat. and regional); Pres. ASSEFAW MEDHIN TEWOLDE (Ethiopia); Sec.-Gen. ANDREA ROSATI (Italy); publ. *News Items* (2 a year).

World Veterinary Association/Association Mondiale Vétérinaire: c/o Dr Lars Holsaae, Emdrupvej 28A, 2100 Copenhagen Ø, Denmark; tel. 38-71-01-56; fax 38-71-03-22; internet www.worldvet.org; f. 1863; mem. organizations in 80 countries, 20 assoc. mems; Pres. Dr HERBERT SCHNEIDER (Namibia); Exec. Sec. Dr LARS HOLSAAE (Denmark); publs *Bulletin* (2 a year), *World Veterinary Directory*.

Arts

Asociación de Lingüística y Filología de América Latina/Latin American Association of Linguistics and Philology: c/o Adolfo Elizaincín, Universidad de la República, CP 1410, 11000 Montevideo, Uruguay; e-mail aelizain@gmail.com; internet www .mundoalfal.org; f. 1964; 1,009 mems; Pres. ALBA VALENCIA ESPINOSA (Chile); Sec.-Gen. ADOLFO ELIZAINCÍN (Uruguay); publs *Actas de los Congresos*, *Revista Lingüística*.

Association for Commonwealth Literature and Language Studies: POB 715, Osmania Univ. Post Office, Hyderabad 500 007, India; tel. (40) 27005301; internet www .aclals.org; f. 1965 as an ind. org.; encourages study in Commonwealth literatures and languages, incl. comparative studies between literatures in English and indigenous literatures and languages, new kinds of English and use of mass media; holds triennial conferences and regional meetings; organizes visits and exchanges; collects source material and publishes creative, critical, historical and bibliographical material; 1,600 mems; Chair. MEENAKSHI MUKHERJEE (India); Vice-Chair. HARISH TRIVEDI (India); Vice-Chair. and Sec. C. VIJAYASREE (India); publ. *Bulletin*.

Commonwealth Association of Museums: POB 30192, Chinook Postal Outlet, Calgary, AB T2H 2V9, Canada; tel. (403) 938-3190; fax (403) 938-3190; e-mail irvinel@ fclc.com; internet www.maltwood.uvic.ca/ cam; f. 1974; maintains and strengthens links between mems of the museum profession; encourages and assists mems to obtain additional training and to attend appropriate confs, seminars; promotes professional excellence; collaborates with nat. and regional museum asscns; runs confs and workshops, internships, distance-learning programme in basic museum studies; nat., institutional and individual mems in 38 countries; gen. assembly every three years with elections; annual

meeting; 315 mems; Pres. MARTIN SEGGER (Canada); Sec.-Gen. LOIS IRVINE (Canada); publs *Bulletin* (irregular), *Conference and Workshop Proceedings*.

Communauté Africaine de Culture: c/o Présence africaine, 25 bis rue des Ecoles, 75005 Paris, France; tel. (1) 43-54-13-74; fax (1) 43-25-96-67; f. 2005 to create unity and friendship among African scholars for the encouragement of their own cultures; mems from 22 countries; Pres. WOLE SOYINKA; Sec.-Gen. Mme YZNDE CHRISTIANE DIOP; publ. *Présence Africaine* (2 a year).

Europa Nostra (Our Europe): Lange Voorhout 35, 2514 EC The Hague, The Netherlands; tel. (70) 3024050; fax (70) 3617865; e-mail info@europanostra.org; internet www .europanostra.org; f. 1991 by merger of Europa Nostra and the Int. Castles Institute; pan-European org. for the protection of Europe's architectural and natural heritage, and the promotion of high standards in architecture and in town and country planning; undertakes campaigns, conferences, research, exhibitions and an annual award scheme; language of instruction French; 1,500 mem. orgs and individuals; Pres. PLÁCIDO DOMINGO; Exec. Pres. DENIS DE KERGORLAY; Sec.-Gen. SNESKA QUAEDVLIEG-MIHAILOVIC; publs *Awards Review* (1 a year), *Europa Nostra Scientific Bulletin* (1 a year), *European Cultural Heritage Review* (1 a year).

European Cultural Foundation/Fondation Européenne de la Culture: Jan van Goyenkade 5, 1075 HN Amsterdam, Netherlands; tel. (20) 573-38-68; fax (20) 675-22-31; e-mail eurocult@eurocult.org; internet www .eurocult.org; f. 1954 as an ind., non-profit org. to promote cultural cooperation in Europe; an operating foundation that initiates and manages its own projects and programmes and gives grants to other bodies for European-level cultural activities; emphasizes the importance of developing a pluralistic civil soc. in Europe by encouraging the linkage of cultural activity and social responsibility; supports a network of nat. cttees based in 23 European countries; Pres. HRH Princess MARGRIET OF THE NETHERLANDS; Dir GOTTFRIED WAGNER; publ. *Beyond Borders* (3 a year).

European Society of Culture/Società Europea di Cultura/Société Européenne de Culture: Villa Hériot, Giudecca 54 P, 30133 Venice, Italy; tel. 041-5230210; fax 041-5231033; e-mail info@ societaeuropeacultura.it; internet www .societaeuropeacultura.it; f. 1950 to unite artists, poets, scientists, philosophers and others through mutual interests and friendship to safeguard and improve the conditions required for creative activity; and to enhance int. collaboration and peace; 1,500 mems; library of 5,000 vols; Pres. VINCENZO CAPPELLETTI (Italy); Premier Vice-Pres. ARRIGO LEVI (Italy); Int. Gen. Sec. MICHELLE CAMPAGNOLO BOUVIER (Italy); publ. *Comprendre* (irregular).

Fédération Internationale des Ecrivains de Langue Française (FIDELF): 3492 ave Laval, Montreal, QC H2X 3C8, Canada; tel. (515) 849-62-39; f. 1982; 18 mem. asscns; Pres. ALIOUNE BADARA BEYE (Senegal); Sec.-Gen. MAMADOU TRAORÉ DIOP (Senegal).

International Amateur Theatre Association—Organization for Understanding and Education through Theatre: Vene 6, 10123 Tallinn, Estonia; tel. 6418-405; fax 6418-406; e-mail secretariat@aitaiata.org; internet www.aitaiata.org; f. 1952; mems in 70 states; composed of nat. centres; organizes int. conferences, colloquia, seminars, work-

shops, festivals incl. world festival of amateur theatre (every 4 years); Administrator ENE JÜRNA; publ. *Bulletin AITA/IATA*.

International Association for Caribbean Archaeology/Association Internationale d'Archéologie de la Caraïbe/Asociación Internacional de Arqueología del Caribe: BP 4030, Terres Sainvilles Cedex, 97254 Fort-de-France, Martinique; tel. 63-65-51; fax 63-65-51; internet museum-server .archanth.cam.ac.uk/iaca.www/iaca.htm; f. 1962; 59 mems; Pres. Dr JAY HAVISER (Netherlands Antilles); Sec. QUETTA KAYE (UK).

International Association of Applied Linguistics/Association Internationale de Linguistique Appliquée: c/o Prof. Daniel Perrin ZHAW Zurich University of Applied Sciences School of Applied Linguistics, 8401 Winterthur, Switzerland; tel. 589346060; e-mail secretariat@aila.info; internet www.aila.info; f. 1964 to promote the application of linguistic theories to the solution of language and language-related problems in society; 8,000 mems; Pres. Prof. MARTIN BYGATE (UK); Sec.-Gen. Prof. DANIEL PERRIN (Switzerland); publs *AILA Book Series* (3 a year), *AILA News* (2 a year), *AILA Review* (1 a year).

International Association of Art: Rosenthaler Str. 11, 10119 Berlin, Germany; tel. (30) 23457666; fax (30) 28099305; e-mail art@igbk.de; internet www.iaa-europe.eu; f. 1954; 81 national cttees; Pres. WERNER SCHAUB.

International Association of Art Critics/Association Internationale des Critiques d'Art: 15 rue Martel, 75010 Paris, France; tel. 1-47-70-17-42; fax 1-47-70-17-81; e-mail office.paris@aica-int.org; internet www.aica-int.org; f. 1949 to promote int. cooperation in the world of plastic arts (painting, sculpture, graphic arts, architecture); consultative status with UNESCO; 3,750 individual mems and 72 National Sections; Pres. HENRY MEYRIC HUGHES (UK); Gen. Sec. RAMON TIO BELLIDO (France); publ. *Annuaire AiCA*.

International Association of Literary Critics/Association Internationale des Critiques Littéraires: 38 rue du Faubourg-St-Jacques, 75014 Paris, France; tel. 1-53-10-12-00; fax 1-53-10-12-12; f. 1969; UNESCO consultative status B; organizes congresses, etc.; Pres. DANIEL LEUVEY; Vice-Pres. SYLVESTRE CLANCIER; publ. *Revue* (1 a year).

International Centre for the Study of the Preservation and Restoration of Cultural Property (ICCROM): Via di San Michele 13, 00153 Rome, Italy; tel. 06-585531; fax 06-58553349; e-mail iccrom@ iccrom.org; internet www.iccrom.org; f. 1959; inter-governmental org.; UNESCO Class A; assembles documentation and disseminates knowledge by way of publications and meetings; coordinates research, organizes training of specialists and short courses; offers technical advice; int. documentation centre; financed by 126 mem. states; library of 100,000 registered references; Dir-Gen. MOUNIR BOUCHENAKI.

International Centre of Films for Children and Young People/Centre International du Film pour l'Enfance et la Jeunesse: Bureau 200, 3774 rue St Denis, Montréal, QC H2W 2M1, Canada; tel. (514) 284-9388; fax (514) 284-0168; e-mail info@ cifej.com; internet www.cifej.com; f. 1955; research centre and clearing-house of information about entertainment films (cinema and television) for children all over the world; 153 mems from 55 countries; Pres. ATHINA RIKAKI (Greece); Sec.-Gen. MONIC

LESSARD (Canada); publ. *CIFEJ Info* (6 a year).

International Committee of Museums and Collections of Arms and Military History (ICOMAM): c/o Dirk Staat, Legermuseum, Korte Geer 1, 2611 CA Delft, Netherlands; tel. (15) 2150500; fax (15) 2150544; e-mail secretary@icomam.icom .museum; internet icomam.icom.museum; f. 1957; officially recoz+nised Int. Committee of the Int. Ccl of Museums; org. to establish contact between museums and other scientific institutions with collns of arms and armour, military equipment, uniforms, etc., that may be visited by the public; to promote the study of relevant groups of objects; triennial confs; 300 instns in 51 countries; Pres. GUY M. WILSON (UK); Sec. MATHIEU WILLEMSEN (acting) (Netherlands); publs *Glossarium Armourum: Arma Defensiva, Repertory of Museums of Arms and Military History, Triennial Reports.*

International Comparative Literature Association/Association internationale de littérature comparée: c/o Prof. Steven P. Sondrup, Brigham Young Univ., HRCB Provo, UT 84602 3168 JFSB, USA; e-mail ailc.icla@gmail.com; internet www.ailc-icla .org; f. 1954; promotes devt of comparative study of literature; 5,000 mems (socs and individuals) in 65 countries; Pres. Prof. STEVEN SONDRUP (USA); Secs Prof. MARC MAUFORT (Belgium), Prof. JOHN BURT FOSTER (USA); publ. *Recherche Littéraire/Literary Research* (2 a year).

International Council for Film, Television and Audiovisual Communication/Conseil International du Cinéma, de la Télévision et de la Communication audiovisuelle: 1 rue Miollis, Bureau B7.2.23–2.25, 75732 Paris Cedex 15; tel. 1-45-68-48-56; e-mail secretariat@ cict-unesco.org; internet www.unesco.org/ iftc; f. 1958 under auspices of UNESCO; seeks to provide a link of information and jt action between member orgs, and to assist them in their int. work in film and television; mems: 36 int. asscns and feds and 12 assocs; Sec.-Gen. LOLA POGGI-GOUJON.

International Council of Graphic Design Associations (ICOGRADA): 455 Saint Antoine Ouest, Suite SS 10, Montréal, QC H2Z 1J1, Canada; tel. (514) 448-4949; fax (514) 448-4948; e-mail info@icograda.org; internet www.icograda.org; f. 1963; collects and exchanges information relating to graphic design; to organize exhibitions and congresses and issues reports and surveys; raises the standards of graphic design and professional practice and the professional status of graphic designers; 71 assoc. mems in 44 countries; library: slide and book library at Design Museum, London, UK; poster and records archives at University of Reading, UK; Pres. RUSSELL KENNEDY (Australia); Sec.-Gen. GRÉGOIRE SERIKOFF (France); Treas. DAVID BERMAN (Canada); Vice-Pres. IVA BABAJA (Croatia); Vice-Pres. JASON FAN (Taiwan); Vice-Pres. DAVID LANCASHIRE (Australia); Vice-Pres. OMAR VULPINARI (Italy); Vice-Pres. XIAO YONG (China); publ. *Board Message* (4 a year).

International Council of Museums (ICOM): Maison de l'UNESCO, 1 rue Miollis, 75732 Paris Cedex 15, France; tel. 1-47-34-05-00; fax 1-43-06-78-62; e-mail secretariat@ icom.museum; internet icom.museum; f. 1946; professional org., open to all mems of the museum profession, established to provide an appropriate org. to advance int. cooperation among museums, and to be the coordinating and representative int. body furthering museum interests; in 117 countries an ICOM Nat. Cttee on int. cooperation among museums has been organized, each as widely representative as possible of museum interests; maintains UNESCO-ICOM Museum Information Centre, a library and information service specializing in the field of museology and museum practice worldwide; 31 int. cttees and 18 int. affiliated asscns on specialized subjects; 26,000 individual and institutional mems in 137 countries; Pres. Dr HANS-MARTIN HINZ (Germany); Dir-Gen. JULIEN ANFRUNS; publs *ICOM News/Nouvelles de l'ICOM/Noticias del ICOM* (4 a year), *Study Series/Cahier d'Etude* (1 a year).

International Council on Monuments and Sites (ICOMOS)/Conseil International des Monuments et des Sites: 49–51 rue de la Fédération, 75015 Paris, France; tel. 1-45-67-67-70; fax 1-45-66-06-22; e-mail secretariat@icomos.org; internet www .international.icomos.org; f. 1965 to promote the study and preservation of monuments and sites; 7,000 mems, 110 national cttees, 22 int. cttees; library: Documentation Centre on preservation and restoration of monuments and sites: 30,000 vols, 350 periodicals, 25,000 slides; Pres. MICHAEL PETZET (Germany); Sec.-Gen. DINU BUMBARU (Canada); publ. *Icomos Scientific Journal.*

International Federation for Theatre Research/Fédération Internationale pour la Recherche Théâtrale: c/o Prof. David Whitton, DELC, Lancaster Univ., Lancaster, LA1 4YN, UK; internet www .firt-iftr.org; f. 1955 by 21 countries at the Int. Conf. on Theatre History, London, UK; int. seminars in theatre history; attached research institute Istituto Internazionale per la Ricerca Teatrale: see Italy chapter; c. 450 mems in approx. 45 countries; Pres. Prof. BRIAN SINGLETON (Ireland); Jt Secs-Gen. Prof. SOPHIE PROUST (France), Prof. DAVID WHITTON (UK); publ. *Theatre Research International* (4 a year).

International Institute for Conservation of Historic and Artistic Works/Institut International pour la Conservation des Objets d'Art et d'Histoire: 6 Buckingham St, London, WC2N 6BA, UK; tel. (20) 7839-5975; fax (20) 7976-1564; e-mail iic@iiconservation.org; internet www .iiconservation.org; f. 1950; permanent org. for coordinating and improving the knowledge, methods and working standards needed to protect and preserve precious materials of all kinds; publishes information on research into all processes connected with conservation, both scientific and technical, and on the devt of those processes; congress held every 2 years; 2,000 individual mems, 400 institutional mems; Pres. JERRY PODANY; Sec.-Gen. JO KIRBY ATKINSON; Exec. Sec. GRAHAM VOCE; publ. *Studies in Conservation* (4 a year).

International Literary and Artistic Association/Association Littéraire et Artistique Internationale: c/o Kimbrough et Associés, 7 bis rue de Monceau, 75008 Paris, France; tel. 1-53-30-24-24; fax 1-53-30-24-25; internet alai.org; f. 1878 at Congress of Paris, presided over by Victor Hugo; seeks to protect the rights and interests of writers and artists of all lands, through the extension of copyright conventions, etc.; mems: nat. groups in Argentina, Austria, Belgium, Canada, Colombia, Croatia, Denmark, Finland, France, Germany, Greece, Hungary, Ireland, Israel, Italy, Japan, Kazakhstan, Mexico, Netherlands, Norway, Portugal, Russia, Spain, Sweden, Switzerland, UK, Uruguay, USA; Pres. VICTOR NABHAN; Sec.-Gen. YVES GAUBIAC.

International Numismatic Commission/Commission internationale de numismatique: Cabinet des Médailles, Bibliothèque Nationale de France, 75084 Paris, France; internet www.inc-cin.org; f. 1927 to facilitate cooperation among individuals and instns in the field of numismatics; mems: nat. orgs in 38 countries; Pres. MICHEL AMANDRY (UK); Sec. Dr CARMEN ARNOLD (USA); publ. *International Numismatic e-News* (irregular).

International PEN (A World Association of Writers): 9–10 Charterhouse Bldgs, Goswell Rd, London, EC1M 7AT, UK; tel. (20) 7253-4308; fax (20) 7253-5711; e-mail intpen@dircon.co.uk; internet www .internationalpen.org.uk; f. 1921 by Mrs Dawson Scott under the presidency of John Galsworthy to promote cooperation between writers all over the world in the interests of literature, freedom of expression and int. goodwill; 138 autonomous centres worldwide; 14,000 mems; Int. Pres. JIRI GRUSA; Int. Sec. TERRY CARLBOM; publ. *PEN International* (2 a year, in English, French and Spanish, in asscn with UNESCO).

International Pragmatics Association (IPrA): POB 33, 2018 Antwerp 11, Belgium; tel. (3) 265-45-63; fax (3) 230-55-74; e-mail ann.verhaert@ua.ac.be; internet ipra.ua.ac .be; f. 1986; aims to create a framework for the discussion and comparison of results of research in all aspects of language use or functions of language and to disseminate knowledge about pragmatic aspects of language; inc. a research centre; 1,400 individual mems; Sec.-Gen. JEF VERSCHUEREN; Exec. Sec. ANN VERHAERT; publ. *Pragmatics* (4 a year).

International Robert Musil Society/Internationale Robert-Musil-Gesellschaft: POB 151150, Univ. des Saarlandes, 66041 Saarbrucken, Germany; tel. (681) 302-3334; fax (681) 302-3034; e-mail info@i-r-m-g.de; internet www.i-r-m-g.de; f. 1974 under the patronage of Bruno Kreisky (Austria), to promote int. cooperation in research and publications on Musil and edns of his writings; 267 mems; organizes colloquia; Pres. Prof. Dr PETER HENNINGER (France); Secs-Gen. Prof. Dr PIERRE BÉHAR (Germany), Prof. Dr ROSMARIE ZELLER (Switzerland); publ. *Musil-Forum* (every 2 years).

International Theatre Institute/Institut International du Théâtre: UNESCO, 1 rue Miollis, 75732 Paris Cedex 15, France; tel. (1) 45-68-48-80; fax (1) 45-68-48-84; e-mail iti@iti-worldwide.org; internet www .iti-worldwide.org/amt; f. 1948 to facilitate cultural exchanges and int. understanding in the domain of the performing arts; conferences, workshops, publs; education and training in performing arts; protection and promotion of cultural diversity; languages of instruction French, English; mems: 102 mem. nations; Pres. RAMENDU MAJUMDAR (Bangladesh); Vice-Pres. ALI MAHDI (Sudan); Vice-Pres. CHRISTINA BABOU-PAGOURELI (Greece); Sec.-Gen. TOBIAS BIANCONE (France); publs *News* (3 a year), *The World of Theatre* (every 2 years), *World Theatre Directory* (online).

International Union of Architects/Union Internationale des Architectes: Tour Maine Montparnasse-B. P. 158, 33 avenue du Maine, 75755 Paris, France; tel. 1-45-24-36-88; fax 1-45-24-02-78; e-mail uia@ uia-architectes.org; internet www .uia-architectes.org; f. 1948; mems in 106 countries

International Union of Cinema/Union Internationale du Cinéma: c/o Jan P. Essing, Lente 33, 8251 NT Dronten, The Netherlands; tel. (321) 319529; fax (321) 312739; e-mail essing.jan@hetnet.nl; internet www.unica-web.com; f. 1937 to encourage devt of art, techniques and critical judgement among amateurs, to facilitate contacts between nat. asscns, and to promote the exchange of films; mems: nat. feds in 35 countries; library of 500 films and video-cassettes; Annual Congress; Sec.-Gen. JAN ESSING; publ. *UNICA News.*

Organization for Museums, Monuments and Sites of Africa/Organisation pour les Musées, les Monuments et les Sites d'Afrique: POB 3343, Accra, Ghana; f. 1975; aims to foster the collection, study and conservation of the natural and cultural heritage of Africa; cooperation between mem. countries through seminars, work-shops, conferences, etc., exchange of person-nel, developing training facilities, and drawing up legislative and admin. measures; mems from 30 countries; Pres. Dr J. M. ESSOMBA (Cameroon); Dir-Gen. Dr CLAUDE MARTIN (Ghana).

World Academy of Art and Science: see under International—Science.

World Crafts Council: El Comendador 1916, Providencia, 6640064 Santiago, Chile; tel. (2) 3545636; fax (2) 2325811; e-mail wis@wccwis.cl; internet www.wccwis.cl; f. 1964; non-profit org. to maintain the status of crafts as a vital part of cultural life and to promote fellowship among the world's crafts-men; offers help and advice to craftsmen, consults with govts, nat. and int. institutions; mem. bodies in approx 90 countries; Pres. MARÍA CELINA RODRÍGUEZ OLEA (Chile); publ. *World Crafts Council—Asia Pacific* (2 a year).

Bibliography

Association for Health Information and Libraries in Africa: c/o WHO Regional Office for Africa, BP 6, Brazzaville, Republic of Congo; tel. 241-39425; fax 241-39673; internet www.ahila.org; f. 1984, name changed 1989; promotes cooperation among African health information centres and libraries, to enhance health information ser-vices and to develop an African *Index Medicus;* Pres. IBRAHIMA BOB; Sec. BACHIR CHAIBOU.

Association of Caribbean University, Research and Institutional Libraries: POB 23317, San Juan, Puerto Rico 00931-3317; tel. (787) 790-8054; fax (787) 763-5685; e-mail acurilsec@yahoo.com; internet acuril .rrp.upr.edu; f. 1969 to facilitate the devt and use of libraries, archives and information services; identification, collection and preser-vation of information resources in support of intellectual and educational endeavours in the area; 200 mems; Pres. ADELE MERRITT BARNARD (Jamaica); Exec. Dir ONEIDA RIVERA DE ORTIZ (Puerto Rico); publs *ACURILEANA* (online), *Conference Proceedings.*

Commonwealth Library Association: POB 144, Mona, Kingston 7, Jamaica; tel. 927-0083; fax 927-1926; e-mail nkpodo@uwimona.edu.jm; f. 1972 to support and encourage library asscns in the Common-wealth; to create and strengthen professional relationships between librarians; to promote the status and education of librarians and the reciprocal recognition of qualifications; to improve libraries; to initiate research pro-jects designed to promote library provision and to advance technical development of libraries in the Commonwealth; language of instruction English; 52 mems incl. 40 nat. asscns, 130 affiliated mems; Pres. (vacant); publ. *COMLA Bulletin* (3 a year).

European Association for Health Infor-mation and Libraries: POB 1393, 3600 BJ Maarssen, Netherlands; fax (346) 550876; e-mail eahil@nic.surfnet.nl; internet www .eahil.net; f. 1987, to bring together and represent health librarians and information officers in Europe; 1,150 mems; Pres. SUZANNE BAKKER (Netherlands); Sec. TONY MCSÈAN (UK); publ. *Journal of EAHIL* (4 a year).

European Theological Libraries/Euro-päische Bibliotheken für Theologie/Bib-liothèques Européennes de Théologie (BETH) Europäische Bibliotheken für Theologie: 5 Swanston Crescent, Edin-burgh, EH10 7BS, UK; tel. (131) 445-1691; e-mail prjhall@aol.com; internet www.beth .be; f. 1961; holds Annual General Assembly; 35 mems (12 ordinary, 14 extraordinary, 10 individuals); Pres. ODILE DUPONT (France); Exec. Sec. Prof. PENELOPE HALL; Treas. VERONIQUE VERSPEURT.

International Association for Mass Com-munication Research/Association inter-nationale des études et recherches sur l'information: c/o Hamid Mowlana, School of International Service, American Univer-sity, 4400 Massachusetts Ave NW, Washing-ton, DC 20016, USA; tel. (202) 885-1621; fax (202) 855-2494; e-mail mowlana@american .edu; internet www.humfak.auc.dk/iamcr; f. 1957 to disseminate information on teaching and research in mass media; to encourage research; to provide a forum for the exchange of information; to bring about improvements in communication practice, policy and research; and to encourage the improvement of training for journalism; over 1,000 mems in 63 countries; Pres. HAMID MOWLANA.

International Association of Agricul-tural Information Specialists/Associ-ation Internationale des Spécialistes de l'Information Agricole: POB 63, Lex-ington, KY 40588-0063, USA; tel. (859) 254-0752; fax (859) 254-8379; e-mail info@iaald .org; internet www.iaald.org; f. 1955; unites agricultural information specialists world-wide, organizes meetings and educational programmes, workshops and annual confs in various parts of world and through social networks, communicates value of knowledge and information, collaborates with partner orgs; 300 mems, representing 80 countries; Pres. Dr BARBARA HUTCHINSON; Sec. and Treas. ANTOINETTE P. GREIDER; publ. *Agri-cultural Information Worldwide* (int. journal for information specialists in agriculture, natural resources and environment, online).

International Association of Biblio-philes/Association Internationale de Bibliophilie: c/o Bibliothèque Nationale de France, Réserve des livres rares, Quai Fran-çois Mauriac, 75706 Paris Cedex 13, France; tel. 1-53-79-54-76; fax 1-53-79-54-60; f. 1963 to form a meeting point for bibliophiles from different countries; int. congresses every 2 years; 450 mems; Pres. T. KIMBALL BROOKER (USA); Sec.-Gen. JEAN-MARC CHATELAIN (France); publ. *Le Bulletin du Bibliophile* (2 a year).

International Association of Law Libraries (IALL)/Association Inter-nationale des Bibliothèques de Droit: ; tel. (1) 8175121; e-mail jaston@lawlibrary.ie; internet www.iall.org; f. 1959 to offer world-wide cooperation in the devt of law libraries and the colln of legal documentation; holds annual conference; 580 mems in 60 coun-tries; Pres. JULES WINTERTON (UK); Sec. JENNEFER ASTON (Ireland); publ. *Inter-national Journal of Legal Information* (3 a year).

International Association of Music Libraries, Archives and Documentation Centres (IAML)/L'Association Inter-nationale des Bibliothèques, Archives et Centres de Documentation Musi-caux/Die Internationale Vereinigung der **Musikbibliotheken, Musikarchive und Musikdokumentationszentren:** c/o Pia Shekhter Gothenburg University Library Music and Drama Library Box 210, 405 30 Gothenburg, Sweden; tel. (31) 786-40-57; e-mail pia.shekhter@gu.se; internet www .iaml.info; f. 1951 to facilitate cooperation between music libraries and information centres, compile music bibliographies, and to promote the professional training of music librarians and documentalists; languages of instruction French, German, English; annual confs, large-scale documentation projects: répertoire internationale des sources musi-cales (RISM), répertoire internationale d'ico-nographie musicale (RIdIM), répertoire internationale de la presse musicale (RIPM), répertoire internationale de lit-térature musicale (RILM); 1,800 mems in 53 countries, incl. 22 nat. brs; Sec.-Gen. PIA SHEKHTER; publ. *Fontes artis musicae* (4 a year).

International Association of Techno-logical University Libraries (IATUL)/ Association Internationale des Bib-liothèques d'Universités Polytechni-ques: c/o Judith Palmer, Radcliffe Science Library, Univ. of Oxford, Parks Rd, Oxford, OX1 3QP, UK; internet www.iatul.org; f. 1955 to promote cooperation between mem. libraries and conduct research on library problems; mems: 200 univ. libraries in 41 countries; Pres. GAYNOR AUSTEN (Australia); Sec. JUDITH PALMER; publs *IATUL News* (4 a year), *IATUL Proceedings* (1 a year).

International Board on Books for Young People (IBBY): Nonnenweg 12, Postfach, 4003 Basel, Switzerland; tel. 612722917; fax 612722757; e-mail ibby@ibby.org; internet www.ibby.org; f. 1953 to support and unify those forces in all countries connected with children's book work; to encourage the pro-duction and distribution of good children's books especially in developing countries; to promote scientific investigation into prob-lems of juvenile books; to organize Int. Children's Book Day and a biennial int. congress; to present the Hans Christian Andersen Award every 2 years to a living author and illustrator whose work is an outstanding contribution to children's litera-ture, and the IBBY-Asahi Reading Promotion Award annually to an org. that has made a significant contribution to children's litera-ture; to make a biennial selection of out-standing books to form the IBBY Honour List; Mems: Nat. Sections and individual mems in 75 countries; Pres. AHMAD REDZA AHMAD KHAIRUDDIN (Malaysia); Exec. Dir LIZ PAGE (Switzerland); publ. *Bookbird* (4 a year).

International Committee for Social Sci-ence Information and Documentation/ Comité International pour l'Informa-tion et la Documentation des Sciences Sociales: c/o Clacso, Callao 875 (3° piso), 1023 Buenos Aires, Argentina; e-mail saugy@clacso.edu.ar; f. 1950 to collect and disseminate information on documentation services in social sciences, help improve documentation, advise socs on problems of documentation and to draw up rules likely to improve the presentation of all documents; mems from int. asscns specializing in social sciences or in documentation, and from other specialized fields; Pres. KRISHANA G. TYAGI (India); Sec.-Gen. CATALINA SAUGY (Argen-tina); publ. *International Bibliography of the Social Sciences* (1 a year, 4 series).

International Council on Archives/Con-seil international des archives: 60 rue des Francs-Bourgeois, 75003 Paris, France; tel. 1-40-27-63-06; fax 1-42-72-20-65; e-mail ica@ica.org; internet www.ica.org; f. 1948; 1,420 mems from 197 countries and territories; Pres. MARTIN BERENDSE (Netherlands); Sec.-Gen. DAVID A. LEITCH (France); publs *COMMA International Journal on Archives* (2 a year), *FLASH* (2 a year).

International Federation of Film Archives/Fédération Internationale des Archives du Film: 1 rue Defacqz, 1000 Brussels, Belgium; tel. (2) 538-30-65; fax (2) 534-47-74; e-mail info@fiafnet.org; internet www.fiafnet.org; f. 1938 to encourage the creation of archives worldwide for the collection and conservation of the film heritage of each country; to facilitate cooperation and exchanges between these film archives; to promote public interest in the art of the cinema; to aid research in this field and to compile new documentation; conducts research; publishes manuals, etc.; holds annual congresses; 108 affiliates in 62 countries; Pres. EVA ORBANZ (Germany); Sec.-Gen. MEG LABRUM (Australia).

International Federation of Library Associations and Institutions (IFLA)/ Fédération Internationale des Associations de Bibliothécaires et des Bibliothèques: POB 95312, 2509 CH, The Hague, Netherlands; tel. (70) 314-08-84; fax (70) 383-48-27; e-mail ifla@ifla.org; internet www.ifla.org; f. 1927; to promote int. library cooperation in all fields of library activity, and to provide a representative body in matters of int. interest; 1,700 mems in 150 countries; Pres. ELLEN TISE (SA); Sec.-Gen. JENNEFER NICHOLSON (Netherlands); publs *IFLA Journal* (4 a year), *IFLA Directory* (every 2 years), *IFLA Professional Reports*, *IFLA Publication Series* (6 a year), *International Cataloguing Bibliographic Control* (4 a year).

Associated Centre:

Metropolitan Libraries Section: State Library Queensland, POB 3488, South Brisbane, Qld 4101, Australia; tel. (7) 38429405; fax (7) 38407860; f. 1967 to encourage int. cooperation between large city libraries, in particular the exchange of books, exhibitions, staff and information and participation in the work of the Int. Fed. of Library Asscns; Pres. LIV SAETEREN (Norway); Sec.-Treas. TAY AI CHENG (Singapore)

International Institute for Children's Literature and Reading Research/Institut für Jugendliteratur/Institut International de Littérature pour Enfants et de Recherches sur la Lecture: 1040 Vienna, Mayerhofgasse 6, Austria; tel. (1) 505-03-59; fax (1) 505-03-59-17; e-mail office@jugendliteratur.net; internet www.jugendliteratur.net; f. 1965 as an int. documentation and advisory centre of juvenile literature; promotes int. research; arranges conferences and exhibitions; compiles recommendation lists; mems: individual and group members in 26 countries; Dir Mag. KARIN HALLER (Austria); publ. *1000 und 1 Buch* (4 a year).

International Society for Knowledge Organization (ISKO): c/o Vivien Petras, Institut für Bibliotheks- und Informationswissenschaft, Unter den Linden 6, 10099 Berlin, Germany; tel. (30) 2093-4325; fax (30) 2093-4335; e-mail secr@isko.org; internet www.isko.org; f. 1989 to promote research, devt, and application of all methods for the org. of knowledge; advises on the construction, perfection and application of classification systems, thesauri, terminologies, etc.; organizes int. conference every 2 years; 400 mems; Pres. H. PETER OHLY (Germany); Sec. and Treas. Prof. VIVIEN PETRAS (Germany); publs *Advances in Knowledge Organization, Ergon* (Proceedings in English, irregular), *Fortschritte der Wissensorganisation, Ergon*

(Proceedings in German, irregular), *Knowledge Organization, Ergon* (4 a year), *Knowledge Organization in Subject Areas 1994–* (irregular).

International Youth Library/Internationale Jugendbibliothek: Schloss Blutenburg, 81247 Munich, Germany; tel. (89) 891211-0; fax (89) 8117553; e-mail info@ijb .de; internet www.ijb.de; f. 1949; an associated project of UNESCO since 1953 Objects: to encourage int. exchange and cooperation in children's book publishing, research, and promotion of reading; to provide information and advice to students, teachers, publishers, etc.; to organize exhibitions; library: largest collection of int. children's literature in the world: 570,000 vols in over 130 languages; Dir Dr CHRISTIANE RAABE; publs *Das Bücherschloss* (report, 1 a year), *Report* (2 a year), *White Ravens* (selection of int. children's and youth literature, 1 a year).

Ligue des Bibliothèques Européennes de Recherche (LIBER): Koninklijke Bibliotheek, National Library of the Netherlands, POB 90407, 2509 The Hague, The Netherlands; tel. 70-314-01-97; e-mail liber@ kb.nl; internet www.libereurope.eu; f. 1971; 360 mems from more than 40 European countries; represents and promotes the interests of research libraries in Europe, particularly to assist them to create a functional research network across nat. boundaries; Pres. HANS GELEIJNSE; Exec. Dir WOUTER SCHALLIER (The Netherlands); publ. *LIBER Quarterly* (online).

Economics, Political Science and Sociology

International Labour Organization (ILO): 4 route des Morillons, 1211 Geneva 22, Switzerland; tel. (22) 799-61-11; fax (22) 798-86-85; e-mail ilo@ilo.org; internet www .ilo.org; f. 1919, became Specialized Agency of UN in 1946; builds a code of int. labour law and practice; is concerned with the safety, health and social security of workers and provides technical expertise where required by member countries; seeks to improve labour conditions, raise living standards and promote productive employment in all countries; library: see under Switzerland; 179 mem. countries; Dir-Gen. JUAN SOMAVIA; publs *Bulletin of Labour Statistics, International Labour Documentation, International Labour Review*, manuals and reports, *Official Bulletin*, studies, *World of Work, Yearbook of Labour Statistics*.

Associated Institutions:

International Institute for Labour Studies: CP 6, 1211 Geneva 22, Switzerland; tel. (22) 799-61-28; fax (22) 799-85-42; e-mail inst@ilo.org; internet www.ilo .org/public/english/bureau/inst; f. 1960 by ILO; provides a global forum for interaction between business, labour, policymakers and academics on emerging labour policy issues; promotes research networks on policy implications of changing relationships between labour, business and the State; develops the research capacities of ministries of labour and employers' and workers' organizations; Dir G. RODGERS.

International Training Centre of the ILO/Centre International de Formation de l'OIT: Viale Maestri del Lavoro 10, 10127 Turin, Italy; tel. 011-693-6111; fax 011-663-8842; e-mail communications@ itcilo.org; internet www.itcilo.org; f. 1964 by International Labour Organization to offer advanced training facilities for managers, trainers and social partners, and

technical specialists from ILO mem. states; Exec. Dir PATRICIA O'DONOVAN

OTHER ORGANIZATIONS

African Training and Research Centre in Administration for Development/ Centre Africain de Formation et de Recherche Administratives pour le Développement (CAFRAD): Pavillon International, Blvd Mohammed V, BP 1796, 90001 Tangier, Morocco; tel. (661) 30-72-69; fax (539) 32-57-85; e-mail cafrad@cafrad.org; internet www.cafrad.org; f. 1964,by African govts, with support of UNESCO; training of African senior civil servants; research into admin. problems in Africa, documentation of results, and the provision of a consultation service for govts and orgs in Africa; holds frequent seminars; mems: Algeria, Angola, Benin, Burkina Faso, Burundi, Cameroon, Cape Verde, Central African Republic, Chad, Congo, Côte d'Ivoire, Dem. Rep. of Congo, Djibouti, Equatorial Guinea, Gabon, Gambia, Ghana, Guinea, Guinea-Bissau, Liberia, Libya, Madagascar, Mali, Mauritania, Morocco, Namibia, Niger, Nigeria, São Tomé e Príncipe, Sierra Leone, Somalia, South Africa, Sudan, Togo, Tunisia, Zambia; UNESCO provided assistance 1964–1970 and UNDP 1971–1983; organizes Pan-African Conf. of Dirs of Schools and Institutes of Public Admin. and Management (ENA/IPA/ IDM); African Day of Administration and Civil Service (23 June each year), seminars; confs and workshops; 37 mem. states; library of 35,000 vols; Pres. S. E. MOHAMED SAÂD EL ALAMI; Dir-Gen. Dr SIMON LELO MAMOSI; publs *African Administrative Studies* (2 a year), *African Public Service Charter, Directory of African Consultants in Public Administration, Directory of African Training and Research Institutions, Proceedings of Pan-African Conference of Ministers of the Civil Service* (every 2 years), *Juelles Verifier et Expedia, Studies and Documents (Series)* (irregular).

American Society for Political and Legal Philosophy: c/o The Sec./Treas., Prof. Jacob T. Levy, Political Science, McGill University, 855 Sherbrooke Ave W, Montreal, QC H3A 2T7, Canada; tel. (514) 398-5519; fax (514) 398-1770; e-mail theasplp@ gmail.com; internet www.political-theory .org/asplp.html; f. 1955; 500 mems; Pres. DONALD HOROWITZ; publ. *NOMOS* (Yearbook).

Association of International Accountants: Staithes 3, The Watermark, Metro Riverside, Newcastle upon Tyne, NE11 9SN, UK; tel. (191) 4930277; fax (191) 4930278; e-mail aia@aiaworldwide.com; internet www.aiaworldwide.com; f. 1928; promotes and supports the advancement of the accountancy profession worldwide; offers a professional qualification for accountants and statutory auditors; 18,000 mems and students; Pres. ANDREW LAMB; Chief Exec. PHILIP TURNBULL; publ. *International Accountant* (6 a year).

Association of Social Anthropologists of the Commonwealth: POB 5230, Hove, BN52 9NB, UK; e-mail admin@theasa.org; internet www.theasa.org; f. 1946; 570 mems; Chair. Prof. RICHARD FARDON; Hon. Sec. Dr IRIS JEAN-KLEIN; publs *ASA Annals, ASA Essays, ASA Methods in Social Anthropology, ASA Studies*.

Centre for Democracy and Development/Centre pour la Démocratie et le Développement: Unit 2L Leroy House, 436 Essex Rd, London, N1 3QP, UK; tel. (20) 7359-7775; fax (20) 7359-2221; e-mail cdd@ cdd.org.uk; internet www.cddwestafrica.org; f. 1997; non-profit NGO dedicated to research, information and exchange of ideas on questions of democratic devt and peace-building in West Africa; offers strategic training in promoting democracy and devt; regional offices in Abuja and Lagos, Nigeria; Dir Dr JIBRIN IBRAHIM; publ. *Democracy and Development: Journal of West African Affairs* (2 a year).

Econometric Society: Dept of Economics, NW Univ., 2003 Sheridan Rd, Evanston, IL 60208-2600, USA; tel. (847) 491-3615; fax (847) 491-5427; internet www .econometricsociety.org; f. 1930 to promote studies on the unification of the theoretical-quantitative and the empirical-quantitative approach to economic problems; 6,700 mems; Exec. Vice-Pres. RAFAEL REPULLO (Spain); Gen. Man. CLAIRE SASHI (USA); publ. *Econometrica*.

European Association for Population Studies/Association Européenne pour l'Étude de la Population: POB 11676, 2502 AR The Hague, Netherlands; tel. (70) 3565200; fax (70) 3647187; e-mail contact@ eaps.nl; internet www.eaps.nl; f. 1983 to promote the study of population in Europe through cooperation between persons interested or engaged in European demographics; mems: demographers and other population scientists from all European countries; Pres. FRANCOIS HERAN (France); Sec.-Gen. and Treas. FRANCESCO BILLARI (Italy); Exec. Sec. HELGA DE VALK; publ. *European Journal of Population/Revue Européenne de Démographie*.

European Centre for Social Welfare Policy and Research: Berggasse 17, 1090 Vienna, Austria; tel. (1) 3194505-0; fax (1) 3194505-19; e-mail ec@euro.centre.org; internet www.euro.centre.org; non-profit autonomous intergovernmental organization affiliated to the UN; conducts research, and provides training and information, in the fields of welfare and social development; library of 8,000 vols; Exec. Dir Prof. Dr BERND MARIN; publ. *Eurosocial Reports Series* (in English, French and German).

European Economic Association: Università Cattolica del Sacro Cuore, 20123 Milan, Italy; tel. 2-72343050; fax 2-72343051; e-mail eea@unicatt.it; internet www.eeassoc.org; f. 1986 to contribute to the devt and application of economics as a science in Europe; to improve communication and exchange between teachers, researchers and students in economics in different European countries; to develop and sponsor cooperation between teaching instns and research instns in Europe; organizes annual congress; 2,700 mems; Pres. Prof. CHRISTOPHER PISSARIDES; Sec. Prof. PIERO TEDESCHI; publ. *Journal of the European Economic Asscn (JEEA)* (6 a year).

European Foundation for Management Development (EFMD): 88 rue Gachard, Boîte 3, 1050 Brussels, Belgium; tel. (2) 629-08-10; fax (2) 629-08-11; e-mail info@ efmd.org; internet www.efmd.be; f. 1971; provides forum for worldwide cooperation in management development; European Quality Initiative (EQUAL) project seeks int. cooperation in assessing quality in management education; mem. orgs (business schools, management centres, companies, consultancies) in 41 countries; Pres. GERARD VAN SCHAIK; Dir-Gen. ERIC CORNUEL; publ. *Forum* (3 a year).

Futuribles International: 47 rue de Babylone, 75007 Paris, France; tel. (1) 53-63-37-70; fax (1) 42-22-65-54; internet www .futuribles.com/home.html; f. 1960; aims to act as an early-warning system to identify major trends and challenges of the future; to undertake research on current economic and social issues; to serve as a consulting group for futures studies and strategic planning; major fields of expertise: development strategies, and multi-disciplinary studies on economic, technological, social and cultural changes in industrialized countries; library and documentation centre containing 90,000 vols; Scientific Council: 41 mems in 15 countries; Pres. JACQUES LESOURNE; Dir-Gen. HUGUES DE JOUVENEL (France); publs *Futuribles* (12 a year), *Vigie Info* (4 a year).

Inter-American Statistical Institute/ Instituto Interamericano de Estadística: c/o INEC, Contraloría General de la República, POB 0816-01521, 0186 Panama, Panama; tel. (507) 510-4890; fax (507) 223-6535; e-mail iasi@indec.mecon.gov.ar; internet www.contraloria.gob.pa/inec/iasi; f. 1940; br. in Buenos Aires; fosters statistical devt in the Western Hemisphere; holds seminars, courses and meetings; 316 mems (226 individual, 34 ex-officio, 16 affiliated (institutional); Pres. Dr LUIS A. ESCOBAR (USA); Technical Sec. Prof. EVELIO O. FABBRONI; publ. *Estadística* (2 a year).

International African Institute (IAI)/ Institut Africain International: School of Oriental and African Studies, Thornhaugh St, Russell Square, London, WC1H 0XG, UK; tel. (20) 7898-4420; fax (20) 7898-4419; e-mail iai@soas.ac.uk; internet www .internationalafricaninstitute.org; f. 1926; encourages the study of African history and society and disseminates the results of research; language of instruction French; Chair. Prof. V. Y. MUDIMBE; Hon. Dir Prof. PHILIP BURNHAM; publs *Africa* (4 a year), *Africa Bibliography* (1 a year).

International Association for South-East European Studies/Association Internationale d'Etudes du Sud-Est Européen (AIESEE): Apt. 18, Nicolae Racota 12–14, 713123 Bucharest, Romania; tel. (21) 2242965; fax (21) 2242964; f. 1963; 23 mem. countries; Pres. Prof. ANDRÉ GUILLOU (France); Sec.-Gen. Prof. RĂZVAN THEODORESCU (Romania); publ. *Bulletin* (1 a year).

International Association for the Study of Insurance Economics/Geneva Association: 53 route de Malagnou, 1208 Geneva, Switzerland; tel. (22) 707-66-00; fax (22) 736-75-36; e-mail secretariat@genevaassociation .org; internet www.genevaassociation.org; f. 1973; non-profit org.; develops research programmes, regular publs and int. meetings; serves as a catalyst for progress in understanding risk and insurance matters; acts as an information creator and disseminator; organizes int. expert networks and manages discussion platforms for insurance execs, specialists, policy-makers, regulators and multilateral orgs; int. insurance 'think tank' for insurance and risk management issues; mems: up to 80 CEOs from the world's insurance companies; Pres. HENRI DE CASTRIES; Sec.-Gen., Man. Dir and Head of Insurance and Finance PATRICK LIEDTKE; Vice Sec.-Gen. and Head of Research Programmes WALTER R. STAHEL; Vice Sec.-Gen. and Head of Progress PROF. MONKIEWICZ; Head of Communications ANTHONY KENNAWAY; publs *The Geneva Papers*, *The Geneva Papers on Risk and Insurance*, *The Geneva Risk and Insurance Review*.

International Association of Schools of Social Work (IASSW): c/o Prof. Lynne Healy, Center for International Social Work Studies, University of Connecticut, School of Social Work, 1798 Asylum Ave, West Hartford, CT 06117, USA; tel. (860) 570-9149; fax (860) 570-9139; e-mail iasswsec@comcast .net; internet www.iassw.soton.ac.uk; f. 1928 to provide int. leadership and encourage high standards in social work education; mems: 1,700 schools of social work in 90 countries and 35 nat. associations of schools; Pres. Prof. TASSE ABYE (France); Sec. Prof. LYNNE HEALY (USA).

International Center for Monetary and Banking Studies/Centre International d'Etudes Monétaires et Bancaires: 11A ave de la Paix, 1202 Geneva, Switzerland; tel. 227349548; fax 227333853; e-mail secretariat@cimb.ch; internet www.icmb.org; f. 1973; ind., associated with the Graduate Institute of Int. and Devt Studies; scientific study of int. monetary, financial and banking issues; organizes conferences, public lectures; Pres. THOMAS JORDAN; Dir Prof. CHARLES WYPLOSZ; publ. *Geneva Reports on the World Economy*.

International Centre for Ethnic Studies: 554/6A Peradeniya Rd, Kandy, Sri Lanka; tel. (81) 2232381; fax (81) 2234892; e-mail icesresch@sltnet.lk; internet www.ices.lk; f. 1982; encourages cross-national comparative research in ethnic policy studies; provides an institutional focus and identity for the study and management of ethnic conflict; library of 6,200 vols, spec. collns on ethnicity and women's issues; Exec. Dir Prof. MATHIAS DEWATRIPONT (Sri Lanka); publs *Ethnic Studies Report* (2 a year), *Nethra* (social issues, 4 a year).

International Commission for the History of Representative and Parliamentary Institutions/Commission Internationale pour l'Histoire des Assemblées d'Etats: c/o Dept of History, 43 North Bailey, Durham, DH1 3EX, UK; tel. (191) 386-4299; fax (191) 334-1041; e-mail j.m .rogister@dur.ac.uk; f. 1936 to encourage research on the origin and history of representative and parliamentary institutions; mems: individuals in 40 countries; languages of instruction French, English, German; organizes annual conferences, publishes monographs; Pres. Prof. J. ROGISTER (UK); Sec. ESTEVÃO DE REZENDE MARTINS (Brazil); publ. *Parliaments, Estates and Representation* (1 a year).

International Centre of Bantu Civilization/Centre International des Civilisations Bantu: BP 770, Libreville, Gabon; tel. 70-40-96; fax 77-50-90; e-mail ciciba@ caramail.com; f. 1983; intergovernmental organization founded by 10 countries containing members of the Bantu peoples: Angola, Central African Republic, Comoros, Democratic Republic of the Congo, Republic of the Congo, Equatorial Guinea, Gabon, Rwanda, São Tomé e Príncipe, Zambia; research and documentation centre for the conservation and promotion of the cultural heritage of the Bantu peoples; activities in all fields of culture, science and education; 50 staff; library of 4,000 vols, and special collection of university theses (microfiche) on 10 member states; Dir-Gen. VATOMENE KUKANDA; publs *CICIBA-Informations* (4 a year), *Muntu* (2 a year).

International Council on Social Welfare/ Conseil International d'Action Sociale/ Consejo Internacional del Bienestar Social: POB 28957, Kampala, Uganda; tel. (414) 32-11-50; e-mail icsw@icsw.org; internet www.icsw.org; f. 1928 to promote forms of social and economic development that aim to reduce poverty, hardship and vulnerability worldwide, especially in developing countries; 104 mem. orgs in 77 countries; Pres. CHRISTIAN ROLLET (France); Exec. Dir DENYS CORRELL; publs *Global Cooperation* (12 a year), *Proceedings of International Conferences on Social Welfare* (every 2 years).

International Federation of Business and Professional Women (BPW Inter-

national)/Federación Internacional de Mujeres de Negocios y Profesionales: POB 568, Horsham, West Sussex, RH13 9ZP, UK; tel. (1403) 739343; fax (1403) 734432; e-mail members@bpw-international .org; internet www.bpwi.org; f. 1930 to promote the interests of business and professional women, and in particular to bring their specialized knowledge and skills to play a more effective part in int. governmental orgs; 250,000 mems; Pres. ANTOINETTE RÜEGG; Exec. Sec. ANN SWAIN.

International Fiscal Association: World Trade Center, Beursplein 37, POB 30215, 3001 DE Rotterdam, Netherlands; tel. (10) 4052990; fax (10) 4055031; e-mail t.gensecr@ ifa.nl; internet www.ifa.nl; f. 1938; to study and advance int. and comparative law with regard to public finance and especially int. and comparative fiscal law and the financial and economic aspects of taxation; 12,000 mems in 105 countries, nat. brs in 62 countries; Pres. M. E. TRON (Mexico); Sec.-Gen. Dr H. A. KOGELS (Netherlands); publs *Cahiers de Droit Fiscal International* (Studies on International Fiscal Law), *Yearbook of the International Fiscal Association.*

International Institute for Ligurian Studies/Istituto Internazionale di Studi Liguri: Via Romana 39, 18012 Bordighera, Italy; tel. (184) 263601; fax (184) 266421; e-mail iisl@istitutostudi.191.it; internet www .iisl.it; f. 1947 to conduct research on ancient monuments and regional traditions in the north-west arc of the Mediterranean; library of 82,000 vols; mems in France, Italy, Spain, Switzerland; Dir Prof. CARLO VARALDO (Italy).

International Institute of Philosophy (IIP)/Institut International de Philosophie: 8 rue Jean-Calvin, 75005 Paris, France; tel. 1-43-36-39-11; fax 1-47-07-77-94; e-mail inst.intern.philo@wanadoo.fr; f. 1937; aims: to clarify fundamental issues of contemporary philosophy in annual meetings, and, by several series of publications, to promote mutual understanding among thinkers of different traditions and cultural backgrounds; a maximum of 115 mems, considered eminent in their field, chosen from all countries and representing different tendencies, are elected; present mems: 106 mems in 47 countries; Pres. TOMÁS CALVO (Spain); Sec.-Gen. Prof. BERNARD BOURGEOIS (France); pubs *Actes des congrès internationaux* (1 a year), *Bibliography of Philosophy* (4 a year, online), *Philosophy of Education, Surveys (Chroniques) of Philosophy.*

International Institute of Sociology/ Institut International de Sociologie: c/o Prof. Karen S. Cook, Dept of Sociology, Stanford University, Stanford, CA 94305, USA; e-mail iisoc@post.tau.ac.il; internet www.tau.sc.il/~iisoc; f. 1893 to advance the study of sociology; 300 mems in 45 countries; Pres. ELIEZER BEN-RAFAEL (Israel); Gen. Sec. and Treas. Prof. KAREN S. COOK (USA); publ. *Annales de l'Institut International de Sociologie / The Annals of the International Institute of Sociology.*

International Monetary Fund Institute: Washington, DC 20431, USA; tel. (202) 623-6660; fax (202) 623-6490; e-mail insinfo@imf .org; internet www.imf.org/external/np/ins/ english/about.htm; f. 1964 to provide specialist training in economic analysis and policy, statistics, public finance, and bank supervision, for officials of mem. countries; courses and seminars in Arabic, English, French and Spanish; library; Dir PATRICK DE FONTENAY; publ. *Courier.*

International Peace Institute: 777 United Nations Plaza, New York, NY 10017-3521, USA; tel. (212) 687-4300; fax (212) 983-8246;

e-mail ipi@ipinst.org; internet www.ipinst .org; f. 1970; acts as independent, int. institution, working closely with the UN and other governmental and non-governmental organizations, to promote the prevention and settlement of armed conflicts between and within states, through policy research and development; Pres. TERJE ROD-LARSEN; Vice-Pres. for External Relations WARREN HOGE; Senior Vice-Pres. for Research and Programs Dr EDWARD LUCK; publs *International Peacekeeping* (co-edited by IPI, 4 a year), *IPI Working Papers.*

International Society for Ethnology and Folklore: Meertens Institute, Joan Muyskenweg 25, 1096 CJ Amsterdam, The Netherlands; tel. (20) 4628500; fax (20) 4628555; e-mail sief@meertens.knaw.nl; internet www .siefhome.org; f. 1964, official seat in Amsterdam since 2001; attached to World Council of Anthropological Assns (WCAA), American Folklore Soc. (AFS) and European Asscn of Social Anthropologists (EASA): collaboration with UNESCO; organizes comms, symposia, congresses; establishes and maintains collaboration between specialists in folklore and ethnology; major int. congress organized every 3 years; 500 mems; Pres. ULLRICH KOCKEL (UK); Exec. Vice-Pres. PETER JAN MARGRY (Netherlands); Vice-Pres. BIRGITTA SVENSSON (Sweden).

International Society for the Study of Medieval Philosophy/Société Internationale pour l'Etude de la Philosophie Médiévale: Secretariat: c/o Prof. Dr Maarten Hoenen, Philosophisches Seminar, Platz der Universität 3, 79085 Freiburg im Breisgau, Germany; tel. (761) 203-2440; fax (761) 203-9260; e-mail siepm.membership@ philosophie.uni-freiburg.de; internet www .siepm.uni-freiburg.de; f. 1958 to promote the study of medieval thought and the collaboration between individuals and institutions engaged in this field; organizes int. congresses every five years and annual colloquium between congresses; 798 mems in 45 countries; Pres. Prof. Dr JOSEP PUIG MONTADA (Spain); Sec.-Gen. Prof. Dr MAARTEN J. F. M. HOENEN (Germany); publ. *Bulletin de Philosophie Médiévale* (1 a year).

International Society for Third-Sector Research (ISTR): Wyman Park Building (Room 559), 3400 N. Charles St, Baltimore, MD 21218-2608, USA; tel. (410) 516-4678; fax (410) 516-4870; e-mail istr@jhu.edu; internet www.istr.org; f. 1992; encourages research relevant to civil society, non-profit orgs, voluntarism and philanthropy; regional research networks in Africa, Asia, Europe, Latin America and the Caribbean, and Arab-speaking countries; conference every 2 years; 675 mems; Pres. BRENDA GAINER (Canada); Exec. Dir MARGERY B. DANIELS; publ. *Voluntas* (4 a year).

International Society of Social Defence and Humane Criminal Policy/Société Internationale de Défense Sociale pour une Politique Criminelle Humaniste: c/o Centro nazionale di prevenzione e difesa sociale, Palazzo comunale delle scienze sociali, Piazza Castello 3, 20121 Milan, Italy; tel. (2) 86460714; fax (2) 72008431; e-mail cnpds.ispac@iol.it; internet www .defensesociale.org; f. 1946; non-governmental org. in consultative status with UN Economic and Social Council; the study of crime-related problems in the perspective of a system of reactions, which through prevention and resocialization of deviants, aims to protect the individuals and society at large; 350 mems; Pres. LUIS ARROYO ZAPATERO (Spain); Sec.-Gen. EDMONDO BRUTI LIBERATI (Italy); publ. *Cahiers de défense sociale* (1 a year, in English, Spanish and French).

Inter-Parliamentary Union/Union Inter-parlementaire: 5 chemin du Pommier, CP 330, 1218 Le Grand-Saconnex, Geneva, Switzerland; tel. 229194150; fax 229194160; e-mail postbox@mail.ipu.org; internet www .ipu.org; f. 1889 to promote contacts among members of the world's parliaments and unite them in common action for int. peace and cooperation; to promote democracy by strengthening and developing the means of action of representative institutions; studies political, economic, social, juridical, cultural and environmental problems of int. significance, notably through conferences; promotes free and fair elections and provides assistance to representative assemblies; helps to solve cases of violation of parliamentarians' rights; promotes status of women in political life; gathers and disseminates information on parliamentary matters; mems: 155 nat. parliaments; Pres. THEO-BEN GURIRAB (Namibia); Sec.-Gen. ANDERS B. JOHNSSON (Sweden); publs *Chronicle of Parliamentary Elections* (1 a year), *IPU Review* (4 a year), *Panorama of Parliamentary Elections* (1 a year), *World Directory of Parliaments* (1 a year).

Italian–Latin American Institute/Istituto Italo-Latino Americano: Piazza B. Cairoli 3, 00186 Rome, Italy; tel. 06-684921; fax 06-6872834; e-mail info@iila.org; internet www.iila.org; f. 1966 to develop and coordinate research and documentation on the problems, achievements and prospects of mem. countries in cultural, scientific, economic, technical and social fields; organizes meetings and promotes activities representative of the development process of Latin America in its social, economic, cultural and technical-scientific aspects; 21 mem. countries; library: library and documentation centre of 90,000 vols, 4,500 periodicals; Sec.-Gen. PAOLO FAIOLA; publ. *Quaderni IILA* (series *Economia, Scienza, Cooperazione*).

Nordic Institute of Asian Studies/Nordisk Institut for Asienstudier: Leifsgade 33, 2300 Copenhagen S, Denmark; tel. 35-32-95-00; fax 35-32-95-49; e-mail sec@nias.ku .dk; internet www.nias.ku.dk; f. 1967; non-profit org. funded through Nordic Council of Ministers; research and documentation centre for modern Asian studies within humanities and social sciences to promote research and publish books on Asia; library of 28,000 vols and 750 current journals; Chair. Dekan LARS BILLE; Dir Dr GEIR HELGESEN.

Organisation for Economic Co-operation and Development (OECD): 2 rue André-Pascal, 75775 Paris Cedex 16, France; tel. 1-45-24-82-00; fax 1-45-24-85-00; e-mail webmaster@oecd.org; internet www.oecd.org; f. 1961; concerned with the impact of science, technology, education and the changing pattern of employment structures on the balance of economic and social development of its member countries (in Europe, North America and the Pacific area) and with the implications of technological development for the environment as well as with the broader aspects of policy to meet new social objectives; it seeks to coordinate its mems' economic and social policies, and aims at being informative, promotional and catalytic through surveys of the current situation, identification of tentative policies and the establishment of a statistical and methodological base in support of government decision-making; serves as an international clearing-house for exchanges of information and provides a forum where experts and policy-makers can discuss common issues and benefit from mutual cooperation; conducts economic analysis of emerging and transition economies; special programmes include the Programme for Educational Building and the Centre for Educational Research and Innovation (*q.v.*); 30 mem. countries; library: online library of books, periodicals and statistics (www.sourceoecd.org); Sec.-Gen. ANGEL GURRÍA; publs note: certain titles are published in more than one language, *Creditor Reporting System on Aid Activities* (6 a year), *Energy Prices and Taxes* (4 a year), *Financial Market Trends* (3 a year), *Higher Education Management and Policy* (3 a year), *International Trade by Commodity Statistics* (5 a year), *Indicators of Industry and Services* (4 a year), *Journal of Business Cycle Measurement and Analysis* (3 a year), *Main Economic Indicators* (12 a year), *Main Science and Technology Indicators* (2 a year), *Monthly Statistics of International Trade, OECD Papers* (12 a year), *OECD Economic Surveys* (18 a year), *OECD Economic Outlook* (2 a year), *OECD Economic Studies* (2 a year), *OECD Journal of Competition Law and Policy* (4 a year), *OECD Journal of Budgeting* (4 a year), *Oil, Gas, Coal and Electricity—Quarterly Statistics, NEA News* (2 a year), *Nuclear Law Bulletin* (2 a year), *PEB Exchange* (3 a year and online), *Quarterly Labour Force Statistics, Quarterly National Accounts, The DAC Journal* (4 a year), *The OECD Observer* (6 a year).

Pan-African Institute for Development/Institut Pan-Africain pour le Développement: BP 4056, Douala, Cameroon; tel. 332-28-06; fax 332-28-06; e-mail ipd.sg@camnet.cm; f. 1964 for the training of African development staff; 2 regional institutes in Cameroon and 1 each in Burkina Faso and Zambia supply support services to development agencies; Sec.-Gen. Dr MBUKI V. MWAMUFIYA; publs *PAID Report* (2 a year), *Yearly Progress Report.*

Society for International Development/Société Internationale pour le Développement: Via Panisperna 207, 00184 Rome, Italy; tel. 06-487-2172; fax 06-487-2170; e-mail info@sidint.org; internet www.sidint.org; f. 1957; a global network of individuals and institutions concerned with devt that is participative, pluralistic and sustainable; mobilizes and strengthens civil society groups by building partnerships among them and with other sectors; fosters local initiatives and new forms of social experimentation; 3,000 mems in 125 countries, with 65 local chapters and 55 institutional mems; Pres. JAN PRONK; Sec.-Gen. ROBERTO SAVIO; publ. *Development* (4 a year).

Statistical Institute for Asia and the Pacific: JETRO-IDE Bldg, 3-2-2 Wakaba, Mihama-ku, Chiba-shi, Chiba 261-8787, Japan; tel. (43) 299-9782; fax (43) 299-9780; e-mail staff@unsiap.or.jp; internet www.unsiap.or.jp; f. 1970; subsidiary body of tUN Economic and Social Comm. for Asia and the Pacific (ESCAP); provides training in official statistics to govt statisticians in the Asia-Pacific region as recommended by resolution 75 (XXIII) of ESCAP; 20 Fellows (Production and Devt of Official Statistics course), 19 Fellows (ICT course), 22 Fellows (Analysis, Interpretation and Use of Official Statistics course), 5 Fellows (Central Asian Countries course); library of 20,000 vols; Dir DAVAASUREN CHULTEMJAMTS.

Stockholm International Peace Research Institute (SIPRI): Signalistgatan 9, 169 70 Solna, Sweden; tel. (8) 6559700; fax (8) 6559733; e-mail sipri@sipri.org; internet www.sipri.org; f. 1966 for research into problems of peace and conflict with particular attention to the problems of disarmament and arms control; library of 52,000 vols; Chair. GÖRAN LENNMARKER (Swe-

den); Dir Dr BATES GILL (USA); publs *SIPRI Fact Sheets and Policy Briefs, SIPRI Insights on Peace and Security, SIPRI policy papers, SIPRI research reports, SIPRI Yearbook.*

UNESCO Institute for Statistics: CP 6128, Succ. Centre-Ville, Montréal, QC H3C 3J7, Canada; tel. (514) 343-6880; fax (514) 343-6882; e-mail information@uis.unesco.org; internet www.uis.unesco.org; f. 1999; primary data source of education and literacy data for leading publs and databases: Education For All Global Monitoring Report, World Devt Indicators, Human Devt Report, State of World's Children; collects and disseminates statistics in education, science and technology, culture and communication; designs new indicators to better reflect policy needs of developing countries; promotes wider use of data for policymaking; Dir HENDRIK VAN DER POL; publ. *Global Education Digest* (1 a year).

United Nations Institute for Training and Research (UNITAR)/Institut des Nations Unies pour la formation et la recherche: Palais des Nations, 1211 Geneva 10, Switzerland; located at: International Environment House, 11–13 chemin des Anémones, 1219 Chatelaine Geneva, Switzerland; tel. 229178455; fax 229178047; internet www.unitar.org; f. 1965 as an autonomous body within the framework of the UN; aims, by training and research, to enhance the effectiveness of the UN in achieving the major objectives of the organization, in particular the maintenance of peace and security and the promotion of economic and social development; conducts seminars for diplomats and others who work in the UN system and carries out training, either at UN headquarters or in the field, which has special relevance for developing countries; conducts research into problems of concern to the UN system; Asst Sec.-Gen. and Exec. Dir MARCEL A. BOISARD (Switzerland); publ. more than 50 titles in English and some in French, Spanish and Russian.

Vienna Institute for International Dialogue and Cooperation/Wiener Institut für Internationalen Dialog und Zusammenarbeit: Moellwaldpl. 5/3, 1040 Vienna, Austria; tel. (1) 7133594; fax (1) 713359473; e-mail office@vidc.org; internet www.vidc.org; f. 1987 as successor to Vienna Institute for Development; aims to disseminate information on problems and achievements of developing countries by all possible means in order to convince the public or industrialized nations of the necessity to increase devt aid and to strengthen int. cooperation; research programmes; organizes cultural exchanges between South and North; engages in anti-racism and anti-discrimination activities in sport at nat. and European levels; Pres. Mag. BARBARA PRAMMER (Austria); Dir Mag. WALTER POSCH.

World Bank Institute: 1818 H St, NW, Washington, DC 20433, USA; tel. (202) 473-1000; fax (202) 477-6391; e-mail wbi_infoline@worldbank.org; internet www.worldbank.org/wbi; f. 1955; provides learning programmes and policy advice in the areas of environment and natural resources, economic policy for poverty reduction, governance, regulation, and finance, human development, knowledge networks and outreach; delivers training activities for policy-makers in 149 countries through direct and distance learning; has formal partnerships with 130 academic and training institutions in developed nations and client countries; Vice-Pres. FRANNIE A. LÉAUTIER; publs *Development Outreach* (4 a year), *WBI News* (3 a year).

World Institute for Development Economics Research of the United Nations University (UNU-WIDER): Katajanokanlaituri 6B, 00160 Helsinki, Finland; tel. (9) 6159911; fax (9) 61599333; e-mail wider@wider.unu.edu; internet www.wider.unu.edu; f. 1984; conducts policy-oriented research into inequality and poverty, global economic development and related issues; Dir Prof. FINN TARP; publ. *WIDER Working Papers.*

World Intellectual Property Organization (WIPO): 34 chemin des Colombettes, 1211 Geneva 20, Switzerland; tel. 223389111; fax 227335428; e-mail wipo.mail@wipo.int; internet www.wipo.int; f. 1970; UN specialized agency; promotes the protection of intellectual property rights worldwide; aims to extend benefits of the int. intellectual property system to all mem. states; main activities are: progressive devt of int. intellectual property law, assisting developing countries and providing services to facilitate the process of obtaining intellectual property rights in multiple countries; 184 mem. states; Dir-Gen. Dr KAMIL IDRIS; publs *Appelations of Origin* (irregular), *International Designs Bulletin* (12 a year), *PCT Newsletter* (12 a year), *WIPO Gazette of International Marks* (52 a year).

World Society for Ekistics: c/o Athens Center of Ekistics, 23 Strat. Syndesmou St, 10673 Athens, Greece; tel. 210-3623216; fax 210-3629337; e-mail ekistics@otenet.gr; internet www.ekistics.org; f. 1965; aims to promote the devt of knowledge and ideas concerning human settlements by research and through publs, conferences, etc.; to encourage the devt and expansion of education in ekistics; to educate public opinion concerning ekistics; to recognize the benefits and necessity of an interdisciplinary approach to the needs of human settlements, and to promote and emphasize such an approach; 200 mems; Pres. Dr MADHAV DEOBHAKTA (India); Sec.-Gen. and Treas. PANAYIS PSOMOPOULOS; publ. conference papers publ. in *Ekistics,* the journal of the Athens Centre of Ekistics.

Education

Academic Cooperation Association (ACA): 15 rue d'Egmontstraat, 1000 Brussels, Belgium; tel. (2) 513-22-41; fax (2) 513-17-76; e-mail info@aca-secretariat.be; internet www.aca-secretariat.be; f. 1993; ind. org. dedicated to management, analysis and improvement of higher education and training cooperation within Europe and between Europe and other parts of world; 22 mems (18 European and 4 non-European), all being major nationally based orgs responsible for the promotion and funding of education cooperation in their countries; Dir BERND WÄCHTER; publ. *ACA Papers on International Cooperation in Education* (monograph series).

African and Malagasy Council for Higher Education/Conseil Africain et Malgache pour l'Enseignement Supérieur (CAMES): 01 BP 134, Ouagadougou 01, Burkina Faso; tel. 50-36-81-46; fax 50-36-85-73; e-mail cames@bf.refer.org; internet www.cames.bf.refer.org; f. 1968 to ensure coordination between member states in the fields of higher education and research; mems: governments of Benin, Burkina Faso, Burundi, Cameroon, Central African Republic, Chad, Republic of Congo, Côte d'Ivoire, Gabon, Guinea, Guinea-Bissau, Madagascar, Mali, Niger, Rwanda, Senegal, Togo; Sec.-Gen. Prof. MAMADOU MOUSTAPHA SALL.

Agence Universitaire de la Francophonie: BP 400 Succ. Côte-des-Neiges, Montréal, QC H3S 2S7, Canada; tel. (514) 343-6630; fax (514) 343-2107; internet www.auf.org; f. 1961; aims: documentation, coordination, cooperation, exchange; Pres. CHARLES GOMBE MBALAWA (Republic of the Congo); Rector MICHÈLE GENDREAU-MASSALOUX (France).

Amazonian Universities Association/ Associação de Universidades Amazônicas (UNAMAZ)/Asociación de Universidades Amazónicas: Trav. 3 de Maio 1573, São Braz, 66063-388 Belém, PA, Brazil; tel. (91) 3229-4478; e-mail secretaria.executiva@unamz.org; internet www.unamaz.org; f. 1987 to promote cultural, technological and scientific cooperation between universities and research instns in the Amazonian region; 69 mem. univs in Bolivia, Brazil, Colombia, Ecuador, Guyana, Peru, Suriname and Venezuela

Arab Bureau of Education for the Gulf States: POB 94693, Diplomatic Quarters, Riyadh 11614, Saudi Arabia; tel. (1) 4800555; fax (1) 4802839; e-mail abegs@abegs.org; internet www.abegs.org; f. 1975 to coordinate and integrate the efforts of the mem. states (Bahrain, Kuwait, Oman, Qatar, Saudi Arabia and the United Arab Emirates) in the fields of education, science and culture; aims to unify the educational system for all the mem. states; Gulf Arab States Educational Research Center: see Kuwait chapter; established Arabian Gulf University in Bahrain; Dir-Gen. Dr ALI AL-KARNI; publ. *Rissalat al-Khaleej al Araby* (Message of the Arab Gulf, 4 a year).

Asian Association of Open Universities: 160 Fuxingmennei St, Beijing, 100031, People's Republic of China; tel. (10) 66490029; fax (10) 66412407; e-mail aaou@crtvu.edu.cn; internet www.aaou.net; Pres. Prof. YAOXUE ZHANG; Sec.-Gen. Prof. YAWAN LI.

Asociación Iberoamericana de Educación Superior a Distancia (AIESAD) (Ibero-American Association for Open University Education): Calle Bravo Murillo 38 (7a Planta), 28015 Madrid, Spain; tel. 91-398-65-49; fax 91-398-65-87; e-mail aiesad@adm.uned.es; internet www.aiesad.org; f. 1980; 13 mem. countries; Pres. Dr JUAN A. GIMENO ULLASTRES; Exec. Sec. ADRIANA LOZADA HERNÁNDEZ.

Associação das Universidades de Língua Portuguesa (AULP) (Association of Portuguese Language Universities): Av. Santos Dumont, 67, 2º, 1050-203 Lisbon, Portugal; tel. (21) 781-63-60; fax (21) 781-63-69; e-mail aulp@aulp.org; internet www.aulp.org; 122 mem. instns in Angola, Brazil, Cape Verde, Guinea-Bissau, Macao, Mozambique, Portugal, São Tomé e Príncipe and Timor-Leste; Pres. JOÃO GUERREIRO; Sec.-Gen. CRISTINA MONTALVÃO SARMENTO; publ. *Actas dos Encontros*.

Association for Teacher Education in Europe: 67 Rue Hobbema, 1000 Brussels, Belgium; fax (2) 502-29-03; e-mail ateesecretariat@gmail.com; internet www.atee1.org; f. 1976 to establish contacts between institutions for teacher education and those responsible for that education; arranges working groups, annual conf., etc.; undertakes consultancy work for European organizations; 120 mems; Pres. Dr JUSTINA ERCULJ; Vice-Pres. Dr JOANA SALAZAR; publ. *European Journal of Teacher Education* (4 a year).

Association Internationale de Pédagogie Universitaire: Service Guidance Étude, Bâtiment B33, Université de Liège au Sart Tilman, 4000 Liège, Belgium; tel. (4) 366-20-73; fax (4) 366-48-96; e-mail mdelhaxhe@ulg

.ac.be; internet www.aipu-assos.org; f. 1979; Francophone org. promoting research and devt in teaching and higher education; 800 mems; Pres. Prof. ABDELLATIF CHIADLI (Maroc); Vice-Pres. Prof. SYLVIE DORÉ; Sec.-Gen. MICHEL DELHAXHE (Belgium); publ. *RIPES* (2 a year).

Association Montessori Internationale: Koninginneweg 161, 1075 CN Amsterdam, Netherlands; tel. (20) 679-8932; fax (20) 676-7341; e-mail info@montessori-ami.org; internet www.montessori-ami.org; f. 1929; propagates ideals and educational methods of Dr Maria Montessori and spreads knowledge on child devt without racial, religious or political prejudice; activities: supervises affiliated training courses for teachers in several countries; sponsors int. congresses and study confs on Montessori education; creates new training centres and offers affiliation to Montessori societies; Pres. A. ROBERFROID; Exec. Dir LYNNE LAWRENCE; publ. *Communications* (2 a year).

Association of African Universities/ Association des Universités Africaines: POB AN5744, Accra-North, Ghana; tel. (21) 774495; fax (21) 774821; e-mail info@aau.org; internet www.aau.org; f. 1967 to collect, classify and disseminate information on higher education and research in Africa; to promote cooperation among African instns in training, research, community services and higher education policy, in curriculum development and in the determination of equivalence in academic degrees; to encourage increased contacts between mems and the int. academic world; to encourage the development and wide use of African languages and support training of univ. teachers and administrators to deal with problems in African education in general; mems: 199 university instns in 45 African countries; Pres. Prof. IS-HAQ OLANREWAJU OLOYEDE (Nigeria); Sec.-Gen. Prof. GOOLAM T. G. MOHAMEDBHAI (Mauritius); publ. *Handbook* (every 2 years).

Association of American International Colleges and Universities: c/o Dr John Bailey, American College of Greece, 6 Gravias St, Aghira Paraskevi, 153 42 Athens, Greece; tel. (210) 600-9800; fax (210) 600-9811; e-mail acg@acg.edu; internet www.acg.edu; f. 1971 to promote cooperation among independent institutions offering int. education in Europe and the Near East; 12 mem. univs and colleges; Pres. Dr JOHN S. BAILEY (Greece); Sec. and Treas. CRAIG SEXSON (Greece).

Association of Arab Universities: POB 401, Jubeyha, Amman, Jordan; tel. 5062048; fax 5062051; e-mail secgen@aaru.edu.jo; f. 1964 to consolidate cooperation between Arab universities and institutions of higher education; mems: 213 universities; Sec.-Gen. Prof. Dr SALEH HASHEM; publs *Bulletin* (6 a year), *Directory of Arab Universities*, *Directory of Teaching Staff of Arab Universities*, *Proceedings of Seminars*.

Association of Caribbean Universities and Research Institutes (UNICA): c/o Prof. Mervyn C. Alleyne, Department of Liberal Arts, University of the West Indies, St Augustine, Trinidad; f. 1968 to foster contact and collaboration between member universities and institutes; conferences, meetings, seminars, etc.; circulation of information through newsletters, bulletins; facilitates cooperation and the pooling of resources in research; encourages exchanges of staff and students; mems: 50 institutions; Sec.-Gen. Prof. MERVYN C. ALLEYNE; publ. *Caribbean Educational Bulletin* (4 a year).

Association of Commonwealth Universities (ACU): Woburn House, 20–24 Tavi-

stock Sq., London, WC1H 9HF, UK; tel. (20) 7380-6700; fax (20) 7387-2655; e-mail info@acu.ac.uk; internet www.acu.ac.uk; f. 1913; promotes contact and cooperation in higher education throughout the Commonwealth; provides assistance with staff and student mobility and devt programmes; researches and disseminates information about univs and relevant policy issues; organizes major meetings of Commonwealth univs and their representatives; provides the secretariats for, and administers, various scholarship and fellowship schemes (incl. the Commonwealth Scholarship Commission in the UK, the Marshall Aid Commemoration Commission and the Commonwealth Univs Study Abroad Consortium; also administers the Commonwealth Foundation Medical Electives Bursaries, the ACU Devt Fellowships, the DFID Shared Scholarship Scheme, the T. H. B. Symons Fellowship, and the Canada Memorial Foundation Scholarships); operates various subject specialist networks for higher education staff; provides an appointments, advertising and publicity service; operates a policy research unit; addresses the gender imbalance in higher education leadership through its women's programme; organizes various training workshops; hosts the Observatory on Borderless Higher Education; provides the secretariat for the Staff and Educational Devt Asscn; hosts an Africa Unit; mems: 525 univs; library of 18,500 vols; Sec.-Gen. Prof. JOHN WOOD.

Association of Southeast Asian Institutions of Higher Learning: c/o Dr Ninnat Olanvoravuth, Jamjuree 1 Bldg, Chulalongkorn Univ., Phayathai Rd, Bangkok 10330, Thailand; tel. (2) 2516966; fax (2) 253-7909; e-mail ninnat.o@chula.ac.th; internet www.seameo.org/asaihl; f. 1956; promotes economic, cultural and social welfare of the people of Southeast Asia by means of educational cooperation and research programmes; fosters the cultivation of a sense of regional identity and interdependence and to cooperate with other regional and int. orgs; serves as a clearing-house for information, provides opportunities for discussion and recognizes distinctive academic achievements; 180 mem. instns from 20 countries; Sec.-Gen. Dr NINNAT OLANVORAVUTH; publs *Handbook, Seminar Proceedings*.

Association of Universities of Asia and the Pacific (AUAP): c/o Centre for International Affairs, Suranaree University of Technology, 111 University Ave, Muang, Nakhon Ratchasima 30000, Thailand; tel. (44) 224143; fax (44) 224140; e-mail auap@sut.ac.th; internet auap.sut.ac.th; f. 1995; 210 regular mems in 19 countries, 3 assoc. mems in 3 countries; Pres. Dr CARMEN Z. LAMAGAN (Bangladesh); Sec. Prof. Dr RUBEN C. UMALY; publ. *Gazette* (4 a year).

Caribbean Network of Educational Innovation for Development (CARNEID): The Towers, 25 Dominica Drive, 3rd Fl., Kingston 5, Jamaica; tel. 427-4771; fax 436-0094; e-mail kingston@unesco.org; internet www.unesco.org/carneid; f. 1981 by UNESCO to advance educational innovation for development through networking among educational institutions and personnel in the Caribbean; publ. *Education Annual*.

Caribbean Regional Council for Adult Education: c/o Azad Hosein, Adult Education Unit, Ministry of Education, 51 Frederick St, Port-of-Spain, Trinidad and Tobago; tel. 625-4091; internet carcae.tripod.com; f. 1978 to promote and facilitate cooperation among national adult education organizations and agencies in non-Spanish-speaking territories of the region; to advocate awareness and recognition of the importance of adult education and to seek funding from governments and other sources; to hold conferences, seminars, training courses, etc.; to advise governments and other bodies on adult education; library of 5,000 vols; Chair. VILMA MCCLENAN (Jamaica); Exec. Sec.-Treas. AZAD HOSEIN.

CEMS—The Global Alliance in Management Education: CEMS Head Office, 1 rue de la Libération, 78350 Jouy-en-Josas, France; tel. 1-39-67-74-57; fax 1-39-67-74-81; e-mail info@cems.org; internet www.cems.org; f. 1988; masters in int. management, provides education and professional experience for multilingual, multicultural postgraduate students; involves academic and corporate partners in the definition and teaching of curriculum, implementation of a series of jt research projects; mems: 26 business schools from 4 continents, 68 corporate partners, 2 social partners (NGOs); Chair. Prof. THOMAS BIEGER (Switzerland); Exec. Dir FRANÇOIS COLLIN; publ. *European Business Forum* (4 a year; print and online, in association with PricewaterhouseCoopers).

Conference of Baltic University Rectors (CBUR): Szczecin University, Al. Jedności Narodowej 22A, 70-453 Szczecin, Poland; tel. (91) 434-25-36; fax (91) 434-29-92; e-mail rektorat@univ.szczecin.pl; f. 1990

Congregazione per l'Educazione Cattolica (Congregation for Catholic Education): Palazzo delle Congregazioni, Piazza Pio XII 3, 00193 Rome; tel. (6) 69884167; fax (6) 69884172; e-mail cec@cec.va; internet www.vatican.va/roman_curia/congregations/ccatheduc; f. 1588; concerned with the direction, temporal admin. and studies of Catholic univs, seminaries, schools and colleges; Prefect Cardinal ZENON GROCHOLEWSKI; Sec. Most Rev. O. P. JEAN-LOUIS BRUGUÈS.

Consejo Superior Universitario Centroamericano (CSUCA) (Higher Council of Central American Universities): Avda Las Américas, 1-03 zona 14, Int. Club Los Arcos, 01014 Guatemala City, Guatemala; tel. 2367-1833; fax 2367-4517; e-mail sg@listas.csuca.org; internet www.csuca.org; f. 1948; exec. body of the Confederación Universitaria Centroamericana; promotes Central American integration and the strengthening of higher education in the region; 18 mem. univs in Belize, Costa Rica, Dominican Republic, El Salvador, Guatemala, Honduras, Nicaragua, Panama; Sec.-Gen. MSc EFRAÍN MEDINA GUERRA; Exec. Sec. ELVIA CHINCHILLA.

Consorcio-Red de Educación a Distancia (Inter-American Distance Education Consortium): c/o Dr Armando Villarroel, Fischler Graduate School of Education and Human Services, Nova Southeastern University, 1750 NE 167th St, N Miami Beach, FL 33162-8569, USA; tel. (954) 262-8569; e-mail axv4@omnibus.ce.psu.edu; internet www.cde.psu.edu/de/cread/cread.html; f. 1990; networks of individuals and instns in North, Central and South America; Exec. Dir Dr ARMANDO VILLARROEL.

Consortium for North American Higher Education Collaboration (CONAHEC): Univ. of Arizona, POB 210300, Tucson, AZ 85721-0300; Univ. of Arizona, 220 W 6th St, University Services Annex Bldg 300A, Room 108, Tucson, AZ 85701; tel. (520) 621-7761; fax (520) 626-2675; internet www.conahec.org; f. 1994; advises and connects instns wishing to establish or strengthen academic collaborative programmes in the N American region; 149 mem. instns (16 in Canada, 69 in Mexico, 44 in the USA and 20 affiliates outside North America); Pres. FERNANDO LEÓN; Exec. Dir FRANCISCO J. MARMOLEJO.

Commonwealth Association of Polytechnics in Africa: c/o Kenya Polytechnic, POB 52428, Nairobi, Kenya; tel. (2) 338232; fax (2) 219689; e-mail polymis@swiftkenya.com; f. 1978 to provide a forum for exchange of professional ideas and practices in technical and business education and training, and to improve the content and methods of polytechnic teaching, to disseminate information through publications and workshops, and to create a data centre and reference library; 135 mem. polytechnics; Sec.-Gen. WILLIAM RWAMBULLA; publ. *CAPA Journal of Technical Education and Training* (2 a year).

Commonwealth of Learning: 1055 W Hasting St, Suite 1200, Vancouver, BC V6E 2E9, Canada; tel. (604) 775-8200; fax (604) 775-8210; e-mail info@col.org; internet www.col.org; f. 1988 by Commonwealth Heads of Govt to promote cooperation among Commonwealth countries, utilizing distance education techniques, incl. communications technologies, to strengthen mem. countries' capacities in human resources devt; works with ministries of education, schools, colleges, univs and NGOs to increase access to opportunities for learning; mems are the 54 Commonwealth countries; library of 7,800 vols; Pres. and CEO Sir JOHN DANIEL; Vice-Pres. and Programme Dir Prof. ASHA S. KANWAR; Dir of Finance, Admin. and Human Resources DORIS B. MCEACHERN; Dir of Technology and Knowledge Management V. BALAJI; publs *Connections/EdTech News* (3 a year), *Three-Year Plan*.

Commonwealth Secretariat, Education Department, Social Transformation Programmes Division: Marlborough House, Pall Mall, London, SW1Y 5HX, UK; tel. (20) 7747-6460; fax (20) 7747-6287; e-mail education@commonwealth.int; internet www.thecommonwealth.org; encourages and supports educational consultation and cooperation between Commonwealth countries through confs, seminars, workshops, meetings of experts, and training courses for educational personnel (with assistance from the Commonwealth Fund for Technical Cooperation); contributes to nat. educational devt through studies of particular problems, handbooks, directories and training manuals, and by providing information on educational subjects; undertakes consultancies for govts on request; triennial conf. of Ministers of Education; Dir Dr SYLVIA ANIE; publ. *LinkIn* (4 a year).

Coordinación Educativa y Cultural Centroamericana (CECC) (Coordinating Body for Education and Culture in Central America): De la Nunciatura, 100 m al norte, casa N° 8815, Rohmoser, San José, Costa Rica; tel. 232-28-91; fax 231-23-66; e-mail sgcecc@racsa.co.cr; internet www.sica.int/cecc; f. 1982; promotes and works for integration in the areas of education and culture in Central America; 7 mem. countries (Belize, Costa Rica, El Salvador, Guatemala, Honduras, Nicaragua, Panama), 1 assoc. country (Dominican Republic); Gen. Sec. MARVIN HERRERA ARAYA.

Council for Cultural Cooperation: Council of Europe, 67075 Strasbourg Cedex, France; tel. 3-88-41-20-00; fax 3-88-41-27-88; f. 1962 to draw up and implement the educational and cultural programme of the Council of Europe; mems: 47 states; publs *EUDISED European Educational Research Yearbook*, *European Heritage*.

Danube Rectors' Conference (DRC)/Donau Rektoren Konferenz: c/o Karolina Bucka, Univ. of Maribor, Int. Relations Office, Slomskov trg 15 2000 Maribor, Slovenia; tel. (2) 235 53 47; fax (2) 235 52 67;

e-mail drc@uni-mb.si; internet drc.uni-mb.si; f. 1983 to improve higher education in teaching and research in the region; has established working groups to address the issues of univ. legislation, curricula and the evaluation of teaching and research; 45 higher education instns in 13 countries; Pres. Rector Prof. Dr FERENC HUDECZ (Hungary).

Education International (EI)/Internationale de l'Education (IE): 5 blvd du Roi Albert II, 1210 Brussels, Belgium; tel. (2) 224-0611; fax (2) 224-0606; e-mail headoffice@ei-ie.org; internet www.ei-ie.org; f. 1993 from the merger of the World Confederation of Organizations of the Teaching Profession (WCOTP/CMOPE) and the International Federation of Free Teachers' Unions (IFFTU/SPIE); to advance the cause of organizations of teachers and education employees, promote status, interests and welfare of mems and defend their trade union and professional rights; to promote free, quality, public education for all; to promote peace, democracy, social justice, equality and the application of the Universal Declaration on Human Rights through the development of education and the collective strength of teachers and education employees; mems: 305 nat. orgs in 155 countries; Pres. THULAS NXESI (South Africa); Gen. Sec. FRED VAN LEEUWEN (Netherlands); publs *Monitor* (in English, French and Spanish), *The Education International Quarterly Magazine* (in English, French and Spanish).

ERASMUS (European Community Action Scheme for the Mobility of University Students): 70 rue Montoyer, 1040 Brussels, Belgium; tel. (32) (2) 233-01-11; fax (32) (2) 233-01-50; e-mail eac-info@ec.europa.eu; internet ec.europa.eu/education/lifelong-learning-programme/doc80_en.htm; f. 1987 by the Council of Ministers of the European Community; aims to encourage greater student and staff mobility throughout the EU and EFTA (European Free Trade Association) countries by means of the creation of a European University Network, the award of 'mobility' grants to students, arrangements for mutual recognition of qualifications and courses, and other supporting measures; publs *ERASMUS and Lingua Action II Directory* (1 a year), *Guidelines for Applicants*.

EuroAsian Universities Association: 119991 Moscow B-106, GSP-1, Moscow State Univ. 'M. V. Lomonosov', Leninskie Gory, Russia; tel. (495) 939-27-69; fax (495) 939-27-69; e-mail eau_msu@rector.msu.ru; internet www.eau.msu.ru; Pres. Acad. VIKTOR SADOVNITCHY.

European Association for International Education: POB 11189, 1001 GD Amsterdam, Netherlands; Herengracht 487, 1017 BT Amsterdam, Netherlands; tel. (20) 3445100; fax (20) 3445119; e-mail eaie@eaie.nl; internet www.eaie.org; f. 1989; non-profit org. with the main aim of stimulating and facilitating the internationalization of higher education in Europe and around the world, and meeting the professional needs of individuals active in int. education; c. 2,000 mems; Pres. BJØRN EINAR AAS (Norway); Dir ALEX OLDE KALTER (Netherlands); publs *Forum, Occasional Papers, Professional Development Series*.

European Association for the Education of Adults: 27 rue Liedts, 1030 Brussels, Belgium; tel. (2) 513-52-05; fax (2) 513-57-34; e-mail eaea-main@eaea.org; internet www.eaea.org; f. 1953 to encourage cooperation between adult education organizations on questions of methods, materials, and exchange of individuals; arranges study sessions and tours; also has offices in Girona (Spain) and Helsinki (Finland); mems in 30 European countries; Gen. Sec. Dr ELLINOR HAASE.

European Association of Distance Teaching Universities: Postbus 2960, 6401 DL Heerlen, Netherlands; Valkenburgerweg 177, 6419 AT Heerlen, Netherlands; tel. (45) 5762214; fax (45) 5741473; e-mail secretariat@eadtu.nl; internet www.eadtu .nl; f. 1987; aims to promote lifelong, open and flexible learning by means of higher distance education, to support bilateral and multilateral contacts between academic staff, to support cooperation in research, course devt, course transfer and credit transfer, to develop new methods for higher distance education, and to organize common projects in cooperation with European authorities; European Open Univ. Network (f. 1995) acts as exec. arm; mems: 11 mem. univs and 15 mem. asscns from European countries, and 3 assoc. mem. univs from S and N America; Pres. DAVID VINCENT; Sec.-Gen. PIET HENDERIKX (Belgium).

European Association of Institutions in Higher Education (EURASHE): Ravensteingalerij 27/3, 1000 Brussels, Belgium; tel. (2) 211-41-97; fax (2) 211-41-99; e-mail eurashe@eurashe.eu; internet www.eurashe .eu; f. 1990; promotes interests of professional higher education in the mem. countries of the EU and in other European countries, in instns that are public or recognized and/or financed by the public authorities of an EU member country or another European country; Pres. LARS LYNGE NIELSEN (Denmark); Sec.-Gen. STEFAN DELPLACE (Belgium).

European Distance and E-Learning Network (EDEN): c/o Budapest Univ. of Technology and Economics, 1111 Budapest, Egry J.u. 1, Hungary; tel. (1) 463-1628; fax (1) 463-1858; e-mail secretariat@eden-online.org; internet www.eden-online.org; f. 1991; to foster devts in flexible, distance and e-learning; 1,078 mems, of which 178 instns, and 900 individuals in the Network of Academics and Professionals; Pres. INGEBORG BØ (Norway); Sec.-Gen. Dr ANDRÁS SZŰCS; publs *Conference Proceedings* (1 a year), *European Journal of Open and Distance Learning* (online).

European Institute of Education and Social Policy: Université Paris IX-Dauphine, 1 place du Maréchal de Lattre de Tassigny, 75775 Paris Cedex 16, France; tel. (1) 44-05-40-01; fax (1) 44-05-40-02; internet www.eiesp.org; f. 1975 by the European Cultural Foundation, the European Commission, the International Council for Educational Development; studies specific issues in education, employment and social policy; policy-oriented and research programmes and seminars undertaken for European governments, int. organizations, universities, or regional and local bodies; Chair. HYWEL CERI JONES; Dir JEAN GORDON; publ. *European Journal of Education* (4 a year, in English).

European University Association/Association Européenne de l'Université: Ave de l'Yser, 1040 Brussels Belgium; tel. (2) 230-55-44; fax (2) 230-57-51; e-mail info@eua.be; internet www.eua.be; f. 2001 through merger of Association of European Universities and Confederation of European Union Rectors' Conferences; represents and supports higher education instns in 46 countries; facilitates partnership in higher education and research within Europe and between Europe and the rest of the world; aims to enhance the contribution of European univs to European integration, principally through the creation of a European Space for Higher Education;

approx. 850 individual, collective mems and affiliates in 46 countries; Pres. Prof. JEAN-MARC RAPP (Switzerland); Sec.-Gen. LESLEY WILSON (Belgium); publ. *EUA News* (online).

Fédération Internationale des Professeurs de Français/International Federation of Teachers of French: 1 ave Léon Journault, 92318 Sèvres Cedex, France; tel. 1-46-26-53-16; fax 1-46-26-81-69; internet www.fipf.org; f. 1969 to unite and assist teachers of French as a first or second language worldwide; mems: 180 associations in 140 countries; Pres. JEAN-PIERRE CUQ (France); Vice-Pres. PEIWHA CHI LEE (Taiwan); Vice-Pres. RAYMOND GEVEART (Belgium); Sec.-Gen. MADELINE ROLLE-BOUMLIC (France); publs *Dialogues and Cultures* (1 a year), *Echanges: Lettre FIPF* (4 a year), *Le Français Dans le Monde* (6 a year).

Federation of the Universities of the Islamic World (FUIW)/Fédération des Universités du monde Islamique (FUMI): ISESCO, Ave des F.A.R., Hay Ryad, POB 2275, 10104 Rabat, Morocco; tel. 37-56-60-52; fax 37-56-60-53; e-mail fumi@ isesco.org.ma; internet www.fuiw.org; part of Islamic Educational, Scientific and Cultural Organization (q.v.); supports univs and higher education instns of comparable level in the Islamic world and encourages cooperation between them; 193 mem. univs; Pres. Dr ABDOLLAH JASSBI; Sec.-Gen. Dr ABDULAZIZ OTHMAN ALTWIJRI.

Institut für den Donauraum und Mitteleuropa (IDM) (Institute for the Danube Region and Central Europe): Hahngasse 6/1/ 24, 1090 Vienna, Austria; tel. (1) 3197258; fax (1) 3197258-4; e-mail idm@idm.at; internet www.idm.at; f. 1953; extramural research think-tank working in the fields of politics, education, research, culture and business; supports the work of embassies, trade missions, cultural institutes and nat. tourist offices in the countries of the Danube region and Central and SE Europe; Chair. Dr ERHARD BUSEK; Gen. Sec. Univ. Prof. Dr LEOPOLD MÄRZ; publs *Buchreihe* (book series), *Info Europa* (journal on the enlarged EU, 5 a year), *Studien* (studies on topical issues).

Instituto Internacional para la Educación Superior en América Latina y el Caribe (IESALC) (International Institute for Higher Education in Latin America and the Caribbean): Avda Los Chorros con Calle Acueducto, Edif. Asovincar, Altos de Sebucán, Caracas, Venezuela; tel. (212) 286-10-20; fax (212) 286-03-26; internet www.iesalc .unesco.org.ve; autonomous body operating as part of UNESCO; contributes to the devt of higher education in the region; Dir ANA LÚCIA GAZZOLA.

Inter-American Organization for Higher Education/Organisation Universitaire Interaméricaine: 3744, rue Jean-Brillant, bureau 592, Montréal, QC H3T 1P1, Canada; tel. (514) 343-6980; fax (514) 344-6454; e-mail secretariat@oui-iohe.qc.ca; internet www.oui-iohe.org; f. 1980; inter-university cooperation and exchange; 305 mems; library of 500 vols; Pres. RAÚL ARIAS LOVILLO (Mexico); Exec. Dir PATRICIA GUDIÑO (Canada).

Inter-University Council for East Africa: 3rd Fl., Plot 4, Nile Ave, East African Development Bank Bldg, POB 7110, Kampala, Uganda; tel. (41) 256251; fax (41) 342007; e-mail info@iucea.org; internet www.iucea.org; f. 1984 as Association of Eastern and Southern African Universities; to encourage and develop mutually beneficial collaboration between mem. universities, and between them and nat. govts and other organizations; helps its mems to contribute

to meeting nat. and regional development needs, to the resolution of problems in every appropriate sector of activity in the region, and to the development of human resource capacity in the academic arena; Chair. Prof. FREDERICK I. B. KAYANJA (Uganda); Exec. Sec. Prof. CHACHA NYAIGOTTI-CHACHA (Kenya).

International Association for Educational and Vocational Guidance/Association Internationale d'Orientation Scolaire et Professionnelle: IAEVG Administration Centre, 202–119 Ross Ave, Ottawa, Ontario, K1Y 0N6 Canada; tel. (613) 729-6164; fax (613) 729-3515; e-mail s .hopkins@iaevg.org; internet www.iaevg.org; f. 1951; contributes to career devt, vocational guidance practice and promote contact between mems across world; organizes int. seminars, colloquial, symposia, confs, congresses, workshops and study tours; promotes professional training of staff and initiates internationally agreed accreditation standards and procedures; 20,000 mems in 48 countries; Pres. LESTER OAKES (New Zealand); Sec.-Gen. LINDA TAYLOR; publ. *International Journal for Educational and Vocation Guidance* (3 a year).

International Association for the Exchange of Students for Technical Experience (IAESTE): IAESTE (UK), British Council, 10 Spring Gardens, London, SW1A 2BN, UK; e-mail iaste@britishcouncil .org; internet www.iaeste.org.uk; f. 1948; arranges technical work experience abroad for science and engineering students; placements in over 80 countries; 62 national committees; Gen. Sec. Dr A. SFEIR.

International Association of Dental Students: c/o FDI World Dental Federation, Tour de Cointrin, Ave Louis Casaï 84 Case Postale 3, 1216 Cointrin, Geneva, Swizerland; tel. 22-560-81-50; fax 22-560-81-40; e-mail president@iads-web.org; internet www.iads-web.org; f. 1951 to promote international contact between dental students, to advance and encourage their interest in the science and art of dentistry, to promote exchanges and int. congresses; mems: 88,000 students globally; Pres. TOMAZ SPINDLER (Slovenia); Sec.-Gen. ZEYAD SALEM (Egypt); Treas. AMIR EL-KHOLI (Egypt); publ. *Bulletin* (2 a year).

International Association of University Presidents (IAUP): c/o Siam University, 235 Petkasem Rd, Phasicharoen, Bangkok 10163, Thailand; tel. (2) 868 6885; fax (2) 868 6879; e-mail siam@siam.edu; internet www .iaups.org; f. 1964 to strengthen the quality of education in higher education instns, and to promote global awareness and competence as well as peace and int. understanding through education; c. 600 mems; Pres. BARHAM MADAIN (Chile); Sec.-Gen. HEITOR GURGULINO DE SOUZA (Brazil).

International Baccalaureate Organization (IBO): 15 route des Morillons, 1218 Grand-Saconnex, Geneva, Switzerland; tel. 227917740; fax 227910277; e-mail ibhq@ibo .org; internet www.ibo.org; f. 1968; non-profit foundation encouraging students to be active learners, well-rounded individuals and engaged world citizens; works with 2,815 schools in 128 countries to develop and offer 3 programmes to more than 775,000 students aged 3 to 19 years; Dir-Gen. JEFFREY BEARD; publs *IB World* (3 a year), *Journal of Research in International Education* (3 a year).

International Bureau of Education: see under UNESCO.

International Centre for Agricultural Education (CIEA)/Internationales Studienzentrum für landwirtschaftliches Bildungswesen: Federal Office of Agriculture, 3003 Berne, Switzerland; tel. 313222619; fax 313222634; internet www .ciea.ch; f. 1958; organizes international courses on vocational education and teaching in agriculture every two years; Dir ROLAND STÄHLI.

International Council for Adult Education: 18 de Julio 2095, apt 301, 11200 Montevideo, Uruguay; tel. and fax (2) 409-79-82; e-mail secretariat@icae.org.uy; internet www.icae.org.uy; f. 1973; global network of NGOs promoting adult and lifelong learning; areas of activity: adult literacy, primary healthcare reform, adult education in prison, global citizenship and gender justice, peace education and conflict resolution, globalization, Adult Learners' Week, education and transformative capacity of work spaces; 800 mems in 50 countries; Pres. PAUL BÉLANGER (Canada); publ. *Convergence* (4 a year).

International Council for Open and Distance Education: Lilleakerveien 23, 0283 Oslo, Norway; tel. 22-06-26-30; fax 22-06-26-31; e-mail icde@icde.org; internet www.icde .org; f. 1938, as Int. Council for Correspondence Education, present name 1982; dedicated to furthering the aims and methods of distance education worldwide by promoting and funding research and scholarly publs, encouraging the formation of regional asscns, facilitating communications and information exchange, and organizing confs and workshops; 7,000 mems in 120 countries; Pres. FRITS PANNEKOEK (Canada); Sec.-Gen. (vacant); publ. *Open Praxis* (2 a year, electronic).

International Federation of Catholic Universities/Fédération Internationale des Universités Catholiques (FIUC)/ Federación Internacional de Universidades Católicas: c/o Institut Catholique, 21 rue d'Assas, 75270 Paris Cedex 06, France; tel. (1) 44-39-52-26; fax (1) 44-39-52-28; e-mail sgfiuc@bureau.fiuc.org; internet www .fiuc.org; f. 1924, officially recognized by the Holy See in 1949; to ensure a strong bond of mutual assistance among all Catholic univs in the search for truth to help to solve problems of growth and devt, and to cooperate with other int. orgs; 206 mems in 52 countries; Pres. ANTHONY J. CERNERA (USA); Sec.-Gen. Prof. Mgr GUY-RÉAL THIVIERGE (France); publs *Idem Aliter* (12 a year), *Journal/Cahiers/Cuadernos*.

International Federation of University Women/Fédération Internationale des Femmes Diplômées des Universités: 10 rue du Lac, 1207 Geneva, Switzerland; tel. 227312380; fax 227380440; e-mail info@ifuw .org; internet www.ifuw.org; f. 1919 to promote understanding and friendship between univ. women irrespective of race, nationality, religion or political opinions, to encourage int. cooperation, to advance the devt of education, to represent univ. women in int. orgs to encourage the full application of their knowledge and skills to the problems that arise at all levels of public life, and to encourage their participation in the resolution of these problems; consultative status with appropriate inter-governmental orgs; offers fellowships and study grants; undertakes studies dealing with the status of women; affiliates in 61 countries; Pres. MARIANNE HASLEGRAVE (UK); Sec.-Gen. LEIGH BRADFORD RATTEREE (Switzerland).

International Federation of Workers' Education Associations: POB 336, Woodstock, 7915, Cape Town, South Africa; tel. (21) 447-1677; fax (21) 447-9244; e-mail ifweasecretariat@lrs.org.za; internet www .ifwea.org; f. 1947 to promote cooperation between nat. non-governmental bodies con-

cerned with adult and workers' education, through clearing-house services, exchange of information, publs, confs, summer schools, etc.; 105 affiliated orgs; Pres. SUSAN SCHURMAN (USA); Gen. Sec. SAHRA RYKLIEF (South Africa); publ. *Workers' Education* (4 a year, in English).

International Institute for Educational Planning: see under UNESCO.

International Phonetic Association (IPA): c/o Dr Katerina Nicolaidis, Dept of Theoretical and Applied Linguistics, School of English, Aristotle Univ. of Thessaloniki, Thessaloniki 54124, Greece; tel. (2310) 997429; fax (2310) 997432; e-mail knicol@ enl.auth.gr; internet www.langsci.ucl.ac.uk/ ipa; f. 1886; promotes scientific study of phonetics and its applications; hosts quadrennial Int. Congress of Phonetic Sciences; offers examinations in phonetics; 400 mems; Vice-Pres. Prof. Dr DANIEL RECASENS (Spain); Sec. Assoc. Prof. Dr KATERINA NICOLAIDIS (Greece); publ. *Journal of the International Phonetic Association* (3 a year).

International Reading Association: 800 Barksdale Rd, POB 8139, Newark, DE 19714-8139, USA; tel. (302) 731-1600; fax (302) 731-1057; e-mail pubinfo@reading.org; internet www.reading.org; f. 1956; sets standards for effective reading instruction; improves the quality of reading instruction through the study of the reading process and teaching techniques; promotes lifetime reading habit and public awareness of global literacy; annual convention, regional conferences, and biennial World Congress; 80,000 mems; library of 6,000 vols; Pres. BARBARA WALKER (USA); Exec. Dir ALAN E. FARSTRUP; publs *Journal of Adolescent and Adult Literature*, *Lectura y Vida* (4 a year), *Reading Research Quarterly*, *The Reading Teacher* (8 a year).

International Schools Association (ISA): c/o Drs Bert Timmermans, Alpenroos 11, 2317 EX Leiden, Netherlands; tel. (715) 210280; fax (715) 727803; internet www .isaschools.org; f. 1951 to coordinate work in International Schools and promote their development; merged in 1968 with the Conference of Internationally-minded Schools (CIS) and now counts in its membership a number of selected national schools; member schools maintain the highest standards and accept pupils of all nationalities, irrespective of sex, race and creed; ISA carries out curriculum research; convenes annual Conferences on problems of curriculum and educational reform; has consultative status with UNESCO, UNICEF, UNHCR, UNEP and ECOSOC; 85 mem. schools worldwide; Chair. CLIVE CARTHEW (Spain); Exec. Dir Drs BERT TIMMERMANS (Netherlands); publ. *Educational Bulletin* (3 a year).

International Society for Business Education/Société Internationale pour l'Enseignement Commercial: 6302 Mineral Point Rd, Ste 100, Madison, WI 53705, USA; tel. (608) 273-8467; e-mail jsutton@ matcmadison.edu; internet www.siec-isbe .org; f. 1901 to organize int. courses and congresses on business education; 1,600 mems organized in 19 nat. groups; Pres. MARGARET SARAGINA (USA); Gen. Sec. Dr JUDITH OLSON-SUTTON (USA).

International Society for Education through Art (InSEA)/Société Internationale pour l'Education Artistique: James H. Sanders III, c/o Dept of Art Education, Ohio State University, 128 N Oval Mall, Columbus, OH 43210, USA; e-mail graham.nash@churchie.com.au; internet www.insea.org; f. 1951 to unite art teachers worldwide, to exchange information and coordinate research into art education; non-

governmental global organization for the study of art education, international congresses, exhibitions and other activities; c. 1,500 mems; Pres. RITA IRWIN (Canada); Sec. GRAHAM NASH (Australia); publ. *InSEA News* (3 a year).

International Union of Students/Union Internationale des Etudiants: POB 58, 17th November St, 1101 Prague 01, Czech Republic; tel. and fax 271731257; e-mail ius@ cfs-fcee.ca; internet www.stud.uni-hannover .de/gruppen/ius; f. 1946 by World Student Congress in Prague; objects: to defend the rights and interests of students, to strive for peace, national independence, academic freedom and democratic education, and to unite the student movement in furtherance of these objectives; activities include conferences, meetings, solidarity campaigns, relief projects, award of scholarships, travel and exchange, sports events, cultural projects, publicity and other activities in the furtherance of the Union's aims; mems: 99 full mem. countries, 25 consultative; Pres. MANISH TEWARI (India); Sec.-Gen. FRAGE SHERIF; publs *Democratization of Education*, various regional and other bulletins (4 a year), *World Student News*.

International Young Christian Workers/ Jeunesse Ouvrière Chrétienne Internationale: 4 Ave Georges Rodenbach, 1030 Brussels, Belgium; tel. (2) 242-18-11; fax (2) 242-48-00; e-mail joci@jociycw.net; internet www.jociycw.net; f. 1925 to train, organize and defend the rights of young workers; develops analysis and action on areas such as informal work, the conditions for young female workers, unemployment, apprenticeships, and temporary and dangerous employment; holds int. councils and training sessions at local, nat. and int. level; mems: nat. orgs in 60 countries; Pres. YOVEL THIRUVALLUVAR; Sec.-Gen. BRIDGET RAUCH.

Islamic Educational, Scientific and Cultural Organization (ISESCO)/Organisation Islamique pour l'Education, les Sciences et la Culture: Ave des F. A. R., Hay Ryad, BP 2275, 10104 Rabat, Morocco; tel. (3) 7-56-60-52; fax (3) 7-56-60-12; internet www.isesco.org.ma; f. 1982 under the aegis of the Islamic Conference Organization to strengthen cooperation between mem. states in the fields of education, culture and science; 51 mems; Islamic Data Bank service (BIDI); Dir-Gen. Dr ABD AL AZIZ OTHMAN AL-TWAIJRI; publs *ISESCO Bulletin* (4 a year), *ISESCO Triennial*, *ISESCO Yearbook*, *Islam Today* (2 a year).

Latin American Institute for Educational Communication/Instituto Latinoamericano de la Comunicación Educativa: Calle del Puente 45, Col. Ejidos de Huipulco, Del. Tlalpan, 14380 México, DF, Mexico; tel. (55) 5728-6500 ext. 2100; e-mail contacto@ilce.edu.mx; internet www.ilce.edu .mx; f. 1956; provides leadership in educational communication and technical assistance to mems; regional cooperation in research, experimentation, production and distribution of audiovisual materials; produces and broadcasts educational television programmes; offers online educational services; training at the Center for Training and Advanced Studies on Educational Communication (CETEC); operates Center of AV Documentation for Latin America (CEDAL); 13 mem. countries; library of 34,000 vols; Dir-Gen. Lic. JOSE LUIS ESPINOSA PIÑA; publ. *Tecnología y Comunicación Educativas* (4 a year).

OECD Centre for Educational Research and Innovation (CERI): 2 rue André Pascal, 75775 Paris Cedex 16, France; tel. 1-45-24-82-00; fax 1-44-30-63-94; e-mail ceri

.contact@oecd.org; internet www.oecd.org/edu/ceri; f. 1968; projects include: future thinking in education, university future, evidence-based policy research in education, national reviews on educational research and development, learning sciences and brain research, formative assessment, systemic innovation; vocational education and training; open educational resources, measuring the social outcomes of learning; globalization and linguistic competencies; promotes generation of forward-looking research analyses and syntheses; identifies and stimulates educational innovation; encourages int. exchange of knowledge and experience; Head of CERI DIRK VAN DAMME.

Organization of Ibero-American States for Education, Science and Culture/Organización de Estados Iberoamericanos para la Educación, la Ciencia y la Cultura (OEI): C/ Bravo Murillo 38, 28015 Madrid, Spain; tel. (91) 594-43-82; fax (91) 594-32-86; internet www.oei.es; f. 1949 as Ibero-American Bureau of Education, name changed 1985; intergovernmental organization for educational, scientific and cultural cooperation within the Ibero-American countries; provides technical assistance to Ibero-American development systems in the above areas; provides information and documentation on the development of education, science and culture; encourages exchanges in these fields; organizes training courses; the General Assembly (at ministerial level) meets every four years; mems: govts of 20 Ibero-American countries; library of 8,000 vols, 500 periodicals; Sec.-Gen. FRANCISCO JOSÉ PIÑÓN.

Organization of the Catholic Universities of Latin America/Organización de Universidades Católicas de América Latina (ODUCAL): c/o Juan Alejandro Tobías, Viamonte 1856, CP 1056, Buenos Aires, Argentina; tel. (11) 4814-9630; fax (11) 4812-4625; internet www.oducal.org; f. 1953; aims to assist the cultural development of Latin America and to promote the activities of Catholic higher education in the region; mems: 34 Catholic univs in Argentina, Brazil, Colombia, Cuba, Ecuador, Mexico, Peru, Puerto Rico, and Venezuela; Pres. JUAN ALEJANDRO TOBIAS; Sec.-Gen. Dr EDUARDO MIRAS.

Pacific Islands Regional Association for Distance Education: c/o Ruby Va'a, University of the South Pacific, (Dir, USP Centre), POB 3014, Apia, Samoa; tel. 20874; fax 23424; e-mail vaa_r@samoa.usp.ac.fj; internet www.col.org/pirade; Pres. RUBY VA'A; Sec. PEPE LUTERU.

Pax Romana: 15 rue du Grand-Bureau, CP 315, 1211 Geneva 24, Switzerland; tel. 228230707; fax 228230708; e-mail miicmica@paxromana.int.ch; internet www.paxromana.org; f. 1921; 2 brs since 1947; student br: *International Movement of Catholic Students* (80 nat. federations); graduate branch: *International Catholic Movement for Intellectual and Cultural Affairs* (60 nat. federations and 5 int. specialized secretariats); Pres. PATRICIO RODE; Sec.-Gen. PAUL ORTEGA; publ. *Convergence* (2 a year, in English, French and Spanish).

Steering Committee for Higher Education and Research (CDESR): c/o Council of Europe, Higher Education Section, 67075 Strasbourg Cedex, France; tel. 3-88-41-20-00; fax 3-88-41-27-06; e-mail katia.dolgova-dreyer@coe.int; internet www.coe.int/higher-education; f. 1978, under the Council for Cultural Cooperation (CDCC), set up within the Council of Europe by the signatories of the European Cultural Convention, to promote cooperation among European countries in the field of higher education and research; the CDESR is a steering cttee under the Committee of Ministers of the Council of Europe; work programme: univ. policy, academic mobility (especially jt Council of Europe-UNESCO network of information centres on equivalences and mobility and a new jt convention on recognition); main contributor to the Bologna Process aiming to establish a European Higher Education Area by 2010; projects on higher education as a public responsibility, higher education governance, the heritage of European univs, intercultural dialogue; assistance in higher education reform in countries of South-Eastern Europe and newly independent states; 96 delegates (2 per country), who are representatives of higher education instns and senior govt officials from the 48 countries party to the European Cultural Convention; Chair. LUC WEBER (Switzerland); Sec. KATIA DOLGOVA-DREYER.

Southeast Asian Ministers of Education Organization (SEAMEO): Mom Luang Pin Malakul Centenary Bldg, 920 Sukhumvit Rd, Bangkok 10110, Thailand; tel. (2) 3910144; fax (2) 3812587; e-mail secretariat@seameo.org; internet www.seameo.org; f. 1965 to promote cooperation among the Southeast Asian nations through its projects and programmes in education, science and culture; 19 regional centres; mem. countries: Brunei Darussalam, Cambodia, Indonesia, Laos, Malaysia, Myanmar, Philippines, Singapore, Thailand, Timor-Leste, Viet Nam; Associate Member Countries: Australia, Canada, France, Germany, Netherlands, New Zealand, Norway, Spain; 3 affiliate mems: ICDE, Univ. of Tsukuba and British Council; library of 2,000 SEAMEO docs; Dir Dato' Dr AHAMAD (bin Sipon); Dir Designate Dato' Dr WITAYA JERADECHAKUL; publs *SEAMEO Accomplishments Report* (1 a year), *SEAMEO Directory* (1 a year), *SEAMEO Education Agenda* (2 a year).

UNESCO European Centre for Higher Education/Centre Européen pour l'Enseignement Supérieur (CEPES): Str. Stirbei Voda 39, 010102 Bucharest, Romania; tel. (21) 313-08-39; fax (21) 312-35-67; e-mail info@cepes.ro; internet www.cepes.ro; f. 1972; centre for policy development and the promotion of international higher education cooperation in Europe, North America and Israel; Secretariat of Joint UNESCO/Council of Europe European Recognition Convention, and of the ENIC Network of Information Centres on Recognition and Mobility in Europe; library of 6,000 books, 135 periodicals, 3,200 documents; Dir Dr JAN SADLAK; publ. *Higher Education in Europe* (4 a year, in English, online in French and Russian).

UNESCO Institute for Information Technologies in Education: Ul. Kedrova 8, Bldg 3, 117292 Moscow, Russia; tel. (095) 129-29-90; fax (095) 129-12-25; e-mail info@iite.ru; internet www.iite.ru; f. 1997; to develop policy and strategy regarding information and communication technologies (ICTs) in education, to monitor and support use of ICTs in education, to provide training for those working in education, and to assist UNESCO member states in problems relating to ICTs; Chair. Prof. Dr SALEH ABD AL RAHMAN AL-ATHEL (Saudi Arabia); Dir VLADIMIR KINELEV.

UNESCO Institute for Lifelong Learning/Institut de l'UNESCO pour l'apprentissage tout au long de la vie/UNESCO-Institut für Lebenslanges Lernen: Feldbrunnenstr. 58, 20148 Hamburg, Germany; tel. (40) 448041-46; fax (40) 4107723; e-mail uil-lib@unesco.org; internet www.uil.unesco.org; f. 1951; an int. research institute of UNESCO; main concern is the content and quality of education in the framework of lifelong learning, with an emphasis on adult learning, non-formal education and adult literacy; main activities are research, dissemination, promotion, research-based training and documentation; a worldwide network for exchange of information on literacy; a research-oriented training programme; library of 61,000 vols, 120 periodicals; spec. collns: sample learning materials on literacy, post-literacy and continuing education from 120 countries; Dir ARNE CARLSEN; publ. *International Review of Education* (6 a year).

UNESCO International Institute for Capacity Building in Africa: POB 2305, Addis Ababa, Ethiopia; tel. (11) 5445284; fax (11) 5514936; e-mail info@unesco-iicba.org; internet www.unesco-iicba.org; f. 1999; the institute's primary responsibility is the development of the capacity of institutions in Africa in the fields of teacher education, curriculum development, educational policy, planning and management, and distance education; Governing Board of 12 mems, sitting for three years each, selected from UNICEF, UNDP, World Bank, OAU, African Development Bank, Association for the Development of Education in Africa, and from representatives of Africa's geographical and linguistic groups; Officer in Charge Dr JULIEN DABOUE.

UNESCO International Institute for Higher Education in Latin America and the Caribbean/Instituto Internacional de la UNESCO para la Educación en América Latina y el Caribe: Edificio Asovincar, Avda Los Chorros con Calle Acueducto, Altos de Sebucán, Apdo Postal 68.394, Caracas 1062-A, Venezuela; tel. (212) 2861020; fax (212) 2860527; internet www.iesalc.unesco.org.ve; seeks to promote cooperation between member states in the region, and their institutions and establishments of higher education, the improvement of higher education systems, comparisons with and research into higher education in other parts of the world, regional integration, development of nat. and regional systems of evaluation and accreditation, the utilization of new information and communication technologies in higher education, and cooperation with UNESCO and implementation of its programmes; library: Documentation and Information Centre founded in 1979: online public catalogue, 11,325 bibliographies, 2,500 abstracts, 900 digital monographs and occasional papers; Dir CLAUDIO RAMA VITALE.

UNESCO-UNEVOC International Centre for Technical and Vocational Education and Training: UN Campus, Hermann-Ehlers-Str. 10, 53113 Bonn, Germany; tel. (228) 815-0100; fax (228) 815-0199; e-mail info@unevoc.unesco.org; internet www.unevoc.unesco.org; f. 2000; assists UNESCO's 193 mem. states strengthen and upgrade their technical and vocational education and training (TVET) systems; offers online services such as highly frequented e-Forum, knowledge-sharing platform TVETipedia and the UNEVOC Network Portal; Dir RUPERT MACLEAN (Australia); publ. *UNESCO-UNEVOC Bulletin* (2 a year, in Arabic, Chinese, English, French, Russian and Spanish).

Union of the Universities of Latin America and the Caribbean/Unión de Universidades de América Latina y el Caribe: Circuito Norponiente del Estadio Olímpico, Ciudad Universitaria, Apdo 70232, Del. Coyoacán, 04510 México, DF, Mexico; tel. (55) 5616-2383; fax (55) 5622-0092; e-mail udual@servidor.unam.mx; internet www.udual.org; f. 1949 to link the Latin American universities and contribute to the cultural and academic integration of the regional nations; organizes General Assemblies and Conferences; permanent statistical work; mems: 185 univs in 21 countries; library of 12,000 vols, 300 serials, records, microforms; Pres. Dr GUSTAVO GARCIA DE PAREDES (Panamá); Sec.-Gen. Dr JOSÉ NARRO ROBLES (Mexico); publs *Boletín UDUAL* (12 a year), *Gaceta UDUAL* (4 a year), *Proceedings of Latin American Universities Conferences*, *Revista Universidades* (4 a year), *Window* (4 a year).

University of the Arctic: POB 122, 96101 Rovaniemi, Finland; tel. (16) 341341; fax (16) 362941; e-mail secretariat@uarctic.org; internet www.uarctic.org; f. 2001; int. cooperating network of 126 'high latitude' universities, colleges and higher education and research institutions; the univ's secretariat, UArctic Int. Secretariat, is hosted by the Univ. of Lapland, Finland; 126 mems; Pres. LARS KULLERUD (Norway); Vice-Pres. OUTI SNELLMAN; Sec. RIITTA AIKIO.

World Association for Educational Research (WAER)/Asociación Mundial de Ciencias de la Educación (AMCE)/ Association Mondiale des Sciences de l'Education (AMSE): c/o Yves Lenoir, Faculté d'Education, Université de Sherbrooke, 2500 blvd de l'Université, Sherbrooke, QC J1K 2R1, Canada; tel. (819) 821-8000 ext. 61339; fax (819) 829-5343; e-mail amseamcewaer@usherbrooke.ca; internet www.amseamcewaer.usherbrooke .ca; f. 1953, present title adopted 2004; aims: to encourage research in educational sciences by organizing congresses, issuing publs, the exchange of information, etc.; 500 individual mems in 32 countries; Pres. YVES LENOIR; Gen. Sec. FOUAD CHAFIQI (Morocco); publ. *Recherche en Education autour du Monde* (2 a year).

World Education Fellowship-International (WEF): 54 Fox Lane, Palmers Green, London, N13 4AL, UK; tel. and fax (20) 8245-4561; e-mail generalsecretary@ wef-international.org; internet www .wef-international.org; f. 1921 to promote the exchange and practice of progressive educational ideas worldwide; organizes workshops and one-day conferences; sections and groups in 22 countries; Chair. CHRISTINE WYKES; Gen. Sec. GUADALUPE G. DE TURNER; publ. *The New Era in Education* (3 a year).

World Maritime University: POB 500, 201 24 Malmö, Sweden; tel. (40) 356300; fax (40) 128442; e-mail info@wmu.se; internet www .wmu.se; f. 1983 by the Int. Maritime Organization (IMO); offers postgraduate programmes in maritime affairs for students from around the world; language of instruction English; library of 18,000 vols (special collection: IMO depository); 300 students; Pres. Dr BJÖRN KJERFVE; publ. *Journal of Maritime Affairs* (2 a year).

World Student Christian Federation (WSCF)/Fédération Universelle des Associations Chrétiennes d'Etudiants: WSCF Inter-Regional Office, 5 route des Morillons, Ecumenical Centre, POB 2100, 1211 Geneva 2, Switzerland; tel. 227916358; fax 227916152; e-mail wscf@wscf.ch; internet www.wscfglobal.org; f. 1895; an ecumenical student, univ. and secondary school org. with participants from all major Christian confessions; consultative status with the UN through ECOSOC and UNESCO; affiliated student Christian movements in 105 countries; languages of instruction French, English, Spanish; Chair. HORACIO MESONES (Uruguay/Argentina); Sec.-Gen. CHRISTINE HOUSEL (USA/Switzerland); publs *Federation News* (2 a year), *Student World* (1 a year), *WSCF Journal*.

World Union of Jewish Students: Rechov King George 58, POB 7114, Jerusalem 91070, Israel; 2nd Fl., Heichal Shlomo, Rechavia, Jerusalem, Israel; tel. (2) 6213444; fax (2) 6251688; e-mail office@wujs .org.il; internet www.wujs.org.il; f. 1924 to act as a global organization for national Jewish student bodies; organizes educational programmes, leadership training seminars, women's seminars and Project Areivim, a service programme for Diaspora communities; divided into 6 regions; organizes Congress every three years; 51 nat. unions; 700,000 students; NGO mem. of UNESCO, youth affiliate of World Jewish Congress, mem. org. of World Zionist Organization; Chair. VIKTORIA DOLBURD; Exec. Dir NIR ORTAL; publs *Heritage and History* (Jewish student activist yearbook), *WUJS Leads*.

ACCREDITATION AND QUALITY ASSURANCE

Arab Network for Quality Assurance in Higher Education (ANQAHE): POB 533, Maadi, Egypt; 13 Bergas St, Garden City, Cairo, Egypt; tel. (2) 25240113; fax (2) 25240343; e-mail secretariat@anqahe.org; internet english.anqahe.org; f. 2007; aims to create a mechanism between the Arab countries to exchange information about quality assurance, construct new quality assurance orgs, develop standards and disseminate good practice, strengthen liaison between quality assurance bodies in the different countries; works in association with the International Network for Quality Assurance Agencies (q.v.) and the Association of Arab Universities (q.v.); Pres. Dr NADIA BADRAWI; Sec.-Gen. Dr TARIQ ALSINDI.

Asia Pacific Accreditation and Certification Commission (APACC): CPSC, Bldg Blk C, DepEd Complex, Meralco Ave, Pasig City 1600, Metro Manila, Philippines; tel. (2) 631-0991; fax (2) 633-8427; e-mail apacc@ cpsctech.org; internet www.apacc4hrd.org; f. 2004 to guide Technical and Vocational Education and Training (TVET) instns in equipping themselves with internationally recognized standards and systems; conduct accreditation and certification of TVET institutions in its member countries; 15 mem. countries (Afghanistan, Bangladesh, Bhutan, Fiji, Indonesia, Republic of Korea, Maldives, Mongolia, Myanmar, Nepal, Pakistan, Papua New Guinea, Philippines, Sri Lanka and Thailand); Pres. Prof. SHYAMAL MAJUMDAR; Jt Coordinator Dr RAJESH KHAMBAYAT; Jt Coordinator Dr THEODORA TESORO-GAYON-DATO.

Asia-Pacific Quality Network (APQN): 202 South Shaan Xi Rd, Shanghai, China; tel. (21) 54032285; fax (21) 54670198; e-mail jiangyq@shec.edu.cn; internet www.apqn .org; f. 2003 to enhance the quality of higher education in the region by promoting the devt of the quality assurance agencies and fostering cooperation between them; 64 mems (25 full, 12 intermediate, 6 assoc., 21 institutional) in 24 countries; Pres. CONCEPCION V. PIJANO (Philippines); Sec./Treas. Dr JIANG YANQIAO (China).

Caribbean Area Network for Quality Assurance in Tertiary Education (CANQATE): 6B Oxford Rd, Kingston 5, Jamaica; tel. 929-7299; fax 929-7312; e-mail elondon@ cwjamaica.com; internet www.canqate.org; f. 2002; 63 mems in 10 territories; Pres. Dr ETHLEY LONDON (Jamaica); Sec. VALDA ALLEYNE (Barbados).

Central and Eastern European Network of Quality Assurance Agencies in Higher Education (CEENet): 1013 Budapest, Krisztina krt. 39/B, Hungary; tel. (1) 344-0134; fax (1) 344-0313; e-mail rozsnyai@ mab.hu; internet www.ceenetwork.hu; f. 2001 as a not-for-profit NGO to share experiences and foster cooperation among member agencies; provides information and best practice examples in quality assurance and quality devt in higher education; provides funds to support projects; organizes events, seminars, workshops, and confs in its field; maintains relations with other European and non-European orgns; 26 mem. agencies in Albania, Austria, Bulgaria, Croatia, Czech Republic, Estonia, Germany, Hungary, Latvia, Lithuania, Macedonia, Poland, Romania, Russia, Slovakia, Slovenia; Sec. Gen. CHRISTINA ROZSNYAI.

Consejo Centroamericano de Acreditación de la Educación Superior (CCA) (Central American Council for Accreditation in Higher Education): 100 m norte y 75 m este de Office Depot, Avda Central, San Pedro, Montes de Oca, San José, Costa Rica; tel. 2202-6133; fax 2224-6903; e-mail cca@ucr.ac.cr; internet www.cca.ucr.ac.cr; f. 2003 to promote the improvement of the quality and the integration of higher education in Central America; Exec. Dir Licda MARIANELA AGUILAR ARCE.

European Association for Quality Assurance in Higher Education (ENQA): Unioninkatu 20–22 / Havis Business Center (3rd Fl.), 00130 Helsinki, Finland; tel. (9) 25225700; fax (9) 25225710; e-mail emmi.helle@enqa.eu; internet www .enqa.eu; f. 2000; disseminates information, experiences and good practices in the field of quality assurance (QA) in higher education to European QA agencies, public authorities and higher education instns; its activities are financed by the European Commission; 40 full mem. agencies (39 nat., 1 European) in 22 countries; Pres. BRUNO CURVALE (France); Sec.-Gen. EMMI HELLE (Finland).

European Consortium for Accreditation in Higher Education (ECA): NVAO, POB 85498, 2508 CD The Hague, Netherlands; tel. (70) 3122352; fax (70) 3122301; e-mail m .frederiks@nvao.net; internet www .ecaconsortium.net; f. 2003 to achieve the mutual recognition of accreditation decisions among the participants, which will contribute to the recognition of qualifications and the mobility of students in Europe; 13 mem. orgs in 9 countries; Coordinator MARK FREDERIKS.

International Network for Quality Assurance Agencies in Higher Education (INQAAHE): POB 85498, 2508 CD The Hague, Netherlands; NVAO, Parkstraat 28, 2514 JK The Hague, Netherlands; tel. (70) 3122300; fax (70) 3122301; e-mail inqaahe@ nvao.net; internet www.inqaahe.org; f. 1991; collects and disseminates information on theory and practice in the assessment, improvement and maintenance of quality in higher education; Pres. Dr DAVID WOODHOUSE (Australia); Sec. GUIDO LANGOUCHE (Netherlands); publs *INQAAHE Bulletin* (4 a year, online), *Quality in Higher Education* (3 a year).

Red Iberoamericana para la Acreditación de la Calidad de la Educación Superior (RIACES) (Iberoamerican Network for Accreditation of Quality in Higher Education): CONEAU, Av. Santa Fe 1385, Piso 4, (C1059ABH), Buenos Aires, Argentina; tel. (11) 4815-1767; fax (11) 4815-0744; e-mail leandroh@coneau.gov.ar; internet www.riaces.net; f. 2003; promotes cooperation and the exchange of information and experiences between Iberoamerican instns concerned with the evaluation and accreditation of quality in higher education; 28 mem. instns in 18 countries; Pres. MARÍA JOSÉ LEMAITRE (Chile).

Engineering and Technology

International Union of Technical Associations and Organizations/Union Internationale des Associations et Organismes Techniques (UATI): 1 rue Miollis, 75732 Paris Cedex 15, France; tel. (1) 45-68-48-28; fax (1) 43-06-29-27; e-mail uati@unesco.org; internet www.unesco.org/uati; f. 1951; activities: working groups and cttees to identify, promote and coordinate actions of mem. asscns in areas of common interest, and to facilitate relations with international bodies, in particular UNESCO, UNIDO and ECOSOC; mems: 25 organizations; Pres. JACQUES ROUSSET (France); Sec.-Gen. ROLAND BRESSON (France); publ. *Convergence* (3 a year).

MEMBER ORGANIZATIONS

International Academy for Production Engineering/Collège International pour la Recherche en Productique: 9 rue Mayran, 75009 Paris, France; tel. 1-45-26-21-80; fax 1-45-26-92-15; e-mail cirp@cirp.net; internet www.cirp.net; f. 1950; aims to promote by scientific research the study of mechanical processing of all solid materials including checks on efficiency and quality of work; 540 mems; Sec.-Gen. Prof. DIDIER DUMUR; publs *Annals–Manufacturing Technology* (2 vols, 1 a year), *Dictionaries of Production Engineering*, *Proceedings of Manufacturing Systems Seminars* (1 a year).

International Association for Hydro-Environment Engineering and Research: Paseo Bajo Virgen del Puerto 3, 28005 Madrid, Spain; tel. (91) 335-79-08; fax (91) 335-79-35; e-mail iahr@iahr.org; internet www.iahr.org; f. 1935; 2,300 individual mems, 200 corporate mems; Exec. Dir Dr C. B. GEORGE; publs *Journal of Hydraulic Research* (6 a year), *Journal of HydroEnvironment Research*, *Journal of River Basin Management* (published in partnership with IAHS and INBO, 4 a year), *Newsflash* (12 a year), *Proceedings of World Congresses* (4 a year).

International Commission of Agricultural Engineering/Commission Internationale du Génie Rural (CIGR): c/o Prof. Dr T. Maekawa, University of Tsukuba, Graduate School of Life and Environmental Sciences, 1-1-1 Tennodai, Tsukuba, 305-8572 Ibaraki, Japan; tel. (81) 29-853-6989; fax (81) 29-853-7496; e-mail biopro@sakura.cc.tsukuba.ac.jp; internet www.cigr.org; f. 1930; application of soil and water sciences to agricultural engineering; conservation, irrigation, land improvement and reclamation; rural construction and equipment; agricultural machinery; distribution of electricity in rural areas and its application in the general energy context; scientific organization of agricultural work; food processing; mem. asscns in 30 countries, individual mems in 6 countries; Pres. Prof. LUIS SANTOS (Portugal); Sec.-Gen. Prof. Dr P. SCHULZE LAMMERS (Germany).

International Commission on Glass (ICG): Instituto de Cerámica y Vidrio (CSIC), c/o Kelsen 5, Campus de Cantoblanco, 28049 Madrid, Spain; tel. 903221678; e-mail psimurka@stonline.sk; internet www.icglass.org; f. 1933; promotes dissemination of information on the art, history, science and technology of glass; mems: nat. socs in 33 countries; Pres. Dr F. NICOLETTI (Italy); Exec. Sec. Dr PETER SIMURKA (Slovakia).

International Commission on Irrigation and Drainage/Commission Internationale des Irrigations et du Drainage: 48 Nyaya Marg, Chanakyapuri, New Delhi 110021, India; tel. (11) 26116837; fax (11) 26115962; e-mail icid@icid.org; internet www.icid.org; f. 1950; to stimulate and promote the devt of the arts, sciences and techniques of engineering, agriculture, economics, ecology and social science in managing water and land resources for irrigation, drainage, flood control and river training applications, incl. research and devt and capacity-building by adopting comprehensive approaches and up-to-date techniques for sustainable agriculture in the world; 65 active mem. countries; 110 Nat. Cttees; Pres. Prof. Dr CHANDRA A. MADRAMOOTOO (Canada); Sec.-Gen. M. GOPALAKRISHNAN (India); Dir VIJAY K. LABHSETWAR; publ. *Irrigation and Drainage—The Journal of the ICID*.

International Commission on Large Dams/Commission Internationale des Grands Barrages: 151 blvd Haussmann, 75008 Paris, France; tel. 1-40-42-68-24; fax 1-40-42-60-71; internet www.icold-cigb.org; f. 1928; mems: national cttees in 80 countries; Pres. C. B. VIOTTI (Brazil); Sec.-Gen. A. BERGERET (France); publs *ICOLD Congress Proceedings and Transactions* (every 3 years), *World Register of Dams*.

International Congress on Fracture (ICF): c/o A. T. Yokobori, Jr, Tohoku University, 1-31-15 Taihoku Aoyama, Sendai, Japan; tel. (22) 795-6894; fax (22) 795-6894; e-mail yokobori@md.mech.tuhoku.ac.jp; internet www.icf11.com; f. 1965; aims to foster research in the mechanics and phenomena of fracture, fatigue, and strength of materials; to promote cooperation among scientists in the field; holds Int. Conference every 4 years; 30 mem. orgs; Founder Pres. Prof. T. YOKOBORI (Japan); Pres. Prof. A. CARPENTER (Italy); Sec.-Gen. A. T. YOKOBORI, JR (Japan); publ. *Proceedings* (every 4 years).

International Dairy Federation: see under Agriculture.

International Federation of Automatic Control (IFAC)/Fédération Internationale de l'Automatique: Schlosspl. 12, 2361 Laxenburg, Austria; tel. (2236) 71447; fax (2236) 72859; e-mail secretariat@ifac-control.org; internet www.ifac-control.org; f. 1957 to promote the science and technology of control in the broadest sense in all systems, e.g. engineering, physical, biological, social and economical, in both theory and application; mems: 49 nat. mems; Pres. ALBERTO ISIDORI (Italy); Sec. KURT SCHLACHER (Austria); publs *Annual Reviews in Control*, *Automatica* (mainly selected papers of IFAC-sponsored symposia, 12 a year), *Control Engineering Practice* (6 a year), *Engineering Applications of Artificial Intelligence*, *Journal of Process Control*, *Mechatronics*.

International Gas Union/Union Internationale de l'Industrie du Gaz: c/o DONG A/S, POB 550, Agern Allé 24–26, 2970 Hoersholm, Denmark; tel. 45-17-12-00; fax 45-17-19-00; e-mail secr.igu@dong.dk; internet www.igu.org; f. 1931; mem. orgs in 65 countries; Pres. GEORGE H. B. VERBERG; Sec.-Gen. PETER K. STORM.

International Institute of Welding/Institut International de la Soudure: Paris Nord 2, 90 rue de Vanesses, BP 51362, Villepinte, 95942 Roissy CDG Cedex, France; tel. 1-49-90-36-08; fax 1-49-90-36-80; e-mail iiw@iiwelding.org; internet www.iiwelding.org; f. 1948; mem societies in 54 countries; Pres. BALDEV RAJ (India); Chief Exec. CÉCILE MAYER (France); publ. *Welding in the World* (6 a year).

International Measurement Confederation (IMEKO)/Confédération Internationale de la Mesure: POB 457, 1371 Budapest, Hungary; tel. 3531-562; fax 3531-562; e-mail imeko@t-online.hu; internet www.imeko.org; f. 1958; promotes the int. exchange of scientific and technical information relating to devts in measuring techniques, instrument design and manufacture and in the application of instrumentation in scientific research and industry; promotes cooperation among scientists and engineers in the field, and with other int. orgs; organizes congresses, symposia, etc.; 39 mem. orgs, 24 technical cttees; Sec.-Gen. Prof. MLADEN BORSIC; Exec. Sec. KAROLINA HAVRILLA; publs *IMEKO Bulletin* (2 a year), *Measurement* (8 a year).

International Navigation Association/Association Internationale de Navigation: Graaf de Ferraris, 11ème étage, Boîte 3, blvd du Roi Albert II 20, 1000 Brussels, Belgium; tel. (2) 553-71-61; fax (2) 553-71-55; e-mail info@pianc-aipcn.org; internet www.pianc-aipcn.org; f. 1885 to promote inland and ocean navigation by fostering and encouraging progress in the design, construction, improvement, maintenance and operation of inland and maritime waterways, ports, and of coastal areas for the benefit of mankind; 2,002 individual mems, 533 corporate mems; Pres. ERIC VAN DEN EEDE; Sec.-Gen. LOUIS VAN SCHEL; publ. *PIANC Bulletin* (4 a year).

International Union of Laboratories and Experts in Construction Materials, Systems and Structures/Réunion Internationale des Laboratoires d'Essais et Experts des Matériaux, systèmes de constructions et ouvrages (RILEM): 157 rue des Blains, 92220 Bagneux Cedex, France; tel. (331) 45-36-10-20; fax (331) 45-36-63-20; e-mail sg@rilem.org; internet www.rilem.net; f. 1947 to advance scientific knowledge related to construction materials, systems and structures and to encourage the transfer and application of this knowledge worldwide; 1,248 mems; Pres. Dr PETER RICHNER (Switzerland); Sec.-Gen. PASCALE DUCORNET; publ. *Materials and Structures—Matériaux et Constructions* (10 a year).

World Energy Council (WEC)/Conseil Mondial de l'Energie (CME): 5th Fl., Regency House, 1–4 Warwick St, London, W1B 5LT, UK; tel. (20) 7734-5996; fax (20) 7734-5926; e-mail info@worldenergy.org; internet www.worldenergy.org; f. 1924 in London as World Power Conference to consider the potential resources and all means of production, transportation, transformation and utilization of energy in all their aspects, and also to consider energy consumption in its overall relationship to the growth of economic activity; collects and publishes data; holds triennial congress; promotes regional symposia and technical studies; mem. cttees in 96 countries; Chair. ANDRÉ CAILLÉ (Canada); Sec.-Gen. GERALD DOUCET (Canada); publs *Energy Efficiency Policies and Indicators* (every 3 years), *Performance of Generating Plant* (every 3 years), *World Survey of Energy Resources* (every 3 years).

World Foundrymen Organization: National Metalforming Centre, 47 Birmingham Rd, West Bromwich, West Midlands B70 6PY, UK; tel. (121) 601-6976; fax (1544) 340332; e-mail secretary@thewfo.com; internet www.thewfo.com; f. 1927 to promote int. cooperation between member asscns and other orgs; congress every 2 years; mems: 28 nat. technical asscns; Pres. Dr Ing. GOTTHARD WOLF (Germany); Sec.-Gen. Ing. ANDREW TURNER (UK); publ. *International Foundry Research* (4 a year).

World Road Association/Association mondiale de la Route: La Grande Arche, Paroi Nord-Niveau 5, 92055 Paris-La

Défense Cedex, France; tel. (1) 47-96-81-21; fax (1) 49-00-02-02; e-mail info@piarc.org; internet www.piarc.org; f. 1909; shares information about roads and transport; 1,640 mems; Pres. ANNE-MARIE LECLERC (Canada); Sec.-Gen. JEAN-FRANÇOIS CORTÉ (France); publs *CD-Route* (technical reports, every 2 years), *E-Newsletter* (4 a year), *Reports to International Winter Road Congress* (every 4 years), *Reports to World Road Congress* (every 4 years), *Routes/Roads* (4 a year).

OTHER ORGANIZATIONS

Arab Petroleum Training Institute: POB 6037, Al Tajeyat, Baghdad, Iraq; tel. (1) 5234100; fax (1) 5210526; f. 1979; training of high-level personnel in all aspects of the oil industry; 11 OAPEC mem. states; library of 5,000 vols, bibliographic and non-bibliographic databases; Dir-Gen. Dr TAL'AT NAJEEB HATTAB.

Council of Academies of Engineering and Technological Sciences (CAETS): c/o William C. Salmon, 112 Pleasant Grove Rd, Locust Grove, VA 22508, USA; tel. (703) 527-5782; fax (703) 526-0570; e-mail caets@nae.edu; internet www.caets.org; f. 1978; promote the devt of engineering and technology worldwide and to provide an int. forum for the discussion of technological and engineering issues; encourages int. engineering efforts to promote economic growth and social welfare; 26 nat. mem. acads; Sec. and Treas. WILLIAM C. SALMON (USA).

European Organization for Civil Aviation Equipment (EUROCAE)/Organisation Européenne pour l'Equipement de l'Aviation Civile: 102 rue Etienne Dolet, 92240 Malakoff, France; tel. (1) 40-92-79-30; fax (1) 46-55-62-65; e-mail eurocae@eurocae.net; internet www.eurocae.eu; f. 1963; studies and advises on problems related to the application of equipment to aviation and prepares minimum performance specifications that administrations in Europe may use for approving equipment; 92 mems; Pres. MICHEL LESAGE; Sec. GILBERT AMATO.

European Society for Engineering Education (SEFI)/Société Européenne pour la Formation des Ingénieurs/Europäische Gesellschaft für Ingenieur-Ausbildung: 119 rue de Stassart, 1050 Brussels, Belgium; tel. (2) 502-36-09; fax (2) 502-96-11; e-mail info@sefi.be; internet www.ntb.ch/sefi; f. 1973 to promote the quality of initial and continuing engineering education and to encourage cooperation throughout Europe; provides services and information about engineering education; encourages exchanges between teachers, researchers and students of engineering; Pres. Prof. Dr ANETTE KOLMOS (Denmark); Sec.-Gen. FRANÇOISE CÔME (Belgium); publs *European Journal for Engineering Education* (4 a year), *SEFI News* (12 a year).

ICHCA International Ltd: Suite 2, 85 Western Rd, Romford, Essex, RM1 3LS, UK; tel. (1708) 735295; fax (1708) 735225; e-mail info@ichcainternational.co.uk; internet www.ichcainternational.co.uk; f. 2003 to promote safety and efficiency in the handling and movement of goods; 900 mems from more than 80 countries; Hon. Pres. JOSÉ ARNAIZ BRÁ (Spain); Chair. JAMES HARTUNG (USA); publ. *Cargo World* (1 a year).

International Association for Bridge and Structural Engineering (IABSE)/Association Internationale des Ponts et Charpentes/Internationale Vereinigung für Brückenbau und Hochbau: Secretariat ETH-Zurich, 8093 Zürich, Switzerland; tel. 446332647; fax 446331241; e-mail secretariat@iabse.org; internet www.iabse.org; f. 1929; aims: international cooperation among scientists, engineers, researchers and manufacturers; interchange of knowledge, ideas and the results of research work in the sphere of bridge and structural engineering in general, whether in steel, concrete or another material; 3,900 mems from 100 countries; Pres. JACQUES COMBAULT (France); Exec. Dir UELI BRUNNER; publs *Conference Report* (irregular), *Structural Engineering Document* (1 a year), *Structural Engineering International* (4 a year).

International Association of Public Transport/Union Internationale des Transports Publics (UITP)/Internationaler Verband für Öffentliches Verkehrswesen: 6 rue Ste Marie, 1080 Brussels, Belgium; tel. (2) 673-61-00; fax (2) 660-10-72; e-mail info@uitp.org; internet www.uitp.org; f. 1885 to study all problems related to the operation of public transportation; 3,400 mems; library of 25,000 vols, 200 journals; online library (MOBI +); Pres. ALAIN FLAUSCH; Sec.-Gen. HANS RAT (Netherlands); publ. *Public Transport International* (6 a year, in English, French, German, Russian, Italian and Spanish).

International Centre for Science and High Technology (ICS): AREA Science Park, Padriciano 99, 34149 Trieste, Italy; tel. 040-9228111; fax 040-9220101; e-mail info@ics.trieste.it; internet www.ics.trieste.it; f. 1988; an int. centre of the United Nations Industrial Development Organization (UNIDO); promotes transfer and application of scientific knowledge and ecofriendly technologies in support of sustainable industrial devt for the benefit of developing countries and countries in economic transition; operates through five thematic fields: renewable energies; biofuels and added value products from biomass; industrial utilization of medicinal and aromatic plants; sustainable industrial devt, food processing and safety; Officer-in-Charge EMILIO VENTO.

International Commission on Illumination (CIE)/Commission Internationale de l'Éclairage: Kegelgasse 27, 1030 Vienna, Austria; tel. (1) 714-31-87-0; fax (1) 714-31-87-18; e-mail ciecb@cie.co.at; internet www.cie.co.at; f. 1900 as Int. Commission on Photometry, reorganized as CIE 1913; objectives: to provide an int. forum for the discussion of all matters relating to science, technology and art in the fields of light and lighting; to develop basic standards and procedures of metrology in the fields of light and lighting; to provide guidance in the application of basic principles and procedures to the devt of int. standards in the fields of light and lighting; to prepare and publish reports and standards; to maintain liaison and technical interaction with relevant int. orgs; 41 Nat. Cttees, 14 supportive mems; Gen. Sec. MARTINA PAUL.

International Council for Research and Innovation in Building and Construction: Postbox 1837, 3014 DB Rotterdam, Netherlands; located at: Kruisplein 25G, 3000 BV Rotterdam, Netherlands; tel. (10) 4110240; fax (10) 4334372; e-mail secretariat@cibworld.nl; internet www.cibworld.nl; f. 1953; facilitates int. cooperation and information exchange between organizations with a research, univ., industry or government background, which collectively are active in all aspects of research and innovation for building and construction; mems: 450 institutes and individuals in 70 countries; Pres. Prof. JOHN MCCARTHY (Australia); Sec.-Gen. Dr WIM BAKENS (Netherlands); publs *CIB Congress and Symposium Proceedings, Directory of Building Research and Development Organizations.*

International Council for Scientific and Technical Information (ICSTI)/Conseil International pour l'Information Scientifique et Technique: 5 rue Ambroise Thomas, 75009 Paris, France; tel. 1-45-25-65-92; fax 1-42-15-12-62; e-mail icsti@icsti.org; internet www.icsti.org; f. 1952 as ICSU Abstracting Board, present name 1984; aims to increase accessibility to and awareness of scientific and technical information, and to foster communication and interaction among participants in the information transfer chain, to take advantage of the progress made independently by each information activity sector; ICSTI is a Scientific Associate of ICSU; 50 nat. and organizational mems in 12 countries; Pres. ROBERTA SHAFFER (USA); Vice-Pres. SIVADAS RAGHAVA (India); Gen. Sec. WENDY WARR (UK); Treas. PAM BJORNSON (Canada).

International Council on Large Electric Systems/Conseil International des Grands Réseaux Électriques (CIGRE): 21 rue d'Artois, 75008 Paris, France; tel. 1-53-89-12-90; fax 1-53-89-12-99; e-mail secretary-general@cigre.org; internet www.cigre.org; f. 1921; electrical aspects of electricity generation, sub-stations and transformer stations, high-voltage electrical lines, interconnection of systems and their operation and protection; 6,653 mems in 85 countries; Pres. ANDRÉ MERLIN (France); Sec.-Gen. JEAN KOWAL (France); publs *Electra* (6 a year, bilingual), *Session Papers and Proceedings* (every 2 years), *Symposium Papers (CD)* (irregular).

International Electrotechnical Commission (IEC)/Commission Electrotechnique Internationale: 3 rue de Varembé, POB 131, 1211 Geneva 20, Switzerland; tel. 229190211; fax 229190300; e-mail info@iec.ch; internet www.iec.ch; f. 1906 to promote int. cooperation in the electrotechnical industry; administers int. conformity assessment schemes in the areas of electrical equipment and components testing and certification (IECEE), quality of electronic components, materials and processes (IECQ), and certification of electrical equipment operated in explosive atmospheres (IECEx); prepares and publishes int. standards for all electrical, electronic and related technologies; creator of the 'International System' (SI) of units of measurement; has compiled a multi-language electronic vocabulary with more than 20,000 terms; Pres. JACQUES RÉGIS (Canada); Gen. Sec. AHARON AMIT (Switzerland); publ. *Bulletin* (6 a year).

International Federation for Housing and Planning (IFHP)/Fédération Internationale pour l'Habitation, l'Urbanisme et l'Aménagement des Territoires (FIHUAT)/Internationaler Verband für Wohnungswesen, Städtebau und Raumordnung (IVWSR): Wassenaarseweg 43, 2596 CG The Hague, Netherlands; tel. (70) 324-45-57; fax (70) 328-20-85; e-mail info@ifhp.org; internet www.ifhp.org; f. 1913; global network of professionals from the field of housing and planning; corporate and individual mems; annual congress; Pres. FRANCESC X. VENTURA I TEIXIDOR (Spain); Sec.-Gen. PAUL J. RŸNAARTS (Netherlands); publ. *Latest Developments in the Field of Housing and Planning* (1 a year).

International Federation for Information Processing: Hofstr. 3, 2361 Laxenburg, Austria; tel. (2236) 73616; fax (2236) 736169; e-mail ifip@ifip.org; internet www.ifip.org; f. 1960; promotes information science and technology by fostering int. cooperation in this field, stimulating research, devt and application of information processing in science and human activity, furthering dissemination and exchange of information about subject, and encouraging education in information processing; 55 mem. orgns in 56 countries; Pres. LEON STROUS (Netherlands); Sec. MARIA RAFFAI (Hungary); publs *Computers in Industry*, *Computers and Security*, *Information Bulletin* (online).

International Federation of Automotive Engineering Societies/Fédération Internationale des Sociétés d'Ingénieurs des Techniques de l'Automobile (FISITA): 1 Birdcage Walk, London, SW1H 9JJ, UK; tel. (20) 7973-1275; fax (20) 7973-1285; e-mail info@fisita.com; internet www.fisita.com; f. 1947 to promote the exchange of information between member societies, ensure standardization of techniques and terms, to publish research on technical and managerial problems, and generally to encourage the technical development of mechanical transport; mem. organizations in 36 countries; Pres. DANIEL M. HANCOCK (USA); Exec. Dir IAN DICKIE (UK); publ. *Global Automotive Network* (6 a year).

International Federation of Operational Research Societies (IFORS): c/o Mary Thomas Magrogan, 7240 Parkway Drive, Suite 300, Hanover, MD 21076, USA; tel. (443) 757-3534; fax (443) 757-3535; e-mail secretary@ifors.org; internet www.ifors.org; f. 1959; devt of operational research as a unified science and its advancement worldwide; comprises nat. Operations Research socs of over 45 countries from four geographical regions: Asia Pacific, Europe, North America, South America; 50 nat. socs, 2 kindred socs; Pres. Prof. DOMINIQUE DE WERRA (Switzerland); Sec. MARY THOMAS MAGROGAN (USA); publs *International Abstracts* (in Operations Research), *International Transactions* (in Operational Research Journal).

International Federation of Robotics: IFR Secretariat, c/o Symap, Maison de la Mécanique, 45 rue Louis-Blanc, 92400 Courbevoie, France; tel. 1-47-17-67-07; fax 1-47-17-67-25; e-mail secretariat@ifr.org; internet www.ifr.org; f. 1987; 25 nat. mem. orgs; Chair. PAUL JOHNSTON (Canada); Sec. HERMAN VERBRUGGE (Germany); publs *Industrial Robotics*, *Service Robotics*, *World Robotics* (1 a year).

International Federation of Surveyors/ Fédération Internationale des Géomètres/Internationale Vereinigung der Vermessungsingenieure: Kalvebod Brygge 31-33, 1780 Copenhagen V, Denmark; tel. 38-86-10-81; fax 38-86-02-52; e-mail fig@fig.net; internet www.fig.net; f. 1878; 9 technical commissions; 73 nat. mem. assocs; Pres. Prof. Dr-Ing. STIG ENEMARK (Denmark); Admin. Dir MARKKU VILLIKKA (Denmark).

International Information Centre for Terminology (Infoterm): Gymnasiumstrasse 50, 1190 Vienna, Austria; tel. (1) 427758026; fax (1) 587-6990; e-mail infopoint@infoterm.org; internet www .infoterm.info; f. 1971 under UNESCO contract; affiliated to Austrian Standards Institute, associated with DPI and ISONETl; consultative status with ECOSOC; operates the secretariat of ISO/TC 37 'Terminology and Other Language and Content Resources'; library of 5,600 vols, 15,000 vocabulary standards at Cologne Univ. of Applied Sciences; 39 nat. and int. corporate bodies and instns; Dir Dr CHRISTIAN GALINSKI; Dir Mag. ANJA DRAME.

International Institute of Communications: 2 Printers Yard, 90A The Broadway, London, SW19 1RD, UK; tel. (20) 8417-0600; fax (20) 8417-0800; e-mail enquiries@iicom

.org; internet www.iicom.org; f. 1969 as Int. Broadcast Inst.; worldwide research and education on telecommunications, broadcasting and information technology; hosts seminars and annual confc; mems in 70 countries; library: 15,000 items, 200 periodicals; Pres. FABIO COLASANTI; Dir-Gen. ANDREA MILLWOOD HARGRAVE; publ. *Intermedia* (5 a year).

International Institute of Refrigeration/ Institut International du Froid: 177 blvd Malesherbes, 75017 Paris, France; tel. 1-42-27-32-35; fax 1-47-63-17-98; internet www .iifiir.org; f. 1908; intergovernmental organization; object: the study of all technical, scientific and industrial issues concerning refrigeration systems, cryogenics, air conditioning, heat pumps and their applications; studies are undertaken, under the direction of a Science and Technology Council, by 10 Commissions; organizes congresses and conferences; large library, also computerized abstract database; provides bibliographical searches; mems: 61 countries and private and corporate members; Dir DIDIER COULOMB (France); publs *Bulletin of the IIR* (bibliographical, in English and French), *International Journal of Refrigeration*, *Proceedings of Conferences*.

International Iron and Steel Institute (IISI)/Institut International du Fer et de l'Acier: 120 rue Col. Bourg, 1140 Brussels, Belgium; tel. (2) 702-89-00; fax (2) 702-88-99; e-mail steel@iisi.be; internet www.worldsteel .org; f. 1967 to promote the interests of the world's steel industries; to undertake research in all aspects of steel industries; to serve as a forum for exchange of knowledge and discussion of problems relating to steel industries; to collect, disseminate and maintain statistics and information; to serve as a liaison body between int. and nat. steel orgs; mems in 50 countries; Chair. KU-TAEK LEE (USA); Sec.-Gen. IAN CHRISTMAS; publs *Crude Steel Production Monthly*, *Iron Production Monthly*.

International Masonry Society: Shermanbury, 6 Church Rd, Whyteleafe, CR3 0AR UK; tel. (20) 8660-3633; fax (20) 8668-6983; e-mail kenneth@fisher5053.fsnet.co .uk; internet www.masonry.org.uk; f. 1986 as British Masonry Soc., changed to International Masonry Soc. 2008; 300 mems; Sec. Dr K. FISHER; publ. *Masonry International* (3 a year).

International Organization for Standardization/Organisation internationale de normalisation: 1 rue de Varembé, CP 56, 1211 Geneva 20, Switzerland; tel. 227490111; fax 227333430; e-mail central@ iso.org; internet www.iso.org; f. 1947 to promote the development of standardization and related activities in the world with a view to facilitating the international exchange of goods and services, and to developing mutual cooperation in the spheres of intellectual, scientific, technological and economic activity; 150 mems; reference library holding full collns of ISO and IEC standards; Pres. HÅKAN MURBY (Sweden); Sec.-Gen. ALAN BRYDEN; publs *ISO Focus* (11 a year), *ISO International Standards*, *ISO Management Systems* (6 a year).

International Society for Photogrammetry and Remote Sensing (ISPRS)/Société Internationale de Photogrammétrie et de Télédétection: c/o Orhan Eltan, ITU Insaat Fakultesi, 34669 Maslak, Istanbul, Turkey; tel. (212) 285-3810; fax (212) 285-6587; internet www.isprs.org; f. 1910; research and information on the application of aerial and space photography and remote sensing to exploration and mapping; federated to ICSU; 90 nat. mem. orgs, 11 assoc.

mems and 12 regional mem. assocs; Pres. IAN DOWMAN (UK); Sec.-Gen. OHRAN ALTAN (Turkey); publs *International Archives of Photogrammetry and Remote Sensing* (6 a year), *ISPRS Highlights* (4 a year), *Journal of Photogrammetry and Remote Sensing* (4 a year).

International Society for Soil Mechanics and Geotechnical Engineering/Société Internationale de Mécanique des Sols et de la Géotechnique: City Univ., Northampton Sq., London, EC1V 0HB, UK; tel. (20) 7040-8154; fax (20) 7040-8832; e-mail secretariat@issmge.org; internet www.issmge.org; f. 1936; 85 mem. socs, 18,000 individual mems; Pres. Prof. JEAN-LOUIS BRIAUD (USA); Sec.-Gen. Prof. R. NEIL TAYLOR (UK).

International Water Association: Alliance House, 12 Caxton St, London, SW1H 0QS, UK; tel. (20) 7654-5500; fax (20) 7654-5555; e-mail water@iwahq.org.uk; internet www.iwahq.org.uk; f. 1999 by the merger of the International Association on Water Quality and the International Water Supply Association; develops effective and sustainable approaches to global water management; members include academic researchers, research centres, energy utilities, consultants, water industry regulators, industrial water users and water equipment manufacturers; Pres. Dr DAVID GARMAN; Exec. Dir PAUL REITER; publs *Hydrology Research* (5 a year), *Journal of Hydroinformatics* (4 a year), *Journal of Water and Climate Change* (4 a year), *Journal of Water and Health* (4 a year), *Journal of Water Supply: Research and Technology—AQUA* (8 a year), *Water Asset Management International* (4 a year), *Water Intelligence Online* (12 a year), *Water Practice and Technology* (4 a year), *Water Policy* (6 a year), *Water Research* (20 a year), *Water Science and Technology* (24 a year), *Water Science and Technology: Water Supply* (6 a year), *Water Utility Management International* (4 a year).

Textile Institute: International Headquarters, 1st Fl., St James's Bldgs, Oxford St, Manchester, M1 6FQ, UK; tel. (161) 237-1188; fax (161) 236-1991; e-mail tiihq@ textileinst.org.uk; internet www.texi.org; f. 1910, Royal Charter 1925 and 1955; the international body for those concerned with any aspect of textiles and related industries; promotion of education and training, professional standards and exchange of information within the industry by means of publications, conferences, meetings and information services; 60 national and regional brs; 8,000 mems in 85 countries; library of 1,500 vols, 120 journals; Professional Affairs Dir HELEN YEOWART; Hon. Sec. M. PARKINSON; publs *Journal* (4 a year), *Textiles* (4 a year), *Textile Horizons* (6 a year), *Textile Progress* (4 a year).

Tin Technology Ltd: Unit 3, Curo Park, Frogmore, St Albans, AL2 2DD, UK; tel. (1727) 875544; fax (1727) 871341; e-mail info@tintechnology.com; internet www .tintechnology.biz; f. 1932; aims to maintain and extend the use and effectiveness of tin in modern technology; its work is directed to develop the use of tin and is based on scientific and technical study of the metal, its alloys and compounds, and of industrial processes that use tin or may provide future markets; 200 mems in 35 countries; Man. Dir DAVID BISHOP.

World Wide Web Consortium (W3C): c/o Massachusetts Institute of Technology, Computer Science and Artificial Intelligence Laboratory (CSAIL), 32 Vassar St, Cambridge, MA 02139, USA; tel. (617) 253-2613; fax (617) 258-5999; internet www.w3.org; f.

1994; provides an open forum for discussing the technical evolution of the World Wide Web; develops technical specifications for the Web's infrastructure; 500 mem. orgs worldwide; Chief Operating Officer STEVE BRATT; Dir TIM BERNERS-LEE.

Law

Hague Academy of International Law: Peace Palace, Carnegieplein 2, 2517 KJ The Hague, Netherlands; tel. (70) 3024242; fax (70) 3024153; e-mail hagueacademy@ registration.nl; internet www.hagueacademy .nl; f. 1923 as a centre of higher studies in international law (public and private) and cognate sciences, in order to facilitate a thorough and impartial examination of questions bearing on international juridical relations; Sec.-Gen. Prof. Y. DAUDET.

Associated Centre:

Centre for Studies and Research in International Law and International Relations: Peace Palace, Carnegieplein 2, 2517 KJ The Hague, Netherlands; tel. (70) 3024242; fax (70) 3024153; e-mail hagueacademy@registration.nl; internet www.hagueacademy.nl; f. 1957; postdoctoral 4-week research courses in August and September after courses held by Academy; open only to participants who are highly qualified by intellectual maturity and experience (12 English-speaking, 12 French-speaking); library: use of Peace Palace Library; Head of Secretariat M. CROESE

Hague Conference on Private International Law/Conférence de La Haye de droit international privé: Scheveningseweg 6, 2517 KT The Hague, Netherlands; tel. (70) 3633303; fax (70) 3604867; e-mail secretariat@hcch.net; internet www.hcch .net; f. 1893 to work for the unification of the rules of private int. law; 72 mems: govts of Albania, Argentina, Australia, Austria, Belarus, Belgium, Bosnia and Herzegovina, Brazil, Bulgaria, Canada, Chile, China, Costa Rica, Croatia, Cyprus, Czech Republic, Denmark, Ecuador, Egypt, Estonia, Finland, France, Georgia, Germany, Greece, Hungary, Iceland, India, Ireland, Israel, Italy, Japan, Jordan, Republic of Korea, Latvia, Lithuania, Luxembourg, former Yugoslav Republic of Macedonia, Malaysia, Malta, Mauritius, Mexico, Monaco, Montenegro, Morocco, Netherlands, New Zealand, Norway, Panama, Paraguay, Peru, Philippines, Poland, Portugal, Romania, Russia, Serbia, Slovakia, Slovenia, South Africa, Spain, Sri Lanka, Suriname, Sweden, Switzerland, Turkey, Ukraine, UK, USA, Uruguay, Venezuela and the European Union; Sec.-Gen. J. H. A. VAN LOON; publs *The Judges' Newsletter–International Child Protection* (2 a year), *Proceedings of the Conference's Sessions/Actes et documents des Sessions de la Conférence*.

Institute of International Law/Institut de Droit International: 24 rue de Morsaint, 1390 Grez-Doiceau, Belgium; tel. 229084407; fax 229086277; e-mail isabelle .gerardi@gmail.com; internet www.idi-iil.org; f. 1873; promotes devt of int. law by endeavouring to formulate general principles in accordance with civilized ethical standards, and by giving assistance to achieve gradual and progressive codification of int. law; 132 mems and assocs worldwide; Sec.-Gen. Prof. JOE VERHOEVEN; publ. *Tableau général des Résolutions*.

Inter-American Bar Association/Federación Interamericana de Abogados/Federação Interamericana de Advogados/ Fédération Inter-Américaine des Avocats: 1211 Connecticut Ave NW, Ste. 202,

Washington, DC 20036, USA; tel. (202) 466-5944; fax (202) 466-5946; e-mail iaba@iaba .org; internet www.iaba.org; f. 1940; mems: 51 bar assocs and individual lawyers in 33 countries; Pres. MERCEDES ARAÚZ DE GRIMALDO; Sec.-Gen. HARRY A. INMAN; publs *Conference Proceedings* (1 a year), *Inter-American Journal of International and Comparative Law* (1 a year).

Intergovernmental Committee of the Universal Copyright Convention: UNESCO, 7 Place de Fontenoy, 75700 Paris, France; tel. 1-45-68-47-11; fax 1-45-68-55-89; internet www.unesco.org/culture/copyright; f. 1952; studies the problems concerning the application and operation of the Universal Copyright Convention; makes preparation for periodic revisions of this Convention; mems: Algeria, Argentina, Austria, Cameroon, China, Croatia, Cuba, France, Greece, Guatemala, India, Israel, Japan, Morocco, Portugal, Russia, Ukraine and USA; Chair. ABDULLAH OUADRHIRI (Morocco); publ. *Copyright Bulletin* (4 a year).

International Association for Penal Law/Association Internationale de Droit Pénal: BP 60118, 33008 Bordeaux Cedex, France; tel. 5-56-06-66-73; fax 1-55-04-92-89; e-mail secretariat@aidp-iapl.org; internet www.penal.org; f. 1924 to promote cooperation between bodies and individuals engaged in the study or practice of criminal law; to study crime, its causes and the means of preventing it, and to advance the theoretical and practical development of int. penal law; 2,000 mems; Pres. Prof. JOSÉ LUIS DE LA CUESTA (Spain); Gen. Sec. Dr H. EPP (Austria); publ. *Revue Internationale de Droit Pénal* (2 a year).

International Association for Philosophy of Law and Social Philosophy (IVR)/ Internationale Vereinigung für Rechts- und Sozialphilosophie: Källerekroken 34, 226 47 Lund, Sweden; tel. (46) 152441; fax (46) 2224444; internet www.cirfid.unibo.it/ ivr; f. 1909 for scientific research in philosophy of law and social philosophy; holds int. congresses every 2 years; 44 nat. sections; 2,300 mems; Pres. (vacant); Sec.-Gen. CHRISTIAN DAHLMAN (Sweden); publ. *Archiv für Rechts- und Sozial-philosophie* (4 a year).

International Association of Democratic Lawyers (IADL)/Association Internationale des Juristes Démocrates: 21 rue Brialmont, 1210 Brussels, Belgium; tel. (2) 223-33-10; fax (2) 223-33-10; e-mail jsharma@del3.vsnl.net.in; internet www .iadllaw.org; f. 1946; aims to facilitate contacts and exchanges of view between lawyers and lawyers' assocs and to foster understanding and goodwill; to work together to achieve the aims of the Charter of the UN; mems in 102 countries; in consultative status with UN Economic and Social Council and UNESCO; Pres. JITENDRA SHARMA (India); Sec.-Gen. BEINUSZ SZMUKLER (Argentina); publ. *Revue Internationale de Droit Contemporain* (2 a year, also published in English and Spanish).

International Association of Lawyers/ Union Internationale des Avocats (UIA): 25 rue du Jour, 75001 Paris, France; tel. 1-44-88-55-66; fax 1-44-88-55-77; e-mail uiacentre@uianet.org; internet www.uianet .org; f. 1927 to promote the independence and freedom of lawyers, and defend their ethical and material interests on an int. level; to contribute to the development of an int. order based on law; mems: 250 organizations, 3,000 individuals; Pres. PASCAL MAURER (Switzerland); Sec.-Gen. MAY-DAPHNE FISHELSON (France); Exec. Dir MARIE-PIERRE RICHARD (France); publ. *Juriste International*.

International Bar Association: 1 Stephen St, 10th Fl., London, W1T 1AT, UK; tel. (20)

7691-6868; fax (20) 7691-6544; e-mail editor@ int-bar.org; internet www.ibanet.org; f. 1947; mems: 195 nat. bar asscns and law socs and 30,000 individual lawyers from 183 countries; Exec. Dir MARK ELLIS; publs *Business Law International* (3 a year), *International Bar News* (6 a year), *Journal of Energy and Natural Resources Law* (4 a year).

International Bureau of Fiscal Documentation (IBFD): POB 20237, 1000 HE Amsterdam, Netherlands; H. J. E. Wenckebachweg 210, 1096 AS Amsterdam, Netherlands; tel. (20) 554-01-00; fax (20) 622-86-58; e-mail customerservice@ibfd.org; internet www.ibfd.nl; f. 1938; an ind. non-profit foundation; supplies information on fiscal law and its application; tax treaties database, European taxation database, and OECD database, on CD-ROM; library of 30,000 vols, 1,000 periodicals; CEO WILLEM FALTER; publs *Asia–Pacific Tax Bulletin* (12 a year), *Bulletin for International Fiscal Documentation* (12 a year), *Derivatives and Financial Instruments* (6 a year), *European Taxation* (12 a year), *International Transfer Pricing Journal* (6 a year), *International VAT Monitor* (6 a year), *Tax News Service* (52 a year).

Attached Academy:

IBFD International Tax Academy: POB 20237, 1000 HE Amsterdam, Netherlands; H.J.E. Wenckebachweg 210, 1096 AS Amsterdam, Netherlands; tel. (20) 554-01-00; fax (20) 620-86-58; e-mail info@ibfd .org; internet www.ibfd.nl; f. 1989; provides education and training on int. and comparative tax law through confs, courses and traineeships; Chair. S. VAN DER FELTZ; Academic Chair. Prof. F. VANISTENDAEL.

International Commission of Jurists/ Commission Internationale de Juristes: POB 91, 33 rue des Bains, 1211 Geneva, Switzerland; tel. 229793800; fax 229793801; e-mail info@icj.org; internet www.icj.org; f. 1952 to promote and protect human rights, and to strengthen the Rule of Law in all its practical manifestations—institutions, legislation, procedures, etc.—and defend it through the mobilization of world legal opinion in cases of general and systematic violation of, or serious threat to, such principles of justice; library of 2,000 vols; Pres. MARY ROBINSON (Ireland); Vice-Pres. JOHN DOWD (Australia); Vice-Pres. PEDRO NIKKEN (Venezuela); Sec.-Gen. WILDER TAYLER; publ. *Attacks on Justice* (online).

International Confederation of Societies of Authors and Composers/Confédération Internationale des Sociétés d'Auteurs et Compositeurs: 20–26 blvd du Parc, 92200 Neuilly sur Seine, France; tel. 1-55-62-08-50; fax 1-55-62-08-60; e-mail cisac@cisac.org; internet www.cisac.org; f. 1926 to ensure more effective protection of the rights of authors and composers, to improve legislation on literary and artistic rights, and to organize research on problems concerning the rights of authors on the internet; participates in preparatory work for inter-governmental conferences on authors' rights; 203 mem. societies in 104 countries; Pres. CHRISTIAN BRÜHN; Dir-Gen. ERIC BAPTISTE; publ. *CISAC News* (4 a year).

International Development Law Organization: Via di San Sebastianello 16, 00187 Rome, Italy; tel. 06-6979261; fax 06-6781946; e-mail idlo@idlo.int; internet www.idli.org; f. 1983 for mid-career training and technical assistance, primarily for developing and transition country lawyers, legal advisers and judges; Rome-based courses and seminars in English and French address legal topics related to economic development and governance, including negotiation, int. contracting and economic law reform; also designs and organizes in-country training workshops on law-related economic development topics; library in process of formation; Dir-Gen. WILLIAM T. LORIS.

International Federation for European Law/Fédération Internationale pour le Droit Européen (FIDE): Via Nicolò Tartaglia 5, 00197 Rome, Italy; fax 80-80-731; f. 1961 to advance studies on European law among members of the European Community by coordinating activities of member societies and by organizing regular colloquies on topical problems of European law; mems: 17 national associations; Pres. Hon. Mr Justice NIALL FENNELLY; Sec.-Gen. PATRICK McCANN.

International Institute for the Unification of Private Law/Institut International pour l'Unification du Droit Privé (Unidroit): Via Panisperna 28, 00184 Rome, Italy; tel. 06-696211; fax 06-69941394; e-mail info@unidroit.org; internet www.unidroit.org; f. 1926, to prepare for the establishment of uniform legislation, to prepare draft uniform laws and int. conventions for adoption by diplomatic conferences, to prepare drafts of int. agreements on private law, to undertake studies in comparative law, and to organize conferences and publish works on such subjects; meetings of organizations concerned with the unification of law; international congresses on private law; mems: governments of 59 countries; library of 235,000 vols; Pres. Prof. BERARDINO LIBONATI (Italy); Sec.-Gen. Prof. HERBERT KRONKE (Germany); publs *Digest of Legal Activities of International Organizations*, *Uniform Law Review* (4 a year).

International Institute of Space Law (IISL)/Institut International de Droit de l'Espace: 8–10 rue Mario-Nikis, 75015 Paris, France; tel. (1) 45-67-42-60; fax (1) 42-73-21-20; e-mail secretary@iafastro-iisl.com; internet www.iafastro-iisl.com; f. 1959 at the XI Congress of the International Astronautical Federation; holds meetings, makes studies on juridical and sociological aspects of astronautics; publishes reports; makes awards; holds an annual Colloquium; mems: 386 individuals elected for life; Pres. Dr N. JASENTULIYANA (USA); Sec. TANJA L. MASSON-ZWAAN (Netherlands); publ. *Proceedings of Colloquia*.

International Juridical Institute/Institut Juridique International: Permanent Office for the Supply of International Legal Information, Spui 186, 2511 BW, The Hague, Netherlands; tel. (70) 346-0974; fax (70) 362-5235; e-mail info@iji.nl; internet www.iji.nl; f. 1918; supplies information in connection with any matter of int. interest, not being of secret nature, respecting int., municipal and foreign law and application thereof; Chair. Prof. A. V. M. STRUYCKEN; Sec. T. HEUKELS; Dir W. G. HUIJGEN.

International Maritime Committee/Comité Maritime International (CMI): Mechelsesteenweg 196, 2018 Antwerp, Belgium; tel. (3) 227-35-26; fax (3) 227-35-28; e-mail admini@cmi-imc.org; internet www.comitemaritime.org; f. 1897 to contribute to the unification of maritime and commercial law, maritime customs, usages and practices; promotes the establishment of national associations of maritime law and cooperates with other int. asscns or organizations having the same object; work includes drafting of conventions on collisions at sea, salvage and assistance at sea, limitation of shipowners' liability, maritime mortgages, etc.; mems: asscns in 51 countries; Pres. JEAN-SERGE ROHART (France); Sec.-Gen. NIGEL FRAWLEY (acting) (Canada); publ. *Year Book*.

World Jurist Association (WJA): 7910 Woodmont Ave, Suite 1440, Bethesda, MD 20814, USA; tel. (202) 466-5428; fax (202) 452-8540; e-mail wja@worldjurist.org; internet www.worldjurist.org; f. 1963 to promote the continued devt of int. law and world order; biennial world conferences, World Law Day, demonstration trials, research programmes and publs have contributed to the growth of law and legal instns by focusing on matters of int. concern; mems: lawyers, jurists and legal scholars in over 150 countries; Pres. VALERIJ O. YEVDOKIMOV (Ukraine); Exec. Vice-Pres. MARGARET M. HENNEBERRY (USA); publs *Law/Technology* (4 a year), *World Jurist* (6 a year).

Affiliated Bodies:

World Association of Center Associates (WACA): 7910 Woodmont Ave, Suite 1440, Bethesda, MD 20814, USA; tel. (202) 466-5428; fax (202) 452-8540; e-mail wja@worldjurist.org; f. 1979 to mobilize interested individuals not in the legal profession to promote the objects of the WJA; Pres. RICK BALTZERSEN (USA).

World Association of Judges (WAJ): 7910 Woodmont Ave, Suite 1440, Bethesda, MD 20814, USA; tel. (202) 466-5428; fax (202) 452-8540; e-mail wja@worldjurist.org; f. 1966 to mobilize judicial leaders on important transnational legal issues and to improve the admin. of justice; over 23 cttees studying int. law; Pres. Prince BOLA AJIBOLA (Nigeria).

World Association of Law Professors (WALP): 7910 Woodmont Ave, Suite 1440, Bethesda, MD 20814, USA; tel. (202) 466-5428; fax (202) 452-8540; e-mail wja@worldjurist.org; f. 1975 to focus the attention of legal scholars and teachers on transnational legal issues, and improve scholarship and education in int. legal matters, incl. training, practice, admin. of justice, human rights, the environment and coordination of legal systems; Pres. SALVADOR B. LAO (Philippines).

World Association of Lawyers (WAL): 7910 Woodmont Ave, Suite 1440, Bethesda, MD 20814, USA; tel. (202) 466-5428; fax (202) 452-8540; e-mail wja@worldjurist.org; f. 1975 to develop transnational law and improve lawyers' expertise in related areas; over 100 cttees studying the devt of int. law; Pres. JACK STREETER (USA)

Medicine and Public Health

World Health Organization/Organisation Mondiale de la Santé: Ave Appia 20, 1211 Geneva 27, Switzerland; tel. 227912111; fax 227913111; e-mail info@who.int; internet www.who.int; f. 1948; WHO, a specialized agency of the UN, is governed by its mem. states, which decide the organization's priorities and monitor its work; WHO has been given the mandate to help all people—in particular the poor and the vulnerable—to achieve the highest possible level of health; WHO's work includes reducing the global burden of disease by taking action against the main diseases of the world, reducing the risk factors for ill health, increasing the knowledge base on health issues through coordinating and supervising research, setting standards and guidelines, and assisting countries in improving their health systems and making them more equitable; 191 mem. states; library: see entry in Switzerland chapter; Dir-Gen. Dr JONG-WOOK LEE (Republic of Korea); publs *Bulletin* (scientific papers: 12 a year, in English; 2 a year, in French and English), *International Digest of Health Legislation* (4 a year, online only), *Weekly Epidemiological Record* (51 a year and online), *WHO Drug Information* (4 a year and online), *World Health Report* (1 a year and online).

OTHER ORGANIZATIONS

Council for International Organizations of Medical Sciences (CIOMS)/Conseil des Organisations Internationales des Sciences Médicales: Secretariat c/o WHO, 20 ave Appia, 1211 Geneva 27, Switzerland; tel. (22) 7913406; fax (22) 7910746; e-mail cioms@who.int; internet www.cioms.ch; f. 1949 to facilitate and coordinate the activities of its mems, to act as a coordinating centre between them and the nat. instns, to maintain collaboration with the UN, to promote int. activities in the field of medical sciences, to serve the scientific interests of the int. biomedical community; mems: 66 int. asscns, nat. academic and research ccls in 30 countries; Pres. Prof. MICHEL B. VALLOTTON; Sec.-Gen. Dr GOTTFRIED KREUTZ; publs *International Ethical Guidelines for Biomedical Research Involving Human Subjects*, *International Guidelines for Ethical Review of Epidemiological Studies*, *International Nomenclature of Diseases*, other publications on diverse aspects of drug safety.

INTERNATIONAL MEMBERS OF CIOMS

FDI World Dental Federation/Fédération Dentaire Internationale (FDI): 13 Chemin du Levant, L'Avant Centre, 01210 Ferney-Voltaire, France; tel. 4-50-40-50-50; fax 4-50-40-55-55; e-mail info@fdiworldental.org; internet www.fdiworldental.org; f. 1900; 1m. individual mems, 144 mem. assocs in 134 countries; Pres. Dr BURTON CONROD (Canada); Pres.-Elect Dr ROBERTO VIANNA (Brazil); Treas. Dr TIN CHUN WONG (Hong Kong); Exec. Dir Dr DAVID C. ALEXANDER (France); publs *International Dental Journal* (6 a year), *Community Dental Health* (4 a year), *Developing Dentistry* (2 a year), *European Journal of Prosthodontics and Restorative Dentistry* (4 a year), *Journal of the International Academy of Periodontology* (4 a year), *Worldental Communiqué* (6 a year).

International Association for the Study of the Liver: c/o c/o Dr K. Rajender Reddy, Dir of Hepatology, Medical Dir of Liver Transplantation, Univ. of Pennsylvania 2 Dulles, 3400 Spruce St, Philadelphia PA 19104, USA; tel. (215) 662-4311; fax (215) 614-0925; e-mail secretariat@iaslonline.com; internet www.iaslonline.com; f. 1958 to foster training of experts in hepatology; encourages research on the liver and its diseases and helps to facilitate prevention, recognition and treatment of liver and biliary tract diseases in the int. community; Pres. DING-SHINN CHEN (Taiwan); Sec. and Treas. Dr K RAJENDER REDDY (USA).

International College of Surgeons/Collège International de Chirurgiens: 1516 North Lake Shore Dr., Chicago, IL 60610, USA; tel. (312) 642-3555; fax (312) 787 1624; e-mail info@icsglobal.org; internet www.icsglobal.org; f. 1935 Geneva, inc. Washington 1940; organized as a worldwide instn to advance the art and science of surgery by bringing together surgeons of all nations, irrespective of nationality, creed or colour; through its Surgical Congresses, Research and Scholarship Project and Surgical Teams Project of volunteers to developing countries, an exchange of surgical knowledge is facilitated in the highest interest of patients; also operates the Int. Museum of Surgical Science located at HQ; 7,000 mems; World Pres. Dr FIDEL RUIZ-HEALY; Exec. Dir MAX C. DOWNHAM; publ. *International Surgery* (6 a year).

International Council of Nurses (ICN)/Conseil International des Infirmières

(CII): 3 place Jean-Marteau, 1201 Geneva, Switzerland; tel. 229080100; fax 229080101; e-mail icn@icn.ch; internet www.icn.ch; f. 1899; works to ensure universal quality nursing care, sound health policies worldwide and advancement of nursing knowledge; Council of National Representatives meets every 2 years; congress every 4 years; mems: 125 national nurses' associations; Pres. CHRISTINE HANCOCK; Exec. Dir JUDITH A. OULTON; publ. *International Nursing Review.*

International Diabetes Federation/Fédération Internationale du Diabète: 166 Chaussée de la Hulpe, 1170 Brussels, Belgium; tel. (2) 538-55-11; fax (2) 538-51-14; e-mail info@idf.org; internet www.idf.org; f. 1949; over 200 mem asscns in 160 countries; holds triennial congresses; Pres. PIERRE LEFÈBVRE (Belgium); Exec. Dir LUC HENDRICKX; publs *Diabetes Atlas* (1 a year), *Diabetes Voice* (3 a year), *Triennial Report.*

International Federation of Clinical Neurophysiology/Fédération Internationale de Neurophysiologie Clinique: c/o Venue Vest Conference Services Ltd, Suite 100, 873 Beatty St, Vancouver, BC V6B 2M6, Canada; tel. (604) 681-5226; fax (604) 681-2503; e-mail ifcn@ifcn.info; internet www.ifcn.info; f. 1949 to attain the highest level of knowledge in the field of electro-encephalography and clinical neurophysiology worldwide; 58 mem. orgs (nat. socs); Pres. HIROSHI SHIBASAKI (Japan); Sec. Prof. REINHARD DENGLER (Germany); publs *Clinical Neurophysiology* (12 a year), *EMG and Motor Control* (6 a year), *Evoked Potentials* (6 a year).

International Federation of Oto-Rhino-Laryngological Societies/Fédération Internationale des Sociétés Oto-rhino-laryngologiques: POB 124, 1135 ZK Edam, Netherlands; fax (299) 373723; e-mail ifos@cest-bien.com; internet www.ifosworld.org; f. 1965; aims: to promote scientific and clinical research into oto-rhino-laryngology; to improve aural health in developing countries; to register educational programmes and promote cooperation; mems from 98 countries and 10 int. socs; Pres. NASSER KOTBY (Egypt); Gen. Sec. JAN J. GROTE (Netherlands).

International Federation of Surgical Colleges/Fédération Internationale des Collèges de Chirurgie: La Panetière, 3 Chemin du Milieu, 1279 Bogis-Bossey, Switzerland;Administration: c/o Asscn of Surgeons of Great Britain and Northern Ireland, RCS, 34–43 Lincoln's Inn Fields, London, WC2A 3PE, UK; tel. (1962) 712-383; fax (1962) 714-614; e-mail rhslane@btinternet.com; internet www.ifsc-net.org; f. 1958 in Stockholm, Sweden; objectives: the improvement and maintenance of the standards of surgery worldwide, by establishment and maintenance of cooperation and interchange of medical and surgical information; encouragement of high standards of education, training and research in surgery and its allied sciences; particularly assisting developing countries in surgical advancement; mems: 70 national colleges or societies and 500 associates; Pres. Prof. S. W. A. GUNN (Switzerland); Sec. R. H. S. LANE (UK); publs *Electronic Journal*, *IFSC News* (2 a year).

International Leprosy Association/Association Internationale contre la Lèpre: c/o ALM Way, Greenway, SC 29601, USA; internet www.leprosy-ila.org; f. 1931 to promote int. cooperation into research on and treatment of leprosy; 1,200 mems; Pres. Dr MARCOS VIRMOND (Brazil); Sec. Prof. INDIRA NATH (India); publ. *International Journal of Leprosy and Other Mycobacterial Diseases* (4 a year).

International Paediatric Association/Association Internationale de Pédiatrie: 17 rue du Cendrier, POB 1726, 1211 Geneva 1, Switzerland; tel. 229069152; fax 227322852; e-mail adminoffice@ipa-world.org; internet www.ipa-world.org; f. 1912; holds regional and int. seminars and symposia; organizes int. paediatric congresses every 3 years; 165 mem. socs; Pres. CHOK WAN CHAN (Hong Kong); Exec. Dir JANE G. SCHALLER (USA); publ. *IPA News* (4 a year).

International Rhinologic Society: c/o Prof. David Kennedy, Univ. of Pennsylvania Medical Center, Dept of ORL, 5th Fl., Ravdin Bldg, 3400 Spruce St, Philadelphia, USA; e-mail kennedyd@uphs.upenn.edu; f. 1965; aims to create a central org. with which all nat. and regional socs of rhinology may be affiliated, to organize int. congresses and courses of instruction, and to encourage study, research and scientific advancement in the field of rhinology and related sciences; nat. and regional soc. mems in 31 countries; Pres. Prof. IN YONG PARK (Republic of Korea); Sec.-Treas. Prof. P. A. R. CLEMENT (Belgium); publs *American Journal of Rhinology*, *Journal of Rhinology*.

International Society of Audiology/Société Internationale d'Audiologie: c/o Dr G. Mencher, 121 Anchor Drive, Nova Scotia B3N 3B9 Halifax, Canada; tel. (902) 477-5360; fax (902) 477-5360; e-mail info@isa-audiology.org; internet www.isa-audiology.org; f. 1952 to advance the study of audiology and protect human hearing; 500 individual mems; Pres. Prof. Dr IEDA RUSSO (Brazil); Sec.-Gen. Prof. Dr G. MENCHER; publs *Audinews* (4 a year), *International Journal of Audiology* (1 a year).

International Society of Internal Medicine/Société Internationale de Médecine Interne: c/o Prof. Hans P. Kohler, Dept of Internal Medicine, RSZ-Bern Hospitals, Zieglerspital, Morillonstrasse 75-91, 3001 Bern, Switzerland; tel. 319707178; fax 319707763; e-mail hanspeter.kohler@spitalnetzbern.ch; internet www.acponline.org/isim; f. 1948 to encourage research and education in internal medicine; sponsors the Int. Congress of Internal Medicine every other year; 61 nat. mem. socs; Pres. Prof. WILLIAM J. HALL (USA); Sec.-Gen. Prof. HANS P. KOHLER.

International Society of Physical and Rehabilitation Medicine (ISPRM): Medicongress, Waalpoel 28–34, 9960 Assenede, Belgium; tel. (9) 344-39-59; fax (9) 344-40-10; internet www.isprm.org; Pres. Prof. LINA-MARA BATTISTELLA (Brazil); Exec. Dir WERNER VAN CLEEMPUTTE.

International Union Against Cancer/Union Internationale contre le Cancer: 62 route de Frontenex, 1207 Geneva, Switzerland; tel. 228091811; fax 228091810; e-mail info@uicc.org; internet www.uicc.org; f. 1933; non-governmental org. devoted to promoting on an int. level the campaign against cancer in its research, therapeutic and preventive aspects; mems: 276 organizations in 85 countries; Pres. Dr JOHN SEFFRIN (USA); Exec. Dir ISABEL MORTARA; publs *International Calendar of Meetings on Cancer* (2 a year), *International Journal of Cancer* (30 a year), *UICC News* (4 a year).

Medical Women's International Association (MWIA): 7555 Morley Dr., Burnaby, BC, Canada; tel. (604) 439-8993; fax (604) 439-8994; e-mail secretariat@mwia.net; internet www.mwia.net; f. 1919 to facilitate contacts between medical women and to encourage their cooperation in matters connected with int. health problems; MWIA Congresses and General Assemblies every 3 years; mems: nat. asscns in 48 countries, with 20,000 mems; Pres. Dr ATSUKO HESHIKI (Japan); Sec.-Gen. Dr SHELLEY ROSS (Canada); publs *Congress Report* (every 3 years), *MWIA Update* (3 a year).

World Allergy Organization (WAO): 555 East Wells St, 11th Fl., Milwaukee, WI 53202-3823, USA; tel. (414) 276-1791; fax (414) 276-3349; e-mail info@worldallergy.org; internet www.worldallergy.org; f. 1951 to advance work in the educational, research and practical medical aspects of allergy diseases; 38,000 mems from 58 nat. and regional socs; Pres. Prof. CARLOS E. BAENA-CAGNANI (Argentina); Sec.-Gen. Prof. G. WALTER CANONICA (Italy); publ. *Allergy & Clinical Immunology International* (6 a year).

World Federation for Medical Education: Faculty of Health Sciences, Københavns Universitet, Panum Institute, Blegdamsvej 3, 2200 Copenhagen N, Denmark; tel. 35-32-71-03; fax 35-32-70-70; e-mail wfme@wfme.org; internet www.sund.ku.dk/wfme; f. 1972 to promote and integrate the study and implementation of medical education worldwide; engaged on programme for worldwide reorientation of medical training; non-governmental relations with WHO, UNICEF, UNESCO, UNDP and the World Bank; 6 regional asscns on a global level; Pres. Prof. STEFAN LINDGREN; Exec. Dir ARNOLD BOON.

World Federation of Associations of Paediatric Surgeons: c/o Prof. J. Boix-Ochoa, Apatado de Correos 3, 08490 Tordera, (Barcelona), Spain; internet www.wofaps.org; f. 1974; 60 mem. asscns worldwide; Pres. S. CYWES (South Africa); Sec. and Treas. Prof. J. BOIX-OCHOA.

World Federation of Neurology: Hill House, Heron Sq, Richmond, TW9 1EP, UK; tel. (208)439-9556; fax (208) 439-9499; e-mail info@wfneurology.org; internet www.wfneurology.org; f. 1957; 96 constituent nat. socs of neurology, representing 24,000 mems; Pres. Dr VLADIMIR HACHINSKI; Vice-Pres. Prof. Dr WERNER HACKE; Sec. and Treas.-Gen. Dr RAAD SHAKIR; publs *Journal of the Neurological Sciences, World Neurology* (4 a year).

World Gastroenterology Organisation: c/o Bridget Barbieri, WGO Exec. Secretariat Medconnect GmbH, Brünnsteinstr. 10, 81541 Munich, Germany; tel. (89) 41419240; fax (89) 41419245; e-mail info@worldgastroenterology.org; internet www.worldgastroenterology.org; f. 1935; raises awareness of the worldwide prevalence and optimal care of digestive disorders through the provision of high-quality, accessible and independent education and training; workshops, global training centres network, global guidelines, World Digestive Health Day research support, int. digestive cancer alliance; 110 nat. societies and 4 regional asscns; Pres. Prof. RICHARD KOZAREK (USA); Sec.-Gen. Prof. CIHAN YURDAYDIN (Turkey); publ. *World Gastroenterology News* (online).

World Heart Federation: 7 rue des Battoirs, 1211 Geneva, Switzerland; tel. 228070320; fax 228070339; e-mail admin@worldheart.org; internet www.worldheart.org; f. 1978; aims to promote the study, prevention and relief of cardiovascular diseases and strokes through scientific and public education programmes, particularly in low- and middle-income countries; organizes the exchange of materials between its affiliated socs and foundations and with related agencies; world congress every 2 years; 196 mems: 159 nat., 8 continental, 29 assocs; Pres. Dr SHAHRYAR A. SHEIKH (Pakistan); CEO JANET VOÛTE (Switzerland); publs

Nature Clincal Practice Cardiovascular Magazine, Prevention and Control (4 a year).

World Medical Association/Association Médicale Mondiale: 13 chemin du Levant, CIB, Bâtiment A, 01210 Ferney-Voltaire, France; tel. 4-50-40-75-75; fax 4-50-40-59-37; e-mail wma@wma.net; internet www.wma.net; f. 1947 to serve humanity by endeavouring to achieve the highest int. standards in medical education, medical science, medical art and medical ethics, and health care for all people; the unit of membership is the nat. medical asscn; has established relations with UNESCO, WHO and other int. bodies; 6 regions; mems: 95 nat. assocs; 797 constituent and assoc. mems; Pres. Dr K. DESAI (India); Sec.-Gen. Dr OTMAR KLOIBER (Germany); publ. *World Medical Journal* (6 a year).

World Psychiatric Association/Association Mondiale de Psychiatrie/Asociación Mundial de Psiquiatría: Geneva Univ. Psychiatric Hospital, 2 chemin du Petit-Bel-Air, 1225 Geneva, Switzerland; tel. 223055737; fax 223055735; e-mail wpasecretariat@wpanet.org; internet www.wpanet.org; f. 1950 at the 1st World Congress of Psychiatry in Paris, France; a not-for-profit charity; aims: to encourage the highest possible standards of clinical practice, to enhance the work of the mem. socs irrespective of their size, to fight stigma and advocate the human right to mental health, to support psychiatrists and other mental health professionals, to disseminate knowledge of the effect of mass violence on mental health, to encourage multi-centre research and enhance standards of training, to promote non-discrimination (parity) in the provision of care of the mentally ill, to organize the World Congress every 3 years and Int. Congresses, and to work with WHO and other governmental agencies to advance public health; 134 mem. socs in 116 countries; Pres. Prof. MARIO MAJ (Italy); Sec.-Gen. Prof. LEVENT COX (UK); publ. *World Psychiatry* (3 a year).

ASSOCIATE MEMBERS OF CIOMS

American College of Chest Physicians: 3300 Dundee Rd, Northbrook, IL 60062-2348, USA; tel. (847) 498-1400; fax (847) 498-5460; e-mail accp@chestnet.org; internet www.chestnet.org; f. 1935; postgraduate medical education; 15,000 mems; Pres. Dr RICHARD S. IRWIN; Exec. Vice-Pres. and CEO ALVIN LEVER; publ. *Chest* (12 a year).

International Committee of Military Medicine/Comité International de Médecine Militaire: Hôpital Militaire Reine Astrid, 1120 Brussels, Belgium; tel. (2) 264-43-48; fax (2) 264-43-67; e-mail info@cimm-icmm.org; internet cimm-icmm.org; f. 1921 to promote world cooperation on questions of military medicine and to foster its international and humanitarian character; holds congress every two years; 104 countries are represented on the Committee; Pres. Lt Brig.-Gen. S. BIN ABDULLAH, (Malaysia); Sec.-Gen. Dr J. SANABRIA (Belgium); publ. *International Review of the Armed Forces Medical Services* (4 a year, in English and French).

International Congress on Tropical Medicine and Malaria/Congrès International de Médecine Tropicale et de Paludisme: c/o Dr E. C. Garcia, Institute of Public Health, University of the Philippines, POB EA-460, Manila, Philippines; Congresses are held triennially; Sec.-Gen. Dr E. C. GARCIA.

International Council on Alcohol and Addictions: CP 189, 1001 Lausanne, Switzerland; tel. 213209865; fax 213209817; e-mail secretariat@icaa.ch; internet www.icaa.ch; f. 1907; aims to reduce and prevent the harmful effects of the use of alcohol and other drugs by the study of addiction problems and the development of programmes in this field, the study of concepts and methods of prevention, treatment and rehabilitation, and the dissemination of knowledge in the interests of public health and personal and social well-being; holds Int. Institute annually and Int. Congress every three or four years, symposia, study courses, training courses on substance abuse in developing countries, etc.; mems: 135 organizations, 500 individuals from 85 countries; library: special collection of 6,000 vols on drug dependence, 12,000 pamphlets, reprints, etc., 120 periodicals; Pres. Dr PETER VAMOS; Exec. Dir Dr SHARAFUDDIN MALIK; publ. *ICAA News* (4 a year).

International Federation of Clinical Chemistry and Laboratory Medicine: Via Carlo Farini 81, 20159 Milan, Italy; tel. 02-66809912; fax 02-60781846; e-mail ifcc@ifcc.org; internet www.ifcc.org; f. 1952; mems: 63 national socs (30,000 individuals); Pres. Prof. MATHIAS M. MÜLLER (Austria); Sec. Dr RENZE BAIS (Australia); publ. *Journal* (6 a year).

International Federation of Medical Students' Associations: c/o WMA, BP 63, 01212 Ferney-Voltaire Cedex, France; fax 4-50-40-59-37; e-mail gs@ifmsa.org; internet www.ifmsa.org; f. 1951 to serve medical students worldwide and to promote int. cooperation; organizes professional exchanges in pre-clinical and clinical fields of medicine; holds Gen. Assembly annually; 63 mem. asscns; Pres. ANDREAS RUDKJØBING; Gen. Sec. STEFANIE BÖTTCHER.

International Society of Blood Transfusion/Société Internationale de Transfusion Sanguine: c/o Jan van Goyenkade 11, 1075 HP Amsterdam, Netherlands; tel. (20) 679-3411; fax (20) 673-7306; e-mail isbt@eurocongres.com; internet www.isbt-web.org; f. 1937; mems: 2,080 in 108 countries; Pres. Dr FRANCINE DÉCARY; Sec.-Gen. Dr PAUL F. W. STRENGERS; publs *Transfusion Today*, *Vox Sanguinis*, *World Directory of Blood Transfusion*.

Rehabilitation International—International Society for Rehabilitation of the Disabled/Société Internationale pour la Réadaptation des Handicapés: 25 E 21st St, New York, NY 10010, USA; tel. (212) 420-1500; fax (212) 505-0871; e-mail ri@riglobal.org; internet www.riglobal.org; f. 1922; world congress and regional conferences every 4 years; Pres. ANNE HAWKER; Sec.-Gen. VENUS ILAGAN; publs *International Rehabilitation Review*, *One in Ten*.

OTHER ORGANIZATIONS

African Medical and Research Foundation: Langata Rd, POB 00506-27691, Nairobi, Kenya; tel. (20) 605220; fax (20) 609518; e-mail fundraising@amrefhq.org; internet www.amref.org; f. 1957; independent, non-profit organization working to improve the health of people in Eastern Africa; funds from governmental and non-governmental aid agencies in Africa, Europe and North America, and private donors; official relations with WHO; activities: primary health care, training, teaching aids, health behaviour and education, airborne medicine, flying doctor service, medical radio communication, ground mobile medicine, emergency intervention in famine and other crises, research, consultancies; library of 6,000 vols, 122 periodicals; Chair. Prof. MIRIAM K. WERE (Kenya); Dir-Gen. Dr MICHAEL SMALLEY (Kenya); publs *AMREF News* (4 a year), *AFYA* (4 a year), *COBASHECA* (4 a year), *Defender* (4 a year), *Helper* (4 a year), *HEN* (4 a year).

Asociación Latinoamericana de Análisis y Modificación del Comportamiento (Latin American Association of Analysis and Behavioural Modification): POB 88754, Bogota, Colombia; f. 1974; professional society for psychology in research and teaching on experimental analysis of behaviour; 1,583 mems; Pres. MIGUEL A. ESCOTET; Vice-Pres. CARLOS M. QUIRCE; publ. *Learning and Behavior* (2 a year).

Association for Medical Education in Europe: Tay Park House, 484 Perth Rd, Dundee, DD2 1LR, Scotland; tel. (1382) 381953; fax (1382) 381987; e-mail amee@dundee.ac.uk; internet www.amee.org; f. 1972 to promote and integrate the study of medical education in the countries of Europe; 1,300 mems: asscns for medical education in most European countries, assoc. corporate mems in countries without nat. asscns, and individual mems worldwide; Pres. MADALENA PATRICIO (Portugal); Gen. Sec. Prof. RONALD M. HARDEN (UK); publ. *Medical Teacher* (12 a year).

Cystic Fibrosis Worldwide: c/o Christine Noke, 210 Park Ave #267, Worcester, MA 10609, USA; tel. (508) 733-6120; e-mail onoke@cfww.org; internet www.cfww.org; f. 2003; promotes access to knowledge and appropriate care to those people living with cystic fibrosis and among medical health professionals and governments worldwide; Pres. MITCH MESSER (Australia); Exec. Dir CHRISTINE NOKE.

European Academy of Anaesthesiology: Waversebaan 319A, 3001 Heverlee, Belgium; tel. and fax (16) 405151; internet eaa.euro-anaesthesiology.org; f. 1978 to improve the standard of training, practice and research in anaesthesiology in Europe; 441 mems (251 full, 190 assoc.); Pres. THOMAS PASCH (Switzerland); Hon. Sec. KLAUS OLKKOLA (Finland); publ. *European Journal of Anaesthesiology*.

European Federation of Internal Medicine: c/o Dr C. Davidson, Department of Cardiology, Royal Sussex County Hospital, Eastern Rd, Brighton, BN2 5BE, UK; tel. (1273) 696955; fax (1273) 684554; e-mail chris.davidson@bsuh.nhs.uk; internet www.efim.org; f. 1996; 27 nat. mem. socs; Pres. Prof. J. MERINO (Spain); Sec.-Gen. Dr C. DAVIDSON (UK); publ. *European Journal of Internal Medicine* (4 a year).

European Society of Cardiology: c/o The European Heart House, 2035 Route des Colles, Les Templiers, BP 179, 06903 Sophia Antipolis, France; tel. 4-92-94-76-00; fax 4-92-94-76-01; e-mail webmaster@escardio.org; internet www.escardio.org; f. 1950; aims to bring together societies of cardiology in all European countries, and to provide a forum for working groups on subjects of common interest; 68,000 mems; Pres. Prof. M. KOMAJDA (France); CEO I. BARDINET (France); publs *Cardiovascular Nursing* (4 a year), *Cardiovascular Research* (14 a year), *European Journal of Cardiovascular Prevention and Rehabilitation* (24 a year), *European Journal of Echocardiography* (6 a year), *European Journal of Heart Failure* (12 a year), *Europace* (12 a year), *The European Heart Journal* (24 a year, plus 10–18 annual supplements).

Inclusion International: KD.2.03 4–6 University Way; Docklands Campus, London E16 2RD, UK; tel. (20) 8223-7709; fax (20) 8223-6081; e-mail info@inclusion-international.org; internet www.inclusion-international.org; f. 1960; advocates for human rights of persons with intellectual disabilities and their families worldwide; furthers cooperation between national bodies, organizes congresses and symposia; consultative status with UNESCO, UNICEF, WHO, ILO, ECOSOC and the Council of Europe; official relations with IIN, the Comm. of the European Communities and various other orgs; mems: 173 socs in 109 countries; 250 mems worldwide (Europe, Asia Pacific, Africa, Americas, Middle East); Pres. KLAUS LACHWITZ; Sec.-Gen. RALPH JONES; publ. *Proceedings*.

International Academy of Cytology/Academie Internationale de Cytologie/ Internationale Akademie für Zytologie/ Academia Internacional de Citología: c/o Dr Volker Schneider, Burgunderstr. 1, 79104 Freiburg, Germany; fax (761) 2923802; e-mail centraloffice@cytology-iac.org; internet www.cytology-iac.org; organizes congresses, International Board of Cytopathology examinations; Pres. Dr MATÍAS JIMÉNEZ-AYALA (Spain); Sec.-Gen. Dr VOLKER SCHNEIDER (Germany); publ. *Acta Cytologica—Journal of Clinical Cytology and Cytopathology* (online).

International Agency for Research on Cancer/Centre International de Recherche sur le Cancer: 150 cours Albert-Thomas, 69372 Lyon Cedex 08, France; tel. 4-72-73-84-85; fax 4-72-73-85-75; f. 1965 as an Agency of the World Health Organization; to promote international collaboration in cancer research; 16 mem. countries; library of 8,200 vols, 211 journals; Dir Dr PETER BOYLE; publ. *Report* (every 2 years).

International Agency for the Prevention of Blindness/Organisation mondiale contre la cécité: L. V. Prasad Eye Institute, L. V. Prasad Marg, Banjara Hills, Hyderabad 500034, India; tel. (40) 23545389; fax (40) 23548271; e-mail iapb@lvpei.org; internet www.iapb.org; f. 1975; umbrella org. in official relationship with WHO; promotes the formation of national cttees and programmes on prevention of blindness and the sharing of information; Chair. and Pres. Dr GULLAPALLI N. RAO (India); Sec.-Gen. Dr LOUIS PIZZARELLO (USA); publ. *IAPB News* (2 a year).

International Association for Child and Adolescent Psychiatry and Allied Professions/Association Internationale de Psychiatrie de l'Enfant et de l'Adolescent et de Professions Associées: Dept of Child and Adolescent Psychiatry, Developmental Psychiatry Section, University of Cambridge, Douglas House, 18B Trumpington Rd, Cambridge, CB2 2AH, UK; tel. (1223) 336098; fax (1223) 746122; e-mail ig104@cus.cam.ac.uk; internet www.iacapap.org; f. 1948 to promote the study, treatment, care and prevention of mental disorders and deficiencies of children, adolescents and their families by promoting research and practice through collaboration with allied professions; mems: nat. asscns and individual mems in 39 countries; Pres. Dr HELMUT REMSCHMIDT (Germany); Sec.-Gen. Dr IAN M. GOODYER (UK); publ. *Yearbooks*.

International Association for Humanitarian Medicine (IAHM): 3 chemin du Milieu, 1279 Bogis-Bossey, Switzerland; tel. 227762161; fax 227766417; e-mail swagunn@bluewin.ch; internet www.iahm.org; f. 1984; aims to promote and deliver health care on the principles of humanitarian medicine through the provision of equitable medical, surgical, nursing and rehabilitation care to patients in or from developing countries; brings relief to disaster victims where health aid is lacking; mobilizes hospitals and health specialists in developed countries to receive and treat such patients free of charge; and advocates humanitarian principles in the practice of medicine, on the principle of health as a human right; limited to 100 on invitation; Pres. Prof. S. WILLIAM A. GUNN (Switzerland); Sec. Prof. LEO KLEIN (Czech Republic); publ. *Journal of Humanitarian Medicine* (4 a year).

International Association for Radiation Research: c/o Dr Fiona Stewart, Experimental Therapy, Plesmanlaan 121, 1066 CX Amsterdam, The Netherlands; tel. (20) 5122036; fax (20) 5122050; e-mail f.stewart@nki.nl; internet cbrl.stanford.edu/brown/index.htm; f. 1962 to advance radiation research in the fields of physics, chemistry, biology and medicine; 3,246 mems; quadrennial congress; Pres. Dr MASAO S. SASAKI (Japan); Sec. and Treasurer Dr FIONA A. STEWART (Netherlands); publ. *Proceedings of International Congresses*.

International Association of Agricultural Medicine and Rural Health/Association Internationale de Médecine Agricole et de Santé Rurale: OALI (NIPCH), 33–35 Szabolcs utca, Budapest 1135, Hungary; tel. (1) 450-1768; fax (1) 439-0473; e-mail iaamrhsecr@oali.hu; internet www.iaamrh.org; f. 1961 to study the problems of medicine in agriculture globally and to prevent diseases caused by agricultural production; 500 mems; Pres. Dr ASHOK PATIL (India); Sec.-Gen. Dr ISTVAN SZILARD (acting) (Hungary); publ. *Journal of International Agricultural Medicine and Rural Health* (4 a year).

International Association of Applied Psychology/Association Internationale de Psychologie Appliquée: c/o Janel Gauthier, Sec.-Gen. Dept of Psychology, Laval Univ., Pavillion Fa Savard, Quebec, G1K7P4, Canada; tel. 91-3943236; fax 91-3510091; e-mail iaap@psy.ulaval.ea; internet www.iaapsy.org; f. 1920 as Association Internationale de Psychotechnique, present name 1955; establishes contacts between those carrying out scientific work on applied psychology, to promote research and the adoption of measures contributing to this work; 2,000 mems; Pres. JOSE M. PEIRO (Spain); Sec.-Gen. JANEL GAUTHIER (Canada); publs *Applied Psychology: An International Review* (4 a year), *Applied Psychology: Health and Wellbeing* (2 a year).

International Association of Asthmology/Association Internationale d'Asthmologie (INTERASMA): internet www.interasma.org; f. 1954 to advance medical knowledge of bronchial asthma and allied disorders; c. 1,000 mems in 52 countries; Pres. RONALD DAHL (Denmark); Sec.-Gen. LAWRENCE DUBUSKE (USA); publ. *News Bulletin* (3 a year).

International Association of Environmental Mutagen Societies: 1821 Michael Faraday Dr., Ste 300, Reston, VA 20190-5348, USA; tel. (703) 438-3103; fax (703) 438-3113; e-mail beidemiller@aim-hq.com; internet www.iaems.net; f. 1973 for the stimulation of scientific activity and exchange of information by means of World Conference every 4 years in the field of environmental mutagenesis and genetic toxicology; 11 mem. socs (12,000 individuals); Pres. STEFANO BONASSI; Vice-Pres. Dr MICHE-LINE KIRSCH-VOLDERS; Vice-Pres. Dr LUCIA RIBEIRO; Exec. Dir Dr BETTY EIDEMILLER (USA); Sec. Dr HESTER VISMER (South Africa).

International Association of Gerontology (IAG): c/o Faculté de Médecine, Institut du Vieillissement, 37 Allées Jules Guesde, Toulouse, 31000, France; tel. 5-61-14-56-39; fax 5-61-14-56-40; e-mail seynes@cict.fr; internet www.iagg.info; f. 1950 to promote research and training in gerontology and geriatrics; 40,000 mems in 70 nat. mem. socs in 65 countries; Pres. Prof. BRUNO VELLAS (France); Sec.-Gen. and Vice-Pres. Prof. ALAIN FRANCO (Canada).

International Association of Hydatidology/Asociación Internacional de Hidatidología: Florida 460, 3° piso, 1005 Buenos Aires, Argentina; tel. (11) 4322-3431 ext. 166; fax (11) 4325-8231; internet iahyd.org; f. 1941; 650 mems in 40 countries; library: specialized library; Pres. ANTÓNIO MENEZES DA SILVA (Portugal); Sec.-Gen. EDUARDO GUARNERA (Argentina); publs *Archivos Internacionales de la Hidatidosis* (every 4 years), *Boletín de Hidatidosis* (4 a year).

International Association of Oral and Maxillofacial Surgeons: 17 West 220 22nd St, Suite 420, Oakbrook Terrace, IL 60181, USA; tel. (630) 833-0945; fax (630) 833-1382; internet www.iaoms.org; f. 1962 to elevate the quality of health care worldwide through the advancement of the art and science of oral and maxillofacial surgery; int. conference every 2 years; promotes collaborative research; educational programmes in developing countries; 3,710 mems; Pres. Dr LARRY NISSEN (USA); Exec. Dir Dr JOHN F. HELFRICK (USA); publ. *International Journal of Oral and Maxillofacial Surgery* (12 a year).

International Brain Research Organization (IBRO): 255 rue Saint Honoré, 75001 Paris, France; tel. 1-46-47-92-92; fax 1-47-46-42-50; e-mail ibro@wanadoo.fr; internet www.ibro.org; f. 1960 to assist all branches of neuroscience; federated to ICSU; 52,000 mems; Pres. Dr A. J. AGUAYO (Canada); Sec.-Gen. JENNIFER LUND (USA); publs *IBRO News* (1 a year), *IBRO Reporter* (12 a year, online), *Neuroscience* (28 a year).

International Cell Research Organization/Organisation Internationale de Recherche sur la Cellule: c/o UNESCO, SC/BES/LSC, 1 rue Miollis, 75732 Paris Cedex 15, France; tel. 1-45-68-58-18; fax 1-45-68-58-16; e-mail icro@unesco.org; internet www.unesco.org/ngo/icro; f. 1962 to create, encourage and promote cooperation between scientists of different disciplines worldwide for the advancement of fundamental knowledge of the cell; organizes international training courses and exchange of scientists, etc.; 400 mems; Chair. Prof. Q. S. LIN (China); Exec. Sec. Prof. G. N. COHEN (France).

International Center of Information on Antibiotics: c/o Prof. M. Welsch, Inst. de Pathologie, Université de Liège, Sart-Tilman, 4000 Liège, Belgium; f. 1961 to gather information on antibiotics and strains producing them; to establish contact with discoverers of antibiotics with a view to obtaining samples and filing information; Dir Prof. M. WELSCH; Senior Scientist in Charge Dr L. DELCAMBE.

International Commission on Occupational Health/Commission Internationale de la Santé au Travail: c/o ISPESL, National Institute for Occupational Safety and Prevention, Via Fontana Candida 1, 00040 Monteporzio Catone (Rome), Italy; tel. 06-94181407; fax 06-94181556; e-mail icohsg@iol.it; internet www.icoh.org.sg; f. 1906 to study new findings in the field of occupational health, to publicize the results of study and investigation in occupational health, and to organize meetings on nat. or int. problems in this field; 2,000 mems in 93 countries; recognized by the UN; official languages: English, French; Pres. Prof. JORMA RANTANEN (Finland); Sec.-Gen. Dr SERGIO IAVICOLI (Italy).

International Council of Ophthalmology: c/o Dr Bruce E. Spivey, International Council of Ophthalmology, 945 Green St, #10, San Francisco, CA 94133, USA; fax (415)

409-8403; e-mail info@icoph.org; f. 1857; 75 affiliated national societies; Pres. Dr BRUCE E. SPIVEY.

International Epidemiological Association/Association Internationale d'Epidémiologie: c/o Prof. Ahmed Mandil, IEA Secretary, 38 Ismailiah St, Apt 201, Mostafa Kamel, Alexandria, Egypt; tel. (3) 5467576; fax (3) 5467576; e-mail ieasecretariat@link .net; internet www.ieaweb.org; f. 1954; int. meetings are held every 3 years in different parts of the world and regional meetings are held regularly throughout the world; 1,500 mems in 100 countries; Pres. Prof. NEIL PEARCE; Sec. Prof. AHMED MANDIL; publ. *International Journal of Epidemiology* (6 a year).

International Federation for Medical and Biological Engineering/Fédération Internationale du Génie Médical et Biologique: c/o Prof. Ratko Magjarevic, Faculty of Electrical Engineering and Computing, University of Zagreb, Unska 3, 10000 Zagreb, Croatia; tel. (1) 6129-938; fax (1) 6129-652; e-mail office@ifmbe.org; internet www.ifmbe .org; f. 1959 to promote international cooperation and communication among societies interested in life and engineering sciences; mem. orgs in 47 countries and 2 transnational orgs; Pres. Prof. JOACHIM NAGEL (Germany); Sec.-Gen. Prof. RATKO MAGJAREVIC (Croatia); publs *Medical and Biological Engineering and Computing* (6 a year), *Proceedings of International Conference on Medical and Biological Engineering* (irregular).

International Federation of Anatomists/ Fédération Internationale des Associations d'Anatomistes: Dept of Anatomy, Medical College of Ohio, POB 10008, Toledo, OH 43699-0008, USA; tel. (419) 381-4111; f. 1903; mems: 52 national and multinational associations; Pres. Prof. Dr LIBERATO J. A. DIDIO (USA); publs *Directory*, Proceedings of each Federative International Congress of Anatomy (every 4 or 5 years).

International Federation of Gynaecology and Obstetrics/Fédération Internationale de Gynécologie et d'Obstétrique: FIGO House, Suite 3, Waterloo Court, 10 Theed St, London, SE15 6DX, UK; tel. (20) 7928-1166; fax (20) 7928-7099; e-mail figo@figo.org; internet www.figo .org; f. 1954; assists and contributes to research in gynaecology and obstetrics; aims to facilitate the exchange of information and perfect methods of teaching; organizes international congresses; 110 nat. socs; Pres. Dr A. ACOSTA (Paraguay); Sec.-Gen. Prof. S. ARULKUMARAN (UK); publ. *International Journal of Gynecology and Obstetrics* (12 a year).

International Federation of Physical Education/Fédération Internationale d'Education Physique (FIEP): CP 837, 85857-970 Foz do Iguaçu, Paraná, Brazil; tel. (45) 3574-1949; e-mail fiep.brasil@uol.com .br; internet www.fiep.net; f. 1923; aims to develop national and international physical education and sport-for-all; organizes congresses and courses; mems in 116 countries; Pres. (vacant); Gen. Sec. Prof. ALMIR ADOLFO GRUHN (Brazil); publ. *FIEP Bulletin* (in English, French and Spanish; Portuguese edition from Brazil).

International Hospital Federation/Fédération Internationale des Hôpitaux: PA Hospital de Loex, Route de Loex 151, 1233 Bernex, Switzerland; tel. 4-50-42-60-00; fax 4-50-42-60-01; e-mail info@ihf-fih.org; internet www.ihf-fih.org; f. 1947; an ind. org. supported by subscribing mems in 45 countries; aims to promote improvements in the planning and management of hospitals and health services through int. conferences, field study courses, training courses, information services, publs and research projects; mems: nat. hospital and health service orgs, governmental and non-governmental; Pres. JOSÉ CARLOS DE SOUSA ABRAHÃO (Brazil); CEO ERIC DE ROODENBEKE (France); publs *Building Quality in Health*, *Care Journal* (2 a year), *International Hospital Federation Reference Yearbook* (1 a year), *World Hospitals and Health Services* (4 a year).

International Institute on Ageing: 117 St Paul's St, Valletta, VLT 1216, Malta; tel. 21243044; fax 21230248; e-mail info@inia.org .mt; internet www.inia.org.mt; f. 1988 by the UN and Government of Malta; Int. training programmes social gerontology; economic and financial aspects of ageing; health promotion, quality of life and well-being; policy formulation, planning, implementation and monitoring of the Madrid Int. Plan of Action on Ageing; demographic aspects of population ageing, its implications for socio-economic devt policies and plans; 'In-Situ' training programmes in developing countries, research and data colln; technical cooperation (advisory services, project design, planning and implementation of training programmes); library of 800 vols; Dir Prof. JOSEPH TROISI; publ. *BOLD* (4 a year).

International League Against Epilepsy/ Ligue Internationale contre l'Epilepsie: 342 N Main St, West Hartford, CT 06117-2507, USA; tel. (860) 586-7547; fax (860) 586-7550; e-mail pberry@ilae.org; internet www .ilae.org; f. 1909 to collect and disseminate information concerning epilepsy, to promote treatment of epileptic patients and to foster cooperation with other int. institutions in similar fields; offices in USA; holds scientific congress every 2 years in conjunction with Int. Bureau for Epilepsy; regional congresses every 2 years; nat. congresses annually by each nat. chapter; 15,000 mems, nat. chapters in 98 countries; Pres. SOLOMON MOSHE; Sec.-Gen. SAMUEL WIEBE; Treas. EMILIO PERUCCA; Vice-Pres. TATSUYA TANAKA; Vice-Pres. MICHEL BAULAC; Chief Staff Officer PETER J. BERRY; publs *Epilepsia* (12 a year), *Epilepsies* (French, 4 a year), *Epilepsy & Behavior* (6 a year), *Epilepsy Research* (15 a year), *Epileptic Disorders*, *Seizure* (8 a year).

International Organization Against Trachoma/Organisation Internationale contre le Trachome: c/o Prof. Georges Cornand, La Bergère, Route de Grenoble, 05140 Aspres-sur-Buëch, France; f. 1923 for the research and study of trachomatous conjunctivitis and ophthalmological tropical and sub-tropical diseases; Pres. Prof. GABRIEL COSCAS (France); Sec.-Gen. Prof. GEORGES CORNAND; publ. *Revue Internationale du Trachome* (4 a year).

International Psychoanalytical Association: 'Broomhills', Woodside Lane, London, N12 8UD, UK; tel. (20) 8446-8324; fax (20) 8445-4729; e-mail ipa@ipa.org.uk; internet www.ipa.org.uk; f. 1910; primary accrediting and regulatory body for psychoanalysis; devt of psychoanalysis for benefit of psychoanalytic patients; 12,000 mems in 70 constituent orgs in 33 countries; Pres. CHARLES HANLY; Sec.-Gen. GUNTHER PERDIGAO; publ. *IPA News Magazine* (1 a year).

International Radiation Protection Association: c/o CEPN, 28 rue de la Redoute, 92260 Fontenay-aux-Roses, France; tel. 1-55-52-19-47; fax 1-40-85-19-21; e-mail irpa.exof@irpa.net; internet www.irpa.net; f. 1966 to promote int. contacts and cooperation among those engaged in health physics and radiation protection; to provide for discussion of the scientific and practical aspects of the protection of mankind and his environment from the hazards caused by ionizing and non-ionizing radiation, facilitating the exploitation of radiation and nuclear energy for the benefit of mankind; 37 mem. socs, 16,000 individual mems; Scientific Assoc. of ICSU, official relations with WHO, ILO, IAEA, ICRP; Pres. KEN KASE (USA); Exec. Officer JACQUES LOCHARD (France).

International Scientific Council for Trypanosomiasis Research and Control/ Conseil Scientifique International pour la Recherche et la Lutte contre les Trypanosomoses: Secretariat OAU/STRC, Ports Authority Bldg, 26/28 Marina, PMB 2359, Lagos, Nigeria; tel. 2633430; fax 2636093; f. 1949 to review the work on tsetse and trypanosomiasis problems carried out by relevant organizations and workers in laboratories and in the field; to encourage further research and discussion and to promote coordination between research workers and organizations in African countries; to provide opportunity for the discussion of related problems and their resolution; Exec. Sec. Prof. JOHNSON A. EKPERE.

International Society for Clinical Electrophysiology of Vision: c/o Daphne L. McCulloch, ISCEV Secretary-General, Dept of Vision Sciences, Glasgow Caledonian University, Glasgow, G4 0BA, UK; tel. (141) 331-3379; e-mail dlmc@gcal.ac.uk; internet www .iscev.org; f. 1958; 400 mems; Pres. Prof. MICHAEL BACH (Germany); Sec.-Gen. Prof. DAPHNE McCULLOCH; publ. *Documenta Ophthalmologica* (6 a year).

International Society for the Psychopathology of Expression and Art Therapy/Société Internationale de Psychopathologie de l'Expression et d'Art-Thérapie: c/o M. Sudres, Université Toulouse-Mirail, U.F.R. Psychologie, 5 allée Antonio Machado, 31058 Toulouse, Cedex 9, France; e-mail sipearther@aol.com; internet online-art-therapy.com; f. 1959 to bring together the various specialists interested in the problems of expression and artistic activities in connection with psychiatric, sociological and psychological research, as well as in the use of methods applied in fields other than that of mental illness; 625 mems; Pres. Prof. L. SCHMITT (France); Sec.-Gen. JEAN-LUC SUDRES (France).

International Society for Vascular Specialists: 900 Cummings Center, 221-U, Beverly, MA 01915, USA; tel. (978) 927-8330; fax (978) 524-8890; internet www .iscvs.vascularweb.org; f. 1950; present name 2003 (comprising members in North and South America, Africa, the Middle East and Australasia); members in Europe and Asia belong to affiliated International Society for Cardiovascular Surgery; promotes the investigation and study of the art, science and therapy of cardiovascular diseases; facilitates the exchange of ideas in the field of vascular diseases through scientific meetings and personal contact between vascular specialists; 2,000 mems; Pres. JAMES MAY; publs *Annals of Vascular Surgery* (6 a year), *Cardiovascular Surgery* (6 a year), *Journal of Vascular Surgery* (12 a year).

International Society of Criminology/ Société Internationale de Criminologie: 12 rue Charles Fourier, 75013 Paris, France; tel. (1) 45-88-00-23; fax (1) 45-88-96-40; e-mail crim.sic@wanadoo.fr; internet perso .wanadoo.fr/societe.internationale.de.criminologie; f. 1938 to promote the development of the sciences in their application to crime; library; 800 mems; Pres. LAWRENCE W. SHERMAN (USA); Sec.-Gen. GEORGES PICCA (France); publ. *Annales Internationales de Criminologie*.

International Society of Haematology/ Société Internationale d'Hématologie: c/o Dr Emin Kansu, Institute of Oncology, Faculty of Medicine, Haceteppe University, Hacettepe, 06100 Ankara, Turkey; tel. (312) 305-28-66; fax (312) 324-20-09; e-mail ekansu@ada.net.tr; internet www.ish-world .org; f. 1946 to promote and foster the exchange and diffusion of information and ideas relating to blood and blood-forming tissues worldwide; to provide a forum for discussion of haematologic problems on an international scale and to encourage scientific investigation of these problems; to promote the advancement of haematology and its recognition as a branch of the biological sciences; to attempt to standardize on an international scale haematological methods and nomenclature; to promote a better understanding of the scientific basic principles of haematology among practitioners of haematology and physicians in general and to foster better understanding and a greater interest in clinical haematological problems among scientific investigators in the field of haematology; Vice-Pres. of European and African Division GAYLE KENOYER (South Africa), FAYZA HAMMOUDA (Egypt); Sec.-Gen. and Treas. of European and African Division EMIN KANSU (Turkey).

International Society of Hypnosis: c/o Dr Eric Vermetten, Department of Military Psychiatry, Central Military Hospital, University Medical Center Utrecht, Heidelberglaan 100, 3584 CX Utrecht, Netherlands; tel. (30) 2502591; fax (30) 2502282; e-mail admin@ish-web.org; internet www.ish-web .org; f. 1973 as an affiliate of the World Federation of Mental Health; to encourage and improve professional research, cooperative relations among scientific disciplines with regard to the study and application of hypnosis; to bring together persons using hypnosis and set up standards for professional training and adequacy; Pres. Dr ERIC VERMETTEN (Netherlands); Sec. and Treas. Dr JULIE LINDEN (USA); publ. *International Journal of Clinical and Experimental Hypnosis* (4 a year).

International Society of Lymphology: Dept of Surgery, Rm 4406, 1501 North Campbell Ave, POB 245200, Tucson, AZ 85724-5200, USA; tel. (520) 626-6118; fax (520) 626-0822; e-mail grace@surgery .arizona.edu; internet www.u.arizona.edu/ ~witte/isl.htm; f. 1966; advances progress in lymphology and related subjects; organizes int. working groups, cooperates with other nat. and int. organizations; int. congresses and postgraduate courses; 400 mems; Pres. RUTTIGER BAUMEISTER; Sec.-Gen. MARLYS WITTE (USA); publs *Lymphology* (4 a year), *Progress in Lymphology* (every 2 years).

International Society of Neuropathology: c/o Dr Seth Love, Dept of Neuropathology, Institute of Clinical Sciences, Frenchay Hospital, Bristol, BS16 1LE, UK; fax (117) 975-3760; e-mail isn@sethlove.co.uk; internet www.intsocneuropathol.com; f. 1972 to initiate and maintain permanent cooperation between nat. and regional socs of neuropathology, to foster links with other int. orgs in the same field, to initiate int. congresses, symposia, etc.; 2,500 mems; Pres. Dr BERNARDINO GHETTI (USA); Sec.-Gen. Dr SETH LOVE (UK); publ. *Brain Pathology* (4 a year).

International Society of Radiology/Société Internationale de Radiologie: 7910 Woodmont Ave, Suite 400, Bethesda, MD 20814, USA; tel. (301) 657-2652; fax (301) 907-8768; internet www.isradiology.org; f. 1953 to develop and advance medical radiology by giving radiologists in different countries an opportunity of personally submitting their experiences, exchanging and discussing their ideas, and forming personal bonds with their colleagues; 3 permanent Int. Commissions: (*a*) on Radiological Protection (ICRP), (*b*) on Radiation Units and Measurements (ICRU), (*c*) on Radiological Education (ICRE); these Commissions meet when necessary; Pres. NICHOLAS GUARTSOYIANNIS (Greece); Exec. Dir OTHA W. LINTON (USA).

International Society of Surgery (ISS)/ Société Internationale de Chirurgie (SIC): Seltisbergerstr. 16, 4419 Lupsingen, Switzerland; tel. 618519666; fax 618114775; e-mail surgery@iss-sic.ch; internet www .iss-sic.ch; f. 1902; organizes congresses; 3,500 mems; Sec.-Gen. Prof. Dr JEAN-CLAUDE GIVEL; publ. *World Journal of Surgery* (12 a year).

International Union against Sexually Transmitted Infections: c/o Dr Raj Patel, Royal South Hants Hospital, Brintons Terrace, Southampton, SO14 0YG, UK; tel. (23) 8082-5152; fax (23) 8082-5122; internet www .iusti.org; f. 1923; administrative and educational activities, public health, and technical aspects of sexually transmitted diseases, esp. HIV/AIDS; 800 individual, 50 nat. and soc. mems; consultative status with WHO; Pres. Dr FRANK JUDSON (USA); Sec.-Gen. Dr RAJ PATEL (UK).

International Union against Tuberculosis and Lung Disease/Union Internationale contre la Tuberculose et les Maladies Respiratoires: 68 Blvd Saint-Michel, 75006 Paris, France; tel. (1) 44-32-03-60; fax (1) 43-29-90-87; e-mail union@ iuatld.org; internet www.iuatld.org; f. 1920 to coordinate the efforts of anti-tuberculosis associations, to promote programmes and research in tuberculosis control, chest diseases and community health, to cooperate in these respects with the World Health Organization, to promote int. and regional conferences on the above subjects, to collect and disseminate relevant information, to assist in developing national programmes in cooperation with national associations; mems: associations in 165 countries; 3,000 individual mems; Pres. Prof. ASMA EL SONY (Sudan); Exec. Dir Dr NILS E. BILLO (Switzerland); Sec.-Gen. Dr MUHAMMAD REZA MASJEDI (Iran); publ. *International Journal of Tuberculosis and Lung Disease* (12 a year, in English).

International Union for Health Promotion and Education/Union Internationale de Promotion de la Santé et d'Education pour la Santé: 42 blvd de la Libération, 93203 St Denis Cedex, France; tel. (1) 48-13-71-20; fax (1) 48-09-17-67; internet www.iuhpe.org; f. 1951; mems: organizations in 21 countries, groups and individuals in 90 countries; Pres. MAURICE MITTELMARK (Norway); Exec. Dir MARIE-CLAUDE LAMARRE (France); publ. *Promotion and Education/International Journal of Health Promotion and Education* (4 a year, in a trilingual edition in English, French and Spanish; special supplement issues throughout the year).

International Vaccine Institute: Kwanak, POB 14, Seoul 151-600, Republic of Korea; tel. (2) 872-2801; fax (2) 872-2803; e-mail iviinfo@ivi.int; internet www.ivi.org; f. 1997; established by the UN Development Programme (UNDP) as an int. centre of research, training and technical assistance for vaccination in the developing world; Chair. Prof. SAMUEL L. KATZ (USA); Dir Dr JOHN D. CLEMENS (Republic of Korea).

Multiple Sclerosis International Federation: Skyline House, 3rd Fl., 200 Union St, London, SE1 0LX, UK; tel. (20) 7620-1911; fax (20) 7620-1922; e-mail info@msif.org; internet www.msif.org; f. 1967 to coordinate and advance the work of nat. multiple sclerosis orgs worldwide, to encourage scientific research in this and related neurological diseases, to collect and disseminate information, and to advise and help in advancing the devt of voluntary nat. multiple sclerosis orgs; Pres. SARAH PHILLIPS (UK); Sec. WEYMAN T. JOHNSON (USA); publs *MSIF Annual Review*, *MS in Focus*.

Organisation Ouest Africaine de la Santé (OOAS)/West African Health Organisation (WAHO): 01 BP 153, Bobo-Dioulasso 01, Burkina Faso; tel. 97-57-75; fax 97-57-72; e-mail wahooas@fasonet.bf; f. 1987 by merger of OCCGE (Organisation de Coordination et de Coopération pour la Lutte contre les Grandes Endémies in Bobo-Dioulaso Burkina Faso) and WAHC (West African Health Community/Communauté Ouest Africaine de la Santé) in Lagos, Nigeria; proactive instrument of regional health integration that enables high-impact and cost-effective interventions; conducts research and trains medical workers; library of 4,072 vols, 21 current serials, 3,196 technical documents; 15 mem. states: Benin, Burkina Faso, Cape Verde, Côte d'Ivoire, Ghana, Guinea, Guinea-Bissau, Liberia, Mali, Niger, Nigeria, Senegal, Sierra Leone, The Gambia, Togo; library of 2,367 vols, 3 current periodicals, 11,010 technical documents; Dir-Gen. Dr PLACIDO M. CARDOSO; publs *Bulletin bibliographique mensuel* (4 a year), *Profil OOAS* (4 a year).

Société de Neurochirurgie de Langue Française (Society of French-Speaking Neurosurgeons): Service de neurochirurgie, Laarbeeklaan 101, 1090 Brussels, Belgium; internet www.snclf.com; f. 1948; 400 mems; Pres. MARC SINDOU; Sec. JEAN D'HAENS; publ. *Neurochirurgie* (6 a year).

Société Internationale de Chirurgie Orthopédique et de Traumatologie/ International Society of Orthopaedic Surgery and Traumatology: Rue Washington 40b 9, 1050 Brussels, Belgium; tel. (2) 648-68-23; fax (2) 649-86-01; e-mail hq@sicot.org; internet www.sicot.org; f. 1929; advances science and art of orthopaedics and traumatology at an int. level for enhancement of patient care; fosters and develops teaching, research and education; facilitates and encourages interchange of professional experience; yearly conference and triennial world congress; 113 mem. countries, 2,000 individual mems; library of 34 vols of *International Orthopaedics*; Pres. Prof. CODY BUNGER (Denmark); Pres.-Elect Prof. MAURICE HINSENKAMP; Sec.-Gen. Prof. JOCHEN EULERT (Germany); Treas. Prof. PATRICIA FUCS; First Vice-Pres. Dr THAMI BENZAKOUR; Assoc. Man. BEA ROFAGHA; publ. *International Orthopaedics* (13 a year).

World Association of Societies of (Anatomic and Clinical) Pathology/Association Mondiale des Sociétés de Pathologie (Anatomique et Clinique): c/o Dept of Clinical Pathology, Koshigaya Hospital, Dokkyo University School of Medicine, 2-1-50 Minamikoshigaya, Koshigaya, Saitama 343, Japan; f. 1947 (formerly International Society of Clinical Pathology) to improve health worldwide by promoting the teaching and practice of all aspects of pathology and laboratory medicine; mems: 50 national associations; Pres. WILLIAM B. ZEILER (USA); Exec. Dir Dr I. SAKURABAYASHI.

World Association of Veterinary Microbiologists, Immunologists and Specialists in Infectious Diseases/Association Mondiale des Vétérinaires Microbiologistes, Immunologistes et Spécialistes des Maladies Infectieuses: Ecole Nationale Vétérinaire d'Alfort, 7 ave du Général de

Gaulle, 94704 Maisons-Alfort Cedex, France; tel. 1-43-96-70-21; fax 1-43-96-70-22; f. 1967 to facilitate international contacts in the field of veterinary microbiologists, immunologists and specialists in infectious diseases; Pres. Prof. CH. PILET (France).

World Confederation for Physical Therapy: Victoria Charity Centre, 11 Belgrave Rd, London, SW1V 1RB, UK; tel. (20) 7931-6465; fax (20) 7931-6494; e-mail info@wcpt .org; internet www.wcpt.org; f. 1951 to encourage improved standards of physical therapy in education and practice; to promote exchange of information between mem. orgs; to assist the development of informed public opinion regarding physical therapy; to cooperate with appropriate agencies of UN and national and int. organizations; 92 mem. organizations; 101 mems; Pres. SANDRA MERCER MOORE; Sec.-Gen. BRENDA MYERS (UK); publ. *WCPT News* (4 a year).

World Council of Optometry: 42 Craven St, London WC2N 5NG, UK; fax (207) 839-6800; e-mail enquiries@worldoptometry.org; internet www.worldoptometry.org; f. 1927; aims to coordinate efforts to provide a high standard of ophthalmic optical (optometric) care worldwide; provides a forum for the exchange of ideas between different countries; a large part of its work is concerned with optometric education, and advice upon standards of qualification; involved in getting legislation approvedin relation to optometry worldwide; 85 mem. orgs in 52 countries; Pres. Prof. ROBERT CHAPPELL (UK); Exec. Dir (vacant); publ. *World Optometry.*

World Federation of Neurosurgical Societies/Fédération Mondiale des Sociétés de Neurochirurgie: c/o Janette A. Joseph, 5 rue du Marché, 1260 Nyon, Vaud, Switzerland; tel. 223624303; fax 223624352; e-mail janjoseph@wfns.ch; internet www .wfns.org; f. 1955 to facilitate the exchange of knowledge and to encourage research; 109 mem. societies and affiliated organizations; Pres. Dr JACQUES BROTCHI; Dir JANETTE A. JOSEPH (Switzerland).

World Federation of Societies of Anaesthesiologists (WFSA)/Federación Mundial de Sociedades de Anestesiólogos/Weltverband der Anaesthesisten-Gesellschaften: 21 Portland Place, London, W1B 1YP, UK; tel. (20) 7631-8880; fax (20) 7631-8882; e-mail wfsahq@ anaesthesiologists.org; internet www .anaesthesiologists.org; f. 1955 to make available the highest standards of anaesthesia, pain treatment, trauma management and resuscitation globally; 122 nat. mem. socs; Hon. Sec. Dr DAVID WILKINSON (UK); Sec. Prof. JOHN MOYERS (USA); publs *Update in Anaesthesia* (2 a year, in 5 languages), *World Anaesthesia* (3 a year, in 3 languages).

Music

International Music Council (IMC)/Conseil International de la Musique: c/o Maison de l'UNESCO, 1 rue Miollis, 75015 Paris, France; tel. 1-45-68-48-50; fax 1-45-68-48-66; e-mail info@imc-cim.org; internet www.imc-cim.org; f. 1949 under the auspices of UNESCO to foster the exchange of musicians, music (written and recorded), and information; to support contemporary composers, traditional music, and young professional musicians; to foster appreciation of music by the public; promotion of diverse music; advancement of music rights; 150 mem. orgs; Sec.-Gen. SILJA FISCHER (France).

MEMBERS OF IMC

European Festivals Association/Association Européenne des Festivals: Kasteel Borluut, Kleine Gentstraat 46, 9051 Gent, Belgium; tel. (9) 241-80-80; fax (9) 241-80-89; e-mail info@efa-aef.eu; internet www.efa-aef .eu; f. 1952 to maintain high artistic standards in festivals, widen the field of operation, organize information and publicity; 106 mem. festivals in Austria, Belgium, Bosnia and Herzegovina, Bulgaria, Croatia, Czech Republic, Denmark, Estonia, Finland, France, Germany, Greece, Hungary, Iceland, Ireland, Israel, Italy, Japan, Lebanon, Lithuania, Luxembourg, former Yugoslav republic of Macedonia, Mexico, Netherlands, Norway, Poland, Portugal, Romania, Russia, Serbia, Slovakia, Slovenia, Spain, Sweden, Switzerland, Turkey, UK; Sec.-Gen. KATHRIN DEVENTER.

International Council for Traditional Music/Conseil International de la Musique Traditionelle: ICTM Secretariat, School of Music, Australian National University, Bldg 100, Canberra, ACT 0200, Australia; tel. (2) 612-51449; fax (2) 612-59775; e-mail secretariat@ictmusic.org; internet www.ictmusic.org; f. 1947 (as International Folk Music Council) to advance the preservation, study, practice and dissemination of traditional music (including dance) worldwide; affiliated to UNESCO; 1,600 mems; Pres. Dr ADRIENNE L. KAEPPLER (USA); Sec.-Gen. Prof. STEPHEN WILD (Australia); publs *Bulletin* (2 a year), *Directory of Traditional Music* (online for mems), *Yearbook for Traditional Music.*

International Federation of Musicians/Fédération Internationale des Musiciens: 21 bis rue Victor Massé, 75009 Paris, France; tel. 1-45-26-31-23; fax 1-45-26-31-57; e-mail office@fim-musicians.org; internet www.fim-musicians.org; f. 1948 to promote and protect the interests of musicians in affiliated unions and to institute protective measures to safeguard musicians against the abuse of their performances; promotes the international exchange of musicians; makes agreements with other international organizations in the interest of member unions and of the profession; mems: 70 unions in 65 countries; Pres. JOHN F. SMITH (UK); Gen. Sec. BENOÎT MACHUEL.

International Music and Media Centre/Internationales Musikzentrum und Medienzentrum: Stiftgasse 29, 1070 Vienna, Austria; tel. (1) 889-03-15; fax (1) 889-03-15-77; e-mail office@imz.at; internet www.imz.at; f. 1961 as a non-profit org. for the promotion and dissemination of opera, dance, concert and music documentaries through the audiovisual media (film, television, radio, gramophone); organizes congresses, seminars and screenings on music in the audiovisual media; organizes competitions to strengthen relations between composers, interpreters and directors, with particular emphasis on the promotion of the young generation; mems: 180 broadcasting orgs and other artistic orgs in 26 countries; Pres. CHRIS HUNT (UK); Sec.-Gen. FRANZ PATAY.

International Musicological Society: see under International Council for Philosophy and Humanistic Studies.

International Research Institute for Media, Communication and Cultural Development (MEDIACULT): Anton-von-Webern-Pl. 1, 1030 Vienna, Austria; tel. (1) 71155-8800; fax (1) 71155-8809; e-mail mediacult@mediacult.mdw.ac.at; internet www.mdw.ac.at/mediacult; f. 1969; library of 1,200 vols; Pres. Prof. RAYMOND WEBER (Luxembourg); Dir Dr ANDREW GEBESMAIR; Sec.-Gen. Dr ALFRED SMUDITS.

International Society for Contemporary Music/Société Internationale pour la

Musique Contemporaine: c/o Muziek Centrum Nederland, Rokin 111, 1012 KN, Amsterdam, Netherlands; tel. (20) 344-60-60; e-mail info@iscm.org; internet www.iscm .org; f. 1922 to promote the devt of contemporary music and to organize annual World Music Days; mem. organizations in 47 countries; Pres. JOHN DAVIS (Australia); Sec. Gen. ARTHUR VAN DER DRIFT; publ. *World New Music Magazine* (1 a year).

International Society for Music Education: POB 909, Nedlands WA 6909, Australia; tel. (8) 9386-2654; fax (8) 9386-2658; e-mail isme@isme.org; internet www.isme .org; f. 1953 to promote music education as a part of general education and community life; organizes int. conferences and seminars; cooperates with other int. music orgs; acts as an advisory body to UNESCO; cooperates with orgs representing other fields of education; 1,650 individual mems, 80000 Assoc. mems; Pres. GRAHAM WELCH; Sec.-Gen. JUDY THÖNELL; publs *Conference and Seminar Proceedings* (every 2 years), *International Journal of Music Education (IJME)* (4 a year).

Jeunesses Musicales International: Palais des Beaux-Arts, 10 rue Royale, 1000 Brussels, Belgium; tel. (32) 2-5139774; fax (32) 2-5144755; e-mail mail@jmi.net; internet www.jmi.net; f. 1945 to enable young people to develop through music across all boundaries; runs a World Orchestra and a World Youth Choir; member organizations in 41 countries; Sec.-Gen. DAG FRANZÉN (acting); publ. *JMI News* (6 a year).

World Federation of International Music Competitions/Fédération Mondiale des Concours Internationaux de Musique: 104 rue de Carouge, 1205 Geneva, Switzerland; tel. 223213620; fax 227811418; e-mail fmcim@iprolink.ch; internet www .wfimc.org; f. 1957; coordinates the activities of members and maintains links between them, arranges the calendar of competitions, helps competition-winners to get to know each other; 118 mem. competitions; Pres. MARIANNE GRANVIG; Sec.-Gen. RENATE RONNEFELD; publ. *Yearbook.*

OTHER ORGANIZATION

Répertoire International de Littérature Musicale (RILM)/International Repertory of Music Literature/Internationales Repertorium der Musikliteratur: RILM International Center, 365 Fifth Avenue, New York, NY 10016-4309, USA; tel. (212) 817-1990; fax (212) 817-1569; e-mail rilm@gc .cuny.edu; internet www.rilm.org; f. 1966; autonomous body sponsored by International Association of Music Libraries, Archives and Documentation Centers, and International Musicological Society; research and gathering of bibliographic references of all significant writings on music, from all nations, for online, printed and CD-ROM database; 63 mem. national committees; library of 1,200 vols, 500 current music journals; Pres. BARBARA DOBBS MACKENZIE; publ. *RILM Abstracts of Music Literature* (1 a year).

Science

Abdus Salam International Centre for Theoretical Physics (ICTP): Strada Costiera 11, 34151 Trieste, Italy; tel. 040-2240111; fax 040-224163; e-mail sci_info@ ictp.it; internet www.ictp.it; f. 1964; administered under a tripartite agreement between UNESCO, the Int. Atomic Energy Agency, and the Italian Govt; primary focus on training and research into high-energy physics, cosmology and astroparticle physics, condensed matter and statistical physics,

Earth system physics, mathematics and applied physics; library of 68,000 vols, 340 journals, 4,000 e-journals, 1,700 electronic books; Dir FERNANDO QUEVEDO.

Academy of Sciences for the Developing World: c/o Abdus Salam International Centre for Theoretical Physics, Strada Costiera 11, 34014 Trieste, Italy; located at: ICTP Enrico Fermi Bldg, 1st Fl., Via Beirut 6, 34014 Trieste, Italy; tel. 040 2240327; fax 040 224559; e-mail info@twas.org; internet www.twas.org; f. 1983 to give recognition and support to research carried out by scientists in developing countries, to facilitate their contacts and foster research in developing countries; awards prizes, research grants, fellowships and associateships to scientists working and living in developing countries; 844 fellows and assoc. fellows; Pres. JACOB PALIS (Brazil); Sec.-Gen. DORAIRAJAN BALASUBRAMANIAN (India); Exec. Dir MOHAMED H. A. HASSAN (Italy); publ. *TWAS Year Book*.

African Academy of Sciences: POB 24916, Nairobi, Kenya; tel. (2) 884401; fax (2) 884406; e-mail aas@aasciences.org; f. 1985 to promote and foster the growth of the scientific community in Africa; activities: mobilization and strengthening of the African scientific community (includes the Network of African Scientific Institutions, profiles and data-bank of African scientists and instns, African Dissertation Internship Programme, assistance to regional orgs); research development and public policy; capacity building in science and technology; 162 Fellows; library of 2,000 vols; Pres. Prof. MOHAMED H. A. HASSAN (Sudan); Exec. Dir Dr Eng. SHEM ARUNGU-OLENDE (Kenya); publs *Discovery and Innovation* (4 a year), *Whydah* (4 a year).

African Association for the Advancement of Science and Technology: c/o Prof. C. Kamala, KNAAS, POB 47288, Nairobi, Kenya; f. 1978; Sec. Prof. C. KAMALA.

African Organization for Cartography and Remote Sensing/Organisation Africaine de Cartographie et Télédétection: BP 102, Hussein Dey, 16040 Algiers, Algeria; tel. (21) 23-17-17; fax (21) 23-33-39; e-mail oact@wissal.dz; internet www.oact.dz; f. 1988 to encourage the development of cartography and of remote sensing by satellite, organize conferences and other meetings, and promote the establishment of training institutions; coordinates four regional training centres, in Burkina Faso, Kenya, Nigeria and Tunisia; 24 mem. countries; Contact MOHAMED SAFAR ZITOUN.

Association for the Taxonomic Study of Tropical African Flora/Association pour l'Etude Taxonomique de la Flore d'Afrique Tropicale: c/o Prof. Dr Sebsebe Demissew, Faculty of Science, Addis Ababa University, POB 3434, Addis Ababa, Ethiopia; tel. (1) 114323; fax (1) 552350; e-mail nat .heb@telecom.net.et; internet www.br.fgov .be/research/meetings/aetfat; f. 1950; language of instruction French; 800 mems from 70 countries; Gen. Sec. Prof. Dr SEBSEBE DEMISSEW; publ. *Bulletin* (1 a year).

Association of Information and Dissemination Centers: POB 3212, Maple Glen, PA 19002-8212, USA; tel. (215) 654-9129; fax (215) 654-9129; e-mail info@asidic.org; internet www.asidic.org; f. 1968; independent organization with 100 centres representing industry, government and academia in the USA, Canada, Europe, Israel, Japan, India, South Africa and Australia; promotes applied technology of information storage and retrieval, and research and development for more efficient use of databases; Pres. MICHAEL WALKER; Sec. DONALD HAWKINS.

BirdLife International: 1 Wellbrook Court, Girton Rd, Girton, Cambridge, CB3 0NA, UK; tel. (1223) 277318; fax (1223) 277200; e-mail birdlife@birdlife.org; internet www.birdlife.org; f. 1922; determines status of bird species worldwide and compiles data on all endangered species; identifies conservation problems and priorities and runs a programme of related field projects; partners and reps in 90 countries; Chair. PETER SCHEI (Norway); Dir and Chief Exec. Dr MARCO LAMBERTINI (UK); publs *Bird Conservation International*, *World Birdwatch*.

Charles Darwin Foundation for the Galapagos Isles/Fundación Charles Darwin para las Islas Galápagos: c/o Fernando Espinoza, Casilla 17-01-3891, Quito, Ecuador; located at: Avda 6 de Diciembre N 36-109 y Pasaje California, Quito, Ecuador; tel. 244-803; fax 443-935; internet www .darwinfoundation.org; f. 1959 to organize and maintain the Charles Darwin Research Station in the Galapagos Islands and to advise the Government of Ecuador on scientific research and conservation in the archipelago; Pres. Dr THOMAS H. FRITTS; Exec. Dir Dr FERNANDO ESPINOZA F.; publ. *Noticias de Galápagos* (2 a year).

Circum-Pacific Council for Energy and Mineral Resources: c/o Michele Redner, Secretariat, 12201 Sunrise Valley Dr., MS-917A, Reston, VA 20192, USA; tel. (703) 648-5042; fax (703) 648-4227; internet www .circum-pacificcouncil.org; f. 1974; non-profit int. org. of earth scientists and engineers; develops and promotes research and cooperation among industry, govt and academics, for the sustainable use of natural resources in the Pacific region; cooperation of 46 int. geoscience orgs; sponsors conferences, meetings and researchincl. the Circum-Pacific Map Project, and int. training schools; Pres. H. GARY GREENE (USA); Chair. EDWARD SAADE (USA); Sec. ERICK MACK (USA).

Commonwealth Geographical Bureau: c/o Department of Geography, University of Otago, POB 56, Dunedin, New Zealand; tel. (3) 479-8774; fax (3) 479-9037; e-mail j.a .binns@geography.otago.ac.nz; internet www .commonwealthgeography.org; f. 1968; encourages the devt of geographical research and study, particularly in developing Commonwealth countries, through assistance to the profession; regional seminars, assistance for study visits; a board of management represents 5 regions: Asia, Africa, Americas, Australasia and Europe

Commonwealth Science Council: Commonwealth Secretariat, Marlborough House, Pall Mall, London, SW1Y 5HX, UK; tel. (20) 7747-6500; fax (20) 7930-0827; e-mail science@commonwealth.int; f. 1975; an intergovernmental body, the Science and Technology Division of the Commonwealth Secretariat; seeks to increase the capability of Commonwealth countries to apply science and technology for social, economic and environmental development; conducts no inhouse research, but provides support for putting into practice the results of research carried out by others and helps to produce knowledge required to solve developmental problems through research; programmes are: biological and genetic resources, renewable energy, water and mineral resources, advanced technologies; runs a fellowship scheme providing short-term placements at training programmes or research institutes in developing countries; runs a travel-grant scheme to help scientists from member countries attend scientific meetings; 37 mems; Sec. Dr KEN LUM; publs *Commonwealth Scientist* (4 a year), *Report* (4 a year).

Council for International Congresses of Entomology/Comité Permanent des Congrès Internationaux d'Entomologie: c/o Dr James Ridsdill-Smith, 75A Birdwood Circus East, Bruce, WA 6157, Australia; tel. (8) 9339-0762; e-mail james.ridsdill-smith@ csiro.au; internet www.ice2012.org; f. 1910 to act as a link between periodic congresses and to arrange the venue for each congress; the committee is also the entomology section of the International Union of Biological Sciences; 23 mems; Chair. Dr HARI SHARMA (India); Sec. Dr JAMES RIDSDILL-SMITH (Australia).

Council of Managers of National Antarctic Programs (COMNAP): COMNAP Secretariat, PMB 4800, Christchurch, New Zealand; Gateway Antarctica, Univ. of Canterbury, Ilam Rd, Christchurch, New Zealand; tel. (64) 3364-2273; fax (64) 3364-2297; e-mail sec@comnap.aq; internet www .comnap.aq; f. 1988; int. asscn brings together National Antarctic Programmes from around the world to develop and promote best practice in managing the support of scientific research in Antarctica; 29 mem. countries; Chair. JOSÉ RETAMALES (Chile); Exec. Sec. MICHELLE ROGAN-FINNEMORE.

European Atomic Energy Community (Euratom): 200 rue de la Loi, 1049 Brussels, Belgium; tel. (2) 235-11-11; internet euratom .org; based on a formal treaty signed in Rome, Italy in March 1957, at the same time as the treaty establishing the EEC; aims to integrate the programmes of member states for the peaceful uses of atomic energy; since 1967 combined with the ECSC and EEC

European Centre for Medium-Range Weather Forecasts: Shinfield Park, Reading, Berks., RG2 9AX, United Kingdom; tel. (118) 949-9000; fax (118) 986-9450; e-mail dg@ecmwf.int; internet www.ecmwf.int; f. 1975; devt of numerical methods for medium-range weather forecasting; colln and storage of data and products, providing operational forecasts to the mem. states and cooperating states, and providing advanced training in numerical weather prediction; 18 mem. states; Dir D. MARBOUTY.

European Geosciences Union: Max-Planck-Str. 13, 37191 Katlenburg-Lindau, Germany; tel. (49) 5556-1440; fax (49) 5556-4709; e-mail egu@copernicus.org; internet www.copernicus.org/egu; f. 2002 by merger of the European Geophysical Society and the European Union of Geosciences; promotes the sciences of the Earth and its environment and of planetary and space sciences, and encourages cooperation between scientists; organizes annual General Assemblies, topical conferences and short courses; Pres. PETER FABIAN; Exec. Sec. Dr ARNE K. RICHTER; publs *Advances in Geosciences*, *Advances in Radio Science*, *Annales Geophysicae*, *Astrophysics and Space Sciences Transactions*, *Atmospheric Chemistry and Physics*, *Atmospheric Chemistry and Physics Discussions*, *Biogeosciences*, *Geophysical Research Abstracts*, *Hydrology and Earth System Sciences*, *Hydrology and Earth System Sciences Discussions*, *Natural Hazards and Earth System Sciences*, *Nonlinear Processes in Geophysics*, *Ocean Science*, *Ocean Science Discussions*, *Social Geography*.

European Institute of Environmental Medicine: Odos Kerasundos 2, Athens 162 32, Greece; tel. 210-7628460; fax 210-7628675; e-mail eiem@otonet.gr; f. 1970 to bring together scientists and scholars with cross-sectional background and research interests and to conduct multi-disciplinary educational and research activities studying the interactions between man and his environment (natural and technical); Dir Prof. C. K. KYRILOV.

European Molecular Biology Laboratory: Meyerhofstr. 1, 69117 Heidelberg, Germany; tel. (6221) 3870; fax (6221) 3878306; e-mail info@embl.de; internet www.embl-heidelberg.de; f. 1974; financed by 15 European states and Israel; basic research in molecular biology; outstations in Hinxton, nr Cambridge (European Bioinformatics Institute), Grenoble, Hamburg and Monterotondo (Rome); library of 22,200 vols; Dir-Gen. Prof. FOTIS C. KAFATOS; publs *Handbook of Statistics* (1 a year), *Research Report* (1 a year).

European Molecular Biology Organization (EMBO)/Organisation Européenne de Biologie Moléculaire: Postfach 1022.40, 69012 Heidelberg, Germany; located at: Meyerhofstr. 1, 69117 Heidelberg, Germany; tel. (6221) 88910; fax (6221) 8891200; e-mail embo@embo.org; internet www.embo.org; f. 1964; promotes excellence in the molecular life sciences in Europe; awards research fellowships; sponsors scientific meetings; awards installation grants to build scientific capacity in selected countries; provides opportunities for career development in the EMBO Young Investigator Programme; offers fellowships and training for scientists outside Europe; offers scientific advice on European science policy; provides quality reviews of national science programmes, and information and online services for life sciences communities; annual life sciences conf.; 1,500 mems; Dir Prof. MARIA LEPTIN; publs *EMBO Journal* (24 a year), *EMBO Molecular Medicine* (12 a year), *EMBO Reports* (12 a year), *Molecular Systems Biology* (26 a year, online).

European Organization for Nuclear Research (CERN)/Organisation Européenne pour la Recherche Nucléaire: 1211 Geneva 23, Switzerland; tel. 227676111; fax 227676555; e-mail cern.reception@cern.ch; internet www.cern.ch; f. 1954; mems: Austria, Belgium, Czech Republic, Denmark, Finland, France, Germany, Greece, Hungary, Italy, Netherlands, Norway, Poland, Portugal, Slovakia, Spain, Sweden, Switzerland and UK; carries out and coordinates research on fundamental particles; research is undertaken mostly by teams of visiting scientists who remain based at their parent instns; in general, the staff is drawn from mem. states, but scientists from any country may be invited to spend a limited period at CERN; research is carried out with the aid of a proton synchrotron of 28 GeV (the PS), the super proton synchrotron (SPS) of 450 GeV and the 27-km LEP electron-positron collider; Pres. of the Council Prof. ENZO IAROCCI; Dir-Gen. Dr ROBERT AYMAR; publ. *CERN Courier* (12 a year, in English and French).

European Physical Society: 6 rue des Frères Lumière, 68060 Mulhouse Cedex, France; tel. 3-89-32-94-40; fax 3-89-32-94-49; internet www.eps.org; f. 1968; aims to promote the advancement of physics in Europe and neighbouring countries by all suitable means; 41 nat. mem. orgs; 6,500 individual mems; 80 assoc. mems; Sec.-Gen. DAVID LEE; publs *European Journal of Physics* (6 a year), *Europhysics News* (6 a year).

European Research Council: Covent Garden Bldg, Pl. Rogier 16, 1049 Brussels; tel. (2) 298-76-31; fax (2) 292-19-75; e-mail erc-press@ec.europa.eu; internet erc.europa .eu; f. 2007; supports investigator-driven frontier research; complements funding activities in Europe; directs scientific strategy, establishes methodologies and procedures; evaluates proposals, scientific reporting and monitoring; Pres. Prof. Dr HELGA NOW-

OTNY (Austria); Vice-Pres. Dr DANIEL ESTÈVE (France); Hon. Pres. Prof. Dr FOTIS C. KAFATOS (UK); Sec. Gen. (vacant); Dir Dr JACK METTHEY.

European Science Foundation: 1 quai Lezay-Marnésia, 67080 Strasbourg Cedex, France; tel. 3-88-76-71-00; fax 3-88-37-05-32; f. 1974; promotes research in all branches of fundamental science and the humanities; advances cooperation in European research; to examine and advise on research and science policy issues; to promote the mobility of research workers and the free flow of information and ideas; to facilitate cooperation in the planning and use of research facilities; to plan and manage collaborative research activities; mems: 78 research-funding agencies from 30 countries; Pres. Prof. IAN HALLIDAY (UK); CEO Prof. MARJA MAKAROW; publ. *ESF Communications* (2 a year).

European Southern Observatory/ Organisation Européenne pour des Recherches Astronomiques dans l'Hémisphère Austral: Karl-Schwarzschild-Str. 2, 85748 Garching bei München, Germany; tel. (89) 320060; fax (89) 3202362; internet www .eso.org; f. 1962; aims: astronomical research in the southern hemisphere, construction and operation of an international observatory in Chile (see under Chile), fostering European cooperation in astronomy; mems: govts of Belgium, Denmark, France, Germany, Italy, The Netherlands, Portugal, Sweden, Switzerland; Dir-Gen. Prof. TIM DE ZEEUW; publ. *The Messenger*.

European Space Agency: 8–10 rue Mario Nikis, 75738 Paris Cedex 15, France; tel. 1-53-69-76-54; fax 1-53-69-75-60; e-mail contact@esa.int; internet www.esa.int; f. 1964, name changed 1975, following merger of ELDO and ESRO, to provide for, and to promote collaboration among, European states in space research and technology and their space applications exclusively for peaceful purposes; provides scientific agencies of the mem. countries with the necessary technical facilities for the carrying out of space experiments, ranging from the study of the near terrestrial environment to that of stellar astronomy; also responsible for a European programme of application satellite projects, including telecommunications and meteorology, also for Spacelab and Ariane Launcher; supports the following establishments: European Space Research and Technology Centre (ESTEC), Noordwijk, Netherlands; European Space Operations Centre (ESOC), Darmstadt, Germany; European Space Research Institute (ESRIN), Frascati, Italy; European Astronaut Centre (EAC), Cologne, Germany; mems: Austria, Belgium, Denmark, Finland, France, Germany, Greece, Ireland, Italy, Luxembourg, Netherlands, Norway, Portugal, Spain, Sweden, Switzerland and UK; Canada is linked by a special cooperation agreement; library: library (ESTEC) of 48,000 vols, 1m. microfiche, 42,000 reports and standards; Dir-Gen. JEAN-JACQUES JORDAIN (France); publs *Bulletin, Connect* (2 a year), *Eurocomp* (1 a year), conference proceedings, scientific and technical reports.

Federation of Arab Scientific Research Councils: Alawayh, POB 13027, Baghdad, Iraq; tel. (1) 5372832; fax (1) 8853923; e-mail fasrc@uruklink.net; f. 1976 to strengthen scientific and technological cooperation and coordination between Arab countries; holds conferences, seminars, workshops and training courses; publishes Directory of Arab Scientific Research Institutions; 15 mem. countries; Sec.-Gen. Dr TAHA TAYIH AL-NAIMI; publs *Computer Research, Proceedings of Scientific Activities*.

Federation of Asian Scientific Academies and Societies (FASAS): c/o Academy of Sciences Malaysia, 902-4 Jalan Tun Ismail, 50480 Kuala Lumpur, Malaysia; tel. (3) 2694-9898; fax (3) 2694-5858; e-mail nasa@akademisains.gov.my; internet www .fasas.com.my; f. 1984 to promote regional cooperation and national and regional self-reliance in science and technology by organizing meetings, training and research programmes, and encouraging exchange of scientists and information; 16 mems (national scientific academies and societies in Afghanistan, Australia, Bangladesh, People's Republic of China, India, Republic of Korea, Malaysia, Nepal, New Zealand, Pakistan, Philippines, Singapore, Sri Lanka, Thailand); Pres. Prof. LEO TAN (Singapore); Sec. Prof. TING-KUEH SOON (Malaysia).

Foundation for International Scientific Coordination/Fondation 'Pour la Science', Centre international de Synthèse: ENS-45, rue d'Ulm, 75005 Paris, France; tel. 1-55-42-83-13; fax 1-55-42-83-19; e-mail fondation.pourlascience.cis@ens.fr; internet www.ehess.fr/acta/synthese; f. 1924; Founder HENRI BERR; Co-Dirs MICHAEL BLAY, ÉRIC BRIAN; publs *Revue de Synthèse* (4 a year), *Revue d'Histoire des Sciences* (4 a year), *Semaines de Synthèse, L'Evolution de l'Humanité*.

Institute of Mathematical Statistics: POB 22718, Beachwood, OH 44122, USA; tel. (216) 295-2340; fax (216) 295-5661; e-mail ims@imstat.org; internet www.imstat .org; f. 1935; 4,000 mems; Pres. THOMAS G. KURTZ; Exec. Sec. ELYSE GUSTAFSON; publs *Annals of Applied Probability* (4 a year), *Annals of Probability, Annals of Statistics* (6 a year), *CBMS Regional Conference Series in Probability and Statistics, IMS Bulletin* (6 a year), *IMS Lecture Notes—Monograph Series, Statistical Science*.

Intergovernmental Oceanographic Commission (IOC) of UNESCO/Commission Océanographique Intergouvernementale de l'UNESCO: c/o UNESCO, 1 rue Miollis, 75015 Paris, France; tel. 1-45-68-39-84; fax 1-45-68-58-10; internet ioc-unesco .org; f. 1960 to promote scientific investigation with a view to learning more about the nature and resources of the oceans through the concerted action of its members; mems: 125 governments; 138 govts mems; Chair. JAVIER ARMANDO VALLADARES (Argentina); Exec. Sec. Dr WENDY WATSON-WRIGHT (Canada); publs *IOC Manuals and Guides, IOC Technical Series, IOC Training Course Reports* (irregular), *IOC Workshop Reports, Summary Reports of Sessions*.

International Academy of Astronautics (IAA)/Académie Internationale d'Astronautique: BP 1268-16, 75766 Paris Cedex 16, France; 6 rue Galilée, 75116 Paris, France; tel. 1-47-23-82-15; fax 1-47-23-82-16; internet www.iaanet.org; f. 1960; aims to foster the development of astronautics for peaceful purposes, recognizing individuals who have distinguished themselves in the field, and provides a programme through which mems can contribute to int. cooperation; liaises with nat. academies of science; developing a multilingual (20 languages) Database; maintains the following cttees: Space Sciences, Int. Space Plans and Policies, Life Sciences, Benefits to Society from Space Activities, Economics of Space Operations, Interstellar Space Exploration, Search for Extraterrestrial Intelligence, Safety and Rescue, Space and Environmental Change, History of Astronautics, Scientific Legal Liaison; mems: 975 in 56 countries; Pres. Prof. E. C. STONE (USA); Vice-Pres Prof. H. CURIEN (France), Prof. K. KASTURIRANGAN (India), Dr Y. N. KOPTEV

(Russia), Dr H. MATSUO (Japan); Sec.-Gen. Dr J. M. CONTANT (France); publs *Acta Astronautica* (12 a year), *Proceedings of Symposia*.

International Association for Mathematics and Computers in Simulation/ Association Internationale pour les Mathématiques et Calculateurs en Simulation: c/o Dept of Computer Science, Hill Center, Busch Campus, Rutgers University, New Brunswick, NJ 08903, USA; internet www.research.rutgers.edu/~imacs; f. 1955 to advance the study of general methods for modelling and computer simulation of dynamic systems; Pres. R. VICHNEVETSKY (USA); Sec.-Gen. R. BEAUWENS (Belgium); publs *Applied Numerical Mathematics* (6 a year), *Mathematics and Computers in Simulation*.

International Association for Plant Physiology (IAPP): USDA—URS, Plant Biology Dept, Univeristy of Illinois, 190 ERML, 1201 W. Gregory Drive Urbana, Illinois, USA 61801-3838; e-mail d-ort@life .uiuc.edu; f. 1955 to promote the development of plant physiology at the international level, especially collaboration between developed and developing nations, through international congresses and symposia and by the publication of plant physiology matters and the promotion of cooperation between national and international associations and scientific journals; represents plant physiologists on the IUBS; mems: 40 national societies of plant physiology and related international groups; Pres. Dr DONALD ORT; Sec.-Gen. Dr D. GRAHAM.

International Association for Plant Taxonomy/Association Internationale pour la Taxonomie Végétale: Bureau for Plant Taxonomy and Nomenclature, Institute of Botany, Univ. of Vienna, Rennweg 14, 1030 Vienna, Austria; tel. (1) 427754098; fax (1) 427754099; e-mail office@iapt-taxon.org; internet www.iapt-taxon.org; f. 1950 to promote the development of plant taxonomy and encourage contacts between people and institutes interested in this work; mems: institutes and individuals in 87 countries; Exec. Sec. Dr ALESSANDRA RICCIUTI LAMONEA (Austria); publs *Regnum vegetabile* (irregular), *Taxon* (24 a year).

International Association for the Physical Sciences of the Ocean (IAPSO)/ Association Internationale des Sciences Physiques de l'Océan: POB 820440, Vicksburg, MS 39182-0440, USA; tel. (601) 636-1363; fax (601) 629-9640; internet www .olympus.net/iapso; f. 1919 to promote the study of scientific problems relating to the oceans, chiefly by the aid of mathematics, physics and chemistry; to initiate, facilitate and coordinate research; to provide for discussion, comparison and publication; 58 mem. states; Pres. Prof. SHIRO IMAWAKI (Japan); Sec.-Gen. Dr FRED E. CAMFIELD (USA); publs *Procès-Verbaux* (every 2–4 years), *Publications Scientifiques* (irregular).

International Association for Vegetation Science/Association Internationale pour l'Etude de la Végétation: c/o Dr J. H. J. Schaminée, Alterra, Green World Research, Postbus 47, 6700 AA Wageningen, Netherlands; tel. (317) 477914; fax (317) 424988; e-mail joop.schaminee@wur.nl; internet www.iavs.org; f. 1937; aims for the development of phytosociology; 1,300 mems; Pres. Prof. E. O. BOX (USA); Sec. Dr J. H. J. SCHAMINÉE; publs *Applied Vegetation Science*, *Journal of Vegetation Science*, *Phytocoenologia*.

International Association of Biological Oceanography: Leigh Marine Laboratory, Univ. of Auckland, POB 349, Warkworth,

New Zealand; e-mail m.costello@auckland.ac .nz; internet www.iabo.org; f. 1966 to promote the study of the biology of the sea; attached to Int. Union of Biological Sciences; Pres. Dr ANNALIES PIERROT-BULTS (Netherlands); Sec.-Gen. Dr MARK J. COSTELLO (New Zealand).

International Association of Geodesy/ Association Internationale de Géodésie: University of Copenhagen, Dept of Geophysics, Juliane Maries Vej 30, 2100 Copenhagen Ø, Denmark; tel. 35-32-06-00; fax 35-36-53-57; e-mail iag@gfy.ku.dk; internet www.gfy .ku.dk/~iag; f. 1922 to promote the study of all scientific problems of geodesy and encourage geodetic research; to promote and coordinate int. cooperation in this field; to publish results; a mem. asscn of IUGG; mems: national cttees in 78 countries; Pres. Prof. G. BEUTLER; Sec.-Gen. Dr C. C. TSCHERNING; publs *Journal of Geodesy* (12 a year), *Travaux de l'AIG* (every 4 years).

International Association of Geomagnetism and Aeronomy (IAGA)/Association Internationale de Géomagnétisme et d'Aéronomie: c/o Prof. Mioara Mandea, Université Paris Diderot, Institut de Physique du Globe de Paris Géophysique spatiale et planétaire, Bâtiment Lamarck Case 7011, 5 rue Thomas Mann, 75205. Paris Cedex 13, France; tel. 1-57-27-84-84; fax 1-57-27-84-82; e-mail iaga_sg@gfz-potsdam.de; f. 1919; study of magnetism and aeronomy of the earth and other bodies of the solar system, and of the interplanetary medium and its interaction with these bodies; mems: countries that adhere to the Int. Union of Geodesy and Geophysics are eligible; Pres. Dr EIGIL FRIIS-CHRISTENSEN (Denmark); Sec.-Gen. Prof. MIOARA MANDEA (France); publs *IAGA Bulletins* (irregular), *Geomagnetic Data* (1 a year), *IAGA News* (1 a year).

International Association of Hydrological Sciences/Association Internationale des Sciences Hydrologiques: c/o Dr Pierre Hubert, UMR Sisyphe, Université Pierre et Marie Curie, case 105, 4 Pl. Jussieu, 75252 Paris Cedex 05, France; tel. 1-64-69-47-40; fax 1-64-69-47-03; e-mail pjy.hubert@free.frr; internet iahs.info; f. 1922; part of IUGG; aims to promote the study of hydrology, to provide means for discussion, comparison and publication of research findings, and the initiation and coordination of research requiring int. cooperation; organizes general assemblies, symposia, etc.; 84 national cttees; Pres. Prof. KUNIYOSHI TAKEUCHI (Japan); Sec.-Gen. Dr PIERRE HUBERT (France); publ. *Hydrological Sciences Journal* (8 a year).

International Association of Meteorology and Atmospheric Sciences (IAMAS)/Association Internationale de Météorologie et de Sciences de l'Atmosphère: c/o Dr Hans Volkert, Institut für Physik der Atmosphäre, Deutsches Zentrum für Luft- und Raumfahrt, DLR-Oberpfaffenhofen, 82234 Wessling, Germany; tel. (8153) 28-2570; fax (8153) 28-1841; e-mail hans .volkert@dlr.de; internet www.iamas.org; f. 1919 to organize research symposia and coordinate research in atmospheric science fields; an Association of the International Union of Geodesy and Geophysics; Pres. Prof. WU, GUOXIONG (China); Sec.-Gen. Dr HANS VOLKERT (Germany); publ. *IAMAP Assembly Proceedings* (every 2 years).

International Association of Sedimentologists: c/o Dr José-Pedro Calvo, Dpto Petrología y Geoquímica, Fac. Ciencias Geológicas, Univ. Complutense, 28040 Madrid, Spain; tel. 91-394-49-05; fax 91-544-25-35; e-mail info@iasnet.org; internet www.iasnet .org; f. 1952; 2,000 mems; Pres. Prof. FINN

SURLYK (Denmark); Sec.-Gen. Dr JOSÉ-PEDRO CALVO; publ. *Sedimentology* (6 a year).

International Society of Limnology/ Association internationale de Limnologie Théorique et Appliquée: c/o Denise L. Johnson, SIL Business Services Coordinator, Univ. of NC, Chapel Hill, NC 27599-7431, USA;located at 135 Dauer Dr., ESE, 148 Rosenau Hall, Chapel Hill, NC 27599-7431 USA; tel. (336) 376-9362; fax (336) 376-8825; e-mail denisej@email.unc.edu; internet www .limnology.org; f. 1922; 3,100 mems; Pres. Prof. Dr BRIAN MOSS (UK); Gen. Sec. and Treas. Prof. Dr MORTEN SØNDERGAARD (Denmark); publs *Inland Waters*, *Verhandlungen*.

International Association of Volcanology and Chemistry of the Earth's Interior (IAVCEI)/Association Internationale de Volcanologie et de Chimie de l'Intérieur de la Terre: c/o S. R. McNutt, Alaska Volcano Observatory, Geophysical Institute UAF, POB 757320, Fairbanks, AK 99775, USA; tel. (907) 474-7131; fax (907) 474-5618; e-mail steve@giseis.alaska.edu; internet www.iavcei.org; f. 1919 to promote scientific investigation and discussion on volcanology and in those aspects of petrology and geochemistry relating to the composition of the interior of the Earth; holds scientific general assemblies; sponsors workshops; participates in IUGG general assemblies; 840 individual mems and nat. correspondents; Pres. Prof. ODED NAVON (Israel); Sec.-Gen. Prof. STEPHEN R. McNUTT (USA); publs *Bulletin of Volcanology*, *Catalogue of the Active Volcanoes of the World*, *Proceedings in Volcanology*.

International Association of Wood Anatomists/Association Internationale des Anatomistes du Bois: c/o Nationaal Herbarium Nederland, Universiteit Leiden Branch, POB 9514, 2300 RA Leiden, Netherlands; fax (71) 527-3511; internet www .kuleuven.ac.be/bio/sys/iawa; f. 1931 for the purpose of study, documentation and exchange of information on the anatomy of wood; 600 mems in 60 countries; Exec. Sec. Dr REGIS B. MILLER (USA); publ. *IAWA Journal* (4 a year).

International Astronautical Federation (IAF)/Fédération Internationale d'Astronautique: 8–10 rue Mario-Nikis, 75015 Paris, France; located at: 94 bis ave de Suffren, 75015 Paris, France; tel. 1-45-67-42-60; fax 1-42-73-21-20; internet www .iafastro.com; f. 1950 to foster the development of astronautics for peaceful purposes at nat. and int. levels; the IAF created the International Academy of Astronautics (IAA), the International Institute of Space Law (IISL) (for information on these bodies, see elsewhere in this chapter), and cttees on activities and membership; Allan D. Emil Award, finances, publications, liaison with int. organizations and developing nations, education, student activities, SYRE, Solar Sail, astrodynamics, Earth observations, satellite communications, natural disaster reduction, life sciences, microgravity science and processes, space exploration, space power, space propulsion, space transportation, space stations, space systems, and materials and structures; annual student awards; mems: 137 nat. astronautical societies in 45 countries; Pres. JAMES V. ZIMMERMAN (USA); Vice-Pres MUKUND RAO (India), STUART W. THOMSON (USA), YUAN JIA-JUN (China), ROBERT C. PARKINSON (UK), YASUNORI MATOGAWA (Japan), VICTOR REGLERO (Spain), ANNE-MARIE MAINGUY (France), VIRENDRA K. JHA (Canada), ANATOLY I. GRIGORIEV (Russia), KLAUS BERGE (Germany); Exec. Dir YVES BEGUIN; publ. *Proceedings* (of Annual Congresses).

International Atomic Energy Agency (IAEA): Vienna International Centre, POB 100, 1400 Vienna, Austria; tel. (1) 2600; fax (1) 2600-7; e-mail info@iaea.org; internet www.iaea.org; f. 1957 by 81 nations; serves as global focal point for nuclear cooperation; assists its mem. States, in context of social and economic goals, in planning for and using nuclear science and technology for various peaceful purposes, incl. generation of electricity, and facilitates transfer of such technology and knowledge in a sustainable manner to developing mem. States; develops nuclear safety standards and, based on these standards, promotes achievement and maintenance of high levels of safety in applications of nuclear energy and protection of human health and environment against ionizing radiation; verifies through its inspection system that States comply with their commitments, under Non-Proliferation Treaty and other non-proliferation agreements, to use nuclear material and facilities only for peaceful purposes; library of 60,000 vols, 40,000 technical reports, 17,000 electronic resources, 950 audiovisual items, 2,300 journals, 1.2m. IAEA, UN and Specialised Agencies documents; 151 mem. states; Dir-Gen. YUKIYA AMANO; publs *Atomic Energy Review (AER)* (4 a year), *IAEA Bulletin* (2 a year, printed and online, www.iaea.org/publications/magazines/bulletin/bull501), *INIS Atomindex* (24 a year), *INIS Database* (www.iaea.org/inisnkm/inis/basis/subscr0.htm), *Meetings on Atomic Energy* (4 a year, online, www.iaea.org/cgi-bin/maeps.page.pl/tableofcontents.htm), *Nuclear Fusion* (12 a year).

International Biometric Society (IBS)/Société Internationale de Biométrie: 1444 I St, NW, Suite 700, Washington, DC 20005, USA; tel. (202) 712-9049; fax (202) 216-9646; e-mail ibs@bostrom.com; internet www.tibs.org; f. 1947; dedicated to the development and application of statistical and mathematical theory and methods in the biosciences; 19 regional organizations and 19 national groups; affiliated to the International Statistical Institute and the World Health Organization, and constitutes the section of Biometry of the International Union of Biological Sciences; mems: 5,200 in more than 70 countries; Pres. GEERT MOLENBERGHS (Belgium); Exec. Dir CLAIRE SHANLEY (USA); publs *Biometrics* (4 a year), *Biometric Bulletin* (4 a year), *Journal of Agricultural, Biological and Environmental Statistics* (4 a year).

International Bureau of Weights and Measures/Bureau International des Poids et Mesures: Pavillon de Breteuil, 92312 Sèvres Cedex, France; tel. (1) 45-07-70-70; fax (1) 45-34-20-21; internet www.bipm.org; f. 1875 for the preservation of standards of the Int. System of Units (SI) and worldwide unification of the units of measurement; determination of nat. standards; precision measurements in physics; establishment of the int. atomic time-scale; 54 mem. states; Pres. Dr B. INGLIS (Australia); Sec. Dr R. KAARLS (Netherlands); Dir Dr M. KÜHNE; publs *Comptes Rendus des Conférences Générales* (every 4 years), *Metrologia*, *Procès-verbaux* (1 a year), *Sessions des dix Comités consultatifs auprès du Comité International* (irregular).

International Centre of Insect Physiology and Ecology: POB 30772-00100, Nairobi, Kenya; tel. (20) 861686; fax (20) 860110; internet www.icipe.org; f. 1970 to develop, through research, plant-borne, human and animal disease management and control strategies, and to promote research and the conservation of arthropods; library of 7,500 vols, 3,500 volumes bound

periodicals, 200 periodicals; Chair. Prof. PETER ESBJERG (Denmark); Dir-Gen. and CEO Dr HANS R. HERREN; publ. *Insect Science and Its Application*.

International Commission for Optics (ICO)/Commission Internationale d'Optique: c/o Angela M. Guzman, Research Assoc. Prof. Physics, Dept Florida Atlantic Univ. 777 Glades Rd, 33431 Boca Raton, USA; tel. (561) 313-8204; fax (561) 297-2662; e-mail angela.guzman@fau.edu; internet www.ico-optics.org; f. 1948; contributes on int. basis to the progress of theoretical and instrumental optics and its application, through confs, colloquia, summer schools, etc.; promotes int. agreement on nomenclature, specifications; 51 mem countries, 6 Int. Soc. mems; Pres. Prof. MARÍA L. CALVO (Spain); Sec.-Gen. Prof. ANGELA GUZMAN (USA).

International Commission for the Scientific Exploration of the Mediterranean Sea/Commission Internationale pour l'Exploration Scientifique de la Mer Méditerranée (CIESM): 16 blvd de Suisse, 98000 Monaco; tel. 93-30-38-79; fax 92-16-11-95; e-mail ciesm@ciesm.org; internet www.ciesm.org; f. 1919 for scientific exploration of the Mediterranean Sea, the study of physical and chemical oceanography, marine geosciences, living resources, marine biodiversity, marine biotechnology, coastal environment; 23 mem. states, 2,500 individual mems; Pres. HSH The Prince ALBERT OF MONACO; Dir-Gen. Prof. FRÉDÉRIC BRIAND; Sec.-Gen. Prof. FRANÇOIS DOUMENGE; publ. *Congress Proceedings* (every 3 years).

International Commission on Zoological Nomenclature/Commission Internationale de Nomenclature Zoologique: c/o The Natural History Museum, Cromwell Rd, London, SW7 5BD, UK; tel. (20) 7942-5653; e-mail iczn@nhm.ac.uk; internet www.iczn.org; f. 1895; the Commission, formerly a standing organ of the Int. Zoological Congresses, now reports to the Gen. Assembly of IUBS; the Commission has judicial powers to determine all matters relating to the interpretation of the *International Code of Zoological Nomenclature* and also plenary powers to suspend the operation of the *Code* where strict application would lead to confusion and instability of nomenclature; the Commission is responsible also for maintaining and developing the *Official Lists of Names in Zoology* and the *Official Indexes of Rejected and Invalid Names in Zoology*; Pres. Prof. D. J. BROTHERS (South Africa); Exec. Sec. Dr E. MICHEL (UK); publ. *Bulletin of Zoological Nomenclature*.

International Confederation for Thermal Analysis and Calorimetry (ICTAC): c/o Prof. M. E. Brown, Chemistry Dept, Rhodes University, Grahamstown 6140, South Africa; tel. (46) 6038254; fax (46) 6225109; e-mail m.brown@ru.ac.za; internet www.ictac.org; f. 1968; 600 mems in 40 countries, 5,000 affiliate mems in 20 affiliated regional and national societies and groups; coordinates these groups and supplies information on their scientific activities; supports national regional seminars and symposia; quadrennial int. conference; Pres. Dr JEAN ROUQUEROL (France); Sec. Prof. MICHAEL E. BROWN (South Africa); publ. *News* (2 a year).

International Council for the Exploration of the Sea (ICES)/Conseil International pour l'Exploration de la Mer: H. C. Andersens Blvd 44-46, 1553 Copenhagen V, Denmark; tel. 33-38-67-00; fax 33-93-42-15; e-mail info@ices.dk; internet www.ices.dk; f. 1902 to promote and encourage research and investigations for the study of

the sea, particularly those related to its living resources; area of interest: the Atlantic Ocean (primarily the N Atlantic) and its adjacent seas; mems: 20 nat. govts; Pres. MICHAEL M. SINCLAIR (Canada); Gen. Sec. GERD HUBOLD; publs *ICES Cooperative Research Reports*, *ICES Fisheries Statistics*, *ICES Journal of Marine Science*, *ICES Marine Science Symposia*, *ICES Techniques in Marine Environmental Sciences*, *Identification Leaflets for Diseases and Parasites of Fish and Shellfish*, *Identification Leaflets for Plankton*, *ICES Insight*.

International Earth Rotation and Reference Systems Service (IERS): Bundesamt für Kartographie und Geodäsie, Richard-Strauss-Allee 11, 60598 Frankfurt am Main, Germany; tel. (69) 6333273; fax (69) 6333425; internet www.iers.org; f. 1988 to replace Int. Polar Motion Service and the earth-rotation section of the Int. Time Bureau; organized jtly by the IAU and IUGG; responsible for defining and maintaining a conventional terrestrial reference system based on observing stations that use the high-precision techniques of space geodesy; defining and maintaining a conventional celestial reference system based on extragalactic radio sources, and relating it to other celestial reference systems; determining the earth orientation parameters connecting these systems; organizing operational activities for observation and data analysis, collecting and archiving appropriate data and results, and disseminating the results; Dir of Central Bureau Dr BERND RICHTER; publ. *IERS Technical Notes*.

International Federation for Cell Biology/Fédération Internationale de Biologie Cellulaire: c/o Dr Denys Wheatley, Hilton College, MG7, Hilton Pl., Aberdeen, AB24 4FA, UK; tel. (1224) 274173; e-mail pat028@abdn.ac.uk; internet www.ifcbiol.org; f. 1972; sponsors an int. congress every 4 years; Pres. Dr CHENG-WEN WU (Taiwan); Sec.-Gen. Dr DENYS WHEATLEY; publ. *Cell Biology International*.

International Federation of Societies for Microscopy/Fédération Internationale des Sociétés de Microscopie: c/o Prof. C. Barry Carter, Dept of Chemical, Materials and Biomolecular Engineering, 191 Auditorium Rd, Unit 3222, Univ. of Connecticut, Storrs, CT 06269-3222, USA; tel. (860) 486-4020; fax (860) 486-2959; e-mail cbcarter@engr.uconn.edu; internet www.ifsm.umn.edu; f. 1955; mems: representative orgs of 39 countries; Pres. Prof. D. COCKAYNE; Sec. Prof. C. B. CARTER.

International Food Information Service: IFIS Publishing, Lane End House, Shinfield, Reading, RG2 9BB, UK; tel. (118) 988-3895; fax (118) 988-5065; e-mail ifis@ifis.org; internet www.ifis.org; f. 1968; governed by CAB International (UK), Institute of Food Technologists (USA), the Centrum voor Landbouwpublikaties en Landbouwdocumentatie (Netherlands) and the Bundesministerium für Landwirtschaft Ernährung und Forsten (represented by Deutsche Landwirtschafts-Gesellschaft eV) in Germany, for the promotion of education and research in food science and technology; Gen. Man. J. SELMAN; publs *Food Science Profiles* (12 a year, in print and on diskette), *Food Science and Technology Abstracts* (12 a year, in print, online, CD-ROM), *Viticulture and Enology Abstracts* (4 a year, in print and online).

International Foundation of the High-Altitude Research Stations, Jungfraujoch and Gornergrat/Fondation internationale des stations scientifiques du Jungfraujoch et du Gornergrat: 5

Sidlerstr, 3012 Bern, Switzerland; tel. 316314052; fax 316314405; e-mail louise .wilson@space.unibe.ch; internet www .ifjungo.ch; f. 1931; Dir Prof. E. FLUECKIGER.

International Genetics Federation: c/o GSA 9560 Rockville Pike, Bethesda, MD 20814-3998, USA; tel. (301) 634-7300; fax (301) 634-7310; e-mail smarts@genetics-gsa .org; internet www.intergenetics.org; f. 1968 to encourage understanding, cooperation and friendship among geneticists worldwide and to plan and support int. congresses of genetics; 37 mem. countries; Exec. Dir Dr SHERRY MARTS (USA).

International Geological Congress/Congrès Géologique International: POB 2694 Solli, 0204 Oslo, Norway; e-mail secretariat@ 33igc.org; internet www.33igc.org; f. 1878 to contribute to the advancement of investigations relating to the study of the Earth and other planets, considered from theoretical and practical points of view; the congress is held every 4 years; Pres. Prof. ARNE BJØR-LYKKE; Sec.-Gen. Prof. ANDERS SOLHEIM; publs *Extended Abstracts*, *General Proceedings*.

International Glaciological Society: Scott Polar Research Institute, Lensfield Rd, Cambridge, CB2 1ER, UK; tel. (1223) 355974; fax (1223) 354931; e-mail igsoc@ igsoc.org; internet www.igsoc.org; f. 1936 to encourage interest in and encourage research into the scientific and technical problems of snow and ice in all countries; sponsors int. symposia; 850 mems; Pres. Prof. ERIC BRUN (Switzerland); Sec.-Gen. MAGNÚS MÁR MAGNÚSSON; publs *Annals of Glaciology* (4 a year), *Ice* (news bulletin, 3 a year), *Journal of Glaciology* (6 a year).

International Hydrographic Organization (IHO)/Organisation Hydrographique Internationale: BP 445, 4 quai Antoine 1er, Monte Carlo, 98011 MonacoCedex; tel. 93-10-81-00; fax 93-10-81-40; e-mail info@ihb.mc; internet www.iho.int; f. 1921 to establish a close and permanent association among the hydrographic offices of its mem. states; to coordinate the activities of the national hydrographic offices of mem. states in order to render maritime navigation easier and safer; to obtain uniformity in nautical charts and documents; to encourage the adoption of the best methods of conducting hydrographic surveys and improvement in the theory and practice of hydrography; to encourage surveying in those areas where accurate charts are lacking; to encourage coordination of hydrographic surveys with relevant oceanographic activities and to provide for cooperation between the IHO and international organizations in the fields of maritime safety and oceanography; to extend and facilitate the application of oceanographic knowledge for the benefit of navigators; 80 mem. states; library of 750 vols, 100 periodicals, 26,000 charts published by member states; Pres. Vice-Adm. ALEXANDROS MARATOS (Greece); Dirs Capt. ROBERT WARD (Australia), Capt. HUGO GORZIGLIA (Chile); publ. online publications (see website).

International Institute for Applied Systems Analysis (IIASA): Schlossplatz 1, 2361 Laxenburg, Austria; tel. (2236) 807; fax (2236) 71313; e-mail inf@iiasa.ac.at; internet www.iiasa.ac.at; f. 1972 on the initiative of the USA and the USSR; nongovernmental research org.; research into issues of global environmental, economic, technological, and social change in the 21st century; orgs from 19 countries; Chair. Prof. Dr PETER LEMKE; Dir Prof. DETLOF VON WINTERFELDT; publ. *Options* (2 a year).

International Institute of Seismology and Earthquake Engineering: Building Research Institute, Ministry of Construction, 1 Tatehara, Tsukuba-shi, Ibaraki Prefecture 305-0802, Japan; tel. (298) 79-0680; fax (298) 64-6777; e-mail iisee@kenken.go.jp; internet iisee.kenken.go.jp; f. 1962 to carry out training and research works on seismology and earthquake engineering for the purpose of fostering these research activities in the developing countries, and undertakes survey, research, guidance and analysis of information on earthquakes and their related matters; 12 mems; Dir TOSHIBUMI FUKUTA; publs *Bulletin of IISEE* (1 a year), *Individual Studies by Participants at the IISEE* (1 a year), *Year Book*.

International Mineralogical Association (IMA): c/o Maryse Ohnenstetter, CNRS-CRPG, 15 rue Notre Dame des Pauvres, BP 20, 54501 Vandoeuvre-lès-Nancy Cedex, France; tel. 3-83-59-42-46; fax 3-83-51-17-98; e-mail mohnen@crpg.cnrs-nancy.fr; internet www.ima-mineralogy.org; f. 1958 to further int. cooperation in the mineralogical sciences; organizes meetings and field excursions; maintains 7 commissions and 5 working groups, which examine and report on certain aspects of mineralogical practice; Commission on New Minerals, Nomenclature and Classification regularly reports on the acceptance of new minerals, and on mineral classification; mems: 38 mineralogical societies or groups in 38 countries; Pres. Prof. TAKAMITSU YAMANAKA (Japan); Sec. MARYSE OHNENSTETTER; publ. *World Directories* (Mineralogists; Mineral Collections).

International Organization of Legal Metrology/Organisation Internationale de Métrologie Légale: 11 rue Turgot, 75009 Paris, France; tel. 1 48-78-12-82; fax 1 42-82-17-27; internet www.oiml.org; f. 1955; documentation and information centre on methods of verifying and checking legal measurements, to study ways of harmonization and to determine the general principles of legal metrology; mems: governments of 59 countries and 54 corresp. mems; Pres. ALAN E. JOHNSTON (acting) (Canada); Dir JEAN-FRANÇOIS MAGAÑA; publs *Bulletin* (4 a year), *International Recommendations and Documents*.

International Ornithological Congress/Congrès International Ornithologique: c/o Prof. Dr Dominique G. Homberger, Dept of Biological Sciences, 202 Life Sciences Bldg, Louisiana State Univ., Baton Rouge, LA 70803-1715, USA; tel. (225) 578-1747; fax (225) 578-2597; internet www.i-o-c.org; f. 1884; int. congress every 4 years; Pres. Prof. Dr JOHN WINGFIELD (USA); Permanent Sec. Prof. Dr DOMINIQUE G. HOMBERGER.

International Palaeontological Association: Palaeontological Institute, Room 121, Lindley Hall, 1475 Jayhawk Blvd, Univ. of Kansas, Lawrence, KA 66045, USA; tel. (785) 864-3338; fax (785) 864-5276; e-mail rmaddocks@uh.edu; internet ipa.geo.ukans .edu; f. 1933 following the meeting of the Int. Geological Congress; affiliated to the Int. Union of Geological Sciences and the Int. Union of Biological Sciences; meets every 4 years at Int. Geological Congress; mems: nat. orgs, research groups; Pres. RICHARD ALDRIDGE (UK); Sec.-Gen. ROSALIE MADDOCKS (USA); publs *Directory of Palaeontologists of the World*, *IPA Fossil Collections of the World*, *Lethaia*.

International Permafrost Association: c/o Dr Hugues Lantuit Alfred, Wegener Institute for Polar and Marine Research, Telefrafenberg A43, 14473 Potsdam, Germany; tel. (331) 288-2162; fax (331) 288-2188; e-mail contact@ipa-permafrost.org; internet ipa-permafrost.org; f. 1983; promotes cooperation among people, nat. and int. orgs engaged in scientific investigation and engineering work on permafrost; outreach activities incl. coordinating int. networks e.g. Global Terrestrial Network for Permafrost (GTN-P) and International Network of Permafrost Observatories (INPO) and Permafrost Young Researchers Network; working groups; 26 mem. countries; Pres. Prof. HANS-W. HUBBERTEN (Germany); Vice-Pres Prof. HANNE H. CHRISTIANSEN (Norway), Prof. ANTONI G. LEWKOWICZ (Canada); publs *Frozen Ground* (Bulletin, 1 a year), contributes a report twice a year in the journal *Permafrost and Periglacial Processes*.

International Society for Human and Animal Mycology (ISHAM)/Société Internationale de Mycologie Humaine et Animale: c/o Dr Malcolm Richardson, Dept of Bacteriology and Immunology, Haartman Institute, University of Helsinki, Haartmaninkatu 3, POB 21, 00014 Helsinki, Finland; tel. (9) 191-26894; fax (9) 26382; e-mail malcolm.richardson@helsinki.fi; internet www.isham.org; f. 1954 to encourage the practice and study of all aspects of medical and veterinary mycology; 990 mems in 74 countries; Pres. Dr DAVID W. WARNOCK (USA); Gen. Sec. Dr MALCOLM RICHARDSON; publs *ISHAM Mycoses Newsletter* (2 a year), *Medical Mycology* (1 a year, in 6 parts).

International Society for Tropical Ecology: c/o Botany Dept, Banaras Hindu University, Varanasi 5, India; tel. (542) 2368399; fax (542) 2368174; f. 1956 to promote and develop the science of ecology in the tropics in the service of man; to publish a journal to aid ecologists in the tropics in communication of their findings; and to hold symposia from time to time to summarize the state of knowledge in particular of general fields of tropical ecology; mems: 500; Pres. Prof. PETER G. MURPHY; Sec. Prof. J. S. SINGH; publ. *Tropical Ecology* (2 a year).

International Society of Biometeorology: c/o Dr Scott Greene, Department of Geography, University of Oklahoma, Norman, OK 73071, USA; tel. (405) 325-4319; fax (405) 447-8455; e-mail jgreene@ou.edu; internet www.biometeorology.org; f. 1956; aims to unite biometeorologists working in the fields of agricultural, botanical, cosmic, entomological, forestry, human, veterinary, zoological and other branches of biometeorology; 243 individual mems in 44 countries; Pres. Dr IAN BURTON (Canada); Sec.-Gen. Dr SCOTT GREENE; publs *Biometeorology Bulletin* (2 a year), *International Journal of Biometeorology* (4 a year), *Progress in Biometeorology*.

International Society of Cryptozoology: POB 43070, Tucson, AZ 85733, USA; located at: Dept of Zoological Collections, International Wildlife Museum, 4800 W. Gates Pass Rd, Tucson, AZ 85745, USA; tel. (520) 884-8369; fax (520) 884-8369; internet www .internationalsocietyofcryptozoology.org; f. 1982 to serve as focal point for the investigation, analysis, publication, and discussion of all matters related to animals of unexpected form or size, or unexpected occurrence in time or space, and to encourage scientific examination of all evidence related to these matters; 800 mems; Pres. Prof. CHRISTINE M. JANIS (acting) (USA); Sec. J. RICHARD GREENWELL (USA); publ. *Cryptozoology* (1 a year).

International Society of Developmental Biologists: c/o Prof. Ben Scheres, Dept of Molecular Cell Biology, Utrecht University, Padualaan 8, 3584 CH Utrecht, Netherlands; tel. (30) 2533133; fax (30) 2513655; internet www1.elsevier.com/homepage/sah/isdb/ f. 1911 as Int. Institute of Embryology; to promote study of developmental biology and to promote int. cooperation among researchers in this field; Developmental Biology Section of the Int. Union of Biological Sciences (*q.v.*); mems: 900 individual, 7 corporate; Pres. Prof. EDWARD M. DE ROBERTIS (USA); Int. Sec. Prof. BEN SCHERES.

International Society of Electrochemistry: rue de Sebeillon 9B, 1004 Lausanne, Switzerland; tel. 216483974; fax 216483975; e-mail info@ise-online.org; internet www.ise-online.org; f. 1949; serves worldwide electrochemical community and that of related disciplines through advancement of electrochemical science and technology, dissemination of scientific and technological knowledge, and promotion of int. cooperation; 2,700 mems in 70 countries; Sec.-Gen. SHARON ROSCOE (Canada); Pres. Prof. Dr M. ORAZEM (USA); publ. *Electrochimica Acta*.

International Society of Exposure Analysis: c/o JSI Research and Training Institute, 44 Farnsworth St, Boston, MA 02210-1211, USA; tel. (617) 482-9485; fax (617) 482-0617; e-mail iseamail@jsi.com; internet www.iseaweb.org; f. 1989 to foster and advance the science of exposure analysis relating to environmental contaminants, both for human populations and ecosystems; holds annual conferences; 400 mems; Pres. Dr CLIFFORD WEISEL; Sec. Dr NATALIE FREEMAN; publ. *Journal of Exposure Science and Environmental Epidemiology* (6 a year).

International Statistical Institute/Institut International de Statistique: Henri Faasdreef 312, POB 24070, 2490 AB The Hague, Netherlands; tel. (70) 3375737; fax (70) 3860025; e-mail isi@cbs.nl; internet isi .cbs.nl; f. 1885; autonomous soc. devoted to the devt and improvement of statistical methods and their application worldwide; provides a forum for the int. exchange of knowledge between mems, and aims to mobilize mems' expertise to play an effective role in the practical solution of global problems; administers int. statistical education programme, incl. statistical education centre in Kolkata, India, and Indian Statistical Institute; conducts statistical research to undertake operational activities in the field of statistics that help to improve the data used in planning and policy formation, to the benefit of the countries concerned; to advance integration of statistics and promote appropriate use of statistical methods in different socio-cultural settings; 2,020 elected mems, also 11 hon., 145 ex-officio, 65 corporate; Pres. JEF TEUGELS (Belgium); Dir Permanent Office ADA VAN KRIMPEN; publs *Bernoulli Journal* (4 a year), *International Statistical Review/Short Book Reviews* (3 a year).

International Union for Quaternary Research (INQUA): c/o Prof. Peter Coxon, Dept of Geography, Museum Bldg, Trinity College, Dublin 2, Ireland; tel. (1) 896-1213; e-mail pcoxon@tcd.ie; internet www.inqua .tcd.ie; f. 1928 Full Scientific Union Member of ICSU; atmospheric sciences, climate change, geography, geology, ocean science, prehistory, palaeontology, palynology, pedology, stratigraphy; 50 mem. countries; Pres. Exec. Comm. Prof. ALLAN CHIVAS (Australia); Sec.-Gen. Prof. PETER COXON; publs *Proceedings of Congresses*, *Quaternary International*.

International Union for the Study of Social Insects/Union Internationale pour l'Etude des Insectes Sociaux: c/o Dr M. Brown, Dept of Zoology, Trinity College Dublin, Dublin 2, Ireland; e-mail wolfgang.h .kirchner@ruhr-uni-bochum.de; internet www.iussi.org; f. 1951; mems: 500 individuals from 24 countries; comprises 7 regional and national sections; Pres. WALTER TSCHINKEL; Sec.-Gen. WOLFGANG H. KIRCHNER; publs *Congress Proceedings*, *Insectes sociaux*.

International Union of Speleology/Union Internationale de Spéléologie: c/o Institute of Karst Research, Titov trg 2, Postojna, Slovenia; internet www.uis-speleo .org; f. 1965; karstology, speleology; 60 mem. countries; Pres. ANDREW JAMES EAVIS (Great Britain); Sec.-Gen. Dr FADI NADER (Lebanon); publs *Bulletin* (1 or 2 a year), *International Journal of Speleology* (1 a year), *Speleological Abstracts* (1 a year).

IUCN, the International Union for Conservation of Nature/UICN, l'Union internationale pour la conservation de la Nature/La UICN, la Unión Internacional para la Conservacion de la Naturaleza: Rue Mauverney 28, 1196 Gland, Switzerland; tel. 229990000; fax 229990002; e-mail mail@iucn.org; internet www.iucn.org; f. 1948 to influence, encourage and assist socs worldwide to conserve the integrity and diversity of nature and to ensure that any use of natural resources is equitable and ecologically sustainable; biodiversity, climate change, energy, human livelihoods and greening the world economy by supporting scientific research, managing field projects all over the world, and bringing governments, NGOs, the UN and companies together to develop policy, laws and best practice; mems: 1,000 mems (govt agencies, NGOs, affiliate orgs and individual scientists) in 160 countries; Pres. ASHOK KHOSLA (India); Dir-Gen. JULIA MARTON-LEFÈVRE (Switzerland); publs *World Conservation* (in English, French and Spanish), *Red Lists: Environmental Policy and Law Papers*, *Best Policy Guidelines*.

NORDITA (Nordic Institute for Theoretical Physics): Roslagstullsbacken 23, 106 91 Stockholm, Sweden; tel. (8) 553-788-81; fax (8) 553-784-04; e-mail info@nordita.org; internet www.nordita.org; f. 1957 as the Nordic Institute for Theoretical Atomic Physics in Copenhagen, Denmark, under the Nordic Council of Ministers, moved to Stockholm, Sweden, in 2007; inter-governmental research institute of Denmark, Finland, Iceland, Norway and Sweden; run jointly by the Royal Institute of Technology (KTH) and Stockholm Univ.; research in astrophysics, condensed matter physics and subatomic physics; Dir LÁRUS THORLACIUS.

OECD Nuclear Energy Agency (NEA)/Agence de l'OCDE pour l'Energie Nucléaire: Le Seine St-Germain, 12 blvd des Îles, 92130 Issy-les-Moulineaux, France; tel. 1-45-24-10-15; fax 1-45-24-11-10; e-mail nea@nea .fr; internet www.nea.fr; f. 1958, name changed 1972; an intergovernmental org. with the primary objective of assisting its mem. countries to maintain and further develop, through int. cooperation, the scientific, technological and legal bases required for a safe, environmentally friendly and economical use of nuclear energy for peaceful purposes, as input to government decisions on nuclear energy policy and to broader OECD policy analyses in areas such as energy and sustainable devt; non-partisan, unbiased source of information, data and analyses, drawing on int. networks of technical experts; mems: 28 countries; Dir-Gen. LUIS ECHÁVARRI; publs *NEA News* (2 a year), *Nuclear Law Bulletin* (2 a year).

Pacific Science Association/Association Scientifique du Pacifique: Bishop Museum, 1525 Bernice St, Honolulu, HI 96817, USA; tel. (808) 848-4124; fax (808) 847-8252; e-mail psa@pacificscience.org; internet www.pacificscience.org; f. 1920 to cooperate in the study of scientific problems relating to the Pacific region; sponsors congresses and inter-congresses; mems: scientists and scientific institutions interested in the Pacific; Pres. Dr R. GERARD WARD (Australia); Exec. Sec. JOHN BURKE BURNETT; publ. *Information Bulletin*.

Pan-American Institute of Geography and History/Instituto Panamericano de Geografía e Historia: Ex-Arzobispado 29, Col. Observatorio, 11860 México, DF, Mexico; tel. (55) 5277-5888; fax (55) 5271-6172; e-mail secretariageneral@ipgh.org; internet www.ipgh.org; f. 1928; encourages, coordinates and promotes the study of cartography, geophysics, geography, history, anthropology, archaeology and other related scientific studies; mems: countries of the Org. of American States; library of 229,062 vols; Sec.-Gen. MSc SANTIAGO BORRERO (Colombia); publs *Boletín de Antropología Americana* (1 a year), *Revista de Arqueología Americana* (1 a year), *Revista Cartográfica* (1 a year), *Revista Geofísica*, *Revista Geográfica* (2 a year), *Revista de Historia de América* (2 a year).

Wetlands International: POB 471, 6700 AL Wageningen, Netherlands; Droevendaalsesteeg 3A, 6708 PB Wageningen, Netherlands; tel. (317) 478854; fax (317) 478850; e-mail post@wetlands.org; internet www .wetlands.org; f. 1954 to sustain and restore wetlands, their resources and biodiversity through worldwide research, information exchange and conservation activities; 58 mem. countries; CEO J. MADGWICK.

World Academy of Art and Science: c/o Dr Walter Truett Anderson, 760 Market St, Suite 315, San Francisco, CA 94102, USA; tel. (415) 915-2449; fax (415) 781-8227; internet www.worldacademy.org; f. 1960; a forum for discussion of the social consequences and policy implications of knowledge; 471 Fellows in 62 countries; Pres. Dr WALTER TRUETT ANDERSON (USA).

World Meteorological Organization/Organisation Météorologique Mondiale: Secretariat CP 2300, 7 bis ave de la Paix, 1211 Geneva 2, Switzerland; tel. 227308111; fax 227308181; e-mail wmo@wmo.int; internet www.wmo.int; f. 1950; objectives: worldwide cooperation in making and standardizing meteorological, climatological, hydrological and related geophysical observations and their exchange and publication; assists in training, research and technology transfer; furthers the application of meteorology to aviation, shipping, water problems, agriculture, environmental problems (incl. climate and climate change) and to sustainable development; constituent bodies: Congress, Executive Council, 6 regional associations, 8 technical commissions; mems: 181 states and 6 territories maintaining their own meteorological or hydrometeorological services; Pres. Dr A. I. BEDRITSKY (Russia); Sec.-Gen. M. JARRAUD (France); publs *WMO Bulletin* (4 a year), *World Climate News* (4 a year).

World Organisation of Systems and Cybernetics/Organisation Mondiale pour la Systémique et la Cybernétique: c/o Dr Alex Andrew, 95 Finch Rd, Earley, Reading, RG6 7JX, UK; tel. (118) 926-9328; e-mail alexandrew@tiscali.co.uk; internet www.cybsoc.org/wosc; f. 1969 to act as focal point for all socs concerned with cybernetics, systems and allied subjects, to aim for the recognition of cybernetics as a bona fide science and to maintain liaison with other int. bodies; holds int. congresses every 3 years; awards Norbert Wiener Memorial Gold Medal; 41 hon. fellows, nat. orgs in more than 20 countries; Pres. Prof. ROBERT VALLÉE; Dir-Gen. Dr ALEX ANDREW; publ. *Kybernetes* (10 a year, online).

PART THREE

Afghanistan–Myanmar

AFGHANISTAN

The Higher Education System

The higher education system in Afghanistan was established with the foundation of Kabul University in 1932. However, during more than 20 years of civil war from 1979 higher education was disrupted by the departure of many teaching staff from Afghanistan. In 1991 there were six institutions of higher education with a total enrolment of 17,000 students. In September 1996 the Islamist Taliban movement gained control of Kabul and issued decrees enforcing their fundamentalist interpretation of Islam, which included banning women from receiving education. In late 2001 a US-led military coalition ousted the Taliban regime following the 11 September terrorist attacks on the USA, which were blamed on the al-Qa'ida organization of Osama bin Laden, a Saudi dissident based in Afghanistan. In March 2002 Kabul University was re-opened for men and women. In 2009 there were 22 universities in operation with some 62,000 students enrolled at the higher education level.

In order to be admitted to higher education students must complete the Baccalauria and pass an entrance examination (Concours). In 2004 The Ministry of Higher Education in cooperation with UNESCO put forward a plan for a four-tier structure of academic institutions: Universities with degree-conferring rights at Bachelors, Masters and Doctoral levels, Technological and Pedagogical Institutes providing the same degrees as universities but within their particular field of specialization, Colleges operating Bachelor degree level programmes and Community Colleges offering courses of up to two years leading to the award of a certificate or diploma. The reform is ongoing. There are also plans to implement a national qualifications framework (NQF) following the Bologna model of three-year Bachelor degree, two-year Masters degree and four-year Doctorate.

In 2009, however, no Afghan universities were in a position to provide teaching at postgraduate level, and no postgraduate degrees were being awarded. In 2006 the USAID-funded Higher Education Project was put into place to rebuild and strengthen the 16 institutions offering four-year teacher education programmes for precisely this reason.

Regulatory and Representative Bodies

GOVERNMENT

Ministry of Education: Mohammad Jan Khan Wat, Kabul; tel. 798801066 (mobile); e-mail attaullah.wahidyar@moe.gov.af; internet www.moe.gov.af; Minister Dr GHU-LAM FAROOQ WARDAK.

Ministry of Higher Education: Karte Char, Kabul; tel. (20) 2500324; e-mail afmohe@hotmail.com; internet www.mohe.gov.af; Minister (vacant).

Ministry of Information and Culture: Mohammad Jan Khan Wat, Kabul; tel. (20) 2101301; fax (20) 2290088; internet www.moic.gov.af; Minister Dr SAYED MAKHDUM RAHEEN.

NATIONAL BODIES

Afghan Rectors' Conference: c/o Kabul Univ., Kabul; e-mail rida_azimi2004@yahoo.com; Pres. Dr DAUD RAWOSH; Sec.-Gen. RIDA AZIMI.

UNESCO Office Kabul: POB 5, UN Compound, Kabul; tel. (2) 214522; fax (2) 214379; e-mail martin.hadlow@undpafg.org.pk; Dir MARTIN HADLOW.

Learned Societies

GENERAL

Academy of Sciences of Afghanistan: Sher Alikhan St, Char Rahe Sher Poor, Kabul; tel. (20) 2102919; fax (20) 2100268; f. 1979; research in science, technology, humanities and culture; 4 main divs: Centre of Natural Sciences (q.v.), Institute of Social Sciences (q.v.), Institute of Languages and Literature (q.v.), Int. Centre for Pashtu Studies (q.v.); Islamic Studies Centre added 2000; further units incl. Int. Research Centre of Kushan Studies and Archaeology, Publication and Literature Dept, Encyclopedia and Dictionaries Dept; library: Central Library of 5,000 vols, Central Archives; Pres. Dr ABDUL BARI RASHID.

UNESCO Office Kabul: POB 5, UN Compound, Kabul; tel. (2) 214522; fax (2) 214379; e-mail martin.hadlow@undpafg.org.pk; Dir MARTIN HADLOW.

LANGUAGE AND LITERATURE

Goethe-Institut: c/o Embassy of the Federal Republic of Germany, POB 83, Kabul; Wazir Akbar Khan, Shahmahmod St, Kabul; tel. (20) 2105200; fax (20) 2105300; e-mail il@kabul.goethe.org; internet www.goethe.de/kabul; promotes cultural exchange with Germany, and contributes to the reconstruction of cultural and educational institutions in Afghanistan; Dir ANNE EBERHARD.

Research Institutes

GENERAL

Afghanistan Research and Evaluation Unit (AREU): Flower St (corner of St 2), Shahr-i-Naw, Kabul; e-mail areu@areu.org.af; internet www.areu.org.af; f. 2002; promotes a culture of research and learning by strengthening analytical capacity in Afghanistan and facilitating reflection and debate; library of 3,000 vols, periodicals, maps, CDs and DVDs; Dir PAUL FISHSTEIN.

Institute of Social Sciences: Kabul; attached to Acad. of Sciences of Afghanistan; philosophy, economics, history, archaeology; Pres. Dr HAKIM HELALI; publs Afghanistan (4 a year in English, French and German), Ariana (4 a year in Pashtu and Dari).

LANGUAGE AND LITERATURE

Institute of Languages and Literature: Kabul; attached to Acad. of Sciences of Afghanistan; linguistics, literature and folklore; study of Pashtu and Dari languages, and Afghanistan dialects; publs Kabul (12 a year, Pashtu), Zayray (48 a year, Pashtu).

International Centre for Pashtu Studies: Kabul; attached to Acad. of Sciences of Afghanistan; research, compilation and translation; publ. Pashtu Quarterly.

MEDICINE

Institute of Public Health: Ansari Wat, Kabul; f. 1962; public health training and research; govt reference laboratory; Dir Dr S. M. SADIQUE; publs Afghan Journal of Public Health (26 a year), books and pamphlets.

NATURAL SCIENCES

General

Centre of Natural Sciences: Kabul; attached to Acad. of Sciences of Afghanistan; institutes of botany, zoology, geology and chemistry, seismology; computer centre, plants museum and botanical garden.

Physical Sciences

Department of Geology and Mineral Survey: Min. of Mines and Industries, Kabul; tel. 25848; f. 1955; research, mapping, prospecting and exploration; library of 8,300 vols; Pres. Dipl. Eng. Haji MOHAMAD NAW-ZADI; publs Journal of Mines and Industries (4 a year), maps and other reference works.

Libraries and Archives

Kabul

Kabul University Library: c/o Min. of Information and Culture, Mohammad Jan Khan Wat, Kabul; tel. 42594; f. 1931; 250,000 vols; Dir Prof. ABDUL RASOUL RAHIN.

Library of the National Bank: c/o Min. of Information and Culture, Mohammad Jan Khan Wat, Kabul; Bank Millie Afghan, Ibn Sina Wat, Kabul; f. 1941; 5,600 vols; Dir A. AZIZ.

Library of the Press and Information Department: c/o Min. of Information and Culture, Mohammad Jan Khan Wat, Kabul; Sanaii Wat, Kabul; f. 1931; 28,000 vols and 800 MSS; Dir MOHAMMED SARWAR RONA.

Ministry of Education Library: c/o Min. of Information and Culture, Mohammad Jan

Khan Wat, Kabul; f. 1920; 30,000 vols; Chief Officer MOHAMAD QASEM HILAMAN; publ. *Erfan* (12 a year journal in Pashtu and Dari).

Nazo Annah Library: c/o Min. of Information and Culture, Mohammad Jan Khan Wat, Kabul; f. 2001 to enable and empower young women through literacy and education; attached to Noor Education Centre; fmrly Women's Welfare Soc. Library; 680 vols.

Public Library: c/o Min. of Information and Culture, Mohammad Jan Khan Wat, Kabul; Charaii-i-Malik Asghar, Kabul; f. 1920; attached to Min. of Information and Culture; 60,000 vols, 433 MSS, 30 current periodicals; Dir MOHAMAD OMAR SEDDIQUI.

Museums and Art Galleries

Ghazni

Ghazni Museum: c/o Min. of Information and Culture, Mohammad Jan Khan Wat, Kabul; Ghazni.

Herat

Herat Museum: c/o Min. of Information and Culture, Mohammad Jan Khan Wat, Kabul; Herat.

Kabul

Kabul Museum: c/o Min. of Information and Culture, Mohammad Jan Khan Wat, Kabul; tel. 42656; f. 1922; archaeology; Dir ORMA KHAN MASSOUDI.

Kandahar

Kandahar Museum: c/o Min. of Information and Culture, Mohammad Jan Khan Wat, Kabul; Kandahar.

Maimana

Maimana Museum: c/o Min. of Information and Culture, Mohammad Jan Khan Wat, Kabul; Maimana.

Mazar-i-Sharif

Mazar-i-Sharif Museum: c/o Min. of Information and Culture, Mohammad Jan Khan Wat, Kabul; Mazar-i-Sharif.

Universities

BALKH UNIVERSITY

Mazar-i-Sharif, Balkh
Telephone: 503487
Fax: 503554
Founded 1988
Pres.: Prof. HABIBULLAH
Number of teachers: 83
Number of students: 4,739
Faculties of economics, engineering, journalism, law, literature, medicine and science.

BAYAZID ROSHAN UNIVERSITY OF NANGARHAR

Darunta, Jalalabad, Nangarhar
Founded 1963 from Medical Faculty of Kabul University, reorganized 1978
State control
Language of instruction: Pashtu
Vice-Chancellor: Dr MOHAMMAD TAYAB
Dean: Prof. ABDUL QADIR FAZLI
Number of teachers: 96
Number of students: 3,263

DEANS

Faculty of Medicine: Prof. ASSADULLAH SHIN-WARI
Faculty of Political Science: MIRWAIS AHMAD-ZAI

HERAT UNIVERSITY

Herat
Internet: heratuniversity.org
Founded 1986
State control
Pres.: Dr MOHAMMAD NAIM ASSAD
Dir of Academic Affairs: MOHAMMAD NASER RAHYAB
Dir of Student Affairs: Dr ABDUL ZAHER O
Librarian: SAID KHALLIL
Library of 2,000 vols
Number of teachers: 210
Number of students: 6,000

Faculties of agriculture, art, computer science, economics, education, engineering, law, literature, medicine, science, theology and Islamic law.

KABUL MEDICAL UNIVERSITY

Kabul
Internet: www.kmu.edu.af
Founded 1932 as Kabul Medical Faculty, initially maintained with collaboration from French and Turkish govts; disrupted under Taliban regime; present name and autonomous univ. status 2005
State control
Dean: Dr OBAIDULLAH OBAID
Library of 20,000 vols
Number of teachers: 213
Number of students: 2,745

Faculties of curative medicine, nursing, paediatrics, stomatology; affiliated teaching hospitals at Aliabad and Maiwand.

KABUL UNIVERSITY

Jamal Mina, Kabul
Telephone: 40341
Internet: www.ku.edu.af
Founded 1932
State control
Academic year: March to January
Language of instruction: Dari
Rector: Prof. MOHAMMAD AKBAR POPAL
Librarian: REYHANA POPALZAI

Library of 200,000 vols
Number of teachers: 450
Number of students: 7,000
Publication: *Natural Science and Social Science* (4 a year)
Faculties of agriculture, economics, engineering, fine arts, history and philosophy, Islamic law, journalism, law, linguistics, pharmacology, psychology, science, social sciences, veterinary science

DEANS

Faculty of Education: Prof. GUL RAHMAN HAKIM
Faculty of Law and Political Science: Prof. IQRAL WASIL
Faculty of Social Sciences: Prof. M. DAUD RAWOSH

ATTACHED RESEARCH CENTRE

National Centre for Policy Research: f. 2003 to promote democracy in Afghanistan; depts of economics, law and political sciences and social science; offers scholarships to Afghani researchers for carrying out postgraduate studies in Germany; financed by Konrad-Adenauer Stiftung (Germany).

KANDAHAR UNIVERSITY

Kandahar
Internet: www.kandaharuniversity.com
Founded 1988
State control
Vice-Pres.: SHAH MAHMUD BARAI
Number of students: 747

UNIVERSITY OF EDUCATION

Kabul
Founded 2002
Number of teachers: 140
Number of students: 1,744

Colleges

Institute of Agriculture: Kabul; f. 1924; veterinary medicine, forestry.

Institute of Arabic and Religious Study: Kabul; Other centres incl. the Najmul-Madares, Nangrahar; the Jamé and Fakhrul Madares, Herat; the Asadia Madrasa, Mazar-i-Sharif; the Takharistan Madrasa, Kunduz; the Zahir Shahi Madrasa, Maimana.

Kabul Art School: Bibi Mahro, near Kabul; music, painting and sculpture courses.

School of Commerce: Kabul; f. 1943; banking, commercial law, economics, business admin., finance.

School of Mechanics: Kabul; for apprentice trainees.

ALBANIA

The Higher Education System

Higher education is offered through universities and higher schools and is governed by legislation enacted in 1999, 2003 and 2007. In 2009 there were nine universities, the oldest of which is the Aleksandër Xhuvani University of Elbasan, founded in 1909. The Law on Higher Education of 1999 introduced and guarantees state funding for public higher education. Albania joined the Bologna Process in 2003, and in the same year implemented a new higher education act that introduced a two-tier Bachelors and Masters degree structure. This new system was scheduled to be fully implemented (with the exception of a few subject areas) by the 2006 academic year. The Law on Higher Education of 2007 governs not only the institutions but also the structure, study programmes and cycles, supervision, students' rights and the financial aspects of higher education. Its enactment marked the official start of the implementation of Bologna degrees. As a result, from 2008/09 all Albanian public universities adopted the new curricula of second and third cycles of studies.

In 2006/07 a total of 86,178 students were enrolled at Albania's institutions of higher education.

University Rectors and Higher School Directors and Headmasters belong to the Conference of Rectors, the highest decision-making body in Albania's higher education system. All universities consist of faculties, which are governed by faculty councils, and sometimes of higher schools; the highest decision-making body in a higher school is the school council. Both faculties and higher schools consist of departments, in which the department council is the highest decision-making body.

Admission to higher education is conducted according to quotas and is subject to main and secondary fees. Main admission fees are proposed by the Ministry of Education and Science, following recommendations from the universities and higher schools, and are approved by the Council of Ministers. Secondary fees are levied for specialist education and can equate to a maximum of 10% of the main fees. Admission to public universities and higher schools is based on competitive examinations which are organized by the Ministry of Education and Science on the advice of the Conference of Rectors. Successful students are then admitted subject to the established fees.

Pre-Bologna (until 2007), there were three levels of university qualifications: Diplomë (Diploma), Kandidat í Shkencave (Candidate of Sciences) and Doktor í Shkencave (Doctor of Sciences). The Diplomë was usually a four-year undergraduate degree, however degrees in engineering, technology and dentistry lasted five years, and courses in medicine lasted six years. The Kandidat í Shkencave was a first postgraduate degree of two to three years. The Doktor í Shkencave was based on a significant period of research. There was no grading system for this level of study. Qualifications from the three military institutions (the Higher Military Academies in Tiranë and Vlora, and the Higher Unified Military School in Tirana) had the same equivalency as civilian qualifications.

Post-Bologna there are six levels of qualification: in the first cycle are the Diplomë Jo-Universitare (Non-University Diploma), which is a higher education award consisting of a study programme of 120 ECTS, in applied subjects, offered at universities and professional colleges (credits can be transferred to a First Level Diploma programme) and the Diplomë í Nivelit te Pare (First Level Diploma), which is a degree awarded after at least three years, of no less than 180 ECTS, and can be issued by universities, academies or professional colleges providing access to second cycle awards. In the second cycle are the Master í Nivelit te Pare (First Level Master), a degree which is an essential requirement for teachers whose first cycle degree is not sufficient, consisting of no less than 60 ECTS, but is not recognized as completion of the second cycle and therefore does not allow access to the third level, and the Diplomë e Nivelit te Dyte (Second Level Diploma), which is a degree awarded after two years' study, involving the attainment of 120 ECTS, allowing entry to the third cycle. In the third cycle are the Master í Nivelit te Dyte (Second Level Master), which is a degree awarded after another one to two years' study and represents the entry requirement to become a university professor, and Doktor í Shkencave (Doctor of Sciences), which takes three to five years and requires completion of 60 ECTS in the first year (although holders of the Second Level Master are exempt), followed by research and defence of a doctoral thesis.

Quality assessment of universities and higher schools and academic accreditation is carried out by the Accrediting Agency and the Accrediting Council, under the authority of the Council of Ministers.

Regulatory and Representative Bodies

GOVERNMENT

Ministry of Education and Science: Rr. Durrësit 23, Tiranë; tel. (4) 2226307; fax (4) 2232002; e-mail mtafaj@mash.gov.al; internet www.mash.gov.al; Minister Prof. Dr MYQEREM TAFAJ.

Ministry of Tourism, Culture, Youth and Sports: Rr. e Kavajës, Tiranë; tel. (4) 2222508; fax (4) 2229120; e-mail informacion@mtkrs.gov.al; internet www.mtkrs.gov.al; Minister FERDINAND XHAFERAJ.

ACCREDITATION

ENIC/NARIC Albania: Drejtoria e Arsimit të Lartë dhe Njohjes së Diplomave, Rr. Durrësit 23, Tiranë; tel. (4) 2227975; fax (4) 2232002; e-mail ecane@mash.gov.al; internet www.mash.gov.al; Specialist EDMOND CANE.

Public Agency for Accreditation of Higher Education: Blvd Zhan 'D' Ark, Pallatet e Lanës, no. 2, Shk 2, Ap. 17, Tiranë; tel. (4) 2266302; fax (4) 2275954; e-mail infoaal@gmail.com; internet www.aaal.edu .al; f. 1999; state funded instn for evaluation of HEIs; conducts evaluations, ranking, preparation of evaluation criteria, procedures, performance indicators and standards, documentation for the council of accreditation; responsible to Ministry of Education and Science; Dir Prof. AVNI MESHI.

NATIONAL BODIES

Albanian Rectors' Conference: c/o Ministry of Education and Science, Rr. e Durrësit 23, Tiranë.

Department of Higher Education and Recognition of Diplomas: c/o Ministry of Education and Science, Rr. e Durrësit 23, Tiranë; tel. (4) 226307; fax (4) 232002; e-mail amucaj@mash.gov.al; internet www.mash .gov.al; Dir of Higher Education Dr AGIM MUÇAJ.

Learned Societies

GENERAL

Academy of Sciences of Albania: Fan. S. Noli Sq., 1000 Tiranë; tel. and fax (42) 230305; e-mail nnati@akad.edu.al; internet www.akad.edu.al; f. 1972; theoretical and practical research in social, natural and technical sciences; facilitates the application of these studies; attached research institutes: see Research Institutes; 28 mems; library of 62,000 vols; Pres. Acad. GUDAR BEQIRAJ; Vice-Pres. Acad. MYZAFER KORKUTI; Scientific Sec. Acad. SALVATOR BUSHATI; publs *Albanian Journal of Natural and Technical Sciences* (2 a year), *Biological Studies* (2 a year), *Folk Culture* (2 a year), *Geographical Studies* (irregular), *Historical Studies* (2 a year), *Ilyria* (2 a year), *Issues of Albanian Folklore* (irregular), *Our Language* (2 a year), *Philological Studies* (2 a year), *Studia Albanica* (2 a year).

Komiteti Shqiptar për Marrëdhënie Kulturore me botën e jashtme (Albanian

Committee for Cultural Relations Abroad): Tiranë; Pres. JORGO MELIKA.

LANGUAGE AND LITERATURE

Alliance Française: Rr. e Barrikadave 122, Tiranë; tel. (4) 2274841; fax (4) 2225697; e-mail info@aftirana.org; internet www .aftirana.org; f. 1991; offers courses and examinations in French language and culture; promotes cultural exchange with France; attached teaching centres in Elbasan, Korçë and Shkodra; Dir DRITA HADAJ; Sec. Gen. GENT BEGA; Head of Treasury IRENA CACI.

British Council: Rr. 'Perlat Rexhepi', Pall 197, Ana, Tiranë; tel. (4) 2240856; fax (4) 2240858; e-mail info@britishcouncil.org.al; internet www.britishcouncil.org/albania; offers British literature and examinations in English language and British culture; promotes cultural exchange with the UK; library of 4,000 vols; Dir CLARE SEARS.

Lidhja e Shkrimtarëve dhe e Artistëve të Shqipërisë (Union of Writers and Artists of Albania): Tiranë; f. 1957; 1,750 mems; Pres. DRITËRO AGOLLI; Secs FEIM IBRAHIMI, PETRO KOKUSHTA, NASI LERA; publs *Drita* (journal, weekly), *Les Lettres Albanaises* (4 a year), *Nëntori* (Review, 12 a year).

PEN Centre of Albania: Rr. 'Ded Gjo Luli', Pallati 5, shk. 3/4, Tiranë; Pres. BESNIK MUSTAFAJ.

NATURAL SCIENCES

Physical Sciences

Shoqata e Gjeologëve te Shqipërisë (Geologists' Association of Albania): Blloku 'Vasil Shanto', Tiranë; tel. (4) 2226597; f. 1989; 450 mems; Chair. ALEKSANDËR ÇINA; Sec.-Gen. ILIR ALLIU; publ. *Buletini i Shkencave Gjeologjike.*

Research Institutes

AGRICULTURE, FISHERIES AND VETERINARY SCIENCE

Instituti i Duhanit (Tobacco Institute): Lagja 2, Pallati 51/2, Cërrik; tel. (581) 2800; f. 1956; library of 1,000 vols; Dir BELUL GIXHARI; publ. *Bulletin des sciences de l'agriculture* (4 a year).

Instituti i Kërkimeve Bujqësore Lushnje (Lushnje Institute of Agricultural Research): Lushnje; tel. (65) 224498; f. 1952; focuses on cultivating new varieties of bread and durum wheat, cotton, sunflower and dry bean; library of 8,000 vols; Dir VLADIMIR MALO.

Instituti i Kërkimeve Pyjore dhe Kullotave (Forest and Pasture Research Institute): Rr. Halil Bego 23, Tiranë; tel. (4) 371242; fax (4) 371237; e-mail ikpk@ albaniaonline.net; f. 1992; Dir SPIRO KARADUMI.

Instituti i Kërkimeve të Foragjere (Forage Research Institute): Fushë-Krujë; tel. (4) 233354; f. 1973; Dir VASILLAQ DHIMA.

Instituti i Kërkimeve të Pemëve Frutore dhe Vreshtave (Institute of Fruit Growing and Vineyard Research): Tiranë; tel. (4) 2229704; f. 1984; library of 70 vols; Dir STEFAN GJOKA; publs *Pemëtaria, Bulletini i Shkencave Bujqësore.*

Instituti i Kërkimeve të Zooteknisë (Institute of Animal Husbandry Research): Laprake, Tiranë; tel. (4) 2223135; f. 1955; library of 1,900 vols; Dir MINA SPIRU.

Instituti i Kërkimeve Veterinare (Institute of Veterinary Research): 'Aleksander Moisiu' St 10, Tiranë; tel. (4) 2372912; fax (4) 2372912; f. 1928; Dir Prof. Dr KRISTAQ BERXHOLI; publ. *Veterinaria* (3 a year).

Instituti i Kerkimit te Bimeve te Arave, Stacioni Eksperimental (Experimental Station of the Research Institute for Arable Farming): Rr. Voskopojës, Korçë; fax (824) 3086; e-mail stacionieksperimental@yahoo .com; f. 1953; attached to Min. of Agriculture, Food and Consumer Protection; library of 600 vols; Dir Dr EQREM MEÇOLLARI.

Instituti i Mbrojtjes Bimeve (Institute of Plant Protection Research): Shkozet, Durrës; tel. (52) 22182; fax (52) 22182; e-mail imb@ anep.al.eu.org; f. 1971; library of 2,410 vols; Dir Dr SKENDER VARRAKU.

Instituti i Perimeve dhe i Patates (Institute of Vegetables and Potatoes): Rr. Skënder Kosturi, Tiranë; tel. (4) 2228422; f. 1980; library of 6,000 vols; Dir XHEVAT SHIMA; publs *Bulletin of Agricultural Sciences, Bulletin of Vegetables, Bulletin of Vegetables and Potatoes.*

Instituti i Studimeve dhe i Projektimeve të Veprave të Kullimit dhe Ujitjes (Institute of Irrigation and Drainage Studies and Designs): Tiranë; f. 1970; Dir DHIMITËR VOGLI.

Instituti i Studimit të Tokave (Institute of Soil Studies): Tiranë; tel. (4) 2223278; fax (4) 2228367; f. 1971; library of 5,000 vols; Dir ALBERT DUBALI.

Instituti i Ullirit dhe i Agrumeve (Institute of Olives and Citrus Plants): 'Uji i Jtohtë', Vlorë; tel. (33) 23225; fax (33) 23225; f. 1971; library of 500 vols; Dir Dr HAIRI ISMAILI.

Qendra e Transferimit te Teknologjive Bujqesore (Agriculture Technologies Transfer Centre (ATTC)): Shkodër; tel. and fax (225) 1200; e-mail qttb_shkoder@yahoo.com; f. 1971 as Institute of Maize and Rice, present name 2006; applied research activity and technology devt; identification, testing, introduction of new methods and materials into agriculture practices; identification, preservation, colln, multiplication of high value authentic genetic resources; preparing of technological package for maize culture and other priority cultures of the region (arboriculture, horticulture, vegetable etc.); production of pre-basic and basic certified seeds and seedlings; activities of technology transfer; laboratory analysis (chemical and biochemical laboratory wide range analysis) of both agriculture and cattle products; 15 mems; library of 4,900 vols; Dir ISMET LLOSHI; publs *Agriculture Science Bulletin* (4 a year), *Albanian Agriculture* (12 a year).

Stacioni i Studimeve dhe i Kërkimeve të Peshkimit (Research Station and Fisheries Research): Rr. 'Skenderbeg', L. Teuta, Durrës; tel. (52) 22552; f. 1960; Dir KASTRIOT OSMANI.

ARCHITECTURE AND TOWN PLANNING

Instituti i Monumenteve të Kulturës (Institute of Cultural Monuments): Rr. Aleksandër Moisiu 76, Tiranë; tel. and fax (4) 2340348; e-mail imk@albmail.com; f. 1965; attached to Min. of Tourism, Culture, Youth and Sports; research and restoration of ancient and medieval architecture, cultural bldgs and artistic monuments; library of 9,000 vols; Dir FATJON DAUTI; publ. *Monumentet* (Monuments, 2 a year).

Instituti i Studimeve e Projektimeve Urbanistikë (Institute of Urban Planning and Design): Rr. M. Gjollesha Istn, Tiranë; tel. (4) 2223361; fax (4) 2223361; f. 1991; library of 400 vols; Dir GJERGJ KOTMILO.

ECONOMICS, LAW AND POLITICS

Albanian Institute for International Studies: Rr. Andon Z, Cajupi 20, Tiranë; tel. (4) 2248853; fax (4) 2270337; e-mail aiis@

aiis-albania.org; internet www.aiis-albania .org; non-profit research and policy institute; areas of research incl. issues in Euro–Atlantic integration, democracy, security and transition, regional security and cooperation; Chair. BESNIK MUSTAFAJ; Exec. Dir ALBERT RAKIPI.

Instituti i Studimeve të Marrëdhënieve Ndërkombëtare (Institute of International Relations): Tiranë; tel. (4) 2229521; fax (4) 2232970; f. 1981; Dir SOKRAT PLAKA; publ. *Politika ndërkombëtare* (International Politics, 4 a year).

EDUCATION

Instituti i Studimeve Pedagogjike (Institute of Pedagogical Studies): Rr. Naim Frashëri 37, Tiranë; tel. (4) 2223860; fax (4) 2223860; f. 1970; Dir Prof. BUJAR BASHA; publs *Albanian Language and Literature in School* (2 a year), *Chemistry and Biology in School* (2 a year), *Elementary School* (1 a year), *Foreign Languages in School* (1 a year), *Mathematics and Physics in School* (2 a year), *Nursery School 3–6* (1 a year), *Revista Pedagogjike* (4 a year), *Social Materials in School* (2 a year), *Vocational Schools* (2 a year), *Yllkat* (12 a year).

FINE AND PERFORMING ARTS

Qendra e Studimeve të Artit (Centre for Art Studies): Rr. Don Bosko 60, Tiranë; tel. (4) 2259667; fax (4) 2228274; e-mail qsa@ akad.edu; f. 1984; research in fine arts, music, choreography, theatre, cinema, art and culture instns; attached to Acad. of Sciences of Albania; Dir Prof. JOSIF PAPAGJONI; publ. *Studime për Artin* (Studies for Art, 2 a year).

HISTORY, GEOGRAPHY AND ARCHAEOLOGY

Instituti i Arkeologjisë (Institute of Archaeology): Bulevardi Dëshmorët e Kombit, Sheshi Nënë Tereza, Tiranë; tel. (4) 2271822; fax (4) 2240712; e-mail instark@ albmail.com; f. 1976; attached to Centre of Albanological Studies; performs archaeological research and excavations in Albania; Dir Prof. ILIRIAN GJIPALI; publs *Candavia* (in Albanian, publ. of the Late Antique and Medieval Dept of the Institute of Archaeology), *Iliria* (in Albanian, English and French, 1 a year).

Instituti i Historisë (Institute of History): Rr. Naim Frashëri 7, Tiranë; tel. (4) 2225869; fax (4) 2225869; e-mail ihistorise@ albaniaonline.net; f. 1972; attached to Acad. of Sciences of Albania; study of ancient and modern Albanian history and people; library of 52,000 vols, 10,000 periodicals; Dir Prof. Dr ANA LALAJ; publ. *Studime Historike* (Historical Studies, 4 a year).

Qendra e Kërkimeve Gjeografike (Centre for Geographical Research): Qendri e Studimeve Hidraulike, Sheshi Fan S. Noli, Tiranë; tel. (4) 2227985; fax (4) 2227985; e-mail geography_albania2003@yahooo.com; f. 1986; attached to Acad. of Sciences of Albania; library of 3,200 vols; Dir Prof. Dr ARQILE BERXHOLI; publ. *Studime Gjeografike* (Geographical Studies, 1 a year).

LANGUAGE AND LITERATURE

Instituti i Gjuhësisë dhe i Letërsisë (Institute of Linguistics and Literature): Rr. Naim Frashëri 7, Tiranë; tel. (4) 2240461; e-mail enver_muhametaj@yahoo.com; f. 1972; attached to Acad. of Sciences of Albania; study of Albanian language and literature; Dir Prof. Dr ENVER MUHAMETAJ; publs *Gjuha Jonë* (Our Language, 1 a year), *Studime Filologjike* (Philological Studies, 2 a year).

Qendra e Enciklopedisë Shqiptare (Centre for the Albanian Encyclopedical Dictionary): Sheshi Fan S. Noli 7, Tiranë; tel. (4) 2250369; fax (4) 2256777; e-mail encikloped@yahoo.com; f. 1988 to prepare revised edn of the *Albanian Encyclopedical Dictionary*; sections of social sciences, natural and technical sciences; attached to the Acad. of Sciences of Albania; Dir Prof. Dr EMIL LAFE.

MEDICINE

Instituti i Mjekësisë Popullore (Institute of Folk Medicine): Tiranë; tel. (4) 2223493; f. 1977; Dir Dr GËZIM BOCARI; publ. *Përmbledhje Studimesh* (Collections of Studies, irregular).

Instituti i Shëndetit Publik (Institute of Public Health): Aleksander Moisiu 80, Tiranë; tel. (4) 2374756; fax (4) 2370058; f. 1969 as Research Institute of Hygiene, Epidemiology and Immunobiological Products; present name 1995; Dir Prof. EDUARD KAKARRIQI; publ. *Revista Mjekesore* (Medical Magazine, 6 a year).

NATURAL SCIENCES

Biological Sciences

Instituti i Kërkimeve Biologjike (Institute of Biological Research): Rr. Sami Frasheri 5, Tiranë; tel. (4) 222638; fax (4) 222638; e-mail ikbiol@albmail.com; f. 1978; attached to Acad. of Sciences of Albania; Dir Prof. EFIGJENI KONGJIKA.

Mathematical Sciences

Instituti i Informatikës dhe i Matematikës së Aplikuar (Institute of Informatics and Applied Mathematics): Rr. Lek Dukagjini 3, Tiranë; tel. (4) 2362968; fax (4) 2362122; e-mail inima@inima.al; f. 1971; attached to Acad. of Sciences of Albania; Dir Prof. Dr GUDAR BEQIRAJ.

Physical Sciences

Instituti i Energjetikës (Institute of Energetics): Tiranë; f. 1982; Dir LLAZAR PAPAJORGJI.

Instituti i Fizikës Bërthamore (Institute of Nuclear Physics): POB 85, Tiranë; tel. (4) 2376341; fax (4) 2362596; e-mail inp@albaniaonline.net; f. 1970; attached to Acad. of Sciences of Albania; Dir Prof. Dr FATOS YLLI.

Instituti i Hidrometeorologjisë (Institute of Hydrometeorology): Rr. e Durrësit 219, Tiranë; tel. (4) 2223518; fax (4) 2223518; e-mail a.selenica@voila.fr; f. 1962, replaced Hydrometeorological Service f. 1949; attached to Acad. of Sciences of Albania; comprises two divs: Department of Meteorology and Department of Hydrology; Dir Prof. Dr AGIM SELENICA; publ. *Hydrometeorological Reports* (periodic review).

Instituti i Sizmologjise (Institute of Seismology): Tiranë; tel. (4) 2228274; fax (4) 2228274; e-mail sizmo@akad.edu.al; f. 1993; attached to Acad. of Sciences of Albania; Dir Prof. Dr SHYQYRI ALIAJ.

Instituti i Studimeve dhe Projektimeve të Gjeologjisë (Geological Research Institute): Blloku 'Vasil Shanto', Tiranë; tel. (4) 2226597; f. 1962; library of 20,000 vols; Dir ALAUDIN KODRA; publ. *Buletini i Shkencave Gjeologjike* (4 a year).

RELIGION, SOCIOLOGY AND ANTHROPOLOGY

Instituti i Kulturës Popullore (Institute of Folk Culture): Rr. Kont Urani 3, Tiranë; tel. (4) 2222323; fax (4) 2224555; e-mail ikp.alb@icc.al.org; f. 1961, present status 1979; depts of ethnology, ethnomusicology and ethnochoreography, prose and poetry; library of 10,000 vols, 1.5m. verses of poetry;

attached to Acad. of Sciences of Albania; Dir Asst Prof. AFËRDITA ONUZI; publ. *Folk Culture* (2 a year).

TECHNOLOGY

Infraproject Consulting SH.p.K.: Rr. Sami Frasheri, Tiranë; tel. (4) 2225206; fax (4) 2228321; road, railway and waterway engineering; library of 900 vols; Dir Gen. VEHIP GURI.

Instituti i Kerkimeve të Ushqimit (Food Research Institute): Rr. 'Muhamed Gjollesha' 56, Tiranë; tel. (4) 2226770; fax (4) 2226770; e-mail iku@anep.al.eu.org; f. 1961; Dir MAKSIM DELIANA; publ. *Përmbledhje Studimesh* (Collections of Studies, irregular).

Instituti i Studimeve dhe i Projektimeve Gjeologjike të Naftës e të Gazit (Institute for Studies and Design of Oil and Gas Geology): Fier; f. 1965; Dir DRINI MEZINI; publ. *Buletini Nafta dhe Gazi* (2 a year, summaries in English).

Instituti i Studimeve dhe i Projektimeve të Hidrocentraleve (Institute of Hydraulic Studies and Design): Tiranë; f. 1966; Dir EGON GJADRI.

Instituti i Studimeve dhe i Projektimeve të Metalurgjise (Institute for Metallurgical Studies and Designs): Elbasan; tel. (54) 55565; fax (54) 55565; f. 1978; metallurgy of iron, chrome, copper, nickel; library of 6,100 vols; Dir ALFRED MALKJA.

Instituti i Studimeve dhe i Projektimeve të Minierave (Mining Research Institute): Blloku 'Vasil Shanto', Tiranë; tel. (4) 2229445; f. 1983; library of 10,000 vols; Dir ENGJELL HOXHAJ; publ. *Buletini i Shkencave Minerare* (2 a year, summaries in English).

Instituti i Studimeve dhe i Projektimeve të Teknologjisë Kimike (Institute of Chemical Studies and Technological Design): Tiranë; f. 1981; Dir GASTOR AGALLIU.

Instituti i Studimeve dhe i Projektimeve të Teknologjisë Mekanike (Institute of Mechanical Technology Studies and Design): Tiranë; f. 1969; Dir ROBERT LAPERI.

Instituti i Studimeve dhe i Projektimeve Teknologjike të Mineraleve (Institute for Studies and Technology of Minerals): Tiranë; tel. (4) 2225582; f. 1979; mineral-processing research; library of 1,480 vols; Dir JLIR LAKRORI.

Instituti i Studimeve dhe i Projektimeve Teknologjike të Naftës e të Gazit (Institute for Studies and Design of Oil and Gas Technology): Tiranë; f. 1981; Dir PERPARIM HOXHA; publ. *Nafta dhe Gazi* (Oil and Gas, 6 a year).

Instituti i Studimeve dhe i Teknologjisë Ndërtimit (Institute of Building Technology Studies): Rr. 'Muhamet Gjollesha', Tiranë; tel. (4) 227498; fax (4) 2223811; f. 1979; library of 1,500 vols; Dir Ing. MUHANEM DELIU.

Instituti i Studimeve dhe Projektimeve Mekanike (Mechanics Research Institute): Rr. 'Ferit Xajko', Tiranë; tel. (4) 2228543; f. 1970; library of 3,000 vols; Dir NEDIM KAMBO.

Qendra e Kerkimeve Hidraulike (Centre of Hydraulic Research): Rr. Sami Frasheri 5, Tiranë; tel. (4) 2227322; fax (4) 2227322; e-mail qekehid@albmail.com; f. 1957; attached to Acad. of Sciences of Albania; Dir Prof. Dr STAVRI LAMI.

Libraries and Archives

Durrës

Durrës Public Library: Durrës; tel. (52) 22281; f. 1945; 180,462 vols; Dir FLORA DERVISHI.

Elbasan

Elbasan Public Library: Elbasan; f. 1934; 284,000 vols.

Gjirokastër

Gjirokastër Public Library: Gjirokastër; 90,000 vols.

Korçë

Korçë Public Library: Korçë; f. 1938; 139,000 vols.

Shkodër

Shkodër Public Library: Shkodër; tel. (2) 2242307; e-mail biboigjo@yahoo.co.uk; internet www.library-shkodra.com; f. 1931; 260,000 vols from the 15th and 16th centuries printed in Germany, Italy, France, Switzerland; collns incl. MSS, Albans-Balkanology, maps and incunabula; Dir GJOVALIN ÇUNI.

Tiranë

Centre for Scientific and Technical Information and Documentation: Rr. Lek Dukagjini 5, Tiranë; tel. and fax (4) 222491; f. 1981; attached to Min. of Education and Science; Dir HYDAI MYFTIU; publ. *Buletin Analitik Fushor* (Disciplinary Analytical Bulletin, 12 a year).

National Library: Sheshi Skenderbej, Tiranë; tel. (4) 223843; fax (4) 223843; e-mail a_plasari@hotmail.com; internet www.bksh.al; f. 1922; 1m. vols; Dir Dr AUREL PLASARI; publs *National Bibliography of Albanian Books* (4 a year), *National Bibliography of Albanian Periodicals* (12 a year).

Scientific Library: Tiranë; f. 1972; attached to Acad. of Sciences of Albania; Dir NATASHA PANO.

State Archives: Rr. 'Jordan Misja', Tiranë; tel. (4) 227959; fax (4) 227959; e-mail dpa@albarchive.gov.al; internet www.albarchive.gov.al; document conservation and research; Dir NIKA NEVILA.

Museums and Art Galleries

Berat

District Historical Museum: Berat; tel. (32) 32595; f. 1948; Dir ARBEM JANPAJ.

Ethnographic Museum: Lagja 13, Shtatori, Berat; tel. (32) 32224; e-mail info@beratmuseum.net; internet www.beratmuseum.net; f. 1979; folk ethnographic culture from Berat and southern Albanian region; Dir KASTRIOT DERVISHI.

'Onufri' Iconographic Museum: Lagja Kala, Berat; tel. (32) 32248; e-mail info@beratmuseum.net; internet www.beratmuseum.net; f. 1986; sited in the town's castle; exhibits incl. icons by the medieval painter Onufri; Dir KASTRIOT DERVISHI.

Durrës

Archaeological Museum: 1st Quartier, Talantia St, Durrës; tel. (52) 22253; f. 1951; exhibits representing life in ancient Durrës; artefacts from ancient Greek, Roman and medieval periods.

Elbasan

Kristoforidhi, K., House-Museum: Elbasan; birthplace of the patriot and linguist; Dir LIMAN VAROSHI.

Fier

Archaeological Museum: Fier; f. 1958; exhibits incl. archaeological items from the fmr town of Apollonia.

District Historical Museum: Fier; tel. (34) 2583; f. 1948; Dir PETRIT MALUSHI.

Korçë

Mio, V., House-Museum: Korçë; house where the painter worked; contains works of art by Mio.

Museum of Education: L 12, Blvd Shen Gjergji, Korçë; tel. (824) 3022; f. 1887 as the first Albanian school of language, converted to museum 1960; displays the history of the Albanian alphabet and devt of education in Albania.

Museum of the Struggle for National Liberation: Blvd Repulika, Korçë; tel. (824) 2888; f. 1977; library of 400 vols.

Muzeu Kombetar i Artit Mesjetar (National Museum of Medieval Art): Korçë; tel. (824) 3022; fax (824) 2022; f. 1980; attached to Min. of Culture, Youth and Sports; 7,000 items; colln of icons by Onufri and Onufer Qiprioti and other anonymous artists of 13th and 14th centuries; Dir LORENC GLOZHENI.

Kruja

National Ethnographic Museum: Fortress of Kruja, Kruja; tel. (53) 22225; f. 1989; objects on display depict the Albanian way of living over 300 years; collns incl. ceramics, cotton, silk, wool; various embroideries.

National Museum 'George Kastriot Skenderbeu': Krujë Castle, Kruja; tel. (53) 22225; f. 1982; memorabilia of the nat. hero; items depicting history of 15th-century Albania.

Përmet

Frashëri Brothers Museum: Përmet; birthplace of the brothers Frashëri.

Shkodër

Gurakuqi, Luigi, House-Museum: Shkodër; house where the patriot lived.

Migjeni House-Museum: Shkodër; where the writer Migjeni lived.

Pascha, Vaso, House-Museum: Shkodër; house where the patriot lived.

Tiranë

Albanian National Culture Museum: Tiranë; attached to Institute of Nat. Culture; exhibits incl. agricultural tools of all periods, stock-breeding equipment, interiors and exteriors, household objects, textiles and customs, local crafts and ceramics up to the present day.

Fine Arts Gallery: Blvd Dëshmorët e Kombit, Tiranë; tel. (4) 2233975; fax (4) 2233975; f. 1952; Dir GËZIM QËNDRO.

National Historic Museum: Blvd 'Deshmoret e Kombit', sheshi Skenderbej, Tiranë; tel. (4) 2228389; fax (4) 2228389; f. 1981; displays 4,750 objects in pavilions representing different periods in Albanian history, heraldic emblems of Albanian princes, cathedral columns, icons by Onufri, Illyrian and Greco-Roman artefacts, history of modern Albania; Dir VILSON KURI.

National Museum of Archaeology: Tiranë; tel. (4) 2226541; f. 1948; attached to the Institute of Archaeology of the Acad. of Sciences of Albania; exhibits from prehistoric and historic times up to Middle Ages; responsible for archaeological museums at Durrës, Apollonia and Butrinti; library of 7,200 vols, film and photograph libraries; Curator ILIR GJIPALI; publ. *Illyria* (2 a year).

Natural Science Museum: Tiranë; attached to Univ. of Tiranë; f. 1948; zoology, botany, geology.

Vlorë

District Historical Museum: Vlorë; tel. (63) 2646; f. 1953; archaeology, history of art, history.

Muzeu Etnografik i Vlorës (Ethnographic Museum): Vlorë; tel. (33) 23514.

Muzeu i Pavarësisë (Independence Museum): Vlorë; tel. (33) 2229419; f. 1936; museum bldg was the site of the Ismail Qemali govt and drafting of the declaration of independence; exhibits incl. objects and documents from the Nat. Renaissance period of Albania, rooms where the first Albanian prime min. worked, the meeting room, a camera from 1912; Chief Officer AGRON SKEHU.

Nushi Brothers Museum: Vuno, Vlorë.

Universities

AKADEMIA E ARTEVE TE BUKURA, TIRANË
(Academy of Fine Arts, Tiranë)

Blvd Dëshmorët e Kombit, Sheshi Nen Tereza, Tiranë
Telephone and fax (4) 2225488
Internet: www.artacademy.al
Founded 1966 as Instituti i Lartë i Arteve (Higher Institute of Arts), univ. status 1990
State control
Rector: Prof. PETRIT MALAJ
Deputy Rectors: Assoc. Prof. ARBEN LLOZO, Assoc. Prof. ARTAN PEQUINI
Library Dir: MIRANDA BAKIASI
Library of 50,000 vols
Number of teachers: 386
Number of students: 947

DEANS

Faculty of Fine Arts: Assoc. Prof. SADIK SPAHIJA
Faculty of Music: Prof. SOKOL SHUPO
Faculty of Scenic Arts (Drama): Prof. KASTRIOT ÇAUSHI

ALEKSANDËR MOISIU UNIVERSITY OF DURRES

Rr. Currilave 1, Durrës
Telephone: (52) 239162
Fax: (52) 239163
E-mail: info@uamd.edu.al
Internet: www.uamd.edu.al
Founded 2005
State control
Languages of instruction: Albanian, English
Academic year: October to July
Rector: Prof. Dr MITHAT MEMA
Deputy Rector: Prof. Dr BARDHYL CEKU
Deputy Rector: ESMERALDA URUCI
Chancellor: ULPIAN HOTI
Head of Int. Relations and Projects Office: BELINA BEDINI
Dir of Library: VENERA ALIAJ
Library of 5,000 vols, foreign scientific periodicals, 26 Albanian periodicals from 1945 to 2003
Number of teachers: 225
Number of students: 6,000
Publication: *Journal of Studies on Economics and Society*

DEANS

Faculty of Business: Prof. Dr BARDHYL CEKU
Faculty of Education: Dr EDI PUKA
Faculty of Information and Technology: Doc. LINDITA MUKLI
Faculty of Integrated Studies with Practice: Dr VLADIMIR MUKA (acting)
Faculty of Juridical and Political Sciences: Dr ALKET HYSENI
Faculty of Professional Studies: KSEANELA SOTIROFSKI (Dir)

UNIVERSITETI 'ALEKSANDËR XHUVANI' ELBASAN

Rinia, Elbasan
Telephone: (54) 52782
Fax: (54) 52593
E-mail: info@uniel.edu.al
Internet: www.uniel.edu.al
Founded 1909
State control
Academic year: October to July
Rector: Prof. Dr JANI DODE
Library of 100,000 vols
Number of teachers: 245
Number of students: 11,000
Publications: *Scientific Bulletin* (4 a year), *Studenti* (magazine)

DEANS

Faculty of Economics: Dr ALBERT DELIMETA
Faculty of Human Sciences: Prof. Dr ROLAND GIJNI
Faculty of Natural Sciences: Prof. Dr PEÇI NAQELLARI
Faculty of Social Sciences: Prof. Dr VILSON KURI

UNIVERSITETI BUJQËSOR I TIRANËS
(Agricultural University of Tiranë)

Kodër-Kamëz, Tiranë
Telephone: (4) 7200873
Fax: (4) 7200874
E-mail: iroaut@yahoo.com
Internet: www.ubt.edu.al
Founded 1951 as Instituti i Lartë Bujqësor (Higher Agricultural Institute), univ. status 1991
State control
Academic year: October to September
Rector: Prof. Dr FATOS HARIZAJ
Vice-Rector for Education: Prof. Dr BIZENA BIJO
Vice-Rector for Research: Prof. Dr VELESIN PEÇULI
Head of Int. Relations office: Prof. Dr ARBEN VERÇUNI
Head of Research and Scientific Cooperation: Prof. Dr ANILA HODA
Library Dir: ERMIRA TOZAJ
Library of 15,000 vols
Number of teachers: 243
Number of students: 9,581
Publication: *Albanian Review of Agricultural Sciences*

DEANS

Faculty of Agriculture and Environment: Prof. Dr ARDIAN MAÇI
Faculty of Biotechnology and Food: Prof. Dr VLASH MARA
Faculty of Economy and Agribusiness: Prof. Dr BAHRI MUSABELLIU
Faculty of Forestry Sciences: Assoc. Prof. VATH TABAKU
Faculty of Veterinary Medicine: Assoc. Prof. DHIMITËR RAPTI

UNIVERSITETI EQREM ÇABEJ

Rr. Shtatori 18, Gjirokastër
Telephone and fax (84) 63776
E-mail: ugjrektori@albmail.com
Internet: www.uogj.edu.al
Founded 1971
State control
Rector: Prof. Dr GËZIM SALA

DEANS

Faculty of Education and Social Sciences: Prof. Dr ROLAND ZISI
Faculty of Natural Sciences: Assoc. Prof. Dr KRISTAQ KIKINA

UNIVERSITETI FAN S. NOLI

Rr. Gjergj Kastrioti, Korçë

Telephone: (82) 42230
Fax: (82) 42580
E-mail: info@unkorce.edu.al
Internet: www.unkorce.edu.al

Founded 1971 as Higher Agricultural Institute, present name and title 1992
State control
Languages of instruction: Albanian, English
Academic year: October to July

Rector: Asst Prof. Dr GJERGJI MERO
Vice-Rector for Tuition: Prof. Dr ALI JASHARI
Vice-Rector for Research: Prof. Dr GJERGJI PENDAVINJI
Chancellor: ILIR SOSOLI
Librarian: EDMOND TOLE

Library of 40,000 books
Number of teachers: 124 full-time and 139 part-time
Number of students: 5,447 (incl. part-time and full-time)

Publication: *Buletin Shkencor* (Scientific Research Bulletin)

DEANS

Faculty of Agriculture: Prof. Dr IRENA KALLÇO
Faculty of Economy: Prof. Dr ELFRIDA ZEFI
Faculty of Education: Asst Prof. Dr ALEKSANDRA PILURI
Br. of Nursing: EDA STASA

PROFESSORS

JASHARI, A., Education
MANOKU, Y., Economics
PENDAVINJI, G., Education
TENEQEXHIU, K., Agriculture
ZEFI, E., Economics

UNIVERSITETI I SHKODRËS 'LUIGJ GURAKUQI'
(University of Shkodra 'Luigj Gurakuqi')

Rektorati, Sheshi 2 Prilli, Shkodër

Telephone: (22) 42235
Fax: (22) 43747
E-mail: iroshkoder@unishk.edu.al
Internet: www.unishk.edu.al

Founded 1991, based on fmr Instituti i Lartë Pedagogjik (Higher Pedagogical Institute), Shkodër (f. 1957)
State control
Languages of instruction: Albanian, French
Academic year: October to July

Chancellor: FLORIAN BJANKU
Rector: Prof. Dr ARTAN HAXHI
Vice-Rector: Prof. Dr FATMIR VADAHI
Librarian: ALIDA LUKA

Library of 1,000 vols in Albanian, catalogue of Albanologist and Balkanologist, 32 rare books dating to the beginning of 16th century
Number of teachers: 909 (incl. 290 full-time, 619 part-time)
Number of students: 10,981 (incl. 8,051 full-time, 2,930 part-time)

Publication: *Scientific Bulletin* (separate series on Natural Sciences, Educational Sciences, Social Sciences and Economic and Law Sciences, 1 a year)

DEANS

Faculty of Economics: Prof. Dr ARJETA TROSHANI
Faculty of Education: Prof. Dr MIT'HAT HOXHA
Faculty of Foreign Languages: Dr RAJMONDA KEÇIRA

Faculty of Law: GASPËR KOKAJ
Faculty of Natural Sciences: Prof. Dr ADEM BEKTESHI
Faculty of Social Sciences: Prof. Dr PAULINA HOXHA

UNIVERSITETI I SPORTEVE TE TIRANËS
(Sports University of Tiranë)

Rr. Muhamet Gjollesha Tiranë

Telephone: (4) 2226652
E-mail: contact@ust.edu.al
Internet: www.ust.edu.al

Founded 1958 as Higher Institute of Physical Education and Sports
Language of instruction: Albanian
Academic year: October to July

Rector: Prof. Dr VEJSEL RIZVANOLLI
Deputy Rector: ARBEN KACURRI

Library of 2,835
Number of teachers: 68
Number of students: 835

DEANS

Faculty of Movement Science: Prof. Dr MEHMET SPAHIU
Faculty of Physical Activity and Recreation: Prof. Assoc. Dr AGRON KASA
Sports Research Institute: Prof. Dr ARTAN SHYTAJ

UNIVERSITETI I TIRANËS
(University of Tiranë)

Blvr Dëshmorët e Kombit, Sheshi Nen Tereza, POB 183, Tiranë

Telephone: (4) 2228402
Fax: (4) 2223981
E-mail: info@unitir.edu.al
Internet: www.unitir.edu.al

Founded 1957
State control
Academic year: September to June

Rector: Prof. Dr DHORI KULE
Vice-Rector: Prof. Dr ELSA KONE
Sec.: MAKLENA ÇABEJ
Library Dir: ARJANA KITA

Library of 700,000 vols
Number of teachers: 750
Number of students: 27,745

Publications: *Buletini i Shkencave Mjekësore* (Medicine, 4 a year), *Buletini i Shkencave të Natyrës* (Natural Sciences, 4 a year), *Përmbledhje studimesh* (Colln of Studies, 4 a year, with Institute of Geological Research)

DEANS

Faculty of Economics: Dr KADRI XHULALI
Faculty of Foreign Languages: Doc. AVNI XHELILI
Faculty of History and Linguistics: Dr PASKAL MILO
Faculty of Law: ZEF BROZI
Faculty of Mechanics and Electronics: Dr GËZIM KARAPICI
Faculty of Medicine: Doc. KRISTO PANO
Faculty of Natural Science: Prof. Dr LLUKAN PUKA
Faculty of Philosophy and Sociology: Doc. LUAN PIRDENI

UNIVERSITETI POLITEKNIK I TIRANËS
(Polytechnic University of Tiranë)

Blvd Dëshmorët e Kombit, Sheshi Nen Tereza, Nr 4, Tiranë

Telephone: (4) 2227996

Fax: (4) 2227914
E-mail: enkjaho@yahoo.com
Internet: www.upt.al

Founded 1951 as Polytechnic Institute, present status 1991
State control

Rector: JORGAQ KACANI
Vice-Rector: AKLI FUNDO

Library of 250,000 vols, 20,000 periodicals
Number of teachers: 470
Number of students: 6,297

DEANS

Faculty of Construction Engineering: ANDREA MALIQARI
Faculty of Electrical Engineering: AIDA SPAHIU
Faculty of Geology and Mining: PERPARIM HOXHA
Faculty of Mechanical Engineering: ANDONAQ LONDO

UNIVERSITETI TEKNOLOGJIK 'ISMAIL QEMAL' VLORË
('Ismail Qemal' Technological University of Vlorë)

Lagija 'Pavaresia', Skele Vlore, Vlorë

Telephone: (63) 24952
Fax: (63) 24952
E-mail: kancelar@univlora.edu.al
Internet: www.univlora.edu.al

Founded 1994 as a Technological University
State control

Rector: EUSTRAT ZHUPA
Chancellor: MIMOZA XHELADINI

Library of 10,100 vols
Number of teachers: 195
Number of students: 15,000

DEANS

Faculty of Economics: Dr ALBERT QARRI
Faculty of Humanities: Dr ENGJELL LICAJ
Faculty of Public Health: Asst Prof. HAJDAR KICAJ
Faculty of Technical Sciences: (vacant)

UNIVERSITY OF NEW YORK TIRANË

Rr. 'Medar Shtylla' prane Kopshtit Botanik, POB 2301, Tiranë

Telephone: (42) 273056
Fax: (42) 273059
E-mail: admissions@unyt.edu.al
Internet: www.unyt.edu.al

Founded 2002, accredited by Min. of Education and Science 2006
Private control
Language of instruction: English
Academic year: September to August

Rector: Dr DIONYSIOS MENTZENIOTIS
Deputy Rector: KONSTANTINOS GIAKOUMIS
Pres. and Founder: ELIAS FOUTSIS

Library of 4,000 vols
Number of teachers: 82
Number of students: 524

DEANS

Faculty of Computer Science: Dr MARENGLEN BIBA
Faculty of Economics and Business: Prof. AGIM KUKELI
Faculty of English: Dr MIMOZA RISTA-DEMA
Faculty of Humanities and Social Sciences: Dr ADAM EHRLICH
Faculty of Mathematics and Natural Sciences: Prof. FEJZI KOLANECI

The Higher Education System

The higher education system in Algeria falls under the authority of the Ministry of Higher Education and Scientific Research. In 2007/08 the number of students receiving higher education was 999,690, and several thousand students also go abroad to study. In addition to the 36 main universities, there are 13 other Centres universitaires and a number of technical colleges.

Students are admitted to higher education on the basis of the Baccalauréat de l'Enseignement Secondaire. The three levels of higher education qualifications are the Diplôme d'études universitaires appliqué (DEUA) or Diplôme d'études supérieures (Licence), Maîtrise and Doctorat d'état. The DEUA is awarded after three years of study, whilst the Licence is usually awarded in scientific fields. Engineering, medicine, dentistry and pharmacy degrees and other professional courses last for five years, while the Doctor of Medicine is awarded after seven years. The second degree level (and first postgraduate) is the Maîtrise. This is a two-year taught course including a thesis. Finally, following a Maîtrise awarded with a grade of at least assez bien, a Doctorat d'état is awarded after three to five years of study.

Students may also undertake technical or vocational training at university level. On completion of basic education, vocational training is offered by Centres de formation professionnelle, and on completion of the three-year course a student is awarded the Certificat d'aptitude professionelle (also called the Certificat de technicien), whilst completion of a four-year course leads to the Brevet de maîtrise.

Instituts de technologie (technological institutes) are educational establishments operated by other ministries or national corporations. Degrees offered include the Diplôme d'études universitaires appliquées (DEUA) (two-and-a-half or three years) and the Diplôme d'ingénieur (five years). These institutes are regulated by the ministry or national corporation responsible, and programmes are not standardized.

Higher education in Algeria is currently undergoing reform. The new system, known as LMD (Licence, Masters, Doctorate) aims to bring Algerian higher education into line with other international education systems, such as the European Bologna model. The first stage, a three-year 180-credit Licence began to be phased in from 2004 and has since been implemented as a pilot project at 10 universities. The second stage, a two-year 120-credit Masters was phased in from 2007/8.

Regulatory and Representative Bodies

GOVERNMENT

Ministry of Culture: BP 100, Palais de la Culture 'Moufdi Zakaria', Plateau des Annassers, Kouba, Algiers; tel. (21) 29-10-10; fax (21) 29-20-89; e-mail contact@m-culture.gov .dz; Minister KHALIDA TOUMI.

Ministry of Higher Education and Scientific Research: 11 chemin Doudou Mokhtar, Ben Aknoun, 16422, Algiers; tel. (21) 91-23-23; e-mail info@mesrs.dz; internet www .mesrs.dz; f. 1968; Min. Prof. RACHID HARAOUBIA; publs *Bulletin Officiel de l'Enseignement Supérieur et de la Recherche Scientifique*, *Bulletin semestriel édité en français et en arabe*.

Ministry of National Education: 8 rue de Pékin, el-Mouradia, Algiers; tel. (21) 60-55-60; fax (21) 60-67-02; e-mail education@men .dz; Minister Prof. BOUBAKEUR BENBOUZID.

Ministry of Training and Vocational Education: rue des Frères Aîssou, Ben Aknoun, Algiers; tel. (21) 91-15-03; fax (21) 91-22-66; e-mail contacts@mfep.gov.dz; internet www.mfep.gov.dz; Minister Dr EL-HADI KHALDI.

NATIONAL BODY

Commission nationale d'Equivalences (National Commission for Credentials Evaluation): c/o Ministry of Higher Education and Scientific Research, 11 chemin Doudou Mokhtar, Ben Aknoun, Algiers; tel. (21) 91-17-96; fax (21) 91-46-01; e-mail mesrs@ist .cerist.dz; internet www.mesrs.edu.dz/ english.

Learned Societies

GENERAL

El-Djazairia el-Mossilia: 1 rue Hamitouche, Algiers; f. 1930; cultural soc., particularly concerned with Arab classical music; 452 mems; Pres. ALI BENMERABET; Sec.-Gen. ABDELHADI MERAOUBI.

HISTORY, GEOGRAPHY AND ARCHAEOLOGY

Société Archéologique du Département de Constantine (Constantine Archaeological Society): Musée Gustave Mercier, Constantine; f. 1852; 250 mems; library of 10,000 vols; Pres. Dr BAGHLI (acting); publ. *Recueil des Notices et Mémoires*.

Société Historique Algérienne (Algerian Historical Society): c/o Faculté des Lettres, Univ. d'Alger, Algiers; f. 1963; 600 mems; publ. *Revue d'Histoire et Civilisation du Maghreb*.

LANGUAGE AND LITERATURE

British Council: British Embassy, 12 rue Slimane Amirate, Hydra, Algiers; tel. (21) 48-09-47; e-mail john.mitchell@britishcouncil .org; offers courses and examinations in English language and British culture and promotes cultural exchange with the UK; Dir JOHN MITCHELL.

Instituto Cervantes: 9 rue Khelifa Boukhalfa, 16000 Algiers; tel. (21) 63-38-02; fax (21) 63-41-36; e-mail cenarg@cervantes.es; internet argel.cervantes.es; f. 1992; offers courses and examinations in Spanish language and culture and promotes cultural exchange with Spain and Spanish-speaking Latin and Central America; Dir FRANCISCO CORRAL SÁNCHEZ-CABEZUDO; Academic Head LUIS ROGER RODRÍGUEZ PANIAGUA; Administrator MARÍA JOSÉ ARTÉS RODRÍGUEZ.

MEDICINE

Union Médicale Algérienne (Algerian Medical Association): POB 8, Aadun St, Algiers; tel. (21) 73-36-00; fax (21) 63-27-77; publ. *Algérie Médicale*.

Research Institutes

GENERAL

Organisme National de la Recherche Scientifique (National Bureau of Scientific Research): Route de Dély Ibrahim, Ben Aknoun, Algiers; main executive body for govt policy; Dir (vacant).

Research Centres:

Centre de Coordination des Etudes et des Recherches sur les Infrastructures, les Equipements du Ministère de l'Enseignement et de la Recherche Scientifique (Centre for the Coordination of Studies and Research on the Infrastructure and Facilities of the Ministry of Higher Education and Scientific Research): 1 rue Bachir Attar, Algiers; Dir A. GUEDIRI.

Centre de Développement des Energies Renouvelables (CDER) (Renewable Energy Development Centre): BP 62, Route de l'Observatoire, Bouzaréah, Algiers; tel. (21) 90-15-03; fax (21) 90-15-60; e-mail belhamel@cder.dz; internet www.cder.dz; f. 1988 as Centre Nat. d'Etudes et de Recherche en Energie Renouvelable (CRENO); solar energy, wind energy, thermal energy, bio-energy, hydro-energy; CEO BELHAMEL MAIOUF; publ. *Revue des Energies Renouvelables*.

Centre d'Etudes et de Recherches en Biologie Humaine et Animale (CERBHA) (Study and Research Centre for Human and Animal Biology): BP 9, Université des Sciences et de la Technologie Houari Boumédienne, Algiers; Dir K. BENLATRACHE.

Centre d'Etudes et de Recherche sur le Développement Régional, Annaba (CERDA) (Annaba Study and Research Centre for Regional Development): Université d'Annaba, Annaba; Dir O. HAM-DAOUI.

Centre d'Etudes et de Recherche sur le Développement Régional, Oran (CERDO) (Oran Study and Research Centre for Regional Development): Université d'Oran, Es-Senia, Oran; Dir M. TALEB.

Centre d'Information Scientifique et Technique et de Transferts Technologiques (CISTTT) (Centre for Scientific and Technical Information and for Technological Transfer): BP 315, blvd Frantz Fanon, Algiers (Gare); Dir M. TIAR (acting).

Centre National d'Astronomie, d'Astrophysique et de Géophysique (CNAAG) (National Centre of Astronomy, Astrophysics and Geophysics): Observatoire de Bouzaréah, Algiers; Dir H. BEN-HALLOU.

Centre National de Documentation et de Recherche en Pédagogie (CNDRP) (National Documentation and Research Centre for Education): Université d'Alger, 2 rue Didouche Mourad, Algiers; Dir M. D. CHABOU.

Centre National d'Etudes et de Recherches pour l'Aménagement du Territoire (CNERAT) (National Centre for Studies and Research in National and Regional Development): 3 rue Professor Vincent, Telemly, Algiers; Dir MESSAOUD TAIEB.

Centre National de Recherches et d'Application des Géosciences (CRAG) (National Centre for Geoscientific Research and Application): 2 rue Didouche Mourad, Algiers; Dir R. ABDELHALIM.

Centre National de Recherche sur les Zones Arides (CNRZA) (National Centre for Research on Arid Zones): Université d'Alger, 2 rue Didouche Mourad, Algiers; Dir N. BOUNAGA (acting).

Centre National de Traduction et de Terminologie Arabe (CNTTA) (National Centre for Arab Translation and Terminology): 3 blvd Franklin Roosevelt, Algiers; Dir A. MEZIANE.

Centre de Recherches Anthropologiques, Préhistoriques et Ethnographiques (CRAPE) (Centre for Anthropological, Prehistoric and Ethnographical Research): 3 rue Franklin Roosevelt, Algiers; f. 1957; Dir M. BELKAID.

Centre de Recherches en Architecture et Urbanisme (CRAU) (Centre for Research in Architecture and Town Planning): BP 2, El-Harrach, Algiers; Dir AMEZIANE IKENE.

Centre de Recherches en Economie Appliquées pour le Développement (CREAD) (Centre for Research in Applied Economics for Development): rue Djamal Eddine El-Afghani, El Hamadia-Bouzareah, Algiers; tel. (21) 94-23-67; fax (21) 94-17-16; e-mail cread@wissal.dz; internet www.cread.edu.dz; f. 1985; Dir MOHAMED YACINE FERFERA; publ. Les Cahiers du CREAD.

Centre de Recherches Océanographiques et des Pêches (CROP) (Centre for Oceanographic and Fisheries Research): Jetée Nord, Amirauté, Algiers; Dir RACHID SEMROUD.

Centre de Recherches sur les Resources Biologiques Terrestres (CRBT) (Centre for Research on Biological Resources of the Land): 2 rue Didouche Mourad, Algiers; Dir (vacant).

Centre Universitaire de Recherches, d'Etudes et de Réalisations (CURER) (University Centre for Research, Study

and Application): Université de Constantine, 54 rue Larbi Ben M'Hidi, Constantine; agriculture, forestry, energy resources; Dir FELLAH LAZHAR.

AGRICULTURE, FISHERIES AND VETERINARY SCIENCE

Institut National de la Recherche Agronomique (INRAA) (National Institute of Agronomic Research): 2 ave des Frères Ouadak, Belfort, El Harrach, Algiers; tel. (21) 75-63-15; f. 1966; library of 6,500 vols; Dir M. BEKKOUCHE; publ. Bulletin d'Agronomie Saharienne.

Institut National de Recherche Forestière (National Institute of Forestry Research): Arboretum de Bainem, Algiers; tel. (21) 79-72-96; fax (21) 78-32-11; f. 1981; library of 4,000 vols; Dir FATEH DAHIEDINE; publ. Annale de la recherche forestière.

BIBLIOGRAPHY, LIBRARY SCIENCE AND MUSEOLOGY

Institut de Bibliothéconomie et des Sciences Documentaires (Institute of Library Economics and Documentation): Univ. d'Alger, 2 rue Didouche Mourad, Algiers; tel. (21) 77-71-08-84-34; fax (21) 93-15-10; e-mail allahoum@yahoo.fr; f. 1975; Dir Prof. RABAH ALLAHOUM.

HISTORY, GEOGRAPHY AND ARCHAEOLOGY

Centre National de Recherches Préhistoriques Anthropologiques et Historiques (National Centre for Prehistorical, Anthropological and Historical Research): 3 rue F. D. Roosevelt, Algiers; tel. and fax (21) 74-79-29; f. 1993; library of 35,000 vols; Dir N. E. SAOUDI; publs Libyca, Madjallat et Tarikh.

Institut National de Cartographie (National Institute of Cartography): 123 rue de Tripoli, BP 69, Hussein-Dey, Algiers; f. 1967; under trusteeship of Min. of Defence; Dir NADIR SAADI; publ. maps (100 to 150 a year).

MEDICINE

Institut National d'Hygiène et de Sécurité (National Institute of Hygiene and Safety): Lotissement Meridja, BP 07, 42395 Saoula; f. 1972; research in the fields of hygiene and safety at work; library of 8,000 vols, 110 periodicals, 45,000 microfiches; Dir-Gen. CHÉRIF SOUAMI; publ. Revue Algérienne de Prévention (4 a year).

Institut Pasteur d'Algérie (Pasteur Institute in Algeria): rue du Dr Laveran, Algiers; tel. (21) 65-88-60; fax (21) 67-25-03; f. 1910; research and higher studies in microbiology, parasitology and immunology; preparation of vaccines and sera in conjunction with the health services of Algeria; library of 47,000 vols, 500 periodicals; Dir Prof. F. BOULAHBAL; publ. Archives (12 a year).

TECHNOLOGY

Commissariat à l'Energie Atomique (Atomic Energy Commissariat): BP 1017, Algiers Gare; tel. (21) 43-44-44; fax (21) 43-42-80; e-mail bibl-crna@crna.dz; f. 1983; research and devt in the field of renewable sources of energy, incl. atomic, solar, wind and geothermal energy; incl. centres for energy conversion and for nuclear and solar studies; Librarian AIDA BAHLOUL.

Office National de la Recherche Géologique et Minière/Service Géologique de l'Algérie (National Office of Geological and Mining Research): Cité Ib Khaldoun, BP 102, Boumerdès 35000; tel. (24) 81-75-99; fax (24) 81-83-79; e-mail orgm-dg@orgm.com.dz;

internet www.orgm.com.dz; f. 1883; 5 regional divs: E (located in Tebessa), Central (Tizi Ouzou), W (Sidi Bel Abbes), SW (Bechar) and S (Tamanrasset); library of 50,000 vols, periodicals, maps and aerial photographs; Gen. Man. ABDELKADER SEMIANI; publs Bulletins du Service Géologique d'Algérie (2 a year), Mémoires du Service Géologique de l'Algérie (1 a year).

Libraries and Archives

Algiers

Archives Nationale d'Algérie (National Archives of Algeria): BP 61, Algiers-Gare; tel. (213) 54-21-60; fax (213) 54-16-16; f. 1971; Dir ABDELMADJID CHIKHI.

Bibliothèque de l'Université d'Alger (Library of the University of Algiers): 2 rue Didouche Mourad, Algiers; tel. (21) 64-02-15; fax (21) 61-31-44; f. 1880; 800,000 vols.

Bibliothèque Nationale (National Library): 1 ave Frantz Fanon, Algiers; tel. (21) 63-06-32; f. 1835; 950,000 vols; spec. collns incl. Africa and the Maghreb; Dir MUHAMMAD AÏSSA-MOUSSA; publs Bibliographie de l'Algérie (2 a year), Publications, several collns in Arabic and French.

Section de Diffusion Scientifique et Technique du Centre Culturel Français d'Alger (Department for the Distribution of Scientific and Technical Information at the French Cultural Centre in Algiers): 7 rue du Médecin Capitaine Hassani Issad, 16000 Algiers; tel. (21) 63-61-83; 25,000 vols, 350 periodicals; Dir MARC SAGAERT.

Constantine

Bibliothèque Municipale (Municipal Library): Hôtel de Ville, Constantine; f. 1895; 25,000 vols.

Museums and Art Galleries

Algiers

Direction du Patrimoine Culturel (Office of Cultural Heritage): Ministère de la Culture et du Tourisme, Kouba, Algiers; f. 1901; gen. admin. of museums, restoration, conservation and archaeological excavations; library of 8,000 vols, 300 periodicals; Dir S. A. BAGHLI; publ. Bulletin d'Archéologie Algérienne (1 a year).

Musée National des Antiquités (National Museum of Antiquities): Parc de la Liberté, Algiers; tel. (21) 74-66-86; fax (21) 74-74-71; f. 1897; library of 3,100 vols, 102 periodicals; Dir DRIAS LAKHDAR; publ. Annales du Musée National des Antiquités.

Musée National des Beaux Arts d'Alger (National Fine Arts Museum of Algiers): pl. Dar-el-Salem, El-Hamma, Algiers; tel. and fax (21) 66-49-16; f. 1930; library of 17,000 vols, 300 periodicals; Dir DALILA ORFALI; publ. Revue (1 a year).

Musée National du Bardo: 3 rue F. D. Roosevelt, Algiers; tel. (21) 74-76-41; fax (21) 74-24-53; f. 1930; prehistory, ethnography; library of 3,000 vols; Dir FATIMA AZZOUG.

Musée National du Djihad: El Madania, Algiers; tel. (21) 65-34-88; f. 1983; contemporary history; publ. Actes du Musée.

Constantine

Musée de Cirta: Blvd de la République, Constantine; f. 1853; archaeology, art; library of 20,000 vols; Dir AHMED GUED-DOUDA; publ. Recueil et Mémoires de la Société Archéologique de Constantine.

Oran

Musée National Zabana: Blvd Zabana, Oran; tel. (41) 34-37-81; f. 1935; prehistory, Roman and Punic archaeology, ethnography, zoology, geology, botany, sculpture and painting; Dir Dr MALKI NORDINE.

Sétif

Musée National de Sétif: Rue de l'A.L.N., 19000 Sétif; tel. (36) 84-35-36; fax (36) 84-58-13; e-mail mns@elhidhab.cerist.dz; f. 1991; prehistoric, Roman, Byzantine and medieval Islamic antiquities; Curator CHERIF RIACHE.

Skikda

Musée de Skikda: Skikda; Punic and Roman antiquities, modern art.

Tlemcen

Musée de Tlemcen: pl. Khemisti, 13000 Tlemcen; tel. (43) 26-55-06; Islamic art, minerals, botany, Numidian and Roman archaeology.

Universities

UNIVERSITÉ 8 MAI 1945 DE GUELMA

BP 401, Guelma 24000
Telephone: (37) 20-49-80
Fax: (37) 20-72-68
E-mail: martridha@gmail.com
Internet: www.univ-guelma.dz
Founded 2001
State control
Faculties of economics and management, humanities and social sciences, law, science and engineering
Rector: Prof. MOHAMED NEMAMCHA
Number of teachers: 137
Number of students: 6,716

UNIVERSITÉ ABDELHAMID IBN BADIS DE MOSTAGANEM

POB 227, Mostaganem 27000
Telephone: (45) 26-54-55
Fax: (45) 26-54-52
E-mail: webmaster@univ-mosta.dz
Internet: www.univ-mosta.dz
Founded 1978
State control
Rector: Prof. SEDDIKI M'HAMED MOHAMED SALAH EDDINE
Publication: *Annales du Patrimoine* (Arabic and French, 2 a year)
Faculties of arts and letters, law and commerce, physical training and sports, science and engineering, social sciences.

UNIVERSITÉ ABOU BEKR BELKAID DE TLEMCEN

22 rue Abi Ayad Abdelkrim, Faubourg Pasteur, BP 119, 13000 Tlemcen
Telephone: (43) 20-31-89
Fax: (43) 20-41-89
E-mail: webcri@univ-tlemcen.dz
Internet: www.univ-tlemcen.dz
Founded 1974 as Centre Universitaire de Tlemcen
State control (by Min. of Higher Education and Scientific Research)
Languages of instruction: Arabic, French
Academic year: September to July
Rector: ZOUBIR CHAOUCHE-RAMDANE
Vice-Rector for External Relations: SIDI MOHAMMED BOUCHENAK-KHELLADI (Teaching)
Vice-Rector for Planning: FOUAD GHOMARI
Vice-Rector for Teaching: GHAOUTI MEKANCHA
Sec.-Gen.: ABDELDJALIL SARI ALI

Librarian: NOUREDDINE HADJI
Library of 66,000 vols
Number of teachers: 1,130
Number of students: 30,036

PROFESSORS
Medicine:
 ALLAL, M. R., Radiology
 BENKALFAT, F. Z., Cardiology
 BENKALFAT, M., General Surgery
 HADJ ALLAL, F., Otorhinolaryngology
Science:
 BABA AHMED, A., Physical Chemistry
 BENMOUANA, M., Nuclear Engineering
 BENYOUCEF, B., Energy Physics
 BOUAMOUD, M., Atomic Physics
 BOUCHERIF, A., Applied Mathematics
 HADJIAT, M., Mathematics
 TALEB BENDIAB, S. A., Chemistry
Social Sciences and Humanities:
 BELMOKADEM, M., Quantitative Technology
 BENDIABDALLAH, A., Management
 BOUCHENAK KHELLADI, S. M., Management
 DENDOUNI, H., Civil Law
 DERRAGUI, Z., Literature
 KAHLOULA, M., Private Law
 KALFAT, C., Criminology
 SOUTI, M., Finance

DIRECTORS
Institute of Arabic Language and Literature: MOHAMMED ABBAS
Institute of Biology: KEBIR BOUCHERIT
Institute of Civil Engineering: MUSTAPHA DJAFFOUR
Institute of Earth Sciences: MOHAMED EL KHAMIS BAGHLI
Institute of Economics: MOHAMMED ZINE BARKA
Institute of Electronics: FETHI TARIK BENDIMERAD
Institute of Exact Sciences: ABDERRAHIM CHOUKCHOU BRAHAM
Institute of Foreign Languages: ZOUBIR DENDEN
Institute of Forestry: RACHID BOUHRAOUA
Institute of Hydraulics: ZINE EL ABIDINE CHERIF
Institute of Law and Administration: MOHAMMED BENAMAR
Institute of Mechanical Engineering: FETHI METALSI-TANI
Institute of Medical Sciences: FOUZI TALEB
Institute of Popular Culture: OKACHA CHAIF
Institute for the Promotion of the Arabic Language and for Intensive Language Training: BOUMÉDIÈNE BENMOUSSAT

UNIVERSITÉ AMAR TELIDJI DE LAGHOUAT

Route de Ghardaia, BP 37G, Laghouat 03000
Telephone: (29) 93-59-75
Fax: (29) 93-26-98
E-mail: rectorat@mail.lagh-univ.dz
Internet: www.lagh-univ.dz
Founded 1986 as Ecole Normale Supérieure de l'Enseignement Technique; univ. status 2001
State control
Languages of instruction: Arabic, French
Academic year: October to July
Faculties of economics and management, engineering science, law and humanities
Rector: Dr AZIB MAKHLOUF
Librarian: NOUIOUA HADJIRA
Library of 65,427 vols, 10 periodicals
Number of teachers: 312
Number of students: 9,417 , 41 foreign students

UNIVERSITÉ BADJI MOKHTAR DE ANNABA

BP 12, 23000 Annaba
Telephone: (38) 87-26-78
Fax: (38) 87-24-36
E-mail: abdelkrim.kadi@univ-annaba.org
Internet: www.univ-annaba.org
Founded 1975
State control
Languages of instruction: Arabic, French
Academic year: September to June
Rector: Prof. ABDELKRIM KADI
Vice-Rector for External Relations: Prof. ABDELMADJID HANOUN
Vice-Rector for Graduate Studies: Prof. MOHAMED MANAA
Vice-Rector for Planning: Prof. MOUSSA OUCHEFOUN
Vice-Rector for Postgraduate Studies and Research: Prof. LOUISA ZOUIOUÉCHE ARIBI
Chief Admin. Officer: AHMED HAMDAOUI
Librarian: HADJ JAHEL
Library of 50,000 vols
Number of teachers: 2,278
Number of students: 40,404
Publications: *El-Tawassol* (humanities and social sciences, 2 a year), *Synthese* (science and technology, 2 a year), *University Journal*

DEANS
Faculty of Earth Sciences: NACER KHÉRICI
Faculty of Economics and Management: BELGACEM MADI
Faculty of Engineering: Prof. KAMEL CHAOUI
Faculty of Law: DJAMEL ABDELNASSER MANAA
Faculty of Letters, Humanities and Social Sciences: FOUAD BOUGUETTA
Faculty of Medicine: RACHID BENALI
Faculty of Science: ABDELAZIZ DOGHMANE

UNIVERSITÉ COLONEL AHMED DRAIA D'ADRAR

Rue 11 Décembre 1960, Adrar 01960
Telephone: (49) 96-59-07
Fax: (49) 96-75-71
E-mail: info@univadrar.org
Internet: www.univadrar.org
Founded 2001
State control
Faculties of arts and humanities, science and engineering, social sciences and Islamic studies
Number of teachers: 35
Number of students: 1,030

UNIVERSITÉ D'ALGER

2 rue Didouche Mourad, Algiers
Telephone: (21) 64-69-70
E-mail: contact@univ-alger.dz
Internet: www.univ-alger.dz
Founded 1879 (reorganized 1909)
Languages of instruction: Arabic, French
State control
Academic year: September to June
Pres.: Prof. TAHAR HADJAR
Deputy-Pres. for Pedagogy: S. BABA-AMEUR
Deputy-Pres. for Planning: RABAH KHIMA
Deputy-Pres. for Postgraduates and Scientific Research: A. E. R. AZZI
Librarian: ABDELLAH ABDI
Number of teachers: 1,400
Number of students: 32,000

UNIVERSITÉ D'ORAN

BP 1524, El-M'Naouer, Oran 31000
Telephone: (41) 58-19-40
Fax: (41) 41-01-57
E-mail: contact@univ-oran.dz
Internet: www.univ-oran.dz

Founded 1967
State control
Languages of instruction: Arabic, French
Academic year: September to July (2 semesters)
Rector: Prof. LARBI CHAHED
Vice-Rector for Pedagogy and Registration: AHMED BENAYED
Vice-Rector for Planning and Equipment: MOHAMMED DELLIL
Vice-Rector for Postgraduate Studies, Research and External Relations: AHMED AMRANI
Sec.-Gen.: MABROUK IKHLEF
Librarian: S. CHAÏB DRAA
Library of 800,000 vols
Number of teachers: 1,200
Number of students: 45,000
Publications: *Al Bahith Ilqtissady* (2 a year), *Cahiers du Centre de Documentation des Sciences Humaines*, *Cahiers de Géographie de l'Ouest Algérien*, *El Moutarjeem* (1 a year), *Proceedings of the Research Unit in Social and Cultural Anthropology*, *Revue des Langues*, *Social Sciences Review* (1 a year), *University Letters* (4 a year)

DIRECTORS
Faculty of Arabic Language, Foreign Languages and Fine Arts: Prof. CHEIKH BOUGUERBA
Faculty of Economics: Prof. BOULANDUAR BACHIR
Faculty of Geography and Land Management: Prof. MEKAHLI LARBI
Faculty of Humanities and Religious Studies: Prof. BEKRI A. KRIM
Faculty of Law and Admin.: Prof. YELLES CHAOUCH BACHIR
Faculty of Medical Studies: Prof. ZOUBIR FOUATIH
Faculty of Sciences: Prof. ABDELGHANI KRALEFAT
Faculty of Social Sciences: Prof. AHMED LALAOUI
IGLAEIL Institute: Prof. MOHAMED MELIANI
Institute of Natural Sciences: ZITOUNI BOUTIBA

UNIVERSITÉ DE BECHAR

BP 417, Kenadsa-Béchar
Telephone: (49) 81-55-81
Fax: (49) 81-52-44
E-mail: webmaster@univ-bechar.dz
Internet: www.univ-bechar.dz
Founded 1986 as Institut National d'Etude Supérieure, present name 2009
Faculties of arts, human and social sciences, languages, law and politics, science and technology
Rector: SLIMANI ABD AL-KADER
Number of teachers: 371
Number of students: 8,461

UNIVERSITÉ DE BEJAIA

Route de Terga Ouzemour, Bejaia 06000
Telephone: (34) 21-43-33
Fax: (34) 21-60-98
E-mail: rectorat@univ-bejaia.dz
Internet: www.univ-bejaia.dz
Founded 1983
State control
Rector: DJOUDI MERABET
Number of students: 3,900

DEANS
Faculty of Arts and Humanities: SALAH DERRADJI
Faculty of Economics and Law: FARID YAICI
Faculty of Natural and Life Sciences: (vacant)

Faculty of Science and Engineering Science: BOUALEM SAIDANI

UNIVERSITÉ DE JIJEL

BP 98, Ouled Aissa, Jijel
Telephone: (34) 50-14-00
Fax: (34) 50-18-65
E-mail: webmaster@univ-jijel.dz
Internet: www.univ-jijel.dz
Founded 1998
State control
Faculties of engineering, law, management, science
Number of teachers: 137
Number of students: 3,757

UNIVERSITÉ DE LA FORMATION CONTINUE D'ALGER
(University of Continuous Education)

BP 41, Bois des Cars, Dely Ibrahim, Algiers
Telephone: (21) 91-06-81
Fax: (21) 91-06-82
E-mail: recteur@ufc.dz
Internet: www.ufc.dz
Founded 1990
Rector: ABDELDJEBAR LEMNOUAR
Vice-Rector for Teaching: ABDELKADER NACERI
Vice-Rector for Communication: BRAHIM BOUKRAA
General Secretary: ABDELKARIM SENIANE.

UNIVERSITÉ DE M'SILA

BP 166, Ichebilia, M'sila 28000
Telephone: (35) 55-04-11
Fax: (35) 55-04-04
E-mail: webcell@univ-msila.dz
Internet: www.univ-msila.dz
Founded as Centre Universitaire de M'sila, present status 2001
State control
Faculties of arts and social sciences, economics, law, management and commercial sciences, science and engineering
Rector: Prof. SLIMANE BARHOUMI
Number of teachers: 246
Number of students: 10,355

UNIVERSITÉ DE MASCARA

BP 305, Route de Mamounia, Mascara 29000
Telephone: (45) 80-41-69
Fax: (45) 80-41-64
E-mail: cum@univ-mascara.dz
Internet: www.univ-mascara.dz
Faculties of arts, commerce and management, economics, languages and languages of the social and human sciences, law and administration, natural and life sciences, science and technology.

UNIVERSITÉ DE TÉBESSA

Tébessa 12002
Telephone: (37) 49-00-62
Fax: (37) 49-02-68
E-mail: cutebessa@ist.cerist.dz
Internet: www.univ-tebessa.dz
Rector: Prof. ABDELKRIM GOUASMIA.

UNIVERSITÉ DES SCIENCES ET DE LA TECHNOLOGIE HOUARI BOUMEDIENE

BP 32, El Alia, Bab Ezzouar, Algiers 16111
Telephone: (21) 24-72-83
Fax: (21) 24-79-04
E-mail: benrect@wissal.dz
Internet: www.usthb.dz
Founded 1974
Languages of instruction: Arabic, French

Academic year: September to July
Rector: Prof. BENALI BENZAGHOU
Vice-Rectors: MALEK BOUHADEF, MAHREZ DRIR, MOHAMED SAIDI, DJAMEL EDDINE AKRETCHE
Sec.-Gen.: REDA DJELLID
Librarian: SOUHILA BENRABAH
Number of teachers: 1,509
Number of students: 20,078 undergraduate, 3,098 postgraduate
Publication: *Annales des Sciences et de la Technologie*

DEANS
Faculty of Biological Sciences: FATIMA LARABA-DJEBARI
Faculty of Chemistry: MOHAMED CHATER
Faculty of Civil Engineering: FARID KAOUA
Faculty of Earth Science, Geography and Management Territory: AZIOUZ OUABADI
Faculty of Electronics and Computer Science: ZAIA ALIMAZIGHI
Faculty of Mathematics: KAMEL BOUKHETALA
Faculty of Mechanical Engineering and Chemical Engineering: RACHIDA MAACHI
Faculty of Physics: MOHAMED BENDAOUD

UNIVERSITÉ DES SCIENCES ET DE LA TECHNOLOGIE MOHAMED BOUDIAF D'ORAN

BP 1505, El M'naouer, Oran
Telephone: (41) 56-03-33
Fax: (41) 56-03-22
E-mail: webmaster@univ-usto.dz
Internet: www.univ-usto.dz
Founded 1975
Languages of instruction: Arabic, French
Academic year: September to July
Rector: Prof. M. BENSAFI
Vice-Rector for Planning and Orientation: MOHAMED TEBBAL
Vice-Rector for Postgraduate Studies, Research and External Relations: BENYOUNES MAZART
Vice-Rector for Teaching and Retraining: MAAMAR BOUDIA
Sec.-Gen.: ELOUADI DORGHAM
Librarian: BACHIR YAKOUBI
Number of teachers: 582
Number of students: 11,491

DEANS
Faculty of Architecture and Civil Engineering: HAMID P. KHELAFI
Faculty of Electrical Engineering: ABDELHAMID MIDOUN
Faculty of Mechanical Engineering: OMAR IMINE
Faculty of Sciences: MOHAMED BENYETTOU

FACULTIES
Faculty of Architecture and Civil Engineering: BP 1505, El M'naouer, Oran; tel. and fax (41) 42-06-82; Depts of Architecture, Civil Engineering, Hydraulics.
Faculty of Electrical Engineering: BP 1505, El M'naouer, Oran; tel. and fax (41) 42-06-81; Depts of Electronics, Electrotechnics.
Faculty of Mechanical Engineering: BP 1505, El M'naouer, Oran; tel. and fax (41) 41-92-69; Depts of Marine Engineering, Mechanical Engineering, Metallurgy.
Faculty of Sciences: BP 1505, El M'naouer, Oran; tel. and fax (41) 42-06-80; Depts of Biology, Computer Sciences, Industrial Chemistry, Languages, Mathematics, Physical Education, Physics.

UNIVERSITÉ DES SCIENCES ISLAMIQUES EMIR ABDELKADER DE CONSTANTINE

Al Kaddour Bumdus, BP 137, Constantine 25000
Telephone: (31) 92-26-94
Fax: (31) 92-53-71
E-mail: a.boukhalkhal@univ-emir.dz
Internet: www.univ-emir.dz

Founded 1984
State control
Academic year: September to June

Faculties of arts and humanities, culture and sharia, fundamentals of Islam, fundamentals of religion

Rector: Dr ABDULLAH BOUKHALKHAL

Library of 16,000 vols
Number of teachers: 112
Number of students: 2,476

UNIVERSITÉ DJILLALI LIABES DE SIDI BEL ABBÈS

BP 89, Sidi Bel Abbès 22000
Telephone: (48) 54-98-88
Fax: (48) 56-95-46
E-mail: rectorat@univ-sba.dz
Internet: www.univ-sba.dz

Founded 1978, present status 1989
State control

Rector: ABDEL NACER TOU

Library of 70,000 vols
Number of students: 15,000

DEANS

Faculty of Economics: M. DANI ELKBIR
Faculty of Engineering: A. KHALFI
Faculty of Humanities: N. SEBBAR
Faculty of Law: B. MEKELKEL
Faculty of Medicine: A. DJADEL
Faculty of Science: M. BENYAHYA
Research Centre: F. TEBBOUNE (Dir)

UNIVERSITÉ DR YAHIA FARÈS DE MÉDÉA

Ain d'Heb, Médéa 26000
Telephone: (25) 58-16-87
Fax: (25) 58-28-11
E-mail: cu.medea@gmail.com
Internet: www.cu-medea.dz

Founded 1989

Director: Dr CHAABAIKI MONKEY

Faculties of arts, commerce and management, economics, languages, law, science and technology, social sciences and humanities.

UNIVERSITÉ DU 20 AOÛT 1955 DE SKIKDA

BP 26, Route d'El-Hadaiek, Skikda 21000
Telephone: (38) 70-10-32
Fax: (38) 70-10-04
E-mail: rectorat@univ-skikda.dz
Internet: www.univ-skikda.dz

Founded 2001
State control

Rector: Prof. ALI KOUADRIA.

UNIVERSITÉ FERHAT ABBAS DE SÉTIF

Route de Scipion, 19000 Sétif
Telephone: (36) 72-10-25
Fax: (36) 92-51-27
Internet: www.univ-setif.dz

Founded 1978
State control
Languages of instruction: Arabic, French
Academic year: September to June

Rector: Prof. CHEKIB-ARSLANE BAKI

Vice-Pres. for Det: Dr LARBI MOKRANI
Vice-Pres. for External Relations and Cooperation: BELKACEM NOUICER
Vice-Pres. for Research and Graduate Studies: Prof. MOHAMMED MOSTEFAI
Vice-Pres. for Undergraduate Studies: Prof. NABIL NANCIB
Gen. Sec.: NOUREDDINE BENHENNI
Librarian: CHÉRIF CHIDEKH

Number of teachers: 594
Number of students: 12,700

Publication: *Annales* (4 a year)

DIRECTORS

Institut d'Architecture: TAHAR BELLAL
Institut de Biologie: RACHID GHARZOULI
Institut de Chimie Industrielle: B. DJELLOULI
Institut de Droit: M. KARMED
Institut d'Electronique: S. BERRETILI
Institut d'Electrotechnique: SAAD BELKHIAT
Institut de Génie Civil: M. MIMOUN
Institut d'Informatique: SAMIR AKROUF
Institut des Langues Etrangères: ABDELKRIM ZEGHAD
Institut des Lettres Arabes: BELKACEM NOUICER
Institut de Mathématiques: BOUBEKEUR MEROUANI
Institut de Mécanique: AHMED MANALLAH
Institut de Physique: ABDELAZIZ MANSOURI
Institut des Sciences Economiques: H. SAHRAOUI
Institut des Sciences Médicales: R. TALBI
Institut de Tronc-Commun et Technologie: MABROUK BENKHEDIMALLAH

UNIVERSITÉ HADJI LAKHDAR DE BATNA

5 ave Chahid Boukhlouf, 05000 Batna
Telephone: (33) 81-41-32
Fax: (33) 82-66-77-114
E-mail: recteur@univ-batna.dz
Internet: www.univ-batna.dz

Founded 1977 as Centre Universitaire de Batna

Rector: Prof. MOUSSA ZEREG
Vice-Rector for External Relations: Dr SALAH BOUBECHICHE
Vice-Rector for Planning: Dr HACENE CHAABANE
Vice-Rector for Postgraduate Students and Research: Dr LAMINE MELKEMI
Vice-Rector for Teaching: Dr HACENE SMADI
Sec.-Gen.: ALI LABOUEL

Library of 60,000 vols

Publications: *Revue des Sciences Agronomiques et Forestières* (1 a year), *Revue Sciences Sociales et Humaines* (1 a year), *Revue II IIA* (1 a year)

Faculties of agronomic and veterinary sciences, economics, humanities and social sciences, hydraulic and civil engineering, medicine, science and technology.

UNIVERSITÉ HASSIBA BENBOUALI DE CHLEF

Hay Salam, route nationale 19, Chlef 02000
Telephone: (27) 72-28-77
Fax: (27) 72-28-77
E-mail: info@univ-chlef.dz
Internet: www.univ-chlef.dz

Founded 1983; present status 2001
State control

Rector: A. OUAGUED

Library of 10,220 vols, 127 periodicals
Number of teachers: 275
Number of students: 12,522

Faculties of earth science and agronomy, humanities and social sciences, science and engineering.

UNIVERSITÉ IBN KHALDOUN DE TIARET

BP 78, 14000 Tiaret
Telephone: (46) 42-42-13
Fax: (46) 42-41-47
E-mail: univ-tiaret@mail.univ-tiaret.dz
Internet: www.univ-tiaret.dz

Founded 1980 as Institut National d'Enseignement Supérieur de Tiaret, became Centre Universitaire de Tiaret 1992, present name and status 2001
Languages of instruction: Arabic, French
Academic year: October to July

Depts of Arabic literature, biology, economics, law, physics, technology; institutes of agronomy, civil engineering, electronic engineering, environment, mechanical engineering, veterinary medicine

Rector: Dr NASREDDINE HADJ-ZOUBIR
Vice-Rector of Planning, Orientation and Information: Dr A. BENAMARA
Vice-Rector of Scientific Research, External Relations and Cooperation: Dr M. HASSANE
Vice-Rector of Studies: K. BOUCHENTOUF
Librarian: ABED MAKHLOUFI

Number of teachers: 229
Number of students: 10,493

UNIVERSITÉ KASDI MERBAH D'OUARGLA

BP 511, Route de Ghardaïa, Ouargla
Telephone: (29) 71-24-68
Fax: (29) 71-51-61
E-mail: info@ouargla-univ.dz
Internet: www.ouargla-univ.dz

Founded 1987 as Ecole Nationale Supérieure; present status 2001
State control
Academic year: September to June

Dir: MOHAMED EL-KHAMES TIDJANI

Number of teachers: 465
Number of students: 10,118

DEANS

Faculty of Law and Economics: NASREDDINE SEMAR
Faculty of Letters and Languages: SALAH KENNOUR
Faculty of Science and Engineering: BELKHEIR DADA MOUSSA

UNIVERSITÉ LARBI BEN MHIDI D'OUM EL-BOUAGHI

BP 358, Oum El-Bouaghi 04000
Telephone: (32) 42-42-12
Fax: (32) 42-10-36
E-mail: chelfaycal@yahoo.fr
Internet: www.univ-oeb.dz

Founded 1983, as Ecole Normale Supérieure d'Oum El-Bouaghi
Academic year: January to December

Rector: Prof. AHMED BOURAS

Number of teachers: 357
Number of students: 16,243

Institutes of economics and management; exact sciences, foreign languages and literature; law and administration; natural sciences; technology; urban technology management.

UNIVERSITÉ M'HAMED BOUGARA DE BOUMERDÈS

Ave de l'indépendance, Boumerdès 35000
Telephone: (24) 81-69-01
E-mail: rectorat@umbb.dz
Internet: www.umbb.dz

Founded 1981.

UNIVERSITÉ MENTOURI DE CONSTANTINE

Route Ain El Bey, 25017 Constantine
Telephone: (31) 81-88-92
Fax: (31) 81-97-11
Internet: www.umc.edu.dz
Founded 1969
Languages of instruction: Arabic, French

Institutes of agriculture and nutrition, Arabic, architecture and town planning, biology, chemistry, civil and mechanical engineering, computer science, earth sciences, economics, electronics, foreign languages, industrial chemistry, law and administration, mathematics, physical education, physics, psychology, social sciences, sociology, technology, veterinary science; also a pre-univ. centre and audiovisual dept

Rector: Prof. ABDELHAMID DJEKOUN
Vice-Rector for Orientation, Planning and Information: EMBAREK FERGAG
Vice-Rector for Postgraduate and Scientific Research: SALAH EDDINE BOUAOUD
Vice-Rector for Teaching: BELKACEM SLATINA
Sec.-Gen.: FOUDIL BELAOUIRA
Librarian: TEBOURA BENKAID-KESBA

Library of 240,000 vols
Number of teachers: 1,503
Number of students: 27,995

UNIVERSITÉ MOHAMED KHIDER DE BISKRA

BP 145, Biskra 07000
Telephone: (33) 74-60-61
Fax: (33) 73-07-30
E-mail: webmaster@univ-biksra.dz
Internet: www.univ-biskra.dz
Founded 1998
State control

Rector: Prof. BELKACEM SELATNIA
Vice Rector: BRAHIM MEZERDI

Number of teachers: 800
Number of students: 28,000

Faculties of economics and management, law and political sciences, literature and foreign languages, science, social sciences, technology.

UNIVERSITÉ MOULOUD MAMMERI DE TIZI-OUZOU

BP 17, Oued-Aissi, Tizi-Ouzou
Telephone: (26) 21-53-14
Fax: (26) 21-29-68
E-mail: univ_tizi@mail.ummto.dz
Internet: www.ummto.dz
Founded 1977; present status 2001
State control

Faculties of arts and humanities, biology and agronomy, construction engineering, economics and management, electrical and computer engineering, law, medicine and science

Rector: Prof. RABAH KAHLOUCHE
Number of students: 37,600

UNIVERSITÉ SAAD DAHLAB DE BLIDA

Route de Soumaa, BP 270, Blida 09000
Telephone: (25) 43-38-65
Fax: (25) 43-38-64
E-mail: contact@univ-blida.dz
Internet: www.univ-blida.edu.dz
Founded 1981 as Centre Universitaire de Blida

Rector: Prof. ABDELLATIF BABA AHMED
Vice-Rector for Devt: DJAMEL BOUKERCH
Vice-Rector for Communication Relations: SALIHA OUKID
Vice-Rector for External Relations: KARIMA MENOUERI

Vice-Rector for Graduate Studies: MAHMOUD CHERGUI
Vice-Rector for Postgraduate Affairs and Scientific Research: MOHAMMED MEGHA-TRIA

Number of teachers: 644
Number of students: 45,491

Publication: *Revue de l'Université*

Depts of aeronautics, agronomy, agricultural engineering, architecture, civil engineering, economics, electronics, industrial chemistry, language and literature, law, mathematics, mechanics, medicine, physics, social sciences, veterinary science.

UNIVERSITÉ TAHAR MOULAY DE SAIDA

BP 138, Cité ENNASR, Saida
Telephone: (48) 47-77-29
Fax: (48) 47-11-24
Internet: www.univ-saida.dz.

UNIVERSITÉ ZIANE ACHOUR DE DJELFA

BP 3117 Cudjelfa, Djelfa 17000
Telephone: (27) 90-02-03
Fax: (27) 90-02-01
E-mail: dg_cud@yahoo.fr
Founded 1990

Institutes of economics, commerce and management, law and administration, literature and languages, natural and life sciences, science and technology, social sciences and humanities.

University Centres

CENTRE UNIVERSITAIRE D'EL OUED

POB 789, Central Valley, El Oued 39000
Telephone: (32) 22-30-07
Fax: (32) 22-30-03
E-mail: administration@mail.univ-eloued.dz
Internet: www.univ-eloued.dz
Founded 1995

Institutes of arts and languages, commerce, economics and management, law and administration, science and technology, social and human sciences

Dir: Dr IZZ AL-DIN HAFTARI
Number of students: 11,435

CENTRE UNIVERSITAIRE D'EL-TARF

BP 73, El-Tarf 36000
Telephone: (38) 60-18-93
Fax: (38) 60-15-28
E-mail: directeur@cuniv-eltaref.edu.dz
Internet: www.cuniv-eltaref.edu.dz
Founded 1992

Institutes of agriculture, biology, Arab language and literature, social science and demography, veterinary science
Number of teachers: 169
Number of students: 3,000

CENTRE UNIVERSITAIRE DE BORDJ BOU ARRÉRIDJ

Bordj Bou Arréridj
Telephone: (35) 66-65-17
Fax: (35) 66-65-21
E-mail: direction_cubba@wissal.dz
Internet: www.centrebba.africa-web.org
Founded 2001

Institutes of computer science, electronics, economics, management
Number of students: 7,000

CENTRE UNIVERSITAIRE DE BOUIRA

Bouira
Telephone: (26) 93-88-43
Fax: (26) 93-09-24
E-mail: cobiblio@yahoo.com
Academic year: September to July

Depts of Arabic language and literature, Berber language and culture, economics and management, human and social sciences, law

Dir: Dr AHMED HIDOUCHE
Number of teachers: 145
Number of students: 12,000

CENTRE UNIVERSITAIRE DE GHARDAIA

Alnoumrat, Ghardaia 47000
Telephone: (29) 87-01-87
Fax: (29) 87-02-10
Internet: www.cu-ghardaia.edu.dz

Institutes of humanities and social sciences, natural and life sciences, trade.

CENTRE UNIVERSITAIRE DE KHENCHELA

Route de Constantine, BP 1252, El Houria, Khenchela 40004
Telephone: (32) 33-19-66
Fax: (32) 33-19-63
E-mail: cuniv_khenchela@cuniv-khenchela.edu.dz
Internet: www.cuniv-khenchela.edu.dz
Founded 2001

Institutes of commerce and management, economics, human and social sciences, law and administration, letters and languages, natural and life sciences, science and technology

Dir: Dr AHMED BAKHOUCHE
Gen. Sec.: YOUCEF HAMADA.

CENTRE UNIVERSITAIRE DE SOUK-AHRAS

Rue Djabar Amor M. Daourouch, Souk-Ahras 41220
Telephone: (37) 32-62-62
Fax: (37) 32-65-65
Internet: www.cu-soukahras.dz
Founded 2001

Institutes of law, science and engineering.

CENTRE UNIVERSITAIRE KHEMIS MILIANA

Route de Theniet El-Had, Khemis Miliana 44225
Telephone: (27) 66-42-32
Fax: (27) 66-48-63
E-mail: cukm@cukm.org
Internet: www.cukm.org

Institutes of science and technology, natural and earth sciences, economics and management, law and administration
Library of 17,968 vols.

National Schools and Institutes

ÉCOLE NATIONALE D'ADMINISTRATION

13 chemin Abdelkader Gadouche, Hydra, Algiers
Telephone: (21) 60-13-50
Fax: (21) 60-49-41
E-mail: ena@wissal.dz
Internet: www.ena.dz
Founded 1964

State control
Dir: HOCINE CHERHABIL
Library of 30,000 vols, 600 periodicals
Publication: *Idara* (52 a year)
Provides training for entry into the civil service.

ÉCOLE NATIONALE D'INFORMATIQUE (ESI)

BP 68M, Oued Smar, El Harrach, Algiers 16309
Telephone: (21) 51-60-77
Fax: (21) 51-61-56
E-mail: de@esi.dz
Internet: www.esi.dz
Founded 2008
Training and research in information science
Dir: M. HENNI.

ÉCOLE NATIONALE POLYTECHNIQUE

Rue des frères Oudak, Hassen Badi El Harrach, Algiers 16200
Telephone: (21) 52-10-27
Fax: (21) 52-29-73
E-mail: omar.stihi@enp.edu.dz
Internet: www.enp.edu.dz
Founded 1925 as Institut Industriel d'Algérie
Depts of basic sciences, chemical engineering, civil engineering, electrical engineering, environmental engineering, hydraulics, industrial engineering, languages, mechanical engineering, metallurgy, mining engineering
Dir: Dr MOHAMED DEBYECHE
Library of 45,000 vols
Number of teachers: 200
Number of students: 1,500 (1,000 undergraduate, 500 postgraduate)

ÉCOLE NATIONALE SUPÉRIEURE AGRONOMIQUE (ENSA)

Hacène Badi, El Harrach, Algiers 16200
Telephone: (21) 52-50-84
Fax: (21) 82-27-29
E-mail: ina@ina.dz
Internet: www.ina.dz
Founded 1905
State control
Dir: M. M. ISSOLATT ROZA
Library of 80,000 vols, 120 periodicals
Number of teachers: 165
Number of students: 1,400
Publication: *Annales* (1 a year).

ÉCOLE NATIONALE SUPÉRIEURE D'HYDRAULIQUE

BP 31, Blida 09000
Telephone: (25) 39-94-47
Fax: (25) 39-94-46
E-mail: miah@ensh.dz
Internet: www.ensh.dz
Founded 1972
State control
Depts of continuing education, core courses, research and postgraduate studies, specialized subjects, training and education
Dir: MOHAMED SAÏD BENHAFID.

ÉCOLE NATIONALE SUPÉRIEURE DES SCIENCES DE LA MER ET DE L'AMÉNAGEMENT DU LITTORAL (ENSSMAL) (National High School of Marine Sciences and Coastal Management)

Campus Universitaire, BP 19, Bois des Cars Dély Ibrahim, 16320 Alger
Telephone: (21) 91-77-74
Fax: (21) 91-77-91
E-mail: dg_enssmal@enssmal.dz
Internet: www.enssmal.dz
Founded 1882
Language of instruction: French
Academic year: September to July
Dir: Dr DJAMEL EDDINE ZOUAKH
Library of 11,500 vols
Number of teachers: 62
Number of students: 1,001 (971 graduates, 30 postgraduates)
Publication: *Pelagos* (irregular).

ÉCOLE NATIONALE SUPÉRIEURE DES TRAVAUX PUBLICS (ENSTP)

Rue Sidi Garidi, BP 32, Algiers 16051
Telephone: (21) 28-68-38
Fax: (21) 28-14-07
E-mail: entp@wissal.dz
Internet: www.entp.edu.dz
Founded 1966
State control
Publication: *Algérie Équipement*.

ÉCOLE NATIONALE SUPÉRIEURE VÉTÉRINAIRE D'ALGER (ENSV)

BP 161, Hacène Badi, El Harrach, Algiers
Telephone: (21) 52-51-32
Fax: (21) 82-44-81
Internet: www.env.dz
Founded 1970
State control
Dir: Prof. LOUARDI GUEZLANE
Library of 8,000 vols, 40 periodicals
Number of teachers: 60
Number of students: 1,050

ÉCOLE NORMALE SUPÉRIEURE D'ENSEIGNEMENT TECHNOLOGIQUE

BP 1523, El-M'naouer, Oran 31000
Telephone: (41) 58-20-64
Fax: (41) 58-20-66
E-mail: benziane_baki@yahoo.fr
Internet: www.enset-oran.dz
Founded 1970
Depts of chemistry, civil engineering, continuing education, electrical engineering, mathematics, mechanical engineering, physics
Dir: BENZIANE BAKI
Library of 34,917 vols
Publication: *COST*.

ÉCOLE NORMALE SUPÉRIEURE DE CONSTANTINE

Plateau du Mansourah, Constantine
Telephone: (31) 61-21-53
Fax: (31) 63-00-75
Internet: www.ens-constantine.dz
Founded 1984
State control
Publication: *Forum de l'enseignant* (1 a year, in Arabic and French).

ÉCOLE NORMALE SUPÉRIEURE DE KOUBA

Bachir El Ibrahimi, BP 92, Kouba 16050
E-mail: webmaster@ens-kouba.dz
Internet: www.ens-kouba.dz
Depts of chemistry, computer science, education, mathematics, music, natural sciences, physics
Dir: Dr ABDELHAMID MERAGHNI.

ÉCOLE POLYTECHNIQUE D'ARCHITECTURE ET D'URBANISME

Route de Beaulieu, El Harrache, BP 177, Algiers 16200
Telephone: (21) 52-47-26
Fax: (21) 52-59-54
E-mail: zerouala54@yahoo.com
Internet: www.epau.edu.dz
Founded 1970
Dir: Prof. MOHAMED SALAH ZEROUALA
Library of 43,000 vols, 296 periodicals
Number of students: 2,804

INSTITUT NATIONAL DE LA PLANIFICATION ET DE LA STATISTIQUE

11 chemin Doudou Mokhtar, Benaknoun, Algiers
Telephone: (21) 91-21-33
Fax: (21) 91-21-39
E-mail: inps-dz@wissal.dz
Internet: www.inps-alger.dz
Founded 1970
State control
Dir: Dr AHMED ZAKANE
Library of 14,089 vols, 430 periodicals
Number of teachers: 122
Number of students: 1,703
3-Year and 5-year undergraduate courses in planning and statistics, 2-year postgraduate course in economics and applied statistics.

Colleges

Conservatoire de Musique et de Déclamation: 2 blvd Ché Guévara, Algiers; f. 1920; library: 6,800 vols; 82 teachers; 2,300 students; Dir-Gen. BACHETARZI MOHIEDDINE; Sec.-Gen. KADDOUR GUECHOUD.

École Supérieure des Beaux-Arts: Blvd Krim Belkacem, Parc Zyriab, Algiers 16200; tel. (21) 74-90-09; fax (21) 74-91-14; f. 1881; painting, sculpture, ceramics, design; library: 9,000 vols; 65 teachers; 350 students; Dir NACER EDDINE KASSAB.

École Supérieure de Commerce d'Alger: 1 Rampe Salah Gharbi, Agha, Algiers; tel. (21) 42-32-31; fax (21) 42-37-32; e-mail contact@esc-alger.com; internet www.esc-alger.com; f. 1900; attached to Univ. of Algiers 1966; 4-year first degree courses, 2-year Masters course; 91 teachers; 1,750 students.

Institut Hydrométéorologique de Formation et de Recherches (IHFR): BP 7019, Séddikia, Oran 31025; tel. (41) 42-28-01; fax (41) 42-13-12; e-mail ihfr@djazair-connect.com; internet www.ihfr.net; f. 1970; library: 15,000 vols; 200 students; Dir A. LAGHA.

Institut des Sciences Politiques et de l'Information: 11 chemin Doudou Mokhtar, Ibn-Aknoun, Algiers; tel. (21) 78-15-18; fax (21) 79-66-41; f. 1948 as result of merger between École Supérieure de Journalisme and Institut d'Études Politiques; attached to Univ. of Algiers; 100 teachers; 2,000 students; Dir Dr ISMAIL DEBECHE.

ANDORRA

The Higher Education System

University-level education is generally undertaken abroad, although there is one university, the Universitat d'Andorra. The University maintains two centres for vocational training, the School of Nursing and the School of Information Technology and Management, and a School of Virtual Learning for distance education. The Ministry of Education, Youth and Sport oversees higher education. In 2005/06 1,066 students were in higher education; 431 students were studying in Andorra, 131 in France and 503 in Spain.

A new baccalaureate examination, which was intended to facilitate direct access for students in the Andorran education system to universities in other European countries, was introduced in 2008.

The Law of Higher Education 12/2008 was passed in June 2008 and a Decree of recognition of foreign qualifications was published in March 2009. With these new regulations, Andorra recognizes levels of qualifications according to the Bologna Process and the Lisbon Convention.

Regulatory and Representative Bodies

GOVERNMENT

Ministry of Education, Youth and Sport: Edif. Molí, 21–23 Avda Rocafort, AD600 Sant Julià de Lòria; tel. 743300; fax 743310; Min. ROSER SUÑÉ PASCUET.

ACCREDITATION

ENIC/NARIC Andorra: Ministra d'Educació, Formació Professional, Joventut i Esports, Edif. el Molí, 4a Planta, 21–23 Avda Rocafort, AD600 Sant Julià de Lòria; tel. 743300; fax 743313; e-mail portal@govern.ad; internet www.govern.ad; Assessor MERITXELL GALLO YANES.

Learned Societies

GENERAL

Amics de la Cultura (Friends of Culture): Plaça Co-Prínceps 4 bis, Despatx no. 1, AD700 Escaldes-Engordany.

Associació Cultural i Artística Els Esquirols (Els Esquirols Cultural and Arts Association): Sala Parroquial, Plaça de l'Església, AD400 La Massana.

Centre de Trobada de les Cultures Pirenenques (Centre for the Understanding of Pyrenean Culture): Edif. Prada Casadet, C/ Prat de la Creu, AD500 Andorra la Vella; tel. 860768; fax 861998; f. 1983; attached to Comunitat de Treball dels Pirineus; database on the Pyrenees; Dir ELISENDA VIVES BALMAÑA.

Cercle de les Arts i de les Lletres (Arts and Letters Circle): 24 Avda Carlemany, AD700 Escaldes-Engordany; tel. 824815; fax 861050; internet www.cercleartsilletres.com; f. 1968; Pres. JOAN BURGUÉS MARTISELLA.

BIBLIOGRAPHY, LIBRARY SCIENCE AND MUSEOLOGY

International Council of Museums, Andorran National Committee: Patrimoni Cultural d'Andorra, Carretera de Bixessarri s/n Aixovall, AD600 Sant Julià de Lòria; tel. 844141; fax 844343; e-mail icom@andorra.ad; internet www.icomandorra.ad; f. 1988; 28 mems; Pres. ISABEL DE LA PARTE CANO.

LANGUAGE AND LITERATURE

Alliance Française: Centre Cultural la Llacuna, Mossèn Cinto Verdaguer 4, AD500 Andorra la Vella; tel. 342852; e-mail alianca-af@andorra.ad; internet www.alliance-francaise-andorre.org; offers courses and examinations in French language and culture and promotes cultural exchange with France.

NATURAL SCIENCES

General

Societat Andorrana de Ciències (Andorra Scientific Society): Centre Cultural la Llacuna, C/ M. C. Verdaguer 4, AD500 Andorra la Vella; tel. 829729; fax 852383; e-mail sac@andorra.ad; internet www.sac.ad; f. 1983; carries out research; organizes talks, conferences and symposiums; 292 mems; Pres. ANGELS MACH; Sec. PERE MUNOZ; Treas. CONXITA NAUDI; publs *Diada Andorrana a la UCE* (1 a year), *El Sac* (12 a year), *Jornades* (1 a year), *Papers de Recerca Històrica* (1 a year), *Recull de Conferències* (1 a year), *Trobades Culturals Pirenenques* (1 a year).

Biological Sciences

Associació per a la Defensa de la Natura (Association for Nature Conservation): Apdo Correus Espanyols 96, AD500 Andorra la Vella; tel. 866086; fax 866586; e-mail adn@andorra.ad; internet www.adn-andorra.org; f. 1986; disseminates information and organizes courses, conferences, school lectures, awareness campaigns about nature and wildlife in Andorra; 300 mems; Pres. ANGELS CODINA FARRÁS; Sec. JORDI PALAUI PUIGVERT; publ. *Aigüerola*.

Research Institutes

GENERAL

Institut d'Estudis Andorrans (Institute of Andorran Studies): Edif. el Molí, 3r pis, 21–23 Avda Rocafort, AD600 Sant Julià de Lòria; tel. 742630; fax 843585; e-mail iea@iea.ad; internet www.iea.ad; f. 1976; centres in Barcelona (Spain) and Toulouse (France); Dir JORDI GUILLAMET.

Attached institutes:

Centre de Biodiversitat (Centre for Biodiversity): Edif. el Molí, 3r pis, 21–23 Avda Rocafort, AD600 Sant Julià de Lòria; tel. 742630; fax 843585; e-mail cbdiea@andorra.ad; f. 1998; study and monitoring of Andorra's biological diversity; library of 450 vols; Dir MARTA DOMÈNECH FERRÉS; publ. *Hàbitats* (2 a year).

Centre d'Estudis de la Neu i de la Muntanya d'Andorra: Edif. el Molí, 3r pis, 21–23 Avda Rocafort, AD600 Sant Julià de Lòria; tel. 742630; fax 843585; e-mail cenma@iea.ad.

Centre de Recerca en Ciències de la Terra (Centre for Earth Sciences Research): Edif. el Molí, 3r pis, 21–23 Avda Rocafort, AD600 Sant Julià de Lòria; tel. 742630; fax 843585; e-mail crecit@andorra.ad; internet www.iea.ad/crecit/index2.html; f. 2001.

Centre de Recerca Sociològica (Centre for Sociological Research): Edif. el Molí, 3r pis, 21–23 Avda Rocafort, AD600 Sant Julià de Lòria; tel. 742630; fax 843585; e-mail cres@iea.ad; internet www.iea.ad/cres/noticies; f. 2000.

Libraries and Archives

Andorra la Vella

Arxiu Nacional d'Andorra (National Archive of Andorra): Edif. Prada Casadet, C/ Prada Casadet, 8–12, AD500 Andorra la Vella; tel. 802288; fax 868645; e-mail ana.gov@andorra.ad; internet www.arxius.ad; f. 1975; 280,000 documents; Head of Service CINTA PUJAL CARABANTES.

Biblioteca Nacional d'Andorra (National Library of Andorra): Placeta de Saint Esteve, Casa Bauró, AD500 Andorra la Vella; tel. 826445; fax 829445; e-mail bncultura.gov@andorra.ad; internet www.bibliotecanacional.ad; f. 1974; legal deposit, Andorran standard book number agency (ISBN); 13,000 vols, 120 periodicals; Chief Librarian PILAR BURGUES MONSERRAT.

Biblioteca Publica del Govern (Government Public Library): Edif. Prada Casadet 2, C/ Prat de la Creu, AD500 Andorra la Vella; tel. 828750; fax 829541; e-mail bibliopublica@andorra.ad; internet www.catalegbiblioteques.ad; f. 1930; 6,076 mems; 55,837 vols; Head INÉS DOMINGO SANCHEZ.

Canillo

Biblioteca Comunal de Canillo (Canillo Community Library): Edif. Telecabina, 3er pis, AD100 Canillo; tel. 753623; e-mail bibliocanillo@andorra.ad; internet www.biblioteques.ad/bibliocanillo; f. 1988; 7,643 items; Librarian DOLORS CALVÓ.

Encamp

Biblioteca Comunal d'Encamp (Encamp Community Library): Complex Esportiu i Sociocultural, AD200 Encamp; tel. 832830;

fax 832903; e-mail biblioteca@encamp.ad; internet www.biblioteques.ad/biblioencamp; f. 1930; 40,000 vols; Librarian CODINA ALFONS.

Escaldes-Engordany

Biblioteca Comunal d'Escaldes-Engordany (Escaldes-Engordany Community Library): Centre Neuràlgic, Parc de la Mola 6, AD700 Escaldes-Engordany; tel. 890875; internet www.biblioteques.ad/biblioescaldes; f. 1971; 33,500 vols; Librarian ALEXIA CARRERAS SIRES.

La Massana

Biblioteca Comunal de la Massana (La Massana Community Library): Avda St Antoni 2, Edif. Telecabina. Plaça del Quart, AD400 La Massana; tel. 838910; fax 736936; e-mail biblioteca@lamassana.ad; internet www.biblioteques.ad/bibliolamassana; f. 1990; 18,367 vols, 45 periodicals; Librarian PAINO GABRIELA; Man. Librarian JOSEFA DIÉGUEZ.

Ordino

Biblioteca Comunal d'Ordino (Ordino Community Library): Edif. la Font, 3a pl., AD300 Ordino; tel. 878136; fax 878137; internet www.biblioteques.ad/bibliordino; f. 1995; 11,000 vols.

Sant Julià de Lòria

Biblioteca Communal de Sant Julià de Lòria (Sant Julià de Lòria Community Library): Centre Cultural i de Congressos Lauredià, Plaça de la Germandat, AD600 Sant Julià de Lòria; tel. 744044; fax 744014; e-mail biblioteca@comusantjulia.ad; internet www.biblioteques.ad/bibliostjulia; f. 1993; 15,522 vols.

Museums and Art Galleries

Andorra la Vella

Casa de la Vall: C/ de la Vall, AD500 Andorra la Vella; tel. 829129; fax 869863; f. 1580.

Canillo

Le Sanctuaire de Meritxell (Meritxell Sanctuary): Meritxell, AD100 Canillo; tel. 851253; fax 851253; historical record of the Andorran people's devotion to their patron saint, the Virgin of Meritxell.

Museu de Les Dues Rodes (Museum of Two Wheels): Ctra. General de Canillo s/n, Al Costat de St Joan de Caselles, AD100 Canillo; tel. 853444; fax 853456; e-mail m2r@canillo.ad; internet www.m2r.ad; motorcycles from the early 20th century to the present day.

Encamp

Electricity Museum: Edif. FEDA, Avda de la Bartra s/n, Sortida d'Escaldes en Direcció a Encamp per la CG2, AD200 Encamp; tel. 739111; fax 739110; e-mail museumw@feda.ad.

Museu d'Art Sacre (Sacred Art Museum): Placeta de Santa Eulàlia, AD200 Encamp; tel. 833551; e-mail casacristo@encamp.ad; colln of liturgical objects from the town's churches, exhibits from 14th century to date.

Museu Nacional de l'Automòbil (National Motor Car Museum): Avda Co-Príncep Episcopal 64, AD200 Encamp; tel. 839760; fax 832266; f. 1988; cars, motorbikes and bicycles from 1898 to 1950, components, miniature cars in porcelain and iron.

Escaldes-Engordany

Andorran Model Museum: Avda de Pessebre 16, AD700 Escaldes-Engordany; tel. 861506; models of prominent Andorran monuments and structures.

Escaldes-Engordany Arts Centre: Avda Carlemany 30, AD700 Escaldes-Engordany; tel. 802255; f. 1934; collns of Josep Viladomat and Andorra Romanesque art.

Museu del Perfum (Perfume Museum): 1era Planta, Avda Carlemany 115, AD700 Escaldes-Engordany; tel. 801926; e-mail museudelperfum@julia.ad; internet www.museudelperfum.ad; history of perfume.

Museu Viladomat d'Escultura (Municipal Cultural Museum): Avda Parc de la Mola 5, Les Escaldes, AD700 Escaldes-Engordany; tel. 829340; fax 829340; e-mail museuviladomat@andorra.ad; f. 1987; Curator GLORIA PUJOL.

La Massana

Casa Rull de Sispony (Rull House of Sispony): C/ Major, Sispony, AD400 La Massana; tel. 836919; fax 835419; e-mail casarull@andorra.ad; family and heritage.

Farga Rossell (Rossell Forge): Avda del Través s/n, AD400 La Massana; tel. 839760; fax 835857; e-mail fargarosell@andorra.ad; internet www.fargarossell.ad; f. 2002.

Ordino

Badge Museum: Ansalonga la Cortinada, AD300 Ordino; tel. 749000; 108,000 different badges relating to significant historical events.

Centre d'Interpretació de la Natura de les Valls d'Ordino (Ordino Valley Nature Interpretation Centre): AD300 Ordino; tel. 837939; fax 837839; e-mail cinvo@andorra.ad; interprets the cultural landscape (nature and culture) of Ordino.

Museu Casa d'Areny-Plandolit (Areny-Plandolit House Museum): C/ Major s/n, AD300 Ordino; tel. 839760; fax 839660; e-mail casa.areny-plandolit@andorra.ad; internet www.patrimonicultural.ad; f. 1987; typical 17th-century house, with later alterations; furniture, porcelain, costumes.

Museu Postal d'Andorra (Andorra Postal Museum): Borda del Raser, C/ Major, AD300 Ordino; tel. 839760; fax 839660; f. 1986, refounded 1998.

Nicolaï Siadristy's Microminiature Museum: Edif. Coma, AD300 Ordino; tel. 838376.

Sant Jordi Iconography and Christianity Museum: Edif. Maragda, AD300 Ordino; tel. 838338; e-mail azorzano@andornet.ad; Christian and Orthodox icons from the main schools in the Ukraine, Russia, Greece and Bulgaria from the 14th to the 19th centuries; 70 polychrome wood statues of Christ from Spanish schools from the 11th to 19th centuries.

Sant Julià de Lòria

Museu del Tabac (Tobacco Museum): Doctor Palau 17, AD600 Sant Julià de Lòria; tel. 741545; fax 842161; e-mail info@museudeltabac.com; internet www.museudeltabac.com; tools, machines, fittings and aromas used in tobacco factories from the 17th century to date; on site of former Reig tobacco factory (1909 to 1957); Dir MARIA MARTÍ.

University

UNIVERSITAT D'ANDORRA

Plaça de la Germandat 7, AD600 Sant Julià de Lòria

Telephone: 743000
Fax: 743043
E-mail: uda@uda.ad
Internet: www.uda.ad
Founded 1997
Language of instruction: Catalan
Vice-Chancellor: DANIEL BASTIDA OBIOLS

DIRECTORS

School of Information Technology and Management: FLORENCI PLA ALTISENT
School of Nursing: ROSA MARI MANDICÓ ALCOBÉ
Centre of Virtual Learning and Univ. Extension: MONTSERRAT CASALPRIM RAMONET

ANGOLA

The Higher Education System

Higher education was established when Angola was still a Portuguese colony, initially with the foundation in 1958 of institutes for training Catholic priests. In 1962 the Estudos Gerais Universitários de Angola was established in Luanda and became the Universidade de Luanda in 1968; a branch was also set up in Huíla. Following independence in 1975 all non-state institutions were closed, and in 1979 the Universidade de Luanda was renamed Universidade de Angola, which in turn became the Universidade Agostinho Neto in 1985; it remains Angola's only public university. Independent Angola's first private university, the Universidade Católica de Angola, was founded in 1992. Currently there are eight private universities operating. In 2004/05 there were 48,184 students in higher education.

Under legislation passed in 1995 full autonomy was conferred on Universidade Agostinho Neto, and staff were empowered to elect organs and officials. Financing for higher education depends on the status of the university: Universidade Agostinho Neto is heavily reliant on state funding, while the private universities rely on students' fees and donations from individuals and non-governmental organizations.

To attend university students must hold the Habilitação Literárias (secondary school leaving certificate), pass the entrance examinations and complete either a period of state employment or pre-university education.

The first undergraduate qualification is the Bacharel, study for which lasts for four years. Students may continue for a further two years, after which the Licenciado is awarded. The Licenciado may also be awarded on completion of a five-year university course, or a six-year course for medical students. A doctorate requires a further two or three years' research following the award of the Licenciado.

Regulatory Bodies

GOVERNMENT

Ministry of Culture: Av. Comandante Gika, Luanda; tel. 222323979; e-mail mincultura@mincultura.gv.ao; internet www.angola-portal.ao/mincult; Minister BOAVENTURA CARDOSO.

Ministry of Education: Av. Comandante Gika, CP 1281, Luanda; tel. 222320653; fax 222321592; internet www.angola-portal.ao/med; Minister ANTÓNIO BURITY DA SILVA NETO.

Ministry of Science and Technology: Ilha do Cabo, Luanda; tel. 222309794; e-mail dgmk@ebonet.com; Minister JOÃO BAPTISTA NGANDAJINA.

Learned Societies

LANGUAGE AND LITERATURE

Alliance Française: Largo da Sagrada Familia, Traversa Barbosa do Bocage 12, CP 1578, Luanda; tel. and fax 222321993; e-mail afluanda@ebonet.net; offers courses and examinations in French language and culture and promotes cultural exchange with France; attached teaching centres in Benguela, Cabinda and Lubango.

União dos Escritores Angolanos (Association of Angolan Writers): CP 2767-C, Luanda; tel. and fax 222323205; e-mail uea@uea-angola.org; internet www.uea-angola.org; f. 1975; 75 mems; library of 2,000 vols; Sec.-Gen. LUANDINO VIEIRA; publs *Criar* (4 a year), *Lavra & Oficina* (12 a year).

Research Institutes

AGRICULTURE, FISHERIES AND VETERINARY SCIENCE

Centro de Investigação Científica Algodoeira (Cotton Scientific Research Centre): Instituto do Algodão de Angola, Estação Experimental de Onga-Zanga, Catete; fibre technology laboratory, agricultural machinery station, crop irrigation station (Bomba-gem); library; Dir Eng. Agr. JOAQUIM RODRIGUES PEREIRA.

Instituto de Investigação Agronómica (Agronomic Research Institute): CP 406, Estação Experimental Agrícola da Chianga, Huambo; f. 1962; incorporates agrarian documentation centre; publs *Comunicações*, *Série Divulgação*.

Instituto de Investigação Veterinária (Institute for Veterinary Research): CP 405, Lubango; tel. 222322094; f. 1965; Dir Dr A. M. POMBAL; publ. *Acta Veterinaria-separatas* (1 a year).

NATURAL SCIENCES

Physical Sciences

Direcção Provincial dos Serviços de Geologia e Minas de Angola (Ángolan Directorate of Geological and Mining Services): CP 1260-C, Luanda; f. 1914; geology, geological mapping and exploration of mineral deposits; library of 40,000 vols; Dir J. TRIGO MIRA; publs *Boletim*, *Carta Geológica de Angola*, *Memória*.

Libraries and Archives

Luanda

Arquivo Histórico Nacional (National Historical Archive): Rua Pedro Félix Machado 49, Luanda; tel. 222333512; fax 222334410; e-mail ahadg@nexus.ao; f. 1977; 20,000 vols, 3,000 periodicals; Dir ROSA CRUZ E SILVA; publ. *Guias de Informação Documental para o Estudo da História de Angola*.

Biblioteca Municipal (Municipal Library): CP 1227, Luanda; tel. 222392297; fax 222333902; f. 1873; 31,470 vols; Dir CUSTA GANHAR FILIPE.

Biblioteca Nacional de Angola (National Library of Angola): Largo António Jacinto, CP 2915, Luanda; tel. 222326331; fax 222326299; e-mail bibliotecanacional@netangola.com; f. 1969; 84,000 vols; IFLA colln legal deposit, nat. deposit for UNESCO and FAO publs; Dir MARIA JOSÉ F. RAMOS.

Museums and Art Galleries

Luanda

Instituto Nacional do Patrimonio Cultural (National Institute for Cultural Heritage): CP 1267, Luanda; tel. 222332575; e-mail ipc@snet.co.ao; nat. antiquities dept; Dir FRANCISCO XAVIER YAMBO.

Affiliated Museums:

Museu Central das Forças Armadas (Central Museum of the Armed Forces): CP 1267, Luanda; Dir SILVESTRE A. FRANCISCO.

Museu do Dundo (Dundo Museum): CP 14, Chitato, Lunda Norte; ethnography; Dir SONY CAMBOL CIPRIANO.

Museu da Escravatura (Museum of Slavery): CP 1267, Luanda; Dir ANICETE DO AMARAL GOURGEL.

Museu Nacional de Antropologia (National Anthropology Museum): CP 2159, Luanda; tel. 222337024; Dir AMERICO A. CUONONOCA.

Museu Nacional de Arqueologia (National Archaeology Museum): CP 79, Benguela; Dir JOAQUIM PAIS PINTO.

Museu Nacional de História Natural (National Museum of Natural History): CP 1267, Luanda; Dir ANA PAULA DOS SANTOS C. VICTOR.

Museu Regional de Cabinda (Cabinda Regional Museum): CP 283, Cabinda; ethnography; Dir TADEU DOMINGOS.

Museu Regional da Huila (Huila Regional Museum): CP 445, Lubango; ethnography; Dir JOSÉ FERREIRA.

Universities

UNIVERSIDADE AGOSTINHO NETO

CP 815, Avda 4 de Fevereiro 7, 2° andar, Luanda
Telephone: 222330517
Fax: 222330520
E-mail: depinf@diee.fe.uan.ao
Internet: www.uan.ao
Founded 1962

Language of instruction: Portuguese
Academic year: October to June
Rector: JOÃO SEBASTIÃO TETA
Number of teachers: 700
Number of students: 6,800

DEANS

Faculty of Agriculture: Dr AMILCAR MATEUS DE OLIVEIRA SALUMBO
Faculty of Economics: Dr LAURINDA DE JESUS FERNANDES HOYGAARD
Faculty of Engineering: CARLOS ALBERTO ABREU SERENO
Faculty of Law: Dr ADERITO CORREIA
Faculty of Medicine: Dr PAULO ADÃO CAMPOS
Faculty of Sciences: Dr ABILO ALVES FERNANDES

AFFILIATED INSTITUTES

Centro Nacional de Investigação Científica: Avda Revolução de Outubro, Luanda; tel. 222350762; Coordinator Dr NANIZEYI KINDUDI ANDRÉ.

Instituto Superior de Ciências da Educação: Rua Salvador Allende, 12, CP 10609, Luanda; tel. 222394979; fax 222394575; internet www.isced-lda.com; Dean Dr DANIEL MINGAS.

UNIVERSIDADE CATÓLICA DE ANGOLA

Rua N. Sra da Muxima 29, CP 2064, Luanda
Telephone: 222331973
Fax: 222398759
E-mail: info@ucan.edu
Internet: www.ucan.edu
Founded 1992
Controlled by Episcopal Conf. of Angola and São Tomé
Academic year: May to December
Faculties of economics, informatics, law, management
Chancellor and Rector: Archbishop DAMIÃO FRANKLIN
Vice-Rector: Fr Dr FILOMENO VIEIRA DIAS
Head of Admin.: Fr Dr MANUEL S. GONÇALVES
Head of Library and Documentation: Fr Dr JOSÉ CACHADINHA
Number of teachers: 99
Number of students: 1,800
Publications: *Revista Academica*, *UCAN Boletim Informativo*.

UNIVERSIDADE JEAN PIAGET DE ANGOLA

Campus Universitário de Viana, Bairro Capalanka, Viana 10365, Brito Godins
Telephone: 222301148
Fax: 222290872
E-mail: info@angola.ipiaget.org
Internet: www.ipiaget.org/campus.asp?id=89
Founded 1998 as a result of collaboration between the Min. for Education and Culture of the Republic of Angola and the Instituto Piaget in Portugal
Courses offered in social sciences and education, science and technology and health.

College

Instituto Médio Industrial de Luanda: Largo de Soweto, CP 2513, Luanda; tel. 222343200; e-mail imil@netangola.com; internet www.netangola.com/imil; f. 1956 as Escola Industrial de Luanda; courses in civil engineering, mechanics, chemistry.

ANTIGUA AND BARBUDA

The Higher Education System

Higher education is provided by an extramural department of the University of the West Indies, which offers several foundation courses leading to higher study at branches elsewhere, and at several other institutes and colleges. Teacher training and technical training are available at the Antigua State College in St John's, which absorbed the Antigua and Barbuda School of Nursing in 2000. There is also an Institute of Technology, a Hotel Training Centre and a private University of Health Sciences.

Admission to tertiary education is usually dependent upon award of the Caribbean Advanced Proficiency Examination (CAPE). Grading in higher education is based on the system used by the University of the West Indies.

Regulatory Bodies

GOVERNMENT

Ministry of Education, Sports, Youth and Gender Affairs: Govt Office Complex, Queen Elizabeth Highway, St John's; tel. 462-4959; fax 462-4970; e-mail doristeen.etinoff@ab.gov.ag; Minister Dr JACQUI QUINN-LEANDRO; Sec. JESSEL EDWARDS; Dir of Education JACINTHA PRINGLE.

Ministry of Tourism, Civil Aviation, Culture and the Environment: Govt Office Complex, Bldg 1, Queen Elizabeth Highway, St John's; tel. 462-0480; fax 462-2483; e-mail mblackman@tourism.gov.ag; Minister HAROLD LOVELL; Minister of State with Responsibility for Culture and Independence Celebrations ELESTON ADAMS.

Learned Societies

BIBLIOGRAPHY, LIBRARY SCIENCE AND MUSEOLOGY

Library Association of Antigua and Barbuda: POB 822, St John's; tel. 462-3500; fax 462-1537; f. 1983; 40 mems; Pres. MOLIVAR SPENCER; Sec. TRACY SAMUEL.

LANGUAGE AND LITERATURE

Alliance Française: POB 2086, St John's; tel. 462-3625; offers courses and examinations in French language and culture and promotes cultural exchange with France.

Archives

St John's

Antigua and Barbuda National Archives: Victoria Park, Factory Rd, St John's; tel. 462-4959; fax 462-4970; e-mail archives@antigua.gov.ag; f. 1982; Dir Dr MARION BLAIR.

Universities

UNIVERSITY OF HEALTH SCIENCES ANTIGUA

Dowhill Campus, Piccadilly, POB 510, St John's

Telephone: 460-1391
Fax: 460-1477
E-mail: admissions@uhsa.edu.ag
Internet: www.uhsa.ag
Founded 1982
Pres.: Dr AKIN OMITOWOJU
Registrar: IVORY TAYLOR
Librarian: (vacant)
Dean, School of Medicine: Dr N. OLOWOPOPO
Library: in process of formation
Number of teachers: 32
Number of students: 203
Schools of liberal arts and sciences, medicine, nursing, veterinary medicine, postgraduate medical education.

Colleges

Antigua and Barbuda International Institute of Technology (ABIIT): POB 736, St John's; tel. 480-2400; fax 480-2411; e-mail info@abiit.edu.ag; internet www.abiit.edu.ag; f. 2001; Pres. GLADWIN HENRY; Dean of Academics EUSTACE HILL.

Antigua State College: POB 193, Golden Grove, St John's; tel. 462-1434; fax 460-9476; f. 1977 by merger of Leeward Islands Teachers' Training College and Golden Grove Technical College, absorbed Antigua and Barbuda School of Nursing in 2000; hospitality and tourism management, teacher training, technical training.

University of the West Indies School of Continuing Studies (Antigua and Barbuda): POB 142, St John's; tel. 462-1355; fax 462-2968; e-mail university@candw.ag; f. 1949; adult education courses, spec. programmes for women, summer courses for children, occasional seminars and workshops; library: 10,000 vols; 23 part-time tutors; 350 students; Resident Tutor Dr ERMINA OSOBA.

ARGENTINA

The Higher Education System

The Federal Law of Education of 1993 decentralized the education system, with administration devolving to each of the 23 individual provinces and to the Municipality of Buenos Aires. The federal Ministry of Education, Science and Technology is responsible for the provision of university education, while each provincial ministry of education is responsible for education provision at post-secondary, non-university level. Technical education is supervised by the Consejo Nacional de Educación Técnica.

Between 2003 and 2007 a number of laws were passed that defined education as a national priority and laid the foundation for developing a state policy. Among these were: the National Education Law (Law No. 26.206, 2007), the Education Finance Act (Law No. 26.075, 2005), the Vocational Technical Education Act (Law No. 26.058, 2005), the Law on National Comprehensive Sex Education (Law No. 26.150, 2006), the Teaching Salary Guarantee Act and 180 days of school (Law No. 25.864, 2003), the Law on the National Teaching Incentive Fund (Law No. 25.919, 2004) and the Law on the Protection of the Rights of Children and Adolescents (Act No. 26.061, 2005).

Admission to higher education is dependent upon successful completion of the secondary qualification. There are two levels of higher qualification: first, a Professional Title (Licenciado), study for which lasts for between four and six years depending on the subject; and second, the Doctorado, which requires a further two years of study. Vocational and professional post-secondary education and training is available at higher technical schools or institutes of technology, also known as polytechnic institutes, and at higher commercial schools. Courses at these institutions are usually two years in length, and successful students are awarded a title such as Técnico Superior or Técnico Universitario in their area of specialization.

Argentina is a member state of the Mercado Común del Sur (MERCOSUR—Southern Common Market) and as such is a participant in its accreditation programme: El Mecanismo Experimental de Acreditación de Carreras del MERCOSUR. This programme has so far accredited Argentine degrees in agronomy, medicine and engineering.

In 2004 there were 1,805,491 students in higher education, of whom 1,273,156 were enrolled at the 37 universities, 512,002 at general non-university institutions and the remaining 20,333 at specialized institutions.

Regulatory and Representative Bodies

GOVERNMENT

Ministry of Education: Pizzurno 935, C1020ACA, Buenos Aires; tel. (11) 4129-1000; e-mail info@me.gov.ar; internet www.me.gov.ar; Minister Prof. ALBERTO SILEONI.

ACCREDITATION

Comisión Nacional de Evaluación y Acreditación Universitaria (CONEAU) (National Commission for University Evaluation and Accreditation): Avda Santa Fe 1385, 4°, C1059ABH, Buenos Aires; tel. (11) 4815-1767; fax (11) 4815-0744; e-mail consulta@coneau.gov.ar; internet www.coneau.gov.ar; f. 1996 to foster improvements in univ. education in Argentina; govt agency under Min. of Education; functions according to the Higher Education Act No. 24.521; composed of 12 mems appointed by the Govt for 4 years; the National Interuniversity Council (CIN), the Federal Senate and the Federal Chamber of Deputies nominate 3 mems each, the Council of Rectors of Private Universities (CRUP), the National Academy of Education and the Min. of Education nominate 1 mem. each; evaluates projects submitted by new public and private univs; performs external evaluation of univs; grants accreditation to govt regulated undergraduate programmes; grants accreditation to graduate programmes; conducts evaluation processes for accreditation of private evaluation and accreditation orgs; serves as Secretariat of Red Iberoamericana para la Acreditación de la Calidad de la Educación Superior (RIACES) and plays an active role in the initiatives carried out by the International Network for Quality Assurance Agencies in Higher Education (INQAAHE); contributes to devt of MERCOSUR experimental accreditation mechanism (MEXA); Pres. FRANCISCO JOSÉ MIGUEL TALENTO CUTRÍN; Sec.-Gen. NÉSTOR RAUL PAN.

NATIONAL BODIES

Academia Nacional de Educación (National Academy of Education): Pacheco de Melo 2084, C1126AAF, Buenos Aires; tel. (11) 4806-2818; fax (11) 4806-8817; e-mail info@acaedu.edu.ar; internet www.acaedu.edu.ar; f. 1984 as Argentine Academy of Education; incl. within the nat. academies rule (Decree number 4362/55) by Min. of Education and Justice (ruling no. 107, dated 27 June 1989; ratified by Decree number 1124, dated 26 October 1989); promotes educational creativity and innovation; Pres. HORACIO SANGUINETTI; Vice-Pres MARÍA CELIA AGUDO DE CÓRSICO, PEDRO SIMONCINI; Sec. MARCELO J. VERNENGO.

Consejo Interuniversitario Nacional (CIN) (National Interuniversity Council): Pacheco de Melo 2084, C1126AAF, Buenos Aires; tel. (11) 4806-2269; e-mail info@cin.edu.ar; internet www.cin.edu.ar; f. 1985; proposes and coordinates policy for mem. univs; defines and coordinates academic, research and management programmes of mem. instns; creates regional orgs for inter-univ. cooperation; consults on creation or closure of nat. univs; generates and supports self-evaluation and external evaluation policies for mems; promotes compatibility and quality assurance of study programmes; Pres. Ing. OSCAR FEDERICO SPADA.

Consejo de Rectores de las Universidades Privadas (CRUP) (Council of Rectors of Private Universities): Montevideo 1910 PB, C1021AAH, Buenos Aires; tel. (11) 4811-6435; fax (11) 4811-0947; internet www.crup.org.ar; representative and consultative org.; coordinates teaching in private univs in conjunction with Min. of Education and the Provincial Ccls of Rectors; fosters collaboration between mem. univs; Pres. Dr HORACIO O'DONNELL; Vice-Pres. Lic. LUIS VELASCO; Vice-Pres. Mgr Dr ALFREDO ZECCA; Sec. Dr HECTOR SAURET.

Learned Societies

AGRICULTURE, FISHERIES AND VETERINARY SCIENCE

Academia Nacional de Agronomía y Veterinaria (Academy of Agronomy and Veterinary Science): Avda Alvear 1711 (2° piso), 1014 Buenos Aires; tel. (11) 4815-4616; fax (11) 4812-4168; internet www.anav.org.ar; f. 1909; 98 mems; library of 3,000 vols; Pres. Dr C. N. CARLOS O. SCOPPA; Sec.-Gen. Ing. Agr. RODOLFO G. FRANK; publ. *Anales* (1 a year).

Asociación Argentina de la Ciencia del Suelo (Argentine Association of Soil Science): Pabellón INGEIS, Ciudad Universitaria, 1428 Buenos Aires; tel. (11) 4783-3021; fax (11) 4783-3024; e-mail consenti@agro.uba.ar; internet www.suelos.org.ar; f. 1958; 800 mems; Pres. GERARDO RUBIO; Sec. PABLO PRYSTUPA; publ. *Ciencia del Suelo* (2 a year).

Sociedad Rural Argentina (Argentine Agricultural Society): Florida 460, 1005 Buenos Aires; tel. (11) 4322-0468; fax (11) 4325-8231; internet www.sra.org.ar; f. 1866; 10,000 mems; library: see Libraries and Archives; Pres. Dr LUCIANO MIGUENS.

ARCHITECTURE AND TOWN PLANNING

Sociedad Central de Arquitectos (Architects' Association): Montevideo 938, C1019ABT Buenos Aires; tel. (11) 4812-3644; fax (11) 4813-6629; e-mail info@socearq.org; internet www.socearq.org; f. 1886; 8,500 mems; library of 9,200 vols, 90 periodicals; Pres. Arq. DANIEL SILBERFADEN; Sec. Arq. LUIS MARÍA ALBORNOZ; publ. *Revista SCA* (6 a year).

BIBLIOGRAPHY, LIBRARY SCIENCE AND MUSEOLOGY

Asociación Argentina de Bibliotecas y Centros de Información Científicos y Técnicos (Argentine Association of Scientific and Technical Libraries and Information Centres): Santa Fe 1145, 1059 Buenos Aires; tel. (11) 4393-8406; f. 1937; 84 mems; Pres. ABILIO BASSETS; Tech. Sec. ERNESTO G. GIETZ; publ. *Union Catalogue of Scientific and Technical Publications.*

Asociación de Bibliotecarios Graduados de la República Argentina (ABGRA) (Association of Argentine Librarians): Tucumán 1424 (8° piso D), C1050AAB Buenos Aires; tel. (11) 4373-0571; fax (11) 4371-5269; e-mail abgra@ciudad.com.ar; internet abgra .sisbi.uba.ar; f. 1953; 1,650 mems; Pres. ANA MARÍA PERUCHENA ZIMMERMANN; Sec.-Gen. ROBERTO JORGE SERVIDIO; publ. *Revista REFERENCIAS* (3 a year).

Comisión Nacional de Museos y de Monumentos y Lugares Históricos (National Commission for Museums and Historic Monuments and Sites): Avda de Mayo 556, 1084 Buenos Aires; tel. (11) 4343-5835; e-mail info@ comisionmonumentos.gov.ar; internet www .monumentosysitios.gov.ar; f. 1938; supervises museums and protects the nat. historical heritage; library; Pres. (vacant); Sec. Arq. JORGE TARTARINI; publ. *Boletín.*

Comisión Nacional Protectora de Bibliotecas Populares (Commission for the Protection of Public Libraries): Ayacucho 1578, 1112 Buenos Aires; tel. (11) 4511-6275; e-mail me@conabip.gov.ar; internet www.conabip.gov.ar; f. 1870; Pres. DANIEL RÍOS; Sec. Prof. ANA T. DOBRA; publ. *Boletín.*

ECONOMICS, LAW AND POLITICS

Academia Nacional de Ciencias Económicas (National Academy of Economic Sciences): Avda Alvear 1790, 1014 Buenos Aires; tel. (11) 4813-2078; fax (11) 4813-2078; f. 1914; 35 mems; library of 13,500 vols; Pres. Dr ADOLFO STURZENEGGER; Sec. Dr FERNANDO H. NAVAJAS; publ. *Anales.*

Academia Nacional de Ciencias Morales y Políticas (National Academy of Moral and Political Sciences): Avda Alvear 1711, PB, 1014 Buenos Aires; tel. (11) 4811-2049; e-mail ancmyp@ancmyp.org.ar; internet www.ancmyp.org.ar; f. 1938; 35 mems; library of 13,536 vols; Pres. Dr JORGE A. AJA ESPIL; Sec. CARLOS A. SÁNCHEZ; publ. *Anales.*

Academia Nacional de Derecho y Ciencias Sociales (National Academy of Law and Social Sciences): Avda Alvear 1711 (1°), 1014 Buenos Aires; tel. (11) 4815-6976; internet www.academiadederecho.org.ar; f. 1874; 25 mems; Pres. Dr JULIO CÉSAR OTAEGUI; Secs Dr SANTOS CIFUENTES, Dr HÉCTOR ALEGRIA; publ. *Anales.*

Academia Nacional de Derecho y Ciencias Sociales (Córdoba) (National Academy of Law and Social Sciences, Córdoba): Artigas 74, 5000 Córdoba; tel. (351) 421-4929; fax (351) 421-4929; e-mail secretaria@ acaderc.org.ar; internet www.acaderc.org.ar; f. 1941; 172 mems; library of 6,578 vols; Pres. Dr LUIS MOISSET DE ESPANÉS; Technical Sec. Dr CHRISTIAN G. SOMMER; publs *Anales, Federalism Journal, History of Law Journal, International Law Journal.*

Colegio de Abogados de la Ciudad de Buenos Aires (Buenos Aires City Bar Association): Montevideo 640, 1019 Buenos Aires; tel. (11) 4371-1110; fax (11) 4375-5442; e-mail info@colabogados.org.ar; internet www.colabogados.org.ar; f. 1913; 1,600 mems; library of 45,000 vols; Pres. ENRIQUE

V. DEL CARRIL; Exec. Dir FERNANDO R. FRÁVEGA; publs *Actualidad* (6 a year), *Revista* (2 a year).

FINE AND PERFORMING ARTS

Academia Nacional de Bellas Artes (National Academy of Fine Arts): Sánchez de Bustamante 2663, 2° piso, 1425 Buenos Aires; tel. (11) 4802-2469; e-mail info@anba .org.ar; internet www.anba.org.ar; f. 1936; 30 mems, 30 foreign corresp. mems; library of 6,000 vols; Pres. JORGE TAVERNA IRIGOYEN; Gen. Sec. OSVALDO SVANASCINI; publs *Anuario, Cuaderno Especial: 'Escenas del Campo Argentino' 1885–1900, Documentos de Arte Argentino, Documentos de Arte Colonial Sudamericano, Monografías de Artistas Argentinos, Serie Estudios de Arte en la Argentina.*

Fondo Nacional de las Artes (National Arts Foundation): Alsina 673, C1087AAI Buenos Aires; tel. (11) 4343-1590; e-mail fnartes@fnartes.gov.ar; internet www .fnartes.gov.ar; f. 1958; promotes and supports the arts; 15 mems; library of 7,000 vols; Pres. Lic. HÉCTOR W. VALLE; publs *Anuario del Teatro Argentino, Bibliografía Argentina de Artes y Letras, Informativo.*

HISTORY, GEOGRAPHY AND ARCHAEOLOGY

Academia Nacional de Geografía (National Academy of Geography): Avda Cabildo 381 (7° piso), C1426AAD Buenos Aires; tel. (11) 4771-3043; fax (11) 4771-3043; e-mail secretaria@an-geografia.org.ar; internet www.an-geografia.org.ar; f. 1956; 32 mems; Pres. Prof. ANTONIO CORNEJO; Sec. HÉCTOR O. J. PENA; publ. *Anales.*

Academia Nacional de la Historia (National Academy of History): Balcarce 139, 1064 Buenos Aires; tel. (11) 4331-5147; fax (11) 4331-4633; e-mail admite@ an-historia.org.ar; internet www.an-historia .org.ar; f. 1893; study of Argentine and American history; 257 mems (34 ordinary, 223 foreign corresp.); Pres. Dr MIGUEL ANGEL DE MARCO; publs *Boletín, Investigaciones y Ensayos.*

Instituto Bonaerense de Numismática y Antigüedades (Buenos Aires Institute of Numismatics and Antiquities): San Martín 336, 1004 Buenos Aires; tel. (11) 449-2659; f. 1872; 107 mems; Pres. HUMBERTO F. BURZIO; publ. *Boletín.*

Junta de Historia Eclesiástica Argentina (Council of Argentine Ecclesiastical History): Reconquista 269, 1003 Buenos Aires; tel. (11) 4343-4397 ext. 309; e-mail info@jhea.org.ar; internet www.jhea.org.ar; f. 1942; 100 mems; Pres. Pbro. Lic. LUIS ALBERTO LAHITOU; Sec. Prof. ANA MARÍA WOITES; publs *Boletín, Revista Archivum* (1 a year).

Sociedad Argentina de Estudios Geográficos (Argentine Society of Geographical Studies): Rodríguez Peña 158 (4° piso Dpto 7), 1020 Buenos Aires; tel. (11) 4373-0588; e-mail informes@gaea.org.ar; internet www .gaea.org.ar; f. 1922; 4,000 mems; library of 12,000 vols; Pres. Dr DARIO CESAR SANCHEZ; Sec. Dra SUSANA MARIA SASSONE; publs *Anales, Contribuciones Científicas, GAEA Boletín, Geografía de la República Argentina.*

LANGUAGE AND LITERATURE

Academia Argentina de Letras (Argentine Academy of Letters): Sánchez de Bustamante 2663, 1425 Buenos Aires; tel. (11) 4802-3814; fax (11) 4802-8340; internet www .aal.universia.com.ar; f. 1931; 77 mems (24 ordinary, 53 corresp.); Pres. PEDRO LUIS

BARCIA; Sec.-Gen. RODOLFO MODERN; publ. *Boletín* (4 a year).

Alliance Française: Avda Córdoba 936–946, 1054 Buenos Aires; tel. (11) 4322-0068; fax (11) 4326-6655; e-mail info@ alianzafrancesa.org.ar; internet www .alianzafrancesa.org.ar; offers courses and examinations in French language and culture and promotes cultural exchange with France; attached teaching offices in Alta Gracia, Azul, Bahia Blanca, Banfield, Baradero, Bell Ville, Bella Vista, Bernal, Bragado, Brandsen, Buenos Aires (Belgrano, Flores and Fortabat), Campana, Campana-Escobar, Chacabuco, Chajari, Chivilcoy, Cinco Saltos, Colon, Comodoro Rivadavia, Concepcion del Uruguay, Córdoba, Coronel-Pringles, Coronel-Suarez, El Trebol, Esperanza, Formosa, Gualeguay, Gualeguaychu, Jesus Maria, Junin, La Plata, Las Varillas, Lincoln, Mar del Plata, Marcos-Juarez, Marcos-Paz, Martinez, Martinez-Olivos, Martinez-San Isidro, Mendoza, Mercedes, Mercedes-Lujan, Neuquén, Neuquén-General Roca, Nogoya, Olavarria, Paraná, Pehuajo, Pergamino, Pigue, Posadas, Quilmes, Rafaela, Reconquista, Resistencia, Rio Cuarto, Rio Gallegos, Rivadavia, Roque Saenz Peña, Rosario, Salta, San Carlos de Bariloche, San Francisco, San Jorge, San Jose, San Juan, San Luis, San Nicolas, San Rafael, San Salvador de Jujuy, Santa Fe, Santa Rosa, Santiago del Estero, Tandil, Trelew, Tres Arroyos, Tucumán, Tuerto, Ushuala, Venado, Vicente Lopez, Vicente Lopez-San Martín, Villa Elisa, Villa Maria, Villa Mercedes and Villaguay; Dir of Operations, Argentina FRANÇOISE COCHAUD.

British Council: Marcelo T. de Alvear 590, C1058AAF Buenos Aires; tel. (11) 4114-8600; fax (11) 4114-8600; e-mail info@ britishcouncil.org.ar; internet www .britishcouncil.org/argentina; offers courses and examinations in English language and British culture and promotes cultural exchange with the UK; Dir HUW JONES.

Goethe-Institut: Avda Corrientes 319, C1043AAD Buenos Aires; tel. (11) 4318-5600; fax (11) 4318-5656; e-mail info@ buenosaires.goethe.org; internet www.goethe .de/buenosaires; offers courses and examinations in German language and culture and promotes cultural exchange with Germany; library of 15,000 vols, 37 periodicals; Dir STEFAN HÜSGEN.

PEN Club Argentino—Centro Internacional de la Asociación PEN (International PEN Centre): Rivadavia 4060, 1205 Buenos Aires; f. 1930; 100 mems; Pres. MIGUEL A. OLIVERA; publ. *Boletín.*

Sociedad Argentina de Autores y Compositores de Música (SADAIC) (Argentine Society of Authors and Composers): Lavalle 1547, 1048 Buenos Aires; tel. (11) 4379-8600; f. 1936; library of 4,000 vols, 13,000 music scores; Pres. ATILIO STAMPONE; Cultural Dir EUGENIO INCHAUSTI.

Sociedad General de Autores de la Argentina (Argentores) (Argentine Society of Authors): Pacheco de Melo 1820, C1126AAB Buenos Aires; tel. (11) 4811-2582; fax (11) 4811-6954; e-mail info@ argentores.org.ar; internet www.argentores .org.ar; f. 1910; 2,000 mems; library of 60,000 vols; Pres. ISAAC AISEMBERG; Sec. AUGUSTO GIUSTOZZI; publ. *Boletín* (4 a year).

MEDICINE

Academia Argentina de Cirugía (Argentine Academy of Surgery): M. T. de Alvear 2416, 1122 Buenos Aires; tel. (11) 4822-2905; fax (11) 4822-6458; internet www .academiaargentinadecirugia.org; f. 1911;

Pres. Dr EDUARDO TRIGO; Gen. Sec. EDUARDO DE SANTIBAÑES.

Academia de Ciencias Médicas de Córdoba: Pueyrredón 59, 2° piso, 5000 Córdoba; tel. (351) 468-5385; f. 1975; 350 mems; Pres. Dr REMO BERGOGLIO; Sec. Dr JESÚS R. GIRAUDO.

Academia Nacional de Medicina (National Academy of Medicine): Las Heras 3092, 1425ASU Buenos Aires; tel. (11) 4805-6890; fax (11) 4806-6638; e-mail acamedbai@acamedbai.org.ar; internet www.acamedbai.org.ar; f. 1822; medical and scientific instn; 35 mems; library of 50,000 vols; Pres. Acad. JUAN M. GHIRLANDA; Pres. Acad. ROBERTO N. PRADIER; publ. *Boletín* (2 a year).

Asociación Argentina de Biología y Medicina Nuclear (Argentine Association for Biology and Nuclear Medicine): Luis Sáenz Peña 250, 6° piso, Of. A, 1110 Buenos Aires; tel. (11) 4382-0583; fax (11) 4382-0583; e-mail aabymn_1@ciudad.com.ar; internet www.aabymn.org.ar; f. 1963; 190 mems; Pres. Dr ARTURO J. SAN MARTÍN; Sec. Dra MARÍA DEL CARMEN ALAK.

Asociación Argentina de Cirugía (Argentine Association of Surgery): Marcelo T. de Alvear 2415, 1122 Buenos Aires; tel. (11) 4822-2905; fax (11) 4822-6458; e-mail info@aac.org.ar; internet www.aac.org.ar; f. 1930; 4,000 mems; Pres. Dr EDUARDO CASSONE; Dir Dr MARTÍN MIHURA; publs *Anuario*, *Boletín Informativo* (24 a year), *Revista Argentina de Cirugía* (8 a year).

Asociación Argentina de Farmacia y Bioquímica Industrial (Argentine Industrial Biochemistry and Pharmacy Association): Uruguay 469 (2° B), 1015 Buenos Aires; tel. (11) 4373-8900; fax (11) 4372-7389; e-mail info@safybi.org; internet www.safybi.org.ar; f. 1952; 1,100 mems; library of 500 vols; Pres. Dr FEDERICO E. MONTES DE OCA; Sec. Dra MIRTA B. FARIÑA; publs *Boletín Informativo* (3 a year), *Revista SAFYBI*.

Asociación Argentina de Ortopedia y Traumatología (Argentine Orthopaedic and Traumatology Association): Vicente López 1878, C1128ABC Buenos Aires; tel. (11) 4801-2320; fax (11) 4801-7703; e-mail gerencia@aaot.org.ar; internet www.aaot.org.ar; f. 1936; 2,944 mems; library of 1,460 vols, 67 periodicals; Pres. Dr GREGORIO M. ARENDAR; Sec. Dr CARLOS F. SANCINETO; publ. *Revista* (4 a year).

Asociación Médica Argentina (Argentine Medical Association): Santa Fe 1171, 1059 Buenos Aires; tel. (11) 4814-2182; fax (11) 4811-3850; e-mail info@ama-med.com; internet www.ama-med.org.ar; f. 1891; 3,520 mems; library of 32,000 vols, 290,000 periodicals; Pres. Dr ELÍAS HURTADO HOYO; Sec. MIGUEL A. GALMÉS; publs *Boletín Informativo* (12 a year), *Revista AMA* (4 a year).

Asociación Odontológica Argentina (Argentine Dental Association): Junín 959, 1113 Buenos Aires; tel. (11) 4961-6141; fax (11) 4961-1110; internet www2.aoa.org.ar; f. 1896; incl. postgraduate school for dentists; 8,000 mems; library of 8,000 vols, 11,300 periodicals; Pres. Dr EDUARDO MAIUCCI; Sec. JUAN CARLOS COMETTI; publ. *Revista*.

Asociación para la Lucha contra la Parálisis Infantil (Association for Combating Infantile Paralysis): San Lorenzo 283 B°, Nueva, Córdoba; tel. (351) 423-2593; fax (351) 422-8183; e-mail alpicordoba@ciudad.com.ar; f. 1943; 30 mems; library of 3,000 vols; Pres. VERÓNICA S. M. DE BUSTO; publ. *Memoria y Balance Anual*.

Federación Argentina de Asociaciones de Anestesia, Analgesia y Reanimación (Argentine Federation of Anaesthesia, Analgesia and Resuscitation Associations): Fragata Sarmiento 541 1er piso, 1405 Buenos Aires; tel. (11) 4431-2547; fax (11) 4431-2463; internet www.anestesia.org.ar; f. 1970; 1,113 mems; Pres. Dr SAÚL SOROTSKI; Gen. Sec. Dr DANIEL CROSARA; publs *Boletín Informativo*, *Revista Argentina de Anestesiología*.

Liga Argentina contra la Tuberculosis (Argentine Anti-Tuberculosis League): Uriarte 2477, C1425FNI, Buenos Aires; tel. (11) 4777-4447; fax (11) 4777-6470; internet www.connmed.com.ar/instituciones/lalac.org.ar; f. 1901; library of 140 series of periodicals; Medical Dir Dr VICENTE DONATO; publs *Revista Argentina del Tórax*, *La Doble Cruz*.

Sociedad Argentina de Ciencias Neurológicas, Psiquiátricas y Neuroquirúrgicas (Argentine Neurological, Neurosurgical and Psychiatric Society): Santa Fe 1171, 1059 Buenos Aires; tel. (11) 441-1633; f. 1920; 400 mems; library of 35,000 vols; Pres. Prof. Dr DIEGO BRAGE; Sec. Prof. Dr CARLOS MÁRQUEZ; publ. *Revista* (12 a year).

Sociedad Argentina de Dermatología (Argentine Society of Dermatology): Avda Callao 852 (2° piso), 1023 Buenos Aires; tel. (11) 4815-4649; fax (11) 4814-4919; e-mail sad@sad.org.ar; internet www.sad.org.ar; f. 1934; 2,100 mems; Pres. Prof. Dr HORACIO CABO; Sec.-Gen. Dra PATRICIA TROIELLI; publ. *Dermatología, Argentina* (5 a year).

Sociedad Argentina de Endocrinología y Metabolismo (Argentine Society of Endocrinology and Metabolism): Avda Díaz Vélez 3889, C1200AAF Buenos Aires; tel. and fax (11) 4983-9800; e-mail info@saem.org.ar; internet www.saem.org.ar; f. 1941; 600 mems; Pres. Dra ALICIA GAUNA; Sec. Dr PABLO KNOBLOVITS; publ. *Revista* (4 a year).

Sociedad Argentina de Farmacología y Terapéutica (Argentine Society of Pharmacology and Therapeutics): Santa Fe 1171, 1059 Buenos Aires; tel. (11) 4811-3580; e-mail info@ama-med.com; f. 1929; 100 mems; Pres. Dr ALFREDO VITALE; Sec. Dra CRISTINA VOLMER.

Sociedad Argentina de Fisiología (Argentine Physiological Society): Solís 453, 1078 Buenos Aires; tel. (11) 4378-1151; fax (11) 4381-0323; e-mail safis@safisiol.org.ar; internet www.safisiol.org.ar; f. 1950; 300 mems; library of 600 vols; mem. of IUPS; Pres. Dr VALERIA RETTORI; Sec. Dr B. FERNANDEZ; publ. *Physiological Mini-Reviews* (12 a year).

Sociedad Argentina de Gastroenterología (Argentine Society of Gastroenterology): Marcelo T. de Alvear 1381 9° piso, C1058AAU Buenos Aires; tel. (11) 4816-9391; fax (11) 4816-9396; e-mail sage@sage.org.ar; internet www.sage.org.ar; f. 1927; 900 mems; Pres. Dr ROBERTO MARTIN MAZURE; Gen. Sec. Dra SILVIA C. GUTIÉRREZ; publ. *Acta Gastroenterológica Latinoamericana*.

Sociedad Argentina de Gerontología y Geriatría (Argentine Gerontological and Geriatrics Society): San Luis 2538, C1056AAD Buenos Aires; fax (11) 4961-0070; e-mail sagg@connmed.com.ar; internet www.sagg.org.ar; f. 1950; 1,500 mems; Pres. Dr ISIDORO FAINSTEIN; Sec. Dr HUGO ALBERTO SCHIFIS; publs *Revista Argentina de Gerontología y Geriatría* (6 a year), *Vivir en Plenitud* (6 a year).

Sociedad Argentina de Hematología (Argentine Society of Haematology): Julian Alvarez 146, C1414DRD Buenos Aires; tel. (11) 4855-2452; e-mail sah@sah.org.ar; internet www.sah.org.ar; f. 1945; 800 mems; Pres. Dr JORGE H. RIVEROS; Sec. Dra MARÍA GABRIELA FLORES.

Sociedad Argentina de Investigación Clínica (Argentine Society of Clinical Research): Combatientes de Malvinas 3150, C1427ARO Buenos Aires; tel. (11) 4523-4963; fax (11) 4523-4963; e-mail secretaria@saic.org.ar; internet www.saic.org.ar; f. 1960; 500 mems; Pres. Dra ADRIANA SEILICOVICH; Sec. Dr RODOLFO REY; publ. *Medicina*.

Sociedad Argentina de Oftalmología (Argentine Ophthalmological Society): Viamonte 1465 7°, C1055ABA Buenos Aires; tel. (11) 4373-8826; fax (11) 4373-8828; e-mail info@sao.org.ar; internet www.sao.org.ar; f. 1920; 2,000 mems; Pres. Dr EDGARDO MANZITTI; Sec. Dr DANIEL WEIL; publ. *Archivos de Oftalmología de Buenos Aires* (12 a year).

Sociedad Argentina de Patología (Argentine Society of Pathology): Pte. Gral. Perón 2234 1° A, C1040AAJ Buenos Aires; tel. (11) 4951-2152; fax (11) 4951-2152; e-mail infosap@patologia.org.ar; internet www.patologia.org.ar; f. 1933; 220 mems; Pres. Dr JULIÁN MOSTO; Gen. Sec. Dra LAURA JUFE; publ. *Archivos*.

Sociedad Argentina de Pediatría (Argentine Paediatric Society): Avda Coronel Díaz 1971, C1425DQF Buenos Aires; tel. (11) 4821-8612; e-mail cdsap@sap.org.ar; internet www.sap.org.ar; f. 1911; 7,500 mems; library of 5,000 vols; Pres. Dra MARGARITA D. RAMONET; Gen. Sec. Dra ANGELA GENTILE; publ. *Archivos Argentinos de Pediatría* (6 a year).

Sociedad de Cirugía de Buenos Aires (Buenos Aires Surgical Society): Santa Fe 1171, 1059 Buenos Aires; tel. (11) 444-0664; Pres. IVAN GOÑI MORENO; Sec.-Gen. GUILLERMO I. BELLEVILLE.

Sociedad de Psicología Médica, Psicoanálisis y Medicina Psicosomática (Society of Medical Psychology, Psychoanalysis and Psychosomatic Medicine): Avda Santa Fe 1171, 1059 Buenos Aires; tel. (11) 4814-2182; e-mail amalia.racciatti@gmail.com; internet www.psicoama.com.ar; f. 1939; 80 mems; Pres. Dr CARLOS GIBERT; Sec. Dra AMALIA RACCIATTI DE MESSUTI.

NATURAL SCIENCES
General

Academia Nacional de Ciencias de Buenos Aires (National Academy of Sciences of Buenos Aires): Avda Alvear 1711 (3° piso), 1014 Buenos Aires; tel. (11) 441-3066; f. 1935; 35 mems; Pres. Dr JULIO H. G. OLIVERA; Sec. Dr HUGO F. BAUZÁ; publs *Anales*, *Escritos de Filosofía* (4 a year).

Academia Nacional de Ciencias (National Academy of Sciences): CC 36, Avda Vélez Sarsfield 229, 5000 Córdoba; tel. (351) 433-2089; fax (351) 421-6350; e-mail secretaria@acad.uncor.edu; internet www.acad.uncor.edu; f. 1869; 79 mems; library of 12,000 vols, 3,800 periodicals; Pres. Dr EDUARDO HUMBERTO STARICCO; Sec. Dr PEDRO J. DEPETRIS; publs *Actas*, *Boletín*, *Miscelánea*.

Academia Nacional de Ciencias Exactas, Físicas y Naturales (National Academy of Exact, Physical and Natural Sciences): Avda Alvear 1711 (4°), 1014 Buenos Aires; tel. (11) 4811-2998; fax (11) 4811-6951; internet www.ancefn.org.ar; f. 1874; 130 mems (36 full voting, 27 nat. corresp., 61 foreign corresp., 6 hon.); library of 400 vols; Pres. Dr ALEJANDRO J. ARVIA; Sec.-Gen. Dr JORGE V. CRISCI; publ. *Anales* (1 a year).

Asociación Argentina de Ciencias Naturales (Argentine Association of Natural Sciences): Avda Angel Gallardo 470, C1405DJR Buenos Aires; tel. (11) 4982-8370; fax (11) 4982-4494; f. 1912; 450 mems; Pres. Dr JUAN CARLOS GIACCHI; Sec. Dra CRISTINA MARINONE; publ. *Physis* (2 a year).

Asociación Argentina para el Progreso de las Ciencias (Association for the

Advancement of Science): Avda Alvear 1711 (4° piso), C1014AAE Buenos Aires; tel. (11) 4811-2998; fax (11) 4811-6951; e-mail secretaria@aargentinapciencias.org; f. 1933; 215 mems (200 ordinary, 15 assoc.); Pres. Dr EDUARDO HERNÁN CHARREAU; Sec. Dr AUGUSTO F. GARCÍA; publ. *Ciencia e Investigación.*

Sociedad Científica Argentina (Argentine Scientific Society): Avda Santa Fe 1145, 1059 Buenos Aires; tel. (11) 4816-4745; fax (11) 4816-5406; e-mail sociedad@cientifica.org.ar; internet www.cientifica.org.ar; f. 1872; affiliations in Santa Fe, La Plata, San Juan; 698 mems; library of 39,600 vols; Pres. Dr ARTURO OTAÑO SAHORES; Sec. Lic. ERNESTO CELMAN; publ. *Anales* (1 a year).

Biological Sciences

Asociación Argentina de Micología (Argentine Mycological Society): Suipacha 531, 2000 Rosario; tel. (341) 480-4592; internet www.asam.org.ar; f. 1960; studies in medical and veterinary mycology, and mycotoxins; 150 mems; library; Pres. Dra LAURA RAMOS; Sec. MARISA BIASOLI; publ. *Revista Argentina de Micología* (3 a year).

Asociación Paleontológica Argentina (Argentine Association of Palaeontology): Maipú 645 (1° piso), C1006ACG Buenos Aires; tel. (11) 4326-7463; fax (11) 4326-7463; e-mail secretaria@apaleontologica.org .ar; internet www.apaleontologica.org .ar; f. 1955; 500 mems; Pres. Dr SERGIO F. VIZCAÍNO; Sec. Dra MARÍA DE LAS MERCEDES DI PASQUO; publ. *Ameghiniana* (4 a year).

Sociedad Argentina de Biología (Argentine Biological Society): Vuelta de Obligado 2490, 1428 Buenos Aires; tel. (11) 4783-2869; e-mail biologia@dna.uba.ar; internet proteus .dna.uba.ar/biologia; f. 1920; 140 mems; Pres. Dra ISABEL LÜTHY; Sec. Dr HÉCTOR COIRINI; publ. *Revista* (1 a year).

Sociedad Argentina de Fisiología Vegetal (Argentine Society of Plant Physiology): Departamento de Agronomía, UNS, 8000 Bahía Blanca; tel. (291) 453-1821; fax (291) 459-5127; internet www.safv.uns.edu.ar; f. 1958; 260 mems; Pres. Dra EDITH TALEISNIK; Sec. Dr LUIS F. HERNANDEZ.

Sociedad Entomológica Argentina (SEA) (Argentine Entomological Society): Miguel Lillo 205, 4107 San Miguel de Tucumán; tel. and fax (381) 423-2965; e-mail seatuc@csnat.unt.edu.ar; internet www.sea .secyt.gov.ar; f. 1925; 400 mems; library of 815 vols, 590 periodicals; located in the Museo de la Plata, Buenos Aires, e-mail bibsea@museo.fcnym.unlp.edu.ar; Pres. MERCEDES LIZARRALDE DE GROSSO; Sec. CARMEN REGUILÓN; publs *Publicación Especial de la Sociedad Entomológica Argentina* (irregular), *Revista de la Sociedad Entomológica Argentina* (2 a year).

Mathematical Sciences

Unión Matemática Argentina (Argentine Mathematical Union): Facultad Ciencias Físico Matemáticas y Naturales, Universidad Nacional de San Luis, Ejército de los Andes 950, 5700 San Luis; tel. (2652) 422803; fax (2652) 430224; f. 1936; 600 mems; Pres. Dr FELIPE ZÓ; Sec. Dr HUGO ALVAREZ; publ. *Revista.*

Physical Sciences

Asociación Argentina Amigos de la Astronomía (Argentine Association for the Friends of Astronomy): Avda Patricias Argentinas 550, C1405BWS Buenos Aires; tel. and fax (11) 4863-3366; internet www .amigosdelaastronomia.org; f. 1929; maintains an observatory and museum; 1,000 mems; library of 6,000 vols; Pres. CARLOS E.

ANGUEIRA VÁZQUEZ; Sec. LUIS MANTEROLA; publ. *Revista Astronómica* (4 a year).

Asociación Argentina de Astronomía (Argentine Astronomy Association): Observatorio Astronómico, B1900FWA La Plata; tel. (221) 423-6593; fax (221) 423-6591; e-mail aaacd@fcaglp.fcaglp.unlp.edu.ar; internet www.astronomiaargentina.org.ar; f. 1958; 312 mems; Pres. MARTA GRACIELA ROVIRA; Sec. ROSA BEATRIZ ORELLANA; publ. *Boletín* (1 a year).

Asociación Argentina de Geofísicos y Geodestas (Argentine Association of Geophysicists and Geodesists): c/o Observatorio Astronómico de La Plata, Paseo del Bosque s/n, 1900 La Plata; e-mail jero@aagg.org.ar; internet www.aagg.org.ar; f. 1959; Pres. Dra MARÍA L. ALTINGER; Sec. Dra MARÍA C. POMPOSIELLO; publs *Boletín* (3 a year), *Geoacta* (1 a year).

Asociación Bioquímica Argentina (Argentine Biochemical Association): Venezuela 1823 3er piso, 1096 Buenos Aires; tel. (11) 4381-2907; fax (11) 4384-7415; e-mail info@aba-online.org.ar; internet www .aba-online.org.ar; f. 1934; Pres. Dr ORLANDO GABRIEL CARBALLO; Sec. Dr ALBERTO VILLAGRA.

Asociación Geológica Argentina (Argentine Geological Association): Maipú 645 (1° piso), C1006ACG Buenos Aires; tel. and fax (11) 4325-3104; e-mail raga@geologica.org.ar; internet www.geologica.org.ar; f. 1945; 1,750 mems; Pres. Dr MIGUEL J. F. HALLER; Sec. Lic. VALÉRIE BAUMANN; publ. *Revista* (4 a year).

Asociación Química Argentina (Argentine Chemical Association): Sánchez de Bustamante 1749, 1425 Buenos Aires; tel. (11) 4822-4886; fax (11) 4822-4886; internet www .aqa.org.ar; f. 1912; 1,000 mems; library of 10,000 vols, 500 periodicals; Pres. Dr EDUARDO A. CASTRO; Sec. Dr EDUARDO J. BOTTANI; publs *Anales de la Asociación Química Argentina* (Scientific), *Industria y Química* (Technical).

Centro Argentino de Espeleología (Argentine Centre of Speleological Studies): Avda de Mayo 651 (1° piso), 1428 Buenos Aires; tel. (11) 4331-6798; f. 1970; 60 mems; library of 250 vols; Pres. JULIO GOYÉN AGUADO; Sec. ROBERTO OSCAR BERMEJO; publ. *Las Brujas* (1 a year).

Grupo Argentino del Color (Argentine Colour Group): c/o Sec. of Research, School of Architecture, Buenos Aires Univ., Ciudad Universitaria, Pav. 3 (4°), C1428BFA Buenos Aires; tel. (11) 4789-6289; fax (11) 4702-6009; e-mail gac@fadu.uba.ar; internet www.fadu .uba.ar/sicyt/color/gac.htm; f. 1979; study of colour science; 159 mems; Pres. Dr MARÍA L. DE MATTIELLO; publ. *GAC Revista* (3 a year).

PHILOSOPHY AND PSYCHOLOGY

Sociedad Argentina de Psicología (Buenos Aires Psychological Society): Callao 435 (1o), 1022 Buenos Aires; tel. (11) 4432-3760; f. 1930; Pres. JUAN CUATRECASAS.

RELIGION, SOCIOLOGY AND ANTHROPOLOGY

Asociación Argentina de Estudios Americanos (Argentine Association of American Studies): Maipú 672, 1424 Buenos Aires; tel. (11) 4392-4971.

Sociedad Argentina de Antropología (Argentine Anthropological Society): Moreno 350, 1091 Buenos Aires; e-mail sociedadargentinaantropologia@yahoo.com; internet www.saantropologia.com.ar; f. 1936; 255 mems; Pres. GUSTAVO POLITIS; Sec. VICTORIA COLL MORITÁN; publ. *Relaciones* (1 a year).

Sociedad Argentina de Sociología: Trejo 241, 5000 Córdoba; tel. (351) 44-5901; f. 1950; Pres. Prof. ALFREDO POVIÑA; Sec.-Gen. Prof. ODORICO PIRES PINTO.

TECHNOLOGY

Asociación Argentina del Frío (Argentine Refrigeration Association): Avda Belgrano (3° piso), Oficina K, C1092AAF Buenos Aires; tel. (11) 4343-1560; fax (11) 4343-1560; e-mail aafrio@aafrio.org.ar; internet www .aafrio.org.ar; f. 1932; 178 mems; small library; Pres. Ing. ROBERTO RICARDO AGUILO; Sec. Ing. CARLOS BRIGNONE; publ. *Clima* (12 a year).

Asociación Electrotécnica Argentina (Argentine Electrotechnical Association): Posadas 1659, C1112ADC Buenos Aires; tel. (11) 4804-3454; internet aea.org.ar; f. 1913; 2,000 mems; library of 2,500 vols; Pres. Ing. JULIO H. DI SALVO; Sec. Ing. ABEL J. CRESTA; publ. *Revista Electrotécnica.*

Centro Argentino de Ingenieros (Argentine Centre of Engineering): Cerrito 1250, C1010AAZ Buenos Aires; tel. (11) 4811-4133; fax (11) 4811-4133; e-mail informes@cai.org .ar; internet www.cai.org.ar; f. 1895; 10,231 mems; library of 11,000 vols; Pres. Ing. ROBERTO P. ECHARTE; publ. *Políticas de la Ingeniería.*

Federación Lanera Argentina (Argentine Wool Federation): Avda Paseo Colón 823, C1063ACI Buenos Aires; tel. (11) 4300-7661; fax (11) 4361-6517; f. 1929; concerned with all aspects of wool trade, from breeding to sales; 50 mems; Pres. RICARDO VON GERSTENBERG; Sec. CLAUDIO ULRICH; publ. *Argentine Wool Statistics* (12 a year).

Research Institutes
GENERAL

Instituto Torcuato Di Tella: Miñones 2159/77, 1° piso, 1428 Buenos Aires; tel. (11) 4783-8630; fax (11) 4783-3061; e-mail salvadororsini@fibertel.com.ar; internet www.itdt.edu; f. 1958; promotes scientific research and artistic creativity on a nat. and int. scale; administers research centres and higher education instns; postgraduate courses in economics, sociology and admin.; library of 85,000 vols; Pres. GREGORIO KLIMOVSKY.

AGRICULTURE, FISHERIES AND VETERINARY SCIENCE

Estación Experimental Agro-Industrial 'Obispo Colombres' ('Obispo Colombres' Agro-Industrial Experimental Research Station): CC 9, Las Talitas, 4101 Tucumán; tel. (381) 452-1000; fax (381) 452-1008; e-mail dt@eeaoc.org.ar; internet www.eeaoc.org.ar; f. 1909 as Agricultural Experiment Station of Tucumán (EEAT), present name since 1978; autonomous unit of the Tucumán provincial govt; research, technological devts. and services for agri-industrial business of North-Western Argentina; library of 8,000 vols, 75,000 periodicals; Pres. and Chair. JUAN JOSÉ BUDEGUER; Technical Dir and CEO Dr LEONARDO DANIEL PLOPER; publs *Avance Agro-Industrial* (4 a year), *Informe Annual EEAOC* (1 a year), *Publicación Especial EEAOC* (irregular), *Revista Industrial y Agrícola de Tucumán* (2 a year).

Instituto Agrario Argentino de Cultura Rural (Argentine Agricultural Institute for Rural Education): Florida 460, 1005 Buenos Aires; tel. (11) 4392-2000; f. 1937; library of 2,000 vols; Dir Dr CORNELIO J. VIERA; Sec. MARÍA LUIS RIVAS; Technical Sec. EURIFUE

ALFREDO VIVANA; publs *Reseñas Argentinas, Reseñas, Comunicados.*

Instituto de Edafología Agrícola (Institute of Agricultural Soil Science): Cerviño 3101, 1425 Buenos Aires; tel. (11) 484-9623; f. 1944; library of 3,200 vols; Dir Ing. Agr. JORGE I. BELLATI; publs *Técnicas Apartados de Artículos Tiradas Internas, Suelos.*

Instituto Nacional de Investigación y Desarrollo Pesquero (National Institute for Fisheries Research and Development): C. C. 175, 7600 Mar del Plata; tel. (223) 486-2586; fax (223) 486-1830; e-mail biblio@inidep.edu.ar; internet www.inidep.edu.ar; f. 1977 from fmr Mar del Plata Marine Biology Institute to perform integral research programmes on fishing grounds, emphasizing the assessment of Argentine fishing resources and sustainable fishing devt; decentralized agency operating under Secretariat of Agriculture, Livestock, Fishing and Food of the Min. of Economy and Production; planning and studies concerning the improvement and devt of catching systems, fishing apparatus and technological processes; devt and colln of growing technologies for raising marine and commercial-interest freshwater organisms, as well as the valorization of fishing crops and marine biodiversity; 300 researchers and assts; library of 4,600 vols, 763 periodicals, 350 theses/dissertations; Dir Lic. OSCAR LASCANO; publs *INIDEP Informe Técnico* (irregular), *Revista de Investigación y Desarrollo Pesquero* (irregular).

Instituto Nacional de Tecnología Agropecuaria (INTA) (National Institute for Agricultural Technology): Rivadavia 1439, 1033 Buenos Aires; tel. (11) 4383-5095; fax (11) 4383-5090; e-mail ctorres@correo.inta.gov.ar; internet www.inta.gov.ar; f. 1956; 42 experimental stations, 13 research institutes; Pres. Ing. Agr. CARLOS CHEPI; Nat. Dir Ing. Agr. ROBERTO BOCHETTO; publs *Idia XXI* (3 a year), *Revista de Investigaciones Agropecuarias* (3 a year).

Main Research Centre:

Centro Nacional de Investigación Agropecuaria (National Centre for Agricultural Research): CC 25, 1712 Castelar, Buenos Aires; tel. (11) 4621-1819; research in all aspects of farming; Dir Dr Vet. HUMBERTO CISALE.

Instituto Nacional de Vitivinicultura (National Vine Growing and Wine Producing Institute): San Martín 430, 5500 Mendoza; tel. (261) 521-6600; internet www.inv.gov.ar/institucional.php?ind=1; f. 1959; library of 20,000 vols, 690 journals; Pres. CPN y Perito Partidor GUILLERMO DANIEL GARCIA; publs *Estadística Vitivinícola* (1 a year), *Exportaciones Argentinas de Productos Vitivinícolas* (1 a year), *Revista Vinifera, Superficie de Vinos por Variedades Implatada en la República Argentina.*

ARCHITECTURE AND TOWN PLANNING

Instituto de Planeamiento Regional y Urbano (IPRU) (Regional and Urban Planning Institute): Calle Posadas 1265 (7°), 1011 Buenos Aires; fax (11) 4815-8673; f. 1952; Dir FERNANDO PASTOR; publs *Cuadernos de IPRU, Plan.*

BIBLIOGRAPHY, LIBRARY SCIENCE AND MUSEOLOGY

Centro de Documentación Bibliotecológica (Centre for Library Science Documentation): Universidad Nacional del Sur, Avda Alem 1253, 8000 Bahía Blanca; tel. (291) 42-8035; fax (291) 455-1447; f. 1962; teaching and research in library science; library of 2,980 vols, 332 periodicals; Chief Librarian

MARTA IBARLUCEA DE RUIZ; publs *Bibliografía Bibliotecológica Argentina 1978–81, Documentación Bibliotecológica, Revista de Revistas.*

Instituto de Bibliografía del Ministerio de Educación de la Provincia de Buenos Aires (Bibliographical Institute of the Ministry of Education of the Province of Buenos Aires): Calle 47 No. 510 (6°), 1900 La Plata; tel. (221) 43-5915; Dir MARÍA DEL CARMEN CRESPI DE BUSTOS; publs *Bibliografía Argentina de Historia, Boletín de Información Bibliográfica.*

ECONOMICS, LAW AND POLITICS

Centro de Investigaciones Económicas (Economic Research Centre): Instituto Torcuato Di Tella, Miñones 2159/77, 1° piso, 1428 Buenos Aires; tel. (11) 5169-7000; fax (11) 5169-7228; e-mail salvadororsini@fibertel.com.ar; internet www.itdt.edu; f. 1960; library of 85,000 vols; Dir ANDRÉS DI TELLA; Gen. Coordinator SALVADOR ORSINI; publ. *Documentos de Trabajo.*

Instituto de Desarrollo Económico y Social (Institute of Economic and Social Development): Aráoz 2838, 1425 Buenos Aires; tel. (11) 4804-4949; fax (11) 4804-5856; e-mail ides@ides.org.ar; internet www.ides.org.ar; f. 1960; library of 15,000 vols; Pres. MARIANO PLOTKIN; Dir JUAN CARLOS TORRE; publ. *Desarrollo Económico—Revista de Ciencias Sociales* (4 a year).

Instituto Nacional de Estadística y Censos (National Institute of Statistics and Censuses): Avda Julio A. Roca 615, 1067 Buenos Aires; tel. (11) 4349-9200; fax (11) 4349-9601; e-mail ces@indec.mecon.gov.ar; internet www.indec.mecon.gov.ar; f. 1894; library of 30,000 vols; Dir ANA MARÍA EDWIN; publs *Anuario Estadístico de la República Argentina* (1 a year), *Comercio Exterior Argentino* (1 a year), *INDEC Informa* (12 a year).

Instituto para el Desarrollo Empresarial en la Argentina (Institute for Management Development): Moreno 1850, 1094 Buenos Aires; tel. (11) 4372-7667; fax (11) 449-6944; f. 1960; library of 10,000 vols, 50 periodicals; Dir RUBEN D. PUENTEDURA; publ. *IDEA.*

Instituto para la Integración de América Latina y el Caribe (Institute for the Integration of Latin America and the Caribbean): Esmeralda 130 (pisos 16 y 17), C1035ABD Buenos Aires; tel. (11) 4320-1850; fax (11) 4320-1865; e-mail int/inl@iadb.org; internet www.iadb.org/intal; f. 1965 following an agreement between the Inter-American Devt Bank and the Govt of Argentina; undertakes research and provides support in all aspects of regional integration and cooperation, incl. infrastructural links among countries, regional devt of border areas, trade liberalization, legal aspects of integration and accession to new agreements; provides technical support for hemispheric integration processes agreed during Summit of the Americas 1994, and to fulfil WTO disciplines; organizes policy-orientated forums for govt officials and other interested parties; library: Documentation Centre of 100,000 documents, 12,000 vols, 400 periodicals; Dir RICARDO CARCIOFI; publs *Caricom Report* (1 a year, in English), *Informe Andino* (Andean Report, 1 a year, in Spanish and English), *Informe Centroamericano* (Central American Report, 1 a year, in Spanish and English), *Informe Mercosur* (Mercosur Report, 1 a year), *Integración & Comercio* (Integration & Trade, 2 a year).

FINE AND PERFORMING ARTS

Instituto Nacional de Estudios de Teatro (National Institute for the Study of Theatre): Avda Córdoba 1199, 1055 Buenos Aires; tel. and fax (11) 4816-7212; f. 1936; library of 16,000 vols, archives; also nat. theatre museum; Dir Prof. CRISTINA LASTRA BELGRANO.

HISTORY, GEOGRAPHY AND ARCHAEOLOGY

Departamento de Estudios Históricos Navales (Department of Naval History Studies): Avda Almirante Brown 401, 1155 Buenos Aires; tel. (11) 4362-1248; fax (11) 4362-1130; e-mail estudioshistoricosnavales@yahoo.com.ar; internet www.ara.mil.ar; f. 1957; large number of publs, also paintings and medals; Dir Capt. GUILLERMO ANDRÉS OYARZABAL.

Dirección Nacional del Antártico (National Antarctic Office): Cerrito 1248, C1010AAZ Buenos Aires; tel. (11) 4813-0072; fax (11) 4813-7807; e-mail dna@dna.gov.ar; internet www.dna.gov.ar; f. 1970; scientific colln; maintains Yubany station at King George Island, Antarctica; library of 15,000 vols; Dir Dr MARIANO A. MEMOLLI; publs *Boletín del SCAR* (3 a year, Spanish edn of SCAR Bulletin), *Contribuciones Científicas* (irregular), *Revista Antártica.*

Attached Institute:

Instituto Antártico Argentino (Argentine Antarctic Institute): Cerrito 1248, C1010AAZ Buenos Aires; tel. and fax (11) 4813-7807; e-mail diriaa@dna.gov.ar; internet www.antartida.gov.ar; f. 1951; Dir Dr SERPIO MAREUSSI.

Instituto Geográfico Militar (Military Geographical Institute): Avda Cabildo 381, 1426 Buenos Aires; tel. (11) 4576-5545; fax (11) 4576-5595; e-mail public@mapas.igm.gov.ar; internet www.igm.gov.ar; f. 1879; topographic survey of Argentina; Dir Coronel FERNANDO MIGUEL GALBÁN; publ. *Revista* (1 a year).

MEDICINE

Administración Nacional de Laboratorios e Institutos de Salud 'Dr Carlos G. Malbran' ('Dr Carlos G. Malbran' National Administration for Laboratories and Institutes of Health): Avda Vélez Sarsfield 563, 1281 Buenos Aires; tel. (11) 4303-1804; fax (11) 4303-1433; e-mail grios@anlis.gov.ar; internet www.anlis.gov.ar; f. 1916; library of 6,500 vols; Dir Dr GUSTAVO RÍOS.

Centro de Investigaciones Neurobiológicas 'Prof. Dr Christfried Jakob' (Christfried Jakob Centre for Neurobiological Research): Avda Amancio Alcorta 1602, 1283 Buenos Aires; tel. and fax (11) 4306-7314; f. 1899; attached to Min. of Public Health and Welfare; neuroscience research; Dir Prof. Dr MARIO-FERNANDO CROCCO; publ. *Folia Neurobiológica Argentina.*

Instituto de Biología y Medicina Experimental (Institute of Biology and Experimental Medicine): Vuelta de Obligado 2490, 1428 Buenos Aires; tel. (11) 4783-2869; fax (11) 4786-2564; e-mail ibyme@dna.uba.ar; internet proteus.dna.uba.ar/ibyme; f. 1944; library of 15,000 vols; Dir Dr EDUARDO H. CHARREAU; publ. *Memoria* (1 a year).

Instituto de Investigaciones Médicas 'Alfredo Lanari' (Alfredo Lanari Institute of Medical Research): Avda Combatientes de Malvinas 3150, C1427ARO Buenos Aires; tel. (11) 4522-1438; e-mail director@lanari.fmed.uba.ar; internet www.lanari.fmed.uba.ar; f. 1957; clinical and basic medical research, teaching; library of 4,185 vols, 6,738 periodicals; Dir Dr DANIEL TOMASONE; publ. *Medicina* (6 a year).

NATURAL SCIENCES

General

Consejo Nacional de Investigaciones Científicas y Técnicas (CONICET) (National Council of Scientific and Technical Research): Avda Rivadavia 1917, 1033 Buenos Aires; tel. (11) 4953-3609; fax (11) 4953-4345; e-mail postmaster@conica.gov.ar; f. 1958; supports 6 regional research centres and 114 research institutes; maintains several scientific services; Pres. ANDRÉS CARRASCO.

Main Research Institutes:

Centro Argentino de Datos Oceanográficos (CEADO) (Argentine Centre of Oceanographic Data): Avda Montes de Oca 2124, 1271 Buenos Aires; tel. (11) 4303-2240; fax (11) 4303-2299; e-mail postmaster@ceado.edu.ar; Dir Capt. ADOLFO GIL VILLANUEVA.

Centro Argentino de Etnología Americana (CAEA) (Argentine Centre for American Ethnology): Avda de Mayo 1437 (1° piso Dpto. A), 1085 Buenos Aires; tel. (11) 4381-1821; e-mail caea@speedy.com.ar; Dir Dr ANATILDE IDOYAGA MOLINA.

Centro Argentino de Primates (CAPRIM) (Argentine Primates Centre): San Cayetano CC 145, 3400 Corrientes; tel. (3783) 42-7790; fax (3783) 42-7790; e-mail ruiz@caprim.edu.ar; Dir Dr JULIO CÉSAR RUIZ.

Centro Austral de Investigaciones Científicas (CADIC) (Southern Centre for Scientific Research): Avda Malvinas Argentinas s/n, CC 92, Ruta Nacional No. 3, Barrio La Misión, Camino Lapataia, 9410 Ushuaia; tel. (2901) 42-2310; fax (2901) 43-0644; e-mail postmaster@cadica.edu.ar; f. 1975; biology, geology, archaeology, anthropology, hydrography, climatology; library of 1,000 vols; Dir Dr EDUARDO B. OLIVERO; publs *Boletín, Contribuciones Científicas del CADIC, Publicaciones especiales del CADIC.*

Centro de Diagnóstico e Investigaciones Veterinarias Formosa (CEDIVEF) (Formosa Centre of Veterinary Diagnosis and Research): Ruta Nacional No. 11, Km 1164, CC 292, 3600 Formosa; fax (3717) 45-1334; Dir Dr CARLOS M. MONZON.

Centro de Ecofisiología Vegetal (CEVEG) (Centre for Plant Ecophysiology): Serrano 669 (pisos 5 y 6), 1414 Buenos Aires; tel. (11) 4856-7110; fax (11) 4856-7110; e-mail postmaster@ceveg.gov.ar; Dir Dr OSVALDO H. CASO.

Centro de Ecología Aplicada del Litoral (CECOAL) (Centre of Coastal Applied Ecology): Ruta Prov. No. 5, Km 2.5, CC 291, 3400 Corrientes; tel. (3783) 45-4418; fax (3783) 45-4421; internet www.cecoal.com.ar; Dir Prof. JUAN JOSÉ NEIFF.

Centro de Estudios e Investigaciones Laborales (CEIL) (Centre of Labour Study and Research): Corrientes 2470 (6° piso, of. 24 y 25), 1046 Buenos Aires; tel. (11) 4952-5273; fax (11) 4952-5273; e-mail postmaster@ceil.edu.ar; f. 1971; Dir Dr JULIO CÉSAR NEFFA; publ. *Boletín-Serie Documentos.*

Centro de Estudios Farmacológicos y Botanicos (CEFYBO) (Centre for Pharmacological Studies and Botany): Serrano 669, 1414 Buenos Aires; tel. (11) 4856-2751; fax (11) 4856-2751; e-mail postmaster@cefybo.edu.ar; f. 1975; Dirs

Dra LEONOR STERIN DE BORDA, Dra MARÍA ANTONIETA DEL PERO.

Centro de Estudios Fotosintéticos y Bioquímicos (CEFOBI) (Centre for Studies in Photosynthesis and Biochemistry): Suipacha 531, 2000 Rosario; tel. (341) 437-1955; fax (341) 437-0044; e-mail carlosandreo@cefobi-conicet.gov.ar; f. 1976; Dir Dr CARLOS S. ANDREO.

Centro de Investigación y Desarrollo en Ciencias Aplicadas 'Dr Jorge J. Ronco' (CINDECA) (Research and Development Centre for Applied Sciences 'Dr Jorge J. Ronco'): Calle 47 No. 257, CC 59, 1900 La Plata; tel. (221) 421-1353; fax (221) 425-4277; e-mail dir-cindeca@quimica.unlp.edu.ar; internet www.cindeca.org.ar; Dir Prof. Dr LUIS ALBERTO GAMBARO; publs *Applied Catalysis, Catalysis Today, Journal of Catalysis, Journal of Material Chemistry.*

Centro de Investigación y Desarrollo en Criotecnología de Alimentos (CIDCA) (Research and Development Centre for Food Cryotechnology): Calles 47 y 116, CC 553, 1900 La Plata; tel. (221) 424-9287; fax (221) 425-4853; Dir Dra MARÍA C. AÑON.

Centro de Investigación y Desarrollo en Fermentaciones Industriales (CINDEFI) (Research and Development Centre for Industrial Fermentation): Calles 47 y 115, 1900 La Plata; tel. (221) 483-3794; fax (221) 425-4533; e-mail voget@biol.unlp.edu.ar; Dir Dr RODOLFO J. ERTOLA.

Centro de Investigación y Desarrollo en Tecnología de Pinturas (CIDEPINT) (Research and Development Centre for Paint Technology): Calle 52 a 121 y 122, 1900 La Plata, Buenos Aires; tel. (221) 421-6214; fax (221) 427-1537; e-mail cielsner@isis.unlp.edu.ar; Dir Dr VICENTE J. D. RASCIO.

Centro de Investigación y Estudios Ortopédicos y Traumatológicos (CINEOT) (Research and Study Centre for Orthopaedics and Traumatology): Potosí 4215, 1199 Buenos Aires; tel. (11) 4958-4011; fax (11) 4981-0991; e-mail cineot@impsat1.com.ar; Dir Dr DOMINGO L. MUSCOLO.

Centro de Investigaciones en Antropología Filosófica y Cultural (CIAFIC) (Centre for Research in Philosophical and Cultural Anthropology): Juramento 142, 1609 Boulogne, Buenos Aires; Federico Lacroze 2100, 1426 Buenos Aires; tel. and fax (11) 4776-0913; e-mail postmaster@ciafic.edu.ar; internet www.ciafic.edu.ar; f. 1976; research into education, philosophy, linguistics, epistemology, anthropology; library of 12,000 vols and periodicals; Sec. Mag. CLOTILDE DE LA BARRA; publs *Archivos* (anthropology, 1 a year), *Servicio de Información Bibliográfica Especializada* (2 a year).

Centro de Investigaciones en Recursos Geológicos (CIRGEO) (Centre for Research into Geological Resources): Ramírez de Velasco 847, 1414 Buenos Aires; tel. (11) 4772-9729; fax (11) 4771-3742; e-mail pompo@cirgeo.edu.ar; f. 1976; library of 6,000 vols, 90 periodicals; Dir Dr BERNABÉ J. QUARTINO.

Centro de Investigaciones Endocrinológicas (CEDIE) (Centre of Endocrinological Research): Gallo 1330, 1425 Buenos Aires; tel. (11) 4963-5931; fax (11) 4963-5930; e-mail biblioteca@cedie.org.ar; Dir Dr HÉCTOR CHEMES; Vice-Dir RODOLFO REY.

Centro de Investigaciones Opticas (CIOP) (Centre for Optical Research): Camino Parque Centenario e/505 y 506,

Gonnet, CC 124, 1900 La Plata, Buenos Aires; tel. (221) 484-0280; fax (221) 453-0189; e-mail postmaster@ciop.edu.ar; Dir Dr MARIO GALLARDO.

Centro de Investigaciones sobre Regulación de Poblacion de Organismos Nocivos (CIRPON) (Centre for Research into Controlling Harmful Organisms): Pasaje Caseros 1050, 4000 San Miguel de Tucumán; tel. and fax (381) 434-6940; e-mail cirponfml@arnetbiz.com.ar; Dir Dr ALBERTO A. P. FIDALGO; Supervisor Prof. MARIANO ORDANO.

Centro de Referencia para Lactobacilos (CERELA) (Reference Centre for Lactobacillus): Chacabuco 145, 4000 San Miguel de Tucumán; tel. (381) 431-1720; fax (381) 431-1720; e-mail crl@cerela.edu.ar; Dir Dra AÍDA A. P. DE RUIZ HOLGADO.

Centro de Tecnología en Recursos Minerales y Cerámica (CETMIC) (Technology Centre for Mineral and Ceramic Resources): CC 49, 1897 Gonnet, Buenos Aires; Camino Centenario y 506, 1897 Gonnet, Buenos Aires; tel. (221) 484-0247; fax (221) 471-0075; e-mail postmaster@cetmic.edu.ar; Dir Dr ENRIQUE PEREIRA.

Centro Experimental de la Vivienda Económica (CEVE) (Experimental Centre for Low-Cost Housing): Igualdad 3585, Villa Siburu, 5003 Córdoba; tel. (351) 489-4442; fax (351) 489-4442; e-mail postmaster@ceve.org.ar; Dir Arq. HORACIO BERRETTA.

Centro Nacional Patagónico (CNP) (National Patagónia Centre): Blvd Alte. Brown s/n, 9120 Puerto Madryn, Chubut; tel. (2965) 45-1375; fax (2965) 47-2885; e-mail postmaster@cenpat.edu.ar; Dir Dr ADAN E. PUCCI.

Instituto Argentino de Investigaciones de las Zonas Aridas (IADIZA) (Argentine Institute for Arid Zones Research): Dr Adrián Ruiz Leal s/n, Parque Gral San Martín, 5500 Mendoza; fax (261) 428-7995; e-mail cricyt@planet.losandes.com.ar; f. 1974; Dir Ing. Agr. JUAN CARLOS GUEVARA (acting); publ. *Boletín Informativo.*

Instituto Argentino de Nivologia, Glaciologia y Ciencias Ambientales (IANIGLA) (Argentine Institute for Snow, Ice and Environmental Sciences): Dr Adrián Ruiz Leal s/n, Parque Gral San Martín, CC 131, 5500 Mendoza; tel. (261) 428-7029; fax (261) 428-7029; e-mail cricyt@planet.losandes.com.ar; Dir Dr WOLFGANG VOLKHEIMER.

Instituto Argentino de Oceanografía (IADO) (Argentine Oceanographic Institute): Edificio E3, Complejo de la Carrindanga, Florida 4000, 8000 Bahía Blanca, Buenos Aires; tel. (291) 42-3555; fax (291) 486-1112; e-mail postmaster@criba.edu.ar; f. 1969; Subdirector-in-Charge Dr JOSÉ KOSTADINOFF; publ. *Contribuciones Científicas IADO.*

Instituto Argentino de Radioastronomía (IAR) (Argentine Institute of Radioastronomy): Casilla de Correo 5, 1894 Villa Elisa, Buenos Aires; tel. (221) 482-4903; fax (221) 425-4909; e-mail biblio@iar.unlp.edu.ar; internet www.iar.unlp.edu.ar; f. 1963; radioastronomy research; electronical equipment devt; library of 11,000 vols, 163 periodicals; Dir Dr MARCELO ARNAL; Dir Dr GUSTAVO ROMERO; publ. *Boletín Radioastronómico.*

Instituto de Botánica del Nordeste (IBONE) (Northeastern Institute of Botany): Sargento Cabral 2131, CC 209, 3400 Corrientes; tel. (3783) 42-7309; fax (3783)

42-7131; e-mail postmaster@unneib.edu.ar; Dir Ing. ANTONIO KRAPOVICKAS.

Instituto de Desarrollo Tecnológico para la Industria Química (INTEC) (Technological Development Institute of the Chemical Industry): Güemes 3450, 3000 Santa Fe; tel. (342) 455-9174; fax (342) 455-0944; e-mail director@intec.unl.edu.ar; Dir Dr ALBERTO E. CASSANO (acting).

Instituto de Geocronología y Geología Isotópica (INGEIS) (Institute of Isotope Geochronology and Geology): Pabellón INGEIS, Ciudad Universitaria, 1428 Buenos Aires; tel. (11) 4784-7798; fax (11) 4783-3024; e-mail postmaster@ingeis.uba.ar; Dir Dr ENRIQUE LINARES.

Instituto de Investigación de Productos Naturales, de Análisis y de Síntesis Orgánica (IPNAYS) (Institute for Research, Analysis and Organic Synthesis of Natural Products): Santiago del Estero 2829, 3000 Santa Fe; tel. (342) 455-3958; fax (342) 456-1146; e-mail rmalizia@fiqus.unl.edu.ar; Dir Ing. J. A. RETAMAR.

Instituto de Investigación Médica 'Mercedes y Martín Ferreyra' (INIMEC) (Mercedes and Martín Ferreyra Medical Research Institute): CC 389, 5000 Córdoba; Friuli 2434, Colinas de V. Sarfield, 5016 Córdoba; tel. (351) 468-1465; fax (351) 469-5163; e-mail immf@immf.uncor.edu; internet www.immf.uncor.edu; f. 1946; scientific research and the development of scientific and technical human resources in medical science; Dir Dr ALFREDO CACERES BEAUGE.

Instituto de Investigaciones Bioquímicas (INIBIBB) (Institute for Biochemical Research): Edificio E1, Complejo de la Carrindanga, Florida 4000, 8000 Bahía Blanca, Buenos Aires; tel. (291) 486-1201; fax (291) 486-1200; e-mail rtfjb1@criba.edu.ar; f. 1975; Dir Prof. Dr FRANCISCO JOSÉ BARRANTES.

Instituto de Investigaciones en Catálisis y Petroquímica (INCAPE) (Catalysis and Petrochemistry Research Institute): Santiago del Estero 2654, 3000 Santa Fe; tel. (342) 453-3858; fax (342) 453-1068; e-mail parera@fiqus.unl.edu.ar; Dir Ing. JOSÉ M. PARERA.

Instituto de Investigaciones Estadísticas (INIE) (Statistical Research Institute): Avda Independencia 1900, CC 209, 4000 San Miguel de Tucumán; tel. (381) 436-4093; fax (381) 410-7548; e-mail inie@herrera.unt.edu.ar; internet www.face.unt.edu.ar; f. 1977; library of 1,132 vols; Dir Dr RAÚL P. MENTZ.

Instituto de Investigaciones Farmacológicas (ININFA) (Pharmacological Research Institute): Junín 956 (5°), 1113 Buenos Aires; tel. (11) 4961-6784; fax (11) 4963-8593; e-mail ininfa@huemul.ffyb.uba.ar; Dir Dra EDDA ADLER DE GRASCHINSKY.

Instituto de Investigaciones Geohistóricas (IIGHI) (Institute of Geohistorical Research): Avda Castelli 930, CC 438, 3500 Resistencia, Chaco; tel. (3722) 42-7798; fax (3722) 43-9983; e-mail postmaster@iighi.gov.ar; Dir Dr ERNESTO J. A. MAEDER.

Instituto de Limnología 'Dr Raul A. Ringuelet' (ILPLA) (Limnology Institute): CC 712, 1900 La Plata, Buenos Aires; tel. (11) 4275-7799; e-mail acapitul@ilpla.edu.ar; internet www.ilpla.edu.ar; f. 1972; library of 1,160 vols; research in limnology, ecology, biodiversity and fisheries; Dir Dr ALBERTO RODRÍGUEZ CAPÍTULO (acting); publs Aquatec (irregular), Biología Acuática (irregular, online).

Instituto de Matemática (INMABB) (Mathematics Institute): Avda Alem 1253, 8000 Bahía Blanca; tel. (291) 43-3382; fax (291) 455-1447; e-mail inmabb@arcriba.edu.ar; f. 1956; Dir Dra AURORA GERMANI.

Instituto de Mecánica Aplicada (IMA) (Institute of Applied Mechanics): Gorriti 43, 8000 Bahía Blanca; tel. (291) 44-5154; fax (291) 455-1447; e-mail ima@criba.edu.ar; Dir Dr PATRICIO A. A. LAURA.

Instituto de Neurobiología (IDNEU) (Neurobiology Institute): Serrano 669, 1414 Buenos Aires; tel. (11) 4855-7674; fax (11) 4856-7108; e-mail postmaster@fuacta.sld.ar; Dir Dr JUAN H. TRAMEZZANI.

Instituto Latinoamericano de Investigaciones Comparadas Oriente y Occidente (ILICOO) (Latin American Institute for Comparative East-West Studies): Callao 853, 1023 Buenos Aires; tel. (11) 4811-2270; e-mail postmaster@uscsoc.edu.ar; f. 1973; library of 2,000 vols, 1,500 periodicals; Dir Prof. MARÍA M. TERREN; publ. Oriente—Occidente.

Instituto Multidisciplinario de Biología Celular (IMBICE) (Multidisciplinary Institute of Cellular Biology): Calle 526, e/ 10 y 11, CC 403, 1900 La Plata, Buenos Aires; tel. (221) 421-0112; fax (221) 425-3320; e-mail biblioteca@imbice.org.ar; internet www.imbice.org.ar; Dir Dr ALEJANDRO DANIEL BOLZÁN.

Instituto Rosario de Investigaciónes en Ciencias de la Educación (IRICE) (Rosario Education Research Institute): Blvd 27 de Febrero 210 'bis', 2000 Rosario; tel. (341) 482-1769; fax (341) 482-1772; e-mail irice@ifir.ifir.edu.ar; Dir Dr NÉSTOR DIRECTORIO ROSELLI.

Fundación Miguel Lillo: Miguel Lillo 251, T4000JFE San Miguel de Tucumán; tel. and fax (381) 433-0868; e-mail direccion@lillo.org.ar; internet www.lillo.org.ar; f. 1931; scientific research in natural sciences and history; incl. institutes of botany, geology and zoology; maintains Geobiological Information Centre of NOA, Cultural Centre 'Alberto Rouges', Study Centre 'Juan Dalma', Lillo Museum of Natural Sciences; library of 210,000 vols; Pres. Dr JORGE L. ROUGÉS; Gen. Dir Lic. ANA MARÍA FRÍAS DE FERNÁNDEZ; Dir, Institute of Botany Lic. MARCELA HERNÁNDEZ DE TERÁN; Dir, Institute of Geology Dra. ANA LÍA AHUMADA; Dir, Institute of Zoology Mg. SUSANA G. ARANDA; Dir, Geobiological Information Centre Trad. ROSALINA CORROTO; Dir, Cultural and Study Centres Prof. MARÍA ELENA PERILLI DE COLOMBRES GARMENDIA; Dir, Lillo Museum of Natural Sciences EDUARDO E. RIBOTTA; publs Acta Geologica Lilloana (2 a year), Actas Jornadas la Generación del Centenario (2 a year), Acta Zoologica Lilloana (2 a year), Extensión Científica y Cultural (irregular), Genera et Species Animalium Argentinorum (2 a year), Genera et Species Plantarum Argentinarum (2 a year), Lilloa (botanical, 2 a year), Miscelánea (2 a year), Opera Lilloana (2 a year), Serie Conservación de la Naturaleza (2 a year), Serie Extensión Científica y Cultural (irregular), also Ensayos y Correspondencia by Alberto Rouges, and biographies of C. R. Schreiter, J. G. Sortheix, J. Padilla and J. Heller.

Biological Sciences

Estación Hidrobiológica (Hydrobiology Station): Avda Alte. Brown s/n, esq. calle 520, 7630 Puerto Quequén, Provincia de Buenos Aires; e-mail ehpog@macn.gov.ar; f. 1928; attached to 'B. Rivadavia' Argentine Museum of Natural Sciences; concerned especially with marine hydrobiology; Dir Lic. GUSTAVO CHIARAMONTE; publ. Trabajos de la Estación Hidrobiológica (irregular).

Instituto de Botánica 'Carlos Spegazzini' ('Carlos Spegazzini' Botanical Institute): Calle 53 No. 477, 1900 La Plata, Buenos Aires; tel. and fax (221) 421-9845; internet www.fcnym.unlp.edu.ar/institutos/spegazzini/indexibs.html; f. 1930; affiliated to Museo de La Plata; mycological research, biodiversity of saprotrophic and biotrophic fungi; mycological collns from Argentina and all South America; germplasm bank of arbuscular mycorrhizal fungi; Dir Prof. Dr MARTA NOEMI CABELLO.

Instituto de Botánica 'Darwinion' (Darwinian Botanical Institute): Labardén 200, CC 22, B1642HYD San Isidro; tel. 4743-4800; fax 4747-4748; e-mail secretaria@darwin.edu.ar; internet www.darwin.edu.ar; f. 1911; attached to the Academia Nacional de Ciencias Exactas, Físicas y Naturales and the Consejo Nacional de Investigaciones Científicas y Técnicas; fields of research: systematic botany, phytogeography, plant anatomy and cytogenetics, palynology, ethnobotany, archaeobotany; library of 160,000 vols, 2,600 periodicals; Dir Dr FERNANDO O. ZULOAGA; publs Hickenia (irregular), Revista Darwiniana (2 a year).

Instituto Municipal de Botánica, Jardín Botánico 'Carlos Thays' (Municipal Botanical Institute, Carlos Thays Botanical Gardens): Sante Fe 3951, 1425 Buenos Aires; tel. (11) 469-3954; f. 1898; library of 1,000 vols, 7,000 periodicals; Dir ANTONIO AMADO GARCÍA; publs Index Seminum, Revista del Instituto de Botánica.

Instituto Nacional de Limnología (National Institute of Limnology): Ciudad Universitaria, Paraje 'El Pozo', 3000 Santa Fe; tel. (342) 451-1645; fax (342) 451-1648; e-mail secretaria@inali.unl.edu.ar; internet www.santafe-conicet.gov.ar/institut/inali; f. 1962; library of 3,000 vols, 385 periodicals; Dir MSc MERCEDES MARCHESE.

Physical Sciences

Comisión Nacional de Actividades Espaciales (CONAE) (National Commission on Space Activities): Avda Paseo Colón 751, 1063 Buenos Aires; tel. (11) 4331-0074; fax (11) 4331-3446; e-mail insti@conae.gov.ar; internet www.conae.gov.ar; f. 1991; develops Argentina's Nat. Space Programme; Exec. and Technical Dir Dr CONRADO FRANCO VAROTTO.

Comisión Nacional de Energía Atómica (National Atomic Energy Commission): Avda del Libertador 8250, 1429 Buenos Aires; tel. (11) 4704-1201; fax (11) 4704-1154; e-mail comunicacion@cnea.gov.ar; internet www.cnea.gov.ar; f. 1950; govt agency; promotes and undertakes scientific and industrial research and applications of nuclear transmutations and reactions; research centres in Buenos Aires, Constituyentes, Ezeiza and Bariloche; information centre: see Libraries; Pres. Lic. NORMA LUISA BOERO; Gen. Man. Dr CARLOS RUBÉN CALABRESE.

Observatorio Astronómico (Astronomical Observatory): Laprida 854, 5000 Córdoba; tel. (351) 433-1064; fax (351) 433-1063; e-mail library@mail.oac.uncor.edu; internet www.oac.uncor.edu; f. 1871; attached to the Univ. of Córdoba; research and undergraduate and postgraduate teaching; library of 5,000 vols; Dir Prof. Dr LUIS A. MILONE; publs Reprints (40 a year), Resultados.

Observatorio Astronómico (Astronomical Observatory): Paseo del Bosque s/n, 1900 La Plata; tel. (221) 423-6593; fax (221) 423-6591; e-mail academic@fcaglp.fcaglp.unlp.edu.ar; internet www.fcaglp.unlp.edu.ar; f. 1883;

library of 25,000 vols, 500 periodicals; Dean Dr JUAN CARLOS MUZZIO.

Servicio Geológico Minero Argentino (Argentine Geological and Mining Service): Avda Julio A. Roca 651, P.B., C1067ABB Buenos Aires; tel. (11) 4349-3200; fax (11) 4349-3198; e-mail veronica@inti.gov.ar; internet www.segemar.gov.ar; f. 1904; attached to the State Secretariat of Mining of the Min. of Economy and Public Works; Pres. Ing. JORGE OMAR MAYORAL; Admin. Dir RODOLFO JORGE SFORZA; publ. *Estadística Minera de la República Argentina* (1 a year).

Servicio Meteorológico Nacional (National Meteorological Service): 25 de Mayo 658, C1002ABN Buenos Aires; tel. (11) 5167-6767; fax (11) 5167-6709; e-mail smn@smn.gov.ar; internet www.smn.gov.ar; f. 1872; library of 45,000 vols; Dir Dr HÉCTOR CIAPPESONI; publs *Boletin Climatológico*, *Boletin Informativo*.

RELIGION, SOCIOLOGY AND ANTHROPOLOGY

Departamento de Estudios Etnográficos y Coloniales (Department of Ethnographical and Colonial Studies): Calle 25 de Mayo 1470, 3000 Santa Fe; tel. (342) 457-3550; fax (342) 457-3550; e-mail etnosfe@ceride.gov.ar; internet www.santafe.gov.ar; f. 1940; Dir Arq. LUIS MARIA CALVO; publ. *America* (1 a year).

Instituto Nacional de Antropología y Pensamiento Latinoamericano (National Institute of Anthropology and Latin American Thought): Calle 3 de Febrero 1378, 1426 Buenos Aires; tel. (11) 4784-3371; fax (11) 4784-3371; e-mail postmaster@bibapl.edu.ar; f. 1943; attached to the Secretariat for Culture at the President's Office; library of 15,000 vols, 1,600 periodicals; Dir Dra DIANA BOLANDI DE PERROT; publ. *Cuaderno*.

TECHNOLOGY

Instituto Argentino de Normalización (IRAM) (Argentine Standards Institute): Perú 552/556, C1068AAB Buenos Aires; tel. (11) 4346-0600; fax (11) 4346-0601; e-mail iram4@vianetworks.net.ar; internet www.iram.com.ar; f. 1935; library of 174,300 standards; Dir-Gen. Ing. JOSÉ F. LÓPEZ; publ. *Boletín IRAM* (12 a year).

Instituto de Mecánica Aplicada y Estructuras (Institute of Applied Mechanics and Structures): Riobamba y Berutti, 2000 Rosario; tel. (341) 480-8538; fax (341) 480-8540; e-mail imaesecr@eie.fceia.unr.edu .ar; internet www.fceia.unr.edu.ar/labinfo; f. 1963; attached to Faculty of Exact Sciences, Engineering and Surveying, Universidad Nacional de Rosario; library of 1,000 vols, 3,000 periodicals; Dir Ing. FERNANDO OSCAR MARTÍNEZ.

Instituto Nacional de Tecnología Industrial (INTI) (National Institute of Industrial Technology): Parque Tecnológico Miguelete, Colectora de Avda General Paz 5445 entre Albarellos y Avda de los Constituyentes, Casilla de correo 157, B1650KNA San Martín, Buenos Aires; tel. (11) 4724-6200; e-mail consultas@inti.gob.ar; internet www.inti.gob .ar; f. 1957; library of 32,000 vols, 2,216 periodicals, 105,000 standards; Pres. Ing. LEÓNIDAS J. F. MONTAÑA; publs *Boletín técnico* (irregular), *Dendroenergía* (2 a year), *Noticiteca* (4 a year).

Research Institutes:

Centro de Investigación de Celulosa y Papel (INTI Celulosa y Papel) (Pulp and Paper Research Centre): Avda Gral Paz 5445, 1650 San Martin, Buenos Aires; tel. (11) 4713-4330; fax (11) 4754-4901; e-mail celulosaypapel@inti.gob.ar; internet www.inti.gob.ar/celulosaypapel; f. 1968; technical studies on pulp and paper industry raw materials, production processes, environmental protection, product properties and product devt; Technical Dir Ing. HUGO VÉLEZ.

Centro de Investigación de los Reglamentos Nacionales de Seguridad para Obras Civiles (Centre for Research for National Regulations on Civil Work Safety): Avda de los Immigrantes 1950 (Of. 22 y 24), 1104 Buenos Aires; Dir Ing. MARTA PARMIGIANI.

Centro de Investigación de Tecnologías de Granos (Centre for Research on Technologies for the Industrialization of Grain Production): Avda Alte. Brown e/ Reconquista y Juan Jose Paso, 6500 Nueve de Julio, Buenos Aires; Dir Ing. NICOLÁS APRO.

Centro de Investigación en Tecnologías de Industrialización de Alimentos (Centre for Research on Technologies for the Industrialization of Food Production): Avda Gral Paz e/ Avda de los Constituyentes y Avda Albarellos 40, CC 157, 1650 San Martin, Buenos Aires; Dir Ing. GUILLERMO CAMBIAZZO.

Centro de Investigación y Asistencia Técnica a la Industria Alimentaria (Centre for Research and Technical Assistance to Food Processing Industry): Avda Mitre y 20 de Junio, 8336 Villa Regina, Rio Negro; tel. (2941) 46-2810; fax (2941) 46-1111; e-mail carlose@ciati.com.ar; internet www.ciati.com.ar; f. 1980; Man. Lic. CARLOS ESPOSITO.

Centro de Investigación y Desarrollo de Carnes (Centre for Meat Research and Development): Avda Gral Paz e/ Avda de los Constituyentes y Avda Albarellos 47, CC 157, 1650 San Martin, Buenos Aires; Dir Ing. NÉLIDA PROLA.

Centro de Investigación y Desarrollo de Electrónica e Informática (Centre for Electronics and Computer Science Research and Development): Avda Gral Paz e/ Avda de los Constituyentes y Avda Albarellos 42, CC 157, 1650 San Martin, Buenos Aires; tel. (220) 4754-4064; fax (220) 4754-5194; Dir Ing. DANIEL LUPI.

Centro de Investigación y Desarrollo de Envases y Embalajes (Centre for Packaging Research and Development): Avda Gral Paz e/ Avda de los Constituyentes y Avda Albarellos 48, CC 157, 1650 San Martin, Buenos Aires; Dir Ing. CARLOS LOMO.

Centro de Investigación y Desarrollo de Ingeniería Ambiental (Centre for Environmental Engineering Research and Development): Paseo Colón 850 (4°), 1063 Buenos Aires; tel. (11) 4345-7541; fax (11) 4331-5362; Dir Ing. LUIS A. DE TULIO.

Centro de Investigación y Desarrollo de la Industria de la Madera y Afines (Centre for the Wood Industry and Related Research and Development): Juana Gorriti 3520, 1708 Hurlingham, Buenos Aires; Dir Ing. GRACIELA RAMIREZ.

Centro de Investigación y Desarrollo del Cuero (Centre for Leather Research and Development): Camino Centenario e/ 505 y 508, CC 6, 1897 Manuel Gonnet, Buenos Aires; tel. (11) 484-1876; fax (11) 484-0244; Dir Ing. ALBERTO SOFÍA.

Centro de Investigación y Desarrollo de Métodos y Técnicas para Pequeñas y Medianas Empresas (Centre for Methods and Techniques Research and Development for Small and Medium-Size Industries): Avda Gral Paz e/ Avda de los Constituyentes y Avda Albarellos 12, CC 157, 1650 San Martin, Buenos Aires; Dir Ing. ROBERTO LÓPEZ.

Centro de Investigación y Desarrollo de Tecnológico de la Industria de los Plásticos (INTI-Plásticos) (Centre for Research and Technological Development of the Plastics Industry): Avda Gral Paz 5445 e/ Avda de los Constituyentes y Avda Albarellos 16, CC 157, B1650WAB San Martin, Buenos Aires; tel. (11) 4724-6373; fax (11) 4753-5773; e-mail plasticos@inti .gob.ar; internet www.inti.gov.ar/plasticos; f. 1978; research and devt; technology transfer; 45 mems; library of 500 vols; Dir Ing. RICARDO GIMÉNEZ.

Centro de Investigación y Desarrollo de Tecnológico de la Industria del Caucho (INTI-Caucho) (Centre for Research and Technological Development of the Rubber Industry): Avda Gral Paz 5445, CPB1650KNA San Martin, Buenos Aires; tel. (11) 4724-6200; fax (11) 4724-6425; e-mail caucho@inti.gob.ar; internet www.inti.gob.ar; f. 1961; physical testing laboratories; chemical laboratory; pilot plants for rubber and latex; adhesive sectors; technical assistance; rubber, latex and adhesives formulations; training courses; 26 mems; Dir Lic. LILIANA REHAK.

Centro de Investigación y Desarrollo en Construcciones (Centre for Construction Research and Development): Avda Gral Paz e/ Avda Albarellos 33/10, CC 157, 1650 San Martin, Buenos Aires; Dir Ing. R. LEONARDO CHECMAREW.

Centro de Investigación y Desarrollo en Física (Centre for Physics Research and Development): Avda Gral Paz e/ Avda de los Constituyentes y Avda Albarellos 3/ 44, CC 157, 1650 San Martin, Buenos Aires; fax (11) 4713-4140; Dir Lic. GUSTAVO RANGUGNI.

Centro de Investigación y Desarrollo en Mecánica (Centre for Mechanics Research and Development): Avda Gral Paz e/ Avda de los Constituyentes y Avda Albarellos 9/46, CC 157, 1650 San Martin, Buenos Aires; tel. (220) 4752-0818; fax (220) 4754-5301; Dir Ing. MARIO QUINTEIRO.

Centro de Investigación y Desarrollo en Química y Petroquímica (Centre for Chemistry and Petrochemistry Research and Development): Avda Gral Paz e/ Avda de los Constituyentes y Avda Albarellos 38, CC 157, 1650 San Martin, Buenos Aires; Dir Lic. GRACIELA ENRIQUEZ.

Centro de Investigación y Desarrollo para el Uso Racional de la Energía (Centre for Research and Development for the Rational Use of Energy): Avda Gral Paz e/ Avda de los Constituyentes y Avda Albarellos 5, CC 157, 1650 San Martin, Buenos Aires; Dir Ing. MARIO OGARA.

Centro de Investigación y Desarrollo sobre Contaminantes Especiales (Centre for Special Pollutants Research and Development): Avda Gral Paz e/ Avda de los Constituyentes y Avda Albarellos 38, CC 157, 1650 San Martin, Buenos Aires; tel. (220) 4754-4074; fax (220) 4753-5749; Dir Ing. ISABEL FRAGA.

Centro de Investigación y Desarrollo sobre Electrodeposición y Procesos Superficiales (Centre for Electroplating and Superficial Processes Research and Development): Avda Gral Paz e/ Avda de los Constituyentes y Avda Albarellos 46, CC 157, 1650 San Martin, Buenos Aires; Dir Ing. ALICIA NIÑO GÓMEZ.

Centro de Investigación y Desarrollo Textil (Centre for Textile Research and Development): Avda Gral Paz e/ Avda de los Constituyentes y Avda Albarellos 15, CC 157, 1650 San Martin, Buenos Aires; Dir Ing. PATRICIA MARINO.

Libraries and Archives

Bahía Blanca

Asociación Bernardino Rivadavia—Biblioteca Popular (People's Library of the Bernardino Rivadavia Association): Avda Colón 31, 8000 Bahía Blanca; tel. (291) 455-4055; fax (291) 455-9677; e-mail abr@abr.org.ar; internet www.abr.org.ar; f. 1882; funded by its members; 4,500 mems; 158,319 vols, 1,000 periodicals, 1,000 video cassettes and a large archive of newspapers; Pres. Dr NÉSTOR J. CAZZANIGA; Sec. MIGUEL A. LALANNE.

Biblioteca Central de la Universidad Nacional del Sur (Central Library of the National University of the South): Avda Alem 1253, B8000CPB Bahía Blanca; tel. (291) 459-5111; fax (291) 459-5110; e-mail unsbc@uns.edu.ar; internet bc.uns.edu.ar; f. 1948; 164,000 vols, 7,293 periodicals; Chief Librarian LUIS A. HERRERA; publs *Memoria Anual*, *Ultimas Adquisiciones*.

Buenos Aires

Archivo General de la Nación (National Archives): Avda Leandro N. Alem 246, 1003 Buenos Aires; tel. (11) 4331-5531; fax (11) 4334-0065; e-mail archivo@mininterior.gov.ar; internet www.mininterior.gov.ar/agn; f. 1821; Supervisor ENRIQUE TANDETER.

Biblioteca Argentina para Ciegos (Argentine Library for the Blind): Lezica 3909, C1202AAA Buenos Aires; tel. (11) 4981-0137; fax (11) 4981-0137 ext. 15; e-mail bac@bac.org.ar; internet www.bac.org.ar; f. 1924; 14,000 vols in Braille, talking books; Dir FERNANDO GALARRAGA; publs *Burbujas* (in Braille, for children), *Con Fundamento* (in Braille, for young people), *Hacia La Luz* (in Braille, for adults).

Biblioteca Central de la Armada (Central Library of the Navy): Estado Mayor General de la Armada, Calle Comodoro Py 2055 PB of 132, 1107 Buenos Aires; tel. (11) 4317-2000 ext. 2301; e-mail esgnbib@ara.mil.ar; f. 1914; 160,000 vols; 50 brs; Dir ALICIA PEREZ; publ. *Revista de Publicaciones Navales*.

Biblioteca Central de la Universidad del Salvador 'Padre Guillermo Furlong' (Fr Guillermo Furlong Central Library of the University of the Saviour): Tte. Gral. Perón 1818, Subsuelo, C1040AAB Buenos Aires; tel. (11) 4371-0422; e-mail uds-bibl@salvador.edu.ar; f. 1956; 55,000 vols; Dir LILIANA LAURA REGA; publ. *Boletín Bibliográfico*.

Biblioteca de la Sociedad Rural Argentina (Library of Argentine Agricultural Society): Florida 460, 1005 Buenos Aires; tel. (11) 4322-3431; fax (11) 4325-8231; f. 1866; 50,000 items; Dir Dr VÍCTOR LUIS FUNES; publs *Anales de la Sociedad Rural Argentina* (4 a year), *Boletín*, *Memoria* (1 a year).

Biblioteca de Leprología 'Dr Enrique P. Fidanza' (Dr Enrique P. Fidanza Leprosy Library): Federación del Patronato del Enfermo de Lepra de la República Argentina, Beruti 2373/77, 1106 Buenos Aires; tel. (11) 483-1815; f. 1930; 4,000 vols, 35,000 cards in its catalogues; museum of histopathology of skin; publ. *Temas de Leprología*.

Biblioteca Prebisch (Prebisch Library): Reconquista 266/250 1° Subsuelo, C1003ABF Buenos Aires; tel. (11) 4348-3772; fax (11) 4348-3771; e-mail biblio@bcra.gov.ar; internet www.bcra.gov.ar; f. 1935; 52,000 vols, 2,600 journals, 280 CDs and 1,865 microfilms; Dir LILIANA MARÍA COVA; publs *Boletín Estadístico* (12 a year), *Boletín*

Monetario y Financiero (4 a year), *Documentos de Trabajo* (irregular), *Información de Entidades Financieras* (12 a year), *Informe Anual del Presidente al Congreso* (1 a year), *Notas Técnicas* (irregular).

Biblioteca del Bibliotecario 'Dr Augusto Raúl Cortazar' (Library of the Librarian Dr Augusto Raúl Cortazar): México 564, 1097 Buenos Aires; f. 1944; a section of the Escuela Nacional de Bibliotecarios (Instituto Superior de Enseñanza); 2,500 vols; Dir RUBY A. ESCANDE.

Biblioteca del Colegio de Escribanos 'José A. Negri' (José A. Negri Library of the College of Notaries): Callao 1540, 1024 Buenos Aires; tel. and fax (11) 4807-1637; e-mail bibnegri@colegio-escribanos.org.ar; internet www.colegio-escribanos.org.ar; f. 1886; law and social science; 32,500 vols; Librarian ANA MARÍA DANZA; publs *Boletín de Legislación*, *Revista del Notariado*.

Biblioteca del Congreso de la Nación (Library of the National Congress): Hipólito Yrigoyen 1750, C1089AAH Buenos Aires; tel. (11) 4010-3000; e-mail coordinacion@bcnbib.gov.ar; internet www.bcnbib.gov.ar; f. 1859; 2m. vols; Pres. Dr JUAN CARLOS GIOJA; Gen. Coordinating Dir BERNARDINO CABEZAS; publ. *Boletín*.

Biblioteca del Ministerio de Relaciones Exteriores y Culto (Ministry of Foreign Affairs and Religion Library): Arenales 761, 1061 Buenos Aires; tel. (11) 441-1498; 50,000 vols; Dir HORACIO R. PIÑEYRO.

Biblioteca del Museo Nacional de Bellas Artes 'Raquel Edelman' (Raquel Edelman Library of the National Museum of Fine Arts): Avda Libertador 1473, C1425AAA Buenos Aires; tel. (11) 4803-0802; fax (11) 4803-8817 ext. 223; e-mail bibliotecamnba@yahoo.com.ar; f. 1910; visual arts; 150,000 vols.

Biblioteca del Servicio Geológico Minero Argentino (Library of the Argentine Mining Geology Service): Avda Julio A. Roca 651 (9°), 1322 Buenos Aires; tel. (1) 349-3200; fax (1) 349-3198; e-mail mjanit@secind.mecon.gov.ar; internet www.segemar.gov.ar; f. 1904; 150,000 vols, 45,000 pamphlets, 15,000 maps; Dir Lic. MARA JANITENS; publs *Anales*, *Boletines*.

Biblioteca Nacional (National Library): Agüero 2502, C1425EID Buenos Aires; tel. (11) 4808-6000; e-mail bibliotecanacional@bn.gov.ar; internet www.bn.gov.ar; f. 1810; 2m. vols, 46,177 MSS; Dir Dr HORACIO GONZÁLEZ.

Biblioteca Nacional de Aeronáutica (National Aeronautics Library): CC 3389, 1000 Buenos Aires; Paraguay 748, 1057 Buenos Aires; tel. (11) 4312-9038; fax (11) 4514-4233; e-mail binae@ciudad.com.ar; internet www.binae.org.ar; f. 1927; aeronautics, astronautics, aeronautical law; 51,010 vols; Dir Brig. MIGUEL ANGEL AGUILAR; Chief Librarian Lic. ANGÉLICA A. LLORCA; publs *Aeroespacio* (6 a year), *Boletín Bibliográfico* (2 a year).

Biblioteca Nacional de Maestros (National Library for Teachers): Pizzurno 953, 1020 Buenos Aires; tel. (11) 4129-1272; fax (11) 4129-1299; e-mail bnminfo@me.gov.ar; internet www.bnm.me.gov.ar; f. 1870; 150,000 vols; general reference and education; Dir Lic. GRACIELA PERRONE.

Biblioteca Nacional Militar 'Agustín P. Justo' (Agustín P. Justo National Military Library): Avda Santa Fe 750, C1059ABO Buenos Aires; tel. (11) 4311-4560; e-mail biblioteca@circulomilitar.org; f. 1938; 150,000 vols; Dir JESÚS PELLEGRINI.

Biblioteca Tornquist (Tornquist Library): Reconquista 266, Hall San Martín—Planta Baja, C1003ABF Buenos Aires; tel. (11) 4348-

3500; e-mail biblio@bcra.gov.ar; internet www.bcra.gov.ar/index.asp; f. 1916; economics and social sciences; 35,842 vols, 1,155 periodicals; Dir JUAN JOSÉ GALLI.

Centro Argentino de Información Científica y Tecnológica (CAICYT) (Argentine Centre of Scientific and Technological Information): Saavedra 15 (1° piso), C1083ACA Buenos Aires; tel. (11) 4951-6975; fax (11) 4951-8334; e-mail postmaster@caicyt.edu.ar; internet www.caicyt-conicet.gov.ar; f. 1958; attached to Consejo Nacional de Investigaciones Científicas y Técnicas; Dir MARIO ALBORNOZ.

Centro de Documentación e Información Internacional (International Centre of Documentation and Information): Dirección Nacional General de Cooperación Internacional, Ministerio de Educación, Agüero 2502 (3°), 1425 Buenos Aires; f. 1959; publs by UN, Organization of American States, etc.; 5,000 vols; Dir FRANCISCO PIÑÓN.

Centro de Información de la Comisión Nacional de Energía Atómica (Information Centre of the National Atomic Energy Commission): Biblioteca Eduardo J. Savino, Edificio Tandar - Sector B, Avda General Paz 1499, 1650 San Martín, Buenos Aires; tel. (11) 6772-7946; e-mail referencia@cnea.gov.ar; internet www.cnea.gov.ar/cac/ci/default.htm; f. 1950; 36,700 vols, 450 current periodicals, 450,000 microcards and reports; Dir ALEJANDRA T. CHAVEZ FLORES; publs *Informes CNEA*, *Memoría CNEA*.

Centro de Información y Estadística Industrial (Centre for Industrial Information and Statistics): c/o INTI, Avda Leandro N. Alem 1067 (1°), 1101 Buenos Aires; attached to Instituto Nacional de Tecnología Industrial; Dir Ing. ALFREDO P. GALLIANO.

Dirección General de Bibliotecas Municipales (Public Libraries Administration): Calle Talcahuano 1261, 1014 Buenos Aires; tel. (11) 4811-9027; fax (11) 4811-0867; f. 1928; comprises 25 public municipal libraries in Buenos Aires with an aggregate of 350,000 vols; Dir-Gen. Prof. JOSEFINA DELGADO; publs *Cuadernos de Buenos Aires*, *Guía Cultural de Buenos Aires*.

Sistema de Bibliotecas y de Información, Universidad de Buenos Aires (Library and Information System of the University of Buenos Aires): Azcuénaga 280 (2°), 1029 Buenos Aires; tel. (11) 4951-1366; fax (11) 4952-6557; e-mail postmaster@sisbi.uba.ar; internet www.sisbi.uba.ar; f. 1941; 17 constituent faculty libraries; Gen. Coordinator ELSA ELENA ELIZALDE (acting).

Córdoba

Biblioteca Mayor de la Universidad Nacional de Córdoba (Main Library of Córdoba National University): Calle Obispo Trejo 242 (1° piso), Casilla de Correo 63, 5000 Córdoba; tel. (351) 433-1072; fax (351) 433-1079; e-mail circu@bmayor.unc.edu.ar; internet www.bmayor.unc.edu.ar; f. 1613; 150,000 vols, 3,890 periodicals and pre-1860 newspapers; partial depository for UN publs; Dir Lic. ROSA M. BESTANI.

Sistema de Bibliotecas de la Universidad Católica de Córdoba (Library of Córdoba Catholic University): Obispo Trejo 323, 5000 Córdoba; tel. (351) 493-8090; fax (351) 493-8091; e-mail bibdir@uccor.edu.ar; internet www.ucc.edu.ar/biblioteca; f. 1956; 85,000 vols, 3,600 periodicals; Dir Mag. SANDRA GISELA MARTÍN; publs *Diálogos Pedagógicos* (2 a year), *Studia Politicae* (2 a year).

La Plata

Biblioteca de la Universidad Nacional de La Plata (Library of La Plata National

University): Plaza Rocha 137, 1900 La Plata; tel. (221) 423-6607; fax (221) 425-5004; e-mail secretaria@biblio.unlp.edu.ar; internet www.biblio.unlp.edu.ar; f. 1884; 450,000 vols, 5,000 periodicals; spec. collns incl. South American newspapers relating to the Independence movement, South American history and geography and first travels in South America; 60 br. libraries within the univ.; Dir Bibl. NORMA MANGIATERRA; publ. *Informaciones*.

Biblioteca del Ministerio de Gobierno de la Provincia de Buenos Aires (Library of the Buenos Aires Province Ministry of the Interior): Casa de Gobierno, 1900 La Plata; law, politics and economics; 20,000 vols.

Biblioteca y Centro de Documentación del Ministerio de Economía de la Provincia de Buenos Aires (Library and Documentation Centre of the Ministry of the Economy of the Province of Buenos Aires): Calle 8 entre 45 y 46 (1° piso Of. 25), 1900 La Plata; tel. (221) 429-4400; 13,800 vols; Dir (vacant); publs *Cuadernos de Economía* (6 a year), *Noticias deEconomia* (6 a year).

Mendoza

Biblioteca Central de la Universidad Nacional de Cuyo (Central Library of the National University of Cuyo): Parque Gral San Martín, 5500 Mendoza; tel. (261) 413-5203; e-mail sid@uncu.edu.ar; f. 1939; 120,000 vols; Dir ISABEL BEATRIZ PIÑEIRO; publs *Boletín Bibliográfico* (irregular), *Cuadernos de la Biblioteca* (irregular).

Biblioteca Pública General San Martín (General San Martín Public Library): Remedios Escalada de San Martín 1843, 5500 Mendoza; tel. (261) 423-1674; f. 1822; 130,000 vols; special collections: local authors, children's books; Dir ANA MARIA GARCIA BUTTINI; publs *BAL* (Biblioteca de Autor Local, 1 a year), *BIL* (Biblioteca Infanto/Juvenil), *Versión II epocá* (1 a year).

Pergamino (Buenos Aires)

Biblioteca Pública Municipal 'Dr Joaquín Menéndez' (Dr Joaquín Menéndez Municipal Public Library): San Martín 838, 2700 Pergamino, Buenos Aires; tel. (2477) 417327; f. 1901; 58,000 vols; Librarian ALICIA D. PARODI.

Resistencia

Centro de Información Bioagropecuaria y Forestal (CIBAGRO) (Bio-Farming and Forestry Information Centre): Dirección de Bibliotecas, Universidad Nacional del Nordeste, Avda Las Heras 727, 3500 Resistencia, Chaco; tel. (3722) 44-3742; fax (3722) 44-3742; e-mail jencinas@bib.unne.edu.ar; f. 1976; 2,500 books, 2,800 pamphlets, 1,000 periodicals; spec. colln: FAO and other int. agricultural orgs; Dir JULIO E. ENCINAS; publs *Agronea*, *Bibliografía Forestal Nacional*, *Bibliografía sobre El Picudo del Algodonero*, *Bibliografía sobre El Quebracho*, *Ciencias Forestales—Bibliografía*.

Forest Information Network for Latin America and the Caribbean (RIFALC): CIBAGRO, Dirección de Bibliotecas, Universidad Nacional del Nordeste, Avda Las Heras 727, 3500 Resistencia, Chaco; tel. and fax (3722) 44-3742; e-mail jencinas@bib.unne.edu.ar; f. 1985; coordinates and integrates at regional level the efforts made by individual networks, and makes accessible in each country all the information available; mems: 19 orgs in 12 countries; Exec. Sec. JULIO E. ENCINAS; publ. *Boletín Informativo*.

Rosario

Biblioteca Argentina 'Dr Juan Alvarez' de la Municipalidad de Rosario (Dr Juan Alvarez Argentine Library of the Municipality of Rosario): Pje Alvarez 1550, 2000 Rosario; tel. (341) 480-2538; fax (341) 480-2561; e-mail biblarg@rosario.gov.ar; f. 1912; 180,000 vols; Dir MARÍA DEL CARMEN D'ANGELO.

Biblioteca Pública 'Estanislao S. Zeballos' (Estanislao S. Zeballos Public Library): Blvd Oroño 1261, 2000 Rosario; tel. (341) 480-2793 ext. 128; fax (341) 480-2797 ext. 110; f. 1915; economics, accountancy, business studies, statistics; 111,000 vols; Dir BEATRIZ LODEZANO; publs *Ciudad y Región* (3 a year), *Revista de la Facultad de Ciencias Económicas y Estadística* (irregular).

San Miguel (Buenos Aires)

Biblioteca de las Facultades de Filosofía y Teología S.I. (Library of the Faculties of Philosophy and Theology): Avda Mitre 3226, 1663 San Miguel, Buenos Aires; tel. (11) 4455-7992; fax (11) 4455-6442; e-mail gerardo@bibusv.edu.ar; f. 1931; central deposit library; 153,000 vols, 700 current periodicals; Librarian Prof. GERARDO LOSADA; publ. *Stromata* (4 a year).

Tucumán

Biblioteca Central de la Universidad Nacional de Tucumán (Central Library of the National University of Tucuman): Lamadrid 817, T4000BEQ San Miguel de Tucumán; tel. (381) 424-7752; fax (381) 424-8025; e-mail bibcen@unt.edu.ar; internet biblio.unt.edu.ar/b_central; f. 1917; 48,000 vols; Dir JUAN RICARDO ACOSTA; publ. *Boletín Bibliográfico*.

Museums and Art Galleries

Buenos Aires

Museo Argentino de Ciencias Naturales 'Bernardino Rivadavia'—Instituto Nacional de Investigación de las Ciencias Naturales (Bernardino Rivadavia Argentine Museum of Natural Sciences—National Research Institute of Natural Sciences): Avda Angel Gallardo 470, C1405DJR Buenos Aires; tel. (11) 4982-0306; fax (11) 4982-5243; e-mail secretaria@macn.gov.ar; internet www.macn.gov.ar; f. 1812; zoology, botany, palaeontology, geology and ecology; library of 500,000 vols; Dir Dr EDGARDO ROMERO; publ. *Revista* (2 or 3 a year).

Museo de Armas de la Nación (National Arms Museum): Maipú 1030, C1059ABO Buenos Aires; tel. (11) 4311-1070; e-mail man@armasdefuego.com.ar; internet www.coleccionables.com.ar/man; f. 1904; library of 1,000 vols; Dir JULIO E. SOLDAINI.

Museo de Arte Español 'Enrique Larreta' (Enrique Larreta Museum of Spanish Art): Juramento 2291 y Obligado 2139, 1428 Buenos Aires; tel. (11) 4784-4040; fax (11) 4783-2640; e-mail museolarreta@ibuenosaires.gob.ar; f. 1962; 13th- to 18th-century wood carvings, gilt objects and painted panels, paintings of Spanish School from 16th to 20th centuries, tapestries, furniture; library of 12,000 vols; Dir MERCEDES DI PAOLA DE PICOT.

Museo de Arte Hispanoamericano 'Isaac Fernández Blanco' (Isaac Fernández Blanco Museum of Spanish-American Art): Suipacha 1422, 1011 Buenos Aires; tel. (11) 4327-0272; e-mail mifb_prensa@buenosaires.gov.ar; internet www.museofernandezblanco.buenosaires.gov.ar; f. 1947; 16th- to 19th-century Spanish- and Portuguese-American art, silver, furniture; library of 5,000 vols; Dir Lic. JORGE COMETTI.

Museo de Arte Moderno de Buenos Aires (Museum of Modern Art): Ave San Juan 350, Buenos Aires; tel. (11) 4342-2970; fax (11) 4342-3001; e-mail mambamail@gmail.com; internet www.museodeartemoderno.buenosaires.gov.ar; f. 1956; modern and contemporary art exhibitions; video art screenings; experimental music concerts; Dir Prof. LAURA BUCCELLATO.

Museo de Bellas Artes de la Boca (Boca Fine Arts Museum): Pedro de Mendoza 1835, 1169 Buenos Aires; tel. (11) 4301-1080; internet www.buenosaires.gov.ar/areas/educacion/programas/quinquela; f. 1933; paintings, sculpture, engravings, and maritime museum; Dir Dr GUILLERMO C. DE LA CANAL.

Museo de la Dirección Nacional del Antártico (Museum of the National Antarctic Administration): Angel Gallardo 470, 1405 Buenos Aires; tel. (11) 4812-7327; natural and physical sciences of the Antarctic; Dir Dr RICARDO CAPDEVILA.

Museo de la Policía Federal Argentina (Argentine Federal Police Museum): San Martín 353 (pisos 7 y 8), 1004 Buenos Aires; tel. (11) 4394-6857; f. 1899; Dir JOSÉ A. GUTIÉRREZ.

Museo Etnográfico 'Juan B. Ambrosetti' (Juan B. Ambrosetti Ethnographical Museum): Moreno 350, 1091 Buenos Aires; tel. (11) 4345-8196; fax (11) 4345-8197; e-mail info.museo@filo.uba.ar; internet museoetnografico.filo.uba.ar; f. 1904; attached to the Faculty of Philosophy and Letters of the Univ. of Buenos Aires; ethnography and archaeology of Argentina, the Americas, Africa, Asia and Oceania; library of 80,000 vols; Dir Dr JOSÉ ANTONIO PÉREZ GOLLÁN; publ. *Runa* (1 a year).

Museo Histórico de la Ciudad de Buenos Aires 'Brigadier-General Cornelio de Saavedra' (Brig.-Gen. Cornelio de Saavedra Historical Museum of the City of Buenos Aires): Calle Crisólogo Larralde 6309, 1431 Buenos Aires; tel. (11) 4572-0746; fax (11) 4574-1328; e-mail museosaavedra_direccion@buenosaires.gov.ar; internet www.museos.buenosaires.gov.ar; f. 1921; library of 5,000 vols; Dir Lic. ALBERTO GABRIEL PIÑEIRO.

Museo Histórico Nacional (National History Museum): Defensa 1600, C1143AAD Ciudad Autónoma de Buenos Aires; tel. (11) 4307-1182; fax (11) 4307-3157; e-mail direccion@mhn.gov.ar; internet www.cultura.gov.ar/direcciones/?info=organismo&i-d=14&idd=5; f. 1889 as City Historical Museum, present status in 1891; library of 15,000 vols, 46,000 artefacts; Dir Dr JOSÉ ANTONIO PÉREZ GOLLÁN; publ. *El Museo Histórico Nacional* (1 a year).

Museo Histórico Sarmiento (Sarmiento History Museum): Juramento 2180, 1428 Buenos Aires; tel. (11) 4782-2989; fax (11) 4782-2354; e-mail info@museosarmiento.gov.ar; internet www.museosarmiento.gov.ar; f. 1938; library of 13,000 vols; Dir Mus. MARTA GERMANI.

Museo Mitre (Mitre Museum): San Martín 336, 1004 Buenos Aires; tel. (11) 4394-7659; fax (11) 4394-8240; internet www.museomitre.gov.ar; f. 1907; preserves the household of Gen. Bartolomé Mitre; antique maps, coins and medals; library of 66,621 vols on American history, geography and ethnology, archive of 80,000 historical documents; Dir Lic. MARÍA GOWLAND.

Museo Nacional de Aeronáutica (National Museum of Aeronautics): Avda Eva Perón 2200, Morón, Buenos Aires; tel. (11) 4697-9769; e-mail mna@uolsinectis.com.ar; internet www.fuerzaaerea.mil.ar/

historia/museo_aeronautico.html; f. 1960; Dir Cmdr (retd) SANTOS A. DOMINGUEZ KOCH.

Museo Nacional de Arte Decorativo (National Museum of Decorative Art): Avda del Libertador 1902, 1425 Buenos Aires; tel. (11) 4801-8248; fax (11) 4802-6606; e-mail museo@mnad.org; internet www.mnad.org; f. 1937; furniture, sculpture, tapestries, European and South American works; library of 2,000 vols; Dir ALBERTO GUILLERMO BELLUCCI.

Museo Nacional de Arte Oriental (National Museum of Oriental Art): Avda del Libertador 1902 (1°), 1425 Buenos Aires; tel. and fax (11) 4801-5988; f. 1966; Asian and African art; library of 1,500 vols, 2,500 periodicals; Dir Lic. MARÍA DEL VALLE GUERRA.

Museo Nacional de Bellas Artes (National Museum of Fine Arts): Avda del Libertador 1473, 1425 Buenos Aires; tel. (11) 4803-0714; fax (11) 4803-4062; f. 1895; Argentine, American and European painting since 19th century, classical painting and sculpture, pre-Columbian art; library of 50,000 vols, 200,000 booklets; Dir Arq. ALBERTO G. BELLUCCI.

Museo Naval de la Nación (National Museum of Naval History): Paseo Victorica 602, Tigre, 1648 Buenos Aires; tel. (11) 4749-0608; e-mail museonaval@hotmail.com; f. 1892; preserves, researches, exhibits and communicates cultural heritage; photo archive; shows history, culture and tradition of naval maritime nation, its evolution, technology and tasks in maritime field; library of 3,000 vols; Dir Capt. ALBERTO JULIO MONGES.

Museo Numismático 'Dr José Evaristo Uriburu' ('Dr José Evaristo Uriburu' Numismatics Museum): Banco Central de la República Argentina, Calle San Martín 216, 1° piso, 1004 Buenos Aires; tel. (11) 4348-3882; fax (11) 4348-3699; e-mail museo@bcra.gob.ar; internet www.bcra.gov.ar; f. 1935; attached to Central Bank of Argentina; Dir DANIEL ANTONIO REY.

Museo Social Argentino (Argentine Museum of Sociology): Avda Corrientes 1723, 1042 Buenos Aires; tel. (11) 4375-4601; fax (11) 4375-4600; f. 1911; library of 80,000 vols; Pres. Dr GUILLERMO GARBARINI ISLAS; publs *Foro Economico* (2 a year), *Foro Político* (3 a year).

Córdoba

Museo Botánico (Botanical Museum): Universidad Nacional de Córdoba, CC 495, 5000 Córdoba; tel. (351) 4332104; fax (351) 4332104; e-mail museo@imbiv.unc.edu.ar; f. 1870; conducts research as a unit of Instituto Multidisciplinario de Biología Vegetal (run by CONICET and Universidad Nacional de Córdoba; library of 8,000 vols; Dir Dr ANA M. ANTON; publs *Kurtziana* (1 a year), *Lorentzia* (irregular).

Museo Provincial de Bellas Artes 'Emilio A. Caraffa' (Emilio A. Caraffa Provincial Museum of Fine Arts): Avda Hipólito Yrigoyen 651, 5000 Córdoba; tel. (351) 433-3412; fax (351) 433-3414; f. 1916; Argentine and foreign paintings, sculptures, drawings and engravings; library and archive; Dir Lic. GRACIELA ELIZABETH PALELLA.

Museo Provincial de Ciencias Naturales 'Bartolomé Mitre' (Bartolomé Mitre Provincial Museum of Natural Sciences): Avda Hipólito Yrigoyen 115, 5000 Córdoba; tel. (351) 422-1428; f. 1919; geology, zoology, botany; library of 3,400 vols and periodicals; Dir MARTA CANO DE MARTIN.

Corrientes

Museo Histórico de Corrientes (Corrientes Historical Museum): Calle 9 de Julio 1044, 3400 Corrientes; tel. (4) 75946; e-mail museohistoricoetes@hotmail.com; internet www.culturo.corrientes.gov.ar; f. 1929; history of Corrientes Province; library of 2,000 vols; Dir MIGUEL FERNANDO GONZÁLEZ AZCOAGA; publ. *Boletín de Extensión Cultural* (4 a year).

La Plata

Museo de La Plata (La Plata Museum): Paseo del Bosque s/n, B1900FWA La Plata; tel. (221) 425-7744; e-mail museo@fcnym.unlp.edu.ar; internet www.fcnym.unlp.edu.ar/abamuse.html; f. 1884; anthropology, archaeology, geology, natural history (incl. palaeontological colln of Patagonian mammalia); library of 60,000 vols, 5,000 periodicals; Dir Dra SILVIA AMETRANO; publs *Anales*, *Notas*, *Novedades*, *Obra del Centenario*, *Obra del Cincuentenario*, *Revista*, *Serie Técnica y Didáctica*.

Luján

Complejo Museografico 'Enrique Udaondo' (Enrique Udaondo Museographic Complex): Lezica y Torrezuri 917, 6700 Luján; tel. (2323) 42-0245; internet www.lujan.gov.ar/cultura/centros/museos; f. 1923; comprises 4 museums: Museo Colonial e Histórico (history, archaeology, silver, paintings, furniture), Museo de Transportes (transport), Museo del Automóvil and Pabellón 'Belgrano' y Depósitos (vintage cars); Dir CARLOS A. SCANNAPIECO.

Mendoza

Museo de Ciencias Naturales y Antropológicas 'Juan Cornelio Moyano' (Juan Cornelio Moyano Museum of Anthropology and Natural Sciences): Extremo Sur del Lago, Parque General San Martín, 5500 Mendoza; tel. and fax (261) 428-7666; f. 1911; library of 18,900 vols on American and Argentine history; Asst Dir Prof. CLARA ABAL DE RUSSO; publ. *Boletín* (2 a year).

Paraná

Museo de Ciencias Naturales y Antropológicas 'Prof. Antonio Serrano' ('Prof. Antonio Serrano' Museum of Anthropology and Natural Sciences): Carlos Gardel 62, E3100FWB Paraná; tel. (343) 420-8894; e-mail biblioserrano@yahoo.com.ar; internet www.museoserrano.com.ar; f. 1917; scientific investigations; papers; editions; exhibitions; library of 35,000 vols; Dir Prof. GISELA BAHLER; publs *Catalogos*, *Memorias*.

Museo Histórico de Entre Rios 'Martiniano Leguizamón' ('Martiniano Leguizamón' Historical Entre Rios Museum): Laprida y Buenos Aires, 3100 Paraná; tel. (343) 420-7869; internet www.parananews.com.ar/museos/museo-historico-martiniano--leguizamon.html; f. 1948; library of 27,000 vols; archive; Dir MARIA ANGEL MATHIEU MAYA.

Rosario

Museo Histórico Provincial de Rosario 'Dr Julio Marc' (Rosario Dr Julio Marc Provincial History Museum): Parque Independencia, 2000 Rosario; tel. (341) 472-1457; fax (341) 472-1457; e-mail museomarc@citynet.net.ar; internet www.santafe.gov.ar/cultura/museos/historo.htm; f. 1939; library of 33,000 vols; Dir Prof. IRMA B. MONTALVAN.

Museo Municipal de Arte Decorativo 'Firma y Odilo Estevez' (Firma y Odilo Estevez Municipal Decorative Arts Museum): Santa Fe 748, 2000 Rosario; tel. (341) 480-2547; fax (341) 480-2547; e-mail museo@museoestevez.gov.ar; internet www.museoestevez.gov.ar; f. 1968; Curator P. A. SINOPOLI.

Museo Municipal de Bellas Artes 'Juan B. Castagnino' (Juan B. Castagnino Municipal Fine Arts Museum): Avda Pellegrini 2202, 2000 Rosario; tel. (341) 480-2542; fax (341) 480-2543; e-mail comunicacion@castagninomacro.org; internet www.museocastagnino.org.ar; f. 1937; library of 2,500 vols; Dir Prof. BERNARDO MIGUEL BALLESTEROS.

San Carlos de Bariloche

Museo de la Patagonia 'Dr Francisco P. Moreno' (Dr Francisco P. Moreno Museum of Patagonia): Centro Cívico, 8400 San Carlos de Bariloche, Río Negro; tel. (944) 22309; fax (944) 22309; e-mail museodelapatagonia@apn.gov.ar; internet www.bariloche.com.ar/museo; f. 1940; political history of Patagonia, ethnology, natural sciences, archaeology; library of 2,500 vols; Dir Lic. CECILIA GIRGENTI; publs *Antropología*, *Diversidad Cultural de la Argentina*.

Santa Fé

Museo de Bellas Artes 'Rosa Galisteo de Rodriguez' (Rosa Galisteo de Rodriguez Museum of Fine Arts): 4 de Enero 1510, 3000 Santa Fe; tel. (42) 596142; fax (42) 596142; internet www.digitalmicrofilm.com.ar/rosagalisteo; f. 1922; contemporary Argentine and modern art; library of 4,200 vols; Dir Arq. MARCELO OLMOS.

Museo Histórico Provincial de Santa Fe (Santa Fe Provincial Museum of History): San Martín 1490, S3000FRH Santa Fe; tel. (342) 457-3529; e-mail info@museohistorico-sfe.gov.ar; internet museohistorico-sfe.gov.ar; f. 1943; Dir Prof. ALICIA TALSKY DE RONCHI.

Museo Provincial de Ciencias Naturales 'Florentino Ameghino' (Florentino Ameghino Provincial Museum of Natural History): 1° Junta 2859, 3000 Santa Fe; tel. (342) 457-3770; fax (342) 457-3730; e-mail ameghino@santafe-conicet.gov.ar; internet www.unl.edu.ar/santafe/museocn.htm; f. 1914; zoology, botany, geology, palaeobiology; library: public library of 50,000 vols; Dir Lic. CARLOS A. VIRASORO.

Santiago del Estero

Museo Provincial de Arqueología 'Wagner' (Wagner Provincial Archaeological Museum): Calle Avellaneda 355, 4200 Santiago del Estero; tel. (385) 4211380; fax (385) 4211380; e-mail museowagnersgo@gmail.com; f. 1917; archaeology of Chaco-Santiagueno and later cultures; Dir ANDRÉS A. CHAZARRETA RUIZ.

Tandil

Museo Municipal de Bellas Artes de Tandil (Tandil Municipal Museum of Fine Arts): Chacabuco 357, 7000 Tandil; tel. (2293) 43-2067; fax (2293) 43-0667; f. 1920; paintings of Classical, Impressionist, Cubist and Modern schools, 20th-century Argentinian art, small statues, furniture, engravings; small library; Dir CRISTIAN SEGURA.

Ushuaia

Museo del Fin del Mundo (The End of the World Museum): Maipú 173, 9410 Ushuaia, Tierra del Fuego; tel. (2901) 42-1863; e-mail museo@tierradelfuego.ml.org; internet www.principiodelmundo.com.ar/museo; f. 1979; history and natural sciences; library of 5,000 vols; Dir OSCAR PABLO ZANOLA; publs *Arqueología de la Isla Grande de Tierra del Fuego*, *Museo Territorial*, *Raíces del Fin del Mundo* (3 a year).

Universities

There are three main categories of Universities in Argentina: National (or Federal), which are supported by the Federal Budget; Provincial (or State), supported by the Provincial Budgets; and Private Universities, created and supported entirely by private initiative, but authorized to function by the Ministry of Education.

National Universities

UNIVERSIDAD DE BUENOS AIRES

Calle Viamonte 430/444, C1053ABJ Buenos Aires

Telephone: (11) 4510-1100
Internet: www.uba.ar

Founded 1821
Academic year: March to November

Rector: Dr RUBEN HALLU
Vice-Rector: Dra BEATRIZ GUGLIELMOTTI
Library Dir: Dra SUSANA SOTO

Number of teachers: 21,688
Number of students: 336,947

Library: see under Libraries

Publications: *Encrucijadas* (4 a year), *Oikos* (4 a year)

DEANS

Faculty of Agriculture (Avda San Martín 4453): Ing. Agr. FERNANDO VILELLA
Faculty of Architecture, Design and Town Planning (Ciudad Universitaria, Pabellón 3, Núñez): Arq. BERARDO DUJOVNE
Faculty of Dentistry (M. T. de Alvear 2142): Dr MÁXIMO GIGLIO
Faculty of Economic Sciences (Avda Córdoba 2122): Dr JUAN CARLOS CHERVATIN
Faculty of Engineering (Paseo Colón 850): Ing. CARLOS ALBERTO RAFFO
Faculty of Exact and Natural Sciences (Ciudad Universitaria, Pabellón 2, Núñez): Dr PABLO MIGUEL JACOVKIS
Faculty of Law and Social Sciences (Avda Pte Figueroa Alcorta 2263): Dr ANDRÉS JOSÉ D'ALESSIO
Faculty of Medicine (Paraguay 2155): Dr SALOMÓN SCHÄCHTER
Faculty of Pharmacy and Biochemistry (Junín 954): Dra REGINA WIGDOROVITZ DE WIKINSKI
Faculty of Philosophy and Letters (Puan 470): Dr FRANCISCO RAÚL CARNESE
Faculty of Psychology (Hipólito Irigoyen 3238/46): Lic. RAÚL COUREL
Faculty of Social Sciences (Marcelo T. de Alvear 2230): Dr FORTUNATO MACIMACCI
Faculty of Veterinary Sciences (Chorroarín 280): Med. Vet. ANÍBAL FRANCO

SELECTED AFFILIATED INSTITUTES

Colegio Nacional de Buenos Aires: Bolívar 263, 1066 Buenos Aires; tel. 331-6777; Rector Dr HORACIO SANGUINETTI.

Escuela Superior de Comercio 'Carlos Pellegrini': Marcelo T. de Alvear 1851, 1122 Buenos Aires; tel. (11) 4811-7547; f. 1890; incorporated in the Univ. of Buenos Aires 1912; 6-year course in commercial education; Rector Dr ABRAHAM LEONARDO GAK.

Hospital de Clínicas 'José de San Martín': Avda Córdoba 2351, Buenos Aires; tel. (11) 4508-3888; Dir Dr JORGE ITALA.

Instituto de Investigaciones Médicas 'Alfredo Lanari': see under Research Institutes.

Instituto Modelo de Clínica Médica 'Luis Agote': Avda Córdoba 2351, 11° piso, Buenos Aires; tel. (1) 961-6001; Exec. Dir Dr FLORENTINO SANGUINETTI.

Instituto de Oncología 'Angel H. Roffo': Avda San Martín 5481, 1417 Buenos Aires; tel. (11) 4580-2800; f. 1966; library of 3,000 vols, 180 periodicals; Dir Dr ALEJO A. L. CARUGATTI.

Instituto de Perfeccionamiento Médico-Quirúrgico 'Prof. Dr José María Jorge': Avda Córdoba 2351, 7° piso, Buenos Aires; tel. (11) 4961-6001; Exec. Dir Dr FLORENTINO SANGUINETTI.

UNIVERSIDAD NACIONAL DE CATAMARCA

Esquiú 612, 4700 Catamarca
Telephone: (3833) 45-6410
E-mail: privadaunca@arnet.com.ar
Internet: www.unca.edu.ar

Founded 1972
Academic year: February to December

Rector: Ing. FLAVIO SERGIO FAMA
Vice-Rector: Lic. ELINA SIVERA DE BUENADE
Sec.-Gen.: Ing. MARCELO FABIÁN VERA
Librarian: MARÍA EMILIA MARTÍNEZ

Number of teachers: 304
Number of students: 14,067

Publication: *Aportes*

DEANS

Faculty of Agricultural Sciences: Ing. Agr. EDMUNDO JOSÉ A. AGUERO
Faculty of Economics and Administration: CPN DANIEL EDUARDO TOLOZA
Faculty of Exact and Natural Sciences: Ing. Qco. BLANCA STELLA SOSA
Faculty of Health Sciences: Dr JORGE DANIEL BRIZUELA DEL MORAL
Faculty of Humanities: Lic. ROLANDO EDGARDO CORONEL
Faculty of Technology and Applied Sciences: Agrim. FÉLIX RAMÓN DOERING
School of Archaeology: Lic. MÓNICA CATOGGIO DE ACOSTA (Dir)
School of Law: Dra IRMA DEL TRÁNSITO ROMERO NIEVA (Dir)
Fray Mamerto Esquiu Higher School: Prof. HORTENCIA DURANTI DE ALVAREZ (Dir)

UNIVERSIDAD NACIONAL DEL CENTRO DE LA PROVINCIA DE BUENOS AIRES

General Pinto 399, B7000GHG Tandil
Telephone: (2293) 42-2000
Fax: (2293) 42-1608
E-mail: rector@rec.unicen.edu.ar
Internet: www.unicen.edu.ar

Founded 1974
State control
Academic year: February to December

Rector: Cr ROBERTO TASSARA
Vice-Rector: Ing. OMAR LOSARDO
Gen. Sec.: Ing. GILLERMO AMILCAR CORRES
Academic Sec.: Profa MABEL PACHECO
Admin. Sec.: Cr JOSÉ LUIS BIANCHINI
Library Dir: Profa ZULEMA GRANDINETTI DE CAGLIOLO

Number of teachers: 1,585
Number of students: 10,427

Publications: *Alternativas*, *Anuario IEHS*

DEANS

Faculty of Agricultural Sciences: Med. Vet. ARNALDO PISSANI
Faculty of Economics: Cr ROBERTO TASSARA
Faculty of Engineering: Ing. EDUARDO F. IRASSAR
Faculty of Humanities: Lic. ALEJANDRO DILLON
Faculty of Sciences: Dr GERY BIOUL

Faculty of Social Sciences: Lic. CRISTINA BACCIN
Faculty of Theatre: Dr CARLOS CATALANO
Faculty of Veterinary Science: Dr PEDRO STEFFAN

UNIVERSIDAD NACIONAL DEL COMAHUE

Buenos Aires 1400, Q8300BCX Neuquén
Telephone: (299) 449-0300
Fax: (299) 449-0351
E-mail: sprector@uncoma.edu.ar
Internet: www.uncoma.edu.ar

Founded 1972
State control
Academic year: March to March

Rector: Dra ANA MARIA PECHEN DE D'ANGELO
Vice-Rector: Dr TERESA VEGA
Sec.-Gen.: OMAR ANTONIO CALVI
Academic Sec.: Prof. LUIS BERTANI
Admin. Sec.: Lic. OSCAR LUSETTI
Librarian: EUGENIA LUQUE

Number of teachers: 1,700
Number of students: 30,000

DEANS

Faculty of Agricultural Sciences: Ing. Ftal. JORGE LUIS GIRARDIN
Faculty of Economics and Administration: Lic. SUSANA GRACIELA LANDRISCINI
Faculty of Education: Lic. GUILLERMO VILLANUEVA
Faculty of Engineering: Ing. DANIEL BOCCANERA
Faculty of Humanities: Lic. PEDRO BARREIRO
Higher School of Languages: Prof. MARÍA ELENA AGUILAR
Faculty of Law and Social Sciences: Dr JUAN MANUEL SALGADO
Faculty of Tourism: Dra ADRIANA OTERO
Bariloche Regional University Centre: Lic. FEDERICO HORACIO PLANAS
Zona Atlantica Regional University Centre: Ing. Agr. MIGUEL ANGEL SILVA

UNIVERSIDAD NACIONAL DE CÓRDOBA

Calle Raúl Haya de la Torre s/n (2° pisopiso), Pabellón Argentina, Ciudad Universitaria, 5000 Córdoba
Telephone: (351) 433-4081
Fax: (351) 433-4081
Internet: www.uncor.edu

Founded 1613, charter received from Philip III of Spain 1622, fully est. by Pope Urban VIII 1634, nationalized 1856
Academic year: February to December

Rector: Ing. JORGE GONZÁLEZ
Vice-Rector: Ing. DANIEL DI GIUSTO
Sec.-Gen.: Ing. GABRIEL TAVELLA
Librarian: Lic. ROSA M. BESTANI

Library: see Libraries and Archives
Number of teachers: 7,753
Number of students: 114,918

Publication: *Revista*

DEANS

Faculty of Agrarian Sciences: Ing. Agr. HECTOR FONTÁN
Faculty of Architecture and Town Planning: Arq. MIGUEL ANGEL ROCA
Faculty of Chemical Sciences: Dr GERARDO FIDELIO
Faculty of Dentistry: Dr NAZARIO KUYUMLIAM
Faculty of Economics: Dr HEBE G. DE ROITTER
Faculty of Exact, Physical and Natural Sciences: Ing. ERNESTO ALVAREZ
Faculty of Languages: Dra CRISTINA ELQUE DE MARTINI
Faculty of Law and Social Sciences: Dra RAMÓN PEDRO YANZI FERREYRA

Faculty of Mathematics, Astronomy and Physics: Dr CRISTIAN URBANO SÁNCHEZ
Faculty of Medicine: Dr PEDRO LEÓN SARACHO CORNET
Faculty of Philosophy and Humanities: Dra SILVIA CAROLINA SCOTTO
Faculty of Psychology: Lic. ANA ALDERETE

UNIVERSIDAD NACIONAL DE CUYO

Centro Universitario, M5502JMA Mendoza
Telephone: (261) 413-5000
Fax: (261) 449-4022
Internet: www.uncu.edu.ar
Founded 1939
State control
Academic year: April to October
Rector: Ing. ARTURO ROBERTO SOMOZA
Vice-Rector: Dr GUSTAVO ANDRÉS KENT
Academic Sec.: ESTELA MARÍA ZALBA DE AGUIRRE
Librarian: Lic. JUAN GUILLERMO MILIA
Library: see Libraries and Archives
Number of teachers: 4,794
Number of students: 31,527
Publication: *Boletín Oficial*

DEANS

Faculty of Agricultural Sciences: Ing. JORGE TACCHINI
Faculty of Applied Science: Ing. ERNESTO MUÑOZ
Faculty of Arts: Prof. ELIO ORTIZ
Faculty of Dentistry: Dr ONOFRE CIPOLLA
Faculty of Economics: RODOLFO SÍCOLI
Faculty of Engineering: Ing. JUAN MANUEL GOMEZ
Faculty of Law: Dr LUIS ABBIATI
Faculty of Medical Sciences: Dr ISAAC RIVERO
Faculty of Philosophy and Letters: Prof. MIGUEL VERSTRAETE
Faculty of Political and Social Sciences: Lic. CARLOS FINOCHIO
Teacher Training College: MARÍA VICTORIA GOMEZ DE ERICE
Zona Sur: Dis. Ind. ADRIANA RUIZ

ATTACHED INSTITUTE

Centro Regional de Investigaciones Científicas y Tecnológicas (CRICYT): Calle Bajada del Cerro s/n, Parque General San Martín, Casilla de Correo 131, 5500 Mendoza; tel. (261) 428-8314; fax (261) 428-7370; Dir Dr RICARDO PAULINO DEI.

UNIVERSIDAD NACIONAL DE ENTRE RÍOS

Eva Perón 24, 3260 Concepción del Uruguay, Entre Ríos
Telephone: (3442) 42-1500
Fax: (3442) 42-1563
E-mail: webmaster@rect.uner.edu.ar
Internet: www.uner.edu.ar
Founded 1973
State control
Academic year: April to March
Rector: EDUARDO FRANCISCO JOSÉ ASUETA
Vice-Rector: Lic. ELOÍSA DE JONG
Gen. Sec.: HIPOLITO B. FINK
Academic Sec.: Lic. SUSANA ESTHER CELMAN
Library Dir: Prof. JORGE TITO MARTÍNEZ
Number of teachers: 1,219
Number of students: 13,204
Publications: *Ciencia, Docencia y Tecnología* (3 a year), *Guía de Carreras*

DEANS

Faculty of Administrative Science: EDUARDO ASUETA
Faculty of Agrarian Sciences: Ing. FRANCISCO RAMÓN ETCHEVERS

Faculty of Bromatology: Lic. SUSANA NOVELLO DE METTLER
Faculty of Economics: JULIO CÉSAR YODICE
Faculty of Education: Prof. MARTHA BENEDETTO DE ALBORNOZ
Faculty of Engineering: Ing. AGUSTÍN CARPIO
Faculty of Health Sciences: Dr JULIO SIMOVICH
Faculty of Nutritional Sciences: Ing. JORGE AMADO GERARD
Faculty of Social Services: A. S. ALICIA MERCEDES GONZÁLEZ ALARCÓN

UNIVERSIDAD NACIONAL DE FORMOSA

Don Bosco 1082, 3600 Formosa
Telephone: (3717) 423-926
Fax: (3717) 423-928
E-mail: adminweb@unf.edu.ar
Internet: www.unf.edu.ar
Founded 1988
State control
Rector: Ing. MARTÍN RENÉ ROMANO
Vice-Rector: Dr ROQUE SILGUERO
Sec.-Gen. (Academic): Lic. OFELIA INÉS FANTÍN
Sec.-Gen. (Science and Technology): Dr CARLOS MONZÓN
Sec. (Management and Devt): LIVIO DANILO PEREIRA (acting)
Sec. (Student Affairs and Univ. Extension): Lic. ARIEL SPEIT
Number of students: 11,937
Library of 12,000 vols

DEANS

Faculty of Economics and Business Administration: Lic. HECTOR CARMELO QUIJANO
Faculty of Health: Dr JOSÉ TRINIDAD ESCOBAR
Faculty of Humanities: Prof. MARÍA DE LA CRUZ COLOMBERA DE CASTAÑEDA
Faculty of Natural Resources: (vacant)

UNIVERSIDAD NACIONAL DE GENERAL SAN MARTÍN

Avda 25 de Mayo y Francia, CP 1650, San Martín, Buenos Aires
Telephone: (11) 4006-1500
Fax: (11) 4006-1511
E-mail: rectorado@unsam.edu.ar
Internet: www.unsam.edu.ar
Founded 1992
State control
Rector: CARLOS RAFAEL RUTA
Vice-Rector: CARLOS GERÓNIMO GIANELLA
Sec.-Gen.: GUILLERMO SCHWEINHEIM
Academic Sec.: JORGE FERNÁNDEZ NIELLO
Admin. Sec.: FRANCISCO HÉCTOR FERNÁNDEZ (acting)
Science and Technology Sec.: ESTEBAN CASSIN
Student Affairs and Univ. Extension Sec.: CARLOS ALMEIDA
Number of students: 7,942
Library of 4,700 vols, 350 periodicals
Publications: *Educación en Ciencias, Educación en Ciencias Sociales, Política y Gestión, Revista de la Escuela de Economía y Negocios*

DEANS

Dan Beninson Institute of Technology: CARLA NOTARI
Institute of Biotechnical Research: ALBERTO FRASCH
Institute of Higher Social Studies: ALEJANDRO GRIMSON
Institute of Industrial Quality: JOAQUÍN VALDÉS
Institute of Rehabilitation Sciences and Movement: HUGO RODRÍGUEZ ISARN
Institute for Research and Environment Engineering: ALBERTO POCHETTINO

Prof. Jorge A. Sabato Institute of Technology: ANA MARÍA MONTI
School of Economics and Business: HORACIO VAL
School of Government and Politics: MARCELO CAVAROZZI
School of Humanities: NORBERTO FERRÉ
School of Postgraduate Studies: ALBERTO POCHETTINO
School of Science and Technology: DANIEL DI GREGORIO

UNIVERSIDAD NACIONAL DE GENERAL SARMIENTO

Campus Universitario, José M. Gutiérrez entre José L. Suárez y Verdi, 1613 Los Polvorines, Buenos Aires
Telephone: (11) 4469-7500
Fax: (11) 4451-4575
E-mail: info@ungs.edu.ar
Internet: www.ungs.edu.ar
Founded 1993
State control
Academic year: October to April
Rector: Lic. SILVIO ISRAEL FELDMAN
Vice-Rector: Ing. MARCELO OSCAR FERNÁNDEZ
Sec.-Gen.: Lic. ALEJANDRO LUIS LOPEZ ACCOTTO
Sec. (Academic): Prof. ELSA BEATRIZ PEREYRA
Sec. (Administration): DANIELA LETICIA GUARDADO
Sec. (Legal and Technical): Lic. HAYDÉE NÉLIDA UGRIN
Sec. (Research): Lic. CARLOS EDUARDO REBORATTI
Library of 18,000 vols, 121 periodicals
Number of students: 5,547

DIRECTORS

Institute of Human Development: Dr EDUARDO RINESI
Institute of Industry: Ing. NÉSTOR BRUNO BRAIDOT
Institute of Science: Lic. ROSA ELENA BELVEDRESI
Institute of Urban Studies: Lic. MAGDALENA GRACIELA CHIARA

UNIVERSIDAD NACIONAL DE JUJUY

Avda Bolivia 1239, 4600 San Salvador de Jujuy
Telephone: (388) 422-1515
Fax: (388) 422-1507
E-mail: info@unju.edu.ar
Internet: www.unju.edu.ar
Founded 1972
State control
Academic year: March to December
Rector: Dr Ing. ENRIQUE MATEO ARNAU
Vice-Rector: Ing. CARLOS GREGORIO TORRES
Secretary for Academic Affairs: Lic. ANGELICA MERCEDES GARAY DE FUMAGALLI
Secretary for Administrative Affairs: PATRICIA CUELLAR DE COMAS
Secretary for Science and Technology: Dr LILIANA LUPO
Secretary for Student Welfare: MARIO VEGA
Secretary for University Extension: Ing. EDUARDO BERRAFATO
Librarian: MARÍA E. C. DE MARTÍNEZ
Library of 18,000 vols
Number of teachers: 700
Number of students: 12,417

DEANS

Faculty of Agriculture: Dra SUSANA MURUAGA DE L'AGENTIER
Faculty of Economics: CPN LUIS SALVADOR FORTUNI
Faculty of Engineering: Ing. ENRIQUE MATEO ARNAU

Faculty of Humanities and Social Sciences: Lic. MARIO RABEY

School of Mining: Ing. Qco ALBERTO CONSTANTINO ALBESA

ATTACHED RESEARCH INSTITUTES

Institute of Geology and Mining: Avda Bolivia 2355, 4600 San Salvador de Jujuy; tel. (388) 422-1593; fax (388) 422-1594; Dir Dra BEATRIZ COIRA.

Institute of Marine Biology: Avda Bolivia No. 2345/55, 4600 San Salvador de Jujuy; tel. (388) 422-1596; fax (388) 422-1597; Dir Lic. MARTHA G. ARCE DE HAMITY.

UNIVERSIDAD NACIONAL DE LA MATANZA

Florencio Varela 1903, B1754JEC San Justo, Buenos Aires

Telephone: (11) 4480-8900

Fax: (11) 4480-8919

E-mail: webmaster@unlam.edu.ar

Internet: www.unlam.edu.ar

Founded 1990

State control

Academic year: March to December (2 semesters)

Rector: Prof. Lic. DANIEL EDUARDO MARTÍNEZ

Vice-Rector: Dr RENÉ NICOLETTI

Sec.-Gen.: Dr JOSÉ PAQUÉZ

Sec. (Academic): Dr GUSTAVO DUEK

Sec. (Admin.): Cdor. ADRIAN SANCCI

Sec. (Information Technology and Communications): Lic. MARCELO PÉREZ GUNTIN

Sec. (Legal and Technical): Dr CRISTIAN JAVIER CABRAL

Sec. (Management and Planning): Dr JORGE NARVAÉZ

Sec. (Postgraduate Affairs): Dr MARIO ENRIQUE BURKÚN

Sec. (Univ. Public Relations): Lic. ROBERTO LUIS AYUB

Number of students: 19,368

DEANS

Economics: Dr ALBERTO LONGO

Engineering and Technological Research: Ing. ALFREDO VÁZQUEZ

Humanities and Social Sciences: Dr FERNANDO LUJÁN ACOSTA

Law and Political Science: Dr ALEJANDRO FINOCCHIARO

UNIVERSIDAD NACIONAL DE LA PAMPA

Cnel. Gil 353, 6300 Santa Rosa, La Pampa

Telephone: (2954) 451-600

E-mail: info@unlpam.edu.ar

Internet: www.unlpam.edu.ar

Founded 1958

Academic year: April to November

Rector: Lic. SERGIO D. MALUENDRES

General Secretary: JUAN JOSÉ COSTA

Academic Secretary: Lic. LUIS MARÍA MORETE

Librarian: Lic. ATILIO DENOUARD

Number of teachers: 632

Number of students: 9,804

DEANS

Faculty of Agronomy: Ing. Agr. GUILLERMO COVAS

Faculty of Economics: CPN ROBERTO OSCAR VASSIA

Faculty of Exact and Natural Sciences: Profa NORA D. ANDRADA DE GUESALAGA

Faculty of Human Sciences: Prof. JOSÉ RUFINO VILLARREAL

Faculty of Veterinary Science: Dr RAÚL ANTONIO ALVAREZ

UNIVERSIDAD NACIONAL DE LA PATAGONIA AUSTRAL

Lisandro de la Torre 860, 9400 Río Gallegos, Santa Cruz

Telephone: (2966) 442-376

Fax: (2966) 442-376

E-mail: rectorad@unpa.edu.ar

Internet: www.unpa.edu.ar

Founded 1994

State control

Rector: Ing. MARÍA EUGENIA MÁRQUEZ

Vice-Rector: Ing. HUGO SANTOS ROJAS

Sec.-Gen. (Academic): Lic. MARÍA JOSÉ LENO

Sec. (Admin. and Finance): Lic. MARCELO MILJAK

Sec. (Planning): Lic. MARIA VICTORIA HERNANDEZ

Sec. (Science and Technology): Dra SANDRA CASAS

Sec. (Univ. Public Relations): Profa VIRGINIA BARBIERI

Number of students: 6,940

CAMPUS DEANS

Caleta Olivia: DANIEL PANDOLFI

Río Gallegos: Dr ALEJANDRO SÚNICO

Río Turbio: MARCELA VILLA

San Julian: CLAUDIA MALIK DE TCHARA

UNIVERSIDAD NACIONAL DE LA PATAGONIA SAN JUAN BOSCO

Ciudad Universitaria, Km 4, 9005 Comodoro Rivadavia, Chubut

Telephone: (297) 455-7856

E-mail: dzonal@unpata.edu.ar

Internet: www.unp.edu.ar

Founded 1980 by merger of Universidad de la Patagonia San Juan Bosco and Universidad Nacional de la Patagonia

Public control

Language of instruction: Spanish

Academic year: February to December

Rector: Lic. ADOLFO DOMINGO GENINI

Vice-Rector: Dra ALICIA BORASO

Academic Sec.: Mag. SUSANA PERALES

Science Sec.: Dra ADRIANA MÓNICA NILLNI

Librarian: Lic. HAYDEE MURGA

Number of teachers: 850

Number of students: 15,952

Library of 40,000 vols

Publication: *Naturalia Patagónica* (4 a year)

DEANS

Faculty of Economics: RICARDO MARIO BARRERA

Faculty of Engineering: Ing. OSCAR RENÉ MIURA

Faculty of Humanities and Social Sciences: Lic. CLAUDIA COICAUD

Faculty of Law: Dr DARDO RUBÉN PETOLI

Faculty of Natural Sciences: Mag. LIDIA BLANCO

REGIONAL FACULTIES

Esquel: Alvear 1021, 3° piso, 9200 Esquel; tel. (2945) 43729; Dir Lic. ROBERTO VIERA; forestry and economics.

Puerto Madryn: Blvd Almirante Brown 3700, CC 164, 9120 Puerto Madryn; tel. (2965) 45-1024; Dir Dr MIGUEL A. HALLER; marine biology, computer science.

Trelew: Faculty of Economics and Faculty of Humanities and Social Sciences, Fontana 488, 9100 Trelew; tel. (2965) 43-1532; fax (2965) 43-1276Faculty of Engineering and Faculty of Natural Sciences, Belgrano 507, 9100 Trelew; tel. (2965) 43-3305; Dir JUAN PÉREZ AMAT.

Ushuaia: CADIC, 9410 Ushuaia; tel. (2901) 43-0892; Dir Dr OSCAR LOBO; tourism, computer science.

UNIVERSIDAD NACIONAL DE LA PLATA

Avda 7 No. 776, 1900 La Plata

Telephone: (221) 423-6804

E-mail: portal@presi.unlp.edu.ar

Internet: www.unlp.edu.ar

Founded 1905

Academic year: March to December

President: Arq. GUSTAVO ADOLFO AZPIAZU

Vice-President: Lic. RAÚL ANIBAL PERDOMO

Gen. Sec.: Arq. FERNANDO ALFREDO TAUBER

Librarian: Dr CARLOS TEJO

Library: see Libraries and Archives

Number of teachers: 6,300

Number of students: 91,135

Publication: *Revista de la Universidad*

DEANS

Faculty of Agriculture: Ing. GUILLERMO MIGUEL HANG

Faculty of Architecture and Town Planning: Arq. JORGE ALBERTO LOMBARDI

Faculty of Astronomy and Geophysics: Prof. CÉSAR AUGUSTO MONDINALLI

Faculty of Dentistry: ALFREDO V. RICCIARDI

Faculty of Economic Sciences: (vacant)

Faculty of Engineering: Ing. LUIS JULIÁN LIMA

Faculty of Exact Sciences: Dr ENRIQUE PEREYRA

Faculty of Fine Arts: Prof. ROBERTO OSCAR ROLLIÉ

Faculty of Humanities and Education: Dr JOSÉ PANETTIERI

Faculty of Juridical and Social Sciences: RICARDO PABLO RECA

Faculty of Medical Sciences: Dr JAIME TRAJTENBERG

Faculty of Natural Sciences: Dr ISIDORO A. SCHALAMUCK

Faculty of Veterinary Sciences: Dr ALBERTO DIBBERN

SELECTED AFFILIATED SCHOOLS AND INSTITUTES

Colegio Nacional 'Rafael Hernández' (National College): Avda 1 y 49, La Plata; Dir Prof. GRACIELA TERESA IBARRA.

Escuela Graduada 'Joaquín V. González' ('Joaquin.V Gonzales' Escuelas Graduadas'): Calle 50 y 119, La Plata; Dir Prof. MARTHA S. BETTI DE MILICHIO.

Escuela Práctica de Agricultura y Ganadería 'María Cruz y Manuel L. Inchausti' ('Maria Cruz y Manuel L. Inchausti' School of Agriculture and Stockbreeding): Estación Valdés, 6660 Veinticinco de Mayo, Pca de Buenos Aires; Dir Dr RICARDO LUIS CABASSI.

Escuela Superior de Periodismo y Comunicación Social (School of Journalism): Avda 44 No. 676, La Plata; Dir Lic. JORGE LUIS BERNETTI.

Instituto de Física de Líquidos y Sistemas Biológicos: Calle 59 No. 789, 1900 La Plata; tel. (221) 44-7545; f. 1981; theoretical and applied research; 9 researchers; library of 582 vols, in process of formation; Dir Dr ANTONIO E. RODRÍGUEZ.

UNIVERSIDAD NACIONAL DE LA RIOJA

Avda Dr Rene Favaloro s/n, 5300 La Rioja

Telephone: (3822) 45-7000

Fax: (3822) 45-7000

E-mail: unlar@unlar.edu.ar

Internet: www.unlar.edu.ar

Founded 1972

State control

Academic year: February to December

Rector: Dr ENRIQUE TELLO ROLDÁN

Vice-Rector: Ing. MANUEL JESÚS MAMANÍ

Administrative Secretary: SANTIAGO ROMERO

Librarian: (vacant)
Library of 23,000 vols
Number of teachers: 1,154
Number of students: 16,519
Publication: *Research Projects* (6 a year)
Faculties of economics, engineering, humanities and arts, social sciences.

UNIVERSIDAD NACIONAL DE LANÚS

29 de Septiembre 3901, 1826 Lanús, Buenos Aires
Telephone: (11) 6322-9200
Fax: (11) 6322-9200
E-mail: info@unla.edu.ar
Internet: www.unla.edu.ar
Founded 1995
State control
Academic year: March to December (two semesters)
Rector: ANA MARÍA JARAMILLO
Vice-Rector and Sec. (Academic): Dr JUAN CARLOS GENEYRO
Sec.-Gen.: JORGE CARTOCIO
Sec. (Admin.): GUILLERMO GROSSKOPF
Sec. (Public Service and Cooperation): Lic. GEORGINA HERNÁNDEZ
Sec. (Research, Science and Technology): Ing. NORBERTO CAMINOA
Librarian: Lic. ELVIRA LOFIEGO
Number of students: 7,079

DIRECTORS

Arts and Humanities: Prof. HECTOR MUZZO-PAPPA
Community Health: Dr DANIEL RODRÍGUEZ
Planning and Public Policy: Dr ALEJANDRO KAWABATA
Production and Labour Development: Dr JORGE MOLINA

UNIVERSIDAD NACIONAL DEL LITORAL

Blvd Pellegrini 2750, S3000ADQ Santa Fe
Telephone: (342) 457-1110
Fax: (342) 457-1110
E-mail: informes@unl.edu.ar
Internet: www.unl.edu.ar
Founded 1919
State control
Academic year: March to December
Rector: Ing. ALBOR CANTARD
Vice-Rector: Dr MARIO T. CADIOTI
Gen.-Sec.: Prof. CLAUDIO LIZÁRRAGA
Academic Sec.: HUGO ERBETTA
Admin. Sec.: Esc. RODOLFO M. R. ACANFORA GRECO
Sec. for International Cooperation: Ing. JULIO C. THEILER
Librarian: MARISA PULIOTTI DE FERRARI
Number of teachers: 2,171
Number of students: 32,924
Publications: *Science and Technology*, *Society and Culture*

DEANS

Faculty of Agrarian Sciences: Ing. Agr. HUGO ARMANDO ERBETTA
Faculty of Architecture, Design and Town Planning: Arq. JULIO ALEJANDRO TALÍN
Faculty of Biochemistry and Biological Sciences: Bioq. EDUARDO RAMÓN VILLARREAL
Faculty of Chemical Engineering: Ing. PEDRO MÁXIMO MANCINI
Faculty of Economics: FRANCISCA SÁNCHEZ DE DUSSO
Faculty of Education: Prof. LEONOR JUANA CHENA
Faculty of Law and Social Sciences: Dr MARIANO T. CANDIOTI
Faculty of Teacher Training: Prof. LEONOR J. CHENA

Faculty of Veterinary Sciences: Med. Vet. EDUARDO BARONI
Faculty of Water Resources Engineering and Sciences: Ing. CRISTÓBAL VICENTE LOZECO

DIRECTORS

Higher Institute of Music: Prof. MARIANO CABRAL MIGNO
Higher School of Health Services: Dr CARLOS PRONO
Higher School of Industry: Ing. JORGE OSVALDO BASILICO
Institute of Food Technology: Ing. HUGO SÁNCHEZ
Institute of Technological Development for the Chemical Industry (INTEC): Dr ALBERTO ENRIQUE CASSANO
School of Agriculture, Stockbreeding and Farming: Ing. Agr. OSVALDO MARIO HERMANN
University School of Food Analysis: Ing. ALEJANDRO BERNABEU
University School of Food Science: Bioq. LUIS MARÍA NICKISH

UNIVERSIDAD NACIONAL DE LOMAS DE ZAMORA

Ruta Provincial No. 4 Km 2, Llavaloll, Buenos Aires
Telephone: (11) 4282-7818
Fax: (11) 4282-8043
E-mail: unlz@unlz.edu.ar
Internet: www.unlz.edu.ar
Founded 1972
State control
Chancellor: GUIDO DI TELLA
Rector: HORACIO GEGUNDE
Vice-Rectors: DIEGO MOLEA (Admin.), HORACIO DAVID CASABE (Academic)
Sec.-Gen.: LEONARDO CLEMENTE
Chief of Staff: NÉSTOR PAN
Librarian: MARIA LUISA ISHIKAWA
Number of teachers: 3,800
Number of students: 35,000

DEANS

Faculty of Agrarian Science: Ing. FERNANDO RUMIANO
Faculty of Economics: Cdr ALEJANDRO KURUC
Faculty of Engineering: Ing. OSCAR PASCAL
Faculty of Law: Dr ALEJANDRO TULLIO
Faculty of Social Sciences: Lic. GABRIEL MARIOTTO

UNIVERSIDAD NACIONAL DE LUJÁN

Ruta 5 y Avda Constitución, 6700 Luján, Buenos Aires
Telephone: (2323) 42-3171
Fax: (2323) 42-5795
E-mail: informes@unlu.edu.ar
Internet: www.unlu.edu.ar
Founded 1973
Academic year: February to December
Rector: Lic. ANTONIO F. LAPOLLA
Vice-Rector: Dr NORBERTO KRYMKIEWICZ
Registrar: Lic. MARCELO BUSALACCHI
Librarian: Lic. EDUARDO ZEISS
Number of teachers: 1,000
Number of students: 18,803
Publications: *Cuadernos de Economía Política*, *Cuadernos de Historia Regional*

DEANS

Department of Basic Sciences: Dr JOSÉ AGUIRRE
Department of Education: Prof. HÉCTOR CUCUZZA
Department of Social Sciences: Lic. AMALIA TESTA
Department of Technology: JUAN TREGONING

UNIVERSIDAD NACIONAL DE MAR DEL PLATA

Diagonal J. B. Alberdi 2695, 7600 Mar del Plata, Pca de Buenos Aires
Telephone: (223) 492-1705
Fax: (223) 492-1711
Internet: www.mdp.edu.ar
Founded 1961
State control
Academic year: March to November
Rector: Lic. FRANCISCO MOREA
Vice-Rector: Dr ARMANDO DANIEL ABRUZA
Sec.-Gen. (Planning and Institutional Development): Arq. ARIEL MAGNONI
Acad. Sec.: Lic. MONICA VAN GOOL
Sec.(Economics and Finance): C. P. JORGE HERRADA
Sec. (Extension): Prof. ADRIANA CORTES
Sec. (Technological Development): Lic. OLGA DELLA VEDOVA
Sec. (University Community): Lic. PAULA PAZ
Librarian: Lic. OSCAR FERNÁNDEZ
Number of teachers: 1,600
Number of students: 27,000
Publication: *Revista de Letras* (3 a year)

DEANS

Faculty of Agriculture: Ing. Agr. JOSÉ LUIS BODEGA
Faculty of Architecture and Town Planning: Arq. MANUEL TORRES CANO
Faculty of Economics and Social Sciences: Cont. OTTORINO OSCAR MUCCI
Faculty of Engineering: Ing. MANUEL LORENZO GONZÁLEZ
Faculty of Exact and Natural Sciences: Dr JULIO LUIS DEL RIO
Faculty of Health Sciences and Social Services: Lic. GRISELDA SUSANA VICENS
Faculty of Humanities: Prof. CRISTINA ROSENTHAL
Faculty of Law: Dr LUIS PABLO SLAVIN
Faculty of Psychology: Lic. MARÍA CRISTINA DI DOMÉNICO

DIRECTORS

Centre for Coastal and Quaternary Geology: Lic. DANIEL MARTINEZ
Institute of Biological Research: Dr JORGE JULIAN SANCHEZ
Institute of Science and Materials Technology Research: Dr SUSANA ROSSO

UNIVERSIDAD NACIONAL DE MISIONES

Ruta Nacional No. 12, Km 7½, N3304 Miguel Lanús, Misiones
Telephone: (3752) 48-0916
Fax: (3752) 48-0500
E-mail: info@unam.edu.ar
Internet: www.unam.edu.ar
Founded 1973
State control
Academic year: February to December
Chancellor: Dr ALDO LUIS CABALLERO
Vice-Chancellor: Aldo M. A. DARÍO MONTINI
Number of teachers: 900
Number of students: 8,800
Publications: *Boletín*, *Revista*

DEANS

Faculty of Arts: Prof. ADA SARTORI DE VENCHARUTTI
Faculty of Economics: JOSE LUIS LIBUTTI
Faculty of Engineering: Ing. OSCAR EDUARDO PERRONE
Faculty of Forestry: Ing. JUAN CARLOS MULARCZUK KOSARIK
Faculty of Humanities and Social Sciences: Prof. ANA MARÍA CAMBLONG
Faculty of Sciences: Ing. RAUL MARUCCI

UNIVERSIDAD NACIONAL DEL NORDESTE

25 de Mayo 868, 3400 Corrientes

Telephone: (3783) 42-5064
Fax: (3783) 42-54678
E-mail: webmaster@unne.edu.ar
Internet: www.unne.edu.ar

Founded 1957

Academic year: March to December

Rector: Arq. OSCAR VICENTE VALDÉS
Vice-Rector: Dr HUGO ALBERTO DOMITROVIC
Sec.-Gen. (Academic Affairs): Arq. OSCAR V. VALDES
Sec.-Gen. (Admin.).: Dr HUGO A. PEIRETTI
Sec.-Gen. (Planning): GABRIEL E. OJEDA
Sec.-Gen. (Science and Technology): Ing. Dr JORGE R. AVANZA
Sec.-Gen (Social Affairs): Dr SERGIO M. FLINTA
Sec.-Gen. (Univ. Extension): Dr LUCIANO R. FABRIS
Librarian: Prof. ITALO JUAN L. METTINI

Number of teachers: 4,327
Number of students: 54,445

Publications: *Cuadernos Serie Agro, Revista de la Facultad de Ciencias Veterinarias, Revista de la Facultad de Derecho, Revista Nordeste, Serie Medicina, Serie Planeamiento*

DEANS

Faculty of Agricultural Industries: Ing. MARÍA ALICIA JUDIS
Faculty of Agricultural Sciences: Ing. Agr. LUIS AMADO MROGINSKY
Faculty of Architecture and Town Planning: Arq. HECTOR LUIS CABALLERO
Faculty of Dentistry: Dr VÍCTOR MENDEZ
Faculty of Economics: EDGARDO MARTÍN AYALA
Faculty of Engineering: Ing. MARIO BRUNO NATALINI
Faculty of Humanities: Prof. ANA MARÍA FOSCHIATTI DE DELL'ORTO
Faculty of Law and Social and Political Sciences: Dr JORGE MARIÑO FAGES
Faculty of Medicine: Dr SAMUEL BLUVSTEIN
Faculty of Natural Sciences and Surveying: Lic. MARÍA SILVIA AGUIRRE
Faculty of Veterinary Sciences: Dr ROBERTO A. JACOBO

UNIVERSIDAD NACIONAL DE QUILMES

Roque Sáenz Peña 180, 1876 Bernal, Buenos Aires

Telephone: (11) 4365-7100
Fax: (11) 4365-7101
E-mail: info@unq.edu.ar
Internet: www.unq.edu.ar

Founded 1989

State control

Rector: Dr MARIO ERMÁCORA
Vice-Rector: Prof. ROQUE DABAT
Sec. (Academic): Dr MARTÍN BECERRA
Sec.(Admin.): CARMEN CHIARADONNA
Sec. (Communication and Information Technology): Lic. SERGIO NAPOLITANO
Sec. (Legal and Technical): Abog. LORENA LAMPOLIO
Sec. (Postgraduate Affairs): Dr DIEGO GOLOMBEK
Sec. (Research): Dra ANAHÍ BALLENT
Sec. (Univ. Public Relations): Lic. MARCELO GÓMEZ
Librarian: LAURA MANZO

Library of 16,000 vols
Number of students: 11,000

Publications: *Prismas, Revista de historía intelectual* (intellectual history), *Redes* (science and technology), *Revista de Ciencias Sociales* (social sciences)

DIRECTORS

Centre for Research and Study: Lic ALBERTO DÍAZ
Department of Science and Technology: Dr DANIEL GHIRINGHELLI
Department of Social Sciences: Prof RODOLFO PASTORE

UNIVERSIDAD NACIONAL DE RÍO CUARTO

Ruta Nacional 36 Km 601, X5804BYA Río Cuarto, Córdoba

Telephone: (358) 467-6200
Fax: (358) 468-0280
E-mail: postmaster@unrc.edu.ar
Internet: www.unrc.edu.ar

Founded 1971

State control

Academic year: February to December

Rector: Ing. OSCAR SPADA
Vice-Rector: Méd. Vet. ANIBA BESSONE
Gen.-Sec.: Méd. Vet. ARMANDO BECERRA
Acad. Sec.: Lic. SILVIA NICOLETTI
Economic Sec.: Lic. JORGE GONZÁLEZ
Extension and Devt Sec.: Lic. RICARDO ROIG
Science and Technology Sec.: Dr ALFREDO BARONIO
Welfare Sec.: Méd. Vet. ENRIQUE BÉRGAMO
Coordinator of Institutional Communication: Arq. LUCÍA FORTUNA
Head of Postgraduate School: Dr Lic. RUBÉN DAVICINO
Librarian: CRISTINA CH. DE FAUDA

Number of teachers: 1,280
Number of students: 20,244

Publications: *Contextos de Educación* (2 a year), *Crónia* (2 a year), *Fundamentos* (2 a year), *Interciencia* (2 a year), *Revista* (2 a year), *Voces de la Universidad* (2 a year)

DEANS

Faculty of Agriculture and Veterinary Science: Luis ROBERTO ROVERE
Faculty of Economics: Lic. ROBERTO TAFANI
Faculty of Engineering: Ing. PEDRO ENRIQUE DUCANTO
Faculty of Exact, Physical, Chemical and Natural Sciences: Lic. GLADYS B. MORI
Faculty of Humanities: Dr ENRIQUE ARTURO GROTE

UNIVERSIDAD NACIONAL DE ROSARIO

Córdoba 1814, 2000 Rosario

Telephone: (341) 480-2620
E-mail: admin@unr.edu.ar
Internet: www.unr.edu.ar

Founded 1968

State control

Academic year: April to November

Rector: Prof. DARIO MAIORANA
Vice-Rector: Lic. EDUARDO SEMINARA
Head of Administration: Dr CARLOS A. DULONG

Number of teachers: 5,741
Number of students: 75,380

DEANS

Faculty of Agricultural Sciences: Ing. LILIANA MARGARITA
Faculty of Architecture, Planning and Design: Dr HÉCTOR DANTE FLORIANI
Faculty of Biochemistry and Pharmacy: Dra CLAUDIA ELIZABETH BALAGUE
Faculty of Dentistry: Dr HÉCTOR DARÍO MASIA
Faculty of Economic Sciences and Statistics: ALICIA INÉS CASTAGNA
Faculty of Exact Sciences, Engineering and Surveying: Ing. DAVID ESTEBAN ASTEGIANO

Faculty of Humanities and Arts: Prof. DARIO MAIORANA
Faculty of Law: Dr RICARDO ISIDORO
Faculty of Medical Sciences: Dra RAQUEL MADIS CHIARA
Faculty of Political Science and International Relations: Lic. FABIÁN ARIEL BACCIRE
Faculty of Psychology: Dr OVIDE JUAN MENIN
Faculty of Veterinary Sciences: Dr CLAUDIO JUAN GIUDICI

UNIVERSIDAD NACIONAL DE SALTA

Buenos Aires 177, 4400 Salta

Telephone: (387) 425-5440
Fax: (387) 425-5535
E-mail: rectora@unsa.edu.ar
Internet: www.unsa.edu.ar

Founded 1972

Academic year: March to December

Rector: Ing. Agr. STELLA MARIS PÉREZ DE BIANCHI
Vice-Rector: Dr CARLOS CADENA
General Secretary: (vacant)
Academic Secretary: Dr MARÍA CELIA ILVENTO
Administrative Secretary: CPN SERGIO ENRIQUE VILLALBA

Library of 57,633 vols, 42,300 periodicals
Number of teachers: 1,390
Number of students: 22,840

DEANS

Faculty of Economics, Juridical and Social Sciences: CPN VICTOR HUGO CLAROS
Faculty of Engineering: Ing. JORGE FÉLIX ALMAZÁN
Faculty of Exact Sciences: Ing. NORBERTO ALEJANDRO BONINI
Faculty of Health Sciences: Lic. NIEVE UBALDINA CHAVEZ
Faculty of Humanities: Lic. FLOR DE MARIA DEL VALLE RIONDA
Faculty of Natural Sciences: Ing. GUILLERMO ANDRES BAUDINO

ATTACHED INSTITUTE

Consejo de Investigación (Research Council): Pres. Ing. EDGARDO LING SHAM.

UNIVERSIDAD NACIONAL DE SAN JUAN

Mitre 396 (E), J5402CWH San Juan

Telephone: (264) 429-5000
E-mail: rector@unsj.edu.ar
Internet: www.unsj.edu.ar

Founded 1973

State control

Academic year: April to March

Rector: Dr Ing. BENJAMÍN RAFAEL KUCHEN
Vice-Rector: Mag. NELLY MARÍA FILIPPA
Admin. and Financial Secretary: Lic. ALEJANDRO LARREA
Librarian: RAÚL I. LOZADA

Number of teachers: 2,001
Number of students: 21,110

DEANS

Faculty of Architecture, Town Planning and Design: Arq. ROMEO BERNABÉ PLATERO
Faculty of Engineering: Ing. ROBERTO ROMUALDO GOMEZ GUIRADO
Faculty of Exact, Physical and Natural Sciences: Ing. JESÚS ABELARDO ROBLES
Faculty of Humanities, Philosophy and Arts: Prof. ZULMA LUCÍA CORZO
Faculty of Social Sciences: Lic. LUIS FRANCISCO MERITELLO

UNIVERSIDAD NACIONAL DE SAN LUIS

Ejército de los Andes 950, D5700HHW San Luis

Telephone: (2652) 42-4027
Fax: (2652) 43-0224
Internet: www.unsl.edu.ar

Founded 1974
Academic year: March to December

Rector: Dr JOSÉ LUIS RICCARDO
Vice-Rector: Lic. NELLY MARÍA MAINERO
Librarian: MIGUEL A. LUCERO

Number of teachers: 255
Number of students: 13,893

DEANS

Faculty of Chemistry, Biochemistry and Pharmacy: Dr ROBERTO OLSINA
Faculty of Education: Lic. NILDA E. PICCO DE BARBEITO
Faculty of Engineering and Business Administration (25 de Mayo 374, 5736 Villa Mercedes, San Luis): Ing. RAÚL A. MERINO
Faculty of Physical, Mathematical and Natural Sciences: Dr JULIO C. BENEGAS

UNIVERSIDAD NACIONAL DE SANTIAGO DEL ESTERO

Avda Belgrano (s) 1912, 4200 Santiago del Estero

Telephone: (385) 450-9500
Fax: (385) 422-2595
E-mail: info@unse.edu.ar
Internet: www.unse.edu.ar

Founded 1973
Academic year: February to December

Rector: Geol. ARNALDO SERGIO TENCHINI
Vice-Rector: LUIS PARADELO
Gen. Sec.: Dra LEONARDA TERESA ROSS
Librarian: JORGE LUJAN GEREZ

Library of 20,000 vols
Number of teachers: 848
Number of students: 11,659

Publications: *Cuadernos de la UNSE*, *Revista de Ciencia y Técnica* (1 a year), *Revista 'Quebracho'* (forestry, 1 a year), *Revista 'Unase'* (6 a year)

DEANS

Faculty of Agriculture and Agricultural Industry: Ing. JOSÉ M. SALGADO
Faculty of Forestry: Ing. VICTORIO MARJOT
Faculty of Humanities: SANTIAGO ÁNGEL DRUETTA
Faculty of Science and Technology: Ing. CARLOS ALBERTO BONETTI

UNIVERSIDAD NACIONAL DEL SUR

Avda Colón 80, B8000FTN Bahía Blanca
Telephone: (291) 459-5015
Fax: (291) 459-5016
E-mail: rector@uns.edu.ar
Internet: www.uns.edu.ar

Founded 1956
Academic year: February to December

Rector: Dr GUILLERMO HÉCTOR CRAPISTE
Vice-Rector: Dr MARÍA DEL CARMEN VAQUERO
Gen.-Sec. (Academic): Dra MARCELO ARMANDO VILLAR
Gen.-Sec. (Culture and University Extension): Lic. CLAUDIA PATRICIA LEGNINI
Gen.-Sec. (Institutional Relations and Planning): Dr OSVALDO ENRIQUE AGAMENNONI
Gen.-Sec. (Scientific and Technological): Dr ALFREDO JUAN
Gen.-Sec. (Student Affairs): Lic. CLAUDIA LEGNINI
Gen.-Sec. (Technical-Administrative): Lic. JUAN CARLOS SCHEFER

Gen.-Sec. (Univ. Superior Council): Abog. DIEGO DUPRAT
Library: see Libraries
Number of teachers: 2,069
Number of students: 22,571

Publications: *Capacitando en Calidad* (3 a year), *Escritos Contables* (2 a year), *Latin American Applied Research* (4 a year), *Reflexiones* (economics), *Revista Diálogos* (4 a year), *Revista Estudios Económicos* (1 a year), *Revista Universitaria de Geografía* (1 a year)

DIRECTORS

Department of Agriculture: Dr MARIO RICARDO SABBATINI
Department of Biology, Biochemistry and Pharmacy: Mag. MARTA AVELDANO
Department of Business Administration: REGINA DEL CARMEN DURÁN
Department of Chemical Engineering: Dr VERÓNICA BUCALÁ
Department of Chemistry: Dr MARÍA SUSANA RODRIGUEZ
Department of Computing Engineering Sciences: Dr RAFAEL GARCÍA
Department of Economics: Mag. ANDREA BARBERO
Department of Electrical Engineering: Dr PEDRO DONATE
Department of Engineering: Dr CARLOS ROSSIT
Department of Geography: Lic. SILVIA GRIPPO
Department of Geology: Dr GRACIELA RAQUEL MAS
Department of Humanities: Lic. ADRIANA CLAUDIA RODRIGUEZ
Department of Law: Abog. ANDRÉS BOUZAT
Department of Mathematics: Dr LILIANA CASTRO
Department of Physics: Dr WALTER RUBÉN CRAVERO

ATTACHED RESEARCH INSTITUTES

Centro de Recursos Naturales Renovables de la Zona Semiárida (CERZOS): Altos del Barrio Palihue, 8000 Bahía Blanca; tel. (291) 486-1127; Dir Dr NÉSTOR CURVETTO.
Centro Regional de Investigaciones Básicas y Aplicadas Bahía Blanca (CRIBABB): Camino La Carrindanga Km 7, 8000 Bahía Blanca; tel. (291) 486-1666; Dir Ing. MARTÍN URBICAIN.
Instituto Argentino de Oceanografía (IADO): Camino La Carrindanga Km 7, 8000 Bahía Blanca; tel. (291) 486-1112; run in conjunction with CONICET; Dir Dra MARÍA CIMTIA PÍCCOLO.
Instituto de Investigaciones Bioquímicas (INIBIBB): Camino La Carrindanga Km 7, 8000 Bahía Blanca; tel. (291) 486-1201; Dir Dr FRANCISCO JOSÉ BARRANTES.
Instituto de Matemática Bahía Blanca (INMABB): Avda Alem 1253, 8000 Bahía Blanca; tel. (291) 459-5116; Vice-Dir Mag. AURORA GERMANI.
Planta Piloto de Ingeniería Química (PLAPIQUI): Camino La Carrindanga Km 7, 8000 Bahía Blanca; tel. (291) 486-1700; Dir Dr ENRIQUE MARCELO VALLÉS.

UNIVERSIDAD NACIONAL DE TRES DE FEBRERO

Avda San Martín 2921, 1678 Caseros, Buenos Aires
Telephone: (11) 4759-9810
Fax: (11) 4759-9810
E-mail: info@untref.edu.ar
Internet: www.untref.edu.ar

Founded 1995
State control
Academic year: March to December

Rector: Lic. ANÍBAL Y. JOZAMI
Vice-Rector: Lic. MARTÍN KAUFMANN
Sec. (Academic): Ing. CARLOS MUNDT
Sec. (Research and Cooperation): Dr FÉLIX PEÑA

Number of students: 4,723

DIRECTORS

Administration and Economics: Dr MARTÍN GRAS
Art and Culture: Lic. FERMÍN FÈVRE
Health Sciences and Social Security: Dr CARLOS TORRES
Mathematics, Statistics and Methodology: Lic. ERNESTO ROSA
Social Sciences: Dr CÉSAR LORENZANO

UNIVERSIDAD NACIONAL DE TUCUMÁN

Ayacucho 491, 4000 San Miguel de Tucumán
Telephone: (381) 424-7762
Fax: (381) 424-8654
E-mail: postmaster@unt.edu.ar
Internet: www.unt.edu.ar

Founded 1914
Language of instruction: Spanish
Academic year: April to December

Rector: JUAN ALBERTO CERISOLA
Vice-Rector: Psic. MARÍA LUISA ROSSI DE HERNÁNDEZ
Gen.-Sec.: JOSÉ HUGO SAAB
Sec. (Academic Affairs): Dra MARTA PESA
Sec. (Admin.): Ing. JUAN CARLOS REIMUNDÍN
Sec. (Planning, Works and Services): MÓNICA INÉS DE LABASTIDA
Sec. (Postgraduate Affairs): Dr SUSANA MAIDANA
Sec. (Science and Technology): Dr DANIEL ENRIQUE CAMPI
Sec. (Student Welfare): Lic. RAMIRO MORENO
Sec. (Univ. Extension): Psic. MANUEL RAÚL ANDUJAR
Dir of International Relations: Dr RAMIRO ALBARRACÍN

Library: see Libraries and Archives
Number of teachers: 3,967
Number of students: 63,291

DEANS

Faculty of Agriculture and Animal Husbandry: Dr CARLOS HUGO BELLONE
Faculty of Architecture and Town Planning: Dr PABLO HOLGADO
Faculty of Biochemistry, Chemistry and Pharmacy: Dr ALICIA BARDÓN
Faculty of Dentistry: Dr GUILLERMO RAIDEN LAZCANO
Faculty of Economics: JUAN ALBERTO CERISOLA
Faculty of Exact Sciences and Technology: Ing. MARIO DONZELLI
Faculty of Fine Arts: Arq. MARCOS FIGUEROA
Faculty of Law and Social Sciences: Prof. PEDRO MARCOS ROUGES
Faculty of Medicine: Dr HORACIO DEZA
Faculty of Natural Sciences and Miguel Lillo Institute: Dr FERNANDO PRADO
Faculty of Philosophy and Letters: Dr ELENA ROJAS
Faculty of Psychology: Prof. MARIA LUISA ROSSI DE HERNANDEZ

UNIVERSIDAD NACIONAL DE VILLA MARÍA

Entre Ríos 1425, 5900 Villa María, Córdoba
Telephone: (353) 453-9100
Fax: (353) 453-9111
E-mail: comunica@unvm.edu.ar
Internet: www.unvm.edu.ar

Founded 1995
State control

Academic year: March to November (2 semesters)

Rector: MARTÍN RODRIGO GILL
Vice-Rector: MARIA CECILIA ANA CONCI
Sec.-Gen.: Abog. GERMÁN CARIGNANO
Sec. (Academic): Dr LUISA MARGARITA SCHWEIZER
Sec. (Finance): PABLO CÉSAR PAGOLA
Sec. (Welfare): Abog. LUIS ALBERTO NEGRETTI
Number of students: 3,000

DIRECTORS

Dr Antonino Sobral University Centre: Lic. SILVIA MARÍA PAREDES
Institute of Basic and Applied Sciences: Cr CARLOS OMAR DOMÍNGUEZ
Institute of Human Sciences: Dr CARLOS DANIEL LASA
Institute of Social Sciences: Lic. DANTE LA ROCCA MARTÍN
University Centre of Mediterranean Studies: Ing. JORGE LUIS FERRERO

UNIVERSIDAD TECNOLÓGICA NACIONAL

Sarmiento 440, C1041AAJ Buenos Aires
Telephone: (11) 5371-5600
Internet: www.utn.edu.ar
Founded 1959
Academic year: April to November
Rector: Ing. HECTOR C. BROTTO
Vice-Rector: Ing. CARLOS E. FANTINI
Academic Sec.: Ing. CIRIO MURAD
Sec. (Finance): Ing. CARLOS RAPP
Sec. (Institutional Relations): Prof. CARLOS RÍOS
Sec. (Student Affairs): Ing. RUBÉN SORO MARTÍNEZ
Sec. (Technological Research): Ing. JORGE FERRANTES
Sec. (Univ. Extension): Ing. DANIEL FERRADAS
Number of teachers: 16,185
Number of students: 70,087
Publication: *Boletín Informativo*.

REGIONAL FACULTIES

Avellaneda: Ing. Marconi 775, 1870 Avellaneda, Buenos Aires; mechanical, electrical and electronic engineering; Dean Ing. HÉCTOR R. GONZÁLEZ.

Bahía Blanca: 11 de Abril 461, 8000 Bahía Blanca, Buenos Aires; construction, electrical and mechanical engineering; Dean Ing. VICENTE EGIDI.

Buenos Aires: Medrano 951, 1179 Buenos Aires; textile, chemical, metallurgical, electronic, construction, electrical and mechanical systems analysis engineering; Dean Arq. LUIS A. DE MARCO.

Concepción del Uruguay: Ing. Pereyra 676, 3260 Concepción del Uruguay, Entre Ríos; electromechanical and construction engineering; Dean Ing. JUAN CARLOS PITER.

Córdoba: Uladíslao Frías s/n, 5000 Córdoba; chemical, metallurgical, mechanical, electronic and electrical engineering; Dean Ing. RUBÉN SORO MARTÍNEZ.

Delta: San Martín 1171, 2804 Campana, Buenos Aires; electrical, mechanical and chemical engineering; Dean Ing. GUSTAVO BAUER.

General Pacheco: Avda Irigoyen 2878, 1617 General Pacheco, Buenos Aires; mechanical engineering; Dean Ing. EUGENIO B. RICCIOLINI.

Haedo: París 532, 1707 Haedo, Buenos Aires; aeronautical engineering, electronics, mechanical engineering; Dean Ing. ELIO BIAGINI.

La Plata: Calle 60 esq. 124, 1900 La Plata, Buenos Aires; chemical, mechanical, elec-

trical and construction engineering; Dean Ing. CARLOS FANTINI.

Mendoza: Rodríguez 273, 5500 Mendoza; construction, electromechanical, chemical, electronic engineering, systems analysis; Dean Ing. JULIO CÉSAR CLETO COBOS.

Paraná: Almafuerte 1033, 3100 Paraná, Entre Ríos; electromechanical and construction engineering; Dean Ing. RAÚL E. ARROYO.

Rafaela: Blvd Roca y Artigas, 2300 Rafaela, Santa Fe; electromechanical and construction engineering; Dean Ing. OSCAR DAVID.

Resistencia: French 414, 3500 Resistencia, Chaco; electromechanical engineering, systems analysis; Dean Ing. SEBASTIÁN VICENTE MARTÍN.

Río Grande: Belgrano 777, 9420 Río Grande, Tierra del Fuego; electronic and industrial engineering; Dean Ing. MARIO FERREIRA.

Rosario: Estanislao Zeballos 1341, 2000 Rosario, Santa Fe; electrical, mechanical, construction, chemical engineering and systems analysis; Dean Ing. DANIEL OSCAR BADÍA.

San Francisco: Avda Gral. Savio 501, 2400 San Francisco, Córdoba; electromechanical engineering, electronics, information technology; Dean Ing. RAÚL C. ALBERTO.

San Nicolás: Colón 332, 2900 San Nicolás, Buenos Aires; electromechanical and metallurgical engineering; Dean Ing. NEORÉN P. FRANCO.

San Rafaél: Comandante Salas 370, 5600 San Rafaél, Mendoza; construction, electromechanical, chemical and civil engineering; Dean Ing. HORACIO P. PESSANO.

Santa Fe: Lavaise 610, 3000 Santa Fe; construction, electrical and mechanical engineering and systems analysis; Dean Ing. RICARDO O. SCHOLTUS.

Tucumán: Rivadavia 1050, 4000 San Miguel de Tucumán; construction, mechanical and civil engineering, information technology; Dean Ing. HUGO E. CELLERINO.

Villa María: Avda Universidad 450, Barrio Bello Horizonte, 5900 Villa María, Córdoba; mechanical and chemical engineering; Dean Ing. CARLOS R. RAPP.

ACADEMIC UNITS

Concordia: Salta 277, 3200 Concordia, Entre Ríos; construction and electromechanical engineering; Dir Ing. JOSÉ BOURREN.

Confluencia: Juan Manuel de Rosas y Juan Soufal, 8318 Plaza Huincul, Neuquén; electronic and chemical engineering; Dir Ing. SUSANA L. TARGHETTA DUR.

La Rioja: Facundo Quiroga y Beccar Varela, 5330 La Rioja; electromechanical engineering; Dir Dr MAURICIO KEJNER.

Rawson: Mitre 764, 9100 Rawson, Chubut; electromechanical and industrial engineering; Dir Ing. ERNESTO A. PASCUALICH.

Reconquista: Freyre 980, 3560 Reconquista, Santa Fe; electromechanical engineering; Dir Ing. OSVALDO DEL VALLE FATALA.

Río Gallegos: Maipú 53, 9400 Río Gallegos, Santa Cruz; electromechanical and industrial engineering; Dir Lic. SERGIO RAÚL RAGGI.

Trenque Lauquen: Villegas y Pereyra Rosas, 6400 Trenque Lauquen, Buenos Aires; electromechanical and construction engineering; Dir Ing. GUILLERMO A. GIL.

Venado Tuerto: Castelli 501, 2600 Venado Tuerto, Santa Fe; electromechanical and construction engineering; Dir Ing. ALFREDO ANÍBAL GUILLAUMET.

Private Universities

PONTIFICIA UNIVERSIDAD CATÓLICA ARGENTINA 'SANTA MARÍA DE LOS BUENOS AIRES'

Alicia Moreau de Justo 1300, C1107AAZ Buenos Aires
Telephone: (11) 4349-0200
Fax: (11) 4349-0246
E-mail: info@uca.com.ar
Internet: www.uca.edu.ar
Founded 1958
Academic year: March to November
Rector: Monseñor Dr ALFREDO HORACIO ZECCA
Vice-Rector: Lic. ERNESTO JOSÉ PARSELIS
Academic Sec.: Dr JORGE NICOLÁS LAFFERRIÈRE
Dir of International Relations: Dr CARLOS EZCURRA
Number of teachers: 3,200
Number of students: 16,800
Publications: *Boletín de Ciencias Económicas* (6 a year), *Colección* (political science, 2 a year), *Letras* (Argentinian and comparative literature, 2 a year), *Prudentia Juris* (2 a year), *Sapientia* (2 a year), *Teología* (2 a year), *Valores* (economics and social ethics, 3 a year)

DEANS

Faculty of Agriculture: Dr CARLOS PACÍFICO
Faculty of Arts and Music: GUILLERMO SCARABINO
Faculty of Canon Law: Lic. VICTOR PINTO
Faculty of Chemistry and Engineering (Mendoza): Lic. LUIS SCOZZINA
Faculty of Economics (Mendoza): Ing. ALFREDO DOMINGO VIOTTI
Faculty of Economic and Social Sciences: Dr LUDOVICO VIDELA
Faculty of Economic Sciences (Rosario): Cr RICARDO PARÍS
Faculty of Health Sciences: Dr CARLOS ALVAREZ
Faculty of Humanities and Education (Mendoza): Prof. ADRIANA MENÉNDEZ DE ZUMER
Faculty of Humanities 'Teresa de Avila' (Paraná): Dr MIGUEL ANGEL NESA
Faculty of Law and Political Sciences: Dr EDUARDO VENTURA
Faculty of Law and Social Sciences (Rosario): Dr GUSTAVO GUILLERMO LO CELSO
Faculty of Philosophy and Letters: Dr HÉCTOR DELBOSCO
Faculty of Physical Sciences, Mathematics and Engineering: Ing. HORACIO CARLOS REGGINI
Faculty of Theology: Dr CARLOS M. GALLI

DIRECTORS

Institute of Bioethics: Dr ALBERTO BOCHATEY
Institute of Social Communication, Journalism and Publicity: Lic. ALICIA PERESON
Institute of Spirituality and Pastoral Action: GUSTAVO LUIS BOQUIN
Institute of University Extension: Dr ALFREDO ZECCA

UNIVERSIDAD DEL ACONCAGUA

Catamarca 147, 5500 Mendoza
Telephone: (261) 520-1600
Fax: (261) 520-1650
E-mail: informes@uda.edu.ar
Internet: www.uda.edu.ar
Founded 1965
Academic year: April to October
Rector: Prof. Dr OSVALDO S. CABALLERO
Secretary-General: OSCAR DAVID CERUTTI
Librarian: HAYDEE TORRES BOUSOÑO
Number of teachers: 451
Number of students: 4,726

DEANS

Faculty of Economics and Commerce: Dr ROLANDO GALLI REY

Faculty of Phono-audiology: Dr GUSTAVO MAURICIO

Faculty of Psychology: Lic. HUGO LUPIAÑEZ

Faculty of Social Sciences and Administration: Dr JUAN FARRES CAVAGNARO

UNIVERSIDAD ARGENTINA DE LA EMPRESA
(Argentine University of Administration Sciences)

Lima 717, C1073AAO Buenos Aires

Telephone: (11) 4372-5454

E-mail: contactcenter@uade.edu.ar

Internet: www.uade.edu.ar

Founded 1962

Academic year: March to December

Rector: Dr JORGE DEL ÁGUILA

Provost: Lic. ANA MARÍA MASS

Sec. (Student Affairs): ROBERTO PEDRAZA

Librarian: RODOLFO LÖHE

Library of 50,000 vols, 865 periodicals

Number of teachers: 750

Number of students: 15,581

Publication: @ UADE (12 a year)

DEANS

School of Communication and Design: Dr OLGA CLAUDIA CORTEZ

School of Economics: Dr RICARDO FELIPE SMURRA

School of Engineering and Exact Sciences: Dr RICARDO OROSCO

School of Legal and Social Sciences: Dr MARIO SERRAFERO

UNIVERSIDAD ARGENTINA 'JOHN F. KENNEDY'

Calle Bartolomé Mitre 1411, 1037 Buenos Aires

Telephone: (11) 4476-4338

Fax: (11) 4476-2271

E-mail: info@kennedy.edu.ar

Internet: www.kennedy.edu.ar

Founded 1961

Rector: Dra MARÍA ELISA HERREN DE DAVID

Vice-Rector: Dr OSCAR ANTONIO CÁMPOLI

Library of 50,000 vols

Number of teachers: 1,800

Number of students: 17,417

UNIVERSIDAD DE BELGRANO

Zabala 1837, 1426 Buenos Aires

Telephone: (11) 4788-5400

Fax: (11) 4576-3912

E-mail: ingresos@ub.edu.ar

Internet: www.ub.edu.ar

Founded 1964

Private control

Language of instruction: Spanish

Academic year: March to November

Rector: Dr AVELINO JOSÉ PORTO

Vice-Rector (Academic Affairs): Prof. BRIGANTE NILDA

Vice-Rector (Institutional Affairs): Prof. ALDO PÉREZ

Vice-Rector (Legal and Technical Admin.): Dr EUSTAQUIO CASTRO

Librarian: MERCEDES PATALANO

Library of 70,043 vols, 2,500 periodicals

Number of teachers: 1,097

Number of students: 10,441

Publications: Académicos (12 a year), Postcátedra (4 a year), UB News (52 a year)

DEANS

Department of Graduate Studies and Continuing Education: Dr CARLOS STEIGER

Faculty of Agriculture: Ing. CARLOS MENDEZ ACOSTA

Faculty of Architecture and Urban Planning: Arq. MÓNICA FERNÁNDEZ

Faculty of Distance Learning: Dr CLARA BONFILL

Faculty of Economics: Dr PATRICIA BONATTI

Graduate School of Economics and International Business: Dr CARLOS STEIGER

Faculty of Engineering and Information Technology: Ing. ALBERTO GUERCI

Faculty of Graduate Studies: Dr ANDRÉS FONTANA

Faculty of Health Sciences: Dr HERNÁN JAVIER ALDANA MARCOS

Faculty of Humanities: Dr SUSANA SEIDMANN

Faculty of Information Technology: Ing. JOHN R. LESTANI

Faculty of Languages and Foreign Studies: Prof. RAQUEL ALBORNOZ

Faculty of Law and Social Sciences: Dr DINO BELLORIO CLABOT

Faculty of Natural and Exact Sciences: Dr HERNÁN JAVIER ALDANA MARCOS

UNIVERSIDAD CAECE

Avda de Mayo 866, 1084 Buenos Aires

Telephone: (11) 5217-7878 ext 286

Fax: (11) 5217-7887

E-mail: informes@caece.edu.ar

Internet: www.caece.edu.ar

Founded 1967

Private control

Rector: Prof. JORGE E. BOSCH

Gen. Vice-Rector: Prof. HENRI BOSCH

Academic Vice-Rector: ROBERTO P. J. HERNÁNDEZ

Chief Admin. Officer: OLGA VILLAVERDE

Librarian: SUSANA BUONO

Library of 9,000 vols

Number of teachers: 300

Number of students: 2,522

Publication: Elementos de Matemática.

UNIVERSIDAD CATÓLICA DE CÓRDOBA

Obispo Trejo 323, 5000 Córdoba

Telephone: (351) 421-9000

Fax: (351) 493-8002

E-mail: info@uccor.edu.ar

Internet: www.ucc.edu.ar

Founded 1956

Academic year: February to December

Chancellor: Mgr CARLOS JOSÉ ÑAÑEZ (Archbishop of Córdoba)

Vice-Chancellor: R. P. ALVARO RESTREPO

Rector: Lic. RAFAEL VELASCO

Vice-Rector (Academic): Dr CARLOS F. SCHICKENDANTZ

Vice-Rector (Economy): Dr JORGE O. PÉREZ

Vice-Rector (Univ. Community): DANIELA GARGANTINI

Academic Sec.: Dr JUAN CARLOS BOGGIO

Dir, Library System: Mag. SANDRA GISELA MARTÍN

Library: see Libraries and Archives

Number of teachers: 1,305

Number of students: 7,156

DEANS

Faculty of Agriculture: Dr JUAN CARLOS BOGGIO

Faculty of Architecture: Arq. ESTEBAN TRISTÁN REMIRO BONDONE

Faculty of Chemical Sciences: Bioq. PAULA MARÍA COOKE

Faculty of Economics and Administration: Mag. CARLOS ORLANDO PÉREZ

Faculty of Education: Dr ENRIQUE NÉSTOR BAMBOZZI

Faculty of Engineering: Ing. RAÚL JUAN VACA NARVAJA

Faculty of Law and Social Sciences: Abog. JOSÉ NARCISO REY NORES

Faculty of Medicine: Mag. CARLOS EMILIO GATTI

Faculty of Philosophy and Humanities: Dr CARLOS FEDERICO SCHICKENDANTZ

Faculty of Political Sciences and International Relations: Lic. MARIO GERMÁN RIORDA

Institute of Administrative Sciences: ADOLFO MARTÍN GUSTAVO BERTOA

UNIVERSIDAD CATÓLICA DE CUYO

Avda Ignacio de la Roza 1516, Rivadavia, 5400 San Juan

Telephone: (264) 429-2300

Fax: (264) 429-2310

E-mail: rectorado@uccuyo.edu.ar

Internet: www.uccuyo.edu.ar

Founded 1953

Private control

Language of instruction: Spanish

Academic year: April to March

Rector: Dr MARÍA ISABEL LARRAURI

Vice-Rector: Dr ALFONSO OSVALDO MARTÍN

Sec.-Gen. (Academic): Prof. CECILIA TRINCADO DE MURÚA

Dir of Library: EUGENIA CARRASCOSA DE YUNES

Library of 32,000 vols

Number of teachers: 910

Number of students: 6,100

Publication: Revista Cuadernos

DEANS

Faculty of Economics and Business: C. P. ALEJANDRO LARGACHA

Faculty of Education: LUCIA GHILARDI DE CARRIZO

Faculty of Food Sciences: CLAUDIO MARCELO LARREA

Faculty of Law and Social Sciences: Dr MIRYAN ANDÚJAR DE ZAMORA

Faculty of Medical Sciences: Dr MERCEDES GÓMEZ DE HERRERA

Faculty of Philosophy and Humanities: Lic. JORGE BERNAT

UNIVERSIDAD CATÓLICA DE LA PLATA

Calle 13 No. 1227, 1900 La Plata

Telephone: (221) 422-7100

Internet: www.ucalp.edu.ar

Founded 1964

Academic year: March to November

Grand Chancellor: Mgr HÉCTOR RUBÉN AGUER

Rector: RAFAEL BREIDE OBEID

Academic Gen.-Sec.: MIGUEL ÁNGEL SARNI

Librarian: GLADYS R. MARDUEL

Number of teachers: 635

Number of students: 3,741

Publication: Revista

DEANS

Faculty of Applied Mathematics: Ing. EDUARDO FULCO

Faculty of Architecture: Arq. CARLOS ALBERTO RUOTOLO

Faculty of Economics: Cr MARIO LUIS SZYCHOWSKI

Faculty of Education: Prof. NANCY DI PIERO DE WARR

Faculty of Law: Dr JORGE O. PERRINO

Faculty of Social Sciences: Dr JORGE O. PERRINO

UNIVERSIDAD CATÓLICA DE SALTA

Ciudad Universitaria, Campo Castañares,
Casilla 18, 4400 Salta
Telephone: (387) 423-3270
E-mail: rectorado@ucasal.net
Internet: www.ucasal.net
Founded 1963
Academic year: March to December
Chancellor: Mgr MARIO ANTONIO CARGNELLO
Rector: Dr ALFREDO GUSTAVO PUIG
Academic Vice-Rector: Prof. GERARDO VIDES
ALMONACID
Admin. Vice-Rector: Ing. MANUEL CORNEJO
TORINO
Sec.-Gen.: Dr LILIAN CONSTANZA DIEDRICH DE
DUBA
Librarian: WARTHA ANSALDI DE VINANTE
Library of 42,000 vols
Number of teachers: 750
Number of students: 19,563

DEANS

Faculty of Architecture and Urban Planning:
Arq. JUAN PEDRO COLOMBO SPERONI
Faculty of Economics and Administration:
Lic. ROBERTO CADAR
Faculty of Engineering and Informatics: Ing.
ERNESTO CLAUDIO MONDADA
Faculty of Law: Dr ARMANDO ISASMENDI
School of Physical Education: Lic. DOLORES
MEDINA BOUQUET
School of Social Service: Lic. SONIA ZAMORA
School of Tourism: Lic. CARLOS FRANCISCO
SÁNCHEZ

UNIVERSIDAD CATÓLICA DE SANTA FE

Echagüe 7151, S3004JBS Santa Fe
Telephone: (342) 460-3030
Fax: (342) 460-3030
E-mail: postmaster@ucsfre.edu.ar
Internet: www.ucsf.edu.ar
Founded 1957
Academic year: February to December
Grand Chancellor: Mgr EDGARDO GABRIEL
STORNI
Rector: Arq. JOSÉ MARÍA PASSEGGI
Vice-Rector for Academic Affairs: Lic. TOMÁS
GUTIERREZ
Vice-Rector for Training: Lic. MARCELO
MATEO
Sec.-Gen.: Dra MARTA D. V. OLMOS
Library Dir: Dr JUAN CARLOS P. BALLESTEROS
Number of teachers: 480
Number of students: 3,864

DEANS

Faculty of Architecture: Arq. RICARDO MARÍA
ROCHETTI
Faculty of Economic Sciences: LUIS ELIO
BONINO
Faculty of Education: Dr JUAN CARLOS PABLO
BALLESTEROS
Faculty of Engineering, Geoecology and the
Environment: Lic. TOMÁS GUTIERREZ
Faculty of Law: Dr RICARDO ANDRÉS VILLA
Faculty of Philosophy: Prof. DANIEL
VASCHETTO (acting)
Faculty of Social Communication: Lic. CAR-
LOS TEALDI

UNIVERSIDAD CATÓLICA DE SANTIAGO DEL ESTERO

Avda Alsina y Dalmacio Vélez Sársfield, 4200
Santiago del Estero
Telephone: (385) 421-1777
Fax: (385) 421-1777
E-mail: postmaster@ucse.edu.ar
Internet: www.ucse.edu.ar
Founded 1960
Language of instruction: Spanish

Academic year: April to November
Grand Chancellor: Mgr GERARDO EUSEBIO
SUELDO
Rector: Ing. JORGE LUIS FEIJÓO
Admin. Dir: Lic. MARÍA ÉLIDA CERRO DE
ÁBALOS
Librarian: Prof. Dr MATIAS ZUZEC
Library of 19,000 vols
Number of teachers: 450
Number of students: 4,000
Publication: *Nuevas Propuestas*

DEANS

Faculty of Applied Mathematics: Ing. OCTA-
VIO JOSÉ MÉDICI
Faculty of Economics: Lic. VÍCTOR MANUEL
FEIJÓO
Faculty of Education: Hna Lic. LILIANA
BADALONI
Faculty of Politics, Social Sciences and Law:
Abogada MARIA TERESA TENTI DE VOLTA

PROFESSORS

Faculty of Applied Mathematics:
CORONEL, J. C., Introduction to Mathemat-
ical Analysis
KORSTANJE, A. P., Operational Research
MARTÍNEZ, E., Systems Evaluation
PASTORINO, M. I., Numerical Methods
TRAJTENBERG, J. O., Introduction to Data
Processing

Faculty of Economics:
ALEGRE, J. C., Bankruptcy Law
BRAVO, W., Auditing
CHAYA, H. N., Administration and Person-
nel
CORONEL, J. C., Budgeting
FERRERO DE AZAR, A. M., Company Law
MARIGLIANO, M., Business Organization
MARTELEUR, R., Introduction to Economics
MORELLINI, P. A., Accounting, Budget
Sheet Analysis
OSTENGO, H., Accounting
PASTORINO, M. I., Statistics
TERUEL, R., General Administration

Faculty of Education:
CASTIGLIONE, J. C., Theology
GELID, T., General Sociology and Sociology
of Education
MUHN, G., Vocational Orientation
RIERA DE LUCENA, E., Philosophical Anthro-
pology, Basic Epistemology
SGOIFO, M. DEL V., Psychology

Faculty of Politics, Social Sciences and Law:
ALEGRE, J. C., Agricultural and Mining
Law
ARGAÑARAZ ORGAZ, C., Administrative Law
ARGUELLO, L. R., Roman Law
ARNEDO, E., Private International Law
AUAD, A., Social Philosophy
BENEVOLE DE GAUNA, T., Legal Consult-
ation
BONACINA, R. A., Introduction to Economics
BRIZUELA, N., General and Social Psych-
ology
BRUNELLO DE ZURITA, A., Civil Law
CASTIGLIONE, J. C., Philosophy of Law
CERRO, F. E., Theory of the State
CHRISTENSEN, E., Finance and Financial
Law
HARO DE SURIAN, E., Economic Geography
LEDESMA, A. E., Civil and Penal Procedural
Law
NAVARRO, J. V., Penal Law
PAZ, G. M., Civil Law
PAZ, M. J., Commercial Law
RETAMOSA, J. R., History of Ideas and
Political Institutions, History of the
World, History of Argentina
RIGOURD, C., Public Law
RIMINI, J. C., Commercial Law
SALERA, J. B., Sociology

VICTORIA, M. A., Agricultural and Mining
Law
ZURITA DE GONZÁLEZ, M., Civil Law

UNIVERSIDAD DE CONCEPCIÓN DEL URUGUAY

8 de Junio 522, E3260ANJ Concepción del
Uruguay, Entre Ríos
Telephone: (3442) 42-5606
Fax: (3442) 42-7721
E-mail: info@ucu.edu.ar
Internet: www.ucu.edu.ar
Founded 1971
Private control
Academic year: February to December
Rector: Dr HÉCTOR CÉSAR SAURET
Vice-Rector: Dra GEORGINA VIERCI
Academic Sec.: CAROLINA THOMPSON
Chief Librarian: Prof. ROSA MURILLO DE
ROUSSEAUX
Library of 4,300 vols
Number of teachers: 222
Number of students: 2,580
Publication: *Ucurrencias*

DEANS

Faculty of Agronomy: Ing. CARMEN BLÁZQUEZ
Faculty of Architecture: Arq. CRISTINA BONUS
Faculty of Communication Sciences and
Education: Dr LUIS A. CERRUDO
Faculty of Economics: Cr MARCELO GRANILLO
Faculty of Judicial and Social Sciences: Dr
FEDERICO LACAVA

UNIVERSIDAD DE LA MARINA MERCANTE
(University of the Merchant Navy)

Avda Rivadavia 2258, C1034ACO Buenos
Aires
Telephone: (11) 4953-9000
Fax: (11) 4953-9000
E-mail: info@udemm.edu.ar
Internet: www.udemm.edu.ar
Founded 1974
Private control
Academic year: March to December
Pres.: Ing. GUSTAVO ZOPATTI
Rector: Dr NORBERTO E. FRAGA
Gen.-Sec.: Lic. MIRKO E. MAYER
Admin. Sec.: Dr DANTE STERRANTINO
Number of teachers: 283
Number of students: 2,164

DEANS

Faculty of Administration and Economics:
Lic. SILVIA ISABEL GÓMEZ MEANA
Faculty of Engineering: Ing. VICENTE GIMÉ-
NEZ
Faculty of Humanities: Lic. CLAUDIA ETKYN
(acting)
Faculty of Law, Social Sciences and Commu-
nication: Lic. HECTOR NAREDO

UNIVERSIDAD DE MENDOZA

Avda Boulogne-sur-Mer 683, 5500 Mendoza
Telephone: (261) 420-2017
Fax: (261) 420-1100
E-mail: rectorado@um.edu.ar
Internet: www.um.edu.ar
Founded 1960
Language of instruction: Spanish
Academic year: March to November
Rector: Dr JUAN C. MENGHINI
Vice-Rectors: Dr Ing. SATURNINO LEGUIZA-
MÓN, Arq. RICARDO PEROTTI
Admin. Officer: ROSA CELESTE
Number of teachers: 785
Number of students: 6,249
Publications: *Idearium, Ideas, Revista*

DEANS

Faculty of Architecture and Town Planning: Arq. RICARDO BEKERMAN
Faculty of Engineering: Dr Ing. SALVADOR NAVARRÍA
Faculty of Health Sciences: Dr JUAN CARLOS BEHLER
Faculty of Law and Social Sciences: Dr EMILIO VÁZQUEZ VIERA

DIRECTORS

Centre of Higher Research: Dr JUAN C. MENGHINI
Department of Evaluation: Arq. CRISTINA INZIRILLO
Department of Scientific Research: Dr Ing. SATURNINO LEGUIZAMÓN
Department of Technology: Ing. DIEGO NAVARRO
Institute of Architectural Technology: Arq. RICARDO BEKERMAN
Institute of Architectural and Urban Culture: Arq. ELIANA BORMIDA
Institute of Design: Dr AURELIO ALVAREZ CAMPI
Institute of Energy: Ing. RUTH GRAVINA
Institute of Environmental, Urban and Regional Research: Arq. RAÚL AMPRIMO
Institute of Informatics: Arq. OSCAR GARCÍA VILA
Institute of Natural Sciences: Prof. RUTH LEITON
Institute of Practical Philosophy: Dr NOLBERTO ESPINOSA
Institute of Private Law: Dra CATALINA A. DERONCHIETTO
Institute of Public Law: (vacant)
Institute of Social Housing: Arq. ALFREDO MÉNDEZ
Institute of Telecommunications: Ing. JORGE MARTÍNEZ
Institute of Virtual Technology: Lic. DANIEL LILLO

UNIVERSIDAD DE MORÓN

Cabildo 134, B1708JPD Morón, Buenos Aires
Telephone: (11) 5627-2000
Fax: (11) 5627-4598
E-mail: postmaster@unimoron.edu.ar
Internet: www.unimoron.edu.ar
Founded 1960
Private control
Academic year: March to December
Rector: Dr HÉCTOR NORBERTO PORTO LEMMA
Sec.-Gen.: Dr JOSÉ MARIA BAÑOS
Sec. (Academic and Research): Dr EDUARDO NÉSTOR COZZA
Sec. (Admin.): Dr JORGE EDUARDO MARCOS
Library Dir: Dr GRACIELA SUSANA PUENTE
Library of 40,000 vols
Number of teachers: 2,000
Number of students: 15,140
Publication: *UM Saber* (24 a year)

DEANS AND DIRECTORS

Faculty of Agronomy and Food Sciences: Ing. Agr. ANTONIO ANGRISANI
Faculty of Architecture, Design, Art and Urban Planning: Arq. OSCAR ANIBAL BORRACHIA
Faculty of Computer Sciences, Communication Sciences and Special Technology: Ing. HUGO RENÉ PADOVANI
Faculty of Economic and Business Sciences: Dr JORGE RAÚL LEMOS
Faculty of Engineering: Dr Ing. EZEQUIEL PALLEJÁ
Faculty of Exact, Chemical and Natural Sciences: Dr AQUILES CARLOS FERRANTI
Faculty of Law, Political and Social Sciences: Dr HÉCTOR NORBERTO PORTO LEMMA
Faculty of Medicine: Dr DOMINGO SANTOS LIOTTA

Faculty of Philosophy, Education and Humanities: Dr ROBERTO MARIO PATERNO
Faculty of Sciences applied to Tourism and Population: Lic. ALEJANDRO GAVRIC
High School of Social Services: Lic. MARÍA CRISTINA DEVITA

UNIVERSIDAD DEL MUSEO SOCIAL ARGENTINO
(University of the Argentine Museum of Sociology)

Avda Corrientes 1723, C1042AAD Buenos Aires
Telephone: (11) 5530-7600
Fax: (11) 5530-7614
E-mail: informes@umsa.edu.ar
Internet: www.umsa.edu.ar
Founded 1912
Rector: Dr GUILLERMO E. GARBARINI ISLAS
Librarian: Lic. GABRIEL MEDINA ERNST
Number of students: 3,591

DEANS

Faculty of Human Recovery Sciences: Lic. ESTELA SALAZAR
Faculty of Information and Opinion Science: Lic. ADRIANA ADAMO
Faculty of Political, Juridical and Economic Sciences: Dr LUIS J. ZABALLA
Faculty of Social Services: Dr GUSTAVO PINARD
School of Economics: ELBA FONT DE MALUGANI
Institute of Political Sciences: Dra MARTA BIAGI
Institute of Professional Training: Lic. MARIA E. PELLANDA
University School of Translation: Lic. ALICIA BERMOLEN

UNIVERSIDAD DEL NORTE SANTO TOMÁS DE AQUINO

9 de Julio 165, T4000IHC San Miguel de Tucumán
Telephone: (381) 430-0698
Fax: (381) 422-4494
E-mail: info@unsta.edu.ar
Internet: www.unsta.edu.ar
Founded 1965
Academic year: March to November
Grand Chancellor: Fr JAVIER POSE
Rector: Dr LUIS RAÚL ALCALDE
Vice-Rector: Ing. RAFAEL ROBERTO CUNSULO
Gen.-Sec.: Ing. JUAN C. MUZZO
Acad. Sec.: Lic. JORGE ABATTE
Dir of the Library: LILIAN GARTNER
Number of teachers: 700
Number of students: 6,282

DEANS

Faculty of Economics and Administration: GUILLERMO JORGE DI LELLA
Faculty of Engineering: (vacant)
Faculty of Humanities: Lic. JUAN JOSE HERRERA
Faculty of Law and Political Sciences: Dra MARIA GILDA PEDICONE DE VALLS
Faculty of Philosophy: Fr JORGE SCAMPINI
Faculty of Psychology and Health Sciences: Dr BERNARDO CARLINO

UNIVERSIDAD NOTARIAL ARGENTINA
(Argentine University for Lawyers)

Avda 51 No. 435, 1900 La Plata
Telephone: (221) 421-9283
Fax: (221) 421-0552
E-mail: uninotlp@universidadnotarial.edu.ar
Internet: www.universidadnotarial.edu.ar
Founded 1964
Academic year: March to November

Chancellor: Not. JORGE F. DUMON
Rector: NÉSTOR O. PÉREZ LOZANO
Vice-Rector: Dr CRISTINA NOEMÍ ARMELLA
General Director: Prof. ALICIA PALAIA
Librarian: Dra DORA C. TÁLICE DE SECO VILLALBA
Number of teachers: 150
Number of students: 2,300
Publication: *Cuadernos Notariales*.

UNIVERSIDAD DEL SALVADOR
(University of the Saviour)

Viamonte 1856, 1056 Buenos Aires
Telephone: (11) 4813-9630
E-mail: uds-secr@salvador.edu.ar
Internet: www.salvador.edu.ar
Founded 1956
Academic year: January to December
Rector: Lic. JUAN ALEJANDRO TOBIAS
Academic Vice-Rector: Lic. JAVIER ALONSO HIDALGO
Vice-Rector (Economics): Dr ENRIQUE A. BETTA
Vice-Rector (Religious Training): Lic. JUAN ALEJANDRO TOBIAS (acting)
Vice-Rector (Research and Devt): Dr FERNANDO LUCERO SCHMIDT
Sec.-Gen.: Prof. PABLO GABRIEL VARELA
Librarian: Lic. LAURA MARTINO
Library: see under Libraries and Archives
Number of teachers: 2,800
Number of students: 16,500
Publications: *Anales*, *Bulletin of Number Theory and Related Topics*, *Signos*

DEANS

Faculty of Administration: Ing. AQUILINO LÓPEZ DIEZ
Faculty of Economics: Dr SERGIO GARCÍA
Faculty of Educational Sciences and Social Communication: Dr GUSTAVO MARTÍNEZ PANDIANJ
Faculty of Law: Dr PRÁXEDES SAGASTA
Faculty of Medicine: Dr ADOLFO LIZARRAGA
Faculty of Philosophy, History and Arts: Dr JUAN CARLOS LUCERO SCHMIDT
Faculty of Psychology and Psychopedagogy: Lic. BERNARDO BÉGUET
Faculty of Science and Technology: Ing. MIGUEL GUERRERO
Faculty of Social Sciences: Lic. EDUARDO SUÁREZ

DIRECTORS

School of Oriental Studies: Prof. LUISA ROSELL
School of Theatre Arts: Prof. ALICE D. DE BEITÍA

National University-Level Institutions
INSTITUTO DE ENSEÑANZA SUPERIOR DEL EJÉRCITO
(Institute of Higher Military Education)

Avda Cabildo 65, 1426 Buenos Aires
Telephone: (11) 4576-5648
E-mail: dieseext@iese.edu.ar
Internet: www.iese.edu.ar
Founded 1990
State control
Dir: Dr LUIS EDUARDO PIERRI
Vice-Rector: Col MIGUEL ANGEL PODESTÁ
Sec.-Gen.: Lt-Col Dr VICTORIO CÁNDIDO FONTANA
Sec. (Academic): Col Dr JULIO HORACIO BERGALLO

Sec. (Evaluation): Col Dr HECTOR EDUARDO GALLARDO

Sec. (Univ. Extension): Col Dr ALEJANDRO ALBERTO DIAZ BESSONE

Depts of distance learning, information technology and modern languages.

CONSTITUENT SCHOOLS

Colegio Militar de la Nación: Avda Matienzo y Ruta 201, 1684 El Palomar, Buenos Aires; tel. (11) 4751-8001; fax (11) 4751-0767; e-mail ingresocmn@ejercito.mil.ar; internet www.colegiomilitar.mil.ar; f. 1869.

Escuela Superior de Guerra: Avda Luis María Campos 480, 1426 Buenos Aires; tel. (11) 4576-5689; fax (11) 4576-5692; e-mail esg@iese.edu.ar; internet www.escuelasuperiordeguerra.iese.edu.ar; f. 1900; library of 30,000 vols, 44 periodicals; Dir Col RAÚL ALBERTO APARICIO; publ. *La Revista* (4 a year).

Escuela Superior Técnica: Avda Cabildo 15, 1426 Buenos Aires, Capital Federal; tel. (11) 4576-5555; fax (11) 4576-5681; e-mail estextuniv@iese.edu.ar; internet www.ingenieriaest.iese.edu.ar; f. 1930; library of 30,000 vols, 100 periodicals; Dir Col JORGE GÓMEZ; publ. *Ingeniería Militar*.

INSTITUTO UNIVERSITARIO AERONÁUTICO

Avda Fuerza Aérea 6500, 5022 Córdoba

Telephone: (351) 568-8800

Fax: (351) 466-1562

E-mail: informes@iua.edu.ar

Internet: www.iua.edu.ar

Founded 1947, integrated into Nat. Univ. System 1971

State control

Language of instruction: Spanish

Academic year: February to December

Rector: Brig. Ing. HÉCTOR EDUARDO RÉ

Vice-Rector (Academic): Cmdr Ing. MIGUEL ANGEL LLABRES

Vice-Rector (Planning): Brig. Ing. ROBERTO ANÍBAL GÓMEZ

Sec.-Gen.: Ing. PEDRO EMILIO MURILLO

Library of 10,000 vols

Associated academic units: Escuela de Aviación Militar, Escuela de Defensa Electrónica, Escuela de Ciencias De La Salud, Escuela De Suboficiales de la Fuerza Aérea;Instituto Nacional de Aviación Civil, Instituto Nacional de Derecho Aeronautico y Espacial, Instituto de Formación Ezeiza; Liceo Aeronáutico Militar, Perfeccionamiento y Experimentación; Unidad de Educación a Distancia en el Exterior.

DEANS

Faculty of Administration: Brig. Ing. ROBERTO ANÍBAL GÓMEZ

Faculty of Engineering: Brig. Ing. FERNANDO ANÍBAL ALVAREZ

INSTITUTO UNIVERSITARIO DE LA POLICÍA FEDERAL ARGENTINA

Rosario 532, 1424 Buenos Aires, Capital Federal

Telephone: (11) 4901-9783

Fax: (11) 4901-9783

E-mail: academica@universidad-policial.edu.ar

Internet: www.universidad-policial.edu.ar

Founded 1974 as Academia Federal de Estudios Policiales; current name and status since 1995

State control

Academic year: March to December (two semesters)

Rector: Dr LUIS MARÍA DESIMONI

Vice-Rector: Lic. CARLOS DANIEL MUSSO

Sec. (Academic): Dr HUGO ALBERTO MÉNDEZ

Sec. (Admin.): Com. Gen. ANGEL JUAN ANTONIO RAMÍREZ

Library of 20,500 vols

Number of students: 3,200

Publication: *Editorial Policial*

DEANS

Faculty of Biomedical Sciences: Dr ENRIQUE LAFRENZ

Faculty of Criminal Sciences: Lic. NORBERTO ANTONIO SANCHEZ

Faculty of Law and Social Sciences: Dr HORACIO TOMAS ARACAMA

Faculty of Security Sciences: Gen. ROBERTO CÉSAR ROSSET

INSTITUTO UNIVERSITARIO DE SEGURIDAD MARÍTIMA

Avda Eduardo Madero 235, 1106 Buenos Aires, Capital Federal

Telephone: (11) 4314-2434

E-mail: arl@arnet.com.ar

Internet: www.prefecturanaval.edu.ar/iupna

Founded 2002

Rector: Prefecto Gen. OSVALDO DANIEL TOURN

Sec. (Academic): Lic. AMALIA INÉS VILLALUSTRE.

INSTITUTO UNIVERSITARIO NACIONAL DEL ARTE

Paraguay 786, 1057 Buenos Aires, Capital Federal

Telephone: (11) 4516-0992

Fax: (11) 4516-0992

Internet: www.iuna.edu.ar

Founded 1996

State control

Rector: Lic. RAÚL OSVALDO MONETA

Sec.-Gen.: Prof. ROBERTO DE ROSE

Publication: *Boletín*.

INSTITUTO UNIVERSITARIO NAVAL

Avda del Libertador 8209, 1429 Buenos Aires, Capital Federal

Telephone: (11) 4704-8200

Fax: (11) 4704-8261

E-mail: administra@inun.edu.ar

Internet: www.inun.edu.ar

Founded 1978 as Instituto Universitario de Estudios Navales y Martimes; current name and status 1991

Controlled by the Armada Argentina (Argentine Navy)

Rector: Ing. JULIO MARCELO PÉREZ

Sec. (Academic): Lic. JULIO E. GROSSO

DIRECTORS

School of Marine Sciences: DANIEL HINDRYCKX

School of Military Naval Studies: CARLOS LUIS MAZZONI

School of Nautical Science: ARMANDO GROSO

School of Navy Officer Studies: EDUARDO OSCAR GUELFO

School of Navy Warfare: PEDRO LUIS DE LA FUENTE

Provincial University

UNIVERSIDAD AUTÓNOMA DE ENTRE RÍOS

Avda Ramírez 1143, 3100 Paraná, Entre Ríos

Telephone: (343) 431-4284

Fax: (343) 420-7880

E-mail: rectorado@uader.edu.ar

Internet: www.uader.edu.ar

Independent control

Rector: Lic. Mag. GRACIELA MINGO DE BEVILACQUA

Sec. (Academic Affairs): Prof SUSANA RIVAS

Sec. (Extension and Student Welfare): ANÍBAL SATTLER

Sec. (Science and Technology): FRANCISCO CACIK.

Colleges

Escuela Nacional de Bibliotecarios: Agüero 2502, 1425 Buenos Aires; tel. (11) 4808-6095; fax (11) 4863-8805; e-mail escuelabib@red.bibnal.edu.ar; internet www.bibnal.edu.ar/paginas/escuelabib.htm; f. 1956; 15 teachers; Rector Prof. JOSÉ EDMUNDO CLEMENTE.

Escuela Nacional de Educación Técnica 'Gral Ing. Enrique Mosconi': Calle Schreiber 892 Cutralco, 8318 Plaza Huincul, Neuquén; tel. (299) 46-3288; f. 1953; specializes in mechanical and petroleum engineering; 600 students; Dir Ing. ARMANDO PARIS.

Instituto Tecnológico de Buenos Aires: Avda Eduardo Madero 399, 1106 Buenos Aires; tel. (11) 4314-7778; fax (11) 4314-0270; e-mail postmaster@itba.edu.ar; internet www.itba.edu.ar; f. 1959; private; library: 16,010 books; 350 teachers; 2,010 students; Rector Almirante Dr ENRIQUE E. MOLINA PICO; publs *Acontecer*, *Boletín General*, *Revista del Instituto Tecnológico de Buenos Aires*.

Schools of Art and Music

Conservatorio Superior de Música 'Manuel de Falla': Gallo 238, 2° piso, Buenos Aires; tel. (11) 4865-9005; f. 1919; 3,000 mems; library: 8,000 scores and vols; Dir AUGUSTO B. RATTENBACH.

Escuela Nacional de Arte Dramático (National School of Drama): French 3614, 1425 Buenos Aires; tel. (11) 4804-7970; f. 1924; 300 students; library: 4,200 vols; Rector CARLOS ALBARENGA.

Escuela Nacional de Bellas Artes 'Prilidiano Pueyrredón': Las Heras 1749, 1018 Buenos Aires; tel. (11) 442-0657; f. 1878; depts of painting, engraving and sculpture; library: 5,923 vols; 373 students; Dir DOMINGO MAZZONE.

Escuela Nacional de Danzas: Esmeralda 285, 1035 Buenos Aires; tel. (11) 445-5478; Rector Prof. GLADYS S. DE MUTTER.

Escuela Superior de Bellas Artes 'Ernesto de la Cárcova': Tristán Achaval Rodríguez 1701, 1107 Buenos Aires; tel. (11) 4361-5144; f. 1923; painting, sculpture, engraving and décors; museum of tracings; library: 4,500 vols; Rector Prof. EDUARDO A. AUDIVERT.

ARMENIA

The Higher Education System

The oldest university in Armenia is the Yerevan State University, which was founded in 1919. Most institutions of higher education were founded while Armenia was a full Union Republic of the Union of Soviet Socialist Republics (USSR). Armenia declared independence from the USSR in 1991. Higher education is overseen by the Ministry of Education and Science, and is governed by the constitution (1995), which states that all citizens have the right to receive an education, and by the Law on Education (1999), which outlines the system's structure. In 2000 the National Assembly approved the State Programme for Education Sector Development 2001–05, which outlined a five-year programme of reforms aimed at rationalizing and modernizing the entire education system. In 2002 the Law on Higher and Postgraduate Professional Education (2002) was passed, outlining the reforms to prepare Armenia for the Bologna Process, which it joined in 2005. The Eurasia International University has fully conformed to the requirements of the Bologna Process since 2007.

To enter higher education students must hold the Mijnakarg Yndhanur Krtoutian Attestat (Certificate of Completed Secondary Education) and pass at least one university entrance examination one month after their high school examinations, depending upon their intended area of study. However, as part of higher education reforms, an independent body is to be established to administer university entrance examinations in place of the ministry.

There are three levels of higher education degrees in Armenia, one undergraduate and two postgraduate. The main undergraduate degree is the Bakalavr (Bachelors), which is usually a four-year programme. In line with the reforms of the Bologna Process the Government has been introducing the European Credit Transfer System (ECTS) since 2002–2003. The Specialist Diploma, meanwhile, is a Soviet-style degree, which lasts for five years and is offered at professional institutions. From 2007–2008 higher education institutions issued the Diploma Supplement to students graduating from first and second cycle programmes. The first postgraduate degree is the Magistros (Masters), a one- or two-year course, admission to which is by examination. The second and final level of postgraduate education is the Aspirantura (Doctorate), which is split into two stages: the Candidate of Science and the Doctor of Science. The first stage lasts for two years and consists of taught and research components, while the second stage is purely research and necessary only for those who wish to pursue a career in higher education.

The first level of non-university technical and vocational education is Preliminary Professional (Vocational) Education and is open to holders of the Himnakan Yndhanur Krtutyan Attestat (Certificate of Basic Education) or the Certificate of Completed Secondary Education. Courses run for between one and three years. The second level of technical and vocational education is known as Middle Level Professional (Vocational) Education and is open to holders of the Certificate of Completed Secondary Education. The principal aim is to train specialists in fields such as the arts, finance, health, the humanities, pedagogy and technology. Training may last between two and five years. Upon qualification students gain the title Junior Specialist. There are also two levels of teacher training: Junior Specialist for primary and basic school teaching; and Bachelors or Specialist Diploma for secondary school teaching.

The Licensing and Accreditation Service, founded in 2000 as a separate unit under the aegis of the Ministry of Education and Science, is responsible for the licensing and accreditation of all public and private institutions under the terms of the Law on Education (1999). The final decision on the licensing and accreditation of an institution, however, lies with the Minister of Education and Science for approval. In 2008/09 114,400 students were enrolled at one of the 90 higher education institutions (including universities).

Regulatory and Representative Bodies

GOVERNMENT

Ministry of Culture: 0010 Yerevan, Republic Sq. 1, Govt House 3; tel. (10) 52-93-49; fax (10) 52-39-22; e-mail mincult@xter.net; Minister HASMIK POGHOSSIAN.

Ministry of Education and Science: 0010 Yerevan, Main Ave, Govt House 3; tel. (10) 52-66-02; fax (10) 52-73-43; e-mail minister@edu.am; internet www.edu.am; Minister ARMEN ASHOTYAN.

ACCREDITATION

ENIC/NARIC Armenia: Nat. Information Centre for Academic Recognition and Mobility, 0070 Yerevan, Vratsyan 73; tel. and fax (10) 57-84-56; e-mail armenic@cornet.am; internet www.armenic.am; f. 2006; provides information, advice and formal decision on recognition of international qualifications; information centre for recognition and internationalization of education; facilitates int. integration of the nat. education system into worldwide educational services; promotes mobility; supports devt of int. cooperation between educational institutions and other sectors; Exec. Dir Dr GAYANE HARUTYUNYAN; Evaluation Expert HASMIK TALALYAN; Evaluation Expert NAREK KOSYAN; Evaluation Expert RAFIK HAKOBYAN.

Learned Societies

GENERAL

National Academy of Sciences of Armenia: 0019 Yerevan, Marshal Baghramyan Ave 24; tel. (10) 52-70-31; fax (10) 56-92-81; e-mail academy@sci.am; internet www.sci.am; f. 1943; depts of Physical, Mathematical and Technological Sciences, Natural Sciences, Humanities; research institutes attached to depts: see Research Institutes; 119 mems; Pres. F. T. SARGASIAN; Acad.-Sec. and Vice-Pres. V. B. BARKHUDARIAN; publs *Astrofizika* (Astrophysics), *Biologicheskii Zhurnal Armenii* (Biological Journal of Armenia), *Doklady* (Reports), *Istoriko-Filologicheskii Zhurnal* (Historical and Philological Journal), *Izvestiya* (Bulletins: Mathematics, Mechanics, Physics, Engineering Sciences, Earth Sciences), *Khimicheskii Zhurnal Armenii* (Chemical Journal of Armenia), *Meditsinskaya Nauka Armenii* (Medical Science of Armenia), *Neirokhimiya* (Neurochemistry), *Soobshcheniya Byurakanskoi Observatorii* (Reports of the Byurakan Astrophysical Observatory), *Vestnik Khirurgii Armenii* (Herald of Armenian Surgery), *Vestnik Obshchestvennykh Nauk* (Herald of Social Sciences).

LANGUAGE AND LITERATURE

Alliance Française: 0010 Yerevan, ul. Aigestan 74; tel. and fax (10) 52-04-01; e-mail alliancefr_arm@hotmail.com; offers courses and examinations in French language and culture and promotes cultural exchange with France.

British Council: 0019 Yerevan, Baghramian Ave 24; tel. (10) 56-99-23; fax (10) 56-99-29; e-mail info@britishcouncil.am; internet www2.britishcouncil.org/armenia.htm; offers courses and examinations in English language and British culture and promotes cultural exchange with the UK; Dir ROGER BUDD.

Research Institutes

GENERAL

Institute of the Arts: 0019 Yerevan, Pr. Marshala Bagramyana 24G; tel. (10) 58-37-02; fax (10) 52-83-18; e-mail instart@sci.am; f. 1958; attached to Nat. Acad. of Sciences of Armenia; depts of Architecture, Fine Arts, Folk Arts, Music, Theatre and Cinema; Dir A. AGHASYAN.

AGRICULTURE, FISHERIES AND VETERINARY SCIENCE

Institute of Hydroponics Problems: 0082 Yerevan, Noragyugh 108; tel. (10) 56-51-62;

fax (10) 56-55-90; e-mail hydrop@netsys.am; internet www.sci.am; f. 1947; attached to Nat. Acad. of Sciences of Armenia; devt of basic science and technology for hydroponic cultivation of valuable, rare and endangered medicinal, aromatic and dye-bearing plants, trees and shrubs; 47 mems; library of 9,500 vols; Dir Dr KHACHATUR MAIRAPETYAN; publ. *Communications of IHP* (every 3 years).

Scientific Centre of Agriculture and Plant Protection: 1110 Echmiadzin, Armavir Marz, St Isy le Moulino St 1; tel. (23) 15-34-54; attached to Min. of Agriculture; 143 staff, 6 depts, 11 laboratories; Dir H. HOVSEPIAN.

ECONOMICS, LAW AND POLITICS

Armenian Centre for National and International Studies: 0033 Yerevan, Yerznkian St 75; tel. (10) 52-87-80; fax (10) 52-48-46; e-mail root@acnis.am; internet www.acnis.am; f. 1994 to research issues of public policy, civic education, foreign relations, conflict resolution and the global environment; 25 mems; library of 4,200 vols; Founder and Pres. Dr RAFFI HOVANNISIAN.

Institute of Economics: 0001 Yerevan, ul. Abovyana 15; tel. (10) 58-19-71; fax (10) 56-92-81; e-mail nas_ie@sci.am; f. 1955; attached to Nat. Acad. of Sciences of Armenia; Dir V. E. KHOJABEKYAN.

HISTORY, GEOGRAPHY AND ARCHAEOLOGY

Institute–Museum of Genocide: 0028 Yerevan, Tsitsernakaberd; tel. (10) 39-09-81; e-mail lbars@sci.am; f. 1995; attached to Nat. Acad. of Sciences of Armenia; Dir L. A. BARSEGHYAN.

Institute of Archaeology and Ethnography: 0025 Yerevan, Charents 15; tel. and fax (10) 55-68-96; f. 1959; attached to Nat. Acad. of Sciences of Armenia; library of 15,000 vols; Dir A. A. KALANTARYAN.

Institute of History: 0019 Yerevan, Pr. Marshala Bagramyana 24G; tel. (10) 52-92-63; fax (10) 56-92-81; e-mail history@sci.am; f. 1943; attached to Nat. Acad. of Sciences of Armenia; Dir A. MELKONYAN.

Institute of Oriental Studies: 0019 Yerevan, Pr. Marshala Bagramyana 24G; tel. (10) 58-33-82; e-mail info@orient.sci.am; internet www.orient.sci.am; f. 1971; attached to Nat. Acad. of Sciences of Armenia; history, sociopolitical, int. and regional relations, culture, religion, problems of nat. minorities and ethnic groups of Middle East, Caucasus and Eastern Asia from antiquity to present; 65 mems; library of 60,000 vols; Dir Dr RUBEN A. SAFRASTYAN; Deputy Dir Dr PAVEL A. CHOBANYAN; publs *Near East: History, Politics, Culture, The Countries and Peoples of the Near and Middle East, Turcic and Ottoman Studies*.

Shirak Armenological Study Centre: 3100 Gyumri, Ankakhutyan Sq. 1; tel. (31) 13-31-73; fax (31) 56-92-81; e-mail academy@sci.am; f. 1997; attached to Nat. Acad. of Sciences of Armenia; Dir S. HAYRAPETYAN.

LANGUAGE AND LITERATURE

Abegyan Institute of Literature: 0015 Yerevan, ul. Grikora Lusavoricha 15; tel. (10) 56-32-54; fax (10) 56-32-54; f. 1943; attached to Nat. Acad. of Sciences of Armenia; Dir A. K. EGHIAZARYAN.

Atcharian Institute of Linguistics: 0001 Yerevan, ul. Abovyana 15; tel. (10) 56-53-37; fax (10) 56-92-81; e-mail inslang@sci.am; f. 1943; attached to Nat. Acad. of Sciences of Armenia; Dir G. B. DJAUKYAN.

MEDICINE

Armenian Institute of Spa Treatment and Physiotherapy: 0028 Yerevan, ul. Bratev Orbeli 41; internet www.medlib.am/spa; f. 1930; library of 30,000 vols; Dir Prof. G. AGADJANIAN.

Armenian Research Centre of Maternal and Child Health Care: 0002 Yerevan, Mesrop Mashtots Ave 22; tel. (10) 53-01-72; fax (10) 53-01-92; internet www.armobgyn.com; f. 1931; library of 25,000 vols; Dir Prof. G. OKOYEV.

Centre of Medical Genetics: 0010 Yerevan, Zakyan St 5/1; tel. (10) 54-43-67; fax (10) 56-92-81; e-mail tamsar@sci.am; f. 1999; attached to Nat. Acad. of Sciences of Armenia; Dir Dr T. F. SARGSIAN.

Centre of Traumatology, Orthopaedics, Burns and Radiology: 0047 Yerevan, Marash 9th St; tel. (10) 65-00-40; fax (10) 65-30-40; internet www.ctooir.narod.ru; f. 1945; fmrly Yerevan Scientific Research Institute of Orthopaedics and Traumatology; functioning depts: acute trauma, polytrauma, post-traumatic complications, infection complication, bone pathology, adult orthopaedics, paediatric orthopaedics, morphology, experimental biology; research depts: bone defect reconstruction, joint replacement, vertebral surgery, bone matrix preparation, bone tumour surgery, complex burns treatment; 28 mems; Dir AIVAZYAN VACHAGAN; publ. *Abstracts of Annual Congress of Traumatologists & Orthopaedic Surgeons of Armenia* (1 a year).

Mikaelian Research Institute of Surgery: Yerevan, Hasratyan 9; tel. (10) 28-19-90; fax (10) 28-22-22; e-mail surgery@netsys.am; f. 1974; library of 5,000 vols; Dir H. S. TAMAZIAN.

Research Centre for Epidemiology, Virology and Medical Parasitology: 0009 Yerevan, ul. Gevorga Kochara 21A; tel. (10) 56-21-02; Dir YU. T. ALEKSANYAN.

NATURAL SCIENCES

Biological Sciences

Buniatian, H., Institute of Biochemistry: 0014 Yerevan, Paruyra Sevak Str. 5/1; tel. (10) 29-73-44; fax (10) 28-19-51; e-mail galoyan@sci.am; f. 1961; attached to Nat. Acad. of Sciences of Armenia; Councillor to the Institute of Biochemistry Prof. Dr ARMEN GALOYAN; publ. *Neurokhimija* (4 a year).

Centre for Ecological–Noosphere Studies: 0025 Yerevan, Abovian 68; tel. (10) 56-93-31; fax (10) 58-02-54; e-mail ecocentr@sci.am; internet www.ecocentre.am; f. 1989; attached to Nat. Acad. of Sciences of Armenia; research area: environment; assessment of natural resources; Dir ARMEN SAGHATELYAN.

Institute of Botany: 0063 Yerevan, Avan; tel. (10) 62-17-81; fax (10) 56-92-81; e-mail academy@sci.am; f. 1939; attached to Nat. Acad. of Sciences of Armenia; Dir A. A. CHARCHOGLYAN.

Institute of Microbiology: 2201 Abovian; tel. and fax (222) 2-00-73; e-mail microbio@sci.am; f. 1961; attached to Nat. Acad. of Sciences of Armenia; library of 5,000 vols; Dir L. S. MARKOSYAN.

Institute of Molecular Biology: 0014 Yerevan, Hasratyan 7; tel. (10) 28-16-26; fax (10) 28-26-22; e-mail aboyajyan@sci.am; internet molbiol.sci.am; f. 1966; attached to Nat. Acad. of Sciences of Armenia; Dir Prof. ANNA BOYAJYAN; Deputy Dir ARSEN ARAKELYAN.

Institute of Zoology: 0044 Yerevan, ul. Paruyra Sevaka 7; tel. (10) 28-14-70; fax (10) 28-13-60; e-mail zool@sci.am; f. 1943;

attached to Nat. Acad. of Sciences of Armenia; Dir S. H. MOVSESIAN.

Orbeli Institute of Physiology: 375028 Yerevan, Orbeli Bros St 22; tel. and fax (10) 27-38-61; fax (10) 27-22-47; e-mail vsargsyan@neuroscience.am; f. 1943; attached to Nat. Acad. of Sciences of Armenia; library of 4,000 vols; Dir V. V. FANARDJIAN.

Sevan Institute of Hydroecology and Ichthyology: 1510 Sevan, ul. Kirova 186; tel. (10) 56-85-54; fax (10) 56-94-11; e-mail rhovan@sci.am; f. 1923; attached to Nat. Acad. of Sciences of Armenia; Dir R. HOVHANNISYAN.

State Microbial Depository Centre: 2201 Abovian; tel. and fax (222) 2-32-40; e-mail microbio@sci.am; internet www.rcdm.am; f. 1993; attached to Nat. Acad. of Sciences of Armenia; library of 22,000 vols; Dir E. G. AFRIKIAN.

Mathematical Sciences

Institute of Mathematics: 0019 Yerevan, Marshala Bagramyana 24B; tel. (10) 52-47-91; fax (10) 52-48-01; e-mail rafayel@instmath.sci.am; internet math.sci.am; f. 1971; 40 mems; attached to Nat. Acad. of Sciences of Armenia; Dir Prof. Dr BAGRAT T. BATIKYAN; Scientific Sec. Dr RAFAYEL H. BARKHUDARYAN; publs *Armenian Journal of Mathematics* (4 a year), *Journal of Contemporary Mathematical Analysis* (6 a year).

Physical Sciences

Byurakan Astrophysical Observatory: 0213 Byurakan, Ashtarak raion; tel. (10) 24-85-75; fax (10) 56-92-81; e-mail ekhach@bao.sci.am; internet www.sci.am/ac/bao.html; f. 1946; attached to Nat. Acad. of Sciences of Armenia; Dir E. KHACHIKIAN.

Garni Geophysical Observatory: 0019 Yerevan, Pr. Marshal Baghramyana 24A; tel. (10) 52-54-61; fax (10) 56-92-81; e-mail romella.pashayan@geology.am; f. 1982; attached to Nat. Acad. of Sciences of Armenia; Dir L. A. HAKHVERDYAN.

Garni Space Astronomy Institute: 2215 Garni, Kotayk; tel. (10) 64-90-01; fax (10) 56-92-81; f. 1982; attached to Nat. Acad. of Sciences of Armenia; Dir G. A. GURZADYAN.

Institute of Chemical Physics: 0014 Yerevan, ul. Paruyra Sevak 5/2; tel. (10) 28-14-81; fax (10) 29-73-09; e-mail tavadyan@ichph.sci.am; internet www.chph.sci.am; f. 1975; attached to Nat. Acad. of Sciences of Armenia; library of 33,410 vols; Dir Prof. LEVOM TAVADYAN.

Institute of Fine Organic Chemistry: 0014 Yerevan, Pr. Azatutyana 26; tel. (10) 28-83-34; fax (10) 28-83-32; e-mail ifoc@msrc.am; f. 1955; attached to Nat. Acad. of Sciences of Armenia; Dir B. T. GHARIBJANIAN.

Institute of General and Inorganic Chemistry: 0051 Yerevan, ul. Fioletova 11110; tel. (10) 23-07-38; fax (10) 23-12-75; f. 1957; attached to Nat. Acad. of Sciences of Armenia; Dir S. S. KARAKHANIAN.

Institute of Geology: 0019 Yerevan, Pr. Marshala Bagramyana 24A; tel. (10) 52-44-26; fax (10) 56-80-72; e-mail hrshah@sci.am; f. 1935; attached to Nat. Acad. of Sciences of Armenia; Dir R. T. JRBASHIAN.

Institute of Geophysics and Engineering Seismology: 3115 Gjumry, Pr. Leningradyana 5; tel. and fax (312) 3-12-61; e-mail as_iges@shirak.am; f. 1961; attached to Nat. Acad. of Sciences of Armenia; Dir S. M. HOVHANNISYAN.

Institute of Organic Chemistry: 0091 Yerevan, ul. Zakaria Kanakertsy 167A; tel. and fax (10) 28-35-21; f. 1935; attached to Nat. Acad. of Sciences of Armenia; Dir SH. H. BADANYAN.

Research Institute of Radiophysical Measurements: 0014 Yerevan, ul. Komitasa 49/4; tel. (10) 23-49-90; Dir P. M. GERUNI.

Yerevan Physics Institute: 0036 Yerevan, ul. Bratev Alikhanyan 2; tel. (10) 34-15-00; fax (10) 35-00-30; internet www.yerphi.am; f. 1942; particle and nuclear physics; library of 10,000 vols; Dir H. ASATRIAN.

PHILOSOPHY AND PSYCHOLOGY

Institute of Philosophy, Sociology and Law: 375010 Yerevan, Aram St 44; tel. (10) 53-05-71; fax (10) 53-10-96; e-mail gevork@sci.am; internet www.ipsol.sci.am; f. 1969; attached to Nat. Acad. of Sciences of Armenia; scientific research on philosophy, history of Armenian philosophy, aesthetics, Armenian law and history, sociology, politology and psychology; library of 6,000 vols; Dir Prof. Dr GEVORG POGHOYSAN; publ. *Science and Society*.

TECHNOLOGY

Institute for Physical Research: 0210 Ashtarak; tel. (10) 28-81-50; fax (10) 56-92-81; f. 1968; attached to Nat. Acad. of Sciences of Armenia; Dir Prof. E. S. VARDANYAN.

Institute of Applied Problems of Physics: 0014 Yerevan, Str. Hr. Nersesian 25; tel. (10) 24-58-96; fax (10) 28-18-65; e-mail amkrtchyan@sci.am; internet www.sci.am/ac/iapp.html; f. 1980; attached to Nat. Acad. of Sciences of Armenia; Dir Dr A. H. MKRTCHYAN; Scientific Sec. GURGEN K. KHACHATURYAN.

Institute of Mechanics: 0019 Yerevan, Pr. Marshala Bagramyana 24B; tel. (10) 52-48-90; fax (10) 56-81-89; e-mail mechins@sci.am; f. 1955; attached to Nat. Acad. of Sciences of Armenia; Dir L. A. AGHALOVIAN.

Institute of Problems in Informatics and Automation: 0014 Yerevan, ul. Paruyra Sevaka 1; tel. and fax (10) 28-58-12; e-mail shouk@sci.am; internet ipia.sci.am; f. 1957; attached to Nat. Acad. of Sciences of Armenia; Dir YU. H. SHOUKOURIAN.

Institute of Radiophysics and Electronics: 0210 Ashtarak, ul. Bratev Alikhanyan; tel. (10) 28-78-50; e-mail office@irphe.am; internet www.irphe.am; f. 1960; library of 12,000 vols; attached to Nat. Acad. of Sciences of Armenia; Dir R. M. MARTIROSYAM.

Special Experimental Design Technological Institute: 3101 Gjumry, Sarkisyana 5A; tel. (312) 4-56-63; fax (10) 56-92-81; e-mail academy@sci.am; f. 1976; attached to Nat. Acad. of Sciences of Armenia; Dir R. Y. SARKISSYAN.

Yerevan Automated Control Systems Scientific Research Institute: 0003 Yerevan, ul. A. Akopyana 3; tel. (10) 27-77-79; internet www.yercsi.am; f. 1992; Dir R. ATOIAN.

Yerevan Computer Research and Development Institute: 0033 Yerevan, Hagop Hagopyan 3; tel. (10) 27-77-79; fax (10) 27-68-52; e-mail ghovhan@ycrdi.am; internet www.ycrdi.am; f. 1956; Dir G. T. HOVHANNISIAN.

Yerevan Telecommunications Research Institute: 0015 Yerevan, Dzorapy 26; tel. (10) 56-60-61; fax (10) 56-17-37; e-mail mark@yetri.am; internet www.yetri.am; f. 1978.

Libraries and Archives
Yerevan

Armenian Scientific-Medical Library: Yerevan; tel. (10) 24-96-77; e-mail staff@medlib.am; internet www.medlib.am; attached to Nat. Acad. of Sciences of Arme-

nia; 500,000 vols, theses, serials, microfiche and audiovisual items; Dir A. E. SHIRINIAN.

Fundamental Scientific Library of the National Academy of Sciences of Armenia: 0019 Yerevan, Baghramyana Ave 24D; tel. and fax (10) 52-47-50; e-mail tigran@flib.sci.am; internet www.flib.sci.am; f. 1935; 3m. vols; Dir Dr TIGRAN ZARGARYAN.

Matenadaran Institute of Ancient Armenian Manuscripts: Yerevan, Mashtots Ave 53; tel. (10) 56-25-78; internet www.matenadaran.am; f. 1959; incorporates research institute of Armenian textology and codicology; 17,000 Armenian MSS dating from 5th to 18th centuries, miniature paintings, 100,000 archival documents and works by Greek, Syrian, Persian, Arabic, Latin, Georgian and Ethiopian authors; Dir S. AREVSHATIAN; publ. *Banber Matenadarani*.

National Centre of Innovation and Entrepreneurship: 0051 Yerevan, Komitas 49/3; tel. (10) 23-67-74; fax (10) 23-80-29; e-mail info@innovcentre.am; internet www.innovcentre.am; f. 1961 as Armenian Centre for Scientific and Technical Information, present name 2009; 22m. vols; 87 mems; Dir H. E. MARGARYAN; publ. *Gitutyun ev Tekhnika* (Science and Technology, online).

National Library of Armenia: 0009 Yerevan, Teryan 72; tel. (10) 58-42-59; fax (10) 52-97-11; e-mail nla@arm.r.am; internet www.nla.am; f. 1919; 6.2m. vols; Dir DAVIT SARGSYAN.

Yerevan State University Library: 0049 Yerevan, ul. Mravyana 1; internet www.ysu.am/~library; 1.5m. vols; Dir V. S. ARSLANIAN.

Museums and Art Galleries
Yerevan

Armenian State Historical Museum: 0010 Yerevan, Republic Sq. 4; tel. (10) 58-27-61; fax (10) 56-53-22; e-mail museum@cln.am; internet www.historymuseum.am; f. 1919; archaeological, ethnographical, documentary and other evidence charting history and culture of Armenia from prehistoric times; Dir ANELKA GRIGORIAN.

Geological Museum of the Institute of Geology: Yerevan, ul. Aboviana 10; tel. (10) 58-06-63; f. 1937; colln mainly from Armenia; Dir G. B. MEZHLUMYAN.

National Gallery of Armenia: 0010 Yerevan, Arami 1; tel. and fax (10) 58-08-12; e-mail galleryarmenia@yahoo.com; internet www.gallery.am; f. 1921; W European, Armenian, Russian and Oriental art; library of 10,330 vols; Dir FARAON MIRZOYAN.

Yegishe Charents State Museum of Literature and Art: Yerevan, Mashtots St 17; tel. (10) 53-55-94; fax (10) 56-36-61; f. 1921; Armenian literature (since 18th century), theatre, cinema and music; library of 84,526 vols, 862,252 MSS; Dir H. BAKHCHINYAN.

Yerevan Children's Picture Gallery: Yerevan, ul. Aboviana 13; tel. (10) 52-78-93; f. 1970; works of art by children of Armenian and other nationalities; Dir H. IKITIAN.

Universities

ABOVIAN ARMENIAN STATE PEDAGOGICAL UNIVERSITY
0070 Yerevan, Khandyjan 5
Telephone: (10) 52-26-04
Fax: (10) 56-00-82
E-mail: armped@netsys.am
Founded 1922; present status 2000
State control

Academic year: September to July
Rector: MISAK DAVTYAN
Number of teachers: 620
Number of students: 4,200
Publication: *Mankavarzh* (12 a year)

DEANS
Armenian Language and Literature: MARTIN GILAVIAN
Art and Aesthetic Education: ARKADIY SHEKUNTS
Biology and Chemistry: MEZHLUM YERITSIAN
Culture: RUBEN MIRZAKHANIAN
History and Geography: POGHOS SIMONIAN
Industrial Pedagogy: KLEMENT ANANIAN
Mathematics and Physics: ALEXANDER GHUSHCHIAN
Primary Education and Defectology: DIMITRIY NAZARIAN
Psychology and Pedagogics: ROBERT DASHIAN
Public Professions: KAMO MKRYTCHIAN

ARMENIAN–RUSSIAN (SLAVONIC) STATE UNIVERSITY
0051 Yerevan, Hovsep Emin Str. 123
Telephone: (10) 28-97-00
Fax: (10) 28-97-01
E-mail: rector@rau.am
Internet: www.rau.am
Founded 1998 by govts of Russia and Armenia
State control
Languages of instruction: Armenian, Russian
Academic year: September to June
Rector: Prof. Dr ARMEN DARBINYAN
Library of 71,000 vols, 2,000 journals
Number of teachers: 290
Number of students: 2,482
Publication: *Vestnik* (2 a year)

DEANS
Faculty of Applied Mathematics and Information Technologies: Dr VLADIMIR YEGIAZARYAN
Faculty of Biomedical Sciences: Prof. Dr HRACHIK VARDAPETYAN
Faculty of Economics: ALBERT VARDANYAN
Faculty of Foreign Languages and Area Studies: Assoc. Prof. ARMINE SIMONYAN
Faculty of Journalism: RAFAEL AIRAPETYAN
Faculty of Law: Dr KAREN SARDARYAN
Faculty of Philology: Prof. ANAID KHACHIKYAN
Faculty of Physics and Technology: Dr HAYK SARKISYAN
Faculty of Politology: Dr VAHAN MELIKYAN
Faculty of Psychology: Dr ASYA BERBERYAN
Faculty of Tourism and Advertisement: Dr NINA KEVORKOVA

FRENCH UNIVERSITY OF ARMENIA
0067 Yerevan, Aigestan 8
Telephone: (10) 57-16-04
Fax: (10) 57-84-57
E-mail: ufa@arminco.com
Internet: www.ufa.am
Founded 2000
State control
Rector: PAUL ROUSSET
Sec.-Gen. and Dir of Studies: LUCIE HUCHOT

DEANS
Faculty of Business: NORAYR SAFARIAN
Faculty of Commerce: ARTAK MELKONIAN
Faculty of Law: GRIGOR BADIRIAN

GAVAR STATE UNIVERSITY
1201 Gavar, Azatutian 1
Telephone: (264) 25775
Fax: (10) 282075
E-mail: mbadalyan@rambler.ru

Internet: www.gsu.am
Founded 1993
State control; attached to RA Min. of Education and Science
Languages of instruction: Armenian, Russian, English
Academic year: September to June
Rector: RUZANNA HAKOBYAN
Vice-Rectors: VARDAN HAYRAPETYAN, ARSEN APROYAN
Librarian: YELIZAVETA BADALYAN
Library of 31,690 vols, yearly collns of the Materials of GSU Scientific Confs
Number of teachers: 147
Number of students: 2,290

DEANS

Faculty of Economics: SAMVEL AMIRKHANYAN
Faculty of Humanities: HAMLET GHAJOYAN
Faculty of Natural Sciences: MARTIN AVAGIAN
Faculty of Part-Time Education: NELLI KUTUZYAN
Faculty of Philology: VIKTOR KATVALYAN

STATE ENGINEERING UNIVERSITY OF ARMENIA

0009 Yerevan, ul. Teryana 105
Telephone: (10) 52-05-20
Fax: (10) 15-10-68
E-mail: president@seua.am
Internet: www.seua.am
Founded 1933
State control
Rector: Y. L. SARKISSIAN
Library of 667,000 vols
Number of teachers: 1,000
Number of students: 8,000
Faculties of Automation and Instrumentation, Chemical Technology and Environmental Engineering, Cybernetics, Electrical Engineering, Informatics and Computer Systems, Machine Building, Mechanics and Machine Science, Mining and Metallurgy, Power Engineering, Radio Technology and Communications Systems, Transport Systems.

YEREVAN STATE MEDICAL UNIVERSITY, 'MKHITAR HERATSI'

0025 Yerevan, Koryun 2
Telephone and fax (10) 58-25-32
E-mail: info@ysmu.am
Internet: www.ysmu.am
Languages of instruction: Armenian, English, Russian
Academic year: September to June
Founded 1920
State control
Rector: DERENIK H. DUMANYAN
Vice Rector for Academic Affairs: VLADIMIR A. SHEKOYAN
Vice-Rector for Clinical Affairs: Prof. Dr MIKAYEL Z. NARIMANYAN
Vice-Rector for Int. Relations: YERVAND S. SAHAKYAN
Vice-Rector for Reforms and Integration: ARMEN G. HARUTYUNYAN
Vice-Rector for Scientific Affairs: Prof. Dr MAGDALINA M. MELKONYAN
Library of 523,359 vols
Number of teachers: 768
Number of students: 4,414
Publications: *New Armenian Medical Journal*, *Apaga Bjishk* (Future Doctor), *Medicine, Science and Education*

DEANS

Faculty of General Medicine: SAMVEL A. AVETISYAN

Faculty of Military Medicine: SAMVEL G. GALSTYAN
Faculty of Pharmacy: HASMIK A. HASRATYAN
Faculty of Postgraduate and Continuing Education: MHER S. BISHARYAN
Faculty of Stomatology: KARINE M. BAROYAN

YEREVAN STATE UNIVERSITY

0025 Yerevan, Alex Manoogian 1
Telephone: (10) 55-46-29
Fax: (10) 55-46-41
E-mail: rector@ysu.am
Internet: www.ysu.am
Founded 1919
State control
Language of instruction: Armenian
Academic year: September to June
Rector: ARAM H. SIMONYAN
Vice-Rector for Academic Affairs: ALEKSANDR K. GRIGORYAN
Vice-Rector for Administrative-Economic Issues: ARARAT TS. MALKHASYAN
Vice-Rector for Scientific Policy and Int. Cooperation: GEGHAM G. GEVORGYAN
Vice-Rector for Students, Alumni and Public Relations: RUBEN L. MARKOSYAN
Dir of Library: ASHOT S. ALEKSANYAN
Number of teachers: 1,571
Number of students: 13,000
Publications: *Physical and Mathematical Sciences* (3 a year), *Proceedings of Yerevan State University*, *Scientific Bulletins* (geology and geography, biology and chemistry, 3 a year)

DEANS

Faculty of Applied Arts: SPARTAK SARGSYAN
Faculty of Armenian Philology: ARTSRUN AVAGYAN
Faculty of Biology: EMIL GEVORGYAN
Faculty of Chemistry: TARIEL V. GHOCHIKYAN
Faculty of Computer Science and Applied Mathematics: VAHRAM ZH. DUMANYAN
Faculty of Economics: HAYK L. SARGSYAN
Faculty of Geology and Geography: MARAT A. GRIGORYAN
Faculty of History: EDIK G. MINASYAN
Faculty of International Relations: GEGHAM H. PETROSYAN
Faculty of Journalism: NAGHASH N. MARTIROSYAN
Faculty of Law: GAGIK S. GHAZINYAN
Faculty of Mathematics and Mechanics: ARTHUR A. SAHAKYAN
Faculty of Oriental Studies: GURGEN V. MELIKIAN
Faculty of Philosophy, Psychology and Sociology: ALEXANDER S. BAGHDASARYAN
Faculty of Physics: ROLAND M. AVAGYAN
Faculty of Radiophysics: YURI L. VARDANIAN
Faculty of Romanic-Germanic Philology: SAMVEL A. ABRAHAMYAN
Faculty of Russian Philology: PAVEL B. BALAYAN
Faculty of Sociology: ARTHUR E. MKRTCHYAN
Faculty of Theology: ANUSHAVAN BISHOP ZHAMKOCHYAN

YEREVAN STATE UNIVERSITY OF LINGUISTICS, 'V. BRUSOV'

0002 Yerevan, Toumanian 42
Telephone: (10) 53-05-52
Fax: (10) 58-55-54
E-mail: yslu@brusov.am
Internet: www.brusov.am
Founded 1935
State control
Faculties of foreign languages, linguistics and inter-cultural communication, Romance and Germanic languages, Russian language and literature

Rector: SUREN ZOLYAN
Number of teachers: 409
Number of students: 4,371

Other Higher Educational Institutes

Armenian Agricultural Academy: 0009 Yerevan, ul. Teryana 74; tel. (10) 52-45-41; fax (10) 52-23-61; e-mail agacad@arminco.com; internet www.arminco.com/homepages/usdaes/acad/acad.htm; f. 1994 from merger of Armenian Agricultural Institute (f. 1930) and Yerevan Zootechnical and Veterinary Institute (f. 1928); faculties of Agrarian Studies, Economics, Technology, Zootechnical and Veterinary Studies, Engineering, Advanced Studies; 152 full professors; 419 teachers; 4,322 students; library: 563,389 vols; Rector A. KHACHATRIAN; publs *Agronews* (52 a year), *Agroscience* (12 a year), *News* (52 a year).

Armenian State Institute of Physical Education: 0070 Yerevan, Alex Manoogian 11; tel. (10) 55-24-31; f. 1945; State control; faculties of Education, Sports; Rector VAHRAM ARAKELIAN.

Gyumri M. Nalbandian State Pedagogical Institute: 3126 Gyumri, Paruir Sevak 4; tel. (312) 3-77-32; fax (312) 3-21-99; e-mail postmaster@shirak.am; f. 1935; state control; faculties of Foreign Languages, History and Philology, Natural Sciences and Geography, Pedagogy, Physical Education, Physics and Mathematics; Rector HOURIK HARUTUNIAN.

Vanadzor State Pedagogical Institute: 2000 Vanadzor, Tigran Mets 36; tel. (322) 4-63-87; fax (322) 2-04-68; e-mail mankocol@hragir.aua.am; f. 1969; state control; faculties of Biology, History and Geography, Mathematics and Physics, Philology and Pre-school Education, Psychology; 310 teachers; 1,900 students; Rector RAFIK YEDOVAN; Vice-Rector SHVAITS SAHAKIAN.

Yerevan Institute of Architecture and Construction: 0009 Yerevan, ul. Teryana 105; tel. (10) 58-01-77; fax (10) 56-59-84; internet yeriac.iatp.irex.am; f. 1989; faculties of Architecture, Construction and Urban Economy, Construction, Hydrotechnical Studies, Industrial and Civil Construction, Transport Construction, Technology; 262 teachers; 1,624 students; library: 1.4m. vols; Rector A. G. BEGLARIAN.

Yerevan Komitas State Conservatoire: 0001 Yerevan, Sayat-Nova 1A; tel. (10) 58-11-64; fax (10) 56-35-40; e-mail ysc@edu.am; f. 1920; orchestral, chamber, choral, folk music; library: 130,000 vols; 386 teachers; 1,045 students; Rector Prof. ARMEN SMHATYAN.

Yerevan State Academy of Fine Arts: 0009 Yerevan, Isahakian 36; tel. (10) 56-07-26; fax (10) 54-27-06; e-mail ysifa@edu.am; internet www.iatp.am/yafa; f. 1945; faculties of Art, Decorative Arts, Design; brs in Gjumri and Dilijan; library: 25,000 vols; 98 teachers; 428 students; Rector Prof. ARAM ISABEKIAN.

Yerevan State Institute of Economics: 0025 Yerevan, Nalbandian St 164; tel. (10) 52-17-21; fax (10) 52-88-64; e-mail ysine@ysine.am; internet www.ysine.am; f. 1975; faculties of Economic Planning, Economics and Organization of Labour, Economics of Labour and Sociology, Economics of Trade and Commodities, Finance and Accounting; 326 teachers; 5,600 students; Rector G. KIRAKOSIAN; publ. *Economics*.

AUSTRALIA

The Higher Education System

In 2009 there were 42 public universities and two private universities, as well as over 100 higher education providers approved by State/Territory to offer specific higher education programmes. In 2008 a total of 1,066,095 students were enrolled in higher education. Under the federal system of government in Australia, the six states and two territories are responsible for providing education services for their own residents. The Australian Constitution, however, empowers the Federal Government to make special-purpose financial grants to the states for education in both government and non-government schools. Responsibility for educational policy rests with the Minister for Education, Science and Training. An education department headed by a Director-General deals with all aspects of education within each state.

The Federal Government is the most important source of funding for universities; in 2003 the Government contributed 41% of accounted funding. Most Australian students contribute to the cost of their courses under the Higher Education Contribution Scheme (HECS), with the amount of the student's contribution depending on the cost of the course and likely future earnings. Financial assistance is available to certain students subject to a means test. In addition, there are a limited number of equity and merit scholarships which exempt students from the HECS charge.

Universities are administered by a Governing Body such as a Council, Senate or Board of Governors, chaired by a Chancellor. A Chief Executive, usually a Vice-Chancellor or President, oversees the day-to-day running of the university and reports to the Governing Body.

In 1990 a Unified National System was established, replacing the previously existing binary system of universities and non-university institutions. The Australian Qualifications Framework (AQF) was introduced in 1995 and implemented by 1999, leading to the development of a comprehensive national framework for post-secondary education and training. The AQF identifies six post-secondary levels of qualification: Diploma, Advanced Diploma, Bachelors degree, Graduate Certificate and Graduate Diploma, Masters degree and Doctoral degree. In May 2009 the Minister for Education announced the creation of a new national regulatory agency, the Tertiary Education Quality and Standards Agency, to come into force in 2012. It was envisaged that its role would be to 'accredit providers, carry out audits, protect the overall quality of the Australian higher education system, encourage best practice and streamline current regulatory arrangements to reduce duplication and provide for national consistency'. It would also decide who qualified for performance funding.

Universities administer their own admissions processes. Admission is usually based on a combination of completion of Year 12, leading to the award of the Senior Secondary Certificate of Education (the name may vary in each state or territory), and entrance test scores. The Diploma and Advanced Diploma, requiring two and three years of study respectively, are sub-degree qualifications that may in certain circumstances allow entry to the second year of a Bachelors degree. The Bachelors degree may be rated either Ordinary/Pass after three years of study or Honours after four years of study. The Graduate Certificate and Graduate Diploma require one or two semesters of full-time study respectively following a Bachelors degree. The Masters degree is awarded after two years of study following an Ordinary/Pass Bachelors or after one year of study following an Honours Bachelors. Finally, the Doctoral degree requires three years of full-time study and research plus submission of a thesis. Other, more recent, Doctoral-level awards include the Professional Doctorate and the Higher Doctorate.

Vocational education and training (VET) is supervised by the Australian National Training Authority, established in 1994. The Australian Recognition Framework approves VET qualifications. VET programmes are offered at upper-secondary schools, Technical and Further Education colleges and State- or Territory-accredited private providers. VET programmes require between one and three years' study depending upon the requirements of the course and the level of qualification sought. The range of VET qualifications is as follows: Certificates I, II, III, IV; Diploma; Advanced Diploma. Teacher training usually requires either a three-year Bachelors degree in the subject to be taught, followed by a one- to two-year (Graduate) Diploma in Education, or the four-year Bachelor of Education.

Regulatory and Representative Bodies

GOVERNMENT

Department of Education, Employment and Workplace Relations: GPOB 9880, Canberra, ACT 2601; 16 Mort St, Canberra, ACT 2601; tel. (2) 6240-8848; internet www.deewr.gov.au; Minister JULIA GILLARD.

Ministerial Council on Education, Employment, Training and Youth Affairs (MCEETYA): POB 202, Carlton South, Vic. 3053; tel. (03) 9639-0588; fax (03) 9639-1790; e-mail enquiries@mceetya.edu.au; internet www.mceetya.edu.au; f. 1993 by merger of the Australian Education Council (AEC), the Council of Ministers of Vocational Education, Employment and Training (MOVEET) and the Youth Ministers Council (YMC); responsible for pre-primary education, primary and secondary education, vocational education and training, higher education, employment and links between employment/labour market programmes and education and training, adult and community education, youth policy programmes and cross-sectoral matters; works in close interaction with the Ministerial Council for Vocational and Technical Education (MCVTE); functions incl. coordination of strategic policy at nat. level, negotiation and devt of nat. agreements on shared objectives and interests (incl. principles for Australian Govt/State relations) in the Council's areas of responsibility, negotiations on scope and format of nat. reporting on areas of responsibility, sharing of information and collaborative use of resources towards agreed objectives and priorities, and coordination of communication with, and collaboration between, related nat. structures; Chair. Dr JANE LOMAX-SMITH.

ACCREDITATION

AEI-NOOSR: Dept of Education, Employment and Workplace Relations, GPOB 1407, Canberra, ACT 2601; tel. (3) 9938-2543; fax (2) 6123-7892; e-mail educational.noosr@deewr.gov.au; internet aei.gov.au/aei/qualificationsrecognition/default.htm; provides official information and advice on the comparability of overseas qualifications with Australian qualifications; Dir of AEI-NOOSR MARGARET PROCTOR.

Australian Qualifications Framework Advisory Board (AQFAB): POB 609, Carlton South, Vic. 3053; Level 3, 15–31 Pelham St, Carlton, Vic. 3053; tel. (3) 9639-1606; fax (3) 9639-1315; e-mail aqfab@aqf.edu.au; internet www.aqf.edu.au; f. 1995 to protect the Australian Qualifications Framework (AQF) qualifications guidelines and to promote and monitor nat. implementation of the AQF; operates as a high-level, cross-sectoral forum; Chair. WARREN GRIMSHAW; Secretariat Exec. Officer Dr JUDY FORSYTH.

Australian Universities Quality Agency: Level 10, 123 Lonsdale St, Melbourne, Vic. 3000; tel. (3) 9664-1000; fax (3) 9639-7377; e-mail admin@auqa.edu.au; internet auqa.edu.au; f. 2000; ind., nat. quality assurance agency responsible for quality audits of higher education instns and accreditation authorities; reports on performance and outcomes and assists in quality enhancement; Exec. Dir Dr DAVID WOODHOUSE.

NATIONAL BODIES

Adult Learning Australia Quest: GPOB 260, Canberra, ACT 2601; tel. (2) 6274-9500; fax (2) 9274-9513; e-mail info@ala.asn.au; internet www.ala.asn.au; f. 1961; mem. of ICAE, ASPBAE, ICEA; coordinates and encourages adult and community education at nat. level; publishes educational books; lobbies govts and appropriate depts; holds nat. conferences; 500 mems, also corporate mems; Pres. GREG PEART; Exec. Dir RON ANDERSON; publs *Adult Learning Australia* (4 a year), *Australian Journal of Adult Learning* (3 a year).

Australian Research Council: GPOB 2702, Canberra, ACT 2601; tel. (2) 6287-6600; fax (2) 6287-6601; e-mail info@arc.gov .au; internet www.arc.gov.au; f. 2001; statutory authority within the Australian Govt's Innovation, Industry, Science and Research (IISR) portfolio; its mission is to advance Australia's research excellence to be globally competitive and deliver benefits to the community; provides advice to the Govt on research matters and manages the National Competitive Grants Programme (NCGP), a significant component of Australia's investment in research and devt, supporting high quality fundamental and applied research and research training through national competition across all disciplines, with the exception of clinical medicine and dentistry; Chief Exec. Prof. MARGARET SHEIL; publs *Discovery* (newsletter, 4 a year), *Strategic Plan* (every 2 years).

Centre for Adult Education (CAE): 253 Flinders Lane, Melbourne, Vic. 3000; tel. (3) 9652-0611; fax (3) 9654-6759; e-mail international@cae.edu.au; internet www.cae .edu.au; f. 1947; statutory body engaged in providing adult education and business training in Vic.; funded in part through the Govt of Vic.; library of 50,000 vols; Dir JOHN WILLS; publs *Dialogue* (every 3 years, catalogue of book, film and music titles available for self-directed learning groups), *Program Guide* (5 a year).

Universities Australia: GPOB 1142, Canberra, ACT 2601; tel. (2) 6285-8100; fax (2) 6285-8101; e-mail contact@ universitiesaustralia.edu.au; internet www .universitiesaustralia.edu.au; f. 1920 as Australian Vice-Chancellors' Cttee; represents Australian univs; Chair. Prof. PETER COALDRAKE; Chief Exec. Dr GLENN WITHERS.

Learned Societies

GENERAL

Academy of the Social Sciences in Australia: GPOB 1956, Canberra, ACT 2601; tel. (2) 6249-1788; fax (2) 6247-4335; e-mail assa .secretariat@anu.edu.au; internet www.assa .edu.au; f. 1971; 447 fellows; Pres. Prof. STUART MACINTYRE; Exec. Dir Dr JOHN BEATON; publs *Dialogue* (3 a year), *Occasional Paper* (irregular).

Australian Academy of the Humanities: GPOB 93, Canberra, ACT 2601; tel. (2) 6125-9860; fax (2) 6248-6287; e-mail enquiries@ humanities.org.au; internet www .humanities.org.au; f. 1969; prehistory and archaeology, European languages and cultures, classical studies, history, fine arts, Asian studies, English, linguistics, philosophy, religion and the history of ideas, cultural and communication studies; 529 mems; Pres. Prof. JOSEPH LO BIANCO; Immediate Past Pres. Prof. IAN DONALDSON; Exec. Dir, Secretariat Dr CHRISTINA PAROLIN; Hon. Sec. Prof. GRAEME CLARKE; Librarian SONJA STEFFEN; publ. *Humanities Australia*.

AGRICULTURE, FISHERIES AND VETERINARY SCIENCE

Australian Institute of Agricultural Science and Technology: Level 2, 21 Burwood Rd, Hawthorn, Vic. 3122; tel. (3) 9815-3600; fax (3) 9815-3633; internet www.aiast.com .au; f. 1935; 2,500 mems; Pres. CHARLES DREW; Exec. Dir ALLAN JONES; publ. *Agricultural Science* (4 a year).

Australian Veterinary Association: Unit 40, 2A Herbert St, St Leonards, NSW 2065; tel. (2) 9431-5000; fax (2) 9437-9068; e-mail members@ava.com.au; internet www.ava .com.au; f. 1921; professional asscn; 5,000 mems; Pres. KERSTI SEKSEL; Chief Exec. MARGARET CONLEY; publ. *Australian Veterinary Journal* (12 a year).

Dairy Industry Association of Australia Inc.: 84 William St, Melbourne, Vic. 3000; tel. (3) 9760-0422; fax (3) 9642-8144; e-mail kmanser@ozemail.com.au; internet www .diaa.asn.au; f. 1946; divisions in each State; 1,600 mems; Pres. JO DAVEY; Sec. KRISTINE MANSER; publs *Australian Dairy Foods* (6 a year), *The Australian Journal of Dairy Technology* (3 a year).

Primary Industries Ministerial Council: Dept of Agriculture, Fisheries and Forestry, Barton, Canberra, ACT 2600; tel. (2) 6272-5216; fax (2) 6272-4772; internet www.affa .gov.au/docs/operating_environment/arm-canz/armcanz.html; f. 2001; mems: Commonwealth, State, Territory and New Zealand ministers responsible for agriculture and rural adjustment; advised by a Standing Committee comprising heads of Commonwealth, State, Territory and New Zealand agencies responsible for agriculture, and representatives from CSIRO and the Bureau of Meteorology; Exec. Dir Dr MAXINE COOPER.

ARCHITECTURE AND TOWN PLANNING

Australian Council of National Trusts: POB 1002, Civic Sq., ACT 2612; tel. (2) 6247-6766; fax (2) 6249-1395; internet www .nationaltrust.org.au; f. 1965; Federal Council of the State and Territory National Trusts established for the conservation of lands and buildings of beauty or of national, historic, scientific, architectural or cultural interest and Aboriginal relics and wildlife; 80,000 mems of the National Trust movement; Chair. SIMON R. MOLESWORTH; Exec. Officer ALAN GRAHAM.

Australian Institute of Architects: POB 3373, Manuka, Canberra, ACT 2603; tel. (2) 6121-2000; fax (2) 6121-2001; e-mail national@raia.com.au; internet www .architecture.com.au; inc. 1930; 8,500 mems; Nat. Pres. KARL FENDER; CEO DAVID PARKEN; ACT Man. SOPHIE CLEMENT; publs *Architecture Australia* (6 a year), occasional newsletters, research papers, seminar and workshop papers, management and law notes.

Australian Institute of Quantity Surveyors: National Office, POB 301, Deakin West, ACT 2600; tel. (2) 6282-2222; fax (2) 6285-2427; e-mail contact@aiqs.com.au; internet www.aiqs.com.au; f. 1971; 3,700 mems; Pres. PETER COX; Gen. Man. TERRY SANDERS; publs *Australian Journal of Construction Economics and Building* (2 a year), *The Building Economist* (4 a year).

Planning Institute of Australia: Unit 8, Level 2, Engineering House, 11 National Circuit, Barton, ACT 2600; tel. (2) 6262-5933; fax (2) 6262-9970; e-mail act@planning .org.au; internet www.planning.org.au; f. 1951; professional asscn for town and regional planners; 3,444 mems; Nat. Pres. MARCUS SPILLER; Pres. CLAIRE MIDDLETON; publs *Australian Planner* (4 a year), *National Office News* (6 a year).

BIBLIOGRAPHY, LIBRARY SCIENCE AND MUSEOLOGY

Australian Library and Information Association: POB 6335, Kingston, ACT 2604; tel. (2) 6215-8222; fax (2) 6282-2249; internet alia.org.au; f. 1937; 6,000 mems; Pres. ROXANNE MISSINGHAM; Exec. Dir SUE HUTLEY; publs *Australian Academic and Research Libraries* (4 a year), *Australian Library Journal* (4 a year), *inCite* (11 a year).

Bibliographical Society of Australia and New Zealand: c/o Dr Chris Tiffin, Hon. Sec. Research Consultant, School of EMSAH, Univ. of Queensland, Brisbane, Qld 4072; tel. (7) 3369-1783; e-mail c.tiffin@uq.edu.au; internet scriptandprint.blogspot.com; f. 1969 to promote research in bibliography; publishes a journal and occasional publs, holds conferences; 200 mems; Pres. Dr JOHN ARNOLD; Treasurer PAM PRYDE; publ. *Script & Print: Bulletin of the Bibliographical Society of Australia and New Zealand* (4 a year).

Museums Australia: POB 266, Civic Sq., ACT 2608; tel. (2) 6273-2437; fax (2) 6273-2451; e-mail director@museumsaustralia.org .au; internet www.museumsaustralia.org.au; f. 1993 to promote museums and galleries to all levels of govt and the community, and to foster high standards in all aspects of museum operations through nat. advocacy, professional devt, training, research, policy formulation, publs, collaborative facilitation and partnerships; 1,500 mems (instns and individuals); Nat. Pres. DARRYL MCINTYRE; Nat. Dir BERNICE L. MURPHY; Man. LEE SCOTT; publ. *Museums Australia Magazine* (4 a year).

ECONOMICS, LAW AND POLITICS

Australian Bar Association: Bar Association of Queensland, Level 5, Inns of Court, 107 North Quay, Brisbane, Qld 4000; tel. (7) 3236-2477; fax (7) 3236-1180; e-mail president@qldbar.asn.au; internet qldbar .asn.au; f. 1962 to advance the interests of barristers; maintains and strengthens the position of the Bar, maintaining its independence and the rule of law; maintains and improves standards of instruction and training of barristers; 3,440 mems; Pres. GLENN MARTIN; Vice-Pres. PETER LYONS; Treas. MARTIN DAUBNEY; Sec. DOUGLAS MURPHY.

Australian Institute of Credit Management: Level 3, 619 Pacific Highway, St Leonards, NSW 2065; tel. (2) 9906-4563; fax (2) 9906-5686; e-mail terry@aicm.com.au; internet www.aicm.com.au; f. 1937 to provide a nat. and professional organization for credit managers and those engaged in the control of credit; 3,000 mems; provides education and qualifications in financial services and credit management; conducts conferences, seminars and workshops; undertakes research and makes submissions to govts on credit; CEO TERRY COLLINS; Nat. Training Man. DEL CSETI; publ. *Credit Management in Australia* (5 a year).

Australian Institute of International Affairs: 32 Thesiger Court, Deakin, ACT 2600; tel. (2) 6282-2133; fax (2) 6285-2334; e-mail ceo@aiia.asn.au; internet www.aiia .asn.au; f. 1933; 1,600 mems; Pres. JOHN MCCARTHY; Exec. Dir MELISSA H. CONLEY TYLER; publs *Australia in World Affairs* (every 5 years), *Australian Journal of International Affairs* (4 a year).

Australian Institute of Management: 181 Fitzroy St, St Kilda, Vic. 3182; tel. (3) 9534-8181; fax (3) 9534-5050; e-mail enquiry@ aimvic.com.au; internet www.aim.com.au; f. 1941; professional management asscn; information and training services; divs in all states; 30,000 professional mems, 7,500 corporate mems; library of 20,000 vols; publ. *National Management Today Magazine* (12 a year).

Australian Political Studies Association: Director's Section, RSSS, ANU, Canberra, ACT 0200; tel. (2) 6125-2257; fax (2) 6125-0502; e-mail mary.hapel@anu.edu.au; internet www.auspsa.org.au; f. 1952; sponsors nat. political science projects; int. exchange programmes with similar asscns; organises an annual conference; workshops; 312 mems; Pres. Prof. ANN CAPLING; Sec. and Treasurer Prof. ROD RHODES; publ. *Australian Journal of Political Science* (4 a year).

Australian Property Institute: 6 Campion St, Deakin, ACT 2600; tel. (2) 6282-2411; fax (2) 6285-2194; internet www.api.org.au; f. 1927; 7,500 mems; Pres. BARRY BRAKEY; Dir GRANT WARNER; publs *Australian & New Zealand Valuation Principles & Standards Manual, Australian Property Journal* (4 a year), *Professional Practice* (1 a year), *Valuation Principles and Practices*.

Committee for Economic Development of Australia: Level 5, 136 Exhibition St, Melbourne, Vic. 3000; tel. (3) 9662-3544; fax (3) 9663-7271; e-mail info@ceda.com.au; internet www.ceda.com.au; f. 1960 to facilitate discussion, research and interdisciplinary communication in the interests of the devt of the nat. economy and the future of Australia; holds more than 250 events, seminars and exec. roundtables each year; 1,000 orgs; Chair. IVAN DEVESON; Chief Exec. DAVID BYERS; publs *Australian Chief Executive* (mem. magazine, 4 a year), *Growth Reports* (multi-author long reports on selected research themes), *Information Papers* (single-author short reports on selected research themes).

Economic Society of Australia: POB 937, St Ives, NSW 2075; tel. (2) 9402-7635; internet www.ecosoc.org.au; f. 1925; 1,400 mems; brs in each State; Pres. NEVILLE NORMAN; Sec. JEFFREY SHEEN; Treas. ANDREW HUGHES; publs *Economic Papers, The Economic Record*.

Institute of Public Affairs: Level 2, 410 Collins St, Melbourne, Vic. 3000; tel. (3) 9600-4744; e-mail ipa@ipa.org.au; internet www.ipa.org.au; f. 1943; non-profit educational org. to study economic and industrial problems and to advance the cause of free enterprise in Australia; supported by 550 companies and 3,500 individuals; Chair. ALAN STOCKDALE; Exec. Dir MIKE NAHAN; publs *Backgrounder* (10 a year), *Current Issues* (5 a year), *IPA Review* (4 a year).

Law Council of Australia: GPOB 1989, Canberra, ACT 2601; 19 Torrens St, Braddon, ACT 2612; tel. (2) 6246-3788; fax (2) 6248-0639; e-mail mail@lawcouncil.asn.au; internet www.lawcouncil.asn.au; f. 1933; 15 constituent bodies representing 50,000 mems; Sec.-Gen. PETER WEBB; publs *Australian Family Lawyer* (4 a year), *Australian Law Management Journal* (4 a year).

Law Society of New South Wales: 170 Phillip St, Sydney, NSW; tel. (2) 9926-0333; fax (2) 9231-5809; internet www.lawsocnsw .asn.au; f. 1884; 20,000 mems; library of 32,000 vols; Sec. C. CAWLEY; publs *Caveat* (irregular), *Law Society Journal* (11 a year).

Local Government Managers Australia: POB 5175, South Melbourne, Vic. 3205; tel. (3) 9682-9222; fax (3) 9682-8977; e-mail national@lgma.org.au; internet www.lgma .org.au; f. 1936; professional local govt assoc. for gen. managers, chief execs and officers employed in management; 2,500 mems; CEO JOHN RAVLIC; publ. *Local Government Manager* (6 a year).

EDUCATION

Australian College of Educators: 42 Geils Court, Deakin, ACT 2600; tel. (2) 6281-1677; fax (2) 6285-1262; e-mail ace@austcolled.com .au; internet www.auscolled.com.au; f. 1959; an independent professional association of educators from every field of education throughout Australia; encourages professional advancement of its members and the nat. development of education; brs and regional groups in each state and territory; conducts nat. and state conferences, surveys and studies, etc.; 6,000 mems; CEO CHERYL O'CONNOR; publs *Education Review* (incl. *ACE Perspectives*, 12 a year), chapter newsletters, *Professional Educator* (4 a year).

IDP Education Australia Ltd: GPOB 2006, Canberra, ACT 2601; tel. (2) 6285-8222; fax (2) 6285-3036; e-mail info@idp.com; internet www.idp.com; f. 1969 as the Int. Development Program of Australian Universities and Colleges Ltd, renamed 1994; 37 mem. Australian univs; an independent company owned by the Australian Universities; seeks to promote Australian education and training services overseas; 53 overseas network offices; Chief Exec. L. HYAM; publ. newsletters in Asia-Pacific languages.

Open and Distance Learning Association of Australia Inc.: POB 594, Stanhope Gardens, NSW 2768; tel. (2) 9837-7240; fax (2) 6773-3510; e-mail executive@odlaa.org; internet www.odlaa.org; f. 1974 to advance the practice and study of distance education in Australia; professional asscn for teachers, developers, researchers, consultants and administrators from Australia and overseas involved in open and distance learning; Pres. Dr ROD SIMS; Vice-Pres. SAM MEREDITH; Exec. Editor for Distance Education Assoc. Prof. SOM NAIDU; publ. *Distance Education* (3 a year).

FINE AND PERFORMING ARTS

Australia Council for the Arts: 372 Elizabeth St, Surry Hills, NSW 2010; tel. (2) 9215-9000; fax (2) 9215-9111; e-mail mail@ australiacouncil.gov.au; internet www .australiacouncil.gov.au; f. 1968; aims to foster the devt of the arts through the programmes of seven funds: Music, Dance, Theatre, Interdisciplinary/New Media Arts, Literature, Visual Arts, Community Partnerships, and one board: Aboriginal and Torres Straits Islander Arts; library of 6,500 vols; Chair. JAMES STRONG; Deputy Chair. JOHN DENTON; CEO KATHY KEELE; publ. *Artery* (4 a year).

Musicological Society of Australia: GPOB 2402, Canberra, ACT 2601; e-mail secretary@msa.org.au; internet www.msa .org.au; f. 1963; the advancement of musicology; 290 mems; Pres. JANE DAVIDSON; National Sec. Dr JONATHAN MACINTOSH; Treas. Dr ROBERT FAULKNER; publ. *Musicology Australia* (2 a year).

Royal Art Society of New South Wales: 25–27 Walker St, North Sydney, NSW 2060; tel. (2) 9955-5752; fax (2) 9925-0064; e-mail lavender@cia.com.au; f. 1880; for the promotion of high standards in Australian art; school for painting (beginners to Diploma RAS of NSW); 400 mems; Pres. RON STANNARD; Sec. CHRISTINE FEHER.

Royal Queensland Art Society Inc.: GPOB 1602, Brisbane, Qld 4001; tel. (7) 3831-3455; fax (7) 3831-3452; e-mail rqasi@ oznetcom.com.au; internet www.rqas .ozevents.com; f. 1887; 500 mems; Sec. KAREN KANE.

Royal South Australian Society of Arts: Institute Bldg, Level 1 N Terrace, Adelaide, SA 5000; tel. (8) 8232-0450; fax (8) 8232-

0450; f. 1856; 702 mems; Pres. BEVERLY M. BILLS; Hon. Sec. JAMES E. G. RAGGATT; publ. *Kalori* (irregular).

Victorian Artists' Society: 430 Albert St, East Melbourne, Vic. 3002; tel. (3) 9662-1484; fax (3) 9662-2343; e-mail vicartists@vicnet .net.au; internet www.vicnet.net.au/ ~vicartists; f. 1870; 1,000 mems; four galleries and a studio; Pres. JOHN HUNT; Sec. TED DANSEY; publ. *Gallery on Eastern Hill*.

HISTORY, GEOGRAPHY AND ARCHAEOLOGY

Australian and New Zealand Association for Medieval and Early Modern Studies (Inc.): c/o Dr Lesley O'Brien, School of Humanities, M208, Univ. of Western Australia, Crawley, WA 6009; fax (8) 6488-1069; e-mail anzamems-membership@arts .uwa.edu.au; internet www.anzamems.arts .uwa.edu.au; f. 1996 by merger of ANZAMRS (Australian and New Zealand Asscn of Medieval and Renaissance Studies) and AHMEME (Australian Historians of Medieval and Early Modern Europe); organizes conferences every 2 years; 230 mems; Pres. CONSTANT MEWS (Monash Univ.); Sec. MEGAN CASSIDY-WELCH (Univ. of Melbourne); publ. *Parergon* (2 a year).

Australian Numismatic Society: POB 366, Brookvale, NSW 2096; tel. (2) 9223-4578; e-mail rodsell@rodsell.com; f. 1913; promotes the study of coins, banknotes and medals with particular reference to Australasia and the Pacific region; monthly meetings in Sydney and Brisbane; 204 mems (incl. overseas); Pres. J. VELTMEYER; Sec. ROD SELL; publs *Report* (2 a year), *NAA Journal* (1 a year).

Geographical Society of New South Wales Inc.: POB 162, Ryde, NSW 1680; tel. (2) 9807-3586; fax (2) 9807-3589; e-mail office@gsnsw.org.au; internet www.gsnsw .org.au; f. 1927; 300 mems; Hon. Sec. E. TARANTO; publ. *Australian Geographer* (3 a year).

Mapping Sciences Institute, Australia: GPOB 1817, Brisbane, Qld 4000; tel. (7) 3343-7706; fax (7) 3219-2281; e-mail msiau@gil.com.au; internet www .mappingsciences.org.au; f. 1952; holds biennial conferences; 1,250 mems; Nat. Pres. JOHN MCCORMACK; Hon. Sec. K. H. SMITH; publ. *Cartography* (2 a year).

Royal Australian Historical Society: History House, 133 Macquarie St, Sydney, NSW 2000; tel. (2) 9247-8001; fax (2) 9247-7854; e-mail history@rahs.org.au; internet www .rahs.org.au; f. 1901; 2,000 mems; library of 30,000 items; Man. MARI METZKE; Librarian DONNA NEWTON; publs *History Magazine* (4 a year), *Journal* (2 a year).

Royal Geographical Society of Queensland Inc.: 237 Milton Rd, Milton, Qld 4064; tel. (7) 3368-2066; fax (7) 3367-1011; e-mail admin@rgsq.org.au; internet www.rgsq.org .au; f. 1885; monthly lectures, geographical trips, organizes Australian Geography Competition; 400 mems; library of 2,500 monographs, 320 periodicals, maps; Administrator KATHRYN BERG; Sec. KEITH SMITH.

Royal Historical Society of Queensland: POB 12057, George St, Brisbane, Qld 4003; tel. (7) 3221-4198; fax (7) 3221-4698; e-mail info@queenslandhistory.org.au; internet queenslandhistory.org.au; f. 1913; Welsby library; research; historical documents preserved and filed; photographic colln; social history; museum; 600 mems; Pres. Dr IAN HADWEN; Man. ALLAN R. BELL; publs *Bulletin* (12 a year), *Journal* (4 a year).

Royal Historical Society of Victoria: 239 A'Beckett St, Melbourne, Vic. 3000; tel. (3)

9326-9288; fax (3) 9326-9477; e-mail office@ historyvictoria.org.au; internet www .historyvictoria.org.au; f. 1909; research; collection of historical material; exhibitions; 1,600 mems; library of 8,000 vols, MSS, photographs, paintings and prints; Pres. Prof. WESTON BATE; Exec. Officer Dr ELIZABETH RUSHDEN; publs *History News* (12 a year), *Journal* (2 a year).

Royal Western Australian Historical Society: Stirling House, 49 Broadway, Nedlands, WA 6009; tel. (8) 9386-3841; fax (8) 9386-3309; e-mail histwest@git.com.au; internet www.histwest.org.au; f. 1926; runs museum, research library and bookshop specialising in W Australian history and archival products; 1,000 mems; Pres. Dr LENORE LAYMAN; publs *Early Days* (1 a year), *History West* (11 a year).

Society of Australian Genealogists: Richmond Villa, 120 Kent St, Sydney, NSW 2000; tel. (2) 9247-3953; fax (2) 9241-4872; e-mail info@sag.org.au; internet www.sag.org.au; f. 1932; 7,500 mems; library of 20,000 vols, 1,000 microfilm reels, 1m. names on microfiche, 40,000 photographs, 30,000 MSS; Exec. Officer H. E. GARNSEY; Librarian ANGELA PHIPPEN; publ. *Descent* (4 a year).

LANGUAGE AND LITERATURE

Alliance Française: 66 McCaughey St, Turner, Canberra, ACT 2601; tel. (2) 6247-5027; fax (2) 6257-6696; e-mail administration@afcanberra.com.au; internet www.alliancefrancaise.com.au; offers courses and examinations in French language and culture and promotes cultural exchange with France; attached teaching centres in Adelaide, Albury, Armidale, Atherton, Ballarat, Blue Mountains, Brisbane, Canberra, Darwin, Davenport, Esperance, Eurobodolla, Geelong, Gold Coast, Gosford, Hobart, Illawarra, Launceston, Lismore, Melbourne, Merimbula, Milton/Ulladulla, Newcastle, Perth, Port Macquerie, Rockhampton, Sunshine Coast, Sydney, Toowoomba, Townsville, Wagga Wagga; Dir BRUNO DUPARC.

Australasian and Pacific Society for Eighteenth-Century Studies: c/o Humanities Research Centre, Australian National University, ACT 0200; f. 1970; a sponsoring body of the David Nichol Smith Seminars; 80 mems; Pres. Prof. IAIN MCCALMAN.

Australian Society of Authors Ltd: POB 1566, Strawberry Hills, NSW 2012; tel. (2) 9318-0877; fax (2) 9318-0530; e-mail asa@ asauthors.org; internet www.asauthors.org; f. 1963; 3,000 mems; Chair. SUSAN HAYES; publ. *The Australian Author* (3 a year).

British Council: POB 88, Edgecliff, NSW 2027; tel. (2) 9326-2022; fax (2) 9327-4868; e-mail enquiries@britishcouncil.org.au; internet www.britishcouncil.org/au.htm; offers courses and examinations in English language and British culture and promotes cultural exchange with the UK; Dir CHRISTOPHER WADE.

English Association Sydney Inc.: POB 91, Wentworth Bldg, Univ. of Sydney, Sydney, NSW 2006; e-mail r.madelaine@unsw.edu .au; f. 1923; organizes confs for teachers and study days for students; 70 mems; Pres. Assoc. Prof. RICHARD MADELAINE; Sec. Dr ROB JACKSON; Treas. CERIDWEN LEE; publ. *Southerly* (3 a year).

Fellowship of Australian Writers NSW Inc.: POB 488, Rozelle, NSW 2039; tel. (2) 9810-1307; e-mail honsecretary@fawnsw.org .au; internet www.fawnsw.org.au; f. 1928; 4,000 nat. mems; brs in all states and territories; Pres. TREVAR LANGLANDS; Sec. COLLEEN PARKER; publ. *Writers' Voice* (every 3 months).

Goethe-Institut: 90 Ocean St, Woollahra, Sydney, NSW 2025; tel. (2) 8356-8333; fax (2) 8356-8314; e-mail info@sydney.goethe.org; internet www.goethe.de/sydney; offers courses and examinations in the German language and promotes German culture and cultural exchange with Germany; Dir KLAUS KRISCHOK.

PEN International (Sydney Centre): Faculty of Humanities and Social Sciences, University of Technology, Sydney, NSW 2007; tel. (2) 9514-2738; fax (2) 9514-2778; e-mail sydney@pen.org.au; internet www .pen.org.au; f. 1926; promotes friendship and intellectual co-operation among writers; 160 mems; Pres. NICHOLAS JOSE; publ. *Newsletter* (4 a year).

MEDICINE

Australasian Association of Clinical Biochemists: POB 278, Mt Lawley, WA 6929; tel. (8) 9370-5224; fax (8) 9370-4409; e-mail office@aacb.asn.au; internet www .aacb.asn.au; f. 1961; 1,400 mems; Chair. MARY CONROY; Sec. CONCHITA KUEK; publs *Clinical Biochemist Newsletter* (4 a year), *Clinical Biochemist Reviews* (4 a year).

Australasian Chapter of Sexual Health Medicine: 145 Macquarie St, Sydney, NSW 2000; tel. (2) 9256-9643; fax (2) 9256-9693; e-mail shmed@racp.edu.au; internet www .racp.edu.au; f. 1988; aims to further the professional devt of medical practitioners in the discipline of sexual health medicine; 190 mems; Pres. Dr. ANNE ROBERTSON; Exec. Officer SUZANNE MARKS.

Australasian College of Dermatologists: POB 3785, Rhodes, NSW 2138; tel. (2) 8765-0242; fax (2) 9736-1174; e-mail admin@ dermcoll.asn.au; internet www.dermcoll.asn .au; f. 1966; undertakes training of dermatologists and scientific research; scientific conferences; provides public education in skin protection; 510 mems; Pres. Dr IAN MCCROSSIN; Hon. Sec. Dr CATHY REID; publ. *The Australasian Journal of Dermatology* (3 a year).

Australian Association of Neurologists: Royal Australasian College of Physicians, 145 Macquarie St, Sydney, NSW 2000; tel. (2) 9256-5443; fax (2) 9241-4083; e-mail aansyd@hotkey.net.au; internet www .medeserv.com.au/aan/index.cfm; f. 1950 to bring together clinical neurologists and scientific workers in the field of the nervous system and its diseases by such means as meetings, provision of special facilities and assistance in any publications on these matters; 450 mems; Pres. Prof. GEOFFREY DONNAN; Hon. Sec. Assoc. Prof. RICHARD MACDONNELL; publ. *Clinical and Experimental Neurology* (1 a year).

Australian Dental Association: 75 Lithgow St, POB 520, St Leonards, NSW 2065; tel. (2) 9906-4412; fax (2) 9906-4676; e-mail adainc@ada.org.au; internet www.ada.org .au; f. 1928 to promote the art and science of dentistry and to promote dental health to the public; 9,500 mems; Chief Exec. ROBERT N. BOYD-BOLAND; publs *Australian Dental Journal* (4 a year), *News Bulletin* (12 a year).

Australian Institute of Holistic Medicine: POB 3079, Success, WA 6964; tel. (8) 9417-3553; fax (8) 9417-1881; f. 1946; education and research in the field of natural medicine; Dean of Studies Dr S. JAYAWARDANA.

Australian Medical Association: 42 Macquarie St, Barton, ACT 2600; tel. (2) 6270-5400; fax (2) 6270-5499; e-mail ama@ama .com.au; internet www.ama.com.au; Sec.-Gen. Dr ROBYN MASON; publs *Australian Medicine*, *Medical Journal of Australia*.

Australian Physiological Society: c/o Dr David Saint, School of Molecular and Biomedical Science, University of Adelaide, Adelaide, SA 5005; tel. (8) 8303-3931; fax (8) 8303-3356; e-mail david.saint@adelaide.edu .au; internet www.aups.org.au; f. 1960 for the advancement of sciences of physiology; 350 mems; Pres. Prof. DAVID ADAMS; National Sec. Dr DAVID SAINT; publ. *Proceedings* (2 a year).

Australian Physiotherapy Association: Level 1, 1175 Toorak Rd, Camberwell, Vic. 3124; tel. (3) 9092-0888; fax (3) 9092-0899; e-mail national.office@physiotherapy.asn.au; internet www.physiotherapy.asn.au; f. 1905; provides postgraduate courses and professional services; 12,000 mems; Nat. Pres. MELISSA LOCKE; CEO CRIS MASSIS; publ. *Journal of Physiotherapy* (4 a year).

Australian Society of Clinical Hypnotherapists: POB 471, Eastwood, NSW 2122; tel. and fax (2) 9874-2776; e-mail secretary@asch.com.au; internet www.asch .com.au; f. 1974; to advance knowledge and practice of hypnosis and to maintain the highest ethical standards in its use; 350 mems; Pres. LYNDALL BRIGGS; Sec. EDWARD ZWICKI; publ. *The Australian Journal of Clinical Hypnotherapy and Hypnosis* (2 a year).

Optometrists Association Australia: POB 185, Carlton South, Vic. 3053; tel. (3) 9663-8533; fax (3) 9663-7478; e-mail oaanat@ optometrists.asn.au; internet www .optometrists.asn.au; f. 1918; promotes optometry and public education on vision care; 3,600 mems; Pres. ANDREW HARRIS; CEO JOSEPH CHAKMAN; publs *Australian Optometry* (12 a year), *Clinical and Experimental Optometry* (6 a year).

Royal Australasian College of Dental Surgeons: 64 Castlereagh St, Sydney, NSW 2000; tel. (2) 9232-3800; fax (2) 9221-8108; e-mail registrar@racds.org; internet www.racds.org; f. 1965; holds scientific meetings and administers examinations; 1,233 fellows; Pres. NEIL J. PEPPITT; Hon. Sec. STEPHEN C. DAYMOND; publs *Annals* (2 a year), *Lecture Notes in Anatomy* (1 a year), *Lecture Notes in Biochemistry* (1 a year), *Lecture Notes in Histology* (1 a year), *Lecture Notes in Microbiology* (1 a year), *Lecture Notes in Pathology* (1 a year), *Lecture Notes in Physiology* (1 a year), *Sedation Guidelines* (irregular).

Royal Australasian College of Physicians: 145 Macquarie St, Sydney, NSW 2000; tel. (2) 9256-5444; fax (2) 9252-3310; e-mail racp@racp.edu.au; internet www.racp .edu.au; f. 1938; charitable, educational and scientific activities; 7,000 fellows; library of 40,000 vols; History of Medicine library containing Ford Collection of rare Australiana; Pres. Dr JILL SEWELL (Vic.); CEO CRAIG PATTERSON; publs *Internal Medicine Journal* (12 a year), *Journal of Paediatrics and Child Health* (6 a year).

Royal Australasian College of Surgeons: College of Surgeons' Gardens, Melbourne, Vic. 3000; tel. (3) 9249-1200; fax (3) 9249-1219; internet www.surgeons.org; CEO Dr DAVID HILLIS; Pres. Dr ANDREW SUTHERLAND; publ. *Australian and New Zealand Journal of Surgery* (12 a year).

Royal Australian and New Zealand College of Ophthalmologists: 94–98 Chalmers St, Surry Hills, Sydney, NSW 2010; tel. (2) 9690-1001; fax (2) 9690-1321; e-mail ranzco@ranzco.edu; internet www.ranzco .edu; f. 1969 (formerly Ophthalmological Society of Australia); 1,322 mems; CEO ROBERT GUEST; Pres. Dr PETER HENDERSON; Vice-Pres. MICHAEL TREPLIN; Hon. Sec. CRAIG

DONALDSON; publ. *Clinical and Experimental Ophthalmology* (6 a year).

The Royal Australian and New Zealand College of Psychiatrists: 309 La Trobe St, Melbourne, Vic. 3000; tel. (3) 9640-0646; fax (3) 9642-5652; e-mail ranzcp@ranzcp.org; internet www.ranzcp.org; f. 1963, present name 1976; 2,429 fellows, 650 trainees; CEO Dr SHARON BROWNIE; publs *Australian and New Zealand Journal of Psychiatry*, *Australasian Psychiatry*.

Royal Australian and New Zealand College of Radiologists: Level 9, 51 Druitt St, Sydney, NSW 2000; tel. (2) 9268-9777; fax (2) 9268-9799; e-mail ranzcr@ranzcr.edu.au; internet www.ranzcr.edu.au; f. 1935; 2,301 mems; CEO DON SWINBOURNE; publ. *Australasian Radiology*.

Royal College of Nursing, Australia: 1 Napier Close, Deakin West, ACT 2600; tel. (2) 6283-3400; fax (2) 6282-3565; e-mail canberra@rcna.org.au; internet www.rcna .org.au; f. 1949; aims to promote improvement in nursing practice through education and research; grants membership to graduates of approved courses; administers nat. scholarships and research grants; conducts policy and devt programme, distance education programme; 10,000 mems; Pres. STEPHANIE FOX-YOUNG; CEO DEBRA CERASA; publs *Collegian* (4 a year), *Nursing Review* (12 a year), *RCNA News* (12 a year).

Royal College of Pathologists of Australasia: Durham Hall, 207 Albion St, Surry Hills, NSW 2010; tel. (2) 8356-5858; fax (2) 8356-5828; e-mail rcpa@rcpa.edu.au; internet www.rcpa.edu.au; f. 1956; 2,700 mems; Pres. Dr PAUL MCKENZIE; CEO Dr DEBRA GRAVES; publ. *Pathology*.

Sydney Medical School Foundation: Edward Ford Bldg A27, University of Sydney, Sydney, NSW 2006; tel. (2) 9351-7315; fax (2) 9036-9182; e-mail smsf@sydney.edu .au; internet sydney.edu.au/medicine/ foundation; f. 1958 previously known as the Medical Foundation; supports all areas of medical research within the Faculty of Medicine at the Univ. of Sydney; focuses on the translation of research knowledge to health outcomes through improved treatment options and prevention of disease; funds research; Pres. ROGER CORBETT; Dir. GEOFF DEAKIN.

NATURAL SCIENCES

General

Australian Academy of Science: GPOB 783, Canberra, ACT 2601; tel. (2) 6201-9400; fax (2) 6201-9494; e-mail eb@science.org.au; internet www.science.org.au; f. 1954; ind. non-profit org. for Australia's leading research scientists, elected for their personal contributions to science; recognizes research excellence, advises government, organizes scientific conferences, publishes scientific books and journals; administers int. exchange programmes and promotes science education and public awareness of science and technology; 420 fellows; Pres. Prof. KURT LAMBECK; Chief Exec. SUE MEEK; Sec. for Biological Sciences Prof. GRAHAM FARQUHAR; Sec. for Education and Public Awareness Prof. JULIE CAMPBELL; Sec. for Physical Sciences Dr PETER HALL; Sec. for Science Policy Dr ROBERT WILLAMSON; Foreign Sec. Prof. JENNY GRAVES; Treasurer Prof. MICHAEL DOPITA; publ. *Records*.

Australian and New Zealand Association for the Advancement of Science (ANZAAS): University of Adelaide, Adelaide, SA 5005; tel. (8) 8303-4965; fax (8) 8177-1732; e-mail mail@anzaas.org.au; internet anzaas.org.au; f. 1886; 1,000 mems;

divs in NSW, Vic., SA, WA, Tas., ACT and NT, also overseas mems; Sec. ROBERT PERRIN; publ. *ANZAAS Mercury* (4 a year).

Australian Conservation Foundation: Floor 1, 60 Leicester St, Carlton, Vic. 3053; tel. (3) 9345-1111; fax (3) 9345-1166; e-mail acf@acfonline.org.au; internet www.acfonline .org.au; f. 1965; non-profit org. working for an ecologically sustainable society; 60,000 mems and supporters; library of 15,000 vols; Pres. Prof. IAN LOWE; Dir DON HENRY; publs *Bilby Bulletin*, *Habitat* (6 a year).

Federation of Australian Scientific and Technological Societies: POB 218, Deakin West, Canberra, ACT 2600; tel. (2) 6257-2891; fax (2) 6257-2897; e-mail fasts@anu .edu.au; internet www.fasts.org; f. 1985 to foster close relations between the scientific and technological socs in Australia and to take concerted action for promoting science and technology in Australia; 60 mem. socs; Pres. Prof. CHRIS FELL; Pres.-Elect Prof. SNOW BARLOW; Exec. Dir BRADLEY SMITH; publ. *FASTS Circular* (12 a year).

Royal Society of New South Wales: 6/142 Herring Rd, North Ryde, POB 1525, Macquarie Centre, NSW 2113; tel. (2) 9887-4448; fax (2) 9887-4448; internet www.science.uts .edu.au/rsnsw; f. 1821; collection of monographs and periodicals relating to the history of Australian science, manuscripts of original research results; 305 mems; Pres. K. F. KELLY; Hon. Sec. Prof. Dr P. A. WILLIAMS; publs *Bulletin* (12 a year), *Journal and Proceedings* (2 a year).

Royal Society of Queensland: POB 6021, St Lucia, Qld 4067; e-mail rsocqld@gmail .com; internet qld.royalsoc.org.au; f. 1884; natural and applied sciences; 100 mems; library of 75,000 vols; Pres. CRAIG WALTON; publ. *Proceedings of the Royal Society of Queensland* (1 a year).

Royal Society of South Australia Inc.: c/o South Australian Museum, North Terrace, Adelaide, SA 5000; e-mail roysocsa@gmail .com; internet www.adelaide.edu.au/rssa; f. 1853; natural sciences; 283 mems; Pres. Dr NICK SOUTER; Hon. Sec. Dr KIM CRITCHLEY; publs *Regional Natural Histories* (irregular), *Transactions* (2 a year).

Royal Society of Tasmania: GPOB 1166, Hobart, Tas. 7001; tel. (3) 6211-4177; fax (3) 6211-4112; e-mail royal.society@tmag.tas .gov.au; internet rst.org.au; f. 1843; 360 mems; library of 40,000 vols; Pres. Prof. JIM REID; Hon. Sec. TONY CULBERG; publ. *Papers and Proceedings* (1 a year).

Royal Society of Victoria: 9 Victoria St, Melbourne, Vic. 3000; tel. (3) 9663-5259; fax (3) 9663-2301; e-mail rsv@sciencevictoria.org .au; internet www.sciencevictoria.org.au; f. 1854; 750 mems; library: large colln of scientific periodicals since 1854; Pres. Prof. LYNNE SELWOOD; Hon. Sec. Dr. WILLIAM D. BIRCH; publ. *Proceedings* (2 a year).

Royal Society of Western Australia: c/o Western Australian Museum, Locked Bag 49, Welshpool DC, WA 6986; tel. (8) 9212-3771; fax (8) 9212-3882; e-mail rswa@museum.wa .gov.au; internet www.ecu.edu.au/pa/rswa; f. 1913; to promote and foster natural and physical science and facilitate interdisciplinary interaction; study of botany, zoology, geology, anthropology, geography, physics and chemistry; 395 mems; Pres. Dr COLIN WALKER; Joint Secs Dr LYNNE MILNE, MARGARET BROCX; publ. *Journal* (4 a year).

Biological Sciences

Australian Society for Fish Biology: WA Marine Research Laboratories, POB 20, North Beach, WA 6020; tel. (8) 9246-8418; e-mail dgaughan@fish.wa.gov.au; internet www.asfb.org.au; f. 1971; promotes the study

of fish and fisheries in Australia and provides a communications medium for Australian fish workers; 530 mems; Pres. Dr DAN GAUGHAN; Sec. and Vice-Pres. KIM SMITH; publ. *Newsletter* (2 a year).

Australian Society for Limnology: Museum of Victoria, GPOB 666, Melbourne, Vic. 3001; tel. (3) 8341-7433; fax (3) 8341-7456; e-mail rmarch@museum.vic.gov.au; internet www.asl.org.au; f. 1961; study and management of inland waters, maintenance of biodiversity, restoration of water quality and wise use of aquatic resources; 288 mems, incl. researchers, managers, engineers, teachers and tertiary-level students; Sec. Dr RICHARD MARCHANT; publ. *ASL Newsletter* (4 a year).

Australian Society for Microbiology Inc.: Unit 23, 20 Commercial Rd, Melbourne, Vic. 3004; tel. (3) 9867-8699; fax (3) 9867-8722; f. 1959; 3,200 mems; Pres. Assoc. Prof. JOHN FINLAY-JONES; Sec. Dr J. LANSER; publs *Microbiology Australia* (5 a year), *Recent Advances in Microbiology* (1 a year).

Australian Society for Parasitology: c/o Heather Koch, Secretary, PO Royal Brisbane Hospital, Brisbane, Qld 4029; tel. (2) 6257-9022; fax (2) 6257-9055; e-mail heather .koch@animalhealthalliance.org.au; internet www.parasite.org.au; f. 1964; all aspects of parasitology, including immunology and vaccinology; 450 mems; 34 fellows; Pres. PETER HOLDSWORTH; Sec. HEATHER KOCH; publ. *International Journal for Parasitology* (12 a year).

Ecological Society of Australia Inc.: POB 1564, Canberra, ACT 2601; tel. (8) 8953-7544; fax (8) 8953-7566; e-mail executiveofficer@ecolsoc.org.au; internet www.ecolsoc.org.au; f. 1960 to promote the scientific study of plants and animals in relation to their environment, and publish the results of research; to facilitate the exchange of ideas among ecologists; to promote the application of ecological principles to the devt, utilization and conservation of Australian natural resources; to advise govt and other agencies; to foster the reservation of natural areas for scientific and recreational purposes; 1,564 mems; Pres. C. CATTERALL; Sec. T. SILBERBAUER; Exec. Officers T. HOWARD, L. MCMILLAN; publs *Austral Ecology* (6 a year), *Bulletin* (4 a year), *Environmental Management and Restoration* (3 a year).

Entomological Society of New South Wales Inc.: Entomology Dept, The Australian Museum, 6–8 College St, Sydney, NSW 2000; e-mail tanya.james@agric.nsw.gov.au; internet entsocnsw.netfirms.com; f. 1953; 180 mems; Pres. MARTIN HORWOOD; Hon. Sec. TANYA JAMES; publ. *General and Applied Entomology* (1 a year).

Entomological Society of Queensland: POB 537, Indooroopilly, Brisbane, Qld 4068; e-mail esq@uqconnect.net; internet www.esq .org.au; ind.; promotes study of entomology; f. 1923; 280 mems; Pres. Dr LYN COOK; Sec. Dr JUDY KING; publs *News Bulletin* (9 or 10 a year), *The Australian Entomologist* (4 a year).

Field Naturalists Club of Victoria: Locked Bag 3, Post Office, Blackburn, Vic. 3130; tel. (3) 9877-9860; fax (3) 9877-9860; e-mail fncv@vicnet.net.au; internet www .vicnet.net.au/~fncv; f. 1880; study of natural history and conservation of environment; 1,000 mems; Pres. KAREN MUSCAT; publs *Field Nats News* (11 a year), *The Victorian Naturalist* (6 a year).

Malacological Society of Australasia: c/o Dept of Malacology, Australian Museum, 6 College St, Sydney, NSW 2010; tel. (2) 9320-6052; fax (2) 9320-6050; e-mail info@

malsocaus.org; internet www.malsocaus.org; f. 1955; promotes the study of molluscs; 170 mems; Pres. Dr RACHEL PRZESLAWSKI; Treasurer Dr DON COLGAN; publs *Malacological Society of Australasia Newsletter* (3 a year), *Molluscan Research* (3 a year).

Royal Australasian Ornithologists Union trading as Birds Australia: Suite 2-05, 60 Leicester St, Carlton, Vic. 3053; tel. (3) 9347-0757; fax (3) 9347-9323; e-mail mail@birdsaustralia.com.au; internet www.birdsaustralia.com.au; f. 1901; for conservation, study and appreciation of native Australasian birds and their habitats; extensive library and database; 8,000 mems; CEO Dr GRAEME HAMILTON; publs *ASG Bulletin, Emu - Austral Ornithology* (4 a year), *Stilt, Wingspan* (4 a year), *Wing Thing*.

Royal Zoological Society of New South Wales: POB 20, Mosman, NSW 2088; tel. (2) 9969-7336; fax (2) 9969-7336; f. 1879; 1,000 mems; Pres. Dr PAT HUTCHINGS; Exec. Officer GILLIAN SIMPSON; publ. *Australian Zoologist* (2 a year).

Royal Zoological Society of South Australia Inc.: Frome Rd, Adelaide, SA 5000; tel. (8) 8267-3255; fax (8) 8239-0637; internet www.zoossa.com.au; f. 1878; maintains public zoo and open-range park; plays an active role in the conservation of endangered species, conservation education and in conservation research; 32,700 mems; library of 4,700 catalogued items; books, audiovisual and digital media, journal articles, photographs; CEO Prof. C. WEST; publ. *Zoo Times* (3 a year).

Wildlife Preservation Society of Australia Ltd: POB 42, Brighton Le Sands, NSW 2216; tel. (2) 9556-1537; fax (2) 9500-0000; e-mail wildlifepreservation@optusnet.com.au; internet www.wpsa.org.au; f. 1909; ind., voluntary, non-profit org., committed to the preservation of Australia's flora and fauna; provides advice to govt agencies and instns regarding environmental and conservation issues; nat. environmental education programmes, political lobbying, advocacy and practical conservation work; 1,000 mems; Pres. SUZANNE MEDWAY; Hon. Sec. PATRICK MEDWAY; publ. *Australian Wildlife Magazine* (4 a year).

Zoological Parks and Gardens Board: POB 74, Parkville, Vic. 3052; tel. (3) 9285-9300; fax (3) 9285-9330; e-mail zpgb@zoo.org.au; internet www.zoo.org.au; f. 1937 as successor to Royal Zoological and Acclimatization Soc. of Victoria (f. 1857); responsible for the management of the Royal Melbourne Zoological Gardens, Healesville Sanctuary and Victoria's Open Range Zoo at Werribee; 9 mems; Chair. TINA McMECKAN.

Mathematical Sciences

Australian Mathematical Society: Dept of Mathematics, La Trobe University, Bundoora, Vic. 3086; tel. (3) 9479-2597; fax (3) 9479-2466; e-mail secretary@austms.org.au; internet www.austms.org.au; f. 1956; 1,000 mems; fosters communication among its members, and organizes and supports mathematical conferences in Australasia; makes grants to promote mathematical investigations; awards prizes; raises community awareness about the importance and benefits of mathematics; Pres. Prof. PETER TAYLOR; Sec. Dr PETER STACEY; Treas. Dr ALGY HOWE; publs *ANZIAM Journal* (4 a year), *Bulletin of the Australian Mathematical Society* (6 a year), *Gazette of the Australian Mathematical Society* (5 a year), *Journal of the Australian Mathematical Society* (6 a year).

Statistical Society of Australia, Inc.: POB 5111, Braddon, ACT 2612; tel. (2) 6249-8266; fax (2) 6249-6558; e-mail admin@statsoc.org.au; internet www.statsoc.org.au; f. 1959; 800 mems; Pres. Prof. KAYE BASFORD; Sec. Dr DOUGLAS SHAW; publs *Australian & New Zealand Journal of Statistics* (4 a year), *SSAI Newsletter* (4 a year).

Physical Sciences

Astronomical Society of Australia: c/o School of Physics, Univ. of Sydney, Sydney, NSW 2006; tel. (2) 9351-3184; fax (2) 9351-7726; e-mail john.obyrne@sydney.edu.au; internet asa.astronomy.org.au; f. 1966 as the Org. of Professional Astronomers in Australia; 500 mems; Pres. Prof. LISTER STAVELEY-SMITH; Sec. Dr JOHN O'BYRNE; Sec. Dr. MARC DULDIG; publ. *Publications of the Astronomical Society of Australia* (online, 4 a year).

Astronomical Society of South Australia Inc.: GPOB 199, Adelaide, SA 5001; tel. (8) 8270-3631; e-mail info@assa.org.au; internet www.assa.org.au; f. 1892; 500 mems; library of 400 vols; Pres. DEAN DAVIDSON; Sec. IAN ANDERSON; publ. *The Bulletin* (12 a year).

Astronomical Society of Tasmania Inc.: c/o The Secretary, POB 1654, Hobart, Tas. 7001; tel. (3) 6323-3777; fax (3) 6323-3776; internet www.ast.net.au; f. 1934; 100 mems; Pres. S. W. MATHERS; Sec. LAURIE PRIEST; publs *Annual Ephemeris for Tasmania, Bulletin* (6 a year).

Astronomical Society of Victoria Inc.: GPOB 1059, Melbourne, Vic. 3001; tel. (3) 9888-7130; internet www.asv.org.au; f. 1922; 18 sections: Astrophotography, Computing, Comet, Cosmology and Astrophysics, Deep Sky, Demonstrators, Historical, Instrument Making, Lunar and Planetary, Outdoor Lighting Improvement, Meteors, Radio Astronomy, Solar, Variable Stars and Nova Search, Club, Diurnals (day group), Junior (for children aged 17 and under) and New Astronomers' Group; 1,000 mems; library of 3,000 vols; Pres. BARRY ADCOCK; Gen. Sec. ANNE WILLIAMS; publs *Crux Magazine* (6 a year), *Yearbook* (1 a year).

Australasian College of Physical Scientists and Engineers in Medicine: Ste 3.13, 247 Coward St, Mascot, NSW 2020; tel. (2) 9700-8522; fax (2) 9693-5145; e-mail secretary@acpsem.org.au; internet www.acpsem.org.au; f. 1977 to promote the devt of the physical sciences as applied to medicine, to facilitate the exchange of information and ideas among mems and others, to disseminate knowledge relating to physical sciences and their application to medicine; 600 mems; Gen. Man. GARY DISHER; Hon. Sec. Dr JOHN R. COLES; publ. *Australasian Physical and Engineering Sciences in Medicine* (4 a year).

Australian Acoustical Society: POB 903, Castlemaine, Vic. 3450; tel. (3) 5470-6381; fax (3) 5470-6381; e-mail watkinsd@castlemaine.net; internet www.acoustics.asn.au; f. 1971; 420 mems; Pres. KEN MIKL; Gen. Sec. D. WATKINS; publ. *Acoustics Australia* (3 a year).

Australian Institute of Physics: 1/21 Vale Street, North Melbourne, Vic. 3051; tel. (3) 9326-6669; fax (3) 9328-2670; internet www.physics.usyd.edu.au/aipaust; f. 1963; 2,500 mems; Pres. Prof. ROBERT ELLMAN; Hon. Sec. Dr IAN BAILEY; publ. *The Physicist* (6 a year).

Geological Society of Australia: Suite 706, 301 George St, Sydney, NSW 2000; tel. (2) 9290-2194; fax (2) 9290-2198; e-mail info@gsa.org.au; internet www.gsa.org.au; f. 1953; 2,300 mems; publs *Alcheringa* (4 a year), *Australian Journal of Earth Sciences* (8 a year).

Royal Australian Chemical Institute: 21 Vale St, North Melbourne, Vic. 3051; tel. (3) 9328-2033; fax (3) 9328-2670; e-mail member@raci.org.au; internet www.raci.org.au; f. 1917, inc. by Royal Charter 1932; it is both the qualifying body for professional chemists and a learned society that aims to promote the science and practice of chemistry in all its branches; 9,500 mems; Pres. DAVID EDMONDS; Hon. Gen. Sec. Dr JANE WEDER; publ. *Chemistry in Australia* (12 a year).

PHILOSOPHY AND PSYCHOLOGY

Australasian Association of Philosophy: POB 1978, Hobart, Tas. 7009; tel. (3) 6294-6319; e-mail elizagoddard@aap.org.au; internet www.aap.org.au; f. 1923; professional org. of academic philosophers in Australia, New Zealand and Singapore; promotes the study of philosophy in Australasia; coordinates professional activities; 400 mems; Chair. Prof. GRAHAM OPPY PRIEST; Exec. Officer ELIZA GODDARD; Sec. Dr TIM OAKLEY; publ. *Australasian Journal of Philosophy* (4 a year).

Australian Psychological Society: POB 38, Flinders Lane, Vic. 8009; 11th Fl., 257 Collins St, Melbourne, Vic. 3000; tel. (3) 8662-3300; fax (3) 9663-6177; e-mail assessments@psychology.org.au; internet www.psychology.org.au; f. 1966; 19,000 mems; Pres. Prof. SIMON CROWE; Exec. Dir Dr LYNDEL LITTLEFIELD; publs *Australian Journal of Psychology* (3 a year), *Australian Psychologist* (3 a year), *In-Psych* (6 a year).

RELIGION, SOCIOLOGY AND ANTHROPOLOGY

The Australian Sociological Association: Institute for Social Research, Swinburne Univ. of Technology, POB 218, Mailbag H28 Hawthorn, Vic. 3122; tel. (3) 9214-5283; fax (3) 9214-8643; e-mail admin@tasa.org.au; internet www.tasa.org.au; f. 1963; aims to promote devt of sociology in Australia, facilitate sociology teaching and research, and enhance the professional devt of mems; holds annual conferences, gives awards; 600 mems; Pres. Dr DEBRA KING; Vice-Pres. Dr JO LINDSAY; Sec. EILEEN CLARK; Treas. Prof. KATIE HUGHES; publs *Health Sociology Review* (4 a year), *Journal of Sociology* (4 a year).

TECHNOLOGY

Australasian Institute of Mining and Metallurgy: Ground Floor, 204 Lygon St, Carlton, Vic. 3053; tel. (3) 9662-3166; fax (3) 9662-3662; e-mail publications@ausimm.com.au; internet www.ausimm.com; f. 1893; incorporated by Royal Charter 1955; 10,300 mems; Pres. IAN GOULD; publ. *The AusIMM Bulletin* (6 a year).

Australian Academy of Technological Sciences and Engineering: Ian McLennan House, 197 Royal Parade, Parkville, Vic. 3052; tel. (3) 9347-0622; fax (3) 9347-8237; e-mail paulaw@atse.org.au; internet www.atse.org.au; f. 1976; promotion of scientific and engineering knowledge for practical purposes; 670 fellows (incl. 8 hon., 9 foreign, 1 Royal); Pres. Dr J. W. ZILLMAN; CEO Dr JOHN DODGSON; publs *Annual Symposia Proceedings, ATSE Focus* (4 a year).

Australian Institute of Energy: POB 268, Toukley, NSW 2263; tel. and fax (2) 4393-1114; e-mail aie@aie.org.au; internet www.aie.org.au; f. 1978; 1,500 mems; Pres. Dr MALCOLM MESSENGER; Sec. COLIN PAULSON; Treasurer Dr DAVID ALLARDICE; publ. *Energy News* (4 a year).

Australian Institute of Food Science and Technology Inc.: Suite 2, Level 2, 191 Botany Rd, Waterloo, NSW 2017; tel. (612) 8399-3996; fax (612) 8399-3997; e-mail aifst@aifst.asn.au; internet www.aifst.asn

.au; f. 1967; nat. asscn for professionals involved in the science and technology of food; Pres. Prof. PAUL BAUMGARTNER; Treasurer Dr JEFF FAIRBROTHER; publ. *Food Australia* (12 a year).

Australian Institute of Nuclear Science and Engineering: PMB No. 1, Menai, NSW 2234; tel. (2) 9717-3376; fax (2) 9717-9268; e-mail ainse@ansto.gov.au; internet www.ainse.edu.au; f. 1958; consortium of Australian univs and the Univ. of Auckland, New Zealand, in partnership with the Australian Nuclear Science and Technology Org.; aims to assist research and training in nuclear science and engineering and to make the facilities of the Lucas Heights Research Laboratories available to research staff and students from mem. institutions; projects in advanced materials, biomedicine, environmental science, applications of nuclear physics, nuclear technology and engineering; organizes Australian Numerical Simulation and Modelling Services and Australian Radioisotope Services; organizes conferences, awards postgraduate studentships and research grants; 49 mems; Pres. Prof. JOHN WHITE; Vice-Pres. Prof. BRIAN O'CONNOR; Scientific Sec. Dr DENNIS MATHER; publ. *AINSE Conference Books*.

Australian Robotics and Automation Association Inc.: GPOB 1527, Sydney, NSW 2001; tel. (2) 9959-3239; fax (2) 9959-4632; internet www.araa.asn.au; f. 1981; professional society concerned with robots, their applications and implications, and related automation technologies; Pres. GORDON WYETH; Vice-Pres. JONATHAN ROBERTS; Sec. MATTHEW DUNBABIN; publ. *Newsletter* (4 a year).

Chartered Institute of Logistics and Transport: POB 4594, Robina, QLD 4230; tel. and fax (7) 5522-7088; e-mail admin@cilta.com.au; internet www.cilta.com.au; f. 1935; professional soc. concerned with logistics and transport; 30,000 mems worldwide; CEO HALL MORRIS; Admin. and Communications Man. HANNA LUCAS; publ. *Australian Transport Review* (2 a year).

Institution of Engineers, Australia trading as Engineers Australia: 11 National Circuit, Barton, ACT 2600; tel. (2) 6270-6555; fax (2) 6273-1488; e-mail memberservices@engineersaustralia.org.au; internet www.engineersaustralia.org.au; f. 1919; incorporates colleges of Biomedical Engineers, Chemical Engineers, Civil Engineers, Electrical Engineers, Environmental Engineers, Information Telecommunications and Electronics Engineers, Mechanical Engineers, and Structural Engineers; 90,000 mems; Chief Exec. PETER TAYLOR; publs *Australian Journal of Civil Engineering*, *Australian Journal of Electrical and Electronics Engineering*, *Australian Journal of Mechanical Engineering*, *Australian Journal of Multidisciplinary Engineering*, *Australian Journal of Water Resources*, *Chemical Engineering in Australia*, *Civil Engineers Australia* (12 a year), *Engineering World* (6 a year), *Engineers Australia* (12 a year), *Transport Engineering in Australia*.

Institution of Surveyors, Australia: 27–29 Napier Close, Deakin, Canberra, ACT 2600; tel. (2) 6282-2282; fax (2) 6282-2576; e-mail info@isaust.org.au; internet www.isaust.org.au; f. 1952; 3,800 mems; CEO JOHN D. CRICKMORE; publs *Geomatics Research Australasia* (2 a year), *The Australian Surveyor* (1 a year), *Trans Tasman Surveyor* (1 a year).

Royal Aeronautical Society, Australian Division: POB 573, Mascot, NSW 2020; tel. (2) 9523-4332; fax (2) 9523-7158; e-mail austdivision@raes.org.au; internet www.raes

.org.au; f. 1927; brs in Adelaide, Brisbane, Canberra, Melbourne, Perth, Sydney; Pres. D. FORSYTH; Hon. Sec. R. D. BARKLA; Treasurer R. H. STEVENS; Admin. Officer PETER BROOKS; publ. *Australian Aeronautics* (every 2 years).

The Australian Ceramic Society: c/o Dept of Applied Physics, Curtin University of Technology, GPOB U1987, Perth, WA 6845; tel. (8) 9266-7544; fax (8) 9266-2377; e-mail j.low@curtin.edu.au; internet www.austceram.com; f. 1961; to promote ceramic science and technology and its applications for Australian ceramic industry and art; 300 mems; Fed. Pres. Dr PHIL WALLS; Fed. Sec. Prof. JIM LOW; publs *Journal of the Australian Ceramic Society* (2 a year), *Newsbulletin of the Australian Ceramic Society* (4 a year).

Research Institutes

AGRICULTURE, FISHERIES AND VETERINARY SCIENCE

Department of Infrastructure, Planning and Natural Resources: GPOB 39, Sydney, NSW 2001; tel. (2) 9228-6111; fax (2) 9228-6455; internet www.dipnr.nsw.gov.au; conservation and management of crown land, rivers and water resources, containment of salinity and acid sulphate soils; Dir-Gen. JENNIFER WESTACOTT.

EDUCATION

Australian Council for Educational Research Ltd: 19 Prospect Hill Rd (PMB 55), Camberwell, Vic. 3124; tel. (3) 9277-5555; fax (3) 9277-5500; e-mail sales@acer.edu.au; internet www.acer.edu.au; f. 1930; ind.; educational research and publishing; books for teachers at all levels, students, parents, psychologists, counsellors, administrators, curriculum writers; educational, psychological and personnel tests; CEO Prof. GEOFFREY MASTERS; publs *Australian Education Index* (subscription database), *Australian Journal of Career Development* (3 a year), *Australian Journal of Education* (3 a year), *Australian Thesaurus of Education Descriptors*, *Education Research Theses* (subscription database), *Professional Education* (4 a year), *Recent Developments* (2 a year), *Teacher* (10 a year).

National Centre for Vocational Education Research (NCVER) Ltd: Level 11, 33 King William St, Adelaide, SA 5000; tel. (8) 8230-8400; fax (8) 8212-3436; e-mail ncver@ncver.edu.au; internet www.ncver.edu.au; f. 1981; ind. org. est. by the Fed., State and Territory ministers responsible for vocational and technical education; Australia's principal provider of vocational education and training (VET) research and statistics; responsible for collecting and managing national VET and New Apprenticeship statistics; provides VET research findings from Australian and int. sources through its VOCED research database; library of 40,000 records; 20,000 full-text; Chair. PETER SHERGOLD; Man. Dir Dr TOM KARMEL; publs *Insight* (news and information, 4 a year), *Vocational Education and Training Research Database (VOCED)* (12 a year).

HISTORY, GEOGRAPHY AND ARCHAEOLOGY

Tasmanian Historical Research Association: POB 441, Sandy Bay, Tas. 7006; tel. (3) 6260-2604; internet www.thra.org.au; f. 1951; 400 mems; Pres. and Chair. Dr ALISON ALEXANDER; Sec. ANDREW MCKINLEY; publ. *Papers and Proceedings* (3 a year).

MEDICINE

Australian Radiation Protection and Nuclear Safety Agency: 619 Lower Plenty Rd, Yallambie, Vic. 3085; tel. (3) 9433-2211; fax (3) 9432-1835; e-mail arpansa@arpansa.gov.au; internet www.arpansa.gov.au; f. 1929; attached to Australian Department of Health and Ageing; works to protect the environment and the health and safety of the public from the harmful effects of radiation; library of 10,000 vols; CEO Dr JOHN LOY; publ. *ARPANSA technical reports* (irregular).

Australian Society for Medical Research: 145 Macquarie St, Sydney, NSW 2000; tel. (2) 9256-5450; fax (2) 9252-0294; e-mail asmr@world.net; internet www.asmr.org.au; f. 1961 to provide a forum for discussion of medical research across disciplinary boundaries, and to encourage recent graduates to consider research as a career; holds Nat. Scientific Conference; 1,400 mems; Hon. Sec. Dr BRONWYN KINGWELL; Hon. Treasurer Dr ROHAN BAKER; publ. *Proceedings*.

Baker IDI Heart and Diabetes Institute: POB 6492, St Kilda Rd Central, Melbourne, Vic. 8008; tel. (3) 8532-1111; fax (3) 8532-1100; e-mail genebank@bakeridi.edu.au; internet www.bakeridi.edu.au; f. 1926; basic, clinical and applied research on cardiovascular disease, physiology, pharmacology, endocrinology, molecular and cell biology; affiliated to WHO, Monash Univ., Alfred Hospital incl. the Alfred Baker Medical Unit (f. 1949); library of 15,000 vols; Pres., Bd of Dirs Prof. ROBERT STEWART; Vice-Pres. PAULA DWYER; publ. *Research*.

CSL Ltd: 45 Poplar Rd, Parkville, Vic. 3052; tel. (3) 9389-1911; fax (3) 9389-1434; f. 1916 for research, production and marketing of biologicals; library: Knowledge Library of 8,500 vols; CEO Dr BRIAN MCNAMEE.

Institute of Dental Research: Westmead Millenium Institute, POB 412, Westmead, NSW 2145; f. 1946; for research into biological problems relating to dental health; Head Prof. NEIL HUNTER (acting).

Institute of Medical and Veterinary Science: Frome Rd, Adelaide, SA 5000; tel. (8) 8222-3000; fax (8) 8222-3538; f. 1938 for purposes of research into diseases of human beings and animals, and to provide a diagnostic pathology service for the Royal Adelaide Hospital and for the State through 12 regional laboratories; teaching is provided for the Univ. of Adelaide Medical School; Dir BARRIE VERON-ROBERTS.

Kolling Institute of Medical Research: Royal North Shore Hospital, Pacific Highway, St Leonards, NSW 2065; tel. (2) 9926-8486; fax (2) 9926-8484; e-mail kolling@med.usyd.edu.au; internet www.kolling.usyd.edu.au; f. 1930; research in allergic diseases, molecular genetics and growth factors; Exec. Officer CAMILLA SCANLAN; Technical Officer HELEN YU.

Mental Health Research Institute: 155 Oak St, Parkville, Vic. 3052; tel. (3) 9388-1633; fax (3) 9387-5061; internet www.mhri.edu.au; f. 1956; studies aspects of the nature and treatment of psychiatric illnesses with a particular emphasis on a neuroscience approach to Alzheimer's Disease and to the major psychoses, especially schizophrenia; Chair. Prof. SANDRA HACKER; Exec. Dir Prof. COLIN MASTERS.

National Health and Medical Research Council: GPOB 9848, Canberra, ACT 2601; tel. (2) 6289-9184; fax (2) 6289-9197; e-mail exec.sec@nhmrc.gov.au; internet www.nhmrc.gov.au; f. 1936 to advise on the achievement and maintenance of the highest practicable standards of individual and public health, and to foster research in the interests of improving those standards; CEO Prof. WARWICK ANDERSON; publ. *Triennial Strategic Plan*.

National Vision Research Institute of Australia: 386 Cardigan St, Carlton, Melbourne, Vic. 3053; tel. (3) 9349-7480; fax (3) 9349-7473; e-mail nvri@optometry.unimelb .edu.au; internet www.optometry.unimelb .edu.au/nvri/nvri.htm; f. 1972; basic, applied and clinical research into vision and visual dysfunction; Chair. S. F. KALFF; Dir of Research Prof. P. R. MARTIN.

Queensland Institute of Medical Research: Locked Bag 2000, Royal Brisbane Hospital, Brisbane, Qld 4029; tel. (7) 3362-0222; fax (7) 3362-0111; e-mail enquiries@ qimr.edu.au; internet www.qimr.edu.au; f. 1946; research into medical problems important in the Australian and Asian Pacific region; current areas are tropical medicine, virology, oncology, cell biology, molecular biology, epidemiology, liver disease, melanoma, mental health, indigenous health; State Medical Research Centre (SMRC) to be constructed by 2012; library of 19,100 vols, 3,000 monographs incl. Eugen Hirschfeld colln of German medical texts dating from 1700s. 600 print journals, 500 online journals and ebooks; Chair. of Council JOHN HAY; Dir Prof. FRANK GANNON.

Walter and Eliza Hall Institute of Medical Research: 1G Royal Parade, Parkville, Vic. 3050; tel. (3) 9345-2555; fax (3) 9347-0852; e-mail information@wehi.edu.au; internet www.wehi.edu.au; f. 1916; research into cellular and molecular immunology, cancer, immunopathology and immunoparasitology, genome science and bioinformatics; 500 staff; library of 20,000 vols; Dir Prof. DOUG HILTON.

NATURAL SCIENCES
General

Commonwealth Scientific and Industrial Research Organisation (CSIRO): Bag 10, Clayton South, Vic. 3169; tel. (3) 9545-2176; fax (3) 9545-2175; e-mail enquiries@csiro.au; internet www.csiro.au; f. 1926; researches all fields of the physical and biological sciences except defence science, nuclear energy and clinical medicine; Sectors: field crops; food processing; forestry, wood and paper industries; horticulture; meat, dairy and aquaculture; wool and textiles; biodiversity; climate and atmosphere; land and water; information technology and telecommunications; built environment; measurement standards; radio astronomy; services; chemicals and plastics; integrated manufactured products; pharmaceuticals and human health; energy; mineral exploration and mining; mineral processing and metal production; petroleum; library: see Libraries and Archives; Chair. CATHERINE LIVINGSTONE; Chief Exec. Dr GEOFF GARRETT; publs *Australian Journal of Agricultural Research* (8 a year), *Australian Journal of Botany* (6 a year), *Australian Journal of Chemistry* (12 a year), *Australian Journal of Experimental Agriculture* (6 a year), *Australian Journal of Invertebrate Taxonomy* (6 a year), *Australian Journal of Marine and Freshwater Research* (6 a year), *Australian Journal of Physics* (6 a year), *Australian Journal of Plant Physiology* (6 a year), *Australian Journal of Reproduction, Fertility and Development* (6 a year), *Australian Journal of Soil Research* (6 a year), *Australian Journal of Wildlife Research* (6 a year), *Australian Journal of Zoology* (6 a year), *Australian Systematic Botany* (4 a year), *ECOS* (4 a year), *The Helix* (6 a year).

National Facility Within CSIRO:

CSIRO–Australia Telescope National Facility: POB 76, Epping, NSW 1710; tel. (2) 9372-4100; fax (2) 9372-4310; e-mail atnf-enquiries@csiro.au; internet www .atnf.csiro.au; f. 1988; a radio telescope array consisting of 6 22-m antennas at the Paul Wild Observatory, Narrabri, NSW, a 22-m antenna at Mopra, west of Coonabarabran, NSW, and a 64-m antenna near Parkes, NSW; Dir Prof. BRIAN BOYLE.

Biological Sciences

Australian Institute of Marine Science: PMB 3, Townsville, MC Qld 4810; tel. (7) 4753-4444; fax (7) 4772-5852; e-mail reception@aims.gov.au; internet www.aims .gov.au; f. 1972; to advance knowledge of the sustainable use and protection of the marine environment, through scientific and technological research; 180 mems; library of 10,000 vols, 1,875 periodicals, 1,544 electronic journals, 450 maps, 55 video cassettes; Chair. WAYNE OSBORNE; CEO Dr IAN R. POINER.

Australian National Botanic Gardens: POB 1777, Canberra, ACT 2601; Clunies Ross St, Black Mountain, Canberra; tel. (2) 6250-9450; fax (2) 6250-9599; e-mail anbg-info@anbg.gov.au; internet www.anbg .gov.au; f. 1970, a few plantings date from 1947; grows a colln of Australian native plants (6,500 species); jtly manages with CSIRO the Centre for Plant Biodiversity Research and Australian National Herbarium with about 1.2m. specimens; manages the Australian Plant Image Index, the largest colln of photographs of Australian native plants; 1,500 mems; library of 13,356 vols, 650 serial titles, 5,000 maps; Dir ANNE DUNCAN; Dir, Centre for Plant Biodiversity Research Dr JUDY WEST.

Royal Botanic Gardens Melbourne: PMB 2000, S. Yarra, Vic. 3141; tel. (3) 9252-2300; fax (3) 9252-2350; e-mail rbg@rbg.vic.gov.au; internet www.rbg.vic.gov.au; f. 1846; 36-ha (94-acre) garden with more than 10,000 different species and cultivars of Australian and exotic plants; herbarium of 1m. specimens; library of 50,000 vols; also Royal Botanic Gardens, Cranbourne, for growing display and study of native Australian plants; also Australian Research Centre for Urban Ecology; Dir Dr PHILIP MOORS; publ. *Muelleria*.

Royal Botanic Gardens Sydney: Mrs Macquaries Rd, Sydney, NSW 2000; tel. (2) 9231-8111; fax (2) 9251-4403; e-mail botanical.is@rbgsyd.nsw.gov.au; internet www.rbgsyd.nsw.gov.au; f. 1816; 470-ha living plant colln in 3 botanic gardens and herbarium of 1m. specimens; library of 50,000 vols; Mount Tomah Botanic Garden for cool-climate plants; Mount Annan Botanic Garden for native plants; specialization in research on Australian native plants; Exec. Dir TIM ENTWISLE; publs *Cunninghamia*, *Telopea*.

Therapeutic Goods Administration Laboratories: POB 100, Woden, ACT 2606; tel. (2) 6232-8400; fax (2) 6232-8442; e-mail tga-information-officer@health.gov .au; internet www.tga.gov.au; f. 1958 as National Biological Standards Laboratories to ensure the quality, safety, efficacy and timely availability of therapeutic goods used in or exported from Australia; part of the Therapeutic Goods Administration, Dept of Health and Aged Care; library of 30,000 vols and 5,000 microfiche; Dir Dr R. J. SMITH; publ. *TGA Laboratory Information Bulletin* (1 a year).

Mathematical Sciences

Australian Bureau of Statistics: Locked Bag 10, Belconnen, ACT 2616; tel. (2) 6252-5000; fax (2) 6251-6009; internet www.abs .gov.au; f. 1905; library of 38,000 vols, 9,600 periodicals; Australian Statistician DENNIS TREWIN; publs *Yearbook Australia* (1 a year), and some 400 other titles listed in *Catalogue of ABS Publications*.

Physical Sciences

Australian Nuclear Science and Technology Organisation (ANSTO): Access ANSTO, PMB 1, Menai, NSW 2234; tel. (2) 9717-3111; fax (2) 9717-9274; internet www .ansto.gov.au; f. 1987; Australia's nat. atomic org.; aims to bring the benefits of atomic science and technology to industry, medicine and the community; research and devt programmes focusing on industrial and other applications of atomic science, environmental science, advanced materials, biomedicine and health; operates nat. facilities, provides technical advice and training; library of 40,000 vols, 900,000 fiches; Chief Exec. Dr ADI PATERSON; publ. scientific papers and reports.

Commonwealth Bureau of Meteorology: GPOB 1289, Melbourne, Vic. 3001; tel. (3) 9669-4000; fax (3) 9669-4699; internet www .bom.gov.au; f. 1908; regional offices in Perth, Adelaide, Brisbane, Sydney, Hobart, Darwin and Melbourne; library of 80,000 vols; Chair. Prof. VICKI SARA; Dir Dr GREG AYERS; publs daily weather bulletins and charts, monthly, seasonal and annual rainfall maps and statistical summaries, publs on spec. subjects, climatological reviews, *Australian Meteorological and Oceanographic Magazine* (4 a year).

Geological Survey of New South Wales: Dept of Mineral Resources, POB 536, St Leonards, NSW 1590; tel. (2) 9901-8888; fax (2) 9901-8777; e-mail webcoord@minerals .nsw.gov.au; internet www.minerals.nsw.gov .au; f. 1874; advice on geology and mineral resources of NSW, incl. preparation of standard series geological, geophysical and metallogenic maps; research studies in tectonics, palaeontology, petrology and selected mineral commodities; Dir.-Gen. ALAN COUTTS; publs *Bulletins*, *Geological and Metallogenic Maps* (with notes), *Geological Memoirs, Mineral Industry, Mineral Resources, Palaeontological Memoirs, Records, Quarterly Notes*.

Geological Survey of Victoria: Dept of Primary Industries, POB 500, East Melbourne, Vic. 3002; tel. (3) 9412-5042; fax (3) 9412-5155; e-mail customer.service@dpi.vic .gov.au; internet www.dpi.vic.gov.au; f. 1852; Man. TOM DICKSON; publ. reports, geological maps, bulletins, etc.

Geological Survey of Western Australia: Mineral House, 100 Plain St, East Perth, WA 6004; tel. (8) 9222-3333; fax (8) 9222-3633; e-mail geological@dmp.wa.gov.au; internet www.dmp.wa.gov.au/gswa; Exec. Dir Dr TIM GRIFFIN; publs *Bulletin, Mineral Resources Bulletin*.

Geoscience Australia (GA): GPOB 378, Canberra, ACT 2601; tel. (2) 6249-9111; fax (2) 6249-9989; e-mail reference.library@ga .gov.au; internet www.ga.gov.au; f. 1946, as Bureau of Mineral Resources; Geology and Geophysics (BMR) to develop a comprehensive, scientific understanding of the geology of Australia, its offshore area, and the Australian Antarctic Territory; library of 43,000 vols, 653 serial titles; CEO Dr CHRIS PIGRAM; publ. *AusGeo News*.

Mineral Resources Tasmania: POB 56, Rosny Park, Tas. 7018; tel. (3) 6233-8333; fax (3) 6233-8338; e-mail info@mrt.tas.gov.au; internet www.mrt.tas.gov.au; f. 1885; library of 10,000 books, 300 periodicals; Chief Geologist A. V. Brown; publs *Explanatory Reports, Geological Survey Maps, Tasmanian Geological Survey Bulletins, Tasmanian Geological Survey Records.*

Mount Stromlo and Siding Spring Observatories: Cotter Rd, Weston Creek, ACT 2611; tel. (2) 6125-0230; fax (2) 6125-0233; e-mail director@mso.anu.edu.au; internet www.mso.anu.edu.au; f. 1924 as Commonwealth Solar Observatory; research in astrophysics, incl. all phases of stellar, galactic and extra-galactic astronomy; transferred to Australian Nat. Univ. 1957; library of 17,000 vols; Dir HARVEY BUTCHER; Sec. PATRICIA THOMSON.

Perth Observatory: 337 Walnut Rd, Bickley, WA 6076; tel. (8) 9293-8255; fax (8) 9293-8138; e-mail perthobs@calm.wa.gov.au; internet www.wa.gov.au/perthobs; f. 1896; astronomy research, education and outreach and information provision; research areas incl. optical astronomy, variable and transient monitoring, photometry, planetary observations, microlens monitoring and minor-body tracking; public star-viewing, guided tours and museum; library of 20,000 vols; Govt Astronomer RALPH MARTIN.

Primary Industries and Resources South Australia: 101 Grenfell St, GPOB 1671, Adelaide, SA 5001; tel. (8) 8463-3000; fax (8) 8204-1880; internet www.pir.sa.gov .au; f. 1892; Geological Survey of S Australia, mining, energy and energy conservation, oil and gas; library of 25,000 vols (spec. colln on early S Australian mining); Chief Exec. JIM HALLION; publs *Geological Survey Bulletin, MESA Journal* (4 a year).

Queensland Department of Natural Resources and Water: GPOB 2454, Brisbane, Qld 4001; 41 George St, Brisbane, Qld 4000; tel. (7) 3224-8790; fax (7) 3224-7571; e-mail library@nrw.qld.gov.au; internet www .nrw.qld.gov.au; f. 1874; climate change, natural resource management, geological mapping, sedimentary basin studies, metallogenic studies, biostratigraphy, geophysics, mineral, petroleum, coal and oil shale resources assessment, extractive industries and environmental management, land use planning, mining safety and technology, energy management, resource economics, computer and information services; library of 8,800 monographs, 27,000 reports, 1,000 serials, records, maps, map commentaries, guidebooks; Dir-Gen. SCOTT SPENCER; publs *DME Reviews, Minerals and Energy Review, Queensland Geology, Queensland Government Mining Journal* (12 a year), *Records.*

Riverview Observatory: Lane Cove, NSW 2066; tel. (2) 9882-8296; fax (2) 9882-8455; e-mail bwmarsh@riverview.nsw.edu.au; f. 1908; meteorological observations, worldwide standard seismograph network station (1962); Dir R. W. MARSH.

RELIGION, SOCIOLOGY AND ANTHROPOLOGY

Australian Institute of Aboriginal and Torres Strait Islander Studies: GPOB 553, Canberra, ACT 2601; tel. (2) 6246-1111; fax (2) 6261-4285; e-mail corporate@ aiatsis.gov.au; internet www.aiatsis.gov.au; f. 1961; statutory body since 1964; provides funds, promotes research and publishes books on all aspects of Aboriginal and Torres Strait Islander studies, traditional and contemporary; library of 11,000 books, 1,220 serial titles, 32,000 book and journal analytics, 2,500 language books, 1,400 rare books, 14,000 pamphlets, 30,000 hours of audio tapes, 9,500 MSS, 650,000 prints and colour slides, 2.5 million feet of film and 5,000 video tapes; Chair. Prof. MICHAEL DODSON; publ. *Australian Aboriginal Studies* (2 a year).

Australian Institute of Archaeology: La Trobe Univ., Vic. 3086; tel. (4) 2159-5966; e-mail director@aiarch.org.au; f. 1946 to investigate discoveries and results that the Institute or any other org. publishes, which relate to the authenticity, historicity, accuracy and inspiration of the Bible; teaching programmes and exhibitions on the ancient Near East and Biblical archaeology; library of 10,000 vols (spec. colln on Palestinian, Egyptian and Mesopotamian archaeology); Dir CHRISTOPHER DAVEY; publ. *Buried History* (1 a year).

Australian Institute of Criminology: GPOB 2994, Canberra, ACT 2601; tel. (2) 6260-9200; fax (2) 6260-9201; e-mail front .desk@aic.gov.au; internet www.aic.gov.au; f. 1973; conducts criminology research, conferences and seminars, provides library and information services, publishes results of research and other materials, and services the Criminology Research Council; library: see Libraries and Archives; Dir Dr ADAM TOMISON; publ. *Trends and Issues in Crime and Criminal Justice* (20 a year).

Elda Vaccari Collection of Multicultural Studies: Library, Victoria Univ. of Technology, POB 14428, Melbourne City Mail Centre, Melbourne, Vic. 8001; tel. (3) 9919-4809; fax (3) 9919-4920; e-mail mark .armstrong-roper@vu.edu.au; internet w2.vu .edu.au/library/specialcollections/vaccari .html; f. 1982; research on immigrant and minority groups in Australia; supported by Vaccari Italian Historical Trust; can be searched online via VU library catalogue at library.vu.edu.au, items prefixed V COLL; library of 4,000 vols; Special Collections Librarian MARK ARMSTRONG-ROPER.

TECHNOLOGY

AMDEL: Level 2, 255 Blackburn Rd, Mount Waverley, Vic. 3149; tel. (3) 8847-0700; fax (3) 8847-0799; internet www.amdel.com; f. 1960; analysis, testing, services in mineral engineering, chemical metallurgy, materials technology, mineralogy and petrology, process control instrument development, petroleum, geoanalysis, chemical analysis; offices and laboratories around Australia and New Zealand and representatives worldwide; 400 staff; Group Gen. Man. RAY DOYLE.

ARRB Group Ltd: 500 Burwood Highway, Vermont South, Vic. 3133; tel. (3) 9881-1555; fax (3) 9887-8104; e-mail info@arrb.com.au; internet www.arrb.com.au; f. 1960; research related to the design, planning, construction, maintenance and use of land transport services; library of 42,000 vols and journals; Man. Dir GERARD WALDRON; Company Sec. SUE ROLLAND; publs *ARRB Briefing, ARRB Research Reports* (irregular), *Australian Transport Index database (ATRI), Proceedings of Biennial Conference, Road and Transport Research* (4 a year), *Special Reports* (irregular), *Transport and Road Update* (12 a year).

Defence Science and Technology Organisation: F2-2-008 Fairbairn Business Park, Canberra, ACT 2600; tel. (2) 6128-6301; fax (2) 6128-6332; e-mail information@dsto .defence.gov.au; internet www.dsto.defence .gov.au; attached to Dept of Defence; Australian Govt's lead agency charged with applying science and technology to protect and defend Australia and its nat. interests; Chief Defence Scientist Dr ROGER LOUGH.

Associated Research Laboratory:

Defence Science and Technology Organisation, Fishermens Bend: 506 Lorimer St, Fishermens Bend, Vic. 3207; f. 1939; incl. divs of Airframes and Engines, Air Operations and Guided Weapons.

Water Research Foundation of Australia: c/o Centre for Resource and Environmental Studies, Australian National Univ., Canberra, ACT 0200; tel. (2) 6125-0651; fax (2) 6125-0757; e-mail office@cres.anu.edu.au; f. 1956; a non-profit research org.; research into the devt, control, use and re-use of Australia's water resources; publ. *Water and the Environment* (6 a year).

Libraries and Archives
Australian Capital Territory

Australian Institute of Criminology, J. V. Barry Library: GPOB 2944, Canberra, ACT 2601; tel. (2) 6260-9264; fax (2) 6260-9299; e-mail jvbarry@aic.gov.au; internet www.aic.gov.au; f. 1974; material is collected in English in the field of criminology and criminal justice; 35,000 monographs, 800 periodicals; articles and monographs of Australian criminological interest are indexed for CINCH–The Australian Criminology Database, publicly available on the Informit network; main objective is to provide information services to researchers at the Institute; Library Man. JANINE CHANDLER.

Australian National University Library: J. B. Chifley Bldg (15), Canberra, ACT 0200; tel. (2) 61252003; fax (2) 61256662; e-mail librarian@anu.edu.au; internet anulib.anu .edu.au; f. 1948; 2.5m. vols; Librarian VIC ELLIOTT.

DEEWR Library, Department of Education, Employment and Workplace Relations: C16MTG, GPOB 9880, Canberra, ACT 2601; tel. (2) 6240-8848; fax (2) 6121-9138; e-mail library@deewr.gov.au; f. 1945; 40,000 vols; Dir KYM HOLDEN (acting).

High Court of Australia Library: POB 6309, Kingston, ACT 2604; tel. (2) 6270-6922; fax (2) 6273-2110; internet www.hcourt.gov .au/library; f. 1903; private library of the Justices of the Court and barristers appearing before it; 149,000 vols in Canberra; Librarian PETAL KINDER.

IP Australia Library: Discovery House, POB 200, Woden, ACT 2606; tel. (2) 6283-2058; fax (2) 6282-5810; e-mail library@ ipaustralia.gov.au; internet www.ipaustralia .gov.au; f. 1904; 15,000 vols, 300 periodicals; Australian and foreign patent specifications from all patent countries, science and technology and intellectual property.

National Archives of Australia: POB 7425, Canberra Mail Centre, ACT 2610; tel. (2) 6212-3600; fax (2) 6212-3699; e-mail archives@naa.gov.au; internet www.naa.gov .au; f. 1945; archival authority of the Commonwealth since 1952; responsible for the management of Commonwealth records: survey, storage, preservation, retention or destruction, retrieval and access; provides information to the public on nature and location of Commonwealth records and on agencies and persons responsible for them; collns of documents, maps, plans, films, photographs, records, paintings, models, microforms and electronic records (487,522 shelf m); holdings date from the early 19th century, but most date from Federation (1901), derived from a variety of sources; offices in Canberra, Darwin and all state capitals; Dir-Gen. ROSS GIBBS; publ. *Memento* (4 a year).

National Library of Australia: Parkes Pl., Canberra, ACT 2600; tel. (2) 6262-1111; fax (2) 6257-1703; e-mail www@nla.gov.au; internet www.nla.gov.au; f. 1901; maintains nat. colln of Australian library materials and provides a gateway to nat. and int. sources of information; 2.9m. vols, 41,031 current serial titles, 643,792 maps, 12,895 m of manuscript material, 16,297 oral history recordings, 189,031 music scores, 64,373 pictures and prints, 750,299 photographs, 860,187 aerial photographs, 3,812 electronic media; Dir-Gen. JAN FULLERTON; publs *APAIS* (online only), *Gateways* (electronic only, 6 a year), *NLA News* (electronic and print, monthly).

University of Canberra Library: The Library, University of Canberra, ACT 2601; tel. (2) 6201-2282; fax (2) 6201-5068; e-mail askalibrarian@canberra.edu.au; internet www.canberra.edu.au/library; f. 1968; 480,000 vols; colln includes audiovisual material, access to electronic information services; Librarian ANITA CROTTY.

New South Wales

Charles Sturt University–Division of Library Services: Locked Bag 7003, Bathurst, NSW 2795; tel. (2) 6338-4732; fax (2) 6338-4986; e-mail soakley@csu.edu.au; internet www.csu.edu.au/division/library; f. 1989 by amalgamation of Mitchell College of Advanced Education (f. 1951) and Riverina-Murray Institute of Higher Education (f. 1947); 624,623 vols, 2010 Aleph EOY report; libraries at Albury-Wodonga, Bathurst, Wagga Wagga, Orange and Dubbo; Burlington (Ontario, Canada); Exec. Dir, Div. of Library Services SHIRLEY OAKLEY.

City of Sydney Library: Customs House Library, Sydney, NSW 2000; tel. (2) 9242-8555; fax (2) 9242-8561; e-mail library@cityofsydney.nsw.gov.au; internet www.cityofsydney.nsw.gov.au; f. 1877; programmes for children and young people, adults, multicultural audiences; local history and user education; home library and inter-library loan services; 8 brs, 2 library links; 500,000 vols, incl. books, CDs, DVDs, audiobooks, magazines, 100 newspaper titles; spec. collns: Australiana, local govt, Olympic Games, Koori (Aboriginal) material; Library Man. DAVID SHARMAN.

Macquarie University Library: Bldg C3C, Macquarie Univ., NSW 2109; tel. (2) 9850-7500; fax (2) 9850-7568; e-mail maxine .brodie@mq.edu.au; internet www.library.mq .edu.au; f. 1964; new Library opens 1 August 2011; 1.3m. vols; Univ. Librarian MAXINE BRODIE.

Newcastle Region Library: War Memorial Cultural Centre, Laman St, Newcastle, NSW 2300; tel. (2) 4974-5300; fax (2) 4974-5396; e-mail library@ncc.nsw.gov.au; internet www.newcastle.nsw.gov.au/library; f. 1948; 406,242 vols, 2,663 periodicals, 121 newspaper titles; spec. facilities: Information Works, Local Studies, Hunter Photo Bank, Earthquake Database; Lending Services Librarian MICHAEL NEWSOME; publs *Monographs* (irregular), *Newcastle Morning Herald Index* (1861–84, 1 a year).

Parliamentary Library of New South Wales: Parliament House, Sydney, NSW 2000; tel. (2) 9230-2383; fax (2) 9231-1932; e-mail libreq@parliament.nsw.gov.au; internet www.parliament.nsw.gov.au; f. 1840; 200,000 vols; Man. of Reference and Information Services DEBORAH BROWN.

State Library of New South Wales: Macquarie St, Sydney, NSW 2000; tel. (2) 9273-1414; fax (2) 9273-1255; e-mail library@sl.nsw.gov.au; internet www.sl.nsw.gov.au; f. 1826; State legal deposit privileges; special collns: Australian, historical pictures, maps, MSS, of Australia and the Pacific; two public reading rooms, specialist client-focused information services; 5m. items incl. 1.1m. photographs; 11.2 linear km of MSS; 234,000 prints, drawings, paintings, maps and oral histories; State Librarian and Chief Exec. REGINA A. SUTTON.

State Records Authority of New South Wales: POB 516, Kingswood, NSW 2747; tel. (2) 9673-1788; fax (2) 9833-4518; e-mail srecords@records.nsw.gov.au; internet www .records.nsw.gov.au; f. 1961; 10,000 vols; incl. Univ. Archives and Heritage Centre; records and archives strategy for the NSW Govt and broader public sector; preservation of the State Archives colln; reference services; reading rooms, online access, enquiry and copying services, exhibitions, publs, talks and tours; Dir ALAN VENTRESS.

University of New England Library: Dixson Library, Univ. of New England, Armidale, NSW 2351; tel. (2) 6773-2165; fax (2) 6773-3943; e-mail unilib@une.edu.au; internet www.une.edu.au/library; f. 1954 Univ. College of Univ. of Sydney, 1938-1954; 908,000 vols; agricultural sciences, Australian law, humanities and social sciences, health, medicine, education; special collns: Campbell Howard (Australian plays in manuscript), Gordon Athol Anderson (music), New England, Royal Soc. of New S Wales, Australian League of Rights, Saunders Colln in War and Peace; Univ. Librarian BARBARA PATON.

University of New South Wales Library: Sydney, NSW 2052; tel. (2) 9385-2615; fax (2) 9385-8002; e-mail information@unsw.edu.au; internet info.library.unsw.edu.au; f. 1949; 2.9m. items at Kensington and other centres; University Librarian ANDREW WELLS.

University of Newcastle Library: Callaghan, NSW 2308; tel. (2) 4921-5851; fax (2) 4921-5833; internet www.newcastle.edu.au/services/library; f. 1965; 1.3m. vols; Librarian GREG ANDERSON.

University of Sydney Library: University of Sydney, NSW 2006; tel. (2) 9351-2993; fax (2) 9351-2890; e-mail loanenq@library.usyd .edu.au; internet www.library.usyd.edu.au; f. 1852; network of 18 libraries containing 5.2m. vols, 68,130 electronic journals and 281,600 electronic books; University Librarian JOHN SHIPP.

Northern Territory

Northern Territory Library: Parliament House, POB 42, Darwin, NT 0801; tel. (8) 8999-7177; fax (8) 8999-6927; e-mail ntlinfo .dlghs@nt.gov.au; internet www.ntl.nt.gov .au; f. 1950 as Darwin Public Library; 140,000 books, 4,132 periodicals, 80,000 photographs, 3,000 maps, 2,500 films and video cassettes, 7,000 microforms; incl. the Northern Territory Colln (1 copy of all types of library material dealing with N and Central Australia, and NT in particular); Dir JO MCGILL; publ. occasional papers.

Queensland

Queensland Parliamentary Library: Parliamentary Annex, Alice St, Brisbane, Qld 4000; tel. (7) 3406-7219; fax (7) 3210-0172; e-mail library.inquiries@parliament .qld.gov.au; f. 1860; research and information service to members of state legislature; statistics, economics, politics, law and education; 120,000 vols; spec. collns incl O'Donovan Colln 19th century parliamentary library; news and audiovisual clippings; Queensland political history; Librarian MARY SEEFRIED; publ. *Queensland Parliamentary Record* (every 3 years).

Queensland University of Technology, Library Services: GPOB 2434, Brisbane, Qld 4001; tel. (7) 3138-1821; fax (7) 3138 9727; e-mail dirlib.pa@qut.edu.au; internet www.library.qut.edu.au; f. 1989; 480,000 vols; 2,800 prints and 80,000 electronic periodicals; Dir JUDY STOKKER.

State Library of Queensland: POB 3488, Brisbane, Qld 4101; tel. (7) 3840-7666; fax (7) 3846-2421; e-mail info@slq.qld.gov.au; internet www.slq.qld.gov.au; f. 1896; State Reference Library, non-lending except for music scores and to libraries, groups and organizations; includes John Oxley Library of Queensland History, James Hardie Library of Australian Fine Arts and Australian Library of Art colln; has library deposit privileges, exhibitions, events; State Librarian LEA GILES-PETERS.

Supreme Court Library:; e-mail susan .sawyer@sclqld.org.au POB 15019, City East, Brisbane, Qld 4002; tel. (7) 3247-4373; fax (7) 3247-9233; e-mail librarian@sclqld.org.au; internet www.sclqld.org.au; f. 1862; 16,000 vols; Librarian ALADIN RAHEMTULA; publs *Qld Legal Indexes*, *Supreme Court History Program Yearbook*.

University of Queensland Library: Qld 4072; tel. (7) 3365-6551; fax (7) 3365-7317; e-mail universitylibrarian@library.uq.edu .au; internet library.uq.edu.au; f. 1911; 2.5m. vols; 10,853 print journals, 47,744 electronic journals, 1,014 networked databases, 370,974 eBooks, 32,645 video cassettes; manuscript, microform and pictorial collns mainly in Australian literature; Librarian KEITH WEBSTER.

South Australia

Flinders University Library: Bedford Park, SA 5042; tel. (8) 8201-2131; fax (8) 8201-2508; e-mail libinfo@flinders.edu.au; internet www.flinders.edu.au/library; f. 1966; 1.5m. vols; Univ. Librarian IAN MCBAIN.

State Library of South Australia: North Terrace, GPOB 419, Adelaide, SA 5001; tel. (8) 8207-7200; fax (8) 8207-7247; e-mail info@ slsa.sa.gov.au; internet www.slsa.sa.gov.au; f. 1884; State general reference library and legal depository; online services incl. networked CD-ROMs; Bray Reference Colln (400,000 vols, 21,000 serial titles, 6,000 current, 109,000 maps); South Australiana Colln (62,000 vols, 12,000 serial titles, 8,000 current, Archival Collns of 4,500 m); spec. collns incl. Children's Literature Research Colln (55,000 vols), Edwardes Colln of Shipping Photographs (8,000), Arbon-Le Maistre Colln of Shipping Photographs (70,000), Mountford-Sheard Colln of Aboriginal Ethnology, Thomas Hardy Wine Library (1,000 vols), Paul McGuire Maritime Library (3,000 vols), Rare Books Colln (92,000 vols), Royal Geographical Soc. of South Australia Inc. Library, J. D. Somerville Oral History Colln (1,500 cassette tapes), Pictorial Colln (350,000 images), Bradman Colln of Cricketing Memorabilia; supports 138 public libraries (1.5m. vols); Dir ALAN SMITH; publ. *Extra Extra* (2 a year).

University of Adelaide Library: University of Adelaide, Adelaide, SA 5005; tel. (8) 8303-5370; fax (8) 8303-4369; e-mail library@ adelaide.edu.au; internet www.adelaide.edu .au/library; f. 1876; 2.1m. items; rare books, spec. collns incl. univ. archives, univ. arts and heritage, univ. press; 2,400,000 vols; Univ. Librarian RAY CHOATE.

University of South Australia Library: Mawson Lakes Blvd, Mawson Lakes, SA 5095; tel. (1300) 137 659; e-mail ocls@unisa .edu.au; internet www.library.unisa.edu.au; libraries located at City East Campus, North Terrace, Adelaide, SA 5000; Mawson Lakes Campus, Mawson Lakes, SA 5095; Magill Campus, Lorne Avenue, Magill, SA 5072; City West Campus, North Terrace, Adelaide, SA 5000; Whyalla Campus, Nicolson Avenue, Whyalla Norrie, SA 5608; f. 1991 (as School of Art 1856); 1m. vols; special collections include Oregon Collection of Theses in Physical Education and Sport, Doris Taylor Collection on Ageing, Gavin Walkley collection on Architectural History; Clearinghouse in Australia for Adult Basic Education and Literacy, Aboriginal and Torres Strait Islander Special Collection, Australian Bureau of Statistics Collection, HOPE Collection; Dir, Library Services HELEN LIVINGSTON.

Tasmania

LINC Tasmania: 91 Murray St, Hobart, Tas. 7000; tel. (3) 6233-7511; fax (3) 6231-0927; e-mail state.library@education.tas.gov .au; internet www.linc.tas.gov.au; f. 1850; 913,032 items; state legal deposit privileges; 46 brs, 4 reference and spec. collns; links adult education, state library of Tasmania, online access centres and the Tasmanian archive and heritage office combining learning, information, literacy, library; Dir SIOBHAN GASKELL.

University of Tasmania Library: PMB 25, GPO Hobart, Tas. 7001; tel. (3) 6226-2223; fax (3) 6226-2878; internet www.utas.edu.au/ library/index.html; f. 1892; 996,832 vols; Sandy Bay Campus libraries: Law, Morris Miller (social sciences and humanities) and Science; Centre for the Arts Library, Hunter St, Hobart; Clinical Library, 43 Collins St, Hobart; Launceston Campus Library, Newnham, Launceston; spec. collns on Quakerism; houses the Royal Soc. of Tasmania Library; Librarian LINDA LUTHER.

Victoria

Commonwealth Scientific and Industrial Research Organisation, Library Network: Bag 10, Clayton South, Vic. 3169; tel. (3) 9518-5940; fax (3) 9518-5959; e-mail thomas.girke@csiro.au; internet www .csiro.au/services/pswn.html; publishes and communicates science information in print, video and multimedia, and electronic databases; disseminates science and research information through CSIRO Library Network, search and inquiry services SEARCH PARTY; archival services for CSIRO research and records; Man. THOMAS GIRKE.

La Trobe University Library: Bundoora, Vic. 3086; tel. (3) 9479-2922; fax (3) 9471-0993; e-mail library@latrobe.edu.au; internet www.lib.latrobe.edu.au; f. 1964; spec. emphasis on humanities and social sciences, allied health sciences; area studies: Latin America, India, Canada; 1.5m. vols; Univ. Librarian Prof. AINSLIE DEWE.

Monash University Library: Monash University, Vic. 3800; tel. (3) 9905-5054; fax (3) 9905-2610; e-mail libweb@lib.monash.edu .au; internet www.lib.monash.edu.au; f. 1961; 2.9m. vols, 17,800 periodicals; also libraries at Caulfield Campus, Caulfield East, Vic. 3145; Peninsula Campus, Frankston, Vic. 3199; Gippsland Campus, Churchill, Vic. 3842; and Berwick Campus, Berwick, Vic. 3806; Pharmacy College, Royal Parade, Parkville, Vic. 3052; Roodepoort 1725, South Africa; Petaling Jaya, 46150 Selangor, Malaysia; Librarian C. HARBOE-REE.

Public Record Office of Victoria: POB 2100, North Melbourne, Vic. 3051; tel. (3) 9348-5600; fax (3) 9348-5656; e-mail ask .prov@dpc.vic.gov.au; internet www.prov.vic .gov.au; f. 1973; 67,074 linear m of public records; Dir and Keeper of Public Records JUSTINE HEAZLEWOOD; publs *Journal* (1 a year, online), *Profile* (4 a year).

State Library of Victoria: 328 Swanston St, Melbourne, Vic. 3000; tel. (3) 8664-7000; fax (3) 9639-4737; e-mail info@slv.vic.gov.au; internet www.slv.vic.gov.au; f. 1854; the oldest publicly funded library in Australia and Victoria's primary gen. reference and research library; legal deposit library responsible for collecting, preserving and making available all published materials and associated material relating to the heritage of the state of Victoria; offers community outreach and learning programmes; works with other library sectors, cultural instns and the education sector to provide access to information and promote Victorian cultural heritage; 2m. vols and periodicals; spec. collns incl. La Trobe Colln (Australiana), art, newspapers, music and performing arts, Anderson Chess Colln, maps, MSS and pictures; digitization of 200,000 items from the Pictures Colln and a broader range of formats incl. text, audio and music are available online; CEO and State Librarian SUE HAMILTON (acting); publs *La Trobe Journal* (2 a year), *State Library of Victoria News* (3 a year).

University of Melbourne Library: Vic. 3010; tel. (3) 8344-9590; fax (3) 8344-9588; internet www.lib.unimelb.edu.au; f. 1855; 3m. vols; spec. collns incl. Australiana, East Asia; responsible for University Archives and Grainger Museum; Librarian HELEN HAYES; publ. *Ex Libris* (4 a year).

Victorian Parliamentary Library: Parliament of Victoria, Spring St, Melbourne, Vic. 3002; tel. (3) 9651-8640; fax (3) 9650-9775; e-mail info@parliament.vic.gov.au; internet www.parliament.vic.gov.au; f. 1851; reference and research service for MPs and associated staff; statistics, economics, politics, law, government publs; Parliamentary Librarian MARION KING; publ. *Victorian Parliamentary Handbook* (every 4 years).

Western Australia

Curtin University of Technology Library: POB U1987, Perth, WA 6845; tel. (8) 9266-7205; fax (8) 9266-3213; e-mail i .garner@curtin.edu.au; internet library .curtin.edu.au; f. 1967; 659,741 vols, 73,254 current serial titles; Univ. Librarian IMOGEN GARNER.

State Library of Western Australia: Perth Cultural Centre, Perth, WA 6000; tel. (8) 9427-3111; fax (8) 9427-3256; e-mail info@ slwa.wa.gov.au; internet www.slwa.wa.gov .au; f. 1887; J. S. Battye Library of W Australian History (f. 1887): 138,000 vols, 16,500 serial and newspaper titles, 16,000 microfilm reels, 29,000 cartographic items, 90,000 ephemeral items, 500,000 pictorial images, 6,000 film and video reels, 13,000 oral history hours, 3,100 m of private archives; gen. reference services: 412,000 vols, 6,000 serial and newspaper titles, 49,000 music scores, 15,000 music recordings, 13,000 microfilm reels, 16,000 video and film titles, 23,000 cartographic items; spec. collns of music business genealogy and Australian children's literature; CEO and State Librarian MARGARET ALLEN (acting); Dir of Public Library Services SUSAN FEENEY; Dir, Resource Services ALISON SUTHERLAND; Dir, Strategic and Corporate Services MARK WOODCOCK; publ. *Statistical Bulletin for Public Libraries in Western Australia* (1 a year).

University of Western Australia Library: 35 Stirling Highway, Crawley, WA 6009; tel. (8) 6488-1777; fax (8) 6488-1012; e-mail uwalibrary@library.uwa.edu.au; internet www.library.uwa.edu.au; f. 1913; 1m. vols; Librarian JOHN ARFIELD.

Museums and Art Galleries

Australian Capital Territory

Australian War Memorial: GPOB 345, Canberra, ACT 2601; tel. (2) 6243-4211; fax (2) 6243-4325; internet www.awm.gov.au; f. 1917; national war memorial, museum, research centre and art gallery illustrating and recording aspects of all wars in which the Armed Forces of Australia have been engaged; dioramas of historical battles, and a total collection of over 3.5m. items; works of art, relics, documentary and audiovisual records; library: books, serials, pamphlets, photographs, maps, film and sound recordings on military history; repository of operational records of Australian fighting units; Dir Maj.-Gen. STEVE GOWER; publ. *Wartime* (4 a year).

National Gallery of Australia: POB 1150, Canberra, ACT 2601; tel. (2) 6240-6411; fax (2) 6240-6529; e-mail information@nga.gov .au; internet www.nga.gov.au; f. 1975; the Nat. Colln has 100,000 works of Australian and int. art; Australian colln incl. fine and decorative arts, folk art, commercial art, architecture and design; other collns incl. arts of Asia and South-east Asia, Oceania, Africa and Pre-Columbian America, European art, also prints, drawings, illustrated books since 1800, photography; colln of Australian archives, colln of oral histories, access to digital pubns on the visual arts; library of 13,000 monograph and exhibition catalogues; 86,000 art and artist files; 53,000 auction sales catalogues 47,000 microfiche titles; 2,400 art related serials; Dir RON RADFORD AO; publ. *Artonview* (4 a year).

National Museum of Australia: POB 1901, Canberra, ACT 2601; tel. (2) 6208-5000; fax (2) 6208-5148; e-mail information@ nma.gov.au; internet www.nma.gov.au; f. 1980; Australian history, Aboriginal and Torres Strait Island cultures, social history and environment; library of 35,000 vols; Dir ANDREW SAYERS (acting).

New South Wales

Art Gallery of New South Wales:; tel. (2) 9225-1700; fax (2) 9221-1701; e-mail artmail@ag.nsw.gov.au; internet www .artgallery.nsw.gov.au; f. 1874; representative collection of Australian art, Aboriginal and Melanesian art; collections of British art since 18th century; European painting and sculpture (since 15th century); Asian art, particularly Chinese and Japanese ceramics and Japanese painting; Australian, British and European prints and drawings, contemporary Australian and foreign art; photography; Pres., Board of Trustees STEVEN LOWY; Dir EDMUND CAPON.

Australian Museum: 6 College St, Sydney, NSW 2010; tel. (2) 9320-6000; fax (2) 9320-6050; e-mail library@austmus.gov.au; internet www.australianmuseum.net.au; f. 1827; natural history, museology, anthropology, palaeontology, mineralogy, biodiversity; library of 100,000 vols; Dir FRANK HOWARTH; publs *Records of the Australian Museum* (4 a year), *Technical Reports of the Australian Museum* (irregular).

Australian National Maritime Museum: POB 5131, Sydney, NSW 2001; tel. (2) 9298-3777; fax (2) 9298-3780; internet www.anmm .gov.au; f. 1985, open 1991; illustrates maritime history as exemplified by the colonial navies, the Royal Australian Navy, merchant shipping and trade, whaling and the fishing industry, explorers and cartographers, immigration, the design and use of leisure and sporting craft and int. competition, surfing, surf life saving and the culture of the beach, and the maritime activities of the Aborigines; models, prints and drawings, glass plate negatives, uniforms, relics, full-size vessels; library of 12,000 vols, 750 periodicals; Chair. PETER SINCLAIR; Dir MARY-LOUISE WILLIAMS; publ. *Signals* (4 a year).

J. T. Wilson, Museum of Human Anatomy: Anderson Stuart Bldg, Dept of Anatomy, Univ. of Sydney, NSW 2006; e-mail hod@anatomy.usyd.edu.au; f. 1886; incl. 1,000 dissected parts and cross-sections of the human body; Curator PETER MILLS.

Macleay Museum: Gosper Lane, off Science Rd, Univ. of Sydney, Sydney, NSW 2006; tel. (2) 9351-2274; fax (2) 9351-5646; e-mail macleay.museum@sydney.edu.au; internet www.usyd.edu.au/museums; f. 1888 based on colln begun in 1790; entomology, zoology, ethnology, 19th-century scientific instruments; Australian photographs since 1850s; Dir DAVID ELLIS.

Museum of Applied Arts and Sciences: 500 Harris St, Ultimo, Sydney, NSW 2007; tel. (2) 9217-0111; fax (2) 9217-0333; e-mail info@phm.gov.au; internet www.powerhousemuseum.com; f. 1880; comprises Powerhouse Museum (decorative arts, history, science and technology), Sydney Observatory astronomical museum, Powerhouse Discovery Centre; colln stored at Castle Hill; Dir Dr DAWN CASEY.

Museum of Contemporary Art: POB R1286, Royal Exchange, NSW 1223; located at: Level 5, 140 George St, Sydney, NSW 2000; tel. (2) 9252-4033; fax (2) 9252-4361; e-mail mail@mca.com.au; internet www.mca.com.au; f. 1991; Dir ELIZABETH ANN MACGREGOR.

Nicholson Museum: Univ. of Sydney, Sydney, NSW 2006; tel. (2) 9351-2812; fax (2) 9351-7305; e-mail nicholsonmuseum@usyd.edu.au; internet www.usyd.edu.au/museums/nicholson; f. 1860; colln of Egyptian, Near Eastern, Cypriot, European, Greek and Roman antiquities; Dir DAVID ELLIS; Senior Curator MICHAEL TURNER.

Northern Territory

Museum and Art Gallery of the Northern Territory: GPOB 4646, Darwin, NT 0801; Conacher St, Bullocky Point, Darwin, NT; tel. (8) 8999-8201; fax (8) 8999-8289; e-mail museum@nt.gov.au; f. 1969; art, history, culture, and natural history of the Northern Territory, particularly Aboriginal visual arts and material culture; South-east Asian and Oceanic art and material culture; maritime archaeology; 5 major permanent galleries; touring gallery; educational facilities for students; library of 10,000 vols, 1,000 serials; Dir ANNA MALGORZEWICZ; publ. *Research Reports* (irregular).

Queensland

Queensland Art Gallery: POB 3686, South Brisbane, Qld 4101; Stanley St, South Brisbane, Qld 4101; tel. (7) 3840-7333; fax (7) 3844-8865; e-mail gallery@qag.qld.gov.au; internet www.qag.qld.gov.au; f. 1895, opened 2nd site, Gallery of Modern Art (GoMA) in 2006, incl. Australian Cinematheque and Children's Art Centre; State colln of Australian and int. paintings, prints, drawings and photographs, sculpture and decorative arts; education and advisory services; holds Asia Pacific Triennial of contemporary art; library of 35,000 books, 500 periodicals, photographs, catalogues, Asia Pacific research colln; Dir TONY ELLWOOD; publ. *Artlines*.

Queensland Herbarium: Brisbane Botanic Gardens Mt Coot-tha, Mt Coot-tha Rd, Toowong, Qld 4066; tel. (7) 3896-9326; fax (7) 3896-9624; internet www.env.qld.gov.au; f. 1874 as Botanic Museum and Herbarium; studies of flora and mapping of vegetation of Queensland, rare and threatened plant species, plant ecology, weeds, poisonous plants and economic botany; 650,000 plant specimens; library of 10,000 vols; Dir G. P. GUYMER; publ. *Austrobaileya* (1 a year).

Queensland Museum: Cultural Centre, South Bank, South Brisbane, Qld 4101; tel. (7) 3840-7555; fax (7) 3846-1918; e-mail inquirycentre@qm.qld.gov.au; internet www.qm.qld.gov.au; f. 1871; zoology, geology, palaeontology, history, anthropology, technology; library of 95,000 vols; Dir Dr IAN GALLOWAY; publ. *Memoirs of the Queensland Museum*.

South Australia

Art Gallery of South Australia: North Terrace, Adelaide, SA 5000; tel. (8) 8207-7000; fax (8) 8207-7070; e-mail agsainformation@artgallery.sa.gov.au; internet www.artgallery.sa.gov.au; f. 1881, present status 1967; comprehensive colln of Australian works of art, British and European painting, prints, drawings and sculpture 16th century to present; British, European and Asian decorative arts; Indian and Indonesian textiles and Japanese art, early South Australian pictures; public programmes; guided tours; education services; library of 37,000 vols; journals, ephemera colln; Dir NICK MITZEVICH; publ. *Articulate* (4 a year).

South Australian Museum: North Terrace, Adelaide, SA 5000; tel. (8) 8207-7500; fax (8) 8203-9805; e-mail marketing@samuseum.sa.gov.au; internet www.samuseum.sa.gov.au; f. 1856; anthropological, geological and zoological material mainly related to S Australia; Australian ethnological colln; education and advisory services; school holiday programme; public exhibitions; Waterhouse art prize; ANZANG nature photography competition; discovery centre; library of 45,000 vols; Dir Dr S. MILLER; publ. *Transactions of the Royal Society of South Australia (incorporating Records of the South Australian Museum)*.

Tasmania

Queen Victoria Museum and Art Gallery: POB 403, Launceston, Tas. 7250; tel. (3) 6323-3777; fax (3) 6323-3776; e-mail enquiries@qvmag.tas.gov.au; internet www.qvmag.tas.gov.au; f. 1891; collns comprise pure and applied art, Tasmanian history, Tasmanian and general anthropology, Tasmanian botany, geology, palaeontology and zoology; library of 11,000 vols; Dir RICHARD MULVANEY; publs *Occasional Paper*, *Records*.

Tasmanian Museum and Art Gallery: 40 Macquarie St, GPOB 1164, Hobart, Tas. 7001; tel. (3) 6211-4177; fax (3) 6211-4112; e-mail tmagmail@tmag.tas.gov.au; internet www.tmag.tas.gov.au; f. 1852; applied science, art and natural and human history, with emphasis on Tasmania and Australia generally; incl. Tasmanian Herbarium, coin collns, early photography, collns relating to the Aboriginal people of Tasmania; collns also at the West Coast Pioneers' Museum at Zeehan (mining, local history and minerals); and the Australasian Golf Museum at Bothwell (golfing memorabilia); Dir BILL BLEATHMAN; publ. *Research Journal—Kanunnah* (1 a year).

Victoria

Museum Victoria: GPOB 666E, Melbourne, Vic. 3001; tel. (3) 8341-7777; fax (3) 8341-7778; e-mail webmaster@museum.vic.gov.au; internet www.museum.vic.gov.au; f. 1854; CEO Dr J. PATRICK GREENE.

Constituent Museums:

Immigration Museum: Old Customs House, 400 Flinders St, Melbourne, Vic. 3000; tel. (3) 9927-2700; fax (3) 9927-2701; e-mail webmaster@museum.vic.gov.au; internet immigration.museum.vic.gov.au; f. 1998.

Melbourne Museum: Carlton Gardens, Carlton, Vic. 3053; tel. (3) 8341-7777; fax (3) 8341-7778; e-mail webmaster@museum.vic.gov.au; internet museumvictoria.com.au/melbournemuseum; f. 2000; science, technology, Australian society, environment, indigenous cultures and human mind and body; incl. Aboriginal Centre, Children's Museum, living forest gallery, IMAX theatre and Royal Exhibition Building.

Scienceworks Museum:; e-mail rastley@museum.vic.gov.au 2 Booker St, Spotswood, Vic. 3015; tel. (3) 9392-4800; fax (3) 9391-0100; e-mail webmaster@museum.vic.gov.au; internet scienceworks.museum.vic.gov.au; f. 1992; science and technology, Melbourne Planetarium, Spotswood Pumping Station.

National Gallery of Victoria: POB 7259, Melbourne, Vic. 8004; tel. (3) 9208-0222; fax (3) 9208-0245; e-mail enquiries@ngv.vic.gov.au; internet www.ngv.vic.gov.au; f. 1861; old masters and depts of prints and drawings, modern European art, Australian art, aboriginal and Oceanic art, decorative art and design, Asian art, antiquities, photography, pre-Columbian art, costume and textiles; library of 45,000 vols, and slides; Dir Dr GERARD VAUGHAN; publs *Art Bulletin of Victoria* (1 a year), *Gallery* (6 a year).

Western Australia

Art Gallery of Western Australia: Perth Cultural Centre, Perth, WA 6000; tel. (8) 9492-6600; fax (8) 9492-6655; e-mail admin@artgallery.wa.gov.au; internet www.artgallery.wa.gov.au; f. 1895; Aboriginal art, Australian and foreign paintings, sculpture, decorative arts and crafts; free guided tours; public and educational programmes; library of 16,000 vols; Dir STEFANO CARBONI.

Western Australian Museum: 49 Kew St, Welshpool, Perth, WA 6106; tel. (8) 9212-3700; fax (8) 9212-3882; e-mail reception@museum.wa.gov.au; internet www.museum.wa.gov.au; f. 1891 as the Geological Museum; present name since 1897; natural history, archaeology, history, earth sciences, anthropology; library of 20,000 vols, 1,500 journal titles; CEO ALEC COLES; Exec. Officer and Foundation Dir JANE HARRIS; publs *Records*, *Records Supplements*.

Universities

AUSTRALIAN CATHOLIC UNIVERSITY

POB 968, North Sydney, NSW 2059

Telephone: (2) 9739-2929
Fax: (2) 9739-2905
E-mail: international@acu.edu.au
Internet: www.acu.edu.au

Founded 1991 by amalgamation of Catholic College of Education, Sydney, Institute of Catholic Education, Victoria, McAuley College, Brisbane, and Signadou College, Canberra

Academic year: February to December

Chancellor: Br JULIAN McDONALD
Pro-Chancellor: EDWARD EXELL
Vice-Chancellor: Prof. GREG CRAVEN
Pro-Vice-Chancellor for Academic Affairs: Prof. GABRIELLE McMULLEN
Pro-Vice-Chancellor for Quality and Outreach: Prof. JOHN O'GORMAN
Pro-Vice-Chancellor for Research and International Relations: Prof. GAIL CROSSLEY (acting)
Exec. Dir., University Services: JOHN CAMERON

Library of 460,903 vols, 2,296 periodicals, 5,415 online journals
Number of teachers: 514
Number of students: 15,279
Publications: *Interlogue* (2 a year), *Journal of Religious Education* (4 a year)

DEANS

Arts and Sciences: Dr GAIL CROSSLEY (acting)
Education: Prof. MARIE EMMITT
Health Sciences: Prof. PAULINE NUGENT

AUSTRALIAN NATIONAL UNIVERSITY

Canberra, ACT 0200
Telephone: (2) 6125-5111
Fax: (2) 6125-9062
E-mail: media@anu.edu.au
Internet: www.anu.edu.au
Founded 1946 for postgraduate research; now consists of Institute of Advanced Studies (postgraduate), the faculties (all levels)
Academic year: March to December
Chancellor: Prof. the Hon. GARETH EVANS
Vice-Chancellor: Prof. IAN CHUBB
Deputy Vice-Chancellor and Vice-Pres.: Prof. LAWRENCE CRAM
Pro-Vice-Chancellor for E-Strategies: Prof. ROBIN STANTON
Pro-Vice-Chancellor for Innovation and Advancement: Prof. MICHAEL CARDEW-HALL
Pro-Vice-Chancellor for Research and Graduate Studies: Prof. MANDY THOMAS
Pro-Vice-Chancellor for Students: Prof. ELIZABETH DEANE
Exec. Dir for Administration and Planning: Dr BROK GLENN
Librarian: VIC ELLIOTT
Number of teachers: 1,578
Number of students: 16,715
Library: See under Libraries and Archives
Publication: *ANU Reporter*.

INSTITUTE OF ADVANCED STUDIES

Institute of Advanced Studies: Chair. of the Institute of Advanced Studies Forum Prof. G. FARQUHAR (acting); number of academic staff: 727; number of postgraduate students: 949.

Constituent Schools:

John Curtin School of Medical Research: Dir Prof. J. WHITWORTH

PROFESSORS

BOARD, P., Molecular Genetics
DULHUNTY, A., Muscle Research
GAGE, P., Membrane Physiology
YOUNG, I., Cytokine Molecular Biology

Research School of Astronomy and Astrophysics: Dir Prof. PENNY D. SACKETT

PROFESSORS

BESSELL, M., Astronomy
BRIGGS, F. H., Astronomy
DA COSTA, G., Astronomy
DOPITA, M. A., Astronomy
FREEMAN, K. C., Astronomy
NORRIS, J. E., Astronomy
SACKETT, P. D., Astronomy
SCHMIDT, B. P., Astronomy

Research School of Biological Sciences: Dir Prof. JONATHAN STONE

PROFESSORS

ANDREWS, T. J., Molecular Genetics
BADGER, M., Photosythetic Functional Genomics
CLARK-WALKER, D., Molecular Genetics
FARQUHAR, G., Environmental Biology

GIBSON, J., Molecular and Poulation Genetics
GRAVES, J., Comparative Genomics
HARDHAM, A., Phytophthora Laboratory
NOBLE, I., Theoretical Ecology
SRINIVASAN, M., Insect Vision
WILLIAMSON, R., Cell Wall Laboratory

Research School of Chemistry: Dean Prof. DENIS EVANS

PROFESSORS

BANWELL, M., Organic Chemistry
COLLINS, M., Physical and Theoretical Chemistry
EASTON, C., Organic Chemistry
EVANS, D., Physical and Theoretical Chemistry
HILL, A., Inorganic Chemistry
KRAUSZ, E., Physical and Theoretical Chemistry
MANDER, L., Organic Chemistry
OTTING, G., Organic Chemistry
RADOM, L., Physical and Theoretical Chemistry
WELBERRY, T., Physical and Theoretical Chemistry
WHITE, J., Physical and Theoretical Chemistry
WILD, S., Inorganic Chemistry
WITHERS, R., Inorganic Chemistry

Research School of Earth Sciences: Dir Prof. MARK HARRISON

PROFESSORS

CHAPPELL, J., Earth Environment
COX, S., Earth Materials
GRIFFITHS, R., Earth Physics
GRUN, R., Earth Environment
JACKSON, I., Earth Materials
KENNETT, B. L. N., Earth Physics
LAMBECK, K., Earth Physics
LISTER, G., Earth Materials
McCULLOCH, M., Earth Environment
O'NEILL, H. ST C., Earth Materials

Research School of Information Sciences and Engineering: Dir Prof. JOHN RICHARDS

PROFESSORS

ANDERSON, B. D. O., Information Engineering
BRENT, R. P., Computer Science
HARTLEY, R., Information Engineering
LLOYD, J., Computer Sciences Laboratory
MOORE, J., Information Engineering

Research School of Pacific and Asian Studies: Dir Prof. J. FOX

PROFESSORS

ANDERSON, A. J., Archaeology and Natural History
BABBAGE, R.
BALL, D. J., Strategic and Defence Studies
BARMÉ, G. R.
BELLWOOD, P.
CROUCH, H.
DENOON, D. J. N., Pacific and Asian History
FANE, G.
FOX, J. J., Anthropology
HILL, H.
HOPE, G.
HORNER, D. M.
JHA, R.
JOLLY, M. A.
KERKVLIET, B. J. T., Political and Social Change
LAL, B.
McCORMACK, G. P., Pacific and Asian History
McKIBBEN, W., Economics
MARR, D.
MOSKO, M.
NELSON, H. N., Pacific and Asian History
PAWLEY, A. K., Linguistics

RAVENHILL, J.
SPRIGGS, M.
TRYON, D.
WARR, P. G., Agricultural Economics

Research School of Physical Sciences and Engineering: Dir Prof. J. WILLIAMS

PROFESSORS

BATCHELOR, M., Theoretical Physics
BAZHANOV, V., Theoretical Physics
DEWAR, R. L., Plasma Physics and Theoretical Physics
DRACOULIS, G. D., Nuclear Physics
ELLIMAN, R. G., Electronic Materials Engineering
HAMBERGER, S. M., Plasma Research
HYDE, S., Applied Mathematics
JAGADISH, C., Electronic Materials Engineering
LUTHER-DAVIES, B., Laser Physics
MARCELJA, S., Applied Mathematics
MITCHELL, D. J., Optical Sciences Centre
MOORE, J. B., Systems Engineering
SPEAR, R. H., Nuclear Physics
WEIGOLD, E., Atomic and Molecular Physics
WILLIAMS, J., Electronic Materials Engineering

Research School of Social Sciences: Dir Prof. F. C. JACKSON

PROFESSORS

BOOTH, A., Economics
BRAITHWAITE, J., Regulatory Institutions Network
BRENNAN, H. G., Economics and Social and Political Theory
CANE, P., Law
CHALMERS, D., Philosophy
CHAPMAN, B., Economics
CHARLESWORTH, H., Regulatory Institutions Network
DAVIES, M., Philosophy
DEACON, D., History
DRAHOS, P., Regulatory Institutions Network
DRYZEK, J. S., Political Science
GODFREY-SMITH, P., Philosophy
GOODIN, B., Philosophy
GRABOSKY, P., Regulatory Institutions Network
GREGORY, R. G., Economics
GUNNINGHAM, N., Regulatory Institutions Network
HAJEK, A., Philosophy
HIGMAN, B., History
HINDESS, B., Political Science
HULL, T., Demography
JACKSON, F. C., Philosophy
JALLAND, P., History
McALLISTER, A., Political Science
McDONALD, P., Demography
McGRATH, A., History
McMILLEN, J., Regulatory Institutions Network
PAGAN, A. R., Economics
RHODES, R., Political Science
RITCHIE, J. D., Australian Dictionary of Biography
SAWER, M., Political Science
SHEARING, C., Regulatory Institutions Network
SNOOKS, G. D., Economic History
STAPLETON, J., Law
STERELNY, K., Philosophy
WAJCMAN, J., Demography and Sociology
WANNA, J., Political Science

School of Mathematical Sciences: Dean Prof. A. L. CAREY

PROFESSORS

BATCHELOR, M., Mathematics
BAXTER, R. J., Mathematics
BAZHANOV, V., Mathematics
DALEY, D., Mathematics

GANI, J., Mathematics
HALL, P. J., Statistics
HEATHCOTE, C., Mathematics
HEYDE, C., Mathematics
HUTCHINSON, J., Mathematics
MCINTOSH, A., Mathematics
NEEMAN, A., Mathematics
NEWMAN, M., Mathematics
OSBORNE, M. R., Advanced Computation
ROBINSON, D., Mathematics
TRUDINGER, N., Mathematics
URBAS, J., Mathematics
WELSH, A., Statistics
WICKRAMASINGHE, D., Mathematics
WILSON, S. R., Statistics

THE COLLEGES

DEANS

College of Arts and Social Sciences: Prof.
TONI MAKKAI
College of Asia and the Pacific: Prof. ANDREW
MACINTYRE
College of Business and Economics: Prof.
KEITH HOUGHTON
College of Engineering and Computer Science: Prof. CHRIS BAKER
College of Law: Prof. MICHAEL COPER
College of Medicine, Biology and Environment: Prof. ANDREW COCKBURN (Dir)
College of Physical and Mathematical Sciences: Prof. AIDAN BYRNE (Dir)

PROFESSORS

College of Arts and Social Sciences:
BELLWOOD, P., Archaeology
CAMPBELL, R. J., Philosophy
CURTHOYS, A., History
GREENHALGH, C. M. B., Art History
GRISHIN, S., Art History
GROVES, C., Archaeology
MERLAN, F. C., Anthropology
MILLER, S., Philosophy
PAPADAKIS, E., Social Sciences
SAIKAI, A., Political Sciences
SITSKY, A., Composition
SPRIGGS, M., Archaeology
WARHURST, J. L., Political Science
WIERZBICKA, A. C., Linguistics
WILLIAMS, D., Visual Arts
WRIGHT, I. R., English
College of Asia and the Pacific:
CORBETT, J., Asian Studies
HOOKER, V., Oriental Studies
LOUIE, K., Chinese Studies
MILNER, A. C., Southeast Asian History
WELLS, K., Korean Studies
College of Business and Economics:
CRAIG, R., Commerce
DOWRICK, S., Economics
GREGOR, S., Business Information Management
HATTON, T., Economics
HEATHCOTE, C. R., Mathematical Statistics
MALLER, R., Finance and Applied Statistics
MONROE, G., Business Information Management
NICHOLLS, D. F., Statistics
O'NEILL, T., Applied Statistics
RICHARDSON, M., Economics
SMITH, T., Applied Statistics
TYERS, R., Economics
College of Engineering and Computer Science:
BLAKERS, A., Engineering
CARDEW-HALL, M., Engineering
CUEVAS, A., Engineering
GEDEON, T., Engineering
JAMES, M., Engineering
MCKAY, B., Engineering
QIN, Q., Engineering
College of Law:
CAMPBELL, T. D., Law

COPER, M. D., Law
DAVIS, J. L. R., Law
DISNEY, J. P., Law
GREIG, D. W., Law
GUNNINGHAM, N. A., Law
HAMBLEY, A. D., Law
PEARCE, D. C., Law
SWEENEY, M. D., Law
ZINES, L. R., Law
College of Physical and Mathematical Sciences:
CLARK, I., Biochemistry
COCKBURN, A., Botany and Zoology
COX, S., Structural Geology
DE DECKKER, P., Geology
ELLIS, D., Igneous Petrology
GUNNINGHAM, N., Resources, Environment and Society
KANOWSKI, P. J., Resources, Environment and Society
KIRK, K., Biochemistry
LEVICK, B., Psychology
MCCLELLAND, D., Physics
PASHLEY, R., Colloid Chemistry
RIDE, D., Geology
STANTON, R., Palaeontology
TURNER, J., Psychology

BOND UNIVERSITY

Qld 4229
Telephone: (7) 5595-1111
Fax: (7) 5595-1140
E-mail: information@bond.edu.au
Internet: www.bond.edu.au
Founded 1987
Private control
Academic year: January to December
Chancellor: HELEN NUGENT
Vice-Chancellor: Prof. ROBERT STABLE
Registrar: ALAN FINCH
Dir of Finance: JOHN LELIEVRE
Dir of Information Services: GRACE SAW
Dir of Marketing and Student Recruitment: ANDREA HARCOURT
Number of teachers: 461
Number of students: 5,370
Publications: *Bond Law Review*, *Revenue Law Journal*

DEANS

Business, Technology and Sustainable Devt: Prof. G. MARCHANT
Health Sciences and Medicine: Prof. C. DEL MAR
Humanities and Social Sciences: Prof. R. MORTLEY
Law: Prof. L. BOULLE

PROFESSORS

Faculty of Business, Technology and Sustainable Devt:
ARIFF, M., Finance
BERTIN, W., Finance
EARL, G., Sustainable Devt
FISHER, C., Management
GASTON, N., Economics
GORDON, R., Business
ISELIN, E., Accounting
KENT, P., Accounting
MOORES, K., Family Business
MORRISON, I., Information Technology
ROBERTS, E., Hotel, Resort and Tourism Management
SHAW, J. B., Human Resource Management
WILLIAMS, B., Finance
Faculty of Health Sciences and Medicine:
CHESS-WILLIAMS, R., Biomedical Sciences
GASS, G., Exercise and Sports Science
HENLY, D., Biomedical Sciences
QUICK, S., Sport Management

VAN DAAL, A., Forensic Sciences
Faculty of Humanities and Social Sciences:
HICKS, R., Psychology
MOLLOY, B., Film and Television
MORTLEY, R., Philosophy
PEARSON, M., Communication and Media
WEBB, S., Australian Studies
WILSON, P., Criminology
Faculty of Law:
BOULLE, L., Medication, Alternative Dispute Resolution
CARNEY, G., Constitutional and Administrative Law
COLVIN, E., Criminal Law
CORKERY, J., Corporate and Taxation Law
FIELD, D., Criminal Law
FORDER, J., Contract Law, Information Technology and Electric Commerce Law
GERRARD, A., Constitutional Law, Admin. Law, Taxation of Business Entities
HISCOCK, M., Contract Law, Int. Law
LESSING, J., Corporations Law, Partnerships
LUPTON, M., Law and Medicine
MARSHALL, B., Restrictive Trade Practices
ONG, D., Equity, Securities Law
SPENCER, L., Franchise Law
SVANTESSON, D., eCommerce, Private Int. Law
WADE, J., Mediation, Negotiation, Family Law
School of Information Technology:
FINNIE, G., Information Systems
KRISHNAN, P., Software Systems

CHARLES DARWIN UNIVERSITY

Darwin, NT 0909
Telephone: (8) 8946-6666
Fax: (8) 8927-0612
E-mail: international@cdu.edu.au
Internet: www.cdu.edu.au
Founded 2003 by the merger of Northern Territory University and Centralian College
Federal control
Academic year: February to November
Chancellor: R. RYAN
Vice-Chancellor: Prof. BARNEY GLOVER
Deputy Vice-Chancellor for Research and International: Prof. ROBERT WASSON
Deputy Vice-Chancellor for Teaching and Learning: Prof. C. WEBB
Exec. Dir of Corporate Services: Dr SCOTT SNYDER
Number of academic staff: 500
Number of students: 21,000

DEANS

Education, Health and Science: Prof. G. PEGG
Law, Business and Arts: Prof. GARY DAVIS (acting)

CHARLES STURT UNIVERSITY

Chancellery, Panorama Ave, Bathurst, NSW 2795
Telephone: (2) 6338-4000
Fax: (2) 6338-6001
E-mail: inquiry@csu.edu.au
Internet: www.csu.edu.au
Founded 1989 by merger of Mitchell College of Advanced Education (f. 1951) with Riverina-Murray Inst. of Higher Education (f. 1947)
State control
Academic year: January to December
Chancellor: LAWRENCE WILLETT
Vice-Chancellor and Pres.: Prof. IAN GOULTER
Deputy Vice-Chancellor for Academic Affairs: Prof. ROSS CHAMBERS

Deputy Vice Chancellor for Research: Prof. SUE THOMAS

Deputy Vice Chancellor for Admin. Services: Prof. LYN GORMAN

Univ. Sec. and Dir Corporate Affairs: MARK BURDACK

Exec. Dir, Library Services: SHIRLEY OAKLEY

Library of 627,163 vols, 51,468 periodicals

Number of teachers: 822

Number of students: 34,611

DEANS

Faculty of Arts: Prof. ANTHONY CAHALAN

Faculty of Business: Prof. LESLEY WHITE

Faculty of Education: Prof. TONI DOWNES

Faculty of Science: Prof. NICHOLAS KLOMP

PROFESSORS

Faculty of Arts (POB 588, Wagga Wagga, NSW 2678; tel. (2) 6933-2861; fax (2) 6933-2868; internet www.csu.edu.au/faculty/arts):

BRADLEY, B., Psychology

CAMPBELL, T., Centre for Applied Philosophy and Public Ethics

CARROLL, J., Communication Research

FARRELL, M., Arts

FRAME, T., Theology

FRYER, D., Social Sciences and Liberal Studies

GOODMAN-DELAHUNTY, J., Psychology and Australian Graduate School of Policing

GREEN, D., Visual and Performing Arts

HAIRE, I., Australian Centre for Christianity and Culture

HUDSON, C., Public and Contextual Theology

KLEINIG, J., Centre for Applied Philosophy and Public Ethics

LUPTON, D., Sociology/Cultural Studies

MAY, L., Social Justice and Applied Ethics

MILLER, S., Philosophy

MILLS, J., Communications

MORAN, C., Humanities and Social Sciences

PAWAR, M., Social Work and Human Services

WECKERT, J., Computing Ethics

Faculty of Business (Panorama Ave, Bathurst, NSW 2795; tel. (2) 6338-4285; fax (2) 6338-4250; internet www.csu.edu.au/faculty/commerce):

BOSSOMAIER, T., Computing Systems

FISH, A., International Business and Human Resource Management

HICKS, J., Economics

JARRATT, D., Marketing

MORRISON, M., Economics and Marketing

OCZKOWSKI, E., Applied Economics

PARTON, K., Strategic Professor– Economics, Agriculture and environmental Science

Faculty of Education (Panorama Ave, Bathurst, NSW 2795; tel. (2) 6338-4444; fax (2) 6338-4182; internet www.csu.edu.au/faculty/educat):

BAIN, A., Education

DALGARNO, B., Information Systems

DOCKETT, S., Early Childhood Education

GREEN, W., Education

HIDER, P., Library and Information Studies

HIGGS, J., Institute of Education for Practice

KEMMIS, S., Education

LOWRIE, T., Education

MARINO, F., Human Movement Studies

MCLEOD, S., Language Acquisition

PERRY, R., Mathematics Education

REID, J., Education

SANTORO, N., Education

SUMSION, J., Early Childhood Education

Faculty of Science (POB 588, Wagga Wagga, NSW 2678; tel. (2) 6933-2864; fax (2) 6933-2868; internet www.csu.edu.au/faculty/science):

ABBOTT, K., Animal and Veterinary Sciences

BALL, P., Rural Pharmacy

BLACKWELL, J., Smart Agricultural Water Technologies

BOWMER, K., Water Policy

BRYANT, R., Dentistry

CHENOWETH, P., Veterinary Reproduction

CHRISTIE, B., Small Animal Medicine

CURTIS, A., Environmental Management

DUFFY, M., Nursing and Midwifery

GURR, G., Applied Ecology

HARDIE, W., Wine Growing Innovation

KEMP, D., Farming Systems

KHAN, S., Hydrology

KLOMP, N., Science

LEMERLE, D., Agricultural Innovation

O'BRIEN, L., Nursing

PARTON, K., Agricultural Economics

PRATLEY, J., Agricultural and Wine Sciences

SANGSTER, N., Pathobiology

SPITHILL, T., Veterinary Parasitology

WANG, L., Clinical Pharmacy/Pharmacology

WILSON, D., Dentistry

WYNN, P., Animal Production

CONSTITUENT CAMPUSES

Albury–Wodonga Campus

POB 789, Albury, NSW 2640

Telephone: (2) 6051-6000

Fax: (2) 6051-6629

E-mail: inquiry@csu.edu.au

Internet: www.csu.edu.au

Founded 1989

Head of Campus: Prof. ALLAN CURTIS

Bathurst Campus

Panorama Ave, Bathurst, NSW 2795

Telephone: (2) 6338-4000

Fax: (2) 6331-9634

E-mail: inquiry@csu.edu.au

Internet: www.csu.edu.au

Founded 1989

Prin.: COLIN SHARP.

Dubbo Campus

Locked Bag 49, Dubbo East, NSW 2830

Telephone: (2) 6885-7300

Fax: (2) 6885-7301

E-mail: inquiry@csu.edu.au

Internet: www.csu.edu.au

Founded 1995

Head of Campus: BEVERLEY MORIARTY (acting).

Orange Campus

POB 883, Orange, NSW

Telephone: (2) 6365-7500

Fax: (2) 6365-7885

E-mail: info@csu.edu.au

Internet: www.csu.edu.au

Prin.: Prof. KEVIN PARTON.

Wagga Wagga Campus

Locked Bag 588, Wagga Wagga, NSW 2678

Telephone: (2) 6933-2000

Fax: (2) 6933-2639

E-mail: inquiry@csu.edu.au

Internet: www.csu.edu.au

Founded 1989

Head of Campus: ADRIAN LINDNER.

Ontario Campus

860 Harrington Court, Burlington, ON Canada L7N 3N4

Telephone: (5) 333-4955

Fax: (5) 333-6562

E-mail: canada@csu.edu.au

Internet: www.charlessturt.ca

Head of Campus: Prof. ROBERT MEYENN.

CQ UNIVERSITY

Bruce Highway, Rockhampton, CQ Mail Centre, Qld 4702

Telephone: (7) 4930-9368

Fax: (7) 4936-1691

E-mail: publicrelations@cqu.edu.au

Internet: www.cqu.edu.au

Founded 1967 as Queensland Institute of Technology (Capricornia); became Capricornia Institute of Advanced Education in 1971; became University College of Central Queensland in 1990 and University of Central Queensland in 1992; became Central Queensland University in 1994; present name 2008

Chancellor: RENNIE FRITSCHY

Vice-Chancellor and Pres.: Prof. JOHN RICKARD

Deputy Vice-Chancellor and Vice-Pres.: Prof. ANGELA DELVES

Deputy Vice Chancellor for Research Scholarship and Industry: Prof. JENNELLE KYD

Exec. Dir for Corporate Services: KEN WINDOW

Exec. Dir for Resources: JOHN NELSON

Dir of Library Services: GRAHAM BLACK

Number of teachers: 321

Number of students: 19,000

DEANS

Faculty of Arts, Business, Informatics, Education: Prof. ELIZABETH TAYLOR

Faculty of Sciences, Engineering and Health: Prof. KEVIN TICKLE

Campuses at Brisbane, Bundaberg, Emerald, Gladstone, Gold Coast, Mackay, Melbourne, Rockhampton and Sydney

CURTIN UNIVERSITY OF TECHNOLOGY

GPOB U1987, Perth, WA 6845

Telephone: (8) 9266-9266

Fax: (8) 9266-2255

Internet: www.curtin.edu.au

Founded 1967 as Western Australian Inst. of Technology; present name and status 1987

Academic year: February to November (2 semesters)

Chancellor: RICHARD TASTULA (acting)

Vice-Chancellor: Prof. LANCE TWOMEY

Sr Deputy Vice-Chancellor: Prof. LESLEY PARKER

Deputy Vice-Chancellor for Research and Devt: Prof. PAUL ROSSITER

Pro Vice-Chancellor for Academic Services: Prof. JANE DEN HOLLANDER

Pro Vice-Chancellor for International and Enterprise: Prof. JEANETTE HACKETT

Exec. Dean, Curtin Business School: Prof. MICHAEL WOOD

Exec. Dean, Engineering, Science and Computing: PETER LEE

Exec. Dean, Health Sciences: Prof. CHARLES WATSON

Exec. Dean, Humanities: Prof. TOM STANNAGE

Exec. Gen. Man., University Resources: PETER WALTON

University Librarian: VICKI WILLIAMSON

Number of teachers: 1,200

Number of students: 40,374

DEANS

Faculty of Built Environment, Art and Design: L. HEVGOLD

Faculty of Education, Language Studies and Social Work: Dr G. DELLAR

Research and Development (Graduate Studies): Prof. L. RENNIE

DEAKIN UNIVERSITY

Gheringhap St, Geelong, Vic. 3217
Telephone: (3) 5227-1100
Fax: (3) 5227-2001
E-mail: enquire@deakin.edu.au
Internet: www.deakin.edu.au
Founded 1974
Academic year: February to November

Chancellor: DAVID MORGAN
Vice-Chancellor: Prof. JANE DEN HOLLANDER
Vice-Pres. for Enterprise and Engagement: KEAN SELWAY
Deputy Vice-Chancellor for Academic Affairs: Prof. PHILLIP CLARKE
Deputy Vice-Chancellor for Int. Relations and Devt: ROBIN BUCKHAM
Deputy Vice-Chancellor for Research: Prof. LEE ASTHEIMER
Librarian: S. MCKNIGHT

Library of 1,586,335 books, 88,776 serials
Number of teachers: 2,600
Number of students: 34,281

Campuses at Melbourne (Burwood), Geelong, Rusden, Toorak, Warrnambool and Geelong Waterfront

DEANS

Faculty of Arts and Education: Prof. JENNIFER RADBOURNE
Faculty of Business and Law: Prof. GAEL MCDONALD
Faculty of Health, Medicine, Nursing and Behavioural Sciences: Prof. JOHN CATFORD
Faculty of Science and Technology: Prof. CHRISTOPHER GRAY

EDITH COWAN UNIVERSITY

270 Joondalup Dr., Joondalup, WA 6027
Telephone: (8) 6304-0000
E-mail: enquiries@ecu.edu.au
Internet: www.ecu.edu.au
Founded 1991
State control
Academic year: February to November (2 semesters)

Chancellor: Hon. Justice R. NICHOLSON
Vice-Chancellor: Prof. KERRY O. COX
Deputy Vice-Chancellor for Academic Affairs: Prof. PATRICK GARNETT
Deputy Vice-Chancellor for Research: Prof. JOHN FINLAY-JONES
Deputy Vice-Chancellor for Students, Advancement and International Affairs: Prof. JOHN WOOD
Pro Vice-Chancellor for Equity and Indigenous Affairs: Prof. BRENDA CHEREDNICHENKO
Pro Vice-Chancellor for Teaching and Learning: Prof. RON OLIVER
Pro Vice-Chancellor for Technology and Information Systems: Prof. TONY WATSON
Vice Pres., Resources and Chief Financial Officer: WARREN SNELL

Number of teachers: 772
Number of students: 23,000

Publications: Digest (4 a year), Handbook (1 a year), Quest (4 a year), Research & Postgraduate Studies (1 a year)

DEANS

Faculty of Business and Law: Prof. ROBERT HARVEY
Faculty of Computing, Health and Science: ANTHONY WATSON
Faculty of Education and Arts: Prof. BRENDA CHEREDNICHENKO
Faculty of Regional Professional Studies: ROBERT IRVINE

FLINDERS UNIVERSITY

GPOB 2100, Adelaide, SA 5001
Telephone: (8) 8201-3911
Fax: (8) 8201-3757
E-mail: central.records@flinders.edu.au
Internet: www.flinders.edu.au
Founded 1966, merged in 1991 with Sturt Campus of South Australian College of Advanced Education
Academic year: March to November (2 semesters)

Chancellor: Sir STEPHEN GEVLACH
Vice-Chancellor: Prof. MICHAEL N. BARBER
Deputy Vice-Chancellor for Academic Affairs: Prof. ANDREW W. PARKIN
Deputy Vice-Chancellor for Int. Relations: Prof. D. FORBES
Deputy Vice-Chancellor for Research: Prof. DAVID DAY
Dir. of Admin.: B. FERGUSSON
Registrar: B. SIMONDSON
Librarian: IAN MCBAIN

Library: see Libraries and Archives
Number of teachers: 625
Number of students: 15,418

Publications: Australian Bulletin of Labour (4 a year), Australian Economic Papers (with Univ. of Adelaide), Australian Journal of Political Science, Health Sociology Review

EXECUTIVE DEANS

Education, Humanities, Law and Theology: Prof. F. H. E. TRENT
Health Sciences: Prof. MICHAEL KIDD
Science and Engineering: Prof. WARREN LAWRANCE
Social and Behavioural Sciences: Prof. PHYLLIS THARENOM

PROFESSORS

AYLWARD, P., Medicine
BARRITT, G. T., Medical Biochemistry
BAUM, F., Public Health
BERSTEN, A. A., Medicine
BLESSING, W. W., Medicine
BULL, M., Biological Sciences
BURGOYNE, L., Biological Sciences
BUTCHER, A. R., Communication Disorders
CATCHESIDE, D. E. A., Biological Sciences
CLARE, J. M. R., Nursing
CLARK, D. J., Law
CONDON, J., Psychiatry
COOPER, L. L., Social Administration and Social Work
COSTA, M., Human Physiology
COSTER, D. J., Ophthalmology
CROCKER, A. D., Psychiatry
CROTTY, M., Rehabilitation, Aged and Extended Care
CURROW, D. C., Palliative Care
DEBATS, D. A., American Studies
DODDS, P. G., Mathematics and Statistics
DUNBAR, J., Rural Health
FAIRWEATHER, P. G., Biological Sciences
FORBES, D. K., Geography
FORSYTH, K. D., Paediatrics and Child Health
GIBBINS, I. L., Anatomy and Histology
GOODMAN, A. E., Biology
GORDON, T. P., Immunology, Allergy and Arthritis
HASSAN, R. U., Sociology
HAY, I. M., Geography
HENDERSON, D. W., Medicine
HOLLEDGE, J., Drama
KALUCY, R. S., Psychiatry
KEIRSE, M., Obstetrics and Gynaecology
KNOWLES, G. P., Computer Systems Engineering
KRISHNAN, J., Surgery
LAWRANCE, W., Chemistry
LAWSON, M. J., Education
LEONARD, D., Economics
LINACRE, A., Forensics

LUSZCZ, M. A., Psychology
MCDONALD, J. M., Economics
MACKENZIE, P. I., Clinical Pharmacology
MACKINNON, A., Medicine
MALTBY, R. G., Screen Studies
MARLIN, C. D., Computer Science
MATISONS, J. G., Chemistry, Physics and Earth Sciences
MAVROMARAS, K., Labour Studies
MINERS, J. O., Clinical Pharmacology
MORLEY, A. A., Haematology
OWEN, H., Anaesthesia and Pain Medicine
PARKIN, A., Political and International Studies
PHILLIPS, P., Medicine
PILLER, N. B., Public Health
PRIDEAUX, D. J., Health Professional Education
RICHARDS, E. S., History
RICHARDSON, S., National Institute of Labour Studies
ROACH ANLEU, S. L., Sociology
ROCHE, A. M., National Centre for Education and Training on Addiction
RODDICK, J. F., Computer Science
RUSH, R. A., Human Physiology
RYALL, R. L., Surgery
SAGE, M. R., Medical Imaging
SHERIDAN, S. M., Women's Studies
SIMMONS, C. T., Groundwater
SMITH, M. D., Medicine
STEWART, A. J., Law
STORER, R., Physics
TEUBNER, P. J. O., Physics
TIGGEMANN, M., Psychology
TOMCZAK, M., Earth Sciences
TONKIN, A. M., Medicine
TOOULI, J., Surgery
TRENT, F. H., Education
TULLOCH, G. J., English
WATSON, D., Surgery
WILLOUGHBY, J. O., Medicine
WING, L. M. H., Medicine
WORLEY, P. S., Rural and Remote Health
YOUNG, G. P., Gastroenterology
ZOLA, H., Medicine

GRIFFITH UNIVERSITY

Qld 4111
Gold Coast Campus: Parklands Dr., Southport, Qld 4215
Telephone: (7) 5552-8800
Fax: (7) 5552-8777
Logan Campus: University Dr., Meadowbrook, Qld 4131
Telephone: (7) 3382-7111
Fax: (7) 3735-7965
Mount Gravatt Campus: Messines Ridge Rd, Mt Gravatt, Qld 4122
Nathan Campus: Kessels Rd, Nathan, Qld 4111
Telephone: (7) 3735-7111
Fax: (7) 3735-7965
Internet: www.griffith.edu.au
(Queensland College of Art, Griffith Univ., 226 Grey St, South Bank, Qld 4101; tel. (7) 3735-3111; fax (7) 3735-3199; f. 1881, became a college of Griffith Univ. 1992)
(Queensland Conservatorium, Griffith Univ., 16 Russell St, South Bank, Qld 4101; tel. (7) 3735-6111; fax (7) 3735-6282; f. 1957, became a college of Griffith Univ. 1991)
Founded 1971
State control
Academic year: February to November

Chancellor: LENEEN FORDE
Vice-Chancellor and Pres.: Prof. IAN O'CONNOR
Deputy Vice-Chancellor for Research and Provost Gold Coast: Prof. NED PANKHURST
Deputy Vice-Chancellor for Academic Affairs: Prof. SUSAN SPENCE

Deputy Vice-Chancellor and Provost: Prof. MARILYN MCMENIMAN
Pro-Vice-Chancellor for Admin.: COLIN MCANDREW
Pro-Vice-Chancellor for Arts, Education and Law: Prof. PAUL MAZEROLLE
Pro-Vice-Chancellor for Business: Prof. MICHAEL POWELL
Pro-Vice-Chancellor for Community Partnerships: Prof. M. STANDAGE
Pro-Vice-Chancellor for Health: Prof. ALLAN CRIPPS
Pro-Vice-Chancellor for Information Services: JANICE RICKARDS
Pro-Vice-Chancellor for Int. Affairs: CHRISTOPHER MADDEN
Pro-Vice-Chancellor for Science, Environment, Engineering and Technology: Prof. SUE BERNERS-PRICE
Academic Registrar: KATHY GRGIC
Dir, Queensland College of Art: Prof. PAUL CLEVELAND
Dir, Queensland Conservatorium: Prof. HUIB SCHIPPERS
Library of 933,959
Number of teachers: 2,966 full-time
Number of students: 42,628
Publication: *Griffith Review* (4 a year)

DEANS

Faculty of Arts: Prof. K. FERRES
Faculty of Education: Prof. C. WYATT-SMITH
Griffith Business School: Prof. W. SHEPHERD (Academic: Prof. L. FULOP (Research: Prof. L. FRAZER (Learning and Teaching)
Griffith Graduate Research School: Prof. J. CUMMING
Griffith Health School: Prof. D. CREEDY (Academic: Prof. K. HALFORD (Research: Assoc. Prof. N. BUYS (Learning and Teaching)
Griffith Law School: Prof. P. BARON
Science, Environment, Engineering and Technology: Assoc. Prof. C. WILD (Academic: G. BUSHELL (Research: D. EDWARDS (Learning and Teaching)

PROFESSORS

AITKEN, L., Nursing
ARTHINGTON, A. H., Environmental Science
AULD, C., Tourism, Leisure, Hotel and Sports Management
BAGNALL, R., Education
BALASUBRAMANIAM, A. B., Engineering
BALFOUR, M., Education
BAMBER, G., Business
BARKER, M., Management
BEACHAM, I., Medical Science
BERNS, S., Law
BORBASI, S., Nursing
BRADDOCK, R., Environmental Sciences
BRAMLEY-MOORE, M., Queensland College of Art
BROWN, L., Environmental Sciences
BROWN, P., Leisure Studies
BUCKLEY, R., Engineering
BUNN, S., Environmental Studies
BURCH, D., Science
BURTON, B., Education
BUSHELL, G., Science
CHABOYER, W., Nursing
CHENOWETH, L., Human Services
CHU, C., Public Health
CLARKE, F., Biomolecular and Physical Sciences
COUCHMAN, P., Management
CREED, P., Psychology
CREEDY, D., Health
CRIPPS, A., Health
CUMMING, J., Education
DALY, K., Criminology and Criminal Justice
DAVIDSON, M. C., Tourism, Leisure, Hotel and Sports Management
DE LEO, D., Suicide Research and Prevention

DEHNE, F., Information and Communication Technology
DEMPSTER, N., Education
DEWAR, J. K., Law
DIMITRIJEV, S., Microelectronic Engineering
DOBSON, J., Science
DRAPER, P., Music
DREW, R., Biomolecular and Physical Sciences
DREW, R., Environmental Studies
DROMEY, R. G., Computing and Information Technology
DYCK, M. J., Business
ELKINS, J., Education
ESTIVILL-CASTRO, V., Information and Communication Technology
FARQHAR, M., International Business and Asian Studies
FERRES, K., Arts
FINNANE, M. J., Arts, Postgraduate Studies
FRAZER, L., Marketing
FULOP, E., Marketing and Management
GAMMACK, J., Management
GIDDINGS, J., Law
GLEESON, B., Environmental Planning
GRIFFITHS, L., Medical Science
GUEST, R., Graduate School of Management
GUILDING, C., Tourism, Leisure, Hotel and Sports Management
HALFORD, G., Psychology
HALFORD, W. K., Health and Applied Psychology
HARRISON, H. B., Microelectronic Engineering
HEAD, B., Law
HEADRICK, J., Medical Science
HEALY, P., Science
HOMEL, R. J., Criminology and Criminal Justice
HOPE, G., Science
HUDSON, C. W., Humanities
HUGHES, J., Environmental Sciences
HUNTER, R., Law
HYDE, M. B., Education
ISLAM, Y., International Business and Asian Studies
IVANOVSKI, S., Dentistry and Oral Health
JENKINS, I., Science
JOHNSON, L., Research
JOHNSON, N. W., Dentistry and Oral Health
JOHNSTONE, R., Law
KANE, J., Politics and Public Policy
KEITH, R., International Business and Asian Studies
KITCHING, R. L., Environmental Science
KNIGHT, A. E., Science
KNIGHT, K., International Business and Asian Studies
KWON, O. Y., International Business and Asian Studies
LAM, A. K., Medicine
LEE, S., Environmental Studies
LISNER, P., Microelectronic Engineering
LOO, Y.-C., Engineering
MCDONALD, J., Law
MACKAY-SIM, A., Biomolecular and Biomedical Sciences
MACKERRAS, C. P., International Business and Asian Studies
MCLURE, R. J., Medicine
MCMENIMAN, M., Education
MCQUEEN, R. I., Law
MCROBBIE, C., Education
MCTAINSH, G., Environmental Studies
MAKIN, A., Accounting, Finance and Economics
MERRILEES, W., Marketing and Management
MIA, L., Accounting and Finance
MORAN, A., Arts
MOYLE, W., Nursing
MUIRHEAD, B. D., Education
NESDALE, A. R., Commerce, Management and Applied Psychology
NG, A. C., Accounting
NGUYEN, D. T.
O'CONNOR, I., Economics

O'FAIRCHEALLAIGH, C. S., Politics and Public Policy
O'TOOLE, J., Education
PALIWAL, K., Microelectronic Engineering
PARRY, K., Management
PATEL, B., Biomolecular and Physical Sciences
PEETZ, D., Industrial Relations
PEGG, D. T., Science
POWELL, M. J., Business
QUINN, R. J., Science
RICKARD, C., Nursing
RICKSON, R., Environmental Studies
ROEMFELDT, P. J., Music
SADLER, D. R., Education
SAMPFORD, C. J., Criminology and Criminal Justice
SATTAR, A., Information Technology
SCHULTZ, J., Public Culture
SCHUMAN, A. D., Business
SCUFFHAM, P., Medicine
SEARLE, J., Medicine
SELVANATHAN, A., International Business and Asian Studies
SELVANATHAN, S., Accounting, Finance and Economics
SHEPHERD, W., International Business and Asian Studies
SHORT, S. D., Public Health
SMITH, C., Accounting, Finance and Economics
SPARKS, B., Tourism and Hotel Management
STANDAGE, M., Science and Health
STEVENSON, J. C., Education
STRACHAN, G., Commerce and Business
SUN, C., Computing and Information Technology
TACON, P., Arts
THIEL, D. V., Microelectronic Engineering
TOH, S. H., Multi-faith Centre
TOMLINSON, R., Environmental Engineering
TOPOR, R. W., Computing and Information Technology
TURNBULL, P. G., Arts
VLACIC, L., Microelectronic Engineering
VON ITZTEIN, M., Biomolecular Science
WALLIS, M., Nursing
WANNA, J., Politics and Public Policy
WELLER, P. M., Politics and Public Policy
WISEMAN, H. M., Science
XU, Z., Environmental Studies
YEO, R., Humanities
ZEVENBERGEN, R., Education

ACADEMIC CENTRES AND INSTITUTES

Centre for Applied Linguistics and Languages: tel. (7) 3735-7089; fax (7) 3875-7090; e-mail call@griffith.edu.au; internet www.griffith.edu.au/centre/call; Dir MARGARET CASEY.

Centre for Applied Studies in Deafness: tel. (7) 5552-8619; e-mail m.hyde@griffith.edu.au; internet www.griffith.edu.au/centre/casd; Dir Prof. MERVYN HYDE.

Centre for Credit and Consumer Law: tel. (7) 3735-4211; fax (7) 3735-5599; e-mail n.howell@griffith.edu.au; internet www.griffith.edu.au/centre/cccl; Dir NICOLA HOWELL.

Centre for Environmental and Population Health: tel. (7) 3735-7458; fax (7) 3735-5318; e-mail c.chu@griffith.edu.au; internet www.griffith.edu.au/centre/ceph; Dir Prof. CORDIA CHU.

Centre for Leadership and Management in Education: tel. (7) 3735-5626; fax (7) 3735-6877; e-mail clme@griffith.edu.au; internet www.griffith.edu.au/centre/clme; Dir (vacant).

Centre for Professional Development: tel. (7) 5552-8452; fax (7) 5552-9076; e-mail b.mclellan@griffith.edu.au; internet www.griffith.edu.au/centre/cpd; Dir Dr M. COOPER.

Griffith Graduate Research School: tel. (7) 3735-5958; e-mail j.cumming@griffith.edu.au; internet www.griffith.edu.au/ggrs; Dir Prof. JOY CUMMING.

Griffith Institute for Higher Education: tel. (7) 3735-5982; fax (7) 3735-5998; e-mail c.birch@griffith.edu.au; internet www.griffith.edu.au/centre/gihe; Dir Prof. KERRI-LEE KRAUSE.

GUMURRII Student Support Centre: tel. (7) 3735-7676; fax (7) 3735-7033; e-mail kerryn.brown@griffith.edu.au; internet www.griffith.edu.au/centre/gumurrii; Dir Prof. B. ROBERTSON.

Institute for Educational Research, Policy and Evaluation: Dir (vacant).

Queensland Centre for Public Health (Griffith Node): tel. (7) 3735-3241; fax (7) 3735-3272; e-mail donald.stewart@griffith.edu.au; internet www.griffith.edu.au/centre/qcph; Dir Prof. DONALD STEWART.

Unit for Italian Studies: Dir C. KENNEDY.

ATTACHED RESEARCH CENTRES

Applied Cognitive Neuroscience Research Centre: tel. (7) 3735-3456; fax (7) 3735-3388; e-mail acnrc@griffith.edu.au; internet www.griffith.edu.au/school/psy/acnrc; Dir Assoc. Prof. DAVID SHUM.

Australian Centre for Intellectual Property in Agriculture: tel. (7) 3346-7506; fax (7) 3346-7480; e-mail acipa@law.uq.edu.au; internet www.acipa.edu.au; Dir Prof. B. SHERMAN.

Australian Institute for Suicide Research and Prevention: tel. (7) 3735-3382; internet www.griffith.edu.au/school/psy/aisrap; Dir Prof. DIEGO DE LEO.

Centre for Applied Language, Literacy and Communication Studies: tel. (7) 3735-5497; fax (7) 3735-5921; Dir Prof. C. WYATT-SMITH.

Centre for Aquatic Processes and Evolution: tel. (7) 5552-9185; fax (7) 5552-8067; e-mail cpp-capp@griffith.edu.au; internet www.griffith.edu.au/centre/capp; Dir Prof. JOE LEE.

Centre for Forestry and Horticultural Research: tel. (7) 3735-6709; fax (7) 3735-7656; e-mail cfhr@griffith.edu.au; internet www.griffith.edu.au/centre/cfhr; Dir Prof. Z. XU.

Centre for Governance and Public Policy: tel. (7) 3735-7723; fax (7) 3735-7737; e-mail p.weller@griffith.edu.au; internet www.griffith.edu.au/centre/cgpp; Dir Prof. PATRICK WELLER.

Centre for Infrastructure Engineering and Management: tel. (7) 5552 8575; fax (7) 5552 8065; internet www.griffith.edu.au/centre/iem; Dir Prof. SHERIF MOHAMED.

Centre for Innovative Conservation Strategies: tel. (7) 5552 9234; internet www.griffith.edu.au/centre/cics/home.html; Dir Assoc. Prof. JEAN MARC HERO (acting).

Centre for Learning Research: tel. (7) 3735-5724; fax (7) 3735-6868; e-mail h.middleton@griffith.edu.au; internet www.griffith.edu.au/centre/clr; Dir Assoc. Prof. HOWARD MIDDLETON.

Centre for Organisational Governance and Performance Management: tel. (7) 3735-6621; fax (7) 3735-7760; e-mail g.warry@griffith.edu.au; internet www.griffith.edu.au/centre/cogap; Dir Assoc. Prof. NAVA SUBRAMANIAN.

Centre for Public Culture and Ideas: tel. (7) 3735-4131; fax (7) 3735-4132; e-mail j.dragisic@griffith.edu.au; internet www.griffith.edu.au/centre/cpci; Co-Dirs Assoc. Prof. A. HAEBICH, Dr F. PAISLEY.

Centre for Quantum Dynamics: tel. (7) 3735-7279; fax (7) 3735-7773; e-mail h.wiseman@griffith.edu.au; internet www.griffith.edu.au/centre/quantumdynamics; Dir Prof. HOWARD WISEMAN.

Centre for Riverine Landscapes: tel. and fax (7) 3735-7403; e-mail a.arthington@griffith.edu.au; internet www.griffith.edu.au/centre/riverlandscapes; Dir Prof. ANGELA ARTHINGTON.

Centre for Wireless Monitoring and Applications: tel. (7) 3735-7192; fax (7) 3735-5198; e-mail d.thiel@griffith.edu.au; internet www.griffith.edu.au/centre/cwma; Dir Prof. DAVID THIEL.

Centre for Work, Leisure and Community Research: tel. (7) 3735-3714; fax (7) 3735-4298; e-mail h.gray@griffith.edu.au; internet www.griffith.edu.au/centre/wlcr; Dir Prof. ADRIAN WILKINSON (acting).

Eskitis, The Institute for Cell and Molecular Therapies: tel. (7) 3735-6006; fax (7) 3735-7656; e-mail eskitis@griffith.edu.au; internet www.griffith.edu.au/centre/eskitis; Dir Prof. RON QUINN.

Forensic Science Research and Innovation Centre: tel. (7) 3735 5069; fax (7) 3735 7773; e-mail dennis.burns@griffith.edu.au; Dir Assoc. Prof. DENNIS BURNS.

Genomics Research Centre: Dir Prof. L. GRIFFITHS.

Griffith Asia Institute: tel. (7) 3735-7370; fax (7) 3735-3731; e-mail gai@griffith.edu.au; internet www.griffith.edu.au/business/griffith-asia-institute; Dir Prof. MICHAEL WESLEY.

Griffith Centre for Coastal Management: tel. (7) 5552-8506; fax (7) 5552-8067; e-mail r.tomlinson@griffith.edu.au; internet www.griffith.edu.au/centre/gccm; Dir Prof. RODGER TOMLINSON.

Griffith Psychological Health Research Centre: tel. (7) 3732-8052; fax (7) 3732-8291; e-mail r.tomlinson@griffith.edu.au; internet www.griffith.edu.au/centre/gphrc; Dir Prof. SHARON DAWE.

Heart Foundation Research Centre: tel. (7) 5552-8314; fax (7) 5552-8802; e-mail m.john@griffith.edu.au; internet www.griffith.edu.au/centre/hfrc; Dir Prof. JOHN HEADRICK.

Institute for Ethics, Governance and Law: tel. (7) 3735-6987; fax (7) 3735-6985; e-mail iegl-enquiry@griffith.edu.au; internet www.griffith.edu.au/centre/iegl; Dir Prof. CHARLES SAMPFORD.

Institute for Glycomics: tel. (7) 5552-7025; fax (7) 5552-8098; e-mail m.vonitzstein@griffith.edu.au; internet www.griffith.edu.au/centre/glycomics; Dir Prof. MARK VON ITZSTEIN.

Institute for Integrated and Intelligent Systems: tel. (7) 3735-3757; fax (7) 3735-4066; e-mail n.dunstan@griffith.edu.au; internet iiis.griffith.edu.au; Dir Prof. ABDUL SATTAR.

International Centre for Ecotourism Research: tel. (7) 5552-8677; fax (7) 5552-8895; e-mail r.buckley@griffith.edu.au; internet www.griffith.edu.au/centre/icer; Dir Prof. RALF BUCKLEY.

International Fruit Fly Research Centre: tel. (7) 3735-3696; fax (7) 3735-3697; e-mail d.drew@griffith.edu.au; internet www.griffith.edu.au/centre/icmpff; Dir Prof. RICHARD DREW.

Key Centre for Ethics, Law, Justice and Governance: tel. (7) 3735-6988; fax (7) 3735-6985; e-mail s.stewart@griffith.edu.au; internet www.griffith.edu.au/centre/kceljag; Dir Prof. ROSS HOMEL.

Nanoscale Science and Technology Centre: tel. (7) 3735-7240; fax (7) 3735-7656; e-mail e.gray@griffith.edu.au; internet www.griffith.edu.au/centre/nstc; Dir Assoc. Prof. EVAN GRAY.

Queensland Conservatorium Research Centre: tel. (7) 3735-6335; fax (7) 3735-6262; e-mail qcrc@griffith.edu.au; internet www.griffith.edu.au/centre/qcrc; Dir Assoc. Prof. HUIB SCHIPPERS.

Queensland Microtechnology Facility: tel. (7) 3735-5053; fax (7) 3735-8021; e-mail barry.harrison@griffith.edu.au; internet www.griffith.edu.au/centre/qmf; Dir Prof. H. BARRY HARRISON.

Research Centre for Clinical Practice Innovation: tel. (7) 5552-8931; e-mail cpi-research@griffith.edu.au; internet www.griffith.edu.au/centre/rccpi; Dir Prof. WENDY CHABOYER.

Service Industry Research Centre: tel. (7) 5552-8790; e-mail c.guilding@griffith.edu.au; internet www.griffith.edu.au/centre/sirc; Dir Prof. CHRIS GUILDING.

Socio-Legal Research Centre: tel. (7) 3735-3747; fax (7) 3735-5169; e-mail slrc@griffith.edu.au; internet www.griffith.edu.au/centre/slrc; Dir Prof. R. JOHNSTONE.

Software Quality Institute: tel. (7) 3735-5209; fax (7) 3735-5207; e-mail sqi@cit.gu.edu.au; internet www.sqi.gu.edu.au; Dir Prof. GEOFF DROMEY.

Urban Research Program: tel. (7) 3735-3742; fax (7) 3735-4026; e-mail j.pascoe@griffith.edu.au; internet www.griffith.edu.au/centre/urp; Dir Prof. BRENDAN GLEESON.

JAMES COOK UNIVERSITY

Townsville, Qld 4811

Telephone: (7) 4781-4111
Fax: (7) 4779-6371
E-mail: vicechancellor@jcu.edu.au
Internet: www.jcu.edu.au

Founded 1970
Academic year: February to November

Chancellor: Lt-Gen. J. GREY
Deputy Chancellor: G. N. WHITMORE
Rector: Prof. SCOT BOWMAN
Vice-Chancellor: Prof. SANDRA HARDING
Deputy Vice-Chancellor: Prof. H. HYLAND
Pro-Vice-Chancellors: B. LILLIS, Prof. R. MCTAGGART, Prof. T. N. PALMER, Prof. A. VANN
Registrar: M. KERN
Librarian: J. W. MCKINLAY

Number of teachers: 444 full-time
Number of students: 15,575

Publications: *Academic Calendar*, *JCU Outlook* (12 a year)

EXECUTIVE DEANS

Faculty of Arts, Education and Social Sciences: Prof. J. D. GREELEY
Faculty of Law, Business and the Creative Arts: Prof. S. SPEEDY
Faculty of Medicine, Health and Molecular Sciences: Prof. I. WRONSKI
Faculty of Science and Engineering: Prof. NED PANKHURST

PROFESSORS

BAXTER, A. G., Biochemistry
BELL, T. H., Earth Sciences
BURNELL, J. N., Biochemistry
CARTER, R. M., Earth Sciences
CLARK, G., Law
COLLINS, B., Tropical Environment
CROZIER, R., Zoology
DAVIS, D. F., Creative Arts
GADEK, P., Tropical Biology
GILBERT, R., Education
GILLIESON, D., Tropical Environment

GLASS, B., Pharmacy
GRAW, S. B., Law
HASSALL, A. J., English
HAVEMANN, P., Law
HAYES, B. A., Nursing
HELMES, E., Psychology
HENDERSON, R. A., Earth Sciences
HERBERT, H. J., Indigenous Australian Studies
HERON, M. L., Physics
HO, Y. H., Medicine
HUGHES, T. P., Marine Biology
KEENE, F. R., Chemistry
KENNEDY, L., Medicine
KINGSFORD, M., Marine Biology
LANKSHEAR, C., Education
LAVERY, B., Information Technology
LAWN, R. J., Tropical Crop Science and CRC for Sustainable Sugar Production
LEAKEY, R., Tropical Biology
LOUGHRAN, J., Engineering
MARSH, H. D., Environmental Science
MILLER, D., Biochemistry and Molecular Biology
NOTT, J., Tropical Environment
OLIVER, N. H. S., Economic Geology
PATTERSON, J. C., Environmental Engineering
PEARCE, P. L., Tourism
PEARSON, R. G., Biological Science
PIERCE, P. F., Australian Literature
PORTER, R., Medicine
PRIDEAUX, B., Business
RANE, A., Medicine
REICHELT, R., CRC Reef Research
SPEARE, R., Public Health and Tropical Medicine
STORK, N. E., CRC Rainforest
SUMMERS, P. M., Tropical Veterinary Science
THORPE, R. M., Social Work
WHITTINGHAM, I., Mathematics and Physics
YELLOWLEES, D., Pharmacy

LA TROBE UNIVERSITY

Bundoora, Vic. 3086
Telephone: (3) 9479-1199
Fax: (3) 9479-3660
E-mail: international@latrobe.edu.au
Internet: www.latrobe.edu.au
Founded 1964
Academic year: March to November
Chancellor: SYLVIA WALTON
Vice-Chancellor: Prof. PAUL JOHNSON
Deputy Vice-Chancellor: Prof. BELINDA PROBERT
Deputy Vice-Chancellor for Research: Prof. TIM BROWN
Pro-Vice-Chancellor for Equity and Access: Prof. K. FERGUSON
Pro-Vice-Chancellor for Information Technology: Prof. E. R. SMITH
Pro-Vice-Chancellor for International Relations: Prof. D. STOCKLEY
University Sec.: D. F. BISHOP
Chief Librarian: AINSLIE DEWE
Number of teachers: 1,253
Number of students: 28,684

DEANS

Education: Prof. LORRAINE LING
Health Sciences: Prof. HAL SWERISSEN
Humanities and Social Sciences: Prof. DAVID DE VAUS
Law and Management: Prof. RAYMOND HARBRIDGE
Science, Technology and Engineering: Prof. D. FINLAY
Albury-Wodonga Campus: LIN CRASE (Dir)
Beechworth Campus: BRIAN MILLAR (Dir)
Bendigo Campus: Prof. ANDREW HARVEY (acting) (Dir)
Mildura Campus: KENT FARRELL (Dir)
Shepparton Campus: ELIZABETH LAVENDER (Dir)

PROFESSORS

AIKHENVALD, A., Research Centre for Linguistics Typology
ALTMAN, D., Politics
ARNASON, J. P., Sociology and Anthropology
BEILHARZ, D. M., Sociology and Anthropology
BERNARD, C., Psychology
BLAKE, B. J., Linguistics
BOLAND, R. C., European Studies
BROWN, D. F., Accounting and Management
CAHILL, L. W., Electronics Engineering
CAMILLERI, J., Politics
CHANOCK, M., Law and Legal Studies
CROUCH, G., Tourism and Hospitality
DILLON, T. S., Computer Science and Computer Engineering
DIXON, R. M. W., Research Centre for Linguistics Typology
DYSON, P., Physics
ENDACOTT, R., Mental Health
FITZGERALD, J. J., Asian Languages
FOOK, J., Health Sciences
FREADMAN, R. B., English
FROST, A. J., History
GATT-RUTTER, J. A., Italian Studies
GAUNTLETT, E., Hellenic Studies
HANDLEY, C., Human Biosciences
HARBRIDGE, R. J., Management
HOFFMAN, A., Genetics and Human Variation
HOOGENRAAD, N. J., Biochemistry
JEFFREY, R., Politics
KAHN, J., Sociology and Anthropology
KELLEHEAR, S., Public Health
KING, J. E., Economics and Finance
LAKE, M., History
LECKEY, R. C. G., Physics
LEDER, G., Education
LIN, V., Health
LINDQUIST, B. I., Occupational Therapy
LUMLEY, J. M., Mothers' and Children's Health
McDONALD, S. J., Midwifery
McDOWELL, G. H., Agriculture
MILLS, T. M., Mathematics
MOOSA, I. A., Economics and Finance
MORRIS, M. E., Physiotherapy
MURPHY, P., Tourism and Hospitality
MURRAY, T. A., Archaeology
NAY, R. M., Nursing
O'MALLEY, P., Law and Legal Studies
PARISH, R. W., Botany
PEARSON, A., Nursing
PERRY, A. R., Human Communication Science
PITTS, M. K., Health and Sexuality
PORTER, R. S., Business
PRATT, C., Psychological Sciences
RAYMOND, K., Pharmacy
REILLY, S., Human Communication Sciences
ROSENTHAL, D. A., Health Sciences
SALMOND, J. A., History
STEPHENSON, D., Zoology
STREET, A. F., Nursing
SUGIMOTO, Y., Sociology and Anthropology
SULLIVAN, P. A., Education
TAMIS, A., Hellenic Studies
THORNTON, M. R., Law and Legal Studies
TORRANCE, C., Nursing
WALKER, G. R., Law and Legal Studies
WHITE, C. M., Graduate School of Management
WILLIS, E. M., Humanities

MACQUARIE UNIVERSITY

Balaclava Rd, North Ryde, NSW 2109
Telephone: (2) 9850-7111
Fax: (2) 9850-7733
E-mail: mqinfo@mq.edu.au
Internet: www.mq.edu.au
Founded 1964 (opened 1967)
Chancellor: Hon. MICHAEL EGAN
Deputy Chancellor: ELIZABETH CROUCH
Vice-Chancellor: Prof. STEVEN SCHWARTZ
Deputy Vice-Chancellor and Provost: Prof. JUDYTH SACHS
Deputy Vice-Chancellor and Chief Operating Officer: Dr PETER DODD
Deputy Vice-Chancellor for International Affairs and Development: CAROLINE TROTMAN
Deputy Vice-Chancellor for Research: Prof. JIM PIPER
Pro-Vice-Chancellor for Social Inclusion: Prof. GAIL WHITEFORD
General Counsel: PAUL LUTTRELL
Academic Registrar: COLIN HAWKINS (acting)
Librarian: MAXINE BRODIE
Number of teachers: 1,098
Number of students: 32,782
Publications: Calendar (1 a year), Research Report (1 a year), Study at Macquarie (1 a year), University News (12 a year)

DEANS

Faculty of Arts: Prof. JOHN SIMONS (Exec.)
Faculty of Business and Economics: Prof. MARK GABBOTT (Exec.)
Faculty of Human Sciences: Prof. JANET GREELEY (Exec.)
Faculty of Science: Prof. STEPHEN THURGATE (Exec.)
Macquarie Graduate School of Management: Dr ROBERT E. WIDING
Macquarie Law School: Prof. NATALIE KLEIN

PROFESSORS

College of Commerce:
ABELSON, P. W., Economics
CROUCHER, J., Statistics
DAVIS, E., Management
EDDEY, P. H., Accounting, Graduate Accounting and Commerce Centre
HARRISON, G. L., Accounting and Finance
HORNE, J., Economics
HUDSON, M., Statistics
JONG, P. DE, Actuarial Studies
O'DONNELL, R., Economics
QUINN, B., Statistics
THROSBY, C., Economics
WOOD, G., Statistics
YUSUF, F., Business

College of Humanities and Social Sciences:
GIBBS, A. M., English and Cultural Studies
GOOT, M., Politics
HAYWARD, P., Contemporary Music Studies
JEFFERY, M., Law
KANAWATI, N., Ancient History
KANE, D., Chinese
LIEU, S. N., History

College of Science and Technology:
BASSETT, J., Biology
BEATTIE, A.
BERGQUIST, P., Biology
BURNS, A., Linguistics
CANDLIN, C., Linguistics
COLTHEART, M., Psychology
COOPER, D., Biological Sciences
CURSON, P., Health and Chiropractice
DEANE, E., Biology
FAGAN, R., Human Geography
JOSS, J., Biology
MATTHIESSEN, C., Linguistics
MURRAY, D., Linguistics
NEWALL, P., Linguistics
O'REILLY, S., Earth and Planetary Sciences
ORR, B., Chemistry
PITMAN, A., Physical Geography
RAPEE, R., Psychology
SMITH, P., Mathematics
STREET, R., Mathematics
VEAL, D., Biology
WALTER, M., Earth and Planetary Sciences
WENDEROTH, P., Psychology
WESTOBY, M., Biology
WILLIAMS, K., Psychology

MONASH UNIVERSITY

Wellington Rd, Clayton, Vic. 3800
Telephone: (3) 9902-6000
Fax: (3) 9905-4007
E-mail: enquiries@adm.monash.edu.au
Internet: www.monash.edu.au

Founded 1958 (opened 1961); merged with Chisholm Institute of Technology and Gippsland Institute of Advanced Education 1990, and with Victorian College of Pharmacy 1992
Academic year: March to November

Chancellor: Dr ALAN FINKEL
Vice-Chancellor and Pres.: Prof. ED BYRNE
Snr Deputy Vice-Chancellor and Deputy Vice-Chancellor for Research: Prof. EDWINA CORNISH
Deputy Vice-Chancellor for Global Engagement: Prof. STEPHANIE FAHEY
Deputy Vice-Chancellor for Education: Prof. ADAM SHOEMAKER
Pres. of the Academic Bd.: Prof. JOHN SHERIDAN
Vice-Pres. for Finance and Chief Financial Officer: DAVID PITT
Vice-Pres. for Advancement: RON FAIRCHILD
Vice-Pres. for Admin.: PETER MARSHALL
Pro-Vice-Chancellor and Pres., Sunway campus, Malaysia: Prof. ROBIN POLLARD
Pro-Vice-Chancellor and Pres., Monash South Africa: Prof. TYRONE PRETORIUS
Pro-Vice-Chancellor and Pres., Gippsland: Prof. HELEN BARTLETT
Pro-Vice-Chancellor: Prof. DAVID COPOLOV
Pro-Vice-Chancellor for Industry Engagement and Commercialisation: Prof. ROD HILL
Pro-Vice-Chancellor for Int. Engagement: Prof. SIMON ADAMS
Pro-Vice-Chancellor for Learning and Teaching: Prof. MARNIE HUGHES-WARRINGTON
Pro-Vice-Chancellor for Planning and Quality: Prof. MERRAN EVANS
Pro-Vice-Chancellor for Research and Research Training: Prof. MAX KING
Pro-Vice-Chancellor for Research and Research Infrastructure: Prof. IAN SMITH
Pro-Vice-Chancellor for Social Inclusion: Prof. SUE WILLIS
Pro-Vice-Chancellor for Campus Coordination and Campus Dir, Berwick and Peninsula: Prof. PHILIP STEELE
Pro-Vice-Chancellor for Student Affairs and Campus Dir, Caulfield and Clayton: Prof. ROB WILLIS
Librarian: CATHRINE HARBOE-REE

Number of teachers: 3,766 (f.t.e.)
Number of students: 59,925

Publications: *Asia-Pacific Journal of Clinical Nutrition* (online), *Eras: School of Historical Studies Online Journal, Journal of Australian Taxation* (6 a year), *Journal of Intercultural Studies* (3 a year), *Monash Bioethics Review* (4 a year), *Monash Law Review* (2 a year)

DEANS

Faculty of Art and Design: Prof. SHANE MURRAY
Faculty of Arts: Prof. RAE FRANCES
Faculty of Business and Economics: Prof. STEPHEN KING (acting)
Faculty of Education: Prof. JOHN LOUGHRAN (acting)
Faculty of Engineering: Prof. TAM SRIDHAR
Faculty of Information Technology: Prof. RON WEBER
Faculty of Law: Prof. ARIE FREIBERG
Faculty of Medicine, Nursing and Health Sciences: Prof. STEVE WESSELINGH
Faculty of Pharmacy and Pharmaceutical Sciences: Prof. WILLIAM CHARMAN
Faculty of Science: Prof. SCOTT O'NEILL

PROFESSORS

Faculty of Art and Design (900 Dandenong Rd, Caulfield East, Vic. 3145; tel. (3) 9903-2707; fax (3) 9903-2845; e-mail enquiries@artdes.monash.edu.au; internet www.artdes.monash.edu.au):

HOFFERT, B. J., Fine Arts
REDMOND, J., Industrial Design
TERSTAPPEN, C., Contemporary Installation and Photography

Faculty of Arts (tel. (3) 9905-2100; fax (3) 9905-2148; e-mail deansec@arts.monash.edu.au; internet www.arts.monash.edu.au):

BENJAMIN, A., Comparative Literature and Cultural Studies
BIGELOW, J. C., Philosophy and Bioethics
BOUMA, G. D., Political and Social Enquiry
BURRIDGE, K., Languages, Cultures and Linguistics
CAINE, B., Historical Studies
COCKLIN, C., Philosophy and Bioethics
DAVISON, G. J., Historical Studies
EDWARDS, I., International Studies
FELIX, U., Languages, Cultures and Linguistics
FITZPATRICK, P., Drama and Theatre Studies
HART, K. J., Comparative Literature and Cultural Studies
JACOBS, J. B., Languages, Cultures and Linguistics
KARTOMI, M. J., Music–Conservatorium
KENT, F. W., Historical Studies
KERSHAW, P. A., Geography and Environmental Science
LE GRAND, H., Philosophy
LIPSIG-MUMME, C., Political and Social Enquiry
LOVE, H. H. R., Literary, Visual and Performance Studies
LYNCH, A., Geography and Environmental Science
MARKUS, A., Jewish Studies
MILNER, A., Comparative Literature and Cultural Studies
MOUER, R., Languages, Cultures and Linguistics
NELSON, B., Languages, Cultures and Linguistics
OPPY, G., Philosophy and Bioethics
PROBYN, C. T., Literary, Visual and Performance Studies
QUARTLY, M., Historical Studies
RUSSELL, L., Australian Indigenous Studies
TAPPER, N., Geography and Environmental Science
VICZIANY, M., Asian Studies
WALTER, J., Political and Social Enquiry

Faculty of Business and Economics (POB 197, Caulfield East, Vic. 3145; tel. (3) 9903-2327; fax (3) 9903-2148; e-mail enquiries.caulfield@buseco.monash.edu.au; internet www.buseco.monash.edu.au):

ARIFF, M., Accounting and Finance
BROOKS, B., Business and Economics
BROOKS, D., Econometrics and Business Statistics
CHENHALL, R. H., Accounting and Finance
CULLEN, R., Business Law and Taxation
DHALIWAL, D., Accounting and Finance
DINGLE, A. E., Economics
DIXON, P. B., Policy Studies
EWING, M., Marketing
FAFF, R., Accounting and Finance
FORSYTH, P. J., Economics
GABBOTT, T. M., Marketing
GODFREY, J. M., Accounting and Finance
HUGHES, O. E., Management
HYNDMAN, R. J., Econometrics and Business Statistics
IN, F., Accounting and Finance
KING, M. L., Business and Economics

LANGFIELD-SMITH, K., Accounting and Finance
MCLAREN, K. R., Econometrics and Business Statistics
MITCHELL, R., Business Law and Taxation
NG, Y., Economics
NYLAND, C., Management
OPPEWAL, H., Marketing
PEARSON, K., Policy Studies
POSKITT, D. S., Econometrics
RAINNIE, A. F., Management
RATNATUNGA, J. T., Accounting and Finance
RICHARDSON, J., Health Programme Evaluation
SARROS, J. C., Management
SILVAPULLE, M., Econometrics and Business Statistics
SKULLY, M. T., Accounting and Finance
SMYTH, R., Economics
SMYTH, R. L., Economics
SOHAL, A., Management
TAM, O. K., MBA Programme
TEICHER, J., Management
VON NESSEN, P., Business Law and Taxation
WEILER, B. V., Management
WILLIS, R. J., MBA Programme
WORTHINGTON, J. S., Marketing
YANG, X., Economics

Faculty of Education (POB 6, Monash University, Clayton, Vic. 3800; tel. (3) 9905-2888; fax (3) 9905-5400; e-mail enquiry@education.monash.edu.au; internet www.education.monash.edu.au):

BURKE, G., Education
FLEER, M., Education
GRONN, P., Education
GUNSTONE, R. F., Education
KENWAY, J., Education
LOUGHRAN, J., Education
MARGINSON, S., Education
SEDDON, T., Education
WILLIS, S. G., Education

Faculty of Engineering (POB 72, Clayton, Vic. 3800; tel. (3) 9905-3404; fax (3) 9905-3409; e-mail enginfo@eng.monash.edu.au; internet www.eng.monash.edu.au):

CURRIE, G., Civil Engineering
DEMIDENKO, S., Electrical and Computer Systems Engineering
EGAN, G. K., Electrical and Computer Systems Engineering
FORSYTH, M., Materials Engineering
HOURIGAN, K., Mechanical Engineering
JARVIS, R. A., Electrical and Computer Systems Engineering
JESSON, D., Materials Engineering
JONES, R., Mechanical Engineering
LEWIS, R. A., Physics
MORGAN, D. L., Electrical and Computer Systems Engineering
MUDDLE, B. C., Materials Engineering
PRINCE, I., Chemical Engineering
PUDLOWSKI, Z. J., UNESCO International Centre for Engineering Education
RHODES, M. J., Chemical Engineering
SHERIDAN, J., Mechanical Engineering
SIMON, G., Materials Engineering
SORIA, J., Mechanical Engineering
SRIDHAR, T., Chemical Engineering
YOUNG, W., Civil Engineering
ZHAO, X.-L., Civil Engineering

Faculty of Information Technology (900 Dandenong Rd, Caulfield East, Vic. 3145; tel. (3) 9903-2433; fax (3) 9903-2745; e-mail admissions@infotech.monash.edu.au; internet www.infotech.monash.edu.au):

ABRAMSON, D., School of Computer Science and Software Engineering
ARNOTT, D. R., School of Information Management and Systems
CROSSLEY, J., School of Computer Science and Software Engineering

DOOLEY, L. S., Gippsland School of Computing and Information Technology
GEORGEFF, M., Dean's Office
GREEN, D., School of Computer Science and Software Engineering
GUPTA, G., Business Systems
KENDALL, E. A., School of Network Computing
McKEMMISH, S. M., School of Information Management Systems
MARRIOTT, K., School of Computer Science and Software Engineering
SCHAUDER, D., School of Information Management and Systems
SCHMIDT, H. W., School of Computer Science and Software Engineering
SHANKS, G., School of Business Systems
SRINIVASAN, B., School of Computer Science and Software Engineering
WALLACE, M., School of Business Systems
WEBB, G., School of Computer Science and Software Engineering
WEBER, R., Dean

Faculty of Law (POB 12, Monash University, Clayton, Vic. 3800; tel. (3) 9905-9335; fax (3) 9905-5868; e-mail law-general@law.monash.edu.au; internet www.law.monash.edu.au):

BOROS, E., Company Law
FOX, R. G., Criminal Law
FREIBERG, A., Dean
GOLDSWORTHY, J., Legal Philosophy and Constitutional Law
HAMPEL, G., Advocacy Training
HODGE, G., Privatization and Public Accountability
JOSEPH, S., International Human Rights and Constitutional Law
KINLEY, D., Human Rights Law
LEE, H. P., Constitutional and Administrative Law
McSHERRY, B., Criminal Law, Mental Health Law and Bioethics
PITTARD, M., Industrial Relations and Employment Law
SCHEEPERS, T., International Development Law
WAINCYMER, J., Taxation and International Trade Law
WILLIAMS, C. R., Criminal Law and Evidence

Faculty of Medicine, Nursing and Health Sciences (Bldg 64, Monash University, Clayton, Vic. 3800; tel. (3) 9905-4327; fax (3) 9905-4302; e-mail enquiries@lmed.monash.edu.au; internet www.med.monash.edu.au):

ABRAMSON, M. J., Epidemiology and Preventive Medicine
ADLER, B., Microbiology
ANDERSON, W. P., Physiology/School of Biomedical Sciences
BERTRAM, J., Anatomy and Cell Biology
BROWN, T., Social Work and Human Services
BROWNE, C., Medical and Health Sciences Education
BURROWS, R. F., Obstetrics and Gynaecology
WESSELINGH, S., Dean
CAMPBELL, D., Health Sciences Research
COLEMAN, G., Psychology
COPPEL, R. L., Microbiology
CORDNER, S. M., Forensic Medicine
CROWE, S., Medicine
DAVIES, J., Microbiology
DAVIS, S. R., Medicine
DE KRETSER, D. M., Reproduction and Development
DOHERTY, R. R., Paediatrics
FRANCIS, K., Nursing
GIBSON, P., Medicine
GODDARD, C. R., Social Work
GODING, J. W., Pathology and Immunology
GOODCHILD, C. S., Anaesthesia
GRIGG, M. J., Surgery
HARDING, R., Physiology

HEALY, D. L., Obstetrics and Gynaecology
HOLDSWORTH, S. R., Medicine
HUMPHREYS, J. S., Rural Health
IRVINE, D., Psychology
JANS, D. A., Biochemistry and Molecular Biology
JENKIN, G., Physiology
JOLLY, B. C., Medical and Health Sciences Education
JUDD, F. K., Psychological Medicine
KOSSMAN, T., Medicine
KRUM, H., Epidemiology and Preventive Medicine
KULKARNI, J., Psychological Medicine
LEWIN, S., Medicine
McGRATH, B., Medicine
MacKINNON, A., Psychological Medicine
McNEIL, J. J., Epidemiology and Preventive Medicine
MEADOWS, G., Psychological Medicine
MITCHELL, C., Biochemistry and Molecular Biology
MULLEN, P. E., Psychological Medicine
NAGLEY, P., Biochemistry and Molecular Biology
OAKLEY-BROWN, M., Psychological Medicine
O'CONNOR, D. W., Psychological Medicine
O'CONNOR, M. M., Nursing
OGLOFF, J., Psychological Medicine
O'HEHIR, R. E., Medicine
PITERMAN, L., General Practice
POLGLASE, A., Surgery
PONSFORD, J. L., Psychology
PRIESTLEY, B. G., Epidemiology and Preventive Medicine
PROSKE, U., Physiology
REUTENS, D., Neurosciences
RICHARDS, J., General Practice
ROOD, J., Microbiology
ROSENFELD, J. V., Neurosurgery
SALEM, H. H., Medicine
SCHMIDT, H., Pharmacology
SMITH, J., Surgery
SOLARSH, G., Rural Health
STOELWINDER, J., Epidemiology and Preventive Medicine
STOREY, E., Neurosciences
SUMMERS, R. J., Pharmacology
THOMSON, N. M., Medicine
TOH, B. H., Pathology and Immunology
TONGE, B. J., Psychological Medicine
TROUNSON, A. O., Early Human Development
WHYTE, G., Bendigo Regional Clinical School
WORKMAN, G., Geriatric Medicine
ZIMMET, P., Biochemistry and Molecular Biology

Faculty of Pharmacy and Pharmaceutical Sciences (381 Royal Parade, Parkville, Vic. 3052; tel. (3) 9903-6000; fax (3) 9903-9581; e-mail info@vcp.monash.edu.au; internet www.pharm.monash.edu.au):

CHAPMAN, C. B., Immunology
CHARMAN, W. N., Pharmaceutics
DOOLEY, M., Pharmacology
NATION, R. L., Pharmaceutics
POUTON, C. W., Pharmaceutics
REED, B. L., Biopharmaceutics
SCAMMELLS, P. J., Biopharmaceutics
STEWART, P. J., Pharmaceutics

Faculty of Science (POB 19, Clayton, Vic. 3800; tel. (3) 9905-4610; fax (3) 9905-5692; e-mail enquiries@sci.monash.edu.au; internet www.sci.monash.edu.au):

ADELOJU, S. B., Applied Sciences
BARBNIK, R. A., Mathematical Sciences
BOND, A., Chemistry
CALLY, P., Mathematical Sciences
CAS, R. A. F., Geosciences
CLAYTON, M., Biological Sciences
CULL, J. P., Geosciences
DEACON, G. B., Chemistry
HAMILL, J. D., Biological Sciences

HEARN, M., Chemistry
JACKSON, R., Chemistry
JACKSON, W. R., Chemistry
JESSON, D., Physics and Material Engineering
KEAYS, R., Geosciences
KLEBANER, F., Mathematical Sciences
LAKE, P. S., Biological Sciences
LEWIS, R., Physics and Material Engineering
MacFARLANE, D. R., Chemistry
MONAGHAN, J. J., Mathematical Sciences
MURRAY, K. S., Chemistry
NORRIS, R., Dean
REEDER, M., Mathematical Sciences
SIMON, G., Physics and Material Engineering
SMYTH, D. R., Biological Sciences
VICKERS-RICH, P., Geosciences

AFFILIATED INSTITUTIONS

Baker Medical Research Institute: Commercial Rd, Melbourne, Vic. 3004; tel. (3) 8532-1111; Dir Prof. G. JENNINGS.

Bureau of Meteorology: 150 Lonsdale St, Melbourne, Vic. 3000; tel. (3) 9669-4915; Dir J. W. ZILLMAN.

MacFarlane Burnet Institute for Medical Research and Public Health Ltd (Burnet Institute): Commercial Rd, Melbourne, Vic. 3004; tel. (3) 9282-2111; Dir Prof. S. WESSELINGH.

Mannix College: Wellington Rd, Monash University, Clayton, Vic. 3800; tel. (3) 9544-8895; Master Rev. K. SAUNDERS.

Mental Health Research Institute of Victoria: Locked Bag No. 11, Parkville, Vic. 3052; tel. (3) 9388-1633; Dir Prof. D. COPOLOV.

Prince Henry's Institute of Medical Research: Monash Medical Centre, Level 4, Block E, 246 Clayton Rd, Clayton, Vic. 3168; tel. (3) 9594-4372; Dir Prof. E. SIMPSON.

MURDOCH UNIVERSITY

South St, Murdoch, WA 6150

Telephone: (8) 9360-6000
Fax: (8) 9360-6847
E-mail: marketing@murdoch.edu.au
Internet: www.murdoch.edu.au

Founded 1973; postgraduate courses began 1974; undergraduate courses began 1975
State control
Academic year: February to November

Chancellor: The Hon. GEOFFREY BOLTON
Pro-Chancellor: Judge KATE O'BRIEN
Vice-Chancellor: Prof. JOHN YOVICH
Pro-Vice-Chancellor for Academic Affairs: Prof. JANETTE THOMAS
Pro-Vice-Chancellor for Regional Development: KATERYNA LONGLEY
Pro-Vice-Chancellor for Research: Prof. ANDRIS STELBOVICS
Pro-Vice-Chancellor for Resource Management: Prof. CRAIG SPENCE (acting)
Pro-Vice-Chancellor for Strategy: GARY MARTIN
Pres., Academic Council: MICHAEL BOROWITZKA
Dir of Library Services: MARGARET JONES

Number of teachers: 455
Number of students: 15,320

Publications: *In Touch* (2 a year), *On Campus* (8 a year), *Research Report* (1 a year), *Synergy* (4 a year)

DEANS

Division of Arts (Information Technology): Assoc. Prof. ARNOLDATHERINE DEPICKERE
Division of Science and Engineering: Exec. Dean Prof. YIANNI ATTIKOUZEL

Division of Social Sciences, Humanities and Education: Exec. Dean Prof. K. LONGLEY

Division of Veterinary and Biomedical Sciences: Exec. Dean Prof. J. YOVICH

School of Education: Prof. DAVID ANDRICH

School of Engineering: Prof. MAURICE ALLEN

School of Health Sciences: Prof. JIM REYNOLDSON (acting)

School of Law: Prof. CHRISTOPHER KENDALL

PROFESSORS

Division of Business, Information Technology and Law (tel. (8) 9360-2414; fax (8) 9360-2994; internet www.murdoch.edu.au/bitl):

    FORBES, R., Law
    MCLEOD, N. D. B., Law
    PENDLETON, M. D., Law
    ROBISON, R., Asian and International Politics
    SIMMONDS, R., Law
    THOMPSON, H. M., Economics

Division of Science (tel. (8) 9360-2161; fax (8) 9360-6304; internet www.science.murdoch.edu.au):

    BLOOM, W. R., Mathematics and Statistics
    CARNEGIE, P., Biotechnology
    DILWORTH, M. J., Biology
    GILES, R. G. F., Organic Chemistry
    HOBBS, R., Environmental Science
    JAMES, I., Mathematics
    JENNINGS, P., Physics, Energy Studies
    JONES, M. G. K., Plant Sciences
    LYONS, T. J., Environmental Science
    NICOL, M. J., Mineral Science
    POTTER, I. C., Animal Biology
    RITCHIE, I. M., Chemistry
    WEBB, J. M., Chemistry

Division of Science and Engineering (Rockingham Campus, Dixon Rd, Rockingham, WA; tel. (8) 9360-7100; fax (8) 9360-7104; internet www.eng.murdoch.edu.au):

    LEE, P. L., Instrumentation and Control Engineering
    ROY, G., Software Engineering

Division of Social Sciences, Humanities and Education (tel. (8) 9360-6045; fax (8) 9360-6367; internet www.sshe.murdoch.edu.au):

    ANDRICH, D., Education
    BALDOCK, C., Sociology
    DE GARIS, B., History
    DUREY, M., History
    FRODSHAM, J. D., English and Comparative Literature
    HILL, B. V., Education
    HILL, D., Asian Studies (Head)
    INNES, M., Psychology
    LOADER, B., Social Enquiry (Head)
    MISHRA, V., English and Comparative Literature
    NEWMAN, P., Science and Technology Policy
    O'TOOLE, L. M., Communication Studies
    RUTHROF, H. G., Philosophy

Division of Veterinary and Biomedical Sciences (tel. (8) 9360-2566; fax (8) 9310-7390; internet www.vet.murdoch.edu.au/home.html):

    HAMPSON, D., Microbiology and Immunobiology
    SWAN, R. A., Veterinary Clinical Studies
    THOMPSON, A., Parasitology
    WILCOX, G. E., Virology

NOTRE DAME UNIVERSITY

19 Mouat St, POB 1225, Fremantle, WA 6959

Telephone: (8) 9433-0533

Fax: (8) 9433-0544

E-mail: international@nd.edu.au

Internet: www.nd.edu.au

Founded 1990 by Act of Parliament

Campuses at Broome, Fremantle and Sydney (Broadway and Darlinghurst)

Private control (Archdiocese of Perth)

Language of instruction: English

Academic year: February to December

Vice-Chancellor: Dr CELIA HAMMOND

Deputy Vice-Chancellor, Broome: Prof. SONIA WAGNER

Deputy Vice-Chancellor, Fremantle and Provost (Broome and Fremantle): Prof. MARK MCKENNA

Deputy Vice-Chancellor and Provost, Sydney Campus: Prof. HAYDEN RAMSEY

Exec. Dir for Admissions and Student Services, Fremantle: ROMMIE MASAREI

Exec. Dir for Admissions and Student Services, Sydney: MARK TANNOCK

Exec. Dir for Resources and Development: WAYNE MCGRISKIN

Number of teachers: 170

Number of students: 3,000

DEANS

Broome and Fremantle Campuses:

    School of Arts and Sciences: Prof. NEIL DREW
    School of Business: Assoc. Prof. SONJA BOGUNOVICH
    School of Education: Prof. MICHAEL O'NEILL
    School of Health Sciences: Prof. HELEN PARKER
    School of Law: Assoc. Prof. JANE POWER
    School of Medicine: Prof. GAVIN FROST
    School of Nursing: Assoc. Prof. SELMA ALLIEX
    School of Philosophy and Theology: Prof. PETER BLACK
    School of Science and Technology: Prof. BRIAN COLLINS

Sydney Campus:

    School of Arts and Sciences: Prof. GERRY TURCOTTE
    School of Business: Prof. JOO-GIM HEANEY
    School of Education: Assoc. Prof. MARK TANNOCK
    School of Law: Prof. GERARD RYAN
    School of Medicine: Prof. JULIE QUINLIVAN
    School of Nursing: Prof. MARGOT KEARNS
    School of Philosophy and Theology: Prof. HAYDEN RAMSAY

QUEENSLAND UNIVERSITY OF TECHNOLOGY

GPOB 2434, Brisbane, Qld 4000

Telephone: (7) 3138-2000

E-mail: qut.information@qut.edu.au

Internet: www.qut.edu.au

Founded 1965; Brisbane CAE merged with the Univ. 1990

State control

Chancellor: Dr C. HIRST

Vice-Chancellor: Prof. P. COALDRAKE

Deputy Vice-Chancellor: Prof. D. GARDINER (acting)

Pro-Vice-Chancellor for Information and Academic Services: T. COCHRANE

Pro-Vice-Chancellor for Research and Advancement: Prof. J. GOUGH (acting)

Exec. Dir of Finance and Resource Planning: STEPHEN PINCUS (acting)

Registrar: Dr C. DICKENSON

Librarian: G. AUSTEN

Library of 672,000 vols

Number of students: 39,359

DEANS

Built Environment and Engineering: Prof. MARTIN BETTS

Business: Prof. PETER LITTLE

Creative Industries: Prof. SUSAN STREET

Education: Prof. WENDY PATTON

Health: Prof. K. J. BOWMAN

Law: Prof. MICHAEL LAVARCH

QUT Carseldine: Prof. RUTH MATCHETT

Science and Technology: Prof. SIMON KAPLAN

PROFESSORS

ABBEY, J., Nursing

ARMSTRONG, H., Design and Built Environment

ARNOLD, N., Advertising, Marketing and Public Relations

ARTHURS, A., Music

BETTS, M., Faculty Office (Built Environment and Engineering)

BOASHASH, B., Electrical and Electronic Systems

BOULTON-LEWIS, G., Learning and Professional Studies

BOWMAN, K., Faculty Office (Health)

BOYCE, G., International Business

BOYD, T., Construction Management and Property

BROMLEY, M., Journalism

CAELLI, W., Data Communications

CARNEY, L., Optometry

CHANG, A., Nursing

CLEMENTS, J., Life Science

COALDRAKE, P., Chancellery

COLLIER, B., Law

COOPER, T., Mathematics, Science and Technology Education

COPE, M., Faculty Office (Law)

CORONES, S., Law Research

COURTNEY, M., Nursing

CRAWFORD, R., Mechanical, Manufacturing and Medical Engineering

CUNNINGHAM, S., Creative Industries Research and Applications Centre

DALE, J., Faculty Office (Science and Technology)

DAWSON, E., Data Communications

DOUGLAS, E., Brisbane Graduate School of Business

DUNCAN, W., Law

EDWARDS, H., Nursing

ENGLISH, L., Mathematics, Science and Technology Education

FERREIRA, L., Civil Engineering

FISHER, D., Law

FITZGERALD, B., Law School

GABLE, G., Information Systems

GARDINER, D., Chancellery

GARDNER, I., Life Science

GEORGE, G., Faculty Office (Science and Technology)

GIBSON, D., Chancellery

GOUGH, J., Research and Advancement

GRIFFIN, M., Faculty Office (Business)

HAMPSON, K., Cooperative Research Centre for Construction

HARDING, S., Faculty Office (Business)

HARTLEY, J., Faculty Office (Creative Industries)

HERINGTON, A., Life Science

HOCKINGS, J., Design and Built Environment

HUDSON, P., Life Science

HURN, A., Economics and Finance

JONES, J., Creative Industries Research and Applications Centre

KABANOFF, B., Management

LANE, W., Law School

LAVERY, P., Creative Industries Faculty Advancement

LAYTON, A., Economics and Finance

LEDWICH, G., Electrical and Electronic Systems

LEHMANN, S., Design and Built Environment

LITTLE, P., Accountancy

MCELWAIN, D., Mathematics

MCGREGOR-LOWNDES, M., Centre of Philanthropy and Non-profit Studies

MCLEAN, V., Faculty Office (Education)

MCROBBIE, C., Mathematics, Science and Technology Education

MCWILLIAM, E., Cultural and Language Studies in Education

MAEDER, A., Electrical and Electronic Systems

MAHENDRAN, M., Civil Engineering
MATCHETT, R., QUT Carseldine
MATHEW, J., Mechanical, Manufacturing and Medical Engineering
MOODY, M., Electrical and Electronic Systems Engineering
NEWMAN, B., Public Health
OLDENBURG, B., Public Health
PARKER, A., Human Movement Studies
PATTI, C., Advertising, Marketing and Public Relations
PATTON, W., Learning and Professional Studies
PEARCY, M., Mechanical, Manufacturing and Medical Engineering
PETTITT, A., Mathematics
PHAM, B., Information Technology
POPE, J., Physical Sciences
RENFORTH, W., Business
RYAN, N., Management
SARA, V., Life Science
SHEEHAN, M., Psychology and Counselling
SIDWELL, A., Construction Management and Property
SKITMORE, R., Construction Management and Property
SRIDHARAN, S., Electrical and Electronic Systems
TAYLER, C., Early Childhood
THAMBIRATNAM, D., Civil Engineering
TOWERS, S., Creative Industries Faculty Academic Programs
TROCKI, C., Humanities and Human Services
TROUTBECK, R., Civil Engineering
WALDERSEE, R., Business
WILLETT, R., Accountancy
WISSLER, R., Research and Advancement
YOUNG, R., Psychology and Counselling

ROYAL MELBOURNE INSTITUTE OF TECHNOLOGY

GPOB 2476V, Melbourne, Vic. 3001
124 La Trobe St, Melbourne, Vic. 3000
Telephone: (3) 9925-2260
Fax: (3) 9663-5029
E-mail: study@rmit.edu.au
Internet: www.rmit.edu.au

Founded 1887; university status 1992
Campuses in Melbourne, Bundoora and Brunswick; int. campuses in Hanoi and Saigon (Ho Chi Minh City)
Academic year: February to November
Chancellor: Prof. DENNIS GIBSON
Vice-Chancellor and Pres.: Prof. MARGARET GARDENER
Pro-Vice-Chancellor for Business: Prof. GILL PALMER
Pro-Vice-Chancellor for Design and the Social Context: Prof. COLIN FUDGE
Pro-Vice-Chancellor for Finance and Business Services: CAMERON MORONEY
Pro-Vice-Chancellor for International Enterprise and Community Development: Dr MADELEINE REEVE
Pro-Vice-Chancellor for Organisational Capability and Development: COLIN SHARP
Pro-Vice-Chancellor for Research and Innovation: Prof. DAINE ALCORN
Pro-Vice-Chancellor for Science, Engineering and Technology: Prof. PETER COLOE
Pro-Vice-Chancellor for Students: Prof. JOYCE KIRK
Pro-Vice-Chancellor for Teaching and Learning: Prof. GAIL HART
Dir, TAFE: ALLAN BALLAGH
Academic Registrar: MADDY MCMASTER
Library Dir.: CRAIG ANDERSON (acting)
Library of 704,322 vols
Number of students: 70,247
Publications: *Research Highlights* (1 a year), *RMIT Openline* (university news, 5 a year)

DEANS
Faculty of Applied Science: Prof. MALCOLM MCCORMICK
Faculty of Art, Design and Communication: Prof. ROBIN WILLIAMS
Faculty of Business: Prof. MARGARET JACKSON
Faculty of Constructed Environment: Prof. BELINDA PROBERT
Faculty of Education, Language and Community Services: Prof. MARY KALANTZIS
Faculty of Engineering: Prof. ROBERT SNOW
Faculty of Life Sciences: Prof. ALEX RADLOFF

SOUTHERN CROSS UNIVERSITY

POB 157, Lismore, NSW 2480
Campuses at Lismore, Coffs Harbour and Tweed Heads
Telephone: (2) 6620-3000
Fax: (2) 6622-1300
E-mail: webmarketing@scu.edu.au
Internet: www.scu.edu.au

Founded 1993 from Northern Rivers and Coffs Harbour components of the University of New England
Academic year: February to November (2 semesters)
Vice-Chancellor: Prof. PETER LEE
Pro-Vice-Chancellors: Prof. B. BAVERSTOCK, Prof. A. C. B. DELVES, Prof. L. Z. KLICH
Exec. Dir and Vice-Pres. for Corporate Services: M. H. MARSHALL
Number of teachers: 350
Number of students: 14,631
Publication: *Research Report* (1 a year)

DEANS
Faculty of Arts and Sciences: JENNY GRAHAM
Faculty of Business and Law: Prof. MICHAEL EVANS

PROFESSORS
ATKINSON, J., Indigenous Australian Peoples
BAVERSTOCK, P., Graduate Research College (and PVC Research)
BRAITHWAITE, R., Tourism and Hospitality Management
DELVES, A., University Enterprise and International Activities (PVC)
GARTSIDE, D. F., Resource Science and Management
GRAHAM, J., Health and Applied Sciences Division (Executive Dean)
HAYDEN, M., Teaching and Learning Unit
HENRY, R. J., Plant Conservation Genetics
JACKSON, J. G., Law and Justice
KLICH, Z., University Academic and Quality Matters (PVC)
KOUZMIN, A., Graduate College of Management
LEIPER, N., Tourism and Hospitality Management
MCCONCHIE, D., Environmental Science and Management
MEREDITH, G., Business Administration
MURUGESAN, S., Multimedia and Information Technology
NECK, P., Business Administration
ROTHWELL, B., Manager, Tweed Gold Coast Campus
SAENGER, P., Environmental Science and Management
SAVERY, L., Business Division (Executive Dean)
SCOTT, D., Commerce and Management
SIMPSON, R., National Marine Science Centre
SPECHT, R., Environmental Science and Management
SPEEDY, G., Teaching and Learning Centre
TAYLOR, B., Nursing and Health Care Practices
THOM, P., Arts Division (Executive Dean)
VANCLAY, J., Environmental Science and Management

WILSON, P., Psychology
YEO, S. M. H., Law and Justice
ZANN, L. P., Environmental Science and Management

SWINBURNE UNIVERSITY OF TECHNOLOGY

POB 218, Hawthorn, Vic. 3122
Telephone: (3) 9214-8000
Fax: (3) 9818-3648
E-mail: study@swinburne.edu.au
Internet: www.swinburne.edu.au

Founded 1908 as Eastern Suburbs Technical College; present name and status 1992
Academic year: March to November
Chancellor: Dr WILLIAM SCALES
Vice-Chancellor: Prof. IAN YOUNG
Deputy Vice-Chancellor for Research: Prof. ANDREW FLITMAN
Deputy Vice-Chancellor for Academic Affairs: Prof. SHIRLEY LEITCH
Divisional Deputy Vice-Chancellor for Technical and Further Education (TAFE Division): LINDA BROWN
Vice-Pres.: STEPHEN BEALL
Librarian: D. WHITEHEAD
Library of 250,000 vols
Number of teachers: 657 (362 Higher Education, 295 TAFE)
Number of students: 38,000 (incl. 14,118 Higher Education, 23,882 TAFE)
Publication: *Research Report*
Campuses at Hawthorn, Wantirna, Croydon, Healesville, Prahran, Lilydale, Sarawak (Malaysia)

DEANS
Faculty of Business and Enterprise: Prof. MIKE DONNELLY
Faculty of Design: Prof. KEN FREIDMAN (acting)
Faculty of Engineering and Industrial Sciences: Prof. JOHN SEYNON
Faculty of Higher Education, Lilydale: Prof. KAY LIPSON
Faculty of Information and Communication Technologies: LEON STERLING (acting)
Faculty of Life and Social Sciences: Prof. RUSSELL CRAWFORD

UNIVERSITY OF ADELAIDE

Adelaide, SA 5005
Telephone: (8) 8313-4455
Fax: (8) 8313-4401
E-mail: council.secretary@adelaide.edu.au
Internet: www.adelaide.edu.au

Founded 1874
Autonomous institution established by Act of Parliament
Academic year: March to December
Chancellor: The Hon. ROBERT HILL
Vice-Chancellor and Pres.: Prof. JAMES MCWHA
Deputy Vice-Chancellor and Vice-Pres. for Academic Affairs: Prof. PASCALE QUESTER MCDOUGALL
Deputy Vice-Chancellor and Vice-Pres. for Research: Prof. MIKE BROOKS
Vice-Pres. for Services and Resources: PAUL DULDIG
Pro-Vice-Chancellor for Int. Affairs: Prof. JOHN TAPLIN
Univ. Librarian: RAY C. CHOATE
Number of teachers: 1,405
Number of students: 24,209
Publications: *Adelaide Law Review* (2 a year), *Australian Economic Papers* (2 a year), *Australian Feminist Studies* (2 a year), *Australian Journal of Legal History* (2 a year), *Australian Journal of Social Research* (4 a year), *Australian Women's*

Studies (1 a year), *Corporate and Business Law Journal* (2 a year), *Economic Briefings* (3 a year), *The Joseph Fisher Lecture in Commerce* (irregular), *Research Report* (1 a year), *Social Analysis* (2 a year)

EXECUTIVE DEANS

Faculty of Engineering, Computer and Mathematical Sciences: Prof. PETER DOWD
Faculty of Health Sciences: Prof. JUSTIN BEILBY
Faculty of Humanities and Social Sciences: Prof. NICK HARVEY
Faculty of the Professions: Prof. CHRISTOPHER FINDLAY (acting)
Faculty of Sciences: Prof. BOB HILL

PROFESSORS

Faculty of Engineering, Computer and Mathematical Sciences (tel. (8) 8303-4700; fax (8) 8303-4361; e-mail eng.cs.maths@adelaide .edu.au; internet www.adelaide.edu.au/ ecms):

BARTER, C. J., Computer Science
BEGG, S. H., Petroleum Engineering and Management
BEHRBRUCH, P., Petroleum Engineering and Management
BRATVOLD, R. B., Petroleum Engineering and Management
BROOKS, M. J., Computer Science
COLE, P. H., Electrical and Electronic Engineering
COUTTS, R. P., Telecommunications
DANDY, G. D., Civil Engineering
GRAY, D. A., Sensor Signal Processing
HANSEN, C. H., Mechanical Engineering
IRELAND, V., Education Centre for Innovation and Commercialisation
KHURANA, A. K., Petroleum Engineering and Management
KING, K. D., Chemical Engineering
LINTON, V. M., Welded Structures (Cooperative Research Centre)
MCLEAN, A. J., Road Accident Research
SARMA, H. K., Petroleum Engineering and Management
WHITE, L. B., Electrical and Electronic Engineering

Faculty of Health Sciences (Medical School North, Frome Rd, Adelaide; tel. (8) 8303-5336; fax (8) 8303-3788; e-mail health .sciences@adelaide.edu.au; internet www .health.adelaide.edu.au):

BARRETT, R. J., Psychiatry
BARTOLD, P. M., Dentistry
BEILBY, J. J., General Practice
BOCHNER, F., Clinical and Experimental Pharmacology
DEKKER, G., Obstetrics and Gynaecology
FREWIN, D. B., Clinical and Experimental Pharmacology
GOLDNEY, R. D., Psychiatry
GOSS, A. N., Dentistry
HENNENBERG, M., Anatomical Sciences
HILLER, J. E., Public Health
HOROWITZ, J. D., Medicine
HOROWITZ, M., Medicine
HOWIE, D. W., Orthopaedics, Trauma
JAMIESON, G. G., Surgery
JONES, N., Surgery
KOTLARSKI, I., Health Sciences Faculty Office
LUDBROOK, G. L., Anaesthesia and Intensive Care
MCFARLANE, A. C., Psychiatry
MACLENNAN, A. H., Obstetrics and Gynaecology
MADDERN, G. J., Surgery
MOYES, D. G., Anaesthesia and Intensive Care
NETTELBECK, T. J., Psychology
NORMAN, R. J., Obstetrics and Gynaecology
ROBERTON, D. M., Paediatrics

ROBINSON, J. S., Obstetrics and Gynaecology
RUFFIN, R. E., Medicine
RUNCIMAN, W. B., Anaesthesia and Intensive Care
SAMPSON, W. J., Dentistry
SAWYER, M. G., Paediatrics
SLADE, G. D., Dentistry
SOMOGYI, A. A., Clinical and Experimental Pharmacology
SPENCER, A. J., Dentistry
TAN, H. L., Paediatrics
TAPLIN, J. E., Psychology
THOMPSON, P. D., Medicine
TIERNEY, A. J., Clinical Nursing
TILLEY, W. D., Medicine
TOWNSEND, G. C., Dentistry
VERNON-ROBERTS, B., Pathology
WHITE, J. M., Clinical and Experimental Pharmacology
WORMALD, P. J., Surgery

Faculty of Humanities and Social Sciences (tel. (8) 8303-5345; fax (8) 8303-4382; e-mail humss.office@adelaide.edu.au; internet www .arts.adelaide.edu.au/arts-web):

BODMAN RAE, C., Music
BOUMELHA, P. A., English
BULBECK, C., Social Inquiry
HARVEY, N., Geographical and Environmental Studies
HUGO, G. J., Social Applications of Geographical Information Systems
JAIN, P. C., Asian Studies
MORTENSEN, C. E., Philosophy
MUHLHAUSLER, P., European Studies, General Linguistics
PREST, W. R., History
SHAPCOTT, T. W., English
WILLIAMS, M. A., Geographical and Environmental Studies

Faculty of the Professions (tel. (8) 8303-3986; fax (8) 8303-4416):

ANDERSON, K., Economics
BRADBROOK, A. J., Law
DETMOLD, M. J., Law
FAIRALL, P. A., Law
MCDOUGALL, F. M., Graduate School of Business
MARJORIBANKS, K. M., Graduate School of Education
NAFFINE, N. M., Law
PARKER, L. D., Commerce
POMFRET, R. W., Economics
QUESTER, P. G., Commerce
RADFORD, A. D., Architecture, Landscape and Urban Design
SHERIDAN, K., Graduate School of Business
SMOLICZ, J. J., Graduate School of Education
TAYLOR, D. W., Commerce

Faculty of Sciences (tel. (8) 8303-5673; fax (8) 8303-4386; internet www.sciences.adelaide .edu.au):

AUSTIN, A. D., School of Earth and Environmental Sciences
BOWIE, J. H., School of Chemistry and Physics
BRUCE, M. I., School of Chemistry and Physics
BURRELL, C. J., School of Molecular and Biomedical Sciences
COVENTRY, D. R., School of Earth and Environmental Sciences
FINCHER, G. B., School of Agriculture and Wine
GREENHALGH, S. A., School of Earth and Environmental Sciences
HILLIS, R. R., Petroleum Geology and Geophysics (National Centre)
HYND, P. I., School of Agriculture and Wine
KALDI, J. G., Petroleum Geology and Geophysics (National Centre)
LANGRIDGE, P., School of Agriculture and Wine

LINCOLN, S. F., School of Chemistry and Physics
MCMILLEN, I. C., School of Molecular and Biomedical Sciences
MILES, T. S., School of Molecular and Biomedical Sciences
MUNCH, J., School of Chemistry and Physics
OWENS, J. A., School of Molecular and Biomedical Sciences
PATON, J. C., School of Molecular and Biomedical Sciences
RANDLES, J. W., School of Agriculture and Wine
RATHJEN, P. D., School of Molecular and Biomedical Sciences
SCHMIDT, O., School of Agriculture and Wine
SEDGLEY, M., School of Agriculture and Wine
SEYMOUR, R. S., School of Earth and Environmental Sciences
SMITH, S. E., School of Earth and Environmental Sciences
TYERMAN, S. D., School of Agriculture and Wine
VINCENT, R. A., School of Chemistry and Physics
WALLACE, J. C., School of Molecular and Biomedical Sciences
WHAN, B., Molecular Plant Breeding (Cooperative Research Centre)

UNIVERSITY OF BALLARAT

POB 663, Ballarat, Vic. 3353
Telephone: (3) 5327-9018
Fax: (3) 5327-9017
E-mail: info@ballarat.edu.au
Internet: www.ballarat.edu.au
Founded 1976 as Ballarat College of Advanced Education; University status acquired 1994

Vice-Chancellor: Prof. DAVID BATTERSBY
Number of students: 22,000 (higher education and Technical and Further Education—TAFE)

DEANS

Arts Academy: Prof. PETER MATTHEWS
School of Behavioural and Social Sciences and Humanities: Assoc. Prof. ROSEMARY GREEN
School of Business: Prof. JULIAN LOWE
School of Business Services—TAFE: RUSSELL BRAY
School of Education: Prof. LAWRIE ANGUS
School of Human Movement and Sport Sciences: Assoc. Prof. LEONIE OTAGO
School of Human Sciences—TAFE: GREG HAINES
School of Information Technology and Mathematical Sciences: Prof. SID MORRIS
School of Manufacturing Services—TAFE: CARLA READING
School of Nursing: Assoc. Prof. HANNELORE BEST
School of Science and Engineering: Prof. MARTIN WESTBROOKE

UNIVERSITY OF CANBERRA

ACT 2601
Telephone: (2) 6201-5111
Fax: (2) 6201-5999
E-mail: international@canberra.edu.au
Internet: www.canberra.edu.au
Founded 1990 from fmr Canberra CAE
Govt control
Academic year: February to December (3 semesters)

Chancellor: JOHN MACKAY
Vice-Chancellor and Pres.: Prof. STEPHEN PARKER

Deputy Vice-Chancellor and Pres. Education: Prof. CAROLE KAYROOZ
Pro Vice-Chancellor for Research: Prof. FRANCES SHANNON
Pro Vice-Chancellor for Devt: Prof. JOHN H. HOWARD
Pro Vice-Chancellor for Int. and Major Projects: ANDREW BAILEY
Registrar: BRUCE LYONS
Univ. Librarian: ANITA R. M. CROTTY
Library: see Libraries and Archives
Number of teachers: 431 (full-time)
Number of students: 12,110

DEANS

Faculty of Applied Science: Prof. ARTHUR GEORGES
Faculty of Arts and Design (Acting): Prof. JEN WEBB
Faculty of Business and Govt: Prof. LAWRENCE PRATCHETT
Faculty of Education: Prof. GEOFFREY RIORDAN
Faculty of Health: Prof. DIANE GIBSON
Faculty of Information Sciences and Engineering: Prof. DHARMENDRA SHARMA
Faculty of Law: Dr MAREE SAINBURY

PROFESSORS

BLOOD, R. W., Professional Communication
BREMNER, C., Architecture
CHO, G., Geoinformatics and the Law
CRAIK, J., Communication
CREAGH, D., Physics
DUNK, A., Accounting
FRITH, S., Architecture
GEORGES, A., Applied Ecology
HALLIGAN, J., Public Administration
HARDING, A.
HAWKINS, S., Health Sciences
HONE, J., Wildlife Management
JONES, G., Freshwater Science
KAYROOZ, C., Education
LEAHY, P.
LENNARD, C., Forensic Studies
MORRISON, P., Nursing
NORRIS, R., Freshwater Ecology
PEGRUM, A., Architecture
PUTNIS, P., Communication
RICHWOOD, D., Psychology
SATHYE, M., Public Administration
SHADDOCK, A., Special Education and Counselling
TAYLOR, P. J., Mathematics Education
TURNER, M., Public Administration
WAGNER, M., Software Engineering
WIDDOWSON, D., International Customs Law and Administration

UNIVERSITY OF MELBOURNE

Melbourne, Vic. 3010
Telephone: (3) 8344-4000
Fax: (3) 8344-5104
E-mail: vc@unimelb.edu.au
Internet: www.unimelb.edu.au
Founded 1853 (opened 1855)
Autonomous institution established by Act of Parliament (State of Victoria) and financed mainly by Commonwealth Government
Academic year: February to December
Chancellor: The Hon. ALEX CHERNOV
Deputy Chancellors: ROSA STORELLI, Justice SUSAN CRENNAN
Vice-Chancellor and Pres.: Prof. GLYN DAVIS
Provost and Deputy Vice-Chancellor for Global Relations: Prof. JOHN DEWAR
Deputy Vice-Chancellor for Research: Prof. PETER RATHJEN
Deputy Vice-Chancellor for Global Engagement: Prof. SUSAN ELLIOTT
Deputy Vice-Chancellor for University Affairs: Prof. WARREN BEBBINGTON
Pro-Vice-Chancellor for Teaching and Learning: Dr PHILIPPA PATTISON

Pro-Vice-Chancellor for Graduate Research: Prof. RICHARD STRUGNELL
Pro-Vice-Chancellor for Research: Prof. LYN YATES
Pro-Vice-Chancellor for Research Partnerships: Prof. JAMES MCCLUSKEY
Pro-Vice-Chancellor for Research Collaborations: Prof. LIZ SONENBERG
Pro-Vice-Chancellors: Prof. GEOFFREY STEVENS, Prof. RON SLOCOMBE
Snr Vice-Prin.: IAN MARSHMAN
Head of University Services: LINLEY MARTIN
Chief Financial Officer: ALLAN TAIT
General Counsel: CHRIS PENMAN
Exec. Dir of Human Resources: NIGEL WAUGH
Exec. Dir of Student Services and Academic Registrar: NIGEL WAUGH
Exec. Dir of Property and Campus Services: CHRIS WHITE
Exec. Dir of Research: DAVID COOKSON
University Sec.: CHRISTOPHER STEWARDSON

Number of teachers: 3,347
Number of students: 35,909

DEANS

Faculty of Architecture, Building and Planning: Prof. T. KVAN
Faculty of Arts: Prof. MARK CONSIDINE
Faculty of Business and Economics: Prof. M. A. ABERNETHY
Faculty of Education: Prof. FIELD RICKARDS
Faculty of Engineering: Prof. IVEN MAREELS (acting)
Faculty of Law: Prof. MICHAEL CROMMELIN
Faculty of Medicine, Dentistry and Health Sciences: Prof. J. ANGUS
Faculty of VCA and Music: Prof. SHARMAN PRETT
Faculty of Science: Prof. ROBERT SAINT
Faculty of Veterinary Science: Prof. KEN HINCHLIFF
Melbourne Business School: Prof. JOHN SEYBOLT (Dir)
Melbourne School of Land and Environment: Prof. R. ROUSH (Chair.)
School of Graduate Studies: Prof. RICHARD STRUGNELL

PROFESSORS

Faculty of Architecture, Building and Planning (tel. (3) 8344-6429; fax (3) 8344-5532; e-mail apb-info@unimelb.edu.au; internet www.arbld.unimelb.edu.au):

BRAWN, G. W., Architecture
BULL, C., Landscape Architecture
DOVEY, K. G., Architecture and Urban Design
FINCHER, R., Urban Planning
GOAD, P., Architecture, Building and Planning
GREEN, R., Landscape Architecture
HUTSON, A., Architecture
KING, R. J., Environmental Planning
LEWIS, M. B.
ROBINSON, J. R. W., Property and Construction
RODGER, A., Architecture, Building and Planning
YENCKEN, D., Architecture, Building and Planning

Faculty of Arts (tel. (3) 8344-6395; fax (3) 9347-0424; e-mail arts-enquiries@unimelb.edu.au; internet www.arts.unimelb.edu.au):

ANDERSON, J., Fine Arts, Classical Studies and Archaeology
AUSTIN, P. K., Linguistics and Applied Linguistics
BUDIMAN, A., Indonesian
CLARKE, A. F., Equine Studies
COALDRAKE, W. H., Japanese
DURING, S., English
ENRIGHT, N. J., Anthropology, Geography and Environmental Studies
FINLAYSON, B., Anthropology, Geography and Environmental Studies

FREIBERG, A., Criminology
GALLIGAN, B. J., Political Science
GELDER, K., English
GRIMSHAW, P. A., History
HAJEK, J., French and Italian Studies
HOLM, D., Chinese
HOLMES, L. T., Political Science
HOME, R. W., History and Philosophy of Science
HURST, A., School of French
JACKSON, A. C., Social Work
LANGTON, M. L., Australian Indigenous Studies
MCINNES, C. V., Higher Education
MACINTYRE, S. F., History
MCPHEE, P. B., History
MALCOLM, E. L., Irish Studies
NETTELBECK, C., School of Languages
O'BRIEN, A., Creative Arts
PIKE, K., Criminology
PRIEST, P. G., Philosophy
RICKLEFS, M., Melbourne Institute of Asian Languages and Societies
RIDLEY, R., History
SEAR, F. B., Classics and Archaeology
STEELE, P. D., English
WALLACE-CRABBE, C. K., English
WEBBER, M. J., Geography

Faculty of Business and Economics (tel. (3) 8344-5328; fax (3) 9347-3986; e-mail commerce-enquiries@unimelb.edu.au; internet www.fbe.unimelb.edu.au):

ABERNETHY, M. A., Accounting and Business Information Systems
BARDSLEY, P., Economics
BORLAND, J., Economics
BROWN, R., Finance
CREEDY, J., Economics
DAVIS, K. T., Finance
DAWKINS, P. J., Melbourne Institute of Applied Economic and Social Research
DICKSON, D., Economics
FREEBAIRN, J. W., Economics
GRIFFITHS, B., Economics
HARDY, C., Management
HOUGHTON, K. A., Accounting
KING, S. P., Economics
KOFMAN, P., Finance
KULIK, C., Management
LEECH, S., Accounting and Business Information Systems
LLOYD, P. J., Economics
MCDONALD, I. M., Economics
MARCHANT, G., Accounting and Business Information Systems
MARTIN, V., Economics
NASSER, S., Accounting and Business Information Systems
NICHOLAS, S., Management
PERKINS, E. J., Economics
SAMSON, D., Management
SHAPIRO, P., Economics
TOURKY, R., Economics
WHEATLEY, S., Finance
WIDING, R. E., Management
WILLIAMS, R. A., Econometrics
WOODEN, M., Melbourne Institute of Applied Economics and Social Research

Faculty of Education (tel. (3) 8344-8628; fax (3) 8344-8529; e-mail enquiries@edfac.unimelb.edu.au; internet www.edfac.unimelb.edu.au):

CALDWELL, B. J., Education (Leadership and Management)
CHRISTIE, F., Language, Literacy and Arts Education
EVANS, G., Learning and Educational Development
GRIFFIN, P. E., Assessment
HILL, P., Education (Leadership and Management)
LAKOMSKI, G., Education
LEE DOW, K., Education
MAGLEN, L. R., Asian Pacific Economics of Education and Training

RABAN-BISBY, B., Early Childhood Studies
RICKARDS, F. W., Education (Learning, Assessment and Special Education)
STACEY, K. C., Science and Mathematics Education
START, B., Learning and Educational Development

Faculty of Engineering (tel. (3) 8344-6703; fax (3) 9349-2182; e-mail eng-info@unimelb .edu.au; internet www.eng.mu.oz.au):

BISHOP, I. D., Geomatics
BOGER, D. V., Chemical Engineering
CHING, M. S., Mechanical and Manufacturing Engineering
EVANS, R. J., Electrical Engineering
FENTON, J. D., Civil and Environmental Engineering
FRASER, C. S., Geomatics
GOOD, M. C., Mechanical and Manufacturing Engineering
HUTCHINSON, G. L., Civil and Environmental Engineering
KOTAGIRI, R., Computer Science and Software Engineering
KRISHNAMURTHY, V., Electrical and Electronic Engineering
MCMAHON, T. A., Environmental Hydrology
MAREELS, I. M. V., Electrical Engineering
MOFFAT, A. M., Computer Science and Software Engineering
MORAN, W., Electronic and Electrical Engineering
STERLING, L. S., Computer Science and Software Engineering
STEVENS, G. W., Chemical Engineering
STUCKLEY, P. J., Computer Science and Software Engineering
TUCKER, R. S., Electrical Engineering
VAN DEVENTER, J., Mineral and Process Engineering
WATSON, H. C., Mechanical and Manufacturing Engineering
WILLIAMSON, I. P., Surveying and Land Information
WOOD, D. G., Engineering
YOUNG, D. M., Engineering Construction Management
ZUCKERMAN, M., Electronic and Electrical Engineering

Faculty of Law (tel. (3) 8344-6164; fax (3) 9347-2392; e-mail post@law.unimelb.edu.au; internet www.law.unimelb.edu.au):

BRYAN, M., Law
CHRISTIE, A. F., Intellectual Property
COLMAN, P. M., Medical Biology
COWMAN, A. F., Medical Biology
CROMMELIN, B. M. L., Law
MCCORMACK, T. L. H., International Humanitarian Law
MITCHELL, R. J., Law
MORGAN, J. J., Law
RAMSAY, I. M., Commercial Law
RICKETSON, S., Law
SAUNDERS, C. A., Law
SKENE, L., Law
SMITH, M. D. H., Asian Law
TRIGGS, G., Law

Faculty of Medicine, Dentistry and Health Sciences (tel. (3) 8344-5894; fax (3) 9347-7854; e-mail medicine-info@unimelb.edu.au; internet www.medfac.unimelb.edu.au/med):

ADAMS, J. M., Medical Biology
ALCORN, D., Anatomy
ANDERSON, I. P., Public Health
ANDERSON, J. N., Public Health
ANDERSON, V., Psychology
BERK, M., Psychiatry
BERKOVIC, S. F., Medicine
BEST, J. D., Medicine
BHATHAL, P. S., Pathology
BLOCH, S., Psychiatry
BOWES, G., Paediatrics
BREARLEY-MESER, L., Paediatrics

BRENNECKE, S. P., Obstetrics and Gynaecology
BROWN, G. V., Medicine
BYRNE, E., Experimental Neurology
CARLIN, J. B., Public Health
CHAN, S. T. F., Surgery
CHIU, E., Psychiatry
CLEMENT, J. G., Forensic Odontology
CORY, S., Medical Biology
CREAMER, M., Psychiatry
DENNERSTEIN, L., Psychiatry
DOHERTY, P., Microbiology and Immunology
DONNAN, G., Medicine
DOWELL, R. C., Otolaryngology
DUNNING, T., Nursing
FAIRLEY, C. K., Sexual Health
FUNDER, J., Medicine
FURNESS, J. B., Anatomy
GALEA, M. P., Physiotherapy
GAYLER, K. R., Biochemistry and Molecular Biology
GETHING, M. J., Biochemistry and Molecular Biology
GIBSON, R. M., Radiology
GOODWIN, A. W., Anatomy
GRAHAM, H. K., Orthopaedic Surgery
GRAVES, S. E., Orthopaedic Surgery
HARRAP, S. B., Physiology
HARRIS, P. J., Physiology
HARRISON, L. C., Medical Biology
HOPPER, J. L., Public Health
JACKSON, H. J., Psychology
KAYE, A. H., Surgery
LOUIS, W. J., Clinical Pharmacology and Therapeutics
MCCALMAN, J. S., Public Health
MCCLUSKEY, J., Microbiology and Immunology
MCMEEKEN, J., Physiotherapy
MANDERSON, L. H., Women's Health
MASTERS, C. L., Pathology
MESSER, H. H., Restorative Dentistry
MESSER, L. J. B., Child Dental Health
MILLGROM, J., Psychology
MORGAN, T. O., Physiology
MORRISON, W. A., Surgery
MULHOLLAND, E. K., Paediatrics
NELSON, S., Nursing
NICHOLSON, G. C., Medicine
NICOLA, N., Medical Biology
NOLAN, T. M., Public Health
O'BOYLE, M. W., Psychology
OLEKALNS, M., Psychology
PARKER, J. M., Postgraduate Nursing
PATTISON, P. E., Psychology
PERMEZEL, J. M. H., Obstetrics and Gynaecology
PIERCE, R., Medicine
PRIOR, M., Psychology
PROIETTO, J., Medicine
REYNOLDS, E. C., Dental Science
ROBINS-BROWN, R. M., Microbiology and Immunology
SCHWEITZER, I., Psychiatry
SHORTMAN, K. D., Medical Biology and Developmental Immunology
SINGH, B. S., Psychiatry
SMALLWOOD, R. A., Medicine
SPEED, T. P., Medical Biology
STRUGNELL, R. A., Microbiology and Immunology
TAYLOR, H. R., Ophthalmology
TILLER, J. W. G., Psychiatry
TRESS, B. M., Radiology
TRINDER, J. A., Psychology
TYAS, M. J., Dental Science
VADJA, F., Medicine
WARD, T., Psychology
WARK, J. D., Medicine
WATTERS, D. A. K., Surgery
WEARING, A. J., Psychology
WETTENHALL, R. E. H., Biochemistry
WICKS, I. P., Medical Biology
WILLIAMS, D. A., Physiology
YEOMANS, N. D., Medicine

YOUNG, D., General Practice
ZAJAC, J. D., Medicine

Faculty of Science (tel. (3) 8344-6404; fax (3) 8344-5803; e-mail science-queries@unimelb .edu.au; internet www.science.unimelb.edu .au):

BACIC, A., Botany
BAKER, A. J. M., Botany
CAMPBELL, G. D., Zoology
CHAN, D. Y. C., Mathematics
CLARKE, A. E., Botany
COLE, B. L., Optometry
FERGUSON, I. S., Forest Science
GHIGGINO, K. P., Chemistry
GRIESER, F., Chemistry
GUTTMANN, A. J., Mathematics
HYNES, M. J., Genetics
KOTAGIRI, R., Computer Science
KLEIN, A. G., Physics
LADIGES, P. Y., Botany
MCBRIEN, N. A., Optometry
MCKELLAR, B. H. J., Theoretical Physics
MCKENZIE, J. A., Genetics
MILLER, C. F., Mathematics
MORRISON, I., Information Systems
NUGENT, K. A., Physics
PICKETT-HEAPS, J. D., Botany
PLIMER, I. R., Geology
RENFREE, M. B., Zoology
RUBINSTEIN, J. H., Mathematics
SCHIESSER, C., Chemistry
SONENBERG, E. A., Information Systems
STERLING, L. S., Computer Science
TAYLOR, G. N., Physics
THOMPSON, C. J., Mathematics
WEDD, A. G., Chemistry

Faculty of VCA and Music (tel. (3) 8344-5256; fax (3) 8344-5346; e-mail enquiries@music .unimelb.edu.au; internet www.vcam .unimelb.edu.au):

BEBBINGTON, W. A., Music
BROADSTOCK, B., Music
GRIFFITHS, J. A., Music

Faculty of Veterinary Science (tel. (3) 8344-7356; fax (3) 8344-7374; e-mail vet-info@ unimelb.edu.au; internet www.vet.unimelb .edu.au):

CAHILL, R. N. P., Veterinary Biology
CAPLE, I. W., Veterinary Medicine
CLARKE, A. F., Equine Studies
SLOCOMBE, R. F., Veterinary Pathology

Melbourne Business School (Leicester St, Carlton, Vic. 3053; tel. (3) 9349-8403; fax (3) 9349-8404; e-mail mbs@unimelb.edu.au; internet www.mbs.unimelb.edu.au):

ALFORD, J. L., Public Sector Management
DAINTY, P., Human Resources Management and Employee Relations
GANS, J. S., Management
GRUNDY, B., Finance
HARPER, I. R., Commerce and Business Administration
KING, S., Economics
LEWIS, G., Strategy
MANN, L., Organizational Behaviour and Decision Making
MISHRA, D., Marketing
OLEKALNS, M., Leadership and Decision Making
RIZZO, P., Finance and Management
SAMSON, D. A., Manufacturing Management
SINCLAIR, A. M. A., Management (Diversity and Change)
SPEED, R., Marketing Management and Advanced Marketing Strategy
WILLIAMS, P. L., Management (Law and Economics)

Melbourne School of Land and Environment (tel. (3) 8344-0276; fax (3) 9348-2156; e-mail enquiries@landfood.unimelb.edu.au; internet www.land-environment.unimelb.edu.au):

BRITZ, M., Food Science

CHAPMAN, D. F., Pasture Science
COUSENS, R. D., Crop Science
EGAN, A. R., Agriculture (Animal Science)
FALVEY, J. L., Agriculture
FERGUSON, I. S., Forest Science
GODDARD, M., Agriculture
HEMSWORTH, P., Agriculture
HILLIER, A. J., Agriculture
KOLLMORGEN, J. F., Agriculture
MACMILLAN, K. L., Agriculture
RICHARDSON, R. A., Land and Food Resources
ROSS, E. W., Agriculture
VINDEN, P., Forest Industries

Victorian College of the Arts (234 St Kilda Rd, Southbank, Vic. 3010; tel. (3) 9685-9300; fax (3) 9682-1841; internet www.vca.unimelb.edu.au):

HULL, A. (Dir)

UNIVERSITY OF NEW ENGLAND

Armidale, NSW 2351
Telephone: (2) 6773-3333
Fax: (2) 6773-3122
E-mail: admissions@une.edu.au
Internet: www.une.edu.au
Founded 1954; previously New England University College (f. 1938); Armidale College of Advanced Education merged with the University in 1989
Commonwealth govt control
Academic year: February to November (2 semesters)
Chancellor: J. CASSIDY
Deputy Chancellor: J. HARRIS
Vice-Chancellor: Prof. ALAN PETTIGREW
Pro-Vice-Chancellor for Academic Affairs: Prof. EVELYN WOODBERRY
Pro-Vice-Chancellor for Research and Development: Prof. R. COOKSEY (acting)
Exec. Dir of Business and Administration: G. DENNEHY ()
Sec. to Council: KIM CULL
Librarian: JACK BEDSON (acting)
Library: see under Libraries and Archives
Number of teachers: 484
Number of students: 18,863
Publications: *Australasian Victorian Studies Journal* (1 a year), *Australian Folklore: A Yearly Journal of Folklore Studies, Journal of Australian Colonial History* (2 a year), *South Asia* (1 a year), *TalentEd* (3 a year), *The University of New England Law Journal* (2 a year), *Wool Technology and Sheep Breeding* (4 a year)

DEANS

Faculty of Arts and Sciences: Prof. M. SEDGLEY
Faculty of the Professions: Prof. V. MINICHIELLO

PROFESSORS

BINDON, B., CRC for Cattle and Beef Quality
BOULTON, A. J., Environmental Sciences and Natural Resources Management
BRASTED, H. V., Classics, History and Religion
BRUNCKHORST, D., Institute for Rural Futures/UNESCO Centre for Bioregional Resource Management
BYRNE, B. J., Psychology
CARRINGTON, K. L., Social Science
CHOCT, M., Rural Science and Agriculture
COLBRAN, S., Law
COOKSEY, R. W., New England Business School
COTTLE, D., Rural Science and Agriculture
DAVIDSON, I., Human and Environmental Studies
DOLLERY, B. E., Economics
ECKERMAN, A.-K., Professional Development and Leadership

FORD, H. A., Environmental Sciences and Natural Resources Management
FORREST, P. R. H., Social Science
FRANZMANN, M., Classics, History and Religion
GEISER, F., Environmental Sciences and Natural Resources Management
GIBSON, J., Rural Science and Agriculture
GODDARD, C. W., Languages, Cultures and Linguistics
GOSSIP, C. J., Languages, Cultures and Linguistics
GUNTER, M. J., Biological and Molecular Sciences
HORSLEY, G. H. R., Classics, History and Religion
HUTCHINSON, P. J., New England Business School
KAUR, A., Economics
KENT, D. A., Classics, History and Religion
KIERNANDER, A. R. D., English, Communication and Theatre
KINGHORN, B. P., Rural Science and Agriculture
LLOYD, C., Economics
MAGNER, E. S., Law
MEEK, V. L., Professional Development and Leadership
NOBLE, W., Psychology
NOLAN, J. V., Rural Science and Agriculture
PEGG, J. E., Education
ROGERS, L. J., Biological, Biomedical and Molecular Sciences
ROWE, J. B., Rural Science and Agriculture
RUVINSKY, A., Rural Science and Agriculture
SAJEEV, A. S. M., Mathematics, Statistics and Computing Science
SCOTT, J. M., Rural Science and Agriculture
SIMPSON, R. D., Environmental Sciences and Natural Resources Management
TAJI, A., Rural Science and Agriculture
THOMPSON, J. M., Rural Science and Agriculture
TREADGOLD, M. L., Economics
UNSWORTH, L., Education
WALMSLEY, D. J., Human and Environmental Studies
WARE, H. R., Professional Development and Leadership
WATSON, K., Biological, Biomedical and Molecular Sciences

UNIVERSITY OF NEW SOUTH WALES

Sydney, NSW 2052
Telephone: (2) 9385-1000
Fax: (2) 9385-2000
E-mail: studentcentral@unsw.edu.au
Internet: www.unsw.edu.au
Founded 1948, incorporated by Act of Parliament 1949
Academic year: February to November (2 sessions)
Chancellor: DAVID GONSKI
Pres. and Vice-Chancellor: Professor FRED HILMER
Deputy Vice-Chancellor for Academic Affairs: Prof. RICHARD HENRY
Deputy Vice-Chancellor for Research: Prof. LES FIELD
Pres. of the Academic Board: Prof. JANET CHAN
Exec. Dir of Finance and Operations: JONATHAN BLAKEMAN
Chief Exec., UNSW Foundation: JENNIFER BOTT
Exec. Dir of Univ. Services: NEIL MORRIS
Univ. Librarian: ANDREW WELLS
Number of teachers: 2,497 (f.t.e.)
Number of students: 46,000

DEANS

Australian School of Business: Prof. ALEC CAMERON
College of Fine Arts: Prof. IAN HOWARD

Faculty of Arts and Social Sciences: Prof. JAMES DONALD
Faculty of the Built Environment: Prof. ALEC TZANNES
Faculty of Engineering: Prof. GRAHAM DAVIES
Faculty of Law: Prof. DAVID DIXON
Faculty of Medicine: Prof. PETER SMITH
Faculty of Science: Prof. MERLIN CROSSLEY
UNSW at the Australian Defence Force Academy: Prof. JOHN BAIRD (Rector)

PROFESSORS

Faculty of Arts and Social Sciences:
ALEXANDER, C., English
ALEXANDER, P., English
ASHCROFT, W., English
BELL, P., History and Philosophy of Science
BELL, R., History
BENNETT, B., Humanities
CAHILL, D., History
CASS, B., Social Policy
CHAN, J., Social Science and Policy
CHANDLER, P., Education
CONDREN, C., Politics and International Politics
COOPER, M., Education
COTTON, J., Humanities
DANIEL, A., Sociology
DENNIS, P., Humanities
DONALD, J., Media, Film and Theatre
EGGERT, P., Humanities
GASCOIGNE, J., History
GREY, J., Humanities
GROSS, M., Education
HALL, R., Social Science and Policy
HUGMAN, R., Social Work
HUMPHREY, M., Sociology
JOHNSON, R., History
KATZ, I., Social Policy
KITCHING, G., Politics and International Relations
LYONS, M., History
OLDROYD, D., History and Philosophy of Science
PATTON, P., Philosophy
PEARSON, M., History
SAUNDERS, P., Social Policy
SCHUSTER, J., Media and Communications
SWELLER, J., Education
THAYER, C., Humanities
TYRRELL, I., History
WILLIAMS, M., Politics and International Relations
WOODMAN, S., Humanities

Faculty of the Built Environment:
CUTHBERT, A., Architecture
LANG, J., Architecture
LOOSEMORE, M., Built Environment
RUAN, X., Architecture
WEIRICK, J., Landscape Architecture

Faculty of Commerce and Economics:
ANDERSON, E., Economics
BALZER, L., Banking and Finance
BROWN, R., Accounting
DWYER, L., Accounting
FELDMAN, D., Banking and Finance
FIEBIG, D., Economics
FOSTER, F., Banking and Finance
FOX, K., Economics
HILL, R., Economics
KOHN, R., Economics
LAYTON, R., Marketing
MORRISON, P., Marketing
MOSHIRIAN, F., Banking and Finance
UNCLES, M., Marketing

Faculty of Engineering:
ACWORTH, R., Civil Engineering
ADESINA, A., Chemical Engineering
ASHBOLT, N., Civil and Environmental Engineering
BRADFORD, M., Civil and Environmental Engineering
CARMICHAEL, D., Civil and Environmental Engineering

CELLER, B., Electrical Engineering
CHATTOPADHYAY, G., Civil and Environmental Engineering
COMPTON, P. J., Computer Science
CROSKY, A., Materials Science and Engineering
DAVIS, T., Chemical Engineering
DOCTORS, L., Mechanical Engineering
DZURAK, A., Electronic Engineering and Telecommunications
FANE, A., Chemical Engineering
FELL, R., Civil and Environmental Engineering
FLEET, G., Chemical Engineering
FOO, N., Computer Science
FORSTER, B., Surveying and Spatial Information Systems
FOSTER, N., Chemical Engineering
GALVIN, J., Mining Engineering
GILBERT, R., Civil and Environmental Engineering
HEBBLEWHITE, B., Mining Engineering
HEISER, G., Computer Science
HOUGH, R., Engineering
JEFFERY, R., Computer Science
KAEBERNICK, H., Mechanical Engineering
KELLY, D., Mechanical Engineering
LEONARDI, E., Mechanical Engineering
MAROSSZEKY, M., Civil and Environmental Engineering
MORRISON, G., Mechanical Engineering
NOWOTNY, J., Materials Science and Engineering
OSTROVSKI, O., Materials Science and Engineering
PINCZEWSKI, W., Petroleum Engineering
RANDALL, R., Mechanical Engineering
RIZOS, C., Surveying and Spatial Information Systems
SAHAJWALLA, V., Materials Science and Engineering
SAMMUT, C., Computer Science
SAVKIN, A., Electrical Engineering
SCHINDHELM, K., Biomedical Engineering
SENEVIRATNE, A., Electrical Engineering
SHARMA, A., Civil and Environmental Engineering
SHAW, J., Computer Science
SKYLLAS-KAZACOS, M., Chemical Engineering
SOLO, V., Electrical Engineering
SORRELL, C., Materials Science and Engineering
TIN LOI, F., Civil and Environmental Engineering
TRIMM, D., Chemical Engineering
TRINDER, J., Surveying and Spatial Information Systems
VALLIAPPAN, S., Civil and Environmental Engineering
WAITE, D., Civil and Environmental Engineering
WENHAM, S., Photovoltaic Engineering
YU, A., Materials Science and Engineering

Faculty of Law:
ARONSON, M., Law
BROWN, D., Law
BYRNES, A., Law
CUNNEEN, C., Law
DISNEY, J., Law
DIXON, D., Law
GREENLEAF, G., Law
KINGSFORD-SMITH, D., Law
KRYGIER, M., Law
REDMOND, P., Law
WILLIAMS, G., Law

Faculty of Medicine:
ANDERSON, D., Medicine
ANDREWS, J., Psychiatry
BARRY, P., Physiology
BENNETT, M., Obstetrics and Gynaecology
BRODATY, H., Psychiatry
CALVERT, G., Medicine
CAMPBELL, T., Medicine
CHESTERMAN, C., Medicine, Pathology

CHISHOLM, D., Medicine, Metabolic Research
CHONG, B., Medicine
COIERA, E., Medical Sciences
COOPER, D., Medicine
CORONEO, M., Ophthalmology
DAY, R., Medicine, Clinical Pharmacology
DEANE, S., Surgery
DICKSON, H., Rehabilitation, Aged and Extended Care
EISENBUCH, I., Medicine
EISMAN, J., Medicine, Bone and Mineral Research
GANDEVIA, S., Medicine
GECZY, C., Pathology
GRAHAM, R., Medicine
HALL, B., Medicine
HARRIS, M., Medicine
HARRISON, G., Anaesthetics
HARVEY, R., Medicine
HENRY, R., Paediatrics
HILLMAN, K., Anaesthetics and Intensive Care
HOGG, P., Pathology
HOLDEN, B. A., Optometry
HOWES, L., Medicine, Physiology
KALDOR, J., Epidemiology
KEARSLEY, J., Surgery
KHACHIGIAN, L., Pathology
KIPPAX, S., HIV Social Research Centre
KRILIS, S., Medicine
KUMAR, R., Pathology
LAWSON, J., Health Services Management
LEE, A., Medical Microbiology
LLOYD, A., Pathology
LORD, R., Surgery
LUMBERS, E., Physiology
MACDONALD, G., Medicine
MCLACHLAN, E., Physiology, Medical Research
MORRIS, D., Surgery
O'ROURKE, M., Medicine
O'SULLIVAN, W., Medical Biochemistry
PARKER, G., Psychiatry
POOLE, M., Surgery
RICHMOND, R., Medicine
ROTEM, A., Medical Education
ROWE, M., Physiology
RUSSELL, P., Medicine
SCHINDHELM, K., Biomedical Engineering
SILOVE, D., Psychiatry
TARANTOLA, D., Medicine
TORDA, T. A., Anaesthetics and Intensive Care
WAKEFIELD, D., Pathology
WHITE, L., Paediatrics
ZWAR, N., Paediatrics
ZWI, A., Paediatrics

Faculty of Science:
ADAMS, M., Biological, Earth and Environmental Science
BALLARD, J., Biotechnology and Biomolecular Science
BISHOP, R., Chemical Sciences
BLACK, D. ST C., Chemical Sciences
BRYANT, R., Psychology
CADOGAN, M., Physics
CAMPBELL, S., Physical, Environmental and Mathematical Sciences
CLARK, R., Physics
COOPER, D., Biological, Earth and Environmental Science
COUCH, W., Physics
COWLING, M., Mathematics
DADDS, M., Psychology
DAIN, S., Optometry
DAWES, W., Biotechnology and Biomolecular Science
DORAN, P., Biotechnology and Biomolecular Science
DUNSMUIR, W., Mathematics
ENGLAND, M., Mathematics
FLAMBAUM, V., Physics
FORGAS, J., Psychology
GAL, M., Physics

GILLAM, B., Psychology
GRAY, P., Biotechnology and Biomolecular Science
HIBBERT, D., Chemical Sciences
HUON, G., Psychology
JACKSON, W., Physical, Environmental and Mathematical Sciences
KEHOE, J., Psychology
KINGSFORD, R., Biological, Earth and Environmental Science
KJELLEBERG, S., Biotechnology and Biomolecular Science
LAMB, R., Chemical Sciences
LESLIE, L., Mathematics
LITTLE, F., Biotechnology and Biomolecular Science
LOVIBOND, P., Psychology
MCCONKEY, K., Psychology
MCLEAN, R., Physical, Environmental and Mathematical Sciences
MCMURTRIE, R., Biological, Earth and Environmental Science
MIDDLETON, J., Mathematics
NEILAN, B., Biotechnology and Biomolecular Science
NEILSON, D., Physics
PASK, C., Physical, Environmental and Mathematical Sciences
ROGERS, C., Mathematics
SAMMUT, R., Physical, Environmental and Mathematical Sciences
SIMMONS, M., Physics
SLOAN, I., Mathematics
STEINBERG, P., Biological, Earth and Environmental Science
STOREY, J., Physics
SUSHKOV, O., Physics
SUTHERLAND, C., Mathematics
SUTHERLAND, P., Mathematics
TAFT, M., Psychology
WAND, M., Mathematics
WARD, C., Biological, Earth and Environmental Science
WEBB, J., Physics
WILKINS, M., Biotechnology and Biomolecular Science
WOLFE, J., Physics

ASSOCIATE COLLEGES

Faculty of the College of Fine Arts: Selwyn St, Paddington, NSW 2021; tel. (2) 9385-0888; f. 1990 following merger of the City Art Institute and the Univ.; Dean and Dir IAN HOWARD.

University College, Australian Defence Force Academy: Northcott Drive, Campbell, ACT 2601; tel. (2) 6268-8111; f. 1981 by agreement between the Commonwealth of Australia and the Univ. of NSW; degree courses started 1986; Rector Prof. ROBERT KING; Exec. Officer T. HODSON.

ASSOCIATED INSTITUTE

Australian Graduate School of Management: Sydney, NSW 2052; tel. (2) 9931-9200; f. 1975; postgraduate MBA and PhD courses, residential courses for execs; 42 faculty mems; library of 25,000 vols; Dir Prof. ROBERT MCLEAN; publ. *Australian Journal of Management*, *AGSM Working Paper Series*.

UNIVERSITY OF NEWCASTLE

University Dr., Callaghan, NSW 2308
Telephone: (2) 4921-5000
Fax: (2) 4985-4200
E-mail: enquirycentre@newcastle.edu.au
Internet: www.newcastle.edu.au
Founded 1965
State control
Academic year: March to November (2 semesters)
Chancellor: Prof. TREVOR WARING

Vice-Chancellor and President: Prof. NICHO-
LAS SAUNDERS
Deputy Vice-Chancellor for Academic and
Global Relations: Prof. KEVIN McCONKEY
Deputy Vice-Chancellor for Research: MIKE
CALFORD
Deputy Vice-Chancellor for University Ser-
vices: Dr SUE GOULD
Pro-Vice-Chancellor, Central Coast Campus:
Dr STEPHEN CRUMP

Library: see under Libraries and Archives
Number of teachers: 800
Number of students: 26,956

Publications: *Cetus* (1 a year), *UniNews*

PRO-VICE-CHANCELLORS

Faculty of Business and Law: Prof. STEPHEN
NICHOLAS
Faculty of Education and Arts: Prof. T. LOVAT
Faculty of Engineering and Built Environ-
ment: Prof. JOHN CARTER
Faculty of Health: Prof. P. DUNKLEY
Faculty of Science and Information Technol-
ogy: Prof. B. HOGARTH

PROFESSORS

Faculty of Business and Law (internet www
.newcastle.edu.au/faculty/bus-law):

BATES, F., Law
BOYCE, G.
BRAY, M., Employment Studies
BURGESS, K.
CATLEY, B., Management
EASTON, S., Finance
MITCHELL, W., Economics
NICHOLAS, S., International Business
Strategy
O'CASS, A., Marketing
WINSEN, J., Commerce
WRIGHT, T., Law

Faculty of Education and Arts (internet www
.newcastle.edu.au/faculty/educ-arts):

ALBRIGHT, J., Education
ALLEN, M., Sociology and Anthropology
BOURKE, S., Education
CAREY, H., History
CRAIG, H., English
EMELJANOW, V., Drama
EWANS, M., Drama
FOLEY, D.
FOREMAN, P., Education
FUERY, P., Film, Media and Cultural Stud-
ies
GORE, J., Curriculum Teaching and Learn-
ing
GRAHAM, A., Fine Art
GRAY, M., Social Work
HOLBROOK, A.
LAURA, R., Education
LOVAT, T., Education
MAYNARD, J., Indigenous History
McDOWELL, J., Theology
PLOTNIKOFF, R.
SCOTT, J.
TARRANT, H., Classics
VELLA, R., Music
WEBB, S.

Faculty of Engineering and Built Environment (internet www.eng.newcastle.edu.au):

BETZ, R., Electrical and Computer Engin-
eering
CARTER, J., Geotechnical Engineering
DLUGOGORSKI, B., Chemical Engineering
EVANS, G., Chemical Engineering
FU, M., Electrical Engineering
GALVIN, K., Chemical Engineering
GOODWIN, G., Electrical Engineering
JAMESON, G., Chemical Engineering
JONES, M., Bulk Solids
KENNEDY, E., Chemical Engineering
KISI, E., Mechanical Engineering
LEHMANN, S., Architecture
MELCHERS, R., Civil Engineering
MIDDLETON, R., Electrical Engineering

MILLER, M., Computer Science and Soft-
ware Engineering
MOGHTADERI, B., Chemical Engineering
MOHEIMANI, S., Electrical and Computer
Engineering
MURCH, G., Materials Engineering
NINNESS, B., Electrical and Computer
Engineering
OSTWALD, M., Architecture
ROBERTS, A., Mechanical Engineering
SHENG, D., Civil Engineering
SLOAN, S., Civil Engineering
STEWART, M., Civil Engineering
WALL, T., Fuels and Combustion Engin-
eering

Faculty of Health (internet www.newcastle
.edu.au/faculty/health):

ASHMAN, L., Medical Biochemistry
ATTIA, J.
BAKER, A.
BURNS, G., Medical Biochemistry
BYLES, J.
CALFORD, M., Human Physiology
CALLISTER, R., Anatomy
DAY, T., Anatomy
DEANE, S.
D'ESTE, C., Public Health
DUNKLEY, P., Medical Biochemistry
FAHY, K., Nursing and Midwifery
FORBES, J.
FOSTER, P., Immunology and Microbiology
GARG, M., Pharmacy and Experimental
Pharmacology
GLEESON, M., Immunology
HAZELTON, M., Nursing
HENSLEY, M., Medicine
HIGGINS, I., Nursing
JONES, A.
JONES, K., Human Physiology
KEATINGE, D., Paediatrics
KELLY, B., Public Health
LI, S., Pharmacy and Experimental
Pharmacology
LUMBERS, E., Pharmacy and Experimental
Pharmacology
POND, D., Medical Practice and Population
Health
RIVETT, D., Physiotherapy
ROSTAS, J.
RYAN, S., Occupational Therapy
SANSON-FISHER, R., Public Health
SCOTT, R., Medical Genetics
SMITH, D., Occupational Health and Safety
SMITH, R.
ZARDAWI, I.

Faculty of Science and Information Technology (internet www.newcastle.edu.au/faculty/
science-it):

AITKEN, J., Biological Sciences
BOLAND, N., Mathematics
BORWEIN, J., Mathematics
DASTOOR, P., Physics
ERSKINE, W., Applied Sciences
GROF, C., Biological Sciences
HEATHCOTE, A., Psychology
HOGARTH, B.
JIN, J., Information Technology
KING, B., Physics
LAWRANCE, G., Chemistry
McCLUSKEY, A., Chemistry
McGUIRK, P., Geography and Environmen-
tal Studies
MENK, F., Physics
O'CONNOR, J., Physics
RAYNER, J., Statistics
RODGER, J., Biological Sciences
ROSE, R., Biological Sciences
STARTUP, M., Psychology
WILLIS, G., Mathematics

UNIVERSITY OF QUEENSLAND

Qld 4072
Brisbane, Qld 4072
Telephone: (7) 3365-1111
Fax: (7) 3365-1199
E-mail: admissionsenquiries@uq.edu.au
Internet: www.uq.edu.au

Founded 1910
Academic year: January to December (2
semesters, and summer semester)

Chancellor: JOHN STORY
Deputy Chancellor: Adjunct Prof. MARY D.
MAHONEY
Vice-Chancellor: Prof. PAUL GREENFIELD
Sr Deputy Vice-Chancellor: Prof. MICHAEL
KENIGER
Deputy Vice-Chancellor for Academic
Affairs: Prof. DEBORAH TERRY
Deputy Vice-Chancellor for External Rela-
tions: Prof. IAN ZIMMER
Deputy Vice-Chancellor for Int. Affairs: Dr
ANNA CICCARELLI
Deputy Vice-Chancellor for Research: Prof.
MAX LU
Pro-Vice-Chancellor: Prof. ALAN RIX
Pro-Vice-Chancellor for Advancement: CLARE
PULLAR
Pro-Vice-Chancellor for Research and Int.
Affairs: Prof. ALAN LAWSON
Exec. Dir of Operations: MAURIE McNARN
Pres. of Academic Board: Prof. SUSAN HAMIL-
TON
Univ. Sec. and Gen. Counsel: (vacant)
Librarian: KEITH WEBSTER

Library: see Libraries and Archives
Number of teachers: 2,615
Number of students: 40,583

Publication: *University News*

EXECUTIVE DEANS

Faculty of Arts: Prof. RICHARD FOTHERINGHAM
(acting)
Faculty of Business, Economics and Law:
Prof. TIM BRAILSFORD
Faculty of Engineering, Architecture and
Information Technology: Prof. GRAHAM
SCHAFFER
Faculty of Health Sciences: Prof. NICK FISK
Faculty of Natural Resources, Agriculture
and Veterinary Science: Prof. ROGER SWIFT
Faculty of Science: Prof. STEPHEN WALKER
Faculty of Social and Behavioural Sciences:
Prof. DAVID DE VAUS (acting)

PROFESSORS

Faculty of Arts (Room E206, Level 2, Forgan
Smith Bldg, St Lucia Campus, Qld 4072; tel.
(7) 3365-1333; fax (7) 3365-2866; e-mail
arts@uq.edu.au; internet www.arts.uq.edu
.au):

ALMOND, P. C., History of European Dis-
courses
BRACANIN, P., Music
CRYLE, P. M., History of European Dis-
courses
ELSON, R., History, Philosophy, Religion
and Classics
GRIFFITHS, P., History, Philosophy, Reli-
gion and Classics
HUNTER, I. R., History of European Dis-
courses
KELLY, V. E., English, Media Studies and
Art History
LATTKE, M. S., History, Philosophy, Reli-
gion and Classics
MOORHEAD, J. A., History, Philosophy,
Religion and Classics
O'REGAN, T., English, Media Studies and
Art History
SUSSEX, R. D., Languages and Comparative
Cultural Studies
TIFFIN, H. M., English, Media Studies and
Art History
TURNER, G., Critical and Cultural Studies

WHITLOCK, G., English, Media Studies and Art History

Faculty of Business, Economics and Law (Room 233, Level 2, Colin Clark Bldg, St Lucia Campus, Qld 4072; tel. (7) 3365-7111; fax (7) 3365-4788; e-mail facbel@bel.uq.edu.au; internet www.bel.uq.edu.au):

ALLAN, J. F. P., Law
ASHKANASY, N. M., Business
BALLANTYNE, R. R., Tourism
BRAILSFORD, T., Business
CALLAN, V. J., Business
CAMPBELL, H. F., Economics
CLARKSON, P., Business
COELLI, T., Economics
COOPER, C., Tourism
CORNWELL, T. B., Business
DE LACY, T., Tourism and Leisure Management
DEVEREUX, J., Law
DODGSON, M., Technology and Innovation Management
FINN, F. J., Business, Economics and Law
FOSTER, J., Economics
GRANTHAM, R. B., Law
GRAY, S., Business
KIEL, G. C., Business
LIESCH, P. W., Business
McCOLL-KENNEDY, J., Business
McLENNAN, A. M, Economics
MANGAN, J. E., Economics
MENEZES, F. M, Economics
O'KEEFE, T., Business
PURI, K., Law
QUIGGIN, J., Economics
RAO, P., Economics
RATNAPALA, A. S., Law
RICKETT, C., Law
SHERMAN, B. G., Law
TOURKY, R., Economics
WILTSHIRE, K. W., Business
ZHANG, J., Economics
ZIMMER, I., Business, Economics and Law

Faculty of Engineering, Architecture and Information Technology (Room S204, Level 2, Hawken Engineering Bldg, St Lucia Campus, Qld 4072; tel. (7) 3365-4777; fax (7) 3365-4444; e-mail admin@epsa.uq.edu.au; internet www.epsa.uq.edu.au):

ADAMS, P., Mathematics
ANDRESEN, B., Architecture
BAILES, P. A., Information Technology and Electrical Engineering
BELL, M. J., Geography, Planning and Architecture
BERGMANN, N., Information Technology and Electrical Engineering
BHATIA, S. K., Chemical Engineering
BIALKOWSKI, M. E., Information Technology and Electrical Engineering
BLACKALL, L. L., Advanced Wastewater Management Centre
BOYCE, R. R., Mechanical Engineering
BRACKEN, A. J., Mathematics
BREMHORST, K., Mechanical Engineering
BRERETON, D., Social Responsibility in Mining
BURRAGE, K., Advanced Computational Modelling Centre
CAMERON, I. T., Chemical Engineering
CHARLES, P. M., Civil Engineering
COLLERSON, K. D., Earth Sciences
CROZIER, S., Information Technology and Electrical Engineering
DARVENIZA, M., Information Technology and Electrical Engineering
DO, D. D., Chemical Engineering
DOBSON, A. J., Population Health
DRUMMOND, P. D., Physics
ECCLESTON, J. A., Physical Sciences
FRANZIDIS, J., Mineral Research Centre
GURGENCI, H., Mechanical Engineering
HAYES, I. J., Information Technology and Electrical Engineering
HECKENBERG, N. R., Physics

INDULSKA, J., Information Technology and Electrical Engineering
KELLER, J., Advanced Wastewater Management Centre
KNIGHTS, P. R., Mining and Minerals Process Engineering
LEVER, P. J. A., Mining and Minerals Process Engineering
LINDSAY, P., Information Technology and Electrical Engineering
McAREE, P. R., Mechanical Engineering
McLACHLAN, G. J., Mathematics
MEMMOTT, P. C., Geography, Planning and Architecture
MORGAN, R., Mechanical Engineering
NIELSEN, L. K., Chemical Engineering
PAILTHORPE, B., Physical Sciences
PANDOLFI, J. M., Earth Sciences
PHINN, S. R., Geography, Planning and Architecture
POLLETT, P. K., Mathematics
RUBINSZTEIN-DUNLOP, H., Physics
RUDOLPH, V., Chemical Engineering
SAHA, T. K., Information Technology and Electrical Engineering
SANDERSON, P., Information Technology and Electrical Engineering
SCHAFFER, G. B., Materials Engineering
SMART, M. K., Mechanical Engineering
STALKER, R. J., Mechanical Engineering
STROOPER, P. A., Information Technology and Electrical Engineering
WILES, J. H., Information Technology and Electrical Engineering
YUAN, Z., Advanced Water Management
ZHOU, X., Information Technology and Electrical Engineering

Faculty of Health Sciences (Level 1, Edith Cavell Bldg, Royal Brisbane Hospital, Herston, Qld; tel. (7) 3365-5342; fax (7) 3365-5533; e-mail healthsciences@uq.edu.au; internet www.uq.edu.au/health):

ABERNETHY, A. B., Human Movement Studies
BAKER, P. G., Medical
BATCH, J. A., Paediatrics and Child Health
BELLAMY, N., Population Health; Medicine
BETT, J., Medicine
BICKEL, M., Dentistry
BLACK, B., Surgery
BOYD, A. W., Experimental Haematology
BROOKS, P., Health Sciences
BROWN, W. J., Human Movement Studies
BURGESS, P., Health Systems Division
BUSH, R., Population Health
CAPRA, M. F., Health Sciences
CAPRA, S. M., Health Sciences
CATTS, S., Psychiatry
CHAN, J., Anaesthesiology and Critical Care
CHAPPELL, M. M., Anaesthesiology and Critical Care
CHENERY, H. J., Health Sciences
CLEGHORN, G. J., Medicine
COMAN, W. B., Surgery
CONNELLY, L. B., Medicine
COULTHARD, A., Medical Imaging
CRAWFORD, D. H., Medicine
CRAWFORD, G. S., Anaesthesiology and Critical Care
DASTAGIR, S. M. N., Anaesthesiology and Critical Care
DAVIS, C. A., Anaesthesiology and Critical Care
DING, Y., Anaesthesiology and Critical Care
DOBSON, A. J., Population Health
DOHERTY, B., Anaesthesiology and Critical Care
ELLIS, N. M., Centre for Military and Veterans' Health
FISK, N. R., Clinical Research
FLORIN, T. H., Medicine
GARDINER, R. A., Surgery

GEORGE, S. A., Anaesthesiology and Critical Care
GORDON, R. D., Medicine
GOTLEY, D., Surgery
GOUGH, I. R., Surgery
GRAY, L., Medicine
HEGNEY, D. G., Nursing and Midwifery
HENDY, R., Health Innovation and Solutions
HEWITT, L., Anaesthesiology and Critical Care
HICKSON, L. M. H., Health and Rehabilitation Sciences
HOSKING, J. A., Anaesthesiology and Critical Care
HOY, W. E., Medicine
ISOARDI, J. C., Anaesthesiology and Critical Care
ISOARDI, K., Anaesthesiology and Critical Care
JACKSON, C. L., Medicine
JOHNSON, D. W., Medicine
JULL, G. A., Health and Rehabilitation Sciences
KENARDY, J. A., Medicine
KOUDOS, P., Anaesthesiology and Critical Care
LAKHANI, S., Molecular and Cellular Pathology
LENTZ, A., Anaesthesiology and Critical Care
LOPEZ, A., Population Health
MACDONALD, D., Human Movement Studies
McINTYRE, H. D., Medicine
MARLEY, J. E., Health Sciences
MARTIN, G., Psychiatry
MARWICK, T., Medicine
MEYERS, I. A., Dentistry
MICHEL, C. A., Anaesthesiology and Critical Care
MONYPENNY, K., Anaesthesiology and Critical Care
MOSER, B., Anaesthesiology and Critical Care
MURDOCH, B. E., Health and Rehabilitation Sciences
NGUI, R. L. C., Population Health
NICHOLLS, K., Anaesthesiology and Critical Care
NIXON, J. W., Paediatrics and Child Health
OCHOLA, J., Anaesthesiology and Critical Care
OWEN, N., Population Health
PANDIE, M. Z., Anaesthesiology and Critical Care
PEARN, J. H., Medicine
PENDER, M. P., Medicine
ROBINSON, L., Health Innovation and Solutions
RYAN, A., Anaesthesiology and Critical Care
SEYMOUR, G. J., Dentistry
SHANNON, C. A., Health Sciences
SHAW, P. N., Pharmacy
SILBURN, P., Surgery
SMITH, M. T., Pharmacy
SOYER, H. P., Medicine
STEWART, D. J., Anaesthesiology and Critical Care
STITZ, R. W., Surgery
STRONG, J., Health and Rehabilitation Sciences
TAYLOR, R. J., Population Health
TETT, S., Pharmacy
TINNING, R. I., Human Movement Studies
TOTH, I., Pharmacy
TUDEHOPE, D. I., Paediatrics and Child Health
TURNER, C. T., Nursing and Midwifery
UNDERWOOD, M., Anaesthesiology and Critical Care
VENKATESH, B., Anaesthesiology and Critical Care
VICENZINO, G. T., Health and Rehabilitation Sciences

WALSH, L. J., Dentistry
WELSH, A., Anaesthesiology and Critical Care
WEST, M. J., Medicine
WHITEFORD, H. A., Health Systems
WILKINSON, D., Medicine
WILLIAMS, G. M., International Health
WILLIAMSON, F., Anaesthesiology and Critical Care
WILLS, C. M., Anaesthesiology and Critical Care
WOOTTON, R., Online Health
WORRALL, L. E., Health and Rehabilitation Sciences

Faculty of Natural Resources, Agriculture and Veterinary Science (N. W. Britton Admin. Bldg (No. 8101), Gatton Campus, Qld; tel. (7) 5460-1276; fax (7) 5460-1204; e-mail nravs.enquiries@uqg.uq.edu.au; internet www.uq.edu.au/nravs):

ANDERSON, G., Veterinary Science
BASFORD, K. E., Land, Crop and Food Sciences
BOSCH, O. J. H., Natural and Rural Systems Management
BRYDEN, W. L., Animal Studies
BURNS, R. G., Land, Crop and Food Sciences
D'OCCHIO, M., Beef Genetic Technologies
FUKAI, S., Land, Crop and Food Sciences
GIDLEY, M., Nutrition and Food Sciences
HAYNES, R. J., Land, Crop and Food Sciences
HILL, J., Veterinary Science
McGOWAN, M. R., Veterinary Science
MENZIES, N. W., Land, Crop and Food Sciences
PHILLIPS, C. J., Animal Welfare and Ethics
RAND, J. S., Veterinary Science
ROSS, H., Natural and Rural Systems Management
ROTHWELL, J., Veterinary Science
SWIFT, R. S., Natural Resources, Agriculture and Veterinary Science
WILLIAMS, R. R., Land, Crop and Food Sciences

Faculty of Science (Room 313, Level 3, Computer Science Bldg, St Lucia Campus, Qld 4072; tel. (7) 3365-1888; fax (7) 3365-1613; e-mail bacs.enquiries@uq.edu.au; internet bacs.uq.edu.au):

ADAMS, D. J., Biomedical Sciences
BIRCH, R., Integrative Biology
BOWLING, F., Molecular and Microbial Sciences
BROAD, T., Biological and Chemical Sciences
CAMPBELL, G. R., Biomedical Sciences
CAMPBELL, J. H., Bioengineering and Nanotechnology
CRITCHLEY, C., Integrative Biology
DEGNAN, B. M., Integrative Biology
DRENNAN, J., Microscopy and Microanalysis
GRESSHOFF, P. M., Integrative Legume Research
GRIGG, G. C., Integrative Biology
HOEGH-GULDBERG, O., Marine Studies
IRWIN, J. A. G., Integrative Biology, Tropical Plant Protection
JENNINGS, M. P., Molecular and Microbial Sciences
KEY, B., Biomedical Sciences
KITCHING, W., Molecular and Microbial Sciences
McEWAN, A., Molecular and Microbial Sciences
McMANUS, M. E., Biological and Chemical Sciences
MINCHIN, R., Biomedical Sciences
NORTON, G. A., Biological Information Technology
O'NEILL, S., Integrative Biology
PETTIGREW, J. D., Vision, Touch and Hearing Research

POSSINGHAM, H., Integrative Biology, Ecology Centre
SMITH, R. W., Molecular and Microbial Sciences
SMITH, S., Molecular and Microbial Sciences
TAYLOR, S. M., Biomedical Sciences
TINDLE, R. W., Clinical Medical Virology Centre
TOTH, I., Molecular and Microbial Sciences
TRAU, M., Bioengineering and Nanotechnology
WENTRUP, C., Molecular and Microbial Sciences
ZALUCKI, M. P., Integrative Biology

Faculty of Social and Behavioural Sciences (Room S423, Level 4, Social Sciences Bldg, St Lucia Campus, Qld 4072; tel. (7) 3365-7487; fax (7) 3346-9136; e-mail sbs@uq.edu.au; internet www.uq.edu.au/sbs):

ALEXANDER, N. M., Australian Centre for Peace and Conflict Studies
ASHMAN, A. F., Education
BALDAUF, R. B. J., Education
BAXTER, J. H., Social Science
BELL, S. R., Political Science and International Studies
BELLAMY, A. J., Political Science and International Studies
BLEIKER, R., Political Science and International Studies
BOREHAM, P., Political Science and International Studies; Social Research
BROMLEY, M. S., Journalism and Communication
GALLOIS, C., Psychology; Social Research in Communication
GILBERT, R. J., Education
GILLIES, R. M., Education
HUMPHREYS, M., Psychology; Human Factors and Applied Cognitive Psychology
KARGER, H., Social Work and Human Services
KENARDY, J. A., Psychology
LAWRENCE, G., Social Science
LEE, C., Psychology
MATTINGLEY, J. B., Psychology
NAJMAN, J. M., Social Science
OEI, T. P. S., Psychology
PETERSON, C. L., Psychology
POWER, C., Education
QUIGGIN, J., Economics
RENSHAW, P. D., Education
SANDERS, M. R., Psychology
SKRBIS, Z., Social Science
SOURDI, T. M., Australian Centre for Peace and Conflict Studies
STIMSON, R. J., Social Research
TRIGGER, D. S., Social Science
VON HIPPEL, W., Psychology
WESTERN, M. C., Social Science
WHITEHOUSE, G. M., Political Science and International Studies
WILSON, J. E., Social Work and Human Services

UNIVERSITY OF SOUTH AUSTRALIA

GPOB 2471, Adelaide, SA 5001
Telephone: (8) 8302-6611
Fax: (8) 8302-2466
Internet: www.unisa.edu.au

Founded 1991 by the merger of the South Australian Institute of Technology and three campuses of the South Australian College of Advanced Education; campuses at City East, City West, Magill, Mawson Lakes, Underdale and Whyalla

Autonomous (established by Act of Parliament)

Academic year: January to December

Chancellor: Dr IAN GOULD
Vice-Chancellor and Pres.: Prof. PETER HØJ

Exec. Dir and Vice-Pres. for Finance and Resources: PAUL BEARD
Exec. Dir and Vice-Pres. for Int. and Devt Affairs: Dr ANNA CICCARELLI
Pro-Vice-Chancellor for Access and Learning Support: Prof. PETER LEE
Pro-Vice-Chancellor for the Division of Business and Enterprise: Prof. GERRY GRIFFIN
Pro-Vice-Chancellor for Education, Arts and Social Sciences: Prof. PAL AHLUWALIA
Pro-Vice-Chancellor for the Division of Health Sciences: Prof. ROBYN McDERMOTT
Pro-Vice-Chancellor for the Division of Information Technology, Engineering and the Environment: Prof. ANDREW PARFITT
Pro-Vice-Chancellor for Organisational Strategy and Change: Prof. HILARY WINCHESTER
Pro-Vice-Chancellor for Research and Innovation: Prof. CAROLINE McMILLEN
Dir of Student and Academic Services: LUCY SCHULZ
Dir of Library Services: HELEN LIVINGSTON

Library: 1m. vols
Number of teachers: 983
Number of students: 34,391

Publication: UniSA Researcher (electronic, 6 a year).

UNIVERSITY OF SOUTHERN QUEENSLAND

Toowoomba, Qld 4350
Telephone: (7) 4631-2100
Fax: (7) 4631-2892
E-mail: international@usq.edu.au
Internet: www.usq.edu.au

Founded 1992 (fmrly the University College of Southern Queensland, founded 1991 from the Darling Downs Institute of Advanced Education)

State control

Academic year: January to December

Chancellor: DONALD STEVENS
Vice-Chancellor: Prof. WILLIAM LOVEGROVE
Deputy Vice-Chancellor for Academic and Global Learning: Prof. JAMES TAYLOR
Pro-Vice-Chancellor for Int. Quality: (vacant)
Pro-Vice-Chancellor for Learning and Teaching: Prof. MAURICE FRENCH
Pro-Vice-Chancellor for Planning and Quality: Prof. WILLIAM MacGILLIVRAY
Pro-Vice-Chancellor for Regional Engagement and Social Justice: Prof. FRANK CROWTHER
Pro-Vice-Chancellor for Research: Prof. GRAHAM BAKER
Provost, Wide Bay Campus: Dr KENNETH STOTT
Gen. Man., Univ. Services: STEVE TANZER
Librarian: M. McPHERSON

Library of 309,000 vols
Number of teachers: 480
Number of students: 26,500

DEANS

Faculty of Arts: Prof. M. FRENCH
Faculty of Business: Assoc. Prof. R. ST HILL
Faculty of Education: Prof. F. CROWTHER
Faculty of Engineering and Surveying: Prof. G. BAKER
Faculty of Sciences: Prof. W. MacGILLIVRAY
School of Transdisciplinary Graduate Studies and Continuing Education: Prof. A. BARNETT

PROFESSORS

BILLINGSLEY, J., Engineering and Surveying
ERWEE, R., Business
FOGARTY, G., Sciences
HEGNEY, D., Sciences
HORSFIELD, B., Arts
McMILLEN, D., Arts
ROBERTS, A., Sciences

Ross, D., Engineering and Surveying
SMITH, R., Engineering and Surveying
TERRY, P., Sciences
TRAN-CONG, T., Engineering and Surveying
VAN ERP, G., Engineering and Surveying

UNIVERSITY OF SYDNEY

Sydney, NSW 2006
Telephone: (2) 9351-2222
Fax: (2) 9351-3111
E-mail: info.centre@sydney.edu.au
Internet: www.usyd.edu.au
Founded 1850
Private control
Academic year: February to December
Chancellor: HE Prof. MARIE BASHIR
Deputy Chancellor: ALAN CAMERON
Vice-Chancellor and Principal: Dr MICHAEL SPENCE
Provost and Deputy Vice-Chancellor: Prof. STEPHEN GARTON
Deputy Vice-Chancellor for Education and Registrar: Prof. DERRICK ARMSTRONG
Deputy Vice-Chancellor for International Affairs: Prof. JOHN HEARN
Deputy Vice-Chancellor for Research: Prof. JILL TREWHELLA
Deputy Vice-Chancellor and CEO: Prof. ANN BREWER
General Counsel: RICHARD FISHER
Univ. Librarian: JOHN SHIPP
Chair. of Academic Bd: Assoc. Prof. PETER MCCALLUM

Library: see under Libraries and Archives
Number of teachers: 3,067
Number of students: 49,061

DEANS

Faculty of Agriculture, Food and Natural Resources: Prof. MARK ADAMS
Faculty of Architecture, Design and Planning: Prof. RICHARD HYDE (acting)
Faculty of Arts: Prof. DUNCAN IVISON
Faculty of Dentistry: Prof. CHRIS PECK
Faculty of Economics and Business: Prof. PETER WOLNIZER
Faculty of Education and Social Work: Prof. ROBERT J. TIERNEY
Faculty of Engineering and Information Technologies: Prof. ARCHIE JOHNSTON
Faculty of Health Sciences: Prof. GWYNNETH LLEWELLYN
Faculty of Law: Prof. GILLIAN TRIGGS
Faculty of Medicine: Prof. BRUCE ROBINSON
Faculty of Nursing and Midwifery: Prof. JILL WHITE
Faculty of Pharmacy: Prof. IQBAL RAMZAN
Faculty of Science: Prof. MITCHELL GUSS (acting)
Sydney College of the Arts: Prof. COLIN RHODES
Sydney Conservatorium of Music: Prof. KIM WALKER

PROFESSORS

Faculty of Agriculture, Food and Natural Resources (tel. (2) 9351-2935; fax (2) 9351-2945; e-mail dean.agriculture@usyd.edu.au):
COPELAND, L., Agriculture
GUEST, D., Horticulture
KENNEDY, I., Agricultural and Environmental Chemistry
MCBRATNEY, A., Soil Science
PARK, R., Cereal Rust Research
SHARP, P., Molecular Plant Breeding
SUTTON, B.
TRETHOWAN, R., Plant Breeding
Faculty of Architecture, Design and Planning (tel. (2) 9351-5924; fax (2) 9351-5665; e-mail slalor@arch.usyd.edu.au):
BLAKELY, E., Urban and Regional Planning
GERO, J., Design Science
HENEGHAN, T., Architecture

HYDE, R., Architectural Science
MAHER, M., Design Computing
Faculty of Arts (tel. (2) 9351-2206; fax (2) 9351-2045; e-mail dean@arts.usyd.edu.au):
School of Languages and Cultures:
DUNSTAN, H., Chinese Studies
EBIED, R., Arabic and Islamic Studies
NEWBIGIN, N., Italian Studies
RIEGEL, J., Languages and Cultures
SANKEY, M., French Studies
VICKERS, A., South East Asian Studies
YANG, M., Asian Studies
School of Letters, Art and Media:
BARNES, G., Medieval Literature
BENJAMIN, R., Art History and Aboriginal Art
CLARK, J., Asian Art History
CLUNIES-ROSS, M., English Language and Early English Literature
DIXON, R., Australian Literature
FOLEY, W., Linguistics
GAY, P., English Literature and Drama
MARTIN, J., Linguistics
School of Philosophical and Historical Inquiry:
ALDRICH, R., European History
CSAPO, E., Classics and Ancient History
FLETCHER, R., Theoretical and World Archaeology
GARTON, S., History
GATENS, M., Philosophy
GAUKROGER, S., History of Philosophy and History of Science
IVISON, D., Political Philosophy
MILLER, M., Classical Archaeology
POTTS, D., Middle Eastern Archaeology
PRICE, H., Philosophy
PROBYN, E., Gender and Cultural Studies
REDDING, P., Philosophy
SLUGA, G., International History
WATERHOUSE, R., Australian History
WHITE, S., American History
WILSON, P., Classics
School of Social and Political Sciences:
AUSTIN-BROOS, D., Anthropology
GILL, G., Government and Public Administration
HAGE, G., Anthropology
HUMPHREY, M., Sociology and Social Policy
JACKSON, M., Government and Public Administration
STILWELL, F., Political Economy
TIFFIN, R., Government and International Relations
WEISS, L., Government and International Relations
Faculty of Dentistry (tel. (2) 9351-8334; fax (2) 9211-5912; e-mail dean@dentistry.usyd.edu.au):
BLINKHORN, A., Dentistry
BRYANT, R., Conservative Dentistry
DARENDELILER, M., Orthodontics
KLINEBERG, I., Prosthodontics
MURRAY, G., Dentistry
SWAIN, M., Biomaterials Science
Faculty of Economics and Business (tel. (2) 9351-3084; fax (2) 9351-4433; e-mail dean@econ.usyd.edu.au):
ANDERSON, E., Decision Sciences
ARENI, C., Marketing
ASPROMOURGOUS, A., Economics
BREWER, A., Organizational Logistics
DEAN, G., Accounting
DUPONT, A., International Security
ELLIOTT, S., Information Systems
FRINO, A., Finance
GALLOP, G., Economics
GRANT, D., Organizational Studies
GRAY, S., International Business
GUTHRIE, J., Accounting
HENSHER, D., Management
JOHNSTONE, D., Finance

JONES, S., Accounting
LANSBURY, R., Work and Organizational Studies
MCKERN, B., International Business
MCLENNAN, A., Economics
O'CONNOR, M., Information Systems
PEARSON, G., Business Law
PITCHFORD, R., Economics
ROBERTS, J., Accounting
SENGUPTA, K., Economics
STOPHER, P., Transport Planning
STYLES, C., Marketing
TIPTON, B., International Business
WALKER, R., Accounting
WOLNIZER, P., Accounting
WOODLAND, A., Econometrics

Faculty of Education and Social Work (tel. (2) 9351-2422; fax (2) 9351-6217; e-mail dean@edfac.usyd.edu.au):
ARMSTRONG, D., Education and Social Work
CONNELL, R., Education and Social Work
FAWCETT, B., Education and Social Work
FREEBODY, P., Education and Social Work
GOODYEAR, P., Education and Social Work
JONES, P., Education and Social Work
MEAGHER, G., Education and Social Work
PALTRIDGE, B., Education and Social Work
REIMANN, P., Education and Social Work
SHERRINGTON, G., History of Education
WELCH, A., Education and Social Work

Faculty of Engineering and Information Technologies (tel. (2) 9351-4739; fax (2) 9351-2111; e-mail engineering@eng.usyd.edu.au):
School of Aerospace, Mechanical and Mechatronic Engineering:
ARMFIELD, S., Aerospace, Mechanical and Mechatronic Engineering
DURRANT-WHYTE, H., Aerospace, Mechanical and Mechatronic Engineering
MAI, Y., Aerospace, Mechanical and Mechatronic Engineering
MASRI, A., Aerospace, Mechanical and Mechatronic Engineering
NEBOT, E., Aerospace, Mechanical and Mechatronic Engineering
TANNER, R., Mechanical Engineering
TONG, L., Aerospace, Mechanical and Mechatronic Engineering
YE, L., Aerospace, Mechanical and Mechatronic Engineering
ZHANG, L., Aerospace, Mechanical and Mechatronic Engineering
School of Chemical and Biomolecular Engineering:
BARTON, G., Chemical and Biomolecular Engineering
COSTER, H., Chemical and Biomolecular Engineering
HAYNES, B., Chemical and Biomolecular Engineering
PETRIE, J., Chemical and Biomolecular Engineering
School of Civil Engineering:
HANCOCK, G., Steel Structures
RASMUSSEN, K., Civil Engineering
SMALL, J., Civil Engineering
School of Electrical and Information Engineering:
AGELIDIS, V., Power Engineering
EADES, P., Software Technology
FENG, D., Electrical and Information Engineering
JOHNSTON, R., Electrical and Information Engineering
MINASIAN, R., Electrical and Information Engineering
PATRICK, J., Language Technologies
VUCETIC, B., Electrical and Information Engineering
YAN, H., Electrical and Information Engineering

ZOMAYA, A., High Performance Computing, Networking and Internetworking

Faculty of Health Sciences (tel. (2) 9351-9161; fax (2) 9351-9412; e-mail fhsuginfo@usyd.edu.au):

BANATI, R., Medical Radiation Sciences
BOHIE, P., Work and Health
BUNDY, A., Occupational Therapy
EINFELD, S., Mental Health
FIATARONE SINGH, M., Exercise and Sport Science
KENDIG, H., Ageing and Health
KENNY, D., Psychology and Music
LLEWELLYN, G., Occupation and Leisure Sciences
MADDEN, R., Classification in Health
MAHER, C., Physiotherapy
MATHEWS, M., Ageing, Health and Disability
ONSLOW, M., Stuttering Research
REFSHAUGE, K., Physiotherapy
VEITCH, C., Community Health
WESTBROOK, J., Health Informatics

Faculty of Law (tel. (2) 9351-0351; fax (2) 9351-0200; e-mail info@law.usyd.edu.au):

ALLARS, M., Law
APPS, P., Public Economics in Law
ASTOR, H., Law
BENNETT, B., Health and Medical Law
BOER, B., Environmental Law
BURNS, L., Taxation Law
BUTT, P., Law
CARNEY, T., Law
CARTER, J., Commercial Law
COOPER, G., Taxation Law
CROCK, M., Public Law
FINDLAY, M., Law
GRAYCAR, R., Law
HILL, J., Law
KINLEY, D., Human Rights Law
MCCALLUM, R., Industrial Law
O'MALLEY, P., Law
PARKINSON, P., Law
SADURSKI, W., Legal Philosophy
STUBBS, J., Criminology
TRIGGS, G., Law
VANN, R., Law

Faculty of Medicine (tel. (2) 9351-6570; fax (2) 9351-3196; e-mail t.rubin@med.usyd.edu.au):

ALLEN, D., Physiology
ALLEN, R., Transplantation Surgery
ANDERSON, C., Stroke Medicine and Clinical Neuroscience
ARMSTRONG, B., Medicine
BANDLER, R., Anatomy and Pain Research
BARTER, P., Medicine
BAUMAN, A., Public Health (Behavioural Epidemiology and Health Promotion)
BAUR, L., Medicine
BAXTER, R., Medicine
BENNETT, M., Physiology
BEREND, N., Respiratory Medicine
BILLSON, F., Clinical Ophthalmology and Eye Health
BISHOP, J., Cancer Medicine
BLACK, J., Medicine
BOKEY, E., Colorectal Surgery
BOOY, R., Medicine
BOYCE, P., Psychological Medicine
BRAITHWAITE, A., Medicine
BRAND-MILLER, J., Medicine
BRITTON, W., Medicine
BURKE, D., Medicine
BYRNE, M., Developmental and Marine Biology
CAMERON, I., Rehabilitation Medicine
CAMPBELL, I., Molecular Biology
CARTER, J., Gynaecological Oncology
CASS, D., Paediatric Surgery
CATERSON, I., Human Nutrition
CELERMAJER, D., Scandrett Cardiology
CHAPMAN, S., Medicine
CHRISTIE, M., Medicine

CHRISTODOULOU, J., Medicine
CHRISTOPHERSON, R., Medicine
CISTULLI, P., Respiratory Medicine
CLARKE, S., Medicine
COATS, A., Medicine
COLAGIURI, S., Metabolic Health
COOK, D., Cellular Physiology
COUSINS, M., Anaesthesia and Pain Management
CRAIG, J., Clinical Epidemiology
CROSSLEY, M., Molecular Genetics
CUMMING, R., Epidemiology and Geriatric Medicine
CUNNINGHAM, A., Medicine
DAMPNEY, R., Cardiovascular Neuroscience
DANDONA, L., International Public Health
DAVIES, M., Medicine
DELBRIDGE, L., Surgery
DOS REMEDIOS, C., Medicine
DREHER, B., Visual Neuroscience
DUNN, S., Psychological Medicine
ELLIOTT, E., Paediatrics and Child Health
FAZEKAS, B., Medicine
FIELD, M., Medicine
FINFER, S., Medicine
FLETCHER, J., Surgery
FRASER, I., Reproductive Medicine
FREEDMAN, S., Cardiology
GAMBLE, J., Vascular Biology
GASKIN, K., Paediatric Nutrition
GEORGE, J., Gastroenterology and Hepatic Medicine
GIBSON, W., Otolaryngology
GILES, W., Medicine
GOTTLIEB, D., Haematology
GÖTZ, J., Molecular Biology
GRAU, G., Vascular Immunology
GUNNING, P., Medicine
GUSS, M., Structural Biology
HABER, P., Medicine
HALL, R., Medicine
HALLIDAY, G., Medicine
HANDELSMAN, D., Reproductive Endocrinology and Andrology
HARPER, C., Neuropathology
HARRIS, D., Medicine
HARRIS, J., Vascular Surgery
HAWKE, S., Medicine
HAZELL, P., Medicine
HEARN, M., Medicine
HICKIE, I., Psychiatry
HORVATH, J., Medicine
HUNT, N., Pathology
HUNYOR, S., Medicine
IRWIG, L., Epidemiology
JEREMY, R., Medicine
JOHNSTON, G., Pharmacology
KAM, C., Anaesthetics
KEECH, A., Medicine, Cardiology and Epidemiology
KEFFORD, R., Medicine
KEMP, A., Paediatric Allergy and Clinical Immunology
KIDD, M., General Practice
KING, N., Medicine
KUCHEL, P., Biochemistry
LAMBERT, T., Psychiatry
LE COUTER, D., Geriatric Medicine
LEEDER, S., Public Health and Community Medicine
LIDDLE, C., Clinical Pharmacology and Hepatology
LINDLEY, R., Geriatric Medicine
LUSBY, R., Surgery
LYLE, D., Rural Health
MCCAUGHAN, G., Gastroenterology and Hepatology
MCINTYRE, P., Medicine
MACINTYRE, R., Medicine
MACMAHON, S., Cardiovascular Medicine and Epidemiology
MCMINN, P., Infectious Diseases
MASON, R., Endocrine Physiology
MAY, J., Surgery
MELLIS, C., Medicine
MINDEL, A., Sexual Health Medicine

MITCHELL, R., Medicine
MITROFANIS, J., Medicine
MORRIS, B., Physiology (Molecular Hypertension)
MORRIS, J., Obstetrics and Gynaecology
MURPHY, C., Histology and Embryology
NANAN, R., Paediatrics
NICHOLSON, G., Medicine
NORTH, K., Paediatrics and Child Health
NORTON, R., Public Health
NUTBEAM, D., Medicine
O'BRIEN, C., Medicine
OUVRIER, R., Paediatric Neurology
PARMENTER, T., Developmental Disability
PEEK, M., Medicine
POLLARD, J., Neurology
POLLOCK, C., Medicine
RASKO, J., Medicine
RASMUSSEN, H., Cardiology
REDDEL, R.
REEVES, P., Microbiology
REICHARDT, J., Molecular Biology (Molecular Medicine)
RICHARDSON, D., Medicine
ROBINSON, B., Medicine (Endocrinology)
ROBINSON, P., Medicine
RUSSELL, P., Medicine
RUSSELL, R., Medical Entomology
RYE, K., Medicine
SALKELD, G., Public Health
SAMBROOK, P., Rheumatology
SEALE, J., Clinical Pharmacology
SEIBEL, M., Endocrinology
SILINK, M., Medicine
SILLENCE, D., Medical Genetics
SIMES, J., Medicine
SIMPSON, J., Biostatistics
SMITH, R., Medicine
SONNABEND, D., Orthopaedic and Traumatic Surgery
SORRELL, T., Clinical Infectious Diseases
STEVENSON, M., Injury Prevention
STOCKER, R., Biochemistry in Vascular Medicine
STONE, J., Retinal and Cerebral Neurobiology
SULLIVAN, C., Medicine
TAM, P., Medicine
TARNOW-MORDI, W., Neonatal Medicine
TATTERSALL, M., Cancer Medicine
THOMPSON, J., Melanoma and Surgical Oncology
TOFLER, G., Preventive Cardiology
TONKIN, M., Hand Surgery
TRENT, R., Medical Molecular Genetics
TREWHELLA, J., Medicine
TRUDINGER, B., Obstetrics and Gynaecology
TRUSCOTT, R., Medicine
USHERWOOD, T., General Practice
VADAS, M., Cancer Medicine and Cell Biology
VAN ASPEREN, P., Paediatric Respiratory Medicine
VAN ZANDWIJK, N., Asbestos Disease
WALL, J., Medicine
WALTER, G., Child and Adolescent Psychiatry
WANG, S., Radiology
WATERHOUSE, P., Medicine
WEBSTER, W., Medicine
WEISS, A., Medicine
WENINGER, W., Dermatology
WILEY, J., Medicine (Haematology)
WILLIAMS, L., Cognitive Neuropsychiatry
YUE, D., Kellion Endocrinology

Faculty of Nursing and Midwifery (tel. (2) 9351-0663; fax (2) 9351-0508; e-mail nursing.enquiries@usyd.edu.au):

LAWLER, J., Nursing
RUDGE, T., Nursing
WHITE, J., Nursing
WHITE, K., Nursing

Faculty of Pharmacy (tel. (2) 9351-2320; fax (2) 9351-4391; e-mail enquiries@pharm.usyd .edu.au):

  ARMOUR, C., Pharmacy
  BENRIMOJ, S., Pharmacy Practice
  BRIEN, J., Clinical Pharmacy
  CHAN, H., Pharmaceutics (Advanced Drug Delivery)
  MCLACHLAN, A., Pharmacy (Aged Care)
  MURRAY, M., Pharmacogenomics (Pharmaceutics)
  RAMZAN, I., Pharmaceutics
  ROUFOGALIS, B., Pharmaceutical Chemistry
  WHITE, L., Pharmacy Management

Faculty of Science (tel. (2) 9351-4123; fax (2) 9351-4124; e-mail dean@science.usyd.edu .au):

          School of Biological Sciences:
  CHAPMAN, G., Marine Ecology
  DICKMAN, C., Terrestrial Ecology
  OLDROYD, B., Behavioural Genetics
  OVERALL, R., Plant Cell Biology
  PARKER, A., Biological Sciences
  SHINE, R., Biological Sciences
  SIMPSON, S., Biological Sciences
  SKURRAY, R., Biology (Genetics)
  THOMPSON, M., Zoology
  UNDERWOOD, A., Experimental Ecology
  WATERHOUSE, P., Biological Sciences

          School of Chemistry:
  CROSSLEY, M., Chemistry (Organic Chemistry)
  HAMBLEY, T., Chemistry
  HARROWELL, P., Chemistry
  KABLE, S., Chemistry
  LAY, P., Chemistry (Inorganic Chemistry)
  WARR, G., Chemistry

          School of Geosciences:
  CLARKE, G., Geosciences
  CONNELL, J., Geosciences
  HATHERLY, P., Mining Geophysics
  HIRSCH, P., Geosciences

     School of Mathematics and Statistics:
  CANNON, J., Mathematical Statistics
  DANCER, E., Pure Mathematics
  JOSHI, N., Applied Mathematics
  ROBINSON, J., Mathematical Statistics
  WEBER, N., Mathematical Statistics

    School of Molecular and Microbial Biosciences:
  BRAND-MILLER, J., Molecular and Microbial Biosciences
  CAMPBELL, I., Molecular Biology
  CATERSON, I., Human Nutrition
  CHRISTOPHERSON, R., Molecular and Microbial Biosciences
  CROSSLEY, M., Molecular and Microbial Biosciences
  KUCHEL, P., Molecular and Microbial Biosciences
  REEVES, P., Molecular and Microbial Biosciences
  WEISS, A., Molecular and Microbial Biosciences

          School of Physics:
  BALDOCK, C., Medical Physics
  BEDDING, T., Astrophysics
  CAIRNS, I., Physics
  DE STERKE, M., Theoretical Physics
  GREEN, A., Physics
  HUNSTEAD, R., Astrophysics
  LENZEN, M., Astrophysics
  MCKENZIE, D., Physics (Material Physics)
  MCPHEDRAN, R., Physics (Electromagnetic Physics)
  MELROSE, D., Physics
  SADLER, E., Physics
  VLADIMIROV, S., Physics

          School of Psychology:
  ANDREWS, S., Psychology
  BLASZCZYNSKI, A., Psychology
  BUTOW, P., Psychology

  MCGREGOR, I., Psychology
  TOUYZ, S., Clinical Psychology

Faculty of Veterinary Science (tel. (2) 9351-8783; fax (2) 9351-3056; e-mail vetsci@vetsci .usyd.edu.au):

  CANFIELD, P., Veterinary Science
  EVANS, G., Veterinary Science
  FULKERSON, W., Veterinary Science
  HUSBAND, A., Veterinary Science
  JEFFCOTT, L., Veterinary Science
  MAXWELL, C., Veterinary Science
  MORAN, C., Veterinary Science
  RAADSMA, H., Veterinary Science
  WARD, M., Veterinary Science
  WHITTINGTON, R., Veterinary Science

Sydney College of the Arts (tel. (2) 9351-1002; fax (2) 9351-119; e-mail sca@usyd.edu .au):

  DUNN, R., Contemporary Visual Art
  RHODES, C., Art

Sydney Conservatorium of Music (tel. (2) 9351-1255; fax (2) 9351-1202; e-mail info@ greenway.usyd.edu.au):

  BOYD, A., Music
  CHARTERIS, R., Historical Musicology
  MARETT, A., Music
  PALLÓ, I., Conducting
  WALKER, K., Music

ATTACHED COLLEGES

Sydney College of the Arts: Dir Prof. RON NEWMAN.

Sydney Conservatorium of Music: Principal Prof. S. E. PRETTY.

UNIVERSITY OF TASMANIA

Hobart campus: POB 252C-52, Hobart, Tas. 7001
Burnie campus: POB 447, Burnie, Tas. 7320
Launceston campus: Locked Bag 1, Launceston, Tas. 7250

Telephone: Hobart campus, (3) 6226-2999; Burnie campus, (3) 6430-4999; Launceston campus, (3) 6324-3999
Fax: Hobart campus, (3) 6226-7871; Burnie campus, (3) 6430-4950; Launceston campus, (3) 6324-3799
E-mail: course.info@utas.edu.au
Internet: www.utas.edu.au
Founded 1991 through merger of the University of Tasmania (f. 1890) and the Tasmanian State Institute of Technology
Academic year: February to October (2 terms)

Chancellor: Dr DAMIAN BUGG
Vice-Chancellor and Principal: Prof. D. LE GREW
Deputy Vice-Chancellor: ROD ROBERTS YVONNE RUNDLE
Pro-Vice-Chancellor for Research: Prof. JOHANNA LAYBOURN-PARRY
Pro-Vice-Chancellor for Teaching and Learning: Prof. GAIL HART
Exec. Dir of Finance and Admin.: A. FERRALL
Academic Registrar: C. P. CARSTENS
Librarian: L. L. LUTHER

Library: see under Libraries and Archives
Number of teachers: 800
Number of students: 18,108

Publication: *Law Review*

DEANS

Faculty of Arts: Prof. SUSAN DODDS
Faculty of Commerce: Prof. P. G. H. CARROLL
Faculty of Education: Prof. IAN HAY
Faculty of Health Science: Prof. A. CARMICHAEL
Faculty of Law: Prof. D. R. C. CHALMERS
Faculty of Science, Engineering and Technology: Prof. J. B. REID
Board of Graduate Studies by Research: Assoc. Prof. C. J. DENHOLM

PROFESSORS
at Hobart campus:

Faculty of Arts (PMB 44, Hobart, Tas. 7001; tel. (3) 6226-1874; fax (3) 6226-7842; e-mail n .foster@utas.edu.au; internet www.arts.utas .edu.au):

  BENNETT, M. J., History and Classics
  BLAND, R., Sociology
  FRANKHAM, N. H., Fine Art
  KELLOW, A. J., Government
  KNEHANS, D., Music
  MALPAS, J. E., Philosophy
  PAKULSKI, J., Sociology
  REYNOLDS, H., History and Classics
  WHITE, R., Sociology and Social Work

Faculty of Commerce (PMB 84, Hobart, Tas. 7001; tel. (3) 6226-2160; fax (3) 6226-2170; e-mail course.info@utas.edu.au; internet www.utas.edu.au/commerce/):

  CARROLL, P. G. H., Accounting and Finance
  GODFREY, J., Accounting and Finance
  KEEN, C. D., Information Systems
  RAY, R., Economics

Faculty of Education (Locked Bag 1308, Launceston, Tas. 7250; tel. (3) 6324-3446; fax (3) 6324-3303; e-mail secretary@utas.edu .au; internet www.educ.utas.edu.au):

  ARNOLD, R. M., Empathic Intelligence and Pedagogy
  HOGAN, D. J., Sociology of Education
  MULFORD, W. R., Educational Leadership
  WILLIAMSON, J. C., Teaching Studies and Teacher Education

Faculty of Health Science (POB 252C-99, Hobart, Tas. 7001; tel. (3) 6226-4757; fax (3) 6226-4747; e-mail shssec@utas.edu.au; internet www.healthsci.utas.edu.au):

  CARMICHAEL, A., Paediatrics and Child Health
  CLARK, M. G., Biochemistry
  CLEMENT, C., Obstetrics and Gynaecology
  DWYER, T., Population Health
  KIRKBY, K. C., Psychiatry
  MUDGE, P., General Practice
  PETERSON, G., Pharmacy
  STANTON, P. D., Surgery
  VICKERS, J. C., Pathology
  WALTERS, H., Medicine

Faculty of Law (PMB 89, Hobart, Tas. 7001; tel. (3) 6226-2066; fax (3) 6226-7623; e-mail secretary@law.utas.edu.au; internet www .law.utas.edu.au):

  CHALMERS, D. R. C., Law
  WARNER, C. A., Law

Faculty of Science, Engineering and Technology (PMB 50, Hobart, Tas. 7001; tel. (3) 6226-2125; fax (3) 6226-7809; e-mail alex .hamiltonsmith@utas.edu.au; internet www .utas.edu.au/scieng):

  BUDD, W. F., Antarctic and Southern Ocean Environment
  BULLEN, F., Engineering
  BUXTON, C. D., Aquaculture and Fisheries
  CANTY, A. J., Chemistry
  CLARK, R. J., Agricultural Science
  CRAWFORD, A., Earth Sciences
  DAVIS, M. R., Civil and Mechanical Engineering
  FORBES, L., Mathematics
  GRIFFIN, R., Cooperative Research Centre for Sustainable Production Forestry
  HADDAD, P. R., Chemistry
  JOHNSON, C., Zoology
  KIRKPATRICK, J. B., Geography and Environmental Studies
  LARGE, R. R., Earth Sciences
  MCMEEKIN, T. A., Agricultural Science
  NGUYEN, D. T., Electrical Engineering and Computer Science
  REID, J. B., Plant Science
  SALE, A., Computing
  SUMMERS, J. J., Psychology

VANCLAY, F., Agricultural Science

at Launceston campus:

Faculty of Arts (PMB 44, Hobart, Tas. 7001; tel. (3) 6226-1874; fax (3) 6226-7842; e-mail n.foster@utas.edu.au; internet www.arts.utas.edu.au):

BLAND, R., Sociology and Social Work
HATLEY, B., Asian Languages and Studies
McGRATH, V. F., Visual and Performing Arts

Faculty of Education (Locked Bag 1308, Launceston, Tas. 7250; tel. (3) 6324-3446; fax (3) 6324-3303; e-mail secretary@utas.edu.au; internet www.educ.utas.edu.au):

MULFORD, W. R., Educational Leadership
WILLIAMSON, J. C., Secondary and Post-compulsory Education

Faculty of Health Science (PMB 99, Hobart, Tas. 7001; tel. (3) 6226-4757; fax (3) 6226-4747; e-mail shssec@utas.edu.au; internet www.healthsci.utas.edu.au):

BALL, M., Biomedical Science
FARRELL, G., Nursing
WALKER, J. H., Rural Health

Faculty of Science, Engineering and Technology (PMB 50, Hobart, Tas. 7001; tel. (3) 6226-2125; fax (3) 6226-7809; e-mail alex.hamiltonsmith@utas.edu.au; internet www.utas.edu.au/scieng):

CHOI, Y. J., Computing
FAY, R., Architecture and Urban Design
PANKHURST, N. W., Aquaculture

UNIVERSITY OF TECHNOLOGY, SYDNEY

POB 123, Broadway, Sydney, NSW 2007
Telephone: (2) 9514-2000
Fax: (2) 9514-1551
E-mail: info.office@uts.edu.au
Internet: www.uts.edu.au

Founded 1965 as NSW Institute of Technology; university status 1988
Academic year: March to December

Chancellor: Prof. VICKI SARA
Deputy Chancellor: KENNETH RENNIE
Vice-Chancellor and President: Prof. ROSS MILBOURNE
Deputy Vice-Chancellor and Vice-Pres. for Academic Affairs: Prof. PETER BOOTH
Pro-Vice-Chancellor and Vice-Pres. for Teaching and Learning: Prof. RICHARD. A. JOHNSTONE
Pro-Vice-Chancellor and Vice-Pres. for Research: Prof. SUSAN ROWLEY
Pro-Vice-Chancellor and Vice-Pres. for International Relations: Prof. DAVID GOODMAN
Registrar: Dr JEFF M. FitzGERALD
Librarian: ALEX BYRNE

Library of 626,983 vols, 37,929 e-journals, 3,775 print journals
Number of teachers: 809 (full-time)
Number of students: 32,254

Publications: *CREArTA* (research and education in the arts, 2 a year), *Cultural Studies Review* (published jtly with Univ. of Melbourne; 2 a year), *Form/Work* (irregular), *Literacy and Numeracy Studies* (education and training of adults, 2 a year), *Locality* (3 a year), *Pacific Rim Property Research Journal* (4 a year), *Public History Review* (1 a year), *UTS Law Review* (1 a year), *UTS Writer's Anthology* (1 a year)

DEANS

Faculty of Arts and Social Sciences: Prof. THEO VAN LEEUWEN
Faculty of Business: Prof. ROY GREEN
Faculty of Design, Architecture and Building: Prof. DESLEY LUSCOMBE

Faculty of Education: Prof. SHIRLEY ALEXANDER
Faculty of Engineering and Information Technology: Prof. ARCHIE JOHNSTON
Faculty of Law: Prof. JILL McKEOUGH
Faculty of Nursing, Midwifery and Health: Prof. JOHN DALY
Faculty of Science: Prof. BRUCE MILTHORPE

UNIVERSITY OF THE SUNSHINE COAST

Locked Bag 4, Maroochydore D.C., Qld 4558
Sippy Downs Dr., Sippy Downs, Qld 4556
Telephone: (7) 5430-1234
Fax: (7) 5430-1111
E-mail: information@usc.edu.au
Internet: www.usc.edu.au

Founded 1996
Academic year: February to December

Vice-Chancellor: Prof. PAUL THOMAS
Deputy Vice-Chancellor: Prof. GREG HILL
Pro-Vice-Chancellor: Prof. ROBERT ELLIOT

Number of teachers: 123 full-time
Number of students: 6,570

DEANS

Faculty of Arts and Social Sciences: Prof. PAM DYER
Faculty of Business: Prof. EVAN J. DOUGLAS
Faculty of Science, Health and Education: Prof. ROD SIMPSON

PROFESSORS

Faculty of Arts and Social Sciences:
ELLIOT, R.
LAMBLE, S.
SCOTT, J.

Faculty of Business:
DOUGLAS, E. J.
HEDE, A.
RALSTON, D.

Faculty of Science, Health and Education:
LOWE, J.
MEYERS, N.
SIMPSON, R.

ATTACHED RESEARCH INSTITUTES

Centre for Healthy Activities, Sport and Exercise (CHASE): Sippy Downs, Qld; tel. (7) 5459-4656; fax (7) 5459-4682; e-mail chase@usc.edu.au; internet www.usc.edu.au/chase; Dir Assoc. Prof. BRENDAN BURKETT.

Centre for Multicultural and Community Development: tel. (7) 5430-1259; fax (7) 5430-2859; e-mail ngopalkr@usc.edu.au; Dir NARAYAN GOPALKRISHNAN.

National Seniors Productive Ageing Centre: POB 1450, Brisbane, Qld 4001; tel. (7) 3321-7074; fax (7) 3321-9339; e-mail info@productiveageing.com.au; internet www.productiveageing.com.au; Dir (vacant).

UNIVERSITY OF WESTERN AUSTRALIA

35 Stirling Highway, Crawley, WA 6009
Telephone: (8) 6488-6000
Fax: (8) 6488-1380
E-mail: general.enquiries@uwa.edu.au
Internet: www.uwa.edu.au

Founded 1911
Academic year: February to October

Chancellor: Dr MICHAEL CHANEY
Pro-Chancellor: Dr PENELOPE FLETT
Vice-Chancellor: Prof. ALAN ROBSON
Sr Deputy Vice-Chancellor: Prof. BILL LOUDEN
Deputy Vice-Chancellor for Research: Prof. ROBYN OWENS
Exec. Dir of Academic Services and Registrar: PETER CURTIS

Exec. Dir of Finance and Resources: GAYE McMATH
Univ. Librarian and Dir of Information Management: Dr MARY DAVIES

Number of teachers: 1,445
Number of students: 22,590

Publication: *Research Expertise*

DEANS

Faculty of Architecture, Landscape and Visual Arts: Prof. SIMON ANDERSON
Faculty of Arts, Humanities and Social Sciences: Prof. KRISHNA SEN
Faculty of Business: Prof. TRACEY HORTON
Faculty of Education: Prof. HELEN WILDY
Faculty of Engineering, Computing and Mathematics: Prof. JOHN DELL
Faculty of Law: Prof. WILLIAM FORD
Faculty of Life and Physical Sciences: Prof. GEORGE STEWART
Faculty of Medicine, Dentistry and Health Sciences: Prof. IAN PUDDEY
Faculty of Natural and Agricultural Sciences: Prof. TONY O'DONNELL
Graduate Research School: Prof. ALAN DENCH
School of Indigenous Studies: Prof. JILL MILROY

PROFESSORS

ABBOTT, L. K., Soil Science and Plant Nutrition
ABBOTT, P. V., Clinical Dentistry
ACKLAND, T. R., Human Movement and Exercise Science
ALMEIDA, O. P., Geriatric Psychiatry
ANDERSON, M., Psychology
ANDRICH, D., Education
ARNOLDA, L. F., Cardiology
ATKINS, C. A., Plant Biology
ATLAS, M. D., Otolaryngology
BADCOCK, D. R., Psychology
BADDELEY, A. J., Mathematics and Statistics
BARLEY, M. E., Earth and Geographical Sciences
BARTLETT, R. H., Law
BASSOM, A., Mathematics and Statistics
BEAZLEY, L. D., Animal Biology
BEILIN, L. J., Medicine
BENNAMOUN, M., Computer Science and Software Engineering
BERNERS-PRICE, S. J., Biological Chemistry
BLAIR, D. G., Physics
BOSWORTH, A. B., Classics and Ancient History
BOSWORTH, R. J. B., History
BOWDLER, S., Archaeology
BRUCE, D. G., Medicine
BUSH, M., Mechanical Engineering
CANTONI, A., Electrical and Electronic Engineering
CASSIDY, M., Offshore Foundation Systems
CAWOOD, P., Tectonic Special Research Centre
CHENG, L., Civil and Resource Engineering
CHISHOLM, J. S., Anatomy and Human Biology
CHRISTIANSEN, F. T., Pathology
CLEMENTS, K. W., Economics
CONSTABLE, I. J., Ophthalmology and Visual Science
CORAM, A. T., Political Science and International Relations
CORDERY, J. L., Management
CROFT, K. D., Medicine
DA SILVA ROSA, R., Financial Studies
DAVIDSON, J. W., Music
DAVIS, T. M. E., Medicine
DAWSON, B. T., Human Movement and Exercise Science
DEEKS, A. J., Civil and Resource Engineering
DELL, J. M., Electrical, Electronic and Computer Engineering
DENCH, A. C., Linguistics
DENTITH, M. C., Geology

DHARMARAJAN, A. M., Anatomy and Human Biology
DYSKIN, A. V., Civil and Resource Engineering
ELLIOTT, B. C., Human Movement and Exercise Science
EMERY, J., General Practice
FAHEY, M., Civil Engineering
FARAONE, L., Electrical and Electronic Engineering
FINN, J. C., Population Health
FORD, W. J., Law
GILES-CORTI, B., Population Health
GILKES, R. J., Soil Science
GRIFFITHS, G., English and Cultural Studies
GROUNDS, M. D., Anatomy and Human Biology
GROVE, J. R., Human Movement and Exercise Science
HALL, J. C., Surgery
HAMMOND, G. R., Psychology
HANDFORD, P. R., Law
HAO, H., Civil and Resource Engineering
HARTMANN, P. E., Biochemistry
HARVEY, A. R., Anatomy and Human Biology
HASKELL, D. J., English
HICKEY, M., Gynaecology
HOLMAN, D., Population Health
HOUGHTON, S. J., Education
HULSE, G. K., Alcohol and Drug Studies
HURLE, B., Oil and Gas Engineering
IMBERGER, J., Water Research
IVEY, G. N., Environmental Systems Engineering
IZAN, H. Y., Financial Studies
JABLENSKY, A. V., Psychiatry
JANCA, A., Psychiatry
JEFFREY, G. P., Medicine
JOHNSON, M. S., Animal Biology
KAKULAS, B. A., Neuropathology
KENNEDY, D. L., Classics and Ancient History
KIRK, T. B., Mechanical Engineering
KIRSNER, P. K., Psychology
KLINKEN, S. P., Clinical Biochemistry
KNUIMAN, M. W., Population Health
LAMBERS, J. T., Plant Biology
LAUTENSCHLAGER, N. T., Geriatric Psychiatry
LEEDMAN, P. J., Cancer Medicine
LEHANE, B. M., Civil and Resource Engineering
LESOUËF, P. N., Paediatrics
LEVINE, M. P., Philosophy
LEWANDOWSKY, S., Psychology
LIU, Y., Materials Engineering
LONDON, G. L., Architecture
LOUDEN, W. R., Education
LOVALLO, D., Management
MCALEER, M., Economics
MCCORMICK, P. G., Materials Engineering
MCEACHERN, D., Research and Innovation
MCGEACHIE, J. K., Anatomy and Human Biology
MACLEOD, C., Psychology
MCMENAMIN, P. G., Anatomy and Human Biology
MCSHANE, S. L., Management
MADDERN, P. C., History
MARTIN, G. B., Animal Biology
MASTAGLIA, F. L., Neurology
MILLER, K., Mechanical Engineering
MILLER, P. W., Economics
MILLWARD, M. J., Clinical Cancer Care
MILNE, G. J., Computer Science and Software Engineering
MITCHELL, H. W., Physiology
MIZERSKI, R. W., Marketing
MORAHAN, G., Diabetes Research
MORGAN, N. A., Law
MURDOCH, C., Rural and Remote Medicine
NEWNHAM, J. P., Maternal–Foetal Medicine
NIVBRANT, B., Surgery
NOAKES, J. L., Mathematics
NORMAN, P. E., Surgery
NURCOMBE, B., Paediatrics
O'DONOGHUE, T. A., Education
O'DONOVAN, J., Law

OLYNYK, J. K., Gastroenterology
OWENS, R. A., Computer Science
PAECH, M., Anaesthesia
PALMER, L., Population Health
PAN, J., Mechanical Engineering
PANNELL, D. J., Agriculture
PATTIARATCHI, C., Water Research
PAUWELS, A., Linguistics
PLATELL, C. F., Surgery
PLOWMAN, D. H., Management
PORTER, P. H., Int. Relations
POULSEN, D. G., Music
PRAEGER, C. E., Pure Mathematics
PRESCOTT, S. L., Paediatrics
PUDDEY, I., Medicine
PUNCH, K. F., Education
RAKOCZY, P. E., Ophthalmology and Visual Science
RANDOLPH, M. F., Civil Engineering
RASTON, C. L., Chemistry
RAVINE, D., Medical Genetics
REGENAUER-LIEB, K., Earth and Geographical Sciences
RENGEL, Z., Soil Science and Plant Nutrition
RHODES, G., Psychology
RILEY, T. V., Microbiology
ROBERTS, J. D., Animal Biology
ROBERTSON, A., Research Initiatives
ROBERTSON, D., Physiology
ROBINSON, B. W. S., Medicine
ROBSON, A. D., Soil Science and Plant Nutrition
SAMPSON, D. D., Electrical and Electronic Engineering
SAUNDERS, C. M., Surgery
SCHMITT, L. H., Anatomy and Human Biology
SHARDA, H., Electrical, Electronic and Computer Engineering
SHELLAM, G. R., Microbiology
SIDDIQUE, K., Agriculture
SIMMER, K., Paediatrics
SINGER, K. P., Surgery
SIVASITHAMPARAM, K., Agriculture
SMETTEM, K. R., Environmental Systems Engineering
SOUTAR, G. N., Management
SPACKMAN, M. A., Chemistry
STACEY, M. C., Vascular Surgery
STACHOWIAK, G. W., Mechanical Engineering
STANLEY, F. J., Paediatrics
STARKSTEIN, S. E., Psychiatry
STEWART, G., Life and Physical Sciences
STEWART, G. A., Microbiology and Immunology
STICK, R., Chemistry
STOCKPORT, G. J., Management
STONE, B. J., Mechanical Engineering
SWEENEY, J. C., Marketing
TAPLIN, J. H. E., Information Management
TAYLOR, W. M., Architecture
TENNANT, M., Oral Biology
TREVELYAN, J. P., Mechanical Engineering
TURKINGTON, D. A., Economics
VENVILLE, G., Education
VRIELINK, A., Biochemistry and Molecular Biology
WADDELL, B. J., Anatomy and Human Biology
WALKER, D. I., Plant Biology
WATTS, G. F., Medicine
WEINSTEIN, P., Population Health
WELLER, R. J., Architecture
WHELAN, J., Biochemistry and Molecular Biology
WHITE, A. H., Chemistry and Crystallography
WHITE, R. S., English and Cultural Studies
WILLIAMS, J. F., Physics
WITHERS, P. C., Animal Biology
WOOD, D. J., Orthopaedics
YEOH, G., Biochemistry and Molecular Biology
ZHENG, M. H., Surgery

UNIVERSITY OF WESTERN SYDNEY

Locked Bag 1797, Penrith, South DC, NSW 2751

Telephone: (2) 9852-5222
Fax: (2) 9678-7160
E-mail: internationalstudy@uws.edu.au
Internet: www.uws.edu.au

Founded 1989
State control
Academic year: March to December

Chancellor: Prof. PETER SHERGOLD
Vice-Chancellor: Prof. JANICE REID
Deputy Vice-Chancellor for Academic Services: Prof. ROBERT COOMBES
Deputy Vice-Chancellor for Devt and Int. Affairs: Prof. CHUNG-TONG WU
Academic Registrar: THEA SEABROOK
Librarian: LIZ CURACH

Library: 1m. vols
Number of teachers: 2,002
Number of students: 39,780

DEANS

College of Arts: Prof. GARY SMITH
College of Business: Assoc. Prof. CRAIG ELLIS (acting)
College of Health and Sciences: Prof. BRANKO CELLER

UNIVERSITY OF WOLLONGONG

Northfields Ave, Wollongong, NSW 2522

Telephone: (2) 4221-3555
Fax: (2) 4221-3477
E-mail: askuow@uow.edu.au
Internet: www.uow.edu.au

Founded 1961 as a College of the Univ. of New South Wales; merged with Wollongong Inst. of Education 1982
Public control
Academic year: March to November (2 sessions), and a summer session from December to February

Chancellor: MICHAEL CODD
Deputy Chancellor: SUE CHAPMAN
Vice-Chancellor and Prin.: Prof. GERARD SUTTON
Vice-Prin. for Admin.: CHRIS GRANGE
Vice-Prin. for Overseas Operations: JAMES LANGRIDGE
Deputy Vice-Prin. for Finance and IT: DAMIEN ISRAEL
Deputy Vice-Chancellor for Academic and Int. Affairs: Prof. ROB CASTLE
Deputy Vice-Chancellor for Operations: Prof. JOHN PATTERSON
Pro-Vice-Chancellor for Research: Prof. MARGARET SHEIL
Dean of Studies: YVONNE KERR
Dir of the Dubai Campus: DAVID ROME (acting)
Registrar: Dr DAVID CHRISTIE (acting)
Librarian: FELICITY MCGREGOR

Library of 708,248 vols, 190,191 journals, 7,063 e-books, 510,944 monographs
Number of teachers: 801
Number of students: 23,171

Publications: *Australian Journal of Information Systems*, *Australian Journal of Natural Resources Law and Policy*, *Boxkite* (creative arts), *Illawarra Unity* (labour history), *International Journal of Forensic Psychology*, *Journal of University Teaching and Learning Practice*, *Rhizome* (2 a year)

DEANS

Faculty of Arts: Prof. JOHN PATTERSON
Faculty of Commerce: Prof. SHIRLEY LEITCH
Faculty of Creative Arts: Prof. AMANDA LAWSON
Faculty of Education: Prof. PAUL CHANDLER

Faculty of Engineering: Prof. CHRIS COOK (acting)
Faculty of Health and Behavioural Sciences: Prof. DON IVERSON
Faculty of Informatics: Prof. JOE CHICHARO
Faculty of Law: Prof. LUKE MCNAMARA
Faculty of Science: Prof. WILL PRICE
Graduate School of Business: Prof. JOHN GLYNN
Graduate School of Medicine: Prof. LIZ FARMER

PROFESSORS

Faculty of Arts:
BEDER, S., Social Sciences, Media and Communication
DODDS, S., English Literature, Philosophy and Languages
HAGAN, J., Arts
KITLEY, P., Social Sciences, Media and Communication
MARSHALL, D., Social Sciences, Media and Communication
MARTIN, B., Social Sciences, Media and Communication
OMMUNDSEN, W., English Literature, Philosophy and Languages
WOLFERS, E., History and Politics

Faculty of Commerce:
BARRETT, M., Management and Marketing
DAWSON, P., Management and Marketing
DOLNICAR, S., Management and Marketing
GAFFIKIN, M., Accounting and Finance
LEWIS, D., Economics and Information Systems
METWALLY, M., Economics
ROSSITER, J., Management and Marketing
SPEDDING, T., Management and Marketing
VILLE, S., Economics

Faculty of Creative Arts:
LAWSON, J., Arts and Design
MILLER, S., Music and Drama
WOOD CONROY, D., Arts and Design

Faculty of Education:
DINHAM, S., Educational Leadership and Pedagogy
FERRY, B., Education
RUSSELL, T., Education
THOMAS, R., Education

Faculty of Engineering:
ARNDT, G., Mechanical Materials and Mechatronics
ARNOLD, P., Mechanical Materials and Mechatronics
BRINSON, G., Mechanical Materials and Mechatronics
BROWN, H., Coating Technology
CHIU, C., Engineering
CHOWDURY, R., Civil Mining and Environmental Engineering
DIPPENAAR, R., Mechanical Materials and Mechatronics
DOU, S., Mechanical Materials and Mechatronics
DUNNE, D., Mechanical Materials and Mechatronics
INDRARATNA, B., Civil Mining and Environmental Engineering
LEWIS, R., Engineering Physics
LIU, H., ISEM
MCCARTHY, G., Civil Mining and Environmental Engineering
METCALFE, P., Engineering Physics
NORRISH, J., Materials Welding and Joining
PERELOMA, E., Mechanical Materials and Mechatronics
PIGHATEL, G., Engineering Physics
ROBINSON, P., Engineering
ROZENFELD, A., Engineering Physics
SEN, G., Civil Mining and Environmental Engineering

SPINKS, G., Mechanical Materials and Mechatronics
TIEU, A., Mechanical Materials and Mechatronics
VARIN, R. A., Mechanical Materials and Mechatronics
ZHANG, C., Engineering Physics

Faculty of Health and Behavioural Sciences:
BARRY, R., Psychology
BUSHNELL, J., Graduate School of Medicine
CALVERT, D., Health Sciences
CARR, N., Graduate School of Medicine
CROOKES, P., Nursing, Midwifery and Indigenous Health
DEANE, F., Psychology
ELSE, P., Health Sciences
FARMER, E., Graduate School of Medicine
HEAVEN, P., Psychology
HOGG, J., Medicine
HUANG, X., Health Sciences
JONES, S., Centre for Health Initiatives
LILLIOJA, S., Health and Behavioural Sciences
MANOHARAN, A., Medicine
STEELE, J., Health Sciences
TAIT, N., Graduate School of Medicine
TAPSELL, L., Biomedical Sciences
WALSH, K., Nursing, Midwifery and Indigenous Health
YEO, W., Graduate School of Medicine

Faculty of Informatics:
BOUZERDOUM, S., Electrical, Computer and Telecommunications Engineering
BUNDER, M., Mathematics and Applied Statistics
CHAMBERS, R., Mathematics and Applied Statistics
DUTKIEWICZ, E., Electrical, Computer and Telecommunications Engineering
EKLUND, P., Information Systems and Technology
FULCHER, J., Computer Science and Software Engineering
GHOSE, A., Computer Science and Software Engineering
GOSBELL, V., Electrical, Computer and Telecommunications Engineering
GRIFFITHS, D. A., Mathematics and Applied Statistics
HILL, J., Mathematics and Applied Statistics
LANDSTAD, M., Mathematics and Applied Statistics
NAGHDY, F., Electrical, Computer and Telecommunications Engineering
OGUNBONA, P., Information Technology and Computer Science
RAEBURN, I., Mathematics and Applied Statistics
SAFAEI, F., Electrical, Computer and Telecommunications Engineering
SEBERRY, J., Information Technology and Computer Science
SOETANTO, D., Electrical, Computer and Telecommunications Engineering
STEEL, D., Mathematics and Applied Statistics
WAND, M., Mathematics and Applied Statistics
ZHU, S., Mathematics and Applied Statistics

Faculty of Law:
ANTONS, C., Comparative Law
CHAPPELL, D., Centre for Transnational Crime Prevention
CHURCHILL, R., ANCORS
FARRIER, M., Natural Resources Law and Policy
TSAMENYI, M., Centre for Maritime Policy

Faculty of Science:
AYRE, D., Biological Sciences
BRADSTOCK, R., Chemistry
BREMNER, J., Chemistry
BUTTEMER, B., Biological Sciences

CHAPPELL, B., Earth and Environmental Sciences
CHIVAS, A., Geosciences
DIXON, N., Chemistry
GRIFFITH, D., Chemistry
HEAD, L., Earth and Environmental Sciences
HULBERT, T., Biological Sciences
KANE-MAGUIRE, L., Chemistry
MORRISION, J., Earth and Environmental Science
MURRAY-WALLACE, C., Earth and Environmental Science
NANSON, G., Geosciences
NE'EMAN, G., Biological Sciences
OFFICER, D., Intelligent Polymer Research Institute
OLSSEN, M., Biological Sciences
PRICE, W., Chemistry
PYNE, S., Chemistry
WALKER, M., Biological Sciences
WALLACE, G., Intelligent Polymer Research Institute
WILSON, M., Biological Sciences
WOODROFFE, C., Earth and Environmental Sciences

VICTORIA UNIVERSITY

POB 14428, Melbourne, Vic. 8001
Telephone: (3) 9919-4000
Fax: (3) 9689-4069
E-mail: graduate@vu.edu.au
Internet: www.vu.edu.au

Founded 1990
Academic year: March to November
Chancellor: GEORGE PAPPAS
Pres. and Vice-Chancellor: Prof. PETER DAWKINS
Deputy Vice-Chancellor and Provost: Prof. LINDA ROSENMAN
Deputy Vice-Chancellor: JON HICKMAN
Deputy Vice-Chancellor and Dir: Dr ANNE JONES
Pro-Vice-Chancellor: Dr ROB BROWN
Pro-Vice-Chancellor: Prof. GREGORY BAXTER
Pro-Vice-Chancellor: Prof. PETER CREAMER
Pro-Vice-Chancellor: Prof. WARREN PAYNE
Vice-Pres. for International Affairs: ANDREW HOLLOWAY
Pro-Vice-Chancellor: Prof. BRIAN KING
Univ. Librarian: RALPH KIEL

Library of 561,341 vols
Number of teachers: 2,607
Number of students: 53,935

Publication: *Journal of Business Systems, Governance And Ethics*

DEANS

Faculty of Arts, Education and Human Devt: Prof. MICHAEL HAMEL GREEN
Faculty of Business and Law: Prof. DAVID LAMOND
Faculty of Health, Engineering and Science: Assoc. Prof. MICHELLE TOWSTOLESS (acting)
Faculty of Technical and Trades Innovation: CORALIE MORRISSEY
Faculty of Workforce Devt: GRANT DREHER
VU College: SUSAN YOUNG

PROFESSORS

ANDERSON, R., Accounting
ANDREWS, N., Law
ARMSTRONG, A., School of Management
ARUP, C., Law
BAKER, H., Nursing
BROCK, D., Psychology
CARLSON, J., Centre for Ageing, Rehabilitation, Exercise and Sport
CARY, J., Key Research Area of Integrated Food Value Chain
CLARK, C., Accounting
DAVIDSON, J., History
DEERY, P., Dept of Asian and Int. Studies

DRAGOMIR, S., Engineering
EADE, R., Arts
FAULKNER, M., Telecommunications
GABB, R., Centre for Educational Devt and Support
GEORGE, G., Accounting
GLASBEEK, H., Business and Law
GREWAL, B., Centre for Strategic Economic Studies
HOUGHTON, J., Centre for Strategic Economic Studies
JAGO, L., Tourism and Hospitality Studies
KALAM, A., Engineering
KING, B., School of Hospitality, Tourism and Marketing
LEUNG, C., Computer Science
MCGRATH, M., Information Systems
MCQUEEN, R., Law
MORRIS, A., Human Devt, Health, Engineering and Science
PATIENCE, A., Arts
POLONSKY, M., Marketing
PRIESTLY, I., Accounting
PRILLELTENSKY, I., Psychology
ROBERTS, T., School of Human Movement, Recreation and Performance
RYAN, M., Education
SEEDSMAN, T., Human Devt, Health, Engineering and Science
SHEEHAN, P., Centre for Strategic Economic Studies
SINCLAIR, J., Arts
THOMAS, I., Centre for Environmental Safety and Risk Engineering
THORPE, G., School of the Built Environment
TURNER, L., School of Applied Economics
WILSON, K., Economics
XIE, M., Engineering
ZHANG, Y., Computer Science

Colleges

Alphacrucis College: POB 125, Chester Hill, NSW 2162; 40 Hector St, Chester Hill, NSW 2162; tel. (2) 9645-9000; fax (2) 9645-9099; e-mail info@alphacrucis.edu.au; internet alphacrucis.edu.au; f. 1948; affiliated to Australian Christian Churches, Assemblies of God and Sydney College of Divinity; campuses in Sydney, Brisbane and Auckland, New Zealand; Pres. Pastor JOHN IULIANO; Prin. Pastor STEPHEN FOGARTY; Acad. Dean Dr JACQUELINE GREY (acting); Dean of Acad. Advancement Dr MARK HUTCHINSON.

Ansto Training: PMB 1, Menai, NSW 2234; tel. (2) 9717-9430; fax (2) 9717-9449; internet www.ansto.gov.au; f. 1964; training arm of the University of NSW and the Australian Nuclear Science and Technology Organisation; short courses in use of radioisotopes, radionuclides in medicine, radiation protection and occupational health and safety; Exec. Dir and Chief Exec. Dr IAN SMITH.

Aquinas College: 1 Palmer Pl., N Adelaide, SA 5006; tel. (8) 8334-5000; fax (8) 8334-5173; e-mail admin@aquinas.edu.au; internet www.aquinas.edu.au; f. 1950; attached to Univ. of Adelaide; residential college; Head Prof. DENIS W. RALPH; College Sec. JUDITH KIRBY; Dean of Studies Bro. JOHN FURLONG.

Australian Film, Television and Radio School: POB 126, North Ryde, NSW 2113; tel. (2) 9805-6611; fax (2) 9887-1030; f. 1973; library: 20,000 vols; 100 full-time students, 3,000 part-time/short course students; courses: 1- and 2-year courses (postgraduate

level), 7-month commercial radio course, short industry courses; Dir MALCOLM LONG; Library Man. MICHELE BURTON.

Australian Maritime College: POB 986, Launceston, Tas. 7250; tel. (3) 6335-4711; fax (3) 6326-6493; e-mail amcinfo@amc.edu.au; internet www.amc.edu.au; f. 1978; library: 36,800 vols; 75 teachers; 1,300 students; Principal Dr NEIL OTWAY; Asst Registrar ELIZABETH VAGG; Dir of Faculty of Fisheries and Marine Environment Dr PAUL MCSHANE; Dir of Faculty of Maritime Transport and Engineering Dr BARRIE LEWARN; Library Officer MICHELLE STEVENS; publs *AMC News*, *Handbook*.

Campion College: POB 3052, Toongabbie East, NSW 2146; 8–14 Austin Woodbury Pl., Old Toongabbie, NSW 2146; tel. (2) 9896-9300; fax (2) 9631-9200; e-mail info@campion.edu.au; internet www.campion.edu.au; f. 2006; offers BA in liberal arts; library: 25,000 vols; 73 students; Pres. Dr DAVID DAINTREE; Deputy Pres. and Registrar TONY HEYWOOD; Librarian ANGELA KOLAR.

Cromwell College: Walcott St, St Lucia, Qld 4067; tel. (7) 3377-1300; fax (7) 3377-1499; e-mail stay@cromwell.uq.edu.au; internet www.cromwell.uq.edu.au; f. 1950, opened in 1954; attached to Univ. of Queensland; 250 students; Chair. BEN DE JONG; Principal ROSS A. SWITZER.

Duchesne College: College Rd, St Lucia, Qld 4067; tel. (7) 3377-2333; fax (7) 3377-2314; e-mail duchesne.college@duchesne.uq.edu.au; internet www.uq.edu.au/duchesne; f. 1937, present status 1959; attached to Univ. of Queensland; 154 students; Principal NANETTE KAY; Vice-Principal Sr KATHLEEN MUIRHEAD; Dean of Students MATTHEW DOWNEY.

Grace College: Walcott St, St Lucia, Qld 4067; tel. (7) 3842-4000; fax (7) 3842-4180; e-mail grace.college@mailbox.uq.edu.au; internet www.uq.edu.au/grace; f. 1970; attached to Univ. of Queensland; residential college for women; Chair. Rev. RAY HERRMANN; Deputy Chair. DENIS BROSNAN; Principal Dr SUE FAIRLEY.

International House: 5 Rock St, St Lucia, Qld 4067; tel. (7) 3721-2480; fax (7) 3721-2476; e-mail admissions@inthouse.uq.edu.au; internet www.internationalhouse.uq.edu.au; f. 1965; attached to Univ. of Queensland; residential college; Pres. BILL MCMILLAN; Dir Dr CARLA TROMANS.

Kathleen Lumley College: 51 Finniss St, N Adelaide, SA 5006; tel. (8) 8267-3270; fax (8) 8239-1705; e-mail klc@adelaide.edu.au; internet www.adelaide.edu.au/klc; f. 1967; attached to Univ. of Adelaide; postgraduate residential college; Master Assoc. Prof. FELIX PATRIKEEFF.

King's College: Upland Rd, St Lucia, Qld 4067; tel. (7) 3871-9600; fax (7) 3871-9666; e-mail kings.college@uq.edu.au; internet www.kings.uq.edu.au/kingscollege.html; f. 1913 at Kangaroo point, present location and present status 1954; attached to Univ. of Queensland; academic residential college for undergraduate and postgraduate male members; Pres. Hon. Justice MARTIN DAUBNEY; Master and Chief Exec. GREGORY C. EDDY; Dean of Students and Deputy Master MATTHEW SHEAHAN; publs *Kingsman Magazine*, *Wyvern*.

Lincoln College: 45 Brougham Pl., N Adelaide, SA 5006; tel. (8) 8290-6000; fax (8) 8267-2942; e-mail admin@lincoln.edu.au;

internet www.lincoln.edu.au; f. 1952; attached to Univ. of Adelaide; residential college; Principal BEC PANNELL; Dean JORDAN BELL.

National Art School: Forbes St, Darlinghurst, NSW 2010; tel. (2) 9339-8744; fax (2) 9339-8740; e-mail nas@det.nsw.edu.au; internet www.nas.edu.au; f. 1843; honours and masters courses offered in ceramics, painting, photography, printmaking, sculpture with painting and art history and art theory; organises a visual arts public programme; 100 teachers; 400 students; Dir BERNARD OLLIS; Deputy Dir GEOFF IRELAND.

National Institute of Dramatic Art: UNSW, Sydney, NSW 2052; tel. (2) 9697-7600; fax (2) 9662-7415; e-mail nida@unsw.edu.au; internet www.nida.edu.au; f. 1958; degree, graduate diploma and advanced diploma courses; library: 28,000 vols, 55 periodicals; 150 full-time students, 5,000 part-time students in Open Program; Dir JOHN R. CLARK.

Roseworthy Residential College: Roseworthy, SA 5371; tel. (8) 8303-7888; fax (8) 8303-7960; e-mail roseworthycollege@adelaide.edu.au; f. 1991; attached to Univ. of Adelaide; library: 33,000 books, 700 journal titles; 250 students; Principal Dr D. TAPLIN.

St Ann's College Inc.: 187 Brougham Pl., N Adelaide, SA 5006; tel. (8) 8267-1478; fax (8) 8267-1903; e-mail info@stannscollege.edu.au; internet www.stannscollege.edu.au; f. 1939; attached to Univ. of Adelaide; residential college; Principal Dr ROSEMARY H. S. BROOKS.

St John's College: College Rd, St Lucia, Qld 4067; tel. (7) 3842-6600; fax (7) 3870-5124; e-mail stjohns.college@uq.edu.au; internet www.uq.edu.au/stjohns; f. 1911 at Kangaroo Point, present location 1954; attached to Univ. of Queensland; residential college for undergraduates and postgraduates; Warden Prof. JOHN MORGAN.

St Leo's College: College Rd, St Lucia, Qld 4067; tel. (7) 3878-0600; fax (7) 3878-0620; internet www.stleos.uq.edu.au; f. 1917 at Wickham Terrace, present location 1961; attached to Univ. of Queensland; residential college for men; Chair. JOAN SHELDON; Rector Bro. VINCE SKELLY; Vice-Rector for Students STEPHEN FOLEY; Vice-Rector for Admin. Bro. GERRY BURKE.

St Mark's College: 46 Pennington Terrace, N Adelaide, SA 5006; tel. (8) 8334-5600; fax (8) 8267-4694; e-mail stmarks@stmarkscollege.com.au; internet www.stmarkscollege.com.au; f. 1925; attached to Univ. of Adelaide; residential college; library: 22,000 vols; Master and CEO ROSE S. ALWYN; Dean JAMES RAW.

The Women's College: College Rd, St Lucia, Qld 4067; tel. (7) 3377-4500; fax (7) 3870-9511; e-mail administration@womens.uq.edu.au; internet www.womens.uq.edu.au; f. 1914 at Kangaroo Point, present location 1958; attached to Univ. of Queensland; residential college for women; Pres. Dr SALLYANNE ATKINSON; Head and CEO Adjunct Prof. IYLA DAVIES; Dean of Students LIZA ALLEN.

Union College: Upland Rd, St Lucia, Qld 4067; tel. (7) 3377-1500; fax (7) 3371-3826; e-mail union.college@uq.edu.au; internet www.uq.edu.au/union; f. 1965; attached to Univ. of Queensland; residential college for undergraduate and postgraduate studies; Chair. CHRIS BURGESS; Head JILL HEWITT.

AUSTRIA

The Higher Education System

Austria's oldest institution is the University of Vienna, established in 1365. Institutes of adult education (Volkshochschulen) are found in all provinces, as are other centres operated by public authorities, church organizations and the Austrian Trade Union Federation. The central controlling and funding body is the Federal Ministry of Education and Research. University-level education is free, and the guiding framework is based on the General Law for University Education (1966) and the University Organization Law (1975). Since 2003 extensive reforms of the higher education system have been enacted. Universities have become quasi-autonomous institutions, independent of state control. A more 'top-down' form of management has been introduced, with university councils responsible for appointing senior managers (Rektorat). Other reforms include the separation of the three medical universities from their parent institutions, the accreditation of private universities and the introduction of competitive hiring practices for recruitment of academic staff. However, reforms have been hampered by the lack of additional funding beyond inflation-level increases.

In 2007 there were 22 universities providing for 209,416 students (excl. private institutions) and 169 tertiary vocational institutions with 28,426 students. Admission to higher education is based on award of the Reifeprüfung (the certificate received upon successful completion of secondary education). In addition, all Austrian citizens over the age of 24 years, and with professional experience, may attend certain university courses in connection with their professional career or trade. However, for certain courses of study offered at Fachhochschulen students may be required to take extra examinations. Students without the Reifeprüfung can gain admission to university study by completing a preparatory course and the Studienberechtigungsprüfung examination. Successful completion of this course gives access to study in the fields in which the examinations were taken.

As one of the original signatories to the Bologna Process, Austria has implemented the two-tier system of undergraduate and graduate Bachelor and Masters level degrees alongside the traditional degrees, with a view to phasing the latter out entirely. However, medical degree programmes and upper-secondary teaching qualifications are exempt from the new system. The following degrees are available: Bakkalaureat, Diplomstudium/Magister, Fachhochschuldiplom and Kurzstudium (all undergraduate); Magisterstudium (Bologna), Aufbaustudium and Doktoratstudium (both postgraduate). The traditional undergraduate degree is the Diplomstudium, leading to the title Magister or Diplom and lasting four to six years. The Bologna equivalent is the Bakkalaureat, lasting three to four years. Students with the Diplom or Magister traditionally proceeded directly to Doctoral studies, which usually lasted between one and three years and required the writing of a thesis and the passing of final examinations, known as Rigorosum. Under the Bologna Process students are now expected to study for up to two years after the Bakkalaureat and earn the Magisterstudium before undertaking doctoral studies.

Non-university higher education is offered in Hochschulen for students, graduates and those who do not have the Reifeprüfung. Fachhochschulen were launched in 1993, entry into which requires the Reifeprüfung. These offer professional training in technology, finance and social affairs which lasts for three to four years and allows admission to doctoral studies. Akademien and Kollegs also offer vocational training.

Regulatory and Representative Bodies

GOVERNMENT

Federal Ministry of Education, Arts and Culture: Minoritenpl. 5, 1014 Vienna; tel. (1) 531200; fax (1) 531203099; e-mail ministerium@bmukk.gv.at; internet www.bmukk.gv.at; Federal Minister Dr CLAUDIA SCHMIED.

Federal Ministry of Science and Research: Minoritenpl. 5, 1014 Vienna; tel. (1) 5312000; fax (1) 531209099; e-mail infoservice@bmwf.gv.at; internet www.bmwf.gv.at; Federal Min. Dr BEATRIX KARL.

ACCREDITATION

Austrian Accreditation Council: Palais Harrach, Freyung 3, 1010 Vienna; tel. (1) 531205673; fax (1) 53120815673; e-mail akkreditierungsrat@bmwf.gv.at; internet www.akkreditierungsrat.at; f. 1999; regulates the private instns offering univ. education in Austria; the Council is an ind. body with full decision powers over the accreditation of private univs; one-half of its mems are Austrians, the other half being experts from other European countries; this guarantees that int. standards are maintained and that the Council remains ind. of nat. conflicts of interest; Pres. Prof. Dr HANS-UWE ERICHSEN; Vice-Pres. Prof. Dr HANNELORE WECK-HANNEMANN.

ENIC-NARIC Austria: Bundesministerium für Wissenschaft und Forschung, Abteilung I/11, Teinfaltstr. 8, 1014 Vienna; tel. (1) 531205921; fax (1) 53120995920; e-mail naric@bmwf.gv.at; internet www.bmwf.gv.at/naric; f. 1981; assessment and recognition of academic qualifications; counselling services for institutions and persons; Dir. Dr HEINZ KASPAROVSKY; Deputy Dir. Dr CHRISTOPH DEMAND.

Fachhochschulrat (FHR) (Accreditation Council for Universities of Applied Sciences): Liechtensteinstrasse 22A, 1090 Vienna; tel. (1) 31950340; fax (1) 319503430; e-mail office@fhr.ac.at; internet www.fhr.ac.at; f. 1993; ind. body responsible for the external quality assurance (accreditation and evaluation) in the Austrian FH sector; operates under Fachhochschule Studies Act (Federal Law Gazette no. 340/1993 as amended); 16 mems, one-half of whom are required to have the relevant post-doctoral lecturing qualification (Habilitation). the other half are required to prove that they have worked in the fields relevant for FH degree programmes for several years; Pres. Prof. DI Dr LEOPOLD MÄRZ; Man. Dir Dr KURT SOHM.

Österreichische Fachhochschul-Konferenz (Austrian Association of Universities of Applied Sciences): Bösendorferstr. 4/11, 1010 Vienna; tel. (1) 890634520; fax (1) 890634560; e-mail kurt.koleznik@fhk.ac.at; internet www.fhk.ac.at; f. 1995; asscn of Austrian Fachhochschulen (Universities of Applied Sciences); supports Fachhochschulen in achieving common educational goals; Pres. Dr HELMUT HOLZINGER; Sec.-Gen. KURT KOLEZNIK.

FUNDING

Fonds zur Förderung der wissenschaftlichen Forschung (Austrian Science Fund): Haus der Forschung, Sensengasse 1, 1090 Vienna; tel. (1) 5056740; fax (1) 5056739; e-mail office@fwf.ac.at; internet www.fwf.ac.at; f. 1967; all Austrian univs with their faculties, the art schools and the Austrian Academy of Sciences are represented, also delegates of non-univ. research instns and professional asscns; Austria's central funding org. for basic research; Pres. Prof. Dr CHRISTOPH KRATKY; publ. *Info Magazine* (German).

NATIONAL BODY

OeAD (Österreichische Austauschdienst) GmbH (Austrian Agency for International Cooperation in Education and Research): Ebendorferstr. 7, 1010 Vienna; tel. (1) 534080; fax (1) 53408999; e-mail info@oead.at; internet www.oead.at; f. 1961 as asscn of the Austrian Rectors' Conf., present name 2009; non-profit-making service org. in the field of int. cooperation in education and research; activities cover gen., academic and vocational education with emphasis on academic mobility; CEO Prof. Dr HUBERT DÜRRSTEIN.

Learned Societies

GENERAL

Österreichische Akademie der Wissenschaften (ÖAW) (Austrian Academy of Sciences (AAS)): Dr Ignaz Seipel-Pl. 2, 1010 Vienna; tel. (1) 515810; fax (1) 5139541; e-mail webmaster@oeaw.ac.at; internet www.oeaw.ac.at; f. 1847; non univ. instn promoting basic research; consists of sections of Mathematics and Natural Sciences (Prof. Dr HELMUT DENK) and Humanities and Social Sciences (Prof. Dr SIGRID JALKOTZY-DEGER (acting)); attached institutes: see under Research Institutes; 673 mems; library: see under Libraries and Archives; Pres. Prof. Dr HELMUT DENK; Vice-Pres. Prof. Dr SIGRID JALKOTZY-DEGER; Sec.Gen. Prof. Dr ARNOLD SUPPAN; Sec. Prof. Dr GEORG STINGL; publs *Almanach, Anzeiger math.-nat. Klasse, Anzeiger phil.-hist. Klasse, Denkschriften der Gesamtakademie, Denkschriften math.-nat. Klasse, Denkschriften phil.-hist. Klasse, Monatshefte für Chemie, Sitzungsberichte math.-nat. Klasse Abt. I, II, Sitzungsberichte phil.-hist. Klasse, Thema: The Magazine* (3 a year).

AGRICULTURE, FISHERIES AND VETERINARY SCIENCE

Österreichische Gesellschaft der Tierärzte (Austrian Society of Veterinary Medicine): Veterinärpl. 1, 1210 Vienna; tel. (1) 250771800; fax (1) 250771890; e-mail dorothea.troxler@vetmeduni.ac.at; internet www.oegt.at; f. 1919; 1,200 mems; Pres. Dr. MONIKA TEINFALT; Vice-Pres. Prof. Dr FRIEDERIKE HILBERT; Sec. Dr BARBARA BOCKSTAHLER; publ. *Wiener Tierärztliche Monatsschrift* (6 a year).

ARCHITECTURE AND TOWN PLANNING

Österreichische Gesellschaft für Raumplanung (Austrian Society for Regional Planning): Technical Univ. of Vienna, Karlspl. 13, 1040 Vienna; tel. (1) 58801280233; fax (1) 5880128099; e-mail oegr@oegr.at; internet www.oegr.at; Pres. Prof. Mag. Dr RUDOLF GIFFINGER; Sec. Dipl.-Ing. JOHN BOCKSTEFL; publs *FORUM Raumplanung* (2 a year), *Schriftenreihe* (irregular).

Österreichischer Ingenieur- und Architekten-Verein (Austrian Society of Engineers and Architects): Eschenbachgasse 9, 1010 Vienna; tel. (1) 5873536; fax (1) 58735365; e-mail office@oiav.at; internet www.oiav.at; f. 1848; 4,000 mems; Pres. Dipl.-Ing. Dr HEINZ BRANDL; Gen. Sec. Dipl.-Ing. PETER REICHEL; publ. *Österreichische Ingenieur- und Architekten-Zeitschrift* (6 a year).

Zentralvereinigung der Architekten Österreichs-ZV (Central Association of Austrian Architects): Salvatorgasse 10, 1010 Vienna; tel. (1) 5334429; e-mail zv@aaf.or.at; internet www.zv-architekten.at; f. 1907; 700 mems; Pres. HANS HOLLEIN.

BIBLIOGRAPHY, LIBRARY SCIENCE AND MUSEOLOGY

Gesellschaft für Landeskunde von Oberösterreich (Upper Austrian Cultural Heritage Association): Haus der Volkskultur, Promenade 33/103–104, 4020 Linz; tel. and fax (732) 770218; e-mail office@ooelandeskunde.at; internet www.ooelandeskunde.at; f. 1833; offers cultural heritage by publs, referats, excursions; visit of exhibitions and museums; 700 mems; Chair. Dr GEORG SPIEGELFELD; Sec. GERTRAUD HAGER; publs *Beiträge zur Landeskunde von Oberösterreich, Jahrbuch, Mitteilungen* (3 a year), *Schriftenreihe*.

Österreichische Gesellschaft für Dokumentation und Information (Austrian Society for Documentation and Information): POB 43, 1022 Vienna; Wollzeile 1–3, 1010 Vienna; e-mail office@oegdi.at; internet www.oegdi.at; f. 1951; organizes vocational training for information professionals, workshops, conferences and lectures in the field of information and library science; 80 mems; Exec. Sec. Dr HERMANN HUEMER.

Vereinigung Österreichischer Bibliothekarinnen und Bibliothekare (Austrian Librarians Association): Fluher str. 4, 6900 Bregenz; tel. (5574) 51144010; fax (5574) 51144095; e-mail voeb@uibk.ac.at; internet www.univie.ac.at/voeb; f. 1945; represents the professional interests and concerns of member librarians; organizes central training event of the academic library system every 2 years; 1,200 mems; Pres. Dr HARALD WEIGEL; Sec. Dr ORTWIN HEIM; publ. *Mitteilungen* (4 a year).

ECONOMICS, LAW AND POLITICS

Nationalökonomische Gesellschaft (Austrian Economics Association): c/o Univ. of Linz, Dept of Economics, Altenberger Str. 69, 4040 Linz; tel. (2) 24688213; fax (2) 24689821; e-mail noeg@jku.at; internet www.noeg.ac.at; f. 1918; non-profit society to promote scientific progress in theoretical and applied economic sciences; 240 mems; Pres. Prof. Dr JOHANN K. BRUNNER; Vice-Pres. Prof. Dr FRITZ BREUSS; Vice-Pres. Prof. Dr MANFRED NERMUTH; Gen. Sec. Prof. Dr GERALD J. PRUCKNER; publ. *Empirica* (applied economics and economic policy, 5 a year).

Österreichische Gesellschaft für Aussenpolitik und die Vereinten Nationen (Foreign Policy and United Nations Association of Austria): Hofburg/Stallburg, Reitschulg, 2/2, OG 1010 Vienna; tel. (1) 5354627; fax (1) 5322605; e-mail office@oegavn.org; internet www.oegavn.org; f. 1945; ind.t org. to inform the Austrian population on Austrian foreign policy and European and int. issues; 700 mems; Pres. Dr WOLFGANG SCHUESSEL; Sec.-Gen. MICHAEL F. PFEIFER; publ. *Global View* (4 a year).

Österreichische Gesellschaft für Kirchenrecht (Austrian Society for Ecclesiastical Law): c/o Institut für Rechtsphilosophie, Religions- und Kulturrecht, Rechtswissenschaftliche Fakultät der Universität Wien, Schenkenstr. 8–10, 4-0438, 1010 Vienna; tel. (1) 427735813; fax (1) 427735899; e-mail harald.baumgartner@univie.ac.at; internet www.univie.ac.at/recht-religion/ogk; f. 1949; scientific asscn to promote research and practice in religion and law; conducts 8 lectures and book presentations in a year; 200 mems; Pres. Hon. Prof. Dr RAOUL KNEUCKER; Vice-Pres. Oberkirchenrat Mag. ROBERT KAUER; Sec. Dr HARALD BAUMGARTNER; publ. *Österreichisches Archiv für Recht und Religion*.

Österreichische Statistische Gesellschaft (Austrian Statistical Society): c/o Statistik Austria, Guglgasse 13, 1110 Vienna; tel. (1) 711287269; fax (1) 711287445; e-mail osg@statistik.gv.at; internet www.osg.or.at; f. 1951; non-profit org; promotes statistical science in all its forms and applications; awards annual scholarships for Masters and diploma theses and dissertations in statistics; 600 mems; Pres. Mag. MARGIT EPLER; publ. *Austrian Journal of Statistics* (3 or 4 a year).

Wiener Juristische Gesellschaft (Vienna Legal Association): Österreichisches Normungsinstitut, Heinestr. 38, 1020 Vienna; tel. (1) 21300605; fax (1) 21300609; e-mail office@wjg.at; internet www.wjg.at; f. 1867; non-political, non-profit org.; promotes and

develops law in theory and practice; 600 mems; Pres. Prof. Dr WALTER BARFUSS; Vice-Pres. Prof. Dr CLEMENS JABLONER; Vice-Pres. Prof. Dr KARL KORINEK; Gen. Sec. Mag. WOLFGANG MÜLLER.

EDUCATION

Österreichische Universitätenkonferenz (Universities Austria): Floragasse 7/7, 1040 Vienna; tel. (1) 31056560; fax (1) 310565622; e-mail office@uniko.ac.at; internet www.uniko.ac.at; f. 1911 as Austrian Rectors' Conf., present name 2008; handles internal coordination of 21 Austrian public univs.; represents the univs in nat. and int. orgs and provides administrative and organizational support to the Nati. Univ. Federation; 21 mems; Pres. Prof. Dr HANS SÜNKEL; Sec.-Gen. HERIBERT WULZ.

Verband der Akademikerinnen Österreichs (Austrian Association of Women Academics): Reitschulgasse 2, 1010 Vienna; tel. (1) 5339080; e-mail office.vaoe-wien@aon.at; internet www.vaoe.at; f. 1922; promotes scientific and professional advancement of univ. women graduates; 650 mems; Pres. Dr INGRID NOWOTNY; Vice-Pres. Mag. ELISABETH GYÖRFY; publ. *VAÖ-Mitteilungen* (4 a year).

FINE AND PERFORMING ARTS

Bundesdenkmalamt (Federal Office for the Care and Protection of Monuments): Hofburg, Säulenstiege, 1010 Vienna; tel. (1) 534159; fax (1) 53415252; e-mail kontakt@bda.at; internet www.bda.at; f. 1850; protection and restoration of historical, artistic and cultural monuments; has control of excavations and art exports; 200 mems; library of 70,000 vols; Pres. Dr BARBARA NEUBAUER; publs *Österreichische-Kunsttopographie, Österreichische Zeitschrift für Kunst und Denkmalpflege*.

Gesellschaft der Musikfreunde in Wien (Society of Friends of Music in Vienna): Bösendorferstr. 12, 1010 Vienna; tel. (1) 5058190; fax (1) 505819094; e-mail office@musikverein.at; internet www.musikverein.at; f. 1812; organizes more than 700 concerts a year; 11,000 mems; choir of 300 mems; library: see under Libraries; Exec. and Artistic Dir Dr THOMAS ANGYAN; publ. *Musikverein* (12 a year).

Internationale Franz Lehár-Gesellschaft (International Franz Lehár Society): Lothringerstr. 20, 1030 Vienna; tel. (1) 7132761; fax (1) 8873967; e-mail alleslehar@aon.at; internet www.franz-lehar-gesellschaft.com; f. 1949; Pres. HELGA PAPOUSCHEK; Gen. Sec. Prof. HARALD SERAFIN.

Johann Strauss-Gesellschaft Wien (Johann Strauss Society of Vienna): Hetzgasse 19/9, 1030 Vienna; tel. and fax (1) 5339194; e-mail office@johann-strauss-gesellschaft.at; internet www.johann-strauss-gesellschaft.at; f. 1936; community for maintenance of music by the Strauss family, other composers of Viennese dance- and operetta-music; 300 mems; Pres. Prof. Mag. PETER WIDHOLZ; Vice-Pres. Prof. WERNER RESEL; Sec.-Gen. Brig. FRIEDRICH FALTUS; publ. *Wiener Bonbons* (4 a year).

Kunsthistorische Gesellschaft (Art History Society):; tel. (1) 427741410; fax (1) 42779414; e-mail eva-maria.grohs@univie.ac.at; f. 1953; mems contribute to the promotion of art historical research and teaching, documentation and publication; 385 mems; Chair. Prof. Dr MICHAEL VIKTOR SCHWARZ; Deputy Chair. Doz. Dr WERNER TELESKO; Sec. Prof. Dr INGEBORG SCHEMPER.

Künstlerhaus (Gesellschaft Bildender Künstler Österreichs) (Austrian Artists

Association): Karlspl. 5, 1010 Vienna; tel. (1) 5879663; fax (1) 5878736; e-mail office@k-haus.at; internet www.k-haus.at; f. 1861; 460 mems; Pres. Arch. DI JOACHIM LOTHAR GARTNER; Dir PETER BOGNER; Sec. KONSTANZE HIMMELBAUER.

Österreichische Gesellschaft für Kommunikationswissenschaft (Austrian Society of Communications): Institut für Kommunikationswissenschaft, Universität Salzburg, Rudolfskai 42, 5020 Salzburg; tel. (662) 80444150; fax (662) 80444190; e-mail oegk@sbg.ac.at; internet www.ogk.at; f. 1976 as Austrian Society for Communication Issues, merged with Austrian Society for Media and Communication Studies in 1999 for present name; encourages cooperation between communication researchers and communication practitioners (journalists, mediaworkers); 140 mems; CEO Dr MICHAEL MANFÉ; Sec. Mag. PETRA STROHMAIER; publ. *Medien Journal* (4 a year).

Österreichische Gesellschaft für Musik (Austrian Music Society): Hanuschgasse 3, 1010 Vienna; tel. (1) 5123143; fax (1) 5124299; e-mail oegm@music.at; f. 1964; lectures, symposia, composer and artist profiles, publications; 1,000 mems; library of 1,000 vols mainly on contemporary music, and records; Pres. Dr WALBURGA LITSCHAUER; Exec. Dir Dr CARMEN OTTNER; publ. *Beiträge* (every 2 years).

Österreichischer Komponistenbund (Association of Austrian Composers): Baumannstr. 8–10, 1031 Vienna; tel. (1) 7147233; fax (1) 714723312; e-mail info@komponistenbund.at; internet www.komponistenbund.at; f. 1913; represents and lobbies for contemporary music composers; initiates musical and artistic projects, concerts, CD and video productions of contests, calls and seminars to international conferences and exchanges; 500 mems; Pres. Univ. Prof. KLAUS AGER; Vice-Pres ALEXANDER KUKELKA, HANNES HEHER; Sec. JOHANNES KRETZ.

Wiener Beethoven Gesellschaft (Vienna Beethoven Society): Heiligenstadt, Probusgasse 6, 1190 Vienna; tel. (1) 3188215; e-mail bjelik@mdw.ac.at; f. 1954; 300 mems; Pres. Prof. ERWIN ORTNER; publ. *Mitteilungsblatt* (4 a year).

Wiener Konzerthausgesellschaft (Vienna Concert Hall Society): Lothringerstr. 20, 1030 Vienna; tel. (1) 24200333; fax (1) 24200111; e-mail wiener@konzerthaus.at; internet www.konzerthaus.at; f. 1913; 6,700 mems; Pres. Dr THERESA JORDIS; Vice-Pres. Dr BURKHARD GANTENBEIN; Vice-Pres. Dr CHRISTOPH KRAUS; publ. *Konzerthaus Nachrichten* (8 a year).

Wiener Secession (Vienna Secession Association of Visual Artists): Friedrichstr. 12, 1010 Vienna; tel. (1) 5875307; fax (1) 587530734; e-mail office@secession.at; internet www.secession.at; f. 1897; promotes exhibitions of contemporary art in its own gallery; 357 mems; Pres. ANDRAS PALFFY; Vice-Pres. CHRISTINA ZURFLUH; Vice-Pres. ANITA WITEK; Sec. MICHAEL KIENZER.

HISTORY, GEOGRAPHY AND ARCHAEOLOGY

Geschichtsverein für Kärnten (Historical Association of Carinthia): Museumgasse 2, 9020 Klagenfurt; tel. (463) 53630573; fax (463) 53630550; e-mail geschichtsverein@landesmuseum-ktn.gu.at; internet www.geschichtsverein-ktn.at; f. 1844; 3,000 mems; Dir Prof. Dr CLAUDIA FRÄSS-EHRFELD; Sec. Prof. Dr GERNOT PICCOTTINI; publs *Archiv für Vaterländische Geschichte und Topographie* (irregular), *Aus Forschung und Kunst* (irregular), *Carinthia I* (1 a year).

Heraldisch-Genealogische Gesellschaft 'Adler' ('Eagle' Heraldry and Genealogy Society): Universitätstr. 6/9B, 1096 Vienna; fax (1) 4092578; e-mail office@adler-wien.at; internet www.adler-wien.at; f. 1870; 700 mems; library of 40,000 vols, 180 journals; Pres. Dr GEORG KUGLER; Sec.-Gen. Dr ANDREAS CORNARO; publs *Jahrbuch, Zeitschrift* (4 a year).

Historische Landeskommission für Steiermark (Historical Commission for Styria): Karmeliterpl. 3/II, 8010 Graz; tel. (316) 8773013; fax (316) 8775504; e-mail office@hlkstmk.at; internet www.hlkstmk.at; f. 1892; 36 mems; Pres. Mag. FRANZ VOVES; Sec. Prof. Dr ALFRED ABLEITINGER; publs *Forschungen und Darstellungen zur Geschichte des Steiermärkischen Landtages, Forschungen zur geschichtlichen Landeskunde der Steiermark, Geschichte der Steiermark, Mitteilungen der Korrespondentinnen und Korrespondenten der Historischen Landeskommission für Steiermark, Quellen zur geschichtlichen Landeskunde der Steiermark, Veröffentlichungen der Historischen Landeskommission für Steiermark.*

Historischer Verein für Steiermark (Styrian Historical Association): Karmeliterpl. 3, 8010 Graz; tel. and fax (316) 8772366; e-mail info@historischerverein.li; internet www.historischerverein.li; f. 1850; 1,360 mems; Chair. Prof. Dr GERHARD PFERSCHY; Sec. MARCO SCHAEDLER; publs *Beiträge zur Erforschung Steirischer Geschichtsquellen, Blätter für Heimatkunde, Zeitschrift.*

Kommission für Neuere Geschichte Österreichs (Commission for Modern Austrian History): Neustiftgasse 47/5, 1070 Vienna; tel. (1) 515817313; fax (1) 515817330; e-mail doris.corradini@chello.at; internet www.oesterreichische-geschichte.at; f. 1900; research into and publishes about modern Austrian history since the 16th century; 28 mems; Chair. Prof. BRIGITTE MAZOHL; Sec. Mag. DORIS CORRADINI; publ. *Veröffentlichungen der Kommission für Neuere Geschichte Österreichs.*

Österreichische Byzantinische Gesellschaft (Austrian Byzantine Society): Institut für Byzantinistik und Neogräzistik, Universität Wien, Postgasse 7/1/3, 1010 Vienna; tel. (1) 427741001; fax (1) 42779410; e-mail byz-neo@univie.ac.at; internet www.byzneo.univie.ac.at/oesterreichische-byzantinische-gesellschaft; f. 1946; attached to Institute of Culture and History, Univ. of Vienna; studies Byzantine history, culture and art; 145 mems; Pres. Prof. Dr JOHANNES KODER; Vice-Pres. Prof. Dr WOLFRAM HÖRANDNER; Sec. ANDREAS KIILZ; publ. *Mitteilungen aus der österreichischen Byzantinistik und Neogräzistik* (1 a year).

Österreichische Geographische Gesellschaft (Austrian Geographical Society): Karl Schweighofer-Gasse 3, 1071 Vienna; tel. and fax (1) 5237974; e-mail kanzlei@oegg.info; internet www.oegg.info; f. 1856; represents and supports interests of Austrian geographers in all professional fields; promotes geography education; organizes lectures, discussions, excursions; 1,400 mems; library: see under Libraries; Pres. Dr CHRISTIAN STAUDACHER; Sec.-Gen. ROBERT MUSIL; publ. *Mitteilungen der Österreichischen Geographischen Gesellschaft* (1 a year).

Österreichische Gesellschaft für Archäologie (Austrian Archaeological Society): c/o Institut für Alte Geschichte, Altertumskunde und Epigraphik, Universität Wien, Dr Karl Lueger-Ring I, 1010 Vienna; e-mail oega@univie.ac.at; internet www.univie.ac.at/oega; f. 1972; publishes on topics relevant

to Austria in archaeology, ancient history and numismatics; public lectures, excursions; 190 mems; Pres. Doz. Dr PETER SCHERRER; Vice-Pres. Dr GUNTER FITZ; Sec. REINHARD LANG; publs *Althistorisch-epigraphische Studien* (irregular), *Austria Antiqua* (irregular), *Römisches Österreich* (1 a year).

Österreichische Gesellschaft für Ur- und Frühgeschichte (Austrian Society for Pre- and Early History): c/o Institut für Ur- und Frühgeschichte, Franz-Klein-Gasse 1, 1190 Vienna; tel. (1) 427740473; fax (1) 42779404; e-mail alexandra.krenn-leeb@univie.ac.at; internet www.oeguf.ac.at; f. 1950; 1,050 mems; Gen. Sec. Mag. Dr ALEXANDRA KRENN-LEEB; publ. *Archäologie Österreichs* (2 a year).

Österreichische Numismatische Gesellschaft (Austrian Numismatic Society): c/o Münze Österreich, Am Heumarkt 1, 1010 Vienna; tel. (1) 525244203; fax (1) 525244299; e-mail office@oeng.at; internet www.oeng.at; f. 1870; organizes exhibitions, lectures, excursions related to numismatics; 400 mems; library of 5,000 vols; Pres. Dr GÜNTHER DEMBSKI; Vice-Pres. DIETMAR SPRANZ; Sec. Dr MICHAEL ALRAM; publ. *Numismatische Zeitschrift* (irregular).

Österreichische Orient-Gesellschaft Hammer-Purgstall (Austrian Orient Society Hammer-Purgstall): Dominikanerbastei 6/6, 1010 Vienna; tel. (1) 5128936; fax (1) 512893617; e-mail office@orient-gesellschaft.at; internet www.orient-gesellschaft.at; f. 1952; informs and educates about people, cultures, politics and soc. in the Middle East; offers courses in oriental languages, talks, lectures, seminars, symposia, cultural evenings and workshops on education, but also on topical issues; Pres. Prof. Dr BERT FRAGNER; Gen. Sec. Dr SIEGFRIED HAAS.

Verband Österreichischer Historiker und Geschichtsvereine (Union of Austrian Historians and Historical Associations): Österreichisches Staatsarchiv Nottendorfergasse 2, 1030 Vienna; tel. (1) 79540100; fax (1) 79540149; e-mail lorenz.mikoletzky@oesta.gv.at; f. 1949; 130 mem. socs; Pres. WILLIBALD ROSNER; Vice-Pres. Prof. Dr LORENZ MIKOLETZKY; Gen. Sec. Dr ERWIN A. SCHMIDL; publ. *Veröffentlichungen des Verbands Österreichischer Historiker und Geschichtsvereine* (every 2 or 3 years).

Verein für Geschichte der Stadt Wien (Association for the History of the City of Vienna): Wiener Stadt- und Landesarchiv, Rathaus, 1082 Vienna; Wiener Stadt- und Landesarchiv, 11, Gugldgasse 14, Gasometer D, 5. Stock, Zimmer 506, 1082 Vienna; tel. (1) 400084815; fax (1) 400084809; e-mail karl.fischer@wien.gv.at; internet www.wien.gv.at/kultur/archiv/kooperationen/vgw/; f. 1853; based in Vienna Municipal and Provincial Archives; researches and publishes on Vienna's history; 1,592 mems; Pres. Dr KARL FISCHER; Vice-Pres. Dr HELMUT KRETSCHMER; Sec. Dr SUSANNE CLAUDINE PILS; publs *Studien zur Wiener Geschichte* (1 a year), *Wiener Geschichtsblätter* (4 a year).

LANGUAGE AND LITERATURE

Austria Esperantista Federacio (Austrian Esperanto Society): POB 39, 1014 Vienna; tel. (1) 8934196; e-mail aef@esperanto.at; internet www.esperanto.at; f. 1935; official national organization of the World Esperanto Association in Austria; works to promote the Esperanto language by serving as a contact, exchanging and disseminating information, operating the website, producing and distributing information material, working with int. or nat. Esperanto orgs, maintaining and sharing experience and contacts; 500 mems; library of 1,500 vols, 1,000 pamphlets; Hon. Pres. Prof. Dr HANS MICHAEL MAITZEN; Chair. BERNHARD TUIDER; Deputy Chair. KATALIN FETES-TOSEGI; publs *Austria-Esperanto-Revuo, Esperanto - Aktuell* (6 a year), *Esperanto-Servo* (4 a year).

British Council: Siebensterngasse 21, 1070 Vienna; tel. (1) 533261677; fax (1) 533261665; e-mail exams@britishcouncil.at; internet www.britishcouncil.at; f. 1946; offers IELTS and Cambridge ESOL English language examinations; promotes cultural exchange with the UK; library contains large colln of modern British fiction, titles on British studies and English language-learning materials; access to British websites, databases and learning software; Dir WILL TODD.

Eranos Vindobonensis: Institut für Klassische Philologie, Mittel- und Neulatein, Universität Wien, Dr Karl Lueger-Ring 1, 1010 Vienna; tel. (1) 4277419; fax (1) 42779419; e-mail andrea.duchac @ univie.ac .at; internet kphil.ned.univie.ac.at/node/ 124629; f. 1876; promotes study of classical archaeology by specialized lectures and presentations, knowledge and experience; 90 mems; Pres. Prof. Dr MARION MEYER; Vice-Pres. Prof. Dr FAROUK F. GREWAL; Sec. and Treas. Prof. Dr PAUL RAIMUND LORENZ.

Gesellschaft für Klassische Philologie in Innsbruck (Classical Philological Society of Innsbruck): Institut für Klassische Philologie, Universität Innsbruck, Innrain 52, 6020 Innsbruck; tel. (512) 5074082; fax (512) 5072982; e-mail klassphil@uibk.ac.at; internet www.uibk.ac.at/sci-org/klassphil; f. 1958; taking philology to the public, offers lectures, readings productions and travels; 200 mems; Chair. SIMON ZUENELLI; Chair. Dr LAV SUBARIC; Chair. Prof. Dr KARL HEINZ TÖCHTERLE; Sec. KATHY ZIPSER; publ. *Acta philologica Aenipontiana*.

Gesellschaft zur Förderung Slawistischer Studien (Society for Slavic Studies): Teschnergasse 4/17, 1180 Vienna; f. 1983; Dir AAGE HANSEN-LÖVE; publs *Journal* (2 a year), *Wiener Slawistischer Almanach*, monograph series (4 a year).

Instituto Cervantes: Schwarzenbergpl. 2, 1010 Vienna; tel. (1) 5052535; fax (1) 505253518; e-mail cenvie@cervantes.es; internet viena.cervantes.es; f. 1991; offers courses and examinations in Spanish language and culture and promotes cultural exchange with Spain and Spanish-speaking Latin and Central America; library of 27,000 vols, 70 periodicals, 920 music CDs, 2,000 VHS-DVDs; Dir JUAN MANUEL CASADO RAMOS; Asst Dir BARBARA STURZEIS.

Österreichische Gesellschaft für Literatur (Austrian Literary Society): Herrengasse 5, 1010 Vienna; tel. (1) 5338159; fax (1) 5334067; e-mail office@ogl.at; internet www .ogl.at; f. 1961; works for promotion and propagation of Austrian literature; presentations, discussions, translations; builds cultural connections; Pres. MARIANNE GRUBER.

Österreichische Goethe-Gesellschaft (Austrian Goethe Society): Prof. Dr. Herbert Zeman, Peterspl. 10/2A, 1010 Vienna; tel. (1) 5336728; e-mail goethe.germanistik@univie .ac.at; internet www.univie.ac.at/goethe/ html; f. 1878 as Wiener Goethen-Verein, present name 2004; conducts readings, lectures, concerts, recitations, symposia, tours, excursions to promote life and work of Johann Wolfgang von Goethe; 300 mems; library of 2,000 books; Pres. Prof. Dr HERBERT ZEMAN; Vice-Pres. Prof. Dr HEINZ KREJCI; Sec. Mag. EMMERICH MAZAKARINI; publ. *Jahrbuch*.

Wiener Humanistische Gesellschaft: Institut für Klassische Philologie, Mittel-

und Neulatein, Univ. Wien, Dr-Karl-Lueger-Ring 1, 1010 Vienna; tel. (1) 427741901; fax (1) 42779419; e-mail kurt.smolak@univie .ac.at; internet www.univie.ac.at/klassphil; f. 1947; philological soc.; promotes humanities; 600 mems; Jt Pres. Prof. HEINRICH STREMITZER; Jt Pres. Prof. KURT SMOLAK; Sec. Dr MARGIT KAMPTNER; Administrator ANDREA DUCHAC; publ. *Wiener Humanistische Blätter*.

Wiener Sprachgesellschaft (Vienna Language Society): Universität Wien, Institut für Sprachwissenschaft, Sensengasse 3A, 1090 Vienna; fax (1) 427741799; e-mail wsg .sprachwissenschaft@univie.ac.at; internet www.univie.ac.at/indogermanistik/wsg; f. 1947; promotes academic study of language in all its forms; 100 mems; Pres. Prof. Dr NIKOLAUS RITT; Exec. Chair. Dr HANS CHRISTIAN LUSCHÜTZKY; Sec. Dr DAVID STIFTER; Sec. CORINNA SALOMON; publ. *Die Sprache* (1 a year).

MEDICINE

Gesellschaft der Ärzte in Wien (Vienna Society of Physicians): Postfach 147, Frankgasse 8, 1090 Vienna; tel. (1) 4054777; fax (1) 4023090; e-mail info@billrothhaus.at; internet www.billrothhaus.at; f. 1837; training, presentation of new medical research findings; organizes scientific events; 2,500 mems; library of 200,000 vols, 25,900 monographs; Pres. Univ. Prof. Dr KARL-HEINZ TRAGL; Secs Univ. Prof. Dr PAUL AIGINGER, Univ. Prof. Dr BEATRIX VOLC-PLATZER; publ. *Wiener Klinische Wochenschrift*.

Gesellschaft der Chirurgen in Wien (Vienna Society of Surgeons): c/o Universitätsklinik für Chirurgie, Klin. Abteilung für Allgemeinchirurgie, Währinger Gürtel 18–20, 1090 Vienna; tel. (1) 404006566; fax (1) 404006566; e-mail chirurgie@billrothhaus.at; internet www.chirurgie-ges.at; f. 1935; 171 mems; Pres. Prof. Dr ADELHEID END; Sec. Prof. Dr BÉLA TELEKY.

Internationale Paracelsus-Gesellschaft: Duerlingerstr. 23, 5020 Salzburg; tel. (662) 826773; e-mail info@paracelsusgesellschaft .com; internet www.paracelsusgesellschaft .at; f. 1951; 315 mems, 27 mem. asscns; scientific society with charitable objectives; founded to deepen and disseminate Paracelsus's findings and investigate the influence of his devt of natural and social sciences; Pres. Prof. Dr HEINZ DOPSCH; Gen. Sec. GERTRAUD WEISS; publ. *Salzburger Beiträge zur Paracelsusforschung* (irregular).

Österreichische Gesellschaft für Anästhesiologie, Reanimation und Intensivmedizin (Austrian Society of Anaesthesiology, Resuscitation and Intensive Care Medicine): Höfergasse 13, 1090 Vienna; tel. (1) 4064810; fax (1) 4064811; e-mail office@oegari.at; internet www.oegari .at; f. 1951; promotes and develops anesthesiology, resuscitation, intensive care, pain management, emergency medicine and disaster medicine; organizes meetings, lectures, scientific meetings, demonstrations, discussions, training programmes; 1,431 mems; Pres. Prof. Dr HELFRIED METZLER; Sec. Dr MANFRED GREHER; publ. *A + IC News* (4 a year).

Österreichische Gesellschaft für Arbeitsmedizin (Austrian Society for Occupational Health): Kaplanhofstr. 1, 4020 Linz; tel. (732) 7815600; fax (732) 784594; internet www.gamed.at; f. 1954; research and identification of work-related health hazards; promotion and devt of workplace health; training programmes for medical and non medical audiences; 350 mems; Pres. Dr CHRISTINE KLIEN.

Österreichische Gesellschaft für Chirurgie (Austrian Society for Surgery): Frankgasse 8, POB 80, 1096 Vienna; tel. (1) 4087920; fax (1) 4081328; e-mail chirurgie@ billrothhaus.at; internet www.chirurgie-ges .at; f. 1958; incl. the associated Austrian socs for traumatology, orthopaedic, thoracic and cardiac surgery, vascular surgery, neurosurgery, obesity surgery, paediatric surgery, plastic, aesthetic and reconstructive surgery, surgical oncology, osteosynthesis, coloproctology, hand surgery, surgical research, Maxillo-Facial surgery, surgical endocrinology, keyhole surgery, medical videography, surgical endoscopy, hernia surgery, implantology and tissue-integrated prosthesis, Austrian Section of the Int. Soc. for Digestive Surgery; 4,892 mems; Pres. Prof. Dr RUDOLF ROKA; publs *Chirurgie* (4 a year), *European Surgery/Acta Chirurgica Austriaca* (6 a year).

Österreichische Gesellschaft für Dermatologie und Venereologie (Austrian Dermatological and Venereologie Society): c/o Wiener Medizinische Akademie, Alser str. 4, 1090 Vienna; tel. (1) 405138320; fax (1) 405138323; e-mail kknob@medacad.org; internet www.oegdv.at/cms; f. 1890; aims for scientific devt and practical implementation in the field to promote specialized disciplines; organizes annual scientific and educational confs and operates a special working group for dermatological training; 876 mems; Pres. Prof. Dr JOSEF AUBÖCK; Vice-Pres. Prof. Dr BEATRIX VOLC-PLATZER.

Österreichische Gesellschaft für Geriatrie und Gerontologie (Austrian Society for Geriatrics and Gerontology): Sozialmedizinisches Zentrum, Apollogasse 19, 1070 Vienna; tel. (1) 521035770; fax (1) 521035779; e-mail ilse.howanietz@wienkav .at; internet www.geriatrie-online.at; f. 1955; researches into aging process, geriatric and gerontologic knowledge; organises scientific meetings and international asscns in the same field; three sections: geriatric, biogerontology and social gerontology; 400 mems; library of 2,000 vols; Pres. Prof. Dr PETER PIETSCHMANN; Vice-Pres. Dr HANNES PLANK; Vice-Pres. Dr MONIKA LECHLEITNER; Sec. ILSE HOWANIETZ; publs *Aktuelle Gerontologie* (12 a year), *European Journal of Geriatrics*, *Geriatrie Praxis Österreich* (6 a year), *Scriptum Geriatricum* (1 a year).

Österreichische Gesellschaft für Hals-, Nasen-, Ohrenheilkunde Kopf- und Halschirurgie (Austrian Society of Ear, Nose and Throat Science, Head and Neck Surgery): Frau Mag. Andrea BALCAR c/o Mondial Congress & Events Operngasse 20B, 1040 Vienna; tel. (1) 58804800; fax (1) 58804185; e-mail sekretariat@hno.at; internet www.hno.at; f. 1892; 640 mems; Pres. Prof. Dr WOLFGANG ZOROWKA; Gen. Sec. Prof. Dr HANS EDMUND ECKEL; publ. *Zeitschrift*.

Österreichische Gesellschaft für Innere Medizin (Austrian Society for Internal Medicine): c/o MAW Freyung 6/3, 1010 Vienna; tel. (1) 5366316; fax (1) 5366361; e-mail oegim@oegim.at; internet www.oegim .at; f. 1901; science and research, education and training in the entire field of internal medicine; promotes and improves the field based on latest medical care; lobbies public instns on matters regarding internal medicine; 400 mems; Pres. Prof. Dr ERNST PILGER; Sec.-Gen. Prof. Dr MARKUS PECK-RADOSAVLJEVIĆ; publ. *Education (Wiener Klinische Wochenschrift)*.

Österreichische Gesellschaft für Kinder- und Jugendheilkunde (Austrian Society for Paediatrics and Adolescent Medicine): Landes-Frauen- und Kinderklinik Linz

Krankenhausstr. 26–30, 4020 Linz; tel. (5055) 46322002; fax (5055) 46322004; e-mail monika.matzinger@gespag.at; internet www.docs4you.at; f. 1962; scientific org. representing interests of its members and providing professional-oriented information; raises awareness consults on policy making in the field; 805 mems; Pres. Prof. Dr KLAUS SCHMITT; Vice-Pres. Prof. Dr REINHOLD KERBL; Exec. Sec. MONIKA MATZINGER; publs *Monatsschrift Kinderheilkunde* (online), *Pädiatrie und Pädologie* (6 a year).

Österreichische Gesellschaft für Klinische Neurophysiologie (Austrian Clinical Neurophysiological Society): Institut für Neurophysiologie der Universität Wien, Währingerstr. 18–20, 1090 Vienna; e-mail mcgraf@aon.at; internet www.oegkn.at; f. 1956; promotes cooperation in fields of electroencephalography and clinical neurophysiology (research and area of application of neurobioelectric appearances); 250 mems; Pres Prof. Dr CHRISTOPH BAUMGARTNER, Prof. Dr EUGEN TRINKA; Secs Prof. Dr IRIS UNTERBERGER, Doz. Dr MARTIN GRAF; publs *EEG/EMG, Thieme* (4 a year).

Österreichische Gesellschaft für Reproduktionsmedizin und Endokrinologie (Austrian Society of Reproductive Medicine and Endocrinology): Kaiser Franz Josef Kai 45, 8010 Graz; tel. (316) 3853810; fax (316) 3854189; e-mail wolfgang.urdl@kfunizgraz.ac.at; internet www.oegrm.at; f. 1983 as Austrian Soc. for In Vitro Fertilization and Assisted Reproduction, present name 1997; umbrella org. for all activities under the reproductive medicine and endocrinology, especially in vitro fertilization and related therapy; Pres. Prof. Dr WOLFGANG URDL; Vice-Pres. Prof. Dr LUDWIG WILDT; Sec. Prof. Dr HERBERT ZECH BREGENZ; Sec. Doz. Dr DIETMAR SPITZER; publ. *Journal für Reproduktionsmedizin und Endokrinologie*.

Österreichische Gesellschaft für Urologie und Andrologie (Austrian Society for Urology and Andrology): Landesklinikum Weinviertel Mistelbach, Liechtensteinstr. 67 2130 Mistelbach; tel. (2572) 33419600; fax (2572) 33414454; e-mail walter.albrecht@mistelbach.lknoe.at; internet www.uro.at; organizes annual training conference, seminars, teaching and training sessions, conducts scientific research and publishes study results; represents interests of the urologists and andrologists in relations with public bodies and institutions; 511 mems; Pres. Dr KLAUS JESCHKE; Sec. Doz. Dr WALTER ALBRECHT; publ. *NÖGU* (2 a year).

Österreichische Ophthalmologische Gesellschaft (Austrian Ophthalmological Society): Schlüsselgasse 9, 1080 Vienna; tel. (1) 4028540; fax (1) 4027935; e-mail oeog@augen.at; internet www.augen.at; f. 1955; promotes ophthalmology and represents the interests of ophthalmologists in Austria and internationally; 730 mems; library of 2,100 vols; Pres. Prof. Dr GÜNTHER GRABNER; Sec. Dr MATTHIAS BOLZ; publ. *Spectrum der Augenheilkunde* (6 a year).

Österreichische Röntgengesellschaft—Gesellschaft für Medizinische Radiologie und Nuklearmedizin (Austrian Radiological Society—Society for Medical Radiology and Nuclear Medicine): Neutorgasse 9/2A, 1010 Vienna; tel. (1) 5334064; fax (1) 5334064448; e-mail office@oerg.at; internet www.oerg.info; f. 1946; 800 mems; Pres. Prof. Dr DIMITER TSCHOLAKOFF; Sec. Prof. Dr CHRISTIAN LOEWE; publ. *ÖRG—Mitteilungen* (4 a year).

Verein für Psychiatrie und Neurologie (Society for Psychiatry and Neurology): Universitätsklinik für Neurologie, AKH, Währinger Gürtel 18–20, 1090 Vienna; tel. (1)

404003514; fax (1) 404003141; internet www.verein-psychiatrie-neurologie.at; f. 1867; promotes the scientific and medical communication between psychiatrists and neurologists; holds regular meetings; bestows research support awards; Pres. Prof. Dr KENNETH THAU; Secs Prof. Dr ANDREAS ERFURTH, Dr JULIA FERRARI.

Wiener Medizinische Akademie für Ärztliche Fortbildung und Forschung (Vienna Academy of Postgraduate Medical Education and Research): Alser str. 4, 1090 Vienna; Spitalgasse 2, Entrance 'Freud Tor 1', Hof, Ehem. Direktionsgebäude, 2nd. Fl., 1090 Vienna; tel. (1) 40513830; fax (1) 405138323; e-mail office@medacad.org; internet www.medacad.org; f. 1924; conf. and asscn management instn for medical non-profit community, providing leadership, organizational guidance, headquarters facilities and staff resources; Pres. Prof. Dr H. GRÜBER; Exec. Dirs JEROME DEL PICCHIA, ROMANA KÖNIG; Secs Prof. Dr W. GRISOLD, Prof. Dr R. DUDCZAK.

NATURAL SCIENCES

General

Naturwissenschaftlicher Verein für Kärnten (Carinthian Association of Natural Sciences): Museumgasse 2, Landesmuseum, 9021 Klagenfurt; tel. (463) 53630574; fax (463) 53630597; e-mail nwv@landesmuseum-ktn.at; internet www.naturwissenschaft-ktn.at; f. 1848; 1,300 mems; Pres. Dr HELMUT ZWANDER; publ. *Carinthia II* (1 a year, with special issues).

Biological Sciences

Österreichische Mykologische (Pilzkundliche) Gesellschaft (Austrian Mycological Society): Rennweg 14, 1030 Vienna; tel. (1) 427754050; fax (1) 42779541; e-mail irmgard.greilhuber@univie.ac.at; internet www.myk.univie.ac.at; f. 1919; 320 mems; library of 1,000 vols; mycological herbarium colln, fungal records online database, excursions, lectures, newsletter; Pres. Dkfm A. HAUSKNECHT; Vice-Pres. IRMGARD GREILHUBER; publ. *Österreichische Zeitschrift für Pilzkunde* (1 a year).

Zoologisch-Botanische Gesellschaft in Österreich (Austrian Zoological-Botanical Society): Althanstr. 14, POB 207, 1091 Vienna; fax (1) 4277542; e-mail wolfgang.punz@univie.ac.at; internet www.univie.ac.at/zoobot; f. 1851; lectures; excursions; library; publs; exchange of publs; nature conservation; botanical illustration courses; confers Walter Fiedler Promotion award; library: spec. library for zoology, botany and ecology; 2,800 periodicals, 4,500 monographs; 610 mems; Pres. Dr ERICH HÜBL; Sec.-Gen. Prof. Mag. Dr WOLFGANG PUNZ; publs *Abhandlungen* (irregular), *Koleopterologische Rundschau* (1 a year), *Verhandlungen* (1 a year).

Mathematical Sciences

Mathematisch-Physikalische Gesellschaft in Innsbruck (Mathematics and Physics Society of Innsbruck): c/o Manfred P. Leubner, Institut für Astrophysik, Universität Innsbruck, Technikerstr. 25, 6020 Innsbruck; tel. (512) 5126060; fax (512) 5122923; e-mail math-phys-ges@uibk.ac.at; f. 1936; 126 mems; Chair. MANFRED P. LEUBNER.

Österreichische Mathematische Gesellschaft (Austrian Mathematical Society): Technische Univ., E104, Wiedner Hauptstr. 8–10, 1040 Vienna; tel. (1) 5880110423; e-mail oemg@oemg.ac.at; internet www.oemg.ac.at; f. 1903; 537 mems; Chair. M. DRMOTA; Sec. F. URBANEK;

publs *International Mathematical News* (3 a year), *Monatshefte für Mathematik* (12 a year).

Physical Sciences

Chemisch-Physikalische Gesellschaft in Wien (Vienna Chemical-Physical Society): Universität Wien, Fakultät für Physik, Strudlhofgasse 4/Boltzmanngasse 5, 1090 Vienna; tel. (1) 427751108; fax (1) 42779732; e-mail christl.langstadlinger@univie.ac.at; internet www.cpg.univie.ac.at; f. 1869; holds meetings, promotes research papers to encourage the spread of skills in chemistry and physics; awards the Loschmidt Prize to support graduates in chemistry or physics; 260 mems; Pres. Prof. Dr PETER MOHN; Sec. CRISTL LANG STADLINGER; publ. *Bulletin* (2 a year).

Gesellschaft Österreichischer Chemiker (Austrian Chemical Society): Nibelungengasse 11/6, 1010 Vienna; tel. (1) 5874249; fax (1) 5878966; e-mail office@goech.at; internet www.goech.at; f. 1897; educational programme for professional advancement in chemistry; 1,900 mems in attached socs; Pres. Prof. Dr HERBERT IPSER; Vice-Pres. Dr PETER JAITNER; Man. Dir Dr ERICH LEITNER; publs *Chemiereport.at* (online at: www.chemiereport.at), *Chemistry–A European Journal* (co-author), *Monatshefte für Chemie*.

Österreichische Geologische Gesellschaft (Austrian Geological Society): Geologische Bundesanstalt, Neulingsgasse 38, 1030 Vienna; tel. (1) 71256740; fax (1) 712567456; e-mail oegg@geologie.ac.at; internet www.geol-ges.at; f. 1907; promotes the science of geology theoretical and practical, especially of the Austrian Alps and surrounding areas; affiliated to American Association of Petroleum Geologists (AAPG); 714 mems; Pres. CHRISTIAN SPÖTL; Vice-Pres. WOLFGANG NACHTMANN; Sec. GERHARD SCHUBERT; publ. *Austrian Journal of Earth Sciences*.

Österreichische Gesellschaft für Analytische Chemie (Austrian Society for Analytical Chemistry):; tel. (1) 427752300; e-mail wolfgang.lindner@univie.ac.at; internet www.asac.at; f. 1948; provides support to research, teaching and application of microchemistry and analytical chemistry; gives awards, scholarships; holds training programmes confs and seminars; 400 mems; Pres. Prof. Dr WOLFGANG LINDNER; Sec. Prof. Dr R. KRSKA; Sec. Prof. Dr M. LÄMMERHOFER.

Österreichische Gesellschaft für Erdölwissenschaften (Austrian Society for Petroleum Sciences): c/o Wirtschaftskammer Österreich, Wiedner Hauptstr. 63, Zimmer 4208, 1045 Vienna; tel. (5) 909004891; fax (5) 909004895; e-mail oegew@oil-gas.at; internet www.oegew.org; f. 1960; promotes science, research, technology and training in exploration, production and storage of petroleum and natural gas; processing and use of petroleum, natural gas and derived products; petrochemistry; also confers the Hans Höfer medal; works with domestic and foreign scientific societies; 502 mems; Pres. REINHART SAMHAT; Sec. SABINE JEHOTEK; publs *Erdöl Erdgas Kohle*, scientific papers.

Österreichische Gesellschaft für Laboratoriumsmedizin und Klinische Chemie (Austrian Society of Laboratory Medicine and Clinical Chemistry): Tullnertalgasse 72, 1230 Vienna; tel. and fax (1) 8896238; e-mail office@oeglmkc.at; internet www.oeglmkc.at; f. 2004; 29 ; Pres. Doz. Dr ALEXANDER C. HAUSHOFER; Vice-Pres. Dr GEORG MUSTAFA.

Österreichische Gesellschaft für Meteorologie (Austrian Meteorological Society): Hohe Warte 38, 1190 Vienna; tel. (1) 360262201; fax (1) 3602672; internet www

.meteorologie.at; f. 1865; metereologcial studies; organizes meetings, lectures, confs; 230 mems; Pres. Prof. Dr FRANZ RUBEL; Sec.-Gen. Dr ERNEST RUDEL; publ. *Meteorologische Zeitschrift* (6 a year).

Österreichische Gesellschaft für Molekulare Biowissenschaften und Biotechnologie (Austrian Association for Molecular Life Sciences and Biotechnology): Institute of Applied Genetics and Cell Biology, Dept of Applied Plant Sciences and Plant Biotechnology, Univ. of Natural Resources and Applied Life Sciences, Muthgasse 18, Haus A, 2. Stock, Zimmer 65 1190 Vienna; tel. (1) 476546394; fax (1) 476546392; e-mail andrea.veitschegger@boku.ac.at; internet www.oegmbt.at; attached to ÖGBT (Austrian Soc. for Biotechnology), ÖGGGT (Austrian Asscn for Genetics and Genetic Engineering) and ÖGBM (Austrian Asscn for Biochemistry and Molecular Biology); promotes research and education in biochemistry, molecular biology and cell biology; 1,000 mems; Pres. JOSEF GLOESSL; Vice-Pres. HANS GRUNICKE; Vice-Pres. ANGELA SESSITSCH; Exec. Sec. ANDREA VEITSCHEGGER; publ. *ÖGBM Nachrichten* (4 a year).

Österreichische Physikalische Gesellschaft (Austrian Physical Society): c/o Dr Karl Riedling, Institute of Sensor and Actuator Systems, TU Vienna, Gusshausstrasse 27/366 1040 Vienna; tel. (1) 5880136658; fax (1) 5880136699; e-mail karl.riedling@tuwien.ac.at; internet www.oepg.at; f. 1950; promotes physical sciences in research, devt and teaching; brings together Austrian physicists and represents them in outside matters; mem. of other int. physicist orgs; 870 mems; Pres. Prof. Dr ERICH GORNIK; Vice-Pres. Prof. Dr MONIKA RITSCH-MARTE; Man. Dir Prof. Dr KARL RIEDLING; publ. *Mitteilungsblatt der ÖPG*.

Österreichischer Astronomischer Verein (Austrian Astronomical Association): Hasenwartgasse 32, 1230 Vienna; tel. (1) 88935410; fax (1) 889354111; e-mail astbuero@astronomisches-buero-wien.or.at; internet www.astronomisches-buero-wien.or.at; f. 1924; astronomical phenomenology; organizes lectures and guided tours; runs a fully automatic fireball station at Martinsberg, Lower Austria and an open air planetarium in Vienna, Georgenberg; 1,500 mems; Pres. Univ. Prof. Dipl.-Ing. Dr ROBERT WEBER; Dir Prof. HERMANN MUCKE; publs *Astronomische Buero: Der Sternenbote* (12 a year), *Der Sternenbote* (12 a year), *Österreichischer Himmelskalender* (1 a year).

PHILOSOPHY AND PSYCHOLOGY

Österreichische Gesellschaft für Parapsychologie und Grenzbereiche der Wissenschaften (Austrian Society for Parapsychology and Frontier Areas of Science): c/o Manfred Kremser, Institute for Social and Cultural Anthropology, Univ. of Vienna, Universitätsstr. 7, 1010 Vienna; tel. (6) 764167190; e-mail office@parapsychologie.ac.at; internet parapsychologie.ac.at; f. 1927; 180 mems; library of 1,200 vols; Pres. Prof. Dr MANFRED KREMSER; Vice-Pres. and Sec.-Gen. Prof. W. PETER MULACZ.

Philosophische Gesellschaft Wien (Philosophical Society of Vienna): Universitätsstr. 7/2/2, 1010 Vienna; tel. (1) 427747402; fax (1) 427747492; f. 1954; 100 mems; Dir Prof. Dr HANS-DIETER KLEIN.

Sigmund Freud Privatstiftung (Sigmund Freud Foundation): Berggasse 19, 1090 Vienna; tel. (1) 3191596; fax (1) 3170279; e-mail office@freud-museum.at; internet www.freud-museum.at; f. 1968; history and application of psychoanalysis; archives; Sigmund Freud museum; 1,000 mems; library of

38,000 vols, 15,000 offprints, 45 journals; Chair. Mag. INGE SCHOLZ-STRASSER.

Wiener Psychoanalytische Vereinigung (Vienna Psychoanalytic Society): Salzgries 16/3, 1010 Vienna; tel. (1) 5330767; e-mail office@wpv.at; internet www.wpv.at; f. 1908; 200 mems; Pres. Dr ELISABETH SKALE; Sec. VIOLA SEIBERT.

RELIGION, SOCIOLOGY AND ANTHROPOLOGY

Anthropologische Gesellschaft in Wien (Vienna Anthropological Society): Burgring 7, 1010 Vienna; tel. (1) 52177569; fax (1) 52177309; e-mail ag@nhm-wien.ac.at; internet ag.nhm-wien.ac.at; f. 1870; 300 mems; Pres. HR. Dr HERBERT KRITSCHER; Sec. HR. Dr ANTON KERN; publs *Anthropologische Forschungen* (irregular), *Mitteilungen der Anthropologischen Gesellschaft in Wien* (1 a year), *Prähistorische Forschungen* (irregular), *Völkerkundliche Veröffentlichungen* (irregular).

Evangelische Akademie Wien (Evangelical Academy in Vienna): Schwarzspanierstr. 13, 1090 Vienna; tel. (1) 4080695; fax (1) 408069533; e-mail akademie@evang.at; internet www.evang-akademie.at; f. 1955; Protestant adult education; documentation on church and soc.; Dir WALTRAUT KOVACIC.

Gesellschaft für die Geschichte des Protestantismus in Österreich (Society for History of Protestantism in Austria): c/o Univ. Prof. Dr Rudolf Leeb, Room 6OG009, Schenkenstr. 8–10, 1010 Vienna; e-mail rudolf.leeb@univie.ac.at; f. 1879; 300 mems; Pres. Prof. Dr RUDOLF LEEB.

Österreichische Gesellschaft für Soziologie (Austrian Sociological Society): Fachbereich Soziologie Technische Universität Wien Paniglgasse 16, 1040 Vienna; tel. (1) 5880127312; e-mail kontakt@oegs.ac.at; internet www.oegs.ac.at; f. 1950; 500 mems; Pres. Prof. Dr JENS DANGSCHAT; publ. *Österreichische Zeitschrift für Soziologie* (4 a year).

Verein für Landeskunde von Niederösterreich (Association for Regional Studies of Lower Austria): Landhauspl. 1, Haus Kulturbezirk 4, 3109 St Pölten; tel. (2742) 90050; fax (2742) 900512060; e-mail post.landnoe@noel.gv.at; internet www.noel.gv.at/bildung/landeskundliche-forschung/verein-fuer-landeskunde.html; f. 1864; 1,300 mems; Pres. Hofrat Dr ANTON EGGENDORFER; Gen. Sec. Mag. Dr WILLIBALD ROSNER; publs *Forschungen zur Landeskunde von Niederösterreich*, *Jahrbuch für Landeskunde von Niederösterreich*, *Unsere Heimat* (4 a year).

Verein für Volkskunde (Society of Ethnography and Popular Culture): Gartenpalais Schönborn, Laudongasse 15–19, 1080 Vienna; tel. (1) 4068905; fax (1) 4085342; e-mail verein@volkskundemuseum.at; internet www.volkskunde.org/index_verein_vk.htm; f. 1894; promotes Austrian folklore; legal representative of Österreichischen Museums für Volkskunde; collaborates with museum in scientific collecting, documentation and research, in exhibitions, event and publishing, maintaining contacts with subject-related companies; 900 mems; Pres. Dr KONRAD KÖSTLIN; Sec. Dr MARGOT SCHINDLER; publs *Österreichische Zeitschrift für Volkskunde* (4 a year), *Volkskunde in Österreich* (12 a year).

Wiener Katholische Akademie (Vienna Catholic Academy): Edith-Stein-Haus, Ebendorferstr. 8/10, 1010 Vienna; tel. and fax (1) 4023917; e-mail wka@edw.or.at; internet www.kath-akademie.at; f. 1945; seminars and lectures, symposia, publications on significant ideological issues; 110 mems; library

of 7,000 vols; Protector Erzbischof Cardinal Dr CHRISTOPH SCHÖNBORN; Gen. Sec. Mag. Dr ELISABETH MAIER; publ. *Schriften der Wiener Katholischen Akademie*.

TECHNOLOGY

Österreichische Gesellschaft für Artificial Intelligence (Austrian Association for Artificial Intelligence): POB 177, 1014 Vienna; tel. (1) 427763117; e-mail anfrage@oegai.at; internet www.oegai.at; f. 1981; promotes exploration of principles, methods and applications in the field of artificial intelligence; represents interests of its members in nat. and int. bodies; awards ÖGAI Prize to young scientists; 150 mems; Pres. ERNST BUCHBERGER; Vice-Pres. SILVIA MIKSCH; Sec. HARALD TROST; publs *AI Communications* (4 a year), *ÖGAI-Journal* (4 a year).

Österreichische Gesellschaft für Vermessung und Geoinformation (Austrian Society for Surveying and Geoinformation): Schiffamtsgasse 1–3, 1020 Vienna; tel. and fax (1) 2167551; e-mail office@ovg.at; internet www.ovg.at; f. 1973; 600 mems; library of 3,000 vols; Pres. Dipl.-Ing. GERT STEINKELLNER; Sec. Dipl.-Ing. KARL HAUSSTEINER; publ. *Österreichische Zeitschrift für Vermessung und Geoinformation* (4 a year).

Österreichische Studiengesellschaft für Kybernetik (Austrian Society for Cybernetic Studies): Freyung 6/6, 1010 Vienna; tel. (1) 5336112; fax (1) 533611220; e-mail sec@ofai.at; internet www.osgk.ac.at; f. 1969; seminars, consulting and funding for cybernetic studies; founding member of International Federation for Systems Research (IFSR); organizes biennial conferences; 1,238 mems (38 ordinary, 1,200 corresp.); Pres. Prof. Dr ROBERT TRAPPL; Sec. Prof. Dr HARALD TROST; publs *Applied Artificial Intelligence: An International Journal* (10 a year), *Cybernetics and Systems: An International Journal* (8 a year), *Reports* (irregular).

Research Institutes
AGRICULTURE, FISHERIES AND VETERINARY SCIENCE

Bundesamt und Forschungszentrum für Landwirtschaft, Wien (Federal Office and Research Centre for Agriculture, Vienna): Straudorfer Str. 1, 2286 Haringsee; tel. (2214) 7100; f. 1995; library of 100,000 vols; Dir-Gen. Hofrat Dipl.-Ing. A. KÖCHL; publs *Die Bodenkultur* (4 a year), *Pflanzenschutz* (4 a year), *Pflanzenschutzberichte* (2 a year).

Bundesamt und Forschungszentrum für Wald (Federal Office and Research Centre for Forests): Seckendorff-Gudent-Weg 8, 1131 Vienna; tel. (1) 878380; fax (1) 878381250; e-mail direktion@bfw.gv.at; internet bfw.ac.at; f. 1874; research and training instn; 6 depts, 2 forestry training centres; research focuses on sustainable multi-functional use, management and protection of forest ecosystems and catchment areas for drinking water supply, long-term changes in ecosystems and biodiversity conservation and enhancement and protection against natural hazards and geo-risk management; library of 1,712,731,805 books and journal vols; Chair. Dipl.-Forstwirt Dr HUBERT DÜRRSTEIN; Vice-Chair. Dr JOHANNES SCHIMA; publ. *BFW-Berichte* (irregular).

Bundesanstalt für Agrarwirtschaft (Federal Institute of Agricultural Economics): Marxergasse 2, 1030 Vienna; tel. (1) 8773651; fax (1) 8773651-7490; e-mail office@awi.bmlfuw.gv.at; internet www.awi.bmlfuw.gv.at; f. 1960; socioeconomic research on issues of agricultural policy, food economics, agricultural enterprises and rural areas; library of 52,193 vols, 442 periodicals; Dir Dipl.-Ing. Dr HUBERT PFINGSTNER; Librarian Mag. HUBERT SCHLIEBER; publs *Agrarpolitische Arbeitsbehelfe* (irregular), *Schriftenreihe der Bundesanstalt* (irregular).

Bundesanstalt für Alpenländische Landwirtschaft, Gumpenstein (Federal Research Institute for Agriculture in Alpine Regions, Gumpenstein): Raumberg 38, 8952 Irdning; tel. (3682) 224510; fax (3682) 2245121; e-mail office@raumberg-gumpenstein.at; internet www.gumpenstein.at/c; f. 1947; research and education facility; research in areas of livestock, animal husbandry, organic farming, plant production and cultural landscape; library of 21,000 vols; Dir Prof. Mag. Dr ALBERT SONNLEITNER; publs *BAL-Berichte, BAL-Veröffentlichungen*.

ARCHITECTURE AND TOWN PLANNING

Institut für Angewandte Mechanik (Institute of Applied Mechanics): Technikerstr. 4/II, 8010 Graz; tel. (316) 8737640; fax (316) 8737641; e-mail gundula.anger@tugraz.at; internet www.mech.tugraz.at; attached to Graz Univ. of Technology; research and teaching in mechanics regarding civil engineering; research focused on simulation of wave propagation phenomena, modelling of porous and granular media, dynamics with friction; Dir Prof. Dr-Ing. MARTIN SCHANZ.

Institut für Architektur und Landschaft (Institute of Architecture and Landscape): Technikerstraße 4/V, 8010 Graz; tel. (316) 8736311; fax (316) 8736809; e-mail ial@tugraz.at; internet www.ial.tugraz.at; attached to Graz Univ. of Technology; covers the mediation of contents and investigation of the interaction between architecture and landscape through training and research; Chair. Prof. Dipl.-Ing. KLAUS K. LOENHART.

Institut für Architektur und Medien (Institute of Architecture and Media): Inffeldgasse 10/II, 8010 Graz; tel. (316) 8734721; fax (316) 8734723; e-mail barbara.rauch@tugraz.at; internet iam.tugraz.at; attached to Graz Univ. of Technology; uses architecture along with media, film and photography; Dir Prof. URS LEONHAND HIRSCHBERG.

Institut für Architekturtechnologie (Institute of Architecture Technology): Rechbauerstr. 12/I , 8010 Graz; tel. (316) 8736301; fax (316) 8736804; e-mail office@at .tugraz.at; internet at.tugraz.at; attached to Graz Univ. of Technology; research into the discipline of building construction, not as an isolated subject but as an integral part of architecture; Dir Prof. Dipl.-Ing. ROGER RIEWE.

Institut für Architekturtheorie, Kunst- und Kulturwissenschaften (Institute of Architectural Theory, History of Art and Cultural Studies): Technikerstr. 4/3, 8010 Graz; tel. (316) 8736276; fax (316) 8736779; e-mail christine.leitgeb@tugraz.at; internet www.kunstundkultur.tugraz.at; attached to Graz Univ. of Technology; conveys knowledge of culture, history and theory of visual arts in the field of architecture; research areas lie in the analysis of architectural and artistic production in culture, media and social science; Dir Prof. Mag. Dr ANSELM WAGNER.

Institut für Baubetrieb und Bauwirtschaft (Institute of Construction Management and Economics): Lessingstr. 25/II, 8010 Graz; tel. (316) 8736251; fax (316) 8736752; e-mail sekretariat.bbw @tugraz.at; internet www.bbw.tugraz.at; attached to

Graz Univ. of Technology; based on the basics of civil engineering; emphasis on the implementation of organizational structures from design to reality; Dir. Prof. Dipl.-Ing. HANS LECHNER.

Institut für Eisenbahnwesen und Verkehrswirtschaft (Institute of Railway Engineering and Transport Economy): Rechbauerstr. 12/II, 8010 Graz; tel. (316) 8736216; fax (316) 816896; e-mail office.ebw@tugraz.at; internet www.ebw.tugraz.at; attached to Graz Univ. of Technology; overall railway system focusing on alignment, feasibility studies of new railway connections, public transport systems and solutions of the logistic problems arising; vehicles under spec. view of the wheel-rail-contact, basic research in the range of the ballast bed; studies on transport economics; Dir Prof. Dipl.-Ing. Dr PETER VEIT.

Institut für Gebäude und Energie (Institute of Buildings and Energy): Rechbauerstr. 12, 8010 Graz; tel. (316) 8734751; fax (316) 8734752; e-mail ige @tugraz.at; internet www.ige.tugraz.at; attached to Graz Univ. of Technology; pursues the goal of energy-efficient architecture; maximizing the energy performance of buildings by optimization of the form and construction; Dir Prof. BRIAN CODY.

Institut für Gebäudelehre (Institute of Architectural Typologies): Lessingstr. 25/IV, 8010 Graz; tel. (316) 8736291; fax (316) 8736297; e-mail r.lenz@tugraz.at; internet www.gl.tugraz.at; attached to Graz Univ. of Technology; architectural research into the concept of building design with regard to growing cities; Dir Prof. Dipl.-Ing. HANS GANGOLY.

Institut für Hochbau und Bauphysik (Institute of Building Construction and Building Physics): Lessingstr. 25/III, 8010 Graz; tel. (316) 8736241; fax (316) 8736740; e-mail office@ihb.tugraz.at; internet www .ihb.tugraz.at; attached to Graz Univ. of Technology; 2 sites; transfers physical principles in the construction industry, which result from theory and experiment; strives to an understanding of building physical relationships through new building materials and construction methods to prevent design errors and construction damage; notified and accredited testing and inspection agency; Dir Prof. Mag. Dr Dipl.-Ing. PETER KAUSCH.

Institut für Ingenieurgeodäsie und Messsysteme (Institute of Engineering Geodesy and Measurement Systems): Steyrergasse 30, 8010 Graz; tel. (316) 8736321; fax (316) 8736820; e-mail sandra.reinbacher @ tugraz.at; internet www.igms.tugraz.at; attached to Graz Univ. of Technology; methodology of engineering geodesy, foundation of the measurement methods in civil engineering, measurement of the geometry and the deformation of objects, monitoring and guidance of processes in civil and geotechnical engineering, measurement systems and sensors, experimental methods and modelling; Head Prof. Dipl.-Ing. Dr FRITZ K. BRUNNER.

Institut für Raumgestaltung (Institute for Spatial Design): Rechbauerstr. 12/II, 8010 Graz; tel. (316) 8736481; fax (316) 8736980; e-mail r.krueger@tugraz.at; internet www .raumgestaltung.tugraz.at; attached to Graz Univ. of Technology; focus on teaching and research; causal analysis of architectural space, perception of space and light; Dir Prof. Mag. IRMGARD FRANK.

Institut für Städtebau (Institute for Urbanism): Rechbauerstr. 12, 8010 Graz; tel. (316) 8736286; fax (316) 8736280; e-mail m.haselbacher-berner@tugraz.at; internet www.staedtebau.tugraz.at; attached to Graz Univ. of Technology; architectural research

focused on city and energy, urban devt and information technology, epistemology; Dir Prof. Dipl.-Ing. Dr JEAN MARIE CORNEILLE MEUWISSEN.

Institut für Strassen- und Verkehrswesen (Institute of Highway Engineering and Transport Planning): Rechbauerstr. 12/II, 8010 Graz; tel. (316) 8736221; fax (316) 8734199; e-mail isv@tugraz.at; internet www.isv.tugraz.at; attached to Graz Univ. of Technology; research on transport planning emphasizing behaviour-based modelling of transport; focus on GIS-based modelling of transport networks of motorized and non-motorized trips in private, public and freight transport; also research in environment-related traffic issues; Dir Prof. Dr-Ing. MARTIN FELLENDORF.

Institut für Tragwerksentwurf (Institute of Structural Design): Technikerstr. 4/IV, 8010 Graz; tel. (316) 8736211; fax (316) 8736712; e-mail tragwerksentwurf@tugraz .at; internet www.ite.tugraz.at; attached to Graz Univ. of Technology; principles of mechanics for bldg constructions and relevant topics; Dir Prof. Dr-Ing. STEFAN PETERS.

Institut für Wasserbau und Wasserwirtschaft (Institute of Hydraulic Engineering and Water Resources Management): Stremayrgasse 10/II, 8010 Graz; tel. (316) 8738861; fax (316) 8738357; e-mail hydro@tugraz.at; internet www.hydro.tugraz.at; f. 1865; attached to Graz Univ. of Technology; study of hydraulic structures and their optimization in engineering, fluid engineering, construction and economy, in conjunction with relevant subject areas (esp. geotechnical), and with the quantitative water management principles in accordance with environmental requirements; Dir Prof. GERALD ZENZ.

Österreichisches Institut für Raumplanung (Austrian Institute for Regional Studies and Spatial Planning): Franz Josefs Kai 27, 1010 Vienna; tel. (1) 53387470; fax (1) 533874766; e-mail oir@oir.at; internet www .oir.at; f. 1957; planning and consulting services for interaction of economic, social, ecological and technical issues in spatial, urban and regional planning; library of 38,000 vols; Chair. REINHOLD DEUßNER; CEO ERICH DALLHAMMER; publ. *RAUM* (4 a year).

ECONOMICS, LAW AND POLITICS

Bundesanstalt Statistik Österreich/Statistik Austria (Statistics Austria): Guglgasse 13, 1110 Vienna; tel. (1) 711280; fax (1) 711287728; e-mail info@statistik.gv.at; internet www.statistik.at; f. 1829, ind. federal instn since 2000; non-personal information system of govt; provides data on economic, demographic, social, ecological and cultural situation in Austria; library of 170,000 vols; Dir-Gens Dr KONRAD PESENDORFER (Statistics Div.), Dr GABRIELA PETROVIĆ (Commerical Div.); publs *Österreichischer Zahlenspiegel* (12 a year), *Statistisches Jahrbuch für Österreich* (1 a year), *Statistische Nachrichten* (12 a year), *Statistische Übersichten* (4 a year).

Dr Karl Kummer Institut für Sozialreform, Sozial- und Wirtschaftspolitik (Institute for Social Reform and Social Politics): Laudongasse 16, 1080 Vienna; tel. (1) 4052674; fax (1) 405267499; e-mail office@kummer-institut.at; internet www .kummer-institut.at; f. 1953; scientific institution to consolidate social and welfare policy supported by Christian ideals; emphasises on corporate social responsibility, work and social partnership, home ownership and middle-sized capital formation, social and health policy, youth and education policy, family and generation politics; Chair. Dr NORBERT

SCHNEDL; Exec. Dirs DORIS PALZ, ALEXANDER RAUNER; publ. *Gesellschaft und Politik* (4 a year).

Forschungsinstitut für Altersökonomie (Research Institute for Economics of Aging): Nordbergstr. 15, Annexe D, 7th Fl., 1090 Vienna; tel. (1) 313365398; fax (1) 31336905398; e-mail aging@wu-wien.ac.at; internet www.wu.ac.at/altersoekonomie; f. 2006; attached to Vienna Univ. of Economics and Business; socio-economic living conditions of older people; economic challenges of an aging society; cost of long-term care; productive contributions of older people; in collaboration with city of Vienna; Dir Prof. ULRIKE SCHNEIDER.

Forschungsinstitut für Familienunternehmen (Research Institute for Family Business): Augasse 2–6, 1090 Vienna; tel. (1) 313365416; e-mail fofu@wu.ac.at; www.wu.ac.at/fofu; attached to Vienna Univ. of Economics and Business; basic and applied research on family businesses; completed projects incl. strategic behaviour and success factors of family; current projects are market orientation in family, success factors and good case studies; Dir Dr HERMANN FRANK.

Forschungsinstitut für Gesundheitsmanagement und Gesundheitsökonomie (Research Institute for Health Care Management and Health Economics): Althanstr. 51, 1090 Vienna; tel. (1) 313364548; e-mail healthcare@wu-wien.ac.at; internet www.wu.ac.at/healthcare; attached to Vienna Univ. of Economics and Business; research on health care facilities as social orgs; effects of management and leadership decisions on staff, business performance indicators and patient outcomes; trains management personnel for health care orgs; Dirs Prof. Dr AUGUST ÖSTERLE, Prof. Dr JOHANNES STEYRER.

Forschungsinstitut für Kooperationen und Genossenschaften (Research Institute for Cooperation and Cooperatives): Augasse 2–6, Upper level 3A, 1090 Vienna; tel. (1) 313364332; fax (1) 31336780; e-mail ricc@wu-wien.ac.at; internet www.wu.ac.at/ricc; attached to Vienna Univ. of Economics and Business; Austrian cooperatives' research unit for business admin; deals with intercompany cooperation, cooperatives and their management; Dir Prof. Dr DIETMAR RÖSSL.

Forschungsinstitut Rechenintensive Methoden (Research Institute for Computational Methods): Augasse 2–6, 1090 Vienna; tel. (1) 313365057; e-mail firm-office@wu.ac.at; internet www.wu.ac.at/firm; attached to Vienna Univ. of Economics and Business; researchers from 4 univ. depts; devt of advanced computational methods in the areas of finance, information systems; Dir Prof. Dr KURT HORNIK.

Institut für Europäische Integrationsforschung (EIF) (Institute for European Integration Research): Strohgasse 45/DG, 1030 Vienna; tel. (1) 515817565; fax (1) 515817566; e-mail eif@oeaw.ac.at; internet www.eif.oeaw.ac.at; f. 1998; attached to Austrian Acad. of Sciences; political science instn dedicated to research on European Union and its policies across multiple levels; research incl. internal EU policies, EU as externally oriented global actor in policy areas, implementation of the various forms of EU law and the resulting effects; Dir Prof. Dr GERDA FALKNER; publs *European Integration online Papers* (online, irregular), *Living Reviews in European Governance*.

Institut für Europäisches Schadenersatzrecht (Institute of European Tort Law): Reichsratsstr. 17/2, 1010 Vienna; tel. (1) 427729651; fax (1) 427729670; e-mail etl@oeaw.ac.at; internet www.etl.oeaw.ac.at; f.

2002, present status 2008; attached to Austrian Acad. of Sciences; comparative legal research in tort law; primary focus European law; examines other jurisdictions like USA, South Africa, Israel, Japan and Korea; library of 11,000 vols; Dir Prof. Dr KEN OLIPHANT; publ. *Journal of European Tort Law* (3 a year).

Institut für Höhere Studien (Institute for Advanced Studies): Stumpergasse 56, 1060 Vienna; tel. (1) 59991-122; fax (1) 59991-162; e-mail communication@ihs.ac.at; internet www.ihs.ac.at; f. 1963; postgraduate training and research in economics and finance, sociology and political science; combines theoretical and empirical research in economics and other social science disciplines; library of 23,500 vols, 500 current periodicals; Dir Prof. Dr BERNHARD FELDERER; publs *Economics, Sociological and Political Science Series*, *Empirical Economics* (4 a year), *European Societies* (4 a year), *German Economic Revue* (4 a year), *Soziale Sicherheit* (12 a year), *Health System Watch* (4 a year).

Österreichische Forschungsstiftung für Internationale Entwicklung (Austrian Research Foundation for International Development): Sensengasse 3, 1090 Vienna; tel. (1) 3174010; fax (1) 3174010150; e-mail office@oefse.at; internet www.oefse.at; f. 1967; documentation and information on devt aid, developing countries and int. devt, particularly relating to Austria; library of 60,000 vols, 200 periodicals; Dir Dr WERNER RAZA; publs *ÖFSE-Edition* (irregular), *ÖFSE-Forum* (irregular), *Österreichische Entwicklungspolitik Analysen-Informationen* (1 a year).

Österreichisches Institut für Wirtschaftsforschung (Austrian Institute of Economic Research): Arsenal, Objekt 20, 1030 Vienna; tel. (1) 7982601; fax (1) 7989386; e-mail office@wifo.ac.at; internet www.wifo.ac.at; f. 1927; analyses economic devts in Austria and internationally; 5 research groups: macroeconomics and European economic policy, labour market, income and social security, industrial economics, innovation and int. competition, structural change and regional devts, environment, agriculture and energy; Dir Prof. Dr KARL AIGINGER; publs *Austrian Economic Quarterly*, *Empirica* (3 a year, with Austrian Economic Asscn), *Monatsberichte* (12 a year).

Spezialforschungsbereich International Tax Coordination (Special Research Program on International Tax Coordination): Nordbergstr. 15, 1090 Vienna; tel. (1) 313364890; fax (1) 31336730; internet www.sfb-itc.at; f. 2003; attached to Vienna Univ. of Business and Economics; issues of int. tax coordination; regional focus on Austria being a gateway between old and new EU member states.

FINE AND PERFORMING ARTS

Abteilung für Inventarisation und Denkmalforschung des Bundesdenkmalamtes (Department of Art Research and Inventory of the Federal Office for the Protection of Monuments): Hofburg, Schweizerhof, Säulenstiege, 1010 Vienna; tel. (1) 53415121; fax (1) 534155120; e-mail denkmalforschung@bda.at; internet www.bda.at; f. 1911; research and documentation on works of art in Austria; library of 22,000 vols; Chief Officer Dr ANDREAS LEHNE; publs *Denkmal Heute*, *Österreichische Zeitschrift für Kunst und Denkmalpflege*.

Gesellschaft für vergleichende Kunstforschung (Society of Comparative Art Research): c/o Mag. Paul Mahringer Bundesdenkmalamt, Abteilung Denkmalverzeichnis, Hofburg Säulenstiege, 1010 Vienna; tel.

(1) 427741425; fax (1) 42779414; e-mail paul.mahringer@vergleichende.at; internet www.vergleichende.at/home.html; f. 1934; conducts research, lectures, courses and excursions related to art and publishes the results; Pres. Dr WALTRAUD NEUWIRTH; Sec.-Gen. Mag. PAUL MAHRINGER; publ. *Mitteilungen* (3 a year).

Institut für Zeitgenössische Kunst (Institute of Contemporary Art): Inffeldgasse 10/II, 8010 Graz; tel. (316) 8734721; fax (316) 8734723; e-mail ikg@tugraz.at; internet izk.tugraz.at; attached to Graz Univ. of Technology; research and practice in the aesthetic field; learning artistic skills and colln of personal experiences in dealing with materials, machines and media with an emphasis on contemporary ways of working; Dir Prof. HANS KUPELWIESER.

Wiener Gesellschaft für Theaterforschung (Viennese Society for Theatre Research): Hofburg, Batthyanystiege, 1010 Vienna; tel. (1) 427748401; fax (1) 42779484; e-mail otto.schindler@univie.ac.at; f. 1944; Pres. Prof. Dr WOLFGANG GREISENEGGER; Gen. Sec. Dr OTTO G. SCHINDLER; publs *Jahrbuch*, *Theater in Österreich* (1 a year).

HISTORY, GEOGRAPHY AND ARCHAEOLOGY

Center for Geosciences: Wohllebengasse 12–14, E.04, 1040 Vienna; tel. (1) 515813630; e-mail andrea.berger@oeaw.ac.at; internet www.oeaw.ac.at/gwz; f. 2007; attached to Austrian Academy for Sciences; coordinates 4 commissions that focus on the earth sciences; initiates interdisciplinary geoscientific research projects; acts as liaison between geoscience research and public; Dir Prof. Dr HANS PETER SCHÖNLAUB.

Forschungsgesellschaft Wiener Stadtarchäologie (Research Unit for Archaeology in Vienna): Apollogasse 7, 1070 Vienna; tel. (676) 7215105; internet www.archaeologie-wien.at; Chair. Doz. Dr ORTOLF HARL; publ. *Onomasticon Provinciarum Europae Latinarum*.

Institut für Angewandte Geowissenschaften (Institute of Applied Geosciences): Rechbauerstr. 12, 8010 Graz; tel. (316) 8736361; fax (316) 8736876; e-mail geomin@egam.tugraz.at; internet www.egam.tugraz.at; attached to Graz Univ. of Technology; institute of engineering geology, mineralogy and hydrochemistry; engineering geology ensures that geological factors that influence the design, construction and operation of engineering structures are correctly identified, interpreted and presented; mineralogy and hydrochemistry includes the devt and use of natural and synthetic mineral materials, water–rock interaction and the genesis and contamination of natural waters; Dir DANIEL SCOTT KIEFFER.

Institut für Demographie (Institute of Demography): Wohllebengasse 12–14, 1040 Vienna; tel. (1) 515817702; fax (1) 515817703; e-mail vid@oeaw.ac.at; internet www.oeaw.ac.at/vid; attached to Austrian Acad. of Sciences; Dir Dr WOLFGANG LUTZ.

Institut für Gebirgsforschung: Mensch und Umwelt (Institute of Mountain Research: Man and Environment): Technikerstr. 21A, Otto Hittmair-Pl. 1, 6020 Innsbruck; tel. (512) 5074941; fax (512) 5074960; e-mail igf-office@oeaw.ac.at; internet www.uibk.ac.at/igf; f. 2006; attached to Austrian Academy of Sciences; inter-and transdisciplinary research in mountain areas across the world with int. group of scientists; focuses on regional sustainability, global change and interdependence of man and environment in the Alpine area; Dir Prof. Dr AXEL BORSDORF; publ. *eco.mont* (2 a year).

Institut für Kulturgeschichte der Antike (IKAnt) (Institute for the Study of Ancient Culture): Bäckerstr. 13, 1010 Vienna; tel. (1) 515813483; fax (1) 515813489; e-mail antike@oeaw.ac.at; internet www.oeaw.ac.at/antike; f. 2000; attached to Austrian Academy of Sciences; comprehensive cultural-historical problems within a supra-regional range; emphasis on living and residing in antiquity and the early middle ages, sepulchral context and collective ideals, urbanism and settlement-historical transformation processes; library of 2,000 vols; Dir Doz. Mag Dr ANDREAS PÜLZ.

Institut für Realienkunde des Mittelalters und der Frühen Neuzeit (Institute for Research into Daily Life and Material Culture in Medieval and Early Modern Times): Körnermarkt 13, 3500 Krems an der Donau; tel. (2732) 84793; fax (2732) 84793-1; e-mail imareal@oeaw.ac.at; internet www.imareal.oeaw.ac.at; f. 1969; attached to Austrian Acad. of Sciences; Dir Dr ELISABETH VAVRA; publs *Forschungen* (every 2 years), *Medium Aevum Quotidianum* (3 or 4 a year), *Veröffentlichungen* (every 2 years).

Institute for Geographic Information Science: Schillerstr. 30, 5020 Salzburg; tel. (662) 80447510; fax (662) 63895260; e-mail office.giscience@oeaw.ac.at; internet www.oeaw.ac.at/giscience; attached to Austrian Academy of Sciences; researches the concepts and methods for modelling, organizing, analysis and communication of geospatial information; Dir JOSEF STROBL.

LANGUAGE AND LITERATURE

Institut für Österreichische Dialekt- und Namenlexika (Institute for Lexicography of Austrian Dialects and Names): Wohllebengasse 12–14, 1040 Vienna; tel. (1) 5158172707292; fax (1) 515817280; e-mail dinamlex@oeaw.ac.at; internet www.oeaw.ac.at/dinamlex; attached to Austrian Acad. of Sciences; f. 1911 as Kommission zur Schaffung des Bayerisch-Österreichischen Wörterbuches und zur Erforschung unserer Mundarten; research in lexicography of dialects and onomastics; major publs written by 7 linguists; has collected a dialect database; Man. Dir Dr INGEBORG GEYER.

MEDICINE

CeMM Research Centre for Molecular Medicine: Lazarettgasse 14, AKH BT 25.3, 1090 Vienna; tel. (1) 4016070011; fax (1) 40160970000; e-mail office@cemm.oeaw.ac.at; internet www.cemm.oeaw.ac.at; attached to Austrian Academy of Sciences; interdisciplinary research centre in molecular medicine; research focus on cancer, inflammation and immune disorders; Man. Dir Dr GERHARD SCHADLER.

Institut für Atemgasanalytik (Breath Research Institute): Dammstr. 22, 6850 Dornbirn; tel. and fax (664) 8051560000; e-mail office-aa@oeaw.ac.at; internet www.oeaw.ac.at/aa; research in the upcoming field of breath analysis enabled diagnosis; Scientific Dir Prof. Dr ANTON AMANN.

Institut für Biomedizinische Altersnforschung (Institute of Biomedical Research on Ageing): Rennweg 10, 6020 Innsbruck; tel. (512) 583919-0; fax (512) 583919-8; e-mail iba@oeaw.ac.at; internet www.iba.oeaw.ac.at; f. 1992; attached to Austrian Acad. of Sciences; aims to study aging processes at the cellular/molecular level and to define measures to postpone/prevent age-related impairments; researches aging through immunology, endocrinology, molecular and cell biology; Dir BEATRIX GRUBECK-LOEBENSTEIN.

NATURAL SCIENCES

General

Institut für Wissenschaft und Kunst (Institute for Science and Art): Berggasse 17/1, 1090 Vienna; tel. and fax (1) 3174342; e-mail iwk.institut@aon.at; internet www.univie.ac.at/iwk; f. 1946; research on women's studies and emigration research; library of 7,000 vols, 100 magazines and newspapers; Pres. Doz. Dr JOHANN DVORAK; publ. *Mitteilungen*.

Institut für Wissenschaftstheorie (Institute for the Philosophy of Science):; tel. (662) 909627; e-mail wissenschaftstheorie@sbg.ac.at; f. 1961; philosophy of science, foundations of logic, mathematics and ethics, philosophy of religion; library of 12,000 vols; Dir Prof. Dr PAUL WEINGARTNER; publ. *Forschungsgespräche* (irregular).

Biological Sciences

Biologische Station Neusiedler See (Biological Station Neusiedler See): Amt d. Burgenl. Landesregierung, Abt. 5, 7142 Illmitz; tel. (2175) 23280; fax (2175) 232810; e-mail biol.stat@aon.at; f. 1971; environmental research, nature conservation, limnology, ornithology, botany, water analysis; Dir Prof. Dr ALOIS HERZIG; publ. *BFB (Biologisches Forschungsinstitut Burgenland)–Berichte* (irregular).

Gregor Mendel Institute of Molecular Plant Biology GmbH: Dr. Bohr-Gasse 3, 1030 Vienna; tel. (1) 790449000; fax (1) 790449001; e-mail office@gmi.oeaw.ac.at; internet www.gmi.oeaw.ac.at; f. 2000; attached to Austrian Academy of Sciences; research in plant molecular biology; covers molecular genetics, basic mechanisms of epigenetics, population genetics, chromosome biology, developmental biology, and stress signal transduction; Science Dir Dr MAGNUS NORDBORG.

Institut für Biophysik und Nanosystemforschung (Institute of Biophysics and Nanosystems Research): Schmiedlstr. 6, 8042 Graz; tel. (316) 4120300; fax (316) 4120390; e-mail ibn.office@oeaw.ac.at; internet www.ibn.oeaw.ac.at; f. 1968; attached to Austrian Acad. of Sciences; focuses on nano-bio-sciences; conducts a flexible programme of interdisciplinary research, interlaced into a network of nat. and int. cooperation; Dir Prof. Dr PETER LAGGNER.

Fakultät Zentrum für Biodiversität an der Universität Wien (Faculty Centre of Biodiversity at University of Vienna): Rennweg 14, 1030 Vienna; tel. (1) 427754100; fax (1) 4277-9541; e-mail botanik@univie.ac.at; internet www.botanik.univie.ac.at; f. 1754 (Garden) and 1844 (Institute), present name 2008; develops an understanding of biodiversity at all relevant ecological and evolutionary dimensions in space and time, and disseminate the knowledge; library of 61,000 vols, 161 periodicals; Dir Prof. Dr TOD F. STUESSY; publs *Neilreichia* (1 a year), *Österreichische Zeitschrift für Pilzkunde* (Austrian Journal of Mycology, 1 a year), *Taxon* (2 a year).

Institut für Limnologie (Institute for Limnology): Herzog Odilo Str. 101, 5310 Mondsee; tel. (6232) 3125; fax (6232) 3578; internet www.oeaw.ac.at/limno; f. 1972; attached to Austrian Acad. of Sciences; performs basic and applied ecological research on inland waters; goal is to understand the structure, function and dynamics of freshwater ecosystems; Dir Dr THOMAS WEISSE.

Institute of Molecular Biotechnology: Dr Bohr-Gasse 3, 1030 Vienna; tel. (1) 79044; fax (1) 79044110; internet www.imba.oeaw.ac.at; attached to Austrian Acad. of Sciences; f.

1999; conducts research on basic biological questions at the molecular level; uses cell biology, structural biology, biochemistry, genomics and genetics to tackle these questions; Scientific Dir Prof. Dr JOSEF PENNINGER; Admin Dir MICHAEL KREBS.

Physical Sciences

Atominstitut der Österreichischen Universitäten (Atomic Institute of the Austrian Universities): Stadion allee 2, 1020 Vienna; tel. (1) 58801141202; fax (1) 5880114199; e-mail office@ati.ac.at; internet www.ati.ac.at; f. 1958; inter-univ. institute for all Austrian univs; research and training in the areas of atomic, nuclear and reactor physics, radiation physics, radiation protection, environmental analytics and radiochemistry, nuclear measurement technology and solid state physics, with quantum physics, quantum optics, low temperature physics and superconductivity as additional focus points of research; Dir Prof. Dipl. Ing. Dr HANNES-JÖRG SCHMIEDMAYER.

BMLFUW Abteilung VII/3–Wasserhaushalt (Federal Ministry of Agriculture, Forestry, Environment and Water Management Sub-Dept VII/3–Water Balance): Marxergasse 2, 1030 Vienna; tel. (1) 711006942; fax (1) 711006851; e-mail wasserhaushalt@bmlfuw.gv.at; internet www.lebensministerium.at; f. 1893; covers the data on water cycle, processes it and stores it in a database; library of 8,000 vols; Head of Division VII/3 Dr Ing. REINHOLD GODINA; publs *Hydrographisches Jahrbuch von Österreich* (1 a year), *Hydrological Atlas of Austria*, *Mitteilungsblatt des Hydrographischen Dienstes von Österreich* (irregular).

Geologische Bundesanstalt (Geological Survey of Austria): Neulinggasse 38, Postfach 127, 1031 Vienna; tel. (1) 7125674-0; fax (1) 712567456; e-mail office@geologie.ac.at; internet www.geologie.ac.at; f. 1849; represents geo-management in Austria's public sector; conducts geoscientific mapping of Austrian territory, manages databases and publishes results; library of 270,270 vols, 2,897 periodicals, 46,575 geological maps, 9,942 aerial photographs, 16,178 archive items, 14,039 microforms; Dir Dr PETER SEIFERT; publ. *Jahrbuch*.

Institut für Astron- und Teilchenphysik, Universität Innsbruck (Institute of Astro- and Particle Physics, University of Innsbruck): Technikerstr. 25, 6020 Innsbruck; tel. (512) 5076061; fax (512) 5072625; e-mail astro@uibk.ac.at; internet astro.uibk.ac.at; f. 1904; attached to Faculty for Mathematics, Computer Science and Physics, Univ. Innsbruck; research in many areas of astrophysics, astroparticle physics and particle physics; talks, seminars, public outreach activities; library of 4,598 vols; Dir Prof. Dr SABINE SCHINDLER; publ. *Mitteilungen* (irregular).

Institut für Astronomie der Universität Wien (Vienna University Observatory): Türkenschanzstr. 17, 1180 Vienna; tel. (1) 427753801; fax (1) 42779538; e-mail astronomie@univie.ac.at; internet www.astro.univie.ac.at; f. 1755; attached to Faculty of Earth Sciences, Geography and Astronomy, Univ. of Vienna; researches into the history of astronomy, various aspects of stars and planets, galaxies and cosmic matter circuit; library of 21,655 vols; Pres. Prof. Mag Dr FRANZ KERSCHBAUM; publ. *Communications in Asteroseismology*.

Associated Body:

Leopold Figl Observatorium für Astrophysik (Leopold Figl Observatory for Astrophysics): Türkenschanzstr. 17, 1180 Vienna; Mitterschöpfl, Altenmarkt an der Triesting, 2571 Vienna; tel. (1) 427751801; fax (1) 4277953895; e-mail admin@astro.univie.ac.at; internet astro .univie.ac.at/foa; f. 1969; astronomical research; lab courses for astronomy programme at Univ of Vienna; public outreach; Head of Science Operations Prof. Dr WERNER W. ZEILINGER.

Institut für Hochenergiephysik (Institute of High Energy Physics): Nikolsdorfer Gasse 18, 1050 Vienna; tel. (1) 5447328; fax (1) 544732854; e-mail ess@hephy.oeaw.ac.at; internet www.hephy.at; f. 1966; attached to Austrian Acad. of Sciences; participates in large experiments at CERN, KEK and in the design of the ILD experiment at the International Linear Collider; studies particle physics; Dir Doz. Dr MANFRED KRAMMER.

Institut für Schallforschung (Acoustics Research Institute): Wohllebengasse 12–14/1st Fl., 1040 Vienna; tel. (1) 51582501; fax (1) 51582530; e-mail konrad.antonicek@oeaw.ac .at; internet www.kfs.oeaw.ac.at; attached to Austrian Acad. of Sciences; active in 5 major areas: computational acoustics, computational hearing, psychoacoustics, acoustic phonetics, audiological acoustics and mathematics and signal processing in acoustics; Dir Prof. Dr WERNER A. DEUTSCH.

Institut für Weltraumforschung (Space Research Institute): Schmiedlstr. 6, 8042 Graz; tel. (316) 4120400; fax (316) 4120490; e-mail office.iwf@oeaw.ac.at; internet www .iwf.oeaw.ac.at; attached to Austrian Acad. of Sciences; f. 1970; covers Austrian activities in solar-system exploration, near-earth space plasma physics and satellite geodesy; involved in int. space projects and nat. space agencies in USA, Japan, France and China; 3 depts: experimental space research, extraterrestrial physics, satellite geodesy; Exec. Dir Prof. Dr WOLFGANG BAUMJOHANN.

Kuffner-Sternwarte (Kuffner Observatory): Johann-Staud-Str. 10, 1160 Vienna; tel. (1) 7295494; fax (1) 729549478; e-mail service.astronomie@vhs.at; internet www .kuffner.ac.at; f. 1883; astronomical observatory; incl. instruments such as the great refractor, the heliometre, the meridian circle and the vertical circle; library of 500 vols; Dir Dr PETER HABISON.

Ludwig Boltzmann Institut für Festkörperphysik (Ludwig Boltzmann Institute for Solid State Physics): Nussdorfer Str. 64, 6th floor, 1090 Vienna; tel. (1) 5132750; fax (1) 5132310; e-mail office@lbg.ac.at; internet www.lbg.ac.at; f. 1965; research into semiconductors, conducting polymers and high-temperature superconductors; Gen. Man. Mag. CLAUDIA LINGNER.

Österreichische Geodätische Kommission (Austrian Geodetic Commission): c/o Norbert Höggerl, Bundesamt für Eich unfd Vermessungswesen, Schiffamtsgasse 1–3, 1020 Vienna; tel. (1) 211102160; fax (1) 211102161; e-mail norbert.hoeggerl@bev.gv .at; internet www.oegk-geodesy.at; f. 1863; represents Austria in the Int. Asscn of Geodesy (IAG); Pres. Prof. Dipl.-Ing. Dr HARALD SCHUH; publ. *Österreichische Zeitschrift für Vermessung und Geoinformation*.

Sonnenobservatorium Kanzelhöhe der Universität Graz (Kanzelhöhe Solar Observatory of the University of Graz): Kanzelhöhe 19, 9521 Treffen; tel. (4248) 2717; fax (4248) 271715; internet www.solobskh.ac.at; f. 1943; attached to Institute of Physics, Univ. of Graz; observatory for solar and environmental research; conducts systematic observations of the sun and the climate; develops instruments; Dir Prof. Dr ARNOLD HANSLMEIER.

Stefan Meyer Institut für Mittelenergiephysik (Stefan Meyer Institute of Medium Energy Physics): Boltzmanngasse 3, 1090 Vienna; tel. (1) 427729701; fax (1) 42779297; e-mail smi@oeaw.ac.at; internet www.oeaw.ac.at/imep; f. 1910, present name 2004; attached to Austrian Acad. of Sciences; basic research in subatomic physics; focuses on study of fundamental symmetries and interactions; specializes in precision spectroscopy of exotic atoms and exotic meson-nucleus bound states as part of int. collaborations at large-scale research facilities; Dir Prof. Dr EBERHARD WIDMANN.

Umweltbundesamt (Environment Agency Austria): Spittelauer Lände 5, 1090 Vienna; tel. and fax (1) 31304; e-mail office@ umweltbundesamt.at; internet www .umweltbundesamt.at; f. 1985; elaboration of scientific studies and basic data for environmental protection policy in Austria; elaboration of recommendations for decision-makers in politics, business and admin. and devt of strategic perspectives and scenarios for the achievement of environmental policy targets in Austria and Europe; library of 20,000 vols, 300 periodicals; Man. Dir GEORGE REBELO.

Zentralanstalt für Meteorologie und Geodynamik (Central Institute for Meteorology and Geodynamics): Hohe Warte 38, 1191 Vienna; tel. (1) 36026; fax (1) 3691233; e-mail dion@zamg.ac.at; internet www.zamg .ac.at; f. 1851; provides nat. weather service; acts in all fields of meteorology except aeronautical field; nat. body responsible for geophysics; library of 80,000 vols; Dir Dr MICHAEL STAUDINGER; Sec. HERMI FUERST; publ. *Österreichische Beitraege zu Meteorologie und Geophysik* (irregular).

PHILOSOPHY AND PSYCHOLOGY

Institut für Kultur- und Geistesgeschichte Asiens (Institute for the Cultural and Intellectual History of Asia): Apostelgasse 23, 1030 Vienna; tel. (1) 51581-6400; fax (1) 51581-6410; e-mail office .ias@oeaw.ac.at; internet ikga.oeaw.ac.at; attached to Austrian Acad. of Sciences; Dir Doz. Dr HELMUT KRASSER.

Konrad-Lorenz-Institut für Vergleichende Verhaltensforschung (Konrad Lorenz Institute of Comparative Behavioural Research): Savoyenstr. 1A, 1160 Vienna; tel. (1) 4515812700; fax (1) 515812800; e-mail initial.name@klivv.oeaw.ac.at; internet www .oeaw.ac.at/klivv; f. 1945; attached to Austrian Acad. of Sciences; Dir Dr DUSTIN PENN.

Psychotechnisches Institut (Psychotechnical Institute): Augasse 9, 2103 Langenzersdorf; tel. (2244) 30996-0; fax (2244) 30996-22; e-mail psychotech@utanet.at; internet www .psychotech.at; f. 1926; institute of industrial psychology and market psychology; conducts psychological group discussions, questionnaire analysis, business interviews, seminars and lectures; Dirs Dr HANS-RICHARD GRÜMM, Dr SUSANNE HACKL-GRÜMM.

RELIGION, SOCIOLOGY AND ANTHROPOLOGY

Institut für Kirchliche Zeitgeschichte (Institute for Contemporary Ecclesiastical History): Mönchsberg 2A, 5020 Salzburg; tel. (662) 842521161; fax (622) 84252118; e-mail kirchliche-zeitgeschichte@ifz.kirchen .net; f. 1961; library of 8,500 vols; Dir Doz. Dr ALFRED RINNERTHALER; publs *Hirtenbriefe aus Deutschland, Österreich und der Schweiz* (1 a year), *Publikationen des Instituts für Kirchliche Zeitgeschichte*.

Institut für Realienkunde des Mittelalters und der frühen Neuzeit (Institute of Material Culture of the Middle Ages and Early Modern Period): Körnermarkt 13, 3500 Krems an der Donau; tel. (2732) 84793; fax (2732) 847931; e-mail imareal@oeaw.ac.at; internet www.imareal.oeaw.ac.at; f. 1969; attached to Austrian Academy of Sciences; research into the diversity of human lifestyles, based on the material culture; basic research in systematic devt of traces of life in the past; in applied research cultural studies are evaluated on the basis of processed material; Dir Dr ELISABETH VAVRA.

Institut für Stadt und Regionalforschung (Institute for Urban and Regional Research): Postgasse 7/4/2, 1010 Vienna; tel. (1) 515813520; fax (1) 515813533; e-mail isr@oeaw.ac.at; internet www.oeaw.ac.at/isr; f. 1946 as Commission for Spatial Research and Reconstruction; present name 1988; attached to Austrian Acad. of Sciences; spatial sciences research institute; focuses on interdisciplinary urban and regional devt on nat. and European scale; Dir Prof. Dr HEINZ FASSMANN.

Kommission für vergleichende Medien- und Kommunikationsforschung (Commission for Comparative Media and Communication Studies): Postgasse 7/4/1, 1010 Vienna; tel. (1) 515813110; fax (1) 515813120; e-mail cmc@oeaw.ac.at; internet www.oeaw.ac.at/cmc; f. 1994 as Commission for Mass Communication History; present name 2005; attached to Austrian Academy of Sciences; interdisciplinary and int. comparative approach in mass media's role; focus on media systems: theory, models and history, media markets: structure, supply and usage, mass media and elections, media and int. relations; Dir Prof. Dr HERBERT MATIS.

Mayr-Melnhof Institut für den Christlichen Osten (Mayr-Melnhof Institute of Eastern Christian Studies): Mönchsberg 2A 5020, Salzburg; tel. (662) 842521141; fax (662) 842521143; e-mail salzburg@ro-oriente .at; internet www.kirchen.net/mmico; f. 1961; research on Christianity in Middle East, India and (S) Eastern Europe through knowledge of cultural characteristics and religious traditions; library of 15,000 vols; Dir Prof. Dr DIETMAR W. WINKLER.

Wiener Institut für Demographie (Vienna Institute of Demography): Wohllebengasse 12–14, 6th Fl., 1040 Vienna; tel. (1) 515817702; fax (1) 515817730; e-mail vid@ oeaw.ac.at; internet www.oeaw.ac.at/vid; attached to Austrian Acad. of Sciences; demographic research in comparative European demography, demography of Austria, population dynamics and forecasting, population economics and health and mortality; Dir Prof. Dr WOLFGANG LUTZ.

TECHNOLOGY

Austrian Standards Institute (Österreichisches Normungsinstitut): Heinestr. 38, 1020 Vienna; tel. (1) 21300; fax (1) 21300-818; e-mail office@as-institute.at; internet www.as-institute.at; f. 1920; private institute for standardization in all fields; library of 236,000 documents (standards) online, 23,000 Austrian, European, int. standards; Pres. Prof. Dr WALTER BARFUSS; Man. Dir Ing. Dr GERHARD HARTMANN; publs *CONNEX* (German, 6 a year), *AS+ top news* (24 a year).

Erich-Schmid-Institut für Materialwissenschaft (Erich Schmid Institute of Solid Material Sciences): Jahnstr. 12, 8700 Leoben; tel. (3842) 804112; fax (3842) 804116; e-mail maria.fliesser@mu-leoben.at; internet www.oeaw.ac.at/esi; f. 1971; attached to Austrian Acad. of Sciences; performs research on new materials concepts; educates students and scientists; collaborates with industrial and scientific partners; Dir Prof. Dr GERHARD DEHM.

Holzforschung Austria (Wood Research Austria): Arsenal, Franz Grillstr. 7, 1030

Vienna; tel. (1) 79826230; fax (1) 798262350; e-mail hfa@holzforschung.at; internet www .holzforschung.at; f. 1948; research institute and accredited testing and inspection body of the Austrian Wood Research Society; conducts seminars, conferences, workshops, training courses, in-house training; library of 35,000 vols; Dir Dipl.-Ing. Dr MANFRED BRANDSTÄTTER; publs *Magazin für den Holzbereich* (4 a year), *Literature Database of the Austrian Wood Research Society* (2 a month).

Institut für Baustatik (Institute for Structural Analysis): Lessingstr. 25/II, 8010 Graz; tel. (316) 8736181; fax (316) 8736185; e-mail ifb@tugraz.at; internet www.ifb.tugraz.at; attached to Graz Univ. of Technology; main research in boundary element method and finite element method; other research priorities are numerical simulation in tunnelling, numerical simulation in physics and computational biomechanics; Dir Prof. Dipl.-Ing. Dr GERNOT BEER.

Institut für Betonbau (Institute of Structural Concrete): Lessingstr. 25, 8010 Graz; tel. (316) 8736191; fax (316) 8736694; e-mail betonbau@tugraz.at; internet www.ibb .tugraz.at; attached to Graz Univ. of Technology; teaching and research in the field of structural concrete construction; static and dynamic analysis of un-reinforced, reinforced and prestressed concrete flaccid structures and their structural perfection; composite structures with a dominant share of concrete and masonry structures; library of 1,700 books and magazines; Dir Prof. Dr-Ing. VIET TUE NGUYEN.

Institut für Bodenmechanik und Grundbau (Institute of Soil Mechanics and Foundation Engineering): Rechbauerstr. 12, 8010 Graz; tel. (316) 8736231; fax (316) 8736232; e-mail margit.rueckert @tugraz.at; internet soil.tugraz.at; attached to Graz Univ. of Technology; research in soil mechanics and foundation engineering; aims to provide a basis for new technologies and methods in design and construction; research activities include laboratory and in-situ tests, devt of constitutive laws for soils and calculations based on numerical methods; Dir Prof. Dipl.-Ing. Dr STEPHAN SEMPRICH.

Institut für Diskrete Mathematik und Geometrie (Institute of Discrete Mathematics and Geometry): Wiedner Hauptstr. 8–10/ 104, 1040 Vienna; tel. (1) 5880110400; fax (1) 5880111499; e-mail michael.drmota@tuwien .ac.at; internet www.dmg.tuwien.ac.at; f. 1999; attached to Austrian Acad. of Sciences; Head Dr MICHAEL DRMOTA.

Institut für Felsmechanik und Tunnelbau (Institute of Rock Mechanics and Tunnelling): Rechbauerstr. 12, 8010 Graz; tel. (316) 8738114; fax (316) 8738618; e-mail tunnel@tugraz.at; internet www.tunnel .tugraz.at; attached to Graz Univ. of Technology; education and research in the field of rock mechanics and tunnelling; partner to contractors, clients, and consultants in questions of rock engineering; emphasises interdisciplinary cooperation; Dir Prof. Dipl.-Ing. Dr WULF SCHUBERT.

Institut für Holzbau und Holztechnologie (Institute of Timber Engineering and Wood Technology): Inffeldgasse 24/I, 8010 Graz; tel. (316) 8734601; fax (316) 8734619; e-mail lignum@tugraz.at; internet www .lignum.at; attached to Graz Univ. of Technology; research in core competencies in the disciplines of timber engineering and wood technology; design and construction sciences in timber engineering and material and structure sciences in wood technology; Dir Prof. Dipl.-Ing. Dr GERHARD SCHICKHOFER.

Institut für Materialprüfung und Baustofftechnologie mit ang TVFA (TVFA, the Institute for Testing and Research in Materials Technology): Stremayrgasse 11, 8010 Graz; tel. (316) 8737151; fax (316) 8737650; e-mail office @tvfa.tugraz.at; internet www .tvfa.tugraz.at; attached to Graz Univ. of Technology; research comprises the whole field of the building materials of building construction, engineering and infrastructure; focus on sustainable construction, structural renovation and propertied of mineral binders; Dir Prof. Dipl.-Ing. Dr PETER MAYDL.

Institut für Quantenoptik und Quanteninformation (Institute for Quantum Optics and Quantum Information): Boltzmanngasse 3, 1090 Vienna; tel. (1) 427729571; fax (1) 427729552; e-mail iqoqi-vienna@oeaw.ac.at; internet iqoqi.at; f. 2003; attached to Austrian Academy of Sciences; 2 branches; theoretical and basic research in quantum optics and quantum information; also focuses on theoretical concepts for realization and implementation of quantum computers, quantum protocols; experimental work is concerned with quantum-optical experiments, realization of quantum computers on basis of individual stored ions; Man. Dir Dr PETER ZOLLER.

Institut für Siedlungswasserwirtschaft und Landschaftswasserbau (Institute of Urban Water Management and Landscape Water Engineering): Stremayrgasse 10/I, 8010 Graz; tel. (316) 8738371; fax (316) 8738376; e-mail office@sww.tugraz.at; internet www.sww.tugraz.at; f. 1975; attached to Graz Univ. of Technology; research focuses on management of sewage water systems, sustainable optimization of water infrastructure, hydrological test areas and urban hydrology and hydraulic optimization of sewer systems and treatment plants; Dir Prof. Dipl.-Ing. Dr HARALD KAINZ.

Institut für Stahlbau und Flächentragwerke (Institute for Steel Structures and Shell Structures): Lessingstr. 25/III, 8010 Graz; tel. (316) 8736201; fax (316) 8736707; e-mail s.pammer@tugraz.at; internet www .stahlbau.tugraz.at; f. 1988; attached to Graz Univ. of Technology; computer oriented design of steel structures, fatigue design of bridges and their components, stability of thin-walled cylindrical structures and the limit load design of beam-columns of steel; Dir Prof. Dipl.-Ing. Dr RICHARD GREINER.

Institut für Technikfolgen-Abschätzung (Institute of Technology Assessment): Strohgasse 45/5, 1030 Vienna; tel. (1) 515816582; fax (1) 7109883; e-mail tamail@oeaw.ac.at; internet www.oeaw.ac.at/ita; f. 1994; attached to Austrian Acad. of Sciences; scientific research at the interface of technology and society; focuses on devt trends, societal consequences and options for shaping technological change; Dir Doz. Dr MICHAEL NENTWICH.

Institut für Wasserbau und Hydrometrische Prüfung (Institute for Hydraulic Engineering and Calibration of Hydrometrical Current-Meters): Severingasse 7, 1090 Vienna; tel. (1) 40268020; fax (1) 402680230; e-mail office.iwb@baw.bmlfuw.gv.at; internet www.iwbhp.at; f. 1913; attached to Federal Agency for Water Management; calculation and implementation of measures concerning the protection and maintenance of waters, as well as flood protection; physical model tests and mathematical models for studies in the field of hydraulic engineering; consulting in hydraulic engineering; devt of ecological bed stabilization methods; library of 5,796 vols, database containing 31,100 articles; Dir Dipl.-Ing. Dr techn. MICHAEL HENGL.

Institute for Integrated Sensor Systems: Viktor Kaplan Str. 2 2700 Wiener Neustadt; tel. (2622) 23420; fax (2622) 23420-99; e-mail office.iiss@oeaw.ac.at; internet www.iiss .oeaw.ac.at; f. 2004; attached to Austrian Academy of Sciences; investigates concepts and methodologies for smart sensors, their design, interconnection, and application; interdisciplinary research in medical technology, electrochemistry, tribology, and micro systems; Head Dipl.-Ing. Dr THILO SAUTER.

Johann Radon Institute for Computational and Applied Mathematics: Altenbergerstr. 69, 4040 Linz; tel. (732) 24685211; fax (732) 24685212; e-mail annette.weihs@ oeaw.ac.at; internet www.ricam.oeaw.ac.at; attached to Austrian Academy of Sciences; basic research in computational and applied mathematics; research groups in computational mathematics for direct field problems, inverse problems, symbolic computation, analysis of partial differential equations, optimization and control, mathematical imaging; Dir Prof. Dr HEINZ W. ENGL.

KMU Forschung Austria (Austrian Institute for SME Research): Gusshausstr. 8, 1040 Vienna; tel. (1) 5059761; fax (1) 5034660; e-mail office@kmuforschung.ac.at; internet www.kmuforschung.ac.at; f. 1952 as Österreichisches Institut für Gewerbeforschung; conducts social and economic research with focus on small and medium-sized enterprises; prepares and supplies information and data to facilitate decision-making for businesses and their advisers, for institutions responsible for economic policy and business promotion as well as for universities, colleges of higher education and other research institutions; member of the Austrian Cooperative Research (ACR) and the European Network for Social and Economic Research (ENSR); 1,563 mems; library of 3,200 vols; Pres. Prof. Dr J. HANNS PICHLER; Dir Dr WALTER BORNETT; Dir Mag. PETER VOITHOFER.

Labor für konstruktiven Ingenieurbau (Laboratory for Structural Engineering): Inffeldgasse 24, 8010 Graz; tel. (316) 8737051; fax (316) 8737061; e-mail lki@ tugraz.at; internet www.lki.tugraz.at; attached to Graz Univ. of Technology; experimental research on the entire field of structural engineering in cooperation with the theoretically working groups of the constructive institute; Dir Dipl.-Ing. Dr BERNHARD FREYTAG.

Österreichisches Forschungsinstitut für Artificial Intelligence (Austrian Research Institute for Artificial Intelligence): Freyung 6/6, 1010 Vienna; tel. (1) 533611260; fax (1) 533611277; e-mail sec@ofai.at; internet www .ofai.at; f. 1984; research institute of the Austrian Soc. for Cybernetic Studies; basic and applied research in language technology, interaction technologies, neural computation and robotics, intelligent music processing and machine learning, intelligent software agents and new media and artificial intelligence and society; library of 3,000 vols; Dir Prof. Dr ROBERT TRAPPL; publs *Applied Artificial Intelligence: An International Journal* (10 a year), *Technical Reports* (irregular).

Österreichisches Forschungsinstitut für Technikgeschichte (ÖFiT) am Technischen Museum in Wien (Austrian Research Institute for the History of Technology at the Museum of Technology in Vienna): Mariahilfer Str. 212, 1140 Vienna; tel. (1) 89998-2500; fax (1) 89998-1111; e-mail helmut.lackner@tmw.at; internet www.tmw.at; f. 1931; Pres. Prof. Dr REINHOLD REITH; publ. *Blätter für Technikgeschichte* (1 a year).

Österreichisches Forschungszentrum Seibersdorf GmbH (Austrian Research Centre, Seibersdorf): 2444 Seibersdorf; tel.

(2254) 7800; fax (2254) 74060; e-mail seibersdorf@zdfzs.arcs.ac.at; f. 1956; contract research and devt in instrumentation and information technology, process and environmental technologies, engineering, life sciences and systems research; library of 15,500 vols; Dir KONRAD FREYBORN; publ. *OEFSZ Reports*.

Österreichisches Giesserei-Institut (Austrian Foundry Research Institute): Parkstr. 21, 8700 Leoben; tel. (3842) 431010; fax (3842) 431011; e-mail office@ogi .at; internet www.ogi.at; f. 1952; research and service institute accredited as a testing facility; services include research and devt, technical advice, material testing, material and component analysis, computed tomography, numerical simulation and seminars and training; library of 2,140 vols; Man. and Tech. Dir Prof. Dr PETER SCHUMACHER; publ. *Giesserei Rundschau* (6 a year).

ÖTI—Institut für Ökologie, Technik und Innovation GmbH (Institute of Ecology, Technology and Innovation GmbH): Spengergasse 20, 1050 Vienna; tel. (1) 54425430; fax (1) 544254310; e-mail office@oeti.at; internet www.oeti.at; f. 1967 as Austrian Carpet Research Institute, present name 2009; accredited testing, inspection and certification institute and notified body in textiles, toys and comforters; int. br. offices; Man. Dir DI Dr ERICH ZIPPEL.

Physikalisch-Technische Versuchsanstalt für Wärme- und Schalltechnik am Technologischen Gewerbemuseum (Physical-technical Institute for Research on Heat and Noise Technology at the Technological Industrial Museum): Währingerstr. 59, 1090 Vienna; tel. (1) 33126411; fax (1) 3305925; research in heat and refrigeration technology, testing of vibrations, indoor acoustics, noise nuisances, absorption and suppression measurement; Dir F. BRUCKMAYER.

Zentrum für Elektronenmikroskopie Graz (Graz Centre for Electron Microscopy): Steyrergasse 17, 8010 Graz; tel. (316) 8738320; fax (316) 811596; e-mail office@felmi-zfe.at; internet www.felmi-zfe.tugraz .at; f. 1959; attached to Austrian Centre for Electron Microscopy and Nanoanalysis at Graz Univ. of Technology; research centre for electron microscopy and nanocharacterization of materials; facilitates interaction between industry and research; provides results from estd and emerging new methods in the field; library of 2,000 vols; Head Prof. Dipl.-Ing. Dr HOFER FERDINAND.

Libraries and Archives

Admont

Bibliothek der Benediktinerabtei (Library of the Benedictine Abbey): 8911 Admont; tel. (3613) 2312602; fax (3613) 2312359; e-mail tomaschek@stiftadmont.at; internet www.stiftadmont.at; f. 1074; library within Admont Benedictine Monastery; has 3-vol. giant Bible and Book of Gospels from 1070; 200,000 vols, 1,400 MSS, 530 incunabula; Librarian Mag. Dr JOHANN TOMASCHEK.

Bregenz

Vorarlberger Landesarchiv (Vorarlberg State Archives): Kirchstr. 28, 6900 Bregenz; tel. (5574) 51145005; fax (5574) 51145095; e-mail landesarchiv@vorarlberg.at; internet www.landesarchiv.at; f. 1898; 25,000 vols; Dir Prof. Dr ALOIS NIEDERSTÄTTER; publ. *Zeitschrift Montfort* (2 a year).

Vorarlberger Landesbibliothek (Vorarlberg State Library): Fluher Str. 4, 6900 Bregenz; tel. (5574) 51144100; fax (5574) 51144095; e-mail info.vlb@vorarlberg.at; internet www.vorarlberg.at/vlb; f. 1904; 450,000 vols, 500 current periodicals, 15,000 postcards, 600 maps, 220,000 photographs; spec. collns incl. late Baroque prayer book MSS, 100 vol. of incunabula; Dir Dr HARALD WEIGEL.

Eisenstadt

Burgenländische Landesbibliothek (Burgenland Provincial Library): Europaplatz 1, Landhaus, 7000 Eisenstadt; tel. (2682) 6002358; fax (2682) 6002058; e-mail post.bibliothek@bgld.gv.at; internet www .burgenland.at/kultur/landesbibliothek; f. 1922; 120,000 vols, 235 periodicals; Library Dir Dr JAKOB MICHAEL PERSCHY; publs *Burgenländische Forschungen* (2 or 3 a year), *Burgenländische Heimatblätter* (4 a year), *Burgenländische Landesbibliographie* (1 a year).

Burgenländisches Landesarchiv (Burgenland Provincial Archives): Europapl. 1, 7000 Eisenstadt; tel. (2682) 6002358; fax (2682) 6002058; e-mail post.archiv@bgld.gv .at; f. 1922; consists of research archives, Burgenländ district court and administrative archive; Head Dr ROLAND ARIES; publs *Burgenländische Forschungen* (2 a year), *Burgenländische Heimatblätter* (4 a year).

Graz

Steiermärkische Landesbibliothek (Styrian Federal State Library): Kalchberggasse 2, Graz; tel. (316) 8774600; fax (316) 8774633; e-mail stlbib@stmk.gv.at; internet www.landesbibliothek.steiermark.at; f. 1811; research library with humanities orientation; collects and preserves Styrian literature; 700,000 vols, 2,800 periodicals, 2,300 MSS; Dir Dr CHRISTOPH BINDER; publs *Arbeiten aus der Steiermärkischen Landesbibliothek* (irregular), *Steirische Bibliographie* (irregular), *Steirische Zeitungsdokumentation* (irregular).

Steiermärkisches Landesarchiv (Styrian Provincial Archives): Karmeliterpl. 3, 8010 Graz; tel. (316) 8772361; fax (316) 8772954; e-mail fa1d@stmk.gv.at; internet www .landesarchiv.steiermark.at; f. 1811; 100,000 vols; Dir Prof. Dr JOSEF RIEGLER; publs *Ausstellungsbegleiter* (irregular), *Mitteilungen* (1 a year), *Quellen aus steirischen Archiven* (irregular), *Styriaca* (irregular), *Veröffentlichungen* (irregular).

Universitätsbibliothek der Technischen Universität Graz (University Library of the Technical University of Graz): Technikerstr. 4, 8010 Graz; tel. (316) 8736151; fax (316) 8736671; e-mail service.bibliothek@tugraz .at; internet www.ub.tugraz.at; f. 1875; technical and scientific literature for research and teaching; 600,000 vols, 1,680 journals; Dir Eva BERTHA.

Universitätsbibliothek Graz (University Library, Graz): Universitätspl. 3A, 8010 Graz; tel. (316) 3803100; fax (316) 384987; e-mail ubgraz@uni-graz.at; internet www .uni-graz.at/en/ubwww.htm; f. 1573; 3.6m. vols, 14,000 electronic journals, 2,203 MSS, 1,150 incunabula; mem. of IFLA, LIBER; spec. colln incl. 300,000 objects before 1900; Dir Dr WERNER SCHLACHER.

Heiligenkreuz bei Baden

Stiftsarchiv des Zisterzienserstiftes (Cistercian Abbey Archives): 2532 Heiligenkreuz; tel. (2258) 8703; fax (2258) 8703-114; e-mail information@stift-heiligenkreuz.at; internet www.stift-heiligenkreuz.at; archives since foundation of the monastery in 1133; Archivist Dr FR ALCUIN SCHACHENMAYR; publs *Analecta Cisterciensia*, *Sancta Crux*.

Innsbruck

Tiroler Landesarchiv (Tyrolese Provincial Archives): Michael-Gaismair-Str. 1, 6020 Innsbruck; tel. (512) 5083502; fax (512) 5083505; e-mail landesarchiv@tirol.gv.at; internet www.tirol.gv.at/landesarchiv; f. 13th century; public archives of Tirol; records from 11th century; 30,000 archival units; Dir Dr JOSEPH LIENER; publs *Tiroler Erbhöfe* (irregular), *Tiroler Geschichtsquellen* (irregular), *Veröffentlichungen des Tiroler Landesarchivs* (irregular).

Universitätsbibliothek Innsbruck (University Library, Innsbruck): Innrain 50, 6010 Innsbruck; tel. (512) 5072401; fax (512) 5072893; e-mail ub-hb@uibk.ac.at; internet www.uibk.ac.at/ub; f. 1746; 3.5m. vols, 6,139 print journals, 1,100 MSS, 2,000 incunabula; Dir Dr MARTIN WIESER.

Klagenfurt

Kärntner Landesarchiv (Carinthian Provincial Archives): St Ruprechter Str. 7, 9020 Klagenfurt; tel. (463) 56234; fax (463) 56234-20; e-mail post.landesarchiv@ktn.gv.at; internet www.landesarchiv.ktn.gv.at; f. 1904; Dir Dr WILHELM WADL; publ. *Das Kärntner Landesarchiv* (1 a year).

Universitätsbibliothek Klagenfurt (University Library, Klagenfurt): Universitätsstr. 65–67, 9020 Klagenfurt; tel. (463) 2700-9580; fax (463) 2700-9599; e-mail info.bibliothek@ uni-klu.ac.at; internet www.uni-klu.ac.at/ub; f. 1775; 820,000 vols; open to the public; Dir Mag. EDELTRAUD HAAS.

Klosterneuburg

Bibliothek des Augustiner-Chorherrenstiftes (Library of the Augustine Abbey): Stiftspl. 1, 3400 Klosterneuburg; tel. (2243) 411-151; fax (2243) 411-156; e-mail info@ stift-klosterneuburg.at; internet www .stift-klosterneuburg.at; f. 1114; 260,000 vols, 1,250 MSS, 836 incunabula; Dir Dr HEINZ RISTORY.

Leoben

Universitätsbibliothek Leoben (University Library, Leoben): Franz-Josef-Str. 18, 8700 Leoben; tel. (3842) 402; fax (3842) 4027702; e-mail office@unileoben.ac.at; internet www.unileoben.ac.at/bibliothek; f. 1840; 265,000 vols, 665 current journals, 4,800 magazine titles; Librarians FRANZ JUREK, Dr CHRISTIAN HASENHÜTTL.

Linz

Bibliothek der Oberösterreichischen Landesmuseen (Library of the Upper Austrian Provincial Museums): Museumstr. 14, 4010 Linz; tel. (732) 774482-41; fax (732) 774482-66; e-mail bibliothek@landesmuseum .at; internet www.landesmuseum.at; f. 1836; 160,000 vols; Chief Librarian WALTRAUD FAISSNER.

Oberösterreichische Landesbibliothek (Federal State Library of Upper Austria): Schillerpl. 2, 4021 Linz; tel. (732) 664071-00; fax (732) 664071-344; e-mail landesbibliothek@ooe.gv.at; internet www .landesbibliothek.at; f. 1774; 450,000 vols; Dirs Dr CHRISTIAN ENICHLMAYR, Dr RUDOLF LINDPOINTNER.

Oberösterreichisches Landesarchiv (Provincial Archives of Upper Austria): Anzengruberstr. 19, 4020 Linz; tel. (732) 772014601; fax (732) 772014619; e-mail landesarchiv@ooe.gv.at; internet www .landesarchiv-ooe.at; f. 1896; Dir Dr GERHART MARCKHGOTT; publs *Beiträge zur Zeitgeschichte Oberösterreichs* (irregular), *Forschungen zur Geschichte Oberösterreichs* (irregular), *Mitteilungen* (irregular), *Quellen zur Geschichte Oberösterreichs* (irregular).

Universitätsbibliothek der Johannes Kepler Universität Linz: Altenberger str. 69, 4040 Linz; tel. (732) 2468 9380; fax (732) 2468 1233; e-mail bibliothek@jku.at; internet www.jku.at/ub/content; f. 1965; 1m. vols, 21,500 periodicals; Dir Dr MONIKA SCHENK.

Melk

Bibliothek des Benediktinerklosters Melk in Niederösterreich (Library of the Melk Benedictine Monastery in Lower Austria): 3390 Stift Melk; tel. (2752) 555; fax (2752) 55552; e-mail bibliothek@stiftmelk.at; internet www.stiftmelk.at; 80,000 vols (mostly pre-19th-century), 1,800 codices, 750 incunabula; Librarian GOTTFRIED GLASSNER.

Salzburg

Bibliothek der Benediktiner Erzabtei St Peter (Library of the Benedictine Abbey of St Peter): St. Peter-Bezirk 1 / Postfach 113, 5010 Salzburg; tel. (662) 844576141; fax (662) 84457680; e-mail bibliothek@erzabtei.at; internet www.stift-stpeter.at; f. 700; 120,000 vols, 1,300 MSS, 899 incunabula, 2,000 journals; Dir Mag. SONJA FÜHRER.

Salzburger Landesarchiv (Salzburg Provincial Archives): Michael Pacher Str. 40, 5020 Salzburg; tel. (662) 80424527; fax (662) 80424661; e-mail landesarchiv@salzburg.gv.at; internet www.salzburg.gv.at/archive.htm; f. 1875; 35,000 photographs, 811 furniture, paintings, crests and seals; 1,000 leaves of graphic arts colln, 1,156 posters and 334 modern calendars; Dir Dr FRITZ KOLLER.

Universitätsbibliothek Salzburg (Salzburg University Library): Hofstallgasse 2–4, 5020 Salzburg; tel. (662) 804477550; fax (662) 8044103; e-mail info.hb@sbg.ac.at; internet www.uni-salzburg.at/bibliothek; f. 1623; 2m. vols, 1,100 MSS, 2,400 incunabula, 564 drawings, 1546 prints; spec. collns incl. 5,600 rare books; Dir Mag. Dr URSULA SCHACHL-RABER.

Sankt Florian

Bibliothek des Augustiner-Chorherrenstiftes (Library of the Augustine Canonical Foundation): Stiftstr. 1, 4490 St Florian; tel. (7224) 890254; fax (7224) 890260; e-mail bibliothek@stift-st-florian.at; internet www.stift-st-florian.at; f. 1071; library of the canons of Saint Augustine's order; reference library; 150,000 vols, 920 MSS, 952 incunabula; Dir Prof. Dr KARL REHBERGER.

Sankt Pölten

Bundesstaatliche Paedagogische Bibliothek beim Landesschulrat für Niederösterreich (Library of the Lower Austrian Education Authority): Rennbahnstr. 29, 3109 St Pöelten; tel. (2742) 2801482; fax (2742) 2801111; e-mail pbn@lsr-noe.gv.at; internet pbn.lsr-noe.gv.at; f. 1923; public open and borrowing library; 160,000 vols, 370 periodicals; Dir Mag. ERNST CHORHERR.

Niederösterreichisches Landesarchiv (Lower Austrian Provincial Archives): Landhauspl. 1, Haus Kulturbezirk 4, 3109 St Pölten; tel. (2742) 9005-12059; fax (2742) 9005-12052; e-mail post.k2archiv@noel.gv.at; internet www.noe.gv.at/bildung/landesarchiv-.html; f. 1513; archives of the province of Lower Austria; preserves state representation, documents, files, manuscripts since its inception; 31,000 vols; Dir Mag. Dr WILLIBALD ROSNER; publs *Mitteilungen, NÖLA*.

Niederösterreichische Landesbibliothek (Lower Austrian Provincial Library): Landhauspl. 1, Haus Kulturbezirk 3, 3109 St Pölten; tel. (2742) 900512847; fax (2742) 900513860; e-mail post.k3@noel.gv.at; internet www.noe.gv.at/landesbibliothek; f.

1813; library of the Lower Austrian provincial govt; has Lower Austria's oldest printed book; 300,000 vols, 4,000 newspapers and periodicals, 20,000 maps; Dir Dr GEBHARD KÖNIG.

Seckau

Bibliothek der Benediktinerabtei (Library of the Benedictine Abbey): 8732 Seckau; f. 1883; 160,000 vols; Dir Dr P. BENNO ROTH.

Vienna

Arbeiterkammer Bibliothek Wien für Sozialwissenschaften (Chamber of Labour Library for Social Sciences): Prinz Eugenstr. 20–22, 1040 Vienna; tel. (1) 501652452; fax (1) 501652229; e-mail bibliothek@akwien.at; internet wien.arbeiterkammer.at/bibliothek; f. 1922; social science specialist library; 450,000 vols, 750 periodicals; Dir Dr HERWIG JOBST.

Archiv, Bibliothek und Sammlungen der Gesellschaft der Musikfreunde in Wien (Archives, Library and Collections of the Society of Friends of Music in Vienna): Bösendorferstr. 12, 1010 Vienna; tel. (1) 505868144; fax (1) 505868166; e-mail office@a-wgm.com; internet www.a-wgm.com; f. 1812; consists of music and letters autographs, music MSS, file archive of the history of society and the conservatory; handwritten and printed books, medieval MSS and tablatures, song books, magazines and other periodicals, libretti, printed documents; historical and non-European musical instruments, music memorabilia, portrait, picture collns, busts, statuettes, reliefs and medals; 23,000 vols; 73,000 scores, historical material; Dir Prof. Dr OTTO BIBA.

Archiv der Universität Wien (Archives of the University of Vienna): Postgasse 9, 1010 Vienna; tel. (1) 427717201; fax (1) 42779172; e-mail archiv@univie.ac.at; internet bibliothek.univie.ac.at/archiv; f. 1365; preserving records of the Univ. of Vienna from 14th to 20th century; Archivist Dr THOMAS MAISEL.

Archiv des Stiftes Schotten (Schotten Abbey Archives): Schottenstift Wien, Musikarchiv, Freyung 6, 1010 Vienna; tel. (1) 53498140; fax (1) 53498105; e-mail archiv.bibliothek@schottenstift.at; internet www.schottenstift.at; f. 1155; archives of the Benedictine monastery; 2,500 handwritten church music compositions, 600 printed music; Archivist Dr MARTIN CZERNIN.

Bibliothek der Akademie der Bildenden Künste (Library of the Academy of Fine Arts): Schillerpl. 3, 1010 Vienna; tel. (1) 588162300; fax (1) 588162399; e-mail b.bastl@akbild.ac.at; internet www.akbild.ac.at; f. 1773; attached to Academy of Fine Arts Vienna; exhibitions, presentation of new books; main collecting areas: visual arts, art history, contemporary art, architecture; 142,000 vols, 128 periodicals, spec. collns incl. 10,000 historical holdings with 5 incunabula; Dir Doz. Dr BEATRIX BASTL.

Bibliothek der Bundesanstalt Statistik Österreich (Library of Statistics Austria): Guglgasse 13, 1110 Vienna; tel. (1) 711287814; fax (1) 71128-7310; e-mail alois.gehart@statistik.gv.at; f. 1829; 180,000 vols; Dir Dr ALOIS GEHART.

Bibliothek der Mechitharisten-Congregation: Mechitaristengasse 4, 1070 Vienna; tel. (1) 5236417; fax (1) 5236417111; e-mail vahanhov58@hotmail.com; internet www.mechitaristen.org; f. 1773; literature related to Armenia; 150,000 vols, 3,000 Armenian MSS, all current Armenian newspapers and periodicals; Dir P. VAHAN HOVAGIMIAN; publ. *Handes Amsorya* (1 a year).

Bibliothek und Archiv der Österreichischen Akademie der Wissenschaften (Library and Archive of the Austrian Academy of Sciences): Dr-Ignaz-Seipel-Pl. 2, 1010 Vienna; tel. (1) 515811262; fax (1) 515811256; e-mail bibliothek@oeaw.ac.at; internet www.oeaw.ac.at/biblio; f. 1847; 361,000 vols; Dir Prof. Dr CHRISTINE HARRAUER.

Bibliothek der Österreichischen Geographischen Gesellschaft (Library of the Austrian Geographical Society): Nottendorfer Gasse 2, 1030 Vienna; tel. (1) 5237974; internet arcims.isr.oeaw.ac.at/website/oegg/oegg.htm; f. 1856; 22,000 vols of monographs, 41,000 maps and globes; Librarian Dr PETER FRITZ.

Bibliothek der Veterinärmedizinischen Universität Wien (Library of Vienna University of Veterinary Medicine): Veterinärpl. 1, 1210 Vienna; tel. (1) 250771414; fax (1) 250771490; e-mail bibliothekinfo@vetmeduni.ac.at; internet www.vu-wien.ac.at/bibl; f. 1777; 208,703 vols, 810 periodicals; Dir Mag. DORIS REINITZER; publ. *RARA-magazin*.

Bibliothek der Wirtschaftskammer Wien (Vienna Chamber of Commerce Library): Stubenring 8–10, 1010 Vienna; tel. (1) 514501370; fax (1) 514501469; e-mail bibliothek@wkw.at; internet portal.wko.at; f. 1849; reference library; contains books from all fields of law, economics and social sciences; 200,000 vols; Dir Dr HERBERT PRIBYL.

Bibliothek des Bundesministeriums für Finanzen (Library of the Ministry of Finance): Hintere Zollamtsstr. 2B, 1030 Vienna; tel. (1) 51433501143; fax (1) 514335907110; e-mail bibliothek@bmf.gv.at; internet www.bmf.gv.at; f. 1810; 200,000 vols; Head of Library Mag. PATRIZIA RABA.

Bibliothek des Bundesministeriums für Land- und Forstwirtschaft, Umwelt und Wasserwirtschaft (Library of the Federal Ministry of Agriculture, Forestry, the Environment and Water Management): Stubenring 1, 1012 Vienna; tel. (1) 71100; fax (1) 7103254; e-mail ingrid.saberi@lebensministerium.at; f. 1868; 127,500 vols; Librarian Mag. INGRID SABERI.

Bibliothek des Bundesministeriums für Soziale Sicherheit, Generationen und Konsumentenschutz (Library of the Federal Ministry for Social Security and Consumer Protection): Stubenring 1, 1010 Vienna; tel. (1) 711006143; fax (1) 718947011-80; e-mail ilga.kubela@bmsg.gv.at; f. 1917; 150,000 vols; Dir ILGA ANNA KUBELA.

Bibliothek des Instituts für Österreichische Geschichtsforschung (Library of the Institute of Austrian Historical Research): Dr Karl Lueger Ring 1, 1010 Vienna; tel. (1) 427727205; fax (1) 42779272; e-mail paul.herold@univie.ac.at; internet www.univie.ac.at/geschichtsforschung/biblio.htm; f. 1854; collns based on the teaching and research environment and the tasks of the institute; institute files since 1854; 75,000 vols, 200 periodicals; Librarian Mag. Dr PAUL HEROLD.

Bibliothek des Österreichischen Patentamtes (Library of the Austrian Patent Office): Dresdner Str. 87, 1200 Vienna; tel. (1) 53424153; fax (1) 53424110; e-mail bibliothek@patentamt.at; internet www.patentamt.at; f. 1899; 26,000,000 vols; Dir Dr INGRID WEIDINGER; publs *Österreichisches Gebrauchsmusterblatt, Österreichischer Markenanzeiger, Österreichischer Musteranzeiger, Österreichisches Patentblatt*.

Bibliothek des Österreichischen Staatsarchivs (Library of the Austrian State Archives): Nottendorfer Gasse. 2, 1030

Vienna; tel. (1) 79540115; fax (1) 79540109; e-mail stabpost@oesta.gv.at; internet www .oesta.gv.at; f. 1984 by combining all libraries in the state archives; history, military history; court and state archives; 800,000 vols; Dir Dr GERHARD ARTL.

Büchereien Wien (Municipal Libraries of Vienna): Urban-Loritz-Pl. 2A, 1070 Vienna; tel. (1) 400084500; fax (1) 40009984510; e-mail post@buechereien.wien.at; internet www.buechereien.wien.at; f. 1945; 1.6m. vols, 250,000 audio media items; central library and 38 brs; Chief Librarian CHRISTIAN JAHL.

Clusterbibliothek—Bibliothek und Dokumentation (Cluster Library—Library and Documentation): Bundesministerium für Wirtschaft, Familie und Jugend, Stubenring 1, 1011 Vienna; tel. (1) 711005483; fax (1) 711002384; e-mail clusterbibliothek@bmwfj .gv.at; internet www.bmwfj.gv.at; interdepartmental cluster library, European Documentation Centre (EDC), publs, policy analysis, documentation; 550,000 vols, 927 journals, 410 loose-leaf editions; Dir Dr BRIGITTA KOHLERT-WINDISCH.

Diözesanarchiv Wien (Vienna Diocesan Archives): Wollzeile 2/3, 1010 Vienna; tel. (1) 51552; fax (1) 515523240; e-mail daw@ edw.or.at; internet www.erzdioezese-wien.at; f. 1936; history of archdiocese of Vienna and of parishes and convents in Vienna and the eastern part of Lower Austria; 45,000 vols, 800 periodicals, 6,000 documents and files; Dir Dr ANNE MARIE FENZL.

Fachbereichsbibliothek Rechtswissenschaften (Faculty Library of Legal Studies): Schottenbastei 10–16, 1010 Vienna; tel. (1) 427716311; fax (1) 427716309; e-mail thomas.luzer@univie.ac.at; internet bibliothek.univie.ac.at/fb-rewi; f. 1922; 238,000 vols, 1,100 periodicals; Dir Dr THOMAS LUZER.

Österreichische Nationalbibliothek (Austrian National Library): Josefspl. 1, POB 308, 1015 Vienna; tel. (1) 53410444; fax (1) 53410437; e-mail awi@onb.ac.at; internet www.onb.ac.at; f. in 14th century; picture archives and graphics dept, map dept, dept of music, literary archives dept of papyri, dept of planned languages, dept of manuscripts and rare books, archives of the Austrian folk song institute; 8 special collns and main library; 8,065,352 vols, 3,625,741 books and periodicals, 8,027 incunabula, 17,241 microforms, 276,592 maps, 644 globes, 133,359 vols of printed music, 41,039 audiovisual items, 2,717,567 pictures, 711,246 other materials (papyri, ex libris and other collns); Dir-Gen. Dr JOHANNA RACHINGER; publs *Ausstellungskataloge* (irregular), *Biblios. Beiträge zu Buch, Bibliothek und Schrift* (2 a year), *Corpus Papyrorum Raineri, Mitteilungen aus der Papyrussammlung* (irregular), *NILUS* (1 or 2 a year), *Profile. Magazin des Literaturarchivs der Österreichischen Nationalbibliothek* (2 or 3 a year), *Sichtungen* (1 a year).

Österreichische Zentralbibliothek für Physik (Austrian Central Library for Physics): Boltzmanngasse 5, 1090 Vienna; tel. (1) 427727600; fax (1) 42779276; e-mail infophysik.ub@univie.ac.at; internet www .zbp.univie.ac.at; f. 1980 as Central Library for Physics in Vienna; present name 2000; attached to Univ. Library of Univ. of Vienna; depository library for USAEC/USDOE report and INIS microfiche colln; regional information centre for IGBP publication; acquires, develops physics-related literature and information sources; 380,000 vols, 2,890 periodicals, 1,175,000 microfiches; Dir Mag. BRIGITTE KROMP.

Österreichisches Staatsarchiv (Austrian State Archives): Nottendorfer Gasse 2, 1030 Vienna; tel. (1) 795400; fax (1) 79540-199; e-mail gdpost@oesta.gv.at; internet www .oesta.gv.at; f. 1945; domestic, Court and State Archives, Gen. Admin. Archives, Finance and Treasury Archives, War Archives, Archives of the Austrian Republic; 177,700 linear m of shelves; Gen. Dir Prof. Dr LORENZ MIKOLETZKY; publ. *Mitteilungen des österreichischen Staatsarchivs*.

Parlamentsbibliothek (Library of Parliament): Dr Karl Renner-Ring 3, 1017 Vienna; tel. (1) 401100; fax (1) 401102825; e-mail bibliothek@parlament.gv.at; internet www .parlament.gv.at/bibliothek; f. 1869; 342,000 vols, 270 journals and newspapers; Dir Dr ELISABETH DIETRICH-SCHULZ; Deputy Dir Dr SIEGLINDE OSIEBE.

Universitätsbibliothek und Universitätsarchiv der Universität für Bodenkultur Wien (Library and Archives of the University of Natural Resources and Applied Life Sciences, Vienna): Peter-Jordanstr. 82, 1190 Vienna; tel. (1) 476542060; fax (1) 476542092; e-mail ub.support@boku.ac.at; internet www.boku.ac.at/bib.html; f. 1872; central archive of the univ.; consists of main library and four departmental libraries; 570,000 vols, 1,300 periodicals, 14,900 dissertations, 3,000 e-journals; Dir Mag. MARTINA HÖRL.

Universitätsbibliothek der Technischen Universität Wien (Vienna University of Technology Library): Resselgasse 4, 1040 Vienna; tel. (1) 58801-44001; fax (1) 58801-44099; e-mail info@ub.tuwien.ac.at; internet www.ub.tuwien.ac.at; f. 1815; 1,325,500 vols; Head Mag. EVA RAMMINGER.

Universitätsbibliothek der Universität für Musik und darstellende Kunst Wien (Library of the Vienna University for Music and Dramatic Art): Lothringerstr. 18, 1030 Vienna; tel. (1) 711558101; fax (1) 711558199; e-mail infobib@mdw.ac.at; internet www.ub.mdw.ac.at; f. 1909; information centre of the univ.; provides required source material for teaching; houses the Bruno Walter archive; 225,000 vols, 52,000 audiovisual media items; Dir Dr SUSANNE ESCHWÉ.

Universitätsbibliothek der Wirtschaftsuniversität Wien (Library of the Vienna University of Economics and Business): Augasse 2–6, 1090 Vienna; tel. (1) 313364990; fax (1) 31336745; e-mail library@wu.ac.at; internet www.wu.ac.at/ library; f. 1898; 800,000 vols; Dir Dr NIKOLAUS BERGER.

Universitätsbibliothek Wien (Vienna University Library): Dr Karl Lueger Ring 1, 1010 Vienna; tel. (1) 42715001; fax (1) 42779150; e-mail direktion@univie.ac.at; internet bibliothek.univie.ac.at; f. 1365; attached to Univ. of Vienna; largest, oldest library in Austria; main library and 10 branch libraries for different depts; 6.6m. vols; Dir Hofrätin Mag. MARIA SEISSL.

Wiener Stadt- und Landesarchiv (Municipal and Provincial Archives of Vienna): Rathaus, 1082 Vienna; Guglgasse 14, Gasometer D, 11 Vienna; tel. (1) 400084808; fax (1) 400084809; e-mail post@m08.magwien.gv .at; internet www.wien.gv.at/kultur/archiv; f. 1889; records since 13th century; documents, books, maps, drafts, photographs and microfilms; 35,000 m of archives; cartographic colln of 50,000 plans, 20,000 photos, 439 MSS, 550 pieces of commemorative sheets; Dir Mag. Dr BRIGITTE RIGELE; publ. *Veröffentlichungen*.

Wiener Stadt- und Landesbibliothek (Vienna City and Provincial Library): Rathaus, 1082 Vienna; tel. (1) 400084920;

fax (1) 40009984915; e-mail post@ wienbibliothek.at; internet www .stadtbibliothek.wien.at; f. 1856; research library; research and documentation of Vienna's history and culture; 550,000 vols, 250,000 MSS, 100,000 musical items, 100,000 MSS musical items, 300,000 posters; Dir Dr SYLVIA MATTL-WURM.

Zentralarchiv des Deutschen Ordens (Central Archive of the Teutonic Order): Singerstr. 7, 1010 Vienna; tel. (1) 5121065261; e-mail zentralarchiv@ deutscher-orden.at; internet www .deutscher-orden.at; f. 1852; information about knights, priests, sisters, offices, administration, business affairs, devt of rules of the Teutonic order, their piety and spirituality; 11,668 vols, 12,000 documents; Archivist Mag. Dipl. FRANK BAYARD.

Zentralbibliothek im Justizpalast (Central Library of the Palace of Justice): Schmerlingpl. 11, 1016 Vienna; tel. (1) 521520; fax (1) 521523710; e-mail ogh .bibliothek@justiz.gv.at; internet www.ogh .gv.at/zentralbibliothek; f. 1829; attached to Supreme Court of Justice; entrance restricted to qualified lawyers (no students); separate reading rooms, one for judges and public prosecutors and one for all other lawyers; 124,000 vols, 180 legal journals; Dir GABRIELE SVIRAK.

Museums and Art Galleries

Bad Deutsch-Altenburg

Archäologisches Museum Carnuntinum (Carnuntinum Archaeological Museum): Badgasse 40–46, 2405 Bad Deutsch-Altenburg; tel. (2165) 216333770; fax (2165) 216333775; internet www.carnuntum.co.at/ park/archaeologisches-museum-carnuntinum; f. 1904; attached to Archaeological Park Carnuntum; museum of Roman archaeology; library of 12,000 vols; Curator Mag. FRANZ HUMER.

Bregenz

Vorarlberger Landesmuseum (Vorarlberg Provincial Museum): Kornmarktpl 1, 6900 Bregenz; tel. (5574) 46050; fax (5574) 4605020; e-mail info@vlm.at; internet www .vlm.at; f. 1857; archaeology, art and folklore of the region; 150,000 objects from the Mesolithic period to the present, 24 oil paintings, 350 graphics; closed for renovation until 2013; Dir TOBIAS G. NATTER; publ. *Jahrbuch*.

Eggenburg

Krahuletz Museum Eggenburg: Krahuletzpl., 3730 Eggenburg; tel. (2984) 3400; fax (2984) 34005; e-mail gesellschaft@ krahuletzmuseum.at; internet www .krahuletzmuseum.at; f. 1902; colln f. 1866; geology, prehistory, ethnology; Dir Dr JOHANNES M. TUZAR; publ. *Katalogreihe*.

Eisenstadt

Burgenländisches Landesmuseum (Burgenland Provincial Museum): Museumgasse 1–5, 7000 Eisenstadt; tel. (2682) 6001234; fax (2682) 6001277; e-mail landesmuseum@bgld .gv.at; internet www.burgenland.at/ landesmuseum; f. 1926; archaeology, geology, history of art, natural history, ethnology, numismatics, history of music, economic history of Burgenland; library of 31,000 vols; Dir Dr JOSEF TIEFENBACH; publ. *Wissenschaftliche Arbeiten aus dem Burgenland*.

Furth bei Göttweig

Graphische Sammlung und Kunstsammlungen Stift Göttweig (Göttweig Abbey Graphic Art Collection): Stift Göttweig, 3511 Furth bei Göttweig; tel. (2732) 85581226; fax (2732) 71848; e-mail graph.kabinett@stiftgoettweig.at; internet www.stiftgoettweig.at; f. 1714; graphic art from the 16th century to the present, music, coins and medals; 30,000 engravings; library of 280,000 vols (history, law, theology, history of art, sciences), 1,110 MSS, 1,120 incunabula, 2,750 archives (1054–1900); Curator Prof. Dr GREGOR MARTIN LECHNER; Deputy Curator Mag. MICHAEL GRÜNWALD.

Graz

Universalmuseum Joanneum: Mariahilferstr. 2–4, 8020 Graz; tel. (316) 80170; fax (316) 80179880; e-mail welcome@museum-joanneum.at; internet www.museum-joanneum.at; f. 1811; 4.5m. objects related to history, archaeology; natural history, art (exhibits housed on several sites); picture and sound archives, incl. Styrian armoury colln, coin cabinet, hunting museum, sculpture park, agriculture museum, etc.; Dir Dr WOLFGANG MUCHITSCH.

Innsbruck

Kaiserliche Hofburg (Imperial Palace): Rennweg 1, 6020 Innsbruck; tel. (512) 587186; fax (512) 58718613; e-mail hofburg.ibk@burghauptmannschaft.at; internet www.hofburg-innsbruck.at; f. 15th century; built as residence of the Tyrolean provincial rulers under Archduke Sigismund the Rich and extended under Emporer Maximilian I(1459–1519); Maria Theresia (1717–80) rebuilt the Palace in the late Viennese baroque style; spec. exhibitions throughout the year; Dir WALTRAUD SCHREILECHNER.

Kunsthistorisches Museum Sammlungen Schloss Ambras (Museum of Fine Art Collections, Ambras Castle): Schloss-str. 20, 6020 Innsbruck; tel. (1) 525244802; fax (1) 525244899; e-mail info.ambras@khm.at; internet www.khm.at/ambras; f. 1580; armour, furniture, pictures, sculpture; Curator Mag. Dr VERONIKA SANDBICHLER.

Museum im Zeughaus (Zeughaus Museum): Zeughausgasse, 6020 Innsbruck; tel. (512) 59489-313; fax (512) 59489-318; e-mail zeughaus@tiroler-landesmuseen.at; internet www.tiroler-landesmuseen.at; f. 1973; geology, history, technology of the Tyrol; Pres. ANDREAS TRENTINI; Dir WOLFGANG MEIGHÖRNER; Curator for Historical Collns Dr CLAUDIA SPORER-HEIS.

Tiroler Landesmuseum Ferdinandeum (Tyrol Provincial Museum): Museumstr. 15, 6020 Innsbruck; tel. (512) 59489; fax (512) 59489109; e-mail sekretariat@tiroler-landesmuseum.at; internet www.tiroler-landesmuseum.at; f. 1823; independent graphics colln established in 1976; historical colln; art history colln divided into older art history and modern; ancient musical instruments, music supplies and materials to Tyrolean music history; natural sciences colln consisting of colln of earth science, botanical, zoological and spec. collns; early provincial roman collns; library of 240,000 vols; Dir Dr WOLFGANG MEIGHÖRNER; publs *Ferdinandea* (4 a year), *Veröffentlichungen des Tiroler Landesmuseums Ferdinandeum* (1 a year).

Tiroler Volkskunstmuseum (Tyrol Folk Art Museum): Universitätsstr. 2, 6020 Innsbruck; tel. (512) 59489510; fax (512) 59489520; e-mail volkskunstmuseum@tirol.gv.at; internet www.tiroler-volkskunstmuseum.at; f. 1929; local folk arts and crafts; focus on arts and crafts,

cottage industries, popular religiosity, masks and costumes of the area; library of 2,940 vols; Dir Dr HERLINDE MENARDI.

Klagenfurt

Landesmuseum für Kärnten (Provincial Museum of Carinthia): Museumgasse 2, 9021 Klagenfurt; tel. (50) 53630599; fax (50) 53630540; e-mail willkommen@landesmuseum.ktn.gv.at; internet www.landesmuseum-ktn.at; f. 1844; history, natural history, archaeology, art, folk arts and crafts; library of 130,000 vols; Dir Mag. ERICH WAPPIS; publs *Archiv für Vaterländische Geschichte und Topographie*, *Carinthia I* (archaeology, history, history of art, and folklore), *Carinthia II* (science), *Kärntner Heimatleben*.

Landesmuseum Kärnten, Kärntner Botanikzentrum (Carinthian Botanic Centre): Prof.-Dr-Kahler-Pl. 1, 9020 Klagenfurt; tel. (463) 50271512; e-mail kbz@landesmuseum.ktn.gv.at; internet www.landesmuseum.ktn.gv.at; f. 1862, present location 1958; cultivation of central and southern Alpine flora; school and adult education in botany and nature conservation; collns of orchids, succulents and carnivorous plants, poisonous and medicinal herbs, spices and useful plants, fossils (4,000 specimens); ethnobotanical and carpological collns; herbarium of 150,000 phanerogams and 50,000 cryptogams; garden for the blind; library of 13,000 vols, 18,000 offprints, slides, biographical and bibliographical collns; Head Mag. Dr ROLAND K. EBERWEIN; publs *Index Seminum* (1 a year), *Wulfenia* (1 a year).

Krems

WEINSTADT Museum (Museum of the Wine City): Körnermarkt 14, 3500 Krems; tel. (2732) 801567; fax (2732) 801576; e-mail museum@krems.gv.at; internet www.weinstadtmuseum.at; f. 1996; located in fmr Dominican monastery; primitive art; Romanesque and Gothic sculptures; Kremser Schmidt's paintings; Dir Dr FRANZ SCHÖNFELLNER.

Kremsmünster

Sternwarte Kremsmünster (Kremsmünster Observatory): Benediktinerstift 4550 Kremsmünster; tel. (7583) 5275; fax (7583) 5275450; e-mail sternwarte.kremsmuenster@telecom.at; internet members.nextra.at/stewar; f. 1748; geological, palaeontological and prehistoric collns; focus on folklore, ethnology, history of civilization; also museum of astronomy; showcases devt of scientific research for quarter of a millennium; library of 25,000 vols; Dir Mag. Dr P. AMAND KRAML; publ. *Naturwissenschaftliche Sammlungen Kremsmünster* (irregular).

Linz

Lentos Kunstmuseum Linz: Ernst-Koref-Promenade 1, 4020 Linz; tel. (732) 70703600; fax (732) 70703604; e-mail info@lentos.at; internet www.lentos.at; f. 1948 as Neue Galerie der Stadt Linz; current name 2003; gallery of contemporary art with paintings (ranging from Klimt, Schiele and Kokoschka to Arnulf Rainter, Karel Appel and Hermann Nitsch), drawings, prints, posters and sculptures since 19th century; 1,600 works of painting, 450 sculpture and art objects; 10,000 graphics, incl. 1,100 photo exhibits; library of 30,000 vols, 25 magazines of visual art; Dir of Art STELLA ROLLIG.

Oberösterreichische Landesmuseen (State Museums for Upper Austria): Museumstr. 14, 4010 Linz; tel. (732) 7744820; fax (732) 77448266; e-mail info@landesmuseum.at; internet www.

.landesmuseum.at; f. 1833; consists of a number of collns in nature, art and culture; 12 locations; library of 130,000 vols; Dir Mag. Dr PETER ASSMANN; publs *Beiträge zur Naturkunde Oberösterreichs*, *Denisia*, *Linzer biologische Beiträge*, *Neues Museum*, *Stapfia*, *Studien zur Kulturgeschichte von Oberösterreich*, *Vogelkundliche Nachrichten aus Oberösterreich*.

Salzburg

Haus der Natur/Museum für Natur und Technik (Natural History Museum): Museumpl. 5, 5020 Salzburg; tel. (662) 8426530; fax (662) 84265399; e-mail office@hausdernatur.at; internet www.hausdernatur.at; f. 1924; zoology, botany, anthropology, geology; science centre, reptile zoo, aquarium, space hall; Dir Dr NORBERT WINDING.

Mozarteum: Schwarzstr. 26, 5020 Salzburg; tel. (662) 889400; fax (662) 8894036; e-mail office@mozarteum.at; internet www.mozarteum.at; f. 1914 by 'Internationale Stiftung Mozarteum'; concert rooms; 2 museums dedicated to life and work of Mozart; autographs, first editions, early prints of selected works and portraits; library of 35,000 vols., 6,000 music sheets, 22,000 sound recordings, 2,800 videos; Man. Dir Dr STEPHAN PAULY.

Mozarts Wohnhaus: Makartpl. 8, 5020 Salzburg; tel. (662) 87422740; fax (662) 872924; e-mail archiv@mozarteum.at; internet www.mozarteum.at; multivision 'Mozart and Salzburg'; the world of Mozart 1773–80; instruments from Mozart's time.

Residenzgalerie Salzburg: Residenzpl. 1, 5010 Salzburg; tel. (662) 8404510; fax (662) 84045116; e-mail office@residenzgalerie.at; internet www.residenzgalerie.at; f. 1923; 16th to 19th century European paintings; focus on 17th century Dutch paintings, 17th and 18th century Italian, French and Austrian paintings; works by 19th century Austrian masters; Dir Dr GABRIELE GROSCHNER.

Salzburg Museum: Neue Residenz, Mozartpl. 1, 5010 Salzburg; tel. (662) 6208080; fax (662) 620808720; e-mail office@salzburgmuseum.at; internet www.salzburgmuseum.at; f. 1834, reopened in 2007; prehistoric and Roman remains, art, coins, musical instruments, costumes, toys; library of 130,000 vols, archives; Dir Mag. PETER HUSTY.

Schloss Hellbrunn (Hellbrunn Palace): 5020 Salzburg; tel. (662) 8203720; fax (662) 8203724931; e-mail info@hellbrunn.at; internet www.hellbrunn.at; f. 1612; furnished 17th-century palace, with water gardens, deer park and open-air theatre; Dir INGRID SONVILLA.

St Pölten

Niederösterreichisches Landesmuseum (Provincial Museum of Lower Austria): Kulturbezirk 5, 3109 St Pölten; tel. (2742) 908090; fax (2742) 908099; e-mail info@landesmuseum.net; internet www.landesmuseum.net; f. 1907; natural history, history of art (since the medieval period); many attached deptl museums located in Lower Austria, incl. Haydn's birthplace at Rohrau; information centre; Dirs BRIGITTE SCHLÖGL, CORNELIA LAMPRECHTER.

Stillfried/March

Museum für Ur- und Frühgeschichte (Museum for Pre- and Early History): Museumsverein Stillfried, Hauptstr. 23, 2262 Stillfried/March (Niederösterreich); tel. (676) 6113979; e-mail stillfried@aon.at; internet www.museumstillfried.at; f. 1914;

local archaeology and palaeontology; Dir Dr WALPURGA ANTL; publ. *Museumsnachrichten* (3 or 4 a year).

Vienna

Albertina: Albertinapl. 1, 1010 Vienna; tel. (1) 534830; fax (1) 53483430; e-mail info@albertina.at; internet www.albertina.at; f. 1805; prints, drawings, posters; classical modern art; 50,000 drawings, 900,000 graphic art works; 50,000 architectural objects; 100,000 objects in photographic colln; library of 100,000 vols; Dir Dr KLAUS ALBRECHT SCHRÖDER.

Department und Sammlungen für Geschichte der Medizin: Währingerstr. 25, 1090 Vienna; tel. (1) 4016026000; fax (1) 40160926000; e-mail sammlungen@meduniwien.ac.at; internet www.meduniwien.ac.at/josephinum; f. 1785 as acad. for military surgeons; 18th-century wax anatomical colln, museum of the Vienna Medical Schools, museum of medical endoscopy and anaesthesia, colln of instruments and pictures; library of 80,000 historical medical books; Co-Head of Dept Mag. Assoc. Prof. Dr SONIA HORN.

Erzbischöfliches Dom- und Diözesanmuseum (Archiepiscopal Cathedral and Diocesan Museum): Stephanspl. 6, 1010 Vienna; tel. (1) 515523300; fax (1) 515523599; e-mail dommuseum@edw.or.at; internet www.dommuseum.at; f. 1933; ecclesiastical art incl. sculpture and painting; fine art with accent on sacral works from St Stephen's Cathedral; 3.000 works of modern art; Dir Dr BERNHARD A. BÖHLER.

Gemäldegalerie der Akademie der Bildenden Künste Wien (Vienna Academy of Fine Arts Gallery): Schillerpl. 3, 1010 Vienna; tel. (1) 588162222; fax (1) 5863346; e-mail gemgal@akbild.ac.at; internet www.akademiegalerie.at; f. 1822; paintings since 14th century; Deputy Dir MARTINA FLEISCHER.

Heeresgeschichtliches Museum (Military History Museum): Arsenal Objekt 1 Vienna; tel. (1) 795610; fax (1) 795611017707; e-mail contact@hgm.or.at; internet www.hgm.or.at; f. 1891; exhibits dating from Thirty Years War to Second World War; library of 70,000 vols; Dir Dr MANFRIED RAUCHENSTEINER.

Kunsthistorisches Museum (Museum of Fine Arts): Maria Theresien-Pl. , 1010 Vienna; tel. (1) 525244025; fax (1) 525409824; e-mail info@khm.at; internet www.khm.at; f. 1891 from Hapsburg Imperial collections; paintings, Egyptian and other antiquities, numismatics, armour, historical costume, plastics and handicrafts, musical instruments, secular and ecclesiastical relics of the Holy Roman Empire and the Hapsburg dynasty, state carriages (at Schönbrunn palace); library of 256,000 vols; Gen. Dir Dr SABINE HAAG.

Kupferstichkabinett der Akademie der Bildenden Künste (Graphic Art Collection of the Academy of Fine Arts): Schillerpl. 3, Raum 113, 1010 Vienna; tel. (1) 588162400; fax (1) 588162499; e-mail m.knofler@akbild.ac.at; internet www.akbild.ac.at/kuka; f. 1689; drawings, prints, photographs, architecture, sculpture gallery; 40,000 drawings, 100,000 prints, 20,000 photographs; reflects central European art education; library: see under Libraries and Archives; Dir Dr MONIKA KNOFLER.

Leopold Museum: Museumspl. 1, 1070 Vienna; tel. (1) 52570-0; fax (1) 52570-1500; e-mail office@leopoldmuseum.org; internet www.leopoldmuseum.org; f. 2001; fmrly private art colln of Rudolf and Elisabeth Leopold; works by Schiele, Klimt, Kokoschka and others; Man. Dir PETER WEINHÄUPL.

Museum für Völkerkunde (Museum of Ethnology): Neue Hofburg, Ringstrassentrakt, 1010 Vienna; tel. (1) 525245052; fax (1) 525245199; e-mail info@ethno-museum.ac.at; internet www.ethno-museum.ac.at; f. 1928; attached to Kunsthistorisches Museum; ethnology of non-European peoples; 220,000 objects, 25,000 historical photographs, 136,000 printed works, 300 km of film; library of 130,000 vols; Dir Prof. Dr CHRISTIAN FEEST; publs *Archiv für Völkerkunde* (1 a year), *Veröffentlichungen zum Archiv für Völkerkunde*.

Museum Moderner Kunst Stiftung Ludwig Wien (Museum of Modern Art Ludwig Foundation Vienna): Museumspl. 1, 1070 Vienna; tel. (1) 52500; fax (1) 525001300; e-mail info@mumok.at; internet www.mumok.at; f. 1962 as Museum des 20 Jahrhunderts; present name 1991; modern and contemporary art, incl. American Pop Art and concurrent European movements; 9,000 works in paintings, sculptures, installations, drawings, graphic works, photographs, videos and films; library of 30,000 items; Dir KAROLA KRAUS.

Naturhistorisches Museum (Natural History Museum): I, Burgring 7, 1010 Vienna; tel. (1) 521770; fax (1) 52177578; e-mail info@hm-wien.ac.at; internet www.nhm-wien.ac.at; f. 1889; 25m. natural objects; ecology, geology, palaeontology, zoology, botany, anthropology, prehistory, speleology; library of 400,000 books; Dir Gen. Prof. Dr CHRISTIAN KÖBERL; publ. *Annalen*.

Österreichische Galerie Belvedere (Austrian Gallery): Oberes Belvedere, Prinz Eugenstr. 27, 1030 Vienna; tel. (1) 795570; fax (1) 79557121; e-mail info@belvedere.at; internet www.belvedere.at; Austrian painting and sculpture from Middle Ages to present, foreign painting and sculpture since 19th century, spec. colln of sculpture by G. Ambrosi; world's largest Gustav Klimt painting colln; library of 80,000 media units; Dir Dr AGNES HUSSLEIN-ARCO; publ. *Belvedere*.

Österreichisches Gesellschafts- und Wirtschafts-Museum (Austrian Museum for Economics and Social Affairs): Vogelsanggasse 36, 1050 Vienna; tel. (1) 5452551; fax (1) 545255155; e-mail wirtschaftsmuseum@oegwm.ac.at; internet www.oegwm.ac.at; f. 1925; archives, maps, photographs; public library on 'Austria Yesterday and Today'; Dir Mag. HANS HARTWEGER; publ. *Österreichs Wirtschaft im Überblick* (1 a year; also in English).

Österreichisches Museum für angewandte Kunst / Gegenwartskunst (Austrian Museum of Applied Arts and Contemporary Art): Stubenring 5, 1010 Vienna; tel. (1) 711360; fax (1) 7131026; e-mail office@mak.at; internet www.mak.at; f. 1864; applied arts from Roman to modern times, incl. furniture and woodwork, textiles and carpets, glass and ceramics, metalwork, the Wiener Werkstätte Archive and contemporary art; library of 200,000 vols, 3,700 magazines, 500,000 prints; Dir MARTINA KANDELER-FRITSCH (acting).

Österreichisches Museum für Volkskunde (Austrian Museum of Folk Life and Folk Art): Laudongasse 15–19, 1080 Vienna; tel. (1) 4068905; fax (1) 4085342; e-mail office@volkskundemuseum.at; internet www.volkskundemuseum.at; f. 1895; historical folk art and folk culture; historical and contemporary lifestyles, cultural expressions of European social and ethnic groups; incl. nat. furniture colln and other spec. collns (housed on separate sites); library of 130,000 ; Dir Dr MARGOT SCHINDLER; publs *Kataloge* (1–3 issues a year), *Österreichische Zeits-*chrift für Volkskunde* (4 a year), *Veröffentlichungen* (irregular).

Österreichisches Theatermuseum (Austrian Theatre Museum): Lobkowitzpl. 2, 1010 Vienna; tel. (1) 525243460; fax (1) 525245399; e-mail info@theatermuseum.at; internet www.theatermuseum.at; f. 1975; 100,000 hand drawings, 1,000 stage design and architectural models, 700,000 photographs, 600 portraits, role, and scene pictures; 600 original costumes with accessories; library of 80,000 vols; Dir Dr THOMAS TRABITSCH.

Schloss Schönbrunn Kultur- und Betriebsges. m.b.H. (Schönbrunn Palace):; e-mail gold@schoenbrunn.at Schönbrunn Palace, 1130, Vienna; tel. (1) 811130; fax (1) 8121106; e-mail info@schoenbrunn.at; internet www.schoenbrunn.at; f. 1992; mid-18th-century fmr Imperial summer residence of the Habsburg dynasty; baroque and botanical gardens; zoological garden opened 1752; placed on UNESCO World Cultural Heritage List in 1996; Dirs Dipl.-Ing. WOLFGANG KIPPES, Dr FRANZ SATTLECKER.

Technisches Museum Wien (Museum of Technology in Vienna): Mariahilferstr. 212, 1140 Vienna; tel. (1) 899980; fax (1) 899983333; e-mail museumsbox@tmw.at; internet www.tmw.at; f. 1909; colln of scientific and technological instruments from 18th century to present; library of 100,000 vols, 750 magazines; Dir Dr GABRIELE ZUNA-KRATKY; publ. *Blätter für Technikgeschichte* (1 a year).

Wien Museum (Vienna Museum): Karlspl., 1040 Vienna; tel. (1) 50587470; fax (1) 50587477201; e-mail office@wienmuseum.at; internet www.wienmuseum.at; f. 1887; local history from prehistoric times to the present; among many associated museums are premises once occupied by Beethoven, Haydn, Mozart, Schubert and Johann Strauss; Dir Dr WOLFGANG KOS.

Universities

All institutions of higher education have university status.

AKADEMIE DER BILDENDEN KÜNSTE WIEN
(Academy of Fine Arts Vienna)

Schillerpl. 3, 1010 Vienna

Telephone: (1) 588160
Fax: (1) 588161898
E-mail: info@akbild.ac.at
Internet: www.akbild.ac.at

Founded 1692
State control
Languages of instruction: German, English
Academic year: October to June

Rector: Prof. Dr STEPHAN SCHMIDT-WULFFEN
Pro-Rectors: Mag. ANDREAS SPIEGL, Mag. ANNA STEIGER
Librarian: BEATRIX BASTL

Library: see under Libraries and Archives

PROFESSORS

ALLIEZ, E., Aesthetics and Sociology of Art
BAATZ, W., Conservation and Restoration
BAUER, U. M., Theory, Practice and Transfer of Contemporary Art
BISCHOF, E., Textile Art
DAMISCH, G., Drawing and Graphic Techniques
GIRONCOLI, B., Sculpture
GRAF, F., Expanded Artistic Environment
GRAF, O., Art History
GREEN, R., Conceptual Art
HASPEL, F., Textile Art

KOGLER, P., Computer and Video Art
LAINER, R., Architectural Design
OBHOLZER, W., Abstract Art
PRUSCHA, C., Architectural Design and Habitat, Environment and Conservation
ROSENBLUM, A., Representational Painting and Drawing
SAMSONOW, E., Philosophical and Historical Anthropology of the Arts
SCHLEGEL, E., Photography and Art
SCHMALIX, H., Art in Public Space
SCHREINER, M., Natural Science and Technology in Art
SCHULZ, J., Textile Arts and Crafts, Tapestry
SLOTERDIJK, P., Cultural Philosophy and Media Theory
WAGNER, K., Construction and Technology
WONDER, E., Stage Design
ZENS, H., Education and Science of Art
ZOBERNIG, H., Sculpture

ALPEN-ADRIA-UNIVERSITÄT KLAGENFURT
(University of Klagenfurt)

Universitätsstr. 65–67, 9020 Klagenfurt
Telephone: (463) 27009200
Fax: (463) 27009299
E-mail: uni@uni-klu.ac.at
Internet: www.uni-klu.ac.at
Founded 1970
State control
Academic year: October to June (2 semesters)
Rector: Prof. Dr HEINRICH C. MAYR
Vice-Rector for Human Resources and Advancement of Women: Prof. Dr SABINE KANDUTH-KRISTEN
Vice-Rector for International Relations: Prof. Dr HUBERT LENGAUER
Vice-Rector for Research: Prof. Dr FRIEDERIKE WALL
Library Dir: Mag. EDEL HAAS
Number of teachers: 600 staff
Number of students: 8,500

DEANS

Faculty of Arts and Sciences: Prof. Dr ALBERT BERGER
Faculty of Interdisciplinary Research and Education: Prof. Ing. Dr VERENA WINIWARTER
Faculty of Economics and Management: Prof. Dr ERICH SCHWARZ
Faculty of Technical Sciences: Prof. Dipl.-Ing. Dr MARTIN HINZ

PROFESSORS

Faculty of Humanities (tel. (463) 27001002):
ARNOLD, U., Philosophy
ASPETSBERGER, F., German Philology
BAMMÉ, A., Educational Science
BERGER, A., German Philology
BRANDSTETTER, A., German Philology
GSTETTNER, P., Educational Science
HEINTEL, P., Philosophy and Group Dynamics
HÖDL, G., Medieval History and Studies Related to History
HOVORKA, H., Special Educational Theory Relating to Disabilities
JAMES, A., English and American Studies
KARMASIN, M., Communications
KLINGLER, J., Educational Theory
KUNA, F. M., English and American Studies
LARCHER, D., Educational Science
LÖSCHENKOHL, E., Psychology and Developmental Psychology
MAYERTHALER, W., General and Applied Philology
MELEZINEK, A., Teaching Methods
MENSCHIK, J., Educational Science
METER, H., Romance Studies

MORITSCH, A., History of Southern and Eastern Europe
NEUHÄUSER, R., Slavic Studies
NEWEKLOWSKY, G., Slavic Studies
OTTOMEYER, K., Social Psychology
POHL, H.-D., General Philology
POSCH, P., Curriculum Studies
RUMPLER, H., Modern Austrian History
SCHAUSBERGER, N., Modern Austrian History
STROBEL, K., Ancient History and Archaeology
STUHLPFARRER, K., History
VÖLKL, F., Educational Psychology
WANDRUSZKA, U., Romance Studies
ZIMA, P. V., General Comparative Literature
Faculty of Technical Sciences (tel. (463) 27005003):
BODENHÖFER, H.-J., Economics of Education
BÖSZÖRMÉNYI, L., Computer Science
DÖRFLER, W., Mathematics
EDER, J., Computer Science
FISCHER, R., Mathematics
FRIEDRICH, G., Computer Science
HELLWAGNER, H., Computer Science
HITZ, M., Computer Science
HORSTER, P., Computer Science
KALSS, S., Law
KALUZA, B., Business Administration
KELLERMANN, P., Sociology of Education
KOFLER, H., Business Administration
KROPFBERGER, D., Business Administration
MAYR, H., Computer Science
MITTERMEIR, R., Computer Science
MÜLLER, W., Mathematics
NADVORNIK, W., Business Administration
NECK, R., Business Administration
PILZ, J., Applied Statistics
POTACS, M., Law
RENDL, F., Mathematics
RIECKMANN, H.-J., Business Administration
RONDO-BROYETTO, P., Business Administration
SAUBERER, M., Geography
SCHNEIDER, D., Business Administration
SCHWARZ, E., Business Administration
SEGER, M., Geography
STETTNER, H., Mathematics

ANTON BRUCKNER PRIVATUNIVERSITÄT
(Anton Bruckner Private University)

Wildbergstr. 18, 4040 Linz
Telephone: (732) 7010000
Fax: (732) 70100030
E-mail: information@bruckneruni.at
Internet: www.bruckneruni.at
Founded 1863
Private control
Academic year: October to September (2 semesters)
Rector: Prof. Dr MARIANNE BETZ
Vice-Rector for Art: JOSEF EIDENBERGER
Univ. Dir: Mag. BRIGITTE MÖSSENBÖCK
Dean of Art Studies: THOMAS KERBL, ERNST KRONSTEINER
Dean for Artistic and Educational Studies
Library Dir: Mag. JOHN LACKINGER
Library of 10,000 vols, 40,000 notes and 2,000 audiovisual media
Number of teachers: 200
Number of students: 850

DONAU-UNIVERSITÄT KREMS/ UNIVERSITÄT FÜR WEITERBILDUNG
(Danube University Krems/University of Continuing Education)

Dr-Karl-Dorrek-Str. 30, 3500 Krems
Telephone: (2732) 8930

Fax: (2732) 8934000
E-mail: info@donau-uni.ac.at
Internet: www.donau-uni.ac.at
Founded 1994
State control
Languages of instruction: German, English
Academic year: October to June
Rector: Prof. Dr JÜRGEN WILLER
Vice-Rector: Prof. Dr VIKTORIA WEBER
Library of 79,312 vols, 24,698 electronic journals
Number of teachers: 1,590
Number of students: 5,692
Publication: Upgrade (4 a year)

PROFESSORS

BAHLI, B., Management and Economics
BAUMGARTNER, P., Interactive Media and Educational Technology
BIFFL, G., Migration, Integration and Security
BRAININ, M., Clinical Medicine and Preventive Medicine
FALKENHAGEN, D., Environmental and Medical Sciences
FILZMAIER, P., Political Communication
FINA, S., European Integration
GARTLEHNER, G., Evidence-based Medicine and Clinical Epidemiology
GENSCH, G., Arts and Management
GRAU, O., Applied Cultural Studies
LEITNER, A., Psychosocial Medicine and Psychotherapy
LEITNER, C., New Public Management and E-Governance
MIKSCH, S., Information and Knowledge Engineering
NEHRER, S., Regenerative Medicine
RISKU, H., Knowledge and Communication Management
STELZEL, M., Interdisciplinary Dentistry and Technology
WAGNER, M., Technology Enhanced Learning and Multimedia
WILLER, J., Interdisciplinary Dentistry and Technology

JOHANNES KEPLER UNIVERSITÄT LINZ
(Johannes Kepler University, Linz)

Altenberger Str. 69, 4040 Linz
Telephone: (732) 24680
Fax: (732) 24688822
E-mail: rektor@jku.at
Internet: www.jku.at
Founded 1966 as Acad. for Social and Economic Sciences, present name and status 1975
State control
Languages of instruction: German, English
Academic year: October to June
Rector: Prof. Dr RICHARD HAGELAUER
Vice-Rector for Academic Affairs: Prof. Dr HERBERT KALB
Vice-Rector for Communication and Foreign Affairs: Prof. Dr FRIEDRICH ROITHMAYR
Vice-Rector for Finance and Resource Management: Dr FRANZ WURM
Vice-Rector for Research: Prof. Dr GABRIELE KOTSIS
Admin. Dir: Dr JOSEF SCHMIED
Library Dir: Dr SUSANNE CASAGRANDA
Library: see under Libraries and Archives
Number of teachers: 2,000
Number of students: 16,000
Publication: UNIVATIONEN—Forschungsmedienservice der Johannes Kepler Universität Linz (4 a year)

DEANS

Faculty of Engineering and Natural Sciences: Prof. Dipl.-Ing. Dr ERICH PETER KLEMENT
Faculty of Law: Prof. Dr MARKUS ACHATZ
Faculty of Social Sciences, Economics and Business: Prof. GERHARD A. WÜHRER

PROFESSORS

Faculty of Engineering and Natural Sciences (Altenberger Str. 69, 4040 Linz; tel. (732) 2468-3220; fax (732) 2468-3225; e-mail tnf-dekanat@jku.at; internet www.tn.jku.at):

AMRHEIN, W., Electrical Drives and Power Electronics
BAUER, G., Semiconductor Physics
BAUER, S., Soft Matter Physics
BÄUERLE, D., Applied Physics
BIERE, A., Formal Models and Verification
BREMER, H., Robotics
BUCHBERGER, W., Analytical Chemistry
CHROUST, G., Systems Engineering and Automation
COOPER, J. B., Functional Analysis
DEL RE, L., Design and Control of Mechatronical Systems
ENGL, H., Industrial Mathematics
FALK, H., Organic Chemistry
FERSCHA, A., Pervasive Computing
GITTLER, P., Fluid Mechanics and Heat Transfer
GRITZNER, G., Chemical Technology of Inorganic Materials
HAGELAUER, R., Integrated Circuits
HOCHREITER, S., Bioinformatics
IRSCHIK, H., Technical Mechanics
JAKOBY, B., Microelectronics
JANTSCH, W., Solid State Physics
JÜTTLER, B., Applied Geometry
KLEMENT, E. P., Fuzzy Logic
KNÖR, G., Inorganic Chemistry
KOTSIS, G., Telecooperation
KROTSCHECK, E., Many Particle Systems
LANGER, U., Computational Mathematics
LARCHER, G., Financial Mathematics
MÖSSENBÖCK, H., System Software
MÜHLBACHER, J., Information Processing and Microprocessor Technology
PAULE, P., Symbolic Computation
PILZ, G., Algebra
POHL, P., Biophysics
SAMHABER, W., Process Engineering
SARICIFTCI, N. S., Physical Chemistry
SCHÄFFLER, F., Semiconductor Physics
SCHEIDL, R., Machine Design and Hydraulic Drives
SCHLACHER, K., Automatic Control and Control Systems Technology
SCHLÖGLMANN, W., Mathematics Education
SCHMIDT, H., Chemical Technology of Organic Materials
SOBCZAK, R., Polymer Science
SPRINGER, A., Communications and Information Engineering
TITULAER, U. M., Condensed Matter Theory
VOLKERT, J., Graphics and Parallel Processing
WAGNER, R., Applied Knowledge Processing
WEIß, P., Stochastics
WIDMER, G., Computational Perception
WINKLER, F., Symbolic Computation
ZAGAR, B., Electrical Measurement Technology
ZEMAN, K., Computer-aided Methods in Mechanical Engineering
ZEPPENFELD, P., Atomic Physics and Surface Science

Faculty of Law (tel. (732) 2468-3201; fax (732) 2468-3205; e-mail re-dekanat@jku.at; internet www.re.jku.at):

ACHATZ, M., Administrative Law and Management
ACHATZ, M., Research Department for Tax Law and Tax Management

APATHY, P., Roman Law
BINDER, B., Administrative Law and Administrative Sciences
BURGSTALLER, A., European and Austrian Civil Procedure Law
DOLINAR, H., Civil Procedure
FLOSZMANN, U., History of Austrian and German Law
FUNK, B.-C., University Law
HAUER, A., Public Law with Special Reference to Austrian Administrative Law
HENGSTSCHLÄGER, J., Constitutional Law and Political Science
JABORNEGG, P., Labour Law and Social Security
KALB, H., Canon Law
KAROLLUS, M., Commercial and Securities Law
KEINERT, H., Commercial and Securities Law
KERSCHNER, F., Civil Law and Environmental Law
KLINGENBERG, G., Roman Law
KÖCK, H., Public International Law and European Law
LEITL, B., Correspondence Course
OBERNDORFER, P., Administrative Law and Administrative Sciences
REISCHAUER, R., Civil Law
RIEDLER, A., Correspondence Course
RUMMEL, P., Civil Law
SPIELBUECHLER, K., Civil Law
WEGSCHEIDER, H., Criminal Law and Procedure
WIDDER, H., Constitutional Law and Political Science
VELTEN, P., Criminal Law and Procedure

Faculty of Social Sciences, Economics and Business (tel. (732) 2468-3211; fax (732) 2468-3215; e-mail sowi-dekanat@jku.at; internet www.sowi.jku.at):

ALTRICHTER, H., Education and Educational Psychology
BACHER, J., Sociology
BATINIC, B., E-learning
BECKER, P., Modern and Contemporary History
BÖHNISCH, W., Business Administration (Management), Human Resources Management
BRUNNER, J., Economics
COCCA, T., Asset Management
DULLECK, U., Economics
DYK, I., Socio-politics
EULER, H. P., Sociology
FELDBAUER-DURSTMÜLLER, B., Business Administration (Accountancy, Auditing, Business Taxation and Controllership)
FRÜHWIRTH-SCHNATTER, S., Applied Statistics and Econometrics
GADENNE, V., Philosophy and Theory of Science
HAUCH, G., Modern and Contemporary History, Gender Studies
KAILER, N., Entrepreneurship and Business Development
LANDESMANN, M., National Economy
MALINSKY, A. H., Environmental Management in Business and Regional Policy
MATZLER, K., Business Administration
MÜLLER, W. G., Applied Statistics
PERNSTEINER, H., Corporate Finance
PILS, M., Data Processing
PÖLL, G., Economics
POMBERGER, G., Software Engineering
ROHATSCHEK, R., Business Administration, Accountancy, Auditing, Business Taxation and Controllership
ROITHMAYR, F., Information Engineering
SANDGRUBER, R., Social and Economic History
SCHAUER, R., Business Administration (Public Administration and Non-Profit Organizations)

SCHNEIDER, F., Economics, Public Economics, Public Choice
SCHREFL, M., Data and Knowledge Engineering
SCHURER, B., Economic and Business Education
SCHUSTER, H., Economics
STARY, C., Communications Engineering
STREHL, F., Business Administration
TUMPEL, M., Business Administration, Accountancy, Auditing, Business Taxation and Controllership
WEIDENHOLZER, J., Social Policy
WINTER-EBMER, R., Economics
WÜHRER, G., Business Administration (Marketing)

KARL-FRANZENS-UNIVERSITÄT GRAZ
(Graz University)

Universitätspl. 3, 8010 Graz
Telephone: (316) 3800
Fax: (316) 3809030
E-mail: info@uni-graz.at
Internet: www.uni-graz.at
Founded 1585
State control
Academic year: October to September (2 terms)

Rector: Prof. Dr ALFRED GUTSCHELHOFER
Vice-Rector for Human Resources Management: Prof. Dr RENATE DWORCZAK
Vice-Rector for International Relations and Interdisciplinary Cooperation: Prof. Dr ROBERTA MAIERHOFER
Vice-Rector for Research and Continuing Education: Prof. Dr IRMTRAUD FISCHER
Vice-Rector for Studies and Teaching: Prof. Dr MARTIN POLASCHEK
Chief Admin. Officer: Dr MARIA EDLINGER
Librarian: Dr WERNER SCHLACHER

Library: see under Libraries and Archives
Number of teachers: 2,563
Number of students: 27,000

Publication: UNIZEIT (4 a year)

DEANS

Faculty of Arts and Humanities: Mag. THERES HINTERLEITNER
Faculty of Environmental and Regional Sciences and Education: Prof. Dr WERNER LENZ
Faculty of Law: Prof. Dr WILLIBALD POSCH
Faculty of Natural Sciences: Prof. Dr KARL CRAILSHEIM
Faculty of Social and Economic Sciences: Prof. Dr WOLF RAUCH
Faculty of Theology: Prof. Dr ANGEL HANS-FERDINAND

PROFESSORS

Faculty of Arts and Humanities (Universitätspl. 3, 8010 Graz; tel. (316) 380-2288; fax (316) 380-9700; e-mail geisteswiss.dekanat@uni-graz.at; internet www.uni-graz.at/en/gewi.htm):

EISMANN, W., Slavic Studies
ERTLER, K.-D., Romance Studies
GOLTSCHNIGG, D., German Studies
GÖPFERICH, S., Translation and Interpreting Studies
HÄRTEL, R., History
HAUG-MORITZ, G., History
HEINEMANN, S., Romance Studies
HELMICH, W., Romance Studies
HIEBEL, H.-H., German Studies
HÖFLECHNER, W., History
HÖLBLING, W., American Studies
HUMMEL, M., Romance Studies
HURCH, B., Linguistics
KASER, K., History
KONRAD, H., History
MAHLER, A., English Studies

MEYER, L., Philosophy
PARNCUTT, R., Music
PIEPER, R., History
PORTMANN, P., German Studies
PRUNC, E., Translation and Interpreting Studies
TOSOVIC, B., Slavic Studies
WALTER, M., Music
WOLF, W., English Studies
ZIEGLER, A., German Studies

Faculty of Environmental and Regional Sciences and Education (Universitätspl. 3 8010 Graz; tel. (316) 380-8020; fax (316) 380-9700; e-mail urbi.dekan@uni-graz.at; internet www.uni-graz.at/en/brek3www.htm):

HACKL, B., Teacher Training
HOPFNER, J., Education
LENZ, W., Education
SCHEIPL, J., Education
STRASSER, U., Geography and Regional Sciences
SUST, M., Sport Science
ZIMMERMANN, F., Geography and Regional Sciences

Faculty of Law (Universitätsstr. 15/A, 8010 Graz; tel. (316) 380-3260; fax (316) 380-9400; e-mail rewi.dekanat@uni-graz.at; internet www.uni-graz.at/en/enredwww):

BENEDEK, W., International Law and International Relations
KOLLER, P., Legal Philosophy, Sociology and Informatics
MARHOLD, F., Labour Law and Social Security Law
MEDIGOVIC, U., Criminology and Criminal Justice
SCHICK, P., Criminology and Criminal Justice
SCHMALENBACH, K., International Law and International Relations
SCHMÖLZER, G., Criminology and Criminal Justice
SOYER, R., Criminology and Criminal Justice
THÜR, G., Roman Law, Ancient Legal History and Modern Legal History

Faculty of Natural Sciences (Universitätspl. 3 8010 Graz; tel. (316) 380-5000; fax (316) 380-9800; e-mail nawi.dekanat@uni-graz.at; internet www.uni-graz.at/nawi/):

ALBERT, D., Psychology
ALKOFER, R., Physics
ARENDASY, M., Psychology
BAUER, R., Pharmacognosy
BLANZ, P., Botany
CRAILSHEIM, K., Zoology
FISCHER, P., Psychology
FRÖHLICH, K.-U., Molecular Biosciences
GATTRINGER, C., Physics
GRUBER, K., Molecular Biosciences
HAASE, G., Mathematics and Scientific Computing
HANSLMEIER, A., Physics
KALLUS, K. W., Psychology
KAPPEL, F., Mathematics
KIRCHENGAST, G., Physics
KOHLWEIN, S.-D., Molecular Biosciences
KRATKY, C., Molecular Biosciences
KRENN, H., Physics
KUNISCH, K., Mathematics and Scientific Computing
LANG, C., Physics
MADEO, F., Molecular Biosciences
MAYER, B. M., Pharmacology and Toxicology
NETZER, F., Physics
NEUBAUER, A., Psychology
NEUPER, C., Psychology
PAECHTER, M., Psychology
PÖTZ, W., Physics
REIDL, J., Molecular Biosciences
RINDERMANN, H., Psychology
ROITSCH, T., Plant Sciences
RÖMER, H., Zoology

SCHAPPACHER, W., Mathematics and Scientific Computing
SCHIENLE, A., Psychology
SCHULTER, G., Psychology
SPAHN-LANGGUTH, H., Pharmaceutical Sciences
STURMBAUER, CH., Zoology
UHLIG, T., Psychology
ZECHNER, R., Molecular Biosciences
ZIMMER, A., Pharmaceutical Sciences

Faculty of Social and Economic Sciences (Universitätsstr. 15/A 8010 Graz; tel. (316) 380-6813; fax (316) 380-9400; e-mail sowi .dekanat@uni-graz.at; internet domino .uni-graz.at/dekanat-extern/main.nsf/ layout_e):

BAIGENT, N., Public Economics
FISCHER, E., Finance
FOSCHT, T., Marketing
HALLER, M., Sociology
LEOPOLD-WILDBURGER, U., Statistics and Operations Research
ORTLIEB, R., Human Resource Management
RAUCH, W., Information Science and Information Systems
REIMANN, M., Production and Operations Management
WETTERER, A., Sociology

Faculty of Theology (Universitätspl. 3 8010 Graz; tel. (316) 380-3150; fax (316) 380-9300; e-mail theologisches.dekanat@uni-graz.at; internet www-theol.uni-graz.at/cms/ziel/ 26669/en/):

BECHMANN, U., World Religions
BUCHER, R.-M., Psychology and Pastoral Theology
ESTERBAUER, R., Theology and Philosophy
FISCHER, I., Old Testament Studies
GROEN, B., Liturgics, Church Music and Christian Art
HEIL, C., New Testament Studies
LARCHER, G., Fundamental Theology

KATHOLISCH-THEOLOGISCHE PRIVATUNIVERSITÄT LINZ (Private Catholic Theological University of Linz)

Bethlehemstr. 20, 4020 Linz
Telephone: (732) 784293
Fax: (732) 7842934155
E-mail: rektorat@ktu-linz.ac.at
Internet: www.ktu-linz.ac.at

Founded 1978
Private control

Rector: Prof. Dr EWALD VOLGGER
Pro-Rector: Prof. Dr MICHAEL ROSENBERGER
Admin. Dir: Mag. MONIKA HOLLER
Library Dir: INGO GLÜCKLER
Library of 180,000 vols, 500 periodicals, 20 MSS, 126 incunabula
Number of teachers: 41

Publications: Kunst und Kirche (4 a year), Theologisch-praktische Quartalschrift (ThPQ) (4 a year).

LEOPOLD-FRANZENS UNIVERSITÄT INNSBRUCK (Innsbruck University)

Christoph-Probst-Pl., Innrain 52, 6020 Innsbruck
Telephone: (512) 5070
Fax: (512) 5072973
E-mail: international-relations@uibk.ac.at
Internet: www.uibk.ac.at

Founded 1669
State control
Academic year: October to July (2 semesters)

Rector: Prof. Dr KARL HEINZ TÖCHTERLE
Vice-Rector for Infrastructure: Prof. Dipl.-Ing. Dr ARNOLD KLOTZ

Vice-Rector for Research: Prof. Dr TILMANN MÄRK
Vice-Rector for Staff and Faculty: Prof. Mag. Dr WOLFGANG MEIXNER
Vice-Rector for Teaching and Students: Prof. Mag. Dr MARGRET FRIEDRICH
Librarian: Dr MARTIN WIESER

Library: see under Libraries and Archives
Number of teachers: 1,541
Number of students: 26,000

Publication: Veröffentlichungen (irregular)

DEANS

Faculty of Architecture: Prof. GABRIELA SEIFERT
Faculty of Biology: Prof. Dr ROLAND PSENNER
Faculty of Catholic Theology: Prof. Dr JÓZEF NIEWIADOMSKI
Faculty of Chemistry and Pharmacy: Prof. Dr ANDREAS BERNKOP-SCHNÜRCH
Faculty of Civil Engineering: Prof. Dr ARNOLD TAUTSCHNIG
Faculty of Economics and Statistics: Prof. Dr HANNELORE WECK-HANNEMANN
Faculty of Education: MICHAEL SCHRATZ
Faculty of Geo- and Atmospheric Sciences: Prof. Dr MARTIN COY
Faculty of Humanities I: Prof. Mag. Dr KLAUS EISTERER
Faculty of Humanities II: Prof. Mag. Dr WALTRAUD FRITSCH-RÖSSLER
Faculty of Law: Prof. Dr BERNHARD ECCHER
Faculty of Mathematics, Computer Sciences and Physics: Prof. Mag. Dr ALEXANDER OSTERMANN
Faculty of Psychology and Sport Science: Prof. Dr WERNER NACHBAUER
School of Management: Prof. ALBERT BECKER
School of Political Science and Sociology: Prof. Dr FRITZ PLASSER

PROFESSORS

Faculty of Arts:

ALBRECHT, R., Cybernetics and Numerical Mathematics
AMBACH, W., Medical Physics
ANDERL, H., Plastic and Restorative Surgery
AXHAUSEN, K. W., Highway Engineering
BARTSCH, G., Urology
BAUER, R., Orthopaedics
BECK, E., Traumatology
BENZER, H., Anaesthesiology and Intensive Care Medicine
BERTEL, C., Austrian Penal Law and Criminology
BICHLER, R., Ancient and Comparative History
BINDER, M., Labour Law and Social Law
BISTER, K., Biochemistry
BOBLETER, O., Radio-chemistry
BODNER, E., Surgery
BONN, G., Analytical Chemistry
BORSDORF, A., Geography
BORTENSCHLAGER, S., Systematic Botany
BRATSCHITSCH, R., Industrial Economics
BÜCHELE, H., Christian Sociology
BURGER, A., Pharmacognosy
CHEN, J. R., Economic Theory and Econometrics
CHESI, G., Geodesy and Photogrammetry
DAPUNT, O., Gynaecology and Obstetrics
DEETJEN, P., Physiology
DEPPERMANN, M., Comparative Literature
DIERICH, M., Hygiene
DORALT, W., Financial Law
EBERT, K., History of German Law and Economy
ECCHER, B., Italian Law
ENDRES, W., Paediatrics
FAISTENBERGER, C., Austrian Civil Law
FETZ, F., Physical Education
FISCHER, G., Old Testament Theology
FRITSCH, P., Dermatology
GAUSCH, K., Dental Medicine

GIENCKE, V., Structural Engineering and Design
GLOSSMANN, H., Biochemical Pharmacology
GÖTTINGER, W., Ophthalmology
GRAEFE, R., Architecture and Preservation of Historic Monuments
GRUBER, J., Physical Chemistry
GRUNICKE, H., Medical Chemistry
GSCHNITZER, F., Surgery
HÄNDEL, P., Classical Philology
HASITSCHKA, M., New Testament Theology
HEINISCH, G., Pharmaceutical Chemistry
HELMBERG, G., Mathematics
HIERDEIS, H., Pedagogics
HINTERHUBER, H., Industrial Economics
HINTERHUBER, H., Psychiatry
HOCHMAIR, E., Applied Physics (Electronics)
HOFSTETTER, G., Theory of Structures
HOLUB, H. W., Political Economy
HUMMER, W., International Law
INGERLE, K., Domestic and Industrial Sanitation
JASCHKE, W., Radiodiagnosis
KAPPLER, E., Management
KAUFER, E., National Economy
KITTINGER, E., Building Physics
KLEINKNECHT, R., Philosophy
KÖBLER, G., History of German Law and Economics
KOLYMBAS, D., Geomechanics and Tunnel Engineering
KÖNIG, B., Legal Procedure in Civil Law
KOPP, E., Railway Construction and Transport System
KORNEXL, E., Physical Education
KRÄUTLER, B., Organic Chemistry
KRIEGBAUM, B., Church History
KRÖMER, W., Romance Philology
KUHN, M., Meteorology and Geophysics
LACKNER, J., Painting, Design and Planning
LANGHOF, C., Town Planning
LARCHER, W., Botany
LASKE, S., Industrial Economics
LEIBOLD, G., Christian Philosophy
LEISCHING, P., Church Law
LESSMANN, H., Building Planning and Estimating
LEXA, H., Industrial Economics
LIEDL, R., Mathematics
LIES, L., Dogmatics
LOOS, O., Mathematics
LUKAS, P., Radiotherapy
MARINELL, G., Statistics
MARKUS, M., English Language and Literature
MASSER, A., Old German Language and Literature
MATHIS, F., Economic and Social History
MAYRHOFER, H., Civil Law
MAZOHL-WALLNIG, B., Austrian History
MEID, W., Comparative Linguistics
MIKUZ, G., Pathological Anatomy
MIRWALD, P., Mineralogy and Palaeontology
MOREL, J., Sociology
MORSCHER, S., Public Law
MOSER, H., German Language and Medieval German Literature
MOSER, K., Construction Statistics
MOSTLER, H., Geology and Palaeontology
MUCK, O., Christian Philosophy
MÜHLBACHER, H., Industrial Economy
MÜHLSTEIGER, J., Church Law
MÜLLER-SALGET, K., New German Language and Literature
NAREDI-RAINER, P., Art History, Architectural Theory
NEUFELD, K., Fundamental Theology
OBERST, U., Mathematics
OHNHEISTER, J., Slavonic Studies
PATSCH, J., Internal Medicine
PAVELKA, M., Histology and Embryology
PELINKA, A., Political Science

PERNTHALER, P., Constitutional and Administrative Law
PETZOLDT, L., European Ethnology
PFEIFFER, K. P., Biostatistics
PFLEIDERER, J., Astronomy
PHILIPPOU, A., Pharmacodynamics and Toxicology
PICHLER, H., Theoretical Meteorology
PLANGG, G., Romance Philology
PLATZER, W., Anatomy
POEWE, W., Neurology
RABER, F., Roman Law
REICHERT-FACILIDES, F., Foreign Law and Austrian Private Law
RICCABONA, G., Nuclear Medicine
RIEDMANN, J., History of the Middle Ages
RIEGER, R., Zoology
RITTER, M., Psychology
RÖD, W., Philosophy
ROITHMAYR, F., System Planning and Information Management
ROTTER, H., Moral Theology
ROTH, G. H., Commercial Law
ROTHLEITNER, J., Theoretical Physics
RUNGGALDIER, E., Philosophy
SCHAUER, E., Building and Layout
SCHAUPP, K., Pastoral Theology
SCHEER, B., Modern English and American Literature
SCHEICHL, S., Austrian Comparative Literature
SCHEITHAUER, R., Forensic Medicine
SCHEUERLEIN, H., Hydraulic Engineering
SCHREDELSEKER, K., Finance
SCHÜLLER, G., Mechanics
SCHÜSSLER, G., Medical Psychology, Psychotherapy
SCHWAGER, R., Dogmatics
SCHWARZHANS, K. E., Inorganic and Analytical Chemistry
SEEBASS, T., Music
SMEKAL, C., Financial Science
SOCHER, K., Political Economy
SPINDLER, K., Late Medieval and Modern Archeology, Urban Archeology
SPRUNG, R., Austrian Civil Court Procedure
STEININGER, R., Current History
STÖFFLER, G., Microbiology
STREHL, F., Business Administration
STRNAD, A., Modern History
THUMFART, W., Otorhinolaryngology
TSCHUPIK, J., Geometry
TSCHEMMERNEGG, F., Steel and Wood Constructions
TWERDY, K., Neurosurgery
UTERMANN, G., Human Genetics
VASS, G., Dogmatics
VON WERLHOF, C., Political Science, Women's Studies and Research
WACHTER, H., Medicinal and Analytical Chemistry
WALDE, E., Classical Archaeology
WAUBKE, N. V., Instruction on Structural Materials and Materials Testing
WEBER, K., Public Law
WECK-HANNEMANN, H., Political Economy
WEIERMAIR, K., Industrial Economics
WEISS, R., Pedagogics
WENSKUS, O., Classical Philology
WICK, G., General and Experimental Pathology
WICKE, M., Reinforced Concrete Construction
WIMMER, N., Austrian Constitutional Law
WINKLER, H., Pharmacology
ZACH, W., English Language and Literature
ZEILINGER, A., Neutron and Solid State Physics
ZOLLER, P., Theoretical Physics

AFFILIATED INSTITUTES

Arbeitskreis für Gleichbehandlungsfragen: Technikerstrasse 13, 6020 Innsbruck.

Forschungsinstitut für Alpenländische Land- und Forstwirtschaft (Dept of Alpine Agriculture and Forestry): Technikerstr. 13, 6020 Innsbruck; f. 1977.

Forschungsinstitut für Alpine Vorzeit: Kaiser-Franz-Josef-Str. 12, 6020 Innsbruck.

Forschungsinstitut 'Brenner-Archiv': Innrain 52, Neubau/VIII, 6020 Innsbruck; f. 1979.

Forschungsinstitut für Hochgebirgsforschung in Obergurgl (Alpine Research Department of the University of Innsbruck in Obergurgl): Innrain 52, 6020 Innsbruck; f. 1951.

Forschungsinstitut für Prophylaxe der Suchtkrankheiten: Krankenhaus Maria Ebene Frastanz, Vorarlberg; f. 1990.

Forschungsinstitut für Textilchemie und Textilphysik: Höchsterstr. 73, 6850 Dornbirn; f. 1982.

Senatsinstitut für Zwischenmenschliche Kommunikation: Sillgasse 8, 6020 Innsbruck; f. 1991.

Sportinstitut: Fürstenweg 185, 6020 Innsbruck; f. 1959.

Universitätsarchiv: Innrain 52, 6020 Innsbruck; f. 1950.

MEDIZINISCHE UNIVERSITÄT GRAZ (Medical University of Graz)

Universitätspl. 3, 8010 Graz

Telephone: (316) 3800
Fax: (316) 3809140
E-mail: rektor@meduni-graz.at
Internet: www.meduni-graz.at
Founded 1863 as Medical Faculty of Graz Univ.; univ. status 2004
State control
Language of instruction: German
Academic year: October to September (2 semesters)

Rector: Prof. Dr JOSEF SMOLLE
Vice-Rector for Financial Management and Organization: Mag. OLIVER SZMEJ
Vice-Rector for Human Resources and Gender Equality: Prof. Dr ANDREA LANGMANN
Vice-Rector for Research: Prof. Dr IRMGARD THERESIA LIPPE
Vice-Rector for Teaching and Studies: Prof. Dr GILBERT REIBNEGGER
Librarian: Dr ULRIKE KORTSCHAK

Library of 370 textbooks, 60,000 vols of journals
Number of teachers: 741
Number of students: 4,058

MEDIZINISCHE UNIVERSITÄT INNSBRUCK (Medical University, Innsbruck)

Christoph-Probst-Pl., Innrain 52, 6020 Innsbruck

Telephone: (512) 5070
E-mail: i-master@i-med.ac.at
Internet: www.i-med.ac.at
Founded 2004 from the medical faculty of the Univ. of Innsbruck
State control
Language of instruction: German
Academic year: October to July

Rector: Prof. Dr HERBERT LOCHS
Vice-Rector for Finance: Dr GABRIELE DÖLLER
Vice-Rector for Human Resources, Human Resources Devt and Gender Equality: Prof. Dr DORIS BALOGH
Vice-Rector for Research: Prof. Dr GÜNTHER SPERK
Vice-Rector for Teaching and Studies: Prof. Dr NORBERT MUTZ
Librarian: Dr MARION BREITSCHOPF

Library of 30,000 vols of journals, 350 current journals
Number of teachers: 1,700
Number of students: 3,500

MEDIZINISCHE UNIVERSITÄT WIEN
(Medical University, Vienna)

Spitalgasse 23, 1090 Vienna
Telephone: (1) 401600
Fax: (1) 40160910000
E-mail: infopoint-meduni@meduniwien.ac.at
Internet: www.meduniwien.ac.at

Founded 1365 as Medical Faculty, Univ. of Vienna; autonomous univ. since 2004
State control
Language of instruction: German
Academic year: October to July (2 semesters)

Rector: Prof. Dr WOLFGANG SCHÜTZ
Vice-Rector for Clinical Affairs: Prof. OSWALD WAGNER
Vice-Rector for Education: Prof. Dr RUDOLF MALLINGER
Vice-Rector for Finance: Mag. PETER SOSWINSKI
Vice-Rector for Human Resource Devt and Women's Issues: Prof. Dr KARIN GUTIÉRREZ-LOBOS
Library Dir: Mag. BRUNO BAUER

Library of 520,000 vols, 2,400 periodicals
Number of teachers: 1,200
Number of students: 7,500

MODUL UNIVERSITY VIENNA

Am Kahlenberg 1, 1190 Vienna
Telephone: (1) 3203555101
Fax: (1) 3203555901
E-mail: office@modul.ac.at
Internet: www.modul.ac.at

Founded 1908
Private control

Pres.: Dr KARL WÖBER
Vice-Pres.: Dr ARNO SCHARL
Man. Dir: Mag. CHRISTIAN HOFFMANN
Librarian: JOHANNA HUBWEBER
Number of students: 250

MONTANUNIVERSITÄT LEOBEN
(University of Leoben)

Franz-Josef Str. 18, 8700 Leoben
Telephone: (3842) 4020
Fax: (3842) 4027702
E-mail: office@unileoben.ac.at
Internet: www.unileoben.ac.at

Founded 1840
Languages of instruction: German, English
Academic year: October to July

Rector: Prof. Dr WOLFHARD WEGSCHEIDER
Vice-Rector for Admin.: Dr MARTHA MÜHLBURGER
Vice-Rector for Finance and Auditing: Prof. Dr HUBERT BIEDERMAN
Librarian: Dr CHRISTIAN HASENHÜTTEL

Library: see under Libraries and Archives
Number of students: 2,338

Publications: *BHM- Berg- und Hüttenmannische Monatshefte* (12 a year), *Triple M* (4 a year)

PROFESSORS

BIEDERMANN, H., Economics, Industrial Management and Industrial Engineering
DANZER, R., Ceramics
EBNER, F., Geology and Mineral Resources
EICHLSEDER, W., Mechanical Engineering
ENGELHARDT, C., Industrial Logistics
FISCHER, D., Mechanics
GALLER, R., Subsurface Engineering
HARMUTH, H., Refractory Materials, Ceramics, Glass and Cement
HEINEMANN, Z., Reservoir Engineering

IMRICH, W., Applied Mathematics
JEGLITSCH, F., Physical Metallurgy and Material Testing
KEPPLINGER, W., Industrial Environmental Protection
KESSLER, F., Conveying Technology
KIRSCHENHOFER, P., Mathematics
KNEISSL, A., Metallography
KRIEGER, W., Ferrous Metallurgy
KUCHAR, F., Physics
LANG, R., Plastics
LANGECKER, G., Plastics Technology
LEDERER, K., Chemistry of Plastics
LORBER, K., Decontamination
MAURITSCH, H., Geophysics
MEISEL, T., Gen. and Analytical Chemistry
MILLAHN, K., Applied Geophysics
O'LEARY, P., Automation
PASCHEN, P., Nonferrous Metallurgy
RUTHAMMER, G., Petroleum Engineering
SACHS, H., Applied Geometry
SITTE, W., Physical Chemistry
STEINER, H., Mineral Processing
VORTISCH, W., Applied Sedimentology
WAGNER, H., Mining Engineering
WEISS, G., Electrical Engineering
WOERNDLE, R., Plastics
WOLFBAUER, J., Business Economics

PARACELSUS MEDIZINISCHE PRIVATUNIVERSITÄT
(Paracelsus Medical University)

Strubergasse 21, 5020 Salzburg
Telephone: (662) 4420020
Fax: (662) 4420021209
E-mail: herbert.resch@pmu.ac.at
Internet: www.pmu.ac.at

Founded 2002
Private control

Rector: Prof. Dr HERBERT RESCH
Honorary Rector: Dr JULIAN FRICK
Vice-Rector: Prof. Dr FELIX SEDLMAYER
Chancellor: Dr MICHAEL NAKE
Dean of Academic Affairs: Prof. Dr MICHAEL STUDNICKA
Dean of Curriculum: Prof. Dr HEINRICH MAGOMETSCHNIGG
Dean of Research: Prof. Dr CHRISTOPH STUPPACK
Dean of Student Affairs: Doz. Dr ROSEMARIE FORSTNER
Library Man.: Mag. CVETKA FLORENTINA LIPUS

Library of 2,000 medical journals, medical databases.

PEF PRIVATUNIVERSITÄT FÜR MANAGEMENT
(PEF Private University of Management)

Brahmspl. 3, 1040 Vienna
Telephone: (1) 534390
Fax: (1) 5343980
E-mail: pef@pef.co.at
Internet: www.pef.at
Private control

Man. Dir: Mag. ANDREA KOBLMÜLLER.

PRIVATUNIVERSITÄT DER KREATIVWIRTSCHAFT—NEW DESIGN UNIVERSITY
(Private University of the Creative Industries—New Design University)

Maria Zeller Str. 97, 3100 St Pölten
Telephone: (2742) 8902418
Fax: (2742) 8902413
E-mail: office@ndu.ac.at
Internet: www.ndu.ac.at

Founded 2004
Private control

DEANS

Faculty of Design: Mag. Dr THOMAS GRONEGGER
Faculty of Engineering: Dipl.-Ing. Dr ANDREAS HASENZAGL

PRIVATUNIVERSITÄT SCHLOSS SEEBURG
(Castle Seeburg Private University)

Seeburgstrasse 8, 5201 Salzburg
Telephone: (6212) 2626
E-mail: info@uni-seeburg.at
Internet: www.uni-seeburg.at

Founded 2007
Private control

Rector: Prof. Dr CHRISTIAN WERNER
Vice-Rector: Prof. Dr FLORIAN KAINZ
Vice-Rector: Prof. Dr WALTER EMBERGER
Number of teachers: 76

DEANS

Faculty of Business Administration: Prof. Dr BIRGIT RENZL
Faculty of Economic Psychology: Prof. Dr JÜRGEN KASCHUBE
Faculty of Sports and Event Management: Prof. Dr PETER KAPUSTIN

SIGMUND FREUD PRIVATUNIVERSITÄT WIEN
(Sigmund Freud Private University Vienna)

Schnirchgasse 9A 1030 Vienna
Telephone: (1) 7984098
Fax: (1) 798409820
E-mail: office@sfu.ac.at
Internet: www.sfu.ac.at

Founded 2003
Private control
Languages of instruction: German, English
Academic year: October to June

Rector: Prof. Dr ALFRED PRITZ
Vice-Rector: Dr JUTTA FIEGL
Vice-Rector for Research: Prof. Dr LUDGER VAN GISTEREN
Vice-Rector for Teaching: Mag. STEFAN HAMPL
Registrar: HEINZ LAUBREUTER
Number of students: 650

TECHNISCHE UNIVERSITÄT GRAZ
(Graz University of Technology)

Rechbauerstr. 12, 8010 Graz
Telephone: (316) 8730
Fax: (316) 8736562
E-mail: info@tugraz.at
Internet: www.tugraz.at

Founded 1811
State control
Academic year: October to July

Rector: Prof. Dr HANS SÜNKEL
Vice-Rector for Academic Affairs: Prof. Dipl.-Ing. Dr HANS MICHAEL MUHR
Vice-Rector for Finances and Personnel: Prof. Dr ULRICH BAUER
Vice-Rector for Infrastructure and Information and Communication Technology: Prof. Dipl.-Ing. Dr HARALD KAINZ
Vice-Rector for Research and Technology: Prof. Dipl.-Ing. Dr FRANZ STELZER
Librarian: Dr WERNER SCHLACHER

Library: see under Libraries and Archives
Number of teachers: 1,376
Number of students: 11,681

Publications: *TU Graz people* (4 a year), *TU Graz research* (2 a year, in English and German)

DEANS

Faculty of Architecture: Prof. LEONARD HIRSCHBERG

Faculty of Chemistry, Chemical and Process Engineering: Prof. Dr FRANK UHLIG

Faculty of Civil Engineering: Prof. Dr MARTIN FELLENDORF

Faculty of Computer Science: Prof. Dr FRANZ WOTAWA

Faculty of Constructional Engineering: Prof. Dr KLAUS RIESSBERGER

Faculty of Electrical and Information Engineering: Prof. Dr HEINRICH STIGLER

Faculty of Mathematical and Physical Engineering: Prof. Dr ROBERT TICHY

Faculty of Mechanical Engineering and Economics: Prof. Dr REINHARD HABERFELLNER

Faculty of Natural Sciences: Prof. Dr HANS VOGLER

PROFESSORS

ARRIGONI, E., Theoretical Physics
AURENHAMMER, F., Basics of Information Processing
BAUER, U., Industrial Management
BEER, G., Building Statics
BERKES, I., Probability Theory and Statistics
BESENHARD, O. J., Inorganic Chemical Technology
BRASSEUR, G., Electrical Measurement and Measurement Signals Processing
BRENN, G., Fluid Mechanics
BRUNNER, F. K., Geodesy
BURKARD, R., Mathematics
CELIGOJ, CH., Strength of Materials
CERJAK, H., Materials Science and Welding
DOURDOUMAS, N., Automatic Control
EICHLSEDER, H., Combustion Engines
ERNST, W., Experimental Physics
FICKERT, L., Electrical Installations
FRANK, A., Manufacturing Technology
FRANK, I., Interior Design
GAMERITH, H., Building and Design
GESCHEIDT-DEMNER, G., Material Testing
GRAMPP, G., Physical Chemistry
GREINER, R., Timberwork and Elevation
GRIENGL, H., Organic Chemistry
HABERFELLNER, R., Management
HEIGERTH, G., Hydraulic Design and Water Resources Management
HEITMEIR, F., Thermo Turbo-Machinery
HIRSCHBERG, W., Automotive Engineering
HOFMANN-WELLENHOF, B., Theoretical Geodesy
JABERG, H., Hydraulic Turbo-machinery
JÜRGENS, G., Machine Principles
KAHLERT, H., Solid State Physics
KAINZ, H., Hydraulics, Agricultural and Industrial Hydraulic Engineering
KERN, G., Analysis and Applications
KNAPP, G., Analytical Chemistry
KOUDELKA, O., Telecommunications
KUBIN, G., Non-linear Signals Processing
KUPELWIESER, H., Artistic Forms
LEBERL, F., Computer-aided Geometry and Graphics
LECHNER, H., Project Envelopment and Project Management
LEITGEB, N., Hospital Technology
MAASS, W., Information Processing
MACHEROUX, P., Biochemistry
MARR, R. J., Process Engineering
MAURER, H., Information Processing
MEUWISSEN, J. M. C., Building and Town Planning
MORITZ, H., Geodesy
MUHR, H. M., Electrical Power Systems and High Voltage Engineering
NIDETSKY, B., Biotechnology
OSER, J., Materials Handling and Mechanical Engineering Design
PFANNHAUSER, W., Food Chemistry
POSCH, R., Applied Information Processing and Communications Technology
RENTMEISTER, M., Electrical Engineering

RIESSBERGER, K., Railways
RÖSCHEL, O., Geometry
SCHUBERT, W., Rock Mechanics and Tunnelling
SCHWAB, H., Biotechnology
SEMPRICH, S., Soil Mechanics and Foundation Engineering
SPAROWITZ, L., Concrete Construction
STADLER, G., Building
STADLOBER, E., Probability Theory and Statistics
STAUDINGER, G., Instrument Construction and Mechanical Techniques
STELZER, F., Chemical Technology of Organic Materials
STIGLER, H., Electricity Economy and Energy Innovation
SÜNKEL, H., Theoretical Geodesy
TICHY, R., Mathematics
TSCHOM, H., Domestic Architecture
VON DER LINDEN, W., Theoretical Physics
VÖSSNER, S., Mechanical Engineering and Industrial Informatics
WACH, P., Theoretical Methods in Mechanical Engineering and Industrial Informatics
WEISS, R., Computer Engineering
WOESS, W., Mathematics
WOHINZ, J., Industrial Management
WOLFBAUER, O., Chemical and Process Engineering
WÜRSCHUM, R., Materials Science and Physical Methods

TECHNISCHE UNIVERSITÄT WIEN
(Vienna University of Technology)

Karlspl. 13, 1040 Vienna
Telephone: (1) 588010
Fax: (1) 5880141099
E-mail: pr@tuwien.ac.at
Internet: www.tuwien.ac.at
Founded 1815
State control
Language of instruction: German
Academic year: October to June (2 semesters)
Rector: Prof. Dr PETER SKALICKY
Vice-Rector: Prof. Dr GERHARD SCHIMAK
Vice-Rector for Academic Affairs: Prof. Dr ADALBERT PRECHTL
Vice-Rector for Finance and Controlling: Dr PAUL JANKOWITSCH
Vice-Rector for Infrastructure and Devt: Prof. Dr GERHARD SCHIMAK
Vice-Rector for Research: Prof. Dr SABINE SEIDLER
Dir: Mag. EVELINE URBAN
Librarian: Dr PETER KUBALEK
Library: see under Libraries and Archives
Number of teachers: 3,020
Number of students: 23,452
Publication: *ZID-Line*

DEANS

Faculty of Architecture and Planning: Prof. Dr KLAUS SEMSROTH
Faculty of Civil Engineering: Prof. Dr JOSEF EBERHARDSTEINER
Faculty of Electrical Engineering and Information Technology: Prof. Dr GOTTFRIED MAGERL
Faculty of Informatics: Prof. Dr GERALD STEINHARDT
Faculty of Mathematics and Geoinformation: Prof. Dr DIETMAR DORNINGER
Faculty of Mechanical Engineering: Prof. Dr BERNHARD GERINGER
Faculty of Physics: Prof. Dr GERALD BADUREK
Faculty of Technical Chemistry: Prof. Dr JOHANNES FRÖHLICH

PROFESSORS

Faculty of Architecture and Planning (Karlspl. 13, 1040 Vienna; tel. (1) 5880125001; fax (1) 5880125099; e-mail

e250@tuwien.ac.at; internet www.rpl-arch.tuwien.ac.at):

ALSOP, W., Building Construction and Building Systems for Architects
BÖKEMANN, D., Town and Country Planning
BRÜLLMANN, K., Residential Building
CERWENKA, P., Transport Systems Planning
DANGSCHAT, J., Urban and Regional Research
FRANCK-OBERASPACH, G., Computer-aided Design and Planning Methods
HIERZEGGER, H., Local Area Planning
JORMAKKA, K. J., Architectural History and Historic Building Survey
JOURDA, F. H., Spatial Design
LESAK, F., Model Construction
MAHDAVI, A., Building Physics and Human Ecology
RICHTER, H., Structural Engineering for Architects
SCHÖNBÄCK, W., Public Finance and Infrastructure Policy
SEMSROTH, K., Urban Design and Planning
STILES, R., Landscape Planning and Garden Architecture
STRAUBE, M., Banking and Securities Law
WEBER, G., History of Art and Cultural Conservation
WEHDORN, M., History of Art, Architectural Conservation, and Industrial Archaeology
WINTER, W., Studies of Structural Design and Timber Construction
WOLFF-PLOTTEGG, M., Building Design and Theory
ZEHETNER, F., Public Law

Faculty of Civil Engineering (Karlspl. 13, 1040 Vienna; tel. (1) 5880120001; fax (1) 5880120099; e-mail info@bauwesen.tuwien.ac.at; internet www.bauwesen.tuwien.ac.at):

BRANDL, H., Foundations
BRUNNER, P. H., Waste Management
DREYER, J., Building Material Sciences, Building Physics and Fire Protection
DROBIR, H., Water Plant Construction, Navigable Waterways and Environmental Hydraulics
GUTKNECHT, D., Hydraulics, Hydrology and Water Supply
JODL, H. G., Construction Practice and Methods
KNOFLACHER, H., Traffic Planning and Engineering
KOLBITSCH, A., Building Construction and Industrial Buildings
KOLLEGGER, J., Reinforced Concrete Construction and Massive Construction
KROISS, H., Water Supply, Sewage Purification and Prevention of Water Pollution
LITZKA, J., Road Engineering and Maintenance
MANG, H., Elasticity and Strength
MATSCHE, N., Water Quality and Waste Management
OBERNDORFER, W. J., Construction and Planning
OGRIS, H., Experimental Hydraulics
RAMBERGER, G., Steel Girder Construction
RUBIN, H., Structural Analysis
SCHIMMERL, J., Rational Mechanics
SCHNEIDER, U., Building Materials
TENTSCHERT, E. H., Geology
ZIEGLER, F., Applied Mechanics

Faculty of Electrical Engineering and Information Technology (Gusshausstr. 25–29, 1040 Vienna; tel. (1) 5880135001; fax (1) 5880135099; e-mail goppenhe@pop.tuwien.ac.at; internet www.info.tuwien.ac.at/et):

BERTAGNOLLI, E., Solid State Electronics
BONEK, E., High Frequency and Communications Technology

BRAUNER, G., Power Systems
CHABICOVSKY, R., Industrial Electronics and Materials Science
DETTER, H., Precision Engineering
DIETRICH, D., Computer Technology
EIER, R., Data Processing
FALLMANN, W., Industrial Electronics and Materials Science
GORNIK, E., Solid State Electronics
HAAS, H., Fundamentals and Theory of Electrical Engineering
KRAUSZ, F., Photonics
LEEB, W., Communications and Radio-Frequency Engineering
MAGERL, G., Electrical Measurement Technology
MECKLENBRÄUKER, W., Low Frequency Technology
PFUNDNER, P., Industrial Electronics and Materials Science
PRECHTL, A., Theory of Electrical Engineering
RUMMICH, E., Electrical Drives and Machines
RUPP, M., Communications and Radio-Frequency Engineering
SCHMIDT, A., Quantum Electronics and Lasers
SCHRÖDL, M., Electrical Machines and Drives
SELBERHERR, S., Software Technology for Microelectronic Systems
VAN AS, H. R., Communication Networks
VELLEKOOP, M., Industrial Electronics and Materials Science
WEINMANN, A., Electrical Control, Navigation and Power Engineering
WEINRICHTER, J., Communications and Radio-Frequency Engineering
ZACH, F., Electrical Drives and Machines
ZEICHEN, G., Flexible Automation
ZIMMERMANN, H., Electrical Measurements and Circuit Design

Faculty of Informatics (Getreidemarkt 9, 1060 Vienna; tel. (1) 5880110000; fax (1) 5880110099; e-mail dek100@mail.zserv.tuwien.ac.at; internet www.cs.tuwien.ac.at):

BREITENEDER, C., Software
BROCKHAUS, M., Information Technology
EITER, T., Information Systems
FLEISSNER, P., Design and Assessment/Social Cybernetics
GOTTLOB, G., Applied Informatics
GRÜNBACHER, H., Computer Engineering (VLSI-Design)
JAZAYERI, M., Information Systems
KAPPEL, G., Software Technology and Interactive Systems
KOPETZ, H., Software Technology
KROPATSCH, W., Design and Manufacturing
KUICH, W., Mathematical Logic and Computer Languages
LEITSCH, A., Computer Languages
MUTZEL, P., Computer Graphics and Algorithms
PURGATHOFER, W., Computer Graphics and Algorithms
SCHILDT, G.-H., Automation Systems
TJOA, A. M., Software Engineering
VIERTL, R., Applied Statistics and Information Science
WAGNER, I., Design and Assessment of Technology

Faculty of Mathematics and Geoinformation (Getreidemarkt 9, 1060 Vienna; tel. (1) 5880110000; fax (1) 5880110099; e-mail dekmug@mail.zserv.tuwien.ac.at; internet www.math.tuwien.ac.at):

BARON, G., Geometry
CARSTENSEN, C., Applied and Numerical Mathematics
DIRSCHMID, H., Analysis and Technical Mathematics
DORNINGER, D., Algebra and Computational Mathematics

DUTTER, R., Technical Statistics
EBEL, H., Technical Physics
FRANK, A., Surveying and Geoinformation
GRUBER, P., Mathematical Analysis
HERTLING, J., Applied and Numerical Mathematics
KAHMEN, H., General Geodesy
KAISER, H., Algebra and Computational Mathematics
KELNHOFER, F., Cartography and Reproduction Technology
KUICH, W., Mathematical Logic and Computer Languages
LANGER, H., Applied Analysis
MLITZ, R., Applied and Numerical Mathematics
POTTMANN, A., Geometry
SCHACHERMAYER, W., Statistics and Probability Theory
SCHNABL, R., Analysis and Technical Mathematics
SCHUH, H., Geodesy and Geophysics
STACHEL, H., Geometry
TROCH, I., Analysis and Technical Mathematics
VANA, N., Dosimetry
VIERTL, R., Applied Statistics and Information Science
WERTZ, W., Financial and Actuarial Mathematics

Faculty of Mechanical Engineering (Karlspl. 13, 1040 Vienna; tel. (1) 5880130001; fax (1) 5880130099; e-mail mrosen@pop.tuwien.ac.at; internet www.tuwien.ac.at/maschinenbau):

BIBERSCHICK, D., Industrial Engineering, Ergonomics and Business Economics
DEGISCHER, H. P., Materials Science and Testing
GAMER, U., Mechanics
GRÖSEL, B., Handling and Transport Technology and General Design Engineering
HASELBACHER, H., Thermal Turbo-Machinery and Power Plants
JÖRGL, H. P., Machine- and Process-Engineering
KLUWICK, A., Hydrodynamics
KOPACEK, P., Handling Devices and Robotics
LENZ, H. P., Internal Combustion Vehicles
LINZER, W., Theory of Heat
LUGNER, P., Mechanics
MATTHIAS, H. B., Water-powered Machines and Pumps
PATZAK, G., Industrial Engineering, Ergonomics and Business Economics
RAMMERSTORFER, F., Light Engineering, Aeroplane Engineering
RINDER, L., Machine Parts
SCHNEIDER, W., Gas and Thermodynamics
SCHUÖCKER, D., Non-conventional Processing, Forming and Laser Technology
SCHWAIGER, W., Accounting and Controlling
SEIDLER, S., Materials Science and Testing
SPRINGER, H., Machine Dynamics and Measurement
STEPAN, A., Industrial Business Management
TROGER, H., Mechanics
UHLIR, H., Industrial Engineering, Ergonomics and Business Economics
VARGA, T., Welding
WESESLINDTNER, H., Computer Integrated Manufacturing
WOJDA, F., Business Management
ZEMAN, J., Pressure Vessel and Plant Technology

Faculty of Physics (Wiedner Hauptstr. 8–10, 1040 Vienna; tel. (1) 5880110000; fax (1) 5880110099; internet www.physik.tuwien.ac.at):

AIGINGER, J., Ionizing Radiation
BADUREK, G., Nuclear Solid State Physics

BALCAR, E., Neutron and Solid State Physics
BENES, E., General Physics
BRÜCKL, E., Geophysics
BURGDÖRFER, J., Theoretical Physics
EBEL, H., Technical Physics
FLECK, M. C., Neutron Physics
KIRCHMAYR, H., Experimental Physics
KRAUS, K., Photogrammetry
KUMMER, W., Theoretical Physics
RAUCH, H., Experimental Nuclear Physics
SCHUH, H., Geodesy and Geophysics
SCHWEDA, M., Theoretical Physics
SKALICKY, P., Applied Physics
WEBER, H. W., Low Temperature Physics
WINTER, H., General Physics

Faculty of Technical Chemistry (Getreidemarkt 9, 1060 Vienna; tel. (1) 5880110000; fax (1) 5880110099; e-mail johannes.froehlich@tuwien.ac.at; internet www.chemie.tuwien.ac.at):

FABJAN, C., Technical Electrochemistry and Solid State Chemistry
GRASSERBAUER, M., Analytical Chemistry
GRUBER, H., Chemical Technology of Organic Materials
HAMPEL, W., Biochemical Technology
HOFBAUER, H., Chemical Engineering, Fuel Technology and Environmental Technology
KNÖZINGER, E., Physical Chemistry
KUBEL, F., Mineralogy, Crystallography and Structural Chemistry
MARINI, I., Chemical Engineering, Fuel Technology and Environmental Technology
SCHMID, R., Inorganic Chemistry
SCHUBERT, U., Inorganic Chemistry
SCHWARZ, K., Physical and Theoretical Chemistry
STACHELBERGER, H., Botany, Technical Microscopy and Organic Raw Materials
WEINBERGER, P., Technical Electrochemistry and Solid State Chemistry
WRUSS, W., Chemical Technology of Inorganic Materials
WURST, F., Applied Botany, Technical Microscopy, and Organic Raw Materials Science

UMIT—PRIVATE UNIVERSITÄT FÜR GESUNDHEITSWISSENSCHAFTEN, MEDIZINISCHE INFORMATIK UND TECHNIK
(Health and Life Sciences University)

Eduard Wallnöfer-Zentrum 1, 6060 Hall

Telephone: (50) 86483000
Fax: (50) 8648673001
E-mail: lehre@umit.at
Internet: www.umit.at

Founded 2002
Private control

Rector: Prof. Dr CHRISTA THEM
Vice-Rector for Finance and Human Resources: PHILIPP UNTERHOLZNER

Library of 7,750 vols, 30 journals, 500 CDs, DVDs and video cassettes
Number of teachers: 270
Number of students: 1,370

UNIVERSITÄT FÜR ANGEWANDTE KUNST IN WIEN
(University of Applied Arts in Vienna)

Oskar Kokoschkapl. 2, 1010 Vienna

Telephone: (1) 711330
Fax: (1) 71133222
E-mail: pr@uni-ak.ac.at
Internet: www.dieangewandte.at

Founded 1867
State control
Academic year: October to September (2 semesters)

Rector: Dr GERALD BAST
Vice-Rector for Facilities Devt and Publication Issues: Prof. Dipl.-Ing Dr WOLF D. PRIX
Vice-Rector for Quality Assurance, Education Issues, Mediation and Communication: Prof. Mag. BARBARA PUTZ-PLECKO
Vice-Rector for Teaching: Prof. Mag. JOSEF KAISER
Chair. of the Academic Senate: Mag. Dr RUTH MATEUS-BERR
Univ. Dir: Dr HEINZ ADAMEK
Head Librarian: Dr GABRIELE JURJEVEC-KOLLER

Library: 400 periodicals, 100,000 monographs, 2,500 video cassettes
Number of teachers: 380
Number of students: 1,800

Publications: exhibition catalogues (6–8 a year), *Prospect* (2 a year).

UNIVERSITÄT FÜR BODENKULTUR WIEN
(University of Natural Resources and Life Sciences, Vienna)

Gregor Mendelstr. 33, 1180 Vienna

Telephone: (1) 476540
Fax: (1) 476542606
E-mail: bdr@boku.ac.at
Internet: www.boku.ac.at

Founded 1872
State control
Academic year: October to June

Rector: Prof. Dr MARTIN H. GERZABEK
Vice-Rector for Education and Internationalisation: Prof. Dr BARBARA HINTERSTOISSER
Vice-Rector for Finances: ANDREA REITHMAYER
Vice-Rector for Research and Int. Research Cooperation: Prof. Dr JOSEF GLÖBL
Vice-Rector for Strategic Devt: Dr GEORG HABENHAUER
Librarian: Mag. MARTINA HÖRL

Library: see Libraries and Archives
Number of teachers: 1,000
Number of students: 10,500

Publications: *Blick ins Land* (12 a year), *Die Bodenkultur*, *Ökoenergie* (6 a year), *Zentralblatt für das gesamte Forstwesen* (4 a year)

PROFESSORS

BERGMEISTER, K.
BERNHARDT, K.
BÜRSTMAYR, H.
BÜRSTMAYR, H.
DÜRRSTEIN, H.
FIEBIG, M.
FLORINETH, F.
FORNECK, A.
FRANK, T.
FREYER, B.
GERZABEK, M.
GERZABEK, M.
GLÖßL, J.
GLÖßL, J.
GRONALT, M.
GRUNDLER, F.
HABERL, R.
HACKLÄNDER, K.
HALTRICH, D.
HASENAUER, H.
HOFREITHER, M.
HOGL, K.
HOLZNER, W.
JEZIK, K.
JUNGWIRTH, M.
KANTELHARDT, J.
KAUL, H.
KNEIFEL, W.
KOSMA, P.
KROMP-KOLB, H.
KRSKA, R.

KUNERT, R.
LECHNER, P.
LICKA, L.
LOISKANDL, W.
MÄRZ, L.
NACHTNEBEL, H.
NOWAK, W.
PRÖBSTL, U.
ROSENAU, T.
SAMMER, G.
SCHIEBEL, W.
SCHNEIDER, G.
SCHNEIDER, J.
SCHOPF, A.
SCHULEV-STEINDL, E.
SLEYTR, U.
SÖLKNER, J.
STERBA, H.
STINGEDER, G.
STÖGER, E.
TEISCHINGER, A.
TREBERSPURG, M.
WEBER, G.
WINCKLER, C.
WINDISCH, W.
WU, W.

UNIVERSITÄT FÜR KÜNSTLERISCHE UND INDUSTRIELLE GESTALTUNG LINZ
(University of Art and Industrial Design, Linz)

Hauptpl. 8, 4010 Linz

Telephone: (732) 78980
Fax: (732) 783508
E-mail: international.office@ufg.ac.at
Internet: www.ufg.ac.at

Founded 1947, present univ. status 1998
State control
Academic year: October to June (2 semesters)

Rector: Prof. Dr RICHARD KANNONIER
Vice-Rector for Central Services: Dr CHRISTINE WINDSTEIGER
Vice-Rector for Research: Dr MANFRED LECHNER
Vice-Rector for Studies and Teaching: Prof. Mag. RAINER ZENDRON
Librarian: Dr MANFRED LECHNER

Library: 200 journals.

UNIVERSITÄT FÜR MUSIK UND DARSTELLENDE KUNST GRAZ
(University of Music and Performing Arts, Graz)

Leonhardstr. 15, Palais Meran, 8010 Graz

Telephone: (316) 3890
Fax: (316) 3891101
E-mail: info@kug.ac.at
Internet: www.kug.ac.at

Founded 1816, conservatory 1920, academy 1963, present status 1998
State control
Language of instruction: German
Academic year: October to June

Rector: Prof. Mag. Dr GEORG SCHULZ
Vice-Rector for Arts and Research: Prof. Mag. Dr ROBERT HÖLDRICH
Vice-Rector for Quality Management, Human Resource Devt, Gender Mainstreaming: Mag. DORIS CARSTENSEN
Vice-Rector for Study: Prof. Mag. EIKE STRAUB
Univ. Dir: Mag. ASTRID WEDENIG
Library Dir: Mag. ROBERT SCHILLER

Library of 210,000 vols incl. books, journals, sheets, records, audio cassettes and other media
Number of teachers: 424
Number of students: 2,000

HEADS OF INSTITUTES

Institute of Aesthetics of Music: Prof. Dr ANDREAS DORSCHEL
Institute of Church Music and Organ: Prof. Dr GUNTHER MICHAEL ROST
Institute of Composition, Music Theory, Music History and Conducting: Prof. Dr PETER REVERS
Institute of Drama: Prof. Dr EVELYN DEUTSCH-SCHREINER
Institute of Early Music and Performance Practice: Prof. Dr KLAUS HUBMANN
Institute of Electronic Music and Acoustics: Dr ALOIS SONTACCHI
Institute of Ethnomusicology: Prof. Dr GERD GRUPE
Institute of Jazz: Prof. ANTHONY PARTYKA
Institute of Jazz Research: Prof. Dr FRANZ KERSCHBAUMER
Institute of Opera: Prof. Dr BARBARA BEYER
Institute of Opera: Prof. FRANK CRAMER
Institute of Music Education: Prof. Mag. GERHARD WANKER
Institute of the Oberschützen Campus: Prof. Dr KLAUS ARINGER
Institute of Piano: Prof. EUGEN JAKAB
Institute of Stage Design: Prof. HANS SCHAVERNOCH
Institute of Strings: Prof. Dr KERSTIN FELTZ
Institute of Voice, Lied and Oratorio: Prof. MARTIN KLIETMANN
Institute of Wind and Percussion Instruments: Prof. Mag. THOMAS EIBINGER

UNIVERSITÄT FÜR MUSIK UND DARSTELLENDE KUNST WIEN
(University of Music and Performing Arts, Vienna)

Anton-von-Webern-Pl. 1, 1030 Vienna

Telephone: (1) 71155
Fax: (1) 71155199
E-mail: rektor@mdw.ac.at
Internet: www.mdw.ac.at

Founded 1817 as Conservatorium der Gesellschaft der Musikfreunde, nationalized 1909
Language of instruction: German
Academic year: October to June

Rector: Prof. Mag. Dr WERNER HASITSCHKA
Vice-Rectors: Prof. Mag. RUDOLF HOFSTÖTTER, Prof. Dr CLAUDIA WALKENSTEINER-PRESCHL, Prof. Mag. GREGOR WIDHOLM
Library Dir: Dr SUSANNE ESCHWÉ

Number of teachers: 800
Number of students: 3,200

DEANS

Office for Instrumental Studies: Prof. Mag. AVEDIS KOUYOUMDJIAN
Office for Music Education Programmes: Prof. Mag. WOLFGANG HEISSLER

HEADS OF INSTITUTES

Bruckner Institute (Theory, Aural Training and Conducting): ALOIS GLASSNER
Film Academy: PETER PATZAK
Hellmesberger Institute (Stringed Instruments): WOLFGANG AICHINGER
Institute of the Analysis, Theory and History of Music: CORNELIA SZABO-KNOTIK
Institute of Chamber Music and Special Ensembles: JOHANNES MEISSL
Institute of Composition and Sound Technology: REINHARD KARGER
Institute of Conducting: THOMAS KREUZBERGER
Institute of Cultural Management: FRANZ-OTTO HOFECKER
Institute of Folk Music Research and Ethnomusicology: GERLINDE HAID
Institute of Keyboard Instruments: MARTIN HUGHES

Institute of Music and Movement Education and Music Therapy: ANGELIKA HAUSER-DELLEFANT
Institute of Music Teaching: PETER RÖBKE
Institute of Organ, Organ Research and Church Music: ERWIN ORTNER
Institute of Research into Musical Style: HARTMUT KRONES
Institute of the Sociology of Music: ALFRED SMUDITS
Institute of Song and Musicals: KARLHEINZ SPITZER
Institute of Stringed Instruments: STEFAN KROPFITSCH
Institute of Wind and Percussion Instruments: BARBARA GISLER
Ludwig van Beethoven Institute (Keyboard Instruments): URSULA KNEIHS
Max Reinhardt Seminar: HUBERTUS PETROLL
Popular Music: WOLFGANG PUSCHNIG
Salieri Institute (Song): MARIA BAYER
Schubert Institute (Wind and Percussion Instruments): WALTER WRETSCHITSCH
Vienna Institute of Sound: WILFRIED KAUSEL

UNIVERSITÄT MOZARTEUM SALZBURG
(University Mozarteum Salzburg)

Schrannengasse 10A, 5020 Salzburg
Telephone: (662) 61980
Fax: (662) 61983033
E-mail: info@moz.ac.at
Internet: www.moz.ac.at
Founded 1841
State control
Academic year: October to June
Depts of brass, wind and percussion studies, conducting, composition and music theory, drama, fine arts, art and craft education, keyboard studies, music and dance education, music education (Innsbruck), music education (Salzburg), music theatre, musicology, stage design, string studies, vocal studies
Rector: Prof. REINHART VON GUTZEIT
Vice-Rector for Artistic Projects: Prof. LUKAS HAGEN
Vice-Rector for Research and Devt: Prof. Dr WOLFGANG GRATZER
Vice-Rector for Resources: Mag. BRIGITTE HÜTTER
Vice-Rector for Teaching: Prof. BRIGITTE ENGELHARD
Dir for Studying: Prof. Mag. Dr FRANZ ZAUNSCHIRM
Librarian: Dr MANFRED KAMMERER
Number of teachers: 490
Number of students: 1,721
Publications: *International Summer Academy Mozarteum Brochure* (1 a year), *Uni-Art* (8 a year).

UNIVERSITÄT SALZBURG
(Salzburg University)

Kapitelgasse 4–6, 5020 Salzburg
Telephone: (662) 80440
Fax: (662) 8044214
E-mail: uni.service@sbg.ac.at
Internet: www.uni-salzburg.at
Founded 1622, closed 1810, College 1810–50, ind. faculty of Catholic Theology 1850–1962, reconstituted 1962
State control
Languages of instruction: German, English
Academic year: October to June (2 semesters)
Rector: Prof. Dr HEINRICH SCHMIDINGER
Vice-Rector for Education: Prof. Dr RUDOLF MOSLER
Vice-Rector for Int. Relations and Communications: Prof. Dr SONJA PUNTSCHER-RIEKMANN

Vice-Rector for Research: Prof. Dr ALBERT DUSCHL
Librarian: Dr URSULA SCHACHL-RABER
Library: see under Libraries and Archives
Number of teachers: 750
Number of students: 14,000

DEANS
Faculty of Catholic Theology: Prof. Dr WOLBERT WERNER
Faculty of Cultural and Social Sciences: Prof. Dr SYLVIA HAHN
Faculty of Law: Prof. Dr FRIEDRICH HARRER
Faculty of Natural Science: Prof. Dr ULRIKE-GABRIELE BERNINGER

PROFESSORS
Faculty of Arts:
  BETTEN, A., German
  BOTZ, G., History
  BRUCHER, G., History of Austrian Art
  DALFEN, J., Classical Philology
  DOPSCH, H., History
  EHMER, J., Modern History
  FABRIS, H., Journalism and Communications
  FELTEN, F., Classical Archaeology
  GOEBL, H., Romance Languages
  GRASSL, H., Ancient History
  GRÖSSING, S., Sport
  HAAS, H., Austrian History
  HAIDER, H., Linguistics
  HASLINGER, A., German
  JALKOTZY, S., Ancient History
  KLEIN, H. M., English
  KNOCHE, M., Journalism and Communications
  KOLMER, L., Medieval History and Historic Auxiliary Sciences
  KRONSTEINER, O., Slavic Languages
  KRUMM, V., Education
  KUON, P., Romance Philology
  MAYER, G., Slavic Languages
  MESSNER, D., Romance Languages
  MORSCHER, E., Philosophy
  MÜLLER, E., Physical Education
  MÜLLER, U., German
  PANAGL, O., Linguistics
  PATRY, J. L., Education
  PETERSMANN, G., Classical Philology
  PIEL, F., Medieval and Modern History of Art
  ROSSBACHER, K., German
  SCHMOLKE, M., Journalism and Communications
  STAGL, J., Sociology
  STENZL, J., Music Science
  TRUCHLAR, L., English
  WEINGARTNER, P., Philosophy
  ZAIC, F., English
Faculty of Catholic Theology:
  BACHL, G., Dogmatics
  BEILNER, W., New Testament Studies
  BUCHER, A., Catechism and Religious Education
  KÖHLER, W., Christian Philosophy and Psychology
  MÖDLHAMMER, J., Ecumenical Theology
  NIKOLASCH, F., Liturgy
  PAARHAMMER, J., Church Law
  PAUS, A., Epistemology and Religious Studies
  SCHLEINZER, F., Pastoral Theology
  SCHMIDINGER, H., Christian Philosophy
  WINKLER, G. B., Church History
  WOLBERT, W., Moral Theology
Faculty of Law:
  BERKA, W., General Theory of the State, Theory of Administration, Constitutional and Administrative Law
  BUSCHMANN, A., German Legal History, German Private and Civil Law
  GRILLBERGER, K., Industrial Law
  HACKL, K., Roman and Civil Law

  HAGEN, J., Sociology of Law
  HAMMER, R., Management
  HARRER, F., Civil and Commercial Law
  KARL, W., International Law
  KOJA, F., General Constitutional Law
  KOPPENSTEINER, H.-G., Austrian and International Commercial Law
  KYRER, A., Economics
  MAYER-MALY, TH., German and Austrian Private Law
  MIGSCH, E., Civil Law
  RAINER, J., Roman and Modern Private Law
  SCHÄFFER, H., Public Law
  SCHMOLLER, K., Austrian Criminal Law
  SCHUMACHER, W., International Commercial Law and Civil Law
  SCHWIMANN, M., International Civil Law
  STOLZLECHNER, H., Public Law
  TRIFFTERER, O., Austrian and International Criminal Law
Faculty of Natural Sciences:
  AMTHAUER, G., Geology
  BAUMANN, U., Psychology
  BENTRUP, F. W., Plant Physiology and Anatomy
  BREITENBACH, M., Molecular Genetics
  CLAUSEN, H., Systems Analysis
  CZIHAK, G., Genetics
  FÜRNKRANZ, D., Botany
  GERL, P., Mathematics
  HERMANN, A., Zoology
  NEUBAUER, G., Geology
  PERNER, J., Psychology
  PFALZGRAF, J., Computer Science
  RIEDL, H., Geography
  SCHWEIGER, F., Mathematics
  STADEL, CH., Geography
  STEINHÄUSLER, F., Biophysics
  STRACK, H.-B., Biochemistry
  WALLBOTT, H., Psychology
  WERNER, H., Sciences Education
  ZINTERHOF, P., Mathematics
Inter-faculty Institutes:
  CROLL, G., Music History of Salzburg
  FAUPEL, K., Political Science
  GACHOWETZ, H., Organizational Psychology
  HAUPTMANN, W., Criminal Psychology
  KOPPENSTEINER, H. G., European Law
  LAUBER, V., Political Science
  MAYER-MALY, TH., Energy Law, Law of Liechtenstein
  MIGSCH, E., Private Insurance Law
  MORSCHER, E., Philosophy, Technology, Economics
  ZINTERHOF, P., Software Technology

UNIVERSITÄT WIEN
(Vienna University)

Dr Karl Lueger-Ring 1, 1010 Vienna
Telephone: (1) 42770
Fax: (1) 42779120
E-mail: public@univie.ac.at
Internet: www.univie.ac.at
Founded 1365
State control
Academic year: October to June (2 semesters)
Rector: Prof. Dr HEINZ W. ENGL
Vice-Rector for Educational Program Devt and Internationalization: Prof. Dr ARTHUR METTINGER
Vice-Rector for Infrastructure, Resources and Library Affairs: Prof. Dr JOHANN JURENITSCH
Vice-Rector for Research and Career Devt: Prof. Dr HEINZ W. ENGL
Vice-Rector for Student Affairs and Continuing Education: Prof. Dr CHRISTA SCHNABL
Librarian: Mag. MARIA SEISSL
Library: see under Libraries and Archives
Number of teachers: 6,747
Number of students: 88,000

DEANS

Faculty of Business, Economics and Statistics: Prof. Dr GERHARD SORGER

Faculty of Catholic Theology: Prof. Dr MARTIN JÄGGLE

Faculty of Chemistry: Prof. Dr BERNHARD KEPPLER

Faculty of Computer Science: Prof. Dr WOLFGANG KLAS

Faculty of Earth Sciences, Geography and Astronomy: Prof. Dr HEINZ FAßMANN

Faculty of Historical and Cultural Studies: Prof. Dr MICHAEL VIKTOR SCHWARZ

Faculty of Law: Prof. Dr HEINZ MAYER

Faculty of Life Sciences: Prof. Dr HORST SEIDLER

Faculty of Mathematics: Prof. Dr HARALD RINDLER

Faculty of Philological and Cultural Studies: Prof. Dr SUSANNE WEIGELIN-SCHWIEDRZIK

Faculty of Philosophy and Educational Sciences: Prof. Dr INES MARIA BREINBAUER

Faculty of Physics: Prof. Dr CHRISTOPH DELLAGO

Faculty of Protestant Theology: Prof. Dr CHRISTIAN DANZ

Faculty of Psychology: Prof. Dr GERMAIN WEBER

Faculty of Social Sciences: Prof. Dr RUDOLF RICHTER

Centre for Molecular Biology: Prof. Dr GRAHAM WARREN (Head)

Centre for Sports Sciences and University Sports: Prof. Dr ARNOLD BACA (Head)

Centre for Translation Studies: Prof. Dr NORBERT GREINER (chemistr)

PROFESSORS

Centre for Sports Sciences and University Sports (tel. (1) 427759001; fax (1) 42779590; e-mail sportwissenschaft@univie.ac.at; internet www.univie.ac.at/sportwissenschaft):

ANKNER, P.
BACHL, N.
BENDA, F.
HACKL-JAGENBREIN, S.
KELLNER, A.
KOLB, M.
MUNZAR, S.
WEIß, O.

Centre for Translation Studies (tel. (1) 427758001; fax (1) 42779580; e-mail translation@univie.ac.at; internet www.univie.ac.at/transvienna):

BUDIN, G.
FRANK, G.
KASTOVSKY, D.
KLAMBAUER, E.
LEIMEIER, C.
MOLDAU, S.
RESCH, R.
SCHÄTTLE, M.
SNELL-HORNBY, M.
WILDMANN, D.

Faculty of Business, Economics and Statistics (tel. (1) 427737030; fax (1) 427737045; e-mail dekanat-win@univie.ac.at; internet www.univie.ac.at/wirtschaftswissenschaften):

ALTENBERGER, O., Business Studies
BONZE, I., Economics
CLEMENZ, G., Economics
DIAMANTOPOULOS, A., Business Studies
DOCKNER, E., Business Studies
FINSINGER, J., Business Studies
FITZSIMONS, C. O., Business Languages
HARTL, J., Business Studies
HEIDENBERGER, K., Business Studies
KUNST, R., Computer Science and Business Informatics
LECHNER, E., Commercial Law
MUELLER, D., Economics
NERMUTH, M., Economics

OROSEL, G., Economics
PFEIFFER, T., Business Studies
PFLUG, G., Statistics and Decision Support Systems
PÖTSCHER, B., Statistics and Decision Support Systems
SORGER, G., Economics
TRAXLER, F., Government
VAN DER BELLEN, A., Economics
WAGENER, A., Economics
WAGNER, U., Business Studies
WEILINGER, A., Commercial Law
WINCKLER, G., Economics
WIRL, F., Business Studies
ZECHNER, J., Business Studies

Faculty of Catholic Theology (tel. (1) 42773001; fax (1) 42779300; internet www.univie.ac.at/ktf):

FEULNER, H.-J., Liturgical Studies
FIGL, J., Study of Religion
GABRIEL, I., Social Ethics
JÄGGLE, M., Religious Education
KÜHSCHELM, R., Ethics and Social Sciences
LANGTHALER, R., Christian Philosophy
MÜLLER, L., Canon Law
PROKSCHI, R., Theology and History of Eastern Churches
REIKERSTORFER, J., Fundamental Theology and Apologetics
SCHLOSSER, M., Theology of Spirituality
STUBENRAUCH, B., Dogmatics
VIRT, G., Moral Theology

Faculty of Chemistry (tel. (1) 427751001; fax (1) 42779510; e-mail chemie.dekanat@univie.ac.at; internet chemie.univie.ac.at):

BRINKER, U., Organic Chemistry
DICKERT, F., Analytical Chemistry and Food Chemistry
DJINOVIĆ-CARUGO, K., Biomolecular Structural Chemistry
FRINGELI, U. P., Biophysical Chemistry
IPSER, H., Inorganic Chemistry
KEPPLER, B., Inorganic Chemistry
KONRAT, R., Biomolecular Structural Chemistry
LINDNER, W., Analytical Chemistry and Food Chemistry
LISCHKA, H., Theoretical Chemistry
MULZER, J., Organic Chemistry
SCHMID, W., Organic Chemistry
SCHUSTER, P., Theoretical Chemistry
SONTAG, G., Analytical Chemistry and Food Chemistry
STEINHAUSER, O., Biomolecular Structural Chemistry

Faculty of Computer Science (tel. (1) 427739001; fax (1) 42779390; internet www.cs.univie.ac.at):

EDER, J., Knowledge and Business Engineering
GROSSMANN, W., Computer Science
HARING, G., Faculty of Computer Science
KARAGIANNIS, D., Knowledge and Business Engineering
KLAS, W., Computer Science
QUIRCHMAYR, G., Distributed and Multimedia Systems
ZIMA, H., Department of Scientific Computing

Faculty of Earth Sciences, Geography and Astronomy (tel. (1) 427753001; fax (1) 42779530; internet www.univie.ac.at/geowissenschaften):

BREGER, M., Astronomy
FAßMANN, H., Geography and Regional Research
FERGUSON, D. K., Palaeontology
HANTEL, M., Meteorology and Geophysics
HENSLER, G., Astronomy
HOFMANN, T., Environmental Geosciences
KAINZ, W., Geography and Regional Research
RABEDER, G., Palaeontology
RICHTER, W., Lithospheric Sciences

STEINACKER, R., Meteorology and Geophysics
STEINHAUSER, P., Meteorology and Geophysics
TILLMANNS, E., Mineralogy and Crystallography
WEICHHART, P., Geography and Regional Research
WOHLSCHLÄGL, H., Geography and Regional Research

Faculty of Historical-Cultural Sciences (tel. (1) 427740001; fax (1) 42779400; e-mail guntram.schneider@univie.ac.at; internet www.univie.ac.at/dekanat-hist-kult):

ASH, M., History
BACH, F. T., Art History
BIETAK, M., Egyptology
BOTZ, G., Contemporary History
BRUCKMÜLLER, E., Social and Economic History
BRUNNER, K., History
DIENST, H., History
DOBESCH, G., Ancient History, Papyrology and Epigraphy
DONNERMAIR, C., Social and Economic History
DREKONJA, G., History
EHMER, J., Social and Economic History
FRIESINGER, H., Prehistoric and Medieval Archaeology
HAHN, W., Numismatics and Monetary History
HASELSTEINER, H., East and Southern European History
KAPPELER, A., East and Southern European History
KLIMBURG-SALTER, D., Art History
KODER, J., Byzantine and Modern Greek Studies
KOHLER, A., History
KÖSTLIN, K., European Ethnology
KRESTEN, O., Byzantine and Modern Greek Studies
KRINZINGER, F., Classical Archaeology
LANGE, A., Jewish Studies
LIPPERT, A., Prehistoric and Medieval Archaeology
LORENZ, H., Art History
MALECZEK, W., History
MEYER, M., Classical Archaeology
PALME, B., Ancient History, Papyrology and Epigraphy
PILLINGER, R., Classical Archaeology
ROSENAUER, A., Art History
SACHSE, C., Contemporary History
SAURER, E., History
SCHMALE, W., History
SCHMIDT-COLINET, A., Classical Archaeology
SCHMITT, O., Eastern and Southern European History
SCHWARZ, M., Art History
SIEWERT, P., Institute of Ancient History, Papyrology and Epigraphy
STELZER, W., History
STEMBERGER, G., Jewish Studies
STERN, F., Contemporary History
STIEFEL, D., Social and Economic History
SUPPAN, A., Eastern and Southern European History
THEIS, L., Art History
WERNER, F., Jewish Studies

Faculty of Law (Schottenbastei 10–16, 1010 Vienna; tel. (1) 427734001; fax (1) 42779340; e-mail dekanat-jur@univie.ac.at; internet www.juridicum.at):

AICHER, J., Commercial Law
BAJONS, E. M., Procedural Law
BENKE, N., Roman Law and Ancient Legal History
BÖHM, P., Civil Procedural Law
BRANDSTETTER, W., Criminal Law and Criminology
BRAUNEDER, W., Austrian and European Legal History

BURGSTALLER, M., Criminal Law and Criminology
DORALT, W., Financial Law
FENYVES, A., Civil Law
FISCHER-CZERMAK, C., Civil Law
FUCHS, H., Criminal Law and Criminology
FUNK, B. CHR., State and Administrative Law
HAFNER, G., International Law and International Relations
HÖPFEL, F., Criminal Law and Criminology
IRO, G., Civil Law
KONECNY, A., Procedural Law
KOPETZKI, C., Commercial and Business Law
KREJCI, H., Commercial Law
LUF, G., Legal Philosophy and Legal Theory
MAYER, H., State and Administrative Law
MAZAL, W., Labour Law and Social Law
MEISSEL, F. S., Roman Law and Antique Legal History
NEUHOLD, H. P., International Law and International Relations
OFNER, H., European, International and Comparative Law
ÖHLINGER, T., State and Administrative Law
PIELER, P. E., Roman Law and History of Ancient Law
POTZ, R., Cultural and Religious Law
RASCHAUER, B., State and Administrative Law
REBHAHN, R., Labour Law and Law of Social Security
RECHBERGER, W., Civil Procedural Law
RIEDL, K., Civil Law
SCHAUER, M., Civil Law
SCHRAMMEL, W., Labour Law and Social Law
SCHREUER, CHR., International Law and International Relations
SIMON, T., Legal and Constitutional History
STELZER, M., State and Administrative Law
TANZER, M., Financial Law
THIENEL, R., State and Administrative Law
VERSCHRÄGEN, B., Comparative Law
WELSER, R., Civil Law
WILHELM, G., Civil Law
WILLVONSEDER, R., Roman Law and Ancient Legal History

Faculty of Mathematics (tel. (1) 427756001; fax (1) 42779560; e-mail dekanat .mathematik@univie.ac.at; internet www .mat.univie.ac.at):

FRIEDMAN, S.-D., Mathematics
GRÖCHENIG, K.-H., Mathematics
KOTH, M., Mathematics
LOSERT, V., Mathematics
MARKOWICH, P., Mathematics
MITSCH, H., Mathematics
MUTHSAM, H., Mathematics
NEUMAIER, A., Mathematics
RINDLER, H., Mathematics
SCHMIDT, K., Mathematics
SCHWERMER, J., Mathematics
SIGMUND, K., Mathematics

Faculty of Philological-Cultural Sciences (tel. (1) 427745001; fax (1) 42779450; internet www.univie.ac.at/dekanat-phil-kult):

ALLGAYER-KAUFMANN, R., Musicology
BESTERS-DILGER, J., Slavonic Studies
BIRKHAN, H., German Studies
CAVIC-PODGORNIK, N. A., Slavonic Studies
CYFFER, N., African Studies
DÖNT, E., Classical Philology, Medieval and Neo-Latin Studies
DORMELS, R., East Asian Studies
DRESSLER, W., Linguistics
EBENBAUER, A., German Studies
EICHNER, H., Linguistics
FAISTAUER, R., German Studies
FROSCH, F., Romance Studies

GREISENEGGER, W., Theatre Arts
GRUBER, G., Musicology
HAIDER, H., Theatre Arts
HARRAUER, C., Classical Philology, Medieval and Neo-Latin Studies
HASSAUER, F., Romance Studies
HOLUBOWSKY, E., East Asian Studies
HUBER, W., English and American Studies
HUNGER, H., Near Eastern Studies
HÜTTNER, J., Theatre Arts
KASPER, C., European and Comparative Literature and Language Studies
KASTOVSKY, D., English and American Studies
KÖHBACH, M., Near Eastern Studies
KREMNITZ, G., Romance Studies
KRUMM, H.-J., German Studies
LAAKSO, J., European and Comparative Literature and Language Studies
LINHART, S., East Asian Studies
LIPOLD-STEVENS, I., English and American Studies
LOHLKER, R., Musicology
MARTINO, A., European and Comparative Literature and Language Studies
MEHLMAUER-LARCHER, B., English and American Studies
MENGEL, E., English and American Studies
METZELTIN, M., Romance Studies
MIKLAS, H., Slavonic Studies
NEWEKLOWSKY, G., Slavonic Studies
NEWERKLA, S. M., Slavonic Studies
POLJAKOV, F., Slavonic Studies
PREISENDANZ, K., South Asian, Tibetan and Buddhist Studies
ROHRWASSER, M., German Studies
RÖMER, F., Classical Philology, Medieval and Neo-Latin Studies
ROSSEL, S. H., European and Comparative Literature and Language Studies
RUBIK, M., English and American Studies
SCHENDL, H., English and American Studies
SCHICHO, W., African Studies
SCHJERVE-RINDLER, R., Romance Studies
SCHMIDT-DENGLER, W., German Studies
SEIDLHOFER, B., English and American Studies
SELZ, G., Near Eastern Studies
SMOLAK, K., Classical Philology, Medieval and Neo-Latin Studies
SODEYFI, H., Slavonic Studies
SOOMAN, I., European and Comparative Literature and Language Studies
STEINKELLNER, E., South Asian, Tibetan and Buddhist Studies
VAN UFFELEN, H., European and Comparative Literature and Language Studies
WAGNER, B., Romance Studies
WEIGELIN-SCHWIEDRZIK, S., East Asian Studies
WIESINGER, P., German Studies
WOLDAN, A., Slavonic Studies
WOYTEK, E., Classical Philology, Medieval and Neo-Latin Studies
ZEMAN, H., German Studies

Faculty of Philosophy and Educational Sciences (tel. (1) 427746001; fax (1) 42779460; internet homehobel.phl.univie.ac.at):

BIEWER, G., Educational Sciences
BREINBAUER, I. M., Educational Sciences
GIAMPIERI-DEUTSCH, P., Philosophy
HÄMMERLE, M., Educational Sciences
HOPMANN, S., Educational Sciences
KAMPITS, P., Philosophy
KLEIN, H.-D., Philosophy
NAGL, H., Philosophy
OESER, E., Philosophy of Science
PIAS, C., Philosophy
POLLMEISTER, K., Educational Sciences
PÖLTNER, G., Philosophy
SWERTZ, C., Educational Sciences
WALLNER, F., Philosophy

Faculty of Physics (tel. (1) 427751001; fax (1) 42779510; e-mail dekanat.physik@univie.ac .at; internet physics.univie.ac.at):

AICHELBURG, P. C., Theoretical Physics
BARTL, A., Theoretical Physics
DELLAGO, C., Experimental Physics
HAFNER, J., Materials Physics
HORVATH, H., Experimental Physics
KARNTHALER, H.-P., Materials Physics
KUTSCHERA, W., Isotope Research and Nuclear Physics
RUPP, R., Experimental Physics
VOGL, G., Materials Physics
YNGVASON, J., Theoretical Physics
ZEILINGER, A., Experimental Physics

Faculty of Protestant Theology (Rooseveltplatz 10, 1090 Vienna; tel. (1) 427732001; fax (1) 42779320; internet www.univie.ac.at/etf):

ADAM, G., Religious Education
DANZ, C., Systematic Theology
DEEG, M., Systematic Theology
HEINE, S., Pastoral Theology and Psychology of Religion
KÖRTNER, U., Systematic Theology
LEEB, R., Christian History, Art and Archaeology
LOADER, J., Old Testament and Biblical Archaeology
PRATSCHER, W., New Testament Studies
WISCHMEYER, W., Christian History, Art and Archaeology

Faculty of Psychology (tel. (1) 427747001; fax (1) 42779470; internet www.univie.ac.at/ psychologie):

BAUER, H., Clinical, Biological and Differential Psychology
FORMANN, A., Psychological Basic Research
HERKNER, W., Psychological Basic Research
KIRCHLER, E., Economic Psychology, Educational Psychology and Evaluation
KRYSPIN-EXNER, I., Clinical, Biological and Differential Psychology
KUBINGER, K., Developmental Psychology and Psychological Assessment
LEDER, H., Psychological Basic Research
SPIEL, C., Economic Psychology, Educational Psychology and Evaluation
VORACEK, M., Psychological Basic Research

Faculty of Social Sciences (tel. (1) 427749001; fax (1) 42779490; internet www.univie.ac.at/ sowi):

AMANN, A., Sociology
BAUER, T. A., Communication
DUCHKOWITSCH, W., Communication
FELT, U., Vienna Interdisciplinary Research Unit for the Study of (Techno) Science and Society
GERLICH, P., Government
GINGRICH, A., Social and Cultural Anthropology
GOTTSCHLICH, M., Communication
GOTTWEIS, H., Political Science
GRIMM, J., Communication
KRAMER, H., Political Science
KREISKY, H. E., Political Science
LANGENBUCHER, W., Communication
RICHTER, R., Sociology
ROSENBERGER, S., Political Science
SAUER, B., Political Science
SCHULZ, W., Sociology
SEGERT, D., Political Science
SEIDL, E., Nursing Science
TÁLOS, E., Government
UCAKAR, K., Government
VITOUCH, P., Communication

VETERINÄRMEDIZINISCHE UNIVERSITÄT WIEN (University of Veterinary Medicine, Vienna)

Veterinärpl. 1, 1210 Vienna
Telephone: (1) 250770

Fax: (1) 250771090
E-mail: rektor@vu-wien.ac.at
Internet: www.vu-wien.ac.at
Founded 1765
State control
Academic year: October to June (2 semesters)
Rector: Dr SONJA HAMMERSCHMID
Vice-Rector for Academic Affairs and Clinical Veterinary Medicine: Prof. Dr PETRA WINTER
Vice-Rector for Resources: Prof. Dr JOSEF EBENBICHLER
Librarian: Mag. DORIS REINITZER
Library: see under Libraries and Archives
Number of teachers: 206
Number of students: 2,300
Publications: *Uni Vet Wien Report* (4 a year), *Wiener Tierärztliche Monatsschrift* (12 a year)

PROFESSORS
ARNOLD, W., Wildlife Biology
AURICH, J. E., Obstetrics, Gynaecology and Andrology
BAMBERG, E., Biochemistry
BAUMGARTNER, W., Internal Medicine and Contagious Diseases of Ruminants and Swine
BÖCK, P., Histology and Embryology
FRANZ, C., Applied Botany
GEMEINER, M., Medical Chemistry
GÜNZBURG, W., Virology
HOFECKER, G., Physiology
KÖNIG, H., Anatomy
MAYRHOFER, E., Radiology
MÜLLER, M., Stock Breeding, Genetics
NIEBAUER, G., Surgery and Ophthalmology
NOHL, H., Pharmacology and Toxicology
ROSENGARTEN, R., Bacteriology, Mycology, Hygiene
SCHMIDT, P., Pathology, Forensic Medicine
SMULDERS, F., Meat Hygiene, Meat Technology, Food Science
STANEK, CH., Orthopaedics in Ungulates
THALHAMMER, J. G., Small Animals and Horses
TROXLER, J., Animal Husbandry, Animal Welfare
WINDISCHBAUER, G., Medical Physics, Biostatistics
ZENTEK, J., Nutrition

WEBSTER UNIVERSITY, VIENNA

Berchtoldgasse 1, 1220 Vienna
Telephone: (1) 26992930
Fax: (1) 269929313
E-mail: info@webster.ac.at
Internet: www.webster.ac.at
Founded 1981
Private control
Academic year: August to July (2 semesters)
Dir: Dr ARTHUR HIRSCH
Lib. Dir: BENJAMIN FASCHING-GRAY
Library of 10,000 vols
Number of teachers: 84
Number of students: 500

WIRTSCHAFTSUNIVERSITÄT WIEN (Vienna University of Economics and Business Administration)

Augasse 2–6, 1090 Vienna
Telephone: (1) 313360
Fax: (1) 31336740
E-mail: lehre@wu.ac.at
Internet: www.wu.ac.at
Founded 1898
State control
Languages of instruction: German, English
Academic year: October to June (2 semesters)
Rector: Prof. Dr CHRISTOPH BADELT

Vice-Rector for Academic Programs and Student Affairs: Prof. Dr KARL SANDNER
Vice-Rector for Financial Affairs: Prof. Dr EVA EBERHARTINGER
Vice-Rector for Infrastructure and Human Resources: Dr MICHAEL HOLOUBEK
Vice-Rector for Research, International Affairs and External Relations: Prof. Dr BARBARA SPORN
Librarian: Dr NIKOLAUS BERGER
Library: see under Libraries and Archives
Number of teachers: 72
Number of students: 26,800
Publication: *Journal für Betriebswirtschaft* (Journal for Business Administration, 6 a year)

PROFESSORS
ABELE, H., Economic Theory and Policy
AFF, J., Economics
ALEXANDER, R. J., English Business Communication
AMBOS, B., International Marketing and Management
BERTL, R., Auditing, Accounting and International Accounting
BOGNER, ST., Department of Corporate Finance
EBERHARTINGER, E., Tax-oriented Business Management
FISCHER, M., Economic and Social Geography
FRANKE, N., Entrepreneurship and Foundation Research
GAREIS, R., Project Management
GRILLER, S., Research Institute for European Affairs
GRÜN, O., Business Organization and Materials Management
HANAPPI-EGGER, E., Gender and Diversity in Organizations
HOLOUBEK, M., Constitutional and Administrative Law
HORNIK, K., Mathematical and Statistical Methods
JAMMERNEGG, W., Industrial Information Processing
JANKO, W., Information Processing and Information Economics
KALSS, S., Business Law
KASPER, H., Management and Management Development
KUBIN, I., International Economics and Development Planning
KUMMER, S., Transportation
LANG, M., International Tax Law
LAURER, H. R., Constitutional and Administrative Law
LIENBACHER, G., Austrian and European Public Law
LUPTÁCIK, M., Economic Theory and Policy
MAUTNER, G., English Business Communication
MAYRHOFER, W., Business and Government Management
MAZANEC, J., Tourism
MEYER, M., Non-profit Management
MOSER, R., International Business
MUGLER, J., Small Business
NEUMANN, G., Business Informatics and New Media
NOWOTNY, C., Commercial Law
NOWOTNY, E., Financial Politics
OBENAUS, W., English Business Communication
OBERMANN, G., Public Finance
PANNY, W., Applied Computer Science
PFEIFFLE, H, Theory of Education
PICHLER, J. H., Economic Theory and Policy
PICHLER, S., Economic Theory and Policy
RAINER, F., Romance Languages
RATHMAYR, R., Slavonic Languages
RIEGLER, C., Integrated Business Accounting
RUNGGALDIER, U., Labour Law, Social Law
SANDNER, K., General Management
SCHEUCH, F., Marketing

SCHLEGELMILCH, B., International Marketing and Management
SCHNEDLITZ, P., Retail Management
SCHNEIDER, U., General Sociology and Economic Sociology
SCHNEIDER, U., Social Policy
SCHUCH, J., International Tax Law
SCHÜLEIN, J. A., General and Economic Sociology
SCHWEIGER, G., Advertising and Market Research
SEICHT, G., Industrial Management
SPECKBACHER, G., Business Management
STEGU, M., Romance Languages
STIASSNY, A., Quantitative Political Economy
STRASSER, H., Experimental Methods of Mathematics and Statistics
TAUDES, A., Industrial Information Processing
VOGEL, G., Technology and Commodity Economics
WALTHER, H., Employment Theory and Policy
WENTGES, P., Business Management

Schools of Applied Science

CAMPUS 02 Fachhochschule der Wirtschaft (CAMPUS 02 University for Applied Sciences): Körblergasse 126, 8021 Graz; tel. (316) 6002177; e-mail info@campus02.at; internet www.campus02.at; f. 2001; degree programmes in automation technology, information technologies and business informatics, innovation management, int. marketing and sales management, financial accounting and management accounting; library: 7,800 printed media; 1,792 students; Man. Dirs Mag Dr. ERIC BRUGGER, Dr ANNETTE ZIMMER.

Fachhochschul-Studiengang Bauingenieurwesen-Baumanagement (School of Applied Construction Engineering and Management): Daumegasse 1, 2nd Fl., 1100 Vienna; tel. (1) 60668772120; fax (1) 60668772129; e-mail bau@fh-campuswien.ac.at; f. 1996; Bachelors and Masters courses in construction engineering and management; Dir Dr DORIS LINK.

Fachhochschul-Studiengang Burgenland GmbH (School of Applied Sciences Burgenland): Campus 1, 7000 Burgenland; tel. (5) 90106090; fax (5) 901060915; e-mail officefh@burgenland.at; internet www.fh-burgenland.at; f. 1994; 2 campuses; Bachelors and Masters courses in economics, environmental and energy management, health studies, information technology and management; Dir Mag. INGRID SCHWAB-MATKOVITS.

Fachhochschul-Studiengang Oberösterreich (School of Applied Sciences of Upper Austria): Franz-Fritsch-Str. 11, 4600 Wels; tel. (7242) 448080; fax (7242) 448877; e-mail info@fh-ooe.at; internet www.fh-ooe.at; f. 1994; Bachelors and Masters courses; campuses in Hagenberg (software, information technology and media), Linz (health and social welfare), Steyr (business and management studies) and Wels (engineering and environment and energy studies); Dir Dr GERALD REISINGER.

Fachhochschul-Studiengang Salzburg (School of Applied Sciences Salzburg): Urstein Süd 1, 5412 Puch/Salzburg; tel. (662) 5022110; fax (662) 5022111099; e-mail press@fh-salzburg.ac.at; internet www.fh-salzburg.ac.at; f. 1995, present status 2004; campuses in Kuchl and Urstein; Bachelors and Masters courses in information technologies, wood and biogene technologies, business and tourism, media and design;

library: 27,800 vols, 170 subscriptions; 100 teachers; 2,262 students; Man. Dirs RAIMUND RIBITSCH, Mag. DORIS WALTER.

Fachhochschul-Studiengänge bfi Wien (School of Applied Science bfi Vienna): Wohlmutstr. 22, 1020 Vienna; tel. (1) 7201286; fax (1) 720128619; e-mail info@fh-vie.at; internet www.fh-vie.ac.at; f. 1996, present status 2002; Bachelors programmes in work design and HR management, banking and finance, European economy and business management, logistics and transport management, project management and information technology, technical sales and distribution management; Masters programmes in banking and finance, European economy and business management, logistics and transport management, project management and organization and quantitative asset and risk management; library: 10,000 media; Man. Dir Dr HELMUT HOLZINGER.

Fachhochschul-Studiengänge Campus Wien (School of Applied Sciences Vienna Campus): Daumegasse 3, 1100 Vienna; tel. (1) 6066877-100; fax (1) 6066877-109; e-mail office@fh-campuswien.ac.at; internet www.fh-campuswien.ac.at; f. 1999; language of instruction: German; diploma courses in bioengineering, biotechnology, information technology and telecommunications, social work, and technical project and process management; Bachelors courses in construction engineering and management; Masters courses in local management and economics, and social management; Dir Ing. WILHELM BEHENSKY; publ. *Aktuell* (12 a year).

Fachhochschul-Studiengänge der Wiener Neustadt (School of Applied Sciences Wiener Neustadt): Johannes Gutenberg Str. 3, 2700 Vienna-Neustadt; tel. (2622) 890840; fax (2622) 89084-99; e-mail office@fhwn.ac.at; internet www.fhwn.ac.at; f. 1994, official status in 1999; Bachelors courses in business consultancy, business and engineering, information technologies, mechatronics and microsystems engineering, aerospace engineering, biomedical analytics, occupational therapy, speech therapy and radiological technology; English language Bachelors and Masters programmes in business consultancy int., aerospace and MedTech; 200 teachers; 3,200 students; CEOs Prof. Dipl.-Ing. Dr GERHARD PRAMHAS, Mag. SUSANNE SCHARNHORST.

Fachhochschul-Studiengänge Kufstein (School of Applied Sciences Kufstein): Andreas Hofer Str. 7, 6330 Kufstein; tel. (5372) 71819; fax (5372) 71819104; e-mail info@fh-kufstein.ac.at; internet www.fh-kufstein.ac.at; f. 1997, present status in 2005; diploma course in property economics and facility management; Bachelors courses in business information technology, sport, culture and event management, European energy economics, facility management and property economics and int. economics and management; Masters courses in crisis management and corporate restructuring, facility and real estate management, int. business studies, European energy, sports, culture and event management; library: 14,000 publs, incl. 80 professional journals, 15 newspapers; 120 teachers; 1,200 students; Exec. Dir Mag. WOLFGANG RICHTER.

Fachhochschul-Studiengänge St Pölten (School of Applied Sciences St Pölten): Matthias Corvinus-Str. 15, 3100 St. Pölten; tel. (2742) 313228333; fax (2742) 313228339; e-mail office@fhstp.ac.at; internet www.fhstp.ac.at; f. 1993 as Society for holding of higher education courses St Pölten; present status in 2004; 9 Bachelors degree programmes in dietetics, railway infrastructure technology, industrial simulation, IT secur-

ity, media and communications consulting, media management, media technology, physiotherapy and social work, 5 Masters programmes in digital media technologies, industrial simulation, information security, media management and social work; 9 training courses in event management, event equipment, photography, IT security, clinical dietetics and nutritional management, MBA programmes in media management, pre-production management and addiction treatment and prevention; library: 16,000 books, DVD, CD-ROM, 150 magazine subscriptions; 260 teachers; 1,800 students; Man. Dirs Dr GABRIELA FERNANDES, Dipl.-Ing. GERNOT KOHL; publ. *FACTS* (2 a year).

Fachhochschul-Studiengänge Technikum Joanneum (School of Applied Sciences Technikum Joanneum): Alte Poststr. 147–154, Eggenberger Allee 9–13, 8020 Graz; tel. (316) 54530; fax (316) 54538801; e-mail info@fh-joanneum.at; internet www.fh-joanneum.at; f. 1995; 3 campuses; 24 Bachelors degree programmes, 18 Masters degree programmes in information, design and technologies, international business, and life, building, environment; language of instruction: German; library: 48,000 books, journals, theses, CD-ROMs, video cassettes and DVDs; Man. Dir Prof. Dipl.-Ing. Dr KARL PETER PFEIFFER.

Fachhochschul-Studiengänge WIFI Steiermark (School of Applied Sciences WIFI Styria): Körblergasse 111–113, 8021 Graz; tel. (316) 6021234; fax (316) 602301; e-mail info@stmk.wifi.at; internet www.stmk.wifi.at; campuses in Graz, Niklasdorf and Unterpremstätten; courses in business management, business studies, modern languages, information technology, civil and mechanical engineering, energy technology, health and welfare, environmental management, tourism and gastronomy, traffic and security systems, personality devt; Pres. Ing. Mag. PETER HOCHEGGER.

Fachhochschule IMC Krems (IMC University of Applied Sciences): Piaristengasse 1, 3500 Krems; tel. (2732) 8020; fax (2732) 8024; e-mail information@fh-krems.ac.at; internet www.fh-krems.ac.at; f. 1994; Bachelors and Masters degree programmes in business studies, life sciences and health studies; library: 50,000 items; 425 teachers; 1,800 students; Rector Prof. EVA WERNER.

Fachhochschule Technikum Kärnten (School of Applied Science Carinthia): Villacher Str. 1, 9800 Spittal; tel. (4762) 905000; fax (4762) 905001110; e-mail info@fh-kaernten.at; internet www.fh-kaernten.at; f. 1995; courses in civil engineering, electronic engineering, geoinformation, healthcare management, medical information technology, public management, social work, network engineering; international Masters degree programmes in communication engineering for information technology, healthcare information technology, integrated systems and circuit design and spatial information manaagement; 5 campuses; library: 40,000 media units in 4 libraries; 2,000 students; Exec. Dir Dipl.-Ing. SIEGFRIED SPANZ.

Fachhochschule Technikum Wien (School of Applied Science Vienna): Mariahilfer Str. 37–39 , 1060 Vienna; tel. (1) 588390; fax (1) 5883949; e-mail info@technikum-wien.at; internet www.technikum-wien.at; f. 1994; present status 2000; 11 Bachelors and 17 Masters programmes in communication technologies and electronic engineering, information technologies and business solutions, engineering and environmental technologies and life science technologies; courses are offered as full-time and/or part-time degree programmes;

library: 10,000 books, theses, magazines and CDs; 2,500 students; Dir Dr MICHAEL WÜRDINGER.

Fachhochschule Vorarlberg (School of Applied Sciences Vorarlberg): Hochschulstr. 1, 6850 Dornbirn; tel. (5572) 7920; fax (5572) 7929500; e-mail info@fhv.at; internet www.fhv.at; f. 1997; 7 Bachelors, 7 Masters courses in technology, business and commerce, design and social work; 6 of these are part-time; library: 48,000 vols, 260 magazines, 2,200 CDs, 2,000 DVDs; 1,027 students; Man. Dir Dr HEDWIG NATTER.

FH Gesundheitsberufe OÖ GmbH (Upper Austria University of Applied Sciences Health Professions): Semmelweisstr. 34/D3, 4020 Linz; tel. (50) 34420000; fax (50) 34420099; e-mail office@fhgooe.ac.at; internet www.fh-gesundheitsberufe.at; f. 2010; Bachelors degrees in biomedical science, dietetics, occupational therapy, midwifery, physical therapy and radiography; Masters degree in management for health professionals and a Masters course in university teaching and learning for health professions; 800 students; Man. Mag. BETTINA SCHNEEBAUER.

FHG—Zentrum für Gesundheitsberufe Tirol GmBH (FHG—Centre for Health Sciences, Tirol GmBH): Innrain 98, 6020 Innsbruck; tel. (50) 86484700; fax (50) 8648674700; e-mail info@fhg-tirol.ac.at; internet www.fhg-tirol.ac.at; f. 2006; Bachelors and Masters courses in biomedical science, dietetics, midwifery, occupational therapy, speech therapy, physiotherapy, osteopathy and radiography; Man. Dir WALTER DRAXL.

FHWien-Studiengänge der WKW (FHWien University of Applied Sciences): Währinger Gürtel 97, 1180 Vienna; tel. (1) 476775744; fax (1) 476775745; e-mail studienzentrum@fh-wien.ac.at; internet www.fh-wien.ac.at; f. 1994; 16 Bachelors and Masters courses in finance, real estate, journalism, communications, marketing, human resources, tourism, organizational and personal devt; 737 teachers; 2,363 students; Dir Mag. MICHAEL HERITSCH.

Holztechnikum Kuchl: Markt 136, 5431 Salzburg; tel. (662) 62445372; fax (662) 624453722; e-mail office@holztechnikum.at; internet www.holztechnikum.at; f. 1943; higher education in the timber processing market; Pres. WIESNER MARKUS.

Lauder Business School: Hofzeile 18–20, 1190 Vienna; tel. (1) 3691818; e-mail office@lbs.ac.at; internet www.lbs.ac.at; f. 2003; Bachelors programme in intercultural business admin. and Masters programme in intercultural management and leadership; also offers Jewish learning programme for Jewish students; Dean Prof. Dr SILVIA KUCERA.

MCI Management Centre Innsbruck—Internationale Hochschule GmbH (MCI Management Centre Innsbruck–International Academy GmbH): Universitaetsstr. 15, 6020 Innsbruck; tel. (512) 20700; fax (512) 20701099; e-mail office@mci.edu; internet www.mci.edu; f. 1996; graduate, non-graduate and postgraduate educational programmes to senior and junior managers from all management levels and brs; 200 teachers; Exec. Dir Prof. Dr ANDREAS ALTMANN.

Other Colleges

Diplomatische Akademie Wien (Diplomatic Academy of Vienna): Favoritenstr. 15A, 1040 Vienna; tel. (1) 5057272; fax (1)

5042265; e-mail info@da-vienna.ac.at; internet www.da-vienna.ac.at; f. 1964; Diploma and Master of advanced int. studies programmes prepare Austrian and foreign graduates for careers in diplomacy, int. business and finance, int. orgs and public admin.; library: 35,000 vols, 330 newspapers in German, English, French, Spanish, Italian and Russian; 82 teachers; 80 students; Dir Dr HANS WINKLER.

Hochschule für Agrar- und Umweltpädagogik Wien (College of Agricultural and Environmental Education Vienna): Angermayergasse 1, 1130 Vienna; tel. (1) 87722660; fax (1) 8772361; e-mail info@agrarumweltpaedagogik.ac.at; internet www.agrarumweltpaedagogik.ac.at; f. 2007; Bachelors in agricultural education, environmental education; Masters in management education in rural areas; library: 11,000 books and periodicals; 58 teachers; Rector Mag. Dr THOMAS HAASE.

Institut für Psychosoziale Intervention und Kommunikationsforschung (Institute for Psychosocial Intervention and Communication Research): Schöpfstr. 3, 6020 Innsbruck; tel. (512) 5070; fax (512) 5078681; e-mail psyko@uibk.ac.at; internet www.uibk.ac.at/psyko; f. 2010; attached to Univ. of Innsbruck; dipl, BA, MA, PhD, training and research in professional intervention methods in psychotherapy; Dir Prof. Dr JOSEF CHRISTIAN AIGNER.

International College for Tourism and Management: Johann Strauss Str. 2, 2540 Bad Vöslau; tel. (2252) 790260; fax (2252) 790470; e-mail office@itm-college.eu; internet www.itm-college.eu; f. 1986; Bachelors programmes in business administration, int. management and hospitality management with tourism; 20 teachers; Dir. of Studies CLAUDIA ROTHWANGL.

Schools of Art and Music

Anton Bruckner Privatuniversität (Anton Bruckner Private University): see under Universities.

Joseph Haydn Konservatorium des Landes Burgenland (Joseph Haydn Conservatory of Burgenland): Glorietteallee 2, 7000 Eisenstadt; tel. (2682) 63734; fax (2682) 637344; e-mail office@haydnkons.at; internet www.haydnkons.at; f. 1929; BMus in instrumental studies, singing, music theory and composition; 40 teachers; 400 students; Dir Prof. Mag WALTER BURIAN.

Kärntner Landeskonservatorium (Carinthian Conservatory of Music): Miesstalerstr. 8, 9020 Klagenfurt; tel. (50) 53640510; fax (50) 53640508; e-mail info@konse.at; internet www.konse.at; f. 1827; Bachelors, Masters courses and doctorates in musicology in cooperation with Alpa Adria Klagenfurt Univ.; 75 teachers; 900 students; Dir Mag. ROLAND STREINER.

Konservatorium Wien Privatuniversität (Conservatory Vienna University): Johannesgasse 4A, 1010 Vienna; tel. (1) 5127747; fax (1) 51277477913; e-mail office@konswien.at; internet www.konservatorium-wien.ac.at; f. 1938; 30 Bachelors and Masters courses in music and dramatic arts; library: 36,000 media, 17,800 songs; 250 teachers; 860 students; Dirs GOTTFRIED EISL, RANKO MARKOVIĆ; publ. *Fidelio* (5 a year).

Tiroler Landeskonservatorium (Tirol Conservatory of Music): Paul-Hofhaimer-Gasse 6, 6020 Innsbruck; tel. (512) 508-6850; fax (512) 508-6855; internet www.tirol.gv.at/konservatorium; f. 1818; 75 teachers; 500 students; library: 100,000 vols and musical notes; Dir Dr THOMAS JUEN; Librarian FRANZ BAUER.

Vienna Konservatorium (Vienna Conservatory): Stiegergasse 15–17, Fenzlgasse 26, 1150 Vienna; tel. (1) 9858112; fax (1) 8922813; e-mail office@viennaconservatory.at; internet www.viennaconservatory.at; Bachelors and Masters programmes in music theory and performance, music theory and composition, classical instruments, classical-vocal, jazz instruments, jazz-vocal; 109 teachers; Dir ROBERT BRANDSTÖTTER.

Vorarlberger Landeskonservatorium GmbH (Vorarlberg State Conservatory GmbH): Reichenfeldgasse 9, 6800 Feldkirch; tel. (5522) 711100; fax (5522) 7111063; e-mail sekretariat@vlk.ac.at; internet www.vlk.ac.at; f. 1856; Bachelor of Arts in Music from Univ. Mozart Salzburg in instrumental, vocal training; library: 4,000 vols, 17,000 notes, 3,800 CDs, 15,000 records, 25 periodicals; 58 teachers; CEO Dr PETER SCHMID.

AZERBAIJAN

The Higher Education System

The higher education system was established when Azerbaijan was a full Union Republic of the Union of Soviet Socialist Republics (USSR). The main language of instruction is Azerbaijani, but there are also Russian-language schools and some teaching in Georgian and Armenian. From 1992 a Turkic version of the Latin alphabet was used in Azerbaijani-language schools (replacing the Cyrillic script). In June 1999 legislation entitled The Programme of Education Reforms of the Republic of Azerbaijan was passed by presidential decree, affecting reforms at all levels of education. In 2005 Azerbaijan signed up to the Bologna Process, under which all European countries were to endeavour to adopt a universal three-tier Bachelors–Masters–Doctorate degree structure. Azerbaijan intended to adopt this system by 2010. In 2008/09 there were 48 state-supported institutions of higher education, including the Azerbaijan State Petroleum Academy, which trains engineers for the petroleum industry, and numerous private universities. In that year a total of 136,587 students were enrolled in higher education.

The State oversees educational policy, dispenses funding and lays down guidelines for quality assurance. Individual institutions are responsible for employing teaching staff and establishing curricula. In 2006 the Ministry of Education established the Standing Commission on Accreditation to act as the main quality assurance body for higher education institutions and secondary specialized institutions. Institutions are subject to inspection every four years. Since 2004/05 entrance examinations for state institutions have been organized by a central body, the Talaba Qabulu üzre Dövlat Komissiyasi (TQDK—State Students Admission Commission). An estimated 20% of school-leavers enter higher education through this process.

The three levels of higher education qualifications are Bachelors, Masters and Doctorates. Study for the Bachelors degree lasts for four years, while the Soviet-style Specialist Diploma, which is still offered in some disciplines, lasts for five years. The Masters degree was introduced in 1997/98 and lasts for up to two years. By 2006 Masters degrees had been introduced in 39 higher institutions throughout Azerbaijan, with approximately 10,000 students enrolled. The Soviet-style Aspirantura and Doctorantura remain the main doctoral degrees, although Bologna Process reforms are being implemented.

Regulatory and Representative Bodies

GOVERNMENT

Ministry of Culture and Tourism: 1000 Baku, Azadlıq meydani 1, House of Govt, 3rd Floor; tel. (12) 493-43-98; fax (12) 493-56-05; e-mail mugam@culture.gov.az; Minister ABULFAZ MURSAL OĞLU KARAYEV.

Ministry of Education: 1008 Baku, Xatai pr. 49; tel. (12) 496-06-47; fax (12) 496-34-83; e-mail office@min.edu.az; internet www.edu .gov.az; Minister MISIR CUMAYIL OĞLU MARDANOV.

Talaba Qabulu üzre Dövlat Komissiyasi (TQDK) (State Students Admission Commission): Baku, Hasan Aliyev str. 17; tel. (12) 440-30-09; e-mail info@tqdk.gov.az; internet www.tqdk.gov.az; directly subordinate to Pres.; centralized org. for management of student admissions; develops regulations for admission to higher and secondary spec. schools; conducts examinations; prepares and implements organizational, scientific and methodical and planning activities; develops proposals for improvement of higher and secondary spec. education on the basis of systemic analysis of admission campaign results; Chair. ABBASZADE MALEYKA MEHDI.

ACCREDITATION

ENIC/NARIC Azerbaijan: Min. of Education, 1008 Baku, Khatai Ave 49; tel. (12) 96-34-14; fax (12) 96-34-90; e-mail a_akhundov@ yahoo.com; internet www.min.edu.az; Sr Expert AZAD AKHUNDOV.

NATIONAL BODY

Council of University Presidents: 370096 Baku, Mehseti 11; tel. (12) 21-79-27; fax (12) 98-93-79; e-mail contact@khazar.org; internet www.khazar.org; Pres. Prof. HAMLET ISAXANLI.

Learned Societies

GENERAL

Azerbaijan National Academy of Sciences: 1141 Baku, F. Ağayev küç. 9; tel. (12) 441-72-81; fax (12) 441-72-81; e-mail secretary@iit.ab.az; internet www.science.az; f. 1945; depts of physical, mathematical and technical sciences (Academician-Sec. A. J. HAJIYEV), chemical sciences (Academician-Sec. A. A. EFENDIYEV), earth sciences (Academician-Sec. A. M. ALIZADEH), biological sciences (Academician-Sec. M. A. MUSAYEV), humanities and social sciences (Academician-Sec. A. A. AKHUNDOV; attached research institutes: see Research Institutes; Pres. M. K. KERIMOV; Academician-Sec. T. N. SHAKHTAKHTINSKIY; publs *Applied and Computational Mathematics* (2 a year), *Azerbaijan and Azerbaijanists* (12 a year, in English and Russian), *Azerbaijan Journal of Chemistry* (4 a year, in Azeri and Russian), *Azerbaijan Journal of Physics* (4 a year, in Azeri, Russian and English), *Journal of Physics* (4 a year, in Azeri, Russian and English), *Journal of Problems of Eastern Philosophy* (2 a year, in Azeri, Arabic, Farsi, Turkish, English, German and French), *Journal of Turkology* (1 a year, in Azeri and Russian), *Proceedings* (4 a year, in Russian and Azeri), *Processes of Petrochemistry and Oil Refining Journal* (6 a year, in Russian and English), *Transactions* (series: physical, mathematical and technical sciences, biological sciences, historical, philosophical and judicial, economics, literature, philology and art, geological).

LANGUAGE AND LITERATURE

British Council: 1010 Baku, 8th Fl., The Landmark III Bldg, 90A Nizami St; tel. (12) 497-20-13; fax (12) 498-92-36; e-mail enquiries@britishcouncil.az; internet www .britishcouncil.org/azerbaijan.htm; office opened 1993; offers courses and examinations in English language and British culture and promotes cultural exchange with the UK; Dir MARGARET JACK.

Research Institutes

AGRICULTURE, FISHERIES AND VETERINARY SCIENCE

Agricultural Research Institute: 1016 Baku, U. Hadjibeyov küç. 40; tel. (12) 497-49-31; fax (12) 497-50-45; f. 1950; attached to Min. of Agriculture; Dir A. MUSAYEV.

Institute of Genetic Resources: 1106 Baku, Azadlyg Ave; tel. (12) 462-94-62; fax (12) 449-92-21; e-mail akparov@yahoo.com; f. 2003; attached to Azerbaijan Nat. Acad. of Sciences; Dir Z. I. AKPAROV; publ. *Transactions* (irregular, in Azeri and Russian).

Institute of Soil Science and Agrochemistry: 1073 Baku, M. Arif küç. 5; e-mail soiman@dcacs.ab.az; tel. (12) 438-32-40; f. 1945; attached to Azerbaijan Acad. of Sciences; Dir M. P. BABAYEV; publ. *Transactions* (1 a year, in Azeri and Russian).

Karaev, A. I., Institute of Physiology: 1100 Baku, Sharif-Zade küç. 2; tel. (12) 432-15-20; e-mail inphys@dcacs.ab.az; f. 1968; attached to Azerbaijan Acad. of Sciences; Dir T. M. AQAYEV; publ. *Transactions* (1 a year, in Azeri and Russian).

Rajably Scientific Research Institute of Horticulture and Sub-Tropical Plants: 4035 Quba, Zardabi; tel. (169) 45-37-17; fax (12) 493-08-84; f. 1926; Dir D. BAYRAMOVA.

ARCHITECTURE AND TOWN PLANNING

Institute of Architecture and Art: 1143 Baku, H. Javid Ave 31; tel. (12) 439-34-94; e-mail ertegin@baku.ab.az; internet www .artandculture.com; f. 1945; attached to Azerbaijan Acad. of Sciences; research in history and theory of architecture; art of Azerbaijan and Turkic culture; Dir. Prof. Dr ARTEGIN SALAMZADE; publs *International Scientific Journal*, *Problems of Art and Culture*.

BIBLIOGRAPHY, LIBRARY SCIENCE AND MUSEOLOGY

'Mähämmäd Füzuli' Institute of Manuscripts (IMANAS): 1001 Baku, Istiglaliyyat küç. 8; tel. (12) 492-31-97; fax (12) 492-83-33; e-mail elyazmalarinstitutu@mail.ru; internet www.elyazmalarinstitutu.com; f. 1950; attached to Azerbaijan Nat. Acad. of Sciences; library of 40,000 MSS, documents and vols; Dir Dr MAMMAD ADILOV; publs *Älyazmalar khäzinäsinda* (irregular), *Kechmishimizdän gälän säslär* (irregular), *Orta äsr älyazmalari vä Azärbaycan mädäniyyäti problemläri* (every 2 years).

ECONOMICS, LAW AND POLITICS

Institute of Economics: 1143 Baku, Pr. H. Javid 31; tel. (12) 439-43-98; fax (12) 435-31-12; e-mail economy@eco.ab.az; f. 1958; attached to Azerbaijan Acad. of Sciences; Dir S. M. MURADOV.

Institute of Philosophy and Law: 1143 Baku, Pr. H. Javid 31; tel. (12) 439-37-28; f. 1945; attached to Azerbaijan Acad. of Sciences; Dir A. ABASOV; publ. *Qendershunaslig* (11 a year, in Azeri and English).

HISTORY, GEOGRAPHY AND ARCHAEOLOGY

Institute of Archaeology and Ethnography: 1143 Baku, Pr. H. Javid 31; tel. (12) 439-36-49; fax (12) 439-39-91; e-mail abbasov@arch.ab.az; attached to Azerbaijan Acad. of Sciences; Dir A. A. ABBASOV.

Institute of Geography: 1143 Baku, Pr. H. Javid 31; tel. (12) 438-29-00; fax (12) 439-35-41; e-mail azgeog@geo.ab.az; f. 1945; attached to Azerbaijan Acad. of Sciences; research into natural resources, industrial and infrastructural problems, desertification, hydrometeorology of the Caspian Sea and its coastal dynamics; 250 mems; library of 53,000 vols; Dir Acad. B. A. BUDAGOV; publ. *Khabarlar* (2 a year).

Institute of History: 1143 Baku, Pr. H. Javid 31; tel. (12) 439-36-15; f. 1940; attached to Azerbaijan Acad. of Sciences; Dep. Dir J. A. BAHRAMOV.

Institute of Oriental Studies: 1143 Baku, Pr. H. Javid 31; tel. (12) 439-23-51; fax (12) 439-23-51; e-mail sharq@lan.ab.az; f. 1958; attached to Azerbaijan Acad. of Sciences; Dir G. B. BAKHSHALIYEVA.

LANGUAGE AND LITERATURE

Nasimi Institute of Linguistics: 1143 Baku, Pr. H. Javid 31; tel. (12) 439-35-71; f. 1932; attached to Azerbaijan Acad. of Sciences; library of 6,000 vols, 50 periodicals; Dir Prof. A. A. AKHUNDOV; publ. *Turkology* (4 a year).

Nizami Institute of Literature: 1143 Baku, 5th Fl., H. Javid 31; tel. (12) 441-74-25; fax (12) 439-56-68; e-mail adib@aas.ab.az; internet www.science.az/en/literature; f. 1932; attached to Azerbaijan Acad. of Sciences; Dir B. A. NABIYEV.

MEDICINE

Azerbaijan Institute of Orthopaedics and Traumatology: 1007 Baku, 32 Abbas Sakhat küç.; tel. (12) 496-62-62.

Azerbaijan Institute of Tuberculosis and Pulmonology: 1001 Baku, 2514 kv., 8 km settlement; tel. (12) 421-22-62.

Azerbaijan Medical Association: 1000 Baku, S. Akhundov küç. 2/1; tel. (12) 31-88-66; fax (12) 31-51-36; e-mail azer.ma@medmail.com; internet azma.aznet.org; f. 1998; 600 mems; Dir NARIMAN SAFARLI.

Azerbaijan Research Institute of Haematology and Blood Transfusion: 1007 Baku, M. Kaskkay 87; tel. (12) 440-53-18; fax (12) 440-63-34; e-mail hajiev_azad@yahoo.com; f. 1943; Dir AZAD HAJIYEV; publ. *Azerbaijan Medical Journal* (4 a year).

Azerbaijan Research Institute of Ophthalmology: 1065 Baku, 6-ya Kommunisticheskaya küç. 5; tel. (12) 421-22-62.

Research Institute of Gastroenterology: 1110 Baku, Leningradsky pr. 111; tel. (12) 464-45-09; f. 1988; Dir B. A. AGAYEV; publ. *Actual Questions of Gastroenterology* (1 a year).

Research Institute of Medical Rehabilitation and Natural Therapeutic Factors: 1008 Baku, Khatai Ave 3; tel. (12) 466-31-93; fax (12) 466-58-35; f. 1936; Dir Prof. Dr A. V. MUSAYEV.

NATURAL SCIENCES

Biological Sciences

Botanical Garden: 1073 Baku, Patamdartskoe shosse 40; e-mail cbg@lan.ab.az; f. 1934; attached to Azerbaijan Acad. of Sciences; Dir O. V. IBADLI.

Institute of Botany: 1073 Baku, Patamdartskoe shosse 40; tel. (12) 439-32-30; fax (12) 439-33-80; e-mail botanica@baku.ab.az; f. 1936; attached to Azerbaijan Acad. of Sciences; Dir V. H. HAJIYEV.

Institute of Microbiology: 1073 Baku, Patamdart Ave 40; f. 1972; attached to Azerbaijan Acad. of Sciences; Dir M. A. SALMANOV; publ. *Transactions* (1 a year, in Azeri and Russian).

Institute of Zoology: 1073 Baku, Proezd 1128, kv. 504, A. Abbasov; tel. (12) 439-73-71; fax (12) 439-73-53; e-mail izb@dcacs.ab.az; f. 1936; attached to Azerbaijan Acad. of Sciences; Dir I.KH. ALAKBAROV; publ. *Transactions* (irregular, in Azeri and Russian).

Mardakan Arboretum: 1044 Baku; tel. (12) 454-30-12; fax (12) 454-03-74; e-mail dendrary@mail.az; f. 1926; attached to Azerbaijan Acad. of Sciences; Dir T. S. MAMEDOV.

Mathematical Sciences

Institute of Mathematics and Mechanics: 1141 Baku, Agaeva küç. 9; tel. (12) 439-39-24; fax (12) 439-01-02; e-mail frteb@aas.ab.az; attached to Azerbaijan Acad. of Sciences; Dir AKIF GADJIEV; publ. *Proceedings* (4 a year, in Azeri, Russian and English).

Physical Sciences

Azerbaijan National Aerospace Agency: 1106 Baku, S. S.Akhundov str. 1; tel. (12) 462-93-87; fax (12) 462-17-38; e-mail a.shirin-zadeh@box.az; f. 1975; Dir-Gen. Prof. ALCHIN SHIRIN-ZADA.

Institute of Chemical Problems: 1143 Baku, Pr. H. Javid 29; tel. (12) 439-29-08; fax (12) 438-77-56; e-mail itpcht@lan.ab.az; f. 1935; attached to Azerbaijan Acad. of Sciences; Dir T. N. SHASKHTAKHTINSKI.

Institute of Geology: 1143 Baku, Pr. H. Javid 29A; tel. (412) 497-52-86; fax (412) 497-52-85; e-mail gia@azdata.net; internet www.gia.az; f. 1938; attached to Azerbaijan Acad. of Sciences; 250 mems; library of 24,000 vols, 70,000 periodicals; Dir A. A. ALI-ZADEH; publs *Proceedings* (1 a year), *Sciences of the Earth* (4 a year).

Institute of Physics: 1143 Baku, Javid Ave, 33; tel. (12) 439-41-51; fax (12) 439-59-61; e-mail director@physics.ab.az; f. 1945; attached to Azerbaijan Nat. Acad. of Sciences; scientific research in the different brs of theoretical and experimental physics; Dir Prof. ARIF GASHIMOV.

Institute of Radiation Problems: 1143 Baku, Pr. H. Javid 31A; tel. (12) 439-33-91; fax (12) 439-83-18; e-mail azerecolab@azerin.com; f. 1969; attached to Azerbaijan Acad. of Sciences; Dir A. A. GARIBOV.

Şamaxı Astro-Physical Observatory: 5600 Şamaxı, Pos. Mamedalieva; tel. (12) 497-52-68; fax (12) 497-52-68; e-mail shao@lan.ab.az; f. 1960; attached to Azerbaijan Acad. of Sciences; Dir A. S. GULUYEV; publ. *The Azerbaijan Astronomical Journal* (4 a year, in Azeri, Russian and English).

TECHNOLOGY

Azerbaijan Petroleum Machinery Research and Design Institute (Azinmash): 1029 Baku, 4 Araz küç.; tel. (12) 467-08-88; fax (12) 467-28-88; e-mail office@azinmash.azeri.com; internet www.azinmash.com; f. 1930; Dir R. DJABBAROV.

Azerbaijan Scientific Gas Research and Projects Institute: 1000 Baku, Yusif Safarov küç. 23; tel. (12) 490-43-59.

Azerbaijan Scientific-Research and Design-Prospecting Power Engineering Institute:; e-mail yusifbayli.n@gmail.com 1012 Baku, Pr. H. Zardabi 94; tel. and fax (12) 432-80-76; e-mail energy_institut@mail.ru; internet www.pei.az; f. 1933; research into power potential and effective use of water resources, power systems, power and automation issues of oil industry, thermodynamics, research of gases less distinctive than ideal gases and committing the generalized case equations of the oil hydrocarbons and their fractions, etc.; library of 59,000 vols; Dir Prof. NURALI ADIL YUSIFBAYLI; publ. *Electroenergetics, Electrotechnics, Electromechanics + Control* (1 a year).

Guliyev, A.M., Institute of Additive Chemistry: 1603 Baku, Beyukshorskoe shosse, kv. 2062; tel. (12) 467-65-33; fax (12) 493-33-64; e-mail aki@lan.ab.az; f. 1965; attached to Azerbaijan Acad. of Sciences; lubricant and fuel additives, cutting fluids and erosion inhibitors; library of 9,000 vols; Dir Dr V. M. FARZALIYEV.

Institute of Cybernetics: 1141 Baku, F. Agaeva str. 9; tel. (12) 439-01-51; fax (12) 439-26-33; e-mail telmancyber@rambler.ru; internet www.telmanaliev.az; f. 1965; attached to Azerbaijan Nat. Acad. of Sciences; Dir Acad. TELMAN ALIEV; publ. *Transactions of National Academy of Sciences* (2 a year).

Institute of Deep Oil and Gas Deposits: 1143 Baku, Pr. H. Javid 33; tel. (12) 439-21-40; fax (12) 497-58-52; e-mail arif.guliyev@lan.ab.az; attached to Azerbaijan Acad. of Sciences; Dir A. M. GULIYEV.

Institute of Information Technology: 1141 Baku, F. Agayev; tel. (12) 439-01-67; fax (12) 439-61-21; e-mail secretary@iit.ab.az; f. 2003; attached to Azerbaijan Acad. of Sciences; Dir R. M. ALGULIYEV.

Institute of Polymer Materials: 5004 Sumqayıt, Samed Vargun küç. 124; tel. (12) 497-60-38; fax (164) 42-04-00; e-mail ipoma@dcacs.ab.az; f. 1966; attached to Azerbaijan Acad. of Sciences; Dir ABASGULU MAMED GULIYEV.

Mamedaliev, Yu. G., Institute of Petrochemical Processes: 1025 Baku, N. Rafiyev 30; tel. (12) 490-24-76; fax (12) 490-35-20; e-mail ipcp@baku-az.net; internet www.science.az/en/oilchemistry; f. 1929; attached to Azerbaijan Acad. of Sciences; Dir M. I. RUSTAMOV; publ. *Process of Petrochemistry and Oil Refining* (6 a year, in Russian and English).

Oil Research and Design Institute (AzNIPIneft): 1033 Baku, Aga Neimatully küç. 39; tel. (12) 493-64-29.

Research and Design Institute for Oil Engineering: 1000 Baku, Aga Neymatully küç. 39; tel. (12) 466-21-69; fax (12) 467-79-39.

Research Institute of Photoelectronics: 1000 Baku, Block 555, Agaeva küç; tel. (12) 439-13-08; f. 1972; library of 1,095 vols; Dir Prof. S. E. YUNISOGLU.

Libraries and Archives
Baku
Azərbaycan Milli Kitabxanası (Azerbaijan National Library): 1000 Baku, Khagani küç. 29; tel. (12) 493-40-03; fax (12) 498-08-22; e-mail contact@anl.az; internet www.anl.az; f. 1923, named M. F. Akhundov State Library of Azerbaijan 1939, awarded Na. Library status 2005; 4,539,598 vols, 30,209 audiovisual items; Dir Dr TAHIROV KARIM MAHAMMAD OĞLU; publs *Azerbaijan Bibliography* (1 a year), *New Books*, *New Literature on Culture, Art and Tourism*, *The Calendar of Significant and Historical Days*.

Azerbaijan Scientific and Technical Library: 1001 Baku, G. Gadzhieva küç. 3; tel. (12) 492-08-07; 9m. vols; Dir G. D. MAMEDOV.

Central Library of the Azerbaijan Academy of Sciences: 1143 Baku, Pr. Narimanova 31; tel. (12) 438-60-17; f. 1925; 2.5m. vols, periodicals and serials; Dir M. M. CASANOVA.

Scientific Library of Baku State University: 1148 Baku, Z. Khalilova küç. 23; tel. (12) 439-06-21; fax (12) 438-33-76; e-mail sara_ibragimova@yahoo.com; f. 1919; 2,458,991 vols; Librarian SARA IBRAGIMOVA; publs *Estestvennikh nauk* (4 a year), *Gumanitarnikh nauk* (4 a year), *Sotsialno-politicheskikh nauk* (4 a year), *Vestnik Bakinskogo Universiteta: Fiziko-Matematicheskikh nauk* (4 a year).

Museums and Art Galleries
Baku
Azerbaijan State Museum of Art: 1001 Baku, Niyazi 9–11; tel. (12) 492-57-89; fax (12) 492-67-69; f. 1920; library of 11,000 vols; Dir A. R. ASRAFILOV.

Baku Museum of Education: 1001 Baku, Niazi küç. 11; tel. (12) 492-04-53; f. 1940; library of 52,000 vols; Dir T. Z. AHMEDZADE.

Huseyn Javid Memorial Flat–Museum: 1000 Baku, Istiglaliyat 8; tel. (12) 492-06-57; f. 1995; attached to Azerbaijan Acad. of Sciences; Dir T. H. JAVID.

Museum of the History of Azerbaijan: 1005 Baku, H. Z. Tagiyev 4; tel. (12) 493-36-48; fax (12) 498-52-11; f. 1920; attached to Azerbaijan Acad. of Sciences; history of the Azerbaijani people since ancient times; Dir N. M. VALIKHANLI.

Nizami Gandjavi State Museum of Azerbaijan Literature: 1001 Baku, Isteglal küç. 53; tel. (12) 492-18-64; f. 1939; history of Azerbaijani literature since ancient times; Dir R. B. HUSEYNOV.

State Museum Palace of Shirvan-Shakh: 1004 Baku, Zamkovski pereulok 76; tel. (12) 492-95-73; fax (12) 492-83-04; e-mail shirvanshah@bakililar.az; internet www.culture.az:8101/museums/shirv/titlerus.htm; f. 1964; historical and architectural museum; Dir SEVDA DADASHEVA.

Stepano-Kert
Stepanakert Museum of the History of Nagornyi-Karabakh: 2600 Xankandi (Stepanakert), Gorkogo küç. 4; history of the Armenian people of Arthakh (Nagornyi Karabakh).

Universities
AZERBAIJAN MEDICAL UNIVERSITY
1022 Baku, Bakizkhanov küç. 23
Telephone: (12) 495-43-13
Fax: (12) 495-38-70
E-mail: info@amu.edu.az
Internet: amu.edu.az
Founded 1930
State control
Rector: AHLIMAN TAPDIQ AMIRASLANOV
Library of 600,000 vols
Number of teachers: 1,620
Number of students: 8,000

DEANS
Admin. for Foreign Students: Assoc. Prof. SEYIDOVA GULER MIR CAFAR
Faculty of Medicine: Assoc. Prof. ISMAYILOV TARIYEL MUSTAFA
Faculty of Pharmacology: AKHMED ŞIXEMMEDOV NURMAMMED
Faculty of Stomatology: Asst Prof. MAMMADOV RIZVAN MOHSUM OGHLU
Medico Preventive and Biology: Assoc. Prof. AYDIN M. MAMEDOV

AZERBAIJAN STATE ECONOMIC UNIVERSITY
1001 Baku, Istiqlaliyyat 6
Telephone: (12) 437-10-86
Fax: (12) 492-59-40
E-mail: aseu@aseu.az
Founded 1930, present name and status 2000
State control
Languages of instruction: Azeri, English, Russian, Turkish
Academic year: September to June
Rector: SHAMSADDIN HAJIYEV
Number of students: 15,190
Faculties of accountancy, commerce, economics, finance, informatics, international economic relations, management, world economy.

AZERBAIJAN STATE PEDAGOGICAL UNIVERSITY 'NASREDDIN TUSI'
1000 Baku, U. Hacjibeyov St 34
Telephone: (12) 493-00-32
Fax: (12) 498-89-33
Founded 1921
State control
Languages of instruction: Azeri, Russian
Pres.: BAHLUL AGAJEV
Number of students: 7,975
Faculties of Azeri language and literature, chemistry and biology, drawing and imitation arts, elementary military education and physical training, geography, history, mathematics, pedagogy and psychology, physics.

AZERBAIJAN STATE UNIVERSITY OF CULTURE AND ART
1065 Baku, Inshaatchilar küç. 9
Telephone: (12) 438-43-10
Fax: (12) 438-93-48
E-mail: info@admiu.edu.az
Internet: www.admiu.edu.az
Founded 1922 as Baku State Turkish School, present status 1945
State control
Academic year: September to July
Rector: TIMUCHIN AFENDIYEV

Vice-Rector: RAFIQ SADIQOV
Library of 80,384 vols
Number of teachers: 190
Number of students: 2,865

DEANS
Faculty of Cultural Studies: ALEKPER MAMMADOV
Faculty of Fine Arts: VEFA ALIYEV
Faculty of Management: BAYRAM HADJIYEV
Faculty of Music: VAMIG MAMMEDALIYEV
Faculty of Painting: DJABBAR HASSANOV
Faculty of Theatre and Cinema: MAMMEDSHAH ATAYEV

AZERBAIJAN UNIVERSITY OF LANGUAGES
1014 Baku, R. Behbudov küç. 60
Telephone: (12) 421-22-31
E-mail: mail@adu.edu.az
Internet: www.adu.edu.az
Founded 1937 as School of Foreign Languages, present name and status 2000
State control
Faculties of English, French, German, international relations and regional studies, Italian, Korean, Philology, Russian, Spanish, translation; 3 campuses
Chancellor: SAMAD I. SEYIDOV
Library of 532,268 vols, 24,303 e-books
Number of teachers: 700
Number of students: 4,573

AZERBAIJAN TECHNICAL UNIVERSITY
1073 Baku, Hussein Javid Ave 25
Telephone: (12) 438-33-43
Fax: (12) 438-32-80
E-mail: aztu@aztukm.baku.az
Internet: www.aztu.az
Founded 1950
State control
Languages of instruction: Azeri, Russian
Academic year: September to July
Rector: Prof. Dr HAVAR AMIR OGLU MAMMADOV
Vice-Rector for Educational Affairs: Assoc. Prof. ISA ALI OGLU KHALILOV
Vice-Rector for Education Work: Assoc. Prof. KHALIG MADJID OGLU YAHUDOV
Vice-Rector for General Affairs: Assoc. Prof. ABUZAR AGAVERDI OGLU MIRZALIYEV
Vice-Rector for Int. Relations: Assoc. Prof. ZAHID MUZAFFAR OGLU SULTANZADEH
Vice-Rector for Learning and Education: Dr K. G. YAHUDOV
Vice-Rector for Research and Devt: Prof. Dr ANAR NADIR OGLU ALIZADEH
Registrar and Chief Admin. Officer: AZIZA B. GASIMLI
Librarian: NARINGUL KHALAFOVA
Library of 700,000 vols
Number of teachers: 695
Number of students: 5,126
Publications: *Research Works* (4 a year), *Ziya* (12 a year)

DEANS
Faculty of Automation and Computing Equipment: Asst Prof. RAUF ALESKER OGLU HASANOV
Faculty of Electrotechnics and Energetics: Dr MAHIR MADJNUN OGLU BASHIROV
Faculty of Engineering Business and Management: Asst Prof. ILHAM ALIDJI OGLU ASLANZADEH
Faculty of Machine-Building: Assoc. Prof. ARASTUN SALMAN OGLU MAMMADOV
Faculty of Metallurgy: Prof. Dr AGIL ISA OGLU BABAYEV

Faculty of Radio Engineering and Communications: Prof. Dr ALSHAN NARMAN OGLU HASANOV

Faculty of Technological and Light Industry Machines: Assoc. Prof. ASIM MIRZAKHAN OGLU MIRZAYEV

Faculty of Transport: Asst Prof. FAZIL ABDULAZIM OGLU HASANOV

Foreign Students Department: Assoc. Prof. ELCHIN RAMIZ OGLU MUSTAFAYEV

PROFESSORS

Faculty of Automation and Computing Technology (tel. (12) 438-94-06):

ABILOV, C. I., Automation
ALIYEV, A. B., Higher Mathematics
ALIZADE, A. N., Applied Mathematics
ASLANOV, G. I., Higher Mathematics
BAYRAMOV, K. T., Computers and Systems
DUNYAMALIEV, M. A., Applied Mathematics
HACHIYEV, M.A., Design and Manufacture of Computers
ISKENDERZADE, Z. A., Applied Physics and Microelectronics
MAMEDOV, H. A., Automation and Control
MELIKOV, A. Z., Automation
NOVRUZBEKHOV, I. G., Applied Mathematics
RZAYEV, T. G., Automation

Faculty of Business and Management for the Engineering Industry (tel. (12) 439-13-96):

ABBASOV, M. A., History
ALIYEV, A. A., Theory of Economics
ALIYEV, A. H., Philosophy and Political Science
ALIYEV, R. Z., Physical Education and Sport
GULIYEV, R. I., Theory of Economics
HUSEYNOV, S. Y., Philosophy and Political Science
ISMAYILOV, R. A., French
JUMSHUDOV, S. Q., Economy and Management of Transportation
NACAFOV, B. I., History
RAMAZANOV, F. F., Philosophy and Political Science
SAMEDZADE, SH. A., Management, Economics and Organization

Faculty of Electrical Engineering and Energy (tel. (12) 439-12-47):

ABDALOV, S. I., Theoretical Electrical Engineering
GURBANOV, M. A., Physics
GURBANOV, T. B., Automation
LAZIMOV, T. M., Automation
NAZIYEV, Y. M., Thermal Engineering and Heating Mechanisms
SHAKHVERDIYEV, A. H., Thermal Engineering and Heating Mechanisms

Faculty of Machine-Building (tel. (12) 439-13-56):

ABBASOV, T. F., Physics
ABBASOV, V. A., Metal-cutting Machines and Tools
EFENDIYEV, SH. M., Physics
GODJAYEV, E. M., Physics
HUSEYNOV, S. O., Hydraulics
MIRZAJANOV, J. B., Machine-building Technology
MOVLAZADE, V. Z., Machine-building Technology
RASULOV, N. M., Machine-building Technology
RUSTAMOV, M. I., Metal-cutting Machines and Tools
SADYKHOV, A. H., Repair Technology of Machines

Faculty of Machine Sciences (tel. (12) 438-94-70):

ABDULLAYEV, A. H., Lift Transport Machines
BAGIROV, SH. M., Mechanical Theory
HUSEYNOV, H. A., Automated Design Systems in Machine-building

KENGERLI, A. M., Mechanical Theory
KHALILOV, A. M., Mechanical Theory
MAMMEDOV, V. A., Mechanical Theory
MUSTAFAYEV, M. R., Mechanical Theory
QAFAROV, A. M., Metrology and Standardization

Faculty of Metallurgy (tel. (12) 438-34-69):

AMIROV, S. T., Construction Materials Technology, Powder Metallurgy and Corrosion
ASKEROV, K. A., Industrial Ecology and Safety
BABAYEV, F. R., Chemistry
EYVAZOV, B. Y., Construction Materials Technology, Powder Metallurgy and Corrosion
HUSEYNOV, R. G., Construction Materials Technology, Powder Metallurgy and Corrosion
MAMEDOV, Z. G., Metallurgy and Science of Metals
MAMMEDOV, A. A., Industrial Ecology and Safety
MAMMEDOV, A. T., Metallurgy and Science of Metals
NOVRUZOV, H. D., Powder Metallurgy and Corrosion
RUSTAMOV, M. A., Chemistry
SHARIFOV, Z. Z., Powder Metallurgy and Science of Metals
SHUKUROV, R. I., Metallurgy and Science of Metals
ZAMANOVA, E. N., Physics

Faculty of Radio-Engineering and Communications (tel. (12) 438-50-13):

EFENDIYEV, C. A., Television and Radio Systems
HASANOV, A. N., Telecommunications
IMAMVERDIYEV, G. M., Electronic Communications
ISMIBEYLI, E. G., Electrodynamics and High Frequency Instruments
KENGERLI, U. S., General Theoretical Radio-Engineering
MAGARRAMOV, V. A., General Theoretical Radio-Engineering
MAMEDOV, F. H., Telecommunications
MAMEDOV, I. R., General Theoretical Radio-Engineering

Faculty of Transportation (tel. (12) 439-12-51):

AHMEDOV, H. M., Road Transport and Road Safety
BAGIROV, S. M., Automation
EFENDIYEV, V. S., Internal Combustion Engine and Refrigeration Machinery
MAKHMUDOV, R. N., Theoretical Mechanics
MIRSALIMOV, V. M., Automechanics of Materials Resistance
NASIBOV, N. E., Theoretical Mechanics
TAGIZADE, A. G., Road Transport and Road Safety

AZERBAIJAN TECHNOLOGICAL UNIVERSITY

2011 Ganja, Heydar Aliyev Ave. 103
Telephone: (22) 57-56-29
Fax: (22) 57-29-61
E-mail: info@aztu-ganja.ws
Internet: aztu-ganja.ws

Founded 1980 as Azerbaijan Technological Institute, present name and status 2000
State control
Rector: Prof. Dr MALIKOV TELMAN GULU OGLU
Dir of Library: GASANOV UMID IMRAN OQLU
Number of students: 1,713
Publications: *Scientific Messages*, *Technologist*

DEANS

Faculty of Economy and Management: Asst Prof. AGAYEVA KHALIDA MEHDI QIZI

Faculty of Foodstuff and Tourism: Asst Prof. HASANOV ARZU NAJAF OQLU
Faculty of Standardization and Technological Machines: Asst Prof. ASKAROV NAMIQ RZA OQLU
Faculty of Technology of Consumer Goods and Examination: Asst Prof. ABBASOV GARAY SURKHAI OQLU

AZERBAIJAN UNIVERSITY

1102 Baku, R. Safarov küç. 17
Telephone: (12) 430-51-79
Fax: (12) 430-49-29
E-mail: office@au.edu.az
Internet: www.au.edu.az

Founded 1991
Private control
Pres.: Prof. AKIF MUSAYEV
Vice-Rector for Gen. Affairs: AGAMALIYEV AGAMALI GULU
Vice-Rector for Science works: Prof. IBRAHIMLI XALEDDIN JALAL
Vice-Rector on Teaching Affairs: BAĞIROV MAJID HEYDAR

Library of 40,603 books
Number of teachers: 133
Number of students: 895

DEANS

Faculty of Economy and Governance: ALIZADEH AKIF VALI
Faculty of Humanities: TINAYEVA ASSIYAT KAMIL

AZERBAIJAN UNIVERSITY OF ARCHITECTURE AND CONSTRUCTION

1073 Baku, 5 A. Sultanova str.
Telephone: (12) 439-05-97
Fax: (12) 498-78-36
E-mail: info@azmiu.edu.az
Internet: www.azmiu.edu.az

Founded 1975 as construction faculty in Baku State Univ., present status 1992, present name 2000
State control
Languages of instruction: Azeri, English, Russian
Academic year: September to June (2 semesters)
Rector: Prof. Dr GULCHOHRA MAMMADOVA
Number of teachers: 632
Number of students: 6,000
Publications: *Ecology and Water Economics*, *Scientific Articles*, *Theoretical and Applied Mechanics*, *Urbanism*

DEANS

Architecture: Prof. TOFIQ ABDULLAYEV
Construction: Prof. HIKMAT MAMMADOV
Construction Economics: Prof. NAZIMA MAMMADOVA
Construction Technology: Prof. NAMIG AGHABAYLI
Mechanization and Automation: Prof. ARIF HAJIYEV
Transporation: Prof. YAGUB PIRIYEV
Water Economics and Engineering Communication Systems: Prof. ZAKIR MUSAYEV

BAKU BUSINESS UNIVERSITY

Baku, H. Zardabi St 88A
Telephone: (12) 431-79-51
Fax: (12) 430-07-80
E-mail: info@bbu.edu.az
Internet: www.bbu.edu.az

Founded 1993
Private control
Rector: Dr IBAD MUSA OGLU ABBASOV

Vice-Rector for Education: SABIR ABUZAR OGLU AMIRKHANOV
Vice-Rector for Scientific Works: AGASALIM KARIM OGLU ALASGAROV
Vice-Rector for Teaching: RAHIM FARAHIM OGLU SADIGOV

Publication: *Audit* (4 a year)

DEANS

School of Business and Management: KHATIRA CINAYEDDIN GIZI MAHMUDOVA
School of Economy and Law: AFIDA IBRAHIM GIZI HASANOVA

BAKU ISLAMIC UNIVERSITY

1000 Baku, Mirza Fatali 7
Telephone: (12) 492-82-23
E-mail: biu_qafqaz@hotmail.com
State control
Rector: Haji SABIR HASANLI.

BAKU SLAVIC UNIVERSITY

1014 Baku, Suleyman Rustam St 25
Telephone and fax (12) 440-27-70
E-mail: bakslavuniver@hotmail.com
Internet: www.bsu-edu.org
Founded 1946 as M. F. Akhundov Azerbaijan State Teacher Training Institute, present name and status 2000
State control
Rector: Prof. Dr KAMAL M. ABDULLAYEV
Vice-Rector for Education: Prof. Dr ASIF A. HAJIEV
Vice-Rector for Educational Work: Dr OKTAY A. SAMEDOV
Vice-Rector for Int. Relations: Prof. Dr SAHIBA A. GAFAROVA
Vice-Rector for Research: Prof. MAMED A. ALIYEV
Library of 500,000 vols
Number of teachers: 469
Publications: *BSU Scientific Works, Mutarjim, Russian Language and Literature in Azerbaijan* (4 a year)

DEANS

International Relations and Regional Studies Faculty: ADIL RAJABLI
Philological Faculty: Assoc. Prof. IBRAHIMPASHA A. BABAYEV
Translation Faculty: Asst Prof. SEYFEL HASANOV

BAKU STATE UNIVERSITY

1148 Baku, Academic Zahid Xalilov St 23
Telephone: (12) 430-32-45
Fax: (12) 498-33-76
E-mail: info@bsu.az
Founded 1919
Academic year: September to July
Rector: ABEL MAMMADALI MAHARRAMOV
Pro-Rector: BAKHRAM MEKHRALI ASKEROV
Pro-Rector: IZZAT ASHRAF RUSTAMOV
Pro-Rector: SHAHVALAD BINNAT KHALILOV
Pro-Rector: VUSAT AMIR EFENDIYEV
Librarian: SARA IBRAGIMOVA
Library: see Libraries and Archives
Number of teachers: 1,380
Number of students: 15,300
Publications: *Estestvennikh nauk* (4 a year), *Gumanitarnikh nauk* (4 a year), *Sotsialno-politicheskikh nauk* (4 a year), *Vestnik Bakinskogo Universiteta: Fiziko–Matematicheskikh nauk* (4 a year)
Depts of applied mathematics, biology, chemistry, commerce, geology and geography, Hebrew studies, int. law and int. relations, journalism, law, library sciences, mathematics, oriental studies, philology, philosophy and psychology, physics, preparatory studies, religion.

GANJA STATE UNIVERSITY

2000 Ganja, Shah Ismail Khatai Ave 187
Telephone: (22) 56-73-10
Internet: www.gsu.az
Founded 1938, present name and status 2000
State control
Languages of instruction: English, Russian
Academic year: September to June
Faculties of chemistry and biology, educational psychology, engineering education, foreign languages, history, mathematics and computer science, philology
Rector: Prof. ELMAN MAMMADOV
Pro-Rector: Dr ASIF CAVADOV
Pro-Rector: FAKRADDIN HASANOV
Pro-Rector: Dr NADIR IBADOV
Pro-Rector: Prof. SALEH SALAHOV
Number of teachers: 554
Number of students: 4,500

KHAZAR UNIVERSITY

370096 Baku, Mehseti St 11
Telephone: (12) 421-10-93
Fax: (12) 498-93-79
E-mail: ashadlinskaya@khazar.org
Internet: www.khazar.org
Founded 1991
Private control
Languages of instruction: Azeri, English, Russian
Academic year: September to June
Pres.: Prof. Dr HAMLET ISAKHANLI
Vice-Pres.: Prof. MOHAMMAD NOURIYEV
Library of 60,000 vols, 87 periodicals
Number of teachers: 200
Number of students: 1,700
Publications: *Azerbaijani Archaeology* (4 a year), *Journal of Azerbaijani Studies* (4 a year), *Khazar Journal of Mathematics*, *Khazar View* (literary and scientific, 24 a year)

DEANS

School of Architecture, Engineering and Applied Science: Assoc. Prof. RAFIG M. AHMADOV
School of Economics and Management: Prof. MAHAMMAD N. NURIYEV
School of Education: ELZA SAMADOVA
School of Humanities and Social Sciences: (vacant)
School of Law: Prof. JABIR Z. KHALILOV
School of Medicine, Dentistry and Public Health: Assoc. Prof. NIGAR ILYASOVNA BAGIROVA

LANKARAN STATE UNIVERSITY

4200 Lankaran, Pr. Azi Aslanov 50
Telephone: (171) 5-25-88
Fax: (171) 5-27-86
E-mail: office@lsu.edu.az
Internet: www.lsu.edu.az
Founded 1991
State control
Faculties of economics, humanities, natural sciences
Rector: ASAF ISKENDEROV
Number of students: 1,369

NAKHCHIVAN STATE UNIVERSITY

7012 Nakhchivan, Mardanov Gardashlari 99
Telephone: (12) 94-99-97
Fax: (12) 95-93-29
E-mail: rector@ndu.edu.az
Internet: www.ndu.edu.az

Founded 1967 as Nakhchivan br. of Azerbaijan State Pedagogical Institute
State control
Language of instruction: Azerbaijani
Academic year: September to July
Rector: Prof. Dr ISA HABBIBBEYLI
Vice-Rector for Admin. and Economy Affairs: ARAZ IBRAHIM ZALOV
Vice-Rector for Educational Affairs: Prof. Dr MAMMAD HUSEYN OGLU RZAYEV
Vice-Rector for Scientific Affairs: Prof. Dr ANAR ALTAY KAZIMOV
Vice-Rector for Teaching Affairs: Prof. HUSEYN MAMMAD OGLU HASHIMLI
Head of Library: PARVIN YAGUB GIZI ALIYEVA
Library of 151,000 vols
Number of teachers: 450
Number of students: 4,000
Publication: *Scientific Works*

DEANS

Architecture: Dr MUBARIZ NURIYEV
Art: Dr ISMAYIL MURSELOV
Economy: Prof. Dr ASIF SHIRALIYEV
History and Philology: Dr IMAN JAFAROV
Int. Relations and Foreign Languages: Dr GURBAN GURBANLI
Law: Dr GARIB ALLAHVERDIYEV
Medical: Dr BAHRUZ MAMMADOV
Nature Study: Dr AKIF MARDANLI
Pedagogy: Dr IBRAHIM RUSTEMOV
Physics and Mathematics: Dr TOFIG NAJAFOV

ODLAR YURDU UNIVERSITY

1072 Baku, Koroglu Rahimov St 13
Telephone: (12) 465-82-00
Fax: (12) 465-67-05
E-mail: fuadhud@yahoo.com
Internet: www.oyu.edu.az
Founded 1995
Private control
Rector: Dr AHMAD VALIYEV
Vice-Rector for Academic Affairs: SAMIR VALIYEV
Vice-Rector for Academic Affairs: FAIK NAGIYEV
Vice-Rector for Financial Issues: MUNIR VALIYEV
Vice-Rector for Int. Relations: RUSLAN SADIRKHANOV
Vice-Rector for Medical Qualifications: AKIF SALEHOV
Library of 50,000 vols

Depts of business and management, engineering ecology, medicine, translations and pedagogics.

QAFQAZ UNIVERSITY

0101 Baku, Sumqayit Rd 16 km, Xirdalan
Telephone: (12) 448-28-62
Fax: (12) 448-28-61
E-mail: info@qafqaz.edu.az
Internet: www.qafqaz.edu.az
Founded 1993
Private control
Academic year: October to June
Rector: Prof. Dr AHMET SANIÇ
Vice-Rector: Assoc. Prof CIHAN BULUT
Vice-Rector: Dr M. MURAT ERGUVAN
Vice-Rector: Dr NIFTAH QOCAYEV
Vice-Rector: Dr ŞAIQ NEBIYEV
Vice-Rector: Dr TAYYAR MUSTAFAYEV
Dir for Library: MEHMET ALI CEYHAN

DEANS

Faculty of Economic and Administrative Sciences: Assoc. Prof. HEZI EYNALOV
Faculty of Engineering: Prof. HEMZAĞA ORUCOV
Faculty of Law: Assoc. Prof. MÜBARIZ YOLÇIYEV

Faculty of Pedagogy: Assoc. Prof. ERDAL KARAMAN

Other Higher Educational Institutes

Azerbaijan Agricultural Institute: 2000 Ganca, Azizbekova küç. 262; tel. (22) 2-10-64; depts of agrochemistry and soil science, agronomy, fruit and vegetable growing, viticulture; animal husbandry, veterinary science, silkworm breeding; mechanization, electrification, economics and management, accounting; library: 200,000 vols; Rector N. A. SAFAROV.

Azerbaijan State Academy for Physical Training and Sports: 1072 Baku, 98 Fatali Khan Khoyski; tel. (12) 498-47-31; fax (12) 493-86-17; e-mail agacanbox@mail.ru; f. 1930; State control; languages of instruction: Azeri, Russian; faculties of physical education, sports; 3,589 students; Rector AGADJAN ABIYEV.

Azerbaijan State Marine Academy: 1000 Baku, Pr. Azerbaijan 18; tel. (12) 493-09-19; fax (12) 493-86-17; e-mail agma@azerin.com; f. 1881; State control; languages of instruction: Azeri, Russian; library: 90,000 vols; 55 doctoral staff; 350 students; Pres. SAMBUR HAMDULLAH.

Azerbaijan State Oil Academy: 1010 Baku, Pr. Azadlyg 20; tel. (12) 493-45-57; fax (12) 498-29-41; e-mail ihm@adna.baku .az; internet www.adna.baku.az; f. 1920; faculties of automation of production, chemical technology, engineering economics, oil and gas exploitation, oil mechanical engineering, power engineering; brs in Sumqayıt and Mingaçevir; library: 860,000 vols; 870 teachers; 6,232 students; Rector S. QARAYEV.

Uzeir Hajibeyov Baku Academy of Music: 1014 Baku, Shamsi Badalbeyli 98; tel. (12) 493-22-48; fax (12) 498-13-30; f. 1920; courses: choral conducting, composition, folk instruments, musicology, orchestral instruments, piano, singing; library: 220,000 vols and 25,000 scores; 290 lecturers; 630 students; Rector F. SH. BADALBEYLI.

BAHAMAS

The Higher Education System

The Bahamas is a contributing country to the University of the West Indies (UWI). The UWI Centre for Hotel and Tourism Management is located in Nassau. Other institutions of higher education include the College of the Bahamas (a community college) and Bahamas Law School (part of the UWI). The Ministry of Education is responsible for education and in 2004 it created the Department of Higher Education and Lifelong Learning, which is responsible for tertiary education and quality assurance. To gain admission to degree programmes students must have at least two GCE A-level subjects or equivalent. Available degrees include Associates, Bachelors, Masters and Doctorates. Associate degrees are taken after GCE O-levels and last for two years. Bachelors degrees last for three years, and Masters degrees last for two years after the Bachelors. A Doctorate takes a further two years after the Masters degree. Associate degrees are mostly available at the College of the Bahamas.

In 2002 there were 3,463 students registered at the College of the Bahamas.

Regulatory Body

GOVERNMENT

Ministry of Education: Thompson Blvd, POB N-3913, Nassau; tel. 502-2700; fax 322-8491; e-mail info@moe.gov.bs; internet moe.gov.bs; Min. DESMOND BANNISTER.

Ministry of Youth, Sports and Culture: Nassau; Minister THOMAS DESMOND BANNISTER.

Learned Societies

GENERAL

Bahamas National Trust: POB N-4105, Nassau; tel. 393-1317; fax 393-2548; e-mail bnt@bnt.bs; internet www.bnt.bs; f. 1959; preservation of bldgs, wildlife and areas of beauty or historic interest; manages 21 nat. parks and protected areas; 2,500 mems; Exec. Dir CHRISTOPHER HAMILTON (acting); publ. *Trust Notes* (6 a year).

HISTORY, GEOGRAPHY AND ARCHAEOLOGY

Bahamas Historical Society: POB SS-6833, Nassau-New Providence; tel. 322-4231; e-mail info@bahamashistoricalsociety.com; internet www.bahamashistoricalsociety.com; f. 1959; 400 mems; collection and preservation of material relating to the history of the Bahamas; Pres. STEPHEN B. ARANHA; Corresp. Sec. JOAN CLARKE; publ. *Bahamas Historical Journal* (1 a year).

LANGUAGE AND LITERATURE

Alliance Française: Suite 60, Grosvernor Close, Shirley St, POB CB-13002, Nassau-New Providence; tel. 356-0961; fax 326-5662; internet alliance-bahamas.com; offers courses and examinations in French language and culture and promotes cultural exchange with France.

Libraries and Archives

Freeport

Sir Charles Hayward Public Lending Library: POB F-40040, Freeport, Grand Bahama; f. 1966; 40,000 vols; Librarian ELAINE B. TALMA.

Nassau

College of the Bahamas–Libraries and Instructional Media Services: POB N-4912, Nassau; tel. 302-4552; fax 326-7803; e-mail library@cob.edu.bs; f. 1974; 75,000 vols; spec. collns incl. Bahamiana, Caribbean dissertations; document delivery and inter-library loans; deposit collns of the UN, WHO and Pan-American Health Organization; Dir WILLAMAE M. JOHNSON; publ. *Library Informer*.

Department of Archives: POB SS-6341, Nassau; tel. 393-2175; fax 393-2855; e-mail archives@batelnet.bs; internet www.bahamasnationalarchives.bs; f. 1971; nat. archival depository; 2,689 linear ft of records; Govt record centre records management, research centre appraisals, conservation and preservation microfilming information technology; Dir M. ELAINE TOOTE; publ. *Preservum* (every 2 years).

Nassau Public Library: POB N-3210, Nassau; f. 1837; 80,000 vols; Dir (vacant).

Museum

Nassau

Bahamia Museum: POB N-1510, Nassau.

Colleges

College of the Bahamas: Thompson Blvd, POB N-4912, Nassau; tel. 323-8550; fax 326-7834; internet www.cob.edu.bs; f. 1974; 4-year college; assoc. degrees in arts, natural and social sciences, business, technology, nursing, teaching; Bachelors degrees in banking and finance, management, accounting, nursing, education; continuing education; 160 teachers; 3,463 students; library: 68,000 vols; Pres. Dr LEON HIGGS; publs *At Random* (1 a year), *COBLA Journal* (2 a year), *College Forum* (2 a year).

University of the West Indies (Bahamas Office): POB N-1184, Nassau; tel. 323-6593; fax 328-0622; e-mail matwilliam@hotmail.com; f. 1965; Representative MATTHEW WILLIAM.

BAHRAIN

The Higher Education System

The University of Bahrain was founded in 1986 by Amiri decree as a merger between University College of Arts, Science and Education and Gulf Polytechnic. The other main institutions of higher education are the College of Health Sciences, founded in 1976, the Arabian Gulf University, founded in 1980 as a joint venture between six (now seven) Arab Governments and the Gulf College of Hospitality and Tourism. Some 29,678 students were enrolled in higher education in 2006/07 and in 2009 about 13,000 students were enrolled at the University of Bahrain alone.

In 2009 there were 12 private tertiary education providers registered with the Higher Education Council. These are a combination of institutions which are wholly owned locally, institutions that have international partners, and institutions that are campuses of universities located in other countries.

Admission to higher education is based on a test score of 70% or higher in the Tawjihiya examinations. The main undergraduate qualifications are the Associate and Bachelors degrees, whilst the main postgraduate qualifications are the Masters degree, Doctorate, and Postgraduate Diploma. The undergraduate degrees are based on the US credits system: Associate degrees last for two years and require 60–70 credits, and Bachelors degrees are four years in length and require 130–140 credits. The Masters degree and Postgraduate Diploma are based on the British Masters degree, and last for two to four years, with an equal division between taught classes and research. Finally, the Doctorate, usually PhD, requires three to five years of full-time study and research. All Bahraini students studying abroad are required to have their degrees submitted for recognition by the Commission for the Evaluation of Academic Degrees. A Quality Assurance Authority affiliated to the Higher Education Council has recently been put into place.

Non-university level education is offered at the University of Bahrain in the form of two-year diploma courses in a number subjects. The admissions criteria are the same as those for a full degree course. The College of Health Sciences offers Certificates, Associate degrees, Post-basic diplomas and Bachelors degrees in mostly medical-related subjects. Vocational and technical training is also offered at the Bahrain Training Institute, the Hotel and Catering Training Centre and the Vocational and Training Centre (the latter being run by the Ministry for Labour and Social Affairs).

From the mid-2000s the implantation of branches of foreign universities gathered pace in Bahrain. For example, construction of the Royal College of Surgeons, within Ireland Medical University of Bahrain at Muharraq, was completed in 2008. Plans to establish a Higher Education City were put into place in 2006. The development was scheduled to become operational by 2011. It was to include a full branch of a leading US university, an international research centre and a specialist academy.

In line with Bahrain's Economic Vision – 2030, in 2008 a Quality Assurance Authority (QAA) affiliated to the Higher Education Council was put into place. It had four main monitoring units: the Schools Review Unit, the Vocational Review Unit, the Higher Education Review Unit and the National Examinations Unit. The QAA is one of the key initiatives of the National Education Reform Initiatives, which aim to develop the education system at all levels. The Initiatives also included the establishment of Bahrain Teacher's College and of Bahrain Polytechnic and the creation of a School Improvement Programme. The Higher Education Review Unit does not have the authority to license or accredit university programmes but it does issue institutional quality review reports on degree programmes from private universities.

Regulatory Body

GOVERNMENT

Ministry of Education: POB 43, Manama; tel. 17680105; fax 17687866; e-mail dir .relations@moe.gov.bh; internet www .education.gov.bh; Minister Dr MAJID BIN ALI AN-NO'AIMI.

ACCREDITATION

Quality Assurance Authority: Bahrain; tel. 17583330; e-mail talsindi@batelco.com .bh; f. 2008; affiliated to Higher Education Ccl; Dir TARIQ ALSINDI.

Learned Societies

ECONOMICS, LAW AND POLITICS

Bahrain Bar Society: POB 5025, Manama; tel. 17720566; fax 17721219; f. 1977; 65 mems; Pres. HASSAN ALI RADHI; publ. *Al Muhami*.

FINE AND PERFORMING ARTS

Bahrain Arts Society: POB 26264, Manama; tel. 17590551; fax 17594211; e-mail info@bahrainartssociety.net; internet www .bahrainartssociety.com; f. 1983; promotes fine arts of Bahrain nationally and internationally; incl. a school of fine arts and art gallery, and the official photography club;

184 mems; library: small library; Pres. ALI AL-MAHMEED.

Bahrain Contemporary Art Association: POB 26232, Manama; tel. 17728046; fax 17723341; e-mail alsaariart@hotmail.com; f. 1970; holds exhibitions; 60 mems; library of 250 vols; Pres. RASHID AL-ORAFI; Dir ABDUL KARIM AL-ORRAYED; Information Officer SAYED HASSAN AL SAARI.

HISTORY, GEOGRAPHY AND ARCHAEOLOGY

Bahrain Historical and Archaeological Society: POB 5087, Manama; tel. 17727895; f. 1953; 143 mems; library: reference library; Pres. Dr ESSA AMIN; Hon. Sec. Dr KHALID KHALIFA; publ. *Dilmun* (2 a year).

LANGUAGE AND LITERATURE

Alliance Française: POB 840, Manama; tel. 17683295; fax 17781137; e-mail info@ afbahrain.com; internet www.afbahrain.com; f. 1969; offers courses and exams in French language and culture and promotes cultural exchange with France; library of 5,000 French books, CDs and DVDs.

Bahrain Writers and Literature Association: POB 1010, Manama; tel. 17274866; f. 1969; 40 mems; library of 700 vols; Pres. ALI AL-SHARGAWI; Sec. FAREED RAMADAN.

British Council: AMA Centre, 146, Shaikh Salman Highway, Manama 356, POB 452;

tel. 17261555; fax 17252269; e-mail bc .enquiries@britishcouncil.org.bh; internet www.britishcouncil.org/me-bahrain.htm; office opened 1959; attached teaching centre; offers courses and exams in English language and British culture and promotes cultural exchange with the UK; library of 9,000 vols; Dir AMANDA BURRELL.

MEDICINE

Bahrain Medical Society: POB 26136, Adliya; tel. 17827818; fax 17827814; f. 1972; 350 mems; library of 300 vols; Pres. Dr ALI MOHD MATAR; Gen. Sec. Dr FAISAL A. ALNASIR; publ. *Journal* (4 a year).

RELIGION, SOCIOLOGY AND ANTHROPOLOGY

Bahrain Society of Sociologists: POB 26488, Manama; tel. 17826309; fax 17727485; f. 1979; 65 mems; library of 423 vols; Pres. Dr AHMED AL-SHARYAN; Sec.-Gen. EBRAHIM ALALAWI.

Islamic Association: POB 22484, Manama; tel. 17671788; fax 17676718; e-mail islamyia@islamyia.org; internet www .islamyia.org; f. 1979; teaches the Qur'an, Fiqh, Hadith, Sunnah; distributes zakat and donations; 200 mems; Pres. Dr ABDULATIF MAHMOUD AL-MAHMOUD.

TECHNOLOGY

Bahrain Information Technology Society: POB 26089, Manama; Villa 6, Gate 1334, Rd 3729, Manama 337; tel. 17741770; fax 17919995; e-mail bits@batelco.com.bh; internet www.bits.org.bh; f. 1981; promotes information technology in the kingdom; 260 mems; Pres. ABDULNABI A. KAL AWADH.

Bahrain Society of Engineers: POB 835, Manama; tel. 17727100; fax 17729819; e-mail mohandis@batelco.com.bh; internet www .mohandis.org; f. 1972; 1,350 mems; Pres. A. MAJEED AL GASSAB; Exec. Man. JAFFAR Y. ALSAMEIKH; publ. *Al-Mohandis* (4 a year).

Research Institute

NATURAL SCIENCES

General

Bahrain Centre for Studies and Research: POB 496, Manama; tel. 17754757; fax 17754678; internet www.bcsr .gov.bh; f. 1981; scientific study and research in economics, politics and strategy, marketing and consumer behaviour, social, educational and tourism studies, int. and inter-civilization studies; library of 6,000 vols, 40 periodicals; Sec.-Gen. Dr HASAN MAHMOOD AL-BASTAKI; publs *Arab Magazine for Food and Nutrition* (2 a year), *Journal of Strategic Research* (irregular).

Libraries and Archives

Isa Town

University of Bahrain Libraries and Information Services: POB 32038, Isa Town; tel. 17838808; fax 17449838; e-mail library@admin.uob.bh; internet libwebserver .uob.edu.bh/assets; f. 1986; 150,000 vols, 700 periodicals; Dir HEDI TALBI.

Manama

Ahmed Al-Farsi Library (College of Health Sciences): POB 12, Manama; tel. 17255555 ext. 5202; fax 17242485; internet www.chs.edu.bh/library; f. 1976; serves Min. of Health staff, also public and reference service; 29,000 vols, 545 periodicals, 375 audiovisual items; Librarian ABBAS AL-KHA-TEM.

Educational Documentation Library: POB 43, Manama; tel. 17710599; fax 17710376; e-mail edudoc@batelco.com.bh; internet www.education.gov.bh/english/ edu-library; f. 1976; part of Min. of Education; 22,000 vols, 197 periodicals, 300 files of documents; Chief Officer FAIQA SAEED AL-SALEH; publs *Acquisitions List* (12 a year), *Bibliographical Lists* (1 a year), *Educational Index of Arabic Periodicals*, *Educational Index of Foreign Periodicals*, *Educational Indicative Abstracts* (3 a year), *Educational Information Abstracts* (3 a year), *Educational Legislation Index*, *Educational Selective Articles* (6 a year).

Historical Documents Centre: POB 28882, Manama; tel. 17664454; fax 17651050; f. 1978; attached to the Crown Prince's Court; maintains historical documents and MSS on the history of Bahrain and the Gulf; 4,000 vols; Pres. SHAIKH ABDULLAH BIN KHALID AL-KHALIFA; Dir Dr ALI ABA-HUSSAIN; publ. *Al-Watheeka* (2 a year).

Manama Central Library: c/o Ministry of Education, POB 43, Manama; tel. 17231105; fax 17274036; e-mail libman@batelco.com.bh; f. 1946; 171,622 vols, 734 periodicals, 1,475 cassettes; Dir of Public Libraries MANSOOR

MOHAMED SARHAN; publ. *Bahrain National Bibliography* (every 4 years).

Museum

Manama

Bahrain National Museum: Ministry of Information, Culture and National Heritage Sector, Museum Directorate, POB 2199, Manama; tel. 17298777; fax 17297871; e-mail musbah@batelco.com.bh; internet www.info.gov.bh/en/culturenationalheritage/ bahrainnationalmuseum; f. 1970; archaeology, ethnography, natural history, art; Dir ABDUL RAHMAN MUSAMAH.

Universities

AHLIA UNIVERSITY

POB 10878, Manama
Telephone: 17298999
Fax: 17290083
E-mail: info@ahlia.edu.bh
Internet: www.ahlia.edu.bh
Private
Founded 2001
Pres.: Prof. ABDULLA Y. AL-HAWAJ
Vice-Pres. for Admin. and Finance: Prof. WAJEEH EL-ALI
Number of students: 1,836
Colleges of arts, science and education; business and finance; engineering; graduate studies and research; information technology; medical and health sciences.

BAHRAIN AMA INTERNATIONAL UNIVERSITY

POB 18041, Salmabad
Telephone: 17787978
Fax: 17879380
E-mail: amaiu@batelco.com.bh
Internet: www.amaiu.edu.bh
Private
Founded 2002
Dir: Dr MARIE REDINA VICTORIA
Registrar: NOLY MANZANO
Librarian: RICHELLE AFINIDAD

DEANS

College of Business Administration: MANOLO ANTO
College of Computer Studies and Engineering: Dr RAMON J. CABIGAO
College of International Studies: Dr ROY TUMANENG

APPLIED SCIENCE UNIVERSITY

POB 5055, Jufair
Telephone: 17728777
Fax: 17728915
E-mail: info@asu.edu.bh
Internet: www.asu.edu.bh
Private
Founded 2004
Pres.: Prof. WAHEEB AHMED AL-KHAJAH.

ARABIAN GULF UNIVERSITY

POB 26671, Manama
Telephone: 17239999
Fax: 17272555
Internet: www.agu.edu.bh
Founded 1980 by the 7 Gulf States
Academic year: September to June
Languages of instruction: Arabic, English

Pres.: Dr KHALID BIN ABDUL-RAHMAN AL OHALY
Dir for Admin. and Financial Affairs: HISHAM ALI AL ANSARI
Head of Personnel Affairs: GHADA ABDULLA AL BOHLASA
Head of Student Affairs: Dr MONA ABDUL AZIZ AL KHALIFA
Registrar: Dr ABDUL HAMEED MARHOON
Librarian: SUAD ALI AL-KHALIFA
Number of teachers: 81
Number of students: 3,623
Publications: *AGU Annual Catalogue*, *Journal of Scientific Research* (3 a year)

DEANS

College of Applied Sciences: (vacant)
College of Education: Prof. FATHI ABD-EL RAHIM (acting)
College of Medicine and Medical Sciences: Prof. FAZAL KARIM DAR
College of Postgraduate Studies: Prof. WALEED KHALIL ZUBARI

PROFESSORS

AD-DIN, M. N., Microbiology
AKBAR, M. M.
AL-AAQIB, AR-R., Water Engineering, Energy
AL-ABADIN, M. Z., Physiology
AL-DIN, N. A.
AL-KHOLY, U.
AL-ANSARI, M. J.
AL-QAISI, K. A., Botany, Algae
ASH-SHAZALI, H., Paediatrics
BANDARANAYAKE, R. C.
BOTTA, G.
FULEIHAN, F., Internal Medicine
GRANGULY, P. K.
GRANT, N. I.
GREALLY, J.
HAMDY, H.
ISSA, A. A.
KHADER, M. H. A., Organic Chemistry
MATHUR, V., Pharmacology
MATHUR, V. S.
NASSER, A. I., Mechanical Engineering
NAYAR, U.
PRASAD, K.
RAHIM, F. AS-A. A., Education and Psychology
RAKHA, I., General Surgery, Orthopaedics
SACHDEVA, U.
SATIR, A. A.
SKERMAN, J. H.

DELMON UNIVERSITY FOR SCIENCE AND TECHNOLOGY

POB 2469, Manama
Telephone: 17294400
Fax: 17292010
E-mail: info@delmon.bh
Internet: www.delmonuniversity.com
Founded 2004
Private
Pres.: Dr HASSAN M. AL-QUADHI
Vice-Pres. for Academic Affairs: Prof. Dr SAAD Z. DARWISH
Dean of Student Affairs: Dr HISHAM OBAIDA
Faculties of economics and administrative sciences, information technology and computer science, law.

GULF UNIVERSITY

POB 26489, Sanad
Telephone: 17620092
Fax: 17692879
E-mail: info@gulfuniversity.net
Internet: www.gulfuniversity.net
Private
Founded 2001
Pres.: Dr MONA RASHID AL-ZAYANI

Vice-Pres. for Admin. and Finance: MOHANNED AL-ANNI
Colleges of business, management and finance, computer engineering sciences, education, engineering, law.

KINGDOM UNIVERSITY

POB 40434, Manama
Telephone: 17238899
Fax: 17271001
E-mail: info@ku.edu.bh
Internet: www.ku.edu.bh
Founded 2001
Private control
Languages of instruction: Arabic, English
Academic year: September to August
Colleges of arts, business and finance, computer and information, engineering, law
Pres.: Dr YOUSEF ABDUL GHAFFAR
Librarian: MOHAMMED AZAHIM SALDEEN
Librarian: HAMDY GHONAIM
Library of 3,250 vols, 20 periodicals
Number of teachers: 35 full-time, 15 part-time, 12 visiting
Number of students: 1,200

DEANS

College of Arts: Dr HANY ALBATAL
College of Business Sciences and Finance: Dr WALEED ABDUL AZIZ
College of Computing and Information Technology: Prof. MUSTAFA ABDUL ATHEEM
College of Engineering: Dr SAMI ALI KAMEL
College of Law: Dr MOHAMMED AL-HITI

ROYAL COLLEGE OF SURGEONS IN IRELAND MEDICAL UNIVERSITY OF BAHRAIN

POB 15503, Adliya
Telephone: 17351450
Fax: 17330806
E-mail: info@rcsi-mub.com
Internet: www.rcsi-mub.com
State; attached to constituent univ. of Royal College of Surgeons, Ireland
Founded 2004

Pres.: Prof. KEVIN O'MALLEY.

ROYAL UNIVERSITY FOR WOMEN

POB 37400, West Riffa
Telephone: 17764444
Fax: 17764445
E-mail: info@ruw.edu.bh
Internet: www.ruw.edu.bh
Founded 2005
Private
Pres.: Prof. MAZIN JUMAH
Librarian: BINDHU NAIR
Library of 10,000 print vols, 21,000 electronic vols, 5,000 periodicals, 100,000 art images

DEANS

Faculty of Art, Design and Computing Science: Dr Z. HADDAD
Faculty of Business Studies: Dr Q. ALI
Faculty of Education: (vacant)

UNIVERSITY OF BAHRAIN

POB 32038, Isa Town
Telephone: 17439996
Internet: www.uob.edu.bh
Founded 1986 by merger of Univ. College of Arts, Science and Education, and Gulf Polytechnic
Autonomous control
Language of instruction: Arabic
Academic year: October to August
Chair. of Bd of Trustees: THE MINISTER OF EDUCATION
Pres.: Dr IBRAHIM MOHAMMED JANAHI
Vice-Pres. for Academic Programmes and Research: Dr NIZAR AL-BAHARNA
Vice-Pres. for Admin. and Finance: Dr SAMIR FAKHRO
Vice-Pres. for Planning and Community Service: Dr GEORGE NAJJAR
Registrar: Dr ISA AL-KHAYAT
Dir of Library and Information Services: WARWICK PRICE
Library: see Libraries and Archives
Number of teachers: 320
Number of students: 6,760

DEANS

College of Arts: (vacant)
College of Business: HAMEEDA JASSIM ABDULLA ABU HUSSAIN
College of Education: KHALIL YOUSIF SULAIMAN ALKHALILI
College of Engineering: NADER MOHAMMED SALEH ALBASTAKI
College of Information Technology: (vacant)
College of Science: HAIFA ALI RASHED AL-MASKATI

Colleges

College of Health Sciences: POB 12, Ministry of Health, Bahrain; tel. 17279664; fax 17251360; e-mail ayousif1@health.gov.bh; internet www.chs.edu.bh; f. 1976; divs of allied health, English, integrated science, nursing; Educational Devt Centre; library: see entry for Ahmed Al-Farsi Library; 111 teachers; Dean Dr SHAWKI ABDULLA AMEEN; Head of Registration and Student Affairs ALI EBRAHIM AL-SAEED; Librarian (Ahmed Al-Farsi Library) ABBAS A. AL-KHATAM.

Gulf College of Hospitality and Tourism: POB 22088, Muharraq; tel. 17320191; fax 17332547; e-mail mancat5@batelco.com.bh; internet www.gulf-college.com; f. 1976; higher nat. diploma and degree courses in hospitality management and travel and tourism; library: 10,000 vols; Dean TONY SPICER; Dir DAVID PATTERSON.

University College of Bahrain: POB 55040, Manama; tel. 17790828; fax 17793858; e-mail ealkhalifa@ucb.edu.bh; internet www.ucb.edu.bh; Private; Pres. Dr KHALID BIN MOHAMMED AL-KHALIFA; Exec. Dir Dr EBRAHIM BIN KHALID AL-KHALIFA; Registrar ISAM AHMED AL-SARAF; Librarian MOUSSA HARB; Schools of business, information technology, media and communication.

BANGLADESH

The Higher Education System

In 2008 there were 26 public and 56 private higher education institutions recognized by the University Grants Commission (UGC). Some 207,577 students were enrolled in universities and 241,336 in technical and vocational institutes. Both public and private universities are governed by the UGC, founded by an Act of Parliament in 1973; private universities are also subject to the Private Universities Act (1992). The Government accounts for 95% of university funding, with the rest coming from students' tuition fees and other compulsory fees. There are four categories of university: General, Special, Open and Affiliating. The President and/or Prime Minister of Bangladesh acts as the Chancellor of a university and appoints the Vice-Chancellors and the academic and executive heads of the universities. The Syndicate is the university's executive body. Its decisions are ratified by the Senate, a board that also approves the accounts. The Academic Council of a university consists of professors and other teaching representatives. Deans of Faculty are either elected by the faculty or appointed by the Academic Council, depending on the institution in question. Most public universities are modelled on the University of London (United Kingdom), consisting of a central department with affiliated colleges and institutions.

Admission is based on completion of 12 years' general education, receipt of the Higher Secondary Certificate, or equivalent, and success in entrance examinations. The main university degrees are the Bachelors, Masters and Doctor of Philosophy. Bachelors degrees from affiliated colleges of public universities are known as 'Pass' degrees and are three years in length; Bachelors degrees from public universities are known as 'Honours' degrees and last four years. Most private universities have adopted the US-style 'major' and 'minor' subject system with a Grade Point Average grading system. A Masters degree requires two years of further study after a 'Pass' degree, and one year after an 'Honours' degree. The Doctorate requires three years of further study and research.

There is a formal system of Islamic education, consisting of a two-year Fazil, roughly equivalent to the Bachelors, and the two-year Kamil, equivalent to the Masters. Students are examined in fields such as Arabic, Hadith and Tafsir (Koranic interpretation). Technical and vocational education is overseen by the Bangladesh Technical Education Board (BTEB). There are three levels of technician award: SSC, HSC and Diploma. The BTEB also administers a four-year diploma.

There is no formal system of accreditation and quality assurance, and institutions are not legally obliged to seek quality assurance. However, there are legislative plans to establish an Accreditation Council, although as of late 2009 this was still in the planning stage.

Regulatory and Representative Bodies

GOVERNMENT

Ministry of Cultural Affairs: Bangladesh Secretariat, Dhaka 1000; tel. (2) 9570667; fax (2) 7169008; e-mail sas-moca@mailcity.com; internet www.moca.gov.bd; Adviser AYUB QUADRI.

Ministry of Education: Bangladesh Secretariat, Bhaban 6, 17th–18th Floors, Dhaka 1000; tel. (2) 7168711; fax (2) 7167577; e-mail info@moedu.gov.bd; internet www.moedu.gov.bd; Minister NURUL ISLAM NAHID; Sec. SYED ATAUR RAHMAN.

FUNDING

University Grants Commission of Bangladesh: Agargaon, Dhaka 1207; tel. (2) 8112629; fax (2) 8122948; e-mail chairmanugc@yahoo.com; internet www.ugc.gov.bd; f. 1973; supervises, maintains, promotes and co-ordinates univ. education; also responsible for maintaining standard and quality in all the public and private univs in Bangladesh; assesses the needs of the public univs in terms of funding and advises Govt on various issues related to higher education; Chair. Prof. NAZRUL ISLAM; Sec. M. KHALED.

NATIONAL BODIES

Association of Universities of Bangladesh (AUB): House 47, Road 10/A, Dhanmondi R/A, Dhaka 1209; tel. (2) 8126101; fax (2) 8126101; e-mail vc-iu@kushtia.com; coordinates activities of all 17 public univs in Bangladesh and liaises with the Govt and the Univ. Grants Comm. in admin. and financial matters; Chair. MUHAMMAD MUSTA-FIZUR RAHMAN; Exec. Sec. S. M. SAIFUDDIN.

Bangaldesh Bureau of Educational Information and Statistics (BANBEIS): 1 Sonargaon Rd, Dhaka 1205; tel. (2) 9665457; e-mail banbeis@bdcom.com; internet www.banbeis.gov.bd; f. 1977; attached to Ministry of Education.

Learned Societies

GENERAL

Society of Arts, Literature and Welfare: Society Park, K. C. Dey Rd, Chittagong; f. 1942; 500 mems; Gen. Sec. NESAR AHMED CHOWDHURY.

UNESCO Office Dhaka: GPOB 57, Dhaka 1207; IDB Bhaban, 16th Fl., E/8-A Rokeya Sharani, Sher-e-Bangla Nagar, Dhaka 1207; tel. (2) 9862073; fax (2) 9871150; e-mail dhaka@unesco.org; internet www.unescodhaka.org; Dir MALAMA MELEISEA.

BIBLIOGRAPHY, LIBRARY SCIENCE AND MUSEOLOGY

Bangladesh Association of Librarians, Information Scientists and Documentalists: CDL, House 67/B, Rd 9/A, Dhanmandi R/A, Dhaka 1209; tel. (2) 8856000; e-mail mmr@northsouth.edu; internet www.balid.org; f. 1986; library professional devt; runs courses in library and information sciences; 550 mems; library of 2,000 vols; Chair. Dr MUHAMMAD MOSTAFIZUR RAHMAN; Sec.-Gen. Dr MUHAMMAD HANIF UDDIN; publ. Informatics (4 a year).

ECONOMICS, LAW AND POLITICS

Bangladesh Bureau of Statistics: E-27/A, Agargaon, Sher-e-Bangla Nagar, Dhaka 1207; tel. (2) 9118045; fax (2) 9111064; e-mail dg@bbs.gov.bd; internet www.bbs.gov.bd; f. 1971; colln, analysis and publ. of statistics covering all sectors of soc. and the economy; Dir-Gen. A. Y. M. EKRAMUL HOQUE; publs Child Nutrition Survey (1 a year), Foreign Trade Statistics (1 a year), Labour Force Survey (1 a year), Statistical Bulletin (12 a year), Statistical Pocket Book (1 a year), Statistical Yearbook (1 a year), Yearbook of Agricultural Statistics (1 a year).

Bangladesh Economic Association: 4/C Eskaton Garden Rd, Dhaka; tel. and fax (2) 9345996; e-mail bea.dhaka@gmail.com; f. 1958; Pres. Dr QAZI KHOLIQUZZAMAN AHMAD; Sec.-Gen. Dr ABUL BARKAT.

LANGUAGE AND LITERATURE

Alliance Française: 26 Mirpur Rd, Dhanmandi, Dhaka 1205; tel. (2) 9675249; fax (2) 8616462; e-mail alliance@afdacca.com; internet www.afdacca.org; offers courses and exams in French language and culture and promotes cultural exchange with France; attached teaching centre in Chittagong; f. 1959; library of 5,600 vols; Pres. M. SADEQ KHAN; Sec. MYRIAM BASSINOT; Treas. M. ARUP KUMAR ROY.

Bangla Academy: Burdwan House 3, Kazi Nazrul Islam Avenue, Ramna, Dhaka 1000; tel. (2) 8619577; fax (2) 8612352; e-mail bacademy@citechco.net; internet www.banglaacademy.org.bd; f. 1972; promotes culture and development of the Bengali language and literature; produces dictionaries, translates scientific and reference works into Bangla; library of 102,000 vols; Pres. Prof. A. NISUZZAMAN; Dir-Gen. Dr ABUL KALAM MANZUR MORSHED; publs Dhan Shaliker Desh (juvenile, 12 a year), Journal (in English, 2 a year), Research Journal, Science Journal (in Bangla, 4 a year), Uttaradhikar (literary, 12 a year).

British Council: 5 Fuller Rd, POB 161, Dhaka 1000; tel. (2) 8618905; fax (2) 8613375; e-mail dhaka.enquiries@bd

.britishcouncil.org; internet www .britishcouncil.org/bangladesh; teaching centre; offers courses and exams in English language and British culture and promotes cultural exchange with the UK; attached teaching centres in Chittagong and Dhaka; Dir Dr JUNE ROLLINSON.

Goethe-Institut: GPOB 903, Dhaka 1000; House 10, Rd 9 (new), Dhanmandi R/A, Dhaka 1205; tel. (2) 9126525; fax (2) 8110712; e-mail info@dhaka.goethe.org; internet www.goethe.de/dhaka; offers courses and exams in German language and culture, and promotes cultural exchange with Germany; library of 4,000 vols, 20 periodicals; Dir Dr TORSTEN OERTEL.

MEDICINE

Bangladesh Medical Association: BMA House, 5/2 Topkhana Rd, Dhaka 1000; tel. (2) 9568714; fax (2) 9566060; e-mail bma@aitlbd .net; internet www.bma.org.bd; f. 1971; 10,000 mems; library of 8,000 vols; Pres. Dr M. A. HADI; Sec.-Gen. Dr A. Z. M. ZAHID HOSSAIN; publ. *Bangladesh Medical Journal* (4 a year).

NATURAL SCIENCES
General

Bangladesh Academy of Sciences: c/o Nat. Science and Technology Museum, Bhaban Agargaon, Dhaka 1207; tel. (2) 9110425; e-mail bas1@bangla.net; internet basbd.org; f. 1973; 59 mems (41 fellows, 9 foreign fellows, 9 expatriate fellows); Pres. Prof. Dr M. SHAMSHER ALI; Vice-Pres. Prof. Dr A. K. M. AMINUL HAQUE, Prof. Dr MESBAHUDDIN AHMED; Treas. Prof. Dr SYED HUMAYUN KABIR; Sec. Prof. Dr NAIYYUM CHOUDHURY; publ. *Journal* (2 a year).

Biological Sciences

Zoological Society of Bangladesh: c/o Dept of Zoology, University of Dhaka, Dhaka 1000; tel. (2) 7168321; fax (2) 8615583; e-mail contact@zsbd.org; internet www.zsbd.org; f. 1972; 1,500 mems; Pres. Prof. M. SOHRAB ALI; Gen. Sec. ABDUR RAHMAN; publs *Bangladesh Journal of Zoology* (2 a year), *Bulletin* (irregular), *Proceedings of National Conference* (every 2 years).

RELIGION, SOCIOLOGY AND ANTHROPOLOGY

Asiatic Society of Bangladesh: 5 Old Secretariat Rd (Nimtali), Ramna, Dhaka 1000; tel. (2) 7168940; fax (2) 7168853; e-mail info@asiaticsociety.org.bd; internet www.asiaticsociety.org.bd; f. 1952; study of Man and Nature of Asia; 1,788 mems; library of 10,000 vols, 500 Urdu and Persian MSS; Pres. Prof. SIRAJUL ISLAM; Gen. Sec. Prof. MAHFUZA KHANAM; publs *Journal of the Asiatic Society of Bangladesh—Humanities* (2 a year), *Journal of the Asiatic Society of Bangladesh—Science* (2 a year).

TECHNOLOGY

Institution of Engineers, Bangladesh: Ramna, Dhaka 1000; tel. (2) 9566336; fax (2) 9562447; e-mail ieb@bangla.net; internet www.iebbd.org; f. 1948; 6,000 mems; library of 4,050 vols; Pres. Eng. A. N. H. AKHTAR HOSSAIN; Vice-Pres. for Academic and International Affairs MUHAMMAD MOHSIN ALI; Vice-Pres. for Admin. and Finance MOHAMMAD REAZUL ISLAM; Vice-Pres. for Human Resources Development MUNIR UDDIN AHMED; Hon. Gen. Sec. Eng. KHAN MANJUR MORSHED; publs *Engineering News* (12 a year), *Journal* (4 a year).

Research Institutes
GENERAL

Bangladesh Council of Scientific and Industrial Research: Dr Qudrat-I-Khuda Rd, Dhanmandi, Dhaka 1205; tel. (2) 8620106; fax (2) 8613022; e-mail info@bcsir .gov.bd; internet www.bcsir.gov.bd; f. 1973; library of 15,000 vols, 100 periodicals; Chair. Prof. Dr MUHAMMAD AKRAM HOSSAIN; publs *Bangladesh Journal of Scientific and Industrial Research*, *Bigganer Joyjattra*, *Purogami Bijnan*, *Science, Technology & Development*, *Scientific & Technological Contributions of BCSIR*.

Attached Research Institutes:

BCSIR Laboratory, Chittagong: Chittagong Cantonment, Chittagong 4220; fax (31) 682505; e-mail ctglab@spnetctg.com; four divisions: chemistry, botany, pharmacology, microbiology; Dir Dr M. MANZUR-I-KHUDA.

BCSIR Laboratory, Dhaka: Dr Qudrat-i-Khuda Rd, Dhanmandi, Dhaka 1205; tel. (2) 8617924; e-mail dhakalab@bcsir.gov.bd; seven divisions: natural products; glass and ceramics; fibres and polymers; leather technology; physical instrumentation; analytical; industrial physics; Dir Dr MIR AMJAD ALI.

BCSIR Laboratory, Rajshahi: Binodpur Bazar, Rajshahi 6206; tel. (721) 750757; fax (721) 750851; four divisions: lac research; fats and oils; fibres; fruit processing and preservation; Dir Dr M. A. KHALEQUE.

Institute of Food Science and Technology, Dhaka: Dr Qudrat-i-Khuda Rd, Dhanmandi, Dhaka 1205; tel. (2) 8621148; e-mail ifst@bcsir.gov.bd; seven divisions: animal food products; biochemistry and applied nutrition; food science and quality control; industrial development; microbiology; plant food products; technology of foodgrains; Dir Dr S. F. RUBBI.

Institute of Fuel Research and Development, Dhaka: Dr Qudrat-i-Khuda Rd, Dhanmandi, Dhaka 1205; tel. (2) 8622908; e-mail ifrd@bcsir.gov.bd; three divisions: biomass and hydrocarbon research; combustion, application and pilot plant; solar energy; Dir Dr M. EUSUF.

Institute of Glass and Ceramic Research and Testing: Dr Qudrat-i-Khuda Rd, Dhanmandi, Dhaka 1205; tel. (2) 9669677; e-mail igcrt@bcsir.gov.bd.

Leather Research Institute: Nayerhat, Savar, Dhaka; tel. (2) 7708754.

Pilot Plant and Process Development Centre: Dr Qudrat-i-Khuda Rd, Dhanmandi, Dhaka 1205; tel. (2) 8622809; e-mail pppdc@bcsir.gov.bd.

AGRICULTURE, FISHERIES AND VETERINARY SCIENCE

Animal Husbandry Research Institute: Comilla; f. 1947; Prin. Scientific Officer SALIL KUMAR DHAR.

Bangladesh Jute Research Institute: Manik Miah Ave, Dhaka 1207; tel. (2) 8121929; fax (2) 9118415; e-mail info@bjri .gov.bd; internet www.bjri.gov.bd; f. 1951; oldest mono-crop research institute; constitutes three main branches: Agricultural, Technological, Marketing and Economic Research on Jute; Dir-Gen. Dr M. FIROZE SHAH SIKDER; Dir of Agriculture M. ASADUZ-ZAMAN; Dir of Technology M. KAMALUDDIN.

BIBLIOGRAPHY, LIBRARY SCIENCE AND MUSEOLOGY

Varendra Research Museum: University of Rajshahi, Aksaya Kumar Maitra Rd, Rajshahi; tel. (721) 752752; f. 1910; under control of University of Rajshahi; museum-based research instn; exhibits from the Indus Valley Civilization, Buddhist and Hindu stone sculptures, Sanskrit, Arabic and Persian scripts and stone inscriptions, indigenous, tribal culture of Rajshahi region; library of 14,000 vols; museum colln; Dir Dr M. SAIFUDDIN CHOWDHURY; publ. *Journal* (1 a year).

ECONOMICS, LAW AND POLITICS

Bangladesh Institute of Development Studies: E-17 Agargaon, Sher-e-Bangla Nagar, GPOB 3854, Dhaka 1207; tel. (2) 9116959; fax (2) 8113023; e-mail dg_bids@ bids.org.bd; internet www.bids.org.bd; f. 1957 as Pakistan Institute of Development Economics (PIDE); present name 1974; divs of agriculture and rural devt, general economic, human resources, industries and physical infrastructures, population studies; provides training in socio-economic analysis and research methodology; 81 mems; library: see Libraries and Archives; Dir-Gen. Dr MUSTAFA KAMAL MUJERI; Sec. Dr SYED NADEEM AHMED; Chief Librarian MUHAMMAD ANWARUL ISLAM; publs *Bangladesh Development Studies* (4 a year), *Bangladesh Unnayan Samikhha* (1 a year, in Bengali).

MEDICINE

Centre for Medical Education (CME): National Health Library Bldg, 3rd Fl., Mohakhali, Dhaka 1212; tel. (2) 8821809; fax (2) 8822563; e-mail director@cmedhaka .gov.bd; internet www.cmedhaka.gov.bd; f. 1983; conducts research related to health care services, health manpower development and the education of health professionals; library of 2,000 vols, 15,000 journals; Dir Dr S. M. MUSTAFA ANOWER.

ICDDR,B: International Centre for Diarrhoeal Disease Research: GPOB 128, Dhaka 1000; 68 Shahid Tajuddin Ahmed Sharani, Mohakhali, Dhaka 1212; tel. (2) 8860523; fax (2) 8823116; e-mail info@icddrb .org; internet www.icddrb.org; f. 1960; funded by 50 countries and NGOs; library of 40,611 vols, 14,600 documents; Exec. Dir Prof. ALEJANDRO CRAVIOTO; Dir of Clinical Sciences Div. Dr MUHAMMAD ABDUS SALAM; Dirof Health Systems and Infectious Diseases Div. (vacant); Dir of Laboratory Sciences Div. Dr HUBERT PH. ENDTZ; Dir of Public Health Sciences Div. (vacant); publs *Health and Science Bulletin* (4 a year), *Journal of Health, Population and Nutrition* (4 a year).

Institute of Epidemiology, Disease Control and Research: Mohakhali, Dhaka 1212; tel. (2) 9898796; fax (2) 8821237; e-mail info@iedcr.org; internet www.iedcr .org; f. 1976; depts of biostatistics, epidemiology, medical entomology and vector bionomics, medical social science, microbiology, parasitology, virology, zoonosis; activities incl. disease surveillance, investigation of known and unknown disease outbreaks with rapid response, management of disease outbreak, training and research for the Nat. Influenza Centre of Bangladesh; library of 6,000 vols; Dir Prof. MAHMUDUR RAHMAN.

NATURAL SCIENCES
Physical Sciences

Geological Survey of Bangladesh: 153 Pioneer Rd, Segun Bagicha, Dhaka 1000; tel. (2) 9349502; fax (2) 9339309; e-mail gsb@

dhaka.agni.com; internet www.gsb.gov.bd; f. 1972; govt org. under Ministry of Energy and Mineral Resources; library of 7,000 vols, 97 journals; Dir-Gen. M. NAZRUL ISLAM; publ. *Records* (irregular).

TECHNOLOGY

Bangladesh Atomic Energy Commission: Paramanu Bhaban, E-12/A, Agargaon, Sher-e-Bangla Nagar, Dhaka 1207; tel. (2) 8130469; fax (2) 8130102; e-mail baec@agni.com; internet www.baec.org.bd; f. 1973; library of 25,375 vols, 192 periodicals; Chair. Dr M. A. MANNAN; publ. *Nuclear Science & Applications* (Series A: Biological Sciences; Series B: Physical Sciences).

Attached Institutes:

Atomic Energy Centre: POB 164, Ramna, Dhaka 2; basic and applied research in physics, electronics and chemistry; library of 10,728 vols, 100 periodicals.

Atomic Energy Research Establishment: Ganakbari, Savar, Dhaka 1349; tel. and fax (2) 7789339; fax (2) 7789620; e-mail siu_aere@yahoo.com; internet www.aere.org.bd; f. 1979; library of 10,000 vols of books; consists of 10 separate institutes: Central Engineering Facilities (CEF), Institute of Computer Sciences (ICS), Institute of Electronics (IE), Institute of Food and Radiation Biology (IFRB), Institute of Nuclear Science and Technology (INST), Nuclear Mineral Unit (NMU), Reactor Operation and Maintenance Unit (ROMU), Scientific Information Unit (SIU), Tissue Banking and Biomaterial Research Unit (TBBRU) and Energy Institute (EI); Senior Librarian SHAMSUL ISLAM.

Beach and Sand Exploration Centre: Coxbazar.

Radiation Testing and Monitoring Laboratory: Chittagong.

Rooppur Nuclear Plant: Pabna; publ. *AERE Annual Technical Report* (1 a year).

Libraries and Archives
Chittagong

Divisional Government Public Library: POB 771, K. C. Dey Rd, Chittagong; tel. (31) 611578; f. 1963; 62,910 vols, 121 periodicals; Senior Librarian A. D. M. ALI AHAMMED.

Dhaka

Bangladesh Central Public Library: 3 Liaquat Ave, Dhaka 1000; tel. (2) 8624713; fax (2) 8610422; internet www.publiclibrary.org.bd; f. 1958; 1m. vols, 2,300 periodicals; spec. colln: depository for UNESCO publs; Dir A. F. M. BADIUR RAHMAN.

Bangladesh Institute of Development Studies Library: E-17, Agargaon, Sher-e-Bangla Nagar, Dhaka 1207; tel. (2) 9140755; fax (2) 9143441; internet www.bids-bd.org; f. 1957; 130,000 vols, 600 peridocals; Chief Librarian SHAHANA PARVEEN (acting).

Bangladesh National Scientific and Technical Documentation Centre (BANSDOC): E-14/Y, Agargaon, Sher-e-Bangla Nagar, Dhaka 1207; tel. (2) 8127744; fax (2) 9140066; e-mail bansdoc@bansdoc.gov.bd; internet www.bansdoc.gov.bd; f. 1963; 19,000 vols, 114 nat. periodicals, 350 foreign periodicals; Dir SETARA BANU CHOWDHURY; Chair. YEAFESH OSMAN; publs *Bangladesh Science and Technology Abstracts* (1 a year), *Current Scientific and Technological Research Projects of Bangladesh* (every 2 years), *National Catalogue of Scientific and Technological Periodicals of Bangladesh* (every 2 years), *Report of the Survey of Research and Development Activities in Bangladesh* (every 2 years).

Directorate of Archives and Libraries: 32 S. M. Murshed Sarani, Sher-e-Bangla Nagar, Agargaon, Dhaka 1207; tel. (2) 9129992; fax (2) 9118704; e-mail nanldirector@gmail.com; internet www.nanl.gov.bd; f. 1971; attached to Min. of Cultural Affairs; coordinating centre for archives and libraries at nat. level; 500,000 vols, 105 Bengali periodicals, 10 foreign periodicals, 20 maps, 3,000 microfilms, 60 rolls of microfiche, 235 issues of National Bibliography (1972–1991); Head Prof. Dr TAIBUL HASAN KHAN.

Institutions under the control of the Directorate:

National Archives of Bangladesh: Nat. Archives Bldg, Sher-e-Bangla Nagar, Agargaon, Dhaka 1207; f. 1972; 225,000 vols of records and documents, 3,500 books, 58 rolls of microfilm, 10,000 press clippings; Head Prof. Dr TAIBUL HASAN KHAN; publs *Annual Reports 1973–84*, *Bulletin of Dissertations and Theses by Bangladeshi Scholars 1947–73*, *SWARBICA Journal Vol III*.

National Library of Bangladesh: Nat. Library Bldg, Sher-e-Bangla Nagar, Agargaon, Dhaka 1207; f. 1972; 550,000 vols, 3,000 maps; Head Prof. Dr TAIBUL HASAN KHAN; publs *Articles Index*, *Bangladesh National Bibliography*.

University of Dhaka Library: Ramna, Dhaka 1000; tel. (2) 9661900; fax (2) 8615583; e-mail duregstr@bangla.net; f. 1921; 5.5m. vols, 30,000 rare MSS and a large number of tracts (booklets, leaflets, pamphlets and puthis) in microfilm format; rare books and reports, puthis, Bengali Tracts and private colln of Buchanan on Bengal have been acquired from the British Museum, UK; Librarian Dr MUHAMMAD SERAJUL ISLAM.

Rajshahi

Rajshahi University Library: Rajshahi; tel. (721) 750666; fax (721) 750064; f. 1953; 250,000 vols, 2,000 journals; Administrator Prof. OBAIDUR RAHMAN PRAMANIK.

Museums and Art Galleries
Dhaka

Ahsan Manzil Museum: Nawab Ahsanulla Rd, Shadarghat, Dhaka; tel. (2) 7391122; fmr home of the Nawab of Dhaka; 23 galleries displaying portraits, furniture and other objects used by the Nawab.

Balda Museum: Dhaka; f. 1927; Bengali art and ancient artifacts; Superintendent MUHAMMAD HANNAN.

Bangabandhu Memorial Museum: House 10 Rd 32, Dhanmandi Residential Area, Dhaka; tel. (2) 8110046; residence of the father of the nation, Bangabandhu Sheikh Mujibur Rahman (1920–75); colln of personal effects and photographs of his lifetime.

Bangladesh National Museum: POB 355, Shahbag, Dhaka 1000; tel. (2) 8619396; fax (2) 8615585; e-mail dgmuseum@yahoo.com; internet www.bangladeshmuseum.gov.bd; f. 1913; history and classical art, ethnography and decorative art, natural history, contemporary art and world civilization; conservation, public education; library of 35,816 vols; Chair. Dr M. AZIZUR RAHMAN; Dir-Gen. PROKASH CHANDRA DAS; publ. *Bangladesh Jadughar Samachar* (Journal of Bangladesh National Museum, 4 a year).

Dhaka Zoo: Mirpur-1, Dhaka; tel. (2) 9002954; f. 1964; attached to Min. of Fisheries and Livestock; colln of more than 2,000 native and non-native animals and wildlife; Curator KAZI FAZLUL HAQUE.

Mukti Juddha Museum: 5 Segun Bagicha, Dhaka; tel. (2) 9559091; fax (2) 9559092; e-mail mukti@citechco.net; f. 1996; concerns Bangladesh's Liberation War (1971); ancient Bengali artefacts, and items from the British Raj period and the Pakistani period, photographs of the war and items used by the freedom fighters during the period; Man. Dir AKKU CHOWDHURY.

National Art Gallery: Shilpakala Academy, Segun Bagicha, Dhaka 1000; tel. (2) 9562801; f. 1965; colln of folk art and paintings by Bangladeshi artists.

National Botanical Garden: Mirpur, 16 Km NW of city, Dhaka; tel. (2) 8018092; e-mail info@bforest.gov.bd; internet www.bforest.gov.bd; f. 1961; attached to Min. of Environment and Forests; colln of 50,000 plants, herbs, shrubs and trees on a 200-acre site.

National Science and Technology Museum: Agargaon, Sher-e-Bangla Nagar, Dhaka 1207; tel. (2) 9112084; fax (2) 9114831; e-mail info@nmst.gov.bd; internet www.nmst.gov.bd; f. 1965; attached to Min. of Science, Information and Communication; library of 4,464 vols; Dir SADARUDDIN AHMED; publ. *Nabin Biggani* (4 a year).

Universities
AHSANULLAH UNIVERSITY OF SCIENCE AND TECHNOLOGY

141–142 Love Rd, Tejgaon Industrial Area, Dhaka 1208

Telephone: (2) 9897311
Fax: (2)9860564
E-mail: vc@aust.edu
Internet: www.aust.edu
Private control, sponsored by Dhaka Ahsania Mission

Founded 1995

Chancellor: PRES. OF THE PEOPLE'S REPUBLIC OF BANGLADESH
Vice-Chancellor: Prof. Dr M. ANWAR HOSSAIN
Registrar: MUHAMMAD AZIZUL HAQUE (acting)
Librarian: MUHAMMAD MOSHARRAF HOSSAIN
Number of students: 2,514

DEANS

Faculty of Architecture and Planning: Prof. Dr M. A. MUKTADIR
Faculty of Business and Social Science: Dr SHYMA PADA BISWAS
Faculty of Education: FATEMA KHATUN
Faculty of Engineering: Prof. Dr ABU MUHAMMAD SHADULLAH

ATTACHED INSTITUTE

Institute of Technical and Vocational Education and Training: ITVET Campus, 20 West Testuri Bazar Rd, Tejgaon, Dhaka 1215; tel. (2) 9130613; f. 1995; offers mid-level programmes in Architecture, Civil Engineering, Computer Technology Engineering, Electrical Engineering, Electronic Engineeringand Textile Engineering.

AMERICAN INTERNATIONAL UNIVERSITY BANGLADESH

House 83 Rd 4, Kamal Ataturk Ave, Banani, Dhaka 1213

Telephone: (2) 9890415

Fax: (2) 881233
E-mail: info@aiub.edu
Internet: www.aiub.edu
Founded 1994
Private control
Academic year: January to December
Number of teachers: 100
Number of students: 2,500
Vice-Chancellor: CARMEN Z. LAMAGNA
Pro-Vice-Chancellor: Prof. Dr ANWAR HOS-SAIN
Number of students: 3,489
Publications: *AIUB Journal of Business and Economics* (2 a year), *AIUB Journal of Science and Engineering* (1 a year)

DEANS

Faculty of Arts and Social Science: Dr CHARLES C. VILLANUEVA
Faculty of Science: Dr A. B. M. SIDDIQUE HOSSAIN

BANGABANDHU SHEIKH MUJIB MEDICAL UNIVERSITY

POB 3048, Dhaka 1000
Telephone: (2) 9661065
Fax: (2) 9661063
E-mail: info@bsmmu.org
Internet: www.bsmmu.org
Founded 1965 as Institute of Postgraduate Medicine and Research; present name and status 1998
Academic year: July to June
Vice-Chancellor: Prof. M. NAZRUL ISLAM
Pro-Vice-Chancellors: Prof. MUHAMMAD CHOUDHURY ALI KAWSER, Prof. MUHAMMAD KAMAL
Registrar: M. A. GAFUR
Chief Librarian: MUHAMMAD SHAHADAT HUS-SAIN
Colleges and Postgraduate Institutes Inspector: Prof. AKRAM HOSSAIN
Founded 1965
Library of 23,000 vols, 100 periodicals
Number of teachers: 200
Number of students: 704
Publications: *Bangladesh Journal of Neurology* (2 a year), *Bangladesh Journal of Psychiatry* (2 a year), *Journal of the Institute of Postgraduate Medicine and Research* (2 a year)

DEANS

Faculty of Basic Medical Sciences: Prof. M. IQBAL ARSLAN
Faculty of Dentistry: Prof. MOTIUR RAHMAN MOLLA
Faculty of Medicine: Prof. K. M. H. S. SIRAJUL HAQUE
Faculty of Surgery: Prof. MOHAMMAD SAIFUL ISLAM

BANGABANDHU SHEIKH MUJIBUR RAHMAN AGRICULTURAL UNIVERSITY

Salna, Gazipur 1703
Telephone: (2) 9252850
Fax: (2) 9252873
E-mail: bsmrau@sdnbd.org
Founded 1983 as Bangladesh College of Agricultural Sciences; became Institute of Postgraduate Studies in Agriculture 1994; present name 1998
State control
Academic year: November to October
Vice-Chancellor: Prof. Dr M. A. HALIM KHAN
Registrar: MOHAMMAD ABUL KALAM AZAD
Asst Librarian: MOHAMMAD ABDUR ROUF MIAN
Number of teachers: 47

Number of students: 394
Publication: *Annals of Bangladeshi Agriculture* (every 2 years)

DEANS

Faculty of Agriculture: Prof. Dr M. A. HALIM KHAN
Graduate Studies: Prof. Dr ABDUL MANNAN AKANDA

BANGLADESH AGRICULTURAL UNIVERSITY

Mymensingh 2202
Telephone: (91) 66846
Fax: (91) 61580
E-mail: registrar@bau.edu.bd
Internet: www.bau.edu.bd
Founded 1961
Autonomous control
Languages of instruction: English, Bengali
Academic year: July to June (two semesters)
Chancellor: MUHAMMAD ZILLUR RAHMAN
Vice-Chancellor: Prof. Dr M. A. SATTAR MANDAL
Registrar: MUHAMMAD NAZIBUR RAHMAN
Public Relations and Pubs Dir: DIWAN RASHIDUL HASSAN
Cttee for Advanced Studies and Research Coordinator: Prof. Dr SULTAN UDDIN BHUIYA
Librarian: PRABIR KUMAR MITRA BISWAS
Library of 193,614 vols
Number of teachers: 513
Number of students: 4,767
Publications: *Bangladesh Journal of Agricultural Economics*, *Bangladesh Journal of Agricultural Engineering*, *Bangladesh Journal of Agricultural Science*, *Bangladesh Journal of Animal Science*, *Bangladesh Journal of Aquaculture*, *Bangladesh Journal of Crop Science*, *Bangladesh Journal of Environmental Science* (1 a year), *Bangladesh Journal of Extension Education*, *Bangladesh Journal of Fisheries* (4 a year), *Bangladesh Journal of Horticulture* (2 a year), *Bangladesh Journal of Plant Pathology*, *Bangladesh Journal of Seed Science and Technology* (2 a year), *Bangladesh Journal of Training and Development*, *Bangladesh Veterinary Journal*, *Journal of Veterinary Medicine*, *Progressive Agriculture*, *The Bangladeshi Veterinarian*

DEANS

Faculty of Agricultural Economics and Rural Sociology: Prof. TOFAZZAL HOSSAIN MIAH
Faculty of Agricultural Engineering and Technology: Prof. Dr M. BURHAN-UD-DIN
Faculty of Agriculture: Prof. Dr MOHAMMAD ABDUL KARIM
Faculty of Animal Husbandry: Prof. Dr M. ALI AKBAR
Faculty of Fisheries: Prof. Dr MUHAMMAD ABDUL WAHAB
Faculty of Veterinary Science: Prof. Dr MUHAMMAD MOTAHAR HUSSAIN MONDAL

PROFESSORS

Faculty of Agricultural Economics and Rural Sociology:
AKBAR, M., Agribusiness and Marketing
AKTERUZZAMAN, M., Agricultural Economics
ALAM, S., Agribusiness & Marketing
ALI, M., Rural Sociology
BASHAR, M., Agricultural Finance
BEGUM, R., Agricultural Statistics
DEBNATH, S., Agricultural Statistics
HAQUE, M., Agricultural Statistics
HOSSAIN, M., Agricultural Statistics
ISLAM, M., Agricultural Economics
JABBAR, M., Agricultural Finance

JAIM, W., Agricultural Economics
MANDAL, M., Agricultural Economics
MIA, M., Agribusiness and Marketing
MIAH, M., Agricultural Economics
MIAH, T., Agricultural Finance
MODAK, P., Agricultural Statistics
MOLLA, A., Agricultural Economics
QUDDUS, M., Agricultural Statistics
RAHA, S., Agribusiness and Marketing
RAHMAN, K., Agricultural Statistics
RAHMAN, M., Agricultural Economics
RASHID, M., Agricultural Economics
SABUR, S., Agribusiness and Marketing
Faculty of Agricultural Engineering and Technology:
ABEDIN, M., Farm Structure
AHMED, M., Irrigation and Water Management
AKHTARUZZAMAN, M., Farm Power and Machinery
ALAM, M., Farm Power and Machinery
ALI, M., Computer Science and Mathematics
ASHRAF, M., Farm Structure
AWAL, A., Farm Structure
BALA, B., Farm Power and Machinery
BASAK, N., Computer Science and Mathematics
BASUNIA, M., Farm Power and Machinery
HAQUE, M., Farm Power and Machinery
HASSNUZZAMAN, K., Irrigation and Water Management
HOQUE, M., Farm Structure
HOQUE, M., Irrigation and Water Management
HOSSAIN, M., Farm Power and Machinery
HUQ, M., Computer Science and Mathematics
HUSSAIN, M., Farm Power and Machinery
HYE, M., Computer Science and Mathematics
ISLAM, M., Food Technology and Rural Industries
ISLAM, M., Irrigation and Water Management
KHAIR, A., Irrigation and Water Management
KHAN, L., Irrigation and Water Management
MOJID, M., Irrigation and Water Management
RAHMAN, K., Farm Structure
RASHID, M., Farm Structure
SARKER, M., Farm Power and Machinery
SATTAR, M., Farm Power and Machinery
SHAMS-UD-DIN, M., Food Technology and Rural Industries
TALUKDER, M., Irrigation and Water Management
UDDIN, M., Food Technology and Rural Industries
ZIAUDDIN, A., Farm Power and Machinery
Faculty of Agriculture:
AHMAD, M., Entomology
AHMAD, M., Plant Pathology
AHMED, K., Entomology
AHMED, Q., Genetics and Plant Breeding
ALAM, M., Genetics and Plant Breeding
ALI, M., Plant Pathology
ASHRAFUZZAMAN, M., Crop Botany
ASHRAFUZZAMAN, M., Plant Pathology
AWAL, M., Crop Botany
BATEN, M., Environmental Science
BEGUM, M., Agronomy
BHUIYA, M., Agronomy
CHOUDHURY, M., Horticulture
CHOWDHURY, A., Agronomy
CHOWDHURY, B., Biochemistry
CHOWDHURY, M., Agricultural Chemistry
FAKIR, M., Crop Botany
FAROOQUE, A., Horticulture
HAQUE, M., Biotechnology
HAQUE, M., Entomology
HAQUE, M.
HASHEM, M., Soil Science

HASSAN, L., Genetics and Plant Breeding
HOSSAIN, A., Soil Science
HOSSAIN, I., Plant Pathology
HOSSAIN, M., Agricultural Extension Education
HOSSAIN, M., Agroforestry
HOSSAIN, M., Biochemistry
HOSSAIN, M., Plant Pathology
HOSSAIN, M., Plant Pathology
HUQUE, M., Agricultural Extension Education
ISLAM, K., Entomology
ISLAM, M., Agricultural Extension Education
ISLAM, M., Genetics and Plant Breeding
ISLAM, M., Crop Botany
ISLAM, M., Soil Science
ISLAM, N., Agronomy
JAHAN, M., Entomology
JAHIRUDDIN, M., Soil Science
KARIM, A., Agricultural Extension Education
KARIM, M., Crop Botany
KARIM, S., Agronomy
KASHEM, M., Agricultural Extension Education
KHAN, A., Entomology
KHAN, M., Crop Botany
MATIN, M., Soil Science
MEAH, M., Plant Pathology
MIAH, M., Agricultural Extension Education
MIAN, M., Soil Science
MIAN, M., Soil Science
MONDAL, M., Horticulture
MOSLEHUDDIN, A., Soil Science
NASIRUDDIN, K., Biotechnology
NEWAZ, M., Genetics and Plant Breeding
NEWAZ, M., Biochemistry
PATWARY, M., Genetics and Plant Breeding
PRAMANIK, M., Crop Botany
PRODHAN, A., Crop Botany
QUDDUS, M., Genetics and Plant Breeding
RABBANI, M., Horticulture
RAHIM, M., Horticulture
RAHMAN, G., Agroforestry
RAHMAN, M., Agricultural Chemistry
RAHMAN, M., Agricultural Extension Education
RAHMAN, M., Agronomy
RAHMAN, M., Crop Botany
RAHMAN, M., Horticulture
RAHMAN, M., Soil Science
RASHID, A., Plant Pathology
RASHID, M., Agricultural Extension Education
RASHID, M., Biochemistry
REZA, M., Biochemistry
ROY, P., Biochemistry
SAHA, K., Physics and Chemistry
SALIM, M., Agronomy
SAMAD, M., Agronomy
SARKAR, M., Agronomy
SATTAR, M., Environmental Science
SEAL, H., Physics and Chemistry
SHAHJAHAN, M., Entomology
SHAMSUDDIN, A., Genetics and Plant Breeding
SIDDIQUA, M., Biochemistry
SIDDQUE, M., Horticulture
WAZUDDIN, M., Genetics and Plant Breeding
ZAMAN, M., Agricultural Chemistry

Faculty of Animal Husbandry:
AKBAR, M., Animal Nutrition
AKHTER, S., Animal Science
ALAM, M., Animal Science
ALI, A., Animal Breeding and Genetics
ALI, M., Poultry Science
AMIN, M., Animal Breeding and Genetics
AMIN, M., Animal Science
BHUIYAN, A., Animal Breeding and Genetics
CHOWDHURY, S., Poultry Science

FARUQUE, M., Animal Breeding and Genetics
HASHEM, M., Animal Science
HASSAN, M., Dairy Science
HOSSAIN, M., Animal Science
HOWLIDER, M., Poultry Science
HUSAIN, S., Animal Breeding and Genetics
ISLAM, M., Dairy Science
KHAN, M., Animal Nutrition
KHAN, M., Animal Science
KHAN, M., Dairy Science
KHANDAKER, M., Animal Breeding and Genetics
KHANDAKER, Z., Animal Nutrition
MOKHTARUZZAMAN, M., Dairy Science
WADUD, A., Dairy Science

Faculty of Fisheries:
AHMED, G., Aquaculture
AHMED, N., Fisheries Management
AHMED, Z., Fisheries Management
ALAM, A., Fisheries Technology
ALAM, M., Fisheries Biology and Genetics
ALI, M., Aquaculture
AMIN, M., Aquaculture
CHAKRABORTY, S., Fisheries Technology
CHANDRA, K., Aquaculture
CHOWDHURY, M., Aquaculture
DAS, M., Aquaculture
FARUK, A., Aquaculture
HABIB, M., Aquaculture
HAQ, M., Fisheries Management
HAQUE, A., National Professor
HAQUE, M., Fisheries Management
HAQUE, S., Fisheries Management
HOSEN, M., Aquaculture
HOSSAIN, M., Fisheries Biology and Genetics
HOSSAIN, M., Fisheries Technology
ISLAM, M., Fisheries Technology
KAMAL, M., Fisheries Technology
KHAN, M., Fisheries Biology and Genetics
KHAN, S., Fisheries Management
MANSUR, M., Fisheries Technology
MIAH, M., Aquaculture
MIAH, M., Fisheries Management
MOLLAH, M., Fisheries Biology and Genetics
RAHMAN, M., Fisheries Management
RAHMATULLAH, S., Aquaculture
RASHID, M., Aquaculture
SALAM, M., Aquaculture
SARDER, M., Fisheries Biology and Genetics
UDDIN, M., Fisheries Technology
WAHAB, M., Fisheries Management

Faculty of Veterinary Science:
AHMAD, N., Physiology
AHMED, J., Surgery and Obstetrics
AHMED, M., Anatomy and Histology
ALAM, M., Surgery and Obstetrics
ASADUZZAMAN, M., Anatomy and Histology
AWAL, M., Anatomy and Histology
AWAL, M., Pharmacology
BAKI, M., Pathology
BARI, A., Pathology
BARI, F., Surgery and Obstetrics
BEGUM, M., Parasitology
BHUIYAN, M., Surgery and Obstetrics
CHOWDHURY, E., Pathology
DAS, P., Pathology
HASHIM, M., Surgery and Obstetrics
HOSSAIN, M., Pathology
HOSSAIN, M., Surgery and Obstetrics
ISLAM, M., Microbiology and Hygiene
ISLAM, M., Pathology
KHAN, M., Anatomy and Histology
KHAN, M., Pathology
KHAN, M., Microbiology and Hygiene
MONDAL, M., Parasitology
MOSTOFA, M., Pharmacology
RAHMAN, M., Medicine
RAHMAN, M., Microbiology and Hygiene
RAHMAN, M., Pathology
RAHMAN, M., Physiology
SAMAD, M., Medicine
SEN, M., Medicine

SHAMSUDDIN, M., Surgery and Obstetrics
UDDIN, M., Physiology

DIRECTORS
Agricultural Museum: Prof. Dr M. ABUL KASHEM
Agricultural University Extension Centre: Prof. Dr M. ABDUL MOMEN MIAH
Agricultural University Research System: Prof. Dr M. SHAHID ULLAH TALUKDER
Central Laboratory: Prof. MUHAMMAD JAHIR UDDIN MIAH
Graduate Training Institute: Prof. M. NAZRUL ISLAM
Seed Pathology Centre: Prof. Dr ISMAIL HOSSAIN
Veterinary Clinic: Prof. Dr FARIDA YEASMIN BARI

CHAIRS
Bureau of Research, Testing and Consultation: Prof. Dr M. BURHAN UDDIN
Bureau of Socio-economic Research and Training: Prof. Dr TOFAZZAL HOSSAIN MIAH

BANGLADESH OPEN UNIVERSITY

Board Bazar, Gazipur 1705
Telephone: (2) 9291112
Fax: (2) 9291130
E-mail: regi@bou.edu.bd
Internet: www.bou.edu.bd

Founded 1992
State control
Chancellor: PRIME MINISTER OF THE PEOPLE'S REPUBLIC OF BANGLADESH
Vice-Chancellor: Prof. Dr R. I. M. AMINUR RASHID
Pro-Vice-Chancellor: Prof. R. I. SHARIF
Registrar: MUHAMMAD MONZUR-E-KHODA TARAFDAR
Librarian: MUHAMMAD SAADAT ALI

Library of 11,000 vols
Number of teachers: 62
Number of students: 103,000

DEANS
Open School: MD. ALINOOR RAHMAN
School of Agriculture and Rural Development: Dr MD. ABU TALEB
School of Business: Prof. ABDUL AWAL KHAN
School of Education: Prof. MONIRA BEGUM HOSSAIN
School of Science and Technology: Prof. Dr MOFIZ UDDIN AHMED
School of Social Science, Humanities and Languages: Prof. Dr ABUL HOSSAIN AHMED BHUIYAN

REGIONAL RESOURCE CENTRES
Resource Centre, Barishal: Rupatali, Post Jaguar, Barishal; tel. (431) 71322; e-mail rcbrisal@bou.bangla.net.

Resource Centre, Bogra: Bangladesh Open University, Bishwa Rd, Banani, Bogra; tel. (51) 72974; e-mail rrcbogra@bou.bangla.net.

Resource Centre, Chittagong: Bangladesh Open University, C. R. B. Rd (Chittagong Stadium), Cothwali, Chittagong; tel. (31) 619633; e-mail rrcctg@bou.bangla.net.

Resource Centre, Comilla: Bangladesh Open University, Dhaka-Chittagong Trunk Rd, Noapara, Durgapur, Comilla; tel. (81) 77557; e-mail rrccom@bou.bangla.net.

Resource Centre, Dhaka: Government Laboratory, School Rd, Dhanmandi, Dhaka 1205; tel. (2) 8616065; e-mail rrcdhaka@bou.bangla.net.

Resource Centre, Faridpur: Beside Nadigabashana Institute, Harokandi, Barishal Rd, Faridpur; tel. (631) 62081; e-mail rrcfarid@bou.bangla.net.

Resource Centre, Jessore: Jessore Upa-Shahar (Dhaka Rd), Jessore; tel. (421) 73250; e-mail rrcjes@bou.bangla.net.

Resource Centre, Khulna: Rd 5, House 51, Sonadanga Residential Area, Khulna 9000; tel. (41) 731795; e-mail rrckhul@bou.bangla.net.

Resource Centre, Mymensingh: Mashkanda (Dhaka–Mymensingh Highway), Mymensingh; tel. (91) 52408; e-mail rrcmyn@bou.bangla.net.

Resource Centre, Rajshahi: Bangladesh Open University, Nohata, Paba, Rajshahi; tel. (721) 761607; e-mail rrcraj@bou.bangla.net.

Resource Centre, Rangpur: Bangladesh Open University, R. K. Rd, Rangpur; tel. (521) 63593; fax (521) 64806; e-mail rrcrnp@bou.bangla.net.

Resource Centre, Sylhet: Bangladesh Open University, Pirijpur, South Surma, Sylhet; tel. (821) 719523; fax (821) 22758; e-mail rrcsyl@bou.bangla.net.

BANGLADESH UNIVERSITY OF ENGINEERING AND TECHNOLOGY

Palassy, Ramna, Dhaka 1000

Telephone: (2) 9665650

Fax: (2) 8613046

E-mail: vc@buet.ac.bd

Internet: www.buet.ac.bd

Founded 1962

State control

Language of instruction: English

Academic year: January to December

Chancellor: PRIME MINISTER OF THE PEOPLE'S REPUBLIC OF BANGLADESH

Vice-Chancellor: Prof. Dr MUHAMMAD ALEE MURTUZA

Registrar: MOHAMMAD SHAHJAHAN

Librarian: MOHAMMAD ZAHIRUL ISLAM

Library of 132,586 vols

Number of teachers: 501

Number of students: 7,773

Publications: *Bangladesh Journal of Water Resource Research, Chemical Engineering Research Bulletin, Electrical and Electronic Engineering Research Bulletin, Industrial and Production Engineering Research Bulletin, Journal of Energy and Environment, Journal of Mechanical Engineering Research and Development, Protibesh Journal of the Dept of Architecture*

DEANS

Faculty of Architecture and Planning: Prof. KHALEDA RASHID

Faculty of Civil Engineering: Prof. Dr MUHAMMAD ABDUR ROUF

Faculty of Electrical and Electronic Engineering: Prof. Dr S. SHAHNAWAZ AHMED

Faculty of Engineering: Prof. Dr A. A. M. REZAUL HAQUE

Faculty of Mechanical Engineering: Prof. Dr MUHAMMAD ABDUR RASHID SARKAR

ATTACHED INSTITUTES

Accident Research Centre: tel. (2) 9669368; fax (2) 8613046; e-mail dirarc@arc.buet.ac.bd; internet www.buet.ac.bd/ari; f. 2002; advancement of safety research in Bangladesh; scientific research and investigation into causes of accidents on roads, railways and waterways; creating awareness on transport safety; Dir Prof. Dr MUHAMMAD SHAMSUL HOQUE.

Bio-Medical Engineering Centre: tel. (2) 9665636; Dir Prof. Dr M. ABU TAHER ALI.

Centre for Energy Studies: tel. (2) 9665650; fax (2) 8613046; e-mail dirces@buet.ac.bd; internet www.buet.ac.bd/ces; f. 1984; Dir Prof. SHAHIDUL ISLAM KHAN.

Centre for Environmental and Resource Management: tel. (2) 9663693; Dir Prof. Dr MUHAMMAD DELWAR HOSSAIN.

Directorate of Continuing Education: tel. (2) 9665633; e-mail dirdce@dce.buet.ac.bd; internet www.buet.ac.bd/dce; f. 1995; Dir Prof. Dr MUHAMMAD ABDUR RASHID SARKAR.

Institute of Appropriate Technology: tel. (2) 9662365; fax (2) 8613026; e-mail iatdir@iat.buet.ac.bd; internet www.buet.ac.bd/iat; Dir Dr MUHAMMAD KAMAL UDDIN.

Institute of Information and Communication Technology: tel. (2) 9665602; fax (2) 9665602; e-mail lutfulkabir@iict.buet.ac.bd; internet www.buet.ac.bd/iict; f. 2001; Dir Prof. Dr S. M. LUTFUL KABIR.

Institute of Water and Flood Management: tel. (2) 9665601; fax (2) 8613046; e-mail diriwfm@iwfm.buet.ac.bd; internet teacher.buet.ac.bd/diriwfm; f. 1974; Dir Prof. ANISUL HAQUE.

BRAC UNIVERSITY

66 Mohakhali C/A, Dhaka 1212

Telephone: (2) 8824051

Fax: (2) 8810183

E-mail: info@bracu.ac.bd

Internet: www.bracuniversity.net

Founded 2001

Private control, under BRAC non-governmental devt org.

Vice-Chancellor: Prof. JAMILUR REZA CHOUDHURY

Registrar: MAHMOOD HASAN

Librarian: HASINA AFROZ

Number of students: 1,659

DEANS

Faculty of Architecture: Prof. FUAD H. MALLICK

Faculty of Computer Science and Engineering: Prof. SAYEED SALAM

Faculty of Economics and Social Sciences: Dr ANWARUL HOQUE

Faculty of English and Humanities: Prof. FIRDOUS AZIM

Faculty of Mathematics and Natural Sciences: Prof. MOFIZ UDDIN AHMED

ATTACHED SCHOOLS AND INSTITUTES

BRAC Business School: Dir Prof. MOJIB U. AHMED.

BRAC Development Institute: Dir Prof. SYED M. HASHEMI.

Centre for Languages: Dhaka 1212; tel. (2) 8824051; e-mail nsabera@bracu.ac.bd; internet www.bracuniversity.net/cfl; Dir SYEDA SARWAT ABED.

Institute of Educational Development: House 113, Block A, Rd 2, Niketon, Gulshan 1, Dhaka 1212; tel. (2) 8824180; fax (2) 8829157; e-mail bu-ied@brac.net; internet www.bracuniversity.net/i&s/ied; Dir Dr MANZOOR AHMED.

Institute of Governance Studies: 40/6 North Ave, Gulshan-2, Dhaka 1212; tel. (2) 8810306; fax (2) 8832542; e-mail igs-info@bracu.ac.bd; internet www.igs-bracu.ac.bd; Dir MANZOOR HASAN.

James P. Grant School of Public Health: Dhaka 1212; tel. (2) 8824051; fax (2) 8823542; e-mail bsph@bracu.ac.bd; internet sph.bracu.ac.bd; Dir ANWAR ISLAM.

School of Law: Dir Dr SHAHDEEN MALIK.

LEARNING CENTRE

Learning Resource Centre: c/o Ayesha Abed Library, BRAC University, 67 Mohakhali, Dhaka 1212; tel. (2) 8824051; e-mail librarian@bracu.ac.bd; internet library.bracu.ac.bd.

CHITTAGONG UNIVERSITY OF ENGINEERING AND TECHNOLOGY

Chittagong 4349

Telephone: (31) 714946

Fax: (31) 714910

E-mail: registrar@cuet.ac.bd

Internet: www.cuet.ac.bd

Founded 1968 as Engineering College, Chittagong; renamed Bangladesh Institute of Technology, Chittagong 1986; present name and status 2003

State control

Language of instruction: English

Vice-Chancellor: Prof. Dr SHYAMAL KANTI BISWAS

Registrar: M. OHIDUZZAMAN

Librarian: M. ABUL HOSSAIN SHAIKH

Number of students: 1,871

DEANS

Faculty of Electrical and Computer Engineering: Prof. Dr PORITOSH KUMAR SHADHU KHAN

Faculty of Engineering: Prof. Dr M. SAIFUL ISLAM

ATTACHED INSTITUTES

Bureau of Research, Testing and Consultation.

Centre for Information and Communication Technology: Chair. Prof. Dr PORITOSH KUMAR SHADHU KHAN.

Earthquake Engineering Research Centre: tel. (31) 714948; fax (31) 714910; e-mail eerc@cuet.ac.bd; Coordinator Prof. Dr M. JAHANGIR ALAM.

Institute of Energy Technology: CUET, Chittagong 4349; tel. (31) 714920; e-mail iet@cuet.ac.bd; internet www.cuet.ac.bd/iet; Dir Prof. Dr MAHMOOD OMAR IMAM.

DHAKA UNIVERSITY OF ENGINEERING AND TECHNOLOGY

Gazipur 1700

Telephone: (2) 9204734

Fax: (2) 9204701

E-mail: duet@duet.ac.bd

Internet: www.duet.ac.bd

Founded 1980; present name and status 2003

State control

Language of instruction: English

Vice-Chancellor: Prof. Dr M. SABDER ALI

Registrar: ALIM DAD

Librarian: M. ANISUR RAHMAN

Library of 25,000

Number of students: 1,519

DEANS

Faculty of Civil Engineering: Prof. Dr MOHAMMAD ABDUR RASHID

Faculty of Electrical and Electronic Engineering: Prof. Dr M. SHAHEEN HASAN CHOWDHURY

Faculty of Mechanical Engineering: Dr MOHAMMED ALAUDDIN

HAJEE MOHAMMAD DANESH UNIVERSITY OF SCIENCE AND TECHNOLOGY

Rangpur, Dhaka Highway, Dinajpur 5200

Telephone: (531) 65429

Fax: (531) 61344

E-mail: vcmdstu@dhaka.net

Internet: www.akashghuri.com/hstu/hstu.htm

Founded 1976; present name and status 2002

State control
Vice-Chancellor: Prof. Dr M. AFZAL HOSSAIN
Registrar: Prof. MOHAMED KHALILUR RAHMAN
Librarian: MOHAMED ALAUDDIN KHAN
Number of students: 903

DEANS

Faculty of Agriculture: Prof. M. ABDUL HAMID
Faculty of Agro-Industrial and Food Processing Engineering: Prof. M. RUHUL AMIN
Faculty of Business Studies: Prof. Dr FAHIMA KHANOM
Faculty of Computer Science and Engineering: Prof. M. ROFIQUL ISLAM MAHMUD (acting)
Faculty of Fisheries: Prof. M. ROFIQUL ISLAM MAHMUD (acting)
Faculty of Postgraduate Studies: Prof. M. ABDUL HAMID

INDEPENDENT UNIVERSITY, BANGLADESH

Plot 16, Block B, Aftabuddin Ahmed Rd, Bashundhara, Dhaka 1229
Telephone: (2) 8401790
Fax: (2) 8401991
E-mail: info@iub.edu.bd
Internet: www.iub.edu.bd
Founded 1992
Private control
Language of instruction: English
Academic year: August to July
Chancellor: PRES. OF THE PEOPLE'S REPUBLIC OF BANGLADESH
Pro-Vice-Chancellor: Prof. OMAR RAHMAN
Vice-Chancellor: Prof. OMAR RAHMAN
Dir of Finance and Accounts: MUHAMMED SAIDUZZAMAN
Assoc. Dean for Undergraduate Admissions: YAZMIN Z. MAHMUD
Registrar: Dr TANVIR AHMED KHAN
Librarian: MUHAMMAD HOSSAM HAIDER CHOWDHURY
Library of 22,700 vols, 72 journal subscriptions
Number of teachers: 205 , (160 full-time, 45 part-time)
Number of students: 3,570 (2,798 undergraduates, 772 graduates)
Publication: *Independent Business Review* (2 a year)

DEANS

School of Business: NADIM JAHANGIR
School of Engineering and Computer Science: MOHAMMED ANWER
School of Environmental Science and Management: HAROUN-ER RASHID
School of Liberal Arts and Social Sciences: NAZRUL ISLAM

PROFESSORS

School of Business (internet sb.iub.edu.bd):
KUMAR SEN, D.
MOHAMMAD ABDUR, R.
School of Engineering and Computer Science:
ANWER, M.
KHODADAT KHAN, A. F. M.
NURUZZAMAN, M.
SUFDERUL HUQ, S.
School of Environmental Science and Management (tel. (2) 9884498; internet www.iub.edu.bd/sesm/sesm.html):
HOSSAIN, M. A.
KAMAL, N.
KARIM, Z.
RAHMAN, M. L.
RAHMAN, O.

School of Liberal Arts and Science (tel. (2) 9881917; internet www.iub.edu.bd/slas/slas.html):
ISLAM, N.

INTERNATIONAL UNIVERSITY OF BUSINESS, AGRICULTURE AND TECHNOLOGY

4 Embankment Drive Rd, Sector 10, Uttara Model Town, Dhaka 1230
Telephone: (2) 8923471
Fax: (2) 8922625
E-mail: info@iubat.edu
Internet: www.iubat.edu
Founded 1991
Private control
Language of instruction: English
Academic year: January to December
Chancellor: PRESIDENT OF THE PEOPLE'S REPUBLIC OF BANGLADESH
Vice-Chancellor: Prof. M. ALIMULLAH MIYAN
Pro-Chancellor: Prof. MAHMUDA KHANUM
Treasurer: SELINA NARGIS
Registrar: Dr M. A. HANNAN
Librarian: MONOWARA SARWAR
Library of 18,317 vols, 14,009 books, 196 journals, 88 periodicals,
Number of teachers: 200
Number of students: 5,500
Colleges of agricultural sciences, arts and sciences, business administration, engineering and technology, health sciences and medical education, nursing, tourism and hospitality management

DEANS

College of Agricultural Sciences: M. A. HANNAN
College of Arts and Sciences: K. R. KAMAL WADOOD
College of Business Administration: M. ALIMULLAH MIYAN
College of Engineering and Technology: MONIRUL ISLAM
College of Health Sciences and Medical Education: A. S. A. MASUD
College of Nursing: KAREN LUND
College of Tourism and Hospitality Management: AMANULLAH

PROFESSORS

ALIMULLAH MIYAN, M.
ALI, F.
AL SIDDIQUE, F.
DEB, S.
HANNAN, M.
HAQUE, E.
HAQUE, R.
ISLAM, R.
JABBER, M.
KAMAL WADOOD, K.
KARIM, S.
KHANUM, M.
LUND, K.
MANNAN, M.
MIAH, S.
MONIRUL ISLAM, M.
NARAYAN GHOSH, S.
RAHMAN, A.
RAQUIB, A.
RASHIDUZZAMAN, A.
RASUL, T.
SAIFULLAH, A.
SUBHAN, A.

ISLAMIC UNIVERSITY

Shantidanga-Dulalpur, Kushtia
Telephone: (71) 54079
Fax: (71) 54400
E-mail: vciu@kushtia.com
Internet: www.shibiriu.org
Founded 1980

Vice-Chancellor: Prof. FAEZ MAHAMMAD SERAJUL HAQUE
Registrar: MUHAMMAD MOSLEM UDDIN
Librarian: (vacant)
Library of 22,000 vols
Number of teachers: 65
Number of students: 9,284

DEANS

Faculty of Social Sciences: Dr M. MAMUN
Faculty of Theology and Islamic Studies: Prof. M. A. HAMID (acting)

ISLAMIC UNIVERSITY OF TECHNOLOGY

Board Bazar, Gazipur 1704
Telephone: (2) 9291250
Fax: (2) 9291260
E-mail: vc@iut-dhaka.edu
Internet: www.iutoic-dhaka.edu
Founded 1981 as Islamic Centre for Technical and Vocational Training and Research; became Islamic Institute of Technology 1994; present name 2001
Subsidiary of the Organization of the Islamic Conference
Academic year: December to September
Vice-Chancellor: Prof. Dr IMTIAZ HOSSAIN
Registrar: MOHAMMAD AHSAN HABIB
Librarian: Dr MIRZA MOHAMMAD REZAUL ISLAM
Library of 32,000 vols, 17 periodicals
Number of teachers: 103
Number of students: 862
Publications: *Journal of Engineering and Technology* (2 a year), *News Bulletin* (1 a year)

PROFESSORS

HOQUE, M. A., Electrical and Electronic Engineering
IQBAL HUSSAIN, A. K. M., Mechanical Engineering
ISLAM, K. K., Electrical and Electronic Engineering
MOTTALIB, M. A., Computer Science and Information Technology
RAZZAQ AKHANDA, M. A., Mechanical Engineering
SADRUL ISLAM, A. K. M., Mechanical Engineering
TAPAN, M. S., Training and General Studies
ULLAH, M. S., Electrical and Electronic Engineering
ZOHRUL KABIR, A. B. M., Mechanical Engineering

JAHANGIRNAGAR UNIVERSITY

Savar, Dhaka 1342
Telephone: (2) 7791045
Fax: (2) 7791052
E-mail: vc@juniv.edu
Internet: www.juniv.edu
Founded 1970
Languages of instruction: Bengali, English
Academic year: July to June (3 terms)
Chancellor: PRES. OF THE REPUBLIC
Vice-Chancellor: Prof. MOHAMMED MUNIRUZZAMAN
Pro-Vice-Chancellor (Academic): Prof. MUHAMMAD ENMUL HUQ KHAN
Pro-Vice-Chancellor (Admin.): Prof. M. IMAMUDDIN
Registrar: ABU BAKR SIDDIQUE (acting)
Librarian: Prof. SUBASH CHANDRA DAS
Library of 103,000 vols, 193 periodicals
Number of teachers: 423
Number of students: 8,105
Publications: *Asian Studies*, *Bangladesh Geoscience Journal*, *Bangladesh Journal of Life Sciences* (Biological and Life Sci-

ences), *Clio* (History), *Copula* (Philosophy), *Harvest* (English Studies), *Jahangirnagar Economic Review, Jahangirnagar Physics Studies, Jahangirnagar Planning Review, Jahangirnagar Review* (Arts and Humanities), *Jahangirnagar Review* (Social Sciences), *Jahangirnagar University Chemical Review, Jahangirnagar University Journal of Sciences* (Mathematical and Physical Sciences), *Journal of Business Research, Journal of Electronic and Computer Science, Journal of Mathematics and Mathematical Sciences, Journal of Statistical Studies, Nre Baggan Patrica* (Anthropology), *Pratnatattva* (Archaeology), *Theatre Studies, Vhasa Shahitta Patra* (Bengali Studies), *Vogal Patrica* (Geography)

DEANS

Faculty of Arts and Humanities: Prof. MUHAMMAD NASIRUDDIN
Faculty of Biological Sciences: Prof. SHAHABUDDIN KABIR CHOWDHURY (Dir)
Faculty of Mathematical and Physical Sciences: Prof. MAHMOODA GHANI AHMED
Faculty of Social Sciences: Prof. AMIN MUHAMMAD ALI

ATTACHED INSTITUTES

Computer Science and Information Technology Institute: e-mail citi@juniv.edu; internet www.juniv.edu/citi.htm; f. 1987; Dir Prof. MAHMOODA GHANI AHMED.
Institute of Remote Sensing: Dir Prof. MUHAMMAD SAJED ASHRAF KARIM.
Language Centre: Dir Prof. U. H. M. SHAMSUN NAHAR.

KHULNA UNIVERSITY

Khulna 9208
Telephone: (41) 721791
Fax: (41) 731244
E-mail: regekuly@bttb.net.bd
Internet: www.ku.ac.bd
Founded 1987
State control
Language of instruction: English
Academic year: July to June
Vice-Chancellor: Prof. Dr M. SAIFUDDIN SHAH
Registrar: MUHAMMAD NAZRUL ISLAM (acting)
Librarian: MOKLESUR RAHMAN (acting)
Library of 30,000 vols
Number of teachers: 154
Number of students: 4,046
Publications: *Business Review* (2 a year), *Khulna University Studies* (2 a year)

DEANS

School of Arts, Humanities and Social Science: Prof. Dr MOHAMED MAHBUBUR RAHMAN
School of Business Administration: Prof. Dr MOHAMED MAHBUBUR RAHMAN
School of Life Science: Prof. MOHAMED ABDUL MALIN
School of Science, Engineering and Technology: Prof. Dr MOHAMED RAZAUL KARIM

KHULNA UNIVERSITY OF ENGINEERING AND TECHNOLOGY

Fulbarigate, Khulna 9203
Telephone: (41) 774584
Fax: (41) 774403
E-mail: registrar@kuet.ac.bd
Internet: www.kuet.ac.bd
Founded 1974 as Khulna Engineering College; became Bangladesh Institute of Technology, Khulna 1986; present name and status 2003
State control

Vice-Chancellor: Prof. Dr M. NAWSHER ALI MORAL
Registrar: (vacant)
Library of 30,000 vols
Number of teachers: 132
Number of students: 1,887

DEANS

Faculty of Civil Engineering: Prof. Dr MUHAMMED ALAMGIR
Faculty of Electrical and Electronic Engineering: Prof. Dr BASHUDEB CHANDRA GHOSH
Faculty of Mechanical Engineering: Prof. Dr M. NAWSHERL ALI MORA

MAWLANA BHASANI UNIVERSITY OF SCIENCE AND TECHNOLOGY

Santosh, Tangail 1902
Telephone: (921) 55399
Fax: (921) 55400
E-mail: registrar@mbstu.ac.bd
Internet: mbstu.ac.bd
Founded 1999
State control
Vice-Chancellor: Prof. Dr M. MONIMUL HUQUE
Registrar: M. NURUL ISLAM MIA

DEANS

Faculty of Computer Science and Engineering: Prof. Dr M. MONIMUL HUQUE
Faculty of Life Sciences: Prof. Dr M. MONIMUL HUQUE

NATIONAL UNIVERSITY

Board Bazar, Gazipur 1704
Telephone: (2) 9291018
Fax: (2) 8110852
E-mail: vc@nu.edu.bd
Internet: www.nu.edu.bd
Founded 1992
State control
Chancellor: PRIME MINISTER OF THE PEOPLE'S REPUBLIC OF BANGLADESH
Vice-Chancellor: Prof. Dr M. MUFAKHARUL ISLAM
Dean of the School of Undergraduate Studies: Prof. FAKIR RAFIQUL ALAM
Dean of Graduate Education, Training and Research: Dr S. M. ABU RAIHAN
Publications: *Jatiya Bishawvidalaya Patrika* (4 a year), *Journal* (4 a year).

NORTH SOUTH UNIVERSITY

12 Banani Commercial Area, Kemal Ataturk Ave, Dhaka 1213
Telephone: (2) 9885611
Fax: (2) 8823030
E-mail: registrar@northsouth.edu
Internet: www.northsouth.edu
Founded 1992
Private control
Academic year: January to December (3 semesters)
Number of teachers: 155 (84 full-time, 71 visiting)
Number of students: 6,488
Vice-Chancellor: Dr HAFIZ G. A. SIDDIQI
Registrar: MOHAMMAD ALI
Dep. Librarian: MUHAMMAD MOSTAFIZUR RAHMAN

DEANS

School of Applied Sciences: Prof. Dr S. A. M. KHAIRUL BASHAR
School of Arts and Social Sciences: Prof. Dr M. ALI RASHID
School of Business: Prof. Dr AMIRUL ISLAM CHOWDHURY

PATUAKHALI UNIVERSITY OF SCIENCE AND TECHNOLOGY

Dumki, Patuakhali 8602
Telephone: (4427) 56011
Fax: (4427) 56009
Internet: www.pstu.ac.bd
Founded 2002
State control
Vice-Chancellor: Prof. Dr SYED SAKHAWAT HUSAIN
Librarian: MOHAMED ANWAR HOSSEIN
Number of students: 578

UNIVERSITY OF CHITTAGONG

University Post Office, Chittagong 4331
Telephone: (31) 682042
Fax: (31) 726310
E-mail: vc-cu@spnetctg.com
Internet: www.cu.ac.bd
Founded 1966
Languages of instruction: Bengali, English
Academic year: July to June
Vice-Chancellor: Prof. M. BADIUL ALAM
Pro-Vice-Chancellor: Prof. Dr MOHAMMED SHAMSUDDIN
Registrar: Prof. IDRIS MIYAN
Librarian: SYED MOHAMED ABU TAHER
Library of 201,514 vols
Number of teachers: 643
Number of students: 14,873

DEANS

Faculty of Arts: Prof. Dr MOHAMMED SIRAJUL ISLAM
Faculty of Commerce: Prof. Dr MONJUR MORSHED MAHMUD
Faculty of Law: Dr MORSHED MAHMUD KHAN
Faculty of Medicine: Prof. CHOWDURY B. MAHMUD
Faculty of Science: Prof. Dr ABU SALEH
Faculty of Social Science: Prof. Dr MUINUL ISLAM
Faculty of Veterinary Medicine: Prof. Dr NITISH CHANDRA DEBNATH

PROFESSORS

Faculty of Arts
    Arabic and Islamic Studies:

AHMED, R.
DOZA, H. M. B
HAQUE, A. F. M. A.
KHATIBI, M. A. H.
QUADER, A. K. M. A.
RASHID, M.

    Bengali:

ALAM, M. S.
AMIN, M. N.
AZIM, A.
AZIZ, M. M.
BISWAS, S. N.
CHOWDHURY, A. U. M. Z. H.
DASTIDAR, S. R.
IQBAL, B. M.
ISLAM, A. K. M. N.
MANIRUZZAMAN, M.
QUASEM, M. A.
SHAHJAHAN
ZAMAN, A. L.

    English:

ALAM, M. U.
BARUA, T. J.
BILLA, Q. M.
CHOWDHURY, G. S.
DUTTA, S. K.
ISLAM, M. S.
MOHMOOD, A. B. M. M.

    Fine Arts:

ALI, S. M. A.
AZIM, F.
BANU, N.
ISLAM, M. S.

KARIM, M. M.
KHALED, S. A.
MANSUR, A.
RAHIM, M.
ROY, A.

History:

CHOWDHURY, M. A.
HOQUE, M.
HOSSAIN, E.
HOSSAIN, H.
KABIR, E.
KHALED, A. M. M. S.
SAYED, A.
SHAH, M.

Islamic History and Culture:

AHMED, A.
AHMED, S.
ALAM, A. Q. M. S.
BHUIYAN, G. K.
CHOWDHURY, M. T. H.
HUQ, M. I.
SHAFIQ ULLAH, S. M.
YUSUF, A.

Oriental Languages:

BARUA, D. S.
BARUA, R. K.
HALDER, S. R.

Philosophy:

AHMED, R.
ALAM, M. S.
ALI, M. A.
ANWAR, A. J.
CHOWDHURY, M. A.
KHALEQUE, A. S. M. A.
RAHMAN, A. K. M. S.
RAHMAN, A. M. M. W.
RAHMAN, M. B.
RAHMAN, M. L.

Faculty of Commerce

Accounting and Information Systems:

AHMED, S.
BHATTACHARJEE, M. K.
CHOWDHURY, R. K.
DAS, S. R.
DATTA, D. K.
MAHMUD, M. M.
MOHIUDDIN, K. M. G.
NAG, A. B.
PURAHIT, K. K.
RASHID, H.
SALAUDDIN, A.
SHARMA, B. K.

Finance and Banking:

HOQUE, M. J.
LOQMAN, M.
MOQTADIR, A. N. M. A.
NABI, K. A.
RASHID, M. H.

Management:

ALAM, M. F.
ALI, A. F. M. A.
ARIF, M. A. A.
ATHER, S. M.
MAMUN, M. A.
MANNAN, M. A.
SIKDER, Z. H.
TAHER, M. A.

Marketing:

BHUIYAN, S. M. S. U.
CHOWDHURY, A. J. M.
KARIM, A. N. M. N.
MEHER, M. S.
SHAHIN, S.
SOLAIMAN, M.

Faculty of Law

Law:

ALAM, M. S.

Faculty of Science

Applied Physics and Electronics:

BHUIYAN, M. A. S.

HOSSAIN, A.
KHAN, M. R. H.
SAHA, S. L.

Biochemistry and Molecular Biology:

ALAUDDIN, M.

Botany:

AHMED, M.
ALAMGIR, A. N. M.
BASET, Q. A.
BHADRA, S. K.
CHOWDHURY, A. M.
GAFUR, M. A.
MRIDHA, M. A.
PASHA, M. K.
RAHMAN, M. A.

Chemistry:

AHMED, M. J.
AHMED, M. S. U.
AKHTAR, S.
BEGUM, S. A.
CHOWDHURY, D. A.
CHOWDHURY, M. Z. A.
DEY, B. K.
HABIB ULLAH, M.
HAZARI, S. K. S.
ISLAM, M.
KABIR, A. K. M. S.
NAZIMUDDIN, M.
PALIT, D.
RAHMAN, K. M. M.
ROY, T. G.
SALAM, M. A.
SALEH, M. A.
UDDIN, M. H.

Computer Science:

MOSTAFA, M. N.

Mathematics:

AHMED, M.
AZAD, A. K.
BHATTACHARJEE, N. R.
ISLAM, M. A.
ISLAM, M. N.
MOHIUDDIN, M.
RAHMAN, M. M.

Microbiology:

ANWAR, M. N.
HAKIM, M. A.

Physics:

AHMED, F. K.
AHMED, M.
BANU, H.
BARUA, B. P.
BEGUM, D. A.
DEB, A. K.
ISLAM, M. N.
MIYA, M. M. H.
NABI, S. R.
PAUL, D. P.
ROY, M. K.
SAFIULLAH, M. A.
SAHA, S. K.
SIDDIQA, N.

Soil Science:

OSMAN, K. T.

Statistics:

ISLAM, S. M. S.
PAUL, J. C.
RAHMAN, M. M.
RASUL, M. A.
ROY, M. K.
SHAMSUDDIN, M.
SHIL, R. N.
YAHYA, N. S. M.

Zoology:

AHMED, B.
AHSAN, M. F.
ALAM, M. S.
ASMAT, G. S. M.
AZADI, M. A.
BANU, Q.
BHUIYAN, A. M.

BHUIYAN, M. A.
HAFIZUDDIN, A. K. M.
ISLAM, M. A.
KHAN, M. A. G.
MEAH, M. I.
NASIRUDDIN, M.
ULLAH, G. M. R.

Faculty of Social Science

Anthropology:

CHOWDHURY, A. F. H.

Economics:

ASHRAF, M. A.
AZAD, A. K.
CHOWDHURY, M. A. M.
DEY, H. K.
DUTTA, J. P.
HOQ, M.
HOQUE, M. S.
HOSSAIN, B.
ISLAM, M.
KHAN, I. K.
KHAN, M. S.
MAHBUB, U.
NAG, N. C.
SALEHUDDIN, M.
TAHERA, B. S.

Political Science:

AHMED, A. N. M. M.
AHMED, S. Z.
AKHTER, M. Y.
ALAM, M. B.
CHOWDHURY, M. H.
CHOWDHURY, S. A.
HAKIM, M. A.
HASSAN, M.
HOQUE, M. E.
KABIR, B. M. M.
KHAN, Z. N.
KHANAM, J.
KHANAM, R.
MUSHRAFI, M. E. M.
SHAMSUDDIN, M.

Public Administration:

AHMED, N. U.
AHMED, T.
AMIN, M. R.
BEGUM, A.
ISLAM, M. N.
MASHREQUE, M. S.
NOOR, A.
WAHHAB, M. A.

Sociology:

ALI, A. F. I.
BHUIYAN, M. A.
CHOWDHURY, A. Q.
CHOWDHURY, H. Z.
CHOWDHURY, I. U.
HUSSAIN, M.
KARIM, M. O.
MAHABUBULLAH, M.
QUDDUS, A. H. G.
SALEHUDDIN, G.
SEN, A.

There are 130 affiliated colleges.

UNIVERSITY OF DHAKA

Ramna, Dhaka 1000
Telephone: (2) 9661900
Fax: (2) 9661920
E-mail: duregstr@bangla.net
Internet: www.univdhaka.edu
Founded 1921
Independent
Languages of instruction: Bengali, English
Academic year: July to June (three terms)
Chancellor: PRESIDENT OF THE PEOPLE'S REPUBLIC OF BANGLADESH
Vice-Chancellor: Prof. A. A. M. S. AREFIN SIDDIQUE
Pro-Vice-Chancellor: Prof. Dr H. RASHID
Treasurer: M. RAHMAN (acting)

Registrar: M. A. HUSSAIN (acting)
Librarian: Dr M. S. ISLAM (acting)
Library: see Libraries and Archives
Number of teachers: 1,492
Number of students: 24,060
Publications: *Dhaka University Studies* (2 a
  year), *Dhaka Viswa Vidyalaya Bartra* (4 a
  year), *Dhaka Viswa Vidyalaya Patrika* (3 a
  year), *Sahitya Patrika* (3 a year)

DEANS

Faculty of Arts: Dr S. AMIN
Faculty of Biological Sciences: Prof. M.
  ABDUL BASHAR
Faculty of Business Studies: Prof Dr A. ALI
  KHAN
Faculty of Earth and Environmental Sci-
  ences: Prof. Dr S. HUQ-HUSSAIN
Faculty of Education: M. SHAH JAHAN
Faculty of Engineering and Technology: Prof.
  Dr S. RAFIQ
Faculty of Law: Prof. Dr B. U. KHAN
Faculty of Medicine: Dr A. Z. M. Z. HOSSAIN
Faculty of Pharmacy: Prof. M. A. RASHID
Faculty of Postgraduate Medical Sciences
  and Research: Prof. T. AHMED
Faculty of Science: Dr T. S. A. ISLAM
Faculty of Social Sciences: H. RASHID (acting)

PROFESSORS

ABDULLAH, A. S. A., Accounting and Informa-
  tion Systems
ABEDIN, K. M., Physics
ABRAR, C. R., International Relations
ABULULAYEE, S. K. M., Philosophy
ADEEB, K., Nutrition and Food Science
ADITYA, S. K., Applied Physics and Electron-
  ics
AFROEZ, D., Psychology
AFTABUDDIN, M., Biochemistry and Molecular
  Biology
AHAD, S. A., Soil, Water and the Environ-
  ment
AHMAD, N., Arabic
AHMED, A., Economics
AHMED, A., Political Science
AHMED, A. F., Public Administration
AHMED, A. I. M. U., Sociology
AHMED, A. K. M. U., Economics
AHMED, A. T. A., Zoology
AHMED, A. U., Nutrition and Food Science
AHMED, E., Chemistry
AHMED, E., International Relations
AHMED, F., Applied Physics and Electronics
AHMED, F., Economics
AHMED, I., Business Administration
AHMED, J. U., Finance
AHMED, K. U., Political Science
AHMED, M., Accounting and Information
  Systems
AHMED, M., Clinical Pharmacy and Pharma-
  cology
AHMED, M., Economics
AHMED, M., Physics
AHMED, M., Public Administration
AHMED, M. F., Finance
AHMED, M. G., Chemistry
AHMED, M. N., Geography and the Environment
AHMED, S., Anthropology
AHMED, S., Economics
AHMED, S., Economics
AHMED, S., Management Studies
AHMED, S. A., Chemistry
AHMED, S. G., Public Administration
AHMED, S. J., Theatre and Music
AHMED, S. U., History
AHMED, S. U., Management Studies
AHMED, W., Bengali
AHMED, Z., History
AHMED MAJIB, U., Accounting and Informa-
  tion Systems
AHMED MAMATAJ, U., Accounting and Infor-
  mation Systems
AHSAN, A., Management Studies
AHSAN, C. R., Microbiology

AHSAN, M., Pharmaceutical Chemistry
AHSAN, M. A., Education and Research
AHSAN, M. Q., Chemistry
AHSAN, R. M., Geography and the Environ-
  ment
AKHTER, N., Botany
AKHTER, R., Philosophy
AKHTER, S. H., Geology
AKHTERUZZAMAN, M., Islamic History and
  Culture
AKKAS, M. A., Management Studies
AKTER, S., Education and Research
ALAM, A. F., Marketing
ALAM, A. M. S., Chemistry
ALAM, B., Physics
ALAM, F., English
ALAM, H. A., Philosophy
ALAM, K. M. U., Geology
ALAM, K. S., Marketing
ALAM, M., Geology
ALAM, M. D., Soil, Water and the Environ-
  ment
ALAM, M. K., Soil, Water and the Environ-
  ment
ALAM, M. M., Economics
ALAM, M. M., Geology
ALAM, M. R., Fine Arts
ALAM, S. S., Botany
ALI, A. H. M. M., Fine Arts
ALI, A. K. M. I., Islamic History and Culture
ALI, A. M., Mass Communication and Jour-
  nalism
ALI, M. A., Education and Research
ALI, M. S., Physics
ALI, M. S., Zoology
ALI, R., Psychology
ALI, S. M. K., Nutrition and Food Science
ALVI, S. A. B., Fine Arts
AMIN, M. R., Islamic Studies
AMIN, S., English
AMIN, S. N., History
AMINUZZAMAN, S. M., Development Studies
ANISUZZAMAN, Philosophy
ANOWAR, A. J., Philosophy
ANOWAR, S. F., Business Administration
ANSARUDDIN, M., Islamic Studies
ARA, R., Philosophy
AREFEEN, H. K. S., Anthropology
ASADUZZAMAN, M., Public Administration
AWAL, A. Z. M. I., History
AZAD, S. A. K., Marketing
AZIM, F., English
AZIZ, A., Botany
BANOO, R., Pharmaceutical Chemistry
BANU, K., Statistics
BANU, N., Zoology
BANU, R., Modern Languages
BANU, S., Mathematics
BANU, S., Psychology
BANU, U. A. B. R. A., Political Science
BAPARY, M. N. A., Political Science
BAQI, A., Islamic Studies
BAQUEE, A. H. M. A., Geography and the
  Environment
BARI, M. E., Law
BARKAT, M. A., Economics
BARMAN, D. C., Peace and Conflict Studies
BARUA, S., Nutrition and Food Science
BASHAR, M. H., Chemistry
BASHER, A., Zoology
BEGUM, A., Islamic History and Culture
BEGUM, A., Physics
BEGUM, F., Sanskrit and Pali
BEGUM, H. A., Education and Research
BEGUM, H. A., Psychology
BEGUM, H. J., Physics
BEGUM, K., Education and Research
BEGUM, L., Philosophy
BEGUM, M., Botany
BEGUM, N., Economics
BEGUM, N., Islamic History and Culture
BEGUM, R., Botany
BEGUM, R., Clinical Psychology
BEGUM, R., Education and Research
BEGUM, R., Marketing
BEGUM, S., Zoology

BEGUM, S. F., Social Welfare and Research
BEGUM, Z. N. T., Botany
BHATTACHARJEE, D. D., Management Studies
BHATTACHARJEE, H., Marketing
BHOWMIK, D. K., Sanskrit and Pali
BHOWMIK, N. C., Applied Physics and Elec-
  tronics
BHUIYAN, G. M., Physics
BHUIYAN, M. A. H., Nutrition and Food
  Science
BHUIYAN, M. M. R., Statistics
BHUIYAN, M. S., Management Studies
BHUIYAN, M. S., Political Science
BHUIYAN, M. Z. H., Marketing
BHUIYAN, S., History
BILLAH, M. M., Statistics
BISWAS, N. C., Sanskrit and Pali
BORHANUDDIN, Geography and the Environ-
  ment
BSAHAR, M. A., Botany
CHAKMA, N. K., Philosophy
CHOWDHURY, A., Zoology
CHOWDHURY, A. A. M. U., Finance
CHOWDHURY, A. B. M. H., Islamic Studies
CHOWDHURY, A. K. A., Clinical Psychology
CHOWDHURY, A. M., History
CHOWDHURY, A. M. S. U., Applied Chemistry
  and Chemical Technology
CHOWDHURY, A. R., Law
CHOWDHURY, A. U., Anthropology
CHOWDHURY, B., Bengali
CHOWDHURY, D. K., Accounting and Informa-
  tion Systems
CHOWDHURY, F., Mathematics
CHOWDHURY, G. M., Business Administration
CHOWDHURY, H. U., Political Science
CHOWDHURY, I. G., Business Administration
CHOWDHURY, L. H., Public Administration
CHOWDHURY, M. A., Economics
CHOWDHURY, M. A. I., Marketing
CHOWDHURY, M. A. M., Management Studies
CHOWDHURY, M. H., Social Welfare and
  Research
CHOWDHURY, M. M., Political Science
CHOWDHURY, M. M. R., Sociology
CHOWDHURY, M. R., Biochemistry and
  Molecular Biology
CHOWDHURY, M. R., Mathematics
CHOWDHURY, M. S., Physics
CHOWDHURY, M. S., Soil, Water and the
  Environment
CHOWDHURY, N., Statistics
CHOWDHURY, N., Women's Studies
CHOWDHURY, P. B., Management Studies
CHOWDHURY, Q. A., Sociology
CHOWDHURY, R. R., Accounting and Informa-
  tion Systems
CHOWDHURY, S., Physics
CHOWDHURY, S. Q., Geology
CHOWDHURY, T. A., Chemistry
DAS, A. K., Chemistry
DATTA, B. K., Pharmaceutical Chemistry
ELAHI, S. F., Soil, Water and the Environ-
  ment
EUSUF, A. Z., Geography and the Environ-
  ment
FAIZ, B., Soil, Water and the Environment
FAIZ, S. M. A., Soil, Water and the Environ-
  ment
FAROUK, A. B. M., Pharmaceutical Technol-
  ogy
FERDAUSI, N., Physics
FERDAUSI, R. R., Mathematics
GHOSH, B., Bengali
GHOSH, S. N., Accounting and Information
  Systems
GOMES, D. J., Microbiology
HADIUZZAM, S., Botany
HAIDER, A. F. M. Y., Physics
HAIDER, A. R. M. A., Islamic Studies
HAKIM, M. A., Accounting and Information
  Systems
HALDER, A. K., Mathematics
HALIM, M. A., International Relations
HANNAN, F., Sociology
HAQ, M., Fine Arts

MOSHIHUZZAMAN, M., Chemistry
MOWLA, S. G., Management Studies
MOYEEN, M. A., Management Studies
MUNSHI, M. S. H., Political Science
MUSA, A. M. M. A., Modern Languages
MUSTAFA, A. I., Applied Chemistry and Chemical Technology
MUTTAQUI, M. I. A., Education and Research
NABI, A. K. M. N., Population Sciences
NABI, M. R., Fine Arts
NAHAR, B., Nutrition and Food Science
NAHAR, L., Nutrition and Food Science
NAHAR, N., Chemistry
NASIRUDDIN, M., Finance
NASREEN, G. A., Mass Communication and Journalism
NAZNEEN, D. R. Z. A., Peace and Conflict Studies
NIZAMI, A. B. M. S. R., Arabic
OSMAN, B., Fine Arts
OSMANY, S. H., History
PAHA, N. A., Chemistry
PARVEEN, K. N., Political Science
PARVEEN, Z., Soil, Water and the Environment
PERVIN, S., Mathematics
QADRI, S. S., Biochemistry and Molecular Biology
QAIS, N., Clinical Pharmacy and Pharmacology
QUADER, M. A., Chemistry
QUASEM, M. A., Philosophy
QUDDUS, M. A., Marketing
QUDDUS, M. A., Mathematics
QUDDUS, M. M. A., Zoology
QUYYUM, M. A., Applied Chemistry and Chemical Technology
RAB, M. A., Geography and the Environment
RABBANI, K. S. E., Physics
RAFIQ, S., Applied Physics and Electronics
RAHIM, K. A., Biochemistry and Molecular Biology
RAHIM, T., Botany
RAHMA, P. K. M. M., Statistical Research and Training
RAHMAN, A., Health Economics
RAHMAN, A., Information Science and Library Management
RAHMAN, A., Modern Languages
RAHMAN, A. H. M. A., Political Science
RAHMAN, A. H. M. H., Finance
RAHMAN, A. H. M. M., Applied Chemistry and Chemical Technology
RAHMAN, A. H. M. M., Soil, Water and the Environment
RAHMAN, A. K. M. M., Information Technology
RAHMAN, A. M. M. H., Modern Languages
RAHMAN, A. S. M. A., Social Welfare and Research
RAHMAN, A. Z. M. A., Accounting and Information Systems
RAHMAN, B. W., Education and Research
RAHMAN, J., Applied Physics and Electronics
RAHMAN, K. M., Nutrition and Food Science
RAHMAN, K. M. M., Statistical Research and Training
RAHMAN, K. R., English
RAHMAN, M., Accounting and Information Systems
RAHMAN, M., Biochemistry and Molecular Biology
RAHMAN, M., Marketing
RAHMAN, M., Public Administration
RAHMAN, M. A., Chemistry
RAHMAN, M. A., Clinical Psychology
RAHMAN, M. A., Law
RAHMAN, M. A., Marketing
RAHMAN, M. A., Mathematics
RAHMAN, M. A., Physics
RAHMAN, M. A., Political Science
RAHMAN, M. F., Arabic
RAHMAN, M. F., Zoology
RAHMAN, M. G., Mass Communication and Journalism
RAHMAN, M. H., Pharmaceutical Technology

RAHMAN, M. H., Sociology
RAHMAN, M. K., Biochemistry and Molecular Biology
RAHMAN, M. K., Soil, Water and the Environment
RAHMAN, M. K., Zoology
RAHMAN, M. L., Computer Science and Engineering
RAHMAN, M. M., Arabic
RAHMAN, M. M., Chemistry
RAHMAN, M. M., Clinical Psychology
RAHMAN, M. M., Marketing
RAHMAN, M. M., Mathematics
RAHMAN, M. M., Microbiology
RAHMAN, M. M., Nutrition and Food Science
RAHMAN, M. M., Philosophy
RAHMAN, M. M., Physics
RAHMAN, M. M., Soil, Water and the Environment
RAHMAN, M. M., Statistics
RAHMAN, M. S., Bengali
RAHMAN, M. S., Education and Research
RAHMAN, M. S., Soil, Water and the Environment
RAHMAN, M. S., Statistics
RAHMAN, M. T., Mathematics
RAHMAN, N., Business Administration
RAHMAN, N., Sociology
RAHMAN, N. N., Pharmaceutical Chemistry
RAHMAN, R., Biochemistry and Molecular Biology
RAHMAN, S. M. L., Bengali
RAHMAN, S. M. M., Banking
RAISUDDIN, A. N. M., Islamic Studies
RASHED, K. B. S., Geography and the Environment
RASHID, A. H. M. H., Philosophy
RASHID, G. H., Soil, Water and the Environment
RASHID, H., Management Studies
RASHID, M. A., Pharmaceutical Chemistry
RASHID, M. H., Accounting and Information Systems
RASHID, M. H., Political Science
RASHID, M. H., Soil, Water and the Environment
RASHID, P., Botany
RASHID, R. I. M. A., Physics
ROY, K. N., English
ROY, P. K., Philosophy
SAHA, M., Applied Chemistry and Chemical Technology
SAHA, M. L., Botany
SAHA, P. K., Education and Research
SAHA, S. K., Accounting and Information Systems
SALAM, S. A., Mass Communication and Journalism
SALAMATULLAH, K., Nutrition and Food Science
SALEH, M. A., Management Studies
SALMA, U., Persian and Urdu
SAMAD, A., Biochemistry and Molecular Biology
SAMAD, M., Social Welfare and Research
SARKER, A. H., Social Welfare and Research
SARKER, A. M., Fine Arts
SARKER, N., Fisheries
SARKER, N. R., Psychology
SARKER, R. H., Botany
SATTER, M. A., Fine Arts
SATTER, M. A., Physics
SEN, K., Statistics
SERAJ, Z. I., Biochemistry and Molecular Biology
SHAFEE, A., Physics
SHAFEE, S., Physics
SHAFI, M., Geology
SHAH, A. K. F. H., Marketing
SHAH, A. S., Fine Arts
SHAHED, S. M., Bengali
SHAHED, S. N., Bengali
SHAHEEN, N., Nutrition and Food Science
SHAHIDULLAH, A. K. M., Political Science
SHAHIDULLAH, K., History
SHAHIDULLAH, S. M., Psychology

SHAHIDUZZAMAN, M., International Relations
SHAMIM, I., Sociology
SHAMSI, S., Botany
SHARIF, M. R. I., Applied Physics and Electronics
SHEIKH, M. D. H., Education and Research
SIDDIQ, A. F. M. A. B., Arabic
SIDDIQ, M. A. B., Arabic
SIDDIQUE, A. A. M. S. A., Mass Communication and Journalism
SIDDIQUE, A. H., Management Studies
SIDDIQUE, S. A., Accounting and Information Systems
SIDDIQUE, T. A., Political Science
SIKDER, S. A., Fine Arts
SUFI, G. B., Zoology
SUKLADAS, J. C., Accounting and Information Systems
SULTANA, A., Mass Communication and Journalism
SULTANA, A., Philosophy
SYED, S., Nutrition and Food Science
TAHER, M. A., Social Welfare and Research
TALUKDER, A. S., Marketing
TASLIM, M. A., Economics
THAKURATA, M. G., International Relations
UDDIN, M. J., Education and Research
ULLAH, A. S. M. O., Geology
ULLAH, S. M., Soil, Water and Environment
WADUD, N., Psychology
WAHID, A. Q. F., Philosophy
YUSUF, H. K. M., Biochemistry and Molecular Biology
ZAFAR, M. A., Bengali
ZAMAN, F., Fine Arts
ZAMAN, N., English
ZAMAN, S. U., Economics

CONSTITUENT AND AFFILIATED COLLEGES

There are 58 constituent colleges and 3 affiliated colleges.

ATTACHED INSTITUTES

Institute of Business Administration: tel. (2) 8617815; fax (2) 8621411; e-mail iba@univdhaka.edu; internet www.iba-du.edu; f. 1966; Dir Prof. M. ZIAULHAQ MAMUN.

Institute of Education and Research: tel. (2) 9661920; fax (2) 8615583; e-mail ier@udhaka.net; internet www.ierdu.5u.com; f. 1960; Dir Prof. SALMA AKHTER.

Institute of Fine Arts: tel. (2) 9661920; fax (2) 9675219; e-mail ifa@udhaka.net; f. 1948; Dir Prof. ABDUS SHAKOOR SHAH.

Institute of Health Economics: tel. (2) 8620952; fax (2) 8615583; e-mail ihedu@citechco.net; f. 1998; Dir Prof. AZIZUR RAHMAN.

Institute of Information Technology: tel. (2) 9661920; fax (2) 8615583; e-mail iit@univdhaka.edu; internet iit.univdhaka.edu; f. 2001; Dir Prof. M. ZULFIQUAR HAFIZ.

Institute of Modern Languages: tel. (2) 8618236; fax (2) 8615583; e-mail hossainanwar@yahoo.com; f. 1964; Dir Dr ANWAR HOSSAIN.

Institute of Nutrition and Food Sciences: tel. (2) 9661900; fax (2) 8615583; e-mail nhassan@bangla.net; f. 1969; Dir Dr NAZMUL HASSAN.

Institute of Social Welfare and Research: tel. (2) 8622860; fax (2) 8615583; e-mail iswr@bttb.net.bd; f. 1973; Dir Dr A. S. M. ATIQUR RAHMAN.

Institute of Statistical Research and Training: tel. (2) 9661920; fax (2) 8615583; e-mail isrt@udhaka.net; internet www.isrt.ac.bd; f. 1964; Dir Dr AZMERI KHAN.

BUREAUX AND RESEARCH CENTRES

Bureau of Business Research.

Bureau of Economic Research.

Bio-Medical Research Centre.

Bose Centre for Advanced Studies and Research in Natural Sciences.

Centre for Advanced Research in Arts and Social Sciences: tel. (2) 8610334; fax (2) 8615583; f. 2005; Dir Prof. Dr A. H. AHMED KAMAL.

Centre for Advanced Research in Physical, Chemical, Biological and Pharmaceutical Sciences: tel. (2) 9661920; fax (2) 8615583; e-mail coe@univdhaka.edu; f. 2003; Dir Prof. SYED SALEHEEN QADRI.

Centre for Advanced Studies and Research in Biological Sciences.

Centre for Advanced Studies in Humanities.

Centre for Advanced Studies in Social Sciences.

Centre for Biotechnology Research: tel. (2) 9661920; fax (2) 8615583; e-mail lailanislam@yahoo.com; f. 2005; Dir Prof. LAILA N. ISLAM.

Centre for Development and Policy Research: f. 1928.

Centre for Disaster Research Training and Management.

Centre for Research in Archives and History.

Delta Study Centre: e-mail dsc@univdhaka .edu; f. 1990; geological studies of Bengal delta region.

Development Centre of Philosophical Research.

Renewable Energy Research Centre: tel. (2) 9661900; fax (2) 8615583; e-mail rerc@univdhaka.edu; f. 1981; Dir Prof. Dr NEEM CHANDRA BHOWMIK.

Semiconductor Technology Research Centre.

UNIVERSITY OF RAJSHAHI

Rajshahi 6205
Telephone: (721) 750041
Fax: (721) 750064
E-mail: rajucc@cilechco.net
Internet: www.ru.ac.bd
Founded 1953
Languages of instruction: English, Bengali
Academic year: July to June (3 terms)
Chancellor: PRES. OF THE PEOPLE'S REPUBLIC OF BANGLADESH
Vice-Chancellor: Prof. SAYEEDUR RAHMAN KHAN
Pro-Vice-Chancellor: Prof. MUMNUNUL KERAMAT
Registrar: Prof. MAHAMMAD SHAFI
Librarian: (vacant)
Library: see Libraries and Archives
Number of teachers: 804
Number of students: 26,691

Publications: *Calendar* (every 2 years), *Rajshahi University Studies* (1 a year)

DEANS

Faculty of Agriculture: Prof. M. ABDUL KHALEQUE
Faculty of Arts: Prof. MOHAMMAD SHAFI
Faculty of Business Studies: Prof. M. OMAR ALI
Faculty of Law: Prof. ASMA SIDDIQUA
Faculty of Life and Earth Science: GOLAM KABIR
Faculty of Medicine: Prof. ABU BAKER SIDDIQUE
Faculty of Science: Prof. M. ABUL HASHEM
Faculty of Social Science: Prof. M. SADIQUL ISLAM

PROFESSORS

Faculty of Agriculture:
  JOARDER, M. O. I., Genetics and Breeding

KABIR, G., Agronomy and Agricultural Extension
KHALEQUE, M. A., Genetics and Breeding

Faculty of Arts:
  ADHIKARY, M. N., Philosophy
  AHMED, K. M., Philosophy
  AHMED, S., Islamic History and Culture
  AHMED, W., History
  ALI, A. K. M. Y., Islamic History and Culture
  ALI, M. A., English
  ALI, M. W., History
  ASADULLAH-AL-GHALIB, M., Arabic
  BARI, M. A., Islamic History and Culture
  CHOWDHURY, N. H., History
  FARUK-UZ-ZAMAN, M., History
  FAZUL, M. A., Bengali
  GHOSE, R. N., Philosophy
  HAMID, M. A., Philosophy
  HAQUE, A., Philosophy
  HAQUE, K. S., Bengali
  HAQUE, M. E., English
  HARUN-OR-RASHID, M., Bengali
  HASSAN, M. A. D., English
  HOSSAIN, K. F., Bengali
  HOSSAIN, S., History
  IBRAHIMI, M. S. A., Arabic
  JALIL, M. A., Bengali
  JALIL, M. A., Folklore
  KHALEQUE, A., Bengali
  KHAN, M. A. A., Arabic
  MATIN, C. Z., Bengali
  MISRA, C. R., History
  MOHIUDDIN, A. K. M., English
  MONDAL, A. A., Philosophy
  NAHAR, S., Islamic History and Culture
  QAIYUM, M. N., History
  QUASEM, M. A., History
  RAHIM, M. A., History
  RAHMAN, A. F. M. S., History
  RAHMAN, A. K. M. A., Bengali
  RAHMAN, M. M., History
  RAHMAN, M. M., Islamic History and Culture
  RAHMAN, Q., Islamic History and Culture
  REHMAN, A. A., English
  ROY, K. L., Languages
  SALAM, M. A., Arabic
  SAMADI, S. S., Bengali
  SARKAR, J. N., Philosophy
  SARKAR, M. S. A., Philosophy
  SHAFI, M., History
  SHAFIQULLAH, M., Islamic Studies
  SHAHIDULLAH, M., English
  SHAHJAHAN, M., Philosophy
  SHAMSUDDIN, Philosophy
  SHIBLY, A. H., History
  TALUKDAR, M. A. H., Philosophy
  TAQI, F. M. A. H., Islamic Studies

Faculty of Business Studies:
  ABDULLAH-AL-HAROON, M., Accounting
  AKAM, M. H. R., Accounting
  ALAM, M. S., Accounting
  ALI, A. S. M. N., Management
  ALI, M. O., Management
  ALI, M. S. N., Management
  ANJUM, M. N., Management
  ANSARI, M. R., Finance and Banking
  DEY, M. M., Accounting
  HOSSAIN, M. M., Accounting
  HOSSAIN, S. Z., Accounting
  ISLAM, M. A., Management
  ISLAM, M. N., Accounting
  MOJID, A. K. M. A., Finance and Banking
  PAUL, P., Accounting
  PRAMANIK, M. A. R., Accounting
  RAHMAN, M. M., Management
  SAHA, A. C., Accounting
  SAHA, S. K., Marketing

Faculty of Law:
  HOSSAIN, M. M.
  RAHMAN, M. H.
  SIDDIQUE, M. A. B.

Faculty of Life and Earth Science:
  AFSARUDDIN, M., Psychology
  AHMED, A., Botany
  AHMED, M., Geology and Mining
  AHMED, M., Psychology
  AHMED, R., Geography and Environmental Studies
  AHMED, S. S., Geology and Mining
  AHMED, S. T., Geology and Mining
  ALAM, M. S., Botany
  ALAM, M. S., Geography and Environmental Studies
  ALI, M. M., Zoology
  ALI, M. S., Zoology
  AMIN, M. N., Botany
  ARA, S., Psychology
  BHUIYAN, M. A. S., Zoology
  FARUK, T., Psychology
  HAQUE, A. B. M. J., Psychology
  HAQUE, M. E., Geography and Environmental Studies
  HAQUE, M. M., Psychology
  HOSSAIN, M. A., Psychology
  HOSSAIN, M. A., Zoology
  HOSSAIN, M. M., Information and Communication Technology
  HOSSAIN, M. MONZUR, Botany
  HOSSAIN, M. MOZAHED, Botany
  HOSSAIN, N., Botany
  HUSSAIN, M. Z., Geography and Environmental Studies
  ISLAM, A. K. M. R., Botany
  ISLAM, M. A., Geology and Mining
  ISLAM, M. B., Geology and Mining
  ISLAM, M. S., Zoology
  JAHAN, M. S., Zoology
  KHALEQUE, M. A., Botany
  KHALEQUZZAMAN, M., Zoology
  KHAN, J. R., Geography and Environmental Studies
  KUNDU, P., Botany
  LATIF, M. A., Psychology
  MAJUMDER, Q. H., Geology and Mining
  MANNAN, M. A., Zoology
  NADERUZZAMAN, A. T. M., Botany
  NAHAR, S., Botany
  PARVEEN, S., Zoology
  PAUL, N. K., Botany
  RAHMAN, A. S. M. S., Zoology
  RAHMAN, M. A., Botany
  RAHMAN, M. A., Geography and Environmental Studies
  RAHMAN, M. A., Zoology
  RAHMAN, M. HABIBUR, Geology and Mining
  RAHMAN, M. HAMIDUR, Geology and Mining
  RAHMAN, M. S., Botany
  RAHMAN, M. S., Zoology
  RAHMAN, M. S., Zoology
  RAHMAN, S. M., Zoology
  RAQUIBUDDIN, M., Geology and Mining
  RUMI, S. R. A., Geography and Environmental Studies
  SALAM, M. A., Zoology
  SHAIKH, M. A. H., Geography and Environmental Studies
  TAHA, M. A., Geography and Environmental Studies
  WAHAB, M. A., Geography and Environmental Studies
  ZAMAN, M., Botany
  ZUBERI, M. I., Botany

Faculty of Science:
  ABEDIN, S., Statistics
  ABSAR, N., Biochemistry
  AHMED, M., Mathematics
  AHMED, N., Chemistry
  AHMED, S. U., Chemistry
  ALI, D. M., Mathematics
  ALI, M. A., Chemistry
  ALI, M. K., Population Science and Human Resource Development
  ALI, M. U., Chemistry
  ALI, M. Y., Chemistry
  ALI, S. M. M., Applied Chemistry and Chemical Technology

ANSARI, M. A., Mathematics
AZAD, M. A. K., Applied Chemistry and Chemical Technology
BAKER, M. A., Applied Chemistry and Chemical Technology
BANU, K., Physics
BASAK, A. K., Physics
BHATTACHARJEE, S., Physics
BHATTACHARJEE, S. K., Mathematics
BHATTACHARJEE, S. K., Statistics
BISWAS, R. K., Applied Chemistry and Chemical Technology
CHAKRAVARTY, P. K., Chemistry
CHOWDHURY, G. M., Physics
DAS, B. K., Chemistry
DEBNATH, R. C., Applied Physics and Electronics
FARUQUI, F. I., Applied Chemistry and Chemical Technology
HAKIM, M. O., Physics
HAQUE, M. E., Chemistry
HAQUE, M. E., Pharmacy
HAQUE, M. E., Physics
HASHEM, M. A., Applied Physics and Electronics
HOSSAIN, M. D., Applied Physics and Electronics
HOSSAIN, M. L., Chemistry
HOWLADER, M. B. H., Chemistry
ISLAM, A. K. M. A., Physics
ISLAM, G. S., Physics
ISLAM, M. A., Chemistry
ISLAM, M. A., Physics
ISLAM, M. F., Applied Chemistry and Chemical Technology
ISLAM, M. N., Chemistry
ISLAM, M. N., Physics
ISLAM, M. S., Applied Chemistry and Chemical Technology
ISLAM, M. S., Chemistry
ISLAM, M. S., Physics
ISLAM, M. W., Mathematics
ISLAM, S. N., Physics
KARMAKER, A. K., Applied Physics and Electronics
KERAMAT, M., Applied Physics and Electronics
KHAN, M. A. R., Chemistry
KHAN, M. K. A., Applied Physics and Electronics
KHAN, M. S. R., Applied Physics and Electronics
LATIF, M. A., Mathematics
MAHATABOALLY, S. Q. G., Physics
MAJUMDER, S., Mathematics
MALLICK, A. K., Mathematics
MIA, M. A. A., Applied Physics and Electronics
MIAH, M. A. B., Statistics
MIAH, M. A. J., Chemistry
MOLLA, M. A. H., Applied Chemistry and Chemical Technology
MONDAL, M. A. S., Physics
MORTUZA, M. G., Physics
MOSTAFA, M. G., Statistics
MOSTOFA, C. H., Applied Chemistry and Chemical Technology
NOOR, A. S. A., Mathematics
NOOR, A. S. A., Population Science and Human Resource Development
PAUL, A. C., Mathematics
PAUL, S. C., Chemistry
RAHMAN, M. A., Applied Chemistry and Chemical Technology
RAHMAN, M. B., Chemistry
RAHMAN, M. L., Chemistry
RAHMAN, M. M., Physics
RAHMAN, M. S., Applied Chemistry and Chemical Technology
RAHMAN, M. Z., Mathematics
RAQIB-UZ-ZAMAN, M., Applied Chemistry and Chemical Technology
RAZZAQUE, M. A., Statistics
SAHA, R. K., Biochemistry
SARKER, M. A. R., Applied Physics and Electronics

SARKER, M. J. A., Physics
SARKER, M. S. A., Mathematics
SATTAR, M. A., Chemistry
SATTAR, M. A., Mathematics
SAYEED, M. A., Applied Chemistry and Chemical Technology
SHAHJAHAN, M., Biochemistry
SOBHAN, M. A., Applied Physics and Electronics
SOBHAN, M. A., Applied Physics and Electronics
TORAFDER, M. T. H., Chemistry

Faculty of Social Science:

AKBAR, M. A., Social Work
ALI, M. M., Economics
BEGUM, H. A., Social Work
BHUIYAN, M. A. Q., Sociology
EUNUS, M., Economics
HABIB, A. H. M. A., Economics
HALIM, M. A., Social Work
HOSSAIN, A. M. M., Economics
HOSSAIN, K. T., Sociology
IMAM, M. H., Sociology
ISLAM, A. S. M. N., Social Work
ISLAM, M. S., Political Science
ISLAM, T. S., Economics
KARIM, A. H. M. Z., Anthropology
KHAN, F. R., Sociology
KHANUM, S. M., Sociology
MIZANUDDIN, M., Sociology
MOAZZEM, M., Economics
MORSHED, G., Political Science
MOSTUFA, S. K., Political Science
NATH, D. K., Economics
NATH, J., Sociology
OBAIDULLAH, A. T. M., Public Administration
QUASEM, M. A., Political Science
QUAYUM, M. A., Economics
RAHMAN, A. H. M. M., Sociology
RAHMAN, M. A., Economics
RAHMAN, M. F., Sociology
RAHMAN, M. M., Political Science
RAHMAN, M. S., Public Administration
RAHMAN, S. M. H., Economics
RAHMAN, S. M. Z., Sociology
SADEQUE, M., Social Work
SAHA, M. S. K., Economics
SARKAR, P. C., Social Work
SIDDIQUI, A. R., Sociology

There are 241 affiliated colleges.

ATTACHED INSTITUTES

Institute of Bangladesh Studies: Rajshahi 6205; tel. (721) 750753; e-mail ibsru@yahoo.com; Dir Prof. M. ABUL BASHAR MIAN.

Institute of Biological Science: Dir Prof. M. WAHIDUL ISLAM.

Institute of Business Administration: Dir Prof. MOHASHIN UL-ISLAM.

Institute of Education and Research: Dir Prof. M. NAZRUL ISLAM.

Institute of Environmental Science: Dir Prof. M. SARWAR ZAHAN.

RAJSHAHI UNIVERSITY OF ENGINEERING AND TECHNOLOGY

Rajshahi Natore Dhaka Rd, Kazla, Rajshahi 6204

Telephone: (721) 6254
Fax: (721) 6254
E-mail: ruetbd@yahoo.com
Internet: www.ruet.ac.bd

Founded 1986 as Engineering College, Rajshahi; present name and status 2003
State control

Vice-Chancellor: Prof. Dr M. FAZLUL BARI
Number of students: 1,763

SHAHJALAL UNIVERSITY OF SCIENCE AND TECHNOLOGY

PO University 3114, Sylhet

Telephone: (821) 713491
Fax: (821) 715257
E-mail: vc@sust.edu
Internet: www.sust.edu

Founded 1987
State control
Languages of instruction: English, Bengali
Academic year: July to June

Chancellor: PRESIDENT OF THE PEOPLE'S REPUBLIC OF BANGLADESH
Vice-Chancellor: Prof. M. AMINUL ISLAM
Registrar: JAMIL AHMED CHOWDHURY
Deputy Librarian: MOHAMED ABDUL HAYEE SAMENI

Library of 41,000 vols
Number of teachers: 307
Number of students: 5,939

Publication: *SUST Studies* (1 a year)

DEANS

School of Agriculture and Mineral Science: Prof. Dr KABIR HUSSAIN (acting)
School of Applied Sciences and Technology: Prof. Dr AKTARUL ISLAM
School of Business Administration: Prof. Dr MUHAMMAD NAZRUL ISLAM (acting)
School of Life Sciences: Prof. Dr M. HABIBUL AHSAN
School of Medical Science: Prof. Dr REZAUL KARIM
School of Physical Sciences: Prof. Dr SYED SAMSUL ALAM
School of Social Sciences: Prof. Dr TULSHI KUMAR DAS

SHER-E-BANGLA AGRICULTURAL UNIVERSITY

Sher-e-Bangla Nagar, Dhaka 1207

Telephone: (2) 9144270
Fax: (2) 8155800
E-mail: vcsau@dhaka.net
Internet: www.sau.ac.bd

Founded 2001
State control

Vice-Chancellor: Prof. Dr M. SHAH-E-ALAM
Registrar: Prof. Dr A. M. M. SHAMSUZZAMAN (acting)
Librarian: MOHAMED ALI (acting)

Library of 45,700 vols
Number of teachers: 20
Number of students: 1,536

Publications: *Journal of Agricultural Education and Technology, Journal of Agricultural Science and Technology, Journal of Sher-e-Bangla Agricultural University*

DEANS

Faculty of Agribusiness Management: Prof. M. ZAKIR HOSSAIN
Faculty of Agriculture: Prof. Dr M. SERAJUL ISLAM BHUIYAN,

PROFESSORS

ABEDIN, M.
AHMED REZA, Z.
AKBAR MIA, A.
AKHTAR, N.
ALI, M.
ALI, M.
BEGUM, J.
BEGUM, R.
CHANDRA SUTRADHAR, G.
FAZLUL KARIM, M.
HAQUE BEG, M.
HOSSAIN BHUIYAN, M.
HOSSAIN, M.
ISLAM BHUIYAN, M.
JAFAR ULLAH, M.
JALIL, G.

KANTI BISWAS, P.
KUMAR PAUL, A.
MAHTABUDDIN, A.
MANDAL, G.
MANNAN MIAH, M.
NAZRUL ISLAM, M.
NURUL ISLAM, M.
RAHMAN MAZUMDER, M.
RAFIQUEL ISLAM, M.
RAFIQUL ISLAM, M.
RASHID BHUIYAN, M.
RUHUL AMIN, A.
RUHUL AMIN, M.
SADRUL ANAM SARDAR, M.
SAROWAR HOSSAIN, M.
SHADAT ULLA, M.
SHAHJAHAN MIAH, M.
SHAMSUL HOQUE, M.

SHAMSUZZAMAN, A.
UDDIN AHMED, K.
ZAHIDUL HAQUE, M.

Colleges

Bangladesh Agricultural Research Institute: Joydebpur, Gazipur 1701; tel. (2) 9252715; fax (2) 9261415; e-mail dg.bari@bari.gov.bd; internet www.bari.gov.bd; f. 1976; library: 28,092 vols, 150 periodicals; Dir-Gen. Dr M. HARUN-UR-RASHID; Sr Librarian A. B. M. FAZLUR RAHMAN; publ. *Bangladesh Journal of Agricultural Research* (4 a year).

Bangladesh College of Leather Technology: 44–50 Hazaribagh, Dhaka 1209; tel. (2) 8617439; fax (2) 8617439; e-mail bclt47@yahoo.com; internet www.bclt.com.bd; f. 1949; constituent college of Univ. of Dhaka under the faculty of engineering and technology; undergraduate degrees in leather technology; 22 teachers; 1,000 students; library: 13,032 vols; Prin. Prof. Dr FAZLUL KARIM.

Bangladesh College of Textile Technology: 92 Shaheed Tajuddin Ahmed Sarani, Tejgaon I/A, Dhaka 1208; tel. (2) 9114260; fax (2) 9124255; internet www.ctet.gov.bd; f. 1950; a constituent college of Univ. of Dhaka; degree courses; 27 teachers; library: 8,535 vols; Prin. Prof. M. A. KASHEM.

BARBADOS

The Higher Education System

The main institution of higher education on the island is a branch campus of the University of the West Indies. Non-university post-secondary education is offered by the Samuel Jackson Prescod Polytechnic and Barbados Community College. In 2006/07 there were 11,405 students enrolled in tertiary education.

Admission to the University is based on satisfactory performance in the Caribbean Advanced Proficiency Examinations. The University offers Associate, Bachelors, Masters and Doctoral degree programmes. The Associate degree lasts for two years, the Bachelors three years, the Masters two years after the Bachelors and the Doctorate two more years after the Masters.

The Samuel Jackman Prescod Polytechnic trade and craft programmes lead to City and Guilds qualifications and Royal Society of Arts qualifications. Two-year Associate degrees are available from the Barbados Community College.

Erdiston Teachers College offers non-graduate teachers a two-year course in primary education, while graduate teachers can pursue further study at the UWI.

A US programme for curriculum reform and the introduction of technology into education, known as Edutech 2000, was implemented in 2010. A National Accreditation Agency was established in 2004, responsible for the registration of post-secondary and tertiary institutions, and for the accreditation of these institutions and their programmes.

Regulatory Body

GOVERNMENT

Ministry of Education and Human Resources Development: Elsie Payne Complex, Constitution Rd, St Michael; tel. 430-2700; fax 436-2411; e-mail mined1@caribsurf.com; internet www.mes.gov.bb; Min. RONALD D. JONES.

Learned Societies

GENERAL

Caribbean Conservation Association: The Garrison, St Michael; tel. 426-5373; fax 429-8483; e-mail admin@cca.net; internet www.cca.net; f. 1967; ind., non-profit-making; preservation and devt of the environment, and conservation of the cultural heritage in the Caribbean as a whole; 200 mems; small library; Pres. ATHERTON MARTIN; Exec. Dir Dr JOTH SINGH.

BIBLIOGRAPHY, LIBRARY SCIENCE AND MUSEOLOGY

Library Association of Barbados: POB 827E, Bridgetown; f. 1968 to unite qualified librarians, archivists and information specialists, and all other persons engaged or interested in information management and dissemination in Barbados, and to provide opportunities for their meeting together; to promote the active development and maintenance of libraries in Barbados and to foster cooperation between them; to interest the general public in the library services available; 60 mems; Pres. SHIRLEY YEARWOOD; Sec. HAZELYN DEVONISH; publ. *Update* (irregular).

HISTORY, GEOGRAPHY AND ARCHAEOLOGY

Barbados Museum and Historical Society: see Museum.

LANGUAGE AND LITERATURE

Alliance Française: POB 357, Cheapside GPO, Bridgetown; tel. 233-3234; e-mail info@afbridgetown.org; internet afbridgetown.unblog.fr; academic year offers courses and examinations in French language and culture and promotes cultural exchange with France; Pres. SIMON HADCHITY-KANNGIESSER.

MEDICINE

Barbados Association of Medical Practitioners: BAMP Complex, Spring Garden, St Michael; tel. 429-7569; fax 435-2328; e-mail bamp@sunbeach.net; internet www.bamp.org.bb; f. 1973; 348 mems; Pres. Dr JEROME WALCOTT; Gen. Sec. RANDOLPH CARRINGTON; publ. *BAMP Bulletin* (5 a year).

Barbados Pharmaceutical Society: POB 820E, St Michael; f. 1948, inc. 1961; 155 mems; Pres. DELORES MORRIS; Sec. GEORGE ALLEYNE; publ. *Pharmacy in Progress*.

Research Institute

GENERAL

Bellairs Research Institute: Holetown, St James; tel. 422-2087; fax 422-0692; e-mail bellairs@caribsurf.com; internet www.mcgill.ca/bellairs; f. 1954; affiliated with McGill University, Canada; field courses, workshops, research and teaching in all aspects of tropical environments; library of 200 vols; Dir Dr BRUCE R. DOWNEY.

Libraries and Archives

Bridgetown

Public Library: Coleridge St, Bridgetown; tel. 436-6081; fax 436-1501; f. 1847; an island-wide service is provided from the central library in Bridgetown by means of 7 brs, 6 centres, and a mobile service to 66 primary schools; acts as a nat. repository for legal deposit printed materials; 165,000 vols; spec. Barbadian and West Indian research colln; Dir JUDY BLACKMAN; publ. *National Bibliography of Barbados* (2 a year with annual cumulations).

University of the West Indies Main Library: POB 1334, Bridgetown; tel. 417-4444; fax 417-4460; e-mail barbara.chase@cavehill.uwi.edu; internet mainlibrary.uwichill.edu.bb; f. 1963; 155,000 vols, special West Indies collection, OAS, UN, UNESCO and World Bank depository library; Librarian BARBARA CHASE.

St James

Department of Archives: Black Rock, St James; tel. 425-5150; fax 425-5911; e-mail archives@sunbeach.net; f. 1963; part of the Prime Minister's Office; 990 linear m of archives, 2,366 vols and pamphlets, 922 serials, 391 microfilm reels, 2,747 fiches, 220 sound recordings; Chief Archivist DAVID WILLIAMS.

Museum

St Ann's Garrison

Barbados Museum and Historical Society: St Ann's Garrison, St Michael; tel. 427-0201; fax 429-5946; e-mail museum@caribsurf.com; internet www.barbmuse.org.bb; f. 1933; collns illustrating the island's geology, prehistory, history, natural history and marine life; European decorative arts, militaria, furniture; library of 5,000 vols; 1,000 mems; Pres. Dr TREVOR CARMICHAEL; Dir ALISSANDRA CUMMINS; publ. *Journal* (1 a year).

University

THE UNIVERSITY OF THE WEST INDIES, CAVE HILL CAMPUS

POB 64, Bridgetown 11000

Telephone: 417-4000
Fax: 425-1327
E-mail: cregoffice@cavehill.uwi.edu
Internet: www.cavehill.uwi.edu

Founded 1963
Language of instruction: English
Academic year: August to May (2 semesters)
Private control

Chancellor: Sir GEORGE ALLEYNE
Vice-Chancellor: Prof. E. NIGEL HARRIS
Pro-Vice-Chancellor and Prin.: Prof. HILARY M. BECKLES
Registrar: JACQUELINE E. WADE
Campus Librarian: ELIZABETH WATSON

Library of 190,000 vols, 2,346 serial titles
Number of teachers: 528 (incl. 363 part-time)
Number of students: 8,342

Publications: *Caribbean Journal of Mathematics* (1 a year), *Caribbean Journal of Science, Economic and Financial Review*, *Caribbean Law Review* (2 a year), *Current Awareness Bulletin*, *Journal of Eastern Caribbean Studies* (4 a year), *The Journal of Carribean Literatures*

DEANS

Faculty of Humanities and Education: Dr
  PEDRO WELCH
Faculty of Law: Hon. Prof. VELMA NEWTON
Faculty of Pure and Applied Sciences: PETER
  GIBBS
Faculty of Social Sciences: Dr GEORGE A. V.
  BELLE
School of Clinical Medicine and Research:
  Prof. HENRY FRASER

PROFESSORS

ANDERSON, W., Int. and off-shore Law
ANTOINE, R., Labour Law and Off-shore Law
BARRITEAU, E., Gender and Public Policy
BARROW, C., Sociology
BRYCE, J., Literature
CARNEGIE, A., Law
CARRINGTON, S., Plant Biology
COBLEY, A., South African and Comparative
  History
CRAIGWELL, R., Financial Economics
FAIDJOE, A., Law
FRASER, H., Medicine and Clinical Pharma-
  cology
HAMBLETON, I., Research
HENNIS, A., Research
HORROCKS, J., Conservation Ecology
HOWARD, M., Economics
IYARE, O., Financial Economics
JOLLIFFE, L., Tourism
KACZOROWSKA, A., European Law
KHAN, J., Public Sector Management
KODILYNE, A., Property Law
LANDIS, C., Research
LAVOIE, M., Microbiology
MAHDI, S., Mathematical Statistics
MAHON, R., Marine Affairs
MAMINGI, N., Economics

MCDOWELL, S., Theoretical and Computa-
  tional Chemistry
MCINTOSH, S., Jurisprudence
O'CALLAGHAN, E., West Indian Literature
OXENFORD, H., Marine Ecology and Fisheries
PUNNETT, B. J., International Business
RAY, T., Theoretical Physics
ROBERTS, P., Creole Linguistics
ROSIN, R. D., Surgery
SAVOLAINEN, H., Surgery
SINGH, U., Condensed Matter Physics
TINTO, W., Organic Chemistry

ATTACHED RESEARCH INSTITUTES

Caribbean Law Institute Centre: POB 64,
Bridgetown 11000; tel. 417-4560; fax 424-
4138; Exec. Dir Prof. RALPH CARNEIGE (acting).

Cave Hill School of Business: POB 64,
Bridgetown 11000; tel. 424-7731; fax 425-
1670; e-mail chsb@uwichill.uwi.edu; internet
www.uwichsb.org; Dir Dr JENNINE COMMA.

**Centre for Gender and Development
Studies:** POB 64, Bridgetown 11000; tel.
417-4490; fax 424-3822; e-mail gender@
uwichill.edu.bb; internet www.cavehill.uwi
.edu/gender; Head JOAN CUFFIE.

**Shridath Ramphal Centre for Inter-
national Trade Law, Policy and Services:** tel. 417-4533; fax 425-1348; e-mail
src@cavehill.uwi.edu; internet www
.shridathramphalcentre.org; Dir Dr KEITH
NURSE.

**Sir Arthur Lewis Institute of Social and
Economic Studies (SALISES):** tel. 417-
4478; fax 424-7291; e-mail salises@cavehill
.uwi.edu; internet www.cavehill.uwi.edu/
salises; Dir Prof. ANDREW DOWNES.

Tertiary Level Institutions Unit: tel. 417-
4506; fax 438-0456; e-mail eriic@cavehill.uwi
.edu; internet www.cavehill.uwi.edu/tliu; Dir
Dr LOUIS. WHITTINGTON.

Colleges

Barbados Community College: 'The
Eyrie', Howell's Cross Rd, St Michael; tel.
426-2858; fax 429-5935; e-mail eyrie@bcc.edu
.bb; internet www.bcc.edu.bb; f. 1968; commerce, liberal arts, health sciences, fine arts,
science, technology, Barbados Language
Centre, Hospitality Institute, general and
continuing education, computer studies,
physical education; library: 35,000 vols; 449
teachers (149 full-time, 300 part-time); 3,697
students; Prin. NORMA J. I. HOLDER; Registrar SYDNEY O. ARTHUR.

Samuel Jackman Prescod Polytechnic:
Wildey, St Michael; tel. 426-1920; fax 426-
0843; e-mail info@sjpp.edu.bb; internet www
.sjpp.edu.bb; f. 1969 in Bridgetown; merged
with Barbados Technical Institute in 1972;
div. of Agriculture est. at Eckstein Village
and main br. relocated in 1975; relocation to
present site 1982; attached to Min. of Education, and Human Resources Devt; divs of
building, electrical engineering, mechanical
engineering and printing, human ecology,
business studies, general studies, agriculture, motor vehicles and welding, distance
and continuing education, open and flexible
learning centre.

BELARUS

The Higher Education System

Until its independence in 1991 Belarus was part of the Union of Soviet Socialist Republics (USSR), and its education system was based on the Soviet model. Following independence the Government began to introduce greater provision for education in the Belarusian language and more emphasis on Belarusian, rather than Soviet or Russian, history and literature. Higher education is the responsibility of the Ministry of Education, while research is coordinated by the National Academy of Sciences of Belarus. All Belarusians have the right to free higher education. By early 2007 there were 43 state-owned and 12 private higher education institutions, including 29 universities, as well as seven academies, 13 institutes, four higher colleges and two theological seminaries. In 2008/09 420,700 students were enrolled in higher education.

The Ministry of Education administers admission to higher education on the joint basis of the Certificate of General Secondary Education (or equivalent) and competitive university entrance examinations. The main undergraduate degree is the Bachelors, taken in conjunction with the Diploma of Higher Education, lasting four to five years. The first level of postgraduate study is the Magister (Masters), requiring one to two years' study, culminating in research and presentation of a thesis. The final level of postgraduate education includes the Aspirantura, leading to the Kandidat Nauk (Candidate of Sciences), and Doctorantura (Doctorate), leading to the title Doctor of Sciences.

Non-university post-secondary education is provided by technical and vocational schools, sometimes known as technicums. Courses vary in length from one to four years, depending on the level of specialization. There are currently 174 technicums, 26 colleges, 49 intermediate professional education institutions, four higher colleges and eight private secondary specialized establishments.

Reform of the higher education system began in 1993, including the introduction of a standardized syllabus and increased institutional autonomy. In 2001 a number of laws were passed to this effect, culminating in 2007 with On Higher Education, which brought the country in line with the Bologna Process, including adoption of the European Credit Transfer System (ECTS) and recognition of foreign degrees. The law also introduced a department of Quality Control within the Ministry of Education.

Regulatory and Representative Bodies

GOVERNMENT

Ministry of Culture: 220004 Minsk, pr. Pobeditelei 11; tel. (17) 203-75-74; fax (17) 223-90-45; e-mail admin@kultura.by; internet kultura.by; Minister ULADZIMIR F. MATVEICHUK.

Ministry of Education: 220010 Minsk, vul. Savetskaya 9; tel. (17) 227-47-36; fax (17) 200-84-83; e-mail root@minedu.unibel.by; internet www.minedu.unibel.by; Minister ALYAKSANDR M. RADZKOW.

ACCREDITATION

Department of Quality Control in Education of the Ministry of Education: 220037 Minsk, 28 Kozlov St; tel. (17) 237-30-18; fax (17) 231-35-45; e-mail gnikon@rambler.ru; Dir VALERIY STEPANOVICH OVSYANIKOV.

ENIC/NARIC Belarus: Foreign Credentials Assessment Dept (Belarusian ENIC), 220007 Minsk, Moskovskaya vul. 15; tel. (17) 228-13-13; fax (17) 222-83-15; e-mail enicbelarus@nihe.niks.by; Head INA MITSKEVICH.

NATIONAL BODIES

Academy of Postgraduate Education: 220040 Minsk, vul. Nekrasova 20; tel. (17) 285-78-28; fax (17) 285-78-68; e-mail tavgen@academy.edu.by; internet www.academy.edu.by; f. 1955; attached to Min. of Education; Rector Prof. ALEH TAUHEN.

National Institute for Higher Education: 220001 Minsk, vul. Moskovskaya 15; tel. (17) 224-66-91; fax (17) 222-83-15; e-mail rector@nihe.niks.by; internet www.nihe.niks.by; Rector Prof. Dr MIKHAIL I. DEMCHUK; Exec. Dir of Belarusian ENIC LUDMILA RUDOVA.

Learned Societies

GENERAL

National Academy of Sciences of Belarus: 220072 Minsk, pr. Nezavisimosti 66; tel. (17) 284-18-01; fax (17) 239-31-63; internet www.ac.by; f. 1929; depts of Biological Sciences (Academician-Sec. I. D. VOLOTOVSKIY, Scientific Sec. V. A. VOINILO), Chemical and Earth Sciences (Academician-Sec. N. P. KRUTKO, Scientific Sec. N. M. LITVINKO), Humanities and Arts (Academician-Sec. P. G. NIKITENKO, Scientific Sec. V. I. LEVKOVICH), Medical Sciences (Academician-Sec. E. D. BELOENKO, Scientific Sec. L. P. MALAEVA), Physical and Technical Sciences (Academician-Sec. S. A. ZHDANOK, Scientific Sec. V. A. GAIKO), and Physics, Mathematics and Information Science (Academician-Sec. S. V. ABLAMEIKO, Scientific Sec. G. A. BUTKIN); 210 mems (94 academicians, 129 corresps, 17 foreign mems, 3 hon. mems); attached research institutes: see Research Institutes; library and archive: see Libraries and Archives; Chair. MIKHAIL V. MYASNIKOVICH (acting); Chief Scientific Sec. NIKOLAI S. KAZAK; publs *Computational Methods in Applied Mathematics* (4 a year), *Doklady* (Reports, 6 a year), *Inzhenerno-Fizicheskii Zhurnal* (Journal of Engineering Physics and Thermophysics, 6 a year), *Litasfera* (Lithosphere, 12 a year), *Materialy, Technologii, Instrumenty* (Materials, Technologies, Tools, 4 a year), *Nonlinear Phenomena in Complex Systems* (4 a year), *Prirodnye Resurcy* (Natural Resources, 4 a year), *Trenie i Iznos* (Friction and Wear, 6 a year), *Vestsi* (Bulletins: Physical-Technical Sciences, Biological Sciences, Biomedical Sciences, Physical-Mathematical Sciences, Humanities, Chemistry, 4 a year), *Zhurnal Prikladnoi Spektroskopii* (Journal of Applied Spectroscopy, 6 a year).

AGRICULTURE, FISHERIES AND VETERINARY SCIENCE

Department of Agricultural Sciences of the National Academy of Sciences of Belarus: 220049 Minsk, vul. Nezavisimosti 1; tel. (17) 284-18-12; fax (17) 284-09-95; attached to Nat. Acad. of Sciences; comprises 16 research institutes and 8 experimental stations; 32 mems (13 academicians, 19 corresp. mems); attached research institutes: see Research Institutes; library: see Libraries and Archives; Pres. VLADIMIR G. GUSAKOV; Scientific Sec. SVETLANA A. KASYANCHIK.

HISTORY, GEOGRAPHY AND ARCHAEOLOGY

Department of Humanitarian Sciences and Arts of the National Academy of Sciences of Belarus: 220072 Minsk, pr. Nezavisimosti 66; tel. (17) 284-07-74; fax (17) 239-31-63; internet www.ac.by/organizations/departments/ogum.html; fields of study include: history; historical geography and cartography; comparative historical and structural-typological studies of Belarusian and other languages; Belarusian literature, poetry and folklore; history of philosophy and politics in Belarus; sociolinguistic and psycholinguistic investigation; Acad.-Sec. Acad. PYOTR G. NIKITENKO.

LANGUAGE AND LITERATURE

Goethe-Institut: 220034 Minsk, vul. Frunze 5; tel. (17) 236-34-33; fax (17) 236-73-14; e-mail info@minsk.goethe.org; internet www.goethe.de/minsk; offers courses and exams in German language and culture and promotes cultural exchange with Germany; library of 8,840 vols; Dir BARBARA FRAENKEL-THONET.

MEDICINE

Department of Medical Sciences of the National Academy of Sciences of Belarus: 220072 Minsk, pr. Nezavisimosti 66; tel. and fax (17) 284-07-78; e-mail medicine@presidium.bas-net.by; internet www.ac.by/organizations/departments/omed.html; develops and coordinates research in the fields of: physiology of self-regulation; devt of a theoretical basis for management of compensatory-recombinatory processes; modern ecosystems and their effects on the physiological state and health of humans; and the devt of medical-biological problems connected with the consequences of the Chornobyl (Chernobyl) nuclear accident in 1986; Acad.-Sec. Acad. EVGENIY D. BELOYENKO.

NATURAL SCIENCES

Department of Biological Sciences of the National Academy of Sciences of Belarus: 220072 Minsk, pr. Nezavisimosti 66; tel. (17) 284-03-79; fax (17) 284-28-21; e-mail biology@presidium.bas-net.by; internet www.ac.by/organizations/ departments/obio.html; fields of study include: biodiversity of plants and animals in Belarus; development of methods of protection of flora and fauna; and reproduction and rational use of biological resources in conditions of anthropogenic pressure; Acad.-Sec. Acad. IGOR D. VOLOTOVSKIY.

Department of Chemistry and Earth Sciences of the National Academy of Sciences of Belarus: 220072 Minsk, pr. Nezavisimosti 66; tel. and fax (17) 284-03-71; e-mail chemistry@presidium.bas-net.by; internet www.ac.by/organizations/ departments/ochi.html; develops and coordinates research in the fields of: chemistry of polymers and their application; organic synthesis of substances with valuable properties; chemistry of inorganic materials; physical chemistry; chemistry of proteins, nucleic acids and low-molecular bioregulators; Acad.-Sec. Acad. NIKOLAI P. KRUTKO.

Department of Physical and Engineering Sciences of the National Academy of Sciences of Belarus: 220072 Minsk, pr. Nezavisimosti 66; tel. (17) 284-03-77; fax (17) 284-03-75; e-mail engine@presidium.bas-net .by; internet www.ac.by/organizations/ departments/ochi.html; develops and coordinates research and applied scientific investigations in the fields of: power engineering; conservation of energy and resources; materials and high-energy technologies; and machine building, modelling and diagnostics; Acad.-Sec. Acad. SERGEI A. ZHDANOK.

Department of Physics, Mathematics and Informatics of the National Academy of Sciences of Belarus: 220072 Minsk, pr. Nezavisimosti 66; tel. and fax (17) 284-03-76; e-mail physics@presidium .bas-net.by; internet www.ac.by/ organizations/departments/ochi.html; develops and coordinates research in the fields of: optics, spectroscopy, laser and plasma physics; atomic and molecular analysis and diagnostics; study and control of the natural environment (incl. laser-sensing and airspace spectrometry); development of materials with electrical, magnetic, optical, and physical-mechanical properties; advanced information technologies (incl. fibre optics, design of automated technical systems); image processing (digital cartography, processing of space images), modelling of intelligent processes (incl. voice-recognition and neurocomputing); Acad.-Sec. Prof. SERGEI V. ABLAMEYKO.

Research Institutes
AGRICULTURE, FISHERIES AND VETERINARY SCIENCE

Belarus Research and Technological Institute of the Meat and Dairy Industry: 220075 Minsk, Partizansky pr. 72; tel. (17) 244-38-52; fax (17) 244-38-91; attached to Acad. of Agricultural Sciences of the Republic of Belarus; Dir NIKOLAY A. PROKO-PEV.

Belarus Research Institute for Potato Cultivation: 223013 Minsk obl., pos. Samokhvalovichi, vul. Kovaleva 2A; tel. (17) 506-61-45; fax (17) 506-70-01; internet mshp .minsk.by/science/kartof; f. 1957; attached to Nat. Acad. of Sciences of Belarus; Dir SERGEI A. BANADYSEV; publ. *Potato Growing* (1 a year).

Belarus Research Institute for Soil Science and Agrochemistry: 220108 Minsk, vul. Kazintsa 62; tel. (17) 277-08-21; fax (17) 277-44-80; e-mail brissa@mail.belpak.by; internet mshp.minsk.by/science/niiagrhru .htm; f. 1931; attached to Acad. of Agricultural Sciences of the Republic of Belarus; Dir Prof. IOSIF M. BOGDEVICH; publs *Soil Investigation and Fertilizer Application* (every 2 years), *Soil Science and Agrochemistry* (1 a year).

Belarus Research Institute of Power Engineering for Agro-industrial Complex: 220024 Minsk, vul. Stebeneva 20; tel. (17) 275-19-07; fax (17) 275-10-20; e-mail energetika@forenet.by; f. 1994; attached to Acad. of Agricultural Sciences of the Republic of Belarus; Dir Prof. VIKENTIY I. RUSAN; publs *Problems in the Development of Power Engineering and Electrification for Agro-industrial Complex, Use of Renewable Energy.*

Grodno Zonal Planting Institute: 231510 Grodno raion, Shchuchin, Akademicheskaya 21; tel. (1514) 2-36-90; fax (1514) 2-36-87; e-mail gznii@tut.by; f. 1910; attached to National Acad. of Sciences of Belarus; 87 mems; library of 22,000 vols; Dir VLADIMIR KURILOVICH.

Institute for Fruit Growing: 223013 Minsk raion, pos. Samokhvalovichi, Kovalevea 2; tel. and fax (17) 506-61-40; e-mail belhort@it.org.by; internet belsad.by; f. 1925; attached to Nat. Acad. of Sciences of Belarus; breeding and introduction of fruit, small fruit, nut bearing and vine crops and their rootstocks for practical use in breeding; genetic resources bank; production and intergovernmental exchange; developing and improving technologies of fruit and small fruit production, storage and processing; diagnostics of virus, virus-like and bacterial pathogens and basic colln creation of virus-free plants; Dir Dr VYACHESLAV A. SAMUS; publ. *Collected articles 'Fruit Growing'* (1 a year).

Institute for Land Reclamation: 220040 Minsk, vul. M. Bogdanovicha 153; tel. (17) 232-49-41; fax (17) 232-64-96; e-mail niimel@ mail.ru; internet www.niimelio.niks.by; f. 1910; attached to Nat. Acad. of Sciences of Belarus; Dir NIKOLAI VAKHONIN; publ. *Reclamation* (2 a year).

Institute of Agricultural Economics: 220108 Minsk, vul. Kazintsa 103; tel. (17) 277-04-11; fax (17) 278-69-21; e-mail agrecinst@mail.belpak.by; f. 1958; attached to Acad. of Agricultural Sciences of the Republic of Belarus; library of 20,000 vols; Dir Dr VLADIMIR G. GUSAKOV; publ. *Agricultural Economics* (12 a year).

Institute of Animal Production: 222160 Minsk obl., Zhodino, vul. Frunze 11; tel. (1775) 3-34-26; fax (1775) 3-52-83; e-mail belniig@tut.by; f. 1949; attached to Nat. Acad. of Sciences of Belarus; library of 68,000 vols; Dir Prof. IVAN P. SHEYKO; publ. *Zootechnic Science of Belarus* (1 a year).

Institute of Experimental Veterinary Medicine 'S. N. Wyshelesski': 223020 Minsk raion, pos. Kuntsevshchina, Vyshelessky 2; tel. and fax (17) 508-81-31; f. 1930; attached to Acad. of Agricultural Sciences of the Republic of Belarus; Dir ALIAKSANDR P. LYSENKA; publ. *Veterinarnaya Nauka-Proisvodstvu* (1 a year).

Institute of Forestry: 246001 Gomel, Praletarskaya vul. 71; tel. (232) 53-73-73; fax (232) 53-53-89; e-mail forinst@server.by; f. 1930; attached to Nat. Acad. of Sciences of Belarus; Dir Prof. Dr VIKTOR A. IPATEV; publ. *Questions in Forest Sciences* (1 a year).

Institute of Plant Protection: 223011 Minsk raion, pos. Priluki, vul. Mira 2; tel. and fax (17) 509-23-39; e-mail entom@izr .belpak.minsk.by; attached to Acad. of Agricultural Sciences of the Republic of Belarus; Dir SERGEY V. SOROKA.

Institute of Vegetable Crops: 220028 Minsk, vul. Mayakovskogo 127A; tel. (17) 221-37-11; e-mail inst@belniio.belpak.minsk .by; internet mshp.minsk.by/science/niiov .htm; attached to Acad. of Agricultural Sciences of the Republic of Belarus; Dir GENNADY I. GANUSH.

Research and Practical Centre for Arable Farming: 222160 Minsk raion, Zhodino, vul. Timiryazeva 1; tel. (1775) 3-25-68; fax (1775) 3-70-66; e-mail izis@tut.by; internet www.izis.by; f. 1928 as Institute of Socialist Agriculture; present name 2006; attached to Nat. Acad. of Sciences of the Republic of Belarus; conducts applied and basic research in arable farming, plant growing, selection, genetics and crop protection; creation of highly productive varieties of agricultural crops, working with resource-saving technologies; library of 70,000 vols; Gen. Dir Dr FEDOR PRIVALOV; publs *Farming and Plant Protection* (6 a year), *Transactions on Arable Farming and Plant Growing in Belarus* (1 a year).

Research Institute of Radiology (RIR): 246000 Belarus, Feduninski St 16; tel. (23) 251-68-21; fax (23) 251-68-22; e-mail office@ rir.by; internet www.rir.by; f. 1986; attached to Acad. of Agricultural Sciences of the Republic of Belarus; brs in Minsk, Brest, Mogilev; research projects and devts in field of nuclear and radiological response and recovery related to consequences of Chernobyl NPP catastrophe of 1986; devt of countermeasures for rehabilitation of affected population and contaminated territories, i.e. affected agricultural sector; recommendations and guidelines for farming on territories affected; scientific supervision of practical application of developed recommendations, and other types of activity; offers laboratory services and postgraduate courses in radiobiology; Dir Dr VIKTOR S. AVERIN; Sec. VICTORIA V. DROBYSHEVSKAYA.

RUE 'Fish Industries Institute: Scientific and Practical Centre of the National Academy of Sciences of Belarus for Animal Husbandry': 220024 Minsk, vul. Stebeneva 22; tel. (17) 275-36-46; fax (17) 275-36-60; e-mail belniirh@tut.by; internet www.belniirh.by; f. 1957; attached to Nat. Acad. of Sciences of Belarus; Dir Dr M. M. RADZKO; publ. *Belarus Fish Industry Problems* (Russian with summary in English, 1 a year).

RUE 'Scientific and Practical Centre of the National Academy of Sciences of Belarus for Agriculture Mechanization': 220049 Minsk, vul. Knorina 1; tel. and fax (17) 266-02-91; e-mail belagromech@tut.by; f. 1947; attached to Nat. Acad. of Sciences of Belarus; devt and implementation of new equipment for crop production and livestock farming, engineering and construction of vegetable storage facilities, creation of technological systems of machinery and equipment for agriculture mechanization; Dir-Gen. VLADIMIR G. SAMOSYUK.

ARCHITECTURE AND TOWN PLANNING

Research and Design Institute of Construction Materials 'BelNIIS': 220114 Minsk, Staroborisovsky tr.; tel. (17) 264-10-01; fax (17) 264-87-92; e-mail lmdp@nsys.by; Dir NADEZHDA N. TSYBULKO.

ECONOMICS, LAW AND POLITICS

Institute for Economic Research of the Ministry of Economics of the Republic of Belarus: e-mail d.niei@mail.by 220086 Minsk, Y; tel. (17) 264-02-78; fax (17) 264-64-40; e-mail niei@main.gov.by; f. 1962; strategic research, elaboration of medium and long-term forecasts and programs, social policy, human potential and social sphere devt, scientific, innovation and investment devt, regional research and devt, economic and mathematic simulation and informatization, world economy research; library of 51,425 vols; Dir AALEXANDER CHERVIAKOV.

Institute of Economics: 220072 Minsk, vul. Surganava 1–2, Korpus 2; tel. (17) 284-24-43; fax (17) 284-07-16; e-mail directorship@economics.basnet.by; internet economics.bas-net.by; f. 1931; attached to Nat. Acad. of Sciences of Belarus; Dir Prof. PETR G. NIKITENKO; publ. *Organizatsiya i upravleniye* (Organization and Management, in Russian, 4 a year).

Institute for State and Law: 220072 Minsk, vul. Surganava 1, Korpus 2; tel. (17) 284-18-64; fax (17) 284-18-24; e-mail philos@bas-net.by; f. 1999; attached to Nat. Acad. of Sciences of Belarus; Dir Dr VLADIMIR P. IZOTKO.

Research Institute of Criminalistics and Forensic Expertise: 220073 Minsk, Kalvariiskaya vul. 43; tel. and fax (17) 226-72-79; e-mail sudexpertiza@adsl.by; internet www.sudexpertiza.by; f. 1929; attached to Ministry of Justice; library of 10,000 vols; Dir Dr ALEXANDER RUBIS; publ. *Issues of Criminalistics, Criminology and Forensic Expertise* (1 a year).

EDUCATION

National Institute of Education: 220004 Minsk, vul. Korolja 16; tel. (17) 220-59-09; fax (17) 220-56-35; f. 1990; library of 20,000 vols; Dir Dr BORIS KRAIKO; publ. *Adulcatsia i Wychawanne.*

HISTORY, GEOGRAPHY AND ARCHAEOLOGY

Institute of History: 220072 Minsk, vul. Akademicheskaya 1; tel. and fax (17) 284-02-19; f. 1929; attached to Nat. Acad. of Sciences of Belarus; Dir Prof. ALEKSANDR A. KOVALENYA (acting).

LANGUAGE AND LITERATURE

Institute of Linguistics 'Ya. Kolas': 220072 Minsk, vul. Surganava 1, Korpus 2; tel. (17) 268-48-84; fax (17) 284-18-85; e-mail inlinasbel@tut.by; f. 1929; attached to Nat. Acad. of Sciences of Belarus; Dir ALEKSANDR A. LUKASHANETS.

Institute of Literature: 220072 Minsk, pr. Nezavisimosti 66; tel. (17) 268-58-86; e-mail inlit@bas-net.by; f. 1931; attached to Nat. Acad. of Sciences of Belarus; Dir VLADIMIR V. GNILOMEDOV.

MEDICINE

N. N. Alexandrov National Cancer Centre of Belarus: e-mail v.chalov@omr.med.by 223040 Minsk, p.o. Lesnoy-2; tel. (17) 287-95-05; fax (17) 265-47-04; e-mail oncobel@omr.med.by; internet omr.med.by; f. 1960 as the N. N. Alexandrov Research Institute of Oncology and Medical Radiology, renamed in March 2008; carries out clinical cancer research; library of 15,000 vols, 55 periodicals; Dir Prof. OLEG G. SUKONKO; publs *Oncological Journal* (4 a year), *Topical Problems in Oncology and Medical Radiology* (1 a year).

Institute of Pulmonology and Phthisiology: 223059 Minsk raion, pos. Novinki; tel. (17) 289-87-95; fax (17) 289-89-50; e-mail niipulm@users.med.by; f. 1923; library of 7,000 vols; Dir VALENTIN V. BORSHCHEVSKIY; publ. *Research Report* (1 a year).

Republican Research and Practical Centre for Epidemiology and Microbiology: e-mail rrpcem@belriem.by 220114 Minsk, vul. Filimonova 23; tel. (17) 267-30-50; fax (17) 267-30-93; e-mail belriem@gmail.com; internet www.belriem.by; f. 1924 as Belarusian Pasteur Institute; research to improve surveillance of infectious diseases, study of molecular mechanisms of pathogenicity of main infectious and immune diseases, devt of immuno- and molecular biologic diagnostic preparations against the agents of main infections, elaboration and implementation into medical practice of up-to-date diagnostic, medical, and vaccine preparations, quality controls of immunobiological products, medical information support in the control of infectious and immune diseases; library of 10,000 vols; Dir Prof. GEORGE M. IGNATYEV (acting).

Republican Scientific Practical Centre of Hygiene: 220012 Minsk, Akademicheskaya 8; tel. (17) 284-13-70; fax (17) 284-03-45; e-mail rspch@rspch.by; internet www.rspch.by; f. 1927; library of 11,982 vols; Dir SERGEY SOKOLOV.

Research Institute for Evaluation of the Working Capacity of Disabled People: 220114 Minsk, Staroborisovsky trakt 24; tel. and fax (17) 264-25-08; f. 1974; library of 35,000 vols; Dir Prof. V. B. SMYCHEK.

Research Institute of Neurology, Neurosurgery and Physiotherapy: 220061 Minsk, vul. Filatova 9; tel. (17) 246-40-88.

Research Institute of Traumatology and Orthopaedics: Minsk, vul. Gorkogo 2.

Scientific Practical Centre 'Cardiology': 220036 Minsk, R. Luxemburg St 110; tel. (17) 286-14-66; fax (17) 286-14-66; e-mail info@cardio.by; internet www.cardio.by; f. 1977; cardiology, cardiosurgery; Dir ALEXANDR MROCHEK.

Skin and Venereological Research Institute: Minsk, Prilukskaya vul. 46A.

NATURAL SCIENCES

Biological Sciences

Central Botanical Garden: 220012 Minsk, vul. Surganava 2A; tel. (17) 284-14-84; fax (17) 284-14-83; e-mail cbg@it.org.by; internet hbc.bas-net.by/cbg; f. 1932; attached to Nat. Acad. of Sciences of Belarus; Dir Acad. VLADIMIR N. RESHETNIKOV.

Institute for Nature Management: 220114 Minsk, 10 F. Skariny Str.; tel. (17) 267-26-32; fax (17) 267-24-13; e-mail nature@ecology.basnet.by; internet www.ecology.basnet.by; f. 1932; attached to Nat. Acad. of Sciences of Belarus; library of 235,500 vols; nature management, environment protection, geotechnology, geoecology, geography and paleogeography, climatology and hydrogeochemistry; Dir ALEXANDER KARABANOV; publs *Natural Resources*, *Nature Management* (2 a year).

Institute of Biochemistry: 230017 Grodno, bul. Leninskogo Komsomola 50; tel. (15) 233-41-61; fax (15) 233-41-21; e-mail val@biochem.unibel.by; f. 1985; attached to Nat. Acad. of Sciences of Belarus; library of 40,000 vols; Dir Prof. PAVEL S. PRONKO.

Institute of Bio-organic Chemistry: 220141 Minsk, vul. Akad. V. F. Kuprevicha 5; tel. (17) 264-87-61; fax (17) 263-71-32; internet iboch.bas-net.by; f. 1974; attached to Nat. Acad. of Sciences of Belarus; Dir Acad. FYODOR A. LAKHVICH.

Institute of Biophysics and Cell Engineering: 220072 Minsk, vul. Akademicheskaya 27; tel. (17) 284-17-49; fax (17) 284-23-57; e-mail ipb@biobel.bas-net.by; internet biobel.bas-net.by/biophys; f. 1973; attached to Nat. Acad. of Sciences of Belarus; Dir Acad. IGOR D. VOLOTOVSKIY; publ. *Godnev's Lectures: Plant Photobiology and Photosynthesis* (1 a year).

Institute of Experimental Botany 'V. Kuprevich': 220072 Minsk, vul. Akademicheskaya 27; tel. (17) 284-15-64; fax (17) 284-18-53; f. 1931; attached to Nat. Acad. of Sciences of Belarus; Dir Prof. Dr NIKOLAI A. LAMAN.

Institute of Genetics and Cytology: 220072 Minsk, vul. Akademicheskaya 27; tel. (17) 284-18-48; fax (17) 284-19-17; internet biobel.bas-net.by/igc; f. 1965; attached to Nat. Acad. of Sciences of Belarus; Dir ALEKSANDR V. KILCHEVSKIY.

Institute of Microbiology: 220141 Minsk, vul. Akad. V. F. Kuprevicha 2; tel. (17) 202-99-46; fax (17) 264-47-66; internet www.mbio.bas-net.by; f. 1975; attached to Nat. Acad. of Sciences of Belarus; Dir EMILIYA I. KOLOMETS.

Institute of Physiology: 220072 Minsk, vul. Akademichnaya 28; tel. (17) 284-24-61; fax (17) 284-16-30; f. 1953; attached to Nat. Acad. of Sciences of Belarus; basic and applied research in biomedicine; Dir VLADIMIR S. ULASHCHYK.

Institute of Radiobiology: 246007 Gomel, Fedyuninskogo Str. 4; tel. and fax (232) 57-07-06; e-mail irb@mail.gomel.by; internet irb.basnet.by; f. 1987; attached to Nat. Acad. of Sciences of Belarus; monitors and forecasts radioactive contamination level of environment; creates new technologies for prophylaxis of diseases with use of bioactive additives and other medical agents; develops protective measures for overcoming the long-term radioecological consequences of Chernobyl accident; researches adaptation mechanisms in organisms, incl. ionizing radiation; offers postgraduate courses in radiation biology and radioecology; Dir Dr ALIAKSANDR NAVUMAV; Scientific Sec. ALEKSANDER NIKITIN.

Institute of Zoology: 220072 Minsk, vul. Akademichnaya 27; tel. (17) 284-22-75; fax (17) 284-10-36; internet biobel.bas-net.by/zoo; f. 1958; attached to Nat. Acad. of Sciences of Belarus; Dir MIKHAIL E. NIKIFOROV.

Mathematical Sciences

Institute of Mathematics: 220072 Minsk, vul. Surganava 11; tel. (17) 284-17-01; fax (17) 284-22-59; internet im.bas-net.by; f. 1959; attached to Nat. Acad. of Sciences of Belarus; Dir Acad. IVAN V. GAISHUN.

Physical Sciences

Institute of Applied Optics: 212793 Mogilev, vul. Bialynitskaga-Biruli 11; tel. and fax (22) 226-46-49; f. 1970; attached to Nat. Acad. of Sciences of Belarus; Dir V. P. REDKO.

Institute of General and Inorganic Chemistry: 220072 Minsk, vul. Surganava 9; tel. (17) 284-27-23; fax (17) 284-27-03; f. 1959; attached to Nat. Acad. of Sciences of Belarus; Dir NIKOLAI P. KRUTKO.

Institute of Molecular and Atomic Physics: 220072 Minsk, pr. Nezavisimosti 70; tel.

(17) 284-16-35; fax (17) 284-00-30; internet imaph.bas-net.by; f. 1992; attached to Nat. Acad. of Sciences of Belarus; Dir Dr SERGEY V. GAPONENKO; publ. *Journal of Applied Spectroscopy*.

Institute of Physical Organic Chemistry: 220072 Minsk, vul. Surganava 13; tel. (17) 284-23-38; fax (17) 284-16-79; e-mail ifoch@ifoch.bas-net.by; internet ifoch.bas-net .by; f. 1929; attached to Nat. Acad. of Sciences of Belarus; Dir Prof. ALEKSANDR V. BILDYUKEVICH (acting).

Institute of Physics 'B. I. Stepanov': 220072 Minsk, pr. Nezavisimosti 68; tel. (17) 284-17-55; fax (17) 284-08-79; internet ifanbel.bas-net.by; f. 1955; attached to Nat. Acad. of Sciences of Belarus; Dir Prof. VLADIMIR V. KABANOV (acting).

Institute of Solid State and Semiconductor Physics: 220072 Minsk, vul. P. Brovki 17; tel. (17) 284-28-14; fax (17) 284-13-13; e-mail ifttpanb@iftt.basnet.minsk.by; f. 1963; attached to Nat. Acad. of Sciences of Belarus; library of 72,000 items; Dir Prof. VALERY M. FEDOSYUK.

PHILOSOPHY AND PSYCHOLOGY

Institute of Philosophy: 220072 Minsk, vul. Surganava 1, korp. 2; tel. (17) 284-18-63; fax (17) 284-29-25; e-mail institute@ philosophy.by; internet www.philosophy.by; f. 1931; attached to Nat. Acad. of Sciences of Belarus; research in the field of theory and methodology of natural scientific and socio-humanitarian cognition, philosophical anthropology, social ecology, ethics and aesthetics; elaboration of innovative strategies of social, spiritual, cultural and scientific progress; study of the actual problems of contemporary socio-political and cultural devt; study and summary of the achievements of the world and nat. philosophical thought; strategic European studies and research in the field of int. humanitarian collaboration; Dir Dr ANATOLY A. LAZAREVICH.

RELIGION, SOCIOLOGY AND ANTHROPOLOGY

Institute of Arts, Ethnography and Folklore: 220072 Minsk, vul. Surganava 1, korp. 2; tel. (17) 239-59-21; f. 1957; attached to Nat. Acad. of Sciences of Belarus; Dir M. P. PILIPENKO.

Institute of Sociology: 220072 Minsk, vul. Surganava 1, korp. 2; tel. (17) 239-48-65; fax (17) 239-59-28; f. 1990; attached to Nat. Acad. of Sciences of Belarus; Dir E. M. BABOSOV.

TECHNOLOGY

A. V. Luikov Heat and Mass Transfer Institute: 220072 Minsk, vul. P. Brovki 15; tel. (17) 284-21-36; fax (17) 292-25-13; internet www.itmo.by; f. 1952; attached to Nat. Acad. of Sciences of Belarus; research and devt on problems of heat and mass transfer in capillary-porous bodies, dispersal systems, rheological and non-equilibrium media, turbulent non-uniform flows, aero-thermo-optical devices and low-temperature generators, laser technologies, hydrogen power engineering, nanomaterials and nano-technologies, plasma and waste treatment, energy and resources saving; Dir Dr OLEG G. PENYAZKOV.

Belarus Institute for the Science, Research and Design of Food Products: 220037 Minsk, Kozlova 29; tel. (17) 285-39-70; fax (17) 285-39-71; f. 2000; library of 20,000 vols; Dir ZENON LOVKIS.

Belarusian Institute of System Analysis and Information Support for Scientific and Technical Sphere (BELISA): 220004 Minsk, pr. Pobeditelei 7; tel. (17) 203-14-87; fax (17) 203-35-40; internet www.belisa.org .by; operated by the State Committee on Science and Technologies of Belarus; Dir VALERJY E. KRATENOK.

Engineering Centre 'Plazmoteg': 220141 Minsk, vul. Akad. V. F. Kuprevicha 1, korp. 3; tel. (17) 263-93-41; fax (17) 263-59-20; e-mail pec@bas-net.by; f. 1990; attached to Nat. Acad. of Sciences of Belarus; Dir EDUARD I. TOCHITSKY.

Institute of Applied Physics: 220072 Minsk, vul. Akademicheskaya 16; tel. (17) 284-17-94; fax (17) 284-10-81; internet iaph .bas-net.by; f. 1963; attached to Nat. Acad. of Sciences of Belarus; physics of non-destructive testing; Dir Prof. Dr NIKOLAI P. MIGUN.

Institute of Chemistry of New Materials: 220141 Minsk, vul. Akad. V. F. Kuprevicha 16; tel. and fax (17) 263-19-23; internet www .ichnm.ac.by; f. 1993; attached to Nat. Acad. of Sciences of Belarus; Dir Acad. VLADIMIR E. AGABEKOV.

Institute of Electronics: 220090 Minsk, Logoiskiy trakt 22; tel. (17) 265-34-13; fax (17) 283-91-51; f. 1973; attached to Nat. Acad. of Sciences of Belarus; Dir YURIY V. TROFIMOV.

Institute of Energetics Problems: 220109 Minsk, vul. Akad. Krasina; tel. and fax (17) 246-70-55; f. 1991; attached to Nat. Acad. of Sciences of Belarus; Dir Dr YURIY V. KLIMENKOV.

Institute of Engineering Cybernetics: 220012 Minsk, vul. Surganava 6; tel. (17) 268-51-71; fax (17) 231-84-03; e-mail cic@ newman.basnet.minsk.by; f. 1965; attached to Nat. Acad. of Sciences of Belarus; Dir Prof. VYACHESLAV S. TANAYEV.

Institute of Machine Mechanics and Reliability: 220072 Minsk, vul. Akademicheskaya 12; tel. (17) 210-07-48; fax (17) 284-02-41; f. 1971; attached to Nat. Acad. of Sciences of Belarus; Dir Dr YURIY V. KLIMENKOV.

Institute of Radiation Physical-Chemical Problems: 220109 Minsk, Akad. Krasina 99; tel. (17) 246-77-50; fax (17) 246-73-17; f. 1991; attached to Nat. Acad. of Sciences of Belarus; Dir SERGEY E. CHIGRINOV.

Institute of Radioecological Problems: 220109 Minsk, Sosny; tel. (17) 246-72-53; fax (17) 246-70-17; e-mail irep@sosny.basnet .minsk.by; f. 1991; attached to Nat. Acad. of Sciences of Belarus; Dir G. A. SHAROVAROV.

Institute of Technical Acoustics: 210023 Vitebsk, ave Lyudnikova 13; tel. and fax (212) 24-39-53; e-mail ita@vitebsk.by; internet www.belpak.vitebsk.by/ita; f. 1995; attached to Nat. Acad. of Sciences of Belarus; library of 43,000 vols; Dir Prof. VASILIY V. RUBANIK.

Institute of Technology of Metals: 212030 Mogilev, vul. Bialynitskaga-Biruli 11; tel. (222) 26-46-43; fax (222) 32-65-93; e-mail inmet@mogilev.unibel.by; internet www.ussr .to/belarus/itm; f. 1992; attached to Nat. Acad. of Sciences of Belarus; Dir Dr EVGENIY MARUKOVICH.

Medical Biotechnological Institute: 220029 Minsk, vul. Varvasheny 17; tel. and fax (17) 234-32-06; internet www.medbiotech .bn.by; f. 1972; 120 mems; Dir VICTOR N. TERECHOV; Dir of Scientific Research K. M. BELIAVSKY.

Metal Polymer Research Institute 'V. A. Belyi': 246050 Gomel, vul. Kirova 32A; tel. (232) 77-52-12; fax (232) 77-52-11; e-mail mpri@mail.ru; internet mpri.org.by; f. 1969; attached to Nat. Acad. of Sciences of Belarus; library of 19,519 vols; Dir Prof. NIKOLAI K. MYSHKIN; publs *Friction and Wear* (6 a year), *Materials, Technologies and Tools* (4 a year).

Non-Traditional Energetics and Energy-Saving Scientific and Engineering Centre: 220109 Minsk, Sosny; tel. (17) 246-76-61; f. 1992; attached to Nat. Acad. of Sciences of Belarus; Dir V. N. YERMASHKEVICH.

Physical-Technical Institute: 220141 Minsk, vul. Akad. V. F. Kuprevicha 10; tel. (17) 264-60-10; fax (17) 263-76-93; e-mail phti@tut.by; internet phti.at.tut.by; f. 1931; attached to Nat. Acad. of Sciences of Belarus; Dir ANATOLIY I. GORDIENKO.

Republican Scientific and Engineering Centre for Environmental Remote Sensing 'Ecomir': 220012 Minsk, vul. Surganava 2; tel. (17) 284-00-49; fax (17) 284-00-47; e-mail ecomir@open.by; internet www .ecomir-eeica.com; f. 1990; attached to Nat. Acad. of Sciences of Belarus; Dir Prof. A. A. KOVALEV.

Scientific-Engineering Republican Unitary Enterprise 'Belavtotraktorostroenie': 220072 Minsk, vul. Akademicheskaya 12; tel. (17) 210-07-49; fax (17) 284-02-41; e-mail bats@ncpmm.bas-net.by; internet www.bats.basnet.by; f. 1993; attached to Nat. Acad. of Sciences of Belarus; Dir Acad. M. S. VYSOTSKY.

Libraries and Archives

Brest

Brest Oblast Library 'M. Gorky': 210601 Brest, bul. Kosmanavtov 48; tel. and fax (162) 22-22-01; e-mail brl@tut.by; internet grl .brest.by; f. 1940; regional centre for 19 central libraries and 818 brs; 740,000 vols; Dir TAMARA P. DANILYUK; publ. *Bibliopanorama* (irregular).

Gomel

Gomel Oblast Universal Library 'V. I. Lenin': 246000 Gomel, pl. Pobedy 2A; tel. (232) 77-36-51; e-mail goub@it.org.by; Dir VALENTINA P. DUBROVA.

Minsk

Belarus Agricultural Library: 220108 Minsk, vul. Kazintsa 86/2; tel. (17) 212-15-61; fax (17) 212-00-66; internet belal.by; f. 1960; attached to Nat. Acad. of Sciences of Belarus; 500,000 vols; Dir VALENTINA YURCHENKO.

Belarus State University Library: 220050 Minsk, pr. Skoriny 4; tel. (17) 220-78-23; fax (17) 226-59-40; e-mail lapo@bsu.by; internet www.library.bsu.by; f. 1921; 2.0m. vols; Dir PETR M. LAPO.

Central Scientific Archive of the National Academy of Sciences of Belarus: 220072 Minsk, pr. Nezavisimosti 66; tel. (17) 284-22-87; fax (17) 284-18-70; f. 1931; Head MARYNA HLEB.

Central Scientific Library of the National Academy of Sciences of Belarus 'Ya. Kolas': 220072 Minsk, vul. Surganava 15; tel. and fax (17) 284-14-28; internet www.csl.bas-net.by; f. 1925; 3.1m. vols; Dir NATALIYA YU. BEREZKINA.

National Library of Belarus: 220114 Minsk, pr. Nezavisimosti 116; tel. (17) 266-37-00; fax (17) 266-37-06; e-mail nlb@nlb .by; internet nlb.by; f. 1922; 8.9m. vols; Dir Prof. ROMAN MATULSKY; publs *Chernobyl: Bibliographical Index* (2 a year), *New Literature on the Culture and Art of Belarus* (12 a year), *Novyja Knigi* (12 a year), *Social Sciences* (12 a year).

Republican Library for Science and Technology of Belarus: 220004 Minsk, pr. Pobediteley 7; tel. and fax (17) 203-31-38; e-mail rlst@rlst.org.by; internet www.rlst.org.by; f. 1977; 2.0m. vols (excl. patents); Dir RAISA SUKHORUKOVA.

Republican Scientific Medical Library: 220007 Minsk, vul. Fabritsiusa 28; tel. (17) 226-21-52; fax (17) 216-20-43; e-mail rsml@rsml.med.by; internet www.rsml.med.by; f. 1941; 860,000 vols; Dir VLADIMIR N. SOROKO.

Mogilev

Mogilev Oblast Library 'V. I. Lenin': 212030 Mogilev, vul. Krylenko 8; tel. and fax (222) 22-51-14; e-mail adm@library.mogilev.by; internet www.library.mogilev.by; f. 1935; Dir ILONA V. SOROKINA; publs *Bibliographic Indices* (irregular), *Bulletin* (irregular).

Vitebsk

Vitebsk Oblast Library 'V. I. Lenin': 210601 Vitebsk, vul. Lenina 8A; tel. (212) 37-45-21; fax (212) 37-30-58; f. 1921; Dir ALEKSANDR SEMKIN.

Museums and Art Galleries

Belovezhskaya Pushcha

'Belovezhskaya Pushcha' National Park Museum: 225063 Brestskaya oblast, Kamenetzky raion; tel. (1631) 5-63-96; fax (1631) 2-50-56; e-mail box@npbprom.belpak.brest.by; internet www.npbp.cis.by; f. 1960; displays flora and fauna of the Belovezhskaya Pushcha Primeval Forest, and shows work being done to preserve the biological diversity in the primeval forest, particularly with respect to the European Bison; Dir NIKOLAI N. BAMBIZA.

Grodno

Grodno State Historical and Archaeological Museum: 230023 Grodno, Zamkovaya vul. 22; tel. and fax (152) 74-08-33; fax (152) 74-08-33; e-mail grodno_museum@tut.by; internet www.history.grodno.museum.by; f. 1920; museum colln contains 190,000 items; library of 35,000 vols; Dir Dr YURY KITURKA; publ. *Krayaznauchya zapiski* (Journal of Regional Studies, every 2 years).

Minsk

Great Patriotic War Museum: 220030 Minsk, pr. Nezavisimosti 25A; tel. and fax (17) 227-11-66; e-mail museumww2@tut.by; internet nacbibl.org.by/war_museum; f. 1943; Soviet Army and partisans' war history 1941–1945; library of 14,000 vols; Dir GENNADIY I. BARKUN.

National Art Museum of the Republic of Belarus:; e-mail artmuseumby@gmail.com 220030 Minsk, Lenin St. 20; tel. and fax (17) 227-71-63; fax (17) 328-68-44; e-mail nmmrb@bk.ru; internet www.artmuseum.by; f. 1939 as State Art Gallery; present name 1993; Belarusian art from 11th century to early 20th century; European art from 16th century to early 20th century; Russian art from 18th century to early 20th century; Oriental Art of the 14th to 20th centuries; temporary exhibitions; Dir VLADIMIR I. PROKOPTSOV.

National Museum of the History and Culture of Belarus: 220030 Minsk, vul. K. Marksa 12; tel. (17) 328-63-75; fax (17) 227-36-65; e-mail histmuseum@tut.by; f. 1957; history and local natural history; archaeological, ethnographical and coin collections; library of 20,000 vols; Dir SERGEJ VECHER.

Universities

BARANOVICHI STATE UNIVERSITY

225404 Baranovichi, vul. Voikova 21

Telephone: (163) 45-78-60

Fax: (163) 45-78-31

E-mail: barsu@brest.by

Internet: www.barsu.by

Founded 2004

Rector: Prof. VASILIY I. KOCHURKO

Library of 266,109 vols
Number of teachers: 562
Number of students: 8,875

DEANS

Faculty of Economy and Law: ELENA IVANOVNA PLATONENKO
Faculty of Education by Correspondence: NATALYA IVANOVNA SHLYAGO
Faculty of Engineering: ALEXANDR VLADIMIROVICH AKULOV
Faculty of Foreign Languages: IRINA VYACHESLAVOVNA PINYUTA
Faculty of Pedagogy: ZOYA NIKOLAYEVNA KOZLOVA
Faculty of Pre-University Training: IGOR VIKTOROVICH DUBEN
Faculty of Persistent Training: MARIYA NIKOLAYEVNA MAKUTA
Institute of Refresher Training and Re-Training: VERA VALERYEVNA KHITRYUK
Lyakhovichi State Agrarian College: VYACHESLAV LUKICH SELMANOVICH (Dir)

BELARUS STATE ECONOMIC UNIVERSITY

220070 Minsk, Partizanski pr. 26

Telephone: (17) 249-40-32

Fax: (17) 249-51-06

E-mail: umoms@bseu.by

Internet: www.bseu.by

Founded 1933

Language of instruction: Russian

State control

Academic year: September to June

Rector: Prof. Dr VLADIMIR SHIMOV

Dean's Office for Int. Students: Dr NATALIA SKRIBA

Library: 1.5m. vols
Number of teachers: 1,200
Number of students: 27,000

Publications: *Belarusian Economic Journal*, *Bookkeeping, Accounting and Analysis*

DEANS

Faculty of Accounting and Economics: VLADIMIR BEREZOVSKY
Faculty of Commerce, Economics and Management: LEXANDER YARTSEV
Faculty of Finance and Banking: NATALIA LESNEVSKAYA
Faculty of International Business Communication: NATALIA POPOK
Faculty of International Economics Relations: GALINA SHMARLOVSKAYA
Faculty of Law: A. SHKLYAREVSKY
Faculty of Management: VALENTINA SIMKHOVICH
Faculty of Marketing: VALERY BORODENYA
Faculty of Pre-University Training: SERGEY KUCHUK
Higher School of Business and Management: SERGEY. KRYCHEVSKIY
Higher School of Tourism: NIKOLAY KABUSHKIN
Special Faculty of Psychology and Pedagogy for Teachers of Economics: BORIS KRAYKO

BELARUS STATE TECHNOLOGICAL UNIVERSITY

220050 Minsk, vul. Sverdlova 13

Telephone: (17) 226-14-32

Fax: (17) 227-62-17

E-mail: root@bstu.unibel.by

Internet: www.bstu.unibel.by

Founded 1930

Rector: IVAN M. ZHARSKIY
Pro-Rector for Academic Affairs: ALEKSANDR S. FEDORENCHIK
Pro-Rector for Administrative Affairs: BORIS V. ALDANOV
Pro-Rector for Economic Affairs: ALEKSANDR I. KUPTSOV
Pro-Rector for Education: GENNADY M. KVESKO
Pro-Rector for Research: PETR A. LYSHCHIK

Library of 1,200,000 vols
Number of teachers: 607
Number of students: 9,103

DEANS

Faculty of Chemical Technology and Engineering: SVETLANA E. OREKHOVA
Faculty of Engineering Economics: MIKHAIL I. BARANOV
Faculty of External Studies: ANDREY R. GORONOVSKIY
Faculty of Forestry: VALERIY K. GVOZDEV
Faculty of Forestry Technology: NIKOLAY P. VYRKO
Faculty of Organic Substance Technology: VALERIY N. FARAFONTOV
Faculty of Publishing and Printing: LEONID M. DAVIDOVICH
Faculty of Qualifications Improvement and Retraining of Specialists: ANDREY I. ROVKACH

BELARUSIAN NATIONAL TECHNICAL UNIVERSITY

220027 Minsk, pr. Nezavisimosti 65

Telephone and fax (17) 232-74-26

E-mail: bntu@bntu.by

Internet: www.bntu.by

Founded 1920

Faculties of architecture, construction, economics and management, instrument-making, mechanics and technology, motor vehicles and tractors, power engineering, road construction, robots and robot systems

Rector: Prof. BORIS M. KHRUSTALEV

Library: 2m. vols
Number of teachers: 2,643
Number of students: 15,000

Publications: *Energetica* (4 a year), *Mir Technologij* (4 a year), *Vestnik BNTU* (4 a year).

BELARUSIAN-RUSSIAN UNIVERSITY

212005 Mogilev, pr. Mira 43

Telephone: (222) 23-61-00

Fax: (222) 22-58-21

E-mail: bru@bru.mogilev.by

Internet: www.bru.mogilev.by

Founded 1961

Rector: IGOR S. SAZONOV
First Pro-Rector: FEDOR G. LOVSHENKO
Pro-Rectors for Academic Affairs: ALEKSANDR A. KATKALO, ALEKSANDR A. ZHOLOBOV
Pro-Rector for Academic, Economic and Int. Affairs: GRIGORIY P. KOSYACHENKO

Library: 1.5 m. vols
Number of teachers: 1,100
Number of students: 6,300

DEANS

Faculty of Automotive and Mechanical Engineering: STANISLAV B. PARTNOV

Faculty of Construction: SERGEY D. GALYUZ-HIN
Faculty of Economics: NIKOLAY S. ZHELTOK
Faculty of Electrotechnology: ALEKSANDR S. KOVAL
Faculty of Machine Building: VIKTOR A. POPKOVSKY

BELARUSIAN STATE AGRARIAN TECHNICAL UNIVERSITY

220023 Minsk, pr. Nezavisimosti 99
Telephone: (17) 264-47-71
Fax: (17) 264-41-16
E-mail: rektorat@batu.edu.by
Internet: www.batu.edu.by

Founded 1954

Faculties of agroenergy, agromechanics, business and management, humanities and ecology in social work, pre-university training and technical service, qualifications improvement and personnel retraining and vocational guidance

Rector: Prof. NIKOLAY V. KAZAROVETS

Library of 381,968 vols
Number of teachers: 519
Number of students: 8,783

BELARUSIAN STATE PEDAGOGICAL UNIVERSITY 'M. TANK'

220050 Minsk, ul. Sovetskaya 18
Telephone: (17) 226-40-20
Fax: (17) 226-40-24
E-mail: rector@bspu.unibel.by
Internet: www.bspu.unibel.by

Founded 1922

Rector: PETR D. KUKHARCHUK
First Pro-Rector: ALEKSANDR I. ANDARALO
Pro-Rector for Academic Affairs: YURIY A. BYKADOROV
Pro-Rector for Admin. Affairs: VLADIMIR V. YADLOVSKIY
Pro-Rector for Education and Social Affairs: SVETLANA I. KOPTEVA
Pro-Rector for Information and Analytical Affairs: VALERIY M. ZELENKEVICH
Pro-Rector for Research: VASILIY V. BUSHCHIK
Librarian: NADEZHDA P. SYATKOVSKAYA

Library: 1.5m. vols
Number of teachers: 1,380
Number of students: 18,000

DEANS

Faculty of Aesthetic Education: TATYANA S. BOGDANOVA
Faculty of Belarusian and Russian Philology: VASILIY D. STARICHENOK
Faculty of History: NIKOLAY N. ZABAVSKIY
Faculty of Mathematics: VLADIMIR V. SHLYKOV
Faculty of Natural Science: NATALYA V. NAYMENKO
Faculty of Physical Education: MIKHAIL M. KRYTALEVICH
Faculty of Physics: VIKTOR I. YANYT
Faculty of Pre-School Training: LIYDMILA N. VORONETSKAYA
Faculty of Pre-University Training: SERGEY V. YAKOVENKO
Faculty of Primary Education: NATALYA V. ZHDANOVICH
Faculty of Psychology: LEONID A. PERGAMENSHCHIK
Faculty of Social Pedagogical Technologies: ALEKSANDR V. KASOVICH
Faculty of Special Education: SVETLANA E. GAIDYKEVICH

BELARUSIAN STATE UNIVERSITY

220050 Minsk, pr. Nezavisimosti 4
Telephone: (17) 209-52-03

Fax: (17) 226-59-40
E-mail: bsu@bsu.by
Internet: www.bsu.by

Founded 1921
State control
Languages of instruction: Belarusan, Russian
Academic year: September to June

Rector: VASILIY I. STRAZHEV
First Pro-Rector: SERGEY K. RAKHMANOV
Pro-Rectors for Academic Affairs: VLADIMIR L. KLYUNYA, VIKTOR V. SAMOKHVAL
Pro-Rector for Admin. and Finance: VLADIMIR V. ROGOVITSKIY
Pro-Rector for Economic and Commercial Affairs: IGOR V. VOYTOV
Pro-Rector for Education and Social Affairs: VLADIMIR V. SUVOROV
Pro-Rector for Int. Affairs: VLADIMIR A. ASTAPENKO

Library: 2m. vols
Number of teachers: 2,400
Number of students: 16,500

Publications: Belarusskiy Universitet (24 a year), Higher School (6 a year), Sociology (4 a year), Vestnik BGU (12 a year)

DEANS

Faculty of Applied Mathematics: P. A. MANDRIK
Faculty of Biology: V. V. LYSAK
Faculty of Chemistry: G. A. BRANITSKY
Faculty of Economics: M. M. KOVALEV
Faculty of Geography: I. I. PIROZHNIK
Faculty of History: S. N. KHODZIN
Faculty of International Relations: A. V. SHARAPO
Faculty of Journalism: V. P. VOROBIOV
Faculty of Law: S. A. BALASHENKO
Faculty of Management and Social Technologies: V. G. BULAVKO
Faculty of Mechanics and Mathematics: N. I. YURCHUK
Faculty of Philology: I. S. ROVDO
Faculty of Philosophy and Social Studies: A. I. ZELENKOV
Faculty of Physics: V. M. ANISCHUK
Faculty of Radiophysics and Electronics: S. G. MULIARCHIK
International Graduate School of Business and Management of Technology: V. V. APANASOVICH

BELARUSIAN STATE UNIVERSITY OF INFORMATICS AND RADIOELECTRONICS

220013 Minsk, ul. Brovska 6
Telephone: (17) 293-89-17
Fax: (17) 293-23-33
E-mail: oms@bsuir.by
Internet: www.bsuir.by

Founded 1964
State control
Accredited by Min. of Education of the Republic of Belarus
Languages of instruction: Russian, Belarusian, English
Academic year: September to May

Rector: Prof. MIKHAIL P. BATURA
First Vice-Rector: Dr ANATOLY OSIPOV
Vice-Rector for Admin.: VLADIMIR I. TARASEVITCH
Vice-Rector for Education: Prof. ALEXANDER A. KHMYL
Vice-Rector for Education: Dr BORIS NIKULSHIN
Vice-Rector for Education: Dr HELENA ZHIVITSKAYA
Vice-Rector for Research and Devt: Prof. ALEXANDER P. KUZNETSOV
Chief Librarian: LUDMILA SIZOVA

Library: 1.5m. vols, 300 periodicals

Number of teachers: 1,000
Number of students: 15,000

Publication: Doklady Bguir

DEANS

Continuous and Distance Education: Dr VASILY BONDARIK
Faculty of Computer-Aided Design: Dr SERGEY DICK
Faculty of Computer Systems and Networks: Dr VALERY PRITKOV
Faculty of Engineering Economics: Dr LUDMILA KNYAZEVA
Faculty of Extramural Training: Dr ALEXANDER V. LOMAKO
Faculty of Information Technologies and Control Systems: Dr ARTUR BUDNIK
Faculty of Military Studies: Col. ALEXANDER DMITRIUK
Faculty of Pre-University Preparation and Occupational Guidance: Dr GALINA F. SMIRNOVA
Faculty of Radioengineering and Electronics: Dr ALEXANDER KOROTKEVICH
Faculty of Telecommunications: Dr OLEG D. TCHERNUKHO

PROFESSORS

ABRAMOV, I., Quantum Mechanics and Statistical Physics
AKSENCHIK, A., Probability Theory
ASAYONOK, I., Psychophysiology
BAKHTIZIN, V., Software Design and Programming Language
BELAYEV, B., Information Protection and Intellectual Property Management
BOBOV, M., Protection of Databases and Software
BORBOTKO, T., Information Protection in Bank Technologies
BORISENKO, V., Nanoelectronics
BRIGIDIN, A., Methods and Devices for Signal Shaping
DASHENKOV, V., Radiotechnical Circuits and Signals
DROBOT, S., Radioelectronics
DVORNIKOV, O., Designing of Integrated Circuits Topology
GAPONENKO, N., Nanophotonics
GASENKOVA, I., Information Protection and Intellectual Property Management
GOLENKOV, V., Mathematical Framework for Artificial Intelligence
GOLIKOV, V., Cryptoprotection of Information in Telecommunications
GULYAKINA, N., General Systems Theory
GURSKY, A., Digital and Microprocessor Units of Gauge Devices
KATKOVSKY, V., Information Protection and Intellectual Property Management
KHATKO, V., General Systems Theory
KIRILLOV, V., Metrological Support
KIRVEL, I., Ecology and Energy Saving, Environmental Economics
KLIUEV, L., Electrical Communication Theory
KOBRINSKY, G., Labour Management
KOLOSOV, S., Algorithmization and Programming
KOMLICHENKO, V., Computer Networks
KONOPELKO, V., Coding Theory
KRIVONOSOVA, T., Programming
KUREYCHIK, K., Computer Architecture
KUZNETSOV, A., Control System Calculation against Random Input
LISTOPAD, N., Transmitter-Receivers, Computer Systems for Data Transfer
LOSIK, G., Cognitive Graphics
LUKIYANETS, S., Automated Control Theory
LYNKOV, L., Information Protection and Intellectual Property Management
MALYKHINA, G., Logics
MUKHA, V., Statistical Methods for Data Processing
MUKHUROV, N., Information Protection and Intellectual Property Management

MURAVYOV, V., Satellite and Radio-Relay Communication Systems

NELAEV, V., Computer-Aided Design Systems in Micro- and Nanoelectronics

NOVIK, E., History of Belarus

PASHUTO, V., Foreign Economic Activities, Labour Management and Rating

PETROV, N., Theory and Methodology of Athletic Training

PRISCHEPA, S., Systems for CAD of Digital Devices

RESHETILOV, A., Electronics and Microcircuitry

SADYKHOV, R., Digital Processing of Signals and Images

SAK, A., Economic Forecasting and Planning

SHILIN, L., Theory of Electrical Circuits

SINITSYN, A., Algorithmization and Programming

SMIRNOV, A., Devices Based on Quantum and Magnetic Effects and Sensors

STOLER, V., Descriptive Geometry and Engineering Graphics

SURIN, V., Engineering Mechanics

TARCHENKO, N., Communication Systems

VILKOTSKY, M., EMC of Radioelectronic Appliances

YARMOLIK, V., Control and Diagnostics of Computer Equipment

YASHIN, K., Novel Production Equipment, Innovative Technologies, Labour Safety

ZABRODSKI, E., Political Science, Human Rights, Ideology of the Belarusian State

BELARUSIAN STATE UNIVERSITY OF PHYSICAL CULTURE

220020 Minsk, pr. Pobediteley 105

Telephone: (17) 250-80-08

Fax: (17) 250-80-08

E-mail: oo@sportedu.by

Internet: www.sportedu.by

Founded 1937

Academic year: September to July

Rector: Prof. Dr MIKHAIL KOBRINSKY

First Vice-Rector: OLGA GUSAROVA

Vice-Rector for Economic Affairs: VALERYI KRIVODUB

Vice-Rector for Education: ALEXEY GATATULLIN

Vice-Rector for Science: TATYANA POLIAKOVA

Number of teachers: 388

Number of students: 7,000 (3,050 full time; 3,950 part time)

Publication: *The World of Sport* (Scientific Journal)

DEANS

Faculty of Health Oriented Physical Training and Tourism: NATALYA MASHARSKAYA

Faculty of Mass Sports: IRYNA GUSLISTOVA

Faculty of Pre-University Education: VLADIMIR LITVINOVICH

Faculty of Sports Games and Combative Sport: ALEXANDR SHAKHLAY

Institute of Tourism: LIUDMILA SAKUN

BELARUSIAN STATE UNIVERSITY OF TRANSPORT

246653 Gomel, ul. Kirova 34

Telephone: (232) 95-20-96

Founded 1953

Rector: Prof. VENIAMIN I. SENKO

First Pro-Rector and Pro-Rector for Academic Affairs: Prof. VIKTOR YA. NEGREY

Pro-Rector for Academic Affairs: SERGEY I. SUKHOPAROV

Pro-Rector for Administrative Affairs: VALERIY V. BABIY

Pro-Rector for Economics: GALINA M. BYCHKOVA

Pro-Rector for Education: GALINA M. CHAYANKOVA

Pro-Rector for Research: Prof. KONSTANTIN A. BOCHKOV

Library of 650,000 vols

Number of teachers: 358

Number of students: 3,390

Publication: *Vestnik BelGUTa: Nauka i Transport* (4 a year)

DEANS

Faculty of Continuing Education: VLADIMIR V. PIGUNOV

Faculty of Electrical Engineering: ALEKSANDR V. GRAPOV

Faculty of Engineering: VIKTOR A. BERBILO

Faculty of Foreign Students: IRINA G. PASHKO

Faculty of Humanities and Economics: YURI P. LYCH

Faculty of Industrial and Civil Construction: ANATOLIY G. TASHNIKOV

Faculty of Mechanical Engineering: YURI G. SAMODUM

Faculty of Military Transportation: Col VLADIMIR V. LEVTRINSKIY

Faculty of Transport Management: NIKOLAY P. BERLIN

Faculty of Vocational Guidance and Pre-University Training: OLEG P. GORAEV

BELARUSIAN TRADE AND ECONOMIC UNIVERSITY OF CONSUMER COOPERATIVES

246029 Gomel, pr. Oktyabrya 50

Telephone: (232) 47-23-71

Fax: (232) 47-80-68

E-mail: priem@bteu.by

Internet: www.i-bteu.by

Founded 1964

Rector: Doc. ALLA A. BYK

First Vice-Rector: VLADIMIR F. PONOMARENKO

Vice-Rectors for Academic Affairs: Doc. VASILIY V. BOGUSH, Doc. LYUBOMIR M. SKORIK

Vice-Rector for Academic Research: Doc. LYUDMILA V. MISNIKOVA

Vice-Rector for Administrative Affairs: Dr YURIY V. BUTOLIN

Pro-Rector for Ideological and Educational Work: Dr ALEKSANDR I. KAPSHTYK

Vice-Rector for Scientific Research: Dr GEORGE S. MITYURICH

Library of 500,000 vols

Number of teachers: 330

Number of students: 10,000

DEANS

Correspondence Faculty of Commerce and Management: GALINA S. HRABAN

Correspondence Faculty of Economics and Accounting: NIKOLAY V. OKSENCHUK

Faculty of Accounting and Finance: VALENTINA A. ASTAFYEVA

Faculty of Business Education: NIKOLAY V. MAKSIMENKO

Faculty of Commerce: KLAVDIYA I. LOKTEVA

Faculty of Economics and Management: TATYANA V. EMELYANOVA

BREST STATE TECHNICAL UNIVERSITY

224017 Brest, vul. Moskovskaya 267

Telephone: (162) 42-33-93

Fax: (162) 42-21-27

E-mail: canc@bstu.by

Internet: www.bstu.by

Founded 1966

Faculties of civil engineering (civil engineering, production of building elements and structures, construction of roads and transport facilities, architecture), economics (accounting, analysis, audit; world economy and international economic relations; marketing), electronic and mechanical engineering (technology, equipment and automation of machine-building; automatic data processing systems; computers, systems and networks), extramural studies and preparatory training, water supply systems and soil conservation (water supply and sewage disposal systems, soil conservation and water resources management)

Rector: Prof. Dr P. S. POJTA

Library of 395,000 vols

Number of teachers: 499

Number of students: 6,438

BREST STATE UNIVERSITY 'A. S. PUSHKIN'

224016 Brest, bul. Kosmonavtov 21

Telephone: (162) 23-33-40

Fax: (162) 23-09-96

E-mail: box@brsu.brest.by

Internet: www.brsu.brest.by

Founded 1945

Rector: Prof. Dr MECHISLAV E. CHESNOVSKIY

First Pro-Rector: Prof. KONSTANTIN K. KRASOVSKIY

Pro-Rector for Academic Affairs: Prof. STANISLAV G. RACHEVSKIY

Pro-Rector for Admin. and Managerial Affairs: SERGEY V. KLIMUK

Pro-Rector for Educational Affairs: Prof. Dr ANNA N. SENDER

Pro-Rector for Educational and Social Affairs: Asst Prof. LIUDMILA A. GODUYKO

Pro-Rector for Scientific Affairs and Economics: Asst Prof. SERGEY A. MARZAN

DEANS

Faculty of Biology: NATALIA M. GOLUB

Faculty of Foreign Languages: SERGEY N. SIEVIERIN

Faculty of Geography: VLADIMIR I. BOYKO

Faculty of History: NATALYA P. GALIMOVA

Faculty of Law: YELENA N. GRIGOROVICH

Faculty of Mathematics: ALEXANDER Y. BUDKO

Faculty of Philology: OLGA A. FIELKINA

Faculty of Physical Education: NIKOLAY I. PRISTUPA

Faculty of Physics: IGOR I. MAKOYED

Faculty of Pre-School Education: LARISA D. GUSAROVA

Faculty of Pre-University Education: YELENA I. MIRSKAYA

Faculty of Psychology and Pedagogy: ALEKSANDER I. OSTAPUK

Faculty of Social Sciences and Pedagogics: ANATOLIY N. GIERASIEVICH

GOMEL STATE MEDICAL UNIVERSITY

224016 Gomel, vul. Lante 5

Telephone: (232) 74-41-21

Fax: (232) 74-98-31

E-mail: medinst@mail.gomel.by

Internet: www.medinstitut.gomel.by

Founded 1990

Public control

Languages of instruction: Russian, Belarusian, English

Rector: Prof. ANATOLY N. LYZIKOV

Vice-Rector for Academic Work: Doc. ALEXANDR A. KOZLOVSKY

Vice-Rector for Admin. and Economic Work: Prof. SERGEY N. GLUSHKOV

Vice-Rector for Education and Ideological Work: Prof. VICTOR M. UMANETS

Vice-Rector for Medical Work: Prof. VLADIMIR V. ANICHKIN

Vice-Rector for Scientific Work: Prof. VALERY P. SITNIKOV

Librarian: SVETLANA M. POLADIEVA

Library of 250,600 vols, 28,400 periodicals

Number of teachers: 490

Number of students: 3,000

Publication: *Problems of Health and Ecology*

DEANS

Faculty of General Medicine: Doc. VYACHE-
SLAV A. PODOLYAKO
Faculty of General Medicine for Overseas
Students: Doc. SVETLANA A. HODULEVA
Faculty of Medical Diagnostics: Doc. ANDREY
L. KALININ
Faculty of Pre-University Education: Doc.
MIHAIL E. ABRAMENKO

PAVEL SUKHOI STATE TECHNICAL UNIVERSITY OF GOMEL

246746 Gomel, pr. Oktyabrya 48
Telephone: (232) 48-16-00
Fax: (232) 47-91-65
E-mail: rector@gstu.by
Internet: www.gstu.by
Founded 1981
Academic year: September to August
Rector: SERGEI I. TIMOSHIN
First Vice-Rector: OLEG D. ASENCHIK
Vice-Rector for Administrative Economic
Operation: GENADII I. AVSEIKOV
Vice-Rector for Education and Educative
Work: VIKTOR V. KIRIENKO
Vice-Rector for Education and Instruction:
ALEKSANDER V. SYCHEV
Vice-Rector for Research: ANDREI A. BOIKA
Library of 538,653 vols
Number of teachers: 397
Number of students: 8,465

DEANS

Faculty of Automation and Information Sys-
tems: GEORGIY I. SELIVESTROV
Faculty of Correspondence: PETR V. LYCHEV
Faculty of Humanities and Economics: RAISA
I. GROMYKO
Faculty of Mechanical Engineering: IGOR B.
ODARCHENKO
Faculty of Power Engineering: MIKHAIL N.
NOVIKOV
Faculty of Pre-University Training: SERGEY
A. YURIS
Faculty of Technology: IGOR B. ODARCHENKO
Faculty of Upgrading and Retraining: YURIY
N. KOLESNIK

GOMEL STATE UNIVERSITY 'F. SKORINA'

246699 Gomel, Sovetskaya vul. 104
Telephone: (232) 56-31-13
Fax: (232) 57-81-11
E-mail: selkin@gsu.unibel.by
Internet: www.gsu.unibel.by
Founded 1969
State control
Languages of instruction: Russian, Belaru-
san
Academic year: September to July
Faculties of biology, economics, foreign lan-
guages, geology and geography, history, law,
mathematics, philology, physical training,
physics, psychology and preparatory train-
ing; France–Belarus Institute of Manage-
ment, Institute of Qualification Improvement
Rector: Prof. Dr MIKHAIL V. SELKIN
First Pro-Rector: ALEKSANDR P. KARMAZIN
Library: 1m. vols
Number of teachers: 570
Number of students: 5,843
Publications: *Belarusan Language*, *Problems
in Algebra*, *University News* (6 a year, in
Belarusan, English and Russian).

GRODNO STATE AGRARIAN UNIVERSITY

230008 Grodno, vul. Tereshkovoy 28
Telephone: (152) 77-01-68
Fax: (152) 72-13-65
E-mail: ggay@uni-agro.grodno.by
Internet: www.uni.agro-grodno.com
Founded 1951
State control
Rector: VITOLD K. PESTIS
First Pro-Rector: ALEKSANDR A. DUDUK
Pro-Rector for Administrative Affairs:
VALERIY N. TRIKUTS
Pro-Rector for Education: FEDOR N. LEONOV
Pro-Rector for Research: ALEKSANDR V. GLAZ
Librarian: NADEZHDA P. KHODOTCHUK
Library of 300,000 vols
Number of teachers: 209
Number of students: 3,842

DEANS

Faculty of Agronomy: FEDOR F. SEDLYAR
Faculty of Economics: IOSIF I. DEGTYAREVICH
Faculty of Plant Protection: GALINA A. ZEZYU-
LINA
Faculty of Pre-University Training: REGINA
K. YANKELEVICH
Faculty of Qualifications Improvement and
Retraining of Agricultural Personnel: OLEG
E. MOLYAVKO (Pro-Rector)
Faculty of Veterinary Medicine: MIKHAIL A.
KAVRUS
Faculty of Zooengineering: EVGENIY A.
DOBRUK

GRODNO STATE MEDICAL UNIVERSITY

E-mail: ief@grsmu.by230009 Grodno, ul.
Gorkogo 80
Telephone: (152) 43-54-51
Fax: (152) 43-53-41
E-mail: mailbox@grsmu.by
Internet: www.grsmu.by
Founded 1958
State control
Rector: VIKTOR A. SNEZHITSKY
First Pro-Rector: VITALY V. VOROBYOV
Pro-Rector for Admin. and Economic Affairs:
VLADIMIR P. KUZMICH
Pro-Rector for Commercial Activities and Int.
Relations: VIKTOR V. ZINCHUK
Pro-Rector for Information and Pedagogical
Affairs: IGOR P. BOGDANOVICH
Pro-Rector for Medical Affairs: VLADIMIR L.
ZVERKO
Pro-Rector for Research: VIKTOR V. ZINCHUK

DEANS

Faculty of Foreign Students: ANDREY R.
PLOTSKY
Faculty of General Medicine: GENNADIY G.
MARMYSH
Faculty of Medical Nurses with Higher Edu-
cation: EVGENY M. TISCHENKO
Faculty of Medical Psychology: TATYANA M.
SHAMOVA
Faculty of Paediatrics: ANDREY L. GURIN

INTERNATIONAL SAKHAROV ENVIRONMENTAL UNIVERSITY

220070 Minsk, St Dolgobrodskaya 23
Telephone: (17) 230-69-98
Fax: (17) 230-68-88
E-mail: info@iseu.by
Internet: www.iseu.by
Founded 1992
State control
Academic year: September to June
Rector: Prof. SEMJON P. KUNDAS

Library of 150,000 vols
Number of teachers: 345
Number of students: 1,370

DEANS

Faculty of Advanced Training and Retrain-
ing: IVAN I. MATVEENKO
Faculty of Environmental Medicine: Asst
Prof. MIKHAIL S. MAROZIK
Faculty of Environmental Monitoring: Prof.
NIKOLAY V. PUSHKAREV
Faculty of Pre-University Training: Asst
Prof. LYUDMILA M. SHEIKO

MINSK STATE LINGUISTIC UNIVERSITY

220034 Minsk, vul. Zakharova 21
Telephone: (17) 284-80-67
Fax: (17) 236-75-04
E-mail: info@mslu.by
Internet: www.mslu.by
Founded 1948
Schools of English, French, German, inter-
cultural communication, retraining and
teacher devt, Russian as a foreign language,
Spanish, translation and interpreting
Rector: NATALYA P. BARANOVA
Library: 1m. vols and periodicals
Number of teachers: 737
Number of students: 7,659
Publications: *Foreign Languages in the
Republic of Belarus* (4 a year), *Method-
ology of Teaching Foreign Languages* (1 a
year), *Studies in Romanic and Germanic
Languages* (1 a year), *Vestnik of MSLU:
History, Philosophy and Economics* (1 a
year), *Vestnik of MSLU: Phylology and
Linguistics* (2 a year), *Vestnik of MSLU:
Psychology, Didactics and Methods of For-
eign Language Teaching* (1 a year).

MOGILEV STATE FOODSTUFFS UNIVERSITY

212027 Mogilev, pr. Shmidta 3
Telephone: (22) 244-03-63
Fax: (22) 244-00-11
E-mail: info@mgup.net
Internet: www.mgup.net
Founded 1973
State control
Rector: Prof. VYACHESLAV SHARSHUNOV
Library of 500,000 vols
Number of teachers: 250
Number of students: 5,530

DEANS

Faculty of Chemical Technology: T. I. PISKUN
Faculty of Economics: NADEZHDA V. ABRAMO-
VICH
Faculty of External Studies: A. V. OBOTUROV
Faculty of Mechanical Engineering: VALERIY
P. CHIRKIN
Faculty of Pre-University Training: ELENA N.
ANDREYCHIKOVA
Faculty of Technology: LIDIYA A. KASYANOVA

MOGILEV STATE UNIVERSITY 'A. A. KULESHOV'

220009 Minsk, vul. Dolgobrodskaya 23
Telephone: (17) 230-69-98
Fax: (17) 230-68-88
E-mail: rector@iseu.by
Internet: msu.mogilev.by
Founded 1913; present name and status 1997
Rector: KONSTANTIN M. BONDARENKO
First Pro-Rector: MIKHAIL I. VISHNEVSKIY
Pro-Rector for Academic Affairs: VLADIMIR I.
POPOV
Pro-Rector for Research: NIKOLAY P. BUZUK

Library of 500,000 vols
Number of teachers: 450
Number of students: 7,600

POLOTSK STATE UNIVERSITY

211440 Novopolotsk, vul. Blokhina 29
Telephone: (214) 53-20-12
Fax: (214) 53-42-63
E-mail: post@psu.by
Internet: www.psu.by
Founded 1968
State control
Rector: DMITRIY N. LAZOVSKIY
First Pro-Rector: NATALYA N. BELORUSOVA
Pro-Rector for Academic Affairs: VASILIY V. BULAKH
Pro-Rector for Admin. Affairs: VLADIMIR P. STRIZHAK
Pro-Rector for Education and Social Affairs: VIKENTIY G. TSYGANOK
Pro-Rector for the Environment: VLADIMIR K. LIPSKIY
Pro-Rector for Information Systems: DMITRIY O. GLUKHOV
Pro-Rector for Innovation: NIKOLAY N. POPOK
Pro-Rector for Int. Affairs: SERGEY V. PESHKUN
Pro-Rector for Maintenance and Construction: VILEN S. LEVIN
Pro-Rector for Research: FEDOR I. PANTALEENKO
Library of 427,000 vols
Number of teachers: 500
Number of students: 6,000

VITEBSK STATE ORDER OF PEOPLES' FRIENDSHIP MEDICAL UNIVERSITY

210023 Vitebsk, pr. Frunze 27
Telephone: (212) 21-04-33
Fax: (212) 37-21-07
E-mail: admin@vgmu.vitebsk.by
Internet: www.vgmu.vitebsk.by
Founded 1934
State control
Academic year: September to July
Languages of instruction: Russian, English
Rector: Prof. VALERY PETROVICH DEIKALO
Vice-Rector for Admin. Affairs: IGOR VASILIEVICH KOSMIN
Vice-Rector for Clinical and Pharmaceutical Affairs: LEONID EGOROVICH KRISHTOPOV
Vice-Rector for Educational Work and Int. Affairs: Prof. Dr NATALLIA YURIEVNA KONEVALOVA
Vice-Rector for Pedagogical and Ideological Affairs: OLGA ARKADIEVNA SYRODOYEVA
Vice-rector for Scientific Research Work: SERGEI ALBERTOVICH SUSHKOV
Library: 1.5m. vols
Number of teachers: 538
Number of students: 6,259
Publications: *Herald* (4 a year), *Immunopathology, Allergology, Infectology* (4 a year), *Maternity and Child Protection* (4 a year), *Pharmacy News* (4 a year), *Surgery News* (4 a year)
VSMU also has a clinic and stomatological polyclinic

DEANS

Faculty for Mastering Skills of Specialists and Collective of Employees Re-training: Prof. RADETSKAYA LYUDMILA YEUGENIEVNA
Faculty of Overseas Students Training: Assoc. Prof. PRISTUPA VADIM VITALIEVICH
Faculty of Pedagogics and Psychology: Prof. KUNTSEVICH ZINAIDA STEPANOVNA
Faculty of Professional Orientation and Preparatory Training: Doc. PASHKOV ALEXANDER ALEXANDROVICH

Medical Faculty: Prof. Dr SEMENOV VALERIY MIHAILOVICH
Pharmaceutical Faculty: Prof. GURINA NATALYA SERGEYEVNA
Stomatological Faculty: Doc. KABANOVA SVETLANA ALEKSEYEVNA

VITEBSK STATE TECHNOLOGICAL UNIVERSITY

210035 Vitebsk, Moskovskiy pr. 72
Telephone: (212) 27-50-26
Fax: (212) 27-74-01
E-mail: vstu@vstu.vitebsk.by
Internet: www.vstu.vitebsk.by
Founded 1959
State control
Rector: Prof. VALERIY S. BASHMETOV
First Pro-Rector: IVAN A. MOSKALEV
Pro-Rector for Admin. Affairs: ALEKSEY N. SHUT
Pro-Rector for Education: ANATOLIY A. BELOV
Pro-Rector for Research: SERGEY M. BASHMETOV
Pro-Rector for Social and Economic Affairs and Construction: BORIS E. RYKLIN
Library of 300,000 vols
Number of teachers: 293
Number of students: 5,500 (incl. 2,500 external)

DEANS

Faculty of Arts and Technology: GALINA V. KAZARNOVSKAYA
Faculty of Civil Engineering and Technology: VITALIY K. SMELKOV
Faculty of Economics: VLADIMIR P. SHARSTNEV
Faculty of External Studies: ANATOLIY M. TIMOFEEV
Faculty of Mechanical Engineering and Technology: VALERIY I. OLSHANSKIY
Faculty of Pre-University Training and Vocational Guidance: ALEKSANDR P. SUVOROV
Faculty of Qualifications Improvement: IGOR M. KONTOROVICH

VITEBSK STATE UNIVERSITY 'P. M. MASHEROV'

210038 Vitebsk, Moskovskiy pr. 33
Telephone: (212) 21-58-66
E-mail: vsu@vsu.by
Internet: www.vsu.by
Founded 1910 as Teacher Training Institute; present name and status 1955
State control
Rector: Prof. ARKADIY V. RUSETSKIY
First Pro-Rector: IOSIF E. ANDRUSHKEVICH
Pro-Rector for Research: GENNADY I. MIKHASYOV
Pro-Rector for Studies: TATYANA G. ALEYNIKOVA
Publications: departmental publications, *My i Chas, Vestnik VGU*

DEANS

Faculty of Belarusian Philology and Culture: VIKTOR I. NESTOROVICH
Faculty of Biology: VITALIY YA. KUZMENKO
Faculty of Graphic Arts: VALENTIN P. KLIMOVICH
Faculty of History: VENIAMIN A. KOSMACH
Faculty of Law: VYACHESLAV I. PUSHKIN
Faculty of Mathematics: NIKOLAY E. BOLSHAKOV
Faculty of Pedagogy: ANATOLIY I. MURASHKIN
Faculty of Philology: LEONID M. VARDOMATSKIY
Faculty of Physics: ILLARION V. GALUZO
Faculty of Social Pedagogy and Psychology: SERGEY A. MOTOROV

YANKA KUPALA STATE UNIVERSITY OF GRODNO

230023 Grodno, vul. Ozheshko 22
Telephone: (152) 73-19-00
Fax: (152) 73-19-10
E-mail: mail@grsu.by
Internet: www.grsu.by
Founded 1940
State control
Academic year: September to June
Rector: Prof. Dr YAUHENI ROUBA
Senior Vice-Rector: Assoc. Prof. Dr SVIATLANA AHIIYAVETS
Vice-Rector for Academic Affairs: Dr ULADZIMIR BARSUKOU
Vice-Rector for Academic Affairs and Economy: Dr VASILI SIANKO
Vice-Rector for Academic Affairs and Quality Management: Dr YURY BIALYKH
Vice-Rector for Academic Affairs (IT and International Cooperation): Dr YURY VAITUKEVICH
Vice-Rector for Research and Innovations: Prof. Dr HENADZ KHATSKEVICH
Library of 716,130 vols
Number of teachers: 835
Number of students: 18,162
Publications: *Vestnik GrGU—Economics* (2 a year), *Vestnik GrGU—History, Philosophy, Political Science, Sociology* (3 a year), *Vestnik GrGU—Law* (4 a year), *Vestnik GrGU—Mathematics, Physics, Informatics, Computer Science and Management, Biology* (3 a year), *Vestnik GrGU—Philology, Pedagogics, Psychology* (3 a year)

DEANS

Faculty of Arts: Dr LIUDMILA CHARNILOUSKAYA
Faculty of Biology and Ecology: Prof. Dr VASILI BURDZ
Faculty of Economics and Management: Dr TCHON LI
Faculty of Engineering and Construction: Assoc. Prof. Dr ALLA VOLIK
Faculty of History and Sociology: Assoc. Prof. Dr EDMUND YARMUSIK
Faculty of Innovative Mechanic Engineering: Prof. Dr VASILI STRUK
Faculty of Law: Assoc. Prof. MIKALAI SILCHANKA
Faculty of Mathematics and Information Science: Dr ALENA LIVAK
Faculty of Pedagogy: Prof. Dr VIKTAR TARANTSEI
Faculty of Philology: Assoc. Prof. INA LISOUSKAYA
Faculty of Physical Training: Assoc. Prof. ANDREI NAVOICHYK
Faculty of Physics and Engineering: Assoc. Prof. Dr HENADZ HACHKO
Faculty of Psychology: Assoc. Prof. Dr. LILIYA DAUKSHA
Faculty of Tourism and Service: Assoc. Prof. Dr SIARHEI DANSKIKH
Military Faculty: Assoc. Prof. ALIAKSANDR DZMITRUK

Other Institutes of Higher Education

Academy of the Ministry of Internal Affairs: 220771 Minsk, pr. Pobeditelei 6; tel. (17) 284-31-15; fax (17) 288-27-58; e-mail info@amia.unibel.by; internet amia.nsys.by; f. 1958; faculties of distance education, forensic medicine, investigation, military studies, officer training and professional training; Rector VITALIY I. APARASEVICH.

Academy of Public Administration of the President of the Republic of

Belarus: 220007 Minsk, vul. Moskovskaya 17; tel. and fax (17) 222-82-05; e-mail rector@pacademy.edu.by; internet www.pacademy.edu.by; f. 1991 as instn of higher and advanced education for the training of public admin. personnel, acquired presidential institution status 1995; 3 constituent institutes: Institute of Civil Service, Institute of Public Admin., Institute of Sr Management Personnel; library: 200,000 vols; Rector PETR KUKHARCHYK; publ. *Issues of Management*.

Belarus State Academy of Arts: 220012 Minsk, pr. Nezavisimosti 81; tel. (17) 232-15-42; fax (17) 232-20-41; e-mail belam@user.unibel.by; internet belam.by.com; f. 1945; faculties of decorative-applied arts, fine arts and design and theatre; postgraduate courses in theatre art, television, cinema and visual arts, fine and decorative-applied arts and architecture, theory of arts, technical aesthetics and design; library: 83,538 vols; Rector Prof. RICHARD B. SMOLSKIY.

Belarus State Agricultural Academy: 213410 Mogilev raion, Gorki, vul. Michurina 5; tel. and fax (2233) 5-14-20; internet www.belagro.org.by; f. 1840; faculties of accounting, agribusiness and law, agroecology, agronomy, animal husbandry, economics, mechanization, land management and hydromelioration; library: 1.0m. vols; 800 teachers; 11,000 students; Rector Prof. ALEKSANDR R. TSYGANOV; publ. collection of research works (1 a year).

Belarusian Medical Academy of Postgraduate Education: 220013 Minsk, vul. P. Brovki 3; tel. and fax (17) 232-25-83; e-mail rector@belmapo.edu.by; internet www.belmapo.edu.by; f. 1931; faculties of dentistry, paediatrics, public health and protection, surgery and therapy; attached Laboratory of Scientific Research; 16,000 students; Rector Prof. GENNADIY Y. KHULUP; Librarian ANNA A. KOLBASKO.

Belarusian State Academy of Music: 220030 Minsk, Internatsionalnaya vul. 30; tel. (17) 227-49-42; fax (17) 206-55-01; e-mail bgam@tut.by; internet www.bgam.edu.by; f. 1932; courses: piano, orchestral and folk instruments, singing, composition, pedagogics, musicology, ethnomusicology, choir and symphony conducting; library: 211,702 vols; 307 teachers; 979 students; Rector M. A. KOZINETS.

Minsk Institute of Management: 220102 Minsk, vul. Lazo 12; tel. (17) 242-97-97; fax (17) 243-67-61; e-mail mik@mikby.com; internet www.miu.by; f. 1991; faculties of accounting and finance, economics and law; Rector Dr NIKOLAY V. SUSHA.

Minsk State Higher Education College of Civil Aviation: 220096 Minsk, vul. Uborevitcha 17; tel. (17) 201-02-81; fax (17) 241-66-32; e-mail aviakollege@ivcavia.com; internet www.avia.by/mgvak_en.shtml; f. 1974; trains specialists in aircraft and engine technical exploitation, lifting and transportation, operation of building and road machinery, technical exploitation of aviation technology (electrical devices and light technical equipment), information technology systems and networks, air traffic control and operation; Head ALEXANDER I. NAUMENKO.

Vitebsk State Academy of Veterinary Medicine: 210026 Vitebsk, vul. 1-ya Dovatora 7/11; tel. (212) 37-20-44; fax (212) 37-02-84; e-mail vet@lib.belpak.vitebsk.by; f. 1924; faculties of correspondence studies, specialist upgrading, veterinary medicine and zooengineering; library: 340,000 vols; 348 teachers; 3,109 students; Rector A. I. YATUSEVICH.

BELGIUM

The Higher Education System

The higher education system in Belgium reflects divisions of language, with separate ministries of education for the Dutch (or Flemish), French (Walloon) and German-speaking communities. This division was enshrined in legislation passed in 1963, under which French was established as the medium of instruction in Wallonia, Flemish in Flanders and German in the East-Cantons (Ostkantone). Brussels, the capital, is officially bilingual (French and Flemish). Both public and private universities are funded through their respective communities, but Roman Catholic institutions are regarded as 'free' and account for about 60% of Belgium's students. In 2007/08 a total of 64,372 students were enrolled in universities. Non-university institutions of higher education provide arts education, technical training and teacher training; in 2007/08 a total of 104,174 students were enrolled in such institutions. A national study fund provides grants where necessary and almost 20% of students receive scholarships.

The requirement for university entrance is the Certificat d'Enseignement Secondaire or Diploma Secundair Onderwijs. Hogescholen (see below) are open to all applicants holding the required certificates or wishing to attend courses as a 'free' student. The latter category of students is only eligible for certificates, not diplomas, after completing part of these studies. Generally, there are no entrance examinations or selective admission systems in use. However, in specific areas like nautical sciences and some art courses (audio-visual arts, music and dance), entrance examinations are compulsory.

The French community controls nine university-level institutions, while the Flemish community controls seven. Courses are divided into a period of general preparation followed by a period of specialization, each lasting two to three years. Belgium began implementing the Bologna Process in the 2004/05 academic year with reforms being carried out by all three communities. The traditional systems were gradually replaced and Bachelors and Masters degrees were fully implemented by 2008/2009. Most universities use the European Credit Transfer and Accumulation System (ECTS) and issue the Diploma Supplement for free. The Bachelors replaces a number of different degrees, notably one-cycle programmes of up to three years which resulted in either Gegradueerde (Flemish) or Graduat (Walloon), and two-cycle programmes of four or more years consisting of Candidat and Licencié (Walloon) or Kandidaat and Licentiaat (Flemish). The first part of the two-cycle degree (Candidat/Kandidaat) provided a general education, and lasted two years, whilst the second part (Licencié/Licentiaat) provided more specialized training over two or more years. The Masters is broadly equivalent to the old degrees of complementary education, the Gediplomeerde in de Aanvullende Studiën (Flemish) and Diplômé d'Etudes Complémentaires (Walloon), and degrees of advanced studies, Diplômé d'Etudes Approfondies (Walloon) and Diploma van Grondige Studies (Flemish). The final, and highest, level of academic degree is the Doctorate, which has no time limit but cannot be awarded until at least two years after completion of the second-cycle degree (now Bachelors).

Previously, non-university post-secondary education was provided by Hautes Ecoles (in Wallonia), Hogescholen (in Flanders) and a number of specialist colleges of technology, agriculture, para-medical studies, economics, social studies and teacher training. In Walloon-controlled institutions, courses were divided into eight subject categories, leading either to a Graduat after a 'short' course of three years or a Licencié after a 'long' course of four years. In 2004/2005 this system changed in line with the Bologna model. Hence, these Haute Ecoles now offer professional Bachelor degrees (180 ECTS) and Masters degrees (60 to 120 ECTS) in conjunction with universities. Furthermore, students can progress to a Diplôme de Spécialisation (DS) of 60 ECTS after the professional Bachelor degree; this is particularly relevant for paramedical subjects.

Programmes in the Hogescholen were also divided into 'long/short' courses of one or two cycles, but have now changed to the Bologna system. Hogescholen can offer professional Bachelor degrees (180 ECTS) and Masters degree programmes in association with a university. Professional Bachelor degrees do not provide direct entry to a Masters degree programme; candidates have to complete a bridging programme of about 45 to 90 ECTS.

Technical and vocational training is available either through an employer or an institution and is divided into three categories: apprenticeship contract; industrial apprenticeship contract; and part-time work and/or training.

The Joint Accreditation Body of the Netherlands and Flanders (NVAO) works within the framework of the European Consortium for Accreditation mutually to recognize the accreditation decisions of its members.

Regulatory and Representative Bodies

GOVERNMENT

Flemish Ministry of Education and Training: Hendrik Consciencegebouw, Koning Albert II-laan 15, 1210 Brussels; tel. (2) 553-86-11; internet www.ond.vlaanderen.be; Min. PASCAL SMET.

Ministry of the French-speaking Community, Office for Education and Social Promotion: pl. Surlet de Chokier 15–17, 1000 Brussels; tel. (2) 801-78-11; e-mail marie-dominique.simonet@cfwb.be; internet gouvernement.cfwb.be/promotion-sociale-0; Min. MARIE-DOMINIQUE SIMONET.

Ministry of the French-speaking Community, Office for Higher Education: rue Belliard 9–13, 1040 Brussels; tel. (2) 213-35-11; fax (2) 213-35-23; internet gouvernement.cfwb.be/enseignement-superieur; Min. JEAN-CLAUDE MARCOURT.

Ministry of the German-speaking Community, Department of Education, Vocational Training and Employment: Gospertstr. 1, 4700 Eupen; tel. (87) 78-96-13; fax (87) 78-67-22; e-mail kab.paasch@dgov.be; Min. OLIVER PAASCH.

ACCREDITATION

Agence pour l'Evaluation de la Qualité de l'Enseignement Supérieur (Higher Education Quality Evaluation Agency): rue Adolphe Lavallée 1, 5ème étage, 1080 Brussels; e-mail presidence@aeqes.be; internet www.aeqes.be; f. 2002, present status 2008; Pres. MARIANNE COESSENS; Vice-Pres. VINCENT WERTZ.

ENIC/NARIC Belgium (French Community): NARIC of the Belgian French Community, Direction générale de l'enseignement non obligatoire et de la recherche scientifique, rue A. Lavallée 1, 1080 Brussels; tel. (2) 690-87-47; fax (2) 690-87-60; e-mail equi.sup@cfwb.be; internet www.enseignement.be; f. 1984; Dir CHANTAL KAUFMANN; Specialist KEVIN GUILLAUME.

NARIC Vlaanderen (Belgium):; e-mail naric@vlaanderen.be NARIC-Flanders, Agency for Quality Control in Education and Training, Division Services APL, Hendrik Consciencegebouw Toren C 2, Koning Albert II-laan 15, 1210 Brussels; tel. (2) 553-89-58; fax (2) 553-98-45; e-mail naric@vlaanderen.be; internet www.naric.be; f. 1984; attached to Flemish Min.istry of Education and Training, Agency for Quality Assurance in Education and Training; equivalences higher education, secondary education, adult education, primary education; application EC— - directive 2005/36 for regulated professions in the Flemish schools; atttestations; information on equivalence matters; Policy Maker ERWIN MALFROY.

REGIONAL AND COMMUNITY BODIES

Conseil des Recteurs des Universités Francophones de Belgique (CReF) (Rectors' Conference of the French-speaking Community of Belgium): rue d'Egmont 5, 1000 Brussels; tel. (2) 504-93-00; fax (2) 504-93-43; e-mail vandevenne@cref.be; internet www.cref.be; f. 1990; Pres. PIERRE DE MARET; Vice-Pres. BERNARD RENTIER; Vice-Pres. BRUNO DELVAUX.

Conseil général des Hautes Écoles (Regional Council of Hautes Écoles): rue Adolphe Lavallée 1, 1080 Brussels; tel. (2) 690-88-24; fax (2) 690-88-46; e-mail brigitte.twyffels@cfwb.be; internet www.enseignement.be; Dir BRIGITTE TWYFFELS (acting).

Conseil Interuniversitaire de la Communauté française de Belgique (CIUF) (Interuniversity Council of the French-speaking Community in Belgium): rue d'Egmont 5, 1000 Brussels; tel. (2) 504-92-91; fax (2) 502-27-68; e-mail info@ciuf.be; internet www.ciuf.be; f. 2003; represents 9 univs. and univ.-level instns in the French-speaking community; advises on education policy; promotes cooperation between univs and univ.-level instns; Pres. BRUNO DELVAUX; Vice-Pres. BERNARD RENTIER; Sec. CLAUDE LALOUT.

Institut d'Encouragement de la Recherche Scientifique et de l'Innovation de Bruxelles/Instituut ter Bevordering van het Wetenschappelijk Onderzoek en de Innovatie van Brussel (Institute for the Encouragement of Scientific Research and Innovation of Brussels): Domaine Latour de Freins, rue Engeland 555, 1180 Brussels (Uccle); tel. (2) 600-50-34; fax (2) 600-50-47; e-mail info@irsib.irisnet.be; internet www.irsib.irisnet.be; f. 2003; promotes, supports and valorizes scientific research and technological innovation; provides financial support.

Vlaamse hogescholenraad (VLHORA) (Flemish Council of University Colleges): Ravensteingalerij 27 bus 3, 1e verd, 1000 Brussels; tel. (2) 211-41-90; fax (2) 211-41-99; e-mail info@vlhora.be; internet www.vlhora.be; f. 1996, awarded statute of public utility institution by decree in 1998; gives advice to the Flemish authorities on all policy aspects regarding college education, scientific project research, social services and the practice of the arts; organizes and stimulates consultation between the institutions on all issues related to the univ. colleges (hogescholen); Chair. Prof. BERT HOOGEWIJS; Sec.-Gen. MARC VANDEWALLE.

Vlaamse Interuniversitaire Raad (VLIR) (Flemish Interuniversity Council): Ravensteingalerij 27, 1000 Brussels; tel. (2) 792-55-00; fax (2) 211-41-99; e-mail administratie@vlir.be; internet www.vlir.be; f. 1976; autonomous body financed by univs; advises on and presents proposals to minister with regard to univ. education; research activities; Chair. Prof. MARC VERVENNE; Sec.-Gen. ROSETTE S' JEGERS.

Learned Societies
GENERAL

Académie Royale des Sciences, des Lettres et des Beaux-Arts de Belgique (Royal Academy of Science, Letters and Fine Arts of Belgium): Palais des Académies, rue Ducale 1, 1000 Brussels; tel. (2) 550-22-12; fax (2) 550-22-05; e-mail academieroyale@cfwb.be; internet www.academieroyale.be; f. 1772; colln of paintings, graphic works, sculptures, letters, memoirs and medals; has video and audio cassette library and archive; 400 mems (200 ordinary, 200 assoc.); library of 600,000 vols; Pres. PIERRE BARTHOLOMÉE; Permanent Sec. HERVE HASQUIN; Librarian GRÉGORY VAN AELBROUCK; Dir for Science Section ALBERT GOLDBETER; Dir for Literature and Moral and Political Sciences Section MARC RICHELLE; Dir for Arts Class LEON WUIDAR; publs *Bulletin de la Classe des Arts* (1 a year), *Bulletin de la Classe des Lettres et des Sciences morales et politiques*, *La Lettre des Académies* (4 a year), *Mémoires de l'Académie Royale de Belgique* (5–10 a year), *Nouvelle Biographie Nationale* (every 2 years).

Académie Royale des Sciences d'Outre-Mer/Koninklijke Academie voor Overzeese Wetenschappen (Royal Academy for Overseas Sciences): ave Louise 231 1050 Brussels; tel. (2) 538-02-11; e-mail kaowarsom@skynet.be; internet www.kaowarsom.be; f. 1928, present name and status 1959; promotes scientific knowledge of overseas countries, esp. with particular devt problems; organizes colloquia, symposia, seminars and confs; 127 mems (61 assoc. mems); Pres. BETTIE VANHOUDT; Permanent Sec. DANIELLE SWINNE; publs *Actes Symposiums/Acta Symposia*, *Biographie belge d'Outre-Mer/Belgische Overzeese Biografie*, *Bulletin des Séances/Mededelingen der Zittingen* (4 a year), *Recueils d'études historiques/Historische bijdragen*.

Koninklijke Vlaamse Academie van België voor Wetenschappen en Kunsten (Royal Flemish Academy of Belgium for Science and the Arts): Paleis der Academiën, Hertogsstraat 1, 1000 Brussels; tel. (2) 550-23-23; fax (2) 550-23-25; e-mail info@kvab.be; internet www.kvab.be; f. 1938; promotes cooperation between different educational institutions; organises scientific and cultural activities; 289 mems (90 ordinary, 30 corresp., 19 hon., 150 foreign assoc.); library of 50,000 vols; Pres. DOMINIQUE WILLEMS; Permanent Sec. Prof. GÉRY VAN OUTRYVE D'YDEWALLE; publs *Academiae Analecta*, *Collectanea Biblica et Religiosa Antiqua*, *Collectanea Hellenistica*, *Collectanea Maritima*, *Fontes Historiae Artis Neerlandicae*, *Iuris Scripta Historica*, *Iusti Lipsi Epistolae*, *Memoirs*.

Attached Institute:

Commission Royale d'Histoire/Koninklijke Commissie voor Geschiedenis (Royal Historical Commission): Palais des Académies, rue Ducale 1, 1000 Brussels; tel. (2) 550-22-20; fax (2) 550-22-05; e-mail luc.moreau@cfwb.be; internet www.kcgeschiedenis.be; f. 1834; researches, analysis and publ. of written sources concerning the history of Belgium; Pres. GUSTAAF JANSSENS; Vice-Pres. CLAUDE BRUNEEL; Sec. and Treas. GUY VANTHEMSCHE; publ. *Instruments de Travail* (irregular).

AGRICULTURE, FISHERIES AND VETERINARY SCIENCE

Fédération Wallonne de l'Agriculture: chaussée de Namur 47, 5030 Gembloux; tel. (81) 60-00-60; fax (81) 60-04-46; e-mail fwa@fwa.be; internet www.fwa.be; f. 2001; protects professional interests.

Attached Institute:

Committee of Agricultural Organizations in the EU (Copa): rue de Trèves 61 1040 Brussels; tel. (2) 287-27-11; fax (2) 287-27-00; e-mail mail@copa-cogeca.eu; internet www.copa-cogeca.eu; f. 1958; 60 mems, 36 partner orgs.; Pres. PADRAIG WALSHE; Sec.-Gen. PEKKA PESONEN.

ARCHITECTURE AND TOWN PLANNING

Association Royale des Demeures Historiques de Belgique (Royal Association for Historic Buildings): rue de Trèves 67, 1040 Brussels; tel. (2) 400-77-08; fax (2) 235-20-08; e-mail administration@demeures-historiques.be; internet www.demeures-historiques.be; f. 1934, present status 1958; Pres. HRH PRINCE LORENZ OF BELGIUM; Pres. Baron CARDON DE LICHTBUER; Sec.-Gen. Baron JOSEPH DE DORLODOT; Treas. DIRK LEERMAKERS; publs *François-Emmanuel de Wasseige*, *La Maison d'Hier et d'Aujourd'hui* (4 a year).

Fédération Royale des Sociétés d'Architectes de Belgique: rue Ernest Allard 21, 1ère étage, 1000 Brussels; tel. (2) 512-34-52; fax (2) 502-82-04; e-mail info@fab-arch.be; internet www.fab-arch.be; f. 1905; Pres. LUC DELEUZE; Sec. GEORGES BRUTSAERT; Treas. PHILEMON WACHTELAER.

Société Centrale d'Architecture de Belgique: Maison des Architectes, rue Ernest Allard 21/4, 1000 Brussels; tel. (2) 511-34-92; fax (2) 611-14-72; e-mail info@scab.be; internet scab.archiscab.be; f. 1872; promotes architecture and town planning; 180 mems; library of 20,000 vols; Pres. SERGE ROOSE; Vice-Pres. RENAUD DARDENNE; Sec. JEAN-PIERRE VIENNE; Treas. LAURENCE MERCIER.

BIBLIOGRAPHY, LIBRARY SCIENCE AND MUSEOLOGY

Archives et Bibliothèques de Belgique: blvd de l'Empereur 4, 1000 Brussels; tel. (2) 519-53-93; fax (2) 519-56-10; e-mail frankd@kbr.be; f. 1907; a sub-cttee of UNESCO, studies methods of standardization of bibliography; 350 mems; Pres. Dr FRANK DAELEMANS; publs *Archives et Bibliothèques de Belgique, Coll* (1 a year).

Association Professionnelle des Bibliothécaires et Documentalistes: Place de la Wallonie, 15, 6140 Fontaine-L'eveque; tel. (71) 52-31-93; fax (71) 52-23-07; internet www.apbd.be; f. 1975; promotes functions of library and information professionals; defends professional interests of librarians and archivists; 300 mems; Pres. LAURENCE BOULANGER; Vice-Pres. ALEXANDRE LEMAIRE; Vice-Pres. ANDRÉ MORUE; Sec. FABIENNE GÉRARD; Treas. GUY TONDREAU.

Service Belge des Echanges Internationaux/Belgische Dienst Internationale Ruil (Belgian International Exchange Service): Keizerslaan, 4 blvd de l'Empereur, 1000 Brussels; tel. (2) 519-53-94; fax (2) 519-54-04; e-mail nathael.istasse@kbr.be; f. 1889; information, documentation, exchange and transmission; Dir Dr NATHAËL ISTASSE; Librarian CHRISTOPHE JOUNIAUX; Librarian NATHALIE GEOFFROIT.

Vereniging van Antwerpse Bibliofielen (Antwerp Bibliophile Society): Museum Plantin-Moretus, Vrijdagmarkt 22, 2000 Antwerp; tel. (3) 221-14-67; fax (3) 221-14-71; e-mail pierre.meulepas@stad.antwerpen.be; internet www.boekgeschiedenis.be; f. 1877; fmrly Maatschappij der Antwerpsche Bibliophilen; conserves typographic heritage; promotes study of history of printed book; organizes excursions; 175 mems; Pres. MARCUS DE SCHEPPER; Vice-Pres. ELLY COCKX-INDESTEGE; Sec. PIERRE MEULEPAS; Treas. NORBERT MOERMANS; publ. *De Gulden Passer* (2 a year).

Vlaamse Museumvereniging (Flemish Museums Association): Europawijk 30/205, 2400 Mol; tel. (14) 71-62-70; fax (14) 72-42-93; e-mail info@museumvereniging.be; internet www.museumvereniging.be; f. 1962, present name and status 1982; defends interests of museums and museum personnel; 650 mems; Pres. WIM DE VOS; Vice-Pres. SOFIER WILDE; Sec. PETER VAN DER PLAETSEN; Treas. ELKE MANSHOVEN; publs *Museumkatern* (4 a year), *VMV Nieuwsbrief*.

ECONOMICS, LAW AND POLITICS

Institut Belge de Science Politique/Belgisch Instituut voor Wetenschap der Politiek (Belgian Political Science Association): place Montesquieu 1/7, 1348 Louvain-la-Neuve; tel. (10) 47-40-48; e-mail absp-cf@uclouvain.be; f. 1951, present status 1996; Pres. BENOÎT RIHOUX; Vice-Pres. CORINNE GOBIN; Sec. RÉGIS DANDOY; Treas. NATHALIE PERRIN.

Société Royale d'Economie Politique de Belgique (Royal Belgian Society of Political Economy): c/o CIFOP, ave Général Michel 1B 6000 Charleroi; tel. (71) 53-29-08; fax (71) 53-29-00; e-mail jf.husson@cifop.be; internet www.cifop.be/groupe.php?id=24; f. 1855, present status 1997; promotes and contributes to progress of political economy; 400 mems; Pres. ETIENNE DE CALLATAY; Vice-Pres. HENRI BOGAERT; Vice-Pres. PAUL-MARIE EMPAIN; Vice-Pres. PHILIPPE EULAERTS; Vice-Pres. ANDRÉ SAPIR; Sec.-Gen. JEAN-FRANÇOIS HUSSON; Treas. JEAN-EDOUARD CARBONNELLE.

Union Royale Belge pour les Pays d'Outre-Mer (Royal Belgian Overseas Union): rue de Stassart 20, 1050 Brussels; tel. (2) 384-37-40; e-mail a.schoro@skynet.be; internet www.urome.be; f. 1912; gathers asscns of fmr colonies, cooperatives and Congolese living in Belgium; protects interests of veterans from Congo, Rwanda and Burundi and member asscns; organizes confs; 10,000 mems; Pres. ANDRÉ DE MAERE; Vice-Pres. GUIDO BOSTEELS; Vice-Pres. PAUL VANNÈS; Admin. and Treas. ELISABETH JANSSENS.

Vereniging voor Politieke Wetenschappen (Institute of Political Science): Van Evenstraat 2B, 3000 Leuven; tel. (16) 32-32-54; fax (16) 32-30-88; e-mail res.publica@soc.kuleuven.be; f. 1958; annual conf. jtly with Dutch Political Science Assn; PhD seminars; 700 mems; Pres. Prof. Dr MARC HOOGHE; publs *Belgian Political Yearbook* (Dutch, English, French), *Res Publica* (Dutch, English, French, 4 a year), *Res Publica Library*.

FINE AND PERFORMING ARTS

Association Belge de Photographie et de Cinématographie asbl: rue de Sévigné, Anderlecht 1A, 1070 Brussels; tel. (47) 214-46-29; e-mail jacques.guilmin@hotmail.com; internet abpc066.hautetfort.com; f. 1874; provides training in photography and cinematography and exhibits works of members; 30 mems; Pres. ROGER WALSCH; Pres. JACQUES MAROQUIN; Vice-Pres. DENISE SCHMIT; Sec. JACQUES GUILMIN; Treas. FATMA LAHBI; publ. *Informations* (5 a year).

HISTORY, GEOGRAPHY AND ARCHAEOLOGY

Académie Royale d'Archéologie de Belgique/Koninklijke Academie voor Oudheidkunde van België (Royal Academy of Archaeology of Belgium): Palais des Académies, rue Ducale 1, 1000 Brussels; e-mail info@acad.be; internet www.acad.be; f. 1842; promotes study of art history of Southern Low Countries, Liège and Belgium; grants Simone Bergmans Award to unpublished study on history of nat. art every 3 years; 100 mems (60 ordinary, 40 corresp.); Pres. Dr CLAIRE DUMORTIER; Vice-Pres. CLAIRE DUMORTIER; Gen. Sec. ALEXANDRA DE POORTER; Treas.-Gen. STÉPHANE DEMETER; publs *Bibliography of the History of the National Art* (online, 1 a year), *Revue Belge d'Archéologie et d'Histoire de l'Art/Belgisch Tijdschrift*

voor Oudheidkunde en Kunstgeschiedenis (1 a year).

Association Egyptologique Reine Elisabeth/Egyptologisch Genootschap Kongingin Elisabeth: Parc du Cinquantenaire 10, 1000 Brussels; tel. (2) 741-73-64; fax (2) 733-77-35; e-mail aere.egke@kmkg-mrah.be; internet www.aere-egke.be; f. 1923; encourages Egyptological and papyrological research; promotes study of history and civilization of Pharaonic, Graeco-Roman and Christian Egypt; 650 mems; library of 30,000 vols; Chair. Comte ARNOUL D'ARSCHOT SCHOONHOVEN; Dir HERMAN DE MEULENAERE; Dir ALAIN MARTIN; Sec.-Gen. LUC LIMME; publs *Bibliographie Papyrologique* (4 a year), *Chronique d'Egypte* (2 a year).

Belgische Vereniging voor Aardrijkskundige Studies/Société Belge d'Etudes Géographiques (Belgian Society for Geographical Studies): W. de Croylaan 42, 3001 Heverlee; tel. (16) 32-24-27; fax (16) 32-29-80; f. 1931; centralizes and coordinates geographical research; 150 mems; Pres. J. CHARLIER; Sec. F. WITLOX; publ. *BELGEO* (2 a year).

Institut Archéologique du Luxembourg (Archaeological Institute of Luxembourg): rue des Martyrs 13–16, 6700 Arlon; tel. (63) 21-28-49; fax (63) 22-47-65; e-mail info@ial.be; internet www.ial.be; f. 1847; deployed between 2 museums; Archaeological Museum covers prehistoric period, Belgian-Roman period, Frankish period; Gaspar Museum displays works by Jean-Marie Gaspar and local art since 16th century; 500 mems; library of 25,000 vols; Pres. LOUIS LEJEUNE; publ. *Annales*.

Institut Archéologique Liégeois: Grand Curtius, quai de Maastricht 13, 4000 Liège; tel. and fax (4) 232-98-60; f. 1850; promotes studies of history and archaeology and related sciences in the Dist. of Liège; 250 mems (200 ordinary, 50 corresp.); Pres. PIERRE GASON; Sec. MAURICE LORENZI.

Institut Géographique National/Nationaal Geografisch Instituut: Abbaye de la Cambre 13, 1000 Brussels; tel. (2) 629-82-82; fax (2) 629-82-83; e-mail sales@ngi.be; internet www.ign.be; f. 1831, present status 1976; land surveying and cartography; performs aerial photographic coverage of the territory; creates database; 267 mems; library of 15,000 maps; Dir-Gen. INGRID VANDEN BERGHE; publ. *Catalog* (1 a year).

Société Archéologique de Namur: Hôtel de Croix, rue Saintraint 3, 5000 Namur; tel. and fax (81) 22-43-62; e-mail soc.arch.namur@scarlet.be; internet www.lasan.be; f. 1845; museum and library; discovery, conservation, implementation and publ. of cultural heritage of Namur; 450 mems; Pres. EMMANUEL BODART; Vice-Pres. JEAN DE WASSEIGE; Sec. JACQUES JEANMART; Treas. MICHEL GILBERT; publ. *Annales* (1 a year).

Société Belge d'Études Byzantines/Belgisch Genootschap voor Byzantijnse Studies: 1 rue Ducale, 1000 Brussels; tel. (9) 264-40-39; fax (9) 264-41-64; e-mail erika.gielen@arts.kuleuven.be; f. 1956; 57 mems; Pres. Prof. KRISTOFFEL DEMOEN; Sec. Dr ERIKA GIELEN; Treas. Prof. ANNE-MARIE DOYEN; publ. *Byzantion*.

Société Royale Belge de Géographie: Laboratoire de géographie humaine, Campus de la Plaine ULB, accès 5, blvd du Triomphe, CP 246, 1050 Brussels; tel. (2) 650-50-72; fax (2) 650-50-92; e-mail srbg@ulb.ac.be; internet www.srbg.be; f. 1876; 110 mems; Pres. Prof. Dr CHRISTIAN VANDERMOTTEN; Sec.-Gen. Dr B. WAYENS; publ. *Belgeo* (4 a year).

Société Royale d'Archéologie de Bruxelles: c/o Université Libre de Bruxelles, CP

175, ave Franklin Roosevelt 50, 1050 Brussels; tel. (2) 650-24-86; fax (2) 650-24-50; internet www.srab.be; f. 1887; prevents destruction of monuments; sections for archaeology, and history of art; other collns in Musées Royaux d'Art et d'Histoire; organizes exhibitions, lectures, tours and excursions; library of 20,000 vols; 450 mems; Pres. A. DIERKENS; Vice-Pres. J. M. DIVOSQUEL; Sec.-Gen. A. VANRIE; publ. *Annales*.

Société Royale de Numismatique de Belgique/Koninklijk Belgisch Genootschap voor Numismatiek (Royal Numismatic Society of Belgium): c/o Cabinet des Médailles, Bibliothèque Royale de Belgique, blvd de l'Empereur 4, 1000 Brussels; tel. (2) 639-00-00; fax (2) 466-86-02; e-mail jm@bvdmc.com; internet www.numisbel.be; f. 1841; promotes numismatics and sigillography through publs and confs; 216 mems (11 hon. mems, 33 instnl mems, 35 foreign mems, 47 working mems, 90 corresp. mems); Pres. JEAN-LUC DENGIS; Vice-Pres. FRANÇOIS DE CALLATAŸ; Vice-Pres. JOHAN VAN HEESCH; Sec. JAN MOENS; Treas. HUGUETTE TAYMANS; publ. *Revue Belge de Numismatique et de Sigillographie* (1 a year).

LANGUAGE AND LITERATURE

Académie Royale de Langue et de Littérature Françaises (Royal Academy of French Language and Literature): Palais des Académies, rue Ducale 1, 1000 Brussels; tel. (2) 550-22-72; fax (2) 550-22-75; e-mail alf@cfwb.be; internet www.arllfb.be; f. 1920; promotes French language and literature; awards literary prizes; 40 mems (incl. 10 foreign mems); Dir YVES NAMUR; Vice-Dir RAYMOND TROUSSON; Permanent Sec. JACQUES DE DECKER; publs *Annuaire*, *Mémoires*.

Alliance Française de Bruxelles-Europe: rue de la Loi 26, 1040 Brussels; tel. (2) 788-21-60; fax (2) 736-47-00; e-mail info@alliancefr.be; internet www.alliancefr.be; f. 1945; offers courses and examinations in French language and culture; attached offices in Antwerp, Condroz-Meuse-Hesbaye, Hainaut, Kortrijk, Limburg, Verviers and Gand; 8 Belgian depts; library of 4,000 vols, 30 periodicals, 400 DVDs, 35 CD-ROMs, 300 brochures, 1,100 audio cassettes and CDs, 450 comics strips, 1,000 video cassettes, 50 exhibits; Dir THIERRY LAGNAU.

Association des Ecrivains Belges de Langue Française (Association of Belgian Writers in the French Language): Maison Camille Lemonnier-Maison des Ecrivains, chaussée de Wavre 150, 1050 Brussels; tel. (2) 512-29-68; fax (2) 502-43-73; e-mail a.e.b@skynet.be; internet www.ecrivainsbelges.be; f. 1902; 500 mems; library of 11,000 vols; awards prizes for essays, poetry and prose; Camille Lemonnier museum; Pres. JEAN-PIERRE DOPAGNE; Vice-Pres. MARIE NICOLAÏ; Vice-Pres. EMILE KESTEMAN; Sec.-Gen. JEAN LACROIX; Treas. JEAN PIRLET; publ. *Nos Lettres* (10 a year).

British Council: Leopold Plaza, rue du Trône 108, 1050 Brussels; tel. (2) 227-08-40; fax (2) 227-08-49; e-mail enquiries@britishcouncil.be; internet www.britishcouncil.org/brussels; offers courses and exams in English language and British culture; promotes cultural exchange with the UK; also responsible for Luxembourg; Dir MARTIN HOPE.

Goethe-Institut: rue Belliard 58, 1040 Brussels; tel. (2) 230-39-70; fax (2) 230-77-25; e-mail info@bruessel.goethe.org; internet www.goethe.de/bruessel; f. 1959; offers courses and examinations in German language and culture; promotes cultural exchange with Germany; library of 20,000 vols, 90 periodicals; Dir Dr BERTHOLD

FRANKE; Sec. ANITA LAMPAERT; Admin. Man. ANNETTE HUERRE.

Instituto Cervantes: ave de Tervurenlaan 64, 1040 Brussels; tel. (2) 737-01-90; fax (2) 735-44-04; e-mail cenbru@cervantes.es; internet bruselas.cervantes.es; offers courses and exams in Spanish language and culture; promotes cultural exchange with Spain and Spanish-speaking Latin and Central America; library of 25,000 documents, incl. books, periodicals, CDs, DVDs, video cassettes and CD-ROMs; Dir MARÍA DE LOS ÁNGELES GONZÁLEZ ENCINAR; Sec. NURIA BLANCO MARTÍNEZ.

International PEN Club, French-speaking Branch: c/o Huguette de Broqueville, ave des Cerfs 10, 1950 Kraainem (Bruxelles); tel. and fax (2) 731-48-47; e-mail huguette .db@skynet.be; internet www.hdebroqueville .be; f. 1922; petitions for writers in prison; literary meeting with int. writers: French, Italy, Russian, German etc.; 540 mems; Pres. HUGUETTE DE BROQUEVILLE; Gen. Sec. ALISON JANE BELL.

International PEN Club, PEN-Centre Belgium: POB 12, King Albertpark, 2600 Antwerp-Berchem; e-mail info@ penvlaanderen.be; internet www .penvlaanderen.be; Dutch-speaking branch; f. 1935; 195 mems; Pres. GEERT VAN ISTENDAEL; Vice-Pres. INGRID VANDER VEKEN; Sec. GUY POSSON; Treas. SUZANNE BINNEMANS; publ. *PEN-Tijdingen* (4 a year).

Koninklijke Academie voor Nederlandse Taal- en Letterkunde (Royal Academy of Dutch Language and Literature): Koningstraat 18, 9000 Ghent; tel. (9) 265-93-40; fax (9) 265-93-49; e-mail secretariaat@ kantl.be; internet www.kantl.be; f. 1886; promotes literary and cultural life in Flanders; encourages research into Dutch language, culture and literature; 74 mems (30 ordinary, 5 extraordinary, 14 hon. mems, 25 foreign hon.); library of 40,000 vols; Pres. WILLY VANDEWEGHE; Vice-Pres. HUGO BREMS; Permanent Sec. Prof. Dr WERNER WATERSCHOOT; Librarian Lic. MARIJKE DE WIT; publ. *Verslagen en Mededelingen* (3 a year).

Société Belge des Auteurs, Compositeurs et Editeurs (Belgian Society of Authors, Composers and Publishers): rue d'Arlon, 75–77, 1040 Brussels; tel. (2) 286-82-11; fax (2) 230-05-89; e-mail frontoffice@ sabam.be; internet www.sabam.be; f. 1922; colln and distribution of copyrights; 25,000 mems; Chair. STIJN CONINX; Vice-Chair. TIMOTHY HAGELSTEIN; Vice-Chair. JAN VAN LANDEGHEM; Man. Dir CHRISTOPHE DEPRETER; publ. *Sabam Magazine* (4 a year).

Société de Langue et de Littérature Wallonnes (Society for Walloon Language and Literature): Université de Liège, place du XX Août 7, 4000 Liège; tel. (86) 34-44-32; e-mail sllw.be@skynet.be; internet users .skynet.be/sllw; f. 1856; promotes local literary productions in Walloon; 400 mems; library of 20,000 vols; Pres. GUY FONTAINE; Sec. MARC DUYSINX; Treas. JEAN BRUMIOUL; publs *Dialectes de Wallonie* (1 a year), *Littérature dialectale d'aujourd'hui* (1 a year), *Mémoire Wallonne* (1 a year), *Wallonnes* (4 a year).

Société d'Etudes Latines de Bruxelles (LATOMUS) absl (Brussels Society for Latin Studies): rue du Palais St Jacques 6, 7500 Tournai; fax (69) 21-47-13; e-mail latomus@belgacom.net; internet users .belgacom.net/latomus; f. 1936; promotes Latin studies, Roman history and archaeology in Belgium by publ. of books and journals; 750 mems; Dir-Gen. M. CARL DEROUX; publs *Collection Latomus*, *Review Latomus* (4 a year).

Société Littéraire de Liège: pl. de la République Française 5, 4000 Liege; tel. (4)

223-71-66; fax (4) 222-48-32; e-mail olivier .hamal@skynet.be; internet www .litteraire-liege.be; f. 1779; maintains archives and runs clubs and circles related to literature, art and history; 500 mems; Pres. OLIVIER HAMAL; Sec. JEAN-MARIE DE COUNE; Treas. BAUDOUIN RABAU.

MEDICINE

Académie Royale de Médecine de Belgique (Royal Academy of Medicine of Belgium): Palais des Académies, rue Ducale 1, 1000 Brussels; tel. (2) 550-22-55; fax (2) 550-22-65; e-mail contact@armb.be; internet www.armb.be; f. 1841, present status 1936; divs of biological sciences, human medicine, immunology, microbiology, parasitology, pharmacy, public health and forensic medicine, surgery and obstetrics, veterinary medicine; 332 mems (51 full, 40 ordinary, 51 hon., 114 hon. foreign, 76 foreign); Pres. Prof. PAUL-PIERRE PASTORET; Vice-Pres. WILLY MALAISSE; Vice-Pres. JEAN-BERNARD OTTE; Permanent Sec. Prof. JANOS FRÜHLING; publ. *Bulletin et Mémoires* (12 a year).

Association Belge de Santé Publique (Belgian Association of Public Health): c/o Scientific Institute of Public Health, rue Juliette Weytsman 14, 1050 Brussels; tel. (2) 642-57-09; fax (2) 642-54-10; e-mail jamila .buziarsist@wiv-isp.be; internet www.baph .be; f. 1938; promotes public health research in Belgium; 200 mems; Pres. Prof. Dr GUIDO VAN HAL; Vice-Pres. VÉRONIQUE TELLIER; Vice-Pres. WILLEM AELVOET; Sec. JAMILA BUZIARSIST; Treas. JOHAN VAN DER HEYDEN; publ. *Archives of Public Health*.

Association Royale des Sociétés Scientifiques Médicales Belges/Koninklijke Vereniging van de Belgische Medische Wetenschappelijke Genootschappen (Royal Association of Medical Scientific Societies of Belgium): ave Winston Churchill 11, bte 30, 1180 Brussels; tel. (2) 374-51-58; fax (2) 374-96-28; e-mail amb@skynet.be; internet www.arsmb-kvbmg.be; f. 1945; promotes Belgian medical socs; 4,000 mems; Pres. Dr D. VAN RAEMDONCK; Vice-Pres. Dr J. P. SQUIFFLET; Sec.-Gen. Dr M. HOOGMARTENS; Treas. Dr PH. KOLH; publs *Acta Anaesthesiologica Belgica* (4 a year), *Acta Chirurgica Belgica* (6 a year), *Acta Neurologica Belgica* (4 a year), *Acta Orthopedica Belgica* (6 a year), *JBR-BTR* (Belgian Journal of Radiology, 6 a year).

Belgian Association for Cancer Research: Department of Medical Oncology, University Hospital Antwerpen, Wilrijkstraat 10, 2650 Antwerp; tel. (3) 821-33-75; fax (3) 825-05-64; e-mail jan.b.vermorken@ uza.be; internet www.bacr.be; Pres. J. B. VERMORKEN; Vice-Pres. V. GREGOIRE; Sec. G. ANDRY; Treas. MARK DE RIDDER.

Koninklijke Academie voor Geneeskunde van België (Belgian Royal Academy of Medicine): Hertogsstraat 1, 1000 Brussels; tel. (2) 550-23-00; fax (2) 550-23-05; e-mail academiegeneeskunde@vlaanderen.be; internet www.academiegeneeskunde.be; f. 1938; promotes scientific research in fields of human medicine, pharmacy, veterinary medicine; awards scientific prizes; organizes meetings and confs.; 168 mems (79 ordinary, 62 foreign corresp., 15 hon., 12 foreign hon.); Pres. Prof. Dr GUY DE BACKER; Sec.-Gen. Prof. Dr BERNARD HIMPENS; publ. *Dissertationes–Series Historica*.

Probio: ave de la Constitution 56/13, 1090 Brussels; tel. (2) 466-22-13; fax (2) 627-45-71; e-mail probio.service@swing.be; internet www.probio.be; f. 1977; promotes and defends profession of biology; determines conditions required to acquire and provide good training for both scientific and educa-

tional, esp. in biology; Pres. CATHERINE LAUMONIER; Vice-Pres. SYLVETTE DESCAMPS; Sec. MARIE DECUYPER; publs *PROBIO Revue* (2 a year), *PROBIO Service* (4 a year).

Société Belge de Médecine Tropicale/ Belgische Vereniging voor Tropische Geneeskunde: Nationalestraat 155, Antwerp; tel. (3) 247-62-12; fax (3) 237-67-31; e-mail dvdr@itg.be; f. 1920; 569 mems (24 Belgian and foreign hon., 66 assoc., 85 titular, 394 corresp.); Sec. Prof. Dr B. GRYSEELS; publ. *Tropical Medicine and International Health* (12 a year).

Société Belge d'Ophtalmologie, section francophone (Belgian Society of Ophthalmology, French-speaking section): c/o Marlene Verlaeckt, Kapucijnenvoer 33, 3000 Louvain; tel. (16) 33-23-98; fax (16) 33-26-78; f. 1896; Sec. Prof. J. M. LEMAGNE; publ. *Bulletin* (4 a year).

NATURAL SCIENCES

General

Association pour la Promotion des Publications Scientifiques (APPS): 26 ave de l'Amarante, 1020 Brussels; tel. (2) 268-29-33; fax (2) 268-25-14; f. 1981; 80 mems and 20 assoc. mems; Pres. Dr JEAN BAUDET; publ. *Ingénieur et Industrie* (12 a year).

Société Royale des Sciences de Liège (Royal Society of Sciences of Liège): Institut de Mathématique de l'Université de Liège, A37, Grande Traverse 12, 4000 Liège; tel. (4) 366-93-71; fax (4) 366-95-47; e-mail srsl@ guest.ulg.ac.be; internet www.srsl-ulg.net; f. 1835; promotes biological, chemical, mathematical, mineral and physical sciences; 200 mems; Pres. THIERRY BASTIN; Vice-Pres. ANDRÉ MATAGNE; Sec.-Gen. Prof. JACQUES AGHION; publ. *Bulletin* (online).

Société Scientifique de Bruxelles: 61 rue de Bruxelles, 5000 Namur; tel. (81) 72-41-36; e-mail anne-martine.baert@fundp.ac.be; f. 1875; 140 mems; Sec.-Gen. GUY DEMORTIER; Admin. ANNE-MARTINE BAERT; publ. *Revue des Questions Scientifiques* (4 a year).

Biological Sciences

Belgian Society of Human Genetics: rue au Bois 22, 1950 Kraainem; e-mail helene .antoine-poirel@uclouvain.be; internet www .beshg.be; f. 2000; promotes research in human genetics; organizes scientific meetings; Pres. HÉLÈNE ANTOINE-POIREL; Sec. THOMY DE RAVEL DE L'ARGENTIÈRE; Treas. GUY VAN CAMP.

Belgische Vereniging voor Microbiologie (Belgische Vereniging voor Microbiologie): Rega Institute, Minderbroedersstraat 10, 3000 Leuven; internet www .belsocmicrobio.be; f. 1996; promotes devt of microbiology; works as forum for Belgian microbiologists; 267 mems; Chair. Prof. ALFONS BILLIAU; Vice-Chair. Prof. PAUL-PIERRE PASTORET; Sec. PAUL DEVOS.

Koninklijke Maatschappij voor Dierkunde van Antwerpen (Royal Zoological Society of Antwerp): Koningin Astridplein 26, 2018 Antwerp; tel. (3) 202-45-40; fax (3) 231-00-18; internet www.kmda.org; f. 1843; zoological and botanical gardens, aquarium, nature reserve, laboratories; educational and cultural services and scientific research; responsible for 3 instns: Antwerp Zoo, Planckendael and Queen Elisabeth Hall (concert hall); 32,000 mems; library of 34,000 vols; CEO DRIES HERPOELAERT; publ. *Zoo* (in Dutch, 4 a year).

Société Belge de Biochimie et de Biologie Moléculaire (SBBBM)/Belgische Vereniging voor Biochemie en Moleculaire Biologie (BVBMB) (Belgian Society of Biochemistry and Molecular Biology): UCL-ICP

74.39, ave Hippocrate 74–75, 1200 Brussels; tel. (2) 764-74-39; fax (2) 762-68-53; e-mail info@biochemistry.be; internet www .biochemistry.be; f. 1951; promotes research in fields of sciences, medicine, pharmacy, agriculture, veterinary medicine; 1,000 mems; Pres. Dr THIERRY ARNOULD; Vice-Pres. Prof. ANNE-MARIE LAMBEIR; Sec. Prof. FRED R. OPPERDOES; Treas. Prof. YVES ENGEL-BORGHS.

Société Belge de Biologie Clinique/Belgische Vereniging voor Klinische Biologie (Belgian Society for Clinical Biology): Laboratoriumgeneeskunde, UZ Gasthuisberg, Herestraat 49, 3000 Leuven; tel. (16) 34-79-02; fax (16) 34-79-31; internet www .bvkb-sbbc.org; f. 1948, present name and status 1997; encourages research in clinical biology; promotes teaching of laboratory medicine; 350 mems; Pres. PIETER VERMEERSCH; Vice-Pres. ANNE DEMULDER; Vice-Pres. ALAIN VERSTRAETE; Sec. DELPHINE MARTINY; Treas. LUC VANDENVULCKE.

Société Royale Belge d'Entomologie/Koninklijke Belgische Vereniging voor Entomologie (Royal Belgian Entomological Society): rue Vautier 29, 1000 Brussels; tel. (2) 627-43-21; fax (2) 627-41-32; e-mail info@srbe-kbve.be; internet www.srbe-kbve.be; f. 1855; promotes study of insects; 250 mems; library of 23,000 vols; Pres. WOUTER DEKONINCK; Vice-Pres. MARC POLLET; Sec. KOEN SMETS; Treas. UGO DALL'ASTA; publs *Bulletin* (2 a year), *Catalogue des Coléoptères de Belgique* (irregular), *Mémoires* (irregular).

Société Royale de Botanique de Belgique/Koninklijke Belgische Botanische Vereniging (Royal Botanical Society of Belgium): c/o Pierre Meerts, chaussée de Wavre 1850, 1160 Brussels; tel. (2) 650-21-64; fax (2) 650-21-25; e-mail inparmen@ulb .ac.be; internet www.botany.be; f. 1862; promotes botany through scientific research, publs, confs and excursions; distributes awards for botanical research; 200 mems; Pres. LUDWIG TRIEST; Vice-Pres. ELMAR ROBBRECHT; Sec. PIERRE MEERTS; Treas. ANN BOGAERTS; publ. *Plant Ecology and Evolution* (2 a year).

Société Royale Zoologique de Belgique/Koninklijke Belgische Vereniging voor Dierkunde (Royal Belgian Zoological Society): Koninklijk Belgisch Instituut voor Natuurwetenschappen, Vautierstaat 29, 1000 Brussels; tel. (2) 650-40-38; fax (2) 650-20-54; e-mail bjz@ua.ac.be; internet www .naturalsciences.be/institute/associations/ rbzs_website; f. 1863; promotes study of zoology; 400 mems; library of 1,500 periodicals; Pres. Dr P. MERGEN; Sec. Prof. Dr H. LEIRS; Treas. Dr E. VERHEYEN; publ. *Belgian Journal of Zoology* (2 a year).

Mathematical Sciences

Belgian Mathematical Society: Campus de la Plaine, CP 218/01, Blvd du Triomphe, 1050 Brussels; tel. (3) 265-39-00; fax (3) 265-37-77; e-mail bms@ulb.ac.be; internet bms .ulb.ac.be; f. 1921; promotion of mathematical activities; defends interests of Belgian mathematicians; 190 mems; library of 200 vols; Pres. Prof. STEFAAN CAENEPEEL; Vice-Pres. FRANÇOISE BASTIN; Sec. JAN VAN CASTEREN; Treas. GUY VAN STEEN; publ. *Bulletin of the Belgian Mathematical Society* (5 a year).

Conseil Supérieur de Statistique: WTCIII, blvd Simon Bolivar 30, 1000 Brussels; tel. (2) 277-71-69; e-mail philippe .mauroy@economie.fgov.be; internet statbel .fgov.be/fr/statistics/organisation/css; f. 1841, present name 1946; supports devt of statistics; ensures quality and unity of statistical work of govt instns; develops regionalized statistics; 36 mems; Pres. MARTINE VAN WOUWE; Sec. PHILIPPE MAUROY; Sec. NADINE BUNTINX.

Physical Sciences

Geologica Belgica: rue Jenner 13, 1000 Brussels; tel. (2) 788-76-30; fax (2) 647-73-59; e-mail wdevos@naturalsciences.be; internet www.ulg.ac.be/geolsed/gb; f. 1887, present name 1973; promotes geological knowledge; has br. in Liege; organizes seminars, confs and field trips; awards prizes and distinctions; 250 mems; Pres. Prof. RUDY. SWENNEN; Sec. Dr ERIC GOEMAERE; Librarian and Treas. Dr WALTER DE VOS; publ. *Geologica Belgica* (2 or 3 a year).

Koninklijk Sterrenkundig Genootschap van Antwerpen/Société Royale d'Astronomie d'Anvers (Royal Astronomical Society of Antwerp): Antverpiagebouw, Sint-Antoniuslei 95, 2930 Brasschaat; tel. (3) 664-28-93; e-mail ksga_inlichtingen@ hotmail.com; f. 1905; dissemination, teaching and aid for promotion of astronomy; 180 mems; Pres. FERDINAND DELATIN; Vice-Pres. WILLY DE KORT; Vice-Pres. ERIC VAN ACKER; publ. *Astronomische Gazet* (6 a year).

Société Astronomique de Liège (Liège Society of Astronomy): ave de Cointe 5, 4000 Liège; tel. (4) 253-35-90; fax (4) 252-74-74; e-mail sal@ societeastronomiquedeliege.be; internet www.societeastronomiquedeliege.be; f. 1938; brings together amateurs of astronomy, and promotes public understanding; 700 mems; library of 1,600 vols; Pres. A. LAUSBERG; Sec. L. PAUQUAY; publ. *Le Ciel* (12 a year).

Société Géologique de Belgique (Geological Society of Belgium): Unité de documentation, B6 allée de la Chimie, 4000 Liège; tel. (4) 366-53-56; fax (4) 366-56-36; e-mail a .anceau@ulg.ac.be; f. 1874; has br. in Brussels; 300 mems; Pres. J. VANDER AUWERA; Sec.-Gen. A. ANCEAU; publ. *Geologica Belgica* (2 a year).

Société Royale Belge d'Astronomie, de Météorologie et de Physique du Globe: ave Circulaire 3, 1180 Brussels; tel. (2) 373-02-53; fax (2) 374-98-22; internet www.srba .be; f. 1894; 800 mems; Pres. GUY STEVINS; Vice-Pres. LOUIS WILLEMS; Vice-Pres. VIVIANE PIERRARD; Sec.-Gen. RENÉ DEJAIFFE; Treas. MARC VANDIEPENBEECK; publ. *Ciel et Terre* (6 a year).

Société Royale de Chimie: ULB, CP 160/ 07, ave F. Roosevelt 50, 1050 Brussels; tel. (2) 650-52-08; fax (2) 650-51-84; e-mail src@ulb .ac.be; internet www.src.be; f. 1887, present name 1904; promotes study of chemistry and highlights contribution of chemistry to sciences; 600 mems; Pres. Prof. Y. MARCHAND; Vice-Pres. ALAIN LAUDET; Sec.-Gen. Prof. JEAN-CLAUDE BRAEKMAN; Treas. PASCAL LAURENT; publ. *Chimie Nouvelle* (3 a year).

PHILOSOPHY AND PSYCHOLOGY

Société Philosophique de Louvain: c/o Institut Supérieur de Philosophie, place du Cardinal Mercier 14, 1348 Louvain-la-Neuve; tel. (10) 47-47-87; fax (10) 47-82-19; e-mail nathalie.frogneux@uclouvain.be; f. 1888; 71 mems; Pres. NATHALIE FROGNEUX; Sec. PIERRE DESTRÉE; Treas. HERVÉ POURTOIS.

RELIGION, SOCIOLOGY AND ANTHROPOLOGY

Institut Belge des Hautes Etudes Chinoises/Belgisch Instituut voor Hogere Chinese Studien: c/o Musées Royaux d'Art et d'Histoire, parc du Cinquantenaire 10, 1000 Brussels; tel. and fax (2) 741-73-55; e-mail inst.chin@kmkg-mrah.be; internet www.china-institute.be; f. 1929; promotes study of Chinese civilization; Sinology and Buddhism; lectures, courses on Chinese art, history, painting and calligraphy; offers scholarships to young Chinese pursuing graduate studies in Belgium; library of 60,000 vols; approx. 300 mems; Pres. ALAIN DAMBREMEZ; Dir JEAN-MARIE SIMONET; publ. *Mélanges Chinois et Bouddhiques* (every 2 years).

Ruusbroecgenootschap/Ruusbroec Institute: Grote Kauwenberg 34, 2000 Antwerp; tel. (3) 275-57-80; fax (3) 220-44-20; e-mail ingrid.deruyte@ua.ac.be; f. 1925, inc. as Centrum voor Spiritualiteit of Universiteit Antwerpen in 1973; soc. of Flemish Jesuits engaged in spiritual studies of Low Countries; library of 115,000 vols (incl. 30,000 old and rare books), 500 MSS, 35,000 devotional prints; Dir Prof. Dr THEO CLEMENS; Sec. INGRID DE RUYTE; Librarian ERNA VAN LOOVEREN; publ. *Ons Geestelijk Erf* (4 a year).

Société des Bollandistes: blvd St Michel 24, 1040 Brussels; tel. (2) 740-24-21; fax (2) 740-24-24; e-mail info@bollandistes.be; internet www.bollandistes.be; f. 1630; research and publs in critical hagiography; library of 500,000 vols, 1,000 periodicals; Dir Dr ROBERT GODDING; publs *Analecta Bollandiana* (critical hagiography, 2 a year), *Subsidia Hagiographica* (irregular), *Tabularium Hagiographicum* (irregular).

Société Royale Belge d'Anthropologie et de Préhistoire/Koninklijke Belgische Vereniging voor Antropologie en Prehistorie (Royal Belgian Society of Anthropology and Prehistory): rue Vautier 29, 1000 Brussels; tel. (2) 627-41-45; fax (2) 627-41-13; e-mail srbap@naturalsciences.be; internet srbap.naturalsciences.be; f. 1882, present name 1931; multidisciplinary study of man and cultures; promotes and disseminates scientific research in these areas; Pres. NATHALIE VANMUYLDER; Vice-Pres. BART VANMONTFORT; Vice-Pres. ROSINE ORBAN; Vice-Pres. DAMIEN FLAS; Sec.-Gen. CAROLINE POLET; Treas. JEAN PIRET; 109 mems; publs *Anthropologie et Préhistoire* (1 a year), *Hominid Remains* (series).

TECHNOLOGY

Bureau de Normalisation (NBN) (Standards Bureau): rue de Birmingham 131, 1070 Brussels; tel. (2) 738-01-11; fax (2) 733-42-64; e-mail info@nbn.be; internet www.nbn.be; f. 1946; Belgian nat. mem. of the CEN (European Cttee of Standardization) and the ISO (Int. Org. for Standardization); establishes outline of standardization programmes; 962 mems; Pres. of Management Cttee MARC DE POORTER; publ. *NBN Revue* (10 a year).

Koninklijke Vlaamse Ingenieursvereniging (Royal Flemish Association of Engineers): Ingenieurshuis, Desguinlei 214, 2018 Antwerp; tel. (3) 260-08-40; fax (3) 216-06-89; e-mail info@kviv.be; internet www.kviv.be; f. 1928; protects professional interests of univ. trained engineers; creates awareness of technical knowledge; promotes technology and engineering; 9,500 mems; Pres. PAUL VERSTRAETEN; Sec.-Gen. Ir P. ERAUW; publs *Het Ingenieursblad* (12 a year), *Ingenieurs in Vlaanderen* (1 a year), *KVIV-Direkt* (12 a year).

Société Belge de Photogrammétrie, de Télédétection et de Cartographie (Belgian Society for Photogrammetry, Remote Sensing and Cartography): C.A.E.-Tour Finances (Bte 38), blvd du Jardin Botanique 50, 1010 Brussels; tel. (2) 210-35-98; f. 1931; 163 mems; Pres. R. THONNARD; Sec. J. VAN HEMELRIJCK; publ. *Bulletin* (4 a year).

Société Royale Belge des Electriciens/Koninklijke Belgische Vereniging der Elektrotechnici: c/o VUB-TW-ETEC, blvd de la Plaine 2, 1050 Brussels; tel. (2) 629-28-

19; fax (2) 629-36-20; e-mail srbe-kbve@vub
.ac.be; internet www.kbve-srbe.be; f. 1884,
present status 1925; organizes seminars;
promotes study and devt of electricity science; 1,600 mems; Sec.-Gen. BRIGITTE
SNEYERS; publ. *Revue E Tijdschrift* (4 a year).

**Société Royale Belge des Ingénieurs et
des Industriels:** Hôtel Ravenstein, rue
Ravenstein 3, 1000 Brussels; tel. (2) 511-58-
56; fax (2) 514-57-95; f. 1885; 2,000 mems;
Pres. PIERRE KLEES; publ. *SRBII info* (12 a
year).

Research Institutes
GENERAL

Antwerp Management School: Sint-
Jacobsmarkt 9–13, 2000 Antwerp; tel. (3)
265-49-89; fax (3) 265-47-34; e-mail info@
antwerpmanagementschool.be; internet
www.antwerpmanagementschool.be;
attached to Univ. of Antwerp; academic and
research support to management field; contributes to creation and dissemination of
knowledge in collaboration with business
world and public and social-profit orgs;
Dean Prof. Dr PHILIP NAERT.

**Centre d'Etudes Nord-Américaines de
l'ULB:** Université Libre de Bruxelles, ave
F. D. Roosevelt 50, CP 175/01, 1050 Brussels;
tel. (2) 650-38-07; fax (2) 650-39-90; e-mail
mlebrun@admin.ulb.ac.be; internet www.ulb
.ac.be/cena; f. 2008; attached to Univ. Libre
de Bruxelles; promotes study of North America, esp. Canada, Mexico and United States;
library of 6,000 vols; Dir SERGE JAUMAIN; Sec.
MIREILLE LEBRUN.

**Centre for International Management
and Development:** Lange Sint Annastraat
7 , 2000 Antwerp; tel. (3) 265-45-25; fax (3)
265-48-53; e-mail filip.debeule@ua.ac.be;
internet www.ua.ac.be/cimda; research
related to investment, devt, multinationals
and transition economies; Chair. Prof. Dr
DANNY VAN DEN BULCKE; Vice-Chair. LUDO
CUYVERS.

**Centre for Research in Finance and
Management:** Rempart de la Vierge 8,
5000 Namur; tel. (81) 72-48-87; fax (81) 72-
48-80; e-mail pierre.giot@fundp.ac.be;
attached to Univ. of Namur; studying aspects
of financial management of company and its
interactions with financial markets, both
empirical and theoretical; Head PIERRE GIOT.

Centrum voor Bedrijfsgeschiedenis:
Prinsstraat 13, 2000 Antwerp; tel. (3) 265-
42-52; fax (3) 265-45-46; e-mail helma
.desmedt@ua.ac.be; attached to Univ. of
Antwerp; research on history of port of
Antwerp in 19th and 20th centuries; history
of stock exchange and banking in Belgium;
Dir Prof. Dr HELMA DE SMEDT.

**Centrum voor Migratie en Intercul-
turele Studies** (Centre for Migration and
Intercultural Studies): Prinsstraat 13, 2000
Antwerp; Lange Nieuwstraat 55, 2000
Antwerp; tel. (3) 265-59-69; fax (3) 265-59-
26; e-mail ina.lodewyckx@ua.ac.be; internet
www.ua.ac.be/cemis; f. 2005; attached to
Univ. of Antwerp; multidisciplinary research
in field of migration and intercultural society; Chair. DIRK VANHEULE; Dir CHRISTIANE
TIMMERMAN.

**Groupe d'Etudes sur le Racisme, les
Migrations et l'Exclusion:** ave F. D.
Roosevelt 50, CP 124, 1050 Brussels; tel. (2)
650-31-82; fax (2) 650-46-59; e-mail germe@
ulb.ac.be; internet www.ulb.ac.be/socio/
germe; f. 1995; attached to Univ. Libre de
Bruxelles; promotes study on migration,
racism; European dimensions of immigration

policy and integration; Dir ANDREA REA; Sec.
CLAUDE LEONIS.

**Instituut voor Ontwikkelingsbeleid en -
beheer** (Institute of Development Policy and
Management): Prinstraat 1, 2000 Antwerp;
Lange Sint-Annastraat 7, 2000 Antwerp; tel.
(3) 265-57-70; fax (3) 265-57-71; e-mail dev@
ua.ac.be; internet www.ua.ac.be/iob;
research on political economy of Great Lakes
Region of Central Africa and devt evaluation
and management, governance and devt,
globalization and devt; library of 25,000
vols; Chair. ROBRECHT RENARD; Vice-Chair.
DANNY CASSIMON; Librarian HANS DE
BACKER; publ. *Annuaire des grands lacs* (1 a
year).

**Instituut voor Samenwerking tussen
Universiteit en Arbeidersbeweging:**
Venusstraat 23, 2000 Antwerp; tel. (3) 265-
58-86; fax (3) 265-59-77; e-mail els.peeters@
ua.ac.be; internet www.ua.ac.be/isua; f. 1970;
attached to Univ. of Antwerp; scientific
research to guard interests of trade unions;
Chair. Prof. MARC RIGAUX; Sec. DOMINIQUE
KIEKENS.

Oostenrijk-Centrum Antwerpen (Austrian Centre Antwerp): Prinsstraat 13, 2000
Antwerp; tel. (3) 220-42-48; fax (3) 220-42-59;
e-mail octant@ua.ac.be; internet www.ua.ac
.be/octant; f. 1993, present status 1999;
attached to Univ. of Antwerp; promotes
cultural dialogue between central and north-
western Europe (BENELUX countries,
France and Germany); plans research projects on topics of relevance to Austria; Man.
Dir EVA STEINDORFER.

Steunpunt Buitenlands Beleid: Lange
Sint-Annastraat 7, 2000 Antwerpen; tel. (3)
265-56-37; fax (3) 265-57-98; e-mail vsbb@ua
.ac.be; internet www.ua.ac.be/vsbbe; f. 2007;
attached to Univ. of Antwerp; scientific
research on European and global relations,
cultural diversity, globalization, devt
cooperation and human rights; research to
provide long-and short-term policy support to
Flemish govt in terms of foreign policy and
int. cooperation; Dir HUGO DURIEUX.

Steunpunt Gelijkekansenbeleid: Lange
Nieuwstraat 55, 2000 Antwerp; tel. (3) 265-
59-63; fax (3) 265-59-26; e-mail
steunpuntgeka@ua.ac.be; internet www.ua
.ac.be/sgk; f. 2002; br. in Hasselt; scientific
and applied research to assess opportunities
in society and to settle and support policies of
Min. of Equal Opportunities; 4 research
pillars linked to groups: women, elderly,
homosexuals and immigrants; Dir Prof. Dr
PETRA MEIER.

**Universitair Wetenschappelijk Instituut
voor Drugproblemen** (University Scientific Institute for Drug Problems): Prinsstraat 13, 2000 Antwerpen; tel. (3) 265-40-
65; fax (3) 265-44-20; e-mail a.uwid@
antwerpen.be; internet www.uwid.be; f.
2003; research, education and service provision in field of drug and substance abuse; Dir
Prof. Dr BOB VERMERGHT.

AGRICULTURE, FISHERIES AND
VETERINARY SCIENCE

Centre des Technologies Agronomiques:
rue de la Charmille 16, 4577 Liege; tel. (85)
27-49-60; fax (85) 51-27-06; e-mail cta.stree@
tiscali.be; internet www.ctastree.be; applied
research-oriented teaching in agricultural
field; Dir CHRISTIAN MARCHE.

**Centre Wallon de Recherches Agrono-
miques** (Walloon Agricultural Research
Centre): rue de Liroux 9, 5030 Gembloux;
tel. (81) 62-65-55; fax (81) 62-65-59; e-mail
cra@cra.wallonia.be; internet www.cra
.wallonie.be; f. 1872, present status 2002;
attached to Regional Government of Wallo-

nia; agricultural research at 8 research
depts; has brs in Libramont and Mussy-la-
Ville; encourages research in agriculture,
horticulture, food processing industries and
environmental sciences; Dir R. BISTON; publ.
Rapport d'activité.

**Centrum voor Onderzoek in Diergen-
eeskunde en Agrochemie/Centre
d'Etude et de Recherches Vétérinaires
et Agrochimiques** (Veterinary and Agrochemical Research Centre): Groeselenberg
99, 1180 Brussels; tel. (2) 379-04-00; fax (2)
379-04-01; e-mail info@var.fgov.be; internet
www.var.fgov.be; f. 1997, merger between
National Veterinary Research Institute
(INRV) and Chemical Research Institute
(IRC); research sites in Brussels, Tervuren
and Machelen; promotes scientific research
in food production, animal health, and public
health; Gen. Man. PIERRE KERKHOFS; publ.
Activiteitsverslag/Rapport d'activité (1 a
year).

ECONOMICS, LAW AND POLITICS

Centre for European Policy Studies:
place du Congrès 1, 1000 Brussels; tel. (2)
229-39-11; fax (2) 219-41-51; e-mail info@
ceps.eu; internet www.ceps.eu; f. 1983;
serves as forum for debate on EU affairs;
organizes task forces, conferences, meetings,
briefings, training seminars; 130 institutional mems, 120 corporate mems; CEO
KAREL LANNOO; Dir DANIEL GROS.

**Centrum voor Beroepsvervolmaking
Rechten:** Venusstraat 23, 2000 Antwerp;
tel. (3) 265-54-48; fax (3) 265-59-79; e-mail
cbr@ua.ac.be; internet www.ua.ac.be/cbr; f.
1985; attached to Univ. of Antwerp; organizes training related to law; Dir PASCALE
BUYCK; Sec. REINHILDE TULKENS; Sec. JUTTA
LEDÈNE.

Europacentrum Jean Monnet: Prinsstraat 13, 2000 Antwerp; tel. (3) 265-40-88;
fax (3) 265-44-20; e-mail evrard.claessens@
ua.ac.be; attached to Univ. of Antwerp; study
of European integration process and EU
devts in Belgium; Dir Prof. Dr EVRARD
CLAESSENS.

**European Centre for Advanced
Research in Economics and Statistics:**
ave F. D. Roosevelt 50, CP 114, 1050 Brussels; tel. (2) 650-30-75; fax (2) 650-44-75;
e-mail ecares@ulb.ac.be; f. 1991, present
name 1999; promotes research in economics,
econometrics and statistics; Head Prof. DAVY
PAINDAVEINE.

Federal Planning Bureau: ave des Arts
47–49, 1000 Brussels; tel. (2) 507-73-11; fax
(2) 507-73-73; e-mail contact@plan.be;
internet www.plan.be; studies and projec-
tions on economic, social and environmental
policy issues and on their integration within
context of sustainable devt; Dir-Gen. MICHEL
ENGLERT; Head of Admin. JAN VERSCHOOTEN.

**Institut de Recherche Multidiscipli-
naire pour la Modélisation et l'Analyse
Quantitative** (Institute for Multidisciplinary Research in Quantitative Modelling and
Analysis): Voie du Roman Pays 34, 1348
Louvain-la-Neuve; tel. (10) 47-43-21; fax (10)
47-43-01; internet www.uclouvain.be/
en-immaq; research in fields of economics,
statistics, biostatistics, actuarial science,
operations; Pres. Prof. RAINER VON SACHS.

**Institut Royal des Relations Internatio-
nales** (Royal Institute for International
Relations): rue de Namur 69, 1000 Brussels;
tel. (2) 223-41-14; fax (2) 223-41-16; e-mail
info@egmontinstitute.be; internet www
.egmontinstitute.be; f. 1947; research in int.
relations, int. economics, int. politics, int.
law, European affairs; documentation centre
covering EU integration, central Africa,

European security and defence policy; archives; 1,000 mems; library of 500 vols; Chair. ETIENNE DAVIGNON; Vice-Chair. DIRK ACHTEN; Dir-Gen. MARC TRENTESEAU; publs *Egmont Papers* (irregular), *Studia Diplomatica* (4 a year).

Studie Centrum voor Onderneming en Beurs: Middelheimlaan 1, 2020 Antwerp; tel. (3) 265-35-38; e-mail frans.buelens@ua.ac .be; internet www.scob.be; f. 1999; attached to Univ. of Antwerp; digitalizing stock exchange information; study of financial data and history of Belgian stock exchanges and companies listed on them; archives of Antwerp Stock Exchange (1858–2002), Liège Stock Exchange and Ghent Stock Exchange (1902–1992); Dir Prof. Dr LUDO CUYVERS.

EDUCATION

Centre for ASEAN Studies: Kipdorp 61, 2000 Antwerp; tel. (3) 275-50-34; fax (3) 275-50-26; e-mail ludo.cuyvers@ua.ac.be; internet webh01.ua.ac.be/cas; attached to Univ. of Antwerp; established jtly by faculty of applied economics and institute of administrative sciences of Univ. of Antwerp (RUCA); promotes inter-university cooperation projects with univs in SE Asia; Dir Prof. Dr LUDO CUYVERS.

Centre for European and International Business Education and Research: Prinsstraat 13, 2000 Antwerp; tel. (3) 265-50-28; fax (3) 265-50-26; e-mail liliane .vanhoof@ua.ac.be; attached to Univ. of Antwerp; Dir Prof. Dr LILIANE VAN HOOF.

Centrum Nascholing Onderwijs: Universiteitsplein 1, 2610 Antwerpen (Wilrijk); tel. (3) 265-29-60; fax (3) 265-29-57; e-mail paul .reynders@ua.ac.be; internet www.ua.ac.be/ cno; organizes training for teachers, middle mans, dirs, secs, CLB staff and others involved in primary, secondary education (ASO, TSO, BSO and KSO) and colleges; Pres. Prof. Dr PETER VAN PETEGEM; Vice-Pres. Prof. Dr ELKE STRUYF; Vice-Pres. Prof. Dr DIRK VAN DYCK; Dir PAUL REYNDERS.

Centrum voor Begaafdheidsonderzoek: Grotesteenweg 40, 2000 Antwerp (Berchem); tel. (3) 297-30-88; fax (3) 297-31-86; e-mail info@cbo-antwerpen.be; internet www .cbo-antwerpen.be; f. 1998, present status 2007; guidance of gifted children and adolescents; organizes training for parents, teachers, dirs, CLB staff, physicians and all others involved in education; research into realization of opportunities for optimal devt of gifted children and adolescents and into difficulties children face at home and esp. at school; Dir TESSA KIEBOOM; publ. *Hoogbegaafd?!*.

Centrum voor Mexicaanse Studiën: Prinsstraat 9, 2000 Antwerpen; tel. (3) 265-44-42; fax (3) 265-44-20; e-mail barbara.ortiz @ ua.ac.be; internet www.ua.ac.be/cms; f. 1990; attached to Univ. of Antwerp; study and research on literature and history of Mexico; library of 15,000 vols; Chair. Prof. Dr JEAN VAN HOUTTE; Dir Prof. Dr ROBERT VERDONK.

Expertise Centrum Hoger Onderwijs: Venusstraat 35, 2000 Antwerp; tel. (3) 265-45-08; fax (3) 265-45-01; e-mail echo@ua.ac .be; internet www.ua.ac.be/echo; attached to Univ. of Antwerp; supports and develops activities aimed at improving and reforming education at Univ. of Antwerp and colleges in asscn (AUHA); organizes workshops and seminars; Dir Prof. Dr PETER VAN PETEGEM.

Instituut voor Joodse Studies (Institute of Jewish Studies): Prinsstraat 13, 2000 Antwerp; Lange Winkelstraat 40–42, 2000 Antwerp; tel. (3) 265-52-43; fax (3) 265-52-41; e-mail ijs@ua.ac.be; internet www.ua.ac.be/ ijs; f. 2001; academic study of Judaism from

historical, philological, cultural, literary, religious, philosophical and sociological perspectives; organizes lectures, language courses; library of 1,500 vols; Dir Prof. Dr VIVIAN LISKA.

Instituut voor Onderwijs- en Informatiewetenschappen: Venusstraat 35, 2000 Antwerp; tel. (3) 265-45-08; fax (3) 265-45-01; e-mail ioiw@ua.ac.be; attached to Univ. of Antwerp; provides scientific research and training in education and library sciences; Pres. PAUL MAHIEU; Vice-Pres. JOZEF COLPAERT.

FINE AND PERFORMING ARTS

Aisthesis: Grote Kauwenberg 18, 2000 Antwerp; tel. (3) 220-43-04; e-mail luc .vandendries@ua.ac.be; f. 1972; attached to Univ. of Antwerp; promotes theatre field studies; Dir Prof. Dr LUK VAN DEN DRIES.

Centre d'Etude de la Peinture du XVe Siècle dans les Pays-Bas Méridionaux et la Principauté de Liège/Studiecentrum voor de 15de-Eeuwse Schilderkunst in de Zuidelijke Nederlanden en het Prinsbisdom Luik (Centre for the Study of 15th Century Painting in the Southern Netherlands and the Principality of Liège): Royal Institute for Cultural Heritage, Jubelpark 1, 1000 Brussels; tel. (2) 739-68-66; fax (2) 732-01-05; e-mail helene.mund@kikirpa.be; internet xv.kikirpa.be; f. 1955; research into 15th-century Flemish painting; collects art historical documentation; photographic archive; language of instruction: French; 14 mems; library of 6,000 vols; Chair. Dr CYRIEL STROO; Vice-Chair. LILIANE MASSCHELEIN-KLEINER; Sec. MYRIAM SERCK-DEWAIDE; Scientific Sec. H. MUND; publs *Contributions*, *Corpus*, *Répertoire*.

LANGUAGE AND LITERATURE

Centrum voor Grammatica, Cognitie en Typologie (Centre for Grammar, Cognition and Typology): Prinsstraat 13, 2000 Antwerp; tel. (3) 220-45-88; fax (3) 220-45-70; e-mail johan.vanderauwera@ua.ac.be; internet webhost.ua.ac.be/cgct; f. 1999; attached to Univ. of Antwerp; research on relationship between morphosyntactic and semantic structure, from functional-cognitive point-of-view; Dir Prof. Dr JOHAN VAN DER AUWERA; Vice-Dir NILSON GABAS JR.

Centrum voor Tekstgenetica (Centre for Manuscript Genetics): Prinsstraat 13, 2000 Antwerp; tel. (3) 265-42-57; fax (3) 265-45-46; e-mail dirk.vanhulle@ua.ac.be; attached to Univ. of Antwerp; study of modern MSS and writing processes; genetic research on authors of second half of 19th and first half of 20th century; emphasis on work of Samuel Beckett and James Joyce; Dir Prof. Dr GEERT LERNOUT; publ. *Genetic Joyce Studies (GJS)* (online).

Computational Linguistics and Psycholinguistics Research Centre: Lange Winkelstraat 40–42, 2000 Antwerp; tel. (3) 265-52-22; fax (3) 265-58-98; e-mail dominiek .sandra@ua.ac.be; internet www.cpl.ua.ac .be; attached to Univ. of Antwerp; research and resources in developmental psycholinguistics, corpus linguistics, and computational linguistics, and investigates interdisciplinary combinations of these disciplines; Dir Prof. Dr DOMINIEK SANDRA.

Instituut voor de Studie van de Letterkunde in de Nederlanden: Prinsstraat 13, 2000 Antwerp; tel. (3) 265-45-67; e-mail rosina.hoydonckx@ua.ac.be; attached to Univ. of Antwerp; researches and provides academic courses in field of Dutch and foreign-language literature in Netherlands; study of Dutch literature and foreign-language literature in low countries, esp. in

French and Latin; Chair. PIET COUTTENIER; Sec. KEVIN ABSILLIS.

International Pragmatics Association: Prinsstraat 13, 2000 Antwerp; tel. (3) 265-45-63; fax (3) 230-55-74; e-mail info@ipra.be; internet ipra.ua.ac.be; f. 1986 as IPrA Research Centre; attached to Univ. of Antwerp; study of language use; research on field of pragmatics as functional (i.e., cognitive, social, and cultural) perspective on language and communication; Pres. SACHIKO IDE; Sec.-Gen. JEF VERSCHUEREN; Exec. Sec. ANN VERHAERT; publ. *Pragmatics* (4 a year).

Studie- en Documentatiecentrum Hugo Claus: Prinsstraat 13, 2000 Antwerp; tel. (3) 265-52-49; fax (3) 265-44-20; e-mail georges .wildemeersch@ua.ac.be; f. 1996; attached to Univ. of Antwerp; study of literature in Netherlands; study of work of Hugo Claus through publ. and organizes scientific and cultural meetings; Dir Prof. Dr GEORGES WILDEMEERSCH.

MEDICINE

Biomedisch Onderzoeksinstituut (Biomedical Research Institute): Agoralaan gebouw A, 3590 Diepenbeek; tel. (11) 26-93-03; fax (11) 26-92-09; e-mail biomed@ uhasselt.be; internet www2.uhasselt.be/ biomed; f. 1999; attached to Hasselt Univ.; research on pathogenic mechanisms of autoimmune diseases and physiopathological mechanisms of cell injury and cell death resulting from stress factors; devt of therapeutic approaches for autoimmune diseases; Dir Prof. Dr PIET STINISSEN; Vice-Dir Prof. Dr MARCEL AMELOOT.

Centrum voor Bekkenbodemkunde: Universiteitsplein 1, 2610 Antwerpen (Wilrijk); tel. (3) 265-25-35; fax (3) 265-25-01; e-mail jeanjacques.wyndaele@ua.ac.be; attached to Univ. of Antwerp; Dir Prof. Dr JEAN-JACQUES WYNDAELE.

Centrum voor de Evaluatie van Vaccinaties (Centre for the Evaluation of Vaccination): Universiteitsplein 1, 2610 Antwerpen-Wilrijk; tel. (3) 265-26-52; fax (3) 265-26-40; e-mail cev@ua.ac.be; internet www.ua.ac.be/ cev; f. 1984, present status 2007; attached to Univ. of Antwerp; research on epidemiology of infectious diseases and economic evaluation of vaccination programmes; Dir Prof. Dr PIERRE VAN DAMME; Sec. EMMY ANGELS.

Centrum voor Huisartsgeneeskunde Antwerpen: Universiteitsplein 1, 2610 Antwerpen (Wilrijk); tel. (3) 265-25-29; fax (3) 265-25-26; e-mail chris.monteyne@ua.ac .be; internet webh01.ua.ac.be/cha; f. 1972; research in primary health care; offers academic services and medical education; Dir Prof. Dr JOKE DENEKENS; Dir Prof. Dr PAUL VAN ROYEN.

Centrum voor Kankerpreventie: Universiteitsplein 1, 2610 Antwerp (Wilrijk); tel. (3) 265-26-53; fax (3) 265-26-40; e-mail rsc@ua .ac.be; attached to Univ. of Antwerp; Dir Prof. Dr JOOST WEYLER.

Centrum voor Thoracale Oncologie Groep Antwerpen: Universiteitsplein 1, 2610 Antwerpen (Wilrijk); tel. (3) 265-26-39; fax (3) 265-25-01; e-mail paul.germonpre@ua .ac.be; attached to Univ. of Antwerp; devt of uniform policy regarding control and treatment of disorders of thoracic oncology; Pres. PAUL GERMONPRÉ; Vice-Pres. ANNEKE LEFEBURE.

Collaborative Antwerp Psychiatric Research Institute: Universiteitsplein 1, 2610 Antwerp (Wilrijk); tel. (3) 265-24-01; fax (3) 265-29-23; e-mail bernard.sabbe@ua.ac .be; internet www.ua.ac.be/capri; attached to Univ. of Antwerp; scientific research in fields of psychiatry, epidemiology, genetics, cognitive neuroscience, experimental psychopathology and psychoneuropharmacology; Dir Prof. Dr BERNARD SABBE; Dir Prof. Dr D. DEBOUTTE.

Direction Opérationnelle Maladies Transmissibles et Infectieuses/Operationele Directie Overdraagbare en Besmettelijke Ziekten (Operational Direction Communicable & Infectious Diseases): rue Engeland 642, 1180 Brussels; tel. (2) 373-31-11; fax (2) 373-32-82; e-mail jmpirotte@wiv-isp.be; internet www.wiv-isp.be/odobz-domti; f. 1900, present name and status by merger between Institute of Hygiene and Epidemiology (IHE) and Pasteur Institute of Brabant (IPB); scientific biomedical research, analyses; has br. at Ixelles; Dir JEAN CONTENT.

Fondation Médicale Reine Elisabeth/Geneeskundige Stichting Koningin Elisabeth (Queen Elisabeth Medical Foundation): ave J. J. Crocqlaan 3, 1020 Brussels; tel. (2) 478-35-56; fax (2) 478-24-13; e-mail fmre.gske@skynet.be; internet www.fmre-gske.be; f. 1926; supports medical research in field of neurobiology through several Belgian univ. laboratories; distributes grants and awards; Hon. Pres. HRH PRINCESS ASTRID; Pres. ALAIN SIAENS; Man. Dir VINCENT PARDOEN; Sec. ERIK DHONDT; Scientific Dir Prof. Dr BARON DE BARSY.

Institut Jules Bordet: blvd de Waterloo 121 1000 Brussels; tel. (2) 541-31-11; fax (2) 541-35-06; e-mail direction@bordet.be; internet www.bordet.be; f. 1939; research on oncology; attached to Univ. Libre de Bruxelles; Pres. Prof. R. TOLLET; Vice-Pres. R. GLINEUR; Gen. Dir O. VAN TIGGELEN.

Institut Neurologique Belge: rue de Linthout 150, 1040 Brussels; tel. (2) 737-85-60; f. 1925; Pres. Comte EDOUARD D'OULTREMONT; publs *Acta Neurologica*, *Psychiatrica Belgica*.

Institut Scientifique de Santé Publique/Wetenschappelijk Instituut Volksgezondheid. (Scientific Institute of Public Health): rue Juliette Wytsman 14, 1050 Brussels; tel. (2) 642-51-11; fax (2) 642-50-01; e-mail ine.vanmarsenille@wiv-isp.be; internet www.wiv-isp.be; promotes scientific research in support of health policy; Belgian rep. at level of EU and World Health Organization, Organisation for Economic Cooperation and Development, and Council of Europe; Gen. Dir Dr JOHAN PEETERS.

Institute Born-Bunge: Universiteitsplein 1, Bldg T, 5th Fl., 2610 Antwerp (Wilrijk); tel. (3) 265-25-96; fax (3) 265-26-69; e-mail jjmneuro@uia.ac.be; internet www.bornbunge.be; f. 1933; attached to Univ. of Antwerp; research in neurological sciences and cardiology; Chair. Prof. Dr P. P. DE DEYN; Vice-Chair. and Man. Dir VAN DEN EYNDE.

Laboratoire d'Investigation et de Recherche Clinique: rue Héger-Bordet 1, CP 401/06, 1000 Brussels; tel. (2) 541-33-99; fax (2) 541-33-97; e-mail data.centre@bordet.be; attached to Université Libre de Bruxelles; diagnosis and treatment of tumours; Dir Prof. JEAN KLASTERSKY.

Rega-Instituut (Rega Institute for Medical Research): Minderbroedersstraat 10, 3000 Leuven; tel. (16) 33-73-41; fax (16) 33-73-40; internet www.kuleuven.be/rega; f. 1954; attached to Katholieke Universiteit van Leuven; consists of deps of medicine and pharmacology; Head GHISLAIN OPDENAKKER.

NATURAL SCIENCES
General

Centre for Research on the Epidemiology of Disasters: Clos Chapelle-aux-Champs, 30.94, 1200 Brussels; tel. (2) 764-33-27; fax (2) 764-34-41; internet www.cred.be; f. 1973; promotes research, training and technical expertise on humanitarian emergencies, with focus on public health and epidemiology; Dir Prof. DEBARATI GUHA-SAPIR.

Institut Royal des Sciences Naturelles de Belgique/Koninklijk Belgisch Instituut voor Natuurwetenschappen (Royal Belgian Institute of Natural Sciences): rue Vautier 29, 1000 Brussels; tel. (2) 627-42-11; fax (2) 627-41-13; e-mail info@naturalsciences.be; internet www.naturalsciences.be; f. 1846; biology, zoology, palaeontology, geology, anthropology; subdivided into 7 depts; library: see under Libraries and Archives; Gen. Dir CAMILLE PISANI; publs *Bulletin: Biology*, *Bulletin: Entomology*, *Bulletin: Palaeontology*, *Study Documents* (irregular).

Biological Sciences

Centrum voor Biomedische Beeldvorming: Groenenborgerlaan 171, 2020 Antwerp; tel. (3) 265-32-30; fax (3) 265-32-33; e-mail annemie.vanderlinden@ua.ac.be; attached to Univ. of Antwerp; Dir Prof. Dr ANNEMIE VAN DER LINDEN.

Institut de Recherche Interdisciplinaire en Biologie Humaine et Moléculaire: route de Lennik 808, CP 602, 1070 Brussels; tel. (2) 555-41-33; fax (2) 555-46-55; e-mail iribhm@ulb.ac.be; internet www.ulb.ac.be/medecine/iribhm; research on molecular genetics, molecular oncology, enzymology and molecular pharmacology, cell biology, theoretical modelling, experimental biology, gene therapy; Dir Prof. GILBERT VASSART.

Jardin Botanique National de Belgique/Nationale Plantentuin van België (National Botanic Garden of Belgium): Domein van Bouchout, Nieuwelaan 38, 1860 Meise; tel. (2) 260-09-20; fax (2) 260-09-45; e-mail office@br.fgov.be; internet www.br.fgov.be; f. 1870, present name 1967; promotes research on tropical and European botany; gene bank of Phaseolinae; herbarium with over 2m. specimens; library of 200,000 vols, 300 journals; Dir Prof. Dr JAN RAMMELOO; publs *Distributiones plantarum africanarum* (irregular), *Dumortiera* (3 a year), *Flore d'Afrique Centrale* (irregular), *Flore illustrée des champignons d'Afrique Centrale* (1 a year), *Icones mycologicae* (irregular), *Opera Botanica Belgica* (irregular), *Scripta Botanica Belgica* (irregular), *Systematics and Geography of Plants* (2 a year).

Referentiecentrum voor Biologische Merkers van Geheugenstoornissen: Universiteitsplein 1, 2610 Antwerp; tel. (3) 265-26-17; fax (3) 265-26-18; e-mail peter.dedeyn@ua.ac.be; attached to Univ. of Antwerp; contributes to devt and characterization of biomarkers for dementia and Alzheimer's disease; develops biomarkers-based diagnostic models that can be used in clinical practice; Dir Prof. Dr PETER DE DEYN.

Vlaams Instituut voor Biotechnologie: Rijvisschestraat 120, 9052 Gent; tel. (9) 244-66-11; fax (9) 244-66-10; e-mail info@vib.be; internet www.vib.be; f. 1996; research on translating scientific results into pharmaceutical, agricultural and industrial applications; Man. Dir JO BURY; Man. Dir RUDY DEKEYSER.

Mathematical Sciences

Centrum voor Proteomics en Massaspectrometrie (Centre for Proteome Analysis and Mass Spectrometry): Groenenborgerlaan 171, 2020 Antwerp; tel. (3) 265-34-21; fax (3) 265-34-17; e-mail suzanne.pooters@ua.ac.be; internet www.ceproma.ua.ac.be; f. 2003; attached to Univ. of Antwerp; laboratory for screening of sequenced and unsequenced species in proteomics; Dir Prof. Dr YVES GUISEZ; Sec. SUZANNE POOTERS.

Direction Générale Statistique et Information Economique/Generaldirektion Statistik und Wirtschaftinformation (Directorate General Statistics and Economic Information): rue du Progrès 50, 1210 Brussels; tel. (2) 277-51-11; fax (2) 277-51-07; e-mail info.eco@economie.fgov.be; internet statbel.fgov.be; f. 1831; collects, processes and disseminates statistical data; Dir-Gen. A. VERSONNEN; publs *Annuaire statistique de la Belgique*, *Bulletin de Statistique* (12 a year).

Departement Moleculaire Genetica (Institute of Molecular Genetics): Universiteitsplein 1, 2610 Antwerpen (Wilrijk); tel. and fax (3) 265-10-02; e-mail gisele.smeyers@ua.ac.be; internet www.molgen.ua.ac.be; attached to Univ. of Antwerp; research in field of human molecular genetics with focus on complex diseases of central and peripheral nervous system; Dir Prof. Dr CHRISTINE VAN BROECKHOVEN.

Physical Sciences

Centre d'Etude de l'Energie Nucléaire/Studiecentrum voor Kernenergie (Belgian Nuclear Research Centre): Boeretang 200, 2400 Mol; tel. (14) 33-21-11; fax (14) 31-50-21; e-mail info@sckcen.be; internet www.sckcen.be; f. 1952, present name 1957; promotes research on nuclear science and technology and ionising radiation; reactor safety; fuel and materials irradiation; characterization and geological disposal of waste; decontamination and dismantling of facilities; radioprotection; nuclear services, incl. irradiation in BR2 and post-irradiation examination; Chair. FRANK DECONINCK; Dir-Gen. ERIC VAN WALLE; Sec.-Gen. CHRISTIAN LEGRAIN; publ. *Scientific Report* (1 a year).

Centrum voor Milieukunde (Centre for Environmental Sciences): Agoralaan gebouw D, 3590 Diepenbeek; tel. (11) 26-83-02; fax (11) 26-83-01; e-mail jaco.vangronsveld@uhasselt.be; internet www.uhasselt.be/cmk; f. 1997; attached to Hasselt Univ.; effects of abiotic stress factors at different biological org. levels: from molecular to ecosystem level; Dir Prof. Dr JACO VANGRONSVELD.

Institut d'Astronomie et d'Astrophysique (Institute of Astronomy and Astrophysics): blvd du Triomphe, CP 226, 1050 Brussels; tel. (2) 650-28-42; fax (2) 650-42-26; e-mail email@ulb.ac.be; internet www.astro.ulb.ac.be; attached to Univ. Libre de Bruxelles; research on nucleosynthesis, nuclear astrophysics, stellar evolution and chemical composition, binary stars, neutron stars; Dir ALAIN JORISSEN; Sec. NANCY TIGNÉE.

Institut d'Aéronomie Spatiale de Belgique/Belgisch Instituut voor Ruimte-Aëronomie (Belgian Institute for Space Aeronomy): ave Circulaire 3, 1180 Brussels; tel. (2) 373-04-04; fax (2) 374-84-23; e-mail info@aeronomie.be; internet www.aeronomie.be; f. 1964; promotes research in field of space aeronomy; disseminates knowledge resulting from application of space investigation methods; library of 3,000 vols and 150 periodicals; Dir Prof. PAUL C. SIMON; Head of Admin. MARC DELANCKER.

Institut Royal Météorologique de Belgique/Koninklijk Meteorologisch Instituut (Royal Meteorological Institute of

Belgium): ave Circulaire 3, 1180 Brussels; tel. (2) 373-05-08; fax (2) 375-12-59; e-mail irni_info@oma.be; internet www.meteo.be; f. 1913; depts for aerology, aerometry, applied meteorology, climatology, geophysics and numerical calculus; Pres. Prof. Dr CH. BOUQUEGNEAU; Dir Dr H. MALCORPS; publs *Bulletin Quotidien du temps* (1 a day), *Climatologie*, *Hydrologie* (1 a year), *Magnétisme terrestre*, *Marées terrestres à Dourbes*, *Observations climatologiques*, *Observations d'ozone* (4 a year), *Observations géophysiques*, *Observations ionosphériques* (12 a year), *Observations synoptiques*, *Rayonnement solaire*.

Instituut voor Milieu & Duurzame Ontwikkeling (Institute of Environment and Sustainable Development): Universiteitsplein 1, 2610 Antwerp (Wilrijk); Fort VI-str. 276, 2610 Antwerp (Wilrijk); tel. (3) 265-21-14; fax (3) 265-21-28; e-mail milieu@ua.ac.be; internet www.ua.ac.be/imdo; research in field of environmental education, environmental management, spatial planning, integrated water management, environmental policy; Pres. Prof. Dr PATRICK MEIRE.

Instituut voor Natuur- en Bosonderzoek (Nature and Forest Research Institute): Kliniekstraat 25, 1070 Brussels; tel. (2) 558-18-11; fax (2) 558-18-05; e-mail info@inbo.be; internet www.inbo.be; research into sustainable management and use of natural resources; supports orgs for nature management, forestry, agriculture, hunting and fisheries; provides data to Flemish govt; has brs in Geraardsbergen, Groenendaal, Linkebeek; Pres. JURGEN TACK; Man. VERONIQUE BIUNKENS.

Observatoire Royal de Belgique/ Koninklijke Sterrenwacht van Belgie (Royal Observatory of Belgium): ave Circulaire 3, 1180 Brussels; tel. (2) 373-02-11; fax (2) 374-98-22; e-mail rob_info@oma.be; internet www.astro.oma.be; f. 1826; astrometry, astrophysics, celestial mechanics, earth tides, fundamental astronomy, gravimetry, radioastronomy, satellite positioning, seismology, solar physics, time service; Dir RONALD VAN DER LINDEN; publs *Annuaire*, *Bulletin Astronomique*, *Communications*.

PHILOSOPHY AND PSYCHOLOGY

Centre for Metaphysics and Culture: Grote Kauwenberg 18, 2000 Antwerp; tel. (3) 265-43-41; fax (3) 265-44-20; e-mail guy .vanheeswijck@ua.ac.be; attached to Univ. of Antwerp; research into history of concept of metaphysics in ancient, medieval, modern and contemporary philosophy and into history of critique of metaphysics; Dir Prof. Dr GUIDO VANHEESWIJCK.

Centre National de Recherches de Logique/Nationaal Centrum voor Navorsingen in de Logica: Fondation Universitaire, rue d'Egmont 11, 1000 Brussels; e-mail cnrlncnl@logic-center.be; internet www .logic-center.be; f. 1955; promotes and coordinates research in logic, philosophical and mathematical, in univs; Pres. M. CRABBÉ; Vice-Pres. R. VERGAUWEN; Vice-Pres. B. LECLERCQ; Sec. B. VAN KERKHOVE; Treas. A. PÉTRY; publs *Cahiers du Centre de Logique*, *Logique et Analyse* (4 a year).

Centrum voor Cultuurfilosofie (Center for Philosophy of Culture): Prinsstraat 13, 2000 Antwerp; tel. (3) 265-45-50; fax (3) 265-44-20; attached to Univ. of Antwerp; research on relation between reason and culture in modern and contemporary society from 3 perspectives: criticism of metaphysics and post-metaphysical thought, criticism of religion and secularisation, modernism and criticism of representation.

Centrum voor Ethiek (Centre for Ethics): Koningstraat 8, 2000 Antwerp; tel. (3) 265-43-12; fax (3) 265-44-20; e-mail willem .lemmens@ua.ac.be; f. 2003; attached to Univ. of Antwerp; research on history of ethics and practical philosophy in early modern and contemporary philosophy and on issues on crossroads between ethics and economics; Head WILLEM LEMMENS.

Centrum voor Filosofische Psychologie (Centre for Philosophical Psychology): Prinsstraat 13, 2000 Antwerp; Office (S) D416, Grote Kauwenberg 18, 2000 Antwerp; tel. (3) 220-43-37; e-mail erik.myin@ua.ac.be; internet www.ua.ac.be/main.aspx?c= .philosophyofmind; f. 1999; attached to Univ. of Antwerp; research on philosophy of perception, linguistic communication, aesthetics and free will; Dir Prof. Dr ERIK MYIN.

RELIGION, SOCIOLOGY AND ANTHROPOLOGY

Centre d'Etudes et de Recherches Arabes: c/o Mme Annie Delsaut, ave Maistriau, 8, 7000 Mons; Université de Mons, pl. du Parc 20, 7000 Mons; tel. (65) 39-45-16; fax (65) 39-45-21; e-mail cerm.umh@gmail.com; internet cermumons.be; f. 1978; incl. Euro–Mediterranean studies section, int. relations section and Arabic language, translation and interpreting (graduate studies); training and research (FTI and ISL) in translation and interpreting; Arabic, English, French (post-graduate studies and Phd); visio-interpreting (e-learning); audiovisual translation: respeaking, subtitling, audiodescription, dubbing and AT/CAT; library of 2,500 vols; Pres. Prof. H. SAFAR; Sec. ANNIE DELSAUT.

Centre Interdisciplinaire d'étude des Religions et de la Laïcité: ave F. D. Roosevelt 17, CP 108, 1050 Brussels; tel. (2) 650-38-49; e-mail bdecharn@ulb.ac.be; internet www.ulb.ac.be/philo/cierl; f. 1965, present name 2003; attached to Univ. Libre de Bruxelles; study of religious phenomena and spirituality in contemporary expressions from ancient polytheism, so-called primitive religions, great monotheistic religions and popular devotions, to beliefs of New Age; library of 226 vols; Dir Prof. BAUDOUIN DECHARNEUX; publs *Divin et Sacré*, *Le Figuier: Annales du Centre interdisciplinaire d'Etude des Religions et de la Laïcité de l'Université libre de Bruxelles*, *Problèmes d'Histoire des Religions*, *Spiritualités et Pensées libres*.

Centrum Pieter Gillis: Prinsstraat 13, 2000 Antwerp; tel. (3) 265-44-77; fax (3) 265-49-38; e-mail nina.vleugels@ua.ac.be; attached to Univ. of Antwerp; promotes respect for, critical approach to and dialogue with other philosophies; promotes research on religious ideas and communities; Chair. GUY VANHEESWIJCK.

Centrum voor Longitudinaal en Levensloop Onderzoek (Research Centre for Longitudinal and Life Course Studies): Sint-Jacobstraat 2, 2000 Antwerp; tel. (3) 265-55-35; fax (3) 265-57-93; e-mail dimitri .mortelmans@ua.ac.be; internet webh01.ua .ac.be/cello; attached to Univ. of Antwerp; colln of panel studies of Belgian households; research on family sociology and sociology of labour; Dir Prof. Dr DIMITRI MORTELMANS.

Centrum voor Rechtssociologie (Centre for Sociology of Law): Sint-Jacobstraat 2, 2000 Antwerp; tel. (3) 265-52-64; fax (3) 265-57-98; e-mail francis.vanloon@ua.ac.be; f. 1972; attached to Univ. of Antwerp; research on interface between law and society; Dir Prof. Dr FRANCIS VAN LOON.

Centrum voor Sociaal Beleid Herman Deleeck (Herman Deleeck Centre for Social Policy): Sint-Jacobstraat 2, 2000 Antwerp; tel. (3) 265-53-74; fax (3) 265-57-98; e-mail ingrid.vanzele@ua.ac.be; internet webhost .ua.ac.be/csb; f. 1972; attached to Univ. of Antwerp; empirical and multidisciplinary research on social inequality and wealth distribution in welfare state; Dir Prof. Dr BEA CANTILLON; Sec. INGRID VAN ZELE.

Centrum voor Stadsgeschiedenis: Prinsstraat 13, 2000 Antwerp; tel. (3) 265-49-54; fax (3) 265-44-20; e-mail stefanie.beghein@ua .ac.be; internet webh01.ua.ac.be/cstadg; attached to Univ. of Antwerp; research on aspects of urban culture, economics, religion, society, politics and instns of Middle Ages to present day to study mutual societies; studies on socio-economic and cultural history; Dir Prof. Dr BERT DE MUNCH; Sec. STEFANIE BEGHEIN; publ. *Stadsgeschiedenis* (2 a year).

Institut d'Etudes du Judaïsme (Institute for the study of Judaism): ave Roosevelt 17, 1050 Brussels; tel. (2) 650-33-48; fax (2) 650-33-47; e-mail iej@ulb.ac.be; internet www.ulb .ac.be/philo/judaism; f. 1959; attached to Université Libre de Bruxelles; studies, publs and documentation on contemporary Judaism; library of 8,000 vols; Pres. Prof. GUY HAARSCHER; Vice-Pres. GEORGES SCHNEK; Dir THOMAS GERGELY; publs *Mosaïque* (1 a year), *Nouvelles* (4 a year).

Institut de Sociologie (Institute of Sociology): ave Jeanne 44, CP 124, 1050 Brussels; tel. (2) 650-34-89; fax (2) 650-35-21; e-mail is@ulb.ac.be; internet is.ulb.ac.be; f. 1902; attached to Univ. Libre de Bruxelles; Dir NATHALIE ZACCAI-REYNERS; Sec. CATHY VANCLEVE; publs *Civilisations*, *L'Année sociale*, *Revue de l'Institut de Sociologie*, *Transitions*.

Ruusbroecgenootschap: Instituut voor de Geschiedenis van de Spiritualiteit in de Nederlanden tot ca. 1750: Prinsstraat 13, 2000 Antwerp; tel. (3) 265-57-80; fax (3) 265-44-20; e-mail theo.clemens@ua.ac .be; f. 1925; attached to Univ. of Antwerp; scientific research of history of Christian spirituality, ascetical and mystical, in Netherlands from conversion to 1750; interpretative and contextual study of religious literature in Netherlands; codicological and historical research on early days of Ruusbroecgenootschap in cultural and social perspectives; library of 150,000 vols, incl. rare books, 500 MSS; Dir Prof. Dr THEO CLEMENS; Sec. INGRID DE RUYTE; Librarian ERNA VAN LOOVEREN; publ. *Ons Geestelijk Erf* (4 a year).

TECHNOLOGY

Antwerp Institute for Enterprise Computing: Prinsstraat 13, 2000 Antwerp; e-mail carlos.debacher@ua.ac.be; attached to Univ. of Antwerp; education, research and services in terms of information technologies and methodologies applied within business context; Dir Prof. Dr CARLOS DE BACKER.

Centrum voor de Economische Studie van Innovatie en Technologie (Centre for Economic Study of Innovation and Technology): Prinsstraat 13, 2000 Antwerp; tel. (3) 220-40-54; fax (3) 220-40-26; e-mail wim .meeusen@ua.ac.be; internet webh01.ua.ac .be/cesit; attached to Univ. of Antwerp; research on technology and innovation; publishes papers and organizes seminars; Dir Prof. Dr WIM MEEUSEN; Dir Prof. Dr JEF PLASMANS.

Centrum voor Micro-en Sporenanalyse (Micro and Trace Analysis Centre): Universiteitsplein, 1, 2610 Antwerp (Wilrijk); tel. (3) 820-23-40; fax (3) 820-23-76; e-mail rene .vangrieken@ua.ac.be; f. 1980; attached to Univ. of Antwerp; research in analytical sciences: trace analysis and microscopic and surface elemental and molecular analysis; fundamental research for better understanding of processes and parameters governing those methods of analysis; devt of methods of analysis; Dir Prof. Dr RENÉ VAN GRIEKEN.

Centrum voor ZorgTechnologie: Universiteitsplein 1, 2610 Antwerp (Wilrijk); tel. and fax (3) 265-23-12; e-mail czt@ua.ac.be; internet www.czt.be; f. 1991; attached to Univ. of Antwerp; devt of technological devices to help people with disabilities.

European Cooperation in Science and Technology (COST): ave Louise 149, 1050 Brussels; tel. (2) 533-38-00; fax (2) 533-38-90; e-mail office@cost.eu; internet www.cost.esf.org; provides platform for European scientists to cooperate on particular projects; nationally-funded research on European level; key domains of research: biomedicine and molecular biosciences, food and agriculture, forests, materials, physics and nanosciences, chemistry molecular sciences and technologies, earth system science and environmental management, information and communication technologies, transport and urban devt, individuals, societies, cultures and health; Pres. Dr ANGELES RODRÍGUEZ-PEÑA.

IMO-IMOMEC: Wetenschapspark 1, 3590 Diepenbeek; tel. (11) 26-88-26; fax (11) 26-88-99; e-mail imo-imomec@uhasselt.be; internet www.uhasselt.be/imo; f. 2001; attached to Hasselt Univ.; collaboration with IMOMEC (Institute for Materials Research in Micro-Electronics), dept of IMEC (Interuniv. Micro Electronics Centre, Louvain); devt and characterization of new material systems with potential use in microelectronics, bioelectronics and nanotechnology; Dir Prof. Dr DIRK VANDERZANDE; Vice-Dir Prof. Dr MARC D'OLIESLAEGER.

Institut Meurice (IIF–IMC–ISI): ave Emile Gryzon 1, 1070 Brussels; tel. (2) 526-73-04; fax (2) 526-73-54; e-mail info@meurice.heldb.be; internet www.heldb.be/he/meurice; f. 1892, present status 1977; research and training centre for industrial engineers in chemistry and biochemistry; library of 80,000 vols, 110 periodicals, 1,000 CD-ROMs; Dir Dr Ir PATRICK DYSSELER.

Institut Scientifique de Service Public: rue du Chéra 200, 4000 Liège; tel. (4) 229-83-12; fax (4) 252-46-65; e-mail direction@issep.be; internet www.issep.be; f. 1990; attached to Walloon Government; applied research, devt and demonstration relating to natural resources, environment, technical and industrial security, solid fuels, radiocommunications; library of 11,000 vols; Gen. Man. M. LAMBERT.

Institute for Reference Materials and Measurements: Retieseweg 111, 2440 Geel; tel. (14) 57-12-11; fax (14) 58-42-73; e-mail jrc-irmm-info@ec.europa.eu; internet irmm.jrc.ec.europa.eu; f. 1957, present name 1993; 1 of 7 institutes of Joint Research Centre (JRC); promotes common and reliable European measurement system; 6 areas of competence: reference materials, food analysis, bioanalysis, chemical reference measurements, radionuclide metrology, neutron physics; Dir KRZYSZTOF MARUSZEWSKI.

Institute for Transport and Maritime Management Antwerp: Keizerstraat 64, 2000 Antwerp; tel. (3) 265-51-51; fax (3) 265-51-50; e-mail frank.vanlaeken@ua.ac.be; internet www.itmma.com; attached to Univ. of Antwerp; research on academic and practice-based maritime and logistics; Pres. Prof. THEO NOTTEBOOM; Dir FRANK VAN LAEKEN.

Instituut voor Mobiliteit: Universiteit Hasselt, Wetenschapspark 5, bus 6, 3590 Diepenbeek; tel. (11) 26-91-11; fax (11) 26-91-99; e-mail imob@uhasselt.be; internet www.uhasselt.be/imob; f. 2003; attached to Hasselt Univ.; research on solutions to problems within domains of mobility, safety and logistics; Dir Prof. Dr GEERT WETS.

Interdisciplinair Instituut voor Breedband Technologie (Interdisciplinary Institute for Broadband Technology): Gaston Crommenlaan 8, POB 102, 9050 Ghent; tel. (9) 331-48-00; fax (9) 331-48-05; e-mail info@ibbt.be; internet www.ibbt.be; promotes innovation in ICT, applications of broadband technology in particular; CEO WIM DE WAELE.

International Medical Equipment Collaborative: Kapeldreef 75, 3001 Leuven; tel. (16) 28-12-11; fax (16) 22-94-00; e-mail bezoek@imec.be; internet www2.imec.be; f. 1984; research in field of nanoelectronics; Pres. and CEO LUC VAN DEN HOVE.

Research Centre for Technology, Energy and Environment: Prinsstraat 13, 2000 Antwerp; tel. (3) 265-49-00; fax (3) 265-49-01; e-mail aviel.verbruggen@ua.ac.be; internet www.ua.ac.be/stem; attached to Univ. of Antwerp; research on processes of scientific and technological innovation to contribute positively to sustainable devt, in its social, economic and ecological dimensions; Chair. Prof. Dr AVIEL VERBRUGGEN.

von Karman Institute for Fluid Dynamics: chaussée de Waterloo 72, 1640 Rhode-St-Genese; tel. (2) 359-96-11; fax (2) 359-96-00; e-mail secretariat@vki.ac.be; internet www.vki.ac.be; f. 1956; multinational postgraduate teaching and research in aerodynamics; supported by countries of NATO; depts of aeronautics/aerospace, turbomachinery and propulsion, environmental fluid dynamics; library of 3,000 vols, 65,000 reports; Dir JEAN MUYLAERT.

Libraries and Archives

Antwerp

AMVC—Letterenhuis (AMVC—House of Literature): Minderbroedersstraat 22, 2000 Antwerp; tel. (3) 222-93-20; fax (3) 222-93-21; e-mail letterenhuis@stad.antwerpen.be; internet www.letterenhuis.be; f. 1933, present name 2002, present status 2004; archives of Flemish literature, theatre, music, arts and culture; files and MSS can be on application; 55,000 files, 2m. letters and MSS, 50,000 posters, 130,000 photographs; Dir LEEN VAN DIJCK.

Erfgoedbibliotheek Hendrik Conscience: Hendrik Conscienceplein 4, 2000 Antwerp; tel. (3) 338-87-10; fax (3) 338-87-76; e-mail consciencebibliotheek@stad.antwerpen.be; internet stadsbibliotheek.antwerpen.be; f. 1481, reorganized 1834; Flemish and Dutch literature, history, humanities, local press; 1m. vols; Dir R. RENNENBERG.

FelixArchief/Stadsarchief (City Archives): Oudeleeuwenrui 29, 2000 Antwerp; tel. (3) 338-94-11; fax (3) 338-94-10; e-mail stadsarchief@stad.antwerpen.be; internet www.felixarchief.be; f. 1796; 21 km of documents concerning the admin. of Antwerp since the 13th century; history, genealogy, heraldry, cartography, sigillography; 11,000 specialized vols, 245 periodicals; Archivist INGE SCHOUPS.

Rijksarchief te Antwerpen/Archives de l'état à Anvers (Antwerp State Archives): Kruibekesteenweg 39/1, 9120 Beveren; tel. (3) 236-73-00; fax (3) 775-26-46; e-mail rijksarchief.antwerpen@arch.be; internet arch.arch.be; f. 1896; history of province of Antwerp; documents from 12th century onwards; 17,000 microfilm colln; Head Dr MICHEL OOSTERBOSCH.

Rubenianum: Kolveniersstraat 20, 2000 Antwerp; tel. (3) 201-15-77; fax (3) 201-15-85; e-mail rubenianum@stad.antwerpen.be; internet www.rubenianum.be; library and documentation centre for study of 16th and 17th century Flemish art, esp. the works of Jordaens, Rubens and Van Dyck; 45,000 vols and exhibition catalogues, books on art, artists and art history, journals, sales catalogues, 150 periodicals; Curator VÉRONIQUE VAN DE KERCKHOF; Librarian UTE STAES; publs *Corpus Rubenianum Ludwig Burchard* (the complete edition of the works of Rubens), *The Rubenianum Quarterly*.

Universiteit Antwerpen—Bibliotheek Campus Drie Eiken: Universiteitsplein 1, 2610 Antwerp; tel. (3) 265-21-45; fax (3) 820-21-59; e-mail helpdesk@lib.ua.ac.be; internet lib.ua.ac.be; f. 1972, fmrly known as Universitaire Instelling Antwerpen, present name 2003; attached to Univ. of Antwerp; 1,380,000 vols; Chief Librarian TRUDI NOORDERMEER.

Universiteit Antwerpen—Bibliotheek Stadscampus: Prinsstraat 13, 2000 Antwerp; tel. (3) 265-44-34; fax (3) 265-44-37; e-mail helpdesk@lib.ua.ac.be; internet lib.ua.ac.be; f. 1852; 1.43m; Chief Librarian TRUDI NOORDERMEER; Librarian VERONIQUE REGA.

Universiteit Antwerpen—Bibliotheek campus Middelheim/Groenenborger: Middelheimlaan 1, 2020 Antwerp; tel. (3) 265-37-94; fax (3) 265-36-52; e-mail helpdesk@lib.ua.ac.be; internet lib.ua.ac.be; f. 1965; 75,000 vols; (mathematics and computer sciences: campus Middelheimlaan 1, 2020; natural sciences: Groenenborgerlaan 171,2620 Antwerp); Librarian TRUDI NOORDERMEER.

Arlon

Archives de l'état à Arlon: Parc des Expositions 9, 6700 Arlon; tel. (63) 22-06-13; fax (63) 22-42-94; e-mail archives.arlon@arch.be; f. 1849; documents concerning Province of Luxembourg since 12th century; 18 km of shelving; 100,000 vols; Archivist VINCENT PIRLOT.

Beveren

Archives de l'état à Beveren: Kruibekesteenweg 39/1, 9120 Beveren; tel. (3) 750-29-77; fax (3) 750-29-70; e-mail rijksarchief.beveren@arch.be; f. 1964; archives for judicial district of Dendermonde; 19th and 20th century archives of creators from provinces of West Flanders, East Flanders, Antwerp and Flemish Brabant; genealogical centre; Head JOHAN DAMBRUYNE.

Bruges

Archives de l'état à Bruges: Academiestraat 14–18, 8000 Bruges; tel. (50) 33-72-88; fax (50) 61-09-18; e-mail rijksarchief.brugge@arch.be; f. 1796; documents on Western Flanders since 12th century; Dept Head Dr MAURICE VANDERMAESEN.

Openbare Bibliotheek Brugge: Kuipersstraat 3, 8000 Bruges; tel. (50) 47-24-00; fax (50) 34-27-05; e-mail bibliotheek@brugge.be; internet www.brugge.be/bibliotheek; f. 1798; colln of medieval MSS, incunabula, old prints, archives, CDs, DVDs, CD-ROMs; Dir SPEECKE LEEN; Librarian CALIS KOEN.

Brussels

Archives de l'état à Bruxelles (Anderlecht): Quai Demets 7, 1070 Brussels (Anderlecht); tel. (2) 524-61-15; fax (2) 520-93-21; e-mail archives.anderlecht@arch.be; f. 2002; repository auxiliary Street Hop; colln of microfilms of church records prior to 1795; public archives of Old Regime; contemporary public records; contemporary and ecclesiastical instns of Ancien Regime; contemporary and ancient notaries; Head LUC JANSSENS.

Archives de l'État dans les Provinces Wallonnes et la Communauté Germanophone: rue de Ruysbroeck 2, 1000 Brussels; tel. (2) 513-76-80; fax (2) 513-76-81; e-mail archives.wallonie@arch.be; Head of Dept CLAUDE DE MOREAU DE GERBEHAYE.

Archives de la Ville de Bruxelles: rue des Tanneurs 65, 1000 Brussels; tel. (2) 279-53-20; fax (2) 279-53-29; e-mail archives@brucity.be; internet archives.bruxelles.be; historical archive of city of Brussels; colln of newspapers and periodicals, maps and plans, posters and advertisements; iconographic colln; cartographic colln; cabinet of medals; 25,000 vols; Archivist ANNE VANDENBULCKE.

Archives du Palais Royal: Rue Ducale 2, 1000 Brussels; tel. (2) 551-20-20; fax (2) 512-56-85; e-mail cap@kppr.be; section of Gen. State Archives and State Archives in Provinces; records of works of depts and services of palace since 1831; colln of maps, illustrations, photographs and medals; works on monarchy and political history of Belgium; part of library of Queen Elizabeth; Head GUSTAAF JANSSENS; publs *Almanach royal*, *Annales administratives et judiciaires de Belgique*, *Moniteur belge*.

Archives et Musée du Centre Public d'Action Sociale de Bruxelles: rue Haute 298A, Brussels; tel. (2) 543-60-55; fax (2) 543-61-06; e-mail archives@cpasbru.irisnet.be; f. 1796; archives, books, objects and art works concerning hospitals, health care and welfare in Brussels since the 12th century; approx. 10 km archives; 15,000 vols; Archivist D. GUILARDIAN.

Archives Générales du Royaume/Algemeen Rijksarchief—Generalstaatsarchiv: rue de Ruysbroeck 2, 1000 Brussels; tel. (2) 513-76-80; fax (2) 513-76-81; e-mail archives.generales@arch.be; internet arch.arch.be; f. 1815; 50 km documents concerning Low Countries, Belgium and Brabant since 11th century; execution of legislation on Public Records; 400,000 vols; Gen. Archivist KAREL VELLE (acting).

Attached Centre:

Centre d'études et de documentation guerre et société contemporaine (CEGES) (Centre for Historical Research and Documentation on War and Contemporary Society): Luchtscheepvaartsquare 29, 1070 Brussels; tel. (2) 556-92-11; fax (2) 556-92-00; e-mail cegesoma@cegesoma.be; internet www.cegesoma.be; f. 1967, present name 1997; colln incl. personal archives, archives of private orgs, of collaborators and collaborationist movements, of resistance fighters and resistance orgs, of official instns and services that existed only between 1939 and 1946; 62,000 vols, 4,000 periodicals; Dir RUDI VAN DOORSLAER; Dir FABRICE MAERTEN (acting); publ. *Cahiers d'Histoire du Temps présent/Bijdragen tot de Eigentijdse Geschiedenis (CHTP/BEG)* (2 a year).

Archives Générales du Royaume et Archives de l'État dans les Provinces: Rue de Ruysbroeck 2, 1000 Brussels; tel. (2) 513-76-80; fax (2) 513-76-81; e-mail archives.generales@arch.be; central br. of state archives in Belgium; acquired govt and private archives; Head KAREL VELLE.

Bibliothèque Artistique, Académie Royale des Beaux-Arts: rue du Midi 144, 1000 Brussels; tel. (2) 506-10-35; fax (2) 506-10-38; e-mail bib.aca@brunette.brucity.be; internet www.brunette.brucity.be/bib/bibp1/bibaca/accueil_ba.html; f. 1886; 18,000 vols, 400 rare books from 17th and 18th centuries; more

than 10,000 books on applied arts from 19th century, collns of photographs from 19th and early 20th centuries (architecture, applied arts, travel); Librarian CHRISTINE FERON.

Bibliothèque d'Art, Ecole Nationale Supérieure des Arts Visuels de la Cambre: abbaye de la Cambre 21, 1000 Brussels; tel. (2) 626-17-86; fax (2) 640-96-93; e-mail bibliotheque@lacambre.be; internet www.lacambre.be; f. 1926; 60,000 vols; Librarian RÉGINE CARPENTIER.

Bibliothèque de l'Institut Royal des Sciences Naturelles de Belgique/Bibliotheek en Documentatiedienst van het Koninklijk Belgisch Instituut voor Natuurwetenschappen (Library and Documentation Service of the Royal Belgian Institute of Natural Sciences): rue Vautier 29, 1000 Brussels; tel. (2) 627-41-89; fax (2) 627-41-13; e-mail bib@naturalsciences.be; internet www.naturalsciences.be; f. 1846; 750,000 vols, Dautzenberg colln with rare vols, 7,000 periodicals, 35,000 geographical, hydrological and geological maps; Dir CAMILLE PISANI; Librarian LAURENT MEESE; publs *Bulletin de l'Institut Royal des Sciences Naturelles de Belgique, Série Biologie, Bulletin de l'Institut Royal des Sciences Naturelles de Belgique, Série Entomologie, Bulletin de l'Institut Royal des Sciences Naturelles de Belgique, Série Sciences de la Terre*.

Bibliothèque des Facultés Universitaires Saint-Louis: blvd du Jardin Botanique 43, 1000 Brussels; tel. (2) 211-79-09; fax (2) 211-79-97; e-mail lib@fusl.ac.be; internet www.bib.fusl.ac.be; f. 1858; specializes in law, economics and social policy; 260,000 vols; Librarian MARIE CLAUDE MINGUET; Librarian NICOLE PETIT.

Bibliothèque, Documentation, Publications du Ministère de l'Emploi et du Travail: Ernesr Blerotst 1, 1070 Brussels; fax (2) 233-44-55; e-mail bibliotheek@werk.belgie.be; internet employment.belgium.be; f. 1896; primarily for staff; open by appointment to outside users; colln on labour and social security, management and org. of work, being at work, occupational safety, occupational health; 150,000 vols, 400 periodicals; Dir JEF CASSIMONS.

Bibliothèque du Parlement Fédéral Belge: rue de la Loi 13, 1000 Brussels; tel. (2) 549-92-12; e-mail bibliotheque@lachambre.be; internet www.lachambre.be/accessible/lachambre_biblio_presentation.htm; f. 1831; colln of documents in law, politics, economics, social sciences, history and parliamentary politics; 500,000 vols, 2,700 periodicals, collns on microfilms, 250,000 monographs, 120 CD-ROM titles; Librarian ROLAND VAN NIEUWENBORGH.

Bibliothèque Espace 27 septembre (Ministère de la Communauté Française): blvd Leopold II 44, 1080 Brussels; tel. (2) 413-31-48; fax (2) 413-33-48; e-mail jean-michel.andrin@cfwb.be; internet www.bibli2709.cfwb.be; f. 1879; contains vols on admin. and law, all brs of science and pedagogy, educational books; open only to teachers and mems of French Dept; 600,000 vols, 900 periodicals; Dir J. M. ANDRIN.

Bibliothèque Fonds Quetelet (Fonds Quetelet Library): 50 Vooruitgangstraat, 1210 Brussels; tel. (2) 277-55-55; fax (2) 277-55-53; e-mail quetelet@economie.fgov.be; internet quetelet.economie.fgov.be; f. 1841; library of the Fed. Public Service Economy, SMEs, Self-Employed and Energy; 1.2m. vols on statistics, economic and social sciences, agriculture, 8,000 periodicals; Chief Librarian STEFAAN JACOBS; publ. *Aanwinsten=Accroissements* (online at www.economie.fgov.be/informations/quetelet/acquisitions_nl.htm).

Bibliothèque Royale de Belgique/Koninklijke Bibliotheek van België (Royal Library of Belgium): blvd de l'Empereur 4, 1000 Brussels; tel. (2) 519-53-11; fax (2) 519-55-33; e-mail info@kbr.be; internet www.kbr.be; f. 1837; nat. depository library; 6 sections of colln: valuable reserve, maps, music, prints, MSS, coins and medals; 5m. vols, 18,000 periodicals, 35,000 MSS, 35,000 rare printed books, 700,000 prints, 140,000 maps, 200,000 coins and medals, 10,000 records, 200,000 maps and plans units; Dir-Gen. PATRICK LEFÈVRE (acting).

Central Library of the European Commission: VM18 1/18, rue Van Maerlant 18, 1049 Brussels; tel. (2) 295-04-28; fax (2) 295-68-26; e-mail roberta.persichelli-scola@ec.europa.eu; internet ec.europa.eu/libraries/doc/index_en.htm; f. 1958; a central library linking a system of specialized library/documentation units; forms part of EC's Directorate-Gen. for Education and Culture; 500,000 vols and periodicals on European integration and EU policies; also br. library in Bech bldg in Luxembourg (tel. 4301-33341); Head of Unit ROBERTA PERSICHELLI-SCOLA.

Hoofdstedelijke Openbare Bibliotheek (Capital City Public Library): Muntplein Prinsenstraat 8, 1000 Brussels; tel. (2) 229-18-40; fax (2) 229-18-50; e-mail info@hob.be; internet www.hob.be; books, CDs, CD-ROMs, video cassettes, DVDs, magazines, community information, newspapers and magazines.

Les Archives et Bibliothèques de l'Université Libre de Bruxelles: ave Franklin D. Roosevelt 50, CP 180, 1050 Brussels; tel. (2) 650-23-70; fax (2) 650-41-86; e-mail bibdir@ulb.ac.be; internet www.bib.ulb.ac.be; f. 1846; 8.5 km linear archives; 1,220,850 vols, 10,856 e-journals, 14,407 audiovisual items; Librarian Prof. JEAN-PIERRE DEVROEY.

NATO Multimedia Library, Public Diplomacy Division: Room Nb 123, 1110 Brussels; tel. (2) 707-44-14; fax (2) 707-42-49; e-mail multilib@hq.nato.int; internet www.nato.int/library; f. 1950; serves the int. staff, int. military staff, delegations and PfP countries; subject areas: int. relations, defence and security, military questions and current world affairs; 14,000 vols, 200 periodicals; incl. NATO audiovisual material; Librarian ISABEL FERNANDEZ; publs *Acquisitions List* (12 a year), *Backgrounders* (12 a year), *Thematic Bibliographies* (10 a year).

SIST-DWTI (Scientific and Technical Information Service): Bâtiment Platinum, ave Louise 231, 1050 Brussels; tel. (2) 238-37-40; fax (2) 238-37-50; e-mail stis@stis.fgov.be; internet www.stis.fgov.be; f. 1964, present name and status 1997; provides information in fields of medicine, science and technology; focal point for library, documentation and information networks (nat. and int.); Dir Dr JEAN MOULIN; Sec. BRIGITTE BLANQUART.

Vrije Universiteit Brussel, Universiteitsbibliotheek: Pleinlaan 2, 1050 Brussels; tel. (2) 629-26-09; fax (2) 629-26-93; e-mail info@biblio.vub.ac.be; internet www.vub.ac.be/biblio; f. 1972; 550,000 vols, 360,000 monographs and 160,000 bound periodicals; Head Librarian Dr PATRICK VANOUPLINES.

Wetenschappelijke Bibliotheek van de Nationale Bank/Bibliothèque Scientifique de la Banque Nationale (Scientific Library of the National Bank of Belgium): Montagne aux Herbes potagères 57, 1000 Brussels; tel. (2) 221-24-10; fax (2) 221-30-42; e-mail documentation@nbb.be; colln of books related to economics, finance and monetary policy; 100,000 vols, 1,300 periodicals.

Courtrai

Archives de l'état à Courtrai: G. Gezelle-straat 1, 8500 Kortrijk; tel. (56) 21-32-68; fax (56) 20-57-42; e-mail rijksarchief.kortrijk@arch.be; f. 1964; records of regional and local govt instns; colln of microfilms of parish registers and records of births of all municipalities in province of West Flanders; colln of journals, reference works and monographs in field of nat., regional and local history; Head MARC THERRY.

Archives de l'état dans les Provinces Flamandes: Guido Gezellestraat 1, 8500 Kortrijk; tel. (56) 22-10-23; fax (56) 20-57-42; e-mail rijksarchief.vlaanderen@arch.be; main dept archive of Flanders; Head of Dept MICHEL NUYTTENS.

Gembloux

Bibliothèque des Sciences Agronomiques: passage des Déportés 2, 5030 Gembloux; tel. (81) 62-21-03; fax (81) 62-25-52; e-mail bib.bsa@ulg.ac.be; internet www.bib.fsagx.ac.be; f. 1860; 100,000 vols, 1,000 journals, 120,000 monographs, 1,000 periodicals; Chief Librarian BERNARD POCHET; publ. *Biotechnologies, Agronomie, Société et Environnement* (4 a year).

Ghent

Rijksarchief te Gent/Archives de l'état à Gand: Geraard de Duivelstraat 1, 9000 Gent; tel. (9) 225-13-38; fax (9) 225-52-01; e-mail rijksarchief.gent@arch.be; f. 1830; 7 km of documents (since 9th century): mainly County of Flanders (until 1795), Diocese of Ghent (until 1801), Province of Oost-Vlaanderen (until 1870), District of Ghent; Head Dr CHANTAL VANCOPPENOLLE.

Liberaal Archief (Liberal Archives): Kramersplein 23, 9000 Ghent; tel. (9) 221-75-05; fax (9) 221-12-15; e-mail info@liberaalarchief.be; internet www.liberaalarchief.be; f. 1982, present status 2002; 6,000 m archives; archives of major liberal orgs; documents of Liberal Int. and Mont Pèlerin soc.; 34,000 vols, 2,300 periodicals; Pres. Prof. Dr JUUL HANNES; Sec. Prof. Dr GUY SCHRANS; Dir LUC PAREYN.

Universiteitsbibliotheek Gent: Rozier 9, 9000 Ghent; tel. (9) 264-38-51; fax (9) 264-38-52; e-mail libservice@ugent.be; internet www.lib.ugent.be; f. 1797; 3m. vols, 5,060 MSS; open to public; Chief Librarian Dr SYLVIA VAN PETEGHEM.

Hasselt

Archives de l'état à Hasselt: Bampslaan 4, 3500 Hasselt; tel. (11) 22-17-66; fax (11) 23-40-46; e-mail rijksarchief.hasselt@arch.be; f. 1869; repository of Limburg State govts and individuals from 1040 to 2000; Head ROMBOUT NIJSSEN.

Bibliotheek van de XIOS Hogeschool: Vildersstraat 5, 3500 Hasselt; tel. (11) 37-06-03; fax (11) 85-95-80; e-mail danny.sneyers@xios.be; internet www.xios.be/bibliotheek; has br. at Diepenbeek; reference books and dictionaries, economics, business studies, social sciences, law, education, linguistics, mathematics, biology, physics, chemistry, engineering, technology, IT; 30,000 vols, 400 journals; Librarian DANNY SNEYERS.

Liège

Archives de l'état à Eupen: Kaperberg 2–4, 4700 Liege (Eupen); tel. (87) 55-43-77; fax (87) 55-87-77; e-mail staatsarchiv.eupen@arch.be; f. 1988; archives of public and private instns; stocks from 14th century; microfilm on church records and civil registers and civil communities in judicial district of Eupen; historical archives (mid-16th to 20th centuries) and newspaper colln (1827 to

present); 30,000 vols; Dir ALFRED MINKE; Archivist ELS HERREBOUT.

Archives de l'état à Liège: rue du Chéra 79, 4000 Liège; tel. (4) 252-03-93; fax (4) 229-33-50; e-mail archives.liege@arch.be; internet arch.arch.be; f. 1794; state archives, Belgian fed. scientific and cultural institute; 22 km of public and private records relating to history of Liège district since 9th century; Dir Prof. Dr SÉBASTIEN DUBOIS; Archivist LAURENCE DRUEZ.

Bibliothèque 'Chiroux-Croisiers': place des Carmes, 8, 4000 Liège; tel. (41) 232-86-86; fax (41) 23-20-62; e-mail chiroux@liege.be; f. 1907; general library; MSS, ancient works - maps; 1,300,000 vols, local history, architecture, Walloon dialectology, 1,000 periodicals; Dir J. P. ROUGE.

Bibliothèque de l'Institut Archéologique Liégeois: Grand Curtius, quai de Maastricht 13, 4000 Liège; tel. and fax (4) 232-98-60; e-mail monique.merland@crmsf.be; f. 1850; archaeology, decorative arts; 27,000 vols (mostly periodicals); Librarian MONIQUE MERLAND; publ. *Bulletin de l'Institut Archéologique Liégeois* (1 a year).

Réseau des Bibliothèques de l'Université de Liège: Grande Traverse 12, bât. B37, 4000 Liège (Sart-Tilman); tel. (4) 366-52-90; fax (4) 366-99-22; e-mail bib.direction@ulg.ac.be; internet www.libnet.ulg.ac.be; f. 1817; institutional repository; spec. collns incl. Fonds Québecois (French Canadian literature and society); 5 depts: law, economics, management and social sciences Leon Graulich, philosophy and letters, agricultural sciences - Gembloux, science and technology, life sciences; 2,600,000 vols and pamphlets (incl. 12,000 current serials, 6,000 MSS and 500 early printed books); Chief Librarian Dr PAUL THIRION; publ. *Bibliotheca Universitatis Leodiensis*.

Louvain

Archives de l'état à Louvain: Vaartstraat 24, 3000 Louvain; tel. (16) 31-49-54; fax (16) 31-49-61; e-mail rijksarchief.leuven@arch.be; f. 2001; records creators based in province of Flemish Brabant; parish registers and civil registration of Flemish Brabant, Brussels and Walloon Brabant; Head HERMAN VAN ISTERDAEL.

Universiteitsbibliotheek—K. U. Leuven: Mgr Ladeuzeplein 21, 3000 Leuven; tel. (16) 32-46-60; fax (16) 32-46-91; e-mail centrale.bibliotheek@bib.kuleuven.be; internet www.bib.kuleuven.be; f. 1636; 4,300,000 vols (of which 3m. in faculty and dept libraries), 1,000 MSS; Chief Librarian Prof. MEL COLLIER; Sec. DENISE DELVAUX.

Louvain-la-Neuve

Archives de l'état à Louvain-la-Neuve: rue Paulin Ladeuze 16, 1348 Louvain-la-Neuve; tel. (10) 23-00-90; fax (10) 23-00-98; e-mail archives.louvain-la-neuve@arch.be; f. 2009; 4 km of archives; regional and local public records of old regime; ecclesiastical, business, notarial, govt and courts archives; scientific and admin. library; Head CATHERINE HENIN.

Bibliothèques de l'Université Catholique de Louvain: Grand Place 45, 1348 Louvain-la-Neuve; tel. (10) 47-81-87; fax (10) 47-82-98; e-mail contact-biul@uclouvain.be; internet www.uclouvain.be/biul.html; has 8 core libraries; 2m. vols, 8,000 current periodicals; Pres. of Central Library C. FOCANT; Chief Librarian CH.-H. NYNS.

Maredsous

Bibliothèque de l'Abbaye de Saint-Benoît: Abbaye de Maredsous, 5198 Denée; tel. (82) 69-91-55; fax (82) 69-83-21; e-mail

biblioteque@maredsous.com; f. 1872; books of learning, esp. history and theology; 400,000 vols, 50,000 brochures; Chief Librarian IGNACE BAISE; publ. *Revue Bénédictine*.

Mechelen

Archdiocesan Archives, Mechelen: Varkensstraat 6, 2800 Mechelen; tel. (15) 29-84-22; fax (15) 21-90-94; e-mail archiv@diomb.be; archives of archdiocese of Mechelen and its predecessors since 12th century; MSS and books; photographs, iconographs, souvenirs; Archivist Drs GERRIT VANDEN BOSCH.

Archief en Stadsbibliotheek: Goswin de Stassartstraat 145, 2800 Mechelen; tel. (15) 20-43-46; fax (15) 21-64-48; e-mail stadsarchief@mechelen.be; f. 1802; archives of city of Malines (Mechelen) since the 13th century and library of Great Ccl of the Netherlands; Archivist WILLY VAN DE VIJVER; publs *Catalogue méthodique de la Bibliothèque de Malines*, *Inventaire des Archives de la ville de Malines*.

Mons

Archives de l'etat à Mons: ave des Bassins 66, 7000 Mons; tel. (65) 40-04-60; fax (65) 40-04-61; e-mail archives.mons@arch.be; internet arch.arch.be; f. 1834; 25,000 vols; archives since 10th century; archives from Abbeys and noble families of Hainaut; records of instns or orgs, families or individuals attached to territory; Head LAURENT HONNORÉ; Archivist JEAN-PIERRE NIEBER.

Bibliothèque de l'Université de Mons: rue Marguerite Bervoets 2, 7000 Mons; tel. (65) 37-30-55; fax (65) 37-30-68; e-mail bibliotheque.centrale@umons.ac.be; internet www.umons.ac.be; f. 1797, present status 1966; collns focus on humanities; heritage collns; 900,000 vols, 3,622 MSS and incunabula, maps, prints; Dir CATHERINE MASSELUS.

Université de Mons—Bibliothèques: Place du Parc 20 , 7000 Mons; tel. (65) 37-30-57; fax (65) 37-45-00; e-mail martine.piens@umons.ac.be; internet www.umons.ac.be; f. 1837; has 9 br. libraries; 900,000 vols, 1,300 journals; Chief Librarian CATHERINE MASSELUS; Sec. MARTINE PIENS.

Namur

Archives de l'etat à Namur: rue d'Arquet 45, 5000 Namur; tel. (81) 65-41-98; fax (81) 65-41-99; e-mail archives.namur@arch.be; internet arch.arch.be; f. 1848; documents concerning county and province of Namur since 8th century; Head EMMANUEL BODART.

Bibliothèque Centrale de la Province de Namur: chaussée de Charleroi 85, 5000 Namur; tel. (81) 77-67-16; fax (81) 77-69-62; e-mail bibliotheques@province.namur.be; central library in province of Namur; Librarian FRANÇOISE DURY.

Bibliothèque Universitaire Moretus Plantin: rue Grandgagnage 19, 5000 Namur; tel. (81) 72-46-46; fax (81) 72-46-45; e-mail direction.bump@fundp.ac.be; internet www.bump.fundp.ac.be; f. 1921; attached to University of Namur; history of W Europe, Classical, Roman and German philology, philosophy, law, economics, art, biomedical sciences, life sciences, earth sciences; 800,000 vols; spec. colln: rare books on natural sciences, 7,000 e-periodicals; Dir KATRIEN BERGÉ.

Sint Niklaas Waas

Bibliotheek voor Hedendaagse Dokumentatie (Library on Contemporary Documentation): Parklaan 2, 9100 Sint Niklaas Waas; tel. (3) 776-50-63; e-mail akses@skynet.be; f. 1964; private political, social and economic library; spec. collns on governmental research, public admin.; US govt documents depository colln; 120,000 vols, 4,000 periodicals, 15,000 maps; Librarian JOHN HESS; publs *Bibliographical Series* (irregular), *Bulletin* (12 a year), *Governmental Publications Survey* (1 a year).

Tournai

Archives de l'État à Tournai: rue des Augustins 20, 7500 Tournai; tel. (69) 22-53-76; fax (69) 54-54-83; e-mail archives .tournai@arch.be; f. 1834; records of external services of the Ministry of Finance; archives of families and enterprises; church archives; microfilms of registers and civil registers of district court; Head BERNARD DESMAELE.

Ypres

Stedelijke Openbare Bibliotheek: Weverijstraat 9, 8900 Ypres; tel. (57) 23-94-20; fax (57) 23-94-29; e-mail bibliotheek@ieper.be; internet www.ieper.be/default .aspx?sgref=26926; f. 1839; gen. interest; colln of encyclopaedias, dictionaries, newspapers, magazines; 120,000 vols, 400 periodicals; Librarian EDDY BARBRY.

Museums and Art Galleries

Antwerp

Etnografisch Museum: Suikerrui 19, 2000 Antwerp; tel. (3) 220-86-00; fax (3) 227-08-71; e-mail etnografisch.museum@stad .antwerpen.be; f. 1988; arts and crafts of preliterate and non-European people; library of 12,000 vols; Dir JAN VAN ALPHEN; publ. *Bulletin van de Vrienden van het Etnografisch Museum Antwerpen.*

FotoMuseum: Waalse Kaai 47, 2000 Antwerp; tel. (3) 242-93-00; fax (3) 242-93-10; e-mail info@fotografie.provant.be; internet www.fotomuseum.be; f. 1965, present name 1980; colln of prints, cameras and photographic objects, and works by nat. and int. photographers; library of 35,000 vols; Dir ELVIERA VELGHE; Curator INGE HENNEMAN; Curator DOMINIQUE SOMERS; publ. *Extra.*

Koninklijk Museum voor Schone Kunsten (Royal Museum of Fine Arts): Leopold De Waelplaats, 2000 Antwerp; tel. (3) 238-78-09; fax (3) 248-08-10; e-mail info@kmska.be; internet www.kmska.be; f. 1890; collns of Flemish Primitives, early foreign schools, Rubens, 16th–17th-century Antwerp School, 17th-century Dutch School, works of Belgian artists since 19th century; important works of De Braekeleer, Ensor, Leys, Magritte, Permeke, Smits, Wouters; from May 2011 to May 2012 colln highlights will be kept on display at Museum aan de Stroom (Museum on the Stream) as well as in other locations in the city; museum will be closed for renovations until December 2017; library of 70,000 vols; Dir Dr PAUL HUVENNE; publs *Antwerp Royal Museum Annual* (2 a year), *Museumkrant* (4 a year), *Restauratie Schone Kunst* (2 a year).

Middelheimmuseum (Openluchtmuseum voor beeldhouwkunst) (Open-air Museum of Sculpture): Middelheimlaan 61, 2020 Antwerp; tel. (3) 288-33-60; fax (3) 288-33-99; e-mail middelheimmuseum@stad .antwerpen.be; internet www .middelheimmuseum.be; f. 1950; important colln of modern and contemporary sculpture, incl. Cragg, Gargallo, Graham, Kirkeby, Maillol, Manzu, Marini, Moore, Muñoz, Rodin and Zadkine; colln of medals, sketches and prints; library of 60,000 vols; Dir MENNO MEEWIS; Curator FILIP JANSSENS; Curator NORA DE SMET; Curator SARA WEYNS.

Museum Brouwershuis: Adriaan Brouwerstraat 20, 2000 Antwerp; tel. (3) 206-03-50; fax (3) 232-65-11; internet museum .antwerpen.be/brouwershuis; f. 1933; closed until further notice; 16th century installations for water-supply to breweries, ccl chamber; Curator F. DE NAVE.

Museum Mayer van den Bergh: Lange Gasthuisstraat 19, 2000 Antwerp; tel. (3) 232-42-37; fax (3) 231-73-35; e-mail museum .mayervandenbergh@stad.antwerpen.be; internet www.museummayervandenbergh .be; f. 1904; paintings from 13th to 18th century, incl. Aertsen, Breughel, Bronzino, de Vos, Heda, Metsys, Mostaert; sculptures from 12th to 18th century; drawings from 16th to 19th century; applied art objects from Gothic age; Chief Curator Dr CLAIRE BAISIER.

Museum Plantin-Moretus/Prentenkabinet/Idem: Vrijdagmarkt 22–23, 2000 Antwerp; tel. (3) 221-14-50; fax (3) 221-14-71; e-mail museum.plantin.moretus@stad .antwerpen.be; internet www .museumplantinmoretus.be; f. 1876; print room f. 1938; UNESCO World Heritage site; 16th–18th century patrician house with ancient printing office and foundry, engravings on copper and wood; typographical collns, drawings, prints and paintings by Rubens; illuminated MSS; rare books and atlases; library of 30,000 rare books (15th–18th century) and modern reference library on humanism and book history, family and business archives (16th–19th century); spec. collns: Max Horn Legacy, Ensemble Emile Verhaeren, 600 MSS; Dir IRIS KOCKELBERGH.

Museum Rockoxhuis (Rockox House Museum): Keizerstraat 10–12, 2000 Antwerp; tel. (3) 201-92-50; fax (3) 201-92-51; e-mail inforockoxhuis@kbc.be; internet www.rockoxhuis.be; f. 1977; colln of furniture, paintings, applied art.

Museum Smidt van Gelder: Lange Nieuwstraat 24, 2000 Antwerp; Belgiëlei 91, 2018 Antwerp; tel. (3) 239-06-52; fax (3) 230-22-81; e-mail museum.smidtvangelder@stad .antwerpen.be; internet museum.antwerpen .be/smidtvangelder; f. 1950; museum is closed temporarily to public; Chinese and European porcelains, 17th century Dutch paintings, 18th century French furniture; Curator CLARA VANDERHENST.

Museum van Hedendaagse Kunst Antwerpen: Leuvenstraat 32, 2000 Antwerp; tel. (3) 260-99-99; fax (3) 216-24-86; e-mail info@muhka.be; internet www .muhka.be; f. 1987; maintains archives; colln Vrielynck; colln of nat. and int. pre-cinema and film hardware; library of 18,000 vols; Dir BART DE BAERE; Exec. Dir ANN CEULEMANS; publs *Afterall, AS.*

Museum Vleeshuis/Klank van de Stad: Vleeshouwersstraat 38–40, 2000 Antwerp; tel. (3) 292-61-00; fax (3) 292-61-29; e-mail vleeshuis@stad.antwerpen.be; internet museum.antwerpen.be/vleeshuis; f. 1913; applied art, archaeology, arms, ceramics, Egyptian, Greek and Roman antiquities, furniture, local history, musical instruments, numismatics, posters, sculpture; colln of Antwerp history; library of 15,000 vols; Curator KAREL MOENS.

Nationaal Scheepvaartmuseum (Steen) (National Maritime Museum): Steenplein 1, 2000 Antwerp; tel. (3) 201-93-40; fax (3) 201-93-41; e-mail scheepmus@stad.antwerpen .be; f. 1952; maritime history, esp. concerning Belgium; colln exhibiting inland navigation, fishing, training ships, 'Belgica' expedition to North Pole, shipbuilding, pleasure craft; library of 43,000 vols; Asst Dir R. JALON.

Rubenshuis (Rubens House): Wapper 9–11, 2000 Antwerp; tel. (3) 201-15-55; fax (3) 227-36-92; e-mail info.rubenshuis@stad .antwerpen.be; internet www.rubenshuis.be; f. 1946; reconstruction of Rubens's house and studio; original 17th-century portico and pavilion; paintings by P. P. Rubens, his collaborators and pupils; 17th-century furnishings; Renaissance architecture and garden; Curator BEN VAN BENEDEN.

Van Mieghem Museum: Ernest Van Dijckkaai 9, 2000 Antwerp; tel. (3) 211-03-30; e-mail van.mieghem.museum@skynet.be; internet www.vanmieghemmuseum.com; colln of works of artist; sculpture and paintings; Curator ERWIN JOOS.

Volkskundemuseum: Gildekamersstraat 2–6, 2000 Antwerp; tel. (3) 220-86-66; fax (3) 220-83-68; f. 1907; folklore of Flemish provinces, esp. folk art and craft; library of 18,000 vols; Curator WERNER VAN HOOF.

Bouillon

Musée Ducal 'Les Amis de Vieux Bouillon': rue du Petit 1–3, 6830 Bouillon; tel. (61) 46-41-89; fax (61) 46-41-99; e-mail courrier@ museeducal.be; f. 1947; archives, historical MSS and documents; archaeology, folklore; exhibition of history of Godefroy de Bouillon; small library; Curator Mme MICHEL GOURDIN.

Bruges

Musea Brugge: Dijver 16, 8000 Bruges; tel. (50) 44-87-11; fax (50) 44-87-78; e-mail musea@brugge.be; internet www .museabrugge.be; 18th century manor house, contains colln of lace and permanent exhibition of works by Frank Brangwyn; umbrella org. for 16 museums subdivided into 3 groups: Groeninge Museum (Artistic Works), Hospitaalmuseum and Bruggemuseum (historical museums); Dir Dr MANFRED SELLINK.

Attached Museums:

Bruggemuseum: Dijver 12, 8000 Bruges; tel. (50) 44-87-11; fax (50) 44-87-78; e-mail musea@brugge.be; internet www.brugge .be/internet/en/musea; f. 1997; 11 brs: Gruuthuse, Onthaalkerk Onze-Lieve-Vrouw, Archeologie, Gentpoort, Belfort, Stadhuis, Brugse Vrije, Volkskunde, Sint-Janshuismolen, Koeleweimolen and Gezelle; library; Curator HUBERT DE WITTE.

Groeningemuseum (Municipal Art Gallery): Dijver 12, 8000 Bruges; tel. (50) 44-87-11; fax (50) 44-87-78; e-mail musea@ brugge.be; internet www.brugge.be/musea/ fr/groeningefrans.htm; Belgian and Dutch paintings and etchings from late medieval times to present; artistic works from 15th to 21st century grouped in Groeninge Museum and Arentshuis; Art Dir MANFRED SELLINK.

Hospitaalmuseum: St John's Hospital, Mariastraat 38, 8000 Bruges; tel. (50) 44-87-11; fax (50) 44-87-78; e-mail musea@ brugge.be; internet www.brugge.be/musea; f. c. 1150; paintings by Hans Memling and Jan Provost, furniture and sculpture from 15th–19th century; mediaeval instruments and books; 17th century pharmacy; colln of records, works of art, applied arts and medical instruments; colln related to healthcare, worship and monastery; has br. O.L.V.-ter-Potterie (Our Lady of the Potteries); Chief Curator EVA TAHON.

Brussels

Bozar Palais des Beaux-Arts (Bozar Centre for Fine Arts): rue Ravensteinstraat 23, 1000 Brussels; tel. (2) 507-82-00; internet www.bozar.be; f. 1928; art exhibition; painting, sculpture, monumental art, applied arts, photography; music concerts; archives; CEO PAUL DUJARDIN.

Horta Museum: rue Américain, 25, 1060 Brussels (Saint-Gilles); tel. (2) 543-04-90; fax (2) 538-76-31; e-mail info@hortamuseum.be; internet www.hortamuseum.be; f. 1969; furniture, utensils and art objects designed by Horta and his contemporaries; Horta's personal archives; photographic archives; Art Nouveau library; Pres. MARTINE WILLE.

Koninklijk Museum voor Midden-Afrika Musée Royal de l'Afrique Centrale/ Musée Royal de l'Afrique Centrale (Royal Museum for Central Africa): Leuvensesteenweg 13, 3080 Tervuren; tel. (2) 769-52-11; fax (2) 769-56-38; e-mail info@africamuseum.be; internet www.africamuseum.be; f. 1897, present name 1960; large collns in fields of prehistory, ethnography, native arts and crafts; geology, mineralogy, palaeontology; zoology (entomology, ornithology, mammals, reptiles); history, economics; archival documents about history of central Africa; library of 110,000 vols; Dir-Gen. GUIDO GRYSEELS; publs *Africana Linguistica, Annales* (5 publs dealing with botany, geology, zoology, humanities and economics), *Journal of Afro-tropical Zoology (JAZ)*.

Musée & Jardins van Buuren (Museum & Gardens van Buuren): ave Léo Errera 41, 1180 Brussels; tel. (2) 343-48-51; fax (2) 347-66-89; e-mail info@museumvanbuuren.be; internet www.museumvanbuuren.com; f. 1975; rare furniture, carpets, stained-glass windows, sculptures and int. masterpieces; art decoration of garden; colln of Flemish and Italian paintings covering 5 centuries of art; open air exhibitions of contemporary sculptures.

Musée d'Ixelles/Museum van Elsene (Museum of Elsene): rue Jean Van Volsem 71, Ixelles, 1050 Brussels; tel. (322) 515-64-21; fax (322) 515-64-24; e-mail musee@ixelles.be; internet www.fading.museumofixelles.be; f. 1892; watercolours, drawings, engravings, sculptures, posters; works of Belgian and foreign schools; colln of works of realist, impressionist, luminist, neo-impressionist and symbolist, fauvism, expressionism, cubism, surrealism and abstraction; library of 3,000 vols (bibliographies); Dir CLAIRE LEBLANC.

Musée Juif de Belgique: rue des Minimes 21, 1000 Brussels; tel. (2) 512-19-63; e-mail z.seewald@mjb-jmb.org; internet www.new.mjb-jmb.org; f. 1946; 20,000 photographs relating to aspects of Jewish life in Belgium, Israel, Israeli-Palestine and Jewish Morocco; Jewish genealogy colln; worship and textile items; archives; music colln; art works; library of 25,000 vols; Pres. BARON SCHNEK; Curator ZAHAVA SEEWALD; Curator DANIEL DRATWA.

Musée René Magritte: rue Esseghem 135, 1090 Brussels; tel. and fax (2) 428-26-26; e-mail info@magrittemuseum.be; internet www.magrittemuseum.be; documents over a biographical journey of artist; mascots, surrealist brochures, adverts, correspondence; drawings, paintings; drawings, sketches, studies, drawings in letters, illustrations in books and graphic works by artist.

Musée Royal de l'Armée et d'Histoire Militaire/Koninklijk Museum van het Leger en de Krijgsgeschiedenis (Royal Museum of the Armed Forces and of Military History): parc du Cinquantenaire 3, 1000 Brussels; tel. (2) 737-78-11; fax (2) 737-78-02; e-mail infocom@klm-mra.be; internet www.klm-mra.be; f. 1910; colln incl. int. military history from 10th century onwards; exhibits arms, uniforms, decorations, paintings, sculpture, maps; photographic and print colln; library of 450,000 vols and archives; Dir-Gen. DOMINQUE HANSON; Curator PIET DE GRYSE; publs *Bulletin du MRA* (1 a year), *Bulletin van het KLM* (1 a year).

Musées Royaux d'Art et d'Histoire: parc du Cinquantenaire 10, 1000 Brussels; tel. (2) 741-72-11; fax (2) 733-77-35; e-mail info@kmkg-mrah.be; internet www.kmkg-mrah.be; f. 1835; Dir-Gen. MICHEL DRAGUET (acting); Sec. DOMINIQUE COUPÉ; Sec. SYLVIE PAESEN; publ. *Musze* (3 a year).

Component Museums:

Musée du Cinquantenaire: parc du Cinquantenaire 10, 1000 Brussels; tel. (2) 741-72-11; fax (2) 733-77-35; e-mail info@kmkg-mrah.be; internet www.kmkg-mrah.be; f. 1835; archaeology of Belgium, the Americas, Asia, the Pacific and Nort-Islamic world, and of ancient Iran and Near East, Egypt, Greece and Rome; European decorative arts; library of 100,000 vols; Dir-Gen. MICHEL DRAGUET; publ. *Musze* (3 a year).

MIM—Musical Instrument Museum: Montagne de la Cour 2, 1000 Brussels; tel. (2) 545-01-30; fax (2) 545-01-77; e-mail info@mim.be; internet www.mim.be; f. 1877; exhibits musical instruments; library of 35,000 vols; Dir-Gen. MICHEL DRAGUET; Art Dir PABLO DIARTINEZ.

Musée d'Extrême-Orient: ave Van Praet 44, 1020 Brussels; tel. and fax (2) 268-16-08; e-mail info@kmkg-mrah.be; internet www.kmkg-mrah.be; Chinese art, porcelain and furniture; Japanese architecture and decorative arts; Dir-Gen. MICHEL DRAGUET.

Pavillon Horta-Lambeaux: parc du Cinquantenaire, 1000 Brussels; tel. (2) 741-72-44; fax (2) 733-77-35; e-mail info@kmkg-mrah.be; internet www.kmkg-mrah.be; f. 1899; temporarily closed; marble relief of Human Passions; Dir-Gen. MICHEL DRAGUET.

Porte de Hal/Hallepoort: blvd du Midi, 1000 Brussels; tel. (2) 534-15-18; e-mail info@kmkg-mrah.be; internet www.kmkg-mrah.be; f. 1835; guild's armor parade of Archduke Albert and his horse naturalized; cradle 'Charles Quint'; painting of Anthonis Sallaert; temporary exhibitions; Dir-Gen. MICHEL DRAGUET.

Musées Royaux des Beaux-Arts de Belgique/Koninklijke Musea voor Schone Kunsten van België (Royal Museums of Fine Arts of Belgium): rue du Musée 9, 1000 Brussels; tel. (2) 508-32-11; fax (2) 508-32-32; e-mail info@fine-arts-museum.be; internet www.fine-arts-museum.be; f. 1801; temporarily closed; Brussels, medieval, Renaissance and modern pictures, drawings and sculpture; public and private collns of archives; library of 164,000 vols, 350,000 monographs and exhibition catalogues, 3,000 periodicals, 50 CD-ROMs; Chief Curator MICHEL DRAGUET; publ. *Bulletin*.

Attached Museums:

Musée Constantin Meunier: rue de l'Abbaye 59, 1050 Brussels; tel. (2) 648-44-49; fax (2) 508-32-32; e-mail info@fine-arts-museum.be; internet www.fine-arts-museum.be; f. 1939; paintings, drawings and sculptures by Constantin Meunier; the artist's house and studio; Dir MICHEL DRAGUET.

Musée d'Art Ancien (Museum of Ancient Art): rue de la Régence 3, 1000 Brussels; tel. (2) 508-32-11; fax (2) 508-32-32; e-mail info@fine-arts-museum.be; internet www.fine-arts-museum.be; f. 1801; 15th–18th-century paintings, drawings and sculpture; Chief Curator MICHEL DRAGUET.

Musée d'Art Moderne (Museum of Modern Art): rue de la Régence 3, 1000 Brussels; tel. (2) 508-32-11; fax (2) 508-32-32; e-mail info@fine-arts-museum.be; internet www.fine-arts-museum.be; f. 1984; paintings since 19th century, drawings and sculpture; Chief Curator MICHEL DRAGUET.

Musée Antoine Wiertz: rue Vautier 62, 1050 Brussels; tel. (2) 648-17-18; fax (2) 508-32-32; e-mail info@fine-arts-museum.be; internet www.fine-arts-museum.be; f. 1868; paintings by Antoine Wiertz; the artist's house and studio; Chief Curator MICHEL DRAGUET.

Musée Magritte Museum: rue de la Régence 3, 1000 Brussels; tel. (2) 508-32-11; fax (2) 508-32-32; internet www.musee-magritte-museum.be; f. 1984; René Magritte colln; paintings, drawings, gouaches, posters, advertising work, letters, photographs, sculptures, films; Gen. Dir MICHEL DRAGUET.

Muséum des Sciences Naturelles (Museum of Natural Sciences): rue Vautier 29, 1000 Brussels; tel. (2) 627-42-11; e-mail info@naturalsciences.be; internet www.naturalsciences.be; f. 1846; colln of minerals, fossils, living animals; temporary exhibitions; dinosaur hall; library.

Museum Erasmus: rue du Chapitre 31, 1070 Brussels; tel. (2) 521-13-83; fax (2) 527-12-69; e-mail info@erasmushouse.museum; internet www.erasmushouse.museum; f. 1932; portraits, books, gothic sculpture, documents, paintings, early edns and MSS relating to Erasmus and other Humanists of 16th century; library of 5,000 vols; Curator Dr ALEXANDER VANAUTGAERDEN; Deputy Curator KATHLEEN LEYS; publ. *Melissa 156* (6 a year).

Charleroi

Musee de la Photographie (Museum of Photography): ave Paul Pastur 11, 6032 Charleroi; tel. (71) 43-58-10; fax (71) 36-46-45; e-mail mpc.info@museephoto.be; internet www.museephoto.be; f. 1987; colln of 80,000 photographs and 3m. negatives; library of 13,000 vols; Dir XAVIER CANONNE; Curator MARC VAUSORT; Curator CHRISTELLE ROUSSEAU.

Musée des Beaux-Arts (Museum of Fine Arts): Place du Manège 1, 6000 Charleroi; tel. (71) 86-11-34; fax (71) 86-11-33; e-mail mba@charleroi.be; internet charleroi-museum.be/wps; works of Belgian artists, from 19th century to today, with links to region; sculptures, paintings, sketches various drawings and archival materials; permanent collns of Museum of Fine Arts.

Courtrai

Musee Paul Delvaux: ave Paul Delvaux laan 42, 8670 Koksijde (St-Idesbald); tel. (58) 52-12-29; fax (58) 51-09-08; e-mail info@delvauxmuseum.com; internet www.delvauxmuseum.com; f. 1982; colln of paintings, drawings, prints by artist and his personal belongings.

Ghent

Design Museum Gent: Jan Breydelstraat 5, 9000 Ghent; tel. (9) 267-99-99; fax (9) 224-45-22; e-mail museum.design@gent.be; internet www.designmuseumgent.be; f. 1903; colln and exhibition of 20th century art and actual design; 17th- and 18th-century furnishings; furniture, glass and ceramics by Alessandro Mendini, Ettore Sottsass, Michele de Lucchi, Massimo Iosa-Ghini, Michael Graves, Marco Zanini, Martine Bedin, Nathalie du Pasquier, Mateo Thun; digital photographic archive; Dir CAREL BEGEER; Curator INGER MOLLIN.

Het Huis Van Alijn (House Of Alijn): Kraanlei 65, 9000 Ghent; tel. (9) 269-23-50; fax (9) 269-23-58; e-mail info@huisvanalijn

.be; internet www.huisvanalijn.be; digital photograph album; sound-recordings and film excerpts; temporary exhibitions; Dir SYLVIE DHAENE.

Kunsthal Sint-Pietersabdij: Sint-Pieters-plein 9, 9000 Ghent; tel. (9) 243-97-30; fax (9) 243-97-34; e-mail drr.sintpietersabdij@gent .be; internet www.gent.be/spa; f. 1958; exhibits works by nat. and int. artists; Dir DOREEN GAUBLOMME (acting).

Museum voor Schone Kunsten (Ghent Museum of Fine Arts): Fernand Scribedreef 1, Citadelpark, 9000 Ghent; tel. (9) 240-07-00; fax (9) 240-07-90; e-mail museum.msk@ gent.be; internet www.mskgent.be; f. 1798; ancient and modern paintings, sculpture, tapestries, prints and drawings; Flemish art from Middle Ages to first half of 20th century; library; Dir ROBERT HOOZEE.

STAM—Stadsmuseum Gent: Godshuizen-laan 2, 9000 Ghent; tel. (9) 267-14-00; fax (9) 267-14-98; e-mail stam@gent.be; internet www.stamgent.be; illustrates history of Ghent; temporary exhibitions; Dir CHRISTINE DE WEERDT.

Stedelijk Museum voor Actuele Kunst (Museum of Contemporary Art): Citadelpark, 9000 Ghent; tel. (9) 240-76-01; fax (9) 221-71-09; e-mail info@smak.be; internet www.smak .be; f. 1975; drawings, etchings, paintings, sculpture; featured movements incl. arte povera, cobra, conceptualism, minimalism, pop art; colln provides an overview of devts in international art from 1945 to present; library of 40,000 vols, 195 periodicals; Dir PHILIPPE VAN CAUTEREN; Man. Dir PHILIPPE VANDENWEGHE; Curator THIBAUT VERHOEVEN; Curator THOMAS CARON.

Liège

Collections Artistiques de l'Université de Liège: place du 20 août 7, 4000 Liège; tel. (4) 366-56-07; fax (4) 366-58-54; e-mail wittert@ulg.ac.be; internet www.ulg.ac.be/ wittert; f. 1903; 30,000 prints and drawings, paintings of 15th and 16th century; modern Belgian paintings, 5,483 coins; colln of Zairian art and craft; works of African art, sculptures; photography colln; Dir Dr JEAN-PATRICK DUCHESNE; Sec. EMMANUELLE GROS-JEAN.

Grand Curtius Museum: quai de Maas-tricht 13, 4000 Liège; tel. (4) 221-68-00; fax (4) 221-68-08; e-mail infograndcurtius@liege .be; internet www.grandcurtius.be; f. 2009; 7,000 years of regional and int. arti-facts; 5,200 items displayed in chronological or thematic order; Dir NICOLE DARDING; Curator CONSTANTIN CHARIOT.

Attached Museums:

Musée Curtius: quai de Maastricht 13, 4000 Liège; tel. (4) 221-83-83; fax (4) 221-94-80; f. 1909; chief sections: prehistory, Romano-Belgian and Frankish, Liège coins, decorative arts (from the Middle Ages to 19th century); annexe: lapidary colln in Palais de Justice; HQ of Archaeo-logical Institute of Liège (q.v.).

Musée d'Ansembourg: Féronstrée 114, 4000 Liège; tel. (4) 221-94-02; f. 1905; collns of 18th-century decorative arts of Liège; reconstituted interiors.

Musée d'Armes: quai de Maestricht 13, 4000 Liege; tel. (4) 221-94-16; fax (4) 221-68-09; e-mail info@museedarms.be; internet www.museedarmes.be; f. 1883; books, specialized articles, archives, photo-graphs; military weapons, hunting and sporting arms, ethnic weapons, ranging from prehistory to present; colln of decor-ations and insignia of knighthood; colln of 600 commemorative medals for Revolution, Consulate and First French Empire; Cur-

ator PHILIPPE JORIS; publ. *Amis du Musée d'Armes de Liège* (4 a year).

Musée d'Art Religieux et d'Art Mosan (Museum of Religious Art and Mosan Museum of Art): rue Mère-Dieu, 4000 Liege; tel. (4) 221-42-25; sculptures from 11th century; plates, fabrics and paintings; works from Flemish school, French school, Brabant school and German school.

Musée du Verre: quai de Maastricht 13, 4000 Liège; tel. (4) 221-94-04; fax (4) 221-94-32; f. 1959; all main centres of produc-tion, from earliest times to present, are represented.

Musées d'Archéologie et d'Arts Déc-oratifs de Liège: Institut Archéologique Liégeois, 13 quai de Maastricht, 4000 Liege; tel. (4) 221-94-04; fax (4) 221-94-32; archaeological collns; Middle Paleolithic stone tools discovered at Spy, in 1885–1886.

Musée d'Art Moderne et d'Art Contem-porain de la Ville de Liege: parc de la Boverie 3, 4020 Liège; tel. (4) 343-04-03; fax (4) 344-19-07; e-mail mamac@skynet.be; internet www.mamac.be; f. 1981; modern paintings, sculptures and abstracts of Bel-gian School, French and foreign masters; collns of paintings and sculptures from 1850 to today; Curator FRANCINE DAWANS; Curator FRANÇOISE DUMONT; Curator FRANÇOISE SAFIN.

Musée de la Vie Wallonne (Museum of Walloon Life): cour des Mineurs 1, 4000 Liège; tel. (4) 237-90-50; fax (4) 237-90-89; e-mail info@viewallonne.be; internet www .viewallonne.be; f. 1913; varied colln covering south Belgium in fields of ethnography, folklore, arts and crafts and history; 450,000 documents; private and public arch-ives; library of 35,000 vols, video cassettes, CD-ROMs, 460 periodicals; Curator MARIE-CLAUDE THURION; publ. *Enquêtes* (1 a year).

Louvain

M-Museum Leuven: Vanderkelenstraat 28, 3000 Leuven; tel. (16) 27-29-29; e-mail m@ leuven.be; internet www.mleuven.be; f. 1823; art works of Leuven and Brabant from Middle Ages to 19th century; Pres. DENISE VANDEVOORT; Vice-Pres. ELS BUELENS; Gen. Dir LUC DELRUE; Chief Curator VERONIQUE VANDEKERCHOVE.

Louvain-la-Neuve

Musée de Louvain-La-Neuve: Place Blaise Pascal 1, 1348 Louvain-la-Neuve; tel. (10) 47-48-41; fax (10) 47-24-13; e-mail accueil-musee@uclouvain.be; internet www .muse.ucl.ac.be; f. 1979; attached to Univer-site Catholique de Louvain; permanent collns focus on 4 areas: ancient sculpture, African art, classical archaeology (primarily from Mainz) and colln of casts; Dir Prof. JOËL ROUCLOUX.

Mariemont

Musée Royal de Mariemont: chaussée de Mariemont 100, 7140 Mariemont (Morlan-welz); tel. (64) 21-21-93; fax (64) 26-29-24; e-mail info@musee-mariemont.be; internet www.musee-mariemont.be; f. 1975; antiqui-ties from Egypt, Greece, Rome, China, Japan; nat. archaeology; Tournai porcelain; bookbindings; library of 130,000 vols, 400 periodicals; Dir MARIE-CÉCILE BRUWIER; Man. Dir DANIEL COURBE; publ. *Les Cahiers de Mariemont* (1 a year).

Mechelen

Stedelijke Musea Mechelen: Minderbroe-dersgang 5, 2800 Mechelen; tel. (15) 29-40-30; fax (15) 29-40-31; e-mail stedelijkemusea@mechelen.be; internet www

.stedelijkemusea.mechelen.be; f. 1844; muni-cipal museum; history, art, applied art; Museum Schepenhuis; Hof van Busleyden; Museum in kinderhanden; closed for renova-tion until mid-2015; Head Curator ALEXAN-DRA PAUWELS.

Namur

Musée Archéologique de Namur: Halle al'Chair, rue de Pont 21, 5000 Namur; tel. (81) 23-16-31; e-mail jean-louis.antoine@ville .namur.be; f. 1855; archaeological collns: pre- and protohistoric, Roman and Merovingian; Head MARTINE GEORGE; Curator JEAN-LOUIS ANTOINE; Curator JACQUES TOUSSAINT.

Musée de Groesbeeck-de Croix: rue Joseph Saintraint 3, 5000 Namur; tel. (81) 24-87-20; fax (81) 24-87-29; e-mail museedecroix@ville.namur.be; furniture and art works of 18th century; paintings, sculp-tures, ceramics, silverware, glassware and crystal; decorative arts; Head MARTINE GEORGE; Curator JOSINE DE FRAIPONT; Cur-ator JACQUES TOUSSAINT.

Musée Félicien Rops: rue Fumal 12, 5000 Namur; tel. (81) 77-67-55; fax (81) 77-69-25; e-mail info@museerops.be; internet www .museerops.be; f. 1964; artist's etchings, drawings, paintings; temporary exhibitions.

Musée Provincial des Arts Anciens du Namurois: Hôtel de Gaiffier d'Hestroy, rue de Fer 24, 5000 Namur; tel. (81) 77-67-54; fax (81) 77-69-24; e-mail musee.arts.anciens@ province.namur.be; internet www .museedesartsanciens.be; f. 1964; colln of paintings by Henri Bles; Trésor d'Oignies; arts of Middle Ages and renaissance of Namur; library of 50,000 vols; Dir and Chief Curator JACQUES TOUSSAINT; publ. *Journal des Musées.*

Sint-Martins-Latem

Museum Dhondt-Dhaenens: Museumlaan 14, 9831 Sint-Martens-Latem (Deurle); tel. (9) 282-51-23; fax (9) 281-08-53; e-mail info@ museumdd.be; internet www.museumdd.be; f. 1968; works by James Ensor, Gust and Leon De Smet, Valerius De Saedeleer, Con-stant Permeke, Albert Servaes, Frits Van den Berghe, Gustave van de Woestyne and contemporary artists; Dir JOOST DECLERCQ; Curator TANGUY EECKHOUT.

Tournai

Musée d'Archéologie (Museum of Archae-ology): rue des Carmes 8, 7500 Tournai; tel. (69) 22-16-72; e-mail musee.archeologie@ tournai.be; internet www.tournai.be/ musee-archeologie; divided into 3 sections: Quaternary, Gallo-Roman and Merovingian; Curator MARIANNE DELCOURT.

Musée d'Armes et d'Histoire Militaire (Museum of Weapons and Military History): rue Roc Saint Nicaise 59–61, 7500 Tournai; tel. (69) 21-19-66; e-mail musee.armes@ tournai.be; internet www.tournai.be/ musee-armes; f. 1930; weapons, military and civilian artefacts; Curator CHARLES DELIGNE.

Musée de Folklore (Folklore Museum): Réduit des Sions 32–36, 7500 Tournai; tel. (69) 22-40-69; e-mail musee.folklore@tournai .be; internet www.tournai.be/musee-folklore; f. 1930; colln exhibits porcelain, tin, printing, medicine, traditions and calendar customs, men's and women's civilian and military clothing evolution; reproduction of a relief ground plan of Tournai in the 17th century made out for King Louis XIV; Curator NICOLE DEMARET.

Musée des Beaux-Arts (Museum of Fine Arts): Enclos Saint-Martin, 7500 Tournai; tel. (11) 33-24-31; e-mail musee.beaux-arts@ tournai.be; internet www.tournai.be/ musee-beaux-arts; f. 1928; architecture, ancient paintings, works of nat. and int. artists; Curator JEAN-PIERRE DE RYCKE.

Musée d'Histoire et des Arts Décoratifs (Museum of History and Decorative Arts): rue Saint-Martin 50, 7500 Tournai; tel. (69) 33-23-53; e-mail musee.histoire.arts .decoratifs@tournai.be; internet www .tournai.be/musee-arts-decoratifs; earthenware of 15th, 16th, 18th centuries; coins minted in Tournai between 12th and 17th centuries; silverware; Curator THOMAS BAYET.

Verviers

Musée d'Archéologie et de Folklore: rue des Raines 42, 4800 Verviers; tel. (87) 33-16-95; e-mail musees.verviers@skynet.be; internet www.lesmuseesenwallonie.be; f. 1959; history of art, archaeology, folklore, local history; Curator MARIE-PAULE DEBLANC.

Musée des Beaux-Arts et de la Céramique: rue Renier 17, 4800 Verviers; tel. (87) 33-16-95; e-mail musees.verviers@skynet.be; internet www.lesmuseesenwallonie.be; f. 1884; sculpture, Belgian paintings; European paintings from 14th to 19th century; ceramics of Europe and Asia; Chinese porcelain and Japanese, Saxony-Meissen, Delft pottery, sandstone Raeren; Dir MARIE-PAULE DEBLANC; publ. *Guide du Visiteur.*

Zulte

Roger Raveel Museum: Gildestraat 2–8, 9870 Zulte (Machelen); tel. (9) 381-60-00; fax (9) 381-60-08; e-mail rrm@ rogerraveelmuseum.be; internet www .rogerraveelmuseum.be; exhibition of works by artist.

Universities

HASSELT UNIVERSITEIT

Campus Diepenbeek Agoralaan, Gebouw D, 3590 Diepenbeek

Telephone: (11) 26-81-11
Fax: (11) 26-81-99
E-mail: info@uhasselt.be
Internet: www.uhasselt.be

Founded 1971, present status 2001
State control
Languages of instruction: Dutch, English
Rector: Prof. Dr LUC DE SCHEPPER
Vice-Rector for Research: PAUL JANSSEN
Vice-Rector for Education: ERNA NAUWE-LAERTS
Permanent Sec.: MARK SMEYERS
Librarian: MARC GOOVAERTS

Library of 70,000 vols
Number of teachers: 530
Number of students: 2,700

DEANS

Faculty of Applied Economics: PIET PAUWELS
Faculty of Law: GUNTER MAES
Faculty of Medicine: PIET STINISSEN
Faculty of Sciences: JEAN MANCA

HOGESCHOOL-UNIVERSITEIT BRUSSEL

Stormstraat 2, 1000 Brussels

Telephone: (2) 210-12-11
Fax: (2) 217-64-64
E-mail: info@hubrussel.be
Internet: www.hubrussel.be

Founded 1968 as Universitaire Faculteiten Sint-Aloysius, became Katholieke Universiteit Brussel 1991, merged with European Univ. College, VLEKHO and HONIM in 2007
Language of instruction: English

Private control
Academic year: October to July
Rector: Prof. Dr DIRK DE CEULAER

Library of 70,000 vols
Number of teachers: 1,000
Number of students: 9,000
Publications: *N9* (4 a year), *Tempo*

DEANS

Department of Economics and Management: G. RASPOET
Department of Germanic Philology: L. TEEUWEN
Department of History: E. DEFOORT
Department of Law: F. FLEERACKERS
Department of Philosophy: J. F. LINDEMANS
Department of Social and Political Sciences: J. DELWAIDE

PROFESSORS

ACX, R., Bank and Credit Sciences
BOUSSET, H., Dutch Literature
BRAEKMAN, W. L., English Literature
CARPENTIER, N.
DE BOECK, A.
DE CLERCQ, M., European Literature and Introduction to Modern Literature
DEFOORT, E., Modern French Texts
DEGADT, J., Economic Science and Social Statistics
DE LATHOUWER, L.
DELWAIDE, J.
DE MARTELAERE, P., Philosophic Anthropology
DEPREEUW, E.
DE SCHRYVER, J.
DESMET, J.
DE VIN, D., Dutch Literature
DEWINTER, L.
ELST, M.
FLEERACKERS, F.
FOBLETS, M.-C.
GEERAERTS, R.
GOOSSENS, W., Historic Introduction to Philosophy
GOTZEN, F., Introduction to Law
HEMMERECHTS, L.
HEYSSE, T.
JAKOBS, D.
JANSSENS, J., History of Medieval Dutch Literature
JANSSENS, P., Modern Times
LINDEMANS, J.-F., Traditional Logics
LOOSVELDT, G., Methods and Techniques of Social Sciences
MOONS, T., History of Antiquity
MUYLLE, J., Art and Cultural History
NELDE, P. H., Germanic Linguistics
OOSTERBOSCH, A., Physics
SCHOENMAECKERS, R.
SWYNGEDOUW, M.
TACQ, J., Sociology
VANDEN BROECKE, S.
VAN DEN WIJNGAERT, M., History of Modern Times
VANDEN WYNGAERD, G.
VAN DE WOESTYNE, I.
VANHEMELRYCK, F., History of Modern Times
VAN HOECKE, M., Introduction to Law
VERRETH, H.
VERSTRAELEN, L., Mathematics
VERTONGHEN, R., Accountancy
WINTGENS, L.

KATHOLIEKE UNIVERSITEIT LEUVEN
(Catholic University of Leuven)

Naamsestraat 22, 3000 Louvain (Leuven)
Telephone: (16) 32-40-10
Fax: (16) 32-40-14
E-mail: info@kuleuven.be
Internet: www.kuleuven.ac.be

Founded 1425, present status 1970

Languages of instruction: Dutch, English
Private control
Academic year: September to September
Rector: Prof. MARK WAER
Vice-Rector for Biomedical Sciences: Prof. MINNE CASTEELS
Vice-Rector for Educational Policy: Prof. LUDO MELIS
Vice-Rector for Humanities and Social Sciences: Prof. FILIP ABRAHAM
Vice-Rector for International Policy: Prof. BART DE MOOR
Vice-Rector for Kortrijk Campus: Prof. JAN BEIRLANT
Vice-Rector for Research Policy: Prof. PETER MARYNEN
Vice-Rector for Science, Engineering and Technology: Prof. KAREN MAEX
Vice-Rector for Student Affairs: Prof. TINE BAELMANS
Gen. Man. for Univ. Admin.: Prof. KOENRAAD DEBACKERE
Librarian: MEL COLLIER
Library: see Libraries and Archives
Number of teachers: 2,600
Number of students: 39,395
Publication: *Campuskrant* (10 a year)

DEANS

Faculty of Arts: Prof. LUK DRAYE
Faculty of Bioscience Engineering: Prof. Dr Ir POL COPPIN
Faculty of Business and Economics: Prof. Dr LUC SELS
Faculty of Canon Law: Prof. RIK TORFS
Faculty of Engineering: Prof. Ir LUDO FROYEN
Faculty of Kinesiology and Rehabilitation Science: Prof. RIK GOSSELINK
Faculty of Law: Prof. PAUL VAN ORSHOVEN
Faculty of Medicine: Prof. Dr BERNARD HIMPENS
Faculty of Pharmaceutical Sciences: Prof. A. VERBRUGGEN
Faculty of Psychology and Educational Sciences: Prof. Dr PATRICK ONGHENA
Faculty of Science: Prof. PETER LIEVENS
Faculty of Social Sciences: KATLIJN MALFLIET
Faculty of Theology: Prof. LIEVEN BOEVE
Institute of Philosophy: ANTOON VANDEVELDE

UNIVERSITÉ CATHOLIQUE DE LOUVAIN
(Catholic University of Louvain)

Place de l'Université 1, 1348 Louvain-la-Neuve

Telephone: (10) 47-21-11
Fax: (10) 47-29-99
E-mail: info-portail@uclouvain.be
Internet: www.uclouvain.be

Founded 1425, present status 1970
Private control
Language of instruction: French
Academic year: September to May
Rector: Prof. BRUNO DELVAUX
Vice-Rector for Health Sciences: Prof. PIERRE GIANELLO
Vice-Rector for Humanities: CAMILLE FOCANT
Vice-Rector for Human Resources Policy: Prof. JACQUES GRÉGOIRE
Vice-Rector for Student Affairs: DIDIER LAMBERT
Vice-Rector for Technology: Prof. PATRICK BERTRAND
Gen. Administrator: DOMINIQUE OPFERGELT
Librarian: CH.-H. NYNS
Library: see Libraries and Archives
Number of teachers: 1,260
Number of students: 21,000

Publication: *Bulletin des Amis de Louvain*

DEANS

Ecole Polytechnique de Louvain: Prof. F. DELANNAY

Faculty of Architecture, Architectural Engineering, Town Planning and Environmental Engineering: Prof. A. DE HERDE

Faculty of Arts and Letters: Prof. P.-A. DEPROOST

Faculty of Bio-engineering, Agronomy and Environment: Prof. J. MAHILLON

Faculty of Economic, Social and Political Sciences: Prof. CL. ROOSENS

Faculty of Law: Prof. B. DUBUISSON

Faculty of Medicine and Dentistry: Prof. A. GEUBEL

Faculty of Motor Sciences: Prof. T. ZINTZ

Faculty of Pharmacy and Biomedical Sciences: Prof. J. LECLERCQ

Faculty of Psychology and Educational Sciences: Prof. M. FRENAY

Faculty of Public Health: Prof. E. DARRAS

Faculty of Sciences (incl. veterinary medicine): Prof. J. GOVAERTS

Faculty of Theology: Prof. A. WÉNIN

Louvain School of Management: VÉRONIQUE SEMINERIO

UNIVERSITÉ DE LIÈGE
(University of Liège)

Place du 20-Août 7, 4000 Liège

Telephone: (4) 366-21-11

Fax: (4) 366-57-00

E-mail: international@ulg.ac.be

Internet: www.ulg.ac.be

Founded 1817, present status 1989

Language of instruction: French

Academic year: October to September

Rector: BERNARD RENTIER

Vice-Rector: ALBERT CORHAY

Vice-Rector for Evaluation and Quality: Prof. FREDDY COIGNOUL

Vice-Rector for Gembloux Agro-Bio Tech: Prof. ERIC HAUBRUGE

Vice-Rector for Int. Relations: Prof. JEAN MARCHAL

Vice-Rector for Research: Prof. PIERRE WOLPER

Gen. Administrator: FRANÇOIS RONDAY

Gen. Dir for Education and Training: MONIQUE MARCOURT-DEFRENE

Library: see Libraries and Archives

Number of teachers: 593

Number of students: 20,000

DEANS

Faculty of Applied Science: Prof. MICHEL HOGGE

Faculty of Law and Political Science—The Jean Constant Criminology School of Liege: Prof. OLIVIER CAPRASSE

Faculty of Medicine: Prof. GUSTAVE MOONEN

Faculty of Philosophy and Letters: Prof. JEAN-PIERRE BERTRAND

Faculty of Psychology and Education: Prof. SERGE BREDART

Faculty of Science: Prof. RUDI CLOOTS

Faculty of Veterinary Medicine: Prof. PIERRE LEKEUX

Gembloux Agro-Bio Tech: PHILIPPE LEPOIVRE

HEC-Management School—ULg: THOMAS FROEHLICHER

Institute for Human and Social Sciences: DIDIER VRANCKEN

PROFESSORS WITH CHAIRS

Faculty of Applied Sciences (chemin des Chevreuils, 1, B52/3 Sart Tilman, 4000 Liege):

BOIGELOT, B., Computer Science

CESCOTTO, S., Mechanics of Materials

CHARLIER, R., Geomechanics and Engineering Geology

CRINE, M., Chemical Engineering

DASSARGUES, A., Hydrogeology and Environmental Geology

DE MARNEFFE, P.-A., Computer Science

DELHEZ, E., General Mathematics

DESTINE, J., Microelectronics

DUYSINX, P., Land Vehicle Engineering

ESSERS, J. A., Aerodynamics

FLEURY, CL., Aerospatial Structures

GERMAIN, A., Industrial Chemistry

GOLINVAL, J.-C., Vibration and Structure Identification

GRIBOMONT, P., Computer Science and Artificial Intelligence

HOGGE, M., Thermomechanics

JASPART, J.-P., Structural Adequacy of Techno-economic Performance and Operation Requirements

LEDUC, G., Computer Networks

MARCHAL, J., Transport Systems and Shipbuilding

PIRARD, E., Mineral Geo-Resources and Geological Imaging

PIRARD, J. P., Applied Physical Chemistry

PONTHOT, J.-P., Non Linear Digital LTAS-Mechanics

SEPULCHRE, R., Systems and Modelling

VERLY, J., Signal and Image Processing

WEHENKEL, L., Systems and Modelling

WOLPER, P., Computer Science

Faculty of Law and Political Science—J. Constant School of Criminology (7 blvd du Rectorat, B 31, Sart Tilman, 4000 Liège):

BIQUET, C., Contract and Credit Law

CAPRASSE, O., Commercial Law

DE LEVAL, G., Civil Law

JACOBS, A., Criminal Law and Criminal Law Procedure

LECOCQ, P., Property and Evidentiary Law

LELEU, Y.-H., Family Law and Medical Law

PARENT, X., Tax Law

WAUTELET, P., Private International Law

Faculty of Medicine (ave de l'hôpital, 1, B 36 Sart Tilman, 4000 Liège):

ADELIN, A., Public Health Science

ANGENOT, L., Pharmacy

ANSSEAU, M., Psychiatry and Medical Psychology

BELAICHE, J., Hepato-gastroenterology

BONIVER, J., Anatomy and Pathological Cytology

BOURS, V., General and Human Genetics

CRIELAARD, J.-M., Physical Skills Evaluation and Conditioning

CROMMEN, J., Drug Analysis

D'ORIO, V., Emergency Medicine

DEFRAIGNE, J.-O., Cardiovascular and Thoracic Surgery

DEFRESNE, M.-P., Histology–Cytology

DE LEVAL, J., Urology

DE MOL, P., Medical Microbiology and Virology

FILLET, G., Haematology

FOIDART, J. M., Gynecology–Obstetrics

GRISAR, T., Human and Pathological Biochemistry and Physiology

HEINEN, E., Human Histology

LIMME, M., Orthodontics and Pedodontics

MALAISE, M., Rhumatology

MEURISSE, M., Abdominal Surgery

MOONEN, G., Normal and Pathological Physiology

PIERARD, L., Cardiology

PIROTTE, B., Pharmaceutical Chemistry

REGINSTER, J.-Y., Epidemiology and Public Health

ROMPEN, E., Bucco-dental Surgery and Periodontics

SCHEEN, A., Diabetology, Nutrition and Metabolic Disorders

SCHOENEN, J., Neuro-anatomy

Faculty of Philosophy and Letters (place du 20-Août, 7, A1 (Centre Ville), 4000 Liège):

ALLART, D., Art History and Archaeology of Modern Times

BAJOMEE, D., Contemporary French Literature

BALACE, F., Contemporary History

BERTRAND, J.-P., 19th and 20th Century French Literature

CURRERI, L., Italian Language and Literature

DELVILLE, M., Modern English and American Literature

DOR, J., Medieval English Language and Literature

DUCHESNE, J.-P., Art History and Contemporary Archaeology

DUMORTIER, J.-L., Romance Language Teacher Training: French, Spanish, Italian

DURAND, P., Cultural Institutions and Information

GIOVANNANGELI, D., History of Modern and Contemporary Philosophy

GOB, A., Museology

KLINKENBERG, J.-M., Rhetoric and Semiology

KUPPER, J. L., History of the Middle Ages and Historical Geography

LAFFINEUR, R., Art History and Archaeology of Classical Antiquity

OTTE, M., Prehistoric Archaeology

RAXHON, P., Historical Criticism

TUNCA, O., Modern English Philology

VROMANS, J., Modern Dutch Language and Synchronic Linguistics

WINAND, J., Egyptology

Faculty of Psychology and Education (5 blvd du Rectorat, B 32 Sart Tilman, 4000 Liège):

BECKERS, J., Professional Teacher Training

BORN, M., Psychology of Criminality and Psycho-Social Development

BREDART, S., Cognitive Psychology

HANSENNE, M., Personality and Individual Differences Psychology

LECLERCQ, D., Economy and Rural Development

LEROY, J.-F., Social Psychology of Groups and Organizations

MEULEMANS, T., Neuropsychology

TIRELLI, E., Behavioural Neuroscience and Experimental Psychopharmacology

Faculty of Science (allée de la Chimie, 5, B6 Sart Tilman, 4000 Liège):

ADELIN, A.

BASTIN, F., Analysis, Functional Analysis, Wavelets

BECKERS, J., Physical Oceanography

BOULVAIN, F., Sedimentary Petrology

BOUQUEGNEAU, J.-M., Oceanology

CLOOTS, R., Structural Inorganic Chemistry

CUGNON, J., Theoretical Physics

DE PAUW, E., Physical Chemistry, Mass Spectrometry

DEMOULIN, V., Algology, Mycology and Experimental Systematics

DOMMES, J., Plant Molecular Biology and Biotechnology

DONNAY, J.-P., Geographic Information Systems and Mapping

FRANSOLET, A. M., Mineralogy

GHOSEZ, P., Theoretical Material Physics

LECOMTE, P., Geometry and Algorithm Theory

LUXEN, A., Synthetic Organic Chemistry

MARTIAL, J., Molecular Biology and Genetic Engineering

MOTTE, P., Functional Genomics and Plant Molecular Imaging

PETIT, F.-F., Geomorphology, Hydrography

RENTIER, B., Basic Virology

SCHOUMAKER-MERENNE, B., Economic Geography

SURDEJ, J., Extragalactic Astrophysics and Space Observation

THOME, J.-P., Animal Ecology and Ecotoxicology

THONART, PH., Microbiology

VANDEWALLE, N., Statistical Physics

VANDEWALLE, P., Functional and Developmental Morphology

Faculty of Veterinary Medicine (20 blvd du Colonster, B 42 Sart Tilman 4000 Liège):
  BALLIGAND, M., Surgery and Surgical Clinical Practice in small animals
  CLERCX, C., Small animal Medical Pathology
  COIGNOUL, F., Pathological Anatomy and Autopsies
  DESMECHT, D., Special Pathology and Autopsies
  GEORGES, M., Animal Genomics
  GODEAU, J. M., Biochemistry
  GUSTIN, P., Pharmacology, Pharmacotherapeutics and Toxicology
  LEKEUX, P., Physiology
  LEROY, P., Information Science Applied to Animal Husbandry
  LOSSON, B., Parasitology and Pathology of Parasitic Diseases
  MAINIL, J., Bacteriology and Pathology of Bacterial Diseases
  SERTEYN, D., General Anesthesiology and Surgical Pathology in Larger Animals
  THIRY, E., Virology, Epidemiology, and Pathology of Viral Diseases
  VANDERPLASSCHEN, A., Immunology and Vaccinology

Gembloux Agro-Bio-Tech (passage des Déportés, 2, 5030 Gembloux; tel. (81) 62-21-11; fax (81) 61-45-44; e-mail gembloux@ulg.ac.be; internet www.fsagx.ac.be):
  BAUDOIN, J.-P., Agricultural Science
  BOCK, L., Environmental Science and Technology
  CLAUSTRIAUX, J.-J., Agricultural Science
  DEBOUCHE, C., Environmental Science and Technology
  DEROANNE, C., Chemistry and Bio-industries
  DESTAIN, M.-F., Environmental Science and Technology
  DU JARDIN, P., Agricultural Science
  HAUBRUGE, E., Agricultural Science
  LEBAILLY, P., Agricultural Science
  LEPOIVRE, P., Agricultural Science
  PAQUOT, M., Chemistry and Bio-Industries
  PORTETELLE, D., Chemistry and Bio-industries
  RONDEUX, J., Environmental Science and Technology
  THEWIS, A., Agricultural Science
  THONART, P., Chemistry and Bio-industries

HEC—ULg School of Management (rue Louvrex, 14, N1, 4000 Liège):
  BAIR, J., International Relations
  CHOFFRAY, J.-M., Computer Decision Support
  CORHAY, A., Accounting and Finance
  CORNET, A., Management of Human Resources and Organizations
  CRAMA, Y., Operational Research and Production Management
  DEFOURNY, J., Social Economy and Economic Systems
  FELD, S., Development Economics
  JURION, B., Political Economy
  PAHUD DE MORTANGES, C., General Marketing
  PICHAULT, F., Human Resource Management
  SURLEMONT, B., International Management–Entrepreneurship

Institute for Human and Social Sciences (blvd du Rectorat, 7, B31, Sart Tilman, 4000 Liège):
  PONCELET, M., Occupational Psychology
  VRANCKEN, D., Sociological Practice

**UNIVERSITÉ DE MONS-HAINAUT
(University of Mons-Hainaut)**

Place du Parc 20, 7000 Mons
Telephone: (65) 37-31-11
Fax: (65) 37-30-54
E-mail: martine.vanelslande@umh.ac.be
Internet: www.umh.ac.be
Founded 1965
Language of instruction: French
State control
Academic year: October to September
Rector: CALOGERO CONTI
Vice-Rector: BERNARD HARMEGNIES
Vice-Rector for Institutional and Regional Devt: GIUSEPPE PAGANO
Vice-Rector for Int. Relations: PIERRE DEHOMBREUX
Vice-Rector for Research: PHILIPPE DUBOIS
Administrator: DANY VINCE
Librarian: RENÉ PLISNIER
Library: see Libraries and Archives
Number of teachers: 250
Number of students: 5,000
Publications: *Elément*, *Polytech.News*, *UMH Dedicace* (4 a year)

DEANS

Faculty of Architecture and Town Planning: NICOLAS PERCSY
Faculty of Engineering: Prof. PAUL LYBAERT
Faculty of Medicine and Pharmacy: Prof. ROBERT N. MULLER
Faculty of Psychology and Education: Prof. AGNÈS VAN DAELE
Faculty of Sciences: Prof. CHRISTIAN MICHAUX
Faculty of Translation and Interpretation: Prof. ALAIN PIETTE
Institute for Language Sciences: BERNARD HARMEGNIES
Warocqué Faculty of Economics and Business Management: Prof. KARIN COMBLE

PROFESSORS

ALEXANDRE, H., Biology and Embryology
BELAYEW, A., Molecular Biology
BIEMONT, E., Astrophysics and Spectroscopy
BREDAS, J.-L., Chemistry of New Materials
BRIHAYE, Y., Theoretical Physics and Mathematics
BRUYÈRE, V., Theoretical Computer Science
BRUYNINCKX, H., Linguistics and Data Processing
CHERON, G., Electrophysiology
COMBLÉ-DARJA, K., Accountancy and Finance
COUVREUR, P., Applied Statistics
DANG, N. N., Probability and Statistics
DE CONINCK, J., Molecular Modelling
DEFRAITEUR, R., Fiscal System
DEPOVER, C., Moulding Technology
DESMET, H., Social and Community Psychology
DONNAY-RICHELLE, J., Clinical Psychology
DOSIERE, M., Physics and Chemistry of Polymers
DUBOIS, P., Polymeric and Composite Materials
DUFOUR, P., Computer Sciences
DUPONT, P., Methodology and Formation
ESCARMELLE, J.-F., Public Economy
FALMAGNE, P., Biological Chemistry
FINET, C., Mathematical Analysis
FORGES, G., Language Teaching
GILLIS, P., Experimental and Biological Physics
GOCZOL, J., Microeconomics and Marketing
GODAUX, E., Neurosciences
HARMEGNIES, B., Metrology in Psychology and Education
HECQ, M., Analytical and Inorganic Chemistry
HERQUET, P., Physics
ISAAC-VANDEPUTTE, M.-T., Historical Bibliography
JANGOUX, M., Marine Biology

LAUDE, L., Solid State Physics
LEBRUN-CARTON, C., Mathematics
LOWENTHAL, F., Cognitive Sciences
LUX, B., Company Management and Economics
MAGEROTTE, G., Education of the Handicapped
MAHY, B., Economic Analysis
MICHAUX, CH., Logic Mathematics
PAGANO, G., Public Finance and Management
PLATTEN, J., General Chemistry
POURTOIS, J.-P., Psychosociology of Family and School Education
RADOUX, C., Mathematics and Number Theory
RASMONT, P., Zoology
SAUSSEZ, S., Anatomy
SPILLEBOUDT-DETERCK, M., Finance
SPINDEL, P., Mechanics and Gravitation
STANDAERT, S., International Economic Analysis
TEGHEM-LORIS, J., Mathematics and Actuarial Science
THIRY, P., Management Information Science
TOUBEAU, G., Histology
TROESTLER, C., Numerical Analysis
VAN DAELE, A., Psychology of Labour
VAN HAVERBEKE, Y., Organic Chemistry
VANSNICK, J.-C., Quantitative Methods
VERHEVE, D., Chemical Technology
WAUTELET, H., Experimental Photonics
WIJSEN, J., Information Systems Science

**UNIVERSITÉ LIBRE DE BRUXELLES
(Free University of Brussels)**

Ave Franklin Roosevelt 50, 1050 Brussels
Telephone: (2) 650-21-11
Fax: (2) 650-36-30
E-mail: inscriptions@admin.ulb.ac.be
Internet: www.ulb.ac.be
Founded 1834, present status 1970
Language of instruction: French
Private control
Academic year: September to July
Rector: DIDIER VIVIERS
Pres.: JEAN-LOUIS VANHERWEGHEM
Vice-Pres.: FABRIZIO BUCELLA
Sec.: MONIQUE TAVERNIER
Librarian: Prof. JEAN-PIERRE DEVROEY
Library: see Libraries and Archives
Number of teachers: 755
Number of students: 24,000
Publication: *Esprit Libre* (4 a year)

DEANS

Faculty of Applied Sciences/Ecole polytechnique: JEAN-CLAUDE MAUN
Faculty of Law and Criminology: ANNEMIE SCHAUS
Faculty of Medicine: SYLVAIN MEURIS
Faculty of Motor Sciences: NATHALIE GUISSARD
Faculty of Pharmacy: JEAN- MICHEL KAUFFMANN
Faculty of Philosophy and Letters: DIDIER VIVIERS
Faculty of Psychology and Education: ALAIN CONTENT
Faculty of Science: MARTINE LABBE
Faculty of Social and Political Sciences: JEAN-MICHEL DE WAELE
Institute of European Studies: MARIANNE DONY
School of Public Health: ALAIN LEVEQUE
Solvay Business School Faculty of Economics and Management: MATHIAS DEWATRIPONT

**UNIVERSITEIT ANTWERPEN
(University of Antwerp)**

Prinsstraat 13, 2000 Antwerp
Telephone: (3) 265-41-11
Fax: (3) 265-44-20

E-mail: info@ua.ac.be
Internet: www.ua.ac.be

Founded 2003 by merger of Universitaire Centrum Antwerpen, Universitaire Faculteiten Sint-Ignatius Antwerpen and Universitaire Insteling Antwerpen

State control
Languages of instruction: Dutch, English
Academic year: September to July

Rector: Prof. Dr ALAIN VERSCHOREN
Pres.: Prof. Dr ANDRE VAN POECH
Chair of Education Council: Prof. Dr JOKE DENEKENS
Chair of Research Council: Prof. Dr JEAN PIERRE TIMMERMANS
Chair of Services Council: Prof. Dr JOHAN MEEUSEN
Man.: Prof. Dr BART HEIJNEN
Librarian: TRUDI NOORDERMEER

Library: see under Libraries and Archives
Number of teachers: 989
Number of students: 13,032

Publications: *Bijdragen tot de Geschiedenis, CSB-Berichten, Economische Didaktiek, Gezelliana, Kroniek van de Gezellestudie, Het Teken van de Ram, In de Steigers, Miscellanea Neerlandica*

DEANS

Faculty of Applied Economics: Prof. Dr KAREL SOUDAN
Faculty of Arts and Philosophy: Prof. Dr BRUNO TRITSMANS
Faculty of Law: Prof. Dr GERT STRAETMANS
Faculty of Medicine: Prof. Dr PAUL VAN DE HEYNING
Faculty of Pharmaceutical, Biomedical and Veterinary Sciences: Prof. Dr FRANS VAN MEIR
Faculty of Political and Social Sciences: Prof. Dr RIA JANVIER
Faculty of Science: Prof. Dr HERWIG LEIRS

UNIVERSITEIT GENT
(Ghent University)

Sint-Pietersnieuwstraat 25, 9000 Ghent
Telephone: (9) 264-31-11
Fax: (9) 264-82-93
E-mail: communicatie@ugent.be
Internet: www.ugent.be

Founded 1817
Language of instruction: Dutch
State control
Academic year: October to July

Rector: Prof. PAUL VAN CAUWENBERGE
Vice-Rector: Prof. LUC MOENS
Govt Commr: YANNICK DE CLERCQ
Chief Academic Admin.: Prof. KOEN GOETHALS
Chief Logistics Administrator: DIRK MANGELEER
Sec. of Board of Govs: DIRK VAN HAELTER

Library: see Libraries and Archives
Number of teachers: 962
Number of students: 32,000

Publication: *Universiteit Gent* (8 a year)

DEANS

Faculty of Arts and Philosophy: FREDDY MORTIER
Faculty of Bioscience Engineering: GUIDO VAN HUYLENBROECK
Faculty of Economics and Business Administration: MARC DE CLERCQ
Faculty of Engineering: LUC TAERWE
Faculty of Law: PIET TAELMAN
Faculty of Medicine and Health Sciences: ERIC MORTIER
Faculty of Pharmaceutical Sciences: STEFAAN DE SMEDT
Faculty of Political and Social Sciences: HERWIG REYNAERT

Faculty of Psychology and Educational Sciences: GEERT DE SOETE
Faculty of Sciences: HERWIG DEJONGHE
Faculty of Veterinary Sciences: HUBERT DE BRABANDER

PROFESSORS

Faculty of Arts and Philosophy (Blandijnberg 2, 9000 Ghent; tel. (9) 264-39-32; fax (9) 264-41-95):

ART, J., Modern History
BOURGEOIS, J., Archaeology and Ancient History of Europe
COMMERS, M., Philosophy and Moral Sciences
DECREUS, F., Latin and Greek
DETREZ, R., Slavonic and East-European Studies
DEVOS, I., Early Modern History
DEVOS, M., Dutch Linguistics
KABUTA, N., African Languages and Cultures
LAUREYS, G., Nordic Studies
LEMAN, M., Art, Music and Theatre Sciences
MOERLOOSE, E., Languages and Cultures of South and East Asia
PINXTEN, H., Comparative Sciences of Culture
ROEGIEST, E., Language and Communication
SLEMBROUCK, S., English
TANRET, M., Languages and Cultures of the Near East and North Africa
THOEN, E., Medieval History
VERHULST, S., Romance Languages (Other than French)
VERVAECK, B., Dutch Literature
WILLEMS, D., French
WILLEMS, K., German

Faculty of Bioscience Engineering (Coupure Links 653, 9000 Ghent; tel. (9) 264-59-01; fax (9) 264-62-45):

DEVLIEGHERE, F., Food Safety and Food Quality
JANSSEN, C., Applied Ecology and Environmental Biology
OTTOY, J., Applied Mathematics, Biometrics and Process Control
PIETERS, J., Biosystems Engineering
REHEUL, D., Plant Production
SORGELOOS, P., Animal Production
STEURBAUT, W., Crop Protection
VAN MEIRVENNE, M., Soil Management
VAN OOSTVELDT, P., Molecular Biotechnology
VERHÉ, R., Organic Chemistry
VERHEYEN, K., Forest and Water Management
VERLOO, M., Applied Analytical and Physical Chemistry
VERSTRAETE, W., Biochemical and Microbial Technology
VIAENE, J., Agricultural Economics

Faculty of Economics and Business Administration (Hoveniersberg 24, 9000 Ghent; tel. (9) 264-34-61; fax (9) 264-35-92):

DE BEELDE, I., Accountancy and Corporate Finance
DE CLERCQ, M., General Economics
HEENE, A., Management, Innovation and Entrepreneurship
OMEY, E., Social Economics
VANDER VENNET, R., Financial Economics
VANHOUCKE, M., Management Information Science and Operation Management
VAN KENHOVE, P., Marketing

Faculty of Engineering (Jozef Plateaustraat 22, 9000 Ghent; tel. (9) 264-79-50; fax (9) 264-95-99):

BRUNEEL, H., Telecommunications and Information Processing
DE BAETS, P., Mechanical Construction and Production

DEGRIECK, J., Materials Science and Engineering
DE ROUCK, J., Civil Engineering
DE ZUTTER, D., Information Technology
KIEKENS, P., Textiles
LEYS, C., Applied Physics
MARIN, G., Chemical Engineering and Technical Chemistry
MELKEBEEK, J., Electrical Energy, Systems and Automation
SIERENS, R., Flow, Heat and Combustion Mechanics
TAERWE, L., Structural Engineering
VAN CAMPENHOUT, J., Electronics and Information Systems
VAN KEER, R., Mathematical Analysis
VAN LANDEGHEM, H., Industrial Management
VERSCHAFFEL, B., Architecture and Urban Planning

Faculty of Law (Universiteitstraat 4, 9000 Ghent; tel. (9) 264-67-62; fax (9) 264-69-99):

BOCKEN, H., Civil Law
BOUCKAERT, B., Legal Theory and Legal History
ERAUW, J., Procedural Law, Arbitration and Private International Law
HUMBLET, P., Labour Law and Social Security Law
MARESCEAU, M., European Institute
SOMERS, E., International Public Law
VAN ACKER, C., Business Law
VAN CROMBRUGGE, S., Tax Law
VENY, L., Public law
VERMEULEN, G., Penal Law and Criminology

Faculty of Medicine and Health Sciences (Campus Heymans, De Pintelaan 185, 9000 Ghent; tel. (9) 332-41-90; fax (9) 332-49-90):

CAMBIER, D., Physical Therapy and Motor Rehabilitation
DE BACKER, G., Public Health
DE CLERCQ, D., Movement and Sports Sciences
DE HEMPTINNE, B., Surgery
DE MAESENEER, J., General Practice and Primary Health Care
DE PAUW, G., Dentistry
DE VOS, M., Internal Medicine
DE WAGTER, C., Radiotherapy and Nuclear Medicine
KESTELYN, P., Opthalmology
LAMBERT, J., Dermatology
LEFEBVRE, R., Pharmacology
MATTHYS, D., Pediatrics and Medical Genetics
MORTIER, E., Anaesthesiology
PIETTE, M., Forensic Medicine
PLUM, J., Clinical Chemistry, Microbiology and Immunology
TEMMERMAN, M., Uro-Gynaecology
THIERENS, H., Basic Medical Sciences
VAN CAUWENBERGE, P., Oto-Rhino-Laryngology
VANDEKERCKHOVE, J., Biochemistry
VAN HEERINGEN, C., Psychiatry and Medical Psychology
VERDONK, R., Physical Medicine and Orthopaedic Surgery
VERSTRAETE, K., Radiology

Faculty of Pharmaceutical Sciences (Campus Heymans, Harelbekestraat 72, 9000 Ghent; tel. (9) 264-80-40; fax (9) 264-81-94):

NELIS, H., Pharmaceutical Analysis
REMON, J., Pharmaceutics
VAN PETEGHEM, C., Bio-Analysis

Faculty of Political and Social Sciences (Universiteitstraat 8, 9000 Ghent; tel. (9) 264-67-80; fax (9) 264-69-86):

BILTEREYST, D., Communication Studies
BRACKE, P., Sociology
COOLSAET, H., Political Science
WALRAET, A., Third World Studies

Faculty of Psychology and Educational Sciences (Henri Dunantlaan 2, 9000 Ghent; tel. (9) 264-63-41; fax (9) 264-64-98):

BROECKAERT, E., Special Education
CLAES, R., Personnel Management, Work and Organizational Psychology
CROMBEZ, G., Experimental Clinical and Health Psychology
DE BIE, M., Social Welfare Studies
DE CORTE, W., Data-Analysis
HARTSUIKER, R., Experimental Psychology
MERVIELDE, I., Developmental, Personality and Social Psychology
SPOELDERS, M., Pedagogy
VALCKE, M., Educational Studies
VERHAEGHE, P., Psychoanalysis and Clinical Consulting

Faculty of Sciences (K. L. Ledeganckstraat 35, 9000 Ghent; tel. (9) 264-50-42; fax (9) 264-53-40):

CLAUWS, P., Solid State Sciences
DE CLERCK, F., Pure Mathematics and Computer Algebra
DE CLERCQ, P., Organic Chemistry
DE MAEYER, P., Geography
DEPICKER, A., Plant Biotechnology and Genetics
DE VOS, P., Biochemistry and Microbiology
HOSTE, S., Inorganic and Physical Chemistry
HUYSSEUNE, A., Biology
JACOBS, P., Geology and Soil Science
RYCKBOSCH, D., Subatomic and Radiation Physics
SARLET, W., Mathematical Physics and Astronomy
STRIJCKMANS, K., Analytical Chemistry
VANDEN BERGHE, G., Applied Mathematics and Computer Science
VAN DER STRAETEN, D., Physiology
VAN ROY, F., Biomedical Molecular Biology

Faculty of Veterinary Sciences (Salisburylaan 133, 9820 Merelbeke; tel. (9) 264-75-03; fax (9) 264-77-99):

DE BACKER, P., Pharmacology, Toxicology and Biochemistry
DE BRABANDER, H., Veterinary Public Health and Food Safety
DE KRUIF, A., Obstetrics, Reproduction and Herd Health
DEPREZ, P., Internal Medicine and Clinical Biology of Large Animals
DUCHATEAU, L., Physiology and Biometry
GASTHUYS, F., Surgery and Anaesthesiology of Domestic Animals
HAESEBROUCK, F., Pathology, Bacteriology and Poultry Diseases
SIMOENS, P., Morphology
VAN BREE, H., Veterinary Medical Imaging and Small Animal Orthopaedics
VAN HAM, L., Medicine and Clinical Biology of Small Animals
VAN ZEVEREN, A., Animal Nutrition, Genetics, Breeding and Ethology
VERCRUYSSE, J., Virology, Parasitology and Immunology

VRIJE UNIVERSITEIT BRUSSEL
(Free University of Brussels)

Pleinlaan 2, 1050 Brussels
Telephone: (2) 629-21-11
Fax: (2) 629-22-82
E-mail: info@vub.ac.be
Internet: www.vub.ac.be

Founded 1834, present status 1970
Languages of instruction: Dutch, English
Private control
Academic year: October to July

Chair.: E. VAN GELDER
Rector: Prof. PAUL DE KNOP
Vice-Rector for Education: Prof. Y. MICHOTTE
Vice-Rector for Research: Prof. L. WYNS

Vice-Rector for Student Policy: Prof. H. CASMAN
Gen. Dir: J. VAN LEEMPUT
Librarian: PATRICK VANOUPLINES
Number of teachers: 1,883
Number of students: 10,198

Publications: *Akademos*, *Nieuw Tijdschrift van de VUB*, *VUB-Press*

DEANS

Department of Teacher Training: NINI VRIJENS
Faculty of Arts and Philosophy: Prof. Dr. PIET VAN DE CRAEN
Faculty of Economic, Political and Social Sciences and Solvay Business School: Prof. Dr JOËL BRANSON
Faculty of Engineering: Prof. Dr JACQUES DE RUYCK
Faculty of Law and Criminology: Prof. Dr G. VAN LIMBERGHEN
Faculty of Medicine and Pharmacy: Prof. A. DUPONT
Faculty of Physical Education and Physiotherapy: Prof. Dr PETER VAN ROY
Faculty of Psychology and Educational Sciences: Prof. Dr ELIAS WILLEM
Faculty of Science and Bio-engineering Sciences: PATRICIA PROVÉ

Institutions with University Status

FACULTÉ POLYTECHNIQUE DE MONS

Rue de Houdain 9, 7000 Mons
Telephone: (65) 37-40-30
Fax: (65) 37-40-34
E-mail: info.polytech@umons.ac.be
Internet: portail.umons.ac.be/fr/universite/facultes/fpms/pages/default.aspx

Founded 1837, present name 1935
State control; attached to Univ. of Mons
Academic year: September to June

Rector: Prof. CALOGERO CONTI
Dean: PAUL LYBAERT
Dept Dir: CHRISTINE MARTENS

Library: see under Libraries and Archives
Number of teachers: 70
Number of students: 1,000

Publications: *Bulletin de l'AIMS* (12 a year), *Mons Mines* (4 a year), *PolyTech News* (4 a year)

PROFESSORS

ANCIA, PH., Mining Engineering
BLONDEL, M., Electromagnetism and Telecommunications
BOUCHER, S., Theoretical Mechanics
BOUQUEGNEAU, C., General Physics
BROCHE, C., Electrotechnics
CONTI, C., Theoretical Mechanics
COUSSEMENT, G., Fluid Mechanics, Applied Mechanics
CRAPPE, R., Microelectronics
DE HAAN, A., General Chemistry, Electrochemistry
DE MEYER, M., Applied Chemistry and Biochemistry
DEHOMBREUX, P., Mechanical Engineering
DELHAYE, M., Electrotechnology
DELVOSALLE, C., Chemical and Biochemical Engineering
DUMORTIER, C., Metallurgy
DUPUIS, C., Geology
DURAND, Y., Mechanical Engineering
DUTOIT, T., Signals Processing
FILIPPI, E., Mechanical Engineering
FORTEMPS, P., Mathematics, Operational Research

FRÈRE, M., Thermodynamics
GUERLEMENT, G., Strength of Materials, Stability of Buildings
HANCQ, J., Signal Processing
HANTON, J., Fluid Mechanics, Applied Mechanics
LAMBLIN, D., Strength of Materials, Stability of Buildings
LAMQUIN, M., Electromagnetism and Telecommunications
LIBERT, G., Computer Science
LIÉNARD, PH., Metallurgy
LOBRY, J., Transport and Distribution of High-Voltage Electricity
LYBAERT, P., Heat Transfer
MACQ, D., Electronics
MANNEBACK, P., Computer Science
MEGRET, P., Electromagnetism and Telecommunications
MOINY, F., General Physics
PILATTE, A., Thermodynamics
PIRLOT, M., Mathematics, Operational Research
QUINIF, Y., Geology
REMY, M., Automation
RENGLET, M., Electronics
RENOTTE, CH., Automation
RIQUIER, Y., Metallurgy
SAUCEZ, PH., Mathematics, Operational Research
TEGHEM, J., Mathematics, Operational Research
TRÉCAT, J., Transport and Distribution of High-Voltage Electricity
TSHIBANGU, J. P., Mining Engineering
TUYTTENS, D., Mathematics, Operational Research
VANDER WOUWER, A., Automation
VANKERKEM, M., Business Administration
VERLINDEN, O., Theoretical Mechanics
WILQUIN, H., Architecture

FACULTÉ UNIVERSITAIRE DE THÉOLOGIE PROTESTANTE DE BRUXELLES/UNIVERSITAIRE FACULTEIT VOOR PROTESTANTSE GODGELEERDHEID TE BRUSSEL (Faculty of Protestant Theology)

Rue des Bollandistes 40, 1040 Brussels
Telephone: (2) 735-67-46
Fax: (2) 735-47-31
E-mail: info@protestafac.ac.be
Internet: www.protestafac.ac.be

Founded 1950
Private control (United Protestant Church)
Languages of instruction: French, Dutch

Head of Admin.: ANNE JOUÉ
Chair. of Admin. Board: PETER TOMSON
Dean of Dutch-speaking Section: Prof. PETER TOMSON
Dean of French-speaking Section: B. HORT
Sec.: DOMINIQUE DESCAMPS
Librarian: ELIANE EVRARD-GRCE

Library of 46,257 vols, 130 periodicals
Number of teachers: 20
Number of students: 110

Publications: *Analecta Bruxellensia* (1 a year), *Belgische Protestantse Biografieën/Biographies Protestantes Belges* (4 a year), *FACtualité/FACtualiteit* (4 a year), *Programme et Horaire des Cours/Studiegids* (1 a year)

PROFESSORS

Dutch-speaking Section:

DE LANGE, J., Practical Theology
REIJNEN, A. M., Ethics
SMELIK, K., Old Testament Studies, Hebrew
TOMSON, P., New Testament Studies, Greek
WIERSMA, J., Dogmatics, Philosophy

WILLEMS, W., Church History, History of Dogma and 16th-century History

French-speaking Section:

HORT, B., Dogmatics, History of Philosophy and Religious Philosophy

MUTOMBO, F., Old Testament Studies and Hebrew

REIJNEN, A. M., Church History, Ethics

ROUVIÈRE, C., Practical Theology

VAN MOERE, R., New Testament Studies

WILLEMS, W., Church History and Methodology

FACULTÉS UNIVERSITAIRES CATHOLIQUES DE MONS

Chaussée de Binche 151, 7000 Mons

Telephone: (65) 32-32-11
Fax: (65) 31-56-91
E-mail: international@fucam.ac.be
Internet: www.fucam.ac.be

Founded 1896 as Institut Supérieur Commercial et Consulaire, univ. status 1965
Private control
Language of instruction: French
Academic year: October to September

Rector: BART JOURQUIN
Vice-Rector: DOMINIQUE HELBOIS

Library of 28,000 vols, 9700 periodicals
Number of teachers: 120
Number of students: 1,200

FACULTÉS UNIVERSITAIRES NOTRE-DAME DE LA PAIX

Rue de Bruxelles 61, 5000 Namur

Telephone: (81) 72-41-11
Fax: (81) 23-03-91
E-mail: info.etudes@fundp.ac.be
Internet: www.fundp.ac.be

Founded 1831
Language of instruction: French
Academic year: September to June

Rector: YVES POULLET
Vice-Rector: PHILIPPE LAMBIN
Gen. Man.: PAUL REDING
Chief Librarian: J. M. ANDRÉ

Library: see under Libraries and Archives
Number of teachers: 210
Number of students: 4,900

DEANS

Faculty of Arts: X. HERMAND
Faculty of Computer Science: J.-M. JACQUET
Faculty of Economics, Social Sciences and Management: A. DE CROMBRUGGHE
Faculty of Law: E. MONTERO
Faculty of Medicine: M. HERIN
Faculty of Sciences: R. SPORKEN

PROFESSORS

Faculty of Arts (rue J. Grafé 1, 5000 Namur; tel. (81) 72-42-07; fax (81) 72-42-03; e-mail dolores.bouchat@fundp.ac.be; internet www.fundp.ac.be/philo_lettres):

ALLARD, A., Classical Philology

BOSSE, A., German and Comparative Literature

BRACKELAIRE, J.-L., Psychology

BURNEZ, L., Prehistoric Art, Archaeology

DELABASTITA, D., English, General and Comparative Literature

DE RUYT, C., History of Ancient Art, Archaeology

DOYEN, A.-M., Greek Language and Literature

GANTY, E., Modern Philosophy

GIOT, J., French Linguistics

HANTSON, A., English Language, Linguistics

LEGROS, G., Romance Philology, Theory of Literature

LEIJNSE, E., Dutch, General and Comparative Literature

LENOIR, Y., History of Music

MARCHETTI, P., Classical Philology, Antiquity and Latin Authors

MORENO, P., Italian Language

NOËL, R., Medieval History

PETERS, M., German Language, Linguistics

PHILIPPART, G., Medieval History

RIZZERIO, L., Ancient Philosophy

SAUVAGE, P., History of the 19th and 20th Centuries

SELDESLACHTS, H., Latin Language, Greek and Latin Linguistics

VANDEN BEMDEN, Y., History of Post-Classical Art, Archaeology

VAN DEN BERGHE, K., Spanish Language

WEISSHAUPT, J., Dutch Language, Linguistics

WYNANTS, P., History of Belgian Institutions

Faculty of Computer Science (rue Grandgagnage 21, 5000 Namur; tel. (81) 72-49-66; fax (81) 72-49-67; e-mail doyen@info.fundp.ac.be; internet www.info.fundp.ac.be):

BERLEUR, J., Informatics and Sciences, Informatics and Rationality (Epistemological questions), Informatics and Society

BODART, F., Information Systems Design, Decision Support System, User/Machine Interface Engineering

BONAVENTURE, O., Computer Architecture, Computer Networks

FICHEFET, J., Graph Theory, Linear Programming, Numerical Analysis, Operations Research, Multicriteria Decision Aid, Management

HABRA, N., Software Engineering, Software Development

HAINAUT, J. L., Database Technology, Database Design, Database Engineering

JACQUET, J.-M., Programming Methodology, Programming Projects, Artificial Intelligence Techniques, Theory of Programming Languages

LE CHARLIER, B., Programming Methodology, Theory of Programming Languages, Abstract Interpretation

LECLERCQ, J.-P., Scientific Methods and Applications, Graph Theory

LESUISSE, R., Organization Design, Strategic Management and Information Systems, Organization Theory

LOBET-MARIS, C., Organization Theories, Psychological Aspects of Information Systems, Communication

NOIRHOMME-FRAITURE, M., Stochastic Processes, Simulation of Systems, Data Mining and Database Analysis, Performance Models and Evaluation

RAMAEKERS, J., Operating Systems, Performance and Measurement of Computer Systems, Computer System Reliability and Security

SCHOBBENS, P.-Y., Artificial Intelligence Techniques, Automatic Testing and Program Testing, Artificial Intelligence in DSSs, Language Theory

Faculty of Economics, Social Sciences and Management (rue de Bruxelles 61, 5000 Namur; tel. (81) 72-48-55; fax (81) 72-48-40; e-mail veronique.gilson@fundp.ac.be; internet www.fundp.ac.be/eco/eco.html):

BALAND, J.-M., Development Economics

BERTELS, K., Information Management

BODART, F., Management Information Systems

BRACKELAIRE, J. L., Psychology

CHEFFERT, J. M., Micro-economics

COLSON, B., Political Sociology and Comparative History of Institutions

DE COMBBRUGGHE DE PICQUENDAELE, A., International Trade Project Evaluation

DESCHAMPS, R., Macro-economics

GLEJSER, H., Econometrics, International and Interregional Economics

GREGOIRE, P., Corporate Finance and Portfolio Management

HOTTE, L., Industrial Economics, Development Economics

JACQUEMIN, J.-C., International Trade, Methods of Economic Investigation

JACQUES, J.-M., Business Policy, International Strategy

JAUMOTTE, CH., Political Economy, Regional and Sectoral Economic Analysis

LEGRAND, M., Epistemology, Philosophical Anthropology

LESUISSE, R., Computer Science

LOUVEAUX, F., Mathematical Statistics, Mathematical Programming, Operations Research

MANIQUET, F., Micro-economics

MIGNOLET, M., Fiscal Policy and Business Strategies, Macro-economics

NIZET, J., Sociology

PLATTEAU, J.-PH., Economic Development, Institutional Economics

PLATTEN, I., Finance and Financial Modelling

REDING, P., Money and Banking, Monetary Theory and Policy, International Monetary Economics

RIGAUX, N., Sociology

SCHEPENS, G., Operations Management, Management Information Systems

VALOGNES, F., Advanced Mathematics

VAN WYMEERSCH, C., Managerial Finance, Business Forecasting, Accounting

VAN YPERSELE, T., Public Economics, Regional Economics

WALLEMACQ, A., Human Resources Management

WUIDAR, J., Mathematics

WYNANTS, B., Introduction to Sociology

WYNANTS, P., History

Faculty of Law (Rempart de la Vierge 5, 5000 Namur; tel. (81) 72-47-94; fax (81) 72-52-00; e-mail secretariat.droit@fundp.ac.be):

COIPEL, N., Methodology and Legal Sources

COIPEL, M., Commercial Law

DIJON, X., Natural Law

DUPLAT, J.-L., Fiscal Law

FIERENS, J., Legal Methodology and Human Rights

KIGANAHÉ, Criminal Law

POULLET, Y., Roman Law

ROBAYE, R., History of Private Law

THIRY, PH., General Theory of Knowledge and Philosophy

THUNIS, X., Comparative Law and Law of Obligation

VUYE, H., Constitutional Law, Dutch Legal Terminology

WÉRY, P., General Principles of Private Law

Faculty of Medicine (rue de Bruxelles 61, 5000 Namur; tel. (81) 72-43-47; fax (81) 72-43-27; e-mail administration-medecine@fundp.ac.be; internet www.fundp.ac.be/medecine):

BOSLY, A., Immunology

DONCKIER, J., Endocrinology

DULIEU, J., Human Anatomy

FLAMION, B., Physiology, Pharmacology

GOFFINET, A., Special Physiology

HÉRIN, M., Histology, Embryology

JADOT, M., Human Biochemistry, General Biochemistry

LALOUX, P., Physiopathology

MARCHANOL, E., Human Physiology

MERCIER, M., Psychology and Medical Psychology

PIRONT, A., General Physiology

POUMAY, Y., General Histology

TRIGAUX, J. P., Radiological Anatomy

VANDERPAS, J., Epidemiology

ZECH, F., Microbiology

Faculty of Sciences (rue de Bruxelles 61, 5000 Namur; tel. (81) 72-54-35; fax (81) 72-53-06; e-mail decanat-sciences@fundp.ac.be; internet www.fundp.ac.be/sciences):

ANDRÉ, J.-M., Quantum Chemistry, Physical Chemistry

BLANQUET, GH., Molecular Infrared Spectroscopy and General Physics

B'NAGY, J., General Chemistry, Spectroscopy

BODART, F., Experimental Physics, Atomic and Nuclear Physics

CALLIER, F., Differential and Integral Calculus, Graph Theory

DE BOLLE, X., Statistics, Biostatistics, Bioinformatics

DELHALLE, J., General Chemistry

DEMORTIER, G., X-ray Physics, General Physics and Nuclear Physics

DEPIEREUX, E., Statistics, Biostatistics, Bioinformatics

DESCY, J.-P., Ecology

DEVOS, P., Endocrinology and Zoology

DUCHENE, J., Philosophy of Science

DURANT, F., Radiocrystallography and General Chemistry

EVRARD, G., Radiocrystallography

GIFFROY, J.-M., Anatomy, Embryology and Ethology of Animals

HALLET, V., Mineralogy, Geology

HARDY, A., Mathematics and Statistics

HENRARD, J., Mathematics, Celestial Mechanics, Astronomy

HEVESI, L., Organic Chemistry

HOUSSIAU, L., Experimental Physics, Thermodynamics

KESTEMONT, P., Ecology

KRIEF, A., Organic Chemistry

LAMBERT, D., Philosophy of Science

LAMBERTS, L., Analytical Chemistry

LAMBIN, P., Analytical Mechanics, Theoretical Physics

LETESSON, J. J., Microbiology, Immunology

LUCAS, A., Theoretical Solid State Physics and Quantum Physics

MAES, A., Mathematics, Differential and Integral Calculus

MASEREEL, B., Pharmaceutical Sciences, Biochemistry and Cytology

MEKHALIF, Z., General Chemistry, Physical Chemistry, Polymers

MESSIAEN, J., General Biology, Vegetal Physiology

MICHA, J.-CL., Ecology

NGUYEN, V. H., Differential and Integral Calculus, Optimization and Applied Mathematics

ORBAN-FERAUGE, F., Geography, Cartography

PAQUAY, R., Animal Physiology

PIREAUX, J.-J., Experimental Physics, Atomic and Molecular Physics

PIRSON, P., Methodology of Chemistry

RAES, M., Biochemistry

RASSON, J.-P., Probabilities

REMACLE, J., Biochemistry

REMON, M., Programming Statistics

ROUSSELET, D., Methodology of Biology

SCHNEIDER, M., Methodology of Mathematics

STOIKEN, R., Physics, Electronics

STRODIOT, J.-J., Optimization

SU, B. L., General Chemistry

THILL, G., Philosophy of Science

THIRAN, J.-P., Numerical Analysis

THIRY, P., Solid State Physics, General Physics

TOINT, PH., Algebra, Numerical Analysis

VAN CUTSEM, P., Biotechnology

VANDENHAUTE, J., Genetics

VERCAUTEREN, D., General Chemistry, Kinetics, Physical Chemistry

VIGNERON, J.-P., Solid State Physics

FACULTÉS UNIVERSITAIRES SAINT-LOUIS

Blvd du Jardin Botanique 43, 1000 Brussels

Telephone: (2) 211-78-11

Fax: (2) 211-79-97

E-mail: webmaster@fusl.ac.be

Internet: www.fusl.ac.be

Founded 1858, present name 1948

Language of instruction: French

Academic year: October to May

Rector: JEAN-PAUL LAMBERT

Vice-Rector: FRANÇOIS OST

Library: see under Libraries and Archives

Number of teachers: 82

Number of students: 2,300

Publications: *Revue interdisciplinaire d'Etudes Juridiques* (2 a year), *Revue internationale des droits de l'Antiquité*

DEANS

Faculty of Economic, Social and Political Sciences: B. HAMAIDE

Faculty of Law: Y. CARTUYVELS

Faculty of Philosophy and Letters: L. VAN EYNDE

PROFESSORS

Faculty of Economic, Social and Political Sciences:

BERTRAND, P., Physics

CALLUT, J. P., English Language

CITTA-VANTHEMSCHE, M., Mathematics

D'ASPREMONT LYNDEN, C., Philosophy and Social Sciences

DE KERCHOVE DE DENTERGHEM, A. M., Economics

DEPRINS, D., Statistics

DE RONGE, Y., Accountancy

DE SAINT-GEORGES, P., Social Communication

DE STEXHE, G., Philosophy and Ethics

EVERAERT-DESMEDT, N., Semiology

FRANCK, C., Political Science

GILLARDIN, J., Introduction to Law

GUERRA, F., Accountancy

HARDY, A., Mathematics

HUBERT, M., Sociology

LAMBERT, J. P., Economics

LECLERCQ, N. C., Civil Law

LEPERS, A., Accountancy

LOUTE, E., Mathematics and Computer Science

MARQUET, J., Sociology

MITCHELL, J., Economics

RIGAUX, M.-F., Introduction to Law, Public Law

SERVAIS, P., Economic and Social History

SIMAR, L., Statistics

SOETE, J. L., Contemporary History

SONVEAUX, E., Chemistry

STREYDIO, J. M., Physics

STRODIOT, J. J., Mathematics

TULKENS, H., Political Economy

VAN CAMPENHOUDT, L., Sociology

VAN RILLAER, J., Social and Industrial Psychology

VERHOEVEN, J., International Law

WIBAUT, S., Political Economy

WITTERWULGHE, R., Political Economy

Faculty of Law:

CARTUYVELS, Y., Introduction to Law

DE BROUWER, J. L., Political Science

DE JEMEPPE, B., Dutch Language

DE THEUX, A., Introduction to Law

DEVILLE, A., Sociology

DILLENS, A. M., Philosophy

DUMONT, H., Public Law

GERARD, P., Introduction to Law

HANARD, G., Roman Law

JACOB, R., Private Law

LORIAUX, C., English

MAHIEU, M., Introduction to Law

NANDRIN, J. P., History

OST, F., Introduction to Law

SEGERS, M. J., Psychology

STROWEL, A., Introduction to Law

VAN DE KERCHOVE, M., Introduction to Law

VAN GEHUCHTEN, P. P., Law

WANTHY, X., Political Economy

Faculty of Philosophy and Letters:

BOUSSET, H., Dutch Authors and Literature

BRAIVE, J., History

BRISART, R., Philosophy

CAUCHIES, J. M., History

CHEYNS, A., Greek Philology and Authors

CUPERS, J.-L., English Authors and Literature

DAUCHY, S., History

DE RUYT, C., Ancient History and History of Art

DUCHESNE, J.-P., History of Art

HEIDERSCHEIDT, J., English Phonetics and Grammar

JONGEN, R., German Phonetics and Grammar, Linguistics

LENOBLE-PINSON, M., Modern French Grammar, Philology

LEONARDY, E., German Literature

LOGE, T., French Literature

LONGREE, D., Latin Philology and Authors

MAESCHALCK, M., Philosophy

MARRANT, A., Latin Authors

MATTENS, W., Dutch Grammar and Philology

RENARD, M. C., French Authors, Modern Literatures, Italian and Spanish

TOCK, B. M., History

WILLEMS, M., Medieval French Literature

XHARDEY, D., History of Greek and Latin Literature and Greek Philology

University Level Institutions

ARCHITECTUURWETENSCHAPPEN VAN DE ARTESIS HOGESCHOOL ANTWERPEN

Mutsaardstraat 31, 2000 Antwerp

Telephone: (3) 205-61-70

Fax: (3) 226-04-11

E-mail: architectuurwetenschappen@artesis.be

Internet: www.artesis.be/architectuurwetenschappen

Founded 1663 by Teniers; ind. 1952

Dept Head: Prof. KOEN VAN DE VREKEN

Publication: *Antwerp Design Sciences Cahiers (ADSC)* (2 a year).

ARTESIS HOGESCHOOL ANTWERPEN

Keizerstraat 15, 2000 Antwerp

Telephone: (3) 213-93-00

Fax: (3) 213-93-41

E-mail: info@artesis.be

Internet: www.artesis.be

Chair.: CAMILLE PAULUS

Vice-Chair.: ROBERT VOORHAMME

Man. Dir: GUY AELTERMAN.

ARTEVELDEHOGESCHOOL

Hoogpoort 15, 9000 Ghent

Telephone: (9) 235-20-00

Fax: (9) 235-20-01

E-mail: info@arteveldehs.be

Internet: www.arteveldehogeschool.be

Languages of instruction: Dutch, English

Academic year: September to June

Chair.: Prof. Dr ERIK DE LEMBRE

Gen. Man.: Prof. Dr JOHAN VEECKMAN

Number of teachers: 1,050

Number of students: 10,000
Publication: *Arteveldemagazine*.

COLLEGE OF EUROPE/COLLÈGE D'EUROPE

Dijver 11, 8000 Bruges
Telephone: (50) 47-71-11
Fax: (50) 47-71-10
E-mail: info@coleurope.eu
Internet: www.coleurope.eu
Founded 1949
Private control
Institute of postgraduate European studies; br. in Natolin (Warsaw)
Languages of instruction: English, French
Academic year: September to June
Pres. of Admin. Board: IÑIGO MENDEZ DE VIGO
Rector: Prof. PAUL DEMARET
Vice-Rector: EWA OŚNIECKA-TAMECKA
Library Dir: ERIC DE SOUZA
Library of 100,000 vols
Number of teachers: 140
Number of students: 300
Publication: *Collegium*

DIRECTORS
Department of Economic Studies: J. PELKMANS
EU International Relations and Diplomacy Studies: S. GSTÖHL
European General Studies: DOMINIK HANF
European Legal Studies: I. GOVAERE
European Political and Administrative studies: J. MONAR

ÉCOLE DES HAUTES ÉTUDES COMMERCIALES

Rue Louvrex 14, 4000 Liège
Telephone: (4) 232-72-11
Fax: (4) 232-72-40
E-mail: info@hec.be
Internet: www.hec.be
Founded 1898
Language of instruction: French
Academic year: September to June
Pres.: YVES NOEL
Dir-Gen.: M. DUBRU
Academic Dir: LOUIS ESCH
Sec.-Gen.: JACQUES DEFER
Librarian: M. A. THOMAS
Library of 12,000 vols
Number of teachers: 217
Number of students: 1,620

ÉCOLE PRACTIQUE DES HAUTES ÉTUDES COMMERCIALES

Ave K. Adenauer 3, 1200 Brussels
Telephone: (2) 772-65-75
E-mail: ephec@ephec.be
Internet: www.ephec.be
Founded 1969
Languages of instruction: English, French
Dir and Pres.: ALAIN GILBERT
Number of teachers: 240
Number of students: 3,000

ERASMUSHOGESCHOOL-BRUSSEL
(Erasmus University College)

Nijverheidskaai 170, 1070 Brussels
Telephone: (2) 523-37-37
Fax: (2) 523-37-57
E-mail: info@ehb.be
Internet: www.erasmushogeschool.be
Founded 1995, merger of 10 colleges in and around Brussels
Private control
Language of instruction: Dutch
Man. Dir: LUC VAN DE VELDE

Admin. Dir: ERIKA EECKHOUT
Number of students: 4,500
Publications: *ehbmagazine*, *Medium—Tijdschrift voor Toegepaste Taalwetenschap* (3 a year), *Tijdschrift voor Bestuurswetenschappen en Publike Recht* (12 a year).

FACULTEIT VOOR VERGELIJKENDE GODSDIENSTWETENSCHAPPEN
(Faculty for Comparative Study of Religions)

Bist 164, 2610 Antwerp (Wilrijk)
Telephone: (3) 830-51-58
Fax: (3) 825-26-73
E-mail: info@antwerpfvg.org
Founded 1980
Languages of instruction: Dutch, English, French, German
Academic year: October to June
Chair. of Board: JEREMY ROSEN
Rector: CHRISTIAAN J. G VONCK
Deans: LYDIA BONTE, JAN VAN REETH, FRANK STAPPAERTS
Librarians: WU JEN, EDDY VAN LAERHOVEN, HUGO PEERLINCK, CHRISTIAN VANDEKERKHOVE
Library of 35,000 vols
Number of teachers: 44
Number of students: 120
Publication: *Acta Comparanda* (1 a year).

GROEP T—INTERNATIONALE HOGESCHOOL LEUVEN
(Group T—International University College Leuven)

Andreas Vesaliusstraat 13, 3000 Leuven
Telephone: (16) 30-10-30
Fax: (16) 30-10-40
E-mail: groept@groept.be
Internet: www.groept.be
Founded 1888
Private control
Languages of instruction: Dutch, English
Pres.: Prof. Dr JOHAN DE GRAEVE
Dir-Gen.: GUIDO VERCAMMEN
Dean of Leuven Education College: STIJN DHERT
Dean of Leuven Engineering College: PATRICK DE RYCK.

HAUTE ÉCOLE ALBERT JACQUARD

Sq. Arthur Masson 1, 5000 Namur
Telephone: (81) 23-43-80
Fax: (81) 26-29-68
E-mail: presidence@heaj.be
Internet: www.heaj.be
Founded 1959, present name and status 1996
Private control
Academic year: September to June
Dir and Pres.: GUY BRIFFOZ.

HAUTE ÉCOLE BLAISE PASCAL

Rue des Déportés 140, 6700 Arlon
Telephone: (63) 23-41-48
Fax: (63) 23-44-38
E-mail: info@hebp.be
Internet: www.hebp.be
Founded 1996
Dir and Pres.: RICHARD JUSSERET
Number of students: 1,300
Publication: *Le Pari*.

HAUTE ÉCOLE CATHOLIQUE CHARLEROI-EUROPE

Pl. Brasseur 6, 6280 Loverval
Telephone: (71) 47-42-70
Fax: (71) 44-10-10

E-mail: peda.loverval@helha.be
Internet: www.hece.eu
Founded 1996
Rector: JEAN-LUC VREUX
Acad. Sec.: BERNARD RIGUELLE.

HAUTE ÉCOLE CHARLEMAGNE

Rue des Rivageois 6, 4000 Liege
Telephone: (4) 254-76-00
Fax: (4) 254-76-20
E-mail: secr.rivageois@hech.be
Internet: www.lesrivageois.be
Founded 1874
Language of instruction: French
Dir and Pres.: CORINE MATILLARD
Number of teachers: 280
Number of students: 2,800

HAUTE ÉCOLE DE BRUXELLES

Chaussée de Waterloo 749, 1180 Brussels
Telephone: (2) 340-12-95
Fax: (2) 347-52-64
E-mail: heb@heb.be
Internet: www.heb.be
Academic year: September to June
Head: MARIANNE COESSENS
Librarian: J. P. GAHIDE
Librarian: O. GALMA
Library of 45,000 vols
Number of teachers: 189
Number of students: 2,200
Publication: *Équivalences* (2 a year)

DIRECTORS
Institute of Economics and Technology: MARIANNE COESSENS
Institute of Teacher-Training: LUC BARBAY
Institute of Translating and Interpreting: FRANS DE LAET

HAUTE ÉCOLE DE LA COMMUNAUTÉ FRANÇAISE DU HAINAUT

Rue Pierre-Joseph Duménil 4, 7000 Mons
Telephone: (65) 34-79-83
Fax: (65) 39-45-25
E-mail: directeur-president@hecfh.be
Internet: www.hecfh.be
Founded 1996
State control
Language of instruction: French
Dir and Pres.: DENIS DUFRANE
Sec.: MICHEL POPIJN
Number of teachers: 333
Number of students: 3,000

HAUTE ÉCOLE DE LA COMMUNAUTÉ FRANÇAISE DU LUXEMBOURG SCHUMAN

Ave de Luxembourg 101, 6700 Arlon
Telephone: (63) 41-00-00
Fax: (63) 41-00-13
E-mail: cel.adm@hers.be
Internet: www.hers.be
State control
Dir and Pres.: MARC FOURNY
Number of teachers: 200
Number of students: 2,000

HAUTE ÉCOLE DE LA COMMUNAUTÉ FRANÇAISE PAUL-HENRI SPAAK

Rue Royale 150, 1000 Brussels
Telephone: (2) 227-35-01
Fax: (2) 217-46-09
E-mail: mejdoubi@he-spaak.be
Internet: www.he-spaak.be
Founded 1995

State control
Dir and Pres.: JACQUES LEBEGGE.

HAUTE ÉCOLE DE LA PROVINCE DE LIÈGE

Ave Montesquieu 6, 4000 Liege
Telephone: (4) 237-96-05
E-mail: hepl@provincedeliege.be
Internet: haute-ecole.prov-liege.be
State control
Dir and Pres.: TONI BASTIANELLI
Number of students: 8,546

HAUTE ÉCOLE DE LA PROVINCE DE NAMUR

Rue Henri Blès 188–190, 5000 Namur
Telephone: (81) 77-67-56
Fax: (81) 77-69-02
Internet: www.hepn.be
State control
Academic year: September to June
Dir and Pres.: FRANÇOISE GASPAR.

HAUTE ÉCOLE DE LA VILLE DE LIÈGE

Rue Hazinelle 2, 4000 Liege
Telephone: (4) 223-28-08
Fax: (4) 221-08-42
E-mail: info@hel.be
Internet: www.hel.be
Founded 1996, by merger of l'Institut d'Enseignement Supérieur Pédagogique, l'École Communale Supérieure de Secrétariat, d'Administration et de Commerce, l'École Supérieure de Logopédie, l'Institut Supérieur d'Enseignement Technologique
Language of instruction: French
Academic year: September to July
Pres.: Dr ANDRÉ NOSSENT
Number of teachers: 250
Number of students: 2,200

HAUTE ÉCOLE DE NAMUR

Rue Saint-Donat 130, 5002 Namur
Telephone: (81) 46-85-00
Fax: (81) 46-85-25
E-mail: info@henam.be
Internet: www.henam.be
Founded 2007, by merger of Haute Ecole Namuroise Catholique and Haute Ecole d'Enseignement Supérieur de Namur
Private control
Language of instruction: French
Academic year: September to June
Dir and Pres.: DANIEL CHAVÉE
Number of students: 4,000

HAUTE ÉCOLE FRANCISCO FERRER DE LA VILLE DE BRUXELLES

Rue de la Fontaine 4, 1000 Brussels
Telephone: (2) 279-57-92
Fax: (2) 279-57-88
E-mail: sec.hefftech@brunette.brucity.be
Internet: www.brunette.brucity.be/heff
Publication: Info-Ferrer.

HAUTE ÉCOLE GALILÉE

Rue des Grands Carmes 23, 1000 Brussels
Telephone: (2) 289-63-30
Fax: (2) 289-63-39
E-mail: directeur.president@galilee.be
Internet: www.galilee.be
Academic year: September to July
Dir and Pres.: MICHEL VAN LIESHOUT
Gen. Sec.: EVELYNE CROUSSE.

HAUTE ÉCOLE LÉONARD DE VINCI

Pl. de l'Alma 2, 1200 Brussels
Telephone: (2) 761-06-80
Fax: (2) 761-06-88
E-mail: info@vinci.be
Internet: www.vinci.be
Founded 1995, by merger of 6 instns: ECAM, Institut Supérieur Industriel, École Normale Catholique du Brabant Wallon, Institut d'Enseignement Supérieur Parnasse-Deux Alice, Institut Libre Marie Haps, Institut Paul Lambin, Institut Supérieur d'Enseignement Infirmier
Academic year: September to June
Dir and Pres.: PAUL ANCIAUX
Sec.: HOURIA ZARKI
Number of teachers: 156
Number of students: 6,457

HAUTE ÉCOLE LIBRE DE BRUXELLES—ILYA PRIGOGINE

Ave Besme 97, 1190 Brussels
Telephone: (2) 349-68-11
Fax: (2) 349-68-31
E-mail: direction.presidence@helb-prigogine.be
Internet: www.helb-prigogine.be
Language of instruction: French
Academic year: September to June
Dir and Pres.: JEAN-MARIE MESKENS.

HAUTE ÉCOLE LIBRE DU HAINAUT OCCIDENTAL

Quai des Salines 20, 7500 Tournai
Telephone: (69) 89-05-05
E-mail: secretariat@helho.be
Internet: www.helho.be
Language of instruction: French
Dir and Pres.: PHILIPPE DE CONINCK
Number of students: 1,500

HAUTE ECOLE LIBRE MOSANE

Mont Saint-Martin 41, 4000 Liege
Telephone: (4) 222-22-00
Fax: (4) 343-30-28
E-mail: info@helmo.be
Internet: www.helmo.be
Founded 2008
Language of instruction: French
Dir and Pres.: ANNE-MARIE MONIOTTE
Sec.-Gen.: ALEXANDRE LODEZ
Librarian: NICOLE GRAVIER
Library of 11,528 vols
Number of teachers: 720
Number of students: 5,600
Publication: Nouvelles de l'Union Gramme (4 a year).

HAUTE ÉCOLE LUCIA DE BROUCKÈRE

Ave Émile Gryzon 1, 1070 Brussels
Telephone: (2) 526-73-00
Fax: (2) 524-30-82
E-mail: info@heldb.be
Internet: www.heldb.be
State control
Language of instruction: French
Academic year: September to June
Dir and Pres.: PATRICK DYSSELER.

HAUTE ÉCOLE PROVINCIALE DE HAINAUT CONDORCET

Chemin du Champ 17, 7000 Mons
Telephone: (65) 40-12-20
Fax: (65) 84-39-18
Internet: www.condorcet.be
Founded 2009

Language of instruction: French
Academic year: September to June
Dir and Pres.: ALAIN SCANDOLO
Number of students: 8,000

HOGERE ZEEVAARTSCHOOL ANTWERPEN/ECOLE SUPÉRIEURE DE NAVIGATION D'ANVERS (Antwerp Maritime Academy)

Noordkasteel Oost 6, 2030 Antwerp
Telephone: (3) 205-64-30
Fax: (3) 225-06-39
E-mail: info@hzs.be
Internet: www.hzs.be
Founded 1834
Languages of instruction: Dutch, English, French
Gen. Man.: PATRICK BLONDÉ
Chair. of Board: PETER RAES
Librarian: HAN JACOBS
Number of students: 686

HOGESCHOOL GENT

Kortrijksesteenweg 14, 9000 Ghent
Telephone: (9) 243-33-33
Internet: www.hogent.be
Founded 1995, by merger of 13 univ. colleges
State control
Language of instruction: Dutch
Academic year: September to May
Prin.: Dr ROBERT HOOGEWIJS
Chair.: FRANS VERHEEKE
Vice-Chair.: DAVID WALGRAEVE
Number of teachers: 2,000
Number of students: 15,000
Publication: Volgende halte: HoGent (8 a year).

HOGESCHOOL SINT-LUKAS BRUSSEL

Paleizenstraat 70, 1030 Brussels
Telephone: (2) 250-11-00
Fax: (2) 250-11-11
E-mail: info@sintlukas.be
Internet: www.sintlukas.be
Founded 1880
Private control
Pres.: JEAN-PIERRE RAMMANT
Vice-Pres.: HUGO CASAER
Number of students: 850

HOGESCHOOL VAN DE PROVINCIE ANTWERPEN

Lange Nieuwstraat 101, 2000 Antwerp
Telephone: (3) 220-57-99
Fax: (3) 220-57-19
E-mail: info@plantijn.be
Internet: www.plantijn.be
Founded 1995
Language of instruction: Dutch
Gen. Man.: ERWIN SAMSON
Number of teachers: 234
Number of students: 3,203

HOGESCHOOL VOOR WETENSCHAP & KUNST (University College for Sciences and Arts)

Koningsstraat 328, 1030 Brussels
Telephone: (2) 250-15-11
Fax: (2) 218-58-39
E-mail: info@wenk.be
Internet: www.wenk.be
Founded 1995
Languages of instruction: Dutch, English
Man. Dir: MARIA DE SMET.

HOWEST: HOGESCHOOL WEST-VLAANDEREN

Marksesteenweg 58, 8500 Kortrijk
Telephone: (56) 24-12-90
Fax: (56) 24-12-92
E-mail: info@howest.be
Internet: www.howest.be
Founded 1995
Private control
Languages of instruction: Dutch, English
Chair.: JAN DURNEZ
Gen. Man.: LODE DE GEYTER
Number of students: 5,500

INSTITUT CATHOLIQUE DES HAUTES ÉTUDES COMMERCIALES

Blvd Brand Whitlock 2, 1150 Brussels
Telephone: (2) 739-37-11
Fax: (2) 739-38-03
E-mail: communication@ichec.be
Internet: www.ichec.be
Founded 1934
Languages of instruction: Dutch, English, French
Rector: BRIGITTE CHANOINE
Gen. Sec.: PIERRE FLAHAUT
Library of 16,000 vols
Number of teachers: 300
Number of students: 2,000
Publication: *Reflets et Perspectives de la Vie Economique*.

INSTITUT COOREMANS

Place Anneessens 11, 1000 Brussels
Telephone: (2) 551-02-10
Fax: (2) 551-02-16
E-mail: heff.economique@he-ferrer.eu
Internet: www.brunette.brucity.be/ferrer/eco
Founded 1911
Academic year: September to June
Courses at Bachelors and Masters degree level in commerce and administration
Pres.: P. LAMBERT
Dir: LUC COOREMANS
Number of teachers: 80
Number of students: 400
Publication: *ECOO* (4 a year).

INSTITUT SUPÉRIEUR D'ARCHITECTURE INTERCOMMUNAL

Site Victor Horta, CP 248, blvd du Triomphe, 1050 Brussels
Telephone: (2) 650-50-52
Fax: (2) 650-50-93
E-mail: isahorta@ulb.ac.be
Internet: horta.ulb.ac.be
Founded 1711
Language of instruction: French
Associated with Free Univ. of Brussels and schools of architecture at Liège and Mons (ISAI); courses in architecture, restoration and heritage conservation, urban design
Academic Dean: FABRIZIO BUCELLA
Dir: JEAN-MARC STERNO
Library of 30,000 vols
Number of teachers: 60
Number of students: 650
Publication: *I.S.A.Br* (12 a year).

INSTITUUT VOOR TROPISCHE GENEESKUNDE/INSTITUT DE MÉDECINE TROPICALE
(Institute of Tropical Medicine)

Nationalestraat 155, 2000 Antwerp
Telephone: (3) 247-66-66
Fax: (3) 216-14-31

E-mail: info@itg.be
Internet: www.itg.be
Founded 1906, Royal Decree 1931
Languages of instruction: French, English
Academic year: September to July
Chair.: CATHY BERX
Vice-Chair.: Prof. Dr ALAIN VERSCHOREN
Dir: Prof. Dr BRUNO GRYSEELS
Librarian: DIRK SCHOONBAERT
Library of 60,000 vols, 5,000 dissertations, 30,000 journals
Number of teachers: 120
Number of students: 650
Publications: *ITGPress* (irregular), *Studies in Health Services Organisation & Policy*, *Tropical Medicine and International Health* (12 a year).

KAREL DE GROTE-HOGESCHOOL

Van Schoonbekestraat 143, 2018 Antwerp
Telephone: (3) 613-13-13
E-mail: info@kdg.be
Internet: www.kdg.be
Founded 1995
Languages of instruction: Dutch, English
Gen. Man.: DIRK BROOS
Library of 130,000 vols, 23,000 audiovisuals
Number of teachers: 1,000
Number of students: 9,000

KATHOLIEKE HOGESCHOOL BRUGGE-OOSTENDE
(Catholic University College of Bruges–Ostend)

Xaverianenstraat 10, 8200 Bruges
Telephone: (50) 30-51-00
Fax: (50) 30-51-01
E-mail: info@khbo.be
Internet: www.khbo.be
Founded 1995
Academic year: September to June
Language of instruction: Dutch
Pres.: WILLIAM DE GROOTE
Gen. Man.: PIET DE LEERSNYDER
Librarian: PATRICK VANDEGEHUCHTE
Number of teachers: 330
Number of students: 3,800

KATHOLIEKE HOGESCHOOL KEMPEN

Kleinhoefstraat 4, 2440 Geel
Telephone: (14) 56-23-10
Fax: (14) 58-48-59
E-mail: info@khk.be
Internet: www.khk.be
Founded 1995
Language of instruction: Dutch
Academic year: September to June
Pres.: KOEN GEENS
Vice-Pres.: LOUIS GENOE
Gen. Man.: MAURICE VAES
Number of students: 7,200
Publication: *Agora* (3 a year).

KATHOLIEKE HOGESCHOOL LEUVEN
(Leuven University College)

Abdij van Park 9, 3001 Heverlee
Telephone: (16) 37-57-00
Fax: (16) 37-57-99
E-mail: info@khleuven.be
Internet: www.leuvenuniversitycollege.be
Chair.: JOS CLIJSTERS
Gen. Dir: TOON MARTENS
Number of teachers: 650
Number of students: 6,500

KATHOLIEKE HOGESCHOOL LIMBURG
(Limburg Catholic University College)

Agoralaan, Gebouw B, bus 1, 3590 Diepenbeek
Telephone: (11) 23-07-70
Fax: (11) 23-07-89
E-mail: informatie@khlim.be
Internet: www.khlim.be
Founded 1994, by merger of 9 schools
Gen. Man.: WILLY INDEHERBERGE
Pres.: NORBERT VAN BROEKHOVEN
Vice-Pres.: KAREL PEETERS
Number of teachers: 700
Number of students: 6,000

KATHOLIEKE HOGESCHOOL SINT-LIEVEN

Gebroeders Desmetstraat 1, 9000 Ghent
Telephone: (9) 265-86-10
Fax: (9) 265-86-25
E-mail: info@kahosl.be
Internet: www.kahosl.be
Founded 1995, by merger of 8 instns
Languages of instruction: Dutch, English
Academic year: September to June
Man. Dir: Prof. Dr FRANK BAERT
Chair.: LUC SANTENS
Number of teachers: 700
Number of students: 6,400

KATHOLIEKE HOGESCHOOL ZUID-WEST-VLAANDEREN

Doorniksesteenweg 145, 8500 Kortrijk
Telephone: (56) 26-41-60
Fax: (56) 26-41-75
E-mail: bachelor@katho.be
Internet: www.katho.be
Founded 1995
Private control
Pres.: ERIC HALSBERGHE
Number of teachers: 520
Number of students: 7,000

LESSIUS ANTWERPEN—MECHELEN

Jozef de Bomstraat 11, 2018 Antwerp
Telephone: (3) 206-04-80
Fax: (3) 206-04-81
E-mail: info@lessius.eu
Internet: www.lessius.eu
Founded 2000, following merger of Handelshogeschool (f. 1923) and Katholieke Vlaamse Hogeschool (f. 1919)
Languages of instruction: Dutch, English
Academic year: September to July
8 Campuses
Chair.: Prof. Dr KOEN GEENS
Man. Dir: JOHAN CLOET
Dir-Gen.: Prof. Dr FLORA CARRIJN
Dir of Finances: PHILIPPE MICHIELS
Number of teachers: 600
Number of students: 10,000
Publication: *Journal of Internationalisation and Localisation*.

LESSIUS MECHELEN
(Lessius University College Mechelen)

Zandpoortvest 13, 2800 Mechelen
Telephone: (15) 36-91-02
Fax: (15) 36-91-09
E-mail: info@mechelen.lessius.eu
Internet: mechelen.lessius.eu
State control
Languages of instruction: Dutch, English
Man. Dir: JOHAN CLOET
Gen. Man.: PHILIPPE MICHIELS

Library of 40,000 vols
Number of students: 4,400

PROVINCIALE HOGESCHOOL LIMBURG

Elfde-Liniestraat 24, 3500 Hasselt
Telephone: (11) 23-88-88
Fax: (11) 23-88-89
E-mail: phl@phl.be
Internet: www.phl.be
Founded 1995 by merger of 6 colleges of higher education
Languages of instruction: Dutch, English
Pres.: Ben Lambrechts
Number of teachers: 620
Number of students: 5,000

DEANS

Dept of Architecture: R. Cuyvers
Dept of Arts: R. Cuyvers
Dept of Bio: M. Schepers
Dept of Business: M. Gaens
Dept of Education: M. Hermans
Dept of Healthcare: R. Nelissen
Dept of Music: L. Leurs

VLERICK LEUVEN GENT MANAGEMENT SCHOOL

Telephone: (9) 210-97-11
Fax: (9) 210-97-00
E-mail: info@vlerick.be
Internet: www.vlerick.com
Founded 1953
Academic year: September to July
Associated with Ghent Univ. and Katholieke Univ. Leuven
Dean: Prof. Philippe Haspeslagh
Librarian: Elke Parrez
Library of 11,000 vols, 30,000 online and printed journals
Number of teachers: 70
Number of students: 480 undergraduate students
Publication: *Vlerick reflect* (4 a year).

XIOS HOGESCHOOL LIMBURG

Agoralaan, Gebouw H, 3590 Diepenbeek
Telephone: (11) 26-00-46
Fax: (11) 26-00-55
E-mail: info@xios.be
Internet: www.xios.be
Private control
Languages of instruction: Dutch, English
Academic year: September to July
Vice-Chancellor: Prof. Dr Dirk Franco
Pres.: Luc Houbrechts
Gen. Man.: Prof. Dr Dirk Franco
Library of 30,000 vols, 400 journals
Number of students: 3,000

Schools of Music, Art and Architecture

Académie des Beaux-Arts et des Arts Décoratifs de Tournai: rue de l'Hôpital Notre-Dame 14, 7500 Tournai; tel. (69) 84-12-63; fax (69) 84-32-53; internet www.actournai.be; f. 1756; courses in drawing, painting, textile design, interior design, advertising, digital arts, comics; Dir Bernard Bay.

Académie Royale des Beaux-Arts de Bruxelles (Brussels Royal Academy of Fine Arts): rue du Midi 144, 1000 Brussels; tel. (2) 506-10-10; fax (2) 506-10-28; e-mail info@arba-esa.be; internet www.arba-esa.be; f. 1711; drawing, engraving, environmental art, illustration, interior design, painting, publicity and visual communication, sculpture, tapestry-textile creation; 80 teachers; 450 students; library: see Libraries and Archives; Dir Marc Partouche.

Conservatoire Royal d'Anvers/Koninklijk Conservatorium (Royal Conservatoire of Antwerp): Desguinlei 25, 2018 Antwerp; tel. (3) 244-18-00; fax (3) 238-90-17; e-mail conservatorium@artesis.be; internet www.artesis.be/conservatorium; f. 1898, present status 1995; languages of instruction: Dutch, English, French, German; 4-year full-time academic education and professional training in theatre and related performing arts; 3 art colleges; 180 teachers; Pres. Pascale De Groote; Admin. Sec. Roger Quadflieg; Librarian Jan Dewilde.

Conservatoire Royal de Bruxelles: rue de la Régence 30, 1000 Brussels; tel. (2) 511-04-27; fax (2) 512-69-79; e-mail info@conservatoire.be; internet www.conservatoire.be; f. 1832; Bachelor and Masters courses in music, theatre and arts; library: 1m. vols, 13,000 MSS, 1,200 periodicals; 250 teachers; 500 students; Dir Frédéric de Roos; Librarian Paul Prospé.

Conservatoire Royal de Mons: rue de Nimy 7, 7000 Mons; tel. (65) 34-73-77; fax (65) 34-99-06; e-mail crm.mons @ sup.cfwb.be; internet www.conservatoire-mons.be; f. 1820; courses in music and theatre; library: 30,000 vols; 420 students; Dir André Foulon.

Conservatoire Royal de Liège: rue Forgeur 14, 4000 Liège; tel. (4) 222-03-06; fax (4) 222-03-84; e-mail info@crlg.be; internet www.crlg.be; f. 1826; 80 professors; students taken from 15 years of age; all branches of music and theatre; Dir Bernard Dekaise; Sec. Nancy Demet; Librarian Philippe Gilson.

École Nationale Supérieure des Arts Visuels de la Cambre: Abbaye de la Cambre 21, 1000 Brussels; tel. (2) 626-17-80; fax (2) 640-96-93; e-mail lacambre@lacambre.be; internet www.lacambre.be; f. 1926; library: see Libraries and Archives; 230 teachers; 631 students; Dir Caroline Mierop.

École Supérieure des Arts Plastiques et Visuels: rue des Sœurs Noires 4A, 7000 Mons; tel. (65) 39-47-60; fax (65) 39-47-61; e-mail esapv.mons@esapv.be; internet www.esapv.be; courses in drawing, digital arts, painting, sculpture, interior architecture; Dir Jean-Pierre Benon; Librarian Lina Vasapolli.

École Supérieure des Arts Saint-Luc: rue d'Irlande 57, 1060 Brussels; tel. (2) 537-08-70; fax (2) 537-00-63; e-mail info@stluc-bruxelles.be; internet www.stluc-bruxelles.be; f. 1863; 130 teachers; 700 students; promotes debate on modern art; research and teaching; Dir Françoise Klein.

École Supérieure des Arts Saint-Luc: blvd de la Constitution 41, 4020 Liege; tel. (4) 341-80-00; fax (4) 341-80-80; e-mail info@saintluc.com; internet www.saintluc-liege.be; courses in practical arts and crafts, graphics, photography, painting, sculpture, interior architecture, industrial design, conservation and restoration of works of arts; 130 teachers; 1,300 students; Dir Eric Van den Berg; Librarian Bruno Vandermeulen.

Etablissement Communal d'Enseignement Supérieur Artistique 'Le 75': ave Jean-François Debecker 10, 1200 Brussels; tel. (2) 761-01-22; fax (2) 761-01-21; e-mail le75@woluwe1200.be; internet www.leseptantecinq.be; f. 1969; courses in visual art, graphics, painting and photography; 230 students; Exec. Sec. Pascale de Coster.

Institut National Supérieur des Arts du Spectacle et Techniques de Diffusion: rue Thérésienne 8, 1000 Brussels; tel. (2) 511-92-86; fax (2) 511-02-79; e-mail info@insas.be; internet www.insas.be; f. 1962; advanced studies in dramatic art, cinema and broadcasting technique, incl. television; library: 6,000 vols, 300 periodicals; Dir Laurent Gross; Admin. Sec. Magali Sonnet.

Institut des Arts de Diffusion: rue des Wallons 77, 1348 Louvain-La-Neuve; tel. (10) 47-80-20; fax (10) 45-11-74; e-mail iad@iad-arts.be; internet www.iad-arts.be; f. 1959; courses in audiovisual and performing arts; Dir Serge Flamé; Vice-Dir Michel Wouters.

Institut Saint-Luc: chaussée de Tournai 7, 7520 Tournai (Ramegnies-Chin); tel. (69) 25-03-04; fax (69) 25-03-82; e-mail secretariat-secondaire@st-luc-tournai.be; internet www.islt.be; courses and technical training in photography, drawing, illustration, advertising; Dir D. Maurage; Asst Dir Dr Wilmart.

Institut Supérieur d'Architecture de la Communauté Française—La Cambre: pl. Eugène Flagey 19, 1050 Brussels; tel. (2) 640-96-96; fax (2) 647-46-55; e-mail isacf@lacambre-archi.org; internet www.lacambre-archi.be; f. 1926; organizes confs, workshops and courses in architecture; library: 17,000 vols, 42 periodicals; Dir Prof. Jean-Louis Genard; Deputy Dir Dr Guy Pilate; Exec. Sec. Samira Barfi; publ. *Pola* (1 a year).

Institut Supérieur de Musique et de Pédagogique: rue Juppin 28, 5000 Namur; tel. (81) 73-64-37; fax (81) 73-95-14; e-mail info@imep.be; internet www.imep.be; f. 1970; research, theoretical and practical training in music; organizes concerts, confs; Dir Guido Jardon; Librarian Thierry Bouillet.

Institut Supérieur Libre des Arts Plastiques/Ecole de Recherche Graphique: rue du Page 87, 1050 Brussels; tel. (2) 538-98-29; fax (2) 539-33-93; e-mail secretariat@erg.be; internet www.erg.be; courses in photography, sculpture, videography, painting, drawing, comics, animation; Dir Yvan Flasse.

Liège Académie Royale des Beaux-Arts de Liège: rue des Anglais 21, 4000 Liege; tel. (4) 221-70-77; fax (4) 221-70-76; e-mail administration@academieroyaledesbeauxart-sliege.be; internet www.academieroyaledesbeauxartsliege.be; f. 1836; courses in tapestry, sculpture, photography, engraving, sketching; organizes workshops.

BELIZE

The Higher Education System

The main institution of higher education is the University of Belize, which was established in 2000 as an amalgam of six previously existing institutions. There is also an extramural branch of the University of the West Indies in Belize. The University of Indianapolis, USA, also awards degrees through Galen University in Cayo District. In 1997/98 there were 2,853 students enrolled in 12 educational institutions, which included technical, vocational and teacher-training colleges.

Admission to university is on the basis of GCE A-level or Caribbean Advanced Proficiency Examination. Holders of the Caribbean Examinations Council Secondary Education Certificate or GCE O-level take a preliminary year before entry to a degree. There are two degree levels, Associate and Bachelors, with the latter available from either the University of Belize or the University of the West Indies. The Associate degree lasts for two years and the Bachelors for three.

Other post-secondary non-university education and training is available either through the workplace or at colleges. Courses can be taken leading to qualifications from City and Guilds, London Chamber of Commerce and the Royal Society of Arts.

The National Accreditation Council of Belize, responsible for evaluating institutions at all levels of education, was due to have begun operations in 2006.

Regulatory Bodies

GOVERNMENT

Ministry of Education: West Block Bldg, Belmopan; tel. 822-2380; fax 822-3389; e-mail moeducation.moes@gmail.com; internet www.moes.gov.bz; Minister PATRICK FABER.

Ministry of National Development, Investment and Culture: New Administration Bldg, Belmopan; tel. 822-2526; fax 822-3673; e-mail finsecmof@btl.net; Minister FRANCIS FONSECA.

Learned Society

NATURAL SCIENCES

Belize Audubon Society: POB 1001, Belize City; fax 223-4985; internet www.belizeaudubon.org; f. 1969; sustainable management of natural resources; manages 8 protected areas; 1,200 mems; Pres. DAVID CRAIG; Hon. Sec. LYDIA WAIGHT; publ. *Newsletter* (4 a year).

Research Institute

NATURAL SCIENCES

Biological Sciences

Carrie Bow Marine Field Station—Caribbean Coral Reef Ecosystems (CCRE): c/o Smithsonian Marine Station, 5612 Old Dixie Highway, Fort Pierce, FL 34946-7303, USA; Carrie Bow Cay, Belize; internet www.mnh.si.edu/biodiversity/ccre.htm; f. 1972; field laboratory; part of the Smithsonian Marine Science Network; attached to the Smithsonian Institution's Nat. Museum of Natural History (USA); Dir Dr VALERIE PAUL.

Libraries and Archives

Belize City

Leo Bradley Library: POB 287, Belize City; Princess Margaret Dr., Belize City; tel. 223-4248; fax 223-4246; f. 1935; nat. library service for Belize; incl. National Collection; 100,000 vols; 40 brs throughout Belize; Chief Librarian JOY YSAGUIRRE.

Belmopan

Belize Archives Department: 26/28 Unity Blvd, Belmopan; tel. 822-2247; fax 822-3140; e-mail archives@btl.net; internet www.belizearchives.org; f. 1965; 150,000 documents; Chief Archivist CHARLES A. GIBSON.

University

UNIVERSITY OF BELIZE

University Dr., POB 340, Belmopan City
Telephone: 223-0256
Fax: 233-0255
Internet: www.ub.edu.bz
Founded 2000
Pres.: Dr CORINTH MORTER-LEWIS
Provost: HENRY ANDERSON

DEANS

Faculty of Agriculture and Natural Science: (vacant)
Faculty of Education and Arts: Dr WILMA WRIGHT
Faculty of Management and Social Science: Dr VINCENT PALACIO
Faculty of Nursing, Health Science and Social Work: Dr ABIGAIL MCKAY
Faculty of Science and Technology: Dr THIPPI THIAGARAJAN

ATTACHED INSTITUTES

Adult and Continuing Education Centre: Freetown Rd, POB 990, Belize City.

Institute of Marine Studies: Freetown Rd, POB 990, Belize City.

Colleges

Corozal Community College: POB 63, Corozal Town; tel. 422-2541; fax 422-3597; internet www.corozal.com/ccc; f. 1978 by merger of Fletcher College and St Francis Xavier College to form an ecumenical (Roman Catholic, Methodist, Anglican) college; 2- and 4-year courses in academic and business studies; 41 teachers; 650 students; Prin. ENDEVORA JORGENSON.

University of the West Indies School of Continuing Studies: POB 229, University Centre, Belize City; tel. and fax 223-2038; e-mail uwibze@btl.net; internet www.uwi.edu/scs; f. 1949; continuing education, particularly adult learning; 20 teachers; 200 students; library: 10,000 vols; Resident Tutor LUZ. M. LONGWORTH.

Wesley College: POB 543, 34 Yarborough Rd, Belize City; tel. 227-6302; fax 227-0278; f. 1882; 4-year arts, science and commercial courses; 20 teachers; 336 students; library: 3,000 vols; Prin. BRENDA J. ARMSTRONG.

BENIN

The Higher Education System

The structure of the higher education system in Benin (known as Dahomey until 1975) is a legacy of its period as a French colony (1890–1960). It is dominated by the Université d'Abomey-Calavi, which was founded in 1970 as Université du Dahomey. The university changed its name to Université Nationale du Bénin in 1975 and adopted its current name in 2001. In 1999/2000 it had approximately 9,000 students. A second university, in Parakou, with a student capacity of approximately 3,000, opened in 2001 and there is now a third university in Porto Novo. In 2005 there were a total of 42,600 students enrolled in further and higher educational institutions. By 2009 there were 15 private institutions, many of which are affiliated to universities in France, Belgium and Canada.

The Ministry of Higher Education and Scientific Research is responsible for the higher education sector. The university rectors are government appointees, but deans of faculty are elected by their peers. State funding for higher education has been affected by economic problems and poor management, with the effect that more specialized private institutions have begun to emerge.

The Baccalauréat is required for admission to university. Qualifications are arranged in three cycles. The first cycle lasts for two years and leads to one of four Diplomas. The second cycle lasts for either one year after the Diplomas for the Licence, or two years for the Maîtrise. Finally, the third cycle is a programme of doctoral research for two or more years leading to the award of Doctorat de Troisième Cycle.

Regulatory Bodies

GOVERNMENT

Ministry of Culture, Tourism and Crafts: 01 BP 2037, Guincomey, Cotonou; tel. 21-30-70-10; fax 21-30-70-31; e-mail sg@tourisme.gouv.bj; internet www.tourisme.gouv.bj; Min. SOUMANOU SEIBOU TOLÉBA.

Ministry of Higher Education and Scientific Research: 01 BP 348, Cotonou; tel. 21-30-06-81; fax 21-30-57-95; e-mail sgm@recherche.gouv.bj; internet www.recherche.gouv.bj; Min. VICENTIA BOCCO.

Research Institutes

GENERAL

Centre Régional de Recherche Sud-Bénin: Attogon; f. 1904; library of 2,000 vols and periodicals; Dir Dr J. DETONGNON.

Institut de Recherches Appliquées: BP 6, Porto Novo; f. 1942; library of 8,000 vols; Dir S. S. ADOTEVI; publ. *Etudes*.

AGRICULTURE, FISHERIES AND VETERINARY SCIENCE

Institut National des Recherches Agricoles du Bénin (INRAB): 01 BP 884, Cotonou; tel. 21-30-37-70; fax 21-30-07-36; internet www.bj.refer.org/benin_ct/rec/inrab/inrab.htm; f. 1992 to replace the Direction de la Recherche Agronomique (DRA); Dir-Gen. DAVID YAO ARODOKOUN.

Station de Recherches sur le Cocotier de Semé-Podji: Semé-Podji; tel. 20-24-07-01; coconut research; f. 1949; attached to Institut des Recherches sur les Huiles et Oléagineux, France; Dir HONORÉ TCHIBOZO.

Station de Recherches sur le Palmier à Huile de Pobe: BP 1, Pobe; tel. and fax 20-25-00-66; f. 1922; palm oil station; attached to Direction de la Recherche Agronomique/Ministère des Affaires Rurales, France; library of 70 vols, 54 reviews; Dir Dr MOÏSE HOUSSOU.

NATURAL SCIENCES

General

Institut de Recherche pour le Développement (IRD): BP 4414, Cotonou; see main entry in France chapter.

TECHNOLOGY

Office Béninois de Recherches Géologiques et Minières: BP 249, Cotonou; tel. 21-31-03-09; fax 21-31-41-20; e-mail obrgm@intnet.bj; f. 1977; branch of Ministry of Mining, Energy and Hydraulics; library of 8,000 vols, 10 current periodicals; Dir-Gen. NESTOR VEDOGBETON; publ. *OBRGM Actu* (4 a year).

Libraries and Archives

Porto Novo

Archives Nationales de la République du Bénin: BP 629, Porto Novo; tel. and fax 20-24-66-09; f. 1914; Dir ELISE PARAISO; publs *Bulletin* (1 a year), *Mémoire du Bénin* (irregular), *Répertoire d'archives* (irregular).

Bibliothèque Nationale: BP 401, Porto Novo; tel. 20-21-25-85; f. 1976; 35,000 vols; Dir H. N. AMOUSSOU.

Museums and Art Galleries

Abomey

Musée Historique d'Abomey: BP 25, Abomey; tel. and fax 22-50-03-14; internet epa-prema.net/abomey/; f. 1943; collection includes craftwork, drawings, jewellery and royal paraphenalia; Curator ZÉPHIRIN DAAVO.

Porto Novo

Musée National: c/o IRA, BP 6, Porto Novo; premises at Cotonou; Curator MARTIN AKABIAMU.

Universities

UNIVERSITÉ D'ABOMEY-CALAVI

Abomey-Calavi, BP 526, Cotonou

Telephone: 21-36-00-74

Fax: 21-30-16-38

Internet: www.bj.refer.org/benin_ct/edu/univ-be/univ-be.htm

Founded 1970 as Université du Dahomey; became Université Nationale du Bénin 1975; present name 2001

State control

Language of instruction: French

Academic year: October to July

Rector: Prof. ISSIFOU TAKPARA

Vice-Rector and Dir of Academic Affairs: TAOFIKI AMINOU

Dir of Admin. and Financial Affairs: EFIOTODJI ACHI NOUMAGNON

Sec.-Gen.: Dr SOUMANOU SEIBOU TOLEBA

Librarian: PASCAL A. I. GANDAHO

Library of 50,000 vols

Number of teachers: 650

Number of students: 18,533

DEANS

Faculty of Agriculture: MATHURIN NAGO

Faculty of Arts, Letters and Humanities: ASCENSION BOGNIAHO

Faculty of Economics and Management: FULBERT GÉRO AMOUSSOUGA

Faculty of Health Sciences: Prof. CÉSAR AKPO

Faculty of Science and Technology: CYPRIEN GNANVO

UNIVERSITÉ DE PARAKOU

BP 123, Parakou

Telephone and fax 23-61-07-12

E-mail: universite_parakou2001@yahoo.fr

Founded 2001

State control

Academic year: October to July

Rector: Prof. ALEXIS HOUNTONDJI

Vice-Rector: Dr AGNÈS THOMAS-ODJO

Registrar: Dr MOUHAMED PARAPE

Librarian: BIO TIKANDE

Library of 3,657 vols

Number of teachers: 28

Number of students: 3,020

DEANS

Faculty of Agricultural Sciences: Dr NESTOR SOKPON

Faculty of Economics: Prof. BARTHÉLÉMY BIAO

Faculty of Law and Policy: Dr OMAR FORTUNÉ ALAPINI

Institute of Technology and Management: Dr SIMÉON FAGNISSE

School of Medicine: Prof. SIMON A. AKPONA

BHUTAN

The Higher Education System

Traditionally, education in Bhutan was purely monastic; the establishment of the contemporary state education system was the result of the reforming zeal of the third King, Jigme Dorji Wangchuck (r. 1952–72). There are five main linguistic groups in Bhutan; Dzongkha, spoken in western Bhutan, is the official language but English is the medium of school instruction. Tertiary education includes various first degree courses offered by institutes under the supervision of the Royal University of Bhutan (RUB), which was established in 2003. Adult literacy and non-formal education (NFE) programmes began in Bhutan in 1992, with the establishment of 10 pilot NFE centres targeting those who had left school before completing the curriculum and those without a formal education. The programme offered a one-year basic literacy programme together with a nine-month post-literacy course in Dzongkha covering practical issues such as agriculture, health and sanitation. By 2008 there were 747 NFEs with some 13,829 adults enrolled.

Admission to higher education is made on the basis of completion of grade 12 and passing of examinations leading to award of either the Indian School Certifcate or Bhutan Higher Secondary Education Certificate. Bachelors which degrees last for three to four years are offered at the RUB as well as other colleges and non-university institutions. The Masters degree is currently offered on a very limited basis. There are no doctoral programmes in Bhutan.

The Department of Human Resources of the Ministry of Labour and Human Resources was founded in 1999 to supervise technical and vocational education and training. Within the Department, the Department of Occupational Standards (formerly Bhutan Vocational Qualifications Authority) has developed a three-tier Bhutan Vocational Qualifications Framework. The grades of occupational training are Apprenticeship Training Programmes, Special Skills Development Programmes and Village Skills Development Programmes. Constituent colleges of the RUB also offer technical and vocational programmes of education.

Regulatory Bodies

GOVERNMENT

Department of Occupational Standards: Ministry of Labour and Human Resources, POB 1036, Thongsel Lam, Lower Motithang, Thimphu; tel. (2) 333867; fax (2) 326731; e-mail sangaydorjee@hotmail.com; internet www.molhr.gov.bt; f. 2000; improves and monitors the quality of vocational skills acquired by individuals through the Bhutan Vocational Qualifications Framework (BVQF); comprises 3 divs: standards and qualifications, assessment and certification, review and audit; Dir SANGAY DORJEE.

Ministry of Education: POB 112, Thimphu; tel. (2) 325325; fax (2) 325183; e-mail p_thinley@hotmail.com; internet www.education.gov.bt; Min. Lyonpo THINLEY GYAMTSHO.

Ministry of Home and Cultural Affairs: Tashichhodzong, POB 133, Thimphu; tel. (2) 322301; fax (2) 324320; internet www.mohca.gov.bt; Min. (vacant).

Libraries and Archives

Thimphu

National Library & Archives of Bhutan:; e-mail sonamnlb@gmail.com POB 185, Thimphu 11001; tel. (2) 324314; fax (2) 322693; e-mail nlb@library.gov.bt; internet www.library.gov.bt; f. 1967; 12,700 Dzongkha/Chokey MSS and block-printed books, 90,000 Dzongkha/Chokey books in other forms; 15,000 foreign (mainly English) books; Eastern branch: Kuenga Rabten, nr Tongsa; Dir HARKA B. GURUNG; publ. *Rigter* (2 a year).

Thimphu Public Library: POB 295 Thimphu; f. 1980; incl. the Jigme Dorji Wangchuk Library (f. 1978); UN depository library; 6,000 vols; Librarian Mrs TSHEWANG ZAM.

Museum and Art Gallery

Paro

National Museum of Bhutan: Ta Dzong, Paro; tel. (8) 271257; fax (8) 271510; e-mail nmb@druknet.net.bt; f. 1968; housed in seven-storey 17th-century fortress; gallery of paintings (Thankas), images, decorative art, arms, jewellery; copper, bronze, wood and bamboo objects, philately, photographs; natural history of Bhutan; reference library with books on Bhutan, Northern Buddhism, Tibetology, museology and conservation; Dir PHUNTSOK TASHI.

University

ROYAL UNIVERSITY OF BHUTAN (RUB)/DRUK GYYELZIN TSHULA LOPDHEY

POB 708, Semtokha, Thimphu
Telephone: (2) 336454
Fax: (2) 336453
E-mail: vc_rub@rub.edu.bt
Internet: www.rub.edu.bt

Founded 2003
State control
Academic year: July to July,February to December (2 sessions)

10 Mem. instns: College of Natural Resources (located in Lobesa, Thimphu), College of Science and Technology (Rinchhending, Phuntsholing), Gaeddu College of Business Studies, Institute of Language and Culture Studies (Semtokha, Thimphu), Jigme Namgyel Polytechnic (Dewathang), National Institute of Traditional Medicine (Thimphu), Paro College of Education (Paro), Royal Institute of Health Science (Thimphu), Samtse College of Education (Samtse), Sherubtse College (Kanglung, Trashigang)

Chancellor: HM JIGME KHESAR NAMGYEL WANGCHUCK
Chair.: Hon. Min. KHANDU WANGCHUCK
Vice-Chancellor: Dr PEMA THINLEY
Dir for Research and External Relations: PHINTSHO CHOEDEN

Number of teachers: 354
Number of students: 5,641 (4,998 full-time, 703 part-time)

Colleges

National Institute of Education: Samtse; tel. (5) 365273; fax (5) 365363; e-mail dorjee@druknet.net.bt; f. 1968; 3-year BEd course, 2-year certificate course, 1-year postgraduate certificate course in Education, 5-year distance-learning course; academic year August to July; 35 teachers; 273 students; library: 15,000 vols, 20 periodicals; Dir DORJEE TSHERING; Prin. TSHEWANG CHHODEN WANGDI.

Royal Bhutan Polytechnic: Dewathang; tel. (7) 260286; f. 1974; 3-year diploma courses in civil, mechanical and electrical engineering; 2-year certificate courses in surveying and draughtsmanship; library: 2,000 vols; Prin. KEZANG CHADOR.

Royal Institute of Management: POB 416, Semtokha, Thimphu; tel. (2) 351013; fax (2) 351029; internet www.rim.edu.bt; f. 1986; training courses for civil service and private sector at certificate, diploma and postgraduate diploma levels; Dir KARMA TSHERING; library: 13,000 vols, 60 periodicals; 32 teachers; 292 students; publ. *dZinchong Rigphel* (2 a year).

Royal Technical Institute: Kharbandi; tel. (5) 252317; fax (5) 252171; e-mail rti@druknet.net.bt; f. 1965; 3- and 5-year certificate courses for electricians, draughtsmen, mechanics, motor mechanics; 42 teachers; 313 students; Principal SANGAY DORJEE.

Sherubtse Degree College: Kanglung, Trashigang; tel. (4) 535208; fax (4) 535129; e-mail shercol@druknet.bt; internet www.sherubtse.edu.bt; f. 1983; affiliated college of Univ. of Delhi (q.v., see India chapter); 3-year honours degree courses in economics, English, geography, Dzongkha and commerce, and general degree courses in sciences; 2-year pre-univ. course in science; language of instruction: English; 46 teachers; 484 students; library: 22,000 vols; Prin. Dr JAGAR DORJI; Asst Prins LOPON JAMPEL CHOGYEL, LHATO JAMBA, NIDUP DORJI; publ. *Sherub Doenme* (journal, in English, 2 a year).

Ugyen Wangchuck University: in process of formation.

BOLIVIA

The Higher Education System

In 2006 there were a total of 69 legally recognised universities offering degree programmes. They fall into one of five categories: Public autonomous universities and members of the Bolivian University System, Public non-autonomous universities, Public non-autonomous universities and members of the Bolivian University System, Universities under special regime, and Private universities.

There are 16 public universities, 10 of which are members of the Comité Ejecutivo de la Universidad Boliviana (CEUB). Ten of these public universities are classified as public autonomous universities as they are self-financing, free to develop their own programmes and undertake research according to the Act of the Constitution of the Bolivian University System. All 10 public autonomous universities are equal in status and offer degrees and research programmes under their own autonomous Sistema de la Universidad Boliviana (SUB). There are also two public non-autonomous universities: Escuela Militar de Ingeniería (Military School of Engineering) and the Universidad Católica Boliviana 'San Pablo' (Catholic University of Bolivia). These are state-funded higher education institutions and members of the CEUB. However, they do not have the authority to offer all types of degrees, which are administered by the Bolivian Army and Catholic Church in this case. There are four public universities which do not participate in the SUB, do not have autonomy and are administered directly by the Ministry of Education and Culture. This group of institutions consists of the Universidad Militar de las Fuerzas Armadas (UMFA), the Universidad Pedagógica Nacional (UPN), the Universidad Públicade El Alto (UPEA) and the Universidad de la Policía Boliviana.

In 2006 there were 52 private universities, which have been offering degrees since the mid-1980s. Most private universities are members of the Asociación Nacional de Universidades Privadas (ANUP), founded in 1992, but are under the supervision of the Ministry of Education and Culture.

One university, the Universidad Andina Simón Bolivar (UASB) has special status in Bolivia. UASB is an international university with campuses in Ecuador, Peru, Venezuela, Colombia and Bolivia. It was established by the Andean Parliament in December 2005 and is considered an international centre of excellence in postgraduate training, research and providing services for the transfer of scientific and technological knowledge. The Bolivian campus in Sucre offers postgraduate programmes in subjects such as medicine, administration and management and law.

The Diploma de Bachiller Científico-Humanístico serves as the principle entry requirement for access to higher education. Unlike some other countries in Latin America, there is no national university entrance examination. Some universities have their own admissions policy which may include passing an entrance examination.

Higher education in Bolivia is offered at four levels: the Técnico Universitario Medio (two years), Técnico Universitario Superior (three years), Bachillerato Universitario (four years) and the Licenciatura (5 years). National standards establishing the general requirements for each of these were set following the Tenth National Congress of Universities in May 2003. Since 2006 these have been applied to all undergraduate degrees at public autonomous universities. At postgraduate level there are four types of degrees: specialist degrees in medical disciplines, specialist degrees in non-medical disciplines, Masters and Doctoral studies. On completion students receive an academic not a professional title. In 2006/07 there were some 346,100 students enrolled in further and higher education.

Accreditation of higher education is carried out by the Consejo Nacional Evaluación y Acreditación de la Educación Superior (CONAES). CONAES was established in 2002 as an independent agency responsible for conducting external evaluation of degree programmes in public and private universities. The system of accreditation is mainly programmatic and not compulsory. As a member of MERCOSUR, CONAES has already established an evaluation committee for first level medical degrees so that these qualifications will be automatically recognised throughout all MERCOSUR member states.

Regulatory and Representative Bodies

GOVERNMENT

Ministry of Education and Culture: Casilla 6500, La Paz; tel. (2) 2203576; internet www.minedu.gov.bo; Min. VÍCTOR CÁCERES RODRÍGUEZ.

NATIONAL BODIES

Comité Ejecutivo de la Universidad Boliviana (CEUB) (Executive Committee of the Bolivian University): Av. Arce esq. Pinilla 2606 y Hnos Manchego 2559, La Paz; tel. (2) 2435302; e-mail rrpp@ceub.edu.bo; internet www.ceub.edu.bo; Nat. Exec. Sec. Dr GONZALO TABOADA LÓPEZ.

Secretaría Nacional de Investigación, Ciencia y Tecnología (Secretariat for Research, Science and Technology): Casilla 11253, La Paz; tel. (2) 2434368; fax (2) 2433929; e-mail sicyt@caoba.entelnet.bo; internet www.ceub.edu.bo/ceub/secretarias/sicyt.html; directs and coordinates activities related to research, science and technology in Bolivian univs; Nat. Sec. Ing. RUBEN MEDINACELI ORTIZ.

Learned Societies

GENERAL

Academia Boliviana (Bolivian Academy): Casilla 4145, La Paz; f. 1927; Corresponding Academy of the Real Academia Española in Madrid; 26 mems; Dir Mons. JUAN QUIRÓS; Permanent Sec. CARLOS CASTAÑÓN BARRIENTOS; Pro-Sec. MARIO FRÍAS INFANTE; publ. *Revista*.

UNESCO Office La Paz: Casilla 5112, La Paz; Edificio del B.B.A. Piso 10, Avda Camacho 1413, La Paz; tel. (2) 2204009; fax (2) 2204029; e-mail la-paz@unesco.org; Dir YVES DE LA GOUBLAYE DE MENORVAL.

AGRICULTURE, FISHERIES AND VETERINARY SCIENCE

Sociedad Rural Boliviana (Agricultural Society): Casilla 786, Edif. El Condor piso 10, Of. 1005, La Paz; f. 1934; 30 assoc. mems; Pres. Ing. JOSÉ LUIS ARAMAYO V.; publs *Cotar, El Surco, IFAP News, Universitas*.

ARCHITECTURE AND TOWN PLANNING

Colegio de Arquitectos de Bolivia: Casilla 8779, La Paz; tel. 39-15-68; fax 39-15-68; f. 1940; architecture and town planning; 3,000 mems; library of 5,000 vols; Pres. FROILÁN CAVERO M.; Sec. JUAN C. BARRIENTOS M.; publs *Arquitectura y Ciudad, CDALP Informa, Punku*.

FINE AND PERFORMING ARTS

Círculo de Bellas Artes (Fine Arts Circle): Plaza Teatro, La Paz; f. 1912; Pres. ERNESTO PEÑARANDA.

HISTORY, GEOGRAPHY AND ARCHAEOLOGY

Academia Nacional de la Historia (National Academy of History): Avda Abel Iturralde 205, La Paz; f. 1929; 18 mems; Pres. Dr DAVID ALVESTEGUI; Sec.-Gen. Dr HUMBERTO VÁZQUEZ-MACHICADO.

Sociedad de Estudios Geográficos e Históricos (Geographical and Historical Society): Plaza 24 de Setiembre, Santa Cruz de la Sierra; f. 1903; Pres. Gral. LUCIO AÑEZ; Vice-Pres. Lic. PLÁCIDO MOLINA B.; Sec. AVELINO PEREDO; publ. *Boletín*.

Sociedad Geográfica de La Paz (La Paz Geographical Society): Casilla 1487, Edif. Santa Mónica, 13 Plaza Abaroa, La Paz; f. 1889; depts of prehistory, history, folklore, geography; 580 mems; Pres. Dr GREGORIO LOZA BALSA; publ. *Boletín* (2 a year).

Sociedad Geográfica y de Historia 'Potosí' (Geographical and Historical Society): Casilla 39, Potosí; tel. (62) 2-27-77; fax (62) 2-27-77; f. 1905; 20 mems; library of 4,000 vols; Pres. Prof. ALFREDO TAPIA VARGS; Sec. WALTER ZAVAL; publ. *Boletín*.

Sociedad Geográfica y de Historia 'Sucre': Plaza 25 de Mayo, Sucre; f. 1887; 8 mems; library of 3,000 vols; Dir Dr JOAQUÍN GANTIER V.; publ. *Boletín*.

LANGUAGE AND LITERATURE

Alliance Française: Calle Guachalla 399—esq. Avda 20 de Octubre, Casilla 10220, La Paz; tel. (2) 2425004; fax (2) 2426293; e-mail adminlpz@afbolivia.org; internet www .afbolivia.org; offers courses and exams in French language and culture and promotes cultural exchange with France; attached teaching offices in Cochabamba, Santa Cruz, Tarija and Sucre; Dir MARIE GRAN-GEON-MAZAT.

Goethe-Institut: Avda Arce 2708, Casilla 2195, La Paz; tel. (2) 2431916; fax (2) 2431998; e-mail info@lapaz.goethe.org; internet www.goethe.de/ins/bo/lap/esindex .htm; offers courses and exams in German language and culture and promotes cultural exchange with Germany; library of 10,000 vols; Dir Dr SIGRID SAVELSBERG.

PEN Club de Bolivia–Centro Internacional de Escritores (International PEN Centre): Calle Goitia 17, Casilla 149, La Paz; f. 1931; 40 Bolivian mems; 7 from other South American countries; Pres. (vacant); Sec. YOLANDA BEDREGAL DE CÓNITZER.

MEDICINE

Ateneo de Medicina de Sucre (Athenaeum of Medicine): Sucre; Pres. Dr AGUSTÍN BENÁVIDES; Vice-Pres. Dr ABERTO MARTÍNEZ; Sec.-Gen. Dr ROMELIO A. SUBIETA.

Sociedad de Pediatría de Cochabamba (Paediatrics Society): Casilla 1429, Cochabamba; f. 1945; 14 mems; Pres. Dr JULIO CORRALES BADANI; Sec. Dr MOISÉS SEJAS.

NATURAL SCIENCES
General

Academia Nacional de Ciencias de Bolivia (Bolivian National Academy of Sciences): Avda 16 de Julio 1732, Paseo El Prado, Casilla de Correos 5829, La Paz; tel. (2) 2363990; fax (2) 2379681; e-mail secretaria@ aciencias.org.bo; internet www.aciencias.org .bo; f. 1960; 42 mems; library of 8,000 vols; Pres. Acad. GONZALO TABOADA LÓPEZ; Gen. Sec. Acad. JOSÉ ANTONIO BALDERRAMA GÓMEZ ORTEGA; Librarian TERESA OCHOA GONZÁLES; publs *Boletín Informativo* (12 a year), *Publicaciones* (irregular), *Revista* (2 a year).

Physical Sciences

Colegio de Géologos de Bolivia: Edif. Sergeomin, calle Federico Zuazo, esq. Reyes Ortiz 1673, Casilla 8941, La Paz; f. 1961 as Sociedad Geológica Boliviana, present name 1996; Pres. Ing. DIONISIO GARZÓN MARTINEZ.

TECHNOLOGY

Asociación de Ingenieros y Geólogos de Yacimientos Petrolíferos Fiscales Bolivianos (AIG—YPFB): Casilla 401, La Paz; f. 1959; 210 mems in 4 brs: La Paz, Camiri, Cochabamba, Santa Cruz; Pres. Ing. JUAN CARRASCO; publ. *Revista Técnica de Yacimientos Petrolíferos Fiscales Bolivianos* (4 a year).

Research Institutes
GENERAL

Institut de Recherche pour le Développement (IRD): CP 9214, La Paz; tel. (2) 784925; fax (2) 782944; e-mail cecilia.ird@ mail.megalink.com; geology, hydrobiology, medical entomology, agronomy, nutrition, hydrology, climatology, social sciences; Dir Dr JEAN-PIERRE CAMOUZE; (see main entry under France).

AGRICULTURE, FISHERIES AND VETERINARY SCIENCE

Sistema Boliviano de Tecnología Agropecuaria (SIBTA): Avda Héctor Ormachea 1000, esq. Calle 12, Piso 3, Obrajes, La Paz; tel. (2) 2786937; fax (2) 2782161; e-mail ucpsa@sibta.gov.bo; f. 1975; 380 mems; library of 47,000 vols, 260 periodicals; Dir Dr GONZALO ROMERO G.

ECONOMICS, LAW AND POLITICS

Instituto Nacional de Estadística (National Institute of Statistics): Calle J. Carrasco 1391, Miraflores, La Paz; tel. (2) 2222333; fax (2) 222693; e-mail ceninf@ine .gov.bo; internet www.ine.gov.bo; f. 1937; nat., economic and social statistics and censuses; library of 10,500 vols, 370 periodicals; Exec. Dir JOSÉ LUIS CARJAVAL B.; publs *Actualidad Estadística* (52 a year), *Actualidad Estadística Departamental* (12 a year), *Anuario Estadístico*, *Encuenta Integrada de Hogares* (1 a year).

HISTORY, GEOGRAPHY AND ARCHAEOLOGY

Instituto Geográfico Militar (Military Institute of Geography): Avda Saavedra 2303, (Estado Mayor), Casilla 7641, La Paz; tel. (2) 2220513; fax (2) 2228329; e-mail igm@ ejercito.mil.bo; internet www.igmbolivia.gov .bo; f. 1936; geodesy, nat. topographical survey; Commandant Col HUGO MÉNDEZ SARAVIA; publ. *Boletín Informativo*.

Instituto Nacional de Arqueología de Bolivia: Calle Tiwanaku 93, Casilla 20319, La Paz; tel. 329624; f. 1975; 26 mems; library of 6,000 vols; Dir CARLOS URQUIZO SOSSA; publ. *Arqueología Boliviana*.

LANGUAGE AND LITERATURE

Instituto Nacional de Estudios Lingüísticos (INEL): Junín 608, Casilla 7846, La Paz; f. 1965; part of *Instituto Nacional de Historia, Literatura y Antropología*; linguistic, social and educational research and teaching; specializations: Quechua and Aymara; library of 1,200 vols; Dir VITALIANO HUANCA TORREZ; publs specialized papers, *Notas y Noticias Lingüísticas* (12 a year), *Yatiñataki*.

MEDICINE

Instituto de Cancerología 'Cupertino Arteaga': Hospital de Clínicas, Plaza de Libertad, Sucre; f. 1947; Dir Dr H. NUNEZ R.

Instituto Médico Sucre (Medical Institute): Calle San Alberto 32, Casilla 82, Sucre; e-mail inmedsuc@yahoo.com; f. 1895; library of 8,000 vols, incl. *Flora Peruviensis* and 16th-century edn of *Aforismos de Hipocrates*, 6,000 pamphlets; research and production of vaccines and sera; Pres. Dr EZEQUIEL L. OSORIO; Sec. Dr JOSÉ AGUIRRE; Librarian Dr GUSTAVO VACA GUZMÁN; publ. *Revista* (4 a year).

Instituto Nacional de Medicina Nuclear (National Institute of Nuclear Medicine): Casilla Postal 5795, La Paz; Calle Mayor Rafael Zubieta 1555, Miraflores, La Paz; tel. (2) 2226116; fax (2) 2112784; e-mail inamen@

caoba.entelnet.bo; f. 1962; Dir Prof. LUIS F. BARRAGÁN M.

NATURAL SCIENCES
Physical Sciences

Observatorio San Calixto: Casilla 12656, La Paz; tel. (2) 2406222; fax (2) 2116723; e-mail oscdrake@entelnet.bo; internet www .observatoriosancalixto.org.bo; f. 1913; meteorology and seismology; library of 11,000 vols; Dir Dr ESTELLA MINAYA.

Servicio Nacional de Geología y Técnico de Minas (SERGEOTECMIN): Federico Zuazo 1673, Casilla 2729, La Paz; tel. (2) 2330766; fax (2) 2391725; e-mail sergeotecmin@sergeomin.gov.bo; internet www.sergeomin.gov.bo; f. 1956 as a nat. dept, reorganized 1965, 1996 and 2004; 136 mems; 10 laboratories; library of 5,124 vols; Exec. Dir ZOILO MONCADA; publs *Boletín Informativo 'Sergeotecmin Informa'* (3 a year), *Boletines Especiales* (technical reports), geological maps.

RELIGION, SOCIOLOGY AND ANTHROPOLOGY

Instituto de Sociología Boliviana (ISBO) (Institute of Sociology): Apdo 215, Sucre; f. 1941; investigates economic, juridical and sociological problems; library of 15,000 vols; Dir TOMÁS LENZ B.; publ. *Revista del Instituto de Sociología Boliviana*.

TECHNOLOGY

Instituto Boliviano de Ciencia y Tecnología Nuclear: Casilla 4821, La Paz; Avda 6 de Agosto 2905, La Paz; tel. (2) 433481; fax (2) 433063; e-mail ibten@datacom-bo.net; f. 1983; Dirs JORGE CHUNGARA CASTRO, FERNANDO BARRIENTOS ZAMORA (acting).

Instituto Boliviano del Petróleo (IBP): Casilla 4722, La Paz; f. 1959 to support and coordinate scientific, technical and economic studies on the oil industry in Bolivia; 50 mems; library of 1,000 technical vols; Pres. Ing. JOSÉ PATIÑO; Gen. Sec. Ing. REYNALDO SALGUEIRO PABÓN; publs *Boletín, Manual de Signos Convencionales*.

Libraries and Archives
Cochabamba

Biblioteca Central Universitaria 'José Antonio Arze' (Universidad Mayor de San Simón): Avda Oquendo esq. Sucre, Casilla 992, Cochabamba; tel. (42) 31733; fax (42) 31691; f. 1930; 30,000 vols; Dir LUIS ALBERTO PONCE; publ. *Boletín Bibliográfico*.

La Paz

Biblioteca Central de la Universidad Mayor de San Andrés: Avda Villazón 1995, La Paz; tel. (2) 359505; internet www .umsa.bo/umsa/app?service=page/ac0300; f. 1930; 121,000 vols; Dir Lic. ALBERTO CRESPO RODAS.

Biblioteca del Instituto Boliviano de Estudio y Acción Social: Avda Arce 2147, La Paz; special collections on social science, Boliviana, education and government documents; 12,000 vols; Dir ELENA PEDDLE.

Biblioteca del Ministerio de Relaciones Exteriores (Library of the Ministry of Foreign Affairs): Plaza Murillo, La Paz; f. 1930; 10,039 vols; private library; Dir Prof. PACÍFICO LUNA QUIJARRO.

Biblioteca Municipal 'Mariscal Andrés de Santa Cruz' (Municipal Library): Zona Central, Plaza del Estudiante, Calle Cañada Strongest esquina México, La Paz; tel. (2) 2378477; fax (2) 2378477; internet saludpublica.bvsp.org.bo/sys/?s2=1; f. 1838; 35,000 vols; Dir YOLOTZIN SALDAÑA.

Biblioteca y Archivo Histórico del Honorable Congreso Nacional (Congress Library): Calle Mercado esquina Ayacucho No. 308, La Paz; tel. (2) 314731; internet www.congreso.gov.bo/5biblioteca; f. 1912; 22,000 vols; Dir VÍCTOR BERNAL SOLARES; Chief Librarian NELLY ARRAYA VASQUEZ; publ. *Reports of Congress*.

Centro Nacional de Documentación Científica y Tecnológica (Bolivian National Scientific and Technological Documentation Centre): Casilla 14538, La Paz; Avda Mariscal Santa Cruz 1175, esquina Calle Ayacucho, La Paz; tel. (2) 359583; fax (2) 359586; e-mail iiicndct@huayna.umsa .edu.bo; internet www.bolivian.com/ industrial/cndct; f. 1967; provides extensive information service for research and devt; attached to Instituto de Investigaciones Industriales, Universidad Mayor de San Andrés; depository library for FAO, WHO and ILO; 9,800 vols; Dir RUBÉN VALLE VERA; publ. *Actualidades* (4 a year).

Potosí

Biblioteca Central Universitaria: Universidad Autónoma 'Tomás Frías', Casilla 54, Avda del Maestro, Potosí; tel. (62) 27313; f. 1942; 43,796 vols, 1,471 periodicals; 1 central library, 8 specialized libraries; Dir JULIA B. DE LÓPEZ; publs *Revista Científica*, *Revista de Ciencias*, *Revista Orientación Pedagógica*.

Biblioteca Municipal 'Ricardo Jaime Freires': Potosí; f. 1920; 30,000 vols; Dir LUIS E. HEREDIA.

Sucre

Biblioteca Central de la Universidad Mayor de San Francisco Xavier: Plaza 25 de Mayo, Apdo 212, Sucre; Dir AGAR PEÑARANDA.

Biblioteca y Archivo Nacional de Bolivia (National Library and Archives): Casilla 338, Sucre; Calle Bolívar, Sucre; tel. (64) 1481; f. 1836; 150,000 vols; Dir GUNNAR MENDOZA.

Museums and Art Galleries

La Paz

Museo 'Casa de Murillo': Calle Apolinar Jaén 790, La Paz; tel. (2) 2280758; f. 1950; folk and colonial art, paintings, furniture, national costume, herb medicine and magic; Dir (vacant).

Museo Costumbrista 'Juan de Vargas': Calle Sucre s/n, esq. Jaén, La Paz; f. 1979; history of La Paz.

Museo de Metales Preciosos Precolombinos: Calle Jaén 777, Casilla 609, La Paz; tel. (2) 2280758; f. 1983; pre-Columbian archaeology (especially gold and silver); Dir JOSÉ DE MESA.

Museo Nacional de Arqueología (National Archaeological Museum): Calle Tihuanaco 93, Casilla oficial, La Paz; tel. (2) 2311621; f. 1846, reinaugurated 1961; archaeological and ethnographical collections; Lake Titicaca district exhibits; Dir JULIO CESAR VELASQUEZ ALQUIZALETH; publ. *Anales*.

Museo Nacional de Arte: Calle Socabaya esq. Calle Comercio, CP 11390, La Paz; tel. (2) 408542; fax (2) 408600; f. 1964; housed in 18th-century baroque palace; colonial art, sculpture and furniture; Bolivian and Latin-American modern art; Dir TERESA VILLEGAS DE ANEIVA.

Potosí

Museo de la Casa Nacional de Moneda (Museum of the National Mint): Calle Ayacucho s/n, Potosí; tel. (2) 6223986; fax (2) 6222777; e-mail cnm@ casanacionaldemoneda.org.bo; internet www .casanacionaldemoneda.org.bo; f. 1938; housed in the 'Casa de Moneda', the Royal Mint, founded 1572, now restored, said to be the most outstanding civic monument of the colonial period in South America; colonial art, 18th-century wooden machinery, coins, historical archives, mineralogy, weapons, Indian ethnography, archaeology, modern art; Dir LUIS ALFONSO FERNÁNDEZ; publ. see under Sociedad Geográfica y de Historia 'Potosí'.

Sucre

Casa de la Libertad: Casilla postal 101, Sucre; Plaza 25 de Mayo 11, Sucre; tel. (4) 6454200; fax (4) 6452690; e-mail cdl@ casadelalibertad.org.bo; internet www .casadelalibertad.org.bo; fmrly Casa de la Independencia; historical collection concerned with Independence, including Bolivian Declaration of Independence; library of 4,000 vols, 1,000 maps; publ. *Memorias*.

Museo Charcas: Universidad Boliviana Mayor, Real y Pontificia de San Francisco Xavier, Calle Bolívar 698, Sucre; tel. (4) 6453285; f. 1944; anthropological collection with pre-Inca archaeology: Dir JAIME URIOSTE ARANA; ethnographical and folklore collection: Dir ELIZABETH ROJAS TORO; colonial and modern art section, including Princesa de la Glorieta collection: Dir MANUEL GIMÉNEZ CARRAZANA; publ. *Boletín Antropológico*.

Universities

UNIVERSIDAD AMAZÓNICA DE PANDO

Calle Enrique Cornejo 77, Pando, Cobija
Telephone: (3) 8422411
Fax: (3) 8429710
E-mail: recuap@hotmail.com
Founded 1993
State control
Rector: ADOLFO MEJIDO.

UNIVERSIDAD AUTÓNOMA DEL BENI 'JOSÉ BALLIVIÁN'

Casilla 38, Trinidad, Beni
Telephone: (46) 20744
E-mail: secretariogeneral@uabjb.edu.bo
Internet: www.uabjb.edu.bo
Founded 1967
State control
Rector: M.Sc. GUILLERMO SUÁREZ ZAMBRANO
Vice-Rector: Dr CARMELO APONTE VÉLEZ
Gen. Sec.: Ing. RUBÉN TORRES TAGLE
Librarian: LORGIA S. DE TANAKA
Library of 9,600 vols
Number of teachers: 155
Number of students: 1,039
Publications: *Boletines de los Institutos de Investigaciones, Ictícola del Beni, Investigaciones Forestales y de Defensa de la Amazonía, Socio-económicas*

DEANS

Faculty of Agriculture: Lic. CASTO PLAZA CUENCA
Faculty of Economics: RODOLFO ARTEAGA CÉSPEDES
Faculty of Stockbreeding: Dr PABLO MEMM DORADO

ATTACHED RESEARCH INSTITUTES

Instituto de Investigaciones Forestales y Defensa del Medio Ambiente de la Amazonia: Casilla 12, Riberalta, Beni; tel. 82484; Dir OSCAR LLANQUE.

Instituto de Investigaciones Icticolas del Beni: Casilla 38, Trinidad, Beni; tel. 21705; Dir Dr RENÉ VASQUEZ PÉREZ.

Instituto de Investigaciones Socio-económicas: Casilla 38, Trinidad, Beni; tel. 21566; Dir Lic. CARLOS NAVIA RIBERA.

UNIVERSIDAD AUTÓNOMA 'GABRIEL RENÉ MORENO'

Plaza 24 de Septiembre, Santa Cruz de la Sierra
Telephone: (3) 3365533
Fax: (3) 3342160
E-mail: uagrmrec@bibosi.scz.entelnet.bo
Internet: www.uagrm.edu.bo
Founded 1879
State control
Language of instruction: Spanish
Academic year: February to December
Rector: Abog. REYMI FERREIRA JUSTINIANO
Vice-Rector: Dr JULIO ARGENTINO SALEK MERY
Sec.-Gen.: Dr JOSÉ MIRTENBAUM KNIEVEL
Univ. Dir of Academic Affairs: Ing. JOSÉ FREDDY SÁNCHEZ SÁNCHEZ
Univ. Dir of Admin. and Finance: Lic. WALDO LOPEZ APARICIO
Univ. Dir of Extension: Arq. ROBERT RIVERA CAMACHO
Univ. Dir of Research: Dr ALFREDO MENACHO VACA
Univ. Dir of Social Welfare: Ing. PILAR DÁVALOS SÁNCHEZ
Librarian: Lic. JOSÉ MELCHOR MANSILLA
Library of 40,000 vols
Number of teachers: 1,019
Number of students: 27,600
Publication: *Universidad*

DEANS

Faculty of Agriculture: Ing. ALFREDO PÉREZ ANGULO
Faculty of Economics and Finance: Lic. ALFREDO JALDÍN FARELL
Faculty of Exact Sciences and Technology: Ing. WALTER YABETA SÁNCHEZ
Faculty of Habitat, Integral Design and Art: Arq. CARLOS BARRERO SUAREZ
Faculty of Health Sciences: Lic. NELSON VILLEGAS ROJAS
Faculty of Humanities: Dr EMILIO DURÁN RIVERA
Faculty of Juridical, Political and Social Sciences: Dr OSVALDO ULLOA PEÑA
Faculty of Veterinary Medicine and Zootechnology: Dr SERGIO SANTA CRUZ GIL
Polytechnic Faculty: Ing. LUIZ ALBERTO VACA PINTO
Polytechnic Faculty of Camiri: Ing. ROBERTO SAAVEDRA ARÉVALO

UNIVERSIDAD AUTÓNOMA 'JUAN MISAEL SARACHO'

Avda Victor Paz 149, CP 51, Tarija
Telephone: (66) 43110
Fax: (66) 43403
E-mail: rector@uajms.edu.bo
Internet: www.uajms.edu.bo
Founded 1946
State control
Academic year: March to December
Rector: Lic. EDUARDO CORTEZ BALDIVIEZO
Number of teachers: 611
Number of students: 12,634
Publications: *Astro Información* (12 a year), *Visión Universitaria* (12 a year)

DEANS

Faculty of Agriculture and Forestry: Ing. WILFREDO BENÍTEZ

Faculty of Dentistry: Dr ALBERTO VARGAS LIRA

Faculty of Economics and Finance: Lic. FRANZ RODRIGUEZ O.

Faculty of Health Sciences: Dra SARA PACHECO

Faculty of Humanities: Lic. EDWIN JIJENA

Faculty of Law and Political Sciences: Dr CARLOS PÉREZ RIVERO

Faculty of Sciences and Technology: Ing. VICTOR MASTAJO R.

UNIVERSIDAD AUTÓNOMA 'TOMÁS FRÍAS'

Casilla 36, Potosí
Avda del Maestro, Avda Civica s/n, Potosí
Telephone: (2) 26227300
Fax: (2) 26226663
E-mail: rector@rect.nrp.edu.bo
Internet: www.uatf.edu.bo
Founded 1892
State control
Academic year: April to November

Rector: Lic. ABDÓN SOZA YÁÑEZ
Vice-Rector: Ing. GERMÁN LIZARAZU PANTOJA
Chief Librarian: Dr CARLOS LOAYZA MENDIZABAL

Number of teachers: 380
Number of students: 7,551

Publication: *Vida Universitaria*

DEANS

Faculty of Agriculture and Stockbreeding: Ing. AMILCAR MARISCAL CORTEZ

Faculty of Arts: Lic. LUIS TORRICO GAMARRA

Faculty of Economics, Finance and Administration: Lic. VALETÍN VIÑOLA QUINTANILLA

Faculty of Engineering: Ing. ALBERTO SCHMIDT QUEZADA

Faculty of Geological Engineering: Ing. DANIEL HOWARD BARRÓN

Faculty of Humanities and Social Sciences: Dr NESTOR GOITIA IRAHOLA

Faculty of Law: Dr JORGE QUILLAGUAMÁN SÁNCHEZ

Faculty of Mining: Ing. EDDY ROMAY MORALES

Faculty of Sciences: Lic. GONZALO POOL GARCÍA

Polytechnic: Téc. Sup. ENRIQUE ARROYO MAMANI

UNIVERSIDAD CATÓLICA BOLIVIANA 'SAN PABLO'

Avda 14 de Septiembre 4807 esq. calle 2 (Obrajes), CP 4805, La Paz
Telephone: (2) 2782222
Fax: (2) 2786707
E-mail: rrppint@ucb.edu.bo
Internet: www.ucb.edu.bo
Founded 1966
Church Control
Language of instruction: Spanish
Academic year: February to December

Grand Chancellor: Mons. EDMUNDO ABASTOFLOR MONTERO
Rector: Dr CARLOS GERKE MENDIETA
Pro-Rector: Ing. HÉCTOR CORDOVA EGUIVAR
Vice-Rector for Admin. and Finance: Lic. FERNANDO MOSCOSCO SALMÓN
Regional Vice-Rector (Cochabamba): Dr RENÉ SANTA CRUZ R.
Regional Vice-Rector (La Paz): Lic. CARLOS MACHICADO
Regional Vice-Rector (Santa Cruz): Dr NABOR DURÁN SAUCEDO
Dir for Academic Planning: Lic. GABRIEL PONCE
Gen. Man.: Lic. JAIME RIVERO

Sec.Gen.: Dr MARIO HOYES
Academic Sec.: Lic. ELIZABETH ALVAREZ R.
Number of teachers: 778
Number of students: 11,000

Publication: *Ciencia y Cultura* (2 a year).

ATTACHED INSTITUTES

Instituto de Investigaciones Socio-Económicas: Avda Hernando Siles 4737, CP 4805, La Paz; tel. (2) 784159; Dir Lic. JUSTO ESPEJO.

Servicio de Capacitación en Radiodifusión para el Desarrollo: Avda Hernando Siles 4737, CP 4805, La Paz; Dir Lic. MARIOLA MATERNA.

UNIVERSIDAD EMPRESARIAL MATEO KULJIS

Calle 24 de Septiembre 444, CP 2321 Santa Cruz
Telephone: (3) 3322211
Fax: (3) 3365173
E-mail: universidad@unikuljis.edu.bo
Internet: www.unikuljis.edu.bo
Founded 2000

Rector: Lic. IVO KULJIS FUTCHNER.

UNIVERSIDAD MAYOR DE SAN ANDRÉS

Monoblock Central, Villazón Av. 1995, La Paz
Telephone: (2) 2352236
E-mail: webmaster@umsa.bo
Internet: www.umsa.bo
Founded 1930
State control
Academic year: January to December

Rector: Dra TERESA RESCALA NEMTALA
Vice-Rector: Ing. JUAN DAVID CASTILLO QUISPE
Gen. Sec.: Lic. JORGE VELASCO ORELLANOS
Librarian: Lic. ELIANA MARTINEZ DE ASBUN
Library: see Libraries
Number of teachers: 2,266
Number of students: 37,109

Publications: *Boletín Tesis, Gaceta Universitaria, Memorias Universitarias*

DEANS

Faculty of Agronomy: Ing. PERCY BAPTISTA
Faculty of Architecture: Arq. DAVID BARRIENTOS ZAPATA
Faculty of Dentistry: Dra NELLY SANDOVAL DE MOLLINEDO
Faculty of Economics and Finance: Lic. CARLOS CLAVIJO VARGAS
Faculty of Engineering: Ing. ADHEMAR DAROCA MORALES
Faculty of Geology: Ing. JOSÉ PONCE VILLAGOMEZ
Faculty of Humanities and Education: Dr RENE CALDERÓN SORIA
Faculty of Law and Political Science: Dr RAMIRO OTERO LUGONES
Faculty of Medicine: Dr BUDDY LAZO DE LA VEGA
Faculty of Pharmacy and Biochemistry: Dr OSWALDO TRIGO FREDERICKSEN
Faculty of Pure and Natural Sciences: Lic. JUAN ANTONIO ALVARADO KIRIGIN
Faculty of Social Sciences: Lic. TERESA MORENO
Faculty of Technology: Lic. LAURENTINO SALCEDO AGUIRRE

ATTACHED RESEARCH INSTITUTES

Centro de Investigaciones Geológicas: Ciudad Universitaria Calle 27 Cota Cota, La Paz; tel. 793392; Dir (vacant).

Instituto de Biología de la Altura: Avda Saavedra 2246, Facultad de Medicina, Piso 11, La Paz; tel. 376675; Dir Dr ENRIQUE VARGAS PACHECO.

Instituto de Ecología: Ciudad Universitaria Calle 27 Cota Cota, Casilla 20127, La Paz; tel. 7924416; Dir CECIL DE MORALES.

Instituto de Ensayo de Materiales: Avda Villazón 1995, Edificio Central, La Paz; tel. 359577; Dir Ing. MARIO TERAN.

Instituto de Genética Humana: Avda Saavedra 2246, Facultad de Medicina Piso 11, La Paz; tel. 359613; Dir Dr JORGE OLIVARES PLAZA.

Instituto de Hidráulica e Hidrología: Ciudad Universitaria Calle 27 Cota Cota, La Paz; tel. 795724; Dir Ing. FREDDY CAMACHO V.

Instituto de Ingenieria Sanitaria: Avda Villazón 1995, Pabellón 103, La Paz; tel. 359519; Dir Ing. JOSÉ DÍAZ BENAVENTE.

Instituto de Investigaciones Arquitectónicas: Calle Lisímaco Gutiérrez, Facultad de Arquitectura, La Paz; tel. 359568; Dir Arq. CRISTINA DAMM PEREIRA.

Instituto de Investigaciones Económicas: Avda 6 de Agosto 2170, Edificio HOY, 5° Piso, La Paz; tel. 359618; Dir Lic. PABLO RAMOS SANCHEZ.

Instituto de Investigaciones Físicas: Ciudad Universitaria Calle 27 Cota Cota, Casilla 8635, La Paz; tel. 792622; Dir Lic. ALFONSO VELARDE.

Instituto de Investigaciones Históricas y Estudios Bolivianos: Avda 6 de Agosto 2080, La Paz; tel. 359602; Dir Lic. RAUL CALDERÓN GENIO.

Instituto de Investigaciones Químicas: Ciudad Universitaria Calle 27 Cota Cota, Casilla 303, La Paz; tel. 792238; Dir Lic. LUIS MORALES ESCOBAR.

UNIVERSIDAD MAYOR DE SAN SIMÓN

Avda Ballivián esq. Reza 591, Casilla 992, Cochabamba
Telephone: (4) 4524769
Fax: (4) 4524772
E-mail: rector@umss.edu.bo
Internet: www.umss.edu.bo
Founded 1832
Language of instruction: Spanish
State control
Academic year: July to December

Rector: JUAN RÍOS DEL PRADO
Vice-Rector: WÁLTER LÓPEZ VALENZUELA
Sec.-Gen.: Arq. CARLOS VALDIVIESO SULFO
Librarian: RUTH VALENCIA

Library: see Libraries and Archives
Number of teachers: 1,700
Number of students: 52,800

Publication: *Guía de Proyectos* (current research projects, 1 a year)

DEANS

Faculty of Agricultural Sciences: Ing. JUAN VILLARROEL SOLIZ
Faculty of Architecture: Arq. CARLOS F. GUZMÁN MONTAÑO
Faculty of Biochemistry and Pharmaceutical Sciences: Dr FÉLIX QUIROGA FLORES
Faculty of Dentistry: Dra WILMA FERRUFINO GUEVARA
Faculty of Economics: Lic. ALEX TORRICO LARA
Faculty of Humanities and Education: Dra ELENA FERRUFINO COQUEUGNIOT
Faculty of Legal and Political Sciences: Dra ANA MARÍA FERNÁNDEZ COCA
Faculty of Medicine: Dr FRANCO IBARRA GÓMEZ
Faculty of Science and Technology: JULIO MEDINA GAMBOA

Faculty of Social Sciences: Lic. ANDRÉS PÉREZ SERÚ

Higher Technical School of Agronomy: Ing. JUAN CARLOS ESCALERA LÓPEZ (Dir)

Nursing Programme: ZUNILDA DURÁN TORANZOS (Dir)

Polytechnical University Institute 'El Valle Alto': Ing. ORLANDO GARNICA (Dir)

RESEARCH INSTITUTES

Banco de Semillas Forestales: Dir (vacant).

Centro de Aguas y Saneamiento Ambiental: tel. (4) 4250660; e-mail aguas@fcyt.umss.edu.bo; Dir Lic. ANA MARÍA ROMERO JALDÍN.

Centro de Biotecnología: Dir Ing. ROBERTO SOTO SOLIZ.

Centro de Desarrollo de Tecnologías de Fabricación: Dir Ing. ANDRES GARRIDO VARGAS.

Centro de Estudios de Población: Dir Lic. ROSSEMARY SALAZAR.

Centro de Estudios Superiores Universitarios: Dir Lic. RENATO CRESPO C.

Centro de Investigación Carrera de Sociologia: Dir Lic. ALBERTO RIVERA PIZARRO.

Centro de Levantamientos Aerospaciales SIG par el Desarrollo Sostenible de los Recursos Naturales: Dir Dr CARLOS VALENZUELA.

Centro de Limnología y Recursos Acuáticos: Dir Lic. MABEL MALDONANDO MALDONADO.

Centro de Medioambiente y Recursos Renovables: Dir Ing. MABEL MAGARIÑOS VILLARROEL.

Centro de Planificación y Gestión: tel. (4) 4542759; e-mail carmenledo@ceplag.umss.edu.bo; Dir Dra CARMEN LEDO GARÍA.

Centro de Tecnologías Agroindustriales: tel. (4) 4232548; fax (4) 4233648; e-mail cta@fcyt.umss.edu.bo; Dir Ing. JOSÉ LUIS BALDERRAMA IDINA.

Centro Universitario de Medicina Tropical: Dir Dr HERNÁN BERMUDEZ PAREDES.

Empresa de Semillas Forrajeras: tel. (4) 4316865; fax (4) 4316947; e-mail sefosam@supernet.com.bo; Dir Ing. GASTÓN SAUMA.

Instituto de Estudios Sociales y Económicos: Dir Lic. CRECENCIO ALBA PINTO.

Instituto de Investigaciones de Arquitectura: Dir Arq. ANTONIO SALINAS MORENO.

Instituto de Investigaciones de la Facultad de Bioquímica y Farmacia: Dir Ing. VICTOR MEÍJA URQUIETA.

Instituto de Investigación de la Facultad de Ciencias Agrícolas y Pecuarias: Dir Ing. CARLOS ROJAS RALDE.

Instituto de Investigaciones de la Facultad de Ciencias y Tecnología: Dir Ing. JOSÉ LUIS VALDERRAMA IDINA.

Instituto de Investigaciones de la Facultad de Humanidades y Ciencias de la Educación: Dir Lic. GUIDO DE LA ZERDA.

Instituto de Investigación de la Facultad de Medicina: Dir Dr WALTER SALINAS ARGANDOÑA.

Instituto de Investigaciones de la Facultad de Odontología: Dir Dr LUIS MORALES ARLANDO.

Instituto de Investigaciones Jurídicas y Políticas: Dir Dra JAROSLAVAB Z. DE BALLÓN.

Instituto de Medicina Nuclear: tel. (4) 4534528; fax (4) 4530765; e-mail nuclear@supernet.com.bo; Dir Dr DANIEL VILLAGRA GONZÁLES.

Laboratorio de Geotecnica: tel. and fax (4) 4236858; e-mail gtumss@bo.net; Dir Ing. GUIDO LEÓN CLAVIJO.

Laboratorio de Hidraúlica: tel. (4) 4226751; e-mail ihumss@comteco.umss.edu.bo; Dir Ing. MAURICIO ROMERO MÉRIDA.

Programa de Alimentos y Productos Naturales: tel. and fax (4) 4251877; e-mail alimentos@fcyt.umss.edu.bo; Dir EDWIN TÓRREZ QUINTEROS.

Unidad de Bioversidad y Genética: tel. and fax (4) 4540364; e-mail biodiv@fcyt.umss.edu.bo; Dir Lic. MILTON FERNÁNDEZ CALATAYUD.

UNIVERSIDAD MAYOR, REAL Y PONTIFICIA DE SAN FRANCISCO XAVIER DE CHUQUISACA

Apdo 212, Sucre
Telephone: (4) 6453308
Fax: (4) 6441541
Internet: www.usfx.info
Founded 1624 by Papal Bull of Gregory XV dated 1621 and Royal Charter of Philip III, 1622
Autonomous control
Academic year: 2 semesters beginning February and August

Rector: Lic. JAIME BARRÓN POVEDA
Vice-Rector: Ing. IVAN ARCIÉNAGA COLLAZOS
Admin. Officer: Lic. JORGE FUENTES
Librarian: Dr RONALD GANTIER LEMOINE

Number of teachers: 1,035
Number of students: 37,000

Publications: *Archivos bolivianos de Medicina*, *Revista del Instituto de Sociología Boliviana*

DEANS

Faculty of Agricultural, Livestock and Forestry Sciences: Ing. CARLOS ANTONIO PÉREZ

Faculty of Chemical, Pharmaceutical and Biochemical Sciences: Dr HUMBERTO SIVILA MOGRO

Faculty of Dentistry: Dr JOSÉ MANUEL CARVAJAL CABALLERO

Faculty of Economics, Administration and Commerce: Lic. MIRKO GARDILCIC

Faculty of Law, Political and Social Sciences: ENRIQUE CORTEZ ROMERO

Faculty of Liberal Arts and Educational Sciences: Lic. JOSÉ ALFREDO CABALLERO ZAMORA

Faculty of Medicine: Dr JOSÉ ARCE ARANCIBIA

Faculty of Public Accountancy and Financial Sciences: Lic. MACEDONIO DELGADO

Faculty of Technology: Ing. EDUARDO RIVERO ZURITA

Technical Faculty: MARCELINO VILLAGOMEZ

ATTACHED INSTITUTES

Banco de Sangre: Urriolagoitia 155, Sucre.

Centro Documental Histórico: Plazuela Ingavi (Inisterio), Sucre.

Centro de Medicina Nuclear: Plaza Libertad 1, Sucre.

Instituto de Anatomía Patológica: Destacamento 111, No 1, Sucre.

Instituto de Cancerología 'Cupertino Arteaga': Plaza Libertad 1, Sucre.

Instituto de Investigaciones Biológicas: Dalence 207, Sucre.

Instituto de Investigaciones Económicas: Grau 117, Sucre.

Instituto de Investigación Mal de Chagas: Dalence 207, Sucre.

Instituto de Investigaciones Tecnológicas: Regimiento Campos 181, Sucre.

Instituto de Sociología Boliviana: Plazuela Ingavi (Inisterio), Sucre.

Instituto Experimental de Biología: Dalence 207, Sucre.

UNIVERSIDAD NACIONAL 'SIGLO XX'

Calle Campero 36, Llallagua
(Office in La Paz: Calle Arturo Costa de la Torre 1367, La Paz)
Telephone: (258) 20222
Fax: (258) 21591
E-mail: webmaster@unsxx.edu.bo
Internet: www.unsxx.edu.bo
Founded 1985

Rector: MILTON GÓMEZ MAMANI
Vice-Rector: EDGAR F. VÁSQUEZ PALENQUE
Chief Admin. Officer: MARIO TÓRREZ MIRANDA
Librarian: FLAVIO FERNÁNDEZ MARISCAL
Academic Coordinator: VICENTE CÁCERES B.
Dir-Gen. for Extension: EDGAR F. VÁSQUEZ P.
Dir-Gen. for Research: DIÓGENES ROQUE T.

Number of teachers: 65
Number of students: 1,526

UNIVERSIDAD TÉCNICA DE ORURO

Avda 6 de Octubre entre Ayacucho y Cochabamba, Oruro
Telephone: (252) 5281745
Internet: www.uto.edu.bo
Founded 1892
Autonomous control
Language of instruction: Spanish
Academic year: January to November

Rector: Ing. JESÚS GUSTAVO ROJAS UGARTE
Vice-Rector: Lic. JUAN MEDINA FLORES
Gen. Sec.: Ing. HECTOR SÁNCHEZ SÁNCHEZ
Admin. Dir: Lic. QUINTÍN MURGUÍA
Librarian: SOFÍA A. ZUBIETA

Number of teachers: 487
Number of students: 10,403

Publications: *Revista de Cultura Boliviana*, *Revista de Derecho*, *Revista de Economía*, *Revista de Mecánica*, *Revista Metalúrgica*, *Revista Universitaria*

DEANS

Faculty of Agricultural Sciences: Ing. HARRY CARREÑO PEREYRA

Faculty of Architecture and Town Planning: Arq. RUBÉN URQUIOLA MURILLO

Faculty of Economics and Finance: Lic. ROLANDO MALDONADO ALFARO

Faculty of Engineering: Ing. EDDY NISTTAHUZ GISBERT

Faculty of Legal, Political and Social Sciences: Dr VIDAL VILLARROEL VEGA

University Polytechnic: HUMBERTO QUISPE GONZALES

Schools of Art and Music

Conservatorio Nacional de Música: Calle Reyes Ortiz 56, La Paz; tel. (2) 373297; fax (2) 361798; f. 1907; state control; library: 420 books, 3,900 scores; Dir ANTONIO ROBERTO BORDA.

Escuela Superior de Bellas Artes 'Hernando Siles': Calle Rosendo Gutiérrez 323, La Paz; tel. (2) 2371141; f. 1926; 18 teachers; 206 students; Dir ALBERTO MEDINA MENDIETA; Registrar WALLY DE MONTALBAN.

BOSNIA AND HERZEGOVINA

The Higher Education System

Bosnia and Herzegovina emerged in its present form from the conflict that, from 1991, engulfed the republics hitherto constituting Yugoslavia. In accordance with the General Framework Agreement for Peace in Bosnia and Herzegovina, signed in 1995, Bosnia and Herzegovina is a single state, which consists of two political entities: the Federation of Bosnia and Herzegovina, principally comprising the Bosniak (Muslim)- and Croat-majority areas, and Republika Srpska, principally comprising the Serb-majority area. Although there is a central (state) Government of Bosnia and Herzegovina, based in Sarajevo, both constituent entities have their own governments. In the Federation of Bosnia and Herzegovina, higher education is the responsibility of the Ministry of Education and Science, based in Sarajevo, and in the Republika Srpska higher education is overseen by the Ministry of Education and Culture, based in Banja Luka. At present, higher education is centrally funded. Although the cantons are responsible for financing higher education, only three of the eight existing cantons coincide with university centres. There are no adequate resources at cantonal level for the financing of higher education.

In 2006/07 in the Federation of Bosnia and Herzegovina, 77,009 students attended 105 higher education institutions. In 2007 there were eight universities, as well as other university faculties, specialist institutes and Visoke skole (high schools). In August 2003 officials of the Federation, Republika Srpska, the cantonal Governments and the Interim District Government of Brčko signed an agreement to replace the country's three ethnically-based education systems with a single unified system. (However, some local authorities remained resistant to the unification of the education system.) In the same year Bosnia and Herzegovina became a signatory to the Bologna Process. However, despite the immediate preparation of a new law pertaining to the implementation of a two-tier higher education system (as well as European Credit Transfer System, ECTS, and the Diploma Supplement), the new Law on Higher Education was not adopted until 2007.

Higher education admission is made on the basis of a Secondary School Leaving Certificate. Higher education has been reorganized and credited according to the ECTS. Although a three-cycle structure has existed for most fields of study in all countries of former Yugoslavia, the new framework clearly corresponds with the Bologna scheme of three cycles of higher education: Bachelor, Masters and Doctoral programmes. There are four university degrees: two at undergraduate level (Diploma Višeg Obrazovanje and Diploma Visokog Obrazovanja) and two at postgraduate level (Magistar and Doktor Nauka). The Diploma Višeg Obrazovanje (Diploma of Higher Education) is a two- to three-year course, resulting in a professional title, but is not a full degree. The Diploma Visokog Obrazovanja (Advanced Diploma of Higher Education) is a full degree course of four to six years leading to a professional title. At postgraduate level, the Magistar (Masters) requires two years of research and defence of a thesis, and the Doktor Nauka (Doctor of Science) requires further research and defence of a thesis, but in a non-specified timeframe.

Regulatory and Representative Bodies

GOVERNMENT

Ministry of Culture and Sports: Obala Maka Dizdara 2, 71000 Sarajevo; tel. (33) 254-100; fax (33) 664-381; e-mail kabinet@fmksa.com; internet www.fmks.gov.ba; Min. GAVRILO GRAHOVAC.

Ministry of Education and Science: Stjepana Radića 33, 71000 Mostar; tel. (36) 355-700; fax (36) 355-742; e-mail info@fmon.gov.ba; internet www.fmon.gov.ba; Min. Prof. MELIHA ALIĆ.

ACCREDITATION

ENIC/NARIC Bosnia and Herzegovina: Min. of Civil Affairs, Sektor za obrazovanje/Education Sector (Unit for Collecting ENIC-NARIC Information), Vilsonovo šetalište 10, 71000 Sarajevo; tel. (33) 655-339; fax (33) 713-956; e-mail miljan.popic@mcp.gov.ba; internet www.mcp.gov.ba; Contact MILJAN POPIĆ.

Learned Societies

GENERAL

Akademija Nauka i Umjetnosti BiH (Academy of Arts and Sciences of Bosnia and Herzegovina): Bistrik 7, 71000 Sarajevo; tel. (33) 206-034; fax (33) 206-033; e-mail akademija@anubih.ba; internet www.anubih.ba; f. 1951 as the Scientific Society, present name and status 1966; attached research institute: see Research Institutes; responsible for the overall devt of science and the arts by organizing scientific research and arts-related events, publishing papers written by its members and associates; 57 mems; library of 50,000 vols; Pres. Dr BOŽIDAR MATIĆ; Vice-Pres. Dr SLOBODAN LOGA; Sec.-Gen. Dr ZIJO PAŠIĆ; publs *Godišnjak* (Annals), *Herbologia*, *Ljetopis* (Yearbook), *Sarajevo Journal of Mathematics* (2 a year).

Hrvatsko Kulturno Društvo 'Napredak' ('Napredak' Croatian Cultural Society): Središnja uprava, Ulica Maršala Tita 56, 71000 Sarajevo; tel. (33) 222-876; fax (33) 663-380; e-mail ured@napredak.com.ba; internet www.napredak.com.ba; f. 1902; Pres. FRANJO TOPIĆ; Sec.-Gen. VANJA RAVEN; 20,000 mems; publ. *Stecak* (cultural and social issues, 12 a year).

Srpske Prosvjetno Kulturno Društvo 'Prosvjeta' Sarajevo ('Prosvjeta' Serbian Cultural Society, Sarajevo): Sime Milutinovića-Sarajlije 1, 71000 Sarajevo; tel. (33) 444-230; fax (33) 444-230; e-mail prosvjeta@bih.net.ba; f. 1902; science, art and literature; 140 mems; library of 3,000 vols; Pres. TEODOR ROMANIĆ; Sec. DRAGAN SELEDA; publ. *Bosanska Vila*.

Udruženje Gradjana Bošnjačka Zajednica Kulture 'Preporod' u BiH ('Preporod' Cultural Association of the Bosniak Community of Bosnia and Herzegovina): Branilaca Sarajeva 30, 71000 Sarajevo; tel. and fax (33) 205-553.

UNESCO Office Sarajevo: Titova 48/4, 71000 Sarajevo; tel. (33) 222-792; fax (33) 222-795; e-mail sarajevo@unesco.org; Dir COLIN KAISER.

AGRICULTURE, FISHERIES AND VETERINARY SCIENCE

Bosnia and Herzegovina Small Animal Veterinary Association: Alipašina St 37, 71000 Sarajevo; tel. (33) 442-303; fax (33) 442-303; e-mail veterins@bih.net.ba; Pres. Dr JOSIP KRASNI.

ARCHITECTURE AND TOWN PLANNING

Društvo Urbanista Bosne i Hercegovine (Society of Town Planning of Bosnia and Herzegovina): Zavod za urbanizam, Aleja bosanskih vladara 6, 75000 Tuzla; tel. (35) 252-038; fax (35) 251-575; f. 1993; 500 ; Pres. ZEHRA MORANKIĆ; publ. *URBO* (1 a year).

BIBLIOGRAPHY, LIBRARY SCIENCE AND MUSEOLOGY

Društvo Arhivskih Radnika Bosne i Hercegovine (Association of Archive Workers of Bosnia and Herzegovina): Franje Ledera 1, 75000 Tuzla; tel. (35) 252-620; fax (35) 252-620; Pres. Dr AZEM KOŽAR; publ. *Glasnik Arhiva i Društva Arhivski Radnika Bosne i Hercegovine* (1 a year).

Društvo Bibliotekara BiH (Librarians' Society of Bosnia and Herzegovina): Zmaja od Bosne 8B, 71000 Sarajevo; tel. (33) 275-325; fax (33) 212-435; f. 1949; 450 mems; Pres. NEVENKA HAJDAROVIĆ; publs *Bibliotekarstvo* (1 a year), *Bilten*.

ECONOMICS, LAW AND POLITICS

Advokatska-Odvjetnicka Komora Federacije Bosne i Hercegovine (Bar Association of the Federation of Bosnia and Herzegovina): Obala Kulina Bana 6, 71000 Sarajevo; tel. (33) 261-090; fax (33) 209-976;

internet www.advokomfbih.ba; 830 mems, incl. 670 attorneys and 160 law trainees; Pres. AMILA KUNOSIĆ-FERIZOVIĆ.

Advokatska Komora Bosne i Hercegovine (Law Society of Bosnia and Herzegovina): Šemaluša 2, 71000 Sarajevo; tel. (33) 471-156; fax (33) 471-156.

Udruženje Sudija i Sudaca u Federacije Bosne i Hercegovine (Association of Judges of the Federation of Bosnia and Herzegovina): Valtera Perića 15, Kancelarija udruženja br. 203, 71000 Sarajevo; tel. and fax (33) 668-035; e-mail usfbih@bih.net.ba; internet www.usfbih.ba; f. 1996; advocacy and training; 320 mems; Pres. VILDANA HELIĆ; Vice-Pres. STJEPAN MIKULIĆ; Vice-Pres. GORAN SALIHOVIĆ; publ. *Mjesečni Časopis*.

Udruženje sudija Republike Srpske (Republic of Srpska Association of Judges): Aleja svetog Save bb, 78000 Banja Luka; tel. (51) 212-801; fax (51) 212-071; e-mail zlatko .kulenovic@pravosudje.ba; f. 2005; annual seminars on criminal and civil and administrative law; 300 mems; Pres. ZLATKO KULE-NOVIĆ; Sec. ŽIVANA BAJIĆ; publs *Seminar Collected Texts* (3 a year), *Bulletin* (6 a year).

EDUCATION

Pedagoško Društvo BiH (Pedagogical Society of Bosnia and Herzegovina): Djure Djakovića 4, 71000 Sarajevo.

FINE AND PERFORMING ARTS

Muzička Omladina Sarajeva BiH (Jeunesses Musicales of Sarajevo): Dalmatinska 2/1, 71000 Sarajevo; tel. (33) 665-713; fax (33) 665-713; e-mail muzomlsa@soros.org.ba; internet jm-sa.open.net.ba; f. 1958; organizes concerts and theatre events; 12,000 mems; library of 1,000 vols, record library of 1,000 items; Pres. REŠAD ARNAUTOVIĆ; Sec. SLAVICA ŠPOLJARIĆ.

Udruženje Muzičkih Umjetnika BiH (Association of Musicians of Bosnia and Herzegovina): Sv. Markovića 1, 71000 Sarajevo.

HISTORY, GEOGRAPHY AND ARCHAEOLOGY

Društvo Istoričara BiH (Historical Society of Bosnia and Herzegovina): Račkog 1, Filozofski fakultet, 71000 Sarajevo.

Geografsko Društvo BiH (Geographical Society of Bosnia and Herzegovina): Prirodnomatematički fakultet, Vojvode Putnika 43A, 71000 Sarajevo; f. 1947; 1,541 mems; Pres. Dr MILOŠ BJELOVITIĆ; Vice-Pres. Dr KREŠIMIR PAPIĆ; publs *Geografski list* (5 a year), *Geografski pregled*, *Nastava geografije* (1 a year).

Geografsko Društvo Republike Srpske (Society of Geographers of Republika Srpska): Bana Lazarevića 1, 78000 Banja Luka; tel. (51) 235-625.

LANGUAGE AND LITERATURE

British Council: Ljubljianska 9, 71000 Sarajevo; tel. (33) 250-220; fax (33) 250-240; e-mail british.council@britishcouncil.ba; internet www.britishcouncil.ba; offers courses and examinations in English language and British culture and promotes cultural exchange with the UK; f. 1996; library of 6,500 vols; Dir MICHAEL MOORE; Deputy Dir GORJANA ŠEVELJ PEĆANAC.

Društvo Pisaca BiH (Association of Writers of Bosnia and Herzegovina): Kranjčevićeva 24, 71000 Sarajevo; tel. (33) 557-940; fax (33) 557-940; e-mail d_pisaca@bih.net.ba; f. 1993; organizes the Int. Festival of Poetry and Sarajevo Poetry days; 165 mems; library of

1,500 vols; Pres. GRADIMIR GOJER; Sec. MUHAMED ČUROVAC; publs *Lica i Život* (4 a year), *Slovo* (12 a year).

Goethe-Institut: Bentbaša 1A, 71000 Sarajevo; tel. (33) 570-000; fax (33) 570-030; e-mail info@sarajevo.goethe.org; internet www.goethe.de/sarajevo; offers courses and examinations in German language and culture and promotes cultural exchange with Germany; f. 2000, present bldg 2004; Dir Dr PETRA RAYMOND; Deputy Dir Dr NINA WICH-MANN.

PEN Centar u BiH (PEN Centre of Bosnia and Herzegovina): Vrazova 1, 71000 Sarajevo; tel. (33) 200-155; fax (33) 217-854; e-mail pencentear@bih.net.ba; internet www .penbih.ba; f. 1992; freedom of expression, dialogue culture, writing without borders, literary critics, and meetings connected to the above-mentioned issues; mem. of the PEN Int. org.; 92 mems; Pres. UGO VLAISAVL-JEVIĆ; Exec. Dir. FERIDA DURAKOVIĆ; publ. *Novi Izraz, Literary and Art Critics Review* (4 a year).

MEDICINE

Društvo Ljekara BiH (Physicians' Society of Bosnia and Herzegovina): Zavod za zdravst-venu zaštitu BiH, Maršala Tita 7, 71000 Sarajevo.

Farmaceutsko društvo Republike Srpske (Pharmaceutical Society of Republika Srpske): Ranka Sipke 32, 78000 Banja Luka; tel. (51) 318-699; e-mail farmacia@teol .net; internet www.farmaceutskodrustvo.org; f. 1996; br. offices in Banja Luka, Doboj, Bijeljina, Foca, Prijedor, Trebinje and Zvornik; training programmes, devt of health education; Pres. RADA AMIDŽIĆ.

Udruga/Udruženje Pedijatara u Bosni i Hercegovini (Paediatric Society in Bosnia and Herzegovina): Sveučilisna klinička bolnica Mostar Klinika za dječje bolest, 88000 Mostar; tel. and fax (36) 343-348; e-mail tajnica@upubih.org; internet www.upubih .org; f. 2006 as legal successor of the Paediatric Asscn of Bosnia and Herzegovina in Sarajevo, registered with the Min. of Justice; disease prevention and health care; Pres. ZELJKO RONCEVIĆ; Vice-Pres. AMIRA SKAKA; Vice-Pres. ZDRAVKO KUZMAN.

Udruženje Farmakologa Federacije Bosne i Hercegovine (Association of Pharmacologists of the Federation of Bosnia and Herzegovina): Čekaluša 90/II, 71000 Sarajevo; tel. (33) 441-813; fax (33) 441-895; e-mail farma@bih.net.ba; f. 1980; 54 mems; library of 5,000 vols; Pres. Prof. Dr NEDŽAD MULABEGOVIĆ; Sec. Asst Prof. SVJETLANA LOGA; publs *Bosnian Journal of Basic Medical Sciences* (6 a year), *Drug Plus* (1 a year).

Udruženje Stomatologa BiH (Dental Association of Bosnia and Herzegovina): School of Dentistry, Bolnička 4A, 71000 Sarajevo; tel. (33) 214-259; fax (33) 214-259; e-mail mganibeg@utic.net.ba; internet www .usfbih.org.ba; f. 1997; 500 mems; Pres. Prof. MAIDA GANIBEGOVIĆ; Vice-Pres. MARINKO TOPIĆ; Gen. Sec. NINA MARKOVIC; publs *Bilten Stomatologa BiH* (in the nat. languages of Bosnia and Herzegovina and in English, 3 a year), *Stomatološki vjesnik* (in the nat. languages of Bosnia and Herzegovina and in English, 2 a year).

NATURAL SCIENCES

General

Društvo Fizičara u BiH (Physical Society in Bosnia and Herzegovina): Zmaja od Bosne 35, zgrada Prirodno-matematički fakultet, 71000 Sarajevo; tel. (33) 653-294; e-mail dfubih@gmail.com; internet www .drustvofizicara.com.ba; organizes competi-

tions, seminars and lectures for the popularization of physics; Pres. RAJFA MUSEMIĆ; Vice-Pres REFIK FAZLIĆ, SLAVICA EREŠ-BRKIĆ, ZALKIDA HADŽIBEGOVIĆ.

Mathematical Sciences

Društvo Matematičara Republike Srpske (Society of Mathematicians of Republika Srpska): Bana Lazarevića 1, 78000 Banja Luka; tel. (51) 268-686.

PHILOSOPHY AND PSYCHOLOGY

Društvo Psihologa BiH (Association of Psychologists of Bosnia and Herzegovina): Aleja lipa 81, 71000 Sarajevo; tel. (33) 659-184.

Društvo Psihologa Republike Srpske (Association of Psychologists of Republika Srpske): Bana Lazarevića 1, treći sprat, soba 47, 78000 Banja Luka; e-mail dprs@ drustvo-psihologa.rs.ba; internet www .drustvo-psihologa.rs.ba; f. 2003; devt and application of theoretical and applied psychology; org. of professional education; Pres. Dr MILENA PASIĆ; Vice-Pres. SINISA LAKIĆ.

Research Institutes

GENERAL

Bošnjački Institut—Fondacija Adila Zulfikarpašića (Bosniak Institute—Adil Zulfikarpašić Foundation): Mula Mustafe Bašeskie 21, 71000 Sarajevo; tel. (33) 279-800; fax (33) 279-777; e-mail bosinst@ bosnjackiinstitut.org; internet www .bosnjackiinstitut.org; f. 1988 in Zurich, in Sarajevo 2001; researches into the history, literature, art, language and religion of the Bosniaks and other people of Bosnia and Herzegovina and the promotion of their cultural heritage; library: reference library of 80,000 vols, open to the public; Exec. Dir AMINA RIZVANBEGOVIĆ DZUVIĆ; Archivist AHMET ZULFIKARPAŠIĆ; Librarian VESNA ČEFO; Librarian NARCISA PULJEK-BUBRIĆ.

Centre for Philosophical Research: Bistrik 7, 71000 Sarajevo; tel. (33) 210-902; fax (33) 206-033; e-mail akademija@anubih.ba; internet www.anubih.ba; attached to Acad. of Arts and Sciences of Bosnia and Herzegovina; Dir ARIF TANOVIĆ; publ. *Dialogue* (4 a year).

Kantonalni Zavod za Zaštitu Kulturno-Historisjkog i Prirodnog Naslijedja Sarajevo (Institute for the Protection of the Cultural, Historical and Natural Heritage of the Canton of Sarajevo): Josipa Štadlera 32, 71000 Sarajevo; tel. (33) 475-020; fax (33) 475-034; e-mail heritsa@bih.net.ba; internet www.spomenici-sa.ba; f. 1965; documentation of monuments; devt projects; surveys and studies; promotes awareness of culture, history and natural heritage; library of 15,000 vols; Dir MUNIB BULJINA; Exec. Dir VALIDA ČELIĆ-ČEMERLIĆ.

Orijentalni Institut u Sarajevu (Oriental Institute, Sarajevo): Zmaja od Bosne 8B, 71000 Sarajevo; tel. (33) 225-353; fax (33) 225-353; e-mail ois@bih.net.ba; internet www .ois.unsa.ba; f. 1950; history, philology and culture of the Ottoman Balkans and the Middle East; library of 10,554 vols, 1,450 periodicals; Scientific Advisor and Dir Dr BEHIJA ZLATAR; Pres. of Steering Cttee HALIL BJELAK; publ. *Prilozi za orijentalnu filologiju/Revue de philologie orientale* (1 a year).

Zavod za Zaštitu Kulturnog, Historijskog i Prirodnog Naslijedja BiH (Institute for the Protection of the Cultural, Historical and Natural Heritage of Bosnia and Herzegovina): Alekse Šantića 8/III, 71000 Sarajevo; tel. (33) 663-299; fax (33) 663-299; e-mail h_c_bih@bih.net.ba; f. 1947; protection and preservation of monuments; conservation, registering of moveable and non-moveable heritage; colln of documents; raising awareness and evaluation of heritage, projects and studies; Dir DŽIHAD PAŠIĆ; publ. *Naše Starine.*

ARCHITECTURE AND TOWN PLANNING

Centar za Islamsku Arhitektura (Centre for Islamic Architecture): Blvr Mese Selimovića 85, 71000 Sarajevo; tel. (33) 459-780; fax (33) 459-700; e-mail centaria@bih.net.ba; internet www.rijaset.ba; f. 1995; attached to Rijaset Islamske Zajednice u Bosni i Hercegovini (Islamic Community in Bosnia and Herzegovina); restoration and reconstruction of damaged and destroyed religious sites; Dir KEMAL ŽUKIĆ.

ECONOMICS, LAW AND POLITICS

Ekonomski Institut Sarajevo (Institute of Economics, Sarajevo): Branilaca Sarajevo 47, 71000 Sarajevo; tel. (33) 565-870; fax (33) 565-874; e-mail ekonomski.institut@efsa.unsa.ba; internet www.eis.ba; f. 1961; economic research for improvement of public policy and business consulting services, increasing competitiveness in the business sector; library of 12,400 vols; Dir Dr ANTO DOMAZET.

Ekonomski Institut Tuzla (Tuzla Institute of Economics): Zvonka Cerića 1, 75000 Tuzla; tel. (35) 214-657; fax (35) 214-336; Dir SEAD BABOVIĆ.

Human Rights Centre: Zmaja od Bosne 8, 71000 Sarajevo; tel. and fax (33) 668-251; e-mail hrc_sa@hrc.unsa.ba; internet www.hrc.unsa.ba; f. 1996; attached to Univ. of Sarajevo; education and training, research and consulting, documentation and information services; library of 582 vols, 5,776 monographs, 928 serials, 600 thesis; Dir SAŠA MADACKI; Librarians AJLA MUHAMEDOVIĆ, AIDA HAJRO, MAJA KALJANAC, NINA KARAĆ.

Institut za istraživanje zločina protiv čovječnosti i međunarodnog prava (Institute for Research of Crimes Against Humanity and International Law): ul. Halida Nazecica 4, 71000 Sarajevo; tel. (33) 561-350; fax (33) 561-351; e-mail info@institut-genocid.ba; internet www.institut-genocid.ba; f. 1992; attached to Univ. of Sarajevo; public scientific institution; provides analysis of crimes against int. law, human rights violations and genocide; Chair. for Board of Management Prof. Dr ISMET DIZDAREVIĆ; Chair. for Scientific Ccl Prof. Dr SMAIL ĆEKIĆ.

HISTORY, GEOGRAPHY AND ARCHAEOLOGY

Institut za Istoriju (Institute of History): Alipašina 9, 71000 Sarajevo; tel. (33) 209-364; fax (33) 217-263; e-mail nauka@bih.net.ba; internet www.iis.unsa.ba; f. 1959; public research institute; deals with research work in field of history; library of 3,000 journals, 12,070 monographs, rare periodicals from the pre-war and 1941–45 period; Dir Dr HUSNIJA KAMBEROVIĆ; Pres. Prof. Dr MUSTAFA IMAMOVIĆ; Sec. ASIDE ŠAHBEGOVIĆ; publ. *Prilozi* (Contributions, 1 a year).

LANGUAGE AND LITERATURE

Institut za Jezik i Književnost (Institute of Language and Literature): Hasana Kikića 12, 71000 Sarajevo; tel. (33) 200-117.

Language Institute: Hasana Kikića 12, 71000 Sarajevo; tel. (33) 200-117; f. 1973; library of 3,200 vols; Dir Dr IBRAHIM ČEDIĆ; publs *Dijalektološki Zbornik* (Dialect Colln,

irregular), *Književni jezik* (Literary Language, 4 a year), *Radovi* (Works, 1 a year).

Media Plan Institute: Antuna Branka Šimića 5/2, 71000 Sarajevo; tel. (33) 717-840; fax (33) 717-850; e-mail mediaplan@mediaplan.ba; internet www.mediaplan.ba; f. 1995; research into and analysis of the media; press clippings; educational projects, media campaigns, communication training; audiovisual productions; Pres. ZORAN UDOVIĆIĆ; Exec. Dir BOJANA ŠUTVIĆ.

NATURAL SCIENCES
Mathematical Sciences

Agencija za Statistiku Bosne i Hercegovine (Agency for Statistics of Bosnia and Herzegovina): Zelenih beretki 26, 71000 Sarajevo; tel. (33) 220-626; fax (33) 220-622; e-mail bhas@bhas.ba; internet www.bhas.ba; f. 1998; dir and two deputies consisting of one Serb, one Croat and one Muslim; documents statistical changes in economic, demographic and social fields, environment and natural resources; Dir ZDENKO MILINOVIĆ; publs *First Release* (12 a year), *Statistical Bulletins* (6–8 a year).

Federalni Zavod za Statistiku (Institute of Statistics of the Federation of Bosnia and Herzegovina): Zeleni beretki 26, 71000 Sarajevo; tel. (33) 664-553; fax (33) 664-553; e-mail fedstat@fzs.ba; internet www.fzs.ba; f. 1997; organizes and conducts statistical research; library of 6,940 vols; Dir DERVIŠ ĐURĐEVIĆ; Sec. SUADA ČUKOJEVIĆ; publs *Federacija BiH u Brojkama* (1 a year), *GDP* (1 a year), *Kanton u Brojkama* (1 a year), *Obrazovanje* (1 a year), *Poljoprivreda* (1 a year), *Pravosudje* (1 a year), *Socjalna Zaštita* (Statistical Bulletin, 1 a year), *Statistički Godisnjak* (1 a year), *Statistički Podaci o Privrednim i Drugim Kretanjima u Federacije BiH* (12 a year), *Statistički Podaci o Privrednim i Drugim Kretanjim o Kantonima* (12 a year), *Zaposlenost i Plaće* (1 a year).

Republički Zavod za Statistiku Republike Srpske (Institute of Statistics of Republika Srpska): Veljka Mlađenovića 12D, 78000 Banja Luka; tel. (51) 450-275; fax (51) 450-279; e-mail stat@rzs.rs.ba; internet www.rzs.rs.ba; f. 1992; attached to Min. of Finance; performs statistical activity for the territory of Republika Srpska; Dir SLAVKO ŠOBOT; publs *Agricultural Statistics Bulletin* (1 a year), *Annual Demographic Review*, *Bulletin of Monthly Statistical Reviews* (12 a year), *Data on Industrial Production* (in Serbian, 1 a year), *Education Statistics Bulletin* (Basic and Secondary Education) (1 a year), *Forestry Statistics Bulletin* (1 a year), *Gender Statistics Bulletin* (1 a year), *Social Welfare Bulletin* (1 a year), *Quarterly Statistical Review*.

Physical Sciences

Federalni Meteorološki Zavod (Federal Hydrometeorological Institute): Bardakčije 12, 71000 Sarajevo; tel. (33) 276-701; fax (33) 276-700; e-mail kontakt@fhmzbih.gov.ba; internet www.fhmzbih.gov.ba; Dir ENES SARAČ.

Geodetski Zavod Bosne i Hercegovine (Geodetic Institute of Bosnia and Herzegovina): Bulevar Meše Selimovića 95, 71000 Sarajevo; tel. (33) 469-357; fax (33) 468-989.

Institute of Meteorology: Hadži Loje 4, 71000 Sarajevo; f. 1891; Dir M. V. VEMIĆ.

Metalurški Institut 'Kemal Kapetanović' (Kemal Kapetanović Metallurgical Institute): Travnička cesta 7, 72000 Zenica; tel. (32) 247-999; fax (32) 247-980; e-mail miz@miz.ba; internet www.miz.ba; f. 1961, fmrly Hasan Brkić; attached to University in

Zenica; depts in physical metallurgy, chemistry, heat engineering, welding, metal casting, electrical engineering and automation; conducts research and devt in natural sciences, technological and architectural engineering, technical testing and analysis, education-related activities; Dir Dr MIRSADA ORUČ.

Zavod za Geologiju (Institute of Geology): Ustanička 11, Ilidža 71210 Sarajevo; tel. (33) 621-567; fax (33) 621-567; e-mail zgeolbih@bih.net.ba; internet www.fzzg.ba; f. 1946 as Geologic Research Institute of the Ministry of Industry and Mining; Asst Dir ALOJZ FILIPOVIĆ.

TECHNOLOGY

Institut za standardizaciju BiH (Institute for Standardization of Bosnia and Herzegovina): V. Radomira Putnika 34, 71123 Sarajevo; tel. (57) 310-560; fax (57) 310-575; e-mail stand@bas.gov.ba; internet www.bas.gov.ba; f. 1992 as Institut za standarde, mjeriteljstvo i intelektualno vlasništvo, present name 2007; proposes the strategy of standardization in Bosnia and Herzegovina; participates in preparing technical regulations, develops and establishes the information system of standards; organizes and carries out specialist education of personnel in standardization area; adopted more than 12,000 int. and European standards by endorsement method; library of 950 vols; Dir GORAN TESANOVIĆ (acting); publ. *Glasnik Standardizacije* (4 a year).

Rudarski Institut: Rudarska 72, 75000 Tuzla; tel. (35) 282-406; fax (35) 282-700; e-mail rituzla@bih.net.ba; internet www.rudarski-institut.com.ba; f. 1960; planning and consulting in mining, electrical, mechanical and civil engineering, geology, geoengineering, occupational safety and environmental protection, testing materials and constructions; Dir Dr RASIM PIRIĆ.

Libraries and Archives
Banja Luka

Arhiv Republike Srpske (Archives of Republika Srpska): ul. Svetog Save 1, 78000 Banja Luka; tel. (51) 340-240; fax (51) 340-231; e-mail arhivrs@inecco.net; internet www.arhivrs.org; f. 1953; attached to Min. of Education and Culture; 2,500 m of records from all periods; 12,000 vols, 15,000 photographs; Dir Prof. LJILJANA RADOSEVIĆ.

Narodna i Univerzitetska Biblioteka Republike Srpske (National and University Library of Republika Srpska): Jevrejska 30, 78000 Banja Luka; tel. (51) 215-894; fax (51) 217-040; e-mail nubrs@urc.bl.ac.yu; internet www.nubrs.rs.ba; f. 1936; organizes continuous educational programmes for librarians; 500,000 vols; Dir RANKO RISOJEVIĆ; Library Sec. LJILJANA BABIĆ; publs *Information Bulletin ISBN/ISMN*, *National Bibliography of Republika Srpska*.

Bihać

Arhiv Unsko-sanskog Kantona Bihać (Una-Sana Canton Archives, Bihać): ul. Bosanskih banova 7, 77000 Bihać; tel. (37) 327-384; fax (37) 327-384; f. 1988; Dir Prof. OSMAN ALTIĆ.

Javna Biblioteka Unsko-sanskog Kantona (Una-Sana Canton Public Library): Trg Slobode 8, 77000 Bihać; tel. (37) 333-372; fax (37) 333-372; f. 1954; Dir REUF MUSTAFIĆ.

Fojnica

Franjevački Samostan Fojnica, Biblioteka (Library of the Franciscan Monastery,

Fojnica): 71270 Fojnica; tel. (30) 832-081; fax (30) 832-082; e-mail samostan.fojnica@gmail.com; internet www.fojnica-samostan.com; f. 1463; 13,000 vols, 15 incunabula, archives incl. documents in Turkish and Bosnian; Guardian Fra NIKICA VUJICA.

Kraljevska Sutjeska

Franjevački Samostan Kraljeva Sutjeska, Biblioteka (Library of the Franciscan Monastery, Kraljeva Sutjeska): 72244 Kraljeva Sutjeska; tel. (32) 771-700; fax (32) 771-705; e-mail urednistvo@kraljeva-sutjeska.com; internet www.kraljeva-sutjeska.com; f. 1350; 11,000 vols, 31 incunabula, archives incl. parish registers and MSS in Bosnian Cyrillic and Turkish; Guardian Fra ILIJA BOZIĆ.

Kreševo

Franjevački Samostan Kreševo, Biblioteka (Library of the Franciscan Monastery, Kreševo): 71260 Kreševo; tel. (30) 806-075; f. 1767; 25,000 vols, archive; Guardian Fra MATO CVIJETKOVIĆ.

Mostar

Arhiv Hercegovine Mostar (Archives of Herzegovina, Mostar): Trg 1 Maj 17, 88000 Mostar; tel. (36) 551-047; fax (36) 551-047; e-mail arhiv@cob.net.ba; f. 1954; records from the 13th century onwards; spec. Oriental colln of 800 MSS and 2,000 documents; 9,000 vols; Dir EDIN ČELEBIĆ; publ. *Hercegovina* (1 a year).

Narodna Biblioteka Mostar (Mostar Public Library): Marsala Tita bb., 88000 Mostar; tel. (36) 551-487; fax (36) 551-487; e-mail biblioteka@mostar.ba; Dir RASIM PRGUDA.

Mrkonjić Grad

Narodna Biblioteka, Mrkonjić Grad (National Library, Mrkonjić Grad): Svetog Save 1, 70260 Mrkonjić Grad; tel. (50) 220-271; e-mail kontakt@junbmg.info; internet www.junbmg.info; f. 1900 as Serbian Orthodox Church-Nikolajević Glee Club, present bldg 1973; activities incl. literary evenings, book promotions, professional and scientific lectures, exhibitions, round tables and workshops; 20,000 books; Dir BILJANA ČELIĆ.

Sarajevo

Arhiv Bosne i Hercegovine (Archive of Bosnia and Herzegovina): Reisa Džemaludina Čauševića 6, 71000 Sarajevo; tel. and fax (33) 206-492; e-mail info@arhivbih.gov.ba; internet www.arhivbih.gov.ba; f. 1947, present name 1965; nat. archive; 11,000 m of documents from the 14th century to the present; 20,000 vols; Dir ŠABAN ZAHIROVIĆ; publ. *Glasnik*.

Arhiv Federacije Bosne i Hercegovine (Archive of the Federation of Bosnia and Herzegovina): Reisa Čauševića 6, 71000 Sarajevo; tel. (33) 214-481; fax (33) 556-905; e-mail info@arhivfbih.gov.ba; internet www.arhivfbih.gov.ba; f. 1994; entity archive; activities incl. archival processing and preservation, devt of archival service; Dir ADAMIRA JERKOVIĆA.

Biblioteka Grada Sarajeva (Sarajevo City Library): Mis Irbina 4, 71000 Sarajevo; tel. (33) 444-580; fax (33) 265-030; e-mail info@bgs.ba; internet www.bgs.ba; f. 1948; colln, restoration, preservation and processing of professional library materials, old and rare books; promotion of information systems; 300,000 vols; Pres. RAMO KOLAR; Dir MESUD SMAJIĆ.

Gazi Husrev-begova biblioteka (Gazi Husrav-Bey Library): Hamdije Kreševljakovića 58, 71000 Sarajevo; tel. (33) 226152; fax (33) 205525; e-mail ghbibl@bih.net.ba; internet www.ghbibl.com.ba; f. 1537; Orien-

tal library; 80,000 vols, incl. 11,000 Islamic MSS; Pres. AHMET ALIBAŠIĆ; Dir Dr MUSTAFA JAHIĆ; Sec. HAMIDA KARČIĆ; publs *Anali Gazi Husrevbegove biblioteke, Katalog arapskih, turskih i perzijskih rukopisa*.

Historijski Arhiv Sarajevo (Sarajevo Historical Archives): Alipašina 19, 71000 Sarajevo; tel. (33) 223-281; fax (33) 209-737; e-mail has@arhivsa.ba; internet www.arhivsa.ba; f. 1948; archive of the canton and city of Sarajevo; 3,000 m of documents; spec. colln of Ottoman MSS; 20,000 vols; Dir Prof. TONČI GRBELJA; publ. *Glas Arhiva Grada Sarajeva*.

Nacionalna i univerzitetska biblioteka Bosne i Hercegovine (National and University Library of Bosnia and Herzegovina): Zmaja od Bosne 8B, 71000 Sarajevo; tel. (33) 275-301; fax (33) 218-431; e-mail nubbih@nub.ba; internet www.nub.ba; f. 1945, destroyed 1992, reconstructed 1995; nat. deposit library; nat. agency for ISSN and ISMN; nat. bibliography centre; centre for permanent education of librarians; nat. centre for cooperative online bibliographic and information system and service; supports univ. research, educational and scientific work; 500,000 vols; Dir Dr ISMET OVČINA.

Zemaljski Muzej Bosne i Hercegovine, Biblioteka (National Museum of Bosnia and Herzegovina, Library): Zmaja od Bosne 3, 71000 Sarajevo; tel. (33) 586-321; fax (33) 262-710; e-mail z.muzej@zemaljskimuzej.ba; internet www.zemaljskimuzej.ba; f. 1888, present bldg 1913; archaeology, ethnology and natural sciences; 250,000 vols; Chief Librarian OLGA LALEVIĆ; publs *Glasnik Zemaljskog muzeja BiH - Arheologija* (scientific reports of the museum of Bosnia and Herzegovina; 3 series: Archaeology, Ethnology, Natural History, in Bosnian and English), *Glasnik Zemaljskog muzeja BiH - Etnologija* (scientific and professional reports of the National Museum of Bosnia and Herzegovina: Ethnology), *Glasnik Zemaljskog muzeja BiH - Natural History* (scientific and professional reports of the National Museum of Bosnia and Herzegovina: Natural History, in Bosnian and English).

Travnik

Kantonalni-Županijski Arhiv Travnik (Cantonal and County Archive, Travnik): ul. Školska bb., 72000 Travnik; tel. (30) 511-580; fax (30) 518-979; f. 1954; 8,900 m of documents; Dir Prof. JASMINA HOPIĆ.

Tuzla

Arhiv Tuzlanskog kantona (Archives of Tuzla Canton): ul. Franje Ledera 1, 75000 Tuzla; tel. (35) 252-620; fax (35) 252-620; e-mail arhiv.tk@bih.net.ba; internet www.arhivtk.com.ba; f. 1954 as Archive of Tuzla, present name 1966; 1,380 m of documents from all periods; 20,000 vols; Dir Dr IZET ŠABOTIĆ; publ. *Archival Practice*.

Narodna i Univerzitetska Biblioteka 'Derviš Sušić' Tuzla (Public and University Library Derviš Sušić, Tuzla): Mihajla i Živka Crnogorčevića 7, 75000 Tuzla; tel. (35) 272-626; fax (35) 266-343; e-mail nubtz@nubtz.ba; internet www.nubtz.ba; f. 1946, present status 1986; gen. reference colln; works in science and arts, literature, history and philosophy, domestic and foreign rarities, doctoral and masters papers, serial publs; 200,000 vols, 10,000 periodicals; Dir ENISA ŽUNIĆ.

Zenica

Opća Biblioteka Zenica (Zenica Public Library): Skolska ul. 6, 72000 Zenica; tel. (32) 407-600; fax (32) 407-664; e-mail biblioze@biblioze.ba; internet www.biblioze

.ba; f. 1954; 78,000 vols; Dir MIDHAT KASAP; Sec. RASMA SEHIC.

Museums and Art Galleries

Banja Luka

Muzej savremene umjetnosti Republike Srpske (Museum of Contemporary Art of Republika Srpska): Trg Srpskih Junaka 2, 78000 Banja Luka; tel. (51) 215-364; fax (51) 215-366; e-mail galrs@inecco.net; internet www.msurs.org; f. 1971; history, archaeology, ethnography, history of art, contemporary art, natural history of Republika Srpska; library of 5,500 vols, 500 journals; Dir LJILJANA LABOVIC-MARINKOVIĆ; Man. MILICA RADOJIČIĆ; Curators BRANKA ŠESTIĆ, DANKA DAMJANOVIĆ, NIKOLA GALIĆ, LANA PAVLOVIĆ, LJILJANA P. MISIRLIĆ, SARITA VUJKOVIĆ; publ. *Zbornik* (irregular).

Bihać

Muzej Unsko-sanskog Kantona (Una-Sana Canton Museum): ul. 5 Korpusa 2, 77000 Bihać; tel. (37) 229-743; f. 1953; archaeology, history, natural history, ethnography; attached museums: Kapetanova kula (The Captain's Tower), Museum of the first Session of AVNOJ; Dir DŽAFER MAHMUTOVIĆ.

Bijeljina

Muzej Semberija (Semberija Museum): Karadjordjeva 1, 76300 Bijeljina; tel. (65) 401-293; fax (65) 471-625; e-mail mbabic@rstel.net; f. 1970; archaeology, history, ethnography; 5,000 artefacts, 2,000 photographs; Resić collns of ceramics, tapestries by Milica Zorić-Čolaković; library of 5,000 vols; Dir MIRKO BABIĆ.

Doboj

Regionalni Muzej Doboj (Doboj Regional Museum): ul. Vidovdanska br. 4, Doboj; tel. (32) 231-220; f. 1956; 16,000 items; archaeology, history, ethnography, photography; Dir DOBRILA BIJELIĆ.

Fojnica

Franjevački Samostan Duha Svetoga Fojnica (Franciscan Monastery Fojnica): ul. Fra Zvizdovića 4, 71270 Fojnica; tel. (30) 832-081; fax (30) 832-082; e-mail samostan.fojnica@gmail.com; internet www.fojnica-samostan.com; spec. colln of church clothes embroidered with gold, bishops' clothing and footwear, Roman and Greek coins; documents relating to the Franciscan order, Fojnica monastery and Fojnica, incl. inventories and parish registers, Ottoman land-related documents, 156 documents in Bosnian Cyrillic and 3,000 Turkish documents; Bosnian ecclesiastical and secular history, education, diaries and autograph letters; library of 12,500 vols, incl. 13 incunabula, Fojnica Arms book, 19th century periodicals; Guardian Fra NIKICA VUJICA.

Kreševo

Franjevački Samostan Kreševo (Franciscan Monastery, Krešovo): 71260 Kreševo; tel. (87) 806-075; f. 1767; library of 17,000 vols, 92 periodicals; Guardian Fra MATO CVIJETKOVIĆ.

Mostar

Muzej Hercegovine (Museum of Herzegovina): Bajatova br. 4, 88000 Mostar; tel. (61) 707-307; fax (36) 551-602; e-mail muzej.herc@bih.net.ba; internet www.muzejhercegovine.com; f. 1950; archaeology, history, ethnography, art, numismatics; Dir ZDRAVKO ZVONIĆ; publ. *Kingdom Magazine*.

Prijedor

Muzej Kozara (Kozara Museum): Nikole Pašića, 79101 Prijedor; tel. (62) 221-334; f. 1953; regional museum; archaeology, history, ethnography, art; collns incl. 400 paintings of the Prijedor school, 900 archaeological exhibits, 5th century Celtic-Illyrian helmets, 400 artefacts from the Kozara region, 2,000 documents relating to the Second World War; Dir MILENKO RADIVOJEC.

Sarajevo

Ars Aevi—Museum of Contemporary Art Sarajevo: Centar Skenderija, Dom mladih, Terezija bb., 71000 Sarajevo; tel. (33) 216-919; fax (33) 216-927; e-mail arsaevi@arsaevi .ba; internet www.arsaevi.ba; f. 1992; contributed works of approx. 120 int. artists form the Ars Aevi Colln; Gen. Dir ENVER HADŽIOMERSPAHIĆ; Exec. Dir AMILA ROMOVIĆ.

Historijski Muzej Bosne i Hercegovine (Historical Museum of Bosnia and Herzegovina): Zmaja od Bosne 5, 71000 Sarajevo; tel. and fax (33) 656-629; fax (33) 656-629; e-mail histmuz@bih.net.ba; internet www.muzej.ba; f. 1945, present name 1993, present bldg 1963; history since medieval times; archive material, objects, academic library, documentation centre (300,000 vols); colln of 2,600 paintings incl. work of artists from all regions of the fmr Yugoslavia; library of 20,000 vols; Dir MUHIBA KALJANAC.

Muzej Književnosti BiH (Literary Museum of Bosnia and Herzegovina): Sime Milutinovića Sarajlije 7, 71000 Sarajevo; tel. (33) 471-828; fax (33) 471-828; literature and theatre arts; collns incl. MSS, documents, photographs, paintings, books and newspaper clippings; Dir ALEKSANDAR LJILJAK; publ. *Baština*.

Muzej Sarajeva (Museum of Sarajevo): Josipa Štedlera 32, 71000 Sarajevo; tel. (33) 475-740; fax (33) 475-749; e-mail info@ muzejsarajeva.ba; internet www .muzejsarajeva.ba; f. 1949; history, archaeology, fine and applied art; Dir MEVLIDA SERDAREVIĆ.

Branch Museums:

Despića Kuća (Despić House): Despićeva 2, 71000 Sarajevo; tel. (33) 215-531; fax (33) 215-532; Serbian merchant's house.

Muzej Jevreja BiH (Jewish Museum of Bosnia and Herzegovina): Velika Avlija bb., 71000 Sarajevo; tel. (33) 535-688; Dir ŽANKA DODIĆ-KARAMAN.

Muzej Sarajevska 1878–1918 (Museum of Sarajevo 1878–1918): Zelenih beretki 1, 71000 Sarajevo; tel. (33) 533-288; used as temporary exhibition space; Curator MIRSAD AVDIĆ.

Svrzina Kuća (Svrzo House): Glodjina 8, 71000 Sarajevo; tel. (33) 535-264; house of the Ottoman period; Curator AMRA MADIŽAREVIĆ.

Muzej Srpsko-pravoslavne Crkve (Museum of the Serbian Orthodox Church): Mula Mustafe Bašeskije 59, 71000 Sarajevo; tel. (33) 534-783; small colln of silver and gold church objects and robes; spec. colln of Cretan and locally-painted icons from 17th century.

Umjetnička galerija Bosne i Hercegovine (Art Gallery of Bosnia and Herzegovina): Zelenih beretki br. 8, 71000 Sarajevo; tel. (33) 266-550; fax (33) 664-162; e-mail info@ugbih.ba; internet www.ugbih.ba; f. 1946; collns of modern art from Serbia and Montenegro and Bosnia and Herzegovina; spec. colln of works by Ferdinand Hodler;

also ancient icons and art; library of 3,000 vols; Dir Prof. MELIHA HUSEDŽINOVIĆ.

Zemaljski Muzej Bosne i Hercegovine (National Museum of Bosnia and Herzegovina): Zmaja od Bosne 3, 71000 Sarajevo; tel. (33) 668-027; fax (33) 262-710; e-mail z .muzej@zemaljskimuzej.ba; internet www .zemaljskimuzej.ba; f. 1888; prehistoric, Roman, Greek and medieval periods, ethnological, botanical, zoological, geological sections; botanical garden; library: see Libraries and Archives; Dir Dr ADNAN BUSULADŽIĆ; publs *Glasnik Zemaljskog muzeja–Arheologija* (1 a year), *GZM–Etnologija* (1 a year), *GZM–Prirodne nauke* (1 a year), *Wissenschaftliche Mitteilungen A (Archäologie)* (irregular), *Wissenschaftliche Mitteilungen B (Volkskunde)* (irregular), *Wissenschaftliche Mitteilungen C (Naturwissenschaft)* (irregular).

Travnik

Zavičajni Muzej Travnik (Regional Museum, Travnik): Memed-paše Kukavice 1, 72270 Travnik; tel. (30) 814-140; e-mail muzej.travnik@bih.net.ba; f. 1950; Dir FATIMA MASLIĆ.

Trebinje

Muzej Herzegovine—Trebinje (Museum of Herzegovina, Trebinje): Stari Grad bb., 88375 Trebinje; tel. (59) 220-220; e-mail muzejhtr@teol.net; internet muzejhercegovine.org; f. 1956; archaeology, history, ethnography, art; library of 8,000 books; Dir VESELJKO SALATIĆ; publ. *Tribunia* (history, archeology, ethnology, art and culture).

Tuzla

Medjunarodna Galerija Portreta Tuzla (Tuzla International Portrait Gallery): ul. Slavka Mičića 13, 75000 Tuzla; tel. (35) 276-150; fax (35) 252-002; e-mail mgptuzla@ inet.ba; internet www.mgp.ba; f. 1964; works by artists from Bosnia and Herzegovina and abroad, incl. int. artists like James Haim Pinto, Adela Bervukić; colln of 200 portraits; spec. colln of works by Izmet Mujezinović, whose studio forms a br. museum; Dir ČAZIM SARAJLIĆ.

Muzej Istočne Bosne Tuzla (Museum of East Bosnia, Tuzla): Džindić mahala 21, 75000 Tuzla; tel. (35) 318321; fax (35) 318320; e-mail muzej.ib@bih.net.ba; f. 1947; 15,000 archaeological artefacts incl. Celtic bronze jewellery, 12,000 historical artefacts from the Second World War; ethnography, natural history, art, numismatics; spec. colln of works by D. Mihajlović; library of 15,000 vols, 30,000 exhibits; Dir Prof. VESNA ISABEGOVIĆ; Curator MIRSAD BAKALOVIĆ; publ. *Članci i gradja za kulturnu historiju istočne Bosne* (Articles and Study Materials for the Cultural History of East Bosnia, 1 a year).

Muzej Solane Tuzla (Tuzla Saltworks Museum): Solanska 1, 75000 Tuzla; tel. (35) 214-167; fax (35) 214-167; devoted to the Tuzla saltworks industry.

Zenica

Muzej Grada Zenice (Zenica Town Museum): Muhameda Seida Serdarevića bb., 72000 Zenica; tel. (32) 209-515; fax (32) 209-518; e-mail zemuzej@bih.net.ba; internet www.zemuzej.ba; f. 1966, present bldg 2007; archaeology, history, ethnography, geology, art; library of 2,000 titles (literature); Dir ADNADIN JAŠAREVIĆ; Sec. SANJA KAIKČIJA.

Universities

SVEUČILIŠTE U MOSTARU
(University of Mostar)

Trg hrvatskih velikana 1, 88000 Mostar
Telephone: (36) 310-778
Fax: (36) 320-885
E-mail: mail@sve-mo.ba
Internet: www.sve-mo.ba

Founded 1977, present name and status 1992
State control
Language of instruction: Croatian
Academic year: September to August

Rector: Prof. Dr VLADO MAJSTOROVIĆ
Pro-Rectors: DRAŽENA TOMIĆ, IVO ČOLAK
Gen.-Sec.: MARINKO JURILJ
Librarian: SLAVICA JUKA

Library of 15,200 vols
Number of teachers: 500
Number of students: 7,500

Publications: *Mostariensia* (2 a year), *Znanstveni glasnik* (2 a year)

DEANS

College of Nursing: LJUBO ŠIMIĆ
Faculty of Agriculture and Food Technology: Dr STANKO IVANKOVIĆ
Faculty of Civil Engineering: Prof. Dr IVO ČOLAK
Faculty of Economics: Prof. Dr IVAN PAVLOVIĆ
Faculty of Education: Prof. Dr ŠIMUN MUSA
Faculty of Law: Prof. Dr DRAGO RADIĆ
Faculty of Mechanical Engineering: Prof. Dr MILENKO OBAD
Faculty of Medicine: Prof. Dr LJERKA OSTOJIĆ

UNIVERZITET U BANJOJ LUCI
(University of Banja Luka)

Blvd vojvode Petra Bojovića 1A, 78000 Banja Luka
Telephone: (51) 321-171
Fax: (51) 315-694
E-mail: uni-bl@blic.net
Internet: www.unibl.org

Founded 1975
State control
Academic year: October to September

Rector: Prof. Dr STANKO STANIĆ
Vice-Rector: Asst Prof. BOZO VAŽIĆ
Vice-Rector: Prof. Dr DRASKO MARINKOVIĆ
Vice-Rector: Prof. Dr SIMO JOKANOVIĆ
Vice-Rector: Prof. Dr VALERIE SAULA
Head of Admin.: DUŠANKA DRAGIĆ
Int. Relations Officer: JELENA ROZIĆ
Librarian: LJILJA PETROVIC ZECIĆ

Library of 185,000 books and 75 scientific magazines
Number of teachers: 1,000
Number of students: 17,000

DEANS

Academy of Arts: Asst Prof. JELENA KARIŠIK
Faculty of Agriculture: Asst Prof. MILANKA DRINIĆ
Faculty of Architecture and Civil Engineering: Prof. Dr MILENKO STANKOVIĆ
Faculty of Economics: Prof. Dr NOVAK KONDIĆ
Faculty of Electrical Engineering: Prof. Dr PETAR MARIĆ
Faculty of Forestry: Asst Prof. ZORAN GOVEDAR
Faculty of Law: Prof. Dr VITOMIR POPOVIĆ
Faculty of Mechanical Engineering: Prof. Dr MIROSLAV ROGIĆ
Faculty of Medicine: Prof. Dr ZDENKA KRIVOKUĆA
Faculty of Mine Engineering: NADEZHDA ČALIĆ
Faculty of Natural Sciences and Mathematics: Prof. Dr RAJKO GNJATO

Faculty of Philosophy: Prof. Dr DRAGO BRAN-KOVIĆ
Faculty of Political Sciences: Prof. Dr NENAD KECMANOVIĆ
Faculty of Physical Education and Sport: Asst Dir GORAN BOŠNJAK
Faculty of Technology: Prof. Dr MILOŠ SORAK
Faculty of Philology: Prof. Dr MLADENKO SADZAK

UNIVERZITET U BIHAĆU
(University of Bihać)

Pape Ivana Pavla II 2/II, 77000 Bihać
Telephone: (37) 222-022
Fax: (37) 222-022
E-mail: rektorat@unbi.ba
Internet: www.unbi.ba
Founded 1997
Public control
Language of instruction: Bosnian
Rector: Prof. REFIK ŠAHINOVIĆ
Gen. Sec.: ASIJA CUCAK
Librarian: HALILAGIĆ DŽENITA
Number of teachers: 400
Number of students: 5,700

UNIVERZITET 'DŽEMAL BIJEDIĆ' MOSTAR
(Džemal Bijedić University of Mostar)

USRC Midhat-Hujdur-Hujka, 88104 Mostar
Telephone: (36) 570-727
Fax: (36) 570-032
E-mail: info@unmo.ba
Internet: www.unmo.ba
Founded 1977
State control
Academic year: October to September
Rector: Dr AHMED DŽUBUR
Vice-Rector for Education: Dr SENAD RAHIMIĆ
Vice-Rector for Int. Relations: MAJA POPOVAC
Vice-Rector for Science and Research: Dr ĐULSA BAJRAMOVIĆ
Sec.-Gen.: ZORAN KAZAZIĆ
Chief Librarian: EDITA MULAOSMANOVIĆ
Publication: Revija za pravo i ekonomiju (Law and Economics Review, 2 a year)
Library of 11,850 vols
Number of teachers: 250
Number of students: 12,000

DEANS

Agromediterranean Faculty: Asst Prof. SEMINA HADŽIABULIĆ
Faculty of Business Management: ARMIN HADROVIĆ
Faculty of Civil Engineering: Dr ADIL TRGO
Faculty of Economics: Dr SAFET SARIĆ
Faculty of Humanities: Dr FUAD CATOVIĆ
Faculty of Information Technology: Dr SUZANA BUBIĆ
Faculty of Law: Asst Prof. MERSIDA MANJGO
Faculty of Mechanical Engineering: Dr SALKO PEZO
Teacher Training Faculty: SALKO PEZO

UNIVERZITET U ISTOČNOM SARAJEVU
(University of East Sarajevo)

Lukavica, Vuka Karadžića br. 30, 71123 Istočno Sarajevo
Telephone: (57) 340-464
Fax: (57) 340-263
E-mail: univerzitet@paleol.net
Internet: www.unssa.rs.ba
Founded 1992 as Univ. of Serb Sarajevo, present name 2005
State control
Language of instruction: Serbian
Rector: Prof. Dr MITAR NOVAKOVIĆ
Vice-Rector for Education and Student Affairs: Prof. Dr ZORAN LJUBOJE

Vice-Rector for International Cooperation: Prof. Dr SLOBODAN MILOVANOVIĆ
Provost for Science and Research: Prof. Dr STEVAN TRBOJEVIĆ
Sec.-Gen.: VOJISLAV SUK
Number of teachers: 919
Number of students: 11,054

DEANS

Academy of Fine Arts: MIRKO TOLJIĆ
Academy of Music: Prof. Dr ZORAN RAKIĆ
Faculty of Agriculture: Prof. MIROSLAV BOG-DANOVIĆ
Faculty of Economics (Brčko): Prof. Dr LJUBOMIR TRIFUNOVIĆ
Faculty of Economics (Pale): Prof. Dr NOVO PLAKALOVIĆ
Faculty of Electrotechnology: Prof. Dr BOŽI-DAR KRSTAJIĆ
Faculty of Law: Prof. Dr RADOMIR LUKIĆ
Faculty of Mechanical Engineering: Prof. Dr DUSAN GOLUBOVIĆ
Faculty of Medicine: Prof. Dr VELJKO MARIĆ
Faculty of Pedagogy: Prof. Dr MOMČILO PELEMIŠ
Faculty of Philosophy: Prof. Dr MILENKO PIKULA
Faculty of Physical Sciences: Prof. Dr DANKO PRŽULJ
Faculty of Production and Management: Prof. Dr RADE IVANKOVIĆ
Faculty of Stomatology: Prof. Dr PETAR GRGIĆ
Faculty of Technology: Prof. Dr MILOVAN JOTANOVIĆ
Faculty of Theology: Prof. Dr PREDRAG PUZO-VIĆ

UNIVERZITET U SARAJEVU
(University of Sarajevo)

Obala Kulina bana 7/II, 71000 Sarajevo
Telephone: (33) 565-118
Fax: (33) 226-379
E-mail: javnost@unsa.ba
Internet: www.unsa.ba
Founded 1949
State control
Academic year: September to September
Rector: Prof. Dr FARUK ČAKLOVICA
Vice-Rectors: Prof. Dr SLAVENKA VOBORNIK, Prof. Dr SAMIR ARNAUTOVIĆ, Prof. Dr HAZIM BAŠIĆ
Sec.-Gen.: ZORAN SELESKOVIĆ
Officers for Int. Cooperation: ADNAN RAHIMIĆ, LJILJANA ŠULENTIĆ JASNA BOŠNJOVIĆ NEAL PUŠINA
Dir for National and Univ. Library: Dr ISMET OVČINA
Number of teachers: 1,302
Number of students: 40,273
Publications: Bulletin (every 2 years), Doctoral Dissertations–Bibliography (1 a year), Pregled (4 a year), Pregled Predavanja (1 a year)

DEANS

Academy of Fine Arts: NUSRET PAŠIĆ
Academy of Music: Prof. Dr IVAN ČAVLOVIĆ
Faculty of Agriculture: Prof. Dr MIRSAD KURTOVIĆ
Faculty of Architecture: Prof. Dr AHMET HADROVIĆ
Faculty of Civil Engineering: Prof. Dr MUHAMED ZLATAR
Faculty of Criminology: Prof. Dr RAMO MASLEŠA
Faculty of Dentistry: Prof. Dr SEAD RED-ŽEPAGIĆ
Faculty of Economics: Prof. Dr VELJKO TRIVUN
Faculty of Education: Prof. Dr UZEIR BAVČIĆ
Faculty of Electrical Engineering: Prof. Dr NARCIS BEHLILOVIĆ
Faculty of Forestry: Prof. Dr FARUK MEKIĆ

Faculty of Health Studies: Prof. Dr DIJANA AVDIĆ
Faculty of Law: Prof. Dr BORISLAV PETROVIĆ
Faculty of Mechanical Engineering: Prof. Dr EJUB DŽAFEROVIĆ
Faculty of Medicine: Prof. Dr BAKIR MEHIĆ
Faculty of Natural Sciences: Prof. Dr RIFAT ŠKRIJELJ
Faculty of Pharmacy: Prof. Dr ELVIRA KOVAČ-BEŠOVIĆ
Faculty of Philosophy: Prof. Dr IVO KOMŠIĆ (acting)
Faculty of Physical Education: Prof. Dr IZET RADJO
Faculty of Political Sciences: Prof. Dr MIRKO PEJANOVIĆ
Faculty of Transportation and Communication: Prof. Dr SAMIR ČAUŠEVIĆ
Faculty of Veterinary Sciences: Prof. Dr ALMEDINA ZUKO
Academy of Performing Arts: Prof. ZIJAD MEHIĆ

DIRECTORS

Centre for Human Rights: SAŠA MADACKI
Centre for Interdisciplinary Postgraduate Studies: Dr TAIDA BEGIĆ-ŠARKINOVIĆ
Institute of Genetic Engineering and Biotechnology: Prof. Dr KASIM BAJROVIĆ
Institute of History: Prof. Dr HUSNIJA KAM-BEROVIĆ
Institute of Oriental Research: Dr BEHIJA ZLATAR
Institute for Research into Crimes against Humanity and Int. Law: Dr SMAIL ČEKIĆ
Univ. Tele-Informatic Centre: Dr SENAD BURAK

UNIVERZITET U TUZLI
(Tuzla University)

Dr Tihomila Markovića 1, 75000 Tuzla
Telephone: (35) 300-500
Fax: (35) 300-547
E-mail: rektorat@untz.ba
Internet: www.untz.ba
Founded 1976
Rector: Prof. Dr ENVER HALILOVIĆ
Vice-Rector for Academic and Student Affairs: Prof. Dr ADMEDINA SAVKOVIĆ
Vice-Rector for Finance and Devt: Prof. Dr SNJEŽANA MARIĆ (acting)
Vice-Rector for Int. Relations: Prof. Dr MIRSAD ĐONLAGIĆ
Vice-Rector for Science and Research: Dr NASER PRLJAČA (acting)
Sec.-Gen.: JASMINA BERBIĆ
Sec. of Senate: DELIĆ MIRSADA
Number of teachers: 737
Number of students: 16,500

DEANS

Academy of Drama: Prof. Dr VLADO KEROŠE-VIĆ
Faculty of Economy: Prof. Dr SAFET KOZAREVI
Faculty of Education and Rehabilitation: Prof. Dr NEVZETA SALIHOVIĆ
Faculty of Electrical Engineering: Doc. Dr AMIR TOKIĆ
Faculty of Mathematics: FEHIM DEDAGIĆ
Faculty of Mechanical Engineering: Doc. Dr IZET ALIĆ
Faculty of Medicine: Prof. Dr FARID LJUCA
Faculty of Mining, Geology, Civil Engineering: Prof. Dr ABDULAH BAŠIĆ
Faculty of Pharmacy: Prof. Dr LEJLA BEGIĆ
Faculty of Philosophy: Prof. Dr ENVER HALI-LOVIĆ (acting)
Faculty of Science: Prof. Dr FEHIM DEDAGIĆ
Faculty of Sport and Physical Education: Prof. Dr BRANIMIR MIKIĆ
Faculty of Technology: Prof. Dr MIRJANA RADIĆ

UNIVERZITET U ZENICI
(University of Zenica)

Fakultetska 3, 72000 Zenica
Telephone: (32) 444-420
Fax: (32) 444-431
E-mail: rektorat@unze.ba
Internet: www.unze.ba
Founded 2000
Languages of instruction: Bosnian, Serbian, Croatian

Rector: Prof. Dr Sabahudin Ekinović
Vice-Rector for Education and Student Affairs: Dr Safet Brdarević
Vice-Rector for Scientific Research, Devt and Int. Cooperation: Dr Darko Petković
Gen. Sec.: Mediha Arnaut

Number of teachers: 210
Number of students: 3,200

Publications: *Didaktički putokazi* (education), *Mašinstvo* (mechanical engineering)

DEANS

Faculty of Economics: Dževad Zečić
Faculty of Education: Refik Catić
Faculty of Health: Sahib Muminagić
Faculty of Law: Salih Jalimam
Faculty of Mechanical Engineering: Prof. Dr Dušan Vukojević
Faculty of Metallurgy and Materials Science: Sulejman Muhamedagić

BOTSWANA

The Higher Education System

Tertiary education is provided by the University of Botswana (which was attended by 15,725 students in 2005) and the Francistown College of Technical and Vocational Education. There are also technical and vocational training centres, including the Botswana College of Agriculture, the Botswana Institute of Administration and Commerce, the Botswana Polytechnic and the Institute of Development Management. The University of Botswana was founded in 1963 as the University of Basutoland (now Lesotho), Bechuanaland (now Botswana) and Swaziland at Roma, in Lesotho. It became the University of Botswana, Lesotho and Swaziland (UBLS) following the independence of Botswana and Lesotho in 1966, and has been known under its current name since 1982. The University of Botswana is funded mainly by the Government and receives some income from students' fees. The Tertiary Education Council is the principal body regulating higher education in Botswana, maintaining a register of accredited programmes from Diploma to Doctoral level at public and private institutions.

Admission to the University of Botswana requires the Botswana General Certificate of Secondary Education, the local variant of the Cambridge Overseas School Certificate, either first or second division, with a credit in English language. The standard undergraduate degree is the Bachelors, which comprises two two-year cycles; the main postgraduate degree is the Masters, taken after the Bachelors. Non-university technical and vocational education and training is mainly provided by institutions affiliated to the University of Botswana, with the most common awards being Diplomas and Certificates.

In 2008 tenders were invited for a public–private partnership to set up the Botswana International University of Science and Technology, due to open in 2011.

Regulatory Bodies

GOVERNMENT

Ministry of Education: PMB 005, Gaborone; tel. 3655400; fax 3655458; e-mail moe.webmaster@gov.bw; internet www.moe.gov.bw/moe/index.html; Min. JACOB NKATE.

Ministry of Youth, Sports and Culture: Gaborone; Min. Maj.-Gen. MOENG PHETO.

Learned Societies

GENERAL

Botswana Society: POB 71, Gaborone; tel. 3919745; e-mail botsoc@info.bw; internet www.botsoc.org.bw; f. 1968, in asscn with the Nat. Museum, Monuments and Art Gallery; encourages knowledge and research on Botswana in all fields; 100 mems; Chair. Dr JOSEPH TSONOPE; Exec. Sec. RAPELANG TSEBE; Vice-Chair. Prof. FRED MORTON; publ. *Botswana Notes and Records* (1 a year).

BIBLIOGRAPHY, LIBRARY SCIENCE AND MUSEOLOGY

Botswana Library Association: POB 1310, Gaborone; tel. 3552295; fax 3957291; f. 1978; 60 mems; Chair. F. M. LAMUSSE; Sec. A. M. MBANGIWA; publs *Botswana Journal of Library and Information Science* (2 a year), *Journal*.

LANGUAGE AND LITERATURE

Alliance Française: POB 1817, Gaborone; tel. 3951650; fax 3584433; e-mail af.gaborone@info.bw; internet www.ibis.bw/~all.francaise/; offers courses and exams in French language and culture and promotes cultural exchange with France.

British Council: British High Commission Bldg, Queen's Rd, The Mall, POB 439, Gaborone; tel. 3953602; fax 3956643; e-mail general.enquiries@britishcouncil.org.bw; internet www.britishcouncil.org/botswana; offers courses and exams in English language and British culture and promotes cultural exchange with the UK; Dir DAVID KNOX.

Research Institute

NATURAL SCIENCES

Physical Sciences

Geological Survey of Botswana: Private Bag 14, Lobatse; tel. 5330327; fax 5332013; internet www.gov.bw/government/geology.htm; f. 1948; library of 2,000 vols, 151 periodicals; Dir TIYAPO NGWISANYI; publs *Bibliography of the Geology of Botswana* (every 5 years), *Bulletin, District Memoir*.

Libraries and Archives

Gaborone

Botswana National Archives and Records Services: Khama Crescent, Government Enclave, POB 239, Gaborone; tel. 3911820; fax 3908545; e-mail kramokate@gov.bw; f. 1967; central govt, district, tribal, business and private archives since c. 1885; audiovisual and machine-readable archives; records management for central govt, districts and parastatal orgs; oral tradition programmes; educational programmes and exhibitions; 14,000 vols; Dir KAGO RAMOKATE; Sr Archivist C. T. NENGOMASHA; Librarian A. R. ADEKANMBI; publ. *Archives Library Accessions List*.

Botswana National Library Service: Private Bag 0036, Gaborone; tel. 3952288; fax 3901149; f. 1968; nationwide public library service; also acts as a nat. library (legal deposit); 282,383 vols; 23 br. libraries, 3 mobile libraries; 286 book box service points; 64 village reading rooms; Dir CONSTANCE B. MODISE; publs *National Bibliography of Botswana* (3 a year), *Quarterly Accessions List, Statistical Bulletin*.

Museums and Art Galleries

Gaborone

National Museum, Monuments and Art Gallery: Independence Ave, Private Bag 00114, Gaborone; tel. 3974616; fax 3902797; e-mail national.museum@gov.bw; internet www.gov.bw/tourism/attractions/thenational.html; f. 1968; provides, through dioramas and graphic displays, a visual education in the development of man in Botswana; preserves and promotes Botswana's cultural and natural heritage; operates mobile education service for rural primary schools; repository for scientific collections relating to Botswana; National Herbarium contains 20,000 plant specimens; art gallery holds a collection of art of all races of Africa south of the Sahara, and exhibits works from the rest of the world; library of 7,000 vols and numerous journals; Dir SUSO R. MWEENDO; publs *The Zebra's Voice* (newsletter), *Zebra's Tales* (4 a year).

Mochudi

Phuthadikobo Museum: POB 367, Mochudi; tel. 5777238; fax 5748920; e-mail phuthadikobo@botsnet.bw; internet www.phuthadikobomuseum.com; f. 1976; archaeology, ethnography, photographic collns, conservation, community and environmental education; Dir VINCENT PHEMELO RAPOO.

University

UNIVERSITY OF BOTSWANA

PMB 0022, Gaborone
Telephone: (35) 50000
Fax: (39) 56591
Internet: www.ub.bw

Founded 1963 as Univ. of Basutoland (now Lesotho), Bechuanaland (now Botswana) and Swaziland at Roma (Lesotho); became Univ. of Botswana, Lesotho and Swaziland (UBLS) following the independence of Botswana and Lesotho in 1966; adopted present name 1982
State control
Language of instruction: English
Academic year: August to May
Vice-Chancellor: Prof. BOJOSI K. OTLHOGILE
Deputy Vice-Chancellor for Academic Affairs: Prof. FRANK YOUNGMAN
Deputy Vice-Chancellor for Finance and Admin.: DAVID BENJAMIN KATZKE
Deputy Vice-Chancellor for Student Affairs: Prof. LYDIA M. SALESHANDO

Library of 456,933
Number of teachers: 878
Number of students: 15,731
Publication: *Pula* (2 a year)

DEANS

Faculty of Business: SATHYAMOORTHI
Faculty of Education: Prof. R. TABULAWA
Faculty of Engineering and Technology: Prof. A. B. NGOWI
Faculty of Health Sciences: Dr T. T. MOKOENA
Faculty of Humanities: Prof. K. H. MOAHI
Faculty of Science: Assoc. Prof. M. P. MODISI
Faculty of Social Sciences: Prof. H. K. SIPHAMBE
School of Graduate Studies: Prof. U. SCHMIDT

Colleges

Botswana College of Agriculture: Content Farm, Sebele, Gaborone; PMB 0027, Gaborone; tel. 3650100; fax 3928753; internet www.bca.bw; f. 1967; associated instn of Univ. of Botswana; library: 29,810 vols, 118 periodicals; 79 teachers; 425 students; Prin. E. J. KEMSLEY.

Botswana Institute of Administration and Commerce: POB 10026, Gaborone; tel. 3956324; fax 3959768; f. 1970; library: 7,000 vols; 73 teachers; Prin. L. L. SEBINA; publ. *Newsletter* (4 a year).

Botswana Polytechnic: PMB 0061, Gaborone; tel. 3952305; fax 3952309; library: 13,000 vols; 120 teachers; 800 students; Prin. A. KERTON; Registrar T. MOGKWATI.

Institute of Development Management: POB 1357, Gaborone; tel. 3952371; fax 3973144; e-mail idm@info.bw; f. 1974; management training in business management, education management, information management, administration of legal services; library: 8,000 vols (incl. spec. World Bank and SADCC cllns); 25 teachers; 965 students; certificate courses; Regional Dir Dr M. KHAKHETLA.

BRAZIL

The Higher Education System

In 2006 there were 2,270 institutions of higher education in Brazil, with total student enrolment of 4,676,646. Universities fall into five categories: federal, state, municipal, private and Catholic. Federal universities are the most popular and competition to enter them is very fierce; they are administered by the federal Government. State universities are funded by the individual states, while municipal universities usually focus on one subject or provide professional training. Private universities are funded by private organizations and students' fees, and Catholic universities, while supported principally by the Catholic Church, are in fact open to students of all denominations. The Ministry of Education has ultimate control of higher education, and the establishment of new institutions is authorized by the Conselho Nacional de Educação (CNE—National Education Council). In 2009 the development began of a new national system of evaluation, the Sistema Nacional da Avaliação da Educação Superior (SINAES). The Commisão Nacional de Avaliação da Educação Superior (CONAES—National Committee for the Evaluation of Higher Education) was established as the national body responsible for coordinating and supervising SINAES.

Both public (federal, state, municipal) and private (including Catholic) universities base admissions on a combination of the secondary school diploma and entrance examinations (Vestibular). There are three qualifications each at undergraduate and postgraduate level. Undergraduate degrees are between four and five years long, and consist of the Bacharel (excludes teacher training), Licenciado (includes teacher training) and Título Profissional (professional title). Parallel to these degrees are cursos següénciais, which are non-degree courses in subjects such as business and management, and the Provão, an obligatory test designed to monitor teaching standards.

Postgraduate qualifications are divided into sensu stricto ('strict sense') and sensu lato ('wide sense'). Sensu stricto encompasses the classical postgraduate schema, consisting of the Mestrado (Masters), which requires two years of study, and the Doutorado (Doctorate), which is awarded after four years of study and research following the Mestrado. Sensu lato covers professional qualifications which do not hold graduate 'credit' but are of value in the private sector; Especialista (Specialist) is the title often bestowed by sensu lato.

The CNE accredits and assesses all federal and private universities at the undergraduate and postgraduate level, while state and municipal universities are accredited and assessed by the respective state council. The Brazilian Higher Education Funding Agency is the body within the Ministry of Education responsible for evaluating graduate programmes, with courses generally requiring a score of three on a scale of seven to meet the minimum requirements.

Vocational and technical training is separate from academic education, and is governed according to the Educational Guidelines Law of 1996, which established three levels of non-university, post-secondary education and training. The three levels are: nivel básico, a first stage open to students of any educational attainment, and leading to a certificate of basic competency in a specific job or skill; nivel técnico, which lasts one to two years, requires at least 11 years of basic education and is regulated by the Ministry of Education or State authorities; and nivel tecnológica, the third and final level, providing vocational education of a higher education standard and lasting two to three years.

In 2010, the International Finance Corporation, a member of the World Bank Group, made a grant to Anhanguera Educacional Participações, the country's leading private post-secondary institution, in order to promote access to higher education in Brazil. Anhanguera Educacional Participações had 250,000 students in 2009, most of whom were people on low incomes who might not have access to public universities.

Regulatory and Representative Bodies

GOVERNMENT

Ministry of Culture: Esplanada dos Ministérios, Bloco B, sala 401, 70068-900 Brasília, DF; tel. (61) 2024-2460; fax (61) 3225-9162; e-mail gm@cultura.gov.br; internet www.cultura.gov.br; f. 1985; Min. João Luiz Silva Ferreira.

Ministry of Education: Esplanada dos Ministérios, Bloco L, 70047-900 Brasília, DF; tel. (61) 2104-8731; fax (61) 2104-9172; e-mail henriquepaim@mec.gov.br; internet www.mec.gov.br; Min. Fernando Haddad.

Instituto Nacional de Estudos e Pesquisas Educacionais Anísio Teixeira (INEP): Inep/MEC, Esplanada dos Ministérios, Bloco L, Anexos I e II, 4° andar, 70047-900 Brasília, DF; tel. (61) 2104-8406; fax (61) 2104-9850; internet www.inep.gov.br; f. 1937; govt agency; promotes study and research of Brazilian education system; supports formation and implementation of education policy; Pres. Reynaldo Fernandes; publ. *Prova Brasil* (irregular).

Secretaria de Educação Superior (SESu): Ministério da Educação, Esplanada dos Ministérios, Bloco L, 70047-903 Brasília, DF; tel. (61) 2104-8012; e-mail sesu@mec.gov.br; internet portal.mec.gov.br/sesu; attached to Min. of Education; Sec. Ronaldo Mota; publ. *Boletim Educação Superior* (digital, 52 a year).

ACCREDITATION

Conselho Nacional de Educação (CNE): SGAS, Av. L/2, Quadra 607, Lote 50, 70200-670 Brasília, DF; tel. (61) 2104-6339; fax (61) 2104-6224; e-mail edsonnunes@mec.gov.br; internet portal.mec.gov.br/cne; f. 1995; Pres. Edson de Oliveira Nunes.

FUNDING

Coordenação de Aperfeiçoamento de Pessoal de Nível Superior (CAPES) (Federal Agency for Postgraduate Education): Ministério da Educação, Anexos I e II, 2° andar, 70359-970 Brasília, DF; tel. (61) 2104-8801; fax (61) 2104-9983; internet www.capes.gov.br; f. 1951; govt agency; funds *sensu stricto* postgraduate study of the sciences in Brazil and abroad; main objects are to deploy the human resources of graduate schools to help govt and public enterprises, to give student grants, to evaluate and coordinate Masters and Doctors courses; funds over half of all eligible postgraduate students in Brazil; library of 126 ; Pres. Jorge Almeida Guimarães; publ. *Revista Brasileira de Pós-Graduação* (3 a year).

NATIONAL BODIES

Associação de Educação Católica do Brasil (Association for Catholic Education in Brazil): SBN Q01, Bloco H, Loja 40, 70040-000 Brasília, DF; tel. (61) 3326-2992; e-mail recepcao@aecbrasil.org.br; internet www.aecbrasil.org.br; f. 1945; supervises 27 sections, with a total of 1,750 schools and seminaries; Pres. Irma Olmira Bernadete Dassoler; publs *Cadernos AEC*, *Revista de Educação AEC* (4 a year).

Conselho de Reitores das Universidades Brasileiras (Council of Brazilian University Rectors): SEP/Norte, Quadra 516, Conj. D, 70770-524 Brasília, DF; tel. (61) 3349-9010; fax (61) 3274-4621; e-mail crub@nutecnet.com.br; internet www.crub.org.br; f. 1966; study of problems affecting higher education; 128 mems; library of 15,000 vols; Pres. Nival Nunes de Almeida; Gen. Sec. Francisco das Chagas Sousa Luna; publ. *Revista Educação Brasileira* (2 a year).

Instituto Brasileiro de Educação, Ciência e Cultura (IBECC) (Brazilian Institute of Education, Science and Culture): UNESCO National Commission, Av. Marechal Floriano 196, 3° andar, Palácio Itamaraty, 20080 Rio de Janeiro, RJ; tel. (21) 516-2458; fax (21) 516-2458; e-mail ibecc@unisys.com.br; f. 1946; library of 1,500 vols; Pres. (vacant); Exec. Sec. Joaquim Caetano

GENTIL NETO; publ. *Boletim: Correio do IBECC*.

Learned Societies
GENERAL

Fundação Bunge (Bunge Foundation): Av. Maria Coelho Aguiar 215, Bloco D, 5° andar, 05804-900 São Paulo, SP; tel. (11) 3741-2170; fax (11) 3741-1288; internet www.fundacaobunge.org.br; f. 1955; to promote the advancement of science, letters and arts in Brazil by granting every year the Bunge Foundation Award and the Bunge Foundation Youth Award, consisting of the following: gold and silver medals, diploma of recognition for outstanding service in any of the scientific, literary or artistic fields, plus a sum of money; Pres. JACQUES MARCOVITCH; Exec. Sec. RENATO WENTER; publ. *Cidadania* (6 a year).

UNESCO Brasilia Office: CP 08563, 70070-000 Brasilia, DF; SAS Quadra 5 Bloco H Lote 6, Edificio CNPQ/IBICT/UNESCO, 9° andar, 70070-914 Brasilia, DF; tel. (61) 2106-3500; fax (61) 321-8577; e-mail grupoeditorial@unesco.org.br; internet www.brasilia.unesco.org; f. 1972; Dir JORGE WERTHEIN; publ. *Unesco News* (4 a year).

AGRICULTURE, FISHERIES AND VETERINARY SCIENCE

Associação Brasileira de Mecânica dos Solos e Engenharia Geotecnica (ABMS) (Brazilian Society for Soil Mechanics and Geotechnical Engineering): Av. Prof. Almeida Prado, 532, prédio 54, Cidade Universitaria, São Paulo, SP 05508-901; tel. (11) 3768-7325; fax (11) 3768-7325; e-mail abms@abms.com.br; internet www.abms.com.br; f. 1950; 1,100 mems; Pres. Dr ARSENIO NEGRO; Sec.-Gen. Dr NILO CESAR CONSOLI; publ. *Soils and Rocks* (int. geotechnical journal, English).

Sociedade Nacional de Agricultura (SNA) (National Agricultural Society): Av. General Justo 171, 7th Floor, 20021-130 Rio de Janeiro, RJ; tel. (21) 3231-6350; fax (21) 2240-4189; e-mail sna@sna.agr.br; internet www.sna.agr.br; f. 1897; undergraduate course in animal science; extension courses in animal husbandry, organic production, gardening; veterinary medicine undergraduate course with Univ. Castelo Branco; campus in Rio de Janeiro acts as a networking org.; annual agribusiness congress; 10,000 mems; library of 45,000 vols; Pres. OCTAVIA ALVARENGA; Vice-Pres. ANTONIO ALVARENGA; publ. *A Lavoura* (6 a year).

BIBLIOGRAPHY, LIBRARY SCIENCE AND MUSEOLOGY

Associação dos Arquivistas Brasileiros: Av. Presidente Vargas 1733 sala 903, 20210-030 Rio de Janeiro, RJ; tel. (21) 2507-2239; fax (21) 3852-2541; e-mail aab@aab.org.br; internet www.aab.org.br; f. 1971; cooperates with the Government, national and international organizations on all matters relating to archives and documentation; organizes national congresses, study courses, conferences, etc.; has achieved national legislation on archives; 300 mems; Pres. LUCIA MARIA VELLOSO DE OLIVEIRA; Secs ISABEL CRISTINA BORGES DE OLIVEIRA, LAURA REGINA XAVIER; publ. *Boletim* (online, 1 a year).

Federação Brasileira de Associações de Bibliotecários, Cientistas da Informação e Instituições (FEBAB) (Brazilian Federation of Library Associations, Information Scientists and Institutions): Rua Avanhandava 40, conj. 110, 01306-000 São Paulo, SP; tel. (11) 3257-9979; fax (11) 3257-9979; e-mail febab@febab.org.br; internet www.febab.org.br; f. 1959 to act for the regional library associations at a national level; to serve as a centre of documentation and bibliography for Brazil; biennial national congress; 27 mem. associations; Pres. SIGRID KARIN WEISS DUTRA; Admin. and Financial Sec. MARIA APARECIDA MACHADO; publ. *Revista Brasileira de Biblioteconomia e Documentação* (online, 2 a year).

ECONOMICS, LAW AND POLITICS

Instituto Brasileiro de Economia (Brazilian Institute of Economics): Fundação Getulio Vargas, Rua Barão de Itambi 607° andar, Botafogo, 22231-000 Rio de Janeiro, RJ; tel. (21) 3799-6799; fax (21) 3799-6774; e-mail dgd@fgv.br; internet www.fgv.br/dgd; f. 1951; Chair. ANTÔNIO SALAZAR P. BRANDÃO; publs *Conjuntura Econômica* (12 a year), *Revista Agroanalysis* (12 a year).

Instituto dos Advogados Brasileiros (Institute of Brazilian Lawyers): Av. Marechal Câmara 210, 5° andar, Centro, 20020-080 Rio de Janeiro, RJ; tel. (21) 2240-3173; fax (21) 2240-3173; internet www.iabnacional.org.br; f. 1843; 1,141 mems; Pres. FERNANDO FRAGOSO; Sec. UBYRATAN CAVALCANTI; library: see Libraries; publs *Folha* (online, 12 a year), *Revista* (1 a year), *Revista Digital* (online, 4 a year).

EDUCATION

Fundação Carlos Chagas: CP 11478, Av. Prof. Francisco Morato 1565, 05513-900 São Paulo, SP; tel. (11) 3723-3000; fax (11) 3721-1059; e-mail fcc@fcc.org.br; internet www.fcc.org.br; f. 1964; activities in the fields of human resources, educational research and educational evaluation; 184 mems; library of 41,000 vols; Pres. Prof. Dr RUBENS MURILLO MARQUES; Sec.-Gen. Prof. Dr NELSON FONTANA MARGARIDO; publs *Cadernos de Pesquisa* (3 a year), *Estudos em Avaliação Educacional* (2 a year).

Fundação Getúlio Vargas: Praia de Botafogo 190, 22253-900 Rio de Janeiro, RJ; tel. (21) 2559-6000; fax (21) 2553-6372; e-mail fgv@fgv.br; f. 1944; technical, scientific, educational and philanthropic activities; includes 3 educational institutes; 385 mems in General Assembly; library: over 120,000 vols; Pres. Dr CARLOS IVAN SIMONSEN LEAL; publs *Agroanalysis* (12 a year), *Conjuntura Econômica* (12 a year), *Correio da UNESCO* (12 a year), *Estudos Históricos* (2 a year), *Revista Brasileira de Economia* (4 a year), *Revista de Administração de Empresas* (6 a year), *Revista de Administração Pública* (4 a year).

HISTORY, GEOGRAPHY AND ARCHAEOLOGY

Instituto Arqueológico, Histórico e Geográfico Pernambucano (Archaeological, Historical and Geographical Institute): Rua do Hospício 130, Boa Vista, Recife, PE; tel. (81) 3222-4952; internet www.institutoarqueologico.com.br; f. 1862; library of 20,000 vols; 50 mems; 130 coresp. mems; 5 hon. mems; Pres. NILZARDO CARNEIRO LEÃO; First Sec. REINALDO JOSÉ CARNEIRO LEÃO; Library Dir FERNANDO ANTÔNIO GUERRA DE SOUZA.

Instituto do Ceará (Ceará Institute): Rua Barão do Rio Branco 1594, 60025-061 Fortaleza, CE; tel. (85) 32316152; fax (85) 32544116; e-mail institutodoceara@secrel.com.br; internet www.institutodoceara.org.br; f. 1887; includes the following commissions: History, Manuscripts and Periodicals, Geography, Anthropology; 40 mems; library of 52,000 vols; Pres. MANUEL EDUARDO PINHEIRO CAMPOS; Gen. Sec. VALDELICE CARNEIRO GIRÃO; publ. *Revista* (1 a year).

Instituto Genealógico Brasileiro (Genealogical Institute): Rua Senador Egidio, 34 2° andar, Centro, 01006-010 São Paulo, SP; tel. (11) 3257-4840; f. 1930; library of 972 vols; Pres. Colonel SALVADOR DE MOYA; Sec. Dr JORGE BUENO DE MIRANDA; publs *Anuário Genealógico Brasileiro*, *Anuário Genealógico Latino*, *Biblioteca*, *Biblioteca Genealógica Brasileira*, *Genealógica Latina*, *Indices Genealógicos Brasileiros*, *Revista Genealógica Brasileira*, *Subsídios Genealógicos*.

Instituto Geográfico e Histórico da Bahia (Bahia Geographical and Historical Institute): Av. Sete de Setembro 94A, Piedade, 40060-001 Salvador, BA; tel. (71) 3329-4463; fax (71) 3329-6336; e-mail ighb@ighb.org.br; internet www.ighb.org.br; f. 1894; 300 mems; library of 35,000 vols; Pres. Profa CONSUELO PONDÉ DE SENA; Sec. SERGIO MATTOS.

Instituto Geográfico e Histórico do Amazonas (IGHA): Rua Bernardo Ramos 135, Centro, 69005-310 Manaus, AM; tel. (92) 232-7077; f. 1917; 120 mems; library of 60,000 vols; Pres. Dr ANA CARLA BRUNO; Gen. Sec. Dr JOSÉ ROBERTO TADROS; Admin. Sec. JOSÉ GERALDO XAVIER DOS ANJOS; publs *Boletim*, *Revista*.

Instituto Geológico (Geological Institute): Av. Miguel Stefano 3900, Água Funda, 04301-903 São Paulo, SP; tel. (11) 5077-1155; fax (11) 5077-2219; e-mail igeologico@igeologico.sp.gov.br; internet www.igeologico.sp.gov.br; f. 1886; 100 mems; library of 8,500 vols, 1,850 periodicals, 10,000 maps; map collection, geological museum; Dir Dr RICARDO VEDOVELLO (acting); publs *Boletim*, *Revista*.

Instituto Histórico e Geográfico Brasileiro (Brazilian Historical and Geographical Institute): Av. Augusto Severo 8, 20021-040 Rio de Janeiro, RJ; tel. (21) 509-5107; fax (21) 252-4430; e-mail ihgbpresidencia@unikey.com.br; f. 1838; library of 560,000 vols; archive of 110,000 documents; museum of 1,100 items; Pres. ARNO WEHLING; Sec. CYBELLE MOREIRA DE IPANEMA; publ. *Revista* (4 a year).

Instituto Histórico e Geográfico de Alagoas (Alagoas Historical Institute): Rua Sol 382, 57000 Maceió, AL; tel. (82) 3223-7797; e-mail webmaster@ihgal.al.org.br; internet www.ihgal.al.org.br; f. 1869; 40 mems; library of 15,000 vols; Pres. JAYME LUSTOSA DE ALTAVILA; Sec. LUIZ NOGUEIRA BARROS; publ. *Revista*.

Instituto Histórico e Geográfico de Goiás (Historical and Geographical Institute): Rua 82, No 455, S. Sul, Goiânia; tel. and fax 3224-4622; e-mail ihgg@hotmail.com; f. 1932; 60 mems; library of 20,000 vols; rare collns of letters and newspapers; Dir Dr COLEMAR NATAL E SILVA; publs *Boletim* (4 a year), *Review* (1 a year).

Instituto Histórico e Geográfico de Santa Catarina (Santa Catarina Historical and Geographical Institute): Praça XV de Novembro/Palácio Cruz e Sousa, CP 1582, Florianópolis, SC; tel. (48) 212-2363 ext. 216; fax (48) 222-5111; e-mail ihgsc@ihgsc.org.br; internet www.ihgsc.org.br; f. 1896; 235 mems; library of 8,000 vols; Pres. Prof. AUGUSTO CÉSAR ZEFERINO; Sec. Prof. JALI MEIRINHO; publs *Anais*, *Boletim* (12 a year), *Coleção Catariniana*, *Coleção Ensaios*, *Revista* (1 a year).

Instituto Histórico e Geográfico de São Paulo (São Paulo Historical and Geographical Institute): Rua Benjamim Constant 158, 01005-000 São Paulo, SP; tel. (11) 3242-8064; e-mail ihgsp@ihgsp.org.br; internet www

.ihgsp.org.br; f. 1894; library of 40,000 vols; Pres. NELLY MARTINS FERREIRA CANDEIAS; Sec. MARIO SAVELLI.

Instituto Histórico e Geográfico de Sergipe (Sergipe Historical and Geographical Institute): Rua Itabaianinha 41, 49010-190 Aracajú, SE; tel. (79) 3214-8491; internet www.ihgse.com.br; f. 1912; library of 43,000 vols; Pres. JOSÉ IBARE COSTA DANTAS; publ. *Revista* (1 a year).

Instituto Histórico e Geográfico do Espírito Santo (Espírito Santo Historical and Geographical Institute): Av. República 374, CP 29020-620, Vitória; tel. (27) 3223-5934; e-mail ihges.vix@zaz.com.br; f. 1916; 400 mems; Pres. Profa LEA BRÍGIDA DE ALVARENGA ROSA; Gen. Sec. VITOR BIASUTTI; publ. *Revista* (1 a year).

Instituto Histórico e Geográfico do Maranhão (Maranhão Historical and Geographical Institute): Edifício Prof. Antônio Lopes, 2° andar, Rua Santa Rita 230, Centro, 65015-430 São Luís, MA; tel. (98) 222-8464; f. 1925; Pres. Profa ENEIDA VIEIRA DA SILVA OSTRIA DE CANEDO; First Sec. RAUL EDUARDO CANEDO; publ. *Revista.*

Instituto Histórico e Geográfico do Pará (Pará Historical and Geographical Institute): Rua d'Aveiro, Cidade Irmã 62, C. Velha, 66020-070 Belém, PA; f. 1900; Pres. Dr JOSÉ RODRIGUES DA SILVEIRA NETTO; First Sec. Dr ALAÚDIO DE OLIVEIRA MELLO.

Instituto Histórico e Geográfico do Paraná (Historical and Geographical Institute of Paraná): Rua José Loureiro 43, 80010-000 Curitiba, PR; tel. (41) 3224-0683; e-mail ayrgcelestino@ig.com.br; f. 1900; Pres. LAURO GREIN FILHO; Sec. NEY FERNANDO PERRACINI DE AZEVEDO; publ. *Boletim.*

Instituto Histórico e Geográfico do Rio Grande do Norte (Rio Grande do Norte Historical and Geographical Institute): Rua da Conceição 622, 59025-270 Natal, RN; tel. (84) 3221-1228; f. 1902; library of 50,000 vols; Pres. Dr ENÉLIO LIMA PETROVICH; Librarian OLAVO DE MEDEIROS FILHO; publ. *Revista.*

Instituto Histórico e Geográfico do Rio Grande do Sul (Rio Grande do Sul Historical and Geographical Institute): Rua Riachuelo 1317, 90010-271 Porto Alegre, RS; tel. and fax (51) 3224-3760; e-mail ihgrgs@terra.com.br; internet www.ihgrgs.org.br; f. 1920; 30 mems; Pres. Prof. GERVÁSIO RODRIGO NEVES; publs *O Pensamento Político* (1 a year), *Revista* (1 a year).

Instituto Histórico e Geográfico Paraíbano (Paraíba Historical and Geographical Institute): Rua Barão do Abiaí 64, Centro, 58013-080 João Pessoa, PB; tel. (83) 3222-0513; internet ihgp.net; f. 1905; library of 30,000 vols; 50 mems; 30 corresp.; Pres. LUIZ HUGO GUIMARÃES; Gen. Sec. ITAPUAN BÔTTO TARGINO.

Sociedade Brasileira de Cartografia (SBC): Av. Presidente Wilson 210, 7° andar, Centro, 20030-021 Rio de Janeiro, RJ; tel. (21) 2240-6901; fax (21) 2262-2823; e-mail sbc.rlk@terra.com.br; internet www.rio.com.br/sbcgfsr; f. 1958; cartography, geodesy, surveying, photogrammetry and remote sensing; 2,000 mems; Pres. Dr Eng. PAULO CESAR TEIXEIRA TRINO; Sec. Eng. JOSÉ HENRIQUE DA SILVA; publs *Boletim* (news and updates, 6 a year), *Proceedings of the Brazilian Congress of Cartography* (every 2 years), *Revista Brasileira de Cartografia* (papers and contributions, irregular).

Sociedade Brasileira de Geografia (Brazilian Geographical Society): Rua Uruguaiana 39, Bloco B, 6° andar, Centro, 20050-093 Rio de Janeiro, RJ; tel. (21) 2224-1223; e-mail sbgrj@socbrasileiradegeografia.com.br; internet www.socbrasileiradegeografia.com.br; f.

1883; library of 13,712 vols; 284 mems; Pres. Prof. Dr WILLIAM PAULO MACIEL; First Sec. Profa ELIANE ALVES DA SILVA; publs *Boletim, Estante Paranista.*

LANGUAGE AND LITERATURE

Academia Amazonense de Letras (Amazonas Academy of Letters): Rua Ramos Ferreira 1009, Manaus, AM; tel. (92) 3234-0584; f. 1918; 40 mems; library of 3,500 vols; Pres. JOSÉ BRAGA; Sec. GENESINO BRAGA; Librarian MÁRIO YPIRANGA MONTEIRO; publ. *Revista.*

Academia Brasileira de Letras (Brazilian Academy of Letters): Av. Presidente Wilson 203, Castelo, 20030-021 Rio de Janeiro, RJ; tel. (21) 3974-2500; e-mail academia@academia.org.br; internet www.academia.org.br; f. 1897; preparing exhaustive *Dictionary of the Portuguese Language*; annual prizes awarded for best Brazilian works in prose, verse and drama; 40 mems; library of 50,000 vols; Pres. CÍCERO SANDRONI; Gen. Sec. IVAN JUNQUEIRA; Librarian BARBOSA LIMA SOBRINHO.

Academia Cearense de Letras (Ceará Academy of Letters): Biblioteca, Rua do Rosario 1, Palacio da Luz, 60055-090 Fortaleza, CE; tel. (85) 253-4275; fax (85) 253-4275; f. 1894; 40 mems; 21 hon. mems; library of 18,000 vols; Pres. PEDRO HENRIQUE SARAIVA LEÃO; Sec.-Gen. VIRGILIO MAIA; publ. *Revista da Academia Cearense de Letras.*

Academia de Letras da Bahia (Bahia Academy of Letters): Av. Joana Angélica 198, Nazaré, 40050 Salvador, BA; tel. (71) 3322-2040; e-mail letrasba@terra.com.br; f. 1917; 40 mems; 19 corresponding in Brazil, 6 abroad; library of 10,000 vols; Pres. CLÁUDIO VEIGA; Vice-Pres. WILSON LINS; Sec. EDIVALDO M. BOAVENTURA; publ. *Revista* (1 a year).

Academia de Letras e Artes do Planalto (Planalto Academy of Arts and Letters): Rua do Santissimo Sacramento 32, 72800-000 Luziânia, GO; tel. (61) 3621-1184; f. 1976; 40 mems; library of 8,000 vols; Pres. MARCO ANTONIO MARTINS DE ARAUJO.

Academia Mineira de Letras (Minas Gerais Academy of Letters): Rua da Bahia 1466, Lourdes, 30160-011 Belo Horizonte, MG; tel. (31) 3222-5764; internet www.academiamineiradeletras.org.br; 40 members; Pres. MURILO BADARÓ; Gen. Sec. Prof. ALOISIO TEIXEIRA GARCIA.

Academia Paraibana de Letras (Paraíba Academy of Letters): Rua Duque de Caxias 25-37, 58000 João Pessoa, PB; tel. (83) 3221.8741; internet www.aplpb.com.br; f. 1941; 40 mems; Pres. ANTÔNIO JUAREZ FARIAS; Gen. Sec. AURÉLIO MORENO DE ALBUQUERQUE; publs *Boletim Informativo, Discursos e Ensaios, Revista.*

Academia Paulista de Letras (São Paulo Academy of Letters): Largo do Arouche 312-324, 01219-000 São Paulo, SP; tel. (11) 3331-7222; e-mail acadsp@terra.com.br; internet www.academiapaulistadeletras.org.br; f. 1909; 40 mems; library of 50,000 vols, 12,000 periodicals, 900 MSS; Pres. JOSÉ RENATO NALINI; publ. *Revista.*

Academia Pernambucana de Letras (Pernambuco Academy of Letters): Av. Rui Barbosa 1596, Graças, 52050-000 Recife, PE; fax (81) 3268-2211; e-mail letraspe@letraspe.com.br; internet apl.iteci.com.br; f. 1901; library of 12,000 vols; 40 mems, unlimited number of hon. and corresp. mems in Brazil and abroad; Pres. WALDENIO FLORENCIO PORTO; Sec. Dr LUCILO VAREJÃO FILHO; publ. *Revista* (irregular).

Academia Piauiense de Letras (Piauí Academy of Letters): Av. Miguel Rosa Sul 3300, Centro, 64001-490 Teresina, PI; tel.

(86) 3221-1566; f. 1917; Pres. MANOEL PAULO NUNES; publ. *Revista.*

Academia Riograndense de Letras (Rio Grande Academy of Letters): Rua Davi Cana Barro 120, 95820-000 General Câmara, RS; 40 mems; publ. *Revista.*

Alliance Française: Rua Duvivier, 43/103 Copacabana, 20020-020 Rio de Janeiro; tel. (21) 2244-6950; fax (21) 2543-7656; e-mail dgafbr@rioaliancafrancesa.com.br; internet www.aliancafrancesa.com; offers courses and exams in French language and culture and promotes cultural exchange with France; attached teaching offices in Aracajú, Batatais, Bauru, Belém, Belo Horizonte, Blumenau, Brasília, Campina Grande, Campinas, Campo Grande, Caxias do Sul, Curitiba, Florianópolis, Fortaleza, Franca, Goiânia, Guarulhos, João Pessoa, Joinville, Juazeiro do Norte, Juíz de Fora, Jundiai, Londrina, Maceió, Manaus, Natal, Niterói, Nova Friburgo, Petrópolis, Porto Alegre, Recife, Resende, Ribeirão Preto, Salvador, Santana do Livramento, Santo André, Santos, São Caetano do Sul, São Carlos, São Gonçalo, São João del Rei, São José dos Campos, São Luís, São Paulo, Sete Lagoas, Sorocaba, Tatuape, Teresopolis, Vicosa and Vitória; Dir of Operations, Brazil LUCE RUDENT.

British Council: Ed. Centro Empresarial Varig, SCN Quadra 04 Bloco B, Torre Oeste Conjunto 202, 70710-926 Brasilia, DF; tel. (61) 2106-7500; fax (61) 2106-7599; e-mail brasilia@britishcouncil.org.br; internet www.britishcouncil.org/brasil.htm; offers courses and exams in English language and British culture and promotes cultural exchange with the UK; attached offices in Curitiba, Recife, Rio de Janeiro (teaching centre) and São Paulo; Dir Dr DAVID COOKE.

Goethe-Institut: Rua Lisboa 974, 05413-001 São Paulo, SP; tel. (11) 3296-7000; fax (11) 3060-8413; e-mail info@saopaulo.goethe.org; internet www.goethe.de/ins/br/lp/ptindex.htm; offers courses and exams in German language and culture and promotes cultural exchange with Germany; attached centres in Curitiba, Porto Alegre, Rio de Janeiro and Salvador/Bahia; library of 15,000 vols, 60 periodicals; Dir and Regional Dir, South America Dr BRUNO FISCHLI.

Instituto Cervantes: Rua do Carmo 27, Segundo Andar, 20011-020 Rio de Janeiro; tel. (21) 3231-6555; fax (21) 2531-9647; e-mail cenrio@cervantes.es; internet riodejaneiro.cervantes.es; offers courses and exams in Spanish language and culture and promotes cultural exchange with Spain and Spanish-speaking Latin and Central America; attached centre in São Paulo; Dir FRANCISCO CORRAL SÁNCHEZ-CABEZUDO.

PEN Clube do Brasil—Associação Universal de Escritores (International PEN Centre): Praia do Flamengo 172, 11° andar, Flamengo, 22210-030 Rio de Janeiro, RJ; tel. (21) 2556-0461; e-mail penclubedobrasil@uol.com.br; internet penclubedobrasil.sites.uol.com.br; f. 1936; 106 mems; monthly free lectures; theatrical performances; Pres. CLÁUDIO MURILO LEAL; Exec. Sec. CLÁUDIO AGUIAR; publ. *Boletim.*

Sociedade Brasileira de Autores (Society of Playwrights): Av. Almirante Barroso 97, 3° andar, 20031-005 Rio de Janeiro, RJ; tel. (21) 25446966; fax (21) 2240-7431; internet www.sbat.com.br; f. 1917; non-profit-making organization; 6,000 mems; library of 6,000 vols, 30,716 plays; Pres. CARLOS EDUARDO NOVÃES; Communications Dir EWA PROCTER; publ. *Revista de Teatro* (6 a year).

MEDICINE

Academia de Medicina de São Paulo (Medical Academy of São Paulo): Av. Brigadeiro Luís Antonio 278, 6° andar—Sala 3, Centro, 01318-901 São Paulo, SP; tel. (11) 3105-4402; fax (11) 3106-5220; e-mail acadmedsp@terra.com.br; internet www .academiamedicinasaopaulo.org.br; f. 1895 as Sociedade de Medicina e Cirurgia; Pres. YVONNE CAPUANO; Gen. Sec. LUIZ CELSO MATTOSINHO FRANÇA.

Academia Nacional de Medicina (National Academy of Medicine): Av. General Justo 365, 7° andar, 20021-130 Rio de Janeiro, RJ; tel. (21) 2524-2164; fax (21) 2240-8673; internet www.anm.org.br; f. 1829; 100 mems; library of 22,000 vols, 1,200 periodicals; Pres. Dr AUGUSTO PAULINO-NETTO; Sec.-Gen. Dr MARCOS F. MORÃES; publ. *Anais* (2 a year).

Associação Bahiana de Medicina (Bahia Medical Society): Rua Baependi, 162, Ondina, 40170-070 Salvador, BA; tel. (71) 2107-9666; internet www.abmnet1.org.br; f. 1894; Pres. Dr JOSÉ SILVEIRA; Sec.-Gen. Dr MENANDRO NOVÃES; publ. *Anais*.

Associação Brasileira de Farmacêuticos (Brazilian Pharmaceutical Association): Rua dos Andradas 96 (10° Andar), Centro 2005-1000, Rio de Janeiro, RJ; tel. (21) 2263-0791; fax (21) 2233-3672; e-mail abf@abf.org.br; internet www.abf.org.br; f. 1916; comprises the following Comms: *Desenvolvimento Cultural* (Cultural Development); *Econômica e Etica Farmacêutica* (Pharmaceutical Economics and Ethics); *Legislação Comercial* (Commercial Legislation); *Legislação de Marcas e Patentes* (Trade Marks and Patents); *Legislação Sanitaria* (Sanitary Legislation); *Legislação Tributaria* (Tax Legislation); *Propaganda e Intercambio Associativo* (Propaganda and Exchange); library; 950 mems (hon. and corresp.); Pres. Dr JORGE CAVALCANTI DE OLIVEIRA; Vice-Pres. Dr JOSÉ LIPORAGE TEIXEIRA; publ. *Revista Brasileira de Farmácia* (3 a year).

Associação Médica Brasileira (Brazilian Medical Association): Rua São Carlos do Pinhal 324, Bela Vista, 01333-903 São Paulo; tel. (11) 3178-6800; fax (11) 3178-6830; e-mail administracao@amb.org.br; internet www.amb.org.br; f. 1951; professional association; 250,000 mems; Pres. JOSÉ LUIZ GOMES DO AMARAL; Gen. Sec. ALDEMIR HUMBERTO SOARES; publs *Boletim AMB* (12 a year), *Jornal AMB* (online, 6 a year), *O Médico & Você* (4 a year), *Revista AMB* (online, 6 a year).

Associação Paulista de Medicina (São Paulo Medical Association): Av. Brig. Luíz Antônio 278, Bela Vista, 01318-901 São Paulo; tel. (11) 3188-4200; e-mail apm@apm .org.br; internet www.apm.org.br; f. 1930; 30,000 active mems; 432 corresp. mems; Pres. JORGE CARLOS MACHADO CURI; publs *Jornal da APM* (12 a year), *Revista Diagnóstico & Tratamento* (4 a year), *Revista Paulista de Medicina* (6 a year).

Sociedade Brasileira de Dermatologia (Brazilian Dermatological Society): Av. Rio Branco 39–18° andar, 20090-003 Rio de Janeiro, RJ; tel. (21) 2253-6747; internet www.sbd.org.br; f. 1912; 16 hon. mems; 56 corresponding mems; 3,800 mems; library of 4,000 vols, 200 periodicals; Pres. OMAR LUPI DA ROSA SANTOS; Gen. Sec. Dr MARIA DE LOURDES VIEGAS; publs *Anais Brasileiros de Dermatologia* (6 a year), *Jornal* (6 a year).

Sociedade de Medicina de Alagoas (Alagoas Medical Society): Rua Barão de Anadia 5, Centro, 57020-630 Maceió, AL; tel. (82) 3223-3463; fax (82) 3223-3463; e-mail someal@matrix.com.br; f. 1917; 1,200 mems;

library of 2,500 vols; Pres. CLÉBER COSTA DE OLIVEIRA; publs *Boletim da SMA*, *Consulta*.

Sociedade de Pediatria da Bahia (Bahia Paediatrics Society): Av. A.C.M. 2487–Sala 1414, Candeal, Salvador, BA; tel. (71) 358-4421; f. 1930; 200 mems; Pres. Dra LÍCIA MOREIRA; publ. *Pediatria e Puericultura*.

NATURAL SCIENCES

General

Academia Brasileira de Ciências (Brazilian Academy of Sciences): Rua Anfilófio de Carvalho 29, 3° andar, 20030-060 Rio de Janeiro, RJ; tel. (21) 3907-8100; fax (21) 3907-8101; e-mail abc@abc.org.br; internet www.scielo.br/aabc; f. 1916; 602 mems; Pres. JACOB PALIS; Vice-Pres. HERNAN CHAIMOVICH GURALNIK; Sec. LUIZ DAVIDOVICH; Sec. JERSON LIMA; Sec. IVÁN IZQUIERDO; Sec. CARLOS HENRIQUE BRITO CRUZ; Sec. EVANDO MIRRA; publ. *Anais da Academia Brasileira de Ciências* (4 a year, also online).

Sociedade Brasileira para o Progresso da Ciência (Brazilian Society for the Advancement of Science): Rua Maria Antonia 294, 4° andar, 01222-010 São Paulo, SP; tel. (11) 3259-2766; fax (11) 3106-1002; e-mail sbpc@sbpcnet.org.br; internet www.sbpcnet .org.br; f. 1948; 3,000 mems; Pres. Dr MARCO ANTÔNIO RAUPP; Sec.-Gen. Prof. Dr ALDO MALAVASI; publs *Anais* (online, 1 a year), *Ciência e Cultura* (4 a year), *Ciência Hoje* (12 a year), *Jornal da Ciência* (26 a year), *Revista Ciência Hoje das Crianças* (12 a year).

Biological Sciences

Sociedade Brasileira de Entomologia (Brazilian Entomological Society): CP 42672, 04299-970 São Paulo, SP; tel. (11) 6161-3504; fax (11) 6161-3504; e-mail sbe@ib .usp.br; internet zoo.bio.ufpr.br/sbe; f. 1937; 400 mems; Pres. PEDRO GNASPINI NETTO; Sec. SÉRVIO TÚLIO PIRES AMARANTE; publ. *Revista Brasileira de Entomologia* (4 a year).

Physical Sciences

Associação Brasileira de Química (Brazilian Chemical Association): Av. Presidente Vargas 633 sala 2208, CEP 20071-004, Rio de Janeiro, RJ; tel. (21) 2224-4480; fax (21) 2224-6881; e-mail abqrj@alternex.com.br; f. 1922; affiliated to IUPAC; 3,000 mems; library of 3,000 vols; regional brs in Amazonas, Bahia, Brasília, Ceará, Maranhão, Pará, Paraíba, Pernambuco, Rio de Janeiro, Rio Grande do Norte, Rio Grande do Sul, and São Paulo; Pres. HARRY SERRUYA; publs *Anais da Associação Brasileira de Química*, *Revista de Química Industrial*.

PHILOSOPHY AND PSYCHOLOGY

Sociedade Brasileira de Filosofia (Brazilian Philosophical Society): Praça da República 54, Rio de Janeiro, RJ; f. 1927; 80 mems; 8 hon., 5 Brazilian corresp., 12 foreign; Pres. Dr HERBERT CANABARRO REICHARDT; Sec.-Gen. Prof. ARNALDO CLARO DE SÃO THIAGO; publ. *Anais*.

RELIGION, SOCIOLOGY AND ANTHROPOLOGY

Comissão Nacional de Folclore (National Folklore Commission): Palácio do Itamaraty, Av. Marechal Floriano 196, 20080-002 Rio de Janeiro, RJ; fax (21) 516-2458; e-mail folclorebrasil@yahoo.com.br; internet www .ibeccunesco-sp.org.br; f. 1947; dept of the Brazilian Institute of Education, Science and Culture (IBECC); Pres. Profa PAULA RIBEIRO; publ. *Boletim*.

Sociedade Hebraico Brasileira Renascença: Rua São Vicente de Paulo 659, Santa

Cecília, 01229-010 São Paulo; tel. (11) 3824-0788; fax (11) 3824-0788; internet www .renascenca.br; f. 1922 as Gymnasio Hebraico-Brasileiro Renascença; Exec. Dir MAX WAINTRAUB.

Attached Faculty:

Faculdades Integradas Hebraico Brasileira Renascença: see separate entry under Colleges.

TECHNOLOGY

Associação Brasileira de Metalurgia, Materiais e Mineração (ABM) (Brazilian Metallurgy, Materials and Mining Association): Rua Antônio Comparato 218, Campo Belo, 04605-030 São Paulo, SP; tel. (11) 5534-4333; fax (11) 5534-4330; e-mail abm@ abmbrasil.com.br; internet www.abmbrasil .com.br; f. 1944; 5,500 mems; library of 5,000 vols, periodicals; Pres. KARLHEINZ POHLMANN; Exec. Dir HORACÍDIO LEAL BARBOSA FILHO; publ. *Metalurgia & Materiais* (12 a year).

Associação de Engenharia Química (Society of Chemical Engineers): Av. Prof. Lineu Prestes 510, Bloco 19, Conjunto das Químicas, Cidade Universitária, 05508-000 São Paulo, SP; tel. (11) 3091-3746; e-mail aeq2005@gmail.com; internet aeq.poli.usp .br; f. 1944; 500 mems; Pres. IGOR ARI TERENNA.

Research Institutes
AGRICULTURE, FISHERIES AND VETERINARY SCIENCE

Centro de Energia Nuclear na Agricultura (CENA) (Centre of Nuclear Energy in Agriculture): CP 96, Av. Centenário 303, Piracicaba, 13400-970 São Paulo, SP; Av. Centenário 303, Piracicaba, 13416-000 São Paulo, SP; tel. (19) 3429-4600; fax (19) 3429-4610; e-mail diretoria@cena.usp.br; internet www.cena.usp.br; f. 1966; attached to Univ. de São Paulo; 52 researchers; animal nutrition, ecology, entomology, electron microscopy, genetic engineering, hydrology, phytopathology, plant biochemistry, plant nutrition, radiochemistry, radiogenetics, radiation protection, soil fertility, soil microbiology, soil physics, water pollution; library of 9,000 vols and 366 periodicals; special collection: IAEA publs on life sciences; Dir Prof. Dr VIRGILIO FRANCO DO NASCIMENTO FILHO; publ. *Scientia Agrícola*.

Centro de Pesquisas Veterinárias 'Desidério Finamor' (Institute of Veterinary Research): CP 2076, 90001-970 Porto Alegre, RS; tel. (51) 481-3711; fax (51) 481-3337; e-mail proehe@ufrgs.br; f. 1949; research and training in all aspects of animal health; library of 1,400 vols; Dir Dr AUGUSTO CÉSAR DA CUNHA; publ. *Pesquisa Agropecuária Gaúcha*.

Empresa Brasileira de Pesquisa Agropecuária (EMBRAPA) (Brazilian Agricultural Research Enterprise): Parque Estacão Biológica s/n, Ed. Sede Plano Piloto, CP 04-0315, 70770-901 Brasília, DF; tel. (61) 3448-4433; fax (61) 3347-1041; e-mail presid@sede .embrapa.br; internet www.embrapa.br; f. 1972; attached to Min. of Agriculture; controls agricultural research throughout the country; library of 120,000 vols; Pres. SILVIO CRESTANA; publs *Cadernos de Ciência e Tecnologia* (4 a year), *Pesquisa Agropecuaria Brasileira* (12 a year), *Textos para Discussão* (irregular).

Research Centres:

Centro de Pesquisa Agroflorestal da Amazônia Ocidental: Rodovia AM-010 km 29, Estrada Manaus/Itacoatiara,

69011-970 Manaus, AM; tel. (92) 621-0300; fax (92) 621-0322; internet www.cpaa .embrapa.br; f. 1975; rubber and oil palm research.

Centro de Pesquisa Agroflorestal da Amazônia Oriental: Travessa Dr Enéas Pinheiro s/n, Bairro do Marco, 66095-100 Belém, PA; tel. (91) 276-6333; fax (91) 276-0323; internet www.cpatu.embrapa.br; f. 1975.

Centro de Pesquisa Agroflorestal de Rondônia: Rodovia BR 364, km 5.5, 78970-900 Porto Velho, RO; tel. (69) 216-6500; fax (69) 216-6543; f. 1976.

Centro de Pesquisa Agroflorestal de Roraima: BR 174, km 08, Distrito Industrial, 69301-970 Boa Vista, RR; tel. (95) 626-7125; fax (95) 626-7104; internet www .cpafrr.embrapa.br; f. 1981.

Centro de Pesquisa Agroflorestal do Acre: Rodovia BR 364, km 14, 69908-970 Rio Branco, AC; tel. (68) 212-3200; fax (68) 212-3284; internet www.cpafac.embrapa .br; f. 1976.

Centro de Pesquisa Agroflorestal do Amapá: Rodovia Juscelino Kubitschek, km 05, (Macapá/Fazendinha), 68903-000 Macapá, AP; tel. (96) 241-1551; fax (96) 241-1480; internet www.cpafap.embrapa .br.

Centro de Pesquisa Agropecuária de Clima Temperado: Rodovia BR 392 km 78, 9° Distrito de Pelotas, 96001-970 Pelotas, RS; tel. (532) 275-8100; fax (532) 275-8221; internet www.cpact.embrapa.br; f. 1975; research on temperate fruit and vegetable crops and food technology.

Centro de Pesquisa Agropecuária do Meio Norte: Av. Duque de Caxias 5.650, Bairro Buenos Aires, 64006-220 Teresina, PI; tel. (86) 225-1141; fax (86) 225-1142; internet www.cnpmn.embrapa.br.

Centro de Pesquisa Agropecuária do Oeste: Rodovia BR 163, km 253.6, 79804-970 Dourados, MS; tel. (67) 425-5122; fax (67) 425-0811; internet www.cpao.embrapa .br; f. 1976.

Centro de Pesquisa Agropecuária do Pantanal: Rua 21 de Setembro 1880, 79320-900 Corumbá, MS; tel. (67) 233-2430; fax (67) 233-1011; internet www .cpap.embrapa.br; research on beef cattle and pasture land.

Centro de Pesquisa Agropecuária dos Cerrados: BR 020 km 18, Rodovia Brasília/Fortaleza, 73301-970 Planaltina, DF; tel. (61) 388-9898; fax (61) 389-9879; internet www.cpac.embrapa.br; f. 1975.

Centro de Pesquisa Agropecuária dos Tabuleiros Costeiros: Av. Beira Mar 3250, 49025-040 Aracaju, SE; tel. (79) 226-1300; fax (79) 226-6145; internet www.cpatc.embrapa.br; f. 1974.

Centro de Pesquisa Agropecuária do Trópico Semi-Árido: Rodovia BR 428 km 152, Zona Rural, 56300-000 Petrolina, PE; tel. (87) 3862-1711; fax (87) 3862-1744; internet www.cpatsa.embrapa.br; f. 1975.

Centro de Pesquisa de Pecuária dos Campos sul Brasileiros: Rodovia 153, km 595, Vila Industrial, Zona Rural, 96400-970 Bagé, RS; tel. (32) 42-8499; fax (32) 42-4395; internet www.cppsul .embrapa.br; f. 1975.

Centro de Pesquisa de Pecuária do Sudeste: Rodovia Washington Luiz km 234, 13560-970 São Carlos, SP; tel. (16) 261-5611; fax (16) 261-5754; internet www .cppse.embrapa.br; f. 1975.

Centro Nacional de Pesquisa de Agrobiologia: Rodovia Rio/São Paulo km 47, BR 465, 23851-970 Seropédica, RJ; tel. (21) 2682-1500; fax (21) 2682-1230; internet www.cnpala.embrapa.br.

Centro Nacional de Pesquisa de Agroindústria Tropical (CNPAT): Rua Dra Sara Mesquita 2270, Bairro Pici, 60511-110 Fortaleza, CE; tel. (85) 299-1800; fax (85) 299-1803; internet www .cnpat.embrapa.br.

Centro Nacional de Pesquisa de Algodão: Rua Osvaldo Cruz 1143, Bairro Centenário, 58107-720 Campina Grande, PB; tel. (83) 341-3608; fax (83) 322-7751; internet www.cnpa.embrapa.br; f. 1975; research on cotton.

Centro Nacional de Pesquisa de Arroz e Feijão: Rodovia Goiânia o Nova Veneza km 12, 75375-000, Santo Antônio de Góias, GO; tel. (62) 533-2110; fax (62) 533-2100; internet www.cnpaf.embrapa.br; f. 1975; research on beans, cowpeas and rice.

Centro Nacional de Pesquisa de Caprinos: Fazenda Três Lagoas/Estrada Sobral/Groaíras km 4, 62010-970 Sobral, CE; tel. (88) 3112-7400; fax (88) 3112-7455; e-mail adriana@cnpc.embrapa.br; internet www.cnpc.embrapa.br; f. 1975; research on goats; Gen. Dir Dr EVANDRO VASCONCELOS HOLANDA Jr; Deputy Gen. Dir Dr MARCO AURELIO DELMONDES BOMFIM.

Centro Nacional de Pesquisa de Embrapa Solos: Rua Jardim Botânico 1024, 22460-000 Rio de Janeiro, RJ; tel. (21) 2179-4500; fax (21) 2274-5291; internet www.cnps.embrapa.br; f. 1974; soil survey and conservation.

Centro Nacional de Pesquisa de Florestas: Estrada da Ribeira km 111, CP 319, 83411-000 Colombo, PR; tel. (41) 666-1313; fax (41) 666-1276; internet www.cnpf .embrapa.br; f. 1978; forest research.

Centro Nacional de Pesquisa de Gado de Corte: Rodovia BR 262 km 04, CP 154, 79002-970 Campo Grande, MS; tel. (67) 3368-2000; fax (67) 3368-2150; internet www.cnpgc.embrapa.br; f. 1976; research on beef cattle.

Centro Nacional de Pesquisa de Gado de Leite: Rua Eugênio do Nascimento 610, Bairro Dom Bosco, 36038-330 Juiz de Fora, MG; tel. (32) 3249-4700; fax (32) 3249-4701; internet www.cnpgl.embrapa.br; f. 1976; dairy research.

Centro Nacional de Pesquisa de Hortaliças: Rodovia BR 060 Brasília-Anápolis km 09, Fazendo Tamandué, 70359-970 Brasília; tel. (61) 385-9000; fax (61) 556-5744; internet www.cnph.embrapa.br; f. 1975; vegetable research.

Centro Nacional de Pesquisa de Mandioca e Fruticultura (National Research Center for Cassava and Fruits):; e-mail sonia@cnpmf.embrapa.br Rua EMBRAPA s/n, 44380-000 Cruz das Almas, Bahia - Brasil; tel. (75) 3312-8071; fax (75) 3312-8097; e-mail chgeral@cnpmf .embrapa.br; internet www.cnpmf .embrapa.br; f. 1975; research on cassava and tropical fruits, with emphasis on banana, pineapple, citrus, papaya, passion fruit, barbados cherry, mango and some regional native fruits; Head Dr DOMINGO HAROLDO REINHARDT.

Centro Nacional de Pesquisa de Milho e Sorgo: Rodovia MG 424, km 65, 35701-970, Sete Lagoas, MG; tel. (31) 3779-1000; fax (31) 3779-1088; internet www.cnpms .embrapa.br; f. 1975; research on maize and sorghum; library of 5,500 vols, 65 periodicals; Head Dr ANTÔNIO FERNANDINO C. BAHIA F.

Centro Nacional de Pesquisa de Monitoramento e Avaliaçao de Impacto Ambiéntal – CNPMA:; e-mail victor@ cnpma.embrapa.br Rodovia SP 340, km 127.5, Bairro Tanquinho Velho, 13820-000 Jaguariúna, SP; tel. (19) 3311-2700; fax (19) 3311-2640; e-mail chgeral@cnpma .embrapa.br; internet www.cnpma .embrapa.br; f. 1982; library of 7,825 vols, 466 journals; Dir Dr CELSO VAINER MANZATO.

Centro Nacional de Pesquisa de Soja: Rodovia Carlos João Strass (Londrina/ Warta), Acesso Orlando Amaral, Distrito de Warta, 86001-970 Londrina, PR; tel. (43) 3371-6000; fax (43) 3371-6100; internet www.cnpso.embrapa.br; f. 1975; research on soya beans and sunflowers.

Centro Nacional de Pesquisa de Suínos e Aves: Rodovia BR 153, km 110, Vila Tamanduá, 89700-000 Concórdia, SC; tel. (49) 442-8555; fax (49) 442-8559; internet www.cnpsa.embrapa.br; f. 1975; research on pigs and poultry; library of 4,000 vols, 800 periodicals.

Centro Nacional de Pesquisa de Tecnologia Agroindustrial de Alimentos: Av. das Americas 29501-B, Guaratiba, 23020-470 Rio de Janeiro, RJ; tel. (21) 2410-9500; fax (21) 2410-1090; internet www.ctaa.embrapa.br; f. 1971; food science and technology centre.

Centro Nacional de Pesquisa de Trigo: Rodovia BR 285 km 174, 99001-970 Passo Fundo, RS; tel. (54) 311-3444; fax (54) 311-3617; internet www.cnpt.embrapa.br; f. 1974; wheat research centre.

Centro Nacional de Pesquisa e Desenvolvimento de Instrumentação Agropecuária: Rua XV de Novembro 1452, Centro, 13561-160 São Carlos, SP; tel. (16) 274-2477; fax (16) 272-5958; internet www .cnpdia.embrapa.br.

Centro Nacional de Pesquisa Tecnológica em Informática para a Agricultura: Cidade Universitária Zeferino Vaz, Campus da Universidade Estadual de Campinas—UNICAMP, Bairro de Barão Geraldo, 13083-970 Campinas, SP; tel. (19) 3789-5700; fax (19) 3789-5711; internet www.cnptia.embrapa.br.

Centro Nacional de Recursos Genéticos e Biotecnologia: Parque Estacão Biológico s/n, Plano Piloto (final W-3 Norte), 70770-900 Brasília, DF; tel. (61) 448-4700; fax (61) 448-3624; internet www .cenargem.embrapa.br; f. 1976.

Embrapa Uva e Vinho:; e-mail katia@ cnpuv.embrapa.br Rua Livramento 515, 95700-000 Bento Gonçalves, RS; tel. (54) 3455-8000; fax (54) 3451-2792; e-mail sac@ cnpuv.embrapa.br; internet www.cnpuv .embrapa.br; f. 1975; research and devt in viticulture, temperate fruit and the wine industry; 165 mems; library of 10,000 vols, 540 journal titles; Gen. Dir Dr LUCAS DA RESSURREICAO GARRIDO.

Núcleo de Monitoramento Ambiental de Recursos Naturais por Satélite: Av. Dr Júlio Soares de Arruda 803, Parque São Quirino, 13088-300 Campinas, SP; tel. (19) 3256-6030; fax (19) 3254-1100; internet www.cnpm.embrapa.br.

Instituto Agronômico (Institute of Agronomy): Av. Barão de Itapura 1481, CP 28, 13012-970 Campinas, SP; tel. (19) 3231-5422; fax (19) 3231-4943; e-mail iacdir@iac.sp.gov .br; internet www.iac.sp.gov.br; f. 1887; basic and applied research on plants, soils, environment, farming methods and agricultural machinery; Divs: agricultural engineering, biology, experimental stations, food plants, industrial plants, soil; Technical Scientific Information Service; library of 200,000 vols; 20 experimental stations in the State of São Paulo; Gen. Dir Dr MARCO ANTÓNIO TEIXEIRA

ZULLO; publs *Bragantia* (2 a year), *O Agronômico* (irregular).

Instituto Brasileiro do Meio Ambiente e dos Recursos Naturais Renováveis (IBAMA) (Brazilian Institute for the Environment and Renewable Natural Resources): SCEN trecho 2, Edifício Sede Ibama, 70818-900 Brasília, DF; tel. (61) 316-1205; fax (61) 226-5094; internet www.ibama.gov.br; f. 1989; library of 65,000 vols; Pres. Dr MARCUS LUIZ BARROSO BARROS.

Instituto de Economia Agrícola (Agricultural Economics Institute): Av. Miguel Stefano 3900, Água Funda, CP 68029, 04301-903 São Paulo, SP; tel. (11) 5067-0526; fax (11) 5073-4062; e-mail iea@iea.sp.gov.br; internet www.iea.sp.gov.br; f. 1942; affiliated to São Paulo Secretariat of Agriculture and Provision; provides information for state and federal govts and other interested bodies; library of 70,000 vols, 2,700 periodicals; Dir Dr VALQUÍRIA DA SILVA; publs *Agricultura em São Paulo* (irregular), *Informações Econômicas* (12 a year), *Informações Estatística da Agricultura* (1 a year).

Instituto de Zootecnia (Institute of Animal Science and Pastures): Rua Heitor Penteado 56, CP 60, 13460-000 Nova Odessa, SP; tel. (19) 3466-9400; fax (19) 3466-6415; e-mail diretoria@iz.sp.gov.br; internet www.iz.sp.gov.br; f. 1905; 92 researchers; beef cattle, dairy cattle, goats, information science, pastures, pigs, reproduction and genetics, sheep, water buffaloes; library of 10,710 vols, 1,610 periodicals; Dir-Gen. ANTONIO ALVARO DUARTE DE OLIVEIRA; publs *Boletim de Indústria Animal* (2 a year), *Boletim Tecnicos*.

Instituto Florestal (Estado de São Paulo) (São Paulo State Forestry Institute): Rua do Horto 931, CP 1322, 02377-000 São Paulo, SP; tel. (11) 6231-8555 ext. 2100; fax (11) 6132-5767; e-mail nuinfo@iflorest.sp.gov.br; internet www.iflorestsp.br; f. 1896; 1,107 staff; library of 7,500 vols, 2,000 periodicals; Dir MARIA CECÍLIA WEY DE BRITO; publs *Revista do Instituto Florestal* (2 a year), *Revista IF-Serie Registros* (irregular).

Organização Nacional de Proteção Fitossanitária (ONPF) (National Plant Protection Organization): Departamento de Sanidade Vegetal, Ministério da Agricultura, Pecuária e Abastecimento, Esplanada dos Ministérios, Bloco D, Anexo B, Sala 303-B, Brasília, DF; tel. (61) 3218-2675; fax (61) 3224-3874; e-mail dsv@agricultura.gov.br; internet www.agricultura.gov.br; f. 2005; Dir JOSÉ GERALDO BALDINI RIBEIRO.

ECONOMICS, LAW AND POLITICS

Centro de Estatística e Informações (Statistics and Information Centre): Centro Administrativo da Bahia, Av. 435 4A, 41750-300 Salvador, BA; tel. (71) 371-9665; fax (71) 371-9664; f. 1983; statistics, natural resources, economic indicators; library of 15,448 vols; Dir RENATA PROSERPIO; publ. *Bahia Análise e Dados* (every 4 months).

EDUCATION

Instituto Nacional de Estudos e Pesquisas Educacionais (National Institute for Educational Studies and Research): INEP/MEC, Esp. dos Ministérios, Bloco L, Anexos I e II (4° andar), 70047-900 Brasília, DF; internet www.inep.gov.br; f. 1938; 130 mems; library of 50,000 vols, 985 periodicals; Pres. Dr MARIA HELENA GUIMARÃES DE CASTRO; publs *Bibliografia Brasileira de Educação*, *Em Aberto*, *Revista Brasileira de Estudos Pedagógicos*.

HISTORY, GEOGRAPHY AND ARCHAEOLOGY

Fundação Instituto Brasileiro de Geografia e Estatística (Brazilian Institute of Geography and Statistics): Av. Franklin Roosevelt 166, 20021-120 Rio de Janeiro, RJ; internet www.ibge.gov.br; f. 1936; produces and analyzes statistical, geographical, cartographic, geodetic, demographic, socioeconomic, natural resources and environmental information; Pres. EDUARDO PEREIRA NUNES; publs *Anuário Estatístico do Brasil*, *Revista Brasileira de Estatística*, *Revista Brasileira de Geografia*.

MEDICINE

Fundação 'Oswaldo Cruz' (Oswaldo Cruz Foundation): Av. Brasil 4365, Manguinhos, CP 926, 21045-900 Rio de Janeiro, RJ; tel. (21) 2598-4242; fax (21) 2270-7444; e-mail ferreirj@fiocruz.br; internet www.fiocruz.br; f. 1900; infectious and parasitic diseases, entomology, epidemiology, history of science, immunology, public health; tropical medicine, virology; library of 800,000 vols, 2,000 current periodicals; Pres. Dr PAULO MARCHIORI BUSS; publs *Cadernos de Saúde Pública* (4 a year), *História, Ciências, Saúde—Manguinhos* (3 a year), *Memórias* (6 a year).

Instituto 'Adolfo Lutz': Av. Dr Arnaldo 355, Pacaembú, 01246-902 01246-902 São Paulo, SP; fax (11) 3085-3505; f. 1892; Central Laboratory of Public Health for the State of São Paulo; library of 50,000 vols, incl. periodicals; Dir.-Gen. CRISTIANO CORRÊA DE AZEVEDO MARQUES; publ. *Revista*.

Instituto 'Benjamin Constant': Av. Pasteur 350/368, Urca, 22290-240 Rio de Janeiro, RJ; tel. (21) 3478-4442; fax (21) 3478-4442; e-mail dirgeral@ibc.gov.br; internet www.ibc.gov.br; f. 1854; educational institute for the blind; library: braille and general library of 15,000 vols; Dir ÉRICA DESLANDES MAGNO OLIVEIRA; publs *Pontinhos* (4 a year), *Revista Benjamin Constant*, *Revista Brasileira para Cegos* (4 a year).

Instituto Brasileiro de Estudos e Pesquisas de Gastroenterologia (IBEPEGE): Rua Dr Seng 320, Bairro da Bela Vista, 01331-020 São Paulo; tel. (11) 3288-2119; fax (11) 3289-2768; f. 1963; study and research in gastroenterology, nutrition and psychosomatic medicine; postgraduate courses; library of 10,000 vols; Pres. Prof. JOSÉ FERNANDES PONTES; Vice-Pres. Dr JOSÉ VICENTE MARTINS CAMPOS; publ. *Arquivos de Gastroenterologia* (4 a year).

Instituto Butantan (Butantan Institute): Av. Vital Brasil 1500, CP 65, 05503-900 São Paulo, SP; tel. (11) 3726-7222; fax (11) 3726-1505; e-mail instituto@butantan.gov.br; internet www.butantan.gov.br; f. 1901; library of 96,000 vols on ophiology and biomedical sciences; famous snake farm; Public Health Institute for research and the production of vaccines, sera, etc.; also research in genetics, virology, pathology, etc.; Hospital Vital Brasil (snake, spider and scorpion accidents); Dir OTÁVIO AZEVEDO MERCADANTE.

Instituto de Saúde (Institute of Health): Rua Santo Antonio 590, Bela Vista, 01314-000 São Paulo, SP; tel. (11) 3293-2244; internet www.isaude.sp.gov.br; f. 1969; degenerative diseases, dermatology, hansenology, nutrition, ophthalmology, organization and supervision of study, phthisiology, research and activities in the fields of mother and child care; library: see Libraries; Dir-Gen. Dr EDMUR F. PASTORELO; publ. *Boletim* (3 a year).

Instituto Evandro Chagas (MS-Fundação Nacional de Saúde): Rodovia BR-316 km 7 s/n, Levilândia, 67030-000 Ananindeua, PA; tel. (91) 3214-2213; fax (91) 3214-2214; e-mail contato@iec.pa.gov.br; internet www.iec.pa.gov.br; f. 1936; research in bacteriology, parasitology, pathology, virology, mycology, medical entomology, human ecology and environment; library of 50,000 vols, 134 current periodicals, 4,000 reprints; Dir ELISABETH CONCEIÇÃO DE OLIVEIRA SANTOS; publ. *Revista Pan-Amazônica de Saúde*.

Instituto Nacional de Cancer, Coordenação de Pesquisa: Rua André Cavalcanti 37/2 andar-Centro, 20231-050 Rio de Janeiro, RJ; tel. (21) 3233-1414; fax (21) 3233-1355; internet www.inca.org.br; f. 1958; cell biology, experimental oncology, genetics, molecular biology, pharmacology; Head of Research Dra MARISA BREITENBACH.

Instituto Oscar Freire (Oscar Freire Institute): Rua Teodoro Sampaio 115, 05405-000 São Paulo, SP; tel. (11) 3085-9677; fax (11) 3085-9677; f. 1918; for instruction and research in forensic medicine; assoc. with Univ. of São Paulo; library of 4,200 vols; Chair. Prof. Dr CLÁUDIO COHEN.

Instituto Pasteur: Av. Paulista 393, 01311-000 São Paulo, SP; tel. (11) 3145-3145; fax (11) 3289-08-31; e-mail pasteur@pasteur.saude.sp.gov.br; internet www.pasteur.saude.sp.gov.br; f. 1903; practical measures and theoretical studies aimed at preventing rabies in humans; 28 staff; library of 5,000 vols and 1,083 periodicals; Technical Dir Dr NEIDE TAKAOKA.

Instituto 'Penido Burnier': Rua Dr Mascarenhas 249, POB 284, 13020-050 Campinas, SP; tel. (19) 3232-5866; fax (19) 3233-4492; e-mail penido@penidoburnier.com.br; f. 1920; anaesthesiology, ophthalmology, otolaryngology; library of 11,585 vols; Chief Librarians Dr HILTON DE MELLO E OLIVEIRA, VANDA REGINA SILVA JUCÁ; publ. *Arquivos IPB* (2 a year).

NATURAL SCIENCES
General

Centro de Ciências, Letras e Artes (Science, Letters and Arts Centre): Rua Bernardino de Campos 989, 13010-151, Campinas, SP; tel. (19) 3231-2567; e-mail ccla@ccla.org.br; internet www.ccla.org.br; f. 1901; library of 120,000 vols; museum and art gallery attached; Pres. Eng. MARINO ZIGGIATTI; Gen. Sec. Dr EDUARDO DA ROCHA E SILVA; Librarian Prof. DUILIO BATTISTONI FILHO; publ. *Revista*.

Conselho Nacional de Desenvolvimento Científico e Tecnológico (CNPq) (National Council of Scientific and Technological Development): SEPN 507, Bloco B, Ed. Sede CNPq, 70740-901 Brasília, DF; tel. (61) 2108-9000; fax (61) 2108-9394; internet www.cnpq.br; f. 1951; an agency of the Ministério da Ciência e Tecnologia; Pres. MARCO ANTONIO ZAGO.

Institut de Recherche pour le Développement (IRD): CP 7091, Lago Sul, 71619-970 Brasília, DF; SHIS, QL 16, Conj. 4, Casa 8, Lago Sul, 71640-245 Brasília, DF; tel. (61) 3248-5323; fax (61) 3248-5378; e-mail bresil@ird.fr; internet www.brasil.ird.fr; f. 1979; headquarters of the Brazilian delegation to Latin America; missions at various univs and research institutes; See main entry under France; Delegate to Brazil JEAN-LOUP GUYOT.

Instituto Nacional de Pesquisas da Amazônia (National Research Institute for Amazonia): Av. André Araújo 2936, Aleixo, 69060-001 Manaus, AM; tel. (92) 3643-3377; fax (92) 3643-3095; internet www.inpa.gov.br; f. 1954; agronomics, biology, ecology, forestry, medicine, technology, and special projects; 1,003 staff; library of 48,000 items; herbarium; wood collection; Dir ADALBERTO LUIS VAL; publ. *Acta Amazônica* (4 a year).

Biological Sciences

Campo de Santana: Praça da República s/n, Centro, 20211-360 Rio de Janeiro, RJ; tel. (21) 2323-3500; internet www.rio.rj.gov.br/fpj/cposantana.htm; laid out 1870 by Auguste F. M. Glaziou, who collected 23,000 plants, including 700 trees; Herbário Glaziou forms the most noteworthy exhibit in the Botanical Division of the National Museum.

Centro de Pesquisa e Gestão de Recursos Pesqueiros Continentais (CEPTA) (Research and Management Centre for Continental Fish Resources): Rod. Pref. Euberto N. P. de Godoy s/n, CP 64, km 6.5, 13630-970 Pirassununga, SP; tel. (19) 3565-1299; fax (19) 3565-1318; f. 1938; library of 26,024 vols; Dir LAERTE BATISTA DE OLIVEIRA ALVES; publ. *Boletim Técnico* (1 a year).

Fundação Ezequiel Dias: Rua Conde Pereira Carneiro 80, Gameleira, 30510-010 Belo Horizonte, MG; tel. (31) 3371-9441; fax (31) 3371-9444; e-mail faleconosco@funed.mg.gov .br; internet www.funed.mg.gov.br; f. 1907; attached to the Minas Gerais state government; health and welfare, biotechnology, immunology research; library; Pres. CARLOS ALBERTO PEREIRA GOMES; Vice-Pres. SILAS PAULO RESENDE GOUVEIA.

Herbário 'Barbosa Rodrigues': Avda Coronel Marcos Konder 800, 88301-302 Itajaí, SC; tel. (47) 3348-8725; e-mail hbr.itajai@gmail.com; internet www.hbr.org.br; f. 1942; botany of southern Brazil, taxonomy, ecology; 186 mems; library of 19,241 vols; Pres. VITUS SCHLICKMANN ROETGER; Dir ADEMIR REIS; publs *Flora Ilustrada Catarinense* (1 a year), *Sellowia* (1 a year).

Instituto Biológico (Biological Institute): Av. Cons. Rodrigues Alves 1252, 40014-002 São Paulo; tel. (11) 5579-4234; fax (11) 5087-1796; e-mail divulgacao@biologico.sp.gov.br; internet www.biologico.sp.gov.br; f. 1927; animal and plant protection; library of 13,000 vols, 105,000 periodicals; Dir-Gen. ANTONIO BATISTA FILHO; publs *Arquivos do Instituto Biológico* (4 a year), *Boletim Técnico* (irregular), *O Biológico* (2 a year).

Instituto de Botânica (Botanical Institute): CP 3005, 01061-970 São Paulo; tel. (11) 5073-600; fax (11) 5073-3678; e-mail biblioteca@ibot.sp.gov.br; internet www.ibot .sp.gov.br; f. 1938; herbarium of 400,000 plants; postgraduate course in plant diversity and the environment; library of 90,000 vols; Dir VERA LUCIA RAMOS BONONI; publs *Boletim* (irregular), *Hoehnea* (4 a year).

Instituto de Pesquisas do Jardim Botânico do Rio de Janeiro: Rua Jardim Botânico 1008, Jardim Botânico, Rio de Janeiro, RJ; tel. (21) 511-0511; fax (21) 259-5041; e-mail jbrj@gov.br; internet www.jbrj .gov.br; f. 1808; attached to Min. of the Environment, Water Resources and Amazonia; botanical research in systematics, wood anatomy (7,148 samples and 17,000 microscope plates), cytomorphology and ecology; botanical garden with 7,800 species and 11,000 specimens; herbarium with 350,000 samples; library of 15,000 vols, 50,000 periodicals, antiquarian collection of 3,000 vols; Dir SERGIO DE ALMEIDA BRUNI; publs *Arquivos*, *Rodriguésia*.

Instituto Estadual do Ambiente (INEA) (State Environmental Institute): Assessoria de Comunicação, Av. Venezuela 110, Rio de Janeiro, RJ; f. 2009 to protect, conserve and restore the Rio de Janeiro State environment and to promote sustainable development; Pres. LUIZ FIRMINO MARTINS PEREIRA; Vice-Pres. PAULO SCHIAVO; publ. *Boletim de Serviço* (online, irregular).

Physical Sciences

Associação Internacional de Lunologia (International Association of Lunology): CP 322, Franca, São Paulo; f. 1969; publishes a review on lunar research carried out by all countries.

Centro Brasileiro de Pesquisas Físicas (Brazilian Centre for Physics Research): Rua Dr Xavier Sigaud 150, 4° andar, Urca, 22290-180 Rio de Janeiro, RJ; tel. (21) 2141-7100; fax (21) 2141-7400; e-mail webmaster@cbpf .br; internet www.cbpf.br; f. 1949; library of 18,951 vols, 811 periodicals; Dir RICARDO MAGNUS OSÓRIO GALVÃO; Sec. IVANILDA GOMES FERREIRA; publs *Ciência e Sociedade*, *Notas de Físicas*, *Notas Técnicas*.

Departamento Nacional da Produção Mineral (National Department of Mineral Production): Setor de Autarquias Norte, Quadra 01, Bloco B, 70041-903 Brasília, DF; tel. (61) 3312-6666; fax (61) 3312-6918; e-mail dir@dnpm.gov.br; internet www .dnpm.gov.br; f. 1907; Dept of Ministry of Mines and Energy; Dir YVAN BARRETTO DE CARVALHO; publs *Anuário Mineral Brasileiro*, *Avulso*, *Balanço Mineral Brasileiro*, *Boletim de Preços*, *Boletim Informativo*.

Instituto Nacional de Meteorologia (National Institute of Meteorology):; e-mail director.inmet@gov.br Eixo Monumental Via S1 Sudoeste, 70680-900 Brasília, DF; tel. (61) 2102-4602; fax (61) 2102-4620; e-mail webmaster.csc@inmet.gov.br; internet www.inmet.gov.br; Dir ANTÔNIO DIVINO MOURA; publ. *Boletim Agroclimatológico*.

Laboratório de Análises (Analytical Laboratory): Av. Rodrigues Alves 81, 20081-250 Rio de Janeiro, RJ; tel. (21) 223-7743; f. 1889; covers organic, inorganic and pharmaceutical chemistry, biochemistry and materials; library of 4,000 vols; Dir Prof. MARCELO DE M. MOURA.

Observatório Nacional do Brasil (National Observatory): Rua General José Cristino 77, São Cristovão, 20921-400 Rio de Janeiro, RJ; tel. (21) 3504-9100; fax (21) 2580-6041; e-mail dir@on.br; internet www .on.br; f. 1827; library; astronomical and geophysical research programmes using 7 refractors, a Time Service at Rio de Janeiro and a Time Station at Brasília; operates 2 magnetic observatories; Dir SERGIO LUIZ FONTES; Sec. MARIA DAS GRAÇAS BRITO DE VARGAS; publs *Contribuições Científicas*, *Efemérides Astronômicas* (1 a year).

PHILOSOPHY AND PSYCHOLOGY

Instituto Neo-Pitagórico (Neo-Pythagorean Institute): CP 1047, 80011-970 Curitiba, PR; Rua Prof. Dario Vellozo 460, Vila Izabel, 80320-050 Curitiba, PR; tel. (41) 3242-1840; e-mail neo@pitagorico.org.br; internet www .pitagorico.org.br; f. 1909; courses in hierology, history of religion, occultism, parapsychology, philosophy, Pythagorean studies, theosophy; 486 mems; library of 21,000 vols; Pres. Dr ANAEL PINHEIRO DE ULHOA CINTRA; Sec. ELIZABETH GARZUZE DA SILVA ARAUJO; publs *A Lâmpada* (4 a year), *Biblioteca Neo-Pitagórica* (1 a year), *Boletim Informativo* (4 a year), *Circulares* (1 a year), *Templo da Paz* (3 a year).

RELIGION, SOCIOLOGY AND ANTHROPOLOGY

Fundação Joaquim Nabuco: Av. 17 de Agosto 2187, Casa Forte, 52061-540 Recife, PE; tel. (81) 3073-6363; fax (81) 3073-6203; fax (81) 441-5600; e-mail relacoespublicas@fundaj.gov.br; internet www.fundaj.gov.br; f. 1949; anthropological, economic, educational, geographical, historical, political, socio-logical, statistical and population studies about Brazil's north and north-east; 600 mems; library: specialized library of 60,238 vols and museum; Pres. FERNANDO SOARES LYRA; publs *Cadernos de Estudos Sociais* (2 a year), *Ciência & Trópico* (2 a year).

TECHNOLOGY

Centro de Pesquisas e Desenvolvimento (CEPED) (Research and Development Centre): Est BA 536, km 0, Entroncamento, 42800-000 Camaçari, BA; tel. (71) 834-7300; fax (71) 832-2095; f. 1969; research in agroindustrial and food technology, analysis, building materials, chemistry and petrochemistry, energy, environmental engineering, metallurgy, ores treatment, materials testing, mineralogy, quality control; library of 26,702 vols; Dir Dr SYLVIO DE QUEIROS MATTOSO; publ. *Tecbahia* (3 a year).

Centro de Pesquisas e Desenvolvimento Leopoldo A. Miguez de Mello (PETROBRAS) (PETROBRAS Research and Development Centre): Av. Jequitibá 950, Cidade Universitária, Ilha do Fundão, Quadra 7, 21941-598 Rio de Janeiro, RJ; tel. (21) 3865-6062; fax (21) 598-6363; e-mail cenpes@cenpes.petrobras.com.br; internet www2 .petrobras.com.br/tecnologia2/port/index .htm; f. 1966; research into exploration, exploitation and refining of petroleum resources; 757 mems; library: specialized library of 35,000 vols, 520 current periodicals; Gen. Man. ANTONIO SERGIO FRAGOMENI; publs *Boletim de Geociências da PETROBRAS* (4 a year), *Boletim Técnico da PETROBRAS* (4 a year), *Ciência-Tecnica-Petróleo*.

Comissão Nacional de Energia Nuclear (CNEN) (Commission for Nuclear Energy): Rua General Severiano 90, Botafogo, 22294-900 Rio de Janeiro, RJ; tel. (21) 2546-2320; fax (21) 2546-2282; internet www.cnen.gov .br; f. 1956; supervisory nuclear agency, coordinates planning and financing of nuclear activities, promotes and executes research programmes, trains scientists and technicians; Pres. JOSÉ MANUO ESTEVES DOS SANTOS.

Attached Institutes:

Centro de Desenvolvimento da Tecnologia Nuclear (CDTN) (Nuclear Technology Development Centre): Belo Horizonte, MG; tel. (31) 3499-3261; fax (31) 3499-3444; e-mail webmaster@urano.cdtn.br; internet www.cdtn.br; f. 1952; environmental and atomic energy research; Coordinator SILVESTRE PAIANO SOBRINHO.

Centro de Energia Nuclear na Agricultura (CENA): see under Agriculture.

Instituto de Engenharia Nuclear (IEN) (Nuclear Engineering Institute): CP 2186, Rio de Janeiro, RJ; tel. (21) 2560-4113; fax (21) 2590-2692; e-mail ien@ien.gov.br; internet www.ien.gov.br; f. 1962; pure and applied research and devt of uses of atomic energy, especially fast breeder reactors, instrumentation and control, cyclotron physics; Dirs LUIZ ALBERTO ILHA ARRIETA, SERGIO CHAVES CABRAL.

Instituto de Pesquisas Energéticas e Nucleares (IPEN) (Energetics and Nuclear Research Institute): Ave Prof. Lineu Prestes 2242, São Paulo-SP, 05508-000; tel. (11) 3133-9000; fax (11) 3812-3546; e-mail webmaster@net.ipen.br; internet www.ipen.br; f. 1956; conducts pure and applied research in energy, mainly in nuclear sector; offers training courses; energy information centre; Dir NILSON DIAS VIERA JR.

Instituto de Radioproteção e Dosimetria (IRD) (Radiation Protection and

Dosimetry Institute): Av. Salvador Allende s/n, Jacarepaguá, CP 37750, 22780-160 Rio de Janeiro, RJ; tel. (21) 2442-1927; fax (21) 2442-1950; internet www.ird.gov.br; f. 1972; research and devt of radiation protection and dosimetry methods and standards; Dir ELIANA AMARAL.

Instituto Brasileiro de Petróleo (Brazilian Institute of Petroleum): Av. Almirante Barroso 52, 26° Andar, 20043, Centro, Rio de Janeiro, RJ; tel. (21) 532-1610; fax (21) 220-1596; internet www.ibp.org.br; f. 1957; holds Brazilian standards for petroleum products and equipment; research in petroleum and petrochemical industries; mems: 146 companies; Pres. GUILHERME DE OLIVEIRA ESTRELLA.

Instituto de Pesquisas Tecnológicas do Estado de São Paulo S.A. (IPT) (Institute for Technological Research of the State of São Paulo): Cidade Universitária Armando de Salles Oliveira, n. 532, 05508-901 São Paulo, SP; tel. (11) 3767-4000; fax (11) 3767-4002; internet www.ipt.br; f. 1899; non-profit-making public corporation, owned by the State of São Paulo; has 8 technical divisions: civil engineering, chemistry, economy and systems engineering, forest products, geology, mechanical and electrical engineering, metallurgy, transport technology; has 4 technical centres: information technology and telecommunications, leather and footwear technology, technological improvement, technological information; library of 98,200 books, 4,315 periodicals, 1,100,000 nat. and int. active and historical standards; Dir Dr GUILHERME ARY PLONSKI; publ. *Tecnologia em dia* (6 a year).

Instituto de Tecnologia do Paraná (Paraná Institute of Technology): Rua Professor Algacyr Munhoz Mader 3775 Cidade Industrial, 81350-010 Curitiba, PR; tel. (41) 3316-3000; fax (41) 3576-1923; e-mail tecpar@tecpar.br; internet www.tecpar.br; f. 1940; research in all aspects of technology for the development of the state; produces vaccines; national and int. exchange with orgs in the same field; library of 8,000 vols, 1,054 periodicals; Pres. ALDAIR TARCISIO RIZZI; publs *Arquivo de Biologia e Tecnologia* (4 a year), *Boletim Técnico* (6 a year).

Instituto Nacional de Pesquisas Espaciais (INPE) (National Institute for Space Research): Av. Dos Astronautas 1758, CP 515, 12227-010 São José dos Campos, SP; tel. (12) 3945-6000; fax (12) 3945-6919; internet www.inpe.br; f. 1961, renamed in 1971; analogic and digital systems, assembly, astrophysics, balloon launching centre, basic meteorology, centre for satellite operation and missions, combustion processes, control and tracking stations, energy supply, environmental analysis, geomagnetism, ground stations, human resources, image production, informatics, integration and tests of space platforms, ionosphere, materials, medium and low atmosphere, meteorological applications, meteorological instrumentation, meteorological satellite services, orbital dynamics and control, payloads for space platforms, plasma physics, qualification of components, remote sensing for forestry and agronomic resources, remote sensing for mineral resources, remote sensing for sea resources, sensors, solar physics, space geodesy, space telecommunications, structure and thermic control of space platforms, systems engineering, technology transfer units and systems for space applications, upper atmosphere; library of 47,000 vols, microforms, CD-ROMs, microfilms and tapes, 1,600 periodicals, 21,000 specialized papers, 10,000 INPE reports, 5,800 maps; Dir Dr GILBERTO CAMARA; publ. *Climanálise*.

Instituto Nacional de Tecnología (National Technological Institute): Av. Venezuela 82, 20081-310 Rio de Janeiro, RJ; tel. (21) 2206-1135; fax (21) 2253-4361; internet www.int.gov.br/principal.html; f. 1922; research in chemical industry, chemistry of natural products, computer-aided projects, corrosion, energy conservation, industrial design, metallurgy, pollution control, rubber and plastics; library of 17,000 vols, 1,000 periodicals, 100,000 microfiches; Dir JOAO LUIZ HANRIOTT SELASCO; publ. *Informativo do INT*.

Instituto Tecnológico do Estado de Pernambuco (ITEP) (Technological Institute of the State of Pernambuco): Av. Prof. Luis Freire 700, Cidade Universitária, Recife, PE; tel. (81) 3272-4399; fax (81) 3272-4272; e-mail itep@itep.br; internet www.itep.br; f. 1942; industrial research; library of 10,000 vols; Pres. FÁTIMA MARIA MIRANDA BRAYER; publ. *Revista Pernambucana de Tecnologia* (2 a year).

Libraries and Archives

Aracajú

Biblioteca Pública Epifânio Dória (Epifânio Dória Public Library): Prolongamento da Vila Cristina, s/n, 49015-000 Aracajú, SE; tel. (79) 224-2127; f. 1851; 15,000 vols; Dir SÔNIA CARVALHO.

Belém

Arquivo Público do Estado do Pará (Pará Public Archives): Rua Campos Sales, 273, 66019-050 Belém, PA; tel. (91) 241-9700; fax (91) 241-9097; f. 1901; 500 vols; special colln of 742 vols; Dir GERALDO MÁRTIRES COELHO; publ. *Anais do Arquivo Público do Pará* (every 2 years).

Biblioteca Central Prof. Dr Clodoaldo Beckmann da Universidade Federal do Pará: Rua Augusto Corrêa 1, Campus Universitário, Guamá, 66075-110 Belém, PA; tel. (91) 3201-7140; fax (91) 3201-7351; e-mail bc@ufpa.br; internet www.ufpa.br/bc; f. 1962; 157,000 vols, 5,000 periodicals; Dir MARIA DAS GRAÇAS DA SILVA PENA.

Biblioteca do Grêmio Literário e Comercial Português (Library of the Portuguese Literary and Commercial Union): Rua Senador Manuel Barata 237, Belém, PA; f. 1867; Sec. ANÍSIO DE SOARES TEIXEIRA; 29,568 vols; exchange service.

Belo Horizonte

Biblioteca Pública Estadual Luiz de Bessa (Public Library): Praça da Liberdade 21, Funcionários, 30140-010 Belo Horizonte, MG; tel. (31) 3269-1166 ext. 100; fax (31) 3261-1311; e-mail sub@cultura.mg.gov.br; f. 1954; 280,000 vols, 5,124 vols of Braille, 300 talking books; 600 brs; Dir MARIA DE FÁTIMA FALCI.

Universidade Federal de Minas Gerais, Biblioteca Universitária/Sistema de Bibliotecas da UFMG: Av. Presidente Antônio Carlos 6627, 31270-901 Belo Horizonte, MG; tel. (31) 499-4611; fax (31) 499-4611; e-mail dir@bu.ufmg.br; internet www.bu.ufmg.br; f. 1927; collection of special documents; 650,000 vols, 6,000 maps, 14,763 rare works, 22,000 periodicals, 15,000 music scores; Dir SIMONE APARECIDA DOS SANTOS.

Brasília

Biblioteca Acadêmico Luiz Viana Filho (Library of the Federal Senate): Senado Federal, Praça dos Três Poderes, Palácio do Congresso (Anexo II—Térreo), 70165-900 Brasília, DF; tel. (61) 3303-4141; internet www.senado.gov.br/sf/biblioteca; f. 1826; specializes in social sciences, law, politics, public administration, legislation; also works on literature, history and geography; 390,000 items; Dir SIMONE BASTOS VIEIRA; publ. *Revista de Informação Legislativa* (online, 4 a year).

Biblioteca Central, Universidade de Brasília: Campus Universitário Darcy Ribeiro, Gleba A, 70910-900 Brasília, DF; tel. (61) 3307-2417; fax (61) 3274-2412; e-mail administracao@bce.unb.br; internet www.bce.unb.br; f. 1962; 530,292 vols, 7,864 periodicals; Dir SELY MARIA DE SOUZA COSTA.

Biblioteca Demonstrativa de Brasília (Public Library): Entrequadras 506/507 W3 Sul, 70350-580 Brasília, DF; tel. (61) 3244-3015; internet www.bdb.org.br; f. 1970; 129,661 vols, 2,400 periodicals on general subjects; also maps, microfilms, slides, pictures; Dir MARIA DA CONCEIÇÃO MOREIRA SALLES.

Biblioteca do Ministério da Justiça (Library of Ministry of Justice): Esplanada dos Ministérios, Ed. Sede Térreo, 70064-900 Brasília, DF; tel. (61) 3429-3323; fax (61) 3429-9910; e-mail biblioteca@mj.br; f. 1941; 130,000 vols, of which many are on law, economics, sociology, labour, and political science; very rare clln of laws of Portuguese colonial period; 6,000-vol. Goethe clln; Dir DOROTI TEREZITA HOF; publ. *Revista Arquivos do Ministério da Justiça*.

Biblioteca do Ministério do Trabalho e Emprego (Library of Ministry of Labour and Employment): Esplanada dos Ministérios, Bloco F, Anexo, Ala B, Térreo, 70059-900 Brasília, DF; tel. (61) 317-6186; fax (61) 226-7536; internet www.mte.gov.br/biblioteca; f. 1871; 18,000 vols; 120 collections of newspapers; Librarian MARIA PAULA GARCIA CAMPOS DE ARAYO; publ. *Relação Anual de Informações Sociais*.

Biblioteca Embaixador Antonio Francisco Azeredo da Silveira (Library of the Ministry of Foreign Affairs): Esplanada dos Ministérios Bloco H, Anexo II, Térreo, 70170-900 Brasília, DF; tel. (61) 3411-9103; fax (61) 3411-6001; e-mail biblio@mre.gov.br; internet www.biblioteca.mre.gov.br; f. 1906; 100,000 vols, 590 periodical titles (history collection in Rio de Janeiro, *q.v.*); law, history, politics and economics; collection of UN documents; Chief Librarian Bib. ELIZABETH MARIA DE MATTOS.

Biblioteca Nacional de Agricultura (BINAGRI) (National Library of Agriculture): CP 02432, Ministério da Agricultura, Pecuária e Abastecimento, Anexos A e B Bl. B, Térreo, 70043-970 Brasília, DF; tel. (61) 3218-2613; fax (61) 3226-8190; f. 1904; central unit of National System of Agricultural Information and Documentation (SNIDA); responsible for establishing State libraries of agriculture in order to decentralize information sources; 300,000 vols, 7,032 serial titles, 216,000 microfiche documents; Coordinator and Librarian NEUZA ARANTES SILVA; publ. *Thesaurus para Indexação/ Recuperação da Literatura Agrícola Brasileira*.

Centro de Documentação e Informação da Câmara dos Deputados do Brasil (Centre for Documentation and Information, Chamber of Deputies, Brazil): Palácio do Congresso Nacional, Camara dos Deputados (Anexo II), 70160-900 Brasília, DF; tel. (61) 3216-5777; fax (61) 3216-5757; e-mail informa.cedi@camara.gov.br; internet www2.camara.gov.br/documentos-e-pesquisa/biblarq; f. 1971; 180,000 vols, 3,500 titles; Dir ADOLFO FURTADO; Dir of Archives Unit FREDERICO DOS SANTOS; Dir of Centre for Documentation and Information ADOLFO FURTADO;

Dir of Cultural Assets and Preservation Unit FRANCISCO CARVALHO; Dir of Information Research Service Unit CHRISTIANE COELHO; Dir of Legislative Studies Unit SYLVIO CARVALHO; Dir of Library Unit PATRICIA MILANI; Dir of Publs Unit MARIA CLARA BIUDO CÉSAR.

Centro de Informação e Biblioteca em Educação: Ministério da Educação, Esplanada dos Ministérios, Bloco L, Térreo, CP 08866, 70047-900 Brasília, DF; tel. (61) 410-9052; fax (61) 223-5137; e-mail cibec@inep .gov.br; internet www.inep.gov.br/cibec; f. 1981; 21,000 vols, 844 periodicals; specialized library on education; Dir ÉRICA MÁSSIMO MACHADO.

Instituto Brasileiro de Informação em Ciência e Tecnologia (IBICT): SAS Quadra 05, Lote 06, Bloco H, 5° andar, 70070-912 Brasília, DF; tel. (61) 3217-6360; fax (61) 3217-6490; internet www.ibict.br; f. 1954 as IBBD, renamed 1976; coordinates scientific and technical information services throughout the country; provides technical assistance, and training; maintains the following databases available for public access, through the Nat. Telecommunications Network: *ACERVO*(library and information science, holds records from 1982 to present, updated daily), *BASES*(directory of Brazilian databases from 1989), *BEN*(directory of Brazilian instns in science and technology, updated daily), *BPS*(union catalogue of serials publications, updated daily), *CIENTE*(scientific and technological policy, updated daily), *EMPRESAS*(directory of software instns), *EVENTOS*(current meetings, updated daily), *FILMES*(Films and videos in science and technology from 1988 to present), *TESES*(theses and dissertations from 1984 to present, updated daily); runs a postgraduate course in information science and a spec. course on scientific documentation; 205,000 vols; Dir (vacant); publ. *Ciência da Informação* (3 a year).

Curitiba

Biblioteca Central da Universidade Federal do Paraná (University of Paraná Library): CP 19051, Rua General Carneiro 370/380, Centro, 81351-990 Curitiba, PR; tel. (41) 3360-5000; fax (41) 3360-5400; e-mail bc@ufpr.br; internet www.ufpr.br; f. 1956; 350,000 vols; 13 specialized libraries; Dir LIGIA ELIANA SETENARESKI.

Biblioteca Pública do Paraná (Paraná Public Library): Rua Cândido Lopes 133, 80020-901 Curitiba, PR; tel. (41) 3221-4900; fax (41) 225-6883; e-mail bppgeral@pr.gov.br; internet www.bpp.pr.gov.br; f. 1954; 530,000 vols, 1,026 periodicals; Dir ROGÉRIO PEREIRA.

Florianópolis

Biblioteca Pública do Estado de Santa Catarina (Santa Catarina State Public Library): Rua Tenete Silveira 343, Centro, 88010-301 Florianópolis, SC; tel. (48) 3028-8063; fax (48) 3028-8061; e-mail biblio@fcc.sc .gov.br; f. 1854; 110,000 vols; collections of rare books, Braille and talking books; Dir ISABELA SALUM FETT.

Fortaleza

Biblioteca Pública Governador Menezes Pimentel (Ceará Public Library): Av. Presidente Castelo Branco 255, Centro, CEP 60010-000, Fortaleza, CE; tel. (85) 3101-2546; fax (85) 3101-2544; e-mail bpublica@ secult.ce.gov.br/ br; f. 1867 as a provincial library; 100,000 vols, incl. books, periodicals, rare books, video cassettes, spoken books, Braille books and CD-ROMs; Man. MARIA HELENA LYRA.

Biblioteca Universitária da Universidade Federal do Ceará: Campus do Pici s/n, CP 6025, 60451-970 Fortaleza, CE; tel.

(85) 3366-9506; fax (85) 3366-9513; internet www.biblioteca.ufc.br; f. 1958, renamed 1982; 164,429 vols; Dir FRANCISCO JONATAN SOARES.

João Pessoa

Biblioteca Pública do Estado da Paraíba (Paraíba Public Library): Rua General Osório 253, Centro, 58000-000 João Pessoa, PB; tel. (83) 3218-4194; f. 1859; 10,000 vols; Dir MARIA RODRIGUES DA SILVA.

Manaus

Biblioteca Pública do Estado (Amazonas Public Library): Rua Barroso 57, Centro, 69010-050 Manaus, AM; tel. (92) 3637-6660; e-mail bpublica@culturamazonas.am.gov.br; internet www.culturamazonas.am.gov.br; 100,000 vols; Dir SHARLES SILVA DA COSTA.

Niterói

Biblioteca Pública do Estado do Rio de Janeiro (Public Library of the State of Rio): Av. Presidente Vargas 1261, Centro, 20071-004 Rio de Janeiro, RJ; tel. (21) 2224-6184; fax (21) 2252-6810; e-mail bibliotecapublica@ bperj.rj.gov.br; internet www.bperj.rj.gov.br; f. 1873; attached to the State Office of Culture; possesses rare early works, newspapers and valuable first editions; 80,000 vols, notably dictionaries, encyclopedias, reference books; Gen. Dir ANA LIGIA MEDEIROS.

Ouro Preto

Biblioteca Dr Amaro Lanari Júnior (Library of the Ouro Preto School of Mines): Campus Universitário, Morro do Cruzeiro, 35400-000 Ouro Preto, MG; tel. (31) 559-1508; e-mail bibem@sisbin.ufop.br; internet www.em.ufop.br/bibliotecas.php; f. 1876; 50,000 vols, 1,900 periodicals; Librarian JORDANA RABELLO SOARES; publ. *Revista*.

Pelotas

Biblioteca Pública Pelotense (Public Library): Praça Coronel Pedro Osório 103, 96015-010 Pelotas, RS; tel. (53) 3222-3856; fax (53) 3222-3856; f. 1875; 150,000 vols; museum, cultural exhibition; Pres. JOAQUIM SALVADOR COELHO PINHO.

Petrópolis

Biblioteca Central Municipal Gabriela Mistral (Municipal Library): Praça Visconde de Mauá 305, Centro, 25685-380 Petrópolis, RJ; tel. (24) 2247-3745; fax (24) 2247-3727; e-mail biblioteca@petropolis.rj.gov.br; internet www.petropolis.rj.gov.br; f. 1871; 140,000 vols; incorporates archive of 300,000 documents concerning admin. history of Petrópolis; Librarian MARIA HELENA DE AVELLAR PALMA.

Porto Alegre

Biblioteca Central da Universidade Federal do Rio Grande do Sul: Av. Paulo Gama 110, Térreo da Reitoria, 90046-900 Porto Alegre, RS; tel. (51) 3316-3065; fax (51) 3316-3984; e-mail bcentral@bc.ufrgs.br; internet www.biblioteca.ufrgs.br; f. 1971; 32 br. libraries; 1,044,830 vols; Dir VIVIANE CARRION CASTANHO.

Biblioteca Pública do Estado do Rio Grande do Sul (Rio Grande do Sul State Public Library): Rua dos Andradas, 736, Centro, Porto Alegre, RS; tel. (51) 3224-5045; fax (51) 3225-9411; e-mail bpe@via-rs .net; internet www.bibliotecapublica.rs.gov .br; f. 1871; 250,000 vols; Dir MORGANA MARCON.

Recife

Biblioteca Central da Universidade Federal de Pernambuco: Av. Prof. Moraes Rego 1235, Cidade Universitária, 50670-901

Recife, PE; tel. (81) 2126-8094; fax (81) 2126-8090; e-mail bcufpe@ufpe.br; internet www .ufpe.br; f. 1968; 405,291 vols (incl. all departmental libraries), 8,603 periodicals; a regional centre for the nat. bibliographic network organized by the Instituto Brasileiro de Informação em Ciência e Tecnologia (*q.v.*); Dir ADELAIDE LIMA; publs *BC-informa* (12 a year), *Sumários de Periódicos* (12 a year).

Biblioteca Pública do Estado de Pernambuco (Pernambuco State Public Library): Rua João Lira s/n, Santo Amaro 50050-550 Recife, PE; tel. (81) 3423-8446; e-mail arles@educacao.pe.gov.br; internet www.biblioteca.pe.gov.br; f. 1852; 250,000 vols, 350,000 periodicals; Dir CLEA DUBEUX PINTO PIMENTEL.

Rio de Janeiro

Arquivo Nacional (National Archives): Rua Azeredo Coutinho 77, 20230-170 Rio de Janeiro, RJ; tel. (21) 2252-2617; fax (21) 2232-8430; e-mail diretorgeral@ arquivonacional.gov.br; internet www .arquivonacional.gov.br; f. 1838; specializes in history of Brazil, technique of archives and legislation; 28,000 vols; 45 shelf-km of documents; Dir-Gen. JAIME ANTUNES DA SILVA; publs *BIBA*, *Revista Acervo*.

Biblioteca Bastos Tigre da Associação Brasileira de Imprensa (Library of Brazilian Press Association): Rua Araújo Porto Alegre 71, 12° andar, 20030-010 Rio de Janeiro, RJ; tel. 2262-9822; fax 2262-3893; e-mail abi@abi.org.br; f. 1908; 40,473 vols, 6,788 periodical titles; Dir MAURÍCIO AZÊDO.

Biblioteca da Sociedade Brasileira de Cultura Inglesa: Rua São Clemente 258 – 3°, 4° e 5° andares, Botafogo, 22260-000 Rio de Janeiro, RJ; tel. (21) 2528-8700; fax (21) 2535-4141; internet www.culturainglesa.net; f. 1934; 3 brs; 34,000 vols; Head Librarian MARIA DE FÁTIMA BORGES GONÇALVES; publ. *Library News*.

Biblioteca do Centro Cultural Banco do Brasil (Library of the Banco do Brasil Cultural Centre): Rua Primeiro de Março 66, 5° andar, Centro, 20010-000 Rio de Janeiro, RJ; tel. (21) 3808-2030; fax (21) 3808-0216; f. 1931; social sciences, literature and arts; 100,000 vols; special collections: rare books, Brazilian music and folklore; Dir KLEUBER DE PAIVA PEREIRA.

Biblioteca do Exército (Army Library): Palácio Duque de Caxias, Ala Marcílio Dias (3° andar), Centro, 20221-260 Rio de Janeiro; tel. (21) 2519-5726; fax (21) 2519-5569; e-mail bibliex@bibliex.com.br; internet www .bibliex.com.br; f. 1881; 60,000 vols; general collections to supply cultural needs of the army; Dir Cel LUIZ EUGÊNIO DUARTE PEIXOTO; publs *Revista A Defesa Nacional* (3 a year), *Revista do Exército Brasileiro* (3 a year), *Revista Militar de Ciência e Tecnologia* (3 a year).

Biblioteca do Instituto dos Advogados Brasileiros (Library of Lawyers' Institute): Av. Marechal Câmara 210, 5° andar, Centro, 20020-080 Rio de Janeiro, RJ; tel. (21) 2240-3921; fax (21) 2240-3173; internet www .iabnacional.org.br; f. 1897; 32,000 vols; Dir ROBERTO DE BASTOS LELIS.

Biblioteca do Ministério da Fazenda no Estado do Rio de Janeiro (Library of the Ministry of Finance of Rio de Janeiro State): Av. Presidente Antônio Carlos 372, 12° andar, sala 1238, Centro, 20020-010 Rio de Janeiro, RJ; tel. (21) 3805-4285; e-mail biblioteca.rj.gra@fazenda.gov.br; f. 1943 by incorporation of various departmental libraries; 145,000 vols, 100 current periodicals; Librarian KATIA APARECIDA TEIXEIRA DE OLIVEIRA; publs *A Legislação Tributária no Brasil, Informe*.

Biblioteca do Ministério das Relações Exteriores no Rio de Janeiro (Library of the Ministry of Foreign Affairs in Rio de Janeiro): Palácio Itamaraty, Av. Marechal Floriano 196, Centro, 20080-002 Rio de Janeiro, RJ; tel. (21) 2253-5730; f. 1906; history; rare books; see also under Brasília; 270,000 vols incl. periodicals; Dir SONIA DOYLE.

Biblioteca do Mosteiro de S. Bento (Library of the St Benedict Monastery): Caixa Postal 2666, 20001-970 Rio de Janeiro, RJ; tel. (21) 2206-8100; fax (21) 2263-5679; e-mail msbrj@osb.org.br; f. 1600; 125,000 vols; Librarian D. MIGUEL VEESER; also in the towns of São Paulo, Salvador (Bahia) and Olinda; publs *Pergunte e Responderemos*, *Liturgia e Vida*.

Biblioteca Nacional (National Library): Av. Rio Branco 219-39, 20040-008 Rio de Janeiro, RJ; tel. (21) 262-8255; fax (21) 220-4173; e-mail infobn@bn.br; internet www.bn.br; f. 1810 with 60,000 vols from the Real Biblioteca brought to Brazil by the Royal Family of Portugal in 1808; 9m. documents; spec. cllns: Col. De Angelis (Brazilian and Paraguayan History), Col. Tereza Cristina Maria (donated by Emperor D. Pedro II, 1891), Col. Alexandre Rodrigues Ferreira (description with illustrations of travels in Amazônia by A. R. Ferreira, 1783–1792); Pres. PEDRO CORREA DO LAGO; publ. *Anais da Biblioteca Nacional*.

Biblioteca Popular do Leblon-Vinicius de Moraes: Av. Bartolomeu Mitre 1297, Gávea, 22431-000, Rio de Janeiro, RJ; tel. (21) 2294-1598; f. 1954; 8,000 vols; Dir MARIA LEONICE DE ALMEIDA.

Biblioteca Pública de Copacabana: Av. N.S. de Copacabana 817, Copacabana, 22050-002 Rio de Janeiro, RJ; tel. (21) 2255-0081; e-mail bibliocopa@pcrj.rj.gov.br; f. 1954; 29,706 vols; Dir ANA MARIA COSTA DESLANDES.

Fundação Casa de Rui Barbosa (Rui Barbosa Foundation): Rua S. Clemente 134, 22260-000 Rio de Janeiro, RJ; tel. (21) 2537-0036; fax (21) 2537-1114; e-mail mario@rb .gov.br; internet www.casaruibarbosa.gov.br; f. 1930, became Foundation 1966; includes a centre for research in law, philology and history, a centre of Brazilian literature (over 50,000 documents), a documentation centre, with a library, Rui Barbosa archive, a microfilm laboratory and a paper restoration laboratory; museum and auditorium; 100,000 vols; Pres. MARIO BROCKMANN MACHADO; Exec. Dir LUIZ EDUARDO CONDE.

Fundação Instituto Brasileiro de Geografia e Estatística – Centro de Documentação e Disseminação de Informações, Divisão de Biblioteca e Acervos Especiais: Rua General Canabarro 706, Térreo Maracanà, 20271-201 Rio de Janeiro, RJ; fax (21) 2142-4933; e-mail ibge@ibge.gov.br; internet www.ibge.gov.br; f. 1977; documentation and dissemination of research and studies in geoscience, environment, demography, social and economic indicators, national accounts, statistics; 48,000 vols, 2,105 periodicals, 20,000 maps, 115,000 photographs; Dir MARIA TERESA PASSOS BASTOS.

Serviço de Documentação da Marinha (Documentation Service of the Navy): Praça Barão de Ladário (Ilha das Cobras), Centro, 20091-000 Rio de Janeiro, RJ; tel. (21) 3870-6721; fax (21) 3870-6716; e-mail admin@sdm .mar.mil.br; internet www.sdm.mar.mil.br; f. 1943; maritime history of Brazil; includes a naval museum and archives; naval library of 110,000 vols; Dir CMG LUIS HENRIQUE DE AZEVEDO BRAGA; publ. *Revista Marítima Brasileira* (3 a year).

Sistema de Bibliotecas e Informação da Universidade Federal do Rio de Janeiro (Library and Information System of the Federal University of Rio de Janeiro): Av. Pasteur 250, Urca, Rm 106, 22295-900 Rio de Janeiro, RJ; tel. (21) 2295-1595 ext. 219; fax (21) 2295-1397; e-mail paulamello@sibi.ufrj .br; internet www.sibi.ufrj.br; f. 1989; coordinates 43 brs; maintains mem. of the Nat. Catalogue of Periodicals Online; 1,567,330 vols, 3,237,673 periodicals; Dir PAULA MARIA ABRANTES COTTA DE MELLO.

Rio Grande

Biblioteca Rio-Grandense (Rio Grande Library): Rua General Osório 454, Bairro Centro, 96200-400 Rio Grande, RS; tel. (53) 231-2842; e-mail contato@ bibliotecariograndense.com.br; internet bibliotecariograndense.com.br; f. 1846; 400,000 vols, 7,600 maps; Pres. Dr JOÃO MARINONIO CARNEIRO LAGES; Dir Dr GILBERTO M. CENTENO CARDOSO.

Rio Negro

Biblioteca Pública Municipal Prof. Wenceslau Muniz (Municipal Library): Rua Getúlio Vargas 680, Centro, 83880-000 Rio Negro, PR; tel. (47) 645-1311; fax (47) 645-1311; e-mail sec.cultura@rno.matrix.com.br.

Salvador

Biblioteca do Gabinete Português de Leitura (Portuguese Reading Room and Library): Praça da Piedade s/n, Centro, 40060-300, Salvador, BA; tel. (71) 3329-3060; fax (71) 3329-1299; f. 1863; 15,000 vols; Librarian AGNÚBIA OLIVEIRA.

Biblioteca Pública do Estado da Bahia (Bahia State Central Library): Rua Gen. Labatut 27, Barris, 40010-100 Salvador, BA; tel. (71) 3328-4555; fax (71) 3328-4555; f. 1811, name changed 1984; 114,698 vols; Dir LÍDIA MARIA BASTISTA BRANDÃO.

São José dos Campos

Biblioteca Pública 'Cassiano Ricardo' ('Cassiano Ricardo' Public Library): Rua XV de Novembro 99, Centro, 12210-070 São José dos Campos, SP; tel. (12) 3921-6330; f. 1968; 70,000 vols and 8,500 periodicals; Dir ANA ELISABETE MARTINELLI GODINHO.

São Luís

Biblioteca Pública Benedito Leite (Benedito Leite Public Library): Praça do Panteon s/n, Centro, 65020-430 São Luís, MA; tel. (98) 3232-9730; fax (98) 3232-9688; e-mail sebpbpbl@cultura.ma.gov.br; f. 1829; 38 mems; 45,000 vols; collns of more than 15,000 engravings, and newspapers since 1821; Dir JOSEANE MARIA DE SOUZA; Librarian ROBERTO TAMARA.

São Paulo

Arquivo do Estado de São Paulo (São Paulo State Archives): Rua Voluntários da Pátria 596, Santana, 02010-000 São Paulo, SP; tel. (11) 6221-2850; fax (11) 6221-4785; e-mail supervisao@arquivoestado.sp.gov.br; internet www.arquivoestado.sp.gov.br; f. 1721; 45,000 vols; 10,000 files of loose documents; 1m. images (negatives, photographs, postcards, caricatures and illustrations); State records, collections of rare books, MSS, periodicals, maps and plans; Dir Dr FAUSTO COUTO SOBRINHO; publ. *Revista Histórica* (print and online, 12 a year).

Biblioteca do Conservatório Dramático e Musical de São Paulo (Library of Academy of Music and Drama): Av. Conselheiro Crispiniano 378, 01037-000 São Paulo, SP; tel. (11) 3337-2111; fax (11) 223-9231; e-mail cdmsp@cdmsp.edu.br; f. 1906; 30,000 vols;

Dir Dr LUÍS CORRÊA FRAGOSO; Sec. JOSÉ RAYMUNDO LOBO.

Biblioteca do Instituto de Saúde (Health Institute Library): Rua Santo Antônio 590, Bela Vista, 01314-000 São Paulo, SP; tel. (11) 3293-2244; internet www.isaude.sp.gov.br; f. 1969; 41,000 vols, valuable collection of works, reviews, maps on dermatology and Hansen's disease, and rare works since 1600; Librarian ASTRID B. WIESEL.

Biblioteca 'George Alexander' (George Alexander Library): Rua da Consolação 896, Prédio 02, Higienópolis, 01302-907 São Paulo, SP; tel. (11) 3236-8302; fax (11) 3236-8302; e-mail biblio.per@mackenzie.com .br; internet www.mackenzie.com.br; f. 1870 as Mackenzie Library, present name 1926; 246,342 vols; Dir KAO SHIN.

Biblioteca Municipal Mário de Andrade (Municipal Library): Rua da Consolação 94, 01302-000 São Paulo, SP; tel. (11) 3241-5630; fax (11) 3259-5728; f. 1925; municipal library; 344,000 vols and 11,000 journal titles; incorporates former Biblioteca Pública do Estado de São Paulo; specialized collections of 40,000 rare editions and MSS, 25,000 drawings and art books, 5,500 maps; microfilms, legislation and multimedia sections; Dir of Municipal Library LUÍS FRANCISCO CARVALHO FILHO; publ. *Revista da Biblioteca Mário de Andrade*.

BIREME—Centro Latino-Americano e do Caribe de Informação em Ciências da Saúde (Latin American and Caribbean Centre on Health Sciences Information): Rua Botucatu 862 São Paulo, SP; tel. (11) 5576-9801; fax (11) 5575-8868; e-mail bireme@ bireme.org; internet www.bireme.org; f. 1967; promotes regional network of health libraries and information centres; aims to index all health literature produced in the region; provides bibliographic searches, document delivery, training, etc.; coordinates and promotes the Virtual Health Library (VHL); coordinates the Latin American and Caribbean Network of Libraries on Health Sciences; 400,000 vols of scientific journals, 3,500 current periodicals, 3,000 discontinued periodicals; Dir PEDRO URRA; publ. *LILACS/ CD-ROM* (3 a year).

British Council Library and Information Centre: Rua Ferreira Araújo, 741 terreo Pinheiros, 05428-000 São Paolo SP; tel. (11) 2126-7560; fax (11) 2126-7564; e-mail centro.info@britishcouncil.org.br; 7,000 vols; Library and Customer Services Officer ANA LUIZA MATTOS.

Discoteca Oneyda Alvarenga: Centro Cultural São Paulo, Rua Vergueiro 1000, Paraíso, 01504-000 São Paulo, SP; tel. (11) 3397-4071; e-mail discoteca@prefeitura.sp.gov.br; internet www.centrocultural.sp.gov.br/ discoteca.asp; f. 1935; study and diffusion of Brazilian and int. classical, folk and popular music; colln of 75,000 records and 62,000 scores music; colln of books, periodical titles in music; museum of folklore; 62,000 music scores and 9,000 books; Librarian JÉSSICA BARRETO.

Sistema Integrado de Bibliotecas da Universidade de São Paulo (São Paulo University Integrated Library System): Av. Prof. Luciano Gualberto, Trav. J, 374-1°andar, 05508-010 São Paulo, SP; tel. (11) 3091-1573; fax (11) 3091-1567; e-mail dtsibi@ usp.br; internet www.usp.br/sibi; f. 1981; 43 libraries, with 7,762,103 vols; Technical Dir ELIANA AZEVEDO MARQUES.

Vitória

Arquivo Público Estadual do Espírito Santo: Rua Pedro Palácios 76, Cidade Alta, 29015-160 Vitória, ES; tel. (27) 3223-7524;

fax (27) 3223-2952; e-mail ape@coplag.es.gov
.br; f. 1855.

Biblioteca Municipal Adelpho Poli Monjardim: Escola de Teatro e Dança, Av.
Jerônimo Monteiro, Centro, Vitória, ES; tel.
(27) 3381-6925; f. 1941; 14,800 vols.

Museums and Art Galleries

Belém

Museu Paraense Emílio Goeldi (Pará
Museum): Av. Magalhães Barata 376, São
Braz, 66040-170 Belém, PA; tel. (91) 3219-
3300; fax (91) 249-3249-0466; e-mail ima@
museu-goeldi.br; internet www.museu-goeldi
.br; f. 1866; part of MCT/CNPq; natural
history, archaeology, anthropology and ethnography of the Amazon region; zoological
and botanical garden; library of 200,000 vols;
collection of rare books; Dir IMA CÉLIA
GUIMARÃES VIEIRA; publs *Boletim* (four separate series on anthropology, botany, geology
and zoology), *Guia*.

Belo Horizonte

Museu Histórico Abílio Barreto (Historical Museum): Av. Prudente de Morais 202,
Barrio Cidade Jardim, 30380-000 Belo Horizonte, MG; tel. (31) 3277-8573; fax (31) 3277-
8572; e-mail mhab@pbh.gov.br; internet
www.pbh.gov.br/cultura; f. 1943; local collection; special collections: original documentation of the Belo Horizonte Construction
Commission, Minas Gerais provincial laws
(1849–89); library; Dir THAÏS VELLOSO COUGO
PIMENTEL.

Campinas

Museu de História Natural (Natural History Museum): Rua Coronel Quirino 2,
Bosque dos Jequitibás, 13025-010 Campinas,
SP; tel. (19) 3295-5850; fax (19) 3251-9849;
e-mail museuaquario@terra.com.br; internet
www.campinas.sp.gov.br/cultura/museus/
mhn; f. 1938; history, folklore and anthropology; Dir TEREZA CRISTINA SILVA MELLO
BORGES.

Campo Grande

Museu das Culturas Dom Bosco (Dom
Bosco Regional Museum): Ave Afonso Pena
7000, Parque das Nações Indígenas, 79010-
200 Campo Grande, MS; tel. (67) 3326-9788;
fax (67) 3312-6489; e-mail info@mcdb.org.br;
f. 1951; ethnographic, shell and insect collns;
Dir Dr AIVONE CARVALHO.

Curitiba

Museu Paranaense (Paraná Museum):
Praça Generoso Marques s/n, 80020-230
Curitiba, PR; tel. (41) 323-1411; fax (41)
222-5824; e-mail museupr@pr.gov.br;
internet www.pr.gov.br/museupr; f. 1876;
historical, ethnographical and archaeological
collections; library of 6,000 vols, 2,200 periodicals; Dir JAYME ANTONIO CARDOSO; publ.
Arquivos do Museu Paranaense.

Fortaleza

Museu do Ceará: Rua São Paulo 51, Centro,
60030-100 Fortaleza, CE; tel. (85) 3101-2610;
fax (85) 3101-2611; e-mail musce@secult.ce
.gov.br; internet www.secult.ce.gov.br/
equipamentos-culturais/museu-do-ceara; f.
1932; history of Fortaleza and Ceará, ethnographical, archeological and literary collns,
abolition of slavery.

Goiânia

Museu Goiano Zoroastro Artiaga (Zoroastro Artiaga State Museum): Praça Cívica

13, Setor Central, 74003-010 Goiânia, GO;
tel. (62) 3201-4676; fax (62) 3201-4675;
e-mail hdefreitas@ig.com.br; internet www
.agepel.go.gov.br/index.html; f. 1946; history,
geology, anthropology, local art, folklore; Dir
Dr HENRIQUE DE FREITAS.

Itu

Museu Republicano 'Convenção de Itu'
(Itu Convention Republican Museum): Rua
Barão de Itaim 67, 13300-160 Centro, SP; tel.
(11) 4023-0240; fax (11) 4023-2525; e-mail
mrci@usp.br; internet www.mp.usp.br/mr; f.
1923; attached to Museu Paulista da Universidade de São Paulo (*q.v.*); historical;
library of 35,000 vols, 113 periodicals, photographs; spec. collns incl. Prudente de Morais
colln, database 1870–1930; Supervisor Prof.
Dr CECÍLIA HELENA DE SALLES OLIVEIRA; Curator Prof. JONAS SOARES DE SOUZA; publ.
Boletim Informativo—SAMUR.

Macapá

Museu Histórico do Amapá (Amapá Historical Museum): Fortaleza de São José de
Macapá, Macapá AP; f. 1948; zoology,
archaeology, ethnography and numismatics;
expeditions; Dir Prof. FERNANDO RODRIGUES.

Olinda

Museu Regional de Olinda (Regional
Museum of Olinda): Rua do Amparo 128,
53120-180 Olinda, PE; tel. (81) 429-0018;
internet www.cultura.pe.gov.br/
museu4_olinda.html; f. 1934; historic and
regional art.

Ouro Preto

Museu da Inconfidência (History of Democratic Ideals and Culture): Praça Tiradentes
139, Centro, Ouro Preto, MG 35400-000; tel.
(31) 3551-1121; fax (31) 3551-1121; e-mail
inconfidencia@veloxmail.com.br; f. 1944;
18th and 19th-century music MSS and works
of art, documents related to Inconfidência
Mineira, documents from the Notary Public's
Office during the Colonial Period; library of
20,000 vols; Dir RUI MOURÃO; publs *Isto é
Inconfidência* (bulletin, 4 a year), *Oficiano do
Inconfidência*, *Revista de Trabalho* (1 a year).

**Museu de Ciência e Técnica da Escola
de Minas** (Science and Technology Museum
of the School of Mines): Praça Tiradentes 20,
Centro, 35400-000 Ouro Preto, MG; tel. (31)
3559-3119; fax (31) 3559-1597; e-mail
museu@ufop.br; internet www.museu.em
.ufop.br/museu; f. 1995; affiliated to the
Universidade Federal de Ouro Preto; Dir
Prof. Dr LEONARDO BARBOSA GODEFROID.

Petrópolis

Museu Imperial (Imperial Museum): Rua
da Imperatriz 220, 25610-320 Petrópolis, RJ;
tel. (24) 2237-8000; fax (24) 2237-8000 ext.
252; internet www.museuimperial.gov.br; f.
1940; 11,024 period exhibits of Brazilian
Empire (1808–89) and Petrópolis history,
notably imperial regalia, jewels and apparel;
library: special library on the history of
Brazil, 35,770 vols; historic archives of
100,000 MSS on Brazilian history in the
19th century; 4,000 photos, 500 maps and
700 iconographic items; Dir MARIA DE
LOURDES PARREIRAS HORTA; publ. *Anuário*.

Porto Alegre

**Museu de Arte do Rio Grande do Sul
Ado Malagoli:** Praça da Alfândega s/n,
90010-150 Porto Alegre, RS; tel. (51) 3227-
2311; fax (51) 3227-2519; e-mail museu@
margs.rs.gov.br; internet www.margs.rs.gov
.br; f. 1954; paintings, statues, prints,
library: art library of 2,500 vols; Dir CÉZAR
PRESTES; publ. *Jornal do MARGS* (11 a year).

Museu 'Julio de Castilhos' (State Historical Museum): Rua Duque de Caxias 1205 e
1231, 90010-283 Porto Alegre, RS; tel. and
fax (51) 3221-3959; f. 1903; 10,100 exhibits of
national history, including the 1835 Revolutionary period, the Paraguayan War, and
collection of Indian pieces; armoury, antique
furniture and slave pieces; library of 5,000
vols; Dir NARA MARIA MACHADO NUNES.

Recife

Museu do Estado de Pernambuco (State
Museum): Av. Rui Barbosa 960, Graças,
52011-040 Recife, PE; tel. (81) 427-9322; fax
(81) 427-0076; internet www.cultura.pe.gov
.br/museu.html; f. 1929; local history, paintings; library of 4,000 vols, 110 periodicals;
Dir SYLVIA PONTUAL.

Rio de Janeiro

**Museu Carpológico do Jardim Botânico
do Rio de Janeiro** (Museum of Carpology of
the Botanical Garden): Rua Pacheco Leão
915, 22460-030 Rio de Janeiro, RJ; tel. (21)
511-2749; fax (21) 511-2749; f. 1915; specializes in botany; collection of 6,200 fruits; Dir
Dra NILDA MARQUETE.

Museu da Fauna (Wildlife Museum): Parque Quinta da Boa Vista s/n, São Cristóvão,
20940-040 Rio de Janeiro, RJ; tel. (21) 3878-
4200; f. 1939; collections include vertebrates,
mammals, birds, butterflies and reptiles from
the principal regions of Brazil; part of Tijuca
National Park; scientific expeditions; publ.
Monograph.

Museu da República (Museum of the
Republic): Rua do Catete 153, Catete,
22220-000 Rio de Janeiro, RJ; tel. (21) 3235-
2650; fax (21) 2285 0795; e-mail museu@
museudarepublica.org.br; internet www
.museudarepublica.org.br; f. 1960; sited in
Catete Palace, built 1858–67, fmr seat of
Government; exhibits of items belonging to
former Presidents; special collections: history
of Brazil, historical archive with 85,000
photographs and documents; library of
10,000 vols; Dir MAGALY CABRAL.

**Museu de Arte Moderna do Rio de
Janeiro** (Museum of Modern Art): Av.
Infante Dom Henrique 85, Parque do Flamengo, 20021-140 Rio de Janeiro, RJ; tel.
(21) 2240-4944; fax (21) 2240-4899; e-mail
mam@mamrio.org.br; internet www.mamrio
.org.br; f. 1948; 12,000 art works; collns
representing different countries; film archive; art exhibition; film screenings; research
and document centre; library of 25,000 vols;
Pres. CARLOS ALBERTO GOUVÊA CHATEAUBRIAND; Curator LUIZ CAMILLO OSÓRIO; Film
Archive Curator GILBERTO SANTEIRO.

Museu de Ciências da Terra, Departamento Nacional da Produção Mineral
(Earth Sciences Museum, National Department of Mineral Production at the Ministry
of Mines and Energy): Av. Pasteur 404, 2°
andar, Praia Vermelha, 22290-240 Rio de
Janeiro, RJ; tel. (21) 2295-6673; fax (21)
2295-4896; e-mail wmuseu@yahoo.com.br;
internet www.dnpm.gov.br; f. 1907; colln of
fossils, minerals, rocks, gems, ore minerals
and meteorites from Brazil and other countries; Dir DIOGENES DE ALMEIDA CAMPOS.

Museu do Índio (Museum of the Indian):
Rua das Palmeiras 55, Botafogo, 22270-070
Rio de Janeiro, RJ; tel. (21) 286-2097; fax (21)
286-8899; internet www.museudoindio.org
.br; f. 1953; ethnology, ethnohistory, museology, linguistics, documentation; conducts
research into Indian societies and cultures;
library of 28,000 vols; scientific archives
(documents, photographs, films and music);
Chair. JOSÉ CARLOS LEVINHO; publs *Boletim*,
Museo ao Vivo.

Museu do Instituto Histórico e Geográ-fico Brasileiro (Museum of the Brazilian Historical and Geographical Institute): Av. Augusto Severo 8, 12º andar, Glória, 20021-040 Rio de Janeiro, RJ; tel. (21) 2252-4430; e-mail info@ihgb.org.br; internet www.ihgb .org.br; f. 1838; history, geography and eth-nography collection; Dir VERA LUCIA BOTTREL TOSTES.

Museu e Arquivo Histórico do Centro Cultural Banco do Brasil (Museum and Historical Archives of the Banco do Brasil Cultural Centre): Rua Primeiro de Março 66, Centro, 20010-000 Rio de Janeiro, RJ; tel. (21) 3808-2353; internet www.bb.com.br/ cultura; f. 1955; collection of banknotes and coins from Brazil and other countries, docu-ments relating to the economic history of Brazil and to the Banco do Brasil; library: see Libraries; Dir KLEUBER DE PAIVA PEREIRA.

Museu Histórico da Cidade do Rio de Janeiro (Historical Museum of the City): Estrada Santa Marinha s/n, Gávea, 22451 Rio de Janeiro, RJ; tel. (21) 2512-2353; e-mail mcrj@pcrj.rj.gov.br; internet www.rio.rj.gov .br/culturas/museus_historico.shtm; f. 1934; art and history of the City; library of 4,000 vols; Dir BEATRIZ DE VICQ CARVALHO.

Museu Histórico Nacional (National His-torical Museum): Praça Marechal Ancora s/n, 20021-200 Rio de Janeiro, RJ; tel. (21) 2550-9221; fax (21) 2550-9220; e-mail mhn02@ visualnet.com.br; internet www .museuhistoriconacional.com.br; f. 1922; collns of coins, medals, ceramics, ivory, vehicles, weapons, furniture, prints, paint-ings, besides historical exhibits; organizes courses in museology, national history, arts; library of 50,000 vols, historical archive; Dir VERA LÚCIA BOTTREL TOSTES.

Museu Nacional (National Museum): Quinta da Boa Vista, 20940-040 Rio de Janeiro, RJ; tel. (21) 254-4320; fax (21) 568-8262 ext. 232; e-mail museu@acd.ufrj.br; internet acd.ufrj.br/museu/; f. 1818; sections: anthropology, botany, entomology, geology and palaeontology, invertebrates and verte-brates, archaeology, ethnolinguistics; 4m. specimens; library of 473,000 vols; Dir Prof. LUIZ FERNANDO DIAS DUARTE; publs *Arquivos* (irregular), *Boletim: Antropologia* (irregular), *Boletim: Botânica* (irregular), *Boletim: Geo-logia* (irregular), *Boletim: Zoologia* (irregu-lar), *Estudos de Antropologia Social* (2 a year).

Museu Nacional de Belas Artes (National Museum of Fine Arts): Av. Rio Branco 199, Centro, 20.040-008 Rio de Janeiro, RJ; tel. (21) 2240-0068; fax (21) 2262-6067; e-mail diretoria@mnba.gov.br; internet www.mnba .gov.br; f. 1937; collections of Brazilian and European paintings and sculpture; graphic arts and furniture; primitive art, numismat-ics, posters, photographs; exhibitions and educational services; library of 12,000 vols; Dir Prof. HELOISA A. LUSTOSA; publ. *Boletim*.

Museus 'Raymundo Ottoni de Castro Maya': R. Murtinho Nobre 93, 20241-050 Santa Teresa, RJ; tel. (21) 3970-1126; fax (21) 3970-1017; e-mail vera.alencar@ museuscastromaya.com.br; f. 1962 by Ray-mundo Ottoni de Castro Maya, now run by the Ministry of Culture; 2 museums: Museu da Chácara do Céu (modern Brazilian and European art, works by Jean Baptiste Deb-ret, Luso-Brazilian furniture, etc.) and Museu do Açude (Chinese pottery and sculp-ture, 17th- to 19th-century Portuguese tiles and sculpture, Luso-Brazilian furniture, etc. in 19th-century manor house); library of 2,000 vols; Dir VERA DE ALENCAR.

Rio Grande

Museu Oceanográfico 'Prof. Eliézer de Carvalho Rios' (Oceanographic Museum): Rua Heitor Perdigão 10, 96200-970, Rio Grande, RS; tel. (53) 232-3496; fax (53) 232-9633; internet www.portoriogrande.com.br/ pt/localizacao/p_turisticos.php; f. 1953; attached to Fundação Universidade Federal do Rio Grande; oceanography, ichthyology, malacology, mammalogy; large shell collec-tion, cetaceans collection; library; Dir Oc. Ms. LAURO BARCELLOS.

Sabará

Museu do Ouro (Gold Museum): Rua da Intendência s/n, Centro, 34505-480 Sabará, MG; tel. (31) 3671-1848; fax (31) 3671-1848; f. 1945; museum housed in a building dated 1730; sections: technical, historical, artistic; antique methods of gold-mining and smelt-ing; gold ingots, 18th-century silverware, 18th-century furniture and typical handi-crafts of the mining districts; library of 3,000 vols, 35,000 documents; Dir SELMA MELO MIRANDA.

Salvador

Museu de Arte da Bahia (Bahia Art Museum): Av. 7 de Setembro 2340, Corredor da Vitória, 40080-001 Salvador, BA; tel. (71) 3117-6902; fax (71) 3336-4583; e-mail mab@ bahia.ba.gov.br; internet www.funceb.ba.gov .br/mab; f. 1918; library of 8,000 vols; 9,209 exhibits; general collection, with emphasis given to art, particularly Bahian Colonial art; Dir LUIZ JASMIN; publ. *Publicações do Museu*.

Museu Henriqueta Catharino (Henri-queta Catharino Museum): Rua Monsenhor Flaviano 2, 40080-150 Salvador, BA; tel. (71) 329-5522; fax (71) 329-5681; e-mail ifbmuseu@terra.com.br; f. 1933; attached to Fundação Instituto Feminino da Bahia; collns of religious art, Brazilian art and feminine apparel; gold, silver, jewellery, clothing, weapons, furniture, porcelain, tex-tiles; Museu de Arte Popular; Dir SONIA MARIA MOREIRA DE SOUZA BASTOS.

São Paulo

Museu de Arqueologia e Etnologia da Universidade de São Paulo e Serviço de Biblioteca e Documentação: Av. Prof. Almeida Prado 1466, CEP 05508-900 São Paulo, SP; tel. (11) 3091-4978; fax (11) 3091-5042; f. 1964; 88 staff; library of 60,000 vols, incl. 19,000 books and 32,000 vols of print periodicals; Museum Dir Dr MURILLO MARA; Library Dir ELIANA ROTOLO; publs *Revista do Museu de Arqueologia e Etnologia* (1 a year), *Sumários de Periódicos* (6 a year).

Museu de Arte Contemporânea da Uni-versidade de São Paulo (Contemporary Art Museum of São Paulo University): Rua da Reitoria 160, CEP 05508-900 São Paulo, SP; tel. (11) 3818-3538; fax (11) 212-0218; e-mail informac@edu.usp.br; internet www .mac.usp.br; f. 1963; a permanent exhibition of international and Brazilian plastic arts; library of 6,000 vols, 30,000 catalogues, 20,500 slides, 4,000 posters; Dir Prof. Dr JOSÉ TEIXEIRA COELHO.

Museu de Arte de São Paulo: Av. Paulista 1578, 01310-200 São Paulo, SP; tel. 251-5644; fax 284-0574; e-mail atendimento@masp.art .br; internet www.masp.art.br; f. 1947; clas-sical and modern paintings, Italian, Spanish, Dutch, Flemish, and French schools; also representative works by Portinari and Lasar Segall; departments of theatre, music, cin-ema, art history, exhibitions, printing, pho-tography and education; library of 60,000 vols about culture and art; Dir JOÃO DA CRUZ VICENTE DE AZEVEDO.

Museu de Arte Sacra: Av. Tiradentes 676, 01102-Luz, São Paulo, SP; tel. (11) 3227-4691; fax (11) 3227-4691; e-mail comunicacao@museuartesacra.org.br; inter-net www.museuartesacra.org.br; f. 1970, for-merly Museu da Curia Metropolitana; sacred art, furniture, numismatics, paintings, sil-verware, jewellery, textiles, etc.; library of 3,400 vols; Dirs MARI MARINO, Dra MARIA THEREZA MCNAIR.

Museu de Zoologia, Universidade de São Paulo (Museum of Zoology, University of São Paulo): Av. Nazaré 481, CP 42694, 04299-970 São Paulo, SP; tel. (11) 6165-8100; fax (11) 6165-8113; e-mail mz@edu .usp.br; internet www.mz.usp.br; f. 1939; 7m. specimens of neotropical and world fauna; library of 104,000 vols; Dir Dr CARLOS ROBERTO FERREIRA BRANDAÕ; publs *Arquivos de Zoologia*, *Papeis Avulsos de Zoologia*.

Museu Florestal 'Octávio Vecchi' (For-estry Museum): Rua do Horto 931, Bairro Horto Florestal, 02377-000, São Paulo, SP; tel. (11) 2231-8555; internet www.iflorestal .sp.gov.br/museu/index.asp; f. 1931; a dependency of the Forestry Institute of the Sec. of State for Environment; forestry and forest technology, collections of local timber; Dir DALMO DIPPOLD VILAR.

Museu Paulista da Universidade de São Paulo (São Paulo University Museum): Parque da Independência s/n, Ipiranga, São Paulo, SP; tel. (11) 6165-8011; fax (11) 6165-8051; e-mail mp@edu.usp.br; internet www .mp.usp.br; f. 1895; history, material culture, historical and numismatic specimens; also collections of furniture and stamps; library of 26,000 vols, 2,300 periodical titles; Dir CECILIA HELENA DE SALLES OLIVEIRA; publs *Anais do Museu Paulista*, *Cadernos de São Paulo*.

Pinacoteca do Estado de São Paulo (State Art Museum): Praça da Luz 02–Luz, 01120-010 São Paulo, SP; tel. (11) 3229-9844; fax (11) 3226-7876; f. 1905; Brazilian art from 19th century to the present; temporary and permanent exhibitions, workshops, lec-tures, int. meetings; library: specialized library of 10,000 vols, 3,440 exhibition cata-logues; Exec. Dir MARCELO MATTOS ARAUJO.

Teresina

Museu do Piauí 'Odilon Nunes': Praça Marechal Deodoro da Fonseca s/n, Centro, 64000 Teresina, PI; tel. (86) 3221-6027; f. 1934; historical, cultural and artistic exhib-itions; Dir SELMA DUARTE FERREIRA; publ. *Boletim*.

Vitória

Museu Solar Monjardim: Av. Paulino Müller s/n, Jucutuquara, 29040-470 Vitória, ES; tel. (27) 3223-0606; f. 1939 as State Museum; inc. Jan. 1967 to Universidade Federal do Espírito Santo; history, sacred art, furniture, porcelain, paintings, arms, books, silverware and photographs; publ. *Boletim* (52 a year).

Universities

CENTRO UNIVERSITÁRIO DE BARRA MANSA—UBM

Rua Vereador Pinho de Carvalho, 267 Cen-tro, 27330-550 Barra Mansa, RJ

Telephone: (24) 3325-0262
Fax: (24) 3323-9565
E-mail: pro.com@ubm.br
Internet: www.ubm.br

Founded 1961 as an instn of higher educa-tion, univ. status and present name 1997
Private control

Rector: GUILHERME DE CARVALHO CRUZ
Pro-Rector for Admin.: FÉRES OSRRAIA NADER
Pro-Rector for Communications: LEANDRO ALVARO CHAVES
Librarian: ANA MARIA DINARDI BARBOSA BARROS

Library of 43,151 books, 500 periodicals

Publications: *Caderno de Cultura Referencia* (4 a year), *Revista Cientifica* (2 a year), *UBM Noticias* (4 a year)

ACADEMIC COORDINATORS

Accountancy: ROSÂNGELA DOS SANTOS
Biological Sciences: ZILANI DE OLIVEIRA MACHADO
Business Administration: JOSE GONCALVES BARBOSA
Communication Disorders and Sciences: DEBORA LUDERS
Computer Engineering: RICARDO DE OLIVEIRA ALVES
Computer Science: JOSE NILTON CANTARINO GIL
Geography: MARIA ILDA FIDÉLIS E SILVA
History: MARIA ILDA FIDÉLIS E SILVA
Letters: MARIA DO CARMO M. BASTOS
Mass Communication: ANA LUCIA CORREA DE SOUZA
Mathematics: JACQUELINE BERNARDO PEREIRA OLIVEIRA
Nursing: SUELI SOLDATI ABRANCHES
Nutrition: MARILENE DE OLIVEIRA LEITE
Pedagogy: MARIA APARECIDA M. GLEIZER
Pharmacy: (vacant)
Physiotherapy: ANDRÉ LUIS VIEIRA CAVALLEIRO
Secondary Teacher Training: ROSA MARIA GOUVEA ESTEVES
Systems Analysis: JOSE CLAUDIO DE A. FILHO
Tourism: MARIA ILDA FIDÉLIS E SILVA
Veterinary Medicine: FRANCISCO RICARDO C. NOGUEIRA
Visual Arts: RONALDO AUAD MOREIRA

CENTRO UNIVERSITÁRIO METODISTA BENNETT

Rua Marquês de Abrantes 55, Flamengo, 22230-060 Rio de Janeiro, RJ
Telephone: (21) 3509-1000
Fax: (21) 3509-1000
E-mail: imb@bennett.br
Internet: www.bennett.br

Founded 1887
Academic year: February to December

Rector: ROBERTO PONTES DA FONSECA
Pro-Rector for Academic Affairs: LINCOLN DE ARAÚJO SANTOS
Library: Libraries with 46,000 vols, 978 periodicals
Number of teachers: 258
Number of students: 3,548

FUNDAÇÃO UNIVERSIDADE FEDERAL DE RONDÔNIA

BR 364 km 9.5, Campus Universitário José Ribeiro Filho, 78900-000 Porto Velho, RO
Telephone: (69) 216-8500
Fax: (69) 216-8506
E-mail: reitoria@unir.br
Internet: www.unir.br

Founded 1982
Federal govt control
Academic year: March to December

Rector: Prof. Dr ENE GLORIA DE SILVEIRA
Vice-Rector: Prof. Dr MIGUEL NENEVÉ
Academic Pro-Rector: FABÍOLA LINS CALDAS
Admin. Pro-Rector: EDUARDO MARTINS
Librarian: LUZIMAR BARBOSA CHAVES

Number of teachers: 260
Number of students: 4,800

Publication: *Presença: Cadernos de Criação* (4 a year)

Faculties of education (depts of letters, geography, mathematics, physical education, teaching), exact sciences (depts of chemistry, computing, engineering), health sciences (depts of biology, nursing, psychology), social sciences (depts of accounting, business administration, economics, law).

PONTIFÍCIA UNIVERSIDADE CATÓLICA DE CAMPINAS

Rodovia Dom Pedro I, km 136, Parque das Universidades, 13086-900 Campinas, SP
Telephone: (19) 3343-7000
Fax: (19) 3343-8477
E-mail: reitoria@puc-campinas.edu.br
Internet: www.puc-campinas.edu.br

Founded 1941
Private control
Language of instruction: Portuguese
Academic year: February to December

Chancellor: Dom BRUNO GAMBERINI
Rector: Prof. WILSON DENADAI
Vice-Rector: Prof. ANGELA DE MENDONÇA ENGELBRECHT
Pro-Rector for Admin.: Prof. ANGELA DE MENDONÇA ENGELBRECHT
Pro-Rector for Extension and Communitarian Subjects: Prof. PAULO DE TARSO BARBOSA DUARTE
Pro-Rector for Research and Graduate and Postgraduate Courses: Prof. VERA ENGLER CURY
Pro-Rector for Undergraduate Courses: Prof. GERMANO RIGACCI JÚNIOR
Sec.-Gen.: Prof. JOSÉ BENEDITO DE ALMEIDA DAVID
Librarian: ROSA MARIA VIVONA B. OLIVEIRA

Library of 294,173 vols
Number of teachers: 1,000
Number of students: 19,618

Publications: *Cadernos da FACECA*, *Cadernos de Extensão*, *Cadernos de Serviço Social*, *Cadernos do CCH*, *Revista Bióikos*, *Revista Comunicarte*, *Revista de Ciências Médicas*, *Revista de Educação*, *Revista de Nutrição*, *Revista Estudos de Psicologia*, *Revista Humanitas*, *Revista Jornalismo*, *Revista Jurídica*, *Revista Letras*, *Revista Notícia Bibliográfica e Histórica*, *Revista Oculum Ensaios*, *Revista Phrónesis*, *Revista Reflexão*, *Revista TransInformação*

DIRECTORS OF CENTRES

Centre for Communication Sciences: Prof. WAGNER JOSÉ GERIBELLO
Centre for Economics and Administration: Prof. EDUARD PRANCIC
Centre for Humanities and Applied Social Sciences (CCHSA): Prof. PAULO SÉRGIO LOPES GONÇALVES
Centre for Life Sciences: Profa MIRALVA APARECIDA DE JESUS SILVA
Centre for Mathematical, Environmental and Technological Sciences: Prof. ORANDI MINA FALSARELLA

DIRECTORS OF FACULTIES

Centre for Communication Sciences (tel. (19) 3343-7192; fax (19) 3343-7191; e-mail clc@puc-campinas.edu.br; internet www.puc-campinas.edu.br/clc):
  Faculty of Advertising and Publicity: Profa FLAILDA BRITO GARBOGGINI
  Faculty of Journalism: Profa ROGÉRIO EDUARDO RODRIGUES BAZI
  Faculty of Letters: Prof. CARLOS DE AQUINO PEREIRA
  Faculty of Public Relations: Profa CLÁUDIA MARIA DE C. CAFVALHO
  Faculty of Tourism: Profa LAURA UMBELINA SANTI

Faculty of Visual Arts: Profa FLÁVIO SHIMODA

Centre for Economics and Administration (tel. (19) 3343-7099; fax (19) 3343-7129; e-mail cea@puc-campinas.edu.br; internet www.puc-campinas.edu.br/cea):
  Faculty of Accounting: Prof. MARCOS FRANCISCO RODRIGUES SOUZA
  Faculty of Admin.: Prof. PAULO ANTÔNIO G. L. ZUCCOLOTTO
  Faculty of Economics: Prof. LINEU CARLOS MAFFEZOLI

Centre for Humanities and Applied Social Sciences (tel. (19) 3343-7299; fax (19) 3343-7298; e-mail cch@puc-campinas.edu.br; internet www.puc-campinas.edu.br):
  Faculty of Education: Profa LUZIA SIQUEIRA VASCONCELOS
  Faculty of History: Prof. JOÃO MIGUEL TEIXEIRA DE GODOY
  Faculty of Law: Prof. LÚIS ARLINDO FERIANI
  Faculty of Library Science: Profa MARIANGELA PISONI ZANAGA
  Faculty of Philosophy: Prof. JOSÉ ANTONIO TRASFERETTI
  Faculty of Physical Education and Sports: Prof. WAGNER ROBERTO BERGAMO
  Faculty of Social Sciences: Prof. PEDRO ROCHA LEMOS
  Faculty of Social Services: Profa VÂNIA MARIA CAIO
  Faculty of Theology and Religious Studies: Prof. ELISIÁRIO CÉSAR CABRAL

Centre for Life Sciences (Av. John Boyd Dunlop s/n, Jardim Ipaussurama, 13060-904 Campinas, SP; tel. (19) 3343-6800; fax (19) 3343-6806; e-mail ccv@puc-campinas .edu.br; internet www.puc-campinas.edu.br/ccv):
  Faculty of Biological Sciences: Profa MARIÂNGELA CAGNONI RIBEIRO
  Faculty of Dentistry: Prof. JOSÉ IGNÁCIO TOLEDO JÚNIOR
  Faculty of Medicine: Prof. JOSÉ ESPIN NETO
  Faculty of Nursing: Profa MARIA APARECIDA GAMPER NUNES
  Faculty of Nutrition: Profa ANGELA DE CAMPOS TRENTIN
  Faculty of Occupational Therapy: Profa LIANA MAURA NAKED TANNUS
  Faculty of Pharmacy: GUSTAVO HENRIQUE DA SILVA
  Faculty of Physical Therapy: Profa ROSANGELA MARIA FRANCO GUERRA DA COSTA
  Faculty of Psychology: Profa HELENA BAZANELLI PREBIANCHI
  Faculty of Speech Therapy and Audiology: Profa MARIENE TERUMI UMEOKA HIDAKA

Centre for Mathematical, Environmental and Technological Sciences (tel. (19) 3343-7314; fax (19) 3343-7315; e-mail ceatec@puc-campinas.edu.br; internet www.puc-campinas.edu.br/ceatec):
  Faculty of Architecture and Urban Planning: Prof. RICARDO DA SOUZA CAMPS BADARÓ
  Faculty of Chemistry: Prof. DALMO MENDELLI
  Faculty of Civil Engineering: Prof. JOÃO CARLOS ROCHA BRAZ
  Faculty of Computer Engineering: Prof. RICARDO LUÍS DE FREITAS
  Faculty of Electrical Engineering: Profa NORMA REGGIANI
  Faculty of Environmental Engineering: Profa SUELI DO CARMO BETTINE
  Faculty of Geography: Prof. DAMARIS PUGA DE MORÃES
  Faculty of Mathematics: Prof. ELIANA DAS NEVES AREAS
  Faculty of Systems Analysis: Prof. JOSÉ ESTEVÃO PICARELLI

PONTIFÍCIA UNIVERSIDADE CATÓLICA DE MINAS GERAIS

Av. Dom José Gaspar 500, Bairro Coração Eucarístico, 30535-610 Belo Horizonte, MG

Telephone: (31) 3319-4444
Fax: (31) 3319-4225
E-mail: central@pucminas.br
Internet: www.pucminas.br

Founded 1958
Academic year: February to December
Chancellor: Dom WALMOR OLIVEIRA DE AZE-
VEDO
Rector: Prof. EUSTÁQUIO AFONSO ARAÚJO
Vice-Rector: Prof. Pe JOAQUIM GIOVANI MOL
GUIMARÃES
Gen. Sec.: FLÁVIO AUGUSTO BARROS
Chief Librarian: CÁSSIO JOSÉ DE PAULA

Library of 200,000 vols
Number of teachers: 2,032
Number of students: 44,043

Publications: *Journal PUC Minas* (12 a year), *No Pique da PUC* (52 a year), *PUC Informa* (52 a year)

DIRECTORS

Institute of Biological and Health Sciences: UBIRATAN BARROS DE MELO
Institute of Continuing Education: Dr MARIA REGINA NABUCO BRANDÃO
Institute of Economic and Managerial Sciences: ÂNGELA MARIA MARQUES CUPERTINO
Institute of Humanities: AUDEMARO TARANTO GOULART
Institute of Informatics: CARLOS BARRETO RIBAS
Institute of Labour Relations: Dr ANTONIO MOREIRA DE CARVALHO NETO
Institute of Psychology: ANA LÚCIA ANDRADE MARÇOLLA
Institute for the Study of Fauna and Flora: MIGUEL ALONSO DE GOUVÊA VALLE
Polytechnic Institute: NILSON DE FIGUEIREDO FILHO
PUC Minas Virtual (Distance Learning): MARIA BATRIZ OLIVEIRA GONÇALVES

AFFILIATED FOUNDATION

Fundação Dom Cabral: Rua Bernardo Guimarães 3071, 30140-083, Belo Horizonte, MG; tel. (31) 275-3466; fax (31) 275-1558; f. 1976; Dean Prof. EMERSON DE ALMEIDA.

PONTIFÍCIA UNIVERSIDADE CATÓLICA DE SÃO PAULO

Rua Monte Alegre 984, Perdizes, 05014-901 São Paulo, SP

Telephone: (11) 3670-8279
Fax: (11) 3670-8504
E-mail: reitoria@pucsp.br
Internet: www.pucsp.br

Founded 1946
Private control
Academic year: February to December (2 semesters)

Grand Chancellor: Dom ODILO PEDRO SCHERER (Archbishop of São Paulo)
Rector: ANTONIO VICO MAÑAS
Vice-Rector for Academic Affairs: Profa RAQUEL RAICHELIS DEGENSZAJN
Vice-Rector for Admin.: Prof. EDUARDO FERNANDES P. MOREIRA
Pro-Rector for Undergraduate Programmes: MARINA FELDMANN
Pro-Rector for Graduate Programmes: ANDRÉ RAMOS TAVARES
Pro-Rector for Culture and Community Relations: HÉLIO DELIBERADOR
Pro-Rector for Continuing Education: HAYDEÉ MARIA ROVERATTI
Pro-Rector for Planning, Development and Management: JOSÉ HELENO MARIANO
Gen. Sec.: CLÁUDIO JOSÉ LANGROIVA PEREIRA

Librarian: ANA MARIA RAPASSI
Library of 250,000 vols
Number of teachers: 1,592
Number of students: 29,015

Publications: *Cadernos Metrópole* (2 a year), *Cognitio* (1 a year), *Delta* (2 a year), *Distúrbios da Comunicação* (2 a year), *Documentação de Estudos em Linguística Teórica Aplicada* (2 a year), *Educação Matemática Pesquisa* (2 a year), *Galáxia* (2 a year), *Hypnos* (2 a year), *Kairós* (2 a year), *Projeto História* (2 a year), *Pesquisa & Debate* (2 a year), *The ESPecialist* (2 a year)

DIRECTORS

Centre of Biological and Medical Sciences: Profa CIBELE ISAAC
Centre of Education: Profa NÁDIA DUMARA RUIZ DA SILVEIRA
Centre of Humanities: Prof. EDISON NUNES
Centre of Law, Economics and Administration: Prof. ADHEMAR DE CAROLI
Centre of Mathematical, Physical and Technological Sciences: Profa TANIA MARIA MENDONÇA CAMPOS

DEANS

Centre of Biological and Medical Sciences (Praça Dr José Ermírio de Morães 290, 18030-230 Sorocaba, SP; tel. (15) 3212-9900; fax (15) 3212-9879; e-mail ccmb@pucsp.br):

Faculty of Biological Sciences: Prof. WALTER BARRELLA
Faculty of Human Sciences and Health: MARIA AMÁLIA ANDERY
Faculty of Medical Sciences and Health: JOSÉ EDUARDO MARTINEZ

Centre of Education (tel. (11) 3670-8258; fax (11) 3670-8161; e-mail faceeducacao@pucsp.br):

Faculty of Education: NEIDE NOFFS

Centre of Humanities (tel. (11) 3670-8306; fax (11) 3670-8289; e-mail centrohumanas@pucsp.br):

Faculty of Communications and Philosophy: SANDRA MRAZ
Faculty of Psychology: Profa MARIA DA GRAÇA MARCHINA GONÇALVES
Faculty of Social Sciences: Profa MARGARIDA LIMENA
Faculty of Social Work: Profa MARIA ROSÂNGELA BATISTONI
Faculty of Theology: VALERIANO DOS SANTOS

Centre of Law, Economics and Administration (tel. (11) 3670-8304; fax (11) 3670-8533; e-mail ccjea@pucsp.br):

Faculty of Economics and Business: JUAREZ TORINO BELLI
Faculty of Law: MARCELO FIGUEIREDO

Centre of Mathematical, Physical and Technological Sciences (Rua Marquês de Paranaguá 111, 01303-050 São Paulo, SP; tel. (11) 3256-1622; fax (11) 3256-1622; e-mail pgedmat@pucsp.br):

Faculty of Mathematical and Physical Sciences: Prof. FERNANDO ANTONIO DE CASTRO GIORNO
Faculty of Sciences and Technology: LUIZ CARLOS CAMPOS

PONTIFÍCIA UNIVERSIDADE CATÓLICA DO PARANÁ

Rua Imaculada Conceição 1155, Prado Velho, CP 16210, 80215-901 Curitiba, PR

Telephone: (41) 330-1515
Fax: (41) 332-5588
E-mail: postmaster@pucpr.br
Internet: www.pucpr.br

Founded 1959
Private control

Academic year: March to December (2 semesters)
Grand Chancellor: PEDRO FEDALTO (Archbishop of Curitiba)
Rector: CLEMENTE IVO JULIATTO
Academic Pro-Rector: Profa NEUZA APARECIDA RAMOS
Admin. Pro-Rector: Prof. ARAMIS DEMETERCO
Community Pro-Rector: ADILSON MORAES SEIXAS
Pro-Rector for Graduate Studies, Research and Extension Services: FLÁVIO BORTO
Pro-Rector for Planning and Devt: ROBERTO BORGES FRANÇA
Registrar: OSVALDO ULYSSES MAZAY
Library Dir: SILVIANE MÜLLER

Number of teachers: 1,241
Number of students: 20,413 (17,721 undergraduate, 2,692 postgraduate)

Publications: *Círculo de Estudos Bandeirantes* (1 a year), *Diálogo Educacional* (2 a year), *Estudos de Biologia* (2 a year), *Estudos de Medicina* (4 a year), *Locus* (1 a year), *Psicologia Argumento* (1 a year), *PUC-PR em Dados* (1 a year), *Revista Acadêmica* (2 a year), *Revista de Filosofia* (1 a year), *Revista de Fisioterapia* (2 a year), *Verba Iuris* (1 a year), *Vida Universitária* (12 a year)

DEANS

Centre for Agronomy and Environmental Sciences: SYLVIO PÉLLICO NETO
Centre for Applied and Social Sciences: SÉRGIO PEREIRA LOBO
Centre for Biological and Health Sciences: ALBERTO ACCIOLY VEIGA
Centre for Exact and Technological Sciences: ROBERT CARLISLE BURNETT
Centre for Humanities and Theological Sciences: ANTÔNIO QUIRINO DE OLIVEIRA
Centre for Juridical and Social Sciences: ROBERTO LINHARES DA COSTA

ATTACHED INSTITUTE

São José dos Pinhais Campus: Seminário dos Sagrados Corações, BR 376, km 14, 83010-500 São José dos Pinhais, Paraná; tel. (41) 283-4434; fax (41) 382-1223; Dir: Prof. SERGIO PEREIRA LOBO

PONTIFÍCIA UNIVERSIDADE CATÓLICA DO RIO DE JANEIRO

Rua Marquês de São Vicente 225, Edif. Pe. Leonel Franca, 8 andar, Gávea, 22453-900 Rio de Janeiro, RJ

Telephone: (21) 3527-1577
Fax: (21) 3527-1094
E-mail: incoming-ccci@puc-rio.br
Internet: www.puc-rio.br

Founded 1941
Private control
Academic year: March to December
Chancellor: Arcebispo Metropolitano do Rio de Janeiro ORANI TEMPESTA
Rector: Fr JOSAFÁ CARLOS DE SIQUEIRA
Vice-Pres.: Fr FRANCISCO IVERN
Vice-Pres. for Academic Affairs: Prof. JOSÉ RICARDO BERGMANN
Vice-Pres. for Admin. Affairs: Prof. LUIZ CARLOS SCAVARDA DO CARMO
Vice-Pres. for Community Affairs: Prof. AUGUSTO LUIZ DUARTE LOPES SAMPAIO
Vice-Pres. for Devt Affairs: Prof. SERGIO BRUNI
Registrar: Prof. WASHINGTON BRAGA
Librarian: Dra DOLORES RODRIGUEZ PERES

Library of 600,000 vols
Number of teachers: 1,162

Number of students: 20,000
Publication: *Anuário*

DEANS

Medical Centre: Prof. Dr HILTON HACKOK
Social Sciences Centre: Profa GISELE GUIMAR-
ÃES CITTADINO
Technical and Scientific Centre: Prof. JOSÉ
ALBERTO DOS REIS PARISE
Theology and Human Sciences Centre: Profa
MARIA CLARA BINGEMER

DIRECTORS OF ATTACHED INSTITUTES

Centre for Telecommunications Research:
Prof. FLAVIO JOSÉ VIEIRA
Dentistry Institute (Postgraduate): Dr
RICARDO GUIMARÃES FISCHER
Institute of International Relations: Profa
SONIA DE CAMARGO
Postgraduate Medical School: Prof. Dr
MAURO MEIRELES PENA
Rio Data Centre (Computer Centre): Prof.
JOSÉ RAIMUNDO LOPES DE OLIVEIRA
Technological Institute: Prof. SÉRGIO LEAL
BRAGA

PONTIFÍCIA UNIVERSIDADE CATÓLICA DO RIO GRANDE DO SUL

Av. Ipiranga 6681, Partenon, CP 1429,
90619-900 Porto Alegre, RS

Telephone: (51) 3320-3500
Fax: (51) 3339-1564
E-mail: gabreit@pucrs.br
Internet: www.pucrs.br

Founded 1948
Private control
Academic year: March to December

Chancellor: Dom DADEUS GRINGS
Rector: Prof. Ir NORBERTO FRANCISCO RAUCH
Pro-Rector for Admin.: Prof. ANTONIO MARIO
PASCUAL BIANCHI
Pro-Rector for Community Affairs: Profa
HELENA WILLHELM DE OLIVEIRA
Pro-Rector for Research and Graduate Stud-
ies: Prof. Dr Mons. URBANO ZILLES
Pro-Rector for Undergraduate Studies: Profa
Dra SOLANGE MEDINA KETZER
Pro-Rector for Univ. Extension: Prof. Dr
PAULO ROBERTO GIRARDELLO FRANCO
Head of Admin.: Prof. MARIO HAMILTON
VILELA
Dir of Uruguaiana campus: Profa MARIA DE
LOURDES SOUZA VILLELA
Librarian: Prof. CÉSAR AUGUSTO MAZZILLO

Number of teachers: 1,896
Number of students: 33,000

Publications: *Agenda PUCRS* (12 a year),
Analise (2 a year), *Anuário* (1 a year),
Biociências (2 a year), *Brasil* (2 a year),
Direito e Justiça (2 a year), *Educação* (2 a
year), *Estudos Ibero-Americanos* (2 a year),
Hifen (2 a year), *Letras de Hoje* (4 a year),
Mundo Jovem (12 a year), *Odontociência* (2
a year), *Psico* (2 a year), *Revista da
FAMECOS* (2 a year), *Revista de Medicina
da PUCRS* (4 a year), *Teocomunicação* (4 a
year), *Veritas* (4 a year)

DIRECTORS

Faculty of Administration, Accountancy and
Computer Science (Uruguaiana campus):
Prof. CLEITON TAMBELLINI BORGES
Faculty of Administration, Accountancy and
Economics: Prof. JORGE ALBERTO FRANZONI
Faculty of Aeronautical Sciences: Profa Me.
MARIA REGINA DE MORAES XAUSA
Faculty of Architecture and Urbanization:
Prof. IVAN GILBERTO BORGES MIZOGUCHI
Faculty of Biosciences: Profa Me. CLARICE
PRADE CARVALHO
Faculty of Chemistry: Prof. Me. ASSIS PEDRO
PERIN PICCINI

Faculty of Computer Science: Profa Dra VERA
LÚCIA STRUBE DE LIMA
Faculty of Dentistry: Prof. JOÃO MIGUEL
MESSINA DA CRUZ
Faculty of Education: Profa Me. MARIA
WALESKA CRUZ
Faculty of Engineering: Prof. Me. EDUARDO
GIUGLIANI
Faculty of Law: Prof. ATTILA SÁ D'OLIVEIRA
Faculty of Law (Uruguaiana campus): Prof.
ROBERTO DURO GICK
Faculty of Letters and Arts: Profa Dra
REGINA ZILBERMANN
Faculty of Mathematics: Profa ALAYDES SAN-
TANNA BIANCHI
Faculty of Medicine: Prof. Dr LUIZ CARLOS
BODANESE
Faculty of Nursing, Nutrition and Physio-
therapy: Profa Me. BEATRIZ SEBBEN OJEDA
Faculty of Pharmacy: Prof. Dr SÉRGIO DE
MEDA LAMB
Faculty of Philosophy and Sciences: Prof. Dr
THADEU WEBER
Faculty of Philosophy, Sciences and Letters
(Uruguaiana campus): Profa MARIA DE
LOURDES SOUZA VILLELA
Faculty of Physical Education and Sport
Sciences: Prof. Dr FRANCISCO CAMARGO
NETTO
Faculty of Physics: Profa Me. MARIA EMILIA
BALTAR BERNASIUK
Faculty of Psychology: Profa Me. JACQUELINE
POERSCH MOREIRA
Faculty of Social Communications: Prof.
JERÓNIMO CARLOS SANTOS BRAGA
Faculty of Social Service: Profa Dra JUSSARA
MARIA ROSA MENDES
Faculty of Theology: Prof. Dr GERALDO LUIZ
BORGES HACKMANN
Faculty of Zootechnics, Veterinary Science
and Agronomy (Uruguaiana campus): Prof.
DOUGLAS DE MENDONÇA THOMPSON

UNIVERSIDADE BANDEIRANTE DE SÃO PAULO

Rua Maria Candida 1813, V. Guilherme,
02071-013 São Paulo, SP

Telephone: (11) 2967-9000
Fax: (11) 2967-9006
E-mail: uniban@ns.uniban.br
Internet: www.uniban.br

Founded 1994
Private control
Academic year: February to December

Rector: HEITOR PINTO FILHO

Library of 400,000 vols, 900 periodicals
Number of teachers: 1,200
Number of students: 30,000

UNIVERSIDADE BRAZ CUBAS

Av. Francisco Rodrigues Filho 1233, Mogilar,
08773-380 Mogi das Cruzes, SP

Telephone: (11) 469-6444
Fax: (11) 4790-3844
Internet: www.brazcubas.br

Founded 1940, univ. status 1986
Private control
Language of instruction: Portuguese
Academic year: February to December

Rector: Prof. MAURÍCIO CHERMANN
Pro-Rector for Administration: Prof. SAUL
GRINBERG
Pro-Rector for Community Affairs: Prof. IRAM
ALVES DOS SANTOS
Pro-Rector for Finance: Prof. ISRAEL ALVES
DOS SANTOS
Secretary-General: PÉRCIO CHAMMA JUNIOR
Librarian: JANDIRA MARIA COUTINHO

Library of 97,000 vols
Number of teachers: 512
Number of students: 10,494

DIRECTORS

Centre for Applied Social Studies: Dr MARCO
ANTONIO RODRIGUES NAHUM
Centre for Exact and Technological Sciences:
Dr BENEDITO LUIZ FRANCO
Centre for Human Sciences, Literature and
Education: Prof. DILSON DEL BEM

UNIVERSIDADE CASTELO BRANCO

Av. Santa Cruz 1631, Realengo, 21710-250
Rio de Janeiro, RJ

Telephone: (21) 3216-7700
Fax: (21) 3216-6090
E-mail: info@castelobranco.br
Internet: www.castelobranco.br

Founded 1994
Private control

Rector: VERA COSTA GISSONI

Library of 33,000 vols
Number of teachers: 167
Number of students: 5,914

UNIVERSIDADE CATÓLICA DE BRASÍLIA
(Catholic University of Brasilia)

QS 07, Lote, 01, EPCT, Águas Claras, 71966-
700 Taguatinga Sul, DF

Telephone: (61) 3356-9000
Fax: (61) 3356-3010
E-mail: ucb@ucb.br
Internet: www.ucb.br

Founded 1974

19 Courses of expertise; 84 ongoing research
projects

Rector: Prof. Fr JOSÉ ROMUALDO DEGASPERI

Library: Libraries with 235,094 vols, 77,038
books; 2,409 periodicals; 1,215 video cassettes; 91 spec. materials: first private
univ. of Brazil, with access to the Portal
Capes/Mec providing 7,900 scientific periodicals and 80 database references
Number of teachers: 831
Number of students: 19,758

Publications: *Direito em Ação* (2 a year),
Revista Brasileira de Ciência e Movimento
(4 a year), *Revista Brasileira de Economia
de Empresa* (3 a year), *Revista Technologia
da Informação* (2 a year).

UNIVERSIDADE CATÓLICA DE GOIÁS

Av. Universitária 1440, Setor Universitário,
74605-010 Goiânia, GO

Telephone: (62) 3946-1000
Fax: (62) 3946-1005
E-mail: reitoria@ucg.br
Internet: www.ucg.br

Founded 1959
Private control
Academic year: March to December

Rector: Prof. WOLMIR THEREZIO AMADO
Vice-Rector for Admin. Affairs: Prof. DANIEL
RODRIGUES BARBOSA
Vice-Rector for Extension and Student Sup-
port: Profa SÔNIA MARGARIDA GOMES SOUSA
Vice-Rector for Institutional Devt: Prof.
EDUARDO RODRIGUES DA SILVA
Vice-Rector for Postgraduate Affairs and
Research: Profa SANDRA DE FARIA
Vice-Rector for Undergraduate Affairs: Profa
HELENIDES MENDONÇA
Registrar: DAGMAR MARTINS DAS GRAÇAS
Librarian: IRENE TOSCANO PASCOAL

Number of teachers: 1,317
Number of students: 22,179

Publications: *Estudos* (6 a year), *Flash* (52 a
year), *Fragmentos de Cultura* (6 a year),
Momento (52 a year)

DIRECTORS

Accounting: NAZARENO ROCHA JÚNIOR
Aeronautical Science: RAUL FRANCÉ MONTEIRO
Architecture: DEUSA MARIA RODRIGUÊS BOAVENTURA
Bilingual Executive Secretariat: ROQUE TOSCANO
Biology: JOSÉ WELLINGTON G. LEMOS
Biomedical Sciences: PAULO ROBERTO DE MELO REIS
Business Administration: JOÃO BOSCO DE BARROS
Computer Engineering: JOSÉ ROLDÃO GONÇALVES BARBOSA
Computer Science: JOSÉ ROLDÃO GONÇALVES BARBOSA
Design: TAI HSUAN NA
Economics: JOSÉ AUGUSTO COSTA
Education: OLGA IZILDA RONCHI
Electrical Engineering: RUI BARBOSA COELHO
Engineering: MANOEL DA SILVA ALVARES
Environmental Engineering: HARLEM INÁCIO DOS SANTOS
Food Science: CLELIA ALVES S. DE SOUZA
History, Geography and Social Sciences: LAÍS APARECIDA MACHADO
Languages: CELINA MARIA DE JESUS
Law: HELENISA M. GOMES
Manufacturing Engineering: PAULO JOSÉ MASCARENHAS RORIZ
Mathematics and Physics: MILTON OLIMPIO ALVES
Nursing: MARIA SALETE S. P. NASCIMENTO
Occupational Therapy: IVONE PORTILHO DO NASCIMENTO
Philosophy and Theology: LUÍZ GIRARDI, UENE JOSÉ GOMES
Physiotherapy: ROSÂNGELA ALVES MOTEFUSCO
Psychology: ANTÔNIO CARLOS G. SANTOS
Speech and Language Therapy: MAIONE MARIA MILÉO
Tourism Management: CARLA BAYLÃO DE CARVALHO
Zootechnics: ROBERTO CAMARGO WASCHECK

UNIVERSIDADE CATÓLICA DE PELOTAS

Rua Félix da Cunha 412, CP 402, 96010-000 Pelotas, RS
Telephone: (53) 284-8000
Fax: (53) 225-3105
E-mail: ucpel@phoenix.ucpel.tche.br
Internet: www.ucpel.tche.br
Founded 1960
Private control
Language of instruction: Portuguese
Academic year: February to December
Chancellor: Dom JAYME HENRIQUE CHEMELLO
Rector: Prof. ALENCAR MELLO PROENÇA
Pro-Rector for Admin.: Cont. CARLOS RICARDO GASS SINNOTT
Pro-Rector for Postgraduate, Research and Extension: Prof. Dr WILLIAM PERES
Pro-Rector for Undergraduate: Profa Dra MYRIAM SIQUIERA DA CUNHA
Library of 91,563 vols
Number of teachers: 443
Number of students: 6,189

DIRECTORS

School of Economics and Business: Prof. RENATO LUIS TAVARES DE OLIVEIRA
School of Education: Profa PAULO DOMINGUES MIERES CARUSO
School of Engineering and Architecture: Prof. DELMAR BROGLIO CARVALHO
School of Environmental Sciences: Profa CLARISSE SIQUEIRA COELHO
School of Informatics: Profa RENATA HAX SANDER REISER
School of Law: Prof. RUBENS BELLORA

School of Medicine: Prof. RENATO AZEVEDO DA SILVA
School of Pharmacy and Biochemistry: Profa IRACI DE LOURDES PACHOLSKI
School of Psychology: Prof. RICARDO AZEVEDO DA SILVA
School of Social Communication: Prof. ANTÔNIO LUIZ OLIVEIRA HEBERLÊ
School of Social Services: Prof. VINI RABASSA SA SILVA

UNIVERSIDADE CATÓLICA DE PERNAMBUCO

Rua do Príncipe 526, Boa Vista, 50050-900 Recife, PE
Telephone: (81) 2119-4000
E-mail: postmaster@unicap.br
Internet: www.unicap.br
Founded 1951
Private control
Academic year: February to December (2 semesters)
Rector: Pe PEDRO RUBENS FERREIRA OLIVEIRA
Pro-Rector for Academic Affairs: Prof. JUNOT CORNÉLIO MATOS
Pro-Rector for Administrative Affairs: LUCIANO JOSÉ PINHEIRO BARROS
Pro-Rector for Community Affairs: Pe MIGUEL DE OLIVEIRA MARTINS FILHO
Registrar: MARIA TERESA BARRETO DE MELO PERETTI
Librarian: ROSILDA MIRANDA DA SILVA
Number of teachers: 575
Number of students: 13,353
Publication: Symposium (2 a year)

DIRECTORS

Centre for Biological and Health Sciences: Prof. ARANILDO RODRIGUES DE LIMA
Centre for Legal Studies: Profa MIRIAN DE SÁ PEREIRA MAIA
Centre for Sciences and Technology: Prof. JOSÉ ORLANDO VIEIRA FILHO
Centre for Social Sciences: Prof. LEONEL FERREIRA DE MORAIS NETO
Centre for Theology and Human Sciences: Profa MARIA DA CONCEIÇÃO BIZERRA

UNIVERSIDADE CATÓLICA DE PETRÓPOLIS

Rua Benjamin Constant 213, Centro, 25610-130 Petrópolis, RJ
Telephone: (24) 2244-4000
Fax: (24) 242-7747
E-mail: reitor@ucp.br
Internet: www.ucp.br
Founded 1961
Private control
Academic year: February to December
Rector: JOSÉ LUIZ RANGEL SAMPAIO FERNANDES
Vice-Rector: Mons. JOSÉ MARIA PEREIRA
Pro-Rector for Academic Affairs: ALEXANDRE SHEREMETIEFF
Pro-Rector for Admin. Affairs: MÁRIO GUARNIDO DUARTE
Registrar: LUIZ HERIQUE SCHAEFFER
Librarian: MARIA DAS NEVES FRANCA LEITE KRÜGER
Number of teachers: 266
Number of students: 3,390
Publications: Informativo UCP (6 a year), O Communitário (12 a year), Revista UCP (3 a year)

DIRECTORS

Faculty of Economics, Accounting and Administration: Prof. CELSO PERMÍNIO SCHIMID
Faculty of Education: Profa SANDRA TEREZA LA CAVA DE ALMEIDA AMADO

Faculty of Law: Prof. LINDOLPHO DE MORAES MARINHO
Institute of Arts and Communication: Profa RUTH M. RANGEL SAMPAIO FERNANDES
Institute of Exact and Natural Sciences: Prof. GUILHERME CRISTÓVÃO NICODEMUS
Institute of Theology, Philosophy and Human Science: Prof. ALFREDO AUGUSTO GARCIA QUESADA
School of Engineering: Prof. RICARDO GRECHI PACHECO
School of Rehabilitation: Prof. GERSON DE AGUIAR LOUREIRO

UNIVERSIDADE CATÓLICA DE SANTOS

Rua Euclides da Cunha 241, Pompéia, 11065-902 Santos, SP
Telephone: (13) 3205-5555
E-mail: secgeral@unisantos.com.br
Internet: www.unisantos.com.br
Founded 1986
Rector: Profa MARIA HELENA DE ALMEIDA LAMBERT
Library of 58,000 vols, 945 periodicals
Number of teachers: 537
Number of students: 7,015

UNIVERSIDADE CATÓLICA DO SALVADOR

Largo do Campo Grande 07, Campo Grande, 40080-121 Salvador, BA
Telephone: (71) 3329-8600
Fax: (71) 3329-8622
E-mail: reitoria@ucsal.br
Internet: www.ucsal.br
Founded 1961
Private control
Languages of instruction: Portuguese, French, English
Chancellor: Cardeal Dom GERALDO MAJELLA AGNELO
Rector: Prof. JOSÉ CARLOS ALMEIDA DA SILVA
Vice-Rector: Profa LILIANA MERCURI DE ALMEIDA
Librarian: SONIA RODRIGUES
Number of teachers: 690
Number of students: 12,000

DIRECTORS

Faculty of Accountancy: (vacant)
Faculty of Economics: (vacant)
Faculty of Education: Profa ITALVA SIMÕES
Faculty of Law: Prof. THOMAS BACELLAR
Faculty of Nursing: Profa MARGARIDA MACHADO
Faculty of Philosophy and Human Sciences: Prof. JURANDYR OLIVEIRA
Institute of Letters: Profa TEREZA CHIANCA
Institute of Mathematics: NILTON CRUZ
Institute of Music: Profa LEDA MARGARIDA DE SOUZA
Institute of Sciences: Profa LYGIA PARAGUASSU
Institute of Theology: Fr ADEMAR DANTOS DE SOUZA
School of Business Administration: Prof. HUGO BELEUS
School of Engineering: Prof. LUIZ GONZAGA MARQUES
School of Physical Education: (vacant)
School of Social Services: Profa EMILIA NORONHA LYRA

UNIVERSIDADE CATÓLICA DOM BOSCO

Av. Tamandaré 6000, Jardim Seminário, 79117-900 Campo Grande, MS
Telephone: (67) 3312-3300
E-mail: reitoria@unibosco.br
Internet: www.unibosco.br

Founded 1993, fmrly Faculdades Unidas Católicas de Mato Grosso

Rector: Pe JOSÉ MARINONI
Pro-Rector for Academic Affairs: Pe Dr GILDASIO MENDES
Pro-Rector for Admin.: Ir RAFFAELE LOCHI

Library of 175,000 vols
Number of teachers: 217

Publications: *Jornal UCDB* (12 a year), *Revista do Direito* (6 a year), *Revista Koembá Pytã* (2 a year).

UNIVERSIDADE CIDADE DE SÃO PAULO

Rua Cesário Galeno 432/448, 03071-000 São Paulo, SP
Telephone: (11) 6190-1200
Fax: (11) 6190-1415
E-mail: gabreit@unicid.br
Internet: www.unicid.br

Founded 1992
Private control

Rector: RUBENS LOPES DA CRUZ
Chancellor: PAULO EDUARDO SOARES DE OLIVEIRA NADDEO

Library of 103,000 vols, 1,200 periodicals
Number of teachers: 535
Number of students: 12,000

UNIVERSIDADE CRUZEIRO DO SUL

Av. Dr Ussiel Cirilo 225, 08060-070 São Paulo, SP
Telephone: (11) 2037-5700
Internet: www.unicsul.br

Founded 1993
Private control

Rector: Profa SUELI CRISTINA MARQUESI
Pro-Rector for Extension and Community Affairs: Prof. Dr RENATO PADOVESE
Pro-Rector for Postgraduate Affairs and Research: Prof. Dr LUIZ HENRIQUE AMARAL
Pro-Rector for Undergraduate Affairs: Prof. Dr CARLOS AUGUSTO BAPTISTA DE ANDRADE

Library of 43,000 vols, 194 periodicals
Number of teachers: 239
Number of students: 9,771

UNIVERSIDADE DA AMAZÔNIA

Av. Alcindo Cacela 287, Umarizal, 66060-902 Belém, PA
Telephone: (91) 4009-3000
Fax: (91) 4009-3909
E-mail: reitor@unama.br
Internet: www.unama.br

Founded 1974
Private control

Rector: Prof. ÉDSON RAYMUNDO PINHEIRO DE SOUZA FRANCO
Vice-Rector: Prof. ANTÔNIO DE CARVALHO VAZ PEREIRA
Pro-Rector for Research, Postgraduate Affairs and Extension: Profa NÚBIA MARIA MACIEL
Pro-Rector for Teaching: Prof. MARIO FRANCISCO GUZZO

Library: Libraries with 121,000 vols, 3,219 periodicals
Number of teachers: 383
Number of students: 10,328

UNIVERSIDADE DA REGIÃO DE CAMPANHA

Av. Tupy Silveira 2099,, 96400-110 Bagé, RS
Telephone: (53) 3242-8244
Fax: (53) 3242-8898
Internet: www.urcamp.tche.br

Founded 1989

Rector: Prof. FRANCISCO ARNO VAZ DA CUNHA

Vice-Rector for Academic Affairs: Profa VIRGÍNIA BRANCATO DE BRUM
Vice-Rector for Administrative Affairs: Prof. JOÃO PAULO LUNELLI
Vice-Rector for Postgraduate Affairs, Research and Extension: Prof. MÁRIO MANSUR FILHO

Library: Libraries with 160,000 vols, 2,350 periodicals
Number of teachers: 578
Number of students: 6,985

UNIVERSIDADE DA REGIÃO DE JOINVILLE

Campus Universitário s/n, Bairro Bom Retiro, CP 246, 89201-972 Joinville, SC
Telephone: (47) 461-9000
Fax: (47) 473-0131
E-mail: reitoria@univille.com.br
Internet: www.univille.br

Founded 1992
State control

Rector: PAULO IVO KOEHNTOPP

Library of 71,000 vols, 1,200 periodicals
Number of teachers: 633
Number of students: 8,532

Publications: *Revista Saúde e Meio Ambiente* (Health and Environmental Journal, 2 a year), *Revista UNIVILLE* (2 a year), *Universo UNIVILLE* (3 a year).

UNIVERSIDADE DE BRASÍLIA

Campus Universitário Darcy Ribeiro, Asa Norte, CP 4399, 70910-900 Brasília, DF
Telephone: (61) 307-2022
Fax: (61) 272-0003
E-mail: unb@unb.br
Internet: www.unb.br

Founded 1961; inaugurated 1962
Under the control of the Fundação Univ. de Brasília
Language of instruction: Portuguese
Academic year: March to December

Rector: LAURO MORHY
Vice-Rector: TIMOTHY MARTIN MULHOLLAND
Dean of Admin. and Finance: ERICO PAULO SIEGMAR WEIDLE
Dean of Community Affairs: THÉRÈSE HOFMANN GATTI
Dean of Extension: DORIS SANTOS DE FARIA
Dean of Graduate Studies and Research: NORAÍ ROMEU ROCCO
Dean of Undergraduate Studies: MICHELÂNGELO GIOTTO S. TRIGUEIRO
Central Library Dir: CLARIMAR ALMEIDA VALLE

Library: see Libraries
Number of teachers: 1,342
Number of students: 25,000

Publications: *Revista Humanidades* (4 a year), *UnB Revista* (4 a year)

DIRECTORS

Faculty of Agricultural Engineering and Veterinary Medicine: EVERALDO A. PEREIRA
Faculty of Applied Social Studies: GILENO FERNANDES MAREELINO (acting)
Faculty of Architecture and Town Planning: GERALDO SÁ NOGUEIRA BATISTA
Faculty of Communications: MURILO CEZAR DE OLIVEIRA RAMOS
Faculty of Education: ERASTO FORKS MENDOZA
Faculty of Health Sciences: REYNALDO FELIPE TARELHO
Faculty of Law: JOSÉ GERALDO DE SOUSA JÚNIOR
Faculty of Medicine: TANIO TORRES ROSA
Faculty of Physical Education: IRAN JUNQUEIRA DE CASTRO

Faculty of Technology: HUMBERTO ABEDALLA JUNIOR
Institute of Arts: SUZETE VENTURELLI
Institute of Biological Sciences: IVONE DOZONDE DIMIZ
Institute of Chemistry: MARCAL DE OLIVEIRA NETO
Institute of Exact Sciences: HAYDÉE WERNECK POUBEL
Institute of Geosciences: NILSON FRANCISQUINI BOTELHO
Institute of Humanities: DENISE BOMTEMPO BIRCHE DE CARVALHO
Institute of Literature: HENRYK SIEVIERSKI
Institute of Physics: ANTONIO LUCIANO DE A. FONSECA
Institute of Political Science and International Relations: VAMIHED CHACON (acting)
Institute of Psychology: MARIA ANGELA GUIMARÃES FEITOSA
Institute of Social Science: ELLEN FENSTERSEIFER WOORTMANN

UNIVERSIDADE DE CAXIAS DO SUL

CP 1352, Rua Francisco Getúlio Vargas 1130, Bairro Petrópolis, 95070-560 Caxias do Sul, RS
Telephone: (54) 212-1133
Fax: (54) 212-1049
E-mail: informa@ucs.tche.br
Internet: www.ucs.tche.br

Founded 1967
Private control
Language of instruction: Portuguese
Academic year: March to December

Rector: Prof. RUY PAULETTI
Vice-Rector: Prof. LUIZ ANTONIO RIZZON
Pro-Rector for Admin.: Prof. EMIR JOSÉ ALVES DA SILVA
Pro-Rector for Extension and Univ. Relations: Prof. ARMANDO ANTONIO SACHET
Pro-Rector for Finance: Prof. ENESTOR JOSÉ DALLEGRAVE
Pro-Rector for Head of Office: Profa GELÇA REGINA LUSA PRESTES
Pro-Rector for Planning: Prof. JOSÉ CARLOS KÖCHE
Pro-Rector for Postgraduates: Profa OLGA MARIA PERAZZOLO
Pro-Rector for Undergraduates: Prof. LUIZ ANTONIO RIZZON
Chief Librarian: LÍGIA GONCALVES HESSELN

Number of teachers: 1,098
Number of students: 27,599

Publications: *Boletim Atos e Fatos, Caderno da Editora da Universidade de Caxias do Sul, Cadernos de Pequisa* (irregular), *Coletânea, Cultura e Saber* (2 a year), *Comunicado* (irregular), *Conjectura* (2 a year), *Guia Acadêmico, Jornal Multicampi e Cadernos de Pesquisa, Revista Chronos, Revista de Ciências Médicas* (2 a year), *Revista do CCET* (2 a year), *Revista Faculdade de Direito* (2 a year), *Revista Jovens Pesquisadores* (1 a year), *Sensu* (2 a year).

UNIVERSIDADE DE CRUZ ALTA

Rua Andrade Neves 308, 98025-810 Cruz Alta, RS
Telephone: (55) 3321-1500
Fax: (55) 3321-1500
E-mail: reitoria@unicruz.edu.br
Internet: www.unicruz.edu.br

Founded 1988

Rector: ELIZABETH FONTOURA DORNELES

Library of 14,000 vols, 864 periodicals
Number of teachers: 236
Number of students: 3,492

UNIVERSIDADE DE CUIABÁ

Av. Beira Rio 3100, 78065-700 Cuiabá, MT
Telephone: (65) 3363-1000
Fax: (65) 3363-1100
Internet: www.unic.br
Founded 1988
Private control
Rector: ALTAMIRO BELO GALINDO
Library: Libraries with 58,000 vols, 261 periodicals
Number of teachers: 408
Number of students: 9,053

UNIVERSIDADE DE FORTALEZA

Av. Washington Soares 1321, Edson Queiroz, 60811-905 Fortaleza, CE
Telephone: (85) 3477-3000
Fax: (85) 3477-3055
E-mail: reitoria@unifor.br
Internet: www.unifor.br
Founded 1973
Private control (Fundação Edson Queiroz)
Chancellor: AIRTON JOSÉ VIDAL QUEIROZ
Rector: FATIMA MARIA FERNANDES VERAS
Librarian: LEONILHA BRASILEIRO DE OLIVEIRA
Library of 87,453 vols
Number of teachers: 601
Number of students: 11,076.

ATTACHED CENTRES

Administrative Sciences Centre: 81 Rua da Paz, Apto 100, Meireles, 60165-180 Fortazela, CE; Dir JOSÉ ALÍPIO FROTA LEITÃO NETO.
CCS: Rua Paschoal de Castro Alves 350/401, 60155-420 Fortaleza, CE; Dir Profa FÁTIMA MARIA FERNANDES VERAS.
Human Sciences Centre: 626 Léa Pompeu St, 60821-490 Fortaleza, CE; Dir EROTILDE HONÓRIO SILVA.
Technological Sciences Centre: 758 Prof. Heráclito St, 60155-440 Fortaleza, CE; Dir RICARDO FIALHO COLARES.

UNIVERSIDADE DE FRANCA

Av. Dr Armando Salles Oliveira 201, Parque Universitário, 14404-600 Franca, SP
Telephone: (16) 3711-8888
Fax: (16) 3711-8886
E-mail: reitoria@unifran.br
Internet: www.unifran.br
Founded 1970
Private control
Rector: CLOVIS GALDIANO CURY
Library of 58,000 vols, 1,300 periodicals
Number of teachers: 221
Number of students: 6,258

UNIVERSIDADE DE ITAÚNA

Rodovia MG 431 km 45, CP 100, 35680-142 Itaúna, MG
Telephone: (37) 3249-3000
E-mail: uit@uit.br
Internet: www.uit.edu.br
Founded 1965
Private control
Academic year: March to December
Pres.: FAIÇAL DAVID FREIRE CHEQUER
Exec. Dir: JOSÉ W. TEIXEIRA DE MELO
Librarian: MARIA DA CONCEIÇÃO APARECIDA CARVALHO CARRILHO
Number of teachers: 200
Number of students: 2,154
Publications: *Cadernos de Extensão, Odonto-Itaúna*

DIRECTORS

Faculty of Dentistry: JAIR RASO

Faculty of Economics: RAIMUNDO DA SILVA RABELLO
Faculty of Engineering: FRANCISCO JOSÉ DE CASTRO BIANCHI
Faculty of Law: GERALDO DOS SANTOS
Faculty of Philosophy, Sciences, Languages and Social Sciences: ANNA ALVES VIERA DOS REIS

UNIVERSIDADE DE MARÍLIA

Campus I, Campus Universitário, 15525-902 Marília, SP
Telephone: (14) 2105-4000
Fax: (14) 3433-8691
E-mail: reitoria@unimar.br
Internet: www.unimar.com.br
Founded 1956
Private control
Academic year: February to December (2 semesters)
Rector: MÁRCIO MESQUITA SERVA
Vice-Rector: REGINA LÚCIA OTTAIANO LOSASSO SERVA
Pro-Rectors: JOSÉ ROBERTO MARQUES DE CASTRO, MARCO ANTONIO TEIXEIRA E SUELY FADUL VILLIBOR FLORY, MARIA BEATRIZ DE BARROS MORAES TRAZZI
Sec.-Gen.: GENI DE ALMEIDA COLLA
Head of Library: MARIA CÉLIA ARANHA RAMOS
Library of 110,000 vols, 15,000 periodicals
Number of teachers: 350
Number of students: 7,000
Publications: *Argumentum* (1 a year), *Asuntamentos Humanos* (1 a year), *Ciências Humanas* (1 a year), *Ciências Odontológicas* (1 a year), *Comunicação Veredas* (1 a year), *Unimar Ciências* (2 a year), *Unimídia* (6 a year), *Uninformativo* (1 a year).

UNIVERSIDADE DE MOGI DAS CRUZES

Av. Dr Cândido Xavier de Almeida Souza 200, 08780-911 Mogi das Cruzes, SP
Telephone: (11) 4798-7000
Fax: (11) 4799-1569
E-mail: reitoria@umc.br
Internet: www.umc.br
Founded 1973
Private control
Language of instruction: Portuguese
Academic year: February to December
Chancellor: Prof. MANOEL BEZERRA DE MELO
Vice-Chancellor: Profa MARIA COELI BEZERRA DE MELO
Rector: Profa REGINA COELI BEZERRA DE MELO NASSRI
Academic Vice-Rector: Prof. JOSÉ AUGUSTO PERES
Admin. Vice-Rector: JORGE KOWALSKI SALVARANI
Pro-Rector for Admin.: JESUS CARLOS PAREDES GONZÁLEZ
Pro-Rector for Research, Graduate Studies and Extension: Prof. LUIZ ROBERTO NUNES
Pro-Rector for Undergraduate Studies: Prof. ELIANA RODRIGUES
Pro-Rector of Fora de Sede Campus: Prof. ANTONIO DE OLIVAL FERNANDES
Registrar: ALINE ALVES DE ANDRADE
Gen. Sec.: CLAUDIO DA SILVA NICOLICHE
Librarian: DECLEIA MARIA FAGANELLO
Library of 168,827
Number of teachers: 787
Number of students: 22,000
Publication: *Entre Nós* (12 a year)

COORDINATORS

Accountancy and Business Admin. (Mogi): Prof. JOSÉ CASTILHO JUNIOR

Accountancy and Business Admin. (São Paulo Campus): Prof. CARLOS FERNANDES FRANCO
Accountancy, Quality and Productivity, Business Management, Personnel Management, Tourism and Hotel Management (São Paulo Campus): Prof. RÔMULO FRANCISCO DE SOUZA MAIA
Admin. (São Paulo Campus): Prof. EDMO ALVES MENINI
Architecture and Town Planning, Civil Engineering (Mogi): Prof. CRISTINA ELIZABETE SILVA RAGAINI
Biology (Mogi): Prof. MOACIR WUO
Chemistry and Chemical Engineering: Prof. ANDRÉ FERNANDO DE OLIVEIRA
Dentistry: Prof. CAMILLO ANAUATE NETTO
Devt of Computer Systems, Internet and Computer Networks Management (São Paulo Campus): Prof. ROBERTO AFFONSO DA COSTA, Jr
Electrical Engineering: Prof. CARLOS MARCELO GURJÃO DE GODOY
Environmental Sciences Technology: Profa JOSÉ ROBERTO KOCHEL DOS SANTOS
Information Systems, Systems Devt Technology, Internet and Computer Networks Management: Prof. HENRIQUE JESUS QUINTINO DE OLIVEIRA
Law: Prof. JOSÉ MOREIRA DE ASSIS
Law (São Paulo Campus): Prof. JOSÉ GERALDO BRITO FILOMENO
Letters (Portuguese, English and Literatures): Profa VERA LÚCIA MEIRA MAGALHÃES
Letters (Portuguese, English and Literatures Pedagogy), (São Paulo Campus): Prof. YÊDA MARIA DA COSTA LIMA VARIOTTA
Mechanical Engineering, Industrial Production Technology and Industrial Automation Technology: Prof. MARCO ANTÔNIO FUMAGALLI
Medicine: Prof. CARLOS MATEUS ROTTA
Nursing: Profa OSVALDO CÉLIO LAGE
Nutrition: Profa SUSANA FONSECA DA SILVEIRA
Pedagogy: Profa MIRIAN APARECIDA ROMANO
Pharmacy: Profa REGINA LÚCIA BATISTA DA COSTA OLIVEIRA
Physical Education: Prof. ZENON SILVA ARANHA FILHO
Physiotherapy: Prof. CESAR AUGUSTO CALONEGO
Psychology: Profa GERALDINA PORTO WITTER
Quality and Productivity, Business Management, Personnel Management, Tourism and Hotel Management (São Paulo Campus): Prof. JOSÉ GALBA DE AQUINO
Social Communications, Design (Visual Programme): Prof. ARMANDO SÉRGIO DA SILVA
Touristic Business Management, Marketing and Sales, Quality and Productivity Management, Enterprising and Business Management: Prof. ROBERTO KANAANE

UNIVERSIDADE DE NOVA IGUAÇU

Av. Augusto Távora 2134, Jardim Redenção, 26275-580 Nova Iguaçu, RJ
Telephone: (21) 2765-4012
Fax: (21) 2765-1687
E-mail: proeg@unig.br
Internet: www.unig.br
Founded 1993
Private control
Rector: JULIO CÉSAR DA SILVA
Pro-Rector for Admin.: JOÃO BATISTA BARRETO LUBANCO
Pro-Rector for Undergraduate Studies: CARLOS HENRIQUE MELO REIS
Pro-Rector for Postgraduate Studies, Research and External Relations: ANTONIO CARLOS CARREIRA FREITAS
Library: Libraries with 59,000 vols, 1,355 periodicals
Number of teachers: 922
Number of students: 12,301

Publications: *Arquivos de Direito*, *In Solidum* (Journal of Faculty of Law and Applied Social Sciences), *InterFace* (Journal of Faculty of Education and Humanities), *Revista de Ciência & Tecnologia*, *Revista de Ciências Biológicas e da Saúde*

DIRECTORS

Faculty of Biological and Health Sciences: UÉLITON VIANNA

Faculty of Education and Humanities: MARIONICE ALEXANDRE BOECHAT

Faculty of Exact Sciences and Technology: JOSÉ CARLOS DA SILVA

Faculty of Law and Applied Social Sciences: JOÃO BATISTA BARRETO LUBANCO

UNIVERSIDADE DE PASSO FUNDO

CP 611, 99052-900 Passo Fundo, RS
BR 285, Bairro São José, Passo Fundo, RS
Telephone: (54) 3316-8100
E-mail: centraldeatend@upf.br
Internet: www.upf.br
Founded 1968
Private control
Academic year: March to November (2 semesters)
Rector: RUI GETÚLIO SOARES
Vice-Rector for Academic Affairs: LORIVAN FISCH DE FIGUEIREDO
Vice-Rector for Admin. Affairs: NELSON GERMANO BECK
Vice-Rector for Extension and Community Affairs: CLÉA BERNADÉTE SILVEIRA NETTO NUNES
Vice-Rector for Research and Postgraduate Affairs: HUGO TOURINHO FILHO
Vice-Rector for Undergraduate Affairs: ELIANE LÚCIA COLUSSI
Registrar: Prof. LUIS DE CESARO
Librarian: WLADEMIR PINTO
Number of teachers: 839
Number of students: 11,409

DIRECTORS

Institute of Arts: Profa MARIA C. DE BRITTO RAMOS

Institute of Biological Sciences: Prof. LORENA GEIB

Institute of Exact and Geosciences: Prof. GERALDO HALLWASS

Institute of Philosophy and Humanities: Prof. TELISA GRAEFF

School of Agronomy: Prof. WALTER BOLLER

School of Dentistry: Prof. RUI GETÚLIO SOARES

School of Economics and Administration: Prof. ACIOLY RÖSING

School of Education: Prof. SELINA MARIA DAL MORO

School of Engineering: Prof. LUIZ FERNANDO PRESTES

School of Law: Prof. LUIZ J. NOGUEIRA DE AZEVEDO

School of Medicine: Prof. LUIZ SÉRGIO DE MOURA FRAGOMENI

School of Physical Education: Prof. CARLOS RICARDO SCHLEMMER

UNIVERSIDADE DE PERNAMBUCO

Av. Agamenon Magalhães s/n, Santo Amaro, 50100-010 Recife, PE
Telephone: (81) 3183-3700
Fax: (81) 423-2248
E-mail: upe@recife.upe.br
Internet: www.upe.br
Founded 1965
Rector: Prof. CARLOS FERNANDO DE ARAÚJO CALADO
Vice-Rector: Prof. REGINALDO INOJOSA CARNEIRO CAMPELLO

Pro-Rector for Admin. Affairs: Prof. Dr PAULO ROBERTO RIO DA CUNHA
Pro-Rector for Extension and Culture: Prof. ÁLVARO VIERA DE MELO
Pro-Rector for Planning: Prof. Dr BÉDA BARKOKÉBAS JÚNIOR
Pro-Rector for Postgraduate Affairs and Research: Profa Dra VIVIANE COLARES SOARES DE ANDRADE AMORIM
Pro-Rector for Undergraduate Affairs: Profa MSc IZABEL CHRISTINA DE AVELAR SILVA
Librarian: LÍDIA PONTUAL
Library of 8,000 vols, 8,302 periodicals (390 titles)
Number of teachers: 879
Number of students: 11,928 (10,968 undergraduate, 350 postgraduate, 610 extension)

DIRECTORS

Amaury de Medeiros Integrated Health Centre: Dr ARINALDO VASCONCELOS DE ALENCAR

Faculty of Administrative Sciences: Prof. ARANDI MACIEL CAMPELO

Faculty of Dentistry: Prof. JOSÉ RICARDO DIAS PEREIRA

Faculty of Medicine: Prof. JOSÉ GUIDO CORREIA DE ARAÚJO

Faculty of Teacher Training (in Garanhuns): Prof. LUIZ TENÓRIO DE CARVALHO

Faculty of Teacher Training (in Petrolina): Prof. JOAQUIM SILVA E SANTANA

Faculty of Teacher Training (in Nazaré da Mata): Prof. LUIZ INTERAMINENSE

Institute of Biological Sciences: Prof. CARLOS ROBERTO DA SILVA

Oswaldo Cruz University Hospital: Dr ÊNIO LUSTOSA CANTARELLI

Polytechnic: Prof. ARMANDO CARNEIRO P. REGO FILHO

School of Nursing: Profa KÁTIA REJANE VERGUEIRO CÉSAR

School of Physical Education: Prof. RENATO MEDEIROS DE MORAES

UNIVERSIDADE DE RIBEIRÃO PRETO

Av. Costábile Romano 2201, Ribeirânia, 14096-900 Ribeirão Preto, SP
Telephone: (16) 3603-6900
Fax: (16) 627-5035
Internet: www.unaerp.br
Founded 1985
Private control
Rector: Profa ELMARA LUCIA DE OLIVEIRA BONINI CORAUCI
Library of 96,000 vols, 796 periodicals
Number of teachers: 399
Number of students: 7,479

UNIVERSIDADE DE SANTA CRUZ DO SUL

Av. Independência 2293, Bairro Universitário, 96815-900 Santa Cruz do Sul, RS
Telephone: (51) 3717-7300
Fax: (51) 3717-1855
E-mail: info@unisc.br
Internet: www.unisc.br
Founded 1964
Rector: VILMAR THOMÉ
Vice-Rector: JOSÉ ANTÔNIO PASTORIZA FONTOURA
Pro-Rector for Admin.: Prof. JAIME LAUFER
Pro-Rector for Extension and Community Relations: Profa ANA LUISA TEIXEIRA DE MENEZES
Pro-Rector for Planning and Institutional Devt: Prof. JOÃO PEDRO SCHMIDT
Pro-Rector for Research and Graduate Courses: Prof. LIANE MÄHLMANN KIPPER

Pro-Rector for Undergraduate Courses: Profa CARMEN LÚCIA DE LIMA HELFER
Library of 26,000
Number of teachers: 548
Number of students: 10,668

UNIVERSIDADE DE SANTO AMARO

Rua Prof. Enéas de Siqueira Neto 340, Jardim das Imbuias, 04829-300 São Paulo, SP
Telephone: (11) 2141-8619
Internet: www.unisa.br
Founded 1968 as Instituição de Ensino Superior; current name 1994
Private control
Rector: DARCI GOMES DO NASCIMENTO
Vice-Rector: JOSÉ DOUGLAS DALLORA
Library of 57,000 vols, 700 periodicals
Number of teachers: 505
Number of students: 7,789

UNIVERSIDADE DE SÃO FRANCISCO

Av. São Francisco de Assis 218, Jd. São José, 12916-900 Bragança Paulista, SP
Telephone: (11) 4034-8170
Internet: www.usf.com.br
Founded 1976, university status 1985
Private control
Language of instruction: Portuguese
Academic year: February to December
Rector: Fr GILBERTO
Vice-Rector: Fr JOSÉ ANTÔNIO CRUZ DUARTE
Pro-Rector for Academic Affairs and Institutional Devt: LEILA PAGNOZZI
Pro-Rector for Admin. Affairs: PAULO CUNHA
Pro-Rector for Community Affairs: EVANDRO RIBEIRO
Gen. Sec.: PAULO POZEBON
Librarian: IVANI BENASSI
Library of 132,000 vols, 1,200 periodicals
Number of teachers: 821
Number of students: 17,561
Publications: *Anais do Encontro de Iniciação Científica e Pesquisadores* (1 a year), *Cadernos do IFAN* (4 a year), *InformIP-PEX* (12 a year), *Informativo USF* (12 a year), *Semeando* (12 a year)

DIRECTORS

Câmpus de Bragança Paulista (Av. São Francisco de Assis 218, CP 163, 12900-000 Bragança Paulista, SP):

Faculty of Dentistry: Prof. ROSSINE AMORIM MACIEL

Faculty of Economics and Administration: Profa HILDA MARIA C. BARROSO BRAGA

Faculty of Law: Prof. JOSÉ NICOLA JANNUZZI

Faculty of Medicine: Prof. SÉRGIO LUIZ MARTIN NARDY

Faculty of Pharmacy: Prof. EDSON RODRIGUES

Faculty of Philosophy, Sciences and Literature: Prof. MIGUEL HENRIQUE RUSSO

Câmpus de Itatiba (Rua Alexandre Rodrigues Barbosa 45, 13251-900 Itatiba, SP):

Faculty of Administrative and Exact Sciences: Prof. FÁBIO ALEXANDRE GAION CASOTTI

Faculty of Engineering: Prof. WERNER MERTZIG

Faculty of Human Sciences: Profa CARMEM BEATRIZ RODRIGUES FABRIANI

Câmpus de São Paulo (Rua Hannemann 352, Pari, 03031-040 São Paulo, SP):

Faculty of Business and Administration: Prof. LUIZ MAURÍCIO DE ANDRADE DA SILVA

Faculty of Education and Social Sciences: Prof. MARINO ANTONIO SEHNEN

Faculty of Law: Prof. MARLON WANDER MACHADO

ATTACHED INSTITUTES

Franciscan Institute of Anthropology: Dir Fr ORLANDO BERNARDI.

Institute for Graduate Research and Extension: Dir Profa JOSIANE MARIA DE FREITAS TONELOTTO.

UNIVERSIDADE DE SÃO PAULO

Cidade Universitária, Rua da Reitoria 109, 05508-900 São Paulo, SP

Telephone: (11) 3091-1000
Fax: (11) 3815-5665
E-mail: gr@usp.br
Internet: www.usp.br

Founded 1934
State control
Academic year: March to November

Rector: Prof. Dra SUELY VILELA
Vice-Rector: Prof. Dr FRANCO MARIA LAJOLO
Pro-Rector for Culture and Univ. Extension: Prof. Dr RUY ALBERTO CORREA ALTAFINE
Pro-Rector for Postgraduate Studies: Prof. Dr ARMANDO CORBANI FERRAZ
Pro-Rector for Research: Prof. Dra MAYANA ZATZ
Pro-Rector for Undergraduate Studies: Profa Dra SELMA GARRIDO PIMENTA
Sec.-Gen.: Profa Dra MARIA FIDELA DE LIMA NAVARRO

Library: see Libraries and Archives
Number of teachers: 5,434
Number of students: 81,179

Publications: *Boletim de Botânica* (1 a year), *Boletim IG/USP—Série Científica* (1 a year), *Brazilian Journal of Veterinary Research and Animal Science* (6 a year), *Educação e Pesquisa—FE* (2 a year), *Estilos da Clínica* (2 a year), *Pesquisa Odontológica Brasileira* (4 a year), *Revista Brasileira de Ciências Farmacêuticas—IQ/FCF* (3 a year), *Revista Brasileira de Oceanografia* (2 a year), *Revista da Escola de Enfermagem* (4 a year), *Revista da Faculdade de Direito* (1 a year), *Revista de Administração* (4 a year), *Revista de Fisioterapia* (2 a year), *Revista de Psicologia USP* (2 a year), *Revista de Saúde Pública* (6 a year), *Revista de Terapia Ocupacional* (4 a year), *Revista do Instituto de Medicina Tropical de SP* (6 a year), *Revista do Museu de Arqueologia e Etnologia* (1 a year), *Revista Paulista de Educação Física* (2 a year), *Revista USP* (4 a year), *Scientia Agrícola—ESALQ* (4 a year), *Sinopses—FAU* (irregular)

DEANS

Faculty of Animal Husbandry and Food Engineering (Pirassununga): Prof. Dr HOLMER SAVASTANO Jr
Faculty of Architecture and Town Planning: Prof. Dr SYLVIO BARROS SAWAYA
Faculty of Dentistry: Prof. Dr CARLOS DE PAULA EDUARDO
Faculty of Dentistry (Bauru): Prof. Dr LUIZ FERNANDO PEGORARO
Faculty of Dentistry (Ribeirão Preto): Prof. Dr OSWALDO LUIZ BEZZON
Faculty of Economics, Administration and Accounting: Prof. Dr CARLOS ROBERTO AZZONI
Faculty of Economics, Administration and Accounting (Ribeirão Preto): Prof. Dr RUDINEI TONETO
Faculty of Education: Profa Dra SONIA TERESINHA DE SOUSA PENIN
Faculty of Law: Prof. Dr JOÃO GRANDINO RODAS
Faculty of Law (Ribeirão Preto): Prof. Dr IGNÁCIO MARIA POVEDA VELASCO

Faculty of Medicine: Prof. Dr MARCOS BOULOS
Faculty of Medicine (Ribeirão Preto): Prof. Dr BENEDITO CARLOS MACIEL
Faculty of Pharmaceutical Sciences: Prof. Dr JORGE MANCINI FILHO
Faculty of Pharmaceutical Sciences (Ribeirão Preto): Prof. Dr AUGUSTO CÉSAR CROPANESE SPADARO
Faculty of Philosophy, Literature and Human Sciences: Profa Dra SANDRA MARGARIDA NITRINI
Faculty of Philosophy, Sciences and Literature (Ribeirão Preto): Prof. Dr SEBASTIÃO DE SOUSA ALMEIDA
Faculty of Public Health: Prof. Dr CHESTER LUIZ GALVÃO CÉSAR
Faculty of Veterinary Medicine and Zootechnics: Prof. Dr JOSÉ ANTONIO VISINTIN
Institute of Biomedical Sciences: Prof. Dr LUIZ ROBERTO GIORGETTI DE BRITTO
Institute of Biosciences: Profa Dra WELLINGTON BRAZ CARVALHO DELITTI
Institute of Chemistry: Prof. Dr HANS VIERTLER
Institute of Chemistry (São Carlos): Prof. Dr EDSON ANTONIO TICIANELLI
Institute of Geophysics, Astronomy and Atmospheric Sciences: Profa Dra MÁRCIA ERNESTO
Institute of Geosciences: Prof. Dr COLOMBO CELSO GAETA TASSINARI
Institute of Mathematical Sciences and Computing Systems (São Carlos): Prof. Dr JOSÉ ALBERTO CUMINATO
Institute of Mathematics and Statistics: Prof. Dr PAULO DOMINGOS CORDARO
Institute of Oceanography: Prof. Dr ANA MARIA S. PIRES VANIN
Institute of Physics: Prof. Dr ALEJANDRO SZANTO DE TOLEDO
Institute of Physics (São Carlos): Prof. Dr GLAUCIUS OLIVA
Institute of Psychology: Profa Dra EMMA OTTA
'Luiz de Queiroz' Higher School of Agriculture: Prof. Dr ANTONIO ROQUE DECHEN
Polytechnic School: Prof. Dr IVAN GILBERTO SANDOVAL FALLEIROS
School of Communication and Arts: Prof. Dr MAURO WILTON DE SOUSA
School of Engineering (Lorena): Prof. Dr NEI FERNANDES DE OLIVEIRA Jr
School of Engineering (São Carlos): Profa Dra MARIA DO CARMO CALIJURI
School of Nursing: Profa Dra ISILIA APARECIDA SILVA
School of Nursing (Ribeirão Preto): Profa Dra MARIA DAS GRAÇAS BOMFIM DE CARVALHO
School of Physical Education and Sport: Prof. Dr GO TANI
School of Physical Education and Sport (Ribeirão Preto): Prof. Dr VALDIR JOSÉ BARBANTI

UNIVERSIDADE DE SOROCABA

Km 92.5, Rod. Raposo Tavares, 18023-000 Sorocaba, SP

Telephone: (15) 2101-7005
Fax: (15) 2101-7112
E-mail: uniso@uniso.br
Internet: www.uniso.br

Founded 1994
Academic year: February to December

Rector: ALDO VANNUCCHI

Library of 128,730 vols, 995 periodicals
Number of teachers: 271
Number of students: 7,212

Publications: *Quaestio—Revista de Estudos de Educação* (2 a year), *Revista de Estudos Universitários* (2 a year).

UNIVERSIDADE DE TAUBATÉ

Rua 4 de Março 432, Centro, 12020-270 Taubaté, SP

Telephone: (12) 3625-4100
Fax: (12) 3632-7660
E-mail: reitoria@unitau.br
Internet: www.unitau.br

Founded 1976
Municipal control
Academic year: March to November

Rector: Profa Dra MARIA LUCILA JUNQUEIRA BARBOSA
Vice-Rector: Prof. Dr JOSÉ RUI CAMARGO
Pro-Rector for Admin.: Prof. Dr FRANCISCO JOSÉ GRANDINETTI
Pro-Rector for Economy and Finance: Profa MARISA DE MOURA MARQUES
Pro-Rector for Extension and Community Relations: Profa Dra ANA APARECIDA DA SILVA ALMEIDA
Pro-Rector for Research and Postgraduate Affairs: Prof. Dr JOSÉ ROBERTO CORTELLI
Pro-Rector for Students: Prof. ARMANDO ANTONIO MONTEIRO DE CASTRO
Pro-Rector for Undergraduates: Profa MARA CRISTINA BICUDO DE SOUZA
Sec.-Gen.: JOSÉ LUIZ RIBEIRO DO VALLE
Chief Librarian: MÁRCIA MARIA DE MOURA RIBEIRO

Library of 214,000 vols
Number of teachers: 700
Number of students: 20,000

Publications: *Ambiente and Água—An Interdisciplinary Journal of Applied Science*, *Caminhos em Lingüística Aplicada*, *Clínica e Pesquisa em Odontologia—UNITAU*, *Revista Biociências*, *Revista Ciências Exatas*, *Revista Ciências Humanas*, *Revista de Extensão da Universidade de Taubaté*, *Revista G&DR*, *Revista Periodontia*

DEANS

Agricultural Sciences: LUCIANO RICARDO MARCONDES DA SILVA
Architecture: MOACYR PAULISTA CORDEIRO
Civil Engineering: ALEX THAUMATURGO DIAS
Dentistry: SANDRA MÁRCIA HABITANTE
Economics, Accounting and Management: Profa MARLENE FERREIRA SANTIAGO
Electrical Engineering: WILTON NEY DO AMARAL PEREIRA
Law: FERNANDO ANTONIO BARBOSA ROMEIRO
Mechanical Engineering: CARLOS ANTONIO VIEIRA
Medicine: ANTONIO CARLOS BARTOLOMUCCI
Nursing: SILVIA MAIRA PEREIRA CINTRA
Physical Education: APARECIDA DE FÁTIMA FERRAZ QUERIDO
Physiotherapy: ULYSSES FERNANDES ERVILHA
Psychology: MARILZA TEREZINHA SOARES DE SOUZA
Social Communications: MARCELO TADEU DOS REIS PIMENTEL
Social Sciences and Languages: SOLANGE TERESINHA RICARDO DE CASTRO
Social Work: MARIA AUXILIADORA ÁVILA DOS SANTOS SÁ

PROFESSORS

ABRAHAM, R.
ABRAO SAAD, W.
ABRUCEZE, S.
ABUD MARCELINO, M.
ABUD MARTINS, A.
AKIYAMA, M.
ALBERNAZ CRESPO, A.
ALEGRE SALLES, V.
ALGADO, A.
ALVES CARRINHO, M.
ALVES CORRÊA, V.
ALVES MARTINS, I.
ALVES SOARES, D.
AMBROSETTI, N.

ANBINDER, A.
ANDRADE BRISOLA, E.
ANTONIO BOVO, L.
APARECIDA RIBEIRO, M.
ARRUDA FILHO, E.
ASSINI BALBUENO, E.
AUXILIADORA PINTO, C.
BARBAGALLO, L.
BARBANERA, M.
BARBERIO, A.
BARBOSA ROMEIRO, F.
BARONE JR, T.
BARROS DINIZ, N.
BARTOLOMUCCI, A.
BASSO SCHMITT, A.
BATISTA TUFFI, V.
BAUAB PUZZO, M.
BOAL TEIXEIRA, M.
BOLL, A.
BORGES GLAUS LEÃO, M.
BRANCO ROMEIRO, R.
BRÁS ROQUE, R.
BRENOL LAGES, R.
BRITTO, M.
BUCHLER ZORRÓN, A.
BUENO COSTA, J.
BURINI, D.
BUSSOLOTTI, J.
CABRAL JR, J.
CAMARGO, J.
CAMARGO ANTONIAZZI, M.
CAMARGO ORTIZ MONTEIRO, P.
CANTANHEDE GUARNIERI, O.
CAPPELLANES, C.
CARDOSO, M.
CARDOSO, N.
CARDOSO JORGE, A.
CARELLI BARRETO, L.
CARLOS PINTO, E.
CARNIELLO, M.
CAVAGLIERI, A.
CAVALCA CORTELLI, S.
CAVALCANTE, K.
CELSO PELLOGIA, M.
CEMBRANELI JR, L.
CERVANTES, J.
CÉSAR JR, C.
CESAR PIRES, O.
CESAR REIS, R.
CÉSAR VIEIRA, M.
CHAVES, C.
CINELLI MOREIRA, P.
CIRELLI, G.
CLARO NEVES, A.
COBO, V.
COIMBRA MAZZINI, R.
CONSTANTINO, E.
CORDEIRO, M.
CORRÊA, J.
CORTELLI, J.
COSTA, V.
COSTA FERRAZ, U.
COSTA NASCIMENTO, L.
COSTA SODRÉ, P.
CRUZ LOURES MERKX, A.
CUSMA PELOGIA, N.
CUSMANICH, K.
CUSTODIO, T.
DA CONCEIÇÃO RIVOLI COSTA, M.
DA COSTA, J.
DA COSTA, L.
DA COSTA E SILVA, L.
DA COSTA REIS, M.
DA COSTA ZÖLLNER, M.
DA CRUZ GALVÃO JÚNIOR, L.
DA CUNHA FILHO, S.
DA CUNHA OLIVEIRA, M.
DA MOTA, A.
DA ROSA, L.
DA SILVA, A.
DA SILVA, A.
DA SILVA, C.
DA SILVA, D.
DA SILVA, E.
DA SILVA, J.

DA SILVA, L.
DA SILVA, M.
DA SILVA, M.
DA SILVA, R.
DA SILVA, R.
DA SILVA, R.
DA SILVA, T.
DA SILVA ALMEIDA, A.
DA SILVA JR, J.
DA SILVA RICHETTO, K.
DA SILVA SANTOS, T.
DA SILVA SOUZA, J.
DA SILVEIRA LUZ, M.
DA TRINDADE SIQUEIRA, M.
DA VEIGA, S.
DALLA VECCHIA GRASSI, A.
DALOMBARDI, J.
DAMILANO, J.
DAORTIZ ABRAHÃO, J.
DAS NEVES CAVALCANTI, B.
DASIMÕES FLORENÇANO, J.
DAVOLI ARIZONO, A.
DE ALBUQUERQUE CAMARA NETO, I.
DE ALMEIDA, A.
DE ALMEIDA, J.
DE ALMEIDA, L.
DE ALMEIDA CANDELÁRIA, L.
DE ALMEIDA MACEDO, E.
DE ALMEIDA NASCIMENTO, E.
DE ALVARENGA, M.
DE ANDRADE, L.
DE AQUINO FREITAS, R.
DE ARANTES GOMES ELLER, R.
DE ARAÚJO, C.
DE ARAÚJO, D.
DE ARAÚJO, R.
DE ARAUJO QUERIDO OLIVEIRA, E.
DE ASSIS CLARO, C.
DE ASSIS COELHO, F.
DE AVILA MOREIRA, M.
DE AZEREDO FREITAS, L.
DE AZEVEDO, A.
DE AZEVEDO, D.
DE BARROS, D.
DE BARROS, J.
DE BARROS REZENDE FILHO, C.
DE BRITO, L.
DE BRITO MARQUES, E.
DE CAMPOS, J.
DE CAMPOS ALMEIDA VIEIRA, C.
DE CARLI BUERI MATTOS, R.
DE CARVALHO, A.
DE CARVALHO, M.
DE CARVALHO, P.
DE CARVALHO ALMEIDA, E.
DE CARVALHO GALIZIA, P.
DE CÁSSIA RIGOTTI VILELA MONTEIRO, R.
DE CASTRO, A.
DE CASTRO, M.
DE CASTRO, P.
DE CASTRO, R.
DE CASTRO, S.
DE CASTRO FOLGUERAS, L.
DE CASTRO MOURA, J.
DE CERQUEIRA, A.
DE FARIA, A.
DE FARIA E SILVA, L.
DE FÁTIMA CAMARGO DIAS FERREIRA, M.
DE FÁTIMA DA SILVA, M.
DE FATIMA FERRAZ QUERIDO, A.
DE FREITAS, D.
DE FREITAS CARPEGEANI, C.
DE JESUS FILHO, J.
DE LEMOS, M.
DE LIMA, J.
DE LIMA E SILVA, M.
DE MATTOS, A.
DE MATTOS MORAES DOS SANTOS, T.
DE MEDEIROS, A.
DE MEDEIROS, J.
DE MELLO, B.
DE MELLO RODE, S.
DE MELO, F.
DE MELO, J.
DE MIRANDA, G.
DE MORAES, M.

DE MORAES, V.
DE MORAES ROCHA MEDEIROS FREITAS LOUR-
ENCO, R.
DE MORAIS, V.
DE MOURA, J.
DE MOURA, L.
DE MOURA MARQUES, M.
DE MOURA RIBEIRO, M.
DE MOURA SANTOS, A.
DE OLIVEIRA, A.
DE OLIVEIRA, A.
DE OLIVEIRA, C.
DE OLIVEIRA, C.
DE OLIVEIRA, E.
DE OLIVEIRA, F.
DE OLIVEIRA, J.
DE OLIVEIRA, L.
DE OLIVEIRA, M.
DE OLIVEIRA, P.
DE OLIVEIRA, T.
DE OLIVEIRA BRAZIL, J.
DE OLIVEIRA CARVALHO, M.
DE OLIVEIRA CHAMON, E.
DE OLIVEIRA FILHO, J.
DE OLIVEIRA MUKAI, A.
DE OLIVEIRA RABAY, F.
DE OLIVEIRA SANCHES, F.
DE OLIVEIRA SILVA, O.
DE PAULA, C.
DE PAULA, M.
DE PAULA, P.
DE PAULA POSSO, I.
DE PAULA POSSO, R.
DE PAULA PRISCO CUNHA, V.
DE REZENDE, A.
DE SA RODRIGUES, C.
DE SÁ RODRIGUES TADEUCCI, M.
DE SANTIS TEIXEIRA, C.
DE SIQUEIRA, O.
DE SIQUEIRA RENDA, V.
DE SOUSA ALMEIDA, R.
DE SOUZA, L.
DE SOUZA, L.
DE SOUZA, M.
DE SOUZA, M.
DE SOUZA, P.
DE SOUZA E SILVA, R.
DE SOUZA QUIRINO, M.
DE SOUZA ROMERO, T.
DE SOUZA SOARES, A.
DE TOLEDO, J.
DE TOLEDO, M.
DE TOLEDO NETTO, A.
DE TOLEDO PIZA FILHO, P.
DE TOLEDO SOUZA, R.
DE VASCONCELLOS, R.
DEL'ARCO JUNIOR, A.
DELLU, M.
DESTRO, M.
DI ANGELIS COELHO, B.
DIAS, A.
DIAS COLOMBO, C.
DIAS RAPOSO FILHO, P.
DO AMARAL PEREIRA, W.
DO NASCIMENTO, A.
DO NASCIMENTO, J.
DO PATROCÍNIO, M.
DO PATROCÍNIO NUNES, L.
DO PRADO, P.
DO PRADO LÁUA, M.
DO REGO, M.
DOLORES ALVES COCCO, M.
DONIZETE GUINALZ, R.
DOS REIS, L.
DOS REIS ERVILHA, F.
DOS REIS PIMENTEL, M.
DOS SANTOS, A.
DOS SANTOS, A.
DOS SANTOS, C.
DOS SANTOS, I.
DOS SANTOS, J.
DOS SANTOS, M.
DOS SANTOS, R.
DOS SANTOS, S.

Dos Santos, S.
Dos Santos, S.
Dos Santos, T.
Dos Santos Araujo, A.
Dos Santos Filho, A.
Dos Santos Sá, M.
Dos Santos Targa, M.
Duarte Abdala, R.
E Santos, R.
E Silva, C.
Echeverria, S.
Effrin Pupio, C.
Elias Junior, M.
Ervilha, U.
Esper Berthoud, C.
Esteves, J.
Esteves Veiga, J.
Faria Neto, A.
Fazenda, A.
Fernandes Barbosa, W.
Fernandes Ferreira, J.
Fernandes Ruivo, G.
Fernandez, J.
Fernando Fisch, G.
Ferreira, F.
Ferreira, L.
Ferreira Nascimento, G.
Ferreira Santiago, M.
Ferreira Santos, A.
Ferreira Viagi, A.
Ferri-De-Barros, J.
Figueiredo Nejar, E.
Filho, N.
Filho, J.
Fiore Jr, M.
Fortes Neto, P.
Fortes Soares d'Azevedo, M.
Fortes Viegas, T.
Franca, H.
Freire, E.
Froio Toledo, M.
Galvão Villela Santos, F.
Galveias Lopes, P.
Garcia Lopes Rossi, M.
Gerasi Cabral, R.
Germano Bassi, D.
Gonçalves, A.
Gonçalves, J.
Gonçalves, J.
Gonçalves, M.
Gonçalves, T.
Gonçalves Cardoso, M.
Gonçalves Contreira, A.
Gonçalves Filho, J.
Gonçalves Franco, D.
Goulart, B.
Goulart, V.
Goulart Gouvea, L.
Gousain Murade, J.
Grandinetti, F.
Guidi Damasceno, A.
Guimarães Azevedo, A.
Guimarães Feliciano, G.
Guimarães Filho, R.
Guioto Abreu, W.
Habitante, S.
Hamzagic, M.
Henriques Luis, P.
Hidenori Enari, E.
Hiroshi Muragaki, W.
Inocente, N.
Israel, E.
Joao Bertoli, C.
Junqueira Barbosa, M.
Kajita, T.
Kalil Kobbaz, A.
Kassab, B.
Kather Neto, J.
Knupp Rodrigues, J.
Komatsu, M.
Labinas, A.
Leonel Galdino, M.
Letícia Alves, G.
Lima, A.
Lima Salgado, F.
Liporoni, P.

Lopes Bonato, L.
Lopes Silva, J.
Lorenzo Acácio, G.
Lourival Ferrazza, J.
Lucarevschi, B.
Lucchesi, M.
Luis Nohara, E.
Luiz Lousada, S.
Luiz Marioto, J.
Luiz Monteiro, R.
Mandelbaun, S.
Manfredini, C.
Marcelo, J.
Marchi, A.
Marchini, L.
Marcitelli, R.
Marcos Valadão, M.
Marques, R.
Martin, I.
Martins, N.
Martins Priante, A.
Mascarenhas Torres, M.
Mauricio, L.
Mazzeo Machado, L.
Medrano Balboa, R.
Melo, G.
Melo Viégas, R.
Mendes Faria, G.
Merli Lamosa, D.
Misailidis Lerena, M.
Monegatti Mattei, S.
Monteiro, R.
Monteiro Arrezze, B.
Monteiro Ilkiu, A.
Moreira, M.
Moreira, M.
Moreira Pinto, J.
Moreira Rosa, L.
Morelli, A.
Moura Lindegger, L.
Mourão, F.
Moure Cícero, C.
Muniz Jr, J.
Natalino Pereira, E.
Naves Silva, T.
Nery Conde Malta, F.
Neto, J.
Nogueira Assad, M.
Nogueira Rezende, P.
Nordi, J.
Okamoto, T.
Osvaldo Cimaschi Neto, E.
Paiva Vianna, L.
Pallos, D.
Panza, E.
Paranhos Gomes Dos Santos, E.
Parquet Bizarria, F.
Parquet Bizarria, J.
Paskewicks, V.
Pastoukhov, V.
Pedro Peres, M.
Pelegrine Guimarães, D.
Pena Matos, A.
Pereira, S.
Pereira, T.
Pereira Cintra, S.
Pereira Iemini, M.
Pereira Leão, M.
Pereira Leite, M.
Perondi Fortes, N.
Pescatore Alves, C.
Pimentel, E.
Pinheiro Werneck, M.
Pinto, C.
Pinto, R.
Pires Clemente, R.
Pirtouscheg, N.
Prado Scherma, A.
Prata Rocha, R.
Prati, A.
Prolungatti Cesar, M.
Púpio Marcondes, M.
Querido, A.
Querido Guisard, R.
Ramos Analio, R.
Ramos Mota, J.

Regina Namura, M.
Rembrandt Gutlich, G.
Reschilian, P.
Rezende, M.
Ribeiro Lara, L.
Ribeiro Peão, G.
Ribeiro Quintairos, P.
Rizzardi Mazzini, X.
Roberto Furlan, M.
Roberto Martins, M.
Rocha, R.
Rocha Jr, A.
Rodrigues, A.
Rodrigues, D.
Rodrigues, E.
Rodrigues Fernandes, T.
Rodrigues Pelogia, A.
Rodrigues Teixeira, F.
Rossi, R.
Ruggeri, C.
Ruv Lemes, M.
Saba, E.
Salim Minhoto, E.
Salles Cauduro, R.
Salvio Carrijo, D.
Sartori, A.
Sashaki, S.
Sebe Tonzar, E.
Serafim, A.
Serafini, F.
Silva Artusi, M.
Silva Lage Marques, J.
Silva Medeiros, H.
Simões Araujo, E.
Soares, R.
Souza Lopes E Silva, A.
Sree Vani, G.
Steinle Camargo, L.
Stellati, C.
Stevanato, E.
Tadeu Iaochite, R.
Tápias Oliveira, E.
Teixeira, M.
Teixeira Batista, G.
Teixeira Branco Costa, M.
Teixeira Brazão, C.
Teixeira Soares, M.
Tonini, A.
Tubaldini Souza, M.
Tuffi, G.
Ueno, M.
Urruchi, W.
Vasconcelos, M.
Velloso, V.
Veneziani Pasin, L.
Vianna Brito, E.
Vieira, C.
Vieira Basili, M.
Vieira Fisch, S.
Villela Chagas, R.
Voltolini, J.
Wanderley Terni, A.
Wellausen Dias, N.
Yoko Uyeno, E.
Zeraik Armani, M.
Zöllner, N.

ATTACHED RESEARCH INSTITUTES

Basic Institute of Biosciences: tel. (12) 3629-7909; Dir Profa Dra Ana Júlia Urias dos Santos Araújo.

Basic Institute of Exact Sciences: tel. (12) 3629-3804; Dir Eurico Arruda Filho.

Basic Institute of Human Sciences: tel. (12) 3622-2474; Dir Maurílio José de Oliveira Camello.

UNIVERSIDADE DE UBERABA

Av. Nenê Sabino 1801, Bairro Universitário, 38055-500 Uberaba, MG

Telephone: (34) 3319-8852
E-mail: divulgacao@uniube.br
Internet: www.uniube.br

Founded 1947 as Faculdade de Odontologia do Triângulo Mineiro; present name 1988

Rector: MARCELO PALMÉRIO

Pro-Rector for Higher Education: Profa INARA BARBOSA PENA ELIAS

Pro-Rector for Research, Postgraduates and Extension: Prof. Dr JOSÉ BENTO ALVES.

UNIVERSIDADE DO BRASIL

Av. Brig. Trompowski s/n, Cidade Universitária, Ilha do Fundão, CP 68536, 21949-900 Rio de Janeiro, RJ

Telephone: (21) 290-2112

Fax: (21) 260-7750

E-mail: reitoria@reitoria.ufrj.br

Internet: www.ufrj.br

Founded 1920 as Univ. do Rio de Janeiro; became Univ. do Brasil 1937 and Univ. Fed. do Rio de Janeiro 1965; reverted to present name 2000

State control

Rector: Prof. PAULO ALCÂNTARA GOMES

Vice-Rector: Prof. JOSÉ HENRIQUE VILHENA DE PAIVA

Sec.-Gen.: Dr IVAN RODRIGUES DA SILVA

Dir of Central Library: MARIZA RUSSO

Library: 42 faculty libraries

Number of teachers: 3,580

Number of students: 40,000

Publications: *Anais, Boletim*

DIRECTORS OF CENTRES

Forum for Science and Culture: Profa MYRIAN DAVELSBERG

Health Sciences Centre: Profa VERA LUCIA RABELO DE CASTRO HALFOUN

Law and Economic Sciences Centre: Prof. CARLOS LESSA

Literature and Arts Centre: Prof. CARLOS ANTONIO KALIL TANNUS

Mathematics and Natural Sciences Centre: Prof. MARCO ANTONIO FRANÇA FARIA

Philosophy and Humanities Centre: Prof. CARLOS ALBERTO MESSEDER PEREIRA

Technology Centre: Prof. OSCAR ACSELRAD

DEANS AND DIRECTORS OF FACULTIES, SCHOOLS AND INSTITUTES

Health Sciences Centre:

Clementino Fraga Filho University Hospital: Prof. AMANCIO PAULINO

Community Health Study Centre: Profa DIANA MAUL DE CARVALHO

Faculty of Dentistry: Prof. NÉLIO VICTOR DE OLIVEIRA

Faculty of Medicine: Profa SYLVIA DA SILVEIRA DE MELLO VARGAS

Faculty of Pharmacy: Prof. JOSÉ CARLOS DA SILVA LIMA

Institute of Biological and Health Sciences: Prof. ANIBAL GIL LOPES

Institute of Biology: Prof. SERGIO LUIS COSTA BONECKER

Institute of Biomedical Sciences: Prof. ANÍBAL GIL LOPES

Institute of Biophysics: Prof. ANTONIO CARLOS CAMPOS DE CARVALHO

Institute of Child Care and Education: Prof. LUÍS AFONSO HENRIQUE MARIZ

Institute of Gynaecology: Prof. PASCHOAL MARTINI SIMÕES

Institute of Microbiology: Prof. SÉRGIO EDUARDO LONGO FRANCALANZZA

Institute of Natural Product Research: Prof. ANTONIO JORGE RIBEIRO DA SILVA

Institute of Neurology: Prof. GIANNI MAURELIO TEMPONI

Institute of Nutrition: Profa REJANE ANDRÉA RAMALHO NUNES DA SILVA

Institute of Psychiatry: Prof. JOÃO FERREIRA DA SILVA FILHO

Institute of Thoracic Diseases: Prof. ALFREDO RISSON PEYNEAU

Maternity School Hospital: Prof. JOFFRE AMIM JUNIOR

São Francisco de Assis School Hospital: Profa SONIA REGINA CARVALHAL GOMES

School of Nursing: Profa IVONE EVANGELISTA CABRAL

School of Physical Education and Sport: Prof. JOSÉ MAURICIO CAPINASSO

Technology Education Institute for Health: Profa ELIANA CLÁUDIA DE OTERO RIBEIRO

Law and Economic Sciences Centre:

Faculty of Business Administration and Accounting: Prof. CARLOS ALBERTO BESSA

Faculty of Law: Prof. AYRTON DA COSTA PAIVA

Graduate School of Business Administration: Prof. AGRÍCOLA DE SOUZA BETHLEM

Institute of Economics: Prof. JOÃO CARLOS FERRAZ

Institute of Research, Regional and Town Planning: Prof. HERMES MAGALHÃES TAVARES

Literature and Arts Centre:

Faculty of Architecture and Town Planning: Profa MARIA ANGELA DIAS ELIAS

Faculty of Literature: Prof. EDIONE TRINDADE DE AZEVEDO

School of Fine Arts: Prof. VICTORINO DE OLIVEIRA NETO

School of Music: Prof. JOSÉ ALVES DA SILVA (Dir)

Mathematics and Natural Sciences Centre:

Computer Science Centre: Prof. EDUARDO PAES

Institute of Chemistry: Prof. ROBERTO MARCHIORI

Institute of Geosciences: Prof. JORGE SOARES MARQUES

Institute of Mathematics: Prof. LUIS PAULO VIEIRA BRAGA

Institute of Physics: Prof. CARLOS ALBERTO ARAGÃO DE CARVALHO FILHO

Valongo Observatory: Profa HELOÍSA MARIA BOECHAT ROBERTY

Philosophy and Humanities Centre:

Faculty of Education: Profa MARLENE DE CARVALHO

Institute of Philosophy and Social Sciences: Profa NEYDE THEML

Institute of Psychology: Profa MARIA INÁCIA D'ÁVILLA NETTO

School of Communications: Prof. ANDRE DE SOUZA PARENTE

School of Social Services: Profa MARIA DURVALINA FERNANDES BASTOS

School of Teacher Training: Prof. MOACYR BARRETO DA SILVA JUNIOR

Technology Centre:

Coordination of Graduate Programmes in Engineering: Prof. SEGEN FARID ESTEFEN

Institute of Macromolecules: Prof. AÍLTON DE SOUZA GOMES

School of Chemistry: Prof. CARLOS AUGUSTO GUIMARÃES PERLINGEIRO

School of Engineering: Prof. HELOI JOSÉ FERNANDES MOURA

UNIVERSIDADE DO CONTESTADO

Rua Itororó 800, 89500-000 Caçador, SC

Telephone: (49) 561-2600

Fax: (49) 561-2600

E-mail: reitoria@unc.br

Internet: www.unc.br

Founded 1990

State control

Rector: WERNER JOSÉ BERTOLDI

Library of 51,400 vols

Number of teachers: 305

Number of students: 5,549

UNIVERSIDADE DO ESTADO DE SANTA CATARINA

Campus Universitário, Av. Madre Benvenuta 2007, CP D-34, Itacorubi, 88035-001 Florianópolis, SC

Telephone: (48) 332-18039

Fax: (48) 332-18001

E-mail: ccii@udesc.br

Internet: www.udesc.br

Founded 1965

State control

Language of instruction: Portuguese

Academic year: March to December

Rector: SEBASTIÃO IBERES LOPES MELO

Chief Academic Officer: SANDRA MAKOWIECKY

Chief Admin. Officer: VINÍCIUS ALEXANDRE PERUCCI

Librarian: LÚCIA MARENGO

Library of 77,930 vols

Number of teachers: 695

Number of students: 12,528

Publication: *Revista da UDESC*

DIRECTORS

Business School: RUBENS DE ARAÚJO

Distance Learning Centre: SONIA MELLO

Faculty of Education: JARBAS JOSÉ CARDOSO

Faculty of Engineering (Joinville): GERSON VOLNEY LAGEMANN

Faculty of Nursing, Nutritional Studies and Zootechnics: ANTÔNIO WALDIMIR LEOPOLDINO DA SILVA

School of Accounting, Information Systems and Sanitary Engineering: JOSÉ CARLOS DE SOUZA

School of Agronomics and Veterinary Medicine: ADIL KNAKFUSS VAZ

School of Architecture and Urbanism Design and Engineering of Fish: JOÃO ROTTA FILHO

School of Fine Arts: ANTÔNIO VARGAS

School of Information Systems and Industrial Mechanical Eng: PIO CAMPOS FILHO

School of Petroleum Engineering: MARIA ESTER MENEGASSO

School of Physical Education: ALEXANDRO ANDRADE

UNIVERSIDADE DO ESTADO DO RIO DE JANEIRO

Rua São Francisco Xavier 524, Maracanã, 20550-900 Rio de Janeiro, RJ

Telephone: (21) 2587-7720

Fax: (21) 2569-4852

E-mail: reitoria@uerj.br

Internet: www.uerj.br

Founded 1950

State control

Language of instruction: Portuguese

Academic year: March to December 2 semesters)

Chancellor: MARCELLO ALENCAR

Rector: RICARDO VIEIRALVES DE CASTRO

Vice-Rector: MARIA CHRISTINA PAIXÃO MAIOLI

Pro-Rector for Extension and Culture: REGINA LÚCIA MONTEIRO HENRIQUES

Pro-Rector for Postgraduate Affairs and Research: MONICA DA COSTA PEREIRA LAVALLE HEILBRON

Pro-Rector for Undergraduate Affairs: LENÁ MEDEIROS DE MENEZES

Librarian: SILVIA MARIA GAGO DA COSTA

Number of teachers: 2,005

Number of students: 17,615

Publications: *Cadernos de Antropologia da Imagem, Em Pauta, Espaço e Cultura, Geo UERJ, Logos, Matraga, Qfwfq, Revista de Enfermagem da UERJ, Revista do Centro de Estudos da Faculdade de Odontologia da UERJ* (2 a year)

SENIOR DIRECTORS

Biomedical Centre: Prof. ELLEN MARCIA PERES

Education and Humanities Centre: Prof. JOSÉ RICARDO DA SILVA ROSA

Faculty of Social Communication: Prof. RICARDO FERREIRA FREITAS

Fernando Rodrigues da Silveira Training College: Profa MARICÉLIA BISPO

Higher School of Industrial Design: Prof. FRANK ANTHONY BARRAL DODD

Social Science Centre: Prof. JOSÉ FLAVIO PESSOA DE BARROS

Technology and Science Centre: Prof. MAURÍCIO JOSÉ FERRARI REY

DEANS

Biomedical Centre:

Faculty of Dentistry: Prof. MILTON SANTOS JABUR

Faculty of Medicine: Prof. JOSÉ AUGUSTO FERNANDES QUADRA

Faculty of Nursing: Profa VERA RODRIGUES OLIVEIRA ANDRADE

Institute of Biology: Prof. ELIZEU FAGUNDES DE CARVALHO

Institute of Nutrition: Profa MARCIA VERONICA DE S. V. BELLA

Institute of Social Medicine: Prof. RICARDO TAVARES

Education and Humanities Centre:

Faculty of Education: Prof. ISAC JOÃO DE VASCONCELLOS

Institute of Letters: Prof. CLAUDIO CEZAR HENRIQUES

Institute of Physical Education and Sport: JOÃO GONZAGA DE OLIVEIRA

Institute of Psychology: Prof. SOLANGE DE OLIVEIRA SOUTO

Social Science Centre:

Faculty of Administration and Finance: Prof. DOMÊNICO MANDARINO

Faculty of Economics: Prof. RALPH MIGUEL ZERKOUVISKY

Faculty of Law: Prof. ANTONIO CELSO ALVES PEREIRA

Faculty of Social Service: Profa ROSANGELA NAIR DE C. BARBOSA

Institute of Philosophy and Human Sciences: Prof. LUIZ EDMUNDO TAVARES

Technology and Science Centre:

Faculty of Engineering: Prof. NIVAL NUNES DE ALMEIDA

Faculty of Geology: Prof. RUI ALBERTO AZEVEDO DOS SANTOS

Faculty of Physics: Prof. JADER BERNUZZI MARTINS

Institute of Chemistry: Prof. ILTON JORNADA

Institute of Geosciences: Profa ANA LÚCIA TRAVASSOS ROMANO

Institute of Mathematics and Statistics: Profa MARINILZA BRUNO DE CARVALHO

UNIVERSIDADE DO ESTADO DO RIO GRANDE DO NORTE

Rua Almino Afonso 478, Centro, 59610-210 Mossoró, RN

Telephone: (84) 3315-2145
Fax: (84) 3315-2770
E-mail: reitoria@uern.br
Internet: www.uern.br

Founded 1968
State control

Rector: Prof. MILTON MARQUES DE MEDEIROS
Chief Admin. Officer: Profa IÊDA MARIA ARAÚJO CHAVES FREITAS
Librarian: ELVIRA FERNANDES DE ARAÚJO

Number of teachers: 400
Number of students: 5,300

Publications: *Contexto* (2 a year), *Expressão* (2 a year), *Terra e Sal* (2 a year)

DEANS

Faculty of Arts: Prof. GILBERTO DE OLIVEIRA SILVA

Faculty of Economic Science: Profa ELIZABETH SILVA VEIGA

Faculty of Education: Profa MARIA DAS DORES LOPES DE PAIVA

Faculty of Law: Profa MARIA HÉLDERI QUEIRÓZ DIÓGENES NEGREIROS

Faculty of Natural and Physical Science: Prof. FRANCISCO VALDOMIRO DE MORAIS

Faculty of Nursing: Profa MARIA DAS GRAÇAS ALVES DE LIMA

Faculty of Philosophy and Social Science: Prof. WILSON BEZERRA DE MOURA

Faculty of Physical Education: Prof. ANTÔNIO DE PÁDUA LOPEZ ALVES

Faculty of Social Service: Profa ZÉLIA MARIA RODRIGUES M. VASCONCELAS

UNIVERSIDADE DO GRANDE RIO

Rua Prof. José de Souza Herdy 1160, Bairro 25 de Agosto, 25071-202 Duque de Caxias, RJ

Telephone: (21) 2672-7777
Fax: (21) 671-4248
E-mail: reitoria@unigranrio.com.br
Internet: www.unigranrio.br

Founded 1994
Private control
Academic year: January to December

Rector: ARODY CORDEIRO HERDY
Pro-Rector for Community and Extension: Profa Dra SONIA REGINA MENDES
Pro-Rector for Postgraduate Affairs and Research: Prof. Dr PROTASIO FERREIRA E CASTRO

Library of 110,535 vols
Number of teachers: 550
Number of students: 10,457

Publications: *Cadernos de Contabilidade e Economia* (2 a year), *Cadernos de Direito* (2 a year), *Cadernos de Educação* (2 a year), *Cadernos de Gestão* (2 a year), *Cadernos de Meio Ambiente* (2 a year), *Cadernos de Odontologia* (2 a year), *Caderno Técnico—Científico da Escola de Medicina Veterinária* (2 a year), *Paidéia: Revista do Instituto de Humanidades* (2 a year).

UNIVERSIDADE DO OESTE DE SANTA CATARINA

Rua Jaime Martins Alves 196, Bairro Flor de Serra, 89600-000, Joaçaba, SC

Telephone: (49) 551-2098
Fax: (49) 551-2100
E-mail: reitor@unoesc.edu.br
Internet: www.unoesc.edu.br

Founded 1968
State control

Rector: ARISTIDES CIMADON

Library of 180,099 vols, 21,633 periodicals
Number of teachers: 766
Number of students: 13,645

UNIVERSIDADE DO OESTE PAULISTA

Rua José Bongiovani 700, 19050-920 Presidente Prudente, SP

Telephone: (18) 3229-1000
Fax: (18) 3229-0200
Internet: www.unoeste.br

Founded 1972
Private control

Rector: ANA CARDOSO MAIA DE OLIVEIRA LIMA
Vice-Rector: ANA CRISTINA DE OLIVEIRA LIMA

Library of 74,000 vols, 43,000 periodicals
Number of teachers: 614
Number of students: 13,744

UNIVERSIDADE DO SAGRADO CORAÇÃO

Rua Irmã Arminda 10–50, 17011-160 Bauru, SP

Telephone: (14) 3235-7000
Fax: (14) 3235-7325
E-mail: reitoria@usc.br
Internet: www.usc.br

Founded 1953
Academic year: February to November
Private control

Rector: Dra Sister JACINTA TUROLO GARCIA
Vice-Rector: Sister ILDA BASSO
Pro-Rector for Academic Affairs: REGINA CÉLIA BELLUZZO
Univ. Sec.: GESIANE MONTEIRO FOLKIS
Librarian: MÔNICA VALÉRIA P. LOSNAK

Library of 110,000 vols
Number of teachers: 353
Number of students: 6,000

Publications: *Boletim Cultural* (cultural studies, 1 a year), *Cadernos de Divulgação Cultural* (Master's theses and doctoral dissertations, 1 a year), *Revista Camoniana* (Portuguese literature studies), *Revista Mimesis* (liberal studies, 2 a year), *Revista Salusvita* (science and health, in Portuguese and English)

DEANS

College of Business Administration: Ir GENI DA SILVA

College of Liberal Arts: Ir EVANIRA DE SOUZA

College of Sciences: Ir MARISABEL LEITE

College of Social Sciences: VALDEIR R. VIDRIK

Committee on Ethics: Dr NILTON AQUILES VON ZUBEN

Lato Sensu Courses: Dr SONIA SEVILHA MARTINS

Research: Dr SÉRGIO AUGUSTO CATANZARO GUIMARÃES

Scientific Initiation Projects: Dr SÉRGIO AUGUSTO CATANZARO GUIMARÃES

UNIVERSIDADE DO SUL DE SANTA CATARINA

Av. José Acácio Moreira 787, Bairro Dehon, 88704-900 Tubarão, SC

Telephone: (48) 621-3000
Fax: (48) 621-3036
E-mail: unisul@unisul.br
Internet: www.unisul.br

Founded 1967
Municipal control
Academic year: March to November

Rector: GERSON LUIZ JONER DA SILVA
Vice-Rector: SEBASTIÃO SALÉSIO HERDT

Library of 161,346 vols
Number of teachers: 1,641
Number of students: 23,113

Publication: *Jornal* (10 a year).

UNIVERSIDADE DO VALE DO ITAJAÍ

Rua Uruguai 458, Centro, CP 360, 88302-202 Itajaí, SC

Telephone: (47) 3341-7500
Fax: (47) 3341-7577
E-mail: reitoria@univali.rsc-sc.br
Internet: www.univali.br

Founded 1970
Municipal control

Rector: Dr JOSÉ ROBERTO PROVESI
Vice-Rector: Dr MÁRIO CESAR DOS SANTOS
Int. Affairs Office Coordinator: Prof. Dr J. M. LUNA

Library of 103,000 vols, 18,000 periodicals
Number of teachers: 1,180
Number of students: 26,100
Publications: *Alcance* (4 a year), *Novos Estudos Jurídicos* (2 a year), *Turismo e Ação* (2 a year).

UNIVERSIDADE DO VALE DO PARAÍBA

Av. Shishima Hifumi 2911, Urbanova, 12244-000 São José dos Campos, SP
Telephone: (12) 3947-1000
Internet: www.univap.br
Founded 1992
Private control
Rector: Prof. Dr BAPTISTA GARGIONE FILHO
Library of 59,000 vols, 539 periodicals
Number of teachers: 269
Number of students: 6,255

UNIVERSIDADE DO VALE DO RIO DOS SINOS

Av. Unisinos 950, CP 275, 93022-000 São Leopoldo, RS
Telephone: (51) 590-8237
Fax: (51) 590-8443
E-mail: unisinos@unisinos.br
Internet: www.unisinos.br
Founded 1969
Private control (Society of Jesus)
Language of instruction: Portuguese
Academic year: February to December
Pres.: Prof. Dr ALOYSIO BOHNEN
Vice-Pres.: Prof. Dr MARCELO FERNANDES DE AQUINO
Dean for Academic Affairs: PEDRO GILBERTO GOMES
Dean for Research and Devt: Prof. LUDGER TEODORO HERZOG
Registrar: EUSÉBIO SCHNEIDER
Library Dir: Dr LODOMILO AUGUSTO MALLMANN
Library of 721,098 vols
Number of teachers: 915
Number of students: 28,051
Publications: *Acta Biologica Leopoldensia* (3 a year), *Acta Geologica Leopoldensia* (2 a year), *Arquitetura revista* (2 a year), *AV: Audio Visual* (2 a year), *Base: revista de Administração e Contabilidade da Unisinos* (3 a year), *Calidoscópio* (3 a year), *Ciências Sociais Unisinos* (3 a year), *Controvérsia* (2 a year), *Cooperativismo* (2 a year), *Educação Unisinos* (3 a year), *Entrelinhas* (3 a year), *Estudos Jurídicos* (3 a year), *Estudos Tecnológicos* (2 a year), *Filosofia UNISINOS* (3 a year), *Fronteiras* (media studies, 3 a year), *História Unisinos* (3 a year), *IHU OnLine* (52 a year), *Jornal UNISINOS* (4 a year), *Perspectiva Econômica* (online, 2 a year), *Scientia* (2 a year), *Verso & Reverso* (3 a year)

DEANS

Communication Sciences: Profa IONE MARIA GHISLENE BENTZ
Economics: Prof. TIAGO WICKSTROM ALVES
Exact and Technological Sciences: Profa SILVIA COSTA DUTRA
Health Sciences: Prof. CORNÉLIA HULDA VOLKART
Human Sciences: Prof. JOSÉ IVO FOLLMANN
Law: Prof. IELBO MARCUS LÔBO DE SOUZA

UNIVERSIDADE ESTÁCIO DE SÁ

Rua do Bispo 83, Rio Comprido, 20261-063 Rio de Janeiro, RJ
Telephone: (21) 3231-0000
Fax: (21) 293-4539
Internet: www.estacio.br

Founded 1988
Private control
Rector: ANTONIO CESAR DA SILVA CALDAS FREIRE
Library of 46,000 vols, 710 periodicals
Number of teachers: 634
Number of students: 17,416

UNIVERSIDADE ESTADUAL DA PARAÍBA

Av. das Baraúnas 351, Campus Universitário, Bodocongó, 58109-753 Campina Grande, PB
Telephone: (83) 3315-3300
Fax: (83) 3315-3300
Internet: www.uepb.edu.br
Founded 1966
Municipal control
Language of instruction: Portuguese
Academic year: March to December
Rector: MARLENE ALVES SOUSA LUNA
Vice-Rector: Prof. ALDO BEZERRA MACIEL
Gen. Sec.: CLEÓMENES LOIOLA CAMINHA
Librarian: IVONETE ALMEIDA GALDINO
Library of 65,000 vols
Number of teachers: 650
Number of students: 10,000
Publications: *Catálogo Geral* (1 a year), *Informativo UEPB*, *Roteiro*

DIRECTORS

Agricultural College 'Assis Chateaubriand': JOSÉ PAULO DE AMORIM FARIAZ
Faculty of Administration and Accounting: FRANCISCO LUIZ DE OLIVEIRA
Faculty of Education, Letters and Social Sciences: ZÉLIA MARIA PEREIRA FERNANDES
Faculty of Law: HARRISON ALEXANDRE TARGINO
Faculty of Nursing: JOSEFA JOSETE DA SILVA SANTOS
Faculty of Odontology: CARLTON FERREIRA NÓBREGA
Faculty of Pharmacy and Biology: LUIZA MARIA BARRETO DA SILVEIRA
Faculty of Philosophy, Sciences and Letters: TANIA PORPINO MARINHO DO NASCIMENTO
Faculty of Physical Education: SIDELENE GONSAGA DE MELO
Faculty of Physiotherapy: LÍDIA MARIA ALBUQUERQUE MARQUES
Faculty of Psychology: GUTEMBERG GERMANO BARBOSA
Faculty of Sciences and Technology: GIVANILDO GONÇALVES DE FARIAS
Faculty of Social Communication: SIMÃO ARRUDA
Faculty of Social Work: MARIA JOSÉ DA COSTA SILVA
School of Agricultural Engineering, Catolé do Rocha: PEDRO FERREIRA NETO

UNIVERSIDADE ESTADUAL DE CAMPINAS

Cidade Universitária 'Zeferino Vaz', 13083-970 Campinas, SP
Telephone: (19) 3788-4720
Fax: (19) 3788-4789
E-mail: gabinete@rei.unicamp.br
Internet: www.unicamp.br
Founded 1966
State control
Academic year: March to December
Rector: Prof. Dr CARLOS HENRIQUE DE BRITO CRUZ
Vice-Rector: Prof. Dr JOSÉ TADEU JORGE
Dean for Extension and Community Matters: Prof. Dr RUBENS MACIEL FILHO
Dean for Graduate Studies: Prof. Dr DANIEL HOGAN

Dean for Research: Prof. Dr FERNANDO FERREIRA COSTA
Dean for Undergraduate Studies: Prof. Dr JOSÉ LUIZ BOLDRINI
Dean for Univ. Devt: Prof. Dr PAULO EDUARDO M. RODRIGUES DA SILVA
Sec.-Gen.: RENATO ATÍLIO JORGE
Librarian: (vacant)
Number of teachers: 1,800
Number of students: 28,000
Publication: *Jornal da Unicamp* (12 a year)

DIRECTORS

Computer Centre: Prof. Dr LUIZ EDUARDO BUZATO
'Gleb Wataghin' Institute of Physics: Prof. Dr DANIEL PEREIRA
Institute of Biology: Prof. Dr MOHAMED HABIB
Institute of Chemistry: Prof. Dr FRANCISCO DE ASSIS MACHADO REIS
Institute of Computer Science: Prof. Dr RICARDO DE OLIVEIRA ANIDO
Institute of Economics: Prof. Dr MARCIO PERCIVAL ALVES PINTO
Institute of Fine Arts: Prof. Dr JOSÉ ROBERTO ZAN
Institute of Geosciences: Prof. Dr ARCHIMEDES PERES FILHO
Institute of Language Studies: Profa Dra CHARLOTTE MARIE CHAMBERLAND GALVES
Institute of Mathematics, Statistics and Computer Science: Prof. Dr JOÃO FREDERICO DA COSTA AZEVEDO MEYER
Institute of Philosophy and Humanities: Prof. Dr RUBEM MURILO LEÃO RÊGO
School of Agricultural Engineering: Prof. Dr ROBERTO TESTEZLAF
School of Chemical Engineering: Prof. Dr MILTON MORI
School of Civil Engineering: Prof. Dr JOÃO ALBERTO VENEGAS REQUENA
School of Dentistry: Prof. Dr THALES ROCHA DE MATTOS FILHO
School of Education: Prof. Dr JORGE MEGID NETO
School of Electrical Engineering: Prof. Dr LÉO PINI MAGALHÃES
School of Food Engineering: Prof. Dr CARLOS ANJOS
School of Mechanical Engineering: Prof. Dr KAMAL ABDEL RADI ISMAIL
School of Medical Sciences: Profa Dra LILIAN TEREZA LAVRAS COSTALLAT
School of Physical Education: Prof. Dr ROBERTO RODRIGUES PAES
Technology Centre: Prof. Dr CLÁUDIO BIANOR SVERZUT

UNIVERSIDADE ESTADUAL DE FEIRA DE SANTANA

Av. Transnordestina s/n, Novo Horizonte, 44036-900 Feira de Santana, BA
Telephone: (75) 3224-8000
Fax: (75) 3224-8001
E-mail: reitor@uefs.br
Internet: www.uefs.br
Founded 1976
State control
Language of instruction: Portuguese
Academic year: March to December
Rector: ANACI BISPO PAIM
Vice-Rector: JOAQUIM PONDÉ FILHO
Academic Pro-Rector: ANACI BISPO PAIM
Admin. Pro-Rector: EUTÍMIO DE OLIVEIRA ALMEIDA
Academic Dir: ANTÔNIO RAIMUNDO BASTOS MELO
Admin. Dir: ROBERTO GOMES DA SILVA NETO
Financial Dir: GILDINCE LIMA FERREIRA
Dir of Student Affairs: ANTONIO ROBERTO SEIXAS DA CRUZ
Librarian: VERA VILENE FERREIRA NUNES
Library of 72,700 vols

Number of teachers: 508
Number of students: 4,253
Publications: *Intercampus, Sitientibus* (2 a year).

UNIVERSIDADE ESTADUAL DE LONDRINA

CP 6001, Campus Universitário, 86055-900 Londrina, PR
Telephone: (43) 371-4000
Fax: (43) 328-4440
E-mail: webadmin@uel.br
Internet: www.uel.br
Founded 1971
Language of instruction: Portuguese
Academic year: February to December
Rector: Profa LYGIA LUMINA PUPATTO
Vice-Rector: EDUARDO DI MAURO
Sec.-Gen.: Profa ANGELA MARIA VEREGUE
Librarian: Profa VILMA APARECIDA GIMENEZ DA CRUZ
Library of 143,756 vols, 5,360 periodicals, 6,442 vols of pamphlets
Number of teachers: 1,643
Number of students: 16,582
Publications: *Biosaúde* (2 a year), *Boletim do CCH* (2 a year), *Boletim Informativo da Biblioteca Central* (12 a year), *Cadernos Difusão* (2 a year), *Crítica—Revista de Filosofia* (4 a year), *Diálogo* (1 a year), *Entretextos* (1 a year), *Informação e Informação* (2 a year), *Olho Mágico* (3 a year), *Paradigmas—Revista de Filosofia Brasileira* (2 a year), *PSI—Revista de Psicologia Social e Institucional* (2 a year), *Revista do Depto de Geociências* (2 a year), *Revista Medicações* (2 a year), *Scientia Iuris* (1 a year), *Semina* (4 a year), *Serviço Social em Revista* (2 a year), *Signum: Estudos da Linguagem* (2 a year), *Signum: Estudos Literarios* (2 a year), *Temática: Estudos de Administração* (2 a year), *Todavia* (1 a year), *Torre de Babel—Reflexões e Pesquisas em Psicologia* (2 a year)

DEANS

Centre of Agrarian Sciences: Prof. ERNST ECKEHARDT MÜLLER
Centre of Applied Social Studies: Prof. MAURO ONIVALDO TICIANELLI
Centre of Biological Sciences: Prof. LUIZ CARLOS BRUSCHI
Centre of Education, Communication and Arts: Profa NÁDINA APARECIDA MORENO
Centre of Exact Sciences: Prof. MARCOS DE CASTRO FALLEIROS
Centre of Health Sciences: Prof. PEDRO ALEJANDRO GORDAN
Centre of Letters and Human Sciences: Profa ESTHER GOMES DE OLIVEIRA
Centre of Physical Education: Profa MARIVAL ANTÔNIO MAZZIO
Centre of Technology and Urbanism: Prof. ANTONIO CARLOS ZANI

UNIVERSIDADE ESTADUAL DE MARINGA

Av. Colombo 5790, Jd. Universitário, 87020-900 Maringá, PR
Telephone: (44) 3261-4040
Fax: (44) 3263-4487
E-mail: fadec@wnet.com.br
Internet: www.uem.br
Founded 1970
Academic year: March to December
Rector: Prof. Dr DÉCIO SPERANDIO
Vice-Rector: Prof. Dr MÁRIO LUIZ NEVES DE AZEVEDO
Pro-Rector for Admin.: Prof. Ms. MARCELO SONCINI RODRIGUES
Pro-Rector for Extension and Culture: Profa Dra WÂNIA REZENDE SILVA

Pro-Rector for Human Resources and Community Affairs: Profa Dra NEUSA ALTOÉ
Pro-Rector for Research and Postgraduate Affairs: Prof. Dr NILSON EVELÁZIO DE SOUZA
Pro-Rector for Teaching: Profa Dra EDNÉIA REGINA ROSSI
Librarian: ANA MARIA MARQUEZINI ALVARENGA
Number of teachers: 1,287
Number of students: 9,804
Publications: *A Economia em Revista, Boletim de Geografia, Caderno da Semana de Geografia, Cadernos de Administração, Caderno de METEP, Jornal Alfabetizando, Revista Apontamentos, Revista de Educação Física, Revista de Psicologia, Revista Diálogos, Revista Enfoque-Reflexão Contábil, Revista Tecnológica, Unimar, Unimar Jurídica, Universidade e Sociedade*

DIRECTORS

Agricultural Sciences Centre: GERALDO TADEU DOS SANTOS
Applied Psychology Centre: MARIA JOSÉ SARAIVA RIBEIRO
Biological Sciences Centre: SANDRA REGINA STÁBILLE
Centre for the Integration of Children and Adolescents: CLEUZA LUCENA
Data Processing Centre: DILVO PAUPITZ
Exact Sciences Centre: LUIZ ROBERTO EVANGELISTA
Health Sciences Centre: MARIA JOSÉ SCOCHI
Humanities and Arts Centre: ROMILDA MARINS CORREA
Languages Institute: CRISTINA MORAES
Socio-Economic Studies Centre: JOSÉ ROBERTO PINHEIRO DE MELO
Technology Centre: MAURO ANTONIO DA SILVA SÁ RAVAGNANI

UNIVERSIDADE ESTADUAL DE MONTES CLAROS

CP 126, 39401-089 Montes Claros, MG
Campus Universitário Prof. Darcy Ribeiro, Vila Mauricéia, 39401-089 Montes Claros, MG
Telephone: (38) 3229-8000
Fax: (38) 3229-8002
E-mail: reitoria@unimontes.br
Internet: www.unimontes.br
Founded 1962
State control
Rector: Prof. PAULO CÉSAR GONÇALVES DE ALMEIDA
Vice-Rector: Prof. JOÃO DOS REIS CANELA
Gen. Sec.: Cont. MARIA JOSÉ VIEIRA ROCHA
Library of 46,000 vols, 2,609 periodicals
Number of teachers: 368
Number of students: 4,667

UNIVERSIDADE ESTADUAL DE PONTA GROSSA

Av. Carlos Cavalcanti 4748, Campus de Uvaranas, 84030-900 Ponta Grossa, PR
Telephone: (42) 220-3232
Fax: (42) 220-3233
E-mail: uepg@uepg.br
Internet: www.uepg.br
Founded 1970
Academic year: March to November
Rector: PAULO ROBERTO GODOY
Vice-Rector: ÍTALO SÉRGIO GRANDE
Pro-Rector for Admin. Affairs: CARLOS LUCIANO SANT'ANA VARGAS
Pro-Rector for Extension and Cultural Affairs: CARLOS ROBERTO BERGER
Pro-Rector for Research and Graduates: ALTAIR JUSTINO
Pro-Rector for Undergraduates: CÂNDIDA LEONOR MIRANDA

Librarian: MARIA LUIZA FERNANDES BERTHOLINO
Number of teachers: 721
Number of students: 11,408
Publications: *Biological Sciences and Health Review* (4 a year), *Exact and Earth Sciences, Agriculture and Engineering Sciences Review* (3 a year), *General Catalogue* (1 a year), *Human Sciences, Applied Social Sciences, Linguistics, Letters and Art Review* (2 a year), *Regional History Review* (2 a year), *Social Emancipation Review* (1 a year), *Teacher Eyes Review* (1 a year), *Uniletras Review* (1 a year), *UPEG em Números* (2 a year)

DIRECTORS

Sector of Agricultural Science and Technology: Prof. VICTOR GEORGE CELINSKI
Sector of Applied Social Sciences: Prof. SILAS GUIMARÃES MORO
Sector of Biological Sciences and Health: Prof. ELIAS ZAHI FADEL
Sector of Exact and Natural Sciences: Prof. JOÃO ALFREDO MADALOZO
Sector of Letters and Human Sciences: Prof. GRACIETE TOZETTO GÓES

ATTACHED INSTITUTES

Augusto Ribas Agricultural High School: Av. Carlos Cavalcanti 4748, Campus de Uvaranas; Principal VERA MÁRCIA MESSIAS.

Centro de Atenção Integral à Criança e ao Adolescente: Av. Carlos Cavalcanti 4748, Campus de Uvaranas; Principal MARY ANGELA TEIXEIRA BRANDALISE.

UNIVERSIDADE ESTADUAL DO CEARÁ

Av. Paranjana 1700, Campus do Itaperi, 60740-000 Fortaleza, CE
Telephone: (85) 3101-9600
Internet: www.uece.br
Founded 1975
State control
Academic year: March to December
Rector: Prof. FRANCISCO DE ASSIS MOURA ARARIPE
Vice-Rector: Prof. ANTÔNIO DE OLIVEIRA GOMES NETO
Registrar: Prof. Dr FÁBIO PERDIGÃO VASCONCELOS
Librarian: ÂNGELA MARIA PINHO DE BARROS
Library of 60,338 vols, 586 periodicals
Number of teachers: 1,071
Number of students: 11,970
Publication: *Revista Lumen Ad Viam*

DIRECTORS

Applied Social Studies Centre: Profa MARIA DA CONCEIÇÃO PIO
Education Centre: Prof. JOSÉ NELSON ARRUDA FILHO
Faculty of Education at Crateús: Prof. Dr JOSÉ OSSIAN GADELHA DE LIMA
Faculty of Education at Itapipoca: Prof. PETRÔNIO AUGUSTO SIMÃO DE SOUZA
Faculty of Education, Sciences and Arts at Iguatu: Prof. Dr EUDÊNIO BEZERRA DA SILVA
Faculty of Education, Sciences and Arts at Inhamuns: Prof. Dr ANTÔNIO CHARLES SILVÉRIO
Faculty of Education, Sciences and Arts at Sertão Central: Prof. Dr JORGE ALBERTO RODRIGUEZ
Faculty of Philosophy 'Dom Aureliano Matos': Prof. HIDELBRANDO DOS SANTOS SOARES
Faculty of Veterinary Science: Prof. CÉLIO PIRES GARCIA
Health Science Centre: Prof. Dr JOSÉ JACKSON COELHO SAMPAIO

Humanities Centre: Prof. Dr MARCOS ANTÔNIO PAIVA COLARES

Science and Technology Centre: Prof. Dr JACKSON SÁVIO DE VASCONCELOS SILVA

UNIVERSIDADE ESTADUAL DO OESTE DO PARANÁ

Rua Universitária 1619, CP 701, Jardim Universitário, 85819-110 Cascavel, PR

Telephone: (45) 3220-3000
Fax: (45) 3224-4590
Internet: www.unioeste.br
Founded 1987
State control

Rector: ALCIBIADES LUIZ ORLANDO
Vice-Rector: BENEDITO MARTINS GOMES

Library: Libraries with 50,000 vols, 741 periodicals
Number of teachers: 393
Number of students: 5,996

UNIVERSIDADE ESTADUAL DO PIAUÍ

Rua João Cabral 2231, Pirajá, 64002-150 Teresina, PI

Telephone: (86) 213-7398
Fax: (86) 213-2733
E-mail: ascom@uespi.br
Internet: www.uespi.br
Founded 1985
State control

Rector: Profa MSc VALÉRIA MADEIRA MARTINS RIBEIRO

Library: Libraries with 59,000 vols, 5,050 periodicals
Number of teachers: 359
Number of students: 7,001

UNIVERSIDADE ESTADUAL DO VALE DO ACARAÚ

Av. da Universidade 850, Campus de Betânia, 62040-370 Sobral, CE

Telephone: (88) 3677-4243
Fax: (88) 3677-1866
E-mail: reitoria@uvanet.br
Internet: www.uvanet.br
Founded 1968
State control

Rector: ANTONIO COLAÇO MARTINS

Library: Libraries with 26,000 vols
Number of teachers: 257
Number of students: 9,717

UNIVERSIDADE ESTADUAL PAULISTA 'JULIO DE MESQUITA FILHO'

Alameda Santos 647, Cerqueira César, 01419-901 São Paulo, SP

Telephone: (11) 3252-0521
Fax: (11) 3252-0316
E-mail: arex@reitoria.unesp.br
Internet: www.unesp.br
Founded 1976, incorporating previous existing faculties in São Paulo State
State control
Academic year: February to December

Rector: MARCOS MACARI
Vice-Rector: HERMAN JACOBUS CORNELIS VOORLWALD
Head of Admin.: KLEBER TOMAS RESENDE
Sec.-Gen.: MARIA DALVA SILVA PAGOTTO
Librarian: MARGARET ALVES ANTUNES

Library: 30 libraries univ.-wide
Number of teachers: 3,329
Number of students: 43,967 , incl. 34,346 undergraduate, 9,621 postgraduate
Publications: Alfa (linguistics, 1 a year), Alimentos e Nutrição (food and nutrition, 1 a year), ARBS (biomedical sciences, 1 a year), ARTunesp (arts, 1 a year), Científica (agronomy, 1 a year), Didática (education, 1 a year), Eclética Química (chemistry, 1 a year), Geociências (geosciences, 2 a year), História (history, 1 a year), Naturália (biological sciences, 1 a year), Perspectivas (social sciences, 1 a year), Revista de Ciêcias Farmacêuticas (pharmaceutical sciences, 2 a year), Revista de Engenharia e Ciências Aplicadas (engineering and applied sciences, 1 a year), Revista de Geografia (geography, 1 a year), Revista de Matemática e Nutrição (mathematics and nutrition, 1 a year), Revista de Odontologia da UNESP (dentistry, 2 a year), Transformação (philosophy, 1 a year), Veterinária e Zootecnia (veterinary and husbandry, 1 a year)

DIRECTORS

Araçatuba Campus:

Faculty of Dentistry (Rua José Bonifácio 1193, 16015-050 Araçatuba, SP; tel. (18) 3236-3203; fax (18) 3636-2638; e-mail diretor@foa.unesp.br; internet www.foa.unesp.br):

Prof. Dr PAULO ROBERTO BOTACIN

Araraquara Campus:

Faculty of Dentistry (R. Humaitá 1680, 14801-903 Araraquara, SP; tel. (16) 3301-6431; fax (16) 3301-6433; e-mail diretor@foar.unesp.br; internet www.foar.unesp.br):

Prof. Dr ROSEMARY ADRIANA CHIÉRICI MARCANTONIO

Faculty of Pharmaceutical Sciences (Rodovia Araraquara–Jaú km 1, 14801-902 Araraquara, SP; tel. (16) 3301-6880; fax (16) 3222-0073; e-mail diretor@fcfar.unesp.br; internet www.fcfar.unesp.br):

Prof. Dr IGUATEMI LOURENÇO BRUNETTI

Faculty of Sciences and Humanities (Rodovia Araraquara–Jaú km 1, 14801-901 Araraquara, SP; tel. (16) 3301-4066; fax (16) 3301-6257; e-mail diretor@fclar.unesp.br; internet www.fclar.unesp.br):

Prof. Dr CLÁUDIO BENEDITO GOMIDE DE SOUZA

Institute of Chemistry (R. Prof. Francisco Degni s/n, Bairro Quitandinha, 14800-900 Araraquara, SP; tel. (16) 3301-6679; fax (16) 3322-2308; e-mail diretor@foar.unesp.br; internet www.iq.unesp.br):

Profa Dra MAYSA FURLAN

Assis Campus:

Faculty of Sciences and Humanities (Av. Dom Antonio 2100, 19800-900 Assis, SP; tel. (18) 3302-5802; fax (18) 3302-5804; e-mail diretor@assis.unesp.br; internet www.assis.unesp.br):

Prof. Dr ANTONIO CELSO FERREIRA

Bauru Campus:

Faculty of Architecture, Arts and Communication (Eng. Luiz Edmundo Carrijo Coube s/n, 17033-360 Bauru, SP; tel. (14) 3103-6050; fax (14) 3101-6051; e-mail diretor@faac.unesp.brr; internet www.faac.unesp.br):

Prof. Dr ANTONIO CARLOS DE JESUS

Faculty of Engineering and Technology (Eng. Luiz Edmundo Carrijo Coube s/n, 17033-360 Bauru, SP; tel. (14) 3221-6100; fax (14) 3221-6101; e-mail diretor@feb.unesp.br; internet www.feb.unesp.br):

Prof. Dr LAURO HENRIQUE MELLO CHUEIRI

Faculty of Sciences (Eng. Luiz Edmundo Carrijo Coube s/n, 17033-360 Bauru, SP; tel. (14) 3103-6070; fax (14) 3103-6071; e-mail diretor@fc.unesp.br; internet www.fc.unesp.br):

Prof. Dr JOSÉ BRÁS BARRETO DE OLIVEIRA

Botucatu Campus:

Faculty of Agronomical Sciences (Fazenda Experimental Lageado, 18610-307 Botucatu, SP; tel. (14) 3811-7150; fax (14) 3811-7139; e-mail diretor@fca.unesp.br; internet www.fca.unesp.br):

Prof. Dr LEONARDO THEODORO BÜLL

Faculty of Medicine (Distrito de Rubião Júnior s/n, 18618-970 Botucatu, SP; tel. and fax (14) 3811-6000; e-mail diretor@fmb.unesp.br; internet www.fmb.unesp.br):

Prof. Dr PASCOAL

Faculty of Veterinary Medicine and Animal Husbandry (Distrito de Rubião Júnior s/n, 18618-970 Botucatu, SP; tel. (14) 3811-6002; fax (14) 3815-4398; e-mail diretor@fmvz.unesp.br; internet www.fmvz.unesp.br):

Prof. Dr LUIZ CARLOS VULCANO

Institute of Biosciences (Distrito de Rubião Júnior s/n, 18618-970 Botucatu, SP; tel. and fax (14) 3811-6160; fax (14) 3811-6160; e-mail diretor@ibb.unesp.br; internet www.ibb.unesp.br):

Prof. Dr JOSÉ ROBERTO CÔRREA SAGGLIETTI

Dracena Campus:

Dracena Campus (R. Bahia 332, 17900-000 Métropole, SP; tel. (18) 3821-8101; fax (18) 3821-8100; internet www.dracena.unesp.br):

Prof. Dr JOSÉ ANTONIO MARQUES

Franca Campus:

Faculty of History, Law and Social Services (R. Major Claudiano 1.488, 14400-690 Franca, SP; tel. (16) 3711-1804; fax (16) 3711-1807; e-mail diretor@franca.unesp.br; internet www.franca.unesp.br):

Prof. Dr HELIO BORGHI

Guaratinguetá Campus:

Faculty of Engineering (Av. Dr Ariberto Pereira da Cunha 333, 12500-000 Guaratinguetá, SP; tel. (12) 3123-2800; fax (12) 3125-2466; e-mail direcao@feg.unesp.br; internet www.feg.unesp.br):

Prof. Dr TÂNIA C. A. M. DE AZEVEDO

Ilha Solteira Campus:

Faculty of Engineering (Av. Brasil Centro 56, 15385-000 Ilha Solteira, SP; tel. (18) 3743-1000; fax (18) 3742-2735; e-mail gd@feis.unesp.br; internet www.feis.unesp.br):

Prof. Dr VICENTE LOPES JUNIOR

Itapeva Campus:

Itapeva Campus (R. Geraldo Alckmin 519, 18049-010 Itapeva, SP; tel. (15) 3524-9100; fax (15) 3524-9107; internet www.itapeva.unesp.br):

Prof. Dr MARCUS TADEU TIBÚRCO GONÇALVES

Jaboticabal Campus:

Faculty of Agricultural and Veterinary Sciences (Prof. Paulo Donato Castellane s/n, 14884-900 Jaboticabal, SP; tel. (16) 322-4250; fax (16) 322-4275; e-mail diretor@fcav.unesp.br; internet www.fcav.unesp.br):

Prof. Dr ROBERVAL VIEIRA

Marília Campus:

Faculty of Philosophy and Sciences (Av. Hygino Muzzi Filho 737, 17525-900 Marília, SP; tel. and fax (14) 3402-1300; e-mail diretor@marilia.unesp.br; internet www.marilia.unesp.br):

Prof. Dr MARIA CANDIDA SOARES DEL MASSO

Ourinhos Campus:

Ourinhos Campus (R. Dom José Marello 749, 19911-760 Vila Perino, SP; tel. (14) 3302-5800; fax (14) 3302-5802; e-mail joaolima@ourinhos.unesp.br; internet www.ourinhos.unesp.br):

Prof. Dr JOÃO LIMA SANT'ANNA NETTO

Presidente Prudente Campus:

Faculty of Science and Technology, Presidente Prudente (R. Roberto Simonsen 305, 19060-900 Presidente Prudente, SP; tel. and fax (18) 229-5300; e-mail dirfct@prudente .unesp.br; internet www.prudente.unesp.br):

Prof. Dr NERI ALVES

Registro Campus:

Registro Campus (R. Tamekeshi Takano 05, 11900-000 Centro, SP; tel. (13) 3822-2230; e-mail benez@registro.unesp.br; internet www.registro.unesp.br):

Prof. SÉRGIO HUGO BENEZ

Rio Claro Campus:

Institute of Biosciences (Av. 24-A 1515, Bela Vista, 13500-900 Rio Claro, SP; tel. and fax (19) 3526-1400; e-mail dirib@rc.unesp.br; internet www.rc.unesp.br):

Prof. Dr AMILTON FERREIRA

Institute of Geosciences and Exact Sciences (Rua Dez 2527, 13500-230 Rio Claro, SP; tel. (19) 534-0326; fax (19) 534-8250; e-mail diretor@caviar.igce.unesp.br):

Profa Dra MARIA RITA CAETANO CHANG

Rosana Campus:

Rosana Campus (Av. dos Barrageiros s/n, 19274-000 Primavera, SP; tel. (18) 3284-9201; fax (18) 3284-9209; e-mail coordenadoria@rosana.unesp.br; internet www.rosana.unesp.br):

Prof. Dr MESSIAS MENGHETTI JÚNIOR

São José do Rio Preto Campus:

Institute of Biosciences, Humanities and Exact Sciences (Ruo Cristóvão Colombo 2265, 15054-000 São José do Rio Preto, SP; tel. (17) 221-2200; fax (17) 221-8692; e-mail diretor@ibilce.unesp.br; internet www.ibilce .unesp.br):

Profa Dr JOHNNY RIZZIERI OLIVEIRA

São José dos Campos Campus:

Faculty of Dentistry (Av. Engenheiro Francisco José Longo 777, 12245-000 São José dos Campos, SP; tel. (12) 3947-9000; fax (12) 3947-9010; e-mail diretor@fosjc.unesp.br; internet www.fosjc.unesp.br):

Profa Dra MARIA AMÉLIA MÁXIMO DE ARAÚJO

São Paulo Campus:

Institute of Arts (Rua Dom Luiz Lasagna 400, Ipiranga, 04266-030 São Paulo, SP; tel. (11) 274-4733; fax (11) 274-2190; e-mail diretor@ia.unesp.br; internet www.ia.unesp .br):

Profa Dra MARISA TRENCH O. FONTERRADA

Institute of Theoretical Physics (Rua Pamplona 145, 01405-900 São Paulo, SP; tel. (11) 3177-9090; fax (11) 215-1371; e-mail gkrein@ iff.unesp.br; internet www.iff.unesp.br):

Profa Dr GASTÃO I. KREIN

São Vicente Campus:

São Vicente Campus (Praça Infante Don Henrique s/n, 011330-205 São Vicente, SP; tel. (13) 3569-9403; fax (13) 3469-7374; e-mail coordenadoria@csv.unesp.br; internet www.csv.unesp.br):

Prof. Dr MARCELO ANTONIO AMARO PINHEIRO

Sorocaba Campus:

Sorocaba Campus (Av. Três de Marco 511, 18087-180 Alto da Boa Vista, SP; tel. (15) 3238-3401; fax (15) 3228-2842; e-mail direcao@sorocaba.unesp.br; internet www .sorocaba.unesp.br):

Prof. Dr GALDENORO BOTURA JÚNIOR

Tupã Campus:

Tupã Campus (Av. Domingas da Costa Lopes 780, 17602-660 Tupã, SP; tel. (14) 3404-4200;

fax (14) 3404-4201; e-mail ejsimon@tupa .unesp.br; internet www.tupa.unesp.br):

Prof. Dr ELIAS JOSÉ MARELLO

COMPLEMENTARY UNITS

Aquaculture Centre: Rodovia Carlos Tonanni km 5, 14870-000 Jaboticabal, SP; tel. (16) 3203-2500; fax (16) 3203-2268; e-mail fatima@caunesp.unesp.br; Dir Profa Dra ELISABETH CRISCUOLO URBINATI.

Centre for Education and Cultural Radio and Television: Av. Eng. Luiz Edmundo Carrijo Coube Ss/n°, 17033-360 Bauru, SP; tel. and fax (14) 230-5486; e-mail dir-rad@faac.unesp.br; Dir Prof. Dr MURILO CÉSAR SOARES.

Centre for Environmental Studies (CEA): Av. 24-A 1.515, 13506-900 Rio Claro, SP; tel. (19) 534-7298; fax (19) 534-2358; e-mail cea@life.ibrc.unesp.br; Dir Prof. Dr NIVAR GOBBI.

Centre of Excellence in Dental Care (CAOE): Rod. Marechal Rondon km 527, 16015-050 Araçatuba, SP; tel. (18) 622-4125 ext. 403; fax (18) 622-2638; e-mail saguiar@ foa.unesp.br; Dir Profa Dra SANDRA MARIA H. C. AVILA DE AGUIAR.

Centre for the Study of Venom and Venomous Animals (CEVAP): Distrito de Rubião Junior s/n°, 18610-000 Botucatu, SP; tel. (14) 6821-2121 ext. 2054; fax (14) 6821-3963; e-mail cevap@botunet.com.br; Dir Prof. Dr CARLOS ALBERTO DE MAGALHÃES LOPES.

Centre for Tropical Root Crops (CERAT): Fazenda Experimental Lageado, CP 237, 18603-970 Botucatu, SP; tel. (14) 6802-7158; e-mail seccerat@fca.unesp.br; internet www.cerat.unesp.br; Dir Profa Dra ELISABETH CRISCUOLO URBINATI.

Institute of Meteorological Research (IPMet): Av. Eng Luiz Edmundo Carrijo Coube s/n, 17033-360 Bauru, SP; tel. (14) 221-6028; fax (14) 230-3649; e-mail ipmet_geral@ipmet.ipmet.unesp.br; Dir Prof. Dr MAURÍCIO DE AGOSTINHO ANTONIO.

Isotopes Centre: Distrito de Rubião Júnior s/n, 18618-000 Botucatu, SP; tel. (14) 6821-1171; fax (14) 6802-6359; e-mail ducatti@ibb .unesp.br; Dir Prof. Dr CARLOS DUCATTI.

AFFILIATED FACULTIES

Faculty of Technology, Americana: Av. Nossa Senhora de Fátima 567, 13465-000 Americana, SP; tel. (149) 468-1049; e-mail douglas@fatecam.com.br; internet www .fatecam.com.br.

Faculty of Technology, Baixada Santista: Av. Bartolomeu de Gusmão 110, 11045-401 Santos, SP; tel. (13) 227-6003; e-mail cpd_fatecbr@ig.com.br.

Faculty of Technology, Guaratinguetá: Praça Conselheiro Rodrigues Alves 48, 12500-000 Guaratinguetá, SP; tel. (12) 532-5110; e-mail fatec@provale.com.br.

Faculty of Technology, Indaiatuba: Rua D. Pedro I 65, 13330-000 Indaiatuba, SP; tel. (19) 834-9168.

Faculty of Technology, Jahu: Rua Frei Galvão s/n°, Jd. Pedro Ometto, 17212-650 Jaú, SP; tel. (14) 622-8533; e-mail fatec.jau@ netsite.com.br; internet www.netsite.com.br/ ccf/fatec.

Faculty of Technology, Ourinhos: Av. Vitalina Marcusso 1400, 19900-000 Ourinhos, SP; tel. (14) 323-3031; e-mail fatec@ fatecou.com.br; internet www.fatecou.com .br.

Faculty of Technology, São Paulo: Praça Coronel Fernando Prestes 110, 01124-060 São Paulo, SP; tel. (11) 227-0105; e-mail secdir@fatecsp.br; internet www.fatecsp.br.

Faculty of Technology, Sorocaba: Av. Eng. Carlos Reinaldo Mendes 2015, 18013-280 Sorocaba, SP; tel. (15) 228-2381; e-mail fatecso@cruzeironet.com.br.

Faculty of Technology, Taquaritinga: Rua Dr Flávio Henrique Lemos 585, Portal Itamaracá, 15900-000 Taquaritinga, SP; tel. (16) 352-5250; e-mail fatec@tq.com.br; internet www.fatectq.com.br.

Faculty of Technology, Zona Leste: Av. Águia de Haia 2633, 03694-6271 São Paulo, SP; tel. (11) 61436271; e-mail fatec-zl@ centropaulasouza.com.br; internet www .fatecsp.br.

UNIVERSIDADE FEDERAL DA BAHIA

Palácio da Reitoria, Rua Augusto Viana s/n, Canela, 40110-909 Salvador, BA

Telephone: (71) 3283-7072
Fax: (71) 3283-7027
Internet: www.ufba.br

Founded 1946
State control

Rector: NAOMAR MONTEIRO DE ALMEIDA FILHO
Vice-Rector: FRANCISCO JOSÉ GOMES MESQUITA
Admin. Officer: LÍGIA JACOBSEN ÁLVARES
Sec.-Gen.: GILKA MIRIAN GHIGNONE DE FIGUEIREDO
Librarian: MARIA DAS GRAÇAS MIRANDA RIBEIRO

Library: Central library and 35 departmental libraries, with 531,000 vols
Number of teachers: 1,812
Number of students: 16,836

Publication: *Universitas*

DIRECTORS

Centre of Afro-Oriental Studies: JEFERSON AFONSO BACELAR
Centre of Bahian Studies: FERNANDO DA ROCHA PEREZ
Centre of Inter-disciplinary Studies for Public Services: DORA LEAL ROSA
Data Processing Centre: MARCIA TEREZA RANGEL DE OLIVEIRA
Faculty of Architecture: SOLANGE SOUZA ARAÚJO
Faculty of Communication: GIOVANDRO MARCUS FERREIRA
Faculty of Dentistry: MARIA ISABEL PEREIRA VIANNA
Faculty of Economics: ANTÔNIO WILSON FERREIRA MENEZES
Faculty of Education: CELI NELZA ZULKE TAFFAREL
Faculty of Fine Arts: RIBEIRO AMANCIO COSTA
Faculty of Law: JONHSON MEIRA SANTOS
Faculty of Medicine: JOSÉ TAVARES CARNEIRO NETO
Faculty of Pharmacy: MARIA SPÍNOLA MIRANDA
Faculty of Philosophy and Humanities: LINA MARIA BRANDÃO DE ARAS
Human Resources Centre: ALBA REGINA NEVES RAMOS
Institute of Biology: JORGE ANTÔNIO MOREIRA DA SILVA
Institute of Chemistry: DIRCEU MARTINS
Institute of Community Health: MARIA DA GLÓRIA LIMA
Institute of Geology: LUIZ ROGÉRIO BASTOS LEAL
Institute of Health Sciences: MARIA THEREZA BARRAL ARAÚJO
Institute of Letters: TERESA LEAL GONÇALVES PEREIRA
Institute of Mathematics: MARCO ANTÔNIO NOGUEIRA FERNANDES
Institute of Physics: ARTHUR MATOS NETO
Maternity Hospital: BENEDITO SOARES METZKER

School of Administration: REGINALDO SOUZA SANTOS
School of Agriculture: WASHINGTON LUIZ COTRIM DUETE
School of Dance: DULCE TAMARA ROCHA LAMEGO DA SILVA
School of Dietetics: IRACEMA SANTOS VELOSO
School of Librarianship: OTHON FERNANDO JAMBEIRO BARBOSA
School of Music: HORST KARL SCHWEBEL
School of Nursing: HELONIZA OLIVEIRA GONÇALVES COSTA
School of Theatre: DANIEL MARQUES DA SILVA
School of Veterinary Medicine: CARLOS ROBERTO FRANKE
University Hospital: ANTONIO CARLOS MOREIRA LEMOS

UNIVERSIDADE FEDERAL DA PARAÍBA

Campus Universitário, 58059-900 João Pessoa, PB

Telephone: (83) 216-7200
Fax: (83) 225-1901
E-mail: gabinete@reitoria.ufpb.br
Internet: www.ufpb.br
Founded 1955
Language of instruction: Portuguese
Academic year: March to December
Rector: JADER NUNES DE OLIVEIRA
Vice-Rector: MÚCIO ANTÔNIO SOBREIRA SOUTO
Registrar: IGUATEMY MARIA DE LUCENA MARTINS
Librarian: BABYNE NEIVA DE G. RIBEIRO
Number of teachers: 1,423
Number of students: 19,203

Publications: *Informação e Sociedade: Estudos* (2 a year), *Nordestina de Biologia* (1 a year), *Revista Brasileira de Ciência da Saúde* (4 a year), *Revista Brasileira de Engenharia Agrícola e Ambiental* (4 a year), *Temas em Educação* (1 a year)

DIRECTORS

Campus I—João Pessoa (58059-900 João Pessoa, PB; tel. (83) 216-7200):
Applied Social Sciences: JOSÉ DÉCIO DE ALMEIDA LEITE
Education: ANEDITE ALMEIDA DE FREITAS
Exact and Natural Sciences: UMBELINO DE FREITAS NETO
Health Sciences: ZORAIDE MARGARET BEZERRA LINS
Human Sciences, Letters and Arts: MARIA YARA CAMPOS MATOS
Law: MANOEL ALEXANDRE CAVALCANTE BELO
Technology: ORLANDO DE CAVALCANTI VILLAR FILHO
Campus II—Areia (58397-000 Areia, PB; tel. (83) 362-2218):
Agricultural Sciences: ALBERÍCIO PEREIRA DE ANDRADE
Campus III—Bananeiras (58220-000 Bananeiras, PB; tel. (83) 363-2621):
Technologist Training Centre: CHATEAUBRIAND BANDEIRA JÚNIOR

UNIVERSIDADE FEDERAL DE ALAGOAS

Campus A. C. Simões, Av. Lourival Melo Mota s/n, Tabuleiro do Martins, 57072-970 Maceió, AL

Telephone: (82) 214-1100
Fax: (82) 322-2345
Internet: www.ufal.br
Founded 1961
State (Federal) control
Language of instruction: Portuguese
Academic year: March to December (2 semesters)

Rector: ANA DAYSE REZENDE DOREA
Vice-Rector: EURICO DE BARROS LÔBO FILHO
Pro-Rector for Extension: EDUARDO SARMENTO DE LYRA
Pro-Rector for Institutional Management: JOÃO CARLOS CORDEIRO BARBIRATO
Pro-Rector for Personnel and Work Management: SÍLVIA REGINA CARDEAL
Pro-Rector for Research and Postgraduate Affairs: JOSEALDO TONHOLO
Pro-Rector for Student Affairs: PEDRO NELSON BONFIM GOMES RIBEIRO
Pro-Rector for Undergraduate Affairs: MARIA DAS GRAÇAS MEDEIROS TAVARES
Number of teachers: 907
Number of students: 6,128

Publication: *Boletim da UFAL*

DIRECTORS

Centre of Agrarian Sciences: PAULO VANDERLEI FERREIRA
Centre of Technology: ALINE DA SILVA RAMOS BARBOZA
Education Centre: ADRIANA ALMEIDA SALES DE MELO
Faculty of Economics, Administration and Accounting: LUIZ ANTONIO PALMEIRA CABRAL
Faculty of Medicine: ROSANA QUINTELLA BRANDÃO VILELA
Institute of Chemistry and Biotechnology: EDSON DE SOUZA BENTO
Institute of Computing: EVANDRO DE BARROS COSTA
Institute of Geography, Development and the Environment: SILVANA QUINTELLA CAVALCANTI CALHEIROS
Institute of Mathematics: AMAURI DA SILVA BARROS

UNIVERSIDADE FEDERAL DE CAMPINA GRANDE

Rua Aprígio Veloso 882, Bodocongó CP 10049, 58109-000 Campina Grande, PB

Telephone: (83) 310-1089
Fax: (83) 310-1089
Internet: www.ufcg.edu.br
Founded 2002, from 4 existing campuses of the Univ. Fed. da Paraíba

Publications: *Ariús–Revista do Centro de Humanidades* (1 a year), *Raizes–Revista do Centro de Humanidades* (2 a year), *Revista Brasileira de Engenharia Agrícola e Ambiental (AGRIAMBI)* (4 a year), *Sheculum* (Revista de História, 1 a year)

DIRECTORS

Cajazeiras Campus (58900-000 Cajazeiras, PB; tel. (83) 531-3046):
Teacher Training Centre: JOSÉ MARIA GURGEL
Campina Grande Campus (58109-000 Campina Grande, PB; tel. (83) 310-1463):
Centre for Biological Sciences and Health: VILMA LÚCIA FONSECA MENDOZA
Centre for Humanities: JOSÉ EDILSON AMORIM
Centre for Science and Technology: BENEDITO GUIMARÃES AGUIAR NETO
Patos Campus (58700-970 Patos, PB; tel. (83) 421-3397):
Centre for Veterinary and Rural Technology: CARLOS PEÑA ALFARO
Sousa Campus (58800-970 Sousa, PB; tel. (83) 521-1363):
Centre for Law and Social Sciences: JOAQUIM CAVALCANTE DE ALENCAR

UNIVERSIDADE FEDERAL DE CIÊNCIAS DA SAÚDE DE PORTO ALEGRE

Rua Sarmento Leite 245, 90050-170 Porto Alegre, RS

Telephone: (51) 3303-9000
Fax: (51) 3303-8810
E-mail: reitoria@ufcspa.edu.br
Internet: www.ufcspa.edu.br
Founded 1953 as Fundação Faculdade Federal de Ciências Médicas de Porto Alegre; present name 2008
State control

Rector: MIRIAM DA COSTA OLIVEIRA
Vice-Rector: CLÁUDIO AUGUSTO MARRONI
Pro-Rector for Admin.: EUGÊNIO STEIN
Pro-Rector for Extension and Community Affairs: LUIS HENRIQUE TELLES DA ROSA
Pro-Rector for Planning: EVELISE FRAGA DE SOUZA SANTOS
Pro-Rector for Research and Postgraduate Affairs: CLAUDIO OSMAR PEREIRA ALEXANDRE
Pro-Rector for Undergraduate Affairs: MARIA TEREZINHA ANTUNES.

UNIVERSIDADE FEDERAL DE GOIÁS

CP 131, Campus Samambaia, 74000-970 Goiânia, GO

Telephone: (62) 3521-1274
Fax: (62) 3521-1193
E-mail: cai@cai.ufg.br
Internet: www.ufg.br
Founded 1960
State control
Language of instruction: Portuguese
Library of 185,350 vols, 104,126 titles, 206,927 periodical titles

Rector: Prof. Dr EDWARD MADUREIRA BRASIL
Pro Rector for Admin. and Finance: Prof. Dr ORLANDO AFONSO VALLE DO AMARAL
Pro Rector for Community Affairs: ERNANDO MELO FILIZZOLA
Pro Rector for Devt and Human Resources: Prof. JEBLIN ANTNIO ABRAO
Pro Rector for Extension: Prof. Dr ANSELMO PESSOA NETO
Pro Rector for Research and Postgraduates: Prof. Dra DIVINA DAS DORES DE PAULA CARDOSO
Pro Rector for Undergraduates: Profa Dra SANDRAMARA MATIAS CHAVES
Librarian: VALRIA MARIA SOLEDADE DE ALMEIDA
Number of teachers: 1,666
Number of students: 14,912

Publications: *Ateli Geogrfico* (4 a year), *Boletim Goiano de Geografia* (2 a year), *Cincia Animal Brasileira* (4 a year), *Histria Revista* (2 a year), *Inter-Ao* (2 a year), *Msica Hodie* (2 a year), *Pensar a Prtica* (4 a year), *Pesquisa Agropecuria Tropical* (2 a year), *Philsophos—Revista de Filosofia* (2 a year), *Revista de Biologia Neotropical* (2 a year), *Revista de Patologia Tropical* (4 a year), *Revista Eletrnica de Enfermagem* (4 a year), *Revista Eletrnica de Farmcia* (4 a year), *Signtica* (2 a year), *Sociedade e Cultura* (2 a year)

DIRECTORS

Centre for Teaching and Applied Research in Education: Profa Dra MARIA JOS OLIVEIRA DE FARIA ALMEIDA
Faculty of Arts: Profa VERA MARIA TIETZMANN SILVA
Faculty of Communication and Library Science: Prof. Dr MAGNO MEDEIROS
Faculty of Dentistry: Prof. Dr GERSINEI CARLOS DE FREITAS
Faculty of Education: Prof. Dr GED GUIMARES

Faculty of Human Sciences And Philosophy: Prof. ANDRE PORTO

Faculty of Law: Prof. Dr CLEULER BARBOSA DAS NEVES

Faculty of Medicine: Prof. Dr VARDELI ALVES DE MORAES

Faculty of Nursing: Prof. Dr MARCELO MEDEIROS

Faculty of Nutrition: Profa Dra MARIA DO ROSRIO GONDIM PEIXOTO

Faculty of Pharmacy: Profa Dra EULA MARIA M. BV

Faculty of Physical Education: Prof. Dr MARCUS FRAGA VIEIRA

Faculty of Visual Arts: Prof. RAIMUNDO MARTINS

Institute of Biological Sciences: Prof. REGINALDO NASSAR FERREIRA

Institute of Chemistry: Prof. Dr NEUCIRIO RICARDO DE AZEVEDO

Institute of Information Science: Prof. Dr CEDRIC LUIZ DE CARVALHO

Institute of Mathematics And Statistics: Prof. Dr GECI JOS PEREIRA DA SILVA

Institute of Physics: Prof. FERNANDO PELEGRINI

Institute of Social and Environmental Studies: Prof. JOO BATISTA DE DEUS

Institute of Tropical Pathology and Public Health: Profa Dra REGINA MARIA BRINGEL MARTINS

School of Agronomy and Food Engineering: Prof. Dr JUAREZ PATRCIO DE OLIVEIRA JNIOR

School of Business and Economics Sciences: Profa Dra MARIA DO AMPARO ALBUQUERQUE AGUIAR

School of Civil Engineering and Environmental Engineering: Prof. OSVALDO LUIZ VALINOTE

School of Electrical Engineering and Computer Science: Prof. Dr REINALDO GONALVES NOGUEIRA

School of Music and Performing Arts: Prof. EDUARDO MEIRINHOS

School of Veterinary Science: Prof. Dr EUGNIO GONALVES DE ARAJO

UNIVERSIDADE FEDERAL DE ITAJUBÁ

Campus Prof. José Rodrigues Seabra, Av. BPS 103, 37500-903 Itajubá, MG

Telephone: (35) 3629-1124

Fax: (35) 3620-1124

E-mail: maua@unifei.edu.br

Internet: www.unifei.edu.br

Founded 1913 as Instituto Eletrotécnico e Mecânico de Itajubá; became Instituto Eletrotécnico de Itajubá 1936 and Escola Federal de Engenharia de Itajubá 1968; present name and status 2002

Rector: Prof. JOSÉ CARLOS GOULART DE SIQUEIRA

Vice-Rector: Prof. FELÍCIO BARBOSA MONTEIRO

Librarian: MARÍA DE FÁTIMA BASTOS

Library of 26,699 vols

Number of teachers: 183

Number of students: 2,581

Publication: Pesquisa e Desenvolvimento Tecnológico (4 a year)

DIRECTORS

Institute of Electrical Engineering: (vacant)

Institute of Mechanical Engineering: Prof. JOSÉ ARNALDO BARRA MONTEVECHI

Institute of Sciences: Prof. Dr FARNEZIO MOREIRA DE CARVALHO FILHO

UNIVERSIDADE FEDERAL DE JUIZ DE FORA

Rua José Lourenço Kelmer s/n, Campus Univ., Bairro São Pedro, 36036-330 Juiz de Fora, MG

Telephone: (32) 2102-3800

E-mail: faleconosco@ufjf.edu.br

Internet: www.ufjf.br

Founded 1960

Federal control

Language of instruction: Portuguese

Academic year: March to December

Rector: HENRIQUE DUQUE DE MIRANDA CHAVES FILHO

Vice-Rector: JOSÉ LUIZ REZENDE PEREIRA

Pro-Rector for Extension and Culture: Prof. ROMÁRIO GERALDO

Pro-Rector for Human Resources: GESSILENE ZIGLER FOINE

Pro-Rector for Planning and Management: ALEXANDRE ZANINI

Pro-Rector for Postgraduate Affairs: Prof. Dr LUIZ CARLOS FERREIRA DE ANDRADE

Pro-Rector for Research: Profa Dra MARTA TAVARES D'AGOSTO

Pro-Rector for Undergraduate Affairs: Prof. EDUARDO MAGRONE

Gen. Sec.: BASILEU PEREIRA TAVARES

Librarian: ADRIANA APARECIDA DE OLIVEIRA

Number of teachers: 1,167

Number of students: 22,336

Publications: Boletim do Centro de Biologia da Reprodução (1 a year), Boletim do Instituto de Ciências Biológicas (1 a year), Educacão em Foco (2 a year), Ética e Filosofia Política (2 a year), Locus (1 a year), Revista do Hospital Universitário (4 a year), Revista do Instituto de Ciências Exatas (1 a year), Revista Eletrônica de História do Brasil (2 a year)

DIRECTORS

Faculty of Dentistry: Prof. ANTÔNIO MÁRCIO RESENDE DO CARMO

Faculty of Economics and Administration: Profa MARIA ISABEL DA SILVA AZEVEDO

Faculty of Education: Prof. DIVA CHAVES SARMENTO

Faculty of Engineering: Prof. JÚLIO CÉSAR TEIXEIRA

Faculty of Law: Prof. MARCOS VINÍCIO CHEIN FERES

Faculty of Letters: MARTA CRISTINA DA SILVA

Faculty of Medicine: Prof. JÚLIO MARIA FONSECA CHEBLI

Faculty of Nursing: Prof. GIRLENE ALVES DA SILVA

Faculty of Pharmacy and Biochemistry: Profa LUCIO GUEDES BARRA

Faculty of Physical Education: Prof. EDNA RIBEIRO HERNANDEZ MARTIN

Faculty of Social Communication: Prof. MARISE PIMENTEL MENDES

Faculty of Social Services: Profa LEILA BAUMGRATZ DELGADO YACOUB

Institute of Biological Sciences: Prof. AMAURY CAIAFA DUARTE

Institute of Exact Sciences: Prof. RUBENS DE OLIVEIRA

Institute of Human Sciences: Profa EDUARDO SALOMÃO CONDÉ

UNIVERSIDADE FEDERAL DE MATO GROSSO

Av. Fernando Corrêa s/n, Coxipó, 78060-900 Cuiabá, MT

Telephone: (65) 3615-8000

Fax: (65) 3628-1219

E-mail: janemar@cpd.ufmt.br

Internet: www.ufmt.br

Founded 1970

Rector: MARIA LÚCIA CAVALLI NEDER

Vice-Rector: FRANCISCO JOSÉ DUTRA SOUTO

Number of teachers: 1,167

Number of students: 9,195

Faculties of agrarian sciences, biological and health sciences, exact sciences, literature and human sciences, social sciences and technology.

UNIVERSIDADE FEDERAL DE MATO GROSSO DO SUL

Cidade Universitária, CP 549, 79070-900 Campo Grande, MS

Telephone: (67) 3345-7000

Fax: (67) 3345-7015

E-mail: reitoria@nin.ufms.br

Internet: www.ufms.br

Founded 1970

Academic year: March to December

Centres of biology, computer studies, education, general studies, physical education; campuses in Aquidaúana, Corumbá, Dourados, Três Lagoas.

UNIVERSIDADE FEDERAL DE MINAS GERAIS

Av. Antônio Carlos 6627, Campus Universitário, Pampulha, CP 1621, 31270-901 Belo Horizonte, MG

Telephone: (31) 3499-4025

Fax: (31) 3499-4530

E-mail: info@cointer.ufmg.br

Internet: www.ufmg.br

Founded 1927

State control

Language of instruction: Portuguese

Academic year: February to December

Rector: Profa ANA LÚCIA ALMEIDA GAZZOLA

Vice-Rector: Prof. MARCOS BORATO VIANA

Vice-Chancellor for Admin.: LUIZ FELIPE VIEIRA CALVO

Vice-Chancellor for Extension: Prof. EDISON JOSÉ CORRÊA

Vice-Chancellor for Planning: Prof. RONALDO TADEU PENA

Vice-Chancellor for Postgraduates: Profa MARIA SUELI DE OLIVEIRA PIRES

Vice-Chancellor for Research: Profa JOSÉ AURÉLIO GARCIA BERGMANN

Vice-Chancellor for Undergraduates: Prof. CRISTINA RIBEIRO ROCHA AUGUSTIN

Dir of Libraries: SIMONE APARECIDA DOS SANTOS

Library of 522,100 vols, 19,400 periodicals

Number of teachers: 2,527

Number of students: 31,000

Publications: Arquivos da Escola de Veterinária da UFMG, Barroco, Diversa (1 a year), Estudos Germânicos, Kriterion, Manuelzão (12 a year), Revista Brasileira de Estudos Políticos

DIRECTORS

Architecture: Prof. LEONARDO BARCI CASTRIOTA

Biological Sciences: Prof. CARLOS ALBERTO PEREIRA TAVARES

Dentistry: Prof. WELLINGTON CORREA JANSEN

Economic Sciences: Prof. CLÉLIO CAMPOLINA DINIZ

Education: Profa ÂNGELA LOUREIRO DE FREITAS DALBEN

Engineering: Prof. RICARDO NICOLAU NASSAR KOURY

Exact Sciences: Prof. BISMARCK VAZ DA COSTA

Fine Arts: Prof. EVANDRO JOSÉ LEMOS DA CUNHA

Geo-Sciences: Prof. ANTÔNIO GILBERTO COSTA

Law: Prof. ALOÍSIO GONZAGA ANDRADE ARAÚJO

Literature: Profa ELIANA AMARANTE DE MENDONÇA MENDES

Medicine: Prof. GERALDO BRASILEIRO FILHO

Music: Prof. LUCAS JOSÉ BRETAS DOS SANTOS
Nursing: Prof. FRANCISCO CARLOS FELIX LANA
Pharmacy: Prof. GERSON ANTÔNIO PIANETTI
Philosophy and Human Sciences: Prof. JOÃO
PINTO FURTADO
Physical Education: Prof. PABLO RUAN GRECO
Veterinary Sciences: Prof. ROBERTO BACARAT
DE ARAÚJO

UNIVERSIDADE FEDERAL DE OURO PRETO

Rua Diogo de Vasconcelos 122, 35400-000
Ouro Preto, MG
Telephone: (31) 3559-1218
Fax: (31) 3551-1689
E-mail: reitoria@ufop.br
Internet: www.ufop.br
Founded 1969
Federal state control
Academic year: February to December
Rector: DIRCEU DO NASCIMENTO
Vice-Rector: MARCO ANTONIO TOURINHO FUR-
TADO
Chief Admin. Officer: MÁRCIO GALVÃO
Librarian: JUSSARA SANTOS SILVA
Number of teachers: 390
Number of students: 5,200   (4,800 under-
graduate, 400 postgraduate)
Publications: *Jornal da UFOP* (12 a year),
Jornal Revirarte, *Revista da Escola de
Minas* (4 a year), *Revista de Historia* (3 a
year), *Revista de Pesquisa da UFOP* (4 a
year), *Revista Juridica* (1 a year).

CONSTITUENT INSTITUTES

Institute of Arts and Culture: Rua Coronel Alves 55, 35400-000 Ouro Preto, MG; f.
1981; Dean GUIOMAR GRAMONT.
**Institute of Exact and Biological Sci-
ences:** Campus Universitario, Morro do
Cruzeiro, 35400-000 Ouro Preto, MG; f.
1982; Dean JOÃO MARTINS.
Institute of Human and Social Sciences:
Rua do Seminário, 35420-000 Mariana, MG;
f. 1979; Dean IVAN A. ALMEIDA.
School of Mines: Praça Tiradentes 20,
35400-000 Ouro Preto, MG; f. 1876; Dean
ANTONIO GOMES.
School of Pharmacy: Rua Costa Sena 171,
35400-000 Ouro Preto, MG; f. 1839; Dean
LISIANE DA SILVEIRA EU.

UNIVERSIDADE FEDERAL DE PELOTAS

Campus Universitário s/n, CP 354, 96010-
900 Pelotas, RS
Telephone: (53) 3275-7104
Fax: (53) 3275-9023
E-mail: reitor@ufpel.edu.br
Internet: www.ufpel.edu.br
Founded 1883 as Imperial Escola de Medi-
cina Veterinária e de Agricultura Prática;
present name 1969
State control
Academic year: March to December
Rector: Dr ANTONIO CESAR GONÇALVES
BORGES
Vice-Rector: Dr TELMO PAGANA XAVIER
Pro-Rector for Admin. Affairs: Eng. FRAN-
CISCO CARLOS GOMES LUZZARDI
Pro-Rector for Extension Services and Cul-
ture: Dr VITOR HUGO BORBA MANZKE
Pro-Rector for Planning and Developmental
Affairs: Prof. ELIO PAULO ZONTA
Pro-Rector for Research and Graduate Stud-
ies: Dr ALCI ENIMAR LOECK
Pro-Rector for Undergraduate Studies: Dr
LUIZ FERNANDO MINELLO
Number of teachers: 948
Number of students: 9,989

Publications: *Cadernos de Educação* (1 a
year), *Dissertatio* (1 a year), *Expresso
Extensão* (1 a year), *História da Educação*
(1 a year), *Jornal da UFPel* (12 a year),
Revista Acadêmica de Medicina (1 a year),
Revista Brasileira de Agrociência (2 a year)

DIRECTORS

College of Agricultural Engineering: Prof.
WOLMER BROD PERES
College of Agronomy: Prof. JOSÉ FRANCISCO
GOMES SCHILD
College of Architecture and Urban Planning:
Profa NIRCE SAFFER MEDVEDOVSKI
College of Education: Prof. AVELINO DA ROSA
OLIVEIRA
College of Home Economics: Profa TÂNIA
ELISA MORALES GARCIA
College of Letters: Prof. PAULO RICARDO
SILVEIRA BORGES
College of Medicine: Prof. FARID IUNAN NADER
College of Meteorology: Prof. JOSÉ HONORATO
DE OLIVEIRA FILHO
College of Nursing: Profa EMILIA NALVA
FERREIRA DA SILVA
College of Nutrition: Prof. JOSÉ BEIRO CAR-
VALHAL
College of Veterinary Medicine: Prof. MARIO
CARLOS ARAÚJO MEIRELES
Faculty of Dentistry: Profa ANGELA MARIA
ANTUNES NUNES
Faculty of Law: Prof. RENATO OSWALDO
FLEISCHMANN
Institute of Arts and Design: Profa ANAIZI
CRUZ ESPÍRITO SANTO
Institute of Biology: Prof. GLADIS AVER
RIBEIRO
Institute of Chemistry and Geosciences: Prof.
SÉRGIO LUIZ DOS SANTOS DO NASCIMENTO
Institute of Human Sciences: Prof. FABIO
VERGARA CERQUEIRA
Institute of Physics and Mathematics: Prof.
ALVARO LEONARDI AYALA FILHO
Institute of Social and Political Sciences:
Prof. ALVARO AUGUSTO DE BORBA BARRETO
School of Music: Profa ISABEL PORTO
NOGUEIRA
School of Physical Education: Profa TÂNIA
BEATRIZ GAMBOA ARAÚJO MORSELLI

UNIVERSIDADE FEDERAL DE PERNAMBUCO

Av. Prof. Moraes Rego 1235, Cidade Uni-
versitária, 50670-901 Recife, PE
Telephone: (81) 2126-8001
Fax: (81) 2126-8029
E-mail: gabinete@ufpe.br
Internet: www.ufpe.br
Founded 1946
Academic year: March to December
Rector: Prof. AMARO HENRIQUE PESSOA LINS
Pro-Rector for Academic Affairs: Profa ANA
MARIA SANTOS CABRAL
Pro-Rector for Extension: Prof. SOLANGE
COUTINHO
Pro-Rector for Personnel Admin. and Quality
of Life: LENITA ALMEIDA AMARAL
Pro-Rector for Planning and Gen.
Coordination: Prof. HERMINO RAMOS DE
SOUZA
Pro-Rector for Research and Postgraduate
Affairs: Prof. ANÍSIO BRASILEIRO
Library: see Libraries and Archives
Number of teachers: 1,787
Number of students: 32,709
Publications: *Boletim Oficial*, *Incampus*
(information bulletin, 12 a year), *Revista
de Estudos Universitários*

DIRECTORS

Centre of Applied Social Sciences: Prof.
SÉRGIO ALVES DE SOUSA

Centre of Arts and Communication: Profa
MARIA VIRGÍNIA LEAL
Centre of Biological Sciences: Profa ÂNGELA
M. ISIDRO DE FARIAS
Centre of Exact and Natural Sciences: Prof.
MANOEL JOSÉ MACHADO SOARES LEMOS
Centre of Health Sciences: Prof. JOSÉ THADEU
PINHEIRO
Centre of Informatics: Profa PAULO ROBERTO
FREIRE CUNHA
Centre of Juridical Sciences: Profa LUCIANA
GRASSANO DE GOUVEA MELO
Centre of Philosophy and Humanities: Profa
MARIA DO SOCORRO FERRAZ BARBOSA
Education Centre: Prof. JOSÉ BATISTA NETO
Technology Centre: Prof. EDMILSON SANTOS
DE LIMA

UNIVERSIDADE FEDERAL DE RORAIMA

BR 174 km 12, Bairro Monte Cristo, 69300-
000 Boa Vista, RR
Telephone: (95) 3621-3102
Fax: (95) 3621-3101
E-mail: robertoramos@ufrr.br
Internet: www.ufrr.br
Founded 1989
Federal control
Rector: Prof. Dr ROBERTO RAMOS SANTOS
Library of 18,000 vols, 980 periodicals
Number of teachers: 278
Number of students: 4,200

UNIVERSIDADE FEDERAL DE SANTA CATARINA

Campus Universitário, CP 476, Bairro Trin-
dade, 88040-970 Florianópolis, SC
Telephone: (48) 331-9000
Fax: (48) 234-4069
Internet: www.ufsc.br
Founded 1960
State control
Language of instruction: Portuguese
Academic year: March to December
Rector: Prof. RODOLFO JOAQUIM PINTO DA LUZ
Vice-Rector: Prof. LÚCIO JOSÉ BOTELHO
Pro-Rector for Academic Affairs: Prof. PEDRO
DA COSTA ARAÚJO
Pro-Rector for Admin.: JOÃO MARIA DE LIMA
Pro-Rector for Extension and Culture: Profa
ROSSANA PACHECO DA COSTA PROENÇA
Pro-Rector for Graduate Education and
Research: Prof. ÁLVARO TOUBES PRATA
Pro-Rector for Undergraduate Education:
Profa SÔNIA MARIA HICKEL PROBST
Number of teachers: 1,658
Number of students: 27,244
Publications: *Biotemas* (biological sciences, 2
a year), *Ciências da Saúde* (health sci-
ences, 2 a year), *Ciências Humanas* (phil-
osophy and human sciences, 2 a year),
Fragmentos (foreign language and litera-
ture, 2 a year), *Geosul* (geosciences, 2 a
year), *Graf & Tec* (graphics, 2 a year), *Ilha
do Desterro* (language studies and literature, 2 a year), *Katalysis* (social services, 2
a year), *Motrivivência—Políticas Públicas*
(physical education, sport and leisure, 2 a
year), *Perspectiva* (education, 2 a year),
Principia (epistemology, 2 a year), *Seqüên-
cia* (politics and law, 2 a year), *Travessia*
(Brazilian literature, 2 a year)

DEANS

Agrarian Sciences Centre: Prof. ÊNIO LUIZ
PEDROTTI
Biological Sciences Centre: Prof. JOÃO DE
DEUS MEDEIROS
Biomedical Sciences Centre: Prof. CARLOS
ALBERTO JUSTO DA SILVA
Communication Centre: Prof. DILVO ILVO
RISTOFF

Education Centre: Profa VERA LÚCIA BAZZO

Engineering and Technology Centre: Prof. ARIOVALDO BOLZAN

Law Sciences Centre: Prof. JOSÉ LUIZ SOBIER-AJSKI

Philosophy and Social Sciences Centre: Prof. JOÃO EDUARDO PINTO BASTO LUPI

Physical Education Centre: Prof. JÚLIO CESAR SCHMITT ROCHA

Physics and Mathematics Centre: Prof. IVAN GONÇALVES DE SOUZA

Social and Economic Sciences Centre: Prof. ERMES TADEU ZAPELINI

UNIVERSIDADE FEDERAL DE SANTA MARIA

Campus Universitário–Camobi, 97105-900 Santa Maria, RS

Telephone: (55) 220-8000
Fax: (55) 220-8001
E-mail: sai@adm.ufsm.br
Internet: www.ufsm.br

Founded 1960
Federal control
Academic year: March to December (2 semesters)

Dean: Prof. FELIPE MARTINS MÜLLER
Vice-Dean: Prof. DALVAN JOSÉ REINERT
Pro-Rector for Admin.: ANDRÉ LUIS KIELING RIES
Pro-Rector for Extension: Prof. JOÃO RODOLPHO FLÔRES
Pro-Rector for Planning: CHARLES JACQUES PRADE
Pro-Rector for Postgraduates and Research: Prof. HELIO LEÃES HEY
Pro-Rector for Student Affairs: Prof. JOSÉ FRANCISCO SILVA DIAS
Pro-Rector for Undergraduates: Prof. ORLANDO FONSECA
Librarian: MARIA INEZ FIGUEIREDO FIGAS

Library of 177,490 vols
Number of teachers: 1,444
Number of students: 18,490 (13,322 undergraduate, 2,262 postgraduate, 2,906 at Technical High School)
Publications: *Animus Revista Interamericana de Comunicação Mediática, Ciência e Ambiente, Ciência e Natura, Ciência Rural, Extensão Rural, Revista Brasilerira de Agroameteorologia*

DIRECTORS OF CENTRES

Arts and Letters: Prof. EDEMUR CASANOVA
Education: Profa HELENISE SANGOI ANTUNES
Health Sciences: Prof. PAULO AFONSO BURMANN
Natural and Exact Sciences: Profa MARTHA BOHRER ADAIME
Rural Science: Prof. THOMÉ LOVATO
Social and Human Sciences: Prof. ROGÉRIO FERRER KOFF
Sports Research Centre: Prof. CARLOS BOLLI MOTA
Technology: Prof. EDUARDO RIZZATTI

ATTACHED INSTITUTES

Faculty of Nursing: Av. Presidente Vargas 2777, 97100 Santa Maria, RS; Dir Ir NOEMI LUNARDI.

Faculty of Philosophy, Sciences and Letters: Rua Andradas 1614, 97100 Santa Maria, RS; Dir Profa MARIA A. MARQUES.

UNIVERSIDADE FEDERAL DE SÃO CARLOS

Rodovia Washington Luiz, km 235, Monjolinho, CP 676, 13565-905 São Carlos, SP

Telephone: (16) 335-18111
Fax: (16) 336-12081
E-mail: reitoria@ufscar.br
Internet: www.ufscar.br

Founded 1970
Federal control
Language of instruction: Portuguese
Academic year: March to December
Campuses in São Carlos, Sorocaba and Araras

Chancellor: FERNANDO HADDAD
Rector: Prof. Dr TARGINO DE ARAÚJO FILHO
Vice-Rector: Prof. Dr PEDRO MANOEL GALETTI, Jr
Chief Admin. Officer: Profa Dra ELISABETH MARCIA MARTUCCI
Librarian: LIGIA MARIA SILVA E SOUZA

Library of 191,500
Number of teachers: 981
Number of students: 12,094
Publications: *Cadernos de Terapia ocupacional, Click Ciência, Revista Brasileira de Fisioterapia, Revista Eletrônica de Educação, Revista Gestão e Produção, Revista Olhar, Revista Universitária do Audiovisual*

DIRECTORS

Araras Campus:

Institute of Agricultural Sciences: Prof. Dr NORBERTO ANTONIO LAVORENTTI

São Carlos Campus:

Institute of Biological and Health Sciences: Prof. Dr JOSÉ EDUARDO DOS SANTOS

Institute of Education and Human Sciences: Profa Dra WANDA AP. M. HOFFMANN

Institute of Sciences and Technology: Prof. Dr PAULO ANTONIO SILVANI CAETANO

UNIVERSIDADE FEDERAL DE SÃO PAULO

Rua Botucatú 740, 5° andar, 04023-900 São Paulo, SP

Telephone: (11) 5576-4000
Fax: (11) 5576-4313
E-mail: reitor@unifesp.br
Internet: www.unifesp.br

Founded 1933 (fmrly Escola Paulista de Medicina)

Rector: WALTER MANNA ALBERTONI
Pro-Rector for Admin.: VILNEI MATTIOLI LEITE
Pro-Rector for Extension: ELEONORA MENICUCCI DE OLIVEIRA
Pro-Rector for Postgraduates and Research: ARNALDO LOPES COLOMBO
Pro-Rector for Undergraduates: MIGUEL ROBERTO JORGE

Library of 9,002 vols, 8,079 journals, 10,600 theses
Number of teachers: 635
Number of students: 3,853
Publication: *A Folha Médica* (4 a year).

UNIVERSIDADE FEDERAL DE SERGIPE

Cidade Universitária, Av. Marechal Rondon s/n, Jardim Rosa Elze, 49100-000 São Cristóvão, SE

Telephone: (79) 2105-6600
Fax: (79) 2105-6474
E-mail: ufs@ufs.br
Internet: www.ufs.br

Founded 1967
Federal control
Language of instruction: Portuguese
Academic year: March to December

Rector: JOSÉ FERNANDES DE LIMA
Vice-Rector: Prof. JOSÉ PAULINO DA SILVA
Pres. of Ccl: Dr LUIZ GARCIA
Librarian: JUSTINO ALVES LIMA

Number of teachers: 448
Number of students: 5,908

Publications: *Jornal* (26 a year), *Relatório Anual de Atividades, Revista* (irregular)

DIRECTORS

Centre of Applied Social Sciences: Prof. NAPOLEÃO DOS SANTOS QUEIROZ
Centre of Biological Sciences and Health (Rua Claudio Batista, Bairro Sanatário, Aracaju, Sergipe): Prof. Dr ANTONIO CESAR CABRAL DE OLIVEIRA
Centre of Education and Humanities: Prof. LUIZ ALBERTO DOS SANTOS
Centre of Exact Sciences and Technology: Prof. JOSÉ AIRTON DOS SANTOS
Centre for Innovation and Technology Transfer: Profa Dra SUZANA LEITÃO RUSSO

UNIVERSIDADE FEDERAL DE UBERLÂNDIA

38400-902 Uberlândia, MG
Avda João Naves de Ávila, n° 2121, Bairro, Santa Mônica

Telephone: (34) 3239-4536
E-mail: reitoria@ufu.br
Internet: www.ufu.br

Founded 1969
Academic year: March to December

Rector: Prof. ALFREDO JÚLIO FERNANDES NETO
Vice-Rector: Prof. DARIZON ALVES DE ANDRADE
Pro-Rector for Extension, Culture and Student Affairs: Prof. Dr ALBERTO MARTINS DA COSTA
Pro-Rector for Human Resources: Dr SINÉSIO GOMIDE JÚNIOR
Pro-Rector for Planning and Admin.: Dr VALDER STEFFEN JÚNIOR
Pro-Rector for Research and Postgraduate Affairs: Dr ALCIMAR BARBOSA SOARES
Pro-Rector for Undergraduate Affairs: Prof. Dr WALDENOR BARROS MORÃES FILHO
Sec.-Gen.: ELAINE DA SILVEIRA MAGALI
Librarian: MARIA DA GRAÇA

Library of 163,631 vols, 5,636 periodicals
Number of teachers: 1,320
Number of students: 12,500
Publications: *Ciência e Engenharia, Economia e Ensaios, Educação e Filosofia, Ensino em Revista, Letras & Letras, Revista do CEBIM, Revista do CETEC, Revista do Direito, Sociedade e Natureza, Veterinária e Notícias*

DIRECTORS

Accounting: Prof. Dr LUCIMAR ANTÔNIO CABRAL DE AVILA
Agrarian Sciences: Prof. Dr REGES EDUARDO FRANCO TEODORO
Architecture: Prof. Dr MARÍLIA MARIA BRASILEIRO TEIXEIRA VALE
Arts: Prof. Dr HUMBERTO APARECIDO DE OLIVEIRA GUIDO
Biological Sciences: Prof. Dr JIMI NAOKI NAKAJIMA
Biomedical Sciences: Prof. Dr MARCO AURÉLIO MARTINS RODRIGUES
Business Administration: Prof. Dr REINALDO CAMPOS ANDRAUS
Chemical Engineering: Prof. Dr CARLOS HENRIQUE ATAÍDE
Chemistry: Prof. Dr MANUEL GONZALO HERNÁNDEZ-TERRONES
Civil Engineering: Prof. Dr MAURO PRUDENTE
Computer Science: Prof. Dr PEDRO FROSI ROSA
Dentistry/Odontology: Prof. Dr JOÃO CARLOS GABRIELLI BIFFI
Economical Sciences: Dr CLÉSIO LOURENÇO XAVIER
Education: Prof. Dr MARA RÚBIA ALVES MARQUES
Electrical Engineering: Prof. Dr MARCELO LYNCE RIBEIRO CHAVES

Geography: Prof. Dr MARLENE TERESINHA DE MUNO COLESANTI

History: Prof. Dr LUCIENE LEMKUHL

International Relations: Prof. Dr JOSÉ RUBENS DAMAS GARLIPP

Journalism: Prof. Dr CARLOS ALBERTO LUCENA

Law: Prof. Dr MÁRCIO ALEXANDRE DA SILVA PINTO

Letters: Prof. Dr CHRISTINA DA SILVA ROQUETTE LOPREATO

Mathematics: Prof. Dr LUÍS ANTONIO BENEDETTI

Mechanical Engineering: Prof. Dr ANTONIO PEDRO CLÁPIS

Medicine: Prof. Dr AGUINALDO COELHO DA SILVA

Physics: Prof. Dr OMAR DE OLIVEIRA DINIZ NETO

Psychology: Prof. Dr ÁUREA DE FÁTIMA OLIVEIRA

Veterinary Medicine: Prof. Dr ROGÉRIO CHAVES VIEIRA

UNIVERSIDADE FEDERAL DE VIÇOSA

Av. P. H. Rolfs s/n, Campus Universitário, CP 384, 36571-000 Viçosa, MG

Telephone: (31) 3899-2796
Fax: (31) 3899-2203
E-mail: reitoria@mail.ufv.br
Internet: www.ufv.br

Founded 1926; frmly Univ. Rural do Estado de Minas Gerais
State control
Language of instruction: Portuguese
Academic year: March to November

Rector: Prof. EVALDO FERREIRA VILELA
Vice-Rector: Prof. FERNANDO COSTA BAÊTA
Pro-Rector for Admin.: Prof. LUIZ EDUARDO FERREIRA FONTES
Pro-Rector for Community Affairs: Prof. LUIZ CLÁUDIO COSTA
Pro-Rector for Extension and Culture: Prof. PAULO CÉSAR STRINGHETA
Pro-Rector for Planning and Budget: Prof. JOSÉ MARIA ALVES DA SILVA
Pro-Rector for Research and Postgraduate: Prof. OG FRANCISCO FONSECA DE SOUZA
Pro-Rector for Undergraduate: Prof. JOSÉ BENÍCIO PAES CHAVES
Chief Admin. Officer: Prof. VICENTE DE PAULA LELIS
Dir of Library: DORIS MAGNA DE AVELAR OLIVEIRA

Number of teachers: 786
Number of students: 9,584 (incl. 815 at high school level)
Publications: *Boletim Técnico de Extensão*, *Economia Rural* (6 a year), *Jornal da UFV* (12 a year), *Revista Brasileira de Armazenamento*, *Revista Brasileira de Zootecnia* (6 a year), *Revista Ceres* (6 a year), *Revista de Ciências Humanas* (2 a year), *Revista de Educação Física* (2 a year), *Revista de Engenharia na Agricultura* (12 a year), *Revista Gláuks* (2 a year), *Revista Oikos* (2 a year)

DIRECTORS

Agricultural Sciences Centre: Prof. MAURINHO LUIZ DOS SANTOS
Biological and Health Sciences Centre: Prof. RICARDO JUNQUEIRA DEL CARLO
Engineering and Technological Sciences Centre: Prof. LUIZ AURELIO RAGGI
Human Sciences and Liberal Arts Centre: Prof. ADRIEL RODRIGUES DE OLIVEIRA

UNIVERSIDADE FEDERAL DO ACRE

CP 500, 69915-900 Rio Branco, AC
Campus Universitario, Rodovia BR 364, km 04, nº 6637, Distrito Industrial, 69915-900 Rio Branco, AC

Telephone: (68) 3901-2500
E-mail: reitoria@ufac.br
Internet: www.ufac.br

Founded 1971

Rector: Profa Dra OLINDA BATISTA ASSMAR
Librarian: VALCI AUGUSTINHO

Library of 46,000 vols
Number of teachers: 274
Number of students: 2,013

UNIVERSIDADE FEDERAL DO AMAZONAS

Av. Gen. Rodrigo Otávio Jordão Ramos 3000, Campus Universitário, Bairro Coroado I, 69077-000 Manaus, AM

Telephone: (92) 644-1620
Fax: (92) 644-1620
E-mail: direx@ufam.edu.br
Internet: www.ufam.edu.br

Founded 1962
Federal control
Academic year: March to December

Rector: Prof. Dr HIDEMBERGUE ORDOZGOITH DA FROTA
Vice-Rector: GERSON SUGIYAMA NAKAGIMA
Pro-Rector for Admin.: NEUZA INÊS LAHAN FURTADO BELÉM
Pro-Rector for Extension: Profa MÁRCIA PERALES
Pro-Rector for Planning and Institutional Devt: Prof. EDMILSON BRUNO DA SILVEIRA
Pro-Rector for Research and Postgraduate Affairs: Prof. Dr ALTIGRAN SOARES DA SILVA
Pro-Rector for Undergraduate Teaching: Prof. BRUCE PATRICK OSBORNE
Library Dir: FLAVIANO LIMA DE QUEIROZ

Number of teachers: 777
Number of students: 15,605
Publications: *Boletim Bibliográfico*, *Boletim Estatístico*, *Caderno de Humanidades e Ciências Sociais*, *Catálogo de Teses*, *Orçamento Programa*, *Plano Diretor*, *Relatório de Atividades*

DIRECTORS

Centre for Arts: Prof. FRANCISCO CARNEIRO DA SILVA FILHO
Centre for Environmental Sciences: Prof. JOSÉ AMÉRICO LEITE
Computer Centre: EDUARDO JAMES PEREIRA SOUTO
Faculty of Law: Prof. JOSÉ RUSSO
Faculty of Health Sciences: Prof. MENA BARRETO SEGADILHA FRANÇA
Faculty of Social Studies: Prof. ROSALVO MACHADO BENTES
Institute of Exact Sciences: Prof. ADEMAR MAURO TEIXEIRA
Institute of Human Sciences and Literature: Prof. MARCO FREDERICO KRÜGER ALEIXO
Institute of Technology: Prof. JORGE ANDRADE FILHO

UNIVERSIDADE FEDERAL DO CEARÁ

Av. da Universidade 2853, Benfica, 60020-181 Fortaleza, CE

Telephone: (85) 3366-7300
Fax: (85) 3366-5383
E-mail: reitor@ufc.br
Internet: www.ufc.br

Founded 1955

Rector: JESUALDO PEREIRA FARIAS
Vice-Rector: HENRY DE HOLANDA CAMPOS
Librarian: FRANCISCO JONATAN SOARES

Number of teachers: 2,359

Number of students: 27,737

UNIVERSIDADE FEDERAL DO ESPÍRITO SANTO

Av. Fernando Ferrar 514, Goiabeiras, 29075-910 Vitória, ES

Telephone: (27) 3335-2244
Fax: (27) 3335-2210
E-mail: reitoria@npd.ufes.br
Internet: www.ufes.br

Founded as State Univ. in 1954, as Federal Univ. in 1961
Federal control
Language of instruction: Portuguese
Academic year: March to December

Rector: JOSÉ WEBER FREIRE MACEDO
Vice-Rector: RUBENS SERGIO RASSELI
Registrar: ELIANA MARA BORTOLONI FRIZERA
Librarian: ANGELA MARIA BECALLI

Number of teachers: 1,036
Number of students: 10,187

Publications: *Caderno de Pesquisa da UFES*, *Dados Estatísticos*, *Jornal Laboratório*, *Journal UFES*, *Primeira Mão*, *RCP—Revista Universo Pedagógico*, *Revista de Cultura da UFES*, *Revista de História*, *Revista Sofia do Departamento de Filosofia*, *Revista Você da Secretaria de Cultura da UFES*

DIRECTORS

Agricultural and Animal Husbandry Centre: WALDIR CINTRA DE JESUS JUNIOR
Arts Centre: CRISTINA ENGEL DE ALVAREZ
Education Centre: MARIA APARECIDA SANTOS CORRÊA BARRETO
Exact Sciences Centre: ARMANDO BIONDO FILHO
Health Sciences Centre: CARLOS ALBERTO REDINS
Human and Natural Sciences Centre: EDEBRANDE CAVALIERI
Law and Economic Sciences Centre: Profa SONIA MARIA DALCOMUNI
North of Espírito Santo University Centre: RENATO PIROLA
Physical Education and Sports Centre: VALTER BRACHT
Technology Centre: Prof. GILBERTO COSTA DRUMOND SOUSA

ATTACHED INSTITUTES

Institute of Dental Medicine: Superintendent RANULFO GIANORDOLI NETO.

Institute of Technology: Superintendent ANNIBAL EWALD MARTINS.

UNIVERSIDADE FEDERAL DO ESTADO DO RIO DE JANEIRO

Av. Pasteur 296, Urca, 22290-240 Rio de Janeiro, RJ

Telephone: (21) 2542-7350
Fax: (21) 2542-5752
E-mail: reitoria@unirio.br
Internet: www.unirio.br

Founded 1979
Federal control

Rector: Profa MALVINA TANIA TUTTMAN
Vice-Rector: Prof. Dr LUIZ PEDRO SAN GIL JUTUCA
Pro-Rector for Admin.: BENEDITO CUNHA MACHADO
Pro-Rector for Graduate Instruction: BRÍGIDA RIBEIRO PONCIANO
Pro-Rector for Planning and Devt: MAURÍCIO DE PINHO GAMA
Pro-Rector for Postgraduate Research and Extension: Prof. Dra ANA MARIA DE BULHÕES CARVALHO
Dir of Central Library: EROTILDES DE LIMA MATTOS

Library: Libraries with 87,000 vols, 204 periodicals
Number of teachers: 575
Number of students: 5,620

DEANS

Centre for Biological Sciences and Health: MARIO BARRETO CORRÊA LIMA
Centre for Humanities: MARIA JOSÉ MESQUITA CAVALLEIRO DE MACEDO WEHLING
Centre for Physical Sciences and Technology: LUIZ PEDRO SAN GIL JUTUCA

DIRECTORS

Centre for Biological Sciences and Health (Rua Silva Ramos 32, Tijuca, 20270-330 Rio de Janeiro, RJ; tel. (21) 2569-6643; fax (21) 2509-0422; e-mail ccbs@unirio.br):

Alfredo Pinto School of Nursing: TERESINHA DE JESUS ESPÍRITO SANTO DA SILVA
Institute of Biomedicine: ANTONIO BRISOLLA DIUANA
School of Biological Sciences: EDUARDO GOMES DOS SANTOS
School of Medicine and Surgery: ANTONIO CARLOS RIBEIRO GARRIDO IGLESIAS
School of Nutrition: MARIA APARECIDA CAMPOS

Centre for Humanities (Av. Pasteur 458 (prédio Pe. José de Anchieta), Urca, 22290-240 Rio de Janeiro, RJ; tel. (21) 2541-1839 ext. 2008; fax (21) 2542-2242; e-mail cch@unirio.br):

Historical Research: MARIA JOSÉ MESQUITA CAVALLEIRO DE MACEDO WEHLING
School of Archaeology: MARIZA BOTINO
School of Education: DAYSE MARTINS HORA
School of Jurisprudence: ÁLVARO REINALDO DE SOUZA
School of Library Studies: MARCOS LUIZ CAVALCANTI DE MIRANDA
School of Museology: JOSÉ MAURO MATHEUS LOUREIRO

Centre for Physical Sciences and Technology (Rua Voluntários de Pátria 107, Botafogo, 22270-000 Rio de Janeiro, RJ; tel. (21) 2266-5694; fax (21) 2266-5694; e-mail ccet@uniriotec.br):

School of Applied Informatics: ASTERIO KYIOSHI TANAKA

UNIVERSIDADE FEDERAL DO MARANHÃO

Av. dos Portugueses s/n, 65085-580 São Luís, MA
Telephone: (98) 2109-2206
Fax: (98) 2109-2203
E-mail: ufmagr@bacanga.ufma.br
Internet: www.ufma.br
Founded 1966
Federal control
Academic year: March to December
Rector: Prof. Dr NATALINO SALGADO FILHO
Vice-Rector: ANTÔNIO JOSÉ SILVA OLIVEIRA
Pro-Rector for Extension: ANTONIO LUIZ AMARAL PEREIRA
Pro-Rector for Human Resources: MARIA ELISA CANTANHEDE LAGO BRAGA BORGES
Pro-Rector for Management and Finance: JOSÉ AMÉRICO DA COSTA BARROQUEIRO
Pro-Rector for Research and Postgraduate Affairs: FERNANDO CARVALHO SILVA
Pro-Rector for Teaching: ALDIR ARAÚJO CARVALHO FILHO
Librarian: MARIA DA GRAÇA MONTEIRO FONTOURA
Number of teachers: 867
Number of students: 8,895

DIRECTORS

Centre of Basic Studies: SEBASTIÃO BARBOSA CAVALCANTI FILHO

Centre of Health Sciences: JAMILE ALVES DE OLIVEIRA
Centre of Social Sciences: RUBEM RODRIGUES FERRO
Centre of Technology: PEDRO JAFAR BERNIZ

UNIVERSIDADE FEDERAL DO PARÁ

CP 479, 66075-110 Belém, PA
Av. Augusto Corrêa 1, Guamá, Belém, PA
Telephone: (91) 3201-7000
Fax: (91) 3201-7675
E-mail: reitor@ufpa.br
Internet: www.ufpa.br
Founded 1957
Federal control
Language of instruction: Portuguese
Academic year: March to December
Rector: Prof. Dr ALEX FIÚZA DE MELLO
Vice-Rector: Profa Dra REGINA FÁTIMA FEIO BARROSO
Central Library Administrator: MARIA DAS GRAÇAS DA SILVA PENA
Number of teachers: 2,179
Number of students: 28,492
Publications: Cadernos de Pós-Graduação em Direito da UFPA, Cadernos do Centro de Filosofia e Ciências Humanas, Humanitas, MOARA, Revista do Centro do Ciências Jurídicas, Revista do Centro Sócio-Econômico, Revista do Tecnológico, Ver a Educação

DIRECTORS

Arts and Literature Centre: (vacant)
Biology Centre: Profa SETSUKO NORO DOS SANTOS
Education Centre: Profa ANA MARIA ORLANDINA TANCREDI CARVALHO
Exact and Natural Sciences Centre: Prof. RENATO BORGES GUERRA
Health Science Centre: Prof. Dr CLÁUDIO JOSÉ DIAS KLAUTAU
Geosciences Centre: Prof. MARCONDES LIMA DA COSTA
Law Sciences Centre: Prof. JOÃO BATISTA KLAUTAU LEÃO
Philosophy and Human Sciences Centre: Prof. JOSÉ ALVES DE SOUZA JÚNIOR
Socio-Economic Centre: Prof. MARIO NAZARENO NORONHA FARIA E SOUZA
Technology Centre: Profa VERA MARIA NOBRE BRÁZ

UNIVERSIDADE FEDERAL DO PARANÁ

Rua 15 de Novembro 1299, CP 441, 80060-000 Curitiba, PR
Telephone: (41) 3360-5343
Fax: (41) 3360-5343
E-mail: internacional@ufpr.br
Internet: www.internacional.ufpr.br
Founded 1912
Academic year: March to December
Rector: ZAKI AKEL SOBRINHO
Vice-Rector: ROGÉRIO ANDRADE MULINARI
Chief Admin. Officer: ANA LÚCIA JANSEN DE MELLO SANTANA
Librarian: LÍGIA ELIANA SETENARESKI
Library: see Libraries and Archives
Number of teachers: 1,800
Number of students: 30,000
Publications: Boletim Paranaense de Geociências (2 a year), Dens (2 a year), Desenvolvimento e Meio Ambiente (2 a year), História: Questões & Debates (2 a year), Nerítica (1 a year), RAEGA (1 a year), Revista de Economia (2 a year), Revista de Faculdade de Direito (2 a year), Revista Letras (2 a year), Scientia Agraria (2 a year)

DIRECTORS

Agriculture: AMADEU BONA FILHO
Applied Social Sciences: Prof. Dr VICENTE PACHECO
Biological Sciences: Prof. Dr JOSÉ MARCELO ROCHA ARANHA
Earth Sciences: Dra CHISATO OKA FIORI
Education: Dra ETTIENE CORDEIRO GUERIOS
Exact Sciences: SILVIA HELENA SOARES SCWAB
Health Sciences: MARIA EMÍLIA DAUDT VON DER HEYDE
Humanities, Letters and Arts: MARIA TARCISA SILVA BEGA
Law: Prof. Dr RICARDO MARCELO FONSECA
Technical School: SÁVIO MARCELO MOREIRA DA SILVA
Technology: MAURO LACERDA SANTOS FILHO

UNIVERSIDADE FEDERAL DO PIAUÍ

Campus Universitário Ministro Petrônio Portella, Bairro Ininga, 64049-550 Teresina, PI
Telephone: (86) 3215-5511
Fax: (86) 3215-2816
E-mail: ufpinet@ufpi.br
Internet: www.ufpi.br
Founded 1968
Controlled by the Fundação Universidade Federal do Piauí
Academic year: March to November
Rector: Prof. Dr LUIZ DE SOUSA SANTOS JÚNIOR
Vice-Rector: Dr EDWAR DE ALENCAR CASTELO BRANCO
Pro-Rector for Administration: FÁBIO NAPOLEÃO DO RÊGO P. DIAS
Pro-Rector for Extension: Profa MARIA DA GLÓRIA CARVALHO MOURA
Pro-Rector for Planning: Prof. Dr JOSÉ ARIMATÉIA DANTAS LOPES
Pro-Rector for Research and Postgraduate Affairs: Prof. Dr SAULO CUNHA DE SERPA BRANDÃO
Pro-Rector for Student and Community Affairs: Profa Dra NADIR DO NASCIMENTO NOGUEIRA
Pro-Rector for Undergraduate Teaching: Profa Dra GUIOMAR DE OLIVEIRA PASSOS
Librarian: MARGARETH DE LUCENA MARTINS LIMA
Library of 88,617 vols
Number of teachers: 1,104
Number of students: 11,612
Publication: Notícias da FUFPI (12 a year)

DIRECTORS

Agrarian Sciences Centre: Prof. Dr WILAMS COSTA NEVES
Educational Sciences Centre: (vacant)
Health Sciences Centre: ANTÔNIO DOS SANTOS ROCHA FILHO
Human Sciences and Letters Centre: Prof. PEDRO VILARINHO CASTELO BRANCO
Natural Sciences Centre: Prof. HELDER NUNES DA CUNHA
Technology Centre: Prof. JACOB MANOEL GAYOSO PEREIRA DA SILVA

UNIVERSIDADE FEDERAL DO RIO GRANDE

Rua Eng. Alfredo Huch 475, Centro, 96201-900 Rio Grande, RS
Telephone: (53) 3233-8600
Fax: (532) 32-3346
E-mail: reitor03@super.furg.br
Internet: www.furg.br
Founded 1969
State control
Language of instruction: Portuguese
Academic year: March to November
Rector: Prof. Dr JOÃO CARLOS BRAHM COUSIN

Vice-Rector: Prof. MSc ERNESTO LUIZ CASARES PINTO
Librarian: MARIA DA CONCEIÇÃO DE LIMA HOHMANN
Library of 75,000 vols
Number of teachers: 647
Number of students: 4,722

UNIVERSIDADE FEDERAL DO RIO GRANDE DO NORTE

Campus Universitário, BR 101, Lagoa Nova, CP 59072-970 Natal, RN
Telephone: (84) 215-3125
Fax: (84) 215-3131
E-mail: gabinete@reitoria.ufrn.br
Internet: www.ufrn.br
Founded 1958
Federal control
Language of instruction: Portuguese
Academic year: March to December
Rector: JOSÉ IVONILDO DO RÊGO
Vice-Rector: NILSEN CARVALHO FERNANDES DE OLIVEIRA FILHO
Librarian: RILDECI MEDEIROS
Number of teachers: 1,679
Number of students: 27,605

DEANS

Administration: LUIZ PEDRO DE ARAÚJO
Extension Programmes: ILZA ARAÚJO LEÃO DE ANDRADE
Graduate Studies: EDNA MARIA DA SILVA
Human Resources: JOÃO CARLOS TENÓRIO ARGOLO
Planning and General Coordination: OSWALDO HAJIME YAMAMOTO
Research: ANANIAS MONTEIRO MARIZ
Undergraduate Studies: ANTÔNIO CABRAL NETO

DIRECTORS

Centre of Applied Social Sciences: Profa MARIA ARLETE DUARTE DE ARAÚJO
Centre of Biosciences: Prof. RANKE DOS SANTOS SILVA
Centre for Earth and Exact Sciences: Prof. JAZIEL MARTINS SÁ
Centre of Health Sciences: Prof. JUAREZ DA COSTA FERREIRA
Centre of Humanities, Letters and Arts: Prof. MÁRCIO MORAES VALENÇA
Centre of Technology: Prof. MANOEL LUCAS FILHO

UNIVERSIDADE FEDERAL DO RIO GRANDE DO SUL

Av. Paulo Gama 110, 90046-900 Porto Alegre, RS
Telephone: (51) 3316-3601
Fax: (51) 3316-3973
E-mail: relinter@ufrgs.br
Internet: www.ufrgs.br
Founded 1934
Federal control
Language of instruction: Portuguese
Academic year: March to November
Rector: Profa WRANA MARIA PANIZZI
Vice-Rector: Prof. JOSÉ CARLOS FERRAZ HENNEMANN
Pro-Rector for Extension: Prof. FERNANDO MEIRELLES
Pro-Rector for Graduate Studies: Profa JOCELIA GRAZIA
Pro-Rector for Human Resources: Prof. DIMITRIOS SAMIOS
Pro-Rector for Infrastructure: Prof. HELIO HENKIN
Pro-Rector, and Sec. for Institutional and Int. Affairs: Profa SILVIA ROCHA (acting)
Pro-Rector for Planning and Admin. and Sec. for Technological Devt: Profa MARIA ALICE LAHORGUE

Pro-Rector for Research: Prof. CARLOS ALEXANDRE NETTO
Pro-Rector and Sec. for Student Affairs: Prof. ANGELO RONALDO PEREIRA DA SILVA (acting)
Pro-Rector for Undergraduate Studies: NORBERTO HOPEN
Registrar: ANDREA BENITES
Librarian: REJANE RAFFO KLAES
Number of teachers: 2,258
Number of students: 29,117 (22,138 undergraduate, 6,979 postgraduate)
Publications: *Análise Econômica* (economics, 2 a year), *Anos 90* (philosophy and humanities, 2 a year), *Arquivos da Faculdade Veterinária* (veterinary science, 2 a year), *Art e Educação em Revista* (arts, 2 a year), *Boletim do Instituto de Biociências* (biosciences, 2 a year), *Caderno de Farmácia* (pharmacy, 2 a year), *Cadernos de Sociologia* (sociology, 2 a year), *Educação e Realidade* (education, 2 a year), *Educação, Subjetividade e Poder* (social and institutional psychology, 2 a year), *Egatea* (engineering, 2 a year), *Em Pauta* (music, 2 a year), *Epistéme* (philosophy and history of science, 2 a year), *Forjamento* (engineering, 2 a year), *Horizontes Antropológicos* (social anthropology, 2 a year), *Humanas* (philosophy and humanities, 2 a year), *Intexto* (communication and information, 2 a year), *Jornal do SAJU* (law, 2 a year), *Napaea* (botany, 2 a year), *Notas Técnicas* (earth sciences, 2 a year), *Organon* (literature, 2 a year), *Pesquisas* (earth sciences, 2 a year), *Porto Artes* (visual arts, 2 a year), *Psicologia: Reflexão e Crítica* (psychology, 2 a year), *Revista da Faculdade de Direito* (law, 2 a year), *Revista da Faculdade de Odontologia* (dentistry, 2 a year), *Revista de Biblioteconomia e Comunicação* (librarianship and communication, 2 a year), *Revista de Informática Teórica e Aplicada* (informatics, 2 a year), *Revista Gaúcha de Enfermagem* (nursing, 2 a year), *Revista HCPA* (Univ. Hospital, 2 a year), *Revista Movimento* (sports, 2 a year), *Revista Perfil* (sports, 2 a year)

DIRECTORS

Faculty of Agriculture: GILMAR ARDUINO BETTIO MARODIN
Faculty of Architecture: Prof. EDSON WALDIR MEDEIROS KREBS
Faculty of Dentistry: Prof. JOÃO JORGE DINIZ BARBACHAN
Faculty of Economic Sciences: Prof. PEDRO CEZAR DUTRA FONSECA
Faculty of Education: Profa MERION CAMPOS BORDAS
Faculty of Law: Prof. PLÍNIO DE OLIVEIRA CORRÊA
Faculty of Librarianship and Communication: Profa MARCIA BENETTI MACHADO
Faculty of Medicine: Prof. WALDOMIRO CARLOS MANFROY
Faculty of Pharmacy: Profa VALQUIRIA LINCK BASSANI
Faculty of Veterinary Medicine: Prof. ANTÔNIO DE PÁDUA FERREIRA DA SILVA FILHO
Institute of Arts: Prof. CIRIO SIMON
Institute of Basic Health Sciences: JOÃO ROBERTO BRAGA MELLO
Institute of Biological Sciences: Prof. JORGE MARIATH
Institute of Chemistry: Prof. DIMITRIOS SAMIOS
Institute of Computer Science: PHILIPPE OLIVIER ALEXANDER NAVAUX
Institute of Food Technology: Prof. MARCO ANTONIO ZACHIA AYUB
Institute of Geological Sciences: Prof. RICARDO NOBERTO AYUP ZOUAIN
Institute of Hydraulic Research: Prof. LUIZ FERNANDO DE ABREU CYBIS

Institute of Letters and Literature: Profa SARA VIOLA RODRIGUES
Institute of Mathematics: Profa ELSA CRISTINA DE MUNDSTOCK
Institute of Philosophy and Humanities: Prof. JOSÉ VICENTE TAVARES DOS SANTOS
Institute of Physics: Prof. CLAUDIO SCHERER
Institute of Psychology: Prof. CLAUDIO S. HUTZ
School of Engineering: Prof. RENATO MACHADA DE BRITO
School of Management: Prof. JOÃO LUIZ BECKER
School of Nursing: Profa IDA HAUNSS DE FREITAS XAVIER
School of Physical Education: Prof. RICARDO DEMÉTRIO DE SOUZA PETERSEN

UNIVERSIDADE FEDERAL FLUMINENSE

Rua Miguel de Frias 9, Icaraí, 24220-900 Niterói, RJ
Telephone: (21) 2629-5000
Fax: (21) 2629-5207
E-mail: gabinete@gar.uff.br
Internet: www.uff.br
Founded 1960 as Fed. Univ. of the State of Rio de Janeiro; present title 1965
Academic year: March to December
Rector: ROBERTO DE SOUZA SALLES
Vice-Rector: EMMANUEL PAIVA DE ANDRADE
Pro-Rector for Academic Affairs: Prof. MARIA HELENA DA SILVA PAES FARIA
Pro-Rector for Extension: Profa AYDIL DE CARVALHO PREIS
Pro-Rector for Planning: Prof. WALTER PINHO DA SILVA FILHO
Pro-Rector for Research and Postgraduates: Prof. MARCOS MOREIRA BRAGA
Chief Admin. Officer: ALDERICO MENDONÇA FILHO
Librarian: JOÃO CARLOS GOMES RIBEIRO
Library: Libraries with 420,000 vols
Number of teachers: 2,637
Number of students: 26,050 (23,982 undergraduate, 2,068 postgraduate)
Publications: *Revista de Ciências Médicas*, *Revista da Faculdade de Educação*

DIRECTORS OF CENTRES

Applied Social Studies Centre: RAUL DE ALBUQUERQUE FILHO
General Studies Centre: ESTHER HERMES LUCK
Ildefonso Bastos Technical Agricultural School: JOSÉ BASTOS CAVICHINI
Medical Sciences Centre: JOSÉ CELESTINO BICALHO DE FIGEIREDO
Nilo Peçanha Agricultural School: FERNANDO GONÇALVES DA CRUZ Jr
Technology Centre: HEITOR LUIZ SALLES SOARES DE MOURA

DIRECTORS OF INSTITUTES

Applied Social Studies Centre:
 Department of Social Service (Campos): GERALDA FREIRE BELLO DE CAMPOS
 Institute of Economics and Administration: ALBERTO SANTOS LIMA FILHO
 Institute of Education: MARIA FELISBERTA BAPTISTA TRINDADE
 Institute of Law: MARIA ARAIR PINTO PAIVA
 School of Social Service: MARIA AUXILIADORA DA COSTA SIMÃO
General Studies Centre:
 Institute of Arts and Social Communications: ANA MARIA LOPES PEREIRA
 Institute of Biology: LUIZ ANTÔNIO BOTELHO ANDRADE
 Institute of Biomedical Science: ALEXANDRE SAMPAIO DE MARTINO
 Institute of Chemistry: LEONOR REISE DE ALMEIDA

Institute of Earth Sciences: WALTER RONALDO NUNES

Institute of Human Sciences and Philosophy: HUMBERTO FERNANDES MACHADO

Institute of Language and Literature: LAURA CAVALCANTI PADILHA

Institute of Mathematics: LUIZ ANTONIO DOS SANTOS CRUZ

Institute of Physics: PAULO ROBERTO SILVEIRA GOMES

Medical Sciences Centre:

Rodolfo Albino University Laboratory: CARLOS DE CASTRO PEREIRA JORGE

School of Dentistry: RAUL FERES MONTE ALTO FILHO

School of Medicine: JOSÉ CARLOS CARRARO EDUARDO

School of Nursing: CARLOS ALBERTO MENDES

School of Nutrition: STELA MARIA PEREIRA DE GREGÓRIO

School of Pharmacy: ANTONIO CARLOS CARRERA FREITAS

School of Veterinary Science: MARIO AUGUSTO RONCONI

Veterinary Experimental Centre (Iguaba): ADEMIL DE SOUZA PINTO

Technology Centre:

School of Architecture and Town Planning: PEDRO ALFREDO MORAES LENTINO

School of Engineering: JOSÉ JAIRO ARAÚJO DE SOUZA

School of Industrial Metallurgy: ANTONIO FONTANA

UNIVERSIDADE FEDERAL RURAL DE PERNAMBUCO

CP 2071, Rua D. Manoel de Medeiros s/n, Dois Irmãos, 52171-900 Recife, PE

Telephone: (81) 3320-6010
E-mail: reitoria@reitoria.ufrpe.br
Internet: www.ufrpe.br

Founded 1912
Federal control
Language of instruction: Portuguese

Rector: Prof. VALMAR CORRÊA DE ANDRADE
Vice-Rector: Prof. REGINALDO BARROS
Admin. Officer: Prof. FRANCISCO RAMOS CARVALHO
Int. Officer: JOSÉ CARLOS B. DUBEUX
Librarian: SR MÁRIO HENRIQUE VAREJÃO

Library of 61,000 vols
Number of teachers: 700
Number of students: 8,000

Publications: Anais (1 a year), Caderno Ômega (irregular), Medicina Veterinária (online), Revista Brasileira de Ciências Agrárias (Brazilian Journal of Agricultural Sciences, online), Revista Custos e Agronegócio (online).

ATTACHED RESEARCH INSTITUTES

Unidade Acadêmica de Garanhuns: Av. Bom Pastor S/N, Boa Vista, 55296-901 Garanhuns; tel. (87) 3761-0882; e-mail diretor.geral@uag.ufrpe.br; internet www.uag.ufrpe.br; f. 2005; Dir Prof. MARCELO MACHADO MARTINS.

Unidade Acadêmica da Serra Talhada: tel. (87) 3831-2206; e-mail diretor.geral@uast.ufrpe.br; internet www.uast.ufrpe.br; f. 2006; Dir CARLOS ROMERO FERREIRA DE OLIVEIRA.

UNIVERSIDADE FEDERAL RURAL DO RIO DE JANEIRO

BR 465 km 7, Antiga Rodovia Rio–São Paulo, 74504, 23825-000 Seropédica, RJ

Telephone: (21) 682-1210
Fax: (21) 682-1120
E-mail: gabinete@ufrrj.br

Internet: www.ufrrj.br

Founded 1910 as Escola Superior de Agronomia e Medicina Veterinária
Federal control
Language of instruction: Portuguese
Academic year: March to December (2 semesters)

Rector: JOSÉ ANTÔNIO DE SOUZA VEIGA
Vice-Rector: MARIA DA CONCEIÇÃO ESTELLITA VIANNI
Chief Admin. Officer: MARCELO SOBREIRO
Librarian: CRISTINA VICTORIA DAL LIN ESTEVES

Library of 44,233 vols
Number of teachers: 612
Number of students: 6,303

Publications: Ciências da Vida (2 a year), Ciências Exatas e da Terra (2 a year), Ciências Humanas (2 a year)

DIRECTORS

Institute of Agronomy: ELSON DE CARVALHO VIEGAS

Institute of Animal Husbandry: NELSON JORGE MORAES MATOS

Institute of Biology: MARCOS ANTONIO JOSÉ DOS SANTOS

Institute of Education: ALDA MARIA MAGALHÃES D'ALMEIDA SILVA

Institute of Forestry: RICARDO DA SILVA PEREIRA

Institute of Humanities: SILVESTRE PRADO DE SOUZA NIETO

Institute of Pure Sciences: ELIZA HELENA DE SOUZA FARIA

Institute of Technology: LUIZ OTÁVIO NUNES DA SILVA

Institute of Veterinary Science: LAERTE GRISI

UNIVERSIDADE GAMA FILHO

Rua Manuel Vitorino 553, Piedade, 20740-900 Rio de Janeiro, RJ

Telephone: (21) 2599-7100
Fax: (21) 289-8394
Internet: www.ugf.br

Founded 1972
Private control
Language of instruction: Portuguese
Academic year: February to December

Chancellor: Prof. Dr PAULO GAMA FILHO
Vice-Chancellors: Prof. LUIZ ALFREDO GAMA FILHO, Prof. PAULO CESAR GAMA FILHO
Rector: Prof. SÉRGIO DE MORAES DIAS
Vice Rector for Academic Affairs: Dr MANOEL JOSÉ GOMES TUBINO
Vice Rector for Admin.: Prof. PREDUÊNCIO FERREIRA
Vice Rector for Community: Prof. PERALVA DE MIRANDA DELGADO
Vice-Rector for Devt: Prof. AYRTON LUIZ GONÇALVES
Vice Rector for Planning and Coordination: Prof. SÉRGIO DE MORAES DIAS
Sec.-Gen.: Dra MARIA CECÍLIA NUNES AMARANTE
Librarian: Profa LÚCIA BEATRIZ R. T. PARANHOS DE OLIVEIRA

Library of 146,000 vols, 130,000 periodicals
Number of teachers: 1,080
Number of students: 15,500

Publications: Artus (2 a year), Ciência (2 a year), Ciência Humana (2 a year), Ciência Social (2 a year)

DEANS

Biological and Health Sciences Centre: Prof. JOAQUIM JOSÉ DO AMARAL CASTELLÕES
Human Sciences Centre: Profa PAULINA CELI GAMA DE CARVALHO
Sciences and Technology Centre: Prof. SÉRGIO FLORES DA SILVA

Social Sciences Centre: Prof. HENRIQUE LUÍS ARIENTE

ATTACHED INSTITUTES

Instituto de Estudos de Linguas Estrangeiras: Rio de Janeiro; Coordinator REGINA LUCIA MORAES MARIN.

Instituto de Pesquisas Gonzaga da Gama Filho: Rio de Janeiro; Admin. Dir Prof. UBIRAJARA PEÇANHA ALVES; Scientific Dir Prof. JOÃO CARLOS DE OLIVEIRA TÓRTORA.

UNIVERSIDADE GUARULHOS

Praça Tereza Cristina 88, Centro, 07023-070 Guarulhos, SP

Telephone: (11) 2464-1650
Fax: (11) 2464-2030
E-mail: reitor@ung.br
Internet: www.ung.br

Founded 1971
Private control
Language of instruction: Portuguese
Academic year: February to December

Provost: Dr ALEXANDRE ESTOLANO
Vice-Provost: LUCIANE PEREIRA, Dr INÊS SANTOS

Library of 146,364 vols, 840 periodicals
Number of teachers: 645
Number of students: 13,650

Publications: Education Magazine (i2 a year, n Portuguese with abstracts in English), Geosciences Magazine (2 a year, in Portuguese with abstracts in English), Health Magazine (2 a year, in Portuguese with abstracts in English), Third Sector Magazine (2 a year, in Portuguese with abstracts in English).

UNIVERSIDADE IBIRAPUERA

Av. Iraí 297, Moema, 04082-000 São Paulo, SP

Telephone: (11) 5091-1155
E-mail: unib@unib.br
Internet: www.unib.br

Founded 1971
Private control

Rector: JORGE BASTOS

Library of 69,000 vols, 1,936 periodicals
Number of teachers: 317
Number of students: 10,829

UNIVERSIDADE JOSÉ DO ROSARIO VELLANO

Rodovia MG 179, km 0, Campus Universitário, CP23, 37130-000 Alfenas, MG

Telephone: (35) 3299-3000
Fax: (35) 3299-3800
E-mail: unifenas@unifenas.br
Internet: www.unifenas.br

Founded 1988 as Univ. de Alfenas, present name 2002
Private control
Academic year: February to December

Rector: MARIA DO ROSARIO ARARIJO VELANO

Library: Libraries with 86,373 vols, 3,593 periodicals
Number of teachers: 896
Number of students: 10,544

Publication: Jornal da UNIFENAS (12 a year).

UNIVERSIDADE LUTERANA DO BRASIL

Av. Farroupilha 8001, Bairro São José, 92425-900 Canoas, RS

Telephone: (51) 3477-4000
Fax: (51) 3477-1313
E-mail: ulbra@ulbra.br

Internet: www.ulbra.br
Founded 1988
Rector: MARCOS FERNANDO ZIEMER
Library: Libraries with 346,000 vols, 1,285 periodicals
Number of teachers: 1,762
Number of students: 17,557

UNIVERSIDADE METODISTA DE PIRACICABA

Rua Rangel Pestana 762, CP 68, 13400-901 Piracicaba, SP
Telephone: (19) 3124-1515
Fax: (19) 3124-1850
E-mail: falecomreitor@unimep.br
Internet: www.unimep.br
Founded 1975
Private control
Languages of instruction: Portuguese, Spanish
Academic year: March to December
Pres.: GUSTAVO JACQUES DIAS ALVIM
Vice-Pres. for Academic Affairs: SERGIO MARCUS PINTO LOPES
Vice-Pres. for Admin.: ARSENIO FIRMINO NOVÃES NETO
Registrar: ENIO TRIERVAILER
Librarian: REGINA FRACETO
Library of 360,000 vols
Number of teachers: 680
Number of students: 15,000
Publications: *Cadernos de Direito* (law), *Impulso* (humanities and social sciences), *Revista Brasileira de Educação Especial* (spec. education), *Revista de Ciência e Tecnologia* (science and technology), *Saúde em Revista* (health sciences), *Revista de Odontologia* (dental medicine)

DIRECTORS

School of Business and Management: Prof. DORGIVAL HENRIQUE
School of Communication: Prof. BELARMINO CESAR COSTA
School of Dental Medicine: Prof. CARLOS W. WERNER
School of Engineering, Architecture and Urban Studies: Prof. GILBERTO MARTINS
School of Health Sciences: Prof. OLNEY L. FONTES
School of Human Sciences: Profa THEREZA B. F. SANTOS
School of Law: Prof. JOÃO MIGUEL RIVERO
School of Natural and Computer Sciences: Profa ANGELA MARIA CORREA
School of Religious Studies: (vacant)

UNIVERSIDADE METODISTA DE SÃO PAULO

Rua do Sacramento, Rudge Ramos 230, CP 5002, 09640-000 São Bernardo do Campo, SP
Telephone: (11) 4366-5600
Fax: (11) 4366-5768
E-mail: reitoria@metodista.br
Internet: www.metodista.br
Founded 1997
Rector: Prof. Dr DAVI FERREIRA BARROS
Library of 97,000 vols, 4,900 periodicals
Number of teachers: 548
Number of students: 11,907

UNIVERSIDADE METROPOLITANA DE SANTOS

Rua da Constituição 374, Vila Mathias, 11015-470 Santos, SP
Telephone: (13) 3226-3400
E-mail: infounimes@unimes.com.br
Internet: www.unimes.com.br

Founded 1968 as Centro de Estudos Unificados Bandeirante; current name 1985
Private control
Rector: Profa RENATA GARCIA DE SIQUEIRA VIEGAS
Pro-Rector for Academic Affairs: Profa VERA APARECIDA TABOADA DE CARVALHO RAPHAELLI
Library of 59,000 vols, 233 periodicals
Number of teachers: 405
Number of students: 5,034

UNIVERSIDADE PARA O DESENVOLVIMENTO DO ESTADO E DA REGIÃO DO PANTANAL

CP 2153, 79003-010 Campo Grande, MS
Rua Ceará 333, Bairro Miguel Couto, Campo Grande, MS
Telephone: (67) 3348-8000
Fax: (67) 3341-9210
E-mail: uniderp@uniderp.br
Internet: www.uniderp.br
Founded 1996
State control
Rector: Prof. Dr GUILHERME MARBACK NETO
Library: Libraries with 100,000 vols, 1,656 periodicals
Number of teachers: 236
Number of students: 5,111

UNIVERSIDADE PAULISTA

Rua Dr Bacelar 1212, Vila Clementino, 04026-002 São Paulo, SP
Telephone: (11) 5586-4000
Fax: (11) 2275-1541
Internet: www2.unip.br
Founded 1988
Private control
Rector: Prof. Dr JOÃO CARLOS DI GENIO
Vice-Rector for Institutional Relations: Prof. Dr HERMÍNIO ALBERTO MARQUES PORTO
Vice-Rector for Planning, Administration and Finance: Prof. FÁBIO ROMEU DE CARVALHO
Vice-Rector for Postgraduate Affairs and Research: Profa Dra SILVIA ANCONA-LOPEZ
Vice-Rector for Undergraduate Affairs: Prof. Dr YUGO OKIDA
Vice-Rector for University Units: Profa MELÂNIA DALLA TORRE
Library of 248,000 vols, 3,300 periodicals
Number of teachers: 2,519
Number of students: 57,064

UNIVERSIDADE POTIGUAR

Av. Nascimento de Castro 1597, Lagoa Nova, 59054-180 Natal, RN
Telephone: (84) 3215-1234
Fax: (84)3 215-1204
E-mail: vicereitoria@unp.br
Internet: www.unp.br
Founded 1981
Private control
Rector: MIZAEL ARAÚJO BARRETO
Library of 32,000 vols, 241 periodicals
Number of teachers: 249
Number of students: 5,813

UNIVERSIDADE PRESBITERIANA MACKENZIE

Rua da Consolação 930, Consolação, 01302-907 São Paulo, SP
Telephone: (11) 2114-8000
Fax: (11) 3214-3102
E-mail: reitoria@mackenzie.br
Internet: www.mackenzie.br
Founded 1870
Private control

Academic year: March to December
Univ. Pres.: Dr MANASSÉS CLAUDINO FONTELES
Vice-Pres.: Dr PEDRO RONZELLI JR
Rector: Dr MANASSÉS CLAUDINO FONTELES
Sec.-Gen.: Prof. NELSON CALLEGARI
Dean for Academic Affairs: Dr ADEMAR PEREIRA
Dean for Extension: Dr HELENA BONITO COUTO PEREIRA
Dean for Graduate Courses and Research: Dr SANDRA MARIA DOTTO STUMP
Librarian: ROSELY BIANCONCINI MULIN
Library of 342,784 vols, 262 periodicals
Number of teachers: 1,488
Number of students: 40,000
Publications: *Horacinho*, *Jornal Análise*, *O Picareta*, *Oráculo*, *Perfil Mackenzie*, *Revista Mackenzie*, *Revista Psicologia: Teoria e Prática*, *Revista Todas as Letras*

DIRECTORS

School of Architecture and Town Planning: Dr. VALTER CALDANA
School of Arts and Communication: Profa MARCIA CRISTINA GONÇALVES DE OLIVEIRA
School of Computer Sciences: Dr ARNALDO R. DE AGUIAR VALLIM FILHO
School of Economics, Administration and Accounting: Dr MOISÉS ARI ZILBER
School of Engineering: Dr MARCEL MENDES
School of Law: Dr NÚNCIO THEÓPHILO NETO
School of Letters and Education: Dr ESMERALDA RIZZO
School of Sciences and Health: Dr BEATRIZ REGINA PEREIRA SAETA
School of Sciences and Humanities: Dr TEREZINHA JOCELEN MASSON
School of Theology: Dr EDSON PEREIRA LOPES

UNIVERSIDADE REGIONAL DE BLUMENAU

Rua Antônio da Veiga 140, Sala A 201, 89012-900 Blumenau, SC
Telephone: (47) 3321-0214
Fax: (47) 3322-8818
E-mail: cri@furb.br
Internet: www.furb.br
Founded 1968
Fundação Universidade Regional de Blumenau
Language of instruction: Portuguese
Academic year: January to December
Rector: Prof. JOÃO NATEL POLLONIO MACHADO
Vice-Rector: Prof. GRISELDES FREDEL BOOS
Pro-Rector and Dean of Admin.: Prof. UDO SCHROEDER
Pro-Rector and Dean of Education: Prof. ANTÓNIO ANDRÉ CHIVANGA BARROS
Pro-Rector and Dean of Research: Prof. MARCOS RIVAIL DA SILVA
Head of Informatics Centre: EMERSON DE PINHO ADAM
Head of Language Laboratory: Prof. MARINA BEATRIZ BORGMANN DA CUNHA
Librarian: GELCI ROSTIROLLA
Library of 481,909 vols
Number of teachers: 850
Number of students: 11,000
Publications: *Dynamis–Revista Tecno-Científica*, *Revista de Divulgação Cultural*, *Revista de Estudos Ambientais*, *Revista de Negócios*, *Revista Jurídica*.

ATTACHED RESEARCH INSTITUTES

Environmental Research Institute: tel. (47) 3321-0540; fax (47) 3321-0556; e-mail ipa@furb.br; internet www.furb.br/2005/ipa.php?secao=1502; Dir Prof. MARCELO DINIZ VITORINO.

Social Research Institute: Rua São Paulo 1525, Ed. Cristiana, Blumenau; tel. (47)

3321-0350; fax (47) 3321-0338; e-mail ips@
furb.br; internet www.furb.br/2005/ips
.php?secao=1837; Dir Prof. CYNTHIA MOR-
GANA BOOS DE QUADROS.
**Technological Research Institute of Blu-
menau:** Rua São Paulo 3250, Bloco I,
Blumenau; tel. (47) 3321-6082; fax (47)
3321-6081; e-mail iptb@furb.br; internet
www.furb.br/2005/iptb.php?secao=1828;
Coordinator Prof. ALBERTO WISNIESKI.

UNIVERSIDADE REGIONAL DO NOROESTE DO ESTADO DO RIO GRANDE DO SUL (UNIJUÍ)

Rua do Comércio, 3000, 98700-000 Ijuí, Rio
Grande do Sul
Telephone: (55) 333-20200
Fax: (55) 333-29100
E-mail: reitoria@unijui.edu.br
Internet: www.unijui.edu.br
Founded 1985
Private control (Fundação de Integração,
Desenvolvimento e Educação do Noroeste
do Estado)
Language of instruction: Portuguese
Academic year: March to December
Rector: MARTINHO LUIS KELM
Vice Rector for Admin.: LAERDE SADY GEHRKE
Vice Rector for Graduate Courses: EVELISE
MORAES BERLEZI
Vice Rector for Undergraduate Courses:
CÁTIA MARIA NEHRING
Academic Sec.: MARISA FRIZZO
Librarian: ELEDA PASSINATO SAUSEN
Library of 327,495 vols
Number of teachers: 569
Number of students: 9,500
Publications: *Coleção Situação de Estudos* (2
a year), *Contabilidade e Informacão* (4 a
year), *Contexto & Educação* (4 a year),
Contexto e Saúde (2 a year), *Desenvolvi-
mento em Questão* (2 a year), *Direito em
Debate* (2 a year), *Educação nas Ciências*
(2 a year), *Espaços da Escola* (4 a year),
Formas & Linguagens (2 a year), *Leitura e
Revista* (2 a year), *Revista AD Homimen
Tomo I* (2 a year), *Revista de Estudos de
Administracão* (2 a year).

UNIVERSIDADE REGIONAL INTEGRADA DO ALTO URUGUAI E DAS MISSÕES

Av. Sete de Setembro 1621, CP 743, 99700-
000 Erechim, RS
Telephone: (54) 3520-9000
Fax: (54) 3520-9090
E-mail: urireitoria@st.com.br
Internet: www.uricer.edu.br
Founded 1992
Rector: Prof. BRUNO ADEMAR MENTGES
Library: Libraries with 204,000 vols, 5,130
periodicals
Number of teachers: 425
Number of students: 8,337

UNIVERSIDADE SALGADO DE OLIVEIRA

Rua Lambari 10, Trindade, 24456-570 São
Gonçalo, RJ
Telephone: (21) 2138-3400
Fax: (21) 701-7444
E-mail: universo@universo.edu.br
Internet: www.universo.edu.br
Founded 1976
Private control
Rector: Profa MARLENE SALGADO DE OLIVEIRA
Library: Libraries with 59,000 vols, 32,859
periodicals

Number of teachers: 426
Number of students: 20,995

UNIVERSIDADE SALVADOR

Campus Costa Azul, Ed. Civil Empresarial,
Rua Doutor José Peroba 251, STIEP,
41770-235 Salvador, BA
Telephone: (71) 3271-8150
Fax: (71) 235-2911
E-mail: areitoria@unifacs.br
Internet: www.unifacs.br
Founded 1972
Private control
Rector: MANOEL JOAQUIM F. DE BARROS
SOBRINHO
Library of 61,000 vols, 485 periodicals
Number of teachers: 151
Number of students: 3,693

UNIVERSIDADE SANTA CECÍLIA

Rua Oswaldo Cruz 277, Boqueirão, 11045-
907 Santos, SP
Telephone: (13) 3202-7100
Fax: (13) 3234-5297
Internet: www.unisanta.br
Founded 1961
Private control
Academic year: February to December
Chancellor: Dr MILTON TEIXEIRA
Pres.: Dra LÚCIA M. TEIXEIRA FURLANI
Vice-Pres.: Profa MARIA CECÍLIA P. TEIXEIRA
Rector: Dra SÍLVIA ÂNGELA TEIXEIRA PEN-
TEADO
Academic Pro-Rector: Profa ZULEIKA DE A.
SENGER GONÇALVES
Admin. Pro-Rector: Dr MARCELO PIRILO TEIX-
EIRA
Community Pro-Rector: Prof. AQUELINO J.
VASQUES
Pro-Rector for Univ. Devt: Profa EMÍLIA
MARIA PIRILO
Gen. Sec.: WALDIR GRAÇA
Chief Librarian: ANA MARIA RACCIOPI SIL-
VEIRA
Library of 84,000 vols
Number of teachers: 640
Number of students: 13,000
Publications: *Ceciliana*, *Revista de Estudo*

COORDINATORS

Bandeirante I Campus: Profa ROSINHA GAR-
CIA DE SIQUEIRA VIEGAS
Bandeirante II Campus: Profa CARMEN LÚCIA
TABOADA DE CARVALHO
Santa Cecília Campus: Profa LÚCIA MARIA
TEIXEIRA FURLANI, Dr MARCELO TEIXEIRA,
Profa MARIA CECÍLIA TEIXEIRA

DEANS

Faculty of Arts and Communication: Prof. A.
J. VASQUES
Faculty of Chemical Engineering: Eng. A. DE
SALLES PENTEADO
Faculty of Civil Engineering: Eng. A. DE
SALLES PENTEADO
Faculty of Commercial and Administrative
Sciences: Prof. A. PORTO PIRES
Faculty of Dance: Prof. L. RACCINI
Faculty of Dentistry: Dr R. G. DE SIQUEIRA
VIEGAS
Faculty of Education and Human Sciences:
Prof. C. M. BAFFA
Faculty of Industrial Engineering: Eng. A. E.
P. FIGUEIREDO
Faculty of Law: Dr R. MEHANNA KHAMIS
Faculty of Physical Education: Prof. V. A.
TABOADA DE CARVALHO RAPHAELLI
Faculty of Sciences and Technology: Prof. R.
PATELLA

UNIVERSIDADE SANTA ÚRSULA

Rua Fernando Ferrari 75, Botafago, 22231-
040 Rio de Janeiro, RJ
Telephone: (21) 2554-2500
E-mail: reitoria@usu.br
Internet: www.usu.br
Founded 1938
Rector: MARIA DO CARMO BITTENCOURT
Library of 123,000 vols, 2,128 periodicals
Number of teachers: 425
Number of students: 7,639

UNIVERSIDADE SÃO JUDAS TADEU

Rua Taquari 546, Mooca, 03166-000 São
Paulo, SP
Telephone: (11) 2799-1677
E-mail: webmaster@saojudas.br
Internet: www.usjt.br
Founded 1985
Private control
Rector: Prof. JOSÉ CHRISTIANO A. SILVA
MESQUITA
Library of 70,000 vols, 2,066 periodicals
Number of teachers: 733
Number of students: 18,410

UNIVERSIDADE SÃO MARCOS

Rua Clóvis Bueno de Azevedo 176, Ipiranga,
04266-040 São Paulo, SP
Telephone: (11) 3491-0500
Fax: (11) 6163-0978
E-mail: info@smarcos.br
Internet: www.smarcos.br
Founded 1970
Private control
Rector: ERNANI BICUDO DE PAULA
Library of 73,000 vols, 347 periodicals
Number of teachers: 309
Number of students: 8,164

UNIVERSIDADE SEVERINO SOMBRA

Praça Martinho Nóbrega 40, Centro, 27700-
000 Vassouras, RJ
Telephone: (24) 2471-8200
Fax: (24) 2471-8225
E-mail: reitoria@uss.br
Internet: www.uss.br
Founded 1969
Private control
Rector: Dr AMÉRICO DA SILVA CARVALHO
Vice-Rector: ANTÓNIO ORLANDO IZOLANI
Pro-Rectors: MARCO ANTÓNIO SOARES DE
SOUZA, PAULO CÉSAR RODRIGUES CASSINO
Library: Libraries with 46,000 vols, 708
periodicals
Number of teachers: 207
Number of students: 2,034

UNIVERSIDADE TIRADENTES

Av. Murilo Dantes 300, Farolândia, 49032-
490 Aracaju, SE
Telephone: (79) 218-2100
Fax: (79) 218-2200
E-mail: asscom@unit.br
Internet: www.unit.br
Founded 1972
Private control
Rector: JOUBERTO UCHÔA DE MENDONÇA
Library of 111,904 vols, 957 periodicals
Number of teachers: 442
Number of students: 11,741
Publication: *Revista Fragmenta* (3 a year).

UNIVERSIDADE VEIGA DE ALMEIDA

Rua Ibituruna 108, Bloco B (3° andar), Tijuca, 20271-020 Rio de Janeiro, RJ

Telephone: (21) 2574-8888

Internet: www.uva.br

Founded 1992

Private control

Rector: Mário Veiga de Almeida Junior

Library: Libraries with 66,000 vols, 1,007 periodicals

Number of teachers: 333

Number of students: 6,864

Colleges
GENERAL

Centro de Ensino Unificado de Brasília: SEPN 707/907, Campus do UniCEUB, Brasília, DF; tel. 340-1878; fax 340-1578; e-mail biblioteca@uniceub.br; internet www .uniceub.br; f. 1968; controls Ciências e Letras do Distrito Federal, Contábeis e Administrativas do Distrito Federal, Faculdade de Ciências da Educacão, Faculdade de Ciências da Saudé, Faculdade de Ciências Econômicas, Faculdade de Ciências Exatas e Tecnologia, Faculdade de Direito do Distrito Federal, Faculdade de Ciências Sociais e Aplicadas, Faculdade de Filosofia; library: 22,000 vols; 710 teachers; 14,000 students; Rector Dr João Herculino de Souza Lopes; publs *Universitas—Biociencias* (2 a year), *Universitas—Jus* (2 a year), *Universitas—Psicologia* (2 a year).

Centro Universitário do Distrito Federal (UDF): SEP/SUL, Eq. 704/904, Conjunto A, 70390-045 Brasília, DF; tel. (61) 3704-8888; e-mail udf@udf.edu.br; internet www.unidf.edu.br; f. 1967; graduate courses in accountancy, administration, advertising, economics, education, information systems, international relations, journalism, law, politics; library: 42,000 vols; 950 teachers; 33,000 students; Pres. Rezende Ribeiro de Rezende.

Centro Universitário Moura Lacerda: Rua Padre Euclides 995, Campos Elíseos, 14085-420 Ribeirão Preto, SP; tel. (16) 2101-1010; fax (16) 2101-1024; internet www .mouralacerda.edu.br; f. 1923; graduate courses in accountancy, administration, architecture and town planning, agronomy, civil, computing and mathematics, economics, education, electronic and production engineering, fashion, international relations, languages and literature, law, philosophy, physical education, social communication, and veterinary medicine; postgraduate courses incl. MBA; campuses in Ribeirão Preto, Jaboticabal and Sertãozinho; library: 50,000 vols; Rector Prof. Dr Glauco Eduardo Pereira Cortez.

Centro Universitário Salesiano de São Paulo—Unidade de Ensino de Lorena: Rua Dom Bosco 284, Centro, 12600-000 Lorena, SP; tel. (12) 3153 2033; fax (12) 3152 1299; internet www.unisal-lorena.br; f. 1985; courses in administration, computer science, education, geography, history, Internet systems technology, law, mathematics, philosophy, psychology, tourism, technology in hotel management; library: 60,000 vols; Dir Dilson Passos Junior; Sec. Getulino do Espírito Santo Maciel; publs *Revista Ciência e Tecnologia*, *Revista de Ciências da Educação*, *Revista Jurídica Direito e Paz*.

Faculdades ASMEC: Av. Dr Professor Antônio Eufrâsio de Tôledo 100, Jardim dos Ypês, 37570-000 Ouro Fino, MG; tel. (35) 3441-1616; e-mail asmec@asmec.br; internet www.asmec.br; f. 1972; run by Associação Sul Mineira de Educação e Cultura; courses in administration, agricultural environmental management, biology, chemistry, education, geography, hotel management, languages and literature, mathematics, nursing, nutrition, physical education, systems analysis and development, tourism; 23 teachers; 1,437 students; library: 8,306 vols, 3,522 periodicals; Gen. Coordinator Bel. Guilherme Bernardes Filho; publ. *Signum*.

Faculdades Integradas Hebraico Brasileira Renascença: Rua Prates 790, Bom Retiro, 01121-000 São Paulo; tel. (11) 3311-0778; fax (11) 3311-0778; e-mail faculdade .br@renascenca.br; internet www.renascenca .br/faculdade; f. 1975; attached to the Sociedade Hebraico Brasileira Renascença; languages of instruction: English, Hebrew, Portuguese, Spanish; academic year January to December (2 terms); library: 41,157 vols, 868 periodicals, 164 video cassettes, 839 theses; 72 teachers; 1,107 students; Dir-Gen. Prof. Bernardo Zweiman Abrão.

Faculdades Oswaldo Cruz: Rua Brigadeiro Galvão 540, Barra Funda, São Paulo, SP; tel. 3825-4266; fax 3825-4266 ext. 236; e-mail faculdades@oswaldocruz.br; internet www.oswaldocruz.br; f. 1966; library: 36,565 vols; 328 teachers; 4,895 students; Dir Carlos Eduardo Quirino Simões de Amorim; Librarian Valdenise Machado Ribeiro Fidelis.

Constituent Institutions:

Escola Superior de Química: Rua Brigadeiro Galvão 540, Prédio I 7° andar, Barra Funda, São Paulo, SP; tel. 3825-4266 ext. 258; fax 3825-4266 ext. 236; e-mail esq@oswaldocruz.br; internet www .oswaldocruz.br; f. 1966; 76 teachers; 1,313 students; courses in engineering, industrial chemistry; Dir Prof. Victor Abou Nehmi.

Faculdade de Ciências Administrativas, Econômicas e Contábeis: Rua Brigadeiro Galvão 540, Prédio I 7° andar, Barra Funda, São Paulo, SP; tel. 3825-4266 ext. 245; fax 3825-4266 ext. 236; e-mail ocfaec@oswaldocruz.br; internet www.oswaldocruz.br; f. 1974; 98 teachers; 2,257 students; courses in accountancy, economics, and management; Dir Prof. Dr Oduvaldo Cardoso.

Faculdade de Ciências Farmacêuticas e Bioquímicas: Rua Brigadeiro Galvão 540, Prédio I 7° andar, Barra Funda, São Paulo, SP; tel. 3825-4266 ext. 259; fax 3825-4266 ext. 236; e-mail farmacia@ oswaldocruz.br; internet www.oswaldocruz .br; f. 1981; courses in biochemistry and pharmacy; 70 teachers; 504 students; Dir Prof. Paulo Roberto Miele.

Faculdade de Filosofia, Ciências e Letras: Rua Brigadeiro Galvão 540, Prédio I 7° andar, Barra Funda, São Paulo, SP; tel. 3825-4266 ext. 243; fax 3825-4266 ext. 236; e-mail ffcl@oswaldocruz.br; internet www.oswaldocruz.br; f. 1969; 84 teachers; 821 students; courses in chemistry, mathematics, pedagogy, physics, Portuguese; Dir Prof. Victor Abou Nehmi.

ECONOMICS, POLITICAL SCIENCE, SOCIOLOGY

Centro Universitário Fundação Santo André: Av. Príncipe de Gales 821, 09060-650 Santo André, SP; tel. (11) 4979-3300; fax (11) 440-2048; internet www.fsa.br; f. 1954; supported by the Fundação Santo André; faculties of economics and administration; engineering; languages and literature, philosophy, sciences; graduate courses in education and MBA; library: 19,340 vols; Rector Prof. Dr Oduvaldo Cacalano.

Escola de Administração de Emprêsas de São Paulo da Fundação Getúlio Vargas: Av. 9 de Julho 2029, Bela Vista, 01313-902 São Paulo, SP; tel. (11) 3281-7777; e-mail mtereza.fleury@fgv.br; internet www .eaesp.fgvsp.br; f. 1954; library: 70,000 books, 1,200 periodicals; business and public administration; 250 teachers; 4,616 students; Dir Maria Tereza Leme Fleury; publs *Relatórios de Pesquisa*, *Revista de Administração de Emprêsas*.

Faculdade de Ciências Políticas e Econômicas de Cruz Alta: Rua Andrade Neves 308, Cruz Alta, RS; f. 1955; independent; library: 4,605 vols; Dir Dario Silveira Netto.

Faculdade de Ciências Sociais Aplicadas do Sul de Minas Gerais: Av. Presidente Tancredo de Almeida Neves 45, Itajubá, MG; tel. (35) 3629-5700; fax (35) 3629-5705; internet www.facesm.br; f. 1965; courses in accountancy, administration and economics; Dir Prof. Guilherme Garnett.

Faculdade Estadual de Ciências Econômicas de Apucarana: Av. Minas Gerais 5021, 86800-970 Apucarana, PR; tel. (43) 3423-7277; fax (43) 3423-7277; internet www .fecea.br; f. 1959; state school; accounting, administration, economics, human sciences, quantitative methods; Dir Prof. Vanderley Ceranto.

Instituto Rio Branco: Ministério das Relações Exteriores, Setor de Administração Federal Sul, Quadra 5–Lotes 2/3, 70170-900 Brasília, DF; tel. (61) 3411-9804; fax (61) 3411-9828; e-mail irbr@mre.gov.br; internet www.irbr.mre.gov.br; f. 1945; official Brazilian Diplomatic Academy; 2-year graduate courses; also courses for foreign students; Dir Min. Andre Mattoso Maia Amado.

Instituto Universitário de Pesquisas do Rio de Janeiro: Rua da Matriz 82, Botafogo, 22260-100, Rio de Janeiro, RJ; tel. (21) 2266-8300; fax (21) 2286-7146; e-mail webmaster@iuperj.br; internet www.iuperj .br; f. 1969; research and graduate training in political science and sociology; 18 teachers; library: 20,000 vols; Exec. Dir José Maurício Domingues; publs *Cadernos de Sociologia e Política* (every 2 years), *Contributions to the History of Concepts* (2 a year), *Dados* (4 a year).

LAW

Faculdade de Direito Cândido Mendes: Rua da Assembléia, 10, sala 416, Centro, Rio de Janeiro, RJ; tel. (21) 2531-2000 ext. 217; e-mail fdcm@candidomendes.edu.br; f. 1953; course in law; library: 10,000 vols; Dir Prof. José Baptista de Oliveira Junior; publ. *Dados*.

Faculdade de Direito de São Bernardo do Campo: Rua Java 425, Jardim do Mar, CP 180, 09750-650 São Bernardo do Campo, SP; tel. and fax 4123-0222; e-mail diretoria@ direitosbc.br; internet www.direitosbc.br; f. 1964; library: 27,000 vols; 57 teachers; 2,486 students; Dir Luiz Antonio Mattos Pimenta Araújo.

Faculdade de Direito de Sorocaba: Rua Dra Ursulina Lopes Torres 123, Vergueiro, 18100 Sorocaba, SP; tel. (15) 2105-1234; fax (15) 2105-1234; internet www.fadi.br; f. 1957; library: 10,000 vols; Dir Dr Helio Rosa Baldy; publ. *Revista*.

MEDICINE

Escola de Farmácia e Odontologia de Alfenas: Rua Gabriel Monteiro da Silva 714, 37130-000 Alfenas, MG; tel. (35) 3299-1062; fax (35) 3299-1063; e-mail grad@efoa.int.br; f. 1914; graduate courses in biochemical and applied pharmacy, biological sciences and nutrition, dentistry, general nursing and obstetrics; 127 teachers; library: 16,059 vols; Dean Prof. MACIRO MANOEL PEREIRA; publ. *Revista*.

Faculdade de Medicina do Triângulo Mineiro: Rua Frei Paulino 30, 38025-180 Uberaba, MG; tel. (34) 3318-5004; fax (34) 3312-1487; e-mail diretoria@diretoria.fmtm .br; internet www.fmtm.br; f. 1953; 185 teachers; 1,383 students; Dir Prof. EDSON LUIZ FERNANDES.

TECHNICAL

Centro Universitário de Lins: Av. Nicolau Zarvos 1925, Jardim Aeroporto, 16401-371 Lins, SP; tel. (14) 3533-3200; fax (14) 3533-3248; internet www.unilins.edu.br; f. 1961; courses in administration, business automation engineering, engineering (civil, computer, electromechanical, electronic, environmental, information), executive secretaryship, information systems, marketing, mechatronics, nursing, social services, technology (in industrial chemistry, in Internet systems, in management processes, in systems analysis); 50 teachers; 650 students; Rector MILTON LÉO; Vice-Rector EDGAR PAULO PASTORELLO.

Centro Universitário do Instituto Mauá de Tecnologia: Praça Mauá, CEP 09580-900, São Caetano do Sul, SP; tel. (11) 4239-3000; fax (11) 4239-3041; e-mail ceum@maua .br; internet www.maua.br; f. 1961; civil, chemical, electrical, environmental and food engineering, mechanical, industrial, mechatronics and packaging technology; library: 60,000 vols; 250 teachers; 4,000 students; Dir OTAVIO DE MATTOS SILVARES.

Escola Superior de Desenho Industrial: Rua Evaristo da Veiga 95, Rio de Janeiro 20031-040; tel. (21) 2240-1790; fax (21) 2240-1890; e-mail diretoria@esdi.uerj.br; internet www.esdi.uerj.br; f. 1962; state school, affiliated to Univ. do Estado do Rio de Janeiro; courses in product and graphic design; 34 teachers; 160 students; Dean GABRIEL PATROCÍNIO.

Faculdade de Ciências de Barretos: Av. Prof. Roberto Frademonte 389, Aeroporto, 14783-226 Barretos, SP; tel. (17) 322-6411; fax (17) 322-6205; e-mail faciba@seb.br; f. 1969; chemistry, food engineering and processing, mathematics, physics; library: 13,300 vols; Prin. LUIZA MARIA PIERINI MACHADO.

Faculdade de Engenharia de Barretos: c/o Fundacão Educacional de Barretos, Av. Prof. Roberto Frade Monte 389, CP 16, 14783-226 Barretos, SP; tel. (17) 3322-6411; fax (17) 3322-6205; e-mail dirgeral@feb.br; internet www.feb.br; f. 1965; part of the Fundação Educacional de Barretos; civil, food and electrical engineering; library: 14,000 vols; 202 teachers; 2,000 students; Academic Dir PATRICIA HELENA RODRIGUES DE SOUZA; Vice-Dir Dr OLIVIO CARLOS NASCIMENTO SOUTO.

Instituto Militar de Engenharia: Praça General Tibúrcio 80, Praia Vermelha, 22290-270 Rio de Janeiro, RJ; tel. (21) 2546-7080; internet www.ime.eb.br; f. 1792; present name 1959; undergraduate, Masters and doctoral courses in sciences and engineering; 200 teachers; 500 students; library: 20,000 vols; Dir-Gen. EMILIO CARLOS ACOCELLA.

Instituto Nacional de Telecomunicações (INATEL): Av. João de Camargo 510, 37540-000 Santa Rita do Sapucaí, MG; tel. (35) 3471-9200; fax (35) 3471-9314; e-mail inatel@ inatel.br; internet telecom.inatel.br; f. 1965; electrical engineering (electronics and telecommunications); library: 13,000 vols; Dir Prof. PEDRO SERGIO MONTI.

Instituto Tecnológico de Aeronáutica: Praça Mal. do Ar Eduardo Gomes 50, Vila das Acácias, 12228-900 São José dos Campos, SP; tel. (12) 3947-5731; fax (12) 3941-3500; e-mail reitor@ita.br; internet www.ita.br; f. 1950; divs of aeronautical engineering, civil and basic engineering, computer engineering, electronic engineering, mechanical engineering; 130 teachers; 800 students; library: 98,841 vols and reports, 135,000 microforms, 2,182 periodicals, 5,000 electronic publs; Rector Prof. MICHAL GARTENKRAUT; Dean Prof. FERNANDO TOSHINORI SAKANE; Admin. Officer Cel. DINO ISHIKURA; publ. *Produção Técnico Científica*.

Instituto Tecnológico e Científico 'Roberto Rios' (INTEC): Av. Prof. Roberto Frade Monte 389, Bairro Aeroporto, 14783-226 Barretos, SP; tel. (17) 3321-6411; fax (17) 3322-6205; e-mail intec@feb.br; internet www.feb.br/intec; f. 1981; courses in administration and business, chemistry, civil engineering, dentistry, electricity and electrical engineering, English, environment, foreign trade, gastronomy, graphic design, health sciences, hotel management, industrial automation, informatics and computer engineering, logistics, networks and infrastructure, safety at work, Web design, welding; Dir Dr GERALDO NUNES CORRÊA.

Universidade Federal Rural da Amazônia: CP 917, 66077-530 Belém, PA; tel. (91) 274-4518; fax (91) 274-4518; e-mail biblioteca@ufra.edu.br; internet www.ufra .edu.br; f. 1951; agronomy, fisheries engineering, forestry and veterinary studies, zootechnics; library: 18,000 vols, 1,343 periodicals; 118 teachers; 1,900 students; Dir Dr MANOEL MALHEIROS TOURINHO; publs *Cartilhas Didáticas* (irregular), *Informe Didático* (irregular), *Informe Técnico* (irregular), *Livros Técnicos* (irregular), *O Trimestre*, *Revista de Ciências Agrárias* (2 a year).

Schools of Art and Music

Centro de Letras e Artes da UNIRIO: Av. Pasteur 436, Urca, 22290-240 Rio de Janeiro, RJ; tel. (21) 2295-2548; fax (21) 2295-1043; internet www.unirio.br/cla; f. 1969; 4-year course in theatre and music, Masters course in theatre and Brazilian music; 96 teachers; 850 students; library: 25,000 vols, 7,000 scores, 3,000 records; Dean EDIR EVANGELISTA GANDRA; Dirs AUSONIA BERNARDES MONTEIRO, NEREIDA DE ASSIS NOGUEIA DE MOURA RANGEL.

Conservatório Brasileiro de Música: Av. Graça Aranha 57, 12° andar, Castelo, 20030-002 Rio de Janeiro; tel. (21) 3478-7600; fax (21) 240-6131; e-mail cbm@cbm-musica.org .br; internet www.cbm-musica.org.br; f. 1936; undergraduate and postgraduate courses; library: 6,000 vols; Gen. Dir CECILIA CONDE; publ. *Revista Pesquisa e Música*.

Conservatório Dramático e Musical de São Paulo: Av. Conselheiro Crispiniano 378, 01037-000 São Paulo; tel. (11) 3337-2111; fax (11) 223-9231; e-mail cdmsp@cdmsp.edu.br; f. 1906; library: 30,000 vols; Dir JÚLIO DA CRUZ NAVEGA NETO (acting).

Escola de Artes Visuais (School of Visual Arts): Rua Jardim Botânico 414, Parque Lage, 22461-000 Rio de Janeiro, RJ; tel. (21) 2538-1879; fax (21) 2538-1879; e-mail eav@ eavparquelage.org.br; internet www .eavparquelage.org.br; f. 1975; linked administratively to the State Dept of Culture; courses in art theory and history, computer art, drawing, painting, photography, sculpture, video cassettes; library: 5,500 vols; 40 teachers; 1,200 students; Dir REYNALDO ROELS, Jr.

Escola de Música da Universidade Federal do Rio de Janeiro: Rua do Passeio 98, Lapa, 20021-290 Rio de Janeiro, RJ; tel. (21) 240-1391; fax (21) 240-1591; f. 1848; 77 teachers; 478 students; library: 100,000 vols of music; museum of 90 antique instruments; Dir Prof. JOSÉ ALVES; Librarian DOLORES BRANDÃO DE OLIVEIRA; publ. *Revista Brasileira de Música* (irregular).

Attached to the School:

> **Centro de Pesquisas Folclóricas:** Rio de Janeiro; f. 1943; collns of traditional music on records; Dir Prof. SAMUEL MELLO ARAÚJO, Jr.

Escola de Música e Belas Artes do Paraná: Rua Emiliano Perneta 179, 80010-050 Curitiba, PR; tel. (41) 3026-0029; fax (41) 3017-2070; e-mail secretaria@embap.pr.gov .br; internet www.embap.pr.gov.br; f. 1948; library: 2,350 vols, also tapes, records; musical instruments, plastic arts, singing; Dir ANNA MARIA LACOMBE FEIJÓ.

Faculdade de Belas Artes de São Paulo: Rua Edmundo Juventino Fuentes 160 (apt 12), Edif. Torino, 03280-000 São Paulo, SP; tel. (11) 6946-1255; fax (11) 6946-1255; f. 1925; architecture, town planning, industrial arts and design, painting, sculpture, etc.; 130 teachers; library: 10,000 vols; Dir PAULO ANTONIO GOMES CARDIM.

Faculdade Santa Marcelina—(FASM): Rua Dr Emílio Ribas 89, Perdizes, 05006-020 São Paulo, SP; tel. (11) 3824-5800; fax (11) 3824-5818; e-mail fasm@fasm.edu.br; internet www.fasm.edu.br; f. 1929; art education, composition, electric-acoustic music, fashion design, international relations, marketing administration, music, musical instruments, nursing, singing, visual arts,; 169 teachers; 1,700 students; library: 50,000 vols; Pres. FILOMENA MARIA PEDONE; Dir ÂNGELA RIVERO.

Fundação Armando Alvares Penteado: Rua Alagoas 903, Higienópolis, 01242-902 São Paulo; tel. (11) 3662-7000; internet www .faap.br; f. 1947; undergraduate, graduate and extension courses; 1,120 teachers; 12,000 students; Pres. CELITA PROCOPIO DE CARVALHO; Exec. Dir Dr ANTONIO BIAS BUENO GUILLON.

BRUNEI

The Higher Education System

The Universiti Brunei Darussalam (founded in 1985) is the principal institution of higher education. A second university, the Universiti Islam Sultan Sharif Ali, was founded in 2007 to offer Islamic education. In the same year the status of the Seri Begawan Training College for Teachers of Islamic Religion was upgraded when it became the Seri Begawan University College for Teachers of Islamic Religion. Malay is the official language of instruction, but courses are also taught in English and Arabic (especially Islamic education). The Ministry of Education is responsible for higher education.

Students with adequate 'A' Level passes are eligible for entry to the Universiti Brunei Darussalam or other tertiary institutions or to be awarded scholarships to study abroad. The Institut Teknologi Brunei provides courses leading to a Higher National certificate (part-time) or a National Diploma (full-time). Bachelors degrees at the Universiti Brunei Darussalam last for four to six years and programmes operate on a US-style 'credit' system, with a minimum number required for graduation. In 2005 there were 4,242 students enrolled in higher education institutions.

Regulatory and Representative Bodies

GOVERNMENT

Ministry of Culture, Youth and Sports: Simpang 336-17, Jalan Kebangsaan, Bandar Seri Begawan BA 1210; tel. 2380667; fax 2380235; e-mail info@kkbs.gov.bn; internet www.kkbs.gov.bn; Min. Pehin Dato' Haji MOHAMMAD BIN DAUD.

Ministry of Education: Old Airport Rd, Jalan Berakas, Bandar Seri Begawan BB 3510; tel. 2382233; fax 2380050; e-mail feedback@moe.edu.bn; internet www.moe .gov.bn; Min. Pehin Dato' Haji ABDUL RAHMAN TAIB.

ACCREDITATION

Brunei Darussalam National Accreditation Council: 2nd Fl., Block B, Ministry of Education, Old Airport Rd , Berakas BB 3510; tel. (2) 381133 ext 2209; fax (2) 381238; e-mail mkpk@moe.edu.bn; internet www .moe.edu.bn/web/moe/dept/highedu/sbnac; f. 1990; ensures and maintains the quality and standard of educational credentials; considers and evaluates the status and quality of qualifications awarded by local and overseas instns; Exec. Sec. ADININ MD SALLEH (acting).

Learned Societies

LANGUAGE AND LITERATURE

Alliance Française: No 1A, Simpang 46, Kg Kiarong, Jalan Dato Ratna, Negara; tel. (2) 654245; fax (2) 652214; e-mail education@ afbrunei.com; internet www.afbrunei.com; offers courses and exams in French language and culture and promotes cultural exchange with France.

British Council: 2nd Fl., Block D, Yayasan Complex, Sultan Haji Hassanal Bolkiah Jalan Pretty, Bandar Seri Begawan BS 8711; tel. (2) 237742; fax (2) 237392; e-mail all.enquiries@bn.britishcouncil.org; internet www.britishcouncil.org/brunei; offers courses and exams in English language and British culture and promotes cultural exchange with the UK; Dir AMANDA GRIFFITHS.

Research Institutes

AGRICULTURE, FISHERIES AND VETERINARY SCIENCE

Brunei Agricultural Research Centre, Department of Agriculture: Dept of Agriculture, Ministry of Industry and Primary Resources, Jalan Tutong, Kilanas BF 2520; tel. (2) 661894; fax (2) 661354; e-mail barc001@brunet.bn; internet www.brunet .bn/gov/doa/barc.htm; f. 1984, present name since 1995; 100 mems; Head of Div. Pengiran Hajah ROSIDAH BINTI PENGIRAN HAJI METUSSIN.

HISTORY, GEOGRAPHY AND ARCHAEOLOGY

Brunei History Centre: Ministry of Culture, Youth and Sports, BS 8610 Bandar Seri Begawan; tel. (2) 240166; fax (2) 241958; e-mail sejarah@brunet.bn; internet www .history-centre.gov.bn; f. 1982; govt dept under the Ministry of Culture, Youth and Sports; research on Brunei's history and genealogies, and history of Brunei's Sultan, royal families, and state dignitaries; Dir Haji MOHAMED JAMIL AL-SUFRI; publs *Pusaka* (Heritage, 2 a year), *Darussalam* (The Abode of the Peace, 1 a year).

Library

Bandar Seri Begawan

Language and Literature Bureau Library: Jalan Elizabeth II, Bandar Seri Begawan; tel. (2) 235501; f. 1961; reference and lending facilities open to the public; 300,000 vols in Malay and English; one central and 4 full-time brs; 5 mobile units; Chief Librarian Haji ABU BAKAR BIN HAJI ZAINAL; publs *Accessions List*, indexes.

Museums and Art Galleries

Bandar Seri Begawan

Brunei Museum: Jalan Kota Batu, Bandar Seri Begawan BD 1510; tel. (2) 244545; fax (2) 242727; e-mail bmdir@brunet.bn; internet www.museums.gov.bn; f. 1965; ethnographical, historical, archaeological displays; natural history, oriental arts and cultural heritage collns; library of 77,813 vols, Borneo colln of 2,492 vols, 63,927 local publs; legal

depository for Brunei; Dir Haji MATASSIM BIN HAJI JIBAH; publs *Berita Muzium* (4 a year), *Brunei Darussalam National Bibliography* (1 a year), *Brunei Museum Journal* (1 a year).

Constitutional History Gallery: Jalan Sultan, Bandar Seri Begawan BD 1510; tel. (2) 238360; fax (2) 242727; f. 1984; Dir Pengiran Haji HASHIM BIN PENGIRAN HAJI MOHAMED JADID.

Malay Technology Museum:; tel. (2) 242861; fax (2) 242727; e-mail bmethno@ brunet.bn; internet www.museums.gov.bn; f. 1988; exhibitions of traditional industries and handicrafts, Malay traditional technologies, research on Brunei indigenous ethnic groups; Curator of Ethnography PUDARNO BIN BINCHIN; Research Officers NORAZAH DAYANGKU BTE PENGIRAN HAJI MUHAMMAD, MASNAH BTE AMIT; Museum Officers BAHRAIN BIN HAJI BOLHASAN, JAHRANI BTE HAJI ABAS; publ. *The Brunei Museum Journal*.

Royal Regalia Building: Jalan Sultan, Bandar Seri Begawan BS 8610; tel. (2) 238360; fax (2) 242727; internet www .museums.gov.bn/bangunan2.htm; f. 1992; Dir Haji MATASSIM BIN HAJI JIBAH.

Universities

UNIVERSITI BRUNEI DARUSSALAM

Jalan Tungku Link, Gadong BE 1410

Telephone: (2) 463001

Fax: (2) 463015

E-mail: office.ipro@ubd.edu.bn

Internet: www.ubd.edu.bn

Founded 1985, the Sultan Hassanal Bolkiah Teachers' College was integrated into the Univ. in 1988, the Institute of Islamic Studies was integrated into the Univ. in 1999, the School of Nursing was integrated into the Univ. in 2008

State control

Languages of instruction: Malay, English

Academic year: August to December,January to May (2 semesters)

Chancellor: HM Sultan Haji HASSANAL BOLKIAH MU'IZZADDIN WADDAULAH

Pro-Chancellor: HRH Crown Prince Pengiran MUDA HAJI AL-MUHTADEE BILLAH

Vice-Chancellor: ZULKARNAIN HANAFI

Registrar and Sec.: Dr Haji AWANG METUSSIN BIN HJ BAKIR

Chief Librarian: HAJI AWG SUHAIMI BIN HAJI ABDUL KARIM

Library of 345,160 vols

Number of teachers: 403

Number of students: 4,728

Publications: *Jare* (1 a year), *Tinjauan* (1 a year), *Ungkayah* (4 a year)

DEANS

Academy of Brunei Studies: Dr SITI NOR-KHALBI BINTI HAJI WAHSALFELAH

Faculty of Arts and Social Science: Dr MOHD GARY JONES

Faculty of Business, Economics and Policy Studies: Dr HAZRI BIN HJ KIFLE

Faculty of Science: Prof. DATO HAJI MOHAMED ABDUL MAJID

Educational Technology Centre: JEREMY PHILIP BROWN

Information, Communication and Technology Centre: LIM SEI GUAN

Institute of Medicine: Dr ANITA BINURUL ZAHRINA AZIZ

Language Centre: Dr HAJI NOOR AZAM BIN OKMB HAJI OTHMAN

Postgraduate Studies and Research: Assoc. Prof. Dr TAN KHA SHENG

Sultan Hassanal Bolkiah Institute of Education: Dr HAJAH ROMAIZAH

Sultan Haji Omar Ali Saifuddien Institute of Islamic Studies: Dr NUROL HUDA

UNIVERSITI ISLAM SULTAN SHARIF ALI (UNISAA)

Jalan Tungku, Gadong BE 1410

Telephone: (2) 463001 ext 1435

Fax: (2) 463065

Internet: www.unissa.edu.bn

Founded 2007

State control

Rector: Pengiran Dato' Seri Setia Dr Haji MOHAMMAD BIN PENGIRAN HAJI ABD RAHMAN

Permanent Academic Advisor: Prof. Dato' Dr MUNIR YAACOB

Registrar: Haji TARIP BIN HAJI MAT YASSIN

Bursar: Haji SULAIMAN BIN LATIP

Dean of Student Affairs: Pengiran Haji SAIFUL BAHRIN BIN PENGIRAN HAJI KULA

DEANS

Faculty of Arabic Language and Islamic Civilization: Prof. Madya Dr ARIF KARKHI ABUKHUDAIRI

Faculty of Business and Management Science: (vacant)

Faculty of Shariah and Law: Dr AYMAN ABDEL RAOUF SALEH

Faculty of Usuluddin: Dr SABER AHMAD TAHA

Colleges

There are Adult Education Centres attached to colleges and schools.

Institut Teknologi Brunei: Tungku Link, Gadong, Bandar Seri Begawan 1410; tel. (2) 461020; fax (2) 461035; internet www.itb.edu.bn; f. 1986; B/TEC HND and BEng courses; library: 35,000 vols; 83 teachers; 483 students; Dir Haji MOHAMED YUSRA BIN HAJI ABDUL HALIM; Registrar Haji MOHAMMAD BIN HAJI HIDUP; Librarian Hajah PUSPARAINI BINTI HAJI THANI.

Jefri Bolkiah College of Engineering: POB 63, Kuala Belait 6000; internet www.brunet.bn/php/chongrms/jbcehome.htm; f. 1970; craft, technical, mathematics and English courses; 78 teachers; 350 students; Principal MICHAEL LIM (acting).

Seri Begawan Religious Teachers' College: Bandar Seri Begawan.

Sultan Saiful Rijal Technical College: POB 914, Simpang 125, Jalan Muara; tel. (2) 331077; fax (2) 343207; e-mail mtssr@brunet.bn; internet www.mtssr.edu.bn; f. 1985; eng. and business courses; 195 teachers; 1,000 students; Dir Pengiran SUHAIMI BIN PENGIRAN HAJI BAKAR (acting).

BULGARIA

The Higher Education System

Higher education is supported by the State through the aegis of the Ministry of Education, Youth and Science. During the mid-1990s the higher education system was extensively reorganized, with a degree system introduced and many foundations renamed. Higher education is governed by the Higher Education Act (amended 1999, 2001 and 2004) and the Academic Degrees and Titles Act (amended 1999). In 2007/08 there were 26,169 students enrolled in colleges and in 2009 there were 246,523 enrolled in 43 universities and equivalent institutions. In mid-1999 tuition fees for university students were introduced.

Admission to higher education is on the basis of the Diploma of Completed Secondary Education and successful entrance examinations. Institutions are allowed to set their own criteria for admission. Under the 2001 and 2004 amendments to the Higher Education Act, Bulgaria has implemented the Bologna Process. The principal undergraduate degree is the Bachelors, which requires four years of study culminating in defence of a thesis. There is also a range of Diploma and Diploma Specialist programmes. The Masters degree requires five years of study (or one more year after the Bachelors) ending with either state examinations or defence of a thesis. Finally, there are three types of Doctorate, each requiring at least three years of study following the Masters: Doctors, Doctor of Sciences, and Doctor Honoris Causa.

Vocational and technical training is mostly implemented at the secondary-school level. The National Evaluation and Accreditation Agency is responsible for evaluating and accrediting institutions of higher education.

Regulatory and Representative Bodies

GOVERNMENT

Ministry of Culture: 'Al. Stamboliiski' Blvd 17, 1040 Sofia; tel. (2) 94-00-900; fax (2) 981-81-45; e-mail press@mc.government.bg; internet www.mc.government.bg; Min. VEZHDI LETIF RASHIDOV.

Ministry of Education, Youth and Science: St Prince Dondukov 2A, 1000 Sofia; tel. (2) 921-77-44; fax (2) 988-26-93; e-mail press_mon@minedu.government.bg; internet www.minedu.government.bg; Min. SERGEY IGNATOV.

ACCREDITATION

ENIC/NARIC Bulgaria: National Centre for Information and Documentation (NACID), 52 A G. M. Dimitrov Blvd, 1125 Sofia; tel. (2) 817-38-62; fax (2) 971-31-20; e-mail naric@nacid.bg; internet www .enic-naric.net/index.aspx?c=bulgaria; Exec. Dir VANYA GRASHKINA.

National Evaluation and Accreditation Agency: 125 Tsarigradsko shose Blvd, Bldg 5, 4th Fl., N Wing, 1113 Sofia; tel. (2) 807-78-11; fax (2) 971-20-68; e-mail info@neaa .government.bg; internet www.neaa .government.bg; statutory body for evaluation, accreditation and monitoring of quality in higher education instns and scientific orgs; 11 mems: 1 chair., 6 reps from higher education instns, 1 from the Bulgarian Acad. of Sciences, 1 from the Nat. Centre of Agricultural Science, 2 reps from the Min. of Education, Youth and Science; Chair. Prof. Dr IVAN PANAYOTOV; Deputy Chair. Prof. DANAIL LAZAROV DANAILOV; Chief Exec. Assoc. Prof. PATRICIA GEORGIEVA.

NATIONAL BODY

Bulgarian Rectors' Conference: Agricultural Univ., 12 Mendeleev Blvd, 4000 Plovdiv; tel. (32) 65-42-00; fax (32) 63-31-57; e-mail rector@au-plovdiv.bg; internet www .au-plovdiv.bg; Rector Prof. Dr DIMITAR GREKOV; Pres. Prof. Dr YORDANKA KUZMANOVA.

Learned Societies

GENERAL

Bulgarian Academy of Sciences: 1040 Sofia; tel. (2) 979-53-33; fax (2) 981-72-62; e-mail presidentbas@cu.bas.bg; internet www.bas.bg; f. 1869 as Bulgarian Learned Society, present name 1911; attached research institutes: see Research Institutes; 224 mems (62 academicians, 89 corresp., 73 foreign); library of 1,956,465 vols; see Libraries and Archives; Pres. STEFAN VODENI-CHAROV; Vice-Pres. Acad. ANGEL GALABOV; Vice-Pres. Sr Dr NIKOLAI MILOSHEV; Sec. Assoc. Dr RAYA KUNCHEVA; Gen. Scientific Sec. Prof. STEFAN HADJITODOROV; publs *Balgaristika/Bulgarica* (2 a year), *Comptes rendus de l'Académie Bulgare des Sciences* (12 a year), *Spisanie na Balgarskata Akademija na Naukite* (Journal of the Bulgarian Academy of Sciences), various spec. publs on science and the arts.

Bulgarian Comparative Education Society: Faculty of Primary and Preschool Education, Blvd Shipchenski prohod 69A, 1574 Sofia; tel. (2) 97-06-240; fax (2) 872-23-21; e-mail npopov@fnpp.uni-sofia.bg; internet bces.home.tripod.com; f. 1991; promotes historical, methodological and practical aspects of comparative education; organizes and supports research; cooperates with scholars, research orgs, instns, societies in Bulgaria and abroad; Pres. Dr Hab. NIKOLAY POPOV.

National Centre of Health Informatics: Acad. Iv. Geshov Blvd 15, 1431 Sofia; tel. (2) 951-53-02; fax (2) 951-52-38; e-mail office@ nchi.government.bg; internet www.nchi .government.bg; specialized authority of the Min. of Healthcare; provides necessary information on healthcare; Dir Assoc. Prof. Dr CHRISTIAN GRIVA; Deputy Dir Eng. PETER AMUDJEV; Deputy Dir KRASSIMIRA DIKOVA; publs *Zdraveopazvane*, *Public Health Statistics* (1 a year).

Union of Publishers in Bulgaria: Alabin St 58, 1000 Sofia; tel. (2) 921-42-04; fax (2) 921-42-31; e-mail office@sib.bg; internet www.sib.bg; f. 2000; non-governmental asscn that defends the freedom of the press, the independence of journalists and encourages their work so that society is objectively informed; 22 mems; Chair. TOSHO TOSHEV; Exec. Dir DESSISLAVA BINEVA.

Union of Scientists in Bulgaria: 39 Madrid Blvd., 2nd Fl., 1505 Sofia; tel. (2) 944-11-57; fax (2) 944-15-90; e-mail science@ usb-bg.org; internet www.usb-bg.org; f. 1944; works in the area of science and research, education, innovations, environment, health care, information, informatics and information technologies, int. cooperation, social assistance, tourism and recreation; 4,000 mems; Pres. Prof. DAMYAN DAMYANOV; Vice-Pres. Prof. ANGEL POPOV; publs *Nauka* (6 a year), *Science* (6 a year).

AGRICULTURE, FISHERIES AND VETERINARY SCIENCE

Scientific and Technical Union of Specialists in Agriculture: G. Rakovski 108, 1000 Sofia; tel. (2) 987-65-13; fax (2) 987-93-60; f. 1965; Pres. Prof. V. VALOV; Sec. DIMITAR RADULOV; publ. *Buletin Vnedreni Novosti*.

Soil Resources Agency: Shose Bankia 7, 1331 Sofia; tel. (2) 824-87-98; fax (2) 824-02-39; e-mail soilsurv@mail.netplus.bg; internet www.soils-bg.org; f. 1959; analytical research of soil; verifies the quality of agricultural land, and applies finding in legal cases; assesses deterioration risks posed by erosion, contamination, salinity, acidity/alkalinity and bogginess; cartographic information and reports; creation and maintenance of the State Digital Map of Soil and Agricultural Land Grades and Soil Resource Geographical Information System, both overseen by the Min. of Agriculture and Forestry; Exec. Dir DAMIAN MIHALEV; Gen. Sec. TSENKA CHERNOGOROVA.

ARCHITECTURE AND TOWN PLANNING

Union of Architects in Bulgaria: Krakra St 11, 1504 Sofia; tel. (2) 943-83-21; fax (2) 943-83-49; e-mail sab@bularch.org; internet www.bularch.org; f. 1965; non-profit asscn; protects professional interests of its mems; develops and extends its professional cooperation with the Chamber of the Architects in Bulgaria and other related Bulgarian, foreign and int. orgs in the area of architecture; creates, distributes and protects cultural values; organizes cultural and educational activities; synchronizes architectural activities with int. professional practice; public discussions, qualification and requalification of the mems in area of architecture; devt of architectural education; documentation and protection of monuments; library of 6,000 vols; 2,200 mems; Pres. Arch. GEORGI BAKALOV; Vice-Pres. Arch. ILKO NIKOLOV; Chair. SPIRIDON GANEV; publs *Architecture* (6 a year), *Bulgarian Architect* (information bulletin, 26 a year).

ECONOMICS, LAW AND POLITICS

Bulgarian Association of Criminology: Vitosha 2, 1000 Sofia; tel. (2) 987-47-51; fax (2) 986-22-70; f. 1986; Pres. Assoc. Prof. Y. BOYADZHIEVA.

Bulgarian Association of International Law: H. C. Belite Brezi, Bldg 6, ap. 31, 1680 Sofia; tel. (2) 859-68-26; fax (2) 869-19-79; e-mail m.ganev@mail.bg; f. 1962; 60 mems; Pres. Prof. ALEXANDER YANKOV; Vice-Pres. Prof. EMIL KONSTANTINOV; Sec.-Gen. Prof. MARGARIT GANEV; publ. *Trudove po Mezhdunarodno Pravo* (every 3 years).

Union of Economists: G. Rakovski 108, 1000 Sofia; tel. (2) 987-18-47; fax (2) 984-43-215; f. 1968; Pres. Assoc. Prof. S. ALEXANDROV; Sec. I. POPOV; publ. *Bjuletin*.

FINE AND PERFORMING ARTS

Union of Bulgarian Actors: 12 Narodno Sabranie Sq., 1000 Sofia; tel. (2) 987-07-25; fax (2) 988-11-78; e-mail office@uba.bg; internet www.uba.bg; f. 1921 as Union of Bulgarian Artists; artistic trade union org. that represents the interests of its members in front of their employers and state authorities; library of 6,000 vols; 600 mems; Chair. HRISTO MUTAFCHIEV; Asst Sec. VELISLAVA SMILIANOVA; publ. *Teatar*.

Union of Bulgarian Artists: Shipka St 6, 1504 Sofia; tel. (2) 944-37-11; fax (2) 946-02-12; e-mail info@sbhart.com; internet www.sbhart.com; f. 1893 as Society for Supporting the Arts in Bulgaria, present name 1953; protects the interests of its members and promotes Bulgarian visual culture nationally and internationally; 2,700 mems; library of 9,000 vols; Chair. Prof. IVAYLO MIRCHEV; Vice-Chair. BOYKO MITKOV; publs *Dekorativno Izkustvo*, *Promishlena Estetika* (Information Bulletin, in Bulgarian only).

Union of Bulgarian Composers: ul. Ivan Vazov, 1000 Sofia; tel. (2) 988-15-60; fax (2) 987-43-78; e-mail mail@ubc-bg.com; internet www.ubc-bg.com; f. 1933 as Contemporary Music Society, present name 1954; encourages composers to use traditional music and recreate it in artistic forms; promotes closer relationships among composers; creates better work conditions for composers; assists financially challenged composers; preserves the memory of composers of merit; 230 mems; library of 25,280 books, scores and recordings; Pres. VELISLAV ZAIMOV; Vice-Pres. STEFAN ILIEV.

Union of Bulgarian Film Makers: Dondukov Blvd 67, 1504 Sofia; tel. and fax (2) 946-10-69; e-mail sbfd@sbfd-bg.com; internet www.filmmakersbg.org; f. 1934; creative professional org; promotes devt of film and audio-visual arts in Bulgaria; 907 mems; Pres. IVAN PAVLOV; Admin. Sec. RENI ZLATANOVA; publ. *KINO* (6 a year).

HISTORY, GEOGRAPHY AND ARCHAEOLOGY

Bulgarian Geographical Society: Tsar Osvoboditel 15, 1000 Sofia; tel. (2) 985-82-61; fax (2) 944-64-87; f. 1918; Pres. Prof. P. V. PETROV; Sec. L. TSANKOVA; publs *Geoecologija*, *Geografija*, *Geografijata Dnes*.

Union of Numismatic Societies: Veliko Tarnovo; tel. (62) 2-37-72; f. 1964; 9,000 mems; Pres. G. HARALAMPIEV; Sec. H. HARITONOV; publ. *Revue Numismatica* (4 a year).

LANGUAGE AND LITERATURE

Alliance Française: Dragan Tsankov St 34A, BP 1015, 4000 Plovdiv; tel. (3) 263-13-42; fax (3) 263-48-07; e-mail afbg@afbg.org; internet www.afbg.org; f. 1904; offers courses and exams in French language and culture and promotes cultural exchange with France; attached offices in Blagoevgrad, Burgas, Kazanlak, Pleven, Stara Zagora, Varna and Veliko Tarnovo; library of 17,000 vols, 40 periodicals, 950 video cassettes, 600 audios, 350 CDs, 105 CD-ROMs; Dir TÉOPHANA BRADINSKA-ANGELOVA; publ. *Alliances* (2 a year).

Balkanmedia Association: Luibotran 96, 1407 Sofia,; tel. (2) 980-70-85; fax (2) 87-16-98; e-mail balkanmedia@internet-bg.net; f. 1990; ind. non-profit org. for mass media and communication culture in the Balkan countries; 36 assoc. mems (from all Balkan countries); Pres. ROSEN MILEV; publ. *Balkanmedia*.

British Council: Krakra St 7, 1504 Sofia; tel. (2) 942-43-44; fax (2) 942-42-22; e-mail bc.sofia@britishcouncil.bg; internet www.britishcouncil.org/bulgaria; f. 1991; offers courses and exams in English language and British culture; promotes cultural exchange with the UK; teaching centre; library of 20,000 vols, 80 periodicals; Dir IAN STEWART.

Bulgarian Philologists' Society: Moskovska 13, 1000 Sofia; tel. (2) 986-25-61; e-mail vessie@biscom.net; f. 1977; Pres. Prof. S. HADZHIKOSEV; Editor-in-Chief Prof. Dr BOIAN VALTCHEV; publ. *Ezik i literatura* (4 a year).

Goethe-Institut: Budapesta St 1, POB 1384, 1000 Sofia; tel. (92) 939-01-00; fax (92) 939-01-99; e-mail info@sofia.goethe.org; internet www.goethe.de/sofia; f. 1989; offers courses and exams in German language and culture; promotes cultural exchange with Germany; library of 10,000 vols; Dir Dr RUDOLF BARTSCH; Sec. OLYA MATEEVA.

Union of Bulgarian Journalists: ul. Graf Ignatiev 4, 1000 Sofia; tel. (2) 987-28-08; fax (2) 988-30-47; f. 1944; 5,500 mems; Pres. MILEN VALKOV.

Union of Bulgarian Writers: Pl. Slavejkova 2A, 1000 Sofia; tel. (2) 88-00-31; fax (2) 88-06-85; f. 1913; 495 mems; Pres. N. HAITOV; publs *Bulgarian Writer*, *Plamak*, *Slavejche*.

Union of Translators in Bulgaria: Slavic 29, 5th Fl., 1000 Sofia; tel. (2) 986-45-00; fax (2) 981-09-60; e-mail office@bgtranslators.org; internet www.bgtranslators.org; f. 1974; non-profit org.; represents and defends the professional and creative rights of its mems; raises the quality of translation; Bureau translation translates about 46 languages; Chair. MARIA PETKOVA; Sec. IVO PANOV; publ. *Panorama*.

MEDICINE

Bulgarian Society of Neurosciences: Zdrave 2, 1431 Sofia; tel. (2) 51-86-23; fax (2) 51-87-83; f. 1987; Pres. Prof. V. OVCHAROV.

Bulgarian Society for Parasitology: Tzar Osvoboditel Blvd 1, 1000 Sofia; tel. (2) 979-23-13; fax (2) 71-01-07; e-mail ieppcom@bas.bg; internet bsparasitology.org; f. 1965 as Soc. of Parasitologists in Bulgaria, present name 1999; conducts research on parasitological aspects of biology, human and veterinary medicine, agriculture and forestry; organizes annual meetings, lectures; Pres. OLGA POLYAKOVA-KRUSTEVA; Sec. IVAN TODEV; Treas. Dr ISKRA RAYNOVA.

Bulgarian Society of Sports Medicine and Kinesitherapy: Dept of Sports Medicine, National Sports Academy, Studentski grad, 1700 Sofia; tel. (2) 962-04-58; e-mail bsssmk@abv.bg; f. 1953; study of the natural

and pathological implications of physical training and sports participation; organizes scientific meetings, courses, congresses, and exhibits in the field of sports medicine; 50 mems; Pres. Assoc. Prof. DIANA DIMITROVA; Vice-Pres. Assoc. Prof. EVGENIA DIMITROVA; Sec. Dr MARIELA SIRAKOVA; publ. *Sports & Science* (12 a year).

Union of the Bulgarian Medical Societies: Nat. Centre of Public Health Protection, 12th Fl., Room 19, 15, Akad. Ivan Geshov Blvd, 1431 Sofia; tel. (2) 954-11-56; fax (2) 80-56-410; e-mail snmd@rtb-mu.com; internet www.medunion-bg.org; f. 1968; promotes research and contributes to maintaining high professional qualities among medical professionals by developing a modern system for continuous medical training; 12,000 mems, 64 mem. socs; Pres. Assoc. Prof TODOR POPOV; Vice-Pres. Prof. RADKA ARGIROVA; Sec-Gen. Prof. SEVDALIN NACHEV; Sec. Prof. RADOSLAV GYRCHEV; publ. *Modern Medicine* (4 a year).

NATURAL SCIENCES

Biological Sciences

Bulgarian Botanical Society: c/o Institute of Botany, Acad. G. Bonchev St., Blvd 23, 1113 Sofia; tel. (2) 871-82-59; fax (2) 71-90-32; e-mail botinst@bio.bas.bg; internet www.bio.bas.bg; f. 1923; Pres. (vacant); Sec. M. ANCHEV.

Bulgarian Society of Natural History: D. Zankov 8, 1164 Sofia; tel. (2) 66-65-94; f. 1896; 1,000 mems; Pres. Prof. D. VODENICHAROV; Sec. S. DIMITROVA; publ. *Priroda i Znanie* (10 a year).

Mathematical Sciences

Union of Bulgarian Mathematicians: Acad. G. Bonchev Blvd 8, 1113 Sofia; tel. (2) 873-80-76; fax (2) 872-11-89; e-mail smb.sofia@gmail.com; internet www.math.bas.bg/smb; f. 1898; 2,000 mems; Pres. Prof. Dr ST. DODUNEKOV; Sec. Dr S. GROZDEV; publ. *Mathematics and Education in Mathematics* (1 a year).

Physical Sciences

Bulgarian Geological Society: Akad. G. Bonchev Str., Bldg 24, 1113 Sofia; tel. (2) 97-93-472; fax 87-246-38; e-mail radnac@geology.bas.bg; internet www.bgd.bg; f. 1925; contributes to the geological studies and protection of the geological heritage of Bulgaria; promotes the activities of its mems and of nat. geology; cooperates with similar nat. and foreign orgs; enhances geological education and professional growth of geologists; protects the professional interests of geoscientists of different generations; supports and helps the competent govt institutions on problems related to the progress of Bulgarian geology; serves as a social corrective of state policy in the field of geology; organizes seminars, confs and geological field trips; 320 mems; library: more than 21,000 books and journals; Pres. Dr RADOSLAV NAKOV; Vice-Pres. Assoc. Prof. Dr EUGENIA TARASOVA; Sec. Assoc. Prof. Dr DARIA IVANOVA; Treas. Dr MOMCHIL DYULGEROV; publ. *Review of the Bulgarian Geological Society* (3 a year).

Union of Physicists in Bulgaria: 5 James Bourchier Blvd, 1164 Sofia; tel. (2) 62-76-60; fax (2) 962-52-76; e-mail upb@phys.uni-sofia.bg; internet www.phys.uni-sofia.bg/~upb/main.html; f. 1971 as Bulgarian Physical Society, present name and status 1989; Pres. Prof. Dr MATEY DRAGOMIROV MATEEV; Exec. Sec. PENKA GANCHEVA LAZAROVA; publ. *Bulgarian Journal of Physics*.

PHILOSOPHY AND PSYCHOLOGY

Bulgarian Pedagogical Society: Shipchenski prohod 69A, 1547 Sofia,; tel. (2) 72-08-93; f. 1975; Pres. Prof. G. BIZHKOV.

Bulgarian Philosophical Association: Tzar Osvoboditel Blvd 15, Sofia Univ., 1504 Sofia; tel. and fax (88) 838-30-73; e-mail ivan_kaltchev@yahoo.com; f. 1968; 320 mems; Pres. Prof. IVAN KALCHEV; Sec. R. KRIKORIAN; publs *Filosofia* (Philosophy, 12 a year), *Filosofski Alternativi* (Philosophical Alternatives, 12 a year), *Filosofski Forum* (Philosophical Forum, 4 a year), *Filosofski Vestnik* (Philosophical News, 4 a year).

Society of Bulgarian Psychologists: Liulin Planina 14, POB 1333, 1606 Sofia; tel. (2) 54-12-95; f. 1969; provides consultation and assistance to its members, institutions and citizens of the country on the ethical issues of the activities of psychologists; develops and applies corrective and disciplinary procedures for investigating and reaching decisions in cases of complaints against its members; Pres. Prof. D. GRADEV; Sec. ZH. BALEV; publ. *Balgarsko Spisanie po Psikhologija*.

RELIGION, SOCIOLOGY AND ANTHROPOLOGY

Bulgarian Sociological Association: Institute for the Study of Societies and Knowledge, Bulgarian Acad. of Sciences, 13A Moskovska St., 1000 Sofia; tel. (2) 980-95-22; fax (2) 980-58-95; e-mail bsa@sociology.bas.bg; internet www.bsa-bg.org; f. 1959 as Sociological Assn, present name 1969; professional non-profit org.; carries out theoretical and empirical research, teaching and publishing activities in the field of sociology in Bulgaria; conducts congresses, confs. and seminars; Pres. SVETLA KOLEVA; Sec. DIANA NENKOVA; publ. *Sociological Problems* (4 a year).

TECHNOLOGY

Bulgarian Astronautical Society: 6 Moskovska St, POB 799, 1000 Sofia; tel. (2) 979-3451; fax (2) 986-1683; e-mail pangelov@space.bas.bg; internet bgastr.hit.bg; f. 1957; astronautics and aeronautics; 300 mems; library of 3,000 vols; Pres. Prof. PETAR GETSOV; Scientific Sec. Prof. PLAMEN ANGELOV.

Federation of the Scientific-Technical Unions in Bulgaria: 108 G. S. Rakovsky St, POB 431, 1000 Sofia; tel. (2) 987-72-30; fax (2) 987-93-60; e-mail info@fnts-bg.org; internet www.fnts-bg.org; f. 1893 as Bulgarian Engineering-Architectural Asscn, present name 1992; non-profit asscn; organizes congresses, confs, symposia, seminars and workshops; participates in the drafting of laws and other normative documents related to science and technology; carries out qualification activity through its Centre for Professional Education and Qualification; 10,000 mems; Pres. Acad. V. SGUREV; publ. *Nauka i Obshestvo* (Scientific newspaper); publ. *Technosphera* (Scientific journal).

Scientific and Technical Union of Civil Engineering: G. Rakovski 108, 1000 Sofia; tel. (2) 988-53-03; fax (2) 987-93-60; f. 1965; Pres. Dr E. MILCHEV; Sec. M. RUSEVA; publs *Stroitel 2000, Stroitelstvo*.

Scientific and Technical Union of Forestry: G. Rakovski 108, 1000 Sofia; tel. (2) 88-36-83; fax (2) 987-93-60; e-mail ntsl@mail.bg; f. 1965; Pres. V. BREZIN; Sec. S. SAVOV; publs *Celuloza i Hartija, Darvoobrabotvashta i mebelna Promislenost*.

Scientific and Technical Union of Mining, Geology and Metallurgy: G. Rakovski 108, 1000 Sofia; tel. (2) 87-57-27; fax (2) 986-13-79; e-mail nts-mdgm@speedbg.net; f.

1965; Pres. Prof. V. STOYANOV; Sec. V. GENEVSKI; publs *Metalurgija, Rudodobiv*.

Scientific and Technical Union of Power Engineers: G. Rakovski 108, 5th Fl., Office 505, 1000 Sofia; tel. (2) 88-41-58; fax (2) 87-93-60; e-mail energy@fnts-bg.org; internet www.ntse-bg.org; f. 1965; carries out vocational training activities and supports the devt of creative ideas and initiatives of its members; participates in the devt and discussion of laws, regulations, rules, instructions and other regulations on energy, environment, protecting people from harmful effects and the protection of tangible property against damage and destruction resulting from the use of energy; conducts scientific and technical events; Pres. Prof. S. BATOV; Sec. Eng. D. TOMOV; publ. *Energetika*.

Scientific and Technical Union of Textiles, Clothing and Leather: G. Rakovski 108, 1000 Sofia; tel. (2) 88-16-41; fax (2) 987-93-60; f. 1965; Pres. Prof. E. KANTCHEV; Sec. I. MECHEV; publs *Kozhi i Obuvki, Tektil i oblekло*.

Scientific and Technical Union of the Food Industry: G. Rakovski 108, 1000 Sofia; tel. (2) 87-47-44; fax (2) 987-93-60; e-mail hvp_magazine@go.com; f. 1965; Pres. A. PETROV; Sec. TODOROV; publ. *Hranitelna promishlenost*.

Scientific and Technical Union of Transport: G. Rakovski 108, 1000 Sofia,; tel. (2) 958-10-36; fax (2) 87-93-60; f. 1965; participates in policy making in the field of transport research and technological devt; Pres. K. ERMENKOV; Sec. ST. GAIDAROV; publs *Patishta, Zelezoрaten Transport*.

Scientific and Technical Union of Water Affairs in Bulgaria: G. Rakovski 108, 1000 Sofia; tel. (2) 988-53-03; fax (2) 987-93-60; f. 1965; Pres. Prof. A. MALINOV; Sec. MARGARITA SJAROVA; publ. *Vodno delo*.

Scientific-Technical Union of Mechanical Engineering: 108 Rakovsky, 1000 Sofia; tel. (2) 987-72-90; fax (2) 986-22-40; e-mail nts-bg@mech-ing.com; internet www.mech-ing.com; f. 1965; supports the industrial devt of Bulgaria; protects and represents the professional, intellectual and social interests of its members; 900 mems; Pres. Prof. GEORGI POPOV; Gen. Sec. DAMIAN DAMIANOV; publ. *International Virtual Journal—Machinery, Technology, Materials* (12 a year).

Union of Chemists in Bulgaria: G. Rakovski 108, 1000 Sofia; tel. and fax (2) 987-58-12; e-mail chem@fnts-bg.org; internet www.unionchem.org; f. 1901; non-profit org.; scientific and technical work; nat. and int. scientific confs. and symposia; Pres. Prof. VENKO NIKOLAEV BESHKOV; Sec. Eng. NAYDEN HRISTOV NAYDENOV; publ. *Bulgarian Chemistry and Industry* (4 a year).

Union of Electronics, Electrical Engineering and Telecommunications: G. Rakovski 108, 1000 Sofia; tel. (2) 987-97-67; fax (2) 987-93-60; e-mail ceec@mail.bg; internet ceec.fnts-bg.org; f. 1965; non-profit org.; scientific and technical events; confs, symposia, seminars, roundtables, discussions; devt of draft laws, regulations, programmes; training activities; int. cooperation; 1,300 mems; Chair. Prof. Prof. IVAN STOYANOV YATCHEV; Deputy-Pres. Assoc. Prof. TODOROV SEFERIN MIRCHEV; Exec. Dir Prof. Dr IVAN VASILEV NIKOLOV; publ. *Elektrotechnica i Elektronica* (12 a year).

Union of Surveyors and Land Managers: G. 108 Rakovski, POB 431, 1000 Sofia; tel. (2) 987-58-52; fax (2) 987-93-60; e-mail geodesy_union@fnts-bg.org; internet geodesy.fnts-bg.org; f. 1922; protects interests of the surveying profession; organises int. and nat.

symposia, confs, seminars, nat. and regional meetings and publishes proceedings and materials of such events; 200 mems; Pres. Prof. Dr Ing. G. MILEV; Sec. ST. BOGDANOV; publ. *Geodesija, Kartografija, Zemeustrojstvo* (6 a year).

Research Institutes

AGRICULTURE, FISHERIES AND VETERINARY SCIENCE

Agricultural Institute: Blvd Simeon Veliki 3, 9700 Shumen; tel. (54) 83-04-48; fax (54) 83-04-55; e-mail agr_inst@abv.bg; internet www.zemedelskiinstitut-shumen.com; f. 2000, by merger of Institute of Buffalo, Institute of Pig Breeding and the Institute of Sugar Beet; research activity in stockbreeding; library of 10,900 vols; Dir TSONKA PEEVA; publs *Bulgarian Journal of Agricultural Science, Genetica i selectija* (4 a year), *Zhivotnovadni Nauki* (8 a year).

Barley Research Institute: 8400 Karnobat; tel. 27-31; fax (559) 58-47; f. 1925; library of 17,000 vols; Dir Assoc. Prof. I. MIHOV.

Canning Research Institute: V. Aprilov 154, 4000 Plovdiv; tel. (32) 95-13-52; fax (32) 95-22-86; e-mail office@canri.org; internet www.canri.org; f. 1962, present status 1974; develops and transfers new technologies and products in canning industry; library of 19,000 vols; Assoc. Dir Dr PAVLINA GEORGIEVA PARASKOVA; Vice-Assoc. Dir Dr GEORGE LEONIDOV BEKYAROV.

Central Medical Veterinary Research Institute: P. Slaveykov 15, 1606 Sofia; tel. (2) 952-12-77; fax (2) 952-53-06; e-mail director@iterra.net; f. 1901; Dir Prof. Dr S. P. MARTINOV.

Dairy Research Institute: 3700 Vidin; tel. 2-32-04; fax 3-46-32; f. 1959; library of 8,000 vols; Dir A. KOZHEV; publs *Advanced Experience* (2 a year), *Dairy Abstracts Bulletin* (12 a year).

Dobrudzha Agricultural Institute: General Toshevo, 9520 Dobrich Dist.; tel. (58) 603125; fax (58) 603183; e-mail dai_gt@dobrich.net; internet www.dai-gt.org; f. 1940; library of 32,000 vols; Dir Prof. Dr IVAN KIRIAKOV.

Field Crops Institute: 55 G. Dimitrov St, 6200 Chirpan; tel. and fax (416) 93133; e-mail iptp@abv.bg; internet www.iptp-chirpan.org; f. 1925, part of the Agricultural Academy at the Min. of Agriculture and Food, Sofia; breeding of high-yielding and high-quality cotton and durum wheat cultivars; devt of cotton and durum wheat cultivation technologies and elements of technologies for main field crops cultivation under irrigation and in dry conditions; laboratory and field experiments with various crops, machinery, fertilizers, pesticides, growth regulators and defoliants; study of technological parameters of cotton fibre and durum wheat grain; information provision; laboratory analysis of soil and plant samples; seed-production of cotton and durum wheat; 115 mems; library of 16,000 vols; Dir Assoc. Prof. Dr NELI VALKOVA; Scientific Sec. Assoc. Prof. Dr GALIA PANAYOTOVA.

Fisheries Industry Institute: Industrialna 3, 8000 Burgas; tel. (56) 84-05-22; fax (56) 4-03-31; f. 1965; Dir Dr ZH. NECHEV.

Forest Research Institute: 132, St. Kliment Ohridski Blvd, 1756 Sofia; tel. (2) 962-04-42; fax (2) 962-04-47; e-mail forestin@bas.bg; internet www.fribas.org; f. 1928; attached to Bulgarian Acad. of Sciences; library of 39,000 vols; Dir Prof. ALEXANDER HARALANOV ALEXANDROV; Deputy-Dir Prof.

HRISTO IVANOV TSAKOV; Scientific Sec. Prof. BOYAN NIKOLOV ROSSNEV; publs *Nauka za gorata* (Forest Science, 4 a year), *Silva Balcanica* (2 a year).

Freshwater Fisheries Research Institute: V. Levski 248, 4003 Plovdiv; tel. (32) 55-60-33; fax (32) 55-39-24; f. 1978; Dir G. GROZEV.

Fruit-Growing Research Institute: 12 Ostromila, 4004 Plovdiv; tel. (32) 69-23-49; fax (32) 67-08-08; e-mail instov@infotel.bg; internet fruitgrowinginstitute.com; f. 1950, present name 1952; attached to Agricultural Acad. at the Min. of Agriculture and Food Supply; research, incl. breeding, genetic resources and biotechnology, fruit growing technologies; extension activities; service in the field of fruit growing; Dir Prof. ARGIR ZHIVONDOV; Deputy Dir ZARYA RANKOVA; Scientific Sec. PETYA GERCHEVA.

Institute for Plant Genetic Resources 'K.Malkov': 4122 Sadovo (Plovdiv District); tel. and fax (32) 62-90-26; f. 1902 as an agricultural experimental station; attached to Nat. Centre for Agrarian Research at Min. of Agriculture and Food Supply; plant genetic resources programme; offers free germplasm exchange, registration and free storage of plant accessions; library of 30,000 vols; Dir Prof. LILIA KRASTEVA.

Institute for the Control of Foot and Mouth Disease and Dangerous Infections: Trakia 75, 8800 Sliven; tel. (44) 2-20-39; fax (44) 2-26-42; f. 1974; Dir R. KASABOV.

Institute of Agricultural Economics: Tsarigradsko Shosse 125, Unit 1, 1113 Sofia; tel. (2) 971-00-14; fax (2) 971-00-13; e-mail office@iae-bg.com; internet www.iae-bg.com; f. 1935; research and devt in economics, org., sociology, ecology and management of agriculture and food–beverage industry; library of 10,850 vols, 5,560 periodicals; Dir RUMEN GROZDANOV POPOV; Deputy Dir QNKA PETRAKIEVA DIMITROVA-SLAVOVA.

Institute of Agriculture: Sofjisko shose St, 2500 Kyustendil; tel. (78) 52-26-12; fax (78) 52-40-36; e-mail iz_kn@abv.bg; internet iz-kyustendil.org; f. 1929; attached to Agricultural Acad. of Min. of Agriculture and Food Supply; research instn for investigation of theoretical and practical problems in agriculture; introduction of Bulgarian and foreign innovations in the area; assistance to the growers; library of 9,000 vols; Dir Prof. Dr DIMITAR DOMOZETOV; Deputy Dir Assoc. Dr ILIYANA RADOMIRSKA; Scientific Sec. Assoc. Prof. Dr ATANAS BLAGOV.

Institute of Animal Science: 2232 Kostinbrod; tel. and fax (721) 68943; e-mail inst_anim_sci@abv.bg; internet www.iasbg .hit.bg; f. 1950 as part of Bulgarian Agricultural Acad.; attached to Nat. Centre of Agricultural Sciences (Min. of Agriculture and Food Supply); basic and applied research in genetics, animal and bee breeding and selection, reproduction, nutritive physiology and biochemistry, feeding technology of farm animals, ecology and quality of animal production; library of 25,200 vols; Dir Assoc. Prof. Dr LAZAR KOZELOV; Deputy Dir of Science and Scientific Sec. Assoc. Prof. Dr MAIA IGNATOVA.

Institute of Cattle and Sheep Breeding: 6000 Stara Zagora; tel. (42) 4-10-76; fax (42) 4-71-48; f. 1942; Dir Prof. GEKO GEKOV.

Institute of Fisheries and Aquaculture: Primorski 4, Blvd 4, POB 72 9000 Varna; tel. (52) 23-18-52; fax (52) 25-78-76; f. 1932; attached to Nat. Center of Agricultural Sciences (Min. for Agriculture and Food Supply); library of 24,000 vols; Dir Dr P. KOLAROV; publ. *Proceedings* (1 a year).

Institute of Forage Crops–Pleven: Gen.-Vladimir Vazov 89 St, 5800 Pleven; tel. (64) 80-58-82; fax (64) 80-58-81; e-mail ifc@elsoft .com; internet www.ifc-pleven.org; f. 1954; attached to Agricultural Acad.; nat. centre for complex scientific and applied researches and devt activities, advises and trains in the field of breeding of forage production, crop technology and animal nutrition; Dir Assoc. Prof. Dr TODOR SIMEONOV KERTIKOV; Scientific Sec. Dr ANELIYA ILIEVA KATOVA.

Institute of Grains and Feed Industry: Kostinbrod 2, 2232 Sofia 2; tel. (721) 20-84; fax (721) 20-84; f. 1965; library of 9,050 vols, 16 periodicals; Dir M. MACHEV.

Institute of Soil Science 'Nikola Poushkarov': Shousse Bankya 7, 1080 Sofia; tel. (2) 824-61-41; fax (2) 824-89-37; e-mail soil@ mail.bg; internet www.iss-poushkarov.org; f. 1947; attached to Agricultural Acad.; research, conservation and restoration of soil resources; management of agriculture and ecosystems; Dir Prof. Dr METODI TEOHAROV; Deputy Dir for Scientific Activities Assoc. Prof. BOZIDAR GEORGIEV; Deputy Dir for Consultancy, Contract and Innovation Activities Assoc. Prof. Dr VICTOR KRUMOV; Scientific Sec. Prof. Dr DIMITRANKA STOICHEVA; publs *Journal of Balkan Ecology* (in English, 4 a year), *Soil Science, Agrochemistry and Ecology* (in Bulgarian with English abstract, 6 a year).

Institute of Soya Bean Growing: POB 8, 5200 Pavlikeni; tel. (610) 22-75; fax (610) 25-41; f. 1925; Dir Dr G. GEORGIEV.

Institute of Viticulture and Oenology: Kala tepe 1, 5800 Pleven; tel. (64) 2-21-61; fax (64) 2-64-70; f. 1902 as State Control Station in Viticulture and Oenology, present name 1944; Dir Prof. P. ABRASHEVA.

Institute of Water Problems: Acad. G. Bonchev St, Bl.1 1113 Sofia; tel. (2) 72-25-72; fax (2) 72-25-77; e-mail santur@iwp.bas.bg; internet www.iwp.bas.bg; f. 1963; attached to Bulgarian Acad. of Sciences; carries out theoretical and applied investigations and develops methods, models, software, technologies and installations concerning water resource use and protection; 73 mems; Dir Prof. Eng. OHANES SANTOURDJIAN; Scientific Sec. Assoc. Prof. Dr Eng. IGOR NIAGOLOV; publ. *Vodni Problemi* (Water Problems, 1 a year).

Maize Research Institute: 3230 Knezha; tel. (9132) 22-11; fax (9132) 27-11; f. 1924; Dir Assoc. Prof. K. ANGELOV.

Maritsa Vegetable Crops Research Institute: Brezovsko shose St 32, 4000 Plovdiv; tel. (32) 95-12-27; fax (32) 96-01-77; e-mail balkanvegetables@gmail.com; f. 1930; attached to Bulgarian Agricultural Acad.; library of 20,500 vols; research emphasizes vegetable quality by improving biological value and sensory characteristics, pest and disease resistance, high temperature and drought tolerance; Dir Assoc. Prof. Dr MASHEVA STOYKA PETKOVA.

Wine and Spirits Research Institute of Bulgaria: Tsar Boris 3rd 134, 1618 Sofia; tel. (2) 818-49-50; fax (2) 855-40-09; e-mail office@wineinbg.org; internet www.wineinbg .org; f. 1952; research incl. chemistry and microbiology of wine and spirits production; Exec. Dir CHRISTO BOEVSKY.

'Obraztsov Chiflik' Institute of Agriculture and Seed Science: 7007 Ruse; tel. (82) 22-57-34; fax (82) 22-58-98; e-mail izsruse@ elits.rousse.bg; f. 1905; Dir Dr GENKA PATENOVA.

Plant Protection Institute: 35 Panayot Volov St, 2230 Kostinbrod, POB 238; tel. (721) 660-61; fax (721) 660-62; e-mail protection@infotel.bg; internet www.ppi-bg

.org; f. 1936, present location 1961; depts of biological and integrated pest control, entomology and radiobiology, prognosis, toxicology, phytopatology and plant immunity, herbology; library of 15,343 vols (incl. 6,744 books, 2,573 periodicals, 6,026 magazines); Dir Assoc. Prof. Dr OLIA EVTIMOVA KARADJOVA; Deputy Dir Assoc. Prof. Dr GANKA STANCHEVA BAEVA; Scientific Sec. Assoc. Prof. Dr HRISTINA TODOROVA KRUSTEVA.

Regional Veterinary Institute: Nezavisimost III, 4000 Plovdiv; tel. (32) 26-08-68; fax (32) 22-33-67; f. 1936; library of 10,000 vols; Dir D. ARNAUDOV.

Regional Veterinary Institute: Slavjanska 5, 5000 Veliko Tarnovo,; tel. 2-16-69; fax 2-16-69; f. 1932; library of 11,840 vols; Dir Assoc. Prof. V. RADOSLAVOV.

Regional Veterinary Research Institute and Centre: Slavyanska 58, 6000 Stara Zagora; tel. (42) 2-67-32; fax (42) 2-31-15; f. 1931; Dir Assoc. Prof. N. IVANOVA.

Research Institute for Irrigation, Drainage and Hydraulic Engineering: Tsar Boris III 136, 1618 Sofia; tel. (2) 56-30-01; fax (2) 55-41-58; e-mail riidhe@bgcict.acad .bg; f. 1953; library of 18,000 vols; Dir Asst Prof. Dr PLAMEN PETKOV; publ. *Proceedings* (every 3 years).

Research Institute for Land Reclamation and Agricultural Mechanization: St Bansko shosse 3, IMM, 1331 Sofia; tel. (2) 825-71-70; fax (2) 824-78-42; e-mail imm_2001@mail.bg; internet www .e-imm2001-ncan-bg.com; f. 1949; nat. centre for strategic and applied research, extension and training in the fields of irrigated agriculture and mechanization of crop husbandry and animal breeding; 135 mems; library of 22,000 vols; Dir Assoc. Prof. Dr NIKOLAY MINKOV MARKOV; Deputy Dir Assoc. Prof. Dr NELI ILIEVA GADJALSKA; Scientific Sec. Assoc. Prof. Dr GEORGI DIMITROV KOSTADINOV; publ. *Agricultural Engineering* (scientific journal, 6 a year).

Research Institute for Roses, Aromatic and Medicinal Plants: Blvd Osvobojdenie 49, 6100 Kazanlak; tel. (431) 2-20-39; fax (431) 4-10-83; f. 1907; library of 3,600 vols; Dir Dr GEORGE CHAUSHEV.

Research Institute of Mountain Stockbreeding and Agriculture: V. Levski 281, 5600 Trojan; tel. (670) 6-28-02; fax (670) 5-30-32; e-mail rimsa@mail.bg; internet www .rimsa.eu; f. 1978; Dir Prof. Dr MARIN METODIEV TODOROV.

Scientific and Production Enterprise with Sugar Beet Research Institute 'Prof. Ivan Ivanov': Carev Brod, 9747 Shumen Dist.; tel. (54) 5-51-02; fax (54) 5-69-06; f. 1926; Dir Assoc. Prof. S. KRASTEV.

Scientific and Production Institute for Veterinary Preparations 'Vetbiopharm': 3000 Vraca; tel. 4-94-81; fax 4-75-30; f. 1942; library of 5,000 vols; Dir Dr T. NIKOLOV.

Tobacco and Tobacco Products Institute: 4108 Plovdiv; tel. (32) 67-23-64; fax (33) 77-51-56; e-mail itti_marcovo@abv.bg; internet www.ttpi-bg.com; f. 1944; library of 40,000 vols; Dir Asst Prof. Dr HRISTO BOZUKOV; publ. *Bulgarian Tobacco* (6 a year).

Veterinary Institute of Immunology Ltd: Bakareno shose 1, 1360 Sofia; tel. (2) 26-31-70; fax (2) 26-24-85; f. 1942; Pres. Prof. Dr STEFANOV.

ARCHITECTURE AND TOWN PLANNING

Centre for Architectural Studies: 1, Akad. G. Bonchev St, 1113 Sofia; tel. and fax (2) 72-46-20; e-mail danizen@iwt.bas.bg; internet www.bas.bg/arch; f. 1949 as Institute for Urbanism and Architecture, present name 1995; attached to Bulgarian Acad. of Sciences; history of architecture and urban planning from ancient period to modern times, architectural stylistic influences, and comparative studies in the larger context of Balkan and European architecture, continuity in architectural traditions through the ages; new ideas in Europe and their impact on world architecture; preservation of architectural heritage and devt of cultural tourism; Dir Prof. Dr KONSTANTIN BOJADJIEV; Research Sec. Dr ANTON GOUGOV.

National Centre for Regional Development and Housing Policy: Alabin 14–16, 1000 Sofia; tel. (2) 980-03-08; fax (2) 980-03-12; f. 1960; library of 9,000 vols; Dir-Gen. Dr V. GARNIZOV; publ. *Series for the Municipalities* (6 a year).

ECONOMICS, LAW AND POLITICS

Institute for Legal Studies: St Serdika 4 1000 Sofia; tel. (2) 987-49-02; fax (2) 989-25-97; e-mail ipn_ban@bas.bg; internet www .ipn-bg.org; f. 1947; attached to Bulgarian Acad. of Sciences; research, activities and training in the field of law; library of 34,187 titles, 20,586 books and 13,601 periodicals; Dir Dr VESSELIN TZANKOV; Deputy Dir Dr VELINA TODOROVA; Scientific Sec. GERGANA MARINOVA (acting); publ. *Pravna Misal* (4 a year).

Institute of Economics: Aksakov St 3, 1040 Sofia; tel. (2) 810-40-10; fax (2) 988-21-08; e-mail ineco@iki.bas.bg; internet www.iki .bas.bg; f. 1949; attached to Bulgarian Acad. of Sciences; nat. research centre for theoretical and scientific-applied studies and training of scientific experts in economy; library of 40,000 vols; Dir Dr MITKO ATANASOV DIMITROV; Scientific Sec. ISKRA BOGDANOVA CHRISTOVA; publs *Ikonomicheska Misal* (6 a year), *Ikonomicheski Izsledvania* (4 a year), *Economic Thought* (1 a year), *Economic Studies* (4 a year).

Research Institute of Forensic Sciences and Criminology: POB 934, 1000 Sofia; tel. (2) 987-82-10; fax (2) 987-82-10; e-mail int .27@mvr.bg; f. 1968; forensic science and criminology studies; Dir Prof. K. BOBEV; publs *News Bulletin* (3 a year), *Scientific Proceedings* (1 a year).

EDUCATION

National Institute for Education – Centre For Higher Education Research: 125 Tsarigradsko shose, Blvd 5, 1113 Sofia; tel. (2) 71-72-24; fax (2) 70-20-62; f. 1996; non-profit org.; supports educational policy, strategy and priorities for change and enhancement of Bulgarian education in the perspective of the wider European integration; library of 100,000 vols; Head Dr ROSITZA PENKOVA; publ. *Strategies for Policy in Science and Education*.

FINE AND PERFORMING ARTS

Institute of Art Studies: Krakra 21, 1000 Sofia; tel. (2) 944-24-14; fax (2) 943-30-92; e-mail office@artstudies.bg; internet artstudies.bg; f. 1947; attached to Bulgarian Acad. of Sciences; carries out studies on ancient, medieval and contemporary art and culture; focuses on collecting and preserving art documentation as well as the analysis of art phenomena, both professional and vernacular, associated with the Bulgarian legacy and its role in the construction of European culture; library of 45,000 vols; Dir Prof. ALEXANDER YANAKIEV; publs *Art Studies Quarterly* (4 a year), *Bulgarian Musicology* (4 a year).

HISTORY, GEOGRAPHY AND ARCHAEOLOGY

Archaeological Institute: Saborna 2, 1000 Sofia; tel. (2) 988-44-06; fax (2) 988-24-05; e-mail naim@naim.bg; internet www.naim .bg; f. 1921; research into prehistory, classical antiquity and the Middle Ages; attached to Bulgarian Acad. of Sciences; Dir Prof. VASIL NIKOLOV; publs *Archaeology* (4 a year), *Reports* (irregular).

Centre for Population Studies: Acad. G. Bonchev St, Bldg 6, 6th Fl., 1113 Sofia; tel. (2) 979-30-30; fax (2) 870-53-03; e-mail cps@ cc.bas.bg; internet cps.bas.bg; f. 2002, fmrly Institute of Demography; attached to Bulgarian Acad. of Sciences; nat. unit for theoretical and applied demographic studies; research on the population of Bulgaria; aim of identifying the laws and determinants of its evolution as well as population strategy and policy concerns within the context of European integration and the global devt trend; Dir Assoc. Prof. Dr GENOVEVA MIHOVA (acting); Scientific Sec. Dr KREMENA BORISSOVA-MARINOVA; publ. *Naselenie*.

Institute of Balkan Studies: 45 Moskovska St, 1000 Sofia; tel. and fax (2) 980-62-97; e-mail balkani@cl.bas.bg; internet www.cl.bas.bg/balkan-studies; f. 1964; attached to Bulgarian Acad. of Sciences; researches on the historical past and contemporary devt of the Balkan states, as well as on issues in the cultural, demographic and linguistic heritage of the Balkan nations; library of 27,000 vols; Dir Prof. Dr AGOP GARABED GARABEDYAN; Deputy Dir Prof. Dr LILIANA VIDENOVA SIMEONOVA; Scientific Sec. Prof. Dr ROUMIANA LACHEZAROVA STANTCHEVA; publ. *Études Balkaniques* (4 a year).

Institute of Geography: Acad. G. Bonchev St, Blvd 3, 1113 Sofia; tel. and fax (2) 870-02-04; e-mail geograph@bas.bg; internet www .geograph.bas.bg; f. 1950; attached to Bulgarian Acad. of Sciences; provides scientific services to the nat., regional, and municipal govts of Bulgaria in the fields of sustainable regional devt, nature protection, and raising the quality of geographic education; library of 17,000 vols; Dir Dr MARIYANA NIKOLOVA; Deputy Dir Prof. Dr CHAVDAR MLADENOV; Sec. Assoc. Prof. ZOYA MATEEVA; publ. *Problems of Geography* (4 a year).

Institute of Historical Studies: Shipchenski prokhod 52 Blvd, Block 17, 1113 Sofia; tel. (2) 870-85-13; fax (2) 870-21-91; e-mail ihistory@ihist.bas.bg; internet www .ihist.bas.bg; f. 1947; attached to Bulgarian Acad. of Sciences; works in the field of theoretical and specialized problems of Bulgarian nat., political, social, religious and cultural history from the establishment of the Bulgarian state to the present day, as well as on problems of world history and int. relations; 106 mems; library of 60,000 vols; Dir Acad. Prof. Dr GEORGI MARKOV; Deputy Dir Prof. Dr VALERY STOYANOW; Scientific Sec. Assoc. Prof. Dr IVAN TANCHEV; publs *Bulgarian Historical Review* (2 a year), *Istoritcheski Pregled* (3 a year).

Prof. Alexander Fol Centre of Thracian Studies: 13 Moskovska St, 1000 Sofia; tel. and fax (2) 981-58-53; e-mail thracologia@ abv.bg; internet www.thracologia.org; f. 1972 as Institute of Thracology; attached to Bulgarian Acad. of Sciences; Thracian history, culture and language; library of 6,000 vols; Dir Prof. SVETLANA YANAKIEVA; Scientific Sec. Prof. Dr IRINA SHOPOVA; publ. *Orpheus* (Journal of Indo-European and Thracian studies, 1 a year).

LANGUAGE AND LITERATURE

Cyrillo-Methodian Research Centre: POB 432, Moskovska St 13, 1000 Sofia; tel.

(2) 987-02-61; fax (2) 986-69-62; e-mail kmnc@bas.bg; internet www.kmnc.bg; f. 1914 as Clement Commission, present name 1980; attached to Bulgarian Acad. of Sciences; comprehensive study and publishing of the translated and original works of Cyril and Methodius, the Slavonic, Greek and Latin sources on the Cyrillo-Methodian activities; Dir Assoc. Prof. Dr SVETLINA NIKOLOVA; Deputy Dir Assoc. Prof. Dr SLAVIA BARLIEVA; Scientific Sec. Assoc. Prof. Dr TATYANA MOSTROVA; publs *Kirilo-Metodievski studii* (Cyrillo-Methodian Studies, 1 a year), *Palaeobulgarica / Starobalgaristica* (4 a year).

Institute for Literature: 52, Blvd Shipchenski prohod, Bldg 17, 7th and 8th Fls, 1113 Sofia; tel. and fax (2) 971-70-56; e-mail director@ilit.bas.bg; internet www.ilit.bas .bg; f. 1948; attached to Bulgarian Acad. of Sciences; researches on Bulgarian literature from the Middle Ages to the present day, in its theoretical, historical, cultural and comparative aspects; library of 114,795 vols; Dir Assoc. Prof. Dr RAYA KUNTCHEVA; Deputy Dir Assoc. Prof. Dr VIHREN CHERNOKOZHEV; Scientific Sec. Assoc. Prof. Dr ELKA TRAYKOVA; publs *Literaturna misal* (literary Thought, print and online, 2 a year), *Scripta & e-Scripta* (journal of interdisciplinary medieval studies, 1 a year), *Starobulgarska literatura* (Old Bulgarian Literature).

Institute for the Bulgarian Language: 52 Shipchenski prohod, Blvd Block 17, 1113 Sofia; tel. and fax (2) 72-23-02; e-mail ibe@ ibl.bas.bg; internet www.ibl.bas.bg; f. 1942, present name 2004; fundamental and applied research on diverse aspects of Bulgarian language; attached to Bulgarian Acad. of Sciences; Dir Dr VASSIL RAINOV; Deputy Dir Dr ELKA MIRCHEVA; Deputy Dir Dr SVETLA KOEV; Scientific Sec. Dr PETYA KOSTADINOVA; publs *Bulgarian Language, Linguistique Balkanique*.

MEDICINE

Centre of Physiotherapy and Rehabilitation: Ovcha Kupel 2B, 1618 Sofia; tel. 56-28-24; fax 55-30-23; f. 1949; Dir Assoc. Prof. P. NIKOLOVA; publ. *Journal*.

Institute of Obstetrics and Gynaecology: Zdrave 2, 1431 Sofia; tel. (2) 51-72-200; fax (2) 51-70-92; f. 1976; library of 2,000 vols; 110 mems; Exec. Dir Assoc. Prof. V. ZLATKOV; publs *Akusherstvo i Ginekologia* (Obstetrics and Gynaecology, 12 a year), *Problems of Obstetrics and Gynaecology* (1 a year).

MHATEM 'N.I. Pirogov': 21 Totleben Blvd, 1606 Sofia; tel. (2) 52-10-77; fax (2) 951-62-68; f. 1951 fmrly Institute 'N.I. Pirogov'; Chair. MATEY MATEEV; Dir DIMITAR RADENKOVSKI; Deputy Finance Dir ANGELO DRENOV; Deputy Admin. Dir LUDMIL DJUNKOV; Deputy Medical Dir PLAMEN STEFANOV; publ. *Emergency Medicine* (magazine).

National Center of Infectious and Parasitic Diseases: 26 Yanko Sakazov Blvd, 1504 Sofia; tel. (2) 944-69-99; fax (2) 943-30-75; e-mail ncipd@ncipd.org; internet www .ncipd.org; f. 1972; courses in epidemiology, microbiology, virology, parasitology and immunology and allergology; training; Dir Prof. HRISTO TASKOV; Vice-Dir Prof. Dr MIRA KOJOUHAROVA; publs *Infektologiya, Problems of Infectious and Parasitic Diseases*.

National Centre of Haematology and Transfusiology: Darvenica, Plovdivsko Pole 6, 1756 Sofia; tel. and fax (2) 9701-235; e-mail tlissitchkov@yahoo.com; f. 1948; Dir Prof. Dr T. LISICHKOV; publ. *Clinical and Transfusional Haematology*.

National Centre of Public Health Protection: Akad. Ivan Ev. Geshov Blvd 15,

1431 Sofia; tel. (2) 805-62-61; fax (2) 954-11-14; e-mail ncphp@ncphp.government.bg; internet www.ncphp.government.bg; f. 2005 by merger of Nat. Centre of Hygiene, Medical Ecology and Nutrition and Nat. Centre of Public Health; 244 mems; research and devt, expert consultancy, methodological and training activities in the field of public health protection; assessment of health risks from occupational and environmental factors, personal behaviour and lifestyle, health promotion and integral diseases prevention, analytical and control services; base org. and coordinator for nat. and int. programmes and projects on public health protection; base for postgraduate and continuation training; library of 32,000 vols; Dir Prof. STEFKA PETROVA; publ. *Bulgarian Journal of Public Health* (4 a year).

National Centre of Radiobiology and Radiation Protection: Sv. G. Sofijski, Blvd 3, House 7, 1606 Sofia; tel. (2) 862-60-36; fax (2) 862-10-59; e-mail ncrrp@ncrrp.org; internet www.ncrrp.org; f. 1963; research, education and training, monitoring and control on occupationally exposed persons and radiological equipment, methodology, diagnostics and prophylaxis of radiation injury, emergency at nuclear accident sites; Dir Prof. Dr RADOSTINA GEORGIEVA (acting).

National Drug Institute: Blvd Yanko Sakazov 26, 1504 Sofia; tel. (2) 943-40-46; fax (2) 943-44-87; e-mail ndi@bg400.bg; f. 1949; registration, analysis and control of drugs; Dir Dr BORISLAV BORISOV.

National Heart Hospital: Konoviza Str. 65, 1309 Sofia; tel. (2) 822-33-49; fax (2) 921-15-61; e-mail cardiosurgery@abv.bg; f. 1972; Dir Dr L. BOYADZHIEV.

National Oncological Centre: Plovdivsko Pole 6, 1756 Sofia; tel. (2) 72-06-54; fax (2) 72-06-51; f. 1952; library of 22,000 vols; Dir Prof. I. CHERNOZEMSKI; publ. *Oncology* (4 a year).

State Institute of Endocrinology and Gerontology: Dame Gruev 6, 1303 Sofia; tel. (2) 987-72-01; fax (2) 87-41-45; f. 1972; Dir Prof. B. LOZANOV.

University Clinical Centre of Gastroenterology – Sofia: UMBAL 'Tsaritsa Giovanna—ISUL', 8 St Bialo more, 1527 Sofia; tel. (2) 943-22-77; fax (2) 43-26-64; e-mail hirurgi@isul.eu; internet www.kcg.medfac-sofia.eu; f. 1959; Dir Prof. Dr DAMIAN DAMIANOV.

University Clinical Dialysis Centre—Sofia: 1st 'St Georgi Sofiiski' Blvd, 1431 Sofia; tel. (2) 923-04-63; fax (2) 923-06-91; e-mail firstkhd_org@yahoo.com; internet www.kcd.medfac-sofia.eu; f. 1967; attached to Clinic of Urology at the Chair of Surgery in the Medical Univ.—Sofia; researches on haemodialysis, peritoneal dialysis and related complications; Head Assoc. Prof. Dr DIANA HRISTOVA YONOVA-IVANCHEVA.

NATURAL SCIENCES

Biological Sciences

Acad. M. Popov Institute of Plant Physiology: Acad. G. Bonchev St, Bldg 21, 1113 Sofia; tel. (2) 979-26-06; fax (2) 873-99-52; e-mail karanov@obzor.bio21.bas.bg; internet www.bio21.bas.bg/ipp; f. 1948 as Institute of Biology, present name 1964; attached to Bulgarian Acad. of Sciences; depts of experimental algology, mineral nutrition and water relations, photosynthesis, plant stress molecular biology, regulation of plant growth and devt; Dir Prof. Dr LOZANKA POPOVA-STAEVSKA; Vice-Dir Prof. Dr KLIMENTINA DEMIREVSKA; Vice-Dir Assoc. Prof. Dr SNEZHANA DONCHEVA; Scientific Sec. Assoc. Prof. Dr LILIANA MASLENKOVA; publ. *General and Applied Plant Physiology*.

Institute of Biodiversity and Ecosystem Research: 2 Yurii Gagarin St, 1113 Sofia; tel. (2) 873-61-37; fax (2) 870-54-98; e-mail iber@iber.bas.bg; internet www.iber.bas.bg; f. 2010, successor of Institute of Zoology, Institute of Botany, and Central Laboratory of General Ecology; attached to Bulgarian Acad. of Sciences; research in theoretical and applied aspects of ecology, biodiversity, environmental conservation and sustainable use of biological resources; training and education in botany, mycology, zoology, ecology, hydrobiology, conservation biology, environmental genetic, parasitology, evolutionary biology and other closely related scientific areas; provides reliable and sound scientific basis and methodological approaches within areas of its research competence; library of 25,500 vols; Dir Assoc. Prof. Dr VALKO BISSERKOV; Scientific Sec. Dr SNEZHANA GROZEVA.

Institute of Biophysics and Biomedical Engineering: Bldg 105 Acad G. Bonchev St, 1113 Sofia; tel. (2) 979-26-30; fax (2) 872-37-87; e-mail ibphbme@bio21.bas.bg; internet www.clbme.bas.bg; f. 2010, by merger of Institute of Biophysics and Centre of Biomedical Engineering; attached to Bulgarian Acad. of Sciences; depts of excitable structures, lipid-protein interactions in biological membranes, photoexcitable membranes, electroinduced and adhesive properties, biomacromolecules and biomolecular interactions, processing and analysis of biomedical data and signals, QSAR and molecular modelling, biomechanics and control of movements, bioinformatics and mathematical modelling; Dir ANDON KOSSEV; Deputy Dir Prof. Dr MIKHAIL MATVEEV; Deputy Dir Assoc. Prof. Dr MAYA VELITCHKOVA; Scientific Sec. Assoc. Prof. Dr TANIA PENCHEVA; publs *Int J Bioautomation* (print and online, 4 a year), *Journal of Geometry and Symmetry in Physics* (4 a year).

Institute of Botany: Acad. Georgi Bonchev St, Bldg 23, 1113 Sofia; tel. (2) 871-82-59; fax (2) 871-90-32; e-mail botinst@bio.bas.bg; internet www.bio.bas.bg/botany; f. 1947; attached to Bulgarian Acad. of Sciences; research in floristic, taxonomic and chemotaxonomic, phytocoenological and ecological, phytogeographical and resource-orientated, historical, anatomical and embryological, biotechnological fields; library of 24,974 vols, 1,5611 periodicals, 9363 books; 98 mems; Dir Prof. Dr DIMITAR PEEV; Deputy Dir Assoc. Prof. Dr DIMITAR IVANOV; Scientific Sec. Assoc. Prof. Dr ANNA GANEVA; publ. *Phytologia Balcanica* (3 a year).

Institute of Experimental Morphology, Pathology and Anthropology with Museum: Acad. G. Bonchev bl. 25, 1113 Sofia; tel. (2) 872-24-26; fax (2) 871-01-07; e-mail iempam@bas.bg; internet www.iempam.bas.bg; f. 1953 as Institute of Morphology, present name 1995, present status 2010; attached to Bulgarian Acad. of Sciences; investigation of contemporary problems in the field of experimental morphology, pathology, cell biology and anthropology; Dir Prof. NINA ATANASSOVA; Deputy Dir Assoc. Prof. Dr DIMITAR KADIYSKY; Scientific Sec. Assoc. Prof. MASHA DIMITROVA; publs *Acta Morphologica et Anthropologica* (1 a year), *Journal of Anthropology* (1 a year).

Institute of Genetics 'Acad. Doncho Kostoff': Tsarigradsko Shose, 13 Km, 1113 Sofia; tel. (2) 974-62-28; fax (2) 978-55-16; e-mail genetika@bas.bg; internet ig.bas.bg; f. 1910, present name 1987; attached to Bulgarian Acad. of Sciences; promotes genetic science and devt; library of 27,069 vols; Dir Prof. Dr KOSTADIN GECHEFF; Deputy Dir Assoc. Prof. Dr LUBOMIR MANOLOV; Deputy Dir Assoc. Prof. Dr ZHIVKO DANAILOV; Scientific Sec. Assoc. Prof. Dr GANKA GANEVA; publ. *Genetics and Breeding* (2 a year).

Institute of Molecular Biology 'Roumen Tsanev': Acad. G. Bonchev St, Bldg 21, 1113 Sofia; tel. and fax (2) 872-80-50; internet www.bio21.bas.bg/imb; f. 1947 as a laboratory of cytology and cytochemistry at the Institute of Applied and Developmental Biology, present status 1960, present name 1979; attached to Bulgarian Acad. of Sciences; research and training in the field of molecular biology and biochemistry; 97 mems; library of 5,000 vols; Dir Prof. ILYA GEORGIEV PASHEV (acting); Deputy Dir Assoc. Prof. G. NACHEVA (acting); Scientific Sec. Assoc. Prof. K. GRANCHAROV (acting).

Institute of Physiology: Acad. G. Bonchev Bldg 23, 1113 Sofia; tel. (2) 71-91-08; fax (2) 71-91-09; f. 1947; attached to Bulgarian Acad. of Sciences; Dir Prof. R. RADOMIROV.

Institute of the Biology and Immunology of Reproduction – Acad. 'K. Bratanov': 73 Tsarigradsko Shose Blvd, 1113 Sofia; tel. (2) 971-13-95; fax (2) 872-00-22; e-mail ibir@abv.bg; internet ibir.bas.bg; f. 1938 as Institute for Artificial Insemination and Breeding Diseases, present name 1994; attached to Bulgarian Acad. of Sciences; fundamental and applied research in the field of animal and human reproductive biology and immunology; Dir Assoc. Prof. MARGARITA MOLLOVA; Deputy Dir Assoc. Prof. DIMITRINKA KACHEVA; Scientific Sec. Assoc. Prof. MARIA STAMENOVA.

Institute of Zoology: 1 Tsar Osvoboditel Blvd, 1000 Sofia; tel. (2) 988-51-15; fax (2) 988-28-97; e-mail zoology@zoology.bas.bg; internet www.zoology.bas.bg; f. 1947, by merger of Zoology and Entomology depts of fmr Royal Institutes of Natural Sciences; attached to Bulgarian Acad. of Sciences; depts of biology and ecology of terrestrial animals, experimental zoology, faunology and zoogeography, hydrobiology, protozoology, taxonomy; library of 15,000 vols, 27,000 periodicals and journals; Dir Prof. Dr PARASKEVA MICHAILOVA; Deputy Dir Assoc. Prof. Dr NASKO ATANASSOV; Scientific Sec. Assoc. Prof. Dr SNEJANA GROZEVA; publs *Acta Zoologica Bulgarica* (3 a year), *Catalogus Faunae Bulgaricae* (1 a year), *Fauna bulgarica* (1 a year).

Stephan Angeloff Institute of Microbiology: Acad. G. Bonchev St 26, 1113 Sofia; tel. 979-31-57; fax 870-01-09; e-mail micb@microbio.bas.bg; internet www.microbio.bas.bg; f. 1947 as Institute of Microbiology; attached to Bulgarian Acad. of Sciences; depts of extremophilic bacteria, immunology, microbial biochemistry, microbial genetics, microbial biosynthesis and biotechnology, microbial ecology, morphology of microorganisms and electron microscopy, mycology, pathogenic bacteria, virology; 121 mems; Dir Prof. Dr ANGEL S. GALABOV; Deputy Dir Assoc. Prof. Dr HRISTO NAJDENSKI; Deputy Dir Assoc. Prof. Dr LUBKA DOUMANOVA; Scientific Sec. Prof. Dr MARIA B. ANGELOVA.

Mathematical Sciences

Institute of Mathematics and Informatics: Acad. Georgi Bonchev St, Block 8, 1113 Sofia; tel. (2) 979-38-28; fax (2) 971-36-49; e-mail office@math.bas.bg; internet www.math.bas.bg; f. 1947; attached to Bulgarian Acad. of Sciences; researches and trains specialists and exercises long-range, consistent policy related to the fundamental trends in the devt of mathematics, computer science and information technologies; Dir Prof. STEFAN DODUNEKOV; Deputy Dir Assoc. Prof. RADOSLAV PAVLOV; Deputy Dir Prof. OLEG MUSKAROV; Scientific Sec. Assoc. Prof. ANDREY ANDREEV; publs *Serdica Journal of*

Computing, Fractional Calculus and Applied Analysis, Mathematica Balkanica, Mathematica Plus, Physico-Mathematical Journal, Pliska, Serdica Mathematical Journal (4 a year).

Physical Sciences

Central Laboratory of Geodesy: Acad. G. Bonchev Bldg 1, 1113 Sofia; tel. and fax (2) 872-08-41; e-mail clgdimi@argo.bas.bg; internet clg.cc.bas.bg; f. 1948; attached to Bulgarian Acad. of Sciences; research in estimation theory and statistics, geodetic astronomy, global, regional and local geodynamics, space geodesy, physical and mathematical geodesy; library of 10,000 vols; Dir Assoc. Prof. Dr DIMITAR DIMITROV; Deputy Dir and Scientific Sec. Assoc. Prof. Dr IVAN GEORGIEV; publ. *Geodesy* (2 a year).

Central Laboratory of Optical Storage and the Processing of Information: 101, Acad. G. Bonchev St, POB 95, 1113 Sofia; tel. (2) 871-00-18; fax (2) 871-91-65; e-mail clospi@optics.bas.bg; internet www.optics.bas.bg; f. 1975; attached to Bulgarian Acad. of Sciences; media and methods for optical and digital holographic recording, optical and digital processing of information clusters and images as well as devt of sensors and measurement equipment for optical metrology; Dir Prof. Dr VENTSESLAV SAINOV; Deputy Dir Assoc. GEORGI MINTCHEV; Deputy Dir KALOYAN ZDRAVKOV; Scientific Sec. Assoc. Prof. Dr ELENA STOYKOVA.

Central Laboratory of Photoprocesses 'Acad. Jordan Malinowski': Acad. G. Bonchev St, Bldg 109, 1113 Sofia; tel. and fax (2) 872-00-73; e-mail clf@clf.bas.bg; internet www.clf.bas.bg; f. 1967; attached to Bulgarian Acad. of Sciences; research into the interaction of condensed matter with light and other irradiations, its application for the devt of new media for information recording, nanotechnologies, optoelectronics, infrared and integral optics, sensor technique; Dir Assoc. Prof. Dr NIKOLAY SPIRIDONONOV STARBOV; Deputy Dir for Research and Devt Assoc. Prof. BORISLAV MEDNIKAROV; Scientific Sec. Assoc. Prof. Dr VESSELINA NIKOLOVA PLATIKANOVA.

Central Laboratory of Solar Energy & New Energy Sources: 72 Tarigradsko Shose Blvd, 1784 Sofia; tel. (2) 877-84-48; fax (2) 875-40-16; e-mail solar@phys.bas.bg; internet www.senes.bas.bg; f. 1977; attached to Bulgarian Acad. of Sciences; specializes in the field of photovoltaics research; 44 mems; Dir Assoc. Prof. Dr PETKO VITANOV; Scientific Sec. Assoc. Prof. Dr MARUSHKA SENDOVA-VASSILEVA.

Geological Institute 'Strashimir Dimitrov': Acad. G. Bonchev St Bldg 24, 1113 Sofia; tel. (2) 872-35-63; fax (2) 872-46-38; e-mail geolinst@geology.bas.bg; internet www.geology.bas.bg; f. 1947; attached to Bulgarian Acad. of Sciences; basic and applied research studies of the geoenvironment of the Bulgarian territory aiming to support the sustainable devt of contemporary society and harmonic safe control of the issues associated with geohazards; library of 73,000 vols; Dir Assoc. Prof. Dr DONCHO KARASTANEV; Deputy Dir for Int. and Information Activities Assoc. Prof. Dr RADOSLAV NAKOV; Admin. Dir ROSIZA DIMITROVA; Scientific Sec. Prof. Dr KRISTALINA STOYKOVA; publs *Geologica Balcanica* (4 a year), *Geochemistry, Mineralogy and Petrology* (1 a year), *Review of the Bulgarian Geological Society* (3 a year).

Georgi Nadjakov Institute of Solid State Physics: 72, Tsarigradsko Shose Blvd, 1784 Sofia; tel. (2) 875-80-61; fax (2) 975-36-32; e-mail director@issp.bas.bg; internet www

.issp.bas.bg; f. 1972, present name 1982; attached to Bulgarian Acad. of Sciences; fundamental and applied research in fields of laser physics, condensed matter physics, microelectronics, spectroscopy and optics; Dir Acad. Prof. Dr ALEXANDER G. PETROV; Deputy Dir Assoc. Prof. Dr STEFAN ANDREEV; Deputy Dir Assoc. Prof. Dr VASSIL ; Scientific Sec. Assoc. Prof. Dr MARINA PRIMATAROWA.

Institute of Catalysis: Acad. G. Bonchev St, Bldg 11, 1113 Sofia; tel. (2) 979-35-63; fax (2) 71-29-67; e-mail icatalys@ic.bas.bg; internet www.ic.bas.bg; f. 1983; attached to Bulgarian Acad. of Sciences; theory and practice of catalysis; elaboration of new catalysts; devt of new catalytic processes; investigation of the kinetics and mechanism of catalytic processes; creation of models of catalytic processes and elementary acts; research and devt of technologies for catalyst manufactures; coordination of the research activities in the field of catalysis in Bulgaria; 78 mems; Dir Prof. Dr SLAVCHO RAKOVSKY; Deputy Dir Prof. Dr SONIA DAMYANOVA; Scientific Sec. Assoc. Prof. Dr ALEXANDER ELIYAS; Deputy Scientific Sec. Assoc. Prof. Dr ELINA MANOVA; publs *Proceedings of the International Symposium on Electron Paramagnetic Resonance, Proceedings of the International Symposium on Heterogeneous Catalysis.*

Institute of Electrochemistry and Energy Systems: Acad. G. Bonchev St, Bldg 10, 1113 Sofia; tel. (2) 872-25-45; fax (2) 872-25-44; e-mail stoynov@bas.bg; internet www.bas.bg/cleps; f. 1967 as Central Laboratory of Electrochemical Power Sources; attached to Bulgarian Acad. of Sciences; depts of electrocatalysis and electrocrystallization, electrochemistry of biocatalytic and metal-air systems, electrochemistry of lead-acid batteries, electrochemical methods, electrochemical scientific instrumentation, lithium systems electrochemistry, nanoscaled materials, solid state electrolytes; Dir Prof. ZDRAVKO STOYNOV; Vice-Dir Prof DARIA VLADIKOVA; Vice-Dir Assoc. Prof. Dr KONSTANTIN PETROV; Scientific Sec. Assoc. Prof. Dr TAMARA PETKOVA; publs *Bulgarian Chemical Communications, EICIS* (online).

Institute of General and Inorganic Chemistry: Acad. Georgi Bonchev St, Bldg 11, 1113 Sofia; tel. (2) 872-48-01; fax (2) 870-50-24; e-mail info@svr.igic.bas.bg; internet www.bas.bg; f. 1960; attached to Bulgarian Acad. of Sciences; Dir Prof. KONSTANTIN HADJIIVANOV; Vice-Dir Prof. ELISAVETA IVANOVA; Vice-Dir Assoc. Prof. PLAMEN STEFANOV; Scientific Sec. Assoc. Prof. EKATERINA ZHECHEVA.

Institute of Geophysics 'Acad. L. Krastanov': Acad G. Bonchev St, Block 3, 1113 Sofia; tel. (2) 971-26-77; fax (2) 971-30-05; e-mail office@geophys.bas.bg; internet www.geophys.bas.bg; f. 1960; attached to Bulgarian Acad. of Sciences; researches physics of the solid Earth and the Earth's environment; activities incl. protection of the population and risk mitigation of unfavourable natural phenomena and disasters; facilitates sustainable devt and use of the natural and raw-material resources of Bulgaria; provides nat. authorities with expert geophysical information; 133 mems; Dir Dr NIKOLAY MILOSHEV; Deputy Dir Dr SV. NIKOLOVA; Deputy Dir Dr D. SOLAKOV; Scientific Sec. Dr DORA PANCHEVA; publ. *Bulgarian Geophysical Journal* (4 a year).

Institute of Mechanics: Acad. G. Bonchev St, Bldg 4, 1113 Sofia; tel. (2) 979-64-20; fax (2) 870-74-98; e-mail office@imbm.bas.bg; internet www.imbm.bas.bg; f. 1977, present name 1993; attached to Bulgarian Acad. of

Sciences; theoretical and experimental research, consultation and experts' reports, metrology measurements, construction of scientific devices and education of highly qualified specialists in theoretical and applied mechanics, biomechanics and mechatronics; main fields of research incl. mechanics of multibody systems, solid mechanics, fluid mechanics, biomechanics and physicochemical mechanics; 158 mems, 100 scientists; library of 8,000 vols; Dir Dr VASIL KAVARDJIKOV; Vice-Dir Prof. NIKOLAY VITANOV, Dr NADIA ANTONOVA; Scientific Sec. VASSIL VASSILEV; publs *Journal of Theoretical and Applied Mechanics* (online), *Series of Biomechanics.*

Institute of Nuclear Research and Nuclear Energy: Tsarigradsko Shose Blvd 72, 1784 Sofia; tel. (2) 974-37-61; fax (2) 975-36-19; e-mail inrne@inrne.bas.bg; internet www.inrne.bas.bg; f. 1972; attached to Bulgarian Acad. of Sciences; scientific research and applications of nuclear science and technologies and studies of their interactions with the environment; Dir Prof. Dr JORDAN STAMENOV; Deputy Dir Assoc. Prof. Dr MITKO GAIDAROV; Deputy Dir Assoc. Prof. Dr PAVLIN PETKOV GRUDEV; Scientific Sec. Assoc. Prof. Dr ANNA ANDREEVA DAMIANOVA; publ. *Proceedings of the International School on Nuclear Physics.*

Institute of Oceanology 'Fridtjof Nansen': POB 152, 9000 Varna; located at: First May Street 40, 9000 Varna; tel. (52) 370-486; fax (52) 370-483; e-mail office@io-bas.bg; internet www.io-bas.bg; f. 1973 as Institute for Marine Research and Oceanology; attached to Bulgarian Acad. of Sciences; research in the field of biology, chemistry, coastal dynamics and ocean technology, geology, ecology marine physics; consulting and expert services; training; library of 10,000 vols; 116 mems; Dir Dr ATANAS PALAZOV; Deputy Dir for Science Dr VESELIN PEICHEV; Deputy Dir for Int. Relations Dr SNEZHANA MONCHEVA; Deputy Dir for Admin. CVETAN SIRAKOV; Scientific Sec. Dr GALINA SHTEREVA; publ. *Proceedings* (irregular).

Institute of Organic Chemistry with Centre of Phytochemistry: Acad. G. Bonchev St, Bldg 9, 1113 Sofia; tel. (2) 960-61-12; fax (2) 870-02-25; e-mail iochem@orgchm.bas.bg; internet www.orgchm.bas.bg; f. 1960; attached to Bulgarian Acad. of Sciences; focuses on clarifying the relationship between synthesis, structure and reactivity of organic compounds; isolation, determination of structure and practical application of natural compounds; determination of structure and the function of proteins, enzymes and peptides; study of the thermal and catalytic transformations of hydrocarbons; Dir Prof. BOJIDAR TCHORBANOV; Deputy Dir Assoc. Prof. JORDAN TSENOV; Deputy Dir Assoc. Prof. Dr BORYANA DAMYANOVA; Scientific Sec. Assoc. Prof. Dr ILIJANA TIMTCHEVA.

Institute of Polymers: Acad. G. Bonchev St, Block 103A, 1113 Sofia; tel. and fax (2) 870-03-09; e-mail instpoly@polymer.bas.bg; internet www.polymer.bas.bg; f. 1960; attached to Bulgarian Acad. of Sciences; research and education in macromolecular sciences relevant to devt and application of polymers and polymeric materials; Dir Prof. Dr KOLIO TROEV; Deputy Dir Assoc. Prof. Dr DARINKA CHRISTOVA; Scientific Sec. Assoc. Prof. Dr NELI KOSEVA.

National Institute of Meteorology and Hydrology (NIMH): Blvd Tsarigradsko chaussee 66, 1784 Sofia; tel. (2) 975-39-96; fax (2) 988-44-94; e-mail office@meteo.bg; internet www.meteo.bg; f. 1890 as the principal meteorological station for Bulgaria; attached to Bulgarian Acad. of Sciences;

main provider of the scientific research and operational activities in meteorology, climatology, agrometeorology and hydrology; library of 25,000 ; Dir-Gen. Assoc. Prof. GEORGI KORTCHEV; Deputy Dir-Gen. Assoc. Prof. Dr VALERY SPIRIDONOV; Deputy Dir-Gen. Assoc. Prof. Dr DOBRI DIMITROV; Scientific Sec. Assoc. Prof. Dr TANIA MARINOVA; publ. *Bulgarian Journal of Meteorology and Hydrology*.

Rostislaw Kaischew Institute of Physical Chemistry: Acad. G. Bonchev St, Bldg 11, 1113 Sofia; tel. and fax (2) 872-75-50; fax (2) 971-26-88; e-mail physchem@ipc.bas.bg; internet www.ipc.bas.bg; f. 1958; attached to Bulgarian Acad. of Sciences; interface colloid science phase formation, crystal growth, electrochemical deposition and metal dissolution; electrochemically obtained materials and corrosion processes; amorphous materials; 102 mems; Dir Prof. Dr IVAN KRASTEV; Deputy Dir Prof. ELENA MILEVA; Scientific Sec. Assoc. Prof. MARIA PETROVA.

Rozhen National Astronomical Observatory: POB 136, 4700 Smoljan; tel. and fax (301) 985-356; e-mail markishki@mail.bg; internet www.nao-rozhen.org; f. 1981; attached to Institute of Astronomy, Bulgarian Acad. of Sciences; fundamental studies in the field of astronomy and astrophysics; library of 5,000 vols; Deputy Dir Dr ANASTAS STINKOV.

Space Research Institute: Moskovska 6, POB 799, 1000 Sofia; tel. (2) 988-35-03; fax (2) 981-33-47; e-mail office@space.bas.bg; internet www.space.bas.bg; f. 1975; attached to Bulgarian Acad. of Sciences; fundamental and applied investigations in space physics, astrophysics, image processing, remote sensing, life sciences, scientific equipment; preparation and realisation of experiments in the region of space investigation and usage from the board of automatic and navigated spacecrafts; investigation on control systems, air- and spacecrafts and equipment for them; activity for creation of cosmic materials and technologies and their transfer in the nat. economy; Dir Prof. Dr PETER STEFANOV GETZOV; Scientific Sec. Prof. GARO MARDIROSSIAN; publ. *Aerospace Research in Bulgaria* (1 a year).

Solar-Terrestrial Influences Laboratory: Block 3 Acad. Georgi Bonchev St, 1113 Sofia; tel. (2) 870-02-29; fax (2) 870-01-78; internet www.stil.bas.bg; f. 1990; attached to Bulgarian Acad. of Sciences; fundamental space research and its application in solar-terrestrial physics; in situ and remote investigation of the geospace, planets and interplanetary space; study of global change and ecosystems and heliobiology and telemedicine and eHealth; Dir Prof. TSVETAN PANTALEEV DACHEV; Deputy Dir Dr DOYNO IVANOV PETKOV; Chair., Scientific Council PETER VELINOV; Scientific Sec. IRINA MITKOVA STOILOVA; publs *Advances in Space Research*, *Comptes Rendus de l'Académie Bulgare des Sciences*, *Journal of Atmospheric and Solar-Terrestrial Physics*.

PHILOSOPHY AND PSYCHOLOGY

Institute for Philosophical Research: 6 Patriarh Evtimij Blvd, 1000 Sofia; tel. and fax (2) 981-07-91; e-mail office@philosophybulgaria.org; internet www .philosophybulgaria.org; f. 1945, as Institute of Philosophy and Education; Institute of Philosophy 1952–88; Institute of Philosophical Sciences 1988–95; present name 1995; attached to Bulgarian Acad. of Sciences; depts of aesthetics and cultural studies, anthropology and religious studies, ethics and bioethics, history of philosophy, logic, ontology and epistemology, philosophy of

science, social philosophy; library of 32,952 vols, incl. 24,929 books and 8,023 periodicals; 65 mems; Dir Prof. Dr VASSIL PRODANOV; Scientific Sec. Assoc. Prof. Dr VESSELIN PETROV; publs *Balkan Journal of Philosophy* (2 a year), *Philosophical Alternatives* (6 a year).

Institute of Psychology: Acad. G. Bonchev St, Bldg 6, Fl. 5, 1113 Sofia; tel. and fax (2) 870-32-17; e-mail bozhi@ipsyh.bas.bg; internet www.ipsyh.bas.bg; f. 1973 as Laboratory of Psychology, present name 1990; attached to Bulgarian Acad. of Sciences; studies the theoretical and practical problems of contemporary psychology; Dir Prof. Dr BOZHIDAR DIMITROV; Deputy Dir Assoc. Prof. DIMITER SHTETINSKY; Scientific Sec. Assoc. Prof. Dr ELIANA PENCHEVA; publ. *Psychological Research*.

RELIGION, SOCIOLOGY AND ANTHROPOLOGY

Ethnographic Institute and Museum: Moskovska 6A, 1000 Sofia; tel. (2) 987-41-91; fax (2) 980-11-62; internet hs41.iccs.bas .bg; f. 1947, present name 1949; attached to Bulgarian Acad. of Sciences; explores different aspects of Bulgarian traditional culture; works on the ethnological problems connected with the role and the specific features of the Bulgarian traditional and modern culture from Slavonic and Balkan perspectives; some aspects of the ethnic devt and ethnic relations between Bulgarians, Christians and Muslims; Dir Assoc. Prof. R. POPOV; publs *Bulgarska Etnologia* (Bulgarian Ethnology), *Ethnologia Balkanica* (1 a year).

Institute of Folklore: Acad. G. Bonchev St., Bldg 6, 1113 Sofia; tel. (2) 71-36-43; fax (2) 870-42-09; e-mail folklor@bas.bg; internet www.folklor.bas.bg; f. 1973; attached to Bulgarian Acad. of Sciences; interdisciplinary research; documents Bulgarian nominations for the UNESCO Representative List of Elements of Intangible Cultural Heritage; library of 4,200 vols, 73 periodicals; Dir Prof. Dr MILA SANTOVA; Scientific Sec. Assoc. Prof. Dr VALENTINA GANEVA-RAJCHEVA; publ. *Bulgarian Folklore* (4 a year).

Institute of Sociology: 13A Moskovska St, 1000 Sofia; tel. (2) 980-90-86; fax (2) 980-58-95; e-mail info@sociology-bg.org; internet sociology-bg.org; f. 1968; attached to Bulgarian Acad. of Sciences; conducts theoretical and applied research in the fields of social communities, social stratification and social mobility, social pathology, sociology of labour, orgs. and politics, sociology of education, science and technologies, ethno-sociology, sociology of religions and everyday life, regional and global devt; Dir Prof. Dr DIMITAR VELKOV DIMITROV; Deputy Dir Prof. Dr VALENTINA ILIEVA ZLATANOVA; Scientific Sec. Assoc. Prof. Dr ANNA IVANOVA MANTAROVA; publ. *Sociological Problems* (4 a year).

TECHNOLOGY

'Acad. Emil Djakov' Institute of Electronics: 72, Tsarigradsko Shose Blvd, 1784 Sofia; tel. (2) 875-00-77; fax (2) 975-32-01; e-mail die@ie.bas.bg; internet www.ie-bas.dir .bg; f. 1963; attached to Bulgarian Acad. of Sciences; applied physics and eng. such as high-tech material fabrication, treatment and analysis, nanosciences and nanotechnologies, nanoelectronics, photonics, optoelectronics, quantum optics, environmental monitoring, biomedical photonics; Dir Assoc. Prof. Dr RADOMIR ENIKOV; Deputy Dir Assoc. Prof. Dr SANKA GATEVA; Deputy Dir Assoc. Prof. Dr NIKOLAY NEDIALKOV; Scientific Sec. Assoc. Prof. Dr KATIA VUTOVA.

Central Laboratory of Applied Physics: 59 St Petersburg Blvd, 4000 Plovdiv; tel. (32)

63-50-19; fax (32) 63-28-10; e-mail ipfban@mbox.digsys.bg; internet www.bas.bg/plovdiv; f. 1979 as Laboratory of Applied Physics, present status and name 1995; attached to Bulgarian Acad. of Sciences; scientific investigation, research and devt work and production in the field of electronics, micro- and optoelectronics, semiconductor sensors and sensor devices and production technologies; Dir Assoc. Prof. Dr ROUMEN KAKANAKOV; Deputy Dir Assoc. Prof. Dr MINKO NESHEV; Scientific Sec. Assoc. Prof. LYDIA BEDIKIAN.

Central Laboratory of Mechatronics and Instrumentation: Acad G. Bonchev, Bldg 1, 1113 Sofia; tel. and fax (2) 872-35-71; internet www.clmi.bas.bg; f. 1994; attached to Bulgarian Acad. of Sciences; research on design, analysis, devt of mechatronic and control systems, robots, specialized and unique devices; Dir Assoc. Prof. TANIO TANEV; Vice-Dir Assoc. Prof. GENCHO STAJNOV; Academic Sec. Assoc Prof. VASSIL TRENEV.

Central Laboratory of Physico-Chemical Mechanics: Georgi Bonchev St, Bldg 1, 1113 Sofia; tel. (2) 871-81-82; fax (2) 870-34-33; e-mail clphchm@clphchm.bas.bg; internet www.clphchm.bas.bg; f. 1972; attached to Bulgarian Acad. of Sciences; nat. coordinator of research in the field of mechanics and technology of non-metallic composite materials for constructions; Dir Assoc. Prof. Dr NIKOLAY BAROVSKY; Asst Dir Eng. ILIYA KRASTEV; Scientific Sec. Prof. Dr RUMIANA KOTSILKOVA; publs *Physico-Chemical Mechanics* (2 a year), *Non-Metallic Composite Materials* (2 a year).

Central Laboratory of Seismic Mechanics and Earthquake Engineering: Acad. G. Bonchev St, Bldg 3, 1113 Sofia; tel. and fax (2) 971-24-07; e-mail clsmseeof@geophys.bas .bg; internet www.clsmee.geophys.bas.bg; f. 1982; attached to Bulgarian Acad. of Sciences; seismic risk assessment of urban areas, buildings and structures; monitors strong ground motion; reduces the effects of earthquakes; elaborates standard documents for design and construction in seismic regions; trains scientific and engineering specialists and improves public earthquake knowledge; Dir Assoc. Prof. Eng. SVETOSLAV SIMEONOV; Vice-Dir Assoc. Prof. Dr Eng. DIMITAR STEFANOV; Scientific Sec. Assoc. Prof. Dr Eng. KIRIL HDJIYSKI.

Institute of Chemical Engineering: Acad. G. Bonchev St, Bldg 103, 1113 Sofia; tel. (2) 870-20-88; fax (2) 870-75-23; e-mail ichemeng@bas.bg; internet www.bas.bg/iceng; f. 1973, present name 1986; attached to Bulgarian Acad. of Sciences; nat. research centre for chemical engineering and bioengineering science; Dir Prof. Dr VENKO BESCHKOV; Scientific Sec. Assoc. Prof. Dr TSVETAN SAPUNDZHIEV.

Institute of Computer and Communication Systems: Acad. G. Bonchev St, Bldg 2, 1113 Sofia; tel. (2) 871-90-97; fax (2) 872-39-05; e-mail diana@iccs.bas.bg; internet iccsweb.isdip.bas.bg; f. 1964 as Institute of Engineering Cybernetics; attached to Bulgarian Acad. of Sciences; comprises 7 depts: architecture of computer and communication systems, dependable computer and communication systems, hierarchical systems, integrated systems for digital processing of information, intelligent computer technologies, real-time control systems, software engineering; Dir Assoc. Prof. Dr ZLATOLILIA ILCHEVA (acting); Scientific Sec. Assoc. Prof. Dr DIMITER LAKOV; publ. *Proceedings of ICCS-BAS*.

Institute of Control and Systems Research 'Saint Apostle and Gospeller Matthew': Acad. G. Bonchev St, Bldg 2, POB

79, 1113 Sofia; tel. (2) 873-26-14; fax (2) 870-33-61; internet www.icsr.bas.bg; f. 1994; attached to Bulgarian Acad. of Sciences; depts of multisensors and robotic systems, knowledge-based control systems, adaptive and robust control hybrid systems and management, modelling and control of ecological systems, and scientific research, applications and training; Dir Prof. Dr CHAVDAR ROUMENIN; Deputy Dir Assoc. Prof. Dr DIMITAR NEDIALKOV; Deputy Dir Assoc. Prof. Dr HRISTO VARBANOV; Scientific Sec. Assoc. Prof. Dr MAYA IGNATOVA.

Institute of Information Technologies: Acad. G. Bonchev St., Block 2, 1113 Sofia; tel. and fax (2) 872-04-97; e-mail office@iit.bas.bg; internet www.iit.bas.bg; f. 1994; attached to Bulgarian Acad. of Sciences; investigates and develops approaches, methods and tools in the modern information technology areas with applications for real problem solving; Dir Assoc. Prof. Dr GEORGI GLUHCHEV (acting); Deputy Dir Assoc. Prof. Dr BOYAN METEV; Deputy Dir Assoc. Prof. Dr IVAN MUSTAKEROV; Scientific Sec. Assoc. Prof. Dr DANAIL DOCHEV; publs *Cybernetics and Information Technologies*, *IIT Working Papers*, *Problems of Engineering Cybernetics and Robotics*.

Institute of Laser Technology: Galichitsa 33A, 1326 Sofia; tel. 68-89-13; fax 68-89-13; f. 1980; Dir Assoc. Prof. I. KHRISTOV.

Institute of Metal Science, Equipment and Technologies with Hydroaerodynamics Centre 'Acad. A. Balevski': Shipchenski prohod 67, 1574 Sofia; tel. (2) 462-62-00; fax (2) 462-63-00; e-mail stvims@ims.bas.bg; internet www.ims.bas.bg; f. 1967; attached to Bulgarian Acad. of Sciences; fundamental and applied research in the field of metal science and heat treatment, casting, crystallization, structure and properties of metals, alloys and composites on metal base, plasticity and fracture of materials, interaction of gases and metal and nonmetal materials, production of high nitrogen steels under high pressures, physics and mechanics of welding processes, ceramics and composites, thermal electric and magnetohydraulic processes in molten metals, ecologically appropriate processes and machines for the production of novel materials and products; Dir Prof. STEFAN VODENICHAROV; Vice-Dir Prof NIKOLAY POPOV; Asst Dir Dr KIRIL STOYCHEV; Scientific Sec. Asst Prof. NIKOLAY LICHKOV; publs *Engineering Sciences* (4 a year), *Journal of Materials Science and Technology* (4 a year).

Institute of Mineralogy and Crystallography 'Acad. Ivan Kostov': Acad. Georgi Bonchev St, Bldg 107, 1113 Sofia; tel. (2) 979-70-55; fax (2) 979-70-56; e-mail mincryst@interbgc.com; internet www.clmc.bas.bg; f. 1984; attached to Bulgarian Acad. of Sciences; basic studies and applied research; consulting; expertise service and analytic activities; practical applications of scientific results and training of highly qualified specialists in the field of mineralogy and crystallography; investigation and modelling of natural and technogenic mineral systems; Dir Dr ZHELYAZKO DAMYANOV; Deputy Dir Dr LUDMIL KONSTANTINOV; Scientific Sec. Dr MIHAIL TARASSOV.

ISOMATIC Labs Ltd: Andrey Lyapchev Blvd 4, 1797 Sofia; tel. (2) 877-45-96; fax (2) 975-30-32; e-mail isomatic@isomatic.com; internet www.isomatic.com; f. 1992; robotics, electronics; Dir Assoc. Prof. G. NACHEV.

Technological Institute of Agricultural Engineering: Blvd Lipnitsa 106, 7005 Ruse; tel. (82) 44-19-21; fax (82) 45-93-82; f. 1962; Dir T. KAYRIAKOV.

Libraries and Archives

Burgas

Library PK Yavorov: Blvd A. Bogoridi 21, 8000 Burgas; tel. and fax (56) 84-27-53; e-mail rl_bourgas@burglib.org; internet www.burglib.org; f. 1888; 560,000 vols; Dir NATALIA KOTSEVA.

Plovdiv

Ivan Vazov National Library: Avksentii Veleshki 17, 4000 Plovdiv; tel. (32) 65-49-01; fax (32) 65-49-02; e-mail nbiv@libplovdiv.com; internet www.libplovdiv.com; f. 1879; 1,313,000 vols, 1,100 periodical titles, 336 MSS, 4,134 incunabula; Dir RADKA KOLEVA; Vice-Dir DIMITAR MINEV; publ. *Plovdivski Kraj* (1 a year).

Ruse

'Lyuben Karavelov' Regional Library: D. Korsakov 1, 7000 Ruse; tel. (82) 82-01-26; fax (82) 82-01-34; e-mail libruse@libruse.bg; internet www.libruse.bg; f. 1888; 700,000 vols; Dir RUMIAN GANCHEV.

Shumen

Public Library 'Stilian Chilingirov': Slavianski Blvd 19, 9700 Shumen; tel. 87-73-32; e-mail libshumen@abv.bg; internet www.libshumen.org; f. 1922; 720,000 vols; Dir Z. KUKUSHKOVA.

Sofia

Archives State Agency: Moskovska 5, 1000 Sofia; tel. (2) 940-01-01; fax (2) 980-14-43; e-mail daa@archives.government.bg; internet www.archives.government.bg; f. 1951; administers 2 central and 6 regional archives; 34,900 vols, 140 periodicals; Chair. Prof. Dr GEORGI BAKALOV; Vice-Chair. BOYKO KIRYAKOV; Vice-Chair. DANIEL HADJIEV; publs *Arhiven pregled / Archives Review* (4 a year), *Arhivite govoryat / The Archives are Talking* (bilingual, French and Bulgarian), *Arhivni Spravochnitzi / Archival Finding Aids*, *Izvestiya na darzhavnite arhivi* (2 a year).

British Council Library and Information Centre: Krakra St 7, Sofia; tel. (2) 942-43-44; fax (2) 942-42-22; e-mail bc.sofia@britishcouncil.bg; internet www.britishcouncil.bg; promotes the teaching of English language, organizes exams and training courses; 7,000 vols; Dir (vacant).

Central Agricultural Library:; e-mail csb@abv.bg Tsarigradsko shose Blvd 125, Block 1, 1113 Sofia; tel. (2) 870-60-81; fax (2) 870-80-78; e-mail csb@abv.bg; internet cnti.hit.bg/cal.htm; f. 1962; attached to Institute of Agricultural Information; documentation centre of nat. and int. literature of the agriculture, food science and forestry industry; 449,483 vols; Dir Assoc. Prof. Dr SIMONA RALCHEVA; Head of Library MARGARITA STAMATOVA; publs *Agricultural Economics and Management*, *Agricultural Engineering*, *Agricultural Science*, *Animal Science*, *Bulgarian Journal Of Agricultural Science*, *Plant Science*, *Soil Science Agrochemistry and Ecology*.

Central Library of the Bulgarian Academy of Sciences: 1, 15 Noemvri St, 1040 Sofia; tel. (2) 987-89-66; fax (2) 986-25-00; e-mail library@cl.bas.bg; internet www.cl.bas.bg; f. 1869; 1,905,253 vols; maintains the book stock of the Central Library and of the 49 special libraries of the acad.; provides information services for the scientific potential of BAS and the country; Dir Assoc. Dr DINCHO KRASTEV; Deputy Dir SABINA ANEVA; publs *Bulgaristika/Bulgarica*, *Informatsionen biuletin*, *Problemi na spetsialnite biblioteki–tematichen sbornik*.

Central Medical Library: St Sofia D. 1, 1431 Sofia; tel. (2) 952-31-71; fax (2) 851-82-65; e-mail mlib@medun.acad.bg; internet www.medun.acad.bg; f. 1918; 25 affiliated libraries; medicine, dental medicine, pharmacy and health care; scientific research and education; exchange of information resources with local and int. scientific instns and orgs; interlibrary loans; publishing and editorial activities; 524,777 vols; Dir Dr LYDIA TACHEVA; publs *Abstracts of Bulgarian Scientific Medical Literature*, *Acupuncture*, *Acta medica Bulgaria* (in English, 2 a year), *Alergology, Clinical Immunology & Clinical Laboratory* (in Bulgarian), *Bulgarian medical journal* (in Bulgarian, 4 a year), *Cardiovascular Diseases* (in Bulgarian), *General Medicine* (in English and Bulgarian, 4 a year), *Medical review* (4 a year), *Nursing* (in Bulgarian), *Pediatrics & Infectious diseases* (in Bulgarian), *Obstetrics and Gynecology*, *Scripta periodica* (in English, 4 a year), *Surgery* (in Bulgarian).

Central Scientific Technical Library at the National Centre for Information and Documentation: NACID, Blvd MD. GM Dimitrov 50, 1125 Sofia; tel. (2) 817-38-41; e-mail ctb@nacid-bg.net; internet www.nacid.bg; f. 1962; collects, stores and makes available various types of Bulgarian and foreign publs, incl. monographs, reference books, encyclopaedias, dictionaries, magazines and periodicals, bibliographic and referral issues, reports from scientific confs held nationally and internationally, and dissertations; 119,000 vols, 13,000 titles of journals and periodicals, bibliographic publs, 76,000 reports of scientific confs, 18,000 UN reports, 13,000 dissertations, 103,000 co literatures, 800 CD-ROMs, DVDs, scientific and technical translations; Dir VALENTINA SLAVCHEVA; publ. *Advances in Bulgarian Science*.

Central State Archives: Moskovska 5, 1000 Sofia; tel. (2) 940-01-04; fax (2) 980-14-43; e-mail cda@archives.government.bg; internet www.archives.government.bg; f. 1952; 110,000 files, documenting the activities of state instns, political parties, state and private cos and enterprises, from the mid-19th century to recent times; personal papers of eminent Bulgarians; Dir GEORGI CHERNEV.

Centre for European Studies: G. M. Dimitrov 52A, 1125 Sofia; tel. and fax (2) 971-24-11; e-mail ces@mail.cesbg.org; f. 1990; European Documentation Centre receiving all official publs of EC; Dir I. SHIKOVA; publ. *Europa* (12 a year).

Institute of Agricultural Information (with Central Agricultural Library): Tsarigradsko shose 125, Bldg 1, 1113 Sofia; tel. (2) 870-55-58; fax (2) 870-80-78; e-mail agrolib@abv.bg; f. 1961; library and information services in agriculture; Dir Assoc. Prof. SIMONA RALCHEVA; Librarian ROUMYANA VASSILEVA; publ. *Bulgarian Journal of Agricultural Science*.

Library of the UBA: 6 Slavyanska St, Sofia; tel. (2) 987-38-72; e-mail library@uba.bg; internet www.uba.bg; plays and drama materials from the end of the 19th and beginning of the 20th centuries; open to mems; 6,000 vols; Librarians IVANKA SHINDAROVA; Librarian VESELA PAVLOVA; publs *Homo Ludens, Theatre magazine*.

National Centre for Information and Documentation (at the Ministry of Industry): G. M. Dimitrov Blvd 52A, 1125 Sofia; tel. (2) 817-38-24; fax (2) 971-31-20; e-mail secretary@nacid.bg; internet www.nacid.bg; f. 1993; attached to Min. of Education, Youth and Science; management models, structure, control and resources ensuring of popular education, higher education, youth and science systems; information products and services in the field of education and science; 4,650,000 vols; Gen. Dir J. KHLEBAROV; CEO VANIA GRASHKINA; publs *Advances in Bulgarian Science* (in English, 1 a year), *Infoswjat* (in Bulgarian, 4 a year), *Scientific and Technical Publications in Bulgaria* (in English, 4 a year).

Scientific Archives of the Bulgarian Academy of Sciences: 15 Noemvri 1, 1040 Sofia; tel. (2) 988-40-46; fax (2) 981-66-29; e-mail archiv2@abv.bg; internet archiv.cl.bas.bg; f. 1947; MSS and 110,000 scientific dossiers; historical archives containing valuable documents on the history of the Bulgarian state; Head Assoc. Prof. ROUZHA SIMEONOVA.

Sofia City Library: 4 Slaveikov Sq., 1000 Sofia; tel. (2)986-21-69; fax (2) 988-22-36; e-mail libsofdir@libsofia.bg; internet www.libsofia.bg; f. 1898, present status 2000; personal library of Dr Constantin Stoilov and Sofia local history colln; 932,428 vols (incl. 866,867 books, 31,304 periodicals, 8,182 black and white drawings, 1,954 maps, 9,075 scores, 13,579 sound records, 269 official editions, 1,833 slides and films and 260 pictures); 9,121 mems; Dir MIHAIL BELCHEV.

St. Cyril and Methodius National Library: Blvd Vasil Levski 88, 1037 Sofia; tel. (2) 988-28-11; fax (2) 843-54-95; e-mail nl@nationallibrary.bg; internet www.nationallibrary.bg; f. 1878, present bldg 1953; holds Slavonic and foreign language MSS, incunabula, rare and valuable edns, Bulgarian historical archives, maps and graphics, official publs, music publs and recordings, foreign books and periodicals, reference books, specialized collns, dept of Oriental collns; 255 staff; 2,863,754 vols and periodicals, 5,536 MSS, 34,187 old and rare publs, 290,093 maps, prints and portraits, 85,418 scores and gramophone records, 292,437 patents and standards, 3,114,876 archival documents; archive of Bulgarian printed material; nat. ISBN and ISSN agency; spec. archive of documents from the period of Ottoman rule, feudalism and the Bulgarian nat. revival; research institute in library science; Dir Prof. Dr BORYANA HRISTOVA; Deputy Dir for Admin. Business SPAS DAMYANOV; Deputy Dir for Library ANETA DONCHEVA; Sec. VIOLETA BOZHKOVA; publs *Biblioteca Journal* (6 a year), *Proceedings* (1 a year).

University Library: 1 Hristo Smirnenski Blvd, 1046 Sofia; tel. (2) 866-52-74; fax (2) 865-68-63; e-mail lib@uacg.bg; internet www.uacg.bg; f. 1942; holds MSS, theses, gray literature, microfilms, spec. colln of art and graphics albums, reference books and encyclopaedias in Bulgarian, English, French, German, Italian, Polish, Russian, Spanish and other Slavonic languages covering areas of architecture, art, agricultural sciences, economics, environmental sciences, geodesy, mathematics, physics, philosophy, political and social sciences, technics; 450,000 vols; Dir PERSIDA TOMOVA RAFAILOVA.

University Library 'St Kliment Ohridski': Tsar Osvoboditel Blvd 15, 1504 Sofia; tel. (2) 846-75-84; fax (2) 846-71-70; e-mail lsu@libsu.uni-sofia.bg; internet www.libsu.uni-sofia.bg; f. 1888; print and electronic library and information services, database access, interlibrary and international interlibrary loans; copying and microfiche services and electronic document delivery services; 2,001,000 vols; Dir Dr ANNA ANGELOVA; Deputy Dir BILIANA YAVRUKOVA; Sec. BISTRA DRAGOLOVA.

Stara Zagora

Regional Library: Tsar Kalojan 50, 6000 Stara Zagora; tel. (42) 64-81-31; e-mail lib-sz@prolink.bg; f. 1954; 419,000 vols; Dir SNEZANA MARINOVA.

Rodina Library: Ruski Blvd 17, 6000 Stara Zagora; tel. (42) 63-01-13; fax (42) 60-39-50; e-mail lib@rodina-bg.org; internet www.rodina-bg.org; f. 1860; 300,000 vols.

Varna

'Pencho Slaveykov' Public Library—Varna: Slivnitsa Blvd 34, 9000 Varna; tel. (52) 65-91-36; e-mail office@libvar.bg; internet www.libvar.bg; f. 1883; depository of Bulgarian nat. literature since 1945; 773,000 vols; Man. Dir EMILIYA STANEVA-MILKOVA.

Veliko Tărnovo

P. R. Slaveykov Regional Public Library: 2 Ivanka Boteva St, 5000 Veliko Tărnovo; tel. and fax (62) 62-02-08; e-mail prs@libraryvt.com; internet www.libraryvt.com; f. 1889; third nat. depository library; 586,873 vols; Dir IVAN ALEXANDROV; Deputy Dir KALINA IVANOVA.

Vidin

Regional library 'Mihalacky Gergiev': Bdintzi pl. 1, Vidin; tel. and fax (94) 60-17-04; e-mail libvidin@vidin.net; internet www.libvidin.net; f. 1863; 282,624 vols of books, periodicals, musical and graphic publs, audiovideo cassettes, CDs, maps.

Museums and Art Galleries

Blagoevgrad

Blagoevgrad Regional History Museum: kvartal Varosha, ul. Rila 1, 2700 Blagoevgrad; tel. (73) 88-53-70; fax (73) 88-53-73; e-mail im_bld@yahoo.com; f. 1951; archaeology, ethnography, fine arts, history, natural history; library of 16,500 vols; Dir K. GRANCHAROVA.

Burgas

Regional Historical Museum, Burgas: Slavianska St 69, 8000 Burgas; tel. (56) 82-03-44; fax (56) 84-25-88; e-mail main@burgasmuseums.bg; internet www.burgasmuseums.bg; f. 1912, present status 2000; organizes research and study of cultural heritage; Dir TSONYA DRAZHEVA; publs *Bulletin* (1 a year), *Bulletin of Museums of Southeast Bulgaria* (1 a year).

Dobrich

Regional Museum of History: 18 Konstantin Stoilov St, p. k. 131, 9300 Dobrich; tel. and fax (58) 60-32-56; e-mail rim_dobrich@abv.bg; internet museum-dobrich.net; f. 1953; holds 150,000 items; depts of archaeology; ethnography; literature and art; modern history, nat. revival period, nature; library of 20,000 vols; Dir DIANA BORISOVA; publ. *Dobrudja* (1 a year).

Haskovo

Regional Museum of History: Pl. Svoboda, 6300 Haskovo; tel. 62-42-37; fax 62-42-37; internet haskovomuseum.com; f. 1952; Dir G. GRAMATIKOV.

Kalofer

Hristo Botev National Museum: Khr. Botev 5, 4370 Kalofer; tel. and fax (3133) 22-71; e-mail musei_botev@abv.bg; f. 1944; birthplace of Hristo Botev, poet, revolution-

ary and rebel against Ottoman rule; objects and clothes showing Bulgarian life in the past; exhibit of rose oil and lace production; Dir A. NIKOLOVA.

Karlovo

'Vasil Levski' Museum – Karlovo: Gen. Kartsov St 57, 4300 Karlovo; tel. and fax (335) 934-89; e-mail v_levski_museum@mail.orbitel.bg; internet www.vlevskimuseum-bg.org; f. 1937; named after Vasil Levski (1837–73), founder of Bulgarian Revolutionary Central Committee, which liberated Bulgaria from Ottoman rule; consists of Levski's birth house, an exhibition hall with personal items, photographs, documents and works of art; and a memorial chapel in which the hair of Vasil Levski is preserved; Dir DORA CHAUSHEVA.

Kazanlak

Shipka-Buzludza National Park Museum: P. R. Slaveljov 8, 6100 Kazanlak; tel. (431) 6-29-18; fax (431) 6-24-95; e-mail shipkamuseum@mail.bg; internet www.shipkamuseum.org; f. 1956; monuments connected with the liberation of Bulgaria from Ottoman rule; Dir DANCHO DANCHEV.

Lovech

Regional Museum of History: Todor Kirkov St 1, 5500 Lovech; tel. (68) 60-13-82; e-mail imlovech@yahoo.com; internet www.lovechmuseum.hit.bg; f. 1895; holds 70,000 exhibits; restoration and conservation activities; photography services; exhibition area for temporary exhibits; Dir IVAN LALEV.

Montana

Regional Museum of History: Tsar Boris III 2, 3400 Montana,; tel. 2-84-81; fax 2-25-36; f. 1953; Dir U. DERAKCHIISKA.

Pazardzhik

Regional Museum of History: Pl. K. Velichkov 15, 4400 Pazardzhik; tel. (34) 44-31-13; fax (34) 44-31-44; e-mail museumpz@yahoo.com; internet www.rimpazar.hit.bg; f. 1911; House Museum of Constantine Velichkov; also incl. historical and ethnographic collns; library of 11,000 vols; Dir BORIS EMILOV HADJIYSKI; publ. *Homeland* (every 2 years).

Stanislav Dospevsky Art Gallery: Pl. K. Velichkov 15, 4400 Pazardzhik; tel. 44-41-52; f. 1963; Dir DOYCHEV.

Pernik

Regional Museum of History: Fizkulturna 2, 2300 Pernik; tel. (76) 60-31-18; e-mail muzeum@rotop.com; f. 1954; sections of archaeology, ethnography, labour movement, socialistic devt, mine and coal devt; Dir O. ASPROV.

Pleven

Regional Historical Museum: Stoyan Zaimov 3, 5800 Pleven; tel. and fax (64) 82-26-23; e-mail plevenmuseum@dir.bg; internet www.plevenmuseum.dir.bg; f. 1903 as Archaeological Society, present location 1984, present name and status 2000; gen. history with a natural science section; units: archaeology, history of Bulgaria from 15th to 19th century, modern history, ethnography, nature, stocks and scientific records, public relations, studio for restoration and conservation, photo-laboratory, library; basic museum colln over 180,000 items; library of 14,122 vols; Dir PETER BANOV; publ. *Museum Studies in North-Western Bulgaria* (1 a year).

Plovdiv

Archaeological Museum: Saedinenie Sq. 1, 4000 Plovdiv; tel. and fax (32) 63-31-06; e-mail ram.plovdiv@gmail.com; internet www.archaeologicalmuseumplovdiv.org; f. 1882, present status 1920; colln of 100,000 museum artefacts related to the history of Plovdiv, prehistoric, Thracian, ancient Greek, Roman medieval, Bulgarian revival art; numismatic colln; library of 13,000 vols; Dir Prof. Dr KOSTADIN KISSIOV; publs *Pulpudeva, Yearbook of the Archaeological Museum.*

City Gallery of Fine Arts: 'Saborna' St 14A, 4000 Plovdiv; tel. (32) 63-53-22; e-mail ghgpl@abv.bg; f. 1952; collects, treasures, and popularizes some of the best works of the Bulgarian fine arts (painting, graphic art, sculpture, applied arts, photography, icon collection, and Mexican art); holds a colln of 6,900 items; Dir KRASIMIR LINKOV.

Ethnographic Museum: Dr Chomakov 2, 4000 Plovdiv; tel. (32) 62-52-57; fax (32) 62-71-32; f. 1917; exhibits traditional material and spiritual culture of the population of Plovdiv and Rodopi; Dir Dr A. YANKOV.

Historical Museum – Plovdiv: Pl. Šaedinenie 1, 4000 Plovdiv; tel. (32) 26-99-55; e-mail ssh@historymuseumplovdiv.com; internet www.historymuseumplovdiv.com; f. 1951; collects, preserves and popularizes historical evidences from the past of Plovdiv and Plovdiv region from 15th to 20th century; Dir SHIVACHEV STEFAN.

Natural Science Museum: Chr. G. Danov 34, 4000 Plovdiv; tel. (32) 63-30-96; fax (32) 62-31-54; e-mail pnm_plovdiv@abv.bg; internet www.rnhm.org; f. 1955; collns in palaeontology, mineralogy, botany; freshwater aquarium with decorative fishes and a few amphibians; colln of Rhodope minerals; library of 7,820 vols; Dir OGNIAN TODOROV.

Rila

Rila Monastery National Museum: Rilski Monastir, 2643 Rila (Sofia District); tel. (70) 54-22-08; fax (70) 54-33-83; e-mail rila_monastery@abv.bg; internet www.rilamonastery.pmg-blg.com; f. 1961; Bulgarian art and architecture during the Ottoman period, Bulgarian history and history of the monastery; Dir P. MITEV.

Ruse

Regional Museum of History: Sq Al. Batenberg 3, POB 60, 7000 Ruse; tel. (82) 82-50-02; fax (82) 82-50-06; e-mail pr@museumruse.com; internet www.museumruse.com; f. 1904; archaeology, ethnography, history of Bulgaria, modern and contemporary history, nature; colln of 130,000 items; library of 15,340 vols; Dir Dr NIKOLAY NENOV; publ. *Izvestija.*

Shumen

Regional Museum of History – Shumen: 17 Slavianski Blvd, 9700 Shumen; tel. and fax (54) 5-74-10; e-mail museum_shumen@abv.bg; internet www.museum-shumen.psit35.net; f. 1904; incl. 6 archaeological reserves and preserved sites; maintains main exhibition in Shumen city museum and 7 smaller museums, specializing in history and/or archaeology of the region; 20 Soc. of the Museum Friends; library of 25,000 vols; Dir GEORGI MAYSTORSKI; publs *Proceedings of the Museum of History, Shumen* (Vols 1–12, 1960–2006), *Yearbook of the Museums of N Bulgaria* (Vols 1–20, 1975–95).

Sofia

Boyana Church National Museum: 1–3 Boyansko Ezero St, 1616 Sofia; tel. and fax (2) 959-29-66; e-mail nmbc@mail.orbitel.bg; internet www.boyanachurch.org; f. 1947; medieval orthodox painting; Dir MARIANA HRISTOVA-TRIFONOVA.

Dimitr Blagoev Museum: L. Koshut 34, 1606 Sofia; tel. (2) 52-31-45; f. 1948; house of the founder of the Bulgarian Social-Democratic Party, containing documents and personal effects; Dir R. RUSSEV.

Georgi Dimitrov National Museum: Opalchenska 66, 1303 Sofia; tel. (2) 32-01-49; f. 1951; Dir VERA DICHEVA.

Ivan Vazov Memorial House: I. Vazov 10, 1000 Sofia; tel. (2) 88-12-70; f. 1926; house in which the Bulgarian poet lived; colln of personal belongings such as clothes, books, presents and awards; his workroom is preserved in its original state; Curator I. BACHEVA.

National Ethnographical Museum: Moskovska 6A, 1000 Sofia; tel. (2) 988-41-91; fax (2) 980-11-62; e-mail eim_bas@mail.bg; internet ethnography.cc.bas.bg; f. 1978; contains elements of Renaissance, Baroque Vienna, reminiscent of French palaces of the 18th century; library of 22,221 vols; Dir Prof. Dr RACHKO POPOV; Deputy Dir Prof. Dr HOPE TENEVA; Sec. Prof. Dr ELYA TSANEVA; publs *Bulgarian Ethnology, Ethnologia Balcanica* (1 a year).

National Gallery of Decorative Arts: Blvd Cerni vrah 2, 1421 Sofia; tel. (2) 963-07-58; fax (2) 963-07-48; f. 1976; works from the 1950s to the present; library of 2,000 vols; Dir ZDRAVKO MAVRODIEV.

National Institute of Archaeology and Museum: Saborna St 2, 1000 Sofia; tel. (2) 988-24-06; fax (2) 988-24-05; e-mail naim@naim.bg; internet www.naim.bg; f. 1892; attached to Bulgarian Acad. of Sciences; permanent exhibitions on prehistory, classical antiquity and the Middle Ages; temporary exhibitions; Dir Dr MARGARITA VAKLINOVA; Deputy Dir Dr LYUDMIL VAGALINSKI; Deputy Dir Dr BISTRA BOZHKOVA; Sec. Dr DIANA GERGOVA; publs *Annual, Archaeology* (4 a year).

National Museum of Bulgarian Literature: ul. Rakovski 138, 1000 Sofia; tel. (2) 988-24-93; f. 1976; Dir DZH. KAMENOV.

National Museum of Ecclesiastical History and Archaeology: Pl. Sv. Nedelya 19, 1000 Sofia; tel. (2) 89-01-15; Dir N. KHADZHIEV.

National Museum of History: 16 Vitoshko lale St, 1000 Sofia; tel. (2) 955-42-80; fax (2) 955-76-02; e-mail nim1973@abv.bg; internet www.historymuseum.org; f. 1973, present location 2000; more than 650,000 exhibits, incl. colln from Paleolithic, Neolithic, Chalcolithic, Bronze, Iron, Roman, Middle–Late Middle ages; numismatics, adornments, jewellery, embroideries, weapons, uniforms and civil clothes and accessories, traditional clothes, applied and fine arts, documents from the nat. revival, modern history of Bulgaria, also maps, printed materials, manufacture samples; 1 br.; Dir Assoc. Prof. Dr BOZHIDA DIMITROV; Deputy Dir Dr IVAN HRISTOV.

National Museum of Military History: Cherkovna St 92, 1505 Sofia; tel. (2) 946-18-05; fax (2) 946-18-06; e-mail m.museum@bol.bg; internet www.militarymuseum.bg; f. 1916; attached to Min. of Defence; more than 1m. artefacts; collects and registers Bulgarian and European military artefacts (arms, uniforms, flags, photographs, etc.); maintains two military mausolea in Sofia; 2 brs in Varna and 1 br. in Krumovo; library of 15,000 vols; Dir Dr SONYA PENKOVA; Deputy Dir Dr DANIELA TSANKOVA-GANCHEVA; publ. *Bulletin* (1 a year).

National Natural History Museum: Tsar Osvoboditel Blvd 1, 1000 Sofia; tel. (2) 987-41-95; fax (2) 988-28-94; internet www.nmnhs.com; f. 1889 as Royal Prince's Natural History Museum; attached to Bulgarian Acad. of Sciences; 1m. specimens and samples, incl. 460 mammal species, 1,990 bird species, reptile and amphibian colln, 480,000 specimens of insects and over 300,000 specimens of other invertebrates; colln also incls mineral species from around the world and more than 30,000 samples of fossil invertebrates; br. at Asenovgrad; library of 7,887 vols of periodicals, 2,427 books; Dir Assoc. Prof. Dr ALEXI POPOV; Scientific Sec. Assoc. Prof. Dr PAVEL STOEV; publ. *Historia naturalis bulgarica* (1 a year).

National Polytechnical Museum: Opulchenska 66, 1303 Sofia; tel. (2) 931-80-18; fax (2) 931-40-46; e-mail polytechnic@abv.bg; internet www.polytechnicmuseum.org; f. 1968; science and technology; library of 10,000 vols; Dir Dr EKATERINA TSEKOVA; publs *Annual of the National Polytechnical Museum, Technitartché.*

Sofia City Art Gallery: 1 Gen. Gurko St, 1000 Sofia; tel. (2) 987-21-81; fax (2) 981-19-44; e-mail sghg@sghg.bg; internet www.sghg.bg; f. 1928, present name and status 1952, present location 1973; conserves, maintains and studies art heritage; modern Bulgarian art; Dir Dr ADELINA FILEVA; Chief Curator Dr MARIA VASSILEVA.

Sofia Museum of History: Exarh Yossif 27, 1000 Sofia; tel. (2) 983-37-55; fax (2) 983-53-51; e-mail p_mitanov@yahoo.com; f. 1952; library of 16,000 vols.

Sopot

Ivan Vazov Museum – Sopot: Vasil Levski 1, 4330 Sopot; tel. (3134) 86-50; fax (3134) 76-60; e-mail vazov-muzeum@sopot-municipality.com; internet www.vazovmuseum.com; f. 1935; birthplace of the writer (1850–1921); Dir C. NEDELCHEVA.

Stara Zagora

Regional Museum of History: 42 Ruski Blvd, 6000 Stara Zagora; tel. (42) 91-92-06; fax (42) 91-94-27; e-mail rim@museum.starazagora.net; internet museum.starazagora.net; f. 1907, present name and status 1953; sections of archaeology, Bulgarian history, folklore, numismatics; library of 7,600 books and periodicals; Dir Assoc. Prof. Dr EUGENIA IVANOVA.

Trjavna

Museum of Wood Carving and Icon Painting: Captain Dyado Nikola Sq. 7, 5350 Tryavna; tel. (677) 22-78; e-mail tryavna_museum@mail.bg; internet www.tryavna-museum.com; f. 1963; woodcarving and icon-painting; library of 4,535 vols; Dir JULIA NINOVA (acting).

Trojan

Museum of Folk Craft and Applied Arts: Pl. Vazrashdane, P.B. 46, 5600 Trojan; tel. 2-20-62; f. 1962; library of 2,700 vols; Dir T. TOTEVSKI; publ. *Cultural and Historical Inheritance of Trojan Region* (1 a year).

Varna

Regional Museum of History: Blvd Maria Luisa 41, 9000 Varna; tel. (52) 68-10-12; fax (52) 68-10-25; internet www.varna-bg.com; f. 1906; br. open-air museums: Roman Baths, Aladzha Monastery, 'Stone Forest' Nat. Park; library of 25,000 vols; Dir Dr VALENTIN PLETNYOV; publ. *Izvestija na narodniya muzei Varna* (1 a year).

Veliko Tărnovo

National Museum of Architecture: Ivan Vazov 35, POB 281, 5000 Veliko Tarnovo; tel. (62) 63-05-87; f. 1979; library of 4,600 vols; Man. Dir T. TEOPHILOV.

Regional Museum of History – Veliko Tărnovo: Nikola Pikolo St 6, 5000 Veliko Tărnovo; tel. and fax (62) 63-69-54; e-mail rimvt@abv.bg; internet www.museumvt.com; f. 1871; comprises Archaeological Museum, Museum of the Bulgarian Revival and Constituent Assembly, Museum of Contemporary History, Museum of Prison, Sarafkina's House, Slaveikov House, Architectural reserve 'Arbanasi', Konstantsalieva's House, Museum of History in the town of Kilifarev, Philip Totyo House, Archaeological reserve 'Nicopolis ad Istrum', Ethnographic complex 'Osenarska reka'; library of 12,000 vols; Dir IVAN TZAROV; publ. *Bulletin* (1 a year).

Vidin

Historical Museum: Tsar Simeon Veliki St 13, 3700 Vidin; tel. (94) 60-17-10; e-mail museumvd@mail.bg; internet museum-vidin .domino.bg; f. 1910; units of archaeology, numismatics, ethnography, modern history, recent history, Bulgarian history (15th to 19th century); library of 4,600 vols; Dir A. BANOVA.

Vratsa

Regional Museum of History: Pl. Hr. Boteva 2, 3000 Vratsa; tel. (92) 2-03-73; f. 1952; Dir I. RAJKINSKY.

Universities

AGRAREN UNIVERSITET PLOVDIV
(Agricultural University Plovdiv)

12 Mendeleev Blvd, 4000 Plovdiv

Telephone: (32) 65-42-00
Fax: (32) 63-31-57
E-mail: inter@au-plovdiv.bg
Internet: www.au-plovdiv.bg

Founded 1945, present status and name 2001
State control
Academic year: October to June

Rector: Assoc. Prof. Dr DIMITAR GREKOV
Pro-Rectors: Prof. IVANKA LECHEVA, Assoc. Prof. CHRISTINA YANCHEVA, Assoc. Prof. VASKO KOPRIVLENSKI
Chief Admin. Officer: VELICHKO RODOPSKI
Chief Librarian: E. ANASTASOVA
Number of teachers: 212
Number of students: 2,950

Publications: *Agricultural Sciences* (2 a year), *Scientific Works of the Agricultural University Plovdiv* (4 a year)

DEANS

Faculty of Agronomy: Assoc. Prof. Dr BOZHIN BOZHINOV
Faculty of Economics: Assoc. Prof. Dr GEORGI DZHELEPOV
Faculty of Plant Protection and Agroecology: Assoc. Prof. Dr YANKO DIMITROV
Faculty of Viticulture and Horticulture: Assoc. Prof. Dr ANGEL IVANOV

PROFESSORS

ALADJADJIYAN, ANNA, Physics
CHOLAKOV, DIMITAR, Horticulture
IVANOV, KRASIMIR, Chemistry
KAMBUROVA, MERI, Chemistry
KOUZMANOVA, IORDANKA, Microbiology
LECHEVA, IVANKA, Entomology
MANDRADZHIEV, SAVA, Agricultural Mechanization
PANDELIEV, SLAVCHO, Viticulture
SPASOV, VELICHKO, Crop Farming

STOYKOV, ALEKSI, Animal Sciences
SVETLEVA, DIANA, Plant Genetics

AMERIKANSKI UNIVERSITET V BULGARIA
(American University in Bulgaria)

1 Georgi Izmirliev Sq., 2700 Blagoevgrad

Telephone: (73) 88-83-06
Fax: (73) 88-83-99
Internet: www.aubg.bg

Founded 1991
Private control
Language of instruction: English
Academic year: August to May

Pres.: DAVID HUWILER
Chair.: GERARD D. VAN DER SLUYS
Chief Admin. Officer: DAVID DURST
Dean of Students: LYDIA KRISE
Assoc. Dean for Academic Affairs: STEVEN SULLIVAN
Assoc. Dean for College of Business: DUDLEY BLOSSOM
Registrar: EVELINA TERZIEVA
Number of teachers: 70
Number of students: 827

Publication: *AUBG Today* (newsletter, 3 a year)

Academic depts: arts, languages and literature; business management; computer science; economics; European studies, history, and political science/int. relations; journalism/mass communication; mathematics and science

PROFESSORS

BRADY, D.
CHRISTOZOV, D.
DURST, D.
FEDHILA, H.
FOULDS, L.
GALLETLY, J.
GREGORY, A.
MATEEV, M.
MIREE, L.
MUTAFCHIEV, L.
NAQVI, N.
POPOV, A.
STEFANOVICH, M.
STOYTCHEV, O.
TOPYAN, K.

BURGAS PROF. ASSEN ZLATAROV UNIVERSITY
(Burgas 'Prof. Assen Zlatarov' University)

Blvd Prof. Yakimov 1, 8010 Burgas

Telephone: (56) 86-00-41
Fax: (56) 88-02-49
E-mail: iroffice@btu.bg
Internet: www.btu.bg

Founded 1963 as Higher Institute of Chemical Technology, present name 1995
State control
Language of instruction: English
Academic year: September to July

Rector: Prof. PETKO PETKO
Assoc. Vice-Rector: Prof. PIPEVA PETRANKA
Vice-Rector for Education): Prof. NIKOLAY RALEV
Vice-Rector for Quality Control: Prof. YONKA BALTADJIEVA
Vice-Rector for Scientific Research and Business: Prof. BOGDAN BOGDANOV
Rector for Int. Cooperation and SDK: Prof. MAGDALENA MAGDALENA
Registrar: IVAN MARKOV
Librarian: IRENA MARKOVSKA
Library of 160,000 vols
Number of teachers: 206
Number of students: 3,918

Publication: *Godishnik*

DEANS

Faculty of Science: Dr RADOSTIN KUTSAROV
Faculty of Social Sciences: Dr IVAN DIMITROV
Faculty of Technical Sciences: Prof. ENCHO BALBOLOV

BURGASKI SVOBODEN UNIVERSITET
(Burgas Free University)

San Stefano St 62, 8000 Burgas

Telephone: (56) 900-400
Fax: (56) 813-912
E-mail: maria@bfu.bg
Internet: www.bfu.bg

Founded 1991
Private control
Academic year: October to June

Pres.: Prof. Dr PETKO CHOBANOV
Rector: Prof. Dr VASIL YANKOV
Vice-Rector for Academic Affairs: Assoc. Prof. Dr MILEN BALTOV
Vice-Rector for Research and Int. Cooperation: Prof. Dr GALYA HRISTOZOVA
Registrar: DARINA DIMITROVA
Librarian: DIANA ADAMOVA
Library of 82,000 vols
Number of teachers: 615
Number of students: 7,000

Publications: *Business Directions*, *Juridical Collection* (2 a year), *University Annual*

DEANS

Faculty of Business Studies: Prof Dr PETKO CHOBANOV
Faculty of Computer Science, Engineering and Natural Studies: Prof. DIMITAR YUDOV
Faculty of Humanities: Assoc. Prof. Dr EVELINA DINEVA
Faculty of Legal Studies: Assoc. Prof. Dr MOMYANA GUNEVA

PROFESSORS

(some professors teach in more than one faculty)
Faculty of Business Studies:
  GROZDANOV, B. K.
  STANKOV, P. C.
  YANKOV, V. N.
Faculty of Computer Science, Engineering and Natural Sciences:
  JUDAH, D. D.
  LAZAROV, A. D.
  STAMOVA, I. M.
Faculty of Humanities:
  HRISTOZOV, G. M.
  LUKOVA, K. G.
Faculty of Legal Studies:
  DRAGIEV, A. D.
  ENCHEV, T. T.
  IVANOV, I. V.
  KYNDEVA-SPIRIDO, E. V.
  ZLATAREV, E. N.

HIMIKO TEHNOLOGIČEN I METALURGIČEN UNIVERSITET
(University of Chemical Technology and Metallurgy)

St Kliment Ohridski Blvd 8, 1756 Sofia

Telephone: (2) 816-31-00
Fax: (2) 868-54-88
E-mail: rector@uctm.edu
Internet: www.uctm.edu

Founded 1953 as Dept of the State Polytechnic, present name 1995, present status 1998
State control
Language of instruction: Bulgarian, some subjects in English, French,German
Academic year: September to July

Rector: Assoc. Prof. Dr BORIS STEFANOV
Sec.: Dr LUDMIL FACHIKOV

Vice-Rector for Education: Prof. Dr SANCHI
NENKOVA
Vice-Rector for Research and Int.
Cooperation: Assoc. Prof. Dr MITKO GEOR-
GIEV
Chief Admin. Officer: Assoc. Prof. Dr LUDMIL
FACHIKOV
Librarian: Ing. MAIA PENCHEVA
Library of 70,000 vols
Number of teachers: 297
Number of students: 3,652

Publication: *Godishnik, now Journal of the
University of Chemical Technology and
Metallurgy* (4 a year, in English)

DEANS

Faculty of Chemical and Systems Engineer-
ing: Assoc. Prof. Dr PESHKO DJAMBOV
Faculty of Chemical Technologies: Prof. Dr
VLADIMIR BOJINOV
Faculty of Metallurgy and Material Science:
Assoc. Prof. Dr IVAN GRUEV
Department of Chemical Sciences: Assoc.
Prof. Dr MARIA MACHKOVA
Department of Humanities: Assoc. Prof. Dr
VENCISLAV GAVRILOV
Department of International Academic
Mobility and Education: Prof. Dr ROSITSA
BECHEVA
Department of Physico-Mathematical and
Technical Sciences: Assoc. Prof. Dr ALEX-
ANDER ALEXANDROV

PROFESSORS

ANGELOVA, D.
BECHEVA, R.
BOJINOV, V.
DISHOVSKI, N.
DOMBALOV, I.
GERGINOV, A.
HADJOV, K.
ILIEVA, M.
IVANOVA, J.
KUMANOVA, B.
NENKOVA, S.
PANEV, S.
PELOVSKI, J.
PENCHEV, I.
TZVETKOV, T.
VEZENKOV, L.

LESOTEHNIČESKI UNIVERSITY
(University of Forestry)

Kl. Ohridski 10, 1756 Sofia
Telephone: (2) 862-16-82
Fax: (2) 862-28-30
Internet: www.ltu.bg

Founded as an ind. institute 1953
State control
Academic year: September to June (2 terms)
Rector: Prof. NINO PETKOV NINOV
Vice-Rectors: Prof. VESELIN STAMENOV BRE-
ZINA, Dr RUMEN IGNATOV TOMOV, Dr PETER
ZHELEV STOYANOV
Registrar: (vacant)
Librarian: JULIANA JOSIFOVA
Number of teachers: 350
Number of students: 3,500

Publications: *Forest Ideas, Management and
Sustainable Development, Propagation of
Ornamental Plants, Woodworking and
Furniture Production*

DEANS

Faculty of Business Administration: Prof.
IVAN PETROV PALIGOROV
Faculty of Forestry: Dr CHRISTOPHER MILKO
MILEV
Faculty of Forestry Industry: Prof. NENO
IVANOV TRICHKOV
Faculty of Veterinary Medicine: Prof. DOR-
OTHEA HRISANOVA
Postgraduate Centre: Prof. EK. PAVLOVA

PROFESSORS

ASPARUCHOV, K., Harvesting Machinery and
Technology
DIMITROV, E., Basis of Forestry
DINKOV, B., Wood Technology
GENCHEVA, S., Ecology and Conservation,
Soil Science
GERASIMOV, SV., Zoology
GRIGOROV, P., Sawing of Timber
KAVALOV, A., Furniture Technology
KOLAROV, D., Plant Physiology
KOVACHEV, G., Veterinary Medicine
KULELIEV, J., Planting Trees and Flowers
KYUCHUKOV, G., Furniture Construction
MICHOV, I., Forest Mensuration
PAVLOV, D., Phytocenology
PAVLOVA, EK., Ecology
PUCHALEV, G., Organization and Planting in
Landscape Architecture
RAICHEV, A., Thermodynamics, Heat and
Mass Transfer
SHECHTOV, CH., Automation of Technological
Processes
SHKTILYANOVA, EL., Floriculture
TASEV, G., Machinery and Technology in
Agronomy
VAKAZELOV, I., Dendrology
VIDELOV, H., Hydrothermal Treatment of
Wood
YOROVA, K., Soil Science
YOSIFOV, N., Particle-Board Technology

MEDICINSKI UNIVERSITET PLEVEN
(Medical University Pleven)

Sveti Kliment Ohridski St 1, 5800 Pleven
Telephone: (64) 88-41-00
Fax: (64) 80-16-03
E-mail: rector@mu-pleven.bg
Internet: www.mu-pleven.bg

Founded 1974
State control
Languages of instruction: Bulgarian, English
Academic year: September to June
Rector: Prof. Dr GRIGOR GORTCHEV
Vice-Rector for Education: Assoc. Prof. Dr
PETYO BOCHEV
Vice-Rector for European Integration and
International Cooperation: Assoc. Prof. Dr
ANGELIKA VELKOVA
Vice-Rector for Quality of Education and
Accreditation: Assoc. Prof. Dr VENETA
LYUBENOVA SHOPOVA
Vice-Rector for Science and Research: Assoc.
Prof. Dr MARIA SREDKOVA
Vice-Rector for Therapeutic Activities: Assoc.
Prof. Dr IVAN LALEV
Vice-Chancellor for Student Affairs: Prof.
PETYO BOCHEV
Chief Librarian: VALENTINA ICHEVA
Library of 82,287 vols, 120 periodicals
Number of teachers: 288
Number of students: 1,661

Publication: *Journal of Biomedical and Clinical Research* (biannual)

DEANS

College of Medical Science: Assoc. Prof. Dr
PAVLINA YORDANOVA (Dir)
Department of Language and Specialized
Training: Assoc. Prof. MARGARITA ALEXAN-
DROVA (Dir)
Faculty of Health Care: Assoc. Prof. Dr
DIMITAR STOYKOV
Faculty of Medicine: Assoc. Prof. Dr DIMITAR
GOSPODINOV
Faculty of Public Health: Assoc. Prof. Dr
GENA GRANCHAROVA

MEDICINSKI UNIVERSITET PLOVDIV
(Medical University of Plovdiv)

15A Vassil Aprilov Blvd, 4002 Plovdiv
Telephone: (32) 60-22-07

Fax: (32) 60-25-34
E-mail: rector@meduniversity-plovdiv.bg
Internet: www.meduniversity-plovdiv.bg

Founded 1945 as Higher Medical Institute
Languages of instruction: Bulgarian, English
Academic year: September to May (2 terms)
Rector: Assoc. Prof. Dr GEORGI PASCALEV
Vice-Rector for Admin. and Economic Affairs:
Dipl. Eng. RADKO STEFANOV
Vice-Rector for Research and Devt: TONKA
VASSILEVA

Library of 170,000 vols
Number of teachers: 636
Number of students: 4,200

Publication: *Folia Medica* (4 a year)

DEANS

Dept for Specialized Medical Education: Dir:
Assoc. Prof. D. MILIEVA
Faculty of Dental Medicine: Assoc.Prof. ST.
VLADIMIROV
Faculty of Medicine: Prof. ILIA YOVCHEV
Faculty of Pharmacy: Assoc. Prof. LUDMIL
LUKANOV
Faculty of Public Health: Dr ROUMEN STEFA-
NOV
Medical College: Dir: Assoc. Prof. N. KRAS-
TEVA

MEDICAL UNIVERSITY 'PROF. DR.
PARASKEV STOYANOV'

'Marin Drinov' St 55, 9002 Varna
Telephone and fax (52) 67-70-20
E-mail: uni@asclep.muvar.acad.bg
Internet: www.mu-varna.bg

Founded 1961
Academic year: September to June
Rector: Prof. Dr ANELIA KLISSAROVA
Vice-Rector for Science and Research: Assoc.
Prof. ROSEN MADJOV
Vice-Rector for Student Affairs: Assoc. Prof.
NEGRIN NEGREV
Vice-Rector for Univ. Hospital Coordination
and Postgraduate Education: Assoc. Prof.
JANETA GEORGIEVA
Chief Librarian: P. A. MILEVA
Library of 200,000 vols
Number of teachers: 382 (172 full profs and
assoc. profs, 210 asst profs and lecturers)
Number of students: 2,360

Publications: *Biomedical Reviews* (1 a year),
Bulgarska koloproktologia (2 a year),
Scripta Scientifica Medica (1 a year),
Syrtse i Byal Drob (Heart and Lung, in
Bulgarian and English, 4 a year)

DEANS

Faculty of Dental Medicine: Assoc. Prof. Dr
VASIL GOSPODINOV SVISTAROV
Faculty of Medicine: Assoc. Prof. Dr MARINKA
TASHKOVA PENEVA
Faculty of Pharmacy: Assoc. Prof. Dr DIMITAR
DIMITROV ATANASOV
Faculty of Public Health: Assoc. Prof. Dr
STOYANKA CVETKOVA POPOVA
Medical College of Dobrich: Assoc. Prof. Dr
N. SPASOVA (Head)
Medical College of Shumen: Assoc. Prof. Dr
N. STOYNOV (Head)
Medical College of Varna: Assoc. Prof. Dr
HRISTO GANCHEV (Dir)

MEDICINSKI UNIVERSITET SOFIA
(Medical University Sofia)

Acad. Ivan Geshov 15, 1431 Sofia
Telephone: (2) 952-37-91
Fax: (2) 953-28-16
E-mail: glavsec@mu-sofia.bg
Internet: mu-sofia.bg

Founded 1972 as the Acad. of Medicine, by
merger of fmr Higher Medical Institute

and the medical research institutes; present name and status 1995
State control
Academic year: September to June

Rector: Prof. VANYO MITEV
Pro-Rector for International Integration: Prof. ANDON FILCHEV
Pro-Rector for Scientific Affairs: Prof. GUENKA PETROVA
Pro-Rector for Students Education: Prof. SASHKA POPOVA
Pro-Rector for Post-graduate Education: Assoc. Prof. VASSIL DIMITROV
Sec.: Prof. Dr ELI GEORGIEVA NIKOLOVA
Gen. Sec.: Assoc. Prof, ALEKSEI ALEKSEEV
Chief Admin. Officer: KHRISTO ANACHKOV
Librarian: Dr DABCHEV

Library of 50,000
Number of teachers: 1,408
Number of students: 5,308
Publication: *Acta Medica Bulgarica* (2 a year)

DEANS

Dental Medical Faculty: Prof. Dr ANDON FILCHEV
Faculty of Medicine: Prof. MARIN MARINOV
Faculty of Nursing: Assoc. Prof. K. YURUKOVA
Faculty of Pharmacy: Assoc. Prof. NIKOLAY LAMBOV
Faculty of Public Health: Prof. Dr SASHKA POPOVA
Faculty of Stomatology: Prof. B. INDZHOV
Free Faculty: Assoc. Prof. N. VRABCHEV

MINNO-GEOLOŽKI UNIVERSITET 'SV. IVAN RILSKI'
(University of Mining and Geology 'St Ivan Rilski')

Studentski grad Hristo Botev St, Sofia
Telephone: (2) 806-03-00
Fax: (2) 962-49-40
E-mail: maillist-mgu@mgu.bg
Internet: www.mgu.bg
Founded 1953
Academic year: October to June (2 terms)

Rector: Prof. Dr IVAN VLADOV MILEV
Vice-Rector for Academic Performance and Quality of Training: NIKOLAI IVANOV DZHERAHOV
Vice-Rector for Research and Int. activities: VENTSISLAV IVANOV SIMEONOV
Registrar: S. IVANOV
Librarian: K. DRAGANOVA

Library of 90,000 vols, 61,000 books, 29,000 periodicals
Number of teachers: 230
Number of students: 2,500
Publication: *Godishnik* (1 a year)

DEANS

Faculty of Geological Prospecting: Dr RADI GEORGIEV RADICHEV
Faculty of Mining Electromechanics: Dr KANCHO IVANOV YORDANOV
Faculty of Mining Technology: Prof. LUBEN IVANOV TOTEV

DIRECTORS

Department of Humanities: MONIKA STOYANOVA HRISTOVA

PROFESSORS

Faculty of Geological Prospecting (tel. (2) 962-72-70 ext. 207; e-mail radirad@mgu.bg):
  GROUDEV, S., Environmental Science
  STAVREV, P., Applied Geophysics
Faculty of Mining Electromechanics (tel. 262-72-28):
  DONCHEV, S., Theory of Mechanics
  FETVADJIEV, G., Mechanization of Mines

Faculty of Mining Technology (tel. (2) 962-72-20 ext. 206; e-mail ltotev@abv.bg):
  KOLEV, K., Rock Mechanics
  KUZEV, L., Mineral Processing
  METODIEV, M., Mineral Processing
  MICHAYLOV, M., Mine Ventilation
  VISOKOV, G., Chemistry
Department of Humanities (tel. (2) 962-72-20 ext. 324):
  STAMATOV, A., Philosophy

NATIONAL MILITARY UNIVERSITY 'VASIL LEVSKI'

Blvd 76, 5006 Veliko Tărnovo
Telephone: (62) 61-88-22
Fax: (62) 61-88-99
E-mail: nvu@nvu.bg
Internet: www.nvu.bg
Founded 1878, present name and status 2002
Library of 149,111 vols.

NOV BULGARKI UNIVERSITET
(New Bulgarian University)

Ovcha Kupel 21, Montevideo St, 1618 Sofia
Telephone and fax (2)8110247
Fax: (2) 8110260
E-mail: info@nbu.bg
Internet: www.nbu.bg
Founded 1990
Private control
Languages of instruction: Bulgarian, French, English

Rector: Assoc. Prof. Dr LJUDMIL GEORGIEV
Vice-Rector for Educational Activities and Accreditation: Assoc. Prof. PLAMEN BOCHKOV
Vice-Rector for Int. Affairs and Public Relations: Prof. TOLYA STOITSOVA
Vice-Rector for Quality, Assessment and Attestation: Assoc. Prof. MORIS GRINBERG
Vice-Rector for Research Activities: Assoc. Prof. Dr LJUDMIL GEORGIEV

Library of 162,300 vols, 1,800 reference works, 480 periodicals
Number of teachers: 500
Number of students: 12,000
Publications: *Kant, Praven Pregled, Sledva*

DEANS

Graduate School: Prof. Dr MARIN MARINOV
School of Basic Education: Assoc. Prof. NIKOLAY ARABADZIYSKI
Undergraduate School: Prof. ATANAS BLIZNAKOV

PLOVDIVSKI UNIVERSITET 'PAISII HILENDARSKI'
(Plovdiv University 'Paisii Hilendarski')

24 Tsar Asen St, 4000 Plovdiv
Telephone: (32) 26-13-63
Fax: (32) 63-50-49
E-mail: ir@uni-plovdiv.bg
Internet: www.uni-plovdiv.bg
Founded 1961, fmrly 'Paisii Hilendarski' Higher Pedagogical Institute, Plovdiv; present status and name 1972
Academic year: October to June

Rector: Prof. IVAN KUTSAROV
Vice-Rector for Univ. Management: MARIYANA MIHAYLOVA
Registrar: D. BOIKOV
Dir of Library: MILKA YANKOVA

Library of 280,000 vols
Number of teachers: 561 (34 full profs, 167 assoc. profs and 360 asst profs
Number of students: 12,500 (7,500 full-time and 5,000 part-time students)

Publications: *Journal Plovdiv University, Nauchni Trudove*

DEANS

Faculty of Biology: Prof. AT. DONEV
Faculty of Chemistry: Prof. AT. VENKOV
Faculty of Economics: Assoc. Prof. M. MIHAILOVA
Faculty of Law: Prof. G. PETROVA
Faculty of Mathematics and Computer Science: Prof. D. MEKEROV
Faculty of Pedagogics: Assoc. Prof. P. RADEV
Faculty of Philology: Prof. Iv. KUTSAROV
Faculty of Physics: Prof. G. MEKISHEV

PROFESSORS

ALEKSANDROV, A.
ANDREEV, G.
ANGELOV, A.
ANGELOV, P., Zoology
ATANASOV, A., Theoretical Physics
BACHVAROV, G.
BALABANOV, N., Nuclear Physics
DIMITROV, R., Technology of Inorganic Chemistry
DRUMEVA, E.
FUTEKOV, L., Analytical Chemistry
GOLEMINOV, C.
GOLEVA, P.
GRUEV, B.
IVANOV, A., Microbiology
IVANOV, S., Technology of Organic Chemistry
JENKINS, D.
KARTALOV, A.
KATSARKOVA, V.
KIRYAKOV, I.
KOLAROV, N.
KUTSAROV, I., Morphology of Modern Bulgarian Language
KUZMANOVA, A.
LAZAROV, K.
MIHAYLOVA, M.
MIHOVSKI, S.
MINKOV, I., Plant Physiology
MITEV, D., Zoology
MOLLOV, T., Algebra
MRACHKOV, V.
NIKOLOVA, M.
PAPANOV, G.
PETROV, P.
POPCHEV, I.
POPOV, P.
SAPAREV, O.
SAPKOVA, I.
SAVOV, E.
TSEKOV, G.
VELCHEV, N., Physics of Dielectrics
VENKOV, A.
YORDANOV, Y

RUSENSKI UNIVERSITET 'ANGEL KANCHEV'
('Angel Kanchev' University of Ruse)

Studentska St 8, 7017 Ruse
Telephone: (82) 88-84-65
Fax: (82) 84-57-08
E-mail: secretary@uni-ruse.bg
Internet: www.ru.acad.bg
Founded 1954 as Institute of Mechanization and Electrification of Agriculture; became Angel Kanchev Higher Technical School 1982 and Angel Kanchev Technical Univ. of Ruse 1990; present name 1995
State control
Academic year: September to July

Rector: Assoc. Prof. Dr HRISTO BELOEV
Vice-Rector for Admission and Degree Programmes: Assoc. Prof. Dr BORISLAV ANGELOV
Vice-Pres. for European Integration and Int. Relations: Assoc. Prof. Dr NIKOLAY MIHAYLOV
Vice-Rector for Scientific and Staff Devt: Assoc. Prof. Dr ANGEL SMRIKAROV

Sec.-Gen.: Assoc. Prof. Dr IORDAN NIKOLOV
Dir of the Int. Relations Dept: Assoc. Prof. Dr
  KIRIL BARZEV
Dir of Library: Mag. Prof. EMILIA KIRILOVA
  LEHOVA
Library of 395,000 vols, incl. 323,000 books,
  41,000 periodicals
Number of teachers: 600
Number of students: 7,700
Publication: *Nauchni Trudove*

DEANS

Faculty of Agricultural Mechanisation:
  Assoc. Prof. PLAMEN KANGALOV
Faculty of Automative and Transport Engin-
  eering: Assoc. Prof. ROSSEN PETROV IVANOV
Faculty of Business and Management: Prof.
  EMIL GEORGIEV TRIFONOV
Faculty of Electrical Engineering, Electron-
  ics and Automation: Assoc. Prof. MIHAIL
  PETKOV ILIEV
Faculty of Law: Assoc. Prof. Dr EMIL MINGOV
Faculty of Mechanical and Manufacturing
  Engineering: Assoc. Prof. VALENTIN GAGOV
Faculty of Pedagogy: Prof. MARGARITA STEFA-
  NOVA TEODOSEVA
Faculty of Pedagogy (Silistra): Assoc. Prof.
  Dr ILIANA GORANOVA
Faculty of Postgraduate Studies and Further
  Education: Assoc. Prof. Dr IULIAN MLADE-
  NOV

DIRECTORS

Branch of the Univ. (Razgrad): Assoc. Prof.
  MILUVKA STANCHEVA
Branch of the Univ. (Silistra): Assoc. Prof.
  DIMO DIMOV

PROFESSORS

Faculty of Agricultural Mechanization:
  ENCHEV, K.
  GUZHGULOV, G.
  MITKOV, A.
  ORLOEV, N.
  PARASHKEVOV, I.
Faculty of Automotive and Transport Engin-
  eering:
  ANDREEV, D.
  ILIEV, L.
  LIUBENOV, SL.
  NENOV, P.
  SIMEONOV, D.
Faculty of Business and Management:
  PAPAZOV, KR.
Faculty of Electrical Engineering, Electron-
  ics and Automatics:
  ANDONOV, K.
Faculty of Law:
  MICHEV, N.
Faculty of Mechanical and Manufacturing
  Engineering:
  IVANOV, V.
  KANEV, M.
  POPOV, G.
  TOMOV, B.
  VELCHEV, S.
  VITLIEMOV, VL.
Faculty of Pedagogy:
  KOZHUKHAROV, K.
Faculty of Pedagogy (Silistra) (Albena 1,
POB 103, 7500 Silistra):
  NEDEV, L.

SHUMENSKI UNIVERSITET 'EPISKOP KONSTANTIN PRESLAVSKI' (Bishop Konstantin Preslavski University of Shumen)

Universitetska St 115, 9712 Shumen
Telephone: (54) 83-04-95
Fax: (54) 83-03-71

E-mail: rector@shu-bg.net
Internet: www.shu-bg.net
Founded 1971
Academic year: September to June
Chair.: Dr KINA VACHKOVA
Deputy Chair.: Dr SONIA BABEV
Rector: Prof. Dr Hab. MARGARITA GEORGIEVA
Vice-Rector of Academic Affairs: Assoc. Prof.
  DIMCHO STANKOV
Vice-Rector of Accreditation: Assoc. Prof.
  BOGDANA GEORGIEVA
Vice-Rector of Int. Relations: Assoc. Prof.
  RUMYANA TODOROVA
Vice-Rector of Research and Projects: Assoc.
  Prof. DRAGOMIR MARCHEV
Library Dir: MARIANA PETEVA
Library of 362,568 vols
Number of teachers: 448
Number of students: 7,389
Publication: *Godishnik* (1 a year)

DEANS

Faculty of Education: Prof. Dr Hab. GEORGI
  KOLEV
Faculty of Humanities: Prof. Dr Hab. IVELINA
  SAVOVA
Faculty of Mathematics and Computer Sci-
  ence: Assoc. Prof. RUSANKA D. PETROVA
Faculty of Natural Sciences: Assoc. Prof.
  DOBROMIR ENCHEV
Faculty of Technical Sciences: Assoc. Prof.
  IVAN CONEV

SOFIISKI UNIVERSITET 'SVETI KLIMENT OHRIDSKY' (Sofia University 'St Kliment Ohridsky')

Tsar Osvoboditel Blvd 15, 1504 Sofia
Telephone: (2) 930-82-00
Fax: (2) 946-02-55
Internet: www.uni-sofia.bg
Founded 1888 as High School, granted char-
  ter 1909
State control
Academic year: September to June (2 terms)
Rector: Prof. IVAN ILCHEV
Asst Rector: KALIN STANUKOV
Vice-Rector for Economic and Investment
  Affairs: Prof. IVAN KOLEV PETKOV
Vice-Rector for Information Affairs and
  Admin.: Assoc. Prof. ZHELYU DECHEV VLA-
  DIMIROV
Vice-Rector for Scientific and Int. Projects:
  Prof. NEDYU IVANOV POPIVANOV
Vice-Rector for Student Affairs: Assoc. Prof.
  MARIYA DELOVA SHISHINYOVA
Vice-Rector for Student Affairs: NEDYALKA
  IGNATOVA VIDEVA
Dir for Int. Relations: R. GRIGOROV
Sec.: R. STANIMIROVA
Dir of Library: Prof. ZH. STOYANOV
Library: see under Libraries
Number of teachers: 1,608
Number of students: 25,454
Publication: *Godishnik*

DEANS

Faculty of Biology: Dr BOZHIDAR GALUTSOV
Faculty of Chemical Engineering: Prof. TONY
  GEORGIEV SPASOV
Faculty of Classical and Modern Philology:
  Prof. PETYA YANEVA
Faculty of Economics: Prof. GEORGI CHOBA-
  NOV
Faculty of Education: Prof. IVAYLO TEPAVI-
  CHAROV
Faculty of Geology and Geography: Assoc.
  Prof. PETAR SLAVEIKOV
Faculty of History: Prof. PLAMEN DIMITROV
  MITEV
Faculty of Journalism: Dr TOTKA MONOVA
Faculty of Law: Dr TENCHO KOLEV DUNDOV

Faculty of Mathematics and Information
  Science: Prof. IVAN SOSKOV
Faculty of Primary and Pre-School Educa-
  tion: Prof. BOZHIDAR ANGELOV
Faculty of Philosophy: Prof. ALEXANDER DIM-
  CHEV
Faculty of Physics: Prof. DIMITAR MARVAKOV
Faculty of Slavonic Philology: Prof. PANAYOT
  KARAGYOZOVA
Faculty of Theology: Dr EMIL TRAICHEV
Medical Faculty: Dr LYUBOMIR SPASSOV

PROFESSORS

Faculty of Biology:
  BOZHILOVA, E., Botany
  IVANOVA, I., Plant Physiology
  KIMENOV, G., Plant Physiology
  KOLEV, D., Biochemistry
  MARGARITOV, N., Hydrobiology and
    Ichthyology
  MINKOV, I., Human and Animal Physiology
  TEMNISKOVA, D., Botany
  VLAHOV, S., General and Industrial Micro-
    biology
Faculty of Chemistry:
  ALEKSANDROV, S., Analytical Chemistry
  BONCHEV, P., Analytical Chemistry
  DOBREV, A., Organic Chemical Technology
  FAKIROV, S., Organic Chemical Technology
  GALABOV, B., Organic Chemical Technology
  IVANOV, I., Physical Chemistry
  KALCHEVA, B., Organic Chemical Technol-
    ogy
  KOSTADINOV, K., Inorganic Chemical Tech-
    nology
  LAZAROV, D., Inorganic Chemical Technol-
    ogy
  MARKOV, P., Organic Chemistry
  PANAYOTOV, I., Physical Chemistry
  PETROV, B., Organic Chemical Technology
  PETSEV, N., Organic Chemistry
  PLATIKANOV, D., Physical Chemistry
  RADOEV, B., Physical Chemistry
  TOSHEV, B., Physical Chemistry
Faculty of Classical and Modern Philology:
  ALEKSIEVA, B., English Philology
  BOEV, E., Eastern Languages
  BOGDANOV, B., Classical Philology
  BOYADZHIEV, D., Classical Philology
  DAKOVA, N., German Philology
  DELIIVANOVA, B., German Philology
  GALABOV, P., Romance Philology
  KANCHEV, I., Ibero-Romance Philology
  PARASHKEVOV, B., German Philology
  PETKOV, P., German Philology
  SHURBANOV, A., English Philology
Faculty of Economics:
  BEHAR, H., History of Economics
  SERGIENKO, R., General Economic Theory
Faculty of Geology and Geography:
  BACHVAROV, M., Geography of Tourism
  ESKENAZI, G., Mineralogy, Petrology and
    Economic Geology
  KANCHEV, D., Economic Geography
  MANDOV, G., Geology and Palaeontology
  PETROV, P., Geography
Faculty of History:
  BAKALOV, G., Byzantine History
  DIMITROV, I., Bulgarian History
  DRAGANOV, D., Modern History
  GEORGIEV, V., Bulgarian History
  GEORGIEVA, I., Ethnography
  GETOV, L., Archaeology
  GYUZELEV, V., Bulgarian History
  ILIEV, I., Modern History
  LALKOV, M., Modern History
  NAUMOV, G., Bulgarian History
  NIKOLOV, J., Medieval History
  OGNYANOV, L., Bulgarian History
  PANTEV, A., Modern History
  POPOV, D., Ancient History and Thracian
    Studies
  SEMKOV, M., Modern History

TACHEVA, M., Ancient History and Thracian Studies
TRIFONOV, S., Modern History

Faculty of Journalism:
DIMITROV, V., Radio Journalism
KARAIVANOVA, P., Journalism
PANAYOTOV, F., History of Journalism
SEMOV, M., Theory of Journalism

Faculty of Law:
BOYCHEV, G., Theory of State Law
GERDZHIKOV, O., Civil Law
MIHAYLOV, D., Criminal Law
PAVLOVA, M., Civil Law
PETKANOV, G., Finance Law
POPOV, P., Civil Law
SREDKOVA, K., Civil Law
STOYCHEV, S., Constitutional and Administrative Law
TSANKOVA, TS., Civil Law
ZAHAROV, V., Theory of State Law
ZIDAROVA, I., International Law

Faculty of Mathematics and Information Science:
BOYANOV, B., Numerical Analysis and Algorithms
DENCHEV, R., Complex Analysis and Topology
GENCHEV, T., Differential Equations
HADZHIIVANOV, N., Education in Mathematics and Computer Sciences
HOROSOV, E., Differential Equations
HRISTOV, E., Complex Analysis and Topology
LILOV, L., Analytical Mechanics
MARKOV, K., Continuous Media Mechanics
POPIVANOV, N., Differential Equations
SKORDEV, D., Mathematical Logic and Applications
STANILOV, G., Education in Mathematics and Computer Sciences
TROYANSKI, S., Mathematical Analysis
ZAPRYANOV, Z., Continuous Media Mechanics

Faculty of Pedagogy:
ANDREEV, M., Didactics
BOYCHEVA, V., History of Pedagogy
DIMITROV, L., Theory of Education
PAVLOV, D., Didactics
STOYANOV, P., History of Pedagogy
VASILEV, D., Didactics

Faculty of Philosophy:
ALEKSANDROV, P., History of Psychology
ANDONOV, A., Philosophy
BOYADZHIEV, T., History of Philosophy
DESEV, L., Social Psychology
DINEV, V., Philosophical Anthropology
FOL, A., History of Culture
GENCHEV, N., History of Culture
GERGOVA, A., Book Science
GINEV, V., Theory of Culture
GRADEV, D., Social Psychology
KARASIMEONOV, G., Political Science
KRUMOV, K., Social Psychology
MIHAILOVSKA, E., Sociology
MITEV, P. E., Political Science
NESHEV, K., Ethics
PETKOV, K., Sociology
RADEV, R., History of Philosophy
SIVILOV, L., Epistemology
STEFANOV, I. I., Sociology
VASILEV, N., Philosophy
VENEDIKOV, Y., Theory of Culture
ZNEPOLOSKY, I., Theory of Culture

Faculty of Physics:
APOSTOLOV, A., Solid State Physics
DENCHOV, G., Geophysics
DINEV, S., Quantum Electronics
GEORGIEV, G., Quantum Electronics
ILIEV, M., Condensed Matter Physics
IVANOV, G., Astronomy
KAMENOV, P., Nuclear Physics and Energetics
KUTSAROV, S., Electronics

LALOV, I., Condensed Matter Physics
LUKYANOV, A., Nuclear Physics and Energetics
MARTINOV, N., Condensed Matter Physics
MATEEV, M., Theoretical Physics
NIKOLOV, N., Plasma Physics
PANCHEV, S., Meteorology and Geophysics
POPOV, A., Semiconductor Physics
SALTIEV, S., Quantum Electronics
SLAVOV, B., Quantum and Nuclear Physics
ZAHARIEV, Z., Theoretical Physics
ZHELYASKOV, I., Plasma Physics

Faculty of Primary and Pre-School Education:
BALTADZHIEVA, A., Special Education
BIZHKOV, G., Primary Education
DOBREV, Z., Special Education
KOLEV, J., Primary Education
PETROV, P., Primary Education
RADEVA, B., Anatomy
TSVETKOV, D., Primary Education
ZDRAVKOVA, S., Primary Education

Faculty of Slavonic Philology:
BIOLCHEV, B., Slavonic Literature
BOEVA, L., Russian Literature
BOYADZHIEV, T., Bulgarian Language
BOYADZHIEV, Z., Linguistics
BRESINSKI, S., Bulgarian Language
BUNDZHALOVA, B., Russian Language
BUYUKLIEV, I., Slavonic Linguistics
CHERVENKOVA, I., Russian Language
CHOLAKOV, Z., Bulgarian Literature
DIMCHEV, K., Teaching Methods of Bulgarian Language and Literature
DOBREV, I., Studies on Cyril and Methodius
GEORGIEV, N., Theory of Literature
HADZHIKOSEV, S., Theory of Literature
MINCHEVA, A., Studies on Cyril and Methodius
NITSOLOVA, R., Bulgarian Language
PASHOV, P., Bulgarian Language
PAVLOV, I., Slavonic Literature
PAVLOVA, R., Russian Language
POPIVANOV, L., Theory of Literature
POPOVA, V., Bulgarian Language
RADEVA, V., Bulgarian Language
TROEV, P., Russian Literature
VASILEV, M., Bulgarian Literature
VIDENOV, M., Bulgarian Language
YANEV, S., Bulgarian Literature
YOTOV, T., Russian Language

Faculty of Theology:
DENEV, I., Practical Theology
HUBANCHEV, A., Christian Philosophy
KIROV, T., Moral Theology
KOEV, T., Dogmatics
MADZHUROV, N., Christian Philosophy
POPTODOROV, R., Canon Law
SHIVAROV, N., Old Testament Studies
SLAVOV, S., Old Testament Studies
STOYANOV, H., Church History

TEHNIČESKI UNIVERSITET GABROVO
(Technical University of Gabrovo)

4 Hadzhi Dimităr, 5300 Gabrovo

Telephone: (66) 82-77-77
Fax: (66) 80-11-55
E-mail: info@tugab.bg
Internet: www.tugab.bg

Founded 1964 as Higher Mechanical and Electrical Engineering Institute of Gabrovo; present name 1990
Academic year: September to June

Rector: Assoc. Prof. DESHKA MARKOVA
Vice-Rector for Research: Assoc. Prof. RAYCHO ILARIONOV
Vice-Rector for Staff Qualification and Int. Cooperation: Assoc. Prof. LYUBOMIR LAZOV
Vice-Rector for Studies: Assoc. Prof. HRISTO HRISTOV
Registrar: NIKOLAY MIRAZCHIEV

Number of teachers: 240
Number of students: 7,219
Publication: *Journal* (2 a year)

DEANS

Faculty of Economics: Assoc. Prof. Dr ANYUTA GEORGIEVA NIKOLOVA
Faculty of Electrical Engineering and Electronics: Assoc. Prof. Dr ANATOLIY TRIFONOV ALEXANDROV
Faculty of Mechanical and Precision Engineering: Assoc. Prof. Dr GEORGI EVSTATIEV RASHEV

TEHNIČESKI UNIVERSITET SOFIA
(Technical University of Sofia)

Blvd Kliment Ohridski 8, 1000 Sofia

Telephone: (2) 965-21-11
Fax: (2) 868-32-15
E-mail: office_tu@tu-sofia.bg
Internet: www.tu-sofia.bg

Founded 1945, present name 1995
Academic year: September to June

Rector: Prof. Prof. KAMEN VESELINOV
Vice-Rector for Academic Affairs: Prof. GEORGI MIHOV SLAVCHEV
Vice-Rector for Academic Staff and Coordination: Dr LYUBOMIR IVANOV MECHKAROV
Vice-Rector for Scientific and Applied activities: Prof. NIKOLA GEORGIEV KALOYANOV
Chief Sec.: VALENTIN DIMITROV IVANOV
Librarian: A. DIMITROVA
Library of 153,517 vols
Number of teachers: 1,309
Number of students: 14,190
Publication: *Nov Tehničeski Avangard* (12 a year)

DEANS

Department of Applied Physics: Prof. UZUNOV IVAN MITEV
Department of Physical Education and Sports: Assoc. Prof. IVAN YORDANOV BOZOV
Department of Telecommunications: Assoc. Prof. VLADIMIR KOSTADINOV PULKOVO
Department of Transportation: Assoc. Prof. TEODOSI PETROV EVTIMOV
DCHEOPL: ANTONIA SLAVEYKOV VELKOVA
Faculty of Applied Mathematics and Information Science: Prof. Eng. KETI GEORGIEVA PEEVA
Faculty of Automation: Assoc. Prof. DIMITAR PETKOV DIMITROV
Faculty of Computer Systems and Control: Assoc. Prof. OGNYAN NAKOV NAKOV
Faculty of Electrical Engineering: Assoc. Prof. VASIL SPASOV GOSPODINOV
Faculty of Electronics and Electronic Technologies: Prof. Dr Eng. MARIN HRISTOV HRISTOV
Faculty of German Engineering Education and Industrial Management: Prof. STEFANOV STEFAN ANGELOV
Faculty of Machine Technology: Assoc. Prof. LUBOMIR DIMITROV VANKOV
Faculty of Management: Prof. G. TSVETKOV
Faculty of Mechanical Engineering Technology: Assoc. Prof. Dr YORDAN GENOV GENOV
Faculty of Power Engineering and Power Machines: Assoc. Prof. YORDANOV VASIL YANEV
English-Language Faculty of Engineering: Assoc. Prof. T. TASHEV
French-Language Faculty of Electrical Engineering: Assoc. Prof. IVAN MOMCHILOV MOMCHEV

TEHNIČESKI UNIVERSITET VARNA
(Technical University of Varna)

Studenska 1, POB 10, 9010 Varna

Telephone: (52) 30-24-44

Fax: (52) 30-27-71
E-mail: rectorat@ms3.tu-varna.acad.bg
Internet: www.tu-varna.bg

Founded 1962 as Institute of Mechanics and Electrics, present name in 1990
Academic year: September to July

Rector: Assoc. Prof. OBED AZARIAH
Vice-Rector for Academic Affairs: Assoc. Prof. STOYANOV DISHKO
Vice-Rector for Accreditation and Devt: Prof. Prof. DIMITAR SVETLOZAROV
Vice-Rector for Int. Cooperation and Integration: Assoc Prof SAVA VASILEV
Vice-Rector for Science and Applied Scientific Research: Dr IVAN VASILEV
Registrar: DIMITAR DIMITRAKIEV
Librarian: D. DIMITROVA
Library of 231,800 vols
Number of teachers: 450
Number of students: 6,500
Publications: *Acta Universitatis Pontica Euxinus* (2 a year), *Annual Proceedings*

DEANS

Department of Foreign Languages: Assoc. Prof. Dr MILENA ALEKSANDROVA PALIY
Faculty of Computing and Automation: Assoc. Prof. Dr PETER IANTONOV
Faculty of Electrical Engineering: Assoc. Prof. Dr MARIA IVANOVA MARINOVA
Faculty of Electronics: Assoc. Prof. Dr JORDAN KOLEV
Faculty of Mechanical Engineering and Technology: Assoc. Prof. Dr ANGEL DIMITROV
Faculty of Marine Sciences and Ecology: Assoc. Prof. Dr ATANAS STEFANOV KRUSHEV
Faculty of Shipbuilding: Assoc. Prof. Dr NIKOLA IVANOV PETROV

PROFESSORS

ALEXANDROV, Z., Theory of Machinery
DIMITROV, D., Electrical Apparatus
GEORGIEV, V., Theoretical Electrical Engineering
GRADINAROV, P., Theoretical Mechanics
IVANOV, I., Law
JOSIFOV, R., Marine Engineering
KANDEVA, E., Law
KOLEV, P., Shipbuilding
KOTSEVA, E., Law
MILANOV, ZH., Law
MILKOV, V., Engineering Mechanics
MINCHEV, N., Engineering Mechanics
MUTAFCHIEV, S., Government
NEDEV, A., Heat Technology
PILEV, D., Transport Machinery and Technology
RUSEV, I., Biology
RUSEV, R, Materials Science
SERAFIMOV, M., Internal Combustion Engine
SHISHKOV, A., Law
SOTIROV, L., Computer Engineering
STAVREV, D., Physical Metallurgy and Metals Engineering
STOYANOV, V., Internal Combustion Engines
VLADIMIROV, R., Law
ZAHAROV, V., Law

TRAKIJSKI UNIVERSITET
(Trakia University)

Students' campus, 6000 Stara Zagora
Telephone: (42) 67-02-04
Fax: (42) 67-20-09
E-mail: rector@uni-sz.bg
Internet: www.uni-sz.bg

Founded 1995, following merger of Higher Institute of Animal Sciences and Veterinary Medicine and Higher Institute of Medicine
State control
Languages of instruction: Bulgarian, English
Academic year: September to July

Rector: Prof. Dr IVAN STANKOV
Asst Rector: Assoc. Prof. Dr DOBRI YARKOV
Vice-Rector for Admin., Economical and Information Activities: Assoc. Prof. Dr IVAN VASHIN
Vice-Rector for Scientific Research and Int. Activities: Prof. Dr VESELINA GADJEVA
Vice-Rector for Student Affairs: Assoc. Prof. Dr KINA SIVKOVA
Chief Sec.: Assoc. Prof. Dr TSONKA KASNAKOVA
Librarian: J. DAKOVSKA
Library of 360,000 vols, monographs, reference books, books and scientific periodicals
Number of teachers: 646
Number of students: 4,000
Publications: *Bulgarian Journal of Veterinary Medicine* (4 a year), *Pro Otology* (4 a year), *Trakia Journal of Sciences* (biomedical sciences and social sciences series, 4 a year)

DEANS

Bulgarian-German Farmers' College: Assoc. Prof. Dr A. ANTONOV (Dir)
Department of Information and In-service Teacher Training: Assoc. Prof. Dr GALYA KOZHUHAORVA
Faculty of Agriculture: Prof. RADOSLAV SLAVOV
Faculty of Medicine: Prof. Dr MAYA VLADOVA GULUBOVA
Faculty of Veterinary Medicine: Prof. Dr DINKO DINEV
Medical College, Haskovo: Dr D. KOSTOV (Dir)
Medical College, Sliven: K. HALACHEVA (Dir)
Medical College, Stara Zagora: Dr K. KOSTOV (Dir)
Technical College, Yambol: Assoc. Prof. KR. GEORGIEVA (Dir)

UNIVERSITET PO ARHITEKTURA, STROITELSTVO I GEODEZIA
(University of Architecture, Civil Engineering and Geodesy)

H. Smirnenski 1, 1046 Sofia
Telephone: (2) 963-52-45
Fax: (2) 865-68-63
E-mail: aceint@uacg.bg
Internet: www.uacg.bg

Founded 1942 as Higher Institute of Architecture and Civil Engineering, present name 1990
State control
Languages of instruction: Bulgarian, English, German
Academic year: September to June

Rector: Assoc. Prof. Dr DOBRIN DENEV DENEV
Vice-Rector for Academic Affairs: Assoc. Prof. Dr KRASIMIR VELKOV PETROV
Vice-Rector for Int. Relations and Postgraduate Qualification: Assoc. Prof. Dr BOYAN MILCHEV GEORGIEV (acting)
Vice-Rector for Management and Devt of Material and Technical Equipment: Assoc. Prof. Dr M. RILSKI
Vice-Rector for Research and Design Affairs: Assoc. Prof. Dr BOGOMIL VESELINOV PETROV
Vice-Rector for Social and Living Affairs: Assoc. Prof. Dr PETAR TODOROV PENEV
Asst Rector: Eng. DIMITAR NIKOLAEV VITANOV
Registrar: S. VASILEVA
Librarian: P. RAFAILOVA
Library of 450,000 vols
Number of teachers: 531 (372 full-time, 159 part-time)
Number of students: 5,300
Publication: *Annals* (1 a year)

DEANS

Department of Applied Linguistics and Physical Culture: BORISLAV NIKOLOV KOLEV

Faculty of Architecture: Assoc. Prof. Dr NEDYALKO IVANOV BONCHEV
Faculty of Geodesy: Assoc. Prof. Dr SLAVEIKO GOSPODINOV
Faculty of Hydrotechnology: Assoc. Prof. Dr STEFAN PARVANOV MODEV
Faculty of Structural Engineering: Prof. TZVETI DAKOV DAKOVSKI
Faculty of Transportation Engineering: Assoc. Prof. Dr STOYO PETKOV TODOROV

PROFESSORS

Faculty of Architecture (tel. (2) 865-31-48; fax (2) 865-68-63; e-mail far@uacg.bg):
DIMITROV, S., Urban Planning
HARALAMPIEV, H., Drawing and Modelling
KRASTEV, T., History of Architecture
TROEVA, D., Urban Planning

Faculty of Geodesy (tel. (2) 866-22-01; fax (2) 866-22-01; e-mail fgs@uacg.bg):
VALEV, G., Geodesy

Faculty of Hydrotechnology (tel. (2) 865-66-48; fax (2) 865-68-63; e-mail fhe@uacg.bg):
ARSOV, R., Water Supply and Sewerage
DIMITROV, G., Water Supply and Sewerage
KALINKOV, P., Water Supply and Sewerage
MARADJIEVA, M., Hydraulics and Hydrology
MLADENOV, K., Theoretical Mechanics

Faculty of Structural Engineering (tel. (2) 865-66-74; fax (2) 865-66-74; e-mail dean_fce@uacg.bg):
BARAKOV, T., Reinforced Concrete Structures
BAYCHEV, I., Building Mechanics
DAKOV, D., Steel, Timber and Plastic Structures
DRAGANOV, N., Steel, Timber and Plastic Structures
GOSPODINOV, G., Building Mechanics
JANCHULEV, A., Organization and Economics of Construction
KIROV, N., Building Technology and Mechanization
NAZARSKI, D., Building Materials and Insulation
STAJKOV, P., Steel, Timber and Plastic Structures

Faculty of Transportation Engineering (tel. (2) 865-50-79; fax (2) 865-68-63; e-mail fte@uacg.bg):
DOULEVSKI, E., Bridges, Tunnels, Harbours
GICHEV, T., Mathematics
KONSTANTINOV, M., Mathematics
TRIFONOV, I., Road Engineering

UNIVERSITET PO HRANITELNI TECHNOLOGII
(University of Food Technology)

Maritsa Blvd 26, 4000 Plovdiv
Telephone: (32) 64-30-05
Fax: (32) 64-41-02
E-mail: uft@uft-plovdiv.bg
Internet: www.uft-plovdiv.bg

Founded 1953 as Higher Institute of Food and Flavour Industries, present name 2003
State control
Academic year: September to July

Rector: Prof. Dr Eng. GEORGE IVANOV VALTCHEV
Vice-Chancellor for Student Affairs and Quality of Training: Prof. Dr GEORGE TODOROV SOMOV
Deputy Rector for Science Activity and Staff Potential: Prof. Prof. KOSTADIN VASILEV VASILEV
Deputy Rector for Int. Cooperation and Public Relations: Prof. Prof. ZHELYAZKO ILIEV SIMOV
Registrar: VOLODYA KAMENOV
Head of Accounts: PENKA PETROVA

Librarian: IVANKA KUNEVA
Library of 150,000 vols
Number of teachers: 222
Number of students: 2,546

Publications: *Scientific Journals in Food Technology* (irregular), *Scientific Works of UFT* (1 a year)

DEANS

Economic Faculty: Assoc. Prof. Dr JORDANKA ALEXIEVA
Technical Faculty: Prof. Dr Eng. MILCHO ANGELOV
Technological Faculty: Prof. Dr Eng. ALBENA STOYANOVA

PROFESSORS

Economic Faculty:
  KONAREV, A., Organization and Management
  STAMOV, S., Catering and Tourism
  ZLATEV, T., Ecology and Environmental Safety
Technical Faculty:
  DICHEV, S., Refrigeration
  GEORGIEV, A., Automatics, Information and Control Equipment
  LAMBREV, A., Technical Equipment in the Food Industry
Technological Faculty:
  KABSEV, J., Technology of Fish and Fish Products
  MARINOV, M., Beverage Technology
  MURGOV, I., Microbiology
  OBRETENOV, T., Organic Chemistry
  VASILEV, K., Technology of Meat and Fish

UNIVERSITET ZA NACIONALNO I SVETOVNO STOPANSTVO
(University of National and World Economics)

Studentski grad 'Hristo Botev', 1700 Sofia
Telephone: (2) 819-52-11
Fax: (2) 962-39-03
E-mail: secretary@unwe.acad.bg
Internet: www.unwe.acad.bg
Founded 1920
Academic year: October to July
Rector: Prof. Dr. BORISLAV BORISOV
Vice-Rector: Assoc. Prof. Dr VALENTIN KISIMOV
Vice-Rector for Continuing Education and Training: Assoc. Prof. Dr MARCHO MARKOV
Vice-Rector for Education in Masters Degree Programmes and Distant Learning: Assoc. Prof. Dr VESELKA PAVLOVA
Vice-Rector for Scientific Research and Int. Projects: Prof. Dr PLAMEN MISHEV
Librarian: DESISLAVA STEFANOVA STEFANOVA
Library of 465,443 vols
Number of teachers: 531
Number of students: 19,556

Publications: *Alternativi* (12 a year), *Trudove* (2 a year)

DEANS

Business Faculty: Assoc. Prof. Dr YORDANKA YOVKOVA
Economics College: Prof. H. KARAKASHEV (Dir)
Faculty of Applied Informatics and Statistics: Assoc. Prof. Dr VALENTIN GOEV
Faculty of Economic Industries: Asst Prof. V. ZLATEV
Faculty of Economics and Infrastructure: Prof. Dr HRISTO PURVANOV
Faculty of Finance and Accounting: Assoc. Prof. Dr OGNYAN SIMEONOV
Faculty of General Economics: Assoc. Prof. Dr ATANAS KAZAKOV
Faculty of International Economics and Politics: Dr GEORGI GENOV

Faculty of Law: Prof. Dr HRISTINA BALABANOVA
Faculty of Management and Administration: Assoc. Prof. Dr VELINA BALEVA
Institute for Postgraduate Studies: Assoc. Prof. B. NEDELCHEVA (Dir)

PROFESSORS

Faculty of Economic Industries:
  GEORGIEV, I., Industrial Business
  ILIEV, I., Industrial Business
  KANCHEV, I., Agrarian Business
  TODOROV, K., Industrial Business
Faculty of Economics:
  BORISOV, B., Economics of Intellectual Property
  KOLEV, B., Sociology
  MIRKOVICH, K., Economics
  NIKOV, A., Economic Psychology and Economic Pedagogy
  YANKOV, G., Politology
Faculty of Economics and Infrastructure:
  IVANOV, T., Economics of National Defence and Security
  KARAKASHEV, H., Public Administration
  LULANSKY, P., Economics of the Social and Cultural Sphere
  VASILEV, E., Economics of Transport
Faculty of Finance and Accounting:
  MLADENOV, M., Finance
  STEFANOVA, P., Finance
Faculty of International Economics and Politics:
  BOEVA, B., International Economics
  MARINOV, V., International Economics
  MIHOV, N., French Language
Faculty of Law:
  BALABANOVA, H., Law
  BOIANOV, G., Law
  KARANIKOLOV, L., Law
  KORENZOV, L., Law
  SUKAREVA, Z., Law
  VASILEV, A., Law
Faculty of Management and Informatics:
  BOGINOV, N., Mathematics
  GEROV, A., Forecasting and Planning
  MANOV, V., Forecasting and Planning
  VLADIMIROVA, K., Marketing

UNIVERSITY OF TRANSPORT 'TODOR KABLESHKOV'

Geo Milev St 158, 1574 Sofia
Telephone: (2) 970-92-40
Fax: (2) 970-92-42
E-mail: office@vtu.bg
Internet: www.vtu.bg
Founded 1922 as State Railway School, present name and status 2000
State control
Rector: Prof. Dr PETAR KOLEV KOLEV
Vice-Rector for Educational Activities: Assoc. Prof. Dr RUMEN KOSTADINOV ULUTCHEV
Vice-Rector for Research and Business Activities: Prof. Dr NENCHO GEORGIEV NENOV
Library of 50,000 vols

DEANS

Faculty of Machinery and Construction Technologies in Transport: Assoc. Prof. Dr VALENTIN ALEKSANDROV NIKOLOV
Faculty of Telecommunications and Electrical Equipment in Transport: Assoc. Prof. Dr IVAN KOSTADINOV MILENOV
Faculty of Transport Management: Assoc. Prof. Dr TOSHO TRIFONOV KACHAUNOV

VARNENSKI SVOBODEN UNIVERSITET
(University of Economics—Varna)

77 Kniaz Boris I Blvd, 9002 Varna
Telephone: (52) 66-02-12
Fax: (52) 23-56-80
E-mail: u_otdel@ue-varna.bg
Internet: www.ue-varna.bg
Founded 1920 as Higher School of Commerce
State control
Academic year: September to June
Rector: Prof. Dr KALYU IVANOV DONEV
Vice-Rector for Academic Affairs: Assoc. Prof. Dr PLAMEN BLAGOV ILIEV
Vice-Rector for IC and Public Relations: Assoc. Prof. Dr BLAGO ANGELOV BLAGOEV
Vice-Rector for PSC and Finance: Assoc. Prof. Dr NIKOLA MILEV BAKALOV
Vice-Rector for Research: Assoc. Prof. Dr ZOJA KOSTOVA MLADENOVA
Registrar: Dr S. IVANOV
Librarian: Mag. T. TSANEVA
Library of 270,000 vols
Number of teachers: 262
Number of students: 8,202

Publications: *Economic Research* (3 a year), *Godishnik, Izvestya*

DEANS

Faculty of Computer Science: Prof. MARIA ZAPRIANOVA KASHEVA
Faculty of Economics: Assoc. Prof. Dr STOYAN ANDREEV STOYANOV
Faculty of Finance and Accounting: Assoc. Prof. NADIA KOSTOVA ENCHEVA
Faculty of Management: Prof. APOSTLE ATANASOV APOSTOLOV

PROFESSORS

ATANASOV, B., Econometrics
DIMITROV, G., Economics of Building
DOCHEV, D., Mathematics
DONEV, K., Auditing
GENOV, G., Accountancy
ILIEV, P., Computer Sciences
KARAMFILOV, Z., Informatics
KOTSEV, T., Finance and Credit
KOVACHEV, Z., Economics
MIKHAILOV, P., Economics
MINCHEV, S., Organic Chemistry
SALOVA, N., Economics and Organization of Trade

VELIKO TURNOVSKI UNIVERSITET 'SV. KIRIL I METODII'
(St Cyril and St Methodius University of Veliko Turnovo)

Teodosii Tarnovski St 2, 5003 Veliko Tarnovo
Telephone: (62) 62-01-89
Fax: (62) 62-80-23
E-mail: mbox@uni-vt.bg
Internet: www.uni-vt.bg
Founded 1963, fmrly 'Kiril i Metodii' Higher Pedagogical Institute, univ. Status 1971
Academic year: October to June
Rector: Prof. Dr PLAMEN ANATOLIEV LEGKOSTUP
Vice-Rector for Education: Assoc. Prof. Dr PETKO STEFANOV PETKOV
Vice-Rector for European Integration and Mobility: Assoc. Prof. Dr BAGRELIYA SABCHEVA BORISOVA
Vice-Rector for Finance and Economic Policy: Assoc. Prof. Dr MARIYA MINKOVA PAVLOVA
Sec.-Gen.: OLEG YANKOV BOZHANOV
Deputy Rector: Assoc. Prof. Dr MILEN VASILEV MIHOV
Dir of Library: Assoc. Prof. Dr SAVA YORDANOV VASILEV
Library of 380,000 vols, 42,000 periodicals, rare and valuable books, electronic and other materials

Number of teachers: 853
Number of students: 14,000

Publications: *Archives of Historical and Geographical Research* (4 a year), *Epochi* (4 a year), *Pir* (1 a year), *Proglas* (4 a year), *Works of the University* (1 a year)

DEANS

Faculty of Arts: Prof. Dr ANTOANETA ANGELOVA ANCHEVA
Faculty of Economics: Prof. Dr Hab. GEORGI STEFANOV IVANOV
Faculty of Education: Assoc. Prof. Dr ZHIVKO TRIFONOV KARAPENCHEV
Faculty of History: Assoc. Prof. Dr ANDREY DIMOV ANDREEV
Faculty of Law: Assoc. Prof. Dr TSVETAN GEORGIEV SIVKOV
Faculty of Modern Languages: Assoc. Prof. Dr BAGRELIA SABCHEVA BORISOVA
Faculty of Orthodox Theology: Assoc. Prof. Dr DIMITAR MARINOV KIROV
Faculty of Philosophy: Assoc. Prof. Dr VIHREN YANAKIEV BUZOV

VISSHE UCHILISHTE PO ZASTRAKHOVANE I FINANSI (VUZF University)

Zh.k. Ovcha Kupel, ul. Gusla No.1, 1618 Sofia
Telephone: (2) 401-58-12
Fax: (2) 401-58-21
E-mail: office@vuzf.bg
Internet: www.vuzf.bg
Founded 2002
Private control
Pres.: Dr GRIGORII VAZOV
Vice-Pres.: CLOVER SMILKOVA
Exec. Dir: RADOSTIN VAZOV
Deputy Rector for Educational Activities and Quality Management: Prof. YORDAN HRISTOSKOV
Deputy Rector for Research and Devt and Institutional Relations: Prof. KOSTADIN KOSTADINOV
Courses in finance; insurance and social insurance; management and marketing.

YUGOZAPADEN UNIVERSITET 'NEOFIT RILSKI' (Southwest University 'Neofit Rilski')

Ivan Michailov St 66, 2700 Blagoevgrad
Telephone: (73) 88-55-05
Fax: (73) 88-55-16
E-mail: info @swu. bg
Internet: www.swu.bg
Founded 1976
State control
Academic year: September to July
Chair.: Prof. Dr ILIA GYUDZHENOV
Rector: Prof. Dr IVAN MIRCHEV
Vice-Rector for Credential Activity, Publs and Information Infrastructure: Prof. Dr IVAN MIRCHEV
Vice-Rector for Int. Relations: Asst Prof. Dr DOBRINKA GEORGIEVA
Vice-Rector for Research and Devt, Practical Training and Professional Qualifications: Assoc. Prof. Dr DIMITAR DIMITROV
Vice-Rector for Teaching: Assoc. Prof. Dr ZDRAVKO GARGAROV
Library of 155,000 vols
Number of teachers: 1,000
Number of students: 10,000

DEANS

Faculty of Arts: Prof. Dr RUMEN POTEROV
Faculty of Economics: Assoc. Prof. Dr CHAVDAR NIKOLOV
Faculty of Law and History: Prof. Dr SOFKA MATEEVA
Faculty of Mathematics and Natural Sciences: Assoc. Prof. Dr BORISLAV YURUKOV
Faculty of Pedagogy: Assoc. Prof. Dr RUSSI RUSSEV
Faculty of Philology: Dr ANTHONY STOILOV
Faculty of Philosophy: Assoc. Prof. GEORGI APOSTOLOV
Faculty of Public Health and Sports: Assoc. Prof. STOIAN IVANOV
Technical College: Assoc. Prof. IVANKA GEORGIEVA (Dir)

Academies and Institutes

Akademija za Muzikalno i Tanzovo Izkustvo (Academy of Music and Dance): T. Samodumov 2, 4025 Plovdiv; tel. (32) 22-83-11; fax (32) 63-16-68; f. 1972; academic year September to July; 105 teachers; 972 students; Rector Assoc. Prof. VASILKA YONCHEVA; Pro-Rector Assoc. Prof. LYUBEN DOSEV; Pro-Rector Prof. SNEJANA SIMEONOVA; Pro-Rector Prof. MILCHO VASILEV; Sec.-Gen. (Man.) K. MECHEV; Librarian V. PAVLOVA; publ. *Collection of Articles* (1 a year).

Bulgaria–Romania Interuniversity Europe Centre: 55 Alexandrovska St, 7000 Ruse; tel. (82) 82-56-67; fax (82) 82-56-62; e-mail brie-bg@ru.acad.bg; internet www.brie.ru.acad.bg; f. 2001 operates through collaboration between the Rusenski Universitet 'Angel Kanchev' and the Academia de Studii Economice (see Romania chapter); attached to Rusenski Universitet 'Angel Kanchev'; offers postgraduate degrees in European studies.

College of Economics and Administration: Blvd Kuklensko Rd 13, Plovdiv; tel. (32) 26-69-35; e-mail ceabul@yahoo.co.uk; internet www.ceabul.net; f. 2003; Chair. Prof. DIMITAR KOSTOV; Rector GEORGI MANOLOV.

College of Tourism: Park Ezero, 8000 Burgas; tel. (56) 85-81-84; fax (56) 81-37-61; e-mail cot@cot.bse.bg; internet www.btu.bg; f. 1967 as Institute of Int. Tourism, present name 1997; attached to Burgas Prof. Assen Zlatarov Univ.; Dir Prof. A. KOKINOV.

European College of Economics and Management: 18 Zadruga St, 4004 Plovdiv; tel. and fax (32) 67-23-62; e-mail office@ecem .org; internet www.ecem.org; f. 2001; offers courses in accountancy and control, business administration, corporate economics, tourist hospitality management; 2,000 students; Pres. Prof. Dr MARIANA MIHAILOVA; Rector Assoc. Prof. Dr TSVETAN KOLEV; Vice-Rector Prof. Dr MARIA KAPITANOVA; Chief Sec. Dr TSVETAN KOTSEV.

G. S. Rakovski National Defence Academy: Evlogi and Hristo Georgiev No. 82, 1504 Sofia; tel. (2) 922-65-10; fax (2) 944-16-57; e-mail rectorrdsc@md.government.bg; internet rdsc.md.government.bg; f. 1912; higher education and scientific research on issues of nat. security and defence; library: 420,000 vols in Academic Library and 250,000 books in Military History Library; 1,000 students; Commandant Major-Gen. GEORGI TANEV GEORGIEV; publ. *Military Journal* (10 a year).

Higher School 'Agricultural College' Plovdiv: Dunav Blvd 78, 4003 Plovdiv; tel. (32) 96-03-60; fax (32) 96-04-06; e-mail agri_college@mail.bg; internet www .agricollege.com; f. 1992, present name 1997, present status 2003; agrotechnologies; technologies in horticulture and wine production; economics of tourism; alternative tourism; agrarian economics; business administration; Rector Assoc. Prof. Dr Eng. DIMITAR DIMITROV; Vice-Rector Assoc. Prof. Dr DIMI-

TAR IV. DIMITROV; Vice-Rector Assoc. Prof. Dr PETAR PETROV; Vice-Rector Assoc. Prof. Dr MARIANA IVANOVA.

Higher School – College Telematics: St Parchevich 26, 6000 Stara Zagora; tel. and fax (42) 63-02-06; e-mail coppk@abv.bg; internet www.telematika-college.com; f. 1989; offers professional courses and specialized language courses, incl. English, French, German, Spanish, Italian, Russian; 470 mems; Rector Prof. Dr CHRISTO SANTULOV.

Higher State School 'College of Telecommunications and Post': Studentski grad 1 Academic Stefan Mladenov St, 1700 Sofia; tel. (2) 862-28-93; fax (2) 806-22-27; e-mail rector@hctp.acad.bg; internet www .hctp.acad.bg; f. 1922; Rector Assoc. Prof. Dr IVAN KURTEV; Deputy Rector for Educational Process Assoc. Prof. TATYANA DAMGOVA; Deputy Rector of PGS and SR Assoc. Prof. Dr STEFAN POPOV.

International University College: Bulgaria St 3, 9300 Dobrich; tel. (58) 65-56-20; fax (58) 60-57-60; e-mail dobrich@vumk.eu; internet www.vumk.eu; f. 1992; library: 12,500 vols; 1,400 students; Rector Prof. TODOR RADEV; Vice-Rector KLARA DIMITROVA; Academic Dir STANISLAV IVANOV; publ. *The European Journal of Tourism Research.*

Medical College: 69 Stefan Stambolov Blvd, 8000 Burgas; tel. (56) 85-81-50; fax (56) 81-32-95; e-mail medcollege@bginfo.net; internet www.btu.bg; f. 1950 as Medical School, present name 1997; attached to Burgas Prof. Assen Zlatarov Univ.; specializes in health care and pharmacy; Dir Asst Prof. M. STOICHEVA.

Ministry of the Interior Academy: c/o Ministry of Interior, 29 Shesti Septemvri St, 1000; tel. (2) 982-50-00; internet www.mvr .bg; f. 2002; attached to Min. of Interior; training state officials, incl. faculties of security, police, fire and emergency safety; organizes nat. and int. confs, seminars and research.

N. Y. Vaptsarov Naval Academy: 73 V. Drumev St, 9026 Varna; tel. (52) 552-228; fax (52) 303-163; e-mail public-rel@naval.acad .bg; internet www.naval-acad.bg; f. 1881 as Machine School for the Navy, present name 1949; trains specialists for the Navy and for the merchant marine in all areas of maritime life; research and devt; Commandant Captain DIMITAR ANGELOV.

National Music Academy 'Prof.Pancho Vladigerov': E. Georgiev 94, 1505 Sofia; tel. (2) 943-34-00; fax (2) 944-14-54; internet www.nma.bg; f. 1921, fmrly State Academy of Music, present name 2006; academic year September to June; faculties of instrumentation, musical theory, composition and conducting, and vocal studies; 220 teachers; 995 students; Rector Prof. Dr DIMITAR MOMCHILOV MOMCHILOV; Vice-Rector for Training's Methodical and Scientific Research Activity Prof. Dr PRAVDA ATANASOVA GORANOV; Vice-Rector for Art Activities and Academic Orchestra Work Prof ANATOLY DOBREV KRASTEV; Vice-Rector for Academic Opera Theatre and Art Activities of the Vocal Faculty Prof. ILKA BORISOVA POPOVA; Dir of Library Dr ELIZABETH PETKOVA; publ. *Godishnik.*

National Sports Academy 'Vassil Levski': Studentski grad, 1700; tel. (2) 962-04-58; fax (2) 62-90-07; internet www.nsa.bg; f. 1942 as Higher School for Physical Education, present name 1999; faculties of physiotherapy, physical education, teachers and coaches training; Rector Prof. Dr LACHEZAR DIMITROV; Vice-Rector for Education Assoc. Prof. Dr PENCHO GESHEV; Vice-Rector for Int. Relations and European Integration Prof. Dr DANIELA DASHEVA; Vice-Rector for Accreditation and Quality of Education Assoc. Prof.

Dr DIMITAR MIHAILOV; Vice-Rector for Science Prof. Dr PETAR BONOV; Vice-Rector for Social and Economic Affairs Prof. Dr KIRIL ANDONOV.

Nacionalna Akademija za Teatralno i Filmovo Izkustvo (National Academy of Theatre and Film Arts): G. S. Rakovski St 108A, 1000 Sofia; tel. (2) 923-12-25; fax (2) 989-73-89; e-mail natfiz@bitex.com; internet natfiz.bg; f. 1948; academic year October to July; offers drama theatre acting, puppet theatre acting, physical theatre, drama theatre directing, puppet theatre directing, stage and screen design; screen arts and stage arts management; incl. faculties of screen arts and stage arts; library: 60,000 vols; 87 teachers; 560 students; Rector Prof. Dr STANISLAV SEMERDJIEV; Registrar STOYAN EVTIMOV; Sec. ILIANA DIMITROVA; Librarian EMILIA BALDZHIYSKA; publ. *108A Magazine*.

Nacionalna Hudojestvena Akademija (National Academy of Art): 1 Shipka St, 1000 Sofia; tel. (2) 988-17-01; fax (2) 987-33-28; e-mail art_academy@yahoo.com; internet www.nha-bg.org; f. 1896, reorganized as an acad. 1995; academic year October to May; offers courses in fine and applied arts, design, conservation and restoration and history and theory of art; 131 teachers; 800 students; Rector Prof. SVETOSLAV KOKALOV; Vice-Rector for Education and Scientific Activities Prof. SVILEN STEFANOV; Vice-Rector for Exhibition and Artistic Activities Prof. ANNA BOYADJIEVA; Vice-Rector for Int. Relations Prof. MITKO DINEV; Librarian DARINKA DIUKMEDJIEVA; publ. *The Art of Drawing* (1 a year).

Pedagogical College in Pleven: c/o Veliko Tărnovski Universitet 'Sv. Kiril i Metodii', T. Tarnovo 2, 5003 Veliko Tărnovo; tel. (62) 61-83-33; fax (62) 62-80-23; internet www.uni-vt.bg; attached to St Cyril and St Methodius Univ. of Veliko Tarnovo; Dir Assoc. Prof. YORDAN MITEV.

Stopanska Akademija 'D. A. Tsenov' ('D. A. Tsenov' Academy of Economics): St Em. Chakarov 2, 5250 Svishtov; tel. (631) 6-62-46; fax (631) 6-09-78; e-mail rectorat@ uni-svishtov.bg; internet www.uni-svishtov .bg; f. 1936 as D. A. Tsenov Higher School of Commerce, present name 1995; State control; academic year September to July; offers courses in economic accounting, finance, management and marketing, production and commercial business; library: 192,748 vols of periodicals, 200,000 vols of books, 15 int. databases; 274 teachers; 12,300 students; Rector Assoc. Prof. Dr VELICHKA ADAMOV IONOV; Vice-Rector for BA Training and Financial Policy Dr GEORGI MARINOV GERGANOVA; Vice-Rector for Social, and Student Information Policy Dr LYUBEN MARINOV KRAEV; Vice-Rector for Research and Int. Cooperation SARKIS AGOP SARKISYAN; Admin. Sec. CNEZHANA DIMITROVA GENKOV; Chief Admin. Officer V. TANEV; Dir of Library ANKA PETKOVA TANEVA; publs *Biznes— Upravlenie* (4 a year), *Dialogue* (online, 4 a year), *Economic World Library* (6 a year), *Narodnostopanski Arhiv* (4 a year).

Technical College: Prof. Yakimov Blvd 1, 8010 Burgas; tel. and fax (56) 88-12-31; e-mail barzov@btu.bg; internet www.btu.bg; f. 1986 as Institute of Mechanical and Electrical Engineering, present name 1997; attached to Burgas Prof. Assen Zlatarov Univ.; machinery and equipment construction, transport equipment and technologies, electrotechnics, electronics, computer systems and technologies, marketing; Dir Prof. P. BARZOV.

Technical College of Lovech: Gr. Lovech, POB 5500, St C Saev 31, Lovech; tel. (68) 60-39-29; fax (68) 60-39-25; e-mail tklovech@ mail.bg; internet www.tklovech.org; f. 1990; attached to Tehničeski Universitet Gabrovo; Dir Assoc. Prof. Dr VASIL KOCHEVSKI.

Theatre College 'Luben Groys': Sq. 'Bulgaria' 1, NDK, Admin. Bldg, 12th Fl., Suite 7A, 1000 Sofia; tel. (2) 986-20-25; fax (2) 916-61-65; e-mail lgroys_college@yahoo.com; internet www.lgrois.50megs.com; f. 1991.

Vratsa College of Education: c/o Veliko Tărnovski Universitet 'Sv. Kiril i Metodii', T. Tarnovo No. 2, 5003 Veliko Tărnovo; tel. (62) 61-83-33; fax (62) 62-80-23; e-mail ; internet www.uni-vt.bg; attached to St Cyril and St Methodius Univ. of Veliko Tarnovo; Dir Assoc. Prof. YORDAN YOTOV.

BURKINA FASO

The Higher Education System

Higher education in Burkina Faso dates from the establishment of a teacher-training institute in 1965 which, after several name changes, became known as the Université de Ouagadougou (UO) in 1972. In addition to the UO there is a polytechnic university at Bobo-Dioulasso and an institute of teacher training at Koudougou; there are also 11 private institutions. The number of students enrolled at tertiary-level institutions in 2006/07 was 33,500. The two state-run universities are government-funded, with additional financial resources provided by bilateral or multilateral agreements and the universities' own revenue streams. Higher education is the responsibility of the Ministry of Secondary and Higher Education and Scientific Research.

The UO and Université Polytechnique de Bobo-Dioulasso have similar, five-tier administrative structures consisting of a Board of Directors, a University Assembly, a University Council, institutions and departments. The Board of Directors consists of representatives from the government ministries, the institution's administrative staff, trade unions' representatives, academic staff and students. The University Assembly decides university policy and is summoned by the Rector at least twice a year. Its members are drawn from the Directors, teaching, administrative and technical staff, students and representatives from government ministries. The Rector (or Chancellor) runs the university with the aid of the Vice-Chancellors and a Secretary-General. Finally, institutions are administered by Directors, who report directly to the Rector.

Admission to higher education is based on the award of the Baccalauréat or Bachelier du second degré. Higher education awards are arranged in three cycles. The first cycle lasts two years and leads to award of the Diplôme d'Études Universitaires Générales (DEUG), Premier Cycle d'Études Médicales (PCEM), Diplôme Universitaire d'Études Littéraires (DUEL), Diplôme Universitaire d'Études Scientifiques (DUES) or Diplôme Universitaire de Technologie. The second cycle lasts one year after the first cycle for the Licence degree, two years for the Maîtrise or three years for Diplôme d'Ingénieur. Finally, the third cycle comprises doctoral-level studies. The Diplôme d'Études Supérieures Spécialisées (DESS) or the Diplôme d'Études Approfondies (DEA) are awarded after one-year courses in subjects such as mathematics, biology, chemistry, law, economics and linguistics, and the Doctorat de Troisième Cycle or Doctorat de Spécialité are awarded following two further years of study after the DEA. In addition to higher education awards, the main vocational award is the Diplôme, which requires two years of study.

Regulatory Bodies

GOVERNMENT

Ministry of Culture, Tourism and Communication: 03 BP 7007, Ouagadougou 03; tel. 50-33-09-63; fax 50-33-09-64; e-mail mcat@cenatrin.bf; internet www.culture.gov.bf; Min. PHILIPPE SAWADOGO.

Ministry of Secondary and Higher Education and Scientific Research: 03 BP 7047, Ouagadougou 03; tel. 50-32-45-67; fax 50-32-61-16; e-mail laya.saw@messrs.gov.bf; internet www.messrs.gov.bf; Min. Prof. JOSEPH PARÉ.

Research Institutes

GENERAL

Centre National de la Recherche Scientifique et Technologique: BP 7047, Ouagadougou 03; tel. 50-32-46-48; fax 50-31-50-03; internet www.cnrst.bf; f. 1950, 1968 incorporated into Ministère de l'Education Nationale, 1978 into Ministère de l'Enseignement Supérieur et de la Recherche Scientifique; basic and applied research in humanities, social sciences, natural sciences, agriculture, energy, medicine; library of 20,000 vols; 102 researchers; Dir-Gen. BASILE L. GUISSOU; publs *Sciences et Technique* (2 a year), *CNRST-Information* (6 a year), *Eurêka* (4 a year).

Institut de Recherche pour le Développement (IRD): BP 182, Ouagadougou 01; tel. 50-30-67-37; fax 50-31-03-85; internet www.ird.bf; f. 1968; hydrology, geography, agronomy, botany, medical entomology, economics, demography, anthropology, pedology, ethnology, geology, sociology; Dir JEAN-PIERRE GUENGANT; (see main entry under France).

AGRICULTURE, FISHERIES AND VETERINARY SCIENCE

Centre de Coopération Internationale en Recherche Agronomique pour le Développement (CIRAD): Ave du Président Kennedy, BP 596, Ouagadougou 01; tel. 50-30-70-70; fax 50-30-76-17; e-mail jacques.pages@cirad.fr; f. 1963; natural resource management and environmental protection; improved crop and livestock production; agroeconomics; remote sensing and geographical information systems; agrifoods; 15 research staff; Regional Dir for continental West Africa JACQUES PAGÈS; publ. *Rapport scientifique* (1 a year).

Institut de l'Environnement et de Recherches Agricoles: BP 8645, Ouagadougou 04; tel. 50-34-71-12; fax 50-34-02-71; e-mail inera.direction@fasonet.bf; f. 1978; research in arable and livestock farming, forestry, agricultural machinery, natural resources, management and farming systems; library of 2,500 vols, 2,500 documents; Dir Prof. HAMIDOU BOLY; publ. *Science et Technique* (2 a year).

EDUCATION

Institut Pédagogique du Burkina: BP 7043, Ouagadougou; tel. 50-33-63-63; f. 1976 by the Min. of Nat. Education, for the devt of methods and courses in primary education; library of 16,000 vols (Min. of Education Library); 150 staff; Dir Gen. JUSTINE TAPSOBA; publ. *Action, Réflexion et Culture* (8 a year).

TECHNOLOGY

Bureau de Recherches Géologiques et Minières (BRGM): BP 86, Ouagadougou; tel. 50-33-50-42; (see main entry under France).

Libraries and Archives

Ouagadougou

Bibliothèque Nationale du Burkina: 03 LP 7007, Ouagadougou 03; tel. 50-32-63-63; internet www.culture.gov.bf/site_ministere/m.c.a.t/ministere/ministere_sr_bn.htm; f. 1988; under Min. of Culture, Tourism and Francophone Affairs; Dir-Gen. ABEL NADIE.

Centre National des Archives: Présidence du Faso, BP 7030, Ouagadougou; tel. 50-33-61-96; fax 50-31-49-26; f. 1970; Dir DIDIER E. OUEDRAOGO.

Museum

Ouagadougou

Musée National: 08 BP 11186, Ouagadougou; located at: Ave Oubritenga, Ouagadougou; tel. 50-30-73-89; fax 50-31-25-09; internet www.culture.gov.bf/site_ministere/textes/etablissements/etablissements_museenational.htm; f. 2003; 4,000 artefacts; Dir Prof. ALIMATA SAWADOGO.

Universities

UNIVERSITÉ POLYTECHNIQUE DE BOBO-DIOULASSO

01 BP 1091, Bobo-Dioulasso 01

Telephone: 20-98-06-35

Fax: 20-98-25-77

E-mail: hamidou.boly@yahoo.fr

Internet: www.univ-bobo.bf

Founded 1997

State control

Academic year: October to July

Pres.: Prof. HAMIDOU BOLY

Vice-Pres. for Teaching and Pedagogic Innovation: Prof. MARIE YVES THÉODORE TAPSOBA

Vice-Pres. for Research, Prospective and Int. Cooperation: Prof. ANTOINE N. SOME
Dir for Int. Cooperation: Dr IRÉNÉE SOMDA
Number of teachers: 101
Number of students: 2,048

DIRECTORS

Ecole Supérieure d'Informatique: Prof. M'BI KABORE
Institut du Développement Rural: Dr HASSAN BISMARCK NACRO
Institut des Sciences Exactes et Appliquées: Dr SADO TRAORE
Institut des Sciences de la Nature et de la Vie: Prof. JULIETTE DIALLO-TRANCHOT
Institut des Sciences de la Santé: Prof. ROBERT T. GUIGUEMDE
Institut Universitaire de Technologie: Dr BETABOALÉ NAHON

UNIVERSITÉ DE OUAGADOUGOU

03 BP 7021, Ouagadougou 03
Telephone: 50-30-70-64
Fax: 50-30-72-42
E-mail: info@univ-ouaga.bf
Internet: www.univ-ouaga.bf
Founded 1969, univ. status 1974

Academic year: October to June
State control
Language of instruction: French
Pres.: JOSEPH PARÉ
Vice-Pres.: JEAN COULIDIATY
Vice-Pres.: GUSTAVE KABRÉ
Vice-Pres.
Sec.-Gen.: MAMIDOU KONE
Librarian: MAÏMOUNA SANOKO
Library of 70,000 vols
Number of teachers: 395
Number of students: 21,309
Publications: *Annales* (2 a year), *Cahiers du Centre d'Etudes, de Documentation et de Recherches Economiques et Sociales* (4 a year), *Revue burkinabé de Droit* (2 a year)

DEANS

Faculty of Economics and Management Sciences: DEMBO GADIAGA
Faculty of Health Sciences: MAMADOU SAWADOGO
Faculty of Law and Politics: G. AUGUSTIN LOADA
Faculty of Letters, Arts, Humanities and Social Sciences: ROSAIRE BAMA, JUSTIN KOUTABA

Faculty of Science and Technology: MARTIN LOMPO

Colleges

Centre d'Etudes Economiques et Sociales d'Afrique Occidentale (CESAO): BP 305, Bobo-Dioulasso; tel. 20-97-10-17; fax 20-97-08-02; e-mail cesao.bobo@fasonet.bf; f. 1960; areas of study incl. the enhancement of rural orgs on an institutional level, the promotion of women, faith and humanity, community health, admin. of the devt of rural communities, environment and land admin., savings and investments in rural areas, devt projects; 16 staff; library: 14,000 vols and 77 periodicals; Dir ROSALIE OUOBA; publ. *Construire Ensemble* (6 a year).

Ecole Inter-Etats d'Ingénieurs de l'Equipement Rural (EIER): BP 7023, Ouagadougou 03; tel. 50-30-20-53; fax 50-31-27-24; f. 1968 by governments of 14 francophone African states; 3-year postgraduate diploma course; hydraulics, civil engineering, refrigeration technology, sanitary engineering; Dir MICHEL GUINAUDEAU.

BURUNDI

The Higher Education System

The main institution of higher education is the Université du Burundi, founded in 1973 following a merger of several institutions, including the Université Officielle de Bujumbura. In 2004/05 17,061 students were enrolled in higher education. The main language of instruction is French. The Minister of Higher Education and Scientific Research is responsible for higher education, although the Université du Burundi enjoys a relative degree of autonomy. There is also a growing private higher education sector.

The Diplôme des Humanités Complètes is the standard secondary education qualification required for admission to higher education. Undergraduate education consists of three stages: the Candidature is a programme of general studies lasting two years; the Diplôme de Licence requires a further two years of study; and in medicine the professional title Docteur en Médecin is awarded after four years of study following the Candidature. The main postgraduate qualification is the Diplôme d'Études Approfondies.

Several institutes of the Université du Burundi also offer higher vocational education, usually courses of three to four years leading to the award of the Diplôme d'Ingénieur Technicien.

Regulatory Bodies

GOVERNMENT

Ministry of Higher Education and Scientific Research: Bujumbura; Min. Dr SAÏDI KIBEYA.

Ministry of Youth, Sports and Culture: Bujumbura; tel. 22226822; Min. JEAN-JACQUES NYENIMIGABO.

Research Institutes

AGRICULTURE, FISHERIES AND VETERINARY SCIENCE

Institut des Sciences Agronomiques du Burundi: BP 795, Bujumbura; tel. 22223390; fax 22225798; e-mail isabu@usan-bu.net; internet www.asareca.org/naris/isabu; f. 1962; agronomical research and farm management; library of 11,500 vols, 120 periodicals; Dir-Gen. Dr JEAN NDIKURANA.

MEDICINE

Laboratoire Médical: Bujumbura; devoted to clinical analyses, physio-pathological research and nutritional studies.

NATURAL SCIENCES

Physical Sciences

Centre National d'Hydrométéorologie: Bujumbura; Dir E. KAYENGAYENGE.

TECHNOLOGY

Direction Générale de la Géologie et des Mines: Ministère de l'Energie et des Mines, BP 745, Bujumbura; tel. 22222278; fax 22223538; Dir-Gen. Dr AUDACE NTUNGICIMPAYE.

Libraries and Archives

Bujumbura

Archives nationales du Burundi: Ministère de la Jeunesse, de la Culture et des Sports, BP 1095 Rohero II, Bujumbura; located at: ave Kunkiko, Bujumbura; tel. 22225051; fax 22226231; 26,000 vols; Dir NICODÈME NYANDWI.

Bibliothèque de l'Université: BP 1320, Bujumbura; tel. 22222857; f. 1961; 192,000 vols, 554 periodicals; Chief Librarian THARLISSE NSABIMANA.

Museums and Art Galleries

Bujumbura

Musée Vivant de Bujumbura: Ministère de la Jeunesse, de la Culture et des Sports, BP 1095 Rohero II, Bujumbura; located at: ave Kunkiko, Bujumbura; tel. 22226852; f. 1977; part of Centre de Civilisation Burundaise attached to Min. of Youth, Sports and Culture; reflects the life of the Burundi people in all its aspects; incl. a reptile house, aquarium, aviary, traditional Rugo dwelling, open-air theatre, fishing museum, botanical garden, herpetology centre, musical pavilion, and crafts village; Dir EMMANUEL NIRAGIRA.

Gitega

Musée National de Gitega: 223 Magarama (Pl. de la Révolution), BP 110, Gitega; tel. 22402359; fax 22219295; e-mail mapfarakoraj@yahoo.com; f. 1955; history, archaeology, ethnography, arts, folk traditions, arms; library: in process of formation (200 vols); Curator JACQUES MAPFARAKORA.

National Universities

UNIVERSITÉ DU BURUNDI

BP 1550, Bujumbura
Telephone: 2242353
Fax: 2223288
E-mail: rectorat@ub.edu.bi
Founded 1960, renamed as Université Officielle de Bujumbura 1964, present name 1974
State control
Academic year: October to September
Language of instruction: French
Pres. of Admin. Ccl: MARC RWABAHUNGU
Rector: Prof. ALEXANDRE HATUNGIMANA
Vice-Rector: Prof. JACQUES BUKURU
Academic Dir: Prof. SYLVIE HATUNGIMANA
Admin. and Finance Dir: VÉNÉRAND NIZIGIYIMANA
Research Dir: Prof. VESTINE NTAKARUTIMANA
Chief Librarian: APOLLINAIRE YENGAYENGE
Number of teachers: 239
Number of students: 8,545

Publications: *Actes de la Conférence des Universités des Etats Membres de la CEPGL* (1 a year), *Actes de la Semaine de l'Université* (1 a year), *Le Flambeau* (1 a year), *Le Héraut* (6 a year), *Revue de l'Université* (4 a year)

DEANS
Faculty of Agriculture: BONAVENTURE NIYOYANKANA
Faculty of Applied Sciences: JOSEPH NZEYIMANA
Faculty of Economic and Administrative Sciences: PASCAL RUTAKE
Faculty of Law: Prof. STANISLAS MAKOROKA
Faculty of Letters and Humanities: Prof. MELCHIOR NTAHONKIRKIYE
Faculty of Medicine: Prof. THEODORE NIYONGABO
Faculty of Psychology and Education: Prof. PAUL NKUNZIMANA
Faculty of Sciences: Prof. DÉO DOUGLAS NIYONZIMA

UNIVERSITÉ DE MWARO

Ave des Etats-Unis, 18, BP 553 Bujumbura
Siège du Campus à Kibumbu, BP 26 Mwaro
Telephone: 22243953
E-mail: info@universitemwaro.org
Internet: www.universitemwaro.org
State control
Faculties of administration and business management and law; 1 institute
Number of teachers: 157 (incl. full-time and part-time)
Number of students: 182

Private Universities

INSTITUT SUPÉRIEUR DE GESTION ET D'INFORMATIQUE (ISGE) (Higher Institute of Business Management)

BP 6624, Bujumbura
Ave de la Révolution No. 38, Bujumbura
Telephone: 22219861
Fax: 22245500
Founded 1987
Private control.

UNIVERSITÉ DE NGOZI

BP 137, Ngozi
Telephone: 22302259

Fax: 22302259
E-mail: info@univ-ngozi.org
Internet: www.univ-ngozi.org
Founded 1999
Private control
Rector: ABBÉ APPOLINAIRE BANGAYIMBAGA
Vice-Rector: BONAVENTURE BANGURAMBONA

Number of teachers: 160 (incl. 38 full-time, 122 part-time)
Number of students: 1,180
Faculties of agronomy; arts and sciences; law, economics and administrative; maths and computer; medicine.

UNIVERSITÉ DU LAC TANGANYIKA
(University of Lake Tanganyika)

BP 5403, Mutanga, Bujumbura
Ave des Palmiers 6, Bujumbura
Telephone and fax 243645
Founded 2000
Private control
Number of students: 2,662
Faculties of law; management science and applied economics; social sciences, policy and administration.

UNIVERSITÉ ESPOIR D'AFRIQUE
(Hope Africa University)

BP 238, Bujumbura
Telephone: 22237973
Internet: hopeafricauniversity.org
Founded 2000 in Nairobi, present location 2003

Private control
Languages of instruction: English, French
Dir: Dr ELIE BUCONYORI
Number of students: 2,500
Faculties of arts and sciences, business and professional studies, educational sciences, engineering, health sciences.

UNIVERSITÉ LUMIÈRE DE BUJUMBURA
(University of Bujumbura Light)

BP 1368, Bujumbura
Telephone: 22248733
E-mail: ntukapaul@yahoo.com
Internet: www.ulbu.info/index.php
Founded 2000
Private control
Pres.: Rev. CHANOINE PAU NTUKAMAZINA
Rector: Dr GRÉGOIRE NJEJIMANA
Sec. Gen.: RUTOMERA PIERRE CLAVER
Number of students: 1,826

DEANS
Faculty of Theology: Rev. DONALD WERNER

UNIVERSITÉ MARTIN LUTHER KING

BP 2393, Bujumbura
Telephone: 243944
E-mail: umlku@yahoo.fr
Private control.

Colleges

Centre Social et Éducatif: Bujumbura; f. 1957; courses in crafts, photography, mechanics; 75 students.

Ecole Normale Supérieure (ENS) (Higher Teachers' Training School): 28th November Blvd, BP 6983, Bujumbura; tel. 22258945; fax 22243356; e-mail ens@cbinf.com; internet www.ens-burundi.org; f. 1965, present status 1999; depts of applied sciences, languages and social sciences, natural sciences; 79 teachers; 2,000 students.

École Supérieure de Commerce du Burundi: BP 1440, Bujumbura; tel. 22224520; f. 1982; 304 students; library: 1,200 vols; Dir PIERRE NZEYIMANA.

Institut Supérieur d'Agriculture: BP 35, Gitega; tel. 22242335; f. 1983; under Min. of Nat. Education; courses in tropical agriculture, stockbreeding, agricultural engineering, food technology; 213 students; Dir (vacant); publ. *Revue des Techniques Agricoles Tropicales* (2 a year).

Institut Supérieur de Techniciens de l'Aménagement et de l'Urbanisme: BP 2720, Bujumbura; tel. 22223694; f. 1983; under the Min. of Public Works and Urban Development; 103 students; library: 863 vols; Dir SALVATOR NAHIMANA.

Lycée Technique: Bujumbura; f. 1949; training apprentices, craftsmen and professional workers; 4 workshops: mechanics, masonry, carpentry, electrical assembling; 450 students.

CAMBODIA

The Higher Education System

The oldest institution of higher education is the Royal University of Phnom-Penh, founded in 1960. The higher education system was greatly affected by the coup of 1975 and the Khmer Rouge regime (1975–79), but has enjoyed a renaissance in recent years with the restoration of pre-Khmer Rouge institutions and foundation of private establishments. Other public institutions of higher education now include universities of agriculture, fine arts and health sciences.

To gain admission to higher education students must possess the Diploma of Upper Secondary Education and pass the competitive national entrance examination. Higher education lasts for up to eight years, including undergraduate and postgraduate study. Until 1993 the most common undergradu-

ate qualification was the Diploma of Higher Education, but since then several other equivalent degree titles have emerged. In 2009 there were 76 higher education institutions; 33 of them were public and 43 were private. There were 168,003 students studying in graduate and postgraduate programmes, and there were 11,694 state public students. In 2009, the Ministry of Education, Youth and Sport (MoEYS) sent 415 students to study overseas and 51 graduates in Cambodia were from overseas. MoEYS admitted 56 foreign students to study in the local universities in that year.

Technical and vocational educational and training courses are one to three years in length, and the Department of Technical Vocational Education and Training (DTVET) has established criteria for certificate- and Diploma-level studies.

Regulatory and Representative Bodies

GOVERNMENT

Ministry of Culture and Fine Arts: 227 blvd Norodom, Phnom-Penh; tel. (23) 217645; fax (23) 725749; e-mail mcfa@cambodia.gov.kh; internet www.mcfa.gov.kh; Minister Prince SISOVAT PANARA SIRIVUDH.

Ministry of Education, Youth and Sport: 80 blvd Norodom, Phnom-Penh; tel. (23) 217253; fax (23) 212512; e-mail moeys@everyday.com.kh; internet www.moeys.gov.kh; Minister KOL PHENG.

ACCREDITATION

Accreditation Committee of Cambodia: 3/F, bldg No. 134, cnr of Monivong and Kampuchea Krom Blvd, Phnom-Penh; tel. (23) 224620; fax (23) 725743; internet www.acc.gov.kh; f. 2003; assures and works to improve the quality of higher education instns in Cambodia; meets int. standards through accreditation; Chair. SOK AN.

Learned Societies

GENERAL

UNESCO Office Phnom-Penh: POB 29, Phnom-Penh; located at: House 38, Samdech Sothearos Blvd, Phnom-Penh; tel. (23) 426726; fax (23) 426163; e-mail phnompenh@unesco.org; internet www.un.org.kh/unesco; Head ANNE LEMAISTRE.

AGRICULTURE, FISHERIES AND VETERINARY SCIENCE

Cambodian Society of Agriculture: c/o CIAP, POB 01, Phnom-Penh; located at: CIAP, 29 Km Highway 3, Phnom-Penh; internet www.bigpond.com.kh/users/ciap/csa.htm; f. 1998; attached to Cambodia-IRRI-Australia Project; 144 mems; Pres. MAK SOLIENG; Sec. TOUCH SAVY; publs *Bulletin* (3 a year), *Cambodian Journal of Agriculture* (irregular).

HISTORY, GEOGRAPHY AND ARCHAEOLOGY

Authority for the Protection and Management of Angkor and the Region of Siem Reap (APSARA): 187 Pasteur St,

Chaktomuk, Daun Penh, Phnom-Penh; tel. (23) 720315; fax (23) 990185 Angkor Preservation Compound, Siem Reap; tel. (63) 760080; fax (63) 760080; e-mail apsara-admin@camnet.com.kh; internet www.autoriteapsara.org; f. 1995; depts of administration, monuments and archaeology 1, monuments and archaeology 2, urbanism and urban planning, Angkor tourist devt, water and forest, demography, public order and cooperation; publs *Journal* (12 a year), *Udaya—Journal of Khmer Studies* (irregular).

Royal Angkor Foundation: POB 255, 1241 Budapest, Hungary; tel. (1) 3224270; fax (1) 3224270; e-mail angkor@hu.inter.net; internet www.angkor.iif.hu; f. 1992; safeguards the monuments and relics of the ancient Khmer civilization, establishing projects and gathering data; Hon. Co-Pres. HM NORODOM SIHANOUK (King of Cambodia); Hon. Co-Pres. ÁRPÁD GÖNCZ (fmr Pres. of Hungary); Chair. of Supervisory Board GÁBOR BARTA.

NATURAL SCIENCES

Biological Sciences

Parks Society of Cambodia: POB 2680, Phnom-Penh; located at: 280B, Street 146, Group 32, Sangkat Toek Laaok II, Khan Toul Kork, Phnom-Penh; tel. (16) 813700; e-mail vibolparkssociety@hotmail.com; internet parkssociety-cambodia.netfirms.com; NGO responsible for community development, environmental education and the preservation of 10 wildlife reserves, 7 national parks, 3 protected landscapes and 3 multiple-use areas.

RELIGION, SOCIOLOGY AND ANTHROPOLOGY

Buddhist Association: c/o Buddhist Institute Library, POB 1047, Phnom-Penh.

Research Institutes

ECONOMICS, LAW AND POLITICS

Cambodia Development Resource Institute: POB 622, Phnom-Penh; 56 St 315, Tuol Kork, Phnom-Penh; tel. (23) 881701; fax (23) 880734; internet www.cdri.org.kh; f. 1990; centre for Peace and Devt programme; research in macroeconomic policy, rural live-

lihoods, governance and decentralization, natural resources and the environment, poverty analysis and monitoring; library of 15,250 vols, 100 periodicals; Dir LARRY STRANGE; Coordinator of the Centre for Peace and Devt ROMDUOL HUY; publs *Annual Development Review* (1 a year), *Cambodia Development Review* (4 a year), *Flash Report on the Cambodian Economy* (12 a year).

Cambodian Institute for Cooperation and Peace: POB 1007, Phnom-Penh; Phum Paung Peay, Sangkat Phnom-Penh Thmey, Khan Sen Sok, Phnom-Penh; tel. (12) 819953; fax (16) 982559; e-mail cicp@everyday.com.kh; internet www.cicp.org.kh; f. 1994; affiliated with ASEAN Institutes of Strategic and International Studies; library of 4,000 vols in Khmer, English and French; Admin. SOTHEARA CHHORN.

Cambodian Institute of Human Rights: POB 550, 30, St 57, Sangk at Boeung Keng Kong 1, Khan Chamcar Morn, Phnom-Penh; tel. (23) 210596; fax (23) 362739; e-mail chir@camnet.com.kh; f. 1993 by UN Transitional Authority in Cambodia; Dir KASSIE NEOU.

Centre for Social Development: POB 1346, Phnom-Penh; House 19, St 57, Sangkat Boeung Trabek, Keng Kang I Khan Chamkar Mon, Phnom-Penh; tel. and fax (23) 364735; internet www.bigpond.com.kh/users/csd; f. 1995; aims to promote democratic values through research, training, advocacy and debate; Pres. CHEA VANNATH; publ. *Bulletin* (12 a year).

MEDICINE

National Institute of Public Health: POB 1300, Phnom-Penh; tel. (23) 880345; fax (23) 880346; e-mail nphri@camnet.com.kh; internet www.camnet.com.kh/nphri; attached to Min. of Health; advises on govt policy and trains senior staff.

RELIGION, SOCIOLOGY AND ANTHROPOLOGY

World Buddhism Association for Development, Cambodia Regional Center: 11c, Rd 1986, Sangkat Phnom-Penh, Termei, Khan Kussey Keo, Phnom-Penh; tel. (23) 368506.

Libraries and Archives
Phnom-Penh

Documentation Centre of Cambodia: POB 110, Phnom-Penh; 70E, King Norodom Sihanouk Blvd, Phnom-Penh; tel. (23) 211875; fax (23) 210358; e-mail dccam@online.com.kh; internet www.dccam.org; f. 1995, as field office of the Cambodian Genocide Program at Yale University, USA; became fully autonomous instn in 1997; information resource centre on the Khmer Rouge regime; Dir YOUK CHHANG.

National Archives of Cambodia: POB 1109, Phnom-Penh; tel. (23) 430582; e-mail archives.cambodia@camnet.com.kh; internet www.camnet.com.kh/archives.cambodia; records of Résidence Supérieure du Cambodge (French colonial administration), 1863–1954; post-colonial govt collns; records of Khmer Rouge regime and 1979 genocide tribunal; periodicals and newspapers in French, Khmer, Vietnamese and Chinese.

National Library of Cambodia: Street 92, Daun Penh District, Phnom-Penh; tel. and fax (23) 430609; f. 1924; 103,635 vols; special collection of original palm-leaf manuscripts, 700 manuscript titles on microfilm; French Indo-China collection; Dir KHLOT VIBOLLA; publ. *Books-in-Print Cambodia*.

Museums and Art Galleries
Phnom-Penh

Museum of Genocide: Tuol Svay Prey Gymnasium, 103rd St, Phnom-Penh; f. 1979; fmr school converted into prison in 1975 after capture of Phnom-Penh by Khmer Rouge, and used as interrogation, torture and execution facility; following fall of the Khmer Rouge in 1979, converted into a museum depicting crimes of the regime.

National Museum of Arts: POB 2341, Phnom-Penh; located at: 13 Street, Phnom-Penh; tel. (23) 24369; f. 1920; main galleries dedicated to bronzes, sculpture, ethnography and ceramics; Dir KHUN SAMEN.

National Universities

BUDDHIST INSTITUTE

POB 1047, Phnom Penh
Sangkat Tonle Basak, Khan Chamkamon, Phnom Penh
Telephone: (23) 212046
Fax: (23) 216779
E-mail: info@budinst.gov.kh
Internet: www.budinst.gov.kh
Founded 1930; attached to Min. of Religion and Cults
State control
Dir: NGUON VAN CHANTHY
Publication: *Kambuja Soriya* (4 a year).

CHEA SIM UNIVERSITY OF KAMCHAYMEAR

GPOB 865, Phnom Penh
Smong Choeung Commun, Kamchay Mear Dist., Prey Veng
Telephone: (17) 888166
E-mail: mvu-camb@forum.org.kh
Internet: www.csuk.edu.kh
Founded 1993 as Maharishi Vedic Univ., present name 2008; attached to Min. of Education, Youth and Sport
State control

Offers Bachelors and Masters courses in agriculture and management; smaller campuses in Kampong Cham and Prey Veng
Pres.: UK THAUN
Dir for Int. Relations: SETH KHAN
Number of students: 3,000

ECONOMICS AND FINANCE INSTITUTE

C/o Min. of Economy and Finance, St 90, Sangkat Wat Phnom, Khan Daun Penh, Phnom Penh
Telephone: (23) 430556
Fax: (23) 430168
E-mail: sengsrengefi@yahoo.co.uk
Internet: efi.mef.gov.kh
Founded 1997; attached to Min. of Economy and Finance
State control
Dir: SENG SRENG
Deputy Sec.-Gen.: Dr HEAN SAHIB.

INSTITUTE OF HEALTH SCIENCE OF ROYAL CAMBODIAN ARMED FORCES

Russian Fed. Blvd, Tek Thla Commun, Russey Keo Dist., Phnom Penh
Telephone: (16) 932876
E-mail: iahs2005@yahoo.com; attached to Min. of Education, Youth and Sport
State control
Dir: Dr SOKHON LON.

INSTITUTE OF TECHNOLOGY OF CAMBODIA

Russian Fed. Blvd., Sangkat Toek leak 1, Khan Tuolkok, Phnom Penh
Telephone: (23) 880370
Fax: (23) 880369
E-mail: direction@itc.edu.kh
Internet: www.itc.edu.kh; attached to Min. of Education, Youth and Sport
State control
Dir: P. HOEURNG SACKONA.

KAMPONG CHAM NATIONAL SCHOOL OF AGRICULTURE

Nat. Rd 7, Veal Vong Commune, Kampong Cham Dist., Kampong Cham
Telephone and fax (42) 340187; attached to Min. of Agriculture, Forestry and Fisheries
State control.

NATIONAL INSTITUTE OF BUSINESS

St 217, Phum Trea, Sangkat Steung Mean Chey, Khan Mean Chey, Phnom Penh
Telephone and fax (23) 424591
E-mail: nib@nib.edu.kh
Internet: www.nib.edu.kh
Founded 1979 as School of Central Commercial Technique, present status 1994, present name 2001; attached to Min. of Education, Youth and Sport
State control
Offers diplomas and Bachelors degrees.

NATIONAL INSTITUTE OF EDUCATION

123, Norodom Blvd, Sangkat Chaktomok, Khan Doun Penh, Phnom Penh
Telephone: (23) 332342
E-mail: nieimkoch@yahoo.com; attached to Min. of Education, Youth and Sport
State control
Dir: IM KOCH
Number of students: 500

NATIONAL POLYTECHNIC INSTITUTE OF CAMBODIA

Phum Sre Reachas, Samrong Krom, Khan DangKor, Phnom Penh
Telephone: (12) 964401
Fax: (23) 353561
E-mail: info@npic.edu.kh
Internet: www.npic.edu.kh
Founded 2005; attached to Min. of Social Affairs, Veterans and Youth Rehabilitation
State control
Offers courses in automobile engineering, CAD/CAM, civil engineering, culinary art (bakery and cookery), electronic engineering, electrical engineering, information technology, mechanical engineering, tourism and hospitality
Dir: HE SOPHOAN PICH
Pres.: HE PHEARIN BUN
Co-Pres.: Prof. Dr SUNG CHUL KIM
Vice-Pres.: Dr YONG WOO LEE.

NATIONAL TECHNICAL TRAINING INSTITUTE

Russian Blvd, Sangkat Teukthla Khan Sensok, Phnom Penh
Telephone and fax (23) 883039
Internet: www.ntti.edu.kh
Founded 1999 as Preach Kossomak Technical and Vocational Training Centre, present name and status 2001; attached to Min. of Labour and Vocational Training
State control
Offer Bachelors and Masters degrees in civil engineering and electrical engineering; diploma courses in business information technology, civil engineering and technology in electricity
Dir: YOK SOTHY.

NATIONAL UNIVERSITY OF MANAGEMENT

Corner of Monivong Blvd. and St 96 (Christopher Howes St), Phnom Penh
Telephone: (23) 428120
Fax: (23) 427105
E-mail: info@num.edu.kh
Internet: www.num.edu.kh; attached to Min. of Education, Youth and Sport
State control
Rector: HE Dr LOR SOCHEAT
Vice-Rector for Academics, Research and Library: HE Dr PIC PHIRUM
Vice-Rector for Accounting: CHHUM CHHONLY
Vice-Rector for Admin. and Personnel: NOU SETHA
Vice-Rector for Int. Relations and Career Placement: SENG BUNTHOEUN
Number of students: 10,000

DEANS

Faculty of Economics: SIM SOVICHA
Faculty of Information Technology: CHHAY PHANG
Faculty of Law: NEAU SARETH
Faculty of Management: SOU PHALLA

PREAH KOSSOMAK POLYTECHNIC INSTITUTE

Russian Blvd, Sangkat Toek Tla, Khan Reusey Keo, Phnom Penh
Telephone: (11) 909148
Fax: (23) 426954
E-mail: ppi@camnet.com.kh
Internet: www.rumdoul.com/ppi
Founded 1965 as Centre de formation Profassionelles des Cardes Technique, present name and status 2001; attached to Min. of Labour and Vocational Training
State control

Languages of instruction: English, French, Khmer

Offers degrees in business administration, civil engineering, electrical engineering, electronic engineering, information technology; diplomas in civil construction, electricity, electronic, information technology

Dir: HEM CHANTHA

Number of teachers: 81

PREK LEAP NATIONAL SCHOOL OF AGRICULTURE

Russey Keo, POB 1319, Phnom Penh

Rd 6A, Prek Leap, Russey Keo, Phnom Penh

Telephone: (23) 219746

E-mail: info@pnsa.edu.kh

Founded 1950, present status 1984; attached to Min. of Agriculture, Forestry and Fisheries

State control

Dir: PHAT MUNY.

ROYAL ACADEMY OF CAMBODIA

Campus 2, Federation of Russia Blvd, Sangkat Tuk Laak 1, Khan Tuol Kok, Phnom-Penh 12156

POB 2070, Phnom-Penh

Telephone: (23) 890180

Fax: (23) 221408

E-mail: hacademy@camnet.com.kh

Internet: www.rac.edu.kh

Founded 1965, disbanded 1975 due to civil war, re-established 1997; attached to Office of the Ccl of Mins

Languages of instruction: Khmer, English

State control

Academic year: October to June

Offers a range of masters and doctoral programmes; promotes research in all major academic areas and organizes scientific forums

Library of 10,000 vols

Pres.: LOK CHUUTEAR KLOT THIDA

Under-General Sec. for Administration and Finance: CHHUN SUM BUN

Under-General Sec. for Training and Research: CHEA NENG.

SUB-INSTITUTES

Institute of Biology, Medicine and Agriculture: tel. (12) 835306; Dir Dr SAM SOPHEAN.

Institute of Culture and Fine Arts: tel. (12) 733336; Dir Dr CHHAY YIHEANG.

Institute of Humanities and Social Sciences: tel. (11) 919044; Dir Dr ROS CHANTRABOT.

Institute of National Language: tel. (12) 836040; Dir (vacant).

Institute of Science and Technology: tel. (11) 951849; Dir Dr CHAN PORN.

ROYAL UNIVERSITY OF AGRICULTURE

POB 2696, Chamkar Daung, Phnom-Penh

Telephone: (23) 219829

Fax: (23) 219690

E-mail: rua@forum.org.kh

Founded 1964, university status since 1999; attached to Min. of Agriculture, Forestry and Fisheries

Rector: HE NARETH CHAN

Vice-Rector: MUNY PHAT

Number of teachers: 217

Number of students: 1,097

DEANS

Agricultural Economics and Rural Development: BORA KATHY

Agricultural Technology and Management: BUNTHAN NGO

Agro-Industry: SOK KUNTHY

Agronomy: SOPHAL CHOUNG

Animal Science and Production: PITH LOAN CHUM

Fisheries: CHHOUK BORIN

Forestry: MONIN VON

Information Technology and Telecommunications: MAO NARA

Land Management and Administration: MAK VISAL

ROYAL UNIVERSITY OF FINE ARTS

Street No. 70, Phnom-Penh

Telephone: (23) 910703

Fax: (23) 986417

E-mail: rufa@camnet.com.kh

Founded 1918 as École des Arts Cambodgiens, merged with Nat. Theatre School 1965, closed 1975, re-opened 1980 as School of Fine Arts 1980, original name and status restored 1993; attached to Min. of Culture and Fine Arts

Faculties of archaeology, architecture and urban studies, choreographic arts, music, plastic arts

Rector: KEOUN TUK

Vice-Rector and Dean of Choreographic Arts: CHHIENG PROEUNG.

ROYAL UNIVERSITY OF LAW AND ECONOMICS

Preah Monivong, Phnom-Penh 12305

Telephone: (23) 211565

Fax: (23) 214953

E-mail: fle@khmerson.com

Internet: www.rule.edu.kh

Founded 1948 as Nat. Institute of Law, Politics and Economics, incorporated into the Univ. of Phnom-Penh as Faculty of Law and Economics 1957, independent univ. status 2003; attached to Min. of Education, Youth and Sport

Language of instruction: Khmer

State control

Academic year: October to July

Faculties of economics and management; law; public administration; graduate schools of law and economics and management

Rector: YUOK NGOY (acting)

Number of teachers: 266 (84 full-time, 112 visiting Cambodian lecturers and 70 foreign visiting lecturers)

Number of students: 4,802

ROYAL UNIVERSITY OF PHNOM-PENH

Russian Federation Blvd, Toul Kork, Phnom-Penh

Telephone: (23) 883-640

Fax: (23) 880116

E-mail: secretary@rupp.edu.kh

Internet: www.rupp.edu.kh

Founded 1960 as Royal Khmer Univ., renamed Phnom-Penh Univ. 1970, closed 1975–1979, re-opened 1980, present name 1996; attached to Min. of Education, Youth and Sport

State control

Languages of instruction: Khmer, English, French

Academic year: September to June

Rector: Prof. LAV CHHIV EAV

Vice-Rector for Academic and Admin. Affairs: PONN CHHAY

Vice-Rector for Curriculum and QA: HE SOK VANNY

Vice-Rector for Gen. Management of CJCC, Youth and Cultural Exchange Programme: OUM RAVY

Vice-Rector for Gen. Management of IFL: SUOS MAN

Vice-Rector for Research, Postgraduate Programme and Int. Relations: HANG CHANTHON

Librarian: SEN SENG

Library of 39,000 vols

Number of teachers: 420

Number of students: 9,000

DEANS

Faculty of Science: ING HENG

Faculty of Social Science and Humanities: KIM SOVANNKIRY

Institute of Foreign Languages: Dr MEAS VANNA

SVAY RIENG UNIVERSITY

Nat. Rd 1, Chambak Village, Sangkat Chek, Svay Rieng

Telephone: (44) 715776

Fax: (44) 715778

E-mail: info@sru.edu.kh

Internet: www.sru.edu.kh

Founded 2006; attached to Min. of Education, Youth and Sport

State control

Faculties of agriculture; art, humanity and foreign language; business administration; science and technology; social science

Rector: TUM SARAVUTH.

UNIVERSITY OF BATTAMBANG

Nat. Rd 5, Prek Preah Sdech Commune, Battambang

Telephone and fax (53) 952905

E-mail: info@ubb.edu.kh

Internet: www.ubb.edu.kh

Founded 2007; attached to Min. of Education, Youth and Sport

State control

Academic year: August to September (2 semesters)

Faculties of agriculture and food processing; arts education and humanities; business administration and tourism; science and technology; sociology and community development

Rector: Dr VISALSOK TOUCH.

UNIVERSITY OF HEALTH SCIENCES

73, Preah Monivong Blvd, Phnom-Penh

Telephone: (23) 430732

Fax: (23) 430129; attached to Min. of Health

Rector: KIM PO VOU.

Private Universities

ANGKOR CITY INSTITUTE

Main Campus, Seam Reap

Telephone: (23) 990424

E-mail: aci@camintel.com; attached to Min. of Education, Youth and Sport

Private control

Dir: SEOUN HOK.

ANGKOR UNIVERSITY

Borey Seang Nam, Phum Khna, Khum Chreav, Srok Siem Reap, Khet Siem Reap, Angkor

Telephone: (92) 256086

Fax: (63) 760340
E-mail: info@angkor.edu.kh
Internet: www.angkor.edu.kh
Founded 2004; attached to Min. of Education, Youth and Sport
Private control
Rector: HE NEAK OKNHA SEANG NAM
Vice-Rector: SHIN HO CHUL
Vice-Rector: YUN LINNE.

ASIA EURO UNIVERSITY

832 ABCD, Kampuchea Krom Blvd, Sangkat Teuk Laak I, Khan Toul Kork, Phnom Penh 12156
Telephone: (11) 757485
Fax: (23) 998124
E-mail: info@aeu.edu.kh
Internet: www.aeu.edu.kh
Founded 2005; attached to Min. of Education, Youth and Sport
Private control
Rector: DUONG LEANG
Dir for Admin: SEANG SOVANN

DEANS

Faculty of Arts, Humanities and Languages: LY BUNSAN

ASIA PACIFIC INSTITUTE

189, Mao Tse Toung Blvd, Khan Chamkarmorn, Phnom Penh
Telephone: (23) 985823
E-mail: steveloun@gmx.net; attached to Min. of Education, Youth and Sport
Private control
Dir: CHHENG LY.

BELTEI INTERNATIONAL INSTITUTE

25A, St 105, Boeng Prolit, Khan 7 Makara, Phnom Penh
Telephone: (12) 823666
Fax: (23) 996889
E-mail: info@beltei.edu.kh
Internet: www.beltei.edu.kh
Founded 2002; attached to Min. of Education, Youth and Sport
Private control
10 Campuses
Dir: HE CHHENG LY.

BUILD BRIGHT UNIVERSITY

Tonle Basac Bldg, Grey Bldg, Samdech Sothearos Blvd, Phnom Penh
Telephone: (23) 987700
Fax: (23) 987900
E-mail: info@bbu.edu.kh
Internet: www.bbu.edu.kh
Founded 2000 as Faculty of Management and Law, present name and status 2002; attached to Min. of Education, Youth and Sport
Private control
Rector: VIRAKCHEAT IN
Pres.: Assoc. Prof. DIEP SEIHA
Vice-Pres. for Academic and Student Affairs: Assoc. Prof. MEAS REN RITH
Vice-Pres. for Admin. Affairs: Asst Prof. IN VIRACHEY
Vice-Pres. for Finance and Property: PROK VEASNA
Vice-Pres. for Legal Affairs and Coordination: Assoc. Prof. LAM CHEA
Vice-Pres. for Postgraduate studies: Prof. Dr TAPAS RANJAN DASH
Number of students: 12,000

DEANS

Faculty of Business Management: SAMRITH CHANHENG

Faculty of Education and Languages: KE CHHUM PANHA
Faculty of Engineering and Architecture: SOK KHOM
Faculty of Law and Social Sciences: OEURN SOKHA
Faculty of Science and Technology: CHI KIM Y
Faculty of Tourism and Hospitality: EM KHEDY

CAMBODIAN MEKONG UNIVERSITY

9B, St 271, Sangkat Tek Thla, Khan Sen Sok, Phnom Penh 12102
Telephone: (23) 882211
Fax: (12) 809191
E-mail: info@mekong.edu.kh
Internet: www.mekong.edu.kh; attached to Min. of Education, Youth and Sport
Private control
Chancellor: ICH SENG
Vice-Chancellor: BAN THERO
Library of 10,000 vols

DEANS

Faculty of Arts, Humanities and Foreign Language: CHENG KIMSAN
Faculty of Economics: LONG SOPHAT
Faculty of Law: PEN PICHSALY
Faculty of Management and Tourism: KON SKAISHANN
Faculty of Science: CHEA CHHOUN HONG
Faculty of Social Science: SUGITA SHIN

CAMBODIAN UNIVERSITY FOR SPECIALTIES

Bldg F, Toul Kork Village, Sangkat Toul Sangke, Khan Russey Keo, Phnom Penh
Telephone: (23) 350828
Fax: (12) 636207
Internet: www.cus.edu.kh; attached to Min. of Education, Youth and Sport
Private control
Campuses in Banteaymeanchey, Battambang, Kamport, Kampong Cham, Kampong Thom
Rector: HE SDOEUNG SOKHOM
Vice-Rector for Admin. Affairs: CHHUN NOCH
Vice-Rector for Foundation and Academic Affairs: SOEUR YAN
Vice-Rector for Research and Devt Affairs: Dr MEAS BORA.

CHAMROEUN UNIVERSITY OF POLY-TECHNOLOGY

88, St 350, Khan Chamkarmorn, Phnom Penh
Telephone: (11) 987795
Fax: (23) 987695
E-mail: cup@camintel.com.kh
Internet: www.cup.edu.kh
Founded 2002; attached to Min. of Education, Youth and Sport
Private control
Rector: HE Dr CHEA CHAMROEUN.

HUMAN RESOURCES UNIVERSITY

Bldg 2, St 163, Sangkat Olympic, Khan Chamkamorn, Phnom Penh
Telephone: (23) 987826
E-mail: info@hru.edu.kh
Internet: www.hru.edu.kh
Founded 1998, present name 2005, present status 2007; attached to Min. of Education, Youth and Sport
Private control
Faculties of arts, humanity and languages; business administration and tourism; law

and political science; science and technology; social science and economics
Rector: SENG PHALLY
Vice-Rector: EK MONOSEN
Vice-Rector: OK SOPHEA.

ICS UNIVERSITY

14, St 214, Sangkat Beoung Raing, Khan Daun Penh, Phnom Penh
Telephone: (23) 724062
Fax: (23) 426104
E-mail: ics@camnet.com.kh; attached to Min. of Education, Youth and Sport
Private control
Rector: KHUON SUDARY.

IIC UNIVERSITY OF TECHNOLOGY

Bldg 650, Nat. Rd 2, Sankat Chak, Angre Krom, Khan Mean Chey, Phnom Penh
Telephone: (23) 425 148
Fax: (23) 425 149
E-mail: info@iic.edu.kh
Internet: www.iic.edu.kh
Founded 1999 as International Institute of Cambodia, present name and status 2008; attached to Min. of Education, Youth and Sport
Private control
Rector: CHHUON CHAN THAN
Number of teachers: 29
Number of students: 500

INSTITUTE FOR BUSINESS EDUCATION

315, St Charles De Gaulle Blvd, Sangkat Orussey II, Khan 7 Makara, Phnom Penh
Telephone: (23) 990980
Fax: (23) 990284
E-mail: info@ibe.edu.kh
Internet: www.ibe.edu.kh
Founded 2006; attached to Min. of Education, Youth and Sport
Private control
Faculties of business and English
Deputy Dir: YOK SETTHA.

INSTITUTE OF CAMBODIA

314, Nat. Rd 5, O Ambel Dist., Bantey Meanchay
Telephone: (12) 737578
Fax: (54) 958505
E-mail: ic.edu.bmc@yahoo.com; attached to Min. of Education, Youth and Sport
Private control
Rector: VIN SOCHEAT.

INSTITUTE OF MANAGEMENT AND DEVELOPMENT

Peal Nhek I, Phtes Prey, Sampov Meas, Pursat
Telephone: (52) 951519
E-mail: mensethy@camintel.com
Internet: www.imd.edu.kh
Founded 2006; attached to Min. of Education, Youth and Sports
Private control
Dir: MEN SETHY.

INSTITUTE OF MANAGEMENT SCIENCE

Monivong St, Khom Kompong Cham, Kompong Cham Dist., Kompong Cham
Telephone: (12) 873539
Fax: (42) 941962; attached to Min. of Education, Youth and Sport
Private control
Rector: SENG LYMENG.

INSTITUTE OF TECHNOLOGY AND MANAGEMENT

St 180, Khan Daun Pen, Phnom Penh
Telephone: (23) 982229
Fax: (23) 210110
E-mail: itm@online.com.kh
Founded 1999; attached to Min. of Education, Youth and Sport
Private control
Dir: SOK BUN LIM.

INTERED INSTITUTE

Level 5 of Phnom Penh Center, Sotheoros Blvd, Khan Chamkarmorn, Phnom Penh
Telephone: (23) 993866
Fax: (23) 994445
E-mail: info@intered.edu.kh; attached to Min. of Education, Youth and Sport
Private control
Rector: UNG DIPOLA.

INTERNATIONAL UNIVERSITY

Corner of Sts 1984 & 1011, Sangkat Phnom Penh Thmey, Khan Russey Keo, Phnom Penh 12100
Telephone: (17) 926969
Fax: (23) 881623
E-mail: iusabo@yahoo.com
Internet: www.iu.edu.kh
Founded 2002; attached to Min. of Education, Youth and Sport
Private control
Languages of instruction: Khmer, French, English
7 Faculties and 1 postgraduate institute; offers 40 degree programmes ranging from assoc. to doctoral degrees
Hon. Chair.: HE Dr OUK RABUN
Pres.: HE Prof. UON SABO
Vice-Pres.: Dr SEUN SAMBATH
Vice-Pres.: HE Prof. SABO OJANO
Dir for Int. Relations: Dr ANBIN EZHILAN
Number of students: 1,250

KHEMARAK UNIVERSITY

Sotheoros Blvd and Preah Sihanouk Blvd corner, Phnom Penh Center, Block D, Phnom Penh
Telephone: (23) 6336296
E-mail: khemarak_university@yahoo.com
Internet: www.khemarak.com; attached to Min. of Education, Youth and Sport
Private control
Faculties of agricultural science and rural development, art and linguistics, business administration and tourism, educational science, humanities, law and economic science, political science and international relation, professional training centre and research, science technology and information
Rector: Dr SOK TOUCH.

KHMER UNIVERSITY OF TECHNOLOGY AND MANAGEMENT

Sangkat 4, Khan Mittapheap, Sihanoukville
Telephone and fax (34) 933718
E-mail: info@kutm-shv.com
Internet: www.kutm-shv.com
Private control
Rector: Dr HONG CHAN SOKHA
Librarian: CHHAY CHANDARET
Librarian: SAM ROTHA.

LIMKOKWING UNIVERSITY OF CREATIVE TECHNOLOGY

120–126, St 1986, Sangkat Phnom Penh Thmei, Khan Sen Sok, Phnom Penh
Telephone: (23) 995733
Fax: (23) 995727
E-mail: enquiry@limkokwing.edu.kh
Internet: www.limkokwing.edu.kh
Founded 1991 in Malaysia
Private control
Campuses in Botswana, People's Republic of China, Indonesia, Lesotho, Malaysia, Swaziland, UK
Pres.: Dr LIM KOK WING.

NEWTON THILAY UNIVERSITY

100, St Pasteur, Psar Tmey 3, Khan Daun Penh, Phnom Penh
Telephone and fax (23) 224807
E-mail: info.ntu@ntu.edu.kh; attached to Min. of Education, Youth and Sport
Private control
8 Faculties and 1 training centre
Rector: CHEA THILAY.

NORTON UNIVERSITY

Corner St 118 & 19 & 130, Sangkat Phsar Chas, Khan Daun Penh, Phnom Penh
Telephone: (23) 982166
Fax: (23) 211273
E-mail: info@norton-u.com
Internet: www.norton-u.com; attached to Min. of Education, Youth and Sport
Private control
Rector: CHAN SOK KHIENG
Dir for Admin. and Personnel: KAO SAM OL
Dir for Information Technology Dept: OUR PHIRUN
Dir for Int. Relations: RODRIGO C. PASCO
Registrar: NGOV SIMRONG
Library of 4,000 vols

DEANS

College of Sciences: HAS BUNTON
College of Social Sciences: TRY SOTHEARITH

PAÑÑĀSĀSTRA UNIVERSITY OF CAMBODIA

92–94, Maha Vithei Samdech Sotheoros, Phnom Penh
Telephone: (23) 990153
Fax: (23) 218909
E-mail: info@puc.edu.kh
Internet: www.puc.edu.kh
Founded 1997; attached to Min. of Education, Youth and Sport
Private control
Faculties of arts, letters and humanities; business and economics; communication and media art; education; law and public affairs; mathematics, science and engineering; medicine and health sciences; social sciences and international art
Pres.: Dr CHEA SAN CHANTHAN
Dir for Library System: MAO KOLAP.

PHNOM PENH INTERNATIONAL UNIVERSITY

Bldg 36, St 169, Sangkat Veal Vong, Khan 7 Makara, Phnom Penh
Telephone: (23) 999908
E-mail: info@ppiu.edu.kh
Internet: www.ppiu.edu.kh
Founded 2006 by merger of Int. Institute of Cambodia and Asean Univ.
Private control
Rector: TEP KOLAP

Vice-Rector: HIN SAM ATH
Vice-Rector for Academic Affairs: KHOV MEAS
Vice-Rector for Admin. and Finance: KEO KUYLY
Number of teachers: 30

DEANS

Art and Languages: PRAK THYLY
Business Studies: KANG SOVANNARA
Information Technology: MEN SARAVUTH
Postgraduate Studies: LY SOKHENG

SACHAK ASIA DEVELOPMENT INSTITUTE

47Eo, St 348, Sangkat Toul Svay Prey I, Kanh Chamkarmon, Phnom Penh
Telephone: (12) 603148
E-mail: info@sadi.edu.kh
Internet: www.sadi.edu.kh
Founded 2004; attached to Min. of Education, Youth and Sport
Private control
Faculties of English, business management, computer science, economics and hotel tourism
Dir: NHEM SACHAK.

SETEC INSTITUTE

92, St 110, Russian Fed. Blvd, Sangkat Teuk Laak I, Khan Toul Kork, Phnom Penh
Telephone and fax (23) 880612
E-mail: info@setecu
Internet: www.setecu.com; attached to Min. of Education, Youth and Sport
Private control
Offers Bachelors degrees in business administration skills and English, computer and local area networking, software engineering, software programming and database management system, website and multimedia development; also offers Masters degrees in business management, database administration, application development, networking technology
Dir: NGOUN SOKVENG
Library of 2,000 books and magazines.

SITC UNIVERSITY

315, St Saldegol, Sangkat Oreushi 2, Khan 7 Makara, Phnom Penh
Telephone: (12) 914321
Fax: (23) 986982
E-mail: sii@online.com.kh; attached to Min. of Education, Youth and Sport
Private control
Vice-Dir: Dr MICHEL YU.

UNIVERSITY OF CAMBODIA

POB 116, Phnom Penh 12000
145, Preah Norodom Blvd, Phnom Penh
Telephone: (23) 993274
Fax: (23) 993284
E-mail: info@uc.edu.kh
Internet: www.uc.edu.kh
Founded 2003; attached to Min. of Education, Youth and Sport
Private control
Chair.: HE Dr AUN PORN MONIROTH
Chancellor: Dr HARUHISA HANDA
Pres.: Dr KAO KIM HOURN
Vice-Pres. for Academic Affairs: Dr ANGUS D. MUNRO
Dir. for Admin.: POR MALIS
Library of 50,000 books, periodicals, magazines
Publication: *Journal of Cambodian Studies*.

UNIVERSITY OF MANAGEMENT AND ECONOMICS

POB 303, Battambang

5 St, Prakpreah sdech Commune, Battambang

Telephone: (17) 868386

Fax: (53) 953160

E-mail: umecambodia@gmail.com

Internet: www.ume.edu.kh

Founded 1998 as Battambang High Education Center, renamed as Institute of Management and Economics 2000, present name 2005; attached to Min. of Education, Youth and Sport

Private control

Hon. Chair.: Dr BUTH KIMSEAN

Chair.: Prof. Dr TEP KHUNNAL

Pres.: Prof. TUN PHEAKDEY

Vice-Pres.: Prof. Dr CHUM LAY

Vice-Pres.: Prof. Dr NORING THA

Vice-Pres.: Prof. Dr PRIEN HIEP

Vice-Pres.: Prof. Dr TUN NARITH

Library of 12,000 vols

Number of teachers: 92 (incl. both part-time and full-time)

Number of students: 3,879

UNIVERSITY OF PUTHISASTRA

55, St 180, Sangkat Boeung Raing, Khan Daun Penh, Phnom Penh

Telephone: (23) 220476

E-mail: info@puthisastra.edu.kh

Internet: www.puthisastra.edu.kh

Founded 2007

Private control

Academic year: October to August

Chair.: Dr HENG VONG BUNCHHAT

Pres.: HE SOK PUTHVYUTH

Vice-Rector for Int. Affairs: STEPHEN PATERSON

Vice-Rector for Student Affairs: KY RAVIKUN

Chief of Admin.: IM PIDO TEVY

Library of 6,000 books, magazines

DEANS

Faculty of Computer Science and Microsoft IT Academy Dept: ONG WITHYARD

Language Department: HENG RATTANA

UNIVERSITY OF SOUTH EAST ASIA

Seam Reap

Telephone: (63) 6901696

E-mail: info@usea.edu.kh

Internet: www.usea.edu.kh

Founded 2006; attached to Min. of Education, Youth and Sport

Private control

Rector: SEIN SOVANNA.

VANDA INSTITUTE OF ACCOUNTING

216–218, Mao Tse Toung Blvd., Sangkat Tomnop Toek, Khan Chamkarmon, Phnom Penh

Telephone: (23) 213563

Fax: (23) 213562

E-mail: vanda@camnet.com.kh

Internet: www.vanda.edu.kh

Founded 1997 as Vanda Centre, present name 2002; attached to Min. of Education, Youth and Sport

Private control

Offers Bachelors and Masters degrees in accounting, auditing and political science

Dir: HENG VANDA

Library of 5,000 vols

Number of students: 2,749

WESTERN UNIVERSITY

15, St 528, Sangkat Boeung kak I, Khan ToulKork, Phnom Penh

Telephone: (23) 998233

Fax: (23) 990699

E-mail: info_wu@western.edu.kh

Internet: www.western.edu.kh/wu

Founded 2003; attached to Min. of Education, Youth and Sport

Private control

Rector: HE TE LAURENT

Vice-Rector for Academic Affairs and Research: HE RONG CHHORNG

Vice-Rector for Admin and Finance: AO VENG

Registrar: TOM BANDOS

Library of 5,000 vols, 100 journals and periodicals

DEANS

Faculty of Arts, Humanities and Language: PRUDENT INJEELI

Faculty of Social Science, Management and Hotel-Tourism: PEH BUNTONG

Graduate School: HE RONG CHHORNG

ZAMAN UNIVERSITY

St 315, No. 8, Boeng Kok 1, Toul Kork, Phnom Penh

Telephone: (23) 996111

E-mail: info@zamanuniversity.com

Internet: www.zamanuniversity.com

Founded 2010

Private control

Academic year: October to September

Faculties of arts, humanities and languages; economics and administrative sciences; engineering; information and computer technologies

Rector: Dr ERKAN POLATDEMIR.

CAMEROON

The Higher Education System

As a result of Cameroon's mixed colonial heritage, there are separate education systems in the former British and French-administered regions. East Cameroon was a French colony from 1916 to 1960, when it became independent and was known as Republic of Cameroon. A merger with the smaller, British-run provinces of Southern Cameroon in the same year led to the creation of United Republic of Cameroon. The official name of the country, Republic of Cameroon, was adopted in 1984. British and French-inspired educational systems now operate in the respective former provinces, and English and French are the respective official languages of instruction. The Université de Yaoundé I (formerly Federal University of Cameroon) was established in 1962 and operates on a decentralized principle, with five regional campuses, each devoted to a different field of study. Five new state universities were created by presidential decree in 1993: Buea, Douala, Dschang, Ngaoundéré and Yaoundé II. The Ministry of Education is responsible for maintaining standards in both the public and private higher education sectors. In 2003 seven private institutions signed 'creation agreements' with the Ministry of Education; such agreements initiate the process by which universities seek authorization for establishment.

Chancellors are government appointees and are the executive heads of universities. The Chancellor oversees the appointments of Deans of faculty, Heads of department and Directors of professional schools in consultation with the Vice-Chancellor. The Governing Council is presided over by the Vice-Chancellor, and includes the Deans, Directors, members of the academic staff and representatives from government and labour organizations.

Admission to university requires the Baccalauréat or two GCE Advanced level examinations and four GCE Ordinary level examinations. University education is divided into three cycles, the first two at undergraduate level and the third at postgraduate level. The first cycle comprises two- or three-year diploma programmes (Diplômes), notably the Diplôme d'Etudes Universitaires Générales (DEUG, two years) and Diplôme d'Etudes Professionnelles Approfondies (three years). The second cycle programmes last for a further one or two years. Awards at this level include the Licence, Bachelors, Maîtrise and Diplôme. The Licence usually requires one year of study after the first cycle, and the Maîtrise two years. The third cycle consists of doctoral studies: two to four years of study after the Maîtrise for the Doctorat du Troisième Cycle; and five years for the award of Doctorat d'Etat.

There are seven universities, six of which are state-owned. There were 120,300 students enrolled at the state-owned universities in 2005/06. Specialist institutions also offer vocational education and technical training in several fields; the most common awards at these institutions are diplomas.

In 2010 the Ministry of Higher Education announced that from 2011 Cameroon students would be offered scholarships by Australia and New Zealand for study at Masters level and at postgraduate level, respectively.

Regulatory Bodies

GOVERNMENT

Ministry of Culture: Quartier Hippodrome, Yaoundé; tel. 2222-6579; fax 2223-6579; Minister AMA TUTU MUNA.

Ministry of Higher Education: Blvd du 20 Mai, BP 1739, Yaoundé; tel. 2222-1907; fax 2222-9724; e-mail elmfouou@yahoo.com; internet www.minesup.gov.cm; Min. Prof. JACQUES FAME NDONGO; publ. *SupInfos* (Note de Conjoncture; Annuaire Statistique).

Ministry of Scientific Research and Innovation: Yaoundé; tel. 2222-1334; fax 2222-1336; e-mail info@minresi.net; internet www.minresi.net; f. 2004; Minister Dr MADELEINE TCHUINTÉ.

Learned Societies

GENERAL

UNESCO Office Yaoundé: POB 12909, Yaoundé; Immeuble Stamatiades, 2e étage, Yaoundé; tel. 2222-5763; fax 2222-6389; e-mail yaounde@unesco.org; internet www.unesco.org/fr/yaounde; f. 1991; designated Cluster Office for Cameroon, Chad and Central African Republic; 19 mems; Dir BERNARD HADJADJ.

LANGUAGE AND LITERATURE

Alliance Française: BP 441, Ngaoundéré; tel. and fax 2225-1826; e-mail alliance.ngaoundere@free.fr; internet alliance.ngaoundere.free.fr; offers courses and exams in French language and culture and promotes cultural exchange with France; attached teaching offices in Bamenda, Buea, Dschang, Garoua and L'Adamaoua; Dir JACQUES LE JOLLEC.

British Council: Immeuble Christo, ave Charles de Gaulle, BP 818 Yaoundé; tel. 2221-1696; fax 2221-5691; e-mail bc-yaounde@britishcouncil.cm; internet www.britishcouncil.org/cameroon; teaching centre; offers courses and exams in English language and British culture and promotes cultural exchange with the UK; attached teaching centre in Douala; Dir JENNY SCOTT; Teaching Centre Man. TOM HINTON.

Goethe-Institut: Quartier Bastos, BP 1067, Yaoundé; tel. 2221-4409; fax 2221-4419; e-mail goethe.il@camnet.cm; internet www.goethe.de/af/yao/deindex.htm; offers courses and exams in German language and culture and promotes cultural exchange with Germany; library of 6,000 vols; Dir ANDREA JACOB.

Research Institutes

GENERAL

Instituts du Ministère de l'Enseignement Supérieur: BP 1457, Yaoundé; tel. 2227-2983; 5 univ. institutes and 5 research institutes; archaeology, botany and vegetal biology, demography, economics, geography, hydrology, nutrition, medical entomology, psycho-sociology, soil science; Sec.-Gen. PIERRE OWONO ATEBA; publs *Annales* (4 a year, in 4 series: languages and literature, human sciences, law, economics), *Revue Science et Technique* (4 a year, in 3 series: agriculture, health sciences, human sciences).

Institut de Recherche pour le Développement (IRD): Représentation ORSTOM, BP 1857, Yaoundé; tel. 2220-1508; fax 2220-1854; e-mail orstyde@ird.uninet.cm; internet www.ird.fr; f. 1944; anthropology, cell biology, demography, geography, hydrology, ecology, linguistics, medical entomology, ornithology, pedology, sedimentology, sociology; see main entry under France; Representative FRANÇOIS RIVIÈRE.

Institut des Sciences Humaines: Yaoundé; f. 1979; part of Min. of Higher Education; Dir W. NDONGKO.

AGRICULTURE, FISHERIES AND VETERINARY SCIENCE

Humid Forest Ecoregional Center: BP 2008, Nkolbisson, Yaoundé; tel. 2223-2644; f. 1980; forestry research; 170 staff (14 researchers); Dir A. M. MAINO.

Institut de la Recherche Agronomique: BP 2123, Yaoundé; tel. 2223-2644; f. 1979; part of Min. of Higher Education; agriculture, agronomy, botany, entomology, phytopathology, pedology; 6 research centres, 16 stations; 314 staff; library of 2,600 vols, 2,500 brochures, 450 periodicals; Dir Dr J.-A. AYUK-TAKEM; publs *Mémoires et Travaux de l'IRA*, *Science et Technique (Series Sciences agronomiques et zootechniques* (4 a year).

Institut de Recherches pour les Huiles et Oléagineux (IRHO): BP 243, Douala; f. 1949; see main entry under France; Dir J. N. REGAUD.

Institut des Recherches Zootechniques et Vétérinaires (IRZV): BP 1457, Yaoundé; tel. and fax 2223-2486; f. 1974; part of Min. of Higher Education; research on livestock, fisheries and wildlife, and environment;

library of 1,800 vols, 358 periodicals; Dir Dr JOHN TANLAKA BANSER; publ. *Science and Technology Review*.

ECONOMICS, LAW AND POLITICS

Institut de Formation et de Recherche Démographiques: BP 1556, Yaoundé; tel. 2222-2471; fax 2222-6793; f. 1972 with the cooperation of the UN; ECA Executing Agency; training and research on demographic phenomena and their links with economic and social factors; library of 17,000 vols; Dir AKOTO ELIWO; publ. *Annales* (3 a year).

Institut des Relations Internationales du Cameroun (IRIC): BP 1637, Yaoundé; tel. and fax 2231-0305; e-mail iric@uycdc.uninet.cm; f. 1971 by the Federal Government, the Carnegie Endowment for International Peace, the Swiss Division for Technical Cooperation and others; a bilingual, postgraduate institute for education, training and research in diplomacy and int. studies, attached to the Univ. of Yaoundé II; library of 65,000 vols; Dir Dr JEAN-EMMANUEL PONDI; Sec.-Gen. SAMUEL ENOH BESONG; publ. *Cameroon Review of International Studies* (1 a year).

EDUCATION

Centre National d'Education: Yaoundé; f. 1979; part of Min. of Higher Education; Dir E. BEBEY.

HISTORY, GEOGRAPHY AND ARCHAEOLOGY

Institut National de Cartographie: BP 157, Ave Mgr.-Vogt, Yaoundé; tel. 2222-2921; fax 2223-3954; e-mail inc@incsdncmr.undp.org; f. 1945; cartography, geography, GIS and remote sensing; Dirs PAUL MOBY ETIA, MICHEL SIMEU KAMDEM.

LANGUAGE AND LITERATURE

Centre Régional de Recherche et de Documentation sur les Traditions Orales et pour le Développement des Langues Africaines (CERDOTOLA): BP 479, Yaoundé; tel. 2230-3144; fax 2230-3189; e-mail cerdotola@yahoo.com; f. 1978; research on African languages, oral literature, traditional music, traditional medicine, traditional arts, African history, African anthropology; 20 mem. countries; library in process of formation; Exec. Sec. Prof. CHARLES BINAM BIKOI.

MEDICINE

Institut de Recherches Médicales et d'Etudes des Plantes Médicinales: Yaoundé; tel. 2223-1361; f. 1979; 250 staff; library of 1,000 vols, 50 periodicals; Dir A. ABONDO; publs *Cahiers*, *Science et Technique* (series *Sciences Médicales*).

NATURAL SCIENCES
Physical Sciences
Direction de la Météorologie Nationale: 33 rue Ivy, BP 186, Douala; tel. and fax 3342-1635; f. 1934; Dir EMMANUEL EKOKO ETOUMANN; publs *Annales climatologiques* (irregular), *Bulletin agrométéorologique décadaire*, *RCM: Résumé climatologique mensuel* (12 a year), *Résumé mensuel du Temps* (12 a year).

TECHNOLOGY

Compagnie Française pour le Développement des Fibres Textiles (CFDT): BP 1699, Douala; brs at Garoua, Maroua, Mora, Touboro and Kaele; textile research.

Institut de Recherches Géologiques et Minières: POB 4110, Yaoundé; tel. and fax 2221-0316; f. 1979; Dir GEORGES E. EKODECK.

Libraries and Archives
Bamenda
British Council Learning and Information Centre: Bamenda Urban Council Library, Commercial Ave, POB 622, Bamenda; tel. 3336-2011; fax 3336-2022; e-mail anyeoscar@yahoo.co.uk; f. 1995; jtly run with Bamenda Urban Ccl; library; learning and information centre; conducts exams; 15,000 vols; Information Officer EMMANUEL NGANG.

Yaoundé
Archives Nationales: BP 1053, Yaoundé; tel. 2223-0078; fax 2223-2010; f. 1952; conserves and classifies all documents relating to the Republic; 15,000 vols; Dir AMADOU POKEKO.

Bibliothèque Nationale du Cameroun: Ministère de la Culture, Yaoundé; tel. and fax 2223-7002; 64,000 vols; Dir NGOTOBO NGOTOBO.

Museums and Art Galleries
Bamenda
International Museum and Library—Akum: POB 389, Bamenda; f. 1948; local and foreign artefacts of interest to researchers and students of sociology, anthropology and archaeology; brasswork, paintings, beaded work, clay figures, animal skins, masks, postage stamps, iron work, sculpture, stools, traditional costumes, films and books; Curator PETER S. ATANGA.

Kumbo-Nso
Musa Heritage Gallery (Mus'Art): POB 21, Kumbo; Bamfem Quarter, Kumbo; tel. 7707-7651; e-mail musartgallery@yahoo.com; internet www.musartgallery.info.ms; f. 1996; named after Cameroonian artists Daniel and John Musa; cultural democratization and heritage preservation of arts, music, arts and crafts of the Western Grassfields region of Cameroon; 400 artefacts; preservation, education and promotion of cultural legacy of the Grass-fields of Cameroon; Dir PETER M. MUSA.

Universities
UNIVERSITÉ DE BUÉA
POB 63, Buea
Telephone: 3332-2134
Fax: 3343-2508
Internet: www.cm.refer.org/edu/ram3/univers/ubuea/ubuea.htm
Founded 1977 (opened 1986) as Buea Univ. Centre, present name and status 1992
State control
Languages of instruction: English, French, Spanish
Academic year: September to June
Chancellor: Dr PETER AGBOR TABI
Pro-Chancellor: Prof. VICTOR ANOMAH NGU
Vice-Chancellor: Dr DOROTHY L. NJEUMA
Deputy Vice-Chancellor for Control: Prof. SAMMY BEBAN CHUMBOW
Deputy Vice-Chancellor for Research and Cooperation: Prof. SAMSON ABANGMA

Deputy Vice-Chancellor for Teaching: Prof. VINCENT P. K. TITANJI
Registrar: Dr HERBERT NGANJO ENDELEY
Librarian: ROSEMARY SHAFACK
Library of 35,000 vols
Number of teachers: 208 (93 full-time, 115 part-time)
Number of students: 3,300
Publication: *Epasa Moto* (1 a year)

DEANS
Faculty of Arts: Prof. EMMANUEL GWAN ACHU
Faculty of Education: Dr GRACE EWENE
Faculty of Health Sciences: Dr THEODOSA McMOLI
Faculty of Science: Dr NZUMBE MESAPE NTOKO
Faculty of Social and Management Sciences: Prof. CORNELIUS LAMBI

CONSTITUENT INSTITUTE
Advanced School of Translators and Interpreters (ASTI): Dir Dr ETIENNE ZÉ AMVELA.

UNIVERSITÉ CATHOLIQUE DE L'AFRIQUE CENTRALE
BP 11628, Yaoundé
Telephone: 2223-7400
Fax: 2223-7402
E-mail: ucac.icy-nk@camnet.cm
Internet: www.cm.refer.org/edu/ram3/univers/ucac/ucac.htm
Founded 1989
Private control (Catholic Church)
Languages of instruction: English, French
Academic year: October to July
Rector: Abbé OSCAR EONE EONE
Vice-Rector: Abbé OLIVIER MASSAMBA LOUBELO
Sec.-Gen.: JOSEPH KONO OWONA
Dir of Devt and Cooperation: GILLES NOUDJAG
Head Librarian: Dr PATRICK ADESO (acting)
Library of 39,341 vols
Number of teachers: 90 and 240 assoc. lecturers
Number of students: 1,692
Publication: *Cahiers de l'U.C.A.C.* (1 a year)

DEANS
Faculty of Social Sciences and Management: Prof. Dr JACQUES FDRY
Faculty of Theology: Père Dr ANTOINE BABÉ
School of Nursing: Soeur RENÉE GEOFFRAY

UNIVERSITÉ DE DOUALA
BP 2701, Douala
Telephone: 3340-6415
Fax: 3340-1134
E-mail: ud@camnet.com
Internet: www.cm.refer.org/edu/ram3/univers/udla/udla.htm
Founded 1977
State control
Languages of instruction: English, French
Academic year: October to July
Rector: Prof. MAURICE TCHUENTE
Deputy Rector: Prof. ROGER GABRIEL NLEP
Sec.-Gen.: THÉRÈSE WANGUE
Librarian: JEREMIE NSANGOU
Number of teachers: 140
Number of students: 6,500
Publications: *Arts Review* (1 a year), *Revue de Sciences Economiques et de Management* (4 a year), *Technologie et Développement* (every 2 years).

CONSTITUENT INSTITUTES

Ecole Normale Supérieure de l'Enseignement Technique: BP 1872, Douala; Dir Dr NDEH NTOMAMBANG NINGO.

Ecole Supérieure des Sciences Economiques et Commerciales: BP 1931, Douala; Dir Dr ROBERT BILONGO.

Faculté des Lettres et des Sciences Humaines: BP 3132, Douala; Dean Prof. SYLVESTRE BOUELET IVAHA.

Faculté des Sciences: BP 24157, Douala; Dean Prof. THÉOPHILE NGANDO MPONDO.

Faculté des Sciences Economiques et de Gestion Appliquée: BP 4032, Douala; Dean Prof. BLAISE MUKOKO.

Faculté des Sciences Juridiques et Politiques: BP 4982, Douala; Dean Dr LEKENE DONFACK.

Institut Universitaire de Technologie: BP 8698, Douala; Dir Dr AWONO ONANA.

UNIVERSITÉ DE DSCHANG

POB 96, Dschang
Telephone: 3345-1092
Fax: 3240-1134
Founded 1993
State control
Languages of instruction: English, French
Academic year: October to July
Rector: Prof. ANACLET FOMETHE
Vice-Rector for Inspection: Prof. LAURE PAULINE FOTSO
Vice-Rector for Research and Cooperation: Prof. JOHN MUCHO NGUNDAM
Vice-Rector for Teaching: Prof. ONGLA JEAN
Sec.-Gen.: Prof. MARTHE ISABELLE ATANGANA ABOLO
Librarian: DJIDERE VALÈRE
Number of teachers: 330
Number of students: 14,000
Publications: *Les Echos* (law and politics, 4 a year), *NKA* (arts and humanities, 2 a year), *Sciences et Développement* (agriculture, 2 a year)

DEANS

Faculty of Agronomy and Agricultural Sciences: Dr MANGELI YACOUBA
Faculty of Economics and Management Sciences: Prof. TAFAH EDOKAT OKI EDWARD
Faculty of Law and Political Science: Prof. FRANÇOIS ANOUKAHA
Faculty of Letters and Social Sciences: Prof. CHARLES ROBERT DIMI
Faculty of Sciences: Prof. PIERRE TANE
Fotso Victor Institute of Technology: MÉDARD FOGUE

UNIVERSITÉ DE NGAOUNDÉRÉ

BP 454, Ngaoundéré
Telephone: 2219-0195
Fax: 3333-0643
E-mail: rectorat_ngaoundere@yahoo.fr
Founded 1977, opened 1982, present name since 1993
State control
Accredited by Min.of Higher Education
Languages of instruction: English, French
Academic year: October to July
Rector: Prof. PAUL-HENRI AMVAM ZOLLO
Vice-Rector for Control and Internal Evaluation: Prof. DAVID BEKOLLÉ
Vice-Rector for Research and Cooperation and Relations with the Business World: Prof. JOSEPH G. KAYEM
Vice-Rector for Teaching, Professionalisation and Devt of Information Technology: Prof. BEDA TIBI
Sec.-Gen.: Prof. ANDRÉ TIENTCHEU NJIAKO
Library of 60,000 vols

Number of teachers: 300
Number of students: 16,000
Publications: *Annales de la Faculté des Arts, Lettres et Sciences Humaines* (1 a year), *Cahiers juridiques et politiques, Ngaoundéré-Anthropos* (social science review, 1 a year), *Revue de la Faculté des Sciences juridiques et politiques* (juridical and political science review, 1 a year)

DEANS

Faculty of Arts, Humanities and Social Sciences: Dr IYA MOUSSA
Faculty of Economics and Management Science: Prof. VICTOR TSAPI
Faculty of Laws and Political Science: Prof. ANDRÉ AKAM AKAM
Faculty of Science: Prof. ISMAIL NGOUNOUNO
Institute of Technology: Dr ALI AHMED
School of Agro-Industrial Sciences: Prof. CARL M. F. MBOFUNG (Dir)
School of Veterinary Medicine and Animal Science: Prof. ANDRÉ ZOLI PAGNAH

PROFESSORS

Faculty of Economics and Management Science:
  FEUDJO, J. R.
  TSAPI, V.
Faculty of Law and Political Science:
  AKAM AKAM, A.
  TIENTCHEU NJIAKO, A.
Faculty of Science:
  AMVAM ZOLLO, P.-H.
  BEKOLLÉ, D.
  LOURA BENGUELLA, B.
  MAPONGMETSEM, P. M.
  NGO BUM, E.
  NGOUNOUNO, I.
  OUMAROU, B.
  TCHUENGUEM FOHOUO, F. N.
School of Agro-Industrial Sciences:
  DZUDIE, T.
  KAMGA, R.
  KAPSEU, C.
  KAYEM, J.
  MBOFUNG, C. M. F.
  NGASSOUM, M. B.
  TCHIEGANG, C.

UNIVERSITÉ DE YAOUNDÉ I

BP 337, Centre Province, Yaoundé
Telephone: 2222-0744
Fax: 2223-5388
E-mail: cdc@uycdc.uninet.cm
Founded 1962
State control
Languages of instruction: English, French
Academic year: October to July
Rector: JEAN TABI-MANGA
Vice-Rector for Inspection: MAURICE AURÉLIEN SOSSO
Vice-Rector for Research and Cooperation: (vacant)
Vice-Rector for Teaching: MAURICE AURÉLIEN SOSSO
Sec.-Gen.: ELIE-CLAUDE NDJITOYAP NDAM
Librarian: ALEXIS EYANGO MOUEN
Library of 90,000 vols
Number of teachers: 929
Number of students: 20,343
Publications: *Annales de la Faculté des Lettres*, *Annales de la Faculté des Sciences*, *Sosongo* (Cameroon review of the arts, annual), *Syllabus* (review of the Ecole Normale Supérieure)

DEANS

Faculty of Arts: Prof. EMMANUEL GWAN ACHU
Faculty of Medicine and Biomedical Science: Prof. AMOUGOU AKOA

Faculty of Sciences: Prof. MAURICE A. SOSSO

FACULTIES AND DEPARTMENTS

Faculty of Arts (POB 755, Yaoundé; Depts of African languages and linguistics, art and archaeology, English, foreign languages, literature and civilization, French, geography, German, history, Negro-African literature, philosophy, psychology, sociology, Spanish).
Faculty of Medicine and Biomedical Science (POB 8290, Yaoundé; tel. 2223-1226; fax 2223-1841; Depts of anatomy and pathology, biomedical sciences, clinical sciences, gynaecology and obstetrics, internal medicine, medical imagery and radiotherapy, ophthalmology, paediatrics, public health, physiology, stomatology, surgery).
Faculty of Science (POB 812, Yaoundé; tel. 2223-5660; Depts of animal biology and physiology, biochemistry, computer science, earth sciences, inorganic chemistry, mathematics, organic chemistry, physics, plant biology and physiology).
Ecole Normale Supérieure (POB 47, Yaoundé; tel. 2222-4934; fax 2222-0913; Depts of biology, chemistry, education, English, French, history and geography, languages, mathematics, philosophy, physics).
Ecole Nationale Supérieure Polytechnique (POB 8290, Yaoundé; tel. 2223-1226; fax 2223-1841; Depts of civil engineering and town planning, computer engineering, electrical engineering, mathematics, physics and chemistry).

UNIVERSITÉ DE YAOUNDÉ II

POB 18, Soa
Telephone: 7220-1154
Fax: 7799-1423
E-mail: info@univ-yde2.org
Internet: www.univ-yde2.org
Founded 1993
State control
Academic year: October to July
Rector: Prof. JEAN TABI MANGA
Vice-Rector for Academic Affairs: Prof. PAUL GÉRARD POUGOUÉ
Vice-Rector for Inspection: Prof. PIERRE OWONA ATEBA
Vice-Rector for Research and Cooperation: Prof. ADOLPHE MINKOA SHE
Sec.-Gen.: Dr LISETTE ELOMO NTONGA (acting)
Number of teachers: 271
Number of students: 13,768
Publications: *African Review of Political Strategy* (1 a year), *Cameroon Review of International Relations* (2 a year), *Fréquence Sud* (2 a year), *Les Cahiers de l'IFORD* (52 a year), *Revue Africaine des Sciences Economiques et de Gestion* (2 a year), *Revue Africaine des Sciences Juridiques* (2 a year)

DEANS

Faculty of Economics and Management: Prof. GEORGES KOBOU
Faculty of Law and Political Science: Prof. VICTOR-EMMANUEL BOKALLI

PROFESSORS

Faculty of Economics and Management:
  BEKOLO, E. B.
  GANKOU, J. M.
  NDJIEUNDE, G.
  TOUNA, M.
Faculty of Law and Political Science:
  ALETUM, M. T.
  ANOUKAHA, F.
  KONTCHOU, K. A.
  MINKOA, S. A.
  NGWAFOR, E. N.
  NTAMARK, P. Y.

OWONA, J.
POUGOUE, P. G.

Advanced School of Mass Communication:
BOYOMO, A. L. C.
CHINJI, K. F.
FAME, N.

International Relations Institute of Cameroon:
OYONO, D.

ATTACHED INSTITUTES

Centre for Study and Research in Economics and Management: tel. 2223-7389; fax 2223-7912; Coordinator Assoc. Prof. SÉRAPHIN FOUDA.

Centre for Study and Research in International Community Law: tel. 2221-4234; fax 2231-3509; Coordinator Assoc. Prof. MAURICE KAMTO.

Colleges

Ecole Nationale d'Administration et de Magistrature: BP 7171, Yaoundé; tel. 2223-1308; f. 1959; training for public admin.; library: 11,000 vols; 85 teachers (10 full-time, 75 part-time); 1,063 students; Dir. V. MOUTTAPA.

Institut d'Administration des Entreprises: BP 337, Yaoundé; 150 students; Dir G. NDJIEUNDE.

CANADA

The Higher Education System

Under legislation passed in 1982, the 10 provinces and three territories enjoy autonomy over higher education; however, the Council of Ministers of Education Canada was created by the provincial and territorial ministers of education to take collective decisions in the national interest. The Association of Universities and Colleges of Canada (AUCC) is the national organization of university executive heads. There are over 200 public and private institutes authorized to offer degrees. Most are conferred by universities and their affiliated and federated institutions, as well as by colleges of applied science and technology. Conservatories and some community colleges are also authorized to offer degrees. There are 113 university-level institutions in the 10 Canadian provinces, 90 of which are public universities and 23 are university colleges federated or affiliated with another university. There are no universities in Canada's three territories. In 2006/07 an estimated 1,059,912 students were enrolled in post-secondary education (not including the Northwest Territories, Nunavut Territory and Yukon Territory). The official languages of Canada are French and English, but English is the language of instruction in most universities except in the province of Québec, where French is used.

The standard administrative structure for a university consists of two governing bodies, a Board of Governors or Regents and a Senate or Academic Council. In addition, a Vice-Chancellor, President, Principal or Rector is responsible for administrative and academic management. Higher education funding varies according to the province or territory in question. The only consistent admissions criteria for university include possession of the secondary school equivalent or, in Québec, the Collège d'enseignement général et professionnel (CEGEP); otherwise, universities are free to set their own criteria.

Though there may be provincial or territorial peculiarities, the university degree system conforms to the Bachelors/Masters/Doctorate schema. The Bachelors (Baccalaureat in Québecois) is a three- to four-year programme the format of which varies from institution to institution, with some following the US-style credits system. Some Bachelors programmes include an element of research and are known as Honours. Following Bachelors are Masters (Maîtrise) programmes of two years, which fall into two classifications: Taught and Research. Finally, the qualification Doctor of Philosophy (PhD, or Philosophiae Doctor) requires three- to five-years' study following the Masters.

Post-secondary technical and vocational education is provided by community and professional colleges; the most common qualifications are the Certificate and Diploma, the latter requiring two- to three-years' study.

There is no central system of accreditation for post-secondary institutions in Canada, only for certain programmes within these institutions. However, procedures and regulations are in place in each province and territory that provide ongoing assessment of the overall quality equivalent to 'accreditation' as it is commonly understood. The Canadian Education and Training Accreditation Commission (CETAC) provides a voluntary system of non-governmental self-regulation of Canada's private post-secondary institutions. There is also the Association of Accrediting Agencies of Canada which provides a national network of professional education accrediting bodies.

Regulatory and Representative Bodies

GOVERNMENT

Council of Ministers of Education, Canada/Conseil des Ministres de l'Éducation (Canada) (CMEC): Suite 1106, 95 St Clair Ave W, Toronto, ON M4V 1N6; tel. (416) 962-8100; fax (416) 962-2800; e-mail info@cmec.ca; internet www.cmec.ca; f. 1967; intergovernmental body of which all 13 provinces and territories are mems; forum to discuss policy issues; mechanism through which to undertake activities, projects and initiatives in areas of mutual interest; means by which to consult and cooperate with nat. education orgs and the federal govt; instrument to represent the education interests of the provinces and territories internationally; provides leadership in education at the pan-Canadian and int. levels and contributes to the fulfilment of the constitutional responsibility for education conferred on provinces and territories; governed by an Agreed Memorandum approved by all mems; current funding C$7.5m. per year, of which provinces and territories provide C$5.7m. through base amount, calculated according to the population of each province and territory, and additional amounts for specific projects and initiatives; Chair. KELLY LAMROCK.

National Research Council Canada: Bldg M58, 1200 Montréal Rd, Ottawa, ON K1A 0R6; tel. (613) 993-9101; fax (613) 952-9907; e-mail info@nrc-cnrc.gc.ca; internet www.nrc.ca; f. 1916; carries out research and devt in engineering, information technology, life sciences, physical sciences, technology and industry support; Pres. Dr PIERRE COLOUMBE; Sec.-Gen. MARIELLE PICHÉ.

ACCREDITATION

Association of Accrediting Agencies of Canada/Association des Agences d'Agrément du Canada: POB 370, 1-247 Barr St, Renfrew, ON K7V 1J6; tel. (613) 432-9491; fax (613) 432-6840; e-mail info@aaac.ca; internet www.aaac.ca; f. 1994; pursues excellence in standards and processes of accreditation to foster the highest quality of professional education; 35 mems; Chair. MARLENE WYATT.

Canadian Education and Training Accreditation Commission (CETAC): Suite 101, 267 Adelaide St W, Toronto, ON M5H 1Y3; tel. (416) 875-8629; fax (416) 977-5612; e-mail info@accreditations.ca; internet www.accreditations.ca; f. 1984; responsible for institutional accreditation of private post-secondary institutions in Canada; provides nat. accrediting service with established nat. standards; Nat. Commissioner BILL RICHES; Nat. Commissioner CAROL LOWTHERS; Nat. Commissioner CHRISTOPHER HOPE; Nat. Commissioner FRANK T. MIOSI; Nat. Commissioner F. RICK KLEIMAN; Nat. Commissioner MICHAEL BARRETT; Nat. Commissioner MONIKA OEPKES; Nat. Commissioner NELLIE BURKE; Nat. Commissioner ROSEMARY BOYD.

Canadian Information Centre for International Credentials (CICIC): Canadian ENIC, 95 St Clair Ave W, Suite 1106, Toronto ON M4V 1N6; tel. (416) 962-9725; fax (416) 962-2800; e-mail info@cicic.ca; internet www.cicic.ca; f. 1990; unit of the Ccl of Mins. of Education, Canada (CMEC); collects, organizes, and distributes information; acts as a nat. clearing house and referral service to support the recognition of Canadian and int. educational and occupational qualifications; promotes int. mobility by advocating wider recognition of higher education and professional qualifications; Nat. Coordinator YVES BEAUDIN; Admin. Officer NOELLINE IP YAM; Project Man. ERIC SCHVARTZ.

NATIONAL BODIES

Association of Atlantic Universities/Association des Universités de l'Atlantique: Suite 403, 5657 Spring Garden Rd, Halifax, NS B3J 3R4; tel. (902) 425-4230; fax (902) 425-4233; e-mail info@atlanticuniversities.ca; internet www.atlanticuniversities.ca; f. 1964; 17 univs in the Atlantic region of Canada and in the W Indies, which offer programmes leading to a degree or have degree-granting status; Exec. Dir PETER HALPIN; Dir of Operations CORINA KENT.

Association of Canadian Community Colleges/Association des Collèges Communautaires du Canada (ACCC): Suite 200, 1223 Michael St N, Ottawa, ON K1J 7T2; tel. (613) 746-2222; fax (613) 746-6721; e-mail info@accc.ca; internet www.accc.ca; f. 1972; nat. voluntary membership org. to represent colleges and institutes to govt, business and industry, both in Canada and worldwide; interacts with fed. depts and agencies on the mems' behalf; links college capabilities to nat. industries; organizes confs and workshops for college staff, students and board mems to facilitate networking and participation in nat. and int. activities such as sector studies, awards programmes and linkages; Pres. and CEO JAMES KNIGHT.

Association of Registrars of the Universities and Colleges of Canada (ARUCC)/ Association des Registraires des Universités et Collèges du Canada: c/o France Myette, Sec. Treas., ARUCC, Univ. de Sherbrooke, 2500 Blvd de l'Université, Sherbrooke QC J1K 2R1; tel. (819) 821-7685; fax (819) 821-7966; e-mail france.myette@usherbrooke.ca; internet www.arucc.unb.ca; f. 1964; approx. 182 mem. instns; mems incl. registrars, admission dirs, student records managers, student services managers and other personnel in the areas of student advice and counselling, student financial aid and student placement; Pres. DAVID HINTON.

Association of Universities and Colleges of Canada (AUCC): 350 Albert St (Suite 600), Ottawa, ON K1R 1B1; tel. (613) 563-1236; fax (613) 563-9745; e-mail info@aucc.ca; internet www.aucc.ca; f. 1911; represents Canadian public and private, not-for-profit univs and univ.-degree level colleges; 95 univ. mems; Pres. and CEO PAUL DAVIDSON; Chair. STEPHEN J. TOOPE.

Canadian Bureau for International Education/Bureau Canadien de l'Education Internationale: 220 Laurier Ave W, Suite 1550, Ottawa, ON K1P 5Z9; tel. (613) 237-4820; fax (613) 237-1073; e-mail info@cbie.ca; internet www.cbie.ca; f. 1966; promotes int. devt and inter-cultural understanding through a broad range of educational activities in Canada and abroad; 3 divs: research, devt and membership, scholarships and awards, centre for central and Eastern Europe; library of 300 vols and journals; 120 institutional mems; Chair. Dr ROBERT MCCULLOCH; publ. *E-Internationalist* (irregular).

Canadian Network for Innovation in Education (CNIE)/Réseau Canadien pour l'Innovation en Education (RCIE): Suite 204, 260 Dalhousie St, Ottawa, ON K1N 7E4; tel. (613) 241-0018; fax (613) 241-0019; e-mail cnie-rcie@cnie-rcie.ca; internet www.cnie-rcie.ca; f. 2007; nat. org. of professionals committed to excellence in the provision of the use of innovation in education in Canada; holds annual conf; Pres. LORRAINE CARTER; Dir of Admin. TIM HOWARD; publs *Canadian Journal of Learning and Technology* (3 a year), *Journal of Distance Education* (3 a year).

Learned Societies

GENERAL

Académie des Lettres du Québec: CP 8888, Succursale Centre-ville, Montréal, QC H3C 3P8; tel. (514) 987-3000; fax (514) 987-8484; e-mail secretariat@academiedeslettresduquebec.ca; internet academiedeslettresduquebec.ca; f. 1944 (fmrly Académie canadienne-française) for the promotion of the French language and culture in Canada; 42 chairs; 38 mems; Pres. JACQUES ALLARD; publ. *Les Ecrits* (3 a year).

Canadian Council for International Co-operation/Conseil Canadien pour la Coopération Internationale: 1 Nicholas St, Suite 300, Ottawa, ON K1N 7B7; tel. (613) 247-7007; fax (613) 241-5302; internet www.ccic.ca; f. 1968 (fmrly Overseas Institute of Canada, f. 1961); coordination centre for voluntary agencies working in int. devt; 115 mems; Chair. JEAN-PIERRE MASSÉ; publs *Directory of Canadian NGOs, Newsletter* (6 a year).

Royal Canadian Academy of Arts: 401 Richmond St West (Suite 375), Toronto, ON M5V 3A8; tel. (416) 408-2718; fax (416) 408-2286; e-mail rcaarts@interlog.com; internet www.rca-arc.ca; f. 1880; visual arts; Pres. ALISON HYMAS.

Royal Canadian Institute for the Advancement of Science: 700 University Ave, H7-D, Toronto, ON M5G 1X6; tel. (416) 977-2983; fax (416) 962-7314; internet www.royalcanadianinstitute.org; f. 1849; promotes knowledge of science; 600 mems; Pres. BRUCE GITELMAN; Sec. DUNCAN JONES; Treas. JOHN GRANT.

Royal Society of Canada: 170 Waller St, Ottawa, ON K1N 9B9; tel. (613) 991-6990; fax (613) 991-6996; e-mail info@rsc.ca; internet www.rsc.ca; f. 1882; 1,800 fellows; academies of Arts (I), Humanities (II) and Science (III); Pres. YVAN GUINDON; Hon. Sec. ROBERT MAJOR; publs *RSC News* (3 a year), *Présentations* (1 a year), *Proceedings* (1 a year).

AGRICULTURE, FISHERIES AND VETERINARY SCIENCE

Agricultural Institute of Canada: Suite 900, 280 Albert St, Ottawa, ON K1P 5G8; tel. (613) 232-9459; fax (613) 594-5190; internet www.aic.ca; f. 1920 to organize and unite all workers in scientific and technical agriculture and to serve as a medium where progressive ideas for improvements in agricultural education, investigation, publicity and extension work can be discussed and recommended for adoption; represents 6,500 scientists and agrologists; publs *Canadian Journal of Animal Science* (4 a year), *Canadian Journal of Plant Science* (4 a year), *Canadian Journal of Soil Science* (4 a year).

Canadian Forestry Association: 185 Somerset St West, Suite 203, Ottawa, ON K2P 0J2; tel. (613) 232-1815; fax (613) 232-4210; e-mail cfa@canadianforestry.com; internet www.canadianforestry.com; f. 1900; conservation org. providing educational materials and programmes to raise awareness of the wise use of forest, wildlife and water resources; 354 mems; Pres. BARRY WAITO; General Manager DAVE LEMKAY.

Canadian Society of Animal Science: Suite 900, 280 Albert St, Ottawa, ON K1P 5G8; tel. (613) 232-9459; fax (613) 594-5190; internet www.csas.net; part of the Agricultural Institute of Canada (*q.v.*); f. 1925 to provide opportunities for discussion of problems, improvement and coordination of research, extension and teaching and to encourage publication of scientific and educational material relating to animal and poultry industries; holds annual meetings, produces occasional papers and presents awards to members; 550 mems; Pres. DUANE MCCARTNEY; Sec.-Treas. CHRISTIANE GIRARD; publs *Canadian Journal of Animal Science* (4 a year), *CSAS Newsletter* (4 a year, mems only).

Canadian Veterinary Medical Association/Association Canadienne des Médecins Vétérinaires: 339 Booth St, Ottawa, ON K1R 7K1; tel. (613) 236-1162; fax (613) 236-9681; e-mail kallen@cvma-acmv.org; internet www.cvma-acmv.org; f. 1948; 4,000 mems; publs *Canadian Journal of Veterinary Research* (4 a year), *Canadian Veterinary Journal* (12 a year).

ARCHITECTURE AND TOWN PLANNING

Canadian Society of Landscape Architects/Association des Architectes Paysagistes du Canada: POB 13594, Ottawa, ON K2K 1X6; tel. (613) 622-5520; fax (613) 622-5870; e-mail info@csla.ca; internet www.csla.ca; f. 1934; 1,100 mems, a federation of seven component asscns; Exec. Dir FRAN PAUZÉ; publs *Bulletin* (6 a year), *Landscapes/Paysages* (4 a year).

Royal Architectural Institute of Canada: 55 Murray St, Suite 330, Ottawa, ON K1N 5M3; tel. (613) 241-3600; fax (613) 241-5750; e-mail info@raic.org; internet www.raic.org; f. 1908; 3,500 mems; Pres. CHRIS FILLINGHAM; Exec. Dir JON F. HOBBS; publs *Bulletin* (online, 12 a year), *Update/En Bref* (4 a year).

BIBLIOGRAPHY, LIBRARY SCIENCE AND MUSEOLOGY

ASTED (Association pour l'Avancement des Sciences et des Techniques de la Documentation) Inc. (Association for the advancement of documentation sciences and techniques): 2065 rue Parthenais, Bureau 387, Montréal, QC H2X 3T1; tel. (514) 281-5012; fax (514) 281-8219; e-mail info@asted.org; internet www.asted.org; f. 1973; a professional organization of libraries, librarians and library technicians; 500 mems; Pres. SYLVIE THIBAULT (acting); Exec. Dir FRANCIS FARLEY-CHEVRIER (acting); publs *Documentation et bibliothèques* (4 a year), *Nouvelles de l'ASTED* (online only).

Bibliographical Society of Canada: POB 575, Postal Station P, Toronto, ON M5S 2T1; e-mail secretary@bsc-sbc.ca; internet www.bsc-sbc.ca/en/bschome.html; f. 1946; 300 mems; Pres. ANNE DONDERTMAN; Sec. GRETA GOLICK; publs *Bulletin* (2 a year), *Papers/Cahiers* (2 a year).

Canadian Association of Law Libraries: POB 1570, Kingston, ON K7L 5C8; tel. (613) 531-9338; fax (613) 531-0626; e-mail office@callacbd.ca; internet www.callacbd.ca; f. 1961 to promote law librarianship, to develop and increase the usefulness of Canadian law libraries, and to foster a spirit of cooperation among them, to provide a forum for meetings and to cooperate with other similar orgs; 500 mems; Pres. JANINE MILLER; Administrative Officer ELIZABETH HOOPER; publs *CALL Newsletter* (5 a year), *Canadian Law Library* (5 a year).

Canadian Library Association: 328 Frank St, Ottawa, ON K2P 0X8; tel. (613) 232-9625; fax (613) 563-9895; e-mail info@cla.ca; internet www.cla.ca; f. 1946; 3,000 mems; Pres. STEPHEN ABRAM; Exec. Dir DON BUTCHER.

Canadian Museums Association/Association des Musées Canadiens: 280 Metcalfe, Suite 400, Ottawa, ON K2P 1R7; tel. (613) 567-0099; fax (613) 233-5438; e-mail info@museums.ca; internet www.museums.ca; f. 1947; advancement of public museums and art galleries services in Canada; 2,000 mems; Exec. Dir JOHN G. MCAVITY; publ. *Muse* (6 a year).

ECONOMICS, LAW AND POLITICS

Canadian Bar Association: 500–865 Carling Ave, Ottawa, ON K1S 5S8; tel. (613) 237-1988; fax (613) 237-0185; e-mail info@cba.org; internet www.cba.org; f. 1914; promotes admin. of justice and uniformity of legislation; also promotes a high standard of legal education, training and ethics; 38,000 mems; Pres. ROD SNOW; Exec. Dir JOHN HOYLES; Treas. ANNETTE HORST; publs *The Canadian Bar Review, The National*.

Canadian Economics Association: c/o Frances Woolley, Dept of Economics, Carleton Univ., 1125 Colonel By Dr., Ottawa, ON K1S 5B6; e-mail frances_woolley@carleton .ca; internet www.economics.ca; f. 1967; non-partisan asscn promoting the advancement of economic knowledge through the encouragement of study and research, the issuing of publs and the furtherance of free and informed discussion of economic questions; 1,400 mems; Pres. GERARD GAUDET; Sec.-Treas. FRANCES WOOLLEY; publs *Canadian Journal of Economics/Revue Canadienne d'Economique, Canadian Public Policy/Analyse de Politique*.

Canadian Institute of Chartered Accountants: 277 Wellington St W, Toronto, ON M5V 3H2; tel. (416) 977-3222; fax (416) 977-8585; internet www.cica.ca; f. 1902; professional and examining body; 70,000 mems; Chair. ALAIN BENEDETT; Pres. and CEO KEVIN J. DANCEY; publ. *CA Magazine* (12 a year).

Canadian Institute of International Affairs: Suite 302, 205 Richmond St W, Toronto, ON M5V 1V3; tel. (416) 977-9000; fax (416) 977-7521; e-mail mailbox@ciia.org; internet www.ciia.org; f. 1928; 1,400 mems in 15 brs; library of 8,000 vols; Chair. The Hon. ROY MACLAREN; Pres. and CEO DOUGLAS GOOLD; publs *Behind the Headlines, International Journal* (4 a year), *Canadian Foreign Relations Index* (CD-ROM, 1 a year; online, 12 a year).

Canadian Political Science Association/Association Canadienne de Science Politique: 260 Dalhousie St, Suite 204, Ottawa, ON K1N 7E4; tel. (613) 562-1202; fax (613) 241-0019; e-mail cpsa-acsp@cpsa-acsp.ca; internet www.cpsa-acsp.ca; f. 1913; organizes annual conf.; awards prizes; runs the Parliamentary Internship Programme and Ontario Legislative Internship Programme; 1,500 mems; Administrator MICHELLE HOPKINS; publ. *Canadian Journal of Political Science/Revue canadienne de science politique* (4 a year).

EDUCATION

Canadian Education Association/Association Canadienne d'Education: 119 Spadina Ave, Suite 705, Toronto, ON M5V 2LI; tel. (416) 591-6300; fax (416) 591-5345; e-mail info@cea-ace.ca; internet www.cea-ace .ca; f. 1891; 300 mems; Chair. CAROLE OLSEN; Vice-Chair. LYNNE ZUCKER; CEO PENNY MILTON; publs *Bulletin* (11 a year), *CEA Handbook/Ki-es-Ki* (1 a year), *Education Canada* (5 a year).

Canadian Society for the Study of Education: Suite 204, 260 Dalhousie St, Ottawa, ON K1N 7E4; tel. (613) 241-0018; fax (613) 241-0019; e-mail csse-scee@csse.ca; internet www.csse-scee.ca; f. 1972; holds annual conf.; promotes educational research; 1,000 mems; Dir of Admin. TIM G. HOWARD; publ. *Canadian Journal of Education* (4 a year).

FINE AND PERFORMING ARTS

Canada Council for the Arts/Conseil des Arts du Canada: POB 1047, 350 Albert St, Ottawa, ON K1P 5V8; tel. (613) 566-4365; fax (613) 566-4390; internet www.canadacouncil .ca; f. 1957; the Council provides grants and services to professional Canadian artists and arts orgs; maintains secretariat for Canadian Commission for UNESCO; administers Public Lending Right Comm. and Canada Council Art Bank; administers Killam Program of prizes and fellowships to Canadian research scholars, and recognizes achievement through a number of prizes, incl.Governor General's Literary Awards, Molson Prizes and Glenn Gould Prize; 90% state-funded; 11

mems; Chair. JOSEPH L. ROTMAN; Vice-Chair. SIMON BRAULT; Dir ROBERT SIRMAN.

Canadian Film Institute: 2 Daly Ave, Suite 120, Ottawa, ON K1N 6E2; tel. (613) 232-6727; fax (613) 232-6315; f. 1935 to encourage and promote the study, appreciation and use of motion pictures and television in Canada; division of Cinémathèque Canada; operates CFI Film Library, renting 6,500 educational films and video cassettes; cinema; Canadian Centre for Films on Art; hosts Ottawa International Animation Festival; Dir TOM MCSORLEY.

Canadian Music Centre (Centre de Musique Canadienne): 20 St Joseph St, Toronto, ON M4Y 1J9; tel. (416) 961-6601; fax (416) 961-7198; e-mail info@musiccentre.ca; internet www.musiccentre.ca; f. 1959; 700 mems; library of 20,000 vols, 15,000 scores; for the collection and promotion, in Canada and abroad, of music by contemporary Canadian composers; produces Canadian concert recordings (Centrediscs); Exec. Dir ELISABETH BIHL.

Sculptors' Society of Canada: c/o Studio 204, 60 Atlantic Ave, Toronto, ON M6K 1X9; 500 Church St, Toronto, ON M4Y 2C8; tel. (647) 435-5858; e-mail gallery@cansculpt .org; internet www.sculptorssocietyofcanada .org; f. 1928; Pres. JUDI MICHELLE YOUNG; Vice-Pres. RICHARD MCNEILL; Treas. ALEX TAVARES.

Society of Composers, Authors and Music Publishers of Canada (SOCAN): 41 Valleybrook Drive, Toronto, ON M3B 2S6; tel. (416) 445-8700; fax (416) 445-7108; e-mail socan@socan.ca; internet www.socan .ca; f. 1990; copyright collective for the communication and performance of musical works; licenses music in Canada; distributes royalties to its members for the use of their music overseas; offices in Dartmouth, Edmonton, Toronto, Montréal, Vancouver, Toronto; 80,000 mems; Pres. PIERRE-DANIEL RHEAULT; publs *Music Means Business/Le Rhytme de vos Affaires* (2 a year), *Words & Music/Paroles & Musique* (4 a year).

Visual Arts Ontario: 1153A Queen St West, Toronto, ON M6J 1J4; tel. (416) 591-8883; fax (416) 591-2432; e-mail info@vao.org; internet www.vao.org; f. 1973; federation of professional artists; 3,600 mems; Exec. Dir HENNIE L. WOLFF; publs *Agenda* (4 a year), *Hidden Agenda* (8 a year).

HISTORY, GEOGRAPHY AND ARCHAEOLOGY

Canadian Association of Geographers: Dept of Geography, McGill Univ., 425-805 Sherbrooke St W, Montréal, QC H3A 2K6; tel. (514) 398-4946; fax (514) 398-7437; e-mail cag@geog.mcgill.ca; internet www .cag-acg.ca; f. 1951; 800 mems; Pres. CHRIS SHARPE; Sec.-Treas. ALAN NASH; publs *The CAG Newsletter* (6 a year), *The Canadian Geographer* (4 a year), *The Directory* (1 a year).

Canadian Historical Association/Société Historique du Canada: 501–130 Albert St, Ottawa, ON K1P 5G4; tel. (613) 233-7885; fax (613) 567-3110; e-mail cha-shc@cha-shc .ca; internet www.cha-shc.ca; f. 1922; 1,200 mems; promotes historical research and public interest in history; annual meeting awards; prizes affiliated committees advocacy; Exec. Dir Dr MICHEL DUQUET; publs *Bulletin* (3 a year), *Canada's Ethnic Groups* (2 a year), *Journal of the CHA/Revue de la SHC* (2 a year), *Register of Dissertations/Répertoire des thèses* (online), *Short Book Series* (2 a year).

Château Ramezay Museum/Musée du Château Ramezay: 280 Notre Dame E,

Old Montréal, QC H2Y 1C5; tel. (514) 861-3708; fax (514) 861-8317; e-mail info@ chateauramezay.qc.ca; internet www .chateauramezay.qc.ca; f. 1895; 250 mems; library of 8,000 books; Dir ANDRÉ J. DELISLE; Sec. SUZANNE LALUMIÈRE; publ. *La Lettre de Ramezay* (Ramezay Letter, 3 a year).

Genealogical Association of Nova Scotia: 3045 Robie St, Suite 222, Halifax, NS B3K 4P6; tel. (902) 454-0322; e-mail gans@ chebucto.ns.ca; internet www.chebucto.ns .ca/recreation/gans; f. 1982; 1,000 mems; Pres. JANICE FRALIC-BROWN; publ. *The Nova Scotia Genealogist* (3 a year).

Genealogical Institute of the Maritimes (Institut Généalogique des Provinces Maritimes): POB 36022, Canada Post Postal Office, 5675 Spring Garden Rd, Halifax, NS B3J 1G0; internet nsgna.ednet.ns.ca/gim; f. 1983; education and research in genealogy; offers certification and registration of individuals undertaking genealogical research for the public; 44 mems.

Institut d'Histoire de l'Amérique Française: 261 Bloomfield Ave, Montréal, QC H2V 3R6; tel. (514) 278-2232; fax (514) 271-6369; e-mail ihaf@ihaf.qc.ca; internet www .ihaf.qc.ca; f. 1946; 1,000 mems; Pres. Prof. ALAIN BEAULIEU; Sec. Prof. BRIGITTE CAULIER; publ. *Revue d'histoire de l'Amérique française* (4 a year).

Ontario Historical Society: 34 Parkview Ave, Willowdale, ON M2N 3Y2; tel. (416) 226-9011; fax (416) 226-2740; e-mail ohs@ ontariohistoricalsociety.ca; internet www .ontariohistoricalsociety.ca; f. 1888; 300 affiliated societies; 3,000 mems; Exec. Dir PATRICIA K. NEAL; publs *OHS Bulletin* (5 a year), *Ontario History* (2 a year).

Royal Canadian Geographical Society: 1155 Lola St, Suite 200, Ottawa ON K1K 4C1; tel. (613) 745-4629; fax (613) 744-0947; e-mail rcgs@rcgs.org; internet www.rcgs.org; f. 1929; 204,000 mems; Pres. JOHN GEIGER; publ. *Canadian Geographic* (10 a year).

Royal Nova Scotia Historical Society: POB 2622, Halifax, NS B3J 3P7; internet nsgna.ednet.ns.ca/rnshs/; f. 1878; history, biography, social studies of provincial past; 350 mems; Pres. JUDITH FINGARD; Sec. R. BARBOUR; publs *Collections* (irregular), *Journal* (1 a year).

Société Généalogique Canadienne Française: 3440 rue Davidson, Montréal, QC H1W 2Z5; tel. (514) 527-1010; fax (514) 527-0265; e-mail info@sgcf.com; internet www .sgcf.com; f. 1943; studies and publications on the origins and history of French Canadian families since 1615; 3,400 mems; library of 21,300 books, 3m. cards on marriages, 4,500 microfilms; Pres. GISÈLE MONARQUE; Dir-Gen. MICHELINE PERREAULT; publ. *Mémoires* (4 a year).

Waterloo Historical Society: c/o Kitchener Public Library, 85 Queen St N, Kitchener, ON N2H 2H1; tel. (519) 743-0271 ext. 252; fax (519) 743-1261; e-mail whs@whs.ca; internet www.whs.ca; f. 1912; local history; colln at Kitchener Public Library; 275 mems; Sec. JOHN ARNDT.

LANGUAGE AND LITERATURE

Alliance Française: 352 MacLaren St, Ottawa, ON K2P 0M6; tel. (613) 234-9470; fax (613) 233-1559; internet www.af.ca; offers courses and examinations in French language and culture and promotes cultural exchange with France; attached offices in Calgary, Edmonton, Halifax, Mississauga, Moncton, North York, Regina, Saskatoon, Toronto, Vancouver, Victoria and Winnipeg; Dir ALAIN LANDRY.

British Council: British High Commission, 80 Elgin St, Ottawa, ON K1P 5K7; tel. (514) 886-5863; e-mail education.enquiries@ca .britishcouncil.org; internet www .britishcouncil.org/canada; promotes education in and cultural exchange with the UK; attached office in Montréal; Dir LILIANA BIGLOU.

Canadian Authors Association: Box 419, Campbellford, ON K0L 1L0; tel. (705) 653-0323; fax (705) 653-0593; e-mail admin@ canauthors.org; internet www.canauthors .org; f. 1921; 600 mems; administers awards; annual conference; workshops and seminars; Pres. JOAN EYOLFSON CADHAM; publ. *The Canadian Writer's Guide* (irregular).

Goethe-Institut: 418 Sherbrooke Est, Montréal, QC H2L 1J6; tel. (514) 499-0159; fax (514) 499-0905; e-mail info@montreal.goethe .org; internet www.goethe.de/montreal; f. 1962; offers courses and examinations in German language and culture and promotes cultural exchange with Germany; attached centres in Ottawa; library of 7,000 vols, 20 periodicals, incl. German newspapers, magazines, CDs and DVDs; Dir MECHTILD MANUS.

PEN Canada: 24 Ryerson Ave, Suite 301, Toronto, ON M5T 2P3; tel. (416) 703-8448; fax (416) 703-3870; e-mail pen@pencanada .ca; f. 1982; international literary association; 125 mems; Pres. ELLEN SELIGMAN; Vice-Pres. CHARLES FORAN.

MEDICINE

Academy of Medicine: c/o Library and Information Services, Univ. Health Network, Toronto General Hospital, 200 Elizabeth St, EN1-418, Toronto, ON M5G 2C4; tel. (416) 340-3259; fax (416) 340-4384; f. 1907; history of medicine; Librarian MARGARET ALIHARAN.

Canadian Association for Anatomy, Neurobiology and Cell Biology/Association Canadienne d'Anatomie, de Neurobiologie et de Biologie Cellulaire: c/o Dr MICHAEL KAWAJA, Dept of Anatomy and Cell Biology, Queen's University, Kingston, ON K7L 3N6; tel. (613) 533-2864; fax (613) 533-2566; e-mail kawajam@post.queensu.ca; f. 1956; 147 mems; Pres. Dr RIC DEVON; Sec. Dr MICHAEL KAWAJA; publ. *The Bulletin* (1 a year).

Canadian Association of Optometrists: 234 Argyle Ave, Ottawa, ON K2P 1B9; tel. (613) 235-7924; fax (613) 235-2025; e-mail info@opto.ca; internet www.opto.ca; f. 1948; Pres. Dr KIRSTEN NORTH; Dir-Gen. GLENN CAMPBELL; Sec.-Treasurer Dr PAUL GENEAU; publ. *The Canadian Journal of Optometry/ La Revue Canadienne d'Optométrie* (4 a year).

Canadian Dental Association: 1815 Alta Vista Drive, Ottawa, ON K1G 3Y6; tel. (613) 523-1770; fax (613) 523-7736; e-mail reception@cda-adc.ca; internet www.cda-adc .ca; f. 1902; Pres. Dr LOUIS DUBÉ; publs *Communiqué* (6 a year), *Journal* (11 a year).

Canadian Lung Association: 3 Raymond St, Suite 300, Ottawa, ON K1R 1A3; tel. (613) 569-6411; fax (613) 569-8860; e-mail info@lung.ca; internet www.lung.ca; f. 1900; 10 provincial member associations (Alberta, British Columbia, Québec, Nova Scotia, Saskatchewan, Manitoba, New Brunswick, Newfoundland and Labrador, Ontario, Prince Edward Island), 1 territorial association (North West Territories); associated professional societies: Canadian Thoracic Society, Canadian Physiotherapy Cardio-Respiratory Society, Canadian Nurses' Respiratory Society, Respiratory Therapy Society; publ. *Canadian Respiratory Journal* (8 a year).

Canadian Medical Association: 1867 Alta Vista Drive, Ottawa, ON K1G 3Y6; fax (613) 236-8864; e-mail pubs@cma.ca; internet www .cma.ca; f. 1867; 60,000 mems; Pres. Dr COLIN MACMILLAN; Sec.-Gen. WILLIAM THOLL; Hon. Treas. Dr JOHN RAPIN; publs *Canadian Association of Radiologists Journal* (6 a year), *Canadian Journal of Emergency Medicine* (4 a year), *Canadian Journal of Rural Medicine* (4 a year), *Canadian Journal of Surgery* (6 a year), *Canadian Medical Association Bulletin* (26 a year), *Canadian Medical Association Journal—CMAJ* (25 a year), *Health Care News* (12 a year), *Journal of Psychiatry and Neuroscience* (5 a year), *Strategy Magazine*.

Canadian Paediatric Society (Société Canadienne de Pédiatrie): 100–2204 Walkley Rd, Ottawa, ON K1G 4G8; tel. (613) 526-9397; fax (613) 526-3332; e-mail info@cps.ca; internet www.cps.ca; f. 1923; 2,000 mems; Pres. C. ROBIN WALKER; publ. *Paediatrics and Child Health* (6 a year).

Canadian Pharmacists Association: 1785 Alta Vista Drive, Ottawa, ON K1G 3Y6; tel. (613) 523-7877; fax (613) 523-0445; e-mail cpha@pharmacists.ca; internet www .pharmacists.ca; f. 1907; 9,000 mems; Pres. GARTH MCCUTCHEON; publs *Compendium of Non Prescription Products* (English only), *Compendium of Pharmaceuticals and Specialties* (English and French edns, 1 a year), *Patient Self-Care* (English only), *Therapeutic Choices* (English only).

Canadian Physiological Society: c/o Canadian Federation of Biological Societies, 305-1750 Courtwood Crescent, Ottawa, ON K2C 2B5; tel. (613) 225-8889; fax (613) 225-9621; internet www.cps.cfbs.org; f. 1936; 300 mems; Pres. Dr CHRIS CHEESEMAN; Sec. Dr C. ELAINE CHAPMAN; Treas. Dr DOUG JONES; publ. *The Canadian Journal of Physiology and Pharmacology* (12 a year).

Canadian Psychiatric Association/Association des Psychiatres du Canada: 141 Laurien Ave West, Suite 701, Ottawa, ON K1P 5J3; tel. (613) 234-2815; fax (613) 234-9857; e-mail cpa@cpa-apc.org; internet www .cpa-apc.org; f. 1951 to promote research into psychiatric disorders and foster high standards of professional practice in clinical care, education and research; 2,950 mems; Chair. Dr BLAKE WOODSIDE; Chief Exec. Officer ALEX SAUNDERS; publ. *The Canadian Journal of Psychiatry* (12 a year).

Canadian Public Health Association: 400-1565 Carling Ave, Ottawa, ON K1Z 8R1; tel. (613) 725-3769; fax (613) 725-9826; e-mail info@cpha.ca; internet www.cpha.ca; f. 1910; represents public health in Canada with links to int. public health community; 1,150 mems; Chair. Dr CORY NEUDORF; CEO DEBRA LYNKOWSKI; publ. *Canadian Journal of Public Health* (6 a year, and online at cjph.cpha.ca).

Canadian Society for Nutritional Sciences: c/o Dr SUSAN WHITING, Div. Nutrition & Dietetics, College of Pharmacy & Nutrition, 110 Science Place, Univ. of Saskatchewan, Saskatoon, SK S7N 5C9; internet www .nutritionalsciences.ca; f. 1957 to extend knowledge of nutrition by research, discussion of research reports, and exchange of information; 340 mems; Pres. SUSAN WHITING; Sec. GUYLAINE FERLAND; publ. *Nutrition/ Forum de Nutrition* (2 a year).

Pharmacological Society of Canada: c/o Dept of Physiology and Pharmacology, M216 Medical Sciences Bldg, Univ. of Western Ontario, London, ON N6A 5C1; e-mail robert.mcneill@usask.ca; internet www .physpharm.med.uwo.ca; f. 1956; 320 mems; Pres. Dr J. ROBERT MCNEILL; Sec. Dr FIONA

PARKINSON; publ. *Canadian Journal of Physiology and Pharmacology*.

Royal College of Physicians and Surgeons of Canada: 774 Echo Dr., Ottawa, ON K1S 5N8; tel. (613) 730-8177; fax (613) 730-8830; e-mail info@rcpsc.edu; internet rcpsc.medical.org; f. 1929; sets standards for postgraduate medical education of specialists in Canada; accredits postgraduate specialist education programmes; acts as nat. examining body to certify medical, surgical and laboratory specialists; offers a professional devt programme; 39,270 mems; CEO Dr ANDREW PADMOS; publ. *Royal College Outlook* (4 a year).

NATURAL SCIENCES
General

Association Francophone pour le Savoir (Acfas): 425 rue de la Gauchetière Est, Montréal, QC H2L 2M7; tel. (514) 849-0045; fax (514) 849-5558; e-mail acfas@acfas.ca; internet www.acfas.ca; f. 1923; aims to popularize science by means of lectures, meetings, awards, publications; 6,000 mems; Pres. CLAIRE V. DE LA DURANTAYE; publs *Découvrir* (6 a year), *Les Cahiers de l'Acfas* (2–3 a year).

Nova Scotian Institute of Science: Ocean Nutrition Canada, 1721 Lower Water St, Halifax, NS B3J 1S5; internet www.chebucto .ns.ca; f. 1862; monthly lecture series; 300 mems; Pres. Dr ARCHIE MCCULLOCH; Vice-Pres. CAROLYN BIRD; Sec. TRUMAN LAYTON; publ. *Proceedings* (irregular).

Biological Sciences

Canadian Phytopathological Society: c/o Joanne McWilliams, KW Neatby Bldg, Agriculture & Agri-Food Canada, 960 Carling Ave, Ottawa, ON K1A 0C6; internet www .cps-scp.ca; f. 1929; 500 mems; Pres. RICHARD MARTIN; Sec. DEENA ERRAMPALLI; publs *Canadian Journal of Plant Pathology* (4 a year), *News* (4 a year).

Canadian Society for Cellular and Molecular Biology: Centre de recherche, Hôtel-Dieu de Québec, 11 Côte du Palais, Quebec, QC G1R 2J6; internet www.csbmcb .ca; f. 1966; 400 mems; Pres. Dr DAVID ANDREWS; Sec. C. CASS; publ. *Bulletin* (3 a year).

Canadian Society for Immunology: c/o Immunology Research Group, University of Calgary, 2500 University Drive NW, Calgary, AB T2N 1N4; tel. (403) 492-0712; fax (403) 439-3439; f. 1966; 400 mems; Pres. Dr JOHN SCHRADER; Sec. and Treas. Dr DONNA CHOW; publ. *Bulletin* (irregular).

Canadian Society of Microbiologists/ Société Canadienne des Microbiologistes: c/o Canadian Federation of Biological Societies, 305-1750 Courtwood Crescent, Ottawa, ON K2C 2B5; tel. (613) 225-8889; fax (613) 225-9621; e-mail info@csm-scm.org; internet www.csm-scm.org; f. 1951; 500 mems; Man. WAFAA ANTONIOUS; publs *CSM Newsletter* (3 a year), *Programme and Abstracts* (1 a year).

Cercles des Jeunes Naturalistes: 4101 Sherbrooke est, Suite 262, Montréal, QC H1X 2B2; tel. (514) 252-3023; fax (514) 254-8744; e-mail cjn@cam.org; internet www.cjn .cam.org; f. 1931; 1,500 mems; Pres.-Gen. YVES BREAULT; Dir LAURE BOUCHARD; publs *Les Naturalistes* (4 a year), *Nouvelles CJN* (12 a year).

Entomological Society of Canada: 393 Winston Ave, Ottawa, ON K2A 1Y8; tel. (613) 725-2619; fax (613) 725-9349; e-mail entsoc .can@bellnet.ca; internet esc-sec.org; f. 1863; 500 mems, 7 affiliated regional socs; Pres. Dr

MAYA EVENDEN; Sec. Dr ANNABELLE FIRLEJ; publ. *The Canadian Entomologist* (6 a year).

Genetics Society of Canada/Société de Génétique du Canada: c/o E. K. Consulting, 53 Slalom Gate Rd, Collingwood, ON L9Y 5B1; tel. (613) 232-9459; fax (613) 594-5190; internet www.life.biology.mcmaster.ca/gsc; f. 1956; 425 mems; Pres. VIRGINIA WALKER; Treasurer JOHN BELL; Sec. CAROLYN J. BROWN; publs *Bulletin* (4 a year), *Genome* (6 a year).

Manitoba Naturalists Society: 401–63 Albert St, Winnipeg, MB R3B 1G4; tel. (204) 943-9029; fax (204) 943-9029; e-mail mns@escape.ca; internet www .manitobanature.ca; f. 1920; 1,500 mems; Pres. LARRY DE MARCH; Exec. Dir GORDON FARDOE; publ. *Bulletin* (10 a year).

Société de Protection des Plantes du Québec: c/o Secretary, 1643 chemin des Lacs, Vincent Phillion, Station de recherches agricoles, CP 480, Saint-Faustin-Lac carré, QC J0T 1J2; e-mail ltartier@sympatico.ca; internet www.sppq.qc.ca; f. 1908; 225 mems; Pres. DANNY RIOUX; Sec. LÉON TARTIER; Treas. GAÉTAN BOURGEOIS; publs *Echos phytosanitaires* (4 a year), *Phytoprotection* (3 a year).

Société Linnéenne du Québec: 1040 Belvédère, Sillery, QC G1S 3G3; tel. (418) 683-2432; fax (418) 683-2893; internet ecoroute .uqcn.qc.ca/group/slq; f. 1929; 800 mems; natural history; Pres. JEAN-PAUL L'ALLIER; Dir AGATHE SAVARD; publ. *Le Linnéen* (4 a year).

Vancouver Natural History Society: POB 3021, Vancouver, BC V6B 3X5; tel. (604) 876-7694; e-mail jpmccall@telus.net; internet www.naturevancouver.ca; f. 1918; promotes interest in nature, conserves natural resources, protects endangered species and ecosystems; 700 mems; Pres. MARGARET COUTTS; Dir and Treas. JEREMY McCALL; publ. *Discovery* (1 a year).

Mathematical Sciences

Canadian Mathematical Society/Société Mathématique du Canada: 209–1725 St Laurent blvd , Ottawa, ON K1G 3V4; tel. (613) 733-2662; fax (613) 733-8994; e-mail office@cms.math.ca; internet www.cms.math .ca; f. 1945, inc. 1979; promotes the discovery, learning and application of mathematics; 960 mems; Pres. JACQUES HURTUBISE; Exec. Dir and Sec. JOHAN RUDNICK; Treas. DAVID RODGERS; publs *Canadian Journal of Mathematics* (6 a year), *Canadian Mathematical Bulletin* (4 a year), *CMS Notes* (6 a year), *CRUX with Mayhem* (8 a year).

Physical Sciences

Canadian Association of Physicists/Association Canadienne des Physiciens et Physiciennes: MacDonald Bldg (Suite 112), 150 Louis Pasteur, Ottawa, ON K1N 6N5; tel. (613) 562-5614; fax (613) 562-5615; e-mail capmgr@uottawa.ca; internet www .cap.ca; f. 1945; 2,000 mems; Pres. Dr HENRY VAN DRIEL; Exec. Dir FRANCINE M. FORD; Sec. and Treas. Dr DAVID LOCKWOOD; publ. *Physics in Canada* (4 a year).

Canadian Meteorological and Oceanographic Society/Société Canadienne de Météorologie et d'Océanographie: Station 'D', POB 3211, Ottawa, ON K1P 6H7; tel. (613) 990-0300; fax (613) 990-1617; e-mail exec-dir@cmos.ca; internet www .cmos.ca; f. 1977; 800 mems; Pres. Dr NORM McFARLANE; Exec. Dir Dr IAN D. RUTHERFORD; publs *Atmosphere-Ocean* (4 a year), *CMOS Bulletin SCMO* (6 a year), *Congress Program and Abstracts* (1 a year).

Canadian Society of Biochemistry, Molecular and Cellular Biology/Société Canadienne de Biochimie et de Biologie Moléculaire et Cellulaire: c/o Dr E. R. Tustanoff, Dept of Biochemistry, University of Western Ontario, London, ON N6A 5C1; tel. (519) 471-1961; fax (519) 661-3175; e-mail etustan@uwo.ca; f. 1958; 1,000 mems; Pres. Dr J. ORLOWSKI; Sec. Dr E. R. TUSTANOFF; publ. *Bulletin* (1 a year).

Canadian Society of Petroleum Geologists: 540 Fifth Ave SW (Suite 160), Calgary, AB T2P 0M2; tel. (403) 264-5610; fax (403) 264-5898; e-mail cspg@cspg.org; internet www.cspg.org; f. 1927; 3,400 mems; Pres. CRAIG LAMB; Business Man. TIM HOWARD; publs *Bulletin of Canadian Petroleum Geology* (4 a year), *Reservoir* (11 a year).

Chemical Institute of Canada: 130 Slater St, Suite 550, Ottawa, ON K1P 6E2; tel. (613) 232-6252; fax (613) 232-5862; e-mail info@ cheminst.ca; internet www.cheminst.ca; f. 1945; 27 local sections, 16 subject divisions, 116 student chapters and 3 constituent societies—Canadian Society for Chemical Engineering, the Canadian Society for Chemical Technology and the Canadian Society for Chemistry; Exec. Dir ROLAND ANDERSSON; publs *Canadian Chemical News* (10 a year), *Canadian Journal of Chemical Engineering* (6 a year).

Geological Association of Canada: c/o Dept of Earth Sciences, Rm ER4063, Memorial University of Newfoundland, St John's, NL A1B 3X5; tel. (709) 737-7660; fax (709) 737-2532; e-mail gac@mun.ca; internet www .gac.ca; f. 1947 to advance the science of geology and related fields of study and to promote a better understanding thereof throughout Canada; 2,500 mems; Pres. Dr STEPHEN JOHNSTON; Sec.-Treas. Dr TOBY RIVERS; publs *Geolog* (4 a year), *Geoscience Canada* (4 a year).

Society of Chemical Industry (Canadian Section): 247 Ridgewood Rd, Toronto, ON M1C 2XC; tel. (416) 708-8924; fax (416) 281-8691; internet www.soci.org; f. 1902; fosters contact between chemical industry, univs and Govt; rewards achievement in industry and universities; promotes int. contact; 150 mems; Administrator BETH GALLOWAY.

Spectroscopy Society of Canada/Société de Spectroscopie du Canada: POB 332, Stn A, Ottawa, ON K1N 8V3; internet www .globalserve.net/~ssccan; f. 1957; 350 mems; provides the annual Herzberg Award, the Barringer Research Award and an award to the Youth Science Foundation; Pres. DIANE BEAUCHEMIN; Sec. TERESA SWITZER; publ. *Canadian Journal of Analytical Sciences and Spectroscopy.*

The Royal Astronomical Society of Canada: 203-4920 Dundas St W, Toronto, ON M9A 1B7; tel. (416) 924-7973; fax (416) 924-2911; e-mail nationaloffice@rasc.ca; internet www.rasc.ca; f. 1890; 29 centres; 4,400 mems; Exec. Dir JO TAYLOR; publs *Journal* (6 a year), *Observers' Handbook* (1 a year).

PHILOSOPHY AND PSYCHOLOGY

Canadian Philosophical Association/Association Canadienne de Philosophie: Saint Paul Univ., 223 Main St, Ottawa, ON K1S IC4; tel. (613) 236-1393; fax (613) 782-3005; e-mail acpa@ustpaul.ca; internet www .acpcpa.ca; f. 1958; promotes philosophical scholarship in Canada and represents Canadian philosophers; 800 mems; Exec. Dir LOUISE MOREL; publ. *Dialogue: Canadian Philosophical Review/Revue canadienne de philosophie* (French and English, 4 a year).

Canadian Psychological Association/Société Canadienne de Psychologie: 151 Slater St, Suite 205, Ottawa, ON K1P 5H3; tel. (613) 237-2144; fax (613) 237-1674; e-mail cpa@cpa.ca; internet www.cpa.ca; f. 1939; 4,500 mems; Exec. Dir Dr JOHN C. SERVICE; publs *Canadian Journal of Behavioural Science* (4 a year), *Canadian Journal of Experimental Psychology* (4 a year), *Canadian Psychology* (4 a year), *Psynopsis* (4 a year).

RELIGION, SOCIOLOGY AND ANTHROPOLOGY

Association for the Advancement of Scandinavian Studies in Canada (AASSC): 643 University College, Winnipeg, MB R3T 2M8; tel. (204) 474-6628; fax (204) 261-5764; f. 1982; 120 mems; Pres. JOHN TUCKER; Sec. KATHY HANSON; publs *Newsbulletin* (2 a year), *Scandinavian-Canadian Studies* (1 a year).

Canadian Association of African Studies/Association Canadienne des Etudes Africaines: CAAS/ACEA Administrator, 4-17E Old Arts Bldg University of Alberta, Edmonton, AB T6G 2E6; fax (780) 492-9125; e-mail caas@ualberta.ca; internet www.arts .ualberta.ca/~caas; f. 1970; 310 mems; promotion of the study of Africa in Canada; aims to improve the Canadian public's knowledge and awareness of Africa; provides a link between Canadian and African scholarly and scientific communities; Admin. LOUISE ROLINGHER; publ. *Canadian Journal of African Studies/Revue Canadienne des Etudes Africaines* (3 a year).

Canadian Association for Latin American and Caribbean Studies/Association Canadienne des Etudes Latino-Américaines et des Caraïbes: CALACS c/o Dept of History, Univ. of Windsor, Windsor ON N9B 3P4; tel. (514) 253-3000; fax (514) 971-3610; e-mail calacs@uwindsor.ca; internet www.can-latam.org; f. 1969; 300 mems; Pres. JUANITA DE BARROS; Treas. STEVEN PALMER; publ. *Canadian Journal of Latin American and Caribbean Studies* (2 a year).

Canadian Society of Biblical Studies: c/o Michele Murray, Dept of Religion, Bishop's University, Lennoxville, QC J1M 1Z7; tel. (819) 822-9600; e-mail mmurray@ubishops .ca; internet www.ccsr.ca/csbs; f. 1933; the promotion of scholarship in Biblical studies; 287 mems; Pres. DAVID HAWKIN; Exec. Sec. M. MURRAY; publ. *Bulletin* (1 a year).

TECHNOLOGY

Canadian Academy of Engineering/Académie Canadienne du Genie: 180 Elgin St, Suite 1100, Ottawa, ON K2P 2K3; tel. (613) 235-9056; fax (613) 235-6861; e-mail acadeng@ccpe.ca; internet www .acad-eng-gen.ca; f. 1987; assesses the changing needs of Canada and the technical resources that can be applied to them; sponsors programmes to meet these needs; provides independent and expert advice on matters of national importance concerning engineering; highlights exceptional engineering achievements; works by cooperation with national and international academies; 260 mems; Pres. RON NOLAN; Sec. and Treas. Dr JOHN McLAUGHLIN; Exec. Dir PHILIP COCKSHUTT; publ. *Newsletter* (4 a year).

Canadian Aeronautics and Space Institute: 1685 Russell Rd, Unit 1R, Ottawa, ON K1G 0N1; tel. (613) 234-0191; fax (613) 234-9039; e-mail casi@casi.ca; internet www.casi .ca; f. 1954; 2,000 mems; Pres. P. WHYTE; Exec. Dir I. ROSS; publs *Canadian Aeronautics and Space Journal* (4 a year), *Canadian Journal of Remote Sensing* (4 a year).

Canadian Council of Professional Engineers: 180 Elgin St, Suite 1100, Ottawa, ON K2P 2K3; tel. (613) 232-2474; fax (613) 230-5759; e-mail info@ccpe.ca;

internet www.ccpe.ca; f. 1936; coordinating body for 12 Provincial and Territorial Licensing Bodies; 152,000 constituent asscns; CEO CHANTAL GUAY.

Canadian Electricity Association: 1155 rue Metcalfe, bureau 1120, Montréal, QC H3B 2V6; tel. (514) 866-6121; fax (514) 866-1880; e-mail info@canelect.ca; internet www .canelect.ca; f. 1891; represents Canada's electric utility industry; 35 corporate utilities, 38 corporate manufacturers, 109 assoc. cos, 2,500 individual mems; Pres. H. R. KONOW; publs *Connections* (10 a year), *Electricity* (1 a year), *Reports* (various).

Canadian Institute of Mining, Metallurgy and Petroleum: Xerox Tower, Suite 1210, 3400 de Maisonneuve blvd West, Montréal, QC H3Z 3B8; tel. (514) 939-2710; fax (514) 939-2714; e-mail cim@cim.org; internet www.cim.org; f. 1898; 10,500 mems; Pres. WARREN HOLMES; Exec. Dir JEAN VAVREK; publs *CIM Bulletin* (10 a year), *CIM Directory* (1 a year), *CIM Reporter* (2 a year), *Journal of Canadian Petroleum Technology* (10 a year).

Engineering Institute of Canada: 1295 Hwy 2E, Kingston, ON K7L 4V1; tel. (613) 547-5989; fax (613) 547-0195; e-mail info@ eic-ici.ca; internet www.eic-ici.ca; f. 1887; 16,000 mems and 13 mem. socs; Pres. Prof. Dr KERRY ROWE; Exec. Dir B. JOHN PLANT.

Research Institutes
GENERAL

Alberta Innovates—Technology Futures: 250 Karl Clark Rd, Edmonton, AB T6N 1E4; tel. (780) 450-5111; fax (780) 450-5333; e-mail referral@albertainnovates .ca; internet www.albertatechfutures.ca; f. 2010 by merger of Alberta Ingenuity, Alberta Research Ccl, iCORE and nanoAlberta; part of Alberta's research and innovation system; helps in bldg healthy, sustainable businesses in the province; provides technical services and funding support to facilitate the commercialization of technologies, to develop new knowledge-based industry clusters and to establish an entrepreneurial-based culture in Alberta; library of 20,000 vols, 3,500 reports, 100 current periodicals; CEO GARY ABACH.

InNOVAcorp: 101 Research Drive, Woodside Industrial Park, Dartmouth, NS B2Y 4T6; tel. (902) 424-8670; fax (902) 424-4679; e-mail corpcomm@innovacorp.ns.ca; f. 1995; library of 20,000 vols; assists firms based in Nova Scotia to develop and market products, particularly in the fields of advanced engineering, information technology and oceans technology; CEO Dr ROSS MCCURDY; publ. *Progress Report* (4 a year).

National Research Council of Canada/ Conseil National de Recherches Canada: 1200 Montréal Rd, Bldg M-58, Ottawa, ON K1A 0R6; tel. (613) 993-9101; fax (613) 952-9907; e-mail info@nrc-cnrc.gc .ca; internet www.nrc-cnrc.gc.ca; f. 1916; integrated science and technology agency of the federal Govt; provides scientific and technological information through Canada Institute for Scientific and Technical Information and industrial support through Industrial Research Assistance Programme; research carried out by 16 research institutes linked to 3 technology groups: biotechnology, information and telecommunications technologies, and manufacturing technologies; Pres. MICHAEL RAYMONT (acting); Sec.-Gen. PAT MORTIMER; publs *Biochemistry and Cell Biology* (6 a year), *Canadian Geotechnical Journal* (6 a year), *Canadian Journal of*

Botany (12 a year), *Canadian Journal of Chemistry* (12 a year), *Canadian Journal of Civil Engineering* (6 a year), *Canadian Journal of Earth Sciences* (12 a year), *Canadian Journal of Fisheries and Aquatic Sciences* (12 a year), *Canadian Journal of Forest Research* (12 a year), *Canadian Journal of Microbiology* (12 a year), *Canadian Journal of Physics* (12 a year), *Canadian Journal of Physiology and Pharmacology* (12 a year), *Canadian Journal of Zoology* (12 a year), *Environmental Reviews* (4 a year), *Genome* (6 a year).

North-South Institute: 55 Murray St, Suite 500, Ottawa, ON K1N 5M3; tel. (613) 241-3535; fax (613) 241-7435; e-mail nsi@ nsi-ins.ca; internet www.nsi-ins.ca; f. 1976; policy-relevant research on issues of relations between industrialized and developing countries; research related to int. cooperation, democratic governance and conflict prevention; library of 10,000 vols, 300 periodicals; Pres. and CEO JOSEPH K. INGRAM; publ. *Canadian Development Report* (1 a year).

Nunavut Research Institute: POB 1720, Iqaluit, NU X0A 0H0; tel. (867) 979-7279; fax (867) 979-7109; e-mail slcnri@nunanet.com; internet pooka.nunanet.com/~research; f. 1978; present name 1995; br. in Igloolik; publ. *Research Compendium* (1 a year).

Process Research ORTECH Corporation: 2350 Sheridan Park Dr., Mississauga, ON L5K 2T4; tel. (905) 822-4941; fax (905) 822-9537; e-mail info@processortech.com; internet www.processortech.com; f. 1928 as Ontario Research Foundation, privatized 1999; contract research in areas of mining, metallurgical, recycling and chemical industries; library of 10,000 vols; Pres. Dr R. SRIDHAR.

RPC (Research and Productivity Council): 921 College Hill Rd, Fredericton, NB E3B 6Z9; tel. (506) 452-1212; fax (506) 452-1395; e-mail info@rpc.ca; internet www.rpc .ca; f. 1962; professional and technical services to help industry develop new products and innovative solutions to operating problems; depts incl. chemical and biotechnical services, engineering materials and diagnostics, food, fisheries and aquaculture, inorganic analytical services, product innovation, and process and environmental technology; library: information centre with 21,000 vols, 250 periodicals, inter-library loan services, access to on-line databases; Exec. Dir Dr P. LEWELL.

Saskatchewan Research Council: 125-15 Innovation blvd, Saskatoon, SK S7N 2X8; tel. (306) 933-5400; fax (306) 933-7446; e-mail info@src.sk.ca; internet www.src.sk.ca; f. 1947; assists the population of Saskatchewan in strengthening the economy and securing the environment by means of research, devt and the transfer of innovative scientific and technological solutions, applications and services; library of 25,000 vols, 5,500 in-house publs and 300 periodicals; Pres. and CEO LAURIER SCHRAMM.

Vizon SciTech Inc.: BC Research Complex, 3650 Wesbrook Mall, Vancouver, BC V6S 2L2; tel. (604) 224-4331; fax (604) 224-0540; internet www.vizonscitech.com; f. 1944 as British Columbia Research Inc. (BCRI), present name 2004; conducts technological research in fields of applied biology, applied chemistry, engineering-physics.

AGRICULTURE, FISHERIES AND VETERINARY SCIENCE

Canadian Forest Service: Ottawa, ON K1A 0E4; f. 1899; forest production, tree improvement, forest statistics and the environmental aspects of forestry, pests, fire, carbon monitoring, industrial competitive-

ness; supports FPInnovations (see Research Institutes, Technology) and research at Canadian forestry schools; Asst Deputy Minister JIM FARRELL; publs *Annual State of Canada's Forests*, *CFS Research Notes*, *Forestry Technical Reports*, *Information Reports Digest*.

Research Establishments:

Great Lakes Forestry Centre: Box 490, 1219 Queen St East, Sault Ste Marie, ON P6A 5M7; Dir-Gen. E. KONDO.

Laurentian Forestry Centre: 1055 rue du P.E.P.S., BP 10380, Ste-Foy, QC G1V 4C7; tel. (418) 648-5847; fax (418) 648-7317; Dir-Gen. N. LAFRENIÈRE.

Maritimes Forestry Service: Box 4000, Fredericton, NB E3B 5P7; Dir-Gen. H. OLDHAM.

Northern Forestry Centre: 5320 122nd St, Edmonton, AB T6H 3S5; Dir-Gen. G. MILLER.

Pacific Forestry Centre: 506 West Burnside Rd, Victoria, BC V8Z 1M5; Dir-Gen. C. WINGET.

Dominion Arboretum: Bldg 72, Central Experimental Farm, Ottawa, ON K1A 0C6; tel. (613) 995-3700; fax (613) 992-7909; f. 1886; part of Agriculture Canada; evaluation of woody plants for cold hardiness and adaptability; display area of 35 ha; special living collections; Dir Dr H. DAVIDSON.

MEDICINE

Canadian Institutes of Health Research: Room 97, 160 Elgin St, Ottawa, ON K1A 0W9; tel. (613) 941-2672; fax (613) 954-1800; e-mail cihr@cihr.ca; internet www.cihr.ca; f. 2000; aims to make Canadian health services and products more effective and to strengthen the health care system; Pres. Dr ALAN BERNSTEIN; publs *Communiqué* (in English and French, 4 a year), *Report of the President* (1 a year).

Cancer Care Ontario: 620 University Ave, Suite 1500, Toronto, ON M5G 2L7; tel. (416) 971-9800; fax (416) 971-6888; e-mail publicaffairs@cancercare.on.ca; internet www.cancercare.on.ca; f. 1943; prevention, diagnosis, treatment, supportive care, education and research in cancer; Pres. and CEO Dr TERRENCE SULLIVAN; publ. *Cancer Care*.

Dentistry Canada Fund: 427 Gilmour Street, Ottawa, ON K2P 0R5; tel. (613) 236-4763; fax (613) 236-3935; e-mail information@dcf-fdc.ca; internet www.dcf-fdc .ca; f. 1902; charity promoting oral health; Pres. and Chair. Dr BERNARD DOLANSKY; Exec. Dir RICHARD MUNRO.

Canadian Cancer Society Research Institute: Suite 200, 10 Alcorn Ave, Toronto, ON M4V 3B1; tel. (416) 961-7223; fax (416) 961-4189; e-mail ccsri@cancer.ca; internet www.cancer.ca/research; f. 1947; research grant-awarding agency; Pres. and CEO Dr PETER GOODHAND; publs *Annual Scientific Report*, *NCIC CBCRI Breast Cancer Bulletin*, *NCIC Update*.

NATURAL SCIENCES
General

Arctic Institute of North America: Univ. of Calgary, 2500 University Dr., NW, Calgary, AB T2N 1N4; tel. (403) 220-7515; fax (403) 282-4609; e-mail arctic@ucalgary.ca; internet www.arctic.ucalgary.ca; f. 1945, became inst. of Univ. of Calgary 1979; multidisciplinary research on physical, biological and social sciences; library of 40,000 vols; Exec. Dir BENOIT BEAUCHAMP; publ. *Arctic* (4 a year).

International Development Research Centre: POB 8500, 150 Kent St, Ottawa,

ON K1G 3H9; tel. (613) 236-6163; fax (613) 238-7230; e-mail info@idrc.ca; internet www .idrc.ca; f. 1970 by act of the Canadian Parliament; supports research in the developing regions of the world in the fields of environment and natural resources; information sciences and systems; health science; social science; training and research utilization; regional offices in Kenya, Senegal, Egypt, Singapore, Uruguay, India; library of 60,000 vols, 5,000 serials, 1,000 pamphlets and annual reports; Pres. Dr DAVID M. MALONE; publs *IDRC Bulletin* (12 a year), *IDRC in_focus Collection.*

Natural Sciences and Engineering Research Council of Canada (NSERC): 350 Albert St, Ottawa, ON K1A 1H5; tel. (613) 995-5992; fax (613) 992-5337; e-mail comm@nserc.ca; internet www.nserc.ca; f. 1978; a Crown corporation of the federal Government reporting to Parliament through the Minister of Industry; supports both basic university research through research grants and project research through partnerships of universities with industry, as well as the advanced training of highly qualified people in both areas; Pres. TOM BRZUSTOWSKI; publ. *NSERC Contact* (newsletter).

Biological Sciences

Huntsman Marine Science Centre: 1 Lower Campus Rd, St Andrews, NB E5B 2L7; tel. (506) 529-1200; fax (506) 529-1212; e-mail huntsman@huntsmanmarine.ca; internet www.huntsmanmarine.ca; f. 1969 with the cooperation of universities and the federal Government; mems incl. several Canadian univs, Fisheries and Oceans Canada, National Research Council of Canada, New Brunswick Depts of Education and of Fisheries and Aquaculture, corporations, organizations and individuals; research and teaching in marine sciences and coastal biology; marine education courses for elementary, high school and univ. groups; centre includes public aquarium with local flora and fauna and Atlantic Reference Centre, which houses a zoological and botanical museum reference colln; Dir W. D. ROBERTSON; publ. *Newsletter (In Depth)* (4 a year).

Jardin Botanique de Montréal: 4101 Sherbrooke St E, Montréal, QC H1X 2B2; tel. (514) 872-1400; fax (514) 872-3765; e-mail jardin_botanique@ville.montreal.qc .ca; internet www.ville.montreal.qc.ca/ jardin; f. 1931; 22,000 plant species and cultivars, 30 thematic gardens; educational, conservation and research activities; affiliated botanical and horticultural socs; library of 29,000 vols on botany, horticulture, landscaping and natural sciences and 60,000 vols of periodicals (500 titles); Botanist-Librarian CELINE ARSENEAULT; publs *Index Seminum* (every 2 years), *Quatre-temps* (Amis du Jardin botanique, 4 a year).

Physical Sciences

Algonquin Radio Observatory: c/o Natural Resources Canada, Geodetic Survey Div., 615 Booth St, Room 440, Ottawa, ON K1A 0E9; tel. (613) 996-4410; fax (613) 995-3215; f. 1959; operated by the Nat. Research Ccl; incl. 150 ft-diameter radiotelescope completed in 1966.

David Dunlap Observatory of the University of Toronto: POB 360, Station A, Richmond Hill, ON L4C 4Y6; tel. (905) 884-2112; fax (905) 884-2672; f. 1935; 50 mems; library of 30,000 vols; Assoc. Dir SLAVEK RUCINSKI.

Dominion Astrophysical Observatory: 5071 West Saanich Rd, Victoria, BC V9E 2E7; tel. (250) 363-0001; fax (250) 363-0045;

f. 1918; part of Nat. Research Ccl Herzberg Inst. of Astrophysics; 70 mems; library of 20,000 vols; Dir Dr JAMES E. HESSER.

Geological Survey of Canada: 601 Booth St, Ottawa, ON K1A 0E8; tel. (613) 996-3919; fax (613) 943-8742; e-mail ess-esic@ nrcan-rncan.gc.ca; internet gsc.nrcan.gc.ca; f. 1842; part of Natural Resources Canada; regional centres in Dartmouth, NS, Ste-Foy, QC, Calgary, AB, Vancouver and Sidney, BC, and associated with Iqaluit, NU, Nunavut Geoscience Centre, NU; nat. geoscience agency providing geological information on Canada's landmass and near-offshore regions to support the sustainable devt of the nation's natural resources, to help mitigate against loss from natural disasters and to inform about environmental stewardship and health issues; carries out studies and provides information relating to bedrock geology at the surface or at depth, and the derived surficial deposits that characterize the geological regions of Canada; carries out research assisted by airborne and ground-based mapping of physical properties of these geological materials; has information on mineral deposits of Canada, including exploration guidelines and techniques, and on mineral potential for land-use planning and policy formulation; provides information and advice on natural hazards and terrain stability influenced by permafrost, glaciation and geomorphology, with spec. emphasis on public safety and the environment; has information on coastal and offshore marine geoscience, hazards and environmental quality of these extensive regions; has geological, geochemical and geophysical information on the coastal zone, seabed, onshore and offshore sedimentary basins and crustal processes; has information on Canada's marine continental margins for UN Convention on Law of the Sea; has geoscience knowledge about oil, gas, coal, coalbed methane and gas hydrate resources throughout Canada, both onshore and offshore; has information on climate change evidence, glaciers, ice caps, glacial history, glacial deposits and drift prospecting; has information on groundwater resources and the sustainability of aquifers for potable water; library services; major cartographic service; has extensive publishing programme for geological, geophysical and geochemical maps and reports; Asst Deputy Min. MARK COREY; publ. *GSC Information Circular.*

Toronto Biomedical NMR Centre: Dept of Medical Genetics and Microbiology, University of Toronto Medical Sciences Building, Rm 1233, Toronto, ON M5S 1A8; fax (416) 978-6885; f. 1970; a national centre for high field NMR spectroscopy servicing industry, universities and the Government; Dir Dr A. A. GREY.

RELIGION, SOCIOLOGY AND ANTHROPOLOGY

Canadian Federation for the Humanities and Social Sciences: Suite 415, 151 Slater St, Ottawa, ON K1P 5H3; tel. (613) 238-6112; fax (613) 238-6114; e-mail fedcan@ fedcan.ca; internet www.fedcan.ca; f. 1941; Exec. Dir PAUL LEDWELL.

International Center for Research on Language Planning/Centre International de Recherche en Aménagement Linguistique: Pavillon De Koninck, Cité Universitaire, Sainte-Foy, QC G1K 7P4; tel. (418) 656-3232; f. 1967; basic research on language planning, description of oral and written Quèbec French, new information technologies, learning of a second language; 19 researchers, 80 graduate students, 4 staff;

library of 6,000 vols, 50 periodicals; Exec. Dir D. DESHAIES.

Social Sciences and Humanities Research Council of Canada/Conseil de Recherches en Sciences Humaines du Canada: 350 Albert St, POB 1610, Ottawa, ON K1P 6G4; tel. (613) 992-0691; fax (613) 992-1787; e-mail info@sshrc-crsh.gc.ca; internet www.sshrc-crsh.gc.ca; f. 1977 to promote research and advanced training in the social sciences and humanities; offers grants for basic and applied research; doctoral and postdoctoral fellowships; scholarly publishing journals and conferences; Pres. Dr CHAD GAFFIELD.

TECHNOLOGY

Atomic Energy of Canada, Ltd (AECL): 2251 Speakman Drive, Mississauga, ON L5K 1B2; tel. (905) 823-9040; fax (905) 823-6120; internet www.aecl.ca; f. 1952; development of economic nuclear power, scientific research and development in the nuclear energy field, and marketing of nuclear reactors; Chair. J. RAYMOND FRENETTE; Pres. and CEO ROBERT VAN ADEL.

Attached Laboratories:

AECL Research, Chalk River Laboratories: Chalk River, ON K0J 1J0; f. 1944; nuclear reactors (NRU, NRX, Pool Test Reactor and ZED-2), Tandem Accelerating Super Conducting Cyclotron, equipment for nuclear research and engineering development.

AECL Research, Whiteshell Laboratories: Pinawa, MB R0E 1L0; f. 1960; I-10/1 Accelerator, Underground Research Laboratory, equipment for nuclear research and engineering development.

BC Advanced Systems Institute: 1048, 4720 Kingsway, Burnaby, BC V5H 4N2; tel. (604) 438-2752; fax (604) 438-6564; e-mail asi@asi.bc.ca; internet www.asi.bc.ca; f. 1986; promotes research and development in high technology areas such as microelectronics and artificial intelligence; Pres. and CEO VICTOR JONES.

Canada Centre for Inland Waters/ Centre Canadien des Eaux Intérieures: 867 Lakeshore Rd, POB 5050, Burlington, ON L7R 4A6; tel. (905) 336-4981; fax (905) 336-6444; f. 1967; jt freshwater research complex of the Depts of Environment and Fisheries and Oceans; freshwater environmental and fisheries research and monitoring; cooperative management by cttee of institutional dirs; 600 mems..

Attached Research Institutes:

Bayfield Institute: 867 Lakeshore Rd, POB 5050, Burlington, ON L7R 4A6; under Dept of Fisheries and Oceans; comprises: Great Lakes Laboratory for Fisheries and Aquatic Sciences; Fisheries and Habitat Management; Canadian Hydrographic Service; Small Craft Harbours br.; and support for shipping. Together with the Freshwater Research Institute in Winnipeg, it provides the federal Fisheries and Oceans programme for the Central and Arctic Region.

National Water Research Institute: 867 Lakeshore Rd, POB 5050, Burlington, ON L7P 3M1; tel. (905) 336-4675; fax (905) 336-6444; e-mail nwriscience.liaison@ec.gc .ca; internet www.nwri.ca; component of Environment Canada's Science and Technology br.; Canada's largest freshwater research facility; staff incl. aquatic ecologists, environmental chemists, hydrologists, modellers, limnologists, physical geographers, research technicians, toxicologists and experts in linking water science to environmental policy; operates

2 main centres: the larger at the Canada Centre for Inland Waters on the shores of the Great Lakes in Burlington, ON; the other at the National Hydrology Research Centre, in the heart of the Canadian Prairies in Saskatoon, SK; also has staff located in Gatineau, QC; Fredericton, NB; and Victoria, BC; works with other govt depts, univs and research orgs to address a variety of water-related issues; conducts a comprehensive programme of ecosystem-based research and devt in the aquatic sciences, generating and disseminating scientific knowledge needed to resolve environmental issues of regional, nat. or int. significance to Canada; brs focus on aquatic ecosystem impacts, protection and management research, science liaison, monitoring and research support; also comprises the Nat. Laboratory for Environmental Testing (NLET) and (since 1974) the program office for the UN's Global Environment Monitoring System (GEMS/Water); 300 mems; library of 58,000 vols, 105 print journals, 105 online journals; Dir-Gen. Dr JOHN H. CAREY; publ. *NWRI Contributions*.

FPInnovations—Forintek Division: Head Office and Western Laboratory, 2665 E Mall, Vancouver, BC V6T 1W5; tel. (604) 224-3221; fax (604) 222-5690; e-mail info@fpinnovations.ca; internet www.fpinnovations.ca; f. 1979, fmrly Forintek Canada Corp.; pulp and paper, forestry and forest products research, contract research and technical services, solid wood products research; Pres. and CEO PIERRE LAPOINTE; Chief Financial Officer Y. NADON.

Institute for Aerospace Studies: 4925 Dufferin St, Toronto, ON M3H 5T6; tel. (416) 667-7700; fax (416) 667-7799; e-mail info@utias.utoronto.ca; internet www.utias.utoronto.ca; f. 1949; attached to Univ. of Toronto; undergraduate and graduate studies; research in aerospace science and engineering, and associated fields; serves industrial research and development needs in government and industry; facilities for experimental and computational research; library of 80,000 vols; Dir Prof. D. W. ZINGG; publ. *Progress Report* (1 a year).

Libraries and Archives

Alberta

Calgary Public Library: 616 Macleod Trail SE, Calgary, AB T2G 2M2; tel. (403) 260-2600; fax (403) 237-5393; e-mail dearlibrary@calgarypubliclibrary.com; internet www.calgarypubliclibrary.com; f. 1912; 2.4m. items; 16 brs; spec. sections on petroleum; Dir GERRY MEEK.

City of Edmonton Archives: 10440 108th Ave, Edmonton, AB T5H 3Z9; tel. (780) 496-8711; fax (780) 496-8732; internet www.edmonton.ca/archives; f. 1971; reference library of 10,000 vols, also MSS, newspapers, slides, city records, photographs and maps of the city; Man. (vacant).

Edmonton Public Library: 7 Sir Winston Churchill Square, Edmonton, AB T5J 2V4; tel. (780) 496-7000; fax (780) 496-7097; internet www.epl.ca; f. 1913; 16 brs; 1,766,809 print items, 242,934 audiovisual items; Dir of Libraries LINDA C. COOK.

Glenbow Library and Archives: 130—9 Ave SE, Calgary, AB T2G 0P3; tel. (403) 268-4204; fax (403) 232-6569; e-mail library@glenbow.org; internet www.glenbow.org; f. 1955; 80,000 vols, 700,000 photographs and a large collection of manuscript materials, chiefly on western and northern Canada.

Legislature Library: 216 Legislature Bldg, 10800 97th Ave, Edmonton, AB T5K 2B6; tel. (780) 427-2473; fax (780) 427-6016; e-mail library@assembly.ab.ca; internet www.assembly.ab.ca/lao/library; f. 1906; 425,000 vols; parliamentary library; extensive colln of most Alberta weekly newspapers; Legislature Librarian VALERIE FOOTZ; publs *New Books in the Library* (10 a year), *Selected Periodical Articles List* (10 a year).

Parkland Regional Library: 5404 56 Ave, Lacombe, AB T4L 1G1; tel. (403) 782-3850; fax (403) 782-4650; e-mail rsheppard@prl.ab.ca; internet www.prl.ab.ca; f. 1959; network of 50 public libraries and 48 school libraries in central Alberta; Dir RONALD SHEPPARD.

Provincial Archives of Alberta: 8555 Roper Rd, Edmonton, AB T6E 5W1; tel. (780) 427-1750; fax (780) 427-4646; e-mail paa@gov.ab.ca; internet culture.alberta.ca/archives/default.aspx; f. 1963; holdings incl. non-current Alberta govt records, private papers, church records, municipal records, photographs, taped oral history interviews, films, video cassettes and maps pertaining to the history of Alberta; regular exhibitions; reference library colln with focus on W Canadiana, local/community histories and archival literature (12,000 vols); Exec. Dir and Provincial Archivist LESLIE LATTA-GUTHRIE.

University of Alberta Library: 5-07 Cameron Library, Edmonton, AB T6G 2J8; tel. (403) 492-3790; fax (403) 492-8302; f. 1909; 4,809,303 vols, 3,690,989 microforms; Chief Librarian ERNIE INGLES; Dir KAREN ADAMS; publ. *Library Editions* (2 a year).

University of Calgary Library: 2500 University Drive NW, Calgary, AB T2N 1N4; tel. (403) 220-5953; fax (403) 282-1218; e-mail libinfo@ucalgary.ca; internet library.ucalgary.ca; f. 1966; 7,678,394 items (2,540,294 print items, 3,528,108 microforms, 1,430,467 maps and aerial photographs, 179,525 audiovisual items), 2,917 m of archives; University Librarian H. THOMAS HICKERSON.

British Columbia

British Columbia Archives: 655 Belleville St, Victoria, BC V8W 9W2; tel. (250) 387-1952; fax (250) 387-2072; e-mail access@bcarchives.gov.bc.ca; internet www.bcarchives.gov.bc.ca; f. 1893; 71,000 items of printed material, 7,000 linear metres of MSS and govt records, 5m. photographs, 9,000 paintings, 35,000 maps, charts and architectural plans, 25,000 hours of sound recordings, 4,000 cans of moving images; Provincial Archivist GARY A. MITCHELL.

Fraser Valley Regional Library: Admin. Centre, 34589 Delair Rd, Abbotsford, BC V2S 5Y1; tel. (604) 859-7141; fax (604) 852-5701; internet www.fvrl.ca; f. 1930; 24 brs, Outreach Services; 900,000 vols, 10,000 talking books, also incl. electronic resources DVDs, CDs, e-books; CEO ROB O'BRENNAN.

Greater Victoria Public Library: 735 Broughton St, Victoria, BC V8W 3H2; tel. (250) 382-7241; fax (250) 382-7125; internet www.gvpl.ca; f. 1864; 940,749 vols; CEO SANDRA ANDERSON.

Legislative Library: Parliament Bldgs, Victoria, BC V8V 1X4; tel. (250) 387-6510; fax (250) 356-1373; e-mail llbc.ref@leg.bc.ca; internet www.llbc.leg.bc.ca; f. 1863; 200,000 vols; Dir PETER GOURLAY.

Public Library InterLINK: 7252 Kingsway, Lower Level, Burnaby, BC V5E 1G3; tel. (604) 517-8441; fax (604) 517-8410; e-mail info@interlinklibraries.ca; internet www.interlinklibraries.ca; f. 1994; federation of 18 autonomous public libraries sharing resources and services and providing open

access to all mem. libraries; spec. services: audiobooks for the visually impaired (46,056 vols), multilingual books, staff training video cassettes, children's educational video cassettes; Man. of Operations RITA AVIGDOR; Exec. Dir MICHAEL BURRIS.

Simon Fraser University, W. A. C. Bennett Library: 8888 University blvd, Burnaby, BC V5A 1S6; tel. (778) 782-3265; fax (778) 782-3023; e-mail libhelp@sfu.ca; internet www.lib.sfu.ca; f. 1965; 1,214,111 vols, 937,181 microforms; Univ. Librarian Dr CHARLES ECKMAN.

University of British Columbia Library: 1961 East Mall, Vancouver, BC V6T 1Z1; tel. (604) 822-6375; fax (604) 822-3893; internet www.library.ubc.ca; f. 1915; 14 brs; 5.5m. vols, 65,000 print and electronic serial subscriptions, 261,000 e-books, 5.2m. microforms; Univ. Librarian Dr W. PETER WARD.

Vancouver Island Regional Library: 6250 Hammond Bay Rd, Box 3333, Nanaimo, BC V9R 5N3; tel. (250) 758-4697; fax (250) 758-2482; internet virl.bc.ca; f. 1936; 37 brs; 1,172,571 vols; Exec. Dir PENNY GRANT.

Vancouver Public Library: 350 West Georgia St, Vancouver, BC V6B 6B1; tel. (604) 331-3603; fax (604) 331-4080; e-mail info@vpl.ca; internet www.vpl.ca; f. 1887; 2,641,444 vols; 22 brs; Chief Librarian SANDRA SINGH.

Vancouver School of Theology Library: 6050 Chancellor Blvd, Vancouver, BC V6T 1X3; tel. (604) 822-9430; fax (604) 822-9372; e-mail gmcleod@vst.edu; internet www.vst.edu; f. 1971; 85,000 vols; Library Dir GILLIAN McLEOD.

Manitoba

Archives of Manitoba: 200 Vaughan St, Winnipeg, MB R3C 1T5; tel. (204) 945-3971; fax (204) 948-2008; e-mail archives@gov.mb.ca; internet www.gov.mb.ca/archives/index.html; f. 1884; 5,500 linear ft private MSS, 65,000 linear ft Manitoba govt and court records, 8,000 linear ft Hudson's Bay Co Archives records, 130,000 architectural drawings, 1.2m. photographs, 32,000 maps, 300 paintings, 5,500 prints and drawings, 7,000 sound records; spec. collns: Red River Settlement and Red River Disturbance, Lt-Governors' papers, Winnipeg General Strike, Canadian Airways Ltd, archives of the Ecclesiastical Province of Rupert's Land, records of local govts and school divs, Archives of Manitoba legal and judicial history; Archivist of Manitoba GORDON DODDS.

Legislative Library of Manitoba: Rm 100, 200 Vaughan St, Winnipeg, MB R3C 1T5; tel. (204) 945-4330; fax (204) 948-1312; e-mail legislative_library@gov.mb.ca; internet www.manitoba.ca/leglib; f. 1870; 1.4m. items; special collns: Canadian, Western Canadian and Manitoba history, economics, political and social sciences, urban, rural and ethnic language newspapers of Manitoba, govt publs; Legislative Librarian (vacant); publs *Monthly Checklist of Manitoba Government Publications* (online), *Selected New Titles* (8 a year, online).

Manitoba Culture, Heritage and Tourism—Public Library Services Branch: 300-1011 Rosser Ave, Brandon, MB R7A 0L5; tel. (204) 726-6590; fax (204) 726-6868; e-mail pls@gov.mb.ca; f. 1972; 45,000 vols, 10,000 e-books; Dir (vacant); publ. *Manitoba Public Library Statistics* (1 a year).

Manitoba Law Library Inc., Great Library: 331—408 York Ave, Winnipeg, MB R3C 0P9; tel. (204) 945-1958; fax (204) 948-2138; internet www.cbsc.org; f. 1877; attached to Law Society of Manitoba; 50,000 vols; Librarian R. GARTH NIVEN.

University of Manitoba Libraries: Winnipeg, MB R3T 2N2; tel. (204) 474-9881; fax (204) 474-7583; e-mail marina_webster@umanitoba.ca; internet www.umanitoba.ca/libraries; f. 1877; collections supporting 18 faculties and 4 schools; spec. collns: Slavic, Icelandic; 2m. vols, 520,000 govt publs, 157,500 other print items (maps, performance music, textbook collection, etc.), 2.7m. microforms, 31,000 audiovisual items, 9,000 serial titles; Dir CAROLYNNE PRESSER.

New Brunswick

Mount Allison University Libraries and Archives: Mount Allison Univ., 49 York St, Sackville, NB E4L 1C6; tel. (506) 364-2562; fax (506) 364-2617; e-mail bgnassi@mta.ca; internet www.mta.ca/library; f. 1840; 454,000 vols, 515,000 microforms, 282,000 documents; Univ. Librarian BRUNO GNASSI.

Bibliothèque Champlain (Université de Moncton): 18 ave Antonine-Maillet, Moncton, NB E1A 3E9; tel. (506) 858-4012; fax (506) 858-4086; internet www.umoncton.ca/umcm-bibliotheque-champlain; f. 1965; gen. academic collns; 649,063 vols, 23,963 periodicals; Head Librarian ALAIN ROBERGE.

Harriet Irving Library: Univ. of New Brunswick, POB 7500, Fredericton, NB E3B 5H5; tel. (506) 453-4740; fax (506) 453-4595; e-mail library@unb.ca; internet www.lib.unb.ca; f. 1790; 1,141,807 vols and 3,103,813 (equivalent vols) microforms; Dir of Libraries JOHN D. TESKEY.

Legislative Library: Box 6000, Fredericton, NB E3B 5H1; tel. (506) 453-2338; fax (506) 444-5889; e-mail library.biblio-info@gnb.ca; f. 1841; 35,000 vols; Librarian MARGARET PACEY.

Provincial Archives of New Brunswick: POB 6000, Fredericton, NB E3B 5H1; tel. (506) 453-2122; fax (506) 453-3288; e-mail provincial.archives@gnb.ca; internet archives.gnb.ca; f. 1968; 25,000 ft of govt and private textual documents, 250,000 photographs, 300,000 cartographic and architectural documents, 4,600 hours audio recordings, 1,800 video cassettes and films, 60,000 microfiches, 14,000 reels microfilm; 20,000 m, 342,000 photographs, 375,000 maps, plans, and drawings, 25,400 microfilm, 555 items documentary art; Provincial Archivist MARION BEYEA.

Newfoundland and Labrador

Newfoundland and Labrador Public Libraries: 48 St George's Ave, Stephenville, NL A2N 1K9; tel. (709) 643-0900; fax (709) 643-0925; internet www.nlpl.ca; f. 1934; 1,300,000 vols at 96 libraries; provides public library services, incl. books, magazines, newspapers, large-print and spoken-word books, DVDs computers with free internet access, digital cameras; Exec. Dir SHAWN TETFORD.

The Rooms Corporation of Newfoundland and Labrador—The Rooms Provincial Archives Division: POB 1800, St John's, NL A1C 5P9; 9 Bonaventure Ave, St John's, NL A1C 5P9; tel. (709) 757-8030; fax (709) 757-8031; e-mail archives@therooms.ca; internet www.therooms.ca; f. 1960, refounded 2005; provincial govt archives, genealogical colln, cartographic and architectural archives, sports archives, film and still images; Provincial Archivist, Newfoundland and Labrador and Dir, The Rooms Provincial Archives Division GREG WALSH.

Provincial Resource Library: Arts and Culture Centre, St John's, NL A1B 3A3; tel. (709) 737-3946; fax (709) 737-2660; f. 1934; Newfoundland Collection open to the public; backup resource library for the provincial

system; 181,604 vols (incl. Newfoundland Collection); Man. MICHELLE WALTERS.

Queen Elizabeth II Library: Memorial University of Newfoundland, St John's, NL A1B 3Y1; tel. (709) 737-7428; fax (709) 737-2153; e-mail lbusby@mun.ca; internet www.library.mun.ca; f. 1925; 1,724,807 vols, 1,977,982 microform units; Librarian LORRAINE BUSBY.

Nova Scotia

Angus L. Macdonald Library: St Francis Xavier Univ., POB 5000, Antigonish, NS B2G 2W5; tel. (902) 867-2267; fax (902) 867-5153; internet library.stfx.ca; f. 1853; 762,000 vols; special collection: Celtic history, literature and language; Librarian LYNNE MURPHY; publ. *The Antigonish Review* (4 a year).

Dalhousie University Libraries: Halifax, NS B3H 4H8; tel. (902) 494-3601; internet www.library.dal.ca; 1,844,000 vols; University Librarian WILLIAM R. MAES.

Halifax Regional Library: 60 Alderney Dr., Dartmouth, NS B2Y 4P8; tel. (902) 490-5744; fax (902) 490-5762; internet www.halifaxpubliclibraries.ca; f. 1996; 898,532 books (fiction, non-fiction, reference, rapid read, multilingual), 51,202 periodicals, 41,099 CDs, 55,471 DVDs, 30,816 video cassettes, 8,440 audio cassettes, 5,613 talking books; CEO JUDITH HARE.

Nova Scotia Archives: 6016 University Ave, Halifax, NS B3H 1W4; tel. (902) 424-6060; fax (902) 424-0628; e-mail nsarm@gov.ns.ca; internet www.gov.ns.ca/nsarm; f. 1929; provincial govt records; family, political, personal and business papers; maps, plans, charts; photographs, paintings; microfilmed files of leading newspapers; film, television and sound archives; research library of 50,000 titles; Dir of Public Services LOIS YORKE; Provincial Archivist (vacant).

Nova Scotia Legislative Library: Province House, 1726 Hollis St, Halifax, NS B3J 2P8; tel. (902) 424-5932; fax (902) 424-0220; e-mail murphymf@gov.ns.ca; internet www.gov.ns.ca/legislature/library; f. 1862; Nova Scotiana Collection; 170,000 vols; Librarian MARGARET MURPHY; publ. *Publications of the Province of Nova Scotia* (12 a year and 1 a year).

Vaughan Memorial Library, Acadia University: POB 4, 50 Acadia St, Wolfville, NS B4P 2P6; tel. (902) 585-1249; fax (902) 585-1748; internet library.acadiau.ca; f. 1843; 1,000,000 vols and govt documents, e-journals; Univ. Librarian SARA LOCHHEAD.

Nunavut Territory

Nunavut Public Library Services: POB 189A, Iqaluit, NU X0A 0H0; tel. (867) 979-5400; fax (867) 979-1373; e-mail nuic@gov.nu.ca; br. libraries in Arctic Bay, Arviat, Baker Lake, Cambridge Bay, Clyde River, Igloolik, Kugluktuk, Pangnirtung, Pond Inlet and Rankin Inlet.

Branch Library:

Iqaluit Centennial Library: POB 189A, Iqaluit, NU X0A 0H0; tel. (867) 979-5400; fax (867) 979-1373; e-mail nuic@gov.nu.ca; T. H. Manning archival collection of polar materials; Librarian TORI-LYNNE EVANS.

Ontario

Canada Institute for Scientific and Technical Information: 1200 Montréal Rd, M-55, Ottawa, ON K1A 0R6; tel. (613) 998-8544; fax (613) 993-7619; e-mail info.cisti@nrc-cnrc.gc.ca; internet cisti-icist.nrc-cnrc.gc.ca; f. 1974, fmrly National Science Library; attached to Nat. Research Ccl Canada; focal point of a national scientific and technical information network; resources

of over 50,000 serial titles are made available through loan, copies and consultation; information services incl. operation of a nat. computerized current awareness service and an online table of contents service (CISTI SOURCE), Customized Literature Search Service providing custom bibliographies on requested topics, MEDLARS coordinator for Canada; Dir-Gen. BERNARD DUMOUCHEL.

Canadian Agriculture Library: Sir John Carling Bldg, Agriculture and Agri-Food Canada, Ottawa, ON K1A 0C5; tel. (613) 759-7068; fax (613) 759-6643; internet www.agr.gc.ca/cal; f. 1910; 1m. vols, 22,200 serials; specializes in agriculture, biology, biochemistry, economics, entomology, food sciences, plant science, veterinary medicine; serves 24 field libraries; Dir DANIELLE JACQUES.

Carleton University Library: 1125 Colonel By Drive, Ottawa, ON K1S 5B6; tel. (613) 520-2735; fax (613) 520-2750; e-mail university.librarian@carleton.ca; internet www.library.carleton.ca; f. 1942; 1,782,483 vols, 10,486 serial subscriptions, 1,513,714 items (microforms, maps, audiovisual items), 12,025 electronic journals; Librarian MARTIN FOSS.

Departmental Library, Indian and Northern Affairs Canada: Ottawa, ON K1A 0H4; tel. (819) 997-0811; fax (819) 953-5491; e-mail reference@ainc-inac.gc.ca; internet www.ainc-inac.gc.ca; f. 1966; 100,600 vols, 20,000 bound periodicals, 2,000 rare books, 3,500 govt documents, 3,000 microfilm reels, incl. records relating to Indian affairs; service to native people, researchers, libraries; br. in Gatineau, Québec; Chief Librarian JULIA FINN.

Earth Sciences Information Centre: 601 Booth St, Ottawa, ON K1A 0E8; tel. (613) 996-3919; fax (613) 943-8742; e-mail esic@nrcan.ac.ca; internet www.nrcan.gc.ca/ess/esic; f. 1842; component of Natural Resources Canada; interlibrary loans, online retrospective searching; 400,000 vols, 260,000 geological maps; Head of ESIC Services PAULINE McDONALD (acting).

Hamilton Public Library: 55 York Blvd, POB 2700, Station A, Hamilton, ON L8N 4E4; tel. (905) 546-3200; fax (905) 546-3202; e-mail kroberts@hpl.ca; internet www.hpl.hamilton.on.ca; f. 1889; special collections of local history, Canadiana to 1950, govt documents; 1,492,467 vols and 1,876 periodicals; 24 br. libraries; 2 bookmobiles; Chief Librarian KEN ROBERTS.

John W. Graham Library, University of Trinity College: 6 Hoskin Ave, Toronto, ON M5S 1H8; tel. (416) 978-2653; fax (416) 978-2797; internet www.trinity.utoronto.ca; f. 1851; 200,000 vols; spec. collns: Anglican Church of Canada Colln, Churchill Colln, G8/G20 Colln, SPCK Colln, Strachan Colln, W. Speed Hill Colln (works of Richard Hooker), Upjohn-Waldie Colln (works of Eric Gill and other fine printing); Nicholls Librarian and Dir of Graham Library LINDA WILSON CORMAN.

Library and Archives Canada: 395 Wellington St, Ottawa, ON K1A 0N4; tel. (613) 996-5115; fax (613) 995-6274; e-mail reference@lac-bac.gc.ca; internet www.collectionscanada.gc.ca; f. 2004, following merger of National Library of Canada (f. 1953) and National Archives of Canada (f. 1872), incl. Canadian Postal Archives; depository of all Canadian publs, public records and historical material; 71,000 films and documentaries, 2.5m. architectural drawings, plans and maps, 21.3m. photographic images, 270,000 hours of audio and visual recordings, 343,000 works of art, Canadian sheet music and 200,000 recordings related to music in Canada, Canadian postal archive, medals, seals, posters and coats of arms, nat., provincial and territorial newspapers, periodicals, MSS, microforms and theses, more than 1m. portraits of Canadians; Librarian and Archivist Dr DANIEL CARON; publ. *Annual Review*.

Library of Parliament: Ottawa, ON K1A 0A9; tel. (613) 995-1166; fax (613) 992-1269; e-mail info@parl.gc.ca; internet www.parl.gc .ca; f. 1867; 407,500 vols in integrated systems, 510,000 microforms; Parliamentary Librarian WILLIAM YOUNG; publs *Quorum* (1 a day, during session), *Radar* (1 a day, during session), *Current Issue Reviews* (12 a year), *Research Publications* (12 a year).

Library of the Pontifical Institute of Mediaeval Studies: 4th Floor, 113 St Joseph St, Toronto, ON M5S 1J4; tel. (416) 926-7146; e-mail pims.library@utoronto.ca; internet www.pims.ca; f. 1929; principal research resource for the Institute's Mellon Fellows, postdoctoral candidates for the Licence in Medieval Studies, and for the faculty and doctoral students of the Univ. of Toronto's Centre for Medieval Studies; 120,000 vols, 210 periodicals, 15 MSS codices, 300 MSS charters, 10,000 folios of MSS on photostats, 250,000 folios of MSS on microfilm; Pres. RICHARD. ALWAY; Dir JONATHAN. BENGTSON.

London Public Library: 251 Dundas St, London, ON N6A 6H9; tel. (519) 661-4600; fax (519) 663-5396; internet www.lpl.london .on.ca; f. 1894; 953,870 vols, 167,975 non-book materials; CEO SUSANNA HUBBARD KRIMMER.

McMaster University Libraries: 1280 Main St West, Hamilton, ON L8S 4L6; tel. (905) 525-9140; fax (905) 546-0625; e-mail libinfo@mcmaster.ca; internet www .mcmaster.ca/library; f. 1887; 1,717,799 vols, 1,488,305 microform items, 175,000 non-print items, 10,976 linear metres archival material, 6,292 serial subscriptions; contains among others Vera Brittain archives, Bertrand Russell archives and 18th-century colln; Librarian GRAHAM R. HILL.

National Defence Headquarters Library: 101 Colonel By Drive, Ottawa, ON K1A 0K2; tel. (613) 995-2213; fax (613) 995-8176; internet www.collectionscanada .ca; f. 1903; library services, inter-library loans, information retrieval; 30,000 vols incl. military Canadiana; Librarian J. BRIAN GRIER.

Natural Resources Canada, Headquarters Library: 580 Booth St, Ottawa, ON K1A 0E4; tel. (613) 996-8282; fax (613) 992-7211; internet www.nrcan-rncan.gc.ca; f. 1958; 65,000 vols and bound periodicals, 3,000 reports; mineral and energy economics, policy, taxation, legislation and statistics, energy conservation; Dir S. E. HENRY.

Ontario Legislative Library: Legislative Bldg, Queen's Park, Toronto, ON M7A 1A9; tel. (416) 325-3900; fax (416) 325-3925; f. 1867; 58,440 monograph titles; Exec. Dir (vacant).

Ottawa City Archives: 1st Floor, Bytown Pavilion, 111 Sussex Drive, Ottawa, ON K1N 1J1; tel. (613) 580-2424; e-mail archives@ ottawa.ca; f. 1976; repository of public records of civic administration and other historical material; special collections: genealogy, heraldry, local railroad history; City Archivist DAVE BULLOCK.

Ottawa Public Library/Bibliothèque Publique d'Ottawa: 120 Metcalfe St, Ottawa, ON; tel. (613) 580-2940; fax (613) 567-4013; e-mail feedback@ biblioottawalibrary.ca; internet www

.bibliottawalibrary.ca; f. 1906; 2.5m. vols; City Librarian BARBARA CLUBB.

Philatelic Collections, Library and Archives Canada: 550 Blvd de la Cité, Gatineau, QC K1A 0N4; tel. (613) 996-5115; fax (613) 995-6274; internet www .collectionscanada.gc.ca/philately-postal; f. 1988 fmrly Canadian Postal Archives; acquisition, preservation, description of philatelic records and related material; Manager PASCAL LEBLOND.

Queen's University Library: Miller Hall, 36 Union St, Kingston, ON K7L 5C4; tel. (613) 533-2519; fax (613) 533-6362; internet library.queensu.ca; f. 1842; 2,380,675 vols, 3,792,624 other items; Univ. Librarian PAUL WIENS; Curator MARK BADHAM.

Supreme Court of Canada Library: 301 Wellington St, Ottawa, ON K1A 0J1; tel. (613) 996-8120; fax (613) 952-2832; e-mail library@scc-csc.gc.ca; internet www.scc-csc .gc.ca; 200,000 vols; Dir ROSALIE FOX.

Toronto Public Library: 789 Yonge St, Toronto, ON M4W 2G8; tel. (416) 393-7131; internet www.tpl.toronto.ca; 99 brs; 1.2m. vols; City Librarian JOSEPHINE BRYANT; publ. *What's On* (4 a year).

University of Ottawa Library Network: 65 University Private, Ottawa, ON K1N 6N5; tel. (613) 562-5883; fax (613) 562-5195; internet www.biblio.uottawa.ca; f. 1848; library contains more than 4.5m. items, incl. more than 1,250,000 monographs, 19,000 current periodicals, 1.9m. microforms; tens of thousands of music scores, sound recordings and audiovisual items; hundreds of thousands of slides, aerial photographs, maps and govt publications; electronic resources; Univ. Chief Librarian LESLIE WEIR.

University of Toronto Libraries: Toronto, ON M5S 1A5; tel. (416) 978-8580; fax (416) 978-7653; e-mail utweb@library.utoronto.ca; internet www.library.utoronto.ca; f. 1891; 10,342,574 vols, 32,485 serials, 5,372,000 microforms, 1,695,060 other non-book items (maps, sound recordings, audiovisual, manuscript titles, aerial photographs, etc.), 32,912 online journals; Chief Librarian CAROLE MOORE.

University of Waterloo Library: 200 University Ave, Waterloo, ON N2L 3G1; tel. (519) 888-4567; fax (519) 888-4320; internet www.lib.uwaterloo.ca; f. 1957; 2,046,934 vol, 1,715,194 microform pieces, 3,998 print titles, 31,585 electronic serials titles; University Librarian K. MARK HASLETT; publ. *Bibliography* (irregular).

University of Western Ontario Libraries: London, ON N6A 3K7; tel. (519) 661-2111; internet www.lib.uwo.ca; f. 1878; 3,546,496 vols, 9,756 print serials subscriptions; 480,985 ebooks, 54,790 electronic journals; 4,062,350 microforms; 1,823,011 audio, video graphic and other spec. materials; Univ. Librarian JOYCE C. GARNETT.

Victoria University Library (E. J. Pratt Library): 71 Queen's Park Crescent East, Toronto, ON M5S 1K7; tel. (416) 585-4471; fax (416) 585-4591; e-mail victoria.library@ utoronto.ca; internet library.vicu.utoronto .ca; f. 1836; 300,000 vols; spec. collns: humanities (gen.), religions and theology; Northrop Frye, S. T. Coleridge, William Blake and his contemporaries, Hogarth Press, Tennyson, V. Woolf, Bloomsbury Group, Wesleyana, Norman Jewison Archive, E. J. Pratt; George Baxter (books and prints); 19th-century Canadian Poetry, French and French-Canadian Literature (Rièse colln); folklore; Senator Keith Davey; posters (Paris riots of 1968); contemporary poets; univ. archives; Chief Librarian Dr ROBERT C. BRANDEIS.

Prince Edward Island

Confederation Centre Public Library: Box 7000, Charlottetown, PE C1A 8G8; tel. (902) 368-4642; fax (902) 368-4652; e-mail ccpl@gov.pe.ca; internet www.library.pe.ca; f. 1773; 72,000 vols; Chief Librarian TRINA O'BRIEN LEGGOTT.

Prince Edward Island Public Library Service: POB 7500, 89 Red Head Rd, Morell, PE C0A 1S0; tel. (902) 961-7320; fax (902) 961-7322; e-mail plshq@gov.pe.ca; internet www.library.pe.ca; f. 1933; 367,000 vols in regional system of 26 public libraries; Provincial Librarian KATHLEEN EATON.

Public Archives and Records Office of Prince Edward Island: POB 1000, Charlottetown, PE C1A 7M4; tel. (902) 368-4290; fax (902) 368-6327; e-mail archives@gov.pe .ca; internet www.gov.pe.ca/archives; f. 1964; Provincial Archivist JILL MACMICKEN-WILSON.

Québec

Bibliothèque de l'Assemblée Nationale du Québec: Edifice Pamphile-Lemay, Québec, QC G1A 1A3; tel. (418) 643-4408; fax (418) 643-3207; e-mail bibliotheque@assnat .qc.ca; internet www.assnat.qc.ca; f. 1802; law and legislation, political science, parliamentary procedure, history, official publs of Québec, newspapers; 955,000 vols; Chief Librarian HÉLÈNE GALARNEAU; publs *Bulletin* (4 a year), *Débats de l'Assemblée législative 1867–1962* (irregular), *Journal des débats: index* (irregular).

Bibliothèque de la Compagnie de Jésus: Collège Jean-de-Brébeuf, L. B4–25, 3200 chemin Côte-Ste-Catherine, Montréal, QC H3T 1C1; tel. (514) 342-9342; f. 1882; books from the 16th to the 18th centuries, Canadiana; philosophy, scripture, theology; 195,000 vols; Dir Dr JOHANNE BIRON.

Bibliothèque de l'Université Laval: Cité Universitaire, Québec, QC G1K 7P4; tel. (418) 656-3344; fax (418) 656-7897; internet www.bibl.ulaval.ca; f. 1852; 5,000,000 vols, 24,452 periodicals, 19,500 films, 140,000 maps; Dir Dr SYLVIE DELORME; publ. *Répertoire des vedettes-matière* (CD-ROM, 2 a year).

Bibliothèques de l'Université de Montréal: CP 6128, Succursale Centre-ville, Montréal, QC H3C 3J7; tel. (514) 343-6905; fax (514) 343-6457; e-mail biblios@bib .umontreal.ca; internet www.bib.umontreal .ca; f. 1928; 3,106,971 vols, 21,087 current periodicals, 1,650,557 microforms, 189,164 audiovisual documents; Dir of Libraries JEAN-PIERRE CÔTÉ.

Bibliothèque de Montréal: 1210 Sherbrooke Est, Montréal, QC H2L 1L9; tel. (514) 872-5171; fax (514) 872-1626; internet www2.ville.montreal.qc.ca/biblio; f. 1902; 2,102,600 vols, of which 51,700 books, 20,757 pamphlets, 43,900 pictures and photographs, 1,547 maps, 3,035 slides and 99,200 microforms related to Canada and its history; 23 brs, 1 sound-recording library and 1 bookmobile; Dir JACQUES PANNETON.

Bibliothèque et Archives Nationales du Québec: 2275 rue Holt, Montréal, QC H2G 3H1; tel. (514) 873-1100; fax (514) 873-9312; e-mail info@banq.qc.ca; internet www.banq .qc.ca; f. 1967; merged with Archives Nationales du Québec (f. 1920) 2006; 4m. vols; Conservation Centre and Grande Bibliothèque in Montréal; 9 archive centres (Chicoutimi, Gatineau, Montréal, Québec, Rimouski, Rouyn-Noranda, Sept-Iles, Sherbrooke,Trois-Rivières); Chair and CEO LISE BISSONNETTE; publ. *A rayons ouverts* (4 a year).

CAIJ—Montréal: Palais de Justice, 17e étage, 1 rue Notre-Dame est, local 17.50,

Montréal, QC H2Y 1B6; tel. (514) 866-2057; fax (514) 879-8592; e-mail mlaforce@caij.qc.ca; f. 1828; 100,000 vols; Librarian MIREILLE LAFORCE.

Concordia University Libraries: 1455 de Maisonneuve Blvd W, Montréal, QC H3G 1M8; tel. (514) 848-2424; fax (514) 848-2882; e-mail libadmin@alcor.concordia.ca; internet library.concordia.ca; f. 1974; 2,730,000 vols; Univ. Librarian GERALD BEASLEY.

Fraser-Hickson Institute Library: 16 Westminster N, Suite 304, Montréal, QC H4X 1Z1; tel. (514) 489-5301; e-mail frances@fraserhickson.ca; internet www.fraserhickson.ca; f. 1870; colln of archives of the Mercantile Library Asscn (Montréal); library currently closed and in storage, pending move to a new site; 150,000 vols; Chief Librarian FRANCES W. ACKERMAN; Reader Services Man. ISABEL RANDALL.

McGill University Libraries: 3459 McTavish St, Montréal, QC H3A 1Y1; tel. (514) 398-4734; fax (514) 398-7356; e-mail doadmin.library@mcgill.ca; internet www.mcgill.ca/library; f. 1855; 13 libraries, 3.6m. vols, 49,897 current periodicals, 1,782,148 microtexts, 676,373 govt documents; Dir JANINE SCHMIDT; Assoc. Dir, Planning and Resources DIANE KOEN.

Osler Library: McGill Univ., McIntyre Medical Sciences Bldg, 3655 Promenade Sir William Osler, 3rd Fl., Montréal, QC H3G 1Y6; tel. (514) 398-4475; fax (514) 398-5747; e-mail osler.library@mcgill.ca; internet www.mcgill.ca/library/library-using/branches/osler-library; f. 1929; history of medicine and allied sciences; 99,511 vols; History of Medicine Librarian PAMELA MILLER.

Saskatchewan

Regina Public Library: 2311 12th Ave, Regina, SK S4P 3Z5; tel. (306) 777-6000; fax (306) 949-7260; internet www.reginalibrary.ca; f. 1908; 9 brs; 665,928 items; Library Dir JEFF BARBER; publs @ the Library (6 a year), Community Information Catalogue, Regina Public Library Film Catalogue, RPL Theatre Calendar (6 a year).

Saskatchewan Legislative Library: 234-2405 Legislative Dr., Regina, SK S4S 0B3; tel. (306) 787-2276; fax (306) 787-1772; e-mail reference@legassembly.sk.ca; internet www.legassembly.sk.ca/leglibrary; f. 1878, present name 1905; 152,500 vols, approx. 522,000 sheets of microfiche; 6,300 reels of microfilm; 3,200 CD-ROMs; 7,600 audio, video and film recordings; social sciences, law and history; noted for its colln of govt documents and W Canadiana; Legislative Librarian MELISSA BENNETT; publ. Checklist of Saskatchewan Government Publications (12 a year).

Saskatchewan Provincial Library and Literacy Office: 409A Park St, Regina, SK S4N 5B2; tel. (306) 787-2972; fax (306) 787-2029; internet www.learning.gov.sk.ca/provinciallibrary; f. 1953; coordinates library services in the province; 97,000 vols, specializing in library science, multilingual books and last copy fiction; Provincial Librarian JOYLENE CAMPBELL.

Saskatoon Public Library System: 311 23rd St East, Saskatoon, SK S7K 0J6; tel. (306) 975-7558; fax (306) 975-7542; internet www.saskatoonlibrary.ca; f. 1913; 7 brs; 828,641 vols, 12,790 audio cassettes, 22,456 video cassettes, 68,189 CDs, 36,171 DVDs, 3,362 talking books; local history room; Dir of Libraries ZENON ZUZAK.

University of Saskatchewan Libraries: 3 Campus Dr., Saskatoon, SK S7N 5A4; tel. (306) 966-5927; fax (306) 966-5932; internet www.library.usask.ca; f. 1909; main library and 6 brs with 1,871,000 vols, 15,423 current journals, 3,054,000 items on microform, 427,902 govt documents and pamphlets, Adam Shortt colln of Canadiana, Conrad Aiken colln of published works; Russell Green music MSS; Dir of Libraries F. WINTER.

Wapiti Regional Library: 145 12th St East, Prince Albert, SK S6V 1B7; tel. (306) 764-0712; fax (306) 922-1516; e-mail wapiti@panet.pa.sk.ca; f. 1950; 53 brs; 5,263,600 vols; Regional Dir JOHN MURRAY.

Museums and Art Galleries

Alberta

Art Gallery of Alberta: 2 Sir Winston Churchill Sq., Edmonton, AB T5J 2C1; tel. (780) 422-6223; fax (780) 426-3105; e-mail info@youraga.ca; internet www.youraga.ca; f. 1924; Canadian and int. drawing, painting, printmaking, sculpture and photography; devt and presentation of original exhibitions of contemporary and historical art from Alberta, Canada and around the world; art education and public programmes; colln of more than 6,000 objects; exhibits, preservation of art and visual culture; Exec. Dir GILLES HEBERT; Deputy Dir CATHERINE CROWSTON.

Banff Park Museum: Box 900, Banff, AB T1L 1K2; tel. (403) 762-1558; fax (403) 762-1565; e-mail banff.vrc@pc.gc.ca; internet www.parkscanada.gc.ca/lnh-nhs/ab/banff/index-e.asp; f. 1895; natural and human history of the park; Historic Sites Supervisor STEVE MALINS.

Buffalo Nations Museum: 1 Birch Ave (Box 850), Banff, AB T1L 1A8; tel. (403) 762-2388; fax (403) 760-2803; e-mail buffalonations@telus.net; f. 1951 as Luxton Museum; promotes education and awareness of the Northern Plains and Canadian Rockies Indians; natural history exhibits; Pres. HAROLD HEALY.

Department of Earth and Atmospheric Sciences Museum, University of Alberta: Edmonton, AB T6G 2E3; tel. (780) 492-2518; fax (780) 492-2030; internet easweb.eas.ualberta.ca; f. 1912; geology, meteorites, mineralogy, invertebrate and vertebrate palaeontology, stratigraphy; Collections and Museums Administrator A. J. LOCOCK.

Glenbow Museum: 130—9 Ave SE, Calgary, AB T2G 0P3; tel. (403) 268-4100; fax (403) 265-9769; e-mail glenbow@glenbow.org; internet www.glenbow.org; f. 1966; western Canadian and foreign cultural history, ethnology, military history, mineralogy and art; library of 100,000 vols, archives of 1,250,000 photos and negatives; Pres. Dr ROBERT R. JANES; Chair., Board of Governors ROBERT G. PETERS; publ. Experience (3 a year).

Medicine Hat Museum and Art Gallery: 1302 Bomford Crescent, Medicine Hat, AB T1A 5E6; tel. (403) 502-8580; fax (403) 502-8589; e-mail mhmag@medicinehat.ca; internet www.city.medicine-hat.ab.ca/cityservices/museum; f. 1967; cultural and natural history, palaeontology, and primitive peoples representative of south-east Alberta; art gallery; monthly exhibits by Canadian and international artists.

Royal Alberta Museum: 12845 102nd Ave, Edmonton, AB T5N 0M6; tel. (780) 453-9100; fax (780) 454-6629; internet www.royalalbertamuseum.ca; f. 1967; Alberta history, geology, natural history; Exec. Dir CHRIS ROBINSON (acting).

Royal Tyrrell Museum of Palaeontology: POB 7500, Highway 838 Midland Provincial Park, Drumheller, AB T0J 0Y0; tel. (403) 823-7707; fax (403) 823-7131; e-mail tyrrell.info@gov.ab.ca; internet www.tyrrellmuseum.com; f. 1985; colln, research, display and interpretation of fossils as evidence for history of life, with emphasis on famous dinosaur fauna of Alberta; resource management, vertebrate and invertebrate palaeontology, palynology, sedimentology, stratigraphy, taphonomy, preparation, illustration, administration; library of 50,000 vols, special biographical collection on Joseph Burr Tyrrell; 110,000 catalogued fossil specimens; field station in Dinosaur Provincial Park; UNESCO World Heritage Site; Dir ANDREW NEUMAN.

British Columbia

H. R. MacMillan Space Centre: 1100 Chestnut St, Vancouver, BC V6J 3J9; tel. (604) 738-7827; fax (604) 736-5665; e-mail tcromwell@spacecentre.ca; internet www.spacecentre.ca; f. 1988; administers the H. R. MacMillan Space Centre, H. R. MacMillan Planetarium and Gordon Southam Observatory; multimedia astronomy shows, laser shows, exhibitions, Observatory activities, lectures; 1,000 mems; Exec. Dir ROB APPLETON; publ. Starry Messenger (4 a year).

Helmcken House Museum: c/o Royal BC Museum, 675 Belleville St, Victoria, BC V8W 9W2; tel. (250) 356-7226; fax (250) 356-8197; internet www.royalbcmuseum.bc.ca; house built in 1852 for the surgeon Dr J. S. Helmcken (1824–1920); historic medical colln; Curator of Human History, Royal BC Museum LORNE HAMMOND.

Museum of Northern British Columbia: 100 First Ave W, Prince Rupert, BC V8J 1A8; tel. (250) 624-3207; fax (250) 627-8009; e-mail mnbc@citytel.net; internet www.museumofnorthernbc.com; f. 1924; exhibits cover 10,000 years of human habitation, incl. First Nations culture, local pioneer history and natural history; art gallery; library of 800 vols (50 rare); Dir ROBIN WEBER; Curator SUSAN MARSDEN.

Royal British Columbia Museum: 675 Belleville St, Victoria, BC V8W 9W2; tel. (250) 356-7226; fax (250) 356-8197; e-mail reception@royalbcmuseum.bc.ca; internet www.royalbcmuseum.bc.ca; f. 1886; contains reference collections and exhibits pertaining to natural history and human history of BC; CEO PAULINE RAFFERTY; publ. Discovery (newsletter, 3 a year).

Vancouver Art Gallery: 750 Hornby St, Vancouver, BC V6Z 2H7; tel. (604) 662-4700; fax (604) 682-1086; e-mail info@vanartgallery.bc.ca; internet www.vanartgallery.bc.ca; f. 1931; Canadian and foreign art by contemporary artists and major historical figures; library of 25,000 vols; Dir KATHLEEN BARTELS; publ. Members' Newsletter (3 a year).

Vancouver Maritime Museum: 1905 Ogden Ave, Vancouver, BC V6J 1A3; tel. (604) 257-8300; fax (604) 737-2621; e-mail director@vancouvermaritimemuseum.com; internet www.vancouvermaritimemuseum.com; f. 1958; maritime history, local and int. heritage vessels, RCMP St Roch Arctic patrol vessel, school programmes, lectures and summer festivals; library of 10,000 vols; Exec. Dir SIMON ROBINSON; publ. Signals (4 a year).

Manitoba

Manitoba Museum of Man and Nature: 190 Rupert Ave, Winnipeg, MB R3B 0N2; tel. (204) 956-2830; fax (204) 942-3679; e-mail info@manitobamuseum.ca; f. 1965; human and natural history of Manitoba; planetarium; 'Touch the Universe' interactive science centre; library of 26,000 vols; Exec. Dir CLAUDETTE LECLERC; publ. *Happenings* (6 a year).

Winnipeg Art Gallery: 300 Memorial Blvd, Winnipeg, MB R3C 1V1; tel. (204) 786-6641; fax (204) 788-4998; e-mail inquiries@wag.ca; internet www.wag.ca; f. 1912; exhibitions, lectures, films, performing arts, education programmes; library of 24,000 vols; Dir Dr STEPHEN BORYS.

New Brunswick

Beaverbrook Art Gallery: POB 605, Fredericton, NB E3B 5A6; tel. (506) 458-8545; fax (506) 459-7450; e-mail emailbag@ beaverbrookartgallery.org; internet www .beaverbrookartgallery.org; f. 1959; paintings; 18th-, 19th- and 20th-century English and continental paintings; 19th- and 20th-century Canadian paintings; 18th- and 19th-century English porcelain; English sculptures; medieval and Renaissance furniture, tapestries; Man. for Public Programming ADDA MILHAILESCU; publ. *Tableau* (2 a year).

Fort Beauséjour (Fort Cumberland National Historic Site of Canada): 111 Fort Beauséjour Rd, Aulac, NB E4L 2W5; tel. (506) 364-5080; fax (506) 536-4399; e-mail fort.beausejour@pc.gc.ca; internet www.pc.gc .ca/lhn-nhs/nb/beausejour/default.asp; f. 1926; semi-restored ruins of star-shaped fort overlooking the Bay of Fundy, built by the French in 1751 to defend their interests in the Isthmus of Chignecto, Acadia; renamed Fort Cumberland by the British; reinforced for the War of 1812, abandoned in 1835 and declared a nat. historic site in 1926; barracks, underground casemates and stone foundations overlooking the Bay of Fundy, the Tantramar marshes and extensive dykes; attached museum and visitor centre; Interpretation Officer and Coordinator JULIETTE BULMER.

Miramichi Natural History Museum: 149 Wellington St, Chatham NB E1N 1L7; fax (506) 773-6509; f. 1880; Curator KEN WEATHERBY.

New Brunswick Museum: 277 Douglas Ave, Saint John, NB E2K 1E5; tel. (506) 643-2300; fax (506) 643-2360; e-mail nbmuseum@nbm-mnb.ca; internet www .nbm-mnb.ca; f. 1842; archives, library, fine art, decorative art, natural science and history; CEO JANE FULLERTON.

York-Sunbury Historical Society Museum: POB 1312, Fredericton, NB E3B 5C8; tel. (506) 455-6041; fax (506) 458-8741; e-mail yorksun@nbnet.nb.ca; f. 1932; domestic and military exhibits of Fredericton and area; housed in British Officers' Quarters of 1840; Exec. Dir KATE MOSSMAN.

Newfoundland and Labrador

The Rooms Corporation of Newfoundland and Labrador—Provincial Museum and Art Gallery: POB 1800, St John's, NL A1C 5P9; 9 Bonaventure Ave, St John's, NL A1C 5P9; tel. (709) 757-8020 (museum); tel. (709) 757-8040 (art gallery); fax (709) 757-8021 (museum); fax (709) 757-8041 (art gallery); e-mail information@therooms.ca; internet www.therooms.ca; f. 2005; colln of over 8,000 works from historical, contemporary, international, crafts and folk art; Canadian works, including a Jean-Paul Riopelle; more than 1m. archeological items and natural history specimens; native artifacts; the world's largest Beothuk colln; Dir of Provincial Museum ANNE CHAFE; Dir of Provincial Art Gallery SHIELA PERRY.

Subsidiary Museums:

Mary March Regional Museum and Loggers' Exhibit: Grand Falls–Windsor, NL; tel. (709) 292-4522; fax (709) 292-4526;

e-mail pwells@nf.aibn.com; internet www .nfmuseum.com; Curator PENNY WELLS.

Southern Newfoundland Seamen's Museum: Grand Bank, NL; tel. (709) 832-1484; fax (709) 832-2053; e-mail gwcrews@nf.aibn.com; internet www .nfmuseum.com; Curator GERALD CREWS.

Nova Scotia

Art Gallery of Nova Scotia: 1723 Hollis St, POB 2262, Halifax, NS B3J 3C8; tel. (902) 424-5280; fax (902) 424-7359; e-mail infodesk@gov.ns.ca; internet www .artgalleryofnovascotia.ca; f. 1975; paintings, drawings, sculpture, prints, colln of Nova Scotia folk art, photography, multimedia; Dir and Chief Curator JEFFREY SPALDING; Dir for Devt BERNARD DOUCET; publ. *The Journal*.

Fort Anne National Historic Site and Museum: POB 9, Annapolis Royal, NS B0S 1A0; tel. (902) 532-2321; fax (902) 532-2232; e-mail information@pc.gc.ca; internet www .pc.gc.ca; f. 1917; Superintendent Operations THERESA BUNBURY.

Fortress of Louisbourg National Historic Site: 259 Park Service Rd, Louisbourg, NS B1C 2L2; tel. (902) 733-2280; fax (902) 733-2362; e-mail louisbourg.info@pc.gc.ca; internet fortress.uccb.ns.ca; f. 1963; reconstruction and restoration project, including 18th-century period rooms and museum complex; archives and library collections of 18th-century French and North American colonial material; District Dir CAROL WHITFIELD.

Maritime Museum of the Atlantic: 1675 Lower Water St, Halifax, NS B3J 1S3; tel. (902) 424-7890; fax (902) 424-0612; e-mail mmalibry@gov.ns.ca; internet museum.gov .ns.ca/mma/; f. 1982; naval and merchant shipping history; *Titanic* and Halifax explosion exhibitions; small boat collection; collection of 20,000 photographs and 5,000 books; Dir MICHAEL MURRAY.

Nova Scotia Museum of Natural History: 1747 Summer St, Halifax, NS B3H 3A6; tel. (902) 424-7370; fax (902) 424-0560; internet nature.museum.gov.ns.ca; f. 1868; collections, research and exhibits relating to natural history of Nova Scotia; Dir D. L. BURLESON.

Ontario

Art Gallery of Hamilton: 123 King St West, Hamilton, ON L8P 4S8; tel. (905) 527-6610; fax (905) 577-6940; e-mail info@ artgalleryofhamilton.com; internet www .artgalleryofhamilton.com; f. 1914; 9,000 works, mainly Canadian paintings, sculpture and graphics; also art from the USA, UK and other European countries; library of 2,000 vols; Pres. and CEO LOUISE DOMPIERRE; publ. *Insights* (members' magazine, 3 a year).

Art Gallery of Ontario: 317 Dundas St W, Toronto, ON M5T 1G4; tel. (416) 979-6648; internet www.ago.net; f. 1900; European and N American art since 15th century; Inuit art in all forms; Henry Moore; research; library of 250,000 vols; Dir and CEO MATTHEW TEITELBAUM; Dir, Collns and Research DENNIS REID; publ. *Art Matters Magazine* (4 a year).

Canada Science and Technology Museum Corporation: POB 9724, Station T, Ottawa, ON K1G 5A3; tel. (613) 991-6090; fax (613) 990-3636; e-mail info@technomuses .ca; internet technomuses.ca; f. 1967; shows Canada's role in science and technology through displays such as: steam locomotives, vintage cars, cycles, carriages, household appliances, computers, communications and space technology, model ships, and through experiments, demonstrations, special exhibitions and educational programmes and an

evening astronomy programme; the Corporation also includes the Canada Aviation Museum and the Canada Agriculture Museum; Pres. and CEO DENISE AMYOT; publs *Collection Profile* (also in electronic edn, 11 a year), *Curator's Choice* (also in electronic edn, irregular), *Material History Review* (2 a year).

Canadian Museum of Nature: POB 3443 Station D, Ottawa, ON K1P 6P4; tel. (613) 566-4700; fax (613) 364-4763; e-mail questions@mus-nature.ca; internet www .nature.ca; f. 1912; research and collns in the areas of botany, evolution, mineralogy, palaeobiology and zoology; houses the Centre for Traditional Knowledge, National Herbarium, the Biological Survey of Canada and the Canadian Centre for Biodiversity; library of 36,000 vols, 2,000 periodical titles (200 active subscriptions); Pres. and CEO JOANNE DICOSIMO.

Collingwood Museum: POB 556, 45 St Paul St, Collingwood, ON L9Y 4B2; tel. (705) 445-4811; fax (705) 445-9004; e-mail museum@collingwood.ca; internet www .collingwood.ca/museum; f. 1904; exhibits, children's programming, adult lectures, display, programming, research, special events; Supervisor SUSAN WARNER.

Dundurn Castle: 610 York Blvd, Hamilton, ON L8R 3H1; tel. (905) 546-2872; fax (905) 546-2875; former home of Sir Allan MacNab, Prime Minister of United Province of Canada 1854–56, built 1834, restored 1967; guided tours, special exhibits, period demonstrations; Curator WILLIAM NESBITT.

Jordan Historical Museum of the Twenty: 3802 Main St, Jordan, ON L0R 1S0; tel. (905) 562-5242; fax (905) 562-7786; f. 1953; a collection illustrating life in the Twenty Mile Creek area since 1776; Curator HELEN BOOTH.

Marine Museum of Upper Canada: Exhibition Place, Toronto, ON M5T 1R5; tel. (416) 392-1765; fax (416) 392-1767; e-mail can-thb@immedia.ca; f. 1959; operated by the Toronto Historical Board; preserves and interprets the marine history of Toronto, Toronto Harbour and Lake Ontario; collections include 1932 steam tug *Ned Hanlan* in dry dock; Curator JOHN SUMMERS.

Museum London: 421 Ridout St N, London, ON N6H 5H4; tel. (519) 661-0333; fax (519) 661-2559; e-mail ramurray@museumlondon .ca; internet www.museumlondon.ca; f. 1940; 25,000 historical artefacts, incl. paintings, prints, drawings and sculptures; undertakes collection and conservation of fine art and artefacts; exhibitions, lectures, films, workshops, tours and live performances; 900 mems; Exec. Dir BRIAN MEEHAN; publ. *At the Museum* (4 a year).

National Arts Centre: 53 Elgin St, Box 1534, Station B, Ottawa, ON K1P 5W1; tel. (613) 947-7000; fax (613) 996-9578; e-mail info@nac-cna.ca; internet www.nac-cna.ca; f. 1969; consists of Southam Hall (2,300 seats), theatre (950 seats), studio (300 seats), 4th stage (140 seats); resident 60-mem. NAC orchestra, English and French theatre, dance, opera, workshops, artist devt; 700 performances a year; Chair. JULIA FOSTER; Pres. and CEO PETER HERNNDORF.

National Gallery of Canada: 380 Sussex Drive, POB 427 Station A, Ottawa, ON K1N 9N4; tel. (613) 990-1985; fax (613) 993-4385; e-mail info@gallery.ca; internet national .gallery.ca; f. 1880; largest colln of Canadian art in the world; collns incl. large and important prints and drawings colln; historical and contemporary Canadian and international photography colln; Canadian art colln; Inuit colln; European colln; large contemporary colln; site incl. Canadian Museum of Contemporary Photography; operates largest travelling exhibition programme in North America; library of 275,000 vols; Dir PIERRE THÉBERGE; publs *National Gallery of Canada Review* (1 a year), *Vernissage* (4 a year).

Ontario Science Centre: 770 Don Mills Rd, Toronto, ON M3C 1T3; tel. (416) 696-1000; fax (416) 696-3124; e-mail webmaster@osc.on .ca; internet www.ontariosciencecentre.ca; f. 1969; more than 600 exhibits in all fields of science and technology; library of 11,000 vols; CEO LESLEY LEWIS; Chief Operating Officer GRANT TROOP.

Queen's University Museums: Miller Hall, Union St, Kingston, ON K7L 3N6; geology dept, tel. (613) 533-6767, f. 1901, Curator M. H. BADHAM; biology dept, tel. (613) 533-6160, f. 1880, Curator A. A. CROWDER; anatomy dept, tel. (613) 533-2600, f. 1854, Curator Dr M. G. JONEJA.

Royal Ontario Museum: 100 Queen's Park, Toronto, ON M5S 2C6; tel. (416) 586-8000; fax (416) 586-5863; e-mail info@rom.on.ca; internet www.rom.on.ca; f. 1912, opened in March 1914; affiliated to the Univ. of Toronto; decorative arts, natural history, anthropology and archaeology, and Canadian historical art; library of 175,000 vols; spec. collns 5,000 vols; Dir WILLIAM THORSELL; publ. *ROM: The Magazine of the Royal Ontario Museum* (3 a year).

Attached Institution:

George R. Gardiner Museum of Ceramic Art: 111 Queen's Park, Toronto, ON M5S 2C7; tel. (416) 586-8080; fax (416) 586-8085; e-mail mail@gardinermuseum .com; internet gardinermuseum.com; f. 1984.

Stephen Leacock Museum: Old Brewery Bay, 50 Museum Rd, Orillia, ON; tel. (705) 329-1908; fax (705) 326-5578; e-mail leacock@mail.transdata.ca; internet www .transdata.ca/~leacock; f. 1957; summer home, correspondence, manuscripts, personal effects of Stephen Butler Leacock 1869–1944; Curator DAPHNE MAINPRIZE.

Tom Thomson Memorial Art Gallery: 840 1st Ave West, Owen Sound, ON N4K 4K4; tel. (519) 376-1932; fax (519) 376-3037; e-mail sreid@e-owensound.com; internet www.tomthomson.org; f. 1967; Tom Thomson paintings, memorabilia; changing exhibitions of historic and contemporary art; Dir and Curator STUART REID; publ. *Newsletter* (4 a year).

Upper Canada Village: R. R. 1, Morrisburg, ON K0C 1X0; tel. (613) 543-3704; fax (613) 543-2847; internet www .uppercanadavillage.com; f. 1961; library of 5,000 vols; living historical site; 45 restored bldgs portraying a rural community c. 1866; spec. colln of 19th-century archival materials, incl. family and business records, photographs and social history documents from the region of eastern Ontario; Man. DAVE DOBBIE (acting).

Prince Edward Island

Confederation Centre Art Gallery and Museum: 145 Richmond St, Charlottetown, PE C1A 1J1; tel. (902) 628-6111; fax (902) 566-4648; e-mail artgallery@ confederationcentre.com; internet www .confederationcentre.com; f. 1964; nat. colln of 15,000 works of Canadian art since 19th century: paintings, drawings, prints, sculpture and photography; Harris Colln (paintings, drawings, MSS and records of Robert Harris, 1849–1919); temporary exhibitions on historical research and the contemporary artist; Dir JON TUPPER; Registrar and Curatorial Man. KEVIN RICE.

Québec

Canadian Museum of Civilization: 100 Laurier St, POB 3100, Station B, Gatineau, QC K1A 0M8; tel. (819) 776-7173; fax (819) 776-7152; e-mail library@civilization.ca; internet www.civilization.ca; f. 1856; archaeology, ethnology, folk culture studies, history of Canada, linguistics, physical anthropology,; study collns open to qualified researchers and gen. public; incl. Archaeological Survey of Canada, Canadian Children's Museum, Canadian Centre for Folk Culture Studies, Canadian Ethnology Service, Canadian Postal Museum, Canadian War Museum and other elements; library of 200,000 vols, of which 70,000 accessible to public; Pres. and CEO Dr VICTOR RABINOVITCH.

Centre Canadien d'Architecture/Canadian Centre for Architecture: 1920 rue Baile, Montréal, QC H3H 2S6; tel. (514) 939-7000; fax (514) 939-7020; e-mail ref@cca.qc .ca; internet www.cca.qc.ca; f. 1979 as a nonprofit org., recognized as a museum in 1989; research centre and museum; aims to advance knowledge and promote public understanding of architecture, its history, theory, practice, and role in soc., through study programmes, exhibitions, publications, seminars, lectures and internships; library of 215,000 printed monographs (incl. rare books); 5,000 runs of periodicals, a number of spec. collns; architecture-related artefacts (such as toys and souvenir models); ephemera; Founding Dir and Pres. of the Board PHYLLIS LAMBERT.

Insectarium de Montréal: 4581 rue Sherbrooke Est, Montréal, QC H1X 2B2; tel. (514) 872-1400; fax (514) 872-0662; e-mail insectarium@ville.montreal.qc.ca; internet www.ville.montreal.qc.ca/insectarium; f. 1990; colln of 160,000 insects; Dir ANNE CHARPENTIER.

McCord Museum of Canadian History: 690 Sherbrooke St West, Montréal, QC H3A 1E9; tel. (514) 398-7100; fax (514) 398-5045; e-mail info@mccord.mcgill.ca; internet www .musee-mccord.qc.ca; f. 1921; museum of Canadian social history with collns of Canadian ethnology, costumes, decorative arts, drawings, documents, paintings, prints, toys; Notman Photographic Archives containing 800,000 glass plates and prints; Exec. Dir Dr VICTORIA DICKENSON.

Montréal Biodôme: 4777 ave Pierre-de-Coubertin, Montréal, QC H1V 1B3; tel. (514) 868-3000; fax (514) 868-3065; e-mail biodome@ville.montreal.qc.ca; internet www .biodome.qc.ca; f. 1992; museum of the environment; live collns, containing more than 4,800 animals of 230 species, and 750 plants species in four recreated ecosystems found in the Americas; housed in the velodrome used for the 1976 Olympic Games; Dir RACHEL LÉGER.

Montréal Museum of Fine Arts: 1379–1380 Sherbrooke St West, Montréal, QC H3G 2T9; tel. (514) 285-1600; fax (514) 844-6042; e-mail webmaster@mbamtl.org; internet www.mmfa.qc.ca; f. 1860; permanent colln of paintings (European and Canadian), sculptures, decorative arts and drawings; art from Asia, Africa and Oceania; library: over 90,000 vols and slide library; Pres. BRIAN M. LEVITT; Dir NATHALIE BONDIL; publ. *M* (3 a year).

Musée d'art contemporain de Montréal: 185 St Catherine St W, Montréal, QC H2X 3X5; tel. (514) 847-6226; fax (514) 847-6291; e-mail info@macm.org; internet www.macm .org; f. 1964; exhibits contemporary Québecois, Canadian and int. art; organizes multimedia events, art videos, art workshops, lectures; library of 38,000 vols and exhibition catalogues, 713 periodicals, 8,000 visual archives, 1,000 video cassettes and audio items, 12,000 artists' files and bibliographic database; Dir PAULETTE GAGNON (acting); Chief Curator MARIE FRASER; publ. *Le Magazine.*

Musée de l'Amérique Française (Museum of French North America): 9 rue de la Vieille-Université, CP 460, succ., Haute-Ville, QC G1R 4R7; tel. (418) 528-0157; fax (418) 692-5206; e-mail archives@mcq.org; internet www.mcq.org; f. 1806, as Musée du Séminaire de Québec, present name 1983; attached to Musée de la Civilisation complex; art and history of French North America; library of 180,000 vols; Museum Dir DANIELLE POIRÉ; Archives Dir PIERRE BAIL.

Musée du Québec/Musée National des Beaux-Arts du Québec: Parc des Champs de Bataille, Québec, QC G1R 5H3; tel. (418) 643-2150; fax (418) 646-3330; e-mail info@ mnba.qc.ca; internet www.mnba.qc.ca; f. 1933; paintings, sculptures, drawings, prints, photographs, decorative art objects, interior design pieces; colln of 24,000 items relating to Québecois art and artists; Exec. Dir Dr JOHN R. PORTER.

Planétarium de Montréal: 1000 rue Saint-Jacques Ouest, Montréal, QC H3C 1G7; tel. (514) 872-4530; fax (514) 872-8102; e-mail info@planetarium.montreal.qc.ca; internet www.planetarium.montreal.qc.ca; f. 1966; astronomy, meteorite colln, museum; Dir PIERRE LACOMBE.

Redpath Museum: 859 Sherbrooke St W, Montréal, QC H3A 2K6; tel. (514) 398-4086; fax (514) 398-3185; e-mail redpath.museum@ mcgill.ca; internet www.mcgill.ca/redpath; f. 1882; promotes biological, geological, and cultural heritage through scientific research, collns-based study and education; Dir DAVID GREEN.

Saskatchewan

MacKenzie Art Gallery: 3475 Albert St, Regina, SK S4S 6X6; tel. (306) 522-4250; fax (306) 569-8191; e-mail mackenzie@uregina .ca; internet www.mackenzieartgallery.ca; f. 1954; permanent colln of Canadian historical and contemporary art, int. art since the 19th century, permanent colln displays and travelling exhibitions; public programmes; library: Resource Centre of 3,500 vols; Exec. Dir STUART REID; Curator TIMOTHY LONG; publs *At the MacKenzie* (3 a year), *@ the MacKenzie* (online, 12 a year).

Mendel Art Gallery and Civic Conservatory (Saskatoon Gallery and Conservatory Corporation): 950 Spadina Crescent East, POB 569, Saskatoon, SK S7K 3L6; tel. (306) 975-7610; fax (306) 975-7670; e-mail mendel@mendel.ca; internet www.mendel .ca; f. 1964; Canadian and int. art, exhibitions, permanent colln; library of 10,000 vols; Exec. Dir and CEO RICHARD MOLDENHAUER (acting); publ. *Folio* (4 a year).

Musée Ukraina Museum: POB 26072, Saskatoon, SK S7K 8C1; tel. (306) 244-4212; fax (306) 384-6310; e-mail ukrainamuseum@sasktel.net; internet www .mumsaskatoon.com; f. 1953; ethnographic collns representing the spiritual, material and folkloric culture of Ukraine; Pres. PATRICIA MIALKOWSKY.

Prince Albert Historical Museum: 10 River St E, Prince Albert, SK S6V 8A9; tel. (306) 764-2992; e-mail historypa@citypa.com; internet www.historypa.com; f. c. 1887 as Saskatchewan Institute, disbanded 1891 when records and artefacts destroyed by fire, re-formed 1923 as Prince Albert Historical Soc.; run by Prince Albert Historical Soc. (also operates the Diefenbaker House Museum, the Evolution of Education Museum and the Rotary Museum of Police and Corrections); local historical exhibits, early settlement, pioneers, Indian life, education, law enforcement; colln of memorabalia relating to Canadian Prime Minister John Diefenbaker; maintains Bill Smiley Archives (12,000 documents, 20,000 photographs and negatives, relating to Prince Albert and area; available for research); Pres. H. S. MAY; Man. JAMES BENSON.

Royal Saskatchewan Museum: College Ave and Albert St, Regina, SK S4P 3V7; tel. (306) 787-2815; fax (306) 787-2820; internet www.gov.sk.ca/rsm; f. 1906; Earth Sciences Gallery depicts 2.5 billion years of Saskatchewan's geological history; First Nations Gallery traces 12,000 years of aboriginal history and culture; Paleo Pit interactive gallery; Megamunch, a roaring robotic Tyrannosaurus rex; Life Sciences Gallery features the flora, fauna and landscapes of Saskatchewan's diverse eco-regions; Dir DAVID BARON.

Saskatchewan Western Development Museum: 2935 Melville St, Saskatoon, SK S7J 5A6; tel. (306) 934-1400; fax (306) 934-4467; e-mail info@wdm.ca; internet www.wdm.ca; f. 1949; exhibit brs at N Battleford, Moose Jaw, Saskatoon, and Yorkton; colln associated with the settlement of the Canadian W; agricultural machinery, early transport and household items; annual summer shows; library: George Shepherd Library of 15,000 historical vols; Exec. Dir DAVID KLATT; publ. *Sparks off the Anvil* (6 a year).

Universities and Colleges

ACADIA UNIVERSITY

15 University Ave, Wolfville, NS B4P 2R6

Telephone: (902) 542-2201

Fax: (902) 585-1072

E-mail: ask.acadia@acadiau.ca

Internet: www.acadiau.ca

Founded 1838

Provincial control

Language of instruction: English

Academic year: September to April

Chancellor: ARTHUR IRVING

Pres.and Vice-Chancellor: Dr RAY IVANY

Academic Vice-Pres.: Dr CYRUS MACLATCHY (acting)

Vice-Pres. for Finance and Transport: GARY DRAPER

Vice-Pres. for Growth and Operations: DOV BERCOVICI

Sr Dir of Communications and Public Affairs: SCOTT ROBERTS

Registrar: ROSEMARY JOTCHAM (acting)

Librarian: SARAH LOCHHEAD

Library: see Libraries and Archives

Number of teachers: 211 full-time, 37 part-time

Number of students: 3,100 full-time, 380 part-time

DEANS

Faculty of Arts: Dr BRUCE MATTHEWS

Faculty of Professional Studies: Dr GARY NESS (acting)

Faculty of Pure and Applied Sciences: Dr PAUL CABILIO (acting)

Faculty of Theology: Dr HARRY GARDNER

Research and Graduate Studies: Dr TOM ELLIS

PROFESSORS

ARCHIBALD, T., Mathematics

ASH, S., Business Administration

ASHLEY, T. R.

BAILET, D., French

BALDWIN, D., History

BARR, S. M., Geology

BAWTREE, M., English

BEDINGFIELD, E. W., Recreation and Kinesiology

BEST, J., French

BISSIX, G., Recreation and Kinesiology

BOOTH, P., Classics

BOWEN, K., Sociology

CABILIO, P., Mathematics

CAMERON, B. W., Geology

CONRAD, M. R., History

DABORN, G. R., Biology

DADSWELL, M., Biology

DAVIES, J. E., Economics

DAVIES, R. A., English

FISHER, S. F., Music

GRIFFITH, B., Education

HERMAN, T. B., Biology

HOBSON, P., Economics

HORVATH, P., Psychology

JOHNSTON, E. M., Nutrition

LATTA, B., Physics

LEITER, M. P., Psychology

LOOKER, E. D., Sociology

MACLATCHY, C. S., Physics

MCLEOD, W., Kinesiology

MATTHEWS, B., History

MOODY, B. M., History

MOUSSA, H., Economics

MULDNER, T., Computer Science

NESS, G., Recreation and Kinesiology

OGILVIE, K. K., Chemistry

OLIVER, L., Computer Science

O'NEILL, P. T. H., Psychology

PARATTE, H. D., French

PIPER, D., Education

PYRCZ, G. E., Political Science

RAESIDE, R. P., Geology

RIDDLE, P. H., Music

ROSCOE, J. M., Chemistry

ROSCOE, S., Chemistry

SACOUMAN, R. J., Sociology

SPARKMAN, R., Business

STEWART, I., Political Science

STEWART, R., English

STILES, D. A., Chemistry

SUMARAH, J., Education

SYMON, S., Psychology

TOEWS, D. P., Biology

TOMEK, I., Computer Science

TOWNLEY, P., Economics

TRITES, A. A., Theology

TRUDEL, A., Computer Science

TUGWELL, M., Economics

VAN WAGONER, N. A., Geology

VERSTRAETE, B. C., Classics

WILSON, R. S., Theology

AFFILIATED COLLEGE

Acadia Divinity College: Wolfville; f. 1968; on campus; under direction of Atlantic United Baptist Convention; degrees granted by the University; Principal L. MCDONALD.

UNIVERSITY OF ALBERTA

Edmonton, AB T6G 2M7

Telephone: (780) 492-3113

Fax: (780) 492-7172

E-mail: info@ualberta.ca

Internet: www.ualberta.ca

Founded 1908

Provincial control

Language of instruction: English (Faculté Saint-Jean: French)

Academic year: September to August

Chancellor: LINDA HUGHES

Pres.: Dr INDIRA V. SAMARASEKERA

Provost and Vice-Pres. for Academic Affairs: Dr CARL G. AMRHEIN

Vice-Pres. for External Relations: DEBRA POZEGA OSBURN

Vice-Pres. for Facilities and Operations: DON HICKEY

Vice-Pres. for Finance and Administration: PHYLLIS CLARK

Vice-Pres. for Research: Dr LORNE BABIUK

Registrar: GERRY KENDAL

Vice-Provost and Chief Librarian: ERNIE INGLES

Associate Vice-Pres. and Registrar: C. BYRNE (acting)

Library: see Libraries

Number of teachers: 3,520

Number of students: 37,588

Publications: *Calendar* (1 a year), *Folio* (23 a year), *Report of tCommunity* (1 a year), *The New Trail* (3 a year)

DEANS

Faculty of Agricultural, Life and Environmental Sciences: JOHN KENNELLY

Faculty of Arts: LESLEY CORMACK (acting)

Alberta School of Business: Prof. MIKE PERCY

Faculty of Education: Dr FERN SNART (acting)

Faculty of Engineering: DAVID LYNCH

Faculty of Extension: Dr KATY CAMPBELL

Faculty of Graduate Studies and Research: Dr MAZI SHIRVANI

Faculty of Law: PHILIP BRYDEN

Faculty of Medicine and Dentistry: PHILIP BAKER

Faculty of Native Studies: Dr ELLEN BIELAWSKI

Faculty of Nursing: Dr ANITA MOLZAHN

Faculty of Pharmacy and Pharmaceutical Sciences: Dr JAMES KEHRER

Faculty of Physical Education and Recreation: Dr KERRY MUMMERY

Faculty of Rehabilitation Medicine: Dr MARTIN FERGUSON-PELL

Faculty of Science: GREGORY TAYLOR

Augustana Campus: Dr ALLEN BERGER

Campus St-Jean: Dr MARC ARNAL

School of Library and Information Studies: Dr LISA M. GIVEN (acting)

School of Public Health: Dr SYLVIE STACHENKO (acting)

AFFILIATED COLLEGES

North American Baptist College: 11525-23 Ave, Edmonton, AB T6J 4T3; affiliated since 1988; offers first-year courses in liberal arts; Pres. Dr M. DEWEY.

St Joseph's College: Edmonton, AB T6G 2J5; affiliated 1926; Roman Catholic; courses in philosophy and Christian theology; Pres. T. SCOTT.

St Stephen's College: Edmonton, AB T6G 2J6; affiliated 1909; theological school of United Church of Canada; offers its own courses to degree level and certain courses open to students of the University; Principal G. ROGER.

ATHABASCA UNIVERSITY

1 Univ. Dr., Athabasca, AB T9S 3A3

Telephone: (780) 675-6100

Fax: (780) 675-6145

Internet: www.athabascau.ca

Founded 1970

Provincial control

Open univ. providing undergraduate and Masters-level courses for adult, non-residential students, with emphasis on distance and online education

Language of instruction: English

Chair., Governing Ccl: JOY ROMERO

Pres.: Dr FRITS PANNEKOEK (acting)

Vice-Pres. for Academic Affairs: Dr MARGARET HAUGHE

Vice-Pres. for Advancement: Dr LORI VAN-ROOIZEN

Registrar: JIM DARCY

Librarian: S. SCHAFER

Library of 143,261

Number of teachers: 258

Number of students: 31,250

Publications: *Aurora* (interviews with leading thinkers and writers), *Electronic Journal of Sociology, Globalization, IRRODDL* (research for Open and Distance Learning), *Radical Pedagogy, Sport and the Human Animal, Theory and Science, Trumpeter*

DIRECTORS

Centre for Computing and Information Systems: KINSHUK
Centre for Distance Education: Dr MOHAMED ALLY
Centre for Global and Social Analysis: DAVID GREGORY
Centre for Graduate Education in Applied Psychology: Dr SANDRA COLLINS
Centre for Innovative Management: ALEX KONDRA
Centre for Language and Literature: VERONICA THOMPSON
Centre for Learning Accreditation: DIANNE CONRAD (acting)
Centre for Nursing and Health Studies: Dr DONNA ROMYN
Centre for Psychology: TREVOR GILBERT
Centre for Science: NORMAN TEMPLE
Centre for State and Legal Studies: JAY SMITH
Centre for Work and Community Studies: LYNDA ROSS
Centre for World and Indigenous Knowledge and Research: PRISCILLA CAMPEAU
School of Business: DAVID ANNAND

BISHOP'S UNIVERSITY

Sherbrooke, QC J1M 1Z7
Telephone: (819) 822-9600
Fax: (819) 822-9661
E-mail: recruitment@ubishops.ca
Internet: www.ubishops.ca
Founded 1843, constituted a univ. by Royal Charter 1853
Academic year: September to May
Language of instruction: English
Chancellor: SCOTT GRIFFIN
Prin.: MICHAEL GOLDBLOOM
Vice-Prin.: Dr MICHAEL CHILDS
Vice-Prin. for Admin. and Finance: HELENE ST AMAND
Registrar and Sec.-Gen.: RUTH SHEERAN
Librarian: WENDY DURRANT
Dean of Student Affairs: BRUCE STEVENSON
Number of teachers: 109 full-time
Number of students: 2,850
Publication: *Journal of Eastern Township Studies* (2 a year)

DEANS

School of Arts and Sciences: Dr JAMIE CROOKS
School of Education: Dr CATHERINE BEAUCHAMP
Williams School of Business: Dr STEVE HARVEY

BRANDON UNIVERSITY

270 18th St, Brandon, MB R7A 6A9
Telephone: (204) 727-9762
Fax: (204) 728-7340
E-mail: president@brandonu.ca
Internet: www.brandonu.ca
Founded 1899; gained full autonomy July 1967
Public control
Language of instruction: English
Academic year: September to April
Chancellor: H. CHAMP
Pres.: Dr DEBORAH POFF
Vice-Pres. for Academic and Research: Dr SCOTT GRILLS
Vice-Pres. for Admin. and Finance: SCOTT J. B. LAMONT

Registrar: Dr LAWRENCE VAN BEEK
Librarian: L. BURRIDGE
Number of teachers: 170
Number of students: 3,200 (full- and part-time)
Publications: *Abstracts of Native Studies, Canadian Journal of Native Studies, Cross Cultural Psychology Bulletin, Ecclectica, Journal of Rural and Community Development*

DEANS AND DIRECTORS

Faculty of Arts: Dr G. BRUCE STRANG
Faculty of Education: JERRY STORIE
Faculty of Science: JANET S. WRIGHT
School of Health Studies: Dr DEAN CARE
School of Music: Dr MICHAEL KIM
Department of Rural Development: Dr ROBERT ANNIS (acting)
First Nations and Aboriginal Counselling Programme: ANDREA HINCH-BOURNS

UNIVERSITY OF BRITISH COLUMBIA

2329 West Mall, Vancouver, BC V6T 1Z4
Telephone: (604) 822-2211
Fax: (604) 822-5785
E-mail: presubc@interchange.ubc.ca
Internet: www.ubc.ca
Founded 1908
Academic year: September to August
Chancellor: SARAH MORGAN-SILVESTER
Pres. and Vice-Chancellor: Prof. STEPHEN J. TOOPE
Vice-Pres. for Academics and Provost: DAVID H. FARRAR
Vice-Pres. for Finance, Resources and Operations: PIERRE OUILLET
Vice-Pres. for Development and Alumni Engagement: BARBARA MILES
Vice-Pres. for External, Legal and Community Relations: STEPHEN OWEN
Vice-Pres. for Research and International: JOHN HEPBURN
Vice-Pres. for Students: BRIAN SULLIVAN
Registrar: R. A. SPENCER
Librarian: INGRID PARENT
Number of teachers: 4,669
Number of students: 50,332
Publications: *BC Asian Review* (1 a year), *BC Studies* (4 a year), *BC Studies: The British Columbian Quarterly* (4 a year), *Canadian Journal of Botany* (4 a year), *Canadian Journal of Civil Engineering* (6 a year), *Canadian Journal of Women and the Law* (1 a year), *Canadian Literature* (4 a year), *PRISM International* (4 a year), *University Calendar* (winter and summer), *Yearbook of International Law*

DEANS

Faculty of Applied Science: TYSEER ABOUL-NASR
Faculty of Arts: GAGE AVERILL
Sauder School of Business: DANIEL F. MUZYKA
Faculty of Dentistry: CHARLES SHULER
Faculty of Education: JON SHAPIRO
Faculty of Forestry: JOHN INNES
Faculty of Graduate Studies: BARBARA EVANS
College for Interdisciplinary Studies: MIKE BURGESS (Principal)
College of Health Disciplines: LOUISE NASMITH (Principal)
Faculty of Land and Food Systems: MURRAY B. ISMAN
Faculty of Law: MARY ANNE BOBINSKI
Faculty of Medicine: GAVIN STUART
Faculty of Pharmaceutical Sciences: ROBERT D. SINDELAR
Faculty of Science: SIMON PEACOCK

DIRECTORS OF SCHOOLS

School of Architecture: Prof. CHRISTOPHER MACDONALD (acting)
School of Audiology and Speech Science: Prof. VALTER CIOCCA
School of Community and Regional Planning: Prof. PENNY GURSTEIN
School of Environmental Health: Prof. PAUL A. DEMERS
School of Human Kinetics: Prof. ROBERT E. SPARKS (acting)
Graduate School of Journalism: Dr MARY LYNN YOUNG
School of Library, Archival and Information Studies: Dr CAROLINE HAYTHORNTHWAITE
School of Music: Prof. RICHARD KURTH
School of Nursing: Prof. SALLY THORNE
School of Population and Public Health: Dr MARTIN SCHECHTER
School of Social Work and Family Studies: Prof. KWONG-IEUNG TANG

PROFESSORS

Faculty of Agricultural Sciences
Department of Agroecology:
BLACK, A.
CHANWAY, C.
CHENG, K.
CHIENG, S.-T.
COPEMAN, R.
CRONK, Q.
ELLIS, B.
ISMAN, M.
JOLLIFFE, P.
LAVKULICH, L.
MCKINLEY, S.
MYERS, J.
RAJAMAHENDRAN, R.
SCHREIER, H.
SHACKLETON, D.
TAYLOR, I.
UPADHYAYA, M.
WEARY, O.

Department of Community and the Environment:
CONDON, P.
PATERSON, D.
QUAYLE, M.

Department of Food, Nutrition and Health:
BARR, S.
CHENG, K.
DURANCE, T.
KITTS, D.
LI-CHAN, E.
THOMPSON, J.
VAN VUUREN, H.
VERCAMMEN, J.

Faculty of Applied Science
Department of Chemical and Biological Engineering:
BERT, J.
BOWEN, B.
CHIENG, S.
DUFF, S.
ENGLEZOS, P.
GRACE, J.
HATZIKIRIAKOS, S.
JIM JIM, C.
KEREKES, R.
LO, K.
OLOMAN, C.
PIRET, J.
SMITH, K.
WATKINSON, P.

Department of Civil Engineering:
ADEBAR, P.
BANTHIA, N.
FANNIN, R.
FOSCHI, R.
HALL, E.
HALL, K. J.
ISSACSON, M.
LAWRENCE, G.

MAVINIC, D.
MINDESS, S.
NAVIN, F.
RUSSELL, A.
SEXSMITH, R.
STEIMER, S.

Department of Electrical and Computer Engineering:

DAVIES, M.
DUMONT, G.
IVANOV, A.
JAEGER, N.
KRISHNAMURTHY, V.
LAWRENCE, P.
LEUNG, C.
LEUNG, V.
PULFREY, D.
SALEH, R.
WARD, R.

Department of Mechanical Engineering:

ALTINTAS, Y.
CALISAL, S.
CHERCHAS, D.
DE SILVA, C.
EVANS, R.
GADALA, M.
GREEN, S.
HILL, P.
HODGSON, M.
HUTTON, S.
RAJAPAKSE, N.
SALCUDEAN, M.
SASSANI, F.
SCHAJER, G.
YELLOWLEY, I.

Department of Metals and Materials Engineering:

DREISINGER, D.
POURSARTIP, A.
REED, R.
TROCZYNSKI, T.
TROMANS, D.

Department of Mining Engineering:

MEECH, J.
SCOBLE, M.
WILSON, W.

Faculty of Arts

Department of Anthropology:

MATSON, R.
MILLER, B.

Department of Art History, Visual Art and Theory:

COHODAS, M.
EDER, R.
GUILBAUT, S.
LUM, K.
O'BRIAN, J.
WATSON, S.
WINDSOR-LISCOMBE, R.

Department of Asian Studies:

DUKE, M.
NOSCO, P.
OBEROI, H.
SCHMIDT, J.
TAKASHIMA, K.-I.

Department of Classical, Near Eastern and Religious Studies:

BARRETT, A. A.
HARDING, P.
SULLIVAN, S.
TODD, R.
WILLIAMS, E.

Department of Economics:

COPELAND, B.
DIEWERT, E.
ESWARAN, M.
EVANS, R.
GREEN, D.
KOTWAL, A.
LEMIEUX, T.
PATERSON, D.

REDISH, A.
RIDDELL, C.

Department of French, Hispanic and Italian Studies:

BOCCASSINI, D.
HODGSON, R.
MCEACHERN, J.
RAOUL, V.
SARKONAK, R.
TESTA, C.
URRELLO, A.

Department of Geography:

BARNES, T.
CHURCH, M.
GREGORY, D.
HIEBERT, D.
LEY, D.
MCCLUNG, D.
MCKENDRY, I.
OKE, T.
PRATT, G.
ROBINSON, J.
SLAYMAKER, O.
STEYN, D.
STULL, R.
WYNN, G.

Department of Germanic Studies:

MORNIN, E.
PETERSEN, K.
PETRO, P.
STENBERG, P.

Department of History:

FRIEDRICHS, C.
KRAUSE, P.
LARY, D.
NEWELL, D.
RAY, A.
UNGER, R.
WARD, P.

Department of Linguistics:

PULLEYBLANK, D.
STEMBERGER, J.
VATIKIOTIS-BATESON, E.

School of Music:

BENJAMIN, W.
BERINAUM, M.
BUTLER, G.
CHATMAN, S.
COOP, J.
DAWES, A.
HAMEL, K.
READ, J.
SHARON, R.
TENZER, M.

Department of Philosophy:

BEATTY, J.
IRVINE, A.
RUSSELL, P.
SAVITT, S.
SCHABAS, M.
WILSON, C.

Department of Political Science:

JOB, B.
JOHNSTON, R.
LASELVA, S.
MARANTZ, P.
MAUZY, D.
RESNICK, P.
TENNANT, P.
TUPPER, A.
WALLACE, M.

Department of Psychology:

ALDEN, L.
CHANDLER, M.
COREN, S.
DUTTON, D.
ENNS, J.
GORZALKA, B.
GRAF, P.
HAKSTIAN, R.
LEHMAN, D.

LINDEN, W.
PINEL, J.
TEES, R.
WALKER, L.
WARD, L.
WERKER, J.

Department of Sociology:

CREESE, G.
CURRIE, D.
ELLIOTT, B.
ERICSON, R.
GUPPY, N.
JOHNSON, G.
JOPPKE, C.
MATTHEWS, D.

Department of Theatre, Film and Creative Writing:

ALDERSON, S.
DURBACH, E.
GARDINER, R.
MCWHIRTER, G.
MAILLARD, K.
WASSERMAN, J.

Faculty of Dentistry

Department of Oral Biological and Medical Sciences:

BRUNETTE, D.
CLARK, C.
DIEWERT, V.
DONALDSON, D.
HANNAM, A.
LARJAVA, H.
LOWE, A.
OVERALL, C.
UITTO, V.-J.
YEN, E.

Department of Oral Health Sciences:

CLARK, C.
DIEWERT, V.
HANNAM, A.
LOWE, A.
MCENTEE, M.

Faculty of Education

Faculty of Curriculum Studies:

CHALMERS, F. G.
ERICKSON, G.
GASKELL, P.
IRWIN, R.
KINDLER, A.
PETERAT, L.
PIRIE, S.

Department of Educational and Counselling Psychology, and Special Education:

AMUNDSON, N.
ARLIN, M.
BORGEN, W.
BUTLER, D.
DANILUK, J.
KAHN, S.
LONG, B.
PORATH, M.
SIEGEL, L.
WESTWOOD, M.
YOUNG, R.
ZUMBO, B.

Department of Educational Studies:

ADAM-MOODLEY, K.
BARMAN, J.
BOSHIER, R.
BROWN, D.
FISHER, D.
KELLY, D.
PRATT, D. D.
ROMAN, L.
RUBENSON, K.
SCHUETZE, H.
SHIELDS, C.
SORK, T.
STRONG-BOAG, V.
UNGERLEIDER, C. S.

Faculty of Forestry:
AVRAMIDIS, S.
BARKER, J.
BARRETT, D.
BUNNELL, F.
CHAFWAY, C.
EL-KASSABY, Y.
EVANS, P.
FANNIN, J.
GUY, R.
HALEY, D.
HOBERG, G.
INNES, J.
KIMMINS, J.
KLINKA, K.
MCLEAN, J.
MARTIN, K.
MURTHA, P.
RITLAND, K.
RUDDICK, J.
VAN DER KAMP, B.

Faculty of Law:
BAKAN, J.
BLACK, W.
BLOM, J.
BOYD, S.
BOYLE, C.
BURNS, P.
ELLIOT, R.
FARQUHAR, K.
GRANT, I.
JACKSON, M.
LEBARON, L. M.
MCDOUGALL, B.
PATERSON, R.
PAVLICH, D.
PUE, W.
SHEPPARD, A.
WEILER, J.
YOUNG, C.

Faculty of Medicine
Department of Anatomy:
BRESSLER, B.
CHURCH, J.
CRAWFORD, B.
EMERMAN, J.
NAUS, C.
OVALLE, W.
SLONECKER, C.
VOGL, A.
WEINBERG, J.

School of Audiology and Speech Sciences:
JOHNSTON, J.
STAPELLS, D.

Department of Biochemistry and Molecular Biology:
BRAYER, G.
BROWNSEY, R.
CULLIS, P.
DEDHAR, S.
FINLAY, B.
MACGILLIVRAY, R.
MCINTOSH, L.
MACKIE, G.
MAUK, A.
MOLDAY, R.
ROBERGE, M.
SADOWSKI, I.

Department of Family Practice:
BASSETT, K.
BATES, J.
CALAM, B.
DONNELLY, M.
GRAMS, G.
GRZYBOWSKI, S.
KHAN, K.
KLEIN, M.
KUHL, D.
LIVINGSTONE, V.
MCKENZIE, D.
SCOTT, I.
TAUNTON, J.
WHITESIDE, C.

WIEBE, C.
WOOLLARD, R.

Department of Healthcare and Epidemiology:
BARER, M.
BLACK, C.
HERTZMAN, C.
KAZANJIAN, A.
KENNEDY, S.
MATHIAS, R.
SCHECHTER, M.
SHEPS, S.
SINGER, J.
TESCHKE, K.

Faculty of Medical Genetics:
BURGESS, M.
EAVES, C.
FIELD, L.
FRIEDMAN, J.
HALL, J.
HIETER, P.
JEFFERIES, W.
JURILOFF, D.
KAY, R.
MCGILLIVRAY, B.
MCMASTER, W.
MAGER, D.
ROSE, A.
SADOVNICK, A.

Department of Medicine:
ABBOUD, R.
BAI, T.
BEATTIE, B.
BIRMINGHAM, C.
BOWIE, W.
BRUNHAM, R.
CAIRNS, J.
CALNE, D.
CHOW, A.
EAVES, A.
EISEN, A.
ESDAILE, J.
FLEETHAM, J.
FREEMAN, H.
HO, V.
HUMPHRIES, R.
KEOWN, P.
KERR, C.
LAM, S.
LUI, H.
MCLEAN, D.
MANCINI, G.
MONTANER, J.
OGER, J.
OSTROW, D.
PAGE, G.
PARÉ, P.
PATY, D.
PELECH, S.
PRIOR, J.
QUAMME, G.
RABKIN, S.
REINER, N.
RIVERS, J.
ROAD, J.
RUSSELL, J.
SCHELLENBERG, R.
SCHRADER, J.
SCHULZER, M.
STEIN, H.
STEINBRECHER, U.
STIVER, H.
STOESSL, J.
SUTTON, R.
TSUI, J.
WALLEY, K.
WANG, Y.
WONG, N.
WRIGHT, J.
YEUNG, M.

Department of Physiology:
BAIMBRIDGE, K.
BUCHAN, A.
FEDIDA, D.

MCINTOSH, C.
NAUS, C. C.
PEARSON, J

Department of Radiology:
COOPERBERG, P.
CULHAM, G.
LI, D.
LYSTER, D.
MACKAY, A.
MÜLLER, N.
MUNK, P.

Department of Surgery:
WARNOCK, G.

Faculty of Science
Department of Botany:
DEWREEDE, R.
DOUGLAS, C.
GANDERS, F.
GLASS, A.
GREEN, B.
GRIFFITHS, A.
MADDISON, W.
TAYLOR, F.
TAYLOR, I.
TOWERS, G.
TURKINGTON, R.

Department of Chemistry:
ANDERSEN, R.
BLADES, M.
BROOKS, D.
BURNELL, E.
COMISAROW, M.
DOLPHIN, D.
DOUGLAS, D.
FLEMING, D.
FRYZUK, M.
FYFE, C.
GERRY, M.
HEPBURN, J.
HERRING, G.
LEGZDINS, P.
MCINTOSH, L.
MITCHELL, K.
ORVIG, C.
PATEY, G.
PIERS, E.
SAWATZKY, G.
SCHEFFER, J.
SHAPIRO, M.
SHERMAN, J.
SHIZGAL, B.
STORR, A.
TANNER, M.
WITHERS, S.

Department of Computer Science:
ASCHER, U.
BOOTH, K.
CONDON, A.
FRIEDMAN, J.
KICZALES, G.
KIRKPATRICK, D.
KLAWE, M.
LAKSHMANAN, L.
LITTLE, J.
LOWE, D.
MACKWORTH, A.
NG, R.
PAI, D.
PIPPENGER, N.
POOLE, D.
ROSENBERG, R.
WOODHAM, R.

Department of Earth and Ocean Sciences:
ANDERSEN, R.
BOSTOCK, M.
BUSTIN, M.
CLARKE, G.
CLOWES, R.
FLETCHER, K.
GROAT, L.
HARRISON, P.
HEALEY, M.

HSIEH, W.
HUNGR, O.
INGRAM, G.
OLDENBURG, D.
RUSSELL, K.
SMITH, L.
SMITH, P.
STEYN, D.
STULL, R.
TAYLOR, M.
ULRYCH, T.
WEIS, D.

Department of Mathematics:

ANSTEE, R.
BLUMAN, G.
BOYD, D.
CARRELL, J.
FOURNIER, J.
GHOUSSOUB, N.
LAM, K.
LOEWEN, P.
MACDONALD, J.
MARCUS, B.
PEIRCE, A.
PERKINS, E.
SEYMOUR, B.
SJERVE, D.
SLADE, G.
WARD, M.

Department of Microbiology and Immunology:

HANCOCK, R. E. W.
JEFFERIES, W. A.
KRONSTAD, J. W.
SMIT, J.
SPIEGELMAN, G.
TEH, H.-S.
WEEKS, G.

Department of Statistics:

HARRY, J.
HECKMAN, N.
PETKAU, J.
VAN EEDEN, C.
ZAMAR, R.
ZIDEK, J.

Department of Zoology:

ADAMSON, M.
BERGER, J.
BLAKE, R.
BROCK, H.
GASS, C.
GOSLINE, J.
GRIGLIATTI, T.
JONES, D.
MILSOM, W.
MOERMAN, D.
MYERS, J.
PAULY, D.
PITCHER, T.
RANDALL, D.
SCHLUTER, D.
SINCLAIR, T.
SMITH, J.
SNUTCH, T.
STEEVES, J.
TETZLAFF, W.
WALTERS, C.

Sauder School of Business

Division of Accounting:

FELTHAM, G.
SIMUNIC, D.

Division of Finance:

GIAMMARINO, R.
HAMILTON, S.
HEINKEL, R.
KRAUS, A.
LEVI, M.

Division of Law:

WAND, Y.

Division of Marketing:

GRIFFIN, D.

WEINBERG, C.

Division of Operations and Logistics:

ATKINS, D.
GRANOT, D.
GRANOT, F.
MCCORMICK, T.
OUM, T.
PUTERMAN, M.
QUEYRANNE, M.
ZHANG, A.
ZIEMBA, W.

Division of Strategy and Business Economics:

ANTWEILER, W.
BOARDMAN, A.
BRANDER, J.
FRANK, M.
HELSLEY, R.
NAKAMURA, M.
NEMETZ, P.
ROSS, T.
SPENCER, B.
VERTINSKY, I.
WINTER, R.

School of Architecture:

BROCK, L.
COLE, R.
CONDON, P.
MACDONALD, C.
PATKAU, P.
WAGNER, G.
WALKEY, R.
WOJTOWICZ, J.

School of Human Kinetics:

CROCKER, P.
FRANKS, I.
MCKENZIE, D.
RHODES, E.
TAUNTON, J.

School of Journalism:

LOGAN, D.

School of Library, Archival and Information Studies:

DURANTI, L.
HAYCOCK, K.
RASMUSSEN, E.

School of Nursing:

ACORN, S.
ANDERSON, J.
BOTTORFF, D.
CARTY, E.
HILTON, A.
JOHNSON, J.
PATERSON, B.
THORNE, S.

School of Social Work and Family Studies:

CHRISTENSEN, C.
MARTIN-MATHEWS, A.
PERLMAN, D.
RUSSELL, M.
WHITE, J.

THEOLOGICAL COLLEGES

Carey Hall and Carey Theological College: 5920 Iona Drive, Vancouver, BC V6T 1J6; tel. 224-4308; internet www.careytheologicalcollege.ca; Baptist; Principal Dr B. F. STELCK.

Regent College: 5800 University Boulevard, Vancouver, BC V6T 2E4; tel. 224-3245; internet www.regent-college.edu; trans-denominational; Pres. ROD WILSON.

St Andrew's Hall: 6040 Iona Drive, Vancouver, BC V6T 2E8; tel. (604) 822-9720; Presbyterian; Dean Rev. B. J. FRASER.

St Mark's College: 5935 Iona Drive, Vancouver, BC V6T 1J7; tel. 224-3311; internet www.stmarkscollege.ca; Roman Catholic; Principal Dr JOHN D. DENNISON.

Vancouver School of Theology: 6000 Iona Drive, Vancouver, BC V6T 1L4; tel. (604) 228-9031; fax (604) 228-0189; internet www.vst.edu; an ecumenical school of theology, incorporated 1971; continues work of the Anglican Theological College of BC and Union College of BC; provides theological education for laymen, for future clergy and for graduates in theology; Principal Dr KENNETH MACQUEEN.

BROCK UNIVERSITY

500 Glenridge Ave, St Catharines, ON L2S 3A1

Telephone: (905) 688-5550
Fax: (905) 688-2789
E-mail: regist@brocku.ca
Internet: www.brocku.ca

Founded 1964
Provincial control
Academic year: September to April
Language of instruction: English

Chancellor: NED GOODMAN
Pres. and Vice-Chancellor: JACK LIGHTSTONE
Provost and Vice-Pres. for Academics: MURRAY KNUTTILA
Vice-Pres. for Admin.: STEVEN PILLAR
Registrar: BARB DAVIS
Librarian: M. GROVE

Library of 2,194,400 vols
Number of teachers: 583
Number of students: 17,877

Publications: *View book* (1 a year), *Surgite* (2 a year)

DEANS

Faculty of Applied Health Sciences: JOANNE MACLEAN
Faculty of Business: PHILIP KITCHEN
Faculty of Education: FOINA BLAIKIE
Faculty of Graduate Studies: MARILYN ROSE
Faculty of Mathematics and Science: RICK CHEEL
Faculty of Social Sciences: THOMAS DUNK

UNIVERSITY OF CALGARY

2500 University Drive NW, Calgary, AB T2N 1N4

Telephone: (403) 220-5110
Fax: (403) 282-7298
E-mail: reginfo@ucalgary.ca
Internet: www.ucalgary.ca

Founded 1945 as a br. of the University of Alberta; gained full autonomy 1966
Language of instruction: English
Academic year: July to June

Chancellor: JIM DINNING
Pres.: Dr ELIZABETH CANNON
Provost and Vice-Pres. for Academic Affairs: ALAN HARRISON
Vice-Pres. for Devt.: GARY DURBENIUK
Assoc. Vice-Pres. for External Relations: CATHERINE BAGNELL STYLES
Vice-Pres. for Facilities Management and Devt.: BOB ELLARD
Vice-Pres. for Finance and Services: JONATHAN GEBERT
Vice-Pres. for Research: Dr ROSE GOLDSTEIN
Registrar: D. B. JOHNSTON
Chief Information Officer for Information Technologies: H. A. ESCHE

Number of teachers: 2,761
Number of students: 29,000

Publications: *Abstracts of English Studies*, *Arctic Journal* (Arctic Institute of North America), *Ariel: Review of International English Literature*, *Calgary Alumni*, *Canadian Energy Research Institute* publs (irregular), *Canadian Ethnic Studies*, *Canadian and International Education* (2 a year), *Canadian Journal of Law and Society* (1 a year), *Canadian Journal of Philosophy* (4 a year), *Classical Views—*

Echos du monde classique, International Journal of Man-Machine Studies (12 a year), *Journal of Child and Youth Care, Journal of Comparative Family Studies, Journal of Educational Thought* (3 a year), *University Gazette* (26 a year)

DEANS

Faculty of Arts: KEVIN MCQUILLAN
Faculty of Education: DENNIS SUMARA
Faculty of Environmental Design: Dr NANCY POLLOCK-ELLWAND
Faculty of Graduate Studies: Dr FRED HALL
Faculty of Kinesiology: Dr WAYNE GILES
Faculty of Law: ALASTAIR R. LUCAS
Faculty of Medicine: Dr TOM FEASBY
Faculty of Nursing (Calgary): DIANNE TAP
Faculty of Nursing (Qatar): SHEILA EVANS
Faculty of Science: Dr KEN BARKER
Faculty of Social Work: Dr GAYLA ROGERS
Schulich School of Engineering: Dr ANIL MEHROTRA
Haskayne School of Business: Dr LEONARD WAVERMAN
Continuing Education: Dr SCOTT MCLEAN (Dir)

PROFESSORS

ADDICOTT, J. F., Biological Sciences
ADDINGTON, D. E. N., Psychiatry
AGOPIAN, E. E., Music
ANDREWS, J. W., Division of Applied Psychology
ARCHER, C. I., History
ARCHER, D. P., Anaesthesia and Clinical Neurosciences
ARCHER, K. A., Political Science
ARCHIBALD, J. A., Linguistics
ARMSTRONG, G. D., Microbiology and Infectious Diseases
ARTHUR, N. M., Division of Applied Psychology
ASTLE, W. F., Surgery
ATKINSON, M. H., Medicine
AUER, R. N., Clinical Neurosciences and Pathology and Laboratory Medicine
AUSTIN, C. D., Social Work
BACK, T. G., Chemistry
BANKES, N. D., Law
BARCLAY, R. M. R., Biological Sciences
BARKER, K. E., Computer Science
BARRY, D., Political Science
BAUWENS, L., Mechanical Engineering
BECH-HANSEN, N. T., Medical Genetics and Surgery
BECKER, W. J., Clinical Neurosciences and Medicine
BEHIE, L. A., Chemical and Petroleum Engineering
BELENKIE, I., Medicine
BELL, A. G., Music
BELL, D. M., Music
BELYEA, B., English
BENEDIKTSON, H., Pathology and Laboratory Medicine
BENNETT, S., English
BENTLEY, L. R., Geology and Geophysics
BERCUSON, D. J., History
BERSHAD, D. L., Art
BEZDEK, K., Mathematics and Statistics
BIDDLE, F. G., Paediatrics and Biochemistry and Molecular Biology and Medical Genetics
BINDING, P. A., Mathematics and Statistics
BIRSS, V. I., Chemistry
BISZTRICZKY, T., Mathematics and Statistics
BLAND, B. H., Psychology
BOND, R. B., English
BOS, L. P., Mathematics and Statistics
BOSETTI, B. L., Education
BOWAL, P. C., Haskayne School of Business
BOYCE, J. R., Economics
BRADLEY, J., Computer Science
BRANNIGAN, A., Sociology
BRANT, R. F., Community Health Sciences
BRAY, R. C., Surgery

BRENKEN, B. A., Mathematics and Statistics
BRENT, D. A., Communication and Culture
BROWDER, L. W., Biochemistry and Molecular Biology and Oncology
BROWN, C. A., Law
BROWN, C. B., Medicine, Oncology, Biochemistry and Molecular Biology
BROWN, J. L. S., Environmental Design
BROWN, J. S., Music
BROWN, K., French, Italian and Spanish
BROWN, R. J., Geology and Geophysics
BROWN, T. G., Civil Engineering
BROWNELL, A. K. W., Clinical Neurosciences and Medicine
BRUCE, C. J., Economics
BRUEN, A. A., Mathematics and Statistics
BRUTON, L. T., Electrical and Computer Engineering
BULLOCH, A. G. M., Physiology and Biophysics
BURET, A. G., Biological Sciences
BURGESS, E. D., Medicine
BURKE, M. D., Mathematics and Statistics
BUTZNER, J. D., Paediatrics
CAIRNCROSS, J. G., Clinical Neurosciences
CAIRNS, K. V., Division of Applied Psychology
CAMERON, E., Art
CAMPBELL, G. W., French, Italian and Spanish
CAMPBELL, N. R. C., Medicine
CANNON, M. E., Geomatics Engineering
CARTER, S. A., History
CAVEY, M. J., Biological Sciences
CERI, H., Biological Sciences
CHACONAS, G., Biochemistry, Molecular Biology, Microbiology and Infectious Diseases
CHADEE, K., Microbiology and Infectious Diseases
CHANG, K.-W., Mathematics and Statistics
CHEN, S. R. W., Physiology, Biophysics, Biochemistry and Molecular Biology
CHINNAPPA, C. C., Biological Sciences
CHIVERS, T., Chemistry
CHUA, J. H., Haskayne School of Business
CHURCH, D. L., Pathology and Laboratory Medicine and Medicine
CHURCH, J. R., Economics
CLARK, A. W., Pathology and Laboratory Medicine and Clinical Neurosciences
CLARK, P. D., Chemistry
CLARKE, M. E., Paediatrics and Psychiatry
CLEVE, R. E., Computer Science
COCKETT, J. R. B., Computer Science
COELHO, V. A., Music
COLE, W. C., Pharmacology and Therapeutics
COLEMAN, H. D. J., Social Work
COLIJN, A. W., Computer Science
COLLINS, D. G., Social Work
COLLINS, J. R., Mathematics and Statistics
CONLY, J. M., Pathology and Laboratory Medicine
COOK, F. A., Geology and Geophysics
COOPER, F. B., Political Science
COPPES, M. J., Oncology and Paediatrics
CORENBLUM, B., Medicine
COUCH, W. E., Mathematics and Statistics
COWIE, R. L., Medicine and Community Health Sciences
CROSS, J. C., Biochemistry, Molecular Biology, Obstetrics and Gynaecology
CURRY, B., Pathology and Laboratory Medicine and Clinical Neurosciences
DAIS, E. E., Law
DANSEREAU, E. D. M., French, Italian and Spanish
DAVIES, J. M., Anaesthesia
DAVIES, W. K. D., Geography
DAVIS, R. C., English
DAVISON, J. S., Physiology and Biophysics
DAY, R. L., Civil Engineering
DEACON, P. G., Art
DELONG, K. G., Music
DEWEY, D. M., Paediatrics
DICKIN, J. P., Faculty of Communication and Culture

DICKINSON, J. A., Family Medicine and Community Health Sciences
DOBSON, K. S., Psychology
DORT, J. C., Surgery
DOWTY, A., Political Science
DRAPER, D. L., Geography
DUCKWORTH, K., Geology and Geophysics
DUGAN, J. S., Drama
DUGGAN, M. A., Pathology, Laboratory Medicine, Obstetrics and Gynaecology
DUNN, J. F., Radiology, Physiology and Biophysics
DUNSCOMBE, P. B., Oncology
DYCK, R. H., Psychology
EAGLE, C. J., Anaesthesia
EATON, B. C., Economics
EBERLY, W. M., Computer Science
EDWARDS, M. V., Music
EGGERMONT, J. J., Physiology and Biophysics and Psychology
EINSIEDEL, E. F., Communications and Culture
EL-BADRY, M. M., Civil Engineering
EL-GUEBALY, M. A., Psychiatry
EL-SHEIMY, N. M., Geomatics Engineering
ELHAJJ, R. S., Computer Science
ELLIOTT, R. J., Haskayne School of Business
ELOFSON, W. M., History
EMES, C. G., Kinesiology
ENGLE, J. M., Music
ENNS, E. G., Mathematics and Statistics
EPSTEIN, M., Mechanical and Manufacturing Engineering
ERESHEFSKY, M. F., Philosophy
ESLINGER, L. M., Religious Studies
FACCHINI, P. J., Biological Sciences
FARFAN, P. C. M., Drama and English
FATTOUCHE, M. T., Electrical and Computer Engineering
FAUVEL, O. R., Mechanical and Manufacturing Engineering
FEDIGAN, L. M., Anthropology
FERRIS, J. R., History
FEWELL, J. E., Obstetrics and Gynaecology, Paediatrics and Physiology and Biophysics
FICK, G. H., Community Health Sciences
FLANAGAN, T. E., Political Science
FLETCHER, W. A., Clinical Neurosciences and Surgery
FONG, T. C., Radiology
FORD, G. T., Medicine
FOREMAN, C. L., Music
FOREMAN, K. J., Drama
FOUTS, G. T., Psychology
FRANCIS, R. D., History
FRANK, A. W., Sociology
FRANK, C. B., Surgery
FRENCH, R. J., Physiology and Biophysics
FRIDERES, J. S., Sociology
FRIESEN, W. J., Faculty of Education
FRITZLER, M. J., Medicine, Biochemistry and Molecular Biology
FUJITA, D. J., Biochemistry and Molecular Biology
GABOR, P. A., Social Work
GAISFORD, J. D., Economics
GEDAMU, L., Biological Sciences
GETZ, D. P., Haskayne School of Business
GHALI, W. A., Medicine and Community Health Sciences
GHANNOUCHI, F., Electrical and Computer Engineering
GHENT, E. D., Geology and Geophysics
GILES, W. R., Physiology and Biophysics and Medicine
GILL, B., French, Italian and Spanish
GILL, M. J., Medicine
GILLIS, A. M., Medicine
GORDON, D. V., Economics
GORDON, T. M., Geology and Geophysics
GOREN, H. J., Biochemistry and Molecular Biology
GORESKY, G. V., Anaesthesia and Paediatrics
GRAHAM, J. R., Social Work
GRAVEL, R. A., Cell Biology and Anatomy

GREEN, F. H. Y., Pathology and Laboratory Medicine
GREENBERG, S., Computer Science
GU, P., Mechanical and Manufacturing Engineering
GUPTA, A., Management
HABIBI, H. R., Biological Science
HAGEN, N. A., Oncology and Medicine
HAJI, I. H., Philosophy
HALL, B. L., Social Work
HANLEY, D. A., Medicine
HANLEY, P. J., Medicine
HARASYM, P. H., Office of Medical Education and Community Health Sciences
HARDER, L. D., Biological Sciences
HARDING, T. G., Chemical and Petroleum Engineering
HARPER, T. L., Environmental Design
HART, D. A., Microbiology and Infectious Diseases, Medicine
HARTMAN, F. T., Civil Engineering
HASLETT, J. W., Electrical and Computer Engineering
HAWE, H. P., Community Health Sciences
HAWKES, R. B., Cell Biology and Anatomy
HAWKINS, R. W., Communication and Culture
HEBERT, Y. M., Faculty of Education
HECKEL, W., Greek and Roman Studies
HELMER, J. W., Archaeology
HENDERSON, C. M., Geology and Geophysics
HERMAN, R. J., Medicine
HERWIG, H. H., History
HERZOG, W., Kinesiology
HETTIARATCHI, J. P. A., Civil Engineering
HEXHAM, I. R., Religious Studies
HEYMAN, R. D., Faculty of Education
HIEBERT, B. A., Division of Applied Psychology
HILLER, H. H., Sociology
HO, M., Microbiology, Infectious Diseases and Medicine
HODGINS, D. C., Psychology
HOGAN, D. B., Medicine and Clinical Neurosciences and Community Health Sciences
HOLLENBERG, M. D., Pharmacology and Therapeutics
HU, B., Clinical Neurosciences, Cell Biology and Anatomy
HUBER, R. E., Biological Sciences
HUGHES, M. E., Law
HULL, R. D., Medicine
HULLIGER, M., Clinical Neurosciences and Physiology and Biophysics
HUNT, J. D., Civil Engineering
HUSHLAK, G. M., Art
HYNES, M. F., Biological Sciences
IRVINE-HALLIDAY, D., Electrical and Computer Engineering
ISMAEL, J. S., Social Work
ISMAEL, T. Y., Political Science
JACOB, J. C., Faculty of Education
JADAVJI, T., Microbiology and Infectious Diseases and Paediatrics
JAMESON, E., History
JARDINE, D. W., Faculty of Education
JARRELL, J. F., Obstetrics and Gynaecology
JEJE, A. A., Chemical and Petroleum Engineering
JENNETT, P. A., Office of Medical Education and Community Health Sciences
JIRIK, F. R., Biochemistry and Molecular Biology
JOHNSON, E. A., Biological Sciences
JOHNSON, J. M., Obstetrics and Gynaecology
JOHNSTON, R. H., Electrical and Computer Engineering
JOHNSTON, R. N., Biochemistry and Molecular Biology
JOLDERSMA, H., Germanic, Slavic and East Asian Studies
JONES, A. R., Medicine and Oncology
JONES, D. C., Faculty of Education
JONES, V. J., Haskayne School of Business
JORDAN, W. S., Music
JOY, M. M., Religious Studies

JULLIEN, G. A., Electrical and Computer Engineering
KALBACH, M. H., Sociology
KALER, K. V. I., Electrical and Computer Engineering
KANTZAS, A., Chemical and Petroleum Engineering
KAPLAN, B. J., Paediatrics
KARGACIN, G. J., Physiology and Biophysics
KARIM, G. A., Mechanical and Manufacturing Engineering
KATZENBERG, M. A., Archaeology
KAUFFMAN, S. A., Biological Sciences, Physics and Astronomy
KAWAMURA, L. S., Religious Studies
KEAY, B. A., Chemistry
KEENAN, T. P., Environmental Design
KEITH, D. W., Chemical and Petroleum Engineering and Economics
KEITH, R. C., Political Science
KELLNER, J. D., Paediatrics, Microbiology and Infectious Diseases
KEREN, M., Communication and Culture and Political Science
KERTZER, A. E., English
KERTZER, J. M., English
KLASSEN, J., Pathology and Laboratory Medicine and Medicine
KLINE, D. W., Psychology
KLINE, T. J., Psychology
KNEEBONE, R. D., Economics
KNOLL, P. J., Law
KNOPFF, R., Political Science
KNUDTSON, M. L., Cardiac Sciences and Medicine
KOOPMANS, H. S., Physiology and Biophysics and Psychology
KOOYMAN, B. P., Archaeology
KOSTYNIUK, R. P., Art
KRAUSE, F. F., Geology and Geophysics
KREBES, E. S., Geology and Geophysics
KUBES, P., Physiology and Biophysics and Medicine
KURTZ, S. M., Education
LACHAPELLE, G. J., Geomatics Engineering
LAFLAMME, C., Mathematics and Statistics
LAFRENIÈRE, R., Surgery
LAI, D. W. L., Social Work
LAING, W. J. H., Art
LAMOUREUX, M. P., Mathematics and Statistics
LANGE, I. R., Obstetrics and Gynaecology
LARTER, S. R., Geology and Geophysics
LAU, D. C. W., Medicine
LAWTON, D. C., Geology and Geophysics
LEAHY, D. A., Physics and Astronomy
LEE, S. S., Medicine
LEE, T. G., Environmental Design
LEES-MILLER, S. P., Biochemistry and Molecular Biology
LEON, L. J., Electrical and Computer Engineering
LEUNG, H. K. Y., Electrical and Computer Engineering
LEVIN, G. J., Music
LEVY, J. C., Law
LEVY, R. M., Environmental Design
LEWKONIA, R. M., Medicine and Paediatrics and Medical Genetics
LINES, L. R., Geology and Geophysics
LOUIE, T. J., Medicine, Microbiology and Infectious Diseases
LOUTZENHISER, R. D., Pharmacology and Therapeutics
LOVE, J. A., Environmental Design
LUCAS, A. R., Law
LUKASIEWICZ, S. A., Mechanical and Manufacturing Engineering
LUKOWIAK, K., Physiology and Biophysics
LYTTON, J., Biochemistry, Molecular Biology, Physiology and Biophysics
MCCALLUM, P. M., English
MCCAULEY, F. E. R., Biological Sciences
MCCLELLAND, R. W., Social Work
MCCONNELL, C. S., Art
MCCREADY, W. O., Religious Studies

MCCULLOUGH, D. T., Drama
MACDONALD, D. L., English
MCGHEE, J. D., Biochemistry and Molecular Biology
MCGILLIS, R. F., English
MCGILLIVRAY, M. D., English
MACINTOSH, B. R., Kinesiology
MACINTOSH, J. J., Philosophy
MCKENZIE, K. J., Economics
MCKEOUGH, A. M., Division of Applied Psychology
MCKINNON, J. G., Surgery and Oncology
MCMORDIE, M. J., Environmental Design, Communication and Culture
MCMULLAN, W. E., Haskayne School of Business
MACNAUGHTON, W. K., Physiology and Biophysics
MCRAE, R. N., Economics
MCWHIR, A. R., English
MAES, M. A., Civil Engineering
MAHER, P. M., Haskayne School of Business
MAHONEY, K. E., Law
MAINI, B. B., Chemical and Petroleum Engineering
MAINS, P. E., Biochemistry and Molecular Biology
MANDIN, H., Medicine
MARTIN, R. H., Paediatrics and Medical Genetics
MARTIN, S. L., Law
MARTINUZZI, R., Mechanical and Manufacturing Engineering
MASH, E. J., Psychology
MATO, D., Art
MAURER, F. O., Computer Science
MEDDINGS, J. B., Medicine
MEEUWISSE, W. H., Kinesiology
MEHROTRA, A. K., Chemical and Petroleum Engineering
MEHTA, S. A., Chemical and Petroleum Engineering
MIDHA, R., Clinical Neurosciences
MILONE, E. F., Physics and Astronomy
MINTCHEV, M. P., Electrical and Computer Engineering
MITCHELL, D. B., Communication and Culture
MITCHELL, I., Paediatrics
MITCHELL, L. B., Cardiac Science and Medicine
MITCHELL, S. H., Education
MOAZZEN-AHMADI, N., Physics and Astronomy
MOCQUAIS, P. Y. A., French, Italian and Spanish
MODY, C. H., Medicine, Microbiology and Infectious Diseases
MOHAMAD, A. A., Mechanical and Maufacturing Engineering
MOLLIN, R. A., Mathematics and Statistics
MOORE, R. G., Chemical and Petroleum Engineering
MORCK, D. W., Biological Sciences
MORTON, F. L., Political Science
MUELLER, J. H., Division of Applied Psychology
MUNRO, M. C., Haskayne School of Business
MURPHREE, J. S., Physics and Astronomy
MURRAY, R. W., Linguistics
MURRAY, S. C., Kinesiology
MUZIK, I., Civil Engineering
MYLES, S. T., Surgery and Clinical Neurosciences
NATION, J. G., Obstetrics and Gynaecology and Oncology
NAULT, B. R., Haskayne School of Business
NEU, D. E., Haskayne School of Business
NEUFELDT, A. H., Faculty of Education
NEUFELDT, R. W., Religious Studies
NICHOLSON, W. K., Mathematics and Statistics
NIELSON, N., Haskayne School of Business
NIGG, B. M., Kinesiology
NKEMDIRIM, L. C., Geography
NORTON, P. G., Family Medicine

NOSAL, M., Mathematics and Statistics
NOSEWORTHY, T. W., Community Health Sciences
OETELAAR, G. A., Archaeology
OKONIEWSKI, M., Electrical and Computer Engineering
OSBORN, G. D., Geology and Geophysics
OSLER, M. J., History
PARKER, J. R., Computer Science
PATTISON, D. R. M., Geology and Geophysics
PAUL, R., Chemistry
PEREIRA ALMAO, P. R., Chemical and Petroleum Engineering
PERL, A. D., Political Science
PERREAULT, J. M., English
PIERS, W. E., Chemistry
PINEO, G. F., Medicine and Oncology
PITTMAN, Q. J., Physiology and Biophysics
POLLAK, P. T., Medicine, Cardiac Sciences, Pharmacology and Therapeutics
PONAK, A. M., Haskayne School of Business
PONTING, J. R., Sociology
POON, M.-C., Medicine and Paediatrics
POST, J. R., Biological Sciences
POWELL, D. G., Family Medicine
PRICE, G. D., Music
PROUD, D., Physiology and Biophysics
PRUSINKIEWICZ, P., Computer Science
PYRCH, T., Social Work
RABIN, H. R., Microbiology, Infectious Diseases and Medicine
RADTKE, H. L., Psychology
RAFFERTY, N. S., Law
RAMRAJ, V. J., English
RANGACHARI, P. K., Pharmacology and Therapeutics
RANGAYYAN, R. M., Electrical and Computer Engineering
RASPORICH, B. J., Communication and Culture
RATTNER, J. B., Cell Biology and Anatomy and Biochemistry and Molecular Biology and Oncology
RAY, D. I., Political Science
RAYMOND, S., Archaeology
REID, D. M., Biological Sciences
REMMERS, J. E., Medicine, Physiology and Biophysics
REVEL, R. D., Environmental Design
REYNOLDS, J. D., Physiology, Biophysics and Medicine
RIABOWOL, K. T., Biochemistry and Molecular Biology
RIEDIGER, C. L., Geology and Geophysics
RITCHIE, J. R. B., Haskayne School of Business
ROBERTSON, S. E., Division of Applied Psychology
ROHLEDER, T. R., Haskayne School of Business
ROKNE, J. G., Computer Science
RONSKY, J. L., Mechanical and Manufacturing Engineering
RORSTAD, O. P., Medicine
ROSS, W. A., Environmental Design
ROTH, S. H., Pharmacology and Therapeutics, and Anaesthesia
ROTHERY, M. A., Social Work
ROUNTHWAITE, H. I., Law
ROWNEY, J. I. A., Haskayne School of Business
ROWSE, J. G., Economics
RUDY, S. A., English
RUHE, G., Computer Science and Electrical and Computer Engineering
RUSSELL, A. P., Biological Sciences
SAINSBURY, R. S., Psychology
SAMUELS, M. T., Division of Applied Psychology
SANDERS, B. C., Physics and Astronomy
SANDS, G. W., Mathematics and Statistics
SANTAMARIA, P., Microbiology and Infectious Diseases
SARNAT, H. B., Paediatrics, Clinical Neurosciences Pathology and Laboratory Medicine

SAUER, N. W., Mathematics and Statistics
SAUNDERS, I. B., Law
SAUVE, R. S., Paediatrics and Community Health Sciences
SCHACHAR, N. S., Surgery
SCHNETKAMP, P. P. M., Biochemistry and Molecular Biology, and Physiology and Biophysics
SCHRYVERS, A. B., Microbiology and Infectious Diseases
SCHULZ, R. A., Haskayne School of Business
SCHWARZ, K.-P., Geomatics Engineering
SCIALFA, C. T., Psychology
SCOLLNIK, D. P. M., Mathematics and Statistics
SCOTT, R. B., Paediatrics
SEGAL, E. L., Religious Studies
SENSEN, C. W., Biochemistry and Molecular Biology
SERLETIS, A., Economics
SESAY, A. B., Electrical and Computer Engineering
SETTARI, A., Chemical and Petroleum Engineering
SEVERSON, D. L., Pharmacology and Therapeutics
SHAFFER, E. A., Medicine
SHANTZ, D. H., Religious Studies
SHAPIRO, B. L., Education
SHARKEY, K. A., Physiology and Biophysics
SHAW, W. J. D., Mechanical and Manufacturing Engineering
SHELDON, R. S., Medicine
SHIELL, A. M., Community Health Sciences
SHRIVE, N. G., Civil Engineering
SICK, G. A., Haskayne School of Business
SIDERIS, M. G., Geomatics Engineering
SIMMINS, G., Art
SINGHAL, N., Paediatrics
SMART, A., Anthropology
SMART, P. J., Anthropology
SMITH, D. D. B., History
SMITH, D. G., Geography
SMITH, D. J., Kinesiology
SMITH, F. R., Physiology and Biophysics
SMITH, G. B., Drama
SMITH, M. R., Electrical and Computer Engineering
SNIATYCKI, J. Z., Mathematics and Statistics
SNYDER, F. F., Paediatrics, Medical Biochemistry and Medical Biology
SOKOL, P. A., Microbiology and Infectious Diseases
SPENCER, R. J., Geology and Geophysics
SPRATT, D. A., Geology and Geophysics
STALKER, M. A., Law
STAM, H. J., Psychology
STAMP, R. M., Education
STAUM, M. S., History
STELL, W. K., Cell Biology and Anatomy and Surgery
STEWART, R. R., Geology and Geophysics
STOCKING, J. R., Art
STOREY, D. G., Biological Sciences
STOUGHTON, N. M., Haskayne School of Business
SUCHOWERSKY, O., Clinical Neurosciences
SUTHERLAND, C. T., Communication and Culture
SUTHERLAND, F. R., Surgery and Oncology
SUTHERLAND, G. R., Clinical Neurosciences
SUTHERLAND, L. R., Medicine and Community Health Sciences
SVRCEK, W. Y., Chemical and Petroleum Engineering
SWAIN, M. G., Medicine
SYED, N. I. S., Cell Biology, Anatomy, Physiology and Biophysics
TARAS, D., Communication and Culture
TARAS, D. G., Haskayne School of Business
TAY, R. S. T., Civil Engineering
TAYLOR, A. R., Physics and Astronomy
TAYLOR, M. S., Economics
TEMPLE, W. J., Surgery and Oncology
TER KEURS, H. E. D., Cardiac Sciences, Medicine, Physiology and Biophysics

TESKEY, G. C., Psychology
TESKEY, W. F., Geomatics Engineering
THOMAS, R. E., Family Medicine
THOMPSON, D. A. R., Environmental Design
THURSTON, W. E., Community Health Sciences
TIELEMAN, D. P., Biological Sciences
TOEWS, J. A., Psychiatry
TOMM, K. M., Psychiatry
TOOHEY, P. G., Greek and Roman Studies
TREBBLE, M. A., Chemical and Petroleum Engineering
TRIGGLE, C. R., Pharmacology and Therapeutics
TRUTE, B., Social Work and Nursing
TSENKOVA, S., Environmental Design
TURNER, L. E., Electrical and Computer Engineering
TURNER, R. W., Cell Biology, Anatomy, Physiology and Biophysics
TUTTY, L. M., Social Work
TYBERG, J. V., Cardiac Sciences, Medicine, Physiology and Biophysics
UNGER, B. W., Computer Science
URBANSKI, S. J., Pathology and Laboratory Medicine
VANBALKOM, W. D., Education
VAN DER HOORN, F. A., Biochemistry and Molecular Biology
VANDERSPOEL, J., Greek and Roman Studies
VAN DE SANDE, J. H., Biochemistry and Molecular Biology
VAN HERK, A., English
VAN ROSENDAAL, G. M. A., Medicine
VEALE, W. L., Physiology and Biophysics
VERBEKE, A. C. M., Haskayne School of Business
VERHOEF, M. J., Community Health Sciences and Medicine
VICKERS, J. N., Kinesiology
VINOGRADOV, O., Mechanical and Manufacturing Engineering
VIOLATO, C., Community Health Sciences
VIZE, P. D., Biological Sciences
VOGEL, H. J., Biological Sciences
VOORDOUW, G., Biological Sciences
VREDENBURG, H., Haskayne School of Business
WAISMAN, D. M., Biochemistry and Molecular Biology
WALKER, D. C., French, Italian and Spanish
WALKER, S., Environmental Design
WALL, A. J., French, Latin and Spanish
WALLACE, J. L., Physiology and Biophysics, and Pharmacology and Therapeutics and Medicine
WALLS, W. D., Economics
WALSH, M. P., Biochemistry and Molecular Biology
WAN, R. G., Civil Engineering
WANG, Y., Electrical and Computer Engineering
WANNER, R. A., Sociology
WARNICA, J. W., Cardiac Sciences and Medicine
WATERS, N. M., Geography
WEBBER, C. F., Education
WEISS, S., Cell Biology and Anatomy and Pharmacology and Therapeutics
WESTRA, H. J., Greek and Roman Studies
WHITE, T. H., Haskayne School of Business
WHITELAW, W. A., Medicine
WIEBE, S., Clinical Neurosciences, Paediatrics and Community Health Sciences
WIERZBA, I., Mechanical and Manufacturing Engineering
WILLIAMS, H. C., Mathematics and Statistics
WILLIAMSON, C. L., Computer Science
WILMAN, E. A., Economics
WILSON, M. G., Social Work
WINCHESTER, W. I. S., Education
WONG, N. C. W., Medicine
WONG, R. C. K., Civil Engineering
WONG, S. L., Biological Sciences
WOODROW, P., Art
WOODROW, R. E., Mathematics and Statistics

Woods, D. E., Microbiology and Infectious Diseases
Wright, L. M., Nursing
Wu, P. P. C., Geology and Geophysics
Wyvill, B. L. M., Computer Science
Yacowar, M., Art
Yang, X. J., Germanic, Slavic and East Asian Studies
Yau, A. W., Physics and Astronomy
Yeung, E. C. J., Biological Sciences
Yong, V. W., Oncology and Clinical Neurosciences
Yoon, J. W., Microbiology and Infectious Diseases and Paediatrics
Young, D. B., Biochemistry, Molecular Biology and Oncology
Zamponi, G. W., Physiology, Biophysics, Pharmacology and Therapeutics
Zanzotto, L., Civil Engineering
Zapf, M. K., Social Work
Zekulin, N. G. A., Germanic, Slavic and East Asian Studies
Ziegler, T., Chemistry
Zochodne, D. W., Clinical Neurosciences
Zvengrowski, P. D., Mathematics and Statistics

CAPE BRETON UNIVERSITY

POB 5300, 1250 Grand Lake Rd, Sydney, NS B1P 6L2

Telephone: (902) 539-5300
Fax: (902) 563-1371
E-mail: welcome@capebretonu.ca
Internet: www.cbu.ca
Founded 1974
State control
Language of instruction: English
Academic year: September to April

Depts of education, mathematics, physics and geology, nutrition, nursing, psychology, public health

Chancellor: Annette Verschuren
Pres. and Vice-Chancellor: John Harker
Vice-Pres. for Academic and Provost: Dr Robert Bailey
Vice-Pres. for External: Dr Keith Brown
Vice-Pres. for Finance and Operations: Gordon MacInnis
Vice-Pres. for Student Services and Registrar: Alexis Manley
Dean of Research: Dr Dale Keefe

Library of 532,290 vols, 800 periodicals
Number of teachers: 153
Number of students: 3,600

DEANS

School of Arts and Social Sciences: Dr Rod Nicholls
School of Graduate and Professional Studies: Dr Robert Bailey (acting)
School of Science and Technology: Dr Allen Britten
Shannon School of Business Studies: John MacKinnon

ATTACHED RESEARCH INSTITUTES

The mailing address is that of the University

Beaton Institute: repository of Cape Breton social, economic, political and cultural history; Dir Wendy Robicheau.

Children's Rights Centre: f. 1996; conducts research and provides public education on children's rights; monitors implementation of UN Children's Rights Convention in Nova Scotia and Canada; Co-Dir Prof. Katherine Covell; Co-Dir Prof. Brian Howe.

Community Economic Development Institute: f. 1996; provides support, training, policy advice and research in community economic devt; Dir Dr Gertrude MacIntyre.

CARLETON UNIVERSITY

1125 Colonel By Drive, Ottawa, ON K1S 5B6

Telephone: (613) 520-2600
Fax: (613) 520-3847
E-mail: infocarleton@carleton.ca
Internet: www.carleton.ca
Founded 1942
Provincial control
Language of instruction: English
Academic year: September to May

Chancellor: Marc Garneau
Pres. and Vice-Chancellor: Dr Richard van Loon
Vice-Pres. for Academic Affairs and Provost: Alan Harrison
Vice-Pres. for Advancement: Lucinda Boucher
Vice-Pres. for Finance and Administration: Duncan Watt
Vice-Pres. for Research: Feridun Hamdullahpur
Asst Vice-Pres. for Development and Alumni: Serge Arpin
Asst Vice-Pres. for Enrolment Management: Susan Gottheil
Librarian: Martin Foss

Library: see Libraries and Archives
Number of teachers: 786
Number of students: 22,535

Publications: *Research and Works* (4 a year), *The President's Report* (1 a year)

DEANS

Faculty of Arts and Social Science: Michael Smith
Faculty of Engineering: Sami Mahmoud
Faculty of Public Affairs and Management: Katherine Graham
Faculty of Science: Jean-Guy Godin
Faculty of Graduate Studies and Research: Roger Blockley

CHAIRS AND DIRECTORS

Faculty of Arts and Social Science (330 Paterson Hall, 1125 Colonel By Drive, Ottawa, ON K1S 5B6; tel. (613) 520-2355; fax (613) 520-4481; internet www.carleton.ca/fass):

Canadian Studies: F. Rocher
English Language and Literature: R. Holton
Environmental Studies: N. Doubleday
French: C. Doutrelepont
Geography: S. Dalby
History: E. P. Fitzgerald
Humanities: S. Wilson
Interdisciplinary Studies: K. Arnup
Philosophy: J. Drydyk
Psychology: J. Logan (acting)
Sociology and Anthropology: C. Gordon
Studies in Art and Culture: B. Gilliingham (acting)
Women's Studies: P. Rankin
Centre for Applied Language Studies: I. Pringle

Faculty of Engineering (3010 Minto Centre, 1125 Colonel By Drive, Ottawa, ON K1S 5B6; tel. (613) 520-5790; fax (613) 520-7481; internet www.carleton.ca/engineeringdesign):

Architecture: G. Haider
Civil and Environmental Engineering: G. Hartley (acting)
Electronics: L. Roy
Industrial Design: L. Frankel
Mechanical and Aerospace Engineering: R. Bell
Systems and Computer Engineering: R. Goubran

Faculty of Public Affairs and Management (D391 Loeb Building, 1125 Colonel By Drive, Ottawa, ON K1S 5B6; tel. (613) 520-3741; fax

(613) 520-3742; e-mail melanie_thompson@carleton.ca; internet www.carleton.ca/pam):

Business: V. Kumar
Criminology and Criminal Justice: B. Wright
Economics: A. Ritter
European and Russian Studies: P. Dutkiewicz
International Affairs: F. Hampson
Journalism and Communication: C. Dornan
Law: C. Swan
Political Economy: R. Mahon
Political Science: C. Brown
Public Administration: L. Pal
Social Work: C. Lundy

Faculty of Science (3239 Herzberg Laboratories, 1125 Colonel By Drive, Ottawa, ON K1S 5B6; tel. (613) 520-4388; fax (613) 520-4389; e-mail odscience@ccs.carleton.ca; internet www.carleton.ca/science):

Biochemistry: M. Smith
Biology: J. Cheetham
Chemistry: G. Buchanan
Computational Sciences: L. Copley
Computer Science: D. Howe
Earth Sciences: C. Schroeder-Adams
Environmental Science: D. Wigfield
Geography: S. Dalby
Integrated Science Studies: I. Munro
Mathematics and Statistics: C. Garner
Physics: P. Kalyndak
Psychology: J. Logan

CONCORDIA UNIVERSITY

Sir George Williams Campus, 1455 de Maisonneuve blvd West, Montréal, QC H3G 1M8

Loyola Campus, 7141 Sherbrooke St West, Montréal, QC H4B 1R6

Telephone: (514) 848-2424
Fax: (514) 848-3494
Internet: www.concordia.ca
Founded 1974 by merger of Sir George Williams Univ. (f. 1948) and Loyola College (inc. 1899)
Provincial control
Language of instruction: English
Academic year: May to April

Chancellor and Univ. Secretariat: Eric Molson
Pres. and Vice-Chancellor: Prof. Frederick H. Lowy
Provost: David Graham
Vice-Provost for Academic Affairs: Robert M. Roy
Vice-Provost for Academic Relations: Rama Bhat
Vice-Provost for Teaching and Learning: Ollivier Dyens
Exec. Dir for Office of the Pres.: Gary Milton
Registrar: Linda Healey
Dir of Libraries: Gerald Beasley
Library: see Libraries and Archives
Number of teachers: 1,837 (884 full-time, 953 part-time)
Number of students: 31,175

Publications: *Canadian Jewish Studies* (1 a year), *Canadian Journal of Irish Studies* (2 a year), *Canadian Journal of Research in Early Childhood Education* (2 a year), *Journal of Canadian Art History/Annales d'Histoire de L'art Canadien* (2 a year), *Journal of Religion and Culture* (1 a year), *Revue de l'Institut Simone de Beauvoir Institute Review* (1 a year)

DEANS

Faculty of Arts and Science: Brian Lewis
Faculty of Engineering and Computer Science: Robin Drew
Faculty of Fine Arts: Catherine Wild

John Molson School of Business: SANJAY SHARMA

School of Graduate Studies and Research: BINA FREIWALD (Dir)

DALHOUSIE UNIVERSITY

Halifax, NS B3H 4H6
Telephone: (902) 494-2450
Fax: (902) 494-1630
E-mail: registrar@dal.ca
Internet: www.dal.ca

Founded 1818; merged with Technical Univ. of Nova Scotia 1997

Private control

Language of instruction: English

Academic year: September to August

Chancellor: Dr FRED FOUNTAIN

Pres. and Vice-Chancellor: THOMAS D. TRAVES

Vice-Pres. for Academic and Provost: A.SHAVER

Vice-Pres. for External: F. DYKEMAN

Vice-Pres. for Finance and Admin: K. BURT

Vice-Pres. for Research: M. CRAGO

Vice-Pres. for Student Services: BONNIE NEUMAN

Registrar: ASA KACHAN

Librarian: W. MAES

Library: see Libraries

Number of teachers: 1,860 (full- and part-time)

Number of students: 11,600 full-time, 3,700 part-time, 1,180 international

DEANS

Faculty of Architecture: C. MACY

Faculty of Arts and Social Sciences: M. E. BINKLEY

Faculty of Computer Science: M. SHEPHERD

Faculty of Dentistry: T. BORAN

Faculty of Engineering: J. LEON

Faculty of Graduate Studies: C. WATTERS

Faculty of Health Professions: WILLIAM WEBSTER

Faculty of Law: PHILLIP SAUNDERS

Faculty of Management: D. WHEELER (acting)

Faculty of Medicine: H. COOK (acting)

Faculty of Science: M. LEONARD

PROFESSORS

Faculty of Architecture (tel. (902) 494-3971; fax (902) 423-6672; e-mail arch.office@dal.ca; internet archplan.dal.ca):

CAVANAGH, E., Architecture
GRANT, J., Planning
KROEKER, R., Architecture
MACKAY-LYONS, B., Architecture
MACY, C., Architecture
PALERMO, F., Planning
POULTON, M., Planning
PROCOS, D., Architecture
WANZEL, J., Architecture

Faculty of Arts and Social Sciences (tel. (902) 494-1440; fax (902) 494-1957; e-mail fass@dal.ca):

APOSTLE, R., Sociology and Social Anthropology
AUCOIN, P. C., Political Science
BAKVIS, H., Political Science
BARKER, W., English
BARKOW, J. H., Sociology and Social Anthropology
BAXTER, J., English
BAYLIS, F., Philosophy
BEDNARSKI, H. E., French
BINKLEY, M. E., Sociology and Social Anthropology
BOARDMAN, R., Political Science
BURNS, S., Philosophy
CAMPBELL, R. M., Philosophy
CROWLEY, J. E., History
CURRAN, J. V., German (Chair.)
DAVIS, J., Political Science

DE MEO, P., French
DIEPEVEEN, L. P., English
FURROW, M. M., English
HANKEY, W., Classics (King's)
HANLON, G., History
HARVEY, F., Political Science
HUEBERT, R., English
KIRK, J. M., Spanish
LI, T. J., Sociology and Social Anthropology
LUCKYJ, C., English
MARTIN, R., Philosophy
MIDDLEMISS, D., Political Science
NEVILLE, C., History (Chair.)
OORE, I., French
OVERTON, D. R., Theatre
PARPART, J., International Development Studies
PEREIRA, N. G. O., History and Russian
PERINA, P., Theatre
RUNTE, H. R., French
SHAW, T. W., Political Science
SCHOTCH, P., Philosophy
SCHROEDER, D., Music
SCHWARZ, H. G., German
SCULLY, S., Classics
SERVANT, G. W., Music
SHERWIN, S., Philosophy
SMITH, J., Political Science (Chair.)
STARNES, C. J., Classics (King's)
STONE, M. I., English
TETREAULT, R., English
THIESSEN, V., Sociology and Social Anthropology
TRAVES, T., History
VINCI, T., Philosophy
WAINWRIGHT, J. A., English and Canadian Studies
WATERSON, K., French

Faculty of Computer Science (tel. (902) 494-2093; fax (902) 492-1517):

BODORIK, P.
BORWEIN, J.
BROWN, J. I.
COX, P.
FARRAG, A.
GENTLEMAN, M.
GRUNDKE, E.
HITCHCOCK, P.
JOST, A.
KEAST, P.
MACDONALD, N.
MILOS, E.
RAU-CHAPLIN, A.
RIORDAN, D.
SAMPALLI, S.
SCRIMGER, J. N.
SHEPHERD, M.
SLONIM, J.
WACH, G.
WATTERS, C. R.

Faculty of Dentistry (tel. (902) 494-2824; fax (902) 494-2527):

LEE, J. M., Applied Oral Sciences
LONEY, R., Dental Clinical Sciences
PRECIOUS, D. S., Oral and Maxillofacial Science
PRICE, R. B. T., Dental Clinical Science
RYDING, H. A., Applied Oral Sciences (Acting Chair.)
SUTOW, E. J., Applied Oral Sciences

Faculty of Engineering (tel. (902) 494-3267; fax (902) 429-3011; e-mail dean.engineering@dal.ca):

ALI, N. A., Civil Engineering
ALLEN, P., Mechanical Engineering
AL-TAWEEL, A., Chemical Engineering
AMYOTTE, P., Chemical Engineering
BASU, P., Mechanical Engineering
BEN-ABDALLAH, N., Biological Engineering (Head)
CADA, M., Electrical and Computer Engineering
CALEY, W. F., Mining and Metallurgical Engineering

CHEN, Z., Electrical and Computer Engineering
CHUANG, J. M., Mechanical Engineering
EL-HAWARY, M., Electrical and Computer Engineering
EL-MASRY, E., Electrical and Computer Engineering (Head)
FELS, M., Chemical Engineering
FENTON, G., Engineering Mathematics
GHALY, A., Biological Engineering
GILL, T., Food Science and Technology
GREGSON, P., Electrical and Computer Engineering
GUNN, E., Industrial Engineering
GUPTA, Y., Chemical Engineering (Head)
HUGHES, F. L., Electrical and Computer Engineering
ISLAM, M., Civil Engineering
KALAMKAROV, A., Mechanical Engineering
KEMBER, G., Engineering Mathematics
KIPOUROS, G., Mining and Metallurgical Engineering
KUJATH, M., Mechanical Engineering
MILITZER, J., Mechanical Engineering
PAULSON, A. T., Food Science and Technology
PEGG, M., Chemical Engineering
PHILLIPS, W., Engineering Mathematics (Head)
RAHMAN, M., Engineering Mathematics
ROBERTSON, W., Engineering Mathematics
ROCKWELL, M., Mining and Metallurgical Engineering
SANDBLOM, C., Industrial Engineering
SATISH, M., Civil Engineering
SPEERS, R. A., Food Science and Technology (Head)
TROTTIER, J.-F., Civil Engineering
UGURSAL, M., Mechanical Engineering
WATTS, K., Biological and Mechanical Engineering
YEMENIDJIAN, N., Mining and Metallurgical Engineering (Head)
ZOU, D. H., Mining and Metallurgical Engineering

Faculty of Health Professions (tel. (902) 494-3327; fax (902) 494-1966; internet healthprofessions.dal.ca):

School of Health and Human Performance:
HOLT, L. E.
LYONS, R. F.
MALONEY, T.
SINGLETON, J.
UNRUH, A.

School of Health Services Administration:
MCINTYRE, L.
NESTMAN, L.
RATHWELL, T. (Dir)

School of Nursing:
BUTLER, L. (Dir)
DOWNE-WAMBOLDT, B. (Dir)
KEDDY, B. A.

School of Occupational Therapy:
TOWNSEND, E. (Dir)

College of Pharmacy:
SKETRIS, I.
YEUNG, P. K. F.

School of Physiotherapy:
KOZEY, C. L.
MAKRIDES, L. (Dir)
TURNBULL, G. I.

Maritime School of Social Work:
DIVINE, D.
WIEN, F. C.

Faculty of Law (tel. (902) 494-3495; fax (902) 494-1316; e-mail lawinfo@dal.ca):

ARCHIBALD, B.
BLACK, V.
DEVLIN, R.
KAISER, H. A.
KINDRED, H. M.

McConnell, M. L.
MacKay, A. W.
Pothier, D. L.
Thomas, P.
Thompson, D. A. R.
Thornhill, E. M. A.
Vanderzwagg, D.
Woodman, F. L.
Yogis, J. A.

Faculty of Management (tel. (902) 494-2582; fax (902) 494-1195; internet www .management.dal.ca):

School of Business Administration:
Brooks, M. R.
Conrad, J.
Duffy, J.
Fooladi, I.
MacLean, L. C.
McNiven, J. D.
Mealiea, L. W.
Oppong, A.
Rosson, P.
Sankar, Y.
Schellinck, D. A.

School of Public Administration:
Aucoin, P. C.
Bakvis, H.
Brown, M. P.
McNiven, J. D.
Siddiq, F.
Sullivan, K.
Traves, T.

School of Resource and Environmental Studies:
Cohen, F. G.
Côté, R.
Duinker, P. (Dir)
Willison, J. H.

Faculty of Medicine (tel. (902) 494-6592; fax (902) 494-7119; e-mail dean.medicine@dal .ca; internet www.medicine.dal.ca):
Alda, H., Psychiatry
Alexander, D., Surgery
Allen, A. C., Paediatrics, Obstetrics and Gynaecology
Anderson, D. R., Medicine, Community Health and Epidemiology
Anderson, P. A., Urology
Anderson, R., Microbiology and Immunology
Armson, A., Obstetrics and Gynaecology
Attia, E., Surgery
Barnes, S., Physiology and Biophysics, Ophthalmology
Baskett, T., Obstetrics and Gynaecology
Baylis, F., Bioethics
Bensted, T., Medicine
Bitter-Suermann, H., Surgery
Blay, J., Pharmacology
Bonjer, H. J., Surgery
Bortolussi, R., Paediatrics
Breckenridge, W. C., Biochemistry
Brown, M. G., Community Health and Epidemiology
Bryson, S., Paediatrics
Byers, D., Paediatrics
Cameron, I., Family Medicine
Camfield, C., Paediatrics
Camfield, P. R., Paediatrics
Casson, A., Surgery and Pathology
Chauhan, B., Ophthalmology, Physiology and Biophysics
Clements, J. C., Biomedical Engineering
Cohen, M. M., Paediatrics
Connolly, J., Medicine
Cook, H. W., Paediatrics
Coonan, T., Anaesthesia (Head)
Cowden, E., Medicine (Head)
Cox, J., Medicine
Crocker, J. F. S., Paediatrics
Croll, R. P., Physiology and Biophysics
Cruess, A. F., Ophthalmology (Chair.)
Currie, R. W., Anatomy and Neurobiology

Daniels, C., Diagnostic Radiology
Devitt, H., Anaesthesia
Doane, B. K., Psychiatry
Dooley, J., Paediatrics
Doolittle, W. F., Biochemistry
Downie, J. W., Pharmacology
Ducharme, J., Emergency Medicine
Duncan, R., Microbiology and Immunology
Dunphy, B., Obstetrics and Gynaecology
Farrell, S., Obstetrics and Gynaecology
Fernandez, L. A. V., Medicine
Ferrier, G. R., Pharmacology
Fine, A., Physiology and Biophysics
Finley, G. A., Anaesthesia
Finley, J. P., Paediatrics
Forward, K., Pathology, Medicine, Microbiology and Immunology
Fox, R. A., Medicine
Frank, B. W., Division of Medical Education
French, A., Biomedical Engineering, Physiology and Biophysics
Gardner, M. J., Medicine
Gajewski, J., Urology
Gass, D. A., Family Medicine
Goldbloom, R., Paediatrics
Graves, G., Obstetrics and Gynaecology (Head)
Gray, M. W., Biochemistry (Head)
Greer, W., Pathology
Gregson, P., Biomedical Engineering
Gross, M., Surgery
Grunfield, E., Medicine, Community Health and Epidemiology
Guernsey, D. L., Pathology, Physiology, Biophysics and Ophthalmology
Haase, D. A., Medicine
Hall, R., Anaesthesia and Pharmacology
Halperin, S., Paediatrics
Handa, S. P., Medicine
Hanly, J. G., Medicine
Hayes, V., Family Medicine
Heathcote, J. G., Ophthalmology and Pathology (Head)
Hirsch, D., Medicine and Psychiatry
Holness, R. O., Surgery
Hopkins, D. A., Anatomy and Neurobiology
Horacek, B. M., Physiology, Biophysics and Biomedical Engineering
Horackova, M., Physiology and Biophysics
Hoskin, D. W., Microbiology, Immunology, and Pathology
Howlett, S., Pharmacology
Hugenholz, H., Surgery
Hung, O. R., Anaesthesia and Pharmacology
Hyndman, J. C., Surgery
Imrie, D., Anaesthesia
Isa, N. N., Obstetrics and Gynaecology
Issekutz, A., Paediatrics and Pathology
Issekutz, T. B., Paediatrics, Microbiology, Immunology and Pathology
Jamieson, C. G., Surgery
Johnston, B. L., Medicine, Community Health and Epidemiology
Johnston, G. C., Microbiology and Immunology (Head)
Johnstone, D. E., Medicine
Kazimirski, J., Division of Medical Education
Kells, C., Medicine
Kelly, M., Pharmacology
Kelly, M. E., Ophthalmology
Kenny, N. P., Paediatrics and Bioethics and Division of Medical Education
Khanna, V. N., Medicine
Kiberd, B. A., Medicine
Kirby, R. L., Medicine and Biomedical Engineering
Kisely, S. R., Community Health and Epidemiology, Psychiatry
Kronick, J., Paediatrics (Head)
Kutcher, S., Psychiatry
Laidlaw, T., Division of Medical Education
Langille, D. B., Community Health and Epidemiology

Langley, G. R., Medicine
LaRoche, G. R., Ophthalmology
Lawen, J. G., Urology
Lazier, C. B., Biochemistry
LeBlanc, R. P., Ophthalmology
Lebron, G., Diagnostic Radiology
Lee, M., Applied Oral Sciences and Biomedical Engineering
Lee, P. W. K., Microbiology, Immunology and Pathology
Lee, T., Microbiology, Immunology and Pathology
Leighton, A. H., Psychiatry
Leslie, R. A., Anatomy, Neurobiology and Psychiatry (Head)
Lo, C. D., Diagnostic Radiology
Ludman, H., Paediatrics
Macaulay, R., Pathology
MacDonald, A. S., Surgery
MacDonald, N., Paediatrics
McDonald, T. F., Physiology and Biophysics
McGrath, P. J., Paediatrics, Psychiatry and Psychology
MacLachlan, R., Family Medicine (Head)
MacLean, L. D., Community Health and Epidemiology
McMillan, D., Paediatrics
Mahony, D. E., Microbiology and Immunology
Malatjalian, D. A., Pathology and Medicine
Mann, K. V., Division of Medical Education
Mann, O. E., Medicine
Marshall, J., Pathology, Microbiology and Immunology
Massoud, E., Surgery
Maxner, C. E., Medicine and Opthalmology
Meinertzhagen, I., Psychology, Physiology and Biophysics
Mendez, I., Surgery
Miller, R. A., Medicine
Miller, R. M., Diagnostic Radiology
Morris, I. R., Anaesthesia
Morris, S. F., Surgery
Mosher, D., Medicine
Moss, M. A., Pathology (Head)
Murphy, P., Physiology and Biophysics (Head)
Murray, T. J., Medicine
Nachtigal, M., Pharmacology
Nashon, B. J., Surgery and Urology
Nassar, B. A., Pathology, Medicine and Urology
Neumann, P. E., Anatomy and Neurobiology
Norman, R., Urology (Head)
O'Neill, B., Medicine, Community Health and Epidemiology
Padmos, M., Medicine
Palmer, F. B. St. C., Biochemistry (Head)
Parkhill, W. S., Surgery
Pelzer, D., Physiology and Biophysics and Division of Medical Education
Peterson, T., Medicine and Pharmacology
Phillips, S., Medicine
Pollak, T., Medicine
Poulin, C., Community Health and Epidemiology
Powell, C., Medicine
Purdy, R. A., Medicine
Ramsey, M., Ophthalmology
Rasmusson, D., Physiology and Biophysics
Renton, K. W., Pharmacology
Ro, H., Biochemistry
Robertson, G. S., Pharmacology and Psychiatry
Robertson, H. A., Pharmacology and Medicine (Head)
Robinson, K. S., Medicine
Rocker, G., Medicine
Rockwood, K., Medicine
Rowden, G., Pathology and Medicine
Rowe, R. C., Medicine

RUSAK, B., Psychiatry, Psychology and Pharmacology
RUTHERFORD, J., Anatomy and Neurobiology
SADLER, R. M., Medicine
SAWYNOK, J., Pharmacology
SCHLECH, W., Medicine
SEMBA, K., Anatomy and Neurobiology
SHUKLA, R. C., Anaesthesia
SIMPSON, D., Medicine
SINCLAIR, D., Emergency Medicine
SINGER, R. A., Biochemistry
STANISH, W. D., Surgery
STEWART, R. D., Anaesthesia, Emergency Medicine and Division of Medical Education
STEWART, S., Psychology
STOKES, A., Psychiatry (Acting Head)
STOLTZ, D. B., Microbiology and Immunology
STONE, R. M., Surgery (Head)
STROINK, G., Biomedical Engineering
STUTTARD, C., Microbiology and Immunology
SULLIVAN, J., Surgery
TURNBULL, G. K., Medicine
VAN DEN HOF, M., Obstetrics and Gynaecology
VANZANTEN, S., Medicine, Community Health and Epidemiology
VAUGHN, P., Division of Medical Education
WALLACE, C. J. A., Biochemistry
WALSH, N., Pathology
WARD, T., Paediatrics
WASSERSUG, R. J., Anatomy and Neurobiology
WEAVER, D., Medicine and Biomedical Engineering
WEST, M. L., Medicine
WILKINSON, M., Physiology, Biophysics, Obstetrics and Gynaecology
WOLF, H. K., Physiology and Biophysics
WRIGHT, J. R., Pathology, Surgery and Biomedical Engineering
YABSLEY, R. H., Surgery

Faculty of Science (tel. (902) 494-2373; fax (902) 494-1123; e-mail science@dal.ca; internet www.science.dal.ca):
BARRESI, J., Psychology
BEAUMONT, C., Oceanography
BENTZEN, P., Biology and Oceanography
BOUDREAU, B. P., Oceanography (Chair.)
BOWEN, A. J., Oceanography
BOYD, R. J., Chemistry (Chair.)
BRADFIELD, F. M., Economics
BROWN, J., Mathematics and Statistics
BROWN, R. E., Psychology
BRYSON, S. E., Psychology
BURFORD, N., Chemistry
BURNELL, D. J., Chemistry
BURTON, P., Economics
CAMERON, T. S., Chemistry
CAMFIELD, C., Psychology
CHATT, A., Chemistry
CLARKE, D. B., Earth Sciences
CLEMENTS, J., Mathematics and Statistics
COLEY, A., Mathematics and Statistics, Physics
CONNOLLY, J. F., Psychology
COXON, J. A., Chemistry
CROLL, R. P., Biology
CULLEN, J., Oceanography
DAHN, J. R., Chemistry and Physics
DARVESH, S., Chemistry
DASGUPTA, S., Economics
DILCHER, K., Mathematics and Statistics
DUNHAM, P. J., Psychology
DUNLAP, R., Physics
FENTRESS, J. C., Biology
FIELD, C. A., Mathematics and Statistics
FINLEY, G. A., Psychology
FOURNIER, R. O., Oceanography
FREEDMAN, W., Biology (Chair.)
GABOR, G., Mathematics and Statistics
GELDART, D. J., Physics

GIBLING, M. R., Earth Sciences (Chair.)
GRANT, J., Oceanography
GREATBATCH, R., Oceanography and Physics
GRINDLEY, B., Chemistry
GUPTA, R. P., Mathematics and Statistics
HALL, B. K., Biology
HAMILTON, D. C., Mathematics and Statistics
HAY, A., Oceanography
HILL, P. S., Oceanography
HILLS, E. L., Biology
HUTCHINGS, J. A., Biology
ISCAN, T., Economics
IVERSON, S. J., Biology
JAMIESON, R. A., Earth Sciences
JERICHO, M. H., Physics
JOHNSTON, M. O., Biology
KAY-RAINING BIRD, E., Psychology
KEAST, P., Mathematics and Statistics (Chair.)
KLEIN, R. M., Psychology
KREUZER, H. J., Physics
KUSALIK, P. G., Chemistry
KWAK, J. C., Chemistry
LANE, P. A., Biology
LEE, R., Biology
LEONARD, M. L., Biology
LESSER, B., Economics (Chair.)
LEWIS, M., Oceanography
LOLORDO, V. M., Psychology
LOUDEN, K. E., Oceanography
LYONS, R., Psychology
MCGRATH, P. J., Psychology
MCMULLEN, P., Psychology
MACRAE, T., Biology
MEINERTZHAGEN, I. A., Psychology
MITCHELL, D. E., Psychology
MOORE, C. L., Psychology
MOORE, R. M., Oceanography
MORIARTY, K., Mathematics and Statistics, and Physics
MYERS, R. A., Biology
NOWAKOWSKI, R., Mathematics and Statistics
O'DOR, R. K., Biology
OSBERG, L. S., Economics
PACEY, P. D., Chemistry
PARÉ, R., Mathematics and Statistics
PATON, B. E., Physics
PATRIQUIN, D. G., Biology
PHILLIPS, D., Psychology
PHIPPS, S. A., Economics
PINCOCK, J. A., Chemistry
POHAJDAK, B., Biology
RAJORA, O. P., Biology
REYNOLDS, P. H., Earth Sciences and Physics
ROBERTSON, H., Psychology
RUDDICK, B., Oceanography
RUSAK, B., Psychology and Psychiatry
SCHEIBLING, R., Biology
SCOTT, D., Earth Sciences
SEMBA, K., Psychology
SHAW, S., Psychology
STEWART, S., Psychology
STROINK, G., Physics (Chair.)
SUTHERLAND, W. R., Mathematics and Statistics
TAN, K. K., Mathematics and Statistics
TAYLOR, K., Mathematics and Statistics
THOMPSON, K., Mathematics and Statistics, and Oceanography
WACH, G. D., Earth Sciences
WALDE, S., Biology
WEAVER, D. F., Chemistry and Division of Neurology
WENTZELL, P. D., Chemistry
WHITE, M. A., Chemistry and Physics
WHITEHEAD, H., Biology
WILLISON, J. H. M., Biology and Resource, Environmental Studies
WOOD, R. J., Mathematics and Statistics
WRIGHT, J. M., Biology
XU, K., Economics
ZWANZIGER, J. W., Chemistry and Physics

Henson College of Continuing Education (tel. (902) 494-2526; fax (902) 494-6875; e-mail henson-info@dal.ca):
BENOIT, J.
FRASER, L.
NOVACK, J.

COLLÈGE DOMINICAIN DE PHILOSOPHIE ET DE THÉOLOGIE

96 Empress Ave, Ottawa, ON K1R 7G3
Telephone: (613) 233-5696
Fax: (613) 233-6064
Internet: www.collegedominicain.com
Founded 1909 as 'Studium Generale' of Order of Friars Preachers in Canada; present name 1967
Private control
Languages of instruction: French, English
Academic year: September to April
Chancellor: YVON POMERLEAU
President and Regent of Studies: GABOR CSEPREGI
Vice-Presidents: MAXIME ALLARD MICHEL GOURGES
Registrar: HERVÉ TREMBLAY
Librarian: MARTIN LAVOIE
Library of 120,000 vols, 500 periodicals
Number of teachers: 25
Number of students: 635 (127 full-time, 508 part-time)

DEANS

Faculty of Theology: MARIE-THÉRÈSE NADEAU
Faculty of Philosophy: EDUARDO ANDUJAR
Institute of Pastoral Theology: DENIS GAGNON (Chair.)

UNIVERSITY OF GUELPH

Guelph, ON N1G 2W1
Telephone: (519) 824-4120
Fax: (519) 766-9481 (for undergraduate studies); (519) 766-0843 (for graduate studies)
Internet: www.uoguelph.ca
Founded 1964 from Ontario Agricultural College, Ontario Veterinary College and Macdonald Institute, formerly affiliated to the University of Toronto
Private/Provincial control
Language of instruction: English

Three semester system

Chancellor: L. M. ALEXANDER
Pres. and Vice-Chancellor: ALASTAIR SUMMERLEE
Provost and Vice-Pres. for Academic Affairs: MAUREEN MANCUSO (acting)
Vice-Pres. for Alumni Affairs and Development: PAMELLA HEALEY (acting)
Vice-Pres. for Finance and Administration: NANCY SULLIVAN
Vice-Pres. for Research: ALAN WILDEMAN
Vice-Provost and Chief Academic Officer: MICHAEL NIGHTINGALE
Librarian: M. RIDLEY

Library: Library of over 2.5m. vols
Number of teachers: 750
Number of students: 14,000

Publications: *Graduate Calendar*, *President's Report*, *Undergraduate Calendar*

DEANS

College of Arts: JACQUELINE MURRAY
College of Biological Science: MICHAEL EMES
College of Physical and Engineering Science: PETER TREMAINE
College of Social and Applied Human Sciences: ALUN JOSEPH
Ontario Agricultural College: CRAIG PEARSON
Ontario Veterinary College: A. H. MEEK
Faculty of Environmental Sciences: M. R. MOSS

Faculty of Graduate Studies: ISOBEL HEATH-COTE

UNIVERSITY OF KING'S COLLEGE

Halifax, NS B3H 2A1
Telephone: (902) 422-1271
Fax: (902) 423-3357
E-mail: admissions@ukings.ns.ca
Internet: www.ukings.ca
Founded 1789 by United Empire Loyalists; granted Royal Charter 1802, entered into asscn with Dalhousie Univ. 1923
Language of instruction: English
Academic year: September to May
Chancellor: MICHAEL MEIGHEN
Pres. and Vice-Chancellor: WILLIAM BARKER
Vice-Pres.: KIM KIERANS
Registrar: E. YEO
Bursar: G. G. SMITH
Librarian: H. DRAKE PETERSEN
Number of teachers: 51
Number of students: 1,158
Publication: *The Hinge* (1 a year)

PROFESSORS

BARKER, W., English
BISHOP, M., French
BURNS, S. A. M., Philosophy
CROWLEY, J., History
HANKEY, W. J., Classics
HUEBERT, R., English
KIMBER, S., Journalism
STARNES, C. J., Classics
VINCI, T., Philosophy

LAKEHEAD UNIVERSITY

955 Oliver Rd, Thunder Bay, ON P7B 5E1
Telephone: (807) 343-8110
Fax: (807) 343-8023
E-mail: commun@lakeheadu.ca
Internet: www.lakeheadu.ca
Founded 1965, fmrly Lakehead College of Arts, Science and Technology, 1956, and Lakehead Technical Institute, 1946
Academic year: September to April
Chancellor: ARTHUR MAURO
Pres.: Dr BRIAN J.R. STEVENSON
Provost and Vice-Pres. for Academic Affairs: Dr MOIRA MCPHERSON
Vice-Pres. for Admin. and Finance: MICHAEL PAWLOWSKI
Vice-Pres. for Student Affairs: MARIAN RYKS-SZELEKOVSZKY
Vice-Pres. for Research: Dr RUI WANG
Registrar: BRENDA WINTER
Librarian: ANNE DEIGHTON
Number of teachers: 240
Number of students: 8,000

DEANS

Faculty of Business Administration: Dr BAHRAM DADGOSTAR
Faculty of Education: Dr JOHN O'MEARA
Faculty of Engineering: Dr HENRI T. SALIBA
Faculty of Graduate Studies: Dr PHILIP HICKS (acting)
Faculty of Health and Behavioural Sciences: Dr LORI LIVINGSTON
Faculty of Medicine: Dr ROGER STRASSER
Faculty of Natural Resource Management: Dr ULF RUNESSON
Faculty of Science and Environmental Studies: Dr ANDREW P. DEAN
Faculty of Social Sciences and Humanities: Dr GILLIAN SIDDALL

LAURENTIAN UNIVERSITY OF SUDBURY

935 Ramsey Lake Rd, Sudbury, ON P3E 2C6
Telephone: (705) 675-1151
Fax: (705) 675-4891
E-mail: admission@laurentian.ca
Internet: www.laurentian.ca
Founded 1960
Provincially assisted, non-denominational
Languages of instruction: French, English(-certain depts offer parallel courses in both languages)
Academic year: September to April

Depts of anthropology, behavioural neuroscience, biology, classical studies, commerce and administration, earth science, education (English), education (French), English, environmental earth science, ethics studies, film studies, folklore, geography, history, liberal science, mathematics and computer science, midwifery, modern languages and literatures, music, native human services, native studies, nursing, philosophy, physics and astronomy, political science, psychology, radiation therapy, religious studies, social work, sociology, sport psychology, sports administration

Pres.: JUDITH WOODSWORTH
Vice-Pres. for Admin.: ROBERT F. BOURGEOIS
Academic Vice-Pres. for Anglophone Affairs: SUSAN SILVERTON
Academic Vice-Pres. for Francophone Affairs: HARLEY D'ENTREMONT
Registrar: RON SMITH
Dir of Library: LIONEL BONIN
Dir for Centre for Continuing Education: DENIS MAYER
Dir for Div. of Physical Education: ROGER COUTURE
Dir for Graduate Studies and Research: PAUL COLILLI
Number of teachers: 377 (full-time)
Number of students: 9,100

DEANS

Humanities and Social Sciences: JOHN ISBISTER
Management: HUGUETTE BLANCO
Professional Schools: ANNE-MARIE MAWHINEY
Sciences and Engineering: PATRICE SAWYER

CONSTITUENT INSTITUTIONS

Algoma University College: 1520 Queen St E, Sault Ste Marie, ON P6A 2G4; internet www.algomau.ca; Pres. C. ROSS; Registrar D. MARASCO.

Collège Universitaire de Hearst: Hearst, ON P0L 1N0; internet www.univhearst.edu; f. 1952; Rector R. TREMBLAY; Registrar J. DOUCET.

FEDERATED UNIVERSITIES

Huntington University: Ramsey Lake Rd, Sudbury, ON P3E 2C6; f. 1960; related to United Church of Canada; Pres.-Principal KEVIN MCCORMICK; Registrar A. HOOD.

Thorneloe University: Ramsey Lake Rd, Sudbury, ON P3E 2C6; Provost S. ANDREWS; Registrar I. MACLENNAN.

University of Sudbury: Ramsey Lake Rd, Sudbury, ON P3E 2C6; f. 1957; conducted by the Jesuit Fathers; Pres. ANDRII KRAWCHUK; Registrar L. BEAUPRÉ.

UNIVERSITÉ LAVAL

Québec, QC G1V 0A6
Telephone: (418) 656-2131
Fax: (418) 656-5920
E-mail: accueil@sg.ulaval.ca
Internet: www.ulaval.ca
Founded 1852, Royal Charter signed December 1852, Pontifical Charter 1876, Provincial Charter 1970
Language of instruction: French
Academic year: September to August
Rector: DENIS BRIÈRE

Vice-Rector for Academic Int. Activities: BERNARD GARNIER
Vice-Rector for Admin. and Finances: JOSÉE GERMAIN
Vice-Rector for Human Resources: MICHEL BEAUCHAMP
Vice-Rector for Research and Creation: EDWIN BOURGET
Deputy Vice-Rector for Research and Creation: CHRISTIANE PICHÉ
Dean of Graduate Studies: MARIE AUDETTE
Dir of Undergraduate Studies: SERGE TALBOT
Dir of Continuing Education: PIERRE DIONNE
Sec.-Gen.: MONIQUE RICHER
Registrar: DANIELLE FLEURY
Librarian: SILVIE DELORME

Library: see Libraries and Archives
Number of teachers: 1,587
Number of students: 37,295 (24,415 full-time, 12,880 part-time)
Publications: *Anthropologie et Sociétés* (anthropology), *Cahiers de Droit* (law), *Cahiers de Géographie du Québec* (geography), *Cahiers de Recherche* (1 a year, economics), *CRIRES* (education), *Communication* (mass communication), *Didaskalia* (2 a year, education), *Ecoscience* (biology), *Ethnologies* (1 a year, journal of Canadian folklore studies), *Études Internationales* (4 a year, international studies), *Études Inuits* (2 a year, Inuit studies), *Études Littéraires* (3 a year, literature), *Langues et Linguistique* (linguistics), *L'Année Francophone Internationale* (L'AFI) (literary), *Laval Théologique et Philosophique* (theology and philosophy), *Les Cahiers du Journalisme* (journalism), *Recherches Féministes* (feminism), *Recherches Sociographiques* (1 a year, Quebec studies), *Rédiger* (1 a year, technical writing), *Relations Industrielles* (industrial relations), *Revue d'Histoire Intellectuelle de l'Amérique Française* (12 a year), *Revue Scientifique* (education), *Service Social* (online, social work), *Visio* (history)

DEANS AND DIRECTORS

Faculty of Administrative Sciences: ROBERT W. MANTHA
Faculty of Agriculture and Food Sciences: JEAN-PAUL LAFOREST
Faculty of Dentistry: ANDRÉ FOURNIER
Faculty of Education: MARCEL MONETTE
Faculty of Forestry and Geomatics: ROBERT BEAUREGARD
Faculty of Law: PIERRE LEMIEUX
Faculty of Letters: THIERRY BELLEGUIC
Faculty of Medicine: PIERRE JACOB DURAND
Faculty of Music: PAUL CADRIN
Faculty of Nursing Sciences: DIANE MORIN
Faculty of Pharmacy: JEAN-PIERRE GRÉGOIRE
Faculty of Philosophy: LUC LANGLOIS
Faculty of Sciences and Engineering: GUY GENDRON
Faculty of Social Sciences: FRANÇOIS BLAIS
Faculty of Theology and Religious Sciences: MARC PELCHAT
Faculty of Urban Planning, Architecture and Visual Arts: RICHARD PLEAU
Québec Institute of Higher International Studies: PAUL GAUTHIER

PROFESSORS

Faculty of Administrative Sciences (Pavillon Palasis-Prince, Bureau 1322, Québec, QC G1K 7P4; tel. (418) 656-2180; fax (418) 656-2624; e-mail fsa@fsa.ulaval.ca; internet www.fsa.ulaval.ca):

AUDET, M., Management
BANVILLE, C., Management Information Systems
BEAULIEU, M.-C., Finance and Insurance
BÉDARD, J., Accounting (Sciences)
BÉLIVEAU, D., Marketing

BELLEMARE, G., Finance and Insurance
BERGERON, F., Management Information Systems
BERNIER, G., Finance and Insurance
BHERER, H., Management
BLAIS, R., Management
BOCTOR, F. F., Operations and Decision Systems
BOIRAL, O., Management
BOULAIRE, C., Marketing
BOURDEAU, L., Management
BRUN, J.-P., Management
CARPENTIER, C., Accounting (School)
CAYER, M., Management
CORMIER, E., Accounting (School)
COULOMBE, D., Accounting (Sciences)
D'AVIGNON, G. R., Operations and Decision Systems
DES ROSIERS, F., Management
DIONNE, P., Management
FISCHER, P. K., Finance and Insurance
GARAND, D. J., Management
GARNIER, B., Management
GASCON, A., Operations and Decision Systems
GASSE, Y., Management
GAUTHIER, A., Operations and Decision Systems
GAUVIN, S., Marketing
GENDRON, M., Finance and Insurance
GOSSELIN, M., Accounting (School)
GRISÉ, J., Management
HASKELL, N., Marketing
KETTANI, O., Operations and Decision Systems
KISS, L. N., Operations and Decision Systems
LACASSE, N., Management
LAI, V. S., Finance and Insurance
LAMOND, B., Operations and Decision Systems
LANDRY, R., Management
LANG, P., Operations and Decision Systems
LEE-GOSSELIN, H., Management
LESCEUX, D., Marketing
LETARTE, P.-A., Management
MANTHA, R. W., Management Information Systems
MARTEL, A., Operations and Decision Systems
MOFFET, D., Finance and Insurance
MONTREUIL, B., Operations and Decision Systems
NADEAU, L., Accounting (School)
NADEAU, R., Operations and Decision Systems
PAQUETTE, S., Accounting (Sciences)
PARÉ, P.-V., Accounting (School)
PASCOT, D., Management Information Systems
POULIN, D., Management
PRÉMONT, P. E., Management Information Systems
RENAUD, J., Operations and Decision Systems
RIDJANOVIC, D., Management Information Systems
RIGAUX-BRICMONT, B., Marketing
ROY, M.-C., Management Information Systems
ROY, M.-J., Management
SAINT PIERRE, J., Finance and Insurance
SEROR, ANN C., Management
SU, Z., Management
SURET, J.-M., Accounting (School)
VERNA, G., Management
VÉZINA, R., Marketing
ZINS, M., Marketing

Faculty of Agriculture and Food Sciences (Pavillon Paul-Comtois, Bureau 1122, Québec, QC G1K 7P4; tel. (418) 656-3145; fax (418) 656-7806; e-mail fsaa@fsaa.ulaval.ca; internet www.fsaa.ulaval.ca):

ALLARD, G., Plant Science
AMIOT, J., Food Science and Nutrition
ANGERS, P., Food Science and Nutrition
ANTOUN, H., Soils and Agricultural Engineering
ARUL, J., Food Science and Nutrition
ASSELIN, A., Plant Science
BAILEY, J. L., Animal Sciences
BEAUCHAMP, C. J., Plant Science
BEAUDOIN, P., Agricultural Economics and Consumer Sciences
BEAUDRY, M., Food Science and Nutrition
BÉLANGER, R., Plant Science
BELZILE, F., Plant Science
BENHAMOU, N., Plant Science
BERGERON, R., Animal Sciences
BERNIER, J.-F., Animal Sciences
BLACKBURN, M., Soils and Agricultural Engineering
BRODEUR, J., Plant Science
CAILLIER, M., Soils and Agricultural Engineering
CALKINS, P., Agricultural Economics and Consumer Sciences
CAREL, M., Agricultural Economics and Consumer Sciences
CARON, J., Soils and Agricultural Engineering
CASTAIGNE, F., Food Science and Nutrition
CESCAS, M. P., Soils and Agricultural Engineering
CHALIFOUR, F. P., Plant Science
CHAREST, P.-M., Plant Science
CHOUINARD, Y., Animal Sciences
COLLIN, J., Plant Science
DANSEREAU, B., Plant Science
DEBAILLEUL, G., Agricultural Economics and Consumer Sciences
DESJARDINS, Y., Plant Science
DESPRES, J.-P., Food Science and Nutrition
DESROSIERS, T., Food Science and Nutrition
DION, P., Plant Science
DOSTALER, D., Plant Science
DOYEN, M., Agricultural Economics and Consumer Sciences
DUFOUR, J. C., Agricultural Economics and Consumer Sciences
EMOND, J.-P., Soils and Agricultural Engineering
FLISS, I., Food Science and Nutrition
FORTIN, J., Soils and Agricultural Engineering
GALIBOIS, I., Food Science and Nutrition
GALLICHAND, J., Soils and Agricultural Engineering
GAUTHIER, S., Food Science and Nutrition
GERVAIS, J.-P., Agricultural Economics and Consumer Services
GOSSELIN, A., Plant Science
GOUIN, D., Agricultural Economics and Consumer Sciences
GOULET, J., Food Science and Nutrition
JACQUES, H., Food Science and Nutrition
KARAM, A., Soils and Agricultural Engineering
LACHANCE, M. J., Agricultural Economics and Consumer Sciences
LAFOREST, J.-P., Animal Sciences
LAGACÉ, R., Soils and Agricultural Engineering
LAMARCHE, B., Food Science and Nutrition
LAMBERT, R., Agricultural Economics and Consumer Sciences
LAPOINTE, G., Food Science and Nutrition
LARUE, B., Agricultural Economics and Consumer Sciences
LAVERDIÈRE, M.-R., Soils and Agricultural Engineering
LEFRANÇOIS, M., Animal Sciences
LEMIEUX, S., Food Science and Nutrition
LEROUX, G., Plant Science
LEVALLOIS, R., Agricultural Economics and Consumer Sciences
LOCONG, A., Food Science and Nutrition
MAKHLOUF, J., Food Science and Nutrition
MARQUIS, A., Soils and Agricultural Engineering
MARTEL, R., Food Science and Nutrition
MARTIN, F., Agricultural Economics and Consumer Sciences
MICHAUD, D., Plant Science
MORISSET, M., Agricultural Economics and Consumer Sciences
OLIVIER, A., Plant Science
OUELLET, D., Food Science and Nutrition
PAQUIN, P., Food Science and Nutrition
PARENT, D., Animal Science
PARENT, L. E., Soils and Agricultural Engineering
PELLERIN, D., Animal Sciences
PERRIER, J.-P., Agricultural Economics and Consumer Sciences
PICARD, G., Food Science and Nutrition
POTHIER, F., Animal Science
POULIOT, Y., Food Science and Nutrition
RATTI, C., Soils and Agricultural Engineering
RIOUX, J.-A., Plant Science
ROBITAILLE, J., Agricultural Economics and Consumer Sciences
ROCHEFORT, L., Plant Science
ROMAIN, R., Agricultural Economics and Consumer Sciences
ROY, D., Food Science and Nutrition
ST-LOUIS, R., Agricultural Economics and Consumer Sciences
SIRARD, M.-A., Animal Science
SUBIRADE, M., Food Science and Nutrition
THÉRIAULT, R., Soils and Agricultural Engineering
TURGEON, S., Food Science and Nutrition
TURGEON-O'BRIEN, H., Food Science and Nutrition
VOHL, J.-C., Food Science and Nutrition
VUILLEMARD, J.-C., Food Science and Nutrition
WEST, E. G., Agricultural Economics and Consumer Sciences
ZEE, J., Food Science and Nutrition

Faculty of Architecture, Planning and Visual Arts (Édifice du Vieux-Séminaire de Québec, 1 Côte de la Fabrique, Bureau 2230, Québec, QC G1R 3V6; tel. (418) 656-2546; fax (418) 656-3325; e-mail faaav@faaav.ulaval.ca; internet www.faaav.ulaval.ca):

BLAIS, M., Architecture
CARRIER, M., Planning
CASAULT, A., Architecture
CHAINE, F., Visual Arts
CLOUTIER, L., Visual Arts
COSSETTE, M. A., Visual Arts
CÔTÉ, P., Architecture
DEMERS, C., Architecture
DESPRÉS, C., Architecture
DUBÉ, C., Planning
GIRARD, G., Visual Arts
JEAN, M., Visual Arts
LAVOIE, C., Planning
LEE-GOSSELIN, M., Planning
LEMIEUX, R., Visual Arts
MALENFANT, N., Visual Arts
MILL, R., Visual Arts
NAYLOR, D., Visual Arts
PICHÉ, D., Architecture
PLEAU, R., Architecture
POTVIN, A., Architecture
POULIOT, S., Visual Arts
ROCHON, A., Visual Arts
RODRIGUEZ-PINZON, M., Planning
TEYSSOT, G., Architecture
THÉRIAULT, M., Planning
TREMBLAY, G.-H., Architecture
VACHON, E., Architecture
VACHON, G., Architecture
VILLENEUVE, P., Planning
ZWIEJSKI, J., Architecture

Faculty of Dentistry (Pavillon de Médecine Dentaire, Bureau 1615, Québec, QC G1K 7P4; tel. (418) 656-2247; fax (418) 656-2720; e-mail fmd@fmd.ulaval.ca; internet www.ulaval.ca/fmd):

BASTIEN, R.
BERNARD, C.

CARON, C.
CHMIELEWSKI, W.
FOURNIER, A.
GAGNON, G.
GAGNON, P.
GAUCHEN, H.
GIASSON, L.
GOULET, J.-P.
GRENIER, D.
LACHAPELLE, D.
MORAND, M.-A.
MORIN, S.
NICHOLSON, L.
PAYANT, L.
PERUSSE, R.
PROULX, M.
ROBERT, D.
ROUABHIA, M.
ROY, S.
VALOIS, M.

Faculty of Education (Pavillon des Sciences de l'Éducation, Québec, QC G1K 7P4; tel. (418) 656-3062; fax (418) 656-7347; e-mail fse@fse.ulaval.ca; internet www.fse.ulaval .ca):

ARRIOLA-SOCOL, M., Foundations and Interventions in Education
BÉLANGER, J.-D., Teaching and Learning Studies
BOISCLAIR, A., Teaching and Learning Studies
BOIVIN, M.-D., Foundations and Interventions in Education
BOUCHARD, P., Foundations and Interventions in Education
BOURASSA, B., Foundations and Interventions in Education
CARDIN, J.-F., Teaching and Learning Studies
CARDU, H., Foundations and Interventions in Education
CLOUTIER, R., Foundations and Interventions in Education
DEBLOIS, L., Teaching and Learning Studies
DENIGER, M.-A., Foundations and Interventions in Education
DÉSAUTELS, J., Teaching and Learning Studies
DESGAGNÉ, S., Teaching and Learning Studies
DIAMBOMBA, M., Foundations and Interventions in Education
DIONNE, J., Teaching and Learning Studies
DRAPEAU, S., Foundations and Interventions in Education
DROLET, J.-L., Foundations and Interventions in Education
FOUNTAIN, R. M. B., Teaching and Learning Studies
FOURNIER, G., Foundations and Interventions in Education
FOURNIER, J.-P., Teaching and Learning Studies
GAGNON, J., Physical Education
GAGNON, R., Teaching and Learning Studies
GAULIN, C., Teaching and Learning Studies
GAUTHIER, C., Teaching and Learning Studies
GERVAIS, F., Teaching and Learning Studies
GIASSON, J., Teaching and Learning Studies
GUAY, F., Foundations and Interventions in Education
GUERETTE, C., Teaching and Learning Studies
GUILBERT, L., Teaching and Learning Studies
HAMEL, T., Foundations and Interventions in Education
JACQUES, M., Teaching and Learning Studies

JEANRIE, C., Foundations and Interventions in Educations
JEFFREY, D., Teaching and Learning Studies
KASZAP, M., Teaching and Learning Studies
LACHANCE, L., Foundations and Interventions in Education
LAFERRIÈRE, T., Teaching and Learning Studies
LANDRY, C., Foundations and Interventions in Education
LAPOINTE, C., Foundations and Interventions in Education
LAROCHELLE, M., Teaching and Learning Studies
LAROSE, S., Teaching and Learning Studies
LE BOSSE, Y., Foundations and Interventions in Education
LECLERC, C., Foundations and Interventions in Education
LEGAULT, M., Teaching and Learning Studies
MARANDA, M.-F., Foundations and Interventions in Education
MARCOUX, Y., Foundations and Interventions in Education
MARTEL, D., Physical Education
MASSOT, A., Foundations and Interventions in Education
MOISSET, J.-J., Foundations and Interventions in Education
MONETTE, M., Foundations and Interventions in Education
MURA, R., Teaching and Learning Studies
NADEAU, G.-A., Physical Education
PAGÉ, P., Teaching and Learning Skills
PELLETIER, P., Teaching and Learning Skills
PLANTE, J., Foundations and Interventions in Education
RATTE, J., Foundations and Interventions in Education
ROY-BUREAU, L., Teaching and Learning Skills
ROYER, E., Teaching and Learning Studies
ST-LAURENT, L., Teaching and Learning Studies
SAMSON, J., Physical Education
SAVARD, C., Physical Education
SIMARD, C., Teaching and Learning Studies
SIMARD, D., Teaching and Learning Skills
SPAIN, A., Foundations and Interventions in Education
TALBOT, S., Physical Education
THERIAULT, G., Physical Education
TROTTIER, C., Foundations and Interventions in Education
VALOIS, P., Foundations and Interventions in Education
VINCENT, S., Teaching and Learning Skills
ZIARKO, H., Teaching and Learning Skills

Faculty of Forestry and Geomatics (Pavillon Abitibi-Price, Bureau 1151, Québec, QC G1K 7P4; tel. (418) 656-3880; fax (418) 656-3177; e-mail ffg@ffg.ulaval.ca; internet www.ffg .ulaval.ca):

ALLARD, M., Geography
BAUCE, E., Wood and Forest Sciences
BEAUDOIN, M., Wood and Forest Sciences
BEAULIEU, B., Geomatics
BEAUREGARD, R., Wood and Forest Sciences
BÉDARD, Y., Geomatics
BÉGIN, J., Wood and Forest Sciences
BÉGIN, Y., Geography
BÉLANGER, L., Wood and Forest Sciences
BELLEFLEUR, P., Wood and Forest Sciences
BERNIER, L., Wood and Forest Sciences
BHIRY, N., Geography
BOULIANNE, M., Geomatics
BOUSQUET, J., Wood and Forest Sciences
BOUTHILLER, L., Wood and Forest Sciences
BRIÈRE, D., Wood and Forest Sciences
CAMIRÉ, C., Wood and Forest Sciences
CHEVALLIER, J.-J., Geomatics

CLOUTIER, A., Wood and Forest Sciences
CONDAL, A., Geomatics
DESROCHERS, A., Wood and Forest Sciences
DESSUREAULT, M., Wood and Forest Sciences
EDWARDS, G., Geomatics
FILION, L., Geography
FORTIN, Y., Wood and Forest Sciences
GODBOUT, C., Wood and Forest Sciences
HERNANDEZ PENA, R., Wood and Forest Sciences
LALONDE, M., Wood and Forest Sciences
LEBEL, L., Wood and Forest Sciences
LOWELL, K., Wood and Forest Sciences
MARGOLLIS, H., Wood and Forest Sciences
MERCIER, G., Geography
MUNSON, A., Wood and Forest Sciences
PICHÉ, Y., Wood and Forest Sciences
PIENITZ, R., Geography
PLAMONDON, A. P., Wood and Forest Sciences
PLANTE, F., Geomatics
POTHIER, D., Wood and Forest Sciences
RIEDL, B., Wood and Forest Sciences
RUEL, J.-C., Wood and Forest Sciences
ST-HILAIRE, M., Geography
SANTERRE, R., Geomatics
STEVANOVIC, J. T., Wood and Forest Sciences
THIBEAULT, J.-R., Wood and Forest Sciences
TREMBLAY, F., Wood and Forest Sciences
VIAU, A., Geomatics

Faculty of Law (Pavillon Charles-DeKoninck, Bureau 2407, Québec, QC G1K 7P4; tel. (418) 656-2131, ext. 6134; fax (418) 656-7230; e-mail fd@fd.ulaval.ca; internet www.ulaval .ca/fd):

ARBOUR, M.
BELLEAU, M.-C.
BOUCHARD, C.
BRETON, R.
BROCHU, F.
COTE-HARPER, G.
CRÊTE, R.
DELEURY, E.
DESLAURIERS, J.
DUPLE, N.
FERLAND, D.
GARDNER, D.
GIROUX, L.
GOUBAU, D.
HALLEY, P.
ISSALYS, P.
LANGEVIN, L.
LAQUERRE, P.
LAREAU, A.
LAUZIÈRE, L.
LEMIEUX, D.
LEMIEUX, P.
MANGANAS, A.
MELKEVILL, B.
NORMAND, S.
OTIS, G.
PRUJINER, A.
RAINVILLE, P.
ROUSSEAU, G.
TREMBLAY, G.
TURGEON, J.

Faculty of Letters (Pavillon Charles-De Koninck, Bureau 3254, Québec, QC G1K 7P4; tel. (418) 656-3460; fax (418) 656-2019; e-mail fl@fl.ulaval.ca; internet www.fl.ulaval .ca):

AUGER, P., Languages and Linguistics
AUGER, R., History
BACZ, B., Languages and Linguistics
BAKER, P., History
BAUDOU, A., Literature
BEAUCHAMP, M., Information and Communication
BEAUDET, M.-A., Literature
BEAUSOLEIL, P., Information and Communication
BELANGER, R., History

BELLEGUIC, T., Literature
BERNIER, J., History
BISAILLON, J., Languages and Linguistics
BOISVERT, L., Languages and Linguistics
BOIVIN, A., Literature
BORGONOVO, C., Languages and Linguistics
BOULANGER, J.-C., Languages and Linguistics
CARANI, M., History
CARDIN, M., History
CAULIER, B., History
CHARRON, J., Information and Communication
CLERC, I., Information and Communication
COSSETTE, J. C., Information and Communication
CUMMINS, S., Languages and Linguistics
DAGENAIS, B., Information and Communication
DAIGLE, J., History
DAVIAULT, A., Literature
DE BONVILLE, J., Information and Communication
DE KONINCK, Z., Languages and Linguistics
DE LA GARDE, R., Information and Communication
DEMERS, F., Information and Communication
DEMERS, G., Languages and Linguistics
DESDOUITS, A.-M., History
DESHAIES, D., Languages and Linguistics
DOLAN, C., History
DUBÉ, P., History
DUFFLEY, P., Languages and Linguistics
DUMONT, F., Literature
ESPANOL, E. M., Languages and Linguistics
FAITELSON-WEISER, S., Languages and Linguistics
FINETTE, L., Literature
FORTIER, A.-M., Literature
FORTIN, M., History
FYSON, D., History
GAGNÉ, M., Literature
GARON, L., Information and Communication
GAUTHIER, G., Information and Communication
GRENIER, D., History
GRIGNON, M., History
GUEVEL, Z., Languages and Linguistics
GUILBERT, L., History
HÉBERT, C., Literature
HERMON, E., History
HUMMEL, K., Languages and Linguistics
HUOT, D., Languages and Linguistics
HUOT-LEMONNIER, F., Languages and Linguistics
JOLICOEUR, L., Languages and Linguistics
JUNEAU, M., Languages and Linguistics
KAREL, D., History
KEGLE, C., Literature
KOSS, B. J., History
KUGLER, M., Information and Communication
LABERGE, A., History
LACHARITÉ, D. P., Languages and Linguistics
LADOUCEUR, J., Languages and Linguistics
LAPOINTE, M., History
LAVIGNE, A., Information and Communication
LEBEL, E., Information and Communication
LEMELIN, B., History
LEMIEUX, J., Information and Communication
LÉTOURNEAU, J., History
LOWE, R., Languages and Linguistics
LUKIC, R., History
MANNING, A., Languages and Linguistics
MARCHAND, J., Information and Communication
MARTIN, P., Languages and Linguistics
MATHIEU, J., History
MERCIER, A., Literature

MOORE, E., History
MOSER VERREY, M., Literature
MOUSSETTE, M., History
NAKOS, D., Languages and Linguistics
NGUYEN-DUY, V., Information and Communication
NIQUETTE, M., Information and Communication
OUELLET, J., Languages and Linguistics
PAQUETTE, G., Information and Communication
PAQUOT, A., Languages and Linguistics
PARADIS, C., Languages and Linguistics
PARKS, S. E., Languages and Linguistics
PELLETIER, E., Literature
PERELLI-CONTOS, I., Literature
PERESTRELO, F., Languages and Linguistics
PICARD, J.-C., Information and Communication
PIETTE, C., History
POIRIER, C., Languages and Linguistics
PONTBRIAND, J.-N., Literature
PRÉVOST, P., Languages and Linguistics
RIVET, J., Information and Communication
ROY, L., Literature
SADETSKY, A., Languages and Linguistics
ST-GELAIS, R., Literature
SAINT JACQUES, D., Literature
SAUVAGEAU, F., Information and Communication
THENON, L., Literature
THÉRY, C., Literature
THOMAS, N. H., Literature
TREMBLAY, G., Geography
TURGEON, L., History
VALLIÈRES, M., History
VAN DER SCHWEREN, É., Literature
VERREAULT, C., Languages and Linguistics
VINCENT, D., Languages and Linguistics
WATINE, T., Information and Communication

Faculty of Medicine (Pavillon Ferdinand-Vandry, Bureau 1214, Québec, QC G1K 7P4; tel. (418) 656-5245; fax (418) 656-2501; e-mail fmed@fmed.ulaval.ca; internet www.fmed.ulaval.ca):

ABDOUS, B., Social and Preventive Medicine
AKOUM, A., Obstetrics and Gynaecology
ALARY, M., Social and Preventive Medicine
ALLEN, T., Family Medicine
AMZICA, F., Anatomy and Physiology
AUBIN, M., Family Medicine
AUDETTE, M., Medical Biology
AUGER, F., Surgery
AYOTTE, P., Social and Preventive Medicine
BACHELARD, H., Medicine
BACHVAROV, D., Medicine
BAIRAM, A., Paediatrics
BAIRATI, I., Surgery
BARDEN, N., Anatomy and Physiology
BASTIDE, A., Obstetrics and Gynaecology
BEAUCHAMP, D., Medical Biology
BEAUCHEMIN, J.-P., Family Medicine
BEAULIEU, A., Medicine
BEDARD, P., Medicine
BÉLANGER, A., Anatomy and Physiology
BÉLANGER, A. Y., Rehabilitation
BÉLANGER, L., Medical Biology
BERGERON, J., Obstetrics and Gynaecology
BERGERON, M. G., Medical Biology
BERGERON, R., Family Medicine
BERNARD, P.-M., Social and Preventive Medicine
BERNATCHEZ, J.-P., Psychiatry
BERNIER, V., Medical Biology
BILODEAU, A., Family Medicine
BISSONNETTE, E., Medicine
BLANCHET, J., Obstetrics and Gynaecology
BLONDEAU, F., Family Medicine
BLONDEAU, L., Medicine
BOGATY, P., Medicine
BOIVIN, G., Medical Biology
BORGEAT, P., Anatomy and Physiology
BOUCHARD, J.-P., Medicine

BOUCHER, F., Paediatrics
BOULAY, M. R., Social and Preventive Medicine
BOULET, L.-P., Medicine
BOURBONNAIS, R., Rehabilitation
BOURGOIN, S.-G., Anatomy and Physiology
BRAILOVSKY, C. A., Family Medicine
BRASSARD, N., Obstetrics and Gynaecology
BRISSON, C., Social and Preventive Medicine
BRISSON, J., Social and Preventive Medicine
CABANAC, M., Anatomy and Physiology
CANDAS, B., Anatomy and Physiology
CAPADAY, C., Anatomy and Physiology
CARRIÈRE, M., Rehabilitation
CARUSO, M., Medical Biology
CHAHINE, M., Medicine
CHAKIR, J., Medicine
CHARRON, J., Medical Biology
CLOUTIER, A., Paediatrics
CORBEIL, J., Anatomy and Physiology
CORMIER, Y., Medicine
CÔTÉ, C., Rehabilitation
CÔTÉ, J., Anaesthesiology
CÔTÉ, L., Medicine
COUET, J., Medicine
CUSAN, L., Anatomy and Physiology
DE KONINCK, M., Social and Preventive Medicine
DE KONINCK, Y., Psychiatry
DE SERRES, G., Medical Biology
DE WALS, P., Social and Preventive Medicine
DELAGE, R., Medicine
DERY, P., Paediatrics
DESCHÊNES, M., Anatomy and Physiology
DESHAIES, Y., Anatomy and Physiology
DESLAURIERS, J., Surgery
DESMEULES, M., Medicine
DEWAILLY, F., Social and Preventive Medicine
DIONNE, C., Rehabilitation
DIONNE, F. T., Social and Preventive Medicine
DODIN, S. D., Obstetrics and Gynaecology
DOILLON, C., Surgery
DORÉ, F. M., Medicine
DORVAL, J., Paediatrics
DOUVILLE, Y., Surgery
DROLET, G., Medicine
DUMESNIL, J.-G., Medicine
DURAND, P.-J., Social and Preventive Medicine
FAURE, R., Paediatrics
FLAMAND, L., Anatomy and Physiology
FOREST, J.-C., Medical Biology
FORTIER, M.-A., Obstetrics and Gynaecology
FORTIN, J.-P., Social and Preventive Medicine
FRADET, Y., Surgery
FRÉMONT, P., Rehabilitation
FRENETTE, J., Family Medicine and Rehabilitation
GAGNON, F., Psychiatry
GAILIS, L., Medicine
GERMAIN, L., Surgery
GERVAIS, M., Rehabilitation
GIRARD, J. E., Social and Preventive Medicine
GLENN, J., Medical Biology
GOSSELIN, J., Anatomy and Physiology
GOVINDAN, M. J., Anatomy and Physiology
GRAVEL, C., Psychiatry
GUAY, G., Medicine
GUÉRIN, S., Anatomy and Physiology
GUIDOIN, R., Surgery
HANCOCK, R., Medical Biology
HUDON, C., Paediatrics
HUOT, J., Medicine
JEANNOTTE, L., Medical Biology
JOBIN, J., Medicine
JULIEN, J.-P., Anatomy and Physiology
JULIEN, P., Medicine
KHANDJIAN, E. W., Medical Biology

KINKEAD, R., Paediatrics
KINGMA, J. G., Medicine
L'ARRIÈRE, M., Rehabilitation
LABBÉ, J., Paediatrics
LABBÉ, R., Medical Biology
LABELLE, Y., Medical Biology
LABERGE, C., Medicine
LABRECQUE, M., Family Medicine
LABRIE, C., Anatomy and Physiology
LABRIE, F., Anatomy and Physiology
LACASSE, Y., Medicine
LAFRAMBOISE, R., Paediatrics
LAGACÉ, R., Medical Biology
LAGASSE, P.-P., Social and Preventive Medicine
LAJOIE, P., Social and Preventive Medicine
LALANNE, M., Medical Biology
LAMBERT, R. D., Obstetrics and Gynaecology
LAMONTAGNE, R., Family Medicine
LANDRY, J., Medicine
LANGELIER, M., Medicine
LANGLOIS, S., Medicine
LANIVIÈLE, R., Medicine
LAROCHELLE, L., Anatomy and Physiology
LATULIPPE, L., Medicine
LAVIOLETTE, M., Medicine
LAVOIE, J., Medical Biology
LEBEL, M., Medicine
LEBLANC, R., Social and Preventive Medicine
LEBLOND, P., Medicine
LECLERC, P., Medical Biology
LEDUC, Y., Family Medicine
LELIÈVRE, M., Paediatrics
LEMAY, A., Obstetrics and Gynaecology
LETARTE, R., Medical Biology
LEVALLOIS, P., Social and Preventive Medicine
LEVESQUE, D., Medicine
LÉVESQUE, R., Medical Biology
LIN, S.-X., Anatomy and Physiology
LUU, T. V., Anatomy and Physiology
MCFADYEN, B. J., Rehabilitation
MAHEUX, R., Obstetrics and Gynaecology
MALOUIN, F., Rehabilitation
MALTAIS, F., Medicine
MARCEAU, F., Medicine
MARCEAU, N., Medicine
MARCHAND, R., Anatomy and Physiology
MARCOUX, H., Family Medicine
MARCOUX, S., Social and Preventive Medicine
MARETTE, A., Anatomy and Physiology
MARTINEAU, R., Medical Biology
MAUNSELL, E., Social and Preventive Medicine
MAURIEGE, P., Social and Preventive Medicine
MAZIADE, M., Psychiatry
MERETTE, C., Psychiatry
MEYER, F., Social and Preventive Medicine
MIRAULT, M.-E., Medicine
MOFFET, H., Rehabilitation
MONTGRAIN, N., Psychiatry
MORISSETTE, J., Anatomy and Physiology
MOSS, T., Medical Biology
MOURAD, M. W., Medicine
MURTHY, M.-R.-V., Medical Biology
NACCACHE, P.-H., Medicine
NADEAU, A., Medicine
NADEAU, L., Medical Biology
NOREAU, L., Rehabilitation
OUELLETTE, M., Medical Biology
PAINCHAUD, G., Psychiatry
PAPADOPOULO, B., Medical Biology
PARENT, A., Anatomy and Physiology
PELLETIER, G.-H., Anatomy and Physiology
PERUSSE, L., Social and Preventive Medicine
PHILIPPE, E., Anatomy and Physiology
PIBAROT, P., Medicine
PIEDBOEUF, B., Paediatrics
POIRIER, D., Anatomy and Physiology
POIRIER, G., Medical Biology
POMERLEAU, G., Psychiatry

POUBELLE, P., Medicine
POULIN, R., Anatomy and Physiology
PUYMIRAT, J., Medicine
RATTÉ, C., Psychiatry
RAYMOND, V., Anatomy and Physiology
RICHARD, D., Anatomy and Physiology
RICHARDS, C. L., Rehabilitation
RIOUX, F., Medicine
RIVEST, S., Anatomy and Physiology
ROBERGE, C., Medical Biology
ROBICHAUD, L., Rehabilitation
ROUILLARD, C., Medicine
ROULEAU, J., Medicine
ROUSSEAU, F., Medical Biology
ROY, M., Obstetrics and Gynaecology
SALESSE, C., Otorhinolaryngology and Ophthalmology
SATO, M., Anatomy and Physiology
SATO, S., Medical Biology
SAUCIER, D., Family Medicine
SAVARD, P., Medicine
SEGUIN, C., Anatomy and Physiology
SERIES, F., Medicine
SHAH, G., Medical Biology
SIMARD, J., Anatomy and Physiology
STERIADE, M., Anatomy and Physiology
SULLIVAN, R., Obstetrics and Gynaecology
TALBOT, J., Medical Biology
TANGUAY, R., Medicine
TEASDALE, N., Social and Preventive Medicine
TESSIER, P., Medical Biology
TETREAULT, S., Rehabilitation
TETU, B., Medical Biology
THIVIERGE, J., Psychiatry
TREMBLAY, A., Social and Preventive Medicine
TREMBLAY, J.-P., Anatomy and Physiology
TREMBLAY, M. J., Medical Biology
TREMBLAY, Y., Obstetrics and Gynaecology
TRUDEL, R., Rehabilitation
VENRREAULT, R., Social and Preventive Medicine
VERRET, S., Paediatrics
VEZINA, M., Social and Preventive Medicine
VILLENEUVE, E., Psychiatry
VINCENT, C., Rehabilitation
VINCENT, C., Medicine

Faculty of Music (Pavillon Louis-Jacques-Casault, Bureau 3312, Québec, QC G1K 7P4; tel. (418) 656-7061; fax (418) 656-7365; e-mail mus@mus.ulaval.ca; internet www.ulaval.ca/mus):

BOULET, M.-M.
CADRIN, P.
DUCHARME, M.
LAFLAMME, S.
MASSON-BOURQUE, C.
MATHIEU, L.
PAPILLON, A.
PARENT, N.
PINSON, J.-P.
RINGUETTE, R.
ROBERGE, M.-A.
STUBER, U.
TEREBESI, G.

Faculty of Nursing Sciences (Pavillon Paul-Comtois, Bureau 4106, Québec, QC G1K 7P4; tel. (418) 656-3356; fax (418) 656-7747; e-mail fsi@fsi.ulaval.ca; internet www.ulaval.ca/fsi):

BLONDEAU, D.
CÔTÉ, E.
DALLAIRE, C.
EBACHER, M.-F.
FILLION, L.
GODIN, G.
HAGAN, L.
LEPAGE, L.
MORIN, D.
O'NEILL, M.
PATENAUDE, L.
PELLETIER, L.
PROVENCHER, H.

VIENS, C.

Faculty of Pharmacy (Pavillon Ferdinand-Vandry, Bureau 2241, Québec, QC G1K 7P4; tel. (418) 656-3211; fax (418) 656-2305; e-mail pha@pha.ulaval.ca; internet www.pha.ulaval.ca):

BEAULAC-BAILLARGEON, L.
BELANGER, P. M.
CASTONGUAY, A.
DALEAU, P.
DESGAGNÉ, M.
DI PAOLO-CHENEVERT, T.
DIONNE, A.
DORVAL, M.
GRÉGOIRE, J.-P.
GUILLEMETTE, C.
JUHASZ, J.
MOISAN, J.
RICHER, M.
TREMBLAY, M.
VÉZINA, C.

Faculty of Philosophy (Pavillon Félix-Antoine-Savard, Bureau 644, Québec, QC G1K 7P4; tel. (418) 656-2244; fax (418) 656-7267; e-mail fp@fp.ulaval.ca; internet www.fp.ulaval.ca):

BÉGIN, L.
BILODEAU, R.
BOSS, G.
CUNNINGHAM, H.-P.
DE KONINCK, T.
KNEE, P.
LAFLEUR, C.
LANGLOIS, L.
NARBONNE, J.-M.
PARIZEAU, M.-H.
PELLETIER, Y.
RICARD, M.-A.
SASSEVILLE, M.
THIBAUDEAU, V.
TOURNIER, F.

Faculty of Sciences and Engineering (Pavillon Alexandre-Vachon, Bureau 1033, Québec, QC G1K 7P4; tel. (418) 656-2163; fax (418) 656-5902; e-mail fsg@fsg.ulaval.ca; internet www.fsg.ulaval.ca):

ADAM, L., Actuarial Science
AIT-KADI, D., Mechanical Engineering
AMIOT, P. L., Physical Engineering and Optics
ANCTIL, F., Civil Engineering
ANDERSON, A., Biology
AUGER, M., Chemistry
BARBEAU, C., Chemistry
BARIBEAU, L., Mathematics and Statistics
BARRETTE, C., Biology
BASTIEN, J., Civil Engineering
BAZIN, C., Mining, Metallurgical and Materials Engineering
BEAUDOIN, G., Geology and Geological Engineering
BEAULIEU, D., Civil Engineering
BEAULIEU, J.-M., Computer Science
BEAUPRÉ, D., Civil Engineering
BÉDARD, D., Actuarial Science
BÉDARD, G., Physical Engineering and Optics
BELISLE, C., Mathematics and Statistics
BELKHITER, N., Computer Science
BERGEVIN, R., Electrical and Computer Engineering
BERNATCHEZ, L., Biology
BORRA, E. F., Physical Engineering and Optics
BOUCHARD, C., Civil Engineering
BOUDREAU, D., Chemistry
BOUKOUVALAS, J., Chemistry
BOURBONNAIS, Y., Biochemistry and Microbiology
BOUSMINA, M. M., Chemical Engineering
BRISSON, J., Chemistry
BUI, M. D., Computer Science
CARDOU, A., Mechanical Engineering

CARMICHAEL, J.-P., Mathematics and Statistics
CASSIDY, C., Mathematics and Statistics
CASSIDY, D. P., Geology and Geological Engineering
CHAIB-DRAA, B., Computer Science
CHARLET, G., Chemistry
CHÉNEVERT, R., Chemistry
CHIN, S. L., Physical Engineering and Optics
CHOUINARD, J.-Y., Electrical and Computer Engineering
CLOUTIER, C., Biology
COSSETTE, H., Actuarial Science
CROS, J., Electrical and Computer Engineering
CURODEAU, A., Mechanical Engineering
D'AMOURS, S., Mechanical Engineering
DARVEAU, A., Biochemistry and Microbiology
DE CHAMPLAIN, A., Mechanical Engineering
DE KONINCK, J.-M., Mathematics and Statistics
DEL VILLAR, R., Mining, Metallurgical and Materials Engineering
DESBIENS, A., Electrical and Computer Engineering
DESCHÊNES, C., Mechanical Engineering
DESHARNAIS, J., Computer Science
DESLAURIERS, N., Biochemistry and Microbiology
DODSON, J., Biology
DORÉ, G., Civil Engineering
DUBE, L. J., Physical Engineering and Optics
DUBÉ, D., Mining, Metallurgical and Materials Engineering
DUCHESNE, J., Geology and Geological Engineering
DUGUAY, M.-A., Electrical and Computer Engineering
DUMAS, G., Mechanical Engineering
DUPUIS, C., Computer Science
DUSSAULT, P., Biochemistry and Microbiology
FAFARD, M., Civil Engineering
FORIERO, A., Civil Engineering
FORTIER, L., Biology
FORTIER, P., Electrical and Computer Engineering
FORTIER, R., Geology and Geological Engineering
FORTIN, A., Mathematics and Statistics
FRENETTE, M., Biochemistry and Microbiology
FYTAS, K., Mining, Metallurgical and Materials Engineering
GAKWAYA, A., Mechanical Engineering
GALSTIAN, T., Physics, Physical Engineering and Optics
GALVEZ-CLOUTIER, R., Civil Engineering
GANGULY, U. S., Electrical and Computer Engineering
GARNIER, A., Chemical Engineering
GAUTHIER, G., Biology
GELINAS, P. J., Geology and Geological Engineering
GENDRON, G., Mechanical Engineering
GENEST, C., Mathematics and Statistics
GERVAIS, J.-J., Mathematics and Statistics
GHALI, E., Mining, Metallurgical and Materials Engineering
GHAZZALI, N., Mathematics and Statistics
GIGUÈRE, M., Actuarial Science
GLOVER, P., Geology and Geological Engineering
GOSSELIN, C., Mechanical Engineering
GOUDREAU, S., Mechanical Engineering
GOULET, V., Actuarial Science
GOURDEAU, F., Mathematics and Statistics
GRANDJEAN, B., Chemical Engineering
GRENIER, D., Electrical and Computer Engineering
GUDERLEY, H., Biology
GUENETTE, R., Mathematics and Statistics

GUERTIN, M., Biochemistry and Microbiology
GUILLOT, M., Mechanical Engineering
HADJIGEORGIOU, J., Mining, Metallurgical and Materials Engineering
HEBERT, R., Geology and Geological Engineering
HIMMELMAN, J., Biology
HODGSON, B. R., Mathematics and Statistics
HODOUIN, D., Mining, Metallurgical and Materials Engineering
HOULE, G., Biology
HUOT, J., Biology
JACQUES, M., Actuarial Science
JOHNSON, L. E., Biology
JONCAS, G., Physics, Physical Engineering and Optics
KALIAGUINE, S., Chemical Engineering
KIRKWOOD, D., Geology and Geological Engineering
KNYSTAUTAS, E., Physics, Physical Engineering and Optics
KONRAD, J.-M., Civil Engineering
KRETSCHMER, D., Mechanical Engineering
KROEGER, H., Physics, Physical Engineering and Optics
LACROIX, R., Chemical Engineering
LAPOINTE, L., Biology
LARACHI, F., Chemical Engineering
LAROCHE, G., Mining, Metallurgical and Materials Engineering
LAROCHELLE, J., Biology
LAROCHELLE, S., Electrical and Computer Engineering
LAURENDEAU, D., Electrical and Computer Engineering
LAVOIE, M. C., Biochemistry and Microbiology
LEBOEUF, D., Civil Engineering
LECLERC, M., Chemistry
LEDUY, A., Chemical Engineering
LE HUY, H., Electrical and Computer Engineering
LEMAY, J., Mechanical Engineering
LEMIEUX, C., Biochemistry and Microbiology
LEMIEUX, G., Biochemistry and Microbiology
LEROUEIL, S., Civil Engineering
LESSARD, P., Civil Engineering
LESSARD, R. A., Physics, Physical Engineering and Optics
LEVASSEUR, M., Biology
LÉVEILLÉ, G., Actuarial Science
LÉVESQUE, B., Mechanical Engineering
LÉVESQUE, C., Mathematics and Statistics
LOCAT, J., Geology and Geological Engineering
LUONG, A., Actuarial Science
MCBREEN, P. H., Chemistry
MCCARTHY, N., Physics, Physical Engineering and Optics
MACIEL, Y., Mechanical Engineering
MALDAGUE, X., Electrical and Computer Engineering
MANOUZI, H., Mathematics and Statistics
MARCEAU, E., Actuarial Science
MARCHAND, J., Civil Engineering
MARCHAND, M., Computer Science
MARCHAND, P., Computer Science
MARLEAU, L., Physics, Physical Engineering and Optics
MARTEL, H., Physics, Physical Engineering and Optics
MASSE, J.-C., Mathematics and Statistics
MATHIEU, P., Physics, Physical Engineering and Optics
MINEAU, G., Computer Science
MOINEAU, S., Biochemistry and Microbiology
MORSE, B., Civil Engineering
MOULIN, B., Computer Sciences
NGUYEN-DANG, T.-T., Chemistry
PALLOTTA, D., Biology
PAQUETTE, N., Biology

PARASZCZAK, J., Mining, Metallurgical and Materials Engineering
PARIZEAU, M., Electrical and Computer Engineering
PAYETTE, S., Biology
PEZOLET, M., Chemistry
PHILIPPIN, G., Mathematics and Statistics
PICARD, A., Civil Engineering
PICHÉ, M., Physics, Physical Engineering and Optics
PIERRE, R., Mathematics and Statistics
PIGEON, M., Civil Engineering
PINEAULT, S., Physics, Physical Engineering and Optics
PLANETA, S., Mining, Metallurgical and Materials Engineering
POMERLEAU, A., Electrical and Computer Engineering
POULIN, R., Mining, Metallurgical and Materials Engineering
RANCOURT, D., Mechanical Engineering
RANSFORD, T.-J., Mathematics and Statistics
RICHARD, M. J., Mechanical Engineering
RITCEY, A.-M., Chemistry
RIVEST, L.-P., Mathematics and Statistics
ROBERT, C., Physics, Physical Engineering and Optics
ROBERT, J.-L., Civil Engineering
ROCHELEAU, M., Geology and Geological Engineering
RODRIGUE, D., Chemical Engineering
ROY, C., Chemical Engineering
ROY, D., Physics, Physical Engineering and Optics
ROY, P.-H., Biochemistry and Microbiology
ROY, R., Physics, Physical Engineering and Optics
RUSCH, L. A., Electrical and Computer Engineering
SEGUIN, M. K., Geology and Geological Engineering
SERODES, J.-B., Civil Engineering
SHENG, Y., Physics, Physical Engineering and Optics
TARASIEWICZ, R., Mechanical Engineering
TAWBI, N., Computer Science
TÊTU, M., Electrical and Computer Engineering
THERRIEN, R., Geology and Geological Engineering
TOURIGNY, N., Computer Science
TREMBLAY, P., Electrical and Computer Engineering
TREMBLAY, R., Physics, Physical Engineering and Optics
TURCOTTE, J., Chemistry
TURMEL, M., Biochemistry and Microbiology
VADEBONCOEUR, C., Biochemistry and Microbiology
VALLÉE, R., Physics, Physical Engineering and Optics
VIAROUGE, P., Electrical and Computer Engineering
VINCENT, W. F., Biology
VO VAN, T., Mining, Metallurgical and Materials Engineering
VOYER, N., Chemistry
WITZEL, B., Physics, Physical Engineering and Optics
ZACCARIN, A., Electrical and Computer Engineering

Faculty of Social Sciences (Pavillon Charles-DeKoninck, Bureau 3456, Québec, QC G1K 7P4; tel. (418) 656-2615; fax (418) 656-2114; e-mail fss@fss.ulaval.ca; internet www.fss.ulaval.ca):

ARCAND, B., Anthropology
AUDET, M., Industrial Relations
BACCIGALUPO, A., Political Science
BAKARY, T., Political Science
BARIBEAU, J., Psychology
BARITEAU, C., Anthropology
BARLA, P., Economics

BARRE, A., Industrial Relations
BEAUCHAMP, C., Sociology
BEAUDREAU, B. C., Economics
BEAUDRY, M., Social Work
BÉLANGER, G., Economics
BÉLANGER, J., Industrial Relations
BÉLANGER, L., Political Science
BERNARD, J.-T., Economics
BERNIER, C., Industrial Relations
BERNIER, J., Industrial Relations
BLAIS, F., Political Science
BLOUIN, R., Industrial Relations
BOISVERT, J.-M., Psychology
BOIVIN, J., Industrial Relations
BOIVIN, M., Psychology
BOLDUC, D., Economics
BOUCHER, N., Social Work
BOUSQUET, N., Sociology
BRETON, G., Political Science
CARMICHAEL, B., Economics
CHALIFOUX, J.-J., Anthropology
CLAIN, O., Sociology
CLOUTIER, R., Psychology
COMEAU, Y., Social Work
CONSTANTANOS, C., Economics
CÔTÉ, P., Political Science
COUILLARD, M.-A., Anthropology
CRÊTE, J., Political Science
DAGENAIS, H., Anthropology
DAMANT, D., Social Work
DARVEAU-FOURNIER, L., Social Work
DECALUWE, B., Economics
DELAGE, D., Sociology
DEOM, E., Industrial Relations
DERRIENNIC, J.-P., Political Science
DESÈVE, M., Sociology
DESROCHERS, S., Psychology
DESSY, S. E., Economics
DIGUER, L., Psychology
DOMPIERRE, J., Industrial Relations
DORAIS, L.-J., Anthropology
DORAIS, M., Social Work
DORÉ, F.-Y., Psychology
DRAINVILLE, A., Political Science
DUCLOS, J.-Y., Economics
DUFORT, F., Psychology
DUHAIME, G., Sociology
DUMAIS, A., Sociology
DUMONT, S., Social Work
ELBAZ, M., Anthropology
EVERETT, J., Psychology
FOREST, P. G., Political Science
FORTIN, A., Sociology
FORTIN, B., Economics
FORTIN, C., Psychology
FORTIN, D., Social Work
GAGNÉ, G., Sociology
GAUTHIER, J., Psychology
GENEST, S., Anthropology
GILES, A. J., Industrial Relations
GINGRAS, A.-M., Political Science
GISLAIN, J.-J., Industrial Relations
GONZALEZ, P., Economics
GORDON, S. F., Economics
GOSSELIN, G., Political Science
GOULET, S., Psychology
GRONDIN, S., Psychology
GUAY, S., Sociology
HERVOUET, G., Political Science
HUDON, R., Political Science
HUNG, N. M., Economics
HURTUBISE, Y., Social Work
IMBEAU, L., Political Science
KHALAF, L. A., Economics
KIROUAC, G., Psychology
LABRECQUE, M.-F., Anthropology
LACOMBE, S., Sociology
LACOUTURE, Y., Psychology
LACROIX, G., Economics
LADOUCEUR, R., Psychology
LAFLAMME, G., Industrial Relations
LAFLAMME, R., Industrial Relations
LAFLEUR, G.-A., Political Science
LAFOREST, G., Political Science
LAMONDE, F., Industrial Relations
LAMOUREUX, D., Political Science

LANDREVILLE, P., Psychology
LANGLOIS, L., Industrial Relations
LANGLOIS, S., Sociology
LAPOINTE, P.-A., Industrial Relations
LAUGRAND, F. B., Anthropology
LAVALLÉE, M., Psychology
LAVOIE, F., Psychology
LEBLANC, G., Economics
LINDSAY, J., Social Work
LORANGER, M., Psychology
MACE, G., Political Science
MARCOUX, R., Sociology
MASSÉ, R., Anthropology
MERCIER, J., Industrial Relations
MERCIER, J., Political Science
MERCURE, D., Sociology
MONTREUIL, S., Industrial Relations
MOREL, S., Industrial Relations
MORIN, C.-M., Psychology
NORMANDIN, L., Psychology
PAQUIN, L., Economics
PELLETIER, R., Political Science
PEPIN, M., Psychology
PETRY, F., Political Science
PICHÉ, C., Psychology
POCREAU, J.-B., Psychology
POIRIER, S., Anthropology
ROLAND, M., Economics
SABOURIN, S., Psychology
SAILLANT, F., Anthropology
SAINT-ARNAUD, P., Sociology
SAINT-YVES, A., Psychology
SAMSON, L., Economics
SAVARD, J., Psychology
SENECAL, C., Psychology
SEXTON, J., Industrial Relations
SHEARER, B., Economics
SIMARD, J.-J., Sociology
SIMARD, M., Social Work
TESSIER, L., Social Work
TESSIER, R., Psychology
THWAITES, J., Industrial Relations
TRUCHON, M., Economics
TRUDEL, F., Anthropology
TURCOTTE, D., Social Work
TURMEL, A., Sociology
VAN AUDENRODE, M., Economics
VEILLETTE, D., Sociology
VEZINA, A., Social Work
VÉZINA, J., Psychology
VINET, A., Industrial Relations
ZYLBERBERG, J., Political Science

Faculty of Theology and Religious Studies
(Pavillon Félix-Antoine-Savard, Bureau 832,
Québec, QC G1K 7P4; tel. (418) 656-3576; fax
(418) 656-3273; e-mail ftsr@ftsr.ulaval.ca;
internet www.ftsr.ulaval.ca):

AUBERT, M.
BRODEUR, R.
CÔTÉ, L.
CÔTÉ, P.-R.
COUTURE, A.
FARRELL, S. E.
FAUCHER, A.
FORTIN, A.
HURLEY, R.
KEATING, B.
LEMIEUX, R.
MAGER, R.
PAINCHAUD, L.
PASQUIER, A.
PELCHAT, M.
POIRIER, P.-H.
RACINE, J.
ROBERGE, R. M.
ROUTHIER, G.
VIAU, M.

UNIVERSITY OF LETHBRIDGE

4401 University Dr., Lethbridge, AB T1K
3M4

Telephone: (403) 320-5700
Fax: (403) 329-5159
E-mail: inquiries@uleth.ca

Internet: www.uleth.ca

Founded 1967
Provincial control
Language of instruction: English
Academic year: September to April (2 semesters), also summer sessions
Chancellor: ROBERT HIRONAKA
Pres. and Vice-Chancellor: WILLIAM HENRY CADE
Provost and Vice-Pres. for Academic Affairs: SEAMUS O'SHEA
Vice-Pres. for Finance and Admin.: NANCY WALKER
Registrar: LESLIE LAVERS
Chief Librarian: JUDY HEAD

Number of teachers: 248 full-time
Number of students: 8,230

Library of 498,000 vols

Publication: *Annual Calendar*

DEANS

Faculty of Arts and Science: CHRISTOPHER NICOL
Faculty of Education: Dr JANE O'DEA
Faculty of Management: Dr JOHN USHER
School of Fine Arts: C. SKINNER
School of Health Sciences: LYNN BASFORD
School of Graduate Studies: ALAM SHAMSUL

MCGILL UNIVERSITY

845 Sherbrooke St W., Montréal, QC H3A 2T5

Telephone: (514) 398-4455
Fax: (514) 398-3594
Internet: www.mcgill.ca

Founded 1821 by legacy of Hon. James McGill
Provincial control
Language of instruction: English
Academic year: September to May (2 terms)

Chancellor: H. ARNOLD STEINBERG
Prin. and Vice-Chancellor: HEATHER MUNROE-BLUM
Provost: Prof. ANTHONY C. MASI
Deputy Provost for Student Life and Learning: Prof. MORTON J. MENDELSON
Vice-Prin. for Admin. and Finance: MICHAEL L. RICHARDS
Vice-Prin. for Devt and Alumni Relations: MARC WEINSTEIN
Vice-Prin. for Health Affairs: Dr RICHARD I. LEVIN
Vice-Prin. for Research and Int. Relations: Prof. RIMA ROZEN
Exec. Head of Public Affairs: VAUGHAN DOWIE
Sec.-Gen.: STEPHEN STROPLE
Registrar and Exec. Dir of Enrolment Services: KATHLEEN MASSEY
Dir of Libraries: DIANE KOEN

Library: see Libraries
Number of teachers: 1,627
Number of students: 35,300

Publications: *McGill Journal of Education* (3 a year), *McGill Journal of Medicine* (2 a year), *McGill Journal of Middle East Studies* (1 a year), *McGill Reporter* (6 a year), *McGill University Health Centre. Annual Report*, *The McGill Journal of Political Economy* (1 a year), *The McGill Journal of Political Studies* (1 a year), *The McGill Law Journal* (4 a year), *MUHC Ensemble*

DEANS

Faculty of Agricultural and Environmental Sciences: Prof. CHANDRA A. MADRAMOOTOO
Faculty of Arts: Prof. CHRISTOPHER P. MANFREDI
Faculty of Dentistry: Dr PAUL ALLISON
Faculty of Education: Dr HÉLÈNE PERRAULT
Faculty of Engineering: CHRISTOPHE PIERRE
Faculty of Law: Prof. DANIEL JUTRAS

Desautels Faculty of Management: Prof. PETER TODD
Faculty of Medicine: Dr RICHARD I. LEVIN
Schulich School of Music: DON MCLEAN
Faculty of Religious Studies: Dr ELLEN AITKEN
Faculty of Science: MARTIN GRANT
Graduate and Postdoctoral Studies: MARTIN KREISWIRTH
Centre for Continuing Education: Dr JUDITH POTTER
Dean of Students: JANE EVERETT

DIRECTORS OF SCHOOLS

Architecture: MICHAEL JEMTRUD
Communication Sciences and Disorders: SHARI R. BAUM
Computer Science: GREGORY DUDEK
Dietetics and Human Nutrition: KRISTINE G. KOSKI
Environment: MARILYN SCOTT
Information Studies: FRANCE BOUTHILLIER
Nursing: HÉLÈNE EZER
Physical and Occupational Therapy: MAUREEN J. SIMMONDS
Social Work: WENDY THOMSON
Urban Planning: DAVID BROWN
Libraries: JANINE SCHMIDT

CHAIRS OF DEPARTMENTS

Faculty of Agricultural and Environmental Sciences (including School of Dietetics and Human Nutrition) (21111 Lakeshore Rd, Ste Anne de Bellevue, QC H9X 3V9; tel. (514) 398-7928; fax (514) 398-7968; e-mail studentinfo@macdonald.mcgill.ca; internet www.mcgill.ca/macdonald):

Agricultural Economics: J. C. HENNING
Agricultural and Biosystems Engineering: G. S. V. RAGHAVAN
Animal Science: X. ZHAO
Biosource Engineering: R. KOK
Food Science and Agricultural Chemistry: W. D. MARSHALL
Natural Resource Sciences: B. CÔTÉ
Plant Science: M. FORTIN

Faculty of Arts (Dawson Hall, 853 Sherbrooke St W, Montréal, QC H3A 2T6; tel. (514) 398-4210; fax (514) 398-8102; e-mail adviser.artsci@mcgill.ca; internet www.mcgill.ca/arts):

Anthropology: M. BISSON
Art History and Communication Studies: W. STRAW
East Asian Studies: G. FONG
Economics: C. GREEN
English: M. KILGOUR
French Language and Literature: F. RICARD
German Studies: K. BAUER
Hispanic Studies: J. PÉREZ-MAGALLÓN
History: B. LEWIS
Italian: L. KROHA
Jewish Studies: E. ORENSTEIN
Linguistics: L. WHITE
Philosophy: R. P. BUCKLEY
Political Science: C. MANFREDI
Russian and Slavic Studies: P. M. AUSTIN
Sociology: S. STRAGGENBORG

Faculty of Education (3700 McTavish St, Montréal, QC H3A 1Y2; tel. (514) 398-7042; fax (514) 398-4679; e-mail sao.education@ mcgill.ca; internet www.education.mcgill.ca):

Educational and Counselling Psychology: S. P. LAJOIE (acting)
Integrated Studies: A. W. PARÉ
Kinesiology and Physical Education: H. PERRAULT

Faculty of Engineering (Macdonald Engineering Bldg, 3rd Floor, 817 Sherbrooke St, Montréal, QC H3A 2K6; tel. (514) 398-7257; fax (514) 398-7379; e-mail information@ engineering.mcgill.ca; internet www.mcgill.ca/engineering):

Chemical Engineering: R. J. MUNZ
Civil Engineering and Applied Mechanics: D. MITCHELL
Electrical and Computer Engineering: D. LOWTHER
Mechanical Engineering: A. K. MISRA
Mining Metals and Materials Engineering: R. A. L. DREW

Faculty of Medicine (6th Floor, McIntyre Medical Bldg, Promenade Sir William Osler, Montréal, QC H3G 1Y6; tel. (514) 398-3515; fax (514) 398-3595; e-mail recep.med@mcgill.ca; internet www.medicine.mcgill.ca):

Anaesthesia: F. CARLI
Anatomy and Cell Biology: J. J. M. BERGERON
Biochemistry: D. Y. THOMAS
Biomedical Engineering: R. E. KEARNEY
Epidemiology and Biostatistics: R. FUHRER
Family Medicine: M. DAWES
Human Genetics: D. S. ROSENBLATT
Medicine: D. GOLTZMAN
Microbiology and Immunology: G. J. MATLASHEWSKI
Neurology and Neurosurgery: R. J. RIOPELLE
Obstetrics and Gynaecology: S. L. TAN
Oncology: G. BATIST
Ophthalmology: M. N. BURNIER, JR
Otolaryngology: M. D. SCHLOSS
Paediatrics: H. J. GUYDA
Pathology: C. COMPTON
Pharmacology and Therapeutics: H. ZINGG
Physiology: A. SHRIER
Psychiatry: J. PARIS
Radiation Oncology: C. R. FREEMAN
Surgery: J. L. MEAKINS

Faculty of Music (Strathcona Music Bldg, Room E203, 555 Sherbrooke St W, Montréal, QC H3A 1E3; tel. (514) 398-4535; fax (514) 398-8061; e-mail undergradadmissions.music@mcgill.ca; internet www.mcgill.ca/music):

Performance: G. FOOTE
Theory: W. WOSZCZYK

Faculty of Science (Dawson Hall, 853 Sherbrooke St W, Montréal, QC H3A 2T6; tel. (514) 398-4210; fax (514) 398-8102; e-mail adviser.artsci@mcgill.ca; internet www.mcgill.ca/science):

Anatomy and Cell Biology: J. J. M. BERGERON
Atmospheric and Oceanic Sciences: J. R. GYAKUM
Biochemistry: D. Y. THOMAS
Biology: P. F. LASKO
Chemistry: R. B. LENNOX
Earth and Planetary Sciences: A. MUCCI
Geography: G. O. EWING
Mathematics and Statistics: K. GOWRISANKAREN
Microbiology and Immunology: G. J. MATLASHEWSKI
Pharmacology and Therapeutics: H. ZINGG
Physics: M. GRANT
Physiology: A. SHRIER
Psychology: K. B. J. FRANKLIN

Centre for Continuing Education (688 Sherbrooke St W, 11th Floor, Montréal, QC H3A 3R1; tel. (514) 398-6200; fax (514) 398-4448; e-mail info@conted.mcgill.ca; internet www.mcgill.ca/conted):

Career and Management Studies: P. MARTUCCI
Education: B. WALKER
General Studies: P. MARTUCCI (acting) (Dir)
Translation Studies: J. ARCHIBALD

INCORPORATED COLLEGES AND CAMPUSES

Macdonald Campus: 21111 Lakeshore Rd, Ste Anne de Bellevue, QC H9X 3V9; site of the Faculty of Agricultural and Environmental Sciences, the School of Dietetics and

Human Nutrition and the School of Environment.

Royal Victoria College: Montréal; non-teaching; provides residential accommodation for women students; Warden F. TRACY.

AFFILIATED BODIES

Montreal Diocesan Theological College: 3473 University St, Montréal, QC H3A 2A8; Prin. J. M. SIMONS.

Presbyterian College: 3495 University St, Montréal, QC H3A 2A8; Prin. J. VISSERS.

United Theological College: 3521 University St, Montréal, QC H3A 2A9; Prin. P. JOUDREY.

MCMASTER UNIVERSITY

Hamilton, ON L8S 4L8
Telephone: (905) 525-9140
Fax: (905) 527-0100
Internet: www.mcmaster.ca
Founded 1887 in Toronto, present location 1930
Private control
Language of instruction: English
Academic year: September to April
Chancellor: Dr L. R. WILSON
Pres. and Vice-Chancellor: Dr PATRICK DEANE
Provost and Vice-Pres. for Academic Affairs: Dr ILENE BUSCH-VISHNIAC
Vice-Pres. for Admin.: ROGER COULDREY
Vice-Pres. for Health Sciences: Dr JOHN KELTON
Vice-Pres. for Research and Int. Affairs: Dr MO ELBESTAWI
Vice-Pres. for Univ. Advancement: MARY WILLIAMS
Registrar: MELISSA POOL (acting)
Librarian: JEFF TRZECIAK
Library: see under Libraries and Archives
Number of teachers: 4,287
Number of students: 26,170
Publications: *Journal of the Bertrand Russell Archives* (4 a year), *McMaster University Library Research News*, *The Research Bulletin* (12 a year)

DEANS

Faculty of Business: Dr ROBERT MCNUTT (acting)
Faculty of Engineering: Dr DAVID WILKINSON
Faculty of Health Sciences: Dr JOHN KELTON
Faculty of Humanities: Dr SUZANNE CROSTA
Faculty of Science: Dr JOHN CAPONE
Faculty of Social Sciences: Dr CHARLOTTE YATES
Graduate Studies: Dr ALLISON SEKULER (acting)
Principal of the Divinity College: Dr STANLEY PORTER

PROFESSORS

Faculty of Engineering:

BAETZ, B. W., Civil Engineering
BEREZIN, A. A., Engineering Physics
CAPSON, D. W., Electrical and Computer Engineering
CASSIDY, D. T., Engineering Physics
CHANG, J. S., Engineering Physics
DEEN, M. J., Electrical and Computer Engineering
DICKSON, J. M., Chemical Engineering
DRYSDALE, R. G., Civil Engineering
ELBESTAWI, M. A., Mechanical Engineering
FRANEK, F., Computing and Software
GARLAND, W. J., Engineering Physics
GERSHMAN, A. B., Electrical and Computer Engineering
GHOBARAH, A., Civil Engineering
HAUGEN, H., Engineering Physics
HRYMAK, A. N., Chemical Engineering

IRONS, G. A., Materials Science and Engineering
JANICKI, R., Computing and Software
JESSOP, P. E., Engineering Physics
JOHARI, G. P., Materials Science and Engineering
KITAI, A. H., Engineering Physics
KLEIMAN, R. N., Engineering Physics
KREYMAN, K., Computing and Software
LOUTFY, R., Chemical Engineering
LUO, Z.-Q., Electrical and Computing Engineering
LUXAT, J. C., Engineering Physics
MACGREGOR, J. F., Chemical Engineering
MAIBAUM, T., Computing and Software
MARLIN, T. E., Chemical Engineering
MASCHER, P., Engineering Physics
PARNAS, D. L., Computing and Software
PELTON, R. H., Chemical Engineering
PETRIC, A., Materials Science and Engineering
PIETRUSZCZAK, S., Civil Engineering
PRESTON, J. S., Engineering Physics
QIAO, S., Computing and Software
REILLY, J. P., Electrical and Computer Engineering
SIVAKUMARAN, K. S., Civil Engineering
SMITH, P. M., Electrical and Computer Engineering
STOLLE, D. F. E., Civil Engineering
SZABADOS, B., Electrical and Computer Engineering
SZYMANSKI, T. H., Electrical and Computer Engineering
TAYLOR, P. A., Computing and Software
TERLAKY, T., Computing and Software
THOMPSON, D. A., Engineering Physics
TODD, T. D., Electrical and Computer Engineering
TSANIS, I. K., Civil Engineering
VLACHOPOULOS, J. A., Chemical Engineering
WEAVER, D. S., Mechanical Engineering
WILKINSON, D. S., Materials Science and Engineering
WONG, K. M., Electrical and Computer Engineering
WOOD, P. E., Chemical Engineering
WU, X., Electrical and Computer Engineering
XU, G., Materials Science and Engineering
ZHU, S., Chemical Engineering
ZIADA, S., Mechanical Engineering
ZUCKER, J. I., Computing and Software

Faculty of Health Sciences:
ADACHI, R., Medicine
ANDREWS, D. W., Biochemistry
ANTONY, M., Psychiatry
ANVARI, M., Surgery
ARNOLD, A., Medicine
ARSENAULT, L., Pathology
ARTHUR, H. M., School of Nursing
ATKINSON, S. A., Paediatrics
BALL, A. K., Pathology
BARR, R. D., Paediatrics
BAUMANN, M. A., School of Nursing
BELBECK, L. W., Medicine
BIRCH, S., Clinical Epidemiology and Biostatistics
BLAJCHMAN, M, Pathology
BOYLE, M. H., Psychiatry
BROWNE, R. M., School of Nursing
BUCHANAN, M. R., Pathology
BUTLER, R. G., Pathology
CAPONE, J. P., Biochemistry
CHAMBERS, L. W., Clinical Epidemiology and Biostatistics
CHEN, V., Pathology
CHERNESKY, M., Paediatrics
CHIRAKAL, R., Radiology
CHURCHILL, D. N., Medicine
CILISKA, D. K., School of Nursing
COATES, G., Radiology
COBLENTZ, C., Radiology
COLLINS, S. M., Medicine

CONNOLLY, S. J., Medicine
COOK, D. J., Medicine
CRANKSHAW, D. J., Obstetrics and Gynaecology
CROITORU, K., Medicine
CUNNINGHAM, C., Psychiatry
DAYA, S., Obstetrics and Gynaecology
DENBURG, J. A., Medicine
DENBURG, S. D., Psychiatry
DICENSO, A., School of Nursing
FAHNESTOCK, M., Psychiatry
FARGAS-BABJAK, A., Anaesthesia
FERNANDES, C., Medicine
FIRNAU, G., Radiology
GAFNI, A. J., Clinical Epidemiology and Biostatistics
GAULDIE, J., Pathology
GERBER, G. E., Biochemistry
GERSTEIN, H. C., Medicine
GINSBERG, J. S., Medicine
GOLDSMITH, C. H., Clinical Epidemiology and Biostatistics
GROVER, A. K., Medicine
GROVES, D., Pathology
GUPTA, R. S., Biochemistry
GUYATT, G. H., Clinical Epidemiology and Biostatistics
HARNISH, D. G., Pathology
HARVEY, J. T., Surgery
HASSELL, J. A., Biochemistry
HATTON, M. W. C., Pathology
HAYNES, R. B., Clinical Epidemiology and Biostatistics
HEIGENHAUSER, G. J. F., Medicine
HENRY, J., Psychiatry
HOLDER, D. A., Medicine
HOLLAND, F. J., Paediatrics
HUCKER, S. J., Psychiatry
HUGHES, D., Obstetrics
HUIZINGA, J. D., Medicine
HUNT, R. H., Medicine
HUTCHISON, B. G., Family Medicine
ISSENMAN, R. M., Paediatrics
JORDANA, M., Pathology
KARMALI, M. A., Pathology
KATES, N., Psychiatry
KAUFMAN, K. J., Family Medicine
KEARON, C., Medicine
KELTON, J. G., Pathology
KILLIAN, K. J., Medicine
KIRBY, T., Medicine
KIRPALANI, H., Paediatrics
KWAN, C. Y., Medicine
LATIMER, E. J., Family Medicine
LAW, M. C., Rehabilitation Science
LEE, R. M. K. W., Anaesthesia
LEVINE, M., Clinical Epidemiology and Biostatistics
LEVITT, C. A., Family Medicine
LONN, E., Medicine
LUDWIN, D., Medicine
LUKKA, H., Medicine
McDERMOTT, M. R., Pathology
MACMILLAN, H., Psychiatry
MACPHERSON, A., Medicine
MAHONY, J., Pathology
MAJUMDAR, B., School of Nursing
McKELVIE, R., Medicine
MANDELL, L., Medicine
MAZUREK, M., Medicine
McQUEEN, M., Pathology
MEYER, R., Medicine
MISHRA, R. K., Psychiatry
MOAYYEDI, P., Medicine
MOHIDE, P. T., Obstetrics and Gynaecology
MOLLOY, D. W., Medicine
MORILLO, C., Medicine
MUGGAH, H. F., Obstetrics and Gynaecology
NAHMIUS, C., Radiology
NEAME, P., Pathology
NEVILLE, A., Medicine
NIEBOER, E., Biochemistry
NILES, L. P., Psychiatry
NORMAN, G. R., Clinical Epidemiology and Biostatistics

O'BYRNE, P., Medicine
OFOSU, F., Pathology
OROVAN, W. L., Surgery
PAES, B. A., Paediatrics
PANJU, A., Medicine
PATTERSON, C. J. S., Medicine
PATTERSON, M., Radiology
PERDUE, M. H., Pathology
PINELLI, J. M., School of Nursing
RADHI, J., Pathology
RATHBONE, M. P., Medicine
RICHARDS, C. D., Pathology
RIDDELL, R., Radiology
RONEN, G. M., Paediatrics
ROSENBAUM, P. L., Paediatrics
ROSENFELD, J. M., Pathology
ROSENTHAL, K. L., Pathology
ROTSTEIN, C. M. F., Medicine
RUSTHOVEN, J., Medicine
RYAN, E., Psychiatry
SALAMAS, S., Pathology
SCHMIDT, B. K., Paediatrics
SCHULMAN, S., Medicine
SEARS, M. R., Medicine
SEGGIE, J., Psychiatry
SHANNON, H. S., Clinical Epidemiology and Biostatistics
SHARMA, A., Medicine
SMAILL, F., Pathology
SNIDER, D., Pathology
SOLOMON, P., School of Rehabilitation Science
SOMERS, S., Radiology
STEER, P., Paediatrics
STEINER, M., Psychiatry
STODDART, G. L., Clinical Epidemiology and Biostatistics
STRATFORD, P., School of Rehabilitation Science
SUR, R., Medicine
SWINSON, R. P., Psychiatry
SZATMARI, P., Psychiatry
SZECHTMAN, H., Psychiatry
TEO, K., Medicine
TOUGAS, G., Medicine
TURNBULL, J. D., Medicine
TURPIE, I. D., Medicine
UPTON, A. R. M., Medicine
VAN DER SPUY, R., Medicine
VERMA, D. K., Family Medicine
VICKERS, J. D., School of Nursing
WALKER, I. R., Medicine
WALTER, S. D., Clinical Epidemiology and Biostatistics
WARKENTIN, T., Pathology
WATTS, J. L., Paediatrics
WAYE, J., Pathology
WEBBER, C., Radiology
WEITZ, J., Medicine
WESSEL, J., Rehabilitation Science
WHELAN, D., Paediatrics
WHITTON, A., Medicine
WITELSON, S. F., Psychiatry
WRIGHT, G. D., Biochemistry
YANG, D. S. C., Biochemistry
YOUNG, E., Pathology
YOUNGLAI, E. V., Obstetrics and Gynaecology
YUSUF, S., Medicine
ZHOROV, B., Biochemistry

Faculty of Humanities:
ADAMSON, J., English
AHMED, A., French
ALLEN, B. G., Philosophy
ALSOP, J. D., History
ARTHUR, R. T. W., Philosophy
BAYARD, C. A., French
BOWERBANK, S., English
CLARK, D. L., English
CROSTA, S., French
DUNBABIN, K. M. D., Classics
FERNS, H. J., English
GAUVREAU, J. M., History
GIROUX, H., English and Communications Studies

GOELLNICHT, D. C., English
GRIFFIN, N. J., Philosophy
HITCHCOCK, D. L., Philosophy
JEAY, M. M., French
JONES, H., Classics
KACZYNSKI, B. M., History
KING, J., English
KOLESNIKOFF, N., Modern Languages and Linguistics
MAGINNIS, H. B. J., School of the Arts
MURGATROYD, P., Classics
NELLES, H. V., History
O'CONNOR, M. E., English
OSTOVICH, H. M., English
RAHIMIEH, N., English and Comparative Literature
RAPOPORT, P., School of the Arts
RENWICK, W., School of the Arts
SILCOX, M., English
STROINSKA, M., Modern Languages and Linguistics
WALMSLEY, P., English
WALUCHOW, W. J., Philosophy
WEAVER, J. C., History
YORK, L. M., English

Faculty of Science:

ALAMA, S., Mathematics and Statistics
ALLAN, L. G., Psychology
BAIN, A. D., Chemistry
BALAKRISHNAN, N., Mathematics and Statistics
BARBIER, J. R. H., Chemistry
BECKER, S., Psychology
BENNETT, P., Psychology
BERLINSKY, A. J., Physics and Astronomy
BRONSARD, L., Mathematics and Statistics
BROOK, M. A., Chemistry
CHETTLE, D. R., Physics and Astronomy
CHOUINARD, V. A., School of Geography and Geology
COUCHMAN, H. M., Physics and Astronomy
CRAIG, W., Mathematics and Statistics
DALY, M., Psychology
DE CATANZARO, D. A., Psychology
DICKIN, A. P., School of Geography and Geology
DRAKE, J. J., School of Geography and Geology
ELLIOTT, S. J., School of Geography and Geology
EYLES, C. H., School of Geography and Geology
EYLES, J. D., School of Geography and Geology
FENG, S., Mathematics
FINAN, T. M., Biology
GAULIN, B. D., Physics and Astronomy
GOLDING, B., Biology
GREEDAN, J. E., Chemistry
GUAN, P., Mathematics and Statistics
HALL, F. L., School of Geography and Geology
HAMBLETON, I., Mathematics and Statistics
HARRIS, R. S., School of Geography and Geology
HARRIS, W. E., Physics and Astronomy
HART, B. T., Mathematics and Statistics
HIGGS, P. G., Physics and Astronomy
HITCHCOCK, A. P., Chemistry
HOPPE, F. M., Mathematics and Statistics
HURD, T. R., Mathematics and Statistics
JACOBS, J. R., Biology
KALLIN, C., Physics and Astronomy
KANAROGLOU, P. S., School of Geography and Geology
KOLASA, J., Biology
KOLSTER, M., Mathematics and Statistics
LEIGH, W. J., Chemistry
LEVY, B. A., Psychology
LEWIS, T. L., Psychology
LIAW, K. L., School of Geography and Geology
LUKE, G. M., Physics and Astronomy
MCCARRY, B. E., Chemistry

MACDONALD, P. D. M., Mathematics and Statistics
MAURER, D. M., Psychology
MIN-OO, M., Mathematics and Statistics
MOORE, G. H., Mathematics and Statistics
MORRIS, W. A., School of Geography and Geology
MOTHERSILL, C. E., Medical Physics and Applied Radiological Science
MURPHY, K. M., Psychology
NICAS, A. J., Mathematics and Statistics
NURSE, C. A., Biology
O'DONNELL, M. J., Biology
PUDRITZ, R. E., Physics and Astronomy
RACINE, R. J., Psychology
RAINBOW, A. J., Biology
ROLLO, C. D., Biology
SAWYER, E. T., Mathematics and Statistics
SCHELLHORN, H., Biology
SCHROBILGEN, G. J., Chemistry
SEKULER, A., Psychology
SHI, A., Physics and Astronomy
SIEGEL, S., Psychology
SINGH, R. S., Biology
STOVER, H., Chemistry
SUTHERLAND, P., Physics and Astronomy
TERLOUW, J. K., Chemistry
TRAINOR, L. J., Psychology
VALERIOTE, M. A., Mathematics and Statistics
VENUS, D., Physics and Astronomy
VIVEROS-AGUILER, R., Mathematics and Statistics
WANG, M. Y. K., Mathematics and Statistics
WELCH, D. L., Physics and Astronomy
WERETILNYK, E. A., Biology
WERSTIUK, N. H., Chemistry
WILSON, C. D., Physics and Astronomy
WILSON, M. I., Psychology
WOLKOWICZ, G. S. K., Mathematics and Statistics
WOO, M. K., School of Geography and Geology
WOOD, C. M., Biology
YIP, P. C. Y., Mathematics and Statistics

Faculty of Social Sciences:

ARCHIBALD, W. P., Sociology
ARONSON, J. H., School of Social Work
BLIMKIE, C. J. R., Kinesiology
BROWN, R. A., Social Work
CAIN, R., Social Work
CANNON, A., Anthropology
CARROLL, B. A., Political Science
CHAN, K. S. Y., Economics
COLARUSSO, J. J., Anthropology
COLEMAN, W. D., Political Science
COOPER, M. O., Anthropology
CUNEO, C. J., Sociology
DENTON, M. A., Gerontology
DOOLEY, M. D., Economics
ELLIOTT, D., Kinesiology
FEIT, H. A., Anthropology
FINSTEN, L., Anthropology
FOX, J. D., Sociology
HERRING, D. A., Anthropology
HICKS, A. L., Kinesiology
HURLEY, J. E., Economics
JACEK, H. J., Political Science
JONES, S. R. G., Economics
KROEKER, P. T., Religious Studies
KUBURSI, A., Economics
LEACH, J. E., Economics
LEE, T. D., Kinesiology
LEVITT, C. H., Sociology
LEWCHUK, W., Economics
LEWIS, T. J., Political Science
MCCARTNEY, N., Kinesiology
MAGEE, L. J., Economics
MENDELSON, A., Religious Studies
MESTELMAN, S., Economics
MIALL, C., Sociology
MULLER, R. A., Economics
PORTER, T., Political Science
RACINE, J., Economics

RICE, J. J., School of Social Work
RODMAN, W. L., Anthropology
SALE, D. G., Kinesiology
SATZEWICH, V., Sociology
SAUNDERS, S. R., Anthropology
SCARTH, W. M., Economics
SCHULLER, E. M., Religious Studies
SHAFFIR, W. B., Sociology
SPENCER, B. G., Economics
SPROULE-JONES, M. H., Political Science
STARKES, J., Kinesiology
STEIN, M. B., Political Science
STUBBS, R. W., Political Science
VEALL, M. R., Economics
WATT, M. S., School of Social Work
WHITE, P. G., Kinesiology
YATES, C. A. B., Political Science

School of Business:

ABAD, P. L., Management Science and Information Systems
AGARWAL, N. C., Human Resources and Management
BABA, V., Business
BART, C. K., Marketing
CHAMBERLAIN, T. W., Finance and Business Economics
CHEUNG, C. S., Finance and Business Economics
COOPER, R. G., Marketing
DEAVES, R., Finance and Business Economics
HACKETT, R. D., Human Resources and Management
KLEINSCHMIDT, E. J., Marketing
KWAN, C. C. Y., Finance and Business Economics
MEDCOF, J. W., Human Resources and Management
MILTENBURG, J. G., Management Science and Information Systems
MOUNTAIN, D. C., Finance and Business Economics
PARLAR, M., Management Science and Information Systems
ROSE, J. B., Human Resources and Management
SHEHATA, M. M., Accounting
STEINER, G., Management Science and Information Systems
WESOLOWSKY, G. O., Management Science and Information Systems
YUAN, Y., Management Science and Information Systems
ZEYTINOGLU, F. I., Human Resources and Management

Divinity College (1280 Main St, W, Hamilton, ON L8S 4R1; tel. (905) 525-9140 ext. 24401; fax (905) 577-4782; internet www.macdiv.ca):

HORNSELL, M. J. A., Old Testament and Hebrew
LONGENECKER, R. N., New Testament
PORTER, S. E., New Testament

ATTACHED RESEARCH INSTITUTES

Centre for Electrophotonic Materials and Devices: Hamilton; research and development; Dir Dr D. A. THOMPSON.

R. Samuel McLaughlin Centre for Gerontological Health Research: Hamilton; research, training and promotion of health and preventive care for the elderly; organizes conferences; publishes reports; Dir Dr L. W. CHAMBERS.

Centre for Health Economics and Policy Analysis: Hamilton; research, consultation, education, liaison; organizes conferences, etc.; publishes health policy commentaries and research reports; Coordinator Dr J. HURLEY.

Centre for Peace Studies: Hamilton; research, graduate and undergraduate courses, seminars, lectures, conferences and other projects in the area of international peace; Dir Dr G. PURDY.

Gerontology Programme: Hamilton; f. 1979; a multidisciplinary unit to promote and develop research and educational programmes on aging; Dir Dr M. DENTON.

McMaster Institute for Energy Studies: Hamilton; f. 1980 to encourage communication between researchers in different fields of energy study; Dir Dr DEAN MOUNTAIN; publ. *Newsletter* (3 a year).

Institute of Environment and Health: Hamilton; research, health surveys and health assessments, identification and evaluation of hazards, development of preventive policies and strategies and of educational programmes; participation in community-based environment and health initiatives; conducts workshops and seminars; Dir Dr B. NEWBOLD (acting).

Brockhouse Institute for Materials Research: Hamilton; research in the chemistry, engineering, metallurgy and physics of solid materials is supplemented through this multidisciplinary unit; principal areas: lattice dynamics, kinetics and diffusion, mechanical properties, microelectric and electro-optic devices, optical materials, phase transformations, thermodynamics, radiation damage, structure determination, surfaces and catalysis; Dir Dr J. S. PRESTON.

Institute of Polymer Production Technology: Hamilton; provides a facility and environment in which univ. staff and technical personnel from industry can do research and development on process technology for polymer production; Dir (vacant).

Office of International Affairs: Hamilton; coordinates institutional international activities; provides leadership in international education and research, and in the provision of professional services by McMaster personnel to the global community; includes Centre for International Health; Dir Dr M. W. L. CHAN.

UNIVERSITY OF MANITOBA

Winnipeg, MB R3T 2N2
Telephone: (204) 474-8880
Fax: (204) 474-7536
E-mail: registrar@umanitoba.ca
Internet: www.umanitoba.ca
Founded 1877
Language of instruction: English
Academic year: September to April (2 terms)
Chancellor: Dr WILLIAM NORRIE
President and Vice-Chancellor: Dr DAVID T. BARNARD
Vice-Pres. for Academic and Provost: JOANNE C. KESELMAN
Vice-Pres. for Admin.: DEBORAH McCALLUM
Vice-Pres. for External: ELAINE GOLDIE
Vice-Pres. for Research: DIGVIR JAYAS (acting)
Dir of Libraries: C. PRESSER
Library of 2,000,000 vols
Number of teachers: 1,142
Number of students: 26,800

DEANS

Faculty of Agricultural and Food Sciences: Dr MICHAEL TREVAN
Faculty of Architecture: Dr DAVID R. WITTY
Faculty of Arts: RICHARD SIGURDSON
Faculty of Dentistry: ANTHONY IACOPINO
Faculty of Education: JOHN WIENS
Faculty of Engineering: DOUGLAS RUTH
Faculty of Graduate Studies: Dr TONY SECCO
Faculty of Environment: LESLIE KING
Faculty of Human Ecology: R. BIRD
Faculty of Law: HARVEY SECTER
Faculty of Management: J. L. GRAY
Faculty of Medicine: B. K. E. HENNEN
Faculty of Nursing: D. M. GREGORY

Faculty of Pharmacy: D. COLLINS
Faculty of Physical Education and Recreation Studies: D. W. HRYCAIKO
Faculty of Science: Dr MARK WHITMORE
Faculty of Social Work: BOB MULLALY

DIRECTORS

School of Agriculture: D. FLATEN
School of Art: D. AMUNDSON
School of Dental Hygiene: S. LAVIGNE
School of Medical Rehabilitation: J. COOPER (Overall Dir: E. ETCHEVERRY (Occupational Therapy: GISELE PEREIRA (Physical Therapy, acting)
School of Music: DALE LONIS
Continuing Education Division: A. PERCIVAL

PROFESSORS

Faculty of Agricultural and Food Sciences:
BALLANCE, G. M., Plant Science
BJARNASON, H., Agribusiness and Agricultural Economics
BLANK, G., Food Science
BOYD, M. S., Agribusiness and Agricultural Economics
BRITTON, M. G., Biosystems Engineering
BRÛLÉ-BABEL, A. L., Plant Science
CAMPBELL, L. D., Animal Science
CENKOWSKI, S., Biosystems Engineering
CONNOR, M. L., Animal Science
DRONZEK, B. L., Plant Science
ENTZ, M., Plant Science
GALLOWAY, T. D., Entomology
GOH, T. B., Soil Science
GUENTER, W., Animal Science
HILL, R. D., Plant Science
HOLLEY, R. A., Food Science
HOLLIDAY, N. J., Entomology
JAYAS, D. S., Biosystems Engineering
KRAFT, D. F., Agribusiness and Agricultural Economics
MACKAY, P. A., Entomology
MacMILLAN, J. A., Agribusiness and Agricultural Economics
McVETTY, P. B. E., Plant Science
MUIR, W. E., Biosystems Engineering
PRITCHARD, M. K., Plant Science
RACZ, G. J., Soil Science
REMPHREY, W. R., Plant Science
ROUGHLEY, R. E., Entomology
SCANLON, M. G., Food Science
SCARTH, R., Plant Science
VESSEY, J. K., Plant Science
WITTENBERG, K. M., Animal Science
ZHANG, Q., Biosystems Engineering

Faculty of Architecture:
COX, M. G., Interior Design
MACDONALD, R. I., Environmental Design
NELSON, C., Landscape Architecture
RATTRAY, A. E., Landscape Architecture
THOMSEN, C. H., Landscape Architecture

Faculty of Arts:
ALBAS, D. C., Sociology
ANNA, T. E., History
ARNASON, D. E., English
BAILEY, P. C., History
BARBER, D. G., Geography
BRIERLEY, J. S., Geography
BUMSTED, J. M., History
BUTEUX, P. E., Political Studies
CAMERON, N. E., Economics
CHERNOMAS, R., Economics
COMACK, A. E., Sociology
COOLEY, D. O., English
COSMOPOULOS, M. B., Classics
DEAN, J. M., Economics
DEBICKI, M., Political Studies
DeLUCA, R., Psychology
EATON, W. O., Psychology
FERGUSON, B. G., History
FINLAY, J. L., History
FINNEGAN, R. E., English
FORTIER, P., French, Spanish and Italian
FRIESEN, G. A., History

GERUS, O. W., History
GONICK, C. W., Economics
GORDON, D. K., French, Spanish and Italian
GREENFIELD, H. J., Anthropology
GRISLIS, E., Religion
HALLI, S. S., Sociology
HELLER, H., History
HINZ, E. J., English
HUM, D., Economics
JOHNSON, C. G., English
JUDD, E. R., Anthropology
KENDLE, J. E., History
KESELMAN, H. J., Psychology
KESELMAN, J. C., Psychology
KINNEAR, E. M., History
KINNEAR, M. S. R., History
KULCHYSKI, P., Native Studies
KWONG, J., Sociology
LeBOW, M. D., Psychology
LEVENTHAL, L. Y., Psychology
LINDEN, E. W., Sociology
LOBDELL, R. A., Economics
LOXLEY, J., Economics
McCANCE, D., Religion
McCARTHY, D. J., Philosophy
MARTIN, D. G., Psychology
MARTIN, G. L., Psychology
MATHESON, C., Philosophy
NAHIR, M., Linguistics
NICHOLS, J. D., Linguistics
NICKELS, J. B., Psychology
NORTON, W., Geography
OAKES, J. E., Native Studies
O'KELL, R. P., English
PEAR, J. J., Psychology
PERRY, R. P., Psychology
PHILLIPS, P. A., Economics
RAMU, G. N., Sociology
REA, J. E., History
REMPEL, H., Economics
ROBERTS, L., Sociology
RUBENSTEIN, H., Anthropology
SCHAFER, A. M., Philosophy
SCHLUDERMANN, E. H., Psychology
SCHLUDERMANN, S., Psychology
SEGALL, A., Sociology
SHAVER, R. W., Philosophy
SHKANDRIJ, M., German and Slavic Studies
SIMPSON, W., Economics
SINGER, M., Psychology
SMIL, V., Geography
SMITH, G. C., Geography
SPRAGUE, D. N., History
STAMBROOK, F. G., History
STEIMAN, L. B., History
SZATHMÁRY, J. E., Anthropology
TAIT, R. W., Psychology
THOMAS, P. G., Political Studies
TODD, D., Geography
TOLES, G. E., English
WALZ, E. P., English
WATERMAN, A. M. C., Economics
WEIL, H. S., English
WIEST, R. E., Anthropology
WILLIAMS, D. L., English
WILSON, L. M., Psychology
WOLF, K., Icelandic
WOLFART, H. C., Linguistics
WORTLEY, J. T., History

Faculty of Dentistry:
BHULLAR, R. P.
BOWDEN, G. H. W.
DAWES, C.
de VRIES, J.
FLEMING, N.
HAMILTON, I. R.
KARIM, A. C.
LAVELLE, C. L. B.
LOVE, W. B.
SCOTT, J. E.
SINGER, D. L.
SUZUKI, M.
WILTSHIRE, W.

Faculty of Education:

BARTELL, R., Educational Administration, Foundations and Psychology

CAP, O., Curriculum, Teaching and Learning

CHINIEN, C., Curriculum, Teaching and Learning

CLIFTON, R. A., Postsecondary Studies, Educational Administration, Foundations and Psychology

FREEZE, D. R., Educational Administration, Foundations and Psychology

GREGOR, A. D., Postsecondary Studies, Educational Administration, Foundations and Psychology

HARVEY, D. A., Curriculum, Teaching and Learning

HLYNKA, L. D., Curriculum, Teaching and Learning

JENKINSON, D. H., Curriculum, Teaching and Learning

KESELMAN, J. C., Educational Administration, Foundations and Psychology

KIRBY, D. M., Postsecondary Studies

LEVIN, B., Educational Administration, Foundations and Psychology

LONG, J. C., Educational Administration, Foundations and Psychology

MAGSINO, R., Educational Administration, Foundations and Psychology

MORPHY, D. R., Postsecondary Studies

PERRY, R. P., Postsecondary Studies

POROZNY, G. H. J., Curriculum, Teaching and Learning

ROBERTS, L. W., Postsecondary Studies

SCHULZ, W. E., Educational Administration, Foundations and Psychology

SEIFERT, K. L., Educational Administration, Foundations and Psychology

STAPLETON, J. J., Educational Administration, Foundations and Psychology

STINNER, A. O., Curriculum, Teaching and Learning

STRAW, S. B., Curriculum, Teaching and Learning

YOUNG, J. C., Educational Administration, Foundations and Psychology

ZAKALUK, B. L., Curriculum, Teaching and Learning

Faculty of Engineering:

BALAKRISHNAN, S., Mechanical and Industrial

BASSIM, M. N., Mechanical and Industrial

BRIDGES, G. E. J., Electrical and Computer

BURN, D. H., Civil and Geological

CAHOON, J. R., Mechanical and Industrial

CARD, H. C., Electrical and Computer

CHATURVEDI, M. C., Mechanical and Industrial

CIRIC, I. M. R., Electrical and Computer

CLAYTON, A., Civil and Geological

GOLE, A. M., Electrical and Computer

GRAHAM, J., Civil and Geological

KINSNER, W., Electrical and Computer

LAJTAI, E. Z., Civil and Geological

LEHN, W., Electrical and Computer

McLAREN, P. G., Electrical and Computer

McLEOD, R. D., Electrical and Computer

MARTENS, G. O., Electrical and Computer

MENZIES, R. W., Electrical and Computer

MUFTI, A. A., Civil and Geological

OLESZKIEWICZ, J. A., Civil and Geological

ONYSHKO, S., Electrical and Computer

PAWLAK, M., Electrical and Computer

POLYZOIS, D., Civil and Geological

POPPLEWELL, N., Mechanical and Industrial

RAGHUVEER, M. R., Electrical and Computer

RUTH, D. W., Mechanical and Industrial

SEBAK, A., Electrical and Computer

SEPEHRI, N., Mechanical and Industrial

SHAFAI, L., Electrical and Computer

SHAH, A. H., Civil and Geological

SHWEDYK, E., Electrical and Computer

SOLIMAN, H. M., Mechanical and Industrial

STIMPSON, B., Civil and Geological

STRONG, D., Mechanical and Industrial

THOMSON, D. J., Electrical and Computer

THORNTON-TRUMP, A. B., Mechanical and Industrial

WOODBURY, A. D., Civil

Faculty of Human Ecology:

BERRY, R. E., Family Studies

BIRD, R. P., Foods and Nutrition

BOND, J. B., Family Studies

ESKIN, N. A. M., Foods and Nutrition

HARVEY, C. D. H., Family Studies

Faculty of Law:

ANDERSON, D. T.

BUSBY, K.

DEUTSCHER, D.

ESAU, A.

GUTH, D. J.

HARVEY, D. A. C.

IRVINE, J. C.

McGILLIVRAY, A.

NEMIROFF, G.

OSBORNE, P. H.

PENNER, R.

SECTER, H. L.

SNEIDERMAN, B.

STUESSER, L.

VINCENT, L.

Faculty of Management:

BARTELL, M., Business Administration

BECTOR, C. R., Business Administration

BHATT, S. K., Business Administration

BRUNING, E. R., Marketing

BRUNING, N. S., Business Administration

ELIAS, N. S., Accounting and Finance

FROHLICH, N., Business Administration

GODARD, J. H., Business Administration

GOOD, W. S., Marketing

GOULD, L. I., Accounting and Finance

GRAY, J. L., Business Administration

HILTON, M. W., Accounting and Finance

HOGAN, T. P., Business Administration

McCALLUM, J. S., Accounting and Finance

NOTZ, W. W., Business Administration

OWEN, B. E., Business Administration

ROSENBLOOM, E. S.

STARKE, F. A., Business Administration

Faculty of Medicine:

ADAMSON, I. Y. R., Pathology

ANDERSON, J., Human Anatomy and Cell Science

ANGEL, A., Medicine and Physiology

AOKI, F. Y., Continuing Medical Education, Medical Microbiology, Medicine, Pharmacology and Therapeutics

ARNETT, J. L., Clinical Health Psychology and Continuing Medical Education

ARTHUR, G., Biochemistry and Medical Genetics

BAKER, S., Medicine

BARAGAR, F., Medicine

BARAKAT, S., Psychiatry

BARAL, E., Medicine, Radiology

BARWINSKY, J., Cardiothoracic Surgery

BEBCHUK, W., Psychiatry

BECKER, A., Paediatrics and Child Health

BEGLEITER, A., Medicine, Pharmacology and Therapeutics

BERCZI, I., Immunology

BLACK, G., Surgery

BLAKLEY, B., Otolaryngology

BOOTH, F., Paediatrics and Child Health

BORODITSY, R., Obstetrics, Gynaecology and Reproductive Sciences

BOSE, D., Anaesthesia, Medicine, Pharmacology and Therapeutics

BOSE, R., Pharmacology and Therapeutics

BOW, E., Medical Microbiology

BOWDEN, G. H., Medical Microbiology

BOWMAN, D. M., Medicine

BOWMAN, W. D., Paediatrics and Child Health

BRANDES, L. J., Medicine, Pharmacology and Therapeutics

BRISTOW, G. K., Anaesthesia

BRUNHAM, R. C., Medical Microbiology, Medicine, Obstetrics, Gynaecology and Reproductive Sciences

BRUNI, J. E., Human Anatomy and Cell Science

CARR, I., Pathology

CARTER, S. A., Medicine and Physiology

CASIRO, O., Paediatrics and Child Health

CATTINI, P., Physiology, Pharmacology and Therapeutics

CHERNICK, V., Paediatrics and Child Health

CHOY, P. C., Biochemistry and Molecular Biology

CHUDLEY, A. E., Continuing Medical Education, Human Genetics, Paediatrics and Child Health

COOMBS, C., Medical Microbiology

COOPER, J., Community Health Sciences

CRAIG, D. B., Anaesthesia

CRISTANTE, L., Surgery

CUMMING, G. R., Paediatrics and Child Health

DANZINGER, R. G., General Surgery

DAVIE, J. R., Biochemistry and Molecular Biology

DEAN, H., Paediatrics and Child Health

DUBO, H. I. C., Medicine

DUKE, P. C., Anaesthesia

EL-GABALAWY, H., Medicine

EVANS, J. A., Community Health Sciences, Human Genetics, Paediatrics and Child Health

FERGUSON, C. A., Paediatrics and Child Health

FINE, A., Medicine

FORESTER, J., Medicine

FORGET, E., Community Health Sciences

GARTNER, J., Immunology, Pathology

GEIGER, J., Pharmacology and Therapeutics

GERRARD, J. M., Paediatrics and Child Health

GLAVIN, G., Pharmacology and Therapeutics

GORDON, R., Radiology

GREENBERG, C. R., Human Genetics, Paediatrics and Child Health

GREWAR, D. A. I., Family Medicine, Paediatrics and Child Health

GUIJON, F., Obstetrics, Gynaecology and Reproductive Sciences

HALL, P. F., Obstetrics, Gynaecology and Reproductive Sciences

HAMERTON, J. L., Paediatrics and Child Health

HAMMOND, G. W., Medical Microbiology, Medicine

HARDING, G. M., Medical Microbiology, Medicine

HARVEY, D. A., Community Health Sciences

HASSARD, T. H., Community Health Sciences

HAVENS, B., Community Health Sciences

HAYGLASS, K. T., Immunology

HELEWA, M., Obstetrics, Gynaecology and Reproductive Sciences

HERSHFIELD, E. A., Community Health Sciences

HERSHFIELD, E. S., Medicine

HOESCHEN, R., Medicine

HOGAN, T. P., Community Health Sciences

HORNE, J. M., Community Health Sciences

HOSKING, D., Surgery

HUDSON, R., Anaesthesia

HUGHES, K. R., Physiology

IRELAND, D. J., Otolaryngology

JAY, F. T., Medical Microbiology

JEFFERY, J., Medicine

JOHNSTON, J. B., Medicine

JORDAN, L. M., Physiology

KARDAMI, E., Human Anatomy and Cell Science
KATZ, P., Psychiatry
KAUFERT, J. M., Community Health Sciences
KAUFERT, P. A., Community Health Services
KAUFMAN, B. J., Medicine
KEPRON, M. W., Medicine
KIRK, P. J., Family Medicine
KIRKPATRICK, J. R., Continuing Medical Education, General Surgery
KREPART, G. V., Obstetrics, Gynaecology and Reproductive Sciences
KROEGER, E. A., Physiology
KRYGER, M., Medicine
LABELLA, F. S., Pharmacology and Therapeutics
LATTER, J., Medicine
LAUTT, W. W., Pharmacology and Therapeutics
LEJOHN, H. B., Human Genetics
LERTZMAN, M., Continuing Medical Education, Medicine
LEVI, C. S., Radiology
LEVITT, M., Medicine
LIGHT, B., Medicine
LIGHT, R. B., Medical Microbiology
LONGSTAFFE, S., Paediatrics and Child Health
LYONS, E. A., Radiology, Obstetrics, Gynaecology and Reproductive Sciences
MCCARTHY, D. S., Medicine
MCCLARTY, B., Radiology
MCCLARTY, G. A., Medical Microbiology
MCCOSHEN, J. A., Obstetrics, Gynaecology and Reproductive Sciences
MCCREA, D. A., Physiology
MCCULLOUGH, D. W., Continuing Medical Education, Otolaryngology
MACDOUGALL, B., Medicine
MCILWRAITH, R., Clinical Health Psychology
MCKENZIE, J. K., Community Health Sciences
MAKSYMIUK, A., Medicine
MINK, G., Medicine
MINUK, G. Y., Medicine, Pharmacology and Therapeutics
MOFFATT, M. E., Community Health Services, Paediatrics and Child Health
MOWAT, M., Biochemistry and Medical Genetics
MURPHY, L. C., Biochemistry and Molecular Biology, Medicine
MURPHY, L. J., Medicine and Physiology
MURRAY, R., Community Health Sciences
MUTCH, A., Anaesthesia
NAGY, J. I., Physiology
NAIMARK, A., Physiology
NANCE, D. M., Pathology
NICOLLE, L., Medicine, Medical Microbiology
OEN, K., Paediatrics and Child Health
OLWENY, C., Medicine
O'NEIL, J. D., Community Health Sciences
ONG, B. Y., Anaesthesia
OPPENHEIMER, L., General Surgery
ORR, F. W., Pathology
PANAGIA, V., Human Anatomy and Cell Science, Physiology
PARKINSON, D., Neurosurgery
PASTERKAMP, H., Paediatrics and Child Health
PATERSON, J. A., Human Anatomy and Cell Science
PEELING, J., Pharmacology and Therapeutics
PEELING, W. J., Radiology
PENNER, B., Medicine
PENNER, S. B., Pharmacology and Therapeutics
PETTIGREW, N., Pathology
PIERCE, G. N., Physiology
PLUMMER, F. A., Medical Microbiology, Medicine

POSTL, B., Community Health Sciences, Paediatrics and Child Health
POSTUMA, R., General Surgery
RAMSEY, E., Surgery
REED, M. H., Continuing Medical Education, Paediatrics and Child Health, Radiology
RENNIE, W., Orthopaedic Surgery
RHODES, R., Pathology
RIESE, K. T., General Surgery and Otolaryngology
RIGATTO, H., Paediatrics and Child Health, Obstetrics, Gynaecology and Reproductive Sciences
ROBERTS, D., Medicine
RONALD, A. R., Community Health Sciences, Medical Microbiology, Medicine
ROOS, L. L., Community Health Sciences
ROOS, N. P., Community Health Sciences
ROY, R., Clinical Health Psychology
RUSH, D., Medicine
SCHACTER, B., Medicine
SCHROEDER, M., Paediatrics and Child Health
SESHIA, M. M. K., Obstetrics, Gynaecology and Reproductive Sciences, Paediatrics and Child Health
SHEFCHY, S., Physiology
SHIU, R. P. C., Physiology
SHOJANIA, A. M., Medicine, Paediatrics and Child Health, Pathology
SIMONS, F. E. R., Immunology, Paediatrics and Child Health
SIMONS, K., Paediatrics and Child Health
SINGAL, P. K., Physiology
SITAR, D., Medicine, Pharmacology and Therapeutics
SMYTH, D., Continuing Medical Education, Pharmacology and Therapeutics
SMYTHE, D., Medicine
SNEIDERMAN, B. M., Community Health Sciences
STANWICK, R. S., Community Health Sciences
STEPHENS, N. L., Physiology
STRANC, M. F., Plastic Surgery
SZATHMÁRY, E. J. E., Human Genetics
TENENBEIN, M., Community Health Sciences, Medicine, Pharmacology and Therapeutics, Paediatrics and Child Health
THLIVERIS, J. A., Human Anatomy and Cell Science
THOMSON, I., Anaesthesia
UNRUH, H. W., Surgery
VRIEND, J., Human Anatomy and Cell Science
WALKER, J., Clinical Health Psychology
WARREN, C. P. W., Continuing Medical Education, Medicine
WARRINGTON, R. J., Immunology and Medicine
WEST, M., Surgery
WILKINS, J. A., Immunology, Medicine, Medical Microbiology
WILLIAMS, T., Medical Microbiology, Paediatrics and Child Health
WOODS, R. A., Human Genetics
WRIGHT, J. A., Biochemistry and Molecular Biology
WROGEMANN, K., Biochemistry and Molecular Biology, Human Genetics
YASSI, A., Community Health Sciences
YOUNES, M., Medicine
YOUNG, T. K., Community Health Sciences
ZELINSKI, T., Biochemistry and Medical Genetics

Faculty of Nursing:
BEATON, J. I.
DEGNER, L. F.
GREGORY, D. M.

Faculty of Pharmacy:
BRIGGS, C. J.
COLLINS, D.
GRYMONPRE, R.

HASINOFF, B.
SIMONS, K. J.
TEMPLETON, J. F.
ZHANEL, G.

Faculty of Physical Education and Recreation Studies:
ALEXANDER, M. J. L.
DAHLGREN, W. J.
GIESBRECHT, G.
HARPER, J.
HRYCAIKO, D. W.
JANZEN, H. F.
READY, A. E.

Faculty of Science:
ABRAHAMS, M., Zoology
AITCHISON, P. W., Mathematics
ARNASON, A. N., Computer Science
AYRES, L. D., Geological Sciences
BALDWIN, W. G., Chemistry
BARBER, R. C., Physics and Astronomy
BELL, M. G., Mathematics
BERRY, T. G., Mathematics
BIRCHALL, J., Physics and Astronomy
BLUNDEN, P., Physics and Astronomy
BOOTH, J. T., Botany
BREWSTER, J. F., Statistics
BUTLER, M., Microbiology
CHARLTON, J. L., Chemistry
CHENG, S. W., Statistics
CHOW, A., Chemistry
CLARK, G. S., Geological Sciences
COLLENS, R. J., Computer Science
DAVISON, N. E., Physics and Astronomy
DICK, T. A., Zoology
DOOB, M., Mathematics
DUCKWORTH, H. W., Chemistry
EALES, J. G., Zoology
ELIAS, R. J., Geological Sciences
ENS, W., Physics and Astronomy
FALK, W., Physics and Astronomy
FU, J. C., Statistics
GERHARD, J. A., Mathematics
GHAHRAMANI, F., Mathematics
GRATZER, G., Mathematics
GUO, B., Mathematics
GUPTA, C. K., Mathematics
GUPTA, N. D., Mathematics
HALDEN, N. M., Geological Sciences
HAWTHORNE, F. C., Geological Sciences
HOSKINS, J. A., Computer Science
HOSKINS, W. D., Mathematics
HRUSKA, F. E., Chemistry
HUEBNER, E., Zoology
HUNTER, N. R., Chemistry
JAMIESON, J. C., Chemistry
JANZEN, A. F., Chemistry
KELLY, D., Mathematics
KENKEL, N. C., Botany
KING, P. R., Computer Science
KLASSEN, G. R., Microbiology
KOCAY, W. L., Computer Science
KRAUSE, G., Mathematics
LAKSER, H., Mathematics
LAST, W. M., Geological Sciences
LOEWEN, P. C., Microbiology
LOLY, P. D., Physics and Astronomy
MACARTHUR, R. A., Zoology
MCKINNON, D. M., Chemistry
MACPHERSON, B. D., Statistics
MAEBA, P. Y., Microbiology
MEEK, D. S., Computer Science
MENDELSOHN, N. S., Mathematics
MOON, W., Geological Sciences
MORRISH, A. H., Physics and Astronomy
O'NEIL, J. D. J., Chemistry
OSBORN, T. A., Physics and Astronomy
PADMANABHAN, R., Mathematics
PAGE, J. H., Physics and Astronomy
PAGE, S. A., Physics and Astronomy
PARAMESWARAN, M. R., Mathematics
PLATT, C., Mathematics
PUNTER, D., Botany
RIEWE, R. R., Zoology
ROBINSON, G. G. C., Botany, Environmental Science Program

ROSHKO, R. M., Physics and Astronomy
SAMANTA, M., Statistics
SCHAEFER, T., Chemistry
SCUSE, D. H., Computer Science
SEALY, S. G., Zoology
SECCO, A. S., Chemistry
SHARMA, K. S., Physics and Astronomy
SHERRIFF, B. L., Geological Sciences
SHIVAKUMAR, P. N., Mathematics
SICHLER, J., Mathematics
SOUTHERN, B. W., Physics and Astronomy
STANTON, R. G., Computer Science
STEWART, J. M., Botany
SUZUKI, I., Microbiology
SVENNE, J. P., Physics and Astronomy
TABISZ, G. C., Physics and Astronomy
TELLER, J. C., Geological Sciences
THOMAS, R. S. D., Mathematics
TRIM, D. W., Mathematics
VAN OERS, W. T. H., Physics and Astronomy
VAN REES, G. H. J., Computer Science
WALLACE, R., Chemistry
WALTON, D. J., Computer Science
WESTMORE, J. B., Chemistry
WIENS, T. J., Zoology
WILLIAMS, G., Physics and Astronomy
WILLIAMS, H. C., Computer Science
WILLIAMS, J. J., Mathematics
WOODS, R. G., Mathematics
WRIGHT, J. A., Microbiology
ZETNER, P. W., Physics and Astronomy

Faculty of Social Work:
FUCHS, D. M.
ROY, R.
TRUTE, B.

School of Art:
AMUNDSON, D. O.
BAKER, M. C.
FLYNN, R. K.
HIGGINS, S. B.
McMILLAN, D. S.
PURA, W. P.
SAKOWSKI, R. C.
SCOTT, C. W.

School of Dental Hygiene:
BOWDEN, G. H. W.
DAWES, C.
FLEMING, N.
HAMILTON, I. R.
JAY, F.
KARIM, A. C.
LAVELLE, C. L. B.
SCOTT, J. E.
SINGER, D. L.

School of Medical Rehabilitation:
ANDERSON, J., Occupational Therapy
COOPER, J. E., Occupational Therapy
LOVERIDGE, B., Physical Therapy

School of Music:
ENGBRECHT, H.
JENSEN, K.
LONIS, D.
WEDGEWOOD, R.

Continuing Education Division:
PERCIVAL, A.

ATTACHED INSTITUTE
Natural Resources Institute: Dir Dr C. EMDAD HAQUE.

AFFILIATED COLLEGES
St Andrew's College: 29 Dysart Rd, Winnipeg, MB R3T 2M7; tel. (204) 474-8995; fax (204) 474-7624; f. 1964 (Ukrainian Orthodox Church); Principal V. OLENDER.

St Boniface College: 200 Cathedral Ave, St Boniface, MB R2H 0H7; tel. (204) 233-0210; fax (204) 237-3240; f. 1818 (Roman Catholic); Rector P. RUEST.

St John's College: 400 Dysart Rd, Winnipeg, MB R3T 2M5; tel. (204) 474-8531; fax

(204) 474-7610; f. 1849 (Anglican); Warden and Vice-Chancellor Dr J. HOSKINS.

St Paul's College: 430 Dysart Rd, Winnipeg, MB R3T 2M6; tel. (204) 474-8575; fax (204) 474-7620; f. 1926 (Roman Catholic); Rector J. J. STAPLETON.

University College: 500 Dysart Rd, Winnipeg, MB R3T 2M8; tel. (204) 474-9522; fax (204) 474-7589; Provost G. WALZ.

MEMORIAL UNIVERSITY OF NEWFOUNDLAND

POB 4200, Elizabeth Ave, St John's, NL A1C 5S7

Telephone: (709) 864-8000
Fax: (709) 864-8699
Internet: www.mun.ca

Founded 1925 by Provincial Government as Memorial University College, university status 1949

Academic year: September to August (3 semesters)

Language of instruction: English

Chancellor: Gen. RICK HILLIER
Pres. and Vice-Chancellor: Dr GARY KACHANOSKI
Vice-Pres. for Academic and Pro Vice-Chancellor: Dr DAVID WARDLAW
Vice-Pres. for Admin.: KENT DECKER
Vice-Pres. for Research: Dr CHRISTOPHER LOOMIS
Vice-Pres. for Grenfell Campus: Dr MARY BLUECHARDT
Registrar: GLENN COLLINS
Librarian: LORRAINE BUSBY
Number of teachers: 2,143
Number of students: 18,746

Publications: *Canadian Folklore Canadien* (2 a year), *Communicator* (4 a year), *Culture and Tradition* (1 a yea), *Echos du Monde Classique / Classical Views* (3 a year), *Gazette* (26 a year), *Labour / Le Travail* (2 a year), *Luminus* (3 a year), *Newfoundland Quarterly* (4 a year), *Regional Language Studies* (1 a year), *Research Matters* (3 a year), *The Muse* (52 a year)

DEANS AND DIRECTORS
Faculty of Arts: Dr NOEL ROY (acting)
Faculty of Business Administration: Dr WILFRED ZERBE
Faculty of Education: Dr ALICE COLLINS (acting)
Faculty of Engineering and Applied Science: Dr JOHN QUAICOE
Faculty of Human Kinetics: Dr ANTHONY CARD
Faculty of Medicine: Dr JAMES ROURKE
Faculty of Science: Dr MARK ABRAHAMS
School of Graduate Studies: Dr NOREEN GOLFMAN
School of Lifelong Learning: KAREN KENNEDY
School of Music: ELLEN WATERMAN
School of Nursing: Dr JUDITH McFERTRIDGE-DURDLE
School of Pharmacy: Dr LINDA HENSMAN
School of Social Work: E. DOW

PROFESSORS
Faculty of Arts:
ALLEN, T. J.
BATH, A. J., Geography
BELL, D. N., Religious Studies
BELL, T. J., Physical Geography
BISHOP, N. B., French and Spanish
BORNSTEIN, C., Philosophy
BRADLEY, J., Linguistics
BRANIGAN, P., Linguistics
BROWN, S. C., Anthropology
BUBENIK, V., Linguistics
BUTLER, K., Physical Geography
BUTRICA, J., Classics
BYRNE, P., English

CATTO, N. R., Physical Geography
CHADWICK, A., French and Spanish
CHERWINSKI, W. J., History
CLARKE, S., Linguistics
CLOSE, D., Philosophy
CROCKER, S., Religious Studies
CULLUM, L., Religious Studies
DEAL, M., Anthropology
DEN OTTER, A. A., History
DEROCHE, M., Religious Studies
DYCK, C., Linguistics
EDINGER, E., Physical Geography
FEEHAN, J. P., Economics
FELT, L. F., Sociology
FISCHER, J., History
GRAHAM, D. E., French and Spanish
HARGER-GRINLING, V. A., French and Spanish
HARRIS, P. F., Linguistics
HART, P., History
HAWKIN, D. J., Religious Studies
HILL, R., Sociology
HILLER, J. K., History
HOUSE, J. D., Sociology
JACOBS, J. D., Geography
JOHNSTONE, F., Sociology
JONES, G. P., English
KENNEDY, J. C., Anthropology
LAI, T. T. L., Philosophy
LATUS, A., Philosophy
LEYTON, E. H., Anthropology
LYNDE, D., English
McKENZIE, M., Linguistics
MANNION, J. J., Geography
MAXWELL, D. V., Philosophy
MAY, J. D., Economics
NARVAËZ, P., Folklore
NICHOL, D. W., English
NICHOL, K., Geography
NURSE, D., Linguistics
O'DEA, S., English
O'DWYER, B., English
PANJABI, R. K., History
PARKER, K. I., Religious Studies
PARKER, M., Classics
PETERS, H., English
POCIUS, G., Folklore
PORTER, J., Religious Studies
RAINEY, L., Religious Studies
RENOUF, P., Anthropology
ROLLMAN, H., Religious Studies
ROSENBERG, N., Folklore
ROY, N., Economics
RYAN, S., History
SCHRANK, B., English
SCHRANK, W. E., Economics
SHARPE, C., Geography
SHAWYER, A. J., Geography
SHORROKS, G., English Language and Literature
SHUTE, M., Religious Studies
SIMMS, A., Geography
SIMMS, E., Geography
SIMPSON, E., Philosophy
SMITH, P., Folklore
STAFFORD, A., Philosophy
STAVELEY, M., Geography
STOREY, C., Economic Geography
TANNER, A., Anthropology
THOMSPON, D., Philosophy
TSOA, E., Economics
TUCK, J. A., Anthropology
WHITE, R. W., Geography
WOOD, C., Geography

Faculty of Business Administration:
BARNES, J. G., Marketing
FASERUK, A. J., Business Administration
KUBIAK, W., Quantitative Methods
PARSONS, J., Information Systems
SAHA, S., Organizational Behaviour
SEXTY, R. W., Management and Policy
SKIPTON, M. D., Management and Policy
SOOKLAL, L. R., Human Resource Management and Organizational Theory
STEWART, D. B., Business Administration

WITHEY, M. J., Organizational Behaviour

Faculty of Education:
BARRELL, B., Education
BROWN, J., Education
BURNABY, B. J., Education
CAHILL, M., Education
CANNING, P., Education
CROCKER, R. K., Education
DOYLE, C. P., Education
GARLIE, N. W., Education
GLASSMAN, M. S., Education
HADLEY, N. H., Education
JEFFREY, G. H., Education
KELLEHER, R. R., Education
KELLY, U., Education
KENNEDY, W., Education
KIM, K. S., Education
MANN, B. L., Education
NESBIT, W. C., Education
OLDFORD-MATCHIM, J., Education
ROBERTS, B. A., Education
SHARPE, D. B., Education
SINGH, A., Education
STEVENS, K., Education
TRESLAN, D., Education

Faculty of Engineering and Applied Sciences:
ABDI, M., Mechanical Engineering
ADLURI, S., Civil Engineering
AHMED, M. H., Electrical and Computer Engineering
BASS, D. W., Mathematics and Statistics and Engineering
BOOTON, M., Mechanical Engineering
BOSE, N., Engineering
BRUCE-LOCKHART, M., Engineering
CLAUDE, D., Engineering
COLES, C., Civil Engineering
GEORGE, G., Electrical and Computer Engineering
GILL, E., Electrical and Computer Engineering
GOSINE, R., Electrical and Computer Engineering
HADDARA, M. M. R., Engineering
HAWBOLDT, K., Civil Engineering
HEYS, H., Electrical and Computer Engineering
HINCHEY, M., Mechanical Engineering
HUSAIN, T., Engineering
IQBAL, T., Electrical and Computer Engineering
JEYASURYA, B., Electrical and Computer Engineering
JORDAAN, I. J., Ocean Engineering
KHAN, F., Mechanical Engineering
KREIN, L., Mechanical Engineering
LI, C., Electrical and Computer Engineering
LYE, L., Engineering
MALONEY, C., Electrical and Computer Engineering
MASEK, V., Electrical and Computer Engineering
NIEFER, R., Engineering
NORVELL, T., Electrical and Computer Engineering
O'YOUNG, S., Electrical and Computer Engineering
PETERS, D., Electrical and Computer Engineering
POPESCU, R., Engineering
QUAICOE, J., Electrical and Computer Engineering
RAHMAN, M., Electrical and Computer Engineering
SABIN, G., Mechanical Engineering
SESHADRI, R., Mechanical Engineering
SHARAN, A., Mechanical Engineering
SHARP, J. J., Engineering
SHIROKOFF, J., Mechanical Engineering
SWAMIDAS, A. S. J., Engineering
VEITCH, B., Engineering
WILLIAMS, F., Engineering

Faculty of Medicine:
BEAR, J. C., Medicine (Genetics)
BROSNAN, J. T., Biochemistry and Medicine
BROSNAN, M. E., Biochemistry and Medicine
CARAYANNIOTIS, G., Medicine and Endocrinology
CORBETT, D. R., Medicine
GADAG, V., Biostatistics
GILLESPIE, L. L., Oncology
HANSEN, P. A., Medicine
HERZBERG, G. R., Biochemistry and Medicine
HOEKMAN, T., Biophysics
HOOVER, R., Biochemistry
HULAN, H., Biochemistry
KEOUGH, K., Biochemistry
LIEPINS, A., Medicine (Cell Sciences)
MARTIN, A. M., Biochemistry
MICHALAK, T. I., Medicine
MICHALSKI, C. J., Medicine (Molecular Biology)
MOODY-CORBETT, F., Physiology
NEUMAN, R. S., Medicine (Pharmacology)
PATER, A., Medicine (Molecular Biology)
PATERNO, G., Medicine (Oncology)
RAHIMTULA, A. D., Biochemistry and Medicine
SCOTT, T. M., Medicine (Anatomy)
VASDEV, S. C., Medicine (Biochemistry)
WEST, R., Pharmacy and Medicine

Faculty of Science:
ADAMEC, R. E., Psychology
ADAMS, R. J., Psychology
AFANASSIEV, I., Physics
AKSU, A. E., Earth Sciences
ANDERSON, R., Psychology
ANDREWS, E., Psychology
ANDREWS, T., Physics
ARLETT, C., Psychology
BARTHA, M., Computer Science
BARTLETT, R., Statistics
BODWELL, G. J., Chemistry
BOURGAULT, D., Physics
BRIDSON, J., Chemistry
BROWN, J. A., Psychology
BRUNNER, H., Mathematics and Statistics
BURDEN, E., Earth Sciences
BURRY, J. H., Mathematics
BURTON, D., Biology
BURTON, M., Biology
BUTTON, C., Psychology
CALON, T. J., Earth Sciences
CARR, S. M., Biology
CHO, C. W., Physics
CLOUTER, M. J., Physics
COLBO, M. H., Biology
COLLINS, M., Biology
COURAGE, M., Psychology
CURNOE, S., Physics
DABINETT, P., Biology
DAVIDSON, W. S., Biochemistry, Molecular Biology
DEBRUYN, J. R., Physics
DEYOUNG, B., Physics
DRIEDZIC, W., Biochemistry, Molecular Biology
DUNBRACK, R. L., Biochemistry, Molecular Biology
DUNNING, G., Earth Sciences
EDDY, R. H., Mathematics and Statistics
EDINGER, E., Biology
EVANS, J., Psychology
FAHRAEUS-VAN RAE, G., Biology
FINNEY-CRAWLEY, J., Biology
FLETCHER, G. L., Ocean Sciences Centre (Biology)
GALE, J. E., Earth Sciences
GAMPERL, K., Biology
GARDNER, G., Biology
GASKILL, H. S., Mathematics
GEORGHIOU, P., Chemistry
GIEN, T. T., Physics
GILLARD, P., Computer Science

GOODAIRE, E. G., Mathematics and Statistics
GOSSE, V., Psychology
GOW, J., Biology
GRANT, M. J., Psychology
GREEN, J. M., Biology
GREEN, J. M., Psychology
HADDEN, K., Psychology
HAEDRICH, R. L., Ocean Sciences Centre (Biology)
HALL, J., Earth Sciences
HANNAH, E., Psychology
HANNAH, T. E., Psychology
HARLEY, C. A., Psychology
HEATH, P. R., Mathematics and Statistics
HERMANUTZ, L., Biology
HISCOTT, R. N., Earth Sciences
HODYCH, J. P., Earth Sciences
HOOPER, R., Biology
HURICH, C. A., Earth Sciences
INDARES, A.-D., Earth Sciences
INNES, D., Biology
JABLONSKI, C. R., Chemistry
JENNER, G., Earth Sciences
JONES, I., Biology
JONES, I., Psychology
KNOECHEL, R., Biology
LAGOWSKI, J., Physics
LARSON, D. J., Biology
LEE, D., Biology
LEITCH, A. M., Earth Sciences
LEWIS, J. C., Physics
LIEN, J., Psychology
LOADER, C. E., Chemistry
LUCAS, C. R., Chemistry
McKIM, W., Psychology
MADDIGAN, R., Psychology
MALSBURY, C., Psychology
MARTIN, G., Psychology
MASON, R. A., Earth Sciences
MEYER, R., Earth Sciences
MILLER, E., Psychology
MILLER, H. G., Earth Sciences
MILLER, T., Biology
MINIMIS, G., Computer Science
MOESER, S., Psychology
MONTEVECCHI, W. A., Psychology
MORROW, M. R., Physics
MURRIN, F., Biology
MYERS, J. S., Earth Sciences
NARAYANASWAMI, P. P., Mathematics and Statistics
PARMENTER, M. M., Mathematics and Statistics
PARSONS, J., Biology
PARSONS, J., Computer Science
PATEL, T. R., Biochemistry and Biology
PENNEY, C. G., Psychology
PETERSEN, C., Psychology
PICKUP, P. G., Chemistry
PODUSKA, K., Physics
POIRIER, R., Chemistry
QUINLAN, G. M., Earth Sciences
QUIRION, G., Physics
RABINOWITZ, F. M., Psychology
REVUSKY, B., Psychology
RICH, N. H., Physics
RIVERS, C. J. S., Earth Sciences
ROSE, B., Psychology
ROSE, G., Marine Institute
SCHNEIDER, D. C., Ocean Sciences Centre
SCOTT, P., Biology
SHAWYER, B. L. R., Mathematics and Statistics
SHERRICK, M., Psychology
SIWEI, L., Computer Science
SKINNER, D., Psychology
SLAWINSKI, M., Earth Sciences
SMITH, F., Physics
SNELGROVE, P., Biology
STAVELY, B. E., Biology
STEIN, A. R., Chemistry
STENSON, G. B., Psychology
STOREY, A. E., Psychology
SUMMERS, D., Mathematics and Statistics

SUTRADHAR, B. C., Mathematics and Statistics
SYLVESTER, P. J., Earth Sciences
TANG, J., Computer Science
THOMPSON, R. J., Ocean Sciences Centre
VOLKOFF, H., Biology
VIDYASANKAR, K., Computer Science
WADLEIGH, M., Earth Sciences
WALSH, D., Physics
WANG, C. A., Computer Science
WARKENTIN, I., Psychology
WHITEHEAD, J. P., Physics
WHITMORE, M. D., Physics
WHITTICK, A., Biology
WILSON, M., Earth Sciences
WILTON, D. H. C., Earth Sciences
WRIGHT, J. A., Earth Sciences
WROBLEWSKI, J. S., Ocean Sciences Centre (Physics)
ZEDEL, L., Physics
ZUBEREK, W. M., Computer Science

School of Nursing:

LARYEA, M., Nursing

School of Pharmacy:

WEST, R., Pharmacy

UNIVERSITÉ DE MONCTON

Moncton, NB E1A 3E9

Telephone: (506) 858-4000
Fax: (506) 858-4585
E-mail: info@umoncton.ca
Internet: www.umoncton.ca

Founded 1864 as St Joseph's Univ., name changed 1963
Language of instruction: French
Public control
Academic year: September to April

Campuses also in Edmundston and Shippagan

Chancellor: LOUIS R. COMEAU
Rector: YVON FONTAINE
Vice-Rector for Academic Research: NEIL BOUCHER
Vice-Rector for Edmundston Campus: PAUL ALBERT
Vice-Rector for Human Resources and Admin.: NASSIR EL-JABI
Vice-Rector for Shippagan Campus: JOCELYNE ROY VIENNEAU
Sec.-Gen.: LYNNE CASTONGUAY (acting)
Librarian: ALAIN ROBERGE

Number of teachers: 389 full-time
Number of students: 5,881 (5,063 full-time, 818 part-time)

Publication: La Revue

DEANS

Moncton Campus:

Faculty of Administration: GASTON LeBLANC
Faculty of Arts and Social Sciences: ISABELLE McKEE-ALLAIN
Faculty of Education: JEAN-FRANÇOIS RICHARD
Faculty of Engineering: PAUL A. CHIASSON
Faculty of Forestry: JEAN-MARIE BINOT
Faculty of Health Sciences and Community Services: PAUL-EMILE BOURQUE
Faculty of Higher Studies and Research: LISA DUBOIS
Faculty of Law: ODETTE SNOW
Faculty of Sciences: FRANCIS LeBLANC

DIRECTORS

Edmundston Campus:

Academic Services: JACQUES PAUL COUTURIER
Arts and Letters: BLANCA NAVARRO-PARDIÑAS
Business Administration: FRANCOIS BOUDREAU
Education: PIERRETTE FORTIN
Human Sciences: LUC VIGNEAULT
School of Nursing: FRANCE L. MARQUIS
Sciences: LUC FRENETTE

Moncton Campus:

School of Kinesiology and Recreology: JEAN-GUY VIENNEAU
School of Nursing: SYLVIE ROUBICHAUD-EKSTRAND
School of Nutrition and Home Economics: SLIMANE BELBRAOUET
School of Psychology: DOUGLAS FRENCH
School of Social Work: HÉLÈNE ALBERT

Shippagan Campus:

Arts and Human Sciences: BENOIT FERRON
Management: ZINE KHELIL
Nursing: SUZANNE OUELLET
Sciences: ELISE MAYRAND

UNIVERSITÉ DE MONTRÉAL

CP 6128, Station Centre-ville, Montréal, QC H3C 3J7

Telephone: (514) 343-6111
Fax: (514) 343-5976
E-mail: international@umontreal.ca
Internet: www.umontreal.ca

Founded 1878
Public control
Language of instruction: French
Academic year: September to August

Chancellor: LOUISE ROY
Rector: GUY BRETON
Vice-Rector for Academic Affairs and Deputy Rector: HÉLÈNE DAVID
Vice-Rector for Development and Graduate Relations: DONAT TADDEO
Vice-Rector for Finance and Infrastructure: ÉRIC FILTEAU
Vice-Rector for Human Resources and Planning: ANNE-MARIE BOISVERT
Vice-Rector for Research and International Relations: JOSEPH HUBERT
Vice-Rector for Student Affairs and Continuing Education: LOUISE BÉLIVEAU
Gen. Sec.: ALEXANDRE CHABOT
Registrar: PIERRE CHENARD
Librarian: RICHARD DUMONT

Library: see Libraries and Archives
Number of teachers: 6,856
Number of students: 56,927

Publications: *Cahiers d'Histoire, Cahiers du Centre d'études de l'Asie de l'Est, Cinémas, CIRCUIT* (North American modern music), *Collection Tiré à part* (School of Industrial Relations), *Criminologie, Études françaises, Géographie physique et Quaternaire, Gestion, L'Actualité Economique, La Gazette des Sciences mathématiques du Québec, Le Médecin vétérinaire du Québec, META, Journal des traducteurs, Paragraphes, Revue Juridique Thémis, Revue des Sciences de l'Education, Sociologie et sociétés, Surfaces, Théologiques*

DEANS

Faculty of Arts and Sciences: GÉRARD BOISMENU
Faculty of Continuing Education: RAYMOND LALANDE (Administrator)
Faculty of Dental Medicine: GILLES LAVIGNE
Faculty of Education Sciences: LOUISE POIRIER
Faculty of Environment Design: GIOVANNI DE PAOLI
Faculty of Graduate Studies: LOUISE BÉLIVEAU
Faculty of Law: GILLES TRUDEAU
Faculty of Medicine: JEAN-LUCIEN ROULEAU
Faculty of Music: SYLVAIN CARON
Faculty of Nursing: FRANCINE GIRARD
Faculty of Pharmacy: PIERRE MOREAU
Faculty of Theology: JEAN-CLAUDE BRETON
Faculty of Veterinary Medicine: RAYMOND S. ROY

PROFESSORS

Faculty of Arts and Sciences

Department of Anthropology:

BEAUCAGE, P.
BERNIER, B.
BIBEAU, G.
CHAPAIS, B.
CHAPDELAINE, C.
CLERMONT, N.
LEAVITT, J.
MEINTEL, D.
MULLER, J.-C.
PANDOLFI, M.
PARADIS, L. I.
SMITH, P.
THIBAULT, P.
TOLSTOY, P.
VERDON, M.

Department of Biology:

ANCTIL, M.
BOISCLAIR, D.
BOUCHARD, A.
BROUILLET, L.
CABANA, T.
CAPPADOCIA, M.
CARIGNAN, R.
HARPER, P.-P.
LEGENDRE, P.
MOLOTCHNIKOFF, S.
MORSE, D.
PINEL-ALLOUL, B.
SAINI, H. S.
SIMON, J.-P.

Department of Chemistry:

BEAUCHAMP, A. L.
BERTRAND, M.
BRISSE, F.
CARRINGTON, T.
CHARETTE, A.
D'AMBOISE, M.
DUGAS, H.
DUROCHER, G.
ELLIS, T. H.
HANESSIAN, S.
HUBERT, J.
LAFLEUR, M.
REBER, C.
ST-JACQUES, M.
WINNIK, F. M.
WUEST, J. D.
ZHU, J.

Department of Classical and Medieval Studies:

FASCIANO, D.

Department of Communication:

CARON, A. H.
GIROUX, L.
LAFRANCE, A. A.
RABOY, M.

Department of Comparative Literature:

CHANADY, A.
GUÉDON, J.-C.
KRYSINSKI, W.
MOSER, W.

Department of Computing Sciences and Operational Research:

ABOULHAMID, E. M.
BRASSARD, G.
CERNY, E.
DSSOULI, R.
FERLAND, J. A.
FLORIAN, M.
FRASSON, C.
GENDREAU, M.
JAUMARD, B.
LAPALME, G.
L'ECUYER, P.
McKENZIE, P.
MARCOTTE, P.
MEUNIER, J.
NGUYEN, S.
POTVIN, J.-Y.

STEWART, N.
VAUCHER, J.

School of Criminology:
BROCHU, S.
BRODEUR, J.-P.
CUSSON, M.
LANDREVILLE, P.
OUIMET, M.
TREMBLAY, P.
TRÉPANIER, J.

Department of Demography:
LAPIERRE-ADAMCYK, E.
PICHÉ, V.

Department of Economics:
BOSSERT, W.
BOYER, M.
BRONSARD, C.
DUDLEY, L.
DUFOUR, J.-M.
GAUDET, G.
GAUDRY, M. J. I.
HOLLANDER, A.
LACROIX, R.
MARTENS, A.
MARTIN, F.
MONTMARQUETTE, C.
POITEVIN, M.
RENAULT, E.
VAILLANCOURT, F.

School of Educational Psychology:
CHARLEBOIS, P.
GAGNON, C.
LARIVÉE, S.
LEBLANC, M.
NORMANDEAU, S.
VAN GIJSEGHEM, H.
VITARO, F.

Department of English Studies:
MARTIN, R. K.

Department of French Studies:
BEAULIEU, J.-P.
CAMBRON, M.
GAUVIN, L.
HÉBERT, F.
LAFLÈCHE, G.
LAROSE, J.
MELANÇON, R.
MICHAUD, G.
NEPVEU, P.
PIERSSENS, M.
SOARE, A.
VACHON, S.

Department of Geography:
BRYANT, C. R.
CAVAYAS, F.
COFFEY, W.
COMTOIS, C.
COMTOIS, P.
COURCHESNE, F.
DE KONINCK, R.
FOGGIN, P. M.
GANGLOFF, P.
GRAY, J. T.
MANZAGOL, C.
MAROIS, C.
RICHARD, P. J. H.
ROY, A. G.
SINGH, B.
THOUEZ, J.-P.

Department of Geology:
BOUCHARD, M. A.
MARTIGNOLE, J.
TRZCIENSKI, W. E.

Department of History:
ANGERS, D.
BOGLIONI, P.
DICKINSON, J. A.
HUBERMAN, M.
KEEL, O.
LÉTOURNEAU, P.
LUSIGNAN, S.

MORIN, C.
PERREAULT, J. Y.
RABKIN, Y.
RAMIREZ, B.
ROUILLARD, J.
SUTTO, C.

Department of History of Art:
DE MOURA SOBRAL, L.
DUBREUIL, N.
GAUDREAULT, A.
KRAUSZ, P.
LAFRAMBOISE, A.
LAMOUREUX, J.
LAROUCHE, M.
LHOTE, J.-F.
MARSOLAIS, G.
NAUBERT-RISER, C.
TOUSIGNANT, S.
TRUDEL, J.

School of Industrial Relations:
BOURQUE, R.
BROSSARD, M.
CHICHA, M.-T.
COUSINEAU, J.-M.
DOLAN, S.
DURAND, P.
GUÉRIN, G.
MURRAY, G.
SIMARD, M.
TRUDEAU, G.

School of Library and Information Sciences:
BERTRAND-GASTALDY, S.
COUTURE, C.
DESCHATELETS, G.
LAJEUNESSE, M.
SAVARD, R.

Department of Linguistics and Translation:
CONNORS, K.
CORMIER, M. C.
FORD, A.
HOSINGTON, B.
JAREMA-ARVANITAKIS, G.
KITTREDGE, R.
MEL'ČUK, I. A.
MÉNARD, N.
MORIN, J.-Y.
MORIN, Y.-C.
NUSELOVICI NOUSS, A.
PATRY, R.
ST-PIERRE, P.
SCHULZE-BUSACKER, E.
SINGH, R.

Department of Literature and Modern Languages:
BOUCHARD, J.
PECK, J.
RÄKEL, H.-H.

Department of Mathematics and Statistics:
ARMINJON, P.
BÉLAIR, J.
BENABDALLAH, K.
BILODEAU, M.
BRUNET, R.
CLÉROUX, R.
DELFOUR, M.
DUFRESNE, D.
FRIGON, M.
GAUTHIER, P.
GIRI, N. C.
GIROUX, A.
HUSSIN, V.
JOFFE, A.
LALONDE, F.
LÉGER, C.
LEPAGE, Y.
LESSARD, S.
PATERA, J.
PERRON, F.
RAHMAN, Q. I.
REYES, G.
ROSENBERG, I.
ROUSSEAU, C.
ROY, R.

SABIDUSSI, G.
SAINT-AUBIN, Y.
SANKOFF, D.
SCHLOMIUK, D.
TURGEON, J.
WINTERNITZ, P.
ZAIDMAN, S.

Department of Philosophy:
BAKKER, E. J.
BODEÜS, R.
DUCHESNEAU, F.
GAUTHIER, Y.
GRONDIN, J.
LAGUEUX, M.
LAURIER, D.
LEPAGE, F.
LÉVESQUE, C.
PICHÉ, C.
ROY, J.
SEYMOUR, M.

Department of Physics:
BASTIEN, P.
CAILLÉ, A.
CARIGNAN, C.
COCHRANE, R. W.
DEMERS, S.
FONTAINE, G.
GOULARD, B.
LAPOINTE, J.-Y.
LAPRADE, R.
LEONELLI, R.
LÉPINE, Y.
LEROY, C.
LESSARD, L.
LEWIS, L. J.
LONDON, D.
MICHAUD, G.
MOFFAT, A.
MOISAN, M.
ROORDA, S.
TARAS, P.
TEICHMANN, J.
VINCENT, A.
WESEMAEL, F.
ZACEK, V.

Department of Politics:
BÉLANGER, A.-J.
BERNIER, G.
BLAIS, A.
BOISMENU, G.
CLOUTIER, É.
DION, S.
DUQUETTE, M.
ÉTHIER, D.
FAUCHER, P.
FORTMANN, M.
JENSON, J.
MONIÈRE, D.
NADEAU, R.
NOËL, A.
SOLDATOS, P.
THÉRIEN, J.-P.

Department of Psychology:
BERGERON, J.
BOUCHARD, M.-A.
BRUNET, L.
CLAES, M.
COMEAU, J.
COSSETTE-RICARD, M.
CYR, M.
DAVID, H.
DOYON, J.
DUBÉ, L.
FAVREAU, O.
FORTIN, A.
GRANGER, L.
HACCOUN, R.
HODGINS, S.
LASRY, J.-C.
LASSONDE, M.
LECOMTE, C.
LEPORE, F.
MATHIEU, M.
NADEAU, L.

PAGÉ, M.
PERETZ, I.
PERRON, J.
ROBERT, M.
SABOURIN, M.
SAVOIE, A.
STRAVYNSKI, A.
TREMBLAY, R. E.
WRIGHT, J.
ZAVALLONI, M.

School of Social Work:

BERNIER, D.
CHAMBERLAND, C.
GROULX, L. H.
LEGAULT, G.
MAYER, R.
PANET-RAYMOND, J.
RINFRET-RAYNOR, M.
RONDEAU, G.

Department of Sociology:

BERNARD, P.
FOURNIER, M.
HAMEL, J.
HAMEL, P.
HOULE, G.
JUTEAU, D.
LAURIN, N.
MCALL, C.
MAHEU, L.
RACINE, L.
RENAUD, J.
RENAUD, M.
ROCHER, G.
SALES, A.
VAILLANCOURT, J.-G.

Faculty of Dental Medicine

Department of Dental Prosthesis:

BALTAJIAN, H.
BOUDRIAS, P.
LAMARCHE, C.
PRÉVOST, A.
TACHÉ, R.

Department of Oral Health:

CHARLAND, R.
JULIEN, M.
KANDELMAN, D.
LAVIGNE, G.
MASSEREDJIAN, V.
REMISE, C.
TURGEON, J.
WECHSLER, M.

Department of Stomatology:

DONOHUE, W. B.
DUNCAN, G.
DUPUIS, R.
DUQUETTE, P.
FOREST, D.
LEMAY, H.
MICHAUD, M.
NANCI, A.

Faculty of Education Sciences

Department of Curriculum and Instruction:

BEER-TOKER, M.
CHARLAND, J.-P.
GAGNÉ, G.
LEMOYNE, G.
PAINCHAUD, G.
PARET, M.-C.
PIERRE, R.
RETALLACK-LAMBERT, N.
SAINT-JACQUES, D.
THÉRIEN, M.
VAN GRUNDERBEECK, N.

Department of Education and Educational Administration Studies:

AJAR, D.
BOURGEAULT, G.
BRASSARD, A.
CHENÉ, A.
CRESPO, M.
DUPUIS, P.
JOFFE-NICODÈME, A.

LESSARD, C.
PELLETIER, G.
PROULX, J.-P.
TARDIF, M.
TRAHAN, M.
VAN DER MAREN, J.-M.

Department of Psychopedagogy and Andragogy:

COMEAU, M.
DUFRESNE-TASSÉ, C.
GAUDREAU, J.
LANGEVIN, J.
LÉVESQUE, M.
MARCHAND, L.
TREMBLAY, N.

Faculty of Environmental Design

School of Architecture:

ADAMCZYK, G.
DALIBARD, J.
DAVIDSON, C. H.
MARSAN, J.-C.

School of Industrial Design:

CAMOUS, R. F.
FINDELI, A.
LECLERC, A.

Department of Kinesiology:

ALAIN, C.
ALLARD, P.
GAGNON, M.
GARDINER, P. F.
LABERGE, S.
LAVOIE, J.-M.
LÉGER, L.
PÉRONNET, F.
PROTEAU, L.

School of Landscape Architecture:

CINQ-MARS, I.
JACOBS, J.
LAFARGUE, B.
POULLAOUEC-GONIDEC, P.

Institute of Urbanism:

BARCELO, A.-M.
BLANC, B.
BOISVERT, M. A.
CARDINAL, A.
GARIÉPY, M.
LESSARD, M.
MCNEIL, J.
PARENTEAU, R.
SOKOLOFF, B.
TRÉPANIER, M.-O.

Faculty of Law:

BENYEKHLEF, K.
BICH, M.-F.
BOISVERT, A.-M.
BRISSON, J.-M.
CHEVRETTE, F.
CIOTOLA, P.
CÔTÉ, P.-A.
CÔTÉ, P. P.
CRÉPEAU, F.
DESLAURIERS, P.
DUMONT, H.
FABIEN, C.
FRÉMONT, J.
GAGNON, J. D.
GOLDSTEIN, G.
GRUNING, D.
HÉTU, J.
KNOPPERS, B. M.
LABRÈCHE, D.
LAJOIE, A.
LAMONTAGNE, D.-C.
LEFEBVRE, G.
LEROUX, T.
LLUELLES, D.
MACKAAY, E.
MOLINARI, P.
NEUWAHI, N.
PINARD, D.
POPOVICI, A.
ROCHER, G.

TALPIS, J.
TREMBLAY, A.
TREMBLAY, L.
TRUDEL, P.
TURP, D.
VIAU, L.
WOEHRLING, J.

Faculty of Medicine

Department of Anaesthesiology:

BLAISE, G.
DONATI, F.
HARDY, J.-F.

Department of Biochemistry:

BOILEAU, G.
BOUVIER, M.
BRAKIER-GINGRAS, L.
BRISSON, N.
CRINE, P.
DAIGNEAULT, R.
DESGROSEILLERS, L.
LANG, F. B.
ROKEACH, L. A.
SKUP, D.
SYGUSCH, J.

Department of Family Medicine:

BEAULIEU, M.-D.
MILLETTE, B.

Department of Health Administration:

BÉLAND, F.
BLAIS, R.
CHAMPAGNE, F.
CONTANDRIOPOULOS, A.-P.
DENIS, J.-L.
DUSSAULT, G.
LAMARCHE, P.
SICOTTE, C.
TILQUIN, C.

Department of Medicine:

AYOUB, J.
BICHET, D.
BRADLEY, E.
BRAZEAU, P.
BUTTERWORTH, R. F.
CARDINAL, J.
CHIASSON, J.-L.
D'AMOUR, P.
DELESPESSE, G. J. T.
DUQUETTE, P.
GOUGOUX, A.
GRASSINO, A.
HALLÉ, J.-P.
HAMET, P.
HUET, M.
LACROIX, A.
LAPLANTE, L.
LECOURS, A. R.
LE LORIER, J.
MALO, J.-L.
MARLEAU, D.
MARTEL-PELLETIER, J.
MATTE, R.
MES-MASSON, A.-M.
NADEAU, R.
NATTEL, S.
PELLETIER, J.-P.
PERREAULT, C.
POITRAS, P.
POMIER-LAYRARGUES, G.
RASIO, E.
SARFATI, M.
SÉNÉCAL, J.-L.
TREMBLAY, J.
VINAY, P.

Department of Microbiology and Immunology:

AUGER, P.
COHEN, É.
DE REPENTIGNY, L.
HALLENBECK, P.
LEMAY, G.
MENEZES, J. P. C. A.
MONTPLAISIR, S.

MORISSET, R.
SEKALY, R.-P.

Department of Nutrition:

DELISLE, H.
DES ROSIERS, C.
GARREL, D.
GAVINO, V.
HOUDE-NADEAU, M.
LÉVY, E.
POEHLMAN, É.
PRENTKI, M.
SERRI, O.
SIMARD-MAVRIKAKIS, S.
VAN DE WERVE, G.

Department of Obstetrics and Gynaecology:

BÉLISLE, S.
DROUIN, P.

Department of Occupational and Environmental Health:

CARRIER, G.
CHAKRABARTI, S. K.
GÉRIN, M.
KRISHNAN, K.
VIAU, C.
ZAYED, J.

Department of Ophthalmology:

BOISJOLY, H.
LABELLE, P.

Department of Paediatrics:

ALVAREZ, F.
BARD, H.
CHEMTOB, S.
FOURON, J.-C.
FRAPPIER, J.-Y.
GAGNAN-BRUNETTE, M.
GAUTHIER-CHOUINARD, M.
LABUDA, D.
LACROIX, J.
LAMBERT, M.
LAPOINTE, N.
RASQUIN-WEBER, A.-M.
ROBITAILLE, P.
ROUSSEAU, É.
SEIDMAN, E.
TEASDALE, F.
VANASSE, M.
VAN VLIET, G.
WEBER, M.
WILKINS, J.

Department of Pathology and Cellular Biology:

BENDAYAN, M.
CHARTRAND, P.
DESCARRIES, L.
GIROUX, L.
KESSOUS, A.
LATOUR, J.-G.
SCHÜRCH, W.

Department of Pharmacology:

CARDINAL, R.
DE LÉAN, A.
DUMONT, L.
DU SOUICH, P.
ÉLIE, R.
GASCON-BARRÉ, M.
LAMBERT, C.
LAROCHELLE, P.
LAVOIE, P.-A.
MOMPARLER, R.
YOUSEF, I.

Department of Physiology:

ANAND-SRIVASTAVA, M.
BERGERON, M.
BERTELOOT, A.
BILLETTE, J.
CASTELLUCCI, V.
COUTURE, R.
DE CHAMPLAIN, J.
DREW, T. B.
FELDMAN, A. G.
GULRAJANI, R.
KALASKA, J. F.

LACAILLE, J.-C.
LAMARRE, Y.
LAVALLÉE, M.
LEBLANC, A.-R.
MAESTRACCI, D.
MALO, C.
READER, T. A.
ROBERGE, F.
ROSSIGNOL, S.
SAUVÉ, R.
SMITH, A.

Department of Preventive and Social Medicine:

BRODEUR, J.-M.
DASSA, C.
FOURNIER, P.
LABERGE-NADEAU, C.
LAMBERT, J.
MAHEUX, B.
PHILIPPE, P.
PINEAULT, R.
POTVIN, L.
SÉGUIN, L.
SIEMIATYCKI, J.

Department of Psychiatry:

AMYOT, A.
CHOUINARD, G.
LALONDE, P.
LEMAY, M.-L.
MONDAY, J.
MONTPLAISIR, J. Y.
SAUCIER, J.-F.
WEISSTUB, D. N.

Department of Radiology, Radio-Oncology and Nuclear Medicine:

BRETON, G.
LAFORTUNE, M.
SAMSON, L.

School of Rehabilitation:

ARSENAULT, B.
BOURBONNAIS, D.
CHAPMAN, C. E.
DUTIL, É.
FERLAND, F.
FORGET, R.
GAUTHIER-GAGNON, C.
GRAVEL, D.
WEISS-LAMBROU, R.

School of Speech Pathology and Audiology:

GAGNÉ, J.-P.
GETTY, L.
JOANETTE, Y.
LE DORZE, G.
SKA, B.

Department of Surgery:

BEAUCHAMP, G.
BERNARD, D.
CAOUETTE-LABERGE, L.
CARRIER, M.
CHARLIN, B.
DALOZE, P.
DUBÉ, S.
DURANCEAU, A.
LABELLE, H.
PAGÉ, P.
PAQUIN, J.-M.
RIVARD, C.-H.
ROBIDOUX, A.
SMEESTERS, C.
VALIQUETTE, L.
WASSEF, R.

Faculty of Music:

BELKIN, A.
DESROCHES, M.
DURAND, M.
EVANGELISTA, J.
GUERTIN, M.
LEFEBVRE, M.-T.
LEROUX, R.
LONGTIN, M.
NATTIEZ, J.-J.
PANNETON, I.

PICHÉ, J.
POIRIER, R.
RIVEST, J.-F.
SMOJE, D.
VAILLANCOURT, L.

Faculty of Nursing:

DUCHARME, F.
DUQUETTE, A.
GAGNON, L.
GOULET, C.
GRENIER, R.
KÉROUAC, S.
REIDY, M.
RICARD, N.

School of Optometry:

BEAULNE, C.
CASANOVA, C.
FAUBERT, J.
KERGOAT, H.
LOVASIK, J. V.
PTITO, M.
SIMONET, P.

Faculty of Pharmacy:

ADAM, A.
BESNER, J.-G.
BISAILLON, S.
BRAZIER, J.-L.
CARTILIER, L.
GAGNÉ, J.
LAURIER, C.
McMULLEN, J.-N.
MAILHOT, C.
ONG, H.
TURGEON, J.
VARIN, F.
WINNIK, F.
YAMAGUCHI, N.

Faculty of Theology:

DUHAIME, J.
NADEAU, J.-G.
PETIT, J.-C.

Faculty of Veterinary Medicine

Department of Clinical Sciences:

BLAIS, D.
BONNEAU, N, H.
BOUCHARD, É.
BRETON, L.
CARRIER, M.
CÉCYRE, A. J.
CHALIFOUX, A.
COUTURE, Y.
CUVELLIEZ, S.
D'ALLAIRE, S.
DI FRUSCIA, R.
DUBREUIL, P.
LAMOTHE, P. J.
LAROUCHE, Y.
LAVERTY, S.
LAVOIE, J.-P.
MARCOUX, M.
PARADIS, M.
VAILLANCOURT, D.
VRINS, A.

Department of Pathology and Microbiology:

BIGRAS-POULIN, M.
DROLET, R.
DUBREUIL, D.
EL AZHARY, Y.
FAIRBROTHER, J. M.
FONTAINE, M.
GIRARD, C.
GOTTSCHALK, M.
HAREL, J.
HIGGINS, R.
JACQUES, M.
LALLIER, R.
LARIVIÈRE, S.
MITTAL, K. R.
MORIN, M.
ROY, R. S.
SCHOLL, D. T.
SILIM, A. N.

Department of Veterinary Biomedicine:
BARRETTE, D.
BISAILLON, A.
DALLAIRE, A.
DEROTH, L.
GOFF, A. K.
LARIVIÈRE, N.
LUSSIER, J. G.
MURPHY, B. D.
SILVERSIDES, D. W.
SIROIS, J.
SMITH, L. C.
TREMBLAY, A. V.

AFFILIATED INSTITUTIONS

Ecole des Hautes Etudes Commerciales:
3000, chemin de la Côte-Sainte-Catherine,
Montréal, QC H3T 2A7; tel. (514) 340-6000; f.
1907; Dir JEAN-MARIE TOULOUSE.

Ecole Polytechnique: 2500 ch. de Polytechnique, Montréal, QC H3T 1J4; tel. (514)
340-4711; f. 1873; Dir RÉJEAN PLAMONDON.

MOUNT ALLISON UNIVERSITY

Sackville, NB E4L 1E4
Telephone: (506) 364-2600
Fax: (506) 364-2262
E-mail: ldillman@mta.ca
Internet: www.mta.ca
Founded 1839
Private control
Language of instruction: English
Academic year: September to May
Chancellor: JOHN BRAGG
Pres. and Vice-Chancellor: Dr ROBERT CAMP-
BELL
Provost and Vice-Pres. for Academics and
Research: Dr STEPHEN MCCLATCHIE
Vice-Pres. for Admin. and Finance: D. J.
STEWART
Registrar: CHRIS PARKER
Librarian: BRUNO GNASSI
Library of 1,200,000 vols
Number of teachers: 130
Number of students: 2,250

DEANS

Faculty of Arts: Dr HANS VANDERLEEST
Faculty of Science: Dr JEFF OLLERHEAD
Faculty of Social Sciences: Dr ROB SUM-
MERBY-MURRAY

PROFESSORS

AIKEN, R., Biology
BAERLOCHER, F. J., Biology
BAKER, C., Mathematics and Computer Sci-
ence
BEATTIE, M., Mathematics and Computer
Science
BEATTIE, R., Mathematics and Computer
Science
BELKE, T., Psychology
BLAGRAVE, M., English
BOGAARD, P., Philosophy
BURKE, R., Fine Arts
COHEN, I., Classics
CRAIG, T., English
FLEMING, B., Sociology
FOX, M., Geography and Environment
HAWKES, B., Physics
HOLOWNIA, T., Fine Arts
HUDSON, R., Commerce
HUNT, W., Political Science
IRELAND, R., Biology
KACZMARSKA, I., Biology
MACMILLAN, C., English
POLEGATO, R., Commerce
ROSEBRUGH, B., Mathematics and Computer
Science
STEWART, J. M., Biochemistry
STRAIN, F., Economics
TUCKER, M., Political Science
VARMA, P., Physics

VERDUYN, C., English
VOGAN, N., Music
WESTCOTT, S., Chemistry

MOUNT SAINT VINCENT UNIVERSITY

Halifax, NS B3M 2J6
Telephone: (902) 457-6117
Fax: (902) 457-6498
E-mail: admissions@msvu.ca
Internet: www.msvu.ca
Founded 1925
Language of instruction: English
Academic year: September to April, 2 sum-
mer sessions
Chancellor: MARY LOUISE BRINK
Pres. and Vice-Chancellor: Dr SHEILA A.
BROWN
Vice-Pres. for Academics: Dr DONNA WOOL-
COTT
Vice-Pres. for Admin.: AMANDA WHITEWOOD
Registrar: J. LYNNE THERIAULT
Univ. Librarian: LILLIAN BELTAOS
Number of teachers: 232 (151 full-time, 81
part-time)
Number of students: 4,500
Publications: *Atlantis* (4 a year), *Folia Mon-
tana*, *The Connection* (12 a year)

DEANS

Arts and Sciences: Dr SHEVA MEDJUCK
Professional Studies: Dr MARY LYON
Student Affairs: Dr CAROL HILL

UNIVERSITY OF NEW BRUNSWICK

UNB Fredericton POB 4400, Fredericton, NB
E3B 5A3
Telephone: (506) 453-4666
Fax: (506) 453-4599
UNB Saint John 100 Tucker Park Rd, POB
5050 Saint John NB E2L 4L5
Telephone: (506) 648-5500
Fax: (506) 648-5691
E-mail: qc2@unb.ca
Internet: www.unb.ca
Founded 1785
Provincial control
Language of instruction: English
Academic year: September to May
Chancellor: RICHARD CURRIE
Pres.: JOHN MCLAUGHLIN
Vice-Pres. for Academic Affairs and Freder-
icton Campus: Dr ANTHONY SECCO (acting)
Vice-Pres. for Finance and Corporate Ser-
vices: DANIEL V. MURRAY
Vice-Pres. for Research: Dr GREGORY S.
KEALEY
Vice-Pres. (Saint John Campus): Dr ROBERT
MACKINNON
Comptroller: LARRY GUITARD
Sec.: STEPHEN STROPLE
Registrar: TOM BUCKLEY
Dir. for Devt and Donor Relations): SUSAN
MONTAGUE
Librarian: JOHN TESKEY
Number of teachers: 679
Number of students: 10,880 (9,430 full-time,
1,450 part-time)
Publications: *Acadiensis*, a historical journal
of the Atlantic provinces (2 a year), *Experi-
ence UNB* (1 a year), *Fiddlehead* (short
stories and poetry, quarterly), *Graduate
Studies Calendar*, *International Fiction
Review*, *Research Inventory* (1 a year),
Studies in Canadian Literature (3 a
year), *Summer School Calendar*, *Under-
graduate Calendar*

DEANS

Fredericton Campus:

Faculty of Administration: DANIEL COLEMAN
Faculty of Arts: Dr JAMES S. MURRAY (acting)

Faculty of Computer Science: ALI GHORBANI
Faculty of Education: SHARON RICH (acting)
Faculty of Engineering: DAVID COLEMAN
Faculty of Forestry and Environmental Man-
agement: IAN METHVEN (acting)
Faculty of Kinesiology: TERRY R. HAGGERTY
Faculty of Law: PHILIP BRYDEN
Faculty of Nursing: CHERYL GIBSON
Faculty of Science: ALLAN SHARP
School of Graduate Studies: GWEN DAVIES
(acting)
Saint John Campus:
Faculty of Arts: Dr JOANNA EVERITT
Faculty of Business: REGENA FARNSWORTH
(acting)
Faculty of Science, Applied Science and
Engineering: Dr RUTH SHAW

PROFESSORS

Fredericton Campus:

Faculty of Administration:
ABEKAH, J.
ANGELES, R.
ARCELUS, F. J.
ASKANAS, W.
BETTS, N.
BOOTHMAN, B.
COLEMAN, D.
DU, D.
DUNNETT, J.
DUPLESSIS, D.
EISELT, H. A.
FLINT, D.
GAUDES, A.
GRANT, S.
HINTON, J.
KABADI, S.
LAUGHLAND, A. R.
LIM, W.
MAHER, E.
MAHER, R.
MITRA, D.
NAIR, K. P. K.
NASIEROWSKI, W.
NEVERS, R.
OTCHERE, I.
OTUTEYE, E.
OUYANG, M.
POST, P.
RAHIM, M. A.
RASHID, M.
RITCHIE, P.
ROY, J. A.
SHARMA, B.
SHEPPARD, R. G.
SIMYAR, F.
SRINIVASAN, G.
THOMAS, M. E.
TOLLIVER, J.
TRENHOLM, B.
WHALEN, H.
WIELMAKER, M.
ZULUAGA, L.

Faculty of Arts:
AHERN, D., Philosophy
ALLEN, J. G., Political Science
ALMEH, R., Sociology
ANDREWS, J., English
AUSTIN, D., English
BALL, J., International Development Stud-
ies
BALL, J. C., English
BEDFORD, A., International Development
Studies
BEDFORD, D., Law and Society
BEDFORD, D., Women's Studies
BEDFORD, D. W., Political Science
BLACK, D., Anthropology
BONNETT, J., History
BOWDEN, G., Sociology
BRANDER, J. R. G., Economics
BROWN, A., French
BROWN, A., Women's Studies
BROWN, J. S., History

BYERS, E. S., Psychology
CAMPBELL, G., History
CANITZ, A. E., English
CARRIERE, M., French
CHARRON, D., French
CHARTERS, D., History
CICHOCKI, W., French
CLARK, D. A., Psychology
CONRAD, M., History
COOK, B. A., Economics
CULVER, K., Law in Society
CULVER, K., Philosophy
CUPPLES, B. W., Philosophy
DAVIES, G., English
D'ENTREMONT, B., Psychology
DICKSON, V., Economics
DOERKSEN, D., English
DONALDSON, A. W., Psychology
DUECK, C., Culture and Language Studies
DUPLESSIS, D., Law in Society
FALKENSTEIN, L., English
FARNWORTH, M., Economics
FERGUSON, B., Economics
FIELDS, D. L., Psychology
FRANK, D., History
GANTS, D. L., English
GEYSSEN, J. W., Classics and Ancient History
HAMLING, A., Women's Studies
HARRISON, D., Sociology
HIEW, C. C., Psychology
HORNE, C., Linguistics
HORNOSTY, J., Women's Studies
HORNOSTY, J. M., Sociology
HOWE, J. M., Sociology
JARMAN, M., English
KEALEY, G. S., History
KEALEY, L., History
KENNEDY, S., History
KERR, W., Classics and Ancient History
KERR, W., Law in Society
KLINCK, A., English
KUFELDT, K., Sociology
LACHAPELLE, D., Psychology
LANTZ, V., Economics
LARMER, R., Philosophy
LAUTARD, E. H., Sociology
LAW, S., Economics
LEBLANC, D., French
LECKIE, R., English
LEMIRE, B., History
LEMIRE, B. J., History
LEVINE, L., Economics
LINTON, M., Culture and Language Studies
LOREY, C., Culture and Language Studies
LOVELL, P. R., Anthropology
LOW, J., Sociology
MCDONALD, T., Economics
MCFARLAND, J., International Development Studies
MCGAW, R. L., Economics
MCTAVISH, L., Women's Studies
MARTIN, R., English
MIEDEMA, B., Sociology
MILLS, M. J., Classics and Ancient History
MILNER, M., History
MITRA, K., International Development Studies
MULLALY, E. J., English
MURRAY, J., Classics and Ancient History
MURRAY, J. S., Classics and Ancient History
MURRAY, K., Political Science
MURRELL, D., Economics
MYATT, A. E., Economics
NASON-CLARK, N., Sociology and Women's Studies
NEILL, W., Philosophy
NEILSON, L., Law in Society
PAPPONET-CANTAT, C., Anthropology and International Development Studies
PARENTEAU, W. M., History
PASSARIS, C. E., Economics
PIERCEY, D., Psychology
PLAICE, E., Anthropology
PLOUDE, R. J., English

POOL, G., International Development Studies
POOL, G. R., Anthropology
POULIN, C., Law in Society
POULIN, C., Psychology
POULIN, C., Women's Studies
RAHMANIAN, A., Philosophy
REHORICK, D. A., Sociology
REID, A., Culture and Language Studies
REZUN, M., Economics, International Development Studies and Political Science
RIDEOUT, V., Sociology
RIMMER, M. P., English
ROBBINS, W., Women's Studies
ROBBINS, W. J., English
ROBINSON, G. B., Psychology
ROWCROFT, J. E., Economics
SCHERF, K., English
SHANNON, C., Women's Studies
SIGURDSON, R., Political Science
SPINNER, B., Psychology
STOPPARD, J. M., Psychology
TASIC, V., Linguistics
THOMPSON, D. G., History
TRYPHONOPOULOS, D., English
TURNER, R. S., History
VAN DEN HOONAARD, W. C., Sociology
VIAU, R., French
VILLIARD, P., Linguistics
WAITE, G. K., History
WHITEFORD, G., International Development Studies
WIBER, M., Anthropology
WISNIEWSKI, L. J., Sociology
WORKMAN, T., Anthropology

Faculty of Computer Science:

BHAVSAR, V. C.
COOPER, R. H.
DEDOUREK, J. M.
DESLONGCHAMPS, G.
DU, W.
EVANS, P.
FRITZ, J.
GHORBANI, A. A.
HORTON, J. D.
KENT, K.
KURZ, B. J.
MACNEIL, D. G.
NICKERSON, B. G.
WASSON, W. D.
ZHANG, H.

Faculty of Education:

ALLEN, P., Adult and Vocational Education
BERRY, K., Educational Foundations
BEZEAU, L., Educational Foundations
BURGE, E., Adult and Vocational Education
CASHION, M., Educational Foundations
CLARKE, G. M., Curriculum and Instruction
COOPER, T. G., Curriculum and Instruction
EYRE, L., Health Education
GILL, B., Educational Administration
HUGHES, A. S., Curriculum and Instruction
LEAVITT, R., Curriculum and Instruction
MYERS, S., Health Education
NASON, P. N., Curriculum and Instruction
OTT, H. W., Educational Foundations
PAUL, L., Curriculum and Instruction
PAZIENZA, J., Curriculum and Instruction
RADFORD, K., Curriculum and Instruction
REHORICK, S., Curriculum and Instruction
SEARS, A., Curriculum and Instruction
SMALL, M. S., Curriculum and Instruction
SOUCY, D. A., Curriculum and Instruction
STEVENSON, M., Electrical and Computer Engineering
STEWART, J. (acting), Educational Foundations
SULLENGER, K., Science Education
WHITEFORD, G., Curriculum and Instruction
WILLMS, J. D., Educational Foundations

Faculty of Engineering:

BENDRICH, G., Chemical Engineering

BIDEN, E., Mechanical Engineering
BISCHOFF, P. H., Civil Engineering
BONHAM, D. J. (acting), Mechanical Engineering
CHANG, L., Electrical and Computer Engineering
CHAPLIN, R. (acting), Chemical Engineering
CHAPLIN, R. A. (acting), Chemical Engineering
COLEMAN, D. J., Geodesy and Geomatics
COLPITTS, B. (acting), Electrical and Computer Engineering
COUTURIER, M. (acting), Chemical Engineering
DARE, P., Geodesy and Geomatics (Chair)
DAWE, J. L. (acting), Civil Engineering
DIDUCH, C. (acting), Electrical Engineering
DORAISWAMI, R., Electrical Engineering
EIC, M., Chemical Engineering
HILL, E. F. (acting), Electrical Engineering
HUDGINS, B., Electrical and Computer Engineering
HUSSEIN, E. (acting), Mechanical Engineering
INNES, J. D., Civil Engineering
IRCHA, M. C., Civil Engineering
LANGLEY, R. B. (acting), Geodesy and Geomatics Engineering
LEE, Y. C., Geodesy and Geomatics
LEWIS, J. E., Electrical Engineering
LISTER, D., Chemical Engineering
LOVELY, D., Electical and Computer Engineering
LOWRY, B. (acting), Chemical Engineering
LUKE, D. M. (acting), Electrical Engineering
LYON, D., Mechanical Engineering
MCLAUGHLIN, J. D. (acting), Geodesy and Geomatics Engineering
MAYER, L., Geodesy and Geomatics Engineering
NI, Y., Chemical Engineering
NICHOLS, S. E. (acting), Geodesy and Geomatics
PARKER, P. A. (acting), Electrical Engineering
ROGERS, R. J., Mechanical Engineering
SHARAF, A. M. M., Electrical Engineering
SOUSA, A. C. M., Mechanical Engineering
SULLIVAN, P., Mechanical Engineering
TAYLOR, J. H. (acting), Electrical Engineering
TERVO, R., Electrical and Computer Engineering
THOMAS, M. D. A. (acting), Civil Engineering
VALSANGKAR, A. J. (acting), Civil Engineering
VANICEK, P., Geodesy and Geomatics Engineering
WAUGH, L. M., Civil Engineering

Faculty of Forestry and Environmental Management:

AFZAL, M. (acting)
ARP, P. A.
BECKLEY, T.
BOURQUE, C.
CHUI, Y.
CUNJAK, R.
CURRY, A.
DAUGHERTY, D.
DIAMOND, T.
ERDLE, T.
FORBES, G.
JAEGER, D.
JORDAN, G.
KEPPIE, D. M.
KERSHAW, J.
KRASOWSKI, M.
LANTZ, V.
LEBLON, B.
MACLEAN, D.
MENG, C.-H.
QUIRING, D. T. W.

ROBAK, E. W.
ROBERTS, M. R.
SAVIDGE, R.
SCHNEIDER, M. H.
SERGEANT, B.
SMITH, I.
ZUNDEL, P.

Faculty of Kinesiology:

BURKARD, J.
HAGGERTY, T. R.
PATON, G. A.
SEXSMITH, J.
STEVENSON, C. L.
WRIGHT, P. H.

Faculty of Law:

BELL, D. G.
BIRD, R. W.
BLADON, G. L.
CHATERJEE, A.
DORE, K. J.
FLEMING, D. J.
GOCHNAUER, M. L.
KUTTNER, T. S.
LAFOREST, A.
MCCALLUM, M. E.
MCEVOY, J. P.
MATHEN, C.
PEARLSTON, K.
PENNEY, S.
SIEBRASSE, N.
TOWNSEND, D.
VEITCH, E.
WILLIAMSON, J. R.

Faculty of Nursing:

ERICSON, P.
GETTY, G.
GIBSON, C.
GILBEY, V. J. U.
LEWIS, K.
OUELLET, L.
RUSH, K. L.
STORR, G.
WIGGINS, N.
WUEST, J.

Faculty of Science:

ADAM, A. G., Chemistry
BALCOLM, B., Chemistry
BANERJEE, P. K., Mathematics and Statistics
BARCLAY, D. W., Mathematics and Statistics
BROSTER, B., Geology
CASHION, P. J., Biology
CHERNOFF, W. W., Mathematics and Statistics
COOMBS, D. H., Biology
COOPER, R., Chemistry
CWYNAR, L., Biology
CULP, J., Biology
CUNJAK, R., Biology
DESLONGCHAMPS, G., Chemistry
DIAMOND, A., Biology
DILWORTH, T. G., Biology
FORBES, G., Biology
GEGENBERG, J., Mathematics and Statistics
HAMZA, A., Mathematics and Statistics
HUSAIN, V., Mathematics and Statistics
INGALLS, C., Mathematics and Statistics
JONES, C., Mathematics and Statistics
KEPPIE, D. M., Biology (also under Faculty of Forestry and Environmental Management)
LENTZ, D., Geology
LINTON, C., Physics
LYNCH, W. H., Biology
MCKELLAR, R., Mathematics and Statistics
MAGEE, D., Chemistry
MARCHAND, E., Mathematics and Statistics
MASON, G. R., Mathematics and Statistics
MATTAR, S., Chemistry
MONSON, B. R., Mathematics and Statistics
MUREIKA, R. A., Mathematics and Statistics
NEVILLE, J., Chemistry

NI, Y., Chemistry
PASSMORE, J., Chemistry
PICKERILL, R. K., Geology
RIDING, R. T., Biology
ROSS, W. R., Physics
SAUNDERS, G., Biology
SEABROOK, W. D., Biology
SHARP, A. R., Physics
SIVASUBRAMANIAN, P., Biology
SPRAY, J., Geology
THAKKAR, A., Chemistry
TIMOTHY, J. G., Physics
TINGLEY, D., Mathematics and Statistics
TUPPER, B. O. J., Mathematics and Statistics
TURNER, T. R., Mathematics and Statistics
VILLEMURE, G., Chemistry
WHITE, J. C., Geology
WHITTAKER, J. R., Biology
WILLIAMS, P. F., Geology
YOO, B. Y., Biology

Saint John Campus:

Faculty of Arts:

BELANGER, L., French
BEST, L., Psychology
BOTH, L., Psychology
BRADLEY, M. T., Psychology
CAMPBELL, M. A., Psychology
CAVALIERE, P. A., History
CHILDS, J., Economics
DARTNELL, M., Political Science
DESSERUD, D., Political Science
DI TOMMASO, E., Psychology
DONNELLY, F., History and Politics
EVERITT, J., Political Science
GENDREAU, P., Psychology
GODDARD, M. J., Psychology
HILL, R., Economics
HILL, V., French
HYSON, S., Political Sciences
JEFFREY, L., Political Sciences
KABIR, M., Social Science
LINDSAY, D., History
MARQUIS, G., History
MOIR, R., Economics
MOSHIRI, S., Economics
NKUNZIMANA, O., French
PONS-RIDLER, S., Humanities and Languages
RIDLER, N. B., Social Science
SELIM, M., Economics
SNOOK, B., Psychology
TAUKULIS, H., Psychology
TONER, P., History and Politics
WHITNEY, R., History
WILSON, A., Psychology

Faculty of Business:

CHALYKOFF, J.
DAVIS, C. H.
DAVIS, G.
GILBERT, E.
MINER, F. C.
PIKE, E.
ROUMI, E.
STERNICZUK, H.
WANG, S.
WONG, J.

Faculty of Science, Applied Science and Engineering:

ALDERSON, H., Mathematical Sciences
ALDERSON, T., Mathematical Sciences
BECKETT, B. A., Physical Sciences
BOONE, C., Engineering
BUCHANAN, J., Nursing (non-professorial Head, acting)
CHOPIN, T., Biology
CHRISTIE, J., Engineering
COTTER, G. T., Engineering (Head)
DE'BELL, K., Mathematical Sciences
FEICHT, A., Chemistry (Chair.)
GAREY, L. E., Mathematics, Statistics and Computer Science
GUPTA, R. D., Mathematics, Statistics and Computer Science

HALCROW, K., Biology
HAMDAN, M., Mathematics, Statistics and Computer Science
HUMPHRIES, R., Physical Sciences
KAMEL, M. T., Mathematics, Statistics and Computer Science
KAYSER, M., Physical Sciences
LEUNG, C.-H., Physical Sciences
LITVAK, M. K., Biology
LOGAN, A., Physical Sciences
MCCULLUM, D., Engineering
MACDONALD, B., Biology
MACLATCHY, D., Biology
MAHANTI, P., Computer Science and Applied Statistics
NUGENT, L., Nursing
PRASAD, R. C., Engineering
PUNNEN, A., Mathematical Sciences
RILEY, E., Engineering
ROCHETTE, R., Biology
SHAW, R., Computer Science and Applied Statistics
SOLLOWS, K., Engineering
STOICA, G., Mathematical Sciences
TERHUNE, J. M., Biology
THOMPSON, C., Computer Science and Applied Statistics (Chair.)
WAGSTAFF, J., Physical Sciences
WALTON, B., Engineering
WILSON, L., Physical Sciences
XU, L.-H., Physical Sciences

ATTACHED COLLEGES

Renaissance College: Dean Dr PIERRE ZUNDEL.

Saint John College: e-mail sjcol@unbsj.ca.

FEDERATED UNIVERSITY

St Thomas University: Fredericton, NB; f. 1910; Pres. DANIEL O'BRIEN.

NIPISSING UNIVERSITY

100 College Dr., Box 5002, North Bay, ON P1B 8L7

Telephone: (705) 474-3450
Fax: (705) 495-1772
E-mail: liaison@nipissingu.ca
Internet: www.nipissingu.ca

Founded 1967 as Nipissing College, affiliated to Laurentian Univ. of Sudbury; merged with North Bay Teachers' College 1973, present status and name 1992
Academic year: September to August
Chancellor: DAVID B. LIDDLE
Pres.: Dr DENNIS R. MOCK
Vice-Pres. of Academic Affairs and Research: Dr. PETER RICKETTS
Vice-Pres. of Admin. and Finance: VICKY PAINE-MANTHA
Dean of Applied and Professional Studies: Dr. RICK VANDERLEE
Dean of Arts and Science: Dr CRAIG COOPER
Dean of Education: Dr RON WIDERMAN
Registrar: ANDREA ROBINSON
Exec. Dir. for Library Services: BRIAN NETTLEFOLD

Number of teachers: 170
Number of students: 7,170

UNIVERSITY OF NORTHERN BRITISH COLUMBIA

3333 University Way, Prince George, BC V2N 4Z9

Telephone: (250) 960-5555
Fax: (250) 960-5543
E-mail: registrar-info@unbc.ca
Internet: www.unbc.ca

Founded 1990; full opening 1994
Language of instruction: English
Academic year: September to May (2 semesters)

Chancellor: Dr JOHN MACDONALD

Pres.: Dr GEORGE IWAMA
Provost: Dr MARK DALE
Vice-Pres. for Admin. and Finance: EILEEN BRAY
Vice-Pres. for External Relations: ROB VAN ADRICHEM
Vice-Pres. for Research: Dr GAIL FONDAHL
Registrar: JOHN DEGRACE
Univ. Librarian: NANCY BLACK
Number of teachers: 178 (full-time); 204 (part-time)
Number of students: 4,177

DEANS

College of Arts, Social and Health Sciences: Dr JOHN YOUNG
College of Science and Management: Dr WILLIAM McGILL
Graduate Programs: Dr IAN HARTLEY
Student Success and Enrolment Management: Dr PAUL MADAK

NOVA SCOTIA AGRICULTURAL COLLEGE

Truro, NS B2N 5E3
Telephone: (902) 893-6722
Fax: (902) 895-5529
E-mail: reg@nsac.ns.ca
Internet: www.nsac.ns.ca
Founded 1905
Under the direction of the Nova Scotia Department of Agriculture and Marketing
President: Dr PHILIP HICKS
Vice-Pres. for Academics: Dr BRUCE GRAY
Vice-President for Admin.: Dr BERNIE MAC-DONALD
Registrar: T. DOLHANTY
Librarian: B. R. WADDELL
Library of 19,000 vols
Number of teachers: 69
Number of students: 900
Publication: *NSAC College Calendar*.

NSCAD UNIVERSITY

5163 Duke St, Halifax, NS B3J 3J6
Telephone: (902) 422-7381
Fax: (902) 425-2420
E-mail: admissions@nscad.ca
Internet: www.nscad.ca
Founded 1887
Academic year: September to April
Pres.: DAVID B. SMITH
Snr Vice-Pres. for Academic Affairs and Research: KENN HONEYCHURCH
Vice-Pres. for Finance and Administration: PETER FLEMMING
Registrar: LAURELLE LeVERT
Library Dir: ILGA LEJA
Library of 50,000 vols, 220 art periodicals, 140,000 colour slides, large holding of films and video cassettes (incl. Canada Council Art Bank colln)
Number of teachers: 53
Number of students: 1,100 (800 full-time, 300 part-time)
Depts of craft, design, fine art, foundation, graduate studies, historical and critical studies, media art
Fine art studios in painting, sculpture, printmaking, ceramics, weaving, video, film, woodworking and metalworking, textiles, fashion, jewellery, photography, digital media; undergraduate programmes include: Bachelor of Arts with major in art history; Bachelor of Design with majors in interdisciplinary design or international major in graphic design, and Bachelor of Fine Arts with majors in interdisciplinary pre-teacher education, ceramics, film, fine art, intermedia, jewellery design and metalwork, photography and textiles; current graduate-level programmes: Master of Design, Master of Design International and Master of Fine Arts.

UNIVERSITY OF OTTAWA

550 Cumberland St, Ottawa, ON K1N 6N5
Telephone: (613) 562-5700
Fax: (613) 562-5103
Internet: www.uottawa.ca
Founded 1848
Independent, provincially assisted
Languages of instruction: French, English
Academic year: September to August (undergraduate 2 semesters, graduate 3 terms)
Chancellor: HUGUETTE LABELLE
Pres. and Vice-Chancellor: ALLAN ROCK (acting)
Vice-Pres. for Academic Affairs: ROBERT MAJOR
Vice-Pres. for Research: MONA NEMER
Vice-Pres. for Resources: VICTOR SIMON
Vice-Pres. for Univ. Relations: (vacant)
Asst Vice-Pres. for Strategic Enrolment Management and Registrar: FRANÇOIS CHAPLEAU
Sec.-Gen.: PIERRE-YVES BOUCHER
Librarian: LESLIE WEIR
Library: see under Libraries and Archives
Number of teachers: 1,737 (936 full-time, 801 part-time)
Number of students: 36,460 (29,800 full-time, 6,660 part-time)

DEANS

Faculty of Arts: GEORGE LANG
Faculty of Education: MARIE JOSÉE BERGER
Faculty of Engineering: CLAUDE LAGUE
Faculty of Health Sciences: DENIS PRUD'HOMME
Faculty of Law: SEBASTIAN GRAMMOND (Acting Dean, Civil Law: BRUCE FELDTHUSEN (Common Law)
Faculty of Medicine: JACQUES E. BRADWEJN
Faculty of Science: ANDRÉ DABROWSKI
Faculty of Social Sciences: FRANCOIS HOULE
Faculty of Graduate and Post-doctoral Studies: GARY SLATER
Telfer School of Management: MICHEÁL J. KELLY

PROFESSORS

Faculty of Arts (internet www.uottawa.ca/academic/arts):

BARBIER, J. A., History
BEHIELS, M. D., History
BERTHIAUME, P., French Literature
BRISSET, A., Translation and Interpretation
BURGESS, R., Classics
CARLSON, D., English
CASTILLO DURANTE, D., French Literature
CHILDS, D., English Literature
CHOQUETTE, R., Religious Studies
CLAYTON, J. D., Russian
CRAM, R., Music
DAIGLE, J.-G., History
DAVIS, D. F., History
DE BRUYN, F., English
DELISLE, J., Translation and Interpretation
DONSKOV, A., Russian
EGERVARI, T., Visual Arts
FERGUSON, S., Communication
FERRIS, I., English
FLOYD, C., Music
FORGET, D., French Literature
FRENCH, H. M., Geography
FROEHLICH, A. J. P., Theatre
GAFFIELD, C. M., History
GAJEWSKI, K., Geography
GELLMAN, S., Music
GEURTS, M.-A., Geography
GILBERT, A., Geography
GIROU-SWIDERSKI, M., French Literature

GOLDENBERG, N., Religious Studies
GOODLUCK, H., Linguistics
GRISE, Y., French Literature
HIRSCHBUHLER, P., Linguistics
HUNTER, D. G., Philosophy
IMBERT, P. L., French Literature
JARRAWAY, D., English Literature
JOHNSON, P. G., Geography
KILMER, M. F., Classics and Religious Studies
KUNSTMANN, P. M. F., French Literature
LABELLE, N., Music
LA BOSSIÈRE, C. R., English Literature
LACHANCE, P. F., History
LAFON, D., French Literature
LANGLOIS, A., Geography
LAPIERRE, A., Linguistics
LAURIOL, B., Geography
LEMELIN, S., Music
LEPAGE, Y. G., French Literature
LEVY, P., Communication
LEWKOWICZ, A. G., Geography
LONDON, A., English Literature
LUGG, A. M., Philosophy
LYNCH, G., English
MAKARYK, I. R., English
MANGANIELLO, D., English
MAYNE, S., English
MERKLEY, P., Music
MOSER, W., Modern Languages and Literature
MOSS, J., English
MUNOZ-LICERAS, J., Modern Languages and Literature
PIVA, M., History
POPLACK, S., Linguistics
PUMMER, R. E., Religious Studies
RADLOFF, B., English
RAMPTON, D. P., English
REID, L., Visual Arts
RIVERO, M. L., Linguistics
ROBERTS, R. P., Translation and Interpretation
RUANO DE LA HAZA, J., Modern Languages and Literature
STROCCHI, L. G., Modern Languages and Literature
SEGUIN, H., Second Language Institute
STAINES, D., Arts
STICH, K. P., English
STOLARIK, M. M., History
VAILLANCOURT, P.-L., French Literature
VANDENDORPE, C., French Literature
VILLA, B. L., History
VON MALTZAHN, N., English
WELLAR, B. S., Geography
WESCHE, M. B., Centre for Second Language Learning
WILSON, K. G., English
YARDLEY, J. C., Classics

Faculty of Education (internet www.uottawa.ca/academic/education):

BÉLAIR, L.
BERGER, M.-J.
BOURDAGES, J. J.
COOK, S.
COUSINS, B.
FORGETTE-GIROUX, R.
FORTIN, J.-C.
GAGNE, E.
GIROUX, A.
HERRY, Y.
JEFFERSON, A. L.
LAVEAULT, D.
LEBLANC, R. N.
MacDONALD, C.
MASNY, D.
MICHAUD, J. P.
ST-GERMAIN, M.
TAYLOR, M.

Faculty of Engineering (internet www.eng.uottawa.ca):

ABOULNASR, T. T., Engineering
ADAMOWSKI, K., Civil Engineering
CHENG, S.-C., Mechanical Engineering

DHILLON, B. S., Engineering Management
DROSTE, R. L., Civil Engineering
EVGIN, E., Civil Engineering
FAHIM, A. E., Mechanical Engineering
GARDNER, N. J., Civil Engineering
GARGA, V. K., Civil Engineering
HADDAD, Y. M., Mechanical Engineering
HALLETT, W. L. H., Mechanical Engineering
KENNEDY, K. J., Civil Engineering
LIANG, M., Mechanical Engineering
MCLEAN, D. D., Chemical Engineering
MUNRO, M. B., Mechanical Engineering
NARBAITZ, R. M., Civil Engineering
NEALE, G. H., Chemical Engineering
NECSULESCU, D.-S., Engineering Management
REDEKOP, D., Mechanical Engineering
SAATCIOGLU, M., Civil Engineering
TANAKA, H., Engineering
TAVOULARIS, S., Mechanical Engineering
THIBAULT, J., Chemical Engineering
TOWNSEND, D. R., Civil Engineering

School of Information Technology and Engineering:

BOCHMANN, G. V.
CADA, M.
CHOUINARD, J.-Y.
DELISLE, G. Y.
DUBOIS, E.
GEORGANAS, N. D.
GIBBONS, D.-T.
HALL, T.
IONESCU, D.
KARMOUCH, A.
MCNAMARA, D. A.
MATWIN, S. J.
MOUFTAH, H. T.
OROZCO, B.-L.
PETRIU, E.
PROBERT, R. L.
RAYMOND, J.
SKUCE, D. R.
STOJMENOVIC, I.
SZPAKOWICZ, S.
URAL, H.
YANG, O. W.
YONGACOGLU, A. M.

Faculty of Health Sciences

School of Human Kinetics:

HARVEY, J.
LAMONTAGNE, M.
ORLICK, T. D.
RAIL, G.
ROBERTSON, G. E.
TRUDEL, P.

School of Nursing:

CRAGG, E. C.
EDWARDS, N.
FOTHERGILL-BOURBONNAIS, F.
O'CONNOR, A.

School of Rehabilitation Sciences:

DURIEUX-SMITH, A., Audiology and Speech-language Pathology

Faculty of Law (internet www.uottawa.ca/academic/droit-law):

Civil Law Section:

ARCHAMBAULT, J.-D.
BEAULNE, J.
BELLEAU, C.
BISSON, A.-F.
BOIVIN, M.
BOUDREAULT, M.
BRAEN, A.
DUPLESSIS, Y.
EMANUELLI, C.
GRONDIN, R.
JODOUIN, A.
LACASSE, J.-P.
MORIN, M.
PELLETIER, B.
PROULX, D.
VINCELETTE, D.

Common Law Section:

DES ROSIERS, N.
JACKMAN, M.
KRISHNA, V.
MCRAE, D. M.
MAGNET, J. E.
MANWARING, J. A.
MENDES, E. P.
MORSE, B. W.
PACIOCCO, D. M.
PERRET, L.
RATUSHNY, E. J.
RODGERS, S.
SHEEHY, E.
SULLIVAN, R.
ZWEIBEL, E.

Faculty of Management:

ADJAOUD, F.
CALVET, A. L.
CARO, D. H. J.
DE LA MOTHE, J.
DOUTRIAUX, J.
GANDHI, D. K.
GOH, S.
HENAULT, G. M.
HENIN, C. G.
JABES, J.
KELLY, M. J.
KERSTEN, G.
KINDRA, G. S.
LANE, D.
MANGA, P.
MICHALOWSKI, W.
NASH, J. C.
SIDNEY, J. B.
WRIGHT, D. J.
ZEGHAL, D.
ZUSSMAN, D.

Faculty of Medicine (internet www.uottawa.ca/academic/med):

ALTOSAAR, I., Biochemistry, Microbiology and Immunology
ANDERSON, P. J., Biochemistry, Microbiology and Immunology
BAENZIGER, J., Biochemistry, Microbiology and Immunology
BERNATCHEZ-LEMAIRE, I., Cellular and Molecular Medicine (Pharmacology)
BROWN, E., Biochemistry, Microbiology and Immunology
CHAN, A. C., Biochemistry, Microbiology and Immunology
CHEN, Y., Epidemiology and Community Medicine
CHEUNG, D. W., Cellular and Molecular Medicine (Pharmacology)
DE BOLD, A. J., Pathology and Laboratory Medicine
DILLON, J. R., Biochemistry, Microbiology and Immunology
DIMOCK, K. D., Biochemistry, Microbiology and Immunology
FRANKS, D., Pathology and Laboratory Medicine
FRYER, J. N., Cellular and Molecular Medicine (Anatomy)
GELFAND, T., History of Medicine
GIBB, W., Obstetrics and Gynaecology
HACHE, R. J. G., Medicine
HAKIM, A. M., Medicine
HÉBERT, R., Medicine
HINCKE, M., Cellular and Molecular Medicine (Anatomy)
JASMIN, B. J., Cellular and Molecular Medicine (Physiology)
KACEW, S., Cellular and Molecular Medicine (Pharmacology)
KRANTIS, A., Cellular and Molecular Medicine (Physiology)
KREWSKI, D., Medicine
LABOW, R., Surgery
LEMAIRE, S., Cellular and Molecular Medicine (Pharmacology)
MCBURNEY, M. W., Medicine

MCDOWELL, I. W., Epidemiology and Community Medicine
MALER, LEONARD, Cellular and Molecular Medicine (Anatomy)
MARCEL, Y. L., Pathology and Laboratory Medicine
MARSHALL, K. C., Cellular and Molecular Medicine (Physiology)
MILNE, R. W., Pathology and Laboratory Medicine
MUSSIVAND, T. F., Surgery
NAIR, R. C., Epidemiology and Community Medicine
PARRY, D. J., Cellular and Molecular Medicine (Physiology)
PETERSON, L. M., Cellular and Molecular Medicine (Physiology)
ROUSSEAUX, COLIN, Cellular and Molecular Medicine
ST JOHN, R. K., Medicine
SATTAR, S. A., Biochemistry, Microbiology and Immunology
SPASOFF, R. A., Epidemiology and Community Medicine
STAINES, W., Cellular and Molecular Medicine (Anatomy)
TANPHAICHITR, N., Obstetrics and Gynaecology
TSANG, B. K., Obstetrics and Gynaecology
TUANA, B. S., Cellular and Molecular Medicine (Pharmacology)
WALKER, P., Medicine
WELLS, G., Medicine
YAO, Z., Biochemistry, Microbiology and Immunology

Faculty of Science (internet www.science.uottawa.ca):

ALVO, M., Mathematics and Statistics
ARNASON, J. T., Biology
BAO, X., Physics
BRABEC, T., Physics
BONEN, L., Biology
BURGESS, W. D., Mathematics and Statistics
CASTONGUAY, C., Mathematics and Statistics
CHAPLEAU, F., Biology
CLARK, I. B., Earth Sciences
CURRIE, D. J., Biology
DABROWSKI, A. R., Mathematics and Statistics
DETELLIER, C. G., Chemistry
DURST, T., Chemistry
FALLIS, A. G., Chemistry
FENWICK, J. C., Biology
FOWLER, A., Earth Sciences
GAMBAROTTA, S., Chemistry
GIORDANO, T., Mathematics and Statistics
HANDELMAN, D. E., Mathematics and Statistics
HATTORI, K., Earth Sciences
HICKEY, D. A., Biology
HODGSON, R. J. W., Physics
IVANOFF, G. B., Mathematics and Statistics
JOOS, B., Physics
KAPLAN, H., Chemistry
LALONDE, A. E., Earth Sciences
LEAN, D. R., Biology
LONGTIN, A., Physics
MCDONALD, D. R., Mathematics and Statistics
MOON, T. W., Biology
MORIN, A., Biology
NEHER, E., Mathematics and Statistics
PERRY, S. F., Biology
PESTOV, V., Mathematics and Statistics
PHILOGÈNE, B. J. R., Biology
RACINE, M. L., Mathematics and Statistics
RANCOURT, D., Physics
RICHESON, D., Chemistry
ROSSMAN, W., Mathematics and Statistics
ROY, D., Mathematics and Statistics
SANKOFF, D., Mathematics and Statistics
SAYARI, A. H., Chemistry
SCAIANO, J. C., Chemistry

SCOTT, P. J., Mathematics and Statistics
STADNIK, Z., Physics
TEITELBAUM, H., Chemistry
VEIZER, J., Earth Sciences

Faculty of Social Sciences (internet www
.uottawa.ca/academic/socsci):
ANDREW, C. P., Political Science
BEAUCHESNE, L., Criminology
CARDINAL, L., Political Science
CELLARD, A., Criminology
CHOSSUDOVSKY, M., Economics
COULOMBE, S., Economics
CRELINSTEN, R., Criminology
DA ROSA, V. M. P., Sociology
DENIS, A. B., Sociology
DENIS, S., Political Science
GABOR, T., Criminology
GRENIER, G., Economics
HASTINGS, J. R., Criminology
HAVET, J. L., Sociology
LACZKO, L., Sociology
LAUX, J. K., Political Science
LAVOIE, M., Economics
LOS, M. J., Criminology
MELLOS, K., Political Science
MOGGACH, D., Political Science
MURPHY, R. J., Sociology
PIRES, A., Criminology
POULIN, R., Sociology
ROBERTS, J., Criminology
SECCARECCIA, M., Economics
TAHON, M.-B., Sociology
THÉRIAULT, J. Y., Sociology
TREMBLAY, M., Political Science
WALLER, I., Criminology

School of Psychology:
BIELAJEW, C.
CAMPBELL, K. B.
CAPPELIEZ, P.
CLEMENT, R.
FIRESTONE, P.
FLYNN, R.
FOURIEZOS, G.
GIRODO, M.
HUNSLEY, J.
JOHNSON, S.
LEDINGHAM, J.
LEE, C.
LEMYRE, L.
MERALI, Z.
MESSIER, C.
MOOK, B.
PELLETIER, L.
RITCHIE, P.
SARRAZIN, G.
SCHNEIDER, B.
TOUGAS, F.
WHIFFEN, V.
YOUNGER, A.

School of Social Work:
CODERRE, C.
HOME, A. M.
ST-AMAND, N.
TOUGAS, F.

FEDERATED UNIVERSITY

Saint Paul University: 223 Main St,
Ottawa, ON K1S 1C4; internet www
.ustpaul.ca; Rector Rev. Prof. DALE SCHLITT

DEANS

Faculty of Canon Law: Rev. ROCH PAGÉ
Faculty of Human Sciences: JEAN-GUY GOU-
LET
Faculty of Theology: Rev. DAVID PERRIN

PROFESSORS

Faculty of Canon Law:
HUELS, J.
MENDONÇA, REV. A.
MORRISEY, REV. F. G.
PAGE, R.

Faculty of Human Sciences:
BÉGIN, B.
DAVIAU, P.
GOULET, J.-G.
MEIER, A.
MOOREN, T.
RIGBY, P.
Faculty of Theology:
COYLE, J. K.
DUMAIS, REV. M.
MARTÍNEZ DE PISÓN, R.
MELCHIN, K.
PAMBRUN, J.
PEELMAN, REV. A.
PROVENCHER, REV. M. N.
SCHLITT, REV. D. M.
VAN DEN HENGEL, REV. J.
WALTERS, G.

UNIVERSITY OF PRINCE EDWARD ISLAND

550 University Ave, Charlottetown, PE C1A
4P3
Telephone: (902) 566-0439
Fax: (902) 566-0795
E-mail: registrar@upei.ca
Internet: www.upei.ca
Founded 1969 by merger of St Dunstan's
University (f. 1855) and Prince of Wales
College (f. 1834)
Academic year: September to May
Chancellor: NORMAN WEBSTER
Pres. and Vice-Chancellor: H. WADE MacLAU-
CHLAN
Vice-Pres. for Academic Devt: VIANNE TIM-
MONS
Vice-Pres. for Finance and Facilities: GARRY
G. BRADSHAW
Registrar: KAREN SMYTHE
Univ. Librarian: LYNN MURPHY
Library: see Libraries
Number of teachers: 192 full-time
Number of students: 3,410 full-time

DEANS

Faculty of Arts: RICHARD KURIAL
Faculty of Business Administration: Dr
ROBERTA MacDONALD
Faculty of Education: Dr GRAHAM PIKE
Faculty of Nursing: Dr IRENE COULSON
Faculty of Science: Dr ROGER GORDON
Faculty of Veterinary Medicine: Dr TIMOTHY
OGILVIE

UNIVERSITÉ DU QUÉBEC

475 rue de l'Eglise, Québec, QC G1K 9H7
Telephone: (418) 657-3551
Fax: (418) 657-2132
E-mail: info-uq@uqss.uquebec.ca
Internet: www.uquebec.ca
Founded 1968
Language of instruction: French
Pres.: PIERRE MOREAU
Vice-Pres. for Admin. and Finance: LOUIS
GENDREAU
Vice-Pres. for Teaching and Research:
DANIEL CODERRE
Sec.-Gen.: MICHEL QUIMPER
Dir of Public Relations: (vacant)
Librarian: (vacant)
Library: Library (network) of 2,340,000 vols
Number of teachers: 2,200
Number of students: 84,700
Publications: *Inventaire de la Recherche
Subventionnée et Commanditée* (1 a year),
Réseau (4 a year).

CONSTITUENT INSTITUTIONS

**Université du Québec en Abitibi-
Témiscamingue**
445 blvd de l'Université, Rouyn-Noranda, QC
J9X 5E4
Telephone: (819) 762-2922
Fax: (819) 797-4727
E-mail: registraire@uqat.ca
Internet: www.uqat.uquebec.ca
Founded 1981 as Centre d'études universi-
taires, name changed 1984
Rector: JULES ARSENAULT
Vice-Rector for Resources: L. BERGERON
Vice-Rector for Teaching and Research:
ROGER CLAUX
Registrar: N. MURPHY
Dir of Services: N. MURPHY
Sec.-Gen.: J. TURGEON
Librarian: A. BÉLAND
Library of 201,000 vols
Number of teachers: 75
Number of students: 911 full-time
Number of students: 1,932 part-time

Université du Québec à Chicoutimi
555 blvd de l'Université, Chicoutimi, QC
G7H 2B1
Telephone: (418) 545-5011
Fax: (418) 545-5049
E-mail: regist@uqac.ca
Internet: www.uqac.ca
Founded 1969
State control
Language of instruction: French
Academic year: September to April
Rector: MICHEL BELLEY
Sec.-Gen.: MARTIN CÔTÉ
Registrar: CLAUDIO ZOCCASTELLO
Librarian: GILLES CARON
Library of 250,000 vols
Number of teachers: 225
Number of students: 6,500 (3,200 full-time,
3,300 part-time)
Publication: *UQACtualité* (4 a year).

Université du Québec en Outaouais
CP 1250, Succursale Hull, Gatineau, QC J8X
3X7
Telephone: (819) 595-3900
Fax: (819) 595-1835
E-mail: registraire@uqo.ca
Internet: www.uqo.ca
Founded 1970
Language of instruction: French
Academic year: September to June
Rector: JEAN VAILLANCOURT
Sec.-Gen.: LUC MAURICE
Registrar: ROBERT BONDAZ
Librarian: HÉLÈNE LAROUCHE
Library of 210,000 vols
Number of teachers: 184
Number of students: 5,492 (2,884 full-time,
2,608 part-time)
Publication: *Savoir Outaouais* (3 a year).

Université du Québec à Montréal
CP 8888, Succ. Centre-ville, Montréal, QC
H3C 3P8
Telephone: (514) 987-3000
Fax: (514) 987-3009
E-mail: registrariat@uqam.ca
Internet: www.regis.uqam.ca
Founded 1969
Rector (vacant)
Vice-Rector for Academics and Research:
LYNN DRAPEAU
Vice-Rector for Academic Services and Tech-
nological Devt: MICHEL ROBILLARD

Vice-Rector for Human Resources and Admin. Affairs: ALAIN DUFOUR
Vice-Rector for Partnership and External Affairs: PAULE LEDUC (acting)
Vice-Rector for Strategic and Financial Planning and Gen. Sec.: LOUISE DANDURAND
Registrar: CLAUDETTE JODOIN
Librarian: JEAN-PIERRE CÔTÉ
Library of 2,388,000 vols
Number of teachers: 903
Number of students: 37,395 (18,406 full-time, 18,989 part-time)

Université du Québec à Rimouski
300 allée des Ursulines, Rimouski, QC G5L 3A1
Telephone: (418) 723-1986
Fax: (418) 724-1525
E-mail: uqar@uqar.uquebec.ca
Internet: www.uqar.qc.ca
Founded 1969
State control
Language of instruction: French
Academic year: September to April (2 semesters)
Rector: MICHEL RINGUET
Vice-Rector for Admin. and Human Resources: MARJOLAINE VIEL
Vice-Rector for Teaching and Research: JEAN-PIERRE OUELLET
Sec.-Gen.: ALAIN CARON
Librarian: DENIS BOISVERT
Library of 334,600 vols
Number of teachers: 200
Number of students: 9,000 (6,100 full-time, 2,900 part-time)
Publication: *UQAR-Info* (8 a year).

ATTACHED CENTRE
Oceanography Centre: Dir V. KOUTITONSKY.

Université du Québec à Trois-Rivières
3351 blvd des Forges, CP 500, Trois-Rivières, QC G9A 5H7
Telephone: (819) 376-5045
Fax: (819) 376-5012
E-mail: crmultiservice@uqtr.ca
Internet: www.uqtr.ca
Founded 1969
Provincial control
Academic year: September to April
Rector: GHISLAIN BOURQUE
Vice-Rector for Admin. and Finance: RENÉ GARNEAU
Sec.-Gen.: ANDRÉ GABIAS
Registrar: NORMAND SHAFFER
Library of 500,000 vols
Number of teachers: 352
Number of students: 11,427 (6,650 full-time, 4,777 part-time)
Publication: *En Tête*.

Ecole Nationale d'Administration Publique
555 blvd Charest Est, Québec, QC G1K 9E5
Telephone: (418) 641-3000
Fax: (418) 641-3060
Founded 1969
Dir-Gen.: PIERRE DE CELLES
Library of 90,000 vols
Number of teachers: 59
Number of students: 1,143

Ecole de Technologie Supérieure
1100 rue Notre-Dame Ouest, Montréal, QC H3C 1K3
Telephone: (514) 396-8800
Fax: (514) 396-8950
Internet: www.etsmtl.ca

Founded 1974
Dir-Gen.: YVES BEAUCHAMP
Library of 65,000 vols
Number of teachers: 126

INRS-Institut Armand-Frappier
531 blvd des Prairies, Laval, QC H7V 1B7
Telephone: (450) 687-5010
Founded 1938
Dir-Gen.: ALAIN FOURMIER
Library of 10,000 vols
Number of teachers: 45
Number of students: 170
Human, animal, environmental health (immunity, infectious diseases, cancer, epidemiology, biotechnologies, toxicology, pharmacodiomistry sciences).

Institut National de la Recherche Scientifique
490 de la Couronne, Québec, QC G1K 9A9
Telephone: (418) 654-2500
Fax: (418) 654-2525
Internet: www.inrs.ca
Founded 1969
Dir-Gen.: DANIEL CODERRE
Library of 58,000 vols
Number of teachers: 154
Number of students: 619 (558 full-time, 61 part-time)

Télé-université
Tour de la Cité, 2600 blvd Laurier, 7e étage, Québec, QC G1V 4V9
Telephone: (418) 657-2262
Founded 1972
Dir-Gen.: A. MARREC
Library of 12,000 vols
Number of teachers: 35
Number of students: 5,716 (258 full-time, 5,458 part-time)
Distance-learning programmes.

QUEEN'S UNIVERSITY AT KINGSTON
99 University Ave, Kingston, ON K7L 3N6
Telephone: (613) 533-2000
Fax: (613) 545-6300
E-mail: liaison@post.queensu.ca
Internet: www.queensu.ca
Founded 1841
Language of instruction: English
Academic year: September to May (2 terms)
Chancellor: Dr DAVID A. DODGE
Vice-Chancellor and Prin.: Dr DANIEL WOOLF
Rector: NICK DAY
Provost and Vice-Prin. for Academics: Dr B. SILVERMAN
Vice-Prin. for Advancement: Dr T. HARRIS
Vice-Prin. for Human Resources: R. MORRISON
Vice-Prin. for Finance and Administration: C. DAVIS
Vice-Prin. for Research: Dr K. ROWE
Registrar: J. BRADY
Librarian: PAUL WIENS
Number of teachers: 2,567
Number of students: 22,477
Publication: *Queen's Quarterly* (4 a year)

DEANS
Faculty of Engineering and Applied Science: Dr K. WOODHOUSE
Faculty of Arts and Science: Dr A. MacLEAN
Faculty of Education: Dr S. ELLIOTT
Faculty of Health Sciences: Dr R. REZNICK
Faculty of Law: W. FLANAGAN
School of Business: Dr D. SAUNDERS
School of Graduate Studies: Dr B. BROUWER
Student Affairs: Dr J. LAKER

PROFESSORS
Some staff teach in more than one faculty.

Faculty of Applied Science (Ellis Hall, Kingston, ON K7L 3N6; tel. (613) 533-2055; fax (613) 533-6500; e-mail appsci@post.queensu.ca; internet appsci.queensu.ca):
AITKEN, G. J. M., Electrical and Computer Engineering
ANDERSON, R. J., Mechanical Engineering
ARCHIBALD, J. F., Mining Engineering
BEAULIEU, N. C., Electrical and Computer Engineering
BIRK, A. M., Mechanical Engineering
BOYD, J. D., Materials and Metallurgical Engineering
BRYANT, J. T., Mechanical Engineering
CAMERON, J., Materials and Metallurgical Engineering
CAMPBELL, T. I., Civil Engineering
CARTLEDGE, J. C., Electrical and Computer Engineering
DANESHMEND, L. K., Mining Engineering
DAUGULIS, A. J., Chemical Engineering
GRANDMAISON, E. W., Chemical Engineering
HALL, K., Civil Engineering
HAMACHER, V. C., Electrical and Computer Engineering
HARRIS, T. J., Chemical Engineering
JESWIET, J., Mechanical Engineering
JORDAN, M. P., Mechanical Engineering
KAMPHUIS, J. W., Civil Engineering
KORENBERG, M., Electrical and Computer Engineering
KRSTIC, V. D., Materials and Metallurgical Engineering
KUEPER, B., Civil Engineering
McKINNON, S. D., Mining Engineering
McLANE, P. J., Electrical and Computer Engineering
MITCHELL, R. J., Civil Engineering
MOUFTAH, H. T., Electrical and Computer Engineering
MULVENNA, C. A., Mechanical Engineering
NEUFELD, R. J., Chemical Engineering
OOSTHUIZEN, P. H., Mechanical Engineering
PICKLES, C. A., Materials and Metallurgical Engineering
POLLARD, A., Mechanical Engineering
ROSE, K., Civil Engineering
SAIMOTO, S., Materials and Metallurgical Engineering
SEN, P. C., Electrical and Computer Engineering
SMALL, C. F., Mechanical Engineering
SURGENOR, B. W., Mechanical Engineering
TAVARES, S. E., Electrical and Computer Engineering
TURCKE, D. J., Civil Engineering
VAN DALEN, K., Civil Engineering
WATT, W. E., Civil Engineering
WYSS, U. P., Mechanical Engineering
YEN, W.-T., Mining Engineering

Faculty of Arts and Science (Mackintosh-Corry Hall, Room F300, Kingston, ON K7L 3N6; tel. (613) 533-2470; fax (613) 533-2067; internet www.queensu.ca/artsci):
AARSSEN, L. W., Biology
AKENSON, D. H., History
AKL, S. G., Computing and Information Science
ATHERTON, D. L., Physics
BAIRD, M. C., Chemistry
BAKAN, A. B., Political Studies
BAKHURST, D., Philosophy
BANTING, K. G., Politics
BEACH, C. M., Economics
BECKE, A. D., Chemistry
BENINGER, R. J., Psychology
BERG, M., English
BERGIN, J., Economics
BERMAN, B. J., Politics
BERNHARDT, D., Economics

BICKENBACH, J. E., Philosophy
BLY, P. A., Spanish and Italian
BOADWAY, R. W., Economics
BOAG, P. T., Biology
BOGOYAVLENSKIJ, O. I., Mathematics and Statistics
BROWN, R. S., Chemistry
BURKE, F., Film
CALLE-GRUBER, M., French
CAMPBELL, H. E. A., Mathematics and Statistics
CARMICHAEL, D. M., Geological Sciences
CARMICHAEL, H. L., Economics
CASTEL, B., Physics
CHRISTIANSON, P., History
CLARK, A. H., Geology
CONAGHAN, C. M., Politics
CORDY, J. R., Computing and Information Science
CRAWFORD, R. G., Computing and Information Science
CRUSH, J., Geography
CUDDY, L. L., Psychology
DALRYMPLE, R. W., Geology
DAVIDSON, R., Economics
DE CAEN, D. J. P., Mathematics and Statistics
DIXON, J. M., Geology
DONALD, M. W., Psychology
DUNCAN, M. J., Physics
du PREY, P. D., Art
ELTIS, D., History
ERDAHL, R. M., Mathematics and Statistics
ERRINGTON, E. J., History
FINLAYSON, J., English
FISHER, A., Music
FLATTERS, F. R., Economics
FLETCHER, R., Physics
FORTIER, S., Chemistry
FOX, M. A., Philosophy
FROST, B. J., Psychology
GEKOSKI, W. L., Psychology
GERAMITA, A. V., Mathematics and Statistics
GILBERT, R. E., Geography
GLASGOW, J., Computing and Information Science
GOHEEN, P. G., Geography
GREGORY, A. W., Economics
GREGORY, D. A., Mathematics and Statistics
GUNN, J. A. W., Politics
HAGEL, D. K., Classics
HAGLUND, D. G., Politics
HAMILTON, R., Sociology
HAMM, J.-J. N., French
HANES, D. A., Physics
HARRISON, J. P., Physics
HARTWICK, J. M., Economics
HELLAND, J., Art
HELMSTAEDT, H., Geology
HENRIKSEN, R. N., Physics
HERZBERG, A. M., Mathematics and Statistics
HEYWOOD, J. C., Art
HIRSCHORN, R. M., Mathematics and Statistics
HODSON, P. V., Biology
HOLDEN, R. R., Psychology
HOLMES, J., Geography
HUGHES, I., Mathematics and Statistics
HUNTER, B. K., Chemistry
JAMES, N. P., Geology
JEEVES, A. H., History
JIRAT-WASIVTYNSKI, V., Art
JOHNSTONE, I. P., Physics
JONKER, L. B., Mathematics and Statistics
KALIN, R., Psychology
KANI, E., Mathematics and Statistics
KILPATRICK, R. S., Classics
KNAPPER, C., Psychology
KNOX, V. J., Psychology
KOBAYASHI, A., Women's Studies
KYMLICKA, W., Philosophy
KYSTER, T. K., Geology
LAKE, K. W., Physics

LAYZELL, D. B., Biology
LEDERMAN, S., Psychology
LEGGETT, W. C., Biology
LEIGHTON, S. R., Philosophy
LELE, J. K., Politics
LESLIE, J. R., Physics
LESLIE, P. M., Politics
LEVISON, M., Computing and Information Science
LEWIS, F. D., Economics
LINDSAY, R. C. L., Psychology
LOBB, R. E., English
LOCK, F. P., English
LOGAN, G. M., English
LOVELL, W. G., Geography
LYON, D., Sociology
MACARTNEY, D. H., Chemistry
McCAUGHEY, J. H., Geography
McCOWAN, J. D., Chemistry
McCREADY, W. D., History
McDONALD, A. B., Physics
McINNIS, R. M., Economics
McKAY, I. G., History
MacKINNON, J. G., Economics
McLATCHIE, W., Physics
MacLEAN, A. W., Psychology
MacLEOD, A. M., Philosophy
McTAVISH, J. D., Art
MALCOLMSON, R. W., History
MANUTH, V., Art
MARSHALL, W. L., Psychology
MEWHORT, D., Psychology
MILNE, F., Economics
MINGO, J. A., Mathematics and Statistics
MONKMAN, L. G., English
MONTGOMERIE, R. D., Biology
MOORE, E. G., Geography
MORRIS, G. P., Biology
MUIR, D. W., Psychology
MURTY, M. R. P., Mathematics and Statistics
NARBONNE, G. M., Geology
NATANSOHN, A. L., Chemistry
O'NEILL, P. J., German
ORZECH, M., Mathematics and Statistics
OSBORNE, B. S., Geography
OVERALL, C. D., Philosophy
PAGE, S. C., Politics
PALMER, B. D., History
PEARCE, G. R. F., Sociology
PEARCE, T. H., Geology
PENTLAND, C. C., Politics
PERLIN, G. C., Politics
PETERS, R. D., Psychology
PIKE, R. M., Sociology
PLANT, R. L., Drama
PLAXTON, W. C., Biology
PRACHOWNY, M. F. J., Economics
PRADO, C. G., Philosophy
PRITCHARD, J., History
QUINSEY, V. L., Psychology
RASULA, J., English
RAY, A., Economics
REEVE, W. C., German
RIDDELL, J. B., Geography
ROBERTS, L. G., Mathematics and Statistics
ROBERTSON, B. C., Physics
ROBERTSON, R. J., Biology
ROBERTSON, R. M., Biology
ROSENBERG, M. W., Geography
SACCO, V. F., Sociology
SAYER, M., Physics
SCHROEDER, F. M., Classics
SHENTON, R. W., History
SILVERMAN, R. A., Sociology
SKILLICORN, D. B., Computing and Information Science
SMITH, G. S., History
SMITH, G. W., Economics
SMOL, J., Biology
SNIDER, D. L., Sociology
SNIECKUS, U. A., Chemistry
SPARKS, G. R., Economics
STAYER, J. M., History
STEVENSON, J. M., Physical and Health Education

STONE, J. A., Chemistry
STOTT, M. J., Physics
SYPNOWICH, C., Philosophy
SZAREK, W. A., Chemistry
TAYLOR, D. R., Physics
TAYLOR, P. D., Mathematics and Statistics
TENNENT, R. D., Computing and Information Science
THOMSON, C. J., Geology
TINLINE, R. R., Geography
VanLOON, G. W., Chemistry
VERNER, J. H., Mathematics and Statistics
WALKER, V. K., Biology
WANG, S., Chemistry
WARDLAW, D. M., Chemistry
WARE, R., Economics
WEISMAN, R. G., Psychology
WIEBE, M. G., English
WOLFE, L. A., Physical and Health Education
YOUNG, P. G., Biology
YUI, N., Mathematics and Statistics
ZAMBLE, E., Psychology
ZAREMBA, E., Physics
ZUK, I. B., Education
ZUREIK, E. T., Sociology

Faculty of Education (tel. (613) 533-6205; fax (613) 533-6203; e-mail regoff@educ.queensu.ca; internet educ.queensu.ca):

HUTCHINSON, N. L.
KIRBY, J. R.
MUNBY, A. H.
O'FARRELL, L.
RUSSELL, T.
UPITIS, R. B.
WILSON, R. J.

Faculty of Health Sciences (tel. (613) 533-2544; fax (613) 533-6884; e-mail jeb8@post.queensu.ca; internet meds.queensu.ca):

ADAMS, M. A., Pharmacology and Toxicology
ANASTASSIADES, T. P., Medicine
ANDREW, R. D., Anatomy and Cell Biology
ARBOLEDA-FLOREZ, J. E., Psychiatry
ASTON, W. P., Microbiology and Immunology
BENNETT, B. M., Pharmacology and Toxicology
BIRTWHISTLE, R. V., Family Medicine
BOEGMAN, R. J., Pharmacology and Toxicology
BRIEN, J. F., Pharmacology and Toxicology
BRUNET, D. G., Medicine
BURGGRAF, G. W., Medicine
BURKE, S. O., School of Nursing
CARSTENS, E. B., Microbiology and Immunology
CHAPLER, C. K., Physiology
CLARK, A. F., Biochemistry
COLE, S. P. C., Pathology
COTE, G. P., Biochemistry
CRUESS, A. F., Ophthalmology
DA COSTA, L. R., Medicine
DAGNONE, L. E., Emergency Medicine
DAVIES, P. L., Biochemistry
DEELEY, R. G., Pathology
DELISLE, G. J., Microbiology and Immunology
DEPEW, W. T., Medicine
DOW, K. E., Paediatrics
DUFFIN, J. M., Health Sciences
DWOSH, I. L., Medicine
EISENHAUER, E. A., Radoncology
ELCE, J. S., Biochemistry
ELLIOTT, B. E., Pathology
FERGUSON, A. V., Physiology
FISHER, J. T., Physiology
FLYNN, T. G., Biochemistry
FORD, P. M., Medicine
FORKERT, P. G., Anatomy and Cell Biology
FROESE, A. B., Anaesthesia
GORWILL, R. H., Obstetrics and Gynaecology
HALL, S. F., Otolaryngology
HEATON, J. P. W., Urology

HOLDEN, J. J. A., Psychiatry
HUDSON, R. W., Medicine
JACKSON, A. C., Medicine
JARRELL, K. F. J., Microbiology and Immunology
JHAMANDAS, K., Pharmacology and Toxicology
JONEJA, M. G., Anatomy and Cell Biology
JONES, G., Biochemistry
KAN, F. W. K., Anatomy and Cell Biology
KISILEVSKY, R., Pathology
KROPINSKI, A. M., Microbiology and Immunology
LAMB, M. W., School of Nursing
LAWSON, J. S., Psychiatry
LILLICRAP, D. P., Pathology
LUDWIN, S. K., Pathology
MCCREARY, B., Psychiatry
MAK, A. S., Biochemistry
MANLEY, P. N., Pathology
MASSEY, T. E., Pharmacology and Toxicology
MERCER, C. D., Surgery
MILNE, B., Anaesthesia
MORALES, A., Urology
MUNT, P. W., Medicine
NAKATSU, K., Pharmacology and Toxicology
NESHEIM, M. E., Biochemistry
NICKEL, J. C., Urology
NOLAN, R. L., Diagnostic Radiology
O'CONNOR, H. M., Emergency Medicine
O'DONNELL, D. E., Medicine
OLNEY, S. J., Rehabilitation Therapy
PANG, S. C., Anatomy and Cell Biology
PATER, J. L., Community Health and Epidemiology
PATERSON, W. G., Medicine
PICHORA, D. R., Surgery
POOLE, R. K., Microbiology and Immunology
PROSS, H. F., Microbiology and Immunology
RACZ, W. J., Pharmacology and Toxicology
RAPTIS, L. H., Microbiology and Immunology
REID, R. L., Obstetrics and Gynaecology
REIFEL, C., Anatomy and Cell Biology
RICHMOND, F. J., Physiology
RIOPELLE, R. J., Medicine
ROSE, P. K., Physiology
SHANKS, G. L., Rehabilitation Medicine
SHIN, S. H., Physiology
SHORTT, S. E. D., Community Health and Epidemiology
SIMON, J. B., Medicine
SINGER, M. A., Medicine
SMITH, B. T., Paediatrics
SZEWCZUK, M. R., Microbiology and Immunology
WALKER, D. M. C., Emergency Medicine
WEAVER, D. F., Medicine
WHERRETT, B. A., Paediatrics
WIGLE, R. D., Medicine
WILSON, C. R., Family Medicine

Faculty of Law (Macdonald Hall, Kingston, ON K7L 3N6; tel. (613) 533-2220; fax (613) 533-6611; e-mail llb@gsilver.queensu.ca; internet gsilver.queensu.ca/law):

ADELL, B. L.
ALEXANDROWICZ, G. W.
BAER, M. G.
BALA, N. C.
CARTER, D. D.
DELISLE, R. J.
EASSON, A. J.
HARVISON YOUNG, A.
LAHEY, K. A.
MAGNUSSON, D. N.
MANSON, A. S.
MULLAN, D. J.
SADINSKY, S.
STUART, D. R.
WEISBERG, M. A.

School of Business (Dunning Hall, Kingston, ON K7L 3N6; tel. (613) 533-2330; fax (613)

533-2013; e-mail info@business.queensu.ca; internet business.queensu.ca):

ANDERSON, D. L.
ARNOLD, S. J.
BARLING, J. I.
COOPER, W. H.
DAUB, M. A. C.
GALLUPE, R. B.
GORDON, J. R. M.
JOHNSON, L. D.
MCKEEN, J. D.
MORGAN, I. G.
NEAVE, E. H.
NIGHTINGALE, D. V.
NORTHEY, M. E.
PETERSEN, E. R.
RICHARDSON, A. J.
RICHARDSON, P. R.
RUTENBERG, D. P.
TAYLOR, A. J.
THORNTON, D. B.

School of Policy Studies (tel. (613) 533-6555; fax (613) 533-6606; e-mail policy@policy.queensu.ca; internet gsilver.queensu.ca/sps):

LEISS, W.
WILLIAMS, T. R.

School of Urban and Regional Planning (tel. (613) 533-2188; fax (613) 533-6905; e-mail williamj@post.queensu.ca; internet info.queensu.ca/surp):

LEUNG, H. L.
QADEER, M. A.
SKABURSKIS, A.

AFFILIATED COLLEGE

Queen's Theological College: Kingston, ON K7L 3N6; f. 1841; Prin. Rev. H. E. LLEWELLYN.

REDEEMER UNIVERSITY COLLEGE

777 Garner Rd East, Ancaster, ON L9K 1J4
Telephone: (905) 648-2131
Fax: (905) 648-2134
E-mail: adm@redeemer.on.ca
Internet: www.redeemer.on.ca

Founded 1976, became Redeemer College 1980, univ. status 1982, present name 2000
Committed to the advancement of Reformed Christian education in all academic disciplines
Language of instruction: English
Private control
Academic year: September to May
Pres.: Dr JUSTIN COOPER
Vice-Pres. for Academics: Dr JACOB ELLENS
Vice-Pres. for Administration and Finance: BILL VAN STAALDUINEN
Registrar: RICHARD WIKKERINK
Librarian: JANNY EIKELBOOM
Library: 100,000 items
Number of teachers: 40
Number of students: 800

FACULTY DIVISION HEADS

Faculty of Arts and Foundations: Dr DOUGLAS LONEY
Faculty of Sciences and Social Sciences: Dr DOUGLAS NEEDHAM

UNIVERSITY OF REGINA

3737 Wascana Pkwy, Regina, SK S4S 0A2
Telephone: (306) 585-4111
Fax: (306) 337-2525
E-mail: admissions.office@leroy.cc.uregina.ca
Internet: www.uregina.ca
Founded 1974 (previously Regina Campus, Univ. of Saskatchewan)
Provincial control
Language of instruction: English

Academic year: September to April (2 terms)
Chancellor: Dr WILLIAM F. READY
Vice-Chancellor and Pres.: Dr VIANNE TIMMONS
Vice-Pres. for Academic Affairs: Dr GARY BOIRE
Vice-Pres. for Admin.: DAVID BUTTON
Vice-Pres. for External Relations: BARBARA POLLOCK
Vice-Pres. for Research and Int. Affairs: Dr DAVID GAUTHIER
Univ. Sec.: ANNETTE REVET
Registrar: JUDY CHAPMAN
Librarian: CAROL HIXSON
Library: 2.4m. items, incl. 655,000 print and electronic vols and periodicals, 626,110 govt publs (incl. 296,000 in microform), 918,000 other items in microform; colln of recordings and materials in other media
Number of teachers: 468
Number of students: 12,179 (9,210 full-time, 2,969 part-time)
Publications: *Carillon* (12 a year), *Degrees* (2 a year), *Wascana Review* (2 a year)

DEANS

Centre for Continuing Education: Dr HARVEY KING (Dir)
Faculty of Arts: Dr THOMAS CHASE
Faculty of Business Admin.: ANNE LAVAK
Faculty of Education: Dr JAMES MCNINCH
Faculty of Engineering: Dr PAITOON TONTIWACHWUTHIKUL
Faculty of Fine Arts: Dr SHEILA PETTY
Faculty of Kinesiology and Health Studies: Dr CRAIG CHAMBERLIN
Faculty of Science: Dr KATHERINE BERGMAN
Faculty of Social Work: Dr DAVID SCHANTZ
Faculty of Graduate Studies and Research: Dr ROD KELLN

PROFESSORS

ALFANO, DENNIS P., Psychology
ANDERSON, LEONA, Religious Studies
ANDERSON, ROBERT, Business Admin.
ASHTON, NEIL W., Biology
ASMUNDSON, GORDON, Kinesiology and Health Studies
AUSTIN, BRYAN J., Business Admin.
BERGMAN, KATHERINE, Geology
BLACKSTONE, MARY, Theatre
BLAKE, RAYMOND, History
BRENNAN, WILLIAM, History
BRIGHAM, R. MARK, Biology
BROAD, DAVID, Social Work
CHAN, CHRISTINE, Engineering
CHANNING, LYNN, Music
CHAPCO, WILLIAM, Biology
CHERLAND, MEREDITH, Education
CHOW, SUI, Psychology
CONWAY, JOHN, Sociology and Social Studies
CRUIKSHANK, JANE, Social Work
DAI, LIMING, Engineering
DIAZ, HARRY, Sociology and Social Studies
DOLMAGE, ROD, Education
DONG, MINGZHE, Engineering
DRURY, SHADIA, Philosophy, Political Science
DURST, DOUG, Social Work
EVANS, DENNIS, Visual Arts
FARENICK, DOUGLAS, Mathematics and Statistics
FISHER, J. C., Mathematics
GAUTHIER, DAVID, Geography
GILLIGAN, BRUCE, Mathematics
GINGRICH, PAUL, Sociology and Social Studies
GRIFFITHS, JOHN, Music
GU, YONGAN, Engineering
HADJISTAVROPOULOS, HEATHER, Psychology
HADJISTAVROPOULOUS, THOMAS, Psychology
HAMILTON, HOWARD, Computer Science
HANDEREK, KELLY, Theatre
HANSEN, PHILLIP, Philosophy
HART, PAUL, Education
HAYFORD, ALISON, Sociology

HEINRICH, KATHERINE, Mathematics and Statistics
HOWARD, WILLIAM, English
HUANG, GUO, Engineering
HUBER, GARTH, Physics
IDEM, RAPHAEL, Engineering
ITO, JACK, Business Admin.
JEFFREY, BONNIE, Social Work
JIN, YEE-CHUNG, Engineering
JOHNSON, SHANTHI, English
KELLN, RODNEY, Chemistry and Biochemistry
KESTEN, CYRIL, Education
KIPLING BROWN, ANN, Education
KIRKLAND, STEPHEN, Mathematics and Statistics
KNUTTILA, K. MURRAY, Sociology and Social Studies
KORTÉ, HERBERT, Philosophy
LAVACK, ANNE, Business Admin.
LEAVITT, PETER, Biology
LEDREW, JUNE, Kinesiology and Health Studies
LEESON, HOWARD, Political Science
LENTON-YOUNG, GERALD, Theatre
LOLOS, GEORGE, Physics
LOUIS, CAMERON, English
MCINTOSH, RICHARD, Mathematics and Statistics
MACLENNAN, RICHARD, Justice Studies
MAEERS, MHAIRI (VI), Education
MAGUIRE, BRIEN, Computer Science
MALLOY, DAVID, Kinesiology and Health Studies
MARCHILDON, GREGORY, Johnson-Shoyama Graduate School of Public Policy
MASLANY, GEORGE, Social Work
MATHIE, EDWARD, Physics
MISSKEY, WILLIAM, Systems Engineering
PALMER, RONALD, Electronic Systems Engineering
PAPANDREOU, ZISIS, Physics
PARANJAPE, RAMAN, Electronic Systems Engineering
PAUL, ALEXANDER, Geography
PETTY, SHEILA, Media Studies
PFEIFER, JEFFREY, Justice, Psychology
PICKARD, GARTH, Education
PITSULA, JAMES, History
QING, HAIRUO, Geology
RAUM, J. RICHARD, Music
RENNIE, MORINA, Business Admin.
ROBINSON, ANNABEL, Classics
RUDDICK, NICHOLAS, English
SAUCHYN, DAVID, Geography
SAXTON, LAWRENCE, Computer Science
SHAMI, JEANNE, English
SHARMA, SATISH, Systems Engineering
SMYTHE, WILLIAM, Psychology
SOIFER, ELDON, Philosophy
STARK, CANNIE, Psychology
STREIFLER, LEESA, Visual Arts
SZABADOS, BELA, Philosophy
TOMKINS, JAMES, Mathematics
TONTIWACHWUTHIKUL, PAITOON, Engineering
TYMCHAK, MICHAEL, Education
WALL, KATHLEEN, English
WATKINSON, AILSA, Social Work
WEE, ANDREW, Chemistry and Biochemistry
WIDDIS, RANDY, Geography
YAKEL, NORM, Education
YANG, XUE-DONG, Computer Science
YAO, YIYU, Computer Science
ZHANG, CHANG, Computer Science
ZIARKO, WOJCIECH, Computer Science

FEDERATED COLLEGES

Campion College: 3737 Wascana Parkway, Regina, SK S4S 0A2; tel. (306) 586-4242; fax (306) 359-1200; e-mail campion.college@uregina.ca; internet www.campioncollege.sk.ca; f. 1917; library of 50,000 vols; Pres. B. FIORE; Academic Dean Dr SAMIRA MCCARTHY.

First Nations University of Canada: 1 First Nations Way, Regina, SK S4S 7K2; tel. (306) 790-5950; fax (306) 790-5994; e-mail info@firstnationsuniversity.ca; internet www.firstnationsuniversity.ca; f. 1975; library of 55,200 vols, incl. the Eeniwuk Colln of 5,000 titles, supporting research in native studies; Pres. CHARLES PRATT (acting); Vice-Pres. for Academic Affairs Dr BERNIE SELINGER.

Luther College: Regina, SK S4S 0A2; tel. (306) 585-5444; fax (306) 585-5267; e-mail lutherreg@uregina.ca; internet www.luthercollege.edu; f. 1913; Pres. Dr BRUCE PERLSON; Academic Dean Dr MARY VETTER.

ATTACHED INSTITUTES

Canadian Institute for Peace, Justice and Security: tel. (306) 585-4779; fax (306) 585-4815; internet www.uregina.ca/arts/cipjs; Dir Dr JEFFREY PFEIFER.

Canadian Plains Research Center: tel. (306) 585-4758; fax (306) 585-4699; e-mail canadian.plains@uregina.ca; internet www.cprc.caRegina; Exec. Dir Dr DAVID GAUTHIER.

Centre for Academic Technologies: tel. (306) 337-2400; fax (306) 337-2401; e-mail cat@uregina.ca; internet www.uregina.ca/cat/home.html; Dir Dr VI MAEERS.

Institut Français: Regina; tel. (306) 585-4828; fax (306) 585-5183; e-mail institut@uregina.ca; internet institutfrancais.uregina.ca/home.htm; Dir DOMINIQUE SARNY.

Organizational and Social Psychology Research Unit: tel. (306) 585-5268; fax (306) 585-4827; e-mail cannie.stark@uregina.ca; internet uregina.ca/~starkc; Dir CANNIE STARK.

Saskatchewan Institute of Public Policy: Univ. of Regina, College Avenue Campus, Regina, SK S4S 0A2; tel. (306) 585-5777; fax (306) 585-5780; e-mail sipp@uregina.ca; internet www.uregina.ca/sipp; Dir IAN PEACH.

Saskatchewan Instructional Development and Research Unit of the Faculty of Education: tel. (306) 585-4537; e-mail contactus@education.uregina.ca; internet education.uregina.ca/index.php?id=38; f. 1985; Dir Dr MICHAEL TYMCHAK.

Saskatchewan Population Health and Evaluation Research Unit (SPHERU): tel. (306) 585-5674; fax (306) 585-5694; e-mail spheru@uregina.ca; internet www.spheru.ca; Dir Dr GEORGE MASLANY (acting).

Social Policy Research Unit: Faculty of Social Work, Univ. of Regina, Regina, SK S4S 0A2; tel. (306) 585-5643; fax (306) 585-5408; e-mail social.policy@uregina.ca; Dir Dr GARSON HUNTER.

Teaching Development Centre: Dir J. MCNINCH.

ROYAL MILITARY COLLEGE OF CANADA

POB 17000 Stn Forces, Kingston, ON K7K 7B4

Telephone: (613) 541-6000
Fax: (613) 542-3565
E-mail: liaison@rmc.ca
Internet: www.rmc.ca

Founded 1876
Languages of instruction: English, French
Academic year: September to May

Chancellor and Pres.: The Min. of Nat. Defence
Commandant: Brig. Gen. J. M. J. LECLERC
Prin. and Director of Studies: Dr J. S. COWAN
Registrar: Cdr DEBORAH A. WILSON
Director of Cadets: Col W. N. PETERS
Chief Librarian: B. CAMERON

Library of 380,000 vols
Number of teachers: 174

Number of students: 865 (760 undergraduate, 105 graduate)

DEANS AND CHAIRMEN OF DIVISIONS

Arts: Dr J. J. SOKOLSKY
Continuing Studies: Dr M. F. BARDON
Engineering: Dr J. A. STEWART
Graduate Studies and Research: Dr B. J. FUGERE
Science: Dr R. F. MARSDEN

PROFESSORS

AKHRAS, G., Civil Engineering
AL-KHALILI, D., Electrical Engineering
ALLARD, P. E., Electrical Engineering
AMAMI, M., Business Administration
AMPHLETT, J. C., Chemistry
ANTAR, Y., Electrical Engineering
BARDON, M. F., Mechanical Engineering
BARRETT, A. J., Mathematics
BATALLA, E., Physics
BATHURST, R. J., Civil Engineering
BEATY, A., Civil Engineering
BENABDALLAH, H., Mechanical Engineering
BENESCH, R., Mathematics
BENNETT, L., Chemistry and Chemical Engineering
BENSON, M., French Studies
BONESS, R. J., Mechanical Engineering
BONIN, H. W., Chemical Engineering
BONNYCASTLE, S., English
BRADLEY, P., Military Psychology and Leadership
BUCKLEY, J., Physics
BUI, T., Chemistry and Chemical Engineering
BUSSIERES, P., Mechanical Engineering
CHAUDHRY, M. L., Mathematics
CHIKHANI, A. Y., Electrical Engineering
CONSTANTINEAU, P., Politics and Economics
CREBER, K., Chemistry and Chemical Engineering
DAVIES BOUCHARD, S., Continuing Studies
DEPLANCHE, D., Electrical and Computer Engineering
DREIZIGER, N. A. F., History
DUNNETT, P., Political and Economic Science
DUQUESNAY, D., Mechanical Engineering
EDER, W. E., Mechanical Engineering
ERKI, M., Civil Engineering
ERRINGTON, J., History
FAROOQ, M., Electrical Engineering
FINAN, J., Politics and Economics
FJARLIE, E. J., Mechanical Engineering
FUGERE, J., Mathematics and Computer Science
GAGNON, Y., Politics and Economics
GAUTHIER, N., Physics
GERVAIS, R., Mathematics
GODARD, R., Mathematics and Computer Science
GRAVEL, P., Mathematics and Computer Science
HADDAD, L., Mathematics and Computer Science
HASSAN-YARI, H., Politics and Economics
HAYCOCK, R. G., History
HEFNAWI, M., Electrical and Computer Engineering
HURLEY, W., Business Administration
ION, A., History
ISAC, G., Mathematics and Computer Science
JENKINS, A. L., Engineering Management
KLEPAK, H., History
LABBE, M., Mathematics and Computer Science
LABONTE, G., Mathematics
LACHAINE, A. R., Physics
LAGUEUX, P.-A., French Studies
LAPLANTE, J. P., Chemistry
LEWIS, B., Chemistry and Chemical Engineering
LUCIUK, L., Politics and Economics
MCDONOUGH, L., Politics and Economics
MCKERCHER, B., History
MALONEY, S., War Studies

MANN, R. F., Chemical Engineering
MOFFATT, W. C., Mechanical Engineering
MONGEAU, B., Electrical Engineering
MUKHERJEE, B. K., Physics
NEILSON, K. E., History
NOEL, J.-M., Physics
POTTIER, R. H., Chemistry
QUILLARD, G., French Studies
RACEY, T. J., Physics
RANGANATHAN, S., Mathematics
REIMER, K., Chemistry and Chemical Engineering
ROBERGE, P. R., Chemistry
ROCHON, P., Physics
ST PIERRE, A., Business Administration
SCHURER, C., Physics
SEGUIN, G., Electrical Engineering
SHEPARD, T., Electrical Engineering
SHOUCRI, R. M., Mathematics
SIMMS, B. W., Engineering Management
SOKOLSKY, J. J., Political Science
SRI, P. S., English
STACEY, M., Physics
STEWART, A., Civil Engineering
TARBOUCHI, M., Electrical and Computer Engineering
THOMPSON, W. T., Chemical Engineering
TORRIE, G. M., Mathematics
TREDDENICK, J. M., Economics
VINCENT, T. B., English
WEIR, R. D., Chemical Engineering
WHELAU, D., Mathematics and Computer Science
WHITEHORN, A. J., Political Science
WILSON, J. D., Electrical Engineering

ROYAL ROADS UNIVERSITY

2005 Sooke Rd, Victoria, BC V9B 5Y2
Telephone: (250) 391-2511
Fax: (250) 391-2500
E-mail: learn.more@royalroads.ca
Internet: www.royalroads.ca

Founded 1995

Pres. and Vice-Chancellor: Dr ALLAN CAHOON
Vice-Pres. for Academic Affairs and Provost: Dr PETER MEEKISON (acting)
Vice-Pres. and Chief Information Officer: DAN TULIP
Vice-Pres. for RRU Foundation and Chief Devt Officer: DAN SPINNER
Vice-Pres. for Univ. Relations: ROBERTA MASON (acting)
Univ. Librarian: (vacant)
Number of students: 3,000

DEANS

Faculty of Management: Dr PEDRO MARQUEZ
Faculty of Social and Applied Science: Dr JIM BAYER
Faculty of Tourism and Hotel Management: Dr NANCY ARSENAULT

RYERSON UNIVERSITY

350 Victoria St, Toronto, ON M5B 2K3
Telephone: (416) 979-5000
Fax: (416) 979-5221
E-mail: international@ryerson.ca
Internet: www.ryerson.ca

Founded 1948 as Ryerson Institute of Technology; became Ryerson Polytechnical Institute 1964 and Ryerson Polytechnic University 1993; present name 2001
Provincial control
Language of instruction: English
Academic year: September to April

Chancellor: G. RAYMOND CHANG
Pres. and Vice-Chancellor: SHELDON LEVY
Provost and Vice-Pres. for Academic Affairs: Dr ALAN SHEPARD
Vice-Provost for Academics: Dr MEHMET ZEYTINOGLU (acting)

Vice-Provost for Faculty Affairs: Dr MICHAEL DEWSON
Vice-Provost for Students: Dr HEATHER LANE VETERE
Vice-Provost for Univ. Planning Office: Dr PAUL STENTON
Vice-Pres. for Admin. and Finance: LINDA GRAYSON
Vice-Pres. for Research and Innovation: Dr TAS VENETSANOPOULOS
Vice-Pres. for Univ. Advancement: ADAM KAHAN
Registrar: KEITH ALNWICK
Chief Librarian: MADELEINE LEFEBVRE
Number of teachers: 771
Number of students: 24,475 (full-time)

DEANS

Faculty of Arts: Dr CARLA CASSIDY
Faculty of Business: TOM KNOWLTON
Faculty of Communication and Design: Dr DANIEL DOZ (acting)
Faculty of Community Services: Dr USHA GEORGE
Faculty of Engineering, Architecture and Science: Dr MOHAMED LACHEMI
School of Graduate Studies: Dr MAURICE YEATES
Ted Rogers School of Management: Dr KEN JONES
The G. Raymond Chang School of Continuing Education: Dr GERVAN FEARON

UNIVERSITÉ SAINTE-ANNE

Church Point, NS B0W 1M0
Telephone: (902) 769-2114
Fax: (902) 769-2930
E-mail: admission@usainteanne.ca
Internet: www.usainteanne.ca

Founded 1890
Language of instruction: French
Academic year: September to April

Chancellor: LOUIS DEVEAU
President: Dr ANDRÉ ROBERGE
Vice-Pres. for Academics: Dr NEIL BOUCHER
Registrar: MURIELLE COMEAU PÉLOQUIN
Librarian: CÉCILE POTHIER-COMEAU

Library of 84,000 vols
Number of teachers: 51
Number of students: 481

Publication: *Port Acadie* (1 a year).

ST FRANCIS XAVIER UNIVERSITY

POB 5000, Antigonish, NS B2G 2W5
Telephone: (902) 867-3931
Fax: (902) 867-5153
E-mail: pr@stfx.ca
Internet: www.stfx.ca

Founded 1853
Language of instruction: English
Academic year: September to May

Chancellor: Most Rev. RAYMOND LAHEY
President: Dr SEAN E. RILEY
Vice-Pres. for Academic Affairs: Dr RON JOHNSON
Vice-Pres. for Administration: RAMSAY DUFF
Vice-Pres. for Student Services: JANA LUKER
Vice-Pres. for University Advancement: PETER FARDY
Vice-Pres. and Director of Coady International Institute: M. COYLE
Director of University Extension: R. WEHRELL
Registrar: J. STARK
Librarian: LYNNE MURPHY

Library: see Libraries and Archives
Number of teachers: 200
Number of students: 5,200 (4,200 full-time, 1,000 part-time)

Publications: *Antigonish Review* (literary), *Xavieran Annual*, *Xavieran Weekly*

DEANS

Faculty of Arts: M. MCGILLIVRAY
Faculty of Science: E. MCALDUFF

PROFESSORS

ANDERSON, A., Earth Sciences
AQUINO, M., Chemistry
ASPIN, M., Modern Languages
BALDNER, S., Philosophy
BECK, J., Chemistry
BELTRAMI, H., Earth Sciences
BERNARD, I., Education
BICKERTON, J., Political Science
BIGELOW, A., Psychology
BILEK, L., Human Kinetics
BROOKS, G. P., Psychology
BUCKLAND-NICKS, J., Biology
CALLAGHAN, T., Psychology
CLANCY, P., Political Science
DEMONT, E., Biology
DEN HEYER, K., Psychology
DOSSA, S. A., Political Science
DUNCAN, C. M., Business Administration
EDWARDS, J., Psychology
EL-SHEIKH, S., Economics
GALLANT, C. D., Mathematics, Statistics and Computer Science
GALLANT, L., Business Administration
GALLANT, M., Human Kinetics
GARBARY, D., Biology
GERGE, A., Music
GERRIETS, M., Economics
GILLIS, A., Nursing
GRANT, J., Education
GRENIER, Y., Political Science
HARRISON, J. F., Political Science
HENKE, P., Psychology
HOGAN, M. P., History
HOLLOWAY, S., Political Science
HUNTER, D., Physics
JACKSON, W., Sociology and Anthropology
JACONO, J., Nursing
JAN, N., Physics
JOHNSON, R. W., Psychology
KLAPSTEIN, D., Chemistry
KOCAY, V., Modern Languages
LANGILLE, E., Modern Languages
LIENGME, B., Chemistry
MCALDUFF, E., Chemistry
MACCAULL, W., Mathematics, Statistics and Computer Science
MACDONALD, B., Religious Studies
MACDONALD, M. Y., Religious Studies
MACEACHERN, A., Mathematics, Statistics and Computer Science
MACFARLANE, E., Nursing
MCGILLIVRAY, M., English
MACINNES, D., Sociology and Anthropology
MADDEN, R. F., Business Administration
MARAGONI, G., Chemistry
MARQUIS, P., English
MARSHALL, W. S., Biology
MELCHIN, M., Earth Sciences
MENSCH, J., Philosophy
MILNER, P., English
MURPHY, J. B., Earth Sciences
NACZK, M., Human Nutrition
NASH, R., Sociology and Anthropology
NEWSOME, G. E., Biology
NILSEN, K., Celtic Studies
NORRIS, J., Education
ORR, J., Education
PALEPU, R., Chemistry
PHILLIPS, P., History
PHYNE, J., Anthropology and Sociology
QUIGLEY, A., Adult Education
QUINN, J., Mathematics, Statistics and Computer Science
QUINN, W. R., Engineering
RASMUSSEN, R., Human Kinetics
SCHUEGRAF, E. J., Mathematics, Statistics and Computer Science
SEYMOUR, N., Biology
SMITH, D., English
SMITH, G., Music

SMITH-PALMER, T., Chemistry
STANLEY-BLACKWELL, L., History
STEINITZ, M. O., Physics
SWEET, W., Philosophy
TAYLOR, J., English
TRITES, G., Information Systems
WALLBANK, B., Physics
WANG, P., Mathematics, Statistics and Computer Science
WEHRELL, R., Extension
WILPUTTE, E., English
WOOD, D., English
WRIGHT, E., Psychology

ATTACHED INSTITUTE

Coady International Institute: POB 5000, Antigonish, NS B2G 2W5; tel. (902) 867-3960; f. 1959; runs leadership and organization development programmes with peoples of Third World countries; diploma and certificate courses in Canada, also training courses and projects overseas; library of 7,000 vols, 90 periodicals; Dir M. COYLE; publ. *Newsletter* (2 a year).

SAINT MARY'S UNIVERSITY

923 Robie St, Halifax, NS B3H 3C3

Telephone: (902) 420-5400
E-mail: public.affairs@smu.ca
Internet: www.smu.ca

Founded 1802
Public control
Academic year: September to May

Chancellor: Dr ROBERT KELLY
Pres. and Vice-Chancellor: Dr J. COLIN DODDS
Vice-Pres. for Academics and Research: Dr DAVID GAUTHIER
Vice-Pres. for Administration: GABRIELLE MORRISON
Vice-Pres. for Finance: LARRY CORRIGAN
Assoc. Vice-Pres. and Registrar: Dr PAUL DIXON
Librarian: MARIE DE YOUNG

Library of 291,000 vols and 27,000 electronic data
Number of teachers: 246
Number of students: 8,539 (6,309 full-time, 2,230 part-time)

DEANS

Faculty of Arts: Dr ESTHER E. ENNS
Faculty of Graduate Studies and Research: Dr KEVIN VESSEY
Faculty of Science: Dr STEVEN SMITH
Sobey School of Business: Dr DAVID WICKS

PROFESSORS

AMIRKHALKHAI, S., Economics
ARYA, P. L., Economics
BARRETT, G., Sociology
BOWLBY, P., Religious Studies
BOYLE, W. P., Engineering
CATANO, V. M., Psychology
CHAMARD, J. C., Management
CHARLES, A., Finance and Management Science
CHENG, T., Accounting
CHESLEY, G. R., Accounting
CHRISTIANSEN-RUFFMAN, L., Sociology and Women's Studies
CLARKE, D., Astronomy and Physics
CONE, D., Biology
DAR, A., Economics
DARLEY, J., Psychology
DAS, H., Management
DAVIS, S., Anthropology
DEUPREE, R., Astronomy and Physics
DIXON, P., Finance and Management Science
DOAK, E. J., Economics
DODDS, J. C., Finance and Management Science
DOSTAL, J., Geology
ELSON, C., Chemistry

EMMS, R., Modern Languages and Classics
ERICKSON, P. A., Anthropology
FARRELL, A., Modern Languages and Classics
FITZGERALD, P., Management
GORMAN, B., Accounting
GUENTHER, D., Astronomy and Physics
HAIGH, E., History
HARTNELL, B., Mathematics and Computing Science
HARVEY, A., Economics
HILL, K., Psychology
HOWELL, C. D., History and Atlantic Canada Studies
KATZ, W., English
KELLOWAY, K., Management and Psychology
KIANG, M.-J., Mathematics and Computing Science
KIM, C., Marketing
KONAPASKY, R., Psychology
LANDES, R., Political Science
LARSEN, M. J., English
LEE, E., Finance and Management Science
LINGRAR, P., Mathematics and Computing Science
McCALLA, R., Geography
MacDONALD, M., Economics and Women's Studies
MacDONALD, R. A., English
McGEE, H., Anthropology
McMULLEN, J., Sociology
MICIAK, A., Marketing
MILLAR, H., Finance and Management Science
MILLS, A., Management
MILLWARD, H., Geography
MITCHELL, G., Astronomy and Physics
MORRISON, J. H., History and Asian Studies
MUIR, P., Mathematics
MUKHOPADHYAY, A. K., Economics
MURPHY, J., Religious Studies
OWEN, V., Geology
PARKER, R., English
PENDSE, S., Management
PE-PIPER, G., Geology
RAND, J., Biology
REID, J. G., History, Atlantic Canada Studies
RICHARDSON, D. H. S., Biology
SASTRY, V., Engineering
SEAMEN, A., English
SIDDIQUI, Q., Geology
STRONGMAN, D., Biology and Forensic Science
SWINGLER, D., Engineering
TARNAWSKI, V., Engineering
THOMAS, G., English
TURNER, D. G., Astronomy and Physics
TWOMEY, R. J., History
VAUGHAN, K., Chemistry
VELTMEYER, H., Sociology, International Development Studies
VESSEY, K., Biology
WAGAR, T., Management
WEIN, S., Philosophy
YOUNG, N., Accounting

UNIVERSITY OF SASKATCHEWAN

105 Administration Pl., Saskatoon, SK S7N 5A2

Telephone: (306) 966-1212
Fax: (306) 966-6730
E-mail: askus@usask.ca
Internet: www.usask.ca

Founded 1907, 2-campus institution 1967 (Saskatoon and Regina), legislation was passed in 1974 creating 2 separate univs
State control
Language of instruction: English
Academic year: September to August

Pres. and Chancellor: R. P. MACKINNON
Provost and Vice-Pres. for Academic Affairs: BRETT FAIRBAIRN
Vice-Pres. for Finance and Resources: RICHARD FLORIZONE
Vice-Pres. for Research: KAREN CHAD
Univ. Sec.: LEA PENNOCK

Registrar: R. ISINGER
Librarian: F. WINTER

Library of 2,046,000 vols
Number of teachers: 1,119
Number of students: 20,515

DEANS

College of Agriculture and Bioresources: M. BUHR
College of Arts and Science: J. R. DILLON
College of Dentistry: G. S. USWAK
College of Education: C. REYNOLDS
College of Engineering: E. BARBER
College of Graduate Studies and Research: L. MARTZ
College of Kinesiology: C. D. RODGERS
College of Law: B. BILSON
College of Medicine: W. ALBRITTON
College of Nursing: J. SAWATZKY (acting)
College of Pharmacy and Nutrition: D. K. GORECKI
College of Veterinary Medicine: C. S. RHODES
Edwards School of Business: D. TARAS

DIRECTOR

School of Physical Therapy: E. L. HARRISON

PROFESSORS

ADAMS, G. P., Veterinary Biomedical Sciences
AKKERMAN, A., Geography
ALBRITTON, W. L., Paediatrics
ALLEN, A. L., Veterinary Pathology
ALTMAN, M., Economics
ANDERSON, D. W., Soil Science
ANGEL, J. F., Biochemistry
ANSDELL, K. M., Geological Sciences
ARCHIBOLD, O. W., Geography
ATKINSON, M., Political Studies
AXWORTHY, C. S., Law
BAILEY, J. V., Large Animal Clinical Sciences
BAKER, C. G., Dentistry
BARANSKI, A. S., Chemistry
BARBER, E. M., Agricultural and Bioresource Engineering
BARBER, S. M., Large Animal Clinical Sciences
BARBOUR, S. L., Civil Engineering
BARTH, A. D., Large Animal and Clinical Sciences
BASINGER, J. F., Geological Sciences
BATTISTE, M., Educational Foundations
BAXTER-JONES, A. D. G., Kinesiology
BELL, K. T. M., Art and Art History
BELL, L. S., Art and Art History
BERENBAUM, S. L., Nutrition and Dietetics
BERGSTROM, D. J., Mechanical Engineering
BETTANY, J. R., Soil Science
BIDWELL, P. M., Languages and Linguistics
BILSON, R. E., Law
BINGHAM, W., Paediatrics
BLACKSHAW, S. L., Psychiatry
BLAKLEY, B. R., Veterinary Biomedical Sciences
BOLTON, R. J., Electrical and Computer Engineering
BONHAM-SMITH, P. C., Biology
BORSA, J., Women's and Gender Studies
BORTOLOTTI, G. R., Biology
BOWDEN, M. A., Law
BOWEN, R. C., Psychiatry
BOYD, C. W., Management and Marketing
BRAWLEY, L., Kinesiology
BREMNER, M., Mathematics and Statistics
BRENNA, D. S., Drama
BRETSCHER, P. A., Microbiology and Immunology
BROOKE, J. A., Mathematics and Statistics
BROWN, W. J., Agricultural Economics
BROWN, Y. M. R., Nursing
BUCHANAN, F. C., Animal and Poultry Science
BUGG, J. D., Mechanical Engineering
BUNT, R. B., Computer Science
BURBRIDGE, B., Medical Imaging
BURNELL, P., History
BURTON, R. T., Mechanical Engineering

Butler, L., Nursing
Calder, R. L., English
Campbell, D. C., Anaesthesia
Campbell, J., Psychology
Campbell, J. R., Veterinary Large Animal Science
Card, C. E., Veterinary Large Animal Science
Card, R. T., Medicine
Carr-Stewart, S., Educational Admin.
Carter, jr, J. A., Computer Science
Casson, A., Psychiatry
Chad, K., Kinesiology
Chapman, D., Anatomy and Cell Biology
Chartrand, P., Law
Chedrese, P. J., Obstetrics, Gynaecology and Reproductive Sciences
Chibbar, R. N., Plant Sciences
Chilibeck, P., Kinesiology
Chilton, N., Biology
Chirino-Trejo, J. M., Veterinary Microbiology
Chivers, D. P., Biology
Clarke, P. L., Industrial Relations and Organizational Behaviour
Classen, H. L., Animal and Poultry Science
Cockcroft, D. W., Medicine
Cooley, R. W., English
Cooper-Stephenson, K. D., Law
Corcoran, M., Anatomy and Cell Biology
Cotter, W. B., Law
Cotton, D. J., Medicine
Coulman, B. E., Plant Science
Crossley, D. J., Philosophy
Crowe, T. G., Agricultural and Bioresource Engineering
Csapo, G., Music
Cuming, R. C. C., Law
Cushman, D. O., Economics
Dabni, C. B., Management and Marketing
Daku, B. L. F., Electrical and Computer Engineering
Dalai, A. K., Chemical Engineering
D'Arcy, C., Psychiatry
Davis, A. R., Biology
Davis, G. R., Physics and Engineering Physics
Dayton, E. B., Philosophy
de Boer, D. H., Geography
Delbaere, L. T. J., Biochemistry
Denham, W. P., English
Denis, W. B., Sociology
Desautels, M., Physiology
Deutscher, T. B., History
Devon, R. M., Anatomy and Cell Biology
Dick, R., Physics and Engineering Physics
Dickinson, H. D., Sociology
Dickson, G., Nursing
Dillon, J. R., Biology
Dodds, D. E., Electrical and Computer Engineering
Doucette, J. R., Anatomy and Cell Biology
Dowling, P. M., Veterinary Biomedical Sciences
Duggleby, W. D., Nursing
Duke, T., Small Animal Clinical Sciences
Dust, W., Surgery
Dyck, L. E., Psychiatry
Dyck, R. F., Medicine
Eager, D. L., Computer Science
Echevarria, E. C., Economics
Ellis, J. A., Veterinary Microbiology
England, G. J., Industrial Relations and Organization Behaviour
Entwistle, G., Accounting
Ervin, A. M., Religious Studies and Anthropology
Fairbairn, B. T., History
Faried, S. O., Electrical and Computer Engineering
Faulkner, R. A., Kinesiology
Ferguson, L. M., Nursing
Findlay, L. M., English
Flannigan, R. D., Law
Flynn, M., Educational Psychology and Special Education

Forsyth, G. W., Veterinary Biomedical Sciences
Fowler, D. B., Plant Sciences
Fowler-Kerry, S. E., Nursing
Franklin, S., Geography
Fulton, M. E., Agricultural Economics
Furtan, W. H., Agricultural Economics
Gander, R. E., Electrical and Computer Engineering
George, G. N., Geological Sciences
Germida, J. J., Soil Science
Giesy, J. P., Veterinary Biomedical Sciences
Gingell, S. A., English
Goldie, H. A., Microbiology and Immunology
Gopalakrishnan, V., Pharmacology
Gordon, J. R., Veterinary Microbiology
Gorecki, D. K. J., Pharmacy
Graham, B. L., Medicine
Grahn, B. H., Small Animal Clinical Sciences
Grant, P. R., Psychology
Gray, R. S., Agricultural Economics
Greer, J. E., Computer Science
Griebel, R. W., Surgery
Gusta, L. V., Plant Sciences
Gusthart, J. L., Kinesiology
Gutwin, C., Computer Science
Haigh, J. C., Veterinary Large Animal Sciences
Haines, D. M., Veterinary Microbiology
Haines, L. P., Educational Psychology and Special Education
Hamilton, D. L., Veterinary Biomedical Sciences
Handy, J. R., History
Harding, A. J., English
Harris, D. I., Music
Harris, R. L., English
Harrison, E. L., Physical Therapy
Harvey, B. L., Plant Sciences
Haug, M. D., Civil and Geological Engineering
Hayes, S. J., Microbiology and Immunology
Hemmings, S. J., Medicine
Henderson, J. R., English
Hendry, M. J., Geological Sciences
Hertz, P. B., Mechanical Engineering
Hiebert, L. M., Veterinary Biomedical Sciences
Hill, G. A., Chemical Engineering
Hirose, A., Physics and Engineering Physics
Hobbs, J. E., Agricultural Economics
Hoeppner, V. H., Medicine
Holm, F. A., Plant Sciences
Hoover, J. N., Dentistry
Howard, S. P., Microbiology and Immunology
Howe, E. C., Economics
Hubbard, J. W., Pharmacy
Hucl, P. J., Plant Sciences
Hull, P. R., Medicine
Hurst, T. S., Medicine
Irvine, D., Family Medicine
Isaac, G., Management and Marketing
Ish, D., Law
Jackson, M. L., Veterinary Pathology
Jelinski, M. D., Large Animal Clinical Sciences
Johnston, G. H. F., Surgery
Juurlink, B. H. J., Anatomy and Cell Biology
Kalra, J., Pathology
Kasap, S. O., Electrical and Computer Engineering
Kasian, G. F., Paediatrics
Keil, J. M., Computer Science
Keith, R. G., Surgery
Kelly, I. W., Educational Psychology and Special Education
Kent, C. A., History (Acting Head)
Kerr, W. A., Agricultural Economics
Kerrich, R. W., Geological Sciences
Khachatourians, G. G., Applied Microbiology and Food Science
Khandelwal, R. L., Medical Biochemistry
Kirk, A., Medicine
Kolb, N. R., Physics and Engineering Physics

Kolbinson, D. A., Diagnostic and Surgical Sciences
Konchak, P. A., Dentistry
Kordan, B., Political Studies
Korinek, V. J., History
Koustov, A. V., Physics and Engineering Physics
Kozinski, J. A., Chemical Engineering
Krahn, J., Pathology
Kreyszig, W. K., Music
Krone, P. H., Anatomy and Cell Biology
Kuhlmann, F.-V., Mathematics and Statistics
Kuhlmann, S., Mathematics and Statistics
Kulshreshtha, S. N., Agricultural Economics
Kulyk, W. M., Anatomy and Cell Biology
Kusalik, A. J., Computer Science
Laarveld, B., Animal and Poultry Science
Laferté, S., Biochemistry
Lee, J. S., Biochemistry
Lehmkuhl, D. M., Biology
Leighton, F. A., Veterinary Pathology
Lepnurm, R., Management and Marketing
Li, P. S., Sociology
Li, X. M., Psychiatry
Llewellyn, E. J., Physics and Engineering Physics
Loh, L. C., Medical Biochemistry
Long, R. J., Industrial Relations and Organization Behaviour
Low, N. H., Applied Microbiology and Food Science
Lowry, N., Paediatrics
Lucas, R. F., Economics
Maaka, R., Native Studies
McCalla, G. I., Computer Science
McCrosky, C., Electrical and Computer Engineering
MacDonald, M. B., Nursing
MacDougall, B., Native Studies
McKay, G., Pharmacy
MacKinnon, J. C., History
McKinnon, J. J., Animal and Poultry Science
MacKinnon, R. P., Law
McLennan, B. D., Biochemistry
MacLennan, J., Professional Communication in Engineering
McMullen, L. M., Psychology
McNeill, D., Music
Majewski, M., Chemistry
Manson, A. H., Physics and Engineering Physics
Mapletoft, R. J., Large Animal and Clinical Sciences
Marciniuk, D. D., Medicine
Martin, J. R., Mathematics and Statistics
Martz, L. W., Geography
Matheson, T. J., English
Maulé, C. P., Agricultural and Bioresource Engineering
Mehta, M. D., Sociology
Merriam, J. B., Geological Sciences
Messier, F., Biology
Meyer, D. A., Archaeology
Michelmann, H. J., Political Studies
Middleton, D., Veterinary Pathology
Miket, M. J., Mathematics and Statistics
Miller, J. R., History
Misra, V., Veterinary Microbiology
Moewes, A., Physics and Engineering Physics
Monture, P. A., Sociology
Moulding, M. B., Restorative and Prosthetic Dentistry
Muhajarine, N., Community Health and Epidemiology
Muir, G. D., Veterinary Biomedical Sciences
Nazarali, A. J., Pharmacy
Neufeld, E. M., Computer Science
Norman, K. E., Law
Ogle, K. D., Family Medicine
Olatunbosun, O. A., Obstetrics, Gynaecology and Reproductive Sciences
Olfert, M. R., Agricultural Economics
Ovsenek, N. C., Anatomy and Cell Biology

PACKOTA, G. V., Dentistry
PAINTER, M., Management and Marketing
PAN, Y., Geological Sciences
PARKINSON, D. J., English
PATERSON, P. G., Nutrition and Dietetics
PATTERSON, W., Geology
PATO, M. D., Medical Biochemistry
PATRICK, G. W., Mathematics and Statistics
PEDRAS, M. S. C., Chemistry
PENG, D.-Y., Chemical Engineering
PENNOCK, D. J., Soil Science
PETERNELJ-TAYLOR, C. A., Nursing
PETRIE, L., Veterinary Large Animal Sciences
PFEIFER, K., Philosophy
PHARR, J. W., Veterinary Anaesthesiology, Small Animal Clinical Sciences
PHILLIPS, B., Management and Marketing
PHILLIPS, F., Accounting
PHILLIPS, P. W. B., Political Studies
PIERSON, R. A., Obstetrics, Gynaecology and Reproductive Sciences
POLLEY, L. R., Veterinary Microbiology
POMEROY, J., Geography
POOLER, J. A., Geography
POPKIN, D. R., Obstetrics, Gynaecology and Reproductive Sciences
POST, K., Small Animal Clinical Sciences
PRATT, B. R., Geological Sciences
PROCTOR, L. F., Curriculum Studies
PUGSLEY, T. S., Chemical Engineering
PYWELL, R. E., Physics and Engineering Physics
QUALTIERE, L. F., Pathology
QUIGLEY, T. L., Law
RALPH, E. G., Curriculum Studies
RANGACHARYULU, C., Physics and Engineering Physics
RANK, G. H., Biology
RAWLINGS, N. C., Veterinary Biomedical Sciences
REED, M. G., Geography
REEDER, B. A., Community Health and Epidemiology
REEVES, M. J., Civil and Geological Engineering
REGNIER, R. H., Educational Foundations
RELKE, D., Women's and Gender Studies
REMILLARD, A. J., Pharmacy
RENAUT, R. W., Geological Sciences
RENIHAN, P. J., Educational Administration
REYNOLDS, C., Educational Administration
RHODES, C. S., Large Animal Clinical Sciences
RICHARDSON, J. S., Pharmacology
ROESLER, W. J., Biochemistry
ROMO, J. T., Plant Sciences
ROSAASEN, K. A., Agricultural Economics
ROSENBERG, A. M., Paediatrics
ROSSER, B. W. C., Anatomy and Cell Biology
ROSSNAGEL, B. G., Crop Development Centre
ROWLAND, G. G., Plant Sciences
RUDACHYK, L., Physical Medicine and Rehabilitation (Acting Head)
RUTLEDGE HARDING, S., Pathology
ST LOUIS, L. V., Economics
SALT, J. E., Electrical and Computer Engineering
SANKARAN, K., Paediatrics
SAWATZKY, J. E., Nursing
SAWHNEY, V. K., Biology
SAXENA, A., Pathology
SCHISSEL, B., Sociology
SCHMUTZ, S. M., Animal and Poultry Science
SCHOENAU, G. J., Mechanical Engineering
SCHONEY, R. A., Agricultural Economics
SCHREYER, D., Anatomy and Cell Biology
SCHWIER, R. A., Curriculum Studies
SCOLES, G. J., Plant Sciences
SEMCHUK, K. M., Nursing
SHAND, P. J., Applied Microbiology and Food Science
SHANTZ, S., Art and Art History
SHARMA, R. K., Pathology
SHERIDAN, D. P., Medicine
SHEVCHUK, Y. M., Pharmacy
SHMON, C. L., Small Animal Clinical Sciences

SHOKER, A., Medicine
SIMKO, E., Veterinary Pathology
SINGH, B., Veterinary Biomedical Sciences
SINGH, J., Veterinary Biomedical Sciences
SINHA, B. M., Religious Studies
SMART, M. E., Small Animal Clinical Sciences
SMITH, B. L., Nursing
SMOLYAKOV, A., Physics and Engineering Physics
SOFKO, G. J., Physics and Engineering Physics
SOTEROS, C. E., Mathematics and Statistics
SPARKS, G. A., Civil and Geological Engineering
SPINK, K. S., Kinesiology
SRINIVASON, R., Mathematics and Statistics
STAMLER, L. R. L., Nursing
STEELE, T. G., Physics and Engineering Physics
STEER, R. P., Chemistry
STEEVES, J. S., Political Studies
STEPHANSON, R. A., English
STEWART, L., History
STEWART, N. J., Nursing
STOICHEFF, R. P., English
STOOKEY, J. M., Veterinary Large Animal Sciences
STORY, D. C., Political Studies
SULAKHE, P. V., Physiology
SUTHERLAND, J. K., Restorative and Prosthetic Dentistry
SUVEGES, L. G., Pharmacy
SZMIGIELSKI, J., Mathematics and Statistics
SZYSZKOWSKI, W., Mechanical Engineering
TAKAYA, K., Electrical and Computer Engineering
TANNOUS, G. F., Finance and Management Science
TAYLOR, S. M., Small Animal Clinical Sciences
TEMPIER, R., Psychiatry
TEPLITSKY, P. E., Restorative and Prosthetic Dentistry
THACKER, P. A., Animal and Poultry Science
THOMLINSON, W., Physics and Engineering Physics
THOMPSON, V. A., Psychology
THORNHILL, J. A., Physiology
THORPE, D. J., English
TOWNSEND, H. G. G., Veterinary Internal Medicine
TREMBLAY, M., Kinesiology
TYLER, R. T., Applied Microbiology and Food Science
TYMCHATYN, E. D., Mathematics and Statistics
VAIDYANATHAN, G., Accounting
VAN REES, K. C. J., Soil Science
VANDENBERG, A., Plant Sciences
VANDERVORT, L. A., Law
VERGE, V. M. K., Anatomy and Cell Biology
VON BAEYER, C. L., Psychology
WAISER, W. A., History
WALDNER, C. L., Large Animal Clinical Sciences
WALDRAM, J. B., Psychology
WALKER, E. G., Anthropology and Archaeology
WALKER, K. D., Educational Administration
WALLEY, F. L., Soil Science
WALTZ, W. L., Chemistry
WARD, A., Curriculum Studies
WARD, D. E., Chemistry
WARRINGTON, R. C., Biochemistry
WASON-ELLAM, L., Curriculum Studies
WATSON, L. G., Mechanical Engineering
WAYGOOD, E. B., Biochemistry
WEST, N. H., Physiology
WETZEL, K. W., Industrial Relations and Organizational Behaviour
WHITE, G. N., Family Medicine
WHITING, S. J., Nutrition and Dietetics
WICKETT, R. E. Y., Educational Foundations
WILSON, D. G., Veterinary Large Animal Sciences
WILSON, T. W., Medicine

WISHART, T. B., Psychology
WOBESER, G. A., Veterinary Pathology
WOODHOUSE, H., Educational Foundations
WORMITH, J. S., Psychology
WOROBETZ, L. J., Medicine
WOTHERSPOON, T. L., Sociology
XIAO, C., Physics and Engineering Physics
XIAO, W., Microbiology and Immunology
YONG-HING, K., Surgery
YU, P. H., Psychiatry
ZELLO, G. A., Nutrition and Dietetics
ZHANG, C., Mechanical Engineering
ZICHY, F. A., English
ZIOLA, B., Pathology

FEDERATED COLLEGE

St Thomas More College: 1437 College Dr., Saskatoon, SK. S7N 0W6; Pres. Rev. G. SMITH.

AFFILIATED COLLEGES

Briercrest College: 510 College Dr., Caronport, SK S0H 0S0; Pres. Rev. D. UGLEM.

Central Pentecostal College: 1303 Jackson Ave, Saskatoon, SK S7H 2M9; Pres. Rev. D. STILLER.

College of Emmanuel and St Chad: 1337 College Dr., Saskatoon, SK S7N 0W6; Principal Rev. W. D. DELLER.

Gabriel Dumont College: Exec. Dir C. RACETTE.

Lutheran Theological Seminary: 114 Seminary Crescent, Saskatoon, SK S7N 0X3; Pres. D. E. BUCK.

St Andrew's College: 1121 College Dr., Saskatoon, SK S7N 0W3; Pres. T. FAULKER.

St Peter's College: POB 10, Muenster, SK S0K 2Y0; Pres. G. KOBUSSEN.

UNIVERSITÉ DE SHERBROOKE

2500 blvd de l'Université, Sherbrooke, QC J1K 2R1

Telephone: (819) 821-7000
Fax: (819) 821-7966
E-mail: information@courrier.usherb.ca
Internet: www.usherbrooke.ca

Founded 1954
Private control
Language of instruction: French
Academic year: September to May

Chancellor: H. E. Mgr JEAN-MARIE FORTIER (Catholic Archbishop of Sherbrooke)
Rector: BRUNO-MARIE BÉCHARD
Vice-Rector for Admin.: LUCE SAMOISETTE
Vice-Rector for Personnel and Students: JEAN DESCLOS
Vice-Rector for Research: EDWIN BOURGET
Vice-Rector for Studies: DENIS MARCEAU
Sec.-Gen.: MARTIN BUTEAU
Registrar: FRANCE MYETTE
Librarian: SYLVIE BELZILE

Library of 1,676,000 vols
Number of teachers: 1,750 (650 full-time, 1,100 part-time)
Number of students: 22,272 (11,259 full-time, 11,013 part-time)

DEANS

Faculty of Administration: ROGER NOËL
Faculty of Applied Sciences: RICHARD J MARCEAU
Faculty of Education: CÉLINE GARANT
Faculty of Law: LOUIS MARQUIS
Faculty of Letters and Human Sciences: BERNARD CHAPUT
Faculty of Medicine: RÉJEAN HÉBERT
Faculty of Physical Education and Sport: PAUL DESHAIES
Faculty of Sciences: JEAN GOULET
Faculty of Theology, Ethics and Philosophy: MICHEL DION

PROFESSORS
Faculty of Administration
Accountancy:
BEAUCHESNE, A.
COMTOIS, J.
GODBOUT, R.
JOLIN, M.
LEMIEUX, P.
MENARD, P.
MORIN, R.
MORIN, R. J.
NOËL, R.

Finance:
BEN-AMOR, A.
GARANT, J.-P.
GARNIER, G.
GUÉRIN, F.
PAGE, J.
PRÉFONTAINE, J.
PREZEAU, C.

Management:
BERGERON, J.-L.
COUPAL, M.
LAFLAMME, M.
LEONARD, H.
PETIT, A.
PRÉVOST, P.
ROBIDOUX, J.
ROY, A. F.
TURCOTTE, P.

Marketing:
BOIVIN, Y.
D'ASTOUS, A.
VALENCE, G.

Quantitative Methods:
BASTIN, E.
BEAUDOIN, P.-H.
INGHAM, J.
MALTAIS, G.
THEORET, A.

Faculty of Applied Sciences
Chemical Engineering:
BOULOS, M.
BROADBENT, A. D.
CHORNET, E.
DEKEE, D.
GRAVELLE, D.
JONES, P.
THÉRIEN, N.

Civil Engineering:
AITCIN, P.-C.
BALLIVY, G.
BRUNELLE, P.-E.
GALLEZ, B.
JOHNS, K. C.
LAHOUD, A.
LEFEBVRE, D.
LEFEBVRE, G. A.
LEMIEUX, P.
LUPIEN, C.
MORIN, J.-P.
NARASIAH, S. K.
NEALE, K. W.
ROHAN, K.

Electrical Engineering and Computer Engineering:
ADOUL, J.-P.
AUBÉ, G.
BÉLAND, B.
BOUTIN, N.
DALLE, D.
DELISLE, J.
DENIS, G.
DUVAL, F.
GOULET, R.
LEROUX, A.
MORISSETTE, S.
RICHARD, S.
THIBAULT, R.

Mechanical Engineering:
BOURASSA, P.-A.

GALANIS, N.
LANEVILLE, A.
MASSOUD, M.
MERCADIER, Y.
NICOLAS, J.
PROULX, D.
ROY, C.
VAN HOENACKER, Y.

Faculty of Education
Counselling and School Administration:
DUPONT, P.
LAFLAMME, CL.
LIMOGES, J.
MARCEAU, D.
MASSE, D.
REID, A.

Pedagogy:
CORMIER, R. A.
HARVEY, V.
HIVON, R.
ROBIDAS, G.
SCHOLER, M.
SERRE, F.
STRINGER, G.

Pre-School and Primary Education:
LAFONTAINE, L.
MARTEL, G.
ROY, G.-R.
THÉRIEN, L.

Special Education:
HADE, D.
LEFEBVRE, R.
OTIS, R.
POULIN, G.
RHEAULT, M.
TARDIF, J.

Faculty of Law:
ANCTIL, J.
BERGERON, J.-G.
BLACHE, P.
BOISCLAIR, C L.
CHARRON, C.
CODÈRE, D.
DUBÉ, J.-L.
DUBÉ, M.
GAGNON, J.
KOURI, R.-P.
LAVOIE, J.-M.
MELANSON, J.
PATENAUDE, P.
PEPIN, R.
PHILIPS-NOOTENS, S.
POIRIER, M. Z.
RATTI, N.
TÉTRAULT, R.

Faculty of Letters and Human Sciences
Economics:
ASCAH, L.-G.
BASTIEN, R.
DAUPHIN, R.
HANEL, P.
LARIN, G.-N.
PELLETIER, G.-R.
ROY, G.
WENER, N.

Geography and Remote Sensing:
BONN, F.
CHOQUETTE, R.
DUBOIS, J.-M.
GAGNON, R.
GWYN, H.
MORIN, D.
NADEAU, R.
PAQUETTE, R.
POULIN, A.
POULIOT, M.

Human Sciences:
BLAIS, M.
CHAPUT, B.
CHOTARD, J.-R.
DE BUJANDA, J.-M.

DUMONT, M.
GAGNON, M.
GIROUX, L.
LACHANCE, A.-L.
LAPERRIÈRE, G.
LEGAULT, G.
LUC, L.
VALCKE, L.
VANDAL, G.

Letters and Communications:
BEAUCHEMIN, N.
BONENFANT, J.
DUPUIS, H.
FOREST, J.
GIGUÈRE, R.
GIROUX, R.
HÉBERT, P.
JONES, D.-G.
LÉARD, J.-M.
MALUS, A.
MARTEL, P.
MICHON, J.
PAINCHAUD, L.
SIROIS, A.
SUTHERLAND, R.
THEORET, M.
TREMBLAY, R.
VINET, M. T.

Psychology:
CHARBONNEAU, C.
LECLERC, G.
L'ECUYER, R.
NORMANDEAU, A.
PAYETTE, M.
ST-ARNAUD, Y.

Social Service:
ALARY, J.
LEFRANÇOIS, R.
MALAVOY, M.

Faculty of Medicine
Anaesthesia:
LAMARCHE, Y.
TÉTREAULT, J. P.

Anatomy and Cellular Biology:
BRIÈRE, N.
CALVERT, R.
MENARD, D.
NEMIROVSKY, M.-S.
NIGAM, V.-N.

Biochemistry:
BASTIN, M.
DE MÉDICIS, M.-E.
DUPUIS, G.
GIBSON, D.
GRANT, A.
LEHOUX, J.-G.
TAN, L.

Biophysics and Physiology:
PAYET, M. D.
RUIZ-PETRICH, E.
SCHANNE, O.
SEUFERT, W. D.

Cardiovascular and Thoracic Surgery:
TEIJEIRA, F. J.

Community Health:
BÉLAND, R.
IGLESIAS, R.
VOBECKY, J.
VOBECKY, J. S.

Diagnostic Radiology:
BRAZEAU-LAMONTAGNE, L.
SCHMUTZ, G.

Family Medicine:
BERNIER, R.
CAUX, R.
GRAND'MAISON, P.

General Surgery:
DEVROEDE, G.
RIOUX, A.

Medicine:

BARON, M., Internal Medicine
BEAUDRY, R., Gastroenterology
BEGIN, R., Pneumology
BELLABARBA, D., Endocrinology
BÉNARD, B., Endocrinology
CÔTÉ, M., Cardiology
DUMAIS, B., Cardiology
HADDAD, H., Gastroenterology
LONGPRÉ, B., Haematology
LUSSIER, A., Rheumatology
MARCOUX, J.-A., Infectious Diseases
MÉNARD, D. B., Gastroenterology
MÉNARD, H., Rheumatology
MONTAMBAULT, P., Nephrology
NAWAR, T., Nephrology
PÉPIN, J.-M., Internal Medicine
PIGEON, G., Nephrology
PLANTE, A., Internal Medicine
PLANTE, G.-E., Nephrology
REIHER, J., Neurology
ROCHON, M., Haematology
ROULEAU, J. L., Cardiology
TÉTREAULT, L., Internal Medicine

Microbiology:

BOURGAUX, D.
BOURGAUX, P.
THIRION, J.-P.
WEBER, J.

Nuclear Medicine and Radiobiology:

JAY-GERIN, J.-P.
SANCHE, L.
VAN LIER, J.

Nursing Sciences:

CHARTIER, L.
LALANCETTE, D.

Obstetrics and Gynaecology:

AINMELK, Y.
BLOUIN, D.
GAGNER, R.

Ophthalmology:

BRUNETTE, J.-R.

Orthopaedic Surgery:

DES MARCHAIS, J. E.

Otorhinolaryngology:

CHARLIN, B.

Paediatrics:

BUREAU, M. A.
LANGLOIS, L.
LEMIEUX, B.
PARÉ, C.
ROLA-PLESZCZYNSKI, M.

Pathology:

COTÉ, R. A.
LAMARCHE, J.
MADARNAS, P.
MASSÉ, S.

Pharmacology:

ESCHER, E.
REGOLI, G.
SIROIS, P.

Faculty of Physical Education and Sport:

BISSONNETTE, R.
CUERRIER, J.-P.
DEMERS, P. J.
DESHAIES, P.
GAUTHIER, P.
LEMIEUX, G.-B.
NADEAU, M.
NADON, R.
OUELLET, J.-G.
QUENNEVILLE, G.
ROY, R.
ROYER, D.
THERRIEN, R.
VANDEN-ABEELE, J.

Faculty of Sciences

Biology:

BEAUDOIN, A.

BEAUMONT, G.
BÉCHARD, P.
BERGERON, J.-M.
CYR, A.
LEBEL, D.
MATTON, P.
MORISSET, J.-A.
O'NEIL, L.-C.
ROBIN, J.

Chemistry:

BANDRAUK, A. D.
BROWN, G. M.
CABANA, A.
DESLONGCHAMPS, P.
GIGUÈRE, J.
JERUMANIS, S.
JOLICOEUR, C.
LESSARD, J.
MÉNARD, H.
MICHEL, A.
PELLETIER, G.-E.
RUEST, L.

Mathematics and Computer Science:

ALLARD, J.
BAZINET, J.
BELLEY, J.-M.
BOUCHER, C.
BRISEBOIS, M.
COLIN, B.
CONSTANTIN, J.
COURTEAU, B.
CUSTEAU, G.
DUBEAU, F.
DUBOIS, J.
FOURNIER, G.
GIROUX, G.
HAGUEL, J.
KRELL, M.
LEDUC, P.-Y.
MORALES, P.
SAINT-DENIS, R.
SAMSON, J.-P.

Physics:

AUBIN, M.
BANVILLE, M.
CAILLÉ, A.
CARLONE, C.
CARON, L. G.
JANDL, S.
LEMIEUX, A.
SIMARD, P.-A.
TREMBLAY, A. M.

Faculty of Theology, Ethics and Philosophy:

BÉDARD, A.
BOISVERT, L.
MELANÇON, L.
OUELLET, F.
RACINE, L.
VACHON, L.
VAILLANCOURT, R.

SIMON FRASER UNIVERSITY

8888 University Dr., Burnaby, BC V5A 1S6
Telephone: (778) 782-3111
E-mail: sfumpr@sfu.ca
Internet: www.sfu.ca
SFU Vancouver: 515 West Hastings St, Vancouver, BC V6B 5K3
Telephone: (778) 782-5000
Internet: www.sfu.ca
SFU, Surrey: 250–13450 102nd Ave, Surrey, BC V3T 0A3
Telephone: (778) 782-7400
Internet: www.sfu.ca
Founded 1963
Provincial control
Language of instruction: English
Academic year: September to August (3 terms of 4 months each)
Chancellor: Dr BRANDT C. LOUIE

Pres. and Vice-Chancellor: Dr MICHAEL STEVENSON
Vice-Pres. for Academic Affairs: Dr JON DRIVER
Vice-Pres. for Research: Dr MARIO PINTO
Registrar and Sec. of Senate: KATE ROSS
Librarian: LYNN COPELAND
Library of 1,000,000 vols
Number of teachers: 942
Number of students: 30,313
Publications: *Canadian Journal of Communication* (4 a year), *International History Review* (4 a year), *West Coast Line* (3 a year)

DEANS

Faculty of Applied Sciences: NIMAL RAJA-PAKSE
Faculty of Arts and Social Sciences: JOHN CRAIG
Faculty of Business Administration: DANIEL SHAPIRO
Faculty of Communication, Art and Technology: CHERYL GEISLER
Faculty of Education: KRIS MAGNUSSON
Faculty of Environment: JOHN PIERCE
Faculty of Health Sciences: JOHN O'NEIL
Faculty of Science: Dr MICHAEL PLISCHKE (acting)
Graduate Studies: WADE PARKHOUSE

PROFESSORS

Faculty of Applied Sciences (9861 Applied Sciences Bldg, Burnaby; tel. (604) 291-4724; fax (604) 291-5802; internet fas.sfu.ca):

School of Communication:

ANDERSON, R. S.
GRUNEAU, R.
HACKETT, R. A.
HARASIM, L. M.
KLINE, S.
LABA, M.
LEWIS, B. S.
LORIMER, R. M.
RICHARDS, W. D.
TRUAX, B. D.

School of Computing Science:

ATKINS, M. S.
BHATTACHARYA, B. K.
BURTON, F. W.
CAMERON, R. D.
DAHL, V.
DELGRANDE, J. P.
FUNT, B. V.
HADLEY, R. F.
HAN, J. W.
HELL, P.
HOBSON, R. F.
KAMEDA, T.
LI, Z. N.
LIESTMAN, A. L.
LUK, W. S.
PETERS, J. G.
POPOWICH, F.
SHERMER, T. C.
YANG, Q.

School of Engineering Science:

BIRD, J. S.
BOLOGNESI, C. R.
CAVERS, J. K.
CHAPMAN, G. H.
DILL, J. C.
GRUVER, W. A.
GUPTA, K. K.
HARDY, R. H. S.
HO, P. K. M.
HOBSON, R. F.
JONES, J. D.
LEUNG, A. M.
PARAMESWARAN, M.
PAYANDEH, S.
RAWICZ, A. H.
SAIF, M.
STAPLETON, S. P.

SYRZYCKI, M.

School of Kinesiology:
BAWA, P. N. S.
DICKINSON, J.
FINEGOOD, D. T.
GOODMAN, D.
HOFFER, J. A.
MACKENZIE, C. L.
MACLEAN, D. R.
MARTENIUK, R. G.
MORRISON, J. B.
PARKHOUSE, W. S.
ROSIN, M.
TIBBITS, G.

School of Resource and Environmental Management Programme:
DE LA MERE, W. K.
GILL, A. M.
GOBAS, F.
PETERMAN, R. M.
WILLIAMS, P. W.

Faculty of Arts (6168 Academic Quadrangle, Burnaby; tel. (604) 291-4414; fax (604) 291-3033; internet www.sfu.ca/arts):

Archaeology:
BURLEY, D. V.
DRIVER, J. C.
FLADMARK, K. R.
GALDIKAS, B. M. F.
HAYDEN, B. D.
NANCE, J. D.
NELSON, D. E.
SKINNER, M. F.

School for the Contemporary Arts:
ALOI, S. A.
DIAMOND, M.
GOTFRIT, M. S.
MACINTYRE, D. K.
SNIDER, G.
TRUAX, B. D.
UNDERHILL, O.

School of Criminology:
BOYD, N. T.
BRANTINGHAM, P. J.
BRANTINGHAM, P. L.
BROCKMAN, J.
BURTCH, B.
CHUNN, D. E.
CORRADO, R. R.
FAITH, K.
GORDON, R. M.
GRIFFITHS, C. T.
JACKSON, M. A.
LOWMAN, J.
MENZIES, R. J.
VERDUN-JONES, S. N.

Economics:
ALLEN, D. W.
BOLAND, L. A.
CHANT, J. F.
DEVORETZ, D. J.
DEAN, J. W.
DOW, G.
EASTON, S. T.
HARRIS, R. G.
JONES, R. A.
KENNEDY, P. E.
MAKI, D. R.
MUNRO, J. M.
OLEWILER, N. D.
SCHMITT, N.
SPINDLER, Z. A.

English:
COE, R. M.
DELANY, P.
DELANY, S.
DJWA, S.
GERSON, C.
MEZEI, K.
MIKI, R. A.
STOUCK, D.
STURROCK, J.

French:
DAVISON, R.
FAUQUENOY, M. C.
VISWANATHAN, J.

Geography:
BAILEY, W. G.
GILL, A. M.
HAYTER, R.
HICKIN, E. J.
PIERCE, J. T.
ROBERTS, A. C. B.
ROBERTS, M. C.

Gerontology Program:
GUTMAN, G.
WISTER, A. V.

History:
BOYER, R. E.
CLEVELAND, W. L.
DEBO, R. K.
DUTTON, P. E.
FELLMAN, M. D.
GAGAN, D. P.
HUTCHINSON, J. F.
JOHNSTON, H. J. M.
LITTLE, J. I.
PARR, J.
STEWART, M. L.
STUBBS, J. O.

Humanities:
ANGUS, I.
DUGUID, S.
DUTTON, P. E.
MEZEI, K.
WALLS, J. W.

Latin American Studies:
BROHMAN, J. A C.

Linguistics:
GERDTS, D. B.
MCFETRIDGE, P.
ROBERTS, E. W.
SAUNDERS, R.

Philosophy:
HANSON, P. P.
JENNINGS, R. E.
ZIMMERMAN, D.

Political Science:
COHEN, L. J.
COHN, T. H.
COVELL, M. A.
ERICKSON, L. J.
GRIFFIN COHEN, M. G.
HOWLETT, M.
MCBRIDE, S.
MEYER, P.
ROSS, D. A.
SMITH, P. J.
STEVENSON, H. M.
WARWICK, P. V.

Psychology:
ALEXANDER, B. K.
BOWMAN, M. L.
HART, S. D.
KIMBALL, M.
KREBS, D. L.
MCFARLAND, C. G.
MISTLBERGER, R.
MORETTI, M. M.
ROESCH, R. M.
WHITTLESEA, B. W. A.

Sociology and Anthropology:
DYCK, N.
GEE, E.
HOWARD, M.
KENNY, M.
MACLEAN, D. R.

Women's Studies:
GRIFFIN COHEN, M. G.
KIMBALL, M. M.
STEWART, M. L.
WENDELL, S.

Faculty of Business Administration (3302 Lohn Building, Burnaby; tel. (604) 291-3708; fax (604) 291-4920; internet www.bus.sfu.ca):
CHOO, E. U.
CLARKSON, P. M.
FINLEY, D. R.
GRAUER, R. R.
LOVE, C. E.
MAUSER, G. A.
MEREDITH, L. N.
PINFIELD, L. T.
POITRAS, G.
RICHARDS, J. G.
SHAPIRO, D. M.
TUNG, R. L.
VINING, A. R.
WATERHOUSE, J. H.
WEDLEY, W. C.
WEXLER, M. N.
WYCKHAM, R. G.
ZAICHKOWSKY, J. L.

Faculty of Education (8622 Education Building, Burnaby; tel. (604) 291-3395; fax (604) 291-3203; internet www.educ.sfu.ca):
BAILIN, S.
BARROW, R.
CASE, R.
DE CASTELL, S. C.
EGAN, K.
GEVA-MAY, I.
GRIMMETT, P. P.
MAMCHUR, C. M.
MARTIN, J.
OBADIA, A. A.
RICHMOND, S.
TOOHEY, K
WINNE, P. H.
WONG, B. Y. L.
ZAZKIS, R.

Faculty of Science (P9451 Shrum Science Centre, Burnaby; tel. (604) 291-4590; fax (604) 291-3424; internet www.sfu.ca/~science):

Biological Sciences:
ALBRIGHT, L. J.
BECKENBACH, A. T.
BORDEN, J. H.
BRANDHORST, B. P.
CRESPI, B. J.
DILL, L. M.
FARRELL, A. P.
GRIES, G. J.
HAUNERLAND, N. H.
LAW, F. C. P.
MATHEWES, R. W.
PUNJA, Z. K.
RAHE, J. E.
ROITBERG, B. D.
WINSTON, M. L.
YDENBERG, R. C.

Chemistry:
BENNET, A. J.
CORNELL, R. B.
D'AURIA, J. D.
GAY, I. D.
HILL, R. H.
HOLDCROFT, S.
JONES, C. H. W.
MALLI, G. L.
PERCIVAL, P. W.
PINTO, B. M.
POMEROY, R. K.
RICHARDS, W. R.
SEN, D.
SLESSOR, K. N.

Earth Sciences:
HICKIN, E. J.
ROBERTS, M. C.

Mathematics:
BERGGREN, J. L.
BORWEIN, J. M.
BORWEIN, P. B.

BROWN, T. C.
GRAHAM, G. A. C.
HELL, P.
LACHLAN, A. H.
LEWIS, A. S.
REILLY, N. R.
RUSSELL, R. D.
SHEN, C. Y.

Molecular Biology and Biochemistry:

BAILLIE, D. L.
BRANDHORST, B. P.
CORNELL, R. B.
DAVIDSON, W. S.
HONDA, B. M.
RICHARDS, W. R.
SEN, D.
SMITH, M. J.

Physics:

BALLENTINE, L. E.
BECHHOEFER, J. L.
BOAL, D. H.
BOLOGNESI, C. R.
CLAYMAN, B. P.
CROZIER, E. D.
ENNS, R. H.
FRINDT, R. F.
HEINRICH, B.
KAVANAGH, K. L.
KIRCZENOW, G.
PLISCHKE, M.
SCHEINFEIN, M. R.
THEWALT, M. L. W.
TROTTIER, H. D.
VETTERLI, M.
WATKINS, S.

Statistics and Actuarial Science:

LOCKHART, R. A.
MACLEAN, D. R.
ROUTLEDGE, R. D.
SCHWARZ, C. J.
SITTER, R. R.
SWARTZ, T. B.

ATTACHED INSTITUTES

Behavioural Ecology Research Group: tel. (604) 291-3664; f. 1989; Dir Dr L. M. DILL.

Canadian Centre for Studies in Publishing: tel. (604) 291-5240; fax (604) 291-5239; f. 1987; Dir Dr R. M. LORIMER.

Centre for Coastal Studies: tel. (604) 291-4653; fax (604) 291-3851; Dir Dr P. GALLAGHER.

Centre for Education, Law and Society: tel. (604) 291-4484; fax (604) 291-3203; f. 1984; Dir Dr W. CASSIDY.

Centre d'Études Francophones Québec-Pacifique: tel. (604) 291-3544; fax (604) 291-5932; Dir Dr G. POIRIER.

Centre for Experimental and Constructive Mathematics: tel. (604) 291-5617; fax (604) 291-4947; f. 1993; Dir Dr J. BORWEIN.

Centre for Innovation in Management: tel. (604) 291-4183; fax (604) 291-5833; Dir Dr E. LOVE.

Centre for Labour Studies: tel. (604) 291-5827; fax (604) 291-3851; Dir Dr M. LEIER.

Centre for Policy Research on Science and Technology: tel. (604) 291-5116; fax (604) 291-5165; f. 1996; Dir R. SMITH.

Centre for Restorative Justice: fax (604) 291-4140; f. 2001; Dirs Dr R. M. GORDON, Dr E. ELLIOTT.

Centre for Scientific Computing: tel. (604) 291-4819; fax (604) 291-4947; Dir Dr R. RUSSELL.

Centre for Scottish Studies: tel. (604) 291-5515; fax (604) 291-4504; Dir Dr S. DUGUID.

Centre for the Study of Government and Business: fax (604) 291-5122; e-mail csgb@csgb.ubc.ca; internet www.csgb.ubc.ca; Co-Dirs Dr T. ROSS, Dr A. R. VINING.

Centre for Systems Science: tel. (604) 291-4588; fax (604) 291-4424; Dir Dr S. ATKINS.

Centre for Tourism Policy and Research: tel. (604) 291-3103; fax (604) 291-4968; f. 1989; Dir Dr P. W. WILLIAMS.

Chemical Ecology Research Group: tel. (604) 291-3646; fax (604) 291-3496; f. 1981; Dir Dr J. H. BORDEN.

Community Economic Development Centre: tel. (604) 291-5849; fax (604) 291-5473; e-mail cedc@sfu.ca; internet www.sfu.ca/cedc; f. 1989; Dir Dr M. ROSELAND.

Cooperative Resource Management Institute: tel. (604) 291-4683; fax (604) 291-4986; f. 1998; Dir R. PETERMAN.

Criminology Research Centre: tel. (604) 291-4040; fax (604) 291-4140; f. 1978; Dir Dr W. GLACKMAN.

David Lam Centre for International Communication: tel. (604) 291-5021; fax (604) 291-5112; f. 1989; Dir Dr J. W. WALLS.

The Dialogue Institute.

Feminist Institute for Studies on Law and Society: f. 1990; Co-Dirs Dr D. CHUNN, Dr W. CHAN.

Gerontology Research Centre: tel. (604) 291-5062; fax (604) 291-5066; f. 1982; Dir Dr G. GUTMAN.

Institute for Canadian Urban Research Studies: tel. (604) 291-3515; fax (604) 291-4140; Dir Dr P. L. BRANTINGHAM.

Institute of Governance Studies: tel. (604) 291-4994; fax (604) 291-4786; Dir P. J. SMITH.

Institute for the Humanities: tel. (604) 291-5516; fax (604) 291-5788; Dir Dr D. GRAYSTON.

Institute of Micromachine and Microfabrication Research: tel. (604) 291-4971; fax (604) 291-4951; Dir Dr A. M. PARAMESWARAN.

Institute for Studies in Criminal Justice Policy: tel. (604) 291-4040; fax (604) 291-4140; f. 1980; Dir Dr M. A. JACKSON.

Institute for Studies in Teacher Education: tel. (604) 291-4937; fax (604) 291-3203; Co-Dirs P. GRIMMETT, Dr M. F. WIDEEN.

International Centre for Criminal Law Reform and Criminal Justice Policy: tel. (604) 822-9875; fax (604) 822-9317; f. 1991; Exec. Dir F. M. GORDON.

Logic and Functional Programming Group: tel. (604) 291-3426; fax (604) 291-3045; f. 1990; Dir Dr V. DAHL.

Mental Health, Law and Policy Institute: tel. (604) 291-3370; fax (604) 291-3427; f. 1991; Dir Dr R. ROESCH.

Pacific Institute for the Mathematical Sciences: tel. (604) 291-4376; fax (604) 268-6657; f. 1996; Dir Dr P. BORWEIN.

Research Institute on South-Eastern Europe: tel. (604) 291-5597; fax (604) 291-5837; Dir Dr A. GEROLYMATOS.

Tri-University Meson Facility (TRIUMF): tel. (604) 222-1047 ext. 6258; Dir Dr A. SHOTTER.

Western Canadian Universities Marine Biological Station (Bamfield): tel. (250) 728-3301; fax (250) 728-3452; f. 1969; Dir Dr A. N. SPENCER.

W. J. VanDusen BC Business Studies Institute: tel. (604) 291-4183; fax (604) 291-5833; f. 1982; Dir Dr E. LOVE.

UNIVERSITY OF TORONTO

27 King's College Circle, Toronto, ON M5S 1A1

Telephone: (416) 978-2011
Fax: (416) 978-5572

Internet: www.utoronto.ca

Founded 1827

Language of instruction: English

Provincially supported, assisted by private funds

Academic year: September to May (May to August, summer session)

Chancellor: The Hon. DAVID R. PETERSON
Pres.: DAVID NAYLOR
Vice-Pres. and Provost: CHERYL MISAK
Vice-Pres. and Chief Advancement Officer: DAVID PALMER
Vice-Pres. for Business Affairs: CATHERINE RIGGALL
Vice-Pres. for Human Resources and Equity: ANGELA HILDYARD
Vice-Pres. for Research: PAUL YOUNG
Vice-Pres. for University Relations: JUDITH WOLFSON
Vice-Pres. and Prin. for Univ. of Toronto at Mississauga: IAN ORCHARD
Vice-Pres. and Prin. for Univ. of Toronto at Scarborough: FRANCO VACCARINO
Chief Librarian: CAROLE MOORE
Library: see Libraries and Archives
Number of teachers: 3,771
Number of students: 73,685

Publications: *Bulletin, Calendars, President's Report, The Graduate, Undergraduate Admission Handbook*

DEANS AND DIRECTORS

Faculty of Applied Science and Engineering: CRISTINA AMON
Faculty of Architecture, Landscape and Design: RICHARD M. SOMMER
Faculty of Arts and Science: MERIC GERTLER
Faculty of Dentistry: DAVID MOCK
Faculty of Forestry: C. T. SMITH
Faculty of Information: SEAMUS ROSS
Faculty of Law: MAYO MORAN
Faculty of Medicine: CATHARINE WHITESIDE
Faculty of Music: RUSSELL HARTENBERGER
Lawrence S. Bloomberg Faculty of Nursing: SIOBAN NELSON
Leslie Dan Faculty of Pharmacy: HENRY J. MANN
Faculty of Physical Education and Health: BRUCE KIDD
Factor-Inwentash Faculty of Social Work: FAYE MISHNA
Ontario Institute of Studies in Education: JANE GASKELL
School of Continuing Studies: MARILYNN BOOTH
School of Graduate Studies: BRIAN CORMAN
Rotman School of Management: ROGER MARTIN
Dalla Lana School of Public Health: JACK MANDEL
School of Public Policy and Governance: MARK STABILE

PROFESSORS

Faculty of Applied Science and Engineering:
AARABI, P., Electrical and Computer Engineering
ABDELRAHMAN, T., Electrical and Computer Engineering
ADAMS, B. J., Civil Engineering
AITCHISON, J., Electrical and Computer Engineering
ALLEN, D., Chemical Engineering
BALKE, S. T., Chemical Engineering
BAWDEN, W., Civil Engineering
BIDLEMAN, T., Chemical Engineering
BIRKEMOE, P. C., Civil Engineering
BONERT, R., Electrical and Computer Engineering
BOOCOCK, D. G. B., Chemical Engineering
BOULTON, P. I. P., Electrical Engineering
BYER, P. H., Civil Engineering
CHAFFEY, C. E., Chemical Engineering
CHARLES, M. E., Chemical Engineering

CHENG, Y., Chemical Engineering
CHOW, P., Electrical and Computer Engineering
CLUETT, W., Chemical Engineering
COBBOLD, R. S. C., Institute of Biomedical Engineering
COLLINS, M. P., Civil Engineering
CORMACK, D. E., Chemical Engineering
COYLE, T., Chemical Engineering
CURRAN, J. H., Civil Engineering
DAVIES, S., Electrical and Computer Engineering
DAVISON, E. J. A., Electrical Engineering
DAWSON, F., Electrical and Computer Engineering
DEWAN, S. B., Electrical Engineering
DIAMOND, M., Chemical Engineering
DIOSADY, L. L., Chemical Engineering
EDWARDS, E., Chemical Engineering
EIZENMAN, M., Electrical and Computer Engineering
ERB, U., Materials Science
EVANS, G., Chemical Engineering
FARNOOD, R., Chemical Engineering
FOULKES, F. R., Chemical Engineering
FOX, M. S., Industrial Engineering
FRANCIS, B. A., Electrical Engineering
FRECKER, R., Electrical and Computer Engineering
FULTHORPE, R., Chemical Engineering
GOLDENBERG, A. A., Mechanical Engineering
GULACK, P., Electrical and Computer Engineering
HATZINAKOS, D., Electrical and Computer Engineering
HERMAN, P., Electrical and Computer Engineering
HOOTON, R., Civil Engineering
IRAVANI, M. R., Electrical and Computer Engineering
JACOBSEN, H.-A., Electrical and Computer Engineering
JAMES, D. F., Mechanical Engineering
JARDINE, A. K. S., Industrial Engineering
JIA, C., Chemical Engineering
JOY, M., Electrical and Computer Engineering
KARNEY, B., Civil Engineering
KAWAJI, M., Chemical Engineering
KIRK, D. W., Chemical Engineering
KONRAD, A., Electrical and Computer Engineering
KORTSCHOT, M., Chemical Engineering
KSCHISCHANG, F., Electrical and Computer Engineering
KUHN, D., Chemical Engineering
KUNOV, H., Biomedical Engineering
KWONG, R. H., Electrical Engineering
LAVERS, J. D., Electrical Engineering
LEE, E. S., Electrical Engineering
LEHN, P., Electrical and Computer Engineering
LEON-GARCIA, A., Electrical Engineering
LI, D., Mechanical Engineering
LO, H.-K., Electrical and Computer Engineering
LUUS, R., Chemical Engineering
MCKAGUE, A., Chemical Engineering
MANDELIS, A., Mechanical Engineering
MANN, S., Electrical and Computer Engineering
MARTIN, K., Electrical Engineering
MEASURES, R. M., Aerospace Studies
MEGUID, S. A., Mechanical Engineering
MILLER, E. J., Civil Engineering
MIMS, C. A., Chemical Engineering
MOHANTY, B., Civil Engineering
OJHA, M., Chemical Engineering
PACKER, J. A., Civil Engineering
PARADI, J., Chemical Engineering
PARK, C., Mechanical Engineering
PASUPATHY, S. P., Electrical Engineering
PEROVIC, D., Materials Science
REEVE, D. W., Chemical Engineering

ROSE, J., Electrical and Computer Engineering
SAIN, M., Chemical Engineering
SALAMA, C. A. T., Electrical Engineering
SANTERRE, J., Chemical Engineering
SARGENT, E., Electrical and Computer Engineering
SAVILLE, B., Chemical Engineering
SEFTON, M. V., Chemical Engineering
SEMLYEN, A., Electrical and Computer Engineering
SEVCIK, K., Electrical and Computer Engineering
SHEIKH, S. A., Civil Engineering
SHOICHET, M., Chemical Engineering
SLEEP, B., Civil Engineering
SMITH, K. C., Electrical Engineering
SMITH, P. W., Electrical Engineering
SODHI, R., Engineering
SOUSA, E., Electrical and Computer Engineering
TERZOPOULOS, D., Electrical and Computer Engineering
TRAN, H. N., Chemical Engineering
TRASS, O., Chemical Engineering
TURKSEN, I. B., Industrial Engineering
VECCHIO, F. J., Civil Engineering
VENETSANOPOULOS, A. N., Electrical Engineering
VENTER, R. D., Mechanical Engineering
VRANESIC, Z. G., Electrical Engineering
WALLACE, J. S., Mechanical Engineering
WANG, Z., Materials Science
WANIA, F., Chemical Engineering
WARD, C. A., Mechanical Engineering
WONHAM, W. M., Electrical Engineering
WOODHOUSE, K., Chemical Engineering
WRIGHT, P. M., Civil Engineering
YAN, N., Chemical Engineering
YIP, C., Chemical Engineering
YOUNG, R., Civil Engineering
ZAKY, S. G., Electrical Engineering
ZANDSTRA, P., Chemical Engineering
ZUKOTYNSKI, S., Electrical Engineering

Faculty of Architecture, Landscape and Design:
CORNEIL, C. S.
EARDLEY, A.

Faculty of Arts and Science:
ABBATT, J., Chemistry
ABOUHAIDAR, M. G., Botany
ABRAHAM, R. G., Astronomy and Astrophysics
ACCINELLI, R. D., History
ADLER, E., Political Science
AIVAZIAN, V. A., Economics
ALLOWAY, T. M., Psychology
ANDERSON, G. M., Geology
ANDERSON, J. B., Botany
ARNHEIM, C., Geography
ARTHUR, J. G., Mathematics
ASTER, S., History
ASTINGTON, J., English
BACCHUS, F., Computer Science
BAILEY, D. C., Physics
BAILEY, R. C., Physics
BAIRD, J., English
BAKER, M., Economics
BAKICH, O., Slavic Languages and Literature
BALDUS, B., Sociology
BARNES, C. J., Slavic Languages and Literature
BARRETT, F. M., Zoology
BARRETT, S. C. H., Botany
BARZDA, V., Physics
BASHKEVIN, S., Political Science
BEINER, R. S., Political Science
BENJAMIN, D., Economics
BERGER, C. C., History
BERKOWITZ, M. K., Economics
BEWELL, A., English
BIERSTONE, E., Mathematics
BINNICK, R. I., Linguistics
BIRGENEAU, R. J., Physics

BISZTRAY, G., Slavic Languages and Literature
BLAKE, T., Botany
BLANCHARD, P. H., History
BLAND, J. S., Mathematics
BLISS, J. M., History
BLOOM, T., Mathematics
BODDY, J., Anthropology
BODEMANN, M., Sociology
BOLTON, C. T., Astronomy
BOND, J., Astronomy and Astrophysics
BOONSTRA, R., Life Sciences
BORODIN, A. B., Computer Science
BOTHWELL, R., History
BOURNE, L. S., Geography
BOYD, M., Sociology
BRAUN, A., Political Science
BRITTON, J., Geography
BROOK, T. J., History, East Asian Studies
BROOKS, D. R., Zoology
BROWN, I. R., Zoology
BROWN, J. R., Philosophy
BROWN, R. M., Humanities
BROWNLEE, J. S., East Asian Studies
BRUDNER, A., Political Science
BRUMER, P. W., Chemistry
BRYAN, R. B., Geography
BRYANT, J., Sociology
BRYM, R. J., Sociology
BUCHWEITZ, R., Mathematics
BUNCE, M., Geography
BURKE, J. F., Spanish and Portuguese
BURTON, F. D., Anthropology
CAMERON, D. R., Political Science
CANFIELD, J. V., Philosophy
CAPOZZI, R., Italian Studies
CARLBERG, R. G., Physical Sciences
CARR, J. L., Economics
CASAS, F. R., Economics
CHAMBERLIN, J. E., English
CHEETHAM, M., Fine Art
CHEN, J., Geography
CHIN, J., Chemistry
CHING, J. C., Religious Studies
CLARKE, W. H., Astronomy
CLIVIO, G. P., Italian Studies
CODE, R. F., Physics
COOK, S. A., Computer Science
CORMAN, B., English Literature
CORNEIL, D. G., Mathematics, Computer Science
CRAWFORD, G., Anthropology
CRUDEN, S., Geology
CUMMINS, W. R., Botany
CUNNINGHAM, F. A., Philosophy, Political Science
DANESI, M., Italian Studies
DAY, R. B., Political Economy
DE KERCKHOVE, D., French
DE QUEHEN, A. H., English
DE SOUSA, R., Philosophy
DEL JUNCO, A., Mathematics
DENGLER, N. G., Botany
DENNY, M. G. S., Economics
DENT, J., History
DESAI, R. C., Physics
DEWAR, M., Classics
DEWEES, D. N., Political Economy
DIAMOND, M., Geography
DION, P.-E., Near Eastern Studies
DONALDSON, D., Chemistry
DONNELLY, M. W., Political Science, East Asian Studies
DRUMMOND, J. R., Physics
DUNLOP, D. J., Physics
EDWARDS, E., Botany
EDWARDS, R. N., Physics
EISENBICHLER, K., Italian
ELLIOTT, G. A., Mathematics
ENRIGHT, W. H., Mathematics, Computer Science
ERICKSON, B. H., Sociology
ESPIE, G., Botany
EVANS, M. J., Statistics
EYLES, N., Physical Sciences
FAIG, M., Economics

FALKENHEIM, V. C., Political Science, East Asian Studies
FARRAR, D., Chemistry
FENNER, A., German
FIUME, E., Computer Science
FOOT, D. K., Economics
FORBES, H. D., Political Science
FORGUSON, L. W.
FRANCESCHETTI, A., Italian Studies
FRIEDLANDER, J. B., Mathematics
FRIEDMANN, H. B., Sociology
FUSS, M. A., Economics
GAD, G. H. K., Geography
GALLOWAY, J. H., Geography
GARTNER, R. I., Sociology
GEORGES, M., Chemistry
GERTLER, M. S., Geography
GERVERS, M., History
GILLIS, A. R., Sociology
GITTINS, J., Geology
GOERING, J., History
GOLDSTEIN, M., Mathematics
GOLDSTICK, D., Philosophy
GOTLIEB, C., Computer Science
GOURIEROUX, C., Economics
GRAHAM, I. R., Mathematics
GREENWOOD, B., Geography
GREENWOOD, B., Geology
GREER, A. R., History
GREINER, P. C., Mathematics
GRIFFEN, P. A., Physics
GROSS, M. R., Zoology
GUNDERSON, M. K., Economics
GWYNNE, D. T., Biology
HAGAN, J. L., Sociology
HALLS, H. C., Geological Sciences
HANNIGAN, J., Sociology
HANSELL, R. I. C., Zoology
HARVEY, D., Geography
HARVEY, E., Sociology
HARVEY, E. R., English
HAYHOE, R., East Asian Studies
HEALEY, A., English
HEATH, M. C., Botany
HEHNER, E. C. R., Computer Science
HELMSTADTER, R. J., History
HIGGINS, V. J., Botany
HIGGS, D. C., History
HINTON, G. E., Computer Science
HIRST, G., Computer Science
HOLDOM, B., Physics
HORGEN, P. A., Botany
HORI, K., Physics
HORTON, S., Economics
HOWARD, K., Geology
HOWARD, P. J., English
HOWELL, N., Sociology
HOWSON, S. K., Social Sciences
HUTCHEON, L. A., English
INGHAM, J. N., History
INWOOD, B. C., Classics, Philosophy
ISRAEL, M., History
IVRII, V., Mathematics
JAAKSON, R., Geography
JACKSON, H., English
JACKSON, K. R., Computer Science
JACOBS, A. E., Physics
JEFFREY, L., Mathematics
JELLINEK, M., Physics
JEPSON, A. D., Computer Science
JOHN, S., Physics
JOHNSON, W. M. L. A., Fine Art
JOHNSTON, A., English
JONES, A., Classics
JONES, C. L., Sociology
JUMP, G. V., Economics
JURDJEVIC, V., Mathematics
KAPRAL, R. E., Chemistry
KAPRANOV, M., Mathematics
KAY, L., Chemistry
KEE, H.-K., Physics
KEITH, W. J., English
KERVIN, J. B., Sociology
KEY, A. W., Physics
KHESIN, B., Mathematics
KHOVANSKII, A., Mathematics

KIM, H., Mathematics
KIM, Y.-B., Physics
KLAUSNER, D. N., English
KLEIN, M. A., History
KLUGER, R. H., Chemistry
KOFMAN, L., Astronomy
KRAMER, C. E., Slavic Languages and Literature
KRIEGER, P., Physics
KRULL, U., Chemistry
KUKLA, A., Psychology, Philosophy
LAMBEK, M. J., Anthropology
LANCASHIRE, A. C., English
LANCASHIRE, D. I., English
LANTZ, K. A., Slavic Languages and Literature
LAUTENS, M., Chemistry
LEDUC, L., Political Science
LEE, M. J., Physics
LEE, R. B., Anthropology
LEGGATT, A. M., English
LEHMAN, A. B., Computer Science
LEVESQUE, H. J., Computer Science
LO, H.-K., Physics
LOGAN, R., Physics
LORIMER, J. W., Mathematics
LUKE, M., Physics
LUONG, H. V., Anthropology, East Asian Studies
LUSTE, G. J., Physics
LYNN, R., East Asian Studies
LYUBICH, M., Mathematics
MCCLELLAND, R. A., Chemistry
MCDONALD, P., Chemistry
MCILWRAITH, T., Geography
MAGEE, J., Classics
MAGILL, D. W., Sociology
MAGNUSSON, L., English
MAGOCSI, P. R., Political Science
MALLOCH, D. W., Botany
MANNERS, I., Chemistry
MARGORIBANKS, R., Physics
MARTIN, J. F., Physics
MARTIN, P. G., Astronomy
MATHEWSON, G. F., Political Economy
MATHON, R. A., Mathematics, Computer Science
MATUS, J., English
MELINO, A., Economics
MENDELSOHN, E., Mathematics, Computer Science
MENDELZON, A. O., Computer Science
MENZINGER, M., Chemistry
MERRILEES, B., French
MIALL, A. D., Geology
MICHELSON, W., Sociology
MIKHALKIN, G., Mathematics
MILKEREIT, B., Physics
MILLER, R., Chemistry
MILLER, R., Physics
MILMAN, P., Mathematics
MIMS, C., Chemistry
MINTZ, J., Economics
MIRON, J. R., Geography
MITROVICHA, J. X., Physics
MOCHNACKI, S., Astronomy
MOGGRIDGE, D. E., Economics
MOORE, G., Physics
MORGAN, K. P., Philosophy
MORRIS, G. K., Zoology
MORRIS, R., Chemistry
MORRIS, S. W., Physics
MORRISON, J. C., Philosophy
MUNK, L., English
MUNRO, D. S., Geography
MURNAGHAN, F., Mathematics
MURRAY, H., English
MURRAY, N., Astronomy
MURTY, V., Mathematics
MYLES, J., Sociology
MYLOPOULOS, J., Computer Science
NACHMAN, A., Mathematics
NEDELSKI, J., Political Science
NETTERFIELD, B., Physics
NEUMAN, S., English
NOYES, J. K., German

O'DAY, D., Zoology
O'DONNELL, P. J., Physics
OLIVER, W. A., French
ORCHARD, A., English
ORCHARD, I., Zoology
ORR, R. S., Physics
ORWIN, C. L., Political Science
OSBORNE, M., Economics
O'TOOLE, R., Sociology
OZIN, G. A., Chemistry
PANGLE, T. L., Political Science
PATERSON, J. M., French
PAULY, P., Political Science, Economics
PEET, A., Physics
PELTIER, W. R., Physics
PERCY, J. R., Astronomy
PERRON, P., French
PIETROPAOLO, D., Italian
PITASSI, T., Computer Science
POLANYI, J. C., Chemistry
POPPITZ, E., Physics
POWELL, J., Chemistry
PRIESTLEY, L. C., East Asian Studies
PRUESSEN, R. W., History
PUGLIESE, G., Italian
RACKOFF, C. W., Computer Science
RAYSIDE, D. M., Political Science
REDEKOP, M., English
REIBETANZ, J. H., English
REID, D., Fine Art
REID, F. J., Economics
REISZ, R. R., Zoology
REITZ, J. G., Sociology
RELPH, T., Geography
REPKA, J. S., Mathematics
RICE, K. D., Linguistics
RICHARDSON, D. S., Fine Art
RISING, J. D., Zoology
ROBIN, P. Y., Geological Science
ROSENTHAL, J., Mathematics
ROSENTHAL, P., Mathematics
ROSSOS, A., History
RUBINOFF, A., Political Science
RUTHERFORD, P., History
SALAFF, J. W., Sociology
SANDBROOK, K. R. J., Political Science
SANDERS, G., East Asian Studies
SAVARD, P., Physics
SCHWARTZ, D. V., Political Science
SCOTT, S. D., Geology
SEAGER, W. E., Philosophy
SEAQUIST, E. R., Astronomy
SEARY, P. D., English
SECO, L., Mathematics
SELICK, P., Mathematics
SELIGER, F., German
SEVCIK, K. C., Computer Science
SHAW, W. D., English
SHEN, V., East Asian Studies
SHEPHERD, T., Physics
SHERK, A., Mathematics
SHERWOOD LOLLAR, B., Geology
SHI, S., Economics
SHUB, M., Mathematics
SIGMON, B. A., Anthropology
SILCOX, P., Political Science
SIMEON, R., Political Science, Law
SIOW, A., Economics
SIPE, J. E., Physics
SKOGSTAD, G. D., Political Science
SMITH, J. J. B., Zoology
SMYTH, D., History
SOECKI, S., English
SOHM, P. L., Fine Art
SOLOMON, P. H., Political Science
SOLOMON, S., Political Science
SPOONER, E. T., Geology
SPRULES, W. G., Zoology
STATT, B., Physics
STEIN, J., Political Science
STEINBERG, A., Physics
STERNBERG, R., Spanish and Portuguese
STEVENS, P., English
STREN, R. E., Political Science
STRONG, K., Physics
SULEM, C., Mathematics

SULLIVAN, R., English
SUMNER, L. W., Philosophy
TAILLEFER, L., Physics
TALL, F. D., Mathematics
TANNER, J., Sociology
TANNY, S., Mathematics
TEICHMAN, J., Political Science
TEPPERMAN, L. J., Sociology
TERZOPOLOUS, D., Computer Science
THOMPSON, J. C., Chemistry
THOMPSON, M., Chemistry
THOMPSON, R. P., Philosophy
THOMSON, L., English
THYWISSEN, J., Physics
TOBE, S. S., Zoology
TOWNSEND, D., English
TREBILOCK, M., Economics
TREFLER, D., Economics
TRISCHUK, W., Physics
TROTT, D., French
TUOHY, C., Political Science
TURNER, D. H., Anthropology
URQUHART, A. I. F., Philosophy
VAN DRIEL, H. M., Physics
VIPOND, R., Political Science
VIRAG, B., Mathematics
WAGLE, N. K., History
WALKER, M. B., Physics
WATERHOUSE, D. B., East Asian Studies
WEI, J., Physics
WEINRIB, L., Political Science
WEISS, W. A., Mathematics
WELLMAN, B. S., Sociology
WESTGATE, J. A., Geology
WHEATON, B., Sociology
WHITE, G., Political Science
WHITE, R. R., Geography
WHITTINGTON, S. G., Chemistry
WILLIAMS, D. D., Life Sciences
WILSON, F. F., Philosophy
WOLFE, D., Political Science
WOOLDRIDGE, T. R., French
WORTMAN, D. B., Computer Science
YOUNG, R. P., Geology
YOUSON, J. H., Zoology
YU, E., Computer Science
ZIMMERMAN, A. M., Zoology

Faculty of Dentistry:
BENNICK, A.
DAVIES, J.
DEPORTER, D. A.
ELLEN, R. P.
FERRIER, J. M.
FREEMAN, E.
HEERSCHE, J. N. M.
LEAKE, J. L.
LEVINE, N.
LEWIS, D. W., Community Dentistry
LOCKER, D.
McCOMB, D.
McCULLOCH, C. A.
MAIN, J. H. P., Oral Pathology
MAYHALL, J. T.
MELCHER, A. H.
MOCK, D.
PILLIAR, R. M.
SANDHAM, H. J.
SESSLE, B. J.
SODEK, J.
SYMINGTON, J. M.
TEN CATE, A. R.
TENENBAUM, H. C.
WATSON, P. A.
ZARB, G. A., Prosthodontics

Faculty of Law:
BEATTY, D. M.
BENSON, P.
BRUDNER, A.
BRUNÉE, J.
CHAPMAN, B.
COOK, R.
COSSMAN, B.
DANIELS, R.
DEWEES, D.
DICKENS, B.

DYZENHAUS, D.
FLOOD, C.
FRIEDLAND, M.
GREEN, A.
HAGAN, J.
JANISCH, H.
LANGILLE, B.
LEE, I.
MACKLEM, P.
NEDELSKY, J.
PHILLIPS, J.
RÉAUME, D.
RIPSTEIN, A.
ROACH, K.
ROGERSON, C.
SIMEON, R.
SOSSIN, R.
TREBILOCK, M.
WADDAMS, S.
WEINRIB, E.
WEINRIB, L.

Faculty of Medicine:
ABEL, S., Otolaryngology
ACKERMANN, U., Physiology
ADAMSON, S., Obstetrics and Gynaecology, Paediatrics
ADELI, K., Pathobiology
ANDERSON, G. H., Nutrition and Food Sciences
ANDREWS, B. J., Medical Genetics and Microbiology
ANDRULIS, I., Pathobiology, Microbiology
ARCHER, M. C., Nutritional Studies
ARROWSMITH, C., Immunology
ASA, S., Pathobiology
ATWOOD, H. L., Physiology
AUBIN, J., Medical Biophysics
AXELRAD, A. A., Medical Biophysics
BAINES, A. D., Clinical Biochemistry
BAKER, R. R., Medicine
BARKER, G., Anaesthesia
BAUMAL, R., Pathology
BAZETT-JONES, D., Biochemistry
BELIK, J., Paediatrics
BENCHIMOL, S., Medical Biophysics
BENSON, L., Paediatrics
BERGERON, C., Pathobiology
BEVAN, D., Anaesthesia
BHAVNANI, B., Obstetrics and Gynaecology
BIGGAR, W. D., Paediatrics
BISSONETEE, B., Anaesthesia
BLAKE, J., Obstetrics and Gynaecology
BLANCHETTE, V., Paediatrics
BLENCOWE, B., Medical Research, Microbiology
BLUMENTHAL, A., Pathobiology
BOCKING, A., Obstetrics and Gynaecology, Physiology
BOGGS, J., Pathobiology
BOGNAR, A., Microbiology
BOHN, D., Anaesthesia
BOONE, C., Medical Research
BOONSTRA, R., Zoology, Physiology
BOUFFET, E., Paediatrics
BOYD, N., Medical Biophysics
BRESLIN, C., Ophthalmology
BRET, P.
BRONSKILL, M., Immunology
BROWN, D., Otolaryngology
BRUBAKER, P., Physiology
BRUNTON, J., Pathobiology
BUNCIC, R., Ophthalmology
BURNHAM, W. M., Pharmacology
BURNS, P., Medical Biophysics
BUSTO, U., Pharmacology
BUTANY, J., Pathobiology
BUTLER, D., Physiology
BYRICK, R., Anaesthesia
CAMERMAN, N., Biochemistry
CAMPBELL, J. B., Microbiology
CARLEN, P. L., Medicine
CASPER, R. F., Obstetrics and Gynaecology
CHALLIS, J., Physiology and Obstetrics
CHAMBERLAIN, D., Pathobiology
CHAN, H. S., Biochemistry

CHAN, S. L., Paediatrics
CHAN, V. L., Microbiology
CHARLTON, M. P., Physiology
CHETTY, R., Pathobiology
CHIANG, L., Pathobiology
CHITAYAT, D., Paediatrics
CHUNG, F. F., Anaesthesia
CLARKE, D., Biochemistry
CLARKE, J. T. R., Paediatrics
COATES, A., Paediatrics, Physiology
COLE, D., Pathobiology
COLE, P., Otolaryngology
COLGAN, T., Pathobiology
COVENS, A., Obstetrics and Gynaecology
CRUZ, T., Pathobiology
CRYSDALE, W. S., Otolaryngology
CUNNANE, S., Nutritional Sciences
CUNNINGHAM, A., Medical Biophysics
DANEMAN, A., Medical Imaging
DANEMAN, D., Paediatrics
DANSKA, J., Medical Biophysics
DEBER, C. M., Medical Biophysics
DEBONI, U., Physiology
DENNIS, J., Pathobiology
DE PETRILLO, A. D., Obstetrics and Gynaecology
DIAMANDIS, E., Pathobiology
DIAMANT, N. E., Physiology
DICK, J. E., Microbiology
DIRKS, F., Medicine
DIRKS, P., Medicine
DIXON, W., Ophthalmology
DORIAN, P., Pharmacology
DOSCH, H., Paediatrics
DOSTROVSKY, J. O., Physiology
DRUCKER, D. J., Pathobiology
DRUTZ, H., Obstetrics and Gynaecology
DUBE, I., Pathobiology
DUFFIN, J., Anaesthesia
DULLIN, J., Medical Biophysics
DURIE, P., Paediatrics
EASTERBROOK, M., Ophthalmology
EDWARDS, A., Medical Research, Microbiology
ELLEN, R., Pathobiology
ELLIS, D., Otolaryngology
EMILI, A., Medical Research, Microbiology
FARINE, D., Obstetrics and Gynaecology
FELDMAN, B. M., Paediatrics
FELDMAN, F., Ophthalmology
FERNIE, G. R., Surgery
FIEDBERG, J., Otolaryngology
FISH, E., Medical Biophysics
FISHER, R. H. G., Family and Community Medicine
FONG, I., Pathobiology
FORNASIER, V., Pathobiology
FORSTNER, G. G., Paediatrics
FORSTNER, J., Biochemistry
FOSTER, F. S., Medical Biophysics
FOX, A., Medical Imaging
FOX, G., Anaesthesia
FRECKER, R., Biomedical Engineering
FREEDMAN, J., Pathobiology
FREEDMAN, M., Paediatrics
FREEDOM, R., Paediatrics
FREEDOM, R., Pathobiology
FREEMAN, J., Otolaryngology
FRIESEN, J., Medical Research
FROM, L., Medicine
GALLIE, B., Ophthalmology
GALLINGER, S., Pathobiology
GANOZA, M. C., Medical Research
GARE, D., Obstetrics and Gynaecology
GARIÉPY, J., Medical Biochemistry
GARVEY, M. B., Medicine
GEARY, D., Paediatrics
GEORGE, S., Pharmacology
GILDAY, D., Medical Imaging
GOLDMAN, B. S., Surgery
GOLDSTEIN, M. B., Medicine
GOTLIEB, A. I., Pathology
GRANT, D., Pharmacology
GREENBERG, G. R., Medicine
GREENBERG, M. L., Paediatrics
GREENBLATT, J. F., Medical Research

GREENWALD, M., Paediatrics
GREENWOOD, C., Nutritional Sciences
GRINSTEIN, S., Biochemistry
GRYNPAS, M., Pathobiology
GUHA, A., Medical Biochemistry
GULLANE, P. J., Otolaryngology
GURD, J., Biochemistry
HALLIDAY, W., Pathobiology
HAMPSON, D., Pharmacology
HANLEY, W., Paediatrics
HANNA, W., Pathobiology
HANNAH, M., Obstetrics and Gynaecology
HARRISON, R., Otolaryngology
HASLAM, R., Paediatrics
HAWKE, M., Pathobiology, Otolaryngology
HAY, J. B., Immunology
HEDLEY, D., Medical Biophysics
HEERSCH, J., Pharmacology
HELM, T., Paediatrics
HENKELMAN, R. M., Medical Biophysics
HERSCHORN, S., Urology
HILL, R., Medical Biophysics
HILLIARD, R., Paediatrics
HINEK, A., Pathobiology
HO PING KONG, Medicine
HOWELL, P., Biochemistry
HUGHES, T., Medical Research
HUNT, J. W., Medical Biophysics
HYDE, M., Otolaryngology
IKURA, M., Medical Biophysics
INABA, T., Pharmacology
INGLES, C. J., Medical Research
ISCOVE, N., Medical Biochemistry
ISENMAN, D. E., Biochemistry
JEEJEEBHOY, K. N., Medicine
JOHNSSTON, K. W., Vascular Surgery
JOHNSTON, M., Pathobiology
JORGENSEN, A. O., Anatomy and Cell Biology
JOTHY, S., Pathobiology
JULIUS, M., Medical Biophysics
KAHN, H. (acting), Pathobiology
KAIN, K., Pathobiology
KALNINS, V. I., Histology
KANDEL, R., Pathobiology
KAPLAN, D., Medical Genetics
KARMALI, M., Pathobiology
KAY, L., Biochemistry
KEELEY, F., Biochemistry, Pathobiology
KERBEL, R., Medical Biophysics, Pathobiology
KHANNA, J. M., Pharmacology
KHOKHA, R., Medical Biophysics, Pathobiology
KISH, S., Pharmacology
KLIP, A., Biochemistry, Paediatrics
KOREN, G., Paediatrics, Pharmacology
KOVACS, K., Pathobiology
KRAFT, S., Ophthalmology
KRAFTCHIK, B., Paediatrics
KRAICER, J., Physiology
KRAUSE, H., Medical Research
KUCHARCZYK, W., Radiology
KUKSIS, A., Medical Research
KUNOV, H., Otolaryngology
LANGER, B., Surgery
LANGILLE, B. L., Pathology
LAWEE, D. H., Family and Community Medicine
LEPOCK, J., Medical Biophysics
LETARTE, M., Medical Biophysics
LEVY, G. A., Medicine
LEWIS, P. N., Biochemistry
LI, R.-K., Pathobiology
LICKLEY, L., Physiology
LICKRISH, G., Obstetrics and Gynaecology
LIEBGOTT, B., Anatomy
LIEW, C. C., Clinical Biochemistry
LINGWOOD, C., Biochemistry
LIU, F.-F., Medical Biophysics, Physiology
LIVINGSTONE, R. A., Obstetrics and Gynaecology
LOGAN, W. J., Paediatrics
LOW, D., Pathobiology
LYE, S., Obstetrics and Gynaecology
MacDONALD, J. F., Physiology

McGEER, A., Pathobiology
McGRAIL, S., Otolaryngology
McINNES, R. R., Paediatrics
MacKAY, M., Biomedical Communications
McKEE, N., Plastic Surgery
MacLENNAN, D. H., Medical Research
MAHURAN, D., Pathobiology
MAK, T.-W., Medical Biophysics
MARKS, A., Neurobiology
MARSDEN, P., Medical Biophysics, Pathobiology
MARSHALL, V. W., Behavioural Science
MAZER, C. D., Anaesthesia
MESSNER, H., Medical Biophysics
MICKLE, D., Pathobiology
MICKLEBOROUGH, L., Cardiac Surgery
MILGRAM, N., Pharmacology
MILLER, F., Physiology
MINDEN, M., Medical Biophysics
MOCK, D., Pathobiology
MOSCARELLO, M., Pathobiology
MORAN, L., Biochemistry
MORAN, M. F., Medical Research
MORGAN, J. E., Obstetrics and Gynaecology
MORTIMER, C. B., Ophthalmology
MROSOVSKY, N., Physiology
NAG, S., Pathobiology
NAGY, A., Medical Genetics
NARANJO, C. A., Pharmacology
NEDZELSKI, J. M., Otolaryngology
NOBLE, W. H., Anaesthesia
NOYEK, A. M., Otolaryngology
O'BRIEN, P., Pharmacology
O'BRODOVICH, H., Paediatrics, Physiology
O'DOWD, B., Pharmacology
OHASHI, P., Medical Biophysics
OHLSSON, A., Paediatrics
OKEY, A. B., Pharmacology
OLIVIERI, N., Paediatrics
OPAS, M., Pathobiology
ORSER, B., Anaesthesia, Physiology
OSMOND, D. H., Physiology
OTTENSMEYER, F. P., Medical Biophysics
PACE-ASCIAK, C., Pharmacology
PAI, E., Biochemistry
PAIGE, C., Medical Biophysics
PANG, C., Physiology
PANG, K., Pharmacology
PANTALONY, D., Pathobiology
PAPPO, A., Paediatrics
PAPSIN, F. R., Obstetrics and Gynaecology
PARKER, J., Ophthalmology
PARKER, J. D., Pharmacology
PAVLIN, C., Ophthalmology
PENCHARZ, P., Paediatrics
PENN, L., Medical Biophysics
PENNINGER, J., Medical Biophysics
PERLMAN, M., Paediatrics
PETERS, W. J., Plastic Surgery
PINKERTON, P. H., Pathology
PLEWES, D., Medical Biophysics
POST, M., Pathobiology, Physiology
PRITZKER, K., Pathobiology
PRUD'HOMME, G., Pathobiology
PULLEYBLANK, D. E., Biochemistry
RABINOVITCH, M., Paediatrics
RACHLIS, A., Pathobiology
RAJALAKSHMI, S., Pathobiology
RAUTH, A., Medical Biophysics
READ, S. E., Paediatrics, Pathobiology
REGAN, M., Ophthalmology
REITHMEIER, R., Biochemistry
RENLUND, R., Physiology
REZNICK, R., General Surgery
RICHARDSON, C., Medical Biophysics
RIDDELL, R., Pathobiology
RITCHIE, J. W. K., Obstetrics and Gynaecology
ROBERTS, E., Paediatrics
ROBINSON, G., Psychiatry
ROIFMAN, C., Paediatrics
ROSE, D., Medical Biophysics
ROTSTEIN, O. D., Surgery
ROWLANDS, J. A., Medical Biophysics
RUTKA, J., Pathobiology

SADOWSKI, P. D., Medical Genetics, Pathobiology
SARMA, D., Pathobiology
SAUDER, D. N., Medicine
SCHATZKER, J., Surgery
SCHIMMER, B. P., Medical Research
SCHLICHTER, L., Physiology
SCHMITT-ULMS, G., Pathobiology
SCULLY, H., Cardiac Surgery
SEGALL, J., Biochemistry, Medical Genetics
SEIDELMAN, W. E., Family and Community Medicine
SELLERS, E. M., Pharmacology
SERMER, M., Obstetrics and Gynaecology
SESSLE, B., Dentistry
SETH, A., Pathobiology
SHAH, C. P., Preventive Medicine and Biostatistics
SHARPE, J. A., Otolaryngology
SHEAR, N., Pharmcology
SHEK, P., Pathobiology
SHERMAN, P., Paediatrics, Pathobiology
SHIER, R. M., Obstetrics and Gynaecology
SHIME, J., Obstetrics and Gynaecology
SHULMAN, H. S., Radiology
SHULMAN, M. J., Immunology, Medical Genetics
SILVERMAN, M., Medicine
SIMOR, A., Pathobiology
SIU, C. H., Medical Research
SLINGER, P., Anaesthesia
SNEAD, III, O. C., Paediatrics
SODEK, J., Biochemistry
SOLE, M. J., Medicine
SONNENBERG, H., Physiology
SPEAKMAN, J., Ophthalmology
SQUARE, P., Speech-Language Pathology
SQUIRE, J., Pathobiology
STEIN, H., Ophthalmology
STEINER, G., Medicine
STEWART, D. J., Pathobiology
STEWART, P. A., Anatomy and Cell Biology
SUN, A., Physiology
TALLETT, S., Paediatrics
TANNOCK, I., Medical Biophysics
TANSWELL, A., Paediatrics
TATOR, C. H., Surgery
TAYLOR, G., Pathobiology
TAYLOR, I. M., Anatomy
TEMPLETON, D. M., Pathobiology
TENENBAUM, H., Pathobiology
TERBRUGGE, K., Medical Imaging
THOMPSON, L., Nutrition
THORNER, P., Pathobiology
TIMMER, V., Botany
TOMLINSON, D., Otolaryngology
TRIMBLE, W. S., Biochemistry
TRITCHLER, D., Medical Biophysics
TROPE, G., Ophthalmology
TSAO, M., Medical Biophysics, Pathobiology
TWEED, D., Physiology
UETECHT, J., Pharmacology
VAN DER KOOY, D. J., Anatomy and Cell Biology
VAN NOSTRAND, P., Otolaryngology
VAN TOL, H., Pharmacology
VAS, S., Pathobiology
VELLEND, H., Medicine
VRANIC, M., Physiology
WADDELL, J. P., Surgery
WALFISH, P. G., Otolaryngology
WANG, Y.-T., Pathobiology
WANLESS, I., Pathobiology
WARSH, J., Pharmacology
WEISBROD, G., Medical Imaging
WEISER, W., Medical Imaging
WEITZMAN, S., Paediatrics
WEKSBERG, R., Paediatrics
WELLS, J., Pharmacology
WELLS, P., Pharmacology
WILLIAMS, D., Biochemistry
WILLINSKY, R., Medical Imaging
WILSON, B., Medical Biophysics
WILSON, G., Pathobiology
WILSON, S., Medical Imaging

WILSON-PAUWELS, L., Biomedical Communications
WITTNICH, C., Cardiac Surgery
WOJTOWICZ, J., Physiology
WOLEVER, T., Nutritional Sciences
WONG, J. T. F., Biochemistry
WONG, P.-Y., Pathobiology
WONG, S., Medical Biophysics
WOOD, L., Medical Biophysics
WOOD, M., Medical Imaging
WOODGETT, J., Medical Biophysics
WOOLRIDGE, N., Biomedical Communications
WU, T. W., Clinical Biochemistry
YAFFE, M., Medical Biophysics
YIP, C. C., Medical Research
YOO, S.-J., Medical Imaging
ZAMEL, N., Otolaryngology
ZHOU, M., Physiology

Faculty of Music:
ARMENIAN, R., Director of Orchestral Activities
HARTENBERGER, R., Percussion, Graduate Coordinator
HATZIS, C., Composition
HAWKINS, J., Theory and Composition
LAUFER, E. C., Music Theory
MACDONALD, L., Voice Studies
SHAND, P. M., Music Education

Faculty of Nursing:
GALLOP, R.
HILLAN, E.
HODNETT, E.
McKEEVER, P.
O'BRIEN-PALLAS, L.
PRINGLE, D.
STEVENS, B.

Faculty of Pharmacy:
O'BRIEN, P. J.
PANG, K. S.
PERRIER, D. G.
ROBINSON, J. B.
SEGAL, H.
STIEB, E. W., History of Pharmacy
THIESSEN, J. J.
UETRECHT, J. P.

Faculty of Social Work:
BARBER, J.
BOGO, M.
HULCHANSKI, D.
LIGHTMAN, E.
McDONALD, L.
NEYSMITH, S.
SHERA, W.

Joseph L. Rothman School of Management:
AIVAZIAN, V., Finance
AMBURGEY, T. (acting), Strategic Management
AMERNIC, J. (acting), Accounting
BAUM, J. (acting), Strategic Management
BEATTY, D. (acting), Strategic Management
BERKOWITZ, M. (acting), Finance
BERMAN, O. (acting), Operations Management
BIRD, R. (acting), Economics
BOOTH, L. (acting), Finance
BORINS, S. (acting), Public Management
BREAN, D. (acting), Business Economics
BROOKS, L. (acting), Business Ethics and Accounting
CALLEN, J. (acting), Accounting
D'CRUZ, J. (acting), Strategic Management
DOBSON, W. (acting), International Business
DUAN, J.-C. (acting), Finance
EVANS, M. (acting), Organizational Behaviour
FELDMAN, M. (acting), Business Economics
FLECK, J. (acting), Business Government Relations
GOLDEN, B. (acting), Strategic Management

GUNZ, H. (acting), Organizational Behaviour
HALPERN, P. (acting), Finance
HORSTMANN, I. (acting), Business Economics
HUGHES, P. (acting), Strategic Management, Space Systems
HULL, J. (acting), Finance
HYATT, D. (acting), Business Economics
KIRZNER, E. (acting), Finance
KOLODNY, H. (acting), Organizational Behaviour
LATHAM, G. (acting), Organizational Effectiveness
McCURDY, T. (acting), Finance
MARTIN, R. (acting), Strategic Management
MENZEFRICKE, U. (acting), Operations Management
MINTZ, J. (acting), Taxation
MITCHELL, A. (acting), Marketing
MOORTHY, S. (acting), Marketing
ONDRACK, D. (acting), Organizational Behaviour
PAULY, P. (acting), Economics
SMIELIAUSKAS, W. (acting), Accounting
SOMAN, D. (acting), Marketing
STARK, A. (acting), Strategic Management
STRANGE, W. (acting), Urban Economics
TOMBAK, M. (acting), Technology Management
TREFLER, D. (acting), Business Economics
WHITE, A. (acting), Finance
WHYTE, G. (acting), Organizational Behaviour
WILSON, T. (acting), Economics

Ontario Institute for Studies in Education:
ACKER, S. (acting), Sociology and Equity Studies in Education, Theory and Policy Studies in Education
ASTINGTON, J., Human Development
BECK, C., Curriculum, Teaching and Learning
BIEMILLER, A. J.
BOGDAN, D., Theory and Policy and Studies in Education
BOYD, D., Theory and Policy Studies in Education
COLE, A., Adult Education
CONNELLY, M., Curriculum, Teaching and Learning
CORTER, C. M.
CUMMING, A., Curriculum, Teaching and Learning
CUMMINS, J., Curriculum, Teaching and Learning
DARROCH-LOZOWSKI, V., Curriculum, Teaching and Learning
DAVIE, L., Curriculum, Teaching and Learning
DEI, G., Sociology and Equity Studies in Education
DIAMOND, P.
EICHLER, M., Sociology and Equity Studies in Education
FARRELL, J., Curriculum, Teaching and Learning, Theory and Policy Studies in Education
GASKELL, J., Sociology and Equity Studies in Education
GEVA, E., Curriculum, Teaching and Learning
GUTTMAN, M. A., Counselling Psychology
HANNAY, L., Curriculum, Teaching and Learning
HARVEY, E., Sociology and Equity Studies in Education
HAYHOE, R., Theory and Policy Studies in Education
HELLER, M., Sociology and Equity Studies in Education
HODSON, D., Curriculum, Teaching and Learning
JENKINS, J., Human Development
JORDAN, A., Curriculum, Teaching and Learning

KEATING, D., Human Development
KNOWLES, J. G., Adult Education
LABRIE, N., Curriculum, Teaching and Learning
LANG, D., Theory and Policy Studies in Education
LAPKIN, S., Curriculum, Teaching and Learning
LEITHWOOD, K., Theory and Policy Studies in Education
LENSKYJ, H., Sociology and Equity Studies in Education
LEVINE, D., Theory and Policy Studies in Education
LEWIS, M., Human Development
LIVINGSTONE, D., Sociology and Equity Studies in Education
McLEAN, R., Curriculum, Teaching and Learning
MIEZITIS, S., Teacher Education
MILLER, J., Curriculum, Teaching and Learning
MISGELD, D., Theory and Policy Studies in Education
MOORE, C., Human Development
NG, R., Adult Education, Sociology and Equity Studies in Education
O'SULLIVAN, E., Adult Education
OATLEY, K., Human Development
OLSON, D., Human Development
PASCAL, C., Theory and Policy Studies in Education
PIERSON, R. R., Sociology and Equity Studies in Education
PIRAN, N., Counselling Psychology
PORTELLI, J., Theory and Policy Studies in Education
QUARTER, J., Adult Education
ROSS, J., Curriculum, Teaching and Learning
RYAN, J., Theory and Policy Studies in Education
SCARDAMALIA, J., Curriculum, Teaching and Learning
SIMON, R., Curriculum, Teaching and Learning
SKOLNIK, M., Theory and Policy Studies in Education
SPADA, N., Curriculum, Teaching and Learning
STANOVICH, K., Curriculum, Teaching and Learning
STERMAC, L., Counselling Psychology
SWAIN, M., Curriculum, Teaching and Learning
THIESSEN, D., Curriculum, Teaching and Learning
TROPER, H., Theory and Policy Studies in Education
VOLPE, R., Human Development
WIENER, J., Human Development
WILLOWS, D., Curriculum, Teaching and Learning
WILSON, D., Curriculum, Teaching and Learning, Theory and Policy Studies in Education

School of Graduate Studies:
ANGENOT, M., Comparative Literature
BEATTIE, J. M., Criminology
BOND, R. J., Theoretical Astronomy
BRYDEN, R., Drama
COHEN, J. S., Graduate Studies
DOOB, A. N., Criminology
HACKING, I. M., History and Philosophy of Science and Technology
HARIANTO, F., International Studies
HEALEY, A. D., Medieval Studies
HERNANDEZ, C., International Studies
KAISER, N., Theoretical Astronomy
LEVERE, T. H., History and Philosophy of Science and Technology
MARKER, L., Drama
MARTIN, P. G., Theoretical Astronomy
NESSELROTH, P. W., Comparative Literature

PESANDO, J. E., Policy Analysis
RIGG, A. G., Medieval Studies
SHEARING, C. D., Criminology
STENNING, P. C., Criminology
STOCK, B. C., Comparative Literature
TREMAINE, S. D., Theoretical Astronomy
VALVERDE, M. V., Criminology
WINSOR, M. P., History and Philosophy of
  Science and Technology

School of Physical Education and Health:
COREY, P.
DONNELLY, P.
FERNIE, G.
GOODE, R.
JACOBS, I.
LEITH, L.
LENSKYJ, H.
MCCLELLAND, J.
MCKEE, N.
PLYLEY, M.
VOLPE, R.

UNIVERSITY COLLEGES

Erindale College/University of Toronto at Mississauga: 3359 Mississauga Rd North, Mississauga, ON L5L 1C6; tel. 828-5211; f. 1964; Prin. IAN ORCHARD.

Innis College: 2 Sussex Ave, Toronto, ON M5S 1J5; tel. 978-7023; fax 978-5503; internet www.utoronto.ca/innis; f. 1964; Prin. F. CUNNINGHAM.

New College: 300 Huron St, Toronto, ON M5S 3J0; tel. 978-2461; fax 978-0554; internet utt2.library.utoronto.ca/www/new_college/index.htm; f. 1962; Pres. DAVID KLANDFIELD.

Scarborough College: 1265 Military Trail, Scarborough, ON M1C 1A4; tel. 287-8872; f. 1964; Prin. R. P. THOMPSON.

University College: 15 King's College Circle, Toronto, ON M5S 3H7; tel. 978-3170; f. 1853; Prin. PAUL J. PERRON.

Woodsworth College: 117–119 St George St, Toronto, ON M5S 1A9; tel. 978-2411; fax 978-6111; e-mail info@wdw.utoronto.ca; f. 1974; Prin. N. M. MELTZ.

FEDERATED UNIVERSITIES

University of St Michael's College: 81 St Mary St, Toronto, ON M5S 1J4; tel. (416) 926-1300; f. 1958; conducted by the Basilian Fathers; Pres. Dr ANNE ANDERSON.

University of Trinity College: 6 Hoskin Ave, Toronto, ON M5S 1H8; tel. (416) 978-2522; f. 1851; Vice-Chancellor and Provost R. PAINTER.

Victoria University, Toronto: 73 Queen's Park Cres., Toronto, ON M5S 1K7; tel. (416) 585-4524; f. 1836; Pres. E. KUSHNER.

FEDERATED COLLEGES

Emmanuel College: 75 Queen's Park Cres., Toronto, ON M5S 1K7; tel. (416) 585-4540; f. 1928; United Church of Canada theological college; Prin. JOHN HOFFMAN.

Knox College: 59 St George St, Toronto, ON M5S 2E5; tel. (416) 978-4500; Presbyterian theological college; Prin. Rev. Dr RAYMOND HUMPHRYES (acting).

Regis College: 15 St Mary St, Toronto, ON M4Y 2R5; tel. (416) 922-5474; f. 1930; Roman Catholic theological college (Society of Jesus); Pres. Rev. JOHN E. COSTELLO.

Wycliffe College: 5 Hoskin Ave, Toronto, ON M5S 1H7; tel. (416) 979-2870; Anglican theological college; Prin. Rev. H. S. HILCHEY (acting).

AFFILIATED INSTITUTES

Massey College: University of Toronto, Toronto, ON M5S 2E1; tel. (416) 978-2895; f. 1963; residential college for graduates and senior scholars engaged in research; Master J. S. DUPRE.

Pontifical Institute of Medieval Studies: 59 Queen's Park Cres. East, Toronto, ON M5S 2C4; affiliated to Univ. of St Michael's College; grants degrees in its own right, offering pontifical Licentiate in Medieval Studies (MSL) and Doctorate in Medieval Studies (MSD); Pres. Prof. M. DIMNIK.

TRENT UNIVERSITY

1600 West Bank Drive, Peterborough, ON K9J 7B8

Telephone: (705) 748-1332
Fax: (705) 748-1629
E-mail: liaison@trentu.ca
Internet: www.trentu.ca

Founded 1963
Language of instruction: English
Academic year: September to April (2 semesters with reading periods intervening; summer sessions also available)

Chancellor: Dr ROBERTA BONDAR
Pres. and Vice-Chancellor: BONNIE M. PATTERSON
Vice-Pres. for Academic Affairs and Provost: SUSAN APOSTLE-CLARK
Vice-Pres. for Administration: DON O'LEARY
Vice-Pres. for External Relations and Advancement: DIANNE LISTER
Registrar: SUSAN SALUSBURY
Senior Director of Public Affairs: DON CUMMING
University Librarian: ROBERT F. CLARKE
Number of teachers: 467 (325 full-time, 142 part-time)
Number of students: 8,050 undergraduates (6,688 full-time, 1,362 part-time), 277 postgraduates

DEANS

Faculty of Arts and Science: CHRISTINE MCKINNON
Faculty of Graduate Studies: DOUGLAS EVANS

PROFESSORS

ARVIN, M. C., Economics
BANDYOPADHYAY, P., Comparative Development Studies
BERRILL, D., School of Education
BERRILL, M., Biology
BISHOP, J., Business Administration
BRUNGER, A. G., Geography
BUTTLE, J., Geography
CHOUDRY, S., Economics
COGLEY, J. G., Geography
CONOLLY, L. W., English Literature
CURTIS, D. C. A., Economics
DAWSON, P. C., Physics
DELLAMORA, R. J., English Literature and Cultural Studies
DILLON, P., Environmental Studies, Chemistry
EVANS, D., Environmental Studies
EVANS, W., Environmental Studies, Physics
FEKETE, J. A., English Literature, Cultural Studies
FOX, M., Environmental Studies, Biology
HAGMAN, R. S., Anthropology
HEALY, P. F., Anthropology
HEITLINGER, A., Sociology
HURLEY, R., Computer Studies, Science
HUXLEY, C. V., Sociology and Comparative Development Studies
JAMIESON, S., Anthropology
JOHNSTON, G. A., English Literature
JONES, E. H., History
JURY, J. W., Physics and Computer Studies
KANE, S., English Literature, Cultural Studies
KATZ, S., Sociology
KEEFER, S., English Literature
KENNETT, D. J., Psychology

KINZL, K. H., Ancient History and Classics
KITCHEN, H. M., Economics
LAFLEUR, P., Geography
LASENBY, D. C., Biology
LEM, W., International Development Studies and Women's Studies
LEWARS, E. G., Chemistry
MCCASKILL, D. N., Native Studies
MCKENNA-NEWMAN, C., Geography
MCKINNON, C., Philosophy
MAXWELL, E. A., Mathematics
METCALFE, C., Environmental Studies
MILLOY, J., Native Studies and History
MITCHELL, O. S., English Literature
MORRISON, D. R., International Development Studies
NADER, G. A., Geography
NEUFELD, J. E., English Literature
NEUMANN, M., Philosophy
NOL, E., Biology
NORIEGA, T. A., Hispanic Studies
PAEHLKE, R. C., Political Studies, Environmental Studies
PALMER, B., Canadian Studies
PARNIS, M., Chemistry
PATTERSON, B., Business Administration
PETERMAN, M., English Literature
PICKEL, A., Political Studies
POLLOCK, Z., English Literature
POOLE, D. G., Mathematics
REKER, G. T., Psychology
SANGSTER, J., History and Women's Studies
SHEININ, D., History
SLAVIN, A. J., Physics
SMITH, C. T., Psychology
SO, J. K.-F., Anthropology
STANDEN, S. D., History
STOREY, I. C., Ancient History and Classics
STRUTHERS, J. E., Canadian Studies, History
SUTCLIFFE, J., Biology
SVISHCHEV, I., Chemistry
TAMPLIN, M., Anthropology
TAYLOR, C., Geography
TAYLOR, G., History
TINDALE, C., Philosophy
TOPIC, J. R., Anthropology
TORGERSON, D., Environmental and Resource Studies
TROMLY, F. B., English Literature
WADLAND, J. H., Canadian Studies
WALDEN, K., History
WERNICK, A. L., Cultural Studies
WHITE, B., Biology
WINOCUR, G., Psychology
ZHOU, B., Mathematics

TRINITY WESTERN UNIVERSITY

7600 Glover Rd, Langley, BC V2Y 1Y1

Telephone: (604) 888-7511
Fax: (604) 513-2061
E-mail: suderman@twu.ca
Internet: www.twu.ca

Founded 1962, university status 1985
Private control
Language of instruction: English
Academic year: September to April

Pres.: Dr JONATHAN RAYMOND
Provost: Dr DENNIS JAMESON
Vice-Pres. for Academic Affairs: Dr DENNIS JAMESON
Vice-Pres. for Advancement: DAVID COONS
Vice-Pres. for Finance: DALE CLARK
Assoc. Provost for Student Life: SHELDON LOEPPKY
Registrar: GRANT MCMILLAN
Librarian: TED GOSHULAK

Library of 430,000 items
Number of teachers: 305 (165 full-time, 140 part-time)
Number of students: 3,500

DEANS

Faculty of Humanities and Social Sciences: Dr ROBERT BURKINSHAW

Faculty of Natural and Applied Sciences-
Graduate School of Theological Studies: Dr
KEN RADANT, Dr KA YIN LEUNG
School of Arts, Media and Culture: Dr DAVID
SQUIRES
School of Business and Economics: ANDREA
SOBERG
School of Graduate Studies: Dr WILLIAM
ACTON
School of Human Kinetics: Dr BLAIR WHIT-
MARSH

UNIVERSITY OF VICTORIA

POB 1700, Victoria, BC V8W 2Y2
Telephone: (250) 721-7211
Fax: (250) 721-7212
E-mail: ucom@uvic.ca
Internet: www.uvic.ca
Founded 1963
Language of instruction: English
Provincial control
Academic year: September to April
Chancellor: MURRAY FARMER
Pres. and Vice-Chancellor: Dr DAVID H.
TURPIN
Vice-Pres. for Academic Affairs and Provost:
Dr REETA TREMBLAY
Vice-Pres. for External Relations: Dr VALERIE
KUEHNE
Vice-Pres. for Finance and Operations:
GAYLE GORRILL
Vice-Pres. for Research: Dr HOWARD BRUNT
Univ. Sec.: Dr JULIA EASTMAN
Admin. Registrar: LAUREN CHARLTON
Univ. Librarian: MARNIE SWANSON

Number of teachers: 790
Number of students: 19,646

Publications: *Calendar* (1 a year), *Malahat Review*

DEANS

Faculty of Business: Dr ALI DASTMALCHIAN
Faculty of Education: Dr TED RIECKEN
Faculty of Engineering: Dr THOMAS TIEDJE
Faculty of Fine Arts: Dr SARAH BLACKSTONE
Faculty of Graduate Studies: Dr AARON
DEVOR
Faculty of Human and Social Development:
Dr MARY ELLEN PURKIS (acting)
Faculty of Humanities: Dr ANDREW RIPPIN
Faculty of Law: Prof. DONNA GRESCHNER
(acting)
Faculty of Science: Dr THOMAS PEDERSON
Faculty of Social Sciences: Dr PETER KELLER

PROFESSORS

AGATHOKLIS, P., Electrical and Computer Engineering
ANDERSON, J., Educational Psychology and Leadership Studies
ANDRACHUK, G. P., Hispanic and Italian Studies
ANTONIOU, A., Electrical and Computer Engineering
ARMITAGE, A., Social Work
AUSIO, J., Biochemistry and Microbiology
AVIO, K. L., Economics
BACHOR, D. G., Psychological Foundations
BALFOUR, W. J., Chemistry
BARCLAY, J. A., Mechanical Engineering
BARNES, C., Earth and Ocean Sciences
BARNES, G. E., Child and Youth Care
BASKERVILLE, P. A., History
BAVELAS, J. B., Psychology
BEDESKI, R. E., Political Science
BENNETT, C., Political Science
BENOIT, C., Sociology
BERRY, E. I., English
BEST, M. R., English
BHARGAVA, V. K., Electrical and Computer Engineering
BHAT, A. K. S., Electrical and Computer Engineering

BLANK, K., English
BOAG, D. A., Faculty of Business
BOHNE, C., Chemistry
BORNEMANN, J., Electrical and Computer Engineering
BORROWS, J., Law
BRADLEY, K. R., Classics
BRENER, R., Visual Arts
BROWNING-MOORE, A., Music
BRUNT, H., Nursing
BRYANT, D., Pacific and Asian Studies
BUB, D., Psychology
BUCKLEY, J. T., Biochemistry and Microbiology
BURKE, R. D., Biology
CAMPBELL, M., Human and Social Development
CARROLL, W. K., Sociology
CASSELS, J. L., Law
CASSWELL, D. G., Law
CELONA, J., Music
CHAPMAN, R., Earth and Ocean Sciences
CHAPPELL, N. L., Sociology
COBLEY, E., English
COCKAYNE, E. J., Mathematics and Statistics
COOPERSTOCK, F. I., Physics and Astronomy
COWARD, H. G., History
CROIZIER, L., Writing
CROIZIER, R. C., History
CUNNINGHAM, J. B., Public Administration
CUTT, J., Public Administration
DEARDEN, P., Geography
DEVOR, H., Sociology
DIACU, F., Mathematics and Statistics
DIMOPOULOS, N., Electrical and Computer Engineering
DIPPIE, B. W., History
DIXON, R. A., Psychology
DJILALI, N., Mechanical Engineering
DOBELL, A. R., Public Administration
DOCHERTY, D., Physical Education
DONALD, L. H., Anthropology
DONG, Z., Mechanical Engineering
DOST, S., Mechanical Engineering
DYSON, L., Psychological Foundations
EDWARDS, A. S., English
EL GUIBALY, F. H., Electrical and Computer Engineering
ENGINEER, M., Economics
ESLING, J., Linguistics
FELLOWS, M., Computer Science
FERGUSON, G. A., Law
FLEMING, T., Education
FOSS, J., Philosophy
FOSTER, H., Law
FOSTER, H. D., Geography
FOWLER, R., Social and Natural Sciences
FRANCE, H., Psychological Foundations
FYLES, T. M., Chemistry
GALAMBOS, N., Psychology
GALLAGHER, Nursing
GALLOWAY, J., Law
GARRETT, C., Physics, Earth and Ocean Sciences
GARTRELL, D., Sociology
GIBSON-WOOD, C., History in Art
GIFFORD, R. D., Psychology
GILES, D. E., Economics
GILLIN, M., Law
GLICKMAN, B., Biology
GOOCH, B. N. S., English
GOUGH, T. E., Chemistry
GRANT, P. J., English
GREGORY, P. T., Biology
GULLIVER, A., Electrical and Computer Engineering
HALL, B., Curriculum and Instruction
HANLEY, B., Curriculum and Instruction
HARKER, W. J., Education
HARRINGTON, D., Chemistry
HARRIS, C., Communication and Social Foundations
HARTWICK, F. D. A., Physics and Astronomy
HARVEY, B., Psychological Foundations
HAWRYSHYN, C., Biology
HEDLEY, R. A., Sociology

HILLS, M., Nursing
HOCKING, M., Chemistry
HODGINS, J., Creative Writing
HOEFER, W. J. R., Electrical and Computer Engineering
HOGYA, G., Theatre
HORITA, R. E., Physics and Astronomy
HORSPOOL, R. N., Computer Science
HOWE, B. L., Physical Education
HOWELL, R. G., Law
HUENEMANN, R. W., Faculty of Business
HULTSCH, D. F., Psychology
ILLNER, R., Mathematics and Statistics
ISHIGURO, E. E., Biochemistry and Microbiology
JOHNSON, T. D., Education
JONES, J. C. H., Economics
KAMBOURELI, S., English
KAY, W. W., Biochemistry and Microbiology
KEELER, R., Physics and Astronomy
KELLER, A., English
KELLER, P., Geography
KERBY-FULTON, K., English
KESS, J. F., Linguistics
KINDERMAN, W., Music
KIRLIN, R. L., Electrical and Computer Engineering
KLUGE, E.-H., Philosophy
KOENIG, D., Sociology
KOOP, B., Biology
KREBS, H., Music
KUEHNE, V., Child and Youth Care
KWOK, H. H. L., Electrical and Computer Engineering
LAI, D. C.-Y., Geography
LANGFORD, J. W., Public Administration
LAPPRAND, M., French Language and Literature
LAZAREVICH, G., Music
LEADBEATER, B., Psychology
LEEMING, D. J., Mathematics and Statistics
LIDDELL, P., Germanic Studies
LIEDTKE, W. W., Education
LINDSAY, D., Psychology
LISCOMB, K., History in Art
LIVINGSTON, N., Biology
LONERGAN, S. C., Geography
LU, W.-S., Electrical and Computer Engineering
McCANN, L., Geography
McDAVID, J. C., Public Administration
McDORMAN, T., Law
McDOUGALL, L., Music
McLAREN, A. G., History
McLAREN, J. P. S., Law
MacGREGOR, J. N., Public Administration
MacPHERSON, G. R. I., History
MAGNUSSON, W., Political Science
MALONEY, M. A., Law
MANNING, E. G., Computer Science, Electrical and Computer Engineering
MARTIN-NEWCOMBE, Y., Communication and Social Foundations
MASSON, M. E. J., Psychology
MATEER, C., Psychology
MAYFIELD, M., Education
MAZUMDER, A., Biology
M'GONIGLE, R., Environmental Studies
MIERS, C. R., Mathematics and Statistics
MILLER, D., Computer Science
MISRA, S., Biochemistry and Microbiology
MITCHELL, D. H., Anthropology
MITCHELL, R. H., Chemistry
MOEHR, J. R., Health Information Service
MOLZAHN, A., Nursing
MORE, B. E., Music
MORGAN, C. G., Philosophy
MOSK, C. A., Economic Relations with Japan
MULLER, H., Computer Science
MURPHY, P., Communication and Social Foundations
MUZIO, J. C., Computer Science
MYRVOLD, W., Computer Science
NANO, F., Biochemistry and Microbiology
NEILSON, W. A. W., Law
NG, I., Business

NICHOLS, D., Physical Education
NIEMANN, O., Geography
OGMUNDSON, R., Sociology
OLAFSON, R. W., Biochemistry and Microbiology
OLESKY, D., Computer Science
OLESON, J. P., Classics
OSBORNE, J., History in Art
PAETKAU, V., Biochemistry
PEARSON, T. W., Biochemistry and Microbiology
PENCE, A. R., Child and Youth Care
PFAFFENBERGER, W. E., Mathematics and Statistics
PHILLIPS, J., Mathematics and Statistics
PICCIOTTO, C. E., Physics and Astronomy
PINDER, W. C., Business
PORTEOUS, J. D., Geography
PRINCE, M. J., Social Policy
PRITCHET, C. J., Physics
PROTTI, D. J., Health Information Science
PROVAN, J. W., Mechanical Engineering
PUTNAM, I., Mathematics and Statistics
RANGER, L., Music
REED, W. J., Mathematics and Statistics
REID, R. G. B., Biology
REITSMA-STREET, M., Child and Youth Care
RICKS, F. A. S., Child and Youth Care
RIEDEL, W. E., Germanic Studies
RING, R. A., Biology
ROMANIUK, P., Biochemistry and Microbiology
ROTH, E., Anthropology
ROTH, W.-M., Social and Natural Sciences
ROY, P., History
RUSKEY, F., Computer Science
RUTHERFORD, M., Economics
SAGER, E. W., History
ST PETER, C., Women's Studies
SCARFE, C. D., Physics and Astronomy
SCHAAFSMA, J., Economics
SCHAARSCHMIDT, G. H., Slavonic Studies
SCHOFIELD, J. A., Economics
SCHULER, R., English
SCHWANDT, E., Music
SCOBIE, S. A. C., English
SERRA, M., Computer Science
SHERWOOD, N., Biology
SHRIMPTON, G., Greek and Roman Studies
SMITH, D., Geography
SOUROUR, A. R., Mathematics and Statistics
SRIVASTAVA, H. M., Mathematics and Statistics
STEPANENKO, Y., Mechanical Engineering
STEPHENSON, P. H., Anthropology
STOBART, S. R., Chemistry
STORCH, J., Nursing
STOREY, V., Communication and Social Foundations
STRAUSS, E., Psychology
STRONG, D. F., Earth and Ocean Sciences
STUCHLY, M., Electrical and Computer Engineering
SYMINGTON, R. T. K., Germanic Studies
THALER, D., French Language and Literature
THATCHER, D. S., English
TUCKER, J., English
TULLER, S., Geography
TULLY, J., Political Science
TUNNICLIFFE, V. J., Earth and Ocean Sciences, Biology
TURNER, N., Environmental Studies
UHLEMANN, M. R., Education
VALGARDSON, W. D., Creative Writing
VAN DEN DRIESSCHE, R., Biology
VAN EMDEN, M., Computer Science
VAN GYN, G., Physical Education
VANCE, J. H., Education
VANDENBERG, D. A., Physics
VICKERS, G. W., Mechanical Engineering
VOGT, B., Music
VON ADERKAS, P., Biology
WADGE, W. W., Computer Science
WALDRON, M. A., Law
WALKER, R. B. J., Political Science
WALTER, G. R., Economics

WAN, P. C., Chemistry
WARBURTON, R., Sociology
WATTON, A., Physics and Astronomy
WEAVER, A., Earth and Ocean Sciences
WELCH, S. A., History in Art
WENGER, H. A., Physical Education
WHITICAR, M., Earth and Ocean Sciences
WILL, H. J., Public Administration
WILLIAMS, T., English
WILSON, J., Political Science
WOLFF, R., Business
WOON, YUEN-FONG, Pacific Asian Studies
WU, Z., Sociology
WYNAND, D., Creative Writing
YORE, L. D., Education
YOUDS, R., Visual Arts
YOUNG, J., Philosophy
ZIELINSKI, A., Electrical and Computer Engineering
ZIMMERMAN, D., History
ZUK, W., Arts in Education

UNIVERSITY OF WATERLOO

Waterloo, ON N2L 3G1
Telephone: (519) 888-4567 ext. 33614
Fax: (519) 746-8088
E-mail: registrar@uwaterloo.ca
Internet: www.uwaterloo.ca
Founded 1957
Provincially supported
Language of instruction: English
Academic year: September to April (Cooperative programmes September to August, Summer Session July to August)
Chancellor: PREM WATSA
Pres. and Vice-Chancellor: DAVID L. JOHNSTON
Vice-Pres. for Academic Affairs and Provost: FERIDUN HAMDULLAHPUR
Vice-Pres. for Admin. and Finance: DENNIS E. HUBER
Vice-Pres. for Univ. Relations: MEG BECKEL
Vice-Pres. for Univ. Research: GEORGE DIXON
Assoc. Provost for Academic and Student Affairs: BRUCE MITCHELL
Assoc. Provost for Graduate Studies: SUE HORTON
Assoc. Provost for Human Resources and Student Services: JANET PASSMORE
Assoc. Provost for Information Systems and Technology: ALAN GEORGE
Registrar: KEN A. LAVIGNE
Univ. Librarian: MARK HASLETT
Library: 2m. vols
Number of teachers: 1,062 (full-time and part-time)
Number of students: 30,861 (full-time and part-time)
Publications: *Alternatives* (6 a year), *Environments Journal* (3 a year), *New Quarterly*

DEANS

Faculty of Applied Health Sciences: ROGER MANNELL
Faculty of Arts: KEN COATES
Faculty of Engineering: Prof. ADEL SEDRA
Faculty of Environmental Studies: Dr H. S. (DEEP) SAINI
Faculty of Mathematics: THOMAS COLEMAN
Faculty of Science: TERRY MCMOHAN

FEDERATED UNIVERSITY

St Jerome's University: Waterloo, ON N2L 3G3; f. 1864; federated 1960; Roman Catholic, conducted by the Congregation of the Resurrection; Pres. D. PERRIN.

AFFILIATED COLLEGES

Conrad Grebel University College: Waterloo, ON N2L 3G6; f. 1961; Mennonite; Pres. H. PAETKAU.

Renison University College: Waterloo, ON N2L 3G4; f. 1959, affiliated 1960; Anglican; Prin. G. CARTWRIGHT.
St Paul's University College: Waterloo, ON N2L 3G5; f. 1962; United Church of Canada; Prin. G. BROWN.

UNIVERSITY OF WESTERN ONTARIO

1151 Richmond St, Suite 2, London, ON N6A 3K7
Telephone: (519) 661-2111
Fax: (519) 661-3710
E-mail: reg-admissions@uwo.ca
Internet: www.uwo.ca
Founded 1878
Academic year: September to April
Chancellor: JOHN THOMPSON
Pres. and Vice-Chancellor: AMIT CHAKMA
Provost and Vice-Pres. for Academic Affairs: J. DEAKIN
Vice-Pres. for External Relations: KEVIN GOLDTHORP
Vice-Pres. for Research and Int. Relations: Dr TED HEWITT
Vice-Pres. for Resources and Operations: GITTA KULCZYCKI
Vice-Provost for Academic Programmes and Students and Registrar: Dr JOHN DOERKSEN
Vice-Provost for School of Graduate and Postdoctoral Studies: L. MILLER
Univ. Librarian: JOYCE GARNETT
Library of 3,546,496 vols
Number of teachers: 1,374 full-time
Number of students: 30,282
Publications: *Alumni Gazette* (magazine, 3 a year), *Dental Journal*, *Gazette* (student daily bulletin), *Mediations*, *Medical Journal*, *Reflections*, *The Business Quarterly*, *The President's Report*, *The Science Terrapin*, *Western News* (52 a year, newspaper)

DEANS

Faculty of Arts and Humanities: Dr D. PENNEE
Faculty of Education: C. BEYNON (acting)
Faculty of Engineering: A. HRYMAK
Faculty of Health Sciences: Dr J. WEESE
Faculty of Information and Media Studies: Dr T. CARMICHAEL
Faculty of Law: Prof. I. HOLLOWAY
Don Wright Faculty of Music: Dr ROBERT WOOD
Faculty of Science: Dr D. WARDLAW (acting)
Faculty of Social Science: Dr B. TIMNEY
Richard Ivey School of Business: C. STEPHENSON
Schulich School of Medicine and Dentistry: M. STRONG

PROFESSORS

Faculty of Arts and Humanities (tel. (519) 661-3043; fax (519) 661-3640; internet www.uwo.ca/arts):

ADAMS, S. J., English
BELL, J. L., Philosophy
BENTLEY, D. M. R., English
BRENNAN, S., Philosophy (Head)
BROWN, C. G., Classical Studies (Head)
BROWN, H., Philosophy
BRUSH, K., Visual Arts
CROWTHER, N. B., Classical Studies
DAVEY, F. W., English
DEMOPOULOS, W. G., Philosophy
ELLIOTT, B., Visual Arts
ESTERHAMMER, A., English, Modern Languages and Literatures
FALKENSTEIN, L., Philosophy
GEDALOF, A., Film Studies
GITTINGS, C., Film Studies (Head)
GOLDSCHLAGER, A. J., French
GRODEN, M. L., English
HARPER, W. L., Philosophy

HOFFMASTER, C. B., Philosophy
KNEALE, J. D., English (Head)
KREISWIRTH, M., English
LEE, A. M., Women's Studies (Head)
LENNON, T. M., Philosophy
LEONARD, J., English
LITTLEWOOD, A. R., Classical Studies
MAHON, P., Visual Arts (Head)
MARRAS, A., Philosophy
MAYNARD, P. L., Philosophy, Visual Arts
MURISON, L., Classical Studies
POOLE, R., English
PURDY, A., French
RAJAN, T., English
RANDALL, M., French
SOMERSET, J. A. B., English
TENNANT, J., French (Head)
THOMSON, C., French

Faculty of Education (tel. (519) 661-3182; internet www.uwo.ca/edu):

CUMMINGS, A.
DICKINSON, G. M.
LESCHIED, A.
MAJHANOVICH, S. E. W.
PEARSON, A. T.

Faculty of Engineering (tel. (519) 661-2128; internet www.eng.uwo.ca):

ADAMIAK, K., Electrical and Computer
BADDOUR, R. E., Civil and Environmental
BARTLETT, F. M. P., Civil and Environmental
BASSI, A., Chemical and Biochemical
BERRUTI, F., Dean's Office, Chemical and Biochemical
BRIENS, C. L., Chemical and Biochemical
DE LASA, H., Chemical and Biochemical
EL NAGGAR, H., Civil and Environmental
FLORYAN, J. M., Mechanical and Materials
GREASON, W. D., Electrical and Computer
HONG, H. P., Civil and Environmental
JIANG, J., Electrical and Computer
JOHNSON, J. A., Mechanical and Materials
JUTAN, A., Chemical and Biochemical
KARAMANEV, D., Chemical and Biochemical
KHAYAT, R. E., Mechanical and Materials
KNOPF, G. K., Mechanical and Materials
PATEL, R. V., Electrical and Computer
ROHANI, S., Chemical and Biochemical
SHANG, J. Q., Civil and Environmental
SHINOZAKI, D. M., Mechanical and Materials
SIDHU, T. S., Electrical and Computer
SIMONOVIĆ, S., Civil and Environmental
SINGH, A. V., Mechanical and Materials
VANFUL, E., Civil and Environmental
ZHU, J., Chemical and Biochemical

Faculty of Health Sciences (tel. (519) 661-4249; internet www.uwo.ca/fhs):

BAKA, R., Kinesiology
BELCASTRO, A. N., Kinesiology
BUCKOLZ, E., Kinesiology
CARRON, A. V., Kinesiology
DOYLE, P., Communication Sciences and Disorders
FORCHUK, C., Nursing
GARLAND, J., Physical Therapy
GOLDENBERG, D., Nursing
HALL, C. R., Kinesiology
IWASIW, C., Nursing
JAMIESON, D., Communication Sciences and Disorders
JOHNSON, C. S., Kinesiology
LASCHINGER, H., Nursing
LEMON, P., Kinesiology
MCWILLIAM, C., Nursing
MEIER, K. V., Kinesiology
MORROW, L. D., Kinesiology
MYERS, A. M., Kinesiology
NOBLE, E., Kinesiology
ORCHARD, C., Nursing (Head)
OVEREND, T., Physical Therapy (Head)
PATERSON, D. H., Kinesiology
PICHÉ, L. A., Kinesiology
SALMONI, A., Kinesiology (Head)

SEEWALD, R. C., Communication Sciences and Disorders
SEMOTIUK, D., Kinesiology
SUMSION, T., Occupational Therapy (Head)
TREVITHICK, J. R., Kinesiology
TRUJILLO, S., Health Sciences (Head)
VANDERVOORT, A. A., Physical Therapy
WATSON, R., Communication Sciences and Disorders (Head)
WEESE, W. J., Kinesiology

Faculty of Information and Media Studies (tel. (519) 661-3542; fax (519) 661-3506; internet www.fims.uwo.ca):

BABE, R. E.
CRAVEN, T. C.
HARRIS, R. M.
PARR, J.
ROSS, C. L.
SPENCER, D.
VAUGHAN, L. Q.
WILKINSON, M. A.

Faculty of Law (tel. (519) 661-3346; fax (519) 850-2412; internet www.law.uwo.ca):

BARTON, P. G.
BROWN, C.
EDGAR, T.
HOLLAND, W. H.
HOLLOWAY, I.
HOVIUS, B.
MCLAREN, R. H.
MERCER, P.
SOLOMON, R.
USPRICH, S. J.
WELLING, B.

Don Wright Faculty of Music (tel. (519) 661-2043; fax (519) 661-3531; e-mail music@uwo.ca; internet www.music.uwo.ca):

BRACEY, J. P., Music Performance Studies
FISKE, H., Music Education
GRIER, J., Music History
HEARD, A., Theory and Composition
KOPROWSKI, P. P., Theory and Composition
MCKAY, J., Music Performance Studies (Head)
NOLAN, C., Theory and Composition (Head)
PARKS, R. S., Theory and Composition
TOFT, R. E., Music History (Head)
WOODFORD, P., Music Education (Head)

Faculty of Science (tel. (519) 661-3040; e-mail science@uwo.ca; internet www.uwo.ca/sci):

BAILEY, R., Biology
BAINES, K. M., Chemistry (Head)
BAIRD, N. C., Chemistry
BARRON, J. L., Computer Science
BATTISTA, J., Medical Biophysics (Head)
BAUER, M. A., Computer Science (Head)
BELLHOUSE, D. R., Statistical and Actuarial Sciences
BOIVIN, A., Mathematics
BRANDL, C., Biochemistry (Head)
CAMPBELL, K., Epidemiology and Biostatistics (Head)
CASS, F. P. A., Mathematics
CAVENEY, S., Biology
CORLESS, R. M., Applied Mathematics; Computer Science; Philosophy (Head, Applied Mathematics)
COTTAM, M. G., Physics and Astronomy
DAY, A. W., Biology
DEAN, P. A. W., Chemistry
DEBRUYN, J. R., Physics and Astronomy (Joint Head)
EATON, D. W. S., Earth Sciences
ELIAS, V. W., Applied Mathematics
ESSEX, G. C., Applied Mathematics
FENTON, M. B., Biology (Head)
FLORYAN, J. M., Applied Mathematics
GUTHRIE, J. P., Chemistry and Biochemistry
HEINICKE, A. G., Mathematics
HICOCK, S. R., Earth Sciences
HOCKING, W. K., Physics and Astronomy
HOLT, R. A., Physics and Astronomy
HUANG, Y., Chemistry

HUNER, N. P. A., Biology
JARDINE, J. F., Mathematics
JEFFREY, D. J., Applied Mathematics
JIN, J., Earth Sciences
JONES, B. L., Physics and Astronomy (Joint Head)
JÜRGENSEN, H., Computer Science
JUTAN, A., Applied Mathematics
KANE, R. M., Mathematics (Head)
KANG, C. Y., Biology
KERR, M. A., Chemistry
KHALKHALI, M., Mathematics
KOVAL, S. F., Earth Sciences, Microbiology and Immunology
KRISHNA, P., Biology
KULPERGER, R. J., Statistical and Actuarial Sciences
LACHANCE, M. A., Biology, Microbiology and Immunology
LAU, L. W. M., Physics and Astronomy
LEAIST, D. G., Chemistry
LEHMAN, M., Anatomy and Cell Biology (Head)
LENNARD, W. N., Physics and Astronomy
LIPSON, R. H., Chemistry
LONGSTAFFE, F. J., Earth Sciences
LUTFIYYA, H., Earth Sciences
MCKEON, D. G. C., Applied Mathematics
MCLEOD, A. I., Statistical and Actuarial Sciences
MCNEIL, J. N., Biology
MADHAVJI, J. W., Computer Science
MARTIN, R. R., Chemistry
MERCER, R. E., Computer Science
MILLAR, J. S., Biology
MILNES, P., Mathematics
MINÀC, J., Mathematics
MIRANSKY, V. A., Applied Mathematics
MITTLER, S., Physics and Astronomy
NESBITT, H. W., Earth Sciences (Head)
NORTON, P. R., Chemistry
PAYNE, N. C., Chemistry
PLINT, A. G., Earth Sciences
PODESTA, R. B., Biology
POTTER, P., History of Medicine (Head)
PROVOST, S., Statistical and Actuarial Sciences
PUDDEPHATT, R. J., Chemistry
RAY, A. K., Applied Mathematics
RENNER, L. E., Mathematics
RILEY, D. M., Mathematics
ROHANI, S., Applied Mathematics
ROSNER, S. D., Physics and Astronomy
RYLETT, R. J., Physiology and Pharmacology (Head)
SECCO, R. A., Earth Sciences
SHAM, T. K., Chemistry
SHAW, G. S., Biochemistry and Chemistry
SHOESMITH, D. W., Chemistry
SICA, R. J., Physics and Astronomy
SINGH, M. R., Physics and Astronomy
SINGH, S. M., Biology
STANFORD, D. A., Statistical and Actuarial Sciences
STILLMAN, M. J., Chemistry
TRICK, C. G., Biology
USSELMAN, M. C., Chemistry
VALVANO, M., Microbiology and Immunology (Head)
WATT, S., Computer Science
WEEDON, A. C., Chemistry
WORKENTIN, M. S., Chemistry
WREN, J. C., Chemistry
YU, P., Applied Mathematics
YU, S., Computer Science
ZHANG, K., Computer Science
ZINKE-ALLMANG, M., Physics and Astronomy

Faculty of Social Science (tel. (519) 661-2053; fax (519) 661-3868; internet www.ssc.uwo.ca):

ABELSON, D., American Studies (Joint Head)
ABELSON, D., Political Science (Head)
ALLAHAR, A., Sociology

ALLEN, N., Psychology
ASHMORE, P. E., Geography
AVERY, D. H., History
AVISON, W. R., Sociology
BEAUJOT, R. P., Sociology
BHATIA, K. B., Economics
BOYER, R. S., Economics
BURGESS, D. F., Economics
CAIN, D. P., Psychology
CARROLL, M., Sociology
CHEN, X., Psychology
CHHEM, R. K., Anthropology
CLARK, S., Sociology
CODE, W. R., Geography
CONNIDIS, I. A., Sociology
CÔTE, J. E., Sociology
CREIDER, C., Linguistics (Joint Head)
CREIDER, C. A., Anthropology (Head)
CYBULSKI, J. S., Anthropology
DARNELL, R., First Nations Studies (Joint Head)
DAVENPORT, P., Economics
DAVIES, J. B., Economics
ELLIS, C., Anthropology
EMERY, G., History
ESSAS, V., Psychology
FISHER, W. A., Psychology
FLEMING, K., Management and Organizational Studies (Head)
FLEMING, M., Political Science
FORSTER, B., History (Head)
GARDINER, M., Sociology
GOODALE, M., Psychology
GRABB, E. G., Sociology
GREEN, M. B., Geography
HAMPSON, E., Psychology
HARSHMAN, R., Psychology
HEAP, D., Linguistics (Joint Head)
HELE, K., First Nations Studies (Joint Head)
HERNANDEZ-SAENZ, L. M., Latin American Studies (Head)
HEWITT, W. E., Sociology
JOHNSTON, A., American Studies (Joint Head)
KATZ, A. N., Psychology
KAVALIERS, M., Psychology
KELLOW, M., International Relations (Head)
KING, R. H., Geography
KNIGHT, J., Economics
KUIPER, N. A., Psychology
LUCKMAN, B. H., Geography
LUPKER, S. J., Psychology
McBEAN, G., Geography, Political Science
McDOUGALL, J. N., Political Science
McQUILLAN, K., Sociology
McRAE, K., Psychology
MARTIN, R. A., Psychology
MAXIM, P. S., Sociology
MEYER, J. P., Psychology
MOLTO, J. E., Anthropology
MORAN, G., Psychology
NEUFELD, R. W. J., Psychology
OLSON, J. M., Psychology
OSSENKOPP, K.-P., Psychology (Head)
PAUNONEN, S. V., Psychology
PEREZ, A., Political Science
RIDDELL-DIXON, E., Political Science
ROBINSON, C. M. G. F., Economics
ROLLMAN, G. B., Psychology
RUSHTON, J. P., Psychology
SANCTON, A. B., Political Science
SELIGMAN, C., Psychology
SHATZMILLER, M., History
SHERRY, D., Psychology
SHRUBSOLE, D., Geography (Head)
SLIVINSKI, A., Economics (Head)
SMART, C. C., Geography
SORRENTINO, R. M., Psychology
SPENCE, M. W., Anthropology
TIMNEY, B. N., Psychology
VERNON, P. A., Psychology
VERNON, R. A., Political Science
WANG, J., Geography
WHALLEY, J., Economics

WHITE, C., Anthropology
WHITE, J., Sociology (Head)
WHITEHEAD, P. C., Sociology
WINTROBE, R. S., Economics
YOUNG, R. A., Political Science

Richard Ivey School of Business (tel. (519) 661-3485; e-mail info@ivey.uwo.ca; internet www.ivey.uwo.ca):

ATHANASSAKOS, G.
BEAMISH, P. W.
BELL, P. C.
CONKLIN, D. W.
DAWAR, N.
DEUTSCHER, T. H.
FISHER, R. J.
FOERSTER, S. R.
GANDZ, J.
HARDY, K. G.
HATCH, J. E.
HENDRICKS, K. B.
HIGGINS, C. A.
HOWELL, J. M.
KALYMON, B.
KONRAD, A. M.
ROTHSTEIN, M. G.
SCHAAN, J. L.
SHACKEL, D. S. J.
VAN DEN BOSCH, M. B.
WHITE, R. W.
WILSON, J. G.
WYNANT, L.

Schulich School of Medicine and Dentistry (tel. (519) 661-3459; internet www.med.uwo.ca):

ADAMS, P. C., Medicine
ALBORES, A., Physiology and Pharmacology
ANG, L. C., Pathology
ARNOLD, J. M. O., Medicine
AVISON, W. R., Paediatrics; Epidemiology and Biostatistics
BAILEY, S. I., Surgery
BALL, E. H., Biochemistry
BANTING, D. W., Dentistry
BARR, R. M., Medicine
BATTISTA, J. J., Oncology
BAUMAN, G., Oncology (Head)
BELL, D. A., Medicine
BEND, J. R., Pathology
BERTRAND, M. A., Obstetrics and Gynaecology
BLAKE, P. G., Medicine
BOLLI, P., Medicine
BORRIE, M. J., Medicine
BOUGHNER, D. R., Medicine
BOURNE, R. B., Surgery
BRANDL, C. J., Biochemistry
BRIDGER, W. A., Biochemistry
BROWN, J. B., Family Medicine
BROWN, J. D., Clinical Neurological Sciences
BROWN, J. E., Medicine
CANHAM, P. B., Medical Biophysics
CECHETTO, D. F., Anatomy and Cell Biology
CERNOVSKY, Z. Z., Psychiatry
CHACONAS, G., Biochemistry
CHAMBERS, A. F., Oncology
CHAN, F. P., Anatomy and Cell Biology
CHANG, D. C. H., Anaesthesia and Perioperative Medicine (Head)
CHERIAN, G. M., Pathology
CHHEM, R. K., Diagnostic Radiology and Nuclear Medicine
CIRIELLO, J., Physiology and Pharmacology
CLARK, W. F., Medicine
COLCLEUGH, R. G., Surgery
COOK, M. A., Physiology and Pharmacology
COOK, R. A., Biochemistry
COOKE, J. D., Physiology and Pharmacology
CORDY, P. E., Medicine
CUNNINGHAM, I. A., Diagnostic Radiology and Nuclear Medicine
DALEY, T. D., Pathology
DEKABAN, G. A., Microbiology and Immunology

DELOVITCH, T. L., Microbiology and Immunology
DENSTEDT, J. D., Surgery (Head)
DIXON, S. J., Physiology and Pharmacology
DONNER, A. P., Epidemiology and Biostatics
DREYER, J. F., Medicine
DRIEDGER, A. A., Medicine
DROST, D. J., Diagnostic Radiology and Nuclear Medicine
DUNN, S. D., Biochemistry
EDMONDS, M. W., Medicine
ELLIS, C. G., Medical Biophysics
FEIGHTNER, J. W., Family Medicine
FELDMAN, R. D., Medicine
FENSTER, A., Diagnostic Radiology and Nuclear Medicine
FERGUSON, G. G., Clinical Neurological Sciences
FINNIE, K. J. C., Medicine
FISHER, W. A., Medicine
FISMAN, S. N., Psychiatry (Head)
FLINTOFF, W., Microbiology and Immunology
FLUMERFELT, B. A., Anatomy and Cell Biology
FOWLER, P. J., Surgery
FRAHER, L. J., Medicine
FREEMAN, T., Family Medicine (Head)
FREWEN, T. C., Paediatrics (Head)
GAGNON, R., Obstetrics and Gynaecology
GARCIA, B. M., Pathology (Head)
GEORGE, C. F. P., Medicine
GERACE, R. V., Medicine
GILBERT, J. J., Pathology
GIROTTI, M. J., Surgery
GIRVAN, D. P., Surgery
GLOOR, G. B., Biochemistry
GOODALE, M. A., Physiology and Pharmacology
GRANT, C. W., Biochemistry
GUENTHER, L. C., Medicine
GUPTA, M. A., Psychiatry
HAASE, P., Anatomy and Cell Biology
HACHINSKI, V., Clinical Neurological Sciences
HAHN, A. F. G., Clinical Neurological Sciences
HAMMOND, J. R., Physiology and Pharmacology
HAMPSON, E., Psychiatry
HAN, V. K. M., Paediatrics
HANIFORD, D. B., Biochemistry
HARRIS, K. A., Surgery
HAYES, K. C., Physical Medicine and Rehabilitation
HEGELE, R. A., Medicine
HENNING, J. L., Physiology and Pharmacology
HERBERT, C. P., Family Medicine
HILL, D. J., Medicine
HOBBS, B. B., Diagnostic Radiology and Nuclear Medicine
HODSMAN, A. B., Medicine
HOFFMASTER, C. B., Family Medicine
HOLLIDAY, R. L., Surgery
HOLLOMBY, D. J., Medicine (Head)
HOOPER, P., Ophthalmology (Head)
HORE, J., Physiology and Pharmacology
HOWARD, J. M., Paediatrics
HRAMIAK, I. M., Medicine
HRYCYSHYN, A. W., Anatomy and Cell Biology
HUANG, G., Physiology and Pharmacology
HUFF, M. W., Medicine
HUMEN, D. P., Medicine
HUNTER, G. K., Dentistry
HURST, L. N., Surgery
JAFFE, P. G., Psychiatry
JAIN, S. C., Psychiatry
JAMIESON, D. G., Medicine
JEVNIKAR, A. M., Medicine
JOHNSON, C., Medicine
JOHNSON, K. C., Epidemiology and Biostatics
JONES, D. L., Physiology and Pharmacology

JUNG, J. H., Paediatrics
KANG, C. Y., Microbiology and Immunology
KARLIK, S. J., Diagnostic Radiology and Nuclear Medicine
KARMAZYN, M., Physiology and Pharmacology
KENNEDY, T. G., Physiology and Pharmacology
KIDDER, G. M., Physiology and Pharmacology
KIERNAN, J. A., Anatomy and Cell Biology
KING, G. J., Surgery
KIRK, M. E., Pathology
KLEIN, G. J., Medicine
KOGON, S. L., Dentistry
KOREN, G., Paediatrics; Medicine
KOROPATNICK, D. J., Oncology
KOSTUK, W. J., Medicine
KRONICK, J. B., Medicine
KVIETYS, P. R., Physiology
LAIRD, D. W., Anatomy and Cell Biology
LAJOIE, G., Biochemistry
LAMPE, H. B., Otolaryngology
LANNIGAN, R., Microbiology and Immunology
LEASA, D. J., Medicine
LEE, D. H., Diagnostic Radiology and Nuclear Medicine
LEE, T. Y., Diagnostic Radiology and Nuclear Medicine
LEFCOE, M. S., Diagnostic Radiology and Nuclear Medicine
LELLA, J. W., History of Medicine
LEUNG, L. W. S., Clinical Neurological Sciences
LEWIS, J. F., Medicine
LINDSAY, R. M., Medicine
LO, T. C., Biochemistry
LOWNIE, S., Clinical Neurological Sciences (Joint Head)
MCCARTHY, G. M., Dentistry
MCCORMACK, D. G., Medicine
MCDONALD, J. W., Medicine
MCFADDEN, D. G., Microbiology and Immunology
MCFADDEN, R. G., Medicine
MCGRATH, P. A., Paediatrics
MCKENZIE, F. N., Surgery
MCLACHLAN, R. S., Clinical Neurological Sciences
MACRAE, D. L., Otolaryngology (Joint Head)
MAO, Y., Epidemiology and Biostatics
MAROTTA, J. T., Clinical Neurological Sciences
MENDONCA, J., Psychiatry
MENKIS, A. H., Surgery
MILLWARD, S. F., Diagnostic Radiology and Nuclear Medicine
MORRIS, V. L., Microbiology
MUIRHEAD, J. M., Medicine
MURKIN, J. M., Anaesthesia and Perioperative Medicine
NARAYANAN, N., Physiology and Pharmacology
NATALE, R., Obstetrics and Gynaecology
NEUFELD, R. W. J., Psychiatry
NICHOLSON, R. L., Diagnostic Radiology and Nuclear Medicine
NICOLLE, D. A., Opthalmology
NISKER, J. A., Obstetrics and Gynaecology
NORMAN, R. M. G., Psychiatry
NORRIS, J. W., Clinical Neurological Sciences
NOVICK, R. J., Surgery
PARNES, L. S., Otolaryngology
PATERSON, N. A. M., Medicine
PAYTON, K. B., Medicine
PERSAD, E., Psychiatry
PETERS, T. M., Diagnostic Radiology and Nuclear Medicine
PETERSEN, N. O., Biochemistry
POTTER, P. M. J., History of Medicine and Science
POZNANSKY, M. J., Biochemistry
PRABHAKARAN, V. M., Biochemistry

PRATO, F. S., Diagnostic Radiology and Nuclear Medicine
RALLEY, F. E., Anaesthesia and Perioperative Medicine
RALPH, E. D., Medicine
RANKIN, R. N., Diagnostic Radiology and Nuclear Medicine (Head)
REID, G., Microbiology and Immunology
REYNOLDS, R. P., Medicine
RICE, G. P. A., Clinical Neurological Sciences
RICHARDSON, B. S., Obstetrics and Gynaecology (Head)
RIEDER, M J., Paediatrics
RODGER, N. W., Medicine
RORABECK, C. H., Surgery
ROTH, J. H., Surgery
RUTLEDGE, F. S., Medicine
RUTT, B. K., Diagnostic Radiology and Nuclear Medicine
RYLETT, R. J., Physiology and Pharmacology
SANDHU, H. S., Dentistry (Head)
SANGSTER, J. F., Family Medicine
SHAW, G. S., Biochemistry
SHERAR, M. D., Oncology
SHKRUM, M. J., Pathology
SHOUKRI, M. M., Epidemiology and Biostatics
SHUM, D. T. W., Pathology
SILCOX, J. A., Obstetrics and Gynaecology
SIMS, S. M., Physiology and Pharmacology
SINGH, B., Microbiology and Immunology
SINGHAL, S. K., Microbiology and Immunology
SOLIMAN, G. L., Medicine
SPENCE, J. D., Clinical Neurological Sciences
STEWART, M. A., Family Medicine
STILLER, C. R., Medicine
STRONG, M. J., Clinical Neurological Sciences (Joint Head)
TAVES, D. H., Diagnostic Radiology and Nuclear Medicine
TEASELL, R. W., Physical Medicine and Rehabilitation (Head)
TEPPERMAN, B. L., Physiology and Pharmacology
THOMPSON, R. T., Diagnostic Radiology and Nuclear Medicine
TRICK, C. G., Microbiology and Immunology
TYML, K., Medical Biophysics
URBAIN, J. L. C. P., Diagnostic Radiology and Nuclear Medicine
VALVANO, M. A., Microbiology and Immunology
VAN DYK, J., Oncology
VILIS, T., Physiology and Pharmacology
VILOS, G., Obstetrics and Gynaecology
VINGILIS, E. R., Family Medicine
WALL, W. J., Surgery
WEAVER, L. C., Physiology and Pharmacology
WESTON, W., Family Medicine
WEXLER, D., Medicine
WHITE, D. J., Surgery
WILLIAMSON, P. C., Psychiatry
WILLIS, N. R., Ophthalmology
WILSON, J. X., Physiology and Pharmacology
WISENBERG, G., Medicine
WRIGHT, E., Otolaryngology (Joint Head)
WRIGHT, J. G., Epidemiology and Biostatistics
WYSOCKI, G. P., Pathology
YANG, K., Obstetrics and Gynaecology
YEE, R., Medicine
YOUNG, G. B., Clinical Neurological Sciences
ZAMIR, M., Medical Biophysics
ZHONG, Z., Surgery

AFFILIATED INSTITUTIONS

Brescia University College: 1285 Western Rd, London, ON N6G 1H2; internet www

.uwo.ca/brescia; f. 1919; arts subjects; Principal T. TOPIĆ

PROFESSORS

SNYDER, J., Philosophy
TOPIC, T., Anthropology

Huron University College: 1349 Western Rd, London, ON N6G 1H3; internet www .huronuc.on.ca; f. 1863; arts and theological college; Principal Dr R. LUMPKIN

PROFESSORS

BLOCKER, J. S., History
CRIMMINS, J. E., Political Science
HAMILTON, G., Theology
HYLAND, P., English
MCCARTHY, D. R., English
READ, C., History
SCHACHTER, J. P., Philosophy
XU, D., Economics

King University College: 266 Epworth Ave, London, ON N6A 2M3; e-mail kings@ uwo.ca; internet www.uwo.ca/kings; f. 1912 (Seminary), 1955 (College); seminary and college of arts; Principal Dr GERALD KILLAN

PROFESSORS

BAHCHELI, T., Political Science
BARUSS, I., Psychology
BROWN, H., Philosophy and Religious Studies
BROWN, J., Social Work
COMPTON-BROUWER, R., History
GORASSINI, D. R., Psychology
HARMAN, L., Sociology
IRVING, A., Social Work
KILLAN, G., History
KOPINAK, K., Sociology
LELLA, J. W., Sociology
MACGREGOR, D., Sociology
O'CONNOR, T., Religious Studies
PATERSON, G. H., English
PRIEUR, M. R., Religious Studies
SKINNER, N. F., Psychology
WERSTINE, P., English

WILFRID LAURIER UNIVERSITY

75 University Ave, Waterloo, ON N2L 3C5
Telephone: (519) 884-1970
Fax: (519) 886-9351
Internet: www.wlu.ca
Founded 1911; formerly Waterloo Lutheran University; name changed 1973
Language of instruction: English
State control
Academic year: September to April (2 terms)
Chancellor: BOB RAE
Pres. and Vice-Chancellor: Dr MAX BLOUW
Vice-Pres. for Academic Affairs: Dr DEBORAH MACLATCHY
Vice-Pres. for Finance and Admin.: JIM BUTLER
Registrar: Dr JOHN METCALFE
Librarian and Archivist: SHARON BROWN
Number of teachers: 838 (410 full-time, 428 part-time)
Number of students: 14,750 (12,700 full-time, 2,050 part-time)
Publications: *Anthropologica* (2 a year), *Canadian Bulletin of Medical History/ Bulletin Canadien D'histoire de la Médecine* (2 a year), *Canadian Social Work Review/Revue Canadienne de Service Social* (2 a Year), *Dialogue: Canadian Philosophical Review/Revue Canadienne de Philosophie* (4 a year), *Leisure/Loisive* (4 a year), *Studies in Religion/Sciences Religieuses* (4 a year), *Toronto Journal of Theology* (4 a year), *Topia: A Canadian Journal of Cultural Studies* (2 a year)

DEANS

Faculty of Arts and Science: Dr ROBERT CAMPBELL

Faculty of Graduate Studies: Dr ADELE REINHARTZ

Faculty of Music: Dr CHARLES MORRISON

Faculty of Science: Dr ARTHUR SZABO

Faculty of Social Work: Prof. LUKE FUSCO

School of Business and Economics: Dr SCOTT CARSON

Waterloo Lutheran Seminary: Dr RICHARD CROSSMAN

UNIVERSITY OF WINDSOR

Windsor, ON N9B 3P4
Telephone: (519) 253-3000
Fax: (519) 973-7050
E-mail: registr@uwindsor.ca
Internet: www.uwindsor.ca
Founded 1857
Provincially assisted
Language of instruction: English
Academic year: September to May (2 semesters)
Chancellor: Dr EDWARD LUMLEY
Vice-Chancellor and Pres.: Dr ALAN WILDEMAN
Vice-Pres. for Admin. and Finance: STEPHEN WILLETTS
Vice-Pres. for Univ. Advancement: MICHAEL SALTER (acting)
Provost and Vice-Pres. for Academics: Prof. NEIL GOLD
Vice-Provost for Students and Registrar: Prof. BRIAN MAZER (acting)
Librarian: GWENDOLYN EBBETT
Number of teachers: 428 (full-time)
Number of students: 16,180 (full-time and part-time)
Publications: *Review*, *The Lance* (52 a year), *Windsor University Magazine* (4 a year)

DEANS

Faculty of Arts and Social Science: Dr CECIL HOUSTON

Faculty of Education: Dr PAT ROGERS

Faculty of Engineering: Dr GRAHAM T. READER

Faculty of Graduate Studies and Research: Dr JIM FRANK

Faculty of Human Kinetics: Dr ROBERT BOUCHER

Faculty of Law: Prof. BRUCE ELMAN

Faculty of Nursing: Dr ELAINE DUFFY

Faculty of Science: Dr MARLYS KOSCHINSKY

Odette School of Business: Dr ALLAN CONWAY

PROFESSORS

Faculty of Arts and Social Science:
AMORE, R. C., Political Sciences
ATKINSON, C. B., English
BABE, R. E., Communication Studies
BALANCE, W. D., Psychology
BAXTER, I., Visual Arts
BÉLANGER, S., Visual Arts
BERTMAN, S., Classical Studies
BIRD, H. W., Classical Studies
BLAIR, J. A., Philosophy
BROOKS, S., Political Science
BROWN-JOHN, C. L., Political Science
BUTLER, E. G., Music
CASSANO, P., French
COHEN, J. S., Psychology
DeANGELIS, J. R., Visual Arts
DeVILLERS, J. P., French
DILWORTH, T. R., English
DITSKY, J. M., English
GOLD SMITH, S. B., Visual Arts
HANSON, J., Music
HAWKINS, F. R., Social Work
HOLOSKO, M. J., Social Work
HOUSEHOLDER, R., Music
KING, J. N., Religious Studies

KINGSTONE, B. D., French
KLINCK, D. M., History
LAKHAN, V. C., Geography
LINTON, J. M., Communication Studies
McCRONE, K. E., History
MacKENDRICK, L. K., English
MADY KELLY, D., Dramatic Art
MURRAY, J., History
PAGE, J. S., Psychology
PALMER, D., Music
PHIPPS, A. G., Geography
PINNELL, W. H., Dramatic Art
REYNOLDS, D. V., Psychology
ROMSA, G. H., Geography
ROURKE, B. P., Psychology
SCHNEIDER, F. W., Psychology
SODERLUND, W. C., Political Science
STARETS, M., French
STEBELSKY, I., Geography
TRENHAILE, A. S., Geography
VAN DEN HOVEN, A., French
WARREN, B., Dramatic Art
WHITNEY, B., Religious Studies
WINTER, J. P., Communication Studies

Faculty of Education:
CRAWFORD, W. J. I.
KUENDIGER, E.
LAING, D. A.
MORTON, L.
WILLIAMS, N. H.

Faculty of Engineering:
AHMADI, M., Electrical Engineering
ALFA, A. S., Industrial Engineering and Manufacturing Systems Engineering
ALPAS, A. T., Mechanical, Automotive and Materials Engineering
ASFOUR, A. A., Civil and Environmental Engineering
BEWTRA, J. K., Civil and Environmental Engineering
BISWAS, N., Civil and Environmental Engineering
BUDKOWSKA, B. B., Cultural and Environmental Engineering
DUTTA, S. P., Industrial Engineering and Manufacturing Systems Engineering
EL MARAGHY, H., Industrial Engineering and Manufacturing Systems Engineering
EL MARAGHY, W., Industrial Engineering and Manufacturing Systems Engineering
FRISE, P. R., Mechanical, Automotive and Materials Engineering
HEARN, N., Civil and Environmental Engineering
KWAN, H. K., Electrical Engineering
LASHKARI, R. S., Industrial Engineering and Manufacturing Systems Engineering
MADUGULA, M. K. S., Civil and Environmental Engineering
MILLER, W. C., Electrical Engineering
NORTH, W., Mechanical, Automotive and Materials Engineering
RAJU, G. R. G., Electrical Engineering
RANKIN, G. W., Mechanical, Automotive and Materials Engineering
READER, G. T., Mechanical, Automotive and Materials Engineering
SID-AHMED, M., Electrical Engineering
SOLTIS, J., Electrical Engineering
TABOUN, S., Industrial Engineering and Manufacturing Systems Engineering
WANG, H., Industrial Engineering and Manufacturing Systems Engineering
WATT, D. F., Mechanical, Automotive and Materials Engineering
WILSON, N. W., Mechanical, Automotive and Materials Engineering

Faculty of Human Kinetics:
BOUCHER, R. L., Athletics and Recreational Studies
MARINO, W., Kinesiology

OLAFSON, G. A., Kinesiology
SALTER, M. A., Kinesiology
WEESE, W. J., Kinesiology

Faculty of Law:
BERRYMAN, J.
BOGART, W. A.
BUSHNELL, I. S.
CARASCO, E. F.
CONKLIN, W.
ELMAN, B.
GOLD, N.
IRISH, M.
MAZER, B. M.
MENEZES, J. R.
MOON, R. J.
MURPHY, P. T.
STEWART, G. R.
WEST, J. L.
WILSON, L. C.
WYDRZYNSKI, C. J.

Faculty of Science
(Some professors are also attached to the Faculty of Engineering)

AL-AASM, I. S., Earth Sciences
ANGLIN, P., Economics
AROCA, R., Chemistry and Biochemistry
ATKINSON, J. B., Physics
BANDYOPADHYAY, S., Computer Science
BARRON, R. M., Mathematics and Statistics
BAYLIS, W. E., Physics
BRITTEN, D. J., Mathematics and Statistics
CAMERON, W. S., Nursing
CARON, R. J., Mathematics and Statistics
CARTY, L., Nursing
CHANDNA, O. P., Mathematics and Statistics
CIBOROWSKI, J. J. H., Biological Sciences
COTTER, D. A., Biological Sciences
DRAKE, G. W., Physics
DRAKE, J. E., Chemistry and Biochemistry
FACKRELL, H. B., Biological Sciences
FAN, Y., Economics
FORTUNE, J. N., Economics
FROST, R. A., Computer Science
FUNG, K. Y., Mathematics and Statistics
GENCAY, R., Economics
GILLEN, W. J., Economics
GLASS, E. N., Physics
HAFFNER, G. D., Biological Sciences
HUDEC, P. P., Earth Sciences
KALONI, P. N., Mathematics and Statistics
KENT, R. D., Computer Science
LEMIRE, F. W., Mathematics and Statistics
LOEB, S. J., Chemistry and Biochemistry
LOVETT DOUST, J. N., Biological Sciences
LOVETT DOUST, L., Biological Sciences
McCONKEY, J. W., Physics
McDONALD, J. F., Mathematics and Statistics
McINTOSH, J. M., Chemistry and Biochemistry
MacISAAC, H. J., Biological Sciences
MAEV, R. G., Physics
MUTUS, B., Chemistry and Biochemistry
PAUL, S. R., Mathematics and Statistics
SALE, P. F., Biological Sciences
SIMPSON, F., Earth Sciences
SMITH, T. E., Earth Sciences
STEPHAN, D. W., Chemistry and Biochemistry
STRICK, J. C., Economics
SUH, S. C., Economics
TAYLOR, N. F., Chemistry and Biochemistry
THOMAS, B. C., Nursing
THOMAS, D., Biological Sciences
TRACY, D. S., Mathematics and Statistics
TUREK, A., Earth Sciences
WARNER, A., Biological Sciences
WONG, C. S., Mathematics and Statistics
ZAMANI, N. G., Mathematics and Statistics

Odette School of Business Administration:
ANDIAPPAN, P.
ANEJA, Y. P.
ARMSTRONG-STASSEN, M.
BRILL, P. H.
CHANDRA, R.
DICKINSON, J. R.
FARIA, A. J.
FIELDS, M.
HUSSEY, R.
KANTOR, J.
LAM, W. P.
MORGAN, A.
OKECHUKU, C.
PUNNETT, B. J.
SINGH, J.
TEMPLER, A.
THACKER, J. W.
WITHANE, S.

FEDERATED UNIVERSITY

Assumption University: 400 Huron
Church Rd, Windsor, ON; Pres. Rev. U. E.
PARÉ.

AFFILIATED COLLEGES

Canterbury College: 172 Patricia Rd,
Windsor, ON; Principal D. T. A. SYMONS.
Holy Redeemer College: Cousineau Rd,
Windsor, ON; Principal Rev. R. CORRIVEAU.
Iona College: Sunset Ave, Windsor, ON;
Principal Rev. D. G. GALSTON.

UNIVERSITY OF WINNIPEG

515 Portage Ave, Winnipeg, MB R3B 2E9

Telephone: (204) 786-7811

Fax: (204) 786-8656

Internet: www.uwinnipeg.ca

Founded 1871, univ. status 1967
Controlled jtly by the Govt of Manitoba and
the United Church of Canada
Language of instruction: English
Academic year: September to April

Chancellor: H. SANDFORD RILEY
Vice-Chancellor and Pres.: LLOYD AXWORTHY
Vice-Pres. for Academic Affairs: BRIAN STE-
VENSON
Vice-Pres. for Finance and Admin.: BILL
BALAN
Vice-Pres. for Human Resources, Audit and
Sustainability: LAUREL REPSKI
Vice-Pres. for Research and Int.: NEIL BES-
NER
Corporate Sec. and Gen. Counsel: VALERIE
GILROY

Number of teachers: 330
Number of students: 9,394

DEANS

Faculty of Arts: DAVID FITZPATRICK
Faculty of Business and Economics: MICHAEL
BENARROCH
Faculty of Continuing Education: ERIN STEW-
ART
Faculty of Education: KEN MCCLUSKEY
Faculty of Science: RODNEY HANLEY
Faculty of Theology: JAMES CHRISTIE
The Collegiate: ROBERT BEND

PROFESSORS

ABD-EL-AZIZ, Chemistry
ABIZADEH, S., Economics
BAILEY, D. A., History
BASILEVSKY, A., Statistics
BECKER, G., Psychology
BOTTERILL, C., Sport Psychology
BRADBURY, H., Psychology
BROWN, J., History
BROWN, W., Economics
BURLEY, D., History
CARLYLE, W. J., Geography
CARTER, T., Geography
CHAN, F. Y., Business Computing

CHEAL, D. J., Sociology
CLARK, J., Psychology
CLOUTIS, E., Geography
DANNEFAER, S., Physics
DAY, P., Religious Studies
DONG, X.-Y., Economics
EVANS, M., English
FEHR, B., Psychology
FORBES, S., Biology
FRIESEN, K., Chemistry
GINSBERG, J., Mathematics
GOLDEN, M., Classics
GRANT, H., Economics
GRANZBERG, G., Anthropology
GREENHILL, P., Women's Studies
HARVEY, C. J., French Studies
HATHOUT, S., Geography
HOWLADER, H., Statistics
HUEBNER, J., Biology
IZYDORCZYK, Z., English
KERR, D. P., Physics
KHAN, R. A., Political Science
KOBES, R., Physics
KUNSTATTER, G., Physics
KYDON, D. W., Physics
LEHR, J., Geography
LEO, C., Political Science
McCORMACK, A. R., History
McCORMACK, R., History
McDOUGALL, I., Classics
McINTYRE, M., Psychology
MAYS, A., Education
MEADWELL, K., French Studies
MEIKLEJOHN, C., Anthropology
MILLS, A., Political Science, Anthropology
MOODIE, G. E. E., Biology
NNADI, J., French Studies
NODELMAN, P. M., English
NORTON, R., Psychology
NOVEK, J., Sociology
PARAMESWARAN, U., English
PEELING, J., Chemistry
PIP, E., Biology
POLYZOI, E., Education
RANNIE, W., Geography
ROCKMAN, G., Psychology
RODRIGUEZ, L., French
SCHAEFER, E., Psychology
SCOTT, G., Geography
SELWOOD, J., Geography
SPIGELMAN, M., Psychology
STANIFORTH, R., Biology
STONE, D. Z., History
STRUB, H., Psychology
TOMCHUK, E., Physics
TOMLINSON, G., Chemistry
VISELLI, S., French Studies
WIEGAND, M., Biology
WRIGHT, C., Political Science
YOUNG, R. J., History

ATTACHED INSTITUTES

Institute of Urban Studies: 515 Portage
Ave, Winnipeg; Dir JINO DISTASIO.
Menno Simons College: 515 Portage Ave,
Winnipeg; Pres. EARL DAVEY.

YORK UNIVERSITY

4700 Keele St, Toronto, ON M3J 1P3

Telephone: (416) 736-2100

Fax: (416) 736-5700

Internet: www.yorku.ca

Founded 1959, ind. 1965
Public control
Language of instruction: English (Glendon
College: English and French)
Academic year: September to April

Chancellor: ROY MCMURTRY
Pres. and Vice-Chancellor: MAMDOUH
SHOUKRI
Pres. and CEO York Univ. Foundation and
Vice-Pres. (Dev) PAUL MARCUS
Vice-Pres. for Academics: SHEILA EMBLETON

Vice-Pres. for Finance and Admin.: GARY
BREWER
Vice-Pres. for Research and Innovation: STAN
SHAPSON
Vice-Pres. for Students and Alumni: ROBERT
J. TIFFIN
Univ. Sec. and Gen. Counsel: HARRIET LEWIS
Number of teachers: 1,415 (full-time)
Number of students: 52,290
Publications: *Profiles* (4 a year), *York Gazette*
(37 a year)

DEANS

Faculty of Education: ALICE PITT
Faculty of Environmental Studies: BARBARA
RAHDER (acting)
Faculty of Fine Arts: BARBRA SELLERS-YOUNG
Faculty of Graduate Studies: DOUGLAS PEERS
Faculty of Liberal Arts and Professional
Studies: MARTIN SINGER
Faculty of Pure and Applied Science: GILLIAN
E. WU
Glendon College: KENNETH MCROBERTS (Prin-
cipal)
Osgoode Hall Law School: PATRICK J. MON-
AHAN
Schulich School of Business: DEZSO HORVATH

PROFESSORS

Faculty of Education:
BRITZMAN, D. P.
BUNCH, G.
EWOLDT, C.
HESHUSIUS, L.
PIPER, T. C.
ROGERS, P. K.
SHAPSON, S.

Faculty of Environmental Studies:
BELL, D. V. J.
DALY, G. P.
FOUND, W. C.
GREER-WOOTTEN, B.
HOMENUCK, H. P. M.
SPENCE, E. S.
VICTOR, P. A.
WEKERLE, G. R.
WILKINSON, P. F.

Faculty of Fine Arts:
BIELER, T., Visual Arts
MÉTRAUX, G. P. R., Visual Arts
MORRIS, P., Film and Video
RUBIN, D., Theatre
SANKARAN, T., Music
TENNEY, J., Music
THURLBY, M., Visual Arts
TOMCIK, A., Visual Arts
WHITEN, T., Visual Arts

Faculty of Liberal Arts and Professional
Studies:
ABRAMSON, M., Mathematics and Statistics
ADELMAN, H., Philosophy
ANISEF, P., Sociology
APPELBAUM, E., Economics
ARMSTRONG, C., History
ARMSTRONG, P., Sociology
ARTHUR, R. G., Humanities
AXELROD, P., Social Science
BARTEL, H., Administrative Studies
BAYEFSKY, A. F., Political Science
BEER, F. F., English
BIALYSTOK, E., Psychology
BIRBALSINGH, F. M., English
BLUM, A. F., Sociology
BORDESSA, R., Geography
BROWN, M. G., Humanities
BURNS, R. G., Mathematics and Statistics
BUTLER, G. R., Humanities
CALLAGHAN, B., English
CARLEY, J., English
CHAMBERS, D., Physical Education
CODE, L. B., Philosophy
COHEN, D., English
COTNAM, J., French Studies

COWLES, M. P., Psychology
CUFF, R. D., History
CUMMINGS, M. J., English
DANZIGER, L., Economics
DARROCH, A. G. L., Sociology
DAVIES, D. I., Social Science and Sociology
DAVIS, C. A., Physical Education
DEWITT, D. B., Political Science
DONNENFELD, S., Economics
DOSMAN, E. J., Political Science
DOW, A. S., Mathematics and Statistics
DRACHE, D., Political Science
DROST, H., Economics
EGNAL, M. M., History
EHRLICH, S. L., Languages, Literatures and Linguistics
ELLENWOOD, W. R., English
EMBLETON, S. M., Languages, Literatures and Linguistics
ENDLER, N. S., Psychology
FAAS, E., Humanities
FANCHER, R. E., Psychology
FICHMAN, M., Humanities
FLEMING, S. J., Psychology
FLETCHER, F. J., Political Science
FLETT, G. L., Psychology
FOWLER, B. H., Physical Education
FREEMAN, D. B., Geography
FROLIC, M. B., Political Science
GILL, S., Political Science
GLEDHILL, N., Physical Education
GRAY, P. T., Humanities
GRAYSON, J. P., Sociology
GREEN, B. S., Sociology
GREEN, L. J. M., Philosophy
GREENBERG, L., Psychology
GREENGLASS, E. R., Psychology
GREER-WOOTTEN, B., Geography
GUIASU, S., Mathematics and Statistics
GUY, G. R., Languages, Literatures and Linguistics
HABERMAN, A., Humanities
HARRIES-JONES, P., Anthropology
HARRIS, L. R., Psychology
HATTIANGADI, J. N., Philosophy
HEIDENREICH, C., Geography
HELLMAN, J., Political Science and Social Science
HELLMAN, S., Political Science
HERREN, M., Classics and Humanities
HILL, A. R., Geography
HOBSON, D. B., Humanities
HOFFMAN, R. C., History
HRUSKA, K. C., Mathematics and Statistics
INNES, C., English
IRVINE, W. D., History
JARVIE, I. C., Philosophy
KANYA-FORSTNER, A. S., History
KAPLAN, H., Political Science and Social Science
KATER, M. H., History
KATZ, E., Economics
KING, R. E., Languages, Literatures and Linguistics
KLEINER, I., Mathematics and Statistics
KOCHMAN, S. O., Mathematics and Statistics
KOHN, P. M., Psychology
LANDA, J. T., Economics
LANPHIER, C. M., Sociology
LENNOX, J. W., English
LEVY, J., Nursing
LEYTON-BROWN, D., Political Science
LIGHTMAN, B. V., Humanities
LIPSIG-MUMMÉ, C., Social Science
LOVEJOY, P. E., History
LUXTON, M., Social Science
MCROBERTS, K. H., Political Science
MADRAS, N. N., Mathematics and Statistics
MAHANEY, W. C., Geography
MAIDMAN, M. P., History
MALLIN, S. B., Philosophy
MANN, S. N., History
MASON, S. N., Humanities
MASSAM, B. H., Geography
MASSAM, H., Mathematics and Statistics

MENDELSOHN, D. J., Languages, Literatures and Linguistics
MOUGEON, R., French Studies
MULDOON, M. E., Mathematics and Statistics
MURDIE, R. A., Geography
NAGATA, J., Anthropology
NELLES, H. V., History
NOBLE, D., Social Science
NORCLIFFE, G. B., Geography
NORTH, L., Political Science
O'BRIEN, G. L., Mathematics and Statistics
OKADA, R., Psychology
OLIN, P., Mathematics and Statistics
OLIVER, P. N., History
ONO, H., Psychology
PANITCH, L., Political Science
PELLETIER, J. M., Mathematics and Statistics
PEPLER, D. J., Psychology
PLOURDE, C., Economics
POLKA, B., Humanities
POPE, R. W. F., Languages, Literatures and Linguistics
PROMISLOW, S. D., Mathematics and Statistics
PYKE, S., Psychology
RADFORD, J. P., Geography
REGAN, D. M., Psychology
RENNIE, D. L., Psychology
ROBBINS, S. G., Physical Education
RODMAN, M. C., Anthropology
ROGERS, N. C. T., History
SALISBURY, T., Mathematics and Statistics
SAUL, J. S., Social Science
SHANKER, S. G., Philosophy
SHTEIR, A. B., Humanities
SHUBERT, A., History
SILVERMAN, M., Anthropology
SIMMONS, H., Political Science
SIMPSON-HOUSLEY, P., Geography
SMITHIN, J. N., Economics
SOLITAR, D., Mathematics and Statistics
STAGER, P., Psychology
STEINBACH, M. J., Psychology
STEPRANS, J., Mathematics and Statistics
SUBTELNY, O., History and Political Science
THOLEN, W., Mathematics and Statistics
UNRAU, J. P., English
VAN ESTERIK, P., Anthropology
WAKABAYASHI, B. T., History
WATSON, W. S., Mathematics and Statistics
WEISS, A. I., Computer Science and Mathematics
WHITAKER, R., Political Science
WHITELEY, W. J., Mathematics and Statistics
WILSON, B. A., Humanities
WONG, M., Mathematics and Statistics
WOOD, J. D., Geography
WU, J., Mathematics and Statistics

Faculty of Pure and Applied Science:

ALDRIDGE, K. D., Earth and Atmospheric Science
ARJOMANDI, E., Computer Science
BARTEL, N. H., Physics and Astronomy
BOHME, D. K., Chemistry
CAFARELLI, E. D., Physical Education
CALDWELL, J. J., Natural Science, Physics and Astronomy
CANNON, W. H., Physics and Astronomy
COLMAN, B., Biology
COUKELL, M. B., Biology
DAREWYCH, J. W., Physics and Astronomy
DAVEY, K. G., Biology
DE ROBERTIS, M. M., Physics and Astronomy
DYMOND, P. W., Computer Science
FENTON, M. B., Biology and Environmental Science
FILSETH, S. V., Chemistry
FORER, A., Biology
FREEDHOFF, H. S., Physics and Astronomy
GLEDHILL, N., Physical Education
GOODINGS, J. M., Chemistry

HARRIS, G. W., Chemistry
HASTIE, D. R., Chemistry
HEATH, I. B., Biology
HEDDLE, J. A. M., Biology
HILLIKER, A. J., Biology
HOLLOWAY, C. E., Chemistry
HOOD, D. A., Physical Education
HOPKINSON, A. C., Chemistry
HORBATSCH, M., Physics and Astronomy
INNANEN, K. A., Physics and Astronomy
JARRELL, R. A., Natural Science
JARVIS, G. T., Earth and Atmospheric Science
KONIUK, R., Physics and Astronomy
LAFRAMBOISE, J. G., Physics and Astronomy
LEE-RUFF, E., Chemistry
LEVER, A. B. P., Chemistry
LEZNOFF, C. C., Chemistry
LICHT, L. E., Biology and Environmental Science
LIU, J. W. H., Computer Science
LOGAN, D. M., Biology and Natural Science
LOUGHTON, B. G., Biology
MCCALL, M., Physics and Astronomy
MCCONNELL, J. C., Earth and Atmospheric Science
MCQUEEN, D. J., Biology and Environmental Science
MALTMAN, K. R., Mathematics and Statistics
MILLER, J. R., Physics and Astronomy
PACKER, L. D. M., Biology
PEARLMAN, R. E., Biology
PRINCE, R. H., Physics and Astronomy
RUDOLPH, J., Chemistry
SALEUDDIN, A. S. M., Biology
SAPP, J. A., Biology
SHEPHERD, G. G., Earth and Atmospheric Science
SIU, K. W. M., Chemistry
SMYLIE, D. E., Earth and Atmospheric Science
STAUFFER, A. D., Mathematics and Statistics, Physics and Astronomy
STEEL, C. G., Biology
TAYLOR, P. A., Earth and Atmospheric Science
TOURLAKIS, G., Computer Science
TSOTSOS, J. K., Computer Science
WEBB, R. A., Biology

Osgoode Hall Law School:

ARTHURS, H. W.
BROOKS, W. N.
GEVA, B.
GRAY, R. J. S.
HASSON, R. A.
HATHAWAY, J. C.
HOGG, P. W.
HUTCHINSON, A. C.
MCCAMUS, J. D.
MANDEL, M. G.
MONAHAN, P. J.
MOSSMAN, M. J.
RAMSAY, I. D.
SALTER, R. L.
SLATTERY, B.
VAVER, D.
WATSON, G. D.
WILLIAMS, S. A.
ZEMANS, F. H.

Schulich School of Business:

BURKE, R. J., Organizational Behaviour, Industrial Relations
BUZACOTT, J., Management Science
COOK, W. D., Management Science
CRAGG, A. W., Business Ethics
DERMER, J. D., Policy
FENWICK, I. D., Marketing
HEELER, R. M., Marketing
HORVATH, D., Policy
LITVAK, I. A., Policy
MCKELLAR, J., Real Property Development
MCMILLAN, C. J., Policy

MORGAN, G. H., Organizational Behaviour, Industrial Relations
OLIVER, C. E., Organizational Behaviour, Industrial Relations
PAN, Y., International Business
PETERSON, R., Policy
PRISMAN, E., Finance
ROBERTS, G. S., Finance
ROSEN, L. S., Accounting
THOMPSON, D. N., Marketing
TRYFOS, P., Management Science
WHEELER, D. C., Business and Sustainability
WILSON, H. T., Policy
WOLF, B. M., Economics

Glendon College:
ABELLA, I. M., History
ALCOCK, J., Psychology
BAUDOT, A., French Studies
DOOB, P. B., English
GENTLES, I. J., History
HORN, M. S. D., History
KIRSCHBAUM, S. J., Political Science
KLEIN-LATAUD, C., Translation
MAHANT, E., Political Science
MORRIS, R. N., Sociology
MOYAL, G. J. D., Philosophy
OLSHEN, B. N., English and Multidisciplinary Studies
ONDAATJE, P. M., English
SHAND, G. B., English
TATILON, C., French Studies
TWEYMAN, S., Philosophy
WALLACE, R. S., English
WHITFIELD, A., Translation

ATTACHED INSTITUTES

Canadian Centre for German and European Studies: 230 York Lanes, York University, 4700 Keele St, Toronto, ON M3J 1P3; Dir J. PECK.

Centre for Atmospheric Chemistry: 006 Steacie Science, York University, 4700 Keele St, Toronto, ON M3J 1P3; Dir G. W. HARRIS.

Centre for Feminist Research: 228 York Lanes, York University, 4700 Keele St, Toronto, ON M3J 1P3; Dir D. KHAYATT.

Centre for Health Studies: 214 York Lanes, York University, Toronto, ON M3J 1P3; Dir G. D. FELDBERG.

Centre for International and Security Studies: 375 York Lanes, York University, 4700 Keele St, Toronto, ON M3J 1P3; Dir D. B. DEWITT.

Centre for Jewish Studies: 260 Vanier College, York University, 4700 Keele St, Toronto, ON M3J 1P3; Dir M. G. BROWN.

Centre for Practical Ethics: 102 McLaughlin, York University, 4700 Keele St, Toronto, ON M3J 1P3; Dir D. SHUGARMAN.

Centre for Public Law and Public Policy: 435 Osgoode, York University, 4700 Keele St, Toronto, ON M3J 1P3; Dir P. J. MONAHAN.

Centre for Refugee Studies: 322 York Lanes, York University, 4700 Keele St, Toronto, ON M3J 1P3; Dir P. PENZ.

Centre for Research in Earth and Space Science: 249 Petrie Science Building, York University, 4700 Keele St, Toronto, ON M3J 1P3; Dir G. SHEPHERD.

Centre for Research on Latin America and the Caribbean: 240 York Lanes, York University, Toronto, ON M3J 1P3; Dir V. PATRONI.

Centre for Research on Work and Society: 276 York Lanes, York University, Toronto, ON M3J 1P3; Dir C. LIPSIG-MUMMÉ.

Centre for the Study of Computers in Education: S869 Ross, York University, 4700 Keele St, Toronto, ON M3J 1P3; Dir R. D. OWSTON.

Centre for Vision Research: 103 Farquharson, York University, 4700 Keele St, Toronto, ON M3J 1P3; Dir J. TSOTSOS.

Joint Centre for Asia Pacific Studies: 270 York Lanes, York University, 4700 Keele St, Toronto, ON M3J 1P3; Dir B. FROLIC.

LaMarsh Centre for Research on Violence and Conflict Resolution: 217 York Lanes, York University, 4700 Keele St, Toronto, ON M3J 1P3; Dir D. J. PEPLER.

Nathanson Centre for the Study of Organized Crime and Corruption: 321A Osgoode, York University, 4700 Keele St, Toronto, ON M3J 1P3; Dir M. BEARE.

Robarts Centre for Canadian Studies: 227 York Lanes, York University, 4700 Keele St, Toronto, ON M3J 1P3; Dir D. DRACHE.

York Centre for Applied Sustainability: 355 Lumbers, York University, 4700 Keele St, Toronto, ON M3J 1P3; Dir D. BELL.

York Institute for Social Research: 242A Schulich School of Business, York University, 4700 Keele St, Toronto, ON M3J 1P3; Dir M. ORNSTEIN.

Schools of Art and Music

Alberta College of Art and Design: 1407 14th Ave NW, Calgary, AB T2N 4R3; tel. (403) 284-7600; fax (403) 289-6682; e-mail admissions@acad.ca; internet www.acad.ab.ca; f. 1926; 4-year degree and diploma programmes in visual arts and design; 100 teachers; 1,000 students; library: 28,578 vols and colln of 124,845 slides, 75 periodical titles; Pres. LANCE CARLSON.

Banff Centre: POB 1020, Banff, AB T1L 1H5; tel. (403) 762-6100; fax (403) 762-6444; internet www.banffcentre.ca; f. 1933; offers programmes in arts (aboriginal arts, audio, press, new media, creative electronic environment, dance, media and visual arts, music, opera, theatre, writing, curatorial practice; leadership development, aboriginal leadership and management, mountain culture, environmental issues; Pres. and CEO MARY E. HOFSTETTER; Senior Vice-President, Programming JOANNE MORROW; Vice-President and CFO J. A NUTT.

Conservatoire de Musique de Montréal: 4750 ave Henri-Julien, Montréal, QC H2T 2C8; tel. (514) 873-4031; fax (514) 873-4601; e-mail cmm@mcc.gouv.qc.ca; internet www.mcc.gouv.ca/conservatoire/montreal.htm; f. 1942; a government-controlled institution, largest of a network of 7 in Québec Province; 76 teachers; 340 students; library: 58,000 books and scores, 125 rare books, 20 MSS, 10,000 recordings and 80 periodicals; Dir ISOLDE LAGACÉ.

Conservatoire de Musique de Québec: 270 rue St-Amable, Québec, QC G1R 5G1; tel. (418) 643-2190; fax (418) 644-9658; e-mail cmq@mcc.gouv.qc.ca; internet www.mcc.gouv.gc.ca/conservatoire/quebec.htm; f. 1944; 50 teachers; 250 students; library: 68,000 vols, recordings, scores and periodicals; Dir GUY CARMICHAEL.

Maritime Conservatory of Performing Arts: 6199 Chebucto Rd, Halifax, NS B3L 1K7; tel. (902) 423-6995; fax (902) 423-6029; e-mail mconservatory@ns.sympatico.ca; f. 1887; 80 teachers; 1,200 students; Dir Dr IFAN WILLIAMS.

Ontario College of Art and Design: 100 McCaul St, Toronto, ON M5T 1W1; tel. (416) 977-6000; fax (416) 977-6006; internet www.ocad.on.ca; f. 1876; library: 24,000 vols, 225 periodical subscriptions, 44,000 pictures, 70,000 slides, etc.; post-secondary education in fine art and design; 200 teachers; 2,329 students; Pres. RON SHUEBROOK; Exec. Vice-Pres. PETER CALDWELL; Financial Aids and Awards Officer KELLY DICKINSON; Dir of Library JILL PATRICK.

Royal Canadian College of Organists: 204 St George St, Suite 204, Toronto, ON M5R 2N5; tel. (416) 929-6400; fax (416) 929-2265; e-mail rcco@the-wire.com; internet www.rcco.ca; f. 1909; Pres. F. ALAN REESOR; Vice-Pres. PATRICIA WRIGHT; Treas. DON TIMMINS; publs Organ Canada (4 a year), The American Organist (12 a year, in asscn with American Guild of Organists).

Royal Conservatory of Music: 273 Bloor St West, Toronto ON M5S 1W2; tel. (416) 408-2824; fax (416) 408-3096; e-mail communityschool@rcmusic.ca; internet www.rcmusic.ca; f. 1886; 350 teachers; 10,000 students; Pres. PETER C. SIMON; Deans JEFF MELANSON, RENNIE REGEHR.

CAPE VERDE

The Higher Education System

Cape Verde has little history of higher education. During five centuries of colonial rule in the archipelago Portugal did not draft any known plans for the establishment of a university for Cape Verde. After the granting of independence in 1975, the number of students enrolled in secondary education increased markedly, and the demand for higher education began to be addressed with the creation of several institutes of higher studies to train teachers and health workers. Most Cape Verdeans studied abroad; in 2002/03 there were 1,743 Cape Verdean students studying at overseas universities. However, the cost of foreign study was high. Thus, as domestic demand increased throughout the 1990s, more concrete plans were made for establishing a university. The Universidade Jean Piaget de Cabo Verde was founded in 2002; in 2005/06 there were 4,567 students in higher education. There is also a higher institute of engineering and marine science, and in 2007 the first professional training centre for mechanics, metalworkers, plumbers, and electricians was opened.

Regulatory Bodies

GOVERNMENT

Ministry of Culture: Praia, Santiago; tel. 261-05-67; Minister MANUEL MONTEIRO DA VEIGA.

Ministry of Education and Higher Education: Palácio do Governo, Várzea, CP 111, Praia, Santiago; tel. 261-05-09; fax 261-27-64; internet www.minedu.cv; Minister FILOMENA DE FÁTIMA RIBEIRO VIEIRA MARTINS.

Learned Society

LANGUAGE AND LITERATURE

Alliance Française: Rua de Santo Antonio, CP 37, Mindelo; tel. 232-11-49; fax 232-11-48; e-mail afmsvcapvert@cvtelecom.cv; internet www.afmindelo.n3.net; offers courses and exams in French language and culture and promotes cultural exchange with France.

Research Institute

ECONOMICS, LAW AND POLITICS

Instituto Nacional de Estatistica de Cabo Verde (Cape Verde National Statistical Institute): CP 116, Praia, Santiago; tel. 261-38-27; e-mail inecv@mail.telecom.cv; internet www.ine.cv; Pres. FRANCISCO FERNANDES TORRES.

Library

Praia

Biblioteca de Assembleia Nacional (National Assembly Library): Achada de Santo António, CP 20-A, Praia, Santiago; tel. 262-32-90; fax 262-26-60; internet www.parlamento.cv/biblioteca; f. 1985; 5,000 vols, 100 periodicals; Dir ALBERTINA GRAÇA.

University

UNIVERSIDADE JEAN PIAGET DE CABO VERDE

Campus Universitário da Cidade da Praia, CP 775, Cidade de Praia, Santiago

Telephone: 262-90-85
Fax: 262-90-89
E-mail: info@caboverde.ipiaget.cv
Internet: www.unipiaget.cv

Founded 2001, attached to Instituto Piaget, Portugal

Academic year: October to July

Courses in architecture, business information, chemistry and physics teaching, civil construction engineering, communications science, hotel and tourism management, education science, economics and management, English language and literature teaching, information systems and engineering, mathematics teaching, nursing, pharmaceutical sciences, physiotherapy, professional education, Portuguese language and literature teaching, psychology, sociology

Rector: Prof. Dr ESTELA PINTO RIBEIRA LAMAS
Vice-Rector: Prof. Dr JORGE SOUSA BRITO
Gen. Administrator: Prof. Dr DAVID RIBEIRO LAMAS

Number of teachers: 50
Number of students: 650

College

Instituto Superior de Engenharia e Ciências do Mar (ISECMAR) (Higher Institute of Engineering and Marine Science): CP 163, Ribeira de Julião, São Vicente; tel. 232-65-61; fax 232-65-63; e-mail info@isecmar.cv; internet www.isecmar.cv; f. 1984; depts of electrical and mechanical engineering, electronic and computer engineering, marine biology and aquatic research, natural and human sciences, nautical sciences; Pres. ELISA FERREIRA SILVA.

CENTRAL AFRICAN REPUBLIC

The Higher Education System

Until the late 1960s higher education was closely linked to the former colonial power, France, from which the Central African Republic (CAR) had gained its independence in 1960. Students either travelled to France to study or attended the Foundation for Higher Education in Central Africa, established by the French to serve the CAR, Gabon, Chad and the Republic of Congo. The state-run Université de Bangui was founded in 1969 and remains the CAR's only university. The provision of state-funded higher education was severely disrupted during the 1990s and early 2000s, owing to the inadequacy of financial resources. The Ministry of Education oversees higher education. In 2006/07 there were 4,462 students in further and higher education.

The University Council is the administrative and executive body of the Université de Bangui, and the Rector is the institutional head. All appointments and promotions are based on recommendations made to the Minister of Education by the University Council.

The secondary school Baccalauréat or Diplôme de Bachelier de l'Enseignement du Second Degré are the main criteria for admission to university. Higher education awards are divided into two cycles. The first cycle results in the award of a Diplôme for which two years of study in an area of specialization (general studies, literature, science, economics, law) are required. The second cycle lasts for a year following this and leads to the award of the Licence degree, after which an additional year of study results in the award of a Maîtrise degree. The only doctoral qualification awarded by the Université de Bangui is the Doctorat en Médecine, which requires six years of study. The Université de Bangui also offers vocational education.

The higher education system in the CAR is beset by numerous and complex challenges. For decades, various governments have failed to provide adequate funding for the education system or regular and decent pay for its workers. Strikes by students and professors have led to the shortening of academic years. The system suffers severe deficiencies in quality and does not satisfy real labour-market demand.

Regulatory Body

GOVERNMENT

Ministry of National Education: BP 791, Bangui; tel. 61-08-38; Minister CHARLES-ARMEL DOUBANE.

Learned Society

LANGUAGE AND LITERATURE

Alliance Française: cnr rue de l'Industrie/rue du Poitou, BP 971, Bangui; tel. 61-49-41; fax 61-90-72; e-mail afbangui@yahoo.fr; offers courses and exams in French language and culture and promotes cultural exchange with France.

Research Institutes

AGRICULTURE, FISHERIES AND VETERINARY SCIENCE

Centre D'Études sur la Trypanosomiase Animale: BP 39, Bouar; stations at Bewiti, Sarki; annexe at Bambari.

Institut de Recherches Agronomiques de Boukoko (Agricultural Research Institute): BP 44, M'Baiki, Boukoko; f. 1948; research into tropical agriculture and plant diseases, fertilization and entomology; library of 2,740 vols; Dir M. GONDJIA.

Institut d'Études Agronomiques d'Afrique Centrale: École Nationale des Adjoints Techniques d'Agriculture de Wakombo, BP 78, M'Baiki; affiliated to Université de Bangui; Dir R. ELIARD.

ECONOMICS, LAW AND POLITICS

Département des Études de Population à l'Union Douanière et Économique de l'Afrique Centrale: BP 1418, Bangui; tel. 61-45-77; f. 1964; Dir JEAN NKOUNKOU.

MEDICINE

Institut Pasteur: BP 983, Bangui; tel. 61-45-76; fax 61-08-66; e-mail ipb@pasteur.cf; f. 1961; research on viral haemorrhagic fevers, polio virus, tuberculosis, HIV/AIDS and simian retroviruses; WHO Regional Centre for poliomyelitis in Africa; 110 researchers; Dir Dr ALAIN LE FAOU.

NATURAL SCIENCES

Station Expérimentale de la Maboké: par M'Baiki; f. 1963 under the direction of the Muséum National d'Histoire Naturelle, Paris; studies in the protection of materials in tropical regions, anthropology, botany, entomology, mycology, parasitology, protection of natural resources, virology, zoology; Dir (vacant).

RELIGION, SOCIOLOGY AND ANTHROPOLOGY

Mission Sociologique Du Haut-Oubangui: BP 68, Bangassou; f. 1954; sociological and archaeological study of socs and cultures from the CAR, espec. from the Gbaya, Nzakara and Zandé countries; historical maps and sociological documents; Head Prof. E. DE DAMPIERRE; publ. *Recherches Oubanguiennes*.

TECHNOLOGY

Institut National de Recherches Textiles et Cultures Vivrières: BP 17, Bambari; Dir GABRIEL RAMADHANE-SAÏD.

Library

Bangui

Bibliothèque Universitaire de Bangui: BP 1450, Bangui; tel. 61-20-00; f. 1980; 26,000 vols, 600 periodicals (Central Library); 9,144 vols (École Normale Supérieure); 5,240 vols, 168 periodicals (Faculty of Health Sciences); Dir JOSEPH GOMA-BOUANGA.

University

UNIVERSITÉ DE BANGUI

ave des Martyrs, BP 1450, Bangui
Telephone: 61-20-00

Fax: 61-78-90
Internet: ww.univ-bangui.info
Founded 1969
Language of instruction: French
Academic year: October to June

Rector: FAUSTIN TOUADÉRA
Vice-Rector: JOSEPH MABINGUI
Sec.-Gen.: GABRIEL NGOUANDJITANGA
Librarian: JOSEPH NGOMA-BOUANGA
Library: See Libraries and Archives
Number of teachers: 243
Number of students: 6,474
Publications: *Annales de l'Université de Bangui Wambesso, Espace Francophone, Revue d'Histoire et d'Archéologie Centrafricaine*

DEANS

Faculty of Health Science: Prof. MAMADOU NESTOR NALI
Faculty of Law and Economics: DAMIENNE NANARE
Faculty of Letters and Humanities: GABRIEL NGOUANDJI-TANGA
Faculty of Science and Technology: Lic. MABOUA BARA

Colleges

École Centrale d'Agriculture: Boukoko.

École Nationale d'Administration et de la Magistrature (ÉNAM) (National School of Administration and Judiciary): BP 1450, Bangui; tel. 61-04-88; state control under Sec.-Gen. of Govt; f. as school for future civil students and magistrates; curriculum now oriented to workshops for benefit of public-sector workers; Dir-Gen. ISAAC EDGAR BENAM.

École Nationale des Arts: BP 349, Bangui; f. 1966; dance, dramatic art, music and plastic arts.

École Territoriale d'Agriculture: Grimari.

CHAD

The Higher Education System

The main institution of higher education is the Université de N'Djamena, which was founded as the Université de Tchad in 1971 and adopted its current name in 1994. In addition, there are several technical colleges. Some 10,468 students were enrolled at further and higher education institutions in 2004/05.

Higher education in Chad is influenced by the French model, in which universities are under direct government supervision. The Ministry of Higher Education, Scientific Research and Professional Training oversees research activities through the National Committee of Scientific and Technical Research. The ministry has power over most education institutions in which teaching and research activities are performed. Some specialized institutions are supervised by other ministries. In 1990 the Government adopted a development strategy entitled Education-Formation-Emploi (EFE—Education-Training-Employment). The strategy, made up of five programmes corresponding to five sectors of the education system, sought to improve the education system's efficiency and increase access to education. It focused on teacher training, curriculum design and the rationalization of management. The Government was committed to improving the management of public resources in an attempt to meet structural adjustment programmes, and directed its attention to investment and basic education. As a result, inadequate resources were allocated to higher education. EFE strategists decided to increase student enrolment, particularly to scientific and technological disciplines. The resulting growth served only to exacerbate existing imbalances. The implementation of EFE strategy has since stalled owing to a lack of resources, and the reforms have yet to yield satisfactory results.

The Baccalauréat is required for admission to university. University-level education consists of two cycles. The first cycle involves two years of study and leads to one of three diplomas, depending on the student's area of specialization: Diplôme Universitaire de Lettres Modernes (humanities), Diplôme Universitaire de Sciences (sciences) and Diplôme Universitaire de Sciences Juridiques, Economiques et de Gestion (social sciences). The second cycle leads to the award of the Licence after one year of study following the award of the Diplôme, and the Maîtrise after a further one or two years of study. The Baccalauréat is also required for admission to non-university higher education and professional training courses.

Regulatory Bodies

GOVERNMENT

Ministry of Culture and the Arts: BP 892, N'Djamena; tel. 52-40-97; fax 52-65-60; Minister DILLAH LUCIENNE.

Ministry of Higher Education, Scientific Research and Professional Training: BP 743, N'Djamena; tel. 51-61-58; fax 51-92-31; Minister Dr OUMAR IDRISS AL-FAROUK.

Research Institutes

AGRICULTURE, FISHERIES AND VETERINARY SCIENCE

Institut de Recherches du Coton et des Textiles Exotiques (IRCT): BP 764, N'Djamena; f. 1939; cotton research (agronomy, entomology and genetics); Head of station at Bebedja M. RENOU; Regional Dir M. YEHOUESSI.

Laboratoire de Recherches Vétérinaires et Zootechniques de Farcha: BP 433, N'Djamena; tel. 52-74-75; fax 52-83-02; f. 1952; veterinary and stock-breeding research and production of vaccines; training; library of 3,500 vols; Dir Dr HASSANE MAHAMAT HASSANE.

EDUCATION

Centre de Recherche, des Archives et de Documentation, Commission Nationale pour l'UNESCO: BP 731, N'Djamena; Sec.-Gen. Dr KHALIL ALIO; publ. *COMNAT: Bulletin d'Information*.

RELIGION, SOCIOLOGY AND ANTHROPOLOGY

Institut National des Sciences Humaines: BP 1117, N'Djamena; tel. 51-62-68; f. 1961; anthropology, ethno-sociology, geography, history, linguistics, oral traditions, palaeontology, prehistory, proto-history, social sciences, sociolinguistics, sociology; 6 researchers; library of 1,000 vols and 400 archive documents; Dir MOUKTHAR DJIBRINE MAHAMAT; Gen. Sec. DJONG-YANG OÜANLARBO; publ. *Revue de Tchad*.

Museum

N'Djamena

Musée National: BP 638, N'Djamena; tel. 51-33-75; fax 51-60-94; f. 1963; attached to Institut National des Sciences Humaines (see above); 100 collections; in process of reformation; depts of ethnography, palaeontology, prehistory and archaeology, scientific archives; Dir DJAMIL MOUSSA NENE.

University

UNIVERSITÉ DE N'DJAMENA (UNDJ)

BP 1117, Ave Mobutu, N'Djamena
Telephone: 51-44-44
Fax: 51-45-81
E-mail: rectorat@intnet.td
Internet: www.undt.info
Founded 1971 as Université de Tchad; present title 1994
State control

Languages of instruction: French, Arabic
Academic year: October to June
Rector: Prof. RODOUMTA KOINA
Vice-Rector: ZAKARIA KHIDIR FADOUL
Sec.-Gen.: MAHAMAT ADOUM DOUTOUM
International Relations Officer: GILBERT LAWANE
Librarian: MAHAMAT SALEH
Library of 30,000 vols
Number of teachers: 203
Number of students: 5,183
Publication: *Annuaire*

DEANS

Faculty of Arts and Human Sciences: AHMED N'GARE
Faculty of Exact and Applied Sciences: AHMAT CHARFADINE
Faculty of Health Sciences: DJADA DJIBRINE ATIM
Faculty of Law and Economics: BENJAMEN DJIKOLOUM BENAN (acting)

Colleges

Ecole Nationale d'Administration: BP 768, N'Djamena; f. 1963; set up by the Government and controlled by an Administrative Council to train students as public servants; Dir N. GUELINA.

Institut Supérieur des Sciences de l'Education: BP 473 N'Djamena; tel. 51-44-87; fax 51-45-50; f. 1992; depts of teacher training for primary education, teacher training for secondary education and teacher training for technical and professional education; Dir MAYORE KARYO.

CHILE

The Higher Education System

There are three types of higher education institution in Chile: public and private universities (universidad publica and universidad privada), professional institutes (instituto profesional) and centres of technical training. In 2007 there were 753,398 students in tertiary education.

Students require the Licencia de Educación Media to be admitted to university, and state-funded universities must hold an entrance examination (Prueba de Aptitud Academica). There are three levels of university qualifications in Chile, one undergraduate and two postgraduate. Undergraduates study for three to five years for the Bachiller (Bachelors), Licenciado or a professional degree. Postgraduates study for two years following the Licenciado to receive the Magister, and then for a further three years for the Doctorado.

Technical and vocational training is coordinated by Instituto Nacional de Capitación Profesional, which administers and accredits qualifications and institutions. Entrance requirements are the same as those for university-level education. Centres of technical training award the title of Técnico Superior in fields of professional education; professional institutes offer training programmes of four to five years, leading to the award of a professional title; and universities award the title of Ingeniero de Ejecucion after four years of full-time study in different fields. Two universities, Universidad de Santiago de Chile and Universidad Técnica 'Federico Santa Maria', offer courses requiring three years of full-time study and leading to the title of Técnico Universitario.

As a MERCOSUR member state Chile is a participant of El Mecanismo Experimental de Acreditación de Carreras del MERCOSUR which has so far accredited Chilean degrees in agronomy, medicine and engineering. At the national level the Comisión Nacional de Acreditación de Pregrado was established in 1999 to ensure national standards are met at undergraduate level. The accreditation process consists of both the accreditation of degrees as well as institutions and is voluntary. Technical committees of university academics assess the standard of degrees. The Comisión Nacional de Acreditación de Posgrado was established in 1999 to monitor standards of postgraduate degrees.

Since 2008 Chile has earned a vast revenue from its copper mines. From this it has paid for many Chileans to earn graduate degrees abroad. The country has also spent millions of dollars on improving its state universities and developing programmes in the humanities, arts, and social sciences—partly in a bid to attract foreign students and professors.

Regulatory and Representative Bodies

GOVERNMENT

Ministry of Education: Alameda 1371, 7°, Santiago; tel. (2) 3904000; fax (2) 3800317; internet www.mineduc.cl; Minister MÓNICA JIMÉNEZ.

National Commission for Culture and the Arts: San Camilo 262, Santiago; tel. (2) 5897824; internet www.consejodelacultura .cl; Minister PAULINA URRUTIA FERNÁNDEZ.

ACCREDITATION

Comisión Nacional de Acreditación (National Accreditation Commission): Avda Ricardo Lyon 1532, Providencia, Santiago; tel. (2) 6201100; fax (2) 6201120; e-mail contacto@cnachile.cl; internet www.cnachile .cl; f. 2006; ind. body set up to verify and promote the quality of univs, professional institutes and self-governing technical training centres, and of the courses and programmes they offer; 13 mems; Pres. EMILIO RODRÍGUEZ PONCE; Exec. Sec. Dr GONZALO ZAPATA LARRAÍN.

Consejo Nacional de Educación (National Council of Education): Marchant Pereira 844, Providencia, Santiago; tel. (2) 3413412; fax (2) 2254616; e-mail consultas@ cned.cl; internet www.cned.cl; f. 1990, fmrly known as Consejo Superior de Educación, reorganized and present name 2009; accredits new univs, professional institutes and technical training centres; promotes devt of research on higher education; Head of Research and Public Information RODRIGO DIAZ; Exec. Sec. DANIELA TORRE GRIGGS; publs *Revista Calidad en la Educación* (2 a year), *Serie Seminarios Internacionales* (1 a year).

NATIONAL BODY

Consejo de Rectores de las Universidades Chilenas (Council of Rectors of Chilean Universities): Alameda 1371, 4° piso, Casilla 14798, Santiago; tel. (2) 6964286; fax (2) 6988436; e-mail cruch@ cruch.cl; internet www.cruch.cl; f. 1954; coordinates the academic activities of its mem. instns, develops policies aimed at enhancing higher-education activities, promotes changes in laws regulating univ. studies and student financial aid; 25 mem. univs; Pres. YASNA PROVOSTE CAMPILLAY; Gen. Sec. CARLOS LORCA AUGER; publ. *Anuario Estadístico* (Statistical Yearbook, 1 a year).

Learned Societies

GENERAL

Instituto de Chile: Almirante Montt 453, 6500445 Santiago; tel. (2) 6854400; internet www.institutodechile.cl; f. 1964; promotes cultural, humanistic and scientific studies; Pres. SERVET MARTÍNEZ AGUILERA; Gen. Sec. MARINO PIZARRO PIZARRO; publ. *Anales*.

Constituent Academies:

Academia Chilena de Bellas Artes (Chilean Academy of Fine Arts): Almirante Montt 453, 6500445 Santiago; tel. (2) 6854418; fax (2) 6337460; e-mail acchbear@ctcinternet.cl; internet www .institutodechile.cl/bellasartes; f. 1964; 40 mems (28 academicians, 11 corresp., 1 hon.); Pres. SANTIAGO VERA RIVERA; Sec. RAMÓN NÚÑEZ VILLARROEL; publ. *Boletín*.

Academia Chilena de Ciencias (Chilean Academy of Sciences): Almirante Montt 454, Santiago; tel. (2) 4812841; fax (2) 4812843; internet www.academia-ciencias .cl; f. 1964; 36 academicians; 21 corresp.; 5 hon. academicians; promotes research in pure and applied sciences; Pres. SERVET MARTÍNEZ AGUILERA; Sec. FRANCISCO HERVE ALLAMAND; publs *Boletín* (irregular), *Figuras señeras de la Ciencia en Chile* (irregular).

Academia Chilena de Ciencias Sociales, Políticas y Morales (Chilean Academy of Social, Political and Moral Sciences): Almirante Montt 454, 6500445 Santiago; tel. (2) 6854416; fax (2) 6385802; e-mail acchcsso@ctcinternet.cl; internet www.institutodechile.cl/cienciassociales; f. 1964; 36 mems; library of 7,000 vols; Pres. JOSÉ LUIS CEA EGAÑA; Sec. JAIME ANTÚNEZ ALDUNATE; publs *Anales* (1 a year), *Boletín* (3 a year), *Folletos*.

Academia Chilena de la Historia (Chilean Academy of History): Almirante Montt 454, 6500445 Santiago; tel. (2) 6854414; fax (2) 6399323; e-mail acchhist@tie.cl; internet www .institutodechile.cl/historia; f. 1933; 36 mems; library of 2,500 vols; Pres. JOSÉ MIQUET BARROS; Sec. RICARDO COUYOUMDJIAN BERGAMALI; publs *Archivo de D. Bernardo O'Higgins* (irregular), *Boletín de la Academia* (2 a year).

Academia Chilena de la Lengua (Chilean Academy of Language): Almirante Montt 453, 6500445 Santiago; tel. (2) 6854413; fax (2) 6640776; e-mail acadchileng@terra.cl; internet www .institutodechile.cl/lengua; f. 1885; fmrly Academia Chilena; coresp. mem. of the Real Academia Española, Madrid; 36 mems; Dir ALFREDO MATUS OLIVIER; Sec. JOSÉ LUIS SAMANIEGO ALDAZÁBAL; publ. *Boletín de la Academia Chilena*.

Academia Chilena de Medicina (Chilean Academy of Medicine): Almirante Montt 453, 6500445 Santiago; tel. (2) 6854417; fax (2) 6388205; e-mail acchmed@tie.cl; internet www .institutodechile.cl/medicina; f. 1964; 75 academicians; 45 hon. foreign mems; library of 900 vols; Pres. ALEJANDRO GOIC

GOIC; Sec. RODOLFO ARMAS MERINO; publs *Boletín*, *Proceedings on the Chilean History of Medicine*.

Regional Bureau for Education in Latin America and the Caribbean/Oficina Regional de Educación para América Latina y el Caribe (OREALC/UNESCO Santiago): Casilla 127, Correo 29, CP 665692 Santiago; Calle Enrique Delpiano 2058, Providencia, Santiago; tel. (2) 4724600; fax (2) 6551046; e-mail santiago@unesco.org; internet www.unesco.org/santiago; f. 1963; dissemination of knowledge, formulation of public policy guidelines, provision of advisory services and technical support to countries of the region, promotion of dialogue, exchange and cooperation; Dir JORGE SEQUEIRA.

AGRICULTURE, FISHERIES AND VETERINARY SCIENCE

Colegio de Ingenieros Forestales de Chile A.G.: San Isidro 22, Of. 503, Santiago Centro; tel. (2) 6393289; fax (2) 6395280; e-mail jsalas@surnet.cl; internet www.cifag.cl; f. 1982; 350 mems; Pres. JAIME SALAS ARANCIBIA; publs *Actas de las Jornadas Forestales* (2 a year), *Renarres* (6 a year).

Sociedad Agronómica de Chile (Agronomical Society of Chile): Calle MacIver 120, Of. 36, Casilla 4109, Santiago; tel. (2) 6384881; fax (2) 6384881; e-mail sociedad.agronomica.chile@gmail.com; internet www.sach.cl; f. 1910; 1,900 mems; library of 1,600 vols; Pres. HORST BERGER; Sec. CHRISTEL OBERPAUR; publ. *Simiente* (3 a year).

Sociedad Chilena de Producción Animal A.G.: c/o Sra Carmen Gallo S., Facultad de Ciencias Veterinarias, Universidad Austral de Chile, Casilla 567, Valdivia; tel. (45) 215706, ext. 299; e-mail mdiaz@inia.cl; internet www.sochipa.cl; f. 1979; 115 mems; Pres. CARMEN GALLO S.; Sec./Treas. DANTE PINOCHET T.

Sociedad Nacional de Agricultura (National Society of Agriculture): Tenderini 187, 8320232 Santiago; tel. (2) 5853300; fax (2) 5853370; e-mail comunicaciones@sna.cl; internet www.sna.cl; f. 1838; library of 3,500 vols; research in agricultural, social and economic problems; controls a plant genetics experimental station and a broadcasting chain with stations in several cities; register of pedigree cattle kept; technical assistance to farmers; annual international and agricultural show since 1869, and home show since 1980; Pres. LUIS SCHMIDT MONTES; Gen. Sec. JUAN PABLO MATTE F.; publs *El Vocero*, *Informe Semanal*, *Revista El Campesino*.

ARCHITECTURE AND TOWN PLANNING

Colegio de Arquitectos de Chile (Chilean College of Architects): Avda Libertador B. O'Higgins 115, Santiago; tel. (2) 6398744; fax (2) 6398769; e-mail central@coarq.com; internet www.arqchile.cl; f. 1942, for all Chilean and foreign architects working in Chile; 5,500 mems; library of 2,000 vols, 2,500 journals; Pres. JOSÉ RAMÓN UGARTE; Gen. Man. ERICO LUEBERT CID; publs *Boletín* (12 a year), *Bienal de Arquitectura* (every 2 years), *Congreso Nacional de Arquitectos* (every 2 years), *Revista CA* (4 a year).

BIBLIOGRAPHY, LIBRARY SCIENCE AND MUSEOLOGY

Colegio de Bibliotecarios de Chile, AG: Diagonal Paraguay 383, Depto 122, Torre 11, Santiago; tel. (2) 2225652; fax (2) 6355023; e-mail cbc@uplink.cl; internet www.bibliotecarios.cl; f. 1969; 1,891 mems; Pres. MARCIA MARINOVIĆ SIMUNOVIĆ; Sec. ANA

MARÍA PINO YÁÑEZ; publs *Documento de Trabajo* (irregular), *Eidisis* (4 a year).

ECONOMICS, LAW AND POLITICS

Servicio Médico Legal (Forensic Medicine Service): Avda La Paz 1012, Independencia, Santiago; tel. (2) 7823500; internet www.sml.cl; f. 1915; attached to Min. of Justice; advises tribunals on forensic medicine; 305 mems; library of 800 vols; Dir Dr PATRICIO BUSTOS; publs *Monografías Servicio Médico Legal* (3 a year), *Revista de Medicina Legal* (3 a year).

FINE AND PERFORMING ARTS

Asociación Plástica Latina Internacional de Chile (APLICH) (Chilean International Plastic Arts Association): Avda P. de Valdivia 1781, Casilla 177, Correo 29, Santiago; tel. (2) 2233444; fax (2) 2233444; internet www.mnba.cl; f. 1990; Pres. ALICIA ARGANDOÑA R.; Gen. Sec. SERGIO JUZAM NUMAN; publ. *APLICH al Día*.

HISTORY, GEOGRAPHY AND ARCHAEOLOGY

Instituto Geográfico Militar (Military Geographical Institute): Nueva Santa Isabel 1640, Santiago; tel. (2) 4606800; fax (2) 4606918; e-mail igm@igm.cl; f. 1922; 400 mems; library of 4,000 vols, 25,000 maps; Dir GDB PABLO GRAN LÓPEZ; publ. *Revista Terra Australis* (1 a year).

Sociedad Chilena de Historia y Geografía (Chilean Society of History and Geography): Casilla 1386, Santiago; Calle Londres 65, Santiago; tel. (2) 6382489; f. 1911; 304 mems; 13 hon.; 70 corresp.; library of 12,600 vols; Pres. SERGIO MARTÍNEZ BOEZA; Vice-Pres. ISIDOROVOZQUEZ DE ACUÑA; Sec.-Gen. ROBERTO COBO DE LA MOZA; publs *Revista Chilena de Historia y Geografía*, related works.

LANGUAGE AND LITERATURE

Alliance Française: Casilla 94, Las Condes, Santiago; Lycée Antoine de Saint-Exupéry, Av. Luis Pasteur 5418, Vitacura, Santiago 10; tel. (2) 8278200; fax (2) 2183287; e-mail serge.buenaventes@lafase.cl; internet www.lafase.cl; offers courses and exams in French language and culture and promotes cultural exchange with France; attached teaching offices in Concepción, Curico, Osorno, Renaca, Santiago, Valparaíso; Head SERGE BUENAVENTES.

British Council: Eliodoro Yáñez 832, Providencia, Santiago; tel. (2) 4106900; fax (2) 4106929; e-mail britishcouncil.cl; internet www.britishcouncil.cl; offers courses and exams in English language and British culture and promotes cultural exchange with the UK; Dir SARAH BARTON.

Goethe-Institut: Esmeralda 650, Santiago; tel. (2) 5711950; fax (2) 5711999; e-mail info@santiago.goethe.org; internet www.goethe.de/ins/cl/sao/esindex.htm; f. 1961; offers courses and exams in German language and culture and promotes cultural exchange with Germany; library of 8,500 vols; Dir JUDITH MAIWORM; Dir REINHARD MAIWORM.

Sociedad Chilena de Lingüística (Chilean Linguistics Society): Casilla 394, Santiago 11; tel. (41) 2203001; internet www.sochil.cl; f. 1971; over 100 mems; Pres. Dr BERNARDO RIFFO; Dir Dr PILAR ALVAREZ-SANTULLANO; publ. *Actas*.

MEDICINE

Colegio de Químico-Farmacéuticos y Bioquímicos de Chile (College of Pharmacists and Biochemists): Casilla 1136, Santiago; Merced 50, Santiago; tel. (2) 6392505;

fax (2) 6399780; internet www.colegiofarmaceutico.cl; f. 1942; 2,500 regional councils in 13 main towns; Pres. Dr ELMER TORRES CORTÉS; Sec. Dra MARÍA ANGÉLICA SÁNCHEZ VOGEL; publ. *Revista*.

Sociedad Chilena de Cancerología y Hematología: Calle Pérez Valenzuela 1520, Of. 502, Providencia, Santiago; tel. (2) 2358357; fax (2) 2051914; internet www.cancersoc.cl; f. 1954; 142 mems; Pres. Dr RAMÓN BAEZA B.; Gen. Sec. Dr MAURICIO CAMUS A.; publ. *Revista Chilena de Cancerología* (4 a year).

Sociedad Chilena de Cardiología y Cirugía Cardiovascular: Alfredo Barros Errázuriz 1954, Oficina 1601, Providencia, Santiago; tel. (2) 2690076; fax (2) 2690207; e-mail sochicar@entelchile.net; internet www.sochicar.cl; f. 1949; Pres. Dr FERNANDO LANAS ZANETTI; publ. *Revista*.

Sociedad Chilena de Dermatología y Venereología: Vitacura 5250, Oficina 202, Vitacura, Santiago; tel. (2) 3781301; fax (2) 3781302; internet www.sochiderm.cl; f. 1938; Pres. Dr ENRIQUE MULLINS; Gen. Sec. Dra IRENA ARAYA.

Sociedad Chilena de Endocrinología y Metabolismo: Bernarda Morín 488, 2° piso, Providencia, Santiago; tel. (2) 2230386; fax (2) 7535556; e-mail sochem@sochem.cl; internet www.sochem.cl; f. 1961; Pres. Dr GILBERTO PÉREZ PACHECO; Sec.-Gen. Dra VERÓNICA ARAYA QUINTANILLA.

Sociedad Chilena de Enfermedades Respiratorias: Santa Magdalena 75, Oficina 701, Providencia, Santiago; tel. (2) 2316292; fax (2) 2443811; e-mail ser@serchile.cl; internet www.serchile.cl; f. 1930; 410 mems; Pres. Dr MANUEL BARROS; Sec. Dra VIVIANA LEZANA; publs *Boletín Informativo* (12 a year), *Revista Chilena de Enfermedades Respiratorias* (4 a year).

Sociedad Chilena de Gastroenterología: El Trovador 4280, Of. 909, Las Condes, Santiago; tel. (2) 3425004; fax (2) 3425005; e-mail schgastr@tie.cl; internet www.socgastro.cl; f. 1938; Pres. Dr FERNANDO FLUXÁ GARCÍA; Exec. Secs Dr FRANCISCO LÓPEZ KOSTNER, Dra PAULA VIAL CERDA; publs *Gastroenterología Latinoamericana*, *Normas de Diagnóstico en Enfermedades Digestivas*.

Sociedad Chilena de Inmunología: Avda Independencia 1027, Santiago 7; tel. (2) 9786347; fax (2) 9786979; e-mail info@sochin.cl; internet www.sochin.cl; f. 1972; 55 active mems; Pres. Dr ÁNGEL OÑATE CONTRERAS; Sec. Biol. DARWIN SÁEZ POBLETE.

Sociedad Chilena de Obstetricia y Ginecología: Román Díaz 205, Oficina 205, Providencia, Santiago; tel. (2) 2350133; fax (2) 2351294; e-mail sochog@entelchile.net; internet www.sochog.cl; f. 1935; 350 mems; Pres. Dr LUIS MARTINEZ; Sec. Dr MAURICIO CUELLO; publ. *Revista Chilena de Obstetricia y Ginecología* (online, 6 a year).

Sociedad Chilena de Oftalmología: Avda Luís Pasteur 5280, Of. 104 Vitacura, Santiago; tel. (2) 2185950; fax (2) 2185950; e-mail sochioft@tie.cl; internet www.sochiof.cl; f. 1931; spec. colln of video cassettes; 600 mems; library of 650 vols; Pres. Dr PEDRO BRAVO C.; Pres. GONZALO MATUS M.; Sec. Dr JAVIER CORVALÁN R.; publs *Archivos Chilenos de Oftalmología* (2 a year), *Revista Informativa* (10 a year).

Sociedad Chilena de Ortopedia y Traumatología: Evaristo Lillo 78, Of. 81, Las Condes, Santiago; tel. (2) 2072151; fax (2) 2069820; e-mail schot@schot.cl; internet www.schot.cl; f. 1949; 508 mems; library of 500 vols; Pres. Dr IGNACIO DOCKENDORFF B.; Sec.-Gen. Dr JORGE VERGARA L.; publ. *Revista*

Chilena de Ortopedia y Traumatología (4 a year).

Sociedad Chilena de Pediatría: CP 6841638, Casilla 593, Correo 11, Santiago; Alcade Eduardo Castillo Velasco 1838, Ñuñoa, Santiago; tel. (2) 2371598; fax (2) 2380046; e-mail contacto@sochipe.cl; internet www.sochipe.cl; f. 1922; 1,230 mems; Pres. Dr OSCAR HERRERA GONZÁLEZ; Sec. Dr CARLOS SAIEH ANDONIE.

Sociedad Chilena de Reumatología: Bernarda Morin 488, Providencia, Santiago; tel. (2) 7535545; fax (2) 2693394; e-mail info@sochire.cl; internet www.sochire.cl; f. 1950; Pres. Dr GONZALO ASTORGA P.; Sec. Dr ALBERTO VALDÉS S.; publ. *Boletín* (4 a year).

Sociedad de Farmacología de Chile: Casilla 70.000, Santiago 7; Avda Independencia 1027, Santiago 7; tel. (2) 6786050; fax (2) 7774216; internet www.sofarchi.cl; f. 1979; 88 mems; Pres. Dra GABRIELA DÍAZ-VÉLIZ.

Sociedad de Neurocirugía de Chile: Esmeralda 678 (2° piso interior), Santiago; tel. (2) 6334149; fax (2) 6391085; e-mail neurocirugia@tie.cl; internet www .neurocirugia.cl; f. 1957; 100 mems; Sec. Dr JEANNETTE VAN SCHUERBECK P.; publ. *Revista Chilena de Neurocirugía* (2 a year).

Sociedad de Neurología, Psiquiatría y Neurocirugía de Chile: Calle Carlos Silva V 1292, Plaza Las Lilas, Providencia, Casilla 251, Correo 35, Santiago; tel. (2) 2329347; fax (2) 2319287; e-mail secretariagral@123.cl; internet www.sonepsyn.cl; f. 1932; Pres. Dr ENRIQUE JADRESIC; publ. *Revista Chilena de Neuro-Psiquiatría* (4 a year).

Sociedad Médica de Concepción (Concepción Medical Society): Casilla 60-C, Concepción; f. 1886; Pres. Dr ENRIQUE BELLOLIOZ; publ. *Anales Médicos de Concepción.*

Sociedad Médica de Santiago (Santiago Medical Society): Casilla 168, Correo Tajamar, Santiago; tel. (2) 7535500; fax (2) 7535599; e-mail smschile@smschile.cl; internet www.smschile.cl; f. 1869; 1,600 mems; library: 50 periodical titles; Pres. Dr HECTOR UGALDE PRIETO; Sec. Dr SYLVIA ECHÁVARRI; Librarian CLAUDIA BELTRAN REINOSO; publ. *Revista Médica de Chile* (12 a year).

Sociedad Odontológica de Concepción: Casilla 2107, Concepción; f. 1924; 300 mems; Pres. Dr EDUARDO NAVARETE; Sec. Dr SERGIO ESQUERRÉ S.; publ. *Anuario.*

NATURAL SCIENCES
General

Academia Chilena de Ciencias Naturales (Chilean Academy of Natural Sciences): Almirante Montt 454, Santiago; tel. (2) 6441030; fax (2) 6332129; f. 1926; Pres. Dr HUGO GUNCKEL L.; Sec. HANS NIEMEYER F.; publ. *Anales.*

Asociación Científica y Técnica de Chile (Scientific and Technical Association of Chile): Carlos Antúnez 1885, Depto 205, Santiago; tel. (2) 2354137; f. 1965; 22 mems; Pres. HÉCTOR CATHALIFAUD ARGANDOÑA; Sec.-Gen. ELENA TORRES SEGUEL.

Corporación para el Desarrollo de la Ciencia: Marcoleta 250, Casilla 10332, Santiago; f. 1978; Pres. FERNANDO DÍAZ A.; Sec.-Gen. HÉCTOR CATHALIFAUD A.; publ. *Revista CODECI.*

Sociedad Científica Chilena 'Claudio Gay' (Chilean Scientific Society): Casilla 2974, Santiago; tel. (2) 7455066; fax (2) 7455176; e-mail ugartepena@itn.cl; f. 1955; 45 mems; library of 5,000 vols; Dir ALFREDO UGARTE-PEÑA.

Biological Sciences

Sociedad de Microbiología de Chile: Canadá 253, piso 3, Of. F, Santiago; tel. (2) 2093503; fax (2) 2258427; e-mail socbiol@manquehue.net; internet somich .biologiachile.cl; f. 1964; 194 mems; Pres. MICHAEL SEEGER PFEIFFER; Sec. GINO CORSINI ACUÑA; publ. *Acta Microbiológica* (2 a year).

Sociedad Chilena de Entomología (Entomological Society): POB 21132, Santiago 21; tel. (2) 6804635; fax (2) 6804602; internet www.insectachile.cl; f. 1922; 170 mems; library of 4,000 periodicals; Pres. Dra FRESIA ESTER ROSAS A.; Sec. Ing. Agr. JOSÉ MONDACA E.; publ. *Revista Chilena de Entomología* (1 a year).

Sociedad de Biología de Chile: Canadá 253, Depto F, Santiago; tel. (2) 2093503; fax (2) 2258427; e-mail socbiol@biologiachile.cl; internet www.biologiachile.cl; f. 1928; 565 mems; Pres. Dr MARCO TULIO NÚÑEZ; Sec. Dr CHRISTIAN GONZÁLEZ; publs *Biological Research* (2 a year), *Noticiario* (12 a year), *Revista Chilena de Historia Natural* (4 a year).

Sociedad de Genética de Chile: Almirante Montt 454, Santiago; tel. and fax (2) 6387046; e-mail sochigen@adsl.tie.cl; internet www .sochigen.cl; f. 1964; 100 mems; Pres. Dra LUCÍA CIFUENTES OVALLE; Sec.-Gen. Prof. PATRICIA PEREZ-ALZOLA; publs *Biological Research*, *Revista Chilena de Historia Natural*.

Sociedad de Vida Silvestre de Chile (Chilean Wildlife Society): Rocío Sanhueza Caba Casilla 164, Valdivia; tel. (63) 215846; e-mail enlace.svsch@surnet.cl; internet svsch .ceachile.cl; f. 1975; 300 mems; Pres. CLAUDIA GIL; Exec. Sec. ROCIO SANHUEZA; publs *Enlace* (1 a year), *Gestión Ambiental* (1 a year).

Mathematical Sciences

Sociedad de Matemática de Chile: Canadá 253, Departamento F, Providencia, Santiago; tel. (2) 2489260; fax (2) 2489260; internet www.somachi.cl; f. 1976; 250 mems; Pres. RUBÍ RODRÍGUEZ MORENO; Sec. MANUEL ELGUETA DEDES; publ. *Boletín* (irregular).

Physical Sciences

Asociación Chilena de Astronomía y Astronáutica: Casilla 3904, Santiago 1; tel. (2) 6327556; f. 1957; union of amateur astronomers; arranges courses and lectures; astronomy, astrophotography, radioastronomy, telescope-making; owns the observatory of Mt Pochoco, near Santiago; 350 mems; library of 1,000 vols; Pres. JODY TAPIA NUÑEZ; Sec. BIANCA DINAMARCA FIERRO; publ. *Boletín ACHAYA* (12 a year).

Asociación Chilena de Sismología e Ingeniería Antisísmica (Chilean Association of Seismology and Earthquake Engineering): Blanco Encalada 2002, piso 4, Santiago; tel. (2) 978-4372; fax (2) 689-2833; e-mail mmualin@ing.uchile.cl; internet www .achisina.cl; f. 1963; Pres. Dr PATRICIO RUIZ.

Comisión Chilena de Energía Nuclear: Amunátegui 95, Casilla 188-D, Santiago; tel. (2) 4702500; fax (2) 4702570; e-mail oirs@cchen.cl; internet www.cchen.gov.cl; f. 1964; research, devt and applications of the nuclear uses of nuclear energy; library of 9,000 vols; Pres. RENATO AGURTO-COLIMA; Exec. Dir Dr JAIME SALAS-KURTE; publ. *Nucleotécnica* (1 a year).

Comité Oceanográfico Nacional (CONA): Casilla 324, Valparaíso; tel. (32) 2266520; fax (32) 2266542; e-mail cona@shoa .cl; internet www.cona.cl; f. 1971; 28 mem. instns; coordinates oceanographic activities among univs and govt research instns; Pres. Capt. PATRICIO J.C. CARRASCO; Exec. Sec.

Capt. FERNANDO J. MINGRAM; publ. *Ciencia y Tecnología del Mar* (2 a year).

Liga Marítima de Chile (Chilean Maritime League): Casilla 1345, Valparaíso; Avda Errázuriz 471, 2° piso, Valparaíso; tel. (32) 2235280; fax (32) 2255179; e-mail ligamar@terra.cl; internet www.ligamar.cl; f. 1914; runs course in nautical education; brs in Iquique, Tocopilla, Santiago, Concepción, Tomé, Valdivia, Puerto Montt and Punta Arenas; 1,350 mems; Pres. Rear Admiral ERI SOLIS OYARZÚN; Exec. Dir Captain ENRIQUE TRUCCO DELÉPINE; publ. *Mar* (1 a year).

Sociedad Chilena de Física: c/o Dr Juan Carlos Retamal, Casilla 307, Correo 2, Santiago; c/o Dr Juan Carlos Retamal, Depto de Física, Universidad de Santiago de Chile, Av. Ecuador 3493 Estación Central, Santiago; tel. (2) 7191200; fax (2) 7769596; e-mail jretamal@lauca.usach.cl; internet fisica .usach.cl; f. 1965; 250 mems; Pres. Dr JUAN CARLOS RETAMAL; Sec. Dr LUIS ROA; publ. *Boletín* (12 a year).

Sociedad Chilena de Fotogrametría y Percepción Remota: Instituto Geográfico Militar, Nueva Santa Isabel 1640, Santiago; tel. (2) 4109314; fax (2) 6990948; e-mail igm@igm.cl; internet www.igm.cl; library of 5,000 vols, 25,000 maps; Pres. Col RODRIGO MATURANA NADAL; publ. *Revista Geografica de Chile: Terra Australis* (1 a year).

Sociedad Chilena de Química: Casilla de Correo 2613, Concepción; tel. (41) 227815; fax (41) 235819; e-mail schq@surnet.cl; internet www.schq.cl; f. 1945; 1,000 mems; library of 1,500 vols and 400 periodicals; Pres. Dr GALO CÁRDENAS; Sec. Dr JUAN GODOY; publ. *Boletin* (4 a year).

Sociedad de Bioquímica de Concepción: Casilla 237, Escuela de Química y Farmacia y Bioquímica, Concepción; f. 1957; Pres. MARIO POZO LÓPEZ; Sec. FROILÁN HERNÁNDEZ CARTES.

Sociedad de Bioquímica y Biología Molecular de Chile: c/o Dr Marcelo López Lastra, Laboratorio de Virología Molecular, Facultad de Medicina, Pontificia Universidad Católica, Marcoleta 391, Santiago; tel. (2) 3548182; fax (2) 6387457; e-mail malopez@med.puc.cl; internet www.sbbmch.cl; f. 1974; 130 mems; Pres. Dr XAVIER JORDANA DE BUEN; Sec. Dr MARCELO LÓPEZ LASTRA.

Sociedad Geológica de Chile: Valentin Letelier 20, Oficina 401, Santiago; tel. (2) 6712415; fax (2) 6980481; e-mail info@sociedadgeologica.cl; internet www .sociedadgeologica.cl; f. 1962; 434 mems; Pres. FRANCISCO HERVÉ; Sec. CÉSAR ARRIAGADA; publs *Comunicaciones* (1 a year), *Revista Geológica de Chile* (2 a year).

TECHNOLOGY

Asociación Interamericana de Ingeniería Sanitaria y Ambiental: Barros Errázuriz 1954, piso 10, Of. 1007, Providencia, Santiago; tel. (2) 2690085; fax (2) 2690087; e-mail aidischi@aidis.cl; f. 1979; Pres. Ing. ALEX CHECHILNITZKY Z.; Sec. JULIO HEVIA MEDEL; publ. *Revista* (4 a year).

Colegio de Ingenieros de Chile, AG: Avda Santa María 0508, Casilla 13745, Santiago; tel. (2) 4221140; fax (2) 4221012; e-mail colegio@ingenieros.cl; internet www .ingenieros.cl; f. 1958; professional engineering asscn; 23,000 mems; Pres. Eng. FERNANDO GARCÍA CASTRO; Gen. Man. Eng. PEDRO TORRES OJEDA; publs *C.I. Informa* (12 a year), *Ingenieros* (4 a year).

Instituto de Ingenieros de Chile (Institute of Chilean Engineers): Casilla 487, Santiago; San Martín N° 352, Santiago; tel. (2) 6984028; fax (2) 6971136; e-mail iing@iing .cl; internet www.iing.cl; f. 1888; 800 mems;

library of 2,100 vols; Pres. MATEO BUDINICH DIEZ; Sec. CARLOS TAPIA ILLANES; publs *Anales*, *Revista Chilena de Ingeniería*.

Instituto de Ingenieros de Minas de Chile: Encomenderos 260, Of. 31, Casilla 14668, Correo 21, Santiago; tel. (2) 2461615; fax (2) 2466387; e-mail iimch@entelchile.net; f. 1930; 1,200 mems; Pres. MARCO ANTONIO ALFARO; Sec. MANUEL VIERA; publ. *Minerales* (6 a year).

Sociedad Chilena de Tecnología en Alimentos (Chilean Society of Food Technology): Echaurren 149, Santiago; tel. (2) 6966236; fax (2) 6974780; e-mail sochital@lauca.usch.cl; internet www.geocities.com/sochital; f. 1963; publ. *Alimentos* (4 a year).

Sociedad Nacional de Minería (National Society of Mining): Avda Apoquindo 3000 (5° piso), Las Condes, Santiago; tel. (2) 8207000; fax (2) 8207053; e-mail sonami@sonami.cl; internet www.sonami.cl; f. 1883; library of 20,000 digital reports, 20,000 plans, 5,000 spec. documents; Pres. ALBERTO SALAS MUÑOZ; Vice-Pres. RAMÓN JARA A; Vice-Pres. PATRICIO CÉSPEDES GUZMÁN; Gen. Sec. HÉCTOR PÁEZ BARAZA; publ. *Boletín Minero*.

Research Institutes

AGRICULTURE, FISHERIES AND VETERINARY SCIENCE

Estación Experimental 'Las Vegas' de la Sociedad Nacional de Agricultura (National Agricultural Society Experimental Station): c/o Sociedad Nacional de Agricultura, Casilla 40-D, Tenderini 187, Santiago; f. 1924; library of 1,000 vols; Dir RAÚL MATTE VIAL; publ. *El Campesino* (12 a year).

Instituto de Fomento Pesquero (Fishery Research Institute): Blanco 839, Valparaíso; tel. (32) 322000; fax (32) 322345; e-mail direccion@ifop.cl; internet www.ifop.cl; f. 1964 for research into fisheries and aquaculture, and to support the regulation of a sustainable marine environment; 400 mems; library of 9,000 vols; Dir GUILLERMO MORENO PAREDES; publ. *Boletín Bibliográfico* (12 a year).

Instituto de Investigaciones Agropecuarias: Casilla 439, Correo 3, Santiago; tel. (2) 5417223; fax (2) 5417667; f. 1964; conducts research on plant and livestock production, horticulture, viticulture, oenology, field crops; 170 research workers; library: see Libraries; Pres. FERNANDO MUJICA CASTILLO; National Dir FRANCISCO GONZÁLEZ DEL RÍO; Dir of Carillanca Agricultural Experiment Station ADRIÁN CATRILEO S.; Dir of Intihuasi Agricultural Experiment Station ALFONSO OSORIO U.; Dir of La Platina Agricultural Experiment Station JORGE VALENZUELA BARNECH; Dir of Kampenaike Agricultural Experiment Station RAÚL LIRA F.; Dir of Quilamapu Agricultural Experiment Station HERNÁN ACUÑA P.; Dir of Remehue Agricultural Experiment Station FRANCISCO LANUZA A.; Dir of Tamelaike Agricultural Experiment Station HERNÁN FELIPE ELIZALDE; publs *Agricultura Técnica* (4 a year), *Bibliografía Agrícola Chilena* (1 a year), *Boletín Técnico* (irregular), *Memoria Anual*, *Tierra Adentro* (6 a year).

Instituto Forestal (Forestry Institute): Casilla 109C, Concepción; Camino a Coronel Km 7.5, Concepción; tel. (41) 2853260; fax (41) 2853265; e-mail oirs@infor.cl; internet www.infor.cl; f. 1961; research and advice in all aspects of forestry; library of 8,000 vols; Exec. Dir HANS GROSSE WERNER; publs *Boletín Estadístico*, *Ciencia e Investigación Forestal*, *Documento de Divulgación*, *Informe Técnico*.

ECONOMICS, LAW AND POLITICS

Instituto Latinoamericano y del Caribe de Planificación Económica y Social (ILPES) (Latin American and Caribbean Institute for Economic and Social Planning): Edif. Naciones Unidas, Avda Dag Hammarskjöld 3477, Vitacura, Casilla 1567, Santiago; tel. (2) 2102507; fax (2) 2066104; e-mail ilpes@cepal.org; internet www.ilpes.cl; f. 1962; permanent body within the Economic Comm. for Latin America and the Caribbean (ECLAC), which in turn forms part of the UN; supports mem. countries in their strategic planning and management of public affairs, by providing training, advisory and research services; library of 60,000 vols, documents and periodicals; Dir JORGE MATTAR; Sec. DANIELA GEBHARD; publs *Panorama de la Gestión Pública*, *Series Gestión Pública*, *Series Manuales*.

Instituto Nacional de Estadísticas (National Statistical Institute): Casilla 498, Correo 3, Santiago; Avda Pdte. Bulnes 418, Santiago; tel. (2) 3667766; fax (2) 6712169; e-mail ine@ine.cl; internet www.ine.cl; f. 1843; library of 16,104 vols; Dir MARIANA SCHKOLNIK CHAMUDES; publs *Compendio Estadístico* (1 a year), *Indicadores Mensuales* (12 a year), *Metodologías*, *Revista Estadística y Economía* (2 a year).

EDUCATION

Centro de Investigación y Desarrollo de la Educación (CIDE): Erasmo Escala 1825, Santiago; tel. (2) 8897100; fax (2) 6718051; e-mail cide@reuna.cl; internet www.cide.cl; f. 1965; attached to the Universidad Alberto Hurtado; aims to provide education relevant to the basic needs of the people; research into education and the family, education and work, education and social values; library of 50,000 vols, 7,000 documents; Pres. FERNANDO MONTES MATTE; Dir JUAN EDUARDO GARCÍA-HUIDOBRO.

Latin American Information and Documentation Network for Education (REDUC): Casilla 13608, Santiago; tel. (2) 6987153; fax (2) 6718051; e-mail reduc@cide .cl; internet www.reduc.cl; f. 1977; network of different educational research institutions; aims to disseminate information on education for research and policy making; 27 mem. instns; documentation centre of 20,000 research summaries; Dir GONZALO GUTIÉRREZ; publ. *Databases* (online).

HISTORY, GEOGRAPHY AND ARCHAEOLOGY

Instituto de Investigaciones Arqueológicas y Museo 'R.P. Gustavo Le Paige, S.J.': San Pedro de Atacama; tel. (55) 851002; fax (55) 851066; e-mail museospa@ucn.cl; f. 1985; affiliated to the Universidad Católica del Norte, Antofagasta; research in archaeology and anthropology; postgraduate courses (MA and PhD); library of books, 5,000 periodicals; Dir Dr AGUSTÍN LLAGOSTERA M.; publ. *Estudios Atacameños* (irregular).

MEDICINE

Instituto de Medicina Experimental del Servicio Nacional de Salud (Institute of Experimental Medicine of the National Health Service): Avda Irarrázaval 849, Casilla 3401, Santiago; tel. (2) 2497930; f. 1937; affiliated to WHO; physiology, neuro-endocrinology and cancer research; maintains tumour bank, available for use by other research centres; 15 mems; library of 6,800 vols; Dir Dr SERGIO YRARRÁZAVAL; Chief Sec. Mrs BERTA IRIBIRRA.

Instituto de Salud Pública de Chile (Chilean Public Health Institute): Avda Marathon 1000, Ñuñoa, Santiago; tel. (2) 3507321; fax (2) 3507578; internet www .ispch.cl; f. 1980; centre for vaccine production, nat. control of pharmaceutical, food and cosmetic products, and for coordination of nat. network of health laboratories; 600 mems; library of 9,142 vols (Central Scientific Library 3,600 vols; Centre of Occupational Health and Air Pollution Library 5,542 vols); Dir JORGE SÁNCHEZ VEGA; publs *Boletín informativo de medicamentos*, *Laboratorio al día*, *Manual de Bioseguridad*, *Manuales de Procedimiento de Laboratorio Clínico*.

NATURAL SCIENCES

General

Centro de Información de Recursos Naturales (CIREN) (Centre for Information on Natural Resources): Avda Manuel Montt 1164, Providencia, 7501556 Santiago; tel. (2) 2008900; fax (2) 2008914; e-mail ciren@reuna .cl; internet www.ciren.cl; f. 1964; privately run corpn; gathers data and provides a central information service in the areas of climate, soil, water, fruit production, afforestation, mining, agricultural resources; holds a landowners register; library of 11,000 vols, 150 journals; Exec. Dir RODRIGO FRANCISCO ALVAREZ SEGUEL.

Physical Sciences

Comité Nacional de Geografía, Geodesía y Geofísica (National Geographical, Geodetic and Geophysical Committee): Nueva Santa Isabel 1640, Santiago; tel. (2) 4606800; fax (2) 4606978; e-mail igm@igm .cl; f. 1935 to encourage and coordinate research in the fields mentioned; 119 mems; Dirs PABLO GRAN LÓPEZ, LUIS ALEGRÍA MATTA, JUAN GUTTIÉRREZ PALACIOS.

Dirección Meteorológica de Chile (Meteorological Bureau): Casilla 140, Sucursal Matucana, Estación Central, Santiago; Avda Portales 3450, Estación Central, Santiago; tel. (2) 4364538; fax (2) 4378212; e-mail dimetche@meteochile.cl; internet www .meteochile.cl; f. 1884; library of 3,000 vols; Dir Col NATHAN MAKUC; publs *Anuario Agrometeorológico*, *Anuario Meteorológico*, *Boletín Agrometeorológico* (12 a year), *Boletín Climatologico* (12 a year), *Boletín de Radiación Ultravioleta*, *Informe Solarimetrico Semestral de Radiación e Insolación*.

European Southern Observatory (ESO): Casilla 19001, Correo 19, Avda Alonso de Córdova 3107, Vitacura, Santiago; tel. (2) 4633000; fax (2) 4633101; internet www.sc .eso.org/santiago/science; f. 1962; ESO is the European organization for astronomical research in the southern hemisphere; ESO operates 3 observational sites in the Chilean Atacama Desert: the Very Large Telescope (VLT), is located on Paranal, a 2600-m high mountain south of Antofagasta; several medium-sized optical telescopes are operated at La Silla, 600 km north of Santiago, at 2400-m altitude; a new submillimetre telescope (APEX) is in operation at the 5000-m high Llano de Chajnantor, near San Pedro de Atacama; a large number of 12-m submillimetre antennas (ALMA) are currently under development; ESO Representative and Head of Science Office in Chile FELIX MIRABEL.

Instituto Antártico Chileno: 1055 Plaza Muñoz Gamero, Punta Arenas; tel. (61) 298100; fax (61) 298149; e-mail inach@inach .cl; internet www.inach.gob.cl; f. 1964; promotes devt of scientific research, technology and innovation in Antarctica following int. standards; participates in the Antarctic Treaty System and related int. forums; strengthening of Punta Arenas as gateway;

organizes activities and evaluation of knowledge regarding Antarctica in the nat. community; advises the Min. of Foreign Affairs in Antarctica matters; 43 mems; library of 4,100 vols, 11,600 periodicals, 3,000 monographs; Dir Dr JOSÉ RETAMALES; publs *Boletín Antártico Chileno* (2 a year), *Programa Nacional de Ciencia Antártica* (1 a year, in English and Spanish).

Instituto Isaac Newton (Isaac Newton Institute): Casilla 8–9, Correo 9, Santiago; tel. (2) 2172013; fax (2) 2172352; e-mail inewton@terra.cl; internet www.ini.cl; f. 1978; promotes astronomy in 9 Eastern European and Eurasian countries; Dir GONZALO ALCAINO; publs *Astronomical Journal* (10 a year), *Astronomy and Astrophysics* (70 a year), *Astrophysical Journal* (10 a year).

Observatorio Astronómico Nacional (National Astronomical Observatory): Universidad de Chile, Departamento de Astronomía, Biblioteca, Casilla 36-D, Santiago 1; tel. (2) 2294002; fax (2) 2293973; e-mail biblio@das.uchile.cl; internet www.das.uchile.cl; f. 1852; attached to Universidad de Chile; Repsold Meridian circle, Transit instrument, Gauthier refractor astrograph, Heyde visual refractor, Danjon astrolabe and Zeiss transit instruments; astronomical station at Cerro El Roble; library of 7,247 vols; Dir Dr MARIO HAMUY.

Observatorio Interamericano de Cerro Tololo (Cerro Tololo Inter-American Observatory): Casilla 603, La Serena; tel. (51) 205200; fax (51) 205212; internet www.ctio.noao.edu; f. 1963; astronomical observation of stars only observable in the southern hemisphere; library of 21,405 vols; Dir Dr ALISTAIR R. WALKER.

Servicio Hidrográfico y Oceanográfico de la Armada de Chile (Hydrographic and Oceanographic Service of the Chilean Navy): Errazuriz 254, Playa Ancha, Valparaíso; tel. (32) 2266666; fax (32) 2266542; e-mail shoa@shoa.cl; internet www.shoa.cl; f. 1874; hydrographic surveys, nautical charts and publs, oceanography, maritime safety, nat. oceanographic data centre; library of 12,700 vols; Dir Capt. PATRICIO J. C. CARRASCO H.; publs *Anuario Hidrográfico* (1 a year), *Boletín de Noticias a los Navegantes* (12 a year), *Derroteros de la Costa de Chile*, *Tablas de Marea de la Costa de Chile* (1 a year).

Servicio Nacional de Geología y Minería: Casilla 10465, Santiago; tel. (2) 7375050; fax (2) 7372026; e-mail msuarez@sernageomin.cl; internet www.sernageomin.cl; f. 1981; geoscience and mining; library of 30,000 vols, 15,000 aerial photographs, 200 satellite photographs, 600 periodical titles, 6,000 maps; Nat. Dir PATRICIO CARTAGENA; publ. *Revista Geológica de Chile* (2 a year).

RELIGION, SOCIOLOGY AND ANTHROPOLOGY

Instituto Latinoamericano de Doctrina y Estudios Sociales: Almirante Barroso 6, Casilla 14446, Correo 21, Santiago; tel. (2) 6714072; fax (2) 6986873; f. 1965; teaching and research in economics and social sciences; in-service courses for teachers and professionals; study, dissemination and renewal of social thought within the Church; 54 mems; Exec. Vice-Dir R. P. GONZALO ARROYO; publs *DOCLA*, *Revista de Análisis Económico*, *Persona y Sociedad*.

TECHNOLOGY

Comisión Nacional de Investigación Científica y Tecnológica (CONICYT) (National Commission for Scientific and Technological Research): Canadá 308, Providencia, Santiago; tel. (2) 3654400; fax (2) 6551396; internet www.conicyt.cl; f. 1969;

govt agency in charge of studying, planning and proposing nat. scientific and technological policy to the govt and developing, promoting and improving science and technology; mem. of ICSU; and FID; library of 4,500 vols; Pres. VIVIAN HEYL CHIAPPINI; Dir of Scientific Information PATRICIA E. MUÑOZ PALMA; publs *C & T* (12 a year, electronic edn only), *Panorama Científico* (12 a year), *Series Bibliografías*, *Series Directorios*, irregular study reports, documentation reports, *Series Información y Documentación*.

Instituto de Investigaciones y Ensayes de Materiales (IDIEM), Universidad de Chile (Institute for Materials Research and Testing): Plaza Ercilla 883, Santiago; tel. (20 9784151; fax (2) 6983166; e-mail idiem@idiem.uchile.cl; f. 1898; library of 8,000 vols; Dir FERNANDO YAÑEZ URIBE.

Instituto Nacional de Normalización (National Institute of Standardization): Matías Cousiño 64, piso 6, Santiago; tel. (2) 4458800; e-mail info@inn.cl; internet www3.inn.cl; f. 1944; library: 160,000 technical standards; Exec. Dir SERGIO TORO GALLEGUILLOS.

Libraries and Archives
Concepción

Universidad de Concepción, Dirección de Bibliotecas: Barrio Universitario, Casilla 1807, 160-C, Correo 3, Concepción; tel. (41) 234985; fax (41) 244796; f. 1919; 425,250 vols, 6,315 periodicals; Dir DIETER OELKER LINK.

Santiago

Archivo Nacional (National Archive): Miraflores 50, Santiago; tel. (2) 3605213; fax (2) 6325735; e-mail archivo.nacional@dibam.cl; internet www.dibam.cl/archivo_nacional; f. 1927; incl. historic and public admin. collns; Dir MARÍA EUGENIA BARRIENTOS.

Biblioteca Central, Instituto de Investigaciones Agropecuarias: Casilla 439 Correo 3, CP 7083150, Santiago; tel. (2) 7575223; fax (2) 5464668; internet alerce.inia.cl; f. 1947; 18,000 vols, 31,800 documents and papers, incl. Chilean colln, 675 current periodicals, 9,764 Chilean univ. theses; Head Librarian SONIA ELSO; publs *Agricultura Técnica* (4 a year, online), *Bibliografía Agrícola Chilena* (online only), *Boletín INIA* (irregular), *Collection Libros INIA* (irregular), *Serie Actas* (irregular), *Tierra Adentro* (6 a year).

Biblioteca del Congreso Nacional (Congress Library): Huérfanos 1117, 2° piso, Clasificador Postal 1199, Santiago; tel. (2) 2701700; fax (2) 2701766; internet www.congreso.cl/biblioteca; f. 1883; 1m. vols and 5,600 periodicals on law, social sciences, politics and economics, human sciences and literature; 13,500 leaflets, 12,000 rare books, 1,353 maps and topographical charts, 4m. Chilean press cuttings, official depository for int. orgs, legal depository for national publs, open to the public; ; Dir XIMENA FELIÚ SILVA; Asst Dir ALICIA ROJAS ESTIBIL; publs *Serie Estudios*, *Alerta Informativa*, *Temas de Actualidad*, *Visión Semanal*.

Biblioteca Nacional de Chile (National Library): Avda Libertador Bernardo O'Higgins 651, Santiago; tel. (2) 3605200; fax (2) 6380461; e-mail biblioteca.nacional@bndechile.cl; internet www.dibam.cl/biblioteca_nacional; f. 1813; 3.5m. vols, 75,000 MSS, 83 incunabula; Dir MARTA CRUZ-COKE M.; publs *Bibliografía Chilena* (1 a year), *Mapocho* (2 a year), *Referencias*

Críticas sobre autores Chilenos, bibliographies, catalogues.

Dirección del Sistema de Bibliotecas de la Universidad de Santiago de Chile: Schatchtebeck 4, Ex-Avenida Oriente, Estación Central, Santiago; tel. (2) 7182603; fax (2) 7763516; e-mail ximena.sobarzo@usach.cl; internet www.biblioteca.usach.cl; f. 1979; 292,175 vols; Dir XIMENA SOBARZO SÁNCHEZ.

Pontificia Universidad Católica de Chile, Sistema de Bibliotecas: Campus San Joaquín, Vicuña Mackenna 4860, Casilla 306, Correo 22, Santiago; tel. (2) 6864615; fax (2) 6865852; f. 1901; 10 university libraries; 1,587,518 vols; Dir MARÍA LUISA ARENAS FRANCO.

Sistema de Servicios de Información y Bibliotecas de la Universidad de Chile (SISIB): Avda Diagonal Paraguay 265, Oficina 703, Santiago; tel. (2) 9782583; fax (2) 9782574; e-mail sisib@uchile.cl; internet www.uchile.cl; f. 1843, reorganized 1936; contains more than 3m. vols, comprising donations from Canada, the UK, the USA and Spain, and from private collns, including those of Pedro Montt and Pablo Neruda; colln of periodicals comprising 14,500 titles, with over 500,000 issues; there are 49 libraries in the univ.; Dir GABRIELA ORTÚZAR FONTT.

Valdivia

Sistema de Bibliotecas, Universidad Austral de Chile: Correo 2, Valdivia; tel. (63) 221290; fax (63) 221360; e-mail biblio@uach.cl; internet www.biblioteca.uach.cl; f. 1962; 167,321 vols, 1,600 periodicals; specializes in science; Dir LUIS VERA CARTES.

Valparaíso

Biblioteca Central de la Universidad Técnica 'Federico Santa María': Avda España 1680, Edificio U, Valparaíso; tel. (32) 2654147; e-mail casa.central@bib.utfsm.cl; internet www.bib.utfsm.cl; f. 1926; 110,000 vols, 2,400 periodicals; audiovisual material: cassettes, video cassettes, maps, microfilms, slides; specializes in science and technology; Dir ALEX ARELLANO CALZADILLA; publs *Gestión tecnológica* (4 a year), *Scientia: Serie A Mathematical Sciences*, *USM Noticias* (12 a year).

Biblioteca de la Pontificia Universidad Católica de Valparaíso: Avda Brasil 2950, Casilla 4059, Valparaíso; tel. (32) 2273261; fax (32) 2273183; e-mail abustos@ucv.cl; internet biblioteca.ucv.cl; f. 1928; 248,000 vols; Dir ATILIO BUSTOS-GONZALEZ; publs *eQuipu Red de Editores Científicos*, *Electronic Journal of Biotechnology*, *Fondo de Etnomusicología Margot Loyola Palacios*.

Biblioteca Publica No. 1 'Santiago Severin' de Valparaíso: Plaza Simón Bolívar, Valparaíso; tel. (32) 213375; fax (32) 213375; f. 1873; incl. a colln of historical books on Chile and America and a colln of 17th- to 19th-century books; 94,149 vols, 166,814 periodicals; Dir YOLANDA SOTO VERGARA.

Museums and Art Galleries
Angol

Museo Dillman S. Bullock: Casilla 8-D, Angol; Km 5 Camino Angol–Collipulli, Angol; tel. (45) 712395; fax (45) 719303; e-mail museodbullock@yahoo.es; f. 1946; general local flora and fauna; extensive local archaeological colln; library of 5,000 vols; undertakes research, scientific expeditions; Dir ALBERTO E. MONTERO.

Antofagasta

Museo Regional de Antofagasta: Bolívar No 188, Casilla 746, Antofagasta; tel. (55) 227016; fax (55) 221109; e-mail museoantof@ terra.cl; f. 1984; archaeology, history, ethnography, geology; small library; Curator IVO KUZMANIĆ PIEROTIĆ.

Arica

Museo Arqueológico San Miguel de Azapa: Museo Universidad de Tarapaca, San Miguel de Azapa, Facultad de Cs. Sociales y Juridicas, Depto de Anthropologia, Casilla 6-D, Arica; tel. (58) 205555; fax (58) 205552; e-mail masma@uta.cl; internet www .uta.cl/masma; f. 1967; univ. museum, belonging to the dept of anthropology; exhibits communicate univ. research on pre-Columbian, colonial and modern native people; library of 8,000 vols; Dir HECTOR GOWZALEZ CORTEZ (acting); publs *Chungara* (Chilean anthropology, 2 a year), *Cuadernos de Trabajo* (irregular).

Cañete

Museo Folklórico Araucano de Cañete 'Juan A. Ríos M.': Casilla 28, Cañete; f. 1968; conserves, exhibits and researches the Mapuche culture from its origins to contact with Spanish culture; recreates the environment that Valdivia saw in 1552 when he built the Tucapel Fort (near the museum); anthropological research of the native Mapuche settlements that still exist; archaeological excavations in the surrounding area; library of 2,000 vols; Curator GLORIA CARDENAS TRONCOSO.

Concepción

Museo de Historia Natural de Concepción (Concepción Natural History Museum): Maipú 2359, Plaza Acevedo, Concepción; tel. (41) 2310932; fax (41) 2310932; e-mail musconce@surnet.cl; internet www.dibam.cl/ sdm_mr_concepcion; f. 1902; library of 6,732 vols; Dir MARCO SÁNCHEZ AGUILERA; publ. *Comunicaciones del Museo de Concepción.*

Museo de Hualpén (Hualpén Museum): Camino Desembocadura s/n, Hualpén; tel. (41) 2426399; f. 1882; collns of Greek, Roman and Egyptian archaeology; Chilean arms and numismatic collns; Oriental art; Chilean and American folk art; Chilean archaeology; 18th- and 19th-century furniture; Dir MARTÍN DOMÍNGUEZ.

Copiapó

Museo Regional de Atacama: Casilla 134, Copiapó; Atacama 98, Copiapó; tel. (52) 212313; fax (52) 212313; e-mail museo .atacama@dibam.cl; internet www.dibam.cl/ sdm_mr_atacama; f. 1973; archaeology, mineralogy, ecology and history; library of 15,000 vols; Dir MIGUEL CERVELLINO.

Iquique

Museo Antropológico de Iquique: c/o Universidad Arturo Prat de Iquique, Calle Grumete Volado 127, Iquique; f. 1987; attached to the Centro de Estudios del Desierto of the Univ.; permanent exhibition showing the cultural devt of the people of the region from 10,000 BC to AD 1900; research in archaeology, rural devt of farming communities, history and ethnography; specialized library; Dir Arq. ÁLVARO ČAREVIĆ RIVERA; publ. research findings.

Museo Regional de Iquique: Calle Baquedano 951, Iquique; tel. (57) 411214; fax (57) 413278; e-mail ftellezc@gmail.com; attached to the Dept of Social Development of the Municipality of Iquique; f. 1960; permanent

exhibition of regional archaeology, ethnography and history; Dir FRANCISCO TÉLLEZ CANCINO.

La Serena

Museo Arqueológico de La Serena (La Serena Archaeological Museum): Calle Cordovez esq. Cienfuegos s/n, La Serena; tel. (51) 224492; fax (51) 550423; e-mail muarse@ entelchile.net; internet www.dibam.cl/ sdm_m_laserena; f. 1943; sections on archaeology, prehistory, physical anthropology, colonial history, ethnology and palaeontology; library of 23,000 vols, 18,043 slides, 28,150 photographs; Dir GONZALO AMPUERO B.

Linares

Museo de Arte y Artesanía de Linares: Casilla Postal 280, Linares; Avda Valentín Letelier 572, Linares; tel. and fax (73) 210662; e-mail mulin@ctcinternet.cl; internet www.museodelinares.cl; f. 1966; arts and crafts from the Inca period to the present; valuable collns, incl. unique clay miniatures; colln of Huaso implements; ceramics; exhibition of history and people of Linares; conferences, lectures, films; library of 2,000 vols; Dir PATRICIO ACEVEDO LAGOS.

Ovalle

Museo del Limari: Covarrubias esq. Antofagasta, Casilla 59, Ovalle; tel. (53) 620029; fax (53) 620029; e-mail mdlim@ctcinternet .net.cl; internet www.mdlim.cl; f. 1963; archaeology (esp. local); Curator DANIELA SERANI ELLIOTT.

Puerto Williams

Museo 'Martín Gusinde': Aragay 1, Puerto Williams, Isla Navarino, XII Región de Magallanes, Antártica Chilena; tel. and fax (61) 621043; e-mail pgrendi@yahoo.com; internet www.dibam.cl; f. 1975; situated on Navarino Island; history and geography of the southernmost archipelagos of the Americas; aboriginal culture, flora, fauna and minerals of the area; library of 500 vols; Curator PAOLA GRENDI ILHARREBORDE.

Punta Arenas

Museo Regional de Magallanes: Centro Cultural Braun-Menéndez, Hernando de Magallanes 949, Punta Arenas; tel. (61) 244216; fax (61) 221387; f. 1983, fmrly Museo de la Patagonia, f. 1967; Patagonian history; library: specialized 3,500 vols; Dir MAURICIO QUERCIA.

Museo Salesiano 'Maggiorino Borgatello' (Salesian Museum 'Maggiorino Borgatello'): Avda Bulnes 336, Casilla 347, Punta Arenas; tel. (61) 221001; e-mail musborga@ hotmail.com; internet www .museomaggiorinoborgatello.cl; f. 1893; scientific and ethnographical (notable relics of extreme South American and Tierra del Fuegan tribes), Patagonic history, Antarctic continent vision, petroleum industry; library of 2,000 vols; Scientific Dir Prof. SALVATORE CIRILLO DAMA.

Santiago

Museo Chileno de Arte Precolombino: Casilla 3687, Bandera 361, Santiago; tel. (2) 6887348; fax (2) 6972779; f. 1981, by the ccl of Santiago City and the Fundación Familia Larraín Echenique; 2,000 items of pre-Columbian art and 1,000 items in ethnographic collns from Mapuche and Aymara cultures; textiles, ceramics, metalwork, stone sculptures; large colln of photographs, slides, video- and audio cassettes; laboratory for textile and pottery conservation; laboratory for archaeological research; research on pre-Columbian music, rock art, Tiahuanaco,

Aymara, Atacama and Araucanian cultures, prehistoric architecture, Andean textiles and symbolism; educational programmes; music archive; library of 6,000 vols, 500 periodicals, spec. colln of pre-Columbian art, conservation and archaeology; Dir CARLOS ALDUNATE DEL SOLAR; publs *Boletín* (1 a year), catalogue of exhibitions (irregular).

Museo de Arte Colonial de San Francisco: Alameda Bernardo O'Higgins 834, Santiago; tel. and fax (2) 6398737; e-mail museosanfrancisco@museosanfrancisco.tie .cl; internet www.museosanfrancisco.cl; f. 1968 by the Franciscan Order; 16th- to 19th-century art (esp. 17th-century paintings); the life of St Francis depicted in 22 pictures; the life of San Diego de Alcalá depicted in 35 pictures; also other religious works of art, furniture, icons, embroidery, sculpture, carving, woodwork and metalwork; Dir ROSA PUGA D.

Museo de Arte Contemporáneo (Contemporary Art Museum): Parque Forestal frente a Calle Mosqueto, Santiago; tel. (2) 6395486; fax (2) 6394945; internet www.uchile.cl/mac; f. 1947; contemporary and fine arts; Dir FRANCISCO BRUGNOLI BAILONI.

Museo de Arte Popular Americano (Museum of American Folk Art): Compañía 2691, Casilla 2100, Universidad de Chile, Santiago; tel. (2) 6821481; fax (2) 6821481; e-mail mapa@uchile.cl; internet www.mapa .uchile.cl; f. 1943; objects of American folk art in pottery, basketware, wood and metal, Araucanian silverware; Dir NURY GONZALEZ.

Museo de Historia Natural de San Pedro Nolasco (Natural History Museum): MacIver 341, Santiago; f. 1922; library of 58,000 vols; spec. collns: Claudio Gay, G. Cuvier, A. E. Brehrm, Ch. Darwin.

Museo de la Educación Gabriela Mistral: Chacabuco 365, Santiago Centro; tel. (2) 6818169; e-mail desarrollo@ museopedagogico.cl; internet www .museodelaeducacion.cl; f. 1941; permanent exhibition on Chilean educational history; central themes of heritage and memory; interactive space for recreational learning; organizes seminars, workshops and training in subjects such as education, culture and soc.; library of 40,000 vols, photographic archive of 6,000 images; Dir Dr MARÍA ISABEL ORELLANA RIVERA.

Museo Histórico Nacional (National Historical Museum): Palacio de la Real Audiencia, Plaza de Armas, Casilla 9764, Santiago; tel. (2) 6381411; fax (2) 6331815; e-mail bdevose@oris.renib.cl; internet www .museohistoriconacional.cl; f. 1911; pre-Hispanic period to the present; costume, iconographic, arms, arts and crafts, and numismatic collections; dept of education; research in textile, paper and photographic restoration; library of 12,000 vols; Dir BARBARA DE VOS EYZAGUIRRE.

Museo Nacional de Bellas Artes (National Museum of Fine Arts): Parque Forestal s/n, Casilla 3209, Correo Central, Santiago; tel. (2) 6391946; fax (2) 6393297; e-mail milan .ivelic@mnba.cl; internet www.dibam.cl; f. 1880; paintings, engravings, etchings and sculpture, Chilean and European paintings; library of 15,000 vols; Dir MILAN IVELIĆ.

Museo Nacional de Historia Natural (National Museum of Natural History): Casilla 787, Santiago; tel. (2) 6804603; fax (2) 6804602; e-mail webmaster@mnhn.cl; internet www.mnhn.cl; f. 1830; depts of zoology, entomology, hydrobiology, botany, mineralogy, palaeontology, anthropology, museology, education; Curator MARÍA ELIANA RAMÍREZ CASALI; publs *Boletín, Noticiario mensual.*

Talca

Museo O'Higginiano y de Bellas Artes de Talca: 1 Norte No. 875, Talca; tel. (71) 210428; fax (71) 227330; e-mail museodetalca@gmail.com; internet www .dibam.cl/sdm_moba_talca; f. 1964; paintings, sculpture, Chilean history, archaeology, religious artefacts, antique furniture, arms; library of 430 vols; video cassettes; Dir ALEJANDRO MORALES YAMAL; publ. *La Casona durante la Colonia.*

Temuco

Museo Regional de la Araucania (Araucania Museum): Avda Alemania 084, Casilla 481, Temuco; tel. (45) 730062; fax (45) 730064; f. 1940; opened to the public 1943; archaeological, artistic and ethnographic exhibits of the Araucanian, or Mapuche, Indians of South Chile, and others relating to the conquest, pacification and colonization of Araucania, as well as the history of Temuco city itself; maintains research section; library: specialized library of 886 vols about Mapuche culture and regional history; 1,400 reprints and maps of Mapuche reservations and foreign colonization; Dir HÉCTOR ZUMAETA ZÚÑIGA; publ. *Bulletin.*

Valdivia

Museo Histórico y Antropológico 'Mauricio Van de Maele': Los Laureles s/n, Isla Teja, Valdivia; tel. and fax (63) 212872; e-mail secmuseologica@uach.cl; internet www.uach.cl/direccion/museologica; f. 1967; attached to Universidad Austral de Chile; centre for conservation of historical monuments, archaeology, museums and historical archives; undertakes teaching, research, training of museum staff, conservation, museology; library of 3,000 vols, 4,000 photographs; Dir LEONOR ADÁN A.

Valparaíso

Museo de Historia Natural de Valparaíso (Natural History Museum): Calle Condell 1546, Valparaíso; tel. (32) 2544840; fax (32) 2544843; e-mail contacto@mhnv.cl; internet www.dibam.cl/sdm_mhn_valpo; f. 1876; natural sciences and anthropology; library of 3,000 vols; Dir CRISTIAN BECKER ALVAREZ; publ. *Anales.*

Vicuña

Museo Gabriela Mistral de Vicuña: Calle Gabriela Mistral 759, Casilla 50, Vicuña; tel. (51) 411223; fax (51) 412524; e-mail mgmistral@entelchile.net; f. 1971; preserves cultural legacy of poet Gabriela Mistral (Nobel Prize for Literature 1945); documents, photographs and personal effects; replica of birthplace of poet, talks, films, music; library of 6,000 vols; Dir RODRIGO IRIBARREN AVILÉS; publ. *Boletín.*

Viña del Mar

Museo Comparativo de Biología Marina: Facultad de Ciencias del Mar y de Recursos Naturales, Universidad de Valparaíso, Casilla 5080 Reñaca, Viña del Mar; tel. (32) 2507824; fax (32) 2507859; e-mail ricardo .bravo@uv.cl; f. 1955; echinoderms, molluscs and other invertebrates; fishes from the coastal regions of the SE Pacific; library for the students of marine biology and oceanic engineering; Curator Dr RICARDO BRAVO; publ. *Revista de Biología Marina y Oceanografía.*

Universities and Technical Universities

UNIVERSIDAD DE ANTOFAGASTA

Avda Angamos 601, Antofagasta
Telephone: (55) 637325
Fax: (55) 637102
E-mail: rectoria@uantof.cl
Internet: www.uantof.cl
Founded 1981
State control
Language of instruction: Spanish
Academic year: March to January

Rector: LUIS ALBERTO LOYOLA MORALES
Vice-Rector for Academic Affairs: HERNÁN BAEZA KUROKI
Vice-Rector for Finance: CARLOS RIVERA DANTAGNAN
Gen. Sec.: MACARENA SILVA BOGGIANO
Dir of Teaching: NELSON HERRERA AVILA
Gen. Dir for Student Affairs: DOMINGO GÓMEZ PARRA
Dir for Admin. and Financial Affairs: OSCAR MORALES CASTILLO
Dir for Computing: RICHARDS ROJAS ARQUERO
Dir for Extension and Communications: CÉSAR TRABUCCO SWANECK
Dir for Graduate Affairs: MARÍA ELISA TABOADA MENESES
Dir for Legal Affairs: FERNANDO FERNÁNDEZ DE LA CERDA
Dir for Studies and Devt: INGRID JAMETT ARANDA
Dir for Research: CARLOS RIQUELME SALAMANCA
Librarian: NORMA MONTERREY
Number of teachers: 320
Number of students: 6,067

Publications: *Estudios Oceanológicos, Hombre y Desierto, Innovación*

DEANS

Faculty of Basic Sciences: GUILLERMO MONDACA
Faculty of Education and Human Sciences: JUAN PANADES VARGAS
Faculty of Engineering: PEDRO CÓRDOVA
Faculty of Health Sciences: MARCOS CIKUTOVIĆ
Faculty of Law: DOMINGO CLAPS
Faculty of Marine Resources: HERNAN BAEZA

ATTACHED INSTITUTES

Instituto del Desierto: research in energy and water resources of Atacama desert; agriculture and solar energy in the desert; Dir RENÉ CONTRERAS.

Instituto de Investigaciones Antropológicas: research in archaeology, anthropology, linguistics and literature of North Chile; Dir PATRICIO NÚÑEZ.

Instituto de Investigaciones Oceanológicas: research in marine life of northern coast of Chile; Dir LUIS RODRIGUEZ.

UNIVERSIDAD ARTURO PRAT

Avda Arturo Prat 2120, Iquique
Telephone: (57) 441208
Fax: (57) 394393
E-mail: j.torres@cec.unap.cl
Internet: www.unap.cl
Founded 1984
State control
Language of instruction: Spanish
Academic year: March to December

Rector: CARLOS MERINO PINOCHET
Vice-Rector for Academic Affairs: CÉSAR ARANCIBIA CÓRDOVA
Admin. Dir: CARLOS LADRIX OSÉS
Librarian: ROBERTO JIMÉNEZ RAMÍREZ

Number of teachers: 500
Number of students: 5,300

UNIVERSIDAD DE ATACAMA

Copayapu 485, Copiapó
Telephone: (52) 206500
Fax: (52) 212662
Internet: www.uda.cl
Founded 1981
State control
Language of instruction: Spanish
Academic year: March to December

Rector: JUAN IGLESIAS DÍAZ
Vice-Rector: GABRIELA PRADO PRADO
Gen. Sec.: TERESA REYES ASPILLAGA
Librarian: MARIANELA VIVANCO CORTÉS

Number of teachers: 95
Number of students: 2,950

Publications: *Revista de Derecho de Aguas* (1 a year), *Revista de Derecho de Minas* (1 a year), *Revista de Ingeniería* (1 a year)

DEANS

Faculty of Engineering: CELSO ARIAS M.
Faculty of Humanities and Education: OSCAR PAINÉAN BUSTAMANTE
Faculty of Law: RODRIGO PÉREZ LISICIC
Faculty of Natural Sciences: RENÉ MAURELIA GÓMEZ

ATTACHED INSTITUTES

Instituto Asistencia a la Minería: Casilla 240, Copiapó; tel. (52) 212006; fax (52) 212662; Dir JUAN NAVEA DANTAGNAN.

Instituto de Investigaciones Científicas y Tecnológicas: Casilla 240, Copiapó; tel. (52) 218770; fax (52) 218770; Dir GERMÁN CÁCERES ARENAS.

Instituto Derecho de Minas y Aguas: Moneda 673, 8° piso, Santiago; tel. (2) 6328290; fax (2) 6383452; Dir ALEJANDRO VERGARA BLANCO.

Instituto Tecnológico: Casilla 240, Copiapó; tel. (52) 206755; fax (52) 206756; e-mail timur.padilla@uda.cl; internet www .tecnologico.uda.cl; Dir TIMUR PADILLA BOCIĆ.

UNIVERSIDAD DEL BÍOBÍO

Avda Collao 1202, Casilla 5-C, Concepción
Telephone: (41) 261200
Fax: (41) 313897
E-mail: rector@ubiobio.cl
Internet: www.ubiobio.cl
Founded 1988
State control
Language of instruction: Spanish
Academic year: March to December

Campus also at Avda Andrés Bello s/n, Chillán

Rector: HILARIO HERNÁNDEZ GURRUCHAGA
Pro-Rector for Chillán Campus: FELIX MARTÍNEZ RODRÍGUEZ
Vice-Rector for Academic Affairs: HÉCTOR GAETE FERES
Vice-Rector for Financial Affairs: CLAUDIO ROJAS MIÑO
Sec.-Gen.: RICARDO PONCE SOTO
Dir for Int. Liaison: ALDO A. BALLERINI

Number of teachers: 603
Number of students: 8,986

Publications: *Arquitecturas del Sur* (3 a year), *Cuadernos de Edificación en Madera* (3 a year), *Maderas: Ciencia y Tecnología* (2 a year), *Memoria Anual Institucional* (1 a year), *Mercado de suelo de Concepción* (3 a year), *Proyección UBB*, *Theoría* (1 a year), *Tiempo y Espacio* (1 a year)

DEANS

Faculty of Architecture, Construction and Design: RICARDO HEMPEL HOLZAPFEL
Faculty of Business Management: LUIS CONTRERAS VILLAR
Faculty of Education and Humanities (Chillán): MARCO AURELIO REYES COCA
Faculty of Engineering: PETER BACKHOUSE ERAZO
Faculty of Health and Food Sciences: NORA PLAZA CEBALLOS
Faculty of Sciences: JORGE PLAZA DE LOS REYES ZAPATA

UNIVERSIDAD DE CHILE

Avda Bernardo O'Higgins 1058, Casilla 10-D, Santiago
Telephone: (2) 6781003
Fax: (2) 6781012
Internet: www.uchile.cl
Founded 1738 as Universidad Real de San Felipe; inaugurated 1843 as Universidad de Chile
State control
Academic year: March to December
Rector: LUIS A. RIVEROS C.
Pro-Rector: LUIS BAHAMONDE BRAVO
Academic Vice-Rector: MARIO SAPAG-HAGAR
Library: see Libraries and Archives
Number of teachers: 2,775 (including all branch institutions)
Number of students: 24,822
Publications: *Actualidad Universitaria* (12 a year), *Anales de la Universidad de Chile* (1 a year), *Anuario Astronómico* (1 a year), *Bizantion Nea Hellas*, *Boletín Chileno de Parasitología* (4 a year), *Boletín de Filología* (2 a year), *Boletín Interamericano de Educación Musical* (1 a year), *Comentarios sobre la Situación Económica*, *Cuadernos de Ciencia Política* (4 a year), *Cuadernos de Historia* (1 a year), *Desarrollo Rural* (2 a year), *Estudios Internacionales* (4 a year), *Ocupación y Desocupación Encuesta Nacional* (2 a year), *Política* (2 a year), *Revista Chilena de Antropología* (1 a year), *Revista Chilena de Historia del Derecho*, *Revista Chilena de Humanidades* (1 a year), *Revista Comunicaciones en Geología* (1 a year), *Revista de Derecho Económico*, *Revista de Derecho Público*, *Revista Económica y Administración* (4 a year), *Revista de Filosofía* (1 a year), *Revista Musical Chilena* (2 a year), *Revista Psiquiátrica Clínica* (1 a year), *Terra Aridae* (2 a year), *U Noticias* (12 a year)

DEANS

Faculty of Agriculture: MARIO SILVA G.
Faculty of Architecture and Town Planning: MANUEL FERNÁNDEZ HECHENLEITNER
Faculty of Chemical and Pharmaceutical Sciences: LUIS NÚÑEZ
Faculty of Dentistry: JOSÉ MATAS COLOM
Faculty of Economic and Administrative Sciences: NASSIR SAPAG
Faculty of Fine Arts: LUIS MERINO MONTERO
Faculty of Forestry: GUILLERMO JULIO A.
Faculty of Law: ANTONIO BASCUÑAN V.
Faculty of Medicine: Dr JORGE LAS HERAS
Faculty of Philosophy and Humanities: MARÍA ISABEL FLISHFISCH
Faculty of Physical and Mathematical Sciences: VÍCTOR PÉREZ VERA
Faculty of Sciences: CAMILO QUEZADA BOUEY
Faculty of Social Sciences: FERNANDO DURÁN
Faculty of Veterinary Sciences and Cattle Breeding: SANTIAGO URCELAY

ATTACHED INSTITUTES

Clinical Hospital of the University of Chile: Avda Santos Dumont 999, Santiago; Dir Dr ITALO BRAGHETTO.

Institute of International Studies: Condell 249, Santiago; Dir JEANETTE IRIGOIN.
Institute of Nutrition and Food Technology: Avda José Pedro Alessandri 5540, Santiago; Dir FERNANDO VIO.
Institute of Public Affairs: María Guerrero 940, Santiago; Dir OSVALDO SUNKEL.

UNIVERSIDAD DE LA FRONTERA

Avda Francisco Salazar 01145, Casilla 54-D, Temuco
Telephone: (45) 325000
Fax: (45) 325950
E-mail: ufro-tco@ufro.cl
Internet: www.ufro.cl
Founded 1981
State control
Academic year: March to December (2 semesters)
Rector: SERGIO BRAVO ESCOBAR
Vice-Rector for Academic Affairs: JUAN MANUEL FIERRO BUSTOS
Vice-Rector for Admin. and Finance: SERGIO CARTER FUENTEALBA
Sec.-Gen.: RICARDO HERRERA LARA
Library Dir: ROBERTO ARAYA NAVARRO
Number of teachers: 645
Number of students: 8,735
Publications: *Cubo* (1 a year), *Chilean Review of Biological Medical Sciences* (2 a year), *International Journal of Morphology* (4 a year), *Vertientes UFRO* (4 a year), *Revista Educación y Humanidades* (education and humanities, 1 a year), *Revista Investigaciones en Educación* (educational research, 1 a year), *Memoria Institucional* (1 a year), *Lengua y Literatura Mapuche* (2 a year), *Revista Médica del Sur* (medicine, 2 a year), *Revista Nuestra Muestra* (2 a year)

DEANS

Faculty of Agricultural and Forestry Sciences: ALIRO CONTRERAS NOVOA
Faculty of Education and Humanities: CARLOS DEL VALLE ROJAS
Faculty of Engineering and Administration: PLINIO DURÁN GARCÍA
Faculty of Medicine: EDUARDO HEBEL WEISS

PROFESSORS

Faculty of Agricultural and Forestry Sciences (Francisco Salazar 01145; tel. (45) 325630; fax (45) 325634; e-mail aliroc@ufro.cl; internet www.agrofor.ufro.cl):

MARÍN, P., Forestry Sciences
SORIANO, R., Agricultural Production
VENEGAS, J., Agricultural Sciences and Natural Resources

Faculty of Education and Humanities (Francisco Salazar 01145; tel. (45) 325370; fax (45) 325379; e-mail hcarrasc@ufro.cl; internet educacionyhumanidades.ufro.cl):

CHÁVEZ, J., Social Sciences
FELMER, L., Psychology
MÉNDEZ, I., Education
RIBERA, E., Language, Literature and Communication
SALAZAR, C., Physical Education, Sports and Recreation
TRABOL, H., Social Work

Faculty of Engineering and Administration (Arturo Prat 321; tel. (45) 325800; fax (45) 325810; e-mail decing@ufro.cl; internet fica.ufro.cl/web):

BARRA, M., Chemical Sciences
BARRERA, A., Mathematics Engineering
BRACHMANN, C., Chemical Engineering
BRICEÑO, I., Electrical Engineering
JARA, F., Administration and Economy
SALAZAR, G., Systems Engineering
SANHUEZA, M., Physical Sciences
VEGA, H., Mathematics and Statistics

VILLASEÑOR, M., Mechanical Engineering
VON-BISCHOFFSHAUSEN, G., Civil Engineering

Faculty of Medicine (Manuel Montt 112; tel. (45) 325700; fax (45) 325710; e-mail decanmed@ufro.cl; internet www.med.ufro.cl):

ARAYA ORÓSTICA, J., Pathology
CONCHA, S., Medicine (specialized)
CORTES, H., Public Health
ESPINOZA, B., Basic Sciences
FERNÁNDEZ, L., Paediatrics and Infant Surgery
FERNÁNDEZ, R., Integral Odontology
FREDES, E., Surgery and Traumatology
FRENE, E., Internal Medicine
FUENTES, L., Mental Health and Psychiatry
GONZÁLEZ, M., Pre-clinical Sciences
VALLEJOS, C., Obstetrics and Gynaecology

UNIVERSIDAD DE LA SERENA

Avda Raúl Bitrán Nachary s/n, La Serena
Telephone: (51) 204000
Fax: (51) 204310
E-mail: uls@userena.cl
Internet: www.userena.cl
Founded 1981
State control
Academic year: March to December
Rector: Dr NIBALDO AVILÉS PIZARRO
Vice-Rector for Academic Affairs: Dr JORGE CATALÁN AHUMADAS
Vice-Rector for Admin.: Dra MARÍA MARCELA AGUIRRE SALGADO
Gen. Dir of Student Affairs: HERNÁN CORTÉS OLIVARES
Sec.-Gen.: Prof. CALIXTO VEAS GAZ
Int. Liaison Officer: Dr RICARDO CASTILLO BOZO
Librarian: Lic. MARÍA A. CALABACERO JIMÉNEZ
Number of teachers: 554
Number of students: 7,694
Publications: *Revista Actas de Logos* (1 a year), *Revista Crisalida* (1 a year), *Revista Humus* (1 a year), *Revista de Investigación y Desarrollo* (1 a year), *Revista Logos* (1 a year), *Revista Omnibus* (1 a year), *Revista Temas de Educación* (1 a year)

DEANS

Faculty of Economics and Business: Dra LUPERFINA ROJAS ESCOBAR
Faculty of Engineering: Dr Ing. ALBERTO CORTÉS ÁLVAREZ
Faculty of Humanities: Dra MARÍA ZÚÑIGA CARRASCO
Faculty of Sciences: Dr GUSTAVO LABBÉ MORALES

UNIVERSIDAD DE LOS LAGOS

Casilla 933, Osorno
Avda Alcalde Fuchslocher 1305, Osorno
Telephone: (64) 333009
Fax: (64) 333501
E-mail: rectoria@ulagos.cl
Internet: www.ulagos.cl
Founded 1993, fmrly Instituto Profesional de Osorno
Public control
Language of instruction: Spanish
Academic year: March to December
Rector: OSCAR GARRIDO ALVAREZ
Vice-Rector for Academic Affairs: JUAN LUIS CARTER
Vice-Rector for Admin. and Finance: BERNARDO AEDO
Vice-Rector for Research and Graduate Studies: EGON MONTECINOS
Vice-Rector for Planning and Devt: OSCAR DIAZ

Gen. Sec.: BRUNO CÁRDENAS
Librarian: ARTURO RUBIO
Library of 40,105 vols
Number of teachers: 220
Number of students: 12,000
Publications: *Alpha* (humanities), *Biota* (aquatic sciences), *Leader* (social sciences).

UNIVERSIDAD DE MAGALLANES

Casilla 113-D, Punta Arenas
Telephone: (61) 212945
Fax: (61) 219276
Internet: www.umag.cl
Founded 1964 (previously branch of Universidad Técnica del Estado)
State control
Language of instruction: Spanish
Academic year: begins in March
Rector: Dr VÍCTOR FAJARDO MORALES
Vice-Rector for Academic Affairs: LUIS OVAL GONZÁLEZ
Sec.-Gen.: FRANCISCO SOTO PIFFAULT
Librarian: ILUMINANDA ROJAS PALACIOS
Number of teachers: 168
Number of students: 3,200
Publications: *Anales del Instituto de la Patagonia, Austrouniversitaria*

DEANS

Faculty of Economics and Law: LUIS POBLETE DAVANZO
Faculty of Engineering: JUAN OYARZO PÉREZ
Faculty of Humanities, Social Sciences and Health Sciences: JUAN YUDIKIS PRELLER
Faculty of Sciences: OCTAVIO LECAROS PALMA

ATTACHED INSTITUTE

Instituto de la Patagonia: Avda Bulnes 01890, Casilla 113-D, Punta Arenas; tel. 217173; fax 212973; f. 1969; scientific, cultural and social development of the South American region; Dir CLAUDIO VENEGAS CANELO.

UNIVERSIDAD DE PLAYA ANCHA

Edificio Puntángeles, piso 6, Avda Playa Ancha 850, Playa Ancha, Valparaíso
Telephone: (32) 2500100
E-mail: mbaxman@upla.cl
Internet: www.upla.cl
Founded 1948
Languages of instruction: Spanish, English, French, German
State control
Academic year: March to December
Rector: PATRICIO SANHUEZA VIVANCO
Pro-Rector: CARMEN IBAÑEZ CASTILLO
Vice-Rector for Academic Affairs: ROLANDO TIEMANN
Vice-Rector for Admin. and Financial Affairs: EDUARDO FAIVOVICH
Vice-Rector for Devt: LUIS BORK
Gen. Sec.: GINETTE BOBILLIER
Librarian: MARIA EUGENIA OLGUIN STEENBECKER
Number of teachers: 328
Number of students: 3,700
Publications: *Diálogos Educacionales, Diccionario Ejemplificado de Chilenismos, Nueva Revista del Pacífico, Notas Históricas y Geográficas, Proyección Universitaria, Revista de Orientación, Visiones Científicas*

DEANS

Faculty of Art: ALBERTO TEICHELMANN SHUTTLETON
Faculty of Education: RENÉ FLORES CASTILLO
Faculty of Humanities: JUAN SAAVEDRA A.
Faculty of Natural and Exact Sciences: JUAN CAMUS

Faculty of Physical Education: ELÍAS MARÍN VALENZUELA

UNIVERSIDAD DE SANTIAGO DE CHILE

Avda Libertador Bernardo O'Higgins 3363, Santiago
Telephone: (2) 7180000
Internet: www.usach.cl
Founded 1849 as Escuela de Artes y Oficios, renamed as Universidad Técnica del Estado 1947, present name 1981
State control
Language of instruction: Spanish
Academic year: March to December
Rector: Dr JUAN MANUEL ZOLEZZI CID
Vice-Rector for Academic Affairs: RODRIGO VIDAL
Vice-Rector for Finances and Management: JUAN PABLO AGUIRRE
Vice-Rector for Research and Devt: Dr MAURICIO ESCUDEY
Sec.-Gen.: GUSTAVO ROBLES
Gen. Dir for Communications: MARGARITA PASTENE
Dir for Int. Relations: MARIA FERNANDA CONTRERAS
Academic Registrar: ENRIQUE SAN JUAN
Librarian: MARÍA ISABEL PARRA
Library of 241,478
Number of teachers: 1,145
Number of students: 20,344
Publications: *Avances en Investigación y Desarrollo, Educación en Ingeniería, Mantención e Industria* (4 a year), *Boletín APYME* (6 a year), *Comunicación Universitaria, Contribuciones Científicas y Tecnológicas, Cuadernos de Humanidades*

DEANS

Faculty of Administration and Economics: SILVIA FERRADA
Faculty of Chemistry and Biology: JUAN LUIS GAUTIER
Faculty of Engineering: RAMÓN BLASCO
Faculty of Humanities: CARMEN NORAMBUENA
Faculty of Medicine: JOSÉ LUIS CÁRDENAS
Faculty of Sciences: SAMUEL NAVARRO
Faculty of Technology: LAURA ALMENDARES
School of Architecture: CARLOS RICHARDS
School of Journalism: MARGARITA PASTENE VALLADARES
School of Psychology: EMILIO MOYANO DÍAZ
Undergraduate Programme: LEOPOLDO SÁEZ GODOY

ATTACHED RESEARCH INSTITUTES

Centre for Innovation and Technology transfer: e-mail mariateresa.santander@usach.cl; Dir MARIA TERESA SANTANDER.

Centre for Innovation Developments in Education: e-mail fidel.oteiza@usach.cl; Dir FIDEL OTEIZA.

Centre for Research in Creativity and Higher Education: e-mail mario.letelier@usach.cl; Dir MARIO LETELIER.

Centre for Studies in Science and Food Technology: e-mail claudio.martinez@usach.cl; Dir CLAUDIO MARTÍNEZ.

Institute for Advanced Studies: e-mail cristian.parker@usach.cl; Dir CRISTIAN PARKER.

UNIVERSIDAD DE TALCA

2 Norte 685, Talca
Telephone: (71) 200101
Fax: (71) 228054
Internet: www.utalca.cl
Founded 1981
State control
Language of instruction: Spanish

Academic year: March to December
Rector: Dr JUAN ANTONIO ROCK TARUD
Vice-Rector for Academic Affairs: LUIS HUERTA
Vice-Rector for Cultural Affairs: PEDRO ZAMORANO PÉREZ
Vice-Rector for Devt: JUAN PABLO PRIETO COX
Vice-Rector for Finance and Admin.: PATRICIO ORTÚZAR RUIZ
Vice-Rector for Student Affairs: PAULINA ARROYO URRIZOLA
Sec.-Gen.: RICARDO SÁNCHEZ VENEGAS
Librarian: RAÚL RAVANAL
Number of teachers: 522 (248 full-time, 274 part-time)
Number of students: 7,989
Publications: *Acontecer* (12 a year), *Ius et Praxis* (2 a year), *Panorama Socio Económico* (1 a year), *Revista de Estudios Constitucionales, Revista de Estudios Seriados en Gestión de Salud, Revista Neuma, Revista Interamericana de Ambiente y Turismo (Riat), Universum* (1 a year)

DEANS

Faculty of Agronomy: HERNÁN PAILLÁN
Faculty of Business Administration: CLAUDIO ROJAS MIÑO
Faculty of Engineering: CLAUDIO TENREIRO LEIVA
Faculty of Forestry Sciences: JUAN FRANCO DE LA JARA
Faculty of Health Sciences: CARLOS GIGOUX CASTELLÓN
Faculty of Juridical and Social Sciences: JORGE DEL PICÓ RUBIO
Faculty of Psychology: EMILIO MOYANO DÍAZ

DIRECTORS

Faculty of Agronomy (Avda Lircay s/n, Casilla 721, Talca; tel. (71) 200210; fax (71) 200362):
School of Agronomy: PAULA MANRÍQUEZ NOVOA
Faculty of Architecture (Avda Lircay s/n, Casilla 727 Talca; tel. (71) 201539; fax (71) 201539):
School of Architecture: GERMÁN VALENZUELA B.
Faculty of Business Administration (Avda Lircay s/n, Casilla 727, Talca; tel. (71) 200310; fax (71) 200358):
Graduate School: PATRICIO SÁNCHEZ CAMPOS
School of Business Data Processing: ANDRÉS RUIZ-TAGLE AVENDAÑO
School of Commercial Engineering: TAMARA TIGERO RICHARDS
School of Public Bookkeeping and Auditing: JOSÉ SALAS ÁVILA
Faculty of Design (Avda Lircay s/n, Casilla 727, Talca; tel. (71) 200200; fax (71)200225):
School of Design: JAIME PARRA MARCHANT
Faculty of Engineering (Camino Los Niches s/n Km 1, , Curico; tel. (75) 201700; fax (75) 325958):
School of Bioinformatics: JOSÉ ANTONIO REYES SUÁREZ
School of Civil and Industrial Engineering: CARLOS TOLEDO
School of Civil Engineering in Computation: FEDERICO MEZA
School of Construction: LEONARDO RISCHMOLLER DELGADO
School of Mechanical Engineering: OSCAR FUENTES MÁRQUEZ
School of Mechatronics Engineering: MARIO FERNÁNDEZ FERNÁNDEZ
Faculty of Forestry Sciences (Avda Lircay s/n, Casilla 727, Talca; tel. (71) 200442; fax (71) 200440):

School of Forestry Engineering: MARCIA VÁSQUEZ SANDOVAL

Faculty of Health Sciences (Avda Lircay s/n, Casilla 727, Talca; tel. (71) 201667; fax (71) 201668):

School of Dentistry: IVONNE BUSTOS

School of Medical Technology: SILVIA VIDAL FLORES

School of Medicine: VERÓNICA MUJICA

School of Physiotherapy: RAMÓN VALDÉS MOYA

School of Speech: EXEQUIEL PLAZA T.

Faculty of Juridical and Social Sciences (Avda Lircay s/n, Casilla 727, Talca; tel. (71) 200299; fax (71) 200410):

School of Law: IVÁN OBANDO CAMINO

Faculty of Psychology (Avda Lircay s/n, Casilla 727 Talca; tel. (71) 200299; fax (71) 200410):

School of Psychology: NADIA RAMOS

School of Music (Avda Lircay s/n, casilla 727, Talca; tel. (71) 201539; fax (71) 201766):

School of Music: MIRTA BUSTAMANTE MÁRQUEZ

UNIVERSIDAD DE TARAPACÁ

Gral Velásquez 1775, Casilla 7-D, Arica
Telephone: (58) 205100
Fax: (58) 232135
E-mail: rec@uta.cl
Internet: www.uta.cl
Founded 1981
State control
Language of instruction: Spanish
Academic year: March to December
Library of 80,242 vols, 499 periodicals
Rector: EMILIO RODRIGUEZ PONCE
Vice-Rector for Academic Affairs: ARTURO FLORES FRANULIC
Vice-Rector for Finance and Admin.: MANUEL DOSONO MUÑOZ
Librarian: INÉS RODRÍGUEZ RIQUELME
Library of 73,300 vols, 622 periodicals
Number of teachers: 237
Number of students: 7,474
Publications: *Chungará* (2 a year), *Diálogo Andino* (2 a year), *Idesia* (2 a year), *Limite* (1 a year), *Revista Facultad de Ingeniería* (1 a year), *Revista de Fisica* (1 a year)

DEANS

Faculty of Agronomy: EUGENIO DOUSSOULIN ESCOBAR

Faculty of Education and Humanities: CARLOS HERRERA SAAVEDRA

Faculty of Engineering: JORGE BENAVIDES SILVA

Faculty of Sciences: HUGO BRAVO AZLAN

Faculty of Social Sciences, Business Administration and Economics: SERGIO PULIDO ROCCATAGLIATA

PROFESSORS

Faculty of Engineering:

ARACENA PIZARRO, D.
BARRAZA SOTOMAYOR, B.
BECK FERNÁNDEZ, H.
BENAVIDES SILVA, J.
BORJAS MONTERO, R.
BUSTOS ANDREU, H.
CAMPOS TRONCOSO, J.
COHEN HORNICKEL, W.
CORREA ARANEDA, E.
DÍAZ ROJAS, H.
DURÁN ARRIAGADA, R.
ESPINOZA VALLEDOR, J.
ESTUPIÑAN PULIDO, E.
FERNÁNDEZ MAGGI, M.
FIGUEROA PÉREZ, H.
FLORES CONDORI, C.
FUENTES HEINRICH, E.

FUENTES ROMERO, R.
GALLEGOS ARAYA, A.
GÁLVEZ SOTO, E.
GODOY RAMSAY, J.
GONZÁLEZ ARAYA, A.
GUÍRRIMAN CARRASCO, R.
HARNISCH VELOSO, I.
JERALDO CASTRO, A.
MARCHIONI CHOQUE, I.
MENDIZABAL JIMÉNEZ, H.
MUÑOZ ESPINOSA, J.
OSSANDON DÍAZ, H.
OSSANDON NUÑEZ, Y.
OVALLE CUBILLOS, R.
PAZ SEGURA, G.
PEDRAJA REJAS, L.
PONCE LÓPEZ, E.
RAMÍREZ VARAS, I.
RODRÍGUEZ ESTAY, A.
SANHUEZA HORMAZABAL, R.
SANZ CANTILLANA, T.
SAPIAÍN ARAYA, R.
TARQUE COSSIO, S.
TORRES ORTÍZ, E.
TORRES SILVA, H.
VALDÉS GONZÁLEZ, H.
VALDIVIA PINTO, R.
VERGARA DÍAZ, J.
VILLALOBOS ABARCA, J.
VILLANUEVA AGUILA, J.
VILLARROEL GONZÁLEZ, C.
ZAMORANO LUCERO, M.

Faculty of Sciences:

ALVAREZ INOSTROZA, L.
BARRIENTOS NUÑOZ, V.
BELTRAN BARRIOS, R.
BOGGIONI CASANOVA, S.
BÓRGUEZ BENITT, CELIA
BRAVO AZLÁN, H.
CABALLERO PETTERSEN, H.
CABELLO FERNÁNDEZ, G.
CALISTO PÉREZ, H.
CAMPOS ORTEGA, H.
CANDIA ANDRADE, M.
CARO ARAYA, M.
CASTRO SANTANDER, F.
CISTERNAS RIVEROS, M.
CORNEJO PONCE, L.
CORRALES MUÑOZ, J.
CORTÉS GAJARDO, W.
CRUZ MARINO, A.
ESPINOZA NAVARRO, O.
FERNÁNDEZ CARVAJAL, I.
FLORES ARAYA, J.
FLORES FRANCULIC, A.
GALAZ LEIVA, S.
GLASS SADIA, B.
GONZÁLEZ FLORES, M.
HERNÁNDEZ VILLASECA, L.
LAIME CONDORI, D.
LAVÍN BECERRA, L.
LAZO NÚÑEZ, E.
LEA RODRÍGUEZ, L.
LEIVA SAJURIA, C.
LOBATO ACOSTA, I.
LÓPEZ PERIC, H.
LORCA PIZARRO, S.
MARTÍN GARCÍA, E.
MEDINA DÍAZ, M.
MENESES VERA, C.
MONTALVO VILLALBA, M.
MOSCOSO ZÁRATE, D.
NARANJO GÁRATE, A. M.
OLIVARES TOLEDO, V.
O'NELL SEQUEIRA, M.
ORTEGA ARAYA, A.
ORTEGA ROJAS, A.
PACHÁ BUSTAMENTE, A.
PALLEROS SANTOS, H.
PEDREROS AVENDAÑO, M.
PÉREZ MORETTI, N.
QUELOPANA DEL VALLE, A.
QUIOZA PALOMINOS, S.
REYES RUBILAR, T.
REY MAS, V.

RIVAS AVILA, M.
ROJAS ESPINOZA, E.
ROJAS TRONCOSO, M.
ROMÁN FLORES, H.
SANHUEZA COLLINAO, M.
UBEDA DE LA CERDA, C.
VALENZUELA ESTRADA, M.
VASQUEZ ROJAS, M. I.
VILAXA OLCAY, A.
VILLANUEVA DÍAZ, H.
VILLEGAS BRAVO, J.
ZÚÑIGA AGUIRRE, J.
ZÚNIGA SALAS, P.

Faculty of Social Sciences, Business Studies and Administration:

ALBURQUENQUE ELIASH, M.
ALFONSO VARGAS, J.
ALFRED ALFARO, F.
ALVAREZ ROSALES, N.
BARRIENTOS BORDOLI, I.
BELMONTE SCHWARZBAUM, E.
BERNAL PERALTA, J.
BRIONES MORALES, L.
BUSSENIUS RISCO, J. C.
CABRALES GÓMEZ, F.
CAYO RIOS, G.
CHACAMA RODRÍGUEZ, J.
CHAIGNEAU ORFANOZ, S.
CISTERNAS ARAPIO, B.
CONTRERAS CORDANO, M.
CÓRDOVA GONZÁLEZ, J.
CUADRA PERALTA, A.
DONOSO MUÑOZ, M.
ESPINOZA VERDEJO, A.
FERREIRA REYES, R.
FIGUEROA GUACHALLA, M.
FLORES TAPIA, E.
GONZÁLEZ CORTÉS, H.
GUTIÉRREZ SAMOHOD, A.
HENRIQUEZ AGUILERA, A.
JIMÉNEZ QUÑONES, P.
KARMELIC PAVLOV, V.
LEAL SOTO, F.
LeBLANC VALENZUELA, L.
MUÑIZ OVALLE, I.
MUÑOZ ABELLA, G.
NAVARRETE ALVAREZ, M.
OCHOA DE LA MAZA, O.
PALMA QUIROZ, A.
PARRA SUAZO, D.
PERALTA MONTECINOS, J.
PULIDO ROCCATAGLIATA, S.
RAMÍREZ HUANCA, D.
RODRÍGUEZ PONCE, E.
ROMERO ROMERO, J.
RUÍZ LARRAL, C.
SALAS PALACIOS, R.
SANTORO VARGAS, C.
STANDEN RAMÍREZ, V.
STOREY MEZA, R.
ULLOA TORRES, H.
VIERA CASTILLO, D.

UNIVERSIDAD DE VALPARAÍSO

Casilla 123-V, Valparaíso
Telephone: (32) 2507000
Fax: (32) 2507143
Internet: www.uv.cl
Founded 1981; previously br. of Univ. of Chile
State control
Academic year: 2 terms, beginning March and August
Rector: ALDO SALVADOR VALLE ACEVEDO
Pro-Rector: OSVALDO CORRALES
Academic Dir-Gen.: OSVALDO BADENIER BUSTAMENTE
Sec.-Gen.: OSVALDO ENRIQUE CORRALES JORQUERA
Number of teachers: 1,189 (322 full-time, 867 part-time)
Number of students: 17,951

Publications: *Boletín Micológico, Revista de Biología Marina, Revista de Ciencias Sociales*

DEANS

Faculty of Architecture: JUAN LUIS MORAGA LACOST
Faculty of Dentistry: Dr OSVALDO BADENIER BUSTAMANTE
Faculty of Economics and Administration: RICARDO BARRIL VILLALOBOS
Faculty of Humanities: CARLOS MARTEL LLANO
Faculty of Law and Social Sciences: ALBERTO BALBONTÍN RETAMALES
Faculty of Marine Sciences and Natural Resources: GERARDO LEIGHTON SOTOMAYOR
Faculty of Medicine: Dr DAVID SABAH JAIME,
Faculty of Pharmacy: MARÍA SOLEDAD LOBOS SALVO
Faculty of Sciences: LUÍS MALDONADO CORTÉS

UNIVERSIDAD METROPOLITANA DE CIENCIAS DE LA EDUCACIÓN

Avda Jose Pedro Alessandri 774, Nunoa, Santiago
Telephone: (2) 2412400
Fax: (2) 2412723
E-mail: prensa@umce.cl
Internet: www.umce.cl
Founded 1889
Rector: JESÚS GONZÁLEZ
Vice-Rector: MAXIMINO FERNANDEZ FRAILE
Dir for Admin.: ROSANA SPROVERA MANRIQUEZ
Librarian: MARÍA ISABEL BRUCE
Number of teachers: 440
Number of students: 4,800
Publications: *Academia, Acta Entomológica chilena, Dimensión histórica de Chile, Educación Física*

DEANS

Faculty of Arts and Physical Education: MILTON COFRE ILUFFI
Faculty of Basic Sciences: MAFALDA SCHIAP-PACASSE COSTA
Faculty of History, Geography and Literature: SILVIA VYHMEISTER TZSCHABRAN
Faculty of Philosophy and Education: JAIME ARAOS SAN MARTIN

UNIVERSIDAD TECNOLÓGICA METROPOLITANA

Calle Dieciocho 161, Casilla 9845, Santiago
Telephone: (2) 7877500
Internet: www.utem.cl
Founded 1981 as Instituto Profesional de Santiago; present name 1993
Rector: HAYDÉE GUTIÉRREZ VILCHES
Vice-Rector for Academic Affairs: JUAN JOSÉ NEGRONI VERA
Vice-Rector for Admin. and Financial Affairs: GERMÁN MOLINA CHÁVEZ
Vice-Rector for Technology Transfer and Extension: MARIO TORRES ALCAYAGA
Gen. Sec.: PATRICIO BASTÍAS ROMÁN
Librarian: XIMENA SÁNCHEZ STAFORELLI
Number of teachers: 458
Number of students: 5,600
Publications: *Anuario Investigación del Departamento de Humanidades, Boletín Investigación del Departamento de Huma-nidades* (4 a year), *Trilogía*

DEANS

Faculty of Administration and Economics: ENRIQUE MATURANA LIZARDI
Faculty of Building and Town and Country Planning: ÁLVARO TORREALBA LÓPEZ
Faculty of Engineering: ARTURO OTT VILLA

Faculty of Humanities and Social Communication Technology: EDUARDO CAMPOS KAHLER
Faculty of Natural Sciences, Mathematics and the Environment: BEATRIZ GÓMEZ HERNÁNDEZ

Private Universities with Public Funding

PONTIFICIA UNIVERSIDAD CATÓLICA DE CHILE
(Catholic University of Chile)

Casilla 114-D, Alameda 340, Santiago
Telephone: (2) 6862415
Fax: (2) 2223116
E-mail: soporte@puc.cl
Internet: www.puc.cl
Founded 1888
Private control
Academic year: March to December
Grand Chancellor: Exmo Rmo Mons. FRAN-CISCO JAVIER ERRÁZURIZ OSSA
Vice-Grand Chancellor: Pbro ANDRÉS ARTEAGA
Rector: PEDRO PABLO ROSSO
Pro-Rector: JUAN IGNACIO VARAS
Vice-Rector: NICOLÁS VELASCO
Gen. Sec.: RAÚL MADRID
Dir of Distance Education: RICHARD WARNER
Librarian: MARÍA LUISA ARENAS
Library: see Libraries and Archives
Number of teachers: 2,100 (1,300 full-time, 800 part-time)
Number of students: 18,000
Publications: *Revista Humanitas* (every 2 years), *Revista Universitaria* (4 a year)

DEANS

Faculty of Agronomy: GUILLERMO DONOSO HARRIS
Faculty of Architecture and Fine Arts: JUAN JOSÉ UGARTE
Faculty of Biological Sciences: RENATO ALBER-TINI BARTOLAMEOLLI
Faculty of Chemistry: LUIS HERNÁN TAGLE DOMÍNGUEZ
Faculty of Communication: FRANCISCA ALES-SANDRI
Faculty of Economics and Management Sciences: FRANCISCO ROSENDE RAMÍREZ
Faculty of Education: GONZALO UNDURRAGA
Faculty of Engineering: HERNÁN DE SOLMINI-HAC
Faculty of History, Geography and Political Sciences: RENÉ MILLAR
Faculty of Law: ARTURO YIRRAZAVAL
Faculty of Mathematics: GUILLERMO MAR-SHALL
Faculty of Medicine: GONZALO GREBE
Faculty of Philosophy: LUIS FLORES
Faculty of Physics: RICARDO RAMÍREZ LEIVA
Faculty of Social Sciences: PEDRO MORANDÉ COURT
Faculty of Theology: R.-P. SAMUEL FERNÁN-DEZ

BRANCH CAMPUS

Sede Regional de Villarrica: Casilla 111; Dir Mons. PAUL WEVERING WEIDEMANN.

PONTIFICIA UNIVERSIDAD CATÓLICA DE VALPARAÍSO

Avda Brasil 2950, Casilla 4059, Valparaíso
Telephone: (32) 2273000
Fax: (32) 2212746
E-mail: rector@ucv.cl
Internet: www.ucv.cl
Founded 1928
Private control

Languages of instruction: Spanish, English
Academic year: March to December
Chancellor: Mgr GONZALO DUARTE GARCÍA DE CORTÁZAR
Rector: Prof. ALFONSO MUGA NAREDO
Vice-Rector for Academic and Student Affairs: EDUARDO ARAYA LEUPÍN
Vice-Rector for Admin. and Financial Affairs: CLAUDIO ELÓRTEGUI RAFFO
Vice-Rector for Devt Affairs: SALVADOR ZAHR MALUK
Vice-Rector for Research and Advanced Studies: SERGIO MARSHALL GONZÁLEZ
Sec.-Gen.: ALAN BRONFMAN VARGAS
Registrar: PAULA DROGUETT MEGE
Librarian: ATILIO BUSTOS GONZÁLEZ
Library: see Libraries and Archives
Number of teachers: 490
Number of students: 12,676
Publications: *Electronic Journal of Biotech-nology* (online), *Revista de Derecho* (online), *Revista de Estudios Histórico-Jurídicos* (online), *Revista Geográfica de Valparaíso* (online), *Revista Investiga-ciones Marinas* (online), *Revista Perspec-tiva Educacional, Revista Philosophica, Revista Signos* (online)

DEANS

Faculty of Agronomy: PEDRO UNDURRAGA MARTÍNEZ
Faculty of Architecture: SALVADOR ZAHR MALUK
Faculty of Basic Sciences and Mathematics: ARTURO MENA LORCA
Faculty of Economics and Admin.: RODRIGO NAVIA CARVALLO
Faculty of Engineering: PAULINO ALONSO RIVAS
Faculty of Law and Social Sciences: ALEJAN-DRO GUZMÁN BRITO
Faculty of Natural Resources: ELEUTERIO YAÑEZ RODRÍGUEZ
Faculty of Philosophy and Education: BALDO-MERO ESTRADA TURRA
Institute of Religious Studies: MARÍA INÉS CONCHA

UNIVERSIDAD AUSTRAL DE CHILE
(Southern University of Chile)

Independencia 641, Valdivia
Telephone: (63) 221277
Fax: (63) 293045
Internet: www.uach.cl
Founded 1954
Private control
Language of instruction: Spanish
Academic year: March to December
Rector: Dr VÍCTOR CUBILLOS GODOY
Vice-Rector for Academic Affairs: Dr OSCAR GALINDO VILLARROEL
Vice-Rector for Economic and Admin. Affairs: AGUSTÍN QUEVEDO GODOY
Sec.-Gen.: Dr JAVIER MILLAR SILVA
Dir of Extension: Prof. ARTURO ESCOBAR VALLEDOR
Dir of Postgraduate Studies: Dr HERNÁN POBLETE WILSON
Dir of Public Relations: PAMELA RADDATZ DELGADO
Dir of Research and Development: Dr ERNESTO ZUMELZU DELGADO
Dir of Student Affairs: Prof. ANGÉLICA AGUI-LAR VIVAR
Dir of Undergraduate Studies: Dr HÉCTOR NORIEGA HERNÁNDEZ
Registrar: MARIA BARRIGA RAMÍREZ
Dir for Library: LUIS VERA CARTES
Library: see Libraries and Archives
Number of teachers: 1,237
Number of students: 12,500
Publications: *AUS, Agro Sur, Archivos de Medicina Veterinaria, Bosque, Cuadernos*

de Cirugía, Estudios Filológicos, Estudios Pedagógicos, Gestión Turística, Revista Austral de Ciencias Sociales

DEANS

Faculty of Agriculture: RICARDO FUENTES PÉREZ
Faculty of Economic and Administrative Sciences: JUAN CARLOS MIRANDA CASTILLO
Faculty of Engineering Sciences: ROGELIO MORENO MUÑOZ
Faculty of Fishery and Oceanography: RENATO WESTERMEIER HITSCHFELD
Faculty of Forestry Sciences: GONZALO PAREDES VELOSO
Faculty of Juridical and Social Sciences: SUSAN TURNER SAELZER
Faculty of Medicine: CLAUDIO FLORES WÜRTH
Faculty of Philosophy and Humanities: YANKO GONZÁLEZ CANGAS
Faculty of Sciences: CARLOS BERTRÁN VIVES
Faculty of Veterinary Science: NÉSTOR TÁDICH BABAIC

UNIVERSIDAD CATÓLICA DE LA SANTÍSIMA CONCEPCIÓN

Caupolicán 491, Concepción
Telephone: (41) 246175
Fax: (41) 212318
E-mail: ucsc@ucsc.cl
Internet: www.ucsc.cl
Founded 1991
Private control; financially supported by the State

Rector: FERNANDO JIMÉNEZ LARRAÍN
Sec.-Gen.: ROLANDO GUTIÉRREZ GONZÁLEZ
Vice-Rector for Academic Affairs: EDUARDO SOUPER ESPINOSA
Vice-Rector for Financial and Admin. Affairs: GABRIEL HIDALGO AEDO

Library of 73,000 vols, 2,311 periodicals
Number of teachers: 263
Number of students: 5,979

DEANS

Faculty of Economics and Administration: JORGE ALAN CLEVELAND
Faculty of Education: FERNANDO SOTO SOTO
Faculty of Engineering: HUBERT MENNICKENT MENA
Faculty of Law: FERNANDO SAENGER GIANONI
Faculty of Medicine: Dr ALVARO LLANCAQUEO VALERI
Faculty of Science: Dr RAMÓN AHUMADA B.

DIRECTORS

School of Journalism: MARIO URZÚA ARACENA
Theological Centre: Dr JUAN CARLOS INOSTROZA LANAS

ATTACHED INSTITUTE

Instituto Tecnológico: Colón 2766, Talcahuano; tel. (41) 735070; fax (41) 735078; internet it.ucsc.cl; Rector FERNANDO JIMÉNEZ LARRAIN.

UNIVERSIDAD CATÓLICA DEL MAULE

Avda San Miguel 3605, CP 617 Talca
Telephone: (71) 203300
Fax: (71) 241767
E-mail: webmaster@hualo.ucm.cl
Internet: www.ucm.cl
Founded 1991
Private control; financially supported by the State

Rector: Dr CLAUDIO ROJAS MIÑO
Vice-Rector for Academic Affairs: HERNÁN MAUREIRA PAREJA
Vice-Rector for Finance and Admin.: MARIANO VARAS HERNÁNDEZ
Sec.-Gen.: ORLANDO ARAVENA AGUILERA

Library of 46,700 vols, 227 periodicals
Number of teachers: 183
Number of students: 5,628

DEANS

Faculty of Agrarian and Forestry Sciences: CLAUDIO RODRÍGUEZ FIGUEROA
Faculty of Education: MARCELO ROMERO MÉNDEZ
Faculty of Engineering: GUSTAVO LEDEZMA MATURANA
Faculty of Health Sciences: HÉCTOR FIGUEROA MARÍN
Faculty of Religion and Philosophy: JAMES MORIN ST ONGE

UNIVERSIDAD CATÓLICA DEL NORTE

Avda Angamos 0610, Casilla 1280, Antofagasta
Telephone: (55) 355002
Fax: (55) 355093
E-mail: mcamus@ucn.cl
Internet: www.ucn.cl
Founded 1956
Language of instruction: Spanish
Private control
Academic year: March to December

Chancellor: Most Rev. PABLO LIZAMA RIQUELME
Rector: MISAEL CAMUS IBACACHE
Vice-Rector for Academic Affairs: JOSE FERNANDO VIAL VALDES
Vice-Rector for Coquimbo Campus: JAIME MERUANE ZUMELZU
Vice-Rector for Economic Affairs: JORGE ALBERTO TABILO ALVAREZ
Gen. Sec.: VICTORIA GONZÁLEZ STUARDO
Head of Admissions Office: OLGA MARIA VALDES DE LA TORRE
Librarian: SERGIO ARCE MOLINA

Library of 113,222 vols
Number of teachers: 372
Number of students: 10,324

Publications: Boletín de Educación, Cuadernos de Arquitectura, Estudios Atacameños, Norte: Revista divulgacíon de ciencias, tecnologia y cultura (science, technology and culture), Revista de Derecho, Revista Proyecciones, Revista Reflejos, Revista Vertiente, Tercer Milenio

DEANS

Antofagasta Campus (tel. (55) 355000; fax (55) 355093):

Faculty of Economics and Management: ANGEL GÓMEZ MORALES
Faculty of Engineering and Construction Science: PABLO REYES FRANZANI
Faculty of Engineering and Geological Sciences: TEODORO POLITIS JARAMIS
Faculty of Humanities: JAIME BARRIENTOS DELGADO
Faculty of Sciences: MIGUEL MURPHY GONZÁLEZ

Coquimbo Campus (Larrondo 1281, Coquimbo; tel. (51) 209701; fax (51) 209707):

Faculty of Marine Sciences: ERNESTO CORTÉS PIZARRO
Faculty of Medicine: Dr NICOLAS VELASCO MORANDÉ

UNIVERSIDAD CATÓLICA DE TEMUCO

Manuel Montt 056, 15-D Temuco
Telephone: (45) 205205
Fax: (45) 234126
E-mail: dara@uct.cl
Internet: www.uct.cl
Founded 1991

Private control; financially supported by the State
Academic year: March to December

Rector: ALBERTO VÀSQUEZ TAPIA
Vice-Rector for Academic Affairs: JAIME MILLÁN HERRERA
Vice-Rector for Finance and Admin.: RICARDO MERY URRUTIA
Vice-Rector for International Affairs: EMILIO GUERRA BUGUEÑO

Library of 61,405 vols, 4,100 periodicals
Number of teachers: 213
Number of students: 4,854

DEANS

Faculty of Agricultural and Forestry Sciences: MARCO ANTONIO FERNÁNDEZ NAVARRETE
Faculty of Agriculture and Veterinary Sciences: ROLANDO VEGA AGUAYO
Faculty of Arts, Humanities and Social Sciences: MARIO SAMANIEGO SASTRE
Faculty of Education: RENÉ MORGAN MELGOSA
Facultiy of Engineering: LUIS DÍAZ ROBLES
Faculty of Science: OSVALDO RUBILAR ALARCÓN
Institute of Theological Studies: JUAN LEONELLI LEONELLI (Dir)
School of Law: RODRIGO COLOMA CORREA (Dir)

ATTACHED RESEARCH INSTITUTES

Centre of Sociocultural Studies: tel. (45) 205626; fax (45) 205626; e-mail tduran@uct.cl; Dir Dra TERESA DURÁN PÉREZ.

Centre of Sustainable Development: tel. (45) 205629; fax (45) 205626; e-mail cds@uct.cl; Dir Dr ANDRÉS YURJEVIC MARSCHAL.

Institute of Regional Studies: tel. (45) 205685; fax (45) 205626; e-mail artufilu@uct.cl; Dir ARTURO HERNANDEZ SALLÁS.

UNIVERSIDAD DE CONCEPCIÓN

Casilla 160-C, Correo 3, Concepción
Telephone: (41) 204000
Fax: (41) 227455
E-mail: foro@udec.cl
Internet: www.udec.cl
Founded 1919
Private control
Language of instruction: Spanish
Academic year: March to January

Rector: SERGIO LAVANCHY MERINO
Vice-Rector for Academic Affairs: ERNESTO FIGUEROA HUIDOBRO
Vice-Rector for Financial Affairs and Personnel: ALBERTO LARRAÍN PRAT
Gen. Sec.: RODOLFO WALTER DÍAZ
Library Dir: OLGA MORA MARDONES

Number of teachers: 1,410
Number of students: 16,800

Publications: Acta Literaria, Agro-Ciencia (2 a year), Atenea (science, art and literature, 12 a year), Gayana, Informativo de Rectoría—PANORAMA (public relations), Revista de Derecho (4 a year), RLA—Revista de Lingüística Aplicada

DEANS

Faculty of Agricultural Engineering: JOSÉ REYES AROCA
Faculty of Agriculture: ALFREDO VERA M.
Faculty of Architecture: RICARDO UTZ BARRIGA
Faculty of Biological Sciences: CARLOS GONZÁLEZ CORREA
Faculty of Chemical Sciences: BERNABÉ RIVAS QUIRÓZ
Faculty of Dentistry: FERNANDO ESCOBAR MUÑOZ
Faculty of Economic and Administrative Sciences: JUAN SAAVEDRA GONZÁLEZ

Faculty of Education: ABELARDO CASTRO HIDALGO
Faculty of Engineering: JOEL ZAMBRANO VALENCIA
Faculty of Forestry Sciences: FERNANDO DRAKE ARANDA
Faculty of Humanities and Art: EDUARDO NÚÑEZ CRISOSTO
Faculty of Law and Social Sciences: SERGIO CARRASCO DELGADO
Faculty of Medicine: OCTAVIO ENRÍQUEZ LORCA
Faculty of Natural Sciences and Oceanography: FRANKLIN CARRASCO VASQUEZ
Faculty of Pharmacy: CARLOS CALVO MONFIL
Faculty of Physical Sciences and Mathematics: JOSÉ SÁNCHEZ HENRÍQUEZ
Faculty of Social Sciences: EDUARDO AQUEVEDO SOTO
Faculty of Veterinary Medicine: RUBÉN PÉREZ FERNÁNDEZ

UNIVERSIDAD TÉCNICA 'FEDERICO SANTA MARÍA'

Avda España 1680, Casilla 110V, Valparaíso
Telephone: (32) 654246
Fax: (32) 654443
E-mail: consultas@utfsm.cl
Internet: www.utfsm.cl
Founded 1926
Private control
Language of instruction: Spanish
Academic year: March to January
Rector: ADOLFO ARATA ANDREANI
Vice-Rector for Academic Affairs: DANIEL ALKALAY LOWITT
Vice-Rector for Economic and Admin. Affairs: GIOVANNI PESCE SANTANA
Sec.-Gen.: FRANCISCO GHISOLFO ARAYA
Library Dir: MARÍA EUGENIA LAULIÉ
Library: see Libraries and Archives
Number of teachers: 456 (237 full-time, 219 part-time)
Number of students: 9,311
Publications: Gestión Tecnológica (2 a year), Revista Industrias (4 a year), Scientia (1 a year).

BRANCH CAMPUSES

Campus Rancagua: Gamero 212, Rancagua; Dir SERGIO ESTAY VILLALÓN.

Campus Santiago: Avda Santa María 6400, Vitacura, Santiago; Dir SERGIO OLAVARRÍA SIMONSEN.

Sede José Miguel Carrera: Avda Federico Santa María 6090, Viña del Mar; Dir ROSENDO ESTAY MARTÍNEZ.

Sede Rey Balduino de Bélgica: Avda Alemparte 943, Talcahuano; Dir ALEX ERIZ SOTO.

Private Universities

UNIVERSIDAD ADOLFO IBÁÑEZ

Balmaceda 1625, Recreo, Viña del Mar
Telephone: (32) 2503500
E-mail: paula.fernandez@uai.cl
Internet: www.uai.cl
Founded 1953
Private control
Language of instruction: Spanish
Academic year: March to December
Rector: ANDRÉS BENÍTEZ
Vice-Rector for Academic Affairs: RAFAEL MACHERONE
Vice-Rector for Economic and Admin. Affairs: CATALINA BOBENRIETH
Gen. Sec.: AGUSTÍN ANTOLA
Dean of Undergraduates: COLIN ROGERS
Librarian: MARÍA ZINA JIMÉNEZ

Number of teachers: 46 full-time
Number of students: 1,444
Publications: Cuadernos Jurídicos (3 a year), Informe Económico (4 a year), INTUS LEGERE: Anuario de Filosofía, Historia y Letras (1 a year)

DEANS

Faculty of Engineering and Science: ALEJANDRO JADRESIC
Faculty of Law: RODRIGO CORREA
Faculty of Liberal Arts: LUCÍA SANTA CRUZ
School of Government: LEONIDAS MONTES
School of Journalism: ASCANIO CAVALLO
School of Management: ALFONSO GÓMEZ
School of Psychology: JORGE SANHUEZA

UNIVERSIDAD CENTRAL

Toesca 1783, Santiago
Telephone: (2) 5826000
E-mail: guia@ucentral.cl
Internet: www.ucentral.cl
Founded 1982
Private control
Language of instruction: Spanish
Academic year: March to January
Rector: LUIS LUCERO ALDAY
Vice-Rector for Academic Affairs: LUIS MERINO MONTERO
Vice-Rector for Admin.: JUAN IGNACIO CARVALLO MARÍN
Vice-Rector for Communication: RAFAEL GARAY PITA
Vice-Rector for Finance: SERGIO ÁLVAREZ MONTOYA
Vice-Rector for Institutional Devt: SILVANA COMINETTI COTTI-COMETTI
Gen. Sec.: OMAR AHUMADA MORA
Librarian: NELLY CORNEJO MENESES
Number of teachers: 662
Number of students: 6,177
Publications: Boletín Informativo, Parthenon (2 a year), Perspectiva, Revista de Arquitectura, Revista de Derecho, Revista de Psicología, Universidad y Sociedad

DEANS

Faculty of Architecture and Town and Country Planning: ELIANA ISRAEL JACARD
Faculty of Communications: BERNARDO DE LA MAZA BAÑADOS
Faculty of Economics and Administration: HUMBERTO VEGA FERNÁNDEZ
Faculty of Education: SELMA SIMONSTEIN FUENTES
Faculty of Law and Social Sciences: ÁNGELA CATTAN ATALA
Faculty of Physical Sciences and Mathematics: SERGIO QUEZADA GONZÁLEZ
Faculty of Politics and Public Administration: ALDO CASSINELLI CAPURRO
Faculty of Social Sciences: LUIS GAJARDO IBÁÑEZ

ATTACHED RESEARCH CENTRES

Centre of Economic and Administrative Research: San Ignacio 414, Santiago; tel. (2) 6954010; fax (2) 6727377; Dir CARLOS RETAMAL UMPIERREZ.

Centre of Housing Research: José Joaquin Prieto 10001, Casilla 6D, San Bernardo; tel. (2) 5585311; fax (2) 5270323; Dir ALFONSO RAPOSO MOYANO.

Centre of Juridical Research: Lord Cochrane 417, Santiago; tel. (2) 6957533; fax (2) 6727377; Dir RUBEN CELIS RODRIGUEZ.

UNIVERSIDAD DIEGO PORTALES

Avda Manuel Rodríguez Sur 415, Santiago 8370179
Telephone: (2) 6762000
Fax: (2) 6762112

E-mail: admsion@udp.cl
Internet: www.udp.cl
Founded 1982
Rector: MANUEL MONTT
Provost: FRANCISCO JAVIER CUADRA
Vice-Rector for Academic Affairs and Research: CARLOS PEÑA
Vice-Rector for Admin., Finance and Devt: HORACIO RÍOS
Dir of Communications and Admission: BÁRBARA FASANI
Librarian: PAULINA GODOY
Number of teachers: 1,208
Number of students: 10,930
Publications: El Portaliano, Noticias Académicas

DEANS

Faculty of Architecture, Design and Art: MATHÍAS KLOTZ
Faculty of Business: MIGUEL LÉON
Faculty of Communication: ANDRÉS VELASCO
Faculty of Engineering: MIGUEL LÉON
Faculty of Health Sciences: FERNANDO MÖNCKEBERG
Faculty of Humanities: CARMEN FARIÑA
Faculty of Human Sciences and Education: JUAN PABLO TORO
Faculty of Industrial Engineering and Data Processing: LUIS COURT
Faculty of Law: ANDRÉS CUNEO

UNIVERSIDAD GABRIELA MISTRAL

Avda Ricardo Lyon 1177, Providencia, Santiago
Telephone: (2) 4144545
Internet: www.ugm.cl
Founded 1981
Academic year: March to January
Rector: ALICIA ROMO ROMÁN
Vice-Rector for Academic Affairs: RICARDO RIESCO JARAMILLO
Vice-Rector for Admin. and Finance: ESTANISLAO GALOFRÉ TERRASA
Librarian: CARMEN BUSQUETS
Number of teachers: 450
Number of students: 3,500

UNIVERSIDAD PEREZ ROSALES

Brown Norte 290, Ñuñoa, Santiago Metropolitana
Telephone: (2) 7571300
Fax: (2) 2238825
E-mail: unitec@uvipro.cl
Internet: www.upper.cl
Founded 1992
Private control
Rector: KARIN RIEDEMANN H.
Sec.-Gen.: ELISA CASTRO P.
Vice-Rector for Academic Affairs: CECILIA IBARRA M.
Vice-Rector for Teaching and Research: MÓNICA HERRERA P.
Dir of Extension Studies and Humanities: PÍA MONTALVA D.
Head Librarian: CLAUDIA GILARDONI.

UNIVERSIDAD SAN SEBASTIÁN

Campus Las Tres Pascualas, General Cruz 1577, Concepción
Telephone: (41) 2400000
E-mail: concepcion@uss.cl
Internet: www.uss.cl
Founded 1989
Private control
Academic year: March to December
Rector: GUIDO ALFREDO MELLER MAYR
Vice-Rector for Academic Affairs: JAIME TORREALBA CUBILLOS

Vice-Rector for Communications: ADOLFO UGARTE ALONSO
Vice-Rector for Devt: LUIS CORDERO BARRERA
Vice-Rector for Economic and Admin. Affairs: LUIS ERNESTO VIDELA BERGUECIO
Vice-Rector for Quality Assurance: KIYOSHI FUKUSHI MANDIOLA
Gen. Sec.: SANDRA GUZMÁN MARTÍNEZ
Librarian: MARGARITA VALDERRAMA CÁCERES

Library of 6,000 vols
Number of teachers: 174
Number of students: 1,714

DEANS

Faculty of Architecture, Art and Design: CRISTIÁN BOZA DÍAZ
Faculty of Dentistry: SERGIO CASTRO ALFARO
Faculty of Economics and Business: ERIK HAINDL
Faculty of Education: JORGE JIMÉNEZ ESPINOZA
Faculty of Engineering and Technology: JUAN BENNETT URRUTIA

Faculty of Health: FERNANDO QUIROGA DUBORNAIS
Faculty of Law: ARMANDO CARTES MONTORY
Faculty of Medicine and Nursing: Dr JAIME SEPÚLVEDA C.
Faculty of Social Services: CARMEN BONNEFOY DIBARRART
Faculty of Veterinary Medicine: NORBERTO BUTENDIECK BURATTINI

Colleges

Escuela Militar del Libertador Bernardo O'Higgins: Los Militares 4500, Las Condes, Santiago; tel. (2) 6615012; fax (2) 6615397; internet www.escuelamilitar.cl; f. 1817 (by General O'Higgins); 90 military instructors and officials, 80 civilian instructors; 700 students; library: 25,000 vols; Dir Col HUMBERTO OVIEDO ARRIAGADA; Librarians OSCAR CORNEJO C., JUAN CARLOS MEDINA V.;

publs *Armas y Servicio, Memorial del Ejército, Revista 'Cien Aguilas'* (1 a year).

Facultad Latinoamericana de Ciencias Sociales (FLACSO): Avda Dag Hammarskjold 3269, Vitacura, Santiago; tel. (2) 2900200; fax (2) 2900263; e-mail flacso@flacso.cl; internet www.flacso.cl; f. 1957; postgraduate training and research centre for Latin America; library: 30,000 vols, 710 periodicals; 16 teachers; 60 students; Dir CLAUDIO FUENTES SAAVEDRA; Librarian MARÍA INÉS BRAVO; publ. *Fuerzas Armadas y Sociedad* (3 a year).

Instituto Agrícola Metodista 'El Vergel' (Methodist Agricultural Institute): Casilla 2-D, Angol; tel. (45) 712103; fax (45) 711202; f. 1919; ornamental plant nursery, fruit nursery, fruit garden, dairy, cattle ranch, apiculture, tourism, workshops, packing; museum; Administrator Rev. MARIO MAYER.

PEOPLE'S REPUBLIC OF CHINA

The Higher Education System

Some of the oldest institutions of higher education in the world are to be found in the People's Republic of China (for example, Hunan University dates back to the establishment of Yuelu Academy in 976). Higher education is dominated by state institutions, although some private universities have been established in recent years, and administration reflects the centralized nature of the State. During the 1950s a number of higher education establishments were designated 'key' institutions and received better staff, facilities and funding. The term 'key institution' is now officially defunct but is still used to denote the highest-rated institutions. The Cultural Revolution (1966–76) led to radical changes in the higher education system, as entrance examinations and continuous assessment were abolished; however, many of the changes were later reversed (the National University Entrance Examination was re-introduced in 1977). Following university unrest in 1989, including the Tianenman Square protests in Beijing, students were required to undergo a year of political 'training' prior to university entrance. Further reforms were launched in 1992, under which institutions were given greater autonomy in decision-making. There was also a trend towards mergers that led to a decrease in the number of higher education institutions, from 1,984 in 1998 to 1,731 in 2004, but this had increased to 1,908 by 2007. In 2008 a total of 20.2m. students were enrolled in higher education. A new higher education reform programme was launched in early 2000, with the aim of modernizing courses and teaching materials and improving pedagogy.

Performance in the National University Entrance Examination represents the main criteria for admission to higher education. Additionally, students may be required to undergo political education and perform some form of industrial or agricultural labour. The examination is conducted on a national basis and students are tested on five core subjects. A score in the range of 550–600 will gain admission to university. The university degree system consists of Xueshi (Bachelors), Shoshi (Masters) and Boshi (Doctorate). Bachelors degree courses last four years and conform to one of the 249 programmes defined by the Ministry of Education. In 1989 it was announced that selection of postgraduate students would also be on the basis of 'moral' and physical fitness. A Masters degree requires two to three years of further study after the Bachelors, including research and submission of a thesis. The Doctorate is awarded after three years of study following the Masters and concludes with submission and defence of a thesis.

Diplomas from technical and vocational education at tertiary level are available from a number of different types of institution, and usually require two to three years of study. Institutions offering technical and vocational education include vocational technology colleges, vocational universities, radio and television universities (Dianda) and spare-time universities (Yeda). Vocational education is supervised by the Department of Education and Labour.

Regulatory and Representative Bodies

GOVERNMENT

Ministry of Culture: 10 Chaoyangmen Bei Jie, Dongcheng Qu, Beijing 100020; tel. (10) 65551432; fax (10) 65551433; e-mail webmaster@whb1.ccnt.com.cn; internet www .ccnt.com.cn; Min. CAI WU.

Ministry of Education: 37 Damucang Hutong, Xidan, Beijing 100816; tel. (10) 66096114; fax (10) 66011049; e-mail webmaster@moe.edu.cn; internet www.moe .edu.cn; Min. YUAN GUIREN.

FUNDING

China Scholarship Council: Level 13, Building A3 No. 9, Chegongzhuang Ave, Beijing 100044; tel. (10) 66093900; fax (10) 88393620; e-mail webmaster@csc.edu.cn; internet www.csc.edu.cn; f. 1994; attached to Ministry of Education; provides financial assistance to Chinese citizens wishing to study abroad and to foreign citizens wishing to study in China; Chair. ZHANG XINSHENG; Sec.-Gen. ZHANG XIUQIN.

NATIONAL BODY

China Education Association for International Exchange: 37 Damucang Hutong, Xicheng Dist., Beijing 100816; 160 Fuxingmen Nei Dajie, Beijing 100031; tel. (10) 66416080; fax (10) 66411885; e-mail info@ ceaie.edu.cn; internet chn.ceaie.edu.cn; f. 1981; not-for-profit org. conducting int. educational exchanges; 159 mem. instns; Pres. ZHANG XINSHENG; Sec.-Gen. Prof. JIANG BO.

Learned Societies

GENERAL

Chinese Academy of Sciences: 52 San Li He Rd, Beijing 100864; tel. (10) 68597289; fax (10) 68512458; internet www.cas.ac.cn; f. 1949; academic divs of chemistry, earth sciences, information technical sciences, life sciences and medicine, mathematics and physics, technological sciences; 633 mems, 13 foreign mems; attached research institutes: see Research Institutes; library: see under Libraries and Archives; Pres. Prof. BAI CHUNLI; Vice-Pres ZHAN WENLONG, DING ZHONGLI, YIN HEJUN; Sec.-Gen. Prof. ZHU XUAN.

Chinese Academy of Social Sciences: 5 Jianguomen Nei Da Jie, Beijing 100732; tel. (10) 65137744; fax (10) 65138154; internet www.cass.net.cn; f. 1977; attached research institutes: see Research Institutes; Pres. WANG WEIGUANG; Sec.-Gen. ZHU JINCHANG.

UNESCO Office Beijing: Waijiaogongyu 5-13-3, Jianguomenwai Compound, Beijing 100600; tel. (10) 65322828; fax (10) 65324854; e-mail beijing@unesco.org; internet www.unescobeijing.org; designated Cluster Office for People's Republic of China, Democratic People's Republic of Korea, Japan, Mongolia and Republic of Korea; Dir YASUYUKI AOSHIMA.

AGRICULTURE, FISHERIES AND VETERINARY SCIENCE

China Society of Fisheries: 31 Minfeng Lane, Beijing 100032; tel. (10) 66020794; fax (10) 66062346; 15,000 mems; library of 12,000 vols; Pres. ZHANG YANXI; publs *Deepsea Fisheries*, *Freshwater Fisheries*, *Journal of Fisheries of China*, *Marine Fisheries*, *Scientific Fish Farming*.

Chinese Academy of Agricultural Sciences: 30 Bai Shi Qiao Rd, Beijing 100081; tel. (10) 62174433; fax (10) 62174142; f. 1957; 40 attached research institutes; library of 650,000 vols, 7,000 periodicals; Pres. LU FEIJIE; publs *Acta Agronomica Sinica*, *Acta Horticulturae Sinica*, *Acta Phyliphulacica Sinica*.

Chinese Academy of Forestry: Wan Shou Shan, Beijing 100091; tel. (10) 62582211; fax (10) 62584229; f. 1958; 4,700 mems; attached research institutes: see Research Institutes; library of 400,000 vols; Pres. JIANG ZEHUI; publs *Chemistry and Industry of Forest Products*, *China Forestry Abstracts*, *Foreign Forest Product Industry Abstracts*, *Foreign Forestry Abstracts*, *Forestry Research*, *Forestry Science and Technology*, *Scientia Silvae Sinicae*, *Wood Industry*, *World Forestry Research*.

Chinese Agricultural Economics Society: Agro-Exhibition, Beijing; Pres. CAI ZIWEI.

Chinese Association of Agricultural Science Societies: Min. of Agriculture, 11 Nongzhanguan Nanli, Beijing 100026; f. 1917; Pres. HONG FUZENG; Sec.-Gen. LI HUAIZHI.

Chinese Sericulture Society: Sibaidu, Zhenjiang, 212018 Jiangsu Province; tel. (511) 5616661; fax (511) 5622507; f. 1963; 10,000 mems; library of 50,000 vols; Pres. XIANG ZHONGHUAI; Sec.-Gen. ZHUANG DAHUAN; publ. *Sericultural Science* (4 a year).

Chinese Society for Horticultural Science: 12 Zhongguancun Nandajie, Beijing 100081; tel. (10) 68919528; fax (10) 62174123; e-mail ivfcaas@public3.bta.net.cn; f. 1930; 3,000 mems; Pres. ZHU DEWEI; publ. *Acta Horticulturae Sinica* (6 a year).

Chinese Society of Agricultural Machinery: 1 Beishatan, Deshengmen Wai, Beijing 100083; tel. (10) 64882231; fax (10) 64883508; e-mail bhmetecj@public3.bta.net.cn; f. 1963; 26,245 mems; library of 1,500,000 vols; Pres. Li Shouren; Sec.-Gen. Gao Yuanen; publs *China Agricultural Mechanization* (6 a year), *Farm Machinery* (12 a year), *Rural Mechanization* (6 a year), *Tractor and Automobile Drivers* (6 a year), *Transactions of the Chinese Society of Agricultural Machinery* (4 a year).

Chinese Society of Forestry: Wanshoushan, Beijing 100091; tel. (10) 62889817; fax (10) 62888312; e-mail csf@csf.forestry.ac.cn; f. 1917; 75,000 mems; Pres. Liu Yuhe; publ. *Scientia Silvae Sinicae* (6 a year).

Chinese Society of Tropical Crops: Baodao Xincun, Danzhou, Hainan Province; tel. and fax (898) 23300157; e-mail scutafao@yahoo.com; f. 1978; 4,474 mems; library of 250,000 vols; Jt Chairs Zeng Yuzhuang, Yu Rangshui; Sec.-Gen. Zheng Wenrong; publ. *Chinese Journal of Tropical Crops* (4 a year).

Crop Science Society of China: Institute of Crop Breeding and Cultivation, 30 Bai Shi Qiao Rd, Beijing 100081; tel. (10) 68918616; fax (10) 68975212; f. 1961; 22,000 mems; Pres. Wang Lianzheng; Sec.-Gen. Chen Xinhua; publs *Acta Agronomica Sinica* (6 a year), *Crops* (6 a year).

Soil Science Society of China: POB 821, Nanjing 210008; tel. (25) 86881532; fax (25) 86881538; e-mail sssc@issas.ac.cn; f. 1945; academic exchange; pub.; scientific popularization; education and training; consultation for decision-making; technical service; int. cooperation; talents recommendation, reward and recognition; 17,600 mems; Pres. Prof. Zhou Jianmin; Vice-Sec.-Gen. Weidong Yan; publs *Acta Pedologica Sinica* (6 a year), *Journal of Soil and Water Conservation*, *Journal of Soil Science* (6 a year), *Pedosphere* (6 a year).

ARCHITECTURE AND TOWN PLANNING

Architectural Society of China: 9 Sanlihe Rd, Beijing 100835; tel. (10) 88082238; fax (10) 88082222; e-mail asc@mail.cin.gov.cn; f. 1953; 30,000 mems; library of 25,000 vols; Pres. Song Chunhua; publs *Architectural Journal* (12 a year), *Architectural Knowledge* (12 a year), *Journal of Building Structure* (6 a year).

Chinese Society for Urban Studies: Bai Wanzhuang, Beijing 100835; tel. (10) 68393424; fax (10) 68313149; e-mail zhaibh@mail.cin.gov.cn; internet www.urbanstudies.org.cn; f. 1984; part of Min. of Housing and Urban-Rural Construction; 30,000 mems; Pres. Zhou Ganshi; Sec.-Gen. Gu Wenxuan; publ. *Urban Studies* (a year).

BIBLIOGRAPHY, LIBRARY SCIENCE AND MUSEOLOGY

Chinese Archives Society: 21 Fengshen Hutong, Beijing; tel. (10) 66175130; fax (10) 66183636; f. 1981; 74 institutional mems, 7,252 individual mems; Chair. Shen Zhengle; publ. *Archive Science Study* (4 a year).

Chinese Association of Natural Science Museums: 126 Tian Qiao South St, Beijing 100050; tel. (10) 67024431; fax (10) 67021254; f. 1979; 1,200 individual mems; 320 group mems; Sec.-Gen. Xie Yenghuan; publ. *China Nature* (6 a year, jtly with Beijing Natural History Museum and China Wildlife Conservation Association).

Chinese Society of Library Science: 39 Bai Shi Qiao Rd, Beijing 100081; tel. (10) 68415566 ext. 5563; fax (10) 68419271; f. 1979; 10,150 mems; Pres. Liu Deyou; publ.

Journal of Library Science in China (in Chinese, every 2 months).

ECONOMICS, LAW AND POLITICS

China Law Society: 6 Xizhi Men Nan Da Jie, Beijing 100035; tel. (10) 66150114; fax (10) 66182128; f. 1982; ind. academic instn for study of the Chinese socialist legal system; 523 corporate mems; 100,000 individual mems; library of 40,000 vols, incl. China Catalogue of Law Books; Pres. Ren Jianxin; Sec.-Gen. Song Shutao; publs *China Law Yearbook*, *Democracy and Law Journal*, *Law of China*.

Chinese Association for European Studies: 5 Jiannei, Beijing 100732; tel. (10) 65138428; f. 1981; 1,000 mems; Chair. Prof. Qiu Yuanlun; publ. *European Studies* (every 2 months, co-edited with Inst. of West European Studies).

Chinese Association of Political Science: c/o Chinese Academy of Social Sciences, 5 Jianguomennei Ave, Beijing; tel. (10) 65125048; f. 1980; asscn of workers in the field of political science; 1,025 mems; Pres. Jiang Liu; Sec.-Gen. Zhang Zhirong; publs *Political Science Abroad* (6 a year), *Studies in Political Science* (6 a year).

Chinese Legal History Society: Law Dept, Beijing University, Haidian District, Beijing 100871; tel. (10) 62561166; f. 1979; studies history of Chinese and foreign legal systems; 300 mems; Pres. Prof. Zhang Guohua; Chief Sec. Rao Xinxian; publs *Communications of Legal History*, *Review of Legal History*.

Chinese Research Society for the Modernization of Management: c/o China Association for Science and Technology, Sanlihe, Xijiao, Beijing; tel. (10) 68318877 ext. 524; f. 1978; Pres. Xie Shaoming; publ. *Modernization of Management*.

Chinese Society of the History of International Relations: 12 Poshangcun, Haidian District, Beijing; Pres. Wang Shengzu.

EDUCATION

Chinese Education Society: 35 Damucang Lane, Beijing 100816; Pres. Zhang Chengxian.

HISTORY, GEOGRAPHY AND ARCHAEOLOGY

Chinese Historical Society: 5 Jianguomennei St, Beijing 100732.

Chinese Society for Future Studies: 32 Baishiqiao Rd, Haidian District, Beijing 100081; f. 1979; 1,000 mems; CEO Du Dagong; publ. *Future and Development* (4 a year).

Chinese Society of Geodesy, Photogrammetry and Cartography: Baiwanzhuang, Beijing; tel. (10) 68992229; f. 1959; 3,000 mems; Pres. Prof. Wang Zhizhuo; Sec.-Gen. Prof. Yang Kai; publ. *Acta Geodetica et Cartographica Sinica*.

Chinese Society of Oceanography: 10 Fuxingmenwai, Beijing; Pres. Peng Deqing.

Geographical Society of China: No. A11, Datun Rd, Beijing 100101; tel. (10) 64870663; fax (10) 64889598; e-mail gsc@igsnrr.ac.cn; internet www.gsc.org.cn; f. 1909; 31 provincial divs; special comms: cartography, climatology, economic geography, environmental geography and chemical geography, geographical information systems, geomorphology and quaternary studies, historical geography, human geography, hydrography, marine geography, medical geography, physical geography, quantative geography, sustained agriculture and rural development, tourist geography, urban geography, world geography; working comms: academic

affairs, edition and publication, geographical education, international scientific and technical cooperation (China National Committee for International Geographical Union—IGU), popularization of geographical knowledge, young geographers; br. socs: coastal open region, Changjiang river research, desert research, environmental remote sensing, glaciology and geocryology, mountain research; geographical construction in the arid and semi-arid region; 18,900 mems; Pres. Lu Dadao; Sec.-Gen. Zhang Guoyou; publs *Acta Geographica Sinica* (6 a year), *China National Geography* (12 a year), *Economic Geography* (6 a year), *Historical Geography* (4 a year), *Human Geography* (6 a year), *Journal of Geographical Sciences* (English edition, 4 a year), *Journal of Glaciology and Geocryology* (6 a year), *Journal of Mountain Science* (6 a year), *Journal of Remote Sensing* (6 a year), *World Regional Studies* (4 a year).

LANGUAGE AND LITERATURE

Alliance Française: 18 Gongtixilu, Guangcai Guojigongyu, Chaoyang District, Beijing 100020; tel. (10) 65532678; fax (10) 65532718; e-mail info.beijing@afchine.org; internet www.alliancefrancaise.org.cn; offers courses and exams in French language and culture and promotes cultural exchange with France; attached teaching centres in Chengdu, Guangzhou, Nanjing, Shanghai and Wuhan.

British Council: Cultural and Education Section, British Embassy, 4th Fl., Landmark Bldg Tower 1, 8 North Dongsanhuan Rd, Chaoyang District, Beijing 100004; tel. (10) 6590-6903; fax (10) 6590-0977; e-mail enquiry@britishcouncil.org.cn; internet www.britishcouncil.org/china; offers courses and exams in English language and British culture and promotes cultural exchange with the UK; attached offices in Shanghai, Guangzou and Chongqing; Dir and Cultural Counsellor Michael O'Sullivan.

Chinese Writers' Association: 2 Shatanbeijie, Beijing 100720; 20,000 mems; Chair. Ba Jin; publs include *People's Literature* (12 a year), *Chinese Writers* (6 a year), *Literature and Arts* (52 a year, newspaper), *Minority Literature* (12 a year), *Poetry* (12 a year).

Goethe-Institut: Cyber Tower, Bldg B, 17th Fl., No. 2, Zhong Guan Cun South Ave, Haidian District, Beijing 100086; tel. (10) 82512909; fax (10) 82512903; e-mail info@peking.goethe.org; internet www.goethe.de/os/pek/deindex.htm; offers courses and exams in German language and culture and promotes cultural exchange with Germany; attached centres in Shanghai; library of 10,000 vols; Dir Dr Ulrich Nowak.

MEDICINE

China Academy of Traditional Chinese Medicine: 18 Beixincang, Dongzhimennei, Beijing 100700; tel. (10) 64014411 ext. 2435; fax (10) 64016387; f. 1955; 12 attached research institutes; library of 300,000 vols; Pres. Fu Shiyuan; publs *Chinese Acupuncture and Moxibustion*, *Chinese Journal of Integrated Traditional and Western Medicine*, *Journal of Traditional Chinese Medicine*.

China Association of Traditional Chinese Medicine: A4 Yinghualu, Hepingli Dongjie, Beijing 100029; tel. (10) 64212828; fax (10) 64220867; f. 1979; 80,000 mems; Chair. Cui Yuli; Gen. Sec. (vacant); publ. *China Journal of Traditional Chinese Medicine* (6 a year).

China Association of Zhenjiu (Acupuncture and Moxibustion): 18 Beixincang Dongcheng Qu, Beijing 100700; tel. (10)

64030611; f. 1979; 13,000 mems; Pres. Hu XIMING; Sec.-Gen. LI WEIHENG; publ. *Chinese Acupuncture and Moxibustion.*

Chinese Academy of Medical Sciences and Peking Union Medical College: 9 Dongdan Santiao, Beijing 100730; tel. 553447; fax 5124876; f. 1917 (College), 1956 (Academy); the two instns have a single governing body; attached research institutes: see Research Institutes; Pres. Dr BA DENIAN; publ. *Chinese Medical Sciences Journal.*

Chinese Anti-Cancer Association: 52 Fucheng, Haidian District, Beijing 100036; tel. (10) 88148749; fax (10) 88148749; e-mail yuhui@caca.org.cn; internet www.caca.org .cn; f. 1985; 40,000 mems; Pres. Dr XU GUANGWEI; publs *Cancer Rehabilitation* (6 a year), *Chinese Journal of Cancer Biotherapy* (4 a year), *Chinese Journal of Cancer Research* (4 a year), *Chinese Journal of Clinical Oncology* (12 a year), *Journal of Practical Oncology* (6 a year), *Research on Prevention and Treatment of Cancer* (6 a year).

Chinese Anti-Tuberculosis Society: 42 Dung-si-xi-da St, Beijing; tel. 553685; Pres. HUANG DINGCHEN; publ. *Bulletin* (4 a year).

Chinese Association for Mental Health: 5 An Kang Hutong, De Wai, Beijing 100088; tel. (10) 82085385; fax (10) 62359838; e-mail camh@camh.org.cn; internet www.camh.org .cn; f. 1985; 30,000 mems; Pres. CAI ZHUOJI; Sec.-Gen. LI ZHANJIANG; publs *Chinese Journal of Clinical Psychology* (4 a year), *Chinese Journal of Health Psychology* (6 a year), *Chinese Mental Health Journal* (12 a year).

Chinese Association of Integrated Traditional and Western Medicine: 18 Beixincang, Dongzhimennei, Beijing; tel. (10) 64010688; fax (10) 64010688; f. 1981; 20,000 mems; Pres. CHEN KEJI; Sec.-Gen. CHEN SHIGUI; publ. *Chinese Journal of Integrated Traditional and Western Medicine* (12 a year in Chinese, 4 a year in English).

Chinese Medical Association: 42 Dongsi Xidajie, Beijing; tel. 551943; tel. (10) 65265331; fax (10) 65265331; f. 1915; library of 80,000 vols; Pres. BAI XIQING; publs *Chinese Journal of Internal Medicine* (12 a year), *Chinese Journal of Surgery* (12 a year), *Chinese Medical Journal* (English edition, 12 a year), *National Medical Journal of China* (12 a year).

Chinese Nursing Association: 42 Dongsi Xidajie, Beijing 100710; tel. (10) 65265331; fax (10) 65265331; f. 1909; Pres. ZENG XIYUAN; publ. *Chinese Journal of Nursing* (12 a year).

Chinese Nutrition Society: Guang'an Men, Xuanwu District, Beijing 100053; tel. (10) 83554781; fax (10) 83554780; e-mail mm@cnsoc.org; internet www.cnsoc.org; f. 1981; 7,026 mems; Pres. GE KEYOU; publ. *Acta Nutrimenta* (Chinese and English, 4 a year).

Chinese Pharmaceutical Association: A38 Lishi Rd N., Beijing 100810; tel. (10) 68316576; f. 1907; Pres. QI MAIJIA.

Chinese Pharmacological Society: 1 Xian Nong Tan St, Beijing 100050; tel. (10) 63013366 ext. 404; fax (10) 63017757; f. 1979; Pres. Prof. ZHANG JUNTIAN; Sec.-Gen. Prof. LIN ZHIBIN; publs *Acta Pharmacologica Sinica, Chinese Journal of Pharmacology and Toxicology, Chinese Pharmacological Bulletin, Pharmacology and Clinics of Chinese Materia Medica.*

NATURAL SCIENCES
General

China Association for Science and Technology (CAST): 3 Fuxing, Beijing 100863;

tel. (10) 68571898; fax (10) 68571897; e-mail cast@public.bta.net.cn; internet www.cast .org.cn; f. 1958; almost all societies in China are affiliated members; organizes academic exchanges, int. conferences and in-service training for scientists, engineers and technicians; library of 50,000 vols; Pres. ZHOU GUANGZHAO.

Chinese Society for Oceanology and Limnology: 7 Nanhai Rd, Qingdao 266071; tel. (532) 2879062 ext. 3402; fax (532) 2870882; f. 1950; 7,000 mems; Pres. QIN YUNSHAN; Sec.-Gen. ZHOU MINGJIANG; publs *Chinese Journal of Oceanology and Limnology* (4 a year, in English), *Oceanologia et Limnologia Sinica* (6 a year, in Chinese).

Chinese Society of the History of Science and Technology: 137 Chao Nei St, Beijing 100010; tel. (10) 64043989; fax (10) 64017637; f. 1980; 1,500 mems; Pres X. ZEZONG, LU YONGXIANG; publs *China Historical Materials of Science and Technology* (4 a year), *Studies in the History of Natural Sciences* (4 a year).

National Natural Science Foundation of China (NSFC): Beijing; tel. (10) 62327001; e-mail bic@nsfc.gov.cn; internet www.nsfc .gov.cn; depts of chemical sciences, earth sciences, eng. and materials science, information sciences, life sciences, management sciences, mathematical and physical sciences; does not have any research entities; directs, coordinates and financially supports basic research and applied basic research, identifies and fosters scientific talents, promotes science and technology; receives research proposals from univs and other institutions, prepares peer reviews and sessions of evaluation panels; provides advisory services on major issues related to the nat. strategic devt of basic and applied basic research in China; supports activities of nat. professional science foundations; develops cooperative relations with scientific orgs in other countries; Pres. CHEN YIYU; Vice-Pres WANG JIE, SHEN WENQING, SUN JIAGUANG, SHEN YAN, YAO JIANNIAN; publ. *Guide to Programs* (1 a year).

Biological Sciences

Biophysical Society of China: 15 Datun Rd, Chaoyang District, Beijing 100101; tel. (10) 64889869; fax (10) 64871293; e-mail bscott@sun5.ibp.ac.cn; internet bsc.org.cn; f. 1980; 2,300 mems; Pres. ZHAO NANMING; Sec.-Gen. Prof. SHEN XUN; publs *Acta Biophysica Sinica* (4 a year), *Progress in Biochemistry and Biophysics* (6 a year).

Botanical Society of China: 20 Naxincun, Xiangshan, Beijing 100093; tel. and fax (10) 62591431; e-mail bsco@public.bta.net.cn; 15,000 mems; Pres. KUANG TINGYUN; publs *Acta Botanica Sinica* (12 a year), *Acta Phytoecologica et Geobotanica Sinica* (4 a year), *Acta Phytotaxomica* (6 a year), *Bulletin of Biology* (12 a year), *Chinese Bulletin of Botany* (4 a year), *Plants* (6 a year).

China Zoological Society: 19 Zhong Guan Cun Lu, Beijing; tel. (10) 62552368; fax (10) 62552368; e-mail czs@panda.ioz.ac.cn; f. 1934; 11,600 mems; Pres. CHEN DAYUAN; publs *Acta Arachnologica Sinica* (2 a year), *Acta Parasitologica et Medica Entomologica Sinica* (4 a year), *Acta Theriologica Sinica* (4 a year), *Acta Zoologica Sinica* (6 a year), *Acta Zootaxonomica Sinica* (4 a year), *Chinese Journal of Zoology* (6 a year).

Chinese Association for Physiological Sciences: 42 Dongsixidajie, Beijing 100710; Pres. CHEN MENGQIN.

Chinese Association of Animal Science and Veterinary Medicine: 33 Nongfengli, Dongdaqiao, Chao Yang District, Beijing 100020; tel. (10) 65005934; fax (10)

65005670; e-mail caavxshb@public.bta.net .cn; f. 1936; 50,000 mems; Pres. WU CHANG-XIN; Sec.-Gen. YAN HANPING; publs *Chinese Journal of Animal and Veterinary Sciences, Chinese Journal of Animal Science, Chinese Journal of Veterinary Medicine.*

Chinese Society for Anatomical Sciences: 42 Dongsi Xidajie, Beijing 100710; tel. (10) 65133311 ext. 247; fax (10) 65123754; f. 1920; 3,000 mems; Pres. XU QUNYUAN; Sec.-Gen. LIU BIN; publs *Acta Anatomica Sinica* (4 a year), *Chinese Journal of Anatomy* (4 a year), *Chinese Journal of Clinical Anatomy* (4 a year), *Chinese Journal of Histochemistry and Cytochemistry* (4 a year), *Journal of Neuroanatomy* (4 a year), *Progress of Anatomical Sciences* (4 a year).

Chinese Society for Microbiology: Zhongguancun, Beijing 100080; tel. (10) 62554677; fax (10) 62554677; e-mail chenggs@sun.im.ac.cn; f. 1952; Pres. WEN YUNMEI; publs *Acta Microbiologica Sinica, Acta Mycologica Sinica, Chinese Journal of Biotechnology, Chinese Journal of Virology, Chinese Journal of Zoonoses, Microbiology.*

Chinese Society of Biochemistry and Molecular Biology: 15 Datun Rd, Chao Yang District, Beijing 100101; tel. (10) 64889859; fax (10) 64872026; e-mail csbmb@ sun5.ibp.ac.cn; internet csbmb.ibp.ac.cn; f. 1979; 1,000 mems; Pres. C. L. TSOU; Sec.-Gen. J. M. ZHOU; publs *Chemistry of Life* (6 a year), *Chinese Journal of Biochemistry and Molecular Biology* (6 a year).

Chinese Society of Environmental Sciences: 115 Xizhimennei Nanxiaojie, Beijing; tel. (10) 661006; f. 1979; 20 industrial/corporate mems; 22,000 individual mems; Pres. LI JINGZHAO; Sec.-Gen. QU GEPING; publs *China Environmental Management, China Environmental Science, Environment, Environmental Chemistry, Environmental Engineering.*

Chinese Society of Plant Physiology: 300 Fongling Rd, Shanghai; tel. (21) 64042090; fax 64042385; f. 1963; 4,000 mems; Chair. Prof. TANG ZHANGCHENG; publs *Acta Phytophysiologica Sinica* (4 a year), *Plant Physiology Communications* (6 a year).

Ecological Society of China: 19 Zhongguancun Lu, Beijing 100080; tel. (10) 62565694; fax (10) 62562775; f. 1979; 5,500 mems; Pres. Prof. WANG ZUWANG; Sec.-Gen. Prof. WANG RUSONG; publs *Acta Ecologica Sinica* (6 a year), *Journal of Applied Ecology* (4 a year), *Journal of Ecology* (6 a year).

Entomological Society of China: 19 Zhongguancun Lu, Haidian, Beijing 100080; tel. (10) 62565687; fax (10) 62630062; e-mail wangmm@panda.ioz.ac.cn; f. 1944; 11,000 mems; Pres. ZHANG GUANGXUE; Gen. Sec. LI DIANMO; publs *Acta Entomologica Sinica* (in Chinese), *Acta Parasitologica et Medica* (in Chinese), *Acta Zootaxonomia Sinica* (in Chinese), *Entomological Knowledge* (in Chinese), *Entomologia Sinica* (in Chinese).

Genetics Society of China: Bldg 917, Datun Rd, Andingmenwai, Beijing 100101; tel. (10) 64919944; fax (10) 64914896; f. 1978; 400 nat. mems, 6,600 mems of local socs; Pres. LI ZHENSHENG; Sec.-Gen. CHEN SHOUYI; publs *Acta Genetica Sinica, Hereditas* (6 a year).

Palaeontological Society of China: 39 E. Beijing Rd, Nanjing 210008; tel. (25) 3612664; fax (25) 3357026; f. 1929; 1,230 mems; Pres. MU XINAN; Sec.-Gen. SUN GE; publ. *Acta Palaeontologica Sinica* (4 a year).

Mathematical Sciences

Chinese Mathematical Society: c/o Institute of Mathematics, Chinese Academy of Sciences, Beijing 100080; tel. (10) 62551022;

fax (10) 62568356; e-mail cms@math08.math
.ac.cn; f. 1935; Pres. K. C. CHANG; Sec.-Gen.
LI WENLIN.

Physical Sciences

Acoustical Society of China: 17 Zhong-guancun St, Beijing 100080; tel. (10) 62553765; fax (10) 62553898; f. 1985; 3,030 mems; Pres. CHEN TONG; Sec.-Gen. HOU CHADHUAN; publs *Acta Acustica* (6 a year), *Applied Acoustics* (4 a year), *Chinese Journal of Acoustics* (4 a year, English version of *Acta Acustica*).

Chinese Academy of Meteorological Sciences: 7 Block 11, Hepingli, Beijing; tel. (10) 64211631; fax (10) 64218703; attached research institutes: see Research Institutes.

Chinese Aerodynamics Research Society: POB 2425, Beijing; Pres. ZHUANG GEN-GGAN.

Chinese Astronomical Society: Purple Mountain Observatory, Nanjing, Jiangsu 210008; tel. (25) 3302147; fax (25) 3301459; f. 1922; 1,611 mems; Pres. FANG CHENG; publs *Acta Astronomica Sinica* (4 a year), *Acta Astrophysica Sinica* (4 a year).

Chinese Chemical Society: POB 2709, Beijing 100080; tel. (10) 62564020; fax (10) 62568157; f. 1932; Pres. XI FU; publs *Acta Chimica Sinica* (12 a year), *Chinese Journal of Chemistry* (6 a year).

Chinese Geological Society: 26 Baiwanzhuang, Beijing 100037; fax (10) 68310894; f. 1922; 71,000 mems; Pres. ZHANG HONGREN; Sec.-Gen. ZHAO XUN; publs *Acta Geologica Sinica*, *Geological Review*.

Chinese Geological Survey: 45 Fu Wai St, Beijing 100037; tel. (10) 58584680; fax (10) 58584681; e-mail netcenter@mail.cgs.gov.cn; internet www.cgs.gov.cn; f. 1959; attached to Ministry of Land and Resources; responsible for the centralized deployment and implementation of China's basic, public and strategic geological investigation and mineral exploration; provides basic geological information and data for the national economy; attached institutes: see Research Institutes; Dir-Gen. MENG XIANLAI; publs *Acta Geologica Sinica*, *Bulletin*, *Geological Review*.

Chinese Geophysical Society: Institute of Geophysics, POB 9701, Beijing 100101; tel. (10) 64889027; fax (10) 64871995; e-mail rxzhu@mail.c-geos.ac.cn; f. 1948; 4,000 mems; Pres. LIU GUANGDING; Sec.-Gen. ZHU RIXIANG; publ. *Acta Geophisica Sinica* (6 a year).

Chinese High-Energy Physics Society: POB 918, Beijing 100039; tel. (10) 68235910; fax (10) 68213374; e-mail zhouxb@alpha02 .ihep.ac.cn; internet www.ihep.ac.cn; f. 1981; 962 mems; Chair. DAI YUANBEN; Sec.-Gen. HUANG TAO; publs *High Energy Physics and Nuclear Physics* (12 a year), *Modern Physics* (6 a year).

Chinese Meteorological Society: 46 Zhongguancun South Ave, Beijing 100081; tel. (10) 68407634; fax (10) 6840682; e-mail cmsams@cms1924.org; internet www .cms1924.org; f. 1924; 21,000 mems; Pres. Prof. Dr QIN DAHE (acting); Sec.-Gen. WANG CHUNYI; publs *Acta Meteorologica Sinica* (24 a year, in English), *Meteorological Knowledge* (12 a year, in Chinese).

Chinese Nuclear Physics Society: POB 275-50, Beijing 102413; tel. (10) 69358003; fax (10) 69357787; e-mail zhusy@ciae.ac.cn; internet www.cnps.ac.cn; f. 1979; 600 mems; Pres. Prof. HUANQIAO ZHANG; Sec.-Gen. Prof. SHENGYUN ZHU; publ. *Nuclear Physics Review* (4 a year).

Chinese Nuclear Society: POB 2125, Beijing 100822; tel. (10) 68531473; fax (10) 68527188; e-mail cns@cnnc.com.cn; internet

www.ns.org.cn; f. 1980; 8,894 mems; Pres. WANG NAIYAN; publ. *Chinese Journal of Nuclear Science and Technology*.

Chinese Physical Society: POB 603, Beijing 100080; tel. (10) 82649019; fax (10) 82649019; e-mail cps@aphy.iphy.ac.cn; internet www.cps-net.org; f. 1932; attached to Chinese Association for Science and Technology; 42,000 mems; Pres. YANG GUO-ZHEN; Sec.-Gen. WANG EN-GE; publs *Acta Physica Sinica* (12 a year, in Chinese), *Chinese Journal of Chemical Physics* (6 a year, in Chinese), *Chinese Physics* (12 a year, in English), *Chinese Physics Letters* (12 a year, in English), *College Physics* (12 a year, in Chinese), *Communications in Theoretical Physics* (12 a year, in English), *Physics Teaching* (12 a year, in Chinese), *Progress in Physics* (4 a year, in Chinese), *Wuli* (Physics, 12 a year, in Chinese).

Chinese Society for Mineralogy, Petrology and Geochemistry: 46 Guanshui Rd, Guiyang 550002, Guizhou Province; tel. and fax (851) 5895823; e-mail csmpg@vip .skleg.cn; internet www.gyig.ac.cn/society; f. 1978; 6,500 mems; library of 10,000 vols and periodicals; Pres. OUYANG ZIYUAN; publs *Acta Mineralogica Sinica* (4 a year), *Acta Petrologica Sinica* (4 a year), *Bulletin of Mineralogy, Petrology and Geochemistry* (4 a year), *Chinese Journal of Geochemistry* (4 a year, in English), *Geochemica* (6 a year), *Journal of Paleography* (4 a year).

Chinese Society for Rock Mechanics and Engineering: POB 9825, Beijing, 100029; tel. and fax (10) 82998163; e-mail csrme@163.com; internet www.csrme.com; f. 1985; 14 corporate mems, 554 individual mems; Pres. Prof. QIAN QIHU (acting); Sec.-Gen. Prof. WU FAQUAN; publs *Chinese Journal of Rock Mechanics and Engineering* (in Chinese), *Chinese Journal of Underground Space and Engineering* (in Chinese), *Journal of Rock Mechanics and Geotechnical Engineering* (in English), *News of Rock Mechanics and Engineering* (4 a year, in Chinese).

Chinese Society of Space Research: 1 Second Southern Ave, Zhongguancun, Beijing 100080; tel. (10) 62559882; f. 1980; Pres. Prof. WANG XIJI; publ. *Chinese Journal of Space Science* (4 a year).

Seismological Society of China: 5 Minzu Daxue Nanlu, Beijing 100081; tel. (10) 68417858; f. 1979; 1,250 mems; Pres. Prof. ZHANG GUOMIN; publ. *Acta Seismologica Sinica* (4 a year, in Chinese and English edns).

PHILOSOPHY AND PSYCHOLOGY

Chinese Psychological Society: Institute of Psychology, Chinese Academy of Sciences, Datun Rd, Jia 10 Hao, Chaoyang District, Beijing 100101; tel. and fax (10) 64855830; e-mail xuehui@psych.ac.cn; internet www .cpsbeijing.org; f. 1921; organizes annual conference on various topics by branch committees; National Congress of Psychology every two years; open lectures to public; promotion of psychological science through the internet; seminars organized for professionals in other fields; 2,000 mems; Pres. Prof. KAN ZHANG; Sec.-Gen. Prof. YUFANG YANG; publs *Acta Psychologica Sinica* (6 a year), *Psychological Science* (6 a year).

RELIGION, SOCIOLOGY AND ANTHROPOLOGY

Chinese Sociological Research Society: c/o Chinese Academy of Social Sciences, 5 Jianguomennei Da Jie, Beijing; f. 1979; Pres. FEI XIAOTONG; Exec. Sec. WANG KANG.

Chinese Study of Religion Society: Xi'anmen Ave, Beijing; Pres. REN JIYU.

Chemical Industry and Engineering Society of China: POB 911, Beijing; tel. (10) 466025; f. 1922; 40,000 mems; Pres. YANG GUANGQI; Sec.-Gen. YIN DELIN; publs *Huagong Jinzhan* (Chemical Engineering Progress, 6 a year), *Huagong Xuebao* (Journal of Chemical Engineering, 4 a year).

China Coal Society: Hepingli, Beijing 100013; tel. (10) 84262776; fax (10) 84261671; f. 1962; 53,000 mems; Pres. FAN WEITANG; Sec.-Gen. PAN HUIZHENG; publs *Journal* (irregular), *Modern Miners* (12 a year).

China Computer Federation: POB 2704, Beijing 100080; tel. (10) 62562503; fax (10) 62567485; e-mail ccf@ns.ict.ac.cn; internet www.ccf.org.cn; f. 1962; fmrly Chinese Information Processing Soc; 40,000 individual mems; Chair. ZHANG XIAOXIANG; Sec.-Gen. CHEN SHUKAI; publs *Chinese Journal of Advanced Software Research*, *Chinese Journal of Computers*, *Journal of Computer Science and Technology* (in English), *Journal of Computer-aided Design and Computer Graphics*, *Journal of Software*.

China Electrotechnical Society: 46 Sanlihe Rd, POB 2133, Beijing 100823; tel. (10) 68595358; fax (10) 68511242; e-mail cesintl@ public.bta.net.cn; internet www.ces.org.cn; f. 1981; 50,000 mems; Pres. WU XIAOHUA; Sec.-Gen. DUAN RUICHUN; publs *Electrical Engineering* (12 a year), *Transactions of China Electrotechnical Society* (12 a year).

China Energy Research Society: 54 San Li He Rd, Beijing 100863; tel. (10) 68511816; fax (10) 68511816; f. 1981; 18,000 mems; Pres. HUANG YICHENG; Sec.-Gen. BAO YUN-QIAO; publ. *Guide to World Energy* (52 a year).

China Engineering Graphics Society: POB 85, Beijing 100083; tel. (10) 82317091; fax (10) 82326420; Pres. TANG RONGXI; publ. *Computer Aided Drafting, Design and Manufacturing* (2 a year).

China Fire Protection Association: 5th Floor, Fire Station, 19A Huawei XiLi, Chaoyang District, Beijing 100021; China Fire, 48, Banbuqiao Road, Xuanwu, Beijing 100054; tel. (10) 51232677; fax (10) 51232676; e-mail english@china-fire.org; internet www.china-fire.com; f. 1984; 30,000 mems; Pres. SUN LUN; publs *Fire Protection in China*, *Fire Science and Technology*, *Fire Technique and Products Information*.

China Society for Scientific and Technical Information: 15 Fuxinglu, Beijing; tel. (10) 68014024; fax (10) 68014025; internet www.cssti.org.cn; f. 1964; organizes academic activities about information science and technology; 13,000 mems; Pres. WU HENG; publ. *Journal of the China Society for Scientific and Technical Information* (6 a year).

Chinese Abacus Association: Sidaokou, Xizhimenwai, Shidaokou, Beijing; tel. (10) 896275; f. 1979; 500,000 mems; Pres. ZHU XI-AN; Sec.-Gen. HU JING; publs *Chinese Abacus* (12 a year), *Chinese Abacus News* (12 a year).

Chinese Academy of Engineering (CAE): POB 3847, Beijing 100038; 3 Fuxing Rd, Beijing; tel. (10) 68530187; fax (10) 68519694; internet www.cae.ac.cn; f. 1994; 616 academicians; Pres. XU KUANGDI; Sec. HE ZHONGWEI.

Chinese Academy of Space Technology: 31 Baishiqiao, POB 2417, Beijing 100081; tel. (10) 68379439; fax (10) 68378237; 4 mems; attached research institutes: see Research Institutes; Pres. QI FAREN.

Chinese Association of Automation: POB 2728, Beijing 100080; tel. (10) 62544415; fax

(10) 62620908; e-mail wangh@iamail.ia.ac.cn; internet www.gongkong.com; f. 1961; 40,000 mems; Pres Prof. CHEN HANFU, Prof. YANG JIACHI, Prof. DAI RUWAI; publs *Acta Automatica Sinica* (6 a year), *Automation Panorama* (6 a year), *Information and Control* (6 a year), *Pattern Recognition and Artificial Intelligence* (4 a year), *Robot* (6 a year).

Chinese Ceramic Society: Bai Wan Zhuang, Beijing 100831; tel. (10) 68313364; fax (10) 68313364; f. 1945; 30,000 mems; Pres. WANG YANMOU; Sec.-Gen. JIANG DONGHUA; publs *Bulletin of the Chinese Ceramic Society* (6 a year), *Journal of the Chinese Ceramic Society* (6 a year).

Chinese Civil Engineering Society: Bai Wan Zhuang, POB 2500, Beijing 100835; tel. (10) 68311313; fax (10) 68313669; f. 1953; Pres. MAO YISHENG; Sec.-Gen. ZHAO XICHUN; publ. *Civil Engineering Journal*.

Chinese Hydraulic Engineering Society: 2-2 Baiguang Rd, Beijing 100053; tel. (10) 63202171; fax (10) 63202154; e-mail ches@mwr.gov.cn; internet www.hwcc.gov.cn; f. 1931; 93,309 mems; Pres. ZHU ERMING; Sec.-Gen. FENG GUANGZHI; publs *China Rural Water and Hydropower* (12 a year), *Journal of Hydraulic Engineering* (12 a year), *Journal of Sediment Research* (12 a year).

Chinese Light Industry Society: B22 Fuchengmenwai Ave, Beijing 100037; tel. 894147; f. 1979; Pres. JI LONG.

Chinese Mechanical Engineering Society: 11th Fl., Bldg 4, Zhuyu Int., 9 Shouti S Rd, Haidian Dist., Beijing 100048; tel. (10) 68799038; fax (10) 68799050; e-mail headquarters@cmes.org; internet www.cmes.org; f. 1936; 180,000 mems; Pres. Dr LU RONGXIANG; Gen. Sec. ZHANG YAN-MIN; publs *Chinese Journal of Mechanical Engineering* (6 a year, in English), *China Mechanical Engineering* (52 a year, in Chinese), *Journal of Mechanical Engineering* (12 a year, in Chinese).

Chinese Petroleum Society: POB 766, Liu Pu Kang, Beijing 100724; tel. (10) 62095615; fax (10) 62014787; f. 1979; academic asscn of petroleum engineers; 60,000 mems; library: 20,000 books, 560 periodicals; Pres. JIN ZHONGCHAO; Sec.-Gen. LU JIMENG; publ. *Acta Petrolei Sinica* (Exploration and Development, and Refining and the Petrochemical Industry, each edition 4 a year).

China Railway Society: 10 Fuxing Rd, POB 2499, Beijing; e-mail yangzm25@yahoo.com.cn; internet www.crs.org.cn; f. 1978; railway transport, construction and rolling stock manufacture; academic exchanges, technological consultation, technical research and devt; 78,000 mems; Chair. SUN YONGFU; Sec.-Gen. LU CHANGQING; publs *Railway Journal*, *Railway Knowledge*.

Chinese Society for Metals: 46 Dongsi Xidajie, Beijing 100711; tel. (10) 65133322; fax (10) 65124122; e-mail csmoffice@csm.org.cn; internet www.csm.org.cn; f. 1956; 100,000 mems; library of 50,000 vols, 20,000 serials, 1,270 periodicals; Pres. WENG YUQING; Sec.-Gen. LI WENXIU; publs *Acta Metallurgica Sinica* (12 a year, in Chinese; 6 a year, in English), *China Metallurgy* (6 a year), *Iron and Steel* (12 a year), *Journal of Materials Science and Technology* (6 a year).

Chinese Society of Aeronautics and Astronautics: 5 Liangguochang Rd, Dongcheng District, Beijing 100010; tel. (10) 84923943; fax (10) 84923942; internet www.csaa.org.cn; f. 1964; 21,800 mems; Pres. LIU GAOZHUO; Sec.-Gen. ZHANG JUEN; publs *Acta Aeronautica et Astronautica Sinica* (6 a year), *Aerospace Knowledge* (12 a year), *Chinese Journal of Aeronautics* (4 a year),

Journal of Aeronautical Materials (6 a year), *Journal of Aerospace Power* (6 a year), *Model Airplane* (6 a year).

Chinese Society of Astronautics (CSA): POB 838, Beijing 100830; 2 Yue Tan Beixiao Tie, Beijing; tel. (10) 68768622; fax (10) 68768624; e-mail csa_heinlein@yahoo.com.cn; internet www.csaspace.org.cn/heinlein/hlindex-en.htm; f. 1979; 10,000 mems; Pres. LIU JIYUAN; Sec.-Gen. Prof. YANG, JUNHUA; publs *Space Exploration*, *Journal*.

Chinese Society of Electrical Engineering: 1 Lane 2, Baiguang Rd, Beijing 10076; Pres. ZHANG FENGXIANG.

Chinese Society of Engineering Thermophysics: POB 2706, Zhong Guan Cun, Beijing; f. 1978; 5,000 mems; Sec.-Gen. Prof. XU JIANZHONG; publ. *Journal of Engineering Thermophysics* (4 a year).

Chinese Society of Naval Architects and Marine Engineers: POB 817, Beijing; tel. (10) 68340527; fax (10) 68313380; f. 1943; Pres. WANG RONGSHENG; Sec.-Gen. WANG SHOUDAO; publs *Naval and Merchant Ships* (12 a year), *Shipbuilding of China* (4 a year, contents and abstracts), *Ship Engineering* (6 a year).

Chinese Society of Theoretical and Applied Mechanics (CSTAM): 15 Zhong-Guan-Cun, Beijing 100080; tel. (10) 62559588; fax (10) 62561284; e-mail cstam@sun.ihep.ac.cn; internet www.cstam.org.cn; f. 1957; 21,000 mems; Dir Prof. BAI YILONG; publs *Acta Mechanica Sinica* (6 a year, in English 4 a year), *Acta Mechanica Solida Sinica* (6 a year, in English 4 a year), *Engineering Mechanics* (4 a year), *Explosion and Shock Waves* (4 a year), *Journal of Computational Mechanics* (4 a year), *Journal of Experimental Mechanics* (4 a year), *Mechanics and Practice* (6 a year).

Chinese Textile Engineering Society: 3 Middle St, Yanjing Li, East Suburb, Beijing 100025; tel. (10) 65016537; fax (10) 65016538; f. 1930; 60,000 mems; Pres. JI GUOBIAO.

Nonferrous Metals Society of China: B12, Fuxing Rd, Beijing 100814; tel. (10) 63971451; fax (10) 63965399; e-mail nfsoc@public.bta.net.cn; internet www.nfsoc.org.cn; f. 1984; 39,000 mems; Pres. KANG YI; Sec.-Gen. NIU YINJIAN; publs *Journal of Nonferrous Metals* (4 a year, with English Abstracts), *Journal of Rare Metals* (4 a year, with English version), *Transactions of Nonferrous Metals Society of China* (4 a year, with English version).

Society of Automotive Engineers of China: 46 Fucheng Rd, Beijing 100036; tel. (10) 68121894; fax (10) 68125556; f. 1963; 1,520 mems; Pres. ZHANG XINGYE; publs *Auto Fan* (12 a year), *Automotive Engineering* (6 a year).

Systems Engineering Society of China: Institute of Systems Science, Zhongyguanycun, Beijing 100080; tel. (10) 62541827; fax (10) 62568364; internet www.amss.iss.ac.cn.sesc; f. 1980; 3,000 individual mems, 150 collective mems; Pres. CHEN, GUANGYA; Sec.-Gen. WANG, SHOUYANG; publs *Journal of Systems Science and Systems Engineering* (4 a year, in English), *Journal of Transportations Systems Engineering and Information Technology* (4 a year, in English), *Systems Engineering* (4 a year, in English), *Systems Engineering—Theory and Practice* (12 a year).

Research Institutes

AGRICULTURE, FISHERIES AND VETERINARY SCIENCE

Chinese Research Institute of the Wood Industry: Wan Shou Shan, Beijing 100091; attached to Chinese Acad. of Forestry.

Forest Economics Research Institute: He Ping Li, Beijing; tel. (10) 64210476; attached to Chinese Acad. of Forestry.

Forest Resource and Insect Research Institute: Kunming, Yunnan Province; attached to Chinese Acad. of Forestry.

Forestry Research Institute: Wan Shou Shan, Beijing 100091; tel. (10) 62888862; fax (10) 62872015; e-mail lumz@www.caf.ac.cn; internet nic6.forestry.ac.cn; f. 1953; attached to Chinese Acad. of Forestry; research into silviculture, tree cultivation, soil science, agroforestry, prevention of desertification, ornamental plants, biotechnology; 148 mems; Dir Prof. Dr LU MENG ZHU; publ. *Forest Research* (6 a year).

Institute of Agricultural Meteorology: 7 Block 11, Hepingli, Beijing; attached to Chinese Acad. of Meteorological Sciences.

Institute of Soil Science: POB 821, Nanjing 210008; tel. (25) 7712572; fax (25) 3353590; f. 1953; attached to Chinese Acad. of Sciences; library of 110,000 vols; Dir Prof. ZHAO QIGUO; publs *Acta Pedologica Sinica*, *Advance of Soil Science*, *Pedosphere*, *Soils*, *Soil Science Research Report*.

Sub-Tropical Forestry Research Institute: Fuyang 311400, Zhejiang Province; attached to Chinese Acad. of Forestry; Dir YANG PEISHOU.

Tropical Forestry Research Institute: Longdong, Guangzhou, Guandong Province 510520; attached to Chinese Acad. of Forestry.

BIBLIOGRAPHY, LIBRARY SCIENCE AND MUSEOLOGY

State Archives Bureau of China: 21 Feng Sheng Hutong, Beijing; tel. (10) 665797; Dir FENG ZIZHI; publ. *Archival Work* (12 a year).

ECONOMICS, LAW AND POLITICS

Academy of Marxism of the Chinese Academy of Social Sciences: Rd Jianguomennei Da jie, No. 5, Beijing; e-mail wangzb@cass.org.cn; internet myy.cass.cn; f. 1980; attached to Chinese Acad. of Social Sciences; Dir SU SHAOZHI; publs *International Thought Review* (in English), *Marxism Digest* (in Chinese), *Study of Marxism* (in Chinese).

Economics Institute: 2 Yuetanxiaojie N., Fuchengmenurai, Beijing 100836; tel. (10) 895323; attached to Chinese Acad. of Social Sciences; Dir ZHAO RENWEI.

Industrial Economics Institute: 2 Yuetanbeixiao Street, Fuchengmenwai, Beijing 100836; f. 1978; attached to Chinese Acad. of Social Sciences; Dir ZHOU SHULIAN.

Institute of American Studies: 3 Zhangzizhong Rd, Beijing 100007; tel. (10) 64039046; fax (10) 64000021; internet ias.cass.cn; f. 1981; attached to Chinese Acad. of Social Sciences; Dir HUANG PING; publ. *American Studies Quarterly*.

Institute of East European, Russian and Central Asian Studies: 3 Zhangzhizhong Rd, Beijing 100007; tel. (10) 64014020; f. 1976; attached to Chinese Acad. of Social Sciences; library of 60,000 vols, 280 periodicals; Dir LI JINGJIE.

Institute of European Studies: 5 Jianguomennei Ave, Beijing 100732; tel. (10) 65138428; fax (10) 65125818; e-mail ies@

cass.net.cn; internet europeanstudies.org; f. 1980; attached to Chinese Acad. of Social Sciences; Dir Prof. ZHOU HONG; publ. *Chinese Journal for European Studies* (6 a year).

Institute of Latin American Studies: POB 1113, Beijing; tel. (10) 64014009; fax (10) 64014011; e-mail latinlat@public.bta.net .cn; f. 1961; attached to Chinese Acad. of Social Sciences; Dir LI MINGDE.

Institute of West Asian and African Studies: 3 Zhangzhizhong Rd, Beijing 100007; f. 1961; attached to Chinese Acad. of Social Sciences; Dir-Gen. Prof. YANG GUANG; publ. *West Asia and Africa* (6 a year).

Japanese Studies Institute: Dong Yuan, 3 Zhangzhizhong Rd, Beijing 100007; f. 1980; attached to Chinese Acad. of Social Sciences; Dir HE FANG.

Law Institute: 15 Shatan St N., Beijing 100720; tel. (10) 64014045; f. 1958; attached to Chinese Acad. of Social Sciences; Dir WANG JIAFU.

Political Science Institute: Shatan Bei Jie, Beijing 100720; f. 1981; attached to Chinese Acad. of Social Sciences; Dir YAN JIAQI.

Quantitative and Technical Economics Institute: 5 Jianguomennei Ave, Beijing 100732; tel. (10) 65137561; fax (10) 65125895; e-mail tswang@mx.cei.gov.cn; internet www.iqte-cass.org; f. 1982; attached to Chinese Acad. of Social Sciences; Dir WANG TONGSAN; publ. *Quantitative and Technical Economics* (12 a year).

Rural Development Institute: Ritan Rd, Beijing; tel. (10) 65275067; fax (10) 65137559; internet www.cass.net.cn/ chinese/s04-nfs/s04-nfs.htm; f. 1978; attached to Chinese Acad. of Social Sciences; Dir Prof. ZHANG XIAOSHAN; publs *Chinese Rural Economy* (12 a year), *Chinese Rural Survey* (6 a year).

Taiwan Studies Institute: 15 Poshangcun, Haidian District, Beijing 100091; tel. (10) 62883311; fax (10) 62880285; f. 1984; attached to Chinese Acad. of Social Sciences; Dir XU SHIQUAN; publ. *Taiwan Studies* (4 a year).

Trade, Finance and Material Supply Institute: 2 Yuetanbeixiao St, Beijing 100836; attached to Chinese Acad. of Social Sciences; Dir ZHANG ZHUOYUAN.

World Economy and Politics Institute: 5 Jianguomennei Ave, Beijing 100732; attached to Chinese Acad. of Social Sciences; Dir PU SHAN.

HISTORY, GEOGRAPHY AND ARCHAEOLOGY

Archaeology Institute: 27 Wangfujing Ave, Beijing 100710; f. 1950; attached to Chinese Acad. of Social Sciences; Dir WANG ZHONGSHU.

Changchun Institute of Geography: 16 Gongnong Rd, Changchun 130021, Jilin Province; tel. (431) 5652931; fax (431) 5652931; f. 1958; attached to Chinese Acad. of Sciences; Dir Prof. HE YAN.

Chinese Academy of Surveying and Mapping, National Bureau of Surveying and Mapping: 16 Bei Tai Ping Lu, Beijing 100039; tel. (10) 68212277; fax (10) 68218654; f. 1959; library of 50,000 vols; Dir LIU XIANLIN; publs *Remote Sensing Information*, *Trends in Science and Technology of Surveying and Mapping*.

History (Chinese) Institute: 5 Jianguomennei Ave, Beijing 100732; attached to Chinese Acad. of Social Sciences; Dir LI XUEQIN.

History (Modern Chinese) Institute: 1 Dongcheng Lane, Wangfu Ave, Beijing

100006; tel. (10) 555400; attached to Chinese Acad. of Social Sciences; Dir WANG QING-CHENG.

History (World) Institute: 1 Dongcheng Lane, Wangfu Ave, Beijing 100006; f. 1964; attached to Chinese Acad. of Social Sciences; Dir ZHANG CHUNNIAN.

Institute of Geography: Bldg 917, Datun Rd, Anwai, Beijing 100101; tel. (10) 64914841; fax (10) 64911844; f. 1940; attached to Chinese Acad. of Sciences; library of 90,000 vols; Dir Prof. ZHENG DU; publ. *Geographical Research* (4 a year).

LANGUAGE AND LITERATURE

Applied Linguistics Institute: 51 Nanxiao Street, Chaoyangmennei, Beijing 100010; tel. (10) 557146; f. 1984; attached to Chinese Acad. of Social Sciences; Dir CHEN YUAN.

Chinese Literature Institute: 5 Jianguomennei Ave, Beijing 100732; attached to Chinese Acad. of Social Sciences; Dir LIU ZAIFU.

Foreign Literature Institute: 5 Jianguomennei Ave, Beijing 100732; attached to Chinese Acad. of Social Sciences; Dir ZHANG YU.

Institute of Ethnic Literature: 5 Jianguomennei Ave, Beijing 100732; tel. (10) 65138025; fax (10) 65134585; e-mail iel-scholarship@cass.org.cn; internet www .ilnm.cass.net.cn; f. 1981; attached to Chinese Acad. of Social Sciences; Dirs TANG XIAOGING, CHAO GEJIN; publ. *Studies of Ethnic Literature* (4 a year).

Institute of Linguistics: 5 Jianguomenei Dajie, Beijing 100732; tel. (10) 65737403; fax (10) 65737403; f. 1950; attached to Chinese Acad. of Social Sciences; Dir SHEN JIAXUAN; publs *Contemporary Linguistics*, *Dialects*, *The Chinese Language and Writing*.

Journalism Institute: 2 Jintai Rd W., Chaoyang District, Beijing 100026; attached to Chinese Acad. of Social Sciences; Dir SUN XUPEI.

MEDICINE

Biomedical Engineering Institute: POB (25) 204, Tianjing 300192; fax (22) 361095; attached to Chinese Acad. of Medical Sciences; Deputy Dir WANG PENGYAN.

Blood Transfusion Institute: Renmin Rd N., Chengdu, Sichuan 61008; tel. (28) 332125; fax (28) 332125; attached to Chinese Acad. of Medical Sciences; Dir YANG CHENG-MIN.

Cancer Institute and Hospital: Faculty of Oncology, Peking Union Medical College, Panjiayuan, Chaoyang District, Beijing 100021; tel. (10) 67781331; fax (10) 67713359; attached to Chinese Acad. of Medical Sciences; Dir DONG ZHIWEI.

Cardiovascular Diseases Institute: A167 Beilishi Rd, Beijing 100037; tel. (10) 68314466; fax (10) 68313012; e-mail fuwaih@public.bta.net.cn; attached to Chinese Acad. of Medical Sciences; Dir GAO RUNLIN.

Clinical Medicine Institute: 1 Shuaifuyuan Lane, Beijing 100730; tel. (10) 65127733; fax (10) 65124875; attached to Chinese Acad. of Medical Sciences; Dir LU ZHADLIN.

Dermatology Institute: 12 Jiangwangmiao St, Nanjing, Jiangsu 210042; tel. (25) 5411040; fax (25) 5411447; attached to Chinese Acad. of Medical Sciences; Dir YE SHUNZHANG.

Haematology Institute: 228 Nanjing Rd, Tianjing 300020; tel. (22) 707939; fax (22) 706542; attached to Chinese Acad. of Medical Sciences; Dir HAO YUSHU.

Health School: Badachu, Xishan, Beijing 100041; tel. (10) 68862233; fax (10) 68864137; attached to Chinese Acad. of Medical Sciences; Dir CHI XINGQIU.

Institute of Basic Medical Sciences: 5 Dongdan Santiao, Beijing 100005; tel. (10) 65134466; fax (10) 65124876; e-mail zheng@ public3.bta.net.cn; attached to Chinese Acad. of Medical Sciences; Dir ZHENG DEXIAN.

Institute of Laboratory Animal Science: 5 Pan Jia Yuan Nan Li, Chao Yang District, Beijing 100021; fax (10) 67780683; attached to Chinese Acad. of Medical Sciences; Dir LIU YINONG.

Institute of Microcirculation: 5 Dongdan Santiao, Beijing 100005; tel. (10) 65126407; fax (10) 62015012; f. 1984; attached to Chinese Acad. of Medical Sciences; Dir Prof. XIU RUIJUAN.

Institute of Plastic Surgery: Badachu, Beijing 100041; tel. (10) 68874826; fax (10) 68864137; f. 1957; attached to Chinese Acad. of Medical Sciences; library of 20,000 vols; Dir Prof. SONG YEGUANG; publ. *Chinese Journal of Plastic Surgery and Burns*.

Materia Medica Institute: 1 Xiannongtan St, Beijing 100050; tel. (10) 63013366; fax (10) 63017757; attached to Chinese Acad. of Medical Sciences; Dir ZHANG JUNTIAN.

Medical Biology Institute: Huahongdong, Kunming 650160, Yunnan Province; f. 1959; attached to Chinese Acad. of Medical Sciences.

Medical Biotechnology Institute: 1 Tiantanxili, Beijing 100050; tel. (10) 757315; fax (10) 63017302; attached to Chinese Acad. of Medical Sciences; Dir ZHANG ZHIPING.

Medicinal Plant Development Institute: 151 Ma Lian Wa North Rd, Haidian District, Beijing 100094; tel. (10) 62896288; fax (10) 62899715; e-mail implad@implad.ac.cn; internet www.implad.ac.cn; f. 1983; attached to Chinese Acad. of Medical Sciences; library of 30,000 vols; Dir Prof. CHEN SHILIN.

Radiation Medicine Institute: POB 71, Tianjin 300192; attached to Chinese Acad. of Medical Sciences.

Shanghai Institute of Materia Medica: 294 Tai-Yuan Rd, Shanghai 200031; tel. (21) 64311833; fax (21) 64370269; f. 1932; attached to Chinese Acad. of Sciences; development of new drugs; library of 80,000 vols, 600 current periodicals; Dir CHEN KAIXIAN; publ. *Acta Pharmocologica Sinica*.

NATURAL SCIENCES

General

Fujian Institute of Research on the Structure of Matter: Xihe, Fuzhou, Fujian 350002; tel. (591) 3714517; fax (591) 3714946; e-mail fjirsm@ms.fjirsm.ac.cn; f. 1960; attached to Chinese Acad. of Sciences; library of 75,000 vols; Dir Prof. HUANG JINSHUN; publ. *Journal on Structural Chemistry* (6 a year).

Institute of Oceanology: 7 Nanhai Rd, Qingdao 266071; tel. (532) 2879062; fax (532) 2870882; e-mail iocas@ms.qdio.ac.cn; f. 1950; attached to Chinese Acad. of Sciences; library of 180,000 vols; Dir XIANG JIANHAI; publs *Chinese Journal of Oceanology and Limnology* (4 a year, in English), *Marine Sciences* (6 a year, in Chinese), *Oceanologia et Limnologia Sinica* (6 a year, Chinese), *Studia Marina Sinica* (Chinese with English abstracts, 1 a year).

Institute of the History of Natural Sciences: 137 Chao Nei St, Beijing 100010; tel. (10) 64043989; fax (10) 64017637; e-mail ihns_2008_@ihns.ac.cn; internet www.ihns .ac.cn; f. 1957; attached to Chinese Acad. of Sciences; library of 150,000 vols; Dir Prof.

DUN LIU; publs *China Historical Materials of Science and Technology* (4 a year), *Studies in the History of Natural Sciences* (4 a year).

Qinghai Institute of Salt Lakes: 7 Xinning Rd, Xinning 810008, Qinghai Province; tel. (971) 44306; fax (971) 46002; f. 1965; attached to Chinese Acad. of Sciences; library of 85,000 vols; Dir LIU DEJIANG; publ. *Journal of Salt Lake Science.*

South China Sea Institute of Oceanology: 164 West Xingang Rd, Guangzhou 510301; tel. (20) 84452227; fax (20) 84451672; internet www.scsio.ac.an; f. 1959; attached to Chinese Acad. of Sciences; library of 95,546 vols; Dir Dr SHI PING; publs *Journal of Tropical Oceanology* (6 a year), *Nanhai Studia Marina Sinica* (irregular, Chinese with English abstracts).

Biological Sciences

Institute of Applied Ecology: POB 417, Shenyang 110015; tel. (24) 3902096; fax (24) 3843313; f. 1954; attached to Chinese Acad. of Sciences; library of 95,000 vols; Dir SUN TIEHANG; publs *Chinese Journal of Applied Ecology, Chinese Journal of Ecology.*

Institute of Biophysics: 15 Datun Rd, Chaoyang District, Beijing 100101; tel. (10) 62022029; fax (10) 62027837; attached to Chinese Acad. of Sciences; Dir WANG SHURONG.

Institute of Botany: 141 Xizhimen Wai St, Beijing 100044; attached to Chinese Acad. of Sciences; Dir ZHANG XINSHI.

Institute of Developmental Biology: POB 2707, Beijing; fax (10) 62561269; f. 1980; attached to Chinese Acad. of Sciences; specializes in biotechnology of fish and mammals; Dir YAN SHAOYI.

Institute of Genetics and Developmental Biology: Datun Rd, Andingmenwai, Beijing 100101; tel. (10) 64889331; fax (10) 64856610; e-mail genetics@genetics.ac.cn; internet www.genetics.ac.cn; attached to Chinese Acad. of Sciences; Dir Prof. JIAYANG LI.

Institute of Hydrobiology: Luojiashan, Wuhan 430072, Hubei Province; tel. (27) 68780789; fax (27) 68780123; e-mail zhh@ihb.ac.cn; internet www.ihb.ac.cn; f. 1930; attached to Chinese Acad. of Sciences; freshwater ecology, fisheries, biotechnology and molecular biology, aquatic environment protection; library of 70,000 vols; fish museum; Dir Dr. GUI JIANFANG; publ. *Acta Hydrobiologica Sinica* (6 a year).

Institute of Microbiology: 13 Beiyitiao, Zhongguancun, Haidian District, Beijing 100080; tel. (10) 62552178; fax (10) 62560912; e-mail gaof@im.ac.cn; internet www.im.ac.cn; f. 1958; attached to Chinese Acad. of Sciences; 380 mems; Dir Prof. GEORGE F. GAO; publs *Acta Microbiologica Sinica* (6 a year), *Chinese Journal of Biotechnology* (6 a year), *Microbiology* (6 a year), *Mycosystema* (4 a year).

Institute of Vertebrate Palaeontology and Palaeo-Anthropology: Academia Sinica, Beijing; f. 1929; attached to Chinese Acad. of Sciences; Dir QIU ZHANXIANG.

Institute of Zoology: Chinese Academy of Sciences, 19 Zhongguancun Rd, Haidian, Beijing 100080; tel. (10) 62552219; fax (10) 62565689; e-mail ioz@panda.ioz.ac.cn; internet panda.ioz.ac.cn; attached to Chinese Acad. of Sciences; Dir Prof. HUANG DAWEI; publs *Acta Entomologica Sinica* (4 a year), *Acta Zoologica Sinica* (6 a year), *Acta Zootaxonomica Sinica* (4 a year), *Chinese Journal of Entomology* (6 a year), *Chinese Journal of Zoology* (6 a year), *Entomologica Sinica* (4 a year, in English).

Kunming Institute of Zoology: Kunming 650223, Yunnan Province; tel. (871) 5190390; fax (871) 51591823; internet english.kiz.cas .cn; f. 1959; attached to Chinese Acad. of Sciences; library of 180,000 vols; Dir Prof. ZHANG YAPING; publ. *Zoological Research* (4 a year).

Nanjing Institute of Geology and Palaeontology: 39 East Beijing Rd, Chi-Ming-Ssu, Nanjing 210008, Jiangsu Province; tel. (25) 7714437; fax (25) 3357026; f. 1951; attached to Chinese Acad. of Sciences; library of 26,000 vols; Dir MU XINAN; publs *Acta Micropalaeontologica Sinica* (4 a year), *Acta Palaeobotanica et Palynologica Sinica* (irregular), *Acta Palaeontologica Sinica* (4 a year), *Bulletin* (irregular), *Journal of Stratigraphy* (4 a year), *Memoirs* (irregular), *Palaeontologia Cathayana, Palaeontologia Sinica* (irregular), *Palaeontological Abstracts* (4 a year), *Palaeoworld* (irregular).

Research Centre for Environmental Sciences: POB 2871, 18 Shuangqing Rd, Haidian, Beijing 100085; tel. and fax (10) 62923549; e-mail zhb@rcees.ac.cn; internet www.rcees.ac.cn; f. 1975; attached to Chinese Acad. of Sciences; 358 mems; library of 20,000 vols; Dir Dr QU JIUHUI; publs *Acta Ecologica Sinica* (24 a year), *Acta Scientiae Circumstantiae* (12 a year, with English abstracts), *Asian Journal of Ecotoxicology* (6 a year), *Chinese Journal of Environmental Engineering* (12 a year), *Huanjing Huaxue* (Environmental Chemistry, 12 a year), *Huanjing Kexue* (Environmental Sciences, 12 a year), *Journal of Environmental Sciences* (12 a year).

Shanghai Institute of Biochemistry: Chinese Academy of Sciences, 320 Yue-Yang Rd, Shanghai 200031; tel. (21) 64374430; fax (21) 64338357; attached to Chinese Acad. of Sciences; Dir Prof. LI BOLIANG.

Shanghai Institute of Cell Biology: 320 Yue-Yang Rd, Shanghai; tel. (21) 64315030; fax (21) 64331090; e-mail jhc@sunm.shcnc.ac .cn; f. 1950; attached to Chinese Acad. of Sciences; Dir Dr GUO LI-HE; publs *Acta Biologiae Experimentalis Sinica, Cell Research, Chinese Journal of Cell Biology.*

Shanghai Institute of Entomology: 225 Chongqing S. Rd, Shanghai 200025; tel. (21) 3282039; f. 1959; attached to Chinese Acad. of Sciences; Dir CHEN YUANGUANG.

Shanghai Institute of Physiology: 320 Yue-Yang Rd, Shanghai; tel. (21) 64370080; fax (21) 64332445; e-mail sls@fudan.ac.cn; f. 1944; attached to Chinese Acad. of Sciences; library of 150,000 vols; Dir XIONG-LI YANG; publ. *Acta Physiologica Sinica* (in Chinese with English abstract, every 2 months).

Shanghai Institute of Plant Physiology: 300 Fongling Rd, Shanghai 200032; tel. (21) 64042090; fax (21) 64042385; f. 1944; attached to Chinese Acad. of Sciences; library of 150,000 vols; Dir Prof. Z. C. TANG.

South China Botanical Garden: Wushan, Guangzhou 510650, Guangdong Province; tel. (20) 37252531; fax (20) 37252711; e-mail sbg@scbg.ac.cn; internet english.scib.cas.cn; f. 1929; attached to Chinese Acad. of Sciences; global change, ecosystem service, environmental degradation, ecological restoration, plant systematic and evolutionary biology, biodiversity, conservation and sustainable utilization, agriculture, food quality and safety, phytochemical resources, sustainable use of plant gene engineering; library of 35,000 vols, 54,000 journals; Dir Dr HONGWEN HUNAG; publ. *Journal of Tropical and Sub-tropical Botany* (24 a year).

Xishuangbanna Tropical Botanical Garden: Menglun, Mengla County 666303,Yunnan Province; tel. (691) 905; f. 1959; attached

to Chinese Acad. of Sciences; library of 50,000 vols; Dir Prof. XU ZAIFU; publs *Collected Research Papers on Tropical Botany* (1 a year), *Tropical Plants Research* (4 a year).

Mathematical Sciences

Institute of Applied Mathematics: Academia Sinica, Box 2734, Beijing 100080; tel. (10) 62562939; fax (10) 62541689; f. 1979; attached to Chinese Acad. of Sciences; Dir ZHANG XIANGSUN.

Institute of Mathematics: Zhongguancun, Beijing 100080; attached to Chinese Acad. of Sciences; Dir YANG LE.

Physical Sciences

562 Comprehensive Geological Brigade: Yanqiaozhen 101601, Sanhe County, Hebei Province; attached to Chinese Acad. of Geological Sciences.

Beijing Observatory: Zhongguancun, Beijing 100080; attached to Chinese Acad. of Sciences; Dir WANG SHOUGUAN.

Changchun Institute of Applied Chemistry: 109 Stalin St, Changchun, Jilin Province; tel. (431) 5682801; fax (431) 5685653; f. 1948; attached to Chinese Acad. of Sciences; library of 120,000 vols; Dir Prof. WANG ERKANG; publs *Analysis Chemistry* (12 a year), *Applied Chemistry* (6 a year).

Changchun Institute of Physics: 1 Yan An Rd, Changchun 130021, Jilin Province; tel. (431) 5952215; fax (431) 5955378; f. 1958; attached to Chinese Acad. of Sciences; luminescence and its application, integrated optics; library of 69,800 vols; Dir JIN YIXIN; publs *Chinese Journal of Liquid Crystal and Displays* (4 a year), *Chinese Journal of Luminescence* (4 a year).

Chengdu Institute of Geology and Mineral Resources: 101 Renmin N. Rd, Chengdu 610082, Sichuan Province; attached to Chinese Acad. of Geological Sciences.

Chinese Institute of Atomic Energy: POB 275, Beijing; tel. (10) 69357487; fax (10) 69357008; f. 1958; attached to Chinese Acad. of Sciences; Dir Prof. SUN ZUXUN; publs *Atomic Energy Science and Technology* (6 a year), *Chinese Journal of Nuclear Physics* (4 a year), *Isotopes* (4 a year), *Journal of Nuclear and Radiochemistry* (4 a year).

Cold and Arid Regions Environmental and Engineering Research Institute: 260 Donggang Rd W., Lanzhou 730000, Gansu Province; tel. (931) 8818203; fax (931) 8885241; e-mail dyj@ns.lzb.ac.cn; f. 1965; attached to Chinese Acad. of Sciences; library of 546,246 vols, 23,968 periodicals; Dir Prof. CHENG GUODONG; publs *Journal of Glaciology and Geocryology* (in Chinese, 4 a year), *Plateau Meteorology* (in Chinese, 4 a year), *Journal of Desert Research* (in Chinese, 4 a year).

Commission for the Integrated Survey of Natural Resources: POB 9717, Beijing 100101; tel. (10) 64889797; fax (10) 64914230; f. 1956; attached to Chinese Acad. of Sciences; co-ordinates the integrated survey teams for the exploitation, utilization, conservation and evaluation of natural resources; multi-disciplinary research; library of 40,096 vols; Dir Prof. CHENG SHENGKUI; publs *Journal of Natural Resources* (with English abstracts, 4 a year), *Resources Science* (6 a year).

Dalian Institute of Chemical Physics: 161 Zhongshan Rd, Dalian; tel. (411) 3631841; fax (411) 363426; f. 1949; attached to Chinese Acad. of Sciences; library of 70,000 vols; Dir YUAN QUAN; publs *Chinese Journal of Chromatography* (6 a year), *Journal of Catalysis* (4 a year).

Guangzhou Institute of Chemistry: Academia Sinica, Guangzhou 510650; tel. (20) 85231815; fax (20) 85231119; e-mail cyha@gic.ac.cn; internet www.gic.ac.cn; f. 1958; attached to Chinese Acad. of Sciences; 270 mems; library of 80,000 vols; Dir CHENGYONG HA; publs *Guangzhou Chemistry* (4 a year), *Journal of Cellulose Science and Technology* (4 a year).

Institute for the Application of Remote Sensing Information: Changsha 410114, Hunan Province; attached to Chinese Acad. of Geological Sciences.

Institute of Acoustics: 17 Zhongguancun St, Beijing 100080; tel. (10) 62553765; fax (10) 62553898; e-mail lig@mail.ioa.ac.cn; internet www.ioa.ac.cn; f. 1964; attached to Chinese Acad. of Sciences; Dir LI QIHU.

Institute of Atmospheric Physics: Qijiahezi, Beijing 100029; tel. (10) 64919693; fax (10) 62028604; f. 1928; attached to Chinese Acad. of Sciences; library of 55,000 vols and periodicals; Dir Prof. ZENG QINGCUN; publs *Advances in Atmospheric Sciences* (4 a year), *Chinese Journal of Atmospheric Sciences* (4 a year), *Collected Papers of the Institute of Atmospheric Physics* (in Chinese), *Scientia Atmospherica Sinica* (in Chinese).

Institute of Atmospheric Sounding: 7 Block 11, Hepingli, Beijing; attached to Chinese Acad. of Meteorological Sciences.

Institute of Chemistry: Zhongguancun, Haidian District, Beijing; tel. (10) 282281; fax (10) 62569564; f. 1956; attached to Chinese Acad. of Sciences; library of 100,000 vols; Dir Prof. HU YADONG.

Institute of Climatology: 7 Block 11, Hepingli, Beijing; attached to Chinese Acad. of Meteorological Sciences.

Institute of Geochemistry: Chinese Academy of Sciences, 73 Guanshui Rd, Guiyang 550002, Guizhou; tel. (851) 5895095; fax (851) 5895574; f. 1966; attached to Chinese Acad. of Sciences; library of 150,000 vols; Dir LIU CONGQIANG; publs *Acta Mineralogica Sinica* (4 a year), *Bulletin of Mineralogy, Petrology and Geochemistry* (4 a year), *Chinese Journal of Geochemistry* (4 a year, in English), *Geology-Geochemistry* (4 a year).

Institute of Geology: 26 Baiwanzhuang Rd, Beijing 100037; attached to Chinese Acad. of Geological Sciences.

Institute of Geomechanics: Fahuasi, Beijing 100081; tel. (10) 68412303; fax (10) 68422326; f. 1956; attached to Chinese Acad. of Geological Sciences; Pres. Prof. WU GANGUO; publ. *Journal of Geomechanics* (4 a year).

Institute of Geophysics: A-11 Datun Rd, Chao Yang District, Beijing 100101; tel. (10) 64871497; attached to Chinese Acad. of Sciences; Dir ZHENG TIANYU.

Institute of Geotectonics: Academia Sinica, Changsha 410013, Hunan Province; tel. (731) 8859150; fax (731) 8859137; internet www.csig.ac.cn; f. 1961; attached to Chinese Acad. of Sciences; library of 36,000 vols; Dir CHEN GUODA; publ. *Geotectonica et Metallogenia* (4 a year).

Institute of High Energy Physics: POB 918, Beijing 100039; tel. (10) 68219643; fax (10) 68213374; e-mail mail@ihep.ac.cn; internet www.ihep.ac.cn; f. 1973; attached to Chinese Acad. of Sciences; Dir Prof. CHEN HESHENG; publs *High Energy Physics and Nuclear Physics* (12 a year), *Modern Physics* (6 a year).

Institute of Karst Geology: 40 Seven Stars Rd, Guilin 541104, Guangxi Autonomous Region; attached to Chinese Acad. of Geological Sciences.

Institute of Mesoscale Meteorology: 7 Block 11, Hepingli, Beijing; attached to Chinese Acad. of Meteorological Sciences.

Institute of Metal Research: Academia Sinica, 72 Wenhua Rd, Shenyang 110015; tel. (24) 3843531; fax (24) 3891320; f. 1953; attached to Chinese Acad. of Sciences; library of 85,000 vols, 2,300 periodicals; publs *Acta Metallurgica Sinica* (12 a year), *Journal of Materials Science and Technology* (6 a year), *Materials Science Progress* (6 a year).

Institute of Mineral Deposits: 26 Baiwanzhuang Rd, Beijing 100037; attached to Chinese Acad. of Geological Sciences.

Institute of Photographic Chemistry: Academia Sinica, Bei Sha Tan, Beijing 100101; tel. (10) 62017061; fax (10) 62029375; f. 1975; attached to Chinese Acad. of Sciences; library of 32,000 vols; Dir CHEN-HO TUNG; publ. *Photographic Science and Photochemistry*.

Institute of Physics: Zhongguancun, Haidian District, Beijing 100080; fax (10) 282271; attached to Chinese Acad. of Sciences; Dir YANG GUOZHEN.

Institute of Process Engineering: 1 Beiertiao, Zhongguancun, Beijing; fax (10) 62561822; internet www.ipe.ac.cn; f. 1958; attached to Chinese Acad. of Sciences; library of 171,500 vols; Dir Prof. JINGHAI LI; publs *Chinese Journal of Process Engineering* (6 a year), *Chinese Journal of Spectroscopy Laboratory* (6 a year), *Computer and Applied Chemistry* (6 a year).

Institute of Rock and Mineral Analysis: 26 Baiwanzhuang Rd, Beijing 100037; tel. (10) 68311550; fax (10) 68320365; f. 1978; attached to Chinese Acad. of Geological Sciences.

Institute of Space Physics: Zhongguancun, Beijing 100080; tel. (10) 288052; attached to Chinese Acad. of Sciences.

Institute of Synoptic and Dynamic Meteorology: 7 Block 11, Hepingli, Beijing; attached to Chinese Acad. of Meteorological Sciences.

Institute of the Corrosion and Protection of Metals: Academia Sinica, 62 Wencui Rd, Shenyang 110015; tel. (24) 3894313; fax (24) 3894149; f. 1982; attached to Chinese Acad. of Sciences; library of 7,000 vols, 500 journals; Dir Prof. WU WEITAO; publ. *Corrosion Science and Protection Technology* (4 a year).

Institute of Theoretical Physics: Academia Sinica, POB 2735, Beijing 100080; tel. (10) 62555058; fax (10) 62562587; f. 1978; attached to Chinese Acad. of Sciences; library of 10,000 vols; Dir OU-YANG ZHONG CAN; publ. *Communications in Theoretical Physics* (12 a year, in English).

Institute of Weather Modification: 7 Block 11, Hepingli, Beijing; attached to Chinese Acad. of Meteorological Sciences.

Lanzhou Institute of Physics: POB Lanzhou 94; attached to Chinese Acad. of Space Technology.

Nanjing Institute of Geology and Mineral Resources: 534 Zhongshan E. Rd, Nanjing 210016, Jiangsu Province; tel. (25) 84600446; e-mail njcgs@cgs.gov.cn; internet www.nanjing.cgs.gov.cn; f. 1962; attached to Chinese Geological Survey; publ. *Resources Survey and Environment*.

Purple Mountain Observatory: 2 West Beijing Rd, Nanjing 210008, Jiangsu Province; tel. (25) 3300818; fax (25) 3300818; f. 1934; attached to Chinese Acad. of Sciences; library of 36,000 vols; Dir LIU BENQUI; publs *Acta Astronomica Sinica* (4 a year), *Publications of Purple Mountain Observatory*.

Shaanxi Astronomical Observatory: POB 18, Lintong, Xian; tel. (29) 3890326; fax (29) 3890196; f. 1966; attached to Chinese Acad. of Sciences; library of 3,500 vols; Dir Prof. LI ZHIGANG; publ. *Time and Frequency* (12 a year).

Shanghai Astronomical Observatory: 80 Nandan Rd, Shanghai 200030; tel. (21) 64384522; fax (21) 64384618; internet www.center.shao.ac.cn; f. 1872; attached to Chinese Acad. of Sciences; library of 80,000 vols; Dir Prof. ZHAO JUNLIANG; publs *Annals of Shanghai Observatory*, *Progress in Astronomy* (4 a year).

Shanghai Institute of Metallurgy: Chinese Academy of Sciences, 865 Changning Rd, Shanghai 200050; tel. (21) 2511070; fax (21) 2513510; f. 1928; attached to Chinese Acad. of Sciences; Dir ZOU SHICHANG.

Shanghai Institute of Nuclear Research: POB 800-204, Shanghai 201800; tel. (21) 59553998; fax (21) 59553021; f. 1959; attached to Chinese Acad. of Sciences; Dir Prof. YANG FUJIA; publs *Journal of Radiation Research and Radiation Processing* (4 a year), *Nuclear Science and Techniques* (4 a year), *Nuclear Technology* (12 a year, in Chinese).

Shanghai Institute of Organic Chemistry: 345 Fenglin Lu, Shanghai 200032; tel. (21) 64163300; fax (21) 64166128; internet www.sioc.ac.cn; f. 1950; attached to Chinese Acad. of Sciences; library of 300,000 vols; Dir Prof. JIANG BIAO; publs *Acta Chimica Sinica* (12 a year, in Chinese), *Chinese Journal of Chemistry* (12 a year, in English), *Organic Chemistry* (12 a year, in Chinese).

Shenyang Institute of Geology and Mineral Resources: Beiling Ave, Shenyang 110032, Liaoning Province; attached to Chinese Acad. of Geological Sciences.

Southwestern Institute of Physics: POB 15, Leshan, 614007 Sichuan; POB 432, Chengdu 610041, Sichuan Province; tel. (28) 2932304 (Chengdu); fax (28) 2932202 (Chengdu); e-mail wb@swip.ac.cn; f. 1965; attached to China Nat. Nuclear Corpn; controlled nuclear fusion and application of intermediate technology; library of 150,000 vols, 630 periodicals; Dir Prof. PAN CHUAN-HONG; publ. *Nuclear Fusion and Plasma Physics* (4 a year).

Tianjin Institute of Geology and Mineral Resources: 4 8th Rd, Dazhigu, Tianjin 300170; tel. (22) 24314386; fax (22) 24314292; f. 1962; attached to Chinese Acad. of Geological Sciences; Dir LU SONG-NIAN; publ. *Progress in Precambrian Research* (4 a year).

Xi'an Institute of Geology and Mineral Resources: 160 Eastern to Youyi Rd, Xian 710054, Shaanxi Province; attached to Chinese Acad. of Geological Sciences.

Yichang Institute of Geology and Mineral Resources: POB 502, Yichang 443003, Hubei Province; attached to Chinese Acad. of Geological Sciences.

Yunnan Observatory: POB 110, Kunming 650011; fax (871) 3911845; e-mail ynao@public.km.yn.cn; f. 1972; attached to Chinese Acad. of Sciences; library of 35,000 vols; Dir Prof. TAN HUISONG; publ. *Publications of Yunnan Observatory* (4 a year).

PHILOSOPHY AND PSYCHOLOGY

Institute of Psychology: POB 1603, Beijing 100101; tel. (10) 64919520; fax (10) 64872070; e-mail yangyf@psych.ac.cn; f. 1951; attached to Chinese Acad. of Sciences; library of 145,000 vols, 1,500 periodicals; Dir Dr YANG YUFANG; publs *Acta Psychologica Sinica* (4 a year), *Journal of Developments in Psychology* (4 a year).

Philosophy Institute: 5 Jianguomennei Ave, Beijing 100732; f. 1977; attached to Chinese Acad. of Social Sciences; Dir XING FONSI.

RELIGION, SOCIOLOGY AND ANTHROPOLOGY

Institute of Population and Labour Economics: 5 Jianguo Mennei Ave, Beijing 100732; tel. (10) 85195417; fax (10) 85195427; e-mail iple@cass.org.cn; internet iple.cass.cn; f. 1980; attached to Chinese Acad. of Social Sciences; 48 mems; library of 10,000 vols; Dir Prof. FANG CAI; publs *China Labour Economics* (4 a year), *Population Science of China* (6 a year).

Institute of World Religions: 5 Jianguo Mennei St, Beijing 100732; tel. (10) 65138523; f. 1964; attached to Chinese Acad. of Social Sciences; Dir Prof. WU YUNGUI; publs *Studies on World Religions* (4 a year), *World Religious Culture* (4 a year).

Nationalities Studies Institute: Baishiqiao, Beijing; attached to Chinese Acad. of Social Sciences; Dir ZHAONA SITU.

Sociology Institute: 5 Jianguomennei Ave, Beijing 100732; f. 1979; attached to Chinese Acad. of Social Sciences; Dir HE JIANZHANG.

TECHNOLOGY

Beijing Institute of Control Engineering: POB 729, Beijing 100080; attached to Chinese Acad. of Space Technology.

Beijing Institute of Spacecraft Systems Engineering: POB 9628, Beijing 100086; attached to Chinese Acad. of Space Technology.

Changchun Institute of Optics and Fine Mechanics: 112 Stalin St, Changchun, Jilin Province; tel. (431) 684692; fax (431) 682346; f. 1950; attached to Chinese Acad. of Sciences; Dir WANG JIAQI; publ. *Optics and Precision Engineering* (6 a year).

Chemical Processing and Forest Products Utilization Research Institute: Longpan Rd, Nanjing, Jiangsu Province; attached to Chinese Acad. of Forestry.

China Coal Research Institute: 5 Qingniangou Rd, Hepingli, Beijing 100013; tel. (10) 84262809; fax (10) 84261671; internet www.ccri.ac.cn; f. 1957; Dir Prof. Dr ZHANG YUZHUO; publs *Coal Science and Technology* (12 a year, in Chinese), *Journal of China Coal Society* (12 a year, in Chinese; 2 a year, in English).

China National Space Administration: POB 2940, Beijing; 8 Fucheng Rd, Haidian District, Beijing 100037; tel. (10) 68516733; fax (10) 68516732; internet www.cnsa.gov.cn; coordinates and implements national space policy and development of space science, technology and industry, and arranges bilateral technical and scientific programmes, incl. launch of space probes; Administrator LUAN ENJIE.

China State Bureau of Technical Supervision (CSBTS): POB 8010, Beijing; tel. (10) 62025835; fax (10) 62031010; f. 1988; research and devt for nat. standards and quality control; colln of nat. standards from 56 countries; Dir-Gen. ZHU YULI; publs *Standards Journal*, *Technical Supervision Journal*.

Institute of Automation: Zhong Guan Cun, Haidian District, Beijing; tel. (10) 62551397; fax (10) 62545229; f. 1956; attached to Chinese Acad. of Sciences; Dir HU FENGFENG; publs *Acta Automatica Sinica* (6 a year, in Chinese), *Chinese Journal of Automation* (4 a year, in English).

Institute of Coal Chemistry: POB 165, Taiyuan 030001, Shaanxi Province; tel. (351) 4041267; fax (351) 4041153; f. 1954; attached to Chinese Acad. of Sciences; Dir Prof. ZHONG BING; publ. *Journal of Fuel Chemistry and Technology* (4 a year).

Institute of Computer Technology: 6 Kexueyuan Nan Lu, Haidian District, Beijing 100080; tel. (10) 62565533; fax (10) 62567724; e-mail wgao@ict.ac.cn; internet www.ict.ac.cn; f. 1956; attached to Chinese Acad. of Sciences; Dir GAO WEN; publs *Computer Research and Development*, *Journal of Computer-aided Design and Graphics*, *Journal of Computer Science and Technology*.

Institute of Computer Technology: 24 Section 2, Sanhao St, Shenyang 110001, Liaoning Province; tel. (24) 7705360; fax (24) 7705319; attached to Chinese Acad. of Sciences; Dir CONG GUANGMIN.

Institute of Electronics: 17 Zhong Guan Cun Rd, POB 2702, Beijing 100080; tel. (10) 62554424; fax (10) 62567363; internet www .ie.ac.cn; f. 1956; attached to Chinese Acad. of Sciences; library of 35,000 vols; Dir Prof. YIN HEJUN; publs *Journal of Electronics and Information Technology* (12 a year, in Chinese), *Journal of Electronics (China)* (6 a year, in English).

Institute of Engineering Mechanics: 9 Xuefu Rd, Harbin 150080; tel. (451) 6662901; fax (451) 6664755; e-mail iem@public.hr.hl .cn; f. 1954; attached to China Seismological Bureau; earthquake and safety engineering; library of 110,000 vols; Dir QUIMIN FENG; publs *Earthquake Engineering and Engineering Vibration* (4 a year), *Journal of Natural Disasters* (4 a year), *World Information on Earthquake Engineering* (4 a year).

Institute of Engineering Thermophysics: 12B Zhongguancun Rd, Beijing; tel. (10) 62554126; f. 1980; attached to Chinese Acad. of Sciences; Dir CAI RUIXIAN; publ. *Journal of Engineering Thermodynamics* (4 a year).

Institute of Hydrogeology and Engineering Geology: Zhengding County 050303, Hebei Province; attached to Chinese Acad. of Geological Sciences.

Institute of Mechanics: 15 Zhongguancun Rd, Beijing 100080; attached to Chinese Acad. of Sciences; Dir ZHENG ZHEMIN.

Institute of Meteorological Instrument Calibration: 7 Block 11, Hepingli, Beijing; attached to Chinese Acad. of Meteorological Sciences.

Institute of Optics and Electronics: POB 350, Shuangliu, Chengdu, Sichuan Province; tel. and fax (28) 85100341; e-mail dangban@ ioe.ac.cn; internet www.ioe.cas.cn; f. 1970; attached to Chinese Acad. of Sciences; library of 90,000 vols; Dir Prof. ZHANG YUDONG; publ. *Opto-Electronics Engineering* (12 a year).

Institute of Semiconductors: POB 912, Beijing 100083; tel. (10) 288131; fax (10) 62562389; f. 1960; attached to Chinese Acad. of Sciences; Dir WANG QIMING.

Institute of Systems Science: 1A Nansi St, Zhongguancun, Beijing 100080; tel. (10) 62541830; fax (10) 62568364; internet www .iss.ac.cn; f. 1979; attached to Chinese Acad. of Sciences; Dir Prof. XIAO-SHAN GAO; publs *Journal of Systems Science and Complexity*, *Journal of Systems Science and Mathematics* (4 a year), *Journal of Systems Science and Systems Engineering* (6 a year).

Science and Technology Development Corporation: 26 Baiwanghuang Rd, Beijing 100037; attached to Chinese Acad. of Geological Sciences.

Shanghai Institute of Ceramics: 1295 Ding Xi Rd, Shanghai 200050; tel. (21) 62512990; fax (21) 62513903; e-mail siccas@ sunm.shcnc.ac.cn; internet www.sic.ac.cn; f. 1959; attached to Chinese Acad. of Sciences; library of 80,000 vols; Dir SHI ERWEI; publ. *Journal of Inorganic Materials* (6 a year).

Shanghai Institute of Optics and Fine Mechanics: POB 800-211, Shanghai, 201800; tel. (21) 69918000; fax (21) 69918800; internet www.siom.ac.cn; attached to Chinese Acad. of Sciences; laser science and technology; Dir Prof. ZHU JIANQING; publs *Acta Optica Sinica* (12 a year, in Chinese), *Chinese Journal of Lasers* (12 a year, in Chinese), *Chinese Optics Letters* (12 a year, in English).

Shanghai Institute of Technical Physics: 500 Yutian Rd, Shanghai 200083; tel. (21) 65420850; fax (21) 63248028; e-mail sitp@mail.sitp.ac.cn; internet www.sitp.ac .cn; f. 1958; attached to Chinese Acad. of Sciences; infrared technology and physics, optoelectronics and remote sensing; library of 40,000 vols; Dir WANG JIANYU; publ. *Chinese Journal of Infrared and Millimetre Waves* (6 a year).

Xian Institute of Optics and Precision Mechanics: Xian, Shaanxi Province; tel. (29) 5261376; fax (29) 5261473; f. 1962; attached to Chinese Acad. of Sciences; library of 120,000 vols; Dir Prof. ZHAO BAOCHANG; publ. *Acta Photinica Sinica* (6 a year).

Xian Institute of Space Radio Technology: POB 165, Xian 710000; tel. (29) 5290500; fax (29) 5290588; f. 1965; attached to Chinese Acad. of Space Technology.

Zhengzhou Institute of the Multi-Purpose Utilization of Mineral Resources: 26 Funu Rd, Zhengzhou 450006, Henan Province; tel. (371) 8984974; fax (371) 8984942; f. 1956; attached to Chinese Acad. of Geological Sciences; library of 200,000 vols; Dir Prof. Dr ZHANG KEREN; publ. *Conservation and Utilization of Mineral Resources* (6 a year).

Libraries and Archives

Baoding

Hebei University Library: 2 Hezuo Rd, Baoding, Hebei Province; tel. (312) 5022922 ext. 417; fax (312) 5022648; f. 1921; 1,960,000 vols, 3,923 current periodicals, 3,000 back copies; special collection: 4,397 vols of Chinese ancient books, incl. local chronicles and family trees; Dir LOU CHENGZHAO; publ. *Journal of Hebei University*.

Beijing

Beijing Normal University Library: Xinjiekouwai Dajie, Beijing 100875; tel. (10) 62208163; fax (10) 62200567; f. 1902; 2,700,000 vols, 14,436 periodicals; rich collection of thread-bound Chinese ancient books, incl. 1,500 titles of remarkable editions, 2,800 titles of local chronicles, 1,300 series; Dir YIU TIANCHI.

Capital Library: 15 Guozijian St, Dongcheng District, Beijing; tel. (10) 64040905; fax (10) 64040905; f. 1913; municipal library; 2,574,000 vols, 142,000 current periodicals; spec. collns incl. traditional opera, folk customs; Dir JIN PEILIN.

Central Archives of China: Wenquan, Haidian District, Beijing; tel. (10) 62556611; f. 1959; revolutionary historical archives from the May 4th Movement of 1919 to the founding of the People's Republic in 1949, and archives of CPC and central government offices; 8,000,000 files; Curator WANG GANG; publs *CPC Documents*, *Central Archives of China Series*, *Collection of PCC Documents*, etc.

Centre for Documentation and Information, Chinese Academy of Social Sci-

ences: 5 Jianguomennei Ave, Beijing 100732; tel. and fax (10) 65126393; e-mail kyc-tsg@cass.org.cn; internet www.lib.cass .org.cn; f. 1985; attached to Chinese Acad. of Social Sciences; administrates Chinese Society of Social Sciences Information; 2,400,000 vols; Dir YANG PEICHAO; publs *Social Sciences Abroad* (6 a year), *Diogenes* (in Chinese, 2 a year).

First Historical Archives of China: Palace Museum inside Xihuamen, Beijing 100031; tel. (10) 63096487; fax (10) 63096489; f. 1925; 10,000,000 files; historical archives of Ming and Qing Dynasties; Curator XING YONGFU; publ. *Historical Archives* (4 a year).

Institute of Medical Information: 3 Yabaolu, Chaoyang District, Beijing 100020; tel. (10) 65122340; fax (10) 85626057; e-mail qianq@imicams.ac.cn; internet www.library .imicams.ac.cn; f. 1958; attached to Chinese Acad. of Medical Sciences and Peking Union Medical Coll.; Dir Prof. DAI TAO.

Institute of Meteorological, Scientific and Technical Information: 7 Block 11, Hepingli, Beijing; attached to Chinese Acad. of Meteorological Sciences.

Institute of Scientific and Technical Information of China (ISTIC): 15 Fu Xing Lu, POB 3827, Beijing 100038; tel. (10) 68514020; fax (10) 68514025; f. 1956; 18,000,000 items from China and abroad, incl. research reports, conference proceedings, periodicals, patents, standards, catalogues and samples and audiovisual material; Dir-Gen. ZHU WEI; publs *Journal of Scientific and Technical Information*, *Review of World Inventions*, *Scientific and Technical Trends Abroad*.

Institute of Scientific and Technological Information on Forestry: Wan Shou Shan, Beijing 100091; tel. (10) 62889713; fax (10) 62882317; e-mail wcli@isti.forestry.ac.cn; internet www.lknet.forestry.ac.cn; f. 1964; attached to Chinese Acad. of Forestry; Deputy Director LI WEIDONG.

Library of the Chinese Academy of Sciences: 33 Beisihuanxilu, Zhongguancun, Beijing 100080; tel. (10) 82626684; fax (10) 82626600; e-mail office@mail.las.ac.cn; internet www.las.ac.cn; f. 1950; 5,200,000 vols, 8,636 current periodicals, 51,000 reports of conference proceedings; spec. collns incl. local chronicles, collected works of the Ming and Qing Dynasties, 40,000 rubbings from stone tablets, 600,000 rare books, 28 web-based databases, 38 CD-rom databases; Chief Deputy Dir ZHANG XIAOLIN; publs *Chinese Biotechnology* (12 a year), *Chinese Mathematical Abstracts* (6 a year), *Chinese Physical Abstracts* (6 a year), *High Technology and Industrialization* (12 a year), *Library and Information Service* (12 a year), *New Technology of Library and Information Service* (12 a year), *Progress in Chemistry* (6 a year), *R&D Information* (12 a year), *Science and Technology International* (12 a year).

Medical Library: 9 Dongdan Santiao, Beijing 100730; tel. (10) 65127733; attached to Chinese Acad. of Medical Sciences; Dir LU RUSHAN.

National Library of China: 33 Zhongguancun Nandajie, Haidian District, Beijing 100081; tel. (10) 88545023; fax (10) 68419271; e-mail interco@publicf.nlc.gov.cn; internet www.nlc.gov.cn; f. 1909; 22,000,000 vols, 21,000 current periodicals, 1,100,000 microforms and audiovisual items; spec. collns incl. 291,696 vols of rare books of imperial libraries in the Southern Song, Ming and Qing dynasties; all kinds of Chinese publs, incl. those in minority languages; foreign books, periodicals and news-

papers, UN publs and govt publs of certain countries; blockprinted editions, books of rubbings, and other antique items; Dir Prof. REN JIYU; publs *Documents* (4 a year), *Journal of the National Library of China* (4 a year), *National Bibliography*.

Peking University Library: Haidian District, Beijing 100871; tel. (10) 62751051; fax (10) 62761008; e-mail office@lib.pku.edu.cn; internet www.lib.pku.edu.cn; f. 1902; 5,736,401 books, 708,424 vols of bound periodicals, spec. colln: 1,600,000 vols of thread-bound Chinese ancient books, incl. 200,000 vols of rare books, 70,000 rubbings, copy of *Complete Works of Shakespeare* (publ. 1623), Dante's *Divine Comedy* (publ. 1896), and plays by Schiller, 529,446 vols of eBooks, 47,010 electronic journal titles, 466 databases.; Dir Prof. QIANG ZHU; publ. *Journal of Academic Libraries* (6 a year).

Renmin University of China Library: 175 Haidian Rd, Beijing; tel. 62511371; fax 62566374; f. 1937; 2,500,000 vols, 2,400 current periodical titles, 400,000 back copies; publs on philosophy, politics, law, economics, etc.; rich collection of philosophy of Marxism, law, economics, modern and contemporary history of China; special collection: Chinese revolutionary documents in liberated and base areas, ancient rare books of Song, Yuan, Ming and Qing Dynasties (2,400 titles); 154 staff; Dir Prof. YANG DONGLIANG; publs *Index to the Complete Works of Marx and Engels*, *Classification of the Renmin University of China Library*, *Index to the ancient rare books of RUC Library*.

Tsinghua University Library: Qinghuayuan, West Suburb, Beijing 100084; tel. (10) 62782137; fax (10) 62781758; e-mail tsg@mail.lib.tsinghua.edu.cn; internet www .lib.tsinghua.edu.cn; f. 1911; 2,500,000 vols, 15,495 periodicals (foreign 5,902); spec. collns: Chinese ancient books 30,000 titles (300,000 vols), including rare editions, only existing copies and handcopies, 3,000 titles (30,000 vols); collns of acad. books and periodicals, conference literature, engineering historical data, local chronicles, collected papers on spec. subjects, major abstract journals, complete set of nearly 200 foreign periodicals; Dir XUE FANGYU; publs *Science Report*, *Tsinghua Journal* (Natural Sciences and Social Sciences edns), *Tsinghua University Selections of Scientific Theses*.

Changchun

Jilin Provincial Library: 10 Xinmin Ave, Changchun, Jilin Province; tel. (431) 5643796; f. 1958; 2,700,000 vols; Dir JIN ENHUI; publ. *Research in Library Science* (6 a year).

Jilin University Library: 117 Jiefang Rd, Changchun 130023, Jilin Province; tel. (431) 8923189; f. 1946; 2,154,000 vols, 3,078 current periodicals, 299,808 back copies; spec. colln: local chronicles, clan trees, Asian Series, documents of Manchurian railways; Dir Prof. WANG TONGCHE.

Northeast Normal University Library: 138 Renmin St, Changchun, Jilin Province; tel. (431) 5684174; f. 1946; 2,300,000 vols, 4,000 current periodicals, 11,600 back copies; publs from time of the War of Resistance Against Japan, rare Chinese ancient books; Dir SUN ZHONGTIAN; publ. *Jilin Libraries of Colleges and Universities* (4 a year).

Changsha

Hunan Provincial Library: 38 Shaoshan Rd, Changsha, Hunan Province; tel. (731) 25653; f. 1904; 3,090,000 vols, 130,000 bound vols of periodicals, 900,000 ancient books.

Chengdu

Sichuan Provincial Library: 6 Lu Zongfu, Chengdu 610016, Sichuan Province; tel. (28) 6659219; f. 1940; 3,760,000 vols, 13,485 periodicals, historical material; Dir WANG ENLAI (acting); publ. *Librarian* (6 a year).

Chongqing

Chongqing Library: 1 Changjiang Rd A, Chongqing, Sichuan Province; tel. (23) 54832; f. 1947; 3,137,198 vols, 690,183 bound periodicals, 65,514 technical reports, 35,000 antique books, historical documents, UN publs; Dir LI PUJIE.

Dalian

Dalian City Library: 7 Changbai, Xigang District, Dalian, Liaoning Province; tel. (411) 3630033; fax (411) 3623796; f. 1907; 2,000,000 vols, 5,502 periodicals; 700 ancient books; Dir LIU ZHENWEI.

Fuzhou

Fujian Provincial Library: 37 Dongfanghong Dajie St, Fuzhou, Fujian Province; tel. (794) 31604; f. 1913; 2,200,000 vols, 4,350 current periodicals, historical material; spec. collns incl. data on Taiwan and Southeast Asia.

Guangzhou

South China Teachers' University Library: Shipai, Tianhe District, Guangzhou, Guangdong Province; tel. (20) 774911; 1,600,000 vols, over 3,000 current periodicals, 7,145 back copies; spec. colln: 180,000 vols of Chinese ancient books, incl. 1,025 titles of local chronicles; 106 staff; Deputy Dir YANG WEIPING.

Zhongshan Library of Guangdong Province: 211 Wenming Rd, Guangzhou, Guangdong Province; tel. (20) 330676; f. 1912; 3,300,000 vols, 6,000 current periodicals, historical documents; spec. collns incl. research materials on Dr Sun Yat-sen; Dir HUANG JUNGUI; publs *Journal of Guangdong Libraries* (4 a year), *Library Tribune* (4 a year).

Guilin

Guilin Library of Guangxi Zhuang Autonomous Region: 15 North Ronghu Rd, Guilin, Guangxi Zhuang Autonomous Region; tel. (773) 223494; f. 1909; 1,380,000 vols, 15,275 current periodicals, historical material; Deputy Dir YANG JIANHONG; publs *Catalogue of Guangxi Local Documents*, *Catalogue of Materials on Guangxi Minority Study* (vols 1–2).

Guiyang

Guizhou Provincial Library: 31 Beijing Rd, Guiyang, Guizhou Province; tel. (851) 25562; f. 1937; 1,270,000 vols, 5,000 periodicals, historical material; publs *Chronological Table of the Historical Calamities of Guizhou Province*, *Collected Papers on the Mineral Products of Guizhou Province*, *Journal* (4 a year).

Hangzhou

Zhejiang Provincial Library: 38 Shuguang Rd, Hangzhou 310007, Zhejiang Province; tel. (571) 87999812; fax (571) 87995860; e-mail bgs@zjlib.net.cn; internet www.zjlib .net.cn; f. 1900; 4,210,000 vols, 7,526 current periodicals; Chief Officer CHENG XIAOLIAN; publ. *Library Science Research and Work* (4 a year).

Hankou

Wuhan Library: 86 Nanjing Rd, Hankou, Hubei Province; tel. (27) 24334; f. 1953; 1,400,000 vols, 2,018 periodicals, 200,000 ancient books, historial material.

Harbin

Heilongjiang Provincial Library: No 218 Changjiang Rd, Nangang Dist., Harbin 150090, Heilongjiang Province; tel. (451) 85990586; fax (451)-85990587; e-mail hljstsg@sina.com; f. 1958; 2,928,193 vols, 2,371,484 books; 133,693 ancient books; 6,602 rare books; 438,675 newspapers and periodicals; 35,866 audiovisual documents and microcopies; 82,168 other documents; spec. collns incl. Russian publs, 1920s–1940s Japanese publs; Dir GAO WENHUA; publ. *Library Development* (12 a year).

Hefei

Anhui Provincial Library: 38 Wuhu Rd, Hefei, Anhui Province; tel. (551) 257602; f. 1913; 2,108,608 vols, 5,400 current periodicals, 30,000 antique books, historical documents; Dir WANG BAO SHENG; publs *Bulletin of Anhui Libraries* (4 a year), *Library Work* (4 a year).

Huhhot

Nei Monggol Autonomous Region Library (Inner Mongolia Autonomous Region Library): People's Park, Huhhot 010020, Nei Monggol Autonomous Region; tel. (471) 27948; f. 1950; 1,260,000 vols, 2,131 current periodicals; spec. collns incl. Mongolia; Dir ZHANG XIANGTANG; publ. *Nei Monggol Library Work* (4 a year, in Mongolian and Chinese).

Jinan

Shandong Provincial Library: 275 Daminhu Rd, Jinan, Shandong Province; tel. (531) 612338; f. 1908; 3,500,000 vols, 3,500 periodicals, ancient books, historical documents.

Shandong University Library: Jinan, Shandong Province; tel. (531) 803861; f. 1901; 2,000,000 vols, 3,000 current periodicals, 260,000 back copies; 77% of holdings are on liberal arts; special collection: rare books, rubbings from stone inscriptions, calligraphy and paintings, revolutionary documents; 118 staff; Dir Prof. XU WEN-TIAN.

Kunming

Yunnan Provincial Library: 2 South Cuihu Rd, Kunming, Yunnan Province; tel. (871) 5298; f. 1950; 2,150,000 vols, 7,172 periodicals, historical material.

Lanzhou

Gansu Provincial Library: 250 Binghedong Rd, Lanzhou, Gansu Province; tel. (931) 28982; f. 1916; 2,400,000 vols, historical material; spec. collns incl. Imperial Library of Qianlong; Dir PAN YINSHENG; publ. *Library and Information* (4 a year).

Nanchang

Jiangxi Provincial Library: 160 North Hongdu Rd, Nanchang, Jiangxi Province; tel. (791) 8517065; f. 1920; 2,200,000 vols, 6,600 periodicals, historical material; publ. *Journal of the Jiangxi Society of Library Science* (4 a year).

Nanjing

Nanjing Library: 66 Chengxian St, Nanjing, Jiangsu Province; tel. (25) 57717619; fax (25) 83372163; e-mail ntbgs@sina.com; internet www.jslib.com.cn; f. 1907; 7,790,000 vols, 8,000 current periodicals, 1,700,000 ancient books; Exec. Dir MA NING; publ. *New Century Library* (6 a year).

Nanjing University Library: 22 Hankou Rd, Nanjing 210093, Jiangsu Province; tel. (25) 3592943; fax (25) 3592943; internet lib .nju.edu.cn; f. 1902; 3,560,000 vols, 5,000 current periodicals, 566,400 bound vols of periodicals; systematic colln of literature,

history, philosophy, economics, law, mathematics, physics, chemistry, astronomy, geology, geography, meteorology, environmental science, computer science, biology and medicine, in Chinese and foreign languages; fairly complete colln of reference books from most countries, colln of major retrieval serials; spec. colln: 1,452 titles of rare books (Song, Yuan, Ming and Qing Dynasties), 10,000 sheets of rubbings from stone inscriptions, many paintings, MSS and handcopies, 4,600 titles (40,000 vols) of local chronicles, mainly of Jiangsu and Sichuan Provinces, also books on orientalism, bibliography and archaeology; Dir Prof. ZHANG YIBING; publ. *Journal of Serials Management and Research* (2 a year).

Second Historical Archives of China: 309 East Zhongshan Rd, Nanjing, Jiangsu Province; tel. (25) 4409996; f. 1951; archive material of the Republic of China (1912–49); 1,740,000 files, 246,000 periodicals; Curator XU HAO; publs *Collected Archives Series of the History of the Republic of China, Republican Archives* (4 a year).

Nanning

Guangxi Zhuang Autonomous Region Library: 61 Minzu Dadao, Nanning, Guangxi Zhuang Autonomous Region; tel. and fax (771) 5860297; e-mail gxlib@mail.nn .gx.cn; internet www.gxlib.org.cn; f. 1931; 2,050,000 vols, 4,575 current periodicals; Dir WANG XUEGUANG; publ. *Library World* (4 a year).

Shanghai

East China Normal University Library: 3663 North Zhongshan Rd, Shanghai; tel. (21) 62579196; f. 1951; 2,640,000 vols, 5,187 current periodicals, 237,000 back copies; notable collns on pedagogy, psychology, geography, classical philosophy, local histories and bibliography; the earliest edns of thread-bound Chinese ancient books are those of the Song Dynasty and of foreign books (publ. 1630); rubbings from stone inscriptions; Dir WANG XIJING; publ. *Library Information* (12 a year).

Fudan University Library: 220 Handan Rd, Shanghai 200433; tel. (21) 65643162; fax (21) 65649814; f. 1918; 3,500,000 vols, incl. remarkable editions of Chinese ancient books; special collections: 709 different editions of *The Books of Songs* and 3,000 titles of collected works of famous writers of Qing Dynasty; Dir Prof. QIN ZENG-FU.

Shanghai Library: Huaihai Rd, Shanghai; tel. (21) 3273176; fax (21) 3278493; f. 1952; 8,200,000 vols, 14,449 periodicals, 152,270 technical reports, early MSS, historical material, microforms, audio-visual material; Dir ZHU QING ZHO; publs *Catalog of Chinese Series* (1959), *Contents of Modern Chinese Journals, Catalog of Shanghai Library Collections of Local Histories, Catalog of Works and Translations by Guo Moruo, National Index of Newspapers and Periodicals*.

Shenyang

Liaoning Provincial Library: Shenyang, Liaoning Province; f. 1948; 1,923,366 vols, 13,307 periodicals.

Taiyuan

Shanxi Provincial Library: 1 Wenguan Lane, South Jiefang Rd, Taiyuan, Shanxi Province; f. 1918; 1,700,000 vols, 9,900 periodicals.

Tianjin

Nankai University Library: 94 Weijin Rd, Tianjin 300071; tel. (22) 23502410; fax (22) 23505633; e-mail tsg@nankai.edu.cn; internet www.lib.nankai.edu.cn; f. 1919;

3,145,805 vols, 3,349 current periodicals, 511,159 bound copies of periodicals; spec. colln: 2,000 titles of rare books, 4,000 titles of local chronicles, 10,000 reference books, complete set of 100 periodicals with back issues of more than 50 years, 5,946 audiovisual items, 1,689 multimedia CD-ROMs, 51 databases; Dir Prof. YAN SHIPING; publs *Catalog of Rare Books Held by Nankai University Library, Catalog of Thread-Bound Ancient Books Held by Nankai University Library*.

Tianjin Library: 12 Chengdedao Rd, Heping District, Tianjin; tel. (22) 315171; f. 1907; 2,800,000 vols, 3,900 current periodicals, 500,000 ancient books; Dir DONG CHANGXU; publ. *Library Work and Research* (4 a year).

Urumqi

Xinjiang Library: 11 South Xinhua Rd, Urumqi, Xinjiang Uygur Autonomous Region; f. 1946; 546,800 vols, 3,723 periodicals, historical documents; spec. collns incl. books in Xinjiang nationality languages.

Wuhan

Central China Teachers' University Library: Mt Guizishan, Wuhan, Hubei Province; tel. (27) 72631; f. 1951; 1,255,000 vols, 6,486 periodicals.

Hubei Provincial Library: 45 Wuluo Rd, Wuchang District, Wuhan 430060, Hubei Province; tel. (27) 871284; f. 1904; 2,605,000 vols, 930,000 vols of periodicals, 50,000 antique books; Dir XIONG JINSHAN; publ. *Library & Information Science Tribune* (4 a year).

Wuhan University Library: Mt Luojiashan, Wuhan, Hubei Province; tel. and fax (27) 7872290; e-mail jwshen@lib.whu.edu.cn; f. 1913; 2,900,000 vols, 6,000 current periodicals, 300,000 back copies; rich colln of works on basic theories, and newspapers and periodicals published before 1949; spec. colln: 180,000 vols of thread-bound local chronicles, over 500 titles of rare books of Yuan, Ming and Qing Dynasties; 141 staff; Dir SHEN JIWU.

Xiamen

Xiamen University Libraries: 422 Siming Nan Rd, Xiamen, Fujian Province; tel. (592) 2186127; fax (592) 2182360; e-mail dehong@ xmu.edu.cn; internet library.xmu.edu.cn; f. 1921; publs on natural and social sciences, esp. economics, biology, chemistry, and data on Southeast Asia and Taiwan; 3,950,000 vols, 2,250,000 items of e-books and e-journals; Dean XIAO DEHONG.

Xian

Shaanxi Provincial Library: 146 Xi Ave, Xian, Shaanxi Province; f. 1909; 2,300,000 vols.

Shaanxi Teachers' University Library: Wujiafen, South Suburb, Xian 710062, Shaanxi Province; tel. (29) 711946, ext. 248; f. 1953; 1,884,487 vols, 2,628 current periodicals, 6,116 back copies; one of the largest univ. libraries of Northwest China; colln of publs on philosophy, social sciences, literature, linguistics and philology, natural sciences, and thread-bound remarkable editions of Chinese ancient books, local chronicles, 7,000 sheets of rubbings from bronze and stone tablets of the Zhou, Qing, Han and Tang Dynasties, el-hi textbooks and materials on pedagogy; 119 staff; Exec. Dir WANG KEJUN.

Xian Jiaotong University Library: Xianning Rd, Xian 710049, Shaanxi Province; tel. (29) 3268102; fax (29) 3237910; e-mail lib@ xjtu.edu.cn; f. 1896; 1,840,000 vols, 4,373 current periodicals, 9,000 back copies; systematic colln of scientific and technical publs, complete sets of 15 world-famous sci-tech periodicals having a history of over 100 years; 143 staff; Dir Prof. LI RENHOU.

Xining

Qinghai Provincial Library: 44 Jiefang Rd, Xining, Qinghai Province; f. 1935; 1,354,000 vols, 2,819 periodicals; publ. *Libraries in Qinghai* (4 a year).

Yinchuan

Ningxia Library: Tongxin Rd N, Yinchuan, Ningxia Hui Autonomous Region; f. 1958; 1,300,000 vols.

Zhengzhou

Henan Provincial Library: 150 Song Shan Nan Rd, Zhengzhou, Henan Province; tel. (371) 7972396; f. 1909; 2,360,000 vols, 4,419 current periodicals, 700,000 antique books, historical material; Dir TONG JIYONG; publ. *Journal of Henan Libraries* (4 a year).

Museums and Art Galleries

Beijing

Arthur M. Sackler Museum of Art and Archaeology: Peking University, School of Archaeology and Museology, Beijing 100871; tel. (10) 62751667; fax (10) 62751667; f. 1993; attached to Peking Univ.; Dir Prof. ZHAO HUI.

Beijing Lu Xun Museum: Ritiao, Gongmenkou, Beijing; Curator LI HELIN.

Beijing Museum of Natural History: 126 Tianqiao South St, Dongcheng Dist., Beijing; tel. (10) 67020641; fax (10) 67021254; e-mail office@bmnh.org.cn; internet www.bmnh.org.cn; f. 1951; specimen collns, scientific researches and scientific popularization in areas as paleontology, biology and anthropology; exhibitions about ancient life, animals, plants and human beings; temporary exhibitions; library of 50,000 vols; Dir MENG QINGJIN; publs *China Nature* (with English contents, jtly with the China Wildlife Conservation Asscn, the Chinese Asscn of Natural Science Museums and Beijing Natural History Museum), *Memoirs* (with English abstract).

China Art Gallery: 1 Wu Si St, East City District, Beijing; tel. (10) 64016234; f. 1958; traditional Chinese painting and sculpture; library of 13,700 vols; Dir LIU KAIQU.

Geological Museum of China: 15 Yangrouhutong, Xisi, Beijing 100034; tel. (10) 66557402; fax (10) 66557477; e-mail ngmc@public2.bta.net.cn; f. 1916; Dir CHENG LIWEI.

Military Museum of the Chinese People's Revolution: 9 Fuxing Rd, Beijing 100038; tel. (10) 68014441; f. 1958; Curator QIN XINGHAN; publ. *Military History* (6 a year).

National Museum of China: 16 East Chang'an Ave, Beijing 100006; tel. (10) 65118983; fax (10) 65118923; e-mail webmaster@chnmuseum.cn; internet www.chnmuseum.cn; f. 2003 by merger of National Museum of Chinese History (f. 1912) and National Museum of the Chinese Revolution (f. 1950); ancient Chinese historical artefacts and documents since prehistoric times; modern Chinese art and history since 1840; archaeology, history and art; Dir LU ZHANGSHEN; publs *Journal of National Museum of China, Modern China and Cultural Relics*.

Palace Museum: 4 Jingshan Qian Jie, Beijing 100009; tel. (10) 65132255; fax (10) 65123119; internet www.dpm.org.cn; f. 1925; paintings, ceramics, bronzes, jades, applied arts, calligraphy, carvings, coins, furniture, arms, decorative arts, musical instruments, clocks, seals, toys; library of 700,000 vols; Dir ZHENG XINMIAO; publs *Forbidden City* (6 a year), *Palace Museum Journal* (6 a year).

Quanzhou

Quanzhou Museum for Overseas Communications History: Quanzhou City, Fujian Province; tel. (595) 226655; f. 1959; Chinese foreign trade and China's int. relations in the fields of culture, science and religion; Curator WANG LIANMAO; publ. *Research into Overseas Communications History* (published jointly with the China Society of Research on Overseas Communications History, 2 a year).

Shanghai

Shanghai Museum: 201 Ren Min Da Dao, Shanghai 200003; tel. (21) 63723500; fax (21) 63728522; e-mail webmaster@shanghaimuseum.net; internet www.shanghaimuseum.net; f. 1952; library of 200,000 vols; Dir CHEN XIEJUN.

Universities and Colleges

ANHUI UNIVERSITY

3 Feixi Rd, Hefei 230039, Anhui Province
Telephone: (551) 5106114
Fax: (551) 5107999
Internet: www.ahu.edu.cn
Founded 1928
Academic year: September to July
Pres.: HUAN DEKUAN
Vice-Pres: WEI SUI, YI YOU MIN, LAN XI JIE, WU LIANG
Heads of Graduate Dept: ZHU SHI QUN, WANG XING HAI
Librarian: XU JUN DA
Number of teachers: 1,100
Number of students: 26,787
Publications: *Anhui University Law Review* (2 a year), *Hui Study* (1 a year), *Journal of Anhui University* (natural sciences, 6 a year), *Journal of Anhui University* (philosophy and social science, 6 a year)

DEANS

Business Administration: ZHOU YA NA
Chinese: TAO XIN MIN
Economics: RONG ZHAO ZI
Electrical Science and Technology: CHEN JUN NING
Foreign Studies: HUANG QING LONG
History: WU CHUN MEI
Law: LI MING FA
Life Science: LI JIN HUA
Management: XIE YANG QUN
Mathematics and Computing Science: JIANG WEI
Philosophy: LI XIA
Physics and Material Science: SHI SHOU HUA

PROFESSORS

BA, ZHAO LIN, Chinese
CAO, ZHUO LIANG, Physics and Material Science
CHEN, DAO GUI, Chinese
CHEN, GUI JING, Mathematics and Computing Science
CHEN, HUA YOU, Mathematics and Computing Science
CHEN, JUN NING, Electrical Science and Technology
CHEN, QIN, Life Science
CHEN, SHENG QING, Law
CHEN, ZHANG JIN, Physics and Material Science
CHENG, JING RONG, Physics and Material Science
DOU, REN SHENG, Physics and Material Science
DU, XIAN NENG, Mathematics and Computing Science
DU, PENG CHENG, Business Administration
FAN, YI ZHENG, Mathematics and Computing Science
FANG, BIN, Electrical Science and Technology
FANG, QING QING, Physics and Material Science
FANG, XIANG ZHENG, Physics and Material Science
FENG, YI MING, Economics
GAO, QING WEI, Electrical Science and Technology
GE, CHUANG LI, Electrical Science and Technology
GE, LI FENG, Electrical Science and Technology
GU, RONG BAO, Mathematics and Computing Science
GU, ZU DAO, Chinese
GUAN, XIN LIN, Business Administration
GUO, JIAN YOU, Physics and Material Science
HAN, JIA HUA, Physics and Material Science
HE, JIA QING, Life Science
HU, GUO GUANG, Physics and Material Science
HU, MAO LIN, Mathematics and Computing Science
HU, SHU HE, Mathematics and Computing Science
HU, YAN JUN, Electrical Science and Technology
HUANG, PEI, Life Science
JIA, HAI JI, Economics
JIANG, WEI, Mathematics and Computing Science
KE, DAO MING, Electrical Science and Technology
KONG, FAN CHAO, Mathematics and Computing Science
LI, CAI FU, Management
LI, JIN HUA, Life Science
LI, MING FA, Law
LI, SHOU SHEN, Economics
LI, XIA, Philosophy
LI, XIAO HUI, Electrical Science and Technology
LI, XIU SONG, History
LI, YU CHENG, Life Science
LIU, XIN FANG, History
LOU, PING, Physics and Material Science
LU, QIN YI, History
LU, RONG SHAN, Economics
LU, YING BIN, Economics
MA, REN JIE, Management
MA, XIU SHUI, Electrical Science and Technology
MING, JUN, Electrical Science and Technology
REN, KAI, Philosophy
RONG, ZHAO ZI, Economics
SHENG, YE SHOU, Life Science
SHENG, ZHAO XUAN, Mathematics and Computing Science
SHI, FU YUAN, Electrical Science and Technology
SHI, SHOU HUA, Physics and Material Science
SHI, XIANG QIAN, Philosophy
SUN, YI KAI, Philosophy
SUN, YU FA, Electrical Science and Technology
SUN, ZHAO QI, Physics and Material Science
TANG, HUA QUAN, Chinese
TANG, QI XUE, History
TAO, XIN MIN, Chinese
WANG, DA MING, Chinese
WANG, DAO MING, Economics
WANG, DAO QING, Chinese
WANG, HUI, Management
WANG, LIANG LONG, Mathematics and Computing Science
WANG, RONG, Law
WANG, XIN YI, History
WANG, YI PING, Life Science

WANG, YIN HAI, Physics and Material Science
WANG, YONG DE, Chinese
WANG, YU, Life Science
WEI, WEI, Economics
WEN, CHUN RU, Philosophy
WU, CHUN MEI, History
WU, JIA RONG, Chinese
XIAO, JIAN, Mathematics and Computing Science
XIAO, YA ZHONG, Life Science
XIE, YANG QUN, Management
XIONG, XIAO QI, Economics
XU, CHANG QING, Mathematics and Computing Science
XU, CHENG ZHI, Chinese
XU, JIAN HUA, Mathematics and Computing Science
XU, JUN DA, Philosophy
XU, ZAI GUO, Chinese
XU, ZHANG CHENG, Physics and Material Science
YAN, PENG FEI, Mathematics and Computing Science
YANG, FANG ZHI, Economics
YANG, SHANG JUN, Mathematics and Computing Science
YANG, XIAO LI, Chinese
YAO, XUE BIAO, Physics and Material Science
YE, LIU, Physics and Material Science
YI, YOU MIN, Physics and Material Science
YONG, XI QI, Mathematics and Computing Science
YU, BEN LI, Physics and Material Science
YUE, FANG SUI, Chinese
YUE, JIE XIAN, Philosophy
ZENG, FAN YIN, Economics
ZHA, XIANG DONG, Life Science
ZHANG, BU CHANG, Life Science
ZHANG, JIAN FENG, Economics
ZHANG, JIN XI, History
ZHANG, LU GAO, Chinese
ZHANG, NENG WEI, Philosophy
ZHANG, QI YOU, Chinese
ZHANG, ZI XIA, History
ZHENG, MING ZHEN, Philosophy
ZHOU, HUAI YU, History
ZHOU, LI ZHI, Life Science
ZHOU, NAN, Law
ZHOU, SHENG MING, Physics and Material Science
ZHOU, YA NA, Business Administration
ZHOU, ZHI YUAN, History
ZHOU, ZHONG ZE, Life Science
ZHU, SHI QUN, Philosophy
ZHU, XUE SHAN, Law
ZHU, ZONG YAN, Economics

BEIJING BROADCASTING UNIVERSITY

Ding Fu Zhuang St, Chao Yang District, Beijing 10024
Telephone: (10) 65779319
Fax: (10) 65779134
Internet: www.cuc.edu.cn

Founded 1954
Min. of Education control
Academic year: August to July

Pres.: LIU JI NAN

Number of teachers: 772
Number of students: 28,000

Publications: *Asia Media and Communication Studies* (1 a year), *Journal of Beijing Broadcasting University* (modern communication, 4 a year), *Journal of Beijing Broadcasting University* (natural science, 4 a year), *Media Studies* (irregular)

DEANS
Advertising Studies: HUANG SHENG MIN
Animation: LU SHENG ZHAN
Film and Television Arts: LI XING GUO
Information Engineering and Science: LI JIAN ZENG

International Communication: XU QIN YUAN
Journalism and Communication: DING JUN JIE
Literature: MIAO DI
Media Management: ZAN YAN QUAN
Presentation Art: LI XIAO HUA
Social Sciences: GAO HUI RAN
Television: GAO XIAO HONG

PROFESSORS
BI, GEN HUI, Film and Television Arts
CAI, CHAO SHI, Information Engineering
CAI, GUO FEN, International Communication
CAI, WEN MEI, Journalism and Communication
CAO, LU, Journalism and Communication
CAO, QING RUI, Film and Television Arts
CHEN, BIAN ZHI, International Communication
CHEN, JING SHENG, Broadcasting
CHEN, WEI XING, International Communication
CHEN, YUAN MENG, International Communication
DING, JUN JIE, Journalism and Communication
DONG, HUA MIAO, Film and Television Arts
DU, HAN FENG, Literature
FENG, SONG CHE, Social Sciences
FU, JUN QING, Journalism and Communication
GAO, FU AN, Film and Television Arts
GAO, FU AN, Media Management
GAO, XIAO HONG, Television
GUAN, LING, Film and Television Arts
GUO, ZHEN ZHI, Television
HA, YAN QIU, Journalism and Communication
HE, LAN, International Communication
HE, SU LIU, Television
HE, XIAO BING, Film and Television Arts
HOU, MIN, Broadcasting
HUANG, JING HUA, Advertising Studies
HUANG, ZHI XUN, Information Engineering
HUO, WEN LI, Television
JIA, FOU, Animation
JIANG, XIU HUA, Information Engineering
JIN, GUI RONG, Film and Television Arts
KE, HUI XIN, Journalism and Communication
LEI, YUE JIE, Journalism and Communication
LI, DONG, Information Engineering
LI, JIAN ZENG, Information Engineering
LI, JIAN ZENG, Science
LI, SHENG LI, Film and Television Arts
LI, XING GUO, Film and Television Arts
LI, ZENG RUI, Information Engineering
LI, ZENG RUI, Science
LI, ZUO FENG, Literature
LIANG, MING, Film and Television Arts
LIANG, YI GAO, Journalism and Communication
LIANG, ZHENG LI, Media Management
LIN, ZHENG BAO, Information Engineering
LIU, JIAN BO, Information Engineering
LIU, JING LIN, Journalism and Communication
LIU, LI WEN, Literature
LIU, LI WEN, Film and Television Arts
LIU, SHU LIANG, Film and Television Arts
LIU, TING, Film and Television Arts
LIU, YE YUAN, Film and Television Arts
LU, GUI ZHEN, Information Engineering
LU, JIAN, Film and Television Arts
LU, SHENG ZHAN, Animation
LU, YING KUN, Film and Television Arts
LUO, LI, Broadcasting
MAO, ZHI JI, Information Engineering
MIAO, DI, Literature
NI, XUE LI, Film and Television Arts
PAN, YE, Film and Television Arts
PENG, HUI GUO, Animation
PU, ZHEN YUAN, Literature
QIN, YU MING, Television
REN, SU QIN, Social Sciences
REN, YUAN, Television

SHENG, QIN, Information Engineering
SHI, MIN YONG, Animation
SHI, XU SHENG, Film and Television Arts
SONG, PEI YI, Film and Television Arts
SONG, PEI YI, Media Management
WANG, CHUN ZHI, Information Engineering
WANG, HONG, Television
WANG, MING YA, Film and Television Arts
WANG, WEI, International Communication
WANG, WU LU, Journalism and Communication
WANG, XIAO HONG, Television
WANG, YA PING, Animation
WEI, YONG ZHENG, Social Sciences
WU, YIN, Television
WU, YU, Broadcasting
XING, XIN, Broadcasting
YANG, FENG JIAO, Television
YANG, LEI, Information Engineering
YANG, LU PING, Television
YANG, XIAO LU, Film and Television Arts
YAO, XIAO OU, Literature
YE, FENG YING, Television
YOU, FEI, Film and Television Arts
YUAN, QING FENG, Film and Television Arts
ZAN, YAN QUAN, Media Management
ZENG, XIANG MIN, Television
ZENG, ZHI HUA, Broadcasting
ZHANG, FEN ZHU, Film and Television Arts
ZHANG, GE DONG, Film and Television Arts
ZHANG, GUI ZHEN, International Communication
ZHANG, JING, Literature
ZHANG, JUN, Animation
ZHANG, QI, Information Engineering
ZHANG, SHU, Journalism and Communication
ZHANG, XIAO FENG, Social Sciences
ZHANG, YAN, Film and Television Arts
ZHANG, YAN, Journalism and Communication
ZHANG, YONG HUI, Information Engineering
ZHANG, YU HUA, Film and Television Arts
ZHAO, SHU PING, Television
ZHAO, XIAO GUANG, Literature
ZHAO, YU MING, Journalism and Communication
ZHONG, TAO, Literature
ZHONG, YI QIAN, Advertising Studies
ZHOU, HONG GUO, Media Management
ZHOU, HUA BIN, Film and Television Arts
ZHOU, JING BO, Film and Television Arts
ZHOU, YONG, Film and Television Arts
ZHOU, YUE LIANG, Film and Television Arts

BEIJING UNIVERSITY OF AERONAUTICS AND ASTRONAUTICS

37 Xueyuan Rd, Beijing 100083
Telephone: (10) 62017251
Fax: (10) 62028356
Internet: www.buaa.edu.cn

Founded 1952
Languages of instruction: Chinese, English
Academic year: September to August
Controlled by the aviation industries of China

Pres.: Prof. SHEN SHITUAN
Vice-Pres: Prof. DENG XUEYING, XU CONGWEI, FEI BINJUN, WU ZHE
Dir, Int. Academic Exchange: CUI DEYU
Librarian: Prof. JIN MAOZHONG

Library of 1,100,000 vols, 98,000 periodicals
Number of teachers: 2,300 (incl. research staff)
Number of students: 12,600 (2,000 postgraduate)

Publications: *Acta Aeronautica et Astronautica Sinica* (12 a year), *Acta Materiae Compositae Sinica* (4 a year), *Aerospace Knowledge* (12 a year), *China Aeronautical Education* (4 a year), *College English* (6 a year), *DADDM* (2 a year), *Journal* (4 a year), *Journal of Aerospace Power* (4 a year), *Journal of Engineering Graphics* (2 a year), *Model World* (4 a year)

DEPARTMENTAL DEANS

Automatic Control: Prof. LI XINGSHAN
Computer Sciences and Engineering: Prof. JIN MAOZHONG
Electronic Engineering: Prof. ZHANG XIAOLIN
Flying Vehicle Design and Applied Mechanics: Prof. WANG JINJUN
Foreign Languages: Prof. LI BAOKUN
Manufacturing Engineering: Prof. TANG XIAOQING
Materials Science and Engineering: Prof. XU HUIBIN
Mechanical and Electrical Engineering: Prof. YANG ZONGXU
Propulsion: Prof. LI QIHAN
Systems Engineering: Prof. YANG WEIMIN

PRINCIPALS

Flying College: Prof. WANG XIAOWAN (Exec. Dir)
Graduate School: Prof. DENG XUEYING
School of Astronautics: Prof. ZHANG ZHENPENG
School of Continuing Education: Prof. WANG BAORAI
School of Haidian Applied Technology: Prof. LIU TIANSHEN
School of Humanities and Social Sciences: Prof. SHENG SHUREN (Dean)
School of Management: Prof. JIANG XIESHENG
School of Science: Prof. GUAN KEYING (Dean)

BEIJING UNIVERSITY OF BUSINESS AND TECHNOLOGY

33 Fu-cheng Rd, Beijing 100037

Telephone: (10) 68904774
Fax: (10) 68417834
Founded 1950
Academic year: September to July
Pres.: Prof. SU ZHIPING
Vice-Pres: LI ZHONG, LIU XIUSHENG, LI DIANFU, WANG ZHONGDE, PAN BANGJIN, NI ZHIHENG
Librarian: GAO YUNZHI

Number of teachers: 700
Number of students: 14,000 (400 graduate)

Publications: *Commercial Economy Research* (12 a year), *Correspondence Department Report* (4 a year), *Journal* (6 a year).

BEIJING UNIVERSITY OF CHEMICAL TECHNOLOGY

15 Bei San Huan East Rd, Chao Yang District, Beijing 100029

Telephone: (10) 64434820
Fax: (10) 64423089
E-mail: office@buct.edu.cn
Internet: www.buct.edu.cn
Founded 1958
Academic year: September to July
Pres.: WANG ZI GAO
Vice-Pres: DING JU YUAN, WANG GUI, ZHAO SU ZHEN, ZUO YU
Head of Graduate Dept: FU ZHI FENG CO
Librarian: ZHANG YU CHUAN

Number of teachers: 1,800
Number of students: 16,900

Publications: *Journal of Beijing University of Chemical Technology* (natural sciences, 6 a year), *Journal of Beijing University of Chemical Technology* (social science, 4 a year)

DEANS

College of Chemical Engineering: ZHANG ZE YAN
College of Economics and Management: YAO FEI
College of Information Science and Technology: ZHAO HENG YONG
College of Life Sciences and Technology: TAN TIAN WEI

College of Literature and Law: FU YU LONG
College of Machine Electricity Engineering: WANG KUI SHENG
College of Materials Science and Engineering: YU DING SHENG
College of Science: JIANG GUANG FENG
Professional Technology Institute: XU XI TANG

PROFESSORS

CAO, LIU LIN, Information Science and Technology
CAO, ZHI QING, Machine Electricity Engineering
CHEN, BIAO HUA, Chemical Engineering
CHEN, CHANG SHU, Literature and Law
CHEN, JIAN FENG, Chemical Engineering
CHEN, XIAO CHUN, Chemical Engineering
CHEN, YAO QI, Literature and Law
CHEN, ZHONG LI, Literature and Law
CUI, WEI QI, Literature and Law
DANG, ZHI MIN, Materials Science and Engineering
DUAN, XUE, Science
FENG, LIAN XUN, Machine Electricity Engineering
GAO, ZHENG MING, Chemical Engineering
GENG, XIAO ZHEN, Machine Electricity Engineering
GUO, FEN, Chemical Engineering
GUO, KAI, Chemical Engineering
HAI, RE TI, Chemical Engineering
HE, JING, Science
HUA, YOU QING, Materials Science and Engineering
HUANG, LI, Materials Science and Engineering
HUANG, MIN LI, Materials Science and Engineering
HUANG, MING ZHI, Materials Science and Engineering
HUANG, XIONG BIN, Chemical Engineering
JI, SHENG FU, Chemical Engineering
JIANG, BO, Machine Electricity Engineering
JIN, RI GUANG, Materials Science and Engineering
LI, CHANG JIANG, Science
LI, CHUN XI, Chemical Engineering
LI, DIAN QING, Science
LI, HANG QUAN, Materials Science and Engineering
LI, HONG GUANG, Information Science and Technology
LI, QI FANG, Materials Science and Engineering
LI, QUN SHENG, Chemical Engineering
LI, WU SI, Economics and Management
LI, XIAO YU, Materials Science and Engineering
LI, XIU JIN, Chemical Engineering
LI, YUE CHENG, Chemical Engineering
LI, ZHI LIN, Materials Science and Engineering
LIU, FENG XIN, Information Science and Technology
LIU, HUI, Chemical Engineering
LIU, JIE, Materials Science and Engineering
LIU, KUN YUAN, Chemical Engineering
LIU, WEI, Chemical Engineering
MA, YUN YU, Life Sciences and Technology
MAO, BING QUAN, Science
MO, DE JU, Information Science and Technology
PAN, LI DENG, Information Science and Technology
PANG, YAN BIN, Information Science and Technology
QIAN, CAI FU, Machine Electricity Engineering
QIAO, JIN LIANG, Materials Science and Engineering
QU, YI XIN, Chemical Engineering
SHENG, WEI YONG, Literature and Law
SONG, HUAI HE, Materials Science and Engineering
SU, HAI JIA, Life Sciences and Technology

SUN, JUN, Economics and Management
TAN, TIAN WEI, Life Sciences and Technology
WANG, FANG, Life Sciences and Technology
WANG, JIAN HONG, Chemical Engineering
WANG, JIAN LIN, Information Science and Technology
WANG, KUI SHENG, Machine Electricity Engineering
WANG, MING MING, Economics and Management
WANG, WEN CHUAN, Chemical Engineering
WANG, XUE WEI, Information Science and Technology
WANG, ZI GAO, Chemical Engineering
WEI, GANG, Materials Science and Engineering
WEI, JIE, Materials Science and Engineering
WU, CHONG GUANG, Information Science and Technology
WU, DE ZHEN, Materials Science and Engineering
WU, GANG, Materials Science and Engineering
WU, XIANG ZHI, Chemical Engineering
WU, YI XIAN, Materials Science and Engineering
XIONG, RONG CHUN, Materials Science and Engineering
XU, CHUN CHUN, Materials Science and Engineering
XU, GUANG JUN, Economics and Management
XU, HONG, Machine Electricity Engineering
XU, PENG HUA, Machine Electricity Engineering
YANG, QI, Science
YANG, RU, Materials Science and Engineering
YANG, WANG TAI, Materials Science and Engineering
YANG, WEN SHENG, Science
YANG, YUAN YI, Science
YANG, ZU RONG, Chemical Engineering
YAO, FEI, Economics and Management
YIN, DENG XIANG, Literature and Law
YU, DING SHENG, Materials Science and Engineering
YUAN, DE YU, Literature and Law
YUAN, QI PENG, Life Sciences and Technology
ZHANG, JING CHANG, Science
ZHANG, LI QUN, Materials Science and Engineering
ZHANG, MEI LING, Machine Electricity Engineering
ZHANG, MING GUO, Literature and Law
ZHANG, PENG, Life Sciences and Technology
ZHANG, WEI DONG, Chemical Engineering
ZHANG, XING YING, Materials Science and Engineering
ZHANG, YING KUI, Economics and Management
ZHANG, YU CHUAN, Materials Science and Engineering
ZHANG, ZE YAN, Chemical Engineering
ZHAO, BAO YUAN, Economics and Management
ZHAO, HENG YONG, Information Science and Technology
ZHAO, SHU QING, Information Science and Technology
ZHAO, SU HE, Materials Science and Engineering
ZHEN, DAN XING, Chemical Engineering
ZHONG, CHONG LI, Chemical Engineering
ZHOU, HENG JIN, Materials Science and Engineering
ZHU, QUN XIONG, Information Science and Technology

BEIJING UNIVERSITY OF CHINESE MEDICINE

11 East Rd, Bei San Huan, Chao Yang District, Beijing 100029

Telephone: (10) 64213841
Fax: (10) 64213817

Internet: www.bjucmp.edu.cn
Founded 1956
Min. of Education control
Academic year: September to July
Pres.: ZHENG SHOU ZE
Vice-Pres: QIAO WANG ZHONG, WANG QING GUO, WEI TIAO MAO, XU XIAO
Heads of Graduate Dept: TU YA, WANG WEI
Librarian: ZHANG QI CHENG
Number of teachers: 2,705
Number of students: 9,925
Publications: *Chinese Medicine Education* (6 a year), *Journal of Beijing University of Chinese Medicine* (6 a year), *Journal of Beijing University of Chinese Medicine* (clinical studies, 4 a year)

DEANS

College of Acupuncture: GU SHI ZE
College of Basic Medicine: GUO XIA ZHEN
College of Chinese Traditional Medicine: LI JIA SHI
College of Nursing: ZHANG MEI
Network Education College: YU YONG JIE

PROFESSORS

BAI, LING MIN, Chinese and Western Medicine
CHEN, JIA XU, Chinese Medicine (Diagnostics)
CHEN, LI XIN, Chinese and Western Medicine
CHEN, MING, Basic Medicine
CHEN, SHU CHANG, Chinese Medicine (Surgery)
CHEN, XIN YI, Chinese and Western Medicine
FENG, QIAN JIN, Chinese and Western Medicine
FU, YAN LING, Basic Medicine
GAO, XUE MIN, Chinese Medicine (Clinical)
GAO, YAN BING, Chinese Medicine
GAO, YING, Chinese Medicine
GU, LI GANG, Chinese and Western Medicine
GU, SHI ZE, Acupuncture
GUO, WEI QIN, Chinese Medicine
GUO, XIA ZHEN, Basic Medicine
GUO, YA JIAN, Chinese Medicine (Traditional)
HAO, RUI FU, Chinese Medicine
HAO, WANG SHAN, Basic Medicine
HOU, JIA YU, Chinese Medicine (Traditional)
HU, LI SHENG, Chinese and Western Medicine
HUANG, QI FU, Chinese and Western Medicine
JI, SHAO LIANG, Chinese Medicine (Diagnostics)
JIANG, LI SHENG, Basic Medicine
JIANG, LIANG GUO, Chinese Medicine
JIN, GUANG LIANG, Basic Medicine
JIN, ZHE, Chinese and Western Medicine
LI, FENG, Chinese Medicine (Diagnostics)
LI, GUO ZHANG, Chinese and Western Medicine
LI, JIA SHI, Chinese Medicine (Traditional)
LI, JIN XIANG, Chinese Medicine
LI, NAI QING, Chinese and Western Medicine
LI, PENG TAO, Chinese and Western Medicine
LI, RI QING, Chinese Medicine (Surgery)
LI, SHI FAN, Basic Medicine
LI, XUE WU, Acupuncture
LI, YU HANG, Basic Medicine
LI, YUN GU, Chinese Medicine (Traditional)
LIANG, RONG, Chinese Medicine (Diagnostics)
LIN, QIAN, Chinese and Western Medicine
LIU, JIN MING, Chinese Medicine
LIU, TIAN JUN, Acupuncture
LIU, TONG HUA, Chinese Medicine
LIU, YAN CHI, Basic Medicine
LU, WEI XING, Chinese and Western Medicine
LU, YUN RU, Chinese Medicine (Traditional)
LU, ZHAO LIN, Basic Medicine
LV, REN HE, Chinese Medicine
MENG, QING GANG, Basic Medicine
NIU, JIAN ZHAO, Chinese and Western Medicine

NIU, XIN, Chinese and Western Medicine
QIAO, YAN JIANG, Chinese Medicine (Traditional)
QIU, QUAN YING, Chinese and Western Medicine
QU, SHUANG QING, Basic Medicine
REN, TIAN CHI, Chinese Medicine (Traditional)
SHI, REN BIN, Chinese Medicine (Traditional)
SONG, NAI GUANG, Basic Medicine
SU, JING, Basic Medicine
SUN, JIAN NING, Chinese Medicine (Traditional)
SUN, YING LI, Chinese and Western Medicine
TANG, QI SHENG, Chinese Medicine
TANG, YI PENG, Chinese and Western Medicine
TIAN, DE LU, Chinese Medicine
TIAN, JING ZHOU, Chinese Medicine
TU, YA, Acupuncture
WANG, HONG TU, Basic Medicine
WANG, JI FENG, Chinese and Western Medicine
WANG, QI, Basic Medicine
WANG, QING GUO, Basic Medicine
WANG, SHUO REN, Chinese and Western Medicine
WANG, TIAN FANG, Chinese Medicine (Diagnostics)
WANG, WEI, Chinese and Western Medicine
WANG, WEN QUAN, Chinese Medicine (Traditional)
WANG, XIN YUE, Chinese Medicine
WANG, YU LAI, Chinese Medicine
WEI, LU XUE, Chinese Medicine (Traditional)
WU, WEI PING, Chinese Medicine
XIAO, PEI GEN, Chinese Medicine (Traditional)
XU, LIN, Chinese and Western Medicine
XU, QIU PING, Chinese Medicine (Traditional)
YAN, JI LAN, Basic Medicine
YAN, JIAN HUA, Basic Medicine
YAN, YU NING, Chinese Medicine (Traditional)
YAN, ZHENG HUA, Chinese Medicine (Clinical)
YANG, JING HUA, Chinese Medicine
YANG, SHU PENG, Chinese Medicine (Traditional)
YE, YONG AN, Chinese Medicine
ZHANG, BING, Chinese Medicine (Clinical)
ZHANG, QI CHENG, Basic Medicine
ZHANG, YAN SHENG, Chinese Medicine (Surgery)
ZHANG, YUN LING, Chinese Medicine
ZHAO, JI PING, Acupuncture
ZHAO, JIN XIN, Chinese Medicine
ZHOU, PING AN, Chinese Medicine
ZHOU, YI HUAI, Chinese Medicine

BEIJING FILM ACADEMY

Xi Tu Cheng Lu 4, Haidian District, Beijing 100088
Telephone: (10) 62012132
Internet: www.bfa.edu.cn
Founded 1950
Pres.: SHEN SONGSHENG
Vice-Pres: XIE FEI, MENG HAIFENG
Deputy Librarians: CHEN WENJING, LU SHIPING
Library of 150,000 vols
Number of teachers: 273
Number of students: 286 (29 postgraduate)
Publication: *Journal*.

BEIJING FOREIGN STUDIES UNIVERSITY

2 North Xisanhuan Ave, Haidian District, Beijing 100089
Telephone: (10) 68916215
Fax: (10) 68423144
E-mail: bwxzb@bfsu.edu.cn
Internet: bfsu.edu.cn

Founded 1941
Academic year: September to July
Chancellor: Prof. CHEN NAIFANG
Vice-Chancellors: Prof. YANG XUEYI, Prof. Dr HE QIXIN, Prof. ZHONG MEISUN, Prof. ZHOU LIE
Library of 600,000 vols
Number of teachers: 700
Number of students: 10,000
Publications: *Foreign Language Teaching and Research*, *Foreign Literatures*, *International Forum*, *Soviet Art and Literature*.

BEIJING FORESTRY UNIVERSITY

Xiaozhuang, Haidian District, Beijing 100083
Telephone: (10) 62338279
Fax: (10) 62325071
Internet: www.bjfu.edu.cn
Founded 1952
Rector: Prof. HE QINGTANG
Registrar: Prof. ZHOU XINCHEN
Librarian: Prof. GAO RONGFU
Library of 560,000 vols
Number of teachers: 700
Number of students: 3,500

BEIJING JIAOTONG UNIVERSITY

Shang Yuan Cun, Xi Zhi Men Wai, Hai Ding District, Beijing 100044
Telephone: (10) 51688421
Fax: (10) 62245827
Internet: www.njtu.edu.cn
Founded 1921
Academic year: September to July
Pres.: TAN ZHEN HUI
Vice-Pres: CHEN FENG, LI XUE WEI, NING BIN, WANG JIA QIONG
Head of Graduate Department: WANG YONG SHENG
Librarian: SHA SHU LI
Number of teachers: 2,500
Number of students: 15,000
Publication: *Journal* (6 a year)

DEANS

School of Civil Engineering and Architecture: XU ZHAO YI
School of Computer and Information Technology: RUAN QIU QI
School of Economy and Management: WANG JIA QIONG
School of Electrical Engineering: ZHENG QIONG LIN
School of Electronics and Information Engineering: ZHANG SI DONG
School of Humanities and Social Science: GUO HAI YUN
School of Mechanical, Electronic and Control Engineering: SUN SHOU GUANG
School of Science: ZHANG PING ZHI
School of Traffic and Transportation: SUN QUAN XIN

PROFESSORS

BI, YING, Humanities and Social Science
CHANG, YAN XUN, Science
CHEN, CHANG JIA, Electronics and Information Engineering
CHEN, HOU JIN, Electronics and Information Engineering
CHEN, JING YAN, Economy and Management
CHEN, SHI RONG, Humanities and Social Science
CHEN, SHU MIN, Humanities and Social Science
CHEN, XI SHENG, Economy and Management
CHEN, YIN HANG, Electronics and Information Engineering
CHENG, ZHEN WEI, Science
DENG, ZHEN BO, Science

DING, HUI PING, Economy and Management
DONG, BAO TIAN, Traffic and Transportation
DU, YAN LIANG, Mechanical Engineering
FAN, YU, Electrical Engineering
FANG, YUE FA, Mechanical Engineering
FENG, QI BO, Science
FENG, YAN QUAN, Science
FENG, YU MIN, Electronics and Information Engineering
GAO, WEN, Humanities and Social Science
GAO, YU CHEN, Civil Engineering and Architecture
GAO, ZI YOU, Traffic and Transportation
GUAN, KE YING, Science
GUAN, ZHONG LIANG, Economy and Management
HAN, BAO MING, Traffic and Transportation
HAO, RONG TAI, Electrical Engineering
HE, QING FU, Mechanical Engineering
HE, SHI WEI, Traffic and Transportation
HOU, YAN BIN, Science
HOU, ZHONG SHENG, Electronics and Information Engineering
HU, SI JI, Traffic and Transportation
HUANG, LEI, Economy and Management
HUANG, MEI, Electrical Engineering
HUANG, SHI HUA, Science
JI, JIA LUN, Traffic and Transportation
JIA, LI, Mechanical Engineering
JIA, LI MIN, Traffic and Transportation
JIA, YUAN HUA, Traffic and Transportation
JIANG, JIU CHUN, Electrical Engineering
JIANG, ZHONG HAO, Science
JIN, XIN MIN, Electrical Engineering
JIN, ZONG ZE, Mechanical Engineering
JU, SONG DONG, Economy and Management
LI, CHENG SHU, Electronics and Information Engineering
LI, DE CAI, Mechanical Engineering
LI, PEI XUAN, Economy and Management
LI, QIANG, Mechanical Engineering
LI, SI ZE, Science
LI, WEN XING, Economy and Management
LI, XUE WEI, Economy and Management
LIN, BO LIANG, Traffic and Transportation
LIN, DAI DAI, Economy and Management
LIU, CHANG BIN, Economy and Management
LIU, JIAN KUN, Civil Engineering and Architecture
LIU, JUN, Traffic and Transportation
LIU, KAI, Traffic and Transportation
LIU, KUN HUI, Science
LIU, MING GUANG, Electrical Engineering
LIU, WEI NING, Civil Engineering and Architecture
LIU, YAN PEI, Science
LIU, YAN PING, Economy and Management
LIU, YI SHENG, Economy and Management
LIU, ZUO YI, Traffic and Transportation
LV, YONG BO, Traffic and Transportation
MA, JIAN JUN, Traffic and Transportation
MAO, BAO HUA, Traffic and Transportation
NIE, YU XIN, Science
NING, TI GANG, Electronics and Information Engineering
NU, YI HONG, Economy and Management
OU, GUO LI, Economy and Management
QIAO, CHUN SHENG, Civil Engineering and Architecture
QU, HONG XIANG, Mechanical
RONG, CHAO HE, Economy and Management
SHA, FEI, Electronics and Information Engineering
SHANG, PENG JIAN, Science
SHAO, CHUN FU, Traffic and Transportation
SHEN, JIN SHENG, Traffic and Transportation
SHENG, XIN ZHI, Science
SHI, DING HUAN, Traffic and Transportation
SHI, MEI XIA, Economy and Management
SHI, ZHI FEI, Civil Engineering and Architecture
SHI, ZHONG HENG, Civil Engineering and Architecture
SONG, SHOU XIN, Economy and Management
SUN, QUAN XIN, Traffic and Transportation
SUN, SHOU GUANG, Mechanical Engineering

TAN, ZHEN HUI, Electronics and Information Engineering
TANG, TAO, Electronics and Information Engineering
TANG, TAO, Electronics and Information Engineering
TANG, ZHEN MIN, Electronics and Information Engineering
WANG, JIA QIONG, Economy and Management
WANG, JUN HONG, Electronics and Information Engineering
WANG, LI DE, Electrical Engineering
WANG, LIAN JUN, Civil Engineering and Architecture
WANG, MENG SHU, Civil Engineering and Architecture
WANG, WEI, Electrical Engineering
WANG, XI SHI, Electronics and Information Engineering
WANG, YAN YONG, Traffic and Transportation
WANG, YAO QIU, Economy and Management
WANG, YI, Electrical Engineering
WANG, YONG SHENG, Science
WANG, YUAN FENG, Civil Engineering and Architecture
WANG, YUE SHENG, Civil Engineering and Architecture
WEI, QING CHAO, Civil Engineering and Architecture
WEI, XUE YE, Electronics and Information Engineering
WU, CHONG QING, Science
WU, LIU, Science
XIA, HE, Civil Engineering and Architecture
XIAO, GUI PING, Traffic and Transportation
XIE, JI LONG, Mechanical Engineering
XIN, SHU MING, Mechanical Engineering
XIU, NAI HUA, Science
XU, TAO BO, Economy and Management
XU, YU GONG, Mechanical Engineering
XU, ZHAO YI, Civil Engineering and Architecture
YAN, FENG PING, Electronics and Information Engineering
YAN, GUI PING, Civil Engineering and Architecture
YAN, HONG SEN, Mechanical Engineering
YANG, HAO, Traffic and Transportation
YANG, QIN SHAN, Civil Engineering and Architecture
YANG, QING XIN, Mechanical Engineering
YANG, SHAO PU, Mechanical Engineering
YANG, ZHAO XIA, Traffic and Transportation
YAO, BIN, Economy and Management
YAO, PEI JI, Economy and Management
YAO, QIAN FENG, Civil Engineering and Architecture
YE, SHU JUN, Economy and Management
YI, XIANG YONG, Traffic and Transportation
YU, LEI, Traffic and Transportation
YU, QING, Traffic and Transportation
YUAN, LU QU, Economy and Management
YUAN, ZHEN ZHOU, Traffic and Transportation
ZHA, JIAN ZHONG, Mechanical, Electronic and Control Engineering
ZHAN, HE SHENG, Economy and Management
ZHANG, CHAO, Traffic and Transportation
ZHANG, GUO WU, Traffic and Transportation
ZHANG, HONG KE, Electronics and Information Engineering
ZHANG, HONG RU, Civil Engineering and Architecture
ZHANG, LEI, Economy and Management
ZHANG, LI, Electrical Engineering
ZHANG, LIN CHANG, Electronics and Information Engineering
ZHANG, LU XIN, Civil Engineering and Architecture
ZHANG, MING YU, Economy and Management
ZHANG, QIU SHENG, Economy and Management
ZHANG, SI DONG, Electronics and Information Engineering
ZHANG, WEN JIE, Economy and Management
ZHANG, XI, Traffic and Transportation

ZHANG, XI QING, Science
ZHANG, XIAO DONG, Electrical Engineering
ZHANG, XIAO QING, Electrical Engineering
ZHANG, XING CHEN, Traffic and Transportation
ZHANG, YI HUANG, Electrical Engineering
ZHANG, YU XIN, Traffic and Transportation
ZHANG, YUN TONG, Economy and Management
ZHANG, ZHI WEN, Traffic and Transportation
ZHANG, ZHONG YI, Traffic and Transportation
ZHANG, ZI MAO, Civil Engineering and Architecture
ZHAO, CHENG GAN, Civil Engineering and Architecture
ZHAO, JIAN, Economy and Management
ZHENG, QIONG LIN, Electrical Engineering
ZHONG, YAN, Traffic and Transportation
ZHOU, LEI SHAN, Traffic and Transportation
ZHOU, XI DE, Electrical Engineering
ZHOU, YU HUI, Electrical Engineering
ZHU, HENG JUN, Mechanical Engineering
ZHU, HONG, Science
ZHU, JIA SHAN, Traffic and Transportation
ZHU, XI, Civil Engineering and Architecture
ZHU, XIAO NING, Traffic and Transportation

BEIJING LANGUAGE AND CULTURE UNIVERSITY

15 Xue Yuan Rd, Haidian Dist., Beijing 100083

Telephone: (10) 82303086
Fax: (10) 82303087
E-mail: zhaosh3@blcu.edu.cn
Internet: www.blcu.edu.cn

Founded 1962
State control
Languages of instruction: Arabic, Chinese, English, French, German, Italian, Japanese, Portuguese, Russian, Spanish, Korean
Academic year: September to July

Pres.: CUI XILIANG
Vice-Pres: HUO MINGJIE
Vice-Pres.: LIN GUOLI
Dir of Int. Students Dept: QU DE NING
Head of Graduate School: HUA ZHANG
Head of Library: KAI ZHANG

Library of 1,000,000 vols
Number of teachers: 760
Number of students: 12,000

Publications: *Chinese Culture Research* (4 a year), *Chinese Teaching in the World* (4 a year), *Language Teaching and Linguistic Studies* (6 a year)

DEANS

College of Advanced Chinese Training: QIU JUN
College of Chinese Language Studies: GUO PENG
College of Foreign Languages: NING YIZHONG
College of Humanities and Social Sciences: HUA XUECHENG
College of Information Sciences: LIU GUILONG
College of Intensive Chinese Studies: CHI LANYING
Continuing (Network) Education College: LI WEI
Int. Business School: LIU KE

PROFESSORS

CHEN, JUAN, Humanities and Social Sciences
CUI, XI LIANG, Humanities and Social Sciences
DU, DAO MING, Humanities and Social Sciences
FAN, LI, Foreign Languages
FANG, MING, Humanities and Social Sciences
HAN, DE MIN, Humanities and Social Sciences
HAN, JING TAI, Humanities and Social Sciences
HU, YU LONG, Foreign Languages

HUANG, ZHUO YUE, Humanities and Social Sciences
JIAO, FENG, Information Sciences
LI, LI CHENG, Chinese Language
LI, YANG, Chinese Language
LI, YAN SHU, Foreign Languages
LI, TIE CHENG, Humanities and Social Sciences
LI, WEI, Finance
LIANG, XIAO SHENG, Humanities and Social Sciences
LIU, XUN, Humanities and Social Sciences
LIU, GUI LONG, Information Sciences
LIU, KE, Finance
LV, WEN HUA, Humanities and Social Sciences
MA, SHU DE, Chinese Language
MA, ZHEN SHENG, Humanities and Social Sciences
NING, YI ZHONG, Foreign Languages
QIU, MING, Foreign Languages
SHEN, ZHI JUN, Chinese Language
SHI, DING GUO, Humanities and Social Sciences
SONG, ROU, Information Sciences
WANG, YE XIN, Chinese Language
WANG, ZHEN YA, Foreign Languages
XU, SHU AN, Humanities and Social Sciences
YAN, CHUN DE, Humanities and Social Sciences
ZHENG, GUI YOU, Humanities and Social Sciences
ZHENG, WANG PENG, Humanities and Social Sciences
ZHU, WEN JUN, Foreign Languages

BEIJING MEDICAL UNIVERSITY

38 Xue Yuan Lu, Northern Suburb, Beijing 100083

Telephone: (10) 62091334
Fax: (10) 62015681
E-mail: dxb@mail.bjmu.edu.cn
Internet: www.bjmu.edu.cn
Founded 1912
Languages of instruction: Chinese, English
Academic year: August to July (2 terms)
19 Research institutes, 11 research centres and 6 affiliated hospitals
Pres.: WANG DEBING
Vice-Pres: CHENG BOJI, HAN QIDE, LIN JIUXIANG, LU ZHAOFENG, WEI LIHUI, WANG YU
Dean for Education: (vacant)
Dir of Libraries: LIAN ZHIJIAN
Library of 730,000 vols, 66,500 periodicals
Number of teachers: 3,721
Number of students: 6,274
Publication: *Journal* (6 a year)

DEANS

First School of Medicine: Prof. ZHANG YOUKANG
School of Basic Medicine: Prof. JIA HONGTI
School of Mental Health: Prof. CUI YUHUA
School of Nursing: Prof. ZHENG XIUXIA
School of Oral Medicine: Prof. YU GUANGYAN
School of Pharmacy: Prof. ZHANG LIHE
School of Public Health: Prof. LI LIMING
Second School of Medicine: Prof. LU HOUSHAN
Third School of Medicine: HOU KUANYONG

BEIJING METALLURGICAL MANAGEMENT INSTITUTE

Guan Zhuang Chao Yang District, Beijing
Telephone: (10) 65762934
Fax: (10) 65762807
Founded 1984
Pres.: MA DEQING
Vice-Pres: HUANG ZHENGYU, LI YAN
Librarian: ZHAO ZONGDE

Library of 70,000 vols
Number of teachers: 126
Number of students: 1,700

BEIJING NORMAL UNIVERSITY

Xinjiekouwai St 19, Beijing 100875
Telephone: (10) 62207960
Fax: (10) 62200074
E-mail: ipo@bnu.edu.cn
Internet: www.bnu.edu.cn
Founded 1902
State control
Academic year: September to July
12 Colleges
Pres.: YUAN GUIREN
Vice-Pres: SHI PEIJUN, DONG QI, ZHENG JUNLI, XIE WEIHE, DAI JIAGANG, ZHENG SHIQU
Librarian: Prof. JIANG LU
Library: see Libraries
Number of teachers: 1,900
Number of students: 16,400 (8,400 full-time, 8,000 part-time)
Publications: *Comparative Education Review* (12 a year), *Foreign Language Teaching in Schools* (12 a year), *Journal* (Natural Science edn, 4 a year; Social Science edition, 6 a year), *Journal of Historiography* (12 a year).

BEIJING UNIVERSITY OF POSTS AND TELECOMMUNICATIONS

10 Xi Tu Cheng Rd, Haidian District, Beijing 100088
Telephone: (10) 62282628
Fax: (10) 62281774
E-mail: faoffice@bupt.edu.cn
Internet: www.bupt.edu.cn
Founded 1954; attached to Min. of Industry and Information Technology
Academic year: September to July
Pres.: ZHU XIANGHUA
Vice-Pres: LIN JINTONG, ZHONG YIXIN, ANG XIUFEN, ZHANG YINGHAI, RENG XIAOMIN, MI JIANHU
Chief Administrative Officer: WANG CHENGCHU
Librarian: MA ZIWEI
Library of 700,000 vols
Number of teachers: 800
Number of students: 8,000
Publications: *Academic Journal of BUPT* (4 a year), *Journal of China University of Posts and Telecommunications*

DEANS

Correspondence College: ANG XIUFEN
Fuzhou Extension: ANG XIUFEN
Graduate School: SONG JUNDE
Management Humanities College: TANG SHOULIAN
Telecommunications College: LIN JINTONG

ATTACHED RESEARCH INSTITUTES

BUPT-BNR (Nortel China) Advanced Telecommunications R&D Centre: 10 Xi Tu Cheng Rd, Beijing 100088; Dir (China) ZHU QILIANG.

Institute of Communications and Optoelectronic Information Processing: 10 Xi Tu Cheng Rd, Beijing 100088; optical fibres, optical wave guides, holography and optical information processing; Dir XU DAXIONG.

Research Institute: 10 Xi Tu Cheng Rd, Beijing 100088; communications systems and networks, information theory and processing, signal processing, artificial intelligence, neural networks and applications; Dir WU WEILING.

BEIJING SPORT UNIVERSITY

Zhong Guan Cun, Hai Ding District, Beijing 100084
Telephone: (10) 62989047
Fax: (10) 62989289
Internet: www.bupe.edu.cn
Founded 1953
State control
Academic year: September to July
Pres.: YANG HUA
Vice-Pres: ZHONG BIN SHU, HE ZHEN WEN, CHI JIAN
Head of Graduate Depnt: CHI JIAN
Librarian: LIU CAI XIA
Number of teachers: 5,000
Number of students: 540
Publications: *China Method of Body Mechanics* (2 a year), *China School Sport* (6 a year), *Journal* (4 a year)

DEANS

School of Gym Education: ZHOU DIAN MIN
School of Gym Management: QIN CHUN LIN
School of Human Sport: XIE MIN HAO
School of Sports Coaching: YUAN ZUO SHENG
School of Wu Shu: LIU BAO CAI

PROFESSORS

GUI, XIANG, Wu Shu
JIN, JI CHUN, Human Sport Science
JIN, YING HUA, Gym Management
LIU, DA QING, Sports Coaching
MEN, HUI FENG, Wu Shu
MENG, WEN DI, Gym Management
QI, GUO YING, Gym Education
QIN, CHUN LIN, Gym Management
SU, PI REN, Gym Education
SUN, BAO LI, Gym Management
WANG, MIN XIANG, Gym Education
WANG, QIAN, Gym Education
WANG, RUI YUAN, Human Sport Science
WANG, WEI, Sports Coaching
XIA, HUAN ZHEN, Gym Education
XIE, MIN HAO, Human Sport Science
XIONG, XIAO ZHENG, Gym Management
XU, SHENG HONG, Sports Coaching
YAO, XIA WEN, Gym Education
YUAN, DAN, Gym Management
YUAN, ZUO SHENG, Sports Coaching
ZHANG, GUANG DE, Wu Shu
ZHAO, LIAN JIA, Gym Education
ZHOU, DENG SONG, Gym Education
ZHU, RUI QI, Wu Shu

BEIJING INSTITUTE OF TECHNOLOGY

7 Bai Shi Giao, Hai Ding District, Beijing 100081
Telephone: (10) 68914246
Fax: (10) 68468035
Internet: www.bit.edu.cn
Founded 1940
State control
Academic year: September to July
Pres: KUANG JINGMING
Vice-Pres: HOU GUANGMING, LI ZHIXIANG, YANG BIN, ZHAO CHANGLU
Head of Graduate Dept: KUANG JINGMING
Librarian: CAO SHU REN
Number of teachers: 3,000
Number of students: 31,000
Publications: *Journal of Beijing Institute of Technology* (natural sciences, 6 a year), *Journal of Beijing Institute of Technology* (social sciences, 6 a year)

DEANS

School of Chemical Engineering and Materials: ZHOU, TONG LAI
School of Computers and Control: HOU, CHAO ZHEN
School of Design Art: ZHANG, NAI REN

School of Humanities and Social Sciences: XI, QIAO JUAN
School of Information Engineering: WANG, YUE
School of Management and Economics: WANG, XIU CUN
School of Mechatronic Engineering: LIU, LI
School of Science and Technology: XU, WEN GUO
School of Software: WANG, SHU WU
School of Vehicle and Transport Engineering: XU, CHUN GUANG

PROFESSORS

AN, JIAN PING, Information and Communication Engineering
BA, YAN ZHU, Optics Engineering
BAI, CHUN HUA, Mechatronic Engineering
BI, SHI HUA, Mechatronic Engineering
CAI, HONG YAN, Material Science and Engineering
CAO, GEN RUI, Apparatus Science and Technology
CAO, YUAN DA, Computer Science and Technology
CHAI, RUI JIAO, Mechatronic Engineering
CHEN, DONG SHENG, Vehicle and Transport Engineering
CHEN, HUI YAN, Vehicle and Transport Engineering
CHEN, JIA BIN, Control Science and Engineering
CHEN, JIE, Control Science and Engineering
CHEN, SHU FENG, Electronic Science and Technology
CHEN, SI ZHONG, Vehicle and Transport Engineering
CHEN, XIANG GUANG, Control Science and Engineering
CUI, ZHAN ZHONG, Mechatronic Engineering
DA, YA PING, Control Science and Engineering
DING, HONG SHENG, Vehicle and Transport Engineering
DONG, YU PING, Material Science and Engineering
DOU, LI HUA, Control Science and Engineering
DU, ZHI MING, Mechatronic Engineering
FAN, NING JUN, Mechatronic Engineering
FAN, TIAN YOU, Applied Mathematics
FAN, XIAO ZHONG, Computer Science and Technology
FEI, YUAN CHUN, Electronic Science and Technology
FENG, CHANG GEN, Mechatronic Engineering
FENG, SHUN SHAN, Mechatronic Engineering
FU, MENG YING, Control Science and Engineering
GAN, REN CHU, Management Science and Engineering
GAO, BEN QING, Electronic Science and Technology
GAO, CHUN QING, Electronic Science and Technology
GAO, MEI GUO, Information and Communication Engineering
GAO, SHI QIAO, Engineering Mechanics
GAO, ZHI YUN, Optics Engineering
GE, WEI GAO, Applied Mathematics
GE, YUN SHAN, Vehicle and Transport Engineering
GOU, BING CONG, Electronic Science and Technology
GU, LIANG, Vehicle and Transport Engineering
GU, ZHI MIN, Computer Science and Technology
GUO, QIAO, Control Science and Engineering
HAN, BAO LING, Vehicle and Transport Engineering
HAN, BO TANG, Management Science and Engineering
HAN, FENG, Mechatronic Engineering
HAN, YUE QIU, Information and Communication Engineering

HE, PEI KUN, Information and Communication Engineering
HOU, CHAO ZHEN, Control Science and Engineering
HOU, GUANG MING, Management Science and Engineering
HU, CHANG WEN, Chemistry
HU, GENG KAI, Solid Mechanics
HUANG, FENG LEI, Mechatronic Engineering
HUANG, RUO, Vehicle and Transport Engineering
JIA, YUN DE, Computer Science and Technology
JIAO, QING JIE, Mechatronic Engineering
JIAO, YONG HE, Vehicle and Transport Engineering
KANG, JING LI, Mechatronic Engineering
KONG, LING JIA, Vehicle and Transport Engineering
KONG, ZHAO JUN, Management Science and Engineering
KUANG, JING MING, Information and Communication Engineering
LI, JIA ZE, Electronic Science and Technology
LI, JIAN, Management Science and Engineering
LI, JIN LIN, Management Science and Engineering
LI, KE JIE, Mechatronic Engineering
LI, LIN, Apparatus Science and Technology
LI, PING, Mechatronic Engineering
LI, SHI YI, Apparatus Science and Technology
LI, SHI YI, Mechatronic Engineering
LI, XIAO LEI, Vehicle and Transport Engineering
LI, ZHI XIANG, Management Science and Engineering
LIAO, NING FANG, Optics Engineering
LIN, YI, Vehicle and Transport Engineering
LIU, LI, Mechatronic Engineering
LIU, YU SHU, Computer Science and Technology
LIU, ZAO ZHEN, Control Science and Engineering
LIU, ZAO ZHEN, Mechatronic Engineering
LIU, ZHAO DU, Vehicle and Transport Engineering
LIU, ZHI WEN, Information and Communication Engineering
LONG, TENG, Information and Communication Engineering
LONG, XIN PING, Mechatronic Engineering
LU, GUANG SHU, Material Science and Engineering
LU, XIN, Electronic Science and Technology
LUO, WEI XIONG, Information and Communication Engineering
LUO, YUN JUN, Material Science and Engineering
MA, BAO HUA, Mechatronic Engineering
MA, BIAO, Vehicle and Transport Engineering
MA, CHAO CHEN, Vehicle and Transport Engineering
MA, SHU YUAN, Apparatus Science and Technology
MAI, XIAO QING, Mechatronic Engineering
MAO, ER KE, Information and Communication Engineering
MEI, FENG XIANG, Applied Mathematics
NING, GUO QIANG, Optics Engineering
NING, JIAN GUO, Mechatronic Engineering
NING, JIAN GUO, Solid Mechanics
OU, YU XIANG, Material Science and Engineering
PENG, ZHENG GUANG, Control Science and Engineering
QI, ZAI KANG, Mechatronic Engineering
QUAN, WEI QI, Optics Engineering
REN, XUE MEI, Control Science and Engineering
SHA, DING GUO, Apparatus Science and Technology
SHAO, BIN, Chemistry
SHENG, TING ZHI, Information and Communication Engineering

SHI, FENG, Computer Science and Technology
SHI, FU GUI, Applied Mathematics
SONG, HAN TAO, Computer Science and Technology
SONG, ZHEN GUO, Mechatronic Engineering
SUI, SHU YUAN, Mechatronic Engineering
SUN, FENG CHUN, Vehicle and Transport Engineering
SUN, GUANG CHUAN, Information and Communication Engineering
SUN, LIANG, Applied Mathematics
SUN, YE BAO, Vehicle and Transport Engineering
SUN, YU NAN, Electronic Science and Technology
TAN, HUI MIN, Mechatronic Engineering
TAN, HUI MIN, Material Science and Engineering
TAO, RAN, Information and Communication Engineering
WANG, BO, Control Science and Engineering
WANG, FU CHI, Material Science and Engineering
WANG, GUO YU, Vehicle and Transport Engineering
WANG, JIAN ZHONG, Mechatronic Engineering
WANG, PEI LAN, Mechatronic Engineering
WANG, QING LIN, Control Science and Engineering
WANG, SHUN TING, Control Science and Engineering
WANG, XIAO LI, Vehicle and Transport Engineering
WANG, XIAO MO, Information and Communication Engineering
WANG, XING WEN, Mechatronic Engineering
WANG, YONG TIAN, Optics Engineering
WANG, YU, Control Science and Engineering
WANG, YUE, Information and Communication Engineering
WU, QI ZONG, Management Science and Engineering
WU, QING HE, Control Science and Engineering
WU, SI LIANG, Information and Communication Engineering
WU, WEN HUI, Material Science and Engineering
XIA, EN JUN, Management Science and Engineering
XIANG, CHANG LE, Vehicle and Transport Engineering
XIE, JING HUI, Optics Engineering
XING, JIAN GUO, Electronic Science and Technology
XU, GENG GUANG, Mechatronic Engineering
XU, XIAO WEN, Electronic Science and Technology
XU, XING ZHONG, Applied Mathematics
XUE, WEI, Optics Engineering
YAN, JI XIANG, Electronic Science and Technology
YANG, JUN, Engineering Mechanics
YANG, RONG JIE, Material Science and Engineering
YANG, SHU YIN, Mechatronic Engineering
YAO, XIAO XIAN, Mechatronic Engineering
YI, JIANG, Mechatronic Engineering
YU, XIN, Electronic Science and Technology
YUAN, SHI HUA, Vehicle and Transport Engineering
ZENG, FENG ZHANG, Management Science and Engineering
ZENG, QING XUAN, Mechatronic Engineering
ZHAN, SHOU YI, Computer Science and Technology
ZHANG, CHENG NING, Vehicle and Transport Engineering
ZHANG, CHUN LIN, Vehicle and Transport Engineering
ZHANG, FU JUN, Vehicle and Transport Engineering
ZHANG, JING LIN, Mechatronic Engineering
ZHANG, PING, Mechatronic Engineering
ZHANG, QI, Mechatronic Engineering

ZHANG, QIANG, Management Science and Engineering
ZHANG, QING MING, Engineering Mechanics
ZHANG, TONG ZHUANG, Vehicle and Transport Engineering
ZHANG, WEI ZHENG, Vehicle and Transport Engineering
ZHANG, YONG FA, Solid Mechanics
ZHANG, YOU TONG, Vehicle and Transport Engineering
ZHANG, YU HE, Control Science and Engineering
ZHANG, YUN HONG, Chemistry
ZHAO, CHANG LU, Vehicle and Transport Engineering
ZHAO, CHANG MING, Electronic Science and Technology
ZHAO, DA ZUN, Optics Engineering
ZHAO, HONG KANG, Electronic Science and Technology
ZHAO, XING QI, Material Science and Engineering
ZHAO, YUE JIN, Apparatus Science and Technology
ZHEN, LIAN, Mechatronic Engineering
ZHENG, HONG FEI, Vehicle and Transport Engineering
ZHENG, LIAN, Control Science and Engineering
ZHONG, QIU HAI, Control Science and Engineering
ZHOU, JIAN, Applied Mathematics
ZHOU, LI WEI, Optics Engineering
ZHOU, TONG LAI, Chemistry
ZHU, DONG HUA, Management Science and Engineering
ZUO, ZHEN XING, Vehicle and Transport Engineering

BEIJING UNIVERSITY OF TECHNOLOGY

100 Ping Le Yuan, Chao Yang District, Beijing 100226
Telephone: (10) 67392239
Fax: (10) 67392675
Internet: www.bjpu.edu.cn
Founded 1960
Academic year: September to July
Pres: FAN, BO YUAN
Vice-Pres: HOU, YI BIN
Head of Graduate Dept: JIANG, YI JIAN
Librarian: FEI, REN YUAN
Number of teachers: 1,100
Number of students: 26,000
Publication: *Journal* (4 a year)

DEANS

College of Applied Science: ZHANG, ZHONG ZHAN
College of Architecture Engineering: HUO, DA
College of Computer Science: ZHANG, SHU JIE
College of Economics and Management: LI, JING WEN
College of Electronic Information and Control Engineering: WANG, PU
College of Energy and Environmental Engineering: MA, CHONG FANG
College of Foreign Languages: WANG, FU XIANG
College of Humanities and Social Sciences: LU, XUE YI
College of Life Science and Bio-Engineering: ZENG, YI
College of Material Science and Engineering: NIE, ZHA REN
College of Mechanical Engineering and Applied Electronics Technology: YANG, JIAN WU
College of Software Engineering: HOU, YI BIN

PROFESSORS

BAO, CHANG CHUN, Electronic Information and Control Engineering
CAO, WANG LIN, Architecture Engineering
CHEN, GUANG HUA, Material Science and Engineering
CHEN, JIAN XIN, Electronic Information and Control Engineering
CHEN, YANG ZHOU, Electronic Information and Control Engineering
CHENG, CAO ZONG, Applied Science and Physics
CHENG, SHUI YUAN, Energy and Environmental Engineering
CUI, PING YUAN, Electronic Information and Control Engineering
DAI, HONG XING, Energy and Environmental Engineering
DI, RUI HUA, Computer Science
DU, XIU LI, Architecture Engineering
DUAN, JIAN MIN, Electronic Information and Control Engineering
FEI, REN YUAN, Mechanical Engineering and Applied Electronics Technology
GUO, BAI NING, Computer Science
HAN, FU RONG, Economics and Management
HE, CUN FU, Mechanical Engineering and Applied Electronics Technology
HE, HONG, Energy and Environmental Engineering
HE, RUO QUAN, Architecture Engineering
HE, ZI NIAN, Energy and Environmental Engineering
HOU, BI HUI, Applied Science and Physics
HOU, YI BIN, Computer Science
HUANG, LU CHENG, Economics and Management
HUANG, TI YUN, Economics and Management
HUO, DA, Architecture Engineering
JIANG, YI JIE, Applied Science and Physics
KANG, BAO WEI, Electronic Information and Control Engineering
KANG, TIAN FANG, Energy and Environmental Engineering
LEI, YONG PING, Material Science and Engineering
LI, DE SHENG, Mechanical Engineering and Applied Electronics Technology
LI, GANG, Laser Engineering
LI, HUI MING, Economics and Management
LI, JING WEN, Economics and Management
LI, SHOU MEI, Applied Science and Physics
LI, XIAO YAN, Material Science and Engineering
LI, ZHEN BAO, Architecture Engineering
LI, ZHI GUO, Electronic Information and Control Engineering
LIAO, HU SHENG, Computer Science
LIU, CHUN NIAN, Computer Science
LIU, XIAO MING, Architecture Engineering
LIU, YOU MING, Applied Science and Physics
LIU, ZHONG LIANG, Energy and Environmental Engineering
LU, XUE YI, Economics and Management
MA, CHONG FANG, Energy and Environmental Engineering
MA, GUO YUAN, Energy and Environmental Engineering
NIE, ZHA REN, Material Science and Engineering
PENG, YONG ZHEN, Energy and Environmental Engineering
REN, FU TIAN, Architecture Engineering
REN, ZHEN HAI, Energy and Environmental Engineering
RUAN, XIAO GANG, Electronic Information and Control Engineering
SHANG, DE GUANG, Mechanical Engineering and Applied Electronics Technology
SHE, YUAN BIN, Energy and Environmental Engineering
SHENG, GUANG DI, Electronic Information and Control Engineering
SHENG, LAN SUN, Electronic Information and Control Engineering

SHI, YAO WU, Material Science and Engineering
SONG, ROU, Computer Science
SUI, YUN KANG, Mechanical Engineering and Applied Electronics Technology
TAO, LIAN JIN, Architecture Engineering
TAO, SHI QUAN, Applied Science and Physics
WAN, SU CHUN, Architecture Engineering
WANG, DA YONG, Applied Science and Physics
WANG, DAO, Energy and Environmental Engineering
WANG, GUANG TAO, Architecture Engineering
WANG, LI, Applied Science and Physics
WANG, PU, Electronic Information and Control Engineering
WANG, SONG GUI, Applied Science and Physics
WU, BIN, Mechanical Engineering and Applied Electronics Technology
WU, GUO WEI, Economics and Management
WU, WU CHEN, Electronic Information and Control Engineering
WU, YONG LUN, Mechanical Engineering and Applied Electronics Technology
XIA, DING GUO, Energy and Environmental Engineering
XUE, LIU GEN, Applied Science and Physics
XUE, SU GUO, Architecture Engineering
YAN, HUI, Material Science and Engineering
YAN, WEI MING, Architecture Engineering
YANG, HONG RU, Applied Science and Physics
YAO, HAI LOU, Applied Science and Physics
YI, BAO CAI, Computer Science
YIN, SHU YAN, Mechanical Engineering and Applied Electronics Technology
YIN, SHU YAN, Material Science and Engineering
YU, JIAN, Energy and Environmental Engineering
YU, KUAN XIN, Applied Science and Physics
YU, YUE QING, Mechanical Engineering and Applied Electronics Technology
ZENG, YI, Energy and Environmental Engineering
ZHANG, AI LIN, Architecture Engineering
ZHANG, HONG BIN, Computer Science
ZHANG, HONG BIN, Electronic Information and Control Engineering
ZHANG, HUI HUI, Mechanical Engineering and Applied Electronics Technology
ZHANG, JIE, Energy and Environmental Engineering
ZHANG, JIU JIE, Material Science and Engineering
ZHANG, WANG RONG, Electronic Information and Control Engineering
ZHANG, WEI, Mechanical Engineering and Applied Electronics Technology
ZHANG, WEN XIONG, Material Science and Engineering
ZHANG, YI GANG, Architecture Engineering
ZHANG, ZE, Applied Science and Physics
ZHANG, ZHEN HAI, Applied Science and Physics
ZHANG, ZHI GANG, Applied Science and Physics
ZHANG, ZHONG ZHAN, Applied Science and Physics
ZHONG, NING, Computer Science
ZHONG, RU GANG, Energy and Environmental Engineering
ZHOU, DA SEN, Energy and Environmental Engineering
ZHOU, MEI LING, Material Science and Engineering
ZHOU, WEI, Architecture Engineering
ZHOU, XI YUAN, Architecture Engineering
ZHOU, YU WEN, Energy and Environmental Engineering
ZONG, GANG, Economics and Management
ZUO, TIE XUN, Applied Science and Physics
ZUO, TIE YONG, Material Science and Engineering

CAPITAL NORMAL UNIVERSITY

105 Xi San Huan, Beijing 100037
Telephone: (10) 68900974
Fax: (10) 68902539
Internet: www.cnu.edu.cn

Founded 1954
Bureau of Education of Beijing
Academic year: September to July

Pres.: XIANG YUAN XU
Vice-Pres: HUI LI GONG, JIAN CHENG LIU, JIAN SHE ZHOU, WAN LIANG WANG
Head of Graduate Dept: JING HE LIANG
Librarian: YUE HU

Number of teachers: 1,147
Number of students: 24,905 (12,786 full-time, 12,119 part-time)
Publications: *Education Art* (12 a year), *Journal of Capital Normal University (Natural Sciences Edition)* (4 a year), *Journal of Capital Normal University (Social Sciences Edition)* (6 a year), *Language Teaching in Middle School* (12 a year), *Middle School Math* (12 a year)

DEANS

College of Biology: HE YIKUN
College of Education: MEN FANHUA
College of Environmental Resources and Tourism: GONG HUILI
College of Fine Arts: SUN ZHIJUN
College of Foreign Languages: YANG YANG
College of Information Technology: WANG WANSEN
College of International Culture: LIU XIAO-TIAN
College of Music: YANG QING
College of Political Sciences and Law: WANG SHUMENG
Department of Chemistry: ZHANG ZHUOYONG
Department of Educational Technology: AI LUN
Department of History: SONG JIE
Department of Mathematics: ZHENG CHON-GYOU
Department of Physics: ZHANG CUNLIN
Elementary Education College: WANG ZHIQIU
Physical Teaching and Research Section: SUN JIANHUI
School of Literature: WU SHIJING
Teaching and Research Division of Marxism: LI SONGLIN
University English Teaching and Research Division: XIE FUZHI

PROFESSORS

AN, YUFENG, Political Sciences and Law
BI, LUO, Environmental Resources and Tourism
CAI, TUANYAO, Biology
CHANG, RUILUN, Fine Arts
CHEN, XINXIA, Political Sciences and Law
CHI, YUNFEI, History
DAI, LIN, Fine Arts
DIAO, YONGZHA, Marxism
DONG, ZHONGXUN, Fine Arts
DU, XIAOSHI, Music
DU, XIXIAN, Fine Arts
FAN, YANNING, Political Sciences and Law
FANG, PING, Education
FANG, YAN, Physics
FU, HUA, Environmental Resources and Tourism
GONG, HUILI, Environmental Resources and Tourism
GU, XUEXIN, Chemistry
HAO, CHUNWEN, History
HE, YIKUN, Biology
HUANG, MEIYING, Music
HUO, LONGGUANG, Mathematics
JIN, QIONGHUA, Chemistry
LAN, WEI, Political Sciences and Law
LEI, DA, Music
LI, AIGUO, Fine Arts
LI, FULI, Physics
LI, JIAYANG, Biology
LI, SHUPEI, Mathematics
LI, SONGLIN, Marxism
LI, XIA, Chemistry
LI, YARU, Marxism
LIAN, SHAOMING, History
LIANG, JINGHE, History
LIN, LI, Foreign Languages
LIU, DACHUN, Mathematics
LIU, LIMIN, Foreign Languages
LU, XIAOMING, Chemistry
MENG, FANHUA, Education
NIE, YUEYAN, Political Sciences and Law
NING, HONG, Education
NING, KE, History
QI, SHIRONG, History
QIU, YUNHUA, Literature
REN, DONG, Biology
SHAO, HUIBO, Chemistry
SHEN, JINGLING, Physics
SHI, SHENGMING, Mathematics
SHUI, SHUFENG, Political Sciences and Law
SONG, JIE, History
SUN, ZHIJUN, Fine Arts
TAN, FENGTAI, Education
TANG, CHONGQIN, Music
TAO, DONGFENG, Literature
TIAN, BAO, Education
WANG, ANGUO, Music
WANG, CHANGCHUN, Education
WANG, DESHENG, Literature
WANG, GUANGMING, Literature
WANG, JIANPING, Education
WANG, LU, Educational Technology
WANG, SHIPING, Physics
WANG, SHUMENG, Political Sciences and Law
WANG, SHUQIN, Political Sciences and Law
WANG, ZHIQIU, Elementary Education
WEI, GUANGQI, History
WEN, LISHU, Political Sciences and Law
WU, JIANGPING, Mathematics
WU, SHIJING, Literature
XIA, JIGUO, History
XIA, LIMIN, Political Sciences and Law
XIE, CHENGREN, History
XING, HONGJUN, Physics
XING, YONGFU, Education
XU, PEIJUN, Physics
XU, YUZHEN, Education
YANG, QING, Music
YANG, SHENGPING, Political Sciences and Law
YANG, YANG, Foreign Languages
YANG, YUE, Biology
YE, XIAOBING, History
YIN, LIPING, Biology
YIN, TIELIANG, Music
YIN, WEIPING, Mathematics
ZHAN, LIJUAN, Music
ZHANG, CUNLIN, Physics
ZHANG, GUOLI, Music
ZHANG, JUNDA, Education
ZHANG, YONGHUA, Chemistry
ZHANG, ZHUOYONG, Chemistry
ZHAO, XUEZHI, Mathematics

CAPITAL MEDICAL UNIVERSITY

10 Xitoutiao, You Anmen, Fengtai Dist., Beijing 100069
Telephone: (10) 83911199
Fax: (10) 83911194
E-mail: guohechu@ccmu.edu.cn
Internet: www.ccmu.edu.cn

Founded 1960
Academic year: September to July

Pres.: LU ZHAOFENG
Vice-Pres.: FAN QI
Vice-Pres.: WANG SONGLING
Vice-Pres.: WANG XIAOMIN
Vice-Pres.: WANG YUHUI
Vice-Pres.: XIAN FUHUA
Head of Graduate Dept: LU ZHAOFENG
Librarian: WANG JIEZHEN

Number of teachers: 2,500

Publications: *Journal* (4 a year), *School of Public Health* (4 a year)

DEANS

Biomedical Engineering Institute: LIU ZHI-CHENG
Eighth Faculty of Clinical Medicine: XI XIUMING
Faculty of Mental Health: CAI ZHUOJI
Faculty of Nursing: LI SHUJIA
Faculty of Obstetrics and Gynaecology: CHEN BAOYING
Faculty of Paediatrics: LI ZHONGZHI
Faculty of Rehabilitation: YOU HONG
Faculty of Stomatology: ZHENG SUN
Fifth Faculty of Clinical Medicine: DAI JIANPING
First Faculty of Clinical Medicine: ZHANG JIAN
Fourth Faculty of Clinical Medicine: LIU HONGBO
Ninth Faculty of Clinical Medicine: ZHAO CHUNHUI
School of Basic Medical Sciences: CHEN TIEJUN
School of Chemical Biology and Pharmaceutical Sciences: PENG SHIQI
School of Chinese Traditional Medicine: QI FANG
School of Health Administration and Education: LIANG WANNIAN
School of Public Health and Family Medical Science: WANG WEI
Second Faculty of Clinical Medicine: GAO DONGCHEN
Sixth Faculty of Clinical Medicine: ZHANG GUANGZHAO
Third Faculty of Clinical Medicine: GAO JUZHONG

PROFESSORS

AN, WEI, School of Basic Medical Sciences
AN, YUNQING, School of Basic Medical Sciences
BAI, YUXING, Faculty of Stomatology
CAI, ZHUOJI, Faculty of Mental Health
CHANG, XHIWEN, Fourth Faculty of Clinical Medicine
CHE, NIANCONG, School of Chinese Traditional Medicine
CHEN, BAOTIAN, Sixth Faculty of Clinical Medicine
CHEN, BAOYING, Faculty of Obstetrics and Gynaecology
CHEN, BIAO, First Faculty of Clinical Medicine
CHEN, HAIYING, School of Chinese Traditional Medicine
CHEN, HUIDE, Third Faculty of Clinical Medicine
CHEN, HUIRU, Fourth Faculty of Clinical Medicine
CHEN, JUN, School of Basic Medical Sciences
CHEN, SHAN, Fourth Faculty of Clinical Medicine
CHEN, TIEJUN, School of Basic Medical Sciences
CHEN, XUESHI, Faculty of Mental Health
CHEN, YILIN, First Faculty of Clinical Medicine
CHEN, YINGCHUN, Sixth Faculty of Clinical Medicine
CHEN, YUPING, Sixth Faculty of Clinical Medicine
CHEN, ZHAN, Sixth Faculty of Clinical Medicine
CUI, GUOHUI, School of Chemical Biology and Pharmaceutical Sciences
CUI, SHUQI, School of Public Health and Family Medical Science
DAI, JIANPING, Fifth Faculty of Clinical Medicine
DAI, XINGHUA, Faculty of Obstetrics and Gynaecology
DAO, HONG, School of Public Health and Family Medical Science

DING, BOTAN, Faculty of Rehabilitation
DING, ZONGYI, Faculty of Paediatrics
DONG, PEIQING, Sixth Faculty of Clinical Medicine
DONG, ZONGJUN, First Faculty of Clinical Medicine
DU, FENGHE, Fifth Faculty of Clinical Medicine
DU, LINDONG, Second Faculty of Clinical Medicine
DUAN, YANPING, School of Chinese Traditional Medicine
DUAN, ZHONGPING, Ninth Faculty of Clinical Medicine
FAN, DONGPO, Fifth Faculty of Clinical Medicine
FAN, MING, School of Basic Medical Sciences
FAN, XUNMEI, Faculty of Paediatrics
FANG, DEYUN, First Faculty of Clinical Medicine
GAO, BAOQIN, Fifth Faculty of Clinical Medicine
GAO, CHUNJIN, Third Faculty of Clinical Medicine
GAO, DONGCHEN, Second Faculty of Clinical Medicine
GAO, FENG, Faculty of Obstetrics and Gynaecology
GAO, JUZHONG, Third Faculty of Clinical Medicine
GAO, MINGZHE, Sixth Faculty of Clinical Medicine
GAO, PEIYI, Fifth Faculty of Clinical Medicine
GAO, WENZHU, Faculty of Rehabilitation
GAO, XIULAI, School of Basic Medical Sciences
GAO, YIMIN, School of Chinese Traditional Medicine
GUAN, DELIN, Third Faculty of Clinical Medicine
GUO, AIMIN, School of Public Health and Family Medical Science
GUO, SONG, Faculty of Mental Health
GUO, XIUHUA, School of Public Health and Family Medical Science
HAN, DEMIN, Fourth Faculty of Clinical Medicine
HAN, LING, Sixth Faculty of Clinical Medicine
HE, YAN, Fifth Faculty of Clinical Medicine
HU, DAYI, Third Faculty of Clinical Medicine
HU, YAMEI, Faculty of Paediatrics
HU, YINYUAN, Faculty of Rehabilitation
HUA, QI, First Faculty of Clinical Medicine
HUANG, JIEYING, Second Faculty of Clinical Medicine
HUANG, SHUZHEN, Faculty of Mental Health
JI, SHURONG, Faculty of Rehabilitation
JIA, HONGTI, School of Basic Medical Sciences
JIA, JIANPING, First Faculty of Clinical Medicine
JIA, JIDONG, Second Faculty of Clinical Medicine
JIANG, BING, School of Health Administration and Education
JIANG, TAO, Fifth Faculty of Clinical Medicine
JIANG, WENHUA, First Faculty of Clinical Medicine
JIANG, ZAIFANG, Faculty of Paediatrics
JIANG, ZUONING, Faculty of Mental Health
JIN, RUI, Ninth Faculty of Clinical Medicine
JU, LIRONG, School of Public Health and Family Medical Science
LI, BIN, Fourth Faculty of Clinical Medicine
LI, CUIYING, Faculty of Stomatology
LI, FEI, First Faculty of Clinical Medicine
LI, HONGPEI, Fifth Faculty of Clinical Medicine
LI, JIANPING, School of Health Administration and Education
LI, KUNCHENG, First Faculty of Clinical Medicine
LI, LIN, First Faculty of Clinical Medicine
LI, LIN, School of Health Administration and Education
LI, PING, Sixth Faculty of Clinical Medicine
LI, REN, Third Faculty of Clinical Medicine
LI, SHUJIA, Faculty of Nursing

LI, SHUREN, Second Faculty of Clinical Medicine
LI, XIA, Biomedical Engineering Institute
LI, YONGJIE, First Faculty of Clinical Medicine
LI, YUJING, Faculty of Stomatology
LI, ZHI'AN, Sixth Faculty of Clinical Medicine
LI, ZHIZIA, Fourth Faculty of Clinical Medicine
LI, ZHONGZHI, Faculty of Paediatrics
LIAN, SHI, First Faculty of Clinical Medicine
LIANG, WANNIAN, School of Health Administration and Education
LING, FENG, First Faculty of Clinical Medicine
LIU, BIN, Fourth Faculty of Clinical Medicine
LIU, CHANGGUI, Second Faculty of Clinical Medicine
LIU, HONGBO, Fourth Faculty of Clinical Medicine
LIU, HONGGANG, Fourth Faculty of Clinical Medicine
LIU, JINGZHONG, Third Faculty of Clinical Medicine
LIU, LEI, Fourth Faculty of Clinical Medicine
LIU, NONG, School of Basic Medical Sciences
LIU, WEIZHEN, School of Basic Medical Sciences
LIU, XICHENG, Faculty of Paediatrics
LIU, YONGBIN, Faculty of Rehabilitation
LIU, ZHICHENG, Biomedical Engineering Institute
LONG, JIE, Fifth Faculty of Clinical Medicine
LU, HUIZHANG, First Faculty of Clinical Medicine
LU, SHIQI, School of Basic Medical Sciences
LUAN, GUOMING, Fifth Faculty of Clinical Medicine
LUO, SHIQI, Fifth Faculty of Clinical Medicine
LUO, SHUQIAN, Biomedical Engineering Institute
MA, BINRONG, Biomedical Engineering Institute
MA, CHANGSHENG, Sixth Faculty of Clinical Medicine
MA, DAQING, Second Faculty of Clinical Medicine
MA, DONGLI, Fourth Faculty of Clinical Medicine
MENG, XU, Sixth Faculty of Clinical Medicine
NI, JIAYI, First Faculty of Clinical Medicine
PAN, JULI, Faculty of Stomatology
PENG, SHIQI, School of Chemical Biology and Pharmaceutical Sciences
QI, FANG, School of Chinese Traditional Medicine
QI, YING, Fourth Faculty of Clinical Medicine
QIAN, YING, School of Chinese Traditional Medicine
QIAO, ZHIHENG, Faculty of Rehabilitation
QU, RENYOU, Third Faculty of Clinical Medicine
SHE, KUNLING, Faculty of Paediatrics
SHEN, LUHUA, Second Faculty of Clinical Medicine
SHEN, YIN, Faculty of Paediatrics
SHI, SHENGGEN, Faculty of Stomatology
SHI, XIAOLIN, School of Basic Medical Sciences
SHI, XIANG'EN, Fifth Faculty of Clinical Medicine
SHI, YUYING, Fourth Faculty of Clinical Medicine
SONG, MAOMIN, Fifth Faculty of Clinical Medicine
SONG, WEIXIAN, Fourth Faculty of Clinical Medicine
SUN, BAOZHEN, Fourth Faculty of Clinical Medicine
SUN, BO, Fifth Faculty of Clinical Medicine
SUN, JIANBANG, First Faculty of Clinical Medicine
SUN, YANQING, Sixth Faculty of Clinical Medicine
SUN, ZHENG, Faculty of Stomatology

TANG, XHAOQU, School of Basic Medical Sciences
TIAN, XHU'EN, Faculty of Mental Health
WANG, BANGKANG, Faculty of Stomatology
WANG, BAOGUO, Fifth Faculty of Clinical Medicine
WANG, CHEN, Third Faculty of Clinical Medicine
WANG, DEXIN, Second Faculty of Clinical Medicine
WANG, ENXHEN, Fifth Faculty of Clinical Medicine
WANG, HUILING, Sixth Faculty of Clinical Medicine
WANG, JIE, Fifth Faculty of Clinical Medicine
WANG, PEIYAN, Third Faculty of Clinical Medicine
WANG, SONGLING, Faculty of Stomatology
WANG, SUQIU, Fifth Faculty of Clinical Medicine
WANG, TIANYOU, Second Faculty of Clinical Medicine
WANG, XHONGCHENG, Fifth Faculty of Clinical Medicine
WANG, WEI, School of Public Health and Family Medical Science
WANG, WENWEI, Fourth Faculty of Clinical Medicine
WANG, XHENFU, Fourth Faculty of Clinical Medicine
WANG, XHIGANG, Second Faculty of Clinical Medicine
WANG, XIAOLIANG, School of Chemical Biology and Pharmaceutical Sciences
WANG, XIAOMIN, School of Basic Medical Sciences
WANG, XIAOYAN, School of Health Administration and Education
WANG, YADONG, School of Health Administration and Education
WANG, YIZHEN, Fifth Faculty of Clinical Medicine
WANG, YONGJUN, Fifth Faculty of Clinical Medicine
WANG, YU, Second Faculty of Clinical Medicine
WANG, ZHONGGAO, First Faculty of Clinical Medicine
WENG, XINAHI, Third Faculty of Clinical Medicine
WENG, YONGZHEN, Faculty of Mental Health
WU, AINGHUA, Sixth Faculty of Clinical Medicine
WU, FENGYI, Third Faculty of Clinical Medicine
WU, HAO, Ninth Faculty of Clinical Medicine
WU, MINYUAN, Faculty of Paediatrics
WU, SHUZENG, Sixth Faculty of Clinical Medicine
WU, XUESHI, Sixth Faculty of Clinical Medicine
WU, ZHAOSU, Sixth Faculty of Clinical Medicine
XI, XIUMING, Eighth Faculty of Clinical Medicine
XIANG, XIUKUN, Fourth Faculty of Clinical Medicine
XIAO, RONG, School of Public Health and Family Medical Science
XU, QUNYAN, School of Basic Medical Sciences
XUE, MING, School of Health Administration and Education
YANG, BAOQIN, School of Chinese Traditional Medicine
YANG, HUI, School of Basic Medical Sciences
YANG, JINKUI, Fourth Faculty of Clinical Medicine
YANG, SHAOXU, Fifth Faculty of Clinical Medicine
YANG, SHENGHUI, Faculty of Stomatology
YANG, YUNPING, Faculty of Mental Health
YAO, CHONGHUA, Sixth Faculty of Clinical Medicine
YAO, TIANQIAO, Sixth Faculty of Clinical Medicine

You, Hong, Faculty of Rehabilitation
You, Kaitao, Third Faculty of Clinical Medicine
Yu, Chunjiang, First Faculty of Clinical Medicine
Yu, Zeli, Fourth Faculty of Clinical Medicine
Yuan, Zhengguo, School of Chinese Traditional Medicine
Yue, Yun, Third Faculty of Clinical Medicine
Zhan, Zhenting, Faculty of Stomatology
Zhang, Binxi, Fourth Faculty of Clinical Medicine
Zhang, Changhuai, Second Faculty of Clinical Medicine
Zhang, Fengxian, Third Faculty of Clinical Medicine
Zhang, Guangzhao, Sixth Faculty of Clinical Medicine
Zhang, Hongyu, Third Faculty of Clinical Medicine
Zhang, Jian, First Faculty of Clinical Medicine
Zhang, Jigu, Faculty of Mental Health
Zhang, Jincai, Faculty of Stomatology
Zhang, Jinrong, Sixth Faculty of Clinical Medicine
Zhang, Jinzhe, Faculty of Paediatrics
Zhang, Jizhi, Faculty of Mental Health
Zhang, Pengtian, Second Faculty of Clinical Medicine
Zhang, Qiuhan, First Faculty of Clinical Medicine
Zhang, Shiji, Faculty of Mental Health
Zhang, Shumin, School of Chinese Traditional Medicine
Zhang, Shuwen, Second Faculty of Clinical Medicine
Zhang, Yu, First Faculty of Clinical Medicine
Zhang, Yuhai, Second Faculty of Clinical Medicine
Zhang, Zhaoguang, Sixth Faculty of Clinical Medicine
Zhang, Zhaoqi, Sixth Faculty of Clinical Medicine
Zhang, Zhitai, Sixth Faculty of Clinical Medicine
Zhao, Chunhui, Ninth Faculty of Clinical Medicine
Zhao, Dong, Sixth Faculty of Clinical Medicine
Zhao, Jizong, Fifth Faculty of Clinical Medicine
Zhao, Ming, School of Chemical Biology and Pharmaceutical Sciences
Zhao, Yadu, Fifth Faculty of Clinical Medicine
Zhao, Yi, Second Faculty of Clinical Medicine
Zhao, Yuanli, Fifth Faculty of Clinical Medicine
Zheng, Banghe, Fourth Faculty of Clinical Medicine
Zheng, Jie, School of Basic Medical Sciences
Zheng, Yi, Faculty of Mental Health
Zhou, Bing, Fourth Faculty of Clinical Medicine
Zhou, Qiwen, Sixth Faculty of Clinical Medicine
Zhou, Yaoting, School of Chinese Traditional Medicine
Zhou, Yujie, Sixth Faculty of Clinical Medicine
Zhu, Xinping, School of Basic Medical Sciences

CENTRAL ACADEMY OF ARTS AND DESIGN

34 North Dong Huan Rd, Beijing 100020
Telephone: (10) 65026391
Founded 1956
Pres.: Chang Shana
Vice-Pres: Wang Ming Zhi, Yang Yong Shan, Wang Zhong Xin
Library Dir: Qiu Chengde
Library of 170,000 vols

Number of teachers: 240
Number of students: 900 (36 postgraduates)
Publications: *College Journal* (12 a year), *Decoration* (4 a year), *Reference on Arts and Crafts* (12 a year).

CENTRAL UNIVERSITY OF FINANCE AND ECONOMICS

39 Xue Yuan Nan Rd, Beijing 100081
Telephone: (10) 62289132
Fax: (10) 62289132
E-mail: wlb@cufe.edu.cn
Internet: www.cufe.edu.cn
Founded 1949
Min. of Education control
Academic year: September to July
Pres.: Wang Guangqian
Vice-Pres: Chen Ming, Li Junsheng, Wang Guohua, Yuan Dong
Head of Graduate Dept: Qi Lan
Librarian: Han Zhiping
Number of teachers: 500
Number of students: 14,000 (6,800 full-time, 7,200 part-time)
Publication: *Journal of the Central University of Finance and Economics* (12 a year)

DEANS

Business School: Sun Guohui
College of Culture and Communication: Wang Qiang
Department of Athletics Economy and Management: Gao Han
Department of Economic Mathematics: Chen Wendeng
Department of Foreign Languages: Wang Xiaohong
Department of Insurance: Hao Yansu
Department of Investment Economics: Wang Yaoqi
Department of Sociology: Li Zhijun
School of Accountancy: Meng Yan
School of Economics: Jin Zhesong
School of Finance: Shi Jianping
School of Information: Wang Lubin
School of Law: Gan Gongen
School of Public Finance and Administration: Ma Haitao

PROFESSORS

Bao, Xiaoguang, Culture and Communication
Chen, Wendeng, Economic Mathematics
Cui, Xinjian, Business
Dong, Chengzhang, Information
Gan, Gongen, Law
Han, Fuling, Finance
Hao, Yansu, Insurance
Hou, Ronghua, Economics
Huo, Pei, Finance
Huo, Qiang, Finance
Jiang, Weizhuang, Public Finance and Administration
Jiang, Xian, Economics
Jin, Zhesong, Economics
Lan, Cuipai, Law
Li, Baoren, Public Finance and Administration
Li, Jian, Finance
Li, Jixiong, Insurance
Li, Junsheng, Public Finance and Administration
Li, Shuang, Accountancy
Li, Xiaolin, Insurance
Li, Yan, Public Finance and Administration
Li, Zhijun, Sociology
Liao, Siping, Culture and Communication
Liu, Heng, Public Finance and Administration
Liu, Hongxia, Accountancy
Liu, Yang, Economics
Ma, Haitao, Public Finance and Administration

Meng, Yan, Accountancy
Miao, Runsheng, Accountancy
Pan, Jinsheng, Finance
Pan, Shengchu, Information
Qi, Huaijin, Accountancy
Qi, Lan, Economics
Shi, Jianping, Finance
Shi, Shulin, Law
Sun, Baowen, Information
Sun, Guohui, Business
Wang, Guohua, Public Finance and Administration
Wang, Jinying, Business
Wang, Juncai, Accountancy
Wang, Kejing, Economics
Wang, Lubin, Information
Wang, Peizhen, Finance
Wang, Qiang, Culture and Communication
Wang, Ruihua, Accountancy
Wang, Yongjun, Public Finance and Administration
Wang, Yongping, Accountancy
Wei, Zhenxiong, Accountancy
Wen, Qian, Economics
Wu, Zhenzhi, Finance
Xi, Shuqin, Accountancy
Xu, Shanhui, Finance
Xu, Xiangyu, Investment Economics
Yang, Jinguang, Accountancy
Yang, Zhiqing, Public Finance and Administration
Yao, Sui, Finance
Zhang, Biqiong, Finance
Zhang, Liqin, Finance
Zhang, Shujun, Business
Zhang, Tiegang, Economics
Zhao, Lifeng, Economics
Zhao, Xueheng, Public Finance and Administration

CENTRAL ACADEMY OF FINE ARTS

8 Hua Jia Di Nan Jie, Chaoyang District, Beijing 100102
Telephone: (10) 64771018
Fax: (10) 64771136
Internet: www.cafa.com.cn
Founded 1950
Min. of Education control
Academic year: September to July
Pres.: Pan Gongkai
Vice-Pres.: Fan Dian
Head of Graduate Department: Chu Di
Librarian: Shen Jiandong
Number of teachers: 141
Number of students: 1,000
Publications: *Art Research* (4 a year), *World Art* (4 a year)

DEANS

Art History Department: Yin Jinan
Art Education Department: Jin Jiazhen
Chinese Painting Department: Tian Liming
First-year Foundation Programme: Wen Guozhang
Mural Painting Department: Sun Jingbo
Oil Painting Department: Dai Shihe
Printmaking Department: Su Xinping
School of Architecture: Lu Pinjing
School of Design: Wang Min
School of Humanities: Yin Jinan
Sculpture Department: Sui Jianguo

PROFESSORS

Cao, Li, Mural Painting
Chao, Ge, Oil Painting
Chen, Wenyi, Mural Painting
Dai, Shihe, Oil Painting
Ding, Yilin, Oil Painting
Fan, Di'an, Humanities
Gao, Rongsheng, Printmaking
Hong, Pengsheng, Humanities
Hu, Jiancheng, Oil Painting
Hu, Wei, Chinese Painting

Hu, Yue, Architecture
Huang, Wei, Architecture
Li, Linzuo, Mural Painting
Lu, Shengzhong, Oil Painting
Lu, Pinjing, Architecture
Luo, Shiping, Humanities
Ma, Lu, Oil Painting
Qiu, Zhenzhong, Chinese Painting
Su, Xinping, Printmaking
Sui, Jianguo, Sculpture
Sun, Jiabo, Sculpture
Sun, Jingbo, Mural Painting
Tan, Ping, Design
Tang, Yongli, Chinese Painting
Tian, Liming, Chinese Painting
Wang, Min, Design
Wang, Yong, Chinese Painting
Wen, Guozhang, First-year Foundation Program
Wu, Changjiang, Printmaking
Yin, Jinan, Art History
Zhou, Zhiyu, Design

CENTRAL CHINA NORMAL UNIVERSITY (HUAZHONG NORMAL UNIVERSITY)

152 Luoyu Rd, Wuhan 430079, Hubei Province

Telephone: (27) 67868133
E-mail: www@ccnu.edu.cn
Internet: www.ccnu.edu.cn

Founded 1903
Min. of Education control
Academic year: September to July

Pres.: Ma Ming
Vice-Pres: Huang Yongling, Le Guangzhou, Li Zongkai, Pang Xiangnong, Yang Zhengnong
Librarian: Zuo Bin

Number of teachers: 1,200
Number of students: 20,000

Publications: Foreign Literature Studies (6 a year), Journal of Central China Normal University (humanities and social science, 6 a year), Journal of Central China Normal University (natural sciences, 6 a year)

DEANS

College of Networking Academy: Zhang Youliang
Department of Computer Science: Tan Liansheng
Department of Information Management: Wang Xuedong
Department of Information Technology: Zhang Guoping
Department of Sociology: Jiang Lihua
School of Chemistry: Yang Guangfu
School of City and Environmental Science: Zeng Juxin
School of Economics: Cao Yang
School of Foreign Language and Literature: Zhang Weiyou
School of History and Culture: Wang Yude
School of Life Science: Chen Qicai
School of Literature: Li Xiangnong
School of Management: Wu Jinsheng
School of Mathematics and Statistics: Deng Yinbin
School of Music: Tian Xiaobao
School of Physics and Technology: Wang Enke
School of Political Science and Law: Lin Jian

PROFESSORS

Bai, Guozhong, Information Management
Cai, Jinquan, History and Culture
Cai, Xu, Physics and Technology
Cao, Yang, Economics
Chen, Chuanli, Mathematics and Statistics
Chen, Guosheng, Life Science
Chen, Hongwei, Foreign Language and Literature
Chen, Jianxian, Literature
Chen, Jisheng, Physics and Technology
Chen, Qicai, Life Science
Chen, Qun, Mathematics and Statistics
Chen, Yin'e, Sociology
Chen, Youlin, Foreign Language and Literature
Chu, Zexiang, Literature
Dai, Jianye, Literature
Deng, Hongguang, History and Culture
Deng, Xianrui, City and Environmental Science
Deng, Yinbin, Mathematics and Statistics
Ding, Mingwu, Chemistry
Ding, Yihua, History and Culture
Feng, Gang, Computer Science
Fu, Huihua, Life Science
Gao, Huaping, Literature
Gong, Shengsheng, City and Environmental Science
Gu, Yongxing, History and Culture
Gu, Zhihua, History and Culture
Guo, Jun, Foreign Language and Literature
Guo, Tuoying, Mathematics and Statistics
Han, Kefang, Physics and Technology
Han, Xunguo, Music
He, Baigen, City and Environmental Science
He, Hongwu, Chemistry
He, Jianming, History and Culture
He, Sui, Mathematics and Statistics
He, Tingting, Computer Science
He, Xuefeng, Sociology
Hong, Huazhu, Life Science
Hou, Fude, Physics and Technology
Hu, Jinzhu, Computer Science
Hu, Xiangming, Physics and Technology
Hu, Yamin, Literature
Hu, Zongqiu, Chemistry
Hua, Xianfa, Foreign Language and Literature
Huang, Huawen, History and Culture
Huang, Qingyang, Life Science
Huang, Wanhui, Computer Science
Huang, Xiaoqun, Foreign Language and Literature
Huang, Xintang, Physics and Technology
Huang, Yonglin, Literature
Huang, Zhengbo, History and Culture
Huang, Zhonglian, Foreign Language and Literature
Jia, Ya, Physics and Technology
Jia, Zhijie, Physics and Technology
Jin, Boxin, City and Environmental Science
Jin, Cong, Computer Science
Jing, Cairui, City and Environmental Science
Li, Bangji, Computer Science
Li, Gaoxiang, Physics and Technology
Li, Jialin, Physics and Technology
Li, Jiaqing, City and Environmental Science
Li, Jiarong, Physics and Technology
Li, Qirong, History and Culture
Li, Taosheng, Mathematics and Statistics
Li, Wenxin, Life Science
Li, Xiangnong, Literature
Li, Xiaoyan, Computer Science
Li, Xingrun, Life Science
Li, Xuebao, Life Science
Li, Yadan, Foreign Language and Literature
Li, Zhiyang, Physics and Technology
Li, Zhonghua, Chemistry
Liang, Miaoyuan, Computer Science
Liao, Meizhen, Foreign Language and Literature
Liao, Zhanru, Chemistry
Lin, Deli, Life Science
Liu, Anhai, Literature
Liu, Feng, Physics and Technology
Liu, Gusheng, History and Culture
Liu, Lianshou, Physics and Technology
Liu, Shaojun, History and Culture
Liu, Shenghua, Chemistry
Liu, Shengjia, City and Environmental Science
Liu, Shengxiang, Life Science
Liu, Shouhua, Literature
Liu, Wei, History and Culture
Liu, Wu, Physics and Technology
Liu, Xianlong, Mathematics and Statistics
Liu, Yonghong, Foreign Language and Literature
Liu, Zhaojie, Chemistry
Lou, Cequn, Information Management
Lu, Guanghan, Chemistry
Lu, Wuqiang, City and Environmental Science
Luo, Bangcheng, Mathematics and Statistics
Luo, Dehui, History and Culture
Ma, Chengwu, Literature
Ma, Min, History and Culture
Meng, Dazhong, Physics and Technology
Mou, Jimei, Physics and Technology
Nie, Zhendao, Foreign Language and Literature
Peng, Changzheng, History and Culture
Peng, Jianxin, Life Science
Peng, Nansheng, History and Culture
Qiu, Baosheng, Life Science
Qiu, Zihua, Literature
Shao, Qingyu, City and Environmental Science
Shen, Jie, Sociology
Shen, Zhengyu, Literature
Su, Baimei, Foreign Language and Literature
Sun, Wenxian, Literature
Tan, Banghe, Literature
Tan, Chuanfeng, City and Environmental Science
Tan, Hong, Mathematics and Statistics
Tan, Liansheng, Computer Science
Tang, Chengchun, Physics and Technology
Tao, Jiayuan, City and Environmental Science
Tian, Songqing, City and Environmental Science
Wan, Jian, Chemistry
Wang, Enke, Physics and Technology
Wang, Guosheng, Literature
Wang, Guoxiu, Life Science
Wang, Lihua, Sociology
Wang, Manjun, Literature
Wang, Qingsheng, Literature
Wang, Qizhou, Literature
Wang, Weijun, Information Management
Wang, Xianpei, Literature
Wang, Xuedong, Information Management
Wang, Yangang, Chemistry
Wang, Younian, Literature
Wang, Yude, History and Culture
Wang, Yufeng, Life Science
Wang, Zelong, Literature
Wei, Changhua, Computer Science
Wu, Gang, Life Science
Wu, Qi, History and Culture
Wu, Yi, Sociology
Wu, Yuanfang, Physics and Technology
Xia, Mingyuan, Mathematics and Statistics
Xia, Xiaobin, Life Science
Xiang, Jiquan, Sociology
Xiao, Debao, Computer Science
Xie, Minyu, Mathematics and Statistics
Xin, Fuyi, Literature
Xin, Laishun, History and Culture
Xiong, Tieji, History and Culture
Xiu, Diao, Literature
Xu, Qiaoli, City and Environmental Science
Xu, Senlin, Mathematics and Statistics
Xu, Zuhua, Literature
Yan, Changhong, History and Culture
Yan, Guozheng, Mathematics and Statistics
Yan, Shaoxiang, History and Culture
Yang, Baoliang, City and Environmental Science
Yang, Chang, History and Culture
Yang, Chunbin, Physics and Technology
Yang, Guangfu, Chemistry
Yang, Shao, Life Science
Yang, Shuanghua, Computer Science
Yang, Xu, Life Science
Yao, Weijun, History and Culture
Yi, Honggen, Foreign Language and Literature

You, LIRONG, Sociology
Yu, GUANGMING, City and Environmental Science
Yu, ZEHUA, Life Science
ZENG, JUXIN, City and Environmental Science
ZENG, LIANMAO, City and Environmental Science
ZENG, QINGQIANG, Foreign Language and Literature
ZHAN, CHANGGUO, Chemistry
ZHAN, ZHENGKUN, Chemistry
ZHANG, AIDONG, Chemistry
ZHANG, CHANGNIAN, Music
ZHANG, FAN, Information Management
ZHANG, GUOPING, Physics and Technology
ZHANG, KAIQUAN, History and Culture
ZHANG, LIDE, Physics and Technology
ZHANG, LONGSHENG, Foreign Language and Literature
ZHANG, QUANMING, History and Culture
ZHANG, SANXI, Literature
ZHANG, SHAOYAN, Economics
ZHANG, WEIYOU, Foreign Language and Literature
ZHANG, YINGLIN, Foreign Language and Literature
ZHANG, YONGJIAN, Literature
ZHANG, YUNENG, Literature
ZHANG, ZHENGMING, History and Culture
ZHAO, YIJUN, Life Science
ZHENG, QUAN, Mathematics and Statistics
ZHENG, XIAOPING, Physics and Technology
ZHOU, DAICUI, Physics and Technology
ZHOU, GUOLIN, History and Culture
ZHOU, JIYUAN, Life Science
ZHOU, XIAOMING, Literature
ZHOU, ZHENGRONG, Mathematics and Statistics
ZHOU, ZONGKUI, Sociology
ZHU, CHANGJIANG, Mathematics and Statistics
ZHU, CHUANFANG, Chemistry
ZHU, XINDE, Chemistry
ZHU, YING, History and Culture
ZOU, SHANGHUI, City and Environmental Science
ZUO, BIN, Sociology

CENTRAL CONSERVATORY OF MUSIC

43 Bao Jia St, Beijing 100031
Telephone: (10) 66425598
Fax: (10) 66413138
E-mail: ccom@ccom.edu.cn
Internet: www.ccom.edu.cn
Founded 1950
Min. of Culture control
Academic year: September to July
Pres.: WANG CIZHAO
Vice-Pres: LI XU, LIU KANGHUA, XU CHANGJUN, ZHOU HAIHONG
Head of Graduate Dept: WANG CIZHAO
Librarian: ZHOU HAIHONG
Number of teachers: 278
Number of students: 1,665
Publication: *Haihong Journal of the Central Conservatory of Music* (4 a year)

DEANS

Composition Department: TANG JIANPING
Conducting Department: YU FENG
General Education Department: LIANG JING
Music Education Department: GAO JIANJIN
Musicology Department: ZHANG BOYU
Orchestral Instruments Department: LIU PEIYAN
Piano Department: YANG MING
Traditional Instruments Department: ZHAO HANYANG
Voice and Opera Department: LIU DONG

PROFESSORS

BIAN, MENG, Piano
CAI, ZHOANGDE, Musicology
CHEN, BIGANG, Piano
CHEN, DANBU, Composition
CHEN, ZIMIN, Musicology
CHENG, DA, Voice and Opera
DU, MINGXIN, Composition
DU, TAIHANG, Piano
DUAN, PINGTAI, Composition
GAO, JIANJIN, Music Education
GUI, XILI, Traditional Instruments
GUO, SHUZHEN, Voice and Opera
GUO, WENJING, Composition
HAN, XIAOMING, Orchestral Instruments
HAN, ZHIHONG, Piano
HAN, ZHONGJIE, Conducting
HE, RONG, Orchestral Instruments
HEI, HAITAO, Voice and Opera
HU, SHIXI, Voice and Opera
HU, ZHIHOU, Traditional Instruments
HUANG, HE, Traditional Instruments
HUANG, PEIYING, Piano
HUANG, XIAOHE, Musicology
LI, GUANGHUA, Traditional Instruments
LI, HENG, Traditional Instruments
LI, JITI, Composition
LI, MENG, Traditional Instruments
LI, QIFENG, Piano
LI, XIANGTING, Traditional Instruments
LI, XINCHANG, Voice and Opera
LI, YINGHUA, Musicology
LI, ZHENGUI, Traditional Instruments
LIANG, DANA, Orchestral Instruments
LIANG, NING, Voice and Opera
LIN, SHICHENG, Traditional Instruments
LIN, YAXIONG, Musicology
LIU, CHANGFU, Traditional Instruments
LIU, DONG, Voice and Opera
LIU, LIN, Composition
LIU, PEIYAN, Orchestral Instruments
LIU, YUAN, Composition
LUO, ZHONGRONG, Composition
MA, HONGHAI, Voice and Opera
PAN, BIXIN, Musicology
PAN, CHUN, Piano
PENG, KANGLIANG, Voice and Opera
PINI, YAXUO, Voice and Opera
SHENG, LIHONG, Composition
SONG, JIN, Musicology
TAI, ER, Piano
TANG, JIANPING, Composition
TIAN, LIANTAO, Musicology
WANG, CIZHAO, Musicology
WANG, SHUHE, Musicology
WANG, XIANLIN, Voice and Opera
WANG, XIUFENG, Voice and Opera
WANG, YAOLING, Orchestral Instruments
WU, SHIKAI, Composition
WU, ZHUQIANG, Composition
XIE, HUAZHEN, Piano
XU, CHANGJUN, Composition
XU, XIN, Conducting
YANG, HONGNIAN, Conducting
YANG, JUN, Piano
YANG, MING, Piano
YAO, HENGLU, Composition
YE, XIAOGANG, Composition
YU, FENG, Conducting
YU, RUNYANG, Musicology
YU, SUXIAN, Composition
YU, ZHIGANG, Musicology
YUAN, JINGFANG, Musicology
ZHANG, BOYU, Musicology
ZHANG, JIANYI, Voice and Opera
ZHANG, LIPING, Voice and Opera
ZHANG, QIAN, Musicology
ZHANG, SHAO, Traditional Instruments
ZHAO, BIXUAN, Voice and Opera
ZHAO, DENGYING, Voice and Opera
ZHAO, HANYANG, Traditional Instruments
ZHAO, RUILIN, Orchestral Instruments
ZHENG, XIAOYING, Conducting
ZHENG, ZHUXIANG, Musicology
ZHONG, ZILIN, Musicology
ZHOU, GUANGREN, Piano
ZHOU, HAIHONG, Musicology
ZHOU, QINGQING, Musicology
ZHU, DUN, Orchestral Instruments
ZHU, YIBING, Orchestral Instruments

CENTRAL UNIVERSITY FOR NATIONALITIES

27 Nan Da Rd, Zhong Guan Village, Haidian District, Beijing 100081
Telephone: (10) 68932544
Fax: (10) 68932544
E-mail: cunofficexz@sina.com
Internet: www.cun.edu.cn
Founded 1951
State Ethnic Affairs Commission control
Academic year: September to July
Pres.: RONG SHIXIANG
Vice-Pres: AI'BI BULA, CHEN LI, GUO WEIPING, HUANG FENGXIAN, JIN YASHENG, REN ZHONGXIA, YAN YUMING
Head of Graduate Dept: CHEN LI
Librarian: LI DELONG
Number of teachers: 700
Number of students: 13,000
Publications: *Journal of The Central University for Nationalities* (natural sciences, 4 a year), *Journal of The Central University for Nationalities* (philosophy and social sciences, 6 a year)

DEANS

School of Arts: YIN HUILI
School of Education: WANG JUN
School of Ethnology and Sociology: YANG SHENGMIN
School of Foreign Language: HE KEYONG
School of Law: ZHU JING'AN
School of Literature, Journalism and Communication: BAI WEI
School of Management: LI JUNQING
School of Music: MENG XINYANG
College of Dance: SU ZIHONG
College of Economics: LIU YONGJI
College of Life and Environment Science: FENG JINZHAO
College of National Minorities: LI JINFANG
College of Science and Engineering: FENG JINZHAO
Department of History: LI HONGBIN
Department of Philosophy and Religion: GONG YUKUAN
Department of Physics: WEI XIAOKANG
Preparatory Department: SONG TAICHENG
Research Institute of Tibet: BANBAN DUOJIE

PROFESSORS

BAI, RUNSHENG, Literature, Journalism and Communication
BAI, WEI, Literature, Journalism and Communication
BAI, YINTAI, National Minority Study
BANBAN, DUOJIE, Tibetan Studies
BI, MUXUN, Literature, Journalism and Communication
BU, ZHONGJIAN, Philosophy and Religion
CHEN, CHANGPING, Ethnology and Sociology
CHEN, FANGYING, Science and Engineering
CHEN, JIANJIAN, Tibetan Studies
CHEN, NAN, History
CUI, GUANZHI, Science and Engineering
DALI, ZHABU, History
DING, HONG, Ethnology and Sociology
DING, SHIQING, National Minority Study
FENG, JINZHAO, Life and Environment Science
FENG, JINZHAO, Science and Engineering
FU, CHENGZHOU, Literature, Journalism and Communication
FU, YIXIN, Education
GEN, SHIMIN, National Minority Study
GENG, YUFANG, Tibetan Studies
GESANG, DUNZHU, Tibetan Studies

GESANG, JUMIAN, Tibetan Studies
GONG, YUKUAN, Philosophy and Religion
HA, JINGXIONG, Education
HAMITI, TIEMUER, National Minority Study
HASHI, E'ERDUN, National Minority Study
HE, JINRUI, Philosophy and Religion
HE, KEYONG, Foreign Languages
HE, QIMIN, Philosophy and Religion
HE, WEI, Science and Engineering
HU, SHAOHUA, History
HU, ZHENHUA, National Minority Study
HUANG, KAI, Science and Engineering
HUOXIGE, TAOKETAO, National Minority
  Study
JI, YONGHAI, National Minority Study
JIAO, YUGUO, Life and Environment Science
JIN, RIGUANG, Music
LI, BINQUAN, Tibetan Studies
LI, GUIZHI, History
LI, HONGBIN, History
LI, JINFANG, National Minority Study
LI, JUNQING, Management
LI, KUI, Arts
LI, XINCHANG, Music
LI, YAN, National Minority Study
LI, YAN, Law
LIN, JING, Music
LIU, BINGJIANG, Arts
LIU, JIANMING, Literature, Journalism and
  Communication
LIU, JINZHEN, Science and Engineering
LIU, YONGJI, Economics
LIU, YONGZHOU, Literature, Journalism and
  Communication
LU, SHAO'EN, Music
MEN, DUHU, National Minority Study
MENG, XINYANG, Music
PIAO, CHANGTIAN, Music
SHANG, YANBIN, History
SHAO, XIANSHU, Ethnology and Sociology
SHEN, JIA, Music
SONG, RUBU, National Minority Study
SU, ZIHONG, Dance
TAO, LIPAN, Literature, Journalism and Com-
  munication
TENG, XING, Education
WANG, JUN, Education
WANG, RAO, Tibetan Studies
WANG, TIANJIN, Economics
WANG, YUANXIN, National Minority Study
WANG, ZHONGHAN, History
WANGMEN, TIEGA, National Minority Study
WEI, FENGRONG, Science and Engineering
WU, LIJI, National Minority Study
XIAO, XIURONG, Management
XING, FUCHON, Science and Engineering
XING, LI, Literature, Journalism and Com-
  munication
XU, LUYA, Foreign Languages
XU, SHOUCHUN, Science and Engineering
XU, WANBANG, Ethnology and Sociology
XU, YONGZHI, History
XU, YONGZHI, Management
YANG, CONG, Economics
YANG, ROOMING, Life and Environment Sci-
  ence
YANG, SHENGMIN, Ethnology and Sociology
YAO, NIANCI, History
YIN, HUILI, Arts
YU, KESEN, Literature, Journalism and Com-
  munication
YU, QIMING, Philosophy and Religion
ZENG, SHIQI, National Minority Study
ZHANG, GONGJIN, National Minority Study
ZHANG, GUANGHUA, Science and Engineering
ZHAO, KANG, Tibetan Studies
ZHAO, SHILIN, Philosophy and Religion
ZHOU, LI, Management
ZHOU, RUNNIAN, Tibetan Studies
ZHU, JING'AN, Law
ZHU, ZHENGYUAN, Science and Engineering

CENTRAL SOUTH UNIVERSITY

Chang Sha 410083, Hunan Province
Telephone: (731) 8879225
Fax: (731) 8830308
E-mail: csuweb@mail.csu.edu.cn
Internet: www.csu.edu.cn
Founded 1952
Academic year: September to July

Pres.: HUANG BOYUN
Vice-Pres: CHEN QIYUAN, CHEN ZHIYA, HU
  TIEHUI, LI GUIYUAN, QIU GUANZHOU
Head of Graduate Dept: LIU YILUN
Librarian: FANG ZHENG

Publications: *International Chinese Nursing
  Journal* (4 a year), *Journal of Central
  South University* (6 a year), *Journal of
  Central South University* (medical sci-
  ences, 6 a year), *Journal of Central South
  University* (social sciences, 6 a year),
  *Transactions of Nonferrous Metals Society
  of China* (6 a year)

DEANS

School of Basic Medical Sciences: WEN JIFANG
School of Business: CHEN XIAOHONG
School of Chemistry and Chemical Engineer-
  ing: HUANG KELONG
School of Civil Engineering and Architecture:
  YU ZHIWU
School of Energy and Power Engineering:
  ZHOU DIAOMIN
School of Fine Arts: DAI DUAN
School of Foreign Languages: TU GUOYUAN
School of Geoscience and Environmental
  Engineering: DAI TAGEN
School of Info-Physics and Geomatics Engin-
  eering: TANG JINGTIAN
School of Information Science and Engineer-
  ing: GUI WEIHUA
School of Law: QI DUOJUN
School of Literature: OU YANG YOUQUAN
School of Materials Science and Engineering:
  YI DANQING
School of Mathematical Sciences and Com-
  puting Technology: ZOU JIEZHONG
School of Mechanical and Electrical Engin-
  eering: WU YUNXIN
School of Medical Technology and Informa-
  tion: GUO QULIAN
School of Metallurgic Science and Engineer-
  ing: LI JIE
School of Nursing: HE GUOPING
School of Pharmaceutical Sciences: LI YUAN-
  JIAN
School of Physics, Sciences and Technology:
  YANG BINGCHU
School of Politics and Public Administration:
  LI JIANHUA
School of Public Health: XIAO SHUIYUAN
School of Resources Processing and Bioengi-
  neering: HU YUEHUA
School of Resources and Safety Engineering:
  LI XIBING
School of Stomatology: JIAN XINCHUN
School of Traffic and Transportation Engin-
  eering: SHI FENG

PROFESSORS

CAI, HONGWEI, Medical Technology and Infor-
  mation
CAI, ZIXING, Information Science and Engin-
  eering
CAO, JIAN, Physics, Sciences and Technology
CAO, XING, Business
CHANG, YETIAN, Medical Technology and
  Information
CHEN, FANGPING, Medical Technology and
  Information
CHEN, FENG, Materials Science and Engin-
  eering
CHEN, HAIBO, Mathematical Sciences and
  Computing Technology
CHEN, HUANXIN, Civil Engineering and Archi-
  tecture

CHEN, HUANXIN, Energy and Power Engin-
  eering
CHEN, JIAN'ER, Information Science and
  Engineering
CHEN, KANGHUA, Powder Metallurgy
CHEN, LIQUAN, Chemistry and Chemical
  Engineering
CHEN, QIYUAN, Chemistry and Chemical
  Engineering
CHEN, SHIZHU, Materials Science and Engin-
  eering
CHEN, SONGQIAO, Information Science and
  Engineering
CHEN, XIAOHONG, Business
CHEN, XIAOQING, Chemistry and Chemical
  Engineering
CHEN, XIAOSONG, Mathematical Sciences and
  Computing Technology
CHEN, XIUFANG, Civil Engineering and Archi-
  tecture
CHEN, YIZHUANG, Politics and Public Admin-
  istration
CHEN, YUEWU, Foreign Languages
CHEN, YUXIANG, Bioscience and Technology
CHEN, ZHENXING, Chemistry and Chemical
  Engineering
CHEN, ZHIGANG, Information Science and
  Engineering
CHEN, ZHONGWEN, Foreign Languages
DAI, BINXIANG, Mathematical Sciences and
  Computing Technology
DAI, DUAN, Fine Arts
DAI, GONGLIAN, Civil Engineering and Archi-
  tecture
DENG, CHAO, Business
DENG, DEHUA, Civil Engineering and Archi-
  tecture
DENG, FEIYAOI, Chemistry and Chemical
  Engineering
DENG, HANWU, Pharmaceutical Sciences
DENG, RUIJIAO, Nursing
DENG, TIANSHENG, Business
DU, YONG, Powder Metallurgy
FAN, XIANGRU, Business
FAN, XIANLONG, Foreign Languages
FAN, XIAOHUI, Resources Processing and
  Bioengineering
FAN, XIAOPING, Information Science and
  Engineering
FANG, LIGANG, Civil Engineering and Archi-
  tecture
FANG, PING, Medical Technology and Infor-
  mation
FANG, YUNXIANG, Pharmaceutical Sciences
FANG, ZHENG, Chemistry and Chemical
  Engineering
FENG, QIMING, Resources Processing and
  Bioengineering
FU, HELIN, Civil Engineering and Architec-
  ture
GAN, SIQING, Mathematical Sciences and
  Computing Technology
GAN, WEIPING, Materials Science and Engin-
  eering
GAO, YANG, Business
GONG, FAN, Chemistry and Chemical Engin-
  eering
GONG, YANPING, Business
GU, JINGHUA, Resources Processing and
  Bioengineering
GU, YINGYING, Chemistry and Chemical
  Engineering
GUAN, LUXIONG, Chemistry and Chemical
  Engineering
GUI, WEIHUA, Information Science and
  Engineering
GUO, GUANGHUA, Physics, Sciences and Tech-
  nology
GUO, QULIAN, Medical Technology and Infor-
  mation
GUO, SHAOHUA, Civil Engineering and Archi-
  tecture
GUO, XIANGRONG, Civil Engineering and
  Architecture
HAN, JINGQUAN, Foreign Languages
HAN, QINGLAN, Business

HAN, XULI, Information Science and Engineering

HAN, XULI, Mathematical Sciences and Computing Technology

HE, BOQUAN, Resources Processing and Bioengineering

HE, GUOPING, Nursing

HE, HONGBO, Physics, Sciences and Technology

HE, HONGQU, Business

HE, JISHAN, Business

HE, XUEWEI, Literature

HE, YUNBO, Foreign Languages

HOU, MANLING, Chemistry and Chemical Engineering

HOU, ZHENTING, Mathematical Sciences and Computing Technology

HU, HUIPING, Chemistry and Chemical Engineering

HU, HUOSHENG, Information Science and Engineering

HU, KAI, Politics and Public Administration

HU, WEIXIN, Bioscience and Technology

HU, YUEHUA, Resources Processing and Bioengineering

HU, ZHENHUA, Business

HUANG, BOYUN, Materials Science and Engineering

HUANG, FANGLIN, Civil Engineering and Architecture

HUANG, JIAN, Chemistry and Chemical Engineering

HUANG, JIANBO, Business

HUANG, JIANREN, Foreign Languages

HUANG, KELONG, Chemistry and Chemical Engineering

HUANG, LANFANG, Chemistry and Chemical Engineering

HUANG, PEIYUN, Materials Science and Engineering

HUANG, PEIYUN, Powder Metallurgy

HUANG, QIZHONG, Powder Metallurgy

HUANG, SHENGSHENG, Resources Processing and Bioengineering

HUANG, YANPING, Politics and Public Administration

HUANG, YONG'AN, Foreign Languages

HUANG, ZHUCHENG, Resources Processing and Bioengineering

HUO, GUOJING, Civil Engineering and Architecture

HUO, YAOHUI, Powder Metallurgy

JIA, WEIJIA, Information Science and Engineering

JIAN, XINCHUN, Stomatology

JIANG, DONGJIU, Nursing

JIANG, DONGMEI, Nursing

JIANG, JINZHI, Chemistry and Chemical Engineering

JIANG, SHAOJIAN, Energy and Power Engineering

JIANG, TAO, Resources Processing and Bioengineering

JIANG, XINHUA, Information Science and Engineering

JIANG, YIMIN, Physics, Sciences and Technology

JIANG, YUREN, Chemistry and Chemical Engineering

JIN, ZHANPENG, Materials Science and Engineering

LAN, XIAOJUN, Medical Technology and Information

LENG, WUMING, Civil Engineering and Architecture

LI, BAIQING, Foreign Languages

LI, DENGQING, Medical Technology and Information

LI, HE, Energy and Power Engineering

LI, HONGJIAN, Physics, Sciences and Technology

LI, HUANDE, Pharmaceutical Sciences

LI, JIANHUA, Politics and Public Administration

LI, JIE, Chemistry and Chemical Engineering

LI, JUNPING, Mathematical Sciences and Computing Technology

LI, LIANG, Civil Engineering and Architecture

LI, LIPING, Business

LI, MINGSHENG, Business

LI, SONGREN, Resources Processing and Bioengineering

LI, XIAOBIN, Energy and Power Engineering

LI, XIAORU, Chemistry and Chemical Engineering

LI, XIBIN, Powder Metallurgy

LI, XUE, Mathematical Sciences and Computing Technology

LI, YANGCHENG, Mathematical Sciences and Computing Technology

LI, YANGSHENG, Fine Arts

LI, YANLIN, Foreign Languages

LI, YIBING, Information Science and Engineering

LI, YIBING, Physics, Sciences and Technology

LI, YIMIN, Powder Metallurgy

LI, YIZHI, Business

LI, YUANGAO, Chemistry and Chemical Engineering

LI, YUANJIAN, Pharmaceutical Sciences

LI, ZIRU, Business

LIANG, HONG, Chemistry and Chemical Engineering

LIANG, LAIYIN, Business

LIANG, XIMING, Information Science and Engineering

LIANG, YIZENG, Chemistry and Chemical Engineering

LIAO, SHENGMING, Civil Engineering and Architecture

LIAO, SHENGMING, Energy and Power Engineering

LIU, AIDONG, Business

LIU, BAOCHEN, Civil Engineering and Architecture

LIU, CHANGQING, Chemistry and Chemical Engineering

LIU, DONGRONG, Business

LIU, GUOPING, Information Science and Engineering

LIU, JIAJIA, Chemistry and Chemical Engineering

LIU, JIANSHE, Resources Processing and Bioengineering

LIU, KAIYU, Chemistry and Chemical Engineering

LIU, LIHANG, Politics and Public Administration

LIU, LIYING, Pharmaceutical Sciences

LIU, MINGJING, Foreign Languages

LIU, QINGTAN, Civil Engineering and Architecture

LIU, SHIJUN, Chemistry and Chemical Engineering

LIU, SUQIN, Chemistry and Chemical Engineering

LIU, WEIJUN, Mathematical Sciences and Computing Technology

LIU, XIAOCHUN, Medical Technology and Information

LIU, XINXING, Resources Processing and Bioengineering

LIU, XIONGFEI, Physics, Sciences and Technology

LIU, YANPING, Bioscience and Technology

LIU, YAZHENG, Business

LIU, YEXIANG, Energy and Power Engineering

LIU, YIRONG, Mathematical Sciences and Computing Technology

LIU, YONGHE, Medical Technology and Information

LIU, YONGMEI, Business

LIU, YOUNIAN, Chemistry and Chemical Engineering

LIU, ZAIMING, Mathematical Sciences and Computing Technology

LIU, ZEMIN, Literature

LIU, ZHIYI, Materials Science and Engineering

LIU, ZHUMING, Materials Science and Engineering

LUO, AIJING, Medical Technology and Information

LUO, AN, Information Science and Engineering

LUO, DAYONG, Information Science and Engineering

LUO, JIAOWAN, Mathematical Sciences and Computing Technology

LUO, WENDONG, Physics, Sciences and Technology

LUO, XIAOLING, Business

LUO, XINXING, Business

LUO, XUEGANG, Basic Medical Sciences

LUO, YIMING, Chemistry and Chemical Engineering

LUO, ZIQIANG, Basic Medical Sciences

LU, HAIBO, Powder Metallurgy

LU, XICHEN, Politics and Public Administration

LU, YAOHUAI, Politics and Public Administration

MA, CHENGYIN, Chemistry and Chemical Engineering

MAN, RUILIN, Chemistry and Chemical Engineering

MAO, XUANGUO, Literature

MEI, MEIZHI, Energy and Power Engineering

MENG, ZE, Foreign Languages

NIU, YINJIAN, Resources Processing and Bioengineering

OU YANG, YOUQUAN, Literature

PAN, QINGLIN, Materials Science and Engineering

PANG, CHUNYAO, Chemistry and Chemical Engineering

PEN, JINDING, Foreign Languages

PENG, JIEYING, Stomatology

PENG, LIMIN, Civil Engineering and Architecture

PENG, PINGYI, Politics and Public Administration

PENG, XIAOQI, Energy and Power Engineering

PENG, XIAOQI, Physics, Sciences and Technology

PENG, YUELIN, Mathematical Sciences and Computing Technology

QIAN, DONG, Chemistry and Chemical Engineering

QIN, XIAOQUN, Basic Medical Sciences

QIU, KEQIANG, Chemistry and Chemical Engineering

QIU, YUNREN, Chemistry and Chemical Engineering

QU, LONG, Chemistry and Chemical Engineering

QU, XUANHUI, Powder Metallurgy

RAO, QIUHUA, Civil Engineering and Architecture

RAO, YUELEI, Business

REN, FENGLIAN, Chemistry and Chemical Engineering

REN, JIFAN, Literature

RUAN, JIANMING, Powder Metallurgy

SHE, XIEBIN, Foreign Languages

SHEN, CHAOHONG, Business

SHEN, MEILAN, Mathematical Sciences and Computing Technology

SHEN, QUNTAI, Information Science and Engineering

SHI, RONGHUA, Information Science and Engineering

SHI, ZHANGMING, Energy and Power Engineering

SHU, WANGEN, Chemistry and Chemical Engineering

SI, SHIHUI, Chemistry and Chemical Engineering

SONG, HUIPING, Bioscience and Technology

SU, YUCHANG, Materials Science and Engineering

SUN, XIANGMING, Fine Arts

SUN, ZHENQIU, Mathematical Sciences and Computing Technology

TAN, DAREN, Medical Technology and Information
TAN, GUANZXHENG, Information Science and Engineering
TAN, MENGQUN, Basic Medical Sciences
TAN, XIPEI, Politics and Public Administration
TAN, YUNJIE, Foreign Languages
TANG, HONG'E, Civil Engineering and Architecture
TANG, RUIREN, Chemistry and Chemical Engineering
TANG, XIANHUA, Mathematical Sciences and Computing Technology
TANG, YOUGEN, Chemistry and Chemical Engineering
TANG, ZHANGUI, Stomatology
TAO, XINLU, Nursing
TU, GUOYUAN, Foreign Languages
TU, LING, Stomatology
WAN, ZHONG, Mathematical Sciences and Computing Technology
WANG, DIANZUO, Resources Processing and Bioengineering
WANG, GUOSHUN, Business
WANG, HANQING, Energy and Power Engineering
WANG, HUI, Chemistry and Chemical Engineering
WANG, JIABAO, Mathematical Sciences and Computing Technology
WANG, JIANQIANG, Business
WANG, JIANXIU, Chemistry and Chemical Engineering
WANG, JIGUI, Medical Technology and Information
WANG, LINGSEN, Powder Metallurgy
WANG, MENGJUN, Civil Engineering and Architecture
WANG, MING'AN, Medical Technology and Information
WANG, MINGMING, Nursing
WANG, MINGPU, Materials Science and Engineering
WANG, SHIPING, Basic Medical Sciences
WANG, SHUHUA, Resources Processing and Bioengineering
WANG, XIAOCHUN, Medical Technology and Information
WANG, XINGHUA, Civil Engineering and Architecture
WANG, YAN, Chemistry and Chemical Engineering
WANG, YIJUN, Information Science and Engineering
WANG, YONGHE, Civil Engineering and Architecture
WANG, YUECHUAN, Literature
WANG, ZHANGHUA, Literature
WANG, ZHIFA, Materials Science and Engineering
WANG, ZHIZHONG, Mathematical Sciences and Computing Technology
WEI, RENYONG, Information Science and Engineering
WEN, JIFANG, Basic Medical Sciences
WEN, YUSONG, Civil Engineering and Architecture
WU, JINMING, Business
WU, KUN, Mathematical Sciences and Computing Technology
WU, LIANGGANG, Business
WU, LIXIANG, Basic Medical Sciences
WU, XIANCHENG, Politics and Public Administration
XIA, CHANGQING, Materials Science and Engineering
XIA, JIAHUI, Bioscience and Technology
XIA, JINLAN, Resources Processing and Bioengineering
XIANG, SHU, Mathematical Sciences and Computing Technology
XIAO, LIMING, Foreign Languages
XIAO, TIEJIAN, Politics and Public Administration
XIAO, XIANZHONG, Basic Medical Sciences

XIAO, XIAODAN, Medical Technology and Information
XIAO, XU, Business
XIAO, ZEQIANG, Energy and Power Engineering
XIE, RUHE, Energy and Power Engineering
XIE, XIAOLI, Stomatology
XIE, YOUJUN, Civil Engineering and Architecture
XIONG, LUMAO, Politics and Public Administration
XIONG, XIANG, Powder Metallurgy
XIONG, YAN, Pharmaceutical Sciences
XU, HUI, Physics, Sciences and Technology
XU, JICHENG, Materials Science and Engineering
XU, QINGSONG, Mathematical Sciences and Computing Technology
XU, ZHISHENG, Civil Engineering and Architecture
YAN, AIMIN, Business
YAN, ZHEN, Literature
YANG, BINGCHU, Physics, Sciences and Technology
YANG, CHANGXIN, Information Science and Engineering
YANG, CHANGYING, Foreign Languages
YANG, DONGLIANG, Chemistry and Chemical Engineering
YANG, GUOLIN, Civil Engineering and Architecture
YANG, HUAMING, Resources Processing and Bioengineering
YANG, JUNSHENG, Civil Engineering and Architecture
YANG, SHOUKANG, Foreign Languages
YANG, WEIWEN, Business
YANG, XINRONG, Information Science and Engineering
YANG, ZHANHONG, Chemistry and Chemical Engineering
YE, BOLONG, Civil Engineering and Architecture
YE, HONGQI, Chemistry and Chemical Engineering
YE, MEIXIN, Civil Engineering and Architecture
YI, DANQING, Energy and Power Engineering
YI, JIANHONG, Powder Metallurgy
YI, MAOZHONG, Powder Metallurgy
YIN, ZHIMIN, Materials Science and Engineering
YIN, ZHOULAN, Chemistry and Chemical Engineering
YU, DEQUAN, Literature
YU, PING, Basic Medical Sciences
YU, SHENGHUA, Mathematical Sciences and Computing Technology
YU, SHOUYI, Information Science and Engineering
YU, ZHIWU, Civil Engineering and Architecture
YUAN, DONGYUAN, Physics, Sciences and Technology
YUAN, JINGEN, Civil Engineering and Architecture
YUAN, LEPING, Business
YUAN, MINGLIANG, Resources Processing and Bioengineering
YUAN, XIUGUI, Mathematical Sciences and Computing Technology
YUE, YIDING, Business
ZENG, CHANGQIU, Politics and Public Administration
ZENG, DONGMING, Chemistry and Chemical Engineering
ZENG, QINGFU, Basic Medical Sciences
ZENG, QINGREN, Basic Medical Sciences
ZENG, QINGYUAN, Civil Engineering and Architecture
ZENG, SUMIN, Materials Science and Engineering
ZENG, YUHUA, Nursing
ZENG, ZHICHENG, Basic Medical Sciences
ZHANG, CHENGPING, Foreign Languages
ZHANG, CONGYI, Foreign Languages

ZHANG, HANJUN, Mathematical Sciences and Computing Technology
ZHANG, HONGYAN, Mathematical Sciences and Computing Technology
ZHANG, HUAILIANG, Fine Arts
ZHANG, JIANXIANG, Basic Medical Sciences
ZHANG, JIASHENG, Civil Engineering and Architecture
ZHANG, JINGSHENG, Resources Processing and Bioengineering
ZHANG, JINRU, Chemistry and Chemical Engineering
ZHANG, LONGKUAN, Foreign Languages
ZHANG, NAN, Civil Engineering and Architecture
ZHANG, PINGMIN, Chemistry and Chemical Engineering
ZHANG, QINGJIN, Resources Processing and Bioengineering
ZHANG, QISEN, Civil Engineering and Architecture
ZHANG, QUAN, Energy and Power Engineering
ZHANG, SENKUAN, Foreign Languages
ZHANG, SHIMIN, Chemistry and Chemical Engineering
ZHANG, SIQI, Materials Science and Engineering
ZHANG, TAIMING, Chemistry and Chemical Engineering
ZHANG, TAISHAN, Information Science and Engineering
ZHANG, XINGXIAN, Foreign Languages
ZHANG, XINMIN, Materials Science and Engineering
ZHANG, XU, Foreign Languages
ZHANG, YAOJUN, Foreign Languages
ZHAO, WANGDA, Civil Engineering and Architecture
ZHAO, YAOLONG, Information Science and Engineering
ZHENG, ZHIQIAO, Materials Science and Engineering
ZHENG, ZHOUSHUN, Mathematical Sciences and Computing Technology
ZHON, HONG, Chemistry and Chemical Engineering
ZHONG, MEIZUO, Medical Technology and Information
ZHONG, SHI'AN, Chemistry and Chemical Engineering
ZHONG, YOUXUN, Literature
ZHOU, CHAOYANG, Civil Engineering and Architecture
ZHOU, CHUNSHAN, Chemistry and Chemical Engineering
ZHOU, DEBI, Chemistry and Chemical Engineering
ZHOU, DIAOMIN, Energy and Power Engineering
ZHOU, FEIMENG, Chemistry and Chemical Engineering
ZHOU, JICHENG, Physics, Sciences and Technology
ZHOU, KECHAO, Powder Metallurgy
ZHOU, KESHENG, Physics, Sciences and Technology
ZHOU, LIUXI, Foreign Languages
ZHOU, MINGDA, Chemistry and Chemical Engineering
ZHOU, NAIJUN, Energy and Power Engineering
ZHOU, PIN, Energy and Power Engineering
ZHOU, QIAN, Energy and Power Engineering
ZHOU, SHIQIONG, Civil Engineering and Architecture
ZHOU, TAO, Chemistry and Chemical Engineering
ZHU, DEQING, Resources Processing and Bioengineering
ZHU, KAICHENG, Physics, Sciences and Technology
ZHU, NIANQIONG, Nursing
ZHUANG, JIANMING, Resources Processing and Bioengineering

Zou, Beiji, Information Science and Engineering
Zou, Jiezhong, Mathematical Sciences and Computing Technology
Zuo, Tieyong, Materials Science and Engineering

CHANG'AN UNIVERSITY

Nan Er Huan Rd, Xian 710064, Shaanxi Province
Telephone: (29) 82334104
Fax: (29) 85261532
Internet: www.xahu.edu.cn
Founded 2000
Min. of Education control
Academic year: September to July
Pres.: Zhou Xu Hong
Vice-Pres: Li Yun Ji, Liu Bo Quan, Liu Jian Chao, Ma Jian
Head of Graduate Dept: Lu Peng Min
Librarian: Sha Ai Min

Number of teachers: 3,438
Number of students: 36,383

Publications: *Automobile Racing Driver* (12 a year), *China Journal of Highway and Transport* (4 a year), *Journal of Chang'an University* (architecture and environmental sciences, 6 a year), *Journal of Chang'an University* (natural sciences, 6 a year), *Journal of Chang'an University* (philosophy and social sciences, 6 a year), *Journal of Earth Sciences and Environment* (4 a year), *Journal of Traffic and Transportation Engineering* (4 a year), *Road Machinery and Construction Mechanization* (12 a year)

DEANS

College of Applied Technology: Hu Xue Mei
College of Construction Engineering: Wang Yi Hong
College of Earth Science and Land Resources Management: Li Yong
College of Environmental Science and Engineering: Wang Wen Ke
College of Foreign Languages: Li Min Quan
College of Geology Engineering and Geomatics: Peng Jian Min
College of Highway Engineering: Xu Yue
College of Information Engineering: He Yi Qu
School of Construction Machinery: Feng Zhong Xu
School of Economics and Management: Zhou Guo Guang
School of Humanities and Social Science: Liu Ji Fa
School of Science: Feng Jian Hu

PROFESSORS

Chen, De Chuan, Highway Management
Chen, Hong, Traffic Engineering
Chen, Kuan Min, Traffic Engineering
Chen, Zhi Xin, Geology Engineering and Geomatics
Chen, Zhong Da, Highways
Dai, Jing Liang, Highways
Dong, Qian Li, Economics and Management
Dou, Ming Jian, Highway Disaster Prevention and Cure
Du, Dong Ju, Geology Engineering and Geomatics
Fan, Wen, Geology Engineering and Geomatics
Feng, Jian Hu, Science
Feng, Zhen Yu, Science
Feng, Zhong Xu, Construction Machinery
Guan, Wei Xing, Environmental Science and Engineering
Guo, Yuan Shu, Information Engineering
Han, Sen, Highways
Hao, Pei Wen, Highways
Hao, Xian Wu, Bridges

He, An Ming, Science
He, Shuang Hai, Bridges
He, Yi Qu, Information Engineering
Hu, Da Lin, Bridges
Hu, Yong Biao, Construction Machinery
Hu, Yue, Bridges
Hu, Zhao Tong, Bridges
Huang, Ping Min, Bridges
Jiang, Chang Yi, Earth Science and Land Resources Management
Jiao, Sheng Jie, Construction Machinery
Ju, Yong Feng, Information Engineering
Lei, Sheng You, Geognosy and Tube Engineering
Li, Pei Cheng, Environmental Science and Engineering
Li, Qing Chun, Geology Engineering and Geomatics
Li, Xiu, Geology Engineering and Geomatics
Li, Yong, Earth Science and Land Resources Management
Li, Yun Feng, Environmental Science and Engineering
Li, Zi Qing, Bridges
Liu, Bao Jian, Geognosy and Tube Engineering
Liu, Ji Fa, Humanities and Social Science
Liu, Jian Xin, Bridges
Liu, Lai Jun, Bridges
Liu, Yong Jian, Bridges
Long, Shui Gen, Construction Machinery
Lu, Kang Cheng, Geognosy and Tube Engineering
Lu, Peng Min, Construction Machinery
Ma, Jiang Ming, Science
Ma, Rong Guo, Traffic Engineering
Ma, Tian Shan, Economics and Management
Mao, Yan Long, Geology Engineering and Geomatics
Men, Yu Ming, Geology Engineering and Geomatics
Ni, Wang Kui, Geology Engineering and Geomatics
Pei, Xian Zhi, Earth Science and Land Resources Management
Peng, Jian Min, Geology Engineering and Geomatics
Qian, Zhuang Zhi, Earth Science and Land Resources Management
Sha, Ai Min, Highways
Shen, Ai Qin, Highways
Shi, Yong Min, Highway Management
Song, Yi Fan, Bridges
Su, Sheng Rui, Geology Engineering and Geomatics
Tan, Cheng Qian, Geology Engineering and Geomatics
Tian, Wei Ping, Highway Disaster Prevention and Cure
Wang, Bin Gang, Highways
Wang, Hu, Science
Wang, Wen Ke, Environmental Science and Engineering
Wang, Xiao Mou, Geognosy and Tube Engineering
Wang, Xuan Cang, Highway Management
Wei, Guang Sheng, Science
Wu, Xiao Guang, Highway Management
Xia, Yong Xu, Geognosy and Tube Engineering
Xie, Yong Li, Geognosy and Tube Engineering
Xu, Hai Cheng, Economics and Management
Xu, Jing Liang, Road Reconnaissance
Xue, Chun Ji, Earth Science and Land Resources Management
Yan, Bao Jie, Traffic Engineering
Yang, Bin Cheng, Bridges
Yang, Shao Wei, Road Reconnaissance
Yang, Xiao Hua, Geognosy and Tube Engineering
Yang, Xing Ke, Earth Science and Land Resources Management
Yi, Guan Sheng, Science
Zhang, Chao, Highways
Zhang, Deng Liang, Highways

Zhang, Jun, Geology Engineering and Geomatics
Zhang, Qin, Geology Engineering and Geomatics
Zhang, Zhi Qiang, Geology Engineering and Geomatics
Zhao, Fa Shuo, Geology Engineering and Geomatics
Zhe, Xue Sen, Geognosy and Tube Engineering
Zheng, Chuan Chao, Highways
Zheng, Nan Xiang, Highways
Zhou, Guo Guang, Economics and Management
Zhou, Wei, Traffic Engineering
Zhou, Xu Hong, Bridges
Zhu, Guang Ming, Geology Engineering and Geomatics

CHANGCHUN UNIVERSITY OF EARTH SCIENCES

6 Ximinzhu St, Changchun 130026, Jilin Province
Telephone: (431) 822391
Founded 1952
Languages of instruction: Chinese, English, Japanese, Russian
Academic year: September to January, March to July
Chancellor: Prof. Zhang Yixia
Vice-Chancellors: Liu Baoren, Ma Zhihong, Prof. Shun Yunsheng
Librarian: Xiang Tianyuan

Library of 800,000 vols
Number of teachers: 830
Number of students: 3,890

Publications: *Geology of the World, Journal.*

CHANGCHUN INSTITUTE OF POSTS AND TELECOMMUNICATIONS

20 Nanhu St, Changchun 130012, Jilin Province
Telephone: (431) 5171220
Fax: (431) 5176342
Founded 1947; attached to Min. of Industry and Information Technology
Language of instruction: Chinese
Academic year: September to July
Pres.: Sun Muqian
Registrar: Liu Yan
Librarian: Yu Jie

Library of 380,000 vols
Number of teachers: 407
Number of students: 2,125 and 2,005 corresponding students

Publication: *Journal of Changchun Institute of Posts and Telecommunications.*

CHENGDU UNIVERSITY OF TECHNOLOGY

1st East Third Rd, Chenghua, Erxianqiao, Chengdu 610059, Sichuan Province
Telephone: (28) 84078898
Internet: www.cdut.edu.cn
Founded 1956
Provincial control
Academic year: September to July
Pres.: Liu Jiaduo
Vice-Pres: Huang Runqiu, Ni Shijun, Tan Shumin, Wang Yingchuan
Librarian: Li Yong

Library of 1,170,000 vols
Number of teachers: 2,021
Number of students: 25,000

Publications: *Computing Techniques for Geophysical Exploration* (4 a year), *Journal* (6 a year), *Journal of Geological Hazards and Environment Preservation* (4 a year), *Journal of Mineralogy and Petrology* (4 a year),

Scientific and Technological Management of Land and Resources (6 a year)

DEANS

Australian Institute of Tourism and Hospitality: LI YUSHENG
College of Applied Techniques and Automation Engineering: GE LIANGQUAN
Commercial College: LI YUSHENG
College of Energy Resources: ZHANG SHAONAN
College of Environment and Civil Engineering: XU QIANG
College of Foreign Languages and Cultures: LUO YIJUN
College of Geosciences: SUN CHUANMIN
College of Humanities and Law: LI QUANHUI
College of Information Engineering: WANG XUBEN
College of Information Management: GUO KE
College of Materials and Bioengineering: WANG LING

PROFESSORS

CAO, JINWEN, College of Information Management
CAO, JUNXING, College of Information Engineering
CHEN, BUKE, College of Energy Resources
CHEN, CHANGQUAN, College of Information Management
CHEN, HONGDE, Geosciences College
CHEN, JUNMING, Australian Institute of Tourism and Hospitality
CHEN, WANJIANG, Commercial College
CHENG, XIA, Commercial College
DENG, LIN, College of Information Engineering
DENG, TIANLONG, College of Materials and Bioengineering
DING, ZHAOYU, Network Education College
FAN, BIWEI, College of Materials and Bioengineering
FANG, FANG, College of Applied Techniques and Automation Engineering:
FENG, WENGUANG, College of Energy Resources
FU, GUANGHAI, Commercial College
FU, RONGHUA, College of Environment and Civil Engineering
FU, RULIN, College of Information Engineering
GE, LIANGQUAN, College of Applied Techniques and Automation Engineering:
GU, XUEXIANG, Geosciences College
GUO, JIANG, College of Information Engineering
GUO, KE, College of Information Management
HE, MINGSHENG, College of Applied Techniques and Automation Engineering:
HE, ZHENGWEI, Geosciences College
HE, ZHENHUA, College of Information Engineering
HONG, ZHIQUAN, College of Information Engineering
HU, GUANGMANG, College of Information Engineering
HU, YUANLAI, College of Information Management
HUANG, DILONG, College of Information Engineering
HUANG, JIJUN, Geosciences College
HUANG, RUNQIU, College of Environment and Civil Engineering
HUANG, SIJING, Geosciences College
JIA, SUYUAN, College of Environment and Civil Engineering
KONG, FANJING, College of Foreign Languages and Cultures
KUANG, JIANCHAO, College of Information Management
LI, HONGMU, College of Applied Techniques and Automation Engineering:
LI, JUCHU, College of Applied Techniques and Automation Engineering:
LI, LIANGMING, Commercial College

LI, LUMING, College of Information Engineering
LI, QUANHUI, College of Humanities and Law
LI, RUI, College of Information Engineering
LI, SHUSHENG, College of Environment and Civil Engineering
LI, TIANBIN, College of Environment and Civil Engineering
LI, WUQUAN, College of Foreign Languages and Cultures
LI, YUSHENG, Commercial College
LI, ZHENGWEN, College of Information Engineering
LI, ZHEQIN, College of Environment and Civil Engineering
LI, ZHIQUAN, College of Information Engineering
LIE, DEXIN, College of Environment and Civil Engineering
LIN, LI, Geosciences College
LIU, DENGZHONG, Geosciences College
LIU, HANCHAO, College of Environment and Civil Engineering
LIU, HONGJUN, College of Information Management
LIU, JIADUO, Geosciences College
LIU, MAOCAI, College of Information Management
LIU, SHUGEN, College of Energy Resources
LIU, XIANFAN, Geosciences College
LU, KUN, College of Applied Techniques and Automation Engineering:
LU, ZHENGYUAN, College of Energy Resources
LUO, MEI, College of Applied Techniques and Automation Engineering:
LUO, RUNTIAN, College of Foreign Languages and Cultures
LUO, SHENGXIAN, College of Information Engineering
LUO, YIJUN, College of Foreign Languages and Cultures
MA, RUNZE, Geosciences College
MA, YUXIAO, College of Applied Techniques and Automation Engineering:
MIAO, FANG, College of Information Engineering
NI, SHIJUN, College of Applied Techniques and Automation Engineering:
PENG, DAJUN, College of Energy Resources
QIE, JINLING, College of Information Engineering
QIU, KEHUI, College of Materials and Bioengineering
REN, GUANGMING, College of Environment and Civil Engineering
SHA, JICHANG, College of Information Management
SHENG, ZHONGMING, College of Energy Resources
SHI, HE, Geosciences College
SHI, ZHEJIN, College of Energy Resources
SUN, CHUANMIN, Geosciences College
SUN, SHUXIA, Network Education College
TAN, JIANXIONG, Geosciences College
TANG, JUXING, Geosciences College
TIAN, JINGCHUN, Geosciences College
TONG, CHUNHAN, College of Applied Techniques and Automation Engineering:
TUO, XIANGUO, College of Information Engineering
WAN, XINNAN, College of Environment and Civil Engineering
WANG, CHENGSHAN, Geosciences College
WANG, HONGFENG, Geosciences College
WANG, HONGHUI, College of Energy Resources
WANG, HUIZHOU, College of Foreign Languages and Cultures
WANG, LANSHENG, College of Environment and Civil Engineering
WANG, LING, College of Materials and Bioengineering
WANG, MOHUI, College of Materials and Bioengineering
WANG, SHITIAN, College of Environment and Civil Engineering

WANG, XIAOCHUN, College of Environment and Civil Engineering
WANG, XINZHUANG, College of Information Management
WANG, XUBEN, College of Information Engineering
WANG, YUNCHENG, College of Energy Resources
WANG, YUNSHENG, College of Environment and Civil Engineering
WANG, ZAIQI, College of Foreign Languages and Cultures
WEI, GUIMING, College of Information Management
WEN, CHUNQI, Geosciences College
WU, SHAN, Geosciences College
XI, DASHUN, College of Information Engineering
XIAN, YUANFU, Geosciences College
XIANG, YANG, College of Energy Resources
XIAO, CIXUN, College of Information Engineering
XING, WENXIANG, College of Information Management
XU, GUOSHENG, College of Energy Resources
XU, MO, College of Environment and Civil Engineering
XU, QIANG, College of Environment and Civil Engineering
YAN, HELIN, Geosciences College
YANG, SHAOGUO, College of Information Engineering
YANG, WUNIAN, Geosciences College
YANG, ZHENGXI, Geosciences College
YI, GUAN, College of Applied Techniques and Automation Engineering:
YI, HAISHENG, Geosciences College
YIN, HUIAN, College of Materials and Bioengineering
ZHANG, CHENGJIANG, College of Applied Techniques and Automation Engineering:
ZHANG, QICHUN, College of Materials and Bioengineering
ZHANG, SHAONAN, College of Energy Resources
ZHANG, ZUOYUAN, College of Environment and Civil Engineering
ZHAO, BING, Geosciences College
ZHAO, QIHUA, College of Environment and Civil Engineering
ZHAO, XIAFEI, College of Energy Resources
ZHAO, XIGUI, College of Energy Resources
ZHAO, ZESONG, Commercial College
ZHEN, HUAN, College of Foreign Languages and Cultures
ZHEN, MINGHUA, Geosciences College
ZHEN, RONGCAI, Geosciences College
ZHONG, BENSHAN, College of Information Engineering
ZHONG, YONGJIAN, Commercial College
ZHOU, JIAJI, College of Information Engineering
ZHOU, RONGSHENG, College of Applied Techniques and Automation Engineering:
ZHOU, SICHUN, College of Applied Techniques and Automation Engineering:
ZHOU, XIXIANG, College of Information Engineering
ZHU, CHUANGYE, Geosciences College
ZHU, JIESHOU, College of Information Engineering

CHENGDU UNIVERSITY OF TRADITIONAL CHINESE MEDICINE

37 Shierqiao Rd, Chengdu 610075
Telephone: (28) 87784542
Fax: (28) 87784606
E-mail: wsc@cdutcm.edu.cn
Internet: www.cdutcm.edu.cn

Founded 1956
State control
Languages of instruction: Chinese, English
Academic year: September to August

Pres.: Prof. ZHU BIDE

Vice-Pres: FU CHUNHUA LIANG FANRONG LUO CAIGUI, XIE KEQING
Chief Administrative Officer: XU, LIAN
Librarian: JIANG YONGGUANG
Library of 602,000 vols
Number of teachers: 1,678
Number of students: 10,095

Publications: *Academic Journal* (4 a year), *Higher Education Research into Traditional Chinese Medicine* (4 a year).

CHINA AGRICULTURAL UNIVERSITY

2 West of Yuanmingyuan Rd, Haidian District, Beijing 100094
Telephone: (10) 62732394
Fax: (10) 62732872
Internet: www.cau.edu.cn
Founded 1905
Academic year: September to July
Pres.: CHEN ZHANGLIANG
Vice-Pres: FU ZETIAN, JIANG SHUREN, MA JIANSHENG, SUN QIXIN, TAN XIANGYONG, ZHANG DONGJUN
Head of Graduate Department: CHEN ZHANGLIANG
Librarian: ZHANG QUAN
Number of teachers: 1,170
Number of students: 18,425

Publications: *Chinese Journal of Veterinary Medicine, Journal* (natural sciences, 6 a year)

DEANS

College of Agronomy and Biotechnology: DAI JINGRUI
College of Animal Science and Technology: LI DEFA
College of Biology Science: WU WEIHUA
College of Economic Management: WANG XIUQING
College of Food Science and Nutritional Engineering: LUO YUNBO
College of Humanities and Development: LI XIAOYUN
College of Information and Electrical Engineering: YANG RENGANG
College of Resource and Environment: ZHANG FUSUO
College of Science: JIAO QUNYING
College of Veterinary Medicine: WANG MING
College of Water Conservation and Civil Engineering: WANG FUJUN
College of International Studies: MENG FANXI

PROFESSORS

AO, GUANGMING, Biological Sciences
CAI, WANZHI, Agronomy and Biotechnology
CAO, YIPING, Resources and the Environment
CAO, ZHIPING, Resources and the Environment
CHANG, JINSHI, Water Conservation and Civil Engineering
CHEN, BAOFENG, Economic Management
CHEN, BU, Agronomy and Biotechnology
CHEN, HUANWEI, Resources and the Environment
CHEN, JIA, Biological Sciences
CHEN, JIANPING, Resources and the Environment
CHEN, MIN, Food Science and Nutritional Engineering
CHEN, QINGYUN, Agronomy and Biotechnology
CHEN, SANFENG, Biological Sciences
CHEN, SHAOJIANG, Agronomy and Biotechnology
CHEN, WENXIN, Biological Sciences
CHEN, YONGFU, Biological Sciences
CHEN, ZHANGLIANG, Agronomy and Biotechnology
CHENG, XU, Agronomy and Biotechnology
CUI, JIANYUN, Food Science and Nutritional Engineering

CUI, SHENG, Biological Sciences
CUI, ZONGJUN, Agronomy and Biotechnology
DAI, JINGRUI, Agronomy and Biotechnology
DENG, NAIYANG, Science
DENG, XIMIN, Agronomy and Biotechnology
DUAN, CHANGQING, Food Science and Nutritional Engineering
FENG, GONG, Humanities and Development
FENG, GU, Resources and the Environment
FENG, KAIWEN, Economic Management
FENG, SHAOYUAN, Water Conservation and Civil Engineering
FU, ZHIYI, Science
GAO, JUNPING, Agronomy and Biotechnology
GAO, QIJIE, Humanities and Development
GAO, WANGSHENG, Agronomy and Biotechnology
GAO, XIWU, Agronomy and Biotechnology
GAO, YANXIANG, Food Science and Nutritional Engineering
GONG, LIMIN, Animal Science and Technology
GONG, YUANSHI, Resources and the Environment
GONG, ZHIZHONG, Biological Sciences
GUO, SHUNTANG, Food Science and Nutritional Engineering
GUO, XIQING, Information and Electrical Engineering
GUO, YANGDONG, Agronomy and Biotechnology
GUO, YUHAI, Agronomy and Biotechnology
GUO, YUYUAN, Agronomy and Biotechnology
GUO, ZEJIAN, Agronomy and Biotechnology
HAN, BEIZHONG, Food Science and Nutritional Engineering
HAN, CHENGGUI, Agronomy and Biotechnology
HAN, JIANGUO, Animal Science and Technology
HAN, YUZHEN, Biological Sciences
HAN, ZHENHAI, Agronomy and Biotechnology
HAO, JINMIN, Resources and the Environment
HE, GUANGWEN, Economic Management
HE, XIURONG, Economic Management
HOU, CAIYUN, Food Science and Nutritional Engineering
HU, XIAOSONG, Food Science and Nutritional Engineering
HU, YUEGAO, Agronomy and Biotechnology
HUANG, GUANHUA, Water Conservation and Civil Engineering
HUANG, WEIDONG, Food Science and Nutritional Engineering
HUANG, WENBIN, Science
HUANG, YUANFANG, Resources and the Environment
HUANG, ZHIYONG, Agronomy and Biotechnology
JI, BAOPING, Food Science and Nutritional Engineering
JI, CHENG, Animal Science and Technology
JI, HAIYAN, Information and Electrical Engineering
JIA, WENSUO, Agronomy and Biotechnology
JIA, ZHIHAI, Animal Science and Technology
JIAN, HENG, Agronomy and Biotechnology
JIANG, RONGFENG, Resources and the Environment
JIANG, SHUREN, Science
JIANG, WEIBO, Food Science and Nutritional Engineering
JIAO, QUNYING, Science
JIAO, SHIYAN, Animal Science and Technology
KANG, DINGMING, Agronomy and Biotechnology
KANG, SHAOZHONG, Water Conservation and Civil Engineering
KE, BINGSHENG, Economic Management
LEI, TINGWU, Water Conservation and Civil Engineering
LENG, PING, Agronomy and Biotechnology
LI, BAOGUO, Resources and the Environment
LI, BAOMING, Water Conservation and Civil Engineering
LI, CHONGJIU, Science

LI, CHUNJIAN, Resources and the Environment
LI, DAWEI, Biological Sciences
LI, DEFA, Animal Science and Technology
LI, GENGLONG, Economic Management
LI, GUANGYONG, Water Conservation and Civil Engineering
LI, GUOHUI, Science
LI, GUOXUE, Resources and the Environment
LI, HUAIFANG, Agronomy and Biotechnology
LI, JI, Resources and the Environment
LI, JIANMIN, Agronomy and Biotechnology
LI, JIANQIANG, Agronomy and Biotechnology
LI, JIANSHENG, Agronomy and Biotechnology
LI, JILUN, Biological Sciences
LI, LITE, Food Science and Nutritional Engineering
LI, LONG, Resources and the Environment
LI, MINZAN, Information and Electrical Engineering
LI, NAN, Science
LI, NING, Biological Sciences
LI, OU, Humanities and Development
LI, PING, Economic Management
LI, SHAOKUN, Agronomy and Biotechnology
LI, SHENGLI, Animal Science and Technology
LI, SHUHUA, Agronomy and Biotechnology
LI, WEIJIONG, Resources and the Environment
LI, XIAOLIN, Resources and the Environment
LI, XIAOYUN, Humanities and Development
LI, XUEFENG, Science
LI, YAN, Biological Sciences
LI, YING, Biological Sciences
LI, ZANDONG, Biological Sciences
LI, ZHAOHU, Agronomy and Biotechnology
LI, ZICHAO, Agronomy and Biotechnology
LIAN, LINSHENG, Animal Science and Technology
LIAN, ZHENGXING, Animal Science and Technology
LIN, CONG, Water Conservation and Civil Engineering
LIN, DEGUI, Veterinary Medicine
LIN, QIMEI, Resources and the Environment
LIN, SHAN, Resources and the Environment
LIU, GUOJIE, Agronomy and Biotechnology
LIU, GUOQIN, Biological Sciences
LIU, LIMING, Resources and the Environment
LIU, QINGCHANG, Agronomy and Biotechnology
LIU, YONGGONG, Humanities and Development
LIU, ZHIYONG, Agronomy and Biotechnology
LOU, CHENGHOU, Biological Sciences
LU, FENGJU, Economic Management
LU, JUAN, Economic Management
LU, YAHAI, Resources and the Environment
LU, ZHIGUANG, Resources and the Environment
LUO, YUNBO, Food Science and Nutritional Engineering
MA, CHANGWEI, Food Science and Nutritional Engineering
MA, CHENGWEI, Water Conservation and Civil Engineering
MAO, DARU, Resources and the Environment
MENG, FANXI, International College
MENG, QINGXIANG, Animal Science and Technology
MI, GUOHUA, Resources and the Environment
MIN, SHUNGENG, Science
NIU, TIANGUI, Food Science and Nutritional Engineering
PAN, SHENQUAN, Agronomy and Biotechnology
PAN, XUEBIAO, Resources and the Environment
PENG, YOULIANG, Agronomy and Biotechnology
QIAO, JUAN, Economic Management
QIAO, ZHONG, Economic Management
QIN, FU, Economic Management
QIN, YAODONG, Resources and the Environment
REN, DONGTAO, Biological Sciences

REN, FAZHENG, Food Science and Nutritional Engineering
REN, LI, Resources and the Environment
REN, SHUMEI, Water Conservation and Civil Engineering
SHEN, DEZHONG, Resources and the Environment
SHEN, JIANZHONG, Veterinary Medicine
SHEN, ZUORUI, Agronomy and Biotechnology
SHI, DAZHAO, Agronomy and Biotechnology
SHI, JIEPING, Food Science and Nutritional Engineering
SHI, YUANCHUN, Resources and the Environment
SONG, YUAN, Biological Sciences
SU, DECHUN, Resources and the Environment
SU, ZHEN, Biological Sciences
SUN, BAOQI, Agronomy and Biotechnology
SUN, CHUANQING, Agronomy and Biotechnology
SUN, JUNSHE, Food Science and Nutritional Engineering
SUN, QIXIN, Agronomy and Biotechnology
SUN, YURUI, Information and Electrical Engineering
SUN, ZHEN, Resources and the Environment
TAN, XIANGYONG, Economic Management
TENG, GUANGHUI, Water Conservation and Civil Engineering
TIAN, WEIMING, Economic Management
WANG, AIGUO, Animal Science and Technology
WANG, BIN, Biological Sciences
WANG, CHUDUAN, Animal Science and Technology
WANG, DEHAI, Humanities and Development
WANG, FANG, Animal Science and Technology
WANG, FUJUN, Water Conservation and Civil Engineering
WANG, GUOYING, Biological Sciences
WANG, HEXIANG, Biological Sciences
WANG, HONGGUANG, Agronomy and Biotechnology
WANG, HUANHUA, Information and Electrical Engineering
WANG, HUAQI, Agronomy and Biotechnology
WANG, HUIMIN, Agronomy and Biotechnology
WANG, JIANHUA, Agronomy and Biotechnology
WANG, JINGGUO, Resources and the Environment
WANG, KU, Information and Electrical Engineering
WANG, MAO, Biological Sciences
WANG, MING, Veterinary Medicine
WANG, PU, Agronomy and Biotechnology
WANG, SHIPING, Food Science and Nutritional Engineering
WANG, SHOUCAI, Agronomy and Biotechnology
WANG, TAO, Biological Sciences
WANG, XIUQING, Economic Management
WANG, XUECHEN, Biological Sciences
WANG, YIMING, Information and Electrical Engineering
WEN, BOYING, Information and Electrical Engineering
WO, YUMING, Animal Science and Technology
WU, PING, Information and Electrical Engineering
WU, WEIHUA, Biological Sciences
WU, WENLIANG, Resources and the Environment
XIA, GUOLIANG, Biological Sciences
XIAO, HAIFENG, Economic Management
XIAO, XINGGUO, Biological Sciences
XIE, GUANGHUI, Agronomy and Biotechnology
XIN, XIAN, Economic Management
XU, HUIYUAN, Economic Management
XU, MINGLIANG, Agronomy and Biotechnology
XU, XUEFENG, Agronomy and Biotechnology
XUE, WENTONG, Food Science and Nutritional Engineering
YAN, TAILAI, Information and Electrical Engineering
YANG, DING, Agronomy and Biotechnology

YANG, HANCHUN, Veterinary Medicine
YANG, JIANCHANG, Agronomy and Biotechnology
YANG, MINGHAO, Information and Electrical Engineering
YANG, NING, Animal Science and Technology
YANG, PEILING, Water Conservation and Civil Engineering
YANG, QIULIN, Economic Management
YANG, RENGANG, Information and Electrical Engineering
YANG, XIAOBING, Agronomy and Biotechnology
YANG, ZHIFU, Resources and the Environment
YE, JINGZHONG, Humanities and Development
YE, ZHIHUA, Agronomy and Biotechnology
YI, MINGFANG, Agronomy and Biotechnology
YU, HUAIJIANG, Humanities and Development
YU, JIALIN, Biological Sciences
YU, RUIPING, Veterinary Medicine
YU, ZHENRONG, Resources and the Environment
YUAN, MING, Biological Sciences
ZANG, RIHONG, Economic Management
ZENG, SHENMING, Animal Science and Technology
ZENG, SHIMAI, Agronomy and Biotechnology
ZHAI, ZHIXI, Agronomy and Biotechnology
ZHANG, BAOGUI, Resources and the Environment
ZHANG, CONG, Resources and the Environment
ZHANG, DAPENG, Biological Sciences
ZHANG, FENGRONG, Resources and the Environment
ZHANG, FUSUO, Resources and the Environment
ZHANG, KEJIA, Veterinary Medicine
ZHANG, LONG, Agronomy and Biotechnology
ZHANG, QIN, Animal Science and Technology
ZHANG, QINGWEN, Agronomy and Biotechnology
ZHANG, RUAN, Animal Science and Technology
ZHANG, SHAOYING, Food Science and Nutritional Engineering
ZHANG, SHUQIU, Biological Sciences
ZHANG, WEI, Information and Electrical Engineering
ZHANG, XIAOMING, Animal Science and Technology
ZHANG, ZHENGHE, Economic Management
ZHANG, ZHENXIAN, Agronomy and Biotechnology
ZHANG, ZHONGJUN, Agronomy and Biotechnology
ZHANG, ZHONGZHI, Veterinary Medicine
ZHAO, DEMING, Veterinary Medicine
ZHAO, GUANGYONG, Animal Science and Technology
ZHAO, LIANGJUN, Agronomy and Biotechnology
ZHAO, MING, Agronomy and Biotechnology
ZHENG, DAWEI, Resources and the Environment
ZHENG, HANG, Biological Sciences
ZHOU, HE, Animal Science and Technology
ZHU, DAOLIN, Resources and the Environment
ZHU, DEHAI, Information and Electrical Engineering
ZHU, DEJU, Resources and the Environment
ZHU, QIZHEN, Humanities and Development
ZHU, SHIEN, Animal Science and Technology
ZUO, QIANG, Resources and the Environment
ZUO, TING, Humanities and Development

CHINA CENTRAL INSTITUTE OF FINE ARTS

5 Xiaowei Hutong, East District, Beijing 100730

Telephone: (10) 65254731

Founded 1950 by merger of Nat. Beijing College of Art and Fine Arts Dep of North China United Univ.

Pres.: JIN SHANGYI
Deputy Pres: DU JIAN, YE YUZHONG
Librarian: TANG CHI

Library: over 170,000 vols (25,000 in foreign languages), 8,500 vols periodicals
Number of teachers: 164
Number of students: 519 (incl. 28 postgraduates)

CHINA FOREIGN AFFAIRS UNIVERSITY

24 Zhanlan Rd, Xicheng, Beijing 100037
Internet: www.cfau.edu.cn

Founded 1955
Academic year: September to July

President: WU JIANMING
Vice-Presidents: QIN YAQING, QU XING
Head of Graduate Department: ZHENG QIRONG
Vice-Librarian: JIAN LEYI

Library of 23,500
Number of teachers: 170
Number of students: 1,600

Publication: *Journal* (4 a year)

DEANS

English: FAN SHOUYI
Foreign Affairs: ZHANG LILI
International Economics: JIANG RUIPING
International Law: JIN KESHENG

PROFESSORS

CHU, GUANGYOU, English
FAN, SHOUYI, English
HUANG, JINQI, English
JIANG, RUIPING, International Economics
QIN, YAQING, English
QU, XING, Foreign Affairs
REN, XIAOPING, English
SU, HAO, Foreign Affairs
WANG, SHAOREN, English
XIONG, ZHIYONG, Foreign Affairs
YANG, XUEYAN, English
YUAN, SHIBING, English
ZHANG, LILI, Foreign Affairs
ZHANG, YITING, English
ZHENG, QIRONG, Foreign Affairs

CHINA UNIVERSITY OF GEOSCIENCES (WUHAN)

Yujiashan, 388 Lumo Rd, Wuhan 430074, Hubei Province

Telephone and fax (27) 87481030
E-mail: xb@dns.cug.edu.cn
Internet: www.cug.edu.cn

Founded 1952
Academic year: September to July

21 Colleges which offer 49 Bachelors degree courses, 65 Masters degree courses and 30 doctoral courses

Pres.: ZHANG, JINGAO
Vice-Pres: OUYANG JIANPING, WANG YANXIN, XING XIANGQIN, YAO SHUZHEN

Library of 1,167,000 vols, 3,852 periodicals
Number of teachers: 2,800
Number of students: 23,600

Publications: *Chinese Journal of Engineering Geophysics, Earth Science, Geological Science and Technology Information, Journal of China University of Geosciences* (in English and Chinese), *Journal of Geoscience Translations*.

CHINA MEDICAL UNIVERSITY

Bei Er Rd, He Ping District, Shenyang 110001, Liaoning Province
Telephone: (24) 23265491

Fax: (24) 23261169
Internet: www.cmu.edu.cn
Founded 1931
Provincial Dept of Education control
Academic year: September to July

Pres.: ZHAO QUN
Vice-Pres: HAN MINTAN, HE QINCHENG, SUN BAOZHI, ZHAO LIKUI
Head of Graduate Dept: ZHAO QUN
Librarian: NENG DIZHI

Number of teachers: 6,126
Number of students: 19,602 (11,094 full-time, 8,508 part-time)

Publications: *Chinese Journal of Health Statistics* (6 a year), *Chinese Journal of Practical Ophthalmology* (12 a year), *Journal* (6 a year), *Journal of China Clinical Medical Imaging* (4 a year), *Liaoning Journal of Pharmacy and Clinical Remedies* (4 a year), *Liaoning Journal of Practical Diabetology* (4 a year), *Paediatric Emergency Medicine* (4 a year), *Practical Journal for Rural Doctors* (6 a year), *Progress of Anatomical Sciences* (4 a year), *Progress in Japanese Medicine* (12 a year)

DEANS

College of Basic Medical Sciences: BAI SHULING
College of Nursing: LI XIAOHAN
College of Public Health: SUN GUIFAN
Department of Information Management and Information Systems: ZHAO YUHONG
Department of Social Science: GUO SHUYING
Faculty of Forensic Medicine: WANG BAOJIE
First Clinical College and First Affiliated Hospital: LI JIGUANG
Fourth Clinical College and Fourth Affiliated Hospital: HAN JIANPING
School of Pharmacy: JIN XIN
School of Stomatology and Affiliated Stomatological Hospital: AI HONGJUN
Second Clinical College and Second Affiliated Hospital: GUO QIYONG
Third Clinical College and Third Affiliated Hospital: XU JIANJUN

PROFESSORS

AI, HONGJUN, Stomatology
AN, XHUNLI, Basic Medical Sciences
BAI, SHULING, Basic Medical Sciences
BAO, ZHONGXIAO, Basic Medical Sciences
CAI, JINGYUAN, First Clinical College
CAI, JIQUN, Basic Medical Sciences
CAI, YUAN, Public Health
CAI, ZHIDAO, First Clinical College
CAO, YAMING, Basic Medical Sciences
CHANG, TIANHUI, Basic Medical Sciences
CHEN, HONGDUO, First Clinical College
CHEN, JUNQING, First Clinical College
CHEN, LIANG, First Clinical College
CHEN, SHUZHENG, Second Clinical College
CHEN, YUHUA, Basic Medical Sciences
CHU, HANG, First Clinical College
CUI, JIANJUN, Second Clinical College
CUI, LEI, Information Management and Information Systems
DAI, XIANWEI, Second Clinical College
DENG, XIANGDONG, First Clinical College
DENG, YAN, Stomatology
DING, LUOLAN, First Clinical College
DING, MEI, Forensic Medicine
DONG, XIAOJIE, Basic Medical Sciences
DONG, YULAN, Basic Medical Sciences
DU, XUEBIN, Social Science
DUAN, ZHIQUAN, First Clinical College
FAN, GUANGYU, First Clinical College
FAN, SHUDUO, Basic Medical Sciences
FANG, JINWU, First Clinical College
FANG, XIUBIN, Basic Medical Sciences
FU, BAOYU, First Clinical College
GAO, DIANWEN, Second Clinical College
GU, CHUNJIU, First Clinical College
GUAN, DAWEI, Forensic Medicine

GUO, DUISHAN, Second Clinical College
GUO, SHUYING, Social Science
HAN, JIANPING, Fourth Clinical College
HAN, YUKUN, Second Clinical College
HE, AN'GUANG, First Clinical College
HE, QINCHENG, Information Management and Information Systems
HE, SANGUANG, First Clinical College
HE, XIUQIN, First Clinical College
HONG, JIAKANG, Basic Medical Sciences
HONG, YANG, Basic Medical Sciences
HOU, XIANGMING, First Clinical College
HUANG, JIANQUN, First Clinical College
JI, SHIJUN, Second Clinical College
JIA, XINSHAN, Basic Medical Sciences
JIANG, RUOLAN, First Clinical College
JIN, CHUNLIAN, Basic Medical Sciences
JIN, WANBAO, Basic Medical Sciences
JIN, XIN, Pharmacy
LI, FUCAO, Basic Medical Sciences
LI, HOUWEN, First Clinical College
LI, JIGUANG, First Clinical College
LI, JINMING, Basic Medical Sciences
LI, LIYUN, First Clinical College
LI, SHAOYING, First Clinical College
LI, SHUQIN, Second Clinical College
LI, XIAOHAN, Nursing
LI, XINGYUAN, Second Clinical College
LI, XIULLING, First Clinical College
LI, YAN, Second Clinical College
LI, YUQUAN, Second Clinical College
LI, ZHENCHUN, Stomatology
LI, ZHENG, Second Clinical College
LI, ZHI, Basic Medical Sciences
LI, ZHUQIN, First Clinical College
LIU, CHUNRONG, First Clinical College
LIU, ENJIE, Basic Medical Sciences
LIU, ENQING, Second Clinical College
LIU, GUOLIANG, First Clinical College
LIU, HONGQIN, Second Clinical College
LIU, JUHUI, Forensic Medicine
LIU, JUNTING, Forensic Medicine
LIU, JUNTING, Pharmacy
LIU, LANQING, Second Clinical College
LIU, LIMIN, Forensic Medicine
LIU, SHUJIE, Stomatology
LIU, XIUMEI, First Clinical College
LIU, YANG, Public Health
LIU, YINGMIN, Second Clinical College
LIU, ZHENLIN, Public Health
LU, CHANGLONG, Basic Medical Sciences
LU, JINGMING, Second Clinical College
LU, SHENGMIN, Second Clinical College
MENG, FANHAO, Pharmacy
MU, HUACHUN, Basic Medical Sciences
PAN, YAPING, Stomatology
PAN, ZHIMIN, First Clinical College
PANG, XINING, Basic Medical Sciences
PEI, ZHUGUO, Second Clinical College
PIAO, AIYING, Second Clinical College
QIU, XUESHAN, Basic Medical Sciences
QU, MING, First Clinical College
REN, CHONG, First Clinical College
SHEN, KUI, First Clinical College
SHI, LIDE, Basic Medical Sciences
SHI, YUXIU, Basic Medical Sciences
SONG, FANGJI, First Clinical College
SONG, JIJIE, Basic Medical Sciences
SONG, JINDAN, Basic Medical Sciences
SONG, MIN, Basic Medical Sciences
SUN, GUIFAN, Public Health
SUN, GUIYUAN, Basic Medical Sciences
SUN, JIANCHUN, Second Clinical College
SUN, KAILAI, Basic Medical Sciences
SUN, LIGUANG, Basic Medical Sciences
TANG, HAO, Basic Medical Sciences
TIAN, XUSHENG, Basic Medical Sciences
WANG, BAOJIE, Forensic Medicine
WANG, CHUN, Fourth Clinical College
WANG, DEWEN, Forensic Medicine
WANG, DEZHI, Second Clinical College
WANG, ENHUA, Basic Medical Sciences
WANG, GUIZHEN, Basic Medical Sciences
WANG, HAIPENG, Basic Medical Sciences
WANG, HAIYI, Second Clinical College
WANG, HE, Basic Medical Sciences

WANG, HONGDA, First Clinical College
WANG, HUAILIANG, Basic Medical Sciences
WANG, HUIZHEN, Second Clinical College
WANG, LIANYING, Second Clinical College
WANG, LIJUN, Second Clinical College
WANG, LIYU, Social Science
WANG, MINGQIAN, Second Clinical College
WANG, SHUBAO, First Clinical College
WANG, SHULAN, First Clinical College
WANG, TIE, Second Clinical College
WANG, WEILIN, Second Clinical College
WANG, XINGDUO, First Clinical College
WANG, XUEYING, Second Clinical College
WANG, YANFENG, Second Clinical College
WANG, YUXIN, Stomatology
WANG, ZHAOGUAN, Second Clinical College
WANG, ZHAOYUAN, Stomatology
WEI, KELUN, Second Clinical College
WU, BAOMIN, Second Clinical College
WU, HUAZHANG, Social Science
WU, JINGTIAN, First Clinical College
WU, KEGUANG, Second Clinical College
WU, YIJIANG, Fourth Clinical College
WU, YINGYU, Second Clinical College
WU, ZHENHUA, Second Clinical College
XIE, HUIFANG, Second Clinical College
XU, ZHAOFA, Public Health
XU, ZHENXING, First Clinical College
XUE, XINDONG, Second Clinical College
XUE, YIXUE, Basic Medical Sciences
YANG, GUORUI, First Clinical College
YANG, JUN, Public Health
YANG, SHILIN, Second Clinical College
YANG, XIANGHONG, Basic Medical Sciences
YANG, XIAODONG, Stomatology
YANG, YUXIU, First Clinical College
YAO, XINGJIA, Public Health
YIN, HONGNIAN, First Clinical College
YIN, SHUGUO, Second Clinical College
YU, BINGXHI, Basic Medical Sciences
YU, RUNJIANG, First Clinical College
YUAN, ZHUANG, Second Clinical College
ZENG, DINGYIN, First Clinical College
ZHA, HONGYAN, Basic Medical Sciences
ZHANG, DAORONG, Basic Medical Sciences
ZHANG, GANZHONG, First Clinical College
ZHANG, HAIPENG, Basic Medical Sciences
ZHANG, HONG, Basic Medical Sciences
ZHANG, JIAXING, Second Clinical College
ZHANG, JINGRONG, First Clinical College
ZHANG, LIFENG, Basic Medical Sciences
ZHANG, SHULAN, Second Clinical College
ZHANG, XUE, Basic Medical Sciences
ZHAO, CHONGZHI, Second Clinical College
ZHAO, GUIZHEN, Second Clinical College
ZHAO, GUOGUI, Second Clinical College
ZHAO, LIJUAN, First Clinical College
ZHAO, SHUFENG, Basic Medical Sciences
ZHAO, SHUXIA, Second Clinical College
ZHAO, YKUN, Basic Medical Sciences
ZHAO, YUHONG, Information Management and Information Systems
ZHONG, MING, Stomatology
ZHOU, BAOSEN, Public Health
ZHOU, WEI, Social Science
ZHOU, XIJING, First Clinical College
ZHOU, YONGDE, Second Clinical College
ZHU, LIPING, Basic Medical Sciences

CHINA UNIVERSITY OF MINING AND TECHNOLOGY

Xuzhou 221008, Jiangsu Province
Telephone: (516) 3885745
Fax: (516) 3888682
Internet: www.cumt.edu.cn
Founded 1909
State control
Academic year: September to July

Pres.: Prof. XIE HEPING
Vice-Pres: Prof. GE SHIRONG, Prof. KE WENJIN, Prof. LUO CHENG XUAN, Prof. SUNG XUEFENG, Prof. WANG JIANPING, Prof. WANG YUEHAN
Registrar: Prof. XING YONGCHANG

Dir of Int. Div.: ZHENG ZHENKANG
Librarian: Prof. TANG YI

Library of 330,000 vols
Number of teachers: 3,817
Number of students: 30,942

Publication: *Journal* (4 a year in Chinese, 2 a year in English)

HEADS OF ACADEMIC DIVISIONS

College of Adult Education: ZHANG FUSHENG
College of Applied Science and Technology: FAN ZHONGQI
Department of Physical Education: CHI ZHONGJUN
School of Architecture and Civil Engineering: ZHOU GUOQING
School of Chemical Engineering: LIU JIONGTIAN
School of Computer Science and Technology: XIA SHIXIONG
School of Environment and Spatial Informatics: HAN BAOPING
School of Foreign Studies: YANG SHU
School of Information and Electrical Engineering: JIANG JIANGUO
School of Mechatronic and Materials Engineering: DUAN XIONG
School of Mineral and Energy Resources Engineering: CAI QINGXIANG
School of Resources and Geoscience: LIN JIAN
School of Management: NIE RUI
School of Politics, Literature and Law: WANG YAN
School of Science: MIAO XIEXIN

CHINA UNIVERSITY OF PETROLEUM

2 North Rd, Dongying 257061, Shandong Province

Telephone: (546) 8392241
Fax: (546) 7366374
Internet: www.hdpu.edu.cn

Founded 1953
State control
Academic year: September to July

Pres.: TONG ZHAOQI
Vice-Pres: SHAN HONGHONG, SUN HAIFENG, TONG XINHUA, WANG RUIHE, ZHA MING
Head of Graduate Dep: WANG RUIHE
Librarian: ZHANG ZHONGXUE

Number of teachers: 1,000
Number of students: 23,500

Publication: *Journal of China University of Petroleum* (6 a year)

DEANS

College of Architecture, Transport and Storage Engineering: ZHANG GUOZHONG
College of Chemistry and Chemical Engineering: JIN YOUHAI
College of Computer and Communication Engineering: DUAN YOUXIANG
College of Economic Administration: ZHANG ZAIXU
College of Foreign Languages: LUAN SHUWEN
College of Geo-Resources and Information: YIN XINGYAO
College of Humanities and Social Science: XIA CHONGYA
College of Information and Control Engineering: TIAN XUEMING
College of Mathematics and Computer Science: LI WEIGUO
College of Mechanical and Electronic Engineering: QI MINGXIA
College of Petroleum Engineering: YAO JUN
College of Physical Education: WEI RULI
College of Physics, Science and Technology: GUAN JITENG

PROFESSORS

BAI, LIANPING, Information and Control Engineering
CHAO, KE, Humanities and Social Science

CHEN, GANGHUA, Geo-Resources and Information
CHEN, JIANMIN, Petroleum Engineering
CHEN, SHIYUE, Geo-Resources and Information
CHEN, YUEMING, Petroleum Engineering
CHENG, YUANFANG, Petroleum Engineering
DAI, JUNSHENG, Geo-Resources and Information
DU, JINLIANG, Humanities and Social Science
FAN, YIREN, Geo-Resources and Information
FANG, JIANHUI, Physics, Science and Technology
GAO, YIFA, Petroleum Engineering
GUAN, ZHICHUAN, Petroleum Engineering
GUANG, JITENG, Physics, Science and Technology
HAN, ZHIYONG, Petroleum Engineering
HE, LIMIN, Architecture, Transport and Storage Engineering
JIA, RUIGAO, Physics, Science and Technology
JIANG, HUA, Humanities and Social Science
JIANG, YOULU, Geo-Resources and Information
JIANG, ZAIXING, Geo-Resources and Information
JIN, QIANG, Geo-Resources and Information
LI, GUOHUA, Physical Education
LI, HANLIN, Geo-Resources and Information
LI, MINGZHONG, Petroleum Engineering
LI, SHURONG, Information and Control Engineering
LI, WEIGUO, Mathematics and Computational Science
LI, YUANCHENG, Physics, Science and Technology
LI, YUXING, Architecture, Transport and Storage Engineering
LI, ZHAOMIN, Petroleum Engineering
LI, ZILI, Architecture, Transport and Storage Engineering
LIANG, JINGUO, Architecture, Transport and Storage Engineering
LIN, CHENGYAN, Geo-Resources and Information
LIU, HUIQING, Petroleum Engineering
LIU, RUNHUA, Information and Control Engineering
LIU, ZHAN, Geo-Resources and Information
LUAN, SHUWEN, Foreign Languages
MA, XIGENG, Information and Control Engineering
MEN, FUDIAN, Physics, Science and Technology
QIU, SHIWEI, Architecture, Transport and Storage Engineering
QIU, ZHENGSONG, Petroleum Engineering
SHAN, YIXIAN, Information and Control Engineering
SHEN, ZHONGHOU, Petroleum Engineering
SHU, HENGMU, Architecture, Transport and Storage Engineering
SONG, DESHENG, Foreign Languages
SUN, BAOJIANG, Petroleum Engineering
SUN, JIANMENG, Geo-Resources and Information
SUN, XIULI, Foreign Languages
TIAN, XUEMIN, Information and Control Engineering
WAN, JIANHUA, Geo-Resources and Information
WANG, HUAQIN, Foreign Languages
WANG, JIANJUN, Humanities and Social Science
WANG, QINGTING, Foreign Languages
WANG, RUIHE, Petroleum Engineering
WANG, SHUTING, Foreign Languages
WANG, WEIFENG, Geo-Resources and Information
WANG, YANJIANG, Information and Control Engineering
WANG, YONGGANG, Geo-Resources and Information
XIA, CHONGYA, Humanities and Social Science
XING, LIANJUN, Physical Education

XU, MINGHAI, Architecture, Transport and Storage Engineering
XU, YIJI, Petroleum Engineering
XUE, SHIFENG, Architecture, Transport and Storage Engineering
YAN, XIANGZHEN, Architecture, Transport and Storage Engineering
YANG, DEWEI, Architecture, Transport and Storage Engineering
YANG, SHAOCHUN, Geo-Resources and Information
YANG, WEI, Physics, Science and Technology
YAO, JUN, Petroleum Engineering
YIN, XINGYAO, Geo-Resources and Information
YU, RANGANG, Architecture, Transport and Storage Engineering
YU, ZHAOXIAN, Physics, Science and Technology
YUAN, HONGCHAN, Foreign Languages
ZHAN, YONGLIANG, Architecture, Transport and Storage Engineering
ZHANG, GUOZHONG, Architecture, Transport and Storage Engineering
ZHANG, JIASHENG, Information and Control Engineering
ZHANG, QI, Petroleum Engineering
ZHANG, RONGHUA, Humanities and Social Science
ZHANG, ZHAOHUI, Information and Control Engineering
ZHAO, FULIN, Petroleum Engineering
ZHAO, XIUTAI, Petroleum Engineering
ZHAO, XIYU, Humanities and Social Science
ZHAO, YONGJUN, Geo-Resources and Information
ZHENG, JINWU, Information and Control Engineering
ZHONG, JIANHUA, Geo-Resources and Information
ZHOU, DETIAN, Humanities and Social Science
ZHOU, XIAOJUN, Petroleum Engineering
ZHOU, YAOQI, Geo-Resources and Information

CHINA PHARMACEUTICAL UNIVERSITY

Xuan Wu Men, Yan Zi Ji, Nanjing 210009, Jiangsu Province

Telephone: (25) 3271319
Fax: (25) 3271101
Internet: www.cpu.edu.cn

Founded 1936
Min. of Education Control
Academic year: September to July

Pres.: WU XIAOMING
Vice-Pres: LI FENGWEN, PAN YUJIAN, WANG GUANGJI, ZHANG XIAOLIAN
Head of Graduate Dept: CHU MINZUO
Librarian: MA SHIPING

Library of 700,000 vols
Number of teachers: 610
Number of students: 8,880

Publications: *Journal of China Pharmaceutical University* (6 a year), *Medical Evolution* (6 a year), *Medicine Annual of China*, *Medicine Education* (4 a year)

DEANS

Basic Institute: TAO LU
Department of Foreign Languages: DU HUI
Institute of Physical Education: WANG YONGTAO
School of Biological Pharmacy: WANG WEN
School of Economics and Economic School of International Medicine: GU HAI
Schools of Medicine and Chinese Traditional Medicine: KONG LINGYI

PROFESSORS

DAI, DEZAI, Medicine
GAO, SHANLIN, Chinese Traditional Medicine
GAO, XIANGDONG, Biological Pharmacy

GU, HAI, Economic School of International Medicine
HU, YUZHU
HUA, WEIYI, Medicine
HUANG, WENLONG, Medicine
JI, HUI, Medicine
JI, MIN, Medicine
KONG, LINGYI, Chinese Traditional Medicine
LIANG, JINGYU, Chinese Traditional Medicine
LIU, JINGJING, Biological Pharmacy
LIU, WENYING, Medicine
LIU, XIAODONG, Chinese Traditional Medicine
LIU, XIAODONG, Medicine
MA, SHIPING, Chinese Traditional Medicine
NI, KUNYI
PENG, SIXUN, Medicine
PING, QINENG, Medicine
QIAN, ZHIYU, Medicine
SHAO, RONG, Economic School of International Medicine
SHEN, ZILONG, Biological Pharmacy
TU, SHUCI, Medicine
WANG, GUANGJI, Medicine
WANG, QIUJUAN, Medicine
WANG, WEN, Biological Pharmacy
WU, WUTONG, Biological Pharmacy
WU, XIAOMING, Medicine
XI, TAO, Biological Pharmacy
XIANG, BINGREN
YANG, ZHONGLIN, Chinese Traditional Medicine
YE, WENCAI, Chinese Traditional Medicine
YOU, QIDONG, Medicine
YU, BOYANG, Chinese Traditional Medicine
ZHANG, LUYONG, Medicine
ZHANG, YIHUA, Medicine
ZHANG, ZHENGHANG, Medicine
ZHOU, JIANPING, Medicine
ZHU, DANNI, Chinese Traditional Medicine
ZHU, JIABI, Medicine

CHINA UNIVERSITY OF POLITICAL SCIENCE AND LAW

Yuanyuan Rd, Chang Ping, Beijing 102249
Telephone: (10) 69745577
Fax: (10) 82228531
Internet: www.cupl.edu.cn
Founded 1952
State control
Academic year: September to July
President: XU XIANMING
Vice-Presidents: JIE ZHANYUAN, MA KANGMEI, ZHANG BAOSHENG, ZHANG GUILIN, ZHANG LIUHUA
Head of Graduate Department: ZHU YONG
Librarian: ZENG ERSHU
Number of teachers: 1,400
Number of students: 21,325
Publications: *Journal of China University of Political Science and Law (Tribune of Political Science and Law)* (6 a year), *Journal of Comparative Law* (6 a year)

DEANS

School of American and Comparative Law: XU CHUANXI
Business School: SUN XUANZHONG
Criminal and Judicial School: WANG MU
School of Foreign Languages: LI LI
School of German and Comparative Law: MI JIAN
International Law School: WANG CHUANLI
Law School: MA HUAIDE
School of Political and Public Management: ZHU WEIJIU

PROFESSORS

CAI, DINGJIAN, Law
CAI, TUO, Political and Public Management
CHE, HU, American and Comparative Law
CHEN, GUANGZHONG, Procedural Law
CHEN, HONGTAI, Political and Public Management

CHEN, LIJUN, Law
CHENG, XIAOXIANG, International Law
CONG, RIYUN, Political and Public Management
CUI, YONGDONG, Law
DING, MEI, German and Comparative Law
DONG, SHUJUN, Criminal and Judicial Law
DU, XINLI, International Law
DUAN, DONGHUI, International Law
FAN, CHONGYI, Procedural Law
FENG, XIA, International Law
GAO, JIAWEI, German and Comparative Law
GU, YONGZHONG, Procedural Law
HAO, WEIHUA, American and Comparative Law
HE, JIAHONG, Procedural Law
HONG, DAODE, Criminal and Judicial Law
HOU, TINGZHI, Business School
HU, WENZHENG, Business School
HUANG, DAOXIU, Foreign Languages
HUANG, YISI, Foreign Languages
JIANG, RUJIAO, International Law
JIAO, HONGCHANG, Law
JIAO, MEIZHEN, Foreign Languages
LANG, PEIJUAN, Law
LE, GUOAN, Criminal and Judicial Law
LI, JUQIAN, International Law
LI, LI, Foreign Languages
LI, MING, Research of Legal Historiography
LI, WEI, International Law
LI, XIAO, Business School
LIN, QIAN, Research of Legal Historiography
LIU, BANGHUI, Criminal and Judicial Law
LIU, CHANGMIN, Political and Public Management
LIU, GENJU, Criminal and Judicial Law
LIU, GUANGAN, Research of Legal Historiography
LIU, HONGYING, Law
LIU, JINGUO, Law
LIU, JUNSHENG, Political and Public Management
LIU, LI, International Law
LIU, MU, Criminal and Judicial Law
LIU, SHANCHUN, Law
LIU, SHEN, Law
LONG, MENGHUI, Foreign Languages
MA, CHENGYUAN, International Law
MA, HUAIDE, Law
MA, ZHIBING, Research of Legal Historiography
MI, JIAN, German and Comparative Law
MO, SHIJIAN, International Law
PAN, QIN, Criminal and Judicial Law
PENG, YANAN, American and Comparative Law
QI, DONGXIANG, American and Comparative Law
QI, XIANGQUAN, International Law
QU, CHAOLI, Political and Public Management
QU, XINJIU, Criminal and Judicial Law
RUAN, QILIN, Criminal and Judicial Law
SHI, XIAOLI, International Law
SHI, YAJUN, Political and Public Management
SHU, GUOYING, German and Comparative Law
SONG, YINGHUI, Procedural Law
SUN, XUANZHONG, Business School
WANG, CHUANLI, International Law
WANG, JIANCHENG, Procedural Law
WANG, JIANXIN, Political and Public Management
WANG, JIE, Law
WANG, MU, Criminal and Judicial Law
WANG, RENBO, Law
WANG, SHUNAN, Criminal and Judicial Law
WU, MINGYANG, Business School
XIAO, JIANHUA, Procedural Law
XIN, CHONGYANG, International Law
XU, CHUANXI, American and Comparative Law
XU, HAIMING, International Law
XU, HAOMING, German and Comparative Law
XU, SHIHONG, Institute of Legal Ancient Books Arrangement

XUAN, ZENGYI, International Law
XUE, GANGLING, Law
YANG, FAN, Business School
YANG, FAN, International Law
YANG, RONGXIN, Procedural Law
YANG, YANG, Political and Public Management
YANG, YUGUAN, Procedural Law, German and Comparative Law
YUE, LILING, German and Comparative Law
ZHANG, GUILIN, Political and Public Management
ZHANG, GUOJUN, Business School
ZHANG, JINFAN, Research of Legal Historiography
ZHANG, LI, International Law
ZHANG, LIYING, International Law
ZHANG, SHENG, Law
ZHANG, SHUYI, Law
ZHANG, XIAOMU, International Law
ZHANG, ZHONGQIU, Research of Legal Historiography
ZHAO, BAOCHENG, Criminal and Judicial Law
ZHAO, WEI, International Law
ZHAO, XIANGLIN, International Law
ZHAO, YIMIN, International Law
ZHENG, XIANWEN, Institute of Legal Ancient Books Arrangement
ZHENG, YONGLIU, German and Comparative Law
ZHOU, JIANHAI, International Law
ZHOU, ZHONGHAI, International Law
ZHU, JIANGENG, International Law
ZHU, WEIJIU, Political and Public Management
ZHU, YONG, Research of Legal Historiography
ZHU, ZIQIN, International Law

CHINA CENTRAL RADIO AND TELEVISION UNIVERSITY

160 Fuxing Men Nei St, Beijing 100031
Telephone: (10) 66412407
Fax: (10) 66419025
E-mail: fao@crtvu.edu.cn
Internet: www.crtvu.edu.cn
Founded 1979 on the 'open university' principle
State control
Academic year: September to July
44 Provincial campuses, 961 br. schools
Pres.: ZHANG YAOXUE
Vice-Pres: RUAN ZHIYONG, SUN LUYI, YAN BING, YU YUNXIU
Library Dir: SUN LUYI
Library of 100,000 vols (CRTVU), 32,869,000 vols (provinces)
Number of teachers: 188 full-time, 565 part-time (CRTVU)
Number of teachers: 42,500 full-time, 31,500 part-time (provinces)
Number of students: 2,300,000
Publication: *Distance Education in China* (6 a year).

CHINESE TRADITIONAL OPERA COLLEGE

3 Li Ren St, Xuan Wu District, Beijing 100054
Telephone: (10) 335156
Founded 1978
Pres.: YU LIN
Vice-Pres: GE SHILIANG, ZHU WENXIANG
Librarian: LIU SHIYUAN
Library of 150,000 vols
Number of teachers: 246
Number of students: 329
Publication: *Traditional Opera Art* (4 a year).

CHONGQING UNIVERSITY

Chongqing, Sichuan Province 630044
Telephone: (23) 65102449
Fax: (23) 65316656
E-mail: fao@cqu.edu.cn
Internet: www.cqu.edu.cn
Founded 1929
State control
Languages of instruction: Chinese, English
Academic year: February to January
Pres.: LIN FEI
Vice-Pres.: WU ZHONGFU
Chief Admin. Officer: CHEN DEWEN
Librarian: TANG YIKE
Number of teachers: 2,000
Number of students: 14,000
Publication: *Journal* (6 a year)

DEANS

College of Business Administration: YANG
 XIUTAI
College of Chemical Engineering: GAN
 GUNANGZHONG
College of Electronic Information Engineer-
 ing: CAO ZEHAN
College of Foreign Languages: JIANG ZHIWEN
College of Resources and Environmental
 Engineering: LI XIAOHONG
College of Trade and Law: HE RONGWEI

CHONGQING UNIVERSITY OF MEDICAL SCIENCES

1 Medicine Rd, Yu Zhong, Chongqing 400046
Telephone: (23) 68804034
Internet: www.cqums.edu.cn
Founded 1956
Academic year: September to July
Pres.: LEI HAN
Vice-Pres: DENG SHIXIONG, DONG ZHI, HUANG
 AILONG, WANG LIHUA, XIE PENG
Librarian: LU CHANGHONG
Library of 570,000 vols
Number of teachers: 4,374
Number of students: 8,923
Publications: *Chinese Journal of Hepatology*
 (6 a year), *Journal of Chongqing Medical
 University* (6 a year), *Journal of Paediatric
 Pharmacy* (6 a year), *Journal of Ultra-
 sound in Clinical Medicine* (6 a year),
 Research in Medical Education (6 a year)

DEANS

College of Basic Medicine: WANG YAPING
Department of Biomedical Engineering:
 WANG ZHIBIAO
Department of Medical Examining: TU ZHI-
 GUANG
Department of Medical Imaging: REN HONG
Department of Reproductive Medical Sci-
 ence: WANG YINGXIONG
Institute of Humanity and Social Science:
 FENG ZHEYONG

PROFESSORS

CHEN, SHOUTIAN, Medical Imaging
CONG, YULONG, Medical Examining
DAI, YONG, Medical Examining
DONG, ZHI, Pharmacy
FENG, ZHEYONG, Humanities and Social Sci-
 ence
HU, GUOHU, Basic Medicine
JIANG, JIKAI, Medical Examining
KANG, GEFEI, Medical Examining
LEI, PEIYING, Medical Imaging
LEI, XIAOKUN, Humanities and Social Science
LI, HUIZHI, Pharmacy
LI, QINGEN, Pharmacy
LI, SHAOLIN, Basic Medicine
LIU, DAWEI, Preventive Medicine
LUO, JIA, Medical Imaging
LUO, YUNPENG, Basic Medicine
LU, CHANGHONG, Basic Medicine

MI, CAN, Basic Medicine
NING, BAODONG, Basic Medicine
PENG, HUIMING, Basic Medicine
QIU, ZONGYING, Pharmacy
QUAN, XUEMO, Medical Imaging
REN, HONG, Medical Imaging
SONG, FANGZHOU, Basic Medicine
SUN, SHANQUAN, Basic Medicine
TANG, SIJIE, Basic Medicine
TANG, WEIXUE, Basic Medicine
TU, ZHIGUANG, Medical Examining
WANG, RUIHUA, Preventive Medicine
WANG, WEIWEI, Basic Medicine
WANG, YANG, Preventive Medicine
WANG, YAPING, Basic Medicine
WANG, YINGXIONG, Reproductive Medical Sci-
 ence
WANG, ZHIBIAO, Biomedical Engineering
WANG, ZHIGANG, Medical Imaging
WU, FENG, Biomedical Engineering
XIANG, LIKE, Basic Medicine
XIE, ZHENGXIANG, Basic Medicine
YANG, ZHENWEI, Basic Medicine
YANG, ZHIBANG, Basic Medicine
YI, YONGFENG, Basic Medicine
YU, YU, Basic Medicine
ZHANG, NENG, Basic Medicine
ZHAO, JIANNONG, Medical Imaging
ZHENG, ZHAOCHUN, Basic Medicine
ZHOU, CHENGHE, Pharmacy
ZHOU, JIANZHONG, Medical Imaging
ZHOU, QIXIN, Basic Medicine
ZHU, DAOYIN, Basic Medicine

DALIAN MARITIME UNIVERSITY

1 Linghai Rd, Dalian 116026, Liaoning Prov-
ince
Telephone: (411) 84727149
Fax: (411) 84727874
E-mail: iceodmu@gmail.com
Internet: www.dlmu.edu.cn
Founded 1909
State control
Academic year: September to July
Pres.: Prof. WU ZHAOLIN
Vice-Pres: Dr SUN LICHENG, Dr SUN PEITING,
 WEN XIAOQIN
Registrar: WANG YUEHUI
Librarian: PANG FUWEN
Number of teachers: 728
Number of students: 12,722
Publications: *Higher Education Research in
 Areas of Communications* (2 a year), *Jour-
 nal* (6 a year), *Liaoning Navigation* (4 a
 year), *World Shipping* (6 a year)

DEANS

Adult Education College: DING YONG
Automation and Electrical Engineering Col-
 lege: WANG XINGCHEN
Business College: FAN HOUMING
Computer Science and Technology College:
 ZHANG WEISHI
Electronic Information College: ZHANG SHU-
 FANG
Environmental Science and Engineering Col-
 lege: DING YONGSHENG
Humanities and Social Sciences College:
 FENG WENHUA
International Cooperation College: ZHANG
 SHIPPING
Law College: QU GUANGQING
Marine Engineering College: REN GUANG
Navigation College: DONG FANG
Shipping Management College: YANG ZHAN

DALIAN UNIVERSITY OF TECHNOLOGY (DUT)

2 Linggong Rd, Ganjingzi District, Dalian
 116023, Liaoning Province
Telephone: (411) 4678300
Fax: (411) 4708116

E-mail: dut@dlut.edu.cn
Internet: www.dlut.edu.cn
Founded 1949 as Dalian Institute of Tech-
 nology
State control
Academic year: September to July
Units incl. 14 schools, 50 research institutes
and 4 Nat. Key Laboratories
Pres.: Prof. CHENG GENGDONG
Vice-Pres: Prof. JIANG DEXUE, Prof. KONG
 XIANJING, Prof. SHEN HONGSHU, Prof.
 WANG LIANSHENG, Prof. XUE GUANG
Librarian: XIE MAOZHAO
Library of 1,840,000 vols, 8,000 periodicals
Number of teachers: 1,297
Number of students: 22,344 (incl. 5,883
 postgraduate)
Publications: *Journal* (6 a year), *Journal of
 Computational Mechanics* (4 a year), *Jour-
 nal of Mathematical Research and Expos-
 ition* (4 a year), *Journal of Social Sciences*
 (4 a year).

DAQING PETROLEUM INSTITUTE

Daqing 151400, Heilongjiang Province
Telephone: (459) 4653232
Fax: (459) 7332415
Internet: www.dqpi.net
Founded 1960
State control
Academic year: September to July
Pres.: LIU YANG
Vice-Pres: LIU YONG JIAN, LU YAN FANG,
 SONG ZHI CHEN, YANG XIAO LONG
Number of teachers: 1,762
Number of students: 10,000
Publications: *Journal* (4 a year), *Petroleum
 Industry Technology* (4 a year)

DEANS

College of Building Construction Engineer-
 ing: SUN JIAN GANG
College of Computing and Information Tech-
 nology: MA RUI MIN
College of Continuing Education: ZHAO JIN
 LIN
College of Earth Sciences: SHI SHANG MING
College of Economics and Management: SHAO
 QIANG
College of Electricity and Information Engin-
 eering: DUAN YU BO
College of Electronic Engineering: WANG
 MING JI
College of Foreign Languages: QIU XUE HE
College of Humanities: KUAN JIN LIN
College of Mathematics: WANG SHOU TIAN
College of Mechanical Science and Engineer-
 ing: WANG ZUN CE
College of Oil Engineering Institute: CUI HAI
 QING

PROFESSORS

AI, CHI, Oil Engineering
BAI, XING HUA, Earth Sciences
CAO, YU QUAN, Electricity and Information
 Engineering
CHANG, YU LIAN, Mechanical Science and
 Engineering
CHEN, TAO PING, Oil Engineering
CHEN, XUE MEI, Mechanical Science and
 Engineering
CUI, HAI QING, Oil Engineering
CUI, ZHEN HUA, Mechanical Science and
 Engineering
DAI, GUANG, Mechanical Science and Engin-
 eering
DU, HONG LIE, Earth Sciences
DUAN, YU BO, Electricity and Information
 Engineering
FAN, HONG FU, Oil Engineering
FU, GUANG, Earth Sciences

FU, GUANG JIE, Electricity and Information Engineering
GAO, BING KUN, Electricity and Information Engineering
GUO, YU FENG, Electronic Engineering
HAN, GUO YOU, Mechanical Science and Engineering
HAN, HONG SHENG, Oil Engineering
HAO, WEN SEN, Mechanical Science and Engineering
JIA, WEN JU, Computing and Information Technology
JIA, ZHEN QI, Oil Engineering
JIANG, MING HU, Mechanical Science and Engineering
JIN, SHAO XIAN, Electronic Engineering
KANG, WANG LI, Oil Engineering
KONG, LING BIN, Mathematics
LI, BAO YAN, Mechanical Science and Engineering
LI, CHUN SHENG, Computing and Information Technology
LI, CONG XIN, Computing and Information Technology
LI, JIE, Earth Sciences
LI, XIAO PING, Mathematics
LI, YAN JIE, Mathematics
LING, JING LONG, Earth Sciences
LIU, JU BAO, Mechanical Science and Engineering
LIU, SU LIN, Mechanical Science and Engineering
LIU, TIE NAN, Electricity and Information Engineering
LIU, XIAO YAN, Earth Sciences
LIU, YANG, Oil Engineering
LIU, YI KUN, Oil Engineering
LIU, YONG JIAN, Oil Engineering
LU, LING JIE, Computing and Information Technology
LU, SHUANG FANG, Earth Sciences
LU, YAN FANG, Earth Sciences
MA, RUI MIN, Computing and Information Technology
MA, SHI ZHONG, Earth Sciences
NUAN, QING DE, Mechanical Science and Engineering
REN, FU SHAN, Mechanical Science and Engineering
REN, WEI JIAN, Electricity and Information Engineering
SHAO, QIANG, Economics and Management
SHI, SHANG MING, Earth Sciences
SONG, KAO PING, Oil Engineering
SONG, YU LING, Humanities
SUN, BO TAO, Foreign Languages
SUN, JIAN GANG, Building Construction Engineering
SUN, YAN BIN, Economics and Management
SUN, YU XUE, Oil Engineering
TANG, GUO WEI, Computing and Information Technology
WANG, DE MING, Oil Engineering
WANG, HENG JIU, Economics and Management
WANG, JING QI, Earth Sciences
WANG, MING JI, Electronic Engineering
WANG, SHOU TIAN, Mathematics
WANG, WEN GUANG, Earth Sciences
WANG, XIU MING, Earth Sciences
WANG, ZUN CE, Mechanical Science and Engineering
WU, WEN XIANG, Oil Engineering
XIA, HUI FENG, Oil Engineering
XU, BU YUN, Mechanical Science and Engineering
XU, SHAO HUA, Computing and Information Technology
YAN, TIE, Oil Engineering
YI, ZHI AN, Computing and Information Technology
ZENG, ZHAO YING, Mathematics
ZHANG, CHANG HAI, Mathematics
ZHANG, DA WEI, Oil Engineering
ZHANG, JI HUA, Foreign Languages
ZHANG, JING, Earth Sciences

ZHANG, YONG HONG, Mechanical Science and Engineering
ZHANG, YU BIN, Mechanical Science and Engineering
ZHAO, WEI MIN, Mechanical Science and Engineering
ZHAO, ZI GANG, Oil Engineering
ZHOU, QING LONG, Mechanical Science and Engineering
ZHU, JUN, Mechanical Science and Engineering

DONGBEI UNIVERSITY OF FINANCE AND ECONOMICS

217 Jianshan St, Shahekou District, Dalian 116025

Telephone: (411) 4691503
Fax: (411) 4691862
E-mail: dufe1952@pub.dl.inpta.net.cn
Internet: www.dufe.edu.cn

Founded 1952
State control
Languages of instruction: Chinese, English
Academic year: September to July

President: Prof. YU YANG
Vice-Presidents: Prof. GUO CHANGLU, Assoc. Prof. LIU JIANMIN, Prof. QIU DONG
President's Assistant: Assoc. Prof. ZHOU LIANSHENG
Librarian: ZHANG LI

Library of 900,000 vols
Number of teachers: 561
Number of students: 11,815 (incl. 5,678 correspondence)

Publication: Research on Finance and Economics Issues

HEADS OF SCHOOLS

School of Accountancy: Prof. LIU YONGZE
School of Adult Education: Prof. CONG JIZENG
School of Business Management: Prof. LIU QINGYUAN
School of Finance and Taxation: Prof. MA GOUQIANG
School of Hotel Management: Assoc. Prof. LI LI
School of International Chinese: Assoc. Prof. ZHANG WENFENG

DONGHUA UNIVERSITY

1882 West Yan-An Rd, Shanghai 200051
Telephone: (21) 62197533
Fax: (21) 62194722
Internet: www.dhu.edu.cn

Founded 1951 as East China Textile Institute of Science and Technology, re-named China Textile Univ. 1985, present name 1999
Academic year: September to July

Pres.: Prof. SHAO SHIHUANG
Vice-Pres: Prof. JIN JIAYOU, Prof. HU XUECHAO, Prof. TAN DEZHONG, Prof. XUE YOUYI, Prof. ZHU SHIGEN
Registrar: Prof. ZHANG JIAYU
Librarian: Prof. YU MING

Library of 810,000 vols and periodicals
Number of teachers: 903
Number of students: 12,081

Publications: Journal (6 a year, English edn 2 a year), Textile Technology Overseas (6 a year)

HEADS OF COLLEGES

Art and Design Institute: Prof. HUANG YUANQING
College of Textile Science and Technology: Prof. ZHU SUKANG
College of Chemistry and Chemicals: Prof. DAI JINJIN
College of Mechanical Engineering: Prof. WANG SHENZE

College of Information Science and Technology: Prof. SONG LIQUN
College of Science: Prof. XIE HANKUN
College of Humanities: ZHANG YI
College of Environmental Science and Engineering: Prof. XI DANLI
College of Materials Science and Engineering: Prof. CHEN YANMO
College of Foreign Languages: Prof. SHEN BAIYAO
Fashion Institute: Prof. ZHANG WEIYUAN
Glorious Sun School of Business Management: Prof. SUN JUNKANG

EAST CHINA NORMAL UNIVERSITY

3663 Zhongshan Rd North, Shanghai 200062
Telephone: (21) 62233333
Fax: (21) 62576217
E-mail: webmaster@ecnu.edu.cn
Internet: www.ecnu.edu.cn

Founded 1951
Controlled by the Min. of Education
Academic year: September to July (two semesters)

Pres.: WANG JIANPAN
Vice-Pres: DU GONGZHUO, MA QINRONG, TANG MINGJIAN, WANG TIEXIAN, YE JIANNONG, YU LIZHONG
Librarian: HUANG XIUWEN

Library of 3,535,000 vols
Number of teachers: 1,647
Number of students: 19,108

Publications: Applied Probability and Statistics (4 a year), East Europe and Central Asia Today (6 a year), Journal of Educational Science (4 a year), Journal of Natural Sciences (4 a year), Journal of Philosophy and Social Sciences (6 a year), Psychological Science (6 a year), Research into the Theory of Ancient Literature (irregular), Theoretical Studies in Literature and Art (6 a year), World Geography Research (2 a year)

DEANS

College of Continuing Education: SUN JIANMING
College of Educational Administration: MA QINRONG
Graduate School: YU LIZHONG
International College of Chinese Culture: WANG TIEXIAN
School of Business: JIN RUNGUI
School of Chemistry and Life Science: XU HONGFA
School of Educational Science and Technology: DING GANG
School of Foreign Languages: ZHANG CHUNBO
School of Humanities: FENG SHAOLEI
School of Literature and Art: HONG BENJIAN
School of Pre-School and Special Education: NIE YOULI
School of Resources and Environmental Science: CHEN ZHONGYUAN
School of Science and Engineering: WANG ZUGENG

EAST CHINA UNIVERSITY OF SCIENCE AND TECHNOLOGY

130 Meilong Rd, Shanghai 200237
Telephone: (21) 4775678
Fax: (21) 4777138
Internet: www.ecust.edu.cn

Founded 1952 (until 1993, East China University of Chemical Technology)

Depts of applied mathematics, applied physics, automatic control and electronic engineering, biochemical engineering, business management, chemical engineering, chemistry, computer science, environmental engineering, English for business, fine chemicals technology, foreign languages, industrial design, inorganic materials, management engineering, mechanical engineering, petroleum processing, polymer materials, social science; research institutes of agrochemical bioregulators, applied chemistry, applied mathematics, biomedical engineering, bioreactors (nat. laboratory) chemical engineering, chemical environmental engineering, chemical physics, chemical reaction engineering (joint laboratory), culture, economic development, fine chemicals technology, heterogeneous reaction engineering (nat. laboratory), higher education, industrial automation, industrial design, inorganic chemical technology, inorganic materials, Marxism and ideological education, materials science, petroleum processing, process equipment and pressure vessels, speciality chemicals, technical chemical physics

Pres.: Prof. WANG XINGYU

Vice-Pres: Prof. DAI GANCE, LIN ZHUYUAN, Prof. ZHANG DONGSHAN, Prof. ZHU ZIBIN

Library of 1,240,000 vols, 4,500 periodicals in 11 languages

Number of teachers: 1,841

Number of students: 8,322

Publication: *Journal* (6 a year).

FUDAN UNIVERSITY

220 Handan Rd, Shanghai 200433

Telephone: (21) 65642222

Internet: www.fudan.edu.cn

Founded 1905, present status 2000, following merger with Shanghai Medical Univ.

State control

Languages of instruction: Chinese, English

Academic year: September to July (2 semesters)

Pres.: Prof. YANG, YULIANG

Exec. Vice-Pres: ZHANG, YIHUAProf. WANG, WEIPING

Vice-Pres.: Prof. CAI, DAFENG

Vice-Pres.: Prof. CHEN, XIAOMAN

Vice-Pres.: Prof. GUI, YONGHAO

Vice-Pres.: LIN, JI

Vice-Pres.: XU, ZHENG

Librarian: Prof. QIN ZENGFU

Library of 4,330,000 vols

Number of teachers: 2,481

Number of students: 26,792 (full-time) and 20,670 studying at the schools of Continuing Education and Online Education

Publications: *Fudan Natural Sciences Journal, Fudan Social Sciences Journal, Mathematics Annals Acta* (6 a year)

DEANS

School of Economics: Prof. HONG YUANPENG

School of Information Science and Engineering

School of Int. Cultural Communication: Prof. ZHU YONGSHENG

School of Int. Relations and Public Affairs: Prof. YONG LONGTU

School of Journalism: Prof. DING GANLIN

School of Law

School of Life Sciences: Prof. LI YUYANG

School of Management: LU XIONGWEN

School of Mathematical Sciences: WANG YONGZHEN (Vice-Dean)

School of Social Devt and Public Policy: Prof. PENG XIZHE

FUJIAN AGRICULTURAL AND FORESTRY UNIVERSITY

Jinshan 350002, Fujian Province

Telephone: (591) 3741721

Fax: (591) 3741251

Internet: www.fjau.edu.cn

Founded 1936

State control

Language of instruction: Chinese

Pres.: Prof. LU LIUXIN

Vice-Pres: PAN TINGGUO, Prof. YE SHANGQING, YOU MINSHENG

Librarian: HU FANPING

Library of 560,000 vols

Number of teachers: 843

Number of students: 3,880

Publications: *Current Communications on Overseas Agricultural Science and Technology, Journal of Entomology in Eastern China, Journal of Fujian Agricultural University, Overseas Agricultural Science: Sugarcane, Wuyi Science*

HEADS OF COLLEGES

College of Adult Education: YE YICHUN

College of Animal Science: HUANG YIFAN

College of Crop Science: LIN YANQUAN

College of Economics and Trade: HUANG JIANCHENG

FUJIAN MEDICAL UNIVERSITY

88 Jiaotong Rd, Fuzhou 350004, Fujian Province

Telephone: (591) 3568821

Internet: www.fjmu.edu.cn

Founded 1937

Pres.: Prof. WU ZHONGFU

Vice-Pres: LIN KEHUA, LUO GUEILIN

Head of Postgraduate Dept: KANG YUANYUAN

Librarian: HUANG HUISHANG

Library of 258,448 vols

Number of teachers: 398

Number of students: 2,306

Publications: *Journal, Medical Education Study.*

FUJIAN NORMAL UNIVERSITY

8 Shang San Rd, Cang Shan Section, Fuzhou 350007, Fujian Province

Telephone: (591) 83456156

Fax: (591) 83425154

Internet: www.fjtu.edu.cn

Founded 1907

Dept of Education of Fujian control

Academic year: September to July

Pres.: LI JIANPING

Vice-Pres: HUANG HANSHENG, LI MIN, WANG ZHENGLU, WANG WENDING, ZHENG YISHU

Head of Graduate Dept: LI JIANPING

Librarian: WAN BAOCHUAN

Number of teachers: 2,500

Number of students: 30,000

Publications: *Journal* (natural sciences, 6 a year), *Journal* (philosophy and social sciences, 6 a year), *Mathematics of Fujian Middle School* (6 a year)

DEANS

College of Physical Education and Sports Science: MEI XUEXIONG

School of Bioengineering: LI MIN

School of Chemistry and Material Science: HU BINGHUAN

School of Economy: LI JIANJIAN

School of Educational Sciences and Technology: YU WENSEN

School of Foreign Languages: LIN DAJIN

School of Geographical Sciences: YANG YUSHENG

School of Humanities: CHEN QINGYUAN

School of Law: GUO TIEMIN

School of Mathematics and Computer Science: LI YONGQING

School of Media: YAN CHUNJUN

School of Music: ZHENG JINYANG

School of Physics and Optoelectronic Technology: XIE SHUSEN

School of Public Administration: HE YILUN

School of Society and History: LIN JINSHUI

School of Software: WENG ZUMAO

School of Tourism: ZHENG YAOXIN

PROFESSORS

CAI, XIULING, Economics

CHAI, YUPING, Public Administration

CHEN, GUIRONG, Public Administration

CHEN, GUORUI, Physical Education and Sports Science

CHEN, HUOPING, Educational Sciences and Technology

CHEN, JUNQIN, Physical Education and Sports Science

CHEN, KAI, Foreign Languages

CHEN, LIANGYUAN, Humanities

CHEN, QINGYUAN, Humanities

CHEN, RONG, Physical Education and Sports Science

CHEN, SHAOHUI, Economics

CHEN, SHAOPING, Chemistry and Material Science

CHEN, TIECHENG, Physical Education and Sports Science

CHEN, WEIZHEN, Foreign Languages

CHEN, YIPING, Bioengineering

CHEN, YONGCHUN, Public Administration

CHEN, YOUQIANG, Bioengineering

CHEN, ZEPING, Humanities

CHEN, ZHENG, Economics

CHENG, LIGUO, Educational Sciences and Technology

DAI, CONGTENG, Foreign Languages

DAI, XIANQUN, Society and History

DU, CHANGZHONG, Foreign Languages

GANG, SONG, Bioengineering

GAO, JIANMIN, Bioengineering

GU, YEPING, Humanities

GUO, TIEMIN, Economics

HE, YILUN, Public Administration

HONG, MING, Educational Sciences and Technology

HONG, YANGUO, Bioengineering

HU, BINGHUAN, Chemistry and Material Science

HU, CANGZE, Society and History

HU, ZHIGANG, Chemistry and Material Science

HUANG, AILING, Educational Sciences and Technology

HUANG, GUANGYANG, Educational Sciences and Technology

HUANG, GUOSHENG, Society and History

HUANG, GUOXIONG, Public Administration

HUANG, HANSHENG, Physical Education and Sports Science

HUANG, JIANZHONG, Bioengineering

HUANG, JIAYE, Economics

HUANG, RENXIAN, Educational Sciences and Technology

HUANG, ZHIGAO, Physics and Optoelectronic Technology

LAN, XUEFEI, Music

LI, HONGCAI, Physics and Optoelectronic Technology

LI, JIANJIAN, Economics

LI, JIANPING, Economics

LI, MIN, Bioengineering

LI, RONGBAO, Foreign Languages

LI, SHUZHEN, Public Administration

LI, XIANGMIN, Public Administration

LIAN, CHENGYE, Society and History

LIAN, RONG, Educational Sciences and Technology

LIN, BENCHUN, Foreign Languages

LIN, DAJIN, Foreign Languages

LIN, GUOPING, Society and History

LIN, JING, Educational Sciences and Technology

LIN, JINHUO, Chemistry and Material Science

LIN, JINSHUI, Society and History

LIN, LIN, Bioengineering

LIN, QING, Economics

LIN, SHANLANG, Economics

LIN, XIUGUO, Public Administration

LIN, ZHANG, Foreign Languages

LIN, ZIHUA, Economics

LIU, HUIYU, Society and History
LIU, JIANQIU, Bioengineering
LIU, RONGFANG, Chemistry and Material Science
LIU, YAMENG, Foreign Languages
LIU, YONGGENG, Humanities
MAO, NING, Bioengineering
MEI, XUEXIONG, Physical Education and Sports Science
PAN, XINHE, Humanities
PAN, YUTENG, Public Administration
QIAO, JIANZHONG, Music
QIU, LING, Foreign Languages
QIU, YISHEN, Physics and Optoelectronic Technology
QIU, YONGQU, Educational Sciences and Technology
SHI, QIAOQIN, Bioengineering
SU, XIAOQING, Physical Education and Sports Science
SU, ZHENFANG, Public Administration
SUN, SHAOZHEN, Humanities
TAN, XUEXHUN, Humanities
TANG, WENJI, Society and History
WANG, GUOHONG, Bioengineering
WANG, HANMIN, Humanities
WANG, JIANDE, Society and History
WANG, KE, Humanities
WANG, YAOHUA, Music
WANG, ZHENGLU, Society and History
WANG, ZHIBO, Public Administration
WEN, RI, Society and History
WENG, JIABAO, Chemistry and Material Science
WENG, YINTAO, Humanities
WENG, ZUMAO, Computer Software
WU, YOUGEN, Economics
WU, ZONGHUA, Chemistry and Material Science
XI, YANG, Humanities
XIAO, HUASHAN, Bioengineering
XIE, BIZHEN, Society and History
XIE, SHUSEN, Physics and Optoelectronic Technology
XU, HONGFENG, Physical Education and Sports Science
XU, MING, Educational Sciences and Technology
XU, YONG, Physics and Optoelectronic Technology
YAN, CHUNJUN, Humanities
YAN, YOUWEI, Educational Sciences and Technology
YANG, KONGCHI, Educational Sciences and Technology
YANG, MINGRU, Bioengineering
YANG, XINHUA, Public Administration
YANG, YUSHENG, Geographical Sciences
YANG, ZHAOFENG, Bioengineering
YE, YIDUO, Educational Sciences and Technology
YOU, YONGLONG, Bioengineering
YU, GECHUN, Public Administration
YU, WENSEN, Educational Sciences and Technology
YUAN, SHUQI, Geographical Sciences
ZENG, CONGSHENG, Geographical Sciences
ZHAN, GUANQUN, Society and History
ZHANG, DINGHUA, Bioengineering
ZHANG, HANJIN, Physical Education and Sports Science
ZHANG, HUARONG, Economics
ZHANG, WENGONG, Chemistry and Material Science
ZHANG, YANDING, Bioengineering
ZHEN, XIAOHUA, Society and History
ZHENG, DAXIAN, Geographical Sciences
ZHENG, JINYANG, Music
ZHENG, YI, Bioengineering
ZHENG, YOUXIAN, Public Administration
ZHU, HEJIAN, Geographical Sciences
ZHU, JIAN, Economics
ZHU, JINZI, Bioengineering
ZHU, LING, Humanities
ZHUANG, HUIRU, Bioengineering
ZHUANG, TAO, Foreign Languages

ZUAN, ZHENGFANG, Public Administration

FUZHOU UNIVERSITY
523 Industry Rd, Fuzhou 350002, Fujian Province
Telephone: (591) 3739513
Fax: (591) 3713866
Internet: www.fzu.edu.cn
Founded 1958
Academic year: September to July
Pres.: WU MIN SHENG
Vice-Pres: CHEN GUO NAN, FAN GENG HUA, FANG ZHEN ZHENG, FU XIAN ZHI
Heads of Graduate Dept: LIN SHU WEN, LIU SONG QING
Librarian: ZHANG WEN DE
Number of teachers: 1,200
Number of students: 20,000
Publications: *Journal* (natural sciences, 6 a year), *Journal* (philosophy, 4 a year)

DEANS

Napier College: XIE LIU HUI
School of Biological Science and Technology: RAO PING FAN
School of Civil Engineering and Architecture: CHEN BAO CHUN
School of Electric Engineering and Automation: CHEN BAO CHUN
School of Environment and Resources: XU HAN QIU
School of Foreign Languages: WU SONG JIANG
School of Humanities and Social Sciences: LIN YI
School of Law: CHEN QUAN SHENG
School of Management: CHEN GUO HONG
School of Materials Sciences and Engineering: CHEN XIAN SHENG
School of Mathematics and Computer Science: WANG XIAO DONG
School of Mechanical Engineering: GAO CHENG HUI
School of Physics and Information Engineering: YU LUN
School of Public Management: WANG JIAN
School of Software: FAN GENG HUA
School of Zhi Cheng: TANG YI ZHU
Sunshine College: CHEN GONG LIN

PROFESSORS

CAI, JIN DING, Electrical Engineering and Automation
CHEN, BAO CHUN, Civil Engineering and Architecture
CHEN, CHONG, Electrical Engineering and Automation
CHEN, FU JI, Public Management
CHEN, GUO HONG, Management
CHEN, LE SHAN, Mechanical Engineering
CHEN, LI, Mechanical Engineering
CHEN, RONG SI, Management
CHEN, SEN, Civil Engineering and Architecture
CHEN, SHU MEI, Mechanical Engineering
CHEN, XIAN SHENG, Materials Science and Engineering
CHEN, XIAO WEI, Foreign Languages
CHEN, XIN, Physics and Information Engineering
CHEN, XIN SHU, Civil Engineering and Architecture
DU, MING, Electrical Engineering and Automation
FANG, ZHEN ZHENG, Civil Engineering and Architecture
GAO, CHENG HUI, Mechanical Engineering
GUO, ZONG REN, Electrical Engineering and Automation
HU, JI RONG, Management
HU, XIAO RONG, Civil Engineering and Architecture
HUANG, KE AN, Management
HUANG, SHU ZHANG, Management

HUANG, WEN XIN, Management
HUANG, YAO ZHI, Mechanical Engineering
HUANG, ZHI GANG, Management
JIAN, WEN BIN, Environment and Resources
LAN, ZHAO HUI, Mechanical Engineering
LEI, DE SEN, Public Management
LIN, GUO RONG, Mechanical Engineering
LIN, QIANG, Physics and Information Engineering
LIN, SHU WEN, Mechanical Engineering
LIN, TONG, Mechanical Engineering
LIN, YI, Humanities and Social Sciences
LIN, YING XING, Management
LIN, YOU WEN, Management
LIN, YUAN QING, Management
LIU, MING HUA, Environment and Resources
LIU, YAN BIN, Mechanical Engineering
PAN, YAN, Management
PENG, DA WEN, Civil Engineering and Architecture
QI, KAI, Civil Engineering and Architecture
QIAN, KUANG WU, Materials Science and Engineering
QIU, GONG WEI, Electrical Engineering and Automation
RAO, PING FAN, Biological Science and Technology
RUAN, YU ZHONG, Materials Science and Engineering
SHENG, FEI MIN, Environment and Resources
SU, KAI XIONG, Physics and Information Engineering
SUN, QIU BI, Management
TANG, DE PING, Materials Science and Engineering
TANG, DIAN, Materials Science and Engineering
TANG, LI HONG, Public Management
TANG, NING PING, Electrical Engineering and Automation
WANG, JIAN, Public Management
WANG, QIN MIN, Physics and Information Engineering
WANG, WEI YI, Management
WANG, YING MING, Public Management
WANG, ZHONG LAI, Biological Science and Technology
WU, HAN GUANG, Electrical Engineering and Automation
WU, SONG JIANG, Foreign Languages
WU, XING NAN, Humanities and Social Sciences
XI, YONG QIN, Public Management
XIE, ZHI XIN, Civil Engineering and Architecture
XU, DOU DOU, Humanities and Social Sciences
XU, HAN QIU, Environment and Resources
YANG, FU WEN, Electrical Engineering and Automation
YANG, XIAO XIANG, Mechanical Engineering
YE, ZHONG HE, Mechanical Engineering
YEA, ZHONG, Management
YU, LUN, Physics and Information Engineering
YUAN, BING LING, Humanities and Social Sciences
ZHANG, BAI, Management
ZHANG, BEI MIN, Electrical Engineering and Automation
ZHANG, QI SHAN, Management
ZHANG, MAO XUN, Mechanical Engineering
ZHANG, QI SHAN, Mechanical Engineering
ZHANG, QIONG, Materials Science and Engineering
ZHANG, YE, Management
ZHENG, JIAN LAN, Civil Engineering and Architecture
ZHENG, SHI BIAO, Physics and Information Engineering
ZHENG, ZHEN, Civil Engineering and Architecture
ZHENG, ZHEN FEI, Civil Engineering and Architecture
ZHOU, RUI ZHONG, Civil Engineering and Architecture

ZHOU, XIAO LIANG, Management
ZHU, YONG CHUN, Civil Engineering and Architecture
ZHU, ZU PING, Mechanical Engineering

GANSU AGRICULTURAL UNIVERSITY

1 Yingmencun, Nanning District, Lanzhou 730070, Gansu Province
Telephone: (931) 7631125
Fax: (931) 7631125
E-mail: wujp@public.lz.gs.cn
Internet: www.gsau.edu.cn
Founded 1958
Academic year: September to July
Pres.: Prof. WANG DI
Vice-Pres: LAN YUZHEN, Prof. LI ZHENXIAO, LU JIANHUA
Dir of Foreign Affairs: Prof. WU JIANPING
Librarian: LIU XI
Library of 500,000 vols
Number of teachers: 600
Number of students: 5,000 (125 postgraduates)
Publications: *Journal of Grassland and Turf* (4 a year), *University Journal* (12 a year)

DEANS

Agricultural Business and Trade: WANG CENGLIN
Agricultural Machinery and Engineering: WU JIANMING
Agronomy: LI WEI
Animal Science: CUI XIAN
Basic Courses: YUAN TONGSHENG
Food Science: YU QUNLI
Forest Science: JIANG ZHIRONG
Grassland Science: CAO ZHIZHONG
Horticulture: YU JIHUA
Plant Protection: ZHANG XINGHU
Social Science: SHANG ZHENHAI
Soil Chemistry: SHI YINGFU
Veterinary Science: LIU YING
Water Conservation: CHENG ZIYONG

GUANGDONG COLLEGE OF MEDICINE AND PHARMACY

40 Guang Han Zhi, Haizhu District, Guangzhou 510224, Guangdong Province
Telephone: 4429040
Founded 1978
Pres.: Prof. DU QI ZHANG (acting)
Vice-Pres: CHENG SHENGHAO, LI TINGJIE
Librarian: LIAO MING QING
Library of 160,000 vols
Number of teachers: 300
Number of students: 1,800
Publication: *Journal*

PROFESSORS

FENGHE, H., Pharmacology
FENGMING, Z., Epidemiology
JINCHENG, H., Pharmaceutical Chemistry
JINGXIAN, J., Internal Medicine
JINGZHI, H., Human Parasitology
JIPENG, L., Pharmacognosy
MUXIAN, L., Biochemistry
PUSHENG, W., Traditional Chinese Medicine
QIHUA, W., Human Anatomy
QIYUN, Y., Phytochemistry
QIZHANG, D., Pharmacology
SHIDE, S., Statistics
YIYUAN, Z., Dermatology
ZHICHENG, C., Hygiene
ZHUHUA, L., Microbiology

GUANGXI NORMAL UNIVERSITY

Yan Shan, Gui Lin 541004, Guangxi Province
Telephone: (773) 5812081
Fax: (773) 5812383

Internet: www.gxnu.edu.cn
Founded 1932
Min. of Education control
Academic year: September to July
Pres.: LIANG HONG
Vice-Pres: LAN CHANGZHOU, LIU JIANBING, LIU MUREN, WANG JIE, YI ZHONG, ZHONG RUITIAN
Librarian: YAO QIAN
Library of 2,060,000 vols
Number of teachers: 1,043
Number of students: 40,000
Publication: *Journal of Guangxi Normal University* (4 a year)

DEANS

College of Foreign Studies: LIU ZHAOZHONG
College of Life Science: QIN XINMING
College of Politics and Public Management: TAN PEIWEN
College of Physics and Information Technology: WANG QIANG
Department of Resources and Environmental Science: HE XINGCUN
Educational Science College: GAO JINLING
School of Chemistry and Chemical Engineering: LIANG FUPEI
School of Culture and Tourism: ZHOU ZUOMING
School of Law and Business: LUO ZHISONG
School of Sports: LIANG ZHUPING

PROFESSORS

CAI, CHANGZHUO, International Culture and Education
CHEN, HONGJIANG, Politics and Public Management
CHEN, JITANG, Foreign Studies
CHEN, QIN, Politics and Public Management
CHEN, XIONGZHANG, Culture and Tourism
CHEN, ZHAOBIN, Physical Education
CHEN, ZHENFENG, Chemistry and Chemical Engineering
CUI, TIANSHUN, Resources and Environmental Science
CUI, YAODONG, Mathematics and Computer Science
DENG, BIYANG, Chemistry and Chemical Engineering
DENG, PEIMING, Mathematics and Computer Science
DING, CHANGMING, Mathematics and Computer Science
FENG, CUNHUA, Mathematics and Computer Science
GUO, LILIANG, Physical Education
HE, LINXIA, Culture and Tourism
HE, XIANGLIN, Foreign Studies
HE, XINGCUN, Resources and Environmental Science
HU, DALEI, Chinese Studies
HUANG, BINLIAN, Physics and Information Technology
HUANG, CHENGMING, Life Science
HUANG, JIESHAN, Social Sciences
HUANG, RUIXIONG, Social Sciences
HUANG, SHEN, Physical Education
HUANG, WEILIN, Chinese Studies
HUANG, ZHUSHENG, Law and Business
JIANG, GUOCHENG, Life Science
JIANG, SHIHUI, Educational Science
JIANG, YIMING, Chemistry and Chemical Engineering
LEI, REI, Chinese Studies
LI, DUNXIANG, Law and Business
LI, FUBO, Chinese Studies
LI, HONGHAN, Educational Science
LI, JIANG, Chinese Studies
LI, LAILONG, Chinese Studies
LI, LU, Educational Science
LI, XIAO, Foreign Studies
LI, YI, Resources and Environmental Science
LI, ZHIQING, Physical Education
LIANG, FUPEI, Chemistry and Chemical Engineering

LIANG, HONG, Chemistry and Chemical Engineering
LIANG, ZHUPING, Physical Education
LIAO, GUOWEI, Chinese Studies
LIN, FENGMIN, Social Sciences
LIN, SHIMIN, Mathematics and Computer Science
LIU, MUREN, Physics and Information Technology
LIU, XIAOLIN, Culture and Tourism
LIU, XINGJUN, Chinese Studies
LIU, YING, International Culture and Education
LIU, ZHAOZHONG, Foreign Studies
LU, XIAO, Physics and Information Technology
LU, YUTAI, Foreign Studies
LUO, GUILIE, Mathematics and Computer Science
LUO, XIAOSHU, Physics and Information Technology
LUO, XINGKAI, Physics and Information Technology
LUO, ZHISONG, Law and Business
MAI, YONGXIONG, Chinese Studies
MO, DAOCAI, Chinese Studies
MO, QIXUN, Chinese Studies
PO, JINZE, Foreign Studies
QI, PEIFANG, Politics and Public Management
QIN, YONGSONG, Mathematics and Computer Science
QIN, ZIXIONG, Physics and Information Technology
QUE, ZHEN, Chinese Studies
REN, GUANWEN, Culture and Tourism
SHEN, JIAZHUANG, Chinese Studies
SHI, GUIYU, Life Science
SU, GUIFA, Chemistry and Chemical Engineering
SUN, JIANYUAN, Chinese Studies
TAN, DEQING, Chinese Studies
TAN, PEIWEN, Politics and Public Management
TAN, ZHAOYI, Culture and Tourism
TANG, DEHUA, Educational Science
TANG, FUCHENG, Mathematics and Computer Science
TANG, GAOYUAN, Foreign Studies
TANG, LING, Culture and Tourism
TANG, ZHAOQING, Life Science
TENG, DINGMING, Chinese Studies
TONG, GUANGZHENG, Law and Business
WANG, CHAOYUAN, Chinese Studies
WANG, CHENGMING, Mathematics and Computer Science
WANG, DEFU, Social Sciences
WANG, DEMING, Chinese Studies
WANG, JIE, Chinese Studies
WANG, QIANG, Physics and Information Technology
WANG, XIANGJUN, Politics and Public Management
WANG, ZHIYING, Chinese Studies
WEI, HAN, Foreign Studies
WENG, JIAQIANG, Physics and Information Technology
WU, DIANHUA, Mathematics and Computer Science
XIE, XIANG, Physical Education
XU, JIWANG, Foreign Studies
XU, XUEFU, Educational Science
XU, XUEYING, Educational Science
XUE, YUEGUI, Life Science
YAN, XIAOWEI, Mathematics and Computer Science
YANG, LIYAN, Law and Business
YANG, QIGUI, Mathematics and Computer Science
YANG, SHANCHAO, Mathematics and Computer Science
YANG, SHUJIE, Chinese Studies
YANG, YONGBING, Physics and Information Technology
YANG, YONGLIANG, Physical Education
YAO, DAILIANG, Chinese Studies
YE, YONGJI, Arts Department

YI, XING, Politics and Public Management
YI, ZHONG, Mathematics and Computer Science
YIN, LINGLING, Physical Education
YU, PING, Mathematics and Computer Science
YUAN, BINYE, Foreign Studies
ZHANG, LIQUN, Chinese Studies
ZHANG, MINGFEI, Chinese Studies
ZHANG, SHICHAO, Mathematics and Computer Science
ZHAO, SHULIN, Chemistry and Chemical Engineering
ZHONG, RUITIAN, Politics and Public Management
ZHOU, LIANGREN, Foreign Studies
ZHOU, QUANLIN, Foreign Studies
ZHOU, SHANYI, Life Science
ZHOU, SHIZHONG, Law and Business
ZHU, CONGBIN, Culture and Tourism
ZHU, JUNQIANG, Law and Business
ZHU, SHOUXING, Chinese Studies

GUANGXI TRADITIONAL CHINESE MEDICAL UNIVERSITY

179 Mingxiudong Rd, Nanning, Guangxi, Zhuang Autonomous Region
Telephone: (771) 3137577
Fax: (771) 317517
Internet: www.gxtcmu.edu.cn
Founded 1956
Pres.: Prof. WEI GUIKANG
Vice-Pres: Prof. LI WEITAI, Assoc. Prof. ZHU HUA, Assoc. Prof. DEN JIAGANG
Librarian: LI JIANGUANG
Library of 300,000 vols
Number of teachers: 296
Number of students: 1,849
Publications: *Guangxi Journal of Traditional Chinese Medicine, Study in Higher Education of Traditional Chinese Medicine.*

GUANGXI UNIVERSITY

10 Xixiangtang Rd, Nanning 530004, Guangxi Zhuang Autonomous Region
Telephone: (771) 3832391
Fax: (771) 3823743
E-mail: gxugjc@public.nn.gx.cn
Internet: www.gxu.edu.cn
Founded 1928
State control
Academic year: September to June
Pres.: Prof. TANG JILIANG
Registrar: Prof. FU ZHENFANG
Librarian: Prof. CHEN DAGUANG
Library of 2,020,000 vols
Number of teachers: 1,735
Number of students: 17,290
Publication: *Guangxi University Journal*

DEANS

College of Adult Education: Prof. HE BAO-CHONG
College of Agronomy: Prof. MO TIANYAN
College of Animal Science and Technology: Prof. YANG NIANSHENG
College of Biological Technology and Sugar Industrial Engineering: Prof. LU JIAJIONG
College of Business: Prof. LIU CHAOMING
College of Culture and Mass Communication: Prof. LIANG YANG
College of Chemistry and Chemical Engineering: Prof. TONG ZHANGFA
College of Civil Engineering: Prof. YAN LIUBIN
College of Computer Science and Information Technology: Prof. LI TAOSHEN
College of Electrical Engineering: Prof. LU ZUPEI
College of Forestry: Prof. JIN DAGANG (Exec. Vice-Dean)

College of Foreign Languages: Prof. ZHOU YI
College of Law: Prof. MENG QINGUO
College of Mechanical Engineering: Prof. LI SHANGPING
College of Natural Resources and the Environment: Prof. MA SHAOJIAN
College of Sciences: Prof. XI HONGJIAN
College of Social Sciences and Management: Prof. XIE SHUN
Department of Physical Education: Prof. XU MINGRONG
Department of Teacher Training: Prof. WANG HAIYIN (Vice-Dean)

GUANGZHOU UNIVERSITY

248 Guang Yuan Zhong Rd, Guangzhou 510405
Telephone: (20) 86394493
Fax: (20) 86370350
E-mail: faogzu@21cn.com
Internet: www.gzhu.edu.cn
Founded 1983, merged with 8 other institutions of higher education 2000
Academic year: September to July
President: Prof. LIN WEIMING
Vice-Presidents: Prof. CHEN WANPENG, Prof. LI XUNGUI, Prof. LONG SHAOFENG, Prof. SHU YANG, Prof. XU CIRONG, Prof. YU GUOYANG
Director of Academic Affairs: Prof. YU QICAI
Director of Academic Research: Prof. XIAN QIAOLING
Director of the Institute for Higher Education Research: Prof. HUANG JIAQUAN
Director of the International Office: Prof. LI YI
Director of Postgraduate Affairs: Prof. YAO PO
Library Director: Prof. ZHANG BAIYING
Library of 182,000 vols
Number of teachers: 2,372
Number of students: 31,333
Publication: *Journal* (12 a year).

GUANGZHOU UNIVERSITY OF TRADITIONAL CHINESE MEDICINE

12 Airport Rd, Guangzhou 510405, Guangdong Province
Telephone: (20) 36588233
Fax: (20) 36585258
Internet: www.gzhtcm.edu.cn
Founded 1956
Dept of Education of Guangdong control
Academic year: September to July
Pres.: FENG XINSONG
Vice-Pres: CHEN YINGHUA, LI JIANJUN, LIN PEICHENG, WANG NINGSHENG, XU ZHIWEI
Head of Graduate Dept: QIU SHIJUN
Librarian: LI JIAN
Number of teachers: 1,025
Number of students: 3,000
Publications: *Journal* (6 a year), *New Journal of Traditional Chinese Medicine* (12 a year), *Traditional Chinese Drug Research and Clinical Pharmacology* (6 a year)

DEANS

First School of Medicine: DENG TIETAO
School of Acupuncture and Massage: CAI TIEQU
School of Basic Medical Sciences: CHEN QUN
School of Chinese Traditional Medicine: CHEN WEIWEN
School of Economy and Administration: QIU HONGZHONG
School of Information Technology: CHEN SU
School of Nursing: HE YANPING
Second School of Medicine: LU YUBO
Third School of Medicine: ZHUANG HONG

PROFESSORS

CAI, TIEQU, Acupuncture and Massage

CHEN, DACAN, Medicine
CHEN, JINGHE, Medicine
CHEN, JIPAN, Medicine
CHEN, QUN, Basic Medical Sciences
CHEN, SU, Information Technology
CHEN, WEIWEN, Chinese Traditional Medicine
CHEN, XHAOFENG, Basic Medical Sciences
CHEN, ZHIQIANG, Medicine
CHENG, YI, Chinese Traditional Medicine
DENG, TIETAO, Medicine
GAO, YOUHENG, Chinese Traditional Medicine
HUANG, SHAOYING, Medicine
I, JIEFEN, Basic Medical Sciences
JIN, RUI, Medicine
LAI, WEN, Basic Medical Sciences
LAI, XINSHENG, Acupuncture and Massage
LI, HANJIN, Basic Medical Sciences
LI, JINGBO, Basic Medical Sciences
LI, RENXIAN, Medicine
LI, RI, Chinese Traditional Medicine
LI, WANYAO, Acupuncture and Massage
LI, WEI, Chinese Traditional Medicine
LI, WEIMIN, Chinese Traditional Medicine
LI, YIWEI, Nursing
LIANG, SONGMIN, Chinese Traditional Medicine
LIN, LI, Chinese Traditional Medicine
LIU, HUANLAN, Basic Medical Sciences
LIU, JUN, Medicine
LIU, SHICHANG, Medicine
LIU, XIAOBIN, Basic Medical Sciences
LUO, RONGJING, Basic Medical Sciences
LUO, YUNJIAN, Medicine
LU, YUBO, Medicine
OU, YONGXIN, Basic Medical Sciences
OUYANG, HUIQING, Medicine
PAN, YI, Basic Medical Sciences
PENG, SHENGQUAN, Medicine
QIU, HEMING, Medicine
QIU, HONGZHONG, Economy and Administration
WANG, HONGQI, Basic Medical Sciences
WU, MIMAN, Basic Medical Sciences
WU, QINGHE, Chinese Traditional Medicine
XIONG, MANQI, Medicine
XU, HONGHUA, Chinese Traditional Medicine
XU, NENGGUI, Acupuncture and Massage
XU, ZHIWEI, Basic Medical Sciences
YANG, SHUNYI, Acupuncture and Massage
YANG, ZHIMIN, Medicine
YUAN, HAO, Medicine
ZHANG, HONG, Acupuncture and Massage
ZHANG, JIAWEI, Acupuncture and Massage
ZHOU, DAIHAN, Medicine
ZHOU, LILING, Chinese Traditional Medicine
ZHUANG, LIXING, Acupuncture and Massage

GUIZHOU UNIVERSITY

Guiyang, Guizhou Province
Telephone: (851) 3851187
Fax: (851) 3851381
Founded 1958 as Guizhou Univ. as successor to institution that had been disbanded in 1953, merged with Guizhou Renmin Univ. (Guizhou People's Univ.) 1993
Colleges: agriculture, arts, biotechnology, humanities, science and engineering, vocational training
Chancellor: XU CAODONG
Vice-Chancellor: LIU CHAOZHENG
Number of teachers: 2,800
Number of students: 10,000

GUIZHOU UNIVERSITY OF TECHNOLOGY

Caijiaguan, Guiyang 550003, Guizhou Province
Telephone: (851) 4731641
Fax: (851) 4731649
E-mail: fao@gut.gy.gz.cn

Founded 1958
Academic year: September to July
President: HU GUOGEN
Registrar: WANG YI
Secretary-General: YUAN HUAJUN
Librarian: HE LIQUAN

Library of 520,000 vols, 1,500 periodicals
Number of teachers: 780
Number of students: 8,000

Publication: *Journal* (6 a year).

HANGZHOU UNIVERSITY OF COMMERCE

29 Jiao Gong Rd, Hangzhou 310035, Zhejiang
Telephone: (571) 8071024
Fax: (571) 8053079
E-mail: huc1@zjpta.net.cn
Internet: www.hzic.edu.cn

Founded 1911
Under control of Min. of Commerce
Academic year: February to July, September to January
Pres.: Prof. HU ZUGUANG
Vice-Pres: DING ZHENGZHONG, HU WEIMIN, Prof. WANG GUANGMING, ZHANG JIANPING, ZHOU DAJUN
Chief Administrative Officer: KE LI
Librarian: ZHU SHANGWU

Library of 620,000 vols
Number of teachers: 326
Number of students: 5,100 full-time, 3,600 part-time

Publications: *Academic Periodical, Economics and Business Administration.*

HARBIN INSTITUTE OF ELECTRICAL TECHNOLOGY

53 Daqing Rd, Harbin 150040, Heilongjiang Province
Telephone: (451) 6221000
Fax: (451) 51623
Founded 1950
Academic year: September to July
Pres.: HE LIAN
Vice-Pres: BAO SHAOXUAN, LIANG YUANHUA, ZHOU SHICHANG
Registrar: LU MINGJUAN
Librarian: BAO SHAOXUAN

Library of 270,000 vols
Number of teachers: 537
Number of students: 2,015 (incl. 95 postgraduates)

Publication: *Journal* (4 a year).

HARBIN ENGINEERING UNIVERSITY

145 Nantong Street, Harbin 150001, Heilongjiang Province
Telephone: (451) 2519212
Fax: (451) 2533090
E-mail: heu@public.hr.hl.cn
Internet: www.hrbeu.edu.cn

Founded 1953
Academic year: September to July
Pres.: Prof. QIU CHANGHUA
Sec. of the Univ. Party Cittee: LIU ZHIGANG

Library of 900,000 vols
Number of teachers: 2,200
Number of students: 23,000

Publications: *Applied Science and Technology, Journal of HEU, Overseas Science and Technology.*

HARBIN MEDICAL UNIVERSITY

194 Nan Gang Section, Xue Fu Rd, Harbin 150086, Heilongjiang Province
Telephone and fax (451) 86671349

Internet: www.hrbmu.edu.cn
Founded 1926
Dept of Education of Heilongjiang Province control
Academic year: September to July
Pres.: YANG BAOFENG
Vice-Pres: CAO DEPIN, LI YUKUI, LIU WENCHUAN, WO ZHENZHONG
Head of Graduate Dept: ZHANG BAOXING
Librarian: YUE WEIPING

Number of teachers: 1,151
Number of students: 9,228 (6,414 full-time, 2,814 part-time)

Publications: *Chinese Journal of Endemiology* (6 a year), *Journal* (6 a year)

DEANS

Branch of Harbin Medical University: ZHANG SHIXUE
Department of Bioinformatics: LI XIA
First School of Medicine: ZHOU JIN
School of Basic Medical Sciences: FU SONGBIN
School of Mouth Cavity Medical Science: ZHANG BIN
School of Nursing: LI JIANFENG
School of Pharmacy: ZHU DALING
School of Public Health: SUN CHANGHAO
Second School of Medicine: ZHANG QIFAN

PROFESSORS

AI, MINGLI, Medicine
BAI, XINZHI, Medicine
BAO, XIUZENG, Pharmacy
BAO, YONGPING, Public Health
BI, WENSHU, Medicine
BI, ZHENGGANG, Medicine
CHEN, BINGQING, Public Health
CHEN, GENGXIN, Medicine
CHEN, LI, Public Health
CHEN, SHUXIANG, Medicine
CHEN, XIUJIE, Pharmacy
CHENG, DEQING, University Branch
CHENG, LIHA, Medicine
CHENG, ZHI, Basic Medical Sciences
CHI, ZIANG, Medicine
CUI, HAO, Medicine
CUI, HONGBIN, Public Health
CUI, LIANBIN, Medicine
CUI, SHI, Medicine
CUI, YUNPU, Medicine
DAI, HAIBIN, Medicine
DAI, QINSHUN, Medicine
DAI, ZE, University Branch
DU, XIUXHEN, Medicine
DU, ZHIMIN, Pharmacy
FAN, LIHUA, Public Health
FU, LU, Medicine
FU, SHIYING, Medicine
FU, SONGBIN, Basic Medical Sciences
GAO, GUANGMING, Dentistry
GAO, GUANGXIN, University Branch
GAO, RUIJU, Medicine
GAO, SHANLING, Medicine
GONG, LINGTAO, University Branch
GU, SUYI, Medicine
GUAN, JINGMING, Medicine
GUAN, YONGMEI, Medicine
GUAN, ZHENZHONG, Medicine
GUO, LUNSHU, University Branch
GUO, ZHENG, Bioinformatics
HAN, DE'EN, Medicine
HAN, DEWEN, University Branch
HAN, FENGPING, Medicine
HAN, MINGZI, Medicine
HAN, XIANGYAN, Medicine
HAO, LI, University Branch
HONG, FENGYANG, Medicine
HONG, WANQING, Medicine
HU, SHUANGJIU, Medicine
HU, XIAOCHEN, Medicine
HUANG, YONGLIN, Medicine
HUANG, ZHENGSONG, Medicine
JI, YUBIN, Pharmacy
JI, ZHUANZHEN, University Branch
JIA, GUODONG, Medicine

JIANG, GUIQIN, Medicine
JIANG, HONGCHI, Medicine
JIANG, LIJING, Medicine
JIANG, XUEHAI, Medicine
LI, BAIXIANG, Public Health
LI, BANQUAN, Medicine
LI, BAOJIE, Medicine
LI, BAOXIN, Pharmacy
LI, BIN, Medicine
LI, BO, Basic Medical Sciences
LI, CHANGXHUN, Medicine
LI, CHUNMING, Medicine
LI, HEYU, Medicine
LI, JIANFENG, Nursing
LI, JIXUE, Medicine
LI, KANG, Public Health
LI, PEILING, Medicine
LI, QIUJIE, Nursing
LI, SHULIN, Medicine
LI, WEIMIN, Medicine
LI, XIA, Bioinformatics
LI, XIA, Pharmacy
LI, XIAOYUN, Medicine
LI, XIULAN, Medicine
LI, YURONG, Basic Medical Sciences
LI, ZHIXU, Medicine
LI, ZUNYI, Medicine
LIN, XUESONG, University Branch
LIN, YIJIA, Medicine
LIU, BAOLIN, Public Health
LIU, BOSONG, Medicine
LIU, DEXIANG, University Branch
LIU, ENZHONG, Medicine
LIU, FENGJI, Medicine
LIU, FENGZHI, Pharmacy
LIU, HAITANG, Medicine
LIU, HONG, Dentistry
LIU, HONGYUAN, Public Health
LIU, JINJIE, University Branch
LIU, RUIHAI, Public Health
LIU, SHUDE, Medicine
LIU, TIEFU, Medicine
LIU, WENZHU, Medicine
LIU, XIANJUN, Medicine
LIU, YUFENG, Medicine
LIU, ZHICHENG, Public Health
LOU, GUIRONG, Medicine
LU, DAGUANG, Medicine
LU, LEI, Medicine
LU, MINGJUN, Public Health
MA, YINGJI, Medicine
MENG, FANCHAO, Medicine
MENG, HUANBIN, Medicine
QI, YOUCHENG, Medicine
QIAO, GUOFENG, Pharmacy
QIN, HUADONG, Medicine
QIU, FENGQIN, Medicine
QIU, ZHONGYI, Medicine
QU, RENHAI, Medicine
QU, XIUFEN, Medicine
QUAN, HUDE, Public Health
SANG, YIMIN, Medicine
SHENG, YUCHEN, Medicine
SHI, YUZHI, Medicine
SI, ZHUANG, Medicine
SONG, CHUNFANG, Medicine
SONG, CUIPING, Medicine
SONG, ZHIMIN, University Branch
SUN, AHIBO, Medicine
SUN, CHANGHAO, Public Health
SUN, GANG, University Branch
SUN, JIANPING, Pharmacy
SUN, KAOXIANG, Pharmacy
SUN, KEMIN, Medicine
SUN, XIANCHAO, Medicine
SUN, YUNQIAO, Medicine
TAN, TIEZHENG, Medicine
TAN, WENHUA, Medicine
TIAN, SULI, Medicine
WANG, BINYOU, Public Health
WANG, BOWEN, Medicine
WANG, CAIXIA, University Branch
WANG, CHUNXIANG, Medicine
WANG, FUJING, Medicine
WANG, GUIZHAO, Medicine
WANG, GUOQING, Medicine

WANG, HUIMIN, Medicine
WANG, JINGHUA, Medicine
WANG, JINGHUA, University Branch
WANG, JUNCHENG, Medicine
WANG, LI, University Branch
WANG, LING, Pharmacy
WANG, LINGSHAN, Medicine
WANG, MENGXUE, Medicine
WANG, MINGJUN, Medicine
WANG, NAIQIAN, Medicine
WANG, SHENGFA, Medicine
WANG, SHOUREN, Medicine
WANG, TAIHE, Medicine
WANG, XIAOFENG, Medicine
WANG, XIUFAN, Medicine
WANG, ZHIBANG, Medicine
WANG, ZHIGUO, Pharmacy
WEI, LINYU, Medicine
WU, DEQUAN, Medicine
WU, KUN, Public Health
WU, LIJIE, Public Health
WU, LINHUA, Pharmacy
WU, QUNHONG, Public Health
WU, YONGWEN, Medicine
XI, ZHENSHAN, Medicine
XING, JIE, University Branch
XU, JUNRU, Medicine
XU, LINSHENG, Medicine
XU, XUGUANG, Medicine
YANG, BAOFENG, Pharmacy
YANG, FUMING, Medicine
YANG, SHIXHUN, Medicine
YANG, WEILIANG, Medicine
YANG, XUEWEI, Medicine
YAO, LI, Medicine
YE, YUANZHU, Medicine
YIN, HUIQING, Medicine
YIN, KESEN, University Branch
YIN, XIAOQIAN, Medicine
YU, BO, Medicine
YU, DANPING, Medicine
YU, JINGHAI, Pharmacy
YU, JINGYUAN, Medicine
YU, WEIGANG, Medicine
YU, WEIPING, Public Health
YU, XIUXIAN, University Branch
YU, ZHONGSHU, Medicine
YUAN, XIZHEN, University Branch
YUAN, FENG, Medicine
YUE, WU, Medicine
ZHANG, BAOKU, Medicine
ZHANG, BIN, Dentistry
ZHANG, FENGMING, Basic Medical Sciences
ZHANG, JUN, University Branch
ZHANG, MINGWEN, Medicine
ZHANG, PENG, Medicine
ZHANG, QIFAN, Medicine
ZHANG, SHUQI, Basic Medical Sciences
ZHANG, SHUTAO, Medicine
ZHANG, TINGDONG, Medicine
ZHANG, XIANGLI, University Branch
ZHANG, XIAOXIAN, Medicine
ZHANG, XICHEN, University Branch
ZHANG, XINYING, Medicine
ZHANG, XIUQI, Medicine
ZHANG, XIYU, Medicine
ZHANG, YAN, Medicine
ZHANG, YINA, Medicine
ZHANG, YUCHENG, Medicine
ZHANG, YUCHUN, Medicine
ZHANG, ZHONGYI, Public Health
ZHAO, CHANGJI, Medicine
ZHAO, SHUZHEN, Medicine
ZHAO, YASHUANG, Public Health
ZHAO, ZHIHAI, Medicine
ZHONG, ZHENYU, Medicine
ZHOU, JIN, Medicine
ZHOU, WENXUE, Medicine
ZHOU, XIAOMING, Medicine
ZHOU, YUQOI, University Branch
ZHOU, ZHONGFANG, Medicine
ZHU, DALING, Pharmacy
ZHU, GUICHUN, Medicine
ZHU, QUAN, Medicine
ZHU, SHUYING, Medicine
ZHU, SIHE, Medicine

ZHU, XIUYING, Medicine
ZHU, YAN, Medicine

HARBIN NORMAL UNIVERSITY

1 Danan Rd, Liming District, Harbin 150080, Heilongjiang Province
Telephone: (451) 86376222
Internet: www.hrbnu.edu.cn
Founded 1951
Academic year: September to July
Pres.: CHEN SHUTAO
Vice-Pres: FU DAOBIN, FU JUNLONG, LU YUSUN, SUN FUGUANG, WANG XUANZHANG, WANG ZHONGQIAO
Librarian: GUO SHIMING
Library of 3,340,000 vols
Number of teachers: 3,695
Number of students: 31,835
Publications: *Continuing Education Research* (6 a year), *Heilongjiang Researches on Higher Education* (6 a year), *Natural Science Journal of Harbin Normal University* (6 a year), *Northern Forum* (6 a year)

DEANS

College of Arts: LU XUSUN
College of Computer Science and Mathematics: WANG YUWEN
College of Education Science and Technology: ZHAO HENIN
College of Life and Environment: ZHAO WENGE
College of Literature: GUO CONGLIN
College of Physics and Chemistry: LU SHUCHENG
College of Politics, Law and Economics Management: XU XIAOFENG
College of Sports Sciences: LIU ZHONGWU
Foreign Language Institute: JIANG TAO

PROFESSORS

CHEN, SHUTAO, Computer Science and Mathematics
DAI, BOQING, Physics and Chemistry
FENG, SUYUN, Literature
FU, DAOBIN, Literature
GAO, HUIMING, Arts
GE, YUNCHENG, Physics and Chemistry
GE, ZHIYI, Literature
GUO, CONGLIN, Literature
HUA, DEZUN, Life and Environment
LI, CHANGYU, Literature
LI, JILIN, Life and Environment
LU, SHUCHENG, Physics and Chemistry
LU, YUSUN, Arts
LUO, ZHENYA, Literature
SONG, WEN, Computer Science and Mathematics
SUN, MUTIAN, Literature
TAO, YABIN, Arts
TIAN, GUOWEI, Life and Environment
WANG, LISAN, Arts
WANG, TONGCHANG, Education Science and Technology
WANG, XUANZHANG, Physics and Chemistry
WANG, YUWEN, Computer Science and Mathematics
WANG, ZHONGQIAO, Literature
XU, GUOLIN, Physics and Chemistry
XU, HENGYONG, Physics and Chemistry
XU, XIANGLING, Life and Environment
XU, XIAOFENG, Literature
YU, LIJIE, Life and Environment
ZHANG, JINGCHI, Literature
ZHANG, JUNMING, Politics, Law and Economics Management
ZHANG, YONGZHENG, Computer Science and Mathematics
ZHAO, HENIN, Education Science and Technology
ZHAO, YUNLONG, Arts
ZHOU, JINXIAN, Literature

HARBIN UNIVERSITY OF SCIENCE AND TECHNOLOGY

57 Xuefu Rd, Nan Gang, Harbin 150080, Heilongjiang Province
Telephone: (451) 86390114
Internet: www.hrbust.edu.cn
Founded 1953
Academic year: September to July
Pres.: ZHAO QI
Vice-Pres: DU GUANGCUN, LI DAYONG, TENG CUNXIAN, WU JUNFENG, ZHAO HONG
Head of Graduate Dept: ZHEN MINLI
Librarian: CHEN JIE
Library of 173,800 vols
Number of teachers: 2,379
Number of students: 19,907
Publications: *Electric Machines and Control* (4 a year), *Journal* (6 a year), *Science, Technology and Management* (6 a year)

DEANS

College of Applied Science: CUI YUNAN
College of Chemistry and Environmental Engineering: LIU BO
College of Computer and Control Science: QIAO PEILI
College of Electrical and Electronic Engineering: WEI XINLAO
College of International Culture Education: ZHAO DAWEI
College of Material Science and Engineering: GUO ERJUN
College of Observation Technology and Communications Engineering: YU XIAOYANG
Foreign Language Institute: LUI LIQUN
School of Economics and Management: XIU GUOYI
School of Law: ZHANG YING
School of Mechanical Engineering: SHAO JUNPENG
Software College: LIU SHENGHUI

PROFESSORS

CHEN, DEYUN, Computer and Control Science
CHEN, DONGYAN, Applied Science
CHEN, GUANGHAI, Applied Science
CHEN, RONGDUO, Economics and Management
CHEN, YUQUAN, Mechanical Engineering
CUI, YUNAN, Applied Science
DENG, CAIXIA, Applied Science
DU, DESHENG, Computer and Control Science
DU, KUNMEI, Electrical and Electronic Engineering
DUAN, TIEQUN, Mechanical Engineering
FAN, JINGYUN, Material Science and Engineering
FAN, YONG, Material Science and Engineering
GAO, ANBANG, Mechanical Engineering
GAO, CHANGYUAN, Economics and Management
GAO, ZHONGWEN, Computer and Control Science
GE, BAOJUN, Electrical and Electronic Engineering
GE, JIANGHUA, Mechanical Engineering
GUO, ERJUN, Material Science and Engineering
GUO, JIANYING, Observation Technology and Communications Engineering
HE, ZHONGXIAO, Computer and Control Science
HU, BAOXIA, Computer and Control Science
JI, DONGHAI, Applied Science
JI, ZHESHENG, Material Science and Engineering
JING, XU, Computer and Control Science
KONG, FANLIANG, Applied Science
LEI, QINGQUAN, Electrical and Electronic Engineering
LI, DAYONG, Material Science and Engineering
LI, DONGMEI, Applied Science

LI, FENGZHEN, Material Science and Engineering
LI, GECHENG, Computer and Control Science
LI, HONGXIA, Economics and Management
LI, LEI, Economics and Management
LI, QUANLI, Computer and Control Science
LI, WEILI, Electrical and Electronic Engineering
LI, YUMING, Chemistry and Environmental Engineering
LI, ZHENJIA, Mechanical Engineering
LI, ZHONGHUA, Electrical and Electronic Engineering
LIANG, JINGXI, Economics and Management
LIANG, YANPING, Electrical and Electronic Engineering
LIN, JIAQI, Applied Science
LIU, BO, Chemistry and Environmental Engineering
LIU, RUNTAO, Applied Science
LIU, SHENGHUI, Computer and Control Science
LIU, WEIJUN, Mechanical Engineering
LIU, WENLI, Electrical and Electronic Engineering
LIU, XIANLI, Mechanical Engineering
LIU, XINGJIA, Mechanical Engineering
LUO, XIAOGUANG, Economics and Management
MA, HONGFEI, Economics and Management
MA, HUAIJIAN, Observation Technology and Communications Engineering
MENG, DAWEI, Electrical and Electronic Engineering
PAN, ZHUANGYUAN, Applied Science
QI, LIANGQUN, Economics and Management
QIAO, PEILI, Computer and Control Science
REN, FUJUN, Mechanical Engineering
SHAO, JUNPENG, Mechanical Engineering
SHAO, TIEZHU, Economics and Management
SHI, LIANSHENG, Material Science and Engineering
SONG, JIASHENG, Economics and Management
SONG, RUNBIN, Material Science and Engineering
SUI, XIULING, Mechanical Engineering
SUN, FENGLIAN, Material Science and Engineering
SUN, LIJIONG, Computer and Control Science
SUN, MINGSONG, Computer and Control Science
SUN, QUANYING, Mechanical Engineering
SUN, XIAOJUN, Chemistry and Envirnomental Engineering
TAN, GUANGYU, Mechanical Engineering
TENG, CUNXIAN, Economics and Management
WAN, GUOQIN, Material Science and Engineering
WANG, HONGQI, Economics and Management
WANG, LIPING, Material Science and Engineering
WANG, MUKUN, Observation Technology and Communications Engineering
WANG, PEIDONG, Computer and Control Science
WANG, TONG, Mechanical Engineering
WANG, XUAN, Applied Science
WANG, XUDONG, Electrical and Electronic Engineering
WANG, YIJIE, Applied Science
WANG, YUDONG, Economics and Management
WEI, XINLAO, Electrical and Electronic Engineering
WEN, JIABIN, Electrical and Electronic Engineering
WU, HONGBO, Economics and Management
WU, JUNFENG, Computer and Control Science
WU, YUBIN, Material Science and Engineering
WU, ZHONGYANG, Computer and Control Science
XIAOXU, Material Science and Engineering
XIU, GUOYI, Economics and Management
XU, LI, Mechanical Engineering
XU, XIAOCUN, Mechanical Engineering

YANG, JIAXIANG, Electrical and Electronic Engineering
YANG, MINGGUI, Mechanical Engineering
YIN, JINGHUA, Applied Science
YOU, BO, Mechanical Engineering
YU, HUILI, Mechanical Engineering
YU, LI, Economics and Management
YU, XIAOYANG, Observation Technology and Communications Engineering
YU, YANDONG, Material Science and Engineering
YUAN, JIANXIONG, Mechanical Engineering
ZHAI, LILI, Economics and Management
ZHANG, CUNXI, Electrical and Electronic Engineering
ZHANG, CUNYI, Mechanical Engineering
ZHANG, DECHENG, Economics and Management
ZHANG, GUOJIE, Economics and Management
ZHANG, JIAZHEN, Mechanical Engineering
ZHANG, LIYONG, Observation Technology and Communications Engineering
ZHANG, XIANYOU, Material Science and Engineering
ZHANG, XIAOHONG, Electrical and Electronic Engineering
ZHANG, YONGDE, Mechanical Engineering
ZHANG, YONGJUN, Mechanical Engineering
ZHANG, ZHONGMING, Mechanical Engineering
ZHAO, DAWEI, Economics and Management
ZHAO, HONG, Electrical and Electronic Engineering
ZHAO, XINLUO, Economics and Management
ZHEN, DIANCUN, Electrical and Electronic Engineering
ZHEN, MINLI, Mechanical Engineering

HARBIN INSTITUTE OF TECHNOLOGY

92 West Dazhi St, Harbin 150001, Heilongjiang Province
Telephone: (451) 6412114
Fax: (451) 6221048
Internet: www.hit.edu.cn
Founded 1920
Pres.: Prof. YANG SHIQIN
Vice-Pres: LIU JIAQU, SHI GUANGJI, WANG SHUGUO, WANG ZUWEN, ZHANG DACHENG
Librarian: SHI HUILAI
Library of 1,000,000 vols
Number of teachers: 2,300
Number of students: 14,843 (incl. 2,652 postgraduates)
Publications: *Higher Engineering Education, Journal, Metal Science and Technology, Studying Computers, Technology of Energy Conservation*

DEANS

School of Astronautics: Prof. JIA SHILOU
School of Computer and Electrical Engineering: Prof. HONG WENXUE
School of Electric Mechanical Engineering: Prof. WANG SHUGUO
School of Energy Science and Engineering: Prof. WANG ZUWEN
School of Humanities and Social Sciences: Prof. JIANG ZHENHUA
School of Management: LI YIJUN
School of Materials Science and Engineering: Prof. ZHAO LIANCHENG
School of Science: Prof. GENG WANZHEN

HEBEI MEDICAL UNIVERSITY

361 Zhongshan East Rd, Shijiazhuang City 050017, Hebei Province
Telephone: (311) 6048177
Fax: (311) 6048177
E-mail: fad@hebmu.edu.cn
Internet: www.hebmu.edu.cn
Founded 1915
Academic year: September to July

Pres.: WEN JINKUN
Vice-Pres: DUAN HUIJUN, JI HAIJIN, WANG RUNTIAN, WANG GENGXIN, WANG YANTIAN, ZHANG ZHANKUI
Head of Graduate School: CONG BIN
Librarian: MO ZHENYUN
Library of 541,000 vols
Number of teachers: 887
Number of students: 12,753
Publications: *Chinese Journal of Ultrasonography* (12 a year), *Clinical Focus* (6 a year), *Journal* (6 a year).

HEBEI UNIVERSITY

1 Hezuo Rd, Baoding 071002, Heibei Province
Telephone: (312) 5079709
E-mail: hbu@mail.hbu.edu.cn
Internet: www.hbu.edu.cn
Founded 1921
Hebei Province control
Academic year: September to July
Pres.: WANG HONGRUI
Vice-Pres: HA MINGHU, LI SHUANGYIN, SUN HANWEN, SUN JINGYUAN, WEI SUI
Head of Graduate College: HA MINGHU
Librarian: LI ZHENGANG
Library of 3,170,000 vols
Number of teachers: 2,500
Number of students: 47,500
Publications: *Journal* (natural sciences, 6 a year), *Journal* (philosophy and social sciences, 6 a year)

DEANS

College of Arts: YANG WENHUI
College of Chemistry and Environment Science: MA FENGRU
College of Economics: GU LIUBAO
College of Education: HE GUOQIN
College of Electronic and Information Engineering: WANG PEIGUANG
College of Foreign Languages: LI ZUOWEN
College of Industry and Commerce: WANG HONGRUI
College of Life Science: REN GUODONG
College of Literature: LI JINSHAN
College of Machinery and Civil Engineering: ZHANG JIANHUI
College of Management: SUN JIANFU
College of Mathematics and Computer Studies: WANG XIZHAO
College of Medicine: YANG GENGLIANG
College of Physics and Technology: HAN LI
College of Political Science and Law: LIU ZHIGANG
College of Quality and Technical Supervision: LI XIAOTING
Faculty of Journalism and Communication: BAI GUI

PROFESSORS

BA, XINWU, Chemistry and Environment Science
BAI, GUI, Journalism and Communication
BAI, SHUQIN, Political Science and Law
BI, WUQIN, Political Science and Law
BIAN, ZHAOLING, Management
CAI, HAIBO, Arts
CAO, MINGLUN, Foreign Languages
CAO, RU, Journalism and Communication
CAO, YUPING, Life Science
CHEN, JUNYING, Education
CHEN, SHUANGXIN, Arts
CHEN, ZHIGUO, Economics
CHENG, CHANGYU, Economics
CHENG, XINXUAN, Management
DING, JIHUI, Machinery and Civil Engineering
DING, XIAOZHENG, Journalism and Communication
DONG, LIFANG, Physics and Technology
DONG, ZHENGXIN, Economics

Du, Hao, Journalism and Communication
Du, Youjun, Journalism and Communication
Fang, Baoan, Management
Fang, Youliang, Machinery and Civil Engineering
Feng, Xiuqi, Education
Feng, Yulong, Life Science
Fu, Songtao, Education
Gao, Jungang, Chemistry and Environment Science
Gao, Shujun, Management
Gu, Liubao, Economics
Gu, Xiaohua, Management
Gu, Zhongliang, Arts
Guo, Baozeng, Electronic and Information Engineering
Guo, Fuliang, Literature
Guo, Jian, Arts
Guo, Jian, Industry and Commerce
Guo, Shixin, Economics
Guo, Xuyuan, Literature
Han, Chengwu, Literature
Han, Li, Physics and Technology
Han, Pangshan, Arts
Han, Panshan, Literature
Han, Xiujing, Economics
He, Guoqin, Education
He, Xueli, Life Science
He, Zhipu, Arts
Hou, Guanying, Journalism and Communication
Hou, Yuhua, Management
Hu, Ning, Arts
Hu, Yan, Management
Hua, Zhuxin, Industry and Commerce
Huang, Gengzhuo, Arts
Huang, Pengzhang, Management
Jian, Min, Arts
Jiang, Jianyun, Literature
Jiang, Jizhi, Life Science
Jiang, Lihua, Economics
Jiao, Guozhang, Journalism and Communication
Jiao, Maolin, Literature
Jie, Yongjun, Arts
Kan, Zhenrong, Life Science
Kang, Shusheng, Economics
Kang, Xianjiang, Life Science
Kong, Linghong, Political Science and Law
Li, Fanghua, Electronic and Information Engineering
Li, Ganshun, Economics
Li, Guohua, Literature
Li, Heping, Political Science and Law
Li, Huarui, Literature
Li, Jinshan, Literature
Li, Jinzheng, Literature
Li, Jitai, Chemistry and Environment Science
Li, Linjie, Economics
Li, Renkai, Literature
Li, Shu, Economics
Li, Shuangjie, Economics
Li, Shuqi, Machinery and Civil Engineering
Li, Sumin, Education
Li, Tongshuang, Chemistry and Environment Science
Li, Wencai, Literature
Li, Wenxiu, Machinery and Civil Engineering
Li, Xiaoting, Quality and Technical Supervision
Li, Xiaowei, Physics and Technology
Li, Yahong, Journalism and Communication
Li, Yanan, Journalism and Communication
Li, Yanbin, Arts
Li, Zuowen, Foreign Languages
Liang, Suzhen, Political Science and Law
Liao, Xiangru, Life Science
Liu, Cuiying, Management
Liu, Huiwen, Journalism and Communication
Liu, Jinzhong, Literature
Liu, Jinzhu, Arts
Liu, Sijin, Literature
Liu, Yongrui, Education

Liu, Yukai, Literature
Liu, Zhigang, Political Science and Law
Liu, Zhiqiang, Physics and Technology
Liu, Zhiqiang, Electronic and Information Engineering
Lu, Hongping, Economics
Lu, Mingfang, Physics and Technology
Lu, Zizheng, Journalism and Communication
Ma, Chenglian, Journalism and Communication
Ma, Yanling, Management
Mao, Zhuoliang, Foreign Languages
Mei, Baoshu, Arts
Meng, Shien, Management
Pei, Guifen, Economics
Peng, Yingcai, Physics and Technology
Peng, Yingcai, Electronic and Information Engineering
Qi, Yi, Arts
Qiao, Yunxia, Journalism and Communication
Ren, Guodong, Life Science
Rong, Xinfang, Foreign Languages
Song, Dengyuan, Electronic and Information Engineering
Song, Ruitian, Physics and Technology
Song, Yaowu, Education
Sun, Hanwen, Chemistry and Environmental Science
Sun, Shengcun, Journalism and Communication
Sun, Zhizhong, Economics
Tao, Dan, Journalism and Communication
Tian, Jianming, Literature
Tian, Junfeng, Mathematics and Computer Science
Wang, Baoxing, Education
Wang, Hongrui, Electronic and Information Engineering
Wang, Hongrui, Industry and Commerce
Wang, Jinying, Economics
Wang, Junjie, Journalism and Communication
Wang, Junli, Life Science
Wang, Peiguang, Electronic and Information Engineering
Wang, Qin, Economics
Wang, Shuhui, Management
Wang, Wenli, Electronic and Information Engineering
Wang, Xizhao, Mathematics and Computer Science
Wang, Yanling, Journalism and Communication
Wang, Yinshun, Physics and Technology
Wang, Zhenchao, Electronic and Information Engineering
Wu, Gengzhen, Journalism and Communication
Wu, Hongcheng, Education
Wu, Yaqing, Economics
Wu, Yongzhen, Management
Xie, Changfa, Education
Xiong, Renwang, Arts
Xu, Jingzhi, Physics and Technology
Xu, Ming, Journalism and Communication
Xue, Kemiu, Literature
Yang, Baozhong, Literature
Yang, Gengliang, Chemistry and Envirnoment Science
Yang, Gengliang, Medicine
Yang, Wenhui, Arts
Yang, Xiuguo, Journalism and Communication
Yang, Xuexin, Industry and Commerce
Yao, Zihua, Chemistry and Environment Science
Zhang, Daochuan, Life Science
Zhang, Deqiang, Chemistry and Environment Science
Zhang, Jianhui, Machinery and Civil Engineering
Zhang, Liping, Life Science
Zhang, Lixin, Education
Zhang, Risheng, Education

Zhang, Shuangcai, Management
Zhang, Wei, Journalism and Communication
Zhang, Wenchuan, Arts
Zhang, Yanjing, Political Science and Law
Zhang, Yuke, Economics
Zhao, Yanyan, Medicine
Zhen, Shuqing, Political Science and Law
Zheng, Yunlong, Physics and Technology
Zheng, Zhiting, Literature
Zhu, Baocheng, Life Science
Zhu, Mingsheng, Life Science

HEBEI UNIVERSITY OF ECONOMICS AND TRADE

Wu Qi Rd, Shijiazhuang 050061, Hebei Province
Telephone: (311) 6039189
Fax: (311) 6039123
Internet: www.heuet.edu.cn
Founded 1982
Pres.: Yu Rengang
Vice-Pres: Cui Yuanmin, Hu Baozhong, Hu Dongyang, Mazhi Zhong, Wu Shengchen, Yao Jingguan
Librarian: Ma Ke
Library of 250,000 vols
Number of teachers: 900
Number of students: 10,000

Publication: *Economics and Management*.

HEBEI NORMAL UNIVERSITY

265 Huadong Rd, Shijiazhuang 030002, Hebei Province
Internet: www.hebtu.edu.cn
Founded 1902
Academic year: September to July
Pres.: Su Baorong
Vice-Pres: Jiang Chunlan, Li Youcheng, Lu Junheng, Wang Changhua, Zhen Shijun
Librarian: Jiao Zhilan
Number of teachers: 3,438
Number of students: 36,185
Publication: *Journal* (4 a year)

DEANS

College of Education Science: Lu Zhongyi
College of Foreign Languages: Pan Binxin
College of Law and Political Science: Zhang Jiliang
College of Life Science: Duang Xianglin
College of Literature: Xing Jiliang
College of Mathematics and Information: Deng Mingli
College of Physics: Liu Jianjun
College of Resources and the Environment: Wang Wei

PROFESSORS

Bai, Ziming, Foreign Languages
Chang, Congqian, Foreign Languages
Chen, Chao, Literature
Chen, Hui, Literature
Cheng, Ruzhen, Mathematics and Information
Cui, Jiyin, Literature
Cui, Zhiyuan, Literature
Deng, Mingli, Mathematics and Information
Di, Zhaoying, Mathematics and Information
Ding, Ren, Mathematics and Information
Dong, Junmin, Foreign Languages
Du, Jianzheng, Education Science
Duan, Xiaoying, Foreign Languages
Duan, Zheren, Foreign Languages
Fan, Shucheng, Law and Political Science
Gao, Shunsheng, Mathematics and Information
Gao, Suogang, Mathematics and Information
Gao, Ting, Mathematics and Information
Gao, Xinfa, Resources and Environment Science

GAO, YUANXIANG, Resources and Environment Science
GAO, ZHIHUAI, Foreign Languages
GE, JINGFENG, Resources and Environment Science
GU, ZHONGQUAN, Foreign Languages
GUI, DINGKANG, Foreign Languages
GUO, BAOLIANG, Literature
GUO, QUNYING, Foreign Languages
HE, ANBAO, Foreign Languages
HE, LIANFA, Mathematics and Information
HU, WENLIANG, Resources and Environment Science
HU, YINGTONG, Foreign Languages
HUANG, HONGQUAN, Foreign Languages
HUANG, HONGXU, Foreign Languages
HUANG, HUAFANG, Resources and Environment Science
JIANG, CHUNLAN, Mathematics and Information
KANG, QINDE, Mathematics and Information
LEI, JIANGUO, Mathematics and Information
LI, SHIJU, Law and Political Science
LI, SUO, Literature
LI, TIANGUI, Law and Political Science
LI, XILONG, Literature
LI, YANNIAN, Literature
LI, ZHENGSHUAN, Foreign Languages
LIANG, YI, Foreign Languages
LIANG, ZHIHE, Mathematics and Information
LIE, WUJUN, Mathematics and Information
LIU, HONG, Education Science
LIU, HUANQUN, Foreign Languages
LIU, MING, Education Science
LIU, SHITIAN, Law and Political Science
LIU, YAN, Resources and Environment Science
LIU, ZHONGMING, Law and Political Science
LU, ZHONGYI, Education Science
LU, ZI, Resources and Environment Science
MA, HENGJUN, Literature
MA, RENHUI, Resources and Environment Science
MA, YUN, Literature
MENG, GUOHUA, Foreign Languages
MI, JUSHENG, Mathematics and Information
NAN, YUESHENG, Resources and Environment Science
PAN, BINXIN, Foreign Languages
QIAN, JINPING, Resources and Environment Science
QIAO, YUYING, Mathematics and Information
SHI, GUOXING, Education Science
SHI, JINGXIU, Literature
SU, BAORONG, Literature
TANG, GUOZENG, Law and Political Science
TIAN, XIUYUN, Law and Political Science
WANG, CHANGHUA, Literature
WANG, DELIN, Education Science
WANG, FENGMIN, Law and Political Science
WANG, FUISHENG, Foreign Languages
WANG, JIANXUN, Foreign Languages
WANG, WEI, Resources and Environment Science
WANG, XIN, Education Science
WANG, YANYING, Mathematics and Information
WANG, ZHENCHANG, Foreign Languages
WU, WEIREN, Foreign Languages
WU, XIUHUA, Literature
WU, ZHENGDE, Mathematics and Information
XIAO, GUIQING, Law and Political Science
XING, JIANCHANG, Literature
XU, JIANPING, Literature
XU, QINGHAI, Resources and Environment Science
YAN, KELE, Education Science
YANG, CHUNHONG, Mathematics and Information
YANG, DONG, Literature
YANG, TONGYONG, Literature
YI, SHENGLEI, Foreign Languages
YI, WEI, Foreign Languages
ZHAI, HONGCHANG, Education Science
ZHAN, YUANJIE, Resources and Environment Science

ZHANG, CHENGZONG, Resources and Environment Science
ZHANG, GUOYING, Foreign Languages
ZHANG, JI, Law and Political Science
ZHANG, JILIANG, Law and Political Science
ZHANG, JUNCAI, Literature
ZHANG, JUNHAI, Resources and Environment Science
ZHANG, WENXIANG, Law and Political Science
ZHANG, YIWEN, Resources and Environment Science
ZHANG, YOUHUI, Mathematics and Information
ZHANG, ZHENGGUO, Mathematics and Information
ZHANG, ZILONG, Mathematics and Information
ZHENG, ZHENFENG, Literature
ZHUANG, BIAO, Literature

HEFEI UNIVERSITY OF TECHNOLOGY

59 Tunxi Rd, Hefei 230009, Anhui Province
Telephone: (551) 4655210
Fax: (551) 4651517
Internet: www.hfut.edu.cn
Founded 1945
15 Depts
Pres.: CHEN XINZHAO
Vice-Pres: LIU GUANGFU, TANG JIAN, WANG DEZE, XU HUIPENG, ZHENG ZHIXIANG
Registrar: ZHOU XU
Librarian: SUN XUANYIN

Number of teachers: 4,513
Number of students: 18,216

Publications: *Engineering Mathematics, Forecasting, Journal, Teaching and Study of Industrial Automation, Techniques Abroad, Tribology Abroad.*

HEILONGJIANG UNIVERSITY OF CHINESE MEDICINE

24 Dongli Section He Ping Rd, Harbin 150040, Heilongjiang Province
Telephone: (451) 82118254
Fax: (451) 82193031
Internet: www.hljucm.net
Founded 1959
Academic year: September to July
Pres.: KUANG HAIXUE
Vice-Pres: CHENG WEI, LI BINGZHI, LI JINGXIAO, WANG XIJUN
Head of Graduate Dept: NING XIE
Librarian: YOU YANJUN

Number of teachers: 370
Number of students: 5,002 (4,817 full-time, 185 part-time)

Publications: *Acts of Chinese Medicine and Pharmacology* (6 a year), *Information on Traditional Chinese Medicine* (6 a year), *Journal of Clinical Acupuncture and Moxibustion* (12 a year)

DEANS

First School of Medicine: TIAN ZHENKUN
School of Basic Medical Sciences: LI YI
School of Human Sciences: TONG ZILIN
School of Pharmacy: LI YONGJI
Second School of Medicine: SUN ZHONGREN

PROFESSORS

AN, LIWEN, Medicine
CHEN, HONGBIN, Basic Medical Sciences
CHENG, WEIPING, Medicine
DAI, TIECHENG, Medicine
DONG, QINGPING, Medicine
DU, XIAOWEI, Pharmacy
DUAN, FUJIN, Basic Medical Sciences
GAO, QUANGUO, Basic Medical Sciences
GONG, ZHANYUE, Medicine
GU, JIALE, Medicine

HAN, BO, Medicine
HOU, LIHUI, Medicine
HUI, XIULI, Medicine
JIA, GUIZHI, Pharmacy
JIANG, DEYOU, Basic Medical Sciences
JIN, SHUYING, Basic Medical Sciences
KANG, GUANGSHENG, Basic Medical Sciences
KUANG, HAIXUE, Pharmacy
LI, JINGXIA, Medicine
LI, LINGGEN, Medicine
LI, QIUHONG, Pharmacy
LI, TINGLI, Pharmacy
LI, YADONG, Basic Medical Sciences
LI, YAN, Medicine
LI, YANBING, Pharmacy
LI, YI, Basic Medical Sciences
LI, YONGJI, Pharmacy
LIU, HANDE, Human Sciences
LIU, HUASHENG, Basic Medical Sciences
LIU, JIANQIU, Medicine
LIU, JILI, Human Sciences
LIU, YUANZHANG, Medicine
LU, BINGWEN, Basic Medical Sciences
LUO, HONGSHI, Medicine
MA, YINGLI, Pharmacy
MENG, RI, Pharmacy
NIE, YUNAHENG, Medicine
QU, JIE, Human Sciences
QUAN, HONG, Pharmacy
SONG, LIQUN, Medicine
SU, LIANJIE, Pharmacy
SU, YUNMING, Basic Medical Sciences
SUN, HUI, Pharmacy
SUN, WEIZHENG, Medicine
SUN, ZHONGREN, Medicine
TIAN, ZHENKUN, Medicine
TIAN, ZHENKUN, Pharmacy
TONG, ZILIN, Human Sciences
WANG, DEMIN, Medicine
WANG, DONG, Pharmacy
WANG, FEI, Basic Medical Sciences
WANG, GANG, Medicine
WANG, HEPING, Pharmacy
WANG, JIANMING, Pharmacy
WANG, LI, Basic Medical Sciences
WANG, TIECE, Basic Medical Sciences
WANG, XIAXIAN, Basic Medical Sciences
WANG, XIJUN, Pharmacy
WANG, XING, Medicine
WANG, XUEHUA, Basic Medical Sciences
WANG, YUMEI, Medicine
WANG, YUXI, Medicine
WU, BOYAN, Basic Medical Sciences
XIE, JINGRI, Medicine
YAN, JING, Pharmacy
YU, JIABIN, Pharmacy
YU, XIAOHONG, Basic Medical Sciences
ZHANG, FULI, Basic Medical Sciences
ZHANG, YOUTANG, Basic Medical Sciences
ZHANG, ZHIMIN, Basic Medical Sciences
ZHAO, WENJING, Basic Medical Sciences
ZHOU, DECHEN, Basic Medical Sciences
ZHOU, LING, Medicine
ZHOU, MIN, Basic Medical Sciences
ZHOU, WI, Medicine
ZHOU, YABIN, Medicine
ZHU, YONGZHI, Medicine
ZHU, ZHIZHEN, Basic Medical Sciences

HENAN UNIVERSITY OF TRADITIONAL CHINESE MEDICINE

1 Jinshui Rd, Zhengzhou 450008, Henan Province
Telephone: (371) 65962930
Fax: (371) 65962930
E-mail: henantcm@gmail.com
Internet: www.henantcm.net
Founded 1958
State control
Language of instruction: Chinese, English
Academic year: September to July
Pres.: Prof. YULING ZHENG
Vice-Pres.: Prof. LI JIANSHENG
Librarian: LAI QIANKAI

Library of 959,000 vols
Number of teachers: 2,842
Number of students: 17,701

Publications: *Henan Traditional Chinese Medicine* (12 a year), *Journal* (6 a year)

PROFESSORS

CHEN, R. F., Internal Medicine
DING, Y., Paediatrics
FENG, M. Q., Traditional Chinese Medicine
GAO, T. S., Traditional Chinese Medicine
HOU, S. L., Traditional Materia Medica
JI, C. R., Traditional Materia Medica
LI, X. W., Traditional Chinese Medicine
LI, Z. H., Traditional Chinese Medicine
LI, Z. S., Internal Medicine
LOU, D. F., Traditional Chinese Medicine for Traumatology
LU, S. C., Qigong
MA, Z. H., Traditional Chinese Medicine
SHANG, C. C., Traditional Chinese Medicine
SHAO, J. M., Acupuncture
SHI, G. Q., Traditional Chinese Medicine
SHUN, L. H., Acupuncture
SUN, C. Q., Physiology
SUN, H. B., Parasitology
SUN, J. Z., Internal Medicine
TANG, S., Traditional Chinese Medicine
WANG, A. B., History of Traditional Chinese Medicine
WANG, R. K., Diagnostics
WANG, Y. M., Pharmaco-Chemistry
YANG, L. Y., Anatomy
YANG, Y. S., Traditional Materia Medica
ZHANG, G. Q., Traditional Materia Medica
ZHENG, J. M., Traditional Chinese Medicine for Paediatrics

HENAN UNIVERSITY

Ming Lun Rd, Kaifeng 475001, Henan Province
Internet: www.henu.edu.cn
Founded 1912
Academic year: September to July

Pres.: GUAN AIHE
Vice-Pres: GUO TIANBANG, HUANG YABIN, LU KEPING, SHI QUANSHENG, WANG FAZENG, ZHAO GUOXIANG
Librarian: LI JINGWEN
Number of teachers: 3,600
Number of students: 240,000

Publications: *Chinese Quarterly Journal of Mathematics*, *Journal* (6 a year), *Journal of Henan University Chemical Research* (4 a year), *Quarterly Journal of Pure and Applied Mathematics*

DEANS

Faculty of History and Culture: ZHANG QIANHONG
College of Arts: ZHAO WEIMING
College of Civil Engineering: BAO PENG
College of Communication and Journalism: LI JIANWEI
College of Economics: DI MINGZAI
College of Environmental Planning: QIN YAOCHEN
College of Foreign Languages: ZHANG KEDING
College of Life Science: SONG CHUNPENG
College of Medicine: MA YUANFANG
School of Business Administration: WEI CHENGLONG
School of Chemistry Engineering: CUI YUANCHENG
School of Computer and Information Engineering: LIU XIANSHENG
School of Mathematics and Information Science: LI QISHENG
School of Physics and Information Optoelectronics: ZHANG WEIFENG

PROFESSORS

CHEN, CHANGYUAN, History and Culture
CHEN, JIAHAI, Arts
CHEN, SHOUXIN, Mathematics and Information Science
CHENG, MINGSHENG, History and Culture
DI, MINGZHAI, Economics
DING, SHENGYAN, Environmental Planning
DING, SHENGYAN, Life Science
DONG, FACAI, Life Science
GAO, HAILIN, History and Culture
GAO, JIANGUO, Economics
GAO, JIANHUA, Environmental Planning
GONG, LIUZHU, History and Culture
GU, YUZONG, Physics and Information Optoelectronics
HOU, XUN, Physics and Information Optoelectronics
HU, CHANGLIU, Mathematics and Information Science
HU, CONGE, Mathematics and Information Science
HU, YUXIN, Life Science
HUANG, YABIN, Physics and Information Optoelectronics
JIA, XINGQIN, Mathematics and Information Science
JIA, YUYING, History and Culture
JU, QINGLIN, Arts
LI, CHENGDE, History and Culture
LI, GUANGYI, History and Culture
LI, GUOQIANG, Mathematics and Information Science
LI, JIANWEI, Communication and Journalism
LI, JIE, Business Administration
LI, MING, History and Culture
LI, QISHENG, Mathematics and Information Science
LI, RUI, Mathematics and Information Science
LI, SUOPING, Life Science
LI, YONGWEN, Environmental Planning
LI, YUJIE, History and Culture
LI, ZHENHONG, History and Culture
LIN, JIAKUN, History and Culture
LIU, BINSHAN, Foreign Languages
LIU, HONG, Arts
LIU, JIANZHONG, Business Administration
LIU, KUNTAI, History and Culture
LU, ZHENGUANG, Communication and Journalism
MA, JIANHUA, Environmental Planning
MA, LING, Arts
MA, XIAOQUAN, History and Culture
MAO, HAITAO, Physics and Information Optoelectronics
MIAO, CHANGHONG, Environmental Planning
MIAO, CHENG, Life Science
MIAO, SHUMEI, History and Culture
MO, YUJUN, Physics and Information Optoelectronics
NIU, JIANQIANG, History and Culture
OU, ZHENGWEN, History and Culture
QI, LING, Economics
QIAN, HUAISUI, Environmental Planning
QIN, MINGZHOU, Environmental Planning
QIN, YAOZHEN, Environmental Planning
SANG, FUDE, Life Science
SHAN, LUN, Life Science
SONG, CHUNPENG, Life Science
SONG, YINGLI, Communication and Journalism
SU, KEWU, Economics
SUN, QIULIN, Environmental Planning
TAN, CHENGLIN, Environmental Planning
TANG, GUIQIN, Arts
WAN, SONGYU, History and Culture
WANG, CHANGSHUN, Physics and Information Optoelectronics
WANG, CHUMING, Economics
WANG, FAZHENG, Environmental Planning
WANG, JILIN, History and Culture
WANG, JINGYE, Communication and Journalism
WANG, JINXIAN, Business Administration
WANG, XINGYU, Business Administration
WANG, YANFA, Arts

WANG, ZHANGUO, Physics and Information Optoelectronics
WANG, ZHENDUO, Communication and Journalism
WEI, CHENGLONG, Economics
WEI, QIANZHI, History and Culture
WENG, YOUWEI, History and Culture
WU, TAO, History and Culture
WU, XUELI, Foreign Languages
XU, XINGYA, Economics
YAN, ZHAOXIANG, History and Culture
YANG, HAIJUN, Communication and Journalism
YANG, XUEZHI, Mathematics and Information Science
YAO, BOHUA, Mathematics and Information Science
YAO, YINGTING, History and Culture
YI, GUOSHENG, Physics and Information Optoelectronics
YI, QIXIANG, History and Culture
YU, BAOLONG, Physics and Information Optoelectronics
YU, JINFU, Economics
ZHANG, DEZONG, History and Culture
ZHANG, JIATAI, History and Culture
ZHANG, JIN, Foreign Languages
ZHANG, KUN, Economics
ZHANG, MINGLIANG, Mathematics and Information Science
ZHANG, QIANHONG, History and Culture
ZHANG, QIUZHOU, History and Culture
ZHANG, RUFA, Communication and Journalism
ZHANG, TAIHAI, Business Administration
ZHANG, TIANDING, Communication and Journalism
ZHANG, WEIFENG, Physics and Information Optoelectronics
ZHANG, XINGMAO, Economics
ZHANG, XIUYING, Business Administration
ZHANG, ZHONGLIANG, Communication and Journalism
ZHANG, ZHONGSUO, Physics and Information Optoelectronics
ZHAO, BINDONG, Environmental Planning
ZHAO, BUYUN, History and Culture
ZHAO, JIANGUO, Communication and Journalism
ZHAO, WEIMING, Arts
ZHAO, ZHENQIAN, Arts
ZHAO, ZHIFA, Economics
ZHENG, HUISHENG, History and Culture
ZHOU, BAOZHU, History and Culture
ZHU, SHAOHOU, History and Culture

HOHAI UNIVERSITY

1 Xikang Rd, Nanjing 210098
Telephone: (25) 3323777
Fax: (25) 3315375
Internet: www.hhu.edu.cn
Founded 1915, fmrly East China Technical Univ. of Water Resources, present name 1985
State control
Languages of instruction: Chinese, English
Academic year: September to July

Pres.: Prof. JIANG HONGDAO
Vice-Pres: Prof. LIU XINREN, Prof. JIN ZHONGQING, Prof. ZHANG CHANG
Librarian: DONG TINGSONG
Number of teachers: 1,343
Number of students: 8,000

Publications: *Advances in the Science and Technology of Water Resources*, *Economics of Water Resources*, *Journal*, *Journal of Higher Education*, *Water Resources Protection*

DEANS

College of Civil Engineering: Prof. ZHUO JIASHOU

College of Computer and Information Engineering: Assoc. Prof. ZHU YAOLONG

College of Electrical Engineering: Prof. YANG JINTANG

College of Harbour, Waterway and Coastal Engineering: Prof. ZHANG CHANGKUAN

College of Mechanical and Electrical Engineering: Prof. JIN YAHE

College of International Industry and Commerce: Assoc. Prof. ZHANG YANG

College of Technical Economics: Prof. ZHENG CHUIYONG

College of Water Conservancy and Hydropower Engineering: Prof. SUO LISHENG

College of Water Resources and Environment: Prof. WANG HUIMIN

HUAQIAO UNIVERSITY

Quanzhou 362011, Fujian

Telephone: (595) 2693630

Fax: (595) 2681940

E-mail: wsc@hqu.edu.cn

Internet: www.hqu.edu.cn

Founded 1960

State control

Academic year: starts September

Pres.: Prof. WU CHENGYE

Vice-Pres: Assoc. Prof. GUAN YIFAN, Prof. GUO HENGQUN, Assoc. Prof. LI JIMIN

Registrar: Prof. HONG SHANGREN

Librarian: Prof. ZHANG WEIBIN

Library of 775,449 vols, 16,235 periodicals

Number of teachers: 542 (full-time)

Number of students: 12,000

Publications: *Journal of Huaqiao University* (Natural science and social science editions, 4 a year, in Chinese), *Research in Higher Education by Overseas Chinese* (in Chinese, 2 a year)

DEANS

College of Economic Management: Prof. YE MINGQIANG

College of Electromechanical Engineering and Automation: Prof. XU XIPENG

College of Foreign Languages: Assoc. Prof. WANG HUAIHUI

College of Information Science and Engineering: Prof. GUO HENGQUN

College of Materials Science and Engineering: Prof. WU JIHUAI

College of Teaching Chinese as a Foreign Language: Assoc. Prof. LI HONG

Fujian Conservatory of Music: Prof. CAI JIKUN

HUAZHONG AGRICULTURAL UNIVERSITY

Shizhishan, Wuhan 430070, Hubei Province

Telephone: (27) 87282026

Fax: (27) 87396057

E-mail: fao@mail.hzau.edu.cn/en.htm

Internet: www.hzau.edu.cn

Founded 1898, present name 1985

State control

Languages of instruction: Chinese, English

Academic year: September to July

Pres.: ZHANG DUANPIN

Vice-Pres: CHEN HUANCHUN, GAO CHI, LI GUIFANG, LI MINGJIA, LIU GUIYOU, WANG CHUANXIN, XIE CONGHUA

Librarian: WAN JIQIN

Library of 620,000 vols

Number of teachers: 2,215

Number of students: 15,000

Publication: *Journal* (4 a year)

DEANS

College of Adult Education: ZHANG DUANPIN

College of Animal Husbandry and Veterinary Science: BI DINGREN

College of Arts and Humanities and Social Science: LI CHONGGUANG

College of Basic Sciences: CHEN CHANGSHUI

College of Economics and Trade: WANG YAPENG

College of Engineering and Technology: ZHANG YANLIN

College of the Fishing Industry: XIE CONGXIN

College of Food Science and Technology: PAN SIYI

College of Horticulture and Forestry Science: BAO MANZHU

College of Land Management: WANG YAPENG

College of Life Sciences and Technology: ZHANG QIFA

College of Plant Science and Technology: ZHANG XIANLONG

College of Resources and Environment: CAI CHONGFA

HUAZHONG UNIVERSITY OF SCIENCE AND TECHNOLOGY

1037 Luoyu Rd, Wuhan 430074, Hubei Province

Telephone: (27) 87542157

Fax: (27) 87547063

E-mail: chengrw@126.com

Internet: www.hust.edu.cn

Founded 1953

Academic year: September to July

Pres.: Prof. FAN MINGWU

Vice-Pres: Prof. CAO SHUQIN, Prof. DING HANCHU, Prof. DING LIEYUN, Prof. FENG XIANGDONG, Prof. FENG YOUMEI, Prof. HUANG GUANGYING, Prof. LI PEIGEN, Prof. LIU XIANJUN, Prof. WANG CHENG, Prof. XIANG JIZHOU

Librarian: Assoc. Prof. WU JINWEI

Library of 2,070,000 vols, 550,000 vols of periodicals in Chinese and foreign languages

Number of teachers: 4,000

Number of students: 50,000

Publications: *Applied Mathematics, China's Organic Chemistry and Cellular Chemistry, Chinese Medicine Digest* (detection and clinical), *Clinical Cardiology, Clinical Gastroenterology, Clinical Haematology, Clinical Otolaryngology, Clinical Urology, Clinic Emergency, Foreign Medicine and Molecular Biology, Foreign Medicine* (social medicine), *Gastroenterology in Combined Traditional Chinese Medicine and Western Medicine, HUST Journal* (in separate natural sciences, social sciences and medical sciences editions), *Hydroelectric Energy, Internal Emergency, Journal of Higher Education, Journal of Solid State Mechanics, Linguistics Study, Medicine and Society, New Architecture, Nursing, Practice of Radiology, Radiant Diagnosis* (Chinese medical digest), *Research in Higher Education of Engineering, Sino–German Tumour Clinic*

DEANS

School of Architecture and Urban Planning: Prof. YUAN PEIHUANG

School of Civil Engineering and Mechanics: Prof. CHEN CHUANYAO

School of Computer Science and Technology: Prof. LU ZHENGDIAN

School of Economics: Prof. XU CHANGSHENG

School of Education: Prof. ZHANG YINGQIANG

School of Electrical and Electronics Engineering: Prof. GU CHENGLIN

School of Energy and Power Engineering: Prof. LIU WEI

School of Environmental Science and Engineering: Prof. SHEN YUNFENG

School of Humanities: Prof. ZHANG SHUGUANG

School of Hydropower and Information Engineering: Prof. WU ZHONGRU

School of Information Technology and Engineering: Prof. HUANG DEXIU

School of Journalism and Information Communication: Prof. WU TINGJUN

School of Law: Prof. LUO YUZHONG

School of Life Science and Technology: Prof. LUO QINGMING

School of Management: Prof. ZHANG JINLONG

School of Materials Science and Engineering: Prof. LI DEQUN

School of Mechanical Science and Engineering: Prof. SHAO XINYU

School of Public Administration: Prof. XIA SHUZHANG

School of Science: Prof. YE ZHAOHUI

School of Software Engineering: Prof. CHEN CHUANBO

School of Traffic Science and Engineering: Prof. ZHAO YAO

Tongji Medical School: Prof. XIANG JIZHOU

HUBEI UNIVERSITY

11 Xueyuan Rd, Wuchang, Wuhan 430062, Hubei Province

Telephone: (27) 88663896

E-mail: xiaoban@hubu.edu.cn

Internet: www.hubu.edu.cn

Founded 1931

Hubei Province control

Academic year: September to July

Pres.: WU CHUANXI

Vice-Pres: GU HAOSHUANG, LI JINHE, YAN MINGMING, ZHOU JIMING

Librarian: ZHANG WEIHUA

Library of 1,520,000 vols

Number of teachers: 1,000

Number of students: 12,700

Publications: *Acta Arachnologica Sinica* (2 a year), *Chinese Journal of Colloids and Polymers* (4 a year), *Journal* (4 a year), *Journal of the Adult Education College of Hubei University* (6 a year)

DEANS

Faculty of Arts: LUN ZUNMING

Faculty of Chemistry and Materials Science: WANG SHIMIN

Faculty of Education: JIN GUOPING

Faculty of Foreign Studies: XU QIUMEI

Faculty of History and Culture: GUO YING

Faculty of Philosophy: DAI MAOTANG

Institute of Physics and Electronic Technology: WANG HAO

School of Business: LIU JIANPING

School of Life Science: CHEN JIAN

School of Resources and the Environment: LI ZHAOHUA

PROFESSORS

BIAN, XIANGYI, Arts

CAO, WANQIANG, Physics and Electronic Technology

CHAN, SHAOHUA, Physics and Electronic Technology

CHANG, SHIYUAN, Chemistry and Materials Science

CHEN, PEIZHI, Chemistry and Materials Science

CHEN, QIUHUI, Mathematics and Computer Science

CHEN, TIANYOU, Business

CHEN, YIHAN, Physics and Electronic Technology

CHEN, YOUQING, Education

CHEN, ZHIHUI, Physics and Electronic Technology

CHEN, ZHUXING, Chemistry and Materials Science

CHENG, CHONGZHEN, Business

CHENG, SIHUI, Education

CHENG, YUANFA, Physics and Electronic Technology

DAI, MAOTANG, Philosophy

FENG, CHUANQI, Chemistry and Materials Science
FENG, HAO, Business
GAO, LU, History and Culture
GONG, GUIFANG, Foreign Studies
GONG, QUN, Philosophy
GU, HAOSHUANG, Physics and Electronic Technology
GU, PEI, History and Culture
GUAN, RONG, Chemistry and Materials Science
GUO, KANGSONG, Arts
GUO, YING, History and Culture
HAN, HUA, Education
HE, PEIXIN, Chemistry and Materials Science
HU, SHUGUANG, Chemistry and Materials Science
HUANG, SHIQIANG, Chemistry and Materials Science
HUANG, YUEHUI, Arts
JIANG, CHANG, Philosophy
JIANG, TAO, Chemistry and Materials Science
JIN, CONG, Mathematics and Computer Science
JIN, KEZHONG, Arts
LEI, TINAN, Education
LI, JUANWEN, Business
LI, JUANWEN, Resources and the Environment
LI, LUOQING, Mathematics and Computer Science
LI, YAN, Chemistry and Materials Science
LI, ZHAOHUA, Resources and the Environment
LI, ZONGRONG, Mathematics and Computer Science
LIU, CHUANE, Arts
LIU, HEGUO, Mathematics and Computer Science
LIU, JIANPING, Business
LIU, SHENGWU, Arts
LIU, ZHUNMING, Arts
LOU, ZHAOWEN, Chemistry and Materials Science
LU, DEPING, Chemistry and Materials Science
LU, ZHILU, Foreign Studies
QIN, ZHAOGUI, History and Culture
SHAO, CHANGGUI, Physics and Electronic Technology
SHI, JINPING, Business
SHU, HUAI, Arts
SONG, KEFU, Arts
TAN, SHUKUI, Business
TIAN, FANJI, Mathematics and Computer Science
TU, HUAIZHANG, Arts
WAN, CHANGGAO, Mathematics and Computer Science
WANG, HAO, Physics and Electronic Technology
WANG, HONGLING, Business
WANG, JIAZHI, Foreign Studies
WANG, SHENGFU, Chemistry and Materials Science
WANG, SHIMIN, Chemistry and Materials Science
WANG, YANG, History and Culture
WANG, ZHENGXIANG, Resources and the Environment
WU, CHUANXI, Mathematics and Computer Science
WU, MIN, Mathematics and Computer Science
XIA, QINGHUA, Chemistry and Materials Science
XIAN, KEN, Mathematics and Computer Science
XIANG, SONG, Foreign Studies
XIAO, DE, Business
XIAO, WEIDONG, Chemistry and Materials Science
XIE, FEIHOU, Education
XIE, JUFANG, Physics and Electronic Technology
XU, QIUMEI, Foreign Studies

XU, XUEJUN, Education
XU, ZHUSHUN, Chemistry and Materials Science
YAN, CUIE, Chemistry and Materials Science
YAN, MEIFU, Education
YAN, MINGMING, Education
YAN, XUEJUN, Business
YANG, JIANBO, Arts
YANG, YAOKUN, Philosophy
YE, YONG, Chemistry and Materials Science
YI, HONGCHUAN, Arts
YOU, WULI, Foreign Studies
ZHANG, BICHENG, Chemistry and Materials Science
ZHANG, HESHENG, Chemistry and Materials Science
ZHANG, JIANMING, Business
ZHANG, QINGZONG, Foreign Studies
ZHANG, TIANJIN, Physics and Electronic Technology
ZHAO, SHAOYI, Mathematics and Computer Science
ZHENG, YUMEI, Mathematics and Computer Science
ZHOU, DEJUN, History and Culture
ZHOU, HAO, Foreign Studies
ZHOU, TAOSHENG, Physics and Electronic Technology
ZHU, JIANZHEN, History and Culture
ZHU, WEIMING, Arts

HUNAN AGRICULTURAL UNIVERSITY

Fu Rong District, Chang Sha 410128, Hunan Province
Telephone: (731) 4618001
Fax: (731) 4611473
Internet: www.hunau.net
Founded 1951
Academic year: September to July
Pres.: ZHOU QINGMING
Vice-Pres: BO LIANYANG, FU SHAOHUI, LU XIANGYANG, PENG KEQIN, ZHU YINGSHENG
Librarian: XIAO QIMING
Library of 909,600 vols
Number of teachers: 978
Number of students: 34,259
Publications: *Crop Research* (4 a year), *Journal* (4 a year)

DEANS

College of Bio-Safety Science and Technology: GAO BIDA
College of Economics Management: ZENG WEI
College of Engineering Technology: SUN SONGLIN
College of Resources and the Environment: DUAN JIANNAN
College of Science: RAO LIQUN
Faculty of Food Science and Technology: XIA YANBIN
Institute of Computing and Information Engineering: SHEN YUE
School of Agriculture: WANG GUOHUAI
School of Literature: QU LINYAN

PROFESSORS

BO, LIANYANG, Bio-Safety Science and Technology
CHEN, JINXIANG, Agriculture
CUI, GUOXIAN, Agriculture
DAI, LIANGYING, Bio-Safety Science and Technology
DENG, FANGMING, Food Science and Technology
DUAN, JIANNAN, Resources and the Environment
FANG, ZHI, Resources and the Environment
GAO, BIDA, Bio-Safety Science and Technology
GAO, YINGWU, Engineering Technology
GUAN, CHUNYUN, Agriculture

GUO, QINGQUAN, Agriculture
HUANG, HUANG, Agriculture
HUANG, YIHUAN, Food Science and Technology
HUANG, ZHENGQUAN, Literature
LAO, LIQUN, Science College
LI, FINGJUN, Bio-Safety Science and Technology
LI, XINGHUI, Food Science and Technology
LI, XUN, Agriculture
LIAO, BOHAN, Resources and the Environment
LIAO, XIAOLAN, Bio-Safety Science and Technology
LIU, DEHUA, Food Science and Technology
LIU, GUOHUA, Agriculture
LIU, QIANG, Resources and the Environment
LIU, ZHONGHUA, Food Science and Technology
LIU, ZHONGSONG, Agriculture
LUO, JUNWU, Food Science and Technology
LUO, KUAN, Bio-Safety Science and Technology
MA, MEIHU, Food Science and Technology
OU YANG, XIRONG, Agriculture
PENG, XILIN, Literature
QU, LINYAN, Literature
RONG, XIANGMING, Resources and the Environment
SHENG, XIAOBANG, Agriculture
SHI, ZHAOPENG, Food Science and Technology
SHUN, HUANLIANG, Agriculture
TAN, JICAI, Food Science and Technology
TAN, JICAI, Bio-Safety Science and Technology
TAN, XINGHE, Food Science and Technology
TANG, CHUYU, Engineering Technology
TANG, QIYUAN, Agriculture
TU, LIAOMEI, Agriculture
WANG, GUOHUAI, Agriculture
WANG, GUOLIANG, Agriculture
WANG, GUOPING, Bio-Safety Science and Technology
WEN, LIZHANG, Bio-Safety Science and Technology
WU, LIYOU, Bio-Safety Science and Technology
XI, YANBIN, Food Science and Technology
XIA, YANBIN, Food Science and Technology
XIAO, QIMING, Bio-Safety Science and Technology
XIAO, TIEGUANG, Bio-Safety Science and Technology
YAN, HEHONG, Agriculture
YANG, RENBIN, Resources and the Environment
YANG, WEILI, Food Science and Technology
YANG, ZHIJIAN, Agriculture
ZENG, FUSHENG, Economics Management
ZENG, QINGRU, Resources and the Environment
ZHANG, FUQUAN, Agriculture
ZHANG, XIWEI, Economics Management
ZHANG, YANGZHU, Resources and the Environment
ZHOU, DONGSHENG, Agriculture
ZHOU, JIHENG, Agriculture
ZHOU, MEILAN, Agriculture
ZHOU, QINGMING, Agriculture
ZHU, QI, Food Science and Technology

HUNAN UNIVERSITY

Yule, Changsha 410082, Hunan Province
Telephone: (731) 8822745
Fax: (731) 8824525
Internet: www.hunu.edu.cn

Founded 976 as Yuelu Acad., became Hunan Institute of Higher Education 1903, Hunan Univ. 1926, Hunan Nat. Univ. 1937, South-Central Institute of Civil Engineering 1953, Hunan Institute of Technology between 1953 and 1959, and Hunan Univ. 1959, merged with Hunan College of Finance and Economics 2000
State control

Pres.: WANG KEMING
Library of 2,380,000 vols
Number of teachers: 1,563
Number of students: 34,000

HUNAN MEDICAL UNIVERSITY

88 Xiang Ya Rd, Changsha 410078, Hunan Province
Telephone: (731) 4471347
Fax: (731) 4471339
Internet: hmu.hypermart.net
Founded 1914
Academic year: September to July
Pres.: Prof. HU DONGXU
Vice-Pres: Prof. CHEN ZHUCHU, Prof. HU TIEHUI, Prof. SUN ZHENGQIU, Prof. TIAN YONGQUAN, Prof. WU ZHONGQI, Prof. ZHOU HONGHAO
Librarian: Assoc. Prof. LIU XIACHUN
Library of 560,000 vols
Number of teachers: 652 (full-time)
Number of students: 3,846 (incl. 585 post-graduates)
Publications: *Bulletin* (6 a year), *Chinese Journal of Endoscopy* (4 a year), *Chinese Journal of General Surgery* (6 a year), *Chinese Journal of Otolaryngological and Craniosacral Surgery*, *Chinese Journal of Psychology* (4 a year), *Higher Medical Education Management* (4 a year), *Journal of Applied Uro-Surgery* (4 a year), *Journal of Foreign Medicine* (sections on Psychiatry, Neurology and Neurosurgery, and Physiology and Pathology), *Journal of Medical Degree and Postgraduate Education* (4 a year), *Journal of Modern Medicine* (12 a year)

DIRECTORS

1st Affiliated Hospital (Clinical Medicine): TIAN YONGQUAN
2nd Affiliated Hospital (Clinical Medicine): LIAO ERYUAN
3rd Affiliated Hospital (Clinical Medicine): LIU XUNYANG
Faculty of Basic Medical Sciences: WEN JIFANG
Faculty of Laboratroy Research: CHEN ZHENGYAN
Faculty of Library and Information Sciences: LIU XIAOCHUN
Faculty of Mental Health: CHEN YUANGUANG
Faculty of Nursing: ZHOU CHANGJU
Faculty of Pharmacology: TANG GUISHAN (Deputy Dir)
Faculty of Preventive Medicine: TANG HONGZHUAN (Deputy Dir)
Faculty of Stomatology: JIAN XINCHUN

PROFESSORS

BAI XIANXIN, Radiology
CAO PING, Internal Medicine (Haematology)
CAO YA, Tumour Molecular Biology
CAO ZHIHAN, Internal Medicine (Kidney Diseases)
CHA GUOZHANG, Clinical Microbiology and Immunology
CHEN DAOJING, General Surgery
CHEN FANGPING, Internal Medicine (Haematology)
CHEN FUWEN, Dermatology
CHEN GANREN, Internal Medicine (Cardiology)
CHEN QIZHI, Anaesthesiology
CHEN SHENGXI, Cardiac Surgery
CHEN SHUZHEN, Microbiology
CHEN YUANGUANG, Psychiatry
CHEN ZHENGYAN, Clinical Biochemistry
CHEN ZHUCHU, Tumour Cellular Biology
CHENG RUIXUE, Pathology
DENG HANWU, Pharmacology
DENG HANXIANG, Biology and Medical Genetics

FAN JUNYUAN, Organic Chemistry
FANG PING, Library and Information Sciences
FU YINYU, Orthopaedic Surgery
GAO JIESHENG, Internal Medicine (Rheumatology)
GONG GUANGFU, Cardiac Surgery
GUO SHISHI, Immunology
GUO ZHAOGUI, Clinical Pharmacology
HAN FENGXIA, Biology
HAN XIUYUN, Internal Medicine (Endocrinology)
HU DONGXU, Cardiac Surgery
HU FUZEN, General Surgery
HU GUOLING, Infectious Diseases
HU JIANGUO, Cardiac Surgery
HU MANLING, Health Chemistry
HU TIEHUI, Cardiac Surgery
HU WEIXIN, Tumour Molecular Biology
HUANG GANCHU, Physics and Chemistry
HUANG XUN, Uro-Surgery
HUANG YIMING, Nutritious Food and Health
HUANG ZHAOMIN, Rebabilitation
HUANG ZHENNAN, Health Statistics
JI LONGZHEN, Internal Medicine (Kidney Diseases)
JIAN XINCHUN, Stomatology
JIANG DEZHAO, Haemophysiology
JIANG XIANZHEN, Uro-Surgery
JIANG YOUQIN, Ophthalmology
JIN YIQIANG, Chinese Traditional Medicine
LI DETAI, Radiology
LI GUIYUAN, Molecular Biology
LI HEJUN, Orthopaedic Surgery
LI JIABANG, Chinese Traditional Medicine
LI JUNCHENG, Physiology
LI LUYUN, Medical Genetics
LI RUIZHEN, Ultrasound Diagnosis
LI XINGQUN, Chinese Traditional Medicine
LI XUERONG, Medical Psychology
LI YUANJIAN, Pharmacology
LIAO ERYUAN, Internal Medicine (Endocrinology)
LIN QIUHUA, Gynaecology and Obstetrics
LIU LIHOU, Anatomy
LIU REN, Uro-Surgery
LIU XIAOCHUN, Library and Information Sciences
LIU XUNYANG, General Surgery
LIU YUNSHENG, Neurosurgery
LIU ZHIRAN, Dermatology
LU BINGQING, Neurology
LU GUANGXIU, Biology and Genetics
LU HANBO, Internal Medicine (Haematology)
LU WENNENG, General Surgery
LU XINSHENG, General Surgery
LU YONGDE, Otorhinolaryngology
LU YINZHU, Internal Medicine (Cardiovascular Diseases)
LUO JIAN, Internal Medicine (Kidney Diseases)
LUO XUEGANG, Anatomy
LUO XUEHONG, Emergency Medicine
MA CHUANTAO, Cardiovascular Physiology
MA ENQING, Burns Medicine
OU YANG KE, Infectious Diseases
OU YANG ZHITING, General Surgery
PAN AIYIN, Isotopes in Medicine
QI FAN, Uro-Surgery
QI SHUSHAN, Internal Medicine (Cardiology)
QI ZHENHUA, Internal Medicine (Haematology)
SHEN PENGFEI, Uro-Surgery
SHEN ZIHUA, Stomatology
SONG HUIPING, Biochemistry
SU JIANZHI, Isotopes in Medicine
SU XIANSHI, Infectious Diseases
SUN MING, Internal Medicine (Cardiovascular Diseases)
SUN XIUHONG, Physiology
SUN ZHENGQIU, Health Statistics
TANG DEMING, Infectious Diseases
TANG MINGDE, Environmental Health
TAO ZHENGDE, Otorhinolaryngology
TIAN YONGQUAN, Otorhinolaryngology
WANG LIZHUANG, Emergency Medicine
WANG QIRU, Haemophysiology

WANG ZHONGLIN, Internal Medicine (Cardiology)
WEN JIFANG, Pathology
WU ESHENG, Internal Medicine (Respiratory Diseases)
WU ZHONGQI, Medical Hyperbaric Oxygen
XIE DINGHUA, Otorhinolaryngology
XIA JIAHUI, Biology and Medical Genetics
XIAO JIANYUN, Otorhinolaryngology
XIE ZHAOXIA, Internal Medicine (Haematology)
XU LILI, Gynaecology and Obstetrics
XU XIUHUA, Infection
XU YOUHENG, Haemophysiology
YANG DESEN, Psychiatry
YANG QIDONG, Neurology
YANG YUJIA, Paediatrics
YAO KAITAI, Experimental Oncology
YE YIYAN, Paediatrics
YI XINYUAN, Parasitology
YI ZHUWEN, Paediatrics
YIN BANGLIAN, Cardiac Surgery
YIN BENYI, Internal Medicine (Cardiology)
YOU JIALU, Pathophysiology
YU XIAOLIANG, Paediatrics
YUAN XIANRUI, Neurosurgery
ZENG XIANFANG, Parasitology
ZHANG GUANGSEN, Internal Medicine (Haematology)
ZHANG XICHUN, Internal Medicine (Digestive Diseases)
ZHANG YANGDE, General Surgery
ZHANG YANXIAN, Pathology
ZHOU CHANGJU, Gynaecology and Obstetrics
ZHAO SHUIPING, Internal Medicine (Cardiology)
ZHAO SHUYING, Children's Health
ZHOU HONGHAO, Pharmacology
ZHOU JIANGNAN, Orthopaedic Surgery
ZHU JIMING, Histology and Embryology
ZHU WEIGUANG, Chinese Traditional Medicine

HUNAN NORMAL UNIVERSITY

36 Lu Shan Rd, He Xi, Changsha 410081, Hunan Province
Telephone: (731) 8883131
Fax: (731) 8851226
E-mail: study@hunnu.edu.cn
Internet: www.hunnu.edu.cn
Founded 1938
Min. of Education control
Academic year: September to July
Pres.: LIU XIANG RONG
Vice-Pres: GONG WEI ZHONG, JIANG JI CHENG, LIANG SONG PING, ZHOU JING MING
Heads of Graduate Dept: CHEN JIAN CHU, SHI OU
Librarian: YAN ZHAO HUI
Number of teachers: 1,000
Number of students: 22,000
Publications: *Ancient Chinese Research* (4 a year), *Chinese Literature Research* (4 a year), *Consumer Economy* (4 a year), *Journal* (education science, 6 a year), *Journal* (medicine, irregular), *Journal* (social science, 6 a year), *Life Science Research* (4 a year), *Modern Law* (4 a year)

DEANS

College of Commerce: LIU MAO SONG
Department of Computer Education: WANG LU YA
School of Chemistry and Chemical Engineering: XIE QING JI
School of Education Science: ZHANG CHUAN SUI
School of Foreign Languages: HUANG ZHEN DING
School of International Chinese Culture: JI XUE FENG
School of Law: JIANG XIN MIAO
School of Life Science: WU XIU SHAN

School of Literature: TAN GUI LIN
School of Mathematics and Computer Science: DONG XIN HAN
School of Medicine: FU XIAO HUA
School of Physical Education: LI YAN LING
School of Tourism: XIE JUN GUI

PROFESSORS

CAI, XUE BING, Law
CHEN, BO, Chemistry and Chemical Engineering
CHEN, CHUAN MIAO, Mathematics and Computer Science
CHEN, HUAN GEN, Mathematics and Computer Science
CHEN, JIA QIN, Life Science
CHEN, LIANG BI, Life Science
CHEN, YUN LIANG, Law
CHEN, ZE, Life Science
CHEN, ZUO HONG, Life Science
CUI, ZHEN HUA, International Chinese Culture
DENG, HONG WEN, Life Science
DENG, LE, Life Science
DENG, LE, Chemistry and Chemical Engineering
DENG, XUE JIAN, Life Science
DONG, XIN HAN, Mathematics and Computer Science
DU, XUE TANG, Mathematics and Computer Science
FANG, KUI, Mathematics and Computer Science
FU, PENG, Life Science
FU, ZAI HUI, Chemistry and Chemical Engineering
GU, YONG GENG, Mathematics and Computer Science
GUO, JING YUN, Mathematics and Computer Science
HAO, SAN RU, Computer Education
HE, DING SHENG, Chemistry and Chemical Engineering
HOU, YAO PING, Mathematics and Computer Science
HUANG, JIAN PING, Computer Education
HUANG, YI NONG, Tourism
HUANG, YUAN QIU, Mathematics and Computer Science
JI, XUE FENG, International Chinese Culture
JIANG, XIAN FU, Law
JIANG, XIAO CHENG, Life Science
JIANG, XIN MIAO, Law
JIN, GUANG HUI, Physical Education
JIN, ZU JUN, Mathematics and Computer Science
LENG, GANG SONG, Mathematics and Computer Science
LI, AI NIAN, Law
LI, FANG CHENG, Life Science
LI, HAI TAO, Chemistry and Chemical Engineering
LI, JIAN ZONG, Life Science
LI, SHUANG YUAN, Law
LI, XIAN BO, Law
LI, YAN LING, Physical Education
LI, ZE LIN, Chemistry and Chemical Engineering
LIANG, SONG PING, Life Science
LIU, HONG, Mathematics and Computer Science
LIU, KE MING, Life Science
LIU, MING YAO, Life Science
LIU, SHAO JUN, Life Science
LIU, YING DI, Life Science
LIU, YUN, Life Science
LIU, ZHEN XIU, Mathematics and Computer Science
LUO, CHEN, Life Science
MA, MING, Chemistry and Chemical Engineering
MA, WEI PING, Physical Education
NUAN, SHENG, Life Science
PENG, XIAN JING, Life Science
QIAN, GUANG MING, Mathematics and Computer Science

QIN, ZHENG DI, Computer Education
QIU, MENG SHENG, Life Science
QIU, XI MIN, Chemistry and Chemical Engineering
QU, FU DONG, Tourism
QUAN, HUI YUN, Mathematics and Computer Science
REN, JI CUN, Chemistry and Chemical Engineering
SHEN, JIAN HUA, Mathematics and Computer Science
SHEN, WEN XUAN, Mathematics and Computer Science
SHI, SHAO RONG, Physical Education
SHI, XIAN LIANG, Mathematics and Computer Science
SHI, YING GUANG, Mathematics and Computer Science
SUN, HONG TAO, Physical Education
TAN, PING PING, Physical Education
WANG, BAO HE, Life Science
WANG, GUI GUO, Law
WANG, GUO QIU, Mathematics and Computer Science
WANG, HONG QUAN, Life Science
WANG, LU YA, Computer Education
WANG, XIAN CHUN, Life Science
WANG, XIAN TAO, Mathematics and Computer Science
WU, XIU SHAN, Life Science
XIA, LI QIU, Life Science
XIANG, KAI NAN, Mathematics and Computer Science
XIAO, BEI GENG, Law
XIAO, XIAO MING, Chemistry and Chemical Engineering
XIE, JING YUN, Life Science
XIE, JUN GUI, Tourism
XIE, QING JI, Chemistry and Chemical Engineering
XU, CHUN XIAO, Tourism
XU, DA, Mathematics and Computer Science
XU, FEI XIONG, Tourism
XU, MAN CAI, Chemistry and Chemical Engineering
XU, MENG LIANG, Life Science
YAN, HENG MEI, Life Science
YANG, XIANG QUN, Mathematics and Computer Science
YANG, XIN JIAN, Mathematics and Computer Science
YAO, SHOU ZHUO, Chemistry and Chemical Engineering
YI, CHANG MIN, Life Science
YIN, DA ZHONG, Life Science
YIN, DONG HONG, Chemistry and Chemical Engineering
YUAN, WU ZHOU, Life Science
ZENG, YUE, Chemistry and Chemical Engineering
ZHANG, BAI ZHEN, Physical Education
ZHANG, JIAN, Life Science
ZHANG, TIAN XIAO, Life Science
ZHANG, XUAN JIE, Life Science
ZHANG, YAO, Mathematics and Computer Science
ZHANG, ZHI GUANG, Life Science
ZHENG, YAN, Tourism
ZHENG, YUAN MIN, Law
ZHOU, GONG JIAN, Life Science
ZHOU, JIAN SHE, Physical Education
ZHOU, TIE JUN, Physical Education
ZHOU, XIN YI, Computer Education
ZHU, QI DING, Mathematics and Computer Science

INNER MONGOLIA UNIVERSITY

235 Daxue West Rd, Huhehaote 010021, Inner Mongolia Autonomous Region
Telephone: (471) 4992241
Fax: (471) 4951761
Internet: www.imu.edu.cn

Founded 1957
Academic year: September to July

Pres.: XU RIGAN
Vice-Pres: CHEN GUOQING, HU GEJILETU, LI YANJUN, LIANG XIXIA, TONG GUOQING
Head of Graduate Dept: LIANG XIXIA
Librarian: A LATANCANG

Number of teachers: 1,447
Number of students: 20,000

Publications: *Journal* (humanities and social sciences, 6 a year), *Journal* (natural sciences, 6 a year), *Journal* (philosophy and social sciences, 6 a year)

DEANS

Academy of Mongolian Studies: BAI YIN-MENDE
College of Art: LI YULIN
College of Chemistry and Chemical Engineering: SU HAIQUAN
College of Computer Science: GAO GUANGLAI
College of Continuing Education: FU WENJUN
College of Economics and Management: GUO XIAOCHUAN
College of Foreign Languages: LI KANING
College of Humanities: QIAN JIANMEI
College of Life Science: YANG JIE
College of Physical Education: YU ZHIHAI
College of Public Administration: JIN HAIHE
College of Science and Technology: BAN SHILIANG
College of Vocational Technology: CHAI JINYI
School of Law: DING WENYING

PROFESSORS

A, LATANCANG, Science and Technology
BAI, XUELIANG, Life Science
BAN, SHILIANG, Science and Technology
BAO, QINGDE, Humanities
BAO, WENHAN, Humanities
BO, YINHUI, Humanities
BU, LINBEILE, Mongolian Studies
BU, RENBATU, Mongolian Studies
CHEN, GUOQING, Science and Technology
CHEN, YOUZUN, Law
CONG, ZHIJIE, Public Administration
DU, LIKE, Humanities
EN, HE, Mongolian Studies
GE, RILETU, Mongolian Studies
GUO, XIAOCHUAN, Economics and Management
HAO, WEIMIN, Mongolian Studies
HE, JIANG, Life Science
HU, TINGMAO, Life Science
JIA, GUISHENG, Public Administration
JIN, HAIHE, Public Administration
LANG, BAORU, Humanities
LI, HONG, Science and Technology
LI, QIANZHONG, Science and Technology
LI, SHUXIN, Humanities
LI, XIAOCHUN, Humanities
LIAN, ZIXIN, Public Administration
LIANG, XIXIA, Science and Technology
LIU, AIHUA, Public Administration
LIU, CHENG, Mongolian Studies
LIU, LIHUA, Public Administration
LIU, XIN, Public Administration
LUO, LIAOFU, Science and Technology
MA, JI, Humanities
MA, ZHANXIN, Economics and Management
MENG, BIN, Economics and Management
MENG, HUIJUN, Economics and Management
MING, YUE, Public Administration
NIU, JIANMING, Life Science
NIU, JINGZHONG, Humanities
QING, GEERTAI, Mongolian Studies
QUAN, FU, Mongolian Studies
REN, WEIDE, Public Administration
REN, YUFENG, Humanities
SHI, ZHENGJI, Humanities
SUN, JIONG, Science and Technology
SUN, KAIMIN, Public Administration
TONG, CHUAN, Life Science
WANG, HONGYAN, Law
WANG, MEICUI, Economics and Management
WANG, YAN, Economics and Management
WANG, YINGCHUN, Life Science

WU, QILATU, Mongolian Studies
WU, YINGJI, Life Science
WU, YUNNA, Public Administration
XU, RIGAN, Life Science
YANG, CHI, Life Science
YANG, JIE, Life Science
YANG, XINMIN, Science and Technology
YU, ZHIHAI, Public Administration
YUN, GUOHONG, Science and Technology
ZHANG, CUIZHEN, Public Administration
ZHANG, FENGMING, Law
ZHANG, ZHIZHONG, Public Administration
ZHAO, MIN, Public Administration
ZHEN, XIUYU, Humanities
ZHOU, QINGSHU, Mongolian Studies

INNER MONGOLIA AGRICULTURAL UNIVERSITY

Xinjian East Rd, Beyong Nanmen, Huhehaote 010018, Inner Mongolia Autonomous Region

Telephone: (471) 4301576
Fax: (471) 4301530
Internet: www.imau.edu.cn

Founded 1952
Provincial control
Academic year: September to July

Pres.: LI CHANGYOU
Vice-Pres: HOU XIANZHI, LI JINQUAN, REN QIANG, WANG LINHE, ZHENG JUNBAO
Library of 750,000 vols
Number of teachers: 1,010
Number of students: 18,800

Publication: *Journal* (4 a year)

DEANS

College of Agriculture: YU ZHUO
College of Animal Science and Animal Medicine: LI JINQUAN
College of Biology Engineering: ZHOU HUANMIN
College of Computing and Information Engineering: PEI XICHUN
College of Ecology and the Environment: WANG MINQIU
College of Economics Management: XIU CHANGBO
College of Forestry: ZHANG QIULIANG
College of Forestry Engineering: WANG XIAOLIANG
College of Humanities and Social Sciences: GAO CHAO
College of Mechanical and Electrical Engineering: WANG CHUNGUANG
College of Water Conservancy and Civil Engineering: JI BAOLIN

PROFESSORS

AN, SHOUQIN, Forestry
AO, CHANGJIN, Animal Science and Medicine
AO, RIGELE, Animal Science and Medicine
BAI, SHULAN, Forestry
CAO, GUIFANG, Animal Science and Medicine
CHANG, JINBAO, Forestry
CHAO, LUNBAGEN, Water Conservancy and Civil Engineering
CHEN, YAXIN, Water Conservancy and Civil Engineering
CUI, ZHIGUO, Animal Science and Medicine
DAO, ERJI, Animal Science and Medicine
DE, LIGEERSANG, Food Science and Engineering
DOU, WEIGUO, Mechanical and Electrical Engineering
DU, WENLIANG, Mechanical and Electrical Engineering
FAN, MINGSHOU, Agriculture
FENG, LIN, Forestry
GA, ERDI, Animal Science and Medicine
GAO, CHAO, Humanities and Social Sciences
GE, RILE, Forestry
GUANG, PINGYUAN, Animal Science and Medicine

GUO, LIANSHENG, Ecology and the Environment
GUO, LIANSHENG, Forestry
HE, YINFENG, Food Science and Engineering
HOU, XIANZHI, Animal Science and Medicine
HU, HEBATEER, Animal Science and Medicine
JIN, SHUGUANG, Animal Science and Medicine
LI, CHANGYOU, Water Conservancy and Civil Engineering
LI, JINQUAN, Animal Science and Medicine
LI, LIANGUO, Agriculture
LI, PEIFENG, Animal Science and Medicine
LI, QINGFENG, Ecology and the Environment
LI, YUNZHANG, Animal Science and Medicine
LIU, DEFU, Ecology and the Environment
LIU, KELI, Agriculture
LIU, YONG, Economics Management
LIU, ZHENGYI, Animal Science and Medicine
MA, SHUOSHI, Mechanical and Electrical Engineering
MA, XUEEN, Animal Science and Medicine
MANG, LAI, Animal Science and Medicine
MO, LIGEN, Biology Engineering
PANG, BAOPING, Agriculture
PEI, XICHUN, Computer and Information Engineering
QI, TONGCHUN, Mechanical and Electrical Engineering
QIAO, CHEN, Agriculture
QIAO, GUANGHUA, Economics Management
QIAO, LING, Animal Science and Medicine
QIN, HUA, Food Science and Engineering
SAI, YINCHAOKETU, Biology Engineering
SHANG, SHIYOU, Mechanical and Electrical Engineering
SHENG, XIANGDONG, Water Conservancy and Civil Engineering
SHENG, ZHIYI, Animal Science and Medicine
SHI, HAIBIN, Water Conservancy and Civil Engineering
SI, YA, Humanities and Social Sciences
TAN, PENZHEN, Humanities and Social Sciences
TIAN, DE, Mechanical and Electrical Engineering
TIAN, ZIHUA, Agriculture
TONG, SHUMIN, Mechanical and Electrical Engineering
WAN, TAO, Biology Engineering
WANG, BINXIU, Economics Management
WANG, CHUNGUANG, Mechanical and Electrical Engineering
WANG, CHUNJIE, Animal Science and Medicine
WANG, HAOFU, Humanities and Social Sciences
WANG, LAI, Biology Engineering
WANG, LIMING, Forestry
WANG, LINHE, Ecology and the Environment
WEN, HENG, Water Conservancy and Civil Engineering
WU, NI, Animal Science and Medicine
WU, SHUQING, Animal Science and Medicine
XIU, CHANGBO, Economics Management
XU, ZHIXIN, Ecology and the Environment
XUE, HERU, Computer and Information Engineering
YAN, SUMEI, Animal Science and Medicine
YAN, WEI, Ecology and the Environment
YAN, WEI, Forestry
YANG, BAOSHOU, Animal Science and Medicine
YANG, MINGSHAO, Mechanical and Electrical Engineering
YANG, XIAOYE, Animal Science and Medicine
YAO, FENGTONG, Economics Management
YAO, YUNFENG, Ecology and the Environment
YU, ZHUO, Agriculture
YUAN, XIUYING, Forestry
YUN, JINGFENG, Ecology and the Environment
YUN, XINGFU, Agriculture
YUN, YUEHUA, Humanities and Social Sciences
ZHANG, DEMIAN, Mechanical and Electrical Engineering

ZHANG, HEPING, Food Science and Engineering
ZHANG, LILING, Animal Science and Medicine
ZHANG, QIULIANG, Forestry
ZHANG, SHAOYING, Agriculture
ZHANG, XINLING, Economics Management
ZHANG, ZHIYI, Mechanical and Electrical Engineering
ZHAO, GENBAO, Computingr and Information Engineering
ZHAO, SHIJIE, Mechanical and Electrical Engineering
ZHAO, YUANFENG, Economics Management
ZHAO, ZHENHUA, Animal Science and Medicine
ZHAO, ZHIGONG, Animal Science and Medicine
ZHOU, HUANMIN, Animal Science and Medicine
ZHOU, HUANMIN, Biology Engineering

INNER MONGOLIA UNIVERSITY FOR NATIONALITIES

22 Huolinhe Rd, Tongliao 028043, Inner Mongolia Autonomous Region

Telephone: (475) 8313292
Fax: (475) 8218937
Internet: www.imun.edu.cn

Founded 1960
Academic year: September to July

Pres.: WANG DINGZHU
Vice-Pres: LIU ZONGRUI, MA GUOWEN, PAN XIANG, XIAO JIANPING
Head of Graduate Dept: XING PENGNIN
Librarian: DONG SHALI

Library of 700,000 vols
Number of teachers: 2,262
Number of students: 31,271

Publications: *Journal* (natural sciences; 6 a year in Chinese, 2 a year in Mongolian), *Journal* (social sciences, 6 a year)

DEANS

College of Arts: (vacant)
College of Education Science: (vacant)
College of Law and History: PU FANDA
College of Literature: XU WENHAI
College of Mathematics and Computer Science: (vacant)
College of Mongolian Medicine: BA GENNA
College of Mongolian Studies: (vacant)
College of Sports: (vacant)

PROFESSORS

A, GULA, Mongolian Medicine
AN, GUANBU, Mongolian Medicine
BA, GENNA, Mongolian Medicine
BA, RIGEQI, Mongolian Medicine
BAI, YANMANDULA, Mongolian Medicine
PU, FANDA, Law and History
XUN, WENHAI, Literature
YANG, AMING, Mongolian Medicine

JIANGNAN UNIVERSITY

1800 Lihu Rd, Wuxi 214122, Jiangsu Province

Telephone: (510) 85913623
Fax: (510) 85913622
Internet: www.jiangnan.edu.cn

Founded 1902
State control
Academic year: September to July

Pres.: CHEN JIAN
Vice-Pres: FENG BIAO, JIANG ZHONGPING, LOU GUODONG, WANG WU, ZHU TUO
Head of Graduate Dept: ZHANG HAO
Librarian: ZHANG YIXIN

Number of teachers: 1,504
Number of students: 19,600

Publication: *Journal of Southern Yangtze University* (editions: food and biotechnology, natural sciences, humanities and social science, 6 a year; beverage and frozen food industry, 4 a year)

DEANS

Department of Art: WANG JIANYAN
Department of Civil Engineering: HUA YUAN
Department of International Studies: GUO XIHUA
Department of Physical Education: YANG RONGLIN
School of Biotechnology: XU YAN
School of Business: FU XIANZHI
School of Chemical and Materials Engineering: FANG YUN
School of Communication and Control Engineering: JI ZHICHENG
School of Continuing Education: HUANG ZHENGMING
School of Design: GUO WEIMIN
School of Education: CHEN MINGXUAN
School of Food Science and Technology: ZHANG HAO
School of Foreign Studies: DONG JIANQIAO
School of Information Technology: WANG SHITONG
School of Law and Politics: ZHU TONGDAN
School of Literature: XU XINGHAI
School of Mechanical Engineering: ZHANG QIUJU
School of Medicine: LI HUAZHONG
School of Science: (vacant)
School of Textiles and Clothing: FANG KUANJUN

PROFESSORS

CAO, GUANGQUN, Chemical and Materials Engineering
CHEN, ANJUN, Mechanical Engineering
CHEN, JIAN, Biotechnology
CHEN, JIONG, Literature
CHEN, ZHENGXING, Food Science and Technology
DENG, ZIMEI, Law and Politics
DING, WEIGUO, Commerce
DING, XIAOLIN, Food Science and Technology
DONG, YUZI, Information Technology
DU, GUOCHENG, Biotechnology
FANG, HANWEN, Literature
FANG, KUANJUN, Textiles
FENG, BIAO, Food Science and Technology
GAO, WEIDONG, Textiles
GE, MINGQIAO, Textiles
GU, GUOXIAN, Biotechnology
GU, WENYING, Food Science and Technology
GU, YAOLIN, Information Technology
GU, YIFAN, Literature
GUO, SHIDONG, Food Science and Technology
HUANG, HUANCHU, Law and Politics
HUANG, WEINING, Food Science and Technology
HUANG, ZHIHAO, Literature
HUANG, ZHONGJING, Law and Politics
JIANG, BO, Food Science and Technology
JIANG, CHENGYONG, Literature
JIN, JIAN, Biotechnology
JIN, QIRONG, Biotechnology
JIN, ZHENGYU, Food Science and Technology
LE, GUOWEI, Food Science and Technology
LI, HUAZHONG, Biotechnology
LI, SHIGUO, Mechanical Engineering
LI, WEIJIANG, Biotechnology
LIU, HUANMING, Law and Politics
LUN, SHIYI, Biotechnology
MA, JIANGUO, Food Science and Technology
MA, QIFAN, Commerce
MAO, ZHONGGUI, Biotechnology
MENG, QING-EN, Law and Politics
PAN, BEILEI, Food Science and Technology
QIU, AIYONG, Food Science and Technology
QUAN, WENHAI, Biotechnology
SHAO, JIYONG, Commerce
SHI, YONGHUI, Food Science and Technology
SIMA, NAN, Literature
SUN, HONG, Literature
SUN, YANTANG, Information Technology
SUN, ZHIHAO, Biotechnology

SUN, ZHOUNIAN, Literature
TANG, JIAN, Food Science and Technology
TAO, BOHUA, Literature
TAO, WENYI, Biotechnology
WANG, SHITONG, Information Technology
WANG, WU, Biotechnology
WANG, YONGFENG, Literature
WANG, ZHANG, Food Science and Technology
WANG, ZHENGXIANG, Biotechnology
WANG, ZHIWEI, Mechanical Engineering
WU, GE, Commerce
WU, GEMING, Literature
WU, PEIZONG, Biotechnology
WU, XIANZHANG, Biotechnology
XIA, WENSHUI, Food Science and Technology
XIE, ZHENRONG, Law and Politics
XU, WENBO, Information Technology
XU, XINGHAI, Literature
XU, YAN, Biotechnology
XU, ZHENGYUAN, Information Technology
YAO, HUIYUAN, Food Science and Technology
YAO, JINMING, Literature
YU, SHIYING, Food Science and Technology
YUAN, HUIXIN, Mechanical Engineering
YUAN, ZHENHUI, Law and Politics
ZENG, YOUXIN, Commerce
ZHANG, GENYI, Food Science and Technology
ZHANG, HEGUAN, Commerce
ZHANG, JIWEN, Information Technology
ZHANG, KECHANG, Biotechnology
ZHANG, MIN, Food Science and Technology
ZHANG, QIUJU, Mechanical Engineering
ZHANG, XINCHANG, Mechanical Engineering
ZHANG, XINGYUAN, Biotechnology
ZHANG, XIQING, Mechanical Engineering
ZHANG, YIXIN, Information Technology
ZHANG, YONGXIN, Literature
ZHANG, YUZHONG, Mechanical Engineering
ZHAO, GUANGAO, Biotechnology
ZHAO, JIANGUO, Biotechnology
ZHAO, YONGWU, Mechanical Engineering
ZHOU, HUIMING, Food Science and Technology
ZHOU, QING, Biotechnology
ZHOU, WUCHUN, Literature
ZHU, TONGDAN, Law and Politics
ZHU, ZHIFENG, Textiles
ZHUGE, HONGYUN, Literature
ZHUGE, JIAN, Biotechnology

JIANGSU UNIVERSITY

301 Xuefu Rd, Zhenjiang 212013, Jiangsu Province
Telephone: (511) 8780048
Fax: (511) 8791785
Internet: www.ujs.edu.cn
Founded 2001
Academic year: September to July
Pres.: YANG JICHANG
Vice-Pres: CAO YOUQING, SONG JINGZHANG, SONG YUQING, SUN YUKUN, XU HUAXI, YUAN SHOUQI, YUAN YINNAN, ZHAO JIEWEN
Head of Graduate Dept: MAO HANPING
Librarian: SONG SHUNLIN
Number of teachers: 900
Number of students: 26,320
Publication: *Journal* (6 a year, editions: higher education, medicine, natural sciences, social sciences)

DEANS

College of Adult Education: XIN JUNKANG
Faculty of Science: TIAN LIXIN
School of Art Education: ZHU ZHENGLUN
School of Automotive and Traffic Engineering: CAI YIXI
School of Biological and Environmental Engineering: WU CHUNDU
School of Chemistry and Chemical Engineering: XIE JIMIN
School of Computer Science and Telecommunications: JU SHIGUANG
School of Electrical and Information Engineering: LIU GUOHAI

School of Energy Resources and Power Engineering: YANG MINGUAN
School of Foreign Languages: LUO XINMIN
School of Humanities and Social Sciences: DA YUANYI
School of Industrial and Business Administration: MEI QIANG
School of Materials Engineering: (vacant)
School of Mechanical Engineering: LI PINGPING
School of Medical Technology: XU WENRONG
School of Medicine: XU HUAXI
School of Normal Education: CHEN LIN
School of Pharmacy: XU XIMING

PROFESSORS

BAO, BINGHAO, Mechanical Engineering
CAI, LAN, Mechanical Engineering
CHEN, CUIYING, Mechanical Engineering
CHEN, GUOXIANG, Humanities and Social Sciences
CHEN, JIN, Mechanical Engineering
CHEN, LIZHEN, Business Administration
CHEN, ZHAOZHANG, Electrical and Information Engineering
CHEN, ZHIGANG, Materials Engineering
CHENG, LI, Electrical and Information Engineering
CHENG, XIANYI, Computer Science and Telecommunications
CHENG, XIAONONG, Materials Engineering
CHONG, KAI, Mechanical Engineering
DAI, QIXUN, Materials Engineering
DING, GUILIN, Mechanical Engineering
DING, JIANNING, Mechanical Engineering
DONG, DEFU, Humanities and Social Sciences
FAN, MING, Business Administration
GE, XIAOLAN, Mechanical Engineering
GU, JINAN, Mechanical Engineering
HE, YOUSHI, Business Administration
HE, ZHIGUO, Art
HUANG, GENLIANG, Materials Engineering
HUANG, XIQUAN, Medical Technology
JIN, LIFU, Humanities and Social Sciences
JU, SHIGUANG, Computer Science and Telecommunications
KONG, YUSHENG, Business Administration
LEI, YUCHENG, Materials Engineering
LI, BOQUAN, Mechanical Engineering
LI, CHANGSHENG, Mechanical Engineering
LI, DETAO, Energy Resources and Power Engineering
LI, PINGPING, Mechanical Engineering
LI, XINCHENG, Mechanical Engineering
LI, YAOMING, Mechanical Engineering
LI, ZHENGMING, Electrical and Information Engineering
LIN, HONGYI, Energy Resources and Power Engineering
LIU, AIZHEN, Foreign Languages
LIU, FENGYING, Computer Science and Telecommunications
LIU, GUOHAI, Electrical and Information Engineering
LIU, JIANYI, Business Administration
LIU, QIUSHENG, Business Administration
LU, ZHANGPING, Mechanical Engineering
LU, ZHENGNAN, Business Administration
LUO, DEFU, Materials Science and Engineering
LUO, TIGAN, Energy Resources and Power Engineering
LUO, XINMIN, Materials Engineering
LUO, ZHIGAO, Mechanical Engineering
MA, LVZHONG, Mechanical Engineering
MAO, HANPING, Mechanical Engineering
MEI, QIANG, Business Administration
QI, HONG, Energy Resources and Power Engineering
QIAO, ZHAOHUA, Humanities and Social Science
QIU, BAIJING, Mechanical Engineering
REN, NAIFEI, Mechanical Engineering
SHAO, HONGHONG, Materials Engineering
SHAO, SHIHE, Medical Technology
SHEN, XIANGQIAN, Materials Engineering

SHI, GUOHONG, Business Administration
SI, NAICHAO, Materials Engineering
SONG, SHUNLIN, Computer Science and Tele-communications
SONG, XINNAN, Energy Resources and Power Engineering
SONG, YUQING, Computer Science and Tele-communications
SUN, JIAGUANG, Computer Science and Tele-communications
SUN, YUKUN, Electrical and Information Engineering
WANG, CUNTANG, Mechanical Engineering
WANG, GANG, Computer Science and Tele-communications
WANG, GUICHENG, Mechanical Engineering
WANG, QIAN, Energy Resources and Power Engineering
WANG, SHULIN, Mechanical Engineering
WANG, SHUQI, Materials Engineering
WANG, ZE, Energy Resources and Power Engineering
WEI, QI, Energy Resources and Power Engineering
WEN, JIANLONG, Energy Resources and Power Engineering
WU, YANYOU, Mechanical Engineering
XIAO, TIEJUN, Computer Science and Tele-communications
XIE, GANG, Humanities and Social Sciences
XU, HUAXI, Medical Technology
XU, WENRONG, Medical Technology
XU, XIMING, Pharmacy
YANG, JICHANG, Mechanical Engineering
YANG, MINGUAN, Energy Resources and Power Engineering
YANG, PING, Mechanical Engineering
YAO, GUANXIN, Business Administration
ZHAN, YONGZHAO, Computer Science and Telecommunications
ZHANG, BINGSHENG, Humanities and Social Sciences
ZHANG, JIAN, Business Administration
ZHANG, RONGBIAO, Electrical and Information Engineering
ZHANG, YONGKANG, Mechanical Engineering
ZHANG, ZHUMEI, Humanities and Social Sciences
ZHAO, BUHUI, Electrical and Information Engineering
ZHAO, DEAN, Electrical and Information Engineering
ZHAO, JIN, Business Administration
ZHAO, XICANG, Business Administration
ZHAO, YANPING, Business Administration
ZHAO, YUTAO, Materials Engineering
ZHOU, HONG, Medical Technology
ZHOU, JIANZHONG, Mechanical Engineering
ZHOU, JUN, Mechanical Engineering
ZHOU, TIANJIAN, Medical Technology
ZHOU, ZHICHU, Humanities and Social Sciences
ZHU, HUANGQIU, Electrical and Information Engineering
ZHU, WEIXING, Electrical and Information Engineering
ZUO, RAN, Energy Resources and Power Engineering

JIANGXI AGRICULTURAL UNIVERSITY

Meiling, Nanchang 330045, Jianxi Province
E-mail: ieojau@yahoo.com.cn
Internet: www.jxau.edu.cn
Founded 1940
Public control
Language of instruction: Chinese
Academic year: September to June
Pres.: Prof. HUANG LUSHENG
Library: over 1,000,000 vols
Number of teachers: 1,500
Number of students: 26,000
Publication: *Journal*.

JILIN UNIVERSITY

10 Qianwei Rd, Changchun 130012
Telephone: (431) 5166885
Fax: (431) 5166570
E-mail: fsc@jlu.edu.cn
Internet: www.jlu.edu.cn
Founded 1946, merged in 2001 with Jilin Univ. of Technology (f. 1955), Norman Bethune Univ. of Medical Sciences (f. 1939), Changchun Univ. of Science and Technology (f. 1951) and Changchun Institute of Posts and Telecommunications (f. 1947), to form new Jilin Univ.
Academic year: September to July (2 semesters).
Colleges: administration studies; art, biology and agricultural engineering; chemistry; clinical medicine;communications engineering; computer science and technology; construction engineering; economics; economics and information; electronics and engineering; environment and resources; foreign languages; geological exploration and information technology; geological sciences; law; life sciences; literature and arts; machinery and engineering; management studies; materials science and engineering; mathematics; motor car engineering; nursing; pharmacy; philosophy and sociology; physical education; physics; public health sciences; stomatology; transport
Pres.: LIU ZHONGSHU
Head of Graduate School: QIU SHILUN
Librarian: BAO CHENGGUAN
Library of 2,510,000 vols
Publications: *Chemical Research in Chinese Universities* (Chinese and English edns), *Higher Education Research and Practice*, *Journal of Demography*, *Journal of Historical Studies*, *Journal of Natural Science*, *Legal Systems and Social Development*, *Mathematics of Northeastern China*, *Modern Japanese Economy*, *Northeast Asian Forum*.

JINAN UNIVERSITY

601 Huangpu West Rd, Guangzhou 510632, Guangdong Province
Telephone: (20) 85220010
E-mail: officex@jnu.edu.cn
Internet: www.jnu.edu.cn
Founded 1906
Academic year: September to July
Pres.: LIU RENHUAI
Vice-Pres: HU JUN, JI ZONGAN, JIA YIMIN, JIANG SHUZHUO, LU DAXIANG, WANG HUA, YE QIN
Head of Graduate Dept: GU WEIFANG
Librarian: ZHU LINA
Number of teachers: 1,477
Number of students: 22,000
Publications: *Chinese Journal of Pathophysiology* (6 a year), *Ecological Science* (4 a year), *Economic Front* (12 a year), *Jinan Higher Education Research* (6 a year), *Journal* (6 a year), *Journal of the College of Chinese Language and Culture of Jinan University* (4 a year), *South-east Asian Studies* (6 a year)

DEANS

College of Chinese Language and Culture: BAO CHAO
College of Continuing Education: HAO ZHAOZHOU
College of Economics: LIU SHAOBO
College of Foreign Studies: LIANG DONGHUA
College of Information Science and Technology: BO YUANHUAI
College of Journalism and Communication: CAI MINGZE
College of Liberal Arts: SUN WEIMING

College of Life Science and Technology: ZHOU TIANHONG
College of Pharmacy: ZHANG RONGHUA
College of Science and Engineering: ZHANG YONGLIN
International School: SUN BOHUA
Management School: SUI GUANGJUN
Medical School: SU BAOGUI
School of Law: ZHOU XIANZHI
Shenzhen College of Tourism: LIU ZEPENG
Zhuhai Special Economic Zone College: HU JUN

PROFESSORS

AO, NINGJIAN, Life Science and Technology
CAI, JIYE, Life Science and Technology
CAI, MINGZE, Journalism and Communication
CAO, BAOLIN, Liberal Arts
CAO, YUNHUA, Law
CHEN, CHUSHENG, Liberal Arts
CHEN, EN, Economics
CHEN, QIAOZHI, Law
CHEN, WEIMING, Liberal Arts
CHEN, XIAOJIN, Liberal Arts
CHEN, XINGDAN, Science and Engineering
CHEN, XUEMEI, Economics
CHEN, YINYUAN, Life Science and Technology
CHEN, YONGLIANG, Economics
CHENG, GUOBIN, Liberal Arts
DENG, QIAOBIN, Chinese
DONG, JIANXIN, Management
DONG, TIANCE, Journalism and Communication
DU, JINMIN, Finance
DUAN, SHUNSHAN, Life Science and Technology
FEI, YONG, Liberal Arts
FENG, BANGYAN, Economics
FENG, XIAOYUN, Economics
GAO, WEINONG, Liberal Arts
GAO, YINGJUN, Science and Engineering
GONG, WEIPING, Economics
GU, GUOYAO, Finance
GUO, SHUHAO, Life Science and Technology
HAN, BOPING, Life Science and Technology
HAN, ZHAOZHOU, Statistics
HE, WENTAO, Finance
HONG, AN, Life Science and Technology
HU, JUN, Management
HU, JUN, Zhuhai SEZ College
HU, SHIZHEN, Economics
HUANG, DEHONG, Management
HUANG, YAOXIONG, Life Science and Technology
JI, MANHONG, Liberal Arts
JI, ZONG-AN, Liberal Arts
JIA, YIMIN, Liberal Arts
JIANG, DUXIAO, Life Science and Technology
JIANG, SHUZHUO, Chinese
JIN, LAHUA, Science and Engineering
LI, BOQIAO, Law
LI, GUISHENG, Life Science and Technology
LI, WEI, Life Science and Technology
LI, YIJUN, Life Science and Technology
LI, YUFANG, Economics
LIN, FUYONG, Zhuhai SEZ College
LIN, LIQIONG, Economics
LIN, RUPENG, Journalism and Communication
LING, WENQUAN, Management
LIU, DEXUE, International Economics and Trade
LIU, JIALIN, Journalism and Communication
LIU, JIANPING, Statistics
LIU, JIESHENG, Life Science and Technology
LIU, RENHUAI, Science and Engineering
LIU, SHAOBO, Finance
LIU, SHAOJIN, Chinese
LIU, YIN, Law
LIU, YINGLIANG, Life Science and Technology
LIU, ZHENGGANG, Liberal Arts
LIU, ZHENGWEN, Life Science and Technology
LU, JUNHUA, Pharmacy
MA, MINGDA, Liberal Arts

MA, QIUFENG, Journalism and Communication
MA, ZHIRONG, Zhuhai SEZ College
MEI, LINHAI, Economics
NIU, DESHENG, Economics
OUYANG, JIANMING, Life Science and Technology
PAN, SHANPEI, Life Science and Technology
PANG, QICHANG, Science and Engineering
QIU, SHUSEN, Liberal Arts
RAO, PENGZI, Chinese
SHAO, JINGMIN, Chinese
SU, BAOHE, Zhuhai SEZ College
SU, DONGWEI, Finance
SUI, GUANGJUN, Management
SUN, BOHUA, International School
SUN, DONGCHUAN, Zhuhai SEZ College
SUN, HANXIAO, Pharmacy
TAN, TIAN, Journalism and Communication
TAN, YUE, Finance
TANG, KAIJIAN, Liberal Arts
TANG, SHUNQING, Life Science and Technology
TANG, SHUZE, Science and Engineering
WANG, CONG, Finance
WANG, FUCHU, Economics
WANG, HUA, Management
WANG, LIEYAO, Liberal Arts
WANG, XIANGPING, Zhuhai SEZ College
WANG, XINMIN, Liberal Arts
WANG, YANKUN, Chinese
WANG, YIFEI, Pharmacy
WANG, YING, Life Science and Technology
WEI, ZHONGLIN, Liberal Arts
WEN, BEIYAN, Law
WU, CHAOBIAO, Statistics
WU, JIANG, Economics
WU, LIGUANG, International Economics and Trade
WU, XIANZHONG, Management
XIA, HONGSHENG, Management
XIANG, JUNJIAN, Life Science and Technology
XIE, QINAN, Statistics
XU, SHIHAI, Life Science and Technology
YANG, QIGUANG, Liberal Arts
YANG, XING, Finance
YANG, YING, Economics
YANG, YUFENG, Life Science and Technology
YAO, XINSHENG, Pharmacy
YE, CHUNLING, Pharmacy
YE, WENCAI, Pharmacy
YIN, HUA, Science and Engineering
YIN, PINGHE, Life Science and Technology
YU, DINGCHENG, Economics
YU, RONGMIN, Pharmacy
YU, YOULONG, Science and Engineering
ZENG, JIANXIONG, Journalism and Communication
ZENG, YAOYING, Life Science and Technology
ZHAN, BOHUI, Chinese
ZHANG, JIE, International Economics and Trade
ZHANG, QIFAN, Liberal Arts
ZHANG, QIZHONG, Life Science and Technology
ZHANG, RONGHUA, Pharmacy
ZHANG, SENWEN, Science and Engineering
ZHANG, SHIJUN, Liberal Arts
ZHANG, XIAOHUI, Liberal Arts
ZHANG, YAOHUI, Zhuhai SEZ College
ZHANG, YONGLIN, Science and Engineering
ZHANG, YUANMING, Life Science and Technology
ZHANG, YUCHUN, Liberal Arts
ZHANG, ZIYONG, Life Science and Technology
ZHAO, JIAMIN, Finance
ZHENG, WENJIE, Life Science and Technology
ZHONG, JINGANG, Science and Engineering
ZHOU, CHANGREN, Life Science and Technology
ZHOU, LIXIN, Life Science and Technology
ZHOU, TIANHONG, Life Science and Technology
ZHOU, XIANZH, Law
ZHU, CHENGPING, Liberal Arts
ZHU, WEIJIE, Life Science and Technology

KUNMING MEDICAL COLLEGE

84 Renmin Xilu, Kunming 650031, Yunnan Province

Telephone: (871) 5339224
Fax: (871) 5311542
Internet: www.kmmc.edu.cn

Founded 1956
Academic year: September to January, March to August

Pres.: Prof. LIANG LIQUAN
Vice-Pres: Prof. CHEN DECHANG, Prof. WANG ZICANG, ZHANG CHAO
Chief Administrative Officer: JIANG RUNSHENG

Library of 170,000 vols, 1,659 periodicals
Number of teachers: 1,200
Number of students: 2,789 (incl. 118 postgraduates)

KUNMING UNIVERSITY OF SCIENCE AND TECHNOLOGY

1 Wenchangxiang, Kunming 650093, Yunnan Province

Telephone: (871) 5144212
Fax: (871) 5158622
Internet: www.kmust.edu.cn

Founded 1954
Academic year: September to July

Pres.: Prof. ZHANG WENBIN
Vice-Pres: Prof. HE TIANCHUN, Prof. TAO HENGCHANG, Prof. XIANG NAIMING
Asst Pres.: Prof. SUN JIALIN
Registrar: Prof. ZHOU RONG
Librarian: Prof. LIU ZHONGHUA

Library of 1,100,000 vols
Number of teachers: 800
Number of students: 8,000

Publications: *Journal, Research in Higher Education in KUST, Science and Technology in KUST*

HEADS OF COLLEGES

College of Adult Education: Prof. XU BAOZHONG
College of Management and Economy: Prof. YANG BAOJIAN
College of Social Science and Art: LI XUEYOU

LANZHOU UNIVERSITY

222 Tianshui Nanlu, Lanzhou 730000, Gansu Province

Telephone: (931) 8912126
Fax: (931) 8625576
Internet: www.lzu.edu.cn

Founded 1909
Academic year: September to July (2 semesters)

Pres.: ZHOU XUHONG
Vice-Pres.: AN LIZHE
Vice-Pres.: CHEN FAHU
Vice-Pres.: GAN HUI
Vice-Pres.: JING TAO
Vice-Pres.: XU SHENGCHENG
Dir for Pres. Office: ZHANG ZHENGGUO
Librarian: SHA YONGZHONG

Number of teachers: 1,779
Number of students: 28,358

Publications: *Collections of Articles on Dunhuang Studies, Historical and Geographical Review of Northwest China.*

LIAONING UNIVERSITY

66 Chongshan Middle Rd, Shenyang 110036, Liaoning Province

Telephone: (24) 86842756
Fax: (24) 62202013
E-mail: office@lnu.edu.cn
Internet: www.lnu.edu.cn

Founded 1948

Min. of Education control
Academic year: September to July

Pres.: CHENG WEI
Vice-Pres: LIU ZHICHAO, MU HUAIZHONG, ZANG SHULIANG, ZHANG WEI
Head of Graduate Dept: XU PING
Librarian: YANG XIAOJUN

Number of teachers: 1,200
Number of students: 23,000

Publications: *Journal* (natural sciences, 4 a year), *Journal* (philosophy and social sciences, 6 a year), *Research of Japan* (4 a year)

DEANS

Asia-Australia College of Business: ZHOU JIE
College of Adult Education: MA YONGJUN
College of Business Management: GAO CHUANG
College of Chemistry and Engineering: SONG XIMING
College of Cultural Communication: GAO KAIZHENG
College of Economics: LIN MUXI
College of Foreign Languages: CHEN FENG
College of Higher Professional Techniques: YU ZHONGCHENG
College of Information Science and Technology: SHI XIANGBIN
College of Law: YANG SONG
College of Philosophy and Public Administration: SHAO XIAOGUANG
College of Radio, Film and Television: HU GUANGHUI
Faculty of Environmental Science: LI FAYUN
Faculty of History: DING HAIBIN
Faculty of Life Sciences: ZHOU RENQING
Faculty of Mathematics: DAI TIANMIN
Faculty of Physics: GUO YONGXIN
Sun Wah International Business School: CHENG WEI

PROFESSORS

BI, XIAOHUI, Philosophy and Public Administration
CHE, WEIYI, Mathematics
CHEN, CHUNGUANG, Information Science and Technology
CHEN, FENG, Foreign Languages
CHEN, XIN, Chemistry and Engineering
DAI, BOXUN, Business Management
DAI, TIANMIN, Mathematics
DING, HAIBIN, History
DING, NING, Information Science and Technology
DONG, SHOUYI, History
DONG, WENCHENG, Cultural Communication
FANG, BAOLIN, Business Management
GAO, CHUANG, Business Management
GAO, KAIZHENG, Cultural Communication
GAO, YANGKUI, Foreign Languages
GU, KUIXIANG, History
GUO, HUOXUN, Philosophy and Public Administration
GUO, JIE, Law
GUO, WENSHENG, Chemistry and Engineering
GUO, YONGXIN, Physics
HAO, JIANSHE, Law
HU, YUHAI, History
JIA, SHUFENG, Foreign Languages
JIAO, RUNMING, History
JIN, LISHUN, Business Management
LI, CHUNGUANG, History
LI, JUEXIAN, Mathematics
LI, LIPING, Information Science and Technology
LI, TIEMIN, Life Sciences
LI, YONGCHANG, History
LIN, MUXI, Economics
LIU, DUCAI, Law
LIU, FULIN, Mathematics
LIU, LIGANG, Business Management
LIU, WEIZHI, Cultural Communication
LIU, XINGZHI, Chemistry and Engineering

LU, JIERONG, Philosophy and Public Administration
LU, DIANZHEN, Chemistry and Engineering
LU, FANG, Mathematics
LU, GUOCHEN, Philosophy and Public Administration
LUO, JUNBO, Mathematics
MA, LIJUAN, Foreign Languages
NIU, BIN, Information Science and Technology
PENG, HAORONG, Business Management
QI, LIQUAN, Chemistry and Engineering
QI, ZHENGHUI, History
QIN, YONGLU, Information Science and Technology
QU, DELAI, Cultural Communication
REN, JI, Law
SHAO, XIAOGUANG, Philosophy and Public Administration
SHEN, GUIFENG, Physics
SHEN, HONGDA, Business Management
SHI, XIANGBIN, Information Science and Technology
SHI, YING, Law
SONG, XIMING, Chemistry and Engineering
SUN, HONGLIE, Mathematics
SUN, LI, Law
TANG, XIAOHUA, Business Management
TIAN, YUFENG, Information Science and Technology
TU, GUANGSHE, Cultural Communication
WANG, CHUNFEI, Cultural Communication
WANG, CHUNRONG, Cultural Communication
WANG, JUN, Chemistry and Engineering
WANG, QIUYU, Life Sciences
WANG, WEI, Cultural Communication
WANG, WEIFAN, Mathematics
WANG, WENCI, Foreign Languages
WANG, XIANGFENG, Cultural Communication
WU, CHUNYU, Physics
WU, WENZHONG, Foreign Languages
WU, XINJIE, Physics
XIAO, SHENG, Business Management
XING, ZHIREN, Law
XU, HAOGUANG, Cultural Communication
XU, ZHIGANG, Cultural Communication
XUE, JIANSHENG, Information Science and Technology
YANG, JIAZHEN, Chemistry and Engineering
YANG, LINRUI, Law
YANG, MING, Law
YANG, SONG, Law
YU, ZHONGZHUO, Business Management
ZANG, SHULIANG, Chemistry and Engineering
ZENG, XIAOFEI, Life Sciences
ZHANG, CHENGHUA, Physics
ZHANG, FENG, Chemistry and Engineering
ZHANG, JIE, History
ZHANG, LIZHEN, History
ZHANG, XIANGDONG, Chemistry and Engineering
ZHANG, YOUHUI, Information Science and Technology
ZHAO, BINGGUI, Law
ZHAO, DEZHI, Philosophy and Public Administration
ZHAO, GUOXING, Information Science and Technology
ZHAO, LINGHE, Cultural Communication
ZHENG, YONGFAN, Mathematics
ZHOU, FEI, Philosophy and Public Administration
ZHOU, RENQING, Life Sciences
ZHU, MINGLUN, Cultural Communication
ZUO, ZHICHENG, Foreign Languages

LIAONING NORMAL UNIVERSITY

Da Lian 116029, Liaoning Province
Telephone: (411) 2158235
Internet: www.lnnu.edu.cn
Founded 1951
Provincial control
Academic year: September to July
Pres.: QU QINGBIAO

Vice-Pres: HAN ZHENGLIN, QU WEI
Librarian: ZHAO YUNSHENG
Library of 1,330,000 vols
Number of teachers: 1,897
Number of students: 25,200
Publication: *Journal* (6 a year)

DEANS

College of the City and Environment: LIN XIANSENG
College of Education: FU WEILI
College of Film and Television Art: GAO GUANGFU
College of Foreign Languages: MA YANGGANG
College of History and Tourism: XIE JINGFANG
College of Law: YU PEILIN
College of Life Science: HOU HESHENG
College of Literature: WANG WEIPING
College of Management: ZHAO ZHONGWEN
College of Physics and Electronic Technology: PAN FENG
College of Politics: SHI YIJUN
College of Sports: HE MINXUE
Faculty of Chemistry and Chemical Engineering: JIAO QIANGZHU
School of Mathematics: HAN YOUFA

PROFESSORS

BI, ZHIGUO, Politics
CAI, MIN, Education
CHANG, JINCHANG, History and Tourism
CHANG, RUOSONG, Education
CHEN, DACHAO, Education
CHEN, LIU, Literature
CHEN, TUYUN, Mathematics
CHENG, XIAOGUANG, Foreign Languages
DIAO, YANBIN, Literature
DONG, GUANGCAI, Foreign Languages
DONG, XUEDONG, Mathematics
DU, LIN, Literature
DU, RUIZHI, Mathematics
DU, XINGZHI, History and Tourism
FAN, YINGHENG, Chemistry and Chemical Engineering
FANG, HONGXIAO, Life Science
FENG, CHUNLIANG, Chemistry and Chemical Engineering
FU, WEILI, Education
GAO, BO, Management
HAN, YOUFA, Mathematics
HAN, YUCHANG, Education
HE, MINXUE, Sports
HOU, HESHENG, Life Science
HOU, LIN, Life Science
HU, ZHENKAI, Education
HUANG, BIN, Sports
JIANG, HUA, Life Science
JIN, CHENGJI, Sports
JIN, HONGYUAN, Education
JIN, RENSHU, Management
LI, CHUNLIN, Literature
LI, JINXIANG, Chemistry and Chemical Engineering
LI, LAIZHI, Management
LI, RENXI, Life Science
LI, TIANJIAN, Mathematics
LI, XUGUANG, Foreign Languages
LI, YAOZHENG, City and Environment Studies
LI, YINGJUN, Chemistry and Chemical Engineering
LIANG, GUIZHI, Literature
LIANG, SHUSHENG, Physics and Electronic Technology
LIN, HUA, Sports
LIN, XIANSHENG, City and Environment Studies
LIU, FANFU, Foreign Languages
LIU, FUGENG, Foreign Languages
LIU, PEIHAN, Politics
LIU, WANQI, Law
LIU, WEN, Education
LIU, XIUCHUN, Politics
LIU, ZHEQING, Mathematics
LUAN, WEIXIN, City and Environment Studies

LU, FENGYING, Law
LU, GUOFENG, Sports
MA, DONGYU, History and Tourism
MA, JIANSHENG, Education
MA, JUNSHAN, Literature
MA, YOUHUI, Life Science
MENG, DEXIU, Foreign Languages
MENG, ZHAOYUAN, Politics
NIU, SHUYUN, Chemistry and Chemical Engineering
PAN, FENG, Physics and Electronic Technology
QI, GUOYING, Physics and Electronic Technology
QU, GUANG, Literature
QU, JIANWU, Politics
QU, QINGBIAO, Politics
QU, WEI, Foreign Languages
SANG, DEJING, Life Science
SHI, LEI, Chemistry and Chemical Engineering
SHI, YIJUN, Politics
SHUN, RENAN, Chemistry and Chemical Engineering
SHUN, YUANGANG, Education
SONG, HUA, History and Tourism
TAO, YAN, Foreign Languages
TIAN, GUANGLIN, History and Tourism
WANG, BING, Foreign Languages
WANG, CHANGSHENG, Chemistry and Chemical Engineering
WANG, GUANLIN, Life Science
WANG, HONG, Sports
WANG, JIPENG, Literature
WANG, LI, Literature
WANG, QIHUA, Life Science
WANG, QINGJIAN, Mathematics
WANG, WEIPING, Literature
WANG, XIUWU, Life Science
WANG, XIUXIANG, Sports
WANG, YAOGUANG, Sports
WANG, YI, Literature
WANG, ZHIWEN, Physics and Electronic Technology
WEI, HUAZHONG, Education
WU, DESHENG, Literature
WU, ZHIHUA, Life Science
XIE, JINGFANG, History and Tourism
XIE, LIN, Mathematics
XIE, MINGJIE, Life Science
XU, YINGJUN, Foreign Languages
YAN, BANGYI, Literature
YAN, ZHILI, Sports
YANG, HONG, Life Science
YANG, LIZHU, Education
YANG, MING, Education
YANG, XIAO, Education
YANG, XIUXIANG, Politics
YANG, YINGJIE, History and Tourism
YANG, ZHONGZHI, Chemistry and Chemical Engineering
YI, HUAINING, City and Environment Studies
YOU, WANSHENG, Chemistry and Chemical Engineering
YU, BING, Literature
YU, DAHUA, History and Tourism
YU, PEILING, Law
YU, WENQIAN, Sports
YUAN, XUEHAI, Mathematics
YUE, ZHONGXING, Physics and Electronic Technology
ZHANG, AIJUN, Politics
ZHANG, GUICHUN, Education
ZHANG, GUIREN, Politics
ZHANG, LIHUA, Education
ZHANG, NINGSHENG, Education
ZHANG, QI, Education
ZHANG, SHUMIN, Chemistry and Chemical Engineering
ZHANG, WEIDONG, Life Science
ZHANG, XIAONING, Foreign Languages
ZHANG, YAOGUANG, City and Environment Studies
ZHAO, YI, History and Tourism
ZHAO, YUBAO, History and Tourism
ZHAO, ZHENYING, History and Tourism

ZHAO, ZHONGWEN, Management
ZHONG, GUIQING, City and Environment Studies
ZHOU, DANHONG, Chemistry and Chemical Engineering
ZHOU, WEI, Life Science
ZHOU, XIAOYAN, Education
ZHOU, ZHIQIANG, Politics
ZHU, NINGBO, Education
ZHU, ZHIJUN, Politics

LIAONING TECHNICAL UNIVERSITY

Fu Xin 3350461, Liaoning
Internet: www.lntu.edu.cn
Founded 1958
State control
Academic year: September to July
Constituent colleges and depts in the following areas: architecture and civil engineering; business management; electrical and information engineering; electrical engineering; foreign languages; geomatics engineering; journalism and communication; materials science and engineering; mechanical engineering; mechanics and engineering sciences; politics and law resources and environmental engineering; software; technology and economics
Pres.: SHI JINFENG
Vice-Pres: MA ZHUANG, PAN YISHAN, SHAO LIANGBIN, WANG JIREN, ZHANG SHUSEN, ZHANG ZUOGANG
Head of Graduate Dept: LIANG BING
Librarian: LIE JIE
Number of teachers: 1,349
Number of students: 25,000
Publications: *Journal* (natural sciences, 6 a year), *Journal* (social sciences, 4 a year)

PROFESSORS

FU, XINGWU, Electrical Engineering
GUO, FENGYI, Electrical Engineering
HUI, XIAOWEI, Electrical and Information Engineering
LI, WEIDONG, Electrical Engineering
LI, XIAOZHU, Electrical Engineering
LI, YIJIE, Electrical and Information Engineering
LI, ZHENGZHONG, Geomatics Engineering
LIU, JIANHUI, Electrical and Information Engineering
LU, SHIKUI, Electrical Engineering
MENG, QINGCHUN, Electrical Engineering
QIAO, YANGWEN, Geomatics Engineering
SONG, WEIDONG, Geomatics Engineering
SUN, JINGUANG, Electrical and Information Engineering
SUN, PENGYONG, Electrical and Information Engineering
WANG, JIAGUI, Geomatics Engineering
WANG, YUFENG, Electrical Engineering
XING, BAOJUN, Electrical Engineering
YE, JINGLOU, Electrical and Information Engineering
YE, JINGLOU, Electrical Engineering
ZHAO, GUOCAI, Electrical Engineering
ZHAO, GUOQIANG, Electrical Engineering
ZHU, HUA, Electrical Engineering

NANCHANG UNIVERSITY

235 Nanjing East Rd, Nanchang 330047, Jiangxi Province
Telephone: (791) 8305499
Fax: (791) 8305835
Internet: www.ncu.edu.cn
Founded 1940
State control
Academic year: September to July
Pres.: ZHOU WENBIN
Vice-Pres: CHENG YANGGUO, FU MINGFU, GAN XIAOQING, LI JIANMIN, LIU SANQIU, SHAO HONG, XIE MINGYONG

Head of Graduate Dept: LI MING
Librarian: HE XIAOPING
Number of teachers: 1,253
Number of students: 45,000
Publications: *Journal* (engineering and technology, 4 a year), *Journal* (humanities and social sciences, 6 a year), *Journal* (natural sciences, 4 a year)

DEANS

Centre for Public Administration Programmes: TAO XUERONG
College of Architectural Engineering: GUI GUOQING
College of Art and Design: XIONG MANLING
College of Information Engineering: CHEN KEN
College of Life Sciences: ZHU YOULIN
College of Mechanics and Engineering: LIU HESHENG
College of Natural Science: LIU NIANHUA
College of Science and Technology: HE JIESHAN
College of Software: LU XIAOYONG
School of Chemistry and Materials Science: ZHOU LANG
School of Economics and Management: YIN JIDONG
School of Environmental Science and Engineering: HU ZHAOJI
School of Foreign Languages: FANG KEPING
School of Humanities and Social Sciences: LI DONGNI

PROFESSORS

BAO, ZHONGXU, Mechanics and Engineering
CAO, DEHE, Humanities and Social Sciences
CAO, YUSHENG, Life Sciences
CHEN, DONGYOU, Humanities and Social Sciences
CHEN, XINLING, Humanities and Social Sciences
DENG, SHUILAN, Economics and Management
DENG, ZEYUAN, Life Sciences
FU, XIAOLONG, Art and Design
GAO, GUOZHEN, Mechanics and Engineering
GAO, YINYU, Life Sciences
GONG, LIANSHOU, Humanities and Social Sciences
GU, XINGBIN, Humanities and Social Sciences
GU, ZHENGSHI, Mechanics and Engineering
HE, CHENGHONG, Mechanics and Engineering
HE, YUN, Economics and Management
HU, PING, Humanities and Social Sciences
HU, QING, Humanities and Social Sciences
HU, ZHAOJI, Environmental Science and Engineering
HUANG, JIHUA, Mechanics and Engineering
HUANG, XIJIA, Economics and Management
HUANG, XINJIAN, Economics and Management
JIANG, BOQUAN, Environmental Science and Engineering
JIANG, SHUISHENG, Mechanics and Engineering
JIN, LAHUA, Environmental Science and Engineering
LI, CHENGGUI, Humanities and Social Sciences
LI, DONGNI, Humanities and Social Sciences
LI, SHENGMEI, Humanities and Social Sciences
LI, XIANTAN, Economics and Management
LIN, BO, Environmental Science and Engineering
LIU, HESHENG, Mechanics and Engineering
LIU, LUNXIN, Humanities and Social Sciences
LIU, NIANHUA, Natural Science
LIU, QIJING, Environmental Science and Engineering
LIU, RENSHENG, Humanities and Social Sciences
LIU, WEIDONG, Mechanics and Engineering
LIU, XIAOHONG, Environmental Science and Engineering

LIU, XIAOQIN, Art and Design
LIU, YING, Mechanics and Engineering
LU, BINGFU, Humanities and Social Sciences
LU, SHENGPING, Art and Design
LU, XIANFENG, Mechanics and Engineering
LU, XIAOYONG, Economics and Management
LU, XIXING, Humanities and Social Sciences
MA, WEI, Economics and Management
NI, YONGNIAN, Life Sciences
PENG, DIYUN, Economics and Management
QIU, ZUMIN, Environmental Science and Engineering
RUAN, RONGSHENG, Life Sciences
SUN, RISHENG, Environmental Science and Engineering
SUN, YONG, Art and Design
WAN, FANGZHEN, Humanities and Social Sciences
WAN, JINBAO, Environmental Science and Engineering
WANG, DEBAO, Humanities and Social Sciences
WANG, LIANGSHENG, Art and Design
WANG, XIANGYANG, Art and Design
WANG, ZHEPING, Humanities and Social Sciences
WEI, LI, Economics and Management
WEN, SHIHUA, Humanities and Social Sciences
WU, LUSHEN, Mechanics and Engineering
WU, XIAOWEI, Humanities and Social Sciences
XIAO, ANKUN, Mechanics and Engineering
XIE, MINGYONG, Life Sciences
XIE, YONG, Economics and Management
XIN, YONG, Mechanics and Engineering
XIONG, JIANXIN, Art and Design
XIONG, MANLING, Art and Design
XIONG, RUIWEN, Mechanics and Engineering
XIONG, XIANGHUI, Mechanics and Engineering
XU, YANG, Life Sciences
YANG, GUOTAI, Mechanics and Engineering
YANG, MINGLANG, Art and Design
YANG, XUECHUN, Mechanics and Engineering
YANG, XUEPIN, Humanities and Social Sciences
YAO, YAPING, Humanities and Social Sciences
YI, PING, Humanities and Social Sciences
YIN, JIDONG, Economics and Management
YIN, XINGFAN, Humanities and Social Sciences
YING, YULONG, Life Sciences
YU, RANGYAO, Humanities and Social Sciences
YUAN, LIHUA, Humanities and Social Sciences
ZHAN, ZHIYOU, Humanities and Social Sciences
ZHANG, HUA, Mechanics and Engineering
ZHANG, NING, Natural Science
ZHANG, RENMU, Humanities and Social Sciences
ZHANG, SHENGYANG, Humanities and Social Sciences
ZHANG, YUMING, Economics and Management
ZHANG, YUSHENG, Humanities and Social Sciences
ZHANG, ZHIYONG, Humanities and Social Sciences
ZHAO, LIQIU, Economics and Management
ZHENG, DIANMO, Environmental Science and Engineering
ZHENG, WEIXIAN, Life Sciences
ZHENG, XIANGQING, Economics and Management
ZHENG, XIAOJIANG, Humanities and Social Sciences
ZHOU, GUOFA, Environmental Science and Engineering
ZHOU, PINGYUAN, Humanities and Social Sciences
ZHOU, SHU, Art and Design
ZHOU, TIANRUI, Mechanics and Engineering
ZHOU, WENBIN, Environmental Science and Engineering

ZHOU, YAOWANG, Humanities and Social Sciences
ZHU, CHUANXI, Natural Science

NANJING UNIVERSITY

22 Hankou Rd, Nanjing 210093, Jiangsu
Telephone: (25) 3593186
Fax: (25) 3302728
Internet: www.nju.edu.cn
Founded 1902
State control
Language of instruction: Chinese
Academic year: September to June
Pres.: JIANG SHUSHENG
Vice-Pres: CHEN JUN, HON YINXING, MIN TIEJUN, SHIN JIANJUN, ZHANG DALIANG, ZHANG YIBIN
Librarian: QIAN CHENGDAN
Number of teachers: 2,400
Number of students: 27,000

Publications: *Approximation Theory and its Application, Contemporary Foreign Literature, Geology in Higher Education, Journal* (humanities and social sciences), *Journal* (natural sciences), *Journal of Computer Science, Journal of Inorganic Chemistry, Mathematics in Higher Education, Mathematics Review* (2 a year), *Progress in Physics, Research in Higher Education*

DEANS

Adult Education School: WANG JIANQIANG
Graduate School: CHEN CHONGQING
International Business School: ZHAO SHUMING
Medical School: HAN XIAODONG
School of Chemistry and Chemical Engineering: PAM YI
School of Foreign Studies: WANG SHOUREN
School of Geoscience: WANG YING
School of Humanities: DONG JIAN
School of Intensive Instruction in Sciences and Liberal Arts: LU DEXIN
School of Law: SHAO JIANDONG (acting)
School of Life Science: ZHANG HONGZU
School of Natural Sciences: GONG CHANGDE
School of Technology: SUN ZHONGXIU

NANJING UNIVERSITY OF AERONAUTICS AND ASTRONAUTICS

29 Yudao Rd, Nanjing 210016, Jiangsu Province
Telephone: (25) 4892424
Fax: (25) 4891512
E-mail: office@nuaa.edu.cn
Internet: www.njmu.edu.cn
Founded 1952
Academic year: September to July
Pres.: HU HAIYAN
Vice-Pres: CHEN XIACHU, LIANG DEWANG, NIE HONG, WANG GUINONG, WANG YONGLIANG, WU QINGXIAN, WU YIZHAO
Head of Graduate Dept: HU HAIYAN
Librarian: HUANG YINHUI
Number of teachers: 1,300
Number of students: 22,725
Publication: *Journal* (6 a year)

DEANS

College of Advanced Vocational Education: JIANG WEI
College of Aerospace Engineering: XU XIWU
College of Art: LIU CANMING
College of Automation Engineering: LIU JIANYE
College of Civil Aviation: SHEN YUANKANG
College of Economics and Management: LIU SIFENG
College of Energy and Power Engineering: ZHANG JINGZHOU

College of Humanities and Social Sciences: WANG YAN
College of Information Science and Technology: BEN DE
College of Material Science and Engineering: TAO JIE
College of Mechanical Engineering: ZHU DI
College of Natural Sciences: YAN XIAOHONG

PROFESSORS

AI, JUN, Aerospace Engineering
AN, YUKUN, Natural Sciences
ANG, HAISONG, Aerospace Engineering
BAO, MING, Aerospace Engineering
BAO, MINGBAO, Humanities and Social Sciences
CAI, QIMING, Economics and Management
CAO, YUNFENG, Automation Engineering
CHANG, HAIPING, Energy and Power Engineering
CHE, GUANGJI, Art
CHEN, DA, Material Science and Engineering
CHEN, DAOLIAN, Automation Engineering
CHEN, GUOPING, Aerospace Engineering
CHEN, HONGQUAN, Aerospace Engineering
CHEN, HUAIHAI, Aerospace Engineering
CHEN, QI, Economics and Management
CHEN, QIAN, Aerospace Engineering
CHEN, RENLIANG, Aerospace Engineering
CHEN, SONGCAN, Information Science and Technology
CHEN, WEI, Energy and Power Engineering
CHEN, XIN, Automation Engineering
CHEN, ZHILIANG, Aerospace Engineering
DANG, YAOGUO, Economics and Management
DENG, ZHIQUAN, Automation Engineering
DING, QIULIN, Information Science and Technology
DING, YUNLIANG, Aerospace Engineering
DU, JIDA, Aerospace Engineering
FAN, YINHE, Energy and Power Engineering
FANG, XIANDE, Aerospace Engineering
GAN, MINLIANG, Civil Aviation
GAO, DEPING, Energy and Power Engineering
GAO, DEPING, Civil Aviation
GAO, ZHENG, Aerospace Engineering
GE, NING, Energy and Power Engineering
GONG, CHUNYING, Automation Engineering
GU, HONGBIN, Civil Aviation
GU, ZHIMING, Natural Sciences
GU, ZHONGQUAN, Aerospace Engineering
GUAN, DE, Aerospace Engineering
GUO, RONGWEI, Energy and Power Engineering
GUO, WANLIN, Aerospace Engineering
HAN, JINGLONG, Aerospace Engineering
HE, JIANGSHENG, Humanities and Social Sciences
HE, JIANPING, Material Science and Engineering
HU, HAIYAN, Aerospace Engineering
HU, JUN, Energy and Power Engineering
HU, MINGHUA, Civil Aviation
HU, MINGMIN, Aerospace Engineering
HUANG, HULIN, Energy and Power Engineering
HUANG, JINQUAN, Energy and Power Engineering
HUANG, MINGGE, Aerospace Engineering
HUANG, SHENGGUO, Civil Aviation
HUANG, SHULA, Art
HUANG, ZAIXING, Aerospace Engineering
HUANG, ZHENGXIN, Humanities and Social Sciences
JI, HONGHU, Energy and Power Engineering
JIANG, BIN, Automation Engineering
JIANG, KESHEN, Economics and Management
LI, BANGYI, Economics and Management
LI, DONG, Humanities and Social Sciences
LI, NAN, Economics and Management
LI, PENGTONG, Natural Sciences
LI, SHUNMING, Energy and Power Engineering
LI, ZIQUAN, Material Science and Engineering
LI, ZONGZHI, Humanities and Social Sciences

LIAN, QIANGUI, Humanities and Social Sciences
LIANG, DAKAI, Aerospace Engineering
LIANG, DEWANG, Energy and Power Engineering
LIU, CANMING, Art
LIU, RENPEI, Material Science and Engineering
LIU, SIFENG, Economics and Management
LIU, WEIHUA, Aerospace Engineering
LIU, XIANBIN, Aerospace Engineering
LIU, YIPING, Economics and Management
LIU, YU, Information Science and Technology
LU, LIZHI, Humanities and Social Sciences
MA, JIE, Humanities and Social Sciences
MENG, FANCHAO, Humanities and Social Sciences
MIAO, JIANJUN, Humanities and Social Sciences
MING, XIAO, Aerospace Engineering
NIE, HONG, Aerospace Engineering
NING, XUANXI, Economics and Management
PENG, CAN, Economics and Management
QIAN, XIAOLIN, Information Science and Technology
RUAN, XINBO, Automation Engineering
SHENG, SONGBO, Natural Sciences
SHI, YUNLONG, Humanities and Social Sciences
SONG, BAOYIN, Aerospace Engineering
SONG, YINGDONG, Energy and Power Engineering
SUN, JIANGUO, Energy and Power Engineering
SUN, JIUHOU, Aerospace Engineering
SUN, LIANGXIN, Aerospace Engineering
TAN, QINGMEI, Humanities and Social Sciences
TANG, DENGBIN, Aerospace Engineering
TAO, JIE, Material Science and Engineering
TONG, MINGBO, Aerospace Engineering
WANG, CAIYONG, Art
WANG, HUAMING, Aerospace Engineering
WANG, JIANDONG, Information Science and Technology
WANG, KAIFU, Aerospace Engineering
WANG, LUJIE, Humanities and Social Sciences
WANG, XINWEI, Aerospace Engineering
WANG, YAN, Humanities and Social Sciences
WANG, YONGLIANG, Aerospace Engineering
WEI, MINXIANG, Energy and Power Engineering
WEN, WEIDONG, Energy and Power Engineering
WU, DAIZHAO, Aerospace Engineering
WU, DINGMIN, Humanities and Social Sciences
WU, WENLONG, Aerospace Engineering
XIA, HONGSHAN, Civil Aviation
XIA, PINQI, Aerospace Engineering
XIAO, JUN, Material Science and Engineering
XIAO, PING, Humanities and Social Sciences
XIE, SHAOJUN, Automation Engineering
XING, YAN, Automation Engineering
XIONG, KE, Aerospace Engineering
XU, DAZHUAN, Information Science and Technology
XU, GUOHUA, Aerospace Engineering
XU, JINFA, Aerospace Engineering
XU, QIANG, Humanities and Social Sciences
XU, ZONGZE, Information Science and Technology
YANG, LILI, Art
YAO, WEIXING, Aerospace Engineering
YE, ZHIFENG, Energy and Power Engineering
YIN, HONGYOU, Natural Sciences
YU, XIONGQING, Aerospace Engineering
YU, XIWU, Aerospace Engineering
YUAN, SHENFANG, Aerospace Engineering
YUE, QIN, Natural Sciences
ZHANG, BUREN, Humanities and Social Sciences
ZHANG, CHENGLIN, Aerospace Engineering
ZHANG, GUODAI, Natural Sciences

ZHANG, JINGZHOU, Energy and Power Engineering
ZHANG, KUNYUAN, Energy and Power Engineering
ZHANG, LINGMI, Aerospace Engineering
ZHANG, LUMING, Natural Sciences
ZHANG, ZENGCHANG, Aerospace Engineering
ZHAO, CHUNSHENG, Aerospace Engineering
ZHAO, JIANXING, Energy and Power Engineering
ZHAO, MIN, Automation Engineering
ZHAO, NING, Aerospace Engineering
ZHAO, YOUQUN, Energy and Power Engineering
ZHENG, QI, Art
ZHENG, SHIJIE, Aerospace Engineering
ZHOU, CHUANRONG, Aerospace Engineering
ZHOU, DEQUN, Economics and Management
ZHOU, JIANJIANG, Information Science and Technology
ZHOU, LI, Aerospace Engineering
ZHU, JIANYING, Civil Aviation
ZHU, JINDONG, Humanities and Social Sciences
ZHU, JINFU, Civil Aviation
ZHU, WUJIA, Information Science and Technology
ZHU, ZHAODA, Information Science and Technology
ZUO, HONGFU, Civil Aviation

NANJING AGRICULTURAL UNIVERSITY

1 Weigang Rd, Nanjing 210095, Jiangsu Province
Telephone: (8625) 84395366
Internet: www.njau.edu.cn
Founded 1952
Min. of Education control
Academic year: September to July
Pres.: ZHENG XIAOBO
Vice-Pres: CAO WEIXING, QU FUTIAN, SUN JIAN, WANG YAONAN, XU XIANG, ZHOU GUANGHONG
Librarian: GAO RONGHUA
Number of teachers: 2,400
Number of students: 24,000
Publications: *Agricultural Education of China* (6 a year), *Agricultural History of China* (4 a year), *Animal Husbandry and Veterinary Science* (6 a year), *Chinese Animal Products and Food* (6 a year), *Journal* (natural sciences, 4 a year), *Journal* (social sciences, 4 a year)

DEANS

College of Adult Education: XU XIANG
College of Agronomy: WAN JIANMIN
College of Animal Science and Technology: WANG TIAN
College of Economics and Management: ZHONG FUNING
College of Engineering: DING WEIMIN
College of Food Science and Technology: LU ZHAOXIN
College of Foreign Studies: XU XIANG
College of Horticulture: XILIN HOU
College of Humanities and Social Sciences: WANG SIMING
College of Information Science and Technology: GAO RONGHUA
College of International Education: YAN ZHIMING
College of Life Sciences: XU LANGLAI
College of Plant Protection: HAN ZHAOJUN
College of Public Management (incorporating College of Land Management): (vacant)
College of Resources and Environmental Sciences: SHEN QIRONG
College of Science: YANG CHUNLONG
College of Veterinary Medicine: ZOU SIXIANG
Graduate School: ZHENG XIAOBO

PROFESSORS

BAO, ENDONG, Veterinary Medicine
BIAN, XINMIN, Agronomy
CAI, QINGSHENG, Agronomy
CAI, QINGSHENG, Life Sciences
CAO, WEIXING, Agronomy
CHEN, FUYAN, Veterinary Medicine
CHEN, JIE, Veterinary Medicine
CHEN, JINFENG, Horticulture
CHEN, MAO, Humanities and Social Sciences
CHEN, QIUSHENG, Veterinary Medicine
CHEN, WANMING, Economics and Management
CHEN, WEIHUA, Veterinary Medicine
CHEN, WENLIN, Humanities and Social Sciences
CHEN, XIAOMIN, Resources and Environmental Sciences
CHENG, CHUNYOU, Foreign Languages
CHU, BAOJIN, Economics and Management
DAI, HAOGUO, Plant Protection
DENG, ZHAOCHUN, Foreign Languages
DING, WEIMIN, Engineering
DONG, MINGSHENG, Food Science and Technology
DONG, SHUANGLIN, Plant Protection
GAI, JUNYI, Agronomy
GAO, GUANG, Land Science
GE, JIQI, Land Management
GONG, YIQIN, Horticulture
GU, HUANZHANG, Economics and Management
GU, ZHENXIN, Food Science and Technology
GUAN, HENGLU, Humanities and Social Sciences
GUO, JIANHUA, Plant Protection
GUO, QIAOSHENG, Horticulture
GUO, SHIRONG, Horticulture
GUO, WEIMING, Horticulture
HAN, ZHAOJUN, Plant Protection
HONG, XIAOYUE, Plant Protection
HOU, GUANGXU, Foreign Languages
HOU, HANQING, Information Science and Technology
HOU, JIAFA, Veterinary Medicine
HOU, XILIN, Horticulture
HU, FENG, Resources and Environmental Sciences
HU, JINBO, Humanities and Social Sciences
HU, QIUHUI, Food Science and Technology
HU, YUANLIANG, Veterinary Medicine
HUANG, KEHE, Veterinary Medicine
HUANG, SHUIQING, Information Science and Technology
HUANG, WEIYI, Resources and Environmental Sciences
HUANG, YAO, Resources and Environmental Sciences
HUI, FUPING, Humanities and Social Sciences
JI, CHANGYING, Engineering
JIANG, HANHU, Food Science and Technology
JIANG, MINGYI, Life Sciences
JIANG, PING, Veterinary Medicine
LAN, YEQING, Land Science
LEI, ZHIHAI, Veterinary Medicine
LI, BAOPING, Plant Protection
LI, SHUNPENG, Resources and Environmental Sciences
LI, XIANGRUI, Veterinary Medicine
LI, YANGHAN, Agronomy
LI, YUEYUN, Economics and Management
LIANG, YONGCHAO, Resources and Environmental Sciences
LIN, MAOSONG, Plant Protection
LIU, BAOJIN, Economics and Management
LIU, DAJUN, Agronomy
LIU, DEHUI, Resources and Environmental Sciences
LIU, HONGLIN, Animal Science and Technology
LIU, LEI, Information Science and Technology
LIU, YOULIANG, Agronomy
LIU, YOUZHAO, Land Management
LIU, ZHAOPU, Resources and Environmental Sciences

LU, CHENGPING, Veterinary Medicine
LU, DAXIN, Engineering
LU, ZHAOXIN, Food Science and Technology
LU, ZUOMEI, Agronomy
LUO, WEIHONG, Agronomy
MA, KAI, Horticulture
MENG, LING, Plant Protection
MENG, LINGJIE, Economics and Management
NIU, YOUQI, Information Science and Technology
OU, MINGHAO, Land Management
PAN, GENXIN, Resources and Environmental Sciences
PAN, JIANJUN, Resources and Environmental Sciences
PENG, JISHENG, Humanities and Social Sciences
PENG, ZENGQI, Food Science and Technology
QIANG, SHENG, Agronomy
QIANG, SHENG, Life Sciences
QIN, LIJUN, Foreign Languages
QU, FUTIAN, Land Management
SHEN, JINLIANG, Plant Protection
SHEN, QIRONG, Resources and Environmental Sciences
SHEN, YIXIN, Animal Science and Technology
SHEN, YONGLIN, Veterinary Medicine
SHEN, ZHENGUO, Agronomy
SHEN, ZHENGUO, Life Sciences
SHENG, BANGYUE, Humanities and Social Sciences
SUN, HANGSHENG, Economics and Management
SUN, JIN, Resources and Environmental Sciences
TANG, YIZU, Agronomy
TU, KANG, Food Science and Technology
WANG, GENLIN, Animal Science and Technology
WANG, GUOJIE, Veterinary Medicine
WANG, HUAIMING, Economics and Management
WANG, JIANMIN, Agronomy
WANG, JINSHENG, Plant Protection
WANG, KAI, Economics and Management
WANG, KERONG, Plant Protection
WANG, LINYUN, Animal Science and Technology
WANG, RONG, Economics and Management
WANG, SIMING, Humanities and Social Sciences
WANG, TIAN, Animal Science and Technology
WANG, WANMAO, Land Management
WANG, XIAOHUA, Engineering
WANG, XIAOLONG, Veterinary Medicine
WANG, YINQUAN, Foreign Languages
WANG, YUQUAN, Land Science
WHONG, ZHIWEI, Resources and Environmental Sciences
WU, QINSHENG, Horticulture
WU, YIDONG, Plant Protection
WU, YULIN, Economics and Management
XIE, ZHUANG, Animal Science and Technology
XU, JIANHUA, Plant Protection
XU, LIANGLAI, Life Sciences
XU, LIREN, Veterinary Medicine
XU, XIANG, Economics and Management
XU, YIWEN, Humanities and Social Sciences
YAN, HUOQI, Humanities and Social Sciences
YAN, PEISHI, Animal Science and Technology
YANG, HONG, Land Science
YANG, LIANFANG, Plant Protection
YANG, LIGUO, Animal Science and Technology
YANG, MINGMIN, Land Science
YANG, QING, Veterinary Medicine
YANG, QING, Life Sciences
YANG, SHIHU, Agronomy
YANG, ZHIMIN, Life Sciences
YE, YIGUANG, Economics and Management
YIN, WENQING, Engineering
YING, RUIYAO, Economics and Management
YU, DEYUE, Agronomy
ZHAI, BAOPING, Plant Protection
ZHANG, BING, Economics and Management
ZHANG, CHUNLAN, Resources and Environmental Sciences

ZHANG, FANG, Humanities and Social Sciences
ZHANG, GUOTAI, Agronomy
ZHANG, HAIBIN, Veterinary Medicine
ZHANG, HONGSHENG, Agronomy
ZHANG, JINGSHUN, Economics and Management
ZHANG, RONGXIAN, Agronomy
ZHANG, SHAOLING, Horticulture
ZHANG, SHUXIA, Veterinary Medicine
ZHANG, TIANZHEN, Agronomy
ZHANG, WEIQIANG, Engineering
ZHANG, ZHEN, Horticulture
ZHAO, RUQIAN, Veterinary Medicine
ZHENG, XIAOBO, Plant Protection
ZHENG, YONGHUA, Food Science and Technology
ZHONG, FUNING, Economics and Management
ZHOU, GUANGHONG, Food Science and Technology
ZHOU, LIXIANG, Resources and Environmental Sciences
ZHOU, MINGGUO, Plant Protection
ZHOU, SHUDONG, Economics and Management
ZHOU, YINGHENG, Economics and Management
ZHU, JUN, Life Sciences
ZHU, SIHONG, Engineering
ZHU, WEIYUN, Animal Science and Technology
ZHU, YUELIN, Horticulture
ZONG, LIANGGANG, Resources and Environmental Sciences
ZOU, SIXIANG, Veterinary Medicine

NANJING UNIVERSITY OF ECONOMICS

128 Tielubeijie, Nanjing 210003
Telephone: (25) 3418207
Fax: (25) 3418207
Internet: www.njue.edu.cn
Founded 1956, present status 1981
State control
Academic year: September to July
President: Dr XU CONGCAI
Vice-Presidents: GAO YADONG, LI SHIHUA, WANG JIAXIN, WANG SUITING, ZHANG ZHENGGANG
Librarian: DING DAKE
Library: over 500,000 vols
Number of teachers: 565
Number of students: 5,600 (incl. correspondence courses 3,000)
Publication: *Journal of Nanjing University of Economics.*

NANJING FORESTRY UNIVERSITY

9 Xinzhuang, Longpan Rd, Nanjing 210037, Jiangsu Province
Telephone: (25) 85427131
Fax: (25) 85412389
E-mail: interpro@njfu.edu.cn
Internet: www.njfu.edu.cn
Founded 1952
Pres.: Prof. YU SHIYUAN
Vice-Pres: Prof. CAI FULIANG, Prof. ZHANG SHUQAN, Prof. SHI JISEN
Librarian: LIU XIUHUA
Library of 600,000 vols
Number of teachers: 731
Number of students: 4,000 (incl. 274 postgraduates)
Publications: *Bamboo Research, China Forestry Science and Technology, Forestry Energy Conservation, Interior Design and Construction, Journal of Nanjing Forestry University*

HEADS OF COLLEGES AND DEPARTMENTS
Adult Education: Prof. GUAN SUQI

Basic Courses Division: Assoc. Prof. WEI SHUGUANG
Chemical Engineering: Prof. AN XINNAN
Civil Engineering: Prof. ZHAO CHEN
Forest Economics and Management: Prof. CHEN GUOLIANG
Forest Resources and Environment: Prof. CAO FULIANG
Graduate Studies: Prof. YE JIANREN
Mechanical and Electronic Engineering: Prof. ZHOU YONGZHAO
Social Sciences Division: Assoc. Prof. WANG GUOPIN
Wood Science and Technology: Prof. TAN SHOUXIA

PROFESSORS
CHEN GUOLIANG, Forest Economics
CHEN ZHI, Chemical Processing of Forest Products
HUA YUKUN, Wood Processing
LI ZHONGZHENG, Chemical Processing of Forest Products
SHEN GUANFU, Forest Mechanics
SU JINYUN, Forest Engineering
XIONG WENYUE, Forest Ecology
ZHU ZHENGDE, Forest Botany

NANJING MEDICAL UNIVERSITY

140 Hanzhong Rd, Nanjing 210029, Jiangsu Province
Telephone: (25) 6649141
Fax: (25) 6612696
E-mail: xiaoban@njmu.edu.cn
Internet: www.njmu.edu.cn
Founded 1934
Academic year: September to July
Pres.: CHEN QI
Vice-Pres: HU GANG, HUANG JUN, QU ZHAOMIN, XU YAOCHU, WANG XINRU
Librarian: ZHANG ZHENGHUI
Library of 1,040,330 vols
Number of teachers: 1,148
Number of students: 7,283
Publications: *Jiangsu Medical Journal* (12 a year), *Journal* (6 a year), *Journal of Clinical Neurology* (6 a year)

DEANS
First Clinical Medical College: HUANG JUN
Second Clinical Medical College: LIU HUI
Third Clinical Medical College: (vacant)
School of Basic Medical Science: ZHU CHANGLIANG
School of Health Policy and Management: MENG GUOXIANG
School of Medicine: ZHU DONGYA
School of Nursing: CUI YAN
School of Public Health: ZHOU JIANWEI

PROFESSORS
BI, ZHIGANG, Clinical Medicine I
BIAN, JIAYI, Medicine
CAI, YI, Clinical Medicine II
CAO, KEJIANG, Clinical Medicine I
CHANG, YI, Clinical Medicine II
CHEN, GUANGMING, Clinical Medicine I
CHEN, GUOYU, Clinical Medicine I
CHEN, RONGHUA, Clinical Medicine II
CHEN, XIWEI, Basic Medical Science
CHEN, YIJIANG, Clinical Medicine I
CHEN, YULIAN, Public Health
CHENG, YUNLIN, Clinical Medicine I
DE, WEI, Basic Medical Science
DING, JIONG, Basic Medical Science
DING, XINSHENG, Clinical Medicine I
FAN, QINHE, Clinical Medicine I
FAN, WEIMING, Clinical Medicine I
FU, CHENGZHANG, Clinical Medicine I
FU, ZHENG, Clinical Medicine I
HU, GUANG, Basic Medical Science
HU, QIN, Medicine
HU, WEIXING, Clinical Medicine I

HUANG, JUN, Clinical Medicine I
HUANG, ZHUHU, Clinical Medicine I
LI, GUOPING, Clinical Medicine I
LI, JIANAN, Clinical Medicine I
LI, JUN, Clinical Medicine II
LI, SHENGNAN, Basic Medical Science
LI, YUEHUA, Basic Medical Science
LI, ZUOHAN, Clinical Medicine II
LIU, CHAO, Clinical Medicine I
LIU, JIAYIN, Clinical Medicine I
LIU, QIZHAN, Public Health
LIU, XUNLIANG, Clinical Medicine I
LU, FENGXIANG, Clinical Medicine I
LUO, DAN, Clinical Medicine I
MA, WENZHU, Clinical Medicine I
MENG, GUOXIANG, Health Policy and Management
MIAO, YI, Clinical Medicine I
NI, CHUNHUI, Public Health
QI, XIAOHONG, Basic Medical Science
SHUN, NANXIONG, Clinical Medicine I
SHUN, YUJIE, Basic Medical Science
TANG, LINGFANG, Public Health
WANG, DEFANG, Clinical Medicine I
WANG, HEMIN, Basic Medical Science
WANG, HONG, Clinical Medicine I
WANG, SHOULIN, Public Health
WANG, XIAOYUN, Clinical Medicine I
WANG, XINRU, Public Health
WANG, XUEHAO, Clinical Medicine I
WANG, YINGWEI, Basic Medical Science
WANG, YONG, Basic Medical Science
WANG, YUBIN, Clinical Medicine I
WEI, BAIQI, Medicine
WU, HAIWEI, Basic Medical Science
WU, HONGFEI, Clinical Medicine I
WU, JINCHANG, Clinical Medicine I
WU, WENXI, Clinical Medicine I
WU, ZHENGYAN, Clinical Medicine I
XIAO, HANG, Public Health
XU, QUNWEI, Medicine
XU, XINRONG, Clinical Medicine I
YIN, KAISHENG, Clinical Medicine I
ZHANG, FUMIN, Clinical Medicine I
ZHANG, HAIDI, Clinical Medicine I
ZHANG, JINAN, Clinical Medicine I
ZHANG, QI, Public Health
ZHANG, YIDONG, Clinical Medicine II
ZHANG, ZHENGDONG, Public Health
ZHANG, ZHONGNAN, Clinical Medicine I
ZHAO, ZHIQUAN, Clinical Medicine I
ZHOU, JIANWEI, Public Health
ZHOU, XUEMIN, Medicine
ZHOU, ZUOMING, Basic Medical Science
ZHU, CHANGLIANG, Basic Medical Science
ZHU, DONGYA, Medicine
ZHU, GUOQING, Basic Medical Science
ZHU, WENYUAN, Clinical Medicine I

NANJING INSTITUTE OF METEOROLOGY

114 Pancheng New Street, Nanjing 210044, Jiangsu Province
Telephone: (25) 8731102
Fax: (25) 7792648
E-mail: nimemail@nim02.njim.edu.cn
Internet: www.njim.edu.cn
Founded 1960
State control
Languages of instruction: Chinese, English
Academic year: September to July
Pres.: SUN ZHAOBO
Vice-Pres.: LU WEISONG
Dean: ZHAO XUEYU
Chief Administrative Officer: XU KAI
Librarian: PANG XINGUO
Library of 500,000 vols
Number of teachers: 450
Number of students: 8,000
Publications: *Journal* (4 a year), *Meteorological Education and Science and Technology* (4 a year).

NANJING NORMAL UNIVERSITY

122 Ninghai Rd, Nanjing 210097, Jiangsu Province

Telephone: (25) 3720999
Fax: (25) 3706565
Internet: www.njnu.edu.cn

Founded 1902
Provincial govt control
Academic year: September to August

Pres.: Prof. GONG PIXIANG
Vice-Pres: Prof. CHEN GUOJUN, Prof. CHEN LINGFU, Prof. HUANG TAO, Prof. LU BINGSHOU, Prof. TU GUOHUA, Prof. WANG XIAOPENG, Prof. ZHU XIAOMAN
Dean of Postgraduate Studies: PAN BAIQI
Librarian: WU JIN

Library of 1,650,000 vols
Number of teachers: 1,100
Number of students: 7,000 (incl. 430 postgraduates)

Publications: *Fine Arts Education in China*, *Periodicals of Nanjing Normal University* (social sciences, natural sciences), *References for Educational Research*, text books.

NANJING UNIVERSITY OF POSTS AND TELECOMMUNICATIONS

66 Xin Mofan Ma Lu, Nanjing 210003, Jiangsu Province

Telephone: (25) 3492038
Fax: (25) 3492349
E-mail: nupt@njupt.edu.cn
Internet: www.njupt.edu.cn

Founded 1942
Academic year: September to July

Pres.: XIE LING
Vice-Pres: TANG JINTU, YIE ZHANGZHAO, ZHANG SHUNYI, ZHANG XIAOQIANG
Librarian: YANG ZHUYING

Library: over 600,000 vols
Number of teachers: 768
Number of students: 7,970 (4,300 undergraduates, 270 postgraduates, 3,400 correspondence)

Publications: *Journal of Social Science*, *NUPT Periodical*

PROFESSORS

BI HOUJIE, Image Communications
CAO WEI, Microwave Communications
CHEN TINGBIAO, Information Engineering
CHEN XI SHENG, Telecommunications Engineering
FENG GUANGZENG, Satellite Communications
HU JIANZHANG, Information Engineering
JU TI, Computer Engineering Science
KAN JIAHAI, Mathematics
LI BIAOQING, Telecommunications Engineering
LUO CHANGLONG, Computer Science
MEI ZHUOCHUN, Communication and Electronic Systems
MI ZHENGKUN, Communications Engineering
QI YUSHENG, Mobile Communication
QIN TINGKAI, Electrical Engineering
SHEN JINLONG, Computer Communication
SHEN YUANLONG, Electrical Engineering
SUN JINLUN, Communications Engineering
TANG JIAYI, Computer Science
WANG SHAOLI, Computer Communication
WANG SHUOPING, Electrical Engineering
WU XINYU, Electrical Engineering
WU ZHIZHONG, Electrical Engineering
XU CHENGQI, Telecommunications Engineering
YANG ZHUYING, Electrical Engineering
YIE ZHANGZHAO, Mathematics
YU ZHAOMIN, Information Engineering
ZHANG LIJUN, Telecommunications Engineering
ZHANG SHUNYI, Computer Communications
ZHANG XIAOQIANG, Communication Systems

ZHANG ZHIYONG, Electrical Engineering
ZHANG ZONGCHENG, Information Engineering
ZHENG BAOYU, Telecommunications Engineering
ZHU XIUCHANG, Information Engineering

NANJING UNIVERSITY OF SCIENCE AND TECHNOLOGY

200 Xiao Lingwei, Nanjing 210094, Jiangsu Province

Telephone: (25) 84315567
Internet: www.njust.edu.cn

Founded 1953
Min. of Industry and Information Technology control
Academic year: September to July

Chair., Univ. Council: GENFU CHEN
Pres.: XIAOFENG WANG
Vice-Pres: DAQING MA, GANG LIU, SHANZHI YANG, WENYU SONG, XIN WANG, YIMIN XUAN, YINKANG XIANG
Head of Graduate Dept: XIN WANG
Librarian: MIN ZHAO

Number of teachers: 1,466
Number of students: 20,283

Publications: *Higher Education Digest* (12 a year), *Journal* (natural sciences, 6 a year), *Journal* (social sciences, 6 a year), *Journal of Ballistics* (4 a year), *Journal of Explosive Materials* (6 a year), *Journal of Optoelectronic Information* (6 a year)

DEANS

Department of Foreign Languages: QUAN ZHANG
Department of Materials Science and Engineering: JINCHUN MEI
School of Adult Education: YUNLEI ZHANG
School of Automation: YUMING BO
School of Chemical Engineering: LIANJUN WANG
School of Computer Science: ZHENMIN TANG
School of Economics and Management: GUANGPING HUI
School of Electronic Engineering and Optoelectronic Technology: QIAN CHEN
School of Humanities and Social Sciences: JIANPING QIAN
School of International Education: WANG QINYOU
School of Joint Education: YUZHEN KE
School of Mechanical Engineering: YONG HE
School of Natural Science: XIAOPING YANG
School of Power Engineering: HAO WANG
Vocational and Technical College: ZHANG YUEXIN

PROFESSORS

AN, LICHAO, Chemical Engineering
BO, LIANFA, Electronic Engineering and Optoelectronic Technology
BO, YUMING, Automation Engineering
CAI, CHUN, Chemical Engineering
CAO, CONGYONG, Mechanical Engineering
CHANG, BENKANG, Electronic Engineering and Optoelectronic Technology
CHEN, GUANG, Materials Science and Engineering
CHEN, GUOLIANG, Materials Science and Engineering
CHEN, HEJUAN, Mechanical Engineering
CHEN, LEI, Electronic Engineering and Optoelectronic Technology
CHEN, QIAN, Electronic Engineering and Optoelectronic Technology
CHEN, QINGWEI, Automation Engineering
CHEN, RUSHAN, Electronic Engineering and Optoelectronic Technology
CHEN, YANRU, Electronic Engineering and Optoelectronic Technology
CHENG, YI, Chemical Engineering
CUI, CHONG, Materials Science and Engineering

DAI, YUEWEI, Automation Engineering
DENG, KAIMING, Natural Science
DU, YULAN, Economics and Management
DUAN, QIJUN, Mechanical Engineering
FAN, BAOCHUN, Power Engineering
FAN, XINMIN, Materials Science and Engineering
FANG, DAGANG, Electronic Engineering and Optoelectronic Technology
FANG, ZHIJIE, Chemical Engineering
FANG, ZILIANG, Mechanical Engineering
FENG, JUNWEN, Economics and Management
GAN, LIREN, Economics and Management
GEN, JIHUI, Power Engineering
GONG, GUANGRONG, Mechanical Engineering
GU, KEQIU, Mechanical Engineering
GU, XIAOHUI, Mechanical Engineering
GUO, ZHI, Automation Engineering
HAN, YUQI, Economics and Management
HAN, ZHIJUN, Economics and Management
HAN, ZIPENG, Power Engineering
HAO, JIANCHU, Chemical Engineering
HE, ANZHI, Natural Science
HE, QIHUAN, Chemical Engineering
HE, YONG, Mechanical Engineering
HE, ZHAOJI, Humanities and Social Sciences
HOU, XIAOXIA, Automation Engineering
HOU, YUANLONG, Mechanical Engineering
HU, KAIJIE, Humanities and Social Sciences
HU, WEILI, Automation Engineering
HUANG, JIN-AN, Automation Engineering
HUANG, YINSHENG, Chemical Engineering
HUANG, ZHENGYA, Chemical Engineering
HUI, JUNMING, Chemical Engineering
HUI, XIAOHUA, Electronic Engineering and Optoelectronic Technology
JIANG, JIANFANG, Automation Engineering
JIANG, LIPING, Electronic Engineering and Optoelectronic Technology
JIANG, RENYUAN, Mechanical Engineering
JIN, ZHONG, Computer Science
KANG, XIAODONG, Economics and Management
LAN, SHAOHUA, Computer Science
LI, BAOMING, Power Engineering
LI, CHENGJUN, Chemical Engineering
LI, DONGBO, Mechanical Engineering
LI, FENGSHENG, Chemical Engineering
LI, HONGCHANG, Chemical Engineering
LI, HUIZHONG, Materials Science and Engineering
LI, XIANGYIN, Natural Science
LI, XIAONING, Mechanical Engineering
LI, XINGGUO, Electronic Engineering and Optoelectronic Technology
LI, YAJUN, Mechanical Engineering
LI, YING, Mechanical Engineering
LI, ZHENHUA, Natural Science
LIANG, RENJIE, Mechanical Engineering
LIU, DABIN, Chemical Engineering
LIU, FENGYU, Computer Science
LIU, HONGYING, Chemical Engineering
LIU, JIACONG, Chemical Engineering
LIU, KUI, Humanities and Social Sciences
LIU, ZHONG, Electronic Engineering and Optoelectronic Technology
LIU, ZULIANG, Chemical Engineering
LOU, LANGHONG, Materials Science and Engineering
LU, CHUNXU, Chemical Engineering
LU, JIAN, Natural Science
LU, JINHUI, Electronic Engineering and Optoelectronic Technology
LU, LUDE, Chemical Engineering
LU, MING, Chemical Engineering
LUO, GUOWEI, Electronic Engineering and Optoelectronic Technology
MA, DAWEI, Mechanical Engineering
MA, YIZHONG, Economics and Management
MENG, YINGJUN, Electronic Engineering and Optoelectronic Technology
MOU, SHANXIANG, Electronic Engineering and Optoelectronic Technology
NI, OUQI, Chemical Engineering
NI, XIAOWU, Natural Science
PAN, GONGPEI, Chemical Engineering

PAN, RENMING, Chemical Engineering
PAN, ZHENGWEI, Mechanical Engineering
PENG, JINHUA, Chemical Engineering
PENG, XINHUA, Chemical Engineering
PU, XIONGZHU, Mechanical Engineering
QIAN, JIANPING, Automation Engineering
QIAN, LINFANG, Mechanical Engineering
SHEN, PEIHUI, Mechanical Engineering
SHEN, RUIQI, Chemical Engineering
SHENG, ANDONG, Automation Engineering
SHI, LIANJIE, Materials Science and Engineering
SHI, TIANHUA, Economics and Management
SHI, XIANGQUAN, Electronic Engineering and Optoelectronic Technology
SONG, YAOLIANG, Electronic Engineering and Optoelectronic Technology
SUN, GUIXIANG, Humanities and Social Sciences
SUN, HUAIJIANG, Computer Science
SUN, JIANPING, Economics and Management
SUN, JINSHENG, Automation Engineering
SUN, JINTAO, Electronic Engineering and Optoelectronic Technology
SUN, YAMIN, Computer Science
SUN, YU, Mechanical Engineering
TAN, LEBIN, Mechanical Engineering
TANG, ZHENMIN, Computer Science
TAO, CHUNKAN, Electronic Engineering and Optoelectronic Technology
WANG, DAYONG, Humanities and Social Sciences
WANG, FENGYUN, Chemical Engineering
WANG, HUAKUN, Mechanical Engineering
WANG, JIANXIN, Electronic Engineering and Optoelectronic Technology
WANG, JIANYU, Automation Engineering
WANG, JINGTAO, Materials Science and Engineering
WANG, JUNDE, Chemical Engineering
WANG, KEHONG, Materials Science and Engineering
WANG, LIANGGUO, Natural Science
WANG, LIANGMING, Power Engineering
WANG, LIANGMO, Mechanical Engineering
WANG, LIANJUN, Chemical Engineering
WANG, NAIYAN, Chemical Engineering
WANG, SHUMEI, Computer Science
WANG, XIAOMING, Mechanical Engineering
WANG, XIN, Chemical Engineering
WANG, YUSHI, Mechanical Engineering
WANG, ZESHAN, Chemical Engineering
WANG, ZHIQUAN, Automation Engineering
WEI, YUNYANG, Chemical Engineering
WEI, ZHIHUI, Natural Science
WEN, CHUNSHENG, Power Engineering
WU, HUIZHONG, Computer Science
WU, JIANG, Materials Science and Engineering
WU, JUNJI, Power Engineering
WU, XIAOBEI, Automation Engineering
XIA, DESHEN, Computer Science
XIAO, HEMING, Chemical Engineering
XIONG, DANGSHENG, Materials Science and Engineering
XU, FUMING, Chemical Engineering
XU, HOUQIAN, Power Engineering
XU, JIANCHENG, Mechanical Engineering
XU, JIANZHONG, Electronic Engineering and Optoelectronic Technology
XU, MING, Chemical Engineering
XU, MINGYOU, Power Engineering
XU, SHENGYUAN, Automation Engineering
XU, WANHE, Mechanical Engineering
XU, ZHENXIANG, Chemical Engineering
XU, ZHILIANG, Automation Engineering
XUAN, YIMIN, Power Engineering
XUE, HENGXIN, Economics and Management
XUE, XIAOZHONG, Power Engineering
YAN, LIANHE, Chemical Engineering
YANG, CHENGWU, Power Engineering
YANG, DETONG, Materials Science and Engineering
YANG, SHUIYANG, Humanities and Social Sciences
YANG, SHULIN, Chemical Engineering

YANG, XIAOPING, Natural Science
YANG, XUJIE, Chemical Engineering
YANG, ZHENYU, Computer Science
YAO, JUN, Humanities and Social Sciences
YE, YOUPEI, Computer Science
YIN, XIAOCHUN, Natural Science
YIN, ZHENGZHOU, Mechanical Engineering
YU, ANPING, Economics and Management
YU, YONGGANG, Power Engineering
YUAN, JUNTANG, Mechanical Engineering
YUAN, YAXIONG, Power Engineering
ZHANG, BAOMIN, Electronic Engineering and Optoelectronic Technology
ZHANG, CHI, Chemical Engineering
ZHANG, FENG, Power Engineering
ZHANG, FUXIANG, Mechanical Engineering
ZHANG, GONGXUAN, Computer Science
ZHANG, HONG, Computer Science
ZHANG, MINGYAN, Economics and Management
ZHANG, SHAOFAN, Power Engineering
ZHANG, TIE, Mechanical Engineering
ZHANG, XI, Mechanical Engineering
ZHANG, XIAOBING, Power Engineering
ZHANG, YOULIANG, Mechanical Engineering
ZHANG, YUE, Mechanical Engineering
ZHANG, YUEJUN, Chemical Engineering
ZHANG, ZHONGLIN, Economics and Management
ZHANG, ZHONGXIONG, Electronic Engineering and Optoelectronic Technology
ZHAO, BAOCHANG, Chemical Engineering
ZHAO, CHUNXIA, Computer Science
ZHAO, HUICHANG, Electronic Engineering and Optoelectronic Technology
ZHENG, JIANGUO, Mechanical Engineering
ZHONG, QIN, Chemical Engineering
ZHOU, BOSEN, Materials Science and Engineering
ZHOU, KEDONG, Mechanical Engineering
ZHOU, SHUGE, Electronic Engineering and Optoelectronic Technology
ZHOU, WEILIANG, Chemical Engineering
ZHOU, XIANZHONG, Automation Engineering
ZHU, JINAN, Mechanical Engineering
ZHU, RIHONG, Electronic Engineering and Optoelectronic Technology
ZHU, XIANCHEN, Economics and Management
ZHU, XIAOHUA, Electronic Engineering and Optoelectronic Technology
ZOU, YUN, Automation Engineering

NANJING UNIVERSITY OF TECHNOLOGY

Gu Lou Section, 5 New Model Rd, Nanjing 210009, Jiangsu Province

Telephone: (25) 83587018
Fax: (25) 83587636
E-mail: xiaoban@njut.edu.cn
Internet: www.njut.edu.cn

Founded 1902
Dept of Education of Jiangsu Province control
Academic year: September to July

Pres.: OUYANG PINGKAI
Vice-Pres: SHU FANG, SUN CHUANSONG, SUN WEIMIN SUN, WANG JINMING, XU NANPING, ZAI JINMIN, ZHU YAO
Head of Graduate Dept: HAN PINGFANG
Librarian: ZHANG ZHENGHUI

Number of teachers: 1,000
Number of students: 23,000

Publications: *Journal* (natural sciences, 6 a year), *Journal* (social sciences, 4 a year)

DEANS

College of Architecture and Urban Planning: WU JILIANG
College of Artistic Design: LIU WEIQING
College of Automation: LIN JINGUO
College of Chemistry and Chemical Engineering: XU NANPING
College of Civil Engineering: CHEN GUOXING

College of Economics and Management: HE HONGJIN
College of Foreign Languages and International Exchange: YIN FULIN
College of Information Science and Engineering: YANG XIAOJIAN
College of Law and Politics: LI BIN
College of Life Sciences and Pharmaceutical Engineering: ZHOU HUA
College of Management Science and Engineering: NIE QIBO
College of Materials Science and Engineering: XU ZHONGZI
College of Mechanical and Power Engineering: TU SHANDONG
College of Sciences: YU BIN
College of Urban Construction, Safety and Environmental Engineering: JIANG JUNCHENG

PROFESSORS

CAI, RUIYING, Information Science and Engineering
CAI, ZHIFU, Mechanical and Power Engineering
CEI, CHENGJIAN, Information Science and Engineering
CHEN, BIAO, Mechanical and Power Engineering
CHEN, CHANGLIN, Chemistry and Chemical Engineering
CHEN, GUOXING, Civil Engineering
CHEN, HONGLING, Chemistry and Chemical Engineering
CHEN, SU, Chemistry and Chemical Engineering
CHEN, XIANYI, Materials Science and Engineering
CUI, KEQING, Mechanical and Power Engineering
CUI, QUN, Chemistry and Chemical Engineering
DAI, SHUHE, Mechanical and Power Engineering
DENG, MIN, Materials Science and Engineering
FAN, YIQUAN, Chemistry and Chemical Engineering
GONG, JIANMING, Mechanical and Power Engineering
GONG, YANFENG, Urban Construction, Safety and Environmental Engineering
GU, BOQIN, Mechanical and Power Engineering
GU, HEPING, Chemistry and Chemical Engineering
GUAN, GUOFENG, Chemistry and Chemical Engineering
GUO, LUCUN, Materials Science and Engineering
HE, HONGJIN, Economics and Management
HE, JIAPENG, Urban Construction, Safety and Environmental Engineering
HUANG, PEI, Chemistry and Chemical Engineering
HUANG, YOUDIAO, Mechanical and Power Engineering
HUANG, ZHENREN, Mechanical and Power Engineering
JIAN, MIAOFU, Materials Science and Engineering
JIANG, JUNCHENG, Urban Construction, Safety and Environmental Engineering
JIANG, JUNCHENG, Mechanical and Power Engineering
JIN, SUMIN, Mechanical and Power Engineering
JIN, WANQIN, Chemistry and Chemical Engineering
LI, BIN, Law and Politics
LI, DONGXU, Materials Science and Engineering
LI, LIQUAN, Materials Science and Engineering
LI, XIANGYING, Foreign Languages and International Exchange

LI, YONGSHENG, Mechanical and Power Engineering
LIN, JINGUO, Automation
LIN, XIAO, Chemistry and Chemical Engineering
LING, XIANG, Mechanical and Power Engineering
LIU, WEIQING, Artistic Design
LIU, XIAOQIN, Chemistry and Chemical Engineering
LIU, ZHONGWEN, Chemistry and Chemical Engineering
LU, JINGUI, Information Science and Engineering
LU, LEI, Materials Science and Engineering
LU, WEILIAN, Automation
LU, XIAOHUA, Chemistry and Chemical Engineering
LU, XIAOPING, Chemistry and Chemical Engineering
LU, YINONG, Materials Science and Engineering
MA, GONGXUN, Mechanical and Power Engineering
MA, ZHENGFEI, Chemistry and Chemical Engineering
PAN, YU, Management Science and Engineering
PAN, ZHIHUA, Materials Science and Engineering
QIAO, XU, Chemistry and Chemical Engineering
QIU, TAI, Materials Science and Engineering
SHEN, LINJIANG, Sciences
SHEN, SHIMING, Mechanical and Power Engineering
SHEN, XIAODONG, Materials Science and Engineering
SHI, JUN, Chemistry and Chemical Engineering
SHI, MEIREN, Chemistry and Chemical Engineering
SUN, WEIMIN, Civil Engineering
TANG, MINGSHU, Materials Science and Engineering
TU, SHANDONG, Mechanical and Power Engineering
WANG, HUI, Information Science and Engineering
WANG, JUN, Chemistry and Chemical Engineering
WANG, TINGWEI, Materials Science and Engineering
WANG, YANRU, Chemistry and Chemical Engineering
WANG, YONGPING, Architecture and Urban Planning
WANG, ZHUOJUN, Law and Politics
WEI, PING, Life Sciences and Pharmaceutical Engineering
WEI, WUJI, Materials Science and Engineering
WU, CHENGZHEN, Materials Science and Engineering
WU, JILIANG, Architecture and Urban Planning
XIAO, WANRU, Sciences
XU, NANPING, Chemistry and Chemical Engineering
XU, YANHUA, Urban Construction, Safety and Environmental Engineering
XU, ZHONGZI, Materials Science and Engineering
YAN, SHENG, Materials Science and Engineering
YANG, XIANNING, Chemistry and Chemical Engineering
YANG, XIAOJIAN, Information Science and Engineering
YAO, CHENG, Sciences
YAO, HUQING, Chemistry and Chemical Engineering
YAO, XIAO, Materials Science and Engineering
YEI, XUCHU, Materials Science and Engineering

YIN, CHENBO, Mechanical and Power Engineering
YIN, FULIN, Foreign Languages and International Exchange
YIN, XIA, Mechanical and Power Engineering
YU, BIN, Sciences
YUN, ZHI, Chemistry and Chemical Engineering
ZENG, CHONGYU, Chemistry and Chemical Engineering
ZENG, YANWEI, Materials Science and Engineering
ZHANG, GANDAO, Life Sciences and Pharmaceutical Engineering
ZHANG, HONG, Mechanical and Power Engineering
ZHANG, JUN, Materials Science and Engineering
ZHANG, LIJING, Urban Construction, Safety and Environmental Engineering
ZHANG, LIXIONG, Chemistry and Chemical Engineering
ZHANG, QITU, Materials Science and Engineering
ZHANG, SHAOMING, Materials Science and Engineering
ZHANG, WEI, Materials Science and Engineering
ZHANG, YAMING, Chemistry and Chemical Engineering
ZHAO, HESHENG, Architecture and Urban Planning
ZHAO, SHILIN, Materials Science and Engineering
ZHAO, YINGKAN, Automation
ZHENG, FENGQIN, Mechanical and Power Engineering
ZHOU, CHANGYU, Mechanical and Power Engineering
ZHOU, HUA, Life Sciences and Pharmaceutical Engineering
ZHU, DUNRU, Chemistry and Chemical Engineering
ZHU, HONG, Materials Science and Engineering
ZHU, XURONG, Chemistry and Chemical Engineering
ZHUANG, JUN, Mechanical and Power Engineering

NANJING UNIVERSITY OF TRADITIONAL CHINESE MEDICINE

282 Hanzhong Rd, Nanjing 210029, Jiangsu Province
Telephone: (25) 86798005
Fax: (25) 86798009
Internet: www.njutcm.edu.cn
Founded 1954
Academic year: September to July
Pres.: XIANG PING
Vice-Pres: CHEN DIPING, LIU SHENLIN, WU MIANHUA
Librarian: JI WENHUI
Library of 4,320,000 vols
Number of teachers: 1,308
Number of students: 6,000
Publication: *Journal* (6 a year)

DEANS

College of Basic Medicine: ZHANG MINGQIN
College of Pharmacy: DING ANWEI
First Clinical Medical College: (vacant)
School of Commercial Management and Trade: (vacant)
School of Foreign Languages: (vacant)
Second Clinical Medical College: LI ZHONGREN

PROFESSORS

BIAN, HUIMIN, Pharmacy
CAI, BAOCHANG, Pharmacy
CHEN, JIANWEI, Pharmacy
DING, ANWEI, Pharmacy

DING, SHUHUA, Clinical Medicine
FANG, TAIHUI, Pharmacy
GUO, LIWEI, Pharmacy
HUANG, YAOZHOU, Pharmacy
LI, XIANG, Pharmacy
LIU, HANQING, Pharmacy
PENG, GUOPING, Pharmacy
QIN, MINGZHU, Pharmacy
WANG, SHOUCHUAN, Clinical Medicine
WU, DEKANG, Pharmacy
WU, HAO, Pharmacy
YAN, DAONAN, Clinical Medicine
YU, XIAOWEI, Clinical Medicine
ZHOU, FUYI, Clinical Medicine
ZHU, QUAN, Pharmacy

ATTACHED RESEARCH INSTITUTES

Adult Education College.

Botanical Refinement Engineering Research Centre: Dir GUO LIWEI.

College of International Education.

Jiangsu Province Research and Development Centre for Marine Pharmaceuticals: Dir WU HAO.

NANKAI UNIVERSITY

94 Weijin Rd, Tianjin 300071
Telephone: (22) 23508208
Fax: (22) 23502208
E-mail: xb@office.nankai.edu.cn
Internet: www.nankai.edu.cn
Founded 1919
Academic year: September to July
Pres.: Prof. HOU ZIXIN
Vice-Pres: CHEN HONG, CHEN XUEQI, CHEN YONGCHUAN, GENG YUNQI, PANG JINJU, ZHANG JING
Librarian: Prof. YAN SHIPING
Library of 2,900,000 vols
Number of teachers: 1,465
Number of students: 23,000
Publications: *Journal* (4 a year), *Nankai Economics Studies* (6 a year), *Nankai Journal* (6 a year), *Nankai Management Review* (6 a year)

DEANS

College of Adult Education: Prof. JING HONGGANG
College of Chemistry: Prof. GUAN NAIJIA
College of Chinese Language and Culture: Prof. SHI FENG
College of Economics: Prof. ZHOU LIQUN
College of Economics and Societal Development: Prof. HOU ZIXIN
College Environmental Science and Engineering: Prof. ZHU TAN
College of Foreign Languages and Literature: Prof. WANG JIANYI
College of History: Prof. LI ZHIAN
College of Ideological and Cultural Education: Prof. LI YI
College of Information Science and Technology: Prof. WU GONGYI
College of International Business: Prof. LI WEIAN
College of Law and Political Science: Prof. ZHU GUANGLEI
College of Life Sciences: Prof. GENG YUNQI
College of Literature: Prof. CHEN HONG
College of Mathematics: Prof. LONG YIMING
College of Medicine: Prof. ZHU TIANHUI
College of Modern Distance Education: Prof. LEI ZONGBAO
College of Occupational Technology: Prof. SU LICHUN
College of Physics: Prof. XU JINGJUN
Software College: Prof. HUANG YALOU
Teda College: Prof. XIAN GUOMING

PROFESSORS

College of Chemistry (tel. (22) 23508470; fax (22) 23502458; e-mail hxx@office.nankai.edu.cn):

Department of Chemistry:

BU XIANHE, Inorganic Chemistry
CAI ZUNSHENG, Physical Chemistry
CAO YURONG, Organic Chemistry
CHENG JINPEI, Inorganic Chemistry
CHENG PENG, Inorganic Chemistry
DENG GUOCAI, Inorganic Chemistry
GUAN NAIJIA, Physical Chemistry
HE JIAQI, Inorganic Chemistry
HE XIWEN, Analytical Chemistry
HU QINGMEI, Organic Chemistry
HUANG JIAXIAN, Polymer Chemistry
HUANG WEIPING, Inorganic Chemistry
HUANG ZHIRONG, Analytical Chemistry
JIANG ZONGHUI, Inorganic Chemistry
LI FANGXING, Polymer Chemistry
LIAO DAIZHENG, Inorganic Chemistry
LIN HUAKUAN, Physical Chemistry
LIU YU, Physical Chemistry
MENG JIBEN, Organic Chemistry
SHEN HANXI, Inorganic Chemistry
SHEN PANWEN, Analytical Chemistry
SONG LICHENG, Organic Chemistry
WANG BAIQUAN, Organic Chemistry
WANG XINSHENG, Organic Chemistry
WANG YONGMEI, Organic Chemistry
WU SHIHUA, Inorganic Chemistry
XU SHANSHENG, Organic Chemistry
YAN SHIPING, Inorganic Chemistry
YAN XIUPING, Analytical Chemistry
YANG GUANGMING, Inorganic Chemistry
YANG XIULIN, Physical Chemistry
YIN LIHUA, Inorganic Chemistry
YOU YINGCAI, Polymer Chemistry
YUAN MANXUE, Physical Chemistry
ZHANG BAOLONG, Organic Chemistry
ZHANG BAOSHEN, Polymer Chemistry
ZHANG GUIZHU, Analytical Chemistry
ZHANG ZHIHUI, Physical Chemistry
ZHAO HONGXI, Physical Chemistry
ZHAO ZUEZHANG, Physical Chemistry
ZHU CHANGYING, Polymer Chemistry
ZHU SHOURONG, Physical Chemistry
ZHU XIAOQING, Organic Chemistry
ZHU ZHIANG, Physical Chemistry
ZUO JU, Polymer Chemistry
ZUO YUMIN, Organic Chemistry

Department of Materials Chemistry:

CHE YUNXIA, Inorganic Chemistry
CHEN JUN, Materials Chemistry
CHEN TIEHONG, Physical Chemistry
GAO XUEPING, Materials Chemistry
LIU SHUANGXI, Physical Chemistry
SONG DEYING, Materials Chemistry
SUN BO, Inorganic Chemistry
TAO KEYI, Physical Chemistry
XIANG SHOUHE, Physical Chemistry
YAN JIE, Materials Chemistry
YUAN HUATUNG, Materials Chemistry
ZHANG WENJUN, Physical Chemistry

College of Chinese Language and Culture (tel. (22) 23501687; fax (22) 23501687; e-mail hy@office.nankai.edu.cn):

CUI JIANXIN, Modern Chinese
GUO JIMAO, Modern Chinese
SHI FENG, Chinese Linguistics
SHI XIANGDONG, Ancient Chinese

College of Economics (tel. (22) 23508981; fax (22) 23500261; e-mail jjxy@office.nankai.edu.cn):

Department of Economics:

HE ZILI, Comparative Economics
JIA GENLIANG, Development Economics
JING WEIMIN, Transitional Economics
LIU CHUNBIN, Agro-economics
LIU JUNMIN, Macroeconomics and Virtual Economics
WANG SHUYING, Industrial Economics
WEN HAICHI, Labour Economics

ZHANG RENDE, Comparative Economics
ZHANG SHIQING, Macroeconomics and Microeconomics
ZHANG TONGYU (acting), Political Economy
ZHAO JIN, History of Economics
ZHU GUANGHUA, Political Economy

Department of Finance:

LI ZHIHUI, International Finance
LIU YUCAO, International Finance
MA JUNLU, International Finance

Department of International Economics and Trade:

GAO LEYONG, International Economic Theories, International Investment
LI KUNWANG, Theory and Policy of International Trade
LIU ZHONGLI, International Trade Management
TONG JIADONG, International Trade, Economics of International Integration
XUE JINGXIAO, International Economics, Japanese Economy
YANG CANYING, Open Economy
ZHANG ZHICHAO, Public Finance, Economics of Development

Department of Risk Management and Insurance:

JIANG SHENGZHONG, Research, Insurance Management
LIU MAOSHAN, Research, Insurance Economics
XIAO YUNRU, Research, Actuarial Mathematics

College of Environmental Science and Engineering (tel. (22) 23508807; fax (22) 23508936; e-mail hjxy@office.nankai.edu.cn):

Department of Environmental Engineering and Management:

BAI ZHIPENG, Air Pollution Chemistry, Environmental Risk Assessment
LIU MAO, Environmental Safety Assessment
WAN QISHAN, Water Pollution Control
ZHU TAN, Environmental Planning and Management
ZHUANG YUANYI, Environmental Engineering

Department of Environmental Science:

CHEN FUHUA, Environmental Chemistry
DAI SHUGUI, Environmental Chemistry
FU XUEQI, Environmental Chemistry
HU GUOCHEN, Environmental Biology
HUANG GUOLAN, Environmental Chemistry
JIN ZHAOHUI, Environmental Chemistry
SUN HONGWEN, Environmental Chemistry, Environmental Pollution Control
ZHANG BAOGUI, Environmental Chemistry, Analytic Chemistry
ZHU LIN, Environmental Biology

College of Foreign Languages and Literature (tel. (22) 23509292; fax (22) 23500497; e-mail wyxy@office.nankai.edu.cn):

Department of English Language and Literature:

CHANG YAOXIN, English Literature
CUI YONGLU, English Translation
GU QI'NAN, English Literature
JIANG HUASHANG, English Literature
LIU SHICONG, English Translation
SU LICHANG, English Linguistics
MA QIUWU, English Linguistics
WANG HONGYIN, English Translation
WANG WENHAN, English Literature
WEI RONGCHENG, English Literature
YAN QIGANG, English Literature
ZHANG MAIZENG, English Linguistics

Department of General Literature:

LI JINGYU, English Language
SUO JUNMEI, English Language
WANG SHIBIN, English Language
XUE CHEN, English Language
ZHANG JUNZHI, English Language

ZHANG WENQI, English Language
ZHOU SHUJIE, English Language

Department of Japanese Language and Literature:

LIU GUIMIN, Japanese Literature and Linguistics
WANG JIANYI, Japanese Literature and Linguistics

Department of Western Languages and Literature:

CHEN XI, Comparative Linguistics
YAN GUODONG, Sino-Russian Cultural Relations, Comparative Culture
ZHANG ZHITING, French Literature

College of History (tel. (22) 23508422; fax (22) 23501637; e-mail lizhian@nankai.edu.cn):

Department of History:

CHANG JIANHUA, Ancient Chinese History
CHEN ZHENJIANG, Modern and Contemporary Chinese History
CHEN ZHIQIANG, Ancient and Medieval World History
FENG ERKANG, Ancient Chinese History
HA QUAN'AN, Ancient and Medieval World History
HOU JIE, Modern and Contemporary Chinese History
JIANG PEI, Modern and Contemporary Chinese History
JIANG SHENGLI, Historiography
LI ZHI'AN, Ancient Chinese History
LI XISUO, Modern and Contemporary Chinese History
LIN HEKUN, Modern and Contemporary World History
LIU MIN, Ancient Chinese History
LIU ZEHUA, Ancient Chinese History
MA SHILI, Modern and Contemporary World History
SUN LIQUN, Ancient Chinese History
WANG DUNSHU, Ancient and Medieval World History
WANG XIANMING, Modern and Contemporary Chinese History
XU TAN, Ancient Chinese History
ZHANG FENTIAN, Ancient Chinese History
ZHANG GUOGANG, Ancient Chinese History

Department of Philosophy:

CHANG JIAN, Western Philosophy
CHEN YANQING, Marxist Philosophy
CUI QINGTIAN, Logical Philosophy
HAN QIANG, Chinese Philosophy
LI NA, Logical Philosophy
LI JIANSHANG, Scientific and Technological Philosophy
LI XIANGHAI, Chinese Philosophy
LIU WENYING, Chinese Philosophy
LU YANG, Aesthetics
REN XIAOMING, Logical Philosophy
WANG NANSHI, Marxist Philosophy
XUE FUXING, Aesthetics
YAN MENGWEI, Marxist Philosophy

Department of Relics and Museum Studies:

LIU YI, Museology
ZHU FENGHAN, Ancient Chinese History

College of Ideological and Cultural Education (tel. (22) 23507985; fax (22) 23507985; e-mail jyxy@office.nankai.edu):

CAO JIE, Marxist Theories and Ideological and Political Education
DING JUN, Political Economics
DOU AIZHI, History of the Chinese Communist Party
LI JIANSONG, Political Economics
LI YI, Marxist Philosophy
LIU JINGQUAN, History of the Chinese Communist Party
SHAO YUNRUI, History of the Chinese Communist Party
WANG YUANMING, Marxist Philosophy

WU DONGSHENG, Marxist Theories and Ideological and Political Education
YANG YONGZHI, Theoretical Thoughts of Deng Xiaopin
ZHANG HONGGUANG, Scientific and Technological Philosophy
ZHAO TIESUO, History of the Chinese Communist Party

College of Information Science and Technology (tel. (22) 23505705; fax (22) 23509054; e-mail nkitnankai.edu.cn):

CHANG SHENGJIANG, Optical Information Processing
CHEN WENJU, Nonlinear Optical Physics and Materials Optoelectronics for Optical Information
DONG YUANYI, Photonics Technology and Modern Optical Communication
FANG ZHILIANG, Optical Information Processing
FU RULIAN, Laser and Biomedical Optics
GENG XINHUA, Photo-electronic Technology and Applications
HAN WEIHENG, Computer Software
LIN MEIRONG, Nonlinear Optical Physics and Materials, Optoelectronics for Optical Information
LIU FULAI, Optical Information Processing
MU GUOGUANG, Optical Information Processing
SHEN JINYUAN, Optical Information Processing
SUN YUN, Photo-electronic Materials and Technology
SUN ZHONGLI, Photo-electronic Technology, Semiconductor Materials and Devices
TANG GUOQING, Molecular Electronic Spectroscopy and Biomedical Photomaps
WANG QINGREN, Pattern Recognition and Intelligent Systems
WANG ZHAOQI, Optical Information Processing
WANG ZONGPAN, Photo-electronic Technology and Applications
XIONG SHAOZHEN, Optoelectronic Devices and Technology, Display Electronics
YUAN SHUZHONG, Fibre Communication and Fibre Sensors
ZHAI HONGCHEN, Institute of Modern Optics
ZHANG GUILAN, Nonlinear Optical Physics and Materials
ZHANG YANXIN, Optical Information Processing, Neural Networks and Pattern Recognition
ZHAO QIDA, Fibre Communication and Fibre Sensors
ZHU XIAONONG, Applications of Femtosecond Laser Science and Technology

Department of Automation:

CHEN QIUSHUANG, Job Shop Schedule Systems, DEDS System
CHEN ZENGQIANG, Adaptive, Predictive and Intelligent Control
SUN YONGHUA, Adaptive Control Systems
TU FENGSHENG, Integrated Computer Manufacturing Systems
WANG XIUFENG, Modelling and Identification, Financial Decision Support Systems
WANG ZHIBAO, Financial Decision Support Systems
YUAN ZHUZHI, Adaptive and Predictive Control, Intelligent Communication

Department of Communications Engineering:

LI WENCHEN, Radio Communications
WU YUE, Radio Communications

Department of Computer Science and Technology:

BAI GANG, Pattern Recognition
LI QINGCHENG, Embedded Operating Systems
LIU JING, Computer Architecture

LU ZHICAI, Intelligent Control and Communication Networks
SUN GUIRU, Software Engineering
WU GONGYI, Computer Networks
YANG YULU, Computer Architecture
YUAN XIAOJIE, Database Technology, Data Warehousing, Data Mining
ZHU YAOTING, Multimedia Technology and Network Teaching

Department of Electronic Information Science and Technology:

LI WEIXIANG, Systems and System Design
YAN SHAOLIN, Superconductor Electronics, Communications Science and Technology
YANG WENXIA, Net Communication

Department of Electronic Science and Technology:

FANG LAN, Superconductivity, Electronics
SHAO SHUMIN, Vacuum Science and Technology, Functional Materials and Devices

Department of Microelectronics:

JIA XIANGLUAN, VLSI and System Design
NIU WENCHENG, Transducer Technology and Systems
NIU XIUQING, VLSI and System Design
QIN SHICAI, VLSI and System Design

College of International Business (tel. (22) 23500603; fax (22) 23501039; e-mail alison41@eyou.com):

Department of Accounting:

FENG YANQI, International Accounting
LIU ZHIYUAN, Managerial Accounting
ZHOU XIAOSU, Financial Accounting

Department of Financial Management:

QI YINFENG, Corporate Finance
WANG QUANXI, Corporate Finance

Department of Human Resource Management:

LI WINJIAN, Human Resource Management
WU GUOCUN, Human Resource Management, Human Resource Development
XIE JINYU, Human Resource Management, Strategic Human Resource Management

Department of Information Systems and Management:

YAN JIANYUAN, Management Information Systems, Logistics Management

Department of International Business:

HAN JINGLUN, Management
JIA LANXIANG, Management
LI FEI, Management
LI GUOJING, Management
QI ANBANG, Management
WANG YINGJUN, Management
ZHANG YULI, Management

Department of Library Science:

LIU YUZHAO, Library Management
WANG ZHIJIN, Library Management

Department of Marketing:

FAN XIUCHENG, Service Marketing Management
HAN DECHANG, Marketing
WU XIAOYUN, Global Marketing Management

Department of Tourism Management:

LI TIANYUAN, Tourism Marketing
QI SHANHONG, Tourism Business Management
WANG JIAN, Tourism Development

College of Law and Political Science (tel. (22) 23501400; fax (22) 23500327; e-mail fzxy@nankai.edu.cn; internet nkfzxy.my163.com):

Department of Law:

BAI HUA, Theory of Law
FU SCHICHENG, Administrative Law
HOU XINYI, Theory of Law
HU SHIKAI, Theory of Law

LI YUNWU, Forensic Medicine
QI DAOMENG, Environmental Law
ZHAO ZHENGQUN, Administrative Law
ZHU JINGAN, International Private Law

Department of Political Science:

CAI TUO, International Relations
GE QUAN, Political Science
SHEN YAPING, Public Administration
WANG ZHENGYI, International Relations
YANG LONG, Political Science
YIN YANJUN, International Relations
ZHANG RUIZHUANG, International Relations
ZHU GUANGLEI, Political Science

Department of Sociology:

GUAN XINPING, Social Policy
HOU JUNSHENG, Applied Sociology
LIU JUNJUN, Applied Sociology
PENG HUAMIN, Social Work
WANG CHUHUI, Applied Sociology
WANG XINJIAN, Social Psychology
YUE GUOAN, Social Psychology

College of Life Sciences (tel. (22) 23501846; fax (22) 23508800; e-mail sky@office.nankai.edu.cn):

Department of Biochemistry:

CAO YOUJIA, Biochemistry and Molecular Biology, Signals Transduction and Apoptosis
CHEN QIMIN, Microbiology and Molecular Genetics, Molecular Virology
DU RONGQIAN, Molecular Biology
GENG YUNQI, Molecular Virology
HUANG XITAI, Biochemistry and Molecular Biology, Structure of Nucleic Acids and Gene Chips
WANG NINGNING, Plant Molecular Biology
WANG SHUFANG, Plant Physiology
WANG YONG, Plant Molecular Biology
YE LIHONG, Protein Biochemistry
YU ZIRAN, Purification and Characterization of Human Growth Hormones Expressed in Insect Cells
YU XINDA, Gene Engineering in Eukaryotic Cells

Department of Biology:

BU WENJUN, Zoological Systematics
CHEN QIANG, Biosensors, Biophysical Chemistry
CHEN RUIYANG, Cytogenetics
GAO YUBAO, Botany and Plant Ecology
LI HOUHUN, Insect Taxonomy, Zoogeography
LIU ANXI, Animal Physiology and Biochemistry
QIU ZHAOZHI, Zootaxy and Parasitology
SONG WENQIN, Molecular Cytogenetics
WANG XINHUA, Systematic Zoology
ZHENG LEYI, Zoological Systematics

Department of Microbiology:

BAI GANG, Molecular Immunology
DIAO HUXIN, Study of Petroleum Microorganisms
LIU FANG, Microbiological Sources and Molecular Biology
LIU RULIN, Microbiology
REN GAIXIN, Insect Microbiology
WANG LEI, Bacterial Genetics and Evolution
XING LAIJUN, Modern Mycology
YANG WENBO, Resource Bacteriology and Engineering

College of Literature (tel. (22) 23508247; fax (22) 23508247; e-mail chinese@wxy.nankai.edu.cn; internet www.nankai.chinese.edu.cn):

Department of Art Design:

XUE YI, Art Design

Department of Basic Cultural Education:

NING JIAYU, Ancient Chinese Literature

Department of Chinese Language and Literature:

CHEN HONG, Ancient Chinese Literature
HONG BO, Ancient Chinese
LI JIANGUO, Ancient Chinese Literature
LIU LILI, Literature and Art Science
LU SHENGJIANG, Ancient Chinese Literature
LUO ZONGQIANG, Ancient Chinese Literature
MA QINGZHU, Modern Chinese
MENG ZHAOLIAN, Ancient Chinese Literature
NING JIAYU, Ancient Chinese Literature
PENG XIUYIN, Literature and Art Science
QIAO YIGANG, Modern and Contemporary Chinese Literature
SHI FENG, Experimental Phonetics
SUN CHANGWU, Ancient Chinese Literature
TAO MUNING, Ancient Chinese Literature
WANG LIXIN, Comparative and World Literature
WANG ZHIGENG, Comparative and World Literature
XING KAI, Languages and Literature of Ethnic Minorities in China
XU XIANGLIN, Ancient Chinese Literature
ZENG XIAOYU, Languages and Literature of Ethnic Minorities in China
ZHANG YI, Ancient Chinese Literature
ZHOU JIAN, Modern Chinese

Department of Eastern Art:

CHEN YUPU, Chinese Painting
FAN ZENG, Chinese Painting
HAN CHANGLI, Chinese Painting
SHEN QUAN, Chinese Painting

Department of Mass Communication:

LUO DERONG, Editorial and Publishing Science
ZHAO HANG, Editorial and Publishing Science

College of Mathematics (tel. (22) 23501233; fax (22) 23506423; e-mail longym@nankai.edu.cn; internet www.math.nankai.edu.cn):

Department of Financial Information and Technology:

CHEN WANYI, Control Theory, Financial Mathematics
WANG GONGSHU, Applied Statistics
WANG HONG, Control Theory

Department of Information and Probability:

FU FANGWEI, Coding Theory, Bioinformation
GUO JUNYI, Stochastic Process, Risk Theory
LIANG PU, Coding Theory, Bioinformation
SHEN SHIYI, Coding Theory, Bioinformation
WANG YONGJIN, Probability, Stochastic Process
WU RONG, Probability, Stochastic Process
ZHOU XINGWEI, Harmonic Analysis, Wavelet Analysis

Department of Mathematics:

DENG SHAOQIANG, Lie Groups and Lie Algebras
DING GUANGGUI, Functional Analysis
GU PEI, Algebra, Group Metahomomorphisms
GUO JINGMEI, Differential Topology
HOU ZIXIN, Lie Groups and Lie Algebras
HUANG YUMIN, Partial Differential Equations
LIANG KE, Lie Groups and Lie Algebras
LIN JINKUN, Algebraic Topology
LIU CHUNGEN, Nonlinear Analysis
MENG DAOJI, Basic Mathematics, Algebra, Lie Therapy

Department of Scientific Computing and Applied Software:

HU JIANGWEI, Numerical Mathematics
TIAN CHUNSONG, Numerical Mathematics

Department of Statistics:

WANG ZHAOJUN, Experimental Design, Statistical Process Control
ZHANG RUNCHU, Experimental Design, Multivariate Analysis, Applied Statistics

College of Medicine (tel. (22) 23509842; fax (22) 23509842; e-mail zhuth@nankai.edu.cn):

LIU WEN, Anatomy
ZHU TIANHUI, Medical Genetics

College of Physics (tel. (22) 23501490; fax (22) 23501490; e-mail physics@nankai.edu.cn; internet www.physics.nankai.edu.cn):

Department of Physics:

CAI CHONGHAI, Evaluation of Nuclear Data
CHEN TIANLUN, Nonlinear Dynamics, Partial Physics Theory
DING DATONG, Nuclear Magnetic Resonance, Computational Materials, Mesoscopic Physics
GAO CHENGQUN, Nuclear Physics
HU BEILAI, Statistical Physics, Plasma Physics
HUANG WUQUN, Nonlinear Dynamics
LI BAOHUI, Nuclear Magnetic Resonance, Computational Physics
LI XUEQIAN, Phenomenology of High Energy Physics
LU ZHENQIU, Inverse Scattering Physics and Imaging Techniques
LUO MA, Perturbative Chromodynamic Power Electronics
MENG XINHE, Particle Physics and the Universe, Mesoscopic Physics
NING PINGZHI, Nuclear Physics
SHEN HONG, Nuclear Physics
WEN JINGSONG, Micro-atmospheric Science Suspension Mechanics
ZHOU WENZHUANG, Crystallology
ZHU YAPING, X-Ray Crystallology

Department of Optical and Electrical Science:

LÜ FUYUN, Photoelectron Laser and Modern Optical Communication
LÜ KECHENG, Photoelectron Laser and Modern Optical Communication
SHENG QIUQIN, Opto-electronics and Optical Fibre Communication, Optical Sensors

Department of Biophysical Science:

YANG WENXIU, Cellular and Molecular Informatics, Cellular and Membrane Biophysics

Software College (tel. (22) 23500526; fax (22) 23500526; e-mail cs@nankai.edu.cn; internet www.cs.nankai.edu.cn):

HUANG YALOU, Intelligent Robot Systems, Intelligent Information Processes

Department of Physical Education (tel. (22) 23502801; e-mail tyb@office.nankai.edu.cn):

WANG YUZHU, Track and Field
XING CHUNGUI, Volleyball
YANG XIANGDONG, Basketball (Dir)
ZHAO SHIJIE, Track and Field

Institute of Ancient Chinese Culture Studies (tel. (22) 23509662; fax (22) 23508247; e-mail chinese@wxy.nankai.edu.cn; internet www.nankai.chinese.edu.cn):

YE JIAYING, Ancient Chinese Literature and Culture

Institute of Economics (tel. (22) 23503997; fax (22) 23501254; e-mail zhoulq@public.tpt.tj.cn):

CAO ZHENLIANG, Regional Economic Theory
CHEN ZHONGSHENG, Socialist Economic Theory
LIU XIN, Capitalist Economic Theory
PANG JINJU, Socialist Economic Theory
WANG YURU, History of Modern Economic Development
ZHOU BING, Socialist Economic Theory
ZHOU LIQUN, Socialist Economic Theory

Institute of Elemento-Organic Chemistry (tel. (22) 23508629; fax (22) 23503438; e-mail yss@office.nankai.edu.cn):

CHEN RUYU, Organic Chemistry
CHENG JUNRAN, Organic Chemistry
FANG JIANXIN, Organic Chemistry
GAO RUYU, Organic Chemistry
HAN JIAXIANG, Organic Chemistry
HUANG RUNQIU, Organic Chemistry
LI JING, Organic Chemistry
LI JINSHAN, Organic Chemistry
LI SHUZHENG, Organic Chemistry
LI ZHENGMING, Organic Chemistry
LIAO RENAN, Organic Chemistry
LIU HUAYIN, Organic Chemistry
LIU LUNZU, Organic Chemistry
TANG CHUCHI, Organic Chemistry
WANG GUANGYUAN, Organic Chemistry
XIE QINGLAN, Organic Chemistry
YANG HUAZENG, Organic Chemistry
ZHANG ZHENGZHI, Organic Chemistry
ZHANG ZUXIN, Organic Chemistry
ZHENG JIANU, Organic Chemistry
ZHOU QILIN, Organic Chemistry

Institute of History (tel. (22) 23508903; fax (22) 23508903; e-mail lg433@eyou.com):

BAI XINLIANG, Ancient Chinese History
DU JIAJI, Ancient Chinese History
LIN YANQING, Ancient Chinese History
NAN BINGWEN, Ancient Chinese History
WANG MAOHE, Ancient Chinese History

Institute of International Economic Law (tel. (22) 23500694; fax (22) 23500327; e-mail shixuey@fm365.com; internet www.nkfzxy.my163.com):

CHENG BAOKU, International Economic Law
SHI XUEYING, International Economic Law

Institute of International Economics (tel. (22) 23508291; fax (22) 23502437; e-mail iitnk@office.nankai.edu.cn):

CHEN LIGAO, Open Economy
DAI JINPING, International Finance
LI RONGLIN, International Trade
QIU LICHENG, International Investment and Business
TENG WEIZAO, International Investment and Business
XIANG GUOMING, International Investment and Business
ZHANG CHENG, International Investment and Business
ZHANG XIAOTONG, Econometrics
ZHANG YANGUI, International Investment and Business

Institute of Modern Research Management (tel. (22) 23508439; fax (22) 23503690; e-mail nkimm@public.tpt.tj.cn):

LE WEIAN, Corporate Governance
ZHANG JINCHENG, Service Management and Strategic Management

Institute of Mathematics (tel. (22) 23501029; fax (22) 23501532; e-mail nim@nankai.edu.cn):

CHEN YONGCHUAN, Combinatorics
FANG FUQUAN, Geometric Topology
FU LEI, Algebraic Geometry
GE MOLIN, Theoretical Physics
LI XUELIANG, Theory of Graphs and Combinatorial Optimizations
LONG YIMING, Nonlinear Analysis
ZHANG WEIPING, Differential Geometry
ZHOU XINGWEI, Harmonic Analysis, Wavelet Analysis

Institute of Molecular Biology (tel. (22) 23501846; fax (22) 23508800; e-mail sky@office.nankai.edu.cn):

CAI BAOLI, Biodegradation and Biotechnology
GAO CAICHANG, Biochemistry and Molecular Biology
LI MINGGANG, Plant Molecular Biology

QIAO MINGQIANG, Molecular Microbiology and Microbial Technology

YU YAOTING, Biomaterials and Enzyme Engineering

ZHANG JINHONG, Enzyme Engineering and Biomedical Materials

ZHANG JU, Medical Genetics

ZHENG JIANYU, Molecular Biology

ZHANG XIAODONG, Tumour Molecular Biology

Institute of Modern Optics (tel. (22) 23502275; fax (22) 23503690; e-mail xxxy@office.nankai.edu.cn):

CHANG SHENGJIANG, Optical Information Processing

CHEN WENJU, Nonlinear Optical Physics and Materials

DONG XIAOYI, Photonics Technology and Modern Optical Communication

FANG ZHILIANG, Optical Engineering

FU RULIAN, Laser and Biomedical Optics

KAI GUIYUN, Fibre Communications and Fibre Sensors

LIN MEIRONG, Nonlinear Optical Physics and Materials

LIU FULAI, Optical Engineering

MU GUOGUANG, Optical Information Processing

SHEN JINYUAN, Optical Information Processing

TANG GUOQING, Molecular Electronic Spectroscopy and Biomedicine Photomaps

WANG ZHAOQI, Optical Information Processing

YUAN ZHUZHONG, Fibre Communications and Fibre Sensors

ZHAI HONGCHEN, Optical Information Processing, Optics Engineering

ZHANG GUILAN, Nonlinear Optical Physics and Materials

ZHANG YANXIN, Optical Information Processing Neural Networks and Pattern Recognition

ZHAO QIDA, Fibre Communications and Fibre Sensors

ZHU XIAONONG, Applications of Femtosecond Laser Science and Technology

Institute of Photoelectronics (tel. (22) 23502778; fax (22) 23502778; e-mail xxxy@office.nankai.edu.cn):

GENG XINHUA, Photoelectronic Technology and Applications

SUN YAN, Photoelectronic Materials and Technology

SUN ZHONGLIN, Photoelectronic Technology, Semiconductor Materials and Devices

WANG ZONGPAN, Photoelectronic Technology and Applications

XIONG SHAOZHEN, Optoelectronic Devices and Technology, Display Electronics

Institute of Polymer Chemistry (tel. (22) 23501386; fax (22) 23503510; e-mail gfzs@office.nankai.edu.cn):

HE BINGLIN, Polymer Chemistry

HUANG WENQIANG, Polymer Chemistry

LI CHAOXING, Polymer Chemistry

LI CHENXI, Polymer Chemistry

LI HONG, Polymer Chemistry

MA JIANBIAO, Polymer Chemistry

MI HUAIFENG, Biochemistry

SHI LINQI, Polymer Chemistry

SHI ZUOQING, Polymer Chemistry

WANG GUOCHANG, Polymer Chemistry

WU QIANG, Polymer Chemistry

YAN HUSHENG, Polymer Chemistry

YUAN ZHI, Polymer Chemistry

ZHANG BANGHUA, Polymer Chemistry

ZHANG ZHENGPU, Polymer Chemistry

Institute of Population and Development (tel. (22) 23508012; fax (22) 23501773; e-mail rks@office.nankai.edu.cn):

LI JIANMIN, Economics of Population and Labour

TAN LIN, Economics of Population and Labour

YUAN XIN, Economics of Population and Labour

APEC Study Centre (tel. (22) 23501573; fax (22) 23500035; e-mail apecnk@office.nankai.edu.cn):

GONG ZHANKUI, Regional Economic Cooperation, International Trade and Investment

Chinese Philology Research Centre (tel. (22) 23507855; fax (22) 23508247; e-mail chinese@wxy.nankai.edu.cn; internet www.nankai.chinese.edu.cn):

HE LEYUE, Chinese Philology

XIANG GUANGZHONG, Chinese Philology

ZHAO XIANCUO, Chinese Philology

Photonics Research Centre (tel. (22) 23503697; fax (22) 23501490; e-mail zhangcp@nankai.edu.cn; internet www.physics.nankai.edu.cn):

LIU SIMIN, Nonlinear Optics, Solid Spectrum

TIAN JIANGUO, Photonics

XU JINGJUN, Condensed Matter Physics and Photonic Devices

ZHANG CHUNPING, Photonics and Biomedical Photonics

ZHANG GUANGYIN, Solid Spectrum, Photonics and Laser Physics

Transnational Studies Centre (tel. (22) 23505235; fax (22) 23502437; e-mail ctsnk@office.nankai.edu.cn):

CHEN LIGAO, Open Economy

DAI JINPING, International Finance

QIU LICHENG, International Investment and Business

XIAN GUOMING, International Investment and Business

ZHANG CHENG, International Investment and Business

ZHANG XIAOTONG, Econometrics

ZHANG YANGUI, International Investment and Business

NINGXIA MEDICAL COLLEGE

Sheng Li South Rd, Yinchuan 750004, Ningxia Province

Telephone: (951) 4095934

Internet: www.nxmc.edu.cn

Founded 1958

Academic year: September to July

Pres.: SHUN TAO

Vice-Pres: CHEN SHENGCHUN, DAI XIUYING, LI ZHENGZHI, SHI WEIZHONG, ZHANG JIANZHONG

Head of Graduate Dept: LI ZHENGZHI

Librarian: WANG HUIFANG

Library of 200,000 vols

Number of teachers: 811

Number of students: 7,500

Publication: *Journal* (6 a year)

DEANS

Department of Basic Medicine: WANG YANRONG

Department of Chinese Medicine: NIU YANG

Department of Clinical Medicine: WANG HUIXING

Department of Dentistry: MA MING

Department of Public Health: SONG QIRU

School of Nursing: ZHANG LIN

School of Pharmacy: ZHANG DONGNIN

PROFESSORS

GAO, WENHUA, Public Health

HOU, LINGLING, Chinese Medicine

HU, SANGPING, Basic Medicine

JIANG, HOUWEN, Chinese Medicine

JIN, ZHIJUN, Public Health

LI, YUCHUN, Chinese Medicine

LI, ZHENGZHI, Public Health

LIU, XIUFANG, Public Health

QIAN, LIQUN, Public Health

SONG, QIRU, Public Health

WANG, YANRONG, Basic Medicine

WANG, ZHONGJIU, Chinese Medicine

WEN, RUNLING, Public Health

ZHANG, YUJIE, Chinese Medicine

ZHANG, ZHENXIANG, Public Health

ZHU, YUDONG, Chinese Medicine

NORTH CHINA ELECTRIC POWER UNIVERSITY

204 Qingnian Rd, Baoding 071003, Hebei Province

Telephone: (312) 5024952

Fax: (312) 5028483

Internet: www.ncepu.edu.cn

Founded 1958

State control

Pres.: LIU JI ZHEN

Vice-Pres: AN LIAN SUO, LEI YING QI, LI HE MING, PENG ZHEN ZHONG

Heads of Graduate Department: AN LIAN SUO, DING CHANG FU

Librarian: KONG ZHENGHUI

Number of teachers: 2,348

Number of students: 20,000

Publications: *Electric Power Higher Education* (4 a year), *Electric Power Information* (4 a year), *Electric Power Record* (4 a year), *Journal* (4 a year), *Modern Electric Power* (6 a year)

DEANS

Department of English: DAI ZHONG XIN

School of Adult Education: AN LIAN SUO

School of Applied Mathematics: LU ZHAN HUI

School of Applied Physics: ZHANG XIAO HONG

School of Automation: (vacant)

School of Computer Science and Technology: ZHU YONG LI

School of Dynamical Engineering: YANG YONG PING

School of Economic Management: QI JIAN XUN

School of Electrical and Communications Engineering: (vacant)

School of Electrical Engineering: CUI XIANG

School of Environmental Engineering: ZHAO YI

School of Humanity and Social Sciences: LI JU YING

School of Mechanical Engineering: (vacant)

School of Physical Education: YAN GUO QIANG

PROFESSORS

AI, XIN, Electrical Engineering

BAO, HAI, Electrical Engineering

CAO, CHUN MEI, Applied Physics

CHEN, SHENG JIAN, Computer Science and Technology

CHEN, WU, Computer Science and Technology

CHEN, YING MIN, Environmental Engineering

CUI, XIANG, Electrical Engineering

DAI, ZHONG XIN, English Department

DONG, XING HUI, Computer Science and Technology

DU, JIAN GUO, Computer Science and Technology

FANG, LU GUANG, Physical Education

FENG, HUI, Environmental Engineering

GUAN, RONG HUA, Applied Physics

GUO, LEI, English Department

HE, YONG GUI, Economics and Management

HU, MAN YIN, Environmental Engineering

HU, ZHI GUANG, Environmental Engineering

HUANG, YUAN SHENG, Economics and Management

JIA, ZHENG YUAN, Economics and Management

JIANG, GEN SHAN, Applied Physics

LI, JU YING, Humanities and Social Sciences
LI, QI, Applied Physics
LI, QUAN HUA, Physical Education
LI, SHOU XIN, Environmental Engineering
LIN, BI YING, Computer Science and Technology
LIU, ZHI YUAN, Humanities and Social Sciences
LU, FANG CHENG, Electrical Engineering
LU, ZHAN HUI, Applied Mathematics
MA, XIN SHUN, Applied Mathematics
NIU, DONG XIAO, Economics and Management
QI, JIAN XUN, Economics and Management
SUN, JIAN GUO, Computer Science and Technology
SUN, WEI, Economics and Management
WAN, SHI WEI, Applied Physics
WANG, BAO YI, Computer Science and Technology
WANG, CUI RU, Computer Science and Technology
WANG, JING MIN, Economics and Management
WANG, MIN, Humanities and Social Sciences
WU, KE HE, Computer Science and Technology
XIAO, XIANG NING, Electrical Engineering
XING, MIAN, Applied Mathematics
YAN, GUO QIANG, Physical Education
YANG, QI XUN, Electrical Engineering
YI, LIAN QING, Environmental Engineering
YI, ZENG QIAN, Applied Physics
YUAN, YONG TAO, Environmental Engineering
ZHANG, SHENG HAN, Environmental Engineering
ZHANG, TIAN XIN, Humanities and Social Sciences
ZHANG, XIAO HONG, Applied Physics
ZHANG, XU ZHEN, Humanities and Social Sciences
ZHANG, ZHEN SHENG, Environmental Engineering
ZHAO, WEN XIA, Applied Mathematics
ZHAO, YI, Environmental Engineering
ZHENG, GU PING, Computer Science and Technology
ZHU, LING, Electrical Engineering
ZHU, YONG LI, Computer Science and Technology

NORTHEAST FORESTRY UNIVERSITY

26 Hexing Rd, Harbin 150040, Heilongjiang Province

Telephone: (451) 2190015
Fax: (451) 2110146
E-mail: faob@public.hr.hl.cn
Internet: www.nefu.edu.cn

Founded 1952
Academic year: September to July

Pres.: Prof. LI JIAN
Vice-Pres: Prof. CHAO JUN, Assoc. Prof. CHEN WENBIN, Assoc. Prof. HU WANYI, Prof. HUO JIANYU, Prof. YANG CHUANPING
Dean of Graduate School: FAN DELIN
Librarian: LIN XISHENG
Library of 570,000 vols
Number of teachers: 846
Number of students: 5,482 (incl. 307 postgraduates)

Publications: *Bulletin of Botany Research* (4 a year), *Chinese Wildlife* (4 a year), *Forest Fire Protection* (4 a year), *Forestry Finance and Accounting* (12 a year), *Forestry Research in Northern China* (4 a year, in English), *Journal of Northeast Forestry University* (4 a year, in English), *Science of Logging Engineering* (6 a year)

HEADS OF COLLEGES AND DEPARTMENTS

College of Civil Engineering: Prof. ZHANG YINGE

College of Electromechanical Engineering: Prof. LI DONGSHENG
College of Foreign Languages: Prof. LIU MENLAN
College of Forest Products: Prof. WANG FENGHU
College of Forest Resources and Environment: Prof. WANG FENGYOU
College of Humanities: Prof. WANG YAOXIAN
College of Information and Computer Engineering: WANG NIHONG
College of Landscape Architecture: Prof. ZHUO LIHUAN
College of Transportation: Prof. WANG LIHAI
College of Wildlife Resources: Prof. JIA JINGBO
Correspondence College: CAO XIAOGUANG
Department of Physical Education: Prof. MO SHONGSHAN
Normal College: Prof. SONG YE

PROFESSORS

DING, B., Silviculture
GE, M., Wood Science, Wood Chemistry
HU, Y., Forest Entomology
HUANG, Q., Plan Statistics
JIANG, M., Forestry Economics
LI, G., Forest Resources
LI JIAN, Wood Science and Technology, Wood Surface Chemistry
LI JINGWEN, Ecosystems, Community Ecology
LIU, G., Financial Accounting
LU, R., Wood and Composites Technology and Manufacturing
MA, J., Wildlife Management, Natural Reserves
MA, L., Forest Machinery
NIE, S., Phytocommunity Ecology, Phytotaxonomy
SHAO, L., Forest Disease Epidemiology, Taxonomy of Pathogenic Fungi
SHI, J., Forest Engineering
WANG, F., Ecosystems, Community Ecology
WANG, Y., Ecosystems, Physical and Chemical Ecology
WANG, Z., High Yield Forests
XIAN, K., Forest Protection, Water and Soil Conservation
XIANG, C., Taxonomy of Pathogenic Fungi, Management of Forest Diseases
YUE, S., Pest Control
ZHOU, X., Ecosystems, Economic Ecology
ZHOU, Y., Phytocommunity Ecology, Phytotaxonomy
ZHU, G., Forestry Vehicles, Sawing Equipment
ZU, Y., Unlinear Phytoecology

NORTHEASTERN UNIVERSITY

No. 11, Lane 3, Wenhua Lu, Heping District, Shenyang 110006, Liaoning Province

Telephone: (24) 3893000
Fax: (24) 3892454
E-mail: neu@ramm.neu.edu.cn
Internet: www.neu.edu.cn

Founded 1923 as Northeastern Univ., became Northeast Univ. of Technology in 1950, reverted to fmr name in 1993
State control
Academic year: September to July (2 semesters)

Pres.: HE JICHENG
Vice-Pres: LIU JIREN, WANG ZHI, YANG PEIZHEN, WANG QIYI, WANG WANSHAN, ZHOU GUANGYOU
Provost: Prof. DUAN YUEHU
Dean of General Affairs: Assoc. Prof. MENG QINGXIAN
Librarian: Prof. YANG HUAI
Library of 1,650,000 vols
Number of teachers: 1,950
Number of students: 18,814 undergraduates, 1,807 postgraduates

Publications: *Basic Automation*, *China Engineer*, *Control and Decision*, *Economics and Management of Metallurgical Enterprise*, *Journal*

DEANS

Adult Education School: Prof. ZHAO LIANGZHEN
College of Business Administration: Prof. BI MENGLIN
College of Gold Metallurgy: Prof. YANG LI
College of Humanities and Law: Prof. PENG DINGAN
College of Information Science and Engineering: Prof. GU SHUSHENG
College of Materials and Metallurgical Engineering: Prof. HAO SHIMING
College of Mechanical Engineering: Prof. WANG DEJUN
College of Resources and Civil Engineering: Prof. CHEN BAOZHI
Graduate School: Prof. HE JICHENG
Liaoning Branch: Prof. MAO TIANYU
Qinhuangdao Branch: Prof. WANG ZHENFAN

NORTHWEST UNIVERSITY

Tai Bai Bei Lu, Xian 710069, Shaanxi Province

Telephone: (29) 8302344
Fax: (29) 7232733
Internet: www.nwu.edu.cn
Founded 1912
Academic year: September to August.

Pres.: Prof. HAO KEGANG
Vice-Pres: CHEN ZONGXING, LIU SHUNKANG, WANG JIAN, WANG SHUANCAI
Librarian: Prof. ZHOU TIANYOU
Library: 1.6m. vols
Number of teachers: 1,135
Number of students: 10,466 (incl. 571 postgraduates)

Publications: *Journal* (arts and social science, natural sciences, 4 a year), *Literature of the Tang Dynasty*, *Middle East*, *Studies in Higher Education*, *Studies in the History of North Western China.*

NORTHWESTERN POLYTECHNICAL UNIVERSITY

Xian 710072, Shaanxi Province
Telephone: (29) 8493119
Fax: (29) 8491000
E-mail: office@nwpu.edu.cn
Internet: www.nwpu.edu.cn
Founded 1938
State control
Languages of instruction: Chinese, English
Academic year: September to July (2 semesters).

Hon. Pres.: Prof. JI WENMEI
Pres.: Prof. JIANG CHENGYU
Vice-Pres: Prof. GAO DEYUAN, Prof. WANG RUNXIAN, Prof. WANG WEI, Prof. YUAN JIANPING
Dean of Studies: Prof. WAN XIANPENG
Dir of Foreign Affairs: Prof. TANG HONG
Librarian: Prof. GOU WENXUAN
Number of teachers: 1,400
Number of students: 28,000, incl. 5,160 postgraduates

Publications: *Journal of Theoretical and Applied Mechanics* (4 a year), *Mechanical Science and Engineering* (4 a year), *University Journal* (4 a year)

DEANS

College of Continuing Education: Prof. WEI SHENGMIN
College of Marine Engineering: SONG BAOWEI
College of Astronautics: Prof. ZHOU JUN

College of Civil Aviation Engineering: Prof. SUN QIN
College of Materials Science: Prof. LI HEJUN
College of Management: Prof. YE ZHENGYIN
Graduate School: Prof. JIANG CHENGYU
School of Mechatronic Engineering: Prof. ZHANG DINGHUA

PROFESSORS

AI, J. L., Aircraft Design
AN, J. W., Aircraft Automatic Control
BAI, C. R., Aerodynamics
CAI, W. D., Computer Application
CAI, Y. H., Aero-engines
CAO, C. N., Physics
CHEN, C. L., Physics
CHEN, G. D., Mechanics
CHEN, K. A., Noise Control
CHEN, M., Gyroscope and Inertial Navigation
CHEN, S. L., Flight Mechanics
CHEN, Z., Metallic Materials and Heat Treatment
CHENG, G., Signal Measuring and Instruments
CHENG, L. F., Physical Metallurgy
CHU, W. L., Aero-engines
CUI, Y. Z., China Revolutionary History
DAI, G. Z., Theory and Application of Automatic Control
DANG, J. B., Solid Mechanics
DENG, Z. C., Mechanics
DING, X. Q., Applied Mathematics
DUAN, Z. M., Signal Circuit and Systems Engineering
FAN, D., Aero-engines
FAN, M. F., China Revolutionary History
FAN, X. D., High Polymer Material
FAN, X. Y., Computer Application
FANG, Q., Flight Mechanics
FANG, Z. D., Mechanical Engineering
FENG, D., Traditional Chinese Painting
FENG, J. L., Linguistics (Japanese)
FU, H. Z., Physical Metallurgy
FU, L. Z., Mathematics
GAN, X. Y., Linguistics (English)
GAO, D. Y., Computer Science and Engineering
GAO, M. T., Drafting
GAO, X. G., Command Systems Engineering
GAO, Z. H., Aerodynamics
GE, W. J., Machinery Design and Manufacturing
GOU, D. B., Track and Field Sports
GOU, W. X., Solid Mechanics
GU, L. X., Guided Missile Design
GUO, H. Z., Metal Forming
GUO, L., Intelligent Signal Processing
GUO, X. P., Physical Metallurgy
HAO, C. Y., Space Vehicle Design
HE, C. A., Theory and Application of Automatic Control
HE, E. M., Aircraft Control
HE, G. Q., Rocket Engine
HE, H. C., Computer and Artificial Intelligence
HE, M. Y., Signal Circuit and Systems Engineering
HE, W. P., Space Flight Manufacturing Engineering
HE, X. S., General Mechanics
HE, Y. Y., Automatic Control
HU, X. L., Physical Chemistry
HU, Z. G., Computer Software
HUANG, J. G., Applied Electronic Technology
HUANG, Q. Q., Structure Intensity
HUANG, W. D., Physical Metallurgy
JIANG, C. Y., Space Flight Manufacturing Engineering
JIANG, D. W., Applied Mathematics
JIANG, J. S., Structural Mechanics
JIANG, Z. J., Computer Software
JIAO, G. Q., Solid Mechanics
JIE, W. Q., Physical Metallurgy
JIN, B. S., Mechanics of Materials
JING, Z. R., Electronic Engineering
KANG, F. J., Automatic Control

KANG, R. K., Machinery Manufacturing
LAI, X. X., Dialectics of Nature
LEI, Y., Signal Processing
LI, B. X., Rocket Engines
LI, E. P., Physics
LI, F. G., Metal Plasticity Processing
LI, F. W., Aerodynamics
LI, H. J., Metallic Materials and Heat Treatment
LI, H. L., Physical Metallurgy
LI, H. X., Aerodynamics
LI, J. L., Mathematics
LI, J. Z., Political Economy
LI, K. Z., Metallic Materials and Heat Treatment
LI, M. Q., Metal Forming
LI, S. J., Magnetos
LI, S. P., Plasticity Processing
LI, T. H., Materials Processing
LI, W. H., Computer Applications
LI, W. J., Aircraft Design
LI, X. Q., Drafting
LI, Y., Space Flight Manufacturing Engineering
LI, Y. J., Guided Missile Automatic Control
LI, Y. L., Fracture Mechanics
LI, Y. Z., Applied Polymer Science
LI, Z. H., Computer Software
LI, Z. S., Underwater Technology
LIAN, B. W., Radio Communication
LIAN, X. C., Aero-engines
LIANG, G. Q., Space Flight Manufacturing Engineering
LIANG, G. Z., Physical and Chemistry Experiment
LIANG, S. X., Equipment Management
LIAO, M. F., Aero-engines Intensity
LIN, H., Electric Technology
LIU, B., Aero-engines
LIU, B. M., Metal Plasticity Processing
LIU, D., Solid Mechanics
LIU, G., Mechanical Design
LIU, J. H., Welding
LIU, L., Physical Metallurgy
LIU, W. G., Electrical Machinery and Control
LIU, X. L., Aircraft Automatic Control
LIU, Z. T., Metallic Materials and Heat Treatment
LU, B. T., Metallic Materials and Heat Treatment
LU, C. D., Machinery Manufacturing
LU, G. Z., Aircraft Structure Intensity
LU, J. C., Automatic Control
LU, S., Engine Structure Intensity
LU, Z. Z., Solid Mechanics
LUO, C. R., Physics
LUO, X. B., Mathematics
MA, R. Q., Electric Engineering
MA, X. Q., Space Flight Manufacturing Engineering
MA, Y. L., Underwater Acoustics Engineering
MAO, G. W., Rocket Engines
MENG, B. A., Track and Field Sports
MENG, J. M., Linguistics (English)
MO, R., Computer Design
MU, D. J., Theory and Application of Automatic Control
NING, R. C., High Polymer Material
NIU, P. C., Mathematics
OU, Y. J., Applied Mathematics
PAN, J. Y., Management Engineering
PAN, Q., Automatic Control
PEI, C. M., Signal Processing
QI, L. H., Metal Art
QI, S. H., High Polymer Material
QIAN, Z. B., Hot Motive Equipment of the Torpedo
QIAO, S. R., Metallic Materials and Heat Treatment
QIAO, Z. D., Computational Aerodynamics
QIN, X. S., Machinery Manufacturing
QIN, Y. Y., Gyroscope and Inertial Navigation
QING, H. Y., Chemistry
QU, S. R., Drafting
REN, X. M., Aero-engines
SHEN, J., Physical Metallurgy

SHI, H. S., Radio Communication
SHI, K. M., Linguistics (German)
SHI, X. F., Administration
SHI, X. H., Mechanical Engineering
SHI, X. Q., Linguistics (French)
SHI, Y. K., Electrical Equipment
SHI, Y. M., Applied Mathematics
SHI, Y. Y., Ergonomics
SHI, Z. K., Theory and Application of Automatic Control
SONG, B. F., Aircraft Design
SONG, B. W., Machinery Manufacturing
SONG, Z. M., Applied Physics
SU, C. W., Applied Mathematics
SU, K. H., Chemistry
SUN, C., Signal Processing
SUN, G. Z., Drafting
SUN, J. C., Applied Acoustics and Noise Control Engineering
SUN, Q., Aircraft Design
SUN, S. D., Machinery Manufacturing
TANG, G. P., Mathematics
TANG, H., Personnel Management
TANG, S., Flight Mechanics
TANG, Y. Z., Aircraft Automatic Control
TAO, H., Space Flight Manufacturing Engineering
TIAN, C. S., Metallic Materials and Heat Treatment
TIAN, Z., Mathematics
TONG, S. R., Equipment Management
TONG, X. Y., Aircraft Design
TU, Q. P., Signal Processing
WAN, X. P., Aircraft Design
WANG, B., Physics
WANG, J., Linguistics (English)
WANG, J. B., Aircraft Manufacture Engineering
WANG, J. F., Financial Accounting
WANG, L., Rocket Engines
WANG, L. D., Physics
WANG, R. M., Compound Materials
WANG, R. X., Numerically Controlled Machine Tools
WANG, S. M., Basic Electrical Training
WANG, S. M., Mechanics
WANG, W., Aircraft Automatic Control
WANG, X. M., Automatic Control and Computer Application
WANG, Y. C., Hot Motive Equipment of the Torpedo
WANG, Y. M., Underwater Acoustics Engineering
WANG, Y. S., Radio Technology
WANG, Z. S., Motive Equipment Control Engineering
WEI, B. B., Physical Metallurgy
WEI, F., Mechanics of Materials
WEI, S. M., Ergonomics
WENG, Z. Q., Navigation Systems
WU, D. Y., Heat Energy Engineering
WU, H., Aero-engines
WU, J., Computer Software
WU, J. J., Space Flight Manufacturing Engineering
WU, X. G., Torpedo Control
WU, Z. Y., Armoured Concrete Systems
XI, D. K., Aerodynamics
XI, S. M., Metallic Materials and Heat Transfer
XIAO, Y. L., Mathematics
XIE, F. Q., Metal Surface Corrosion
XIN, K., Linguistics (English)
XU, D. M., Torpedo Automatic Control
XU, J. D., Microwave and Antenna Technology
XU, M., Aerodynamics
XU, W., Applied Mathematics
XU, Y. D., Physical Metallurgy
XU, Z., Applied Mathematics
YAN, J., Aircraft Navigation Control
YAN, J. G., Automatic Control
YANG, G. C., Physical Metallurgy
YANG, H., Space Flight Technology
YANG, H. C., Computer Design
YANG, J., Aircraft Automatic Control

YANG, N. D., Systems Engineering
YANG, S. Q., Welding
YANG, Y. F., Linguistics (English)
YANG, Y. N., Aerodynamics
YANG, Y. Q., Metallic Materials and Heat Transfer
YANG, Y. S., Electrical Technology
YANG, Z. C., Solid Mechanics
YANG, Z. Y., Computer Applications
YAO, Z. K., Metal Forming
YE, Z. L., Applied Mathematics
YE, Z. Y., Aerodynamics
YU, H. X., Radio Communication
YUAN, J. P., Flight Mechanics
YUAN, W. Z., Machinery Manufacturing
YUAN, Z. K., Dialectics of Nature
YUE, Z. F., Aircraft Design
ZHANG, A., Command Systems Engineering
ZHANG, B. Q., Aerodynamics
ZHANG, D., Guided Missile Design
ZHANG, D. H., Ergonomics
ZHANG, D. S., Structural Mechanics
ZHANG, H. C., Theory and Application of Automatic Control
ZHANG, H. F., Thermal and Solar Energy Engineering
ZHANG, H. G., Linguistics (German)
ZHANG, H. S., Signal Circuit and Systems Engineering
ZHANG, K. S., Solid Mechanics
ZHANG, K. Y., Applied Mathematics
ZHANG, L. T., Physical Metallurgy
ZHANG, Q. X., Physical Metallurgy
ZHANG, Q. Y., High Polymer Material
ZHANG, S. S., Equipment Engineering
ZHANG, W. G., Aircraft Navigation Control
ZHANG, W. H., Space Flight Manufacturing Engineering
ZHANG, X. A., Building Structure
ZHANG, X. K., Space Flight Manufacturing Engineering
ZHANG, X. M., Detonator Technology
ZHANG, Y. M., Torpedo Design
ZHANG, Y. Y., Computer Software
ZHANG, Y. Z., Automatic Control
ZHAO, J. L., Modern Optics Application
ZHAO, J. W., Sound Electronic Engineering of Water
ZHAO, R. C., Signal and Graph Processing
ZHAO, S. Z., Machinery Manufacturing
ZHAO, X. A., Linguistics (English)
ZHAO, X. M., Mathematics
ZHAO, X. P., Solid Mechanics
ZHAO, Y. S., General Mechanics
ZHAO, Z. W., Computer Software
ZHI, B. S., Automatic Control
ZHI, X. Z., General Mechanics
ZHOU, D. Y., Command Systems Engineering
ZHOU, J., Aircraft Navigation Control
ZHOU, J. H., Analysis and Design of Control Systems
ZHOU, Q., Automatic Control
ZHOU, W. C., Physical Metallurgy
ZHOU, X. S., Computer Applications
ZHOU, Y. H., Physical Metallurgy
ZHOU, Z., Flight Mechanics
ZHU, H. R., Heat Energy Engineering
ZHU, J. Q., Aero-engines
ZHU, M. Q., Measurement Control in Mechanical Engineering
ZHU, X. P., Automatic Control
ZHU, Y. A., Computer Applications
ZOU, G. R., Materials Processing Engineering

PEKING UNIVERSITY

5 Yiheyuan Rd, Haidian, Beijing 100871
Telephone: (10) 62752114
Fax: (10) 62751207
Internet: www.pku.edu.cn
Founded 1898
Languages of instruction: Chinese, English
Academic year: September to June
President: ZHOU QIFENG

Vice-Presidents: CHEN ZHANGLIANG, CHI HUISHENG, HAN QIDE, HAO PING, HE FANG-CHUAN, LII ZHAOFENG, LIN JIUXIANG, LIN JUNJING, MIN WEIFANG
Registrar: LI KE'AN
Librarian: DAI LONGJI
Library of 4,610,000 vols
Number of teachers: 4,537
Number of students: 55,000
Publication: *Peking University Academic Journal.*

PEKING UNION MEDICAL COLLEGE

9 Dong Dan San Tiao, Dongcheng District, Beijing 100730
Telephone: (10) 65295912
Fax: (10) 65133086
E-mail: liudp@pumc.edu.cn
Internet: www.pumc.edu.cn
Founded 1917
Academic year: September to July
President: LIU DEPEI
Vice-Presidents: HE WEI, LIU QIAN, LU CHONGMEI, QI KEMING, SONG XUEMIN
Head of Graduate Department: LIU DEPEI
Librarian: WANG ZHAOLING
Number of teachers: 3,328
Publications: *Acta Academiae Medicinae Sinicae* (6 a year), *Bilingual Journal of Medicine International* (6 a year), *Chinese Chemical Letters* (12 a year), *Journal of Asian Natural Products Research* (4 a year)

DEANS

Cancer Hospital: ZHAO PING
Fu Wai Hospital: HU SHENGSHOU
Institute of Materia Medica: WANG XIAOLIANG
Institute of Medical Biology Technology: JIANG JIANDONG
Orthopaedic Surgery Hospital: QI KEMING
Peking Union Medical College Hospital: LIU QIAN
School of Basic Medical Sciences: ZHENG DEXIAN
School of Nursing: SHEN NING

PROFESSORS

BAO, XIULAN, Peking Union Medical College Hospital
CAI, BOQIANG, Peking Union Medical College Hospital
CAI, LIXING, Peking Union Medical College Hospital
CAI, WEIMING, Cancer Hospital
CAO, JIMIN, School of Basic Medical Sciences
CHEN, CUANXIA, Peking Union Medical College Hospital
CHEN, DECHANG, Peking Union Medical College Hospital
CHEN, GUOZHANG, Orthopaedic Surgery Hospital
CHEN, HONGSHAN, Institute of Medical Biology Technology
CHEN, JIE, Peking Union Medical College Hospital
CHEN, TINGYUAN, Peking Union Medical College Hospital
CHEN, XI, Fu Wai Hospital
CHU, DATONG, Cancer Hospital
DAI, JINGLEI, Cancer Hospital
DAI, YUHUA, Peking Union Medical College Hospital
DONG, JINGWU, Peking Union Medical College Hospital
DONG, YI, Peking Union Medical College Hospital
FAN, JINCAI, Orthopaedic Surgery Hospital
FANG, DEFU, School of Basic Medical Sciences
FANG, QI, Peking Union Medical College Hospital
GAO, JUZHEN, Cancer Hospital
GAO, RUNLIN, Fu Wai Hospital

GU, DAZHONG, Cancer Hospital
GU, DONGFENG, Fu Wai Hospital
GUAN, YAN, Peking Union Medical College Hospital
GUANG, YAO, Peking Union Medical College Hospital
GUI, LAI, Orthopaedic Surgery Hospital
GUO, HUIYUAN, Institute of Medical Biology Technology
GUO, YUZHEN, Peking Union Medical College Hospital
HA, XIANGWEN, Cancer Hospital
HAO, YUZHI, Cancer Hospital
HE, ZHAMA, Fu Wai Hospital
HE, ZHUGEN, Cancer Hospital
HONG, FENGYI, Cancer Hospital
HONG, WANJUN, Cancer Hospital
HU, JINGQUN, Cancer Hospital
HU, SHENGSHOU, Fu Wai Hospital
HUANG, GUOJUN, Cancer Hospital
HUANG, HANYUAN, Peking Union Medical College Hospital
HUANG, LIANG, Institute of Materia Medica
HUANG, XIZHEN, Peking Union Medical College Hospital
HUANG, YIRONG, Cancer Hospital
HUI, RUTAI, Fu Wai Hospital
JI, BAOHUA, Peking Union Medical College Hospital
JI, XIAOCHENG, Peking Union Medical College Hospital
JIANG, JIANDONG, Institute of Medical Biology Technology
JIANG, MING, Peking Union Medical College Hospital
JIANG, XIUFANG, Peking Union Medical College Hospital
JIANG, ZHUMING, Peking Union Medical College Hospital
JIAO, HAIYAN, Peking Union Medical College Hospital
JIN, LAN, Peking Union Medical College Hospital
LI, CHANGLING, Cancer Hospital
LI, DIANDONG, Institute of Medical Biology Technology
LI, HANHONG, Peking Union Medical College Hospital
LI, JIAXIU, Cancer Hospital
LI, KUI, Cancer Hospital
LI, LIHUAN, Fu Wai Hospital
LI, LING, Cancer Hospital
LI, LONGYU, Peking Union Medical College Hospital
LI, QINGHONG, Cancer Hospital
LI, SENKAI, Orthopaedic Surgery Hospital
LI, TAISHENG, Cancer Hospital
LI, ZEJIAN, Peking Union Medical College Hospital
LIANG, XIAOTIAN, Institute of Materia Medica
LIANG, ZHIQUAN, School of Basic Medical Sciences
LIU, DAWEI, Peking Union Medical College Hospital
LIU, DEPEI, School of Basic Medical Sciences
LIU, FUSHENG, Cancer Hospital
LIU, GENTAO, Institute of Materia Medica
LIU, JINGSHENG, School of Basic Medical Sciences
LIU, LIYING, Cancer Hospital
LIU, QIAN, Peking Union Medical College Hospital
LIU, RUIXUE, Peking Union Medical College Hospital
LIU, SHUFAN, Cancer Hospital
LIU, TONGHUA, Peking Union Medical College Hospital
LIU, XINFAN, Cancer Hospital
LIU, YULING, Institute of Materia Medica
LIU, YUQING, Fu Wai Hospital
LIU, ZHONGXUN, Institute of Medical Biology Technology
LOU, ZHIXIAN, Institute of Medical Biology Technology
LU, CHONGMEI, School of Nursing
LU, NING, Cancer Hospital

LU, WEIXUAN, Peking Union Medical College Hospital
LUO, HUIYUAN, Peking Union Medical College Hospital
LUO, WEICI, Peking Union Medical College Hospital
MIAO, YANJUN, Cancer Hospital
OU YANG, HAN, Cancer Hospital
PAN, QINJING, Cancer Hospital
PAN, YANRUO, Peking Union Medical College Hospital
PU, JIELIN, Fu Wai Hospital
QI, KEMING, Orthopaedic Surgery Hospital
QI, MEIFU, Peking Union Medical College Hospital
QI, YONGFA, Cancer Hospital
QIANG, TUNAN, Cancer Hospital
QIAO, SHUBIN, Fu Wai Hospital
QIN, DEXING, Cancer Hospital
QIU, GUIXING, Peking Union Medical College Hospital
QIU, HUIZHONG, Peking Union Medical College Hospital
REN, YUZHU, Peking Union Medical College Hospital
SHAO, YONGFU, Cancer Hospital
SHEN, NING, School of Nursing
SHI, MULAN, Cancer Hospital
SHI, YUANKAI, Cancer Hospital
SONG, ZONGLU, Peking Union Medical College Hospital
SU, XUEZENG, Cancer Hospital
SUN, GENGTIAN, Cancer Hospital
SUN, JIANHENG, Cancer Hospital
SUN, LI, Cancer Hospital
SUN, LIXHONG, Fu Wai Hospital
SUN, NIANGU, Peking Union Medical College Hospital
SUN, YAN, Cancer Hospital
SUN, YINGLONG, Fu Wai Hospital
TANG, BANGCI, Peking Union Medical College Hospital
TANG, PINGZHANG, Cancer Hospital
TANG, WEISONG, Peking Union Medical College Hospital
TU, GIYI, Cancer Hospital
WANG, DANHUA, Peking Union Medical College Hospital
WANG, JIAQI, Orthopaedic Surgery Hospital
WANG, JINWAN, Cancer Hospital
WANG, LIANGJUN, Cancer Hospital
WANG, LUHUA, Cancer Hospital
WANG, MEI, Cancer Hospital
WANG, QILU, Cancer Hospital
WANG, SHIZHEN, Peking Union Medical College Hospital
WANG, XHISHI, Peking Union Medical College Hospital
WANG, XIAOMING, School of Basic Medical Sciences
WANG, YIPENG, Peking Union Medical College Hospital
WEI, MIN, Peking Union Medical College Hospital
WU, AIRU, Cancer Hospital
WU, NING, Cancer Hospital
WU, NING, Peking Union Medical College Hospital
WU, YANGFENG, Fu Wai Hospital
XI, ZHI, Cancer Hospital
XU, BINGHE, Cancer Hospital
XU, BINGZE, Cancer Hospital
XU, CHENGSU, School of Basic Medical Sciences
XU, GUOZHEN, Cancer Hospital
XU, JINGQIN, Peking Union Medical College Hospital
XU, LETIAN, Peking Union Medical College Hospital
XU, ZHENGANG, Cancer Hospital
YANG, GONGHUAN, School of Basic Medical Sciences
YANG, LIN, Cancer Hospital
YANG, YAOJIN, Fu Wai Hospital
YANG, ZIBIN, School of Basic Medical Sciences

YE, QIBIN, Peking Union Medical College Hospital
YIN, WEIBO, Cancer Hospital
YOU, KAI, Peking Union Medical College Hospital
YU, DEQUAN, Institute of Materia Medica
YU, GAOZHI, Cancer Hospital
YU, GUORUI, Cancer Hospital
YU, HONGZHAO, Cancer Hospital
YU, MENGXUE, Peking Union Medical College Hospital
YU, XHIHAO, Cancer Hospital
YUE, JILIANG, Orthopaedic Surgery Hospital
ZENG, XIAOFENG, Peking Union Medical College Hospital
ZENG, XUAN, School of Basic Medical Sciences
ZHAN, RUGANG, Cancer Hospital
ZHANG, BAONING, Cancer Hospital
ZHANG, DAWEI, Cancer Hospital
ZHANG, DECHANG, School of Basic Medical Sciences
ZHANG, DECHAO, Cancer Hospital
ZHANG, DELI, Peking Union Medical College Hospital
ZHANG, FENCHUN, Peking Union Medical College Hospital
ZHANG, HONGXING, Cancer Hospital
ZHANG, HUILAN, Fu Wai Hospital
ZHANG, JIANXI, Peking Union Medical College Hospital
ZHANG, SHIYUAN, Peking Union Medical College Hospital
ZHANG, WENHUA, Cancer Hospital
ZHANG, XHIXIAN, Cancer Hospital
ZHANG, XIANGRU, Cancer Hospital
ZHANG, XUE, School of Basic Medical Sciences
ZHANG, YOUJU, Peking Union Medical College Hospital
ZHANG, ZHENHAN, Peking Union Medical College Hospital
ZHANG, ZHIPING, Institute of Medical Biology Technology
ZHAO, MIN, Orthopaedic Surgery Hospital
ZHAO, PING, Cancer Hospital
ZHAO, SHIHUA, Fu Wai Hospital
ZHAO, SHIMIN, Peking Union Medical College Hospital
ZHAO, YAN, Peking Union Medical College Hospital
ZHAO, YUPEI, Peking Union Medical College Hospital
ZHEN, YONGSU, Institute of Medical Biology Technology
ZHENG, DEXIAN, School of Basic Medical Sciences
ZHONG, SHOUGUANG, Peking Union Medical College Hospital
ZHOU, JICHANG, Cancer Hospital
ZHOU, QIAN, Peking Union Medical College Hospital
ZHOU, XHUNWU, Cancer Hospital
ZHOU, YANMIN, Peking Union Medical College Hospital
ZHU, CHUANQIU, Peking Union Medical College Hospital
ZHU, DAHIA, School of Basic Medical Sciences
ZHU, GUANGJI, School of Basic Medical Sciences
ZHU, JUN, Fu Wai Hospital
ZHU, LI, Peking Union Medical College Hospital
ZHU, WENLING, Peking Union Medical College Hospital
ZHU, XIAODONG, Fu Wai Hospital
ZHUANG, HONGXING, Orthopaedic Surgery Hospital
ZHUI, YUANYU, Peking Union Medical College Hospital

QINGHAI NATIONALITIES COLLEGE

25 Ba Yi Rd, Xining 810007, Qinghai Province
Telephone: (971) 76803
Founded 1949

Pres.: DUO JIE JIAN ZAN
Vice-Pres: SHAO DESHAN, Assoc. Prof. YU DEYUAN, ZHUO MA CAI DAN
Librarian: YAO KERANG
Library of 550,000 vols
Number of teachers: 330
Number of students: 1,572
Publications: *Journal of Qinghai Nationalities Institute, Qinghai Nationalities Research*

PROFESSORS

FENG, Y., Theory of Arts
HU, A., Ancient Chinese
MI, Y., History of Chinese
ZHU, K., Modern Literature

QUFU NORMAL UNIVERSITY

57 Jingxuanxi Rd, Qufu 273165, Shandong Province
Telephone: (537) 4458831
Fax: (537) 4455669
Internet: www.qfnu.edu.cn
Founded 1955
Academic year: September to July
Pres.: TIAN DEQUAN
Librarian: DU YU
Library of 1,880,000 vols
Number of teachers: 2,200
Number of students: 42,000
Publications: *Journal* (4 a year), *Qilu Journal* (6 a year)

DEANS

College of Literature: XUE YONGWU
College of Mathematics Science: (vacant)

PROFESSORS

CHEN, KESHOU, Literature
CHEN, QINGPING, Literature
DAN, CHENGBIN, Literature
GAO, SHANGQU, Literature
LIU, FENGGUANG, Literature
LIU, XINSHENG, Literature
LIU, YAOJIN, Literature
PU, ZHAOLIN, Literature
QIAN, JIAQING, Literature
TANG, XUENING, Literature
XU, ZHENGUI, Literature
XUE, YONGWU, Literature
ZHANG, LIANRANG, Literature
ZHANG, QUANZHI, Literature
ZHAO, DONGSHUAN, Literature
ZHAO, LIMING, Literature
ZHENG, JIEWEN, Literature

ATTACHED RESEARCH INSTITUTE

Adult Education College: Dir DU YIDE.

RENMIN UNIVERSITY OF CHINA

39 Haidian Rd, Haidian District, Beijing 100872
Telephone: (10) 62563399
Fax: (10) 62566374
Internet: www.ruc.edu.cn
Founded 1937
State control
Academic year: starts September
President: LI WENHAI
Vice-Presidents: DU HOUWEN, LI KANGTAI, LI SHAOGONG, LUO GUOJIE, MA SHAOMENG, YANG DEFU, ZHENG HANGSHENG
Librarian: DAI YI
Number of teachers: 1,595
Number of students: 14,289 (incl. 1,284 postgraduates)
Publications: *Archival News* (6 a year), *Economic Theory and Business Management, Information Service News, International Journalism World* (4 a year), *Learned Journal of the People's University of China*

(6 a year), *Population Research*, *Teaching and Research*, *The History of Qing Dynasty Research Newsletter*.

SHAANXI NORMAL UNIVERSITY

199 Chang'an South Rd, Xian 710062, Shaanxi Province
Telephone: (29) 85308992
Fax: (29) 85307025
Internet: www.snnu.edu.cn
Founded 1944
Min. of Education control
Academic year: September to July
Pres.: FANG YU
Vice-Pres: XIAO ZHENGHONG, ZHANG JIANXIANG, ZHAO BIN, ZHOU DEMING
Head of Graduate Dept: LI JIKAI
Librarian: YANG ENCHENG
Number of teachers: 2,600
Number of students: 40,000
Publications: *Journal* (natural sciences, 4 a year), *Journal* (philosophy and social sciences, 6 a year)

DEANS

College of Arts: HU YUKANG
College of Chemistry and Materials Science: ZHANG CHENGXIAO
College of Chinese Language and Literature: LI XIJIAN
College of Computer Science: FENG DEMIN
College of Educational Science: YOU XUJUN
College of Food Engineering: CHEN JINPING
College of Foreign Languages: MA ZHENYI
College of Further Education: JIA WENXING
College of History and Civilization: JIA ERQIANG
College of International Business: LI ZHONGMIN
College of Life Sciences: WANG ZHEZHI
College of Mathematics and Information Science: WU JIANHUA
College of News and Media: LIU LU
College of Physical Education: LI ZHENBIN
College of Physics and Information Technology: ZHAO WEI
College of Political Economy: WANG ZHENYA
College of Teachers and Administrators: GONG JIANGUO
College of Tourism and the Environment: HUANG CHUNCHANG
e-College: LU JIURU

PROFESSORS

CAO, HAN, Computer Science
CAO, HUAIXIN, Mathematics and Information Science
CAO, WEIAN, History and Civilization
CHANG, JINCANG, History and Civilization
CHEN, FENG, History and Civilization
CHEN, JINPING, Life Science
CHEN, JINPING, Food Engineering
CHEN, XIAORUI, Educational Science
CHEN, YASHAO, Chemistry and Materials Science
DANG, HUAIXING, Chinese Language and Literature
DU, HONGKE, Mathematics and Information Science
DU, JIULIN, Physics and Information Technology
DU, WENYU, History and Civilization
DUAN, YUFENG, Food Engineering
FANG, YU, Chemistry and Materials Science
FENG, DEMING, Computer Science
FENG, WENLOU, Chinese Language and Literature
FU, SHAOLIANG, Chinese Language and Literature
GUO, MIN, Computer Science
GUO, QINNA, Chinese Language and Literature
HAO, WENWU, Educational Science

HE, JUHOU, Computer Science
HU, ANSHUN, Chinese Language and Literature
HU, DAODAO, Chemistry and Materials Science
HU, JI, History and Civilization
HU, MANCHENG, Chemistry and Materials Science
HUANG, QIN-AN, Mathematics and Information Science
HUANG, YUAN, Life Science
HUO, SONGLIN, Chinese Language and Literature
HUO, YOUMING, Chinese Language and Literature
JI, GUOXING, Mathematics and Information Science
JIA, ERQIANG, History and Civilization
LI, BAOLIN, Chemistry and Materials Science
LI, BAOXIN, Chemistry and Materials Science
LI, GUOQING, Educational Science
LI, HONGWU, Educational Science
LI, HUISHI, Mathematics and Information Science
LI, JIANFENG, Food Engineering
LI, JIKAI, Chinese Language and Literature
LI, QUANLU, Physics and Information Technology
LI, SHENGGANG, Mathematics and Information Science
LI, WANSHE, Mathematics and Information Science
LI, XIJIAN, Chinese Language and Literature
LI, YONGFANG, Physics and Information Technology
LI, YONGMING, Mathematics and Information Science
LI, YUMIN, History and Civilization
LI, ZHEN, Chinese Language and Literature
LIAN, ZHENMIN, Life Science
LIANG, DAOLI, Chinese Language and Literature
LIN, SHUYU, Physics and Information Technology
LIU, FENGDAO, Chinese Language and Literature
LIU, JING, Chinese Language and Literature
LIU, LU, News and Media
LIU, PENG, Physics and Information Technology
LIU, XINKE, Educational Science
LIU, XINPING, Mathematics and Information Science
LIU, ZHAOTIE, Chemistry and Materials Science
LIU, ZONGHUAI, Chemistry and Materials Science
LU, JIURU, Chemistry and Materials Science
LUO, ZENGRU, Mathematics and Information Science
MA, GEDONG, Chinese Language and Literature
MA, ZHENDUO, Foreign Languages
MIAO, RUNCAI, Physics and Information Technology
NIU, YONG, Physics and Information Technology
QIU, GUOYONG, Computer Science
QIU, NONGXUE, Food Engineering
QIU, XUENONG, Life Science
QU, YAJUN, Chinese Language and Literature
REN, YI, Life Science
RUN, QINGSHENG, Chinese Language and Literature
SHANG, ZHIYUAN, Physics and Information Technology
SHE, XIAOPING, Life Science
SUN, RUNGUANG, Physics and Information Technology
TANG, YIGONG, History and Civilization
TIAN, CHENRUI, Life Science
TIAN, JIANRONG, Educational Science
WANG, BO, Chemistry and Materials Science
WANG, CHENRUI, Food Engineering

WANG, GUOJUN, Mathematics and Information Science
WANG, HUI, History and Civilization
WANG, SHUANGHUAI, History and Civilization
WANG, WENLIANG, Chemistry and Materials Science
WANG, XIAOAN, Life Science
WANG, XIAOMING, Computer Science
WANG, XILI, Computer Science
WANG, XIN, Physics and Information Technology
WANG, YINGZONG, Physics and Information Technology
WANG, YINHUI, Computer Science
WANG, ZHEZHI, Life Science
WANG, ZHIWU, Chinese Language and Literature
WEI, GENGYUAN, Chinese Language and Literature
WEI, JIANGUO, Chinese Language and Literature
WEI, JUNFA, Chemistry and Materials Science
WU, BAOWEI, Mathematics and Information Science
WU, HONGBO, Mathematics and Information Science
WU, JIANHUA, Mathematics and Information Science
WU, YANSHENG, Chinese Language and Literature
WU, ZHENQIANG, Computer Science
XI, GENGSI, Life Science
XIAO, ZHENGHONG, History and Civilization
XING, XIANGDONG, Chinese Language and Literature
XUE, PINGSHUAN, History and Civilization
YANG, CUNTANG, History and Civilization
YANG, ENCHENG, Chinese Language and Literature
YANG, HEQING, Chemistry and Materials Science
YANG, HONGKE, Chinese Language and Literature
YANG, WANMIN, Physics and Information Technology
YANG, ZUPEI, Chemistry and Materials Science
YIN, SHENGPING, History and Civilization
YOU, XILIN, Chinese Language and Literature
YOU, XUQUN, Educational Science
YUAN, LIN, History and Civilization
ZANG, ZHEN, History and Civilization
ZHANG, CHENGXIAO, Chemistry and Materials Science
ZHANG, GUOJUN, Chinese Language and Literature
ZHANG, JIANHUA, Mathematics and Information Science
ZHANG, JIANMIN, Physics and Information Technology
ZHANG, JIANZHONG, Mathematics and Information Science
ZHANG, MAORONG, History and Civilization
ZHANG, XIAOLING, Chemistry and Materials Science
ZHANG, XINKE, Chinese Language and Literature
ZHANG, XUEZHONG, Chinese Language and Literature
ZHANG, YUHU, Chemistry and Materials Science
ZHANG, ZHIQI, Chemistry and Materials Science
ZHANG, ZHUJUN, Chemistry and Materials Science
ZHAO, BIN, Mathematics and Information Science
ZHAO, SHICHAO, History and Civilization
ZHAO, WANGQIN, Chinese Language and Literature
ZHENG, XINGWANG, Chemistry and Materials Science
ZHENG, ZHEMIN, Life Science
ZHOU, TIANYOU, History and Civilization

SHAANXI UNIVERSITY OF SCIENCE AND TECHNOLOGY

49 Renmin West Rd, Xianyang 712081, Shaanxi Province
Telephone: (910) 3579500
Fax: (910) 3579700
Internet: www.sust.edu.cn
Founded 1958
Academic year: September to July
Pres.: LUO HONGJIE
Vice-Pres: CAO JUJIANG, CUI JIHUA, SHEN YIDING, ZHANG MEIYUN
Head of Graduate Dept: ZHANG XIAOLEI
Librarian: GAO DONGQIANG
Number of teachers: 900
Number of students: 18,000
Publications: *Journal* (6 a year), *The Future* (6 a year)

DEANS

College of Chemistry and Chemical Engineering: ZHANG GUANGHUA
College of Computer and Information Engineering: CHEN HUA
College of Design: YANG JUNSHUN
College of Electrical and Electronic Engineering: MENG YANJING
College of Electromechanical Engineering: DANG XINAN
College of Life Sciences and Engineering: CHEN HE
College of Management: YAN YUJIE
College of Materials Science and Engineering: WANG XIUFENG
College of Paper Manufacture Engineering: ZHANG MEIYUN
College of Resources and the Environment: MA JIANZHONG
College of Science: LIN XIAOLIN
College of Vocational Technology (Xian): LI WENHAN
College of Vocational Technology (Xianyan): ZHANG WEIPING
Department of Foreign Languages: LI XIAOHONG

PROFESSORS

CHEN, HE, Life Sciences and Engineering
CHEN, HUA, Computer and Information Engineering
CHEN, JUNZHI, Chemistry and Chemical Engineering
CHEN, MANRU, Design
CHEN, TAILUN, Science
CHENG, FENGXIA, Resources and the Environment
DANG, HONGSHE, Electrical and Electronic Engineering
DANG, SISHAN, Science
DANG, XIN-AN, Electromechanical Engineering
DONG, WENBIN, Life Sciences and Engineering
DU, RUIQING, Foreign Languages
GAN, JIANZHI, Design
GONG, TAISHENG, Resources and the Environment
HOU, ZAIEN, Science
LI, GUOXING, Science
LI, LINSHENG, Chemistry and Chemical Engineering
LI, XI, Electrical and Electronic Engineering
LI, XIAORUI, Chemistry and Chemical Engineering
LI, ZHONGJIN, Chemistry and Chemical Engineering
LIN, XIAOLIN, Computer and Information Engineering
LIU, SHUXING, Life Sciences and Engineering
LU, JIALI, Life Sciences and Engineering
LU, XINGFANG, Resources and the Environment
LUO, CANGXUE, Life Sciences and Engineering
LUO, HONGJIE, Materials Science and Engineering
MA, JIANZHONG, Resources and the Environment
MENG, YANJING, Electrical and Electronic Engineering
MIAO, HONGYAN, Materials Science and Engineering
NING, DUO, Electrical and Electronic Engineering
QI, XIANGJUN, Life Sciences and Engineering
QIANG, XIHUAI, Resources and the Environment
SHAN, JINGMIN, Design
SHEN, YIDING, Chemistry and Chemical Engineering
SONG, HONGXIN, Life Sciences and Engineering
SUN, YU, Electrical and Electronic Engineering
TIAN, SANDE, Life Sciences and Engineering
WANG, DEZHONG, Design
WANG, FENG, Materials Science and Engineering
WANG, HONGRU, Resources and the Environment
WANG, JIANGEN, Resources and the Environment
WANG, LIANJIE, Life Sciences and Engineering
WANG, MENGXIAO, Electrical and Electronic Engineering
WANG, QUANJIE, Resources and the Environment
WANG, XIUFENG, Materials Science and Engineering
WANG, XUECHUAN, Resources and the Environment
XU, JIANZHONG, Foreign Languages
XU, MUDAN, Life Sciences and Engineering
YANG, JIANZHOU, Chemistry and Chemical Engineering
YANG, JUNSHUN, Design
YU, CONGZHEN, Resources and the Environment
YU, DAYUAN, Electrical and Electronic Engineering
ZHANG, CHUANBO, Resources and the Environment
ZHANG, GUANGHUA, Chemistry and Chemical Engineering
ZHANG, XIAOLEI, Resources and the Environment
ZHANG, ZHENGXI, Computer and Information Engineering
ZHENG, ENRANG, Electrical and Electronic Engineering
ZHOU, LIAN, Materials Science and Engineering
ZHU, ZHENFENG, Materials Science and Engineering

SHANDONG UNIVERSITY

Shanda Nanlu, Shandong 250100, Jinan Province
Telephone: (531) 8364701
Fax: (531) 8565657
Internet: www.sdu.edu.cn
Founded 1901
Min. of Education control
Academic year: September to July
Pres.: ZHAN TAO
Vice-Pres: FAN HONGJIAN, FANG HONGJIAN, HU JIACHEN, LI CHENGJUN, WANG QILONG, YU XIUPING, ZHANG YONGBING
Head of Graduate Dept: WANG QILONG
Librarian: SU WEIZHI
Number of teachers: 3,154
Number of students: 50,000
Publications: *Folk Custom Research* (4 a year), *Journal of Literature, History and Philosophy* (6 a year), *Journal of Shandong University* (editions: philosophy and social sciences; natural sciences; health science; engineering science, 6 a year), *Studies of Zhouyi* (6 a year), *Young Thinker* (6 a year)

DEANS

School of Business Administration: XU XIANGYI
School of Chemistry and Chemical Engineering: JIANG JIANZHUANG
School of Civil Engineering: CAO SHENGLE
School of Computer Science and Technology: MENG XIANGXU
School of Continuing Education: ZHUANG PING
School of Control Science and Engineering: JIA LEI
School of Dentistry: YANG PISHAN
School of Economics: ZANG XUHENG
School of Electrical Engineering: ZHAO JIANGUO
School of Energy and Power Engineering: PAN JIHONG
School of Environmental Science and Engineering: GAO BAOYU
School of Fine Arts: LI XIAOFENG
School of Foreign Languages and Literature: WANG SHOUYUAN
School of History and Culture: WANG YUJI
School of Information Science and Engineering: YUAN DONGFENG
School of Law: CHEN JINZHAO
School of Life Sciences: QU YINBO
School of Literature and Journalism: CHEN YAN
School of Marxist Theory of Education: ZHOU XIANGJUN
School of Materials Science and Engineering: JIANG MINHUA
School of Mathematics: LIU JIANYA
School of Mechanical Engineering: LI JIANFENG
School of Medicine: ZHANG YUN
School of Nursing: LOU FENGLAN
School of Pharmacy: LOU HONGXIANG
School of Philosophy and Social Development: FU YOUDE
School of Physics and Microelectronics: XIE SHIJIE
School of Political Science and Public Administration: LIU YUAN
School of Public Health: ZHAOS ZHONGTANG

PROFESSORS

BAI, ZENGLIANG, Life Sciences
BAO, SITAO, Literature and Journalism
BAO, XIAOMING, Life Sciences
BAO, YIFEI, Civil Engineering
BIAN, XIUFANG, Materials Science and Engineering
BU, YUXIANG, Chemistry and Chemical Engineering
CAI, LUZHONG, Information Science and Engineering
CAI, ZHENGTING, Chemistry and Chemical Engineering
CAO, CHENGBO, Chemistry and Chemical Engineering
CAO, QINGJIE, Mathematics
CAO, SHENGLE, Civil Engineering
CHAO, ZHONGCHEN, History and Culture
CHEN, CHUANZHONG, Materials Science and Engineering
CHEN, DAIRONG, Chemistry and Chemical Engineering
CHEN, GUANJUN, Life Sciences
CHEN, HONG, Foreign Languages and Literature
CHEN, JIGUANG, Civil Engineering
CHEN, KAOSHAN, Life Sciences
CHEN, LIANBI, Medicine
CHEN, QINGLAI, Civil Engineering
CHEN, SHANGSHENG, History and Culture
CHEN, SHAOZHU, Mathematics
CHEN, SHENHAO, Chemistry and Chemical Engineering

CHEN, XIAO, Chemistry and Chemical Engineering
CHEN, XISHEN, Materials Science and Engineering
CHEN, YAN, Literature and Journalism
CHEN, ZENGJING, Mathematics
CHEN, ZHIJUN, Business Administration
CHEN, ZIAN, History and Culture
CHENG, XINGKUI, Physics and Microelectronics
CHENG, ZHAOLIN, Mathematics
CHI, ZHENMING, Life Sciences
CONG, YAPING, Foreign Languages and Literature
CUI, DAYONG, History and Culture
CUI, XI, Public Health
CUI, XING, Medicine
CUI, ZHAOJIE, Environmental Science and Engineering
DING, RONGGUI, Business Administration
DING, SHILIANG, Physics and Microelectronics
DING, SHILIANG, Chemistry and Chemical Engineering
DING, YUANMING, Philosophy and Social Development
DUAN, QI, Mathematics
EHRLICH, M. A., Philosophy and Social Development
FAN, JINXUE, Law
FAN, XIULING, Business Administration
FANG, HUI, History and Culture
FANG, LEI, Political Science and Public Administration
FENG, DACHENG, Chemistry and Chemical Engineering
FENG, DIANMEI, Law
FENG, MEILI, Nursing
FENG, SHENGYU, Chemistry and Chemical Engineering
FU, YONGJUN, Philosophy and Social Development
FU, YOUDE, Philosophy and Social Development
GAN, YING, Business Administration
GAO, BAOYU, Chemistry and Chemical Engineering
GAO, BAOYU, Environmental Science and Engineering
GAO, JIANGUO, Philosophy and Social Development
GAO, PEIJI, Life Sciences
GAO, RUWEI, Physics and Microelectronics
GAO, YINGMAO, Medicine
GAO, ZHENMING, Information Science and Engineering
GE, BENYI, Literature and Journalism
GENG, HAORAN, Materials Science and Engineering
GENG, JIANHUA, Literature and Journalism
GENG, ZUNJING, Civil Engineering
GONG, YAOQIN, Medicine
GU, LUANZHAI, History and Culture
GU, QINGMIN, Medicine
GU, YUEZHU, Chemistry and Chemical Engineering
GUAN, SHAOJI, History and Culture
GUAN, XIAOJUN, Materials Science and Engineering
GUO, DAJUN, Mathematics
GUO, JIDE, Foreign Languages and Literature
GUO, YANLI, Literature and Journalism
HAN, SHENGHAO, Physics and Microelectronics
HAO, AIYOU, Chemistry and Chemical Engineering
HAO, JINGCHENG, Chemistry and Chemical Engineering
HE, MAO, Physics and Microelectronics
HE, ZHONGHUA, Philosophy and Social Development
HONG, XIAOGUANG, Computer Science and Technology
HOU, WANGUO, Chemistry and Chemical Engineering

HOU, XUEYUAN, Information Science and Engineering
HU, JIFAN, Physics and Microelectronics
HU, PEICHU, Mathematics
HU, WEICHENG, Medicine
HU, WEIQING, History and Culture
HU, WENRONG, Environmental Science and Engineering
HU, XINSHENG, History and Culture
HU, ZHENGMING, Business Administration
HUANG, FAYOU, Literature and Journalism
HUANG, FENG, Life Sciences
HUANG, QINGZHI, Political Science and Public Administration
HUANG, SHENG, Civil Engineering
HUANG, WANHUA, Literature and Journalism
HUANG, XIRONG, Chemistry and Chemical Engineering
JI, AIGUO, Pharmacy
JI, FAHAN, Literature and Journalism
JI, PEIRONG, Political Science and Public Administration
JI, YUNXIA, Foreign Languages and Literature
JIA, LEI, Control Science and Engineering
JIA, ZHIPING, Computer Science and Technology
JIANG, BAOFA, Public Health
JIANG, JIANZHUANG, Chemistry and Chemical Engineering
JIANG, MINHUA, Materials Science and Engineering
JIANG, QINGLI, Environmental Science and Engineering
JIANG, SHENG, History and Culture
JIANG, SHOULI, Mathematics
JIANG, YONG, Philosophy and Social Development
JIN, WENRUI, Chemistry and Chemical Engineering
KONG, FANJIN, Literature and Journalism
KONG, JIAN, Life Sciences
KONG, LINGREN, History and Culture
LI, CHUANLIN, Computer Science and Technology
LI, DAIBIN, Control Science and Engineering
LI, DAXING, Mathematics
LI, FENGXIAN, Environmental Science and Engineering
LI, GANZUO, Chemistry and Chemical Engineering
LI, GUOJUN, Mathematics
LI, HONGWEI, Life Sciences
LI, HUA, Physics and Microelectronics
LI, JIANFENG, Literature and Journalism
LI, JIE, Public Health
LI, JINGZHOU, Computer Science and Technology
LI, JINYU, Physics and Microelectronics
LI, JUN, Business Administration
LI, MUSEN, Materials Science and Engineering
LI, QIN, Philosophy and Social Development
LI, QINGZHONG, Computer Science and Technology
LI, QIQIANG, Control Science and Engineering
LI, SHAOMING, Foreign Languages and Literature
LI, SHUCAI, Civil Engineering
LI, WEI, History and Culture
LI, XIAO, History and Culture
LI, XIAOYAN, Chemistry and Chemical Engineering
LI, XUEQING, Computer Science and Technology
LI, XUEZHEN, Foreign Languages and Literature
LI, YAJIANG, Materials Science and Engineering
LI, YUCHEN, Computer Science and Technology
LI, YUEZHONG, Life Sciences
LI, ZHENZHONG, Medicine
LI, ZHONGYOU, Materials Science and Engineering
LIANG, HUIXING, Law

LIANG, ZUOTANG, Physics and Microelectronics
LIAO, QUN, Literature and Journalism
LIE, JIE, Philosophy and Social Development
LIE, JIE, Computer Science and Technology
LIN, JIANQIANG, Life Sciences
LIN, JUREN, Philosophy and Social Development
LIN, LU, Mathematics
LIN, MING, Law
LIN, XINYING, Public Health
LIU, BAOYU, Law
LIU, CHENGBO, Chemistry and Chemical Engineering
LIU, FENGJUN, History and Culture
LIU, GANG, Business Administration
LIU, GUIZHEN, Mathematics
LIU, HONGWEI, Business Administration
LIU, JIANYA, Mathematics
LIU, JIAZHUANG, Mathematics
LIU, JU, Information Science and Engineering
LIU, KAI, Medicine
LIU, LUPENG, Philosophy and Social Development
LIU, PING, History and Culture
LIU, RONGXING, Computer Science and Technology
LIU, SHIGUO, Law
LIU, SHUMEI, Foreign Languages and Literature
LIU, SHUTANG, Control Science and Engineering
LIU, SHUWEI, Medicine
LIU, TIANLU, History and Culture
LIU, XIANXI, Medicine
LIU, XINLI, Philosophy and Social Development
LIU, YIHUA, Physics and Microelectronics
LIU, YU-AN, Political Science and Public Administration
LIU, YUFENG, History and Culture
LIU, YUNGANG, Control Science and Engineering
LIU, YUTIAN, Electrical Engineering
LIU, ZHAOLI, Mathematics
LIU, ZHAOXU, Nursing
LIU, ZHENQIAN, Foreign Languages and Literature
LIU, ZHIYU, Medicine
LIU, ZONGLIN, Chemistry and Chemical Engineering
LOU, FENGLAN, Nursing
LOU, HONGXIANG, Pharmacy
LU, JUNWEI, History and Culture
LU, WEIZHONG, Foreign Languages and Literature
LU, YAO, History and Culture
LUAN, FENGSHI, History and Culture
LUO, FUTENG, Literature and Journalism
MA, FENGSHU, Political Science and Public Administration
MA, GUANGHAI, Philosophy and Social Development
MA, HONGLEI, Physics and Microelectronics
MA, JUN, Computer Science and Technology
MA, LIXIAN, Medicine
MA, LONGQIAN, Literature and Journalism
MA, RUIFANG, Literature and Journalism
MA, SHAOHAN, Mathematics
MEI, LIANGMO, Physics and Microelectronics
MENG, LIRONG, Computer Science and Technology
MENG, XIANGCAI, History and Culture
MENG, XIANGXU, Computer Science and Technology
MIAO, JUNYING, Life Sciences
MIAO, QINGHAI, Physics and Microelectronics
MIAO, RUNTIAN, Philosophy and Social Development
MIAO, XINGWEI, Foreign Languages and Literature
MIN, GUANGHUI, Materials Science and Engineering
MO, WENCHUAN, Business Administration
NING, FEI, Computer Science and Technology

NIU, YUNQING, Literature and Journalism
PAN, AILING, Business Administration
PANG, SHOUYING, Literature and Journalism
PENG, SHIGE, Mathematics
PENG, YUHUA, Information Science and Engineering
PENG, ZHIZHONG, Business Administration
QI, GUIJIE, Business Administration
QI, YANPING, Law
QIAN, ZENGYI, Literature and Journalism
QIAO, YIZHENG, Control Science and Engineering
QIAO, YOUMEI, History and Culture
QU, YINBO, Life Sciences
REN, DENGYI, Materials Science and Engineering
REN, QUAN, Information Science and Engineering
REN, XIANGHONG, History and Culture
RUI, HONGXING, Mathematics
SHANG, QINGSEN, Civil Engineering
SHANG, YU, Philosophy and Social Development
SHAO, LIHUA, Public Health
SHENG, YUQI, Literature and Journalism
SHI, BING, Computer Science and Technology
SHI, KAIQUAN, Mathematics
SHI, LIANYUN, Business Administration
SHI, YUMING, Mathematics
SONG, GANG, Medicine
SUI, QINGMEI, Control Science and Engineering
SUN, DEJUN, Chemistry and Chemical Engineering
SUN, HONGJIAN, Chemistry and Chemical Engineering
SUN, JILIN, Literature and Journalism
SUN, KANGNING, Materials Science and Engineering
SUN, NAZHENG, Mathematics
SUN, SIXIU, Chemistry and Chemical Engineering
SUN, TONGJING, Control Science and Engineering
SUN, WENSHENG, Medicine
SUN, XINQIANG, Law
SUN, YINGCHUN, Foreign Languages and Literature
SUN, ZIMEI, Literature and Journalism
TAN, HAOZHE, Literature and Journalism
TAN, SHIBAO, History and Culture
TAN, YEBANG, Chemistry and Chemical Engineering
TANG, ZIHENG, Literature and Journalism
TIAN, GUOHUI, Control Science and Engineering
TIAN, XUELEI, Materials Science and Engineering
WAN, JIANCHENG, Computer Science and Technology
WANG, CHENGRUI, Physics and Microelectronics
WANG, CHUNLEI, Physics and Microelectronics
WANG, DEGANG, Business Administration
WANG, FENGSHAN, Pharmacy
WANG, FUTAI, Business Administration
WANG, HAIYANG, Computer Science and Technology
WANG, HUAIJING, Medicine
WANG, JIANMIN, Political Science and Public Administration
WANG, JIANWU, Chemistry and Chemical Engineering
WANG, JIAYE, Mathematics
WANG, JIEZHEN, Public Health
WANG, JINFENG, Physics and Microelectronics
WANG, JINXING, Life Sciences
WANG, JIYANG, Materials Science and Engineering
WANG, JUNJU, Foreign Languages and Literature
WANG, KEMING, Physics and Microelectronics
WANG, KEMING, Materials Science and Engineering

WANG, LILI, Foreign Languages and Literature
WANG, LIPING, Law
WANG, PEIYUAN, Literature and Journalism
WANG, PENG, Life Sciences
WANG, PING, Literature and Journalism
WANG, QILONG, Chemistry and Chemical Engineering
WANG, QING, Civil Engineering
WANG, QINGYOU, Information Science and Engineering
WANG, QUANJUAN, Civil Engineering
WANG, RENQING, Life Sciences
WANG, RUBIN, Pharmacy
WANG, SHANBO, Philosophy and Social Development
WANG, SHAOXING, Political Science and Public Administration
WANG, SUMEI, Public Health
WANG, TIANHONG, Life Sciences
WANG, WEI, Mathematics
WANG, WENCHENG, Literature and Journalism
WANG, WENQIAO, Mathematics
WANG, XIAOSHU, Literature and Journalism
WANG, XIAOYI, History and Culture
WANG, XIAOYUN, Mathematics
WANG, XINCHUN, Philosophy and Social Development
WANG, XINGYUAN, Business Administration
WANG, XINNIAN, Physics and Microelectronics
WANG, XUEDIAN, History and Culture
WANG, YIMING, Business Administration
WANG, YOUZHI, Civil Engineering
WANG, YUJI, History and Culture
WANG, YUZHEN, Control Science and Engineering
WANG, ZHIFU, Materials Science and Engineering
WANG, ZHIYU, Public Health
WANG, ZHOUMING, Literature and Journalism
WANG, ZUNONG, Life Sciences
WANG, ZUOCHENG, Materials Science and Engineering
WEI, ZHONGLI, Mathematics
WEN, SHULIN, Materials Science and Engineering
WU, AIHUA, Business Administration
WU, JIAN, Chemistry and Chemical Engineering
WU, RUNTING, Literature and Journalism
WU, XIAOJUAN, Information Science and Engineering
WU, YAOHUA, Control Science and Engineering
WU, YOUSHI, Materials Science and Engineering
WU, ZHEN, Mathematics
XIA, GUANGMIN, Life Sciences
XIA, HAIRUI, Physics and Microelectronics
XIA, YUEYUAN, Physics and Microelectronics
XIANG, FENGNING, Life Sciences
XIAO, JINMING, Law
XIAO, MIN, Life Sciences
XIAO, XIA, Foreign Languages and Literature
XIE, HONGXIANG, Literature and Journalism
XIE, HUI, Law
XIE, KEQIN, Public Health
XIE, QUBING, Physics and Microelectronics
XIE, SHIJIE, Physics and Microelectronics
XIONG, ZHIPING, Civil Engineering
XU, BIN, Materials Science and Engineering
XU, CHAO, Literature and Journalism
XU, DONG, Materials Science and Engineering
XU, GUIFA, Public Health
XU, GUIYING, Chemistry and Chemical Engineering
XU, MINGYU, Mathematics
XU, PING, Life Sciences
XU, QIULIANG, Computer Science and Technology
XU, WENFANG, Pharmacy
XU, XIANGYI, Business Administration
XU, YANSHENG, Civil Engineering

YAN, BINGGANG, Philosophy and Social Development
YANG, DANPING, Mathematics
YANG, HUIXIN, Business Administration
YANG, JINGHE, Chemistry and Chemical Engineering
YANG, LIANZHONG, Mathematics
YANG, LUHUI, Political Science and Public Administration
YANG, RUIZHI, Literature and Journalism
YANG, XUEJIN, Business Administration
YANG, YANZHAO, Chemistry and Chemical Engineering
YI, HONGXUN, Mathematics
YIN, YANSHENG, Materials Science and Engineering
YU, GUANG, Business Administration
YU, GUANGHAI, History and Culture
YU, HONGXIA, Public Health
YU, XIUPING, Medicine
YUAN, DONGFENG, Information Science and Engineering
YUAN, SHISHUO, Literature and Journalism
YUAN, YIRANG, Mathematics
YUE, QINGYAN, Environmental Science and Engineering
ZENG, GUANGZHOU, Computer Science and Technology
ZENG, ZHENYU, History and Culture
ZHAN, TAO, Mathematics
ZHANG, CAIMING, Computer Science and Technology
ZHANG, CHANGKAI, Life Sciences
ZHANG, CHENGHUI, Control Science and Engineering
ZHANG, CHUNGUANG, Chemistry and Chemical Engineering
ZHANG, CHUNLING, Public Health
ZHANG, HENG, Medicine
ZHANG, HUAZHONG, Computer Science and Technology
ZHANG, JIANYE, Medicine
ZHANG, JINLONG, History and Culture
ZHANG, JUREN, Life Sciences
ZHANG, KELI, Literature and Journalism
ZHANG, LIHENG, History and Culture
ZHANG, LINING, Medicine
ZHANG, NAIJIAN, Physics and Microelectronics
ZHANG, PEILIN, Physics and Microelectronics
ZHANG, PEIZHONG, Civil Engineering
ZHANG, QINGFAN, Control Science and Engineering
ZHANG, QINGZHU, Pharmacy
ZHANG, RUILIN, Physical Education
ZHANG, SHUNHUA, Mathematics
ZHANG, SHUXUE, History and Culture
ZHANG, SHUZHENG, Literature and Journalism
ZHANG, TAO, History and Culture
ZHANG, TIQIN, Business Administration
ZHANG, XIEN, Political Science and Public Administration
ZHANG, XINGYU, Information Science and Engineering
ZHANG, XIUMEI, Medicine
ZHANG, XIWEI, History and Culture
ZHANG, XUEJUN, Literature and Journalism
ZHANG, XUEYAO, Physics and Microelectronics
ZHANG, YULIN, Control Science and Engineering
ZHANG, YUZHEN, Life Sciences
ZHANG, YUZHONG, Life Sciences
ZHAO, AIGUO, History and Culture
ZHAO, BINGXIN, Business Administration
ZHAO, GUOQUN, Materials Science and Engineering
ZHAO, JIANGUO, Electrical Engineering
ZHAO, JINGHUA, Business Administration
ZHAO, SHENGZI, Information Science and Engineering
ZHAO, WEIMIN, Medicine
ZHAO, XIAOFAN, Life Sciences
ZHAO, ZHONGTANG, Public Health
ZHENG, CHUN, Literature and Journalism
ZHENG, FENGLAN, Literature and Journalism

ZHENG, LIQIANG, Chemistry and Chemical Engineering
ZHENG, PEIXIN, History and Culture
ZHENG, XUNZUO, Literature and Journalism
ZHONG, MAIYING, Control Science and Engineering
ZHONG, WEILIE, Physics and Microelectronics
ZHOU, GENYAN, Medicine
ZHOU, GUANGYUAN, History and Culture
ZHOU, HONGXING, Mathematics
ZHOU, LAIXIANG, Literature and Journalism
ZHOU, XIAOYU, History and Culture
ZHU, DAMING, Computer Science and Technology
ZHU, RUIFU, Materials Science and Engineering
ZHU, WEISHEN, Civil Engineering

SHANDONG AGRICULTURAL UNIVERSITY

61 Dai Zong St, Taian 271018, Shandong Province
Telephone: (538) 8242291
Fax: (538) 8226399
E-mail: xb@sdau.cdu.cn
Internet: www.sdau.edu.cn

Founded 1906
Dept of Education of Shandong control
Academic year: September to July

Pres.: WEN FUJIANG
Vice-Pres: DONG SHUTING, YAO LAICHANG, ZHANG JINGHE, ZHANG XIANSHENG
Head of Graduate Dept: WANG ZHENLIN
Librarian: ZHANG XIANIQI

Number of teachers: 1,151
Number of students: 20,000

Publications: *Journal* (natural sciences, 4 a year), *Journal* (social sciences, 4 a year), *Shandong Journal of Animal Husbandry and Veterinary Science* (6 a year)

DEANS

College of Agricultural Resources and Environment: SHI YANXI
College of Agronomy: WANG HONGGANG
College of Animal Technology: TAN JINGHE
College of Chemistry and Materials Science: ZHOU JIE
College of Economy and Management: HU JILIAN
College of Food Science and Engineering: DONG HAIZHOU
College of Foreign Languages: LI ZHILING
College of Forestry: MU ZHIMEI
College of Horticulture: WANG XIUFENG
College of Humanities and Law: SUN YANQUAN
College of Hydrology and Civil Engineering: LIU FUSHENG
College of Information Science and Technology: WANG YUNCHENG
College of Life Sciences: ZHENG CHENGCHAO
College of Mechanical and Electronic Engineering: ZHENG WEI
College of Plant Protection: LI DUOCHUAN
College of Science: ZHOU JIE

PROFESSORS

AI, SHIYUN, Chemistry and Materials Science
CAI, TONGJIE, Animal Technology
CHANG, WEISHAN, Animal Technology
CHEN, XUESEN, Horticulture
CHENG, SHUHAN, Information Science and Technology
CUI, DECAI, Life Sciences
CUI, WEI, Humanities and Law
CUI, WEIZHENG, Forestry
CUI, YANSHUN, Animal Technology
CUI, ZHIZHONG, Animal Technology
DIAO, YOUXIANG, Animal Technology
DING, AIYUN, Plant Protection
DING, SHIFEI, Information Science and Technology

DONG, HAIZHOU, Food Science and Engineering
DONG, JINLING, Economy and Management
DONG, SHUTING, Agronomy
DU, SHOUJUN, Humanities and Law
FAN, WEIXING, Animal Technology
FAN, ZHICHENG, Horticulture
FENG, CHENGMING, Electromechanical Engineering
FENG, YONGJUN, Agricultural Resources and Environment
GAO, HUA, Information Science and Technology
GAO, HUA, Science
GAO, HUIYUAN, Life Sciences
GAO, QINGRONG, Agronomy
GAO, RONGQI, Agronomy
GUANGLIANG, DONGYE, Agricultural Resources and Environment
GUO, HUABEI, Information Science and Technology
GUO, HUABEI, Science
GUO, XINMIN, Electromechanical Engineering
HA, YIMING, Science
HE, MINGRONG, Agronomy
HU, CHANGHAO, Agronomy
HU, JILIAN, Economy and Management
HU, YANJI, Agronomy
JIANG, LIN, Chemistry and Materials Science
JIANG, YONGBIN, Economy and Management
JIN, XIANG, Chemistry and Materials Science
KANG, JINGFENG, Electromechanical Engineering
KONG, LINGRANG, Agronomy
LI, ANFEI, Agronomy
LI, DEQUAN, Life Sciences
LI, DUOCHUAN, Plant Protection
LI, FUCHANG, Animal Technology
LI, JIRONG, Horticulture
LI, JIYE, Hydrology and Civil Engineering
LI, QIANG, Plant Protection
LI, QINGQI, Agronomy
LI, RUXIN, Electromechanical Engineering
LI, TONGSHU, Animal Technology
LI, XIANGDONG, Agronomy
LI, XIANGDONG, Plant Protection
LI, XIANLI, Horticulture
LI, ZENGJIA, Agronomy
LI, ZHAOHUI, Plant Protection
LI, ZHENSHENG, Plant Protection
LIANG, XUETIAN, Hydrology and Civil Engineering
LIN, HAI, Animal Technology
LIN, HONGXIAO, Hydrology and Civil Engineering
LIN, QUANYE, Forestry
LING, CHENGHOU, Electromechanical Engineering
LIU, CHUANBAO, Hydrology and Civil Engineering
LIU, CHUNSHENG, Agricultural Resources and Environment
LIU, FUSHENG, Hydrology and Civil Engineering
LIU, KAIQI, Plant Protection
LIU, LIANWE, Science
LIU, LIANWEI, Chemistry and Materials Science
LIU, SHIDANG, Animal Technology
LIU, XIAOGUANG, Plant Protection
LIU, YAN, Foreign Languages
LIU, ZHONGXIANG, Animal Technology
LU, FUSUI, Chemistry and Materials Science
LU, FUSUI, Science
LUO, WANCHUN, Plant Protection
MA, SHUSHENG, Hydrology and Civil Engineering
MENG, QINGWEI, Life Sciences
MENG, XIANGDONG, Horticulture
MIAO, LIANG, Information Science and Technology
MU, LIYI, Plant Protection
MU, ZHIMEI, Forestry
NIE, JUNHUA, Agricultural Resources and Environment

PANG, QINGJIANG, Hydrology and Civil Engineering
PEIZHENG, ZHANG, Food Science and Engineering
QI, SHUJUN, Foreign Languages
QU, XIANGJIN, Science
SHAN, LUN, Agronomy
SHEN, XIANG, Horticulture
SHI, JIANMIN, Economy and Management
SHI, PEI, Agronomy
SHI, YANXI, Agricultural Resources and Environment
SHU, HUAIRUI, Horticulture
SHUHAN, CHENG, Science
SONG, JIANCHENG, Agronomy
SU, LANZHEN, Agronomy
SUN, MINGGAO, Forestry
SUN, XUGEN, Forestry
SUN, YANQUAN, Humanities and Law
SUN, ZHONGXU, Horticulture
TAN, JINGHE, Animal Technology
TIAN, BO, Plant Protection
TIAN, JICHUN, Agronomy
TIAN, QIZHUO, Agronomy
WAN, JIACHUAN, Economy and Management
WAN, YONGSHAN, Agronomy
WANG, DECHUN, Economy and Management
WANG, HANZHONG, Life Sciences
WANG, HONGGANG, Agronomy
WANG, HONGMO, Economy and Management
WANG, HUIMING, Electromechanical Engineering
WANG, KAIYUN, Plant Protection
WANG, LIQIN, Horticulture
WANG, SHUYING, Animal Technology
WANG, XIANZE, Life Sciences
WANG, XIUFENG, Horticulture
WANG, YUNCHENG, Information Science and Technology
WANG, YUNCHENG, Science
WANG, ZELI, Life Sciences
WANG, ZHENLIN, Agronomy
WANG, ZHONGHUA, Animal Technology
WEI, JIANGCHUN, Plant Protection
WEN, FUJIANG, Life Sciences
XING, SHIYAN, Forestry
XU, HONGFU, Plant Protection
XU, KUN, Horticulture
XU, WEIAN, Plant Protection
XUE, XINGLI, Economy and Management
XUESONG, HUANG, Food Science and Engineering
YAN, YANCHUN, Life Sciences
YAN, ZHENYUAN, Hydrology and Civil Engineering
YANG, DI, Humanities and Law
YANG, HONGQIANG, Horticulture
YANG, JIHUA, Forestry
YANG, QUANMING, Animal Technology
YANG, XUECHENG, Economy and Management
YANG, ZAIBIN, Animal Technology
YIN, XIANGCHU, Plant Protection
YIN, XUNHE, Animal Technology
YIN, YANPING, Agronomy
YU, SONGLIE, Agronomy
YU, XIANCHANG, Horticulture
YU, YIMIN, Hydrology and Civil Engineering
YU, YUANJIE, Agronomy
YU, ZHENWEN, Agronomy
YUE, YONGSHENG, Animal Technology
ZENG, YONGQING, Animal Technology
ZHAI, HENG, Horticulture
ZHANG, CHUNQING, Agronomy
ZHANG, GUANGMIN, Plant Protection
ZHANG, LIANGCHENG, Hydrology and Civil Engineering
ZHANG, MIN, Agricultural Resources and Environment
ZHANG, TIANYU, Plant Protection
ZHANG, XIANSHENG, Life Sciences
ZHANG, XIAOHUI, Electromechanical Engineering
ZHANG, ZHIGUO, Agricultural Resources and Environment
ZHAO, GENGXING, Agricultural Resources and Environment

ZHAO, HONGKUN, Animal Technology
ZHAO, LANYONG, Forestry
ZHAO, TANFANG, Agronomy
ZHENG, CHENGCHAO, Life Sciences
ZHENG, GUOSHENG, Life Sciences
ZHOU, JIE, Chemistry and Materials Science
ZHOU, JIE, Science
ZHOU, YANPING, Economy and Management
ZHU, FENGGANG, Chemistry and Materials Science
ZHU, FENGGANG, Science
ZHU, LUSHENG, Agricultural Resources and Environment
ZHU, RUILIANG, Animal Technology
ZOU, QI, Life Sciences

SHANDONG INSTITUTE OF ECONOMICS

4 East Yanzishan Rd, Jinan 250014, Shandong

Telephone: (531) 8934161
Internet: www.china-sd.com/business/sdjjxy/home2e.htm
Founded 1958
Pres.: Prof. HU JIJIAN
Vice-Pres: LI RENQUAN, Prof. LIU SHIFAN, Prof. REN HUI
Librarian: LI ZIRUI
Number of teachers: 322
Number of students: 2,118
Publications: *Accountant, Shandong Economy, Statistics and Management.*

SHANDONG NORMAL UNIVERSITY

88 Wen Hua East Rd, Jinan 250014, Shangdong Province

Telephone: (531) 6180018
Fax: (531) 6180017
E-mail: xiaoban@sdnu.edu.cn
Internet: www.sdnu.edu.cn
Founded 1950
Provincial control
Academic year: September to July
Pres.: ZHAO YANXIU
Vice-Pres: QI WANXUE, TANG BO, WANG ZHAOLIANG, WANG ZHIMIN, ZHANG QINGGANG
Head of Graduate Dept: ZHANG WEIJUN
Librarian: SHEN DAGUANG
Number of teachers: 1,150
Number of students: 37,300 (24,300 full-time, 13,000 part-time)
Publications: *China Population, Resources and Environment* (6 a year), *Journal* (humanities and social sciences, 6 a year), *Journal* (natural sciences, 4 a year), *Journal of the School of Foreign Languages of Shandong Teachers' University* (4 a year), *Shandong Foreign Languages Journal* (6 a year)

DEANS

College of Broadcasting: MENG XIANGZENG
College of Chemistry, Chemical Engineering and Materials Science: DONG YUBIN
College of Chinese Language and Literature: ZHOU JUNPING
College of Educational Science: ZHANG WENXIN
College of Fine Arts: KONG XINMIAO
College of Foreign Languages: YANG MIN
College of History, Culture and Social Development: WANG WEI
College of Information and Management: LIU XIYU
College of Legal Science: HAN YUGUI
College of Life Sciences: AN LIGUO
College of Mathematical Science: FU XILIN
College of Music: ZHANG ZHUN
College of Physical Education: YU TAO

College of Physics and Electronics: WANG CHUANKUI
College of Population, Resources and the Environment: REN JIANLAN

PROFESSORS

AN, LIGUO, Life Sciences
BI, HUALIN, Chemistry, Chemical Engineering and Materials Science
CAI, JINLING, Chemistry, Chemical Engineering and Materials Science
CAO, CHUNCHUN, Foreign Languages
CAO, DAOPING, Life Sciences
CAO, MINGHAI, Chinese Language and Literature
CHEN, DEZHAN, Chemistry, Chemical Engineering and Materials Science
CHEN, HAIHONG, History, Culture and Social Development
CHEN, HUANZHEN, Mathematical Science
CHEN, QING, Broadcasting
CHEN, XIULAN, Physics and Electronics
CHEN, YIMING, Music
CHENG, DAOPING, Population, Resources and the Environment
CHENG, JIEMIN, Population, Resources and the Environment
CHENG, XHUANFU, Physics and Electronics
DAI, SHIJUN, Chinese Language and Literature
DENG, HONGMEI, Chinese Language and Literature
DIAO, PEIJUN, Legal Science
DONG, SHAOKE, Chinese Language and Literature
DONG, YUBIN, Chemistry, Chemical Engineering and Materials Science
DU, GUICHEN, Chinese Language and Literature
FAN, XIJUN, Physics and Electronics
FU, HAILUN, Mathematical Science
FU, RONGRU, Life Sciences
FU, XILIN, Mathematical Science
GAO, FENGQIANG, Educational Science
GAO, HUA, Foreign Languages
GAO, JINGZHEN, Mathematical Science
GAO, TIEJUN, Physics and Electronics
GAO, YIQING, Fine Arts
GUO, CHENGSHAN, Physics and Electronics
GUO, GENSHENG, Broadcasting
HAN, HONGFEI, Physical Education
HAN, MEI, Population, Resources and the Environment
HAN, YUGUI, Legal Science
HE, JIAMEI, Population, Resources and the Environment
HE, JINGLIANG, Physics and Electronics
HONG, XUEBIN, Broadcasting
HOU, FULIN, Life Sciences
HOU, KANGWEI, Music
HUANG, MINGSHUI, Music
JI, GUANGMAO, Chinese Language and Literature
JIANG, CHONGQIU, Chemistry, Chemical Engineering and Materials Science
JIANG, ZHENCHANG, Chinese Language and Literature
JIANG, ZHONGYING, Broadcasting
JIANG, ZIWEN, Mathematical Science
KONG, XINMIAO, Fine Arts
LI, AIHUA, Legal Science
LI, HONGRUI, Chemistry, Chemical Engineering and Materials Science
LI, HUAIXIANG, Chemistry, Chemical Engineering and Materials Science
LI, JIAN, Physics and Electronics
LI, LAIZHONG, Chemistry, Chemical Engineering and Materials Science
LI, PING, Population, Resources and the Environment
LI, QIAN, Mathematical Science
LI, SHIZHENG, Mathematical Science
LI, TAOXIN, Educational Science
LI, XIAOLIN, Chemistry, Chemical Engineering and Materials Science
LI, XUEMIN, Mathematical Science

LI, YANXHU, Chinese Language and Literature
LI, YUJIANG, Population, Resources and the Environment
LI, YUNLONG, Life Sciences
LI, ZHIHUA, Chemistry, Chemical Engineering and Materials Science
LIANG, FANZHEN, Chemistry, Chemical Engineering and Materials Science
LIN, SHENGLU, Physics and Electronics
LIU, CHUNYING, Foreign Languages
LIU, FANG'AI, Information and Management
LIU, FENGLING, Chemistry, Chemical Engineering and Materials Science
LIU, HAIYAN, Educational Science
LIU, HONG, Information and Management
LIU, PEIYU, Information and Management
LIU, TAO, Physical Education
LIU, WENXIAN, Physics and Electronics
LIU, XIAOLIAN, Physical Education
LIU, XIYU, Information and Management
LIU, YANSHENG, Mathematical Science
LIU, ZAISHENG, Music
LU, HONG, Broadcasting
MA, SHUNYE, Mathematical Science
MA, YONGQING, Legal Science
MAN, BAOYUAN, Physics and Electronics
MENG, XIANGZENG, Broadcasting
NIE, QINGXIANG, Physics and Electronics
QI, WANXUE, Educational Science
QU, MINGWEN, Foreign Languages
QU, WENGUANG, Mathematical Science
QUAN, CHAOLU, Educational Science
REN, JIANLAN, Population, Resources and the Environment
SHENG, DAZHONG, Chemistry, Chemical Engineering and Materials Science
SHI, JINGMIN, Chemistry, Chemical Engineering and Materials Science
SHI, ZHIQIANG, Chemistry, Chemical Engineering and Materials Science
SONG, FENGGUANG, Fine Arts
SONG, JIGUO, Fine Arts
SONG, LILI, Music
SUN, LEI, Mathematical Science
SUN, XIHUA, Population, Resources and the Environment
TANG, BO, Chemistry, Chemical Engineering and Materials Science
TANG, BO, Life Sciences
TANG, NING, Music
TIAN, JIANGUO, Mathematical Science
TIAN, SHUFENG, Broadcasting
TONG, DIANMIN, Physics and Electronics
WAN, GUANGXIA, Legal Science
WANG, BAOSHAN, Life Sciences
WANG, BING, Educational Science
WANG, CHUANKUI, Physics and Electronics
WANG, HONGJIAN, Chemistry, Chemical Engineering and Materials Science
WANG, HONGQI, Chinese Language and Literature
WANG, HUAIYOU, Chemistry, Chemical Engineering and Materials Science
WANG, HUAXUE, Chinese Language and Literature
WANG, KUIYONG, Information and Management
WANG, QINGXIN, Foreign Languages
WANG, SHENGHAI, Physical Education
WANG, WANSEN, Chinese Language and Literature
WANG, WEI, History, Culture and Social Development
WANG, YOUBANG, Population, Resources and the Environment
WANG, ZEXIN, Chemistry, Chemical Engineering and Materials Science
WANG, ZHIMING, Chinese Language and Literature
WEI, JIAN, Chinese Language and Literature
WEI, WEI, Educational Science
WU, QINGFENG, Chinese Language and Literature
WU, QUANYUAN, Population, Resources and the Environment

Wu, Yiqin, Chinese Language and Literature
Xia, Zhifang, Chinese Language and Literature
Xiang, Yang, Music
Xiao, Longfu, Foreign Languages
Xu, Changjun, Music
Xu, Qingpu, Legal Science
Xu, Qingru, Music
Xu, Xinzhai, Mathematical Science
Xu, Yaotong, Population, Resources and the Environment
Yan, Baoqiang, Mathematical Science
Yang, Guoliang, Physical Education
Yang, Min, Foreign Languages
Yang, Shousen, Chinese Language and Literature
Yu, Jinjiang, Foreign Languages
Yu, Quanxun, Physics and Electronics
Yu, Tao, Physical Education
Zhang, Congshan, Broadcasting
Zhang, Enyi, Broadcasting
Zhang, Fuji, Legal Science
Zhang, Guorong, Chemistry, Chemical Engineering and Materials Science
Zhang, Hui, Life Sciences
Zhang, Jinghuan, Educational Science
Zhang, Jinping, Broadcasting
Zhang, Qinggang, Physics and Electronics
Zhang, Qinghua, Chinese Language and Literature
Zhang, Shufeng, Educational Science
Zhang, Shuqin, Foreign Languages
Zhang, Wenxin, Educational Science
Zhang, Xijie, Fine Arts
Zhang, Yufen, Mathematical Science
Zhang, Yuhong, Life Sciences
Zhang, Zhide, Chemistry, Chemical Engineering and Materials Science
Zhang, Zhulu, Population, Resources and the Environment
Zhang, Zhun, Music
Zhao, Chengfu, Educational Science
Zhao, Jian, Population, Resources and the Environment
Zhao, Jie, Physics and Electronics
Zhao, Qinguo, Fine Arts
Zhao, Qingzhen, Information and Management
Zhao, Yanxiu, Life Sciences
Zheng, Mingchun, Information and Management
Zheng, Xinqi, Population, Resources and the Environment
Zhou, Bo, Chinese Language and Literature
Zhou, Junping, Chinese Language and Literature
Zhou, Zhichen, Chemistry, Chemical Engineering and Materials Science
Zhu, Defa, Chinese Language and Literature
Zhu, Junkong, Physics and Electronics
Zhuang, Wan, Mathematical Science
Zhuang, Wenzhong, Life Sciences
Zhuo, Zhuang, Physics and Electronics

SHANGHAI INTERNATIONAL STUDIES UNIVERSITY

550 Dalian Rd West, Shanghai 200083
Telephone: (21) 65360599
Fax: (21) 65313756
E-mail: oisasisu@mail.online.sh.cn
Internet: www.shisu.edu.cn
Founded 1949
Academic year: September to July
President: Dai Weidong
Vice-Presidents: Sheng Yuliang, Tan Jinghua, Wu Youfu, Zhu Jianguo
Head of Graduate Department: Feng Qinghua
Librarian: Zhu Lei
Number of teachers: 300
Number of students: 8,300
Publications: *Educational Technology for Foreign Language Teaching* (6 a year),

Journal (6 a year), *The Arab World* (6 a year)

DEANS

College of Eastern Languages: Lu Peiyong
College of International Business Administration: Lin Xunzi
College of International Cultural Exchange: Xu Baomei
College of International Education: Shi Huili
College of Japanese Culture and Economy: Pi Xigeng
College of Journalism and Communication: Hu Shuzhong
College of the English Language: Shi Zhikang
College of the Russian Language: Zheng Tiwu
College of Western Language and Literature: Wei Maoping
Graduate Institute of Interpretation and Translation: Chai Mingjiong
School of Law: Yu Jianhua

PROFESSORS

Cai, Yousheng, Western Language and Literature
Cao, Deming, Western Language and Literature
Chai, Mingjiong, Graduate Institute of Interpretation and Translation
Chen, Huizhong, International Cultural Exchange
Chen, Xiaochun, Western Language and Literature
Dai, Huiping, Graduate Institute of Interpretation and Translation
Dai, Weidong, English
Dou, Hui, Law
Du, Yunde, Graduate Institute of Interpretation and Translation
Feng, Qinghua, English
He, Zhaoxiong, English
Hu, Long, Journalism and Communication
Hu, Shuzhong, Journalism and Communication
Li, Weiping, English
Lu, Jingsheng, Western Language and Literature
Lu, Loufa, Graduate Institute of Interpretation and Translation
Lu, Peiyong, Eastern Languages
Lu, Yongchang, Russian
Lu, Guangdan, English
Mei, Deming, English
Pi, Xigeng, Japanese Culture and Economy
Qian, Peixin, Western Language and Literature
Qiu, Maoru, English
Shen, Yucheng, Japanese Culture and Economy
Shi, Huili, International Education
Shi, Zhikang, English
Shi, Zhikang, Graduate Institute of Interpretation and Translation
Shu, Shengpeng, Western Language and Literature
Tan, Jinghua, Japanese Culture and Economy
Wei, Maoping, Western Language and Literature
Wu, Dagang, Japanese Culture and Economy
Wu, Dingbo, English
Xie, Tianzhen, Graduate Institute of Interpretation and Translation
Xu, Yulong, English
Yang, Jinhua, International Cultural Exchange
Yu, Jianhua, Law
Zhang, Shihua, Western Language and Literature
Zhang, Weiliang, English
Zhang, Yonghua, Journalism and Communication
Zhang, Zhuxin, Journalism and Communication

Zheng, Tiwu, Russian
Zhou, Ping, Japanese Culture and Economy
Zhou, Shen, English
Zhou, Wenju, Eastern Languages

SHANGHAI JIAOTONG UNIVERSITY

1954 Hua Shan Rd, Shanghai 200030
Telephone: (21) 62812444
Fax: (21) 62821369
E-mail: wangxuanban@yahoo.com.cn
Internet: www.sjtu.edu.cn
Founded 1896
Academic year: September to July
President: Zhang Jie
Vice-Presidents: Chen Gang, Lin Zhongqin, Ye Quyuan, Yin Jie, Zhang Shimin, Zhang Wenjun, Zhu Zhenggang
Director of President's Office: Zhang Wei
Librarian: Chen Zhaonen
Library of 1,826,000 vols
Number of teachers: 2,889
Number of students: 36,100 (incl. 18,100 postgraduates)
Publication: *Journal* (6 a year, also in English)

HEADS OF SCHOOLS

Department of Physical Education: Sun Qiling
Department of Plasticity Technology: Ruan Xueyu
School of Chemistry and Chemical Engineering: Tang Xiaozheng
School of Civil Engineering and Mechanics: Liu Zhengxing
School of Electric Power Engineering: Hou Zhijian
School of Electronics and Information Technology: Xi Yugeng
School of Foreign Languages: Zheng Shutang
School of Humanities and Social Sciences: Ye Dunping
School of Life Sciences and Technology: Tang Zhangcheng
School of Machinery Engineering: Yan Junqi
School of Management: Zhang Xiang
School of Materials Science and Engineering: Wu Jiansheng
School of Naval Architecture and Ocean Engineering: Li Runpei
School of Power and Energy Resources Engineering: Xu Jijun
School of Science: Shi Zhongci

SHANGHAI NORMAL UNIVERSITY

100 Guilin Rd, Nanjing 200234, Jiangsu Province
Telephone: (21) 64322881
Fax: (21) 64360512
Internet: www.shtu.edu.cn
Founded 1954
Academic year: September to July
Pres.: Yu Lizhong
Vice-Pres: Jiang Weiyi, Liu Zhigang, Lu Jianping, Xiang Jiaxiang
Librarian: Cao Xu
Library of 2,600,000 vols
Number of teachers: 1,181
Number of students: 40,000
Publications: *Chinese University Academic Abstracts* (6 a year), *Journal* (6 a year)

DEANS

Architecture Engineering College: Liu Jianxin
Engineering College of Machinery and Electronics Information: Lin Xiaoyun
Fine Arts College: Xu Wangyao
Life and Environmental Sciences College: Li Hexing

Mathematics and Science College: ZHANG JIZHOU
School of Arts: XIE JING
School of Commerce: FU HONGCHUN
School of Education: LU JIAMEI
School of European Culture and Trade: MAO XUNCHENG
School of Foreign Languages: GU DAXIN
School of Law and Politics: SHANG HONGRI
School of Literature: SUN XUN
School of Music: DAI DINGCHENG
Sports College: LU CHANGYA

PROFESSORS

CAI, LONGQUAN, Foreign Languages
CAO, TONG, Life and Environmental Sciences
CAO, XU, Literature
CEN, GUOZHEN, Education
CHEN, KEJIAN, Law and Politics
CHEN, MINGZHENG, Arts
CHEN, WEI, Literature
CHEN, WEIPING, Law and Politics
CHENG, XINGHUA, Foreign Languages
CHENG, ZHEHUAN, Law and Politics
DAI, DINGCHENG, Music
DENG, MINGDE, Foreign Languages
FAN, KAITAI, Literature
FAN, WUYUN, Literature
FANG, GUANGCHANG, Law and Politics
FEI, HELIANG, Mathematics and Science
FU, HONGCHUN, Commerce
GAN, FENG, Law and Politics
GAO, HUIZHU, Law and Politics
GAO, JIANHUA, Mathematics and Science
GU, DAXI, Foreign Languages
GU, HAIGEN, Education
HE, YUNFENG, Law and Politics
HONG, XIAOXIA, Law and Politics
HUANG, BAOHUA, Literature
JIA, HUANZHEN, Arts
JIANG, CHUANGUANG, Law and Politics
KANG, AISHI, Arts
LI, HEXING, Life and Environmental Sciences
LI, JIAHOU, Arts
LI, SHENG, Law and Politics
LI, SHI, Literature
LI, WEIHUI, Commerce
LI, WEIMING, Sports
LI, XIAOYUN, Machinery and Electronics Information Engineering
LI, YIZHEN, Life and Environmental Sciences
LI, ZHIGUO, Commerce
LIU, DANQING, Literature
LIU, JIANXIN, Architecture
LIU, YANYAN, Law and Politics
LU, CHANGYA, Sports
LU, JIAMEI, Education
LU, RUOPING, Arts
LU, RUZHAN, Literature
MA, DELING, Law and Politics
MEI, ZIHAN, Literature
MI, ZHENG, Arts
QI, LUYANG, Literature
REN, ZHONGLUN, Literature
SHANG, HONGRI, Law and Politics
SHAO, YONG, Literature
SHEN, HEBO, Life and Environmental Sciences
SHI, YONGBING, Mathematics and Science
SHUN, XUN, Literature
SUN, JINGRAO, Literature
SUN, XUSHENG, Sports
SUN, YUWEI, Law and Politics
TAN, WEIGUO, Foreign Languages
TANG, LIXING, Literature
TAO, BENYI, Literature
WANG, CUIYING, Sports
WANG, GUORONG, Mathematics and Science
WANG, JIREN, Literature
WANG, TIANQU, Literature
WANG, XIAODUN, Literature
WANG, XINQIU, Foreign Languages
WANG, YANMING, Mathematics and Science
WEI, SHIXIAN, Arts
WENG, MINHUA, Literature
WU, HONGLIN, Arts

WU, JINGDONG, Law and Politics
WU, JUNMING, Life and Environmental Sciences
WU, QUANXI, Life and Environmental Sciences
WU, XIAQIN, Life and Environmental Sciences
XIA, HUIXIAN, Education
XIE, LIMIN, Education
XU, SHIYI, Literature
XU, WEIHONG, Arts
XUE, HESHENG, Commerce
XUE, SIJIA, Life and Environmental Sciences
YAN, GWENHU, Literature
YANG, DONG, Sports
YANG, JIANLONG, Literature
YANG, ZHONGHUA, Mathematics and Science
YANG, ZHONGNAN, Life and Environmental Sciences
YE, HUANIAN, Foreign Languages
YE, HUANIAN, Literature
YU, XIBING, Life and Environmental Sciences
YUAN, BING, Literature
YUAN, FENG, Law and Politics
YUE, RONGXIAN, Mathematics and Science
ZHANG, JIZHOU, Mathematics and Science
ZHANG, ZIQIANG, Machinery and Electronics Information Engineering
ZHAO, XIAONAN, Arts
ZHENG, KELU, Literature
ZHOU, GENYU, Life and Environmental Sciences
ZHOU, ZHONGZHI, Law and Politics
ZHU, SHUNQUAN, Mathematics and Science
ZHU, XIANSHENG, Literature

SHANGHAI SECOND MEDICAL UNIVERSITY

280 South Chongqing Rd, Shanghai 200025
Telephone: (21) 63846590
Fax: (21) 63842916
Internet: www.shsmu.edu.cn
Founded 1952
Languages of instruction: Chinese, English, French
Academic year: September to July
Chancellor: FAN GUANRONG
Vice-Chancellors: Prof. CHEN ZHIXING, Prof. QIAN GUANXIANG, Prof. ZHUANG MENGHU, Assoc. Prof. ZHU ZHENGGANG
Registrar: Prof. CAI WEI
Librarian: Assoc. Prof. ZHANG WENHAO
Library of 420,000 vols
Number of teachers: 3,379
Number of students: 5,000

Publications: *Chinese Journal of Endocrinology and Metabolism* (in Chinese), *Journal of Clinical Paediatrics* (in Chinese), *Journal of Shanghai Second Medical University* (in Chinese and English), *Shanghai Journal of Immunology* (in Chinese)

DEANS

College of Basic Medical Sciences: Prof. LU YANG
Department of Social Sciences: XIANG YANG
Faculty of Clinical Medicine in Ren Ji Hospital: Prof FAN GUANRONG
Faculty of Clinical Medicine in Rui Jin Hospital: Prof. LI HONGWEI
Faculty of Clinical Medicine in No. 6 People's Hospital: Prof. LIN FAXIONG
Faculty of Paediatrics and Clinical Medicine in Xin Hua Hospital: Prof. SHEN XIAOMIN
Junior Medical College in Bao Gang Hospital: JUN SHENGJI
Health School: Assoc. Prof. WU XIANGQIAN
School of Stomatology: Prof. ZHANG ZHIYUAN

SHANGHAI TIEDAO UNIVERSITY

450 Zhennan Lu, Shanghai 200333
Telephone: (21) 2506812

Fax: (21) 2506812
Internet: www.shtdu.edu.cn
Founded 1995 by merger of Shanghai Institute of Railway Technology and Shanghai Railway Medical College
State control
Academic year: September to July (2 terms)
Pres.: Prof. CHEN GUANMAO
Vice-Pres: Prof. LI MENG, Prof. MA WENZENG, Prof. MAO YONGJIANG, Assoc. Prof. SUN ZHANG, Prof. XU LONG, Prof. ZHU GUANGJIE
Registrar: Prof. MIAO RUNSHEN
Librarian: Prof. WU WENQI
Library of 850,000 vols, 2,900 periodicals
Number of teachers: 1,164
Number of students: 6,354

Publication: *Journal*

PROFESSORS

AI, Y., Hygienics
CAI, N., Physiology
CAI, T., Surgery
CHAO, X., Bridge, Tunnel and Structural Engineering
CHEN, D. L., Dermatology
CHEN, D. Y., Fluid Drive
CHEN, H., Mechanical Engineering
CHEN, J., Railway Locomotives and Rolling Stock
CHEN, S., Railway Locomotives and Rolling Stock
CHENG, S., Pathology
DENG, N., Internal Medicine
DU, Q., Electrification and Automation
FAN, P., Mechanical Engineering
FENG, Z. Q., Histology and Embryology
FENG, Z. Z., Railway Vehicles
GONG, J., Railway Locomotives and Rolling Stock
GUO, D. F., Railway Location and Construction
GUO, D. P., Orthopaedics
HOU, H., Neuropathology
HU, B., Anatomy
HU, K., Bridge, Tunnel and Structural Engineering
HU, M., Computer Communication
HUA, W., English
HUANG, S., Transport Management
JI, L., Transport Management
JIANG, E., Internal Combustion Engines
LE, S., Stomatology
LI, D., Surgery
LI, H., Mathematics
LI, J., Ophthalmology
LI, M., Applied Computer Technology
LI, S., Internal Medicine
LI, Y., Mechanics
LIN, Z., Ultrasonic Diagnosis
LIU, C., Internal Medicine
LIU, Q., Hydraulic Pressure Technology
LIU, X., Railway Automation
LIU, Y., Electrical Appliances
LIU, Z., Paediatrics
LU, G., Civil Engineering
LU, Y., Civil Engineering
NIE, C., Fluid Drive and Control
PAN, K., Stomatological Surgery
PENG, Y. O., Economics
QI, W., Internal Combustion Engines
QIU, W., Medical Genetics
REN, J., Transport Management
RUAN, Y., Computer Engineering
SHAO, B., Power Electronics Technology
SHEN, P., Railway Locomotives and Rolling Stock
SHEN, Z., Infectious Diseases
SHI, S., Stomatology
SONG, J., Anaesthesia
SUN, P., Surgery
SUN, Q., Railway Location and Construction
SUN, S., Parasitology
SUN, Y., Laboratory Testing
TAN, B., Mechanical Engineering
TAO, S., Computer Engineering

TAO, Z., Fluid Drive
TONG, D., Wheel-rail System
WANG, B., Applied Computer Technology
WANG, B., Surgery
WANG, D., Telecommunications
WANG, F., Railway Vehicles
WANG, Q., Railway Electrification and Automation
WANG, R., Mathematics
WANG, W., Railway Engineering
WANG, Y., Biochemistry
WU, F., Telecommunications
WU, J., Railway Location and Construction
WU, W. Q., Transport Signals and Control
WU, W. Y., Psychiatry
WU, X., Railway Location and Construction
WU, Z. K., Electrical Appliances
WU, Z. R., Civil Engineering
XIA, Y., Mechanics
XIONG, W., Mechanics
XU, T., Mechanics
YANG, G., Mechanics
YANG, H. C., Histology and Embryology
YANG, H. Y., Transport Management
YANG, X., Civil Engineering
YE, E., Hygienics
YIN, L., Mechanics
YU, W., Pharmacology
YUAN, S., Stomatology
ZHANG, D. X., Railway Locomotives and Rolling Stock
ZHANG, D. Z., Railway Locomotives and Rolling Stock
ZHANG, J., Gynaecology and Obstetrics
ZHANG, S. C., Stomatology
ZHANG, S. J., Telecommunications and Information Processing
ZHANG, W. C., Civil Engineering
ZHANG, X., Mechanics
ZHANG, Y. J., Electrical Technology
ZHANG, Y. Z., Internal Medicine
ZHANG, Z., Railway Locomotives and Rolling Stock
ZHAO, S., Politics
ZHENG, G., Stomatology
ZHENG, T., Power Electronics Technology
ZHOU, Z., Stomatological Surgery
ZHU, J., Railway Location and Construction
ZHU, M., Mechanics
ZHU, P., Theoretical Physics
ZHU, X., Mathematics
ZONG, G., Structural Engineering

SHANGHAI UNIVERSITY OF FINANCE AND ECONOMICS

777 Guoding Rd, Shanghai 200433
Telephone: (21) 65903505
Fax: (21) 65100561
Internet: www.shufe.edu.cn
Founded 1917
Ministry of Education control
Academic year: September to July
President: TAN MIN
Vice-Presidents: CONG SHUHAI, HUANG LIN-FANG, SUN ZHENG, WANG HONGWEI, ZHOU ZHONGFEI
Head of Graduate Department: FENG ZHENG-QUAN
Librarian: LI XIAOYE
Number of students: 20,000

Publications: *Economics and Management of Foreign Countries* (12 a year), *Higher Education of Finance and Economics* (4 a year), *Journal* (6 a year), *Journal of Finance and Economics* (12 a year)

DEANS

Department of Foreign Languages: WANG XIAOQUN
Department of Information Management: LIU LANJUAN
Department of Physical Education: CHEN XIAO
Department of Statistics: HAN XIAOLIANG

School of Accountancy: CHEN XINYUAN
School of Applied Mathematics: CHEN QIHONG
School of Economics: TIAN GUOQIANG
School of Finance: DAI GUOQIANG
School of Humanities: ZHANG XIONG
School of International Business Management: SUN HAIMING
School of Law: ZHOU ZHONGFEI
School of MBA Programmes: LUO ZUWANG
School of Public Economy Administration: JIANG HONG

PROFESSORS

BIAN, ZUWU, Statistics
CHANG, NING, Statistics
CHAO, GANGLING, Marketing
CHE, WEIHAN, International Economics
CHEN, HUIQIN, Statistics
CHEN, QIHONG, Applied Mathematics
CHEN, QIJIE, Marketing
CHEN, WENHAO, Accountancy
CHEN, XIAO, Physical Education
CHEN, XINKANG, Marketing
CHEN, XINYUAN, Accountancy
CHEN, YUN, Public Economy Administration
CHENG, ENFU, Economics
CHU, MINWEI, Public Economy Administration
CHU, YIYUN, Accountancy
CONG, SHUHAI, Public Economy Administration
DAI, GUOQIANG, Banking
DING, BANGKAI, Law
DONG, FENGGU, Statistics
DOU, JIANMING, Statistics
DU, XUNCHENG, Economics
FEI, FANGYU, International Finance
GAN, CHUNHUI, Industry Economics
GU, GUIDING, Applied Mathematics
GU, GUOZHU, Humanities
GUO, SHIZHENG, Public Economy Administration
GUO, YUDAN, International Trade
HAN, QING, Economics
HAN, XIAOLIANG, Statistics
HE, JIANMIN, Tourism Management
HE, YUCHANG, Economics
HU, JINGBEI, Economics
HU, YIJIAN, Public Economy Administration
HU, YIMING, Accountancy
HU, YONGGANG, Economics
HUO, WENWEN, Finance
JIANG, HONG, Public Economy Administration
JIANG, YIHONG, Accountancy
JIN, DEHUAN, Finance
LAN, YISHENG, International Trade
LI, XIAOYE, Humanities
LI, XIAOYU, Statistics
LI, XIN, Economics
LIANG, ZHIAN, Applied Mathematics
LIAO, YINLIN, Statistics
LIN, JUE, International Economics
LIU, HANLIANG, Statistics
LIU, LIJUAN, Resource Management
LIU, YONGMING, Banking
LU, PINYUE, Humanities
LU, SHIMIN, Banking
LU, WANZHONG, Statistics
LUO, ZUWANG, Humanities
MA, GUOXIAN, Public Economy Administration
MI, WENZHAN, Humanities
PAN, FEI, Accountancy
PEI, YIRAN, Humanities
PENG, JIAQIANG, Humanities
QI, ZHIXIANG, Humanities
QU, WEIDONG, International Finance
SHAO, JIANLI, Statistics
SHENG, BANGHE, Humanities
SHI, BINGCHAO, Banking
SHI, XIQUAN, International Finance
SU, JUNHE, Statistics
SUN, HAIMING, Industry Economics
SUN, YUNWU, Statistics

SUN, ZHENG, Accountancy
TAN, MIN, Economics
TAN, ZHENG, Information Management
TAO, TINGFANG, Tourism Management
WANG, DEFA, Statistics
WANG, HONGWEI, Public Economy Administration
WANG, HUILING, Statistics
WANG, LIMING, Statistics
WANG, LIYA, Foreign Languages
WANG, SONGNIAN, Accountancy
WANG, XIAOMING, Statistics
WANG, XIAOQUN, Foreign Languages
WANG, XINXIN, Marketing
WANG, XUEMIN, Statistics
WANG, YU, Business Management
WU, LONGSHENG, Resource Management
XI, JUNYANG, International Finance
XIA, JIANMING, Business Management
XIE, ZHIGANG, Finance
XU, DAJIAN, Humanities
XU, GUOXIANG, Statistics
XU, JIANPING, Humanities
XU, JINLIANG, Finance
XU, ZHENDAN, Accountancy
XUE, HUACHENG, Information Management
YAN, GUANGHUA, Business Management
YANG, DAKAI, Public Economy Administration
YANG, GONGPU, Industry Economics
YANG, JUNCHANG, Public Economy Administration
YANG, NAN, Statistics
YIN, CHENGYUAN, Applied Mathematics
YING, SHICHANG, Finance
YOU, JIARONG, Accountancy
YU, DINGWEI, Statistics
YU, ZHIYOU, Finance
YUAN, HONGQI, Accountancy
YUE, YAOXING, International Trade
ZAN, TINGQUAN, Information Management
ZHANG, CHUN, Accountancy
ZHANG, JUE, Humanities
ZHANG, MIAO, Statistics
ZHANG, MING, Accountancy
ZHANG, MINGFANG, Statistics
ZHANG, XIONG, Humanities
ZHANG, YAN, Humanities
ZHANG, YAOTING, Economics
ZHANG, YINJIE, Economics
ZHAO, JIANYONG, Accountancy
ZHAO, XIAOJU, Banking
ZHAO, XIAOLEI, Economics
ZHAO, XIAOSHENG, Foreign Languages
ZHOU, ZHONGFEI, Law
ZHU, BAOHUA, Economics
ZHU, GUOHUA, Industry Economics
ZHU, JIANZHONG, Statistics
ZHU, MINGXIONG, Statistics
ZHU, PINGFANG, Economics
ZHU, RONGEN, Accountancy
ZHU, YINGPING, Humanities
ZHU, ZHONGDI, International Economics

SHANGHAI UNIVERSITY

1220 Xin Zha Rd, Shanghai 200041
Telephone: (21) 2553062
Fax: (21) 2154780
Internet: www.shu.edu.cn
Founded 1983

Chancellor: Prof. WANG SHENGHONG
Deputy Chancellor: Prof. LIN JIONGRU
Vice-Chancellors: Prof. CAO ZHONGXIAN, Prof. LI MINGZHONG
University Dean: Prof. WENG SHIRONG
University Coordinator for Foreign Affairs and International Programmes: ZHONG GUOXIANG

Number of teachers: 1,200, incl. 296 profs
Number of students: 7,500

Publications: *Journal, Secretariat, Sociology*

PRESIDENTS

College of Business: Prof. JIANG JIAJUN
College of Engineering: Prof. MA GUOLIN
College of Fine Arts: Prof. LI TIANXIANG
College of International Business: Prof. LU GUANQUAN
College of Liberal Arts: Prof. WANG XIMEI
College of Political Science: Prof. WANG XIMEI

SHANTOU UNIVERSITY

243 University Rd, Shantou 515063, Guangdong Province
Telephone: (754) 2902350
Fax: (754) 2510509
Internet: www.stu.edu.cn

Founded 1981
Provincial control
Academic year: September to July

Pres.: XU XIAOHU
Vice-Pres: LI YUGUANG, WU GUANGGUO, XIANG BING, XIAO ZELI, ZHENG YI
Head of Graduate Dept: WANG ZHAN
Librarian: HUANG TING

Number of teachers: 630
Number of students: 12,868 (8,254 full-time, 4,614 part-time)

Publications: *Chinese Literature* (6 a year), *Journal* (4 a year), *Journal* (humanities and social sciences edition, 6 a year), *Journal* (natural science edition, 4 a year)

DEANS

College of Business: XUE YUNKUI
College of Engineering: GONG LEIGUANG
College of Law: ZHOU WEI
College of Literature: FENG SHANG
College of Medicine: LI YUGUANG
College of Science: LI DAN
Department of Physical Education: XU BIN
Department of Social Science: CHENG JIAMING
School of Art and Design: JIN DAIQIANG
School of Journalism and Communication: CHEN WANYING

PROFESSORS

CAO, BINGYUAN, Science
CHEN, FANGJING, Literature
CHEN, GUOQIANG, Science
CHEN, HANWEN, Business
CHEN, HONGLIN, Science
CHEN, MAOHUAI, Medicine
CHEN, WANYING, Journalism and Communication
CHEN, YAN, Art and Design
CHENG, JIAMING, Social Science
DING, XIAOJUN, Medicine
DING, ZHAOKUN, Science
DU, DANMING, Business
DU, GANGJIAN, Law
DU, LUNLUN, Literature
DUAN, MINGKE, Medicine
FANG, JIE, Science
GAO, KUNSHAN, Science
GONG, LEIGUANG, Engineering
GUO, XIANGUO, Medicine
GUO, XISHEN, Science
HAN, YALI, Science
HANG, JIAN, Art and Design
HE, SHAOHENG, Medicine
HERFORD, P. M., Journalism and Communication
HU, XINGRONG, Journalism and Communication
HUANG, CHANGJIANG, Science
HUANG, DONGYANG, Medicine
HUANG, XUELAN, Law
HUANG, YAN, Business
HUANG, YUANMING, Science
HUO, XIA, Medicine
JIANG, XUEWU, Medicine
JIN, DAIQIANG, Art and Design
KONG, KANGMEI, Medicine
LAN, SHENG, Science

LI, DAN, Science
LI, ENMIN, Medicine
LI, GUICANG, Literature
LI, KANGSHENG, Medicine
LI, PING, Law
LI, QING, Art and Design
LI, SHENGPING, Engineering
LI, YUGUANG, Medicine
LIN, FURONG, Science
LIN, SHUNCHAO, Medicine
LIU, JIANBIN, Engineering
LIU, XIAOHUA, Science
LOU, ZENGJIAN, Science
LUO, WENHONG, Medicine
MA, WENHUI, Science
MAI, JIEHUA, Science
MO, YAN, Literature
NI, ZHENHUA, Engineering
QI, DAQING, Business
QI, WEILI, Medicine
QIAN, SHUANRU, Medicine
QIAN, ZHIQIANG, Art and Design
QIN, DANIAN, Medicine
QIU, HANYING, Medicine
QIU, QINGCHUN, Science
SHEN, MINFEN, Engineering
SHI, GANGGANG, Medicine
SU, MIN, Medicine
TIAN, DONGPING, Medicine
WANG, CHEN, Medicine
WANG, FUREN, Literature
WANG, HUIGE, Medicine
WANG, JUNMING, Science
WANG, SHOUZHI, Art and Design
WANG, YINHE, Science
WANG, ZIYUAN, Science
WU, GUANGFUO, Science
WU, JIANXHONG, Medicine
WU, RENHUA, Medicine
WULAN, HASHI, Science
XIANG, BING, Business
XIAO, TAN, Science
XIE, HUICAI, Engineering
XIE, ZHUANGNING, Engineering
XU, JIANHENG, Medicine
XU, LUHANG, Law
XU, XIAOHU, Medicine
XU, ZONGLING, Business
XUE, YUNKUI, Business
YANG, SHOUZHI, Science
YANG, ZHONGQIANG, Science
YE, RUISONG, Science
YIN, YEGAO, Science
YUAN, ZHOU, Journalism and Communication
ZHAO, XIAOHUA, Engineering
ZHENG, XHIPEI, Medicine
ZHENG, YI, Engineering
ZHOU, WEI, Law

SHANXI AGRICULTURAL UNIVERSITY

Taigu 030801, Shaanxi Province
Telephone: (354) 6288211
Fax: (354) 6222942
E-mail: sxauxb@sxau.edu.cn
Internet: www.sxau.edu.cn

Founded 1950
Provincial control
Academic year: September to July

Pres.: DONG CHANGSHENG
Vice-Pres: CUI KEYONG, WANG JUNDONG, YUE WENBIN
Librarian: KANG CHENGYE

Number of teachers: 602
Number of students: 7,300

Publications: *Journal* (natural sciences, 4 a year), *Journal* (social sciences, 4 a year), *Study of Agriculture in Higher Education* (6 a year)

DEANS

College of Adult Education: REN JIAYAN
College of Agriculture: LI SHENGCAI

College of Animal Technology: LI HONGQUAN
College of Economics and Trade: (vacant)
College of Engineering Technology: (vacant)
College of Food Science and Engineering: HAO LIPING
College of Forestry: (vacant)
College of Horticulture: REN JIAYAN
College of Life Sciences: (vacant)
College of Resources and Environmental Science: SUN TAISEN
College of Social Science: (vacant)
Department of Modern Education and Technology: (vacant)

PROFESSORS

BAI, ZHONGKE, Resources and Environmental Science
CHANG, MINGCHANG, Food Science and Engineering
DONG, CHANGSHENG, Animal Technology
FAN, WENHUA, Resources and Environmental Science
HAN, JUCAI, Agriculture
HAO, JIANPING, Agriculture
HAO, LIN, Food Science and Engineering
HAO, LIPING, Food Science and Engineering
HE, YUNCHUN, Agriculture
HONG, JIANPING, Resources and Environmental Science
LI, BINGLIN, Agriculture
LI, HONGQUAN, Animal Technology
LI, SHENGCAI, Agriculture
LIN, DAYI, Resources and Environmental Science
LIU, HUIPING, Agriculture
LU, XIN, Resources and Environmental Science
MA, LIZHEN, Food Science and Engineering
PANG, QUANHAI, Animal Technology
SUN, TAISEN, Resources and Environmental Science
TANG, CHAOZHONG, Animal Technology
WANG, HONGFU, Agriculture
WANG, JUNDONG, Animal Technology
WANG, RUFU, Food Science and Engineering
WANG, SHENGUI, Resources and Environmental Science
WANG, YUGUO, Agriculture
WANG, ZHIRUI, Animal Technology
WANG, ZHIYA, Resources and Environmental Science
WEN, WEIYE, Animal Technology
WU, CAI-E, Food Science and Engineering
XIE, YINGHE, Resources and Environmental Science
YANG, JINZHONG, Agriculture
YANG, WUDE, Agriculture
ZHANG, HENG, Resources and Environmental Science
ZHAO, LIZHI, Agriculture

SHANXI UNIVERSITY

36 Wu Cheng Rd, Taiyuan 030006, Shanxi Province
Telephone: (351) 7010944
Fax: (351) 7011981
E-mail: xiaoban@sxu.edu.cn
Internet: www.sxu.edu.cn

Founded 1902
Provincial control
Academic year: September to July

Pres.: GUICHUN GUI
Vice-Pres: JIA SUOTANG, LIU WEIQI, LIU ZHENSHENG, QI FENG, XING LONG
Head of Graduate Dept: GAO CE
Librarian: LI JIALIN

Number of teachers: 1,105
Number of students: 18,817 (11,905 full-time, 6,912 part-time)

Publications: *Acta Sinica Quantum Optica* (philosophy and social sciences, 4 a year), *Journal* (natural sciences, 4 a year), *Journal* (philosophy and social sciences, 4 a year), *Journal of Teachers' College of Shanxi University* (4 a year), *Shanxi Library Journal* (6 a year)

DEANS

College of Fine Arts: WANG ERXI
College of Music: WANG LIANG
College of Physical Education: LI JIANYING
College of Physics and Electronics Engineering: LIANG JIUQING
Department of History: LI SHUJI
Department of Mathematics: LI SHENGJIA
School of Chemistry and Engineering: ZHAO YONGXIANG
School of Chinese Language and Literature: QIAO QUANSHENG
School of Computer Science and Information Technology: LIANG JIYE
School of Economics: LIU JIANSHENG
School of Education Science: HOU HUAIYIN
School of Environmental Science and Resources: GUO DONGSHENG
School of Foreign Languages: NIE JIANZHONG
School of Law: WANG JIJUN
School of Life Science and Technology: MA ENBO
School of Management: CAO LIJUN
School of Philosophy and Sociology: QIAO RUIJIN
School of Political Science and Public Administration: LI LUQU

PROFESSORS

AN, XIMENG, Philosophy and Sociology
BI, FUSHENG, Philosophy and Sociology
CAO, LIJUN, Management
CHEN, JINSHENG, Law
CHEN, SHIBIN, Music
CHEN, ZHAOBIN, Chemistry and Engineering
CHENG, RENGAN, History
DENG, BING, Chemistry and Engineering
DONG, CHUAN, Chemistry and Engineering
DONG, YUMING, Law
FAN, WENBIAO, Environmental Science and Resources
FAN, YINGFANG, Chemistry and Engineering
GAO, XING, Music
GONG, RONGDE, Fine Arts
GUO, DONGSHENG, Environmental Science and Resources
GUO, GUICHUN, Philosophy and Sociology
GUO, YUXIANG, Fine Arts
HAN, JIANRONG, Life Science and Technology
HAN, XIANGMING, Education Science
HAN, ZHIMO, Fine Arts
HAO, JIANGRUI, Physics and Electronics Engineering
HONG, LIANGZHEN, Chinese Language and Literature
HOU, HUAIYIN, Education Science
HU, JIANHUA, Physical Education
HU, MINGLIANG, Foreign Languages
HUANG, FENGCHUN, Chemistry and Engineering
HUANG, SHUPING, Chemistry and Engineering
JIA, LIANFENG, Physics and Electronics Engineering
JIA, SHUOTANG, Physics and Electronics Engineering
JIA, XINCHUN, Mathematics
JIA, XIUYING, Foreign Languages
JIN, WEIJUN, Chemistry and Engineering
KANG, JINSHENG, Chinese Language and Literature
LAI, YUNZHONG, Physics and Electronics Engineering
LAN, HUANG, Chinese Language and Literature
LI, DEREN, Fine Arts
LI, FUYI, Mathematics
LI, JIANYING, Physical Education
LI, JINLONG, Physical Education
LI, LUQU, Political Science and Public Administration

LI, RUINING, Physics and Electronics Engineering
LI, SHENGJIA, Mathematics
LI, SHUJI, History
LI, WENDE, Chemistry and Engineering
LI, YUE'E, Foreign Languages
LI, ZHENGMIN, Chinese Language and Literature
LI, ZHIQIANG, Economics
LI, ZHONGHAO, Physics and Electronics Engineering
LIANG, JIAHUA, Management
LIANG, JIUQING, Physics and Electronics Engineering
LIANG, JIYE, Computer Science and Information Technology
LIANG, LIPING, Political Science and Public Administration
LIANG, ZHANDONG, Mathematics
LIU, BO, Chemistry and Engineering
LIU, CHAO, Music
LIU, GUIHU, Chinese Language and Literature
LIU, HAILIANG, Foreign Languages
LIU, HONGBING, Music
LIU, JIANSHENG, Economics
LIU, SHUQING, Chinese Language and Literature
LIU, WENSEN, Physics and Electronics Engineering
LIU, XHENSHENG, Chemistry and Engineering
LIU, XIAOHUI, Life Science and Technology
LIU, XIAOLI, Physical Education
LIU, YEPING, Fine Arts
LIU, ZHENSHENG, Chemistry and Engineering
MA, AIPING, Law
MA, ENBO, Life Science and Technology
MA, GUIBIN, Chemistry and Engineering
MA, HAILIANG, Foreign Languages
MA, WEIHUA, Law
MA, YONGMING, Chemistry and Engineering
MA, YUSHAN, History
MENG, ZIQIANG, Life Science and Technology
MIAO, DUOQIAN, Mathematics
NIE, HONGYIN, Chinese Language and Literature
NIE, YIXIN, Physics and Electronics Engineering
PAN, JINGHAO, Chemistry and Engineering
PAN, QING, Physics and Electronics Engineering
PANG, RENJI, Foreign Languages
PEI, CHENGFA, Economics
PEI, CHENGFA, Management
PENG, KUIXI, Physics and Electronics Engineering
PENG, YUNYE, Law
QIAO, DECAI, Physical Education
QIAO, QUANSHENG, Chinese Language and Literature
QIAO, RUIJIN, Philosophy and Sociology
QIN, XUEMEI, Chemistry and Engineering
REN, JIANGUO, Chemistry and Engineering
SHI, YAN, Physical Education
SHUANG, SHAOMIN, Chemistry and Engineering
SONG, BINGYAN, Philosophy and Sociology
SU, CHUNSHENG, Chinese Language and Literature
TIAN, YANNI, Chemistry and Engineering
WANG, HAI, Physics and Electronics Engineering
WANG, JIJUN, Law
WANG, JUNMIN, Physics and Electronics Engineering
WANG, LAN, Life Science and Technology
WANG, LIANG, Music
WANG, RONGSHENG, History
WANG, SHIYING, Mathematics
WANG, XIANMING, History
WANG, YI, Law
WANG, YINTIAN, History
WANG, YUANZHI, Law
WANG, ZHENGREN, Foreign Languages
WEI, GUANHLAI, History
WU, GAOSHOU, Philosophy and Sociology

WU, MIN, Political Science and Public Administration
WU, MINZHONG, Political Science and Public Administration
XIA, XHIXHONG, Chemistry and Engineering
XIANG, LILING, Management
XIE, CHANGDE, Physics and Electronics Engineering
XIE, JIAOLIANG, Life Science and Technology
XIE, SHULIAN, Life Science and Technology
XIE, YINGPING, Life Science and Technology
XING, LONG, History
XU, BINGSHENG, Chinese Language and Literature
XU, GENQI, Mathematics
XU, YONGMIN, Philosophy and Sociology
YAN, FENGWU, Chinese Language and Literature
YAN, JURANG, Mathematics
YANG, BINSHENG, Chemistry and Engineering
YANG, JUPING, History
YANG, LIAN, Chinese Language and Literature
YANG, PIN, Chemistry and Engineering
YANG, SUPING, Life Science and Technology
YI, HUILAN, Life Science and Technology
YU, GUODONG, Foreign Languages
YUE, QIANHOU, History
ZHANG, CUIYING, Management
ZHANG, FENG, Life Science and Technology
ZHANG, HENG, Chinese Language and Literature
ZHANG, JINGSHI, Education Science
ZHANG, JINTUN, Environmental Science and Resources
ZHANG, KUANSHOU, Physics and Electronics Engineering
ZHANG, MIN, Chinese Language and Literature
ZHANG, MINGYUAN, Fine Arts
ZHANG, RU, Chinese Language and Literature
ZHANG, RUIRONG, Music
ZHANG, SHENGWAN, Chemistry and Engineering
ZHANG, TIANCAI, Physics and Electronics Engineering
ZHANG, XIAOGE, Music
ZHANG, XINWEI, Management
ZHANG, YIXIAN, Life Science and Technology
ZHANG, ZHAO, Chemistry and Engineering
ZHANG, ZHUANGHUA, Life Science and Technology
ZHAO, AIMIN, Mathematics
ZHAO, JIANGUO, Chinese Language and Literature
ZHAO, RUIMIN, History
ZHAO, XIAOJUN, Law
ZHAO, YONGXIANG, Chemistry and Engineering
ZHAO, YUXIA, Philosophy and Sociology
ZHAO, ZHAOMING, Life Science and Technology
ZHOU, GUOSHENG, Physics and Electronics Engineering

SHENYANG AGRICULTURAL UNIVERSITY

120 Dongling Rd, Shenyang 110161, Liaoning Province
Telephone: (24) 88421121
Fax: (24) 88417415
Internet: www.syau.edu.cn
Founded 1952
Academic year: September to July
Pres.: ZHANG YULONG
Vice-Pres.: LI TIANLAI
Vice-Pres.: LIU GUANGLIN
Vice-Pres.: MENG QINGCHENG
Head of Graduate Dept: JIN BAOLIAN
Librarian: DUAN YUXI
Number of teachers: 859
Number of students: 20,105

Publications: *Chinese Journal of Soil Science*
(6 a year), *Higher Agricultural Education*
(12 a year), *Journal* (natural sciences, 6 a
year), *Journal* (social sciences, 4 a year),
Journal of Pig Rearing (6 a year), *New
Agriculture* (12 a year)

DEANS

College of Agronomy: CAO MINJIAN
College of Biological Science and Technology:
ZHANG LIJUN
College of Economics and Trade: FANG TIAN-
KUN
College of Engineering: LI CHENGHUA
College of Food Science: LIU CHANGJIAN
College of Forestry: LIU MINGGUO
College of Horticulture: LI ZUOXUAN
College of Information and Electrical Engin-
eering: PU ZAILIN
College of Land and the Environment: WANG
QIUBING
College of Plant Protection: FU JUNFAN
College of Practical Technology: YANG YIN-
SHAN
College of Science and Technology: (vacant)
College of Veterinary Science: HU JIANMING
College of Water Resources: WANG TIELIANG

PROFESSORS

BEI, NAXIN, Plant Protection
BIAN, QUANLIAN, Veterinary Science
CAO, MINJIAN, Agronomy
CAO, YUANYIN, Plant Protection
CAO, ZHIQIANG, Agronomy
CHEN, ENFENG, Land and the Environment
CHEN, JIE, Plant Protection
CHEN, WENFU, Agronomy
CHEN, XIAOFEI, Water Resources
CHEN, XISHI, Land and the Environment
CHEN, ZHENWU, Agronomy
CHENG, GUOHUA, Biological Science and Tech-
nology
CHENG, YULAI, Food Science
CHI, DAOCAI, Water Resources
CONG, BIN, Plant Protection
DAI, PENGJUN, Economics and Trade
DONG, WENXUAN, Horticulture
DU, GUANGMING, Horticulture
DU, SHAOFAN, Veterinary Science
DUAN, YUXI, Plant Protection
FANG, TIANKUN, Economics and Trade
FENG, HUI, Horticulture
FU, JUNFAN, Plant Protection
GAO, DESAN, Biological Science and Technol-
ogy
GAO, GUOPING, Forestry
GAO, XINGLIAN, Engineering
GUAN, LIANZHU, Land and the Environment
GUO, XIUWU, Horticulture
GUO, YUHUA, Agronomy
HAN, XIAORI, Land and the Environment
HE, JUNSHI, Water Resources
HE, LILI, Horticulture
HOU, LIBAI, Agronomy
HU, JIANMIN, Veterinary Science
HUANG, RUIDONG, Agronomy
HUI, SHURONG, Basic Education
JI, JIANWEI, Information and Electrical
Engineering
JI, MINGSHAN, Plant Protection
JI, MINGXI, Water Resources
JI, SHUJUAN, Food Science
JIANG, QILIANG, Plant Protection
LAN, QINGGAO, Economics and Trade
LI, BAOFA, Engineering
LI, BAOHUA, Basic Education
LI, BAOJIANG, Horticulture
LI, BINGCHAO, Basic Education
LI, CHENGHUA, Engineering
LI, GUOJIE, Insititute of Higher Education
LI, JIANNAN, Biological Science and Technol-
ogy
LI, TIANLAI, Horticulture
LI, XINHUA, Food Science
LI, YONGKUI, Engineering
LI, YUXIA, Basic Education

LI, ZUOXUAN, Horticulture
LIANG, CHENGHUA, Land and the Environ-
ment
LIANG, JINGYI, Plant Protection
LIN, GUOLIN, Land and the Environment
LIU, CHANGJIANG, Food Science
LIU, MINGGUO, Forestry
LIU, RONGHOU, Engineering
LIU, ZHIHENG, Plant Protection
LIU, ZHONGQIN, Economics and Trade
LU, GUOZHONG, Plant Protection
LU, JIE, Economics and Trade
LU, SHUXIA, Biological Science and Technol-
ogy
LUO, GUANGBIN, Veterinary Science
MAO, TAO, Food Science
MENG, XIANJUN, Food Science
MI, YONGNING, Water Resources
NIU, SHEN, Centre for Analysis and Testing
PU, ZAILIN, Information and Electrical Engin-
eering
QIN, LI, Biological Science and Technology
QIU, LICHUN, Engineering
REN, WENTAO, Engineering
SHEN, XIANGQUN, Horticulture
SHI, ZHENSHENG, Agronomy
SI, LONGTING, Horticulture
SUN, JUNDE, Land and the Environment
TANG, YONG, Biological Science and Technol-
ogy
WANG, BOLUN, Agronomy
WANG, CHUNPING, Economics and Trade
WANG, HONGPING, Plant Protection
WANG, HUICHENG, Engineering
WANG, JINGKUAN, Land and the Environment
WANG, JINMIN, Agronomy
WANG, LIXUE, Water Resources
WANG, QINGXIANG, Agronomy
WANG, QIUBING, Land and the Environment
WANG, SHAOBIN, Agronomy
WANG, XIAOQI, Plant Protection
WANG, XUEYING, Biological Science and Tech-
nology
WEI, YUTANG, Horticulture
WU, LUPING, Horticulture
WU, YUANHUA, Plant Protection
XIAO, SHENGAN, Social Science
XIE, FUTI, Agronomy
XU, XIAOMING, Physical Education
XU, ZHENGJIN, Agronomy
YAN, HONGWEI, Forestry
YANG, GUIQIN, Veterinary Science
YANG, SHOUREN, Agronomy
YANG, YONG, Information and Electrical
Engineering
YI, YANLI, Land and the Environment
YIN, MINGFANG, Forestry
YU, ZHONGTAO, Social Science
ZHAI, YINLI, Economics and Trade
ZHANG, BAOSHI, Agronomy
ZHANG, KAIBIN, Horticulture
ZHANG, LIJUN, Biological Science and Tech-
nology
ZHANG, LONGBU, Agronomy
ZHANG, SHUSHEN, Plant Protection
ZHANG, XIURAN, Information and Electrical
Engineering
ZHANG, YONGMING, Social Science
ZHANG, YULIN, Social Science
ZHANG, YULONG, Land and the Environment
ZHANG, ZHIHONG, Horticulture
ZHANG, ZULI, Engineering
ZHAO, YUJUN, Veterinary Science
ZHOU, BAOLI, Horticulture
ZHOU, HONGFEI, Agronomy
ZHOU, QILONG, Information and Electrical
Engineering
ZHOU, YANMING, Centre for Analysis and
Testing

SHENZHEN UNIVERSITY

Nanhai Rd 3688, Shenzhen 518060, Guangdong Province

Telephone and fax (755) 26534940

E-mail: szufao@szu.edu.cn
Internet: www.szu.edu.cn
Founded 1983
State control
Academic year: September to July
Pres.: ZHANG BIGONG
Vice-Pres.: DU HONGBIAO
Vice-Pres.: LI FENGLIANG
Vice-Pres.: Prof. LI YONGHUA
Vice-Pres.: Prof. RUAN SHUANGCHEN
Vice-Pres.: Prof. XING FENG
Vice-Pres.: Prof. XING MIAO
Registrar: XU CHEN
Librarian: HUANG WEIPING
Library: 3.8m. vols, incl. 2.69m. journals and
books, 1.26m. e-books
Number of teachers: 1,221
Number of students: 28,000
Publications: *Shenzhen University Journal*
(social sciences and humanities), *Shenzhen
University Journal* (natural sciences),
World Architecture Review

DEANS

Department of English: Prof. CAO YIAJUN
Faculty of Adult Education: Prof. YANG
ZHONGXIN
Faculty of Architecture and Civil Engineer-
ing: Prof. XU ANZHI
Faculty of Art: Prof. LIAO XINGQIAO
Faculty of Arts: Prof. YU LONGYU
Faculty of Economics: Prof. CAO LONGQI
Faculty of Engineering Technology: Prof.
ZHU QIN
Faculty of Golf Sport and Management: Prof.
LIN ZUJI
Faculty of Information Engineering: Prof.
YONG ZHENGZHENG
Faculty of Science: Prof. SHU QIQING
Sports Department: Prof. CHEN XIAORONG
Teachers' College: Prof. ZHANG BIGONG

SICHUAN AGRICULTURAL UNIVERSITY

12 Xinkang Rd, Yaan 625014, Sichuan Province

Telephone: (835) 2882233
Fax: (835) 2883166
Internet: www.sicau.edu.cn
Founded 1906 as Sichuan Tong Sheng Agri-
cultural School, subordinated to Nat.
Sichuan Univ. in 1935, present name 1985
Academic year: September to July
Pres.: WEN XINTIAN
Vice-Pres: REN ZHENGLONG, YANG WENYU,
ZHANG QIANG, ZHENG YOULIANG, ZHU QING
Librarian: XIA JIMING
Schools and Faculties: agronomy, animal
science, economical management in agricul-
ture and forestry, environmental engineer-
ing, forestry and grass science, humanities
and social sciences, information and engin-
eering technology, land resource manage-
ment, life science, plant protection,
veterinary science, vocational technology;
Further Education College
Library of 2,000,000 vols
Number of teachers: 1,500
Number of students: 28,000

Publication: *Journal* (4 a year).

SICHUAN UNION UNIVERSITY

Jiuyanqiao, Chengdu 610064, Sichuan Province

Telephone: (28) 5412233
Fax: (28) 5410187
E-mail: scuu@sun.scuu.cdnet.edu.cn
Founded 1994 by merger of Sichuan Univ.
and Chengdu Univ. of Science and Tech-
nology
State control

Language of instruction: Chinese
Academic year: September to July

Pres.: LU TIECHENG
Vice-Pres.: CHEN JUNKAI
Vice-Pres.: LIU YINGMING
Vice-Pres.: LI ZHIQIANG
Vice-Pres.: LONG WEI
Vice-Pres.: YANG JIRUI
Vice-Pres.: ZHANG YIZHENG
Registrar: XIAO DINGQUAN
Librarians: CAI SHUXIAN, FENG ZESI, LIU YINGMING

Library of 3,650,000 vols
Number of teachers: 3,660
Number of students: 19,150

Publications: *Journal of Atomic and Molecular Physics, Oil-field Chemistry, Polymeric Material Science and Technology, Religion Studies, Sichuan Union University Journal of Natural Science, Sichuan Union University Journal of Social Science, Sichuan Union University Journal of Engineering Science, South Asian Studies Quarterly*

DEANS

College of Chemical Science and Engineering: ZHU JIAHUA
College of Economics and Management: CHEN GAOLIN
College of Energy Resources Science and Engineering: (vacant)
College of Fine Art: DENG SHENGQING
College of Foreign Languages: (vacant)
College of Humanities: CAO SHUNQING
College of Information Science and Engineering: TAO FUZHOU
College of Journalism: QIU PEIHUANG
College of Law: TANG LEI
College of Life Sciences and Engineering: CHEN FANG
College of Light Science and Engineering: WU DACHENG
College of Manufacturing Science and Engineering: (vacant)
College of Materials Science and Engineering: GU YI
College of Sciences: (vacant)
College of Urban and Rural Construction and Environmental Protection: LUO TEJUN
School of Adult Education and Vocational Education: WANG ZHONGMING

SICHUAN UNIVERSITY

24 South Section 1, Yihuan Rd, Chengdu 610065, Sichuan Province

Telephone: (28) 85402443
Fax: (28) 85403260
Internet: www.scu.edu.cn

Founded 1896
State control
Academic year: September to July

Pres.: ZHAO YANXIU
Vice-Pres: LI ZHIQIANG, LIU YINGMING, TANG DENGXUE, XIE HEPING, YANG JIRUI, ZHANG WEIGUO, ZHAO ZHAODA
Head of Graduate Dept: LIU YINGMING
Librarian: LI BINGYAN

Library of 4,847,300 vols
Number of teachers: 1,035
Number of students: 44,003

Publication: *Journal* (edns: natural sciences, 6 a year; engineering, 12 a year; medicine, 4 a year; philosophy and social sciences, 4 a year)

DEANS

College of Art: (vacant)
College of Chemistry: HU CHANG WEI
College of Economics and Management: ZHOU GUANG YAN
College of Foreign Languages and Cultures: SHI JIAN

College of Literature and Journalism: CAO SHUNQING
College of Mathematics: LI AN MIN
College of Physical Science and Technology: GONG MIN
College of Politics: WANG GUO MIN
College of Polymer Science and Engineering: YANG MING BO
College of Software Engineering: ZHOU JI LIU
College of Water Resources and Hydropower: LIANG CHUAN
School of Architecture and the Environment: FAN YU BO
School of Chemistry and Engineering: ZHU JIA HUA
School of Community and Sanitation: MA XIAO
School of Computer Science and Engineering: (vacant)
School of Electricity and Electronic Information: ZHAO ZHUO YAO
School of History and Culture: WANG TING ZHI
School of Law: (vacant)
School of Life Sciences: CHEN FANG
School of Manufacturing Science and Engineering: YIN GUO FU
School of Materials Science and Engineering: (vacant)
School of Physical Education: TANG CHENG
School of Pre-Clinical and Forensic Medicine: HOU YI PING
School of Tourism: (vacant)
West China College of Stomatology: ZHOU XUE DONG
West China School of Pharmacy: ZHANG ZHI RONG

PROFESSORS

AI, NAN SHAN, Architecture and the Environment
AO, FAN, Foreign Languages and Cultures
CAO, GUANG FU, Mathematics
CAO, YI PING, Electronics and Information Engineering
CAO, YI, Life Sciences
CAO, YU RONG, Politics
CENG, ZONG YONG, Life Sciences
CHEN, DAO BANG, Pre-Clinical and Forensic Medicine
CHEN, DE BEN, Chemistry
CHEN, GAO LIN, Economics and Management
CHEN, GUO DI, Pre-Clinical and Forensic Medicine
CHEN, HONG CHAO, Chemistry
CHEN, JIAN KANG, Water Resources and Hydropower
CHEN, JUN KAI, Architecture and the Environment
CHEN, KANG YANG, Law
CHEN, QIAN DE, Architecture and the Environment
CHEN, QIAO, Pre-Clinical and Forensic Medicine
CHEN, TIAN LANG, Chemistry
CHEN, WEN JUN, Chemistry
CHEN, YONG GE, Law
CHEN, ZE FANG, Chemistry
CHEN, ZHONG RONG, Foreign Languages and Cultures
CHENG, LI, Tourism
CHENG, XI LIN, Foreign Languages and Cultures
DAI, ZONG KUN, Electronics and Information Engineering
DAN, DE ZHONG, Architecture and the Environment
DENG, XIAO KANG, Pre-Clinical and Forensic Medicine
DENG, ZHEN HUA, Pre-Clinical and Forensic Medicine
DOU, HOU SONG, Chemistry
FAN, HONG, Architecture and the Environment
FAN, YU BO, Architecture and the Environment

FANG, GUO ZHEN, Chemistry
FANG, SHU XIN, History and Culture
FENG, YI JUN, Chemistry
FENG, ZE HUI, Foreign Languages and Cultures
FU, HE JIAN, Chemistry
FU, HUA LONG, Life Sciences
GAO, CHUN HUA, Manufacturing Science and Engineering
GAO, RONG, Life Sciences
GU, BIN, Life Sciences
GU, ZHONG BI, Electronics and Information Engineering
GUAN, PENG, Pre-Clinical and Forensic Medicine
HE, CHANG RONG, Water Resources and Hydropower
HE, JIANG DA, Water Resources and Hydropower
HE, JING XU, Law
HE, PEI YU, Electronics and Information Engineering
HE, PING, Foreign Languages and Cultures
HE, QING, History and Culture
HE, XING JIN, Life Sciences
HE, YA PING, Pre-Clinical and Forensic Medicine
HE, YU EN, Chemistry
HOU, XIAN DENG, Chemistry
HU, HUO ZHEN, Life Sciences
HU, JIA YUAN, Chemistry
HU, JUN MEI, Pre-Clinical and Forensic Medicine
HUANG, DE CHANG, Economics and Management
HUANG, FA LUN, Mathematics
HUANG, GUANG LIN, Chemistry
HUANG, NAN JING, Mathematics
HUANG, NIAN CI, Electricity and Electronic Information
HUANG, NING, Pre-Clinical and Forensic Medicine
HUANG, SHAN, Electricity and Electronic Information
HUANG, YING, Pre-Clinical and Forensic Medicine
JIANG, BO, Chemistry
JIANG, CHENG FA, Chemistry and Engineering
JIANG, WEN JU, Architecture and the Environment
JIN, MING, Law
JING, DONG, Electricity and Electronic Information
JU, XIAO MING, Water Resources and Hydropower
KANG, ZHEN HUANG, Architecture and the Environment
KE, JI GUI, Foreign Languages and Cultures
LEI, YONG XUE, Politics
LI, AN MIN, Mathematics
LI, BO HUAI, Tourism
LI, DE YU, Architecture and the Environment
LI, FANG, Chemistry
LI, FU HAI, Economics and Management
LI, GUO CHENG, Electricity and Electronic Information
LI, HONG, Pre-Clinical and Forensic Medicine
LI, HUI, Chemistry and Engineering
LI, JIAN MING, Chemistry and Engineering
LI, JIAO, Foreign Languages and Cultures
LI, JIE, Politics
LI, JU CAI, Chemistry
LI, KE FENG, Water Resources and Hydropower
LI, LIANG, Pre-Clinical and Forensic Medicine
LI, MENG LONG, Chemistry
LI, PING, Law
LI, RUI XIANG, Chemistry
LI, SHI YAN, Economics and Management
LI, TAO, History and Culture
LI, XIAO SONG, Infrastructure and Sanitation
LI, YAO ZHONG, Chemistry
LI, YING BI, Pre-Clinical and Forensic Medicine

LI, YING, Chemistry
LI, ZAN, Law
LI, ZHANG ZHENG, Architecture and the Environment
LI, ZHI SHU, Computer Science and Engineering
LI, ZHONG FU, Mathematics
LI, ZHONG MING, Polymer Science and Engineering
LIANG, BING, Chemistry and Engineering
LIANG, JI HUA, Mathematics
LIANG, YUAN DI, Economics and Management
LIAO, LIN CHUAN, Pre-Clinical and Forensic Medicine
LIN, BI GUO, Foreign Languages and Cultures
LIN, DA QUAN, Manufacturing Science and Engineering
LIU, CHANG JUN, Electronics and Information Engineering
LIU, DONG QUAN, Software Engineering
LIU, FEI PENG, Electricity and Electronic Information
LIU, GUANG ZHONG, Economics and Management
LIU, JIA YONG, Electronics and Information Engineering
LIU, LI MIN, Foreign Languages and Cultures
LIU, MIN, Pre-Clinical and Forensic Medicine
LIU, NIAN, Electricity and Electronic Information
LIU, QI CHAO, Software Engineering
LIU, RONG ZHONG, Manufacturing Science and Engineering
LIU, SHAN JUN, Water Resources and Hydropower
LIU, SHENG QING, Manufacturing Science and Engineering
LIU, TIAN QI, Electricity and Electronic Information
LIU, TING HUA, Polymer Science and Engineering
LIU, YI FEI, History and Culture
LIU, YU SHENG, Electricity and Electronic Information
LONG, JIAN ZHONG, Electronics and Information Engineering
LONG, KUI, Foreign Languages and Cultures
LONG, WEI, Manufacturing Science and Engineering
LONG, YUN FANG, Infrastructure and Sanitation
LONG, ZONG ZHI, Law
LUO, DI LUN, Foreign Languages and Cultures
LUO, LIN, Water Resources and Hydropower
LUO, LIN, Architecture and the Environment
LUO, MAO KANG, Mathematics
LUO, MEI MING, Chemistry
LUO, SU QIONG, Infrastructure and Sanitation
LUO, TE JUN, Architecture and the Environment
LUO, WAN BO, Computer Science and Engineering
LUO, XIANG LIN, Polymer Science and Engineering
LV, GUANG HONG, Computer Science and Engineering
LV, TAO, Mathematics
MA, HONG, Mathematics
MA, LI TAI, Foreign Languages and Cultures
MENG, YAN FA, Life Sciences
MU, CHUN LAI, Mathematics
NIE, GANG, Politics
NING, YUAN ZHONG, Electricity and Electronic Information
PEI, JUE MIN, Architecture and the Environment
PENG, BANG BEN, History and Culture
PENG, LIAN GANG, Mathematics
QI, JIAN GUO, Pre-Clinical and Forensic Medicine
QIN, SHI LUN, Architecture and the Environment

QIU, WANG SHENG, Foreign Languages and Cultures
QU, ZHAO YANG, Pre-Clinical and Forensic Medicine
SHI, JIAN, Foreign Languages and Cultures
SHI, YING PING, Tourism
SHU, QIN, Electricity and Electronic Information
SONG, HANG, Chemistry and Engineering
SONG, WEI, Economics and Management
SUN, CHENG JUN, Infrastructure and Sanitation
SUN, JIN QUAN, History and Culture
SUN, QI, Mathematics
TAN, DA LU, Architecture and the Environment
TAN, XIAO PING, Architecture and the Environment
TAN, YANG, Pre-Clinical and Forensic Medicine
TANG, JIA LING, Polymer Science and Engineering
TANG, LEI, Law
TANG, NING JIU, Computer Science and Engineering
TANG, YA, Architecture and the Environment
TAO, LI, Economics and Management
TU, SHANG YIN, Foreign Languages and Cultures
TU, YUAN ZHAO, Electricity and Electronic Information
WAN, JIA YI, Chemistry
WANG, DAO HUI, Electricity and Electronic Information
WANG, FAN, Pre-Clinical and Forensic Medicine
WANG, GUO MIN, Politics
WANG, JIAN PING, Law
WANG, LEI, Pre-Clinical and Forensic Medicine
WANG, LI, Water Resources and Hydropower
WANG, LI, Life Sciences
WANG, QI ZHI, Architecture and the Environment
WANG, QING YUAN, Architecture and the Environment
WANG, SHU YU, Foreign Languages and Cultures
WANG, XIAO LU, Foreign Languages and Cultures
WANG, YA JING, Pre-Clinical and Forensic Medicine
WANG, YING HAN, Polymer Science and Engineering
WANG, ZHEN XUE, Electronics and Information Engineering
WEI, XIN PING, Water Resources and Hydropower
WEI, ZHONG HAI, Politics
WEN, CHU AN, Foreign Languages and Cultures
WU, JIANG, Chemistry
WU, JIN, Pre-Clinical and Forensic Medicine
WU, QING, Pre-Clinical and Forensic Medicine
WU, XIAN HONG, Foreign Languages and Cultures
WU, ZHI HUA, Polymer Science and Engineering
XIA, SU LAN, Chemistry and Engineering
XIANG, TAO, Pre-Clinical and Forensic Medicine
XIANG, ZHAO YANG, Law
XIAO, AN FU, Foreign Languages and Cultures
XIAO, SHEN XIU, Chemistry
XIAO, XU, Politics
XIE, BANG HU, Polymer Science and Engineering
XIONG, FENG, Architecture and the Environment
XU, DAO YI, Mathematics
XU, HENG, Life Sciences
XU, LAN, Electronics and Information Engineering
XUE, YING, Chemistry

YANG, FANG JU, Pre-Clinical and Forensic Medicine
YANG, GANG, Polymer Science and Engineering
YANG, HONG GENG, Electricity and Electronic Information
YANG, HONG YU, Computer Science and Engineering
YANG, JIANG, Economics and Management
YANG, JIE, Chemistry
YANG, JUN LIU, Architecture and the Environment
YANG, SHI WEN, History and Culture
YANG, SUI QUAN, Law
YANG, WAN QUAN, Electronics and Information Engineering
YANG, WU NENG, Foreign Languages and Cultures
YANG, YI, Manufacturing Science and Engineering
YANG, YI, Life Sciences
YANG, ZHEN ZHI, Tourism
YANG, ZHENG GUANG, Politics
YE, GUANG DOU, Polymer Science and Engineering
YI, DAN, Foreign Languages and Cultures
YI, XU FU, Pre-Clinical and Forensic Medicine
YIN, HUA QIANG, Architecture and the Environment
YIN, YONG XIANG, Chemistry and Engineering
YOU, XIAN GUI, Chemistry and Engineering
YU, JIAN HUA, Architecture and the Environment
YU, ZHONG DE, Software Engineering
YUAN, DAO HUA, Computer Science and Engineering
YUAN, DE CHENG, Foreign Languages and Cultures
YUAN, DE QI, Chemistry
YUAN, LI HUA, Chemistry
YUAN, PENG, Water Resources and Hydropower
YUAN, YONG MING, Chemistry
YUAN, ZHI RUN, Architecture and the Environment
YUE, LI MIN, Pre-Clinical and Forensic Medicine
ZENG, CHENG MING, Life Sciences
ZENG, LING FU, Infrastructure and Sanitation
ZHANG, CHAO, Electricity and Electronic Information
ZHANG, DAI RUN, Electricity and Electronic Information
ZHANG, DE XUE, Mathematics
ZHANG, GUANG KE, Water Resources and Hydropower
ZHANG, HONG WEI, Computer Science and Engineering
ZHANG, HUA, Electricity and Electronic Information
ZHANG, JIAN ZHOU, Computer Science and Engineering
ZHANG, KE RONG, Infrastructure and Sanitation
ZHANG, LIN, Water Resources and Hydropower
ZHANG, PIN, Pre-Clinical and Forensic Medicine
ZHANG, WEI NIAN, Mathematics
ZHANG, WEI, Pre-Clinical and Forensic Medicine
ZHANG, XIN PEI, Architecture and the Environment
ZHANG, XU, Mathematics
ZHANG, YI ZHONG, Electricity and Electronic Information
ZHANG, YONG KUI, Chemistry and Engineering
ZHAO, CHANG SHEN, Polymer Science and Engineering
ZHAO, CHENG YU, Life Sciences
ZHAO, SHI PING, Manufacturing Science and Engineering
ZHAO, YUN, Life Sciences

ZHENG, CHANG YI, Chemistry
ZHENG, HUA, Politics
ZHONG, SHU LIN, Chemistry
ZHONG, YIN PING, Polymer Science and Engineering
ZHOU, AN MIN, Electronics and Information Engineering
ZHOU, BO, Architecture and the Environment
ZHOU, BU XIANG, Electricity and Electronic Information
ZHOU, GUANG YA, Foreign Languages and Cultures
ZHOU, JI LIU, Software Engineering
ZHOU, JIAN LUE, Chemistry
ZHOU, LI MING, Pre-Clinical and Forensic Medicine
ZHOU, WEI, Law
ZHOU, XUE, Pre-Clinical and Forensic Medicine
ZHOU, YI, Tourism
ZHU, HUI, Foreign Languages and Cultures
ZHU, XIN MIN, Economics and Management
ZHU, YUN MIN, Mathematics
ZHUANG, CHENG SAN, Computer Science and Engineering
ZUO, WEI MIN, Law

SOOCHOW UNIVERSITY

1 Shi Xin St, Suzhou 215006, Jiangsu Province
Internet: www.suda.edu.cn
Founded 1900
Academic year: September to July
Pres.: QIAN PEIDE
Vice-Pres: BAI LUN, GE JIANYI, ZHANG XUE-GUANG, ZHU XIULIN
Head of Graduate Dept: ZHU SHIQUN
Librarian: WANG GUOPING
Library of 3,320,000 vols
Number of teachers: 1,200
Number of students: 32,300

Publication: *Journal of Suzhou University* (editions: engineering sciences, medical science, 6 a year; natural sciences, philosophy and social science, 4 a year)

DEANS

College of Politics and Public Management: ZHOU KEZHEN
Institute of Pollution and Public Health: TONG JIAN
Material Engineering Institute: CHEN GUOQIANG
School of Agricultural Science and Technology: SHEN WEIDE
School of Chemistry and Chemical Engineering: JI SHUNJUN
School of Computer Science and Technology: ZHU QIAOMING
School of Electronic Information: ZHAO HEMING
School of Foreign Languages: WANG LABAO
School of Life Sciences: ZHANG XUEGUANG
School of Literature Department: LUO SHIJIN
School of Mathematical Sciences: WANG LABAO
School of Mechanical and electronic Engineering: RUI YANNIAN
School of Medicine: WU AIQIN
School of Physical Education and Sports: WANG JIAHONG
School of Social Science: WANG LABAO

PROFESSORS

BAO, SHIQIAO, Medicine
CAO, YONGLUO, Mathematical Sciences
CAO, YONGLUO, Mechanical and Electronic Engineering
CHEN, LINSEN, Computer Science and Technology
CHEN, QINGGUAN, Mechanical and Electronic Engineering
CHEN, ZIXING, Medicine

CUI, ZHIMING, Mechanical and Electronic Engineering
FENG, ZHIHUA, Mechanical and Electronic Engineering
FU, GEYAN, Mechanical and Electronic Engineering
GAO, FANGYING, Social Science
GAO, QI, Medicine
GU, ZHENLUN, Medicine
GU, ZONGJIANG, Medicine
GUI, SHIHE, Mechanical and Electronic Engineering
HONG, FASHUI, Life Sciences
HU, HUACHENG, Medicine
HUA, RENDE, Art
HUANG, QIANG, Medicine
JIANG, WENKAI, Physical Education and Sports
JIANG, XINGHONG, Medicine
JIN, WEIXING, Social Science
LAN, QING, Medicine
LI, DECHUN, Medicine
LIANG, JUN, Art
LIAO, LIANGYUN, Art
LIU, CHUNFENG, Medicine
LIU, ZHIHUA, Medicine
LU, HUIMIN, Medicine
LU, JIAN, Social Science
MA, WEIZHONG, Literature
QIAN, HAIXIN, Medicine
QIN, ZHENGHONG, Medicine
RUI, YANNIAN, Mechanical and Electronic Engineering
SHEN, YULIANG, Mathematical Sciences
SHEN, ZHENYA, Medicine
SHI, GUANGYU, Mechanical and Electronic Engineering
SHI, SHIHONG, Mechanical and Electronic Engineering
SONG, HUICHUN, Life Sciences
SUN, JUNYING, Medicine
SUN, MINZHI, Physical Education and Sports
TANG, TIANSI, Medicine
TANG, ZHENGPEI, Social Science
TANG, ZHINGMING, Mathematical Sciences
TIAN, JIUMAI, Physical Education and Sports
TU, YIFENG, Chemistry and Chemical Engineering
WAN, JIEQIU, Commerce
WANG, GUANGWEI, Commerce
WANG, GUOPING, Social Science
WANG, JIAHONG, Physical Education and Sports
WANG, ZHAOYUE, Medicine
WEI, XIANGDONG, Social Science
WEN, DUANGAI, Medicine
WU, DEPEI, Medicine
WU, HAORONG, Medicine
WU, JINCHANG, Medicine
XIA, CHAOMING, Medicine
XIA, CHUNLIN, Medicine
XU, HAOWEN, Physical Education and Sports
XUE, YONGQUAN, Medicine
YAN, CHUNYIN, Medicine
YANG, JICHENG, Medicine
YANG, XIANGJUN, Medicine
YIN, YUNXING, Mechanical and Electronic Engineering
YU, HONGBING, Mathematical Sciences
YU, TONGYUAN, Social Science
YU, ZHENG, Social Science
ZANG, ZHIFEI, Social Science
ZHANG, LIN, Physical Education and Sports
ZHANG, MING, Social Science
ZHANG, PENGCHUAN, Art
ZHANG, RI, Medicine
ZHANG, SHIMING, Medicine
ZHANG, XIQING, Medicine
ZHANG, XUEGANG, Life Sciences
ZHANG, XUEGUANG, Medicine
ZHANG, ZHAOYU, Social Science
ZHAO, ZENGYAO, Commerce
ZHONG, KANGMIN, Mechanical and Electronic Engineering
ZHOU, DAI, Medicine

ZHOU, JIANPENG, Chemistry and Chemical Engineering
ZHU, CONGBING, Social Science
ZHU, JIANG, Life Sciences
ZHUGE, HONGXIANG, Medicine
ZHUGE, KAI, Art

SOUTH CHINA AGRICULTURAL UNIVERSITY

Wushan, Guangzhou 510642, Guangdong Province
Telephone: (20) 85280007
Fax: (20) 85282693
E-mail: office@scau.edu.cn
Internet: www.scau.edu.cn
Founded 1909
State (provincial) control
Academic year: September to July

Pres.: Prof. LUO SHIMING
Vice-Pres.: Prof. CHEN BEIGUANG
Vice-Pres.: Assoc. Prof. CHEN CHANGSHENG
Vice-Pres.: Prof. LUO XIWEN
Librarian: YE JINGHUA

Library of 700,000 vols
Number of teachers: 753
Number of students: 12,501

Publications: *Guangdong Agricultural Sciences* (jtly published with Guangdong Acad. of Agricultural Science, 12 a year), *Journal* (4 a year), *Poultry Husbandry and Disease Control* (12 a year)

DEANS

College of Adult Education: Prof. NIU BAOJUN
College of Biotechnology: Prof. PENG XINXIANG
College of Economics and Trade: Prof. LI DASHENG
College of Forestry: Prof. CHEN XIMU
College of Liberal Arts: Prof. ZHANG WENFANG
College of Resources and Environment: Prof. LI HUAXING
College of Science: Prof. ZHANG GUOQUAN
Department of Agronomy: Prof. ZHANG GUIQUAN
Department of Animal Medicine: Prof. ZENG ZHENLING
Department of Animal Science: Prof. FENG DINGYUAN
Department of Food Science: Assoc. Prof. LI BIN
Department of Horticulture: Assoc. Prof. CHEN RIYUAN
Department of Physical Education: Assoc. Prof. WANG CHANGQING
Department of Sericulture: Assoc. Prof. XU XINGYAO
Polytechnic College: Prof. OU YINGGANG

PROFESSORS

BI, Y. Z., Animal Nutrition and Immunology
CAO, Y., Silkworm Biotechnology
CHEN, B.G., Forest Ecology
CHEN, D. C., Pomology
CHEN, W. K., Insect Toxicology
CHEN, W. X., Post-harvest Physiology of Fruit and Vegetables
CHEN, X. M., Plant Systematics and Evolution
CHEN, Y. S., Animal Genetics and Breeding
CHEN, Y. Q., Food Biochemistry
CHEN, Z. L., Veterinary Medicine
CHEN, Z. Q., Crop Genetics and Breeding
FAN, H. Z., Plant Pathology
FAN, X. L., Soil Chemistry
FENG, D. Y., Animal Nutrition and Feed Science
FENG, Q. H., Veterinary Medicine
FU, C., Economic Policy and Development
FU, W. L., Animal Physiology
GAO, X. B., Plant Pathology
GU, D. J., Insect Ecology

GUO, Z. F., Plant Physiology and Molecular Biology
HONG, T. S., Agricultural Mechanization
HUANG, B. Q., Insecticide
HUANG, H. B., Fruit Tree Physiology
HUANG, Q. Y., Veterinary Microbiology
HUANG, X. Y., Food Nutrition
HUANG, Z. L., Biochemistry
JI, Z. L., Agricultural Product Storage and Processing
JIAN, Y. Y., Plant Biotechnology
JIANG, H., Agricultural Economics and Management
JIANG, Z. D., Plant Pathology
KONG, X. M., Veterinary Pathology
LAN, S. F., Ecological Energy and Value of Energy
LI, B. T., Plant Taxonomy
LI, D. S., Economics of Agricultural Engineering
LI, G. Q., Veterinary Parasitology
LI, H. X., Soil Science
LI, J. P., Soil Chemistry
LI, K. F., Wood Science
LI, M. Q., Plant Physiology
LI, Z. L., Crop Cultivation
LIANG, G. W., Insect Ecology
LIANG, J. N., Crop Cultivation
LIAO, Z. W., Soil Science and the Environment
LIN, J. R., Silkworm Genetics and Breeding
LIN, S. Q., Pomology
LIN, Y. G., Genetic Engineering
LU, Y. G., Plant Genetics
LUO, B. L., Agricultural Economics and Management
LUO, F. H., Forest Management
LUO, S. M., Agroecology
LUO, X. W., Agricultural Mechanization
MEI, M. T., Plant Biotechnology
OU, Y. G., Agricultural Engineering
PAN, Q. H., Plant Pathology
PANG, X. F., Insect Ecology and Taxonomy
PENG, X. X., Plant Physiology and Molecular Biology
REN, S. X., Insect Ecology
SUN, Y. M., Food Chemistry
TAN, Z. W., Plant Genetics and Breeding
TIE, L. Y., Fashion Design
WAN, B. H., Plant Genetics and Breeding
WANG, D. L., Tea Science
WANG, J., Forest Pathology
WANG, S. Z., Landscape Gardening
WANG, Z. S., Animal Ecology
WANG, Z. Z., Plant Pathology
WEN, S. M., Agricultural Economics and Management
WU, H., Botany
WU, Q. T., Agricultural Environment Protection
XIAO, H. G., Plant Pathology
XIN, C. A., Poultry Disease
XU, F. C., Plant Physiology
XU, H. H., Insect Toxicology
XU, X. Y., Silkworm Pathology
YAN, X. L., Plant Nutrition
YANG, G. F., Animal Genetics and Breeding
YANG, Y. S., Genetic Engineering
ZENG, L., Insect Ecology
ZENG, Z. L., Veterinary Pharmacology
ZHANG, G. Q., Crop Genetics and Breeding
ZHANG, T. L., Agricultural Mechanization
ZHANG, W. F., Agricultural Economics and Management
ZHANG, X. Q., Animal Genetics and Breeding
ZHANG, Y. H., Agricultural Economics and Management

SOUTH CHINA NORMAL UNIVERSITY

Shipai, Guangzhou 510631, Guangdong Province

Telephone: (20) 85210169
Fax: (20) 85210991
Internet: www.scnu.edu.cn

Founded 1933
Academic year: September to July
Pres.: WANG GUOJIAN
Vice-Pres: HU SHEJUN, HUANG LIYA, LI YONGJIE, LIU MING, MO LEI, QIAN XIANBIN, WU YINGMIN
Head of Graduate Dept: XIAO HUA
Librarian: ZHU JIANLIANG
Number of teachers: 2,400
Number of students: 60,600
Publications: *High School Physics Education* (12 a year), *Journal* (6 a year), *Journal of Physical Education* (6 a year), *Oriental Culture* (6 a year)

DEANS

College of Economics and Management: LI YONGJIE
College of Educational Information Technology: XU FUYING
College of Foreign Languages: (vacant)
College of Humanities: KE HANLING
College of International Culture: LI SHENGBING
College of Life Sciences: MA GUANGZHI
College of Optoelectronics Technology: LIU SONGHAO
College of Physics and Telecommunications Engineering: LIU QIONGFA
College of Politics and Law: HU ZEHONG
College of Sports Science: ZHOU AIGUANG
Department of Art: HUANG LIYA
Department of Chemistry: ZENG HEPING
Department of Computer Science: BAO SUSU
Department of Geography: XU XIANGJUN
Department of Mathematics: HUANG ZHIDA
Department of Music: CHENG JIANPING
Department of Tourism Management: GAN QIAOLIN
School of Continuing Education: HUANG ZHIYING
School of Education Science: MO LEI

PROFESSORS

BAO, ZONGTI, Physics and Telecommunications Engineering
BIN, JINHUA, Life Sciences
CHANG, HONGSEN, Physics and Telecommunications Engineering
CHEN, HAO, Physics and Telecommunications Engineering
CHEN, HUOWANG, Computer Science
CHEN, JUNFANG, Physics and Telecommunications Engineering
CHEN, QI, Sports Science
CHEN, XIANGLIN, Life Sciences
CHEN, XINMIN, Economics and Management
CHEN, YAOSHENG, Economics and Management
CHEN, YONGSHAO, Mathematics
CHEN, YUQUN, Mathematics
CHEN, ZHANGHE, Life Sciences
DENG, SHUXUN, Sports Science
DING, SHIJIN, Mathematics
DING, XIN, Educational Information Technology
DONG, WULUN, Economics and Management
FANG, XINGQI, Economics and Management
FENG, YOUHE, Mathematics
GAN, QIAOLIN, Tourism Management
GAO, SHIAN, Mathematics
HAO, XUANMING, Sports Science
HE, ZHENGJIANG, Physics and Telecommunications Engineering
HU, LIAN, Physics and Telecommunications Engineering
HU, XIAOMING, Sports Science
HUANG, KUANROU, Sports Science
HUANG, LIREN, Mathematics
HUANG, WENFANG, Life Sciences
HUANG, YUSHAN, Sports Science
LI, DONGFENG, Life Sciences
LI, HONGQING, Life Sciences
LI, JIANYING, Economics and Management
LI, JIDONG, Economics and Management
LI, KEDONG, Educational Information Technology
LI, LING, Life Sciences
LI, SHAOSHAN, Life Sciences
LI, SHIJIE, Mathematics
LI, WEISHAN, Chemistry
LI, WEN, Mathematics
LI, YIJUN, Sports Science
LI, YONGJIE, Economics and Management
LI, YUNLIN, Educational Information Technology
LIN, CHANGHAO, Mathematics
LIN, YONG, Economics and Management
LING, JIANGHUAI, Economics and Management
LIU, BOLIAN, Mathematics
LIU, CHENGYI, Sports Science
LIU, QIONGFA, Physics and Telecommunications Engineering
LIU, SONGHAO, Optoelectronics
LIU, YUQIANG, Mathematics
LU, YUANZHEN, Sports Science
MO, LEI, Education Science
PAN, RUICHI, Life Sciences
PENG, BIYU, Economics and Management
SANG, XINMIN, Educational Information Technology
SHEN, WENHUAI, Mathematics
SUN, DAOCHUN, Mathematics
SUN, RUYONG, Life Sciences
TAN, HUA, Sports Science
TANG, SHANGYONG, Mathematics
TANG, ZAIXIN, Economics and Management
TANG, ZHILIE, Physics and Telecommunications Engineering
TONG, QINGXI, Geography
WANG, ANLI, Life Sciences
WANG, LINQUAN, Mathematics
WANG, QIAN, Sports Science
WANG, WEINA, Life Sciences
WANG, XIAOJING, Life Sciences
WENG, PEIXUAN, Mathematics
WU, CHAOLIN, Economics and Management
XIA, HUA, Physics and Telecommunications Engineering
XIAO, GUOQIANG, Sports Science
XIAO, PENG, Life Sciences
XIONG, JIANWEN, Physics and Telecommunications Engineering
XIONG, JINCHENG, Mathematics
XU, FUYING, Educational Information Technology
XU, JIE, Life Sciences
XU, XIAOYANG, Sports Science
XU, XUAN, Chemistry
YANG, WENXUAN, Sports Science
YANG, YONGHUA, Economics and Management
YE, QINGSHENG, Life Sciences
YI, FAHUAI, Mathematics
YU, YING, Chemistry
YUAN, GUANLING, Physics and Telecommunications Engineering
ZENG, HEPING, Chemistry
ZHENG, ZHI, Chemistry
ZHANG, JIANWU, Economics and Management
ZHANG, JUNPENG, Physics and Telecommunications Engineering
ZHANG, MOUCHENG, Mathematics
ZHANG, ZHIYONG, Sports Science
ZHAO, XUEZENG, Economics and Management
ZHOU, AIGUANG, Sports Science
ZHU, JIANJUN, Life Sciences
ZUO, ZAISHI, Mathematics

SOUTH CHINA UNIVERSITY OF TECHNOLOGY

Wushan, Guangzhou 510641, Guangdong Province

Telephone: (20) 87110000
Fax: (20) 85516386
Internet: www.scut.edu.cn

Founded 1952
State control

Academic year: September to July
Pres.: LIU HUANBIN
Vice-Pres: HAN DAJIAN, HUANG SHISHENG, JIA XINZHEN, LIU SHUDAO, CHEN NIANQIANG
Registrar: LIN YANGSU
Librarian: LI JIANBIN

Library of 1,350,000 vols
Number of teachers: 2,200
Number of students: 14,000

Publications: *Control Theory and Applications, Journal*

DEANS

School of Adult Education: WU MAN
School of Business Administration: SUN DONGCHUAN
School of Chemical Engineering: CHEN HUANQIN
School of Electrical Communication: ZHU XUEFENG
School of Electric Power: WU JIE
School of Light Chemical Engineering and Food Engineering: GAO DAWEI
School of Materials Science and Engineering: JIA DEMIN

SOUTHEAST UNIVERSITY

Si Pai Lou 2, Nanjing 210096
Telephone: (25) 83792412
Fax: (25) 83615736
E-mail: oic@seu.edu.cn
Internet: www.seu.edu.cn

Founded 1902
State control

Pres.: Prof. YI HONG
Vice-Pres.: Prof. LIU BO
Vice-Pres.: Prof. PU YUEPU
Vice-Pres.: Prof. ZHAO QIMAN
Vice-Pres.: Prof. HU MINQIANG
Vice-Pres.: Prof. ZHENG JIAMAO
Vice-Pres.: Prof. SHEN JIONG
Vice-Pres.: Prof. WANG BAOPING

Library: 3.3m. vols
Number of teachers: 2,269
Number of students: 41,090

Publication: *Journal*

DIRECTORS

Chien-shiung Wu College: Prof. LI AIQUN
College of Continuing Education: ZHUANG BAOJIE
College of Integrated Circuits: Prof. SHI LONGXING
College of International Students: Prof. HUANG KAI
Department of Mathematics: Prof. LIU JIJUN
Department of Physics: Prof. YANG YONGHONG
Department of Physical Education: Prof. CAI XIAOBO
Research Institute of SEU in Changzhou: Prof. LIU JINGNAN
Research Institute of SEU in Suzhou: HU MINQIANG
School of Architecture: Prof. WANG JIANGUO
School of Arts: Prof. WANG TINGXIN
School of Automation: Prof. FEI SHUMIN
School of Biological Science and Medical Engineering: Prof. GU NING
School of Computer Science and Engineering: Prof. LUO JUNZHOU
School of Chemistry and Chemical Engineering: Prof. LIN BAOPING
School of Civil Engineering: Prof. WU GANG
School of Economics and Management: Prof. XU KANGNING
School of Electrical Engineering: Prof. HUANG XUELIANG
School of Electronic Science and Engineering: Prof. SHI LONGXING
School of Energy and Environment: Prof. JIN BAOSHENG

School of Foreign Languages: Prof. LI XIAOXIANG
School of Humanities: Prof. FAN HEPING
School of Information Science and Engineering: Prof. YOU XIAOHU
School of Instrument Science and Engineering: Prof. SONG AIGUO
School of Material Science and Engineering: Prof. PAN YE
School of Mechanical Engineering: Prof. TANG WENCHENG
School of Medicine: Prof. TENG GAOJUN
School of Public Health: Prof. LIU PEI
School of Transportation: Prof. WANG WEI

SOUTH WESTERN UNIVERSITY OF FINANCE AND ECONOMICS

55 Guanghua St, Chengdu 610074, Sichuan Province
Telephone: (28) 7352937
Fax: (28) 7352355
Internet: www.swufe.edu.cn

Founded 1950
State control
Academic year: September to July

Pres.: WANG YUGUO
Vice-Pres: FENG XIDE, LIU CAN, ZHAO DEWU
Head of Graduate Dept: ZHAO ZHENXIAN
Librarian: LIU FANGJIAN

Library of 1,000,000 vols
Number of teachers: 1,300
Number of students: 14,000

Publications: *Finance and Economics* (6 a year), *The Economist*

DEANS

Department of Economical Mathematics: XIANG KAILI
School of Accounting: PENG SHAOBING
School of e-Commerce: PU GUOQUAN
School of Economics: LI PING
School of Economic Information Engineering: SHAOBING SONG
School of Finance: YIN MENGBO
School of Insurance: AI SUNLIN
School of International Business: CHENG MINXUAN
School of Law: GAO JINKANG
School of Public Administration: YIN QINGSHUANG
School of Public Finance and Taxation: WANG GUOQING
School of Statistics: SHI DAIMIN

PROFESSORS

AI, SUNLIN, Insurance
CAI, CHUN, Accounting
CAO, TINGGUI, Finance
CHEN, MINGLI, Law
CHEN, SUYU, Law
CHEN, YONGSHENG, Finance
CHEN, YUANHONG, Accounting
CHENG, MINXUAN, International Business
CHENG, QIAN, Public Finance and Taxation
DENG, GUANJUN, e-Commerce
DING, RENZHONG, Economics
DU, ZHIHAN, Economic Mathematics
FAN, XINGJIAN, Accounting
FENG, JIAN, Accounting
FENG, XIDE, Economics
FENG, YADONG, Law
FU, DAIGUO, Accounting
FU, HONGCHUN, Economics
GAO, JINKANG, Law
GUO, FUCHU, Accounting
HE, ZERONG, Finance
JIANG, LING, Economics
JIANG, YUMEI, Law
KUANG, SONG, Economic Information Engineering
LI, NANCHENG, Statistics
LI, PING, Economics
LI, SHI, Statistics

LIN, WANXIANG, Accounting
LIN, YI, Insurance
LIU, CAN, Economics
LIU, RONG, Public Finance and Taxation
LIU, SHIBAI, Economics
MA, XIAO, Public Finance and Taxation
MU, LIANGPING, Economics
NI, KEQIN, Finance
PAN, XUEMO, Accounting
PANG, HAO, Statistics
PENG, SHAOBING, Accounting
REN, ZHIJUN, Economics
SHEN, XIAOMEI, Public Administration
SHI, DAIMIN, Statistics
SUN, RONG, Insurance
TU, KAIYI, International Business
WANG, GUOQING, Public Finance and Taxation
WANG, XIANGXI, e-Commerce
WANG, YONGXI, Economics
WANG, YUGUO, Economics
WANG, ZHIAN, Accounting
XIANG, KAILI, Economic Mathematics
XIANG, RONGMEI, Statistics
XIE, JIANMIN, e-Commerce
XIE, SHENGZHI, Economic Information Engineering
XIE, ZHILONG, e-Commerce
XING, QIANGGUO, Public Administration
XU, LANG, Statistics
YIN, MENGBO, Finance
YIN, QINGSHUANG, Public Administration
YIN, YINPIN, Public Finance and Taxation
YIN, ZHONGMING, International Business
YUAN, WENPING, Economics
YUE, CAISHEN, Law
ZENG, KANGLIN, Finance
ZENG, XIAOLING, Accounting
ZHANG, HEJIN, Finance
ZHANG, KUANHAI, Economic Information Engineering
ZHANG, QIAOYUN, Finance
ZHANG, WEI, Economics
ZHANG, XINCAI, e-Commerce
ZHAO, DEWU, Accounting
ZHENG, JINGJI, Economics
ZHONG, CHENG, e-Commerce
ZHOU, GUANGDA, Statistics
ZHOU, HONGYUAN, Finance
ZHOU, QIHAI, Economic Information Engineering
ZHOU, XIAOLIN, Public Finance and Taxation
ZHU, MINGXI, Public Finance and Taxation
ZHUO, ZHI, Insurance

SOUTHWEST JIAOTONG UNIVERSITY

111 North 1, Er Huan Rd, Chengdu 610031, Sichuan Province
Telephone: (28) 87600114
Fax: (28) 87600502
Internet: www.swjtu.edu.cn

Founded 1896
State control
Academic year: September to July

Pres.: ZHOU BENKUAN
Vice-Pres: CHEN ZHIJIAN, HUANG QING, JIANG GEFU, LIN ANLIN, PU DEZHANG, YANG LIZHONG
Head of Graduate Dept: HUANG QING
Librarian: DONG DEZHEN

Number of teachers: 1,961
Number of students: 20,000

Publication: *Journal* (natural sciences, in Chinese and English, 6 a year)

DEANS

College of Foreign Languages: XIA WEIRONG
College of Traffic and Transportation: ZHANG DIANYE
Faculty of Software: WU GUANG
School of Art and Communication: WANG SHUNHONG
School of Architecture: QIU JIAN

School of Civil Engineering: LI QIAO
School of Computer Science and Communications Engineering: FAN PINGZHI
School of Economics and Management: JIA JIANMIN
School of Electrical Engineering: LI QUNZHEN
School of Environmental Science and Engineering: LIU BAOJUN
School of Material Science and Engineering: HUANG NAN
School of Mechanical Engineering: XU MINGHENG

PROFESSORS

CAI, HUAI, Computer Science and Communications Engineering
CAI, YING, Civil Engineering
CEN, MINYI, Civil Engineering
CHE, HUIMIN, Civil Engineering
CHEN, JUNYING, Material Science and Engineering
CHEN, XIANGDONG, Computer Science and Communications Engineering
CHEN, XIAOCHUAN, Electrical Engineering
CHENG, QIANGONG, Civil Engineering
DAI, GUANGZE, Material Science and Engineering
DENG, RONGGUI, Civil Engineering
DENG, YOUQIANG, Economics and Management
DENG, YUCAI, Civil Engineering
DIAO, MINGBI, Economics and Management
FAN, HONG, Computer Software
FAN, LILI, Economics and Management
FAN, PINGZHI, Computer Science and Communications Engineering
FANG, XUMING, Computer Science and Communications Engineering
FENG, BO, Material Science and Engineering
FENG, QUANYUAN, Computer Science and Communications Engineering
FENG, XIAOYUN, Electrical Engineering
FU, YONGSHENG, Environmental Science and Engineering
GAO, BO, Civil Engineering
GAO, LONGCHANG, Economics and Management
GAO, SHIBIN, Electrical Engineering
GUAN, BAOSHU, Civil Engineering
GUO, JIN, Computer Science and Communications Engineering
GUO, YAOHUANG, Economics and Management
HE, CHUAN, Civil Engineering
HE, DAKE, Computer Science and Communications Engineering
HE, GUANGHAN, Civil Engineering
HU, HOUTIAN, Civil Engineering
HU, PEI, Economics and Management
HU, XIEWEN, Civil Engineering
HUANG, DENGSHI, Economics and Management
HUANG, DINGFU, Civil Engineering
HUANG, NAN, Material Science and Engineering
HUANG, ZEWEN, Material Science and Engineering
JIA, JIANMIN, Economics and Management
JIA, ZHIYONG, Economics and Management
JIANG, GUANLU, Civil Engineering
JIANG, QI, Material Science and Engineering
JIANG, SHIZHONG, Civil Engineering
JIN, WEIDONG, Electrical Engineering
LAO, YUANCHANG, Civil Engineering
LENG, YONGXIANG, Material Science and Engineering
LI, CHENGHUI, Civil Engineering
LI, CHENGZHONG, Computer Science and Communications Engineering
LI, JUN, Economics and Management
LI, QIAO, Civil Engineering
LI, QUNZHEN, Electrical Engineering
LI, XIAOHONG, Material Science and Engineering
LI, YADONG, Civil Engineering
LI, YONGSHU, Civil Engineering

LI, YUANFU, Civil Engineering
LI, ZHI, Electrical Engineering
LIAO, HAILI, Civil Engineering
LIU, DAN, Environmental Science and Engineering
LIU, HANWEI, Material Science and Engineering
LIU, XUEYI, Civil Engineering
LIU, ZHENGPING, Civil Engineering
LU, CHANGJIANG, Civil Engineering
LU, HELIN, Civil Engineering
LU, YANG, Civil Engineering
LU, ZHENQIN, Civil Engineering
LUO, BIN, Computer Science and Communications Engineering
LUO, YUANLIANG, Economics and Management
MA, YONGQIANG, Computer Science and Communications Engineering
MOU, RUIFANG, Environmental Science and Engineering
PAN, WEI, Computer Science and Communications Engineering
PENG, DAIYUAN, Computer Science and Communications Engineering
PENG, QIYUAN, Traffic and Transportation
PU, JINHUI, Civil Engineering
QI, TAIYUE, Civil Engineering
QIAN, DONGSHENG, Civil Engineering
QIANG, YONGJIU, Civil Engineering
QIU, WENGE, Civil Engineering
QUE, YANJUN, Civil Engineering
SHI, BENSHAN, Economics and Management
SU, BIN, Computer Software
SUN, LINFU, Civil Engineering
TANG, XIAOHU, Computer Science and Communications Engineering
WAN, FUGUANG, Civil Engineering
WANG, BEN, Electrical Engineering
WANG, CHENGZHANG, Economics and Management
WANG, JIN, Material Science and Engineering
WANG, JUNSHI, Material Science and Engineering
WANG, MINGNIAN, Civil Engineering
WANG, PING, Civil Engineering
WANG, QIAN, Economics and Management
WANG, YONG, Material Science and Engineering
WONG, JIE, Material Science and Engineering
WU, GUANG, Civil Engineering
WU, GUANG, Environmental Science and Engineering
WU, GUANG, Computer Software
WU, GUANGNING, Electrical Engineering
WU, ZHENYE, Economics and Management
XIA, WEIRONG, Foreign Languages
XIAO, JIAN, Electrical Engineering
XIE, QIANG, Civil Engineering
XU, JIANPING, Electrical Engineering
YAN, CHUANPENG, Material Science and Engineering
YANG, BANGCHENG, Material Science and Engineering
YANG, CHUAN, Material Science and Engineering
YANG, JIMEI, Economics and Management
YANG, LIZHONG, Civil Engineering
YANG, LIZHONG, Environmental Science and Engineering
YANG, PING, Material Science and Engineering
YANG, SHUNSHENG, Environmental Science and Engineering
YANG, YONGGAO, Computer Software
YAO, LINGKAN, Civil Engineering
YE, ZIRONG, Economics and Management
YI, SIRONG, Civil Engineering
YIN, ZHIBEN, Computer Science and Communications Engineering
YIN, ZHIBEN, Computer Software
ZENG, HUASANG, Computer Science and Communications Engineering
ZHANG, CUIFANG, Computer Science and Communications Engineering

ZHANG, DIANYE, Traffic and Transportation
ZHANG, JIANQIANG, Environmental Science and Engineering
ZHANG, JIASHU, Computer Science and Communications Engineering
ZHANG, JICHUN, Civil Engineering
ZHANG, KUNLUN, Electrical Engineering
ZHANG, WEI, Economics and Management
ZHANG, XIYAN, Material Science and Engineering
ZHAO, LEI, Civil Engineering
ZHAO, RENDA, Civil Engineering
ZHAO, SHANRUI, Civil Engineering
ZHAO, YUGUANG, Civil Engineering
ZHENG, KAIFENG, Civil Engineering
ZHOU, DEPEI, Civil Engineering
ZHOU, GUOHUA, Economics and Management
ZHOU, RONGHUI, Computer Science and Communications Engineering
ZHOU, SHAOBING, Material Science and Engineering
ZHOU, ZHONGRONG, Material Science and Engineering
ZHOU, ZUOWAN, Material Science and Engineering
ZHU, BING, Civil Engineering
ZHU, CHANGJIN, Computer Science and Communications Engineering
ZHU, DEGUI, Material Science and Engineering
ZHU, FENG, Electrical Engineering
ZHU, WENHAO, Material Science and Engineering
ZHUANG, SHENGXIAN, Electrical Engineering

SOUTHWEST PETROLEUM UNIVERSITY

Chengdu, Nanchong 637001, Sichuan Province

Telephone: (817) 2642301
Internet: aa.swpu.edu.cn/en

Founded 1958
Provincial control
Academic year: September to July

Pres.: DU ZHIMIN
Vice-Pres: CHEN CICHANG, SUN YIPING, ZHAO JINZHOU, ZHOU MAO
Librarian: REN HAO
Library of 1,473,000 vols
Number of teachers: 888
Number of students: 15,951

Publications: *Higher Petroleum Education* (4 a year), *Journal* (4 a year)

DIRECTORS

College of Computer Science: CHEN WENBIN (Deputy Dir)
College of Electronics and Information Engineering: DU JIAN
College of Resources and Environment Engineering: ZHAN FAN
Department of Basic Experimental Education: LAI TIANHUA
Department of Foreign Languages: LONG SHIWEN
Department of Physical Education: YANG XUEMING
School of Civil Engineering and Architecture: YAO ANLING
School of Chemistry and Chemical Engineering: HUANG ZHIYU
School of Continuing Education: DENG YU
School of Economics and Management: LIU XIANTAO
School of Humanities and Social Sciences: YANG BOWEN
School of Law: SUN PING
School of Materials Science and Engineering: ZENG MINGYOU
School of Mechanical Engineering: LIANG ZHENG
School of Petroleum Engineering: ZHANG LIEHUI

School of Sciences: XIE XIANGJUN
School of Vocational and Technical Education: DENG HONGBO

PROFESSORS

BENG, JUN, Resources and the Environment
CHEN, JINGSHAN, Petroleum Exploration
CHEN, PING, Petroleum Engineering
CHENG, SHIQI, Resources and the Environment
DENG, JIANMING, Petroleum Engineering
DU, ZHIMIN, Petroleum Engineering
DUAN, DARONG, Electronic Information
GUO, XIAOYANG, Petroleum Engineering
HONG, QINYU, Depositation
HU, XINGQI, Electronic Information
HUANG, BINGGUANG, Petroleum Engineering
HUANG, LINJI, Petroleum Engineering
HUANG, ZHIYU, Electronic Information
JIANG, PING, Resource Science and Engineering
KANG, YILI, Petroleum Engineering
LI, BINGYUAN, Petroleum Engineering
LI, CHANGJUN, Petroleum Engineering
LI, CHUANLIANG, Petroleum Engineering
LI, CHUNFU, Resource Science and Engineering
LI, QIAN, Petroleum Engineering
LI, SHILUN, Petroleum Engineering
LI, YINGCHUAN, Petroleum Engineering
LI, YUN, Petroleum Engineering
LI, ZHIPING, Petroleum Engineering
LIAN, ZHANGHUA, Petroleum Engineering
LIANG, ZHENG, Resource Science and Engineering
LIAO, XIMING, Resources and the Environment
LIEHUI, Petroleum Engineering
LIU, CHONGJIAN, Petroleum Engineering
LUO, MINGGAO, Resources and the Environment
LUO, PINGYA, Petroleum Engineering
MA, DEKUN, Resource Science and Engineering
PU, XIAOLIN, Petroleum Engineering
QIN, QIRONG, Resources and the Environment
SHEN, ZHAOGUO, Survey and Exploration of Mineral Products
SHI, TAIHE, Petroleum Engineering
SUN, LIANGTIAN, Petroleum Engineering
WANG, TINDONG, Resources and the Environment
WANG, XINZHI, Resources and the Environment
WANG, YUAN, Petroleum Engineering
YAN, QIBIN, Survey and Exploration of Mineral Products
YANG, SHIGUANG, Electronic Information
YAO, ANLIN, Building Engineering
YUAN, ZONGMING, Petroleum Engineering
ZHANG, BAILIN, Resources and the Environment
ZHANG, FAN, Resources and the Environment
ZHANG, MINGHONG, Resource Science and Engineering
ZHANG, PENG, Resource Science and Engineering
ZHANG, TINSHAN, Resources and the Environment
ZHAO, JINZHOU, Petroleum Engineering
ZHAO, LIQIANG, Petroleum Engineering
ZHAO, LIZHI, Electronic Information
ZHOU, KAIJI, Petroleum Engineering

SOUTHWEST UNIVERSITY OF POLITICAL SCIENCE AND LAW

2 Zhuangzhi Rd, Shapingba, Chongqing 400031
Telephone: (23) 65382114
Fax: (23) 65383284
Internet: www.swupl.edu.cn
Founded 1953
Academic year: September to July

President: LONG ZONGZHI
Vice-Presidents: FU ZITANG, LI CHUNRU, LIU JUN, WANG JIANHUA
Head of Graduate Department: YANG SHUMING
Librarian: ZOU YULI
Library of 800,000 vols
Number of teachers: 1,000
Number of students: 20,000
Publications: *Contemporaneity Law School* (6 a year), *Journal* (6 a year)

DEANS

School of Administration: CAO DAYOU
School of Administrative Law: (vacant)
School of Applied Law: LI WEI
School of Civil and Business Law: ZHAO WANYI
School of Criminology: GUAN GUANGCHENG
School of Economic and Trade Law: TANG QINGYANG
School of Economics: LIU LUJI
School of Foreign Languages: SONG LEI
School of Law: CHEN ZHONGLIN
School of Media: ZHAO ZHONGJI
School of Politics and Public Affairs: RAN ZHI

PROFESSORS

BAI, SHENG, Administration
CAO, DAYOU, Administration
CHANG, YI, Law
CHEN, JINQUAN, Administrative Law
CHEN, WEI, Civil and Business Law
CHEN, ZHONGLIN, Law
DENG, RUIPING, Economic and Trade Law
FU, ZITANG, Economic and Trade Law
FU, ZITANG, Law
GAO, SHAOXIAN, Law
GUAN, GUANGCHENG, Criminology
HAN, TIANSEN, Economic and Trade Law
HU, GUANGZHI, Economic and Trade Law
HU, RUKUI, Politics and Public Affairs
HU, SHICHENG, Criminology
HUI, YIN, Environment and International Law
LAI, DAQING, Economic and Trade Law
LI, CHANGQI, Economic and Trade Law
LI, JINRONG, Economic and Trade Law
LI, KAIGUO, Civil and Business Law
LI, PEIZE, Law
LI, SHENGYU, Administrative Law
LI, WEI, Law Application
LI, YONGSHENG, Law
LI, ZUJUN, Law
LIAO, ZHONGHONG, Law
LIN, RUIYING, Politics and Public Affairs
LIU, LUJI, Economics
LIU, XIANGSHU, Economic and Trade Law
LONG, ZONGZHI, Law
LU, DAIFU, Economic and Trade Law
RAN, ZHI, Politics and Public Affairs
REN, ZUYAO, Economics
SHI, HUIRONG, Civil and Business Law
SONG, LEI, Foreign Languages
SONG, YUBO, Administration
SUN, CHANGYONG, Law
TIAN, PINGAN, Law
WAN, YINGZHONG, Economics
WANG, LIRONG, Law
WANG, SHIHU, Civil and Business Law
WANG, XUEHUI, Administrative Law
WEN, ZHENGBANG, Administrative Law
WU, YUE, Economic and Trade Law
XIAO, YUNSHU, Foreign Languages
XU, JINGCUN, Law
XU, MINGYUE, Economic and Trade Law
YANG, SHUMING, Economic and Trade Law
YU, RONGGEN, Law
ZENG, DAIWEI, Administrative Law
ZENG, FANYUE, Politics and Public Affairs
ZHANG, GENG, Civil and Business Law
ZHANG, QIAN, Administrative Law
ZHANG, SHIDI, Media
ZHANG, YUMIN, Civil and Business Law
ZHAO, MING, Administrative Law

ZHAO, WANYI, Civil and Business Law
ZHAO, XUEQING, Economic and Trade Law
ZHAO, ZHONGJI, Media
ZHENG, CHUANKUN, Administrative Law
ZHONG, MINGZHAO, Economic and Trade Law
ZHU, JIANHUA, Law
ZUO, KAIDA, Politics and Public Affairs

SUN YAT-SEN UNIVERSITY

135 Xingang Rd, Guangzhou 510275, Guangdong Province
Telephone: (20) 84111583
Fax: (20) 84039173
E-mail: adpo@sysu.edu.cn
Internet: www.sysu.edu.cn
Founded 1924
State control
Academic year: September to July

Pres.: HUANG DAREN
Vice-Pres.: CHEN RUZHU
Vice-Pres.: CHEN WEILING
Vice-Pres.: CHEN YUCHUAN
Vice-Pres.: LIANG QINGYIN
Vice-Pres.: LI PING
Vice-Pres.: WANG JIANPING
Vice-Pres.: XU JIARUI
Vice-Pres.: XU NINGSHENG
Vice-Pres.: XU YUANTONG
Vice-Pres.: YAN GUANGMEI
Vice-Pres.: YU SHIYOU
Librarian: CHENG HUANWEN
Library of 4,170,000 vols
Number of teachers: 7,700
Number of students: 41,000
Publications: *Journal* (natural sciences and social sciences edns, each 4 a year), *Journal of the Graduates*, *Pearl River Delta Economy*, *South China Population*

HEADS OF SCHOOLS

College of Continuing Education: Prof. ZHAO GUODU
Graduate School: Prof. HUANG DAREN
Guang Hua School of Stomatology: Prof. LING JUNQI
Lingnan (University) College: Prof. SHU YUAN
School of Business: Prof. WEI MINGHAI
School of Chemistry and Chemical Engineering: Prof. CHEN XIAOMING
School of Environmental Science and Engineering: Prof. SUN XIAOMING
School of Foreign Languages: Prof. HUANG GUOWEN
School of Geographical Science and Planning: Prof. BAO JIGANG
School of Humanities: Prof. CHEN CHUNSHENG
School of Information Science and Technology: Prof. HUANG JIWU
School of Law and Political Science: Prof. REN JIANTAO
School of Life Sciences: Prof. XU ANLONG
School of Mathematics and Computational Science: Prof. ZHU XIPING
School of Physics and Engineering: Prof. XU NINGSHENG
School of Nursing: Prof. YOU LIMING
School of Overseas Educational Exchange: Prof. XU NINGSHENG
School of Pre-Clinical Medicine: Prof. XIE FUKANG
School of Public Health: LING WENHUA

SUN YAT-SEN UNIVERSITY OF MEDICAL SCIENCES

74 Zhongshan Rd II, Guangzhou 510089, Guangdong Province
Telephone: (20) 778223
Fax: (20) 765679
Internet: www.gzsums.edu.cn
Founded 1866

State control
Languages of instruction: Chinese, English
Pres.: LU GUANGQI
Vice-Pres.: GU JIANHUI
Vice-Pres.: TAN XUCHANG
Vice-Pres.: ZHU JIAKAI
Vice-Pres.: ZHUO DAHONG
Librarian: HUANG RUXUEN

Library of 545,900 vols
Number of teachers: 1,101
Number of students: 3,825 (incl. 489 post-graduates)

Publications: *Academic Journal, Cancer, Chinese Journal of Microsurgery, Chinese Journal of Nephrology, Chinese Journal of Neurology and Psychiatry, Family Doctor, New Chinese Medicine, Ophthalmic Science*

DEANS

Faculty of Stomatology: REN CAI-NIAN
First School of Clinical Medicine: XIAO GUANHUI
School of Basic Sciences: LI GUIYUN
School of Public Health: CHENG CHENZHANG
Second School of Clinical Medicine: ZHANG XUMING
Third School of Clinical Medicine: GU CAIRAN

There are 8 research institutes, 30 research laboratories, an attached ophthalmic centre, 4 hospitals, and an affiliated school of nursing.

TAIYUAN UNIVERSITY OF TECHNOLOGY

West Fen River Park, Taiyuan, Shanxi Province
Telephone: (351) 6010140
Fax: (351) 6041236
Internet: www.tyut.edu.cn
E-mail: xiaoban@tyut.edu.cn

Founded 1902
Academic year: September to July
Pres.: XIE KECHANG
Vice-Pres: GUO MINTAI, HAO JIANGGONG, HU BOYAN, LU MING, LU ZHENGUANG, MA FUCHANG, XU BINGSHE
Head of Graduate Dept: LING KAICHENG
Librarian: WANG SHENGKUN

Library of 1,830,000 vols
Number of teachers: 1,506
Number of students: 15,659

Publications: *Coal Transformation* (4 a year), *Journal* (natural sciences, 6 a year; social sciences, 4 a year), *Journal of Social Science of Shanxi High Schools* (12 a year), *Journal of Systemic Dialectics* (4 a year)

DEANS

College of Architecture and Environmental Engineering: (vacant)
College of Chemical Engineering and Technology: (vacant)
College of Economics Management: NIU CHONGHUAI
College of Electrical and Power Engineering: BU QINGHUA
College of Humanities: (vacant)
College of Information Engineering: XIE KEMING
College of Materials Science and Engineering: XU BINGSHE
College of Mechanical Engineering: (vacant)
College of Mining Engineering: KANG LIXUN
College of Science: (vacant)
College of Textile Engineering and Arts: (vacant)

PROFESSORS

BU, QINGHUA, Electrical and Power Engineering

CHEN, JUNJIE, Information Engineering
DUAN, FU, Information Engineering
DUAN, KANGLIAN, Mining Engineering
FANG, JINGHUA, Electrical and Power Engineering
GUO, YONGYI, Mining Engineering
HAN, FUCHUN, Electrical and Power Engineering
JIA, XIAOCHUAN, Electrical and Power Engineering
KANG, LIXUN, Mining Engineering
LI, XUEZHONG, Mining Engineering
NIU, CHONGHUAI, Economics Management
REN, PINGZHAO, Electrical and Power Engineering
SONG, JIANCHENG, Electrical and Power Engineering
TIAN, QUZHEN, Mining Engineering
WANG, HANBIN, Economics Management
ZHANG, JIANPING, Economics Management
ZHAO, YIFANG, Mining Engineering
ZHAO, YUHUAI, Electrical and Power Engineering

TIANJIN CONSERVATORY OF MUSIC

57 11th Meridian Rd, Hedong District, Tianjin 300171
Telephone: (22) 412882
Internet: www.tjcm.edu.cn

Founded 1958
Pres.: Prof. YANG JINHAO (acting)
Vice-Pres: Prof. CHEN JIXU
Vice-Pres: Assoc. Prof. SHI WEIZHENG
Vice-Pres: Assoc. Prof. XU YONGKUN
Librarian: Assoc. Prof. WANG ZHIJIAN

Library of 99,106 vols, 20,000 records
Number of teachers: 178
Number of students: 344 (incl. 9 postgraduates)

Publication: *Music Study and Research* (4 a year)

DEANS

Chinese Traditional Music: Assoc. Prof. SONG GUOSHENG
Composition: Prof. CHEN ENGUANG
Education: Assoc. Prof. YANG LIZHONG
Orchestra: Prof. YAN ZHENGPING
Vocal: Assoc. Prof. XIA ZHONGHENG

TIANJIN MEDICAL UNIVERSITY

22 Qi Xiang Tai Rd, Heping District, Tianjin 300070
Telephone: (22) 341234
Fax: (22) 319429
Internet: www.tijmu.edu.cn

Founded 1951
Pres.: WU XIANZHONG
Vice-Pres.: CUI YITAI
Vice-Pres.: FANG PEIHUA
Vice-Pres.: LI JINGFU
Vice-Pres.: XING KEHAO
Chief Librarian: BAI JINGWEN

Library of 284,000 vols
Number of teachers: 761
Number of students: 1,883

Publications: *Foreign Medicine* (4 a year), *Journal of Tianjin Medical College* (4 a year), *Medical Education Research* (2 a year), *Medical Inquiry* (6 a year), *Medical Translation* (4 a year)

CHAIRMEN

Biomedical Engineering: LI YUANMING
Medicine: ZHANG NAIXIN
Nursing: ZOU DAOHUI
Public Health: LAI ZEMIN
Stomatology: SHI SHUJUN

PROFESSORS

Dermatology:
FU ZHIYI
SHEN JIANMING

Endocrinology:
LI LIANGE
MA LIYUN
PANG ZHILING

Internal Medicine:
CHENG YUQIAN
DU WENBIN
HUANG NAIXIA
HUANG TIGANG
HUANG XIANGQIAN
SHI YUSHU
WANG PEIXIAN
YIN WEI
ZHOU JINTAI

Isotope:
FANG PEIHUA
LU TIZHANG
ZHENG MIAORONG

Neurology:
CHEN SHIJUN
PU PEIYU
JIANG DEHUA
XUE QINGCHENG
YANG LUCHUN

Obstetrics and Gynaecology:
JIAO SHUZHU
ZHAI ZHANCAN

Ophthalmology:
SONG GUOXIANG
WANG YANHUA
YING SHIHAO
YUAN JIAQING
ZHANG LIANJING

Otorhinolaryngology:
GUO QIXIN
WANG YANYOU
YAN CHENGXIAN

Paediatrics:
HUANG HONGHAI
LIU YUJI

Radiology:
HE NENGSHU
LIAN ZHONGCHENG
LI JINGXUE
WU ENHUI
YANG TIANEN
ZHAO CHANGJIANG

Stomatology:
HOU ZHIYAN
SUN XUEMIN

Surgery:
DAI ZHIHUA
DONG KEQUAN
GUO SHIFU
LI QINGRUI
LIU ZIKUAN
SHENG XIKUN
WANG PENGZHI
WU XIANZHONG
YU SONGTING

TIANJIN NORMAL UNIVERSITY

241 Weijing Rd, Tianjin 300074
Telephone: (22) 23540025
Fax: (22) 23541665
E-mail: msk@mail.tjnu.edu.cn
Internet: www.tjnu.edu.cn

Founded 1958
Academic year: September to July
Pres.: GAO YUBAO
Vice-Presidents: WANG GUILIN, WANG YAOJIN, XU JIANDONG

Library of 2,140,000 vols
Number of teachers: 2,113

Number of students: 30,000
Publication: *Journal* (4 a year)

DEANS

College of Basic Education: WANG GONGLIANG
College of Biology and Chemistry: GU BIN-
HONG
College of Chemistry and Environment Sci-
ence: (vacant)
College of Computer and Information Engin-
eering: (vacant)
College of Economics: (vacant)
College of Education Science: GAO HENGLI
College of Foreign Languages: GU GANG
College of History and Culture: HOU JIANXIN
College of Literature: MENG ZHAOYI
College of Management: (vacant)
College of Mathematics: (vacant)
College of News and Communication: LIU
WEIDONG
College of Physical Culture and Science:
ZHANG JINNIAN
College of Physics and Electronic Informa-
tion: CHANG XIANGRONG
College of Politics and Public Administration:
GAO JIAN
Institute of Arts: SHUN GUANGJUN

PROFESSORS

BA, XINSHENG, History and Culture
BAO, YUANKAI, Arts
BI, GUANGJI, Physics and Electronic Informa-
tion
CHANG, SHIYAN, Politics and Public Adminis-
tration
CHEN, SHANGWEI, Politics and Public Admin-
istration
CHEN, XU, Biology and Chemistry
CHEN, YAN, Literature
CHEN, YUANLONG, Arts
CUI, FENGFU, Mathematics
DING, WEIMING, Economics
DONG, SIDAI, Politics and Public Administra-
tion
DUO, LIAN, Biology and Chemistry
FENG, JINCHENG, Biology and Chemistry
GAO, HENGWEN, Literature
GAO, JIAN, Politics and Public Administration
GAO, JIE, Management
GE, LUNHONG, Foreign Languages
GONG, ZUOMING, Chemistry and Environment
Science
GU, BINHONG, Biology and Chemistry
GU, GANG, Foreign Languages
GU, WEIQING, Management
GUO, JIAN, Mathematics
GUO, QINGZHU, Foreign Languages
HAO, GUISHENG, Politics and Public Adminis-
tration
HAO, JINKU, Biology and Chemistry
HE, CHENGQUAN, Chemistry and Environ-
ment Science
HONG, SONGLING, Economics
HOU, JIANXIN, History and Culture
HOU, RUNSHENG, Physical Culture and Sci-
ence
LI, BAOYI, Mathematics
LI, DAPENG, Literature
LI, HUA, Literature
LI, JIECHUAN, History and Culture
LI, LONGZHU, Management
LI, PEIWU, Chemistry and Environment Sci-
ence
LI, XUEZHI, History and Culture
LI, YI, Physics and Electronic Information
LI, YIJIN, Literature
LI, YUNXING, Foreign Languages
LI, ZHENGANG, Physics and Electronic Infor-
mation
LIAO, QIBING, Physical Culture and Science
LIU, CHUNMAO, Management
LIU, DONGHUA, Biology and Chemistry
LIU, HONG, Economics
LIU, LILI, Biology and Chemistry
LIU, QIANG, Biology and Chemistry

LIU, SHIMING, Politics and Public Adminis-
tration
LIU, WEIDONG, News and Communication
LIU, XIANGJUN, Biology and Chemistry
LIU, XIAOLAN, Biology and Chemistry
LIU, YUZHEN, Foreign Languages
LONG, XIUQING, History and Culture
LU, GUANGYUAN, Physics and Electronic
Information
MA, DEPU, Politics and Public Administration
MA, JUNMING, History and Culture
MA, RUIJIANG, History and Culture
MA, YI, News and Communication
MAO, JIANYAO, Mathematics
MENG, ZHAOYI, Literature
MIU, FANGMING, Biology and Chemistry
PAN, RONG, History and Culture
PANG, ZHUOHENG, History and Culture
PENG, JINRONG, Economics
PENG, YONGKANG, Biology and Chemistry
PING, HUIYUAN, Literature
RONG, CHANGHAI, Politics and Public Admin-
istration
SHEN, LAIFAN, Arts
SHUN, HUIMIN, Economics
SHUN, QIFENG, Arts
SONG, CHANGLI, Literature
SONG, YI, Arts
TIAN, QINGJUN, Physics and Electronic Infor-
mation
WAN, QUAN, Economics
WAN, TANGMING, Literature
WANG, FU, Arts
WANG, GUANGMING, Mathematics
WANG, GUOSHOU, Literature
WANG, JIANING, Foreign Languages
WANG, JINGAN, Biology and Chemistry
WANG, JINLING, Biology and Chemistry
WANG, TONGQI, Politics and Public Adminis-
tration
WANG, XINHUA, Economics
WANG, XIUGE, Politics and Public Adminis-
tration
WANG, YAN, Basic Education College
WANG, YAPING, History and Culture
WANG, YONGCHENG, Physics and Electronic
Information
WANG, YUBEN, Mathematics
WANG, ZHENYING, Biology and Chemistry
WEI, WENYUAN, Mathematics
WEI, ZIGUANG, Biology and Chemistry
WU, CHUNHUA, Politics and Public Adminis-
tration
XIA, XIAOYANG, Physics and Electronic Infor-
mation
XIAO, LIJUN, History and Culture
XU, DATONG, Politics and Public Administra-
tion
XU, DELING, Economics
XU, LIMIAO, Chemistry and Environment
Science
XU, RONGKUN, Arts
XU, YONGLONG, Management
XU, ZHELIN, Mathematics
YAN, YONGXIN, Management
YANG, JIALING, Biology and Chemistry
YANG, XIYUN, History and Culture
YOU, ZHEQING, Physics and Electronic Infor-
mation
YU, JINCHENG, Politics and Public Adminis-
tration
ZENG, YUEXIN, Physics and Electronic Infor-
mation
ZHAI, CHANGMING, Politics and Public Admin-
istration
ZHANG, FUYE, Arts
ZHANG, JIER, Mathematics
ZHANG, JINGNIAN, Physical Culture and Sci-
ence
ZHANG, LINJIE, Literature
ZHANG, QIYING, Economics
ZHANG, WENHUI, Biology and Chemistry
ZHANG, XIN, Biology and Chemistry
ZHANG, ZHIYONG, Physics and Electronic
Information
ZHAO, DENGYING, Arts

ZHAO, JIE, Physics and Electronic Informa-
tion
ZHAO, LIMING, Literature
ZHAO, LIZHU, Foreign Languages
ZHENG, LIANBING, Biology and Chemistry
ZHONG, YUXIU, Foreign Languages
ZHU, SHAOHONG, Mathematics

TIANJIN POLYTECHNIC UNIVERSITY

63 Chenglinzhuang Rd, Hedong District,
Tianjin 300160
Telephone: (22) 24528000
Fax: (22) 24528001
E-mail: zxb@tjpu.edu.cn
Internet: www.tjpu.edu.cn
Founded 1958
Academic year: September to July

Pres.: Prof. ZHANG, HONGWEI
Vice-Pres.: Prof. JIANG XIUMING
Vice-Pres.: Prof. XIAO CHANGFA
Vice-Pres.: Assoc. Prof. YANG HONG
Vice-Pres.: YANG JIDI
Dirs of Int. Office: Prof. CHENG BOWEN, Prof.
LI YUXIANG
Librarian: HANG GUANGFENG
Library of 700,000 vols, 2,100 periodicals
Number of teachers: 1,086
Number of students: 23,600
Publication: *Journal* (6 a year)

HEADS OF SCHOOLS AND COLLEGES

College of Adult Education: Prof. YANG
XIULAN
College of Vocational Technology: Prof. YANG,
XIULAN
School of Accounting: Prof. WEI, YAPING
School of Art Design: Prof. XU, DONG
School of Computer Technology and Automa-
tion: Prof. HANG, QUIRI
School of Economics: Prof. ZHAO, HONG
School of Foreign Languages: Assoc. Prof.
YU, XIAODAN
School of Humanities and Law: Prof. ZHANG,
CHUNHONG
School of Information and Communications
Engineering: Prof. MIAO, CHANYUN
School of International Culture: Prof. LI
YUXIANG
School of Management: Assoc. Prof. WU,
ZHONGYUAN
School of Material Science and Chemical
Engineering: Prof. CHENG, LI
School of Mechanical and Electronic Engin-
eering: Prof. WU BAOLIN
School of Science: Prof. SUN MINGZHU
School of Textiles and Clothing: Prof. WANG,
RUI
Institute of Function Fibre: Prof. MA, YAJING
Institute of Laser Processing: Prof. YANG,
XICHEN
Institute of Membrane Technology: Prof. LI,
XINMIN
Institute of Textile Composite Material: Prof.
LI, JIALU

There are 38 research institutes and laboratories.

TIANJIN UNIVERSITY

92 Weijin Rd, Tianjin 300072
Telephone: (22) 27406148
Fax: (22) 23358706
Internet: www.tju.edu.cn
Founded 1895
State control
Academic year: August/September to July (2
semesters)

Pres.: Prof. SHAN PING
Vice-Pres.: Prof. GAO WENXIN
Vice-Pres.: Prof. HU XIAOTANG
Vice-Pres.: Prof. KOU JISONG
Vice-Pres.: Prof. WANG YULIN
Vice-Pres.: Prof. YU DAOYIN

Sec.-Gen.: Prof. SU QUANZHONG (Deputy)
Dean of Studies: Prof. CHEN RONGJIN
Chief for Gen. Affairs: Prof. LI JINPU
Librarian: Prof. YANG JIACHENG
Library of 1,740,000 vols, 148,854 periodicals
Number of teachers: 2,438
Number of students: 18,000

Publications: *Collection of Research Achievements*, *Journal* (4 a year), various departmental publs

DEANS

Graduate School: Prof. YU DAOYIN
School of Adult Education: Prof. CHEN RONGJIN
School of Architecture: Prof. ZHANG QI
School of Chemical Engineering: Prof. ZHAO XUEMING
School of Constructional Engineering: Prof. GU XIAOLU
School of Electrical Automation and Energy Resources Engineering: Prof. SUNG YUGENG
School of Electronic Information Engineering: RING RUNTAO
School of Letters: Assoc. Prof. LIU YUSHAN
School of Management: Prof. ZHANG SHIYING
School of Materials Science and Engineering: Prof. LI JIAJUN
School of Mechanical Engineering: Prof. ZHANG CE
School of Petrochemical Engineering: Prof. CHEN HONGFANG (Dir)
School of Precision Instruments and Opto-Electronics Engineering: Prof. JIN SHIJIU
School of Sciences: JIANG ENYONG

TIANJIN UNIVERSITY OF COMMERCE

East Entrance of Jinba Road, Beichen District, Tianjin 300134
Telephone: (22) 26667666
Fax: (22) 26675789
Internet: www.tjuc.edu
Founded 1980
President: Prof. LIU SHUHAN
Library of 400,000 vols, 1,817 periodicals
Number of teachers: 839
Number of students: 15,000
Publication: *University Journal*

DEANS

College of Administration: ZHANG GUOWANG
College of Biological Technology and Food Science: PANG GUANGCHANG
College of Economy and Trade: BAI LING
College of Information Engineering: LIU DUO
College of International Exchange: KOU XIAOXUAN
College of Law and Politics: SHI RUIJIE
College of Mechanical Engineering: (vacant)
College of Science: YU YILIANG
College of Tourism Administration: WANG WENJUN
School of Foreign Languages: PAUL CHILTON

TIANJIN UNIVERSITY OF LIGHT INDUSTRY

1038 Dagu Nanlu, Tianjin 300222
Telephone: (22) 8340538
Fax: (22) 8341536
E-mail: tjili@tju.edu.cn
Founded 1958
State control
Languages of instruction: Chinese, English
Pres.: TAN GUOMIN
Vice-Pres: CHANG RUXIANG
Vice-Pres: LI JUN
Vice-Pres: XU MINLIANG
Vice-Pres: YANG SHUHUI
Chief Admin. Officer: LI ZHENG

Library of 450,000 vols
Number of teachers: 552
Number of students: 5,109
Publication: *Journal*

Divs of applied liberal arts and sciences, biotechnology and food technology, chemistry and chemical engineering, industrial art engineering, management and systems engineering, mechanical and electrical engineering.

TIBET UNIVERSITY

Lhasa, Tibet Autonomous Region
Telephone: (891) 6324482
E-mail: master@utibet.edu.cn
Internet: www.utibet.edu.cn
Founded 1951, as Tibet Cadres School, current name and status 1985, based on Tibet Teachers' College
State control
Library of 22,000 vols
Number of teachers: 320
Number of students: 1,400

Main degree areas: biology and geography, chemistry, Chinese and English, economics and management, mathematics and physics, politics and history, Tibetan art and music, Tibetan language.

TONGJI MEDICAL UNIVERSITY

13 Hang Kong Lu, Wuhan 430030, Hubei Province
Telephone: (27) 83692777
Fax: (27) 3643050
Internet: www.tjmu.edu.cn
Founded 1907
State control
Languages of instruction: Chinese, English, German
Academic year: September to July
Chancellor: Prof. LIU SHUMAO
Pres.: Prof. XUE DELIN
Vice-Pres.: Prof. LI GUOCHENG
Vice-Pres.: Prof. LIU SHENGYUAN
Vice-Pres.: Prof. WANG CAIYUAN
Vice-Pres.: Prof. WANG XIMING
Vice-Pres.: Prof. WANG ZUQIN
Vice-Pres.: Prof. WEN LIYANG
Registrar: Prof. LUO WUJIN
Deputy Librarian: Prof. XU FENGYING

Library of 400,000 vols
Number of teachers: 2,692
Number of students: 7,962

Publications: *Acta Universitatis Medicinae Tongji* (Chinese and English, 6 a year), *China Higher Medical Education* (Chinese, 6 a year), *Journal* (Chinese, 4 a year), various departmental publs

DIRECTORS

College of Basic Medicine: Prof. SHI YOU'EN
College for Continuing Medical Education: Prof. XIANG CHUNTING
College of Pharmacy: Prof. TIAN SHIXIONG
College of Public Health: Prof. CHEN XUEMIN
Faculty of Foreign Languages: Prof. ZHANG HONGQING
Faculty of Forensic Medicine: Prof. QIN QISHENG
Faculty of Maternal and Child Health: Prof. LIU XIAOXIAN
Faculty of Medical Library and Information Sciences: Prof. LI DAOPING (Deputy Dir)
Faculty of Paediatrics: Prof. HONG GUANGXIANG
Faculty of Social Sciences: Prof. HU JICHUN
First College of Clinical Medicine: (vacant)
Second College of Clinical Medicine: Prof. HONG GUANG XIANG

TONGJI UNIVERSITY

1239 Siping Rd, Shanghai 200092
Telephone: (21) 65982200
Fax: (21) 65983803
Internet: www.tongji.edu.cn
Founded 1907
Pres.: PEI GANG
Vice-Pres.: CHEN YIYI
Vice-Pres.: CHEN XIAOLONG
Vice-Pres.: DONG QI
Vice-Pres.: JIANG CHANGJUN
Vice-Pres.: LI YONGSHENG
Vice-Pres.: WU JIANG
Vice-Pres.: ZHENG HUIQIANG
Librarian: SHEN JINHUA

Number of teachers: 6,350 6350 (incl. 645 profs)
Number of students: 77,516 (incl. 14,312 postgraduates)
Publications: *Tongji Journal*, several technical publications

DEANS

College of Architecture and Urban Planning: CHEN BINZHAO
College of Computer Science: XUAN GUORONG
College of Economics and Management: HUANG YUXIANG
College of Environmental Engineering: LIU SUIQING
College of Humanities and Law: DENG WEIZHI
College of Mechanical Engineering: MAO QINGXI
College of Structural Engineering: FAN LICHU
Graduate School: WU QIDI
Professional Education and Correspondence School: WU QIDI
Sino-German School: WU QIDI

TSINGHUA UNIVERSITY

1 Qing Hua Yuan, Haidian Dist., Beijing 100084
Telephone: (10) 62782015
Fax: (10) 62771134
E-mail: lbzhz@tsinghua.edu.cn
Internet: www.tsinghua.edu.cn
Founded 1911 as Tsinghua Xuetang; renamed Tsinghua School 1912; univ. section added 1925; became Nat. Tsinghua Univ. 1928; re-structured 1952
State control
Languages of instruction: Chinese, English
Academic year: September to January, February to June (2 semesters)
Pres.: Prof. GU BINGLIN
Vice-Pres.: Prof. CHEN JINING
Vice-Pres.: Prof. CHENG JIANPING
Vice-Pres.: Prof. KANG KEJUN
Vice-Pres.: Prof. QIU YONG
Vice-Pres.: Prof. XIE WEIHE
Vice-Pres.: Prof. YUAN SI
Vice-Pres.: Prof. ZHANG FENGCHANG
Provost: Prof. YUAN SI
Librarian: Prof. DENG JINGKANG

Library: 3.76m. vols
Number of teachers: 7,186
Number of students: 31,643

Publications: *China MediaTech* (in Chinese), *Computer Education* (in Chinese), *Decorative Arts* (in Chinese), *Experimental Technology and Management* (in Chinese), *Frontiers of Environmental Science & Engineering in China* (in English), *Journal of Tsinghua University (Philosophy and Social Science)* (in Chinese), *Journal of Tsinghua University (Science and Technology)* (in Chinese), *Modern Education Technology* (in Chinese), *Physics and Engineering* (in Chinese), *Tsinghua Journal of Education* (in Chinese), *Tsinghua Law Review* (in Chinese), *Tsinghua Sci-*

ence and Technology (in English, 6 a year), *Word Architecture* (in Chinese)

DEANS

Academy of Art and Design: Prof. FENG YUAN, Prof. ZHENG SHUYANG
Graduate School: Prof. GU BINGLIN
Institute of Nuclear and New Energy Technology: Prof. ZHANG ZUOYIN
School of Aerospace: WANG YONGZHI, Prof. LIANG XINGANG
School of Architecture: Prof. ZHU WENYI
School of Civil Engineering: Prof. CHEN YONGCAN
School of Economics and Management: Prof. QIAN YINGYI
School of Humanities and Social Sciences: Prof. LI QIANG
School of Information Science and Technology: Prof. SUN JIAGUANG
School of Journalism and Communication: Prof. FAN JINGYI, Prof. YIN HONG
School of Law: Prof. WANG ZHENMIN
School of Life Sciences: Prof. SHI YIGONG
School of Marxism: Prof. XING BENSI, Prof. AI SILIN
School of Mechanical Engineering: Prof. YOU ZHENG
School of Medicine: Prof. WU JIEPING, Prof. SHI YIGONG
School of Public Policy and Management: Prof. XUE LAN
School of Sciences: Prof. ZHU BANGFEN
Teaching and Research Division of Physical Education: Prof. CHEN WEIQIANG

UNIVERSITY OF ELECTRONIC SCIENCE AND TECHNOLOGY OF CHINA

4 North Jian She Rd, Chengdu 610054, Sichuan Province
Telephone: (28) 3202353
Fax: (28) 3202365
E-mail: whfu@uestc.edu.cn
Internet: www.uestc.edu.cn

Founded 1956
Academic year: September to July
8 Colleges, 16 departments, 10 research institutes, and 6 centres.
Pres.: Prof. LIU SHENGGANG
Dir of the Int. Office: Prof. FU WENHAO
Librarian: Prof. WU WEIGONG
Library of 1,000,000 vols
Number of teachers: 1,380
Number of students: 20,000 (2,000 postgraduate)
Publication: *University Journal* (6 a year).

UNIVERSITY OF INTERNATIONAL BUSINESS AND ECONOMICS

10 Hui Xin East St, Chao Yang District, Beijing 100029
Telephone: (10) 64492001
E-mail: zhaoban@uibe.edu.cn
Internet: www.uibe.edu.cn

Founded 1951
State control
Academic year: September to July
Pres.: CHEN ZHUN MIN
Vice-Pres: HU FU YIN, LIU YA, WANG ZHENG FU, XU ZI JIAN
Heads of Graduate Dept: YANG CHANG CHUN, YANG FENG HUA
Librarian: QIU XIAO HONG
Number of teachers: 1,600
Number of students: 20,000
Publications: *International Trade Problem Research* (4 a year), *Japanese Study and Research* (4 a year), *Journal* (6 a year), *Logistics World* (4 a year)

DEANS

Haier Business School: ZHANG XIN MIN
Institute of Executive Development: XU ZI JIAN
International College of Excellence: CEHN SU DONG
School of Continuing Education: XIE YI BIN
School of Finance: WU JUN
School of Foreign Studies: YANG YAN HONG
School of Higher Vocational Education: XIE WEI FANG
School of Humanities and Politic Administration: ZHENG JUN TIAN
School of Information Technology and Management Engineering: CHEN JIN
School of Insurance: CHEN XIN
School of International Business and Economics: ZHANG XIN MIN
School of International Education: (vacant)
School of International Studies: LI PING
School of International Trade and Economics: LIN GUI JUN
School of Law: SHENG SI BAO
School of Long-Distance Education: XIE YI BIN
School of Physical Education: LI FENG QIAO
Sino-American School of International Management: LIU BAO CHENG
Sino-French School of International Management: LIU BAO CHENG
Sino-German Institute: CHEN JIAN PING

PROFESSORS

BAI, SHU QIANG, International Trade and Economics
CHANG, LI, International Studies
CHANG, YU TIAN, International Studies
CHE, HONG BO, Humanities and Political Administration
CHEN, GONG HE, Information Technology and Management Engineering
CHEN, JIAN PING, Chinesisch-Deutsches Institut
CHEN, JIN, Information Technology and Management Engineering
CHEN, XIN, Insurance
DU, QI HUA, International Trade and Economics
FAN, LI BO, International Business and Economics
FENG, LI CHENG, International Trade and Economics
FU, HUI FEN, International Business and Economics
GE, TIE YING, Foreign Studies
GUO, FEI, International Trade and Economics
GUO, MING HUA, Chinesisch-Deutsches Institut
HAN, QI, International Trade and Economics
HUANG, JING YANG, Insurance
JIA, HUAI QIN, International Business and Economics
JIA, WEN HAO, International Studies
JIANG, PING, International Business and Economics
JIANG, XIAN JING, International Studies
JIN, BING YUN, Foreign Studies
KONG, SHU HONG, International Trade and Economics
LI, AI WEN, Foreign Studies
LI, BO JIE, Chinesisch-Deutsches Institut
LI, DA FENG, Information Technology and Management Engineering
LI, PING, International Studies
LI, QING, International Trade and Economics
LI, SHI, International Trade and Economics
LI, XIAO, Information Technology and Management Engineering
LIANG, PEI, International Trade and Economics
LIN, GUI JUN, International Trade and Economics
LIN, HAN QUAN, International Business and Economics

LIU, SHU LIN, International Trade and Economics
LIU, YUAN, International Trade and Economics
LIU, ZI AN, International Business and Economics
LU, JIN YONG, International Trade and Economics
LU, YONG, Foreign Studies
MA, CHUN GUANG, International Business and Economics
MEN, MING, International Trade and Economics
RONG, ZHEN, Humanities and Political Administration
SANG, BAI CHUAN, International Trade and Economics
SHENG, SI BAO, Law
SHENG, SU PING, International Studies
SHI, YAN PING, International Trade and Economics
TANG, YI HONG, International Trade and Economics
WANG, EN MIAN, International Studies
WANG, GUAN FU, International Studies
WANG, JIAN, International Trade and Economics
WANG, LIN SHENG, International Trade and Economics
WANG, SHAO XI, International Trade and Economics
WANG, TIAN QING, Foreign Studies
WANG, XIAO LIN, International Trade and Economics
WANG, XIU LI, International Business and Economics
WANG, ZHENG FU, Chinesisch-Deutsches Institut
WU, FEN, International Studies
WU, GE, International Business and Economics
WU, JUN, Finance
XI, NING HUA, Information Technology and Management Engineering
XU, YONG BIN, Foreign Studies
XU, ZI JIAN, International Business and Economics
XUE, RONG JIU, International Trade and Economics
YANG, CHANG CHUN, International Trade and Economics
YANG, YAN HONG, Foreign Studies
YAO, LI PING, Foreign Studies
YE, DONG YA, International Trade and Economics
YU, LI JUN, International Studies
YU, XU LIAN, International Business and Economics
ZHANG, JIAN PING, International Business and Economics
ZHANG, JIE, International Business and Economics
ZHANG, JING, Foreign Studies
ZHANG, MI, Foreign Studies
ZHANG, WEI, International Trade and Economics
ZHANG, XIN MIN, International Business and Economics
ZHANG, ZUO QI, Information Technology and Management Engineering
ZHAO, JUN, International Business and Economics
ZHAO, ZHONG XIU, International Trade and Economics
ZHENG, JUN TIAN, Humanities and Political Administration
ZHU, KAI, Foreign Studies
ZHU, MING XIA, International Trade and Economics

UNIVERSITY OF INTERNATIONAL RELATIONS

12 Po Shang Cun, Hai Ding District, Beijing 250014
Telephone: (10) 62861310

Fax: (10) 62861660
Internet: www.uir.edu.cn
Founded 1949
Academic year: September to July
Number of teachers: 1,000
Schools: continuing education, culture and communication, English language, Japanese and French language, law, Marxism and Leninism, national economy, national politics, science and technology information.

UNIVERSITY OF SCIENCE AND TECHNOLOGY BEIJING

30 Xueyuan Lu, Beijing 100083
Telephone: (10) 62332312
Fax: (10) 62327283
Internet: www.ustb.edu.cn
Founded 1952, present name 1988
Pres.: Prof. YANG TIANJUN
Vice-Pres.: Prof. XU JINWU
Head of Foreign Relations: LIU YONGCAI
Library of 837,000 vols
Number of teachers: 2,849
Number of students: 5,122 undergraduates, 1,424 graduates
Publications: *Higher Education Research, Journal of UST Beijing.*

UNIVERSITY OF SCIENCE AND TECHNOLOGY OF CHINA

96 Jinzhai Rd, Hefei 230026, Anhui Province
Telephone: (551) 3601000
Fax: (551) 3631760
E-mail: iao@ustc.ac.cn
Internet: www.ustc.edu.cn
Founded 1958 by Chinese Acad. of Sciences
Academic year: September to January, March to July
Schools of: chemistry and materials science, computer science and technology, continuing education, earth and space sciences, engineering science, the gifted young, humanities and social science, information science and technology, life sciences, management, nuclear science and technology, physical sciences, software engineering
Pres.: ZHU QINGSHI
Vice-Pres: CHENG YI, HOU JIANGUO, LI DING, LI GUODONG, XU WU
Sec.-Gen.: WANG KEQIANG
Dir of Foreign Affairs: ZHANG MENGPING
Library of 1,620,000 vols, 230,000 periodicals
Number of teachers: 1,162 (full-time)
Number of students: 15,500 (incl. 8,100 postgraduates)
Publications: *Chinese Journal of Low Temperature Physics, Education and Modernization, Experimental Mechanics, Journal, Journal of Chemical Physics.*

WEST CHINA CENTRE OF MEDICAL SCIENCES

17 Renminnanlu 3 Duan, Chengdu 610044, Sichuan Province
Telephone: (28) 85501047
Fax: (28) 85502321
E-mail: dff@wcums.ecu.cn
Internet: www.wcums.edu.cn
Founded 1910
State control; attached to Sichuan Union Univ.
Languages of instruction: Chinese, English
Academic year: September to January, February to July
Pres.: XIE HEPING
Vice-Pres.: BAO LANG
Vice-Pres.: LI HONG
Vice-Pres.: ZHANG ZHAODA
Chief Admin. Officer: BU HONG

Librarian: LI BINYAN
Library of 650,000 vols
Number of teachers: 1,057
Number of students: 4,998
Publications: *Chinese Journal of Medical Genetics, Chinese Journal of Ocular Fundus Diseases, Chinese Journal of Reparative and Reconstructive Surgery, Journal of West China University of Medical Sciences, Modern Preventive Medicine, West China Journal of Pharmaceutical Sciences, West China Journal of Stomatology, West China Medical Journal*

DEANS

School of Basic Medical Sciences: Dr HOU YIPING
School of Continued Education: Dr HUO TINGFU
School of Medicine: Dr SHI YINGKANG
School of Pharmacy: WANG FENGPENG
School of Public Health: Dr MA XIAO
School of Stomatology: Dr ZHOU XUEDONG

DISTINGUISHED PROFESSORS

Faculty of Forensic Medicine:
WU MEIYUN, Forensic Medicine

School of Basic Medical Sciences:
BAO LANG, Pathophysiology
CAI MEIYING, Immunology
CHEN HUAIQING, Biomedical Engineering
CHEN JUNJIE, Biochemistry
CHEN MANLING, Biochemistry
DAI BAOMIN, Pathophysiology
FU MINGDE, Biochemistry
HU XIAOSHU, Parasitology
LI RUIXIANG, Anatomy
LIU BINGWEN, Biochemistry
LU ZHENSHAN, Histology and Embryology
OU KEQUN, Histology and Embryology
WANG BOYAO, Pathophysiology
WU LIANGFANG, Histology and Embryology
ZHU BIDE, Histology and Embryology

School of Pharmacy:
LI TUN, Pharmaceutics
LIAO GONGTIE, Pharmaceutics
LU BIN, Pharmaceutics
WANG FENGPENG, Chemistry of Natural Medicinal Products
WANG XIANKAI, Pharmaceutical Chemistry
WENG LINGLING, Pharmaceutical Chemistry
XU MINGXIA, Pharmaceutical Chemistry
ZHENG HU, Pharmaceutical Chemistry
ZHONG YUGONG, Pharmaceutical Chemistry

School of Public Health:
LI CHANGJI
LI XIAOSONG, Health Statistics
NI ZONGZAN
PENG SHUSHENG, Nutrition and Food Hygiene
SUN MIANLING, Environmental Health
WANG RUISHU, Nutrition and Hygiene
WANG ZHIMING, Occupational Health and Occupational Diseases
WU DESHENG, Environmental Health
YANG SHUQIN, Health Statistics
ZHANG CHAOWU
ZHANG CHENLIE, Occupational Health and Occupational Diseases

School of Stomatology:
CAO YONGLIE, Orthodontics
DU CHUANSHI, Prosthodontics
LI BINGQU, Oral Medicine
LI SHENWEI, Maxillofacial Surgery
LIU TIANJIA, Oral Medicine
LUO SONGJIAO, Orthodontics
MAO ZHUYI, Maxillofacial Surgery
WANG DAZHANG, Maxillofacial Surgery
WANG HANZHANG, Maxillofacial Surgery
WEI ZHITONG, Orthodontics
WEN YUMING, Maxillofacial Surgery

YUE SONGLING, Oral Medicine
ZHANG YUNHUI, Oral Medicine
ZHAO YUNFENG, Orthodontics
ZHOU XIUKUN, Orthodontics

West China School of Medicine:
CAO ZEYI, Obstetrics and Gynaecology
CAO ZHONGLIANG, Infectious Diseases
CHEN WENBIN, Internal Medicine
DENG XIANZHAO, Genito-Urinary Surgery
FANG QIANXUN, Ophthalmology
GAO LIDA, Neural Surgery
HU TINGZE, Paediatric Surgery
HUANG DEJIA, Diagnostic Imaging
HUANG MINGSHENG, Psychiatry and Mental Health
LEI BINGJUN, Infectious Diseases
LI GANDI, Pathology
LI XIUJUN, Internal Medicine
LIAO QINGKUI, Paediatrics
LIN DAICHENG, Otolaryngology
LIU XIEHE, Psychiatry and Mental Health
LUO CHENGREN, Ophthalmology
LUO CHUNHUA, Paediatrics
MIN PENGQIU, Diagnostic Imaging
OUYANG QIN, Gastroenterology
PENG ZHILAN, Obstetrics and Gynaecology
SHEN WENLU, General Surgery
SHI YINGKANG, Cardiological Surgery
TANG TIANZHI, Nuclear Medicine
TANG ZEYUAN, Paediatrics
WANG SHILANG, Obstetrics and Gynaecology
WANG ZENGLI, Internal Medicine
WEI FUKANG, Paediatric Surgery
XIAO LUJIA, General Surgery
YAN LUNAN, General Surgery
YAN MI, Ophthalmology
YANG GUANGHUA, Pathology
YANG YURU, Genito-Urinary Surgery
YANG ZHIMING, Orthopaedics
ZHANG ZIZHONG, Medical Genetics
ZHANG ZHAODA, General Surgery
ZHAO LIANSAN, Infectious Diseases

WUHAN UNIVERSITY

Wuhan 430072, Hubei Province
Telephone: (27) 87882547
Fax: (27) 87882661
E-mail: wupo@whu.edu.cn
Internet: www.whu.edu.cn
Founded 1893
Academic year: September to July
Pres.: Prof. LIU JINGNAN
Vice-Pres.: Prof. CHEN ZHAOFANG
Vice-Pres.: Prof. HUANG CONGXIN
Vice-Pres.: Prof. HU DEKUN
Vice-Pres.: Prof. LI QINGQUAN
Vice-Pres.: Prof. LIU JINGNAN
Vice-Pres.: Prof. LI WENXIN
Vice-Pres.: Prof. LONG XIAOLE
Vice-Pres.: Prof. WU JUNPEI
Sec.-Gen.: Prof. REN XINNIAN
Dir of Foreign Affairs Office: Assoc. Prof. PENG YUANJIE
Librarian: Prof. YAN JINWEI
Number of teachers: 5,000
Number of students: 40,000
Publications: *Economic Review* (6 a year), *French Studies* (every 2 years), *Journal* (humanities edn, in Chinese; social sciences edn, in Chinese; natural sciences edn, in English; engineering edn, in Chinese; information sciences edn, in English and Chinese; medical science edn, in Chinese), *Journal of Analytical Science* (6 a year), *Journal of Audiology and Speech Pathology* (4 a year), *Journal of Mathematical Medicine* (6 a year), *Journal of Mathematics* (4 a year), *Knowledge of Library Information* (4 a year), *Law Review* (6 a year), *Stroke and Nervous Diseases* (4 a year), *Writing* (12 a year)

DEANS

Business: Prof. ZHOU MAORONG
Chemistry and Molecular Science: Prof. PANG DAIWEN
Civil Engineering: Prof. ZHU YIWEN
Computer Science: Prof. HE YANXIANG
Dynamics and Mechanics: Prof. WU QINGMING
Electrical Engineering: Prof. CHEN YUNPING
Foreign Languages: Prof. WANG XIUZHEN
Geomatics: Prof. LI JIANCHENG
Humanities: Prof. GUO QIYONG
Information Management (Library and Information Science): Prof. MA FEICHENG
International Relations: (vacant)
Journalism and Communications: Prof. LUO YICHENG
Law: Prof. ZENG LINGLIANG
Life Science: Prof. HE GUANGCUN
Materials Science and Engineering: (vacant)
Mathematics and Probability: Prof. CHEN HUA
Medicine: Prof. FAN MINGWEN
Pharmacy: (vacant)
Photoelectronics and Information Service: Prof. KE HENGYU
Physics: Prof. SHI JING
Political Science and Management: Prof. TAN JUNJIU
Public Health: (vacant)
Public Management: Prof. DENG DASONG
Remote Sensing and Information Engineering: Prof. WANG YOUCHUAN
Resources and Environmental Science: Prof. LIU YAOLIN
Stomatology: Prof. FAN MINGWEN
Urban Studies: Prof. ZHAO BING
Water Resources and Hydropower Engineering: Prof. TAN GUANGMING

WUHAN UNIVERSITY OF TECHNOLOGY

122 Luoshi Rd, Wuhan 430070, Hubei Province
Telephone: (27) 87658253
Internet: www.whut.edu.cn
Founded 1945
State control
Academic year: September to July

Schools: economics, material science and engineering, literature and law, international studies, arts and design, natural sciences, resources and environmental engineering, mechatronic engineering, automotive engineering, automation, computer science and technology, information engineering, civil engineering and architecture, transportation, navigation, energy and power engineering, management sciences; Deps: logistics engineering, humanities, chemical engineering, physical education, Institutes: continuing education, network education

Pres.: ZHOU ZUDE
Vice-Pres: CHEN DONGSHENG, LI HAIYING, TAO DEXIN, YAN XINGPING, ZHANG LIANMENG, ZHANG QINGJIE
Librarian: XIAO JINSHENG
Library of 2,720,000 vols
Number of teachers: 2,400
Number of students: 37,000
Publication: Journal (editions: management and information engineering; material sciences (in English); social sciences; transportation science and engineering)

PROFESSORS

CAI, CHANGXIU, Mechanical Design and Theory
CHANG, ZHIHUA, Automotive Engineering
CHEN, BINKANG, Ship-Building and Marine Structure Design
CHEN, DINGFANG, Manufacturing Engineering and Automation
CHEN, GONGYU, Management Science and Engineering
CHEN, GUOHONG, Management Science and Engineering
CHEN, MINGZHAO, Marine Engineering
CHEN, TIEQUN, Automotive Engineering
CHEN, WEN, Material Physics and Chemistry
CUI, KERUN, Marine Engineering
DENG, CHUNAN, Automotive Engineering
DENG, MINGRAN, Management Science and Engineering
FENG, ENDE, Ship-Building and Marine Structure Design
FU, ZHENGYI, Material Processing Engineering
GAO, XIAOHONG, Marine Engineering
GONG, WENQI, Mineralogy
GU, BICHONG, Mechanical Design and Theory
HU, RONGQIANG, Mechanical Design and Theory
HU, SHUGUANG, Material Science and Engineering
HU, SHUHUA, Management Science and Engineering
JIANG, CANGRU, Structural Engineering
JIANG, DESHENG, Material Science and Engineering
JIANG, ZHENGFENG, Mechanical Design and Theory
LI, BIQING, Management Science and Engineering
LI, GANGYAN, Mechanical Design and Theory
LI, HAIYING, Management Science and Engineering
LI, LAYUAN, Transportation Information Engineering and Control
LI, QIANG, Material Physics and Chemistry
LI, SHIPU, Material Science and Engineering
LI, ZHIMING, Mechanical Design and Theory
LI, ZHUOQIU, Structural Engineering
LIN, QITAI, Mineralogy
LIN, ZONGSHOU, Material Science and Engineering
LIU, GUOXIN, Management Science and Engineering
LIU, HANXING, Material Physics and Chemistry
LIU, ZUOMING, Mechanical Design and Theory
LIU, ZUYUAN, Fluid Mechanics
LU, KAISHENG, Marine Engineering
LU, LING, Transportation Information Engineering and Control
MEI, BINGCHU, Material Processing Engineering
MO, YIMIN, Mechanical Design and Theory
NAN, CEWEN, Material Physics and Chemistry
OU YANG, SHIXI, Material Science and Engineering
PAN, CHUNXU, Material Processing Engineering
PENG, SHAOMIN, Structural Engineering
QU, WEILIAN, Structural Engineering
SHEN, CHENWU, Ship-Building and Marine Structure Design
SUN, GUOZHENG, Mechanical Design and Theory
TAO, DEXIN, Manufacturing Engineering and Automation
WAN, JUNKANG, Management Science and Engineering
WANG, CENGFANG, Ship-Building and Marine Structure Design
WANG, DEXUN, Fluid Mechanics
WANG, JIEDE, Ship-Building and Marine Structure Design
WANG, LUNKANG, Fluid Mechanics
WANG, SHAOMEI, Mechanical Design and Theory
WANG, ZHONGFAN, Automotive Engineering
WU, BOLIN, Material Physics and Chemistry
WU, DAIHUA, Structural Engineering
XIA, YUANYOU, Structural Engineering
XIAO, HANLIANG, Application Engineering for Load-Carrying Equipment
XIAO, JINSHENG, Marine Engineering
XIE, KEFAN, Management Science and Engineering
XIONG, QIANXING, Transportation Information Engineering and Control
XUE, YIYU, Automotive Engineering
YAN, SHILIN, Structural Engineering
YAN, XINGPING, Application Engineering for Load-Carrying Equipment
YAN, YUHUA, Material Physics and Chemistry
YANG, MINGZHONG, Mechanical Design and Theory
YUAN, CHUXIONG, Mineralogy
YUAN, RUNZHANG, Material Science and Engineering
ZHANG, LEWEN, Fluid Mechanics
ZHANG, LIANMENG, Material Processing Engineering
ZHANG, QINGJIE, Material Science and Engineering
ZHANG, SHIXIONG, Mineralogy
ZHANG, YOULING, Automotive Engineering
ZHANG, ZHONGPU, Mechanical Design and Theory
ZHAO, XIUJIAN, Material Physics and Chemistry
ZHONG, LUO, Structural Engineering
ZHOU, YICHEN, Marine Engineering
ZHOU, ZAOJIAN, Ship-Building and Marine Structure Design
ZHOU, ZUDE, Manufacturing Engineering and Automation
ZHU, MEIQI, Ship-Building and Marine Structure Design
ZHU, RUIGENG, Mineralogy
ZHU, XICHAN, Automotive Engineering

XIAMEN UNIVERSITY

422 Siming Rd S, Xiamen 361005, Fujian Province
Telephone: (592) 2182229
Fax: (592) 2086526
E-mail: xmupo@xmu.edu.cn
Internet: www.xmu.edu.cn
Founded 1921
Academic year: September to July

Pres.: CHEN CHUANHONG
Vice-Pres.: PAN SHIMO
Vice-Pres.: SUN SHIGANG
Vice-Pres.: WU SHUIPENG
Vice-Pres.: ZHU CONGSHI
Foreign Affairs Office: SU ZIXING
Registrar: YANG BING
Librarian: CHEN MINGGUANG
Library of 2,180,000 vols
Number of teachers: 2,589
Number of students: 12,125
Publications: China's Social Economics (4 a year), Xiamen University Journal (philosophy and social sciences edn and natural sciences edn, both 4 a year)

DEANS

Adult Education College: YANG YOUTING
College of Art Education: WU PEIWEN
College of Economics: QIU HUABING
College of Foreign Languages and Cultures: LIAN SHUNENG
College of Humanities: CHEN ZHIPING
College of Life Science: PEN XUANXIAN
Medical College: LIN YANLIN
Overseas Education College: ZHAN XINLI
School of Chemistry and Chemical Engineering: WAN HUILIN
School of Computer and Information Engineering: CHEN HUIHUANG
School of Law: LIAO YIXIN
School of Management: WU SHILONG
School of Oceanography and Environment: YAN DONGXING
School of Physics and Machinery Electronic Engineering: CHEN JINCAN
Vocational Technical College: YANG SHENYUN

HEADS OF DEPARTMENTS AND INSTITUTES

College of Art Education (tel. (592) 2182404; fax (592) 2181499):

Fine Arts: HE SHIYANG
Music: YANG ZHEN

College of Economics (tel. (592) 2181387):

Economics: CHEN YONGZHI
Finance and Banking: LEI GENGQIANG
International Trade: ZHANG DINGZHONG
Planning and Statistics: DAI YIYI

College of Foreign Languages and Cultures (tel. (592) 2186380; fax (592) 2182476):

Asian and European Language and Literature: FENG SHOULONG
Foreign Languages: ZHANG LILONG
Foreign Language Teaching: GUO YONGHUI

College of Humanities (tel. (592) 2181932):

Chinese: ZHU SHUIYONG
History: DAI YIFENG
Journalism and Communication: ZHU JIANQIANG
Philosophy: CHEN XICHENG
Sociology: ZHANG YOUQIN

College of Life Science (tel. (592) 2185360; fax (592) 2186392):

Biology: HUANG HEQING

School of Chemistry and Chemical Engineering (tel. (592) 2182430):

Chemical Engineering: LI QINGBIAO
Chemistry: ZHU YAXIAN
Materials: FENG ZUDE

School of Computer and Information Engineering (tel. (592) 2183127):

Architecture: LING SHIDE
Automation: CAI JIANLI
Computing: LU WEI
Electronic Engineering: XIE TINGGUI

School of Law (tel. (592) 2186653):

Law: XU CONGLI
Politics: ZHU RENXIAN

School of Management (tel. (592) 2182873):

Accounting: CHEN HANWEN
Business Administration: SHEN WEITAO

School of Oceanography and Environment (tel. (592) 2183064):

Oceanography: PAN WEIRAN

School of Physics and Machinery Electronic Engineering (tel. (592) 2182454; fax (592) 2189426):

Electronic Engineering for Machinery: ZHU LIMIAO
Physics: LIN GUOXING

XIAN INTERNATIONAL STUDIES UNIVERSITY

437 South Changan Rd, Xian 710061, Shaanxi Province

Telephone: (29) 85309274
Fax: (29) 85261350
Internet: www.xisu.edu.cn
Founded 1952
Provincial control
Academic year: September to July
Pres.: DU RUIQING
Vice-Pres: CHU CHU, HU XISHE, LIU YUELIAN
Head of Graduate Dept: YANG XIWEN
Librarian: YANG YONGCAI
Library of 901,000 vols
Publications: *Foreign Language Education* (6 a year), *Human Geography* (6 a year), *Journal of Xian Foreign Languages Institute* (4 a year)

DEANS

Department of French: ZHANG PING
Department of German: WEN RENBAI
School of Audiovisual Communication: QIN YAMING

School of Culture and Communication: HU RUIHUA
School of Eastern Languages and Culture: ZHANG SEHNGYU
School of Economics: PAN HUIXIA
School of Tourism: DANG JINXUE

PROFESSORS

DANG, JINXUE, Tourism
FENG, GUANG, Audiovisual Communication
GAO, YAOTING, German Studies
HU, RUIHUA, Culture and Communication
LI, QIUQUAN, Tourism
LIN, KAI, Audiovisual Communication
LIU, JIANQIANG, Eastern Languages and Culture
MA, YONGPING, Eastern Languages and Culture
WANG, XINGZHONG, Tourism
WANG, XINRONG, Eastern Languages and Culture
WEI, GENYUAN, Audiovisual Communication
WEN, RENBAI, German Studies
YAO, BAORONG, Tourism
YUAN, JIANPING, Russian Studies
ZHANG, BAONING, Culture and Communication
ZHANG, CONG, Culture and Communication
ZHANG, SHENGYU, Eastern Languages and Culture
ZHENG, MINGJIANG, Culture and Communication

XIAN JIAOTONG UNIVERSITY

28 West Xianning Rd, Xian 710049

Telephone: (29) 2668234
Fax: (29) 3234781
E-mail: mailxjtu@xjtu.edu.cn
Internet: www.xjtu.edu.cn
Founded 1896
State control
Academic year: September to July (two semesters)
Pres.: ZHENG NANNING
Registrar: LI NENGGUI
Admin. Officer: LIU BIN
Librarian: ZHOU JINGEN
Number of teachers: 3,241
Number of students: 26,410 (incl. 5,504 postgraduate)
Publications: *Applied Mechanics* (4 a year), *Engineering Mathematics* (4 a year), *Journal* (4 a year), *Journal of Economic Sciences* (4 a year), *Journal of Medical Sciences* (4 a year), *Journal of Social Sciences* (4 a year)

DEANS

Graduate School: XU TONGMO
School of Accountancy: XHANG TIANXI
School of Architectural Engineering and Mechanics: CHEN YIHENG
School of Continuing Education: SUN BI
School of Economics and Finance: XUE MOUHONG
School of Electrical and Communications Engineering: ZHU SHIHUA
School of Electrical Engineering: WANG ZHAOAN
School of Energy and Power Engineering: HUI SHEN
School of Environmental and Chemical Engineering: CHENG GUANGXU
School of Foreign Languages: BAI YONGQUAN
School of Humanities and Social Science: LIU YONGFU
School of Life Sciences and Technology: WAN MINGXI
School of Management: XI YOUMIN
School of Materials Science and Engineering: XU KEWEI
School of Mechanical Engineering: XING JIANDONG

School of Medical Science: YAN JIANQUN
School of Network Education: YU DEHONG
School of Science: XU ZONGBEN
School of Stomatology: (vacant)

There are 64 research institutes and 126 research laboratories.

XIAN MEDICAL UNIVERSITY

205 Zhuquedajie, Nanjiao, Xian 710061, Shaanxi Province

Telephone: (29) 5261609
Fax: (29) 5267364
E-mail: mail1@irix.xamu.edu.cn
Founded 1937
Min. of Health
Language of instruction: Chinese
Academic year: September to January, March to July (3-year, 4-year, 5-year and 7-year courses)
Pres.: Prof. REN HUIMIN
Vice-Pres.: Prof. CHEN HENGYUAN
Vice-Pres.: Prof. FAN XIAOLI
Library Dir: MA XINGFU
Number of teachers: 4,972
Number of students: 4,000
Publications: *Abstracts of Medicine, Academic Journal of Xian Medical University* (Chinese and English editions), *Journal, Journal of Audio-Visual Medical Education, Journal of Children's Health, Journal of Chinese Medical Ethics, Journal of Maternity and Child Health Overseas, Journal of Medical Education in Northwest China, Journal of Medical Geography Overseas, Journal of Modern TCM* (Traditional Chinese Medicine), *Journal of Pharmacy in Northwest China, P.R. China* (dermatology)

DEANS

Faculty of Biomedical Engineering: JIN JIE
Faculty of Foreign Languages: BAI YONGQUAN
Faculty of Health Administration: GAO JIANMIN
Faculty of Maternal and Child Care: ZHANG MINGHUI
Faculty of Nursing: SHAO WEIWEI
First Clinical Medical School: PAN CHENGEN
Pre-clinical Medical School: GAO HONGDE
Secondary Health School: NI KAI
Second Clinical Medical School: CHEN JUNCHANG
School of Adult Training: FENG XINZHOU
School of Forensic Medicine: LI SHENGBIN
School of Pharmacy: YANG SHIMI
School of Public Health: YAN HONG
School of Social Medicine: LI JINSUO
School of Stomatology: HU YONGSHENG

PROFESSORS

BAI YONGQUAN, English
CHEN JUNCHANG, Surgery
CUI CHANGZONG, Internal Medicine
DENG YUNSHAN, Dermatology
DIAO GUIXIANG, Pathology
DING DONGNING, Chemistry
DING HUIWEN, Cardiology
DONG LEI, Digestive Medicine
FANG XIAOLI, Physiology
FENG XUELIANG, Internal Medicine
FENG YINQUN, Orthopaedics
GU JIANZHANG, Paediatrics
GUO YINGCHUN, Cardiology
HE LANGCHONG, Pharmaceutical Analysis
HU GUOYING, Isotopes
HU HAOBO, Health Administration
HU YONGSHENG, Stomatology
JI ZONGZHENG, Surgery
JIN JIE, Physics
KONG XIANGZHEN, Pathophysiology
LEI LIQUAN, Pathophysiology
LEI XIAOYING, Ultrasonic

LI GUOWEI, Surgery
LI RONG, Oncology
LI SHUXI, Digestive Medicine
LI YIMING, Surgery
LI YINGLI, Pharmacognosy
LI ZHE, Parasitology
LI ZHONGMIN, Internal Medicine
LIU HONGTAO, English
LIU HUIXI, Gynaecology and Obstetrics
LIU JINYAN, Internal Medicine
LIU SHANXI, Internal Medicine
LIU XIAOGONG, Surgery
LIU ZHIQUAN, Internal Medicine
LU GUILIN, Gynaecology and Obstetrics
LU ZHUOREN, Cardiology
MA AIQUN, Internal Medicine
MA XIUPING, Endocrine Medicine
MEI JUN, Physiology
MEN BOYUAN, Epidemics
NAN XUNYI, Urology
PAN CHENGEN, Surgery
PANG ZHIGONG, Analytical Chemistry
PIAN JANPING, Health Care of Children
QIN ZHAOYIN, Surgery
QIU SHUDONG, Histology and Embryology
QU XINZHONG, Gynaecology and Obstetrics
REN HUIMIN, Anatomy
RUAN MEISHENG, Stomatology
SHI JINGSEN, Surgery
SHI WEI, Neurology
SONG TIANBAO, Histology and Embryology
SU MIN, Pathological Anatomy
SUN NAIXUE, Ophthalmology
TAN SHENGSHUN, Dermatology
TAN TINGHUA, Physical Chemistry
WANG BAOQI, Inorganic Chemistry
WANG BINGWEN, Pharmacology
WANG HUI, History of the Communist Party
WANG JINGUI, Physical Education
WANG KUNZHENG, Orthopaedics
WANG QIANG, Stomatology
WANG SHICHEN, Internal Medicine
WANG SHIYING, Stomatology
WANG XUELIANG, Epidemics
WANG ZEZHONG, Radiology
WANG ZIMING, Urology
WU YINGYUN, Respiratory Medicine
XU WENYOU, Pharmacology
YANG DINGYI, Internal Medicine
YANG GUANGFU, Radiological Diagnosis
YE PINGAN, Anaesthesiology
YU BOLANG, Medical Image Diagnosis
YUAN BINGXIANG, Pharmacology
YUE JINSHENG, Infectious Diseases
ZHANG AHUI, Chemistry
ZHANG HUAAN, Pharmacology
ZHANG MINGHUI, Gynaecology and Obstetrics
ZHANG QUANFA, Cardiology
ZHANG SHULIN, Infectious Diseases
ZHANG YONGHAO, Parasitology
ZHANG ZHEFANG, Radiology
ZHAO GENRAN, Anatomy
ZHAO JUNYONG, Biochemistry
ZHAO ZHONGRONG, Radiology
ZHU HONGLIANG, Otorhinolaryngology
ZHU JIAQING, Cardiology

XIAN PETROLEUM INSTITUTE

18 Dian Zi Er Lu, Xian 710061, Shaanxi Province
Telephone: (29) 5253253
Fax: (29) 5263449
Founded 1958
Nat. Petroleum Corpn
Language of instruction: English
Pres.: LIN RENZI
Vice-Pres: XIN XIXIAN, XUE ZHONGTIAN, YANG ZHENGYI
Registrar: WANG XIAOQUAN
Librarian: XIE KUN
Library of 280,000 vols, 2,000 periodicals
Number of teachers: 558
Number of students: 4,000

Publications: *Journal* (natural science and social science editions), *Petroleum Library and Information*, *Supervision of Petroleum Industry Technology*

PROFESSORS
CHEN XIAOZHENG, Petroleum Economics
FU XINGSHENG, Earth Strata Slope Angles, Well-Logging Methods and Instruments
GAO CHENGTAI, Well-testing
GAO JINIAN, Applied Electric-Hydraulic Control Technology
HU QI, Petroleum Instruments
LI DANG, Mechanism of High-Energy Gas Fracturing
LU JIAO, Petroleum Instruments
PANG JUFENG, Physics and Nuclear Well Logging
SHENG DICHENG, Walking Beam Pumping Units
WANG JIAHUA, Computers
WANG SHIQING, Mechanical Engineering
WANG YIGONG, Management Systems of Petroleum Machinery
WU KUN
WU YIJIONG, Pumping Wells
ZHANG SHAOHUAI, Drilling
ZHANG ZONGMING, Petroleum Tectonics of China
ZHAO GUANGCHANG, Economics and Management

XIAN UNIVERSITY OF ARCHITECTURE AND TECHNOLOGY

13 Yanta Rd, Xian 710055, Shaanxi
Telephone: (29) 2202121
Fax: (29) 5522471
E-mail: jianda@webmail.xauat.edu.cn
Internet: www.xauat.edu.cn
Founded 1956
Academic year: September to July
Pres.: Prof. XU DELONG
Vice-Pres: Prof. DUAN ZHISHAN, Prof. GAN ANSHENG, Prof. WANG XIAOCHANG, Assoc. Prof. MA JIANHUA
Head of the Graduate School: Assoc. Prof. YUAN SHOUQIAN
Librarian: Prof. LIU JIAPING
Library of 1,000,800 vols
Number of teachers: 2,100
Number of students: 22,518

Publications: *Journal* (4 a year), *Science and Technology of Xian University of Architecture and Technology* (4 a year), *Study of Higher Education*

HEADS OF COLLEGES AND DEPARTMENTS
College of Architecture: Prof. LIU KECHENG
College of Civil Engineering: Prof. BAO GUOLIANG
College of Environmental and Municipal Engineering: Prof. WANG XIAOCHANG
College of Management: Prof. LUO FUZHOU
College of Metallurgy Engineering: Prof. LAN XINZHE
College of Information and Auto-control Engineering: Prof. ZHAO WENJING
College of Mechanical and Electrical Engineering: Prof. ZHANG XIAOLONG
College of Materials Science and Engineering: Prof. XU QIMING
College of Humanities and Chinese Literature: Prof. ZHANG TONGLE
College of Science: Prof. LI DONGLIANG
College of Environmental Arts: Prof. YANG HAOZHONG
College of Vocational Technology: Prof. LI HUIMIN
Department of Foreign Studies: Assoc. Prof. TANG YIFAN

XIAN UNIVERSITY OF SCIENCE AND TECHNOLOGY

58 Yanta Rd, Mid Sector, Xian 710054, Shaanxi Province
Telephone: (29) 5583033
Fax: (29) 5583719
E-mail: iecc@xust.sn.cn
Internet: www.xust.sn.cn
Founded 1958
Academic year: September to July
Pres.: Prof. CHANG XINTAN
Vice-Pres.: Prof. HAN JIANGSHUI
Vice-Pres.: Prof. LU JIANJUN
Vice-Pres.: Prof. MA HONGWEI
Vice-Pres.: Prof. YANG GENGSHE
Librarian: Prof. WANG TINGMAN
Library of 580,000 vols
Number of teachers: 750
Number of students: 14,200

Publications: *Higher Education Research* (6 a year), *Journal* (12 a year), *Scientech Talent Market* (6 a year).

XIAN UNIVERSITY OF TECHNOLOGY

5 Jinhua Rd (South), Xian 710048, Shaanxi Province
Telephone: (29) 82312541
Fax: (29) 83230026
E-mail: xzb@mail.xaut.edu.cn
Internet: www.xaut.edu.cn
Founded 1949, until 1993, Shaanxi Institute of Mechanical Engineering
Jt Min. of Education and Provincial control
Academic year: September to July
Pres.: Prof. CHEN ZHIMING
Vice-Pres.: Prof. CUI DUWU
Vice-Pres.: Prof. FU YOUMING
Vice-Pres.: Prof. LIU DING
Vice-Pres.: Prof. ZHANG MIAOFENG
Librarian: Prof. SHI JUNPING
Library of 800,000 vols
Number of teachers: 1,050
Number of students: 26,200

Publications: *Foundry Technology* (6 a year), *Journal of Shaanxi Water Power* (4 a year), *Journal of Xian University of Technology* (4 a year)

DEANS
Faculty of Automation Engineering and Information Science: Prof. GAO YONG
Faculty of Computer Science and Engineering: Prof. ZHANG YIKUN
Faculty of Humanities and Social Sciences: Prof. LI QINGMING
Faculty of Management: Prof. DANG XINHUA
Faculty of Materials Science and Engineering: Prof. FAN ZHIKANG
Faculty of Mechanical Engineering: Prof. LI YAN
Faculty of Printing and Packaging Engineering: Prof. WANG JIAMIN
Faculty of Science: Prof. HE QINXIANG
Faculty of Water Conservancy and Hydroelectric Power: Prof. LUO XINGQI
Polytechnic College: Prof. WANG HUI

XIANGTAN UNIVERSITY

Yanggutang, Xiangtan 411105, Hunan Province
Telephone: (732) 8292130
Fax: (732) 8292282
E-mail: ecc@xtu.edu.cn
Internet: www.xtu.edu.cn
Founded 1975
State control
Language of instruction: Chinese
Pres.: Prof. LUO HE'AN
Number of teachers: 1,309
Number of students: 31,600

Publications: *Journal* (social science and natural science editions), *Journal* (philosophy and social sciences series, 6 a year), *Journal* (natural science series, 4 a year), *Transaction of Chinese Verse* (4 a year).

XIDIAN UNIVERSITY

2 South Tai Bai Rd, Xian 710071, Shaanxi Province

Telephone: (29) 8202221
Fax: (29) 8201620
E-mail: master@xidian.edu.cn
Internet: www.xidian.edu.cn

Founded 1937
State control
Academic year: September to July

Pres.: DUAN BAOYAN
Vice-Pres: CAO TIANSHUN, CHEN YONG, HAO YUE, LI RUFENG, YU NANNAN
Librarian: FAN LAIYAO

Library of 860,000 vols
Number of teachers: 1,900
Number of students: 15,000

Publication: *Journal* (editions: physical and social sciences)

DEANS

School of Computer Science and Engineering: WU BO
School of Economics and Management: ZHAO PENGWEI
School of Electronic Engineering: JIAO LICHENG
School of Humanities: ZHAO BOFEI
School of Mechatronics: JIA JIANYUAN
School of Science: WU ZHENSEN
School of Technical Physics: AN YUYING
School of Telecommunications Engineering: LI JIANDONG

PROFESSORS

BAI, BAOMING, Telecommunications Engineering
CAI, XIQIAO, Software Engineering
CHEN, BOXIAO, Electronic Engineering
CHEN, JIANJUN, Mechatronic Engineering
CHEN, PING, Computer Science and Engineering
DUAN, ZHENHUA, Computer Science and Engineering
FENG, DAZHENG, Electronic Engineering
FU, FENGLIN, Telecommunications Engineering
GAO, XINBO, Electronic Engineering
GAO, YOUXING, Computer Science and Engineering
GONG, JIEMIN, Software Engineering
GONG, SHUXI, Electronic Engineering
GUO, BAOLONG, Mechatronic Engineering
HU, QIYING, Economics and Management
HUANG, LIYU, Electronic Engineering
JI, HONGBING, Electronic Engineering
JIA, JIANYUAN, Mechatronic Engineering
JIANG, ZHEXIN, Economics and Management
JIAO, LICHENG, Electronic Engineering
JIAO, YONGCHANG, Electronic Engineering
LI, BINGBING, Telecommunications Engineering
LI, HUA, Economics and Management
LI, WEIYING, Telecommunications Engineering
LI, YUSHAN, Electronic Engineering
LI, ZHIWU, Mechatronic Engineering
LIANG, CHANGHONG, Electronic Engineering
LIU, FANG, Computer Science and Engineering
LIU, HONGWEI, Electronic Engineering
LIU, HONGWEI, Science
LIU, JIAN, Software Engineering
LIU, MING, Mechatronic Engineering
LIU, QIZHONG, Electronic Engineering
LIU, ZHIJING, Computer Science and Engineering

MA, JIANFENG, Computer Science and Engineering
MA, JINPING, Electronic Engineering
NIU, ZHONGQI, Electronic Engineering
QIU, YANG, Mechatronic Engineering
QIU, YUANYING, Mechatronic Engineering
REN, ZHICHUN, Economics and Management
SHI, GUANGMING, Electronic Engineering
SUN, XIAOZI, Electronic Engineering
WANG, ANMIN, Economics and Management
WANG, BAOSHU, Computer Science and Engineering
WANG, JIALI, Mechatronic Engineering
WANG, LI, Software Engineering
WEN, XIAONI, Economics and Management
WEN, YOUKUI, Economics and Management
WEN, ZHENGZHONG, Mechatronic Engineering
WU, SHUNJUN, Electronic Engineering
XIE, YONGJUN, Electronic Engineering
XING, MENGDAO, Electronic Engineering
XU, CHUNXIANG, Economics and Management
XU, GUOHUA, Economics and Management
XU, LUPING, Electronic Engineering
YANG, WANHAI, Electronic Engineering
ZENG, PING, Computer Science and Engineering
ZENG, XINGWEN, Telecommunications Engineering
ZHANG, FUSHUN, Electronic Engineering
ZHANG, HUI, Telecommunications Engineering
ZHANG, JUNYING, Computer Science and Engineering
ZHANG, PING, Mechatronic Engineering
ZHANG, SHIXUAN, Electronic Engineering
ZHANG, SHOUHONG, Electronic Engineering
ZHANG, YONGRUI, Mechatronic Engineering
ZHAO, GUOQING, Electronic Engineering
ZHAO, KE, Mechatronic Engineering
ZHAO, PENGWEI, Economics and Management
ZHAO, WEI, Economics and Management
ZHAO, WENPING, Economics and Management
ZHAO, YIGONG, Electronic Engineering
ZHI, BOQING, Mechatronic Engineering
ZHOU, WEI, Mechatronic Engineering

XINJIANG UNIVERSITY

14 Sheng Li Rd, Urumqi 830046, Xinjiang Uygur Autonomous Region

Telephone: (991) 8582221
Fax: (991) 8581249
E-mail: wsc@xju.edu.cn

Founded 1924; merged with Xinjiang Engineering Institute 2000
Academic year: September to July

Rector: ANIWER AMUT
Vice-Rector: AZHAT SULITAN
Vice-Rector: TASHPLAT TYIP
Vice-Rector: ZHANG XIAOFAN
Librarian: WANG KAIYUAN

Library of 1,330,000 vols
Number of teachers: 1,830
Number of students: 39,000 (incl. 784 postgraduate)

Publication: *Xinjiang University Journal* (natural sciences and social sciences versions)

Teaching units: College of Adult Education; College of Chemistry and Chemical Engineering; College of Construction Engineering; College of Electrical Engineering; College of Foreign Languages; College of Information Science and Engineering; College of Liberal Arts; College of Mechanical Engineering; College of Science and Technology; Department of Physics; Department of Textile Engineering; Institute of Life Sciences and Technology; Institute of Mathematics and Systematic Science; Institute of Resources and Environmental Science; Higher Vocational and Technical College; School of Economics and Management; School of Law

Research Institutes: Institute of Altaic Study; Institute of Applied Chemistry; Institute of Architectural Design; Institute of Arid Ecology; Institute of Central Asian Culture; Institute of Demography; Institute of Economics; Institute of Mathematical Theory.

YANBIAN UNIVERSITY

88 977 Gongyuan Rd, Yanji 133002, Jilin Province

Telephone: (433) 2713167
Fax: (433) 2719618
Internet: www.ybu.edu.cn

Founded 1949
Provincial control
Academic year: September to July

Pres.: JIN BINMIN
Vice-Pres: GAI TONGXIANG, LI SHUIJIN, PIAO YONGHAO, YU YONGHE
Head of Graduate Dept: CUI XIONGHAN
Librarian: HAN ZHE

Library of 1,400,000 vols
Number of teachers: 1,345
Number of students: 16,447

Publications: *Chinese Studies, Collection of Papers on Korean Issues, Collection of Papers on Korean Nationality, Collection of Papers on North and South Korean Studies, Dongjiang* ('Eastern Border'), *Journal* (editions: agricultural, medical, sciences and engineering and social science), *Oriental Philosophy Research*

DEANS

College of Agriculture: ZHANG SHOUFA
College of Art: JIANG GUANGXUN
College of Chinese Language and Culture: (vacant)
College of Economics and Management: XUAN DONGRI
College of Foreign Languages: (vacant)
College of Medicine: CUI JIONGMO
College of Nursing: JIN DONGXU
College of Pharmacy: CUI JIONGMO
College of Physical Education: LIU QIXIAO
College of Science and Engineering: WU XUE
College of Science and Technology: WU XUE
Normal College: CUI CHENGRI
School of Law: CHEN ZHENMING

PROFESSORS

AN, GUOFENG, Chinese Language and Culture
BAI, HONGAI, Foreign Languages
CAI, MEIHUA, Normal College
CAO, XIULING, Chinese Language and Culture
CHEN, YANQIU, Agriculture
CUI, CHENGXUE, Normal College
CUI, RONGYI, Science and Technology
CUI, SHENGYUN, Science and Technology
CUI, TAIJI, Chinese Language and Culture
CUI, YONGCHUN, Art
FANG, HAOFAN, Normal College
FANG, MEISHAN, Art
FANG, NANZHU, Agriculture
FEI, HONGGEN, Normal College
FU, WEIJIE, Agriculture
GU, GUANGRUI, Science and Technology
GUO, ZHENPING, Science and Technology
HE, YUNPENG, Law
HUANG, ZHENJI, Chinese Language and Culture
JIANG, HAISHUN, Law
JIANG, JIJIAN, Agriculture
JIANG, LONGFAN, Normal College
JIANG, RISHAN, Science, Technology and Engineering
JIANG, YONGZHE, Physical Education
JIANG, YUN, Normal College
JIN, BINGHUO, Normal College
JIN, BINGMIN, Normal College
JIN, CHENGGAO, Normal College

JIN, CHUNZHI, Physical Education
JIN, DONGRI, Science and Technology
JIN, HAIGUO, Agriculture
JIN, HELU, Law
JIN, HEWAN, Pharmacy and Nursing
JIN, HEYAN, Normal College
JIN, HUALIN, Economics and Management
JIN, HUXIONG, Normal College
JIN, JIANGLONG, Agriculture
JIN, JISHI, Normal College
JIN, JUNCHENG, Art
JIN, KUANXIONG, Normal College
JIN, LONGZHE, Physical Education
JIN, QIANGYI, Normal College
JIN, XIANGHUA, Chinese Language and Culture
JIN, XINGGUANG, Agriculture
JIN, XINGSAN, Art
JIN, XUECHUN, Law
JIN, YINGXIONG, Physical Education
JIN, YONGCHUN, Law
JIN, YONGHAO, Science and Technology
JIN, YONGSHOU, Foreign Languages
JIN, YUANZHE, Medicine
JIN, ZHEHUA, Normal College
JIN, ZHEHUI, Foreign Languages
JIN, ZHENGYI, Normal College
JIN, ZHEZHU, Normal College
LI, AISHUN, Art
LI, BAOQI, Law
LI, CHUNYU, Pharmacy and Nursing
LI, GUANFU, Normal College
LI, MINDE, Foreign Languages
LI, MINZI, Art
LI, SHANJI, Science and Technology
LI, SHENGLONG, Art
LI, WUJI, Foreign Languages
LI, YUNJUN, Science and Technology
LI, ZONGXUN, Normal College
LIAN, ZHEMAN, Science and Technology
LIN, CHENGHU, Foreign Languages
LIN, JINSHU, Economics and Management
LIU, XIANHU, Agriculture
LU, CHENG, Agriculture
LU, LONGSHI, Agriculture
MA, JINKE, Normal College
MENG, FANPING, Medicine
NAN, CHENGYU, Foreign Languages
PAN, CHANGHE, Normal College
PIAO, CHENGXIAN, Economics and Management
PIAO, XIUHAO, Economics and Management
PU, SHIZHEN, Law
PU, TAIZHU, Normal College
PU, XIANGFAN, Science and Technology
PU, YUMING, Normal College
PU, ZHE, Medicine
PU, ZHENGYANG, Normal College
QU, BOHONG, Agriculture
QUAN, LONGHUA, Foreign Languages
QUAN, XUEXI, Normal College
QUAN, YU, Foreign Languages
QUAN, ZONGXUE, Science and Technology
SHAO, JINGBO, Science and Technology
SUN, DEBIAO, Normal College
SUN, DONGZHI, Medicine
SUN, SHU, Medicine
TIAN, GUANRONG, Science, Technology and Engineering
WANG, GUIFEN, Science and Technology
WANG, KEPING, Chinese Language and Culture
WANG, XIAOBO, Normal College
WEI, ZHIFANG, Normal College
WEN, ZHAOHAI, Normal College
WU, MINGGEN, Agriculture
WU, XUE, Science, Technology and Engineering
XIANG, KIAMING, Art
XU, JI, Normal College
XU, MINGZHE, Normal College
XU, WENYI, Medicine
XU, YUANXIAN, Law
XUAN, DONGRI, Economics and Management
YAN, CHANGGUO, Agriculture

YIN, BINGZHU, Science, Technology and Engineering
YIN, TAISHUN, Law
YU, CHUNHAI, Normal College
YU, CHUNXI, Foreign Languages
YU, YANCUN, Normal College
ZHANG, JINGZHONG, Normal College
ZHANG, MIN, Agriculture
ZHANG, SHOU, Science and Technology
ZHANG, SHOUFA, Agriculture
ZHANG, ZHENAI, Foreign Languages
ZHAO, ENHUA, Physical Education
ZHAO, JINGCHUN, Foreign Languages
ZHAO, LIANHUA, Science and Technology
ZHENG, DAHAO, Agriculture
ZHENG, RINAN, Normal College
ZHENG, XIANRI, Foreign Languages
ZHENG, YONGZHEN, Normal College
ZHOU, ZHIYUAN, Normal College

YANGZHOU UNIVERSITY

88 Daxue Rd South, Yangzhou 225009, Jiangsu Province
Telephone: (514) 7971850
Fax: (514) 7352262
Internet: www.yzu.edu.cn
Founded 1902
Provincial control
Academic year: September to July
Pres.: GUO RONG
Vice-Pres: FANG HONGJIN, FENG CHAONIAN, HU JIAXING, LIU CHAO, YANG JIADONG, ZHOU XINGUO
Head of Graduate Dept: YUAN JIANLI
Librarian: ZHANG ZHENGHUI
Number of teachers: 2,000
Number of students: 46,000 (30,000 full-time, 16,000 part-time)
Publications: *Journal* (editions: higher education study, humanities and social sciences, 6 a year; agricultural and life sciences, natural sciences, 4 a year), *Journal of Taxation College of Yangzhou University* (4 a year)

DEANS

Guangling College: LIU YANQING
School of Agriculture: WANG YULONG
School of Animal Science and Technology: CHEN GUOHONG
School of Architectural Science and Engineering: LIU PING
School of Arts: ZHANG MEILIN
School of Biological Sciences and Biotechnology: JIAO XIN'AN
School of Chemistry and Chemical Engineering: HU XIAOYA
School of Chinese Language and Literature: YAO WENFANG
School of Economics: JIANG NAIHUA
School of Educational Science and Technology: CHEN JIALILN
School of Environmental Science and Engineering: FENG KE
School of Foreign Languages: YU HONGLIANG
School of Information Engineering: CHEN LING
School of Law: JIAO FUMIN
School of Management: CHEN YAO
School of Mathematical Sciences: WANG HONGYU
School of Mechanical Engineering: ZHOU YIPING
School of Medicine: TANG YAO
School of Physical Education: TONG ZHAOGANG
School of Physical Science and Technology: CHEN XIAOBING
School of Social Development: ZHOU JIANCHAO
School of Tourism and Food Science: LU XINGUO
School of Veterinary Science: QIN AIJIAN

School of Water Conservation and Hydraulic Engineering: CHEN JIANKANG

PROFESSORS

BAN, JIQING, Chinese Language and Literature
BAO, ZHENQIANG, Information Engineering
BI, QIAO, Physical Science and Technology
CAI, CHUANREN, Mathematical Science
CAO, JINHUA, Social Development
CHANG, HONG, Animal Science and Technology
CHEN, GUOHONG, Animal Science and Technology
CHEN, JIALILN, Educational Science and Technology
CHEN, JIANKANG, Water Conservancy and Hydraulic Engineering
CHEN, JIANMIN, Biological Sciences and Biotechnology
CHEN, LING, Information Engineering
CHEN, RONGFA, Mechanical Engineering
CHEN, XIAOBING, Physical Science and Technology
CHEN, XIAOMING, Management
CHEN, YAO, Management
CHENG, JILIN, Water Conservancy and Hydraulic Engineering
CHENG, YONG, Veterinary Science
CHOU, BAOYUN, Water Conservancy and Hydraulic Engineering
CHOU, ZHIGANG, Physical Education
CHU, XUN, Water Conservancy and Hydraulic Engineering
DAI, XHIYI, Agriculture
DIAO, SHUREN, Social Development
DING, JIATONG, Animal Science and Technology
DING, LI, Medicine
DONG, GUOYAN, Chinese Language and Literature
ER, RONGBEN, Chinese Language and Literature
FAN, MING, Management
FANG, HONGYUAN, Water Conservancy and Hydraulic Engineering
FANG, WENLI, Foreign Languages
FEI, XUN, Social Development
FENG, KE, Environmental Science and Engineering
FENG, YONGSHAN, Medicine
GAO, HUIMING, Medicine
GAO, SONG, Veterinary Science
GE, XIAOQUN, Medicine
GU, FENG, Chinese Language and Literature
GU, NONG, Chinese Language and Literature
GU, RUIXIA, Tourism and Food Science
GU, SHILIANG, Agriculture
GUO, XIA, Chemistry and Chemical Engineering
HE, DAREN, Physical Science and Technology
HU, JINGGUO, Physical Science and Technology
HU, RONG, Medicine
HU, XIAOYA, Chemistry and Chemical Engineering
HU, XUENONG, Information Engineering
HU, XUEQIN, Economics
HUA, CHANGYOU, Social Development
HUANG, CHENG, Economics
HUANG, QIAN, Medicine
HUANG, QIANG, Chinese Language and Literature
HUANG, SHUCHENG, Economics
HUANG, SHUCHENG, Tourism and Food Science
HUO, WANLI, Arts
JI, MINGCHUN, Medicine
JI, SUYUE, Mathematical Science
JIANG, NAIHUA, Economics
JIAO, FUMIN, Law
JIAO, WENFENG, Social Development
JIAO, XIN'AN, Biological Sciences and Biotechnology
JIN, YINGEN, Biological Sciences and Biotechnology

JIN, YU, Physical Education
LI, BICHUN, Animal Science and Technology
LI, CHANGJI, Chinese Language and Literature
LI, CUNHUA, Information Engineering
LI, GUOLI, Medicine
LI, HOUDA, Veterinary Science
LI, JIANJI, Veterinary Science
LI, JINYU, Animal Science and Technology
LI, SHIHAO, Agriculture
LIANG, JIANSHENG, Biological Sciences and Biotechnology
LIN, ZHIGUI, Mathematical Science
LIU, CHAO, Water Conservancy and Hydraulic Engineering
LIU, CHENG, Social Development
LIU, GANG, Management
LIU, HONG, Chinese Language and Literature
LIU, MOXIANG, Medicine
LIU, PING, Architectural Science and Engineering
LIU, XIUFAN, Veterinary Science
LIU, YAN, Architectural Science and Engineering
LIU, YANQING, Medicine
LIU, YONGJUN, Physical Science and Technology
LIU, ZHUHAN, Mathematical Science
LIU, ZONGPING, Veterinary Science
LU, JIANFEI, Agriculture
LU, LINGUANG, Water Conservancy and Hydraulic Engineering
LU, XINGUO, Tourism and Food Science
MAO, YUYANG, Tourism and Food Science
MO, YUEPING, Information Engineering
PAN, XHAOWEI, Physical Education
PIAO, PING, Medicine
QIANG, JIANYA, Tourism and Food Science
QIANG, JING, Medicine
QIANG, ZHONGHAO, Economics
QIN, AIJIAN, Veterinary Science
QIN, XINGFANG, Economics
SHAO, YAOCHUN, Physical Science and Technology
SHEN, JIE, Information Engineering
SHI, MINGYI, Medicine
SHI, YONGFAN, Physical Education
SU, PEIQING, Medicine
SUN, GUORONG, Biological Sciences and Biotechnology
SUN, HUAICHANG, Veterinary Science
TIAN, HANYUN, Chinese Language and Literature
TONG, ZHAOGANG, Physical Education
WANG, BAO'AN, Veterinary Science
WANG, HANDONG, Veterinary Science
WANG, HONGRONG, Animal Science and Technology
WANG, HONGYU, Mathematical Science
WANG, JIANJUN, Medicine
WANG, JUN, Chinese Language and Literature
WANG, LINSUO, Water Conservancy and Hydraulic Engineering
WANG, LONGTAI, Mechanical Engineering
WANG, QINGREN, Social Development
WANG, XINGCHI, Management
WANG, XINGLONG, Animal Science and Technology
WANG, YEMING, Architectural Science and Engineering
WANG, YONGPING, Chinese Language and Literature
WANG, YONGPING, Social Development
WANG, YOUPING, Biological Sciences and Biotechnology
WANG, YULONG, Agriculture
WANG, ZHAOLONG, Biological Sciences and Biotechnology
WANG, ZONGYUAN, Veterinary Science
WEI, JUN, Physical Education
WEI, SHANHAO, Chinese Language and Literature
WEI, WANHONG, Biological Sciences and Biotechnology
WU, JIAN, Management

WU, SHANZHONG, Social Development
WU, YANTAO, Veterinary Science
WU, ZHOUWEN, Chinese Language and Literature
XIAO, SHUFENG, Chinese Language and Literature
XIONG, DEPING, Economics
XU, DEMING, Chinese Language and Literature
XU, JIANZHONG, Chinese Language and Literature
XU, LICHUN, Medicine
XU, MINGLIANG, Biological Sciences and Biotechnology
XU, WEIPING, Social Development
XU, YIMIN, Veterinary Science
YAN, JUN, Physical Education
YANG, BENHONG, Social Development
YANG, JIADONG, Economics
YANG, QIANPU, Social Development
YANG, SHUHE, Mechanical Engineering
YAO, WENFANG, Chinese Language and Literature
YIN, SHIXUE, Environmental Science and Engineering
YIN, XINCHUN, Information Engineering
YU, HAIPENG, Economics
YUAN, JIANLI, Architectural Science and Engineering
YUAN, XINMING, Water Conservancy and Hydraulic Engineering
ZENG, LI, Mechanical Engineering
ZHANG, HONGCHENG, Agriculture
ZHANG, HONGLIANG, Chinese Language and Literature
ZHANG, HONGQUAN, Medicine
ZHANG, JUN, Physical Education
ZHANG, MIANG, Chemistry and Chemical Engineering
ZHANG, MINLI, Architectural Science and Engineering
ZHANG, PEIJIAN, Medicine
ZHANG, QIJUN, Chinese Language and Literature
ZHANG, QING, Law
ZHANG, RUIHONG, Mechanical Engineering
ZHANG, TIANPING, Information Engineering
ZHANG, ZHENGANG, Medicine
ZHAO, GUOQI, Animal Science and Technology
ZHAO, ZONGFANG, Agriculture
ZHOU, JIANCHAO, Social Development
ZHOU, MINGYAO, Water Conservancy and Hydraulic Engineering
ZHOU, XIAOXIA, Medicine
ZHOU, XINTIAN, Social Development
ZHOU, YIPING, Mechanical Engineering
ZHOU, YIPING, Social Development
ZHU, XIASHI, Chemistry and Chemical Engineering
ZHU, YONGZE, Medicine
ZHUANG, LIN, Social Development

YANSHAN UNIVERSITY

438 Hebei Ave, Qinhuangdao 066004, Hebei Province

Telephone: (335) 8057100
Fax: (335) 8051148
E-mail: headmaster@ysu.edu.cn
Internet: www.ysu.edu.cn

Founded 1960
Provincial control
Academic year: September to July
Pres.: LIU HONGMIN
Vice-Pres: KONG XIANGDONG, LI QIANG, LIU BIN, WANG YONGCHANG, XING GUANGZHONG, YANG YULIN
Head of Graduate Dept: ZHAO YONGSHENG
Librarian: ZHANG FUCHENG
Library of 600,000 vols
Number of teachers: 1,321
Number of students: 28,000

Publication: *Journal* (editions: natural science, philosophy and social sciences, 4 a year)

DEANS
College of Civil Engineering and Mechanics: (vacant)
College of Economic Administration: YUAN YE
College of Electrical Engineering: GUAN XINPING
College of Environmental and Chemical Engineering: BAI MINGHUA
College of Fine Art: ZHANG JIAXIN
College of Foreign Languages: (vacant)
College of Humanities and Law: WU YONG
College of Information Science and Engineering: KONG LINGFU
College of Material Science and Engineering: TIAN YONGJUN
College of Mechanical Engineering: ZHANG QING
College of Science: JIN XILI

PROFESSORS
AN, ZIJUN, Mechanical Engineering
BAI, MINGHUA, Environmental and Chemical Engineering
BI, WEIHONG, Information Science and Engineering
CHANG, DANHUA, Information Science and Engineering
CUI, YUNQI, Mechanical Engineering
DONG, HONGXUE, Foreign Languages
DONG, SHIMIN, Mechanical Engineering
DU, FENGSHAN, Mechanical Engineering
FANG, BAOGUO, Humanities and Law
GAO, DIANKUI, Mechanical Engineering
GAO, DIANRONG, Mechanical Engineering
GAO, FENG, Mechanical Engineering
GAO, SHIYOU, Mechanical Engineering
GAO, YINGJIE, Mechanical Engineering
GONG, JING'AN, Mechanical Engineering
GUO, BAOFENG, Mechanical Engineering
GUO, JINGFENG, Information Science and Engineering
GUO, XIJUAN, Information Science and Engineering
HAN, DECAI, Mechanical Engineering
HAN, PEIFU, Information Science and Engineering
HAN, XIAOJUAN, Mechanical Engineering
HOU, LANTIAN, Information Science and Engineering
HU, GUODONG, Mechanical Engineering
HU, ZHANQI, Mechanical Engineering
HUANG, ZHEN, Mechanical Engineering
HUI, JIXING, Humanities and Law
JIANG, SHIPING, Mechanical Engineering
JIANG, WANLU, Mechanical Engineering
JIN, ZHENLIN, Mechanical Engineering
JING, TIANFU, Material Science and Engineering
KONG, LINGFU, Information Science and Engineering
KONG, XIANGDONG, Mechanical Engineering
LI, BAODONG, Humanities and Law
LI, FULIANG, Humanities and Law
LI, JINLIANG, Mechanical Engineering
LI, JIUTONG, Mechanical Engineering
LI, KUIYING, Material Science and Engineering
LI, QIANG, Mechanical Engineering
LI, WEIMIN, Mechanical Engineering
LI, XIANKUI, Mechanical Engineering
LI, YUPENG, Mechanical Engineering
LIAN, JIACHUANG, Mechanical Engineering
LIU, GUOHUA, Information Science and Engineering
LIU, HONGMIN, Mechanical Engineering
LIU, RIPING, Material Science and Engineering
LIU, XIPING, Mechanical Engineering
LIU, YONGSHAN, Information Science and Engineering
LIU, ZEQUAN, Foreign Languages

LIU, ZHUBO, Mechanical Engineering
LU, XIUCHUN, Mechanical Engineering
LU, YI, Mechanical Engineering
NIE, SHAOMIN, Mechanical Engineering
PAN, MINGHAN, Information Science and Engineering
PENG, YAN, Mechanical Engineering
QIAO, CHANGSUO, Mechanical Engineering
QIN, SIJI, Mechanical Engineering
REN, YUNLAI, Mechanical Engineering
SHEN, GUANGXIAN, Mechanical Engineering
SHEN, LIMIN, Information Science and Engineering
SHEN, XIAOMEI, Humanities and Law
SHENG, YIPING, Environmental and Chemical Engineering
SHI, RONG, Mechanical Engineering
SONG, GUOSEN, Information Science and Engineering
SUN, HUIXUE, Mechanical Engineering
SUN, XUGUANG, Mechanical Engineering
TANG, JINGLIN, Mechanical Engineering
WANG, CHENGRU, Information Science and Engineering
WANG, FUSHENG, Foreign Languages
WANG, HAIRU, Mechanical Engineering
WANG, JUN, Mechanical Engineering
WANG, QINGXUE, Humanities and Law
WANG, XINSHENG, Information Science and Engineering
WANG, YIQUN, Mechanical Engineering
WANG, YONGCHANG, Mechanical Engineering
WEI, LIBO, Humanities and Law
WEN, DESHENG, Mechanical Engineering
WU, XIAOMING, Mechanical Engineering
WU, YONG, Humanities and Law
WU, YUEMING, Mechanical Engineering
XIAO, HONG, Mechanical Engineering
XU, CHENGQIAN, Information Science and Engineering
XU, HONGXIANG, Mechanical Engineering
XU, LIZHONG, Mechanical Engineering
XU, RUI, Material Science and Engineering
YANG, YULIN, Mechanical Engineering
YE, DEQIAN, Information Science and Engineering
YU, DESHENG, Information Science and Engineering
YU, DONGLI, Material Science and Engineering
YU, ENLIN, Mechanical Engineering
YU, JIANPING, Foreign Languages
YU, RONGJIN, Information Science and Engineering
YU, YUFENG, Information Science and Engineering
ZHANG, HAI, Mechanical Engineering
ZHANG, LIYING, Mechanical Engineering
ZHANG, QING, Mechanical Engineering
ZHANG, QISHENG, Mechanical Engineering
ZHANG, TAO, Mechanical Engineering
ZHANG, TONGYI, Mechanical Engineering
ZHANG, WEIDONG, Foreign Languages
ZHANG, WENZHI, Mechanical Engineering
ZHANG, ZHONGYI, Humanities and Law
ZHAO, JINGYI, Mechanical Engineering
ZHAO, JUN, Mechanical Engineering
ZHAO, TIESHI, Mechanical Engineering
ZHAO, YONGHE, Mechanical Engineering
ZHAO, YONGSHENG, Mechanical Engineering
ZHENG, SHENGXUAN, Information Science and Engineering
ZHOU, CHAO, Mechanical Engineering
ZHOU, QINGTIAN, Mechanical Engineering
ZHU, GUANGRONG, Humanities and Law
ZOU, MUCHANG, Information Science and Engineering

YANTAI UNIVERSITY

Yantai 264005, Shandong Province
Telephone: (535) 6888995
Fax: (535) 6888801
Internet: www.ytu.edu.cn
Founded 1984

State control
Languages of instruction: Chinese, English
Degree programmes in applied mathematics, applied physics, architecture, biochemical engineering, chemical engineering, Chinese language and literature, electronics and computing, finance and economics and management, fisheries industry, foreign languages and literature, industrial and civil engineering, international business, law, machine design and manufacture, physical education
Pres.: ZHANG JIANYI
Registrar: LU XUEMING
Librarian: SUN JILIANG

Library of 40,000 vols
Number of teachers: 450
Number of students: 3,839

Publication: *Journal*.

YUNNAN FINANCE AND TRADE INSTITUTE

Shangmacun, North Suburb, Kunming 650221, Yunnan Province
Telephone: (871) 5122394
Fax: (871) 5163384
Founded 1981
Pres.: Prof. WU JIANAN
Vice-Pres: Assoc. Prof. MA GUANGBI, WU TANXUE, YANG LIZHI
Registrar: ZHOU ANFAN
Librarian: LIU SHUNDE

Library of 280,000 vols
Number of teachers: 289
Number of students: 2,620

Publications: *Foreign Economic Theory and Administration*, *Journal*.

YUNNAN INSTITUTE FOR THE NATIONALITIES

420 Huanchengbei Rd, Kunming 650031, Yunnan Province
Telephone: (871) 5154308
Fax: (871) 5154304
Internet: www.ynni.edu.cn
Founded 1951
State control
Languages of instruction: Chinese, English, Thai, Burmese and some minority languages
Academic year: September to July
Pres.: ZHAO JIAWEN
Vice-Pres: HUANG HUIKUN, PU TONGJIN, ZHAO JUNSHAN
Chief Admin. Officer: DI HUAYI
Librarian: DUAN SHENG'OU

Library of 430,000 vols, 28 special collns
Number of teachers: 385
Number of students: 4,969

Publication: *Journal* (social sciences edn and science edn, 4 a year).

YUNNAN UNIVERSITY

2 North Cuihu Rd, Kunming 650091, Yunnan Province
Telephone: (871) 5148533
Fax: (871) 5153832
Internet: www.ynu.edu.cn
Founded 1923
State control
Academic year: September to July
Pres.: Prof. WU SONG
Vice-Pres: Prof. WANG RONG, Prof. HONG PINJIE, Prof. LIN CHAOMIN, Prof. NI HUIFANG, Prof. ZHANG KEQIN, Prof. CHEN SHIBO
Registrar: Prof. YANG JIAHE
Librarian: Prof. WANG WENGGUAN

Library of 1,170,000 vols
Number of teachers: 888

Number of students: 7,160
Publication: *The Ideological Front* (6 a year)

PROFESSORS
Dianchi School (tel. (871) 5172513):
    WU JIANGUO, Chemistry
School of Adult Education (tel. (871) 5147702):
    DU CHAO, Analytical Chemistry
    SHI PENGFEI, Ancient Chinese Literature
    WANG JIALIN, Analytical Chemistry
    WANG SHIDONG, Fluxional Dynamic Systems
School of Computer Science (tel. (871) 5031597):
    LI TAILING, Electronic Circuits and Communication
    LI TIANMU, Electronics and Information Systems
    LIU WEIYI, Fuzzy Database Theory
    TIAN ZHILIANG, Management Operating Systems
    ZHENG WENXING, Correspondence
School of Development Research (tel. (871) 5031453):
    CHEN LIN, Systems Engineering
    LIAO HONGZHI, Systems Engineering
    MAO YUGONG, Management Science
    XIAO XIAN, History of International Relations
    YANG MANSU, History of International Relations
    YANG SHOUCHUANG, Ethnic History
School of Economics (tel. (871) 5033613):
    CHEN JIANBO, Economic Statistics
    GUO SHUHUA, Finance
    HONG HUAXI, Economics
    HU QIHUI, Economics
    JIN RONG, Economics
    LI DEPU, Economics
    LU ZHAOHE, Demology
    MA JUN, Accountancy
    PAN JIANXING, Mathematical Statistics
    SHI BENZHI, Investment
    SHI LEI, Economic Statistics
    SUN WENSHUANG, Mathematical Statistics
    WANG XUEREN, Economics
    XU GUANGYUAN, Economics
    YENG XIANMING, Finance
    ZHANG JIANHUA, Foreign Trade
    ZHANG JIN, Economic Statistics
    ZHU YINGGENG, Ideological History of Western Economics
School of Foreign Languages (tel. (871) 5033629):
    GONG NINGZHU, Lao, Vietnamese
    LI JIGANG, English
    XU FENG
    ZHANG XINHE, English
School of Humanities (tel. (871) 5033607):
    JIN DANYUAN, Aesthetics
    LI CONGZONG, Modern Literature
    LI JIABIN, Ancient World History
    LI YAN, History of the Chinese Feudal Economy
    LIN CHAOMIN, Ethnic History
    QIAO CHUANZAO, Writing
    SUN QINHUA, Literary Language
    TANG MIN, Modern World History
    WANG KAILIAN, Classical Chinese Language
    XU KANGMING, Modern World History
    YANG ZHENKUN, Modern Literature
    YOU ZHONG, History of Chinese Minorities
    ZHANG FUSAN, Ethnic and Folk Literature
    ZHANG GUOQING, Classical Chinese Writings
    ZHANG XINCHANG, History and Archives of Chinese Minorities
    ZHU HUIRONG, Historical Geography
School of Law (tel. (871) 5184816):
    CHEN ZIGUO, Civil Law

Xu ZHISHAN, Constitution

School of Life Sciences and Chemistry (tel. (871) 5031412):

Dai Shushan, Physics and Chemistry
He Senquan, Organic Chemistry
Hong Pinjie, Microwave Plasma
Hu Zhihao, Botany
Huang Suhua, Botany
Li Liang, Organic Chemistry
Li Qiren, Plant Cell Engineering
Liu Fuchu, Organic Chemistry
Liu Songyu, Analytical Chemistry
Liu Xinhua, Soil Ecology
Tao Yuanqi, Quantum Organic Chemistry
Wang Changyi, Organic Chemistry
Xu Qiheng, Analytical Chemistry
Yang Chunjin, Inorganic Chemistry
Yang Pipeng, Organic Chemistry
Yin Jianguo, Inorganic Chemistry
Zan Ruiguang, Cell Biology
Zheng Zhuo, Microbiology
Zuo Yangxian, Invertebrates

School of Public Administration (tel. (871) 5033609):

Chen Guoxing, Socialism
Cui Yunwu, Public Administration
Gao Li, Ethics
Hou Yihong, Management Psychology
Jiang Zihua, Politics
Jin Ziqiang, Current Chinese Politics
Kuang Zhiming, Politics
Li Bin, Philosophy
Liu Jiazhi, Philosophy
Liu Yunhang, Aesthetics
Wang Yanbing, Sociology
Xiong Siyuan, Economics
Yang Jiqiong, Current Chinese Politics
Zeng Jian, Dialectics
Zhou Ping, Politics

School of Tourism and Business Administration (tel. (871) 5034561):

Guang Ningshen, Tourism Administration
Li Hao, Tourism Administration
Liu Xueyu, Business Management
Tian Weiming, Tourism Administration
Wang Jianpin, Econometrics
Xue Qunhui, Tourism Administration
Yang Guihua, Tourism Administration
Zhang Mingan, Business Management
Zhang Xiaopin, English

School of Sciences (tel. (871) 5032012):

Cao Kefei, Physics
Chen Zhongzhang, Physics
Cong Lianli, Earth Sciences
Guo Shicang, Earth Sciences
Guo Xiaojiang, Mathematics
Guo Yuqi, Mathematics
He Daming, Earth Sciences
He Xiangpang, Mathematics
Hu Jiafu, Earth Sciences
Hu Wenguo, Physics
Ju Jianhua, Earth Sciences
Li Jianpin, Mathematics
Li Yaotang, Mathematics
Li Yongkun, Mathematics
Lin Lizhong, Physics
Liu Zhengrong, Mathematics
Luo Yaohuang, Physics
Mei Dongcheng, Physics
Peng Kuangding, Physics
Peng Shouli, Physics
Tang Xinghua, Mathematics
Tien Xinshi, Physics
Wang Weiguo, Earth Sciences
Wen Xiaomin, Physics
Wu Xinghui, Material Sciences
Xie Yingqi, Atmospheric Science, Mathematics
Yan Guangxiong, Mathematics
Yan Huasheng, Earth Sciences
Yang Deqing, Physics
Yang Huakang, Mathematics
Yang Xuesheng, Earth Sciences
Yang Yu, Material Sciences

Zhang Li, Physics
Zhang Zhongmin, Physics
Zhao Xiaohua, Mathematics
Zheng Baozhong, Material Sciences
Zheng Xiyin, Mathematics
Zhou Qing, Physics

ZHEJIANG UNIVERSITY

38 Zheda Rd, Hangzhou 310027, Zhejiang Province
Telephone: (571) 87951846
Fax: (571) 87951358
E-mail: zupo@zju.edu.cn
Internet: www.zju.edu.cn
Founded 1897, merged with Hangzhou Univ., Zhejiang Agricultural Univ. and Zhejiang Medical Univ. 1998
State control
Languages of instruction: Chinese, English(for foreign students)
Academic year: September to June
Pres.: Prof. Pan Yunhe
Exec. Vice-Pres.: Prof. Ni Mingjiang
Vice-Pres.: Prof. Bu Fanxiao
Vice-Pres.: Prof. Chu, Jian
Vice-Pres.: Prof. Hu Jianmiao
Vice-Pres.: Prof. Lai Maode
Vice-Pres.: Prof. Si, Jianmin
Vice-Pres.: Prof. Zhu, Jun
Dir of Int. Programmes Office: Prof. Qiu Jizhen
Librarian: Zhu Haikang
Number of teachers: 3,285
Number of students: 90,475 (43,222 full-time, 30,571 part-time, 16,682 distance learning)

Publications: *Applied Mathematics of Chinese Universities* (in Chinese and English), *Applied Psychology* (in Chinese), *China Higher Medical Education* (in Chinese), *Engineering Design* (in Chinese), *Journal of Zhejiang University (Agricultural and Life Sciences)* (in Chinese), *Journal of Zhejiang University (Humanities and Social Science)* (in Chinese), *Journal of Zhejiang University (Medicine)* (in Chinese), *Journal of Zhejiang University (Natural Science)* (in Chinese), *Journal of Zhejiang University (Sciences)* (in Chinese and English), *Materials Science and Engineering* (in Chinese), *Management Engineering* (in Chinese), *Population and Eugenics* (in Chinese), *Practical Oncology* (in Chinese), *Spatial Structures* (in Chinese).

ZHEJIANG UNIVERSITY OF TECHNOLOGY

District 6, Zhaohui Xincun, Hangzhou 310032, Zhejiang Province
Telephone: (571) 88320114
Fax: (571) 88320272
E-mail: webmaster@zjut.edu.cn
Internet: www.zjut.edu.cn
Founded 1953
Academic year: September to July
Pres.: Prof. Shen Yinchu
Vice-Pres.: Prof. Ma Chun'an
Vice-Pres.: Prof. Xiao Ruifeng
Vice-Pres.: Prof. Xuan Yong
Vice-Pres.: Prof. Zhang Libin
Librarian: Prof. He Limin
Library of 1,002,000 vols
Number of teachers: 2,600
Number of students: 18,000

Publication: *Journal* (separate edns for natural sciences and social sciences, each 6 a year)

DEANS

College of Architecture and Civil Engineering: Prof. Zheng Jianjun
College of Arts and Humanities: Prof. Sun Liping
College of Biological and Environmental Engineering: Prof. Chen Jianmeng
College of Business Administration: Prof. Cheng Huifang
College of Chemical Engineering: Prof. Ji Jianbing
College of Electrical and Mechanical Engineering: Prof. Chai Guozhong
College of Foreign Languages: Prof. Liao Fei
College of Information Engineering: Prof. Cai Jiamei
College of Law: Prof. Zhang Xu
College of Pharmaceutical Sciences: Prof. Qian Junqing
College of Sciences: Prof. Cheng Cheng
College of Vocational and Technical Education: Prof. Du Shigui

ZHENGZHOU UNIVERSITY

100 Kexue St, Zhengzhou 450001, Henan Province
Telephone: (371) 7763036
Fax: (371) 7763036
E-mail: headmaster@zzu.edu.cn
Internet: www.zzu.edu.cn
Founded 1956
Provincial control
Academic year: September to July
Pres.: Shen Changyu
Vice-Pres: Gao Danying, Jiao Liucheng, Song Maoping, Xu Zhenlu, Zheng Yuling
Head of Graduate Dept: Zhu Chengshen
Librarian: Zhang Leishun
Library of 3,900,000 vols
Number of teachers: 2,200
Number of students: 44,000

Publication: *Journal* (edns: science, natural sciences, 4 a year; philosophy and social science, medical science, 6 a year)

DEANS

College of Nursing: (vacant)
College of Public Health: Hu Dongsheng
College of Chemical Engineering: Wei Xinli
Department of Bioengineering: Kang Qiaozhen
Department of Chemistry: Liu Hongmin
Department of History and Archaeology: Jiang Jianshe
Department of Management Engineering: (vacant)
Department of Mathematics: Chen Shaochun
Department of Music: Gong Wei
Institute of Physical Science and Technology: Wang Zhongyong
School of Applied Technology: Li Shuxin
School of Basic Medical Science: Dong Ziming
School of Civil Engineering: Liu Lixin
School of Economics: Du Shuyun
School of Education: Wang Zongmin
School of Electrical Engineering: Chen Tiejun
School of Environment and Water Conservancy: Wang Fuming
School of Foreign Languages: Shen Nana
School of Information Management: Ke Ping
School of Journalism and Communication: Dong Guangan
School of Law: Tian Tucheng
School of Liberal Arts: Zhang Hongsheng
School of Materials Science and Engineering: Guan Shaokang
School of Mechanical Engineering: Zhang Luoming
School of Physical Education: Wu Lanying
School of Pharmacy: Rao Yaogang

School of Physical Science and Technology: LI YUXIAO
School of Public Administration: (vacant)
School of Tourism Management: MAO ANFU

PROFESSORS

AN, GUOLOU, History and Archaeology
AN, YUHUI, Basic Medical Science
CAO, SHAOKUI, Materials Science and Engineering
CEN, SHAOCHENG, Mechanical Engineering
CHAN, JIE, Basic Medical Science
CHEN, HUAI, Civil Engineering
CHEN, JINGBO, Materials Science and Engineering
CHEN, JINZHOU, Materials Science and Engineering
CHEN, TAN, Public Health
CHEN, TIEJUN, Electrical Engineering
CHEN, YILANG, Chemical Engineering
CHENG, BAOSHAN, Law
CUI, JING, Basic Medical Science
CUI, JINGBIN, Basic Medical Science
CUI, LIUXIN, Public Health
CUI, XIULING, Chemistry
DONG, GUANGAN, Journalism and Culture
DONG, MINGMIN, Bioengineering
DONG, QIWU, Chemical Engineering
DONG, ZIMING, Basic Medical Science
DU, CHENXIA, Chemistry
DU, SHUYUN, Economic School
DU, XIANTANG, Bioengineering
DUAN, GUANGCAI, Public Health
FAN, MING, Information Engineering
FAN, XIQING, Physical Science and Technology
FAN, YAOTING, Chemistry
FANG, WENJI, Chemical Engineering
FENG, DONGQING, Electrical Engineering
FENG, LIYUN, Public Health
FU, CHUNJING, Basic Medical Science
FU, RUNFANG, Basic Medical Science
GAO, JIANHUA, Chemistry
GAO, JINFENG, Electrical Engineering
GAO, XIAOQUN, Basic Medical Science
GAO, ZHENGYAO, Physical Science and Technology
GONG, JUNFANG, Chemistry
GUAN, HUILING, Mechanical Engineering
GUAN, SHAOKANG, Materials Science and Engineering
GUAN, XINXIN, Chemistry
GUO, SHILING, Chemical Engineering
GUO, XIANJI, Chemistry
GUO, YANCHUN, Chemistry
GUO, YINGJIAN, Foreign Languages
GUO, YIQUN, Chemistry
GUO, YUANCHENG, Civil Engineering
HAN, GUOHE, History and Archaeology
HAN, JIE, Mechanical Engineering
HAN, QIAO, Chemistry
HAN, WEICHENG, Chemistry
HE, ZHANHANG, Chemistry
HOU, HONGWEI, Chemistry
HOU, ZONGYUAN, Law
HU, DONGSHENG, Public Health
HU, JIANLI, Chemistry
HUA, SHAOJIE, Mechanical Engineering
HUO, YUPING, Physical Science and Technology
JIA, HANDONG, Chemistry
JIA, XIAOLIN, Materials Science and Engineering
JIANG, DENGGAO, Chemical Engineering
JIANG, JIANCHU, Law
JIANG, JIANSHE, History and Archaeology
JIANG, MAYUN, Education
JIANG, YUANLI, Chemical Engineering
KE, PING, Information Management
LI, DAWANG, Civil Engineering
LI, GANG, Chemistry
LI, HAIMEI, Materials Science and Engineering
LI, JIANJUN, Chemistry
LI, JIANKE, Bioengineering
LI, LIMIN, Chemistry

LI, TIAN, Civil Engineering
LI, WENJIE, Public Health
LI, XIAOWEN, Basic Medical Science
LI, XINFA, Materials Science and Engineering
LI, YINGDAN, Public Health
LI, YUEBAI, Basic Medical Science
LI, YUXIAO, Physical Science and Technology
LI, ZHIMIN, Public Health
LI, ZHONGJUN, Chemistry
LIANG, ERJUN, Physical Science and Technology
LIANG, FENGRONG, Law
LIAO, XINCHENG, Chemistry
LIN, LIN, Chemistry
LIU, DAZHUANG, Chemical Engineering
LIU, DEFA, Law
LIU, GUOJI, Chemical Engineering
LIU, HONGMIN, Chemistry
LIU, HONGXIA, Chemistry
LIU, HUALIAN, Public Health
LIU, JINDUN, Chemical Engineering
LIU, JINXIA, Chemistry
LIU, LIXIN, Civil Engineering
LIU, MINYING, Materials Science and Engineering
LIU, PU, Chemistry
LIU, SHOUCHANG, Chemistry
LIU, XIANGWEN, Law
LIU, XIANLIN, Electrical Engineering
LIU, XINTIAN, Materials Science and Engineering
LIU, YUNBO, Foreign Languages
LU, MEIYI, History and Archaeology
LU, SONGYUE, Law
LU, TAIFENG, Law
LU, WENGE, Public Health
LU, XINGUANG, Materials Science and Engineering
LU, ZUHUI, Physical Science and Technology
LUO, DAPENG, Public Health
MA, SHENGGANG, Mechanical Engineering
MA, XIAOJIAN, Chemical Engineering
MAO, LUYUAN, Materials Science and Engineering
MIAO, HUIQING, Economic School
MIAO, LIANYING, Law
NING, JINCHENG, Law
NING, ZHENHUAN, Physical Science and Technology
NIU, YUNYIN, Chemistry
PEI, BINGNAN, Information Engineering
PEI, YINGXIN, Public Health
QI, YUANMING, Bioengineering
QIAO, HAILING, Basic Medical Science
QIN, GUANGYONG, Physical Science and Technology
QU, CHUANZHI, Basic Medical Science
QU, LINGBO, Chemistry
RAO, YAOGANG, Pharmacy
REN, BAOZENG, Chemical Engineering
REN, CUIPING, Chemistry
SHEN, GUIMING, Law
SHEN, KAIJU, Law
SHEN, NANA, Foreign Languages
SHEN, NINGFU, Materials Science and Engineering
SHEN, XIANZHANG, Electrical Engineering
SHEN, XIAOCHENG, Bioengineering
SHI, JIE, Chemistry
SHI, MAOSHENG, Law
SHI, QIUZHI, Chemistry
SHI, XUEZHONG, Public Health
SHUI, TINGLIANG, Chemical Engineering
SONG, MAOPING, Chemistry
SU, JINGXIANG, Information Engineering
SU, YUNLAI, Chemistry
SUN, PEIQIN, Chemical Engineering
SUN, YUFU, Materials Science and Engineering
TAN, XINMIN, Education
TANG, KEYONG, Materials Science and Engineering
TANG, MINGSHENG, Chemistry
TAO, JINGCHAO, Chemistry
TIAN, TUCHENG, Law
TONG, LIPING, Civil Engineering

WANG, DONGWEI, Civil Engineering
WANG, FENG, Law
WANG, FUAN, Chemical Engineering
WANG, GUANGLONG, Chemical Engineering
WANG, GUOLING, Education
WANG, HONGXING, Chemistry
WANG, HONGYING, Materials Science and Engineering
WANG, JIE, Electrical Engineering
WANG, JINGWU, Materials Science and Engineering
WANG, LIANFENG, Law
WANG, LIDONG, Bioengineering
WANG, MINCAN, Chemistry
WANG, MINGCHEN, Basic Medical Science
WANG, XIANGYU, Chemistry
WANG, XIKE, Materials Science and Engineering
WANG, XINGGUANG, History and Archaeology
WANG, XINLING, Civil Engineering
WANG, YAN, Chemical Engineering
WANG, YUDONG, Materials Science and Engineering
WANG, YUNZHI, History and Archaeology
WANG, ZHONGQUAN, Basic Medical Science
WANG, ZHONGYONG, Information Engineering
WEI, XINLI, Chemical Engineering
WU, FENG, Basic Medical Science
WU, MIN, Public Health
WU, MINGJIAN, Chemical Engineering
WU, XIAOLING, Mechanical Engineering
WU, YANGJIE, Chemistry
WU, YIMING, Public Health
WU, YOULIN, Physical Science and Technology
XIAO, GUOXING, Law
XIAO, QIANGANG, Law
XU, HAISHENG, Chemical Engineering
XU, QILOU, Civil Engineering
XU, QUN, Materials Science and Engineering
XU, SHUN, Chemistry
XU, XIUCHENG, Chemical Engineering
XU, YAN, Chemistry
XU, YOULI, History and Archaeology
XUE, CHANGGUI, Basic Medical Science
XUE, LEXUN, Bioengineering
YAN, SUQING, Public Health
YANG, CHANGCHUN, Chemistry
YANG, GUANYU, Chemistry
YANG, JIUJUN, Materials Science and Engineering
YANG, SHENGLI, Basic Medical Science
YANG, TIANYU, History and Archaeology
YANG, YUANHUI, Electrical Engineering
YE, BAOXIAN, Chemistry
YE, YANGDONG, Information Engineering
YU, XIANGDONG, History and Archaeology
YU, YANGUANG, Information Engineering
YUAN, SIGUO, Chemical Engineering
YUAN, ZULIANG, History and Archaeology
ZENG, ZHIPING, Chemical Engineering
ZHANG, AFANG, Materials Science and Engineering
ZHANG, BAOLIN, Chemical Engineering
ZHANG, BINGLIN, Physical Science and Technology
ZHANG, GUOSHUO, History and Archaeology
ZHANG, HAOQIN, Chemical Engineering
ZHANG, HENG, Mechanical Engineering
ZHANG, HONGQUAN, Public Health
ZHANG, HONGYUN, Chemistry
ZHANG, JIANMIN, Chemistry
ZHANG, LINNA, Mechanical Engineering
ZHANG, MINFU, History and Archaeology
ZHANG, PING, Basic Medical Science
ZHANG, QIAN, Basic Medical Science
ZHANG, QINXIAN, Basic Medical Science
ZHANG, RUI, Materials Science and Engineering
ZHANG, RUIQIN, Chemistry
ZHANG, SHUSHENG, Chemistry
ZHANG, SHUYUAN, Chemistry
ZHANG, XIUQUAN, Law
ZHANG, XUHUA, History and Archaeology
ZHANG, YADONG, Chemical Engineering
ZHANG, ZHAO, Basic Medical Science

ZHANG, ZHIHONG, Information Engineering
ZHAO, JIANWEN, Law
ZHAO, QINGXIANG, Materials Science and Engineering
ZHAO, WENEN, Chemical Engineering
ZHAO, XINGTAI, Education
ZHAO, YUFEN, Chemistry
ZHENG, YONGFU, History and Archaeology
ZHOU, CAIRONG, Chemical Engineering
ZHOU, CHUXIAN, Chemistry
ZHOU, DAPENG, Chemistry
ZHOU, PENG, Information Engineering
ZHOU, QINGLEI, Information Engineering
ZHOU, YUANFANG, Public Health
ZHU, CHENGSHEN, Materials Science and Engineering
ZHUANG, LEI, Information Engineering
ZHUANG, YINFENG, Materials Science and Engineering

ZHONGNAN UNIVERSITY OF ECONOMICS AND LAW

114 Wu Luo Rd, Wuhan 430064, Hubei Province

Telephone: (27) 88044332
Fax: (27) 88044339
E-mail: xz@znufe.edu.cn
Internet: www.znufe.edu.cn

Founded 1948
Academic year: September to July

Pres.: WU HANDONG
Vice-Pres: LI HANCHANG, TAN YOUTU, ZHANG ZHONGHUA, ZHAO LINGYUN
Head of Graduate Dept: ZHU YANFU
Librarian: HU YUANMIN
Number of teachers: 1,173
Number of students: 35,200

Publications: *Journal* (6 a year), *Studies in Law and Business* (6 a year)

DEANS

School of Accounting: LUO FEI
School of Banking and Insurance: ZU XINGRONG
School of Business Administration: ZHANG XINGUO
School of Economics: LU XIANXIANG
School of Finance and Public Administration: YANG CANMING
School of Foreign Languages: XIE QUN
School of Humanities: WANG YUCHEN
School of Information Science: YANG YUNYAN
School of Journalism and Mass Media: YIN XIULIN
School of Law: QI WENYUAN
School of Public Administration: ZHAO MAN
School of Public Security: YANG ZONGHUI

PROFESSORS

CAI, HONG, Law
CAI, LING, Economics
CAO, SHIQUAN, Law
CHAO, LONGQI, Banking and Insurance
CHEN, CHIBO, Business Administration
CHEN, DAJIE, Finance and Public Administration

CHEN, GUANGYAN, Finance and Public Administration
CHEN, JINLIANG, Law
CHEN, XIAOJUN, Law
CHENG, LIHUA, Humanities
CHENG, QIZHI, Economics
CHENG, QUANMING, Finance and Public Administration
CUI, MINGXIA, Law
DAI, WUTANG, Economics
DU, XINGCHAI, Economics
DUAN, NINGHUA, Information Science
FAN, ZHONGXI, Law
FANG, SHIRONG, Law
GU, YUANQING, Economics
GUO, DAOYANG, Accounting
HU, XIANSHUN, Information Science
HUANG, SHIPING, Humanities
JIA, QIYU, Information Science
JIANG, HAISU, Business Administration
KU, KEJIAN, Business Administration
LEI, XINGHU, Law
LI, CHANGQING, Banking and Insurance
LI, DAMING, Finance and Public Administration
LI, DAORONG, Humanities
LI, GEFEI, Banking and Insurance
LI, GUANGZHONG, Accounting
LI, JIANXUN, Public Security
LI, MAONIAN, Information Science
LI, NAINZHAO, Banking and Insurance
LI, QINGZHI, Public Security
LI, WEINING, Economics
LI, XIANPEI, Business Administration
LI, XUANJU, Information Science
LIANG, YUXIA, Law
LIN, HANCHUAN, Economics
LIU, DAHONG, Law
LIU, KEFENG, Humanities
LIU, LIELONG, Economics
LIU, LUANSHENG, Humanities
LIU, MAOLIN, Law
LIU, SIHUA, Economics
LIU, TENGHONG, Information Science
LIU, XIANFAN, Humanities
LU, XIANXIANG, Economics
LU, ZHONGMEI, Law
LUO, FEI, Accounting
LUO, SHENGBAO, Business Administration
MEI, ZIHUI, Banking and Insurance
MOU, BINGHUA, Information Science
NI, PINGSONG, Finance and Public Administration
NIE, HUAMING, Banking and Insurance
OUYANG, XUCHU, Business Administration
PANG, FENGXI, Finance and Public Administration
PENG, XINGLV, Business Administration
PENG, YONGXING, Information Science
PENG, ZHENGHUI, Law
QI, WENYUAN, Law
QIN, YOUTU, Law
QIU, JIAWU, Information Science
QU, GUANGQIN, Law
SHEN, BENZHU, Law
SHONG, QINGHUA, Banking and Insurance
SU, SHAOZHI, Economics
SUN, XIAOFU, Law

SUN, XIAOMEI, Humanities
TANG, GUOPING, Accounting
TANG, WEIBEN, Economics
TANG, WUYUN, Economics
TONG, ZHIWEI, Law
WAN, HOUFEN, Business Administration
WANG, FULIN, Humanities
WANG, JUNPING, Public Security
WANG, QUANXIN, Law
WANG, SHOU'AN, Information Science
WANG, XINGYUAN, Information Science
WU, GUANGBING, Economics
WU, HANGDONG, Law
WU, JUNPEI, Finance and Public Administration
WU, LIANLIAN, Humanities
WU, YIJUN, Business Administration
WU, ZHIZHONG, Law
XIA, CHENGCAI, Accounting
XIA, XINYUAN, Economics
XIA, YONG, Law
XIONG, SHENGXU, Business Administration
XU, DUNKAI, Economics
XU, GUOXIN, Economics
XU, JIANGUO, Finance and Public Administration
XU, RENZHANG, Finance and Public Administration
YAN, DEYU, Accounting
YAN, LIDONG, Business Administration
YAN, QIZHONG, Business Administration
YAN, RICHU, Information Science
YANG, CANMING, Finance and Public Administration
YANG, JIAZHI, Economics
YANG, KAIHAN, Information Science
YANG, YUNYAN, Economics
YANG, ZONGHUI, Public Security
YAO, HUIYUAN, Economics
YAO, LI, Law
YE, QING, Finance and Public Administration
YU, XIYAN, Business Administration
YU, ZONGQI, Humanities
YUAN, JICHENG, Humanities
ZENG, QINGWEI, Information Science
ZHAN, CAILI, Accounting
ZHANG, CHAOQUN, Finance and Public Administration
ZHANG, FULIN, Humanities
ZHANG, HUAIFU, Finance and Public Administration
ZHANG, LONGPING, Accounting
ZHANG, SHIJING, Humanities
ZHANG, SHUZHEN, Law
ZHANG, YU, Public Security
ZHANG, YUANHUANG, Public Security
ZHANG, ZHENGLING, Humanities
ZHAO, LINGYU, Economics
ZHAO, MAN, Finance and Public Administration
ZHENG, ZHUJUN, Law
ZHOU, JUN, Banking and Insurance
ZHU, HAIFANG, Accounting
ZHU, YANFU, Economics
ZOU, LIGANG, Law
ZU, XINGRONG, Banking and Insurance

HONG KONG

Regulatory and Representative Bodies

GOVERNMENT

Education Bureau: 15th Fl., Wu Chung House, 213 Queen's Rd E, Wan Chai; tel. (852) 28910088; fax (852) 28930858; e-mail edbinfo@edb.gov.hk; internet www.edb.gov.hk; Sec. for Education MICHAEL M. Y. SUEN; Permanent Sec. for Education RAYMOND H. C. WONG.

Leisure and Cultural Services Department: Leisure and Cultural Services HQ, 1–3 Pai Tau St, Sha Tin; tel. (852) 24145555; fax (852) 26030642; e-mail enquiries@lcsd.gov.hk; internet www.lcsd.gov.hk; attached to Home Affairs Bureau; Dir BETTY FUNG CHING SUK-YEE; Deputy Dir for Cultural Services CHUNG LING-HOI; Deputy Dir for Leisure Services BOBBY CHENG KAM-WING.

ACCREDITATION

Hong Kong Council for Accreditation of Academic & Vocational Qualifications: 10th Fl., Cambridge House, Taikoo Pl., 979 King's Rd, Quarry Bay; tel. (852) 36580000; fax (852) 28459910; e-mail info@hkcaavq.edu.hk; internet www.hkcaavq.edu.hk; f. 1990; Chair. Dr YORK LIAO; Exec. Dir Prof. YIU-KWAN FAN.

NATIONAL BODIES

Heads of Universities Committee: The Hong Kong Polytechnic Univ., Hung Hom, Kowloon; tel. (852) 27665168; fax (852) 23631349; e-mail pphucom@polyu.edu.hk; internet www.polyu.edu.hk; Convenor Prof. WAY KUO.

Hong Kong Examinations and Assessment Authority: Southorn Centre, 12th–14th Fl., 130 Hennessy Rd, Wan Chai; tel. (852) 36288833; fax (852) 36288088; e-mail tsa1@hkeaa.edu.hk; internet www.hkeaa.edu.hk; 17 mems; Chair. EDDIE NG HAK-KIM; Deputy Chair. HUI CHIN-YIM; Sec.-Gen. Dr FRANCIS CHEUNG.

University Grants Committee: 7th Fl., Shui On Centre, 6–8 Harbour Rd, Wan Chai; tel. (852) 25243987; fax (852) 28451596; e-mail ugc@ugc.edu.hk; internet www.ugc.edu.hk; f. 1965; 30 mems; Chair. Hon. LAURA M. CHA; Sec.-Gen. MICHAEL V. STONE.

Vocational Training Council: VTC Tower, 27 Wood Rd, Wan Chai; tel. (852) 28361000; fax (852) 28380667; e-mail vtcmailbox@vtc.edu.hk; internet www.vtc.edu.hk; f. 1982; 13 mem. instns; Chair. Hon. ANDREW LEUNG KWAN-YUEN; Exec. Dir Dr CARRIE WILLIS.

Learned Societies

GENERAL

Royal Asiatic Society Hong Kong Branch: PO Box 3864, Central; tel. and fax (852) 28137500; e-mail info@royalasiaticsociety.org.hk; internet www.royalasiaticsociety.org.hk; f. 1847, re-established 1959; encourages history, arts, science and literature in relation to Asia, particularly Hong Kong and China and their cultures; lectures and social activities; 720 mems (incl. 150 overseas mems); library of 5,500 books, 140,000 index cards; Pres. ROBERT NIELD; Vice-Pres. Dr ELIZABETH SINN; Vice-Pres. PETER STUCKEY; Hon. Sec. DAVID McKELLAR; Hon. Treas. Dr PETER HALLIDAY; Hon. Librarian JULIA CHAN; publ. *Journal of the Hong Kong Branch of the Royal Asiatic Society* (1 a year).

BIBLIOGRAPHY, LIBRARY SCIENCE AND MUSEOLOGY

Hong Kong Library Association: POB 10095, Gen. Post Office; e-mail hkla@hkla.org; internet www.hkla.org; f. 1958; promotes librarianship; offers professional growth, networking and community service; develops policies promoting provision of information and library services in Hong Kong; 694 mems; Pres. PETER SIDORKO; Vice-Pres. MARY CHENG; Hon. Sec THOMAS HUNG; Hon. Treas. MANDY IP; publ. *Journal* (irregular).

University of Hong Kong Museum Society: Univ. Museum and Art Gallery, Univ. of Hong Kong, 94 Bonham Rd, Pokfulam; tel. (852) 22415500; fax (852) 25469659; e-mail info@hkums.com; internet www.hkums.com; f. 1988; attached to Univ. of Hong Kong; supports the Univ. of Hong Kong Museum and Art Gallery; promotes Chinese arts and antiquities; sponsors art and educational programmes in the community; 500 mems; Chair. BONNIE KWAN HUO; Vice-Chair. YVONNE CHOI; Sec. WINNIE TONG; Treas. AUDY MAK; publ. *MVSE News* (5 a year).

ECONOMICS, LAW AND POLITICS

Hong Kong Institute of Certified Public Accountants: 37th Fl., Wu Chung House, 213 Queen's Rd E, Wan Chai; tel. (852) 22877228; fax (852) 28656603; e-mail hkicpa@hkicpa.org.hk; internet www.hkicpa.org.hk; f. 1973, fmrly Hong Kong Society of Accountants; registers and grants practising certificates to Certified Public Accountants in Hong Kong; mems earn description Certified Public Accountant and designatory letters CPA; assures the quality of entry into the profession through its postgraduate CPA Qualification Programme; promulgates financial reporting, auditing and ethical standards in Hong Kong; 28,000 mems; 13,000 students; Pres. WILSON FUNG; Vice-Pres. FOOK AUN CHEW; Vice-Pres. PHILIP TSAI WING CHUNG; Chief Exec. and Registrar WINNIE C. W. CHEUNG; publs *APlus* (12 a year), technical bulletin, guides and other publs online.

Hong Kong Management Association: 14th Fl., Fairmont House, 8 Cotton Tree Dr., Central; tel. (852) 25266516; fax (852) 28684387; e-mail hkma@hkma.org.hk; internet www.hkma.org.hk; f. 1960; non-profit org.; offers management training courses, management consultancy services, library information, seminars, forums, awards and competitions; 12,000 mems; Chair. Hon. DAVID K. P. LI; Deputy Chair. Dr DENNIS SUN; Deputy Chair. HENRY H. L. FAN; Deputy Chair. Dr IAN FOK; Dir-Gen. Dr ELIZABETH S. C. SHING; publ. *The Hong Kong Manager* (4 a year).

The Law Society of Hong Kong: 3rd Fl., Wing On House, 71 Des Voeux Rd, Central; tel. (852) 28460500; fax (852) 28450387; e-mail sg@hklawsoc.org.hk; internet www.hklawsoc.org.hk; f. 1907; professional assn for solicitors in Hong Kong; ensures compliance by solicitors with relevant laws, codes, regulations and practice directions; supports and protects the character, status and interests of solicitors; 6,122 mems; Pres. HUEN WONG; Vice-Pres. JUNIUS K. Y. HO; Vice-Pres. DIETER YIH; Sec.-Gen. RAYMOND C. K. HO; Deputy Sec.-Gen. HEIDI K.P. CHU; publ. *Hong Kong Lawyer*.

LANGUAGE AND LITERATURE

Alliance Française: 1st and 2nd Fl., 123 Hennessy Rd, Wan Chai; tel. (852) 25277825; fax (852) 28653478; e-mail afinfo@alliancefrancaise.com.hk; internet www.alliancefrancaise.com.hk; f. 1953; offers courses and examinations in French language and culture and promotes cultural exchange with France; Pres. R. A. V. RIBERO; Dir-Gen. JEAN-PIERRE DUMONT; Treas. THIERRY MÉQUILLET; publ. *Paroles*.

British Council: 3 Supreme Court Rd, Admiralty; tel. (852) 29135100; fax (852) 29135102; e-mail enquiries@britishcouncil.org.hk; internet www.britishcouncil.org.hk/index.asp; f. 1948; teaching centre; offers courses and examinations in English language and British culture and promotes cultural exchange with the UK; Dir RUTH GEE; Deputy Dir, Teaching Centre GEORGINA PEARCE.

Goethe-Institut: 14th Fl., Hong Kong Arts Centre, 2 Harbour Rd, Wan Chai; tel. (852) 28020088; fax (852) 28024363; e-mail info@hongkong.goethe.org; internet www.goethe.de/hongkong; f. 1963; offers courses and examinations in German language and culture and promotes cultural exchange with Germany; library of 7,400 vols, incl. audio-visual materials; Dir MICHAEL MÜLLER-VERWEYEN; Deputy Dir and Head of Language Courses MARTIN BODE; Head of Library and Information Service GABRIELE SANDER.

Hong Kong Chinese Speaking PEN Centre: Flat F, 4th Fl., Tower 6, Jubilant Pl. 99, Paucheung St, Kowloon; f. 1955; 92 mems; library of 1,600 vols; Pres. YU HOI FU; Sec. S. B. TENG; publ. *PEN News* (52 a year, in Chinese).

MEDICINE

Hong Kong Medical Association: Duke of Windsor Social Service Bldg, 5th Fl., 15 Hennessy Rd; tel. (852) 25278285; fax (852) 28650943; e-mail hkma@hkma.org; internet www.hkma.org; f. 1920, fmrly Hong Kong Chinese Medical Assn; promotes welfare and protects the lawful interests of the medical profession; promotes cooperation with nat. and int. medical socs; works for the advancement of medical science; 8,400 mems; Pres. Dr TSE HUNG HING; Vice-Pres. Dr ALVIN CHAN YEE SHING; Vice-Pres. Dr CHIN CHOW PAK; Hon. Sec. Dr ERNIE LO CHI FUNG; Hon. Treas. Dr CHI CHU LEUNG; Chief Exec. YVONNE LEUNG; publs *HKMA CME Bulletin* (12 a year), *Hong Kong Medical Journal* (6 a year), *HKMA News* (12 a year).

Research Institutes

MEDICINE

Institute of Chinese Medicine: 2nd and 3rd Fl., Science Centre E Block, Chinese Univ. of Hong Kong, Sha Tin, New Territories; tel. (852) 31634370; fax (852) 26035248; e-mail icm@cuhk.edu.hk; internet www.icm.cuhk.edu.hk/icm/en; f. 2000, fmrly Chinese Medicinal Material Research Centre; attached to Chinese Univ. of Hong Kong; conducts scientific research to modernize, commercialize and promote Chinese medicine; sections in clinical trials, drug devt, standardization and safety of Chinese medicine, natural products; Chair. Prof. JACK CHENG; Dir Prof. P. C. LEUNG; Dir Prof. K. P. FUNG.

NATURAL SCIENCES

Hong Kong Observatory: 134A Nathan Rd, Kowloon; tel. (852) 29268200; fax (852) 23119448; e-mail mailbox@hko.gov.hk; internet www.hko.gov.hk; f. 1883, renamed

Royal Observatory, Hong Kong 1912, original name restored 1997; attached to the Govt of the Hong Kong Special Administrative Region; govt dept that operates weather forecasting, cyclone warning and other meteorological and geophysical services; library of 40,000 vols; Dir Dr Boo-ying Lee; publs *Daily Weather Chart*, *Hong Kong Observatory Almanac* (1 a year), *Hong Kong Observatory Calendar*, *Hong Kong Tide Tables* (1 a year), *Monthly Weather Summary*, *Occasional papers* (irregular), *Summary of Meteorological Observations in Hong Kong* (1 a year), *Technical Notes* (irregular), *Technical Notes (local)* (irregular), *Tropical Cyclones* (1 a year).

Libraries and Archives
Hong Kong

Hong Kong Central Library: 66 Causeway Rd, Causeway Bay; tel. (852) 31501234; fax (852) 28815500; e-mail hkcl_ref@lcsd.gov.hk; internet www.hkpl.gov.hk; f. 2001; attached to Hong Kong Public Libraries, Leisure and Cultural Services Dept; 2.4m. vols, incl.books, audiovisual materials, newspapers, periodicals, CD-ROM databases, microforms and maps; largest library facility in the Hong Kong Public Libraries system; depository library for publs of Asian Devt Bank, European Union, ILO, Int. Maritime Org., UN, UNESCO, World Bank, World Trade Org. and World Food Programme; Chief Librarian Rochelle Lau.

Hong Kong Public Libraries: c/o Hong Kong Central Library, Moreton Terrace, Causeway Bay; tel. (852) 29210208; e-mail enquiries@lcsd.gov.hk; internet www.hkpl .gov.hk; f. 1962; attached to Leisure and Cultural Services Dept; promotes literary arts and literary research in Hong Kong; cultivates public interest in creative writing and literary research; encourages literary writing and cultural exchange; central reference library of 6 subject depts; toy library; a young adult library; exhibition gallery and lecture theatre; provides a network of 66 br. libraries and 10 mobile libraries; 12.47m. items, incl. books, audiovisual materials, newspapers, periodicals, CD-ROM databases, microforms and maps.

Pao Yue-kong Library–Hong Kong Polytechnic University: Hung Hom, Kowloon; tel. (852) 27666863; fax (852) 27658274; e-mail lbinf@polyu.edu.hk; internet www.lib .polyu.edu.hk; f. 1972 as The Univ. Library, present name 1995; inter-library loan and document delivery services; reference and personal information consultancy services, information skills workshops, online information literacy programmes; 1,267,609 monographs, 247,328 series bound vols, 646 electronic databases, 32,603 full-text e-journal titles, 225,033 e-books and 249 electronic learning programmes; spec. collns: Industrial Standards (online, 55,967 vols); Slide Colln (260,398 items); local TV programmes (24,913); digital images (online, 47,211); audio-visual material (63,960 items); 387,643 microfiches; 2,394 reels of microfilm; PolyU examination paper database, PolyU course scheme database, PolyU electronic theses, Hongkongiana online, video-on-demand, online audio libraries, newspaper clippings image database; Univ Librarian Steve O'Connor; publ. *Directory of Professional Associations and Learned Societies in Hong Kong*.

Public Records Office: 3rd Fl., Hong Kong Public Records Bldg, 13 Tsui Ping Rd, Kwun Tong, Kowloon; tel. (852) 21957700; fax (852) 28046413; e-mail proinfo@grs.gov.hk; internet www.info.gov.hk/pro; f. 1972; attached to Govt Records Service (f. 1997);

22,000 Hong Kong Govt publs; newspapers colln, photographs colln, map colln; 800,000 archival records and library items.

University Library System: Tin Ka Ping Bldg 2 Fl., Sha Tin, New Territories; tel. (852) 26097305; fax (852) 26036952; e-mail library@cuhk.edu.hk; internet www.lib.cuhk .edu.hk; f. 1963; attached to Chinese Univ. of Hong Kong; coordinates the collns and services of the Univ. Library (f. 1965) and the 7 br. libraries; spec. collns: Careers colln; CUHK theses submitted since 1967; Chinese Overseas colln; History of Medicine of Hong Kong, China and the Asia-Pacific region; Hong Kong Govt documents; Hong Kong Studies; Instructional Materials colln; Modern Chinese Drama colln; rare Chinese books from the Yuan to the Qing dynasties; 2,541,000 vols incl. 1,031,250 vols of books and bound journals in East Asian languages, 1,343,543 vols of books and bound journals in Western languages, more than 9,700 active print serials, 106,000 e-journals, 1.88m. e-books, 650 e-databases; Univ. Librarian Dr Colin Storey; Deputy Librarian Rita Wong; publ. *Annotated Bibliography of Rare Books in the CUHK Libraries*.

University of Hong Kong Libraries: 4th Fl. Main Library, Univ. of Hong Kong Pokfulam; tel. (852) 28592203; fax (852) 28589420; e-mail hkulref@hkucc.hku.hk; internet www.lib.hku.hk; f. 1912; main library and 6 brs; spec. collns incl. Hong Kong Colln, Morrison Colln, Hong Kong Tourist Asscn Colln, Republic of China Govt Publs, Taiwan Studies, Univ. of Hong Kong Theses; 2,796,653 print vols in East Asian and Western languages, 9,173 current print journals, 62,568 e-journals on subscription, 2,427,681 e-books and 3,280 audiovisual items and 1,574,060 materials in microform; Librarian Peter E. Sidorko; Deputy Librarian Dr Y. C. Wan (acting).

Museums and Art Galleries
Hong Kong

Art Museum: Institute of Chinese Studies, Chinese Univ. of Hong Kong, Sha Tin, New Territories; tel. (852) 26097416; fax (852) 26035366; e-mail artmuseum@cuhk.edu.hk; internet www.cuhk.edu.hk/ics/amm; f. 1971; attached to Institute of Chinese Studies, Chinese Univ. of Hong Kong; collects, preserves, researches and exhibits artefacts representing the rich art and cultural heritage of ancient and pre-modern China; promotes Chinese culture and heritage; facilitates academic exchange between China and the West; collaborates with univ. dept of Fine Arts for practice in museology and teaching in art history.

Hong Kong Film Archive: 50 Lei King Rd, Sai Wan Ho; tel. (852) 27392139; fax (852) 23115229; e-mail hkfa@lcsd.gov.hk; internet www.filmarchive.gov.hk; f. 1993; attached to Leisure and Cultural Services Dept; acquires and conserves films made in Hong Kong; catalogues and maintains archival colln; provides information related to cinema and the Hong Kong film industry; organizes thematic retrospectives, exhibitions, symposia and seminars on cinema; publ. *Oral History Series*.

Hong Kong Heritage Museum: 1 Man Lam Rd, Sha Tin; tel. (852) 21808188; fax (852) 21808111; e-mail hkhm@lcsd.gov.hk; internet www.heritagemuseum.gov.hk; attached to Leisure and Cultural Services Dept; colln of local history relics, natural history relics, performing art relics, folk art and popular culture artefacts (toys and comics); art colln: contemporary art, design

and Chinese fine art (Chinese paintings, calligraphy and Chinese antiquities); houses 6 permanent galleries: Orientation Theatre, New Territories Heritage Hall, Cantonese Opera Heritage Hall, T. T. Tsui Gallery of Chinese Art, Chao Shao-an Gallery, Children's Discovery Gallery and 6 thematic galleries; 3 br. museums: Hong Kong Railway Museum (Tai Po), Sam Tung Uk Museum (Tsuen Wan), Sheung Yiu Folk Museum (Sai Kung).

Hong Kong Maritime Museum: Ground Fl., Murray House, Stanley Plaza, Stanley; tel. (852) 28132322; fax (852) 28138033; e-mail info@hkmaritimemuseum.org; internet www.hkmaritimemuseum.org; non-profit org.; stimulates public interest in ships and the sea particularly the South China coast and adjacent seas; promotes the growth of Hong Kong as a major port and int. maritime centre; 2 galleries: ancient and modern displaying c. 500 exhibits incl. ceramics, ships models, paintings, trade goods and ships manifests; Chair. Anthony J. Hardy; Dir Dr Stephen Davies; Exec. Man. and Curator Catalina Chor.

Hong Kong Museum of Art: 10 Salisbury Rd, Tsim Sha Tsui, Kowloon; tel. (852) 27210116; fax (852) 27237666; e-mail enquiries@lcsd.gov.hk; internet www.lcsd .gov.hk/hkma; f. 1962, present bldg 1991; attached to Leisure and Cultural Services Dept; 15,000 art objects; Chinese antiquities, incl. the Henry Yeung colln; historical paintings, prints and drawings of Hong Kong, Macao and China, incl. Chater, Sayer, Law and Ho Tung collns; contemporary works by local artists; Chinese paintings and calligraphy, incl. the Xubaizhai Colln; 1 br. museum: Museum of Tea Ware; Chief Curator Christina Chu.

Branch Museum:

Museum of Tea Ware: 10 Cotton Tree Dr., Central; tel. (852) 28690690; fax (852) 28100021; f. 1984; displays famous Yixing teapots; conducts tea gatherings and lecture programmes to promote ceramic art and Chinese tea drinking culture.

Hong Kong Museum of History: 100 Chatham Rd South, Tsimshatsui, Kowloon; tel. (852) 27249042; fax (852) 27249090; e-mail hkmh@lcsd.gov.hk; internet hk .history.museum; f. 1962 as City Museum and Art Gallery, present status and name 1975, present location 1998; attached to Leisure and Cultural Services Dept; archaeology, ethnography, natural history and history of Hong Kong; historical photographs and documents; postal history and numismatics colln; brs at Lei Cheng Uk Han Tomb Museum, Law Uk Folk Museum, Hong Kong Museum of Coastal Defence, Dr. Sun Yat-sen Museum and Fireboat Alexander Grantham Exhibition Gallery; permanent exhibition: 'The Hong Kong Story'; Chief Curator Esa Leung Kit-Ling.

Branch Museums:

Dr Sun Yat-sen Museum: 7 Castle Rd, Central; tel. (852) 23676373; fax (852) 35800498; e-mail sysm@lcsd.gov.hk; internet hk.drsunyatsen.museum; f. 2006; life and career of Dr Sun Yat-sen; Hong Kong's role in reform movements and revolutionary activities in the 19th–20th centuries; 2 permanent exhibitions display historical artefacts.

Fireboat Alexander Grantham Exhibition Gallery: Quarry Bay Park; tel. (852) 23677821; fax (852) 35800498; displays unique fire fighting artefacts; documents marine rescue work in Hong Kong.

Hong Kong Museum of Coastal Defence: 175 Tung Hei Rd, Shau Kei Wan; tel. (852) 25691500; fax (852)

25691637; e-mail hkmcd@lcsd.gov.hk; internet hk.coastaldefence.museum; f. 2000, fmrly the Lei Yue Mun Fort; preserves and presents 600–year history of coastal defence in Hong Kong.

Law Uk Folk Museum: 14 Kut Shing St, Chai Wan; tel. (852) 28967006; fax (852) 27249090; 18th-century Hakka village house.

Lei Cheng Uk Han Tomb Museum: 41 Tonkin St, Sham Shui Po, Kowloon; tel. (852) 23862863; fax (852) 23612105; f. 1988 declared as gazetted monument, tomb discovered 1955; tomb closed to public; displays pottery and bronze wares excavated from the tomb, texts, graphics, photos, maps, video cassettes, models of the tomb; 2 exhibitions 'Lei Cheng Uk Han Tomb' and 'Han Culture in South China'.

Hong Kong Science Museum: 2 Science Museum Rd, Tsim Shat Tsui E, Kowloon; tel. (852) 27323232; fax (852) 23112248; e-mail enquiries@hk.science.museum; internet hk.science.museum; f. 1991; attached to Leisure and Cultural Services Dept; 500 exhibits on permanent display, temporary thematic exhibitions; 16 galleries; education and extension activities; lecture hall and spec. rental exhibition hall; Chief Curator MICHAEL WONG HING-IAN; Sr Man. KATHLEEN MA KA-LIN.

Hong Kong Space Museum: 10 Salisbury Rd, Tsim Sha Tsui, Kowloon; tel. (852) 27210226; fax (852) 23115804; e-mail spacem@space.lcsd.gov.hk; internet hk.space.museum; f. 1980; attached to Leisure and Cultural Services Dept; promotes interest in astronomy and related sciences by exhibitions, lectures, films, Omnimax and sky shows; 100 staff; library of 1,700 vols, also films and video cassettes; Curator CHAN KI HUNG; publ. *Astrocalendar* (1 a year).

Hong Kong Visual Arts Centre: 7A Kennedy Rd, Central; tel. (852) 25213008; fax (852) 25014703; internet www.lcsd.gov.hk/ce/museum/apo/en/vac.html; f. 1992; attached to Art Promotion Office, Leisure and Cultural Services Dept; provides studios for trained artists practising in the fields of sculpture, printmaking and ceramics; organizes art activities incl. workshops, exhibitions, demonstrations, lectures and artist-in-residence programmes.

Ping Shan Tang Clan Gallery and Heritage Trail Visitors Centre: Hang Tau Tsuen, Ping Shan, Yuen Long, New Territories; tel. (852) 26171959; fax (852) 26170925; internet www.lcsd.gov.hk/ce/museum/monument/en/ping_shan.php; f. 1993 as Ping Shan Heritage Trail, present name and staus 2007, converted from the Old Ping Shan Police Station built in 1899; attached to Antiquities and Monuments Office, Leisure and Cultural Services Dept; displays various relics belonging to members of the Tang Clan who personally relate their history, customs and cultural life; introduces monuments and bldgs along the Ping Shan Heritage Trail; spec. thematic exhibitions on history and culture of the New Territories.

University Museum and Art Gallery: Univ. of Hong Kong, 94 Bonham Rd, Pokfulam; tel. (852) 22415500; fax (852) 25469659; e-mail museum@hkusua.hku.hk; internet www.hku.hk/hkumag/main.html; f. 1953 as Fung Ping Shan Museum of Chinese Art and Archaeology, present name and bldg 1996; attached to Univ. of Hong Kong; 1,000 items of Chinese antiquities, ceramics, bronzes and paintings; colln incl. items dating from the Neolithic period to the Qing dynasty; bronze colln incl. works from the Shang to the Tang dynasties; largest colln of Yuan dynasty Nestorian crosses in the world;

carvings in jade, wood and stone; colln of Chinese oil paintings; attached tea gallery promotes Chinese tea culture; Dir YEUNG CHUN-TONG; Curator for Art TINA YEE-WAN PANG; Curator for History ANITA YIN-FONG WONG.

Universities

CHINESE UNIVERSITY OF HONG KONG

Sha Tin, New Territories
Telephone: (852) 26097000
Fax: (852) 26035544
E-mail: cpr@cuhk.edu.hk
Internet: www.cuhk.edu.hk

Founded 1963
Public control
Languages of instruction: Chinese, English
Academic year: August to July
Chancellor: CHIEF EXEC. OF THE HONG KONG SPEC. ADMIN. REGION
Chair. of Council: VINCENT H. C. CHENG
Vice-Chancellor and Pres.: Prof. JOSEPH J. Y. SUNG
Pro-Vice-Chancellor, Vice-Pres. and Provost: Prof. BENJAMIN W. WAH
Pro-Vice-Chancellor and Vice-Pres.: Prof. HENRY N. C. WONG
Pro-Vice-Chancellor and Vice-Pres.: Prof. PAK-CHUNG CHING
Pro-Vice-Chancellor and Vice-Pres.: Prof. JACK C. Y. CHENG
Pro-Vice-Chancellor and Vice-Pres.: Prof. KENNETH YOUNG
Pro-Vice-Chancellor and Vice-Pres.: Prof. MICHAEL K. M. HUI
Pro-Vice-Chancellor and Vice-Pres.: Prof. YANGSHENG XU
Assoc. Pro-Vice-Chancellor: Prof. TUNG FUNG
Univ. Dean of Students: Prof. DENNIS K. P. NG
Bursar: TERENCE C. W. CHAN
Registrar: ERIC S. P. NG
Sec.: JACOB S. K. LEUNG
Treas.: ROGER K. H. LUK
Librarian: Dr COLIN STOREY
Library of 2,300,000 vols
Number of teachers: 1,436
Number of students: 14,347

Publications: *Annals of Contemporary Diagnostic Pathology* (1 a year), *Asian Anthropology* (1 a year), *Asian Economic Journal* (4 a year), *Asian Journal of Counselling* (2 a year), *Asian Journal of English Language Teaching* (1 a year), *Asian Journal of Mathematics* (4 a year), *Chinese Academic Journal* (every 2 years), *Chinese Journal of Communication* (4 a year), *Chinese Language Newsletter* (4 a year), *Chinese Language Studies* (2 a year), *Comparative Literature and Culture* (1 a year), *Communication and Society* (4 a year), *Communications in Information and Systems* (4 a year), *Crosslinks in English Language Teaching* (every 2 years), *Education Journal* (2 a year), *Education Journal in Chinese* (2 a year), *Educational Research Journal* (2 a year), *Geographic Information Sciences* (2 a year), *Global Chinese Journal on Computers in Education* (2 a year), *Journal of Basic Education* (2 a year), *Journal of Chinese Philosophy and Culture* (2 a year), *Journal of Chinese Studies* (2 a year), *Journal of Contemporary Chinese Education* (2 a year), *Journal of Phenomenology and Contemporary Philosophy* (1 a year), *Journal of Phenomenology and the Human Sciences* (1 a year), *Journal of Translation History* (1 a year), *Journal of Translation Studies* (2 a year), *Methods and Application of Analysis* (4 a

year), *Phenomenology and the Human Sciences* (1 a year), *Renditions* (2 a year), *Southeast Asia Bulletin of Mathematics* (6 a year), *The China Review* (2 a year), *Twenty-first Century* (6 a year), *University General Education Bulletin* (1 a year)

DEANS
Faculty of Arts: Prof. HSIUNG PING-CHEN
Faculty of Business Administration: Prof. WONG TAK-JUN
Faculty of Education: Prof. ALVIN S. M. LEUNG
Faculty of Engineering: Prof. C. P. WONG
Faculty of Law: Prof. MIKE MCCONVILLE
Faculty of Medicine: Prof. FOK TAI-FAI
Faculty of Science: Prof. NG CHEUK-YIU
Faculty of Social Science: Prof. PAUL S. N. LEE
Graduate School: Prof. WONG WING-SHING

PROFESSORS
BAKER, H. D. R., Humanities
BANIASSAD, E., Architecture
BOND, M. H., Psychology
CHAN, A. T. C., Clinical Ontology
CHAN, H. C., Physiology
CHAN, J. C. N., Medicine and Therapeutics
CHAN, K. L., Medicine and Therapeutics
CHAN, K. M., Orthopaedics and Traumatology
CHAN, N. H., Statistics
CHAN, R. H. F., Mathematics
CHEN, H. C., Psychology
CHENG, J. C. Y., Orthopaedics and Traumatology
CHEUNG, F. M. C., Psychology
CHEUNG, S. H. N., Chinese Language and Literature
CHING, P. C., Electronic Engineering
CHIU, H. F. K., Psychiatry
CHO, C. H., Pharmacology
CHOW, M. S. S., Pharmacy
CHUNG, T. K. H., Obstetrics and Gynaecology
COCKRAM, C. S., Medicine and Therapeutics (Medicine)
FAURE, D., History
FOK, T. F., Paediatrics
FUNG, K. P., Biochemistry
GIN, T., Anaesthesia and Intensive Care
GRIFFITHS, S., Public Health
HAZLETT, C. B., Medical Education
HO, S. S., Community and Family Medicine
HUI, M. K. M., Marketing
KEMBER, D. R., Learning Enhancement
KUNG, H. F., Virology
LAM, D. S. C., Ophthalmology and Visual Sciences
LANG, L. H. P., Finance
LAU, J. W. Y., Surgery
LAU, K. S., Mathematics
LAU, L. J., Economics
LAU, L. W. M., Physics (Materials Science)
LAU, S. K., Sociology
LAW, S. K., Management
LEE, K. H., Marketing
LEE, L. O. F., Humanities
LEE, R. P. L., Sociology
LEE, S. S., Infectious Diseases
LEE, S. Y., Statistics
LEE, T. T., Information Engineering
LEE, V. H. L., Pharmacy
LEUNG, Y., Geography and Resource Management (Geography)
LEUNG, Y. S., History
LI, R. S. Y., Information Engineering
LIN, C., Information Engineering, Electronic Engineering (Photonics)
LIU, P. W., Economics
LO, D. Y. M., Chemical Pathology
LO, L. N. K., Educational Admin. and Policy
MCCONVILLE, M., Law
MCNAUGHT, C. M., Learning Enhancement
MIRRLEES, J. A., Distinguished Professor-at-Large

NG, H. K., Anatomical and Cellular Pathology
NG, P. C., Paediatrics
NGAN, K. N., Electronic Engineering
PARKER, D. H., English
POON, W. S., Surgery
SHUN, K. L., Philosophy
So, B. K. L., History
So, J. F. S., Fine Arts
SUN, S. S. M., Biology
SUNG, J. J. Y., Medicine and Therapeutics
TANG, K. L., Social Work
VAN HASSELT, C. A., Surgery (Otorhinolaryngology)
WONG, H. N. C., Chemistry
WONG, K. S., Medicine and Therapeutics
WONG, L. K. P., Translation
WONG, T. J., Accountancy
WONG, W. S., Information Engineering
WOO, J., Medicine and Therapeutics (Medicine)
WU, C., Chemistry
XIE, Z., Chemistry
XIN, Z. P., Mathematics
XU, L., Computer Science and Engineering
XU, Y., Automation and Computer-Aided Engineering
YANG, C. N., Distinguished Professor-at-Large
YAO, A. C. C., Distinguished Professor-at-Large
YAO, D. D. W., Systems Engineering and Engineering Management
YAU, S. T., Distinguished Professor-at-Large
YEUNG, C. K., Surgery
YEUNG, W. H., Information Engineering
YEW, D. T. W., Anatomy
YIM, A. P. C., Surgery
YOUNG, K., Physics
YOUNG, L., Finance
YUM, P. T. S., Information Engineering
ZHANG, J., Economics
ZHOU, X., Systems Engineering and Engineering Management

CITY UNIVERSITY OF HONG KONG

83 Tat Chee Ave, Kowloon
Telephone: (852) 34427654
Fax: (852) 27881167
E-mail: webmaster@cityu.edu.hk
Internet: www.cityu.edu.hk
Founded 1984 as City Polytechnic of Hong Kong, present name and status 1994
Autonomous control, financed by the Univ. Grants Committee
Language of instruction: English
Academic year: September to August
Pres.: Prof. WAY KUO
Provost: Prof. ARTHUR B. ELLIS (acting)
Vice-Pres. for Devt and External Relations: Prof. RODERICK S. C. WONG
Vice-Pres. for Research and Technology: Prof. GREGORY B. RAUPP (acting)
Vice-Pres. for Student Affairs: Prof. PAUL KWAN-SING LAM (acting)
Librarian: Prof. STEVE CHING (acting)
Library of 945,600 vols of books, 200,700 vols of bound periodicals, 2,620 print serials
Number of teachers: 926 full-time
Number of students: 17,597 (12,247 full-time, 5,350 part-time)
Publications: *Bulletin* (12 a year), *CityU Today* (3 a year), *Linkage* (4 a year)

DEANS

Chow Yei Ching School of Graduate Studies: Prof. GREGORY B. RAUPP (acting)
College of Business: Prof. KWOK-KEE WEI
College of Humanities and Social Sciences: Prof. MARTIN PAINTER (acting)
College of Liberal Arts and Social Sciences: Prof. GREGORY BARRY LEE (acting)

College of Science and Engineering: Prof. JIAN LU (acting)
School of Creative Media: Prof. JEFFREY SHAW
School of Energy and Environment: Prof. JOHNNY CHUNG-LEUNG CHAN
School of Law: Prof. GUIGUO WANG

HONG KONG BAPTIST UNIVERSITY

Kowloon Tong, Kowloon
Telephone: (852) 34117400
Fax: (852) 23387644
E-mail: aaco@hkbu.edu.hk
Internet: www.hkbu.edu.hk
Founded 1956
State control
Languages of instruction: English, Chinese
Academic year: September to June
Pres. and Vice-Chancellor: Prof. ALBERT CHAN
Vice-Pres. for Academic Affairs: Prof. FRANKLIN LUK
Vice-Pres. for Admin. and Sec.: ANDY LEE SHIU CHUEN
Vice-Pres. for Research and Institutional Advancement: Prof. TSOI AH-CHUNG
Academic Registrar: Dr TONG CHONG-SZE
Librarian: Dr TERRY WEBB
Library of 1,045,530 vols, 132,586 audio-visual materials and microforms, 221,990 e-books, 34,644 e-journals, 3,901 serials, 210 e-databases
Number of teachers: 561 (full-time)
Number of students: 8,720
Publications: *Contemporary Historical Review* (4 a year), *Journal of the History of Christianity in Modern China* (1 a year), *Journal of Physical Education and Recreation* (2 a year), *Sino Humanitas* (2 a year)

DEANS

Academy of Visual Arts: Prof. WAN QINGLI
Faculty of Arts: Prof. CHUNG LING
Faculty of Science: Prof. RICK WONG
Faculty of Social Sciences: Prof. ARIAN BAILEY
Graduate School: Prof. TANG TAO (Dir)
School of Business: Prof. STEPHEN Y. L. CHEUNG
School of Communication: Prof. XINSHU ZHAO (acting)
School of Continuing Education: Dr SIMON WONG
School of Chinese Medicine: Prof. LIU LIANG

HONG KONG POLYTECHNIC UNIVERSITY

Yuk Choi Rd, Hung Hom, Kowloon
Telephone: (852) 27665111
Fax: (852) 27643374
E-mail: paadmin@inet.polyu.edu.hk
Internet: www.polyu.edu.hk
Founded 1937 as Govt Trade School, became Hong Kong Technical College 1947 and Hong Kong Polytechnic 1972, present name and status 1994
Autonomous control, financed by the Univ. Grants Cttee
Language of instruction: English
Academic year: September to August
Chancellor: CHIEF EXEC. OF THE HONG KONG SPEC. ADMIN. REGION
Pres.: Prof. TIMOTHY W. TONG
Deputy Pres. and Provost: Prof. PHILIP C. H. CHAN
Exec. Vice-Pres.: NICHOLAS W. YANG
Vice-Pres. for Academic Devt: Prof. WALTER W. YUEN
Vice Pres. for Institutional Advancement and Partnership: Prof. ANGELINA YUEN
Vice Pres. for Int. and Exec. Education: Prof. JUDY TSUI
Vice Pres. for Management: Ir Prof. ALEX WAI

Vice-Pres. for Research Devt: Prof. ALBERT S.C. CHAN
Vice-Pres. with Special Duties: Ir Prof. KO JAN-MING
Univ. Librarian: STEVE O'CONNOR
Library: see Libraries and Archives
Number of teachers: 1,200
Number of students: 28,000
Publications: *PolyU Milestones* (2 a year), *University Calendar* (1 a year)

DEANS

College of Professional and Continuing Education: Prof. PETER P. YUEN
Faculty of Applied Science and Textiles: Prof. K. Y. WONG
Faculty of Business: Prof. HOWARD DAVIES (acting)
Faculty of Communication: Prof. T. P. LEUNG
Faculty of Construction and Land Use: Prof. JIN-GUANG TENG
Faculty of Engineering: Prof. CHARLES SURYA (acting)
Faculty of Health and Social Sciences: Prof. MAURICE YAP
Faculty of Humanities: Prof. CHU-REN HUANG

HONG KONG UNIVERSITY OF SCIENCE AND TECHNOLOGY

Clear Water Bay, Kowloon
Telephone: (852) 23586000
Fax: (852) 23580537
E-mail: webmaster@www.ust.hk
Internet: www.ust.hk
Founded 1988, first student intake 1991
State control
Language of instruction: English
Academic year: September to July
Chancellor: CHIEF EXEC. OF THE HONG KONG SPEC. ADMIN. REGION
Pres.: Prof. Dr TONY F. CHAN
Vice-Pres. for Academic Affairs: Prof. Dr WEI SHYY
Vice-Pres. for Administration and Business: Prof. Dr YUK-SHAN WONG
Vice-Pres. for Institutional Advancement: Dr EDEN WOON
Vice-Pres. for Research and Graduate Studies: Prof. Dr JOSEPH HUN-WEI LEE
Univ. Librarian: Dr SAMSON SOONG
Library of 687,000 print vols, 357,000 microforms, 36,000 audiovisual items, 165,000 electronic books, 26,100 electronic journals, 317 databases
Number of teachers: 497
Number of students: 9,881
Publications: *Academic Calendar*, *HKUST Facts and Figures*

DEANS

Business and Management: Prof. LEONARD K. CHENG
Engineering: Prof. KHALED BEN LETAIEF
HKUST Fok Ying Tung Graduate School: Prof. LIONEL M. NI
Humanities and Social Science: Prof. JAMES Z. LEE
Science: Prof. NANCY YUK-YU IP
Undergraduate Education: KAR YAN TAM

PROFESSORS

ADAVAL, R., Marketing
ALTMAN, M., Physics
ARYA, S., Computer Science and Engineering
AU, O., Electronic and Computer Engineering
BAARK, E., Environment
BAARK, E., Social Science
BANFIELD, D., Biology
BARFORD, J., Chemical and Biomolecular Engineering
BEN LETAIEF, K., Electronic and Computer Engineering

BENSAOU, B., Computer Science and Engineering

BERMAK, A., Electronic and Computer Engineering

CAI, L., Mechanical Engineering

CAI, N., Industrial Engineering and Logistics Management

CAI, Y., Social Science

CAO, X., Electronic and Computer Engineering

CHAN, A., Biochemistry

CHAN, C., Chemical and Biomolecular Engineering

CHAN, C., Civil and Environmental Engineering

CHAN, C., Environment

CHAN, C., Humanities

CHAN, C., Physics

CHAN, G., Computer Science and Engineering

CHAN, H., Physics

CHAN, K., Finance

CHAN, K., Humanities

CHAN, K., Mathematics

CHAN, M., Electronic and Computer Engineering

CHAN, T., Computer Science and Engineering

CHAN, T., Mathematics

CHANG, C., Civil and Environmental Engineering

CHANG, H., Mathematics

CHAO, C., Mechanical Engineering

CHAO, M., Management

CHASNOV, J., Mathematics

CHATTOPADHYAY, P., Management

CHAU, Y., Chemical and Biomolecular Engineering

CHEN, B., Mathematics

CHEN, G., Chemical and Biomolecular Engineering

CHEN, G., Civil and Environmental Engineering

CHEN, J., Humanities

CHEN, K., Accounting

CHEN, K., Electronic and Computer Engineering

CHEN, K., Mathematics

CHEN, L., Computer Science and Engineering

CHEN, L., Humanities

CHEN, P., Accounting

CHEN, P., Electronic and Computer Engineering

CHEN, S., Economics

CHEN, T., Accounting

CHEN, Y., Social Science

CHENG, J., Civil and Environmental Engineering

CHENG, L., Economics

CHENG, R., Electronic and Computer Engineering

CHENG, S., Computer Science and Engineering

CHENG, S., Mathematics

CHEUNG, K., Information Systems, Business Statistics and Operations Management

CHEUNG, M., Civil and Environmental Engineering

CHEUNG, S., Computer Science and Engineering

CHEUNG, S., Humanities

CHEUNG, Z., Biochemistry

CHEW, S., Economics

CHIANG, Y., Mathematics

CHIGRINOV, V., Electronic and Computer Engineering

CHIN, R., Computer Science and Engineering

CHO, H., Social Science

CHOI, C., Biology

CHOI, D., Finance

CHONG, J., Social Science

CHONG, K., Humanities

CHOW, K., Biology

CHUNG, A., Computer Science and Engineering

CHUNG, K., Biochemistry

CLARK, T., Information Systems, Business Statistics and Operations Management

COOK, D., Economics

DAI, W., Chemistry

DALTON, A., Marketing

DASGUPTA, S., Finance

DING, C., Computer Science and Engineering

DING, F., Finance

DING, X., Social Science

DU, D., Finance

DU, S., Physics

DUCLOS, R., Marketing

FARH, L., Management

FENG, W., Biochemistry

FOREMAN, B., Physics

FU, F., Humanities

FUNG, J., Environment

FUNG, J., Mathematics

FUNG, P., Electronic and Computer Engineering

FUNG, Y., Humanities

GALLI, M., Marketing

GAN, J., Environment

GAN, J., Finance

GAN, J., Mathematics

GAO, F., Chemical and Biomolecular Engineering

GAO, Y., Mechanical Engineering

GEORGE, E., Management

GHIDAOUI, M., Civil and Environmental Engineering

GOLIN, M., Computer Science and Engineering

GONG, Y., Management

GOONETILLEKE, R., Industrial Engineering and Logistics Management

GOYAL, V., Finance

GU, L., Computer Science and Engineering

GUO, L., Marketing

GUO, Z., Chemistry

HA, A., Information Systems, Business Statistics and Operations Management

HAMDI, M., Computer Science and Engineering

HAN, L., Social Science

HAN, Y., Physics

HARRISON, P., Environment

HAYNES, R., Chemistry

HE, J., Management

HE, W., Social Science

HE, X., Mathematics

HELSEN, K., Marketing

HILARY, G., Accounting

HO, S., Biology

HO, V., Humanities

HOLZ, C., Social Science

HONG, J., Industrial Engineering and Logistics Management

HONG, J., Marketing

HORNER, A., Computer Science and Engineering

HOSSAIN, T., Economics

HSIEH, C., Accounting

HSING, I., Chemical and Biomolecular Engineering

HSU, C., Accounting

HSU, C., Mechanical Engineering

HU, I., Information Systems, Business Statistics and Operations Management

HU, J., Mathematics

HUA, X., Economics

HUANG, A., Accounting

HUANG, H., Electronic and Computer Engineering

HUANG, J., Mathematics

HUANG, P., Biology

HUANG, X., Chemistry

HUANG, Z., Management

HUI, D., Chemical and Biomolecular Engineering

HUI, K., Accounting

HUI, K., Information Systems, Business Statistics and Operations Management

HUNG, C., Humanities

IP, N., Biochemistry

JAISINGH, J., Information Systems, Business Statistics and Operations Management

JAMES, L., Information Systems, Business Statistics and Operations Management

JIA, G., Chemistry

JIANG, W., Industrial Engineering and Logistics Management

JING, B., Mathematics

JONEJA, A., Industrial Engineering and Logistics Management

JU, N., Finance

KARHADE, P., Information Systems, Business Statistics and Operations Management

KATAFYGIOTIS, L., Civil and Environmental Engineering

KI, W., Electronic and Computer Engineering

KIKKERT, G., Civil and Environmental Engineering

KIM, J., Mechanical Engineering

KIM, K., Economics

KIM, S., Computer Science and Engineering

KO, R., Biochemistry

KU, A., Social Science

KUANG, J., Civil and Environmental Engineering

KUNG, J., Social Science

KURSUN, V., Electronic and Computer Engineering

KWOK, H., Electronic and Computer Engineering

KWOK, J., Computer Science and Engineering

KWOK, Y., Mathematics

LAI, E., Economics

LAI, K., Biochemistry

LAM, D., Mechanical Engineering

LAM, H., Chemical and Biomolecular Engineering

LAM, J., Chemistry

LAU, A., Civil and Environmental Engineering

LAU, A., Environment

LAU, A., Mathematics

LAU, D., Biology

LAU, K., Electronic and Computer Engineering

LAU, S., Biology

LAU, V., Electronic and Computer Engineering

LEA, C., Electronic and Computer Engineering

LEE, C., Industrial Engineering and Logistics Management

LEE, D., Computer Science and Engineering

LEE, J., Social Science

LEE, K., Biology

LEE, N., Industrial Engineering and Logistics Management

LEE, O., Biology

LEE, R., Mechanical Engineering

LEE, Y., Mechanical Engineering

LENG, Y., Mechanical Engineering

LENNOX, C., Accounting

LEUNG, C., Civil and Environmental Engineering

LEUNG, P., Physics

LEUNG, S., Economics

LEUNG, S., Mathematics

LEUNG, W., Chemistry

LI, B., Computer Science and Engineering

LI, J., Management

LI, J., Mathematics

LI, K., Mathematics

LI, N., Biology

LI, Q., Information Systems, Business Statistics and Operations Management

LI, W., Mathematics

LI, X., Chemistry

LI, Y., Information Systems, Business Statistics and Operations Management

LI, Z., Civil and Environmental Engineering

LI, Z., Electronic and Computer Engineering

LI, Z., Mechanical Engineering

LIANG, C., Biochemistry

LIN, F., Computer Science and Engineering

LIN, N., Physics

LIN, Y., Social Science
LIN, Z., Chemistry
LING, S., Mathematics
LIU, H., Biology
LIU, H., Environment
LIU, G., Humanities
LIU, L., Finance
LIU, Q., Industrial Engineering and Logistics Management
LIU, T., Humanities
LIU, Y., Computer Science and Engineering
LO, A., Information Systems, Business Statistics and Operations Management
LO, H., Civil and Environmental Engineering
LO, I., Civil and Environmental Engineering
LOCHOVSKY, F., Computer Science and Engineering
LORTZ, R., Physics
LOY, M., Physics
LU, Z., Humanities
LUI, F., Economics
LUO, Q., Computer Science and Engineering
LUONG, H., Electronic and Computer Engineering
MA, J., Humanities
MA, J., Social Science
MCKAY, G., Chemical and Biomolecular Engineering
MCKAY, M., Electronic and Computer Engineering
MACKAY, P., Finance
MAK, B., Computer Science and Engineering
MAK, H., Industrial Engineering and Logistics Management
MARKLE, A., Management
MENG, G., Mathematics
MI, Y., Chemical and Biomolecular Engineering
MILLER, A., Biology
MOK, P., Electronic and Computer Engineering
MOW, W., Electronic and Computer Engineering
MOY, A., Mathematics
MU, M., Mathematics
MUKHOPADHYAY, A., Marketing
MUPPALA, K., Computer Science and Engineering
MURCH, R., Electronic and Computer Engineering
MUTHUKRISHNAN, A., Marketing
NASON, E., Management
NG, C., Civil and Environmental Engineering
NG, K., Chemical and Biomolecular Engineering
NG, K., Humanities
NG, S., Information Systems, Business Statistics and Operations Management
NG, T., Physics
NG, W., Computer Science and Engineering
NI, L., Computer Science and Engineering
NI, S., Finance
NOVOSELOV, K., Accounting
PALOMAR, D., Electronic and Computer Engineering
PAPADIAS, D., Computer Science and Engineering
PATCHELL, G., Environment
PATCHELL, G., Social Science
PENG, H., Biology
PING GAO, P., Chemical and Biomolecular Engineering
PONG, T., Computer Science and Engineering
POON, A., Electronic and Computer Engineering
POON, R., Biochemistry
QI, R., Biochemistry
QI, X., Industrial Engineering and Logistics Management
QIAN, P., Biology
QIAN, T., Mathematics
QIU, H., Mechanical Engineering
QIU, L., Electronic and Computer Engineering
QU, H., Computer Science and Engineering
QU, J., Electronic and Computer Engineering

QUAN, L., Computer Science and Engineering
RENNEBERG, R., Chemistry
SANDER, P., Computer Science and Engineering
SAUTMAN, B., Social Science
SEASHOLES, M., Finance
SEN, R., Finance
SENGUPTA, J., Marketing
SHANG, C., Civil and Environmental Engineering
SHAO, Q., Mathematics
SHARIF, N., Social Science
SHEN, H., Computer Science and Engineering
SHEN, V., Computer Science and Engineering
SHENG, P., Physics
SHI, B., Electronic and Computer Engineering
SHI, L., Electronic and Computer Engineering
SHIMOKAWA, S., Social Science
SHUM, S., Information Systems, Business Statistics and Operations Management
SIN, J., Electronic and Computer Engineering
SIN, R., Information Systems, Business Statistics and Operations Management
SING, M., Social Science
SO, A., Social Science
SO, M., Information Systems, Business Statistics and Operations Management
SO, R., Industrial Engineering and Logistics Management
SOU, I., Physics
STAM, W., Management
SULLIVAN, B., Management
SUN, J., Humanities
SUN, Q., Mechanical Engineering
SZETO, K., Physics
TAI, C., Computer Science and Engineering
TAKEUCHI, R., Management
TAM, K., Information Systems, Business Statistics and Operations Management
TAM, K., Social Science
TAM, W., Physics
TANAKA, M., Economics
TANG, B., Chemistry
TANG, C., Computer Science and Engineering
TANG, K., Mechanical Engineering
TANG, Z., Physics
THONG, J., Information Systems, Business Statistics and Operations Management
TONG, P., Physics
TSANG, D., Electronic and Computer Engineering
TSANG, S., Biochemistry
TSENG, M., Industrial Engineering and Logistics Management
TSIM, K., Biology
TSUI, C., Electronic and Computer Engineering
TSUNG, F., Industrial Engineering and Logistics Management
TU, J., Social Science
TUNG, Y., Civil and Environmental Engineering
VISARIA, S., Economics
WAN, J., Biochemistry
WAN, X., Information Systems, Business Statistics and Operations Management
WANG, G., Civil and Environmental Engineering
WANG, H., Management
WANG, J., Civil and Environmental Engineering
WANG, J., Physics
WANG, N., Physics
WANG, P., Economics
WANG, S., Accounting
WANG, S., Economics
WANG, W., Biology
WANG, X., Humanities
WANG, X., Mathematics
WANG, X., Physics
WANG, Y., Civil and Environmental Engineering
WANG, Y., Economics

WEI, K., Finance
WEI, Z., Biochemistry
WEN, W., Physics
WEN, Z., Biochemistry
WILLIAMS, I., Chemistry
WONG, A., Electronic and Computer Engineering
WONG, E., Management
WONG, G., Physics
WONG, J., Biology
WONG, K., Physics
WONG, L., Humanities
WONG, M., Electronic and Computer Engineering
WONG, M., Mathematics
WONG, M., Physics
WONG, R., Computer Science and Engineering
WONG, R., Social Science
WONG, S., Humanities
WONG, W., Biochemistry
WONG, Y., Biochemistry
WONG, Y., Biology
WU, D., Computer Science and Engineering
WU, H., Chemistry
WU, J., Mechanical Engineering
WU, L., Mathematics
WU, X., Social Science
WU, Y., Chemistry
WU, Z., Biochemistry
XIA, J., Biochemistry
XIANG, Y., Marketing
XIANG, Y., Mathematics
XIE, D., Economics
XIE, Y., Biology
XIJUN HU, X., Chemical and Biomolecular Engineering
XU, B., Chemistry
XU, C., Computer Science and Engineering
XU, J., Economics
XU, J., Electronic and Computer Engineering
XU, K., Mathematics
XU, S., Information Systems, Business Statistics and Operations Management
XU, Y., Information Systems, Business Statistics and Operations Management
XUE, H., Biochemistry
YAN, M., Mathematics
YAN, Y., Chemistry
YANG, H., Civil and Environmental Engineering
YANG, Q., Computer Science and Engineering
YANG, S., Chemistry
YANG, Z., Physics
YAO, S., Mechanical Engineering
YE, W., Mechanical Engineering
YEE, A., Humanities
YEUNG, D., Computer Science and Engineering
YEUNG, K., Chemical and Biomolecular Engineering
YI, K., Computer Science and Engineering
YIK, M., Social Science
YIP, K., Humanities
YIU, C., Humanities
YOU, H., Accounting
YU, J., Chemistry
YU, J., Environment
YU, M., Information Systems, Business Statistics and Operations Management
YU, S., Information Systems, Business Statistics and Operations Management
YU, T., Mechanical Engineering
YU, W., Electronic and Computer Engineering
YUAN, G., Electronic and Computer Engineering
YUEN, M., Mechanical Engineering
ZANG, A., Accounting
ZENG, B., Electronic and Computer Engineering
ZHANG, C., Computer Science and Engineering
ZHANG, C., Finance
ZHANG, G., Accounting

ZHANG, H., Information Systems, Business Statistics and Operations Management
ZHANG, J., Industrial Engineering and Logistics Management
ZHANG, L., Civil and Environmental Engineering
ZHANG, M., Accounting
ZHANG, M., Biochemistry
ZHANG, M., Humanities
ZHANG, M., Information Systems, Business Statistics and Operations Management
ZHANG, N., Computer Science and Engineering
ZHANG, Q., Computer Science and Engineering
ZHANG, R., Industrial Engineering and Logistics Management
ZHANG, T., Mechanical Engineering
ZHANG, X., Civil and Environmental Engineering
ZHANG, Y., Accounting
ZHANG, Z., Physics
ZHAO, J., Civil and Environmental Engineering
ZHAO, T., Mechanical Engineering
ZHAO, Y., Marketing
ZHENG, R., Information Systems, Business Statistics and Operations Management
ZHENG, S., Information Systems, Business Statistics and Operations Management
ZHOU, R., Marketing
ZHU, G., Biochemistry
ZHU, J., Management
ZHU, K., Industrial Engineering and Logistics Management
ZHU, T., Economics
ZHU, X., Humanities
ZHU, Y., Mathematics
ZHU, Y., Social Science
ZWEIG, D., Social Science

LINGNAN UNIVERSITY

8 Castle Peak Rd, Tuen Mun, New Territories
Telephone: (852) 26168888
Fax: (852) 24638363
E-mail: oiapa@ln.edu.hk
Internet: www.ln.edu.hk
Founded 1888 as Christian College in China, as Lingan College Co Ltd 1967, self-accrediting status 1998, present name 1999
Academic year: September to August
Chancellor: Hon DONALD YAM-KUEN TSANG
Pres.: Prof. CHAN YUK-SHEE
Vice-Pres.: Prof. SEADE JESÚS
Comptroller: HERDIP SINGH
Dean of Students: Prof. LEE HUNG-KAI
Registrar: Prof. WILLIAM LEE
Univ. Librarian: Dr FREDERICK NESTA
Library of 470,246 vols
Number of teachers: 170
Number of students: 2,592

DEANS

Faculty of Arts: Prof. STEPHEN CHAN
Faculty of Business: Prof. DEAN TJOSVOLD
Faculty of Social Sciences: Prof. PETER BAEHR

OPEN UNIVERSITY OF HONG KONG

30 Good Shepherd St, Homantin, Kowloon
Telephone: (852) 27112100
Fax: (852) 27150760
E-mail: infoctr@ic.ouhk.edu.hk
Internet: www.ouhk.edu.hk
Founded 1989 as Open Learning Institute of Hong Kong, present location 1996, present name and status 1997
Public control
Chancellor: Hon. CHIEF EXEC. OF THE HONG KONG SPEC. ADMIN. REGION
Pres.: Prof. JOHN LEONG CHI-YAN

Vice-Pres. for Academic Affairs: Prof. DANNY WONG
Vice-Pres. for Technology and Devt: Prof. LEUNG CHUN-MING
Registrar: LEE SHU WING
Librarian: MOK WONG WAI-MAN
Library of 500,000 vols, 133,000 printed and multimedia items, 20,200 e-books, 980 printed serials, 18,200 electronic serials
Number of teachers: 590 full-time, 1,060 part-time
Number of students: 17,000 (full-time and distance learning)

DEANS

School of Arts and Social Sciences: Prof. TAM KWOK-KAN
School of Business and Administration: Prof. IP YIU-KEUNG
School of Education and Languages: YVONNE FUNG SHI YUK-HANG
School of Science and Technology: Prof. HO KIN CHUNG

UNIVERSITY OF HONG KONG

Pokfulam Rd, Pokfulam
Telephone: (852) 28592111
Fax: (852) 28582549
E-mail: cpao@hku.hk
Internet: www.hku.hk
Founded 1912
Academic year: September to June
Chancellor: CHIEF EXEC. OF THE HONG KONG SPEC. ADMIN. REGION
Pro-Chancellor: Dr The Hon. DAVID LI KWOK PO
Vice-Chancellor and Pres.: Prof. LAP-CHEE TSUI
Deputy Vice-Chancellor: Prof. RICHARD Y. C. WONG
Pro-Vice-Chancellor and Vice-Pres. for Infrastructure: Prof. JOHN GRAHAM MALPAS
Pro-Vice-Chancellor and Vice-Pres. for Research: Prof. PAUL K. H. TAM
Pro-Vice-Chancellor and Vice-Pres. for Staffing: Prof. JOSEPH H. W. LEE
Pro-Vice-Chancellor and Vice-Pres. for Teaching and Learning: Prof. AMY B. M. TSUI
Pro-Vice-Chancellor and Vice-Pres. for Univ. Relations: Prof. SHEW-PING CHOW
Treas.: PAUL M. Y. CHOW (acting)
Registrar: HENRY W. K. WAI
Librarian: Dr A. W. FERGUSON
Number of teachers: 2,001 full-time
Number of students: 21,652
Publications: *Bulletin* (3–4 a year), *Centennial Campus Newsletter* (4 a year), *Convocation Newsletter* (4 a year), *Journal of Oriental Studies* (2 a year)

DEANS

Faculty of Architecture: Prof. RALPH LERNER
Faculty of Arts: Prof. LOUIE KAM HUNG (acting)
Faculty of Business and Economics: Prof. ERIC C. CHANG (acting)
Faculty of Dentistry: Prof. L. P. SAMARANAYAKE
Faculty of Education: Prof. FREDERICK K. S. LEUNG (acting)
Faculty of Engineering: Prof. CHEW WENG CHO
Faculty of Law: Prof. JOHANNES CHAN MAN MUN
Faculty of Medicine: Prof. LEE SUM-PING
Faculty of Science: Prof. KWOK SUN
Faculty of Social Sciences: Prof. IAN HOLLIDAY

PROFESSORS

ABERNETHY, A. B., Human Performance
AU, T. K. F., Psychology

BRAY, T. M., Education
BURNS, J. P., Politics and Public Administration
CHAN, D. K. O., Zoology
CHAN, M. M. W., Medicine
CHAN, V. N. Y., Medicine
CHANG, E. C., Business
CHAU, K. W., Real Estate and Construction
CHE, C. M., Chemistry
CHEAH, K. S. E., Biochemistry
CHENG, K. M., Education
CHENG, K. S., Physics
CHIN, F. Y. L., Computer Science and Information Systems
CHO, C. H., Pharmacology
CHOW, N. W. S., Social Work and Social Administration
CHOW, S. P., Orthopaedic Surgery
CHWANG, A. T. Y., Mechanical Engineering
DUGGAN, B. J., Mechanical Engineering
FAN, S. T., Surgery
FANG, H. H. P., Civil Engineering
FREWER, R. J. B., Architecture
FUNG, P. C. W., Medicine
GHAI, Y. P., Law
GOLDSTEIN, L., Philosophy
HAGG, E. U. O., Dentistry
HANSEN, C., Philosophy
HEDLEY, A. J., Community Medicine
HO, P. C., Obstetrics and Gynaecology
IP, M. S. M., Medicine
JIM, C. Y., Geography
KO, R. C. C., Zoology
KUMANA, C. R., Medicine
KUNG, H., Molecular Biology
LAI, C. L., Medicine
LAI, K. N., Medicine
LAM, E., Botany
LAM, K. S. L., Medicine
LAM, S. K., Medicine
LAM, T. H., Community Medicine
LAM, W. K., Medicine
LAU, A. H. L., Business
LAU, C. P., Medicine
LAU, Y. L., Paediatrics and Adolescent Medicine
LEE, C. F., Civil Engineering
LEE, J. H. W., Civil Engineering
LI, V. O. K., Electrical and Electronic Engineering
LI, W. K., Statistics and Actuarial Science
LIANG, R. H. S., Medicine
LIE KEN JIE, M. S. F., Chemistry
LO, C. M., Surgery
LUK, K. D. K., Orthopaedic Surgery
MALPAS, J. G., Earth Sciences
MAN, R. Y. K., Mathematics
MOK, N., Mathematics
NG, T. S., Electrical and Electronic Engineering
NUNAN, D. C., English Centre
SAMARANAYAKE, L. P., Dentistry
SHERRIN, C. H., Professional Legal Education
TAM, P. K. H., Surgery
TAMBLING, J. C. R., Comparative Literature
TANG, S. W., Psychiatry
TIDEMAN, H., Dentistry
TONG, H., Statistics
TSE, D. K. C., Business
TSUI, A. B. M., Education
WEI, W. I., Surgery
WONG, J., Surgery
WONG, R. Y. C., Economics and Finance
WONG, S. L., Sociology
WU, F. F., Electrical and Electronic Engineering
YAM, V. W. W., Chemistry
YANG, E. S., Electrical and Electronic Engineering
YEH, A. G. O., Urban Planning and Environmental Management
YUEN, K. Y., Microbiology
ZHANG, F., Physics

Colleges

Chung Chi College: Taipo Rd, New Territories; tel. (852) 26098009; e-mail ccc@cuhk .edu.hk; internet www.cuhk.edu.hk/ccc; f. 1951, present location 1956, present status 1963; attached to Chinese Univ. of Hong Kong; depts of arts, business administration, education, engineering, law, medicine, science and social science; 2,807 students; Head Prof. YUEN-SANG LEUNG; Dean of Gen. Education Prof. KWOK-NAM LEUNG; Dean of Students Prof. WING-PING FONG; Librarian KEVIN LEUNG; publs *Chung Chi Alumni* (4 a year, electronic), *Chung Chi Campus Newsletter*.

Hong Kong Academy for Performing Arts: 1 Gloucester Rd, Wan Chai; tel. (852) 25848500; fax (852) 28024372; e-mail aso@ hkapa.edu; internet www.hkapa.edu; f. 1984, present status 1992; schools of dance, drama, film and television, music, theatre and entertainment arts and Chinese traditional theatre; library: 18,000 vols of Chinese books, 48,000 vols of English books, 1,900 books in other languages, 25,000 music scores, 36,000 audiovisual items, 329 printed journals, 2,100 titles in archives, 600 slide sets and kits, 7,400 electronic plays, 5,200 e-books, 1,300 electronic journal titles, 40 reference and aggregator databases; 453 teachers (79 full-time, 374 part-time); 749 students; Pres. CHIEF EXEC. OF THE HONG KONG SPEC. ADMIN. REGION; Dir Prof. KEVIN THOMPSON; Assoc. Dir for Admin. and Registrar Dr HERBERT HUEY; Assoc. Dir for Operations PHILIP SODEN; Librarian LING WAI-KING; publ. *Dramatic Arts* (1 a year).

Hong Kong Design Institute: Planning Team Office, Room 735, VTC Tower, 27 Wood Rd, Wan Chai; tel. (852) 28361912; fax (852) 35204185; e-mail hkdi@vtc.edu.hk; internet www.hkdi.edu.hk; f. 2007; attached to Vocational Training Ccl; depts of designs, engineering, fashion and textiles, printing and digital media, toy design and multimedia exhibition design; at present all programmes are delivered at IVE campuses; new HKDI campus at Tiu Keng Leng opens in 2010–11; Exec. Dir Dr CARRIE WILLIS; publ. *D. I Winners*.

Hong Kong Institute of Education: 10 Lo Ping Rd, Tai Po, New Territories; tel. (852) 29488888; fax (852) 29486000; e-mail info@ ied.edu.hk; internet www.ied.edu.hk; f. 1994 by merger of four colleges of education and the Institute of Language in Education, present location 1997, self-accrediting status 2004; faculties of arts and sciences, education studies, languages; library: 605,914 vols; 412 teachers; 7,153 students; Pres. Prof. ANTHONY B. L. CHEUNG; Vice-Pres. for Academic Affairs Prof. LEE WING ON; Vice-Pres. for Admin. Prof. CHRIS MONG CHAN; Vice-Pres. for Research and Devt Prof. CHENG YIN CHEONG; publs *Education Focus*, *Education Matters*, *Joy of Learning* (bilingual magazine).

IVE Morrison Hill: 6 Oi Kwan Rd, Wan Chai; tel. (852) 25745321; fax (852) 25729847; e-mail csivemh@vtc.edu.hk; internet www.vtc.edu.hk/ti/mhti/homepage/ english/; f. 1969, fmrly Morrison Hill Technical Institute; attached to Vocational Training Ccl; depts of business administration, construction, information and communications technology, real estate and facilities management; library: 50,000 books, 200 periodicals; 300 full-time teachers; 6,260 students; Prin. DANIEL KWOH KAI HING.

Maritime Services Training Institute: 23 Castle Peak Rd, Tai Lam Chung, Tuen Mun, New Territories; tel. (852) 24583833; fax (852) 24400308; e-mail msti@vtc.edu.hk; internet www.vtc.edu.hk/vtc/web/template/ about_the_centr.jsp?fldr_id=498; f. 1988; attached to Vocational Training Ccl; programmes for new entrants and professionals in marine-related and shore-based industry.

New Asia College: Sha Tin, New Territories; tel. (852) 26097609; fax (852) 26035418; e-mail nac@cuhk.edu.hk; internet www3 .cuhk.edu.hk/na; f. 1949 as Asia Evening College of Arts and Commerce, present name 1950, present status and location 1973; attached to Chinese Univ. of Hong Kong; 2,800 students; Head Prof. HENRY WONG; Dean of Gen. Education Prof. S. O. CHAN; Dean of Students Prof. MARIA S. M. TAM; publs *Ch'ien Mu Lectures in History and Culture* (monograph series), *New Asia College Academic Bulletin*, *New Asia Life Monthly*.

Shaw College: LG1, Wen Lan Tang; tel. (852) 26097363; fax (852) 26035427; e-mail shaw-college@cuhk.edu.hk; internet www5 .cuhk.edu.hk/shaw; f. 1990; attached to Chinese Univ. of Hong Kong; Head Prof. JOSEPH J. Y. SUNG; Dean of Gen. Education Prof. HO PUI-YIN; Dean of Students Prof. FREEDOM Y. K. LEUNG; publs *Shaw Link*, *Shaw Net*.

United College: 2nd Fl., Tsang Shiu Tim Bldg, Chinese Univ. of Hong Kong, Sha Tin, New Territories; tel. (852) 26097575; fax (852) 26035412; e-mail unitedcollege@cuhk .edu.hk; internet www2.cuhk.edu.hk/uc; f. 1956 by merger of five colleges: Canton Overseas, Kwang Hsia, Wah Kiu, Wen Hua and Ping Jing College of Accountancy, present status 1959, present location 1971; attached to Chinese Univ. of Hong Kong; faculties of arts, business administration, education, engineering, law, medicine, science and social science; 2,931 students; Head Prof. FUNG KWOK-PUI; Dean of Gen. Education Prof. JIMMY C. M. YU; Dean of Students Prof. STEPHEN H. S. WONG; Librarian YIFENG WU; publs *United Bulletin*, *United College Alumni Newsletter* (4 a year), *United We Advance*.

MACAO

Regulatory Body

NATIONAL BODY

Gabinete de Apoio ao Ensino Superior (Tertiary Education Services Office): Avenida do Dr. Rodrigo Rodrigues No. 614A-640, Edif. Long Cheng, 5° a 7° andares; tel. (853) 28345403; fax (853) 28318401; e-mail info@ gaes.gov.mo; internet www.gaes.gov.mo; f. 1992; govt dept in charge of higher education affairs under the leadership of the Sec. for Social Affairs and Culture; formulates policies for the devt of higher education; helps in the evaluation of higher education instns; Dir Dr KUOK SIO LAI (acting); publs *Data of Higher Education in Macao (Numbers of Staff and Students)* (1 a year, in Chinese, online version in English), *Higher Education Bursaries* (1 a year, in Chinese), *Guidebook for Higher Education in Macao* (1 a year, in Chinese), *Q&A: Studying in a Higher Education Institution of Macao* (1 a year, simplified Chinese).

Learned Societies

GENERAL

Fundação Macau (Macao Foundation): Ave da República 6; tel. (853) 28966777; fax (853) 28968658; e-mail info@fm.org.mo; internet www.fmac.org.mo; conducts research on cultural, social, economic, educational, scientific, academic, philanthropic activities for the promotion of Macao; Pres. CHUI SAI ON; Pres. for Admin. VITOR NG.

ARCHITECTURE AND TOWN PLANNING

Architects Association of Macau:tel. (853) 28703458; fax (853) 28704089; e-mail info@macaoarchitects.com; internet www .macaoarchitects.com; f. 1980 as Macau Association of Architects in Private Practice, present name 1988; Dir EDDIE Y. K. WONG; Gen-Sec. JOY TIN TIN CHOI.

ECONOMICS, LAW AND POLITICS

Associação de Ciências Sociais de Macau (Macao Society of Social Sciences): Estrada Adolfo Loureiro 3A, Edif. Tak On, 3rd Floor A, POB 957; tel. (853) 28319880; fax (853) 28319880; f. 1985; studies and serves the society of Macao; 40 mems; Pres. HUANG WEI-WEN; Sec. CHEONG CHOK FU; publ. *Huo Keng* (Mirror of Macao, 2 a year).

FINE AND PERFORMING ARTS

Instituto Cultural do Governo da R. A. E. de Macau (Cultural Affairs Bureau): Praça do Tap Seac, Edif. do Instituto Cultural; tel. (853) 83996699; fax (853) 28366899; e-mail postoffice@icm.gov.mo; internet www.icm.gov.mo; f. 1982, fmrly Cultural Institute of Macao, reorganized to present status 1994; cultural studies; classes for music, drama and ballet; promotion of cultural events; also oversees the Macao Historical Archives, the Macao Central Library and the Macao Museum; Pres. Dra HEIDI HO; publ. *Revista de Cultura* (in English, Chinese and Portuguese, 4 a year).

LANGUAGE AND LITERATURE

Alliance Française: 4/F Travessa do Bom Jesus R/C; tel. (853) 28965342; fax (853) 28962697; e-mail info.macao@afchine.org;

internet www.alliancefrancaise.org.mo; f. 1987; offers courses and examinations in French language and culture and promotes cultural exchange with France; 11 mems; Pres. JOAQUIM JORGE PERESTRELO NETO VALENTE; Dir (vacant); Head of Studies PATRICIA BERTONECHE.

MEDICINE

Nurses Association of Macao: Ave Macao 1-1B, E Sunrise House 2-D Block; tel. (853) 28525614; fax (853) 28581787; e-mail naom@macau.ctm.net; internet www.naom.org.mo; f. 1986; improves professional standards of care and promotes basic rights of nurses; 650 mems; Pres. LI XUE-PING; Vice-Pres. SHU-CHEN HUANG; Chair. TIAN JIE BING; Sec.-Gen. MAO XIAONI.

Research Institutes

GENERAL

Instituto Ricci de Macau (Macau Ricci Institute): Ave Cons. Ferreira de Almeida 95-E; tel. (853) 28532536; fax (853) 28568274; e-mail info@riccimac.org; internet www.riccimac.org; f. 1999, present status 1999; non-profit org.; studies and research dedicated to fostering mutual understanding between China and the world community; library of 10,198 Chinese books, 7,782 Western books, 343 periodicals; Dir ARTUR WARDEGA; Vice-Dir LUÍS SEQUEIRA; Gen.-Sec. JERÓNIMO HUNG; Sec. SANDY LEI HAO WENG; publs *Chinese Cross Currents* (in Chinese and English, 4 a year), *Macau Ricci Institute Studies*.

ECONOMICS, LAW AND POLITICS

Social, Economic and Public Policy Research Centre: Rua de Luís Gonzaga Gomes; tel. (853) 85996267; fax (853) 28704200; e-mail cepes@ipm.edu.mo; internet www.ipm.edu.mo/cepes; f. 2007; attached to Macao Polytechnic Institute; research areas incl. gambling industry of Macao, devt of economy, society, govt and public policy in Macao; provides consultancy services to Macao Spec. Admin. Region Govt; Exec. Deputy Dir Prof. CHEN QINGYUN.

MEDICINE

Institute of Chinese Medical Sciences: c/o Univ. of Macao, Ave Padre Tomás Pereira SJ, Taipa; tel. (853) 83974698; fax (853) 28841358; e-mail icms.enquiry@umac.mo; internet www.umac.mo/icms; f. 2002; attached to Univ. of Macao; develops postgraduate education; trains management and scientific research professionals in medical science; researches in medicine and pharmacology; networks with int. instns and orgs; promotes traditional Chinese medicine; Dir YITAO WANG.

Macau Institute for Applied Research in Medicine and Health: Macau Univ. of Science and Technology, Ave Wai Long, Taipa; tel. (853) 88972633; fax (853) 28822799; e-mail miar@must.edu.mo; internet www.mustf-miar.org.mo; attached to Macau Univ. of Science and Technology; provides educational service, clinical practice and various biological research and devt for the Faculty of Chinese Medicine (Macau Univ. of Science and Technology); also provides a platform in Macao for biotechnology industrialization, modernization and internationalization of Chinese medicine; Dir Dr TIMOTHY MING WAI CHAN; Deputy Dir Dr BRAD W. C. LAU.

Libraries and Archives
Macao

Arquivo Histórico de Macau (Macao Historical Archives): Praca do Tap Seac, Edif. do Instituto Cultural; tel. (853) 28592919; fax (853) 28561495; e-mail info.ah@icm.gov.mo; internet www.archives.gov.mo; f. 1952 as Macao Gen. Archives, renamed and restructured 1979; attached to Instituto Cultural do Governo da R.A.E. de Macau (Cultural Affairs Bureau); promotes research; holds govt gazettes, original records, microfilms of rare works on Macao's history and Portugal's relations with the Far East; 7,000 vols; Dir MARIE IMELDA MACLEOD; publ. *Boletim do Arquivo Histórico de Macau*.

Biblioteca Central de Macau (Macao Central Library): Largo de Sto. Agostinho, No.3; tel. (853) 28371623; fax (853) 28314456; e-mail inf.bc@icm.gov.mo; internet www.library.gov.mo; f. 1895; attached to Instituto Cultural do Governo da R.A.E. de Macau (Cultural Affairs Bureau of the Macao SAR Government); public network of main library and 6 brs; gen. colln; Chinese Books (Sir Robert Ho Tung); highlights traditional culture and encourages leisure reading through reading activities, exhibitions and lectures; participates in Library Week; 750,000 vols; Dir NG, KENT; Sec. CATHERINE LO; publs *Boletim Bibliográfico de Literatura Portuguesa*, *Boletim Bibliográfico de Macau*, *Boletim de Literatura Infantil*.

Biblioteca da Ilha Verde (Ilha Verde Library): Ave de Concórdia 281, 4th Floor Edif. 'May Fair Garden' II Fase; tel. (853) 28225783; fax (853) 28225474; internet www.library.gov.mo/pt/general/library_3.aspx; f. 1995; attached to Macao Central Library; cultural and educational centre for dissemination of entertainment and information; 34,000 vols of monographs, 2,400 multimedia material, 72 newspaper titles and 435 journals.

Biblioteca de Coloane (Library of Coloane): Rua de 5 de Outubro, Coloane; tel. and fax (853) 28882254; internet www.library.gov.mo/pt/general/library_5.aspx; f. 1983; attached to Macao Central Library; 8,700 vols of monographs, 16 newspaper titles and 59 magazine titles.

Biblioteca de Mong Há (Mong Ha Library): Bairro de Mong Há, near the Pavilion de Mong Ha; tel. (853) 28317288; fax (853) 28481963; internet www.library.gov.mo/pt/general/library_4.aspx; f. 1988; attached to Macao Central Library; 21,000 vols incl. monographs, 51 journal titles and 229 magazines.

Biblioteca do Edifício do IACM (IACM Building Library): Ave de Almeida Ribeiro 163, Edif. do IACM; tel. (853) 28572233; fax (853) 28312772; internet www.library.gov.mo/pt/general/library_6.aspx; f. 1929 fmrly Biblioteca do Leal Senado; attached to Macao Central Library; spec. collns incl. historical and scholarly works on China and Portuguese rule in the Far East and Africa; 30,000 vols, 19,000 monographs, 22 journals, 99 newspapers.

Biblioteca Sir Robert Ho Tung (Sir Robert Ho Tung Library): Largo do Sto. Agostinho 3; tel. (853) 28377117; fax (853) 28314456; internet www.library.gov.mo/pt/general/library_2.aspx; f. 1958; attached to Macao Central Library; largest public library in Macao; 100,000 vols, incl. 5,000 ancient Chinese books, 79,924 other books, 4,925 multimedia materials, 74 journals, 732 magazines, 23 newspaper titles; Librarian SAM CHAN FAI; publ. *Boletim Bibliográfico de Macau*.

Museums and Art Galleries
Macao

Macao Tea Culture House: Lou Lim Ieoc Garden, Ave do Conselheiro Ferreira de Almeida; tel. (853) 28827103; fax (853) 28827102; e-mail dic@iacm.gov.mo; internet www.iacm.gov.mo/museum; f. 2005; attached to Civic and Municipal Affairs Bureau; represents China's tea culture; Macao's role in the history of Chinese tea propagation and trade.

Macau Maritime Museum: 1 Largo do Pagode da Barra; tel. (853) 28595481; fax (853) 28512160; e-mail museumaritimo@marine.gov.mo; internet www.museumaritimo.gov.mo; f. 1987, present bldg 1990; plans and drawings of old Portuguese vessels such as ships of war, merchant ships and fishing vessels; photographs dating from 1920; library of 2,500 vols.

Museu das Comunicações (Communications Museum): Estrada D. Maria II 7; tel. (853) 28718570; fax (853) 28718018; e-mail info@macao.communications.museum; internet macao.communications.museum; f. 2006; stimulates interest in philatelic colln, stamp colln; promotes Macao philately and scientific and technical knowledge of telecommunications.

Museu de Arte de Macau (Macao Museum of Art): Centro Cultural de Macau, Ave Xian Xing Hai s/n Nape; tel. (853) 287919814; fax (853) 28751317; e-mail artmuseum@iacm.gov.mo; internet www.artmuseum.gov.mo; f. 1999; attached to Civil and Municipal Affairs Bureau; collns incl. Shi Wan ceramics, Chinese painting and calligraphy, historical pictures, Macao contemporary art, ceramics and stoneware excavated from Heisha in Macao, seal cutting from Guangdong, Western historical paintings, poster design, photographic works; attached auditorium and library; Dir CHAN HOU SENG.

Museu de Macau (Museum of Macao): Praceta do Museu de Macau 112; tel. (853) 28357911; fax (853) 28358503; e-mail info.mm@icm.gov.mo; internet www.macaumuseum.gov.mo; f. 1998; attached to Instituto Cultural do Governo da R.A.E. de Macau; promotes understanding and interest in Macao's history and cultural heritage; creates and develops collns related to archaeology, history, natural history, ethnography and ethnology; serves as a centre for learning through research and study; preserves and records materials of historical and cultural significance; library of 3,000 vols; Dir CHAN IENG HIN; publ. *Museum of Macao* (magazine).

Nature and Agriculture Museum: Seac Pai Van Park, Coloane Island; tel. (853) 28870277; fax (853) 28870271; e-mail decn@iacm.gov.mo; internet nature.iacm.gov.mo.

Temporary Exhibition Gallery of the Civic and Municipal Affairs Bureau (IACM): Ave Almeida Ribeiro 163, 'Leal Senado' Bldg; tel. (853) 89884100; internet www.iacm.gov.mo/museum; f. 1985; attached to Civic and Municipal Affairs Bureau; housed in historically significant 'Leal Senado' bldg; exhibits works of local and Chinese artists.

Universities

UNIVERSIDADE DE CIÊNCIA E TECNOLOGIA DE MACAU
(Macau University of Science and Technology)

Avenida Wai Long, Taipa
Telephone: (853) 28881122
Fax: (853) 28880022
E-mail: enquiry@must.edu.mo
Internet: www.must.edu.mo

Founded 2000
Private control

Chancellor: Dr LIU CHAK WAN
Rector: Prof. XU AO AO
Vice Rector: Acad. LIU REN HUAI
Vice Rector: Prof. CHAN LAI KOW
Registrar: Prof. KEITH ROBERT BARCLAY MORRISON
Univ. Librarian: Prof. DAI LONG JI

Library of 100,000 vols, 15,000 periodicals, electronic database

DEANS

Faculty of Arts and Humanities: Dr CHEN NAI CHI
Faculty of Chinese Medicine: Prof. XIANG PING
Faculty of Health Sciences: Prof. LAM WAI KEI
Faculty of Information Technology: Prof. DING LI YA
Faculty of International Tourism: Prof. ALIANA LEONG MAN WAI
Faculty of Law: Prof. MI JIAN
Faculty of Management and Administration: Prof. CHAN LAI KOW
School of Graduate Studies: Prof. TANG HUNG LIAN

UNIVERSIDADE DE MACAU
(University of Macao)

Ave Padre Tomás Pereira, Taipa
Telephone: (853) 28831622
Fax: (853) 28831694
E-mail: info@umac.mo
Internet: www.umac.mo

Founded 1981 as Univ. of East Asia, present name 1991
State control
Languages of instruction: Chinese, Portuguese, English
Academic year: September to June

Chancellor: CHIEF EXEC. OF MACAO SPEC. ADMIN. REGION
Rector: Prof. WEI ZHAO
Vice-Rector for Academic Affairs: Prof. SIMON SHUN MAN HO
Vice-Rector for Admin.: Dr ALEX LAI IAT LONG
Vice-Rector for Research: Prof. RUI PAULO DA SILVA MARTINS
Librarian: Dr PAUL POON WAH TUNG

Library: 3m. vols, 300,000 periodicals, 13,000 vols old Chinese edns, 1m. ebooks, 35,000 online journals
Number of teachers: 407
Number of students: 6,791

Publications: *Boletim da Faculdade de Direito* (in Chinese and Portuguese, 2 a year), *Journal of Macau Studies* (6 a year)

DEANS

Faculty of Business Administration: Prof. JACKY YUK CHOW SO
Faculty of Education: Prof. GEORGE CHENG CHUN WAI
Faculty of Law: Prof. ZENG LINGLIANG
Faculty of Science and Technology: Prof. PHILIP CHEN CHUN LUNG

Faculty of Social Sciences and Humanities: Prof. HAO YUFAN
Honours College: Prof. MOK KAI MENG
Institute of Chinese Medical Sciences: Prof. WANG YI TAO

Colleges

Instituto de Formação Turística (Institute for Tourism Studies): Colina de Mong-Há; tel. (853) 28561252; fax (853) 28519058; e-mail iftpr@ift.edu.mo; internet www.ift.edu.mo; f. 1995, governed by Sec. for Social Affairs and Culture of the Macao Spec. Admin. Region Govt; offers degree programmes in heritage, hospitality, tourism, tourism event and tourism retail, marketing management; Pres. Prof. FANNY VONG.

Instituto Politécnico de Macau (Macao Polytechnic Institute): Rua Luis Gonzaga Gomes; tel. (853) 28578722; fax (853) 28308801; e-mail webadmin@ipm.edu.mo; internet www.ipm.edu.mo; f. 1991; programmes in Chinese–English translation and interpretation, Chinese–Portuguese translation and interpretation, accounting and finance, computer studies, design, e-commerce, management, music, nursing and biomedical science, public administration, physical education and sports, social work, visual arts; 500 teachers; 2,800 students; Pres. Prof. LEI HEONG IOK; Vice-Pres. Prof. YIN LEI; Sec.-Gen. RAYMOND CHAN; publs *Journal of MPI* (in Chinese and English, 4 a year), *Journal of Sino-Western Cultural Studies* (2 a year).

COLOMBIA

The Higher Education System

The Roman Catholic Church pioneered higher education in Colombia, with the establishment of the Pontificia Universidad Javeriana in 1622, and remained the driving force behind universities until the 1930s. In 1994 the Educational Law (No. 115) put the Ministry of National Education in charge of public and private education. In 2002 there were an estimated 321 higher education institutes (including universities) in Colombia. In 2006/07 some 1,372,700 students were enrolled in higher education. Other university-level institutions include centros, corporaciones, escuelas, fundaciones, institutos and colegios.

Admission to higher education is on the basis of the secondary school certificate (Bachillerato) and, from March 2000, a new version of the State Higher Education Entrance Examination. The basic university degree structure consists of Licenciado (equivalent to Bachelors), Magister (Masters) and Doctorado (Doctorate) degrees. Undergraduates study for four to five years for the Licenciado or professional title. At postgraduate level the Diploma de Especialización (Diploma of Specialization) requires one to four years of study, usually in a professional or applied discipline. The Magister is awarded after two years of study following Licenciado, while a Doctorado requires two to three years of study in an area of specialization.

Public and private institutos tecnológicas (technical institutes) offer post-secondary technical and vocational education. The title Técnico Profesional Intermedio is awarded after two years of study following the Bachillerato, and a Título de Tecnólogo or a Técnico de Alto Nivel is awarded by technical institutes and some universities after three years of study. Another qualification is the Tecnólogo Especializado, which requires two years of study.

Regulatory and Representative Bodies

GOVERNMENT

Ministry of Culture: Calle 8, No 6-97, Bogotá, DC; tel. (1) 3424100; fax (1) 3421721; e-mail servicioalcliente@mincultura.gov.co; internet www.mincultura.gov.co; Minister PAULA MARCELA MORENO ZAPATA.

Ministry of National Education: Centro Administrativo Nacional (CAN), Of. 501, Calle 45, Avda El Dorado, Bogotá, DC; tel. (1) 2222800; fax (1) 2224578; e-mail dci@mineducacion.gov.co; internet www.mineducacion.gov.co; Minister CECILIA MARÍA VÉLEZ WHITE.

ACCREDITATION

Consejo Nacional de Acreditación (National Accreditation Council): Calle 19, No 6-68 Piso 17, Bogotá; tel. (1) 3411050; fax (1) 2863416; e-mail cna@cna.gov.co; internet www.cna.gov.co; f. 1992; directs and organizes the accreditation of programmes and instns; Coordinator HAROLD JOSÉ RIZO OTERO.

FUNDING

Instituto Colombiano de Crédito Educativo y Estudios Técnicos en el Exterior (ICETEX) (Colombian Institute for Educational Loans and Advanced Studies Abroad): Carrera 3A, No 18–24, Apdo Aéreo 5735, Bogotá; tel. (1) 2867780; fax (1) 2843510; f. 1950; provides undergraduate and postgraduate grants; selects Colombian students for foreign scholarships, and finances foreign postgraduate students in Colombia; information and documentation centres; library of 15,000 vols; Dir Dr CARLOS A. BURITICÁ GIRALDO.

NATIONAL BODIES

Asociación Colombiana de Universidades (Colombian Universities Association): Calle 93, No 16–43, Bogotá; tel. (1) 6231580; fax (1) 2185098; e-mail ascun@ascun.org.co; internet www.ascun.org.co; f. 1957; Pres. Monseñor LUIS FERNANDO RODRÍGUEZ VELÁSQUEZ; Sec.-Gen. Dr CARLOS HERNANDO FORERO ROBAYO.

Instituto Colombiano para el Fomento de la Educación Superior (ICFES) (Colombian Institute for the Promotion of Higher Education): Calle 17, No 3–40, Bogotá; tel. (1) 3387338; e-mail direcciondelicfes@icfes.gov.co; internet www.icfes.gov.co; attached to Min. of Nat. Education; assesses the Colombian educational system at all levels; implements policies to promote higher education and assessment; promotes the devt of research in higher education instns; Dir MARGARITA PEÑA BORRERREO; Gen. Sec. GENISBERTO LÓPEZ CONDE.

Learned Societies

GENERAL

Academia Colombiana de la Lengua (Colombian Academy): Apdo Aereo 13922, Bogotá; f. 1871; corresp. of the Real Academia Española (Madrid); 29 mems; 50 corresp. and hon. mems; library of 40,000 vols; Dir JAIME POSADA DÍAZ; Exec. Sec. JAIME BERNAL LEONGÓMEZ; publ. Boletín.

Casa de la Cultura de la Costa (House of Caribbean Coast Culture): Carrera 3, No 19–60, Of. 401, Bogotá; tel. (1) 2433898; f. 1981; study centre for devt of the Colombian coastal regions and int. Caribbean studies; 36 companies and individuals, 86 congressmen from the coast; library of 2,000 vols; Pres. MARCO ANTONIO CONTRERAS; Sec. GERARDO MORA MEDINA; publ. Revista Caribe Internacional (12 a year).

AGRICULTURE, FISHERIES AND VETERINARY SCIENCE

Sociedad de Agricultores de Colombia (Colombian Farmers' Society): Carrera 7, No 24–89, 44° piso, Apdo Aéreo 3638, Bogotá; tel. (1) 2821989; fax (1) 2844572; internet www.sac.org.co; f. 1871; consultative body for the Govt; 400 mems; library of 5,500 vols, 435 periodical titles; Pres. RAFAEL MEJIA LÓPEZ; Sec. RICARDO SÁNCHEZ LÓPEZ; publs Documentos Independientes, El Editorial Agrario (irregular), Revista Nacional de Agricultura (4 a year).

BIBLIOGRAPHY, LIBRARY SCIENCE AND MUSEOLOGY

Asociación Colombiana de Bibliotecarios (ASCOLBI) (Colombian Association of Librarians): Calle 10, No 3–16, Apdo Aéreo 30883, Bogotá; tel. (1) 2694219; f. 1942; 1,200 mems; Pres. SAUL SANCHEZ TORO; Gen. Sec. B. N. CARDONA DE GIL; publ. Boletín (4 a year).

Centro Regional para el Fomento del Libro en América Latina y el Caribe (CERLALC) (Regional Centre for the Promotion of Books in Latin America and the Caribbean): Calle 70, No 9–52, Apdo Aéreo 57348, Bogotá; tel. (1) 3217501; fax (1) 3217503; internet www.cerlalc.com; f. 1972, by UNESCO and Colombian Govt, later joined by most states in the area; promotes production and circulation of books, and devt of libraries; provides training; promotes protection of copyright; 21 mem. countries; library of 5,600 documents, 100 periodicals; Dir ALMA BYINGTON DE ARBOLEDA; publs Boletín Informativo CERLALC (4 a year), El Libro en América Latina y el Caribe (4 a year).

Fundación para el Fomento de la Lectura—(FUNDALECTURA): Dg 40A bis No 16–46, Apdo 48902, Bogotá; tel. (1) 3201511; fax (1) 2877071; e-mail contactenos@fundalectura.org.co; internet www.fundalectura.org; f. 1984; promotes reading, and children's and juvenile literature; library of 40,200 vols; Dir CARMEN BARVO; publs Nuevas Hojas de Lectura (3 a year), Revista Latinoamericana de Literatura Infantil y Juvenil (2 a year, online at www.relalij.com).

ECONOMICS, LAW AND POLITICS

Academia Colombiana de Jurisprudencia (Colombian Academy of Jurisprudence): Carrera 9 No 74–08, Oficina 203, Bogotá; tel. (1) 2124315; f. 1894; 50 mems; Pres. HERNANDO MORALES M.; publs Anuario, Revista (2 a year).

Sociedad Colombiana de Economistas: Carrera 20 No 36–41, Apdo Aéreo 8429,

Bogotá; tel. (1) 2459637; f. 1957; promotes improvement of the teaching of economic sciences and economics as a profession, for the economic and social devt of the country; 5,500 mems; library of 25,000 vols; Pres. Dr Sergio Entrena López; publ. *Revista* (6 a year).

HISTORY, GEOGRAPHY AND ARCHAEOLOGY

Academia Antioqueña de Historia (Antioquia Academy of History): Carrera 43, No 53–37, Apdo Aéreo 7175, Medellín; tel. (942) 395576; f. 1903; 60 mems; Pres. Jaime Sierra Garcia; Sec. Alicia Giraldo Gómez; publs *Bolsilibros, Repertorio Histórico* (3 a year).

Academia Boyacense de Historia (Boyaca Academy of History): Casa del Fundador, Tunja; tel. (9792) 3441; f. 1905; publication and encouragement of historical, literary and anthropological studies in Boyaca; 30 mems; library of 1,000 vols, 600 MSS from the period 1539–1860; Pres. Javier Ocampo Lopez; Sec. Ramón Correa; publ. *Repertorio Boyacense* (2 a year).

Academia Colombiana de Historia (Colombian Academy of History): Calle 10 No 8–95, Apdo Aéreo 14428, Bogotá; f. 1902; 40 mems, excluding Colombian and foreign corresp. mems; library of 45,000 vols; Pres. Dr Germán Arciniegas; Sec. Roberto Velandia; Library Dir Dr Rafael Serrano Camargo; publ. *Boletín de Historia y Antigüedades*.

Academia de la Historia de Cartagena de Indias (Cartagena Academy of History): Casa de la Inquisición, Plaza Bolívar, Cartagena; tel. (59) 645432; f. 1918; spec. collns on history of Cartagena and Colombia; 24 mems, and 48 Colombian and 48 foreign corresponding mems; library of 10,000 vols; Pres. Leon Trujillo Velez; Sec.-Gen. Jorge Perz Villa; publ. *Boletín Historial* (4 a year).

Sociedad Bolivariana de Colombia: Calle 19A, No 4–40E, Apdo 11812, Bogotá; tel. (1) 2431166; f. 1924; 20 hon. mems; library of 1,000 vols, specialized bibliography on Simón Bolívar; Pres. Col Alberto Lozano; publ. *Revista Bolivariana* (3 a year).

Sociedad Geográfica de Colombia (Colombian Geographical Society): Observatorio Astronómico Nacional, Apdo 2584, Bogotá; tel. (1) 2348893; f. 1903; 40 mems; Pres. Clemente Garavito; Sec. Rafael Convers Pinzon; publs *Boletín* (3 a year), *Cuadernos de Geografía Colombiana*; branch socs in Barranquilla, Medellín, Pasto, Sibundoy, Tunja.

LANGUAGE AND LITERATURE

Alliance Française: Carrera 7A, No 84–72, Bogotá; tel. (1) 2563197; fax (1) 6556045; e-mail alfradir@neutel.com.co; internet www .alianzafrancesa.org.co; offers courses and examinations in French language and culture and promotes cultural exchange with France; attached teaching offices in Armenia, Barranquilla, Bogatá-Centro, Bucuramanga, Cali, Cartagena, Manizales, Medellín, Pereira, Popayán and Santa Marta.

British Council: Carrera 9, No 76–49, piso 5, Bogotá DC; tel. (1) 3259090; fax (1) 3259091; e-mail customer.services@ britishcouncil.org.co; internet www .britishcouncil.org/colombia; offers courses and examinations in English language and British culture and promotes cultural exchange with the UK; separate teaching centre in Bogotá; library of 7,500 vols, 60 periodicals; Dir Robert Ness.

Goethe-Institut: Carrera 7, No 81–57, Bogotá; tel. (1) 2547600; fax (1) 2127167; e-mail vl@bogota.goethe.org; internet www .goethe.de/hn/bog/deindex.htm; offers courses and examinations in German language and culture and promotes cultural exchange with Germany; Dir Katja Kessing.

Instituto Caro y Cuervo: Carrera 10, No 4–69, Apdo Aéreo 51502, Bogotá; tel. (1) 3422121; fax (1) 2170243; e-mail contactenos@caroycuervo.gov.co; internet www.caroycuervo.gov.co; f. 1942; attached to Min. of Culture; Hispanic philology and literature; library of 102,491 vols, 102,000 vols of periodicals; Dir Hernando Cabarcas Antequera; Sec.-Gen. Liliana Rivera Orjuela; publs *Aguas Vivas, Anuario Bibliográfico Colombiano, Archivo Epistolar Colombiano, Atlas Lingüístico-Etnográfico de Colombia, Biblioteca de Publicaciones del Instituto, Biblioteca Colombiana, Biblioteca 'Ezequiel Uricoechea', Clásicos Colombianos, Cuadernos del Seminario Andrés Bello, Diccionario de Construcción y Régimen de la Lengua Castellana, Filólogos Colombianos, La Granada Entreabierta, Litterae, Noticias Culturales* (6 a year), *Poesia Rescatada, Thesaurus* (3 a year).

PEN Internacional, Colombia: Calle 88, 11A-20, Apdo 302, Bogotá; tel. (1) 6919627; e-mail pencolombia@cable.net.co; f. 1936; 50 mems; library of 1,000 vols; Pres. Emeritus Dr Cecilia Balcázar; Pres. Enrique Santos-Molano; Sec.-Gen. Prof. Rubén Darío Flórez.

MEDICINE

Academia Nacional de Medicina de Colombia (Colombian National Academy of Medicine): Carrera 7, No 69–05, Bogotá; tel. (1) 3458890; fax (1) 2128670; e-mail acadmed@cable.net.co; internet www .fepafem.org/anm; f. 1873; 557 mems; library of 10,000 vols; Pres. Dr Juan Mendoza-Vega; Perm. Sec. Dr Hernando Groot; publs *Medicina* (4 a year), *Temas Médicos* (1 a year).

Asociación Colombiana de Facultades de Medicina—ASCOFAME (Colombian Association of Medical Faculties): Carrera 14, No 101–53, Barrio Rincón de Chicó, Bogotá; tel. (1) 7425380; fax (1) 7425386; e-mail ascofame@ascofame.org.co; internet www.ascofame.org.co; f. 1959; furthers higher education and research in medicine; divs of education, evaluation, health and social security, information; 24 medical faculties (institutional mems), 4,500 individuals, 7 affiliated mems; library of 3,500 vols, 100 periodicals and audiovisual materials; Pres. Jose Maria Maya; Exec. Dir Julio Enrique Ospina; publs *Boletín del Centro de Etica Médica y Bioética, Boletín de Medicamentos y Terapéutica* (4 a year), *Cuadernos de Actualización Médica Permanente, Gaceta Médica, Revista de ASCOFAME*.

Asociación Colombiana de Fisioterapia: Carrera 23 No. 47–51, Of. 3N-06-D, Bogotá; tel. (1) 2876106; f. 1953; 950 mems; library of 300 vols; Pres. Elisa Jaramillo de Lopez; Exec. Sec. Clara Ines de Amaya; publ. *Revista* (1 a year).

Asociación Colombiana de Psiquiatría: Carrera 18 No. 84–87, Oficina 403, Bogotá; tel. (1) 2561148; fax (1) 2563549; e-mail acp@ psiquiatria.org.co; internet www.psiquiatria .org.co; f. 1961; 854 mems; Pres. Dr Carlos Alberto Miranda Bastidas; Sec. Dr Ramón Eduardo Lopera Lopea; publs *Cuadernos de Psiquiatría Enlace* (4 a year), *Revista Colombiana de Psiquiatría* (4 a year).

Asociación Colombiana de Sociedades Científicas: Carrera 14, No 127–10, Oficina 206, Bogotá; tel. (1) 6481928; fax (1) 6335961; e-mail sociedadsc@col.net.co; internet www .sociedadescientificas.com; f. 1957; present name 1970; health sciences; 3,692 mems;

Exec. Dir Dr Fabio Loaiza D.; publ. *Boletín* (4 a year).

Capitolo Colombiano de las Federaciones Latinoamericanas de Asociaciones de Cancer (Colombian Chapter of Latin American Cancer Asscns): Clínica del Country, Carrera 15 No. 84–13, Bogotá; tel. (1) 2361168; f. 1983; Pres. Calixto Noguera.

Federación Médica Colombiana: Carrera 7, No 82–66, Oficinas 218/219, Bogotá; fax (1) 8050073; e-mail federacionmedicacolombiana@encolombia .com; internet www.encolombia.com/ federamedicolom.htm; f. 1935; Pres. Dr Sergio Isaza Villa; Sec. Sergio Robleda Riaga; publ. *Directorio Médico Asistencial* (1 a year).

Instituto Nacional de Medicina Legal y Ciencias Forenses (National Institute of Legal Medicine and Forensic Sciences): Calle 7a, A 12–61, Santafé de Bogotá; tel. (1) 233854; f. 1914; staff of 800; library of 30,000 vols; Dir Ricardo Mora Izquierdo; publ. *Revista*.

Sociedad Colombiana de Cardiología (Colombian Cardiological Society): Avda 19, No 97–31, Of. 401, Apdo Aéreo 1875, Bogotá; tel. and fax (1) 6234603; f. 1950; 245 mems; Pres. Dr Ricardo Rozo Uribe; Sec. Dra Margarita Blanco de Escobar; publ. *Revista SCC* (4 a year).

Sociedad Colombiana de Cirugía Ortopédica y Traumatología: Calle 134 No. 7B-83, Oficina 201, Bogotá; tel. (1) 6257445; fax (1) 6257417; e-mail secretaria@sccot.org.co; internet www.sccot.org.co; f. 1946; 961 mems; Pres. Dr Nicolás Restrepo; Gen. Sec. Dr Fernando Helo; publ. *Carta de Ortopédica* (12 a year).

Sociedad Colombiana de Obstetricia y Ginecología: Carrera 23, No. 39–82, Apdo Aéreo 34188, Bogotá; tel. (1) 2681485; f. 1943; 300 mems; library of 1,000 vols; Pres. Dr Jaime Ferro Camargo; Vice-Pres. Dra Maria Teresa Peralta Abello; Sec.-Gen. Dr Pio Iván Gómez Sánchez; publ. *Revista Colombiana de Obstetricia y Ginecología* (4 a year).

Sociedad Colombiana de Patología: Dpto de Patología, Universidad del Valle, Cali; f. 1955; to improve all aspects of pathology studies; 155 mems; Pres. Dr Edgar Duque; Sec. and Treas. Dr José A. Dorado.

Sociedad Colombiana de Pediatría (Colombian Paediatrics Society): Avdo 4 Norte, No. 16–23, Apdo 3124, Cali; tel. (2) 611407; fax (2) 673614; f. 1917; 150 mems; library of 2,300 vols; Pres. Cesar A. Villamizar Luna; Sec. Alberto Levy F.; publs *Acta Pediatrica Colombiana, Pediatría* (4 a year).

Sociedad Colombiana de Radiología (Radiological Society): Carrera 13a No. 90–18, Of. 208, Bogotá; tel. (1) 6183895; fax (1) 6183775; f. 1945; 400 mems; library of 3,000 vols, collections of journals; Pres. Cayo Duarte; Sec. Patricia Castro S.

NATURAL SCIENCES
General

Academia Colombiana de Ciencias Exactas, Físicas y Naturales (Colombian Academy of Exact, Physical and Natural Sciences): Carrera 28a, No. 39A–63, Apdo Aéreo 44763, Bogotá DC; tel. (1) 2683290; fax (1) 2443486; internet www.accefyn.org.co; f. 1933; 40 active mems (98 corresp., 6 hon.); Pres. Jaime Rodriguez Lara; Sec. José A. Lozano; publ. *Revista* (4 a year).

Biological Sciences

Sociedad Colombiana de Biología: Calle 73, No 10–10, Apartamento 301, Bogotá; Pres. Dr Gonzalo Montes; Sec. Margaret Ordóñez Smith.

Mathematical Sciences

Sociedad Colombiana de Matemáticas: Apdo Aéreo 2521, Bogotá 1; tel. (1) 3165000; f. 1955; 800 mems; library of 7,000 vols; Pres. LEONARDO RENDÓN ARBELÁEZ; publs *Lecturas Matemáticas*, *Revista Colombiana de Matemáticas*.

Physical Sciences

Sociedad Colombiana de Ciencias Químicas: Univ. Nacional de Colombia, sede, Unidad Camilo Torres, Bloque C Modulo 7, Oficina 202, Bogotá; tel. (1) 2216920; fax (1) 3150751; e-mail info@socolquim.com; internet www.socolquim.com; f. 1941; promotes chemical research in Colombia; upholds professional ethical standards; serves as an advisory body for public and private orgs, to maintain relations with similar instns at home and abroad; 350 mems; Pres. FABIAN PARADA ALFONSO; Vice-Pres. BARBARA MORENO MURILLO; Sec. MYRIAM MUNOZ; Treas. CESAR SIERRA AVILA; publ. *Química e Industria* (2 a year).

TECHNOLOGY

Asociación Colombiana de Industrias Gráficas—ANDIGRAF (Graphic Industry National Association): Carrera 4a No. 25B–46, Apdo Aéreo 45243, Bogotá; tel. (1) 2819611; f. 1975; 200 company mems; Pres. JOSE GRANADA RODRIGUEZ; publs *Boletín Informativo* (12 a year), *Colombia Gráfica* (1 a year).

Asociación Colombiana de Informática y Comunicaciones (Colombian Association of Information Technology and Communication): Avda Estación 5B Norte, 73 Oficina 205, Santiago de Cali; tel. (2) 6675595; e-mail acvcsurocci@telesat.com.co; internet www .acvc.org.co; f. 1970; 400 company mems; library of 1,500 documents; Pres. JOSE GUILLERMO JARAMILLO G.; Exec. Dir CESAR AUGUSTO SALAZAR U.; publs *ACUC Noticias* (6 a year), *Boletín El Usuario* (52 a year), *Catálogo Nacional de Software—Guía de Servicios Informáticos* (1 a year).

Sociedad Colombiana de Ingenieros (Colombian Society of Engineers): Carrera 4, No. 10–41, Apdo 340, Bogotá; tel. (1) 2862200; fax (1) 2816229; f. 1887; 2,000 mems; library of 5,000 vols; Pres. HERNANDO MONROY VALENCIA; Exec. Dir SANTIAGO HENAO PÉREZ; publ. *Anales de Ingeniería* (4 a year).

Research Institutes

GENERAL

Instituto Colombiano para el Desarrollo de la Ciencia y la Tecnología 'Francisco José de Caldas' (Colciencias): Transversal 9a No. 133–28, Apdo Aéreo 051580, Santafé de Bogotá; tel. (1) 2169800; fax (1) 6251788; f. 1968 to promote scientific and technical development; coordinates and finances projects; library of 15,000 vols, 225 periodicals, 10,000 databases; Dir LUIS FERNANDO CHAPARRO OSORIO; Sec.-Gen. JUAN RICARDO MORALES ESPINEL; publs serials: *Carta de Colciencias* (12 a year), *Colombia Ciencia y Tecnología* (4 a year).

AGRICULTURE, FISHERIES AND VETERINARY SCIENCE

Instituto Colombiano Agropecuario (Colombian Agricultural and Livestock Institute): Apdo Aéreo 7984, Calle 37 No. 8–43 (4° y 5° pisos), Bogotá; tel. (1) 2855520; fax (1) 2884169; internet www.iica-saninet/ica/ica .htm; f. 1962 to promote, coordinate and carry out research, teaching and develop-

ment in agriculture and animal husbandry; library: see Libraries and Archives; Dir-Gen. ALVARO JOSÉ ABISAMBRA ABISAMBRA; publ. *Informe Anual*.

ECONOMICS, LAW AND POLITICS

Centro de Estudios sobre Desarrollo Económico (Centre for Economic Development Studies): Universidad de los Andes, Carrera 1E No. 18A–10, Apdo Aéreo 4976, Bogotá; tel. (1) 3324495; fax (1) 3324492; e-mail infocede@uniandes.edu.co; internet economia.uniandes.edu.co; f. 1958; library of 35,000 vols; Dir ROBERTO STEINER; publ. *Desarrollo y Sociedad* (2 a year).

Departamento Administrativo Nacional de Estadística (National Statistics Department): Transversal 45 No. 26–70 Interior 1 CAN, Apdo Aéreo 80043, Bogotá; tel. (1) 5978300; fax (1) 5978384; e-mail dane@dane .gov.co; internet www.dane.gov.co; f. 1953; library of 12,000 vols, 850 periodicals received; Dir CÉSAR AUGUSTO CABALLERO REINOSO; publs *Anuario de Comercio Exterior* (1 a year), *Anuario de Industria Manufacturera* (1 a year), *Atlas Sociodemográfico de Colombia*, *Bases de Contabilidad*, *Boletín Mensual de Estadística* (12 a year), *Colombia Estadística*, *Cuentas Nacionales de Colombia*, *DIVIPOLA*, *Estudios Censales*, *Indicadores de Coyuntura*, *Metodología Cuentas Departamentales*, *Mujeres con Hijos Habitantes de la Calle*, *Plan Estadístico de Cundinamarca*.

EDUCATION

Centro de Investigación y Educación Popular: Carrera 5 No 33A-08, Apdo 25916, Bogotá; tel. (1) 2858977; fax (1) 2879089; f. 1962; private, non-profit org. specializing in social sciences education, and analysis of the Colombian system; library of 25,000 vols; Dir Dr MAURICIO GARCIA-DURAN; publs *Cien Días* (4 a year), *Controversia* (2 a year).

Instituto Colombiano para el Fomento de la Educación Superior: Calle 17 No. 3–40, Apdo Aéreo 6319, Bogotá; tel. (1) 2819311; fax (1) 2868045; e-mail snies@icfes .gov.co; f. 1968; branch of the Min. of National Education; govt body supervising the running of higher education; coordinates the country's distance education system; library: documentation centre specializing in higher, distance and 'open' education, and nat. film colln: 9,200 vols, 2,500 documents, 2,527 periodicals, 1,015 films, audiovisual items and video cassettes; Dir LUIS CARLOS MUÑOZ URIBE; publs *Estadísticas de la Educación Superior*, *Memorias de Eventos Científicos*, *Revista ICFES* (irregular).

HISTORY, GEOGRAPHY AND ARCHAEOLOGY

Instituto Colombiano de Antropología e Historia (Colombian Institute of Anthropology and History): Calle 12 No. 2–41, Apdo Aéreo 407, Bogotá; tel. (1) 3418849; fax (1) 2811051; f. 1941; research in fields of history, archaeology and anthropology; oversees cultural, archaeological and anthropological patrimony of Colombia, and administers national archaeological parks; publishes editions of 'Flora of the Botanic Expedition' of the New Kingdom of Granada; library of 30,000 vols (open to public); Dir MARÍA VICTORIA URIBE-ALARCÓN; publs *Fronteras de la Historia* (1 a year), *Revista Colombiana de Antropología* (1 a year).

Instituto Geográfico 'Agustín Codazzi': Apdo 6721, Carrera 30 No. 48–51, Santafé de Bogotá; tel. (1) 3694053; fax (1) 3694099; e-mail webpage@igac.gov.co; internet www .igac.gov.co; f. 1935; prepares topographical,

cadastral, sectional, national, and agricultural maps of the country, and geophysical, cadastral and geodetic surveys; prepares geographical studies of Colombia; library of 10,000 vols; Dir IVAN DARIO GOMEZ GUZMÁN.

MEDICINE

Instituto Nacional de Cancerología: Calle 1, No. 9–85, Bogotá 1; tel. (1) 3342474; fax (1) 3341844; e-mail biblioteca@ incancerologia.gov.co; internet www .incancerologia.gov.co; f. 1934; diagnosis, therapy, control, teaching and research in cancer; adviser instn to Min. of Health, designs and implements national policies and programmes to control the spread of cancer; library of 26,000 vols; Dir-Gen. CARLOS VICENTE RADA ESCOBAR; publ. *Revista Colombiana de Cancerología*.

Instituto Nacional de Salud (National Institute of Health): Avda el Dorado Carrera 50, Apdo Aéreo 80334, Bogotá; tel. (1) 2221059; fax (1) 2220194; f. 1968; library of 10,000 vols, 500 periodicals; Dir Dr MOISES WASSERMAN; publs *Biomédica*, *Boletín Epidemiológico*, *Informe Quincenal de Casos y Brotes de Enfermedades* (26 a year).

NATURAL SCIENCES

Biological Sciences

Instituto de Ciencias Naturales (Institute of Natural Sciences): Universidad Nacional de Colombia, Apdo 7495, Bogotá; tel. (1) 3165305; fax (1) 3165365; e-mail inscien_bog@unal.edu.co; internet www.icn .unal.edu.co; f. 1936; 11 groups of research; library of 8,000 vols; Dir Dr JAIME AGUIRRE; publs *Biblioteca José Jerónimo Triana*, *Caldasia*, *Colombia Diversidad Biotica*, *Fauna de Colombia*, *Flora de Colombia*.

Instituto de Investigaciones Marinas y Costeras 'José Benito Vives de Andreis' (INVEMAR): Apdo Aéreo 1016, Santa Marta; tel. (327) 211380; fax (327) 211377; e-mail bibliote@invemar.org.co; internet www.invemar.org.co; f. 1963; institute of Colciencias (*q.v.*); aims to study and preserve the marine wildlife of the Colombian Caribbean; library of 8,850 vols; Dir Dr FRANCISCO ARMANDO ARIAS ISAZA; publ. *Anales*.

Physical Sciences

Observatorio Astronómico Nacional (National Astronomical Observatory): Carrera 8, Calle 8, Apdo Aéreo 2584, Bogotá; tel. (1) 2423786; f. 1803; library of 3,000 vols; Dir JORGE ARRAS DE GREIFF; publs *Anuario del Observatorio*, occasional publications.

TECHNOLOGY

Instituto Colombiano de Geologia y Mineria (INGEOMINAS) (Institute for Research and Information in the Geosciences, Mining, the Environment and Nuclear Physics): Diagonal 53, No 34–53, Apdo Aéreo 4865, Bogotá; tel. (1) 2221811; fax (1) 2220797; internet www.ingeominas .gov.co; f. 1940 as Nat. Geological Survey, present name 1969; library of 6,000 books, 104 current periodicals, 2,400 technical reports; Dir Dr JULIAN VILLARRUEL TORO; publs *Boletín de Actividad Sismica*, *Boletin de Vocanes Colombianos*, *Boletín Geológico* (3 vols, 1 a year), *Informe de Actividades Anuales*, *Revista Ingeominas*.

Instituto Colombiano de Normas Técnicas y Certificación (ICONTEC): Carrera 37, No. 52–95, Bogotá; tel. (1) 6078888; fax (1) 2221435; e-mail cliente@icontec.org .co; internet www.icontec.org.co; f. 1963; 1,200 mems; library of 800,000 vols; Exec. Dir Ing. FABIO TOBÓN; Admin. Dir RICARDO TOBO; publ. *Normas y Calidad* (4 a year).

Instituto Colombiano del Petróleo (Colombian Petroleum Institute): Autopista Piedecuesta Km 7, Apdo Aereo 4185, Bucaramanga; tel. (57) 76445420; fax (57) 76445444; internet www.icp.ecopetrol.com .co; exploration and development of oil reserves; library of 19,000 vols, 500 periodicals and newspapers, 1,000 audiovisual items, 8,000 documents; Dir JAIME CADAVID CALVO; publ. *GT & F Magazine*.

Instituto de Ciencias Nucleares y Energías Alternativas (Institute for Nuclear Sciences and Alternative Energy): Avda Eldorado, Carrera 50, Apdo Aéreo 8595, Santafé de Bogotá, DC; tel. (1) 2220071; fax (1) 2220173; f. 1959 to study the application of atomic and nuclear energy for peaceful uses, devt of alternative energy sources and efficient use of energy; library of 18,000 vols, 60 periodicals, 70,000 reprints, 120,000 microforms; Dir Dr CESAR HUMBERTO ARIAS PABON.

Libraries and Archives

Barranquilla

Biblioteca Pública Departamental Meira Delmar: Calla 38, No. 38B–21, Barranquilla; tel. (95) 3307020; e-mail baguilar@ atlantico.gov.co; internet www.cultura .atlantico.gov.co/biblioteca.asp; f. 1923; 40,000 vols; Dir BEATRIZ EUGENIA AGUILAR CADAVID.

Bello

Biblioteca del Marco Fidel Suárez: Avda Suárez, Bello, Antioquia; tel. (942) 750774; f. 1957; public library and regional centre; 2,615 vols; Dir WALTER GIL.

Bogotá

Archivo Nacional de Colombia: Archivo General de la Nación, Calle 24 No. 5–60, 4° piso, Bogotá; tel. (1) 416015; f. 1868; 40,600 vols and 3,135 metres of documents; Dir JORGE PALACIOS PRECIADO; publs *Catálogos, Revista.*

Biblioteca Agropecuaria de Colombia: Inst. Colombiano Agropecuario, Apdo Aéreo 240142, Santafé de Bogotá; tel. (1) 3443000 ext. 1253; fax (1) 3443000 ext. 1248; e-mail fsalazar@corpoica.org.co; internet www .corpoica.org.co; f. 1954; 46,000 vols devoted to agriculture and livestock, 46,300 pamphlets, 1,900 journals, 29,560 documents, 170 maps, 150 audiovisual titles, 497 audio cassettes; Dir FRANCISCO SALAZAR ALONSO.

Biblioteca Central de la Pontificia Universidad Javeriana: Carrera 7a, No. 41–00, Bogotá; tel. (1) 3208320 ext. 2132; fax (1) 2850973; f. 1931; 287,000 vols; Dir LUZ MARIA CABARCAS SANTOYA.

Biblioteca 'Luis-Angel Arango' del Banco de la República (Bank of the Republic Library): Carrera 5 No. 11–68, Apdo Aéreo 3531, Bogotá; tel. (1) 3431202; fax (1) 2863551; e-mail wbiblio@banrep.gov .co; internet www.lablaa.org; f. 1932; includes Museo Botero and Museo de Artes del Banco de la Republica; 1,050,000 vols, 23,000 periodicals, 14,000 maps, 102,000 slides, 4,000 original works of art, 25,000 sound recordings, 9,000 video recordings; Dir JORGE ORLANDO MELO; publ. *Boletín Cultural y Bibliográfico* (3 a year).

Biblioteca Nacional de Colombia (National Library): Calle 24, No. 5–60, Apdo 27600, Bogotá; tel. (1) 3414029; fax (1) 3414030; f. 1777; 800,000 vols, 22,000 periodicals; rare book section (28,000 vols); Dir CARLOS JOSÉ REYES POSADA; publ. *Revista Senderos.*

Biblioteca Seminario Conciliar de San José (Library of the San José Seminary): Carrera 7 No. 94–80, Bogotá 8; tel. (1) 6440405; fax (1) 2181096; e-mail semmayorbogota@hotmail.com; internet www.seminariobogota.org; f. 1581; 40,000 vols specializing in philosophy and theology; Dir Rev. CESAR BARACALDO VEGA.

Dirección de Bibliotecas—Sede Bogotá, Universidad Nacional de Colombia: Ciudad Universitaria, Apdo Aéreo 14490, Santafé de Bogotá; tel. and fax (1) 3165000; e-mail jensanchezsal@unal.edu.co; internet www.sinab.unal.edu.co/bog; f. 1867; 900,000 vols; Dir JENNIFER SÁNCHEZ SALAZAR.

División de Documentación e Información Educativa, Ministerio de Educación Nacional (Educational Documentation and Information Division, Ministry of National Education): Avda El Dorado, CAN, Bogotá; tel. (1) 222800; coordinates the Educational Documentation and Information Sub-system, the School Libraries National Programme and runs the National Educational Documentation Centre; 10,000 vols, 300 pamphlets, 6,000 documents, 300 periodicals; Dir MARY LUZ ISAZA; publs *Correo Educativo, Memorias del Ministro de Educación al Congreso Nacional* (1 a year).

Cali

Biblioteca Centenario: Avda Colombia Cl. 4 Oeste, Calí; tel. (2) 8932908; f. 1910; 22,000 vols; Dir ORIETTA LOZANO.

Biblioteca Departamental de Calí: Calle 14 Norte No 9–45, Calí; tel. (2) 6613018; fax (2) 6618214; 54,000 vols; Dir ELISA INÉS ARBOLEDA MAYORK.

Cartagena

Centro de Información y Documentación Biblioteca Fernández de Madrid, Universidad de Cartagena: Centro Cerrera 6, No. 36–100, Cartagena; tel. (95) 6646182; fax (95) 6697778; f. 1827; 50,000 vols; Librarian LUIS EDUARDO ESPINAL A.

Manizales

Biblioteca Central, Universidad de Caldas: Apdo Aéreo 275, Calle 65 No. 26-10, Manizales, Caldas; tel. (968) 861250 ext. 115; fax (968) 862520; internet biblio.ucaldas.edu .co; f. 1958; 53,000 vols, 5,500 documents, 1,300 periodicals; Librarian SAUL SANCHEZ TORO; publs *HIPSIPILA – Revista Cultural de la Universidad* (2 a year), *Revista de Agronomía* (4 a year), *Revista de Educación Física y Recreación* (2 a year), *Revista de Medicina Veterinaria y Zootecnia* (2 a year), *Revista de la Universidad de Caldas* (2 a year).

Biblioteca Pública Municipal: Calle 23 No. 20–30, Manizales; tel. (968) 831697; f. 1931; 8,100 vols; Librarian NELLY AGUIRRE DE FIGUEROA.

Medellín

Biblioteca de la Universidad Pontificia Bolivariana: Apdo Aéreo 56006, Medellín; tel. (4) 4159075; fax (4) 4118513; internet biblio.upb.edu.co; f. 1936; 139,000 vols, 3,000 periodicals, 12,779 pamphlets, 150,000 audiovisual records; Librarian Lic. OLGA BEATRIZ BERNAL LONDOÑO; publs *Comunicación UPB, Cuestiones Teológicas, Revista de la Facultad de Derecho y Ciencias Políticas, Revista de la Facultad de Filosofía, Revista de la Facultad de Medicina, Revista de la Facultad de Trabajo Social, Revista Universidad Pontificia Bolivariana.*

Biblioteca Pública Piloto de Medellín (Pilot Public Library of Medellín): Carrera 64 con Calle 50 No. 50–32, Apdo Aéreo 1797, Medellín; tel. (4) 2302422; fax (4) 2305389; f. 1954 under the auspices of UNESCO; 85,000 vols; spec. collns: Antioquia and Antioquian authors, UNESCO depository; Dir GLORIA INES PALOMINO L.

Departamento de Bibliotecas, Universidad de Antioquia: Apdo Aéreo 1226, Medellín; tel. (4) 2105140; fax (4) 2116939; internet biblioteca.udea.edu.co; f. 1935; 13 br. libraries; 662,000 vols, 7,000 periodicals; Dir NORA HELENA LÓPEZ CALLE; publs *Ex-Libris* (4 a year), *Leer y Releer* (4 a year).

Popayán

Departamento de Bibliotecas, Universidad del Cauca: Apdo Nacional 113, Calle 5 No 4–70, Popayán; tel. (2) 8209800; internet biblio.unicauca.edu.co; f. 1827; 70,000 vols; Dir JOSÉ MARÍA SERRANO PRADA; publs *Catálogo del Archivo Central del Cauca, Boletín Bibliográfico, Boletín Informativo, Cuadernos de Medicina, Boletín del Comité de Investigaciones Científicas, Revista Cátedra.*

Tunja

Universidad Pedagógica y Tecnológica de Colombia, Biblioteca Central, Tunja: Apdo Aéreo 1234, Tunja; tel. (98) 400668; f. 1932; 68,000 vols; 1,800 periodical titles; spec. collns: theses, Fondo E. Posada, rare books, learned works; Dir BARBARA MARTIN MARTIN; publs *Lista de Canje, Apuntes del CENES, Educación y Ciencia, Cuadernos de Lingüística hispánica-UPTC, Agricultura y Ciencia, Perspectiva Proceso Salud-Enfermedad, Inquietud Empresarial, Revista Facultad de Ingeniería, Revista de Ciencias Sociales.*

Museums and Art Galleries

Bogotá

Casa Museo 'Jorge Eliécer Gaitán': Calle 42, No. 15–23, Bogotá; tel. (1) 2450368; fax (1) 2879093; f. 1948; collection relating to the history of Bogotá; run by the Centro Jorge Eliécer Gaitán; Dir GLORIA GAITÁN.

Casa Museo Quinta de Bolívar (Bolívar Museum): Calle 20, No. 2–91 Este, Bogotá; tel. (1) 3366419; fax (1) 3366410; e-mail quintadebolivar@excite.com; f. 1919 in the country house occupied by Simón Bolívar from 1820 to 1830, where relics of the Liberator and his epoch are exhibited; is administered by the Ministry of Culture and the Sociedad de Mejoras y Ornato de Bogotá; Dir DANIEL CASTRO BENÍTEZ.

Jardín Botánico de Bogotá 'José Celestino Mutis': Calle 63 No. 68–95, Bogotá; tel. (1) 4377060; fax (1) 6305075; e-mail bogotanico@jbb.gov.co; internet www.jbb.gov .co; f. 1955; research and conservation of biodiversity in the Andean ecosystem; library of 6,000 vols; Dir HERMAN MARTÍNEZ GÓMEZ; Gen. Sec EDNA PATRICIA RANGEL BARRAGÁN; publ. *Pérez-Arbelaezia* (2 a year).

Museo Colonial (Museum of the Colonial Period): Carrera 6, No. 9–77, Bogotá; tel. (1) 3416017; fax (1) 2866768; e-mail colonial@ mincultura.gov.co; f. 1942; paintings, sculpture, furniture, gold and silver work, drawings, etc., of the Spanish colonial period (16th, 17th and 18th centuries); library of 1,000 vols in education dept; installed in a building erected by the Jesuits in 1604 to house the first Javeriana University; Dir CONSTANZA TOQUICA CLAVIJO; publ. *Cuadernos de Estudio* (1 a year).

Museo del Oro (Gold Museum): Calle 16, No 5–41, Parque de Santander, Bogotá; tel. (1)

3431414; fax (1) 2847450; e-mail wmuseo@
banrep.gov.co; internet www.banrep.gov.co/
museo/home.htm; f. 1939; 36,000 pre-Columbian gold objects representing the gods,
myths and customs of the Quimbaya, Muisca,
Tairona and other native Indian cultures;
Dir CLARA ISABEL BOTERO CUERVO.

Museo Nacional (National Museum): Carrera 7, No. 28–66, Bogotá; tel. (1) 3342129;
fax (1) 3347447; e-mail info@museonacional
.gov.co; internet www.museonacional.gov.co;
f. 1823; archaeology, ethnology, history since
Spanish conquest; collections of portraits,
arms, banners, medals, coins, ceramics, fine
arts; theatre; exhibition gallery; Dir ELVIRA
CUERVO DE JARAMILLO.

Museo Nacional de Antropología
(National Museum of Anthropology): Calle
8, No. 8-87, Bogotá; tel. (1) 2462481; fax (1)
2330960; f. 1941; ceramics, stone carvings,
gold objects, textiles, etc., from all districts of
Colombia; is a department of the Instituto
Colombiano de Antropología; Dir MYRIAM
JIMENO SANTOYO; publs *Informes Antropológicos, Revista Colombiana de Antropología*.

Medellín

**Museo de Ciencias Naturales del Cole-
gio de San José** (Natural Science Museum):
Apdo Aéreo 1180, Medellín; f. 1913; natural
history in general, zoology, botany, mineralogy, anthropology; library of 500 vols and
1,000 magazines; Dir H. MARCO A. SERNA D.;
publs *Avancemos* (12 a year), *Boletín Cultural* (4 a year), *El Colombiano* (1 a day),
catalogues.

**Museo Filatélico del Banco de la Repú-
blica:** Edif. Banco de la República, Parque de
Berrío, Medellín; tel. (4) 5767400; fax (4)
2515488; e-mail grincogo@banrep.gov.co; f.
1977; collns of Colombian postage stamps,
and stamps from other countries; Dir GON-
ZALO RINCÓN GÓMEZ; publ. *Revista*.

Museo Universitario: Universidad de Antioquia, Apdo Aéreo 1226, Medellín; tel. (4)
2105180; fax (4) 2638282; internet quimbaya
.udea.edu.co/~museo; f. 1942; sections:
anthropology, university history, natural sciences, visual arts, the human being, interactive exhibition; Dir ROBERTO L. OJALVO
PRIETO; publ. *Códice* (scientific and cultural
journal).

Roldanillo

Museo Omar Rayo: Calle 8A, 8–53, Rolda-
nillo, Valle del Cauca; tel. (92) 2298623; fax
(92) 2297290; e-mail museorayo@hotmail
.com; internet www.museorayo.net; f. 1976,
opened 1981; run by Fundación Museo Rayo;
specializes in modern works on or with
paper, fundamentally graphic art and design,
by Latin American artists or those working
in Latin America; a large colln has been
donated by the artist Omar Rayo; library of
2,003 vols; Pres. of Foundation and Dir-Gen.
OMAR RAYO REYES; publ. *Ediciones Embalaje*.

National Universities

ESCUELA SUPERIOR DE ADMINISTRACIÓN PÚBLICA

Apdo Aéreo 29745, Diagonal 40 No. 46A–37,
Santafé de Bogotá
Telephone: (1) 2224700
Fax: (1) 2224356
Internet: www.esap.edu.co
Founded 1958
State control
Academic year: February to November
Dir-Gen.: SAMUEL OSPINA MARÍN

Academic Deputy Dir: TITO ANTONIO HUERTAS
PORRAS
Admin. Deputy Dir: GUILLERMO LEÓN REY
Sec.-Gen.: GERMÁN PUENTES GONZÁLEZ
Librarian: MARÍA CRISTINA ESCOBAR DE ARA-
NGO

Library of 27,000 vols
Number of teachers: 91
Number of students: 905

Publications: *Administración y Desarrollo* (2
a year), *Documentos ESAP*

DEANS

Faculty of Advanced Studies: OCTAVIO BAR-
BOSA CARDONA
Faculty of Political and Administrative Sci-
ences: TITO ANTONIO HUERTAS PORRAS

POLITÉCNICO COLOMBIANO JAIME ISAZA CADAVID

Carrera 48 No. 7–151, Avenida Las Vegas
Medellín- Colombia-Suramé
Telephone: (574) 3197900
Fax: (574) 2680067
E-mail: rectoria@elpoli.edu.co
Internet: www.politecnicojic.edu.co
Founded 1964
State control
Rector: Dr JUAN CAMILO RUIZ PÉREZ
Sec.-Gen.: IVÁN ECHEVERRI VALENCIA
Vice-Rector for Admin.: JUAN GUILLERMO
VILLADA ARANGO
Vice-Rector for Extension: GILBERTO GIRALDO
BUITRAGO
Vice-Rector for Teaching and Research: GIO-
VANI OROZCO ARBELÁEZ
Number of teachers: 880
Number of students: 13,500
Regional campus in Rionegro

DEANS

Faculty of Administration: FABIO TORRES
LOZANO
Faculty of Basic, Social and Human Sciences:
ELMER JOSÉ RAMÍREZ MACHADO
Faculty of Engineering: JAIRO MIGUEL VER-
GARA ÁVILA

DIRECTORS

School of Agriculture: JAIME LEÓN BOTERO
AGUDELO
School of Audiovisual Communication: JOSÉ
SAMUEL ARANGO MARTÍNEZ
School of Physical Education, Recreation and
Sport: GONZALO JARAMILLO HERNÁNDEZ

UNIVERSIDAD DE ANTIOQUIA

Apdo Aéreo 1226, Ciudad Universitaria,
Medellín, Antioquia
Telephone: (4) 2198332
Fax: (4) 2191012
E-mail: wwwmgr@www.udea.edu.co
Internet: www.udea.edu.co
Founded 1822
State control
Academic year: January to November
Rector: ALBERTO URIBE CORREA
Vice-Rector for Academic Affairs: OSCAR
SIERRA RODRÍGUEZ
Vice-Rector for Admin.: RUBEN ALBERTO
AGUDELO SIERRA
Vice-Rector for Extension: MARÍA HELENA
VIVAS LÓPEZ
Vice-Rector for Gen. Affairs: MARTINIANO
JAIME CONTRERAS
Vice-Rector for Research: JAIRO HUMBERTO
RESTREPO ZEA
Sec.-Gen.: LUQUEGI GIL NEIRA
Librarian: MARÍA TERESA ARBELAEZ GARCES
Library: see Libraries and Archives
Number of teachers: 1,043

Number of students: 21,337
Publications: *Revista Estudios de Derecho* (2
a year), *Revista Iatreia* (4 a year), *Revista
Lecturas de Economia* (2 a year), *Revista
Universidad de Antioquia* (4 a year)

DEANS AND DIRECTORS

Faculty of Arts: CLARA MÓNICA ZAPATA JAR-
AMILLO
Faculty of Communications: EDISON DARÍO
NEIRA PALACIO
Faculty of Dentistry: CARLOS MARIO URIBE
SOTO
Faculty of Economics: MAURICIO ALVIAR
RAMÍREZ
Faculty of Education: CARLOS ARTURO SOTO
LOMBANA
Faculty of Engineering: CARLOS ARROYAVE
POSADA
Faculty of Exact and Natural Sciences:
NÉSTOR LÓPEZ ARISTIZÁBAL
Faculty of Law and Political Science: MARTA
NUBIA VELÁSQUEZ RICO
Faculty of Medicine: LUIS JAVIER CASTRO
NARANJO
Faculty of Nursing: ASTRID ELENA VALLEJO
RICO
Faculty of Pharmaceutical Chemistry:
AMANDA INÉS MEJÍA GALLÓN
Faculty of Social and Human Sciences: LUZ
STELLA CORREO BOTERO
Faculty of Veterinary Medicine and Animal
Husbandry: LUIS JAVIER ARROYAVE MOR-
ALES
Institute of Philosophy: ALFONSO MONSALVE
SOLÓRZANO
Institute of Physical Education and Sports:
ALAIN PEDRO BUSTAMANTE SIMÓN
Institute of Political Sciences: MANUEL
ALBERTO ALONSO ESPINAL
Institute of Regional Studies: DIEGO HERRERA
GÓMEZ
National Faculty of Public Health: OSCAR
SIERRA RODRÍGUEZ
School of Bacteriology and Clinical Labora-
tory: ANGELA MARÍA ARANGO RAVE
School of Languages: ADRIANA GONZÁLEZ
MONCADA
School of Nutrition and Dietetics: DORA
NICOLASA GÓMEZ CIFUENTES

ATTACHED INSTITUTE

**Escuela Interamericana de Biblioteco-
logía** (Interamerican School of Librarianship): Apdo Aéreo 1307, Medellín; f. 1956;
training in librarianship to postgraduate
level; technical assistance on administration
and organization of information centres and
libraries; 15 staff (10 full-time; 5 part-time);
292 students; library of 16,000 vols; Dir
MARÍA TERESA MÚNERA TÓRRES; publ. *Revista
Interamericana de Bibliotecología*.

UNIVERSIDAD DE CALDAS

Apdo Aéreo 275, Calle 65 No. 26-10, Mani-
zales, Caldas
Telephone: (68) 861250 ext. 114
Fax: (68) 8862732
E-mail: biblio@ucaldas.edu.co
Internet: www.ucaldas.edu.co
Founded 1943
State control
Languages of instruction: English, Spanish
Academic year: February to December (2
semesters)
Rector: RICARDO GÓMEZ GIRALDO
Vice-Rector for Academic Affairs: LUZ AMALIA
RIOS VASQUEZ
Registrar: ALEJANDRO GUTIÉRREZ DÍAZ
Librarian: HECTOR MARIO CASTILLO
Library: see Libraries and Archives
Number of teachers: 488
Number of students: 3,620

Publications: *Altamira* (fine arts, 1 a year), *Boletín Científico Museo de Historia* (1 a year), *Cuadernos Filósofos Literarios* (1 a year), *IDEE Revista* (education, 2 a year), *Revista Luna Azul* (ecology, 2 a year)

DEANS

Faculty of Agriculture: Dr JOSE FERNANDO KOGSON QUINTERO
Faculty of Arts and Humanities: Dr CARLOS ALBERTO OSPINA HERRERA
Faculty of Engineering: Dra CARLOS ALBERTO RUIZ VILLA
Faculty of Exact and Natural Sciences: Dr MARIA YOLANDA AGUIRRE OSPINA
Faculty of Health Sciences: Dr DOLLY MAGNOLIA GONZALEZ HOYOS
Faculty of Juridical and Social Sciences: Dra EDGARD DAVID SERRANO MOYA

UNIVERSIDAD DE CARTAGENA

Apdo Aéreo 1382, Cartagena, Bolívar
Telephone: (59) 654480
Fax: (59) 650426
Internet: www.unicartagena.edu.co
Founded 1827
State control
Academic year: February to December
Pres. of the Council: Dr GUILLERMO PANIZA RICARDO
Rector: Dra BEATRIZ BECHARA DE BORGE
Academic Vice-Rector: Dr JAIME BARRIOS AMAYA
Admin. Dir: Dr CLARET BERMUDEZ CORONEL
Chief Admin. Officer: Dr EDGAR REY SINNING
Librarian: PERLA ECHEVERRI LEMA
Library: see Libraries and Archives
Number of teachers: 560
Number of students: 4,310
Publications: *Boletín Informativo*, *Revista Ciencia*, *Revista Facultad de Medicina*, *Revista Facultad de Economía*, *Prospecto Universidad*, *Tecnología y Educación*

DEANS

Faculty of Dentistry: Dr LUIS ALVAREZ GARCIA
Faculty of Economics: Dr GUILLERMO QUINTANA SOSSA
Faculty of Engineering: Dr ALVARO CUBAS MONTES
Faculty of Law: Dr ALCIDES ANGULO PASSOS
Faculty of Medicine: Dr ROBERTO GUERRERO FIGUEROA
Faculty of Nursing: Lic. YADIRA FERREIRA DE SIERRA
Faculty of Pharmaceutical Chemistry: Dra THELMA DEL CASTILLO DE SALAZAR
Faculty of Social Work: Lic. NATACHA MORILLO DE RODRIGUEZ

UNIVERSIDAD DE CÓRDOBA

Apdo Aéreo 354, Carrera 6 No. 76–103, Córdoba
Telephone: (4) 7800381
E-mail: rectoria@unicordoba.edu.co
Internet: www.unicordoba.edu.co
Founded 1964
Public control
Language of instruction: Spanish
Academic year: February to December
Rector: Dr EMIRO JESÚS MADERA REYES
Academic Vice-Rector: Dr GUILLERMO ARRÁZOLA PATERNINA
Admin. Dir: Dr CARLOS FRASSER ARRIETA
Library Dir: JULIO ALVAREZ
Number of teachers: 900 (400 full-time, 500 part-time)
Number of students: 11,355
Publications: *Revista MVZ Córdoba*, *Revista Facultad Ciencias de la Salud*, *Temas Agrarios*

DEANS

Faculty of Agricultural Engineering: Dr MAXIMILIANO ESPINOSA PERALTA
Faculty of Education: Dr JOSÉ MORALES MANCHEGO
Faculty of Nursing: Dra GISELLE FERRER FERRER
Faculty of Science: Dr AQUILES GONZÁLEZ SALAZAR
Faculty of Veterinary Medicine and Animal Husbandry: Dr FRANCISCO AGUILAR MADERA

UNIVERSIDAD DE CUNDINAMARCA

Diagonal 18 No. 20–29, Fusagasugá, Cundinamarca
Telephone: (91) 8672144
Fax: (91) 8677898
E-mail: rectoria@udecund.edu.co
Internet: www.udecund.edu.co
Founded 1969
State control
Rector: Dr ALFONSO SANTOS MONTERO.

UNIVERSIDAD DE LA AMAZONIA

Avda Circunvalación Barrio El Porvenir, Florencia, Caquetá
Telephone: (98) 4340851
Fax: (98) 4358231
E-mail: rectoria@uniamazonia.edu.co
Internet: www.uniamazonia.edu.co
Founded 1971 as Instituto Tecnológico Universidad Surcolombiana; present name and status 1982
State control
Rector: Dr OSCAR VILLANUEVA ROJAS
Sec.-Gen.: MEYER HURTADO PARRA
Number of students: 4,000

DEANS

Faculty of Accountancy: (vacant)
Faculty of Agricultural Sciences: Mgr OSCAR ALFREDO MORELES GAMBOA
Faculty of Basic Sciences: JOSE ANTONIO MARÍN PEÑA
Faculty of Education: (vacant)
Faculty of Engineering: Ing. JULIO CESAR LUNA
Faculty of Law: LUIS FERNANDO URREGO CARVAJAL

UNIVERSIDAD DE LA GUAJIRA

Apdo Aéreo 172, Riohacha
Internet: www.uniguajira.edu.co
Founded 1976
State control
Academic year: February to July,August to November
Rector: FRANCISCO JUSTO PÉREZ VAN-LEENDEN
Vice-Rector: ROSALBA CUESTA LÓPEZ
Chief Admin. Officer: CRISTÓBAL VEGA GUTIÉRREZ
Librarian: MARINELA MENGUAL MEZA
Number of teachers: 107
Number of students: 1,258
Publications: *Anuario Estadístico*, *Revista Universidad de La Guajira*, *WOUMMAINPA*

DEANS

Faculty of Business Administration: ISIDORO OSPINO MERIÑO
Faculty of Education: JOSÉ CLEMENTE MARTÍNEZ
Faculty of Industrial Engineering: JAIRO SALCEDO DAVILA

UNIVERSIDAD DE LOS LLANOS

Km 12 Vía Puerto López, Villavicencio, Meta
Telephone: (98) 6616800
Fax: (98) 6616800-196
E-mail: rectoria@unillanos.edu.co
Internet: www.unillanos.edu.co
Founded 1974 as Universidad Tecnológica de Los Llanos Orientales; present name and status 1992
State control
Academic year: February to December
Rector: OSCAR DOMINGUEZ GONZÁLEZ
Sec.-Gen.: HERNANDO PARRA CUBEROS
Library of 45,000 vols
Number of teachers: 350
Number of students: 6,000
Publications: *Boletín*, *Boletín Estadístico*, *Catálogo*, *Revista Orinoquia*
Faculties of health sciences, agricultural sciences and natural resources, human sciences and education; faculty of economics.

UNIVERSIDAD DE NARIÑO

Ciudad Universitaria Torobajo, Pasto, Nariño
Telephone: (27) 7313605
Fax: (27) 7313605
Internet: www.udenar.edu.co
Founded 1827 as Colegio Provincial by General Francisco de Paula Santander; later named Colegio Académico; university status 1964
First degree courses
Rector: JAIRO MUÑOZ HOYOS
Vice-Rector: JAMIE HERNAN CABRERA
Vice-Rector for Admin.: VICENTE PARRA
Vice-Rector for Research, Postgraduates and Int. Relations: CARLOS CORDOBA
Dir of Planning: ARMANDO MUÑOZ
Gen. Sec.: JUAN ANDRES VILLOTA RAMOS
Librarian: SEGUNDO BURBANO L.
Library: central library of 10,000 vols; agronomy library of 15,000 vols
Number of teachers: 700
Number of students: 8,000
Publications: *Awarca*, *Foro Universitario*, *Revista de Ciencias Agrícolas Meridiano*, *Revista de Investigaciones*, *Revista de Zootecnia*

DEANS

Faculty of Agroindustrial Engineering: NELSON ARTURO
Faculty of Agronomy: GERMÁN ARTEAGA MENESES
Faculty of Arts: ALVARO ZAMBRANO
Faculty of Economics and Administration: LUIS ALBERTO ARCOS
Faculty of Education: ALVARO TORRES
Faculty of Engineering: JAIRO GUERRERO GARCÍA
Faculty of Human Sciences: CARLOS SANTAMARIA
Faculty of Law: MANUEL CORAL PABON
Faculty of Natural Sciences and Mathematics: ARSENI HIDALGO TROYA
Faculty of Stockbreeding: HECTOR FABIO VALENCIA

UNIVERSIDAD DE PAMPLONA

Ciudad Universitaria 'El Buque', Pamplona, Santander del Norte
Telephone: (7) 5685303
Fax: (7) 5682750
E-mail: rectoria@unipamplona.edu.co
Internet: www.unipamplona.edu.co
Founded 1960, univ. status 1970
State control
Academic year: February to December
Rector: ÁLVARO GONZÁLEZ JOVES

Vice-Rector for Academic Affairs: Luis
Alberto Gualdrón Sánchez
Vice-Rector for Research: Yolanda Albarra-
cín Contreras
Vice-Rector for Social Devt: Luis Gustavo
Araque
Admin. Dir: Jairo Agustín Acevedo Bau-
tista
Sec.-Gen.: Rosalba Omaña Bonilla
Number of teachers: 215 (145 full-time, 70
part-time)
Number of students: 4,560
Publications: *Bistua* (natural and techno-
logical sciences, 2 a year), *Faria* (arts and
humanities, 2 a year), *Zulima* (business
and economics, 2 a year)

DEANS

Arts and Humanities: Flor Delia Púlido C.
Business and Economics: Jairo del Carmen
Olmos S.
Education: Inés Romero Martínez
Health: Pedro Leon Peñaranda L.
Natural and Technological Sciences: Jairo
Alonso Mendoza Suárez

UNIVERSIDAD DE SUCRE

Apdo Aéreo 406, Cra. 28 No. 5-267, Sincelejo,
Sucre
Telephone: (52) 821240
Fax: (52) 821240
Internet: www.unisucre.edu.co
Founded 1977
State control
Academic year: February to December
Rector: Gustavo Vergara Arrázola
Chief Admin. Officer: Victor Raúl Castillo
Jiménez
Sec.-Gen.: Amira Valdés Altamar
Librarian: Irma Ochoa de Fonseca
Library of 12,000 vols
Number of teachers: 65
Number of students: 910

DEANS

Faculty of Engineering: Pablo Alfonso Caro
Rettiz
Faculty of Health Sciences: Carmen Cecilia
Alvis de Puentes
Faculty of Sciences and Humanities: Carmen
Payares Payares
Faculty of Stockbreeding: Julio Alejandro
Hernández

UNIVERSIDAD DEL ATLÁNTICO

Km 7 Vía Puerto Colombia, Apdo Aéreo 1890,
Barranquilla, Atlántico
Telephone: (5) 3599458
Internet: www.uniatlantico.edu.co
Founded 1941
Undergraduate courses
Rector: Ana Sofía Mesa De Cuervo
Sec.-Gen.: Roberto Noriega
Librarian: Eduardo Pinzon
Number of teachers: 845
Number of students: 17,910
Publications: *Cuadernos de literatura del
Caribe e Hispanoamérica Nº 4, Economía,
Historia Caribe Vol. iv Nº 12*

DEANS

Faculty of Architecture: Wilson Annichiar-
ico
Faculty of Economics: Fernando Cabarcas
Charris
Faculty of Education: Janeth Tovar Guerra
Faculty of Fine Arts: Guillermo Carbo
Ronderos
Faculty of Law and Political Science: Guil-
lermo Carbo Ronderos

Faculty of Nutrition and Dietetics: Sonia
Saavedra Arenas
Faculty of Pharmacy and Chemistry: Clara
Fay Vargas Lascarro

UNIVERSIDAD DEL CAUCA

Apdo Nacional 113, Calle 5 No. 4–70, Popa-
yán, Cauca
Telephone: (2) 8209900
E-mail: rectoria@ucauca.edu.co
Internet: www.unicauca.edu.co
Founded 1827
State control
Academic year: January to December
Rector: Rafael Eduardo Vivas Lindo
Vice-Rector for Academic Affairs: Konny
Elizabeth Campo Sarzosa
Vice-Rector for Culture and Welfare: Evialra
Castrillón
Vice-Rector for Research: Juan Martín
Velasco M.
Pres. of Supreme Council: Temistocles
Ortega
Gen. Sec.: Guillermo Muñoz Velásquez
Admin. Dir: José María Arboleda Castril-
lón
Planning Head: César Osorio Vera
Library Dir: Amparo Prado
Library: see Libraries and Archives
Number of teachers: 600
Number of students: 7,000

DEANS

Faculty of Accountancy, Administration and
Economics: Dr Enrique Peña Forero
Faculty of Arts: Lic. Matilde Chávez de Toba
Faculty of Civil Engineering: Ing. Margarita
Polanco
Faculty of Education Sciences: Dr Gerardo
Naundorf Saez
Faculty of Electronic Engineering: Ing. Fran-
cisco J. Terán Cuaran
Faculty of Health Sciences: Jaime A. Nates
Burbano
Faculty of Humanities: Dr Héctor Ortega
Burbano
Faculty of Law, Political and Social Sciences:
Dr Alvaro Hurtado Tejada

DIRECTORS OF POSTGRADUATE INSTITUTES

Accounting: Luis A. Colvo
Civil Engineering: Ing. Fernando Hurtado
Electronics and Telecommunications: Ing.
Pedro Vera Vera
Health Sciences: Alonso Ruiz Perea
Human Sciences: Luciano Rivera
Law: Carlos Ignacio Mosquera U.

UNIVERSIDAD DEL MAGDALENA

Carrera 32 No. 22-08, Santa Marta, Magda-
lena
Telephone: (57) 4301692
Fax: (57) 4303621
E-mail: vicedocencia@unimagdalena.edu.co
Internet: www.unimag.edu.co
Founded 1958
State control
Academic year: February to December (2
semesters)
Rector: Dr Ruthber Escorcia Caballero
Librarian: Milvida Suárez
Library of 67,506 vols
Number of teachers: 772
Number of students: 9,163
Publications: *Revista Agronómica, Revista
Económica, Revista Facultad Ingeniería
Pesquera*

DEANS

Basic Sciences: Miguel Cantillo
Economic and Managerial Sciences: Jaime
Morón

Education: Erick Hernández
Engineering: Gerardo Angulo
Health Sciences: Guillermo Trout

UNIVERSIDAD DEL PACÍFICO

Avda Simón Bolívar 54A-10, Buenaventura
Telephone: (92) 2439789
Fax: (92) 2431461
E-mail: info@unipacifico.edu.co
Internet: www.unipacifico.edu.co
Founded 1988
State control
Rector: Dr Omar Barona Murillo
Sec.-Gen.: Dra Maria Carmela Quiñonez.

UNIVERSIDAD DEL QUINDÍO

Cerrera 15, Cl. 12N, Avda Bolívar, Apdo
Aéreo 460, Armenia, Quindío
Telephone: (7) 460112
Fax: (7) 460222
Internet: www.uniquindio.edu.co
Founded 1960
State control
Academic year: February to June, August to
November
Rector: Alfonso Londoño Orozco
Vice-Rector for Academic Affairs: Orlando
Salazar Salazar
Vice-Rector for Admin.: Clara Ines Aristiza-
bal Roa
Sec.-Gen.: Franceline Barrero
Dean of Research Cttee: Patricia Landazury
Registrar: Nelly Restrepo Sánchez
Librarian: Lic. Miryam Garcia
Library of 26,250 vols
Number of teachers: 844
Number of students: 12,320
Publications: *Revista Facultad de Formación
Avanzada e Investigaciones, Revista de la
Universidad del Quindío*

DEANS

Faculty of Agricultural Industry Sciences:
Jaime Botero
Faculty of Basic and Technological Sciences:
Eduardo Arango
Faculty of Civil Engineering: Jose Fenando
Echeverry
Faculty of Education and Pedagogy: Dario
Alvarez
Faculty of Health Sciences: Roberto Stefan
Faculty of Human Sciences: William Garcia
Faculty of Management and Economics Sci-
ences: Fabiola Restrepo

UNIVERSIDAD DEL TOLIMA

Apdo Aéreo No. 546, Santa Elena, Ibagué,
Tolima
Telephone: (98) 2649219
Fax: (98) 2644869
E-mail: ut@ut.edu.co
Internet: www.ut.edu.co
Founded 1945
State control
Academic year: January to December
Rector: Jesús Ramón Rivera Bulla
Vice-Rector for Academic Affairs: José Her-
man Muñoz Nungo
Vice-Rector for Admin.: Luis Evelio Guzmán
Diaz
Vice-Rector for Devt and Educational
Resources: Fabio Alfonso Sandoval
Patarroyo
Registrar: Luz Angela Calle Barrero
Librarian: Cielo Urueña Lozano
Number of teachers: 201
Number of students: 10,130
Publication: *Revista Panorama Universitario*

DEANS

Faculty of Agricultural Engineering: CARLOS ANTONIO RIVERA BARRERO
Faculty of Business Administration: GERMÁN RUBIO GUERRERO
Faculty of Educational Science: LUIS ALBERTO MALAGÓN PLATA
Faculty of Forestry Engineering: RAFAEL VARGAS RÍOS
Faculty of Health Sciences: FRANCIA HELENA DE BETANCOURTH
Faculty of Science: RAMIRO URIBE KAFFURE
Faculty of Technology: ALBERTO MEJÍA RENGIFO
Faculty of Veterinary Medicine and Zootechnics: FRANCISCO SEGURA CANIZALES
Institute of Distance Education: LUCÍA DURÁN PINILLA

UNIVERSIDAD DEL VALLE

Ciudad Universitaria, Meléndez, Apdo Aéreo 25360, Apdo Nacional 439, Calí, Valle del Cauca

Telephone: (2) 392310
Fax: (2) 398484
Internet: www.univalle.edu.co

Founded 1945
State control
Academic year: January to June,August to December

Rector: JAIME E. GALARZA SANCLEMENTE
Vice-Rector for Academic Affairs: CARLOS E. DULCEY BONILLA
Vice-Rector for Admin.: Dr ALBERTO LOPEZ SANCHEZ
Vice-Rector for Research: Dr HUMBERTO REY VARGAS
Vice-Rector for Univ. Welfare: Dra CECILIA MADRIÑAN POLO
Library Dir: Lic. ISABEL ROMERO DE DULCEY
Library of 267,656 vols
Number of teachers: 962
Number of students: 14,640 (9,640 full-time; 5,000 part-time)
Publications: *Boletín Socioeconómico, Colombia Médica, Cuadernos de Administración, Historia y Espacio, Heurística, Humboltia, Fin de Siglo, La Palabra, Lenguaje, Praxis Filosófica, Planta Libre, Pliegos Administrativos, Poligramas, Revista de Ciencias, Revista Estomatología, Revista Universidad del Valle*

DEANS

Faculty of Administrative Science: Dr BERNARDO BARONA
Faculty of Architecture: Dr CARLOS ENRIQUE DULCEY BONILLA E.
Faculty of Economics and Social Sciences: Dr LUGARDO ALVAREZ AGUDELO
Faculty of Education: Dr MARIO DIAZ
Faculty of Engineering: Dr SILVIO DELVASTO
Faculty of Health: Dr HECTOR RAUL ECHAVARRIA ABAD
Faculty of Humanities: Dr HUMBERTO VÉLEZ RAMÍREZ
Faculty of Science: Dr LUIS FERNANDO CASTRO

UNIVERSIDAD DISTRITAL 'FRANCISCO JOSÉ DE CALDAS'

Carrera 7, No. 40–53, Bogotá
Telephone: (1) 3239300
Fax: (1) 3239300 ext. 2002
E-mail: spral@udistrital.edu.co
Internet: www.udistrital.edu.co
Founded 1950
Number of teachers: 600
Number of students: 7,200
Rector: LUIS CARLOS MOLINA MARIÑO

Faculties of education and science; engineering; environment and natural resources; technology.

UNIVERSIDAD FRANCISCO DE PAULA SANTANDER

Avda Gran Colombia 12E–96, Barrio Colsag, Apdo Aéreo 1055, Cúcuta, Norte de Santander

Telephone: (75) 753172
Internet: www.ufps.edu.co
Founded 1962
State control
Affiliated to the Universidad Nacional
Undergraduate courses

Chancellor: PATROCINIO ARARAT DÍAZ
Sec.-Gen.: ALVARO ORLANDO PEDROZA ROAJS
Admin. Dir: HÉCTOR MIGUEL PARRA LÓPEZ
Academic Vice-Chancellor: JOSÉ LUIS TOLOSA CHACÓN
Librarian: GLORIA MATILDE MELO SALCEDO
Library of 5,000 vols
Number of teachers: 350
Number of students: 6,500

DEANS

Faculty of Basic Sciences: JOSÉ LUIS MALDONADO
Faculty of Business Studies: JOSÉ RAMÓN VARGAS TOLOSA
Faculty of Education, Arts, Humanities and Sciences: RICARDO GARCIA
Faculty of Engineering: HUGO ALBERTO PORTILLA DUARTE
Faculty of Environmental Sciences: CIRO ESPINOSA
Faculty of Health Sciences: FANNY MARTINEZ

UNIVERSIDAD INDUSTRIAL DE SANTANDER

Apdo Aéreo 678, Bucaramanga, Santander
Telephone: (7) 6344000
Internet: www.uis.edu.co
Founded 1947
Academic year: February to June,August to December

Rector: JORGE GÓMEZ DUARTE
Vice-Rector for Academic Affairs: GERMÁN OLIVEROS VILLAMIZAR
Vice-Rector for Admin.: HUMBERTO PRADILLA ARDILA
Sec.-Gen.: Dra LILIA AMANDA PATIÑO DE CRUZ
Research Dir: LUIS ALFONSO MALDONADO CERÓN
Librarian: ESPERANZA MÉNDEZ BRAVO
Number of teachers: 455
Number of students: 9,684

DEANS

Faculty of Distance Education: GLORIA INÉS MARÍN MUÑOZ
Faculty of Health: GERMAN GAMARRA HERNÁNDEZ
Faculty of Human Sciences: EMILIA ACEVEDO DE ROMERO
Faculty of Physical/Chemical Sciences: CARLOS JULIO MONSALVE MORENO
Faculty of Physical/Mechanical Sciences: ROBERTO MARTÍNEZ ANGEL
Faculty of Sciences: AUGUSTO LÓPEZ ZAGARRA

UNIVERSIDAD MILITAR NUEVA GRANADA

Carrera 11 No. 101-80, Bogotá
Telephone: (1) 6343200
Fax: (1) 2159679
E-mail: rectoria@unimilitar.edu.co
Internet: www.umng.edu.co
Founded 1982
State control

Language of instruction: Spanish
Academic year: January to December
Rector: EDUARDO ANTONIO HERRERA BERBEL
Vice-Rector for Academic Affairs: Dra MARHA BAHAMON JARA
Vice-Rector for Admin.: EDGAR CEBALLOS
Vice-Rector for General Affairs: ALBERTO BRAVO SILVA
Vice-Rector for Research: Dr JOSE RICARDO CURE HAKIM
Number of teachers: 270
Number of students: 15,400

DEANS

Biology and Basic Sciences: Dr FERNANDO CANTOR
Economics and Business Admin.: Dra MARTHA ELENA CASTAÑEDA
Engineering: Dr ERNESTO VILLAREAL
Law: Dr BERNARDO VANEGAS
Medicine: Dr JUAN MIGUEL ESTRADA

UNIVERSIDAD NACIONAL ABIERTA Y A DISTANCIA

Calle 14 sur No. 14–23, Bogotá
Telephone: (1) 3443700
Fax: (1) 3444120
E-mail: sgeneral@unad.edu.co
Internet: www.unad.edu.co
Founded 1981 as Unidad Universitaria del Sur de Bogotá; current name and status 1997
State control
Academic year: February to December
Rector: Dra JAIME LEAL AFANADOR
Vice-Rector for Academic Affairs: LETICIA ESCOBAR CEDANO
Vice-Rector for Finance and Admin.: SEHIFAR BALLESTEROS MORENO
Sec.-Gen.: ROBERTO SALAZAR RAMOS

DEANS

Faculty of Administrative Sciences: ROQUE JULIO RODRIGUEZ PARRA
Faculty of Agricultural Sciences: DOMINGO ALIRIO MONTAÑO ARIAS
Faculty of Basic Sciences and Engineering: JOSE HUMBERTO GUERRERO RODRIGUEZ
Faculty of Social, Human and Educational Sciences: CARLOS BERNAL GRANADOS

UNIVERSIDAD NACIONAL DE COLOMBIA

Ciudad Universitaria, Apdo Aéreo 14490, Bogotá
Telephone: (1) 3165000
Fax: (1) 2219891
E-mail: secgener@unal.edu.co
Internet: www.unal.edu.co
Founded 1867
Academic year: February to December
Campuses in Manizales, Medellín, Palmira, Arauca, San Andrés and Leticia
Rector: MARCO PALACIOS
Vice-Rector for Arauca Campus: MARÍA SARA MEJÍA DE TAFUR
Vice-Rector for Leticia Campus: ADRIANA SANTOS MARTÍNEZ
Vice-Rector for Manizales Campus: GERMAN PALACIO CASTAÑEDA
Vice-Rector for Medellín Campus: JORGE EDUARDO HURTADO GÓMEZ
Vice-Rector for Palmira Campus: ARGEMIRO ECHEVERRY CANO
Vice-Rector for San Andrés Campus: ALEXIS DE GREIFF
Library: see Libraries and Archives
Number of teachers: 3,055
Number of students: 43,159
Publications: *Acta Bibliográfica, Agronomía Colombiana, Alimentos, Anuario Colom-*

biano de Historia, Anuario del Observatorio Astronómico Nacional, Boletín de Matemáticas, Caldasia (natural science), *Cuadernos de Economía, Forma y Función* (philology and languages), *Geografía Geología Colombiana, Ideas y Valores, Ingeniería e Investigación, Lozania* (natural science), *Maguaré* (anthropology), *Mutisia* (natural science), *Revistas* (Faculty publications)

DEANS

Faculty of Agronomy: FABIO LEYVA BARÓN
Faculty of Arts: FERNANDO MONTENEGRO LIZARRALDE
Faculty of Dentistry: GLADYS NÚÑEZ BARRERA
Faculty of Economics: LUIS IGNACIO AGUILAR
Faculty of Engineering: JULIO COMENARES MONTAÑEZ
Faculty of Humanities: GERMAN MELENDEZ ACUÑA
Faculty of Law and Political and Social Sciences: ADOLFO SALAMANCA CORREA
Faculty of Medicine: JAIME GALLEGO ARBELÁEZ
Faculty of Nursing: CLARA BEATRIZ SÁNCHEZ HERRERA
Faculty of Science: MOISES WASSERMAN LERNER
Faculty of Veterinary Science and Animal Husbandry: RAMÓN FAYAD NAFAH

OTHER CAMPUSES

Medellín Campus: Apdo Aéreo 568, Medellín

DEANS

Faculty of Architecture: OCTAVIO URIBE TORO
Faculty of Humanities: CATALINA REYES CÁRDENAS
Faculty of Mining: GONZALO JIMÉNEZ CALAD
Faculty of Sciences: MARIO ARIAS ZABALA
Faculty of Stockbreeding: DIEGO HOYOS DUQUE

Manizales Campus: Carrera 27 No. 64-60, Manizales

DEANS

Faculty of Architecture and Engineering: JOSÉ JAIRO BOTERO ANGEL
Faculty of Science and Administration: GONZALO DE JESÚS SÁNCHEZ

Palmira Campus: Apdo Aéreo 237, Palmira

DEANS

Faculty of Stockbreeding: EUGENIO ESCOBAR HANRIQUE

UNIVERSIDAD PEDAGÓGICA NACIONAL

Apdo Aéreo 75144, Calle 73, No. 11–73, Santafé de Bogotá
Telephone: (1) 3473562
Fax: (1) 3473535
Internet: www.pedagogica.edu.co
Founded 1955
State control
Languages of instruction: Spanish, English
Academic year: January to December (2 semesters)
Rector: Dr ADOLFO RODRÍGUEZ BERNAL
Vice-Rector for Academic Affairs: Dr MANUEL ERAZO PARGA
Vice-Rector for Admin.: Dr HERNÁN VÁSQUEZ ROCHA
Librarian: Dr CAMILO ROJAS LEÓN
Number of teachers: 660
Number of students: 4,190
Publications: *Pedagogica y Saberes, Revista Colombiana de Educación*

DEANS

Faculty of Education: Dra MYRIAM PARDO TORRES
Faculty of Humanities: Dra GLORIA RINCÓN CUBIDES
Faculty of Science and Technology: Dr RAFAEL HUMBERTO RAMÍREZ GIL

ATTACHED INSTITUTE

Instituto Pedagógico Nacional: Calle 127 No. 12A-20, Santafé de Bogotá; 2,178 students; Dir LUIS ERNESTO OJEDA SUÁREZ.

UNIVERSIDAD PEDAGÓGICA Y TECNOLÓGICA DE COLOMBIA

Apdo Aéreo 1094 y 1234, Carretera Central del Norte, Tunja, Boyacá
Telephone: (8) 7422175
Fax: (8) 7424311
Internet: www.uptc.edu.co
Founded 1953
State control
Academic year: February to December
Rector: OLMEDA VARGAS HERNÁNDEZ
Vice-Rector for Academic Affairs: MANUEL FRANCISCO CAICEDO RUIZ
Vice-Rector for Admin.: FRANCISCO MANOSALVA CERON
Sec.-Gen.: NUBIA ELENA PEDRAZA VARGAS
Librarian: BARBARÁ MARTÍN MARTÍN
Number of teachers: 520
Number of students: 15,850
Publications: *Acción Pedagógica* (education, 2 a year), *Agenda P & G* (planning and management, 2 a year), *Agrodesarrollo* (agriculture, 2 a year), *Anuario de Investigaciones* (research, 1 a year), *Apuntes del Cenes* (economics and business administration, 2 a year), *Boletín de Acuerdos* (2 a year), *Boletín UPTC en Cifras* (university statistics, annual), *Ciencia en Desarrollo* (science, 2 a year), *Ciencia y Agricultura* (2 a year), *Cuadernos de Lingüística* (Hispanic linguistics, 1 a year), *EPG Geografía* (2 a year), *Matemáticas y Educación* (2 a year), *Observatorio Urbano* (project management, 3 a year), *Pensamiento y Acción* (2 a year), *Perspectiva Geográfica* (2 a year), *Perspectiva Salud y Enfermedad* (health sciences, 2 a year), *Revista Metalurgia y Ciencia de Materiales* (2 a year), *Terra Nostra* (project management, 4 a year)

DEANS AND DIRECTORS

Faculty of Agricultural Sciences: MAGNOLIA DEL PILAR CANO ORTIZ
Faculty of Economics and Business Administration: VÍCTOR HERMES BARRERA GODOY
Faculty of Education: ANA MARGARITA SANTAFÉ CALDERÓN
Faculty of Engineering: LUIS EDUARDO VARGAS CARMONA
Faculty of Health Sciences: CARLOS ALBERTO JIMÉNEZ ESPINEL
Faculty of Law and Social Sciences: GERMÁN BERNAL CAMACHO
Faculty of Sciences: CARLOS NORBERTO GÓMEZ GÓMEZ
Sectional Faculty, Chiquinquirá: MANUEL HUMBERTO RESTREPO DOMÍNGUEZ
Sectional Faculty, Duitama: ALVARO CALVACHE ARCHILA
Sectional Faculty, Sogamoso: RAFAEL BALCAZAR COLLO
Institute of Open Learning and Correspondence Courses: FAUSTO RENAN MASTRODOMENICO CORREDOR
Centre of Educational Research: MARÍA NUBIA ROMERO BALLEN

UNIVERSIDAD POPULAR DEL CÉSAR

Apdo Aéreo 590, Sede Balneario Hurtado, Valledupar, César
Telephone: (95) 5736203
Fax: (95) 5735877
E-mail: univer@teleupar.net.co
Internet: www.unicesar.edu.co
Founded 1973 as Instituto Tecnológico del César; present name and status 1976
State control
Academic year: February to December (2 semesters)
Faculties of business administration, economics and accountancy, education, engineering and technology, health sciences, and law, politics and social sciences
Rector: Dr OSCAR PACHECO HERNANDEZ
Library of 17,000 vols.

UNIVERSIDAD SURCOLOMBIANA

Avda Pastrana Borrero con Carrera 1A, Neiva, Huila
Telephone: (88) 745444
Internet: www.usurcolombia.com
Founded 1970
State control
Academic year: February to December
Rector: ALVARO LOZANO OSORIO
Vice-Rector for Academic Affairs: CARLOS BOLIVAR BONILLA
Vice-Rector for Admin.: MARIA BEATRIZ PAVA MARÍN
Chief Admin. Officer: EFRAÍN POLANÍA VIVAS
Sec.: JOSÉ PIAR IRIARTE VELILLA
Librarian: LUIS ALFREDO PINTO
Number of teachers: 450
Number of students: 4,500

DEANS

Faculty of Accountancy and Administration: ALFONSO MANRIQUE MEDINA
Faculty of Educational Science: FABIO LOSADA PÉREZ
Faculty of Engineering: ALFONSO ORTÍZ
Faculty of Medicine and Health: ANTONIO ACEVEDO A.

UNIVERSIDAD TECNOLÓGICA DE PEREIRA

Apdo Aéreo 97, Pereira, Risaralda
Telephone: (6) 63213292
Fax: (6) 63215839
E-mail: relint@utp.edu.co
Internet: www.utp.edu.co
Founded 1958
State control
Academic year: February to December
Rector: LUIS ENRIQUE ARANGO JIMÉNEZ
Vice-Rector for Academic Affairs: GERMÁN LÓPEZ QUINTERO
Vice-Rector for Admin.: FERNANDO NOREÑA JARAMILLO
Registrar: DIEGO OSORIO
Gen. Sec.: CARLOS ALFONSO ZULUAGA ARANGO
Librarian: MARGARITA FAJARDO
Library of 30,000 vols, 1,400 periodicals
Number of teachers: 700
Publications: *Revista de Ciencias Humanas* (3 a year), *Revista Médica de Risaralda, Scientia et Technica* (2 a year)

DEANS

Faculty of Basic Sciences: JOSÉ GÓMEZ ESPÍNDOLA
Faculty of Education: Licda MARÍA TERESA ZAPATA SALDARRIAGA
Faculty of Electrical Engineering and Computer Science: Ing. OMAR IVÁN TREJOS BURITICÁ

Faculty of Environmental Sciences: Dr SAMUEL DARIO GUZMÁN LÓPEZ

Faculty of Fine Arts and Humanities: JUAN HUMBERTO GALLEGO RAMÍREZ

Faculty of Industrial Engineering: Ing. WILSON ARENAS VALENCIA

Faculty of Mechanical Engineering: Ing. WALDO LIZCANO ARIAS

Faculty of Medicine: Dr SAMUEL EDUARDO TRUJILLO HENAO

Faculty of Technology: Ing. JOSÉ REINALDO MARÍN BETANCOURTH

UNIVERSIDAD TECNOLÓGICA DEL CHOCÓ 'DIEGO LUIS CÓRDOBA'

Carrera 2A, No 25–22, Quibdó, Chocó

Telephone: (57) 711589

Internet: www.utch.edu.co

Founded 1972

State control

Academic year: February to June

Rector: HECTOR D. MOSQUERA BENITEZ

Vice-Rector for Academic Affairs: ALVARO GIRALDO GOMEZ

Vice-Rector for Admin.: VICTOR RAUL MOSQUERA BENITEZ

Registrar: LEONILA BLANDÓN ASPRILLA

Librarian: ZAHILY SARRAZOLA MARTINEZ

Number of teachers: 125

Number of students: 1,500

Publications: *Libros Tecnicos en diferentes areas del Conocimieto*, *Obras Literarias*

DEANS

Faculty of Education: EFRAIN MORENO RODRIGUEZ

Faculty of Health and Social Security: MELIDA MORENO MURILLO

Faculty of Technology: LORENZO PORTOCARRERO SIERRA

Private Universities

FUNDACIÓN UNIVERSIDAD CENTRAL

Carrera 5A, No 21–38, Bogotá

North Bogotá branch: Calle 75 No. 15–91, Bogotá

Telephone: (1) 3134537

Fax: (1) 3134720

E-mail: webpage@ucentral.edu.co

Internet: www.ucentral.edu.co

Founded 1966

Academic year: January to December

Faculties of accounting, business administration, economics, electronic engineering, environmental engineering industrial engineering, marketing and advertising, mechanical engineering, musical studies, social communication and journalism, systems engineering, and water resources; postgraduate programmes

Rector: Dr RUBÉN AMAYA REYES

Vice-Rector for Academic Affairs: Dra GLORIA RINCÓN CUBIDES

Vice-Rector for Admin. and Finance: Dr FERNANDO ALVAREZ MORALES

Sec.-Gen.: Dr BILLY ESCOBAR PÉREZ

Number of teachers: 700

Number of students: 12,000

Publications: *Cuadernos del Cine Club* (2 a year), *Hojas Universitarias* (2 a year), *Magazin Mercadológico* (2 a year), *Nómadas* (2 a year), *NotiCentral* (4 a year).

FUNDACIÓN UNIVERSIDAD DE BOGOTÁ 'JORGE TADEO LOZANO'

Apdo Aéreo 34185, Carrera 4, No. 22–61, Bogotá

Telephone: (1) 3341777

Fax: (1) 2826197

E-mail: btadeo12@andinet.lat.net

Internet: www.utadeo.edu.co

Founded 1954

Private control

Academic year: February to December (2 semesters)

Pres.: GUILLERMO RUEDA MONTAÑA

Rector: EVARISTO OBREGON GARCES

Vice-Rector for Academic Affairs: JUAN MANUEL CABALLERO PRIETO

Vice-Rector for Admin.: FANNY MESTRE DE GUTIERREZ

Vice-Rector for Postgraduate Studies: MIGUEL BERMUDEZ PORTOCARRERO

Sec.-Gen.: OSCAR AZUERO RUIZ

Librarian: MARIA CONSUELO MONCADA CAMACHO

Number of teachers: 1,020

Number of students: 11,500

Publications: *Agenda cultural*, *Ecotropica*, *La Tadeo*, *Tadeísta*

DEANS

Faculty of Agriculture and Stockbreeding Administration: INES ELVIRA TAMARA

Faculty of Agrology: Dr TOMAS LEON SICARD

Faculty of Business Administration: Dra CONSUELO VIDAL DE BRUGGEMAN

Faculty of Computer Science: JUAN ORLANDO LIZCANO

Faculty of Economic Sciences: JOAQUIN FLOREZ TRUJILLO

Faculty of Fine Arts: NATALIA GUTIERREZ E.

Faculty of Food Technology: JANETH LUNA

Faculty of Geographic Engineering: Dr JAIME VILLAREAL MORALES

Faculty of Graphic Design: Dra PASTORA CORREA DE AMAYA

Faculty of Industrial Design: Dr FERNANDO CORREA MUÑOZ

Faculty of Interior Design: Dr DICKEN CASTRO DUQUE

Faculty of International Commerce: HUGO VILLAMIL P.

Faculty of International Relations: ESTHER LOZANO DE REY

Faculty of Law: CAMILO NOGUERA

Faculty of Marine Biology: IVAN REY CARRASCO

Faculty of Marketing: JESUS ANTONIO POVEDA

Faculty of Public Accountancy: Dra GENOVEVA CAMACHO DE CONSTAIN

Faculty of Publicity: Dr CHRISTIAN SCHRADER

Faculty of Social Communication: Dr MARGOTH RICCI DE GOSSAIN

Food Business Management: PEDRO LUIS JIMENEZ

Health Services Management: ALFONSO LEON CANCINO

International Business Management: CIRO AREVALO Y.

Workers' Health: LEONARDO CAÑON ORTEGON

DIRECTORS

Agro-industrial Marketing: ISMAEL PEÑA DIAZ

Commercial Logistics: JORGE URIBE ROLDAN

History and Fine-Art Criticism: FRANCISCO GIL TOVAR

International Relations: DIEGO URIBE VARGAS

Marketing Management: ALEJANDRO SCHNARCH KIRBERG

Regional Development Planning: CARLOS A. GONZALEZ PARRA

PONTIFICIA UNIVERSIDAD JAVERIANA

Carrera 7 No. 40–76, Apdo Aéreo 56710, Bogotá

Telephone: (1) 3208320

Fax: (1) 2853348

E-mail: puj@javeriana.edu.co

Internet: www.javeriana.edu.co

Founded 1622 by the Jesuit Fathers; reestablished 1931, present status 1937

Academic year: January to November (2 semesters)

Grand Chancellor: Fr P.-H. KOLVENBACH

Vice-Grand Chancellor: Fr GABRIEL IGNACIO RODRÍGUEZ

Rector: Fr GERARDO REMOLINA

Vice-Rector for Academic Affairs: Dr JAIRO H. CIFUENTES

Vice-Rector for Admin.: Ing. ROBERTO ENRIQUE MONTOYA

Vice-Rector for Univ. Affairs: Fr MIGUEL ROZO

Rector for Calí Section: Fr JOAQUÍN SÁNCHEZ

Sec.-Gen.: Fr JAIME BERNAL

Library: see Libraries and Archives

Number of teachers: 3,958

Number of students: 28,611

Publications: *Cuadernos de Agroindustria y Economía Rural*, *Cuadernos de Administración*, *Ingeniería y Universidad*, *Memoria y Sociedad*, *Papel Político*, *Revista Ibero-Latinoamericana de Seguros*, *Signo y Pensamiento* (2 a year), *Theologica Xaveriana*, *Universitas Canonica*, *Universitas Economica*, *Universitas Humanistica*, *Universitas Jurídica*, *Universitas Médica* (4 per year), *Universitas Odontologica*, *Universitas Philosophica*, *Universitas Psychologica* (2 a year), *Universitas Scientiarum*

DEANS

Faculty of Architecture: Arq. ALVARO BOTERO

Faculty of Arts: M. JUAN ANTONIO CUÉLLAR

Faculty of Canon Law: Dr RAFAEL GÓMEZ

Faculty of Communication and Language: Dr JÜRGEN HORLBECK

Faculty of Dentistry: Dr ALEJANDRO ZAPATA

Faculty of Economic and Administrative Sciences: Dr GUILLERMO GALÁN

Faculty of Economic and Administrative Sciences (in Calí): Dr BERNARDO BARONA

Faculty of Education: Dr JOSÉ BERNARDO TORO

Faculty of Engineering: Ing. FRANCISCO JAVIER REBOLLEDO

Faculty of Engineering (in Calí): Dr JORGE FRANCISCO ESTELA

Faculty of Environmental and Rural Studies: Dr LUIS MIGUEL RENJIFO

Faculty of Humanities and Social Sciences (in Calí): Dr ESTEBAN OCAMPO

Faculty of Law: Fr LUIS FERNANDO ALVAREZ

Faculty of Medicine: Dr IVAN SOLARTE

Faculty of Nursing: Dra ROSAURA CORTÉS DE TÉLLEZ

Faculty of Philosophy: Dr ALFONSO FLÓREZ

Faculty of Psychology: Dra ANGELA MARÍA ROBLEDO

Faculty of Political Sciences and International Relations: Dra CLAUDIA DANGOND

Faculty of Sciences: Dra ANGELA UMAÑA

Faculty of Social Sciences: Dra CONSUELO URIBE

Faculty of Theology: Fr VÍCTOR MARTÍNEZ

Department of Languages: Dra NELLY ESPERANZA TORRES

UNIVERSIDAD AUTÓNOMA DE BUCARAMANGA

Calle 48, 39-234, Apdo Aéreo 1642, Bucaramanga

Telephone: (97) 6436161

Fax: (97) 6474488

E-mail: mcamargoa@unab.edu.co
Internet: www.unab.edu.co
Founded 1952
Private control
Academic year: January to November
Pres.: Dr ALBERTO MONTOYA PUYANA
Vice-Pres. for Academic Affairs: Dra EULALIA
GARCIA
Vice-Pres. for Admin.: Dr GILBERTO RAMIREZ
Dir of Int. Relations: MARIA T. CAMARGO
Librarian: ELENA UVAROVA

Library of 65,664 vols, 3,099 journals
Number of teachers: 454
Number of students: 7,362

Publications: *Periódico 15*, *Revista Cues-
tiones*, *Revista Facultad de Contaduría*,
Revista Medunab, *Revista Prospectiva*,
Revista Reflexiones, *Revista Temas Socio-
Jurídicos*

DEANS

Faculty of Accountancy: FERNANDO CHAPARRO
Faculty of Business Administration: JUAN
CARLOS HEDERICH MARTÍNEZ
Faculty of Business Psychology: LILIANA
STELLA QUIÑONEZ TORRES
Faculty of Communication: IVAN DARIO MON-
TOYA
Faculty of Economics: CATHERINNE GIOHANNA
MÉDINA ARÉVALO
Faculty of Education: AMPARO GALVIS DE
ORDUZ
Faculty of Energy Engineering: GERMAN
OLIVEROS
Faculty of Finance Engineering: MARTHA
INES BLANCO
Faculty of Hospitality and Tourism Admin-
istration: ALVARO MORALES
Faculty of Law: JORGE CASTILLO RUGELES
Faculty of Marketing Engineering: LUIS
ALFREDO ROJAS
Faculty of Mechanical and Electronic Engin-
eering: GERMAN OLIVEROS
Faculty of Medicine: LUZ MARINA CORSO
Faculty of Music: JESÚS ALBERTO REY MARIÑO
Faculty of Nursing: OLGA GOMEZ
Faculty of Systems Engineering: WILSON
BRICEÑO PINEDA
Faculty of Visual Arts Production: CARLOS
ACOSTA

UNIVERSIDAD AUTÓNOMA LATINOAMERICANA

Carrera 55 (Tenerife) No. 49–51, Apdo 3455,
Medellín
Telephone: (4) 5112199
Fax: (4) 5123418
E-mail: info@unaula.edu.co
Internet: www.unaula.edu.co
Founded 1966
Private control with state supervision
Academic year: February to November
President: Dr LUCIANO SANÍN ARROYAVE
Rector: Dr JAIRO URIBE ARANGO
Vice-Rector for Academic Affairs: Dr ANÍBAL
VÉLEZ MUÑOZ
Vice-Rector for Admin.: Dr JOSÉ RAÚL JAR-
AMILLO RESTREPO
Sec.-Gen.: Dr ÁLVARO OCHOA MORALES
Registrar: Dr VICENTE IGLESIAS ESCORCE
Librarian: Dr ALONSO GUILLERMO MERINO G.

Number of teachers: 250
Number of students: 2,000

Publications: *Actividad Contable* (1 a year),
Apuntes de Economía (1 a year), *Boletín
Informativo* (12 a year), *Círculo de Huma-
nidades* (4 a year), *Ratio Juris* (2 a year),
Revista Unaula (1 a year), *Sociología* (1 a
year), *Visión Autónoma* (2 a year)

DEANS

Faculty of Accountancy: Dr JORGE ALBERTO
SÁNCHEZ GIRALDO
Faculty of Economics: Dr ÁLVARO JAVIER
CORREA VÉLEZ
Faculty of Education and Social Sciences: Dr
FERNANDO CORTÉS GUTIÉRREZ
Faculty of Industrial Engineering: Dr ANÍBAL
VÉLEZ MUÑOZ
Faculty of Law: Dr FERNANDO SALAZAR MEJÍA
Faculty of Sociology: Dr FRANCISCO MÚNERA
DUQUE
Faculty of Postgraduate Studies: Dr HÉCTOR
ORTIZ CAÑAS

UNIVERSIDAD CATÓLICA DE MANIZALES

Apdo 357, Carrera 23 No. 60–63, Manizales
Telephone: (68) 860019
Fax: (68) 860575
E-mail: sucatomz@col2.telecom.co
Internet: www.ucatolicamz.edu.co
Founded 1954
Private control
Academic year: February to June, July to
November
Rector: JUDITH LEON GUEVARA
Vice-Rector for Admin.: Sis. CECILIA GOMEZ
JARAMILLO
Vice-Rector for Higher Teaching: SILVIO
CARDONA GONZALEZ
Vice-Rector for Planning and Devt: JORGE
OSWALDO SANCHEZ BUITRAGO
Vice-Rector for Professional Teaching:
GLORIA ARRIETA DE PLATA
Vice-Rector for Research: MARCO FIDEL CHICA
LASSO
Vice-Rector for Univ. Environment: Sis.
BEATRIZ PATINO GARCIA
Registrar: FANNY CASTELLANOS TORO
Librarian: Dr GABRIEL DEL ROSARIO

Number of teachers: 248
Number of students: 2,567

Publications: *Boletín Informativo*, *Protocolo*,
Revista de Investigaciones.

UNIVERSIDAD CATÓLICA POPULAR DEL RISARALDA

Avda de las Américas, Frente al Parque
Metropolitano del Café, Apdo Aéreo 2435,
Pereira
Telephone: (96) 3127722
Fax: (96) 3127613
E-mail: ucpr@ucpr.edu.co
Internet: www.ucpr.edu.co
Founded 1975
Private control
Academic year: January to November
Grand Chancellor: Mgr FABIO SUESCÚN
MUTIS
Rector: Fr ALVARO EDUARDO BETANCUR JIMÉ-
NEZ
Vice-Rector: Dr JAIME MONTOYA FERRER
Admin. Dir: Dr HÉCTOR FABIO LONDOÑO
PARRA
Librarian: Dra JUDITH GÓMEZ GÓMEZ

Number of teachers: 250
Number of students: 1,850

Publication: *Páginas de la UCPR* (5 a year)

DEANS

Faculty of Architecture: Dr EDGAR SALOMÓN
CRUZ MORENO
Faculty of Business Administration: Dr
ARIEL GALVIS GONZÁLEZ
Faculty of Industrial Design: Dra CARMEN
ADRIANA PÉREZ CARDONA
Faculty of Industrial Economics: Dr HEDMAN
ALBERTO SIERRA SIERRA
Faculty of Psychology: Dra BEATRIZ MARÍN
LONDOÑO

Faculty of Religious Studies: Dr HÉCTOR
CÓRDOBA VARGAS
Faculty of Social Communication and Jour-
nalism: Dra CRISTINA BOTERO SALAZAR

UNIVERSIDAD DE LA SABANA

Km 21, Autopista Norte de Bogotá D.C.,
Apdo Aéreo 140013, Bogotá
Telephone: (1) 8615555
Fax: (1) 8614220
E-mail: universidad.de.la.sabana@unisabana
.edu.co
Internet: www.unisabana.edu.co
Founded 1979
Private control
Languages of instruction: Spanish, English
Academic year: February to November
Chancellor: JAVIER ECHEVARRÍA RODRÍGUEZ
Rector: Dr ALVARO MENDOZA RAMIREZ
Vice-Rector for Academic Affairs: Dra LILI-
ANA OSPINA DE GUERRERO
Vice-Rector for Institutional Devt: Dra LAURA
ELVIRA POSADA NÚÑEZ
Vice-Rector for Univ. Welfare: Dra MERCEDES
SINISTERRA POMBO
Registrar: LUZ ANGELA VANEGAS
Sec.-Gen.: Dr JAVIER MOJICA SÁNCHEZ
Head of Admin.: Dr MAURICIO ROJAS PÉREZ
Academic Sec.: Dra LUZ ANGELA VANEGAS DE
SÁNCHEZ
Librarian: Dra NELLY VÉLEZ SIERRA

Number of teachers: 491
Number of students: 8,872

Publications: *Pensamiento y Cultura* (1 a
year), *Persona y Bioética* (1 a year)

DEANS

Faculty of Economic and Business Sciences:
Dr HERNÁN DARÍO SIERRA ARANGO
Faculty of Education: Dra JULIA GALOFRE
CANO
Faculty of Engineering: Dra GLORIA GONZÁ-
LEZ MARIÑO
Faculty of Law: Dr OBDULIO VELÁSQUEZ
OSADA
Faculty of Medicine: Dr EDUARDO BORDA
CAMACHO
Faculty of Nursing: Dra LEONOR PARDO
NOVOA
Faculty of Psychology: Dra MARÍA EUGENIA DE
BERMÚDEZ
Faculty of Social Communication and Jour-
nalism: Dr CESAR MAURICIO VELÁSQUEZ
OSSA

UNIVERSIDAD DE LA SALLE

Apdo Aéreo 28638, Bogotá
Telephone: (1) 2842606
Fax: (1) 2815064
Internet: www.lasalle.edu.co
Founded 1964
Academic year: February to May
Rector: Bro. JOSE VICENTE HENRY VALBUENA
Vice-Rector for Academic Affairs: Bro. LUIS
HUMBERTO BOLÍVAR RODRÍGUEZ
Vice-Rector for Admin.: Dr ORLANDO ORTIZ
PEÑA
Vice-Rector for Promotion and Human Devt:
Bro. JOSE ANTONIO RODRÍGUEZ OTERO
Sec.-Gen.: Dr JUAN GUILLERMO DURÁN MAN-
TILLA
Librarian: Dr NAPOLEÓN MUÑOZ NEDA

Number of teachers: 1,000
Number of students: 11,300

Publications: *Ciencia Animal*, *Ensayo en
Administración*, *Reflejos*

DEANS

Faculty of Accountancy: Dr JESÚS MARÍA
PEÑA BERMÚDEZ

Faculty of Agricultural Administration: Dr CARLOS ARTURO GONZÁLEZ
Faculty of Architecture: Dr TOMÁS FERNANDO URIBE
Faculty of Business Administration: Dr JESÚS SANTOS AMAYA
Faculty of Civil Engineering: Dr MIGUEL ORTEGA RESTREPO
Faculty of Economics: Dr SEBASTIÁN ARANGO FONNEGRA
Faculty of Education: Dra LUZ AMPARO MARTÍNEZ R.
Faculty of Food Engineering: LUIS FELIPE MAZUERA
Faculty of Library Science and Archives: Dr HUGO NOEL PARRA FLÓREZ
Faculty of Optometry: Dr CARLOS HERNANDO MENDOZA
Faculty of Philosophy and Letters: Dr LUIS ENRIQUE RUÍZ LÓPEZ
Faculty of Sanitary Engineering: Dr CAMILO H. GUÁQUETA R.
Faculty of Social Work: Dra ROSA MARGARITA VARGAS
Faculty of Stockbreeding: Dr GERMÁN SERRANO QUINTERO
Faculty of Veterinary Medicine: Dr GONZALO LUQUE FORERO
Division of Advanced Training: Dr FELIPE REYES DE LA VEGA

UNIVERSIDAD DE LOS ANDES

Carrera 1, No. 18A-70, Bogotá
Telephone: (1) 3394949
Fax: (1) 3324448
E-mail: uniandes@uniandes.edu.co
Internet: www.uniandes.edu.co
Founded 1948
Private control
Languages of instruction: Spanish, English
Academic year: January to December
Pres.: DIEGO PIZANO
Rector: CARLOS ANGULO
Vice-Rector for Academic Affairs: JOSÉ RAFAEL TORO
Vice-Rector for Admin.: CONSUELO CARRILLO
Vice-Rector for Research: CARL LANGEBAEK
Sec.-Gen.: MARÍA TERESA TOBÓN
Registrar: ALEJANDRO RICO RESTREPO
Librarian: ANGELA MARÍA MEJÍA DE RESTREPO
Library of 409,700 vols
Number of teachers: 1,320 (full- and part-time)
Number of students: 15,500
Publications: *Colombia Internacional* (4 a year), *Hipótesis* (2 a year), *Historia Crítica* (2 a year), *Nota Uniandina* (3 a year), *Revista de Estudios Sociales* (2 a year), *Revista de Ingeniería* (2 a year)

DEANS

Faculty of Admin.: JAVIER SERRANO
Faculty of Architecture and Design: ALBERTO MIANI
Faculty of Arts and Humanities: CLAUDIA MONTILLA
Faculty of Economics: ALEJANDRO GAVIRIA
Faculty of Engineering: ALAIN GAUTHIER
Faculty of Law: EDUARDO CIFUENTES
Faculty of Medicine: MARIO BERNAL
Faculty of Sciences: CARLOS MONTENEGRO
Faculty of Social Sciences: CARL LANGEBAEK

UNIVERSIDAD DE MEDELLÍN

Apdo Aéreo 1983, Carrera 87, No 30–65, Belén Los Alpes, Medellín, Antioquia
Telephone: (4) 3405555
Fax: (4) 3414913
E-mail: udem@guayacan.udem.edu.co
Internet: www.udem.edu.co
Founded 1950
Academic year: February to December

Rector: NÉSTOR HINCAPIÉ VARGAS
Sec.-Gen.: RAFAEL SOSA
Admin. Dir: MARIA TRINIDAD PINEDA CUERVO
Academic Dir: VICENTE ALBÉNIZ LACLAUSTRA
Dir for Postgraduate Studies: CARLOS TULIO MONTOYA HERRERA
Librarian: MARTA LUZ TAMAYO PALACIO
Number of teachers: 623
Number of students: 8,801
Publications: *Revista Con-Textos* (2 a year), *Revista Universidad de Medellín* (2 a year)

DEANS

Faculty of Administrative Sciences: JORGE LEÓN JARAMILLO MOLINA
Faculty of Civil Engineering: ARTURO ALBERTO ARISMENDY JARAMILLO
Faculty of Communication and Corporate Relations: LUIS MARIANO GONZALEZ AGUDELO
Faculty of Educational Sciences: JAIRO PÉREZ ARROYAVE
Faculty of Environmental Engineering: JUAN CARLOS BUITRAGO BOTERO
Faculty of Industrial Economy: JAIRO PÉREZ ARROYAVE
Faculty of Law: JUAN CARLOS VASQUEZ RIVERA
Faculty of Public Accountancy: ESTELLA SABA LOPEZ
Faculty of Statistics and Informatics: MARTA CECILIA MEZA PELÁEZ
Faculty of Systems Engineering: MARTA CECILIA MESA

UNIVERSIDAD DE SAN BUENAVENTURA

Trans. 26, No 172–08, Apdo Aéreo 50679, Bogotá, D.C.
Telephone: (1) 6671090
Fax: (1) 6773003
Internet: www.usbbog.edu.co
Founded 1708, present status 1961
Private control
Academic year: February to November
Rector Gen.: Fr LUIS JAVIER URIBE MUÑOZ
Sec.-Gen.: Fr LUIS ARMANDO ROMERO GAONA.

CAMPUSES

Bogotá, D.C. Campus

Transversal 26, No. 172–08, Apdo Aéreo 75010, Bogotá
Telephone: (1) 6671090
Fax: (1) 6773003
Internet: www.usbbog.edu.co
Rector: Fr PABLO CASTILLO NOVA
Academic Dir: Dr BLANCA DE PINILLA
Admin. Dir: Dr RENÁN RODRIGUEZ CÁRDENAS
Librarian: Lic. JOSÉ BUELVAS
Number of teachers: 400
Number of students: 4,000
Publications: *Franciscanum* (3 a year), *Ingenium* (2 a year), *Itinerario Educativo* (3 a year), *Management* (2 a year)

DEANS

Faculty of Business Sciences: Dr JORGE GALEANO
Faculty of Education: Dr LUIS JAVIER CLARO
Faculty of Engineering: Ing. JAIME LEAL
Faculty of Gerontology: Dr OMAR PEÑA
Faculty of Philosophy: Fr MIGUEL ANGEL BUILES
Faculty of Psychology: Dr CLEMENCIA RAMÍREZ
Faculty of Theology: Fr FERNANDO GARZÓN

Calí Campus

La Umbría, Carretera a Pance, Apdo Aéreo 25162, Calí
Telephone: (23) 552007
Fax: (23) 552006

Internet: www.usb.edu.co
Rector: Fr LUIS JAVIER URIBE MUÑOZ
Academic Dir: Dr DELIO MERINO ESCOBAR
Admin. Dir: Dr FRANCISCO VELASCO VELEZ
Librarian: CICILIA LIBREROS
Number of teachers: 360
Number of students: 5,041
Publications: *Architectura*, *Boletín Institucional* (26 a year), *Derecho* (2 a year), *Economía* (2 a year), *Educación* (2 a year), *Contaduria* (2 a year), *Ingeniería de Sistemas* (2 a year)

DEANS

Faculty of Accountancy: Dr JUAN GUILLERMO OCAMPO
Faculty of Agroindustrial Engineering: Dr RAÚL SALAZAR
Faculty of Architecture: Dr JUAN MARCO ANGEL
Faculty of Business Administration: Dr DIDIER NAVARRO
Faculty of Economics: Dr FRANCISCO JOSÉ RIZO
Faculty of Education: Dr OCTAVIO CALVACHES
Faculty of Electronic Engineering: Dr HAROLD PEDROZA
Faculty of Industrial Engineering: Dr ARTURO HERNÁNDEZ
Faculty of Law: Dr JORGE LUIS ROMERO
Faculty of Psychology: Dr JOEL OTERO
Faculty of Systems Engineering: Dr RICARDO LLANO

Cartagena Campus

Calle Real de Ternera, Apdo Aéreo 7833, Cartagena
Telephone: (53) 610465
Fax: (53) 630943
Internet: www.usbctg.edu.co
Rector: Fr ALBERTO MONTEALEGRE GONZÁLEZ
Academic Dir: Dr NICANOR ESPINOSA
Admin. Dir: Dr SILVIO MONTIEL
Sec.-Gen.: Fr MARIO RAMOS
Number of teachers: 68
Number of students: 961

DEANS

Faculty of Accountancy: Dr DEMÓSTENES BARRIOS
Faculty of Architecture: Dr GUSTAVO LEMAITRE
Faculty of Bacteriology: Dr LOURDES BENITEZ
Faculty of Business Administration: Dr LUIS MOSQUERA
Faculty of Chemical Engineering: Dr IGNACIO BURGOS
Faculty of Food Engineering: Dr MAYRA AYUZ
Faculty of Law: Dr HERNANDO URIBE
Faculty of Physical Therapy: Dra SANDRA DÍAZ
Faculty of Psychology: Dr BERTHA NUÑEZ
Faculty of Systems Engineering: Dr JORGE BUSTOS

Medellín Campus

Carrera 56c No. 51–90, Apdo Aéreo 5222-7370, Medellín
Telephone: (4) 5113600
Fax: (4) 2316191
Internet: www.usb-med.edu.co
Rector: Fr HERNANDO ARIAS RODRÍGUEZ
Admin. Dir: Dr EDGAR HINCAPIÉ
Sec.-Gen.: Fr ANDRÉS BOTERO
Number of teachers: 249
Number of students: 2,640

DEANS

Faculty of Architecture: Dr MARCO BAQUERO
Faculty of Business Science: Dr HERNÁN ARIAS
Faculty of Education: Dr LUIS ALBERTO RADA
Faculty of Engineering: Dr JESÚS LONDOÑO

Faculty of Law: Dr JUAN SÁNCHEZ
Faculty of Psychology: Dr ENRIQUE ARBELÁEZ
Faculty of Sociology: Dr GUILLERMO RIVERA

UNIVERSIDAD DEL NORTE

Km 5 Via Puerto Colombia, Barranquilla, Atlántico, Apdo Aéreo 1569-51820
Telephone: (5) 3509509
Fax: (5) 3598852
E-mail: webmaster@uninorte.edu.co
Internet: www.uninorte.edu.co
Founded 1966
Languages of instruction: Spanish, English
Academic year: January to December
Rector: JESÚS FERRO BAYONA
Vice-Rector for Academic Affairs: ALBERTO ROA VARELO
Vice-Rector for Admin.: ALMA LUCÍA DIAZ GRANADOS
Dean of Students: GINA PEZZANO
Dir, International Cooperation and Devt: CARMEN H. JIMENEZ DE PEÑA
Librarian: LUIS TARAZONA
Library of 89,238 vols, 1232 periodicals
Number of teachers: 855
Number of students: 10,721
Publications: *Derecho* (2 a year), *Eidos* (2 a year), *Ingenieria y Desarollo* (2 a year), *Investigacion y Desarrollo* (4 a year), *Pensamiento y Gestion* (2 a year), *Psicología desde el Caribe* (2 a year), *Revista Salud Uninorte* (2 a year)

DEANS

Division of Administrative Sciences: DIEGO CARADONA MADARIAGA
Division of Basic Sciences: JOACHIM HAHN
Division of Engineering: JAVIER PAEZ SAAVE-DRA
Division of Health Sciences: HERNANDO BAQUERO LATOME
Division of Humanities and Social Sciences: JOSE AMAR AMAR
Division of Law: SILVIA GLORIA DE VIVO
Institute of Studies in Economics: LEONOR JARAMILLO DE CERTAIN

UNIVERSIDAD DEL ROSARIO – COLEGIO MAYOR DE NUESTRA SEÑORA DEL ROSARIO

Calle 14, No. 6-25, Bogotá
Telephone: (1) 2970200
Fax: (1) 2818583
E-mail: orelaint@urosario.edu.co
Internet: www.urosario.edu.co
Founded 1653
Private control
Languages of instruction: Spanish, English
Academic year: February to November
Rector: HANS-PETER KNUDSEN QUEVEDO
Vice-Rector: Dr JOSÉ MANUEL RESTREPO ABONDANO
Sec.-Gen.: Dr LUIS ENRIQUE NIETO A.
Librarian: Dra MARGARITA LISOWSKA
Library of 62,735 vols, 2,143 periodicals, 16,267 e-books, 99 databases
Number of teachers: 1,044 (251 full-time, 134 half-time, 659 part-time)
Number of students: 13,382 (7,423 undergraduates, 5,959 graduates)
Publications: *Revista Desafíos, Revista de Economía del Rosario, Revista Estudios Sociojurídicos, Revista Universidad—Empresa* (2 a year)

DEANS

Faculty of Business: LUIS FERNANDO RESTREPO PUERTA
Faculty of Economics: HERNÁN JARAMILLO SALAZAR

Faculty of Human Development: LEONARDO PALACIOS SÁNCHEZ
Faculty of Human Sciences: FRANCISCO RODRIGUEZ LATORRE
Faculty of International Relations: EDUARDO BARAJAS SANDOVAL
Faculty of Law: ALEJANDRO VENEGAS FRANCO
Faculty of Medicine: LEONARDO PALACIOS SÁNCHEZ
Faculty of Political Science: EDUARDO BARAJAS SANDOVAL
Faculty of Science and Mathematics: LEONARDO PALACIOS SÁNCHEZ

UNIVERSIDAD EAFIT

Avda Las Vegas, Carrera 49 No. 7 Sur-50, Medellín
Telephone: (4) 2619600
Fax: (4) 2664284
Internet: www.eafit.edu.co
Founded 1960
Private control
Academic year: January to December
Rector: JUAN LUIS MEJÍA ARANGO
Registrar: MARÍA EUGENIA HOYOS
Academic Provost: MAURICIO VÉLEZ U.
Librarian: MARÍA CRISTINA RESTREPO LÓPEZ
Library of 40,000 vols
Number of teachers: 759
Number of students: 8,000
Publications: *AD Minister* (2 a year), *Cuadernos de Investigación, Eafitense* (12 a year), *Ecos de Economía* (2 a year), *Lúdica* (social communication), *Nuevo Foro Penal* (3 a year), *Revista Universidad Eafit* (4 a year), *Ruido Blanco* (2 a year), *Yesca y Pedernal* (4 a year)

DEANS

School of Administration and Accountancy: FRANCISCO LÓPEZ G.
School of Engineering: ALBERTO RODRÍGUEZ G.
School of Law: HUGO ALBERTO CASTAÑO Z.
School of Sciences and Humanities: LUCIANO ANGEL T.

UNIVERSIDAD EXTERNADO DE COLOMBIA

Calle 12, No. 1–17 Este, Bogotá
Telephone: (1) 3420288
Fax: (1) 2843769
E-mail: uextpub3@impsat.net.co
Internet: www.uexternado.edu.co
Founded 1886
Private control
Academic year: February to December
Rector: Dr FERNANDO HINESTROSA
Sec.-Gen.: Dr HERNANDO PARRA NIETO
Librarian: Dra LINA ESPITALETA DE VILLEGAS
Number of teachers: 639
Number of students: 7,000
Publications: *Boletín Tiempo y Turismo, Contexto* (4 a year), *Colección de Estudios en Derecho Penal—Cuadernos de Conferencias y Artículos* (3 a year), *Derecho del Estado* (2 a year), *Derecho Económico, Derecho Penal y Criminología* (3 a year), *Derecho y Vida, Documentos para la Historia del Constitucionalismo Colombiano* (2 a year), *Filosofía del Derecho* (4 a year), *Lúdica* (social communication), *Revista de Derecho Privado* (2 a year), *Revista de Economía Institucional, Notas de Coyuntura Económica, Oasis—Observatorio de Análisis de los Sistemas Internacionales, Revista Zero, Temas de Derecho Público* (4 a year)

DEANS

Faculty of Business Administration: Dra DIANA CABRERA
Faculty of Economics: Dr MAURICIO PÉREZ
Faculty of Education: Dra MIRYAM OCHOA PIEDRAHITA
Faculty of Finance, Government and International Relations: Dr ROBERTO HINESTROSA
Faculty of Furniture Restoration: Dra HELENA WIESNER
Faculty of Hotel Management and Tourism: Dr LUIS CARLOS CRUZ CORTÉS
Faculty of Law: Dr FERNANDO HINESTROSA
Faculty of Public Finance: Dr HERNANDO PÉREZ DURÁN
Faculty of Social Communication and Journalism: Dr MIGUEL MÉNDEZ CAMACHO
Faculty of Social Sciences and Humanities: Dra LUCERO ZAMUDIO

UNIVERSIDAD ICESI

Calle 18, 122–135, Calí, Valle del Cauca
Telephone: (2) 5552334
Fax: (2) 5552345
E-mail: wwwmgr@icesi.edu.co
Internet: www.icesi.edu.co
Founded 1979
Private control
Language of instruction: Spanish
Pres.: FRANCISCO PIEDRAHITA
Sec.-Gen.: MARÍA CRISTINA NAVIA K.
Librarian: MARTA CECILIA LORA
Number of teachers: 260
Number of students: 2,580 (2,124 undergraduates, 456 graduates)
Publications: *Estudios Gerenciales* (3 a year), *Innovando* (52 a year), *Precedente* (3 a year), *Revista Interacción* (3 a year), *Sistemas y Telemática* (52 a year)

DEANS

Faculty of Economics and Administration: Dr HÉCTOR OCHOA DÍAZ
Faculty of Engineering: Dr HENRY ARANGO
Faculty of Law and Social Sciences: Dr LELIO FERNANDEZ

UNIVERSIDAD INCCA DE COLOMBIA

Apdo Aéreo 14817, Bogotá
Telephone: (2) 865200
Fax: (2) 824932
Internet: www.unincca.edu.co
Founded 1955
Private control
Academic year: January to December
Rector: Dra LEONOR GARCIA DE ANDRADE
Vice-Rector: Dra MARUJA GARCIA DE CORDOBA
Vice-Rector for Admin.: Dr JORGE ROJAS ALARCON
Academic Registrar: Dr MOISES NAJAR SANABRIA
Gen. Sec.: Dr JOSE LUIS ROBAYO LEON
Librarian: MARTHA ISABEL ANGEL GIRALDO
Number of teachers: 520
Number of students: 6,700

DEANS

Faculty of Basic and Natural Sciences: Mgr OVER QUINTERO CASTILLO
Faculty of Economic and Management Sciences: JULIO SILVA COLMENARES
Faculty of Human and Social Sciences: Mgr MESTOR BRAVO SALINAS
Faculty of Judicial and State Sciences: Dr OSCAR DUEÑAS RUIZ
Faculty of Postgraduate Studies: Mgr GERMAN PACHON OVALLE
Faculty of Technical and Engineering Sciences: Ing. Sis. MARIO MARTINEZ ROJAS

UNIVERSIDAD LA GRAN COLOMBIA

Carrera 6A, No 13–40, Apdo Aéreo 7909, Bogotá

Telephone: (1) 2868200
Fax: (1) 2828386
E-mail: rectorjg@colomsat.net.co
Internet: www.ugrancolombia.edu.co
Founded 1953
Private control
Academic year: January to November (2 semesters)

Rector: JOSÉ GALAT NOUMER
Vice-Rector: RAFAEL BELTRAN BAJARANO
Gen. Sec.: RAÚL PACHECO BLANCO
Librarian: CONSTANZA GOMEZ DE NOVOA
Number of teachers: 661
Number of students: 9,650

DEANS

Faculty of Accountancy: JOSE DONADO UCROS
Faculty of Architecture: LUIS ALFREDO QUIÑONES SARMIENTO
Faculty of Civil Engineering: MANUEL RICARDO RUIZ ROMERO
Faculty of Economics: VICTOR MANUEL PEREZ ARGUELLEZ
Faculty of Law: CARLOS FREDY NAVIA PALACIOS
Faculty of Postgraduate Courses and Continuing Education: SERAFIN CRISANTO PEÑA MURCIA
Faculty of Sciences: AURA FELISA PEÑA

UNIVERSIDAD LIBRE DE COLOMBIA
(Colombia Free University)

Calle 8 No. 5–80, Bogotá

Telephone: (1) 2820389
Fax: (1) 2823580
Internet: www.unilibre.edu.co
Founded 1923
Rector: FERNANDO DJANON RODRIGUEZ
Number of teachers: 2,500
Number of students: 32,000

Faculties of accountancy, business administration, economics, education, engineering, law, medicine; campuses in Barranquilla, Calí, Cartagena, Cúcuta, Pereira, Socorro.

UNIVERSIDAD LIBRE, SECCIONAL DE PEREIRA

Apdo Aéreo 1330, Calle 40 No. 7–30, Pereira

Telephone: (63) 366025
Internet: www.ulibrepei.edu.co
Founded 1971
Academic year: February to December
Rector: JAIME ARIAS LOPEZ
Librarian: LUZ MARIA HINCAPIE
Number of teachers: 121
Number of students: 1,311
Publication: Boletín del Centro de Investigaciones (4 a year)

DEANS

Faculty of Economics: BERNARDO VÁSQUEZ CORREA
Faculty of Law: RODRIGO RIVERA CORREA

UNIVERSIDAD PONTIFICIA BOLIVARIANA

Apdo Aéreo 56006, Circular 1A, No 70–01, Medellín, Antioquia

Telephone: (4) 4159015
Fax: (4) 2502080
E-mail: secretaria@logos.upb.edu.co
Internet: www.upb.edu.co
Founded 1936
Private control
Academic year: January to December

Chancellor: Mgr ALBERTO GIRALDO JARAMILLO
Rector: Mgr GONZALO RESTREPO RESTREPO
Vice-Rector for Academic Affairs: JORGE IVÁN RAMÍREZ AGUIRRE
Vice-Rector for Admin. and Finance: Econ. OSCAR VELÁSQUEZ URIBE
Vice-Rector for Pastoral Affairs: Mgr CARLOS LUQUE AGUILERA
Sec.-Gen.: Abog. CARMEN HELENA CASTAÑO CARDONA
Library Dir: OLGA BEATRIZ BERNAL LONDOÑO
Library: see Libraries and Archives
Number of teachers: 1,746
Number of students: 7,462

Publications: Administración UPB (1 a year), Boletín de Programación de Radio Bolivariana (6 a year), Comunicación Social UPB (1 a year), Cuestiones Teológicas y Filosóficas (2 a year), Escritos (philosophy, irregular), Pensamiento Humanista (1 a year), Revista Contaminación Ambiental (2 a year), Revista de la Facultad de Derecho y Ciencias (1 a year), Revista de la Facultad de Trabajo Social UPB (1 a year), Revista de Medicina UPB (2 a year), Revista Universidad Pontificia Bolivariana (2 a year)

DEANS

Graduate School: Ing. AUGUSTO URIBE MONTOYA
School of Advertising: MARÍA PATRICIA VÉLEZ BERNAL
School of Architecture: Arq. CARLOS MARIO RODRÍGUEZ
School of Basic Science: Ing. BERNARDO LOPERA VILLA
School of Business Administration: Admor. ÁLVARO GÓMEZ FERNÁNDEZ
School of Chemical Engineering: Ing. MARÍA ELENA SIERRA VÉLEZ
School of Communications: JORGE ALBERTO VELÁSQUEZ BETANCUR
School of Design, Philosophy and Humanities: RESTREPO POSADA CLEMENCIA
School of Divinity: GUILLERMO LEÓN ZULETA SALAS
School of Economics: Econ. ROBERTO ZAPATA VILLEGAS
School of Education: Mgr OLGA OSORIO RAMÍREZ
School of Electrical Engineering: Ing. MARISOL OSORIO CÁRDENAS
School of Electronic Engineering: Ing. MARISOL OSORIO CÁRDENAS
School of Humanities: Mgr. CARLOS LUQUE AGUILERA
School of Law: Abog. JOSÉ ALFREDO TAMAYO JARAMILLO
School of Mechanical Engineering: Ing. JORGE MANRIQUE HENAO
School of Medicine: MARTA BETANCUR GÓMEZ
School of Nursing: GLORIA ANGEL JIMÉNEZ
School of Philosophy: ALVARO MURILLO CASTAÑO
School of Psychology: JAIRO RESTREPO RINCÓN
School of Social Work: OLGA CECILIA OSPINA DE GIRALDO
School of Textile Engineering: Ing. JORGE MANIQUE HENAO

UNIVERSIDAD SANTIAGO DE CALÍ

Apdo Aéreo 4102, Calle 5 No. 62-00 (Pampalinda), Calí, Valle del Cauca

Telephone: (2) 5183000
Fax: (2) 5516567
E-mail: secgener@usaca.edu.co
Internet: www.usc.edu.co
Founded 1958
Private control
Languages of instruction: Spanish, English
Academic year: January to December
Rector: HEBERT CELÍN NAVAS

Vice-Rector: JOSÉ IGNACIO ZAMUDIO FRANCO
Admin. Dir: CARLOS JULIO BARRERO SANMIGUEL
Dir for Univ. Welfare: WILSON LÓPEZ ARAGÓN
Gen. Sec.: JORGE ELIÉCER TAMAYO MARULANDA
Academic Registrar: LUZ MARIA CANO ARIAS
Library Dir: JAVIER SALDARRIAGA ARANGO
Number of teachers: 1,368
Number of students: 13,469

UNIVERSIDAD SANTO TOMÁS

Carrera 9, No 51–11, Bogotá

Telephone: (1) 3484141
Fax: (1) 5740383
E-mail: admisiones@correo.usta.edu.co
Internet: www.usta.edu.co
Founded 1580, restored 1965
Academic year: February to December
Rector: Fr EDUARDO GONZÁLEZ GIL
Vice-Rector for Academic Affairs: Fr FAUSTINO CORCHUELO ALFARO
Vice-Rector for Admin.: Fr VICENTE BECERRA REYES
Sec.-Gen.: HÉCTOR FABIO JARAMILLO SANTAMARIA
Librarian: Fr ADALBERTO CARDONA GÓMEZ
Library of 69,800 vols
Number of teachers: 660
Number of students: 12,961

Publications: Análisis, Cuadernos de Filosofía Latinoamericana, Educación y Pedagogía (research and education, 2 a year), Revista Activos, Revista Ciencia, Tecnología y Ambiente (science, technology and the environment, 2 a year), Revista CIFE, Revista de Psicología, Revista Interamericana de Investigación (research and education, 2 a year)

DEANS

Faculty of Civil Engineering: Ing. CARLOS ALBA MENDOZA
Faculty of Economics: Dr GILBERTO ENRIQUE HERAZO CUETO
Faculty of Electronic Engineering: Ing. CLAUDIA PATRICIA PÉREZ ROMERO
Faculty of Law: Dra LUZ AMPARO SERRANO QUINTERO
Faculty of Mechanical Engineering: JORGE ENRIQUE HERRERA FLAUTERO
Faculty of Philosophy: ALBERTO CÁRDENAS PATIÑO
Faculty of Physical Culture, Entertainment and Sports: PATRICIA CASALLAS REYES
Faculty of Psychology: EMILIO ESPEJO MOLANO
Faculty of Public Accounting: FERNANDO ARTURO RODRÍGUEZ MARTÍNEZ
Faculty of Social Communication: P. ADALMIRO ARIAS AGUDELO
Faculty of Sociology: RICARDO ARTURO ARIZA LÓPEZ
Faculty of Telecommunications Engineering: MAURICIO SAMUDIO LIZCANO

POSTGRADUATE INSTITUTES

Administration: Dir HERNÁN BOJACÁ MARTÍN.

Administration and Management of Quality Systems: Dir GERMÁN DARÍO MARÍN SEGURA.

Administrative Law: Dir MARIA EUGENIA SAMPER.

Business and Commercial Law: Dir HERNANDO ACOSTA RODRÍGUEZ.

Clinical and Family Psychology: Dir JAIRO ESTUPIÑAN MOJICA.

Economics: Dir DANILO TORRES REINA.

Electronic Instrumentation: Dir LUIS ALFONSO INFANTE.

Family Law: Dir LUZ AMPARO SERRANO QUINTERO.

Finance: Dir HERNÁN BOJACÁ MARTÍN.

Health Auditing: Dir Dr CARLOS IVÁN RODRÍGUEZ MELO.

International Business Management: Dir Dr JAVIER OSWALDO GUECHA MARIÑO.

Juridical Psychology: Dir FERNANDO DÍAZ COLORADO.

Latin-American Philosophy: Dir CARMENZA NEIRA.

Management of Health and Social Security Institutions: Dir Dr CARLOS IVÁN RODRÍGUEZ MELO.

Penal Law: Dir YESID REYES ALVARADO.

Political Sociology and Governmental Administration: Dir Dra ANA MEDINA DE RUÍZ.

Public Accounting: Dir TAYRON ROA VARGAS.

Socioeconomic Planning: Dir Dr DIEGO GIRALDO SAMPER.

Strategic Management of Financial Institutions: Dir DANILO TORRES REINA.

Systematic Family Supervision: Dir JAIRO ESTUPIÑAN MOJICA.

Systems Auditing: Dir Dr JAVIER OSWALDO GUECHA MARIÑO.

Tax Auditing: Dir TAYRON ROA VARGAS.

Technical Management of Electronic Engineering Projects: Dir LUIS ALFONSO INFANTE.

OTHER CAMPUSES

Bucaramanga Campus

Carrera 18, No. 9–27, Apdo Aéreo 75010, Bucaramanga

Telephone: (976) 712970

Fax: (976) 717067
E-mail: ustabuca@coll.telecom.com.co
Internet: www.usta.edu.co
Academic year: February to December
Sectional Rector: Fr CARLOS ARTURO DÍAZ RODRÍGUEZ
Vice-Rector for Academic Affairs: Fr PEDRO JOSÉ DÍAZ CAMACHO
Vice-Rector for Admin.: Fr JESÚS ANTONIO CEBALLOS GIRALDO
Gen. Sec.: Dr JOSÉ PABLO SANTAMARÍA
Library of 46,887 vols
Number of teachers: 423
Number of students: 4,500
Publications: *Iusticia* (law, 2 a year), *Temas* (humanities, 2 a year)

Tunja Campus

Calle 1, No. 11–64, Apdo Aéreo, Tunja
Telephone: (8) 7445847
Fax: (8) 7445851
E-mail: rectoria@ustatunja.edu.co
Internet: www.usta.edu.co
Academic year: January to December
Sectional Rector: Fr JOSÉ ANTONIO BALAGUERA CEPEDA
Vice-Rector for Academic Affairs: Fr SAMUEL ELIAS FORERO BUITRAGO
Vice-Rector for Admin.: Fr CARLOS ARIEL BETANCOURT OSPINA
Gen. Sec. (vacant)
Library of 6,800 vols
Number of teachers: 114
Number of students: 1,500
Publications: *Colecciones Investigando* (1 a year), *Iter Veritatis* (2 a year), *Principia Iuris* (2 a year).

Schools of Art and Music

Conservatorio de Música de la Universidad del Atlántico: Calle 68, No. 53–45, Apdo Aéreo 1890, Barranquilla; f. 1939; 21 teachers; 400 students; Dir Prof. GUNTER RENZ.

Conservatorio Nacional de Música (National Conservatory of Music): Dpto de Música, Facultad de Artes, Universidad Nacional, Carrera 30 No. 45–03 Bogotá; tel. (1) 3165000; fax (1) 3681551; e-mail consermu_farbog@unal.edu.co; internet www .facartes.unal.edu.co/conservatorio; f. 1882 as Academia Nacional de Música, present name 1910; basic and university-level courses; 60 teachers; 900 students; library: 11,000 vols, scores and records; Dir MARIO ALBERTO SARMIENTO RODRÍGUEZ.

Conservatorio del Tolima: Carrera 1, Calle 9, No 1–18, Ibagué; tel. (82) 618526; fax (82) 615378; e-mail info@ conservatoriodeltolima.edu.co; internet www .conservatoriodeltolima.edu.co; f. 1906, present name 1920; 121 teachers; 2,135 students; library: 3,216 vols, 100 DVDs, 35 LDs, 150 CDs, 200 cassettes, 1,700 LPs, 150 VHS; Rector Dr LUZ ALBA BELTRÁN AGUDELO.

Escuela de Música: Universidad de Nariño, Calle 21 No. 23-90, Pasto, Nariño; Dir FAUSTO MARTINEZ.

Escuela de Pintura y Artes Plásticas: Universidad del Atlántico, Calle 68, No. 53–54, Barranquilla; f. 1961; teaching of plastic arts; staff of 11; library: 1,900 vols; Dir Dr EDUARDO VIDES CELIS.

Instituto Musical de Cartagena: Apdo Aéreo No. 17–67, Cartagena, Bolívar; f. 1890; 12 teachers; 340 students; library: 1,500 vols; Dir Prof. JIRI PITRO M.

COMOROS

The Higher Education System

The Comoros declared their independence from France in 1975. French is one of the official languages, along with Comorian and Arabic. For many years higher education in the Comoros was limited to a number of programmes in teacher training, agriculture and health sciences at colleges and schools. Many students left the Comoros to study abroad; the World Bank estimated that 1,000 students did so in 1995. The Government provided scholarships for these students, but relied on funds from international donors to do so. The islands' first university, the Université des Comores, opened in December 2003 and 2,600 students were enrolled there in 2005/06.

Illiteracy, especially among females, poses serious difficulties for the Comoros (as in many African countries). The development of higher education is hampered by the absence of a viable primary and secondary education system. In the Comoros more than one-third of school-age children have no access to six-year formal education; of those who do have access only one-tenth continue to lower-secondary education. Enrolment levels at primary, secondary and post-secondary education are estimated at 64%, 11% and just 2%, respectively.

Regulatory Body

GOVERNMENT

Ministry of National Education, Research, Culture, and the Arts: Moroni; Minister MOHAMED ISSIMAILA.

Research Institute

AGRICULTURE, FISHERIES AND VETERINARY SCIENCE

Institut National de la Recherche pour L'Agriculture, La Pêche et l'Environ-ment (INRAPE): Moroni; tel. 736688; fax 736357; agricultural and environmental research; Dir-Gen. ABOUBACAR ALLAOUI.

Library

Moroni

Centre National de Documentation et de Recherche Scientifique (CNDRS): BP 169, Moroni; tel. 744187; fax 744189; f. 1979; incorporates the national library and archives, national museum and research centre (human and natural sciences); Dir Dr DJAFFAR MMADI.

University

UNIVERSITÉ DES COMORES

route de la corniche, BP 2585, Moroni
Telephone: 734227
E-mail: univ_com@snpt.km
Internet: www.univ-comores.com
Founded 2003
State control
Pres.: MOHAMED RACHADI.

DEMOCRATIC REPUBLIC OF THE CONGO

The Higher Education System

Prior to independence from Belgium in 1960, the country was known as Belgian Congo. Following independence it became the Democratic Republic of the Congo, and then Zaire in 1971; in 1997 the name reverted to Democratic Republic of the Congo. The oldest university is the Université de Kinshasa (formerly Université Lovanium), which was founded in 1954 by the Université Catholique de Louvain (Belgium). Between 1971 and 1981 the Université de Kinshasa was merged with the Université de Kisangani (formerly the Protestant-run Université Libre du Congo, founded 1963) and the Université de Lubumbashi (founded 1955) to form the National University of Zaire (UNAZA). Since 1981 these three state-run universities have reverted to autonomous institutions. There are also private universities at Kinshasa, Bas-Congo, Bakavu, Butembo and Goma. Other institutions of higher education include technical institutes and teaching institutes. In 2002/03 there were an estimated 60,341 students in tertiary education.

In 1997 the former ministries of primary, secondary, technical and higher education were merged into a supra-Ministry of Higher and University Education. As a result of the prolonged civil conflict in the late 1990s and early 2000s, government funding for education was effectively suspended, contributing to a decline in enrolment. In 2002 an emergency programme for education, at an estimated cost of US \$101m., was introduced to restore access to basic education. Administration of higher education is split between government ministries: the Ministry of Finance controls budget allocation; the Ministry of the Civil Service controls personnel; and the Ministry of Planning oversees the use of human resources. Senior administrative and academic figures, such as the Rector and heads of department, are appointed by the President and/or the Minister of Higher and University Education.

The Diplôme d'Etat d'Etudes Secondaires du Cycle Long is required for admission to university education. University degree programmes are divided into three cycles. The first cycle lasts three years and leads to the award of Graduat; the second cycle lasts two to three years and results in the award of the Licence, although some programmes, such as medicine and veterinary medicine, may require longer; and the third cycle is a two- to four-year programme of postgraduate study resulting in either the award of a Diplôme d'Études Spéciales (DES) or of a Diplôme de Spécialiste. Doctorates in agriculture are also available.

Technological and teaching-training institutes attached to universities provide three-year courses of higher vocational education, leading to the award of the Gradué.

Regulatory Bodies

GOVERNMENT

Ministry of Culture and the Arts: BP 8541, Kinshasa 1; tel. (12) 31005; Minister ESDRAS KAMBALE.

Ministry of Higher and University Education: Kinshasa; Min. LÉONARD MASUGA RUGAMIRA.

Learned Societies

GENERAL

UNESCO Office Kinshasa: Immeuble Losonia, Blvd du 30 juin, POB 7248, Kinshasa; tel. 8848253; fax 8848252; e-mail kinshasa@unesco.org; Head of Office CATHERINE OKAI.

BIBLIOGRAPHY, LIBRARY SCIENCE AND MUSEOLOGY

Association des Archivistes, Bibliothécaires et Documentalistes: BP 805, Kinshasa 11; f. 1973, to assist the Government in the planning and organization of archives, libraries and documentation centres; professional training and seminars.

HISTORY, GEOGRAPHY AND ARCHAEOLOGY

Société des Historiens: BP 7246, Lubumbashi; f. 1974; attached to Min. of Higher Education and Univ.; brings about a better understanding of the nation's past; organizes meetings, etc. for historians; preserves the national archives, works of art, and archaeological remains; Pres. Prof. NDAYWEL È NZIEM; Sec.-Gen. Prof. Dr TSHIBANGU MUSAS KABET; publs *Etudes d'Histoire Africaine* (1 a year), *Likundoli* (2 a year).

LANGUAGE AND LITERATURE

Alliance Française: 11, Ave Lubefu, Commune de la Gombe, BP 5404, Kinshasa 10; tel. 8803221; fax 8804707; offers courses and exams in French language and culture and promotes cultural exchange with France; attached teaching centres in Boma, Bukavu, Kananga, Kikwit, Kisangani, Lubumbashi and Matadi.

Research Institutes

GENERAL

Centre de Recherche en Sciences Humaines (CRSH): BP 3474, Kinshasa-Gombe; f. 1985 by fusion of IRS and ONRD; administration, economics, education, history, law, linguistics, literature, philosophy, psychology, social sciences, sociology; library of 4,000 vols and 12,000 periodicals; Dir-Gen. MAKWALA MA MAVAMBU YE BEDA; publs *Cahier Zaïrois de Recherche en Sciences Humaines* (4 a year), *IRS—Information*.

AGRICULTURE, FISHERIES AND VETERINARY SCIENCE

Institut National pour l'Etude et la Recherche Agronomique (INERA): BP 2037, Kinshasa 1; tel. 32332; f. 1933; agronomical study and research; 2,250 staff; library of 38,428 vols; Pres. Dr Ir. MASIMANGO NDYANABO; publs *Bulletin Agricole du Zaïre* (2 a year), *Bulletin Agroclimatologique* (1 a year), *Info-INERA* (12 a year), *Programme d'Activités* (1 a year).

HISTORY, GEOGRAPHY AND ARCHAEOLOGY

Institut Géographique: 106 Blvd du 30 Juin, BP 3086, Kinshasa-Gombe; f. 1949; geodetic, topographical, photogrammetric and cartographic studies; small library; Dir-Gen. Major LUBIKU LUSIENSE BELANI.

MEDICINE

Institut de Médecine Tropicale: BP 1697, Kinshasa; f. 1899; clinical laboratory serving Hôpital Mama Yemo with reference laboratory functions for other medical services in Kinshasa; Dir Dr DARLY JEANTY.

NATURAL SCIENCES

Biological Sciences

Institut Congolais pour la Conservation de la Nature: BP 868, Kinshasa 1; tel. 31401; f. 1925; 2,295 staff; library of 2,500 vols; Man. Dir EULALIE BASHIGE; publ. *Revue Leopard*.

TECHNOLOGY

Bureau de Recherches Géologiques et Minières (BRGM): BP 1974, Kinshasa 1; copper mining; see main entry under France; Dir G. VINCENT.

Centre de Recherches Géologiques et Minières: 44 Ave des Huileries, BP 898, Kinshasa 1; tel. 9928982; e-mail crgm@cedesurk.refer.org; f. 1939; staff of 120 undertake mineral exploration and geological mapping; library of 7,305 vols; Dir-Gen. Prof. NTOMBI MUEN KABEYA; publ. *Revue* (52 a year).

Commissariat Général à l'Energie Atomique: BP 868-184, Kinshasa XI; f. 1959; scientific research in peaceful applications of atomic energy; 140 staff; library of 3,000 vols; Commissary Gen. Prof. MALU WA KALENGA; publs *Bulletin d'Information Scientifique et Technique* (4 a year), *Rapport de Recherche* (1 a year).

Libraries and Archives

Kinshasa

Archives Nationales: BP 3428, 42A Ave de la Justice, Kinshasa-Gombe; tel. 31083; f.

1947; 3,000 vols; Curator KIOBE LUMENGA-NESO.

Bibliothèque Centrale de l'Université de Kinshasa: BP 125, Kinshasa 11; f. 1954; 300,000 vols; Chief Librarian (vacant); publs *Liste des Acquisitions*, *Nouvelles du Mont Amba* (52 a year).

Bibliothèque Publique: BP 410, Kinshasa; f. 1932; 24,000 vols; Librarian B. MONGU.

Kisangani

Bibliothèque Centrale de l'Université de Kisangani: BP 2012, Kisangani; tel. 2948; f. 1963; 90,000 vols; Chief Librarian MUZILA LABEL KAKES.

Lubumbashi

Bibliothèque Centrale de l'Université de Lubumbashi: POB 2896, Lubumbashi; f. 1955; 300,000 vols, 1,000 periodicals, 500,000 microfiches and microfilms; Librarian MUBADI SULE MWANANSUKA; publs *Cahiers Philosophiques Africains* (6 a year), *Lettres*, *Likundoli* (irregular), *Séries A.*

Museums and Art Galleries

Kananga

Musée National de Kananga: 160 Ave Kinkole, BP 612, Kananga.

Kinshasa

Musée National de Kinshasa: BP 4249, Kinshasa.

Lubumbashi

Musée National de Lubumbashi: BP 2375, Lubumbashi.

Universities

UNIVERSITÉ DE KINSHASA

BP 127, Kinshasa 11
Telephone: 30123
Internet: www.unikin.cd
Founded 1954 as the Université Lovanium by the Université Catholique de Louvain in collaboration with the Government; reorganized 1971 and 1981
Language of instruction: French
Academic year: October to July
Rector: BOGUO MAKELI
Sec.-Gen.: KAPETA NZOVU
Library: see Libraries and Archives
Number of teachers: 536
Number of students: 5,800
Publications: *Annales* (faculty publs, 2 a year), *Cahiers Economiques et Sociaux* (4 a year)

DEANS

Faculty of Economics: KINTAMBO MAFUKU
Faculty of Law: KISAKA KIA KOY
Faculty of Medicine: Dr NGALA KENDA
Faculty of Pharmacy: MULUMBA BIPI
Faculty of Sciences: MUKANA WA MURANA
Polytechnic Faculty: ANDRE DE BOECK

ATTACHED RESEARCH INSTITUTES

Centre de Cardiologie.

Centre de Recherches pour le Développement.

Centre de Recherche pour l'Exploitation de l'Energie Renouvelable (CREER).

Centre de Recherche Interdisciplinaire pour le Droit de l'Homme.

Centre Interdisciplinaire d'Etudes et de Documentation Politiques (CIE-DOP).

Centre Interdisciplinaire pour le Développement et l'Education Permanente (CIDEP): BP 2307, Kinshasa 1; training courses in management; branches at Kisangani, Lubumbashi and Karanga; politics and administration, commerce, social sciences, applied education, applied technology; 1,785 students; Sec.-Gen. MBULAMOKO ZENGE MOVOAMBE.

Institut d'Etudes et de Recherche Historique du Temps Présent.

Institut de Recherches Economiques et Sociales (IRES): BP 257, Kinshasa 11; Dir ILUNGA ILUKAMBA.

Institut des Sciences et Techniques de l'Information (ISTI): BP 14.998, Kinshasa 1; first degrees and doctorates; 15 staff; 103 students; Dir-Gen. MALEMBE TAMANDIAK.

Institut Supérieur d'Arts et Métiers (ISAM): BP 15.198, Kinshasa 1; f. 1968; management training for the clothing industry; 18 staff, 101 students; Dir OMONGA OKAKO DENEWADE.

Institut Supérieur de Commerce, Kinshasa: BP 16.596, Kinshasa 1; 37 staff; 600 students; Dir-Gen. PANUKA D'ZENTEMA.

Institut Supérieur des Bâtiments et Travaux Publics (IBTP): BP 4.731, Kinshasa 2; 83 staff; 916 students; Dir-Gen. BUTASNA BU NIANGA.

Institut Supérieur de Techniques Appliquées (ISTA): BP 6593, Kinshasa 31; tel. 20727; f. 1971; technical training; 513 staff; 5,814 students; library of 3,443 vols, 2,486 periodicals, 2,789 dissertations; Dir-Gen. Prof. MUKANA WA MUANDA.

Institut Supérieur des Techniques Médicales (ISTM): BP 774, Kinshasa 11; tel. 22113; f. 1981; 80 staff, 1,005 students; Dir-Gen. Dr PHAKA MBUMBA.

Laboratoire d'Analyses des Médicaments et des Aliments.

UNIVERSITÉ DE KISANGANI

BP 2012, Kisangani
Telephone: 2152
Founded 1963; present name 1981
State control
Language of instruction: French
Academic year: October to July (three terms)
Rector: MWABILA MADELA
Admin. Sec.: GUDIJIGA A. GIKAPA
Academic Sec.: BOKULA MOISO
Budget Administrator: LINDONGA TEMELE-ZEMAKA
Library: see Libraries and Archives
Number of teachers: 216
Number of students: 2,439
Publication: *Le Cahier du CRIDE*
Faculties of administration, medicine, political science, science, social sciences.

ATTACHED RESEARCH INSTITUTES

Bureau Africain des Sciences de l'Education (BASE): BP 14, Kisangani; Dir A. S. MUNGALA.

Centre de Recherche Interdisciplinaire pour le Développement de l'Education (CRIDE): BP 1386, Kisangani; Dir KALALA NKUDI.

Institut Facultaire des Sciences Agronomiques (IFA): BP 1232, Kisangani; f. 1973; first degrees and doctorates in agriculture; 38 teachers; 683 students; library of 7,141 vols, 14,574 periodicals; Rector Dr Ir Prof. MAMBANI BANDA; publ. *Annales.*

Institut Supérieur de Commerce, Kisangani: BP 2.012, Kisangani; Dir KABAMBI MULAMBA.

Institut Supérieur d'Etudes Agronomiques de Bengamisa: BP 202, Kisangani; 31 staff; 328 students; Dir-Gen. LUMPUNGU KABAMBA.

UNIVERSITÉ DE LUBUMBASHI

BP 1825, Lubumbashi
Telephone: 225285
E-mail: unilu@unilu.net
Internet: www.unilu.ac.cd
Founded 1955; reorganized 1971 and 1981
Language of instruction: French
State control
Academic year: October to July (October–February, March–July)
Rector: Prof. KAUMBA LUFUNDA
Sec.-Gen. for Academic Affairs: Prof. HUIT MULONGO
Sec.-Gen. for Admin.: CHABU MUMBA
Chief Librarian: SUKA MUBADI
Number of teachers: 442
Number of students: 13,158
Publications: *Cahiers Philosophiques Africains*, *Cahiers d'Études Politiques et Sociales* (2 a year), *Études d'Histoire Africaine* (2 a year), *Likundoli* (2 a year), *Mitunda* (African cultures, 2 a year), *Prospective et Perspective* (2 a year), *Recherches Linguistiques et Littéraires* (2 a year), various faculty publs

DEANS

Faculty of Agricultural Science: Prof. MICHEL NGONGO LUHEMBWE
Faculty of Economics: Prof. KASANGANA MWALABA
Faculty of Law: Prof. MALEMBA M. N'SAKILA
Faculty of Letters: Prof. KASHALA KAPALOWA
Faculty of Medicine: Prof. MUTETA WA PA MANDA
Faculty of Psychology and Pedagogy: (vacant)
Faculty of Sciences: Prof. BYAMUNGU BIN RUSANGIZA
Faculty of Social, Administrative and Political Sciences: Prof. ELENGESA NDUNGUNA
Faculty of Veterinary Medicine: Prof. KASHALA KAPAWOLA
Polytechnic Faculty: Prof. KALENGA NGOY

AFFILIATED RESEARCH INSTITUTES

École Supérieur de Commerce (ESC): Dir Prof. KIZOBO O'OBWENG O.

École Supérieure d'Ingénieur (ESI): Dir Prof. NGOIE NSENGA.

Institut Supérieur d'Etudes Sociales de Lubumbashi: BP 825, Lubumbashi 1; tel. 4315; f. 1956; 18 full-time staff, 785 students; Dir KITENGE YA.

Institut Supérieur de Statistique (ISS): BP 2471, Lubumbashi (Shaba); tel. 3905; f. 1967; 72 staff, 700 students; library of 3,000 vols, 10 periodicals; Dir-Gen. Prof. Dr MBAYA KAZADI; Sec.-Gen. for Academic Affairs Prof. Dr ANYENYOLA WELO; Sec.-Gen. for Admin. Lic. BIHINI YANKA; publ. *Annales.*

Institut Supérieur des Techniques Médicales: Dir Prof. MALONGA KAJ.

UNIVERSITÉ DE MBUJI-MAYI
(University of Mbuji-Mayi)

BP 225, Ave de l'Université, Campus de Tshikama, Dibindi, Mbuji-Mayi, Kasaï Oriental
Telephone: 8854890
Fax: 8854111
E-mail: univmayi@yahoo.fr
Internet: www.fundp.ac.be/~itshiman/um/html

Founded 1990
Private control (Catholic Church)
Language of instruction: French
Academic year: November to July
Faculties of applied science, economics, human medicine and law
Rector: RAPHAËL MBOWA KALENGAYI
Library of 14,000 vols, 75 periodicals
Number of teachers: 134
Number of students: 904

UNIVERSITÉ KONGO

BP 202, Mbanza-Ngungu, Bas-Congo
Telephone: 232132
Founded 1990 as Univ. de Bas-Zaïre

Private control
Language of instruction: French
Rector: Prof. B. LUTULALA MUMPHASI
Sec.-Gen.for Academic Affairs: Prof. PHUKU PHUATI
Sec.-Gen. for Admin.: F. KITUBA MAKUNSA
Number of teachers: 154
Number of students: 816

DEANS

Faculty of Agronomy: Prof. K. MAFWILA
Faculty of Economics and Management: Prof. KAMIANTAKO MIYAMWENI
Faculty of Law: Prof. K. BUKA
Faculty of Literature and Social Communication: (vacant)

Faculty of Medicine: Prof. Dr MBANZULU PITA
Polytechnic Faculty: Prof. PHUKU PHUATI

Colleges

Académie des Beaux-Arts (ABA): BP 8.349, Kinshasa 1; 44 staff; 248 students; Dir BEMBIKA NKUNKU.

Institut National des Arts (INA): BP 8332, 1 Ave du Commerce, Zone en Gombé, Kinshasa 1; 72 staff; 147 students; Dir Prof. BAKOMBA KATIK DIONG.

REPUBLIC OF CONGO

The Higher Education System

Higher education was established while the Republic of Congo was under French administration (it was then part of French Equatorial Africa), through the foundation of an Institute for Advanced Studies and a Centre for Advanced Administrative and Technical Studies. Following independence in 1960 the Fondation de l'Enseignement Supérieur en Afrique Centrale was created, which comprised several centres and schools. It was dissolved in 1971 and in the same year the Université de Brazzaville was inaugurated; in 1977 it adopted its current name, Université Marien-Ngouabi. In 2000 there were some 20,000 students enrolled at the Université Marien-Ngouabi, which is the only state university. In 2002/03 the total number of students in further and higher education was estimated at 12,456. Public education exists at two levels: university and non-university. Private initiatives are also increasingly moving into the higher education system, providing mainly technical and professional training in subjects such as business management. Some Congolese students also attend further education establishments abroad. In September 2004 the World Bank approved a grant of US $20m. to assist with the reconstruction of the country's educational sector, which had been severely damaged by years of civil conflict.

The four types of higher educational establishment—public and private universities, training schools and institutions of continuing education—are stipulated in the 1990 law related to education, which was modified by the November 1995 law (008/90) defining the organizational structures of the Congolese educational system. This law also stipulates a number of depositions, among them equality in access, free public education, the Government's responsibility for the organization of education and the recognition of the private sector.

Admissions to the Université Marien-Ngouabi are determined by ministerial decree. Generally, the university accepts candidates of Congolese nationality and foreigners holding a high school degree (baccalauréat) or its equivalent in return for an application fee. University-level qualifications are divided into two cycles: first, either the Diplôme Universitaire d'Études Littéraires (DUEL) in arts and humanities or the Diplôme Universitaire d'Études Scientifiques (DUES) in the sciences is awarded after two years of study; second, the Licence is awarded after an additional two years of study after DUEL/DUES, with an option of studying a further two years for the Diplôme des Études Supérieures (DES). There are no Masters or doctoral programmes. There are also professional institutes and schools that award the DES, usually after two-year courses of study.

Regulatory Bodies

GOVERNMENT

Ministry of Culture and the Arts: BP 20480, Brazzaville; tel. 81-02-35; fax 81-40-25; Minister JEAN-CLAUDE GAKOSSO.

Ministry of Higher Education: Ancien Immeuble de la Radio, BP 169, Brazzaville; tel. 81-08-15; fax 81-52-65; Minister HENRI OSSEBI.

Ministry of Scientific Research and Technical Innovation: Ancien Immeuble de la Radio, Brazzaville; tel. 81-03-59; Minister PIERRE ERNEST ABANDZOUNOU.

Ministry of Technical Education and Vocational Training: BP 2076, Brazzaville; tel. 81-17-27; fax 81-56-82; e-mail metp_cab@yahoo.fr; Minister PIERRE MICHEL NGUIMBI.

Learned Societies

GENERAL

Union Panafricaine de la Science et de la Technologie (UPST): Ave E. P. Lumumba, BP 2339, Brazzaville; tel. 83-65-35; fax 83-21-85; f. 1987; coordinates research into scientific and technological devt; 409 mem. instns (asscns, academies, socs and research institutes); Pres. Prof. EDWARD S. AYENSU; publ. *Nouvelles de l'UPST* (4 a year).

LANGUAGE AND LITERATURE

PEN Centre of Congo: BP 2181, Brazzaville; tel. 81-36-01; fax 81-36-01; Pres. E. B. DONGALA.

Research Institutes

GENERAL

Direction Générale de la Recherche Scientifique et Technique: BP 2499, Brazzaville; tel. 81-06-07; f. 1966; spec. commissions for industrial and technological sciences, medical science, natural sciences, social sciences and agricultural sciences; library of 4,500 vols; Dir-Gen. Prof. MAURICE ONANGA; publ. *Sciences et Technologies*.

Institut de Recherche pour le Développement (IRD): BP 1286, Zone Industrielle, Pointe-Noire; tel. 94-02-38; fax 94-39-81; f. 1950; biological and physical oceanography, botany, nematology, pedology, plant ecology, plant physiology; library; see main entry under France; Dir LAURENT VEYSSEYRE.

Institut de Recherche pour le Développement (IRD–DGRST): BP 181, Brazzaville; tel. 83-26-80; fax 83-29-77; f. 1947; bioclimatology, botany, demography and sociology, entomology, hydrology, medical epidemiology, microbiology, nutrition, phytopathology, soil science; see main entry under France; library of 16,000 vols; Dir C. REICHENFELD.

AGRICULTURE, FISHERIES AND VETERINARY SCIENCE

Centre de Recherche Forestière du Littoral: BP 764, Pointe-Noire; tel. and fax 94-39-12; f. 1992; forestry research; Dir Dr MAURICE DIABANGOUAYA.

Centre d'Etudes sur les Resources Végétales (CERVE): BP 1249, Brazzaville; tel. 81-21-83; f. 1985; attached to Min. of Scientific Research; catalogues plant species of the Congo; promotes traditional phytotherapy; develops indigenous and exotic fodder plants; library of 100 vols; Dir Prof. LAURENT TCHISSAMBOU.

Station Fruitière du Congo: BP 27, Loudima; f. 1963; Dir C. MAKAY.

HISTORY, GEOGRAPHY AND ARCHAEOLOGY

Centre de Recherche Géographique et de Production Cartographique: Ave de l'OUA, BP 125, Brazzaville; tel. 81-07-80; f. 1945; attached to Min. of Scientific Research and Technical Innovation; library of 2,786 vols; Dir F. ELONGO.

MEDICINE

Direction de la Médecine Préventive: BP 236, Brazzaville; tel. 81-43-51; f. 1978; attached to Ministry of Health and Social Affairs; responsible for carrying out policy on endemo-epidemic illnesses; 98 staff; Dir Dr RÉNÉ CODDY-ZITSAMELE; publ. various reports and research papers.

TECHNOLOGY

Centre de Recherche et d'Initiation des Projets de Technologie (CRIPT): BP 97, Brazzaville; tel. 51-44-95; fax 81-03-30; f. 1986; under the Min. of Scientific Research and Technical Innovation; aims to develop farming and forestry, to promote the creation of industry, to set up projects concerned with industrial science and technology, and to adapt imported technology for local requirements; Dir Dr GASTON GABRIEL ELLALY.

Libraries and Archives

Brazzaville

Bibliothèque Nationale Populaire: BP 1489, Brazzaville; tel. 83-34-85; f. 1971; 15,000 vols (7,000 in brs); Dir PIERRE MAYOLA.

Bibliothèque des Sciences de la Santé et Centre de Documentation/AFRO Health Sciences Library and Documentation Centre: BP 6, Brazzaville; tel. 241-39425; fax 241-39673; f. 1952; 7,000 vols; Librarian MARIE-PAULE KABORE.

Bibliothèque Universitaire, Université Marien-Ngouabi: BP 2025, Brazzaville; tel. 83-14-30; f. 1992; 78,000 vols; Chief Librarian INNOCENT MABIALA; publs *Cahiers congolais d'anthropologie et d'histoire*, *Cahiers de la Jurisprudence, Congolaise de Droit, Revue.*

Centre d'Information des Nations Unies: BP 1018, Ave Foch, Brazzaville; tel. 83-50-90; fax 83-61-40; f. 1983; affiliated to UN Dept of Information in New York; 4,378 vols (mostly NGO publs); Dir ISMAEL A. DIALLO; publs *Notes d'Information*, monthly list of acquisitions.

Museums and Art Galleries

Brazzaville

Musée National: BP 994, Brazzaville; tel. 81-03-30; f. 1965; ethnographic colln and nat. history; library of 285 vols; Dir JEAN GILBERT JULES KOULOUFOUA.

Kinkala

Musée Régional André Grenard Matsoua: BP 85, Kinkala; tel. 85-20-14; f. 1978; under the Min. of Culture and the Arts; ethnography; 5 staff; library; Curator BIVINGOU-NZEINGUI.

Pointe Noire

Musée Régional Ma-Loango Diosso: BP 1225, Pointe-Noire; tel. 94-15-79; f. 1982; attached to Min. of Culture and the Arts; collects historical, ethnographical, scientific, artistic materials as a source of information on Congolese culture; Curator JOSEPH KIM-FOKO-MADOUNGOU.

University

UNIVERSITÉ MARIEN-NGOUABI

BP 69, Brazzaville
Telephone and fax 81-01-41
E-mail: unimariengouabi@yahoo.fr
Founded 1961 as Fondation de l'Enseignement Supérieur en Afrique Centrale, became Université de Brazzaville 1971, present name 1977
State control
Language of instruction: French
Rector: Prof. ARMAND MOYIKOUA
Library: see Libraries and Archives
Number of teachers: 595
Number of students: 20,259
Publications: *Annales de l'Université Marien NGOUABI, Revue médicale du Congo* (6 a year)

DEANS

Faculty of Arts and Humanities: DIEUDONNÉ TSOKINI
Faculty of Economics: HERVÉ DIATA
Faculty of Health Sciences: JEAN ROSAIRE IBARA
Faculty of Law: PLACIDE MOUDOUDOU

Faculty of Science: JEAN-MAURILLE OUAMBA

DIRECTORS OF SCHOOLS

École Normale d'Administration et de Magistrature (ENAM): ALPHONSE OKO
École Normale Supérieur (ENS): PASCAL ONGOKA
École Normale Supérieure Polytechnique (ENSP): DÉSIRÉ LILONGA-BOYENGA

ATTACHED INSTITUTES

Institut du Développement Rural (IDR): BP 69, Brazzaville; f. 1976; Dir FULBERT AKOUANGO.

Institut Supérieur d'Education Physique et Sportive (ISEPS): BP 1100, Brazzaville; f. 1976; Dir PIERRE BAZOLO.

Institut Supérieur de Gestion (ISG): BP 2469, Brazzaville; f. 1976; Dir FILA HYACINTHE DEFOUNDOUX.

Colleges

Collège d'Enseignement Technique Agricole: BP 30, Sibiti; f. 1943; Dir JEAN BOUNGOU.

Collège Technique, Commercial et Industriel de Brazzaville (et Centre d'Apprentissage): Brazzaville; f. 1959; Dir HUBERT CUOPPEY.

Ecole Supérieure Africaine des Cadres des Chemins de Fer (Higher School for Railway Engineers): Brazzaville; f. 1977; management and technical courses.

COSTA RICA

The Higher Education System

The Universidad de Costa Rica is the oldest institution of higher education in Costa Rica. It was founded in 1843 by the Roman Catholic Church as Universidad de Santo Tomás, closed in the 1880s and refounded under its current name in 1940. The Ministry of Public Education controls the formal education system under the aegis of the Consejo Superior de Educación (Higher Council of Education). The supervisory body of public universities is the Consejo Nacional de Rectores (National Council of Rectors). Private universities are under the control of the Consejo Nacional de Educación Superior de Universidades Privadas (National Council of Higher Education for Private Universities).

The administrative structure of a university consists of an Asamblea General (legislative body), Concejo Universitario (board of directors), Rectoría (president) and Vicerrectorías (vice-presidents). Faculties are the top academic divisions, and are subdivided into departments. There are also attached research centres and institutes.

The Bachiller or Bachillerato is the main undergraduate qualification, for which a student is required to accrue 120–144 credits over four to five years; an additional 30–36 credits lead to the award of the Licenciado. At postgraduate level, following Bachiller or Bachillerato, a Maestría is awarded after two years of study or 60–72 credits. Finally, the Doctorado requires three-and-a-half years of study or 100–120 credits (including those accrued for the Maestría). In 2004/05 there were 110,717 students enrolled in higher education.

Technical and vocational education is offered by public and private 'para-universities'. Courses last for two to three years and lead to the award of the Diplomado or Técnico Superior.

Regulatory and Representative Bodies

GOVERNMENT

Ministry of Culture, Youth and Sport: Avdas 3 y 7, Calles 11 y 15, frente al parque España, San José; tel. 2221-3806; fax 2221-1759; e-mail mcarballo@mcj.go.cr; internet www.mcjdcr.go.cr; Minister MARÍA ELENA CARBALLO.

Ministry of Public Education: Edif. Antigua Embajada, Apdo 10087, 1000 San José; tel. 2258-3745; fax 2258-3745; e-mail contraloriaservicios@mep.go.cr; internet www.mep.go.cr; Minister LEONARDO GARNIER.

ACCREDITATION

Sistema Nacional de Acreditación de la Educación Superior (SINAES) (National System of Accreditation in Higher Education): Apdo 1174-1200 Pavas, San José; tel. 2290-3325, ext. 3317; fax 2290-8653; e-mail sinaes@sinaes.ac.cr; internet www.sinaes.ac.cr; f. 1999; Pres. GUILLERMO VARGAS SALAZAR; Vice-Pres. Dra SONIA MARTA MORA ESCALANTE.

NATIONAL BODY

Consejo Nacional de Rectores (CONARE) (National Council of Rectors): Apdo 1174-1200, San José; tel. 2290-3325; fax 2296-5626; e-mail conare@conare.ac.cr; internet www.conare.ac.cr; f. 1974; responsible for co-ordinating decision-making regarding the state university education system; composed of the rectors of the Universidad de Costa Rica, Instituto Tecnológico de Costa Rica, Universidad Nacional and Universidad Estatal a Distancia; Pres. OLMAN SEGURA BONILLA.

Learned Societies

GENERAL

UNESCO Office San José: Apdo 220-2120, San Francisco de Guadalupe, San José; Paseo Colon, Avda 1 bis, Calle 28, Casa Esquinera 2810, San José; tel. 2258-7625; fax 2258-7458; e-mail san-jose@unesco.org; designated Cluster Office for Costa Rica, El Salvador, Guatemala, Honduras, Mexico, Nicaragua and Panama; Dir ALEJANDRO ALFONZO.

HISTORY, GEOGRAPHY AND ARCHAEOLOGY

Academia de Geografía e Historia de Costa Rica (Costa Rican Academy of Geography and History): Apdo 4499, 1000 San José; tel. 2234-7629; fax 2234-7629; f. 1940; 32 mems; Pres. Dra MARÍA EUGENIA BOZZOLI; Sec. EUGENIA IBARRA; publ. *Anales*.

LANGUAGE AND LITERATURE

Academia Costarricense de la Lengua (Costa Rican Academy of Language): Apdo 157, 1002 Paseo de los Estudiantes, San José; internet www.acl.ac.cr; f. 1923; corresp. of the Real Academia Española (Madrid); 18 mems; Dir ALBERTO F. CAÑAS ESCALANTE; Sec. FERNANDO DURÁN AYANEGUI; publ. *Boletín*.

Alliance Française: Avda 7, Calle 5, Apdo 10195, 1000 San José; tel. 2222-2283; fax 2233-5819; e-mail alcultfr@racsa.co.cr; internet www.alianzafr.ac.cr; offers courses and exams in French language and culture and promotes cultural exchange with France; Dir PATRICK LACOMBE.

MEDICINE

Colegio de Médicos y Cirujanos de Costa Rica: Sabana Sur, San José; tel. 2232-3433; fax 2232-2406; e-mail info@medicos.sa.cr; internet www.medicos.sa.cr; f. 1857; promotes devt of medical profession through medical research, interchange between mem. asscns and cooperation with nat. and int medical authorities; 45 mem. asscns; Pres. Dr ARTURO ROBLES ARIAS; Sec. Dr ABDÓN CASTRO BERMÚDEZ; publs *Acta Médica Costarricense* (4 a year), *Medicine, Vida y Salud*.

Member Associations:

Asociación Costarricense de Cardiología (Costa Rican Cardiology Association): Apdo 527, Pavas, San José; tel. 2253-8868; fax 2272-4214; f. 1978; 36 mems; library of 50 vols; Pres. Dr ANDRES BENAVIDES SANTOS.

Asociación Costarricense de Cirugía (Costa Rican Surgery Association): POB 548, 1000 San José; tel. 2231-0301; fax 2233-4165; f. 1954; 150 mems; Pres. Dr EDUARDO FLORES MONTERO; Sec. Dr LUIS MORALES ALFARO.

Asociación Costarricense de Medicina Interna (Association of Internal Medicine): Hospital San Juan de Díos, San José; tel. 2257-5252; fax 2235-1308; Pres. Dr RODOLFO LEAL VEGA.

Asociación Costarricense de Pediatría (Costa Rican Paediatrics' Association): Apdo 1654, 1000 San José; tel. 2221-6821; fax 2221-6821; e-mail acope@hnn.sa.cr; f. 1951; organizes nat. conf. annually in October; 370 mems; Pres. Dr EFRAÍN ARTAVIA LORÍA; Sec. Dra JULIA FERNÁNDEZ MONGE; publ. *Acta Pediátrica Costarricense*.

Asociación de Obstetricia y Ginecología de Costa Rica (Obstetrics and Gynaecology Association): Apdo 1011–1116, La Y Griega, San José; tel. 8911-4555; fax 2227-3300; e-mail rmontielarios@gmail.com; internet www.aogcr.com; f. 1956; 220 mems; Pres. Dr CAM LIM BADILLA.

Research Institutes

GENERAL

Consejo Nacional para Investigaciones Científicas y Tecnológicas (CONICIT): Apdo 10318, 1000 San José; tel. 2224-4172; fax 2225-2673; e-mail conicit@conicit.go.cr; internet www.conicit.go.cr; f. 1973; promotes devt of science and technology; makes available funds for research; works in cooperation with the Min. of Nat. Planning and Economic Policy, and Min. of Science and Technology; library of 3,500 vols; spec. colln: UNISIST program; Pres. Dr RONALD MELÉNDEZ; Exec. Sec. Lic. ALVARO BORBÓN; publ. *Memoria Anual CONICIT*.

AGRICULTURE, FISHERIES AND VETERINARY SCIENCE

Centro Agronómico Tropical de Investigación y Enseñanza (CATIE): 7170 Turrialba; tel. 2558-2000; fax 2558-2060; e-mail comunicacion@catie.ac.cr; internet www.catie.ac.cr; f. 1973 by the IICA and the Costa Rican Govt as a non-profit-making scientific and educational asscn for research and graduate education in devt, conservation and the sustainable use of natural resources in Belize, Colombia, Costa Rica, Dominican Republic, El Salvador, Guatemala, Honduras, Mexico, Nicaragua, Panama and Venezuela; library of 92,000 vols, 5,000 current periodicals; Dir Dr PEDRO FERREIRA ROSSI; publs *Informe Anual, Revista Manejo Integrado de Plagas* (plant protection and public health, 4 a year), *Revista Agroforestería en las Américas, Revista Forestal Centroamericana*.

ECONOMICS, LAW AND POLITICS

Instituto Latinoamericano de las Naciones Unidas para la Prevención del Delito y Tratamiento del Delincuente (ILANUD) (UN Latin American Institute for Crime Prevention and Treatment of Offenders): Apdo 10071, 1000 San José; tel. 2257-5826; fax 2233-7175; e-mail ilanud@ilanud.or.cr; internet www.ilanud.or .cr; f. 1975 as a UN regional agency; training, advice and research in the fields of law and criminology, crime prevention and treatment of offenders; specialized library and data bank for int. use; arranges symposia, ministerial meetings; projects include standardization of criminal statistics, human rights in the admin. of justice, female and juvenile crime, 'white-collar' crime; Dir Dr ELÍAS CARRANZA; publ. *ILANUD* (2 a year).

Instituto Nacional de Estadística y Censos: Apdo 10163, 1000 San José; de la Rotonda de La Bandera, 450 metros oeste, Calle Los Negritos, Edificio Ana Lorena, Mercedes de Montes de Oca, San José; tel. 2280-9280; fax 2224-2221; e-mail informacion@inec.go.cr; internet www.inec .go.cr; f. 1883; 250 mems; library of 8,500 items; Dir Licda MARÍA ELENA GONZÁLEZ QUESADA; publs *Anuario Estadístico de Costa Rica* (1 a year), *Cifras Básicas sobre Fuerza de Trabajo* (1 a year), *Cifras Básicas sobre Pobreza e Ingresos* (1 a year), *Costa Rica: Cálculo de Población por Provincia, Cantón y Distrito* (2 a year), *Costo de la Canasta Básica de Alimentos* (12 a year), *Encuesta de Hogares de Propósitos Múltiples, Módulo de Empleo* (1 a year), *Estadísticas de Comercio Exterior* (2 a year), *Estadísticas de la Construcción* (2 a year), *Estadísticas Vitales: Población, Nacimientos, Defunciones, Matrimonios* (1 a year), *Indicadores Demográficos* (1 a year), *Indice de Precios al Consumidor* (12 a year), *Indices de Precios de los Insumos Básicos de la Industria de la Construcción* (12 a year), *Mortalidad Infantil y Evolución Reciente* (2 a year).

EDUCATION

Fundación Omar Dengo: Apdo 1032-2050, 1000 San José; tel. 2527-6000; fax 2527-6010; e-mail info@fod.ac.cr; internet www.fod.ac.cr; f. 1987 to promote the economic, social and human development of Costa Rica, implementing innovative programs to improve the quality of education; Pres. ALFONSO GUTIÉRREZ; publ. *Estado de la Nación* (irregular).

HISTORY, GEOGRAPHY AND ARCHAEOLOGY

Instituto Geográfico Nacional: Apdo 2272, 1000 San José; Avda 20, Calle 5/7, San José; tel. 2523-2630; fax 2221-0087; e-mail lbenavides@mopt.go.cr; internet www .mopt.go.cr/ign; f. 1944; library of 3,000 vols; Dir MAX LOBO HERNÁNDEZ.

MEDICINE

Centro Internacional de Investigación y Adiestramiento Médico de la Universidad del Estado de Louisiana (Louisiana State University International Centre for Medical Research and Training): Apdo 10155, 1000 San José; tel. 2280-5149; fax 2224-7236; e-mail icmrtlsu@sol.racsa.co.cr; f. 1962; research on viral diseases; library of 4,000 vols; Dir Dr RONALD B. LUFTIG.

Instituto Costarricense de Investigación y Enseñanza en Nutrición y Salud (Institute of Research and Teaching in Nutrition and Health): Apdo 4, Tres Ríos, Cartago; La Unión, Cartago; tel. 2279-9911; fax 2279-5546; e-mail msolis@incensa.sa.cr; internet www.incensa.sa.cr; f. 1977; attached to Min. of Public Health and affiliated to the Univ. of Costa Rica; library of 4,500 vols; Dir LISSETTE NAVAS ALVARADO; publ. *Boletín INCIENSA* (3 a year).

NATURAL SCIENCES

Biological Sciences

Organization for Tropical Studies: Apdo 676, 2050 San Pedro; tel. 2524-0607; fax 2524-0608; e-mail cro@ots.ac.cr; internet www.ots.ac.cr; f. 1963; promotes education, research and the responsible use of natural resources in the tropics; operates 3 biological stations: Las Cruces, incorporating Wilson Botanical Garden (premontane forest), Palo Verde (dry forest) and La Selva (tropical wet forest); consortium of 58 univs and research instns in the USA, Latin America and Australia; library of 10,000 vols, 50 current periodicals; Dir Dr JORGE JIMÉNEZ; publ. *Liana* (Spanish and English edns, each 2 a year).

Tropical Science Centre: Apdo 83870, 1000 San José; tel. 2253-3267; fax 2253-4963; e-mail cct@cct.or.cr; internet www.cct .or.cr; f. 1962; private non-profit asscn; research and training in tropical science; consultation on tropical ecology, land use capability and planning, environmental assessments; biological reserve and field station at Monteverde Cloud Forest; library of 7,000 vols; Exec. Dir JULIO CALVO ALVARADO; publ. *Occasional Paper Series* (irregular).

Physical Sciences

Instituto Meteorológico Nacional: Apdo 5583, 1000 San José; Frente a Antiguo Emergencias del Hospital Calderón Guardia, Barrio Aranjuez, San José; tel. 2222-5616; fax 2223-1837; e-mail imn@imn.ac.cr; internet www.imn.ac.cr; f. 1888; climatology, hydrometeorology, agrometeorology, synoptic and aeronautical meteorology; Dir PAULO MANSO SAYAO; publ. *Boletín Meteorológico* (12 a year).

TECHNOLOGY

Comisión de Energía Atómica de Costa Rica (National Atomic Energy Commission): San Fco. de Goicoecheca, 25 Este de la Escuela Claudio Cortés, Oficentro el Solar de la Abadía, 2° Piso, Local 4, 1000 San José; tel. 2248-1591; fax 2221-8680; e-mail coatom@racsa.co.cr; internet www.cea.go.cr; f. 1969; Pres. Ing. MARIO CONEJO SOLÍS; Dir LILLIANA SOLÍS DÍAZ.

Libraries and Archives

San José

Archivo Nacional de Costa Rica: Apdo 41-2020, Zapote, San José; 900 metros sur y 150 oeste de Plaza del Sol Curridabat, San José; tel. 2283-1400; fax 2234-7312; e-mail ancost@ ice.co.cr; internet www.archivonacional.go .cr; f. 1881; 5,000 vols, 8.5 shelf-km of documents; Dir-Gen. Lic. VIRGINIA CHACÓN ARIAS; publs *Archívese* (bulletin, 4 a year), *Cuadernillos del Archivo Nacional* (2 or 3 a year), *Revista del Archivo Nacional* (1 a year).

Biblioteca Instituto Diplomático: Apdo 10027, 1000 San José; tel. 2223-7555; fax 2257-8401; e-mail biblioteca@rree.go.cr; internet www.rree.go.cr; f. 1991; attached to Min. of Foreign Relations; int. affairs, diplomacy, foreign policy, law; 20,000 vols historical memories, official diary, texts; Librarian LUIS GONZÁLEZ CALVO; publ. *Revista Costarricense de Política Exterior*.

Biblioteca 'Mark Twain'–Centro Cultural Costarricense-Norteamericano: Apdo 1489, 1000 San José; tel. 2207-7574; fax 2224-1480; e-mail bibmarktwain@cccncr .com; internet www.cccncr.com; f. 1945; 18,000 vols and documents; Librarian ANDREA SOLIS; publ. *CCCNoticias* (6 a year).

Biblioteca Nacional Miguel Obregón Lizano: Apdo 10008, 1000 San José; Calles 15 y 17, Av. 3 y 3B, San José; tel. 2221-2436; fax 2223-5510; e-mail dibinacr@racsa.co.cr; internet www.mcjdcr.go.cr/ sistema_bibliotecas/biblioteca_nac.html; f. 1888; 270,000 vols; Dir GUADALUPE RODRIGUEZ MÉNDEN; publ. *Bibliografía Nacional*.

Centro de Información 'Alvaro Castro Jenkins': Avda Central y Primera, Calles 2 y 4, San José; tel. 2243-4460; fax 2243-4583; e-mail centroinf@bccr.fi.cr; internet www .bccr.fi.cr/ci; f. 1950; attached to the Central Bank; specializes in economics; 43,028 vols; Librarian DEYANIRA VARGAS DE BONILLA.

Departamento de Servicios Bibliotecarios, Documentación e Información de la Asamblea Legislativa: Apdo 75-1013, San José; tel. 2243-2394; fax 2243-2400; e-mail jvolio@congreso.aleg.go.cr; internet www .asamblea.go.cr/biblio; f. 1953; social sciences; 40,000 vols, 800 periodicals; Dir Lic. JULIETA VOLIO GUEVARA; publs *C. R. Leyes, decretos* (index of Costa Rican legislation, 12 a year), *Revista Parlamentaria* (4 a year).

Sistema de Bibliotecas, Documentación e Información: Ciudad Universitaria Rodrigo Facio, 2060 San Pedro de Montes de Oca, San José; tel. 2253-6152; fax 2234-2809; e-mail mbriceno@sibdi.ucr.ac.cr; internet sibdi.bldt.ucr.ac.cr; f. 1946; attached to Univ. de Costa Rica; 443,853 vols, 13,425 periodicals, 48,059 theses, 23,212 audiovisual items, 5,615 maps and atlases; Dir Licda MA. EUGENIA BRICEÑO MEZA.

Museums and Art Galleries

Alajuela

Museo Histórico Cultural Juan Santamaría: Apdo 785, 4050 Alajuela; tel. 2441-4775; fax 2441-6926; e-mail mhcjscr@ice.co .cr; internet www.museojuansantamaria.go .cr; f. 1974; attached to Min. of Culture and Youth; 19th-century colln; library of 2,000 vols; Dir Prof. RAÚL AGUILAR PIEDRA; publ. *11 de Abril: Cuadernos de Cultura*.

San José

Museo de Arte Costarricense: Apdo 378, Fecosa 1009, San José; Parque Metropolitano de La Sabana, San José; tel. 2222-7155; fax 2222-7247; e-mail info@musarco.go.cr; internet www.musarco.go.cr; attached to Ministry of Culture and Youth; f. 1977; collects and exhibits representative works of Costa Rican art; promotes artistic work through workshops and grants; supervision and preservation of state art collns; library of 5,000 vols; Dir ELIZABETH BARQUERO.

Museo Indígeno (Native Museum): Seminario Central, San José; f. 1890; library of

40,000 vols; Dir Rev. WALTER E. JOVEL CASTRO.

Museo Nacional de Costa Rica: Apdo 749, 1000 San José; Calle 17, Avda Central y 2, San José; tel. 2257-1433; fax 2233-7427; e-mail informacion@museocostarica.go.cr; internet www.museocostarica.go.cr; f. 1887; gen. museum: pre-Columbian art, colonial and republican history, nat. herbarium, natural history, culture; library of 70,000 vols; Dir MELANIA ORTIZ VOLIO; publs *Brenesia* (natural sciences), *Trees and Seeds from the Neotropics*, *Vínculos* (anthropology, 2 a year).

Affiliated Museums:

Museo de Insectos: Faculty of Agricultural Sciences, Univ. de Costa Rica, San Pedro, San José; internet www.miucr.ucr.ac.cr; f. 1962; 1m. specimens of butterflies and other insects.

Museo de Zoología: Dpto de Biología, Univ. de Costa Rica, San José; mammals, herpetology, fish; small library.

Universities

ESCUELA DE AGRICULTURA DE LA REGION TROPICAL HÚMEDA (UNIVERSIDAD EARTH)

Apdo Postal 4442 SJ, San José
Telephone: 2713-0000
Fax: 2713-0001
E-mail: admision@earth.ac.cr
Internet: www.earth.ac.cr

Founded 1986
Private control
Language of instruction: Spanish
Academic year: January to December

Rector: Dr JOSÉ A. ZAGLUL SLON
Provost: Dr DANIEL SHERRARD
Vice-Pres. for Admin. and Finance: Ing. ALEX MATA
Librarian: JOSÉ RUPERTO ARCE

Library of 47,000 vols
Number of teachers: 45
Number of students: 410

Publication: *Tierra Tropical: Sostenibilidad, Ambiente y Sociedad*.

UNIVERSIDAD AUTÓNOMA DE CENTRO AMERICA

Apdo 7637-1000, San José
Campus Los Cipreses, 1 km al Norte del Servicentro La Galera, Curridabat, San José
Telephone: 2272-9100
Fax: 2271-2046
E-mail: info@uaca.ac.cr
Internet: www.uaca.ac.cr

Founded 1976
Private control
Language of instruction: Spanish
Academic year: January to December (3 terms)

Rector: Lic. GUILLERMO MALAVASSI VARGAS
Chancellor: GONZALO GALLEGOS J.
Vice-Chancellor: LISETTE MARTÍNEZ L.
Registrar: PABLO ARCE
Librarian: JULISSA MÉNDEZ M.

Number of teachers: 250
Number of students: 5,000

Publications: *Acta Académica* (2 a year), *Ordenanzas y Anuario Universitario*.

CONSTITUENT COLLEGES

Colegio Andrés Bello: Apdo 2393-2050, San Pedro, San José; tel. 2272-9102; fax 2271-3839; e-mail abello@uaca.ac.cr; Dean Lic. HERBERTH SASSO.

Colegio de Ciencias Clorito Picado: 2393-2050, San Pedro, San José; tel. 2272-9100; fax 2271-3839; e-mail ccp@uaca.ac.cr.

Colegio Iñigo de Loyola: Apdo 12345-1000, San José; tel. 2225-5413; fax 2225-5413; Dean ELIO BURGOS.

Colegio Leonardo da Vinci: Apdo 44-1009, San José; tel. 2290-2552; fax 2290-2728; e-mail davinci@racsa.co.cr; Dean TERESITA BONILLA.

Collegium Academicum: Apdo 2393-2050, San Pedro, San José; tel. 2272-9102; fax 2271-3839; e-mail academicum@uaca.ac.cr; Dean GASTÓN CERTAD.

Stvdivm Generale Costarricense: Apdo 7651-1000, San José; tel. 2271-2100; fax 2271-2015; e-mail stvdivm@uaca.ac.cr; Dean Lic. MARIO GRANADOS.

UNIVERSIDAD DE COSTA RICA

Ciudad Universitaria 'Rodrigo Facio', San Pedro de Montes de Oca, San José
Telephone: 2207-4000
Fax: 2224-8214
E-mail: consultas.odi@ucr.ac.cr
Internet: www.ucr.ac.cr

Founded 1843, refounded 1940
Autonomous control
Language of instruction: Spanish
Academic year: March to November

Rector: Dra YAMILETH GONZÁLEZ GARCÍA
Vice-Rector for Admin.: Dr HERMANN HESS
Vice-Rector for Research: Dr HENNING JENSEN PENNINGTON
Vice-Rector for Student Life: MSc ALEJANDRINA MATA
Vice-Rector for Teaching: Dra LIBIA HERRERO URIBE
Registrar: Sr JORGE RECOBA VARGAS (acting)
Librarian: Lic. AURORA ZAMORA GONZÁLEZ (acting)
Library: see Libraries and Archives

Number of teachers: 3,800
Number of students: 28,986

DEANS

Faculty of Agronomy: Dr MANUEL ZELEDÓN
Faculty of Dentistry: Dr FERNANDO SAÉNZ FORERO
Faculty of Economics: Dr JUSTO AGUILAR FONG
Faculty of Education: ALEJANDRINA MATA SEGREDA
Faculty of Engineering: Ing. FERNANDO SILESKY GUEVARA
Faculty of Fine Arts: Dr LUIS DIEGO HERRA RODRÍGUEZ
Faculty of Law: Dr RAFAEL GONZÁLEZ BALLAR
Faculty of Letters: M. L. ENRIQUE MARGERY PEÑA
Faculty of Medicine: Dr GUIDO ULATE
Faculty of Microbiology: Dr MARIO CHAVES VILLALOBOS
Faculty of Pharmacy: Dra LIDIETTE FONSECA GONZÁLEZ
Faculty of Science: Dr OLDEMAR RODRÍGUEZ ROJAS
Faculty of Social Sciences: Dr ROBERTO SALOM ECHEVERRIA (acting)
Graduate Studies: Dra MAIA PÉREZ YGLESIAS
There are 21 research institutes attached to the various faculties.

REGIONAL CENTRES

Centro Regional del Atlántico: internet www.sa.ucr.ac.cr; Dir Ing. CARLOS CALVO PINEDA.

Centro Regional de Guanacaste: Dir Ing. RAFAEL MONTERO ROJAS.

Centro Regional de Limón: Dir Dr ENRIQUE ZAPATA DUARTE.

Centro Regional del Occidente: internet www.so.ucr.ac.cr; Dir Dr ELIAM CAMPOS BARRANTES.

Centro Regional del Pacífico: internet www.srp.ucr.ac.cr; Dir SUSAN CHEN MOK.

UNIVERSIDAD EMPRESARIAL DE COSTA RICA

Apdo 12640-1000, San José
Telephone: 2253-5952
Fax: 2225-5141
E-mail: info@unem.edu
Internet: www.unem.edu

Founded 1992 as International Postgraduate School affiliated with Universidad de San Jose; became independent and adopted present name 1997
Private control
Languages of instruction: Spanish, English
Academic year: January to December

Rector: Dr RAFAEL ANGEL PÉREZ CORDOVA
Registrar: ELAINE PÉREZ
Librarian: RODOLFO MARTÍNEZ

Number of teachers: 62
Number of students: 895

Publication: *Gazetta Empresarial*

Faculties of administrative sciences, biological sciences, education and humanities, psychology and behavioural sciences, social sciences, postgraduate studies; school of languages.

UNIVERSIDAD ESTATAL A DISTANCIA (Open University)

Apdo 474, 2050 San Pedro de Montes de Oca, San José
Telephone: 2527-2000
Fax: 2253-4990
Internet: www.uned.ac.cr

Founded 1977
State control
Language of instruction: Spanish
Academic year: March to November

Rector: RODRIGO ARIAS CAMACHO
Academic Vice-Rector: JOSÉ LUIS TORRES
Exec. Vice-Rector: LUIS GUILLERMO CARPIO MALAVASSI
Vice-Rector for Planning: SILVIA ABDELNOUR ESQUIVEL
Dir of Information Technology, and Communications: MSc VIGNY ALVARADO CASTILLO
Librarian: RITA LEDEZMA

Number of teachers: 235
Number of students: 12,000

DIRECTORS

School of Business Administration: RODOLFO TACSAN CHEN
School of Education: (vacant)
School of Exact and Natural Sciences: Ing. OLMAN DÍAZ SÁNCHEZ
School of Social Sciences and Humanities: GERARDO ESQUIVEL MONGE

There are 28 regional centres where students can register, receive instruction, sit examinations and use library facilities

UNIVERSIDAD FIDELITAS

Apdo 8063-1000, San José
Telephone: 2253-0262
Fax: 2253-2186
E-mail: informacion@ufidelitas.ac.cr
Internet: www.ufidelitas.ac.cr

Founded 1980 as Collegium Fidélitas; present name 1994
Private control

Rector: JESÚS MERINO SERNA
Gen. Man.: MIGUEL MARÍN VALENCIANO

Courses in advertising design, business administration, civil engineering, computer systems engineering, electrical engineering, electromechanical engineering, industrial engineering, law, pre-school education, psychology, public finance, teaching of English.

UNIVERSIDAD INTERNACIONAL DE LAS AMERICAS

Apdo 1447–1002, San José
Barrio Aranjuez, Calle 23 (Avenidas 7 y 7bis), El Carmen, San José
Telephone: 2258-0220
Fax: 2222-3216
E-mail: correo@uia.ac.cr
Internet: www.uia.ac.cr
Founded 1986
Private control
Library of 25,000 vols

Schools of administration, advertising, computer engineering, dentistry, education, electromechanical engineering, industrial engineering, international business, international relations, journalism, languages, law, medicine, pharmacy, public finance, tourism.

UNIVERSIDAD LATINA DE COSTA RICA

Apdo 1561-2050, San Pedro, San José
Telephone: 2283-2611
Fax: 2225-2801
Internet: www.ulatina.ac.cr
Founded 1981
Private control
Rector: ARTURO JOFRÉ VARTANIÁN
Vice-Rector for Academic Affairs: LUIS ALBERTO CHAVES MONGE

Campuses in Cañas, Grecia, Guápiles, Limón, Palmares, Paso Canoas, Puntarenas, San Isidro del General, Santa Cruz and Turrialba

Courses in economics and business administration, education, tourism and environmental science, engineering and architecture, health sciences, social sciences.

UNIVERSIDAD LATINOAMERICANA DE CIENCIA Y TECNOLOGIA (ULACIT)

Apdo 10235, 1000 San José
Telephone: 2523-4000
Fax: 2256-5609
E-mail: info@ulacit.ac.cr
Internet: www.ulacit.ac.cr
Founded 1987
Languages of instruction: English, Spanish
Private control
Academic year: January to December
Pres.: Dr SYLVIA CASTRO
Vice-Pres. for Academic Affairs: Dr ILEANA CONTRERAS
Vice-Pres. for Int. Affairs: MAUREEN VILLALOBOS
Vice-Provost for Research and Devt: EDGAR SALGADO
Registrar: Ing. JOANNE BARNETT
Librarian: FANNY MORALES
Library of 25,000 vols
Number of teachers: 275
Number of students: 3,000

DEANS

Graduate School: ROSMERY HERNÁNDEZ

School of Business Administration: LAURA BRAVO
School of Engineering: ERIC GREGORY
School of Dentistry: Dr MARIELA PADILLA
School of Education: Lic. NELLY SANTIAGO
School of Industrial Engineering: ORLANDO TORRES
School of Law: Dr ALFONSO NAVAS
School of Psychology: Lic. MARÍA ANTONIETA CAMPOS

UNIVERSIDAD NACIONAL

Apdo 86-3000, Heredia
Telephone: 2261-0101
Fax: 2237-7593
E-mail: jmora@una.ac.cr
Internet: www.una.ac.cr
Founded 1973
State control
Language of instruction: Spanish
Academic year: February to November
Rector: Dra SONIA MARTA MORA ESCALANTE
Vice-Rector for Academic Affairs: Dr CARLOS LÉPIZ JIMÉNEZ
Vice-Rector for Devt: MARCO TULIO FALLAS DÍAZ
Vice-Rector for Student Affairs: HERIBERTO VALVERDE CASTRO
Library Dir: Lic. MARGARITA GARCÍA
Number of teachers: 1,200
Number of students: 12,000

Publications: *ABRA* (2 a year), *Relaciones Internacionales* (4 a year), *Repertorio Americano* (2 a year), *Revista Ciencias Ambientales*, *Revista de Historia* (2 a year), *Uniciencia* (2 a year), *Vida Silvestre Neotropical* (2 a year)

DEANS

Faculty of Earth and Sea Sciences: Dr MARÍA DE LOS ANGELES ALVAREZ FERNÁNDEZ
Faculty of Exact and Natural Sciences: Dr LUIS MANUEL SIERRA SIERRA
Faculty of Health Sciences: Dr PEDRO UREÑA BONILLA
Faculty of Philosophy and Letters: JORGE ALFARO PERÉZ
Faculty of Social Sciences: JOSÉ CARLOS CHINCHILLA COTO
Centre of General Studies: Dr CARLOS ARAYA GUILLÉN
Centre for Research and Teaching in Education: IRMA ZÚÑIGA LEÓN
Centre for Research, Teaching and Extension in Fine Arts: ELSA FLORES MONTERO
Brunca Regional Centre: Lic. JUAN RAFAEL MORA CAMACHO

UNIVERSIDAD DE SAN JOSE

Apdo 7446, 1000 San José
Telephone: 2218-0747
E-mail: info@usanjose.ac.cr
Internet: www.usanjose.ac.cr
Founded 1976 as Colegio Académicum; present name and status 1992
Private control
Language of instruction: Spanish
Academic year: January to December (3 terms)
Rector: MANUEL SANDI MURILLO
Registrar: Lic. RÓGER SEGNINI ESQUIVEL
Librarian: JOSÉ SEGNINI
Number of teachers: 175
Number of students: 1,800

Publication: *Revista Universitaria*

Schools of business administration, computer science, education and psychology, humanities, international trade, law, social science; international postgraduate school.

UNIVERSIDAD VERITAS

Apdo 1380–1000, San José
Telephone: 2283-4747
Fax: 2225-2907
E-mail: info@uveritas.ac.cr
Internet: www.uveritas.ac.cr
Private control
Academic year: January to December (3 semesters)
Rector: Ing. JOSÉ JOAQUIN SECO
Number of teachers: 95
Number of students: 1,100
Faculties of art, architecture and design.

Colleges

INCAE Business School: Apdo 960, 4050 Alajuela; tel. 2437-2200; fax 2433-9101; e-mail library@incae. edu; internet www .incae.edu/es/biblioteca/sistema-bibliotecas/ costa-rica/crbiblio.php; f. 1964 in Nicaragua with technical assistance from Harvard Univ.; Costa Rica campus opened 1983; (see also under Nicaragua); 2-year MBA programmes in English and Spanish; exec. education programmes; management research and consulting; library: 32,600 vols in fields of business admin., economic devt, natural resources, tourism and Latin American economic and social conditions; Rector Dr ARTURO CONDO; Librarian Lic. THOMAS BLOCH.

Instituto Centroamericano de Administración Pública (ICAP): Apdo 10025-1000, 100 sur, 75 oste de la Heldería Pop's, Curridabat, San José; tel. 2234-1011; fax 2225-2049; e-mail info@icap.ac.cr; internet www.icap.ac.cr; f. 1954 as Escuela Superior de Administración Pública (ESAPAC) by a jt project of the govts of Costa Rica, El Salvador, Guatemala, Honduras and Nicaragua (Panama inc. 1961); Masters degree programmes in public management; training courses for managers and technical personnel; advisory services; Centre for Information Technology; Dir Dr HUGO ZELAYA CÁLIX; publ. *Revista Centroamerica de Administración Pública* (2 a year).

Instituto Tecnológico de Costa Rica: Apdo 159-7050 Cartago; tel. 2552-5333; fax 2551-5348; e-mail archivo@itcr.ac.cr; internet www.itcr.ac.cr; f. 1971; State control; language of instruction: Spanish; academic year February to December; Rector EUGENIO TREJOS; Vice-Rector for Academic Affairs Dr LUIS GERARDO MEZA CASCANTE; Vice-Rector for Academic Services and Students JEANNETTE BARRANTES M.; Vice-Rector for Admin. JOSÉ RAFAEL HIDALGO; Vice-Rector for Research and Extension Dr JUAN FERNANDO ALVAREZ CASTRO; Registrar WILLIAM VIVES BRENES; Librarian CRISTINA GÓMEZ MOLINA; depts of agricultural engineering, agricultural management engineering, agronomy, architecture and town planning, biology, business administration, chemistry, computer science, communication, construction engineering, culture and sport, electromechanical engineering, electronic engineering, forestry engineering, industrial design, industrial production engineering, materials science and engineering, mathematics, physics; safety and hygiene at work, social sciences; library: 54,000 vols; 455 teachers; 6,000 students; publs *Comunicación* (2 a year), *Espacio Virtual de la Física*, *Kurú: Revista Forestal*, *Revista Virtual Matemática Educación e Internet*, *Tecnología en Marcha* (3 a year).

CÔTE D'IVOIRE

The Higher Education System

Côte d'Ivoire was a province in French West Africa before gaining its independence in 1960. The Université de Cocody in Abidjan is the oldest university, founded in 1958 as Centre d'Enseignement Supérieur d'Abidjan; in 1964 it became the Université Nationale de Côte d'Ivoire, and it acquired its current name in 1995. There are also two other universities, at Abodo-Adjamé (also in Abidjan) and at Bouaké. Some 96,681 students were enrolled in tertiary education in 1998/99. Education in the north of the country was badly disrupted following the failed coup in 2002. The Ministry of Higher Education and Scientific Research oversees the universities. There are also two administrative bodies, the Council of Higher Education Teaching and the Standing Board of Higher Education Teaching. The universities are run by Councils.

The Baccalauréat is the secondary school qualification required for admission to university. After the first two years of undergraduate studies, a diploma is awarded based on the academic path being followed: arts and humanities (Diplôme Universitaire d'Études Littéraires—DUEL), sciences (Diplôme Universitaire d'Études Scientifiques—DUES), law (Diplôme Universitaire d'Études Juridiques—DUEJ), economics (Diplôme Universitaire d'Études Économiques Générales—DUEEG) or general studies (Diplôme d'Études Universitaires Générales—DEUG). After the Diplôme, a further year of study leads to the Licence. However, five years of study are required for the Diplôme d'Ingénieur. At postgraduate level, the Maîtrise is awarded following one year of study after the Licence. A further year of study leads to the Diplôme d'Études Approfondies (DEA). A final year of postgraduate study results in the award of either the Diplôme d'études Supérieures or the Doctorat de Spécialité de Troisième Cycle. Vocational and technical education is provided by several schools and institutes.

Regulatory Bodies

GOVERNMENT

Ministry of Culture and Francophone Affairs: 22e étage, Tour E, Tours Administratives, BP V39, Abidjan; tel. 20-21-40-34; fax 20-21-33-59; e-mail culture.ci@ci.refer.org; Minister KOMOÉ AUGUSTIN KOUADIO.

Ministry of Higher Education and Scientific Research: 20e étage, Tour C, Tours Administratives, BP V151, Abidjan; tel. 20-21-57-73; fax 20-21-22-25; Minister IBRAHIMA CISSÉ.

Learned Societies

LANGUAGE AND LITERATURE

Alliance Française: AFI N'Gokro, BP 1899, Yamoussoukro; tel. and fax 30-64-25-30; e-mail afi_yakro@yahoo.fr; offers courses and exams in French language and culture and promotes cultural exchange with France; attached teaching offices in Abengourou, Korhogo and San Pedro.

Goethe-Institut: Cocody, rue C27, par ave C16 Jean Mermoz prolongée, BP 982, Abidjan; tel. 22-44-14-22; fax 22-44-96-89; e-mail verw@abidjan.goethe.org; internet www.goethe.de/af/abi/deindex.htm; offers courses and exams in German language and culture and promotes cultural exchange with Germany; library of 7,750 vols; Dir FRIEDRICH ENGELHARDT.

Research Institutes

GENERAL

Institut de Recherche pour le Développement (IRD): rue du Chevalier de Clieu, Zone 4, 15 BP 917, Abidjan 15; tel. 21-24-37-79; fax 21-24-65-04; e-mail rep@ird.ci; internet www.ird.ci; f. 1946; health education, economic devt, environmental management; (see main entry under France); Rep. ALAIN MORLIÈRE.

AGRICULTURE, FISHERIES AND VETERINARY SCIENCE

Centre de Co-opération Internationale en Recherche Agronomique pour le Développement (CIRAD): see entry in Burkina Faso.

Centre National de Recherche Agronomique (CNRA) (National Centre for Agricultural Research): Adiopodoumé, KM17 Route de Dabou, 01 POB 1740, Abidjan 01; tel. 23-47-24-24; fax 23-47-24-11; e-mail info@cnra.ci; internet www.cnra.ci; f. 1998; 140 mems; Dir-Gen. Dr KOFFI SIE; publ. *CNRA-Info* (4 a year).

ECONOMICS, LAW AND POLITICS

Centre Ivoirien de Recherches et d'Etudes Juridiques: blvd Latrille, opp. Eglise St Jean, Cocody 01, BP 3811, Abidjan; tel. 22-44-60-54; f. 1973; strategic research into problems affecting the judiciary in Côte d'Ivoire; Dir KOMENAN ZAPKA.

Centre de Recherche et d'Action pour la Paix (CERAP): 08 BP 2088, Abidjan 08; tel. 22-40-47-20; fax 22-44-84-38; e-mail iddh@cerap-inades.org; internet www.cerap-inades.org; f. 1962 by the Soc. of Jesus; promotes the devt of newly ind. countries; research and training in human rights, peace, politics, economics; library of 50,000 vols, 230 periodicals; Gen. Dir Prof. DENIS MAUGENEST; publs *Débats: Courrier d'Afrique de l'Ouest* (12 a year), *La Lettre de l'IDDH, Bulletin sur les Droits de l'homme en Afrique de l'Ouest* (4 a year).

MEDICINE

Institut Pasteur de Côte d'Ivoire: 01 BP 490, Abidjan 01; tel. 23-45-33-92; fax 23-45-76-23; f. 1972; research laboratories for the study of viral diseases, including yellow fever, poliomyelitis, rabies, influenza, hepatitis, HIV/AIDS; clinical analysis laboratories used by the Centre Hospitalier Universitaire, Cocody; small library in process of formation; Dir MIREILLE DOSSO.

Institut Pierre Richet: BP1500, Bouaké; tel. 30-63-37-46; fax 30-63-27-38; e-mail ipr@ird.ci; f. 1973; research into tropical endemic diseases, incl. malaria, sleeping sickness, dengue fever and yellow fever; part of l'Organisation de Co-opération et de Co-ordination de la Lutte contre les Grandes Endémies en Afrique de l'Ouest (OCCGE); training on 2 levels: technician in medical entomology, and medical entomologist; missions and field studies carried out as required by member countries of OCCGE; library containing spec. colln and field data; Dir P. CARNEVALE.

NATURAL SCIENCES

General

Centre de Recherches Océanographiques: 29 rue des Pêcheurs, BP V18, Abidjan; tel. 21-35-50-14; fax 21-35-11-55; e-mail abe@cro.ird.ci; internet www.refer.ci/ivoir_ct/rec/cdr/cro/accueil.htm; f. 1958; biological oceanography, hydrobiology, physics and chemistry; 40 staff; library of 30,000 vols; Dir Dr JACQUES ABE; publs *Archives Scientifiques, Journal Ivoirien d'Océanologie et de Limnologie*.

Physical Sciences

Station Géophysique de Lamto: BP 31, N'Douci; tel. 31-62-90-95; fax 31-62-92-20; e-mail lamtogeo@aviso.ci; f. 1962; atmospherical and climatological, seismological, infrared studies; Dir Prof. MAMADOU FOFANA; publ. *Bulletin of Teleseisms* (52 a year).

RELIGION, SOCIOLOGY AND ANTHROPOLOGY

Centre des Sciences Humaines: BP 1600, Abidjan; f. 1960; ethnological and sociological research, especially in the cultural and religious field; museology, conservation, exhibitions; Dir Dr B. HOLAS; see also Musée des Civilisations.

TECHNOLOGY

Bureau de Recherches Géologiques et Minières (BRGM): 01 BP 1335, Abidjan 01; gold-mining stations at Bondoukou, Fetekio, Ity, Toulepleu, Yaouré.

Société pour le Développement Minier de la Côte d'Ivoire (SODEMI): 01 BP 2816, 31 blvd Latrille Abidjan 01; tel. 22-44-29-95; fax 22-44-08-21; e-mail sodemi@aviso.ci; f. 1962; carries out a programme of geological and geophysical minerals prospecting; mineral mining; library of 5,435 vols, 28 current periodicals, 2,556 geological or prospecting reports, 3,500 topographic and geological maps; Dir-Gen. J. N'ZI.

Libraries and Archives
Abidjan

Archives de Côte d'Ivoire: BP V126, Abidjan; tel. 20-32-41-58; f. 1913; Dir (vacant).

Bibliothèque Centrale de la Côte d'Ivoire: BP 6243, Abidjan-Treichville; f. 1963; a service of the Ministry of National Education; public lecture service; 14,000 vols; founded with help of UNESCO; Librarian P. ZELLI ANY-GRAH.

Bibliothèque Centrale de l'Université de Cocody: BP V34, Abidjan 01; tel. 22-44-08-47; f. 1963; 95,000 vols, 1,650 periodicals; Librarian FRANÇOISE N'GORAN.

Bibliothèque du Centre Culturel Français: 01 BP 3995, 01 Abidjan; tel. 20-22-56-28; fax 20-22-71-32; 32,014 vols (adult library), 6,352 vols (children's library), and 5,000 vols in African Documentation section; 197 periodicals and reviews; Dir MICHEL JANNIN; Librarian GÉRARD AUDOUIN.

Bibliothèque Nationale: BP V180, Abidjan; tel. 20-21-38-72; f. 1968; scientific library of 75,000 vols and 135 current periodicals; part of the former centre of the Institut Français d'Afrique Noire; Dir COFFIE TIBURCE; publ. *Bibliographie de la Côte d'Ivoire* (1 a year).

Museum
Abidjan

Musée des Civilisations: BP 1600, Abidjan 01; fmrly Musée de la Côte d'Ivoire; exhibits of ethnographical, sociological, artistic and scientific nature; attached to the Centre des Sciences Humaines; Dir MEMEL SILVIE KASSI.

Universities

UNIVERSITÉ D'ABOBO-ADJAMÉ

BP 801, Abidjan 02
Telephone: 22-37-81-22
Fax: 22-37-81-18
E-mail: abobo-adj@abobo.edu.ci
Internet: www.abobo.edu.ci
Founded 1957 as Centre d'Enseignement Supérieur; became part of Université Nationale de Côte d'Ivoire 1964; ind. status and present name 1992
State control
Units of basic sciences, food technology and higher education; school of health sciences; centres for advanced training and ecology
Pres.: ETIENNE EHOUAN EHILÉ
Library of 14,000
Number of teachers: 50
Number of students: 5,000

UNIVERSITÉ DE BOUAKÉ

BP V 18, Bouaké 01
Telephone: 30-63-48-57
Fax: 30-63-59-84
Internet: www.refer.ci/ivoir_ct/edu/sup/uni/bke/accueil.htm
Founded 1960, became part of Université Nationale de Côte d'Ivoire 1964, present status 1994
State control

Units of communication, environment and society, economics and development, higher education, law, administration and development and medical sciences; centres for development research and lifelong education
Pres.: FRANÇOIS KOUAKOU N'GUESSAN
Sec.-Gen.: GERMAIN ADJA-DIBY.

UNIVERSITÉ DE COCODY

BP V34, Abidjan 01
Telephone: 22-44-90-00
Fax: 22-44-14-07
E-mail: acceuil@ucocody.ci
Internet: www.ucocody.ci
Founded 1958 as the Centre d'Enseignement Supérieur d'Abidjan; became part of Université Nationale de Côte d'Ivoire 1964; present name 1995
State control
Language of instruction: French
Academic year: September to July
Pres.: CÉLESTIN TÉA GOKOU
Gen. Sec.: JÉRÔME TOTO BALOUBI
Librarian: FRANÇOISE N'GORAN
Number of teachers: 1,081
Number of students: 37,500
Publications: *En-Quête* (Humanities), *Repères* (Humanities), *Revues Médicales* (4 a year), *Revues Sociales* (2 a year)

DEANS

Faculty of Biosciences: VALENTIN N'DOUBA
Faculty of Construction Engineering and Technology: MARIE-CHANTAL KOUASSI-GOFFRI
Faculty of Criminology: ZÉPHIRIN BOLIGA
Faculty of Earth Sciences and Mining Resources: JEAN BIENI
Faculty of Economic Sciences: GILBERT-MARIE AKE NGBO
Faculty of Human and Social Sciences: IGNACE ZASSELI BIAKA
Faculty of Information, Art and Communication: AUGUSTE AGHI BAHI
Faculty of Language, Literature and Civilization: FRANÇOIS ASSI ADOPO
Faculty of Law: DJEDRO MELEDJE
Faculty of Mathematics and Computer Science: KONIN KOUA
Faculty of Medicine: ISIDORE MOHÉNOU DIOMANDE
Faculty of Odontostomatology: SIAKA TOURÉ
Faculty of Pharmacy: ANGLADE KLA MALAN

PROFESSORS

Faculty of Biosciences:
ACHY SEKA, A., Atmospheric Physics
AIDARA, D.
ASSA, A.
BOKRA, Y.
DEGNY, E.
DJAKOURE, A. L.
EBBY, N.
EHILE, E. E.
HONENOU, P.
KAMENAN, A.
KOPOH, K.
KOUAKOU, G.
KOUASSI, N., Zoology
KRA, G.
LOROUGNON, G.
N'DIAYE, A. S., Cell Biology
NEZIT, P., Mathematics
N'GUESSAN, Y. T., Organic Chemistry
OFFOUMOU, A. M.
SERI, B.
TOURE, S., Mathematics
TOURE, V., Organic Chemistry

Faculty of Economic Sciences:
ATSAIN, A.
ALLECHI, M.
KOULIBALY, M.

Faculty of Language, Literature and Civilization:
ANO, N., Oral Literature
BOKA, M., The African Novel in French
DIBI, K., Metaphysical Philosophy
HAUHOUOT, A., Geography
KODJO, N., History
KOMENAN, A. L., Philosophy
KONATE, Y., Philosophy
KONE BONI, T., Philosophy
LEZOU, D. G., The Francophone African Novel South of the Sahara, Semiotics
M'BRA, E., History
N'DA, P., The Francophone Novel
NIAMKET, K., Philosophy
NIANGORAN, B., Ethnology
SEMI-BI, Z., History
TANO, J., Differential Psychology

Faculty of Law:
BLEOU, D. M., Public Law
DEGNI-SEGUI, R., Public Law
ISSA, S., Private Law
SARASSORO, H., Private Law
WODIE, V. F., Public Law
YAO-N'DRE, P., Public Law

Faculty of Medicine:
ANDOH, J.
ATTIA, Y. R.
BAMBA, M.
BEDA, Y. B.
BOUHOUSSOU, K. M.
COULIBALY, O. A.
DAGO, A. B. A.
DJEDJE, M.
DOSSO, B. M.
EHOUMAN, A.
GADEGBEKU, A. S.
KADIO, A.
KANGA, J. M.
KANGA, M.
KEITA, A. K.
KONE, N.
KOUAKOU, N. M.
KOUAME, K. J.
LAMBIN, Y.
MOBIOT, M. L.
N'DORI, R.
N'DRI, K. D.
N'GUESSAN, K. G.
NIAMKET, E. K.
ODEHOURI, K. P.
ODI, A. M.
ROUX, C.
SANGARE, A.
SANGARE, I. S.
SOMBO, M. F.
TIMITE ADJOUA, M.
WAOTA, C.
WELFFENS-EKRA, C.

Faculty of Odontostomatology:
ANGOA, Y.
BAKAYOKO, L. R.
BROU, K. E.
EGNANKOU, K.
ROUX, H.
TOURE, S.

Faculty of Pharmacy:
BAMBA, M.
KONE, M.
MARCY, R.
OUATTARA, L.
YAPO, A. E.

DIRECTORS

Institute of African History of Art and Archaeology: ZAN SEMI-BI
Institute of African Literature and Aesthetics: (vacant)
Institute of Applied Linguistics: ASSY ADOPO
Institute of Ethnosociology: (vacant)
Institute of Teacher-training and Teaching Research: ADOU AKA

Centre for Architectural and Urban Research: (vacant)

Centre for Communication Teaching and Research: REGINA SERIE TRAORE

University Centre for French Studies: N'GUESSAN KOUASSI

Colleges

Académie Régionale des Sciences et Techniques de la Mer: BP V158, Abidjan; tel. 20-37-18-23; f. 1975 by 17 African countries; merchant shipping, training for radio officers, marine management; library; Dir-Gen. AKA ADOU.

Ecole Nationale d'Administration: BP V 20, Abidjan; tel. 22-41-52-25; fax 22-41-49-63; e-mail ena@globe.access.net; f. 1960; 954 students; library: 11,676 vols, 15 periodicals; Dir GUILLAUME KOUACOU DJAH.

Ecole Nationale des Postes et Télécommunications: BP 1501, Abidjan; tel. 21-25-54-94; fax 21-25-99-05.

Ecole Nationale Supérieure de Statistique et d'Economie Appliquée: Cnr blvd François Mitterand and blvd des Grandes Ecoles, Campus Universitaire de Cocody, 08 BP3, Abidjan 08; tel. 22-44-08-40; fax 22-44-39-88; e-mail ensea@ensea.ed.ci; internet www.ensea.refer.ci; f. 1961; 20 teachers; 120 students; library: 13,268 vols; Dir KOFFI N'GUESSAN.

Ecole Nationale Supérieure des Travaux Publics: BP 1083, Yamoussoukro; tel. 30-64-01-00; fax 30-64-03-06; f. 1963; comprises l'Ecole Préparatoire, l'Ecole Nationale Supérieure des Ingénieurs, le Centre de Formation Continue, l' Ecole Nationale des Techniciens Supérieurs; library: 60,000 vols; 97 teachers; 567 students; Dir SYLVAIN KACOU.

Ecole Supérieure d'Agronomie: BP 1313, Yamoussoukro; tel. 30-64-07-70; fax 30-64-17-49; e-mail esayakro@africaonline.ci; f. 1965; training of agricultural managers; research into agricultural production; 75 teachers; 600 students; library: 6,000 vols; Dir Dr KAMA BERTÉ.

Ecole Supérieure Interafricaine de l'Electricité/Interafrican Electrical Engineering College: BP 311, Bingerville; tel. 22-40-33-12; fax 22-40-35-07; f. 1979; bilingual (English and French) training to graduate level in electrical engineering for students sponsored by power-supply authorities or private companies from all over Africa; Dir-Gen. ABDOU KARIM DIAGNE.

Institut National Polytechnique Félix Houphouët-Boigny: BP 1093, Yamoussoukro; tel. 30-64-05-41; fax 30-64-04-06; f. 1975; technical and vocational training; comprises l' Ecole de Formation Continue et de Perfectionnement des Cadres, l' Ecole Supérieure d'Agronomie, l' Ecole Supérieure de Commerce et d'Administration d'Entreprises, l' Ecole Supérieure d'Industrie, l' Ecole Supérieure des Travaux Publics; library: 20,000 vols; 350 teachers; 3,500 students; Dir-Gen. ADO GOSSAN; publs *Akounda* (1 a year), *Leader* (4 a year).

CROATIA

The Higher Education System

Before gaining independence in 1991 Croatia was a federal republic of the former Yugoslavia. The oldest university is Sveučilište u Zagreb (University of Zagreb), which was founded in 1669. Higher education is administered according to the Higher Education Law of 1996, and is the responsibility of the Ministry of Science, Education and Sports. In 2007/08 a total of 143,410 students were enrolled at 115 institutions of higher education in Croatia, including seven universities (in Zagreb, Rijeka, Osijek, Zadar, Pula, Dubrovnik and Split). In 2008 the Dubrovnik International University was founded.

Higher education institutions set their own admissions requirements, with the approval of the Ministry of Science, Education and Sports. Students are usually required to possess the requisite secondary school qualifications and sit an entrance exam. In 2001 Croatia signed up to the Bologna Process and aimed to have implemented most prescribed changes by 2010; the traditional undergraduate degrees, the

Vise Obrazovanje (two to three years' study) and Visoko Obrazovanja (four to six years' study), have been phased out in favour of the Bachelors (four years). Study for a Magistar (Masters degree) in either arts or science subjects includes a magistarski rad (Masters thesis). The Doctorate is the highest postgraduate qualification, study for which includes the research and defence of a doktorski rad (doctoral thesis).

Tertiary-level technical and vocational education consists of one- to four-year programmes in industrial, trade and craft occupations. Students who complete a postgraduate course in art at a polytechnic may attain the professional title of Master of Arts in accordance with a separate law.

Both higher education institutions and study programmes must undergo an evaluation process in order to be accredited for operation in Croatia. The request for accreditation is submitted to the Ministry of Science, Education and Sports which requests a recommendation from the National Council for Higher Education.

Regulatory and Representative Bodies

GOVERNMENT

Ministry of Culture: Runjaninova 2, HR-10000 Zagreb; tel. (1) 4866-666; fax (1) 4866-280; e-mail kabinet@min-kulture.hr; internet www.min-kulture.hr; Min. BOŽO BIŠKUPIĆ.

Ministry of Science, Education and Sports: Donje Svetice 38, HR-10000 Zagreb; tel. (1) 4569-000; fax (1) 4594-301; e-mail office@mzos.hr; internet www.mzos.hr; Min. RADOVAN FUCHS.

ACCREDITATION

ENIC/NARIC Croatia: Croatian ENIC/NARIC Office, Donje Svetice 38/5, HR-10000 Zagreb; tel. (1) 6274-888; fax (1) 6274-889; e-mail enic@azvo.hr; internet www.azvo.hr/default.aspx?sec=110; f. 2004; information centre for academic mobility and recognition of foreign higher education qualifications; part of European Network of nat. information centres on recognition and mobility; Head of Office MARINA CVITANUSIĆ.

NATIONAL BODIES

Agencija za znanost i visoko obrazovanje (Agency for Science and Higher Education): Donje Svetice 38/5, HR-10000 Zagreb; tel. (1) 6274-800; fax (1) 6274-801; e-mail ured@azvo.hr; internet www.azvo.hr; f. 2004; legal entity which autonomously and independently performs activities within the scope and authorities determined under the Scientific Activity and Higher Education Act, the Act on Quality Assurance in Higher Education and Science, and the Act on Recognition of Foreign Educational Qualifications; activities incl. quality assurance and improvement in higher education and science; full mem of Int. Network for Quality Assurance Agencies in Higher Education since 2006; Pres Prof. MILE DŽELALIJA; Dir Prof. JASMINA HAVRANEK (acting).

Hrvatska akademska i istraživačka mreža (CARNet) (Croatian Academic and Research Network): Josipa Marohnića 5, HR-10000 Zagreb; tel. (1) 6661-616; fax (1) 6661-

615; e-mail ured@carnet.hr; internet www.carnet.hr; f. 1991; attached to Min. of Science, Education and Sports; develops advanced information technology and infrastructure for the academic and research community to improve higher education and to promote the design, introduction and implementation of new technologies in Croatia; 250 mem. instns in 382 locations; Chair. of the Board Prof. Dr MARIO KOVAČ; CEO ZVONIMIR STANIĆ.

Rektorski zbor (Rectors' Conference): Trg Sr. Trojstra 3, HR-31000 Osijete; tel. (31) 224-102; fax (31) 207-015; e-mail rc@unizg.hr; internet www.unizg.hr/rz; promotes implementation of the Bologna Declaration; Pres. Prof. Dr GORDANA KRALIK; Sec.-Gen. Prof. Dr BRANKO JEREN.

Vijeće Veleučilišta i Visokih škola Hrvatske (Croatian Council of Institutions of Higher Professional Education): Martićeva 13, HR-10000 Zagreb; tel. (1) 5495-762; fax (1) 5495-769; e-mail vijece@zvu.hr; f. 2002; Pres. Prof. Dr MARKO JELIĆ.

Learned Societies

GENERAL

Društvo za Proučavanje i Unapredenje Pomorstva (Society for Research and Promotion of Maritime Sciences): Riva 16/V, POB 301, HR-51000 Rijeka; tel. (51) 334-210; fax (51) 334-210; e-mail dpuprh@inet.hr; f. 1962; research divided into 9 sections: economics, ethnology, history, law, literature, medicine, natural sciences, nautical sciences, technology; 323 elected mems; Pres. Prof. Dr BLANKA KESIĆ; Sec. Dr DUŠAN VRUS; publ. *Pomorski Zbornik* (Maritime Annals, 1 a year).

Hrvatska Akademija Znanosti i Umjetnosti (Croatian Academy of Sciences and Arts): Zrinski Trg 11, HR-10000 Zagreb; tel. (1) 4895-111; fax (1) 4819-979; e-mail kabpred@hazu.hr; internet www.hazu.hr; f. 1861; depts of fine arts, literature, mathematical, medical sciences, music, natural sciences, philology, physical and chemical sciences, social sciences, technical sciences;

15 scientific ccls and 8 cttees; 136 mems, 91 assoc. mems, 135 corresponding mems; library: see Libraries and Archives; Pres. Prof. ZVONKO KUSIĆ; Vice-Pres. Prof. JAKŠA BARBIĆ; Vice-Pres. Prof. VELIMIR NEIDHARDT; Sec.-Gen. Prof. PAVAO RUDAN; publs *Ljetopis*, *Rad* (Memoirs).

BIBLIOGRAPHY, LIBRARY SCIENCE AND MUSEOLOGY

Hrvatsko Knjižničarsko Društvo (Croatian Library Association): c/o Nat. and Univ. Library, Hrvatske bratske zajednice 4, HR-10000 Zagreb; tel. and fax (1) 6159-320; e-mail hkd@nsk.hr; internet www.hkdrustvo.hr; f. 1940; promotes library services and the profession of librarianship; publishes journals and other literature; organizes professional meetings; creates library legislation; promotes devt of libraries and general literacy; raises public awareness of the need to preserve and protect cultural heritage; 1,200 mems; Pres. ZDENKA SVIBEN; Vice-Pres. ANICA ŠABARIĆ; Vice-Pres. BRUNO DOBRIĆ; Sec. SANJA ŽUNIĆ; Treas. VESNA GOLUBOVIĆ; publs *HKD Novosti* (4 a year, online), *Vjesnik bibliotekara Hrvatske* (4 a year).

Hrvatsko Muzejsko Društvo (Croatian Museum Association): c/o Muzej za umjetnost i obrt, Trg Maršala Tita 10, HR-10000 Zagreb; tel. (1) 4851-808; fax (1) 4851-977; e-mail hmd@hrmud.hr; internet www.hrmud.hr; f. 1946 as Association of the Employees and Associates of Museums, Galleries and Conservation Institutes in People's Republic of Croatia, present name 1998; non-profit org.; promotes growth and advancement of museum profession and protects the common interests of museum workers; 500 mems; Pres. DUBRAVKA OSREČKI JAKELIĆ; Sec. DORA BOŠKOVIĆ; publ. *News of Museum Custodians and Conservators of Croatia* (4 a year).

EDUCATION

Hrvatski pedagoško-književni zbor (Croatian Pedagogic-Literary Association): Trg Maršala Tita 4, HR-10000 Zagreb; tel. (1) 4855-713; fax (1) 4810-396; e-mail hpkz@zg.t-com.hr; internet www.hpkz-napredak.hr; f. 1871; brs in Slavonski Brod, Križevci,

Vukovar, Dubrovnik, Split, Petrinja, Sibenik and Zagreb; 2,000 mems; Pres. VESNA BUDINSKI; Vice-Pres. NEVIO ŠETIÆ; Sec. KRISTINA ŠNIDARŠIĆ-VLAŠIĆ; publ. *Napredak* (4 a year).

HISTORY, GEOGRAPHY AND ARCHAEOLOGY

Geografija (Croatian Geographic Society): Marulićev Trg 19, POB 595, HR-10000 Zagreb; tel. (1) 4895-402; fax (1) 4895-451; e-mail geografija.hr@gmail.com; internet www.geografija.hr; f. 1897; 600 mems; library of 6,550 vols, 9,570 in spec. collns; Pres. ALEKSANDAR LUKIĆ; publs *Geografski glasnik* (1 a year), *Geografski horizont* (4 a year).

Hrvatsko numizmatičko društvo (Croatian Numismatic Society): Habdelićeva 2, POB 181, HR-10000 Zagreb; tel. (1) 431-426; internet www .hrvatskonumizmatickodrustvo.hr; f. 1928; 500 mems; library of 1,600 vols; Pres. DAMIR KOVAČ; Sec. Prof. BORIS PRISTER; Sec. BERISLAV KOPAC; publs *Numizmatičke vijesti* (1 a year), *Numizmatika, Obol* (1 a year).

LANGUAGE AND LITERATURE

Alliance Française: Ante Kovačića 4, HR-10000 Zagreb; tel. and fax (1) 4818-292; e-mail alliance-francaise@zg.htnet.hr; internet www.alliance-francaise.hr; offers courses and examinations in French language and culture and promotes cultural exchange with France; attached offices in Dubrovnik and Split.

British Council: Illica 12, PP55, HR-10001 Zagreb; tel. (1) 4899-500; fax (1) 4833-955; e-mail zagreb.info@britishcouncil.hr; internet www.britishcouncil.hr; offers courses and examinations in English language and British culture and promotes cultural exchange with the UK; library of 7,500 vols, 60 periodicals, 2,500 DVDs; Dir ROY CROSS.

Goethe-Institut: ul. Grada Vukovara 64, HR-10000 Zagreb; tel. (1) 6195-000; fax (1) 6274-355; e-mail info@zagreb.goethe.org; internet www.goethe.de/ms/zag/deindex .htm; offers courses and examinations in German language and culture and promotes cultural exchange with Germany; library of 10,000 vols, 20 periodicals; Dir JULIANE STEGNER; Head Librarian MAJA ANTUNOVIĆ.

MEDICINE

Hrvatskog Liječničkog Zbora (Croatian Medical Association): Šubićeva ul. 9, HR-10000 Zagreb; tel. (1) 4693-300; fax (1) 4655-066; e-mail tajnistvo@hlz.hr; internet www .hlz.hr; f. 1874; 26 regional brs, 121 mem. socs, 10,400 individual mems; Pres. Prof. Dr ŽELJKO METELKO; Vice-Pres. Prof. Dr ZELJKO KRZNARIĆ, HRVOJE PEZO; Gen. Sec. Prof. Dr TOMISLAV BOŽEK; publs *Acta Stomatologica Croatica*, *Liječničke Novine* (Medical News), *Liječnički Vjesnik* (Medical Journal).

Hrvatsko Farmaceutsko Društvo (Croatian Pharmaceutical Society): Masarykova 2, HR-10000 Zagreb; tel. (1) 4872-849; fax (1) 4872-853; e-mail hfd-fg-ap@zg.t-com.hr; internet www.hfd-fg.hr; f. 1858, present name 1946; asscn of pharmacists to improve professional and scientific work in the field of pharmacy in Croatia, organizes educational courses, professional and scientific events; 1,040 mems; library of 2,000 vols; Chair. KREŠIMIR RUKAVINA; Sec.-Gen. MAJA JAKŠE-VAC MIKŠA; publs *Acta Pharmaceutica* (4 a year), *Farmaceutski glasnik* (12 a year).

NATURAL SCIENCES
General

Hrvatsko Prirodoslovno Društvo (Croatian Society of Natural Sciences): Frankopanska 1/I, POB 258, HR-10001 Zagreb; tel. (1) 4831-224; fax (1) 4831-223; e-mail hpd@hpd.hr; internet www.hpd.hr; f. 1885; organizes meetings and scientific platforms for the promotion of natural sciences; Pres. Prof. Dr NIKOLA LJUBEŠIĆ; Vice-Pres. MLADEN JURAČIĆ; Sec. Dr LIDIJA SUMAN; publs *Periodicum Biologorum* (scientific journal with papers on biomedicine and biochemistry, 6 a year), *Priroda* (Nature, 12 a year).

TECHNOLOGY

Hrvatski Savez Građevinskih Inženjera (Croatian Association of Civil Engineers): Berislavićeva 6, HR-10000 Zagreb; tel. (1) 4872-498; fax (1) 4828-053; e-mail dgiz@zg .t-com.hr; internet www.hsgi.org; f. 1970; promotes scientific research work in the field of architecture; organizes lectures, confs and symposia; 3,017 mems; library of 5,000 vols; Chief Officer Prof. Dr Ing. ERVIN NONVEILLER; publ. *Gradevinar* (online at www.casopis-gradjevinar.hr).

Research Institutes
GENERAL

Zavod za povijest i filozofiju znanosti u Zagrebu (Institute for the History and Philosophy of Science in Zagreb): Ante Kovačića 5, HR-10000 Zagreb; tel. (1) 4698-231; internet info.hazu.hr/ zavod_za_povijest_i_filozofiju_znanosti; f. 1992 by merger of the Institute for Te History of Natural, Mathematical and Medical Sciences (f. 1960) and the Institute for the Philosophy of Science and Peace; attached to Hrvatske Akademije Znanosti i Umjetnosti (Croatian Acad. of Sciences and Arts); comprises divs for the history of natural and mathematical sciences, philosophy of science and history of medical sciences; incorporates Institute of the History of Pharmacy of the Croatian Pharmaceutical Soc., Institute for the History of Medicine, Medical Faculty, Univ. of Zagreb, Cabinet for the History of Veterinary Medicine, Museum of the Soc. of Physicians of Croatia and Institute for the Philosophy of Sciences; scientific institution to foster research into the history of science, espec. that of the Croats; plans to study problems of methodology, to organize at Zagreb higher education the study of the history of science, to collaborate with analogous institutes at home and abroad; library of 8,000 vols; Dir Prof. Dr ŽARKO DADIĆ; publ. *Rasprave i Gradja za Povijest Nauka* (1 a year).

Zavod za Znanstveni i Umjetnički u Splitu (Institute for Scientific and Artistic Work in Split): Trg Braće Radića 7, POB 100, HR-42000 Split; tel. (21) 348-599; fax (21) 348-599; e-mail hazu.zavod.split@st.t-com .hr; internet info.hazu.hr/ zavod_za_znanstveni_i_umjetnicki_rad_u_s-plitu; f. 1925 as Institute of Maritime and Social Sciences, reconstituted to present status 1981; attached to Hrvatske Akademije Znanosti i Umjetnosti (Croatian Acad. of Sciences and Arts); performs scientific and other expert research in the areas of the humanities, social and bio-technical sciences (history, archaeology, viticulture, wine production, ecological food production and tourism); initiates and organizes scientific meetings, symposia, exhibitions; publishes the results of scientific work and research;

library of 6,000 vols; Hon. Dir Prof. Dr DAVORIN RUDOLF; publ. *Adrias*.

AGRICULTURE, FISHERIES AND VETERINARY SCIENCE

Institut za oceanografiju i ribarstvo (Institute of Oceanography and Fisheries): Setalište Ivana Meštrovića 63, HR-21000 Split; tel. (21) 408-000; fax (21) 358-650; e-mail office@izor.hr; internet www.izor.hr; f. 1930; conducts research in hydrography, geology, marine biology, mariculture and fishery technology, marine fisheries, ichthyology, mariculture and fishery technology, oceanography; postgraduate study in fisheries; has a hatchery and a research vessel; library of 15,000 vols; Dir Dr IVONA MARASOVIĆ; Pres. of Scientific Council Dr IVICA VILIBIĆ; publs *Acta Adriatica, Notes*.

Poljoprivredni Institut Osijek (Osijek Agricultural Institute): Južno Predgrade 17, POB 334, HR-31001 Osijek; tel. (31) 515-501; fax (31) 515-509; e-mail institut@poljinos.hr; internet www.poljinos.hr; f. 1916; agricultural and scientific research into breeding of wheat, barley, corn, soybeans, sunflowers and alfalfa; 160 mems; library of 5,380 vols; Dir Dr ZVONIMIR ZDUNIĆ; publ. *Poljoprivreda* (Agriculture, 2 a year).

ARCHITECTURE AND TOWN PLANNING

Kabinet za Arhitekturu i Urbanizam (Cabinet for Architecture and Urban Planning): Hebrangova 1, HR-10000 Zagreb; tel. (1) 4825-406; e-mail arlikum@hazu.hr; internet info.hazu.hr/ kabinet_za_arhitekturu_i_urbanizam; f. 1952; attached to Arhiv za lLikovne Umjetnosti Hrvatska Akademija Znanosti i Umjetnosti (Fine Art Archives of the Croatian Academy of Sciences and Arts); scientific study of the history of architecture and town planning and methods of protection, conservation and presentation of monuments; holds seven collns: catalogue colln, author files, exhibition files, periodicals colln, artist's correspondence, personal archives, archives of art societies and photograph colln; 5 mems; library of 2,000 vols, 30 periodicals; Hon. Dir VELIMIR NEIDHARDT; publs *Bulletin Razreda za likovne umjetnosti* (2 a year), *Monographs* (irregular), *Rad JAZU* (irregular).

BIBLIOGRAPHY, LIBRARY SCIENCE AND MUSEOLOGY

City of Zagreb, City Institute for the Conservation of Cultural and Natural Heritage: Kuševićeva 2, HR-10000 Zagreb; tel. (1) 6101-970; fax (1) 6101-896; e-mail zastita.spomenika@zagreb.hr; f. 1991; attached to City of Zagreb Govt; tasks related to cultural and natural heritage and cultural property; research on architectural heritage, analysing, assessing or reassessing buildings of artistic and historical interest; initiates projects, incl. measures for conservation-restoration of movable and immovable cultural heritage, monitors and evaluates restorative and reconstructive interventions related to art objects; approves architectural plans and documentation in the process of issuing bldg permits; issues permits for export of cultural goods; catalogues private collns; protects natural environment and natural values, nature parks, forest parks, monuments of park architecture, important landscapes, prescribes nature protection measures and conditions; library of 1,400 vols, photographic colln of 54,000 negatives, 10,000 charts; Prin. SILVIJE NOVAK; publ. *Godišnjak zaštite spomenika kulture Hrvatske* (Yearbook of Protection of Croatian Cultural Monuments).

Hrvatski restauratorski zavod (Croatian Conservation Institute): Nike Grskovica 23, HR-10000 Zagreb; tel. (1) 4684-599; fax (1) 4683-289; e-mail uprava@h-r-z.hr; internet www.h-r-z.hr; f. 1997 by merger of Institute for the Conservation of Objects of Art (f. 1948) and the Conservation Institute of Croatia (f. 1966); restoration of and research into the conservation of paintings, historic architecture, wooden sculpture, furniture, stucco, stone, mosaics, wall paintings, architectural monuments, paper and leather, textiles, metal and other archaeological finds; underwater archaeological research; Dir Prof. FERDINAND MEDER.

Regionalni zavod za zaštitu spomenika kulture (Regional Institute for the Protection of Historic Monuments): Poljudsko šetalište 15, POB 191, HR-21000 Split; tel. (21) 342-327; f. 1854; library of 12,000 vols and periodicals, 130,000 photographs and negatives; Dir Dr JOŠKO BELAMARIĆ; Sec. NEIRA STOJANAC; publ. *Prilozi povijesti umjetnosti u Dalmaciji.*

ECONOMICS, LAW AND POLITICS

Institute for International Relations: POB 303, ul. Lj. Farkaša Vukotinovića 2/II, HR-10000 Zagreb; tel. (1) 4877-460; fax (1) 4828-361; e-mail ured@irmo.hr; internet www.imo.hr; f. 1963 as Africa Research Institute, name changed to Institute for Developing Countries 1971, present name and status 1996; attached to Min. of Science, Education and Sports; interdisciplinary study of devt processes and economic and int. relations, and cooperation in the field of economics, culture, science, environmental protection and politics; organizes seminars, int. confs and specialist training programmes; library of 9,000 vols, 400 periodicals; Pres. of Management Ccl Dr MLADEN ANDRLIĆ; Dir Dr SANJA TIŠMA; publs *Croatian International Relations Review* (4 a year, in English), *Culturelink* (3 a year and spec. issue in English), *Euroscope* (6 a year, in Croatian).

Jadranski zavod (Adriatic Institute): Frane Petrića 4/1, HR-10000 Zagreb; tel. and fax (1) 481-2703; e-mail jz@hazu.hr; internet www.hazu.hr/jzavod; f. 1945, inc. as research institute of Yugoslav Academy of Sciences and Arts (now Croatian Acad. of Sciences and Arts) 1948, renamed Institute of Maritime Law, History and Economics 1974, present bldg 1992, present name 1994; attached to Hrvatske akademije znanosti i umjetnosti (Croatian Acad. of Sciences and Arts); maritime law and the law of the sea, with particular emphasis on the carriage of goods by sea, maritime safety, insurance, protection of the marine environment and maritime delimitations; library of 15,000 vols, 117 periodicals, 2,500 documents; Dir Prof. Emeritus VLADIMIR-DJURO DEGAN; Sec. VLATKA ŽIVOJNOVIĆ; publ. *Poredbeno pomorsko pravo* (Comparative Maritime Law, 1 a year, in English and Croatian).

LANGUAGE AND LITERATURE

Leksikografski Zavod 'Miroslav Krleža' ('Miroslav Krleža' Lexicographic Institute): Frankopanska 26, HR-10000 Zagreb; tel. (1) 4800-398; fax (1) 4800-399; e-mail lzmk@lzmk.hr; internet www.lzmk.hr; f. 1951; collects and processes MSS for encyclopaedic, lexicographic, bibliographic, monographic and other scientific edns; publishes results of research and cooperates with similar institutions abroad; 10,000 contributors, specialists in all fields; library: specialized library of 35,000 vols; Dir-Gen. Prof. BOGIŠIĆ BLAISE; Dir BRUNO KRAGIĆ.

Staroslavenski institut (Old Church Slavonic Institute): Demetrova 11, HR-10000 Zagreb; tel. (1) 4851-380; fax (1) 4851-377; e-mail info@stin.hr; internet www.stin.hr; f. 1902, as Old Church Slavonic Academy, present name 1952; research of the Croatian Glagolitic heritage: language, literature and palaeography; library of 20,000 vols, 11,820 book titles, 482 periodicals; Dir Dr MARICA ČUNČIĆ; Sec. MARINA ŠANTIĆ; publ. *Slovo* (1 a year).

MEDICINE

Institut za medicinska istraživanja i medicinu rada (Institute for Medical Research and Occupational Health): Ksaverska cesta 2, POB 291, HR-10001 Zagreb; tel. (1) 4673-188; fax (1) 4673-303; e-mail uprava@imi.hr; internet mimi.imi.hr; f. 1947 as Institute of Occupational Hygiene; ind. status 1958, present name 1959; attached to Min. of Science, Education and Sports; conducts research on working and living environment, hygiene, health and dissemination of knowledge on industrial hygiene, environmental pollution and radiation; seeks to implement research results in industry and runs a number of projects of national interest; scientists of the institute teach in postgraduate and undergraduate programmes, primarily at the Univ. of Zagreb; library of 8,000 books, 75 journals; Dir Dr ANA LUCIĆ VRDOLJAK; Chair. VLASTA DREVENKAR; publ. *Arhiv za higijenu rada i toksilologiju* (Archives of Industrial Hygiene and Toxicology, 4 a year, in English and Croatian).

NATURAL SCIENCES

General

Institut 'Rudjer Bošković' (Rudjer Bošković Institute): Bijenička cesta 54, POB 1016, HR-10000 Zagreb; tel. (1) 4561-111; fax (1) 4680-084; e-mail info@irb.hr; internet www.irb.hr; f. 1950; attached to Univ. of Osijek, Univ. of Rijeka and Univ. of Zagreb; research in physics (biophysics, medical, nuclear and atomic, theoretical), chemistry (biochemistry, organic and physical), biology (biomedicine, molecular biology), electronics; marine research centres in Rovinj and Zagreb; 82 laboratories; library of 37,000 vols, 760 print journals and access to 16,000 electronic journals; Dir-Gen. Dr DANICA RAMLJAK; Sec. JADRANKA KUČAN; Head of Library BOJAN MACAN.

Biological Sciences

Bureau for Nature Conservation: Ilica 44/II, HR-10000 Zagreb; tel. (1) 432-022; fax (1) 431-515; f. 1961; photographic colln of 12,200 negatives, 12,000 photographs and 1,240 colour slides; 16 mems; library of 5,400 vols; Dir Prof. Dr MIHO MILJANIĆ.

Physical Sciences

Državni hidrometeorološki zavod (Meteorological and Hydrological Service): Grič 3, HR-10000 Zagreb; tel. (1) 4565-666; fax (1) 4851-901; e-mail dhmz@cirus.dhz.hr; internet meteo.hr; f. 1947; meteorology, climatology, ecological studies, hydrology; maintains Marine Meteorological Centre in Split; library of 7,000 vols, 45 periodicals; Dir IVAN CACIČ; publs *Bilten* (meteorological and hydrological bulletin, 12 a year), *Croatian Meteorological Journal* (1 a year).

RELIGION, SOCIOLOGY AND ANTHROPOLOGY

Institut za Društvena Istraživanja Zagreb (Institute for Social Research Zagreb): Amruševa 11/II, HR-10000 Zagreb; tel. (1) 4810-264; fax (1) 4810-263; e-mail idiz@idi.hr; internet www.idi.hr; f. 1964;

attached to Univ. of Zagreb; research in all fields of sociology, social anthropology, psychology; library of 16,400 vols and periodicals; Dir. RUŽA FIRST-DILIĆ; publs *Revija za Sociologiju* (Sociology Review), *Sociologija Sela* (Rural Sociology, 4 a year).

Institut za etnologiju i folkloristiku (Institute of Ethnology and Folklore Research): Šubićeva 42, HR-10000 Zagreb; tel. (1) 4596-700; fax (1) 4596-709; e-mail institut@ief.hr; internet maief.ief.hr; f. 1948 as Institute of Folk Art; 185,000 items of archives and documentation; spec. colln of ethnographic materials: 1,800 text collns and music annotations, 19 dance collns, 374 kinetograms, 57 drawing collns with 2,000 panels, 3,300 audio cassette recordings (music recordings and narratives); record library (770 sound recordings); photographic and slide library (4,700 items); 970 video cassettes and 51 films; library of 28,100 vols, 19,000 books and offprints, 9,100 bound periodicals; Dir IVAN LOZICA; Sec. SANJA LESIĆ; Librarian ANAMARIJA STARCEVIĆ-STAMBUK; publs *Narodna Umjetnost* (2 a year), *Nova etnografija* (Series).

TECHNOLOGY

Končar–Institut za elektrotehniku d.d. (Končar–Electrical Engineering Institute): Fallerovo šetalište 22, HR-10002 Zagreb; tel. (1) 3667-315; fax (1) 3667-317; e-mail info@koncar-institut.hr; internet www.koncar-institut.hr; f. 1991; research and devt division within Končar Group of companies; research and devt in all fields of electrical engineering; library of 30,000 vols, 350 periodicals; Chair. Dr STJEPAN CAR.

Libraries and Archives

Dubrovnik

Znanstvena knjižnica Dubrovnik (Scientific Library of Dubrovnik): Cvijete Zuzorić 4, HR-20000 Dubrovnik; tel. (20) 323-911; fax (20) 323-767; e-mail znanstvena@dkd.hr; internet www.dkd.hr; f. 1936; 267,000 vols, 7,000 vols of periodicals, 77 incunabula, 928 MSS, 10,490 books belonging to the Republic of Dubrovnik up to 1808 (Old Ragusina), collection of 14,000 vols (New Ragusina); Chief Officer MIRJANA URBAN.

Pula

Sveučilišna knjižnica u Puli (University Library of Pula): Herkulov prolaz 1, HR-52100 Pula; tel. (52) 213-888; fax (52) 214-603; e-mail skpu@unipu.hr; internet www.skpu.hr; f. 1861; publicly accessible central library for the Juraj Dobrila Univ. of Pula; Antonio Smareglia memory room; spec. colln of the Istrian Area; marine library; colln of Eduard Ćalić; Mijo Mirković memory room; Biblioteca Provinciale; music colln; graphic colln; 300,000 vols, 120,000 periodicals; spec. collns: the Istrian area 15,000 vols, Austro-Hungarian Naval Library (20,000 vols); Marine Library: 20,000 vols (131,716 monographs, 6,655 journals, annals and newspapers); 200 vols of incunabula and books from the 16th and 17th centuries; 2,400 audio recordings, 541 maps, postcards and plaques; Dir TIJANA BARBIĆ DOMAZET; publ. *Nova Istra* (literary review, 4 a year).

Rijeka

Sveučilišna knjižnica Rijeka (University Library Rijeka): Dolac 1, POB 132, HR-51000 Rijeka; tel. (51) 336-911; fax (51) 332-006; e-mail ravnatelj@svkri.hr; internet www.svkri.hr; f. 1948, as Scientific Library of Rijeka, present name and status 1979; legal deposit library; spec. collns of material on the

Primorsko-Goranska region and on the Glagolitic script; repository of Univ. of Rijeka publs and dissertations; 400,000 vols, 20,000 online magazines, heritage colln: 100,000 vols; Dir SENKA TOMLJANOVIĆ.

Split

Sveučilišna knjižnica u Splitu (Split University Library): Ruđera Boškovića 31, HR-21000 Split; tel. (21) 434-800; fax (21) 434-801; e-mail svkst@svkst.hr; internet www.svkst.hr; f. 1903; 3,000 mems; material on Split and the surrounding area; 400,000 vols, 12,000 periodicals, 700 MSS, 5,000 rare books, maps and atlases, sheet music, sound recordings and graphic material; Dir Prof. PETAR KROLO; Head Librarian SANJA BRBORA.

Varaždin

Gradska knjižnica i čitaonica 'Metel Ožegović' (City Library 'Metel Ožegović'): Trg Slobode 8A, HR-42000 Varaždin; tel. and fax (42) 212-767; e-mail gknjizmo@vz.htnet.hr; internet library.foi.hr/metel; f. 1838; 190,000 vols; Dir MARIO SOŠTARIĆ; Deputy Dir JASMINKA ŠTIMAC.

Zadar

Znanstvena Knjižnica Zadar (Research Library of Zadar): Ante Kuzmanića bb, HR-23000 Zadar; tel. (23) 211-365; fax (23) 312-129; e-mail zkzd@zkzd.hr; internet www.zkzd.hr; f. 1855 as Biblioteca Comunale Paravia; deposit library; spec. colln: Dalmatica (20,000 vols); 815,000 vols, collns incl. 372 parchments, 34 incunabula, 1,140 MS, 1,460 rare books, 236 Masters and Doctoral theses, colln of 2,398 photographs and 300 negatives on glass plates, 2,250 maps and atlases, 2,250 music scores; Dir MIRO GRUBIĆ; Sr Librarian MILENKA BUKVIĆ; publ. *Knjižno blago Naučne biblioteke u Zadru* continued as *Knjižno blago Znanstvene knjižnice Zadar.*

Zagreb

Hrvatski državni arhiv (Croatian State Archives): Marulićev Trg 21, HR-10000 Zagreb; tel. (1) 4801-999; fax (1) 4829-000; e-mail hda@arhiv.hr; internet www.arhiv.hr; f. 1643; records of central govt archives, other public instns and nat. cinematographic production; incl. 24,000 linear m of records since 10th century, concerning the history of Croatia; 20,000 km of film; 160,000 vols, 90,000 books, 70,000 magazines and newspapers, 600,000 photographs; Dir Dr STJEPAN ĆOSIĆ; publs *Arhivski vjesnik* (Archives Bulletin), *Fontes: Izvori za hrvatsku povijest* (Fontes: Sources for Croatian history).

Knjižnica Hrvatske akademije znanosti i umjetnosti (Library of the Croatian Academy of Sciences and Arts): Strossmayerov Trg 14, HR-10000 Zagreb; tel. (1) 4895-113; fax (1) 4895-134; e-mail library@hazu.hr; internet knjiznica.hazu.hr; f. 1867; 400,000 vols, 1,000 current periodicals; Dir VEDRANA JURIČIĆ.

Knjižnice Grada Zagreba (Zagreb City Libraries): Starčevićev Trg 6, HR-10000 Zagreb; tel. (1) 4572-344; fax (1) 4572-089; e-mail kgz@kgz.hr; internet www.kgz.hr; f. 1967, beginning of library network with merger of City Library of Zagreb and Silvije Strahimir Kranjčević Library; network of public libraries; comprises the City Library of Zagreb (f. 1907) and the Božidar Adžija Library (f. 1927) both holding the largest collns, the County Research and Devt Dept, 12 br. libraries with a network of 31 attached brs in 45 locations; bookmobile service; Dir DAVORKA BASTIĆ; publ. *Književni petak* (Literary Friday).

Nacionalna i sveučilišna knjižnica u Zagrebu (National and University Library in Zagreb): ul. Hrvatske bratske zajednice 4, POB 550, HR-10000 Zagreb; tel. (1) 6164-111; fax (1) 6164-186; e-mail nsk@nsk.hr; internet www.nsk.hr; f. 1611, present name 1874, present bldg 1995; generates and organizes Croatian nat. colln of library holdings and supervises acquisition of publs on the nat. level, and on behalf of the Univ. of Zagreb; acts as the nat. bibliographic office; keeps and renews/updates the library's holdings in accordance with int. programme; promotes Croatian books and other publs; performs bibliographic and information activities, incl. inter-library lending; performs scientific research in the area of librarianship and information science; is also involved in publishing, exhibition and promotional activities; 2.5m. vols; average annual acquisition: 12,000 books, 4,800 magazines and newspapers, 8,800 gen. items and 1,000 pieces of electronic material; spec. collns: MSS and old books, print colln, music and map collns; Chair. MILIVOJ ZENIĆ; Dir-Gen. Prof. TIHOMIL MAŠTROVIĆ; Sr Librarian Dr SLAVKO HARNI; publ. *Hrvatska bibliografija* (Croatian Bibliography, 12 a year).

Museums and Art Galleries

Dubrovnik

Dubrovacki muzeji (Dubrovnik Museums): Pred dvorom 3, HR-20000 Dubrovnik; tel. (20) 321-422; fax (20) 322-096; internet www.mdc.hr/dubrovnik; f. 1872 as the Dubrovnik Regional Museum; comprises 6 museums; Head Dir PAVICA VILAC.

Attached Museums:

Archaeological Museum: Brace Andrijica 7, Dubrovnik; tel. (20) 324-041; e-mail dubrovacki.muzeji1@du.t-com.hr; internet www.mdc.hr/dubrovnik/nj/arheoloski; f. 1991; reference library; museums holdings divided into the prehistoric, antique, early medieval collns, colln from 13th century to the 1667 earthquake, Egyptian, vase and coin collns; Dir ROMANA MENALO.

Cultural Historical Museum: Pred Dvorom 3, HR-20000 Dubrovnik; tel. (20) 321-422; fax (20) 322-096; internet www.mdc.hr/dubrovnik/kulturnopovijesni; Rector's palace: seat of govt and residence of the Prince (Rector) of the Dubrovnik Republic; colln of paintings, ceramics, icons, metalwork, textiles, furniture, glassware, photography, postcards, documents, instruments, clocks and watches; Head Dir and Sr Curator PAVICA VILAĆ; Sr Curator LJILJANA IVUSIĆ.

Ethnographic Museum—The 'Rupe' Museum: Od Rupa 3, Dubrovnik; tel. (20) 412-545; internet www.mdc.hr/dubrovnik/nj/etnografski; f. 1991; 5,000 exhibits on permanent display; collns incl. traditional folk costumes, folklore, textiles, lace; Dir MIRJANA ZEC.

Marin Drzic House: Siroka ul. 7, Dubrovnik; tel. (20) 420-490; internet www.mdc.hr/dubrovnik/nj/marindrzic; f. 1989; theatrical museum, scientific-documentary institute and exhibition space; collns of posters, programmes and photographs of Marin Drzic's plays in Croatia and abroad; display of post-modern installations reconstructing the Renaissance period during which Drzic lived; puppets, posters and stage props; audio guides with excerpts from Drzic texts; Dir IVANA JASIĆ.

Maritime Museum: St John's Fortress, HR-20000 Dubrovnik; tel. (20) 323-904; fax (20) 322-096; internet www.mdc.hr/ dubrovnik/nj/pomorski; f. 1941, admin by Yugoslav Acad. of Arts and Sciences 1949, present status 1987; Dubrovnik's maritime past; ship models from the 17th, 18th and 19th centuries; flags, cannons and other weapons, figureheads, nautical instruments and log books; library of rare books and archival materials; library of 10,027 vols; Dir Prof. ĐIVO BAŠIĆ; Curator Prof. LJERKA DUNATOV; Curator Prof. ANA KAZNAĆIĆ.

Modern History Museum: Poljana Paska Milicevica 1, Dubrovnik; tel. and fax (20) 324-856; e-mail msp@dumus.hr; internet www.mdc.hr/dubrovnik/nj/suvremenapovijest; f. 1956; colln of documents from the Second World War, memoirist writings on the Croatian Homeland War; Dir Prof. VARINA JURICA TURK; publ. *The city-That is you.*

Muzej Srpske Pravoslavne Crkve (Museum of the Serbian Orthodox Church): Od Puća 2, HR-20000 Dubrovnik; f. 1953; colln of portraits, and over 170 icons from Serbia, Crete, Corfu, Venice, Russia, Greece, Dubrovnik, Boka-Kotorska; the palace that houses the colln is also of historical interest; library of 25,000 vols.

Umjetnička Galerija Dubrovnik (Museum of Modern Art Dubrovnik): Frana Supila 23, HR-20000 Dubrovnik; tel. (20) 426-590; fax (20) 432-114; e-mail info@ugdubrovnik.hr; internet www.ugdubrovnik.hr; f. 1945; exhibitions of modern and contemporary art and exhibitions from its rich holdings of modern and contemporary art; 2,449 items; library of 1,157 vols; Dir ANTUN MARAČIĆ; Curator ROZANA VOJVODA; Curator PETRA GOLUŠIĆ.

Rijeka

Muzej Moderne i Suvremente Umjetnosti, Rijeka (Museum of Modern and Contemporary Art, Rijeka): Dolac 1/II, HR-51000 Rijeka; tel. (51) 492-611; fax (51) 492-623; e-mail mmsu-rijeka@ri.t-com.hr; internet www.mmsu.hr; f. 1948; paintings, sculptures, prints, posters, photographs, installations, new media from Croatia and other countries; publs catalogues; colln of over 5,000 artwork, covering periods from the end of the 19th century to present day; 18 mems; library of 30,000 books and catalogues; Dir Dr JERICA ZIHERL.

Prirodoslovni muzej Rijeka (Natural History Museum Rijeka): Lorenzov Prolaz 1, HR-51000 Rijeka; tel. and fax (51) 553-669; e-mail info@prirodoslovni.com; internet www.prirodoslovni.com; f. 1876; on permanent display: geological history of the Adriatic; inorganic, zoological and botanical collns (90,000 specimens); library of 4,024 vols; Dir MILVANA ARKO PIJEVAC; Sec. TANJA CICAVARIĆ.

Slavonski Brod

Brlić House (Ivana Brlić-Mažuranić Memorial): Titov Trg 8, HR-55000 Slavonski Brod; f. 1933; private family house containing archives, furniture showing the evolution of a Croatian middle-class family over 300 years; Ivana Brlić (1874–1938) was a writer and first female mem. of the Yugoslav Acad. of Sciences and Arts; library of 8,000 vols; Curator VIKTOR RUŽIĆ.

Split

Arheološki muzej u Splitu (Archaeological Museum Split): Zrinjsko-Frankopanska 25, HR-21000 Split; tel. (21) 329-345; fax (21) 329-360; e-mail info@armus.hr; internet www.mdc.hr/split-arheoloski; f. 1820, present bldg 1914; prehistoric collns, relics from the Greek colonies on the east shore of the Adriatic Sea; Roman and Christian relics from Salonae and Dalmatia; Croatian medieval monuments from 9th to 13th century; numismatic colln; library of 50,000 vols incl. 8 incunabula and 170 16th-century books, spec. colln: Dalmatica; Dir ZRINKA BULJEVIĆ; Museum Consultant MAJA BONACIC MANDINIĆ (Coin Colln); Museum Consultant BRANKO KIRIGIN (Graeco-Hellenistic Colln); Head of Library ARSEN DUPLANCIĆ; publ. *Vjesnik za arheologiju i povijest dalmatinsku* (Bulletin of Dalmatian Archaeology and History, 1 a year).

Etnografski muzej Split (Ethnographical Museum of Split): Iza Vestibula 4, HR-21000 Split; tel. (21) 344-164; fax (21) 344-108; e-mail etnografski-muzej-st@st.t-com.hr; internet www.etnografski-muzej-split.hr; f. 1910; 19,500 items; nat. costumes, jewels, weapons, and traditional technological objects from Dalmatia, Dinaric Alps area and other neighbouring regions; illustrations section; library of 3,000 vols; Dir SILVIO BRAICA; Librarian IVA MESTROVIĆ.

Galerija umjetnina Split (Art Gallery Split): ul. kralja Tomislava 15, HR-21000 Split; tel. (21) 350-110; fax (21) 350-111; e-mail galerija-umjetnina@galum.hr; internet www.galum.hr; f. 1931; 2,300 paintings and sculptures (ancient and modern); library of 14,000 vols; Dir Prof. BOŽO MAJSTOROVIĆ; Sr Curator IRIS SLADE; Sr Curator JASMINKA BABIĆ.

Muzej grada Splita (City Museum of Split): Papalićeva 1, HR-21000 Split; tel. (21) 360-171; fax (21) 344-917; e-mail muzej-grada-st@st.tel.hr; internet www.mdc .hr/splitgr; f. 1946; political and cultural history of Split; library of 8,000 vols; Dir ELVIRA ŠARIĆ KOSTIĆ; Librarian JASNA ČUBELIĆ; publ. *Editions.*

Muzegi Ivana Meštrovića (Ivan Meštrović Museums): Šetalište Ivana Meštrovića 46, HR-21000 Split; tel. (21) 340-800; fax (21) 340-810; e-mail mim@mestrovic.hr; internet www.mdc.hr/mestrovic; f. 1991 as Ivan Meštrović Foundation with admin. HQ in Zagreb, present status 2007; protects and promotes Ivan Meštrović's life and work; permanent exhibition of sculptures of Ivan Meštrović (1883–1962); Dir ANDRO KRSTULOVIĆ OPARA; Sr Curator DANICA PLAZIBAT.

Attached Museums:

Church of the Most Holy Redeemer: HR-22322 Otavice; tel. (22) 872-630; e-mail mim@mestrovic.hr; f. 1952; Ivan Meštrović's family vault and mausoleum; permanent display of stone reliefs carved in the altar and lateral niches and on lateral walls, bas-reliefs of religious themes; spec. wall display: *Annunciation with the Archangel Gabriel and Virgin Mary, Soul of a Dead Man* and *Soul of a Dead Woman*; Curator MAJA ŠEPAROVIĆ PALADA.

Crikvine—Kaštelet: Setaliste Ivana Mestrovica 39, HR-21000 Split; tel. (21) 358-185; e-mail mim@mestrovic.hr; f. 1952; fmr summerhouse of the Capogrosso family built in the early 16th century; bought by Meštrović in 1939; on display in the Holy Crucifix Church: reliefs and artwork inspired by the life of Christ; Curator MAJA ŠEPAROVIĆ PALADA.

Meštrović Atelier: Mletacka 8, HR-10000 Zagreb; tel. (1) 485-1123; fax (1) 485-1126; e-mail mim@mestrovic.hr; f. 1959; works from first four decades of Meštrović's artistic life incl. portraits with the recurring theme of mother and child, female nudes, religious and mythological themes, monuments and historical figures; sculptures in marble, stone, wood and bronze; drawings and graphics; Museum Advisor LJILJANA ČERINA; Sr Curator DANICA PLAZIBAT.

Meštrović Gallery: Setaliste I. Mestrovica 46, HR-21000 Split; tel. (21) 340-800; fax (21) 340-810; e-mail mim@mestrovic .hr; f. 1952; colln of 192 sculptures, 583 drawings, 4 paintings, 291 architectonic plans made by Ivan Meštrović (1898–1961), 2 furniture sets based on Meštrović's sketches; documentation relating to Meštrović's life and work; Curator MAJA ŠEPAROVIĆ PALADA.

Prirodoslovni muzej i zoološki vrt (Museum of Natural Sciences and Zoo): Kolombatovićevo šetalište 2, HR-21000 Split; tel. (21) 322-988; fax (21) 322-990; e-mail prirodoslovni@prirodoslovni.hr; internet www.prirodoslovni.hr; f. 1924; contains more than 130,000 exhibits of mineralogical, palaeontological, botanical and zoological specimens from Dalmatia and the Adriatic Sea; collns of minerals, fossils, Coleoptera, marine invertebrates and vertebrates, plants, mammals, reptiles and birds (mostly Dalmatian); library of 7,000 vols; Dir Prof. NEDILJKO ŽEVRNJA; Library Man. BOŽE KOKAN; publs *Museum of Natural Sciences, Zoological Garden.*

Zagreb

Arheološki muzej u Zagrebu (Archaeological Museum of Zagreb): Trg Nikole Šubića Zrinskog 19, POB 13, HR-10000 Zagreb; tel. (1) 4873-101; fax (1) 4873 102; e-mail amz@amz.hr; internet www.amz.hr; f. 1846; museum of archaeological finds from neolithic times to 13th century, incl. prehistoric colln, Egyptian colln, Greek, Roman and medieval collns, numismatic colln; Lapidarium in courtyard, featuring stone monuments from Roman era; colln of nearly 400,000 varied artefacts and monuments; library of 45,000 vols; Dir Prof. ANTE RENDIĆ-MIOČEVIĆ; Head Librarian ROLAND HEIDE; publ. *Vjesnik Arheološkog Muzeja u Zagrebu* (1 a year).

Etnografski muzej Zagreb (Ethnographic Museum Zagreb): Mažuranićev Trg 14, HR-10000 Zagreb; tel. (1) 4826-220; fax (1) 4880-320; e-mail emz@emz.hr; internet www.emz .hr; f. 1919; exhibitions, cultural traditions of the 3 ethnographic regions of Croatia: Pannonic, Dinaric, Adriatic; dept of world cultures; collns of folks costumes, small decorated wood items, pottery and wickerwork, house inventory items, musical instruments, traditional adornments, textiles, traditional economy and items related to customs and beliefs; library of 15,000 vols; Dir DAMODAR FRLAN; publ. *Ethnographic Researches* (1 a year).

Glyptothèque HAZU: Medvedgradska 2, HR-10000 Zagreb; tel. (1) 4686-060; fax (1) 4686-052; e-mail gliptoteka@hazu.hr; internet info.hazu.hr/the_glyptotheque; f. 1937; colln of medieval frescos and plaster casts of ancient, medieval and modern sculptures and architecture; originals of Croatian sculptures since 19th century; Hon. Dir IVAN KOŽARIĆ; Dir Prof. ARIANA KRALJ.

Hrvatski muzej naivne umjetnosti (Croatian Museum of Naïve Art): Sv. Cirilometodska 3, Gornji grad, HR-10000 Zagreb; tel. (1) 4851-911; fax (1) 4852-125; e-mail info@ hmnu.org; internet hmnu.org; f. 1952 as the Peasant Art Gallery, present name 1994; 1,700 works of art, paintings, sculptures, drawings and prints; permanent display: *Naïve Art as a Segment of Modern Art*; works of ind. Croatian artists and artists from the Hlebine School; Dir Prof. VLADIMIR CRNKOVIĆ; Sr Curator Prof. MIRA FRANCETIĆ MALČIĆ; Sr Curator Prof. SVJETLANA SUMPOR; Sec. KSENIJA PAVLINIĆ-TOMASEVAGOVIĆ.

Hrvatski povijesni muzej (Croatian History Museum): Matoševa 9, HR-10000

Zagreb; tel. (1) 4851-900; fax (1) 4851-909; e-mail hismus@hismus.hr; internet www .hismus.hr; f. 1846; history of Croatia; 200,000 artefacts arranged into stone monuments, paintings, prints and sculptures, 20th-century fine art, religious artefacts, objects from everyday life, flags and uniforms, heraldry and sphragistics, decorations, plaques, medals and badges, edged weapons and fire-arms, maps, first and second documentary, varia and photographs, films and negatives; library of 43,000 vols; Dir Prof. ANKICA PANDŽIĆ; Librarian Prof. ZORA GAJSKY.

Hrvatski prirodoslovni muzej (Croatian Natural History Museum): Demetrova 1, HR-10000 Zagreb; tel. (1) 4851-700; fax (1) 4851-644; e-mail hpm@hpm.hr; internet www.hpm .hr; f. 1846; depts of botany, geology and palaeontology, mineralogy and petrography, zoology; library of 40,000 vols; Dir Dr TATJANA VLAHOVIĆ; Sec. NARCISA ANTONIOLI; publ. *Natura Croatica* (2 a year).

Hrvatski školski muzej (Croatian School Museum): Trg m. Tita 4, HR-10000 Zagreb; tel. (1) 4855-716; fax (1) 4855-825; e-mail hsm@hsmuzej.hr; internet www.hsmuzej.hr; f. 1901 as the Croatian Pedagogic-Literary Soc., present name and status 1901; history of the school system and education in Croatia; collns of teaching aids, teaching materials and school equipment, student and teacher writings, textbooks and handbooks, school regulations, archival colln of documents, colln of photographs and a record file on schools; library of 37,000 vols on the history of schools and education in gen.; Dir and Sr Curator Prof. BRANKA MANIN; Sr Librarian STEFKA BATINIĆ; publ. *Anali za povijest odgoja* (Annals of the History of Education, 1 a year).

Kabinet Grafike (Department of Prints and Drawings): Hebrangova 1, HR-10000 Zagreb; tel. and fax (1) 4922-374; e-mail kabgraf@ hazu.hr; internet www.kabinet-grafike.hazu .hr; f. 1916 as Arts dept of the fmr Yugoslav Acad. of Sciences and Arts, present status 1951; 17,500 inventory units divided into 4 collns: old colln of drawings and prints (15th–19th century), colln of 20th and 21st centuries (drawings and prints), colln of posters and colln of chalcographic plates; Hon. Dir IGOR FISKOVIĆ; Dir SLAVICA MARKOVIĆ; Sec. TANJA LISEC.

Moderna Galerija (Gallery of Modern Art): Andrije Hebranga 1, HR-10000 Zagreb; tel. (1) 6041-040; fax (1) 6041-044; e-mail moderna-galerija@zg.t-com.hr; internet www .moderna-galerija.hr; f. 1905; Croatian arts since 19th century; collns of painting, sculpture and graphic arts; 1,945 medals; library of 5,922 vols; Dir BISERKA RAUTER PLANČIĆ; Librarian VIŠNJA KOVAČEVIĆ.

Muzej grada Zagreba (Zagreb City Museum): Opatička 20, HR-10000 Zagreb; tel. (1) 4851-361; fax (1) 4851-359; e-mail mgz@mgz.hr; internet www.mgz.hr; f. 1907; exhibits on Zagreb since prehistoric times; 5 collns: prehistoric archaeology, medieval archaeology, colln and flat of the architect Viktor Kovačić, Bela and Miroslav Krleža memorial space, Dr Ivan Ribar and Cata Dujšin-Ribar colln; library of 11,000 vols; Dir Prof. VINKO IVIĆ; Sec. BRANKO BEŠTAK; Librarian SLOBODANKA RADOVČIĆ; publ. *Iz starog i novog Zagreba* (from Old and New Zagreb, irregular).

Muzej Suvremene Umjetnosti Zagreb (Museum of Contemporary Art Zagreb): Ave Dubrovnik 17, HR-10000 Zagreb; tel. (1) 6052-700; fax (1) 6052-798; e-mail msu@ msu.hr; internet www.msu.hr; f. 1954; collns of drawings, graphics, prints and art on paper, 456 films and video cassettes, photographs after the 1950s developed at the Centre for Photography, Film and Television (CEFFT); sculpture colln: 561 artworks, 1,200 works by Croatian and int. artists; Tošo Dabac archive: 200,000 negatives, 2,000 enlargements, photography equipment, newspaper clippings; Seissel Donation: paintings and architectural designs by Josip Seissel; Richter colln: 182 works of art by Vjenceslav Richter dating 1964–2002; Benko Horvat colln: 611 paintings, graphic art dating 15th–18th centuries; library of 12,500 vols; Dir and Sr Curator SNJEŽANA PINTARIĆ.

Muzej za umjetnost i obrt (Museum of Arts and Crafts): Trg maršala Tita 10, HR-10000 Zagreb; tel. (1) 4882-111; fax (1) 4828-088; e-mail muo@muo.hr; internet www.muo.hr; f. 1880; fine and applied arts since 14th century; furniture, textiles, ceramics, glass, metalwork, sculpture, paintings, photography, costumes, clocks and watches, ivory, architecture, design and posters; library: art library of 60,000 vols; Dir Prof. MIROSLAV GAŠPAROVIĆ.

Strossmayerova galerija starih majstora (Strossmayers' Gallery of Old Masters): Trg Nikole Šubića Zrinskog 11, HR-10000 Zagreb; tel. (1) 4813-344; fax (1) 4819-979; e-mail sgallery@hazu.hazu.hr; internet www.mdc.hr/strossmayer; f. 1861, opened to public 1884; art from 14th to 19th centuries; library of 10,000 titles in art and cultural history, archeology, ethnology, 400 journals, reference colln; Dir Prof. ĐURO VANDURA; Curators Prof. BORIVOJ POPOVCAK, SANJA CVETNIĆ; Librarian Prof. INDIRA CVEK FLASCHAR; publs *Bulletin, HAZU, Razreda za likovne umjetnosti.*

Tehnički muzej Zagreb (Technical Museum Zagreb): Savska cesta 18, HR-10000 Zagreb; tel. (1) 435-446; fax (1) 428-431; e-mail tehnicki-muzej@zg.tel.hr; internet www.tehnicki-muzej.hr; f. 1954, present bldg 1959; colln of over 5,000 exhibits pertaining to various technical fields; library of 6,000 vols; Dir BOZICA SKULJ; Sr Curator VESNA DAKIĆ; Sr Curator MIROSLAV MIRKOVIĆ; Sr Curator NEDA STAKLAREVIĆ.

Universities

MEDUNARODNO SVEUČILIŠTE U DUBROVNIKU
(Dubrovnik International University)

Sv. 4 Dominika, HR-20000 Dubrovnik

Telephone: (20) 414-111
E-mail: diu@diu.hr
Internet: www.diu.hr
Private control
Language of instruction: English
Pres.: Prof. Dr MIOMIR ŽUŽUL
Rector: Prof. Dr JANICE MCCORMICK
Provost: Prof. Dr MARGARET MELADYAccepts only 100 students each year

DEANS

School of International Business: Prof. Dr GARY O'CALLAGHAN
School of Diplomacy: Prof. Dr THOMAS P. MELADY

SVEUČILIŠTE JOSIPA JURJA STROSSMAYERA U OSIJEKU
(Josip Jurja Strossmayer University of Osijek)

Trg sv. Trojstva 3, HR-31000 Osijek

Telephone: (31) 224-102
Fax: (31) 207-015
E-mail: rektorat@unios.hr
Internet: www.unios.hr

Founded 1975
State control
Academic year: October to September
Rector: Prof. Dr GORDANA KRALIK
Vice-Rectors: Prof. Dr DRAGO ŽAGAR, Prof. Dr DRAŽEN BARKOVIĆ, Prof. Dr IVAN SAMARDŽIĆ, Prof. Dr RUDOLF EMERT
Sec.-Gen.: ZDENKA BARIŠIĆ
Librarian: DRAGUTIN KATALENAC
Number of teachers: 523
Number of students: 13,214

Publications: *Ekonomski vjesnik* (Economic Courier), *Medicinski vjesnik* (Medical Courier), *Poljoprivreda* (Agriculture), *Pravni vjesnik* (Law Courier), *Sveučilišni Glasnik* (University Newsletter), *Tehnički vjesnik* (Technical Courier)

DEANS

Faculty of Agriculture: VLADO GUBERAC
Faculty of Civil Engineering: DAMIR MARKULAK
Faculty of Economics: ŽELJKO TURKALJ
Faculty of Electrical Engineering: RADOSLAV GALIĆ
Faculty of Food Technology: DRAGO ŠUBARIĆ
Faculty of Law: IGOR BOJANIĆ
Faculty of Mechanical Engineering: DRAŽAN KOZAK
Faculty of Medicine: ALEKSANDAR VČEV
Faculty of Philosophy: VIŠNJA PAVIČIĆ TAKAČ (acting)
Department of Mathematics: RUDOLF SCITOVSKI
Teacher-Training College: ANĐELKA PEKO

PROFESSORS

Faculty of Agriculture (tel. (31) 224-200; fax (31) 207-017; e-mail nastava@suncokret.pfos.hr; internet www.pfos.hr):

BERTIĆ, B., Agrochemistry, Fertilizers
BUKVIĆ, Ž., Mechanization in Livestock Farming and Crop Production
EMERT, R., Agricultural Machinery and Maintenance
GUBERAC, V., Plant Breeding, Seed Science
IVEZIĆ, M., Entomology with Phytopharmacy and Plant Protection, Nematology
JOVANOVAC, S., General Livestock, Genetics of Domestic Animals
JURIĆ, I., Principles of Agriculture, Tropical Agriculture
JURKOVIĆ, D., Plant Protection, Phytopharmacy
KALINOVIĆ, I., Storage and Technology of Agricultural Products
KNEŽEVIĆ, I., Cattle Breeding
KNEŽEVIĆ, M., Botany
KOVAČEVIĆ, V., Cereal Crop Production
KRALIK, G., Husbandry of Swine, Poultry and Fur-bearing Animals
KRISTEK, A., Industrial Crops
MADJAR, S., Agricultural Improvement, Irrigation
MILAKOVIĆ, Z., Microbiology
RASTIJA, T., General Cattle and Horse Raising
SENČIĆ, Đ., Pig Breeding, Livestock Breeding
STEINER, Z., Nutrition of Domestic Animals
STJEPANOVIĆ, M., Forage Crops
VUKADINOVIĆ, V., Plant Physiology, Agricultural Mechanization
ZIMMER, R., Mechanization in Farming, Processing Technology and Storing
ŽUGEC, I., General Crop Production, Alternative Agriculture

Faculty of Civil Engineering (Drinska 16A, HR-31000 Osijek; tel. (31) 274-377; fax (31) 274-444; e-mail dekan@gfos.hr; internet www.gfos.hr):

ANIČIĆ, D., Surveying, Earthquake Engineering
MEDANIĆ, B., Construction Management

SIGMUND, V., Construction Stability and Dynamics, Resistance of Materials
TAKAČ, S., Wooden Buildings, Bricklaying

Faculty of Economics (Gajev Trg 7, HR-31000 Osijek; tel. (31) 224-400; fax (31) 211-604; internet www.efos.hr):

BABAN, LJ., Theory of Marketing, International Economics
BARKOVIĆ, D., Operational Research
CRNJAC, M., Mathematics
JELINIĆ, S., Commercial Law
KARIĆ, M., Microeconomics, Cost Management, Accounting
LAMZA-MARONIĆ, M., Management and Information Systems
LAUC, A., Sociology of Management
MELER, M., Introduction to Marketing, Marketing Management
NOVAC, B., Finance Management, Financial Markets
PROKLIN, P., Accounting
SEGETLIJA, Z., Business Logistics, Branch Marketing
SINGER, S., Strategic Management
SRB, V., Finance, Public Finance, Banking
TURKALJ, Ž., Business Organization

Faculty of Electrical Engineering (Kneza Trpimira 2B, HR-31000 Osijek; tel. (31) 224-600; fax (31) 224-605; e-mail etf@etfos.hr; internet www.etfos.hr):

FLEGAR, I., Electronics, Networking Theory, Electrical Compatibility
GODEC, Z., Metrology, Monitoring
JOVIĆ, F., Information and Communications, Computers and Processes, Computer and Terminal Networks, Artificial Intelligence
ŠTEFANKO, S., Fundamentals of Electrical Engineering, Theoretical Electrical Engineering
ŠVEDEK, T., Electronic Components, Microelectronics, High-Frequency Electronics
VALTER, Z., Fundamentals of Electromechanical Engineering

Faculty of Food Technology (F. Kuhača 20, HR-31000 Osijek; tel. (31) 224-300; fax (31) 207-115; e-mail office@ptfos.hr; internet www.ptfos.hr):

MANDIĆ, M., Quality Control, Sensor Analyses, Fundamentals of Food Technology, Food Science
PILIŽOTA, V., Raw Materials in Food Industry, Technology of Fruit and Vegetable Preserving and Processing
ŠERUGA, M., Physical Chemistry, Packing Materials, Methods of Analysis by Instrument
UGARČIĆ-HARDI, Ž, Raw Materials in Food Industry, Flour Production and Processing

Faculty of Law (S. Radića 13, HR-31000 Osijek; tel. (31) 224-500; fax (31) 224-540; e-mail office@pravos.hr; internet www.pravos.hr):

BABAC, B., Administrative Law, Administrative Science
BELAJ, V., Civil Law
JELINIĆ, S., Commercial Law, Social Law, Copyright
KLASIČEK, D., International Law
LAUC, Z., Constitutional Law
LJUBANOVIĆ, V., Criminal Procedural Law
MECANOVIĆ, I., Constitutional Law, Informatics for Lawyers
ROMŠTAJN, I., Transport Law, Insurance Law
SRB, V., Financial Law and Sciences, Banking and Credit

Faculty of Mechanical Engineering (Trg I. B. Mažuranić 18, HR-35000 Slavonski Brod; tel. (35) 446-188; fax (35) 446-446; internet www.sfsb.hr):

BUDIĆ, I., Foundry, Processing Technology, Assembling Technology, Design

GRIZELJ, B., Metal Forming, Technology, Tools

HNATKO, E., Heat Engines and Devices

KATALINIĆ, B., Automation, Flexible Systems

KLJAJIN, M., Machine Elements, Technical Drafting

KRUMES, D., Materials, Heat Processing, Tribology, Surface Engineering, Tools

MAJDANDŽIĆ, N., Computers and Information Systems, Production Process, Artificial Intelligence, Planning Methods

MATEJIČEK, F., Mechanics, Engine Dynamics

RAOS, P., Polymer Processing, Machine Maintenance

VITEZ, I., Materials, New Technologies

Faculty of Medicine (J. Huttlera 4, HR-31000 Osijek; tel. (31) 512-800; fax (31) 512-833; e-mail ured@mefos.hr; internet www.mefos .hr):

BELICZA, B., History of Medicine, Medical Ethics

KOSTOVIĆ-KNEŽEVIĆ, LJ., Histology, Embryology

ŠESTO, M., Internal Medicine

SOLDO, I., Infectious Diseases

TUCAK, A., Urology, Civil War Medicine

Faculty of Philosophy (L. Jägera 9, HR-31000 Osijek; tel. (31) 211-400; fax (31) 212-514):

APARAC-JELUŠIĆ, T., Library Science, Informatics and Communication

BRLENIĆ-VUJIĆ, B., Comparative Literature

JERKOVIĆ, J., Conducting, Choir

MARIJANOVIĆ, S., Croatian Literature

NIKČEVIĆ, M., Methodology of Scientific Work, Methodics of Literature Teaching

OBAD, V., German Literature

ŽIVKOVIĆ, P., Medieval History

Department of Mathematics (Trg Lj. Gaja 6, HR-31000 Osijek; tel. (31) 224-800; fax (31) 224-801; e-mail math@mathos.hr; internet www.mathos.hr):

BUTKOVIĆ, D., Linear Algebra

SCITOVSKI, R., Numerical Mathematics, Computer Exercises II

SVRTAN, D., Theoretical Mechanics, Discrete Mathematics

VOLENEC, V., Geometry Models, Metric Geometry

Teacher-Training College (L. Jägera 9, HR-31000 Osijek; tel. (31) 200-602; fax (31) 200-604; e-mail helpdesk@ufos.hr; internet www .ufos.hr):

BABIĆ, N., Pre-School Education, Teaching Methods in Pre-School Education, Education Communication

SVEUČILIŠTE JURJA DOBRILE U PULI
(Juraj Dobrila University of Pula)

Preradovićeva 1/1, HR-52100 Pula

Telephone: (52) 377-000

Fax: (52) 216-416

E-mail: ured@unipu.hr

Internet: www.unipu.hr

Founded 2006

Public control

Languages of instruction: Croatian, Italian, English

Academic year: September to June

Rector: Prof. Dr ROBERT MATIJAŠIĆ

Vice-Rector for Education and Students: Prof. Dr ĐENI DEKLEVA RADAKOVIĆ

Vice-Rector for Finance and Business Relationships: LOVRE BOZINA

Vice-Rector for Int. Cooperation: Prof. Dr IVAN JURKOVIĆ

Vice-Rector for Scientific Research: MARLI GONAN BOZAC

Library: see under Libraries and Archives

Number of teachers: 230

Number of students: 3,000

DEANS

Dept of Humanities: Prof. Dr GORAN FILIPI

Dept of Music: BASHKIM SHEHU

Dept of Pre-School and Primary School Teaching: Prof. Dr IGOR MEDICA

Dept of Studies in the Italian Language: Prof. Dr ELIS DEGHENGHI OLUJIĆ

Interdisciplinary Marine Science: Prof. Dr RENATO BATEL

Interdisciplinary Culture and Tourism: Prof. Dr MAURO DUJMOVIĆ

SVEUČILIŠTE U RIJECI
(University of Rijeka)

Trg braće Mažuranića 10, HR-51000 Rijeka

Telephone: (51) 406-500

Fax: (51) 406-588

E-mail: ured@uniri.hr

Internet: www.uniri.hr

Founded 1973

State control

Language of instruction: Croatian (and some courses in Italian)

Academic year: October to July

Rector: Prof. Dr PERO LUČIN (acting)

Vice-Rector: Prof. Dr GORAN KALOGJERA

Vice-Rector: Prof. Dr NEVENKA OŽANIĆ

Vice-Rector: Prof. Dr SNJEŽANA PRIJIĆ-SAMARŽIJA

Sec.-Gen.: ROBERTA HLAČA MLINAR

Librarians: BRUNO DOBRIĆ (Pula), SENKA TOMLJANOVIĆ (Rijeka)

Number of teachers: 928

Number of students: 19,139

Publications: *Gaudeamus* (irregular), *Sveučilišni vodič* (guide to curriculums, 1 a year)

DEANS

Academy of Applied Arts: Prof. ANTE VLADISLAVIĆ

Faculty of Civil Engineering in Rijeka: Prof. Dr ALEKSANDRA DELUKA-TIBLJAS

Faculty of Economics and Tourism 'Dr Mijo Mirković' in Pula: Prof. Dr HERI BEZIĆ

Faculty of Economics in Rijeka: Prof. Dr VINKO KANDŽIJA

Faculty of Engineering in Rijeka: Prof. Dr TONČI MIKAC

Faculty of Law in Rijeka: Prof. Dr MIOMIR MATULOVIĆ

Faculty of Maritime Studies: Prof. SERDO KOS

Faculty of Medicine in Rijeka: Prof. Dr ALAN ŠUSTIĆ

Faculty of Philosophy in Pula: Assoc. Prof. Dr ROBERT MATIJAŠIĆ

Faculty of Philosophy in Rijeka: Prof. Dr PREDRAG ŠUSTAR

Faculty of Teacher Education: Prof. VINKA UZELAC

SVEUČILIŠTE U SPLITU
(University of Split)

Livanjska 5/I, HR-21000 Split

Telephone: (21) 558-200

Fax: (21) 348-163

E-mail: rektorat.office@unist.hr

Internet: www.unist.hr

Founded 1974

State control

Languages of instruction: Croatian, English

Academic year: October to September

Rector: Prof. Dr IVAN PAVIĆ

Vice-Rector: Prof. Dr SIMUN ANDJELINOVIĆ

Vice-Rector: Prof. Dr BRANKA RAMLJAK

Vice-Rector: Prof. Dr ROKO ANDRICEVIĆ

Vice-Rector: Prof. Dr DRAGAN BOLANCA

Sec.-Gen.: JOSIP ALAJBEG

Library of 369,000 vols

Number of teachers: 1,500

Number of students: 23,000

Publications: *Sveučilišni godišnjak, Universitas* (12 a year)

DEANS

Academy of Arts: Dr BRANKO MATULIĆ

Faculty of Catholic Theology: Dr NEDILJKO ANTE ANČIĆ

Faculty of Chemistry and Technology: Dr MLADEN MILOŠ

Faculty of Civil Engineering and Architecture: Dr BERNARDIN PEROŠ

Faculty of Economics: Dr BRANKO GRČIĆ

Faculty of Electrical, Mechanical and Naval Engineering: Dr TOMISLAV KILIĆ

Faculty of Kinesiology: BORIS MALEŠ

Faculty of Law: Dr BORIS BUKLIJAŠ

Faculty of Medicine: Dr MATKO MARUŠIĆ

Faculty of Natural Sciences, Mathematics and Education: Dr ANKA GOLEMAC

Faculty of Philosophy: MARKO TROGRLIĆ

Faculty of Tourism and Foreign Trade (Dubrovnik): Dr DJURO BENIĆ

Maritime Faculty (Dubrovnik): Dr JOSIP LOVRIĆ

PROFESSORS

Academy of Arts (Glagoljaška bb, HR-21000 Split; tel. (21) 348-622; e-mail office@umas .hr; internet www.umas.hr):

BATOVIĆ, Š., Prehistoric Archaeology

BELOŠEVIĆ, J., Medieval Archaeology

CAMBJ, N., Classical and Old Christian Archaeology

ĆOSIĆ, V., French Language

DUKAT, Z., Greek Language and Literature

FRANIĆ, A., Modern Croatian Literature

GERERSDORFER, V., French Language and Medieval Literature

GRGIN, T., General and Systematic Psychology

JURIĆ, B., Political Economy and National Economic History

KALENIĆ, A. S., Latin Language and Literature

KOLUMBIĆ, N., Old Croatian Literature

MANENICA, I., Systematic Psychology

MIKIĆ, P., German Language

OBAD, S., Modern History

PEDERIN, S., German Literature

PETRICIOLI, I., Art History

SKLEDAR, N., Sociology

ŽELIĆ, I., Visual Arts, Teaching Methods

ŽIVKOVIĆ, P., Croatian History up to 1918

Faculty of Chemistry and Technology (Teslina 10/V, HR-21000 Split; tel. (21) 329-420; fax (21) 329-461; e-mail office@ktf-split .hr; internet www.ktf-split.hr):

KOVAČIĆ, T., Polymers

KRSTULOVIĆ, R., Chemistry and Technology of Non-Metals

MEKJAVIĆ, I., Physical Chemistry

PETRIĆ, N., Thermodynamics

RADOŠEVIĆ, J., Electrochemistry

ROJE, U., Organic Industry – Technological Processes; Catalysis; Polymerization

VOJNOVIĆ, I., Materials and Energy Balance

ŽANETIĆ, R., Measuring and Process Operation

Faculty of Civil Engineering and Architecture (Matice Hrvatske 15, HR-21000 Split; tel. (21) 303-333; fax (21) 465-117; e-mail dekan@gradst.hr; internet www.gradst.hr):

BONACCI, O., Hydrology

DAMJANIĆ, F., Technical Mechanics

JOVIĆ, V., Hydromechanics

MARGETA, J., Water Supply

MAROVIĆ, P., Strength of Materials, Testing of Structures

MIHANOVIĆ, A., Mechanics, Stability and Dynamics of Structures

MILIČIĆ, J., Construction and Construction Machines
ŠESTANOVIĆ, S., Geology and Petrology
ŠKOMRLJ, J., Technology and Organization of Construction
STOJIĆ, P., Hydrotechnical Systems
VOJNOVIĆ, J., Building Construction
VRDOLJAK, B., Mathematics

Faculty of Economics (Matice Hrvatske 31, HR-21000 Split; tel. (21) 430-600; fax (21) 430-701; e-mail dekanat@efst.hr; internet www.efst.hr):

ANDRIJIĆ, S., Macroeconomics, Econometrics
BUBLE, M., Organization Design, Job Evaluation
DOMANČIĆ, P., International Finance
DULČIĆ, A., Economics of Trade and Tourism
JELAVIĆ, A., Business Economics
LUKŠIĆ, B., Business Economics
ŠTAMBUK, D., Regional Economics

Faculty of Electrical, Mechanical and Naval Engineering (Ruđera Boškovića bb, HR-21000 Split; tel. (21) 305-777; fax (21) 463-877; e-mail dekanat@fesb.hr; internet www.fesb.hr):

DEŽELIĆ, R., Materials Technology
GRISOGONO, P., Industrial Furnaces and Fuels, Industrial Transportation
JADRIĆ, M., Electromagnetic Theory and Electrical Machinery
KURTOVIĆ, M., Asynchronous Machines, Electric Motor Plants, General Theory of Electric Machines
PILIĆ, L., Fluid Mechanics
SLAPNIČAR, P., Circuits

Faculty of Law (Domovinskog rata 8, HR-21000 Split; tel. (21) 393-500; fax (21) 393-572; e-mail dekanat@pravst.hr; internet www.pravst.hr):

BILIĆ, I., Political Economy
BORKOVIĆ, I., Administrative Law
BOSNIĆ, P., International Private Law
CARIĆ, A., Criminal Law
CVITAN, O., Administrative Sciences
DUJIĆ, A., Modern Political Systems
GRABOVAC, I., Maritime and Transport Law
PETRIĆ, I., Economic Politics
PETRINOVIĆ, I., History of Political Theories
RUDOLF, D., International Public Law
ŠMID, V., Civil Law
VISKOVIĆ, N., Theory of State and Law

Faculty of Natural Sciences, Mathematics and Education (Teslina 12/III, HR-21000 Split; tel. (21) 385-133; fax (21) 384-086; e-mail dekanat@pmfst.hr; internet www.pmfst.hr):

JAKELIĆ, P., Graphic Design
KALOGJERA, A., Methods of Education
KRSTULOVIĆ, I., Painting
MARASOVIĆ, T., Croatian and European Medieval Art
MIDŽOR, A., Sculpture
MILAT, J., General Pedagogy
OMAŠIĆ, V., History

Faculty of Tourism and Foreign Trade (Dubrovnik):

KONJHODŽIĆ, H., International Finance
MARKOVIĆ, M., Economics and Business Organization
PAPARELA, I., International Finance and Business Finance
REŠETAR, M., Travel Agency Management; Business Analysis
ŽABICA, T., Economic and Tourist Geography

Maritime Faculty (Zrinsko-Frankopanska 38, HR-21000 Split; tel. (21) 380-762; internet www.pfst.hr):

FABRIS, O., Thermodynamics, Ships' Refrigerating Plants
LOVRIĆ, J., Ship Maintenance

SJEKAVICA, I., Terrestrial Navigation

SVEUČILIŠTE U DUBROVNIKU
(University of Dubrovnik)

Branitelja Dubrovnika 29, HR-20000 Dubrovnik
Telephone: (20) 445-744
Fax: (20) 435-590
E-mail: rektorat@unidu.hr
Internet: www.unidu.hr
Founded 2003
Public control

Rector: MATEO MILKOVIĆ
Head Librarian: ANA PUJO

Library of 10,000 monographs, 4,000 projects, Masters and Doctoral dissertations, 43 Croatian magazines and 37 foreign-language magazines
Number of teachers: 160
Number of students: 2,600

Offers undergraduate programmes in art and restoration, aquaculture, economics and business studies, electrical engineering and computing and maritime studies, engineering; graduate programmes in communication technologies, media, public relations.

SVEUČILIŠTE U ZADRU
(University of Zadar)

Mihovila Pavlinovića bb, HR-23000 Zadar
Telephone: (23) 200-501
Fax: (23) 200-605
E-mail: rektorat@unizd.hr
Internet: www.unizd.hr
Founded 2003
State control
Academic year: October to June

Depts of agriculture and Mediterranean aquaculture, archaeology, classical philology, Croatian and Slavic studies, economy, English language and literature, ethnology and cultural antrophology, French language and literature, geography, German language and literature, health studies, history, history of art, information and communication studies, Italian language and literature, linguistics, librarianship and information studies, pedagogy, philosophy, psychology, sociology, teacher and pre-school teacher-training, transport and maritime studies

Rector: Prof. Dr ANTE UGLEŠIĆ
Pro-Rector: Prof. Dr STIPE BELAK
Pro-Rector: Prof. Dr SREĆKO JELUŠIĆ
Pro-Rector: Prof. Dr VLADIMIR SKRAČIĆ
Pro-Rector: ANA PROROKOVIĆ
Sec.-Gen.: ANTONELLA LOVRIĆ
Librarian: MIRTA MATOŠIĆ

Library of 110,000 vols, 22,000 periodicals, 1,050 MSS
Number of teachers: 365
Number of students: 5,945

SVEUČILIŠTE U ZAGREBU
(University of Zagreb)

Trg maršala Tita 14, pp 407, HR-10000 Zagreb
Telephone: (1) 4564-111
Fax: (1) 4830-602
E-mail: unizg.info@unizg.hr
Internet: www.unizg.hr
Founded 1669
Academic year: October to September
Language of instruction: Croatian

Rector: Prof. ALEKSA BJELIŠ
Vice-Rector for Devt and Spatial Planning: Prof. BOJAN BALETIĆ
Vice-Rector for Financing: Prof. TONKO ČURKO
Vice-Rector for Int. and Inter-Institutional Cooperation: Prof. KSENIJA TURKOVIĆ

Vice-Rector for Science and Technology: Prof. MELITA KOVACEVIĆ
Vice-Rector for Teaching and Quality Assurance: Prof. LJILJANA PINTER
Chief Admin. Officer: ANA RUŽIČKA
Number of teachers: 5,250
Number of students: 63,000
Publication: Sveučilišni vjesnik (University Herald)

DEANS

Academy of Dramatic Arts: Prof. ENES MIDŽIĆ
Academy of Fine Arts: Prof. SLAVOMIR DRINKOVIĆ
Academy of Music: Prof. MLADEN JANJANIN
Agriculture: Prof. DAVOR ROMIĆ
Architecture: Prof. LENKO PLEŠTINA
Catholic Theology: Dr JOSIP OSLIĆ
Chemical Engineering and Technology: Prof. STANISLAV KURAJICA
Civil Engineering: Prof. MLADEN RADUJKOVIĆ
Defectology: Dr BRANKO RADOVANČIĆ
Dental Medicine: DRAGUTIN KOMAR
Economic Sciences: Dr IVAN LOVRINOVIĆ
Education and Rehabilitation Sciences: DRAŽENKA BLAŽI
Electrical Engineering and Computing: Prof. VEDRAN MORNAR
Food Technology and Biotechnology: Prof. DAMIR JEŽEK
Forestry: Prof. ANDRIJA BOGNER
Geodesy: Prof. STANISLAV FRANGEŠ
Geotechnical Engineering (in Varaždin): Prof. MLADEN BOŽIČEVIĆ
Graduate School of Economics and Business: VLADIMIR ŠIMOVIĆ
Graphic Arts: Prof. DIANA MILČIĆ
Kinesiology: Prof. IGOR JUKIĆ
Law: Prof. ŽELJKO POTOČNJAK
Mechanical Engineering and Naval Architecture: Prof. IZVOR GRUBIŠIĆ
Medical School: Prof. DAVOR MILIČIĆ
Medicine: Dr DAVOR MILIČIĆ
Metallurgy (in Sisak): Prof. FARUK UNKIĆ
Mining, Geology and Petroleum Engineering: Dr BILJANA KOVAČEVIĆ-ZELIĆ
Natural Sciences and Mathematics: Dr IVAN VICOKOVIĆ
Organization and Informatics (in Varaždin): Dr TIHOMIR HUNJAK
Pharmacy and Biochemistry: Dr NIKOLA KUJUNDŽIĆ
Philosophy: Prof. DAMIR BORAS
Physical Education: Dr MATO BARTOLUCI
Political Sciences: Prof. VLATKO CVRTILA
School of Dental Medicine: Prof. DRAGUTIN KOMAR
Science: Prof. MLADEN JURAČIĆ
Stomatology: Dr VLADO CAREK
Teacher Education: Prof. VLADIMIR ŠIMOVIĆ
Textile Technology: Prof. DARKO UJEVIĆ
Transport and Traffic Engineering: Prof. Dr IVAN DADIĆ
University Centre for Croatian Studies: Prof. ZVONIMIR ČULJAK, (Head)
Veterinary Medicine: Prof. VELIMIR SUSIĆ

College

Američka visoka škola za management i tehnologiju (American College of Management and Technology): Don Frana Bulića 6, HR-20000 Dubrovnik; tel. (20) 433-000; fax (20) 433-001; e-mail american.college@acmt.hr; internet www.acmt.hr; f. 1997 by the Min. of Science, Education and Sports in collaboration with the Rochester Institute of Technology (USA); Private control; undergraduate programmes in service management and information technology and postgraduate programmes in human resource development and service leadership and innovation; 1,500 students; Pres. and Dean DON HUDSPETH.

Inter-University Centre Dubrovnik: Don Frana Bulića 4, HR-20000 Dubrovnik; tel. (20) 413-626; fax (20) 413-628; e-mail iuc@iuc.hr; internet www.iuc.hr; f. 1972; ind. instn for int. cooperation in teaching and research; courses in crime prevention through criminal law and security studies, organization theory, social philosophy and philosophy of science; library: 10,000 vols; Chair. of Council FRANK LAUBERT (University of Hamburg, Germany); Dir-Gen. Prof. KRUNOSLAV PISK (University of Dubrovnik, Croatia); Deputy Dir-Gen. Prof. PETER KAMPITS (University of Vienna, Austria).

Međunarodna diplomska škola za poslovno upravljanje Zagreb (International Graduate Business School Zagreb): Trg J. F. Kennedya 7, HR-10000 Zagreb; tel. (1) 2314-990; fax (1) 2335-165; e-mail mba@igbs.hr; internet www.igbs.hr; Private control; offers courses in business ethics and law, corporate finance, entrepreneurship and strategic management, European economic policy, financial and managerial accounting, human resources, int. financial strategy and intermediation, int. macroeconomics, investments, managerial economics, marketing strategy, new product management, operations management, quantitative analysis, retailing; Dean ZLATAN FRÖHLICH.

Visoko Gospodarsko Učilište u Križevcima (College of Agriculture at Križevci): Milislava Demerca 1, HR-48260 Križevci; tel. (48) 681-597; fax (48) 682-790; e-mail dekan@vguk.hr; internet www.vguk.hr; f. 1860; graduate and professional programmes in farm management, plant production and zoology; library: 10,000 vols; Dean Dr VINKO PINTIĆ; Head of Library SANDRA KANTAR.

Polytechnics

Tehničko veleučilište u Zagrebu (Technical Polytechnic in Zagreb): Vrbik 8, HR-10000 Zagreb; tel. (1) 5603-900; fax (1) 5603-999; e-mail tvz@tvz.hr; internet www.tvz.hr; f. 1998; programmes in computing and mechanical engineering, construction, electrical engineering, informatics; 5,400 students; Dean Dr MLADEN PETRIČEC.

Veleučilište 'Marko Marulić' u Kninu (Marko Marulić Polytechnic in Knin): Petra Krešimira IV 30, HR-22300 Knin; tel. (22) 664-450; fax (22) 661-374; e-mail info@veleknin.hr; internet www.veleknin.hr; f. 2005; Public control.

Veleučilište u Karlovcu (Karlovac University of Applied Sciences): *Campus 1*: Ivana Meštrovića 10, HR-47000 Karlovac; *Campus 2*: Josipa Juraja Strossmayera 9, HR-47000 Karlovac; tel. (47) 843-500; fax (47) 843-579; e-mail dekanat@vuka.hr; internet www.vuka.hr; Public control; depts of business, food technology, hunting and nature production, mechanical engineering, security and protection, textiles; Dean Prof. Dr ANTUN ALEGRO; Sec.-Gen. MILAN VIGNJEVIĆ.

Veleučiliste u Požegi (Požega Polytechnic): Vukovarska 17, HR-34000 Požega; tel. (34) 271-018; fax (34) 271-008; e-mail knjiznica@vup.hr; internet www.vup.hr; Public control; f. 1998; depts of agriculture and social sciences; library: 32,000 books; 2,000 students; Dean IVAN BUDIĆ; Sec. JASMINA SMOLČIĆ; Librarian Prof. ANTONIO VALEŠIĆ.

Veleučilište u Rijeci (Rijeka Polytechnic): Trpimirova 2/V, HR-51000 Rijeka; tel. (51) 321-300; fax (51) 211-270; e-mail ured@veleri.hr; internet www.veleri.hr; Private control; f. 2008; depts of business, traffic, agriculture and security studies; library: 3,600 vols, 14 foreign and 30 domestic periodicals; Dean Prof. Dr DUŠAN RUDIĆ; Sec. BORIS SERGOVIĆ.

Veleučilište u Šibeniku (Šibenik Polytechnic): Trg Andrije Hebranga 11, Šibenik; tel. (22) 311-060; fax (22) 216-716; internet www.vus.hr; Public control; depts of administration, management and traffic studies.

Veleučilište u Varaždinu (Varaždin Polytechnic): Križanićeva 33, HR-42000 Varaždin, Varaždinska; tel. (42) 493-338; fax (42) 493-333; e-mail tajnistvo@velv.hr; internet www.velv.hr; Private control; f. 2001; programmes in automation, construction, design and implementation, electrical engineering, multimedia, nursing, production engineering; Dean Dr MARIN MILKOVIĆ.

Veleučilište Velika Gorica (Velika Gorica University of Applied Sciences): Zagrebačka cesta 5, HR-10410 Velika Gorica; tel. (1) 6222-501; fax (1) 7897-645; e-mail info@vvg.hr; internet www.vvg.hr; Private control; professional programmes in computer systems maintenance, crisis management, aircraft maintenance, motor vehicle maintenance and eye optics; spec. programmes in crisis management and logistics, information systems; 920 students; Dean Prof. IVAN TOTH.

CUBA

The Higher Education System

The oldest university is the Universidad de la Habana, which was founded in 1728 while Cuba was governed by Spain. Control of the island was ceded to the USA in 1898 and independence was gained in 1902. Most universities have been founded since 1959, when guerrilla forces led by Dr Fidel Castro Ruz seized control of government. State education in Cuba is universal and free at all levels. Education is based on Marxist-Leninist principles and combines study with manual work. Higher education institutions include universities, centros universitarios (university centres), institutos superiores politécnicos (higher polytechnic institutes) and institutos superiores (higher institutes). Workers attending university courses receive a state subsidy to provide for their dependants. Courses at intermediate and higher levels lay an emphasis on technology, agriculture and teacher training. In 2008/09 there were an estimated 710,978 students in tertiary education.

Admission to higher education is based on completion of upper secondary education and results of the national competitive entrance examination. The main undergraduate qualification is the Licenciado, which is awarded after five years of study. Courses may also lead to a professional title, such as Ingeniero (Engineer), Contador (Accountant), Estomatólogo (Dentist) or Arquitecto (Architect). Between undergraduate and doctoral-level studies there is a Masters-level qualification, Título de Máster. The first doctoral-level qualification is the Doctor en Ciencias Específicas, which requires three to four years' study. The second (and final) doctoral-level degree is the Doctor en Ciencias, awarded after additional years of research, published and defended before a jury. Technical and vocational education is offered at the secondary level and higher.

The Junta de Acreditación Nacional (JAN) was established in 1999 as the national umbrella organization responsible for quality assurance, accreditation and evaluation of all tertiary institutions and programmes.

Regulatory and Representative Bodies

GOVERNMENT

Ministry of Culture: Calle 2, No 258, entre 11 y 13, Plaza de la Revolución, Vedado, Havana 10400; tel. (7) 55-2260; fax (7) 66-2053; e-mail atencion@min.cult.cu; internet www.min.cult.cu; Minister ABEL ENRIQUE PRIETO JIMÉNEZ.

Ministry of Education: Obispo 160, Havana; tel. (7) 61-4888; internet www .rimed.cu; Min. ENA ELSAVELÁZQUEZ COBIELLA.

Ministry of Higher Education: Calle 23, No 565 Of, esq. a F, Vedado, Havana; tel. (7) 55-2335; fax (7) 33-4390; e-mail vecino@ reduniv.edu.cu; internet www.mes.edu.cu; Min. MIGUEL MARIO DIAZ-CANEL BERMÚDEZ.

NATIONAL BODY

Consejo Nacional de Universidades (National University Council): Ministerio de Educación Superior, Ciudad Libertad, Havana 1; f. 1960; coordinating body for educational and scientific activities and for the admin. of the 4 nat. univs; Pres. JOSÉ RAMÓN FERNÁNDEZ; Sec. Ing. MIGUEL MARRERO VALLET.

Learned Societies

GENERAL

Academia de Ciencias de Cuba (Cuban Academy of Sciences): Industria y San José, Capitolio Nacional, Habana Vieja, Havana 12400; tel. (7) 862-6545; fax (7) 867-0599; e-mail alejandro@academiaciencias.cu; internet www.academiaciencias.cu; f. 1861; attached research institutes: see Research Institutes; National Archive: see Libraries and Archives; Pres. Dr ISMAEL CLARK; publs *Actas Botánicas Cubanas* (1 a year), *Anuario L.L. sobre estudios Lingüísticos, Anuario L.L. sobre estudios Literarios, Boletín Climática* (1 a year), *Boletín del Archivo Nacional* (1 a year), *Boletín de Síntesis, Boletín Meteorológico Marino* (3 a year), *Boletín Oficial de la ONIITEM* (1 a year), *Boletín Señal* (52 a year), *Cablegráfica* (12 a year), *Datos Astronómicos para Cuba* (1 a year), *Datos Astronómicos para el Caribe* (2 a year), *Directorio Biotec* (1 a year), *Estudios de Historia de la Ciencia y la Tecnología* (1 a year), *Estudios de Política Científica y Tecnología* (1 a year), *Físicas y Matemáticas* (2 a year), *Poeyana* (1 a year), *Resumen Climático de Cuba* (1 a year), *Revista Ciencias Biológicas* (2 a year), *Revista Ciencia de la Información* (4 a year), *Revista Ciencias de la Tierra y del Espacio* (2 a year), *Revista Ciencias Técnicas, Revista Cubana de Ciencias Sociales* (2 a year), *Revista Cubana de Meteorología* (2 a year), *Tablas de Mareas* (1 a year).

Ateneo de La Habana (Havana Athenaeum): San Martín 258, Havana; f. 1902; Sec. Dr JOSÉ ENRIQUE HEYMANN Y DE LA GÁNDARA.

Casa de las Américas (House of the Americas): Calle 3ra esquina a G, El Vedado, Havana 10400; tel. (7) 838-2706; fax (7) 834-4554; e-mail presidencia@casa.cult.cu; internet www.casa.cult.cu; f. 1959; cultural instn supporting Latin American literature, art and science; organizes festivals, exhibitions, conferences; maintains the 'José Antonio Echeverría' public library; documentary centre; Pres. ROBERTO FERNÁNDEZ RETAMAR; publs *Anales del Caribe* (1 a year), *Boletín de Música* (2 a year), *Casa de las Américas* (3 a year), *Conjunto* (4 a year), *Criterios* (1 a year).

EDUCATION

UNESCO Office Havana and Regional Bureau for Culture in Latin America and the Caribbean: Calzada 551–Esq. a D, Vedado, Havana; tel. (7) 32-2840; fax (7) 33-3144; e-mail habana@unesco.org; internet www.unesco.org.cu; f. 1950; designated Cluster Office for Cuba, Dominican Republic and Haiti; Dir FRANCISCO JOSÉ LACAYO PARAJON.

LANGUAGE AND LITERATURE

Academia Cubana de la Lengua (Cuban Academy of Language): Centro Cultural Dulce María Loynaz, Calle E 502, entre calles 17 y 19, Vedado, 10400 Havana; tel. (7) 835-2732; e-mail acadcuba@cenyai.inf.cu; f. 1926; corresp. of the Real Academia Española (Madrid); Dir ROBERTO FERNÁNDEZ RETAMAR; Sec. MARLEN DOMÍNGUEZ HERNÁNDEZ.

Alliance Française: Calle J N° 302 esq. a 15 Vedado, Havana; tel. (7) 833-3370; fax (7) 833-1105; e-mail dgafcuba@enet.cu; offers courses and exams in French language and culture and promotes cultural exchange with France; attached office in Santiago; Prin. ANDRE DE UBEDA.

British Council: 7ma Avda, e/ Calle 34 y 36, Miramar, Havana; tel. (7) 207-9605; fax (7) 214-2218; e-mail information@cu .britishcouncil.org; internet www .britishcouncil.org/cuba; offers courses and exams in English language and British culture and promotes cultural exchange with the UK; Dir JENNY WHITE.

Unión de Escritores y Artistas de Cuba (Writers' and Artists' Union of Cuba): Calle 17 No. 351, Vedado, Havana; tel. (7) 53-5081; fax (7) 33-3158; internet www.uneac.com; f. 1961; 4,589 mems; Pres. CARLOS MARTÍ BRENES; Exec. Sec. MARTIZA HERNANDEZ; publs *Ediciones Unión* (12 a year), *La Gaceta de Cuba* (4 a year), *Literatura Cubana* (2 a year).

MEDICINE

Sociedad Cubana de Historia de la Medicina (Cuban Society for the History of Medicine): Calle L No. 406 esq. 23 y 25, Vedado, Havana 4; e-mail amaro@abril.sld .cu; Pres. Dr RUBÉN RODRÍGUEZ GAVALDÁ; Sec. Dra MARÍA DEL CARMEN AMARO CANO; publ. *Cuadernos.*

Sociedad Cubana de Imagenología (Cuban Imagenology Society): Calle L 406 esq. 23 y 25, Vedado, Havana 10400; tel. (7) 876-1150; e-mail jrxdigestivo@hha.sld.cu; internet www.sld.cu/sitios/imagenologia; f. 2007; 600 mems; Pres. Prof. ORLANDO VALLS PÉREZ; Sec. Prof. MIGUEL A. RODRÍGUEZ ALLENDE.

Research Institutes

AGRICULTURE, FISHERIES AND VETERINARY SCIENCE

Centro de Investigaciónes para el Mejoramiento Animal (Research Centre for the Improvement of Livestock): Carretera Central Km 21½, Loma de Tierra, Cotorro, Havana 14000; tel. and fax (7) 57-9408; f. 1970; library of 4,600 vols; Dir José R. MORALES; publ. *Revista Cubana de Reproducción Animal* (2 a year).

Centro de Investigaciones Pesqueras (Fisheries Research Centre): Barlovento, Santa Fé, Playa, Havana; tel. (2) 09-7875; fax (2) 04-9827; f. 1959; research on fisheries, marine aquaculture, fish-processing technology; training courses; library of 4,230 vols, 1,500 periodicals; Gen. Dir Dr TIZOL CORREA RAFAEL; publs *Ciencia y Tecnología Pesquera* (4 a year), *Revista Cubana de Investigaciones Pesqueras*.

Estación Experimental Apícola (Experimental Station for Beekeeping): Arroyo Arenas, El Cano, La Lisa, Havana 19190; tel. (7) 202-0027; fax (7) 202-0950; e-mail eeapi@ceniai.inf.cu; f. 1982; library of 2,443 vols; Dir MSc ADOLFO M. PÉREZ PIÑEIRO; publs *Apiciencia* (research, 3 a year), *Boletín Apicienia* (for beekeepers, 4 a year).

Instituto Cubano de Investigaciones de los Derivados de la Caña de Azúcar (ICIDCA) (Cuban Institute for Research on Sugar Cane By-Products): Vía Blanca y Carretera Central 804, Apdo 4026, San Miguel del Padrón, Havana; tel. (7) 55-7015; fax (7) 98-8653; e-mail icidca@ceniai.inf.cu; internet www.icidca.cu; f. 1963; library of 7,000 vols; Dir LUIS O. GÁLVEZ TAUPIER; publ. *Sobre los derivados de la Caña de Azúcar* (4 a year).

Instituto de Investigaciones Agropecuarias 'Jorge Dimitrov' (Jorge Dimitrov Livestock Research Institute): Carretera a Manzanillo Km 16½, Gaveta Postal 2140, Bayamo, Granma; tel. (23) 5239; e-mail dimitrov@dimitrov.granma.inf.cu; attached to Cuban Acad. of Sciences; Dir Dr ISMAEL LEONARD ACOSTA.

Instituto de Investigaciones Avícolas (Poultry Research Institute): Gaveta Postal 1, 17200 Santiago de las Vegas, Havana; tel. (7) 683-9040; fax (7) 683-9034; e-mail viiacan@ceniai.inf.cu; internet www.iia.cu; f. 1976; Dir Dr SAÚL AMIGO DELGADO; publ. *Revista Cubana de Ciencia Avícola* (2 a year).

Instituto de Investigaciones de Sanidad Vegetal (Plant Health Research Institute): Calle 110 No. 514 entre 5ta B y 5ta F, Miramar, Playa, Havana CP 11600; tel. (7) 202-2516; fax (7) 202-9366; e-mail administrador@inisav.cu; internet www.inisav.cu; f. 1970; Dir Dr JORGE OVIES DIAZ; publ. *Fitosanidad* (4 a year).

Instituto de Investigaciones en Viandas Tropicales (Research Institute for Tropical Vegetables): Apdo 6, Santo Domingo 53000, Villa Clara; tel. (42) 40-3103; fax (42) 40-3689; e-mail inivit@ip.etecsa.cu; f. 1967; tropical root and tuber crops, bananas and plantains; library of 14,439 vols; Dir Dr SERGIO RODRIGUEZ MORALES; publ. *Agrotecnia de Cuba*.

Instituto de Investigaciones Forestales (Institute of Forestry Research): Calle 174 No. 1723 e/ 17-B y 17-C, Siboney, Playa, Havana; tel. (7) 208-2189; e-mail direccion@forestales.co.cu; f. 1969; attached to Cuban Acad. of Sciences; library of 10,000 vols; Dir HUMBERTO GARCÍA CORRALES; publ. *Revista Forestal Baracoa* (2 a year).

Instituto de Investigaciones Fundamentales en Agricultura Tropical 'Alejandro de Humboldt' (Alexander von Humboldt Institute of Basic Research in Tropical Agriculture): Calle 2, esq. a 1, Santiago de las Vegas, Havana 17200; tel. (7) 57-9010; fax (7) 57-9014; e-mail yamiletrst@inifat.esihabana.cu; f. 1904; library of 2,600 vols; Dir Dr ADOLFO RODRÍGUEZ NODALS; publ. *Agrotecnia de Cuba*.

Instituto de Investigaciones Porcinas (Pig Research Institute): Carretera del Guatao Km 5½, Punta Brava, Bauta, Havana; e-mail iip00@ceniai.inf.cu; internet www.iip.co.cu; f. 1972.

HISTORY, GEOGRAPHY AND ARCHAEOLOGY

Instituto de Geografía Tropical (Institute of Tropical Geography): Calle 13 No. 409 esquina F. Vedado, Plaza de la Revolución, Havana 10400; tel. (7) 832-4295; fax (7) 836-3174; e-mail geotrop@ama.cu; internet www.geotech.cu; f. 1962; attached to Min. of Science, Technology and the Environment; Dir Dra MARLEN MARTHA PALET RABAZA.

LANGUAGE AND LITERATURE

Instituto de Literatura y Lingüística 'José Antonio Portuondo Valdor' (José Antonio Portuondo Valdor Institute of Literature and Linguistics): Ave Salvador Allende 710 e/ Soledad y Castillejo, Centro, Havana 10300; tel. (7) 878-6486; fax (7) 873-5718; e-mail ill@ceniai.inf.cu; internet www.ill.cu; f. 1965; attached to Min. of Science, Technology and the Environment; Dir Dra NURIA GREGORI TORADA; publs *Anuario* (linguistics edition, 1 a year), *Anuario* (literature edition, 1 a year).

MEDICINE

Centro Ingeniería Genética y Biotecnología de Cuba (Centre for Genetic Engineering and Biotechnology of Cuba): Ave 31E 160 y 190, Rpto Cubanacán, Playa, Havana; internet www.cigb.edu.cu; f. 1986; research, devt, production and commercial applications of biotechnology; vaccine research; Dir-Gen. Dr LUIS HERRERA MARTINEZ; publ. *Biotecnología Aplicada*.

Centro Nacional de Información de Ciencias Médicas (CNICM) (National Centre for Information on Medical Science): Calle E No. 454 e/ 19 y 21, El Vedado, 10400 Havana; tel. (7) 32-2004; fax (7) 33-3063; e-mail webmaster@infomed.sld.cu; internet www.sld.cu/cnicm.html; Dir Dr JEREMÍAS HERNÁNDEZ OJITO; publ. *Revista Cubana de Medicina*.

Instituto Nacional de Higiene, Epidemiología y Microbiología (National Institute of Hygiene, Epidemiology and Microbiology): Infanta 1158 e/ Llinás y Clavel, Centro, 10300 Havana; tel. (7) 870-5723; fax (7) 33-3063; internet www.sld.cu/webs/epidem; f. 1943; attached to Min. of Public Health; library of 3,000 vols; Dir Dr MARIANO BONET.

Instituto Nacional de Oncología y Radiobiología de La Habana (National Institute of Oncology and Radiobiology in Havana): Calle 29 y F, Vedado, 10400 Havana; tel. (7) 55-2577; fax (7) 55-2587; e-mail dinor@infomed.sld.cu; f. 1961; library of 2,700 vols; Dir Dr ALBERTO CÉSPEDES CARRILLO; publ. *Revista Cubana de Oncología*.

NATURAL SCIENCES

General

Centro Nacional de Investigaciones Científicas (National Centre for Scientific Research): Ave 25 No. 15202 esq. 158, Reparto Cubanacán, Playa, 12100 Havana; tel. (7) 271-4453; fax (7) 208-0497; internet www.cnic.edu.cu; f. 1969; natural, biomedical and technological sciences, development of medicines and medical equipment; postgraduate education; library of 100,000 vols; Dir Dr CARLOS GUTIERREZ CALZADO; publs *Revista CENIC Ciencias Biológicas* (3 a year), *Revista CENIC Ciencias Químicas* (3 a year).

Instituto de Oceanología (Institute of Oceanology): Ave 1ra. No. 18406 entre 184 y 186, Rpto. Flores, Playa, 12100 Havana; tel. (7) 21-6008; fax (7) 33-9112; e-mail oceano@oceano.inf.cu; f. 1965; attached to Min. of Science, Technology and the Environment; Dir Lic. JUAN PÉREZ; publ. *Avicennia*.

Biological Sciences

Centro Nacional de Producción de Animales de Laboratorio (CENPALAB) (National Centre for the Production of Laboratory Animals): Carretera El Cacahual Km 2½ AP 3, Bejucal, La Habana; e-mail ccalidad@cenpalab.inf.cu; f. 1982; attached to Cuban Acad. of Sciences; Dir Dr LEONARDO CABEZAS RODRÍGUEZ.

Mathematical Sciences

Centro de Estudios de Población y Desarrollo (CEPDE) (Centre for Population and Development Studies): Oficina Nacional de Estadísticas, Paseo 60 e/ 3ra y 5ta, Vedado, Plaza de la Revolución, 10400 Havana; tel. (7) 830-0053; e-mail oneweb@one.gov.cu; attached to National Statistical Office; Dir Dr JUAN CARLOS ALFONSO FRAGA.

Physical Sciences

Centro de Investigaciones para la Industria Minero-Metalúrgica (Research Centre for Mining and Metallurgy): Finca la Luisa, Carretera Varona 12028, Boyeros, A. P. 8067, Havana; tel. (7) 644-2315; fax (7) 643-8082; e-mail cipimm@cipimm.minbas.cu; f. 1967; attached to Min. of Basic Industry; research in geology, mining, chemical analysis, metallurgy; Dir Dr EDUARDO ACEVEDO DEL MONTE.

Centro Nacional de Investigaciones Sismológicas (CENAIS (National Centre for Seismological Research): Ministerio de Ciencia Tecnología y Medio Ambiente, Calle 17 No. 61 e/ 4 y 6, Vista Alegre, 90400 Santiago de Cuba; tel. (226) 4-1623; fax (226) 4-1579; e-mail cenais@cenais.ciges.inf.cu; f. 1992; Dir Ing. LUIS SIERRA QUESADA.

Instituto de Cibernética, Matemática y Física (ICIMAF) (Institute of Cybernetics, Mathematics and Physics): Calle 15 No. 551 e/ C y D, Vedado, Havana; tel. (7) 832-7764; fax (7) 833-3373; e-mail icimaf@icmf.inf.cu; internet www.icmf.inf.cu; f. 1964; attached to Cuban Acad. of Sciences; Dir Ing. RAIMUNDO FRANCO PARELLADA.

Instituto de Geofísica y Astronomía (Institute of Geophysics and Astronomy): Calle 212 No. 2906, Marianao, Havana; tel. (7) 271-4331; e-mail lpalacio@iga.cu; internet www.iga.cu; f. 1974; attached to Min. of Science, Technology and the Environment; library of 1,000 vols; Dir Dra LOURDES PALACIO SUÁREZ; publ. *Datos Astronómicos para Cuba* (1 a year).

Instituto de Meteorología (INSMET) (Institute of Meteorology): Apdo 17032, Loma de Casablanca, Regla, 11700 Havana; tel. (7) 61-7500; fax (7) 867-0711; e-mail meteoro@met.inf.cu; internet www.met.inf.cu; attached to Min. of Science, Technology and the Environment; Dir Dr TOMÁS GUTIERREZ PÉREZ; publs *Boletín Meteorológico Marino* (2 a year), *Revista Cubana de Meteorología* (2 a year).

PHILOSOPHY AND PSYCHOLOGY

Instituto de Filosofía (Institute of Philosophy): Calzada No. 251 esq. J., Vedado, Havana 10400; tel. (7) 832-1887; e-mail instituto@filosofia.cu; internet www.filosofia .cu; f. 1966; attached to Cuban Acad. of Sciences; library of 3,000 vols; Dir Dra CONCEPCIÓN NIEVES AYÚS; publs *Revista Cubana de Ciencias Sociales* (2 a year), *Revista Cubana de Filosofía* (online, 3 a year).

RELIGION, SOCIOLOGY AND ANTHROPOLOGY

Centro de Antropología (Centre for Anthropology): Calzada de Buenos Aires 111 e/ Agua Dulce y Diana, Cerro, 10600 Havana; tel. (7) 33-5514; fax (7) 33-8054; e-mail antropol@ceniai.inf.cu; attached to Min. of Science, Technology and the Environment; Dir Dra LOURDES SERRANO PERALTA.

Centro de Investigaciones Psicológicas y Sociológicas (CIPS) (Centre for Research in Psychology and Sociology): Calle B No. 352 esq. 15, Vedado, Havana; tel. (7) 830-1451; fax (7) 33-4327; internet www.cips.cu; attached to Min. of Science, Technology and the Environment; undertakes socio-psychological surveys which relate to social politics in Cuba and the means of ensuring the participation of workers in the different levels of social planning; Dir Lic. ANGELA CASAÑAS MATA.

TECHNOLOGY

Centro de Desarrollo Científico de Montañas (Centre for the Scientific Development of Mountainous Regions): Matazón, Sabaneta, El Salvador, Guantanamo; tel. (21) 9-9230; attached to Cuban Acad. of Sciences; Dir Ing. FRANCISCO VELÁZQUEZ RODRÍGUEZ.

Centro de Desarrollo de Equipos e Instrumentos Científicos (CEDEIC) (Centre for the Development of Scientific Equipment and Instruments): Luz 375 e/ Compostela y Picota, 10100 Havana; tel. (7) 61-2846; fax (7) 33-8707; e-mail cedeic@ ceniai.inf.cu; attached to Cuban Acad. of Sciences; laser technology and its application in medicine, nutrition and electronics; Dir Ing. LUIS EMILIO GARCÍA MAGARINO.

Centro de Diseño de Sistemas Automatizados de Computación (CEDISAC) (Centre for the Design of Automated Computer Systems): Ave. 47 e/ 18A y 20, Aptdo Postal 604, Miramar, 11300 Havana; tel. (7) 23-5153; fax (7) 24-8202; e-mail cdisac@ ceniai.inf.cu; attached to Cuban Acad. of Sciences; Dir Dra BEATRIZ ALONSO BECERRA.

Centro de Investigaciones de Energía Solar (Centre for Research into Solar Energy): Micro 3 Reparto 'Abel Santamaría', Santiago de Cuba 90800; tel. and fax (226) 7-1131; e-mail relinter@cies.ciges.inf.cu; f. 1986; attached to Min. of Science, Technology and the Environment; Dir Ing. ORLANDO LASTRES DANGUILLECOURT.

Centro de Investigaciones para la Industria Minero Metalúrgica (Research Centre of the Metal-Mining Industry): Finca 'La Luisa' Km 1½, Carretera Varona No. 12028, Apdo 8067, Boyeros, Havana; tel. and fax (7) 57-8082; internet www.camaracuba .cu; f. 1967; library of 4,000 vols; Dir Dr EDUARDO ACEVEDO; publs *Infomin* (bulletin, 12 a year), *Resenas*, *Revista Tecnológica* (3 a year).

Libraries and Archives

Havana

Archivo Nacional de Cuba (Cuban National Archive): Compostela 906 esq. a San Isidro, Havana 10100; tel. (7) 862-9436; fax (7) 33-8089; e-mail arnac@ceniai.inf.cu; internet www.ceniai.inf.cu/ciencia/citma/aid/ archivo; f. 1840; 25,000 linear metres of archive material; 12,834 vols, 675 periodicals; Dir Dra BERARDA SALABARRÍA ABRAHAM; publ. *Boletín* (1 a year).

Biblioteca Central 'Rubén Martínez Villena' de la Universidad de la Habana (Rubén Martínez Villena Central Library of the University of Havana): Calle San Lázaro y L, Municipio Plaza de la Revolución, Havana; tel. (7) 78-1230; fax (7) 33-5774; e-mail susan@dict.uh.cu; internet www.dict .uh.cu; f. 1728; 945,000 vols; Dir Lic. BÁRBARA SUSANA SÁNCHEZ VIGNAU; publs *Revista Cubana de Educación Superior* (3 a year), *Revista Cubana de Física* (2 a year), *Revista Cubana de Psicología* (3 a year), *Revista Debates Americanos* (2 a year), *Revista de Biología* (1 a year), *Revista de Ciencias Matemáticas* (2 a year), *Revista del Jardín Botánico Nacional* (1 a year), *Revista de Investigaciones Marinas* (3 a year), *Revista Economía y Desarrollo* (2 a year), *Revista Investigación Operacional* (3 a year), *Revista Universidad de la Habana* (2 a year).

Biblioteca del Instituto Pre-universitario de La Habana (Library of the Havana Pre-University Institute of Education): Zuleta y San José, Havana; f. 1894; 32,000 books, newspaper library; Dir JOSÉ MANUEL CASTELLANOS RODILES.

Biblioteca 'Fernando Ortiz' del Instituto de Literatura y Lingüística (Fernando Ortiz Library of the Institute of Literature and Linguistics): Salvador Allende 710 entre Soledad y Castillejo, Havana 10300; tel. (7) 878-5405; fax (7) 873-5718; e-mail ill@ceniai .inf.cu; f. 1793; 1m. items; Librarian Lic. Ma. ELOISA DÍAZ FAURE.

Biblioteca Histórica Cubana y Americana 'Francisco González del Valle' (Francisco González del Valle Library of Cuban and American History): Tacón 1 e/ Obispo y O'Reilly, Havana; tel. (7) 861-5001; e-mail biblioteca@patrimonio.ohch.cu; internet www.ohch.cu; f. 1938.

Biblioteca 'José Antonio Echeverría' (José Antonio Echeverría Library): G y 3ra, Havana; tel. (7) 838-2706; e-mail biblioservicios@casa.cult.cu; internet biblio .casadelasamericas.org; f. 1959; Caribbean and Latin American books; 150,000 vols, 8,500 journals; Dir ERNESTO SIERRA; publ. *Boletín* (12 a year).

Biblioteca 'Manuel Sanguily' (Manuel Sanguily Library): Cuchillo de Zanja 19, Primer Piso, entre Rayo y San Nicolás, Centro Havana; tel. (7) 63-3232; f. 1960; 29,512 vols, 3,200 periodicals; Dir ESTRELLA GARCÍA.

Biblioteca Nacional 'José Martí' (José Martí National Library): Apdo 6670, Avda de Independencia e/20 de Mayo y Aranguren, Plaza de la Revolución José Martí, Havana; tel. (7) 881-2428; e-mail direccion@bnjm.cu; internet www.bnjm.cu; f. 1901; 4,242,936 items; Dir ELIADES ACOSTA MATOS; publs *Bibliografía Cubana* (1 a year), *Bibliotecas: Anales de Investigación, Catálogo Cuba en Publicaciones Extranjeras, Indice General de Publicaciones Periódicas Cubanas, Revista de la Biblioteca Nacional José Martí.*

Biblioteca Provincial 'Rubén Martínez Villena' (Rubén Martínez Villena Provincial Library): Plaza de Armas, Centro Histórico, La Habana Vieja, Havana; tel. (7) 862-9035;

e-mail database@bpvillena.ohc.cu; internet www.bpvillena.ohc.cu; f. 1960; 94,328 vols; spec. braille colln; Dir Lic. ANA MARÍA SÁNCHEZ RODRÍGUEZ.

Centro de Información Bancaria y Económica, Banco Central de Cuba (Banking and Economic Information Centre, Central Bank of Cuba): Cuba 410 e/ Amargua y Lamparilla, 10100 Havana; tel. (7) 62-8318; fax (7) 66-6661; e-mail cibe@bc.gov.cu; internet www.bc.gov.cu; f. 1950; 33,000 vols; Man. ARACELIS CEJAS RODRÍGUEZ; Library Dept Chief JORGE FERNÁNDEZ PÉREZ; publs *Cuba: Half Yearly Economic Report, Economic Report* (1 a year), *Revista del Banco Central* (Journal of the Central Bank of Cuba).

Centro de Información y Documentación Agropecuario (Livestock Information and Documentation Centre): Gaveta postal 4149, Havana 4; tel. (7) 81-8808; fax (7) 33-5086; f. 1971; 20,000 vols, 1,400 journals; Dir Dr DAVID WILLIAMS CANTERO; publs numerous journals.

Instituto de Información Científica y Tecnológica (IDICT) (Institute of Scientific and Technical Information): Apdo postal 2213, 10200 Havana; Capitolio de La Habana, Prado entre Dragones y San José, La Habana Vieja, Havana; tel. (7) 862-6531; fax (7) 860-8813; e-mail tere@idict.cu; internet www.idict.cu; f. 1963; attached to Min. of Science, Technology and the Environment; 150,000 vols, 8,000 journals; Gen. Dir CARMEN SÁNCHEZ ROJAS; publs *Boletín FID / CLA* (4 a year), *Ciencia, Innovación y Desarrollo* (4 a year), *Ciencias de la Información* (4 a year).

Santiago

Biblioteca Central de la Universidad de Oriente (Central Library of the University of Oriente): Avda Patricio Lumumba s/n, 90500 Santiago de Cuba; tel. (226) 3-1973; f. 1947; 42,000 vols; Librarian Lic. MAURA GONZÁLEZ PÉREZ; publs *Revista Cubana de Química, Revista Santiago.*

Biblioteca Provincial 'Elvira Cape' (Elvira Cape Provincial Library): Calle Heredia 258 e/ Pío Rosado y Hartman, 90100 Santiago de Cuba; tel. (22) 65-4836; e-mail bpcape@lib.cultstgo.cult.cu; internet www .cultstgo.cult.cu/biblioteca/index.htm; f. 1899; 169,000 vols, 1,760 periodicals; Dir DAYMA SERPA LÓPEZ; publ. *Boletín Electrónico.*

Museums and Art Galleries

Camagüey

Museo Ignacio Agramonte (Ignacio Agramonte Museum): Camagüey; tel. (32) 28-2425; e-mail cmqcppatrimonia@pprincips .cult.cu; f. 1955; paintings, furniture, textiles and relics from the colonial period; Dir YOLANDA GUTIÉRREZ CAMPOS.

Cárdenas

Museo Municipal 'Oscar M. de Rojas' (Oscar M. de Rojas Muncipal Museum): Calle Calzada 4 e/ Echeverría y Martí, Cárdenas; f. 1903; exhibits relating to Martí and other aspects of Cuban history, malacology, insects, butterflies and colonial weaponry; library; Curator OSCAR M. DE ROJAS Y CRUZAT.

Havana

Acuario Nacional de Cuba (National Aquarium of Cuba): Ave 1ra y Calle 60, Miramar, Playa, Havana 11300; tel. (7) 203-6401; fax (7) 204-1442; e-mail comercial@

acuarionacional.cu; internet www .acuarionacional.cu; f. 1960; attached to Min. of Science, Technology and the Environment; library of 3,000 vols; Dir Lic. GUILLERMO GARCÍA MONTERO.

Archivo Histórico Municipal (Muncipal Historical Archive): Tacón 1 e/ Obispo y O'Reilly, Havana; tel. (7) 861-5001; e-mail archivo@patrimonio.ohch.cu; internet www .ohch.cu; f. 1938; historical items since 1550.

Jardín Botánico Nacional de Cuba (National Botanical Garden of Cuba): Carretera del Rocío Km 3½, CP 19230, Calabazar, Boyeros, Havana; tel. (7) 697-9310; fax (7) 697-9160; f. 1968; administered by Universidad de la Habana; library of 4,700 vols, 1,253 periodicals; herbarium; 100,000 specimens; Cuban flora colln: fungi, pteridophytes, gymnosperms and angiosperms; postgraduate training on vegetal anatomy, morphology and systematics; Masters degree in botany; Dir-Gen. Dra ANGELA LEIVA SÁNCHEZ; publ. *Revista Jardin Botanico Nacional* (1 a year).

Museo Antropológico Montané (Montané Anthropological Museum): Edif. Felipe Poey, Plaza Ignacio Agramonte, Colina Universitaria, Havana; tel. (7) 879-3488; f. 1903; colln of pre-Columbian artefacts; library of 5,000 vols; Dir Dr ANTONIO J. MARTÍNEZ FUENTES.

Museo Casa Natal José Martí (House Museum of José Martí): Calle Leonor Pérez 314 e/ Calles Egido y Picota, Havana; internet www.cnpc.cult.cu/cnpc/museos/ marti; f. 1925; relics of José Martí and his works; Curator MARIA DE LA LUZ RAMIREZ ESTRADA.

Museo de Arte Colonial de la Habana (Havana Museum of Colonial Art): San Ignacio 61, Plaza de la Catedral, Havana; tel. (7) 862-6440; e-mail colonial@bp .patrimonio.ohc.cu; internet www.ohch.cu; f. 1969; housed in mansion built 1720; Dir MARGARITA SUÑAREZ GARCÍA.

Museo de Historia Natural 'Felipe Poey' (Felipe Poey Museum of Natural History): Facultad de Biología, Universidad de La Habana, Calle 25 e/J e I, Vedado, 10400 Havana; tel. (7) 879-3488; fax (7) 832-1321; e-mail museopoey@fbio.uh.cu; internet www .uh.cu/museos/poey/index.html; f. 1842; zoology; library of 80,520 vols; Dir Dr ALEJANDRO BARRO CAÑAMERO.

Museo Ernest Hemingway (Ernest Hemingway Museum): Finca Vigía, San Francisco de Paula, Havana 19180; tel. (7) 91-0809; fax (7) 55-8090; f. 1962; house, library and personal items of Ernest Hemingway who lived at the address 1939–60; Dir DANILO M. ARRATE HERNÁNDEZ.

Museo Municipal de Guanabacoa (Guanabacoa Muncipal Museum): Calle Martí 108 e/ Versalles y San Antonio, Guanabacoa, Havana; tel. (7) 797-9117; e-mail musgbcoa@cubarte.cult.cu; f. 1964; popular Cuban religions of African origin; Dir MARIA CRISTINA PEÑA REIGOSA.

Museo Nacional y Palacio de Bellas Artes (National Museum and Palace of Fine Arts): Trocadero entre Zulueta y Monserrate, Havana Vieja 10200; tel. (7) 63-9042; fax (7) 62-9626; e-mail musna@cubarte.cult .cu; internet www.museonacional.cult.cu; f. 1913; ancient Egyptian, Greek and Roman art, 16th- to 19th-century European art, Cuban art from the colonial period to the present; Dir MORAIMA CLAVIJO COLOM.

Attached Museums:

Castillo de la Real Fuerza de la Havana (Castle of the Royal Garrison of Havana): O'Reilly entre Avda del Puerto y Tacón, Plaza de Armas, Havana Vieja 10100; tel. (7) 61-6130; fax (7) 61-3857; f. 1977; modern ceramic exhibits housed in a 16th-century fortification; Dir ALEJANDRO G. ALONSO.

Museo de Artes Decorativas (Museum of Decorative Arts): Calle 17, No. 502 entre D y E, Vedado, Havana 10200; tel. (7) 32-0924; fax (7) 61-3857; f. 1964; European and Oriental decorative art since 17th century; Dir KATIA VARELA.

Museo Napoleónico (Napoleonic Museum): San Miguel 1159 esq. Ronda, Plaza de la Revolución, Havana; tel. (7) 79-1460; fax (7) 79-1412; e-mail musnap@cubarte.cult.cu; internet www.cnpc.cult.cu; f. 1961; historical objects and works of art of Revolutionary and Imperial France; specialized library.

Museo Numismático (Numismatic Museum): Obispo 305 e/ Aguiar y Habana, Havana 1; tel. (7) 861-5811; e-mail numismatica@cultural.ohch.cu; internet www.ohch.cu; f. 1975; coins, banknotes, medals and decorations; library; Dir INÉS MORALES GARCÍA.

Parque Zoológico Nacional (National Zoological Garden): Carretera de Varona Km 3½, Boyeros, Havana; tel. (7) 44-7616; fax (7) 57-8054; e-mail pzn@ceniai.inf.cu; f. 1984; attached to Min. of Science, Technology and the Environment; library of 1,300 vols; Dir TOMÁS ESCOBAR HERRERA; publ. *Revista Cubazos*.

Matanzas

Museo Provincial de Matanzas (Matanzas Provincial Museum): Palacio de Junco, Calle Milanés e/ Magdalena y Ayllón, Plaza de la Vigía, Matanzas; tel. (52) 24-3195; f. 1959; history, natural history, decorative arts, weaponry, archaeology and ethnology; library of 1,000 vols; Dir Lic. GONZALO DOMÍNGUEZ CABRERA; publ. *Museo* (2 a year).

Remedios

Museo de Remedios 'José Maria Espinosa' (José Maria Espinosa Museum in Remedios): Maceo 32, Remedios; f. 1933; history, science, art; Dir. ALBERTO VIGIL Y COLOMA.

Santiago

Museo Emilio Bacardi Moreau (Emilio Bacardi Moreau Museum): Pío Rosado esq. Aguilera, 90100 Santiago; tel. (7) 62-8402; e-mail cppatrim@cultstgo.cult.cu; f. 1899; history, art; Curators JOSÉ A. AROCHA ROVIRA, FIDELIA PÉREZ GONZÁLEZ.

Universities

UNIVERSIDAD DE CAMAGÜEY

Carretera de Circunvalación Norte Km 5½, 74650 Camagüey

Telephone: (32) 28-1363
Fax: (32) 26-1587
E-mail: dri@reduc.edu.cu
Internet: www.reduc.edu.cu

Founded as a branch of University of Havana 1967; present name 1974
State control
Academic year: September to July

Rector: Dra C. LIANET GOYAS CÉSPEDES
Vice-Rector for Academic Affairs: Dra ANGELA PALACIOS HIDALGO
Vice-Rector for Administration and Services: MSc. FRANCISCO PRÉSTAMO
Vice-Rector for Extension: Ing. PEDRO RODRÍGUEZ
Vice-Rector for Financial Affairs: Dra ANA FERNÁNDEZ
Vice-Rector for Research and Postgraduate Affairs: Dra HILDA OQUENDO
Registrar: Lic. RAÚL GARRIGA CORZO

Librarian: Lic. SARA ARTILES VISBAL
Number of teachers: 450
Number of students: 3,200
Publications: *Revista de Producción Animal*, *Revista La Nueva Gestión Organizacional*, *Revista Retos de la Dirección*

DEANS

Faculty of Animal Sciences: Dr JOSÉ BERTOT
Faculty of Communication: MSc. TEL PINO SOSA
Faculty of Computer Science: Dr LUIS CORRALES BARRIOS
Faculty of Construction: Dr ELIO PÉREZ
Faculty of Economics and Business: Dra ANA DE DIOS
Faculty of Electromechanics: Dr LUIS CORRALES BARRIOS
Faculty of Food Chemistry: Dr PABLO GALINDO
Faculty of Languages: MSc. NORMA MOREDO
Faculty of Law: Dra MARÍA ELENA PRADO
Faculty of Social and Humanistic Sciences: Dra FLOR DE MARÍA FERNÁNDEZ FIFONTES

UNIVERSIDAD DE CIEGO DE AVILA

Km 9 Carretera de Ciego de Avila a Morón, Ciego de Ávila 69450

Telephone: (33) 22-4544
Fax: (33) 26-6365
E-mail: webmaster@rect.unica.cu
Internet: www.unica.cu

Founded 1978 as Instituto Superior Agrícola de Ciego de Avila; current name and status since 1996
Faculties of agronomy, economics, humanities, computer science and engineering

Rector: Dr MARIO ARES SÁNCHEZ
Library Dir: JORGE ANTONIO GÓMEZ CORDERO
Library of 41,963 vols
Number of teachers: 1,451
Number of students: 6,061
Publication: *Fidelia* (4 a year)

UNIVERSIDAD DE CIENFUEGOS 'CARLOS RAFAEL RODRÍGUEZ'

Carretera de Rodas Km 4, Cuatro Caminos, Cienfuegos 59430

Telephone: (432) 2-1521
Fax: (432) 2-2762
E-mail: rector@ucfinfo.ucf.edu.cu
Internet: www.ucf.edu.cu

Founded 1979 as Instituto Superior Técnico de Cienfuegos; university status 1994; current name since 1998
State control

Rector: Dr ANDRÉS OLIVERA RANERO
Vice-Rector for Academic Affairs: Dr ABEL QUIÑONEZ URQUIJO
Vice-Rector for Admin.: MAGDIEL E. CHAVIANO DÍAZ
Vice-Rector for Research and Postgraduates: Dra MIRIAN IGLESIAS LEÓN
Vice-Rector for Standardization of Higher Education: LOURDES POMARES CASTELLÓN
Sec.-Gen.: Lic. BLAS JUANES RAMÍREZ
Librarian: Dr LÁSARO S. DIBUT TOLEDO
Library of 50,000 vols
Number of teachers: 363
Number of students: 2,600
Publication: *Anuarios Científico* (1 a year)

DEANS

Faculty of Computer Science: Dr MARIO ALVAREZ GUERRA PLACENCIA
Faculty of Economics and Business: FRANCISCO BECERRA
Faculty of Humanities: Dr MARIANELA MORALES CALATAYUD
Faculty of Mechanics: Dr JUAN B. COGOLLOS MARTÍNEZ

Faculty of Physical Education: OSCAR MUÑOZ HERNÁNDEZ

ATTACHED RESEARCH INSTITUTES

Centro de Estudios y Desarrollo de la Oleohidráulica y la Neumática (CEDON): e-mail lmcglez@fmec.ucd.edu.cu; Dir Dr LUIS M. CASTELLANOS GONZÁLEZ.

Centre de Estudios de Didáctica y Dirección de la Educación Superior (CEDDES): e-mail mcaceres@rectorado.ucf.edu.cu; Dir Dra MARITZA CÁCERES MESA.

Centro de Estudios de Energía y Medio Ambiente (CEEMA): e-mail marmas@fmec.ucf.edu.cu; Dir Dr MARCOS DE ARMAS TEIRA.

Centro de Estudio Socioculturales de Cienfuegos (CESOC): e-mail lmartin@fmec.ucf.edu.cu; Dir Dra LILIAN MARTÍN BRITO.

Centro de Estudio Para la Transformación Agraria Sostenible (CETAS): e-mail asocorro@fmec.ucf.edu.cu; Dir Dr ALEJANDRO RAFAEL SOCORRO CASTRO.

UNIVERSIDAD DE GRANMA

Carretera de Manzanillo Km 17.5, Bayamo, Granma

Telephone: (23) 9-2130
Fax: (23) 9-2131
E-mail: antonia@udg.granma.inf.cu
Internet: www.udg.co.cu

Founded 1967
State control

Rector: Dra ANTONIA MARÍA CASTILLO RUÍZ

Number of teachers: 316
Number of students: 2,300

Faculties of accountancy and finance, agriculture, engineering, social and human sciences and veterinary medicine.

UNIVERSIDAD AGRARIA DE LA HABANA

Autopista Nacional y Carretera de Tapaste San José de las Lajas, La Habana

Telephone: (64) 6-3014
Fax: (64) 6-3395
E-mail: rector@main.isch.edu.cu
Internet: www.isch.edu.cu

Founded 1976

Rector: Dr JULIÁN RODRÍGUEZ RODRÍGUEZ

Number of teachers: 447
Number of students: 2,300

Faculties of agronomy, mechanization of agricultural production and veterinary science; department of Marxism-Leninism; campus on Isla de la Juventud.

UNIVERSIDAD DE LA HABANA

Zarezka Martínez Remigio, Gen.-Sec., Havana

Telephone: (7) 879-1313; (7) 78-3231
E-mail: webmaster@uh.cu
Internet: www.uh.cu

Founded 1728, reorganized 1976
Academic year: September to July

Rector: Dr GUSTAVO COBREIRO SUÁREZ
Gen. Sec.: Dra ZAREZKA MARTÍNEZ REMIGIO
Library: see under Libraries and Archives
Number of teachers: 2,974
Number of students: 27,537

Publications: *Boletín Universitario, Universidad de la Habana*, various scientific and technical publs

DEANS

Faculty of Accounting and Finance: Dra MARICELA VICTORIA REYES ESPINOSA
Faculty of Arts and Letters: Dr JOSÉ ANTONIO BAUJÍN

Faculty of Biology: Dra ALICIA OTAZO SÁNCHEZ
Faculty of Chemistry: Dr JOSÉ MANUEL NIETO VILLAR
faculty of Communication: FRANCISCO GONZÁLEZ GARCÍA
Faculty of Distance Education: ANTONIO MIRANDA JUSTINIANI
Faculty of Foreign Languages: Dr ROBERTO ESPÍ VALERO
Faculty of Geography: Dra NANCY PÉREZ RODRÍGUEZ
Faculty of Law: Dr JOSÉ LUIS TOLEDO SANTANDER
Faculty of Mathematics and Computing: Dr LUIS RAMIRO PIÑEIRO DIAZ
Faculty of Philosophy and History: Dr JOSÉ CARLOS VÁZQUEZ LÓPEZ
Faculty of Physics: Dra MARIA SÁNCHEZ COLINA
Faculty of Planning for the National Economy: Dra VILMA HIDALGO DE LOS SANTOS
Faculty of Psychology: M.Sc. KARELYN LÓPEZ SÁNCHEZ
Spanish Language for Non-Spanish Speaker: Dra HILDA LEÓN CASTELLANOS
Faculty of Tourism: Dra LOURDES CISNEROS MUSTELIER
Institute of Pharmacy and Food: Dr OSCAR ROS LÓPEZ
San Gerónimo de la Habana School: FÉLIX JULIO ALFONSO LÓPEZ

UNIVERSIDAD DE HOLGUÍN 'OSCAR LUCERO MOYA'

Avda 20 Aniversario, Nuevo Holguín, Gaveta Postal 57, 80100 Holguín

Telephone: (24) 48-1302
Fax: (24) 48-1662
E-mail: acristina@ict.uho.edu.cu
Internet: www.uho.edu.cu

Founded 1976 as Centro Universitario de Holguín; became Instituto Superior Técnico de Holguín 1982; current name and status 1995

Rector: Dr SEGUNDO PACHECO TOLEDO
Librarian: MATILDE RIVERON HERNÁNDEZ

Library of 90,980 vols
Number of teachers: 376
Number of students: 3,276

Publications: *Ambito* (4 a year), *Diéresis* (1 a year)

DEANS

Faculty of Engineering: MANUEL VEGA ALMAGUER
Faculty of Economics: MIGUEL TORRES PEREZ

UNIVERSIDAD CENTRAL 'MARTA ABREU' DE LAS VILLAS

Carretera a Camajuaní Km 5½, 54830 Santa Clara, Villa Clara

Telephone: (42) 28-1519
Fax: (42) 28-1449
E-mail: rector@uclv.edu.cu
Internet: www.uclv.edu.cu

Founded 1952
Academic year: September to July

Rector: Dr JOSÉ RAMÓN SABORIDO LOIDI
Vice-Rector for Academic Affairs: Dra MIRIAM NICADO GRACIA
Vice-Rector for Administrative Affairs: Dr OSVALDO FERNÁNDEZ MARTÍNEZ
Vice-Rector for Economic and Financial Management: Dr JOSÉ RAMÓN CASTELLANOS CASTILLO
Vice-Rector for Extension: Dr JUAN JOSÉ HERNÁNDEZ SANTANA
Vice-Rector for Research and Postgraduate Affairs: Dr ANGEL RUBIO GONZÁLEZ
Gen. Sec.: Dr SAMUEL RODRÍGUEZ GARCÍA
Librarian: Ing. JOSÉ RIVERO DÍAZ

Library of 386,000 vols
Number of teachers: 1,187
Number of students: 5,132

Publications: *Centro Agrícola, Centro Azúcar, Biotecnología Vegetal* (4 a year), *Islas* (4 a year)

DEANS

Faculty of Agricultural Sciences: Dr ANDRÉS CASTRO ALEGRÍA
Faculty of Building: Dr GILBERTO QUEVEDO SOTOLONGO
Faculty of Chemistry and Pharmacy: Dr RONALDO SANTOS HERRERO
Faculty of Economics: Dr INOCENCIO RAUL SÁNCHEZ
Faculty of Electrical Engineering: Dr FÉLIX ÁLVAREZ PALIZA
Faculty of Humanities: M.Sc. ANA IRIS DÍAZ MARTÍNEZ
Faculty of Industrial Engineering and Tourism: Dr HUGO GRANELA MARTÍN
Faculty of Information Science and Education: M.Sc. ROBERTO VICENTE RODRÍGUEZ
Faculty of Law: Dr YADIRA GARCÍA RODRIGUEZ
Faculty of Mathematics, Computing and Physics: Dra YANET RODRÍGUEZ SARABIA
Faculty of Mechanical Engineering: Dr ANGEL SILVIO MACHADO RODRÍGUEZ
Faculty of Psychology: Dra OSANA MOLERIO PÉREZ
Faculty of Social Sciences: Dra MELY DEL ROSARIO GONZÁLEZ ARÓSTEGUI

UNIVERSIDAD DE MATANZAS 'CAMILO CIENFUEGOS'

Autopista a Veradero Km 3, Matanzas

Telephone: (53) 52-62222
Fax: (53) 52-53101
E-mail: info@umcc.cu
Internet: www.umcc.cu

Founded 1972

Library of 80,000 vols
Number of teachers: 381
Number of students: 3,020

Rector: Ing. JORGE RODRÍGUEZ PÉREZ
Vice-Rector for Admin. and Services: Ing. JOSÉ R. DÍAZ
Vice-Rector for Research and Postgraduate Studies: Dr ROBERTO VIZCÓN TOLEDO
Vice-Rector for Teaching: Ing. MIGUEL SARRAF GONZÁLEZ

Publications: *Revista de Investigaciones Turísticas, Revista Pastos y Forrajes*

DEANS

Faculty of Agronomy: Dr SERGIO RODRÍGUEZ JIMÉNEZ
Faculty of Chemistry and Mechanics: Dr ROBERTO VIZCÓN TOLEDO
Faculty of Computer Science: Dr JULIO TELOT GONZÁLEZ
Faculty of Economics and Industry: Lic. BENITA N. GARCÍA GUTIÉRREZ
Faculty of Physical Education: Lic. FÉLIX MOYA
Faculty of Social Sciences and Humanities: Lic. ZOE DOMINGUEZ GARCÍA

ATTACHED RESEARCH INSTITUTES

Centro de Estudios de Anticorrosión y Tensioactivos (CEAT): Dir CARLOS A. ECHEVERRÍA LAGE.

Centro de Estudios de Combustión y Energía (CECYEN): e-mail barroso@quimec.umcc.cu; Dir JORGE ÁNGEL BARROSO ESTÉBANEZ.

Centro de Estudio y Desarrollo Educacional (CEDE): e-mail gerardo.ramos@umcc.cu; Dir Dr GERARDO RAMOS SERPA.

Centro de Estudios de Medioambiente (CEMAN): Dir Dra JUANA ZOILA JUNCO HORTA.

UNIVERSIDAD DE ORIENTE

Avda Patricio Lumumba s/n, 90500 Santiago de Cuba

Telephone: (22) 63-1860
Fax: (22) 63-2689
E-mail: marcosc@rect.uo.edu.cu
Internet: www.uo.edu.cu

Founded 1947

Academic year: September to July

Rector: Dr MARCOS CORTINA VEGA
Vice-Rectors: MSc ELIO CASTELLANOS, Dra ZAIDA VALDÉS ESTRADA, Dr SERGIO CANO ORTIZ, Dr JUAN BORY REYES, Dr PEDRO A. BEATÓN SOLER
Sec.-Gen.: Arq. SONIA QUESADA
Librarian: Dr BAYARDO DUPOTEY RIBAS
Library: see Libraries and Archives
Number of teachers: 842
Number of students: 24,500 (5,500 undergraduate, 19,000 postgraduate and continuing education)
Publications: *Revista Cubana de Química* (3 a year), *Revista Santiago* (2 a year), *Tecnología Química* (3 a year)

DEANS

Faculty of Building Construction: MSc ALEJANDRO FAJARDO
Faculty of Chemical Engineering: Dra ANA SÁNCHEZ DEL CAMPO LAFFITA
Faculty of Computing Sciences and Mathematics: MSc ALEJANDRO GARCÉS CALVELO
Faculty of Distance Learning: Dra ROSARIO LEÓN ROBAINA
Faculty of Economics: MSc ULISES PACHECO FERIA
Faculty of Electrical Engineering: MSc EMILIO SOTO MORLÁ
Faculty of Humanities: Dra ETNA SANZ
Faculty of Law: Dra JOSEFINA MÉNDEZ
Faculty of Mechanical Engineering: Dr ROBERTO ZAGARÓ ZAMORA
Faculty of Natural Sciences: Dr PEDRO MUNÉ BANDERA
Faculty of Social Sciences: Dra MARÍA JULIA JIMÉNEZ FIOL

UNIVERSIDAD DE PINAR DEL RÍO

Calle J. Martí 272 esq. a 27 de Noviembre, Pinar del Río 20100

Telephone and fax (48) 77-9353
E-mail: mfdez@vrect.upr.edu.cu
Internet: www.upr.edu.cu

Founded 1972

State control

Academic year: September to July

Rector: Dr ANDRÉS ERASMO ARES ROJAS

Vice-Rector for Admin.: Dr YORKY MAYOR HERNÁNDEZ
Vice-Rector for Community Relations: Dra MAYRA CARMONA GONZÁLEZ
Vice-Rector for Research: Dra MARISELA GONZÁLEZ PÉREZ
Vice-Rector for Teaching: Dra TERESA DE LA C. DÍAZ DOMÍNGUEZ
Sec.-Gen.: Lic. MAGALYS GONZÁLEZ HERNÁNDEZ
Librarian: Lic. MABEL RODRÍGUEZ
Number of teachers: 2,528
Number of students: 13,621
Publication: *Anuario Científico*

DEANS

Faculty of Agronomy and Forestry: Dr JORGE LUÍS CUE
Faculty of Economics: YOSVANY BARRIOS HERNÁNDEZ
Faculty of Geology and Mechanics: Lic. JORGE SÁNCHEZ
Faculty of Humanities: ANA ROSA ANDINO RUIBAL
Faculty of Mountain Agronomy: Dr JOSÉ REYNALDO DÍAZ
Faculty of Telecommunications and Informatics: Dr WILFREDO FALCÓN URQUIAGA

AFFILIATED INSTITUTES

Centre of Agroecology: Universidad de Pinar del Río, Facultad de Forestal y Agronomía Pinar del Río; tel. (48) 75-5452; e-mail mariol@af.upr.edu.cu; Dir Dra MARIOL MOREJÓN.

Centre for Forestry Sciences: e-mail betancourt@af.upr.edu.cu; Dir Dr YNOCENTE BETANCOURT FIGUERAS.

Centre for Higher Education Research: e-mail tdiaz@vrect.upr.edu.cu; Dir Dra TERESA DE LA C. DÍAZ.

Centre for Management and Tourism Studies: e-mail diana@eco.upr.edu.cu; Dir Dra DIANA DE LA NUEZ HERNÁNDEZ.

Centre of Natural Resources and the Environment: e-mail mcasas@eco.upr.edu.cu; Dir Dra MAYRA CASAS VILARDELL.

Centre for the Study of Co-operatives: e-mail arivera@eco.upr.edu.cu; Dir Dr CLAUDIO A. RIVERA.

Colleges

Instituto Superior de Ciencias Médicas de Camagüey: Carretera Central Oeste esquina a Madame Curie, Camagüey; tel. (32) 9-2100; e-mail romulo@finlay.cmw.sld.cu; f. 1981 from medical faculty of Univ. of Camagüey; schools of dentistry, medicine, nursing; biomedical, clinical and sociomedical research; 587 teachers; 3,500 students; Rector Dr RÓMULO RODRÍGUEZ RAMOS; publ. *Revista de Ciencias Médicas de Camagüey* (2 a year).

Instituto Superior de Relaciones Internacionales 'Raul Roa García': Calle Calzada 308 esq. H, Vedado, Havana 10400; tel. (7) 831-9495; fax (7) 838-1359; e-mail isri@isri.minrex.gov.cu; internet www.isri.cu; f. 1971; library: 14,000 vols; special collection containing the personal library of Dr Raúl Roa García; 61 teachers; Rector Embajadora Lic. ISABEL ALLENDE KARAM; Gen. Sec. Dr RENÉ OCHOA FÚNEZ.

Instituto Superior Politécnico 'José Antonio Echeverría': Calle 114 No. 11901 entre 119 y 127, CUJAE, Marianao, CP 19390, Havana; tel. (7) 261-4932; fax (7) 267-2694; e-mail rosy@tesla.cujae.edu.cu; internet www.cujae.edu.cu; f. 1976, fmrly Faculty of Technology of University of Havana; faculties of architecture, chemical engineering, civil engineering, electrical engineering, industrial engineering, information engineering, mechanical engineering; advanced education centre, biomedical engineering centre, hydraulic research centre, innovation and maintenance study centre, management techniques study centre, microelectronic research centre, renewable energy technology study centre, process engineering centre, systems engineering study centre, tropical architecture and construction centre; library: 157,370 vols; 1,012 teachers; 5,299 students; Rector Dr GUSTAVO COBREIRO SUÁREZ; Sec. Ing. RAÚL CAPETILLO ALVAREZ; publs *Arquitectura y Urbanismo* (3 a year), *Ingeniería Electrónica, Automática y Telecomunicaciones* (3 a year), *Ingeniería Energética* (3 a year), *Ingeniería Hidráulica y Ambiente* (3 a year), *Ingeniería Industrial* (3 a year), *Ingeniería Mecanica* (3 a year).

Schools of Art and Music

Academia Nacional de Bellas Artes 'San Alejandro' (National Academy of Fine Arts): Avenida 31 y Calle 100 No. 10006, Obelisco de Marianao, 11400 Havana; tel. (7) 260-9234; e-mail sanalejandro@cubarte.cult.cu; internet www.sanalejandro.cult.cu; f. 1818 as Academia de San Alejandro; formerly Escuela de Pintura, organized by the French painter Jean Baptiste Vermay; 800 students; Dir DOMINGO RAMOS ENRÍQUEZ.

Conservatorio Alejandro García Caturla: Avda 31 y Calle 82, Marianao, Havana.

Conservatorio de Música Amadeo Roldán: Rastro y Lealtad, Havana.

CYPRUS

The Higher Education System

Cyprus was governed by the United Kingdom form 1878 until it achieved independence in 1960, following a guerrilla campaign by Greek Cypriots seeking unification (Enosis) with Greece. Government was subsequently on the basis of a power-sharing agreement between the Greek and Turkish communities, but in 1963 the Turks withdrew from central government. In 1974, after Greek officers of the Cypriot National Guard had staged a coup, the Turkish army occupied the northern third of the island, where Turkish Cypriots subsequently established a de facto Government and, in 1975, declared a Turkish Federated State of Cyprus (TFSC). In 1983 the TFSC unilaterally declared an independent Turkish Republic of Northern Cyprus (TRNC). The Greek Cypriot administration, meanwhile, claims to be the Government of all Cyprus, and is generally recognized as such. Until 1965 each community in Cyprus managed its own schooling through a Communal Chamber. On 31 March of that year, however, the Greek Communal Chamber was dissolved and a Ministry of Education (now Ministry of Education and Culture) was established to take its place. Inter-communal education has been placed under this Ministry.

Cyprus:

The University of Cyprus, in Nicosia, was founded in 1989. There were a total of 38 higher education institutions in 2006/07, including professional institutes and colleges for art, forestry and management. In 2007/08 25,688 students (including 7,752 foreign pupils) were enrolled in tertiary education, while a total of 22,530 students from the Greek Cypriot area were studying at universities abroad, mainly in Greece, the USA and the United Kingdom.

Students must hold the main secondary school qualification (Apolytirion) and sit a competitive entrance examination to gain admission to the University of Cyprus. Cyprus became a signatory to the Bologna Process in 2001, and a two-tier Bachelors and Masters degree system has been implemented. Non-university higher education consists of one- to four-year Certificate, Diploma and Higher Diploma programmes, offered by the University of Cyprus and private institutions in professional fields of study. Private higher education institutions are registered and accredited by the Ministry of Education and Culture, in accordance with Law 67 (I) 96, introduced in September 1997.

The first university degree level is the undergraduate Bachelors degree, which is awarded after four years' study. Students must accumulate 120–180 credit units in eight semesters. Both of the postgraduate degrees, Masters and Doctor of Philosophy (PhD), require 30 credit units.

Post secondary technical and vocational education is offered by both public and private institutions.

Turkish Republic of North Cyprus:

The international community, including the UN and EU, does not recognize the TRNC as a separate self-governing country. The Republic of Cyprus is recognized as having *de jure* sovereignty over the whole island. The Greek Cypriot Government, which legally remains the competent authority for all of Cyprus, does not recognize or accredit Turkish Cypriot higher education institutions.

The education system in the TRNC follows the Turkish model, and those institutions recognized by the Turkish Government can be expected to have a comparable standard of education to the Turkish mainland.

Cyprus's first university, the Eastern Mediterranean University, which is located near Gazi Mağusa (Famagusta), was opened in 1979 as the Higher Technological Institute and was elevated to full university status under its current name in 1986. A total of 13,809 students attended the university in 2007/08. The European University of Lefke was founded in 1990. In 2007/08 43,021 students were studying at universities in the TRNC, while 1,815 students were pursuing higher education studies abroad, mainly in Turkey, the USA and the United Kingdom. All schools and educational institutes are administered by the Ministry of Education and Culture (with a few exceptions of professional institutes attached to the appropriate Ministry). Education in the Turkish Cypriot zone is divided into two sections, formal and adult (informal) education. Formal education covers nursery, primary, secondary and higher education. Adult education caters for special training outside the school system. In 1982 an International Institute of Islamic Banking and Economics was opened to provide postgraduate training.

Completion of the Lise Bitirme Diplomasi or equivalent is required for entry to university. The organization of undergraduate degrees is based on the US-style 'credit' and grade-point average (GPA) system. The Bachelors degree lasts eight semesters (four years) and students require at least 120 credits and a GPA of 2.0 to graduate. A two-year Diploma course is also available. Masters programmes such as the Master of Arts (MA), Master of Business Administration (MBA) and Master of Science (MSc) take 1–2 years' study following the Bachelors, and require between 21 (MSc) and 42 (MBA) credits. A Masters is required for admission onto the Doctor of Philosophy (PhD) programme, which is a combination of core coursework and original research; candidates for a PhD must submit a research thesis.

Technical and vocational education is provided by several colleges and institutes, admission to which is dependent upon the Lise Bitirme Diplomasi.

Regulatory and Representative Bodies

GOVERNMENT

Ministry of Education and Culture: Kimonos and Thoukydidou, Akropolis, 1434 Nicosia; tel. 22800931; fax 22305117; e-mail moec@moec.gov.cy; internet www.moec.gov.cy; Minister ANDREAS DEMETRIOU.

Ministry of Education and Culture: Lefkosa, TRNC, via Mersin 10, Turkey; tel. 2283136; fax 2282344; internet www.moec.gov.cy.

ACCREDITATION

Cyprus Council of Educational Evaluation—Accreditation (CEEA): POB 12592, 2251 Nicosia; tel. 22402476; fax 22305513; e-mail sekap@cytanet.com.cy; internet www.moec.gov.cy/sekap; Pres. GEORGE PHILOKYPROU.

ENIC/NARIC Cyprus: Cyprus Council for the Recognition of Higher Education Qualifications, POB 12758, 2252 Nicosia; tel. 22402472; fax 22402481; e-mail info@kysats.ac.cy; internet www.kysats.ac.cy; Chair. Prof. CONSTANTINOS CHRISTOU.

Learned Societies

GENERAL

Etaireia Kypriakon Spoudon (Society of Cypriot Studies): 1508, POB 21436, Nicosia; tel. 22432578; fax 22343439; e-mail cypriotstudies@gmail.com; internet www.cypriotstudies.org; f. 1936; colln, preservation and study of material concerning all periods of the history, dialect and folklore of Cyprus; maintains Museum of Cypriot Folk Art; library of Kypria, Cypriot studies; 1,050 mems; library of 5,000 vols; Pres. CHRISTODOULOS HADJICHRISTODOULOU; Sec. Dr CHARALAMPOS CHOTZAKOGLOU; publ. *Kypriakai Spoudai* (Cypriot Studies, 1 a year).

BIBLIOGRAPHY, LIBRARY SCIENCE AND MUSEOLOGY

Kypriake Enose Vivliothikonomon—Epistemonon Pleroforeses (Cyprus Association of Librarians—Information Scientists): POB 21100, 1501 Nicosia; e-mail kebepcy@gmail.com; internet kebep.blogspot .com; f. 1984; 150 mems; Pres. CHRYSANTHI STAVROU; Treas. DESPINA LAMBROU.

HISTORY, GEOGRAPHY AND ARCHAEOLOGY

Cyprus Geographical Association: POB 23656, Nicosia; tel. 22368981; f. 1968; research and study of the geography of Cyprus; aims to improve the teaching of geography, and safeguard professional interests of geographers; 200 mems; library of 500 vols; Pres. Prof. PANAYIOTIS ARGYRIDES; publ. *The Geographical Chronicles* (1 a year).

LANGUAGE AND LITERATURE

Alliance Française: 10 Panagi Lappa, POB 56681, 3309 Limassol; tel. 25877784; fax 25662633; e-mail aflima@spidernet.com.cy; internet www.aflimassol.eu; offers courses and exams in French language and culture and promotes cultural exchange with France; Pres. NIKI PAPA.

British Council: POB 21175, 1503 Nicosia; 1–3 Aristotelous St, 1011 Nicosia; tel. 22585000; fax 22585129; e-mail enquiries@ cy.britishcouncil.org; internet www .britishcouncil.org/cyprus.htm; offers courses and exams in English language and British culture and promotes cultural exchange with the UK; Dir PETER SKELTON.

Research Institutes

GENERAL

Cyprus Research and Publishing Centre: 3B Abdi Cavus, Lefkosa, TRNC, via Mersin 10, Turkey; tel. 2272592; f. 1984; research in the fields of ethnography, history, language and literature, society; publ. *New Cyprus* (12 a year).

Kentron Epistemonikōn Erevnōn (Cyprus Research Centre): POB 22687, 1523 Nicosia; tel. 22668848; fax 22667816; e-mail kykem@cytanet.com.cy; f. 1967; attached to Min. of Education and Culture; promotes scientific research in Cyprus with spec. reference to the historico-philological disciplines and the social sciences; research library; sections: (a) Historical Section: editing and publ. of the sources of the history of Cyprus; (b) Ethnographic Section: colln, preservation, and publ. of materials relating to the local culture of the island; (c) Philological and Linguistic Section: colln of lexicographic materials, the preparation of a historical dictionary of the Cypriot dialect, and the editing of literary and dialect texts; (d) Oriental Section: promotion of oriental studies in Cyprus, with spec. reference to Ottoman studies; (e) Archives Section: colln and preservation of MSS and documents relating to all aspects of the society of Cyprus; Dir CHRISTOS LACOVOU; publs *Epeteris* (1 a year), *Texts and Studies of the History of Cyprus.*

HISTORY, GEOGRAPHY AND ARCHAEOLOGY

Cyprus American Archaeological Research Institute: 11 Andreas Demetriou St, 1066 Nicosia; tel. 22456414; fax 22671147; e-mail librarian@caari.org.cy; internet caari.org; f. 1978; one of the American Schools of Oriental Research; promotes the study of archaeology and related disciplines in Cyprus; encourages communication among scholars interested in Cyprus and provides residence facilities; library of 8,300 books, 110 current periodicals; representative ceramic, geological, lithic, archaeometallurgical and faunal reference collections, slide archive; Dir Dr THOMAS W. DAVIS; Librarian EVI KARYDA.

Libraries and Archives

Famagusta

Municipal Library: POB 41, Famagusta; f. 1954; reference and lending sections, incl. many books on Cyprus and in several languages; the Famagusta Municipal Art Gallery, with a historical maps section, is attached; 18,000 vols; Librarian and Curator CH. CHRISTOFIDES.

Limassol

Municipal Library: 352 St Andrew St, 3035 Limassol; tel. 25362155; f. 1945; 12,000 vols; Librarian A. KYRIAKIDES.

Nicosia

Cyprus Library: Eleftheria Sq., 1011 Nicosia; tel. 22303180; fax 22304532; e-mail cypruslibrary@cytanet.com.cy; internet www .cypruslibrary.gov.cy; f. 1987; 125,000 vols, 2,164 CDs and DVDs, 285 video cassettes, 1,111 microforms; spec. colln: Cypriot studies; Librarian Dr ANTONIS MARATHEFTIS; publ. *Bulletin of the Cyprus Bibliography.*

Cyprus Museum Library: POB 2024, Nicosia; tel. 22865848; fax 22303148; e-mail antiquitieslibrary@da.mcw.gov.cy; f. 1883; inc. in Dept of Antiquities 1934; 20,000 vols (excl. bound periodicals), 220 periodicals, Pierides colln of 1,400 vols; Librarian MARIA DEMETRIOU-ECONOMIDOU.

Cyprus Turkish National Library: Kızılay Ave, Lefkoşa, TRNC, via Mersin 10, Turkey; tel. 22283257; f. 1961; 56,000 vols; Chief Librarian FATMA ÖNEN.

Library of the Archbishop Makarios III Foundation: POB 21269, 1505 Nicosia; tel. 22430008; fax 22346753; internet www .makariosfoundation.org.cy; f. 1983; research library of 65,000 vols relating mostly to Greek, Byzantine and post-Byzantine studies, Christian theology and recent political history of Cyprus; incorporates the library of Phaneromeni, the library of the Holy Archbishopric of Cyprus, the library of the Society of Cypriot Studies, and the Foundation library; Dir Dr M. STAVROU.

Library of the Institute of Education: Macedonia Avenue, Latsia, 2250 Nicosia; tel. 22402300; fax 22480505; e-mail papandreou@cyearn.pi.ac.cy; internet athena .pi.ac.cy; f. 1972; 60,000 vols, mainly on education; Dir ANDREAS PAPANDREOU.

State Archives of the Republic of Cyprus: Min. of Justice and Public Order, 1461 Nicosia; tel. 22451045; fax 22667680; e-mail statearchives@sa.mjpo.gov.cy; internet www.mjpo.gov.cy; f. 1978; place of deposit for public records received from govt depts and other bodies, subject to the State Archives Law; makes these records publicly available for research; 13,165 vols; 159,000 Secretariat Archives files, 9,200 km of linear shelving of archival holdings; State Archivist EFFY PARPARINOU.

Museums and Art Galleries

Ayia Napa

Marine Life Museum: 25 Ayias Mavris St, Ayia Napa; tel. 23723409; fax 23722607; f. 1922.

Gazimagosa

St Barnabas Archaeology Icon Museum: Gazimagosa, TRNC, via Mersin 10, Turkey; tel. 3648331; fax 3660685; f. 1974; St Barnabas monastery dating from 5th century; colln of icons from 18th century; works of art from Neolithic to Roman periods; bronze and marble pieces; library of 5,000 vols; Famagusta Dept of Antiquities Dir HASAN TEKEL.

Larnaca

Larnaca Municipal Museum of Natural History: Leoforos Grigori Afxentiou, Larnaca; collns of local reptiles, insects, birds, animals, fossils and rock formations; marine life and plants from Cyprus and neighbouring countries; colln of insects and endemic plants.

Lefkosa

Dervish Pasha Mansion: Belig Pasha St, Lefkosa, TRNC, via Mersin 10, Turkey; tel. 2281922; fax 2281934; colln of Ottoman artefacts.

National Struggle Museum: Old Bishopric, Lefkosa, TRNC, via Mersin 10, Turkey; f. 1989; documents, photographs and other memorabilia of the 1955–1959 National Liberation Struggle and from the 1974 Turkish invasion.

Limassol

Cyprus Medieval Museum: Kolossi Castle, Limassol; tel. 25305419; f. 1987; rich colln of local and imported pottery from the Early Christian, Byzantine and medieval periods; unique collns of medieval tombstones, coats of arms and architectural exhibits from palaces, castles and churches; coins, arms, cannons, etc.

Cyprus Wine Museum: Pafos St, Erimi, Limassol; tel. 25873808; fax 25821718; e-mail cypruswinemuseum@cytanet.com.cy; internet www.cypruswinemuseum.com; Dir ANASTASIA GUY.

Municipal Folk Art Museum: 253 Agiou Andreou St, Limassol; tel. 25362303; f. 1985; exhibits of national costumes, tapestry, embroidery, wooden chests, waistcoats, men's jackets, necklaces, a variety of light clothes, town costumes, country tools.

Nicosia

Archbishop Makarios III Foundation Art Galleries: Plateia Archiepiskopou Kyprianou, Nicosia; tel. 22430008; internet www.makariosfoundation.org.cy.

Cyprus Folk Art Museum: POB 21436, 1508 Nicosia; tel. 22432578; fax 22343439; e-mail cypriotstudies@gmail.com; internet www.cypriotstudies.org; f. 1937 by mems of the Society of Cypriot Studies; Cyprus arts and crafts from early to recent times; mainly Cypriot Greek items; 950 mems; Dir Dr CHARALAMPOS CHOTZAKOGLOU; publ. *Cypriot Studies* (1 a year).

Cyprus Historical Museum and Archives: Pentelis 50, Strovolos, Nicosia; f. 1975; a private enterprise to create a cultural centre; aims to tape-record accounts of historical events in Cyprus, to photocopy all existing historical material about Cyprus, to liaise with the Ministry of Education and Culture and Greek historians, to find and publicize historical treasures in private collns; library of 3,000 vols; Pres. PETROS STYLIANOU; Gen. Sec. CLEITOS SYMEONIDES.

Cyprus Museum: POB 22024, Nicosia; tel. 22865888; fax 22303148; f. 1882; incorporated in Dept of Antiquities 1934; collns: (1) pottery from the Neolithic and Chalcolithic periods to the Graeco-Roman Age; (2) terracotta figures of the Neolithic Age to Graeco-Roman times, including the Ayia Irini group; (3) limestone and marble sculpture from the Archaic to the Graeco-Roman Age; (4) jewellery from the Neolithic period, especially Mycenaean (1400–1200 BC), to early Byzantine times, and coins from the 6th century BC to Roman times; (5) misc. collns, incl. inscriptions (Cypro-Minoan, Phoenician, Cypro-syllabic, Latin, Greek); bronzes, glass, alabaster, bone, etc.; exhibitions of jewellery, seals, coins; reconstructed tombs; extensive reserve collns are available for students; an archaeological library (see above) is housed in the Cyprus Museum bldg and is open to all; Dir Dr MARIA HADJICOSTI.

Universities

GREEK CYPRIOT UNIVERSITIES

CYPRUS UNIVERSITY OF TECHNOLOGY

POB 50329, Lemesos
Telephone: 25002500
Fax: 25002450
E-mail: administration@cut.edu.tr
Internet: www.cut.ac.cy
Public control
Accredited by Cyprus Council of Educational Evaluation–Accreditation (CEEA)
Pres.: ELPIDA KERAVNOU
Vice-Pres.: GEORGIOS CHARALAMBIDES
Vice-Pres: IOANNIS MANTAS

Faculties of applied arts and communication, engineering and technology, geotechnical sciences and environmental management, management and economics.

OPEN UNIVERSITY OF CYPRUS

Yiannou Kranidioti Ave 33, 2220 Nicosia
Telephone: 22411600
Fax: 22411601
E-mail: info@ouc.ac.cy
Internet: www.ouc.ac.cy
Founded 2003
Public control
Languages of instruction: Greek, English
Academic year: September to June
Chair.: Prof. PANOS RAZIS
Vice-Pres.: Prof. GEORGIOS PHILOKIPROU
Dir for Admin. and Finance: CHRISTOPHOROS CHRISTODOULIDES
Librarian: PANAGIOTIS THEMISTOCLEOUS
Library of 7,400 vols, 102 int. databases
Number of teachers: 138, incl. academic research personnel and part-time educational personnel
Number of students: 2,000

UNIVERSITY OF CYPRUS

Univ. House 'Anastasios G. Leventis', POB 20537, 1678 Nicosia
Telephone: 22894000
E-mail: info@ucy.ac.cy
Internet: www.ucy.ac.cy
Founded 1989
State control
Languages of instruction: Greek, Turkish
Academic year: September to June
Rector: Prof. CONSTANTINOS CHRISTOFIDES

Vice-Rector for Academic Affairs: Prof. STELIOS GEORGIOU
Vice-Rector for Int. Affairs, Finance and Admin.: Prof. MARIOS MAVRONICOLAS
Dir for Admin. and Finance: ANDREAS CHRISTOFIDES
Dir for Library: PHILIPPOS TSIMPOGLOU
Number of teachers: 285
Number of students: 6,500

DEANS

Faculty of Economics and Management: Prof. LOUIS N. CHRISTOFIDES
Faculty of Engineering: Prof. PANOS PAPANASTASIOU
Faculty of Humanities: Prof. ANDREAS PAPAPAVLOU
Faculty of Letters: Prof. MICHALIS PIERIS
Faculty of Pure and Applied Sciences: Prof. CONSTANTINOS PATTICHIS
Faculty of Social Sciences and Education: Prof. ATHANASIOS GAGATSIS

PROFESSORS

Faculty of Economics and Management:
CHARALAMBOUS, C., Public and Business Administration
CHARITOU, A., Public and Business Administration
CHRISTOFIDES, L., Economics
LEONIDOU, L., Public and Business Administration
MAMUNEAS, T., Economics
MICHAEL, M., Economics
MICHAELIDES, A., Public and Business Administration
PASHARDES, P., Economics
TRIGEORGIS, L., Public and Business Administration
TSOUKAS, H., Public and Business Administration
VAFEAS, N., Public and Business Administration
ZENIOS, S., Public and Business Administration

Faculty of Engineering:
ALEXANDROU, A., Mechanical and Manufacturing Engineering
CHARALAMBOUS, C., Electrical and Computer Engineering
DOUMANIDIS, C., Mechanical and Manufacturing Engineering
PAPANASTASIOU, P., Civil and Environmental Engineering
POLYCARPOU, M., Electrical and Computer Engineering

Faculty of Humanities:
AGAPITOS, P., Byzantine and Modern Greek Studies
ANGELATOS, D., Byzantine and Modern Greek Studies
IACOVOU, M., History and Archaeology
MICHAELIDES, D., History and Archaeology
PANAYOTOU-TRIANTAPHYLLOPOULOU, A., Classics and Philosophy
PIERIS, M., Byzantine and Modern Greek Studies
RIZOPOULOU-EGOUMENIDOU, E., History and Archaeology
TAIFACOS, I., Classics and Philosophy
VOUTOURIS, P., Byzantine and Modern Greek Studies

Faculty of Letters:
AGAPITOS, P., Byzantine and Modern Greek Studies
ANGELATOS, D., Byzantine and Modern Greek Studies
IACOVOU, M., History and Archaeology
MICHAELIDES, D., History and Archaeology
PANAYOTOU-TRIANTAPHYLLOPOULOU, A., Classics and Philosophy
PIERIS, M., Byzantine and Modern Greek Studies

RIZOPOULOU-EGOUMENIDOU, E., History and Archaeology
TAIFACOS, I., Classics and Philosophy
VOUTOURIS, P., Byzantine and Modern Greek Studies

Faculty of Pure and Applied Sciences:
ALEXANDROU, C., Physics
CHRISTOFIDES, C., Physics
CHRISTOFIDES, T., Mathematics
CONSTANTINOU, A., Biology
DAMIANOU, P., Mathematics
DELTAS, C., Biology
EFSTATHIOU, A., Chemistry
EVRIPIDOU, P., Computer Science
GEORGIOU, G., Mathematics
KAKAS, A., Computer Science
KARAGEORGHIS, A., Mathematics
KERAVNOU-PAPAILIOU, E., Computer Science
KOUMANDOS, S., Mathematics
MAVRONICOLAS, M., Computer Science
PANAGOPOULOS, C., Physics
PAPADOPOULOS, G., Computer Science
PAPARODITIS, E., Mathematics
PATRICKIOS, C., Chemistry
PATTICHIS, C., Computer Science
PITSILLIDES, A., Computer Science
RAZIS, P., Physics
SAMARAS, G., Computer Science
SCHIZAS, C., Computer Science
THEOCHARIS, C., Chemistry
TSERTOS, H., Physics
VIDRAS, A., Mathematics

Faculty of Social Sciences and Education:
CHRISTOU, C., Education
DEMETRIOU, A., Psychology
GAGATSIS, A., Education
IOANNIDES KOUTSELINI, M., Education
JOSEPH, J., Social and Political Sciences
KAPARDIS, A., Law
KATSIKIDES, S., Social and Political Sciences

UNIVERSITY OF NICOSIA

46 Makedonitissas Ave, 1700 Nicosia
Telephone: 22841500
Fax: 22357481
E-mail: info@gau.edu.tr
Internet: www.unic.ac.cy
Founded 1980 as Intercollege, univ. status 2007
Private control
Accredited by Cyprus Ccl of Educational Evaluation–Accreditation (CEEA) for Private Univs; schools of business, education, humanities, social sciences and law
Number of students: 4,000 in Nicosia, 500 on Limassol and Larnaca campuses
Publication: *Cyprus Review* (2 a year).

TURKISH CYPRIOT UNIVERSITIES

CYPRUS INTERNATIONAL UNIVERSITY

Haspolat, Nicosia, TRNC, via Mersin 10, Turkey
Telephone: 26711111
Fax: 26711122
E-mail: info@ciu.edu.tr
Internet: www.ciu.edu.tr
Founded 1997
Private control
Accredited by Turkish Higher Educational Board
Pres.: Prof. Dr MEHMET ALI YÜKSELEN
Vice-Pres.: Prof. Dr NÜKET SARACEL

DEANS

Faculty of Arts and Sciences: Prof. Dr METIN KARADAĞ

Faculty of Communications: Prof. Dr HIKMET SEÇIM

Faculty of Economics and Administrative Sciences: Prof. Dr NÜKET SARACEL

Faculty of Education: Prof. Dr AHMET PEHLIVAN

Faculty of Engineering: Prof. Dr BOZOK OZERDIM

Faculty of Fine Arts: Prof. Dr ATILLA YUCEL

DIRECTORS

Institute of Sciences: Asst Prof. Dr MEHMEDI EGEMEN

Institute of Social Sciences: Prof. Dr HIKMET SEÇIM

School of Applied Sciences: Asst Prof. Dr SALIH KARANFIL

School of Foreign Languages: Assoc. Prof. Dr MEHMET ALI YAVUZ

School of Tourism and Hotel Management: Asst Prof. Dr EBRU GÜNEREN

Vocational School: Asst Prof. Dr ERTAN AKÜN

EASTERN MEDITERRANEAN UNIVERSITY

POB 95, Gazi Mağusa, TRNC, via Mersin 10, Turkey

Telephone: 26301111
Fax: 23654479
E-mail: info@emu.edu.tr
Internet: www.emu.edu.tr

Founded 1979 as Higher Technological Institute; univ. status 1986
Language of instruction: English
State control
Academic year: September to June (two semesters)

Pres.: Prof. Dr UFUK TANERI
Vice-Rector for Academic Affairs: Prof. Dr DERVIŞ Z. DENIZ
Vice-Rector for Financial and Technical Affairs: Asst Prof. Dr ERALP BEKTAŞ
Vice-Rector for Int. Affairs: Asst Prof. Dr BAHIR E. ÖZAD
Vice-Rector for Student Affairs: Asst Prof. Dr KADIR ATLANSOY
Sec.-Gen.: GÜROL ÖZKAYA
Registrar: HÜSEYIN ÜNSAL YETINER
Librarian: OSMAN SOYKAN

Library of 125,000 vols, 600 periodical subscriptions and 25 electronic networks
Number of teachers: 641 full-time, 141 part-time
Number of students: 14,256

Publications: EMU Tourism Research Journal (in English), Journal of Cyprus Studies (in English), Review of Social, Economic and Business Studies (in English), Woman 2000 (in English)

DEANS

Faculty of Architecture: Prof. Dr IBRAHIM NUMAN

Faculty of Arts and Sciences: Prof. Dr OSMAN YILMAZ

Faculty of Business and Economics: Prof. Dr ÖZAY MEHMET

Faculty of Communication and Media Studies: Assoc. Prof. Dr TUGRUL ILTER

Faculty of Education: Assoc. Prof. Dr NECDET OSAM

Faculty of Engineering: Prof. Dr HASAN AMCA

Faculty of Law: Prof. Dr ESIN KOPNANC

DIRECTORS

Distance Education Institute: Asst Prof. Dr ISIK AYBAY

Institute of Advanced Technology Research and Development: Prof. Dr SENER UYSAL

Institute for Graduate Studies and Research: Prof. Dr ELVAN YILMIZ

School of Foreign Languages: HUSEYIN DEMIREL

School of Computing and Technology: Asst Prof. Dr MUSTAFA ILKAN

School of Tourism and Hospitality Management: Asst Prof. Dr ILKAY YORGANCI MALONEY

EUROPEAN UNIVERSITY OF LEFKE

Gemıkonağı, Lefke, TRNC, via Mersin 10, Turkey

Telephone: 26602000
Fax: 27277528
E-mail: international@lefke.edu.tr
Internet: www.lefke.edu.tr

Founded 1990 by Cyprus Science Foundation; accredited by Higher Education Council of Turkey
Languages of instruction: English, Turkish
Academic year: October to June

Rector: Prof. Dr M. TURGAY ERGUN
Gen. Sec.: METIN BAYTEKIN
Registrar: MEHMET YALÇIN
Librarian: ELIF BILOKÇUOĞLU

Library of 30,000 vols, 70 periodicals
Number of teachers: 120
Number of students: 2,800

Publication: Laü'nün Sesi Journal (6 a year)

DEANS

Faculty of Agricultural Sciences: Assoc. Prof. Dr ULRICH KERSTING

Faculty of Architecture and Engineering: Prof. Dr K. BALASUBRAMANIAN

Faculty of Arts and Sciences: Prof. Dr GÜNAY KARAAĞAÇ

Faculty of Communication Sciences: Prof. Dr FARUK KALKAN

Faculty of Economics and Administrative Sciences: Assoc. Prof. Dr FIKRET KUTSAL (acting)

PROFESSORS

Faculty of Agricultural Sciences (tel. (392) 7146781; fax (392) 7146783):

Horticultural Production and Marketing: Asst Prof. Dr İLHAMI TOZLU

Faculty of Architecture and Engineering:

Architecture and Interior Architecture: Prof. Dr BOZOK ÖZERDIM

Civil Engineering: Asst Prof. Dr KONSTANTIN SOBOLEV

Computer Sciences: Prof. Dr K. BALASUBRAMANIAN (acting)

Electrical and Electronic Engineering: (vacant)

Faculty of Arts and Sciences:

English Language Teaching: Asst Prof. Dr SÜLEYMAN GÖKER

History: Asst Prof. Dr MEHMET DEMIRYÜREK

Turkish Language and Literature: Prof. Dr GÜNAY KARAAĞAÇ (acting)

Faculty of Communication Sciences:

Journalism: Assoc. Prof. Dr FILIZ SEÇIM

Public Relations and Advertising: Asst Prof. Dr FAIK KARTELLI

Radio, Television and Cinema: Prof. Dr FARUK KALKAN (acting)

Faculty of Economics and Administrative Sciences:

Business: Asst Prof. Dr SERDAR SAYDAM

Economics: Assoc. Prof. Dr FIKRET KUTSAL

International Relations: Asst Prof. Dr SUPHI GALIP

GIRNE AMERICAN UNIVERSITY

University Dr., Girne, TRNC, via Mersin 10, Turkey

Telephone: 26502000
Fax: 26502062
E-mail: info@gau.edu.tr

Internet: www.gau.edu.tr

Founded 1985
Private control

Rector: Prof. Dr YILDIRIM ONER
Chancellor: SERHAT AKPINAR
Vice-Rector for Academic Affairs: SADIK ULKER

Publication: GAU Journal of Social and Applied Science

DEANS

Faculty of Architecture: Asst Prof. Dr SERDAR SAYDAM (acting)

Faculty of Business and Economics: Asst Prof. Dr OSMAN ALTAY (acting)

Faculty of Communication: Prof. Dr ALPAY ATAOL

Faculty of Educational Science: Prof. Dr TANJU GÜRKAN

Faculty of Engineering: Asst Prof. Dr ZAFER AĞDELEN

Faculty of Humanities: Prof. Dr NESRIN KALE

MIDDLE EAST TECHNICAL UNIVERSITY, NORTH CYPRUS CAMPUS

Kalkanlı, Güzelyurt, TRNC, via Mersin 10, Turkey

Telephone: 26612000
Fax: 26612009
E-mail: ncc@metu.edu.tr
Internet: www.ncc.metu.edu.tr

Founded 2000
Private control

Pres.: Prof. Dr AHMET ACAR
Vice-Pres: Prof. Dr AYSE ÇIĞDEM ERÇELEBI, Prof. Dr HASAN NEVZAT ÖZGÜVEN, Prof. Dr MEHMET TUNCAY BIRAND
Number of students: 1,280

DEANS

Faculty of Architecture: HALUK PAMIR
Faculty of Arts And Sciences: CÜNEYT CAN
Faculty of Economic and Administrative Sciences: YASAR EYÜP ÖZVEREN
Faculty of Education: MERAL AKSU
Faculty of Engineering: ZAFER DURSUNKAYA

PROFESSORS

ABDULLAH, O.
ABDURRAHIM, Y.
ADNAN, Y.
AĞACIK, Z.
AHMET, G.
AHMET, I.
AHMET, R.
AHMET, S.
AHMET, G.
AHMET BÜLENT, D.
AHMET CAN, B.
AHMET CEVDET, Y.
AHMET DEMIR, B.
AHMET HALIS, A.
AHMET NEDIM, E.
AHMET NURI, Y.
AHMET ORHAN, E.
AHMET ORHAN, Y.
AHMET RAŞIT, K.
AHMETŞ Ş., U.
AHMETŞ ŞINASI, A.
ALAEDDIN, T.
ALEV, B.
ALI, C.
ALI, E.
ALI, G.
ALI, K.
ALI, K.
ALI, U.
ALI, U.
ALI, T.
ALI, Y.
ALI, T.
ALI BÜLENT, E.

ALI DURSUN, K.
ALI İHSAN, U.
ALI NEZIH, G.
ALI SADI, G.
ALI SAHIR, A.
ALI TAYFUN, A.
ALI TUĞRUL, T.
ALI ÜNAL, S.
ALPAY, A.
ALTAN, B.
ALTUNKAN, H.
AMDULLA, M.
ARIİ, D.
ARIF, E.
ASUMAN, T.
ASUMAN, D.
ATALAY, K.
ATİLA, E.
AYDA, E.
AYDAN, E.
AYDIN, E.
AYHAN, I.
AYKUT, C.
AYKUT, K.
AYMELEK, O.
AYŞE, A.
AYŞE, G.
AYŞE, K.
AYŞE, K.
AYŞE ÇIĞDEM, E.
AYŞE FERIDE, A.
AYŞE GÜNIZ, G.
AYŞE NURHAN, S.
AYŞE TÜLAY, O.
AYSEL, A.
AYŞEN, A.
AYŞEN, E.
AYŞEN, Y.
AYŞIL, Y.
AYSIT, T.
BAYRAM, K.
BEAR AYTEN, C.
BEGÜM, O.
BEHÇET MURAT, E.
BILGEHAN, O.
BILGIN, K.
BILGIN, K.
BIROL, D.
BÜLENT, C.
BÜLENT, K.
BÜLENT EMRE, P.
BÜLENT GÜLTEKIN, A.
BÜLENT HULUSİ, E.
BUYURMAN, B.
ÇAĞLAR, G.
ÇAHIT, C.
ÇAHT, E.
CANAN, T.
CANAN, O.
CARNOT EDWARD, N.
CELAL, G.
CELAL, K.
CELAL FERDI, G.
CEM, T.
CENGIZ, O.
CENGIZ, B.
CENGIZ, E.
ÇETIN, Y.
ÇETN, H.
ÇEVDET, K.
CİHAN, E.
CIHANGIR, T.
CÜNEYT, C.
DEAN WALLACE, O.
DEMET, G.
DEMIR, A.
DENIZ, U.
DENIZ, Z.
DOĞAN, T.
DOĞAN H., A.
DURAN IHSAN, D.
DUYGU, K.
EDUARD, E.
EKREM, S.
EMEL, A.
EMIN, O.

EMINE NEVIN, S.
ENDER, O.
ENGIN, S.
ENGIN, K.
ENGIN SADIK, K.
ENGIN UMUT, A.
ERDAL, C.
ERDAL, B.
ERDAL, O.
ERDIN, B.
ERES, S.
ERGIN, A.
ERHAN ONUR, I.
ERKAN AHMET, K.
ERKUT, G.
EROL, T.
EROL, K.
EROL HASAN, C.
ERSAN, A.
ERSIN, T.
ESIN, T.
ESRA M., Y.
FAIKA DILEK, S.
FARUK, G.
FARUK, P.
FARUK, A.
FARUK ESEN, O.
FARUK TAHSIN, B.
FATIH, C.
FATIH, Y.
FATMA CANAN, C.
FATOŞ TÜNAY, V.
FERAL, E.
FERHUNDE, O.
FERIDE, S.
FERIT, B.
FERRUH, O.
FERSUN AYŞE, P.
FETHİ PAYIDAR, G.
FEVZI, G.
FEVZİ SUAT, K.
FEZA, K.
FIKRET, S.
FILIZ BENGÜ, D.
GENCAY, S.
GERHARD, R.
GERHARD WILHELM, W.
GIRAY, B.
GÖKSEL NIYAZII, D.
GÖKTÜRK, U.
GÖNÜL, E.
GÖNÜL, S.
GÖTZ JOCHEN, R.
GÖZDE, A.
GÜLAY, O.
GÜLAY, O.
GÜLBİN, D.
GÜLERMAN, S.
GÜLHAN, O.
GÜLİN, G.
GÜLIN AYŞE, B.
GÜLSER, G.
GÜLSER, K.
GÜLSÜN, G.
GÜNERI, A.
GÜNERI NEVZAT, G.
GÜNEY, O.
GÜNGÖR, G.
GÜRBÜZ, D.
GÜRDAL, T.
GÜRKAN, K.
GÜRKAN HASAN, T.
GÜRSEVIL, T.
GÜZIN, E.
HACER CEYHAN, K.
HAFIT, Y.
HAKAN, G.
HAKKI POLAT, G.
HALE, G.
HALIL, K.
HALIL, O.
HALIM, D.
HALUK, G.
HALUK, P.
HALUK, A.
HALUK, A.

HALUK, D.
HALUK, E.
HALUK, H.
HALUK, S.
HAMIDE, E.
HAMIT, Y.
HASAN, T.
HASAN, S.
HASAN, Y.
HASAN CENGİZ, G.
HASAN NEVZAT, O.
HASAN ÜNAL, N.
HAYRETTIN, Y.
HAYRI, O.
HAYRIYE CANAN, S.
HİLMI ÖNDER, O.
HÜROL, F.
HURŞIIT, O.
HÜSEYIN, I.
HÜSEYIN, B.
HÜSEYIN, V.
HÜSEYIN AVNI, O.
HÜSEYIN KAMIL, B.
HÜSEYIN ÖZTAŞ, A.
HÜSNÜ, O.
HÜSNÜ, E.
İBRAHIM, G.
İBRAHIM SINAN, A.
İBRAHIM YURDAHAN, G.
İHSAN, A.
İLHAN, T.
İLKER, O.
İNCİ, E.
İNCI, T.
İSHAK, K.
IŞIK, O.
ISMAIL, T.
İSMAIL HAKKI, T.
İSMAIL HAKKI, T.
İSMAIL ŞUAYIP, G.
İSMET, E.
İSMİHAN, A.
JALE, H.
JALE ADILE, E.
KADRI FATIH, I.
KADRI SINAN, B.
KAHRAMAN, U.
KAHRAMAN, A.
KEMAL, A.
KEMAL, P.
KEMAL, I.
KEMAL, O.
KERIM, D.
LEMI, T.
LEVENT, Y.
LEVENT, P.
LEVENT A., B.
LEVENT KAMIL, T.
LEYLA, A.
MACIT, O.
MAHINUR, A.
MAHMUT, K.
MAHMUT, P.
MAHMUT VEDAT, A.
MARAT, A.
MARGARETA, O.
MEHMET, Y.
MEHMET, Z.
MEHMET, A.
MEHMET, C.
MEHMET, K.
MEHMET, P.
MEHMET, T.
MEHMET, U.
MEHMET CEMAL, G.
MEHMET CEVDET, C.
MEHMET KADRI, A.
MEHMET KAYHAN, M.
MEHMET KAZIM, A.
MEHMET KEMAL, L.
MEHMET POLAT, S.
MEHMET TUNCAY, B.
MEHMET UFUK, E.
MEHMET ZEKI, C.
MEHMET ZÜLFÜ, A.
MEHPARE, B.

MELIH, E.
MELIH ALI, Y.
MELIHA, A.
MELTEM, S.
MERAL, Y.
MERAL, A.
MERAL, C.
MERAL, A.
MESUDE, I.
METE, S.
METIN, D.
METIN, G.
METIN, G.
METIN, B.
METIN, Z.
METIN, A.
MEYDA, M.
MIRZAHAN, H.
MOTI LAL, T.
MUAMMER, E.
MÜBECCEL, D.
MUHAMMET YAŞAR, O.
MUHARREM, T.
MUHITTIN CEM, S.
MUHTAR, O.
MÜNEVVER, T.
MURAT, T.
MURAT, B.
MURAT, A.
MURAT, D.
MURAT, K.
MÜRVET, V.
MUSA, D.
MÜSLIM, B.
MUSTAFA, K.
MUSTAFA, T.
MUSTAFA, D.
MUSTAFA, S.
MUSTAFA, T.
MUSTAFA, G.
MUSTAFA, K.
MUSTAFA İLHAN, G.
MUSTAFA TURGUT, O.
MUSTAFA VERŞAN, K.
NACI, S.
NACI, B.
NACIYE CAN, M.
NAFI GÜRDAL, A.
NAFIZ, A.
NAIL, B.
NAZIFE, B.
NAZIFE SUZAN, K.
NAZIM KADRI, E.
NAZIYET, G.
NEBI, S.
NECATI, P.
NEŞE, Y.
NESRIN, H.
NEVIN, S.
NEVZAT, O.
NEVZAT, Y.
NEZIHE NILGÜN, K.
NIGAR, A.
NIHAD BEKIR, P.
NILGÜN, G.
NILGÜN, K.
NILGÜN, G.
NIZAMI, H.
NUMAN, T.
NUR EVIN, O.
NURAY AYŞE, K.
NURKAN, K.
NURSEL, I.
OĞUZ, O.
OKAY, C.
OLCAY, O.
OLCAY, I.
ÖMER, G.
ÖMER, A.
ÖMER, T.
ÖMER, G.
ÖMER, K.
ÖMÜR, B.
ORHAN, A.
OSMAN, S.
OSMAN, S.

OSMAN, Y.
OSMAN YAVUZ, A.
OZAN, T.
ÖZDEMIR, A.
ÖZDEMIR, D.
ÖZKAN BENGI, O.
PINAR, C.
PULAT, O.
RAIF ORHAN, Y.
RAMAZAN, A.
RAMAZAN, S.
RAŞIT, T.
REHA, A.
REŞAT, U.
REŞIT, S.
RIKKAT, C.
RIZA, G.
RÜKNETTIN, O.
RUŞEN, K.
RUŞEN, G.
RÜVEYDE SEZER, A.
RÜYAL, E.
SABRI KURTULUŞ, K.
SADIK, K.
ŞAFAK, A.
ŞAHINDE, D.
ŞAIM, O.
ŞAKIR, E.
ŞAKIR, B.
SAVAŞ, K.
ŞAZIYE, G.
SEÇIL, A.
SELAHATTIN, O.
SELMIN, T.
SEMIH, Y.
SEMIH, B.
SEMRA, K.
SEMRA, T.
ŞENAY, K.
SENCER, A.
SERGEY, F.
SERHAT, A.
SERPIL, S.
SERVET GÜLÜM, S.
SEVGI, A.
SIBEL, B.
SINAN, K.
ŞINASI, E.
ŞITKI, D.
SONER, G.
SUAT, U.
SÜHA, B.
SÜHA, O.
ŞÜKRIYE, R.
ŞÜKRÜ, K.
ŞÜKRÜ SELÇUK, B.
SÜLEYMAN, T.
SÜLEYMAN, O.
SYEDA NAZLI, W.
TAKHMASSIB, A.
TALAT MUSTAFA, B.
TAMER, T.
TANJU, M.
TANSEL, T.
TANSI, S.
TARIK, O.
TAYFUN, A.
TAYFUR, O.
TEMEL, O.
TEMEL ENGIN, T.
TEO, G.
TEOMAN, T.
TEOMAN NURIDDIN, N.
TEVFIK, G.
TIMUR, D.
TUĞRUL, A.
TÜLAY, Y.
TÜLIN, G.
TÜLIN, G.
TUNA, B.
TURGUT, T.
TURGUT SAMI, T.
TURHAN Y., E.
TÜRKER, M.
TÜRKER, G.
UFUK, B.

UFUK, G.
UĞUR, H.
UĞURLU NURAY, S.
ÜLKÜ, Y.
ÜLKÜ, Y.
ÜMIT, K.
ÜMIT MUSTAFA, A.
ÜNSAL, Y.
URAL, A.
UYGUR, S.
VACIT, I.
VASIF NEJAT, H.
VEDAT, T.
VEDAT, D.
VOLKAN, A.
WOLF KURT, K.
YAHYA ÖNDER, Y.
YAKIN, E.
YAKUP, K.
YAKUP CEVDET, A.
YALÇIN, M.
YALÇIN, T.
YAŞAR EYÜP, O.
YASEMIN, Y.
YASIN, C.
YAVUZ, Y.
YAVUZ ALI, T.
YAVUZ SAMIM, U.
YENER, O.
YERLI MERYEM, B.
YILDIRAY, O.
YILDIRIM, Y.
YILDIZ, W.
YILDIZ, E.
YILMAZ, A.
YURDANUR, T.
YUSUF, O.
YUSUF ZIYA, O.
ZAFER, E.
ZAFER, N.
ZAFER, U.
ZAFER, D.
ZEKI, K.
ZUHAL, K.

NEAR EAST UNIVERSITY

Near East Ave, Nicosia, TRNC, via Mersin 10, Turkey

Telephone: 22236464
Fax: 22236461
E-mail: info@neu.edu.tr
Internet: www.neu.edu.tr

Founded 1988
Private control

Faculties of architecture, arts and sciences, Ataturk education, communication, dentistry, economics and admin. sciences, engineering, fine arts and design, health sciences, law, maritime studies, medicine, performing arts, pharmacy; schools of physical education and sports, tourism and hotel management; Graduate School of Applied Sciences; institutes of educational sciences, health sciences, social sciences

Rector: Prof. Dr UMIT HASSAN
Pres.: Dr SUAT İ. GÜNSEL
Dir for Public Relations: ERDOGAN SARACO-GLU.

Colleges

Americanos College: POB 22425, 1521 Nicosia; tel. 22661122; fax 22664118; e-mail college@ac.ac.cy; internet www.ac.ac.cy; f. 1975; private control; accredited by Cyprus Council of Educational Evaluation–Accreditation (CEEA); Diplomas, Bachelors and Masters degrees.

Arte Music Academy: POB 21207, 1504 Nicosia; tel. 22676823; fax 22665695; internet www.artemusic.org; f. 2002; private control; accredited by Cyprus Council of Educational Evaluation–Accreditation (CEEA); Bachelors degree in music; Dir PITSA SPYRIDAKI; Artistic Dir MARTINO TIRIMO; Academic Registrar KLERI AGGELIDOU; Librarian ANTRI SPYRIDAKI.

CDA College: POB 21972, 1515 Nicosia; tel. 22661104; fax 22671387; e-mail cdaadm@spidernet.com.cy; internet www.cdacollege.ac.cy; private control; accredited by Cyprus Council of Educational Evaluation–Accreditation (CEEA); Bachelors degree in business studies; programmes in information and communication technology, interior design and architectural drawing, travel and tourism admin. secretarial studies; brs in Limassol and Larnaca; 800 students; Prin. D. A. CHRISTOFOROU.

College of Tourism and Hotel Management: POB 20281, 2150 Nicosia; tel. 22462846; fax 22336295; e-mail cothm@spidernet.com.cy; internet www.cothm.ac.cy; private control; accredited by Cyprus Council of Educational Evaluation–Accreditation (CEEA); Pres. ANTONIS CHARALAMBIDES; Dir SAVVAS ADAMIDES.

CTL Eurocollege: POB 51938, 3509 Limassol; tel. 25736501; fax 25736629; e-mail college@ctleuro.ac.cy; internet www.ctleuro.ac.cy; private control; accredited by Cyprus Council of Educational Evaluation–Accreditation (CEEA); Bachelors degree and Diploma programmes in business, computing, hospitality and tourism, law.

Cyprus College: POB 22006, 1516 Nicosia; tel. 22713000; fax 22662051; internet www.cycollege.ac.cy; f. 1961; 2-year assoc. degree courses, 3- and 4-year Bachelors degree courses in social sciences, business admin., computer science, MBA programme; 51 teachers; 1,020 students; library: 35,000 vols; Dir NICOS ANASTASIOU; publ. *Journal of Business and Society*.

Cyprus College of Art: 23 Mehmet Ali St, 6026 Larnaca; tel. 25341387 *UK Office* (all enquiries): 27 Holywell Row, London, EC2A 4JB, UK; e-mail enquiries@artcyprus.org; internet www.artcyprus.org; f. 1969; one-year foundation courses in art and design; undergraduate degree programmes in asscn with partner orgs in the UK; postgraduate courses in fine art; 8 teachers; 40 students; Dir STASS PARASKOS.

Cyprus Forestry College: Prodromos, 4841 Limassol; tel. 25813606; fax 25462646; e-mail forcollege@fc.moa.gov.cy; internet www.moa.gov.cy/fc; f. 1951; technical-level and advanced training in forestry; library: 2,000 vols, 7 periodicals; 7 teachers; 20 students; Prin. CHR. ALEXANDROU.

Cyprus International Institute of Management: 21 Akademias Ave, Aglandjia, POB 20378, Nicosia; tel. 22462246; fax 22331121; e-mail ciim@ciim.ac.cy; internet www.ciim.ac.cy; f. 1990; 1-year full-time and 2-year part-time courses leading to MBA and MPSM degrees and Advanced Diploma; MSc in science; executive education; library: 3,000 vols; Dir Dr JIM LEONTIADES.

Frederick Institute of Technology: 7 Frederickou St, Palouriotisa, 0136 Nicosia; tel. 22431355; fax 22438234; e-mail info@fit.ac.cy; internet www.fit.ac.cy; f. 1966; private control; accredited by Cyprus Council of Educational Evaluation–Accreditation (CEEA); campus in Limassol; Bachelors degrees and Diploma programmes in business, engineering, computers, technology, design, education and human sciences.

Global College: 245 Eleonon St, Strovolos, 2048 Nicosia; tel. 22814555; fax 22814580; e-mail gic@cytanet.com.cy; internet www.globalcollege.com.cy; f. 1972; private control; accredited by Cyprus Council of Educational Evaluation–Accreditation (CEEA); secretarial studies, business admin., computer studies; Gen. Dir GEORGE KRITICOS.

Intercollege (International College): 46 Makedonitissa Ave, POB 24005, 1700 Nicosia; tel. 22841500; fax 22352067; e-mail nicosia@intercollege.ac.cy; internet www.intercollege.ac.cy; f. 1980; private control; instruction in English; undergraduate and postgraduate courses lead to qualifying examinations for local, British and US degrees; also centres at Limassol and Larnaca; library: 70,000 vols; 203 teachers (112 full-time, 91 part-time); 5,000 students (incl. 613 at Limassol and 566 at Larnaca); Rector Dr VAN COUFOUDAKIS; publ. *Cyprus Review* (2 a year).

KES College: 5 Kallipolis Ave, 1055 Nicosia; tel. 22875737; fax 22756562; internet www.kes.ac.cy; f. 1971; private control; accredited by Cyprus Ccl of Educational Evaluation–Accreditation (CEEA); programmes in office

admin. and secretarial studies, beauty therapy, medical representatives courses; Dir THEO P. STYLIANOU.

Mediterranean Institute of Management: POB 20536, 1679 Nicosia; tel. 22806000; fax 22376872; e-mail info@kepa.mlsi.com.cy; internet www.kepa.gov.cy; f. 1976; int. component of Cyprus Productivity Centre (a dept of Min. of Social and Labour Insurance); postgraduate management diploma course; research and management consultancy projects; library: 8,000 vols; 30 teachers; 90 students; Dir Dr IOANNIS MODITIS.

PA College: Larnaca; tel. 24021555; fax 24628860; e-mail information@pacollege.ac.cy; internet www.pacollege.ac.cy; private control; accredited by Cyprus Council of Educational Evaluation–Accreditation (CEEA); BA degree in business admin.; BSc in business computing; Dir Dr ANDREAS Z. PATSALIDES.

Philips College: POB 28008, Strovolos, 2090 Nicosia; 4–6 Lamias St, 2001 Nicosia; tel. 22441860; fax 22315222; e-mail admissions@philips.ac.cy; internet www.philips.ac.cy; private control; accredited by Cyprus Council of Educational Evaluation–Accreditation (CEEA); accounting and finance, business studies, computing and information systems, public relations, social studies; Pres. Prof. PHILIPPOS CONSTANTINOU.

REA College: POB 50625, 3608 Nicosia; 2 Pasikratous St, 3085 Nicosia; tel. 25381095; fax 25383360; internet www.reacollege.ac.cy; f. 1986; private control; accredited by Cyprus Council of Educational Evaluation–Accreditation (CEEA); BSc degrees in aesthetics, dietetics, nutrition.

Susini College: POB 3502, 3502 Limassol; 10 Tagmatarchou Pouliou St, 3020 Limassol; tel. 25366196; fax 25369702; e-mail susini@spidernet.com.cy; internet www.susini.ac.cy; f. 1982; private control; accredited by Cyprus Council of Educational Evaluation–Accreditation (CEEA); beauty therapy; Dir of Studies PHANIE ANTONIADOU-POUPOUTSI.

Vladimiros Kafkarides School of Drama: Nicosia; tel. 2421609; fax 2493450; private control; accredited by Cyprus Council of Educational Evaluation–Accreditation (CEEA); Dir DEMETRIOS LAZARIDES.

CZECH REPUBLIC

The Higher Education System

Higher education institutions predate the foundation of the former Czechoslovakia in 1918, with the oldest being Univerzita Karlova, which was founded in 1348. In 1990, following the removal of the communist Government, which had been in power since 1948, Czechoslovakia was replaced by the Czech and Slovak Federative Republic (CzSFR). In turn, the CzSFR was dissolved in 1993 and the Czech Republic and Slovakia became independent, sovereign states. Higher education reforms in both states were initiated under Act 172, passed in 1990; the Higher Education Act of 1998 (amended 2001) and a new education law in 2005 have also come into force. In 2007/08 some 344,180 students attended 70 universities. Higher education is financed by the Ministry of Education, Youth and Sport.

The secondary school leaving certificate (Maturita) is the main requirement for admission to higher education. Precise entry requirements vary among institutions, and students may have to sit an entrance examination. Legislation passed in 1998, and amended in 2001, brought the Czech Republic into line with the Bologna Process. The Bakalár is the main undergraduate degree, and lasts for three to four years. The first postgraduate degree, Magistr, is awarded after two to three years' study following the Bakalár. Some disciplines involve integrated undergraduate and postgraduate programmes lasting five to six years, leading to professional qualifications; these include engineering, architecture and medicine. Finally, following Magistr, doctoral studies take three to four years and result in the award of the title Doktor.

Post-secondary technical and vocational education dates from the establishment of vyšší odborná škola (tertiary technical schools) in 1992. There are now about 150 such establishments offering education and training in vocational fields. The period of study is two to three-and-a-half years, and students are awarded the Diplomovaný Specialista.

The quality of higher education is overseen by the Accreditation Commission.

Regulatory and Representative Bodies

GOVERNMENT

Ministry of Culture: Maltéské nám. 471/1, 118 11 Prague 1; tel. 257085111; fax 224318155; e-mail posta@mkcr.cz; internet www.mkcr.cz; Min. JIŘÍ BESSER.

Ministry of Education, Youth and Sport: Karmelitská 8, 118 12 Prague 1; tel. 234811111; fax 234811790; e-mail info@msmt.cz; internet www.msmt.cz; Min. JOSEF DOBEŠ.

ACCREDITATION

Akreditační komise (Accreditation Commission): Ministry of Education, Youth and Sports, Higher Education Dept, Karmelitská 7, 118 12 Prague 1; tel. 234811488; fax 234811351; e-mail smrckaj@msmt.cz; internet www.akreditacnikomise.cz; f. 1990; evaluates teaching, scholarly, scientific, research, devt and innovative, artistic and other creative activities of higher education instns; 21 mems (academic and professional experts); Chair. Prof. Dr VLADIMÍRA DVOŘÁKOVÁ; Sec. Dr JIŘÍ SMRČKA.

ENIC/NARIC Czech Republic: U Dvou Srpů 2024/2, 15 000 Prague 5; tel. 257011335; fax 257531672; e-mail skuhrova@csvs.cz; internet www.naric.cz; Head ŠTEPÁNKA SKUHROVÁ.

NATIONAL BODIES

Česká konference rektorů (Czech Rectors' Conference): Masarykova univerzita, Zerotínovo nám. 9, 601 77 Brno; tel. 549491121; fax 549491122; e-mail crc@muni.cz; internet crc.muni.cz; Pres. Prof. Ing. JAN HRON; Gen. Sec. Dr MARIE FOJTÍKOVÁ.

Rada vysokých škol (Council of Higher Education Institutions): José Martího 31, 162 52 Prague 6; tel. (2) 20560221; fax (2) 20560221; e-mail arvs@ftvs.cuni.cz; internet www.radavs.cz.

Learned Societies

GENERAL

Akademie věd České republiky AV ČR (Academy of Sciences of the Czech Republic): Národní tř. 3, 117 20 Prague 1; tel. 221403111; fax 224240512; e-mail kavcr@kav.cas.cz; internet www.avcr.cz; f. 1992; the Academy is a network of 60 autonomous research institutes which conduct theoretical and applied research in three broad sections: chemical and life sciences (Dir Prof. HELENA ILLNEROVÁ), humanities and social sciences (Dir Dr VILÉM HEROLD), mathematics, physics and earth sciences (Dir Dr KAREL JUNGWIRTH); attached research institutes: see Research Institutes; library and archive: see Libraries and Archives; Pres. Prof. JIŘÍ DRAHOŠ; Pres. of Scientific Council Asst Prof. Dr KAREL OLIVA; publ. *Akademický bulletin* (newsletter, 12 a year).

Rada vědeckých společností České republiky (Council of Scientific Societies of the Czech Republic): Středisko společných činností Akademie věd ČR, Národní tř. 3, 117 20 Prague; tel. and fax 221403478; e-mail rvs@kav.cas.cz; internet www.cas.cz/rvs; coordinates 70 scientific socs, representing natural science, medicine and the social, and technical sciences; 34,000 mems; Pres. Prof. Dr IVO HÁNA.

AGRICULTURE, FISHERIES AND VETERINARY SCIENCE

Česká Akademie Zemědělských Věd (Czech Academy of Agricultural Sciences): Těšnov 65/17, 117 05 Prague 1; tel. 222320582; fax 222328898; e-mail cazv@cazv.cz; internet www.cazv.cz; f. 1924; sections of agricultural engineering, energy and devt (Chair. Ing. JAROSLAV KÁRA), animal production (Chair. Doc. Ing. VĚRA SKŘIVANOVÁ), economics, management, sociology and information technology (Chair. Doc. Ing. JAN HRON), food technology and technique (Chair. Ing. JAN DRBOHLAV), forestry (Chair. Ing. VILÉM PODRÁZSKÝ), human nutrition and food quality (Chair. Ing. SLAVOMÍRA VAVRERINOVÁ), plant production (Chair. Dr SLAVOJ PALÍK), plant protection (Chair. Dr JAN NEDĚLNÍK), soil science (Chair. Ing. RADIM VÁCHA), veterinary medicine (Chair. Prof. Dr MIROSLAV TOMAN), water management (Chair. Doc. Ing. MILOSLAV JANEČEK; agricultural research, devt and education; 610 mems; Pres. Mgr JAN LIPAVSKÝ; Vice-Pres. Prof. Ing. JAN HRON; Sec. VACLAV HRUBY; publs *Genetika a šlechtění* (Czech Journal of Genetics and Plant Breeding, 4 a year), *Journal of Forest Science* (12 a year), *Ochrana rostlin* (Plant Protection Science, 4 a year), *Potravinářské vědy* (Czech Journal of Food Sciences, 6 a year), *Plant, Soil and Environment* (12 a year), *Soil and Water Research* (4 a year), *Veterinární Medicína* (Veterinary Medicine, 12 a year), *Horticultural Science* (Horticultural Science, 4 a year), *Zemědělská ekonomika* (Agricultural Economics, 12 a year), *Zemědělská technika* (Research in Agricultural Engineering, 4 a year), *Živočišná výroba* (Czech Journal of Animal Science, 12 a year).

ARCHITECTURE AND TOWN PLANNING

Obec architektů (Society of Architects): Revoluční 23, 110 00 Prague 1; tel. (2) 57535025; fax (2) 57535033; e-mail obecarch@architekt.cz; internet www.architekt.cz; f. 1989; 1,000 mems; Pres. JIŘÍ MOJŽÍŠ; publ. *Architekt* (12 a year).

ECONOMICS, LAW AND POLITICS

Česká společnost ekonomická (Czech Economic Society): Politických vězňů 7, 110 00 Prague 1; e-mail cse@cse.cz; internet www.cse.cz; f. 1962; 180 mems; Pres. Dr MICHAL SKOREPA; publ. *Bulletin* (3 a year).

Česká společnost pro mezinárodní právo (Czech Society for International Law): Národní tř. 18, 116 91 Prague 1; tel. 224933494; e-mail sturma@prf.cuni.cz; f. 1969 as Czechoslovak Society of International Law, present status 1993; attached to Acad. of Sciences of the Czech Republic; non-profit org. of academics and professionals in the field of int. law; cooperates with the Czech br. of the Int. Law Asscn and with foreign societies of int. law; represents, through its mems, the Czech doctrine of int. law in int. scientific orgs; organizes lectures and discussions, research conferences and publishes non-periodical books and periodicals; 96 mems; Pres. Prof. Dr PAVEL ŠTURMA; Scientific Sec. Dr VERONIKA BÍLKOVÁ; First Vice-Pres. Prof. Dr DALIBOR JÍLEK.

Česká společnost pro politické vědy (Czech Association for Political Sciences): Nám. W. Churchilla 4, 130 67 Prague 3; tel. (2) 24095204; fax (2) 24220657; e-mail cabada@kap.zcu.cz; internet www.cspv.cz; f. 1964; 160 mems; Pres. Assoc. Prof. LADISLAV CABADA; Sec. Dr HELENA HRICOVÁ; Sec. LINDA PIKNEROVÁ; publ. *Politologická Revue* (2 a year).

EDUCATION

Česká komise pro UNESCO (Czech Commission for UNESCO): Rytirska 31, 110 00 Prague 1; tel. 221610126; fax 221610122; e-mail unesco@mzv.cz; internet www.mzv.cz/unesco; f. 1994, as part of Ministry of Foreign Affairs, subsidiary advisory body of govt; Sec.-Gen. Ing. MILAN KUNA.

Česká pedagogická společnost (Czech Pedagogical Society): Poříčí 31, 603 00 Brno; tel. 549493645; fax 543232722; e-mail sekretar@cpds.cz; internet www.cpds.cz; f. 1964; 240 mems; Pres. Dr TOMÁŠ ČECH; Sec. Dr MARTA RYBIČKOVÁ; publ. *Pedagogická orientace* (4 a year).

FINE AND PERFORMING ARTS

Asociace hudebních umělců a vědců (Association of Musicians and Musicologists): Radlická 99, 150 00 Prague 5; tel. and fax 251553996; e-mail ahuv@seznam.cz; internet www.ahuv.cz; f. 1990; 1,200 mems; Pres. Prof. JIŘÍ HLAVÁČ; Exec. Sec. MARCELA POSEJPALOVÁ; publ. *Hudební rozhledy* (12 a year).

Česká hudební společnost (Czech Music Society): Radlická 99, 150 00 Prague 5; tel. and fax 251552453; e-mail mila.smetackova@volny.cz; f. 1973; 5,000 mems; Pres. MÍLA SMETÁČKOVÁ; Sec.-Gen. EVA STRAUSOVÁ; publs *CHS News* (2 a year), *Josef Suk Society News* (2 a year), *Vítězslav Novák Society News* (1 a year).

Český filmový a televizní svaz (FITES) (Czech Film and Television Association): Pod Nuselskými schody 1721/3, 120 00 Prague 2; tel. 222562331; fax 222562331; e-mail info@fites.cz; internet www.fites.cz; f. 1966; 720 mems; Pres. MARTIN SKYBA; publ. *Synchron* (6 a year).

Český spolek pro komorní hudbu (Czech Chamber Music Society): c/o Česká filharmonie Rudolfinum, 1, Alšovo nábřeží 12, 110 00 Prague; tel. 227059343; fax 227059226; e-mail cskh@cfmail.cz; internet www.ceskafilharmonie.cz; f. 1894; 3,500 mems; Chair. Ing. IVAN ENGLICH.

Divadelní ústav (Theatre Institute): Celetná 17, 110 00 Prague 1; tel. 224809132; fax 224810278; internet www.divadlo.cz; f. 1956; research and documentation on Czech theatre; Czech centre of the International Theatre Institute (ITI); library of 100,000 vols; Dir ONDŘEJ ČERNÝ; publs *Divadelní noviny* (24 a year), *Divadelní revue* (4 a year), *Informační servis Divadelního ústavu* (12 a year), *Loutkář* (10 a year), *Ročenka českých divadel* (1 a year), *Theatre Czech* (1 a year).

Společnost pro estetiku (Society for Aesthetics): Dept of Aesthetics, Faculty of Philosophy, Charles Univ., Celetná 20, 110 00 Prague 1; tel. 224491384; e-mail ondrej .dadejik@ff.cuni.cz; internet www.cas.cz/rvs/index_gb.html; f. 1969; 85 mems; Pres. Dr ONDREJ DADEJIK; Sec. KATERINA NOVOTNÁ.

Unie výtvarných umělců (Union of Creative Artists): Masarykovo nábř. 250, 110 00 Prague 1; tel. and fax 541213555; e-mail uvucr@uvucr.cz; internet www.uvucr.cz; f. 1990; supports the professional interests of visual artists; acts as an information centre and coordinates the activities of its members; keeps a register of professional visual artists working in the Czech Republic; 3,000 mems; Pres. VÁCLAV KUBÁT; Exec. Vice-Pres. VÍT WEBER; publs *Art Folia* (1 a year), *Atelier* (26 a year), *Technologia Artis* (1 a year), *Výtvarné umění* (4 a year).

HISTORY, GEOGRAPHY AND ARCHAEOLOGY

Česká archeologická společnost (Czech Archaeological Society): Letenská 4, 118 01 Prague 1; tel. 224317913; fax 221619730; e-mail zuzana.blahova@ff.cuni.cz; internet www.archaeology.cz/cas; f. 1919; organizes annual colloquiums, publs, lectures, excursions about new archaeological excavations; 580 mems; Pres. Dr KAREL SKLENÁŘ; Sec. Dr ONDŘEJ CHVOJKA; publs *Archeologie Moravy a Slezska* (Archaeology of Moravia and Silesia, 1 a year), *Studia Hercynia* (1 a year), *Zprávy* (Bulletin, irregular).

Česká demografická společnost (Czech Demographic Society): Albertov 6, 128 43 Prague 2; tel. 221951418; fax 224920657; e-mail demodept@natur.cuni.cz; internet www.natur.cuni.cz/~demodept/cds; f. 1964; 450 mems; Pres. JITKA RYCHTAŘÍKOVÁ; Sec. FELIX KOSCHIN.

Česká geografická společnost (Czech Geographical Society): Albertov 6, 128 43 Prague 2; tel. 221951383; fax 224920657; e-mail perlin@natur.cuni.cz; internet www .geography.cz; f. 1894; 500 mems; Pres. Prof. TADEUSZ SIWEK; Scientific Sec. Dr RADIM PERLÍN; Sec. Dr DANA FIALOVÁ; publs *Geografické rozhledy* (Geographical perspective, 5 a year), *Geografie* (Geography, scientific journal, 4 a year), *Informace CGS* (2 a year).

Matice moravská (Moravian Society of History and Literature): Arne Nováka 1, 602 00 Brno; tel. 549493552; e-mail matice@phil.muni.cz; internet www .matice-moravska.cz; f. 1849; 560 mems; Pres. Prof. Dr JIŘÍ L. MALÍŘ; Sec. Dr BRONISLAV CHOCHOLÁČ; publ. *Časopis Matice moravské* (2 a year).

LANGUAGE AND LITERATURE

Alliance Française: c/o French Embassy in the Czech Republic, Štěpánská 35, 111 21 Prague 1; tel. 221401063; fax 222230576; e-mail michel.wattremez@diplomatie.gouv .fr; internet www.alliancefrancaise.cz; offers courses and exams in French language and culture and promotes cultural exchange with France; attached offices in Brno, České Budějovice, Hradec Králové, Kladno, Kroměříž, Liberec, Louny, Ostrava, Pardubice, Plzeň, Pribram, Ustí nad Labem and Zlín; General Coordinator MICHEL WATTREMEZ.

British Council: Bredovský dvůr, Politických vězňů 13, 110 00 Prague 1; tel. 221991160; fax 224933847; e-mail info .praha@britishcouncil.cz; internet www .britishcouncil.cz; teaching centre; offers courses and exams in English language and British culture and promotes cultural exchange with the UK; attached teaching centre in Pilsen; Dir NIGEL BELLINGHAM; Deputy Dir STEVE OXLEY.

Český esperantský svaz (Czech Union of Esperantists): c/o Pavel Polnicky, Na Vinici 110/10, 290 01 Podebrady; e-mail cea .polnicky@quick.cz; internet www.esperanto .cz; tel. 325615651; f. 1969; 800 mems; Pres. JANA MELICHÁRKOVÁ; Sec. PAVEL POLNICKÝ; publ. *Starto* (4 a year).

Czech Centre of International PEN: POB 123, 110 00 Prague 1; Klementinum 190 (Nat. Library Bldg), 5 Fl., 110 00 Prague; tel. and fax (2) 24234343; e-mail centrum@pen .cz; internet www.pen.cz; f. 1924; Writers in Prison Cttee; regular authors' readings, exhibitions, spring and autumn literary festivals, discussions with writers in schools, clubs and civic facilities; awards Karel Čapek Prize and PEN Club Lifetime Achievement Prize every 2 years; 197 mems, incl. 13 hon. mems; Pres. Mgr JIRI DĚDEČEK; Dir Ing. LIBUŠE LUDVIKOVÁ; Sec. DANA MOJŽÍŠOVÁ.

Goethe-Institut: Masarykovo nábřeží 32, 110 00 Prague 1; tel. 221962111; fax 221962250; e-mail info@prag.goethe.org; internet www.goethe.de/ins/cz/pra/; offers courses and exams in German language and culture and promotes cultural exchange with Germany; library of 14,000 vols; Dir Dr STEPHAN NOBBE.

Literárněvědná společnost (Literary Society): Katedra slavistiky PF Univerzity Hradec Králové, Rokitanského 62, 500 03 Hradec Králové; tel. 493333160; e-mail oldřich .richterek@uhk.cz; f. 1934; 285 mems; Pres. Prof. Dr OLDŘICH RICHTEREK.

Obec spisovatelů (Society of Czech Writers): Železná 18, 110 00 Prague 1; tel. 224234060; fax 224234060; e-mail obecspis@volny.cz; internet www.obecspisovatelu.cz; f. 1989; seminars, debates and conferences; 700 mems; Hon. Pres. VÁCLAV HAVEL; Pres. VLADIMÍR KŘIVÁNEK; publ. *Dokořán* (4 a year).

MEDICINE

Česká imunologická společnost (Czech Society for Immunology): Vídeňská 1083, 142 20 Prague 4; e-mail cis@biomed.cas.cz; internet www.biomed.cas.cz/cis/; f. 1986; 600 mems; Pres. Prof. Dr ALEŠ MACELA; Sec. Dr MARTIN BILEJ; publ. *Imunologický zpravodaj* (3 a year).

Česká lékařská společnost J. E. Purkyně (J. E. Purkyně Czech Medical Association): Sokolská 31, 120 26 Prague 2; tel. 224266201; fax 224266212; e-mail cls@cls.cz; internet www.cls.cz; f. 1947; 34,500 mems; Pres. Prof. Dr JAROSLAV BLAHOŠ; Scientific Sec. Prof. Dr JIŘÍ HOMOLKA; publs *Acta Chirurgiae Plasticae* (in English, 4 a year), *Anesteziologie a intenzivní medicína* (Anaesthesiology and Intensive Critical Care Medicine, 6 a year), *Časopis lékařů českých* (Journal of Czech Physicians, 12 a year), *Česká a slovenská farmacie* (Czech and Slovak Pharmacy, 6 a year), *Česká a slovenská gastroenterologie a hepatologie* (Czech and Slovak Gastroenterology and Hepatology, 6 a year), *Česká a slovenská neurologie a neurochirurgie* (Czech and Slovak Neurology and Neurosurgery, 6 a year), *Česká a slovenská oftalmologie* (Czech and Slovak Ophthalmology, 6 a year), *Česká a slovenská psychiatrie* (Czech and Slovak Psychiatry, 8 a year), *Česká gynekologie* (Czech Gynaecology, 6 a year), *Česká radiologie* (Czech Radiology, 6 a year), *Česká revmatologie* (Czech Rheumatology, 4 a year), *Česká stomatologie a Praktické zubní lékařství* (Czech Stomatology and Practical Dentistry, 6 a year), *Česko-slovenská dermatologie* (Czech-Slovak Dermatology, 6 a year), *Česko-slovenská patologie a Soudní lékařství* (Czech-Slovak Pathology and Forensic Medicine, 4 a year), *Česko-slovenská pedjatrie* (Czech-Slovak Paediatrics, 12 a year), *Česko-slovenská fyziologie* (Czechoslovak Physiology, 4 a year), *Epidemiologie, mikrobiologie, imunologie* (Epidemiology, Microbiology, Immunology, 4 a year), *Hygiena* (Hygiene, 4 a year), *Klinická biochemie a metabolismus* (Clinical Biochemistry and Metabolism, 4 a year), *Klinická onkologie* (Clinical Oncology, 6 a year), *Lékař a technika* (Physician and Technology, 6 a year), *Otorinolaryngologie a foniatrie* (Otorhinolaryngology and Phoniatrics, 4 a year), *Pracovní lékařství* (Occupational Medicine, 4 a year), *Praktický lékař* (The Generalist, 12 a year), *Rehabilitace a fyzikální lékařství* (Rehabilitation and Physical Medicine, 4 a year), *Rozhledy v chirurgii* (Surgical Review, 12 a year), *Vnitřní lékařství* (Internal Medicine, 12 a year), *Revizní a posudkové lékařství* (Health Insurance and Medical Revision, 4 a year), *Endoskopie* (Endoscopy, 4 a year), *Transfuze a hematologie dnes* (Transfusion and Haematology Today, 4 a year).

NATURAL SCIENCES
General

Český svaz vědeckotechnických společností (Czech Association of Scientific and Technical Societies): Novotného lávka 5, 116 68 Prague 1; tel. 221082247; fax 222221780; e-mail poriz@csvts.cz; internet www.csvts.cz; f. 1990; promotes professional interests of mems; organizes educational programmes, training courses in technical and general fields of education, and congresses, confs, workshops and seminars; 136,000 mems; Pres. Doc. Ing. DANIEL HANUS; Exec. Sec. Ing. VLADIMIR PORIZ; publs *Bio Prospect* (irregular), *Chemical Papers (Prague)* (6 a year), *Glass Paper* (irregular), *Plant Physician* (4 a year), *Reporter* (4 a year), *Silicate Reporter* (irregular).

Společnost pro dějiny věd a techniky (Society of the History of Sciences and Technology): Kostelní 42, 170 78 Prague 7; tel. 220399208; fax 233371801; e-mail barvikova@archiv.cas.cz; internet dvt .hyperlink.cz; f. 1965; 300 mems; Pres. Prof. PETR SVOBODNY; Sec. Dr MILADA SEKYRKOVÁ; publs *Acta historiae rerum naturalium necnon technicarum* (1 a year), *Dějiny věd a techniky* (4 a year), *Práce z dějin techniky a přívodních věd* (Treatise on the History of Technology and Sciences, irregular).

Biological Sciences

Česká botanická společnost (Czech Botanical Society): Benátská 2, 128 01 Prague 2; tel. 221951664; e-mail botspol@natur .cuni.cz; internet www.natur.cuni.cz/cbs; f. 1912; 787 mems; library of 3,000 vols, 1,400 periodicals; Chair. Dr LUBOMÍR HROUDA; Sec. Dr J. ŠTĚPÁNEK; publs *Preslia* (4 a year), *Zprávy ČBS* (irregular).

Česká parazitologická společnost (Czech Society for Parasitology): c/o Institute of Postgraduate Medical Education, 10, Ruská 85, 100 05 Prague; tel. 271019254; fax 272740458; e-mail fajfrlik@fnplzen.cz; internet www.parazitologie.cz; f. 1993; 199 mems; Pres. Dr LIBUSE KOLÁŘOVÁ; Sec. Dr KAREL FAJFRLÍK; publ. *Zprávy České parazitologické společnosti* (4 a year).

Česká společnost bioklimatologická (Czech Society for Bioclimatology): Kroftova 43, 616 67 Brno; tel. 267103321; fax 272761549; e-mail jstr@ig.cas.cz; internet www.cbks.cz; f. 1965; 75 mems; Pres. Dr J. ROŽNOVSKÝ; Sec. J. STŘEŠTIK; publ. *Digests of Science Reports* (1 a year).

Česká společnost entomologická (Czech Entomological Society): Vinicna 7, 128 00 Prague 2; tel. 224923535; e-mail klapagenda@centrum.cz; internet www .entospol.cz; f. 1904; 750 mems; library of 20,500 vols; Pres. Dr JOSEF JELINEK; Sec. Dr KLARA FARKACOVA; publ. *Klapalekiana* (2 a year).

Česká společnost histo- a cytochemická (Czech Society for Histo- and Cytochemistry): Kamenice 3, 625 00 Brno; tel. 549493701; fax 549491320; e-mail pdubovy@med.muni.cz; internet www.med.muni.cz/hcspol; f. 1962; associated with the International Federation of Societies for Histochemistry and Cytochemistry; 120 mems; Pres. Prof. Dr PETR DUBOVÝ; Sec. Prof. Dr SVATOPLUK ČECH.

Česká společnost pro biomechaniku (Czech Society for Biomechanics): FTVS–Katedra anatomie a biomechaniky, J. Martiho 31, 160 00 Prague 6; tel. and fax 220560225; e-mail otahal@ftvs.cuni.cz; internet biomech.ftvs.cuni.cz/csb; f. 1990; 168 mems; Pres. Prof. STANISLAV OTÁHAL; Sec. Asst Prof. MIROSLAV SOCHOR; publ. *Bulletin* (2 a year).

Česká společnost zoologická (Czech Zoological Society): Viničná 7, 128 44 Prague; tel. 221951860; e-mail chalupsk@natur.cuni.cz; internet www.natur.cuni.cz/zoospol; f. 1927; 220 mems; library of 18,050 vols; Pres. Dr VÁCLAV PIŽL; Sec. Dr M. ŠVÁTORA; Sec. Dr M. SKUHRAVÁ; publ. *Acta Societatis Zoologicae Bohemicae* (4 a year).

Česká vědecká společnost pro mykologii (Czech Scientific Society for Mycology): POB 106, 111 21 Prague 1; tel. 533435238; e-mail cvsm@natur.cuni.cz; internet www .natur.cuni.cz/cvsm; f. 1946; voluntary org. for professional and amateur mycologists; organizes mycological lectures for the public, mycological excursions (mushroom-picking, micromycetes), seminar meetings; 200 mems; library of 900 vols, 135 journals; Pres. Dr VLADIMÍR ANTONÍN; Sec. Dr ALENA KUBÁTOVÁ; publs *Czech Mycology* (in English, 2 a year), *Mykologické Listy* (in Czech with English summary, 4 a year).

Československá biologická společnost (Czechoslovak Biological Society): Tomešova 12, 602 00 Brno; tel. and fax 549492394; e-mail rjanisch@med.muni.cz; internet www .med.muni.cz/biolspol; f. 1922; 1,902 vols; Pres. Prof. Dr V. MORNSTEIN; Sec. Prof. Dr R. JANISCH; publ. *Zpravodaj Čs. Biologické společnosti* (Bulletin of the Czechoslovak Biological Society, in Czech, 2 a year).

Československá společnost mikrobiologická (Czechoslovak Society for Microbiology): Vídeňská 1083, 142 20 Prague 4; tel. 296442494; fax 296442396; e-mail gabriel@biomed.cas.cz; internet www.cssm.info; f. 1928; organizes int. and nat. conferences in the field of basic and applied microbiology, molecular biology and genetics; courses for both undergraduate and postgraduate students; 1,000 mems from Czech Republic and Slovakia; Pres. Dr JIRI GABRIEL; Sec.-Gen. Dr JIRI MATEJU; publs *Bulletin* (Czech, Slovak, 4 a year), *Folia microbiologica* (English, 6 a year).

Mathematical Sciences

Jednota českých matematiků a fyziků (Union of Czech Mathematicians and Physicists): Žitná 25, 117 10 Prague 1; tel. 222211100; e-mail predseda@jcmf.cz; internet www.jcmf.cz; f. 1862; 2,300 mems; Pres. JOSEF KUBÁT; Sec. JIRI FIALA; publs *Matematika-Fyzika-Informatika* (12 a year), *Pokroky matematiky, fyziky a astronomie* (4 a year), *Rozhledy matematicko-fyzikální* (4 a year), *Učitel matematiky* (4 a year).

Physical Sciences

Česká astronomická společnost (Czech Astronomical Society): Královská obora 233, 170 21 Prague 7; tel. (2) 33377204; e-mail info@astro.cz; internet www.astro.cz; f. 1917; 700 mems; Pres. Dr JIŘÍ BOROVIČKA; Sec. Dr MILOSLAV ZEJDA; publ. *Kosmické rozhledy* (irregular).

Česká geologická společnost (Czech Geological Society): V Holešovičkách 41, 182 09 Prague 8; tel. 266009323; fax 266410649; e-mail budil@cgu.cz; internet www .geologickaspolecnost.cz; f. 1923; 500 mems; Pres. Dr PETR BUDIL; Sec. BLANKA ČIZKOVÁ; publ. *Journal* (4 a year).

Česká meteorologická společnost (Czech Meteorological Society): Na Šabatce 17, 143 06 Prague; tel. 221912548; fax 221912533; e-mail kmop@mff.cuni.cz; internet www .cmes.cz; f. 1958; provides information on meteorology and climatology, history of meteorology, and meteorological bibliography and terminology; 215 mems; Pres. Doc. Dr TOMÁŠ HALENKA; Sec. Dr MILAN ŠÁLEK; Treas. PETR SKALAK.

Česká společnost chemická (Czech Chemical Society): Novotneho lavka 5, 116 68 Prague 1; tel. 221082383; fax 222220184; e-mail csch@csch.cz; internet www.csch.cz; f. 1866; 3,480 mems; Pres. Prof. Dr JITKA ULRICHOVÁ; publs *Bulletin* (4 a year), *Chemické Listy* (12 a year).

Spektroskopická společnost J. Marca Marci (J. Marcus Marci Spectroscopic Society): Thákurova 7, 166 29 Prague 6; Masarykova univerzita, Přírodovědecká fakulta, Kotlářská 2, 611 37 Brno; tel. (54) 9491436; fax (54) 9492494; e-mail immss@spektroskopie.cz; internet www .spektroskopie.cz; f. 1949; 970 mems; Chair. Prof. Dr VIKTOR KANICKÝ; Scientific Sec. Prof. Dr JAN HÁLA.

Vědecká společnost pro nauku o kovech (Metals Science Society): Ke Karlovu 5, 121 16 Prague 2; tel. 221911362; fax 221911490; e-mail vsnk@met.mff.cuni.cz; f. 1966; 120 mems; Pres. Prof. VLADIMÍR CÍHAL; Sec. Prof. VLADIMÍR ŠÍMA.

PHILOSOPHY AND PSYCHOLOGY

Filozofický ústav Akademie věd České republiky (Institute of Philosophy of the Czech Academy of Sciences): Jilská 1, 110 00 Prague 1; tel. 222220099; fax 222220108; e-mail flusekr@site.cas.cz; internet www.flu .cas.cz; f. 1990; 250 mems; Dir Dr PAVEL BARAN; publs *Acta Comeniana* (in English, French and German), *Filosofický časopis* (Philosophical Journal, 6 a year, summaries in English and German), *Teorie vedy* (Theory of Science, 4 a year, in Czech and English).

RELIGION, SOCIOLOGY AND ANTHROPOLOGY

Česká společnost antropologická (Czech Anthropological Society): Viničná 7, 128 44 Prague 2; internet anthropology.cz; f. 1964; 180 mems; Pres. Dr J. JELÍNEK; Sec. Doc. Dr V. NOVOTNÝ; publ. *Zprávy* (4 a year).

Masarykova česká sociologická společnost (Masaryk Czech Sociological Association): Husova 4, 110 00 Prague 1; tel. 222220631; fax 222220631; e-mail mcss@seznam.cz; internet www.ceskasociologicka .org; f. 1964; supports devt of all aspects of Czech sociology on nat. and regional level; 310 mems; Pres. Doc. Dr JIŘÍ ŠUBRT.

Národopisná společnost (Ethnographical Society): Národní třída 3, 117 20 Prague 1; e-mail valka@phil.muni.cz; f. 1893; 280 mems; Pres. Dr MIROSLAV VÁLKA; publs *Národopisný věstník* (1 a year), *Zpravodaj Národopisné Společnosti* (3 a year).

TECHNOLOGY

Česká společnost pro kybernetiku a informatiku (Czech Society for Cybernetics and Informatics): Pod Vodárenskou věží 2, 182 07 Prague 8; tel. 266053901; fax 286585789; e-mail cski@utia.cas.cz; internet www.cski.cz; f. 1966; 350 mems; Pres. Prof. OLGA ŠTĚPÁNKOVÁ; Sec. DAGMAR HARMANCOVÁ; publs *Kybernetika* (in English, 6 a year), *Zpravodaj* (12 a year).

Česká společnost pro mechaniku (Czech Society for Mechanics): Dolejškova 5, 182 00

Prague 8; tel. 266053045; e-mail csm@it.cas .cz; internet www.csm.cz; f. 1966; 580 individual mems, 18 organizational mems; Pres. Prof. Ing. MILOSLAV OKROUHLÍK; Sec. Ing. JITKA HAVLÍNOVÁ; publ. *Bulletin* (3 a year).

Česká společnost pro vědeckou kinematografii (Czech Society for Scientific Cinematography): Zemědělská 1665/1, 613 00 Brno-Černá Pole; tel. 545135021; fax 545135013; e-mail rygl@mendelu.cz; f. 1923; 150 mems; Pres. Ing. V. BOUČEK; Sec. Ing. L. RYGL; publ. *Bulletin* (1 a year).

Research Institutes

ARCHITECTURE AND TOWN PLANNING

ABF—Nadace pro rozvoj architektury a stavitelství (Architecture and Building Foundation): Václavské nám. 833/31, 110 00 Prague 1; tel. 224225001; fax 224233136; e-mail fibiger@abf-nadace.cz; internet www .abf-nadace.cz; f. 1991; incl. Česká stavební akademie (Czech Bldg Acad.); organizes 2 evaluative competions: Stavba roku (Bldg of the year) and Vyrok-technologie roku (Product-technology of the year); organizes spec. exibitions; library of 10,000 vols; Dir Dr JAN FIBIGER; Sec. PETRA PROKOPOVA; publs *ABF Forum* (4 a year), *Building Products Review* (1 a year), *Forum of Architecture and Building* (12 a year).

ECONOMICS, LAW AND POLITICS

CERGE-EI: POB 882, Politických vězňů 7, 111 21 Prague 1; tel. 224005123; fax 224227143; e-mail office@cerge-ei.cz; internet www.cerge-ei.cz; f. 1991; attached to Acad. of Sciences of the Czech Republic and to Charles Univ.; conducts US-style PhD programme in economics; library of 100,000 vols; depository for World Bank publs; Dir Dr STEPAN JURAJDA; publs *CERGE-EI Working Papers*, *Working Papers* (12 a year).

Ústav státu práva AV ČR (Institute of State and Law AS CR): Národní 18, 116 91 Prague 1; tel. 221990711; fax 224933056; e-mail ilaw@ilaw.cas.cz; internet www.ilaw .cas.cz; attached to Acad. of Sciences of the Czech Republic; library of 40,000 vols, 100 periodicals; Dir Dr JAROSLAV ZACHARIÁŠ; publ. *Právník* (12 a year).

FINE AND PERFORMING ARTS

Ústav dějin umění AV ČR, v.v.i. (Institute of Art History AS CR, v. v. i.): Husova 4, 110 00 Prague 1; tel. 222222144; fax 222221654; e-mail arthist@site.cas.cz; internet www.udu .cas.cz; f. 1953; attached to Acad. of Sciences of the Czech Republic; Dir Dr LUBOMIR KONEČNÝ; publs *Estetika: The Central European Journal of Aesthetics* (2 a year), *Fontes Historiae Artium* (book series, irregular), *Studia Rudolphina* (1 a year), *Umění* (6 a year).

HISTORY, GEOGRAPHY AND ARCHAEOLOGY

Archeologický ústav AV ČR, Brno (Archaeological Institute AS CR, Brno): Královopolská 147, 612 64 Brno; tel. 541514101; fax 541514123; e-mail archeo@iabrno.cz; internet www.iabrno.cz; attached to Acad. of Sciences of the Czech Republic; Dir Dr PAVEL KOUŘIL; publs *Fontes Archeologicae Moravicae* (irregular), *Studie Archeologického ústavu* (1 a year).

Archeologický ústav AV ČR, Praha (Archaeological Institute AS CR, Prague): Letenská 4, 118 01 Prague 1; tel. 257530922; fax 257532288; e-mail jiran@arup.cas.cz; internet www.arup.cas.cz; f. 1919; attached to Acad. of Sciences of the Czech Republic;

Dir Dr LUBOŠ JIRÁŇ; publs *Archeologické rozhledy* (4 a year), *Památky archeologické* (2 a year).

Historický ústav AV ČR (Institute of History AS CR): Prosecká 76, 190 00 Prague 9; tel. 286887513; fax 286887513; e-mail bucharova@hiu.cas.cz; internet www.hiu.cas .cz; f. 1921; attached to Acad. of Sciences of the Czech Republic; Dir Dr MILOSLAV POLÍVKA; publs *Český časopis historický* (4 a year), *Folia Historica Bohemica* (irregular), *Historia Europae Centralis* (1 a year), *Historica* (Historical Sciences in the Czech Republic, annual), *Historická geografie* (every 2 years), *Mediaevalia Historica Bohemica* (1 a year), *Moderní dějiny* (1 a year), *Slovanské historické studie* (1 a year), *Slovanský přehlad* (4 a year).

Kabinet pro klasická studia FLÚ AV ČR, v. v. i. (Institute for Classical Studies AS CR): Na Florenci 3, 110 00 Prague 1; tel. 222828303; fax 222828305; e-mail uks@ics .cas.cz; internet www.ics.cas.cz; f. 1953; attached to Acad. of Sciences of the Czech Republic; researches classical traditions and impact of ancient civilizations on cultural life of Bohemia since its beginning to 21st century; library of 60,000 vols; Head Dr JIŘÍ BENEŠ; publs *Eirene, Studia Graeca et Latina* (on classical studies, 1 a year), *Listy filologické, Folia philologica* (Folia Philologica, 2 a year).

Orientální ústav AV ČR (Oriental Institute AS CR): Pod vodárenskou věží 4, 182 08 Prague 8; tel. 266053111; fax 286581897; e-mail orient@orient.cas.cz; internet www .orient.cas.cz; f. 1922; attached to Acad. of Sciences of the Czech Republic; research in history, religious and philosophical systems, languages, literatures and cultures of Asia and Africa; library of 210,000 vols; Dir Dr STANISLAVA VAVROUŠKOVÁ; Sec. PAVEL HONS; publ. *Archiv orientální* (4 a year).

Slovanský ústav AV ČR (Institute of Slavonic Studies AS CR): Valentinská 1, 110 00 Prague 1; tel. 224800251; fax 224800252; e-mail slu@slu.cas.cz; internet www.slu.cas .cz; f. 1922; attached to Acad. of Sciences of the Czech Republic; Dir Prof. VLADIMÍR VAVŘÍNEK; publs *Byzantinoslavica* (2 a year), *Germanoslavica* (2 a year), *Slavia* (4 a year).

Ústav pro soudobé dějiny AV ČR v.v.i. (Institute of Contemporary History AS CR v.v.i.): Vlašská 9, 118 40 Prague 1; tel. 257286362; fax 257531121; e-mail usd@usd .cas.cz; internet www.usd.cas.cz; f. 1990; attached to Acad. of Sciences of the Czech Republic; Czech and Slovak history from 1938–2000; library of 35,000 vols; Dir Dr OLDŘICH TÚMA; publ. *Soudobé dějiny*.

Výzkumný ústav geodetický, topografický a kartografický (VUGTK) (Research Institute of Geodesy, Topography and Cartography): 250 66 Zdiby 98; tel. 284890351; fax 284890056; e-mail vugtk@vugtk.cz; internet www.vugtk.cz; f. 1954; library of 70,000 vols; Dir Dr Ing. VÁCLAV SLABOCH; publ. *Proceedings of Research Works* (every 2 years).

LANGUAGE AND LITERATURE

Ústav pro českou literaturu AV ČR (Institute of Czech Literature AS CR): Na Florenci 3/1420, 110 00 Prague 1; tel. 234612111; fax 224818437; e-mail literatura@ucl.cas.cz; internet www.ucl.cas .cz; f. 1947; attached to Acad. of Sciences of the Czech Republic; library of 130,000 vols; Dir Dr PAVEL JANOUŠEK; publ. *Česká literatura* (6 a year).

Ústav pro jazyk český AV ČR (Czech Language Institute AS CR): Letenská 4, 118

51 Prague 1; tel. 257533756; fax 257531761; e-mail ujc@ujc.cas.cz; internet www.ujc.cas .cz; f. 1911; attached to Acad. of Sciences of the Czech Republic; Dir Dr KAREL OLIVA; publs *Acta Onomastica* (1 a year), *Bibliografie české lingvistiky* (1 a year), *Časopis pro moderní filologii* (2 a year), *Linguistica Pragensia* (2 a year), *Naše řeč* (5 a year), *Slovo a slovestnost* (4 a year).

MEDICINE

Farmakologický ústav AV ČR (Institute of Pharmacology AS CR): 4–Krč, Vídeňská 1083, 142 20 Prague; tel. 261710024; e-mail fkuavcr@biomed.cas.cz; internet www.cas.cz; attached to Acad. of Sciences of the Czech Republic; Dir Dr EVŽEN BUCHAR.

Ústav experimentální medicíny AV ČR (Institute of Experimental Medicine AS CR): Vídeňská 1083, 142 20 Prague 4; tel. 241062230; fax 241062782; e-mail uemavcr@biomed.cas.cz; internet uemweb .biomed.cas.cz; f. 1975; attached to Acad. of Sciences of the Czech Republic; Dir Prof. EVA SYKOVÁ.

NATURAL SCIENCES

General

Ústav geoniky AV ČR (Institute of Geonics AS CR): Poruba, Studentská 1768, 708 00 Ostrava; tel. 596979352; fax 596919452; e-mail geonics@ugn.cas.cz; internet www .ugn.cas.cz; f. 1982; attached to Acad. of Sciences of the Czech Republic; Dir Prof. RADIM BLAHETA; publ. *Moravian Geographical Report* (4 a year).

Biological Sciences

Biofyzikální ústav AV ČR (Institute of Biophysics AS CR): Královopolská 135, 612 65 Brno; tel. 541517111; fax 541211293; e-mail ibp@ibp.cz; internet www.ibp.cz; f. 1955; attached to Acad. of Sciences of the Czech Republic; Dir Dr STANISLAV KOZUBEK.

Botanický ústav AV ČR, V. V. I. (Institute of Botany AS CR): Zámek 1, 252 43 Průhonice; tel. 271015233; fax 271015105; e-mail ibot@ibot.cas.cz; internet www.ibot.cas.cz; attached to Acad. of Sciences of the Czech Republic; Dir Dr JAN KIRSCHNER; publs *Folia Geobotanica* (4 a year), *Index Seminum et Plantarum* (1 a year).

Biologické centrum AV ČR, v.v.i., Entomologický ústav (Biology Centre AS CR v.v.i., Institute of Entomology): Branišovská 1160/31, 370 05 České Budějovice; tel. 385310350; fax 385310354; e-mail entu@ entu.cas.cz; internet www.entu.cas.cz; f. 1962, part of Biology Centre AS CR since 2006; attached to Acad. of Sciences of the Czech Republic; basic and applied research on insects as models for biological research or as pests or species important for environment monitoring; Dir Prof. in FRANTIŠEK SEHNAL; Head Dr JAN ŠULA; publ. *European Journal of Entomology* (4 a year).

Fyziologický ústav AV ČR, v.v.i. (Institute of Physiology AS CR): Vídeňská 1083, 142 20 Prague 4; tel. 241062424; fax 241062488; e-mail fgu@biomed.cas.cz; internet www.biomed.cas.cz; f. 1954; attached to Acad. of Sciences of the Czech Republic; Dir Dr JAROSLAV KUNEŠ; publ. *Physiological Research* (6 a year).

Hydrobiologický ústav AV ČR (Hydrobiological Institute AS CR): Na sádkách 7, 370 05 České Budějovice; tel. 387775881; fax 385310248; e-mail hbu@hbu.cas.cz; internet www.hbu.cas.cz; attached to Acad. of Sciences of the Czech Republic; Dir Dr JOSEF MATÉNA.

Mikrobiologický ústav AV ČR (Institute of Microbiology AS CR): Vídeňská 1083, 142

20 Prague 4; tel. 244472272; fax 244471286; e-mail mbu@biomed.cas.cz; internet www .biomed.cas.cz/mbu; f. 1962; attached to Acad. of Sciences of the Czech Republic; Dir Prof. RNDr BLANKA ŘÍHOVÁ; publ. *Folia Microbiologica* (6 a year).

Parazitologický ústav AV ČR (Institute of Parasitology AS CR): Branišovská 31, 370 05 České Budějovice; tel. 387775403; fax 385310388; e-mail paru@paru.cas.cz; internet www.paru.cas.cz; f. 1962; attached to Acad. of Sciences of the Czech Republic; Dir Dr TOMÁŠ SCHOLZ; publ. *Folia Parasitologica* (4 a year).

Ústav biologie obratlovců AV ČR, v.v.i (Institute of Vertebrate Biology AS CR, v.v.i): Květná 8, 603 65 Brno; tel. 543422538; fax 543211346; e-mail ubo@ivb.cz; internet www .ivb.cz; f. 1954; 50 mems; attached to Acad. of Sciences of the Czech Republic; library of 36,371 vols of zoology; Dir Dr Ing. MARCEL HONZA; publs *Biennial Report IVB, Folia Zoologica* (4 a year).

Ústav experimentální botaniky AV ČR (Institute of Experimental Botany AS CR): Rozvojová 263, 165 02 Prague 6; tel. 225106453; fax 225106456; e-mail zazimalova@ueb.cas.cz; internet www.ueb .cas.cz; f. 1962; attached to Acad. of Sciences of the Czech Republic; Dir Asst Prof. Doc. EVA ZAŽÍMALOVÁ; publs *Biologia Plantarum* (irregular), *Photosynthetica* (irregular).

Ústav fyziky plazmatu AV ČR (Institute of Plasma Physics AS CR): Za Slovankou 3, 182 21 Prague 8; tel. 266052052; fax 286586389; e-mail ipp@ipp.cas.cz; internet www.ipp.cas .cz; f. 1959; attached to Acad. of Sciences of the Czech Republic; Dir Prof. Dr Ing. PAVEL CHRÁSKA.

Ústav molekulární biologie rostlin AV ČR, v.v.i. (Institute of Plant Molecular Biology AS CR, v.v.i.): Branišovská 31, 370 05 České Budějovice; tel. 385310357; fax 385310356; e-mail umbr@umbr.cas.cz; internet www.umbr.cas.cz; f. 1991; attached to Biology Centre, Acad. of Sciences of the Czech Republic; Dir Prof. Dr J. ŠPAK.

Ústav molekulární genetiky AV ČR, v.v.i. (Institute of Molecular Genetics AS CR, v.v.i.): Vídeňská 1083, 142 20 Prague 4; tel. 241063215; fax 224310955; e-mail office@ img.cas.cz; internet www.img.cas.cz; f. 1961 as Institute of Experimental Biology and Genetics; joined with several biochemical laboratories of the Institute of Organic Chemistry and Biochemistry and renamed Institute of Molecular Genetics 1977; public research instn 2007; attached to Acad. of Sciences of the Czech Republic; basic and applied research in molecular biology and genetics and in cell biology, incl. molecular and cellular immunology, functional genomics and bioinformatics, virology, oncogene biology, apoptosis, molecular biology of development, mechanisms of receptor signalling and cell differentiation, biology of cytoskeleton, epigenetic mechanisms, genome stability, and structural biology; Dir Prof. VÁCLAV HOŘEJŠÍ.

Ústav organické chemie a biochemie AV ČR (Institute of Organic Chemistry and Biochemistry AS CR): Flemingovo nám. 2, 166 10 Prague 6; tel. 220183333; fax 220183578; e-mail uochb@uochb.cas.cz; internet www.uochb.cas.cz; f. 1950; attached to Acad. of Sciences of the Czech Republic; Dir Dr ZDENĚK HAVLAS; publ. *Collection of Czechoslovak Chemical Communications* (12 a year).

Ústav půdní biologie AV ČR (Institute of Soil Biology AS CR): Na sádkách 7, České Budějovice; tel. 385310134; fax 385300133; e-mail upb@upb.cas.cz; internet www.upb

.cas.cz; f. 1979; attached to Acad. of Sciences of the Czech Republic; Dir Dr VÁCLAV PIŽL.

Ústav živočišné fyziologie a genetiky AV ČR (Institute of Animal Physiology and Genetics AS CR): Rumburská 89, 277 21 Liběchov; tel. 206639511; fax 206697186; e-mail uzfg@iapg.cas.cz; internet www.iapg .cas.cz/uzfg; attached to Acad. of Sciences of the Czech Republic; Dir Prof. Dr IVAN MÍŠEK.

Mathematical Sciences

Český statistický úřad (Czech Statistical Office): Na padesátém 81, 100 82 Prague 10; tel. and fax 274054070; internet www.czso .cz; f. 1899; library of 27,500 vols; Pres. JAN FISCHER; publs *ČZSO Monthly Statistics, Selected Economic and Social Indicators of the Czech Republic* (4 a year), *Statistical Bulletin* (4 a year).

Matematický ústav AV ČR (Institute of Mathematics AS CR): Žitná 25, 115 67 Prague 1; tel. 222090711; fax 222090701; e-mail mathinst@math.cas.cz; internet www .math.cas.cz; f. 1947; attached to Acad. of Sciences of the Czech Republic; Dir Dr PAVEL KREJČÍ; publs *Applications of Mathematics* (6 a year), *Czechoslovak Mathematical Journal* (4 a year), *Mathematica Bohemica* (4 a year).

Physical Sciences

Astronomický ústav AV ČR (Astronomical Institute AS CR): Fricova 298, 251 65 Ondřejov; tel. 323620113; fax 323620117; e-mail sekretariat@asu.cas.cz; internet www .asu.cas.cz; f. 1950; attached to Acad. of Sciences of the Czech Republic; Dir Dr PETR HEINZEL; publs *Scripta Astronomica* (irregular), *Time and Latitude* (4 a year).

Česká geologická služba (Czech Geological Survey): 118 21 Prague 1, Klárov 3; tel. 257089500; fax 257531376; e-mail secretar@cgu.cz; internet www.geology.cz; f. 1919; library: see Libraries and Archives; Dir Mgr. ZDENĚK VENERA; publs *Bulletin of Geosciences* (4 a year), *Geological Bibliography of the Czech Republic* (1 a year), *Geoscience Research Reports* (1 a year), *Journal of Geological Sciences* (1 a year), *Special Papers* (1 a year).

Fyzikální ústav AV ČR (Institute of Physics AS CR): Na Slovance 2, 182 21 Prague 8; tel. 266053111; fax 286890527; e-mail secretary@fzu.cz; internet www.fzu.cz; f. 1954; attached to Acad. of Sciences of the Czech Republic; Dir Dr KAREL JUNGWIRTH; publs *Československý časopis pro fyziku* (6 a year), *Czechoslovak Journal of Physics* (12 a year), *Jemná mechanika a optika* (Fine Mechanics and Optics, 12 a year).

Geofyzikální ústav AV ČR (Geophysical Institute AS CR): Boční II/1401, 141 31 Prague 4; tel. 267103111; fax 272761549; e-mail gfu@ig.cas.cz; internet www.ig.cas.cz; f. 1953; attached to Acad. of Sciences of the Czech Republic; Dir Dr ALEŠ ŠPIČÁK; publs *Bulletin of the Czechoslovak Seismological Stations* (1 a year), *Studia Geophysica et Geodaetica* (4 a year), *Travaux Géophysiques* (1 a year).

Geologický ústav AV ČR, v.v.i. (Institute of Geology AS CR, v.v.i.): Rozvojová 269, 165 00 Prague 6; tel. 233087111; fax 220922670; e-mail inst@gli.cas.cz; internet www.gli.cas .cz; f. 1957; attached to Acad. of Sciences of the Czech Republic; library of 10,000 vols; geology, esp. petrology, mineralogy, basin analysis and tectonics, palaeontology, environmental geology and geochemistry, karstology, pedology; Dir Dr VÁCLAV CÍLEK; publs *Geolines* (2 a year), *Institute Research Reports* (1 a year).

Společná laboratoř chemie pevných látek AV ČR a Univerzity Pardubice (Joint Laboratory of Solid State Chemistry

of the Institute of Macromolecular Chemistry of AS CR and Pardubice University): Studentská 84, 532 10 Pardubice; tel. 406036150; fax 406036011; e-mail slchpl@ upce.cz; internet slchpl.upce.cz; f. 1986; attached to Acad. of Sciences of the Czech Republic; Head Dr LADISLAV TICHÝ.

Státní úřad pro jadernou bezpečnost (State Office for Nuclear Safety): Senovážné nám. 9, 110 00 Prague 1; tel. 221624111; fax 221624704; e-mail podatelna@sujb.cz; internet www.sujb.cz; f. 1993; regulatory activities in nuclear safety, radiation protection, inspection of materials and technologies of dual use for nuclear, biological and chemical weapons; Chair. DANA DRÁBOVÁ.

Ústav analytické chemie AV ČR (Institute of Analytical Chemistry AS CR): Veveří 97, 602 00 Brno; tel. 532290182; fax 541212113; e-mail uiach@iach.cz; internet www.iach.cz/uiach; f. 1956; attached to Acad. of Sciences of the Czech Republic; research in analytical chemistry, devt of theory, methodology, and instrumentation for analytical chemistry; Head Prof. LUDMILA KRIVANKOVA; publ. *Research Activities and Future Trends* (irregular).

Ústav anorganické chemie AV ČR, v.v.i. (Institute of Inorganic Chemistry AS CR, v.v.i.): 250 68 Husinec-Řež; tel. 220940158; fax 220941502; e-mail sekretar@iic.cas.cz; internet www.iic.cas.cz; f. 1959; attached to Acad. of Sciences of the Czech Republic; basic and applied research, preparation of inorganic compounds and materials and their applications in the field of inorganic chemistry; branches of inorganic chemistry, incl. physical chemistry, solid state physics, polymer chemistry, and ecology; bio-inorganic chemistry; attached laboratories of inorganic materials and low temperatures located in Prague; Dir Ing. JANA BLUDSKÁ; publs *Bulletin* (1 a year), *Ceramics–Silikáty* (6 a year).

Ústav chemických procesů AV ČR (Institute of Chemical Process Fundamentals AS CR): Rozvojová 135, 165 02 Prague 6; tel. 220390111; fax 220920661; e-mail icecas@ icpf.cas.cz; internet www.icpf.cas.cz; f. 1960; attached to Acad. of Sciences of the Czech Republic; Dir Prof. JIŘÍ DRAHOŠ.

Ústav fyzikální chemie J. Heyrovského AV ČR, v.v.i. (J. Heyrovský Institute of Physical Chemistry AS CR, v.v.i.): Dolejškova 3, 182 23 Prague 8; tel. 286583014; fax 286582307; e-mail director@jh-inst.cas.cz; internet www.jh-inst.cas.cz; f. 1972; attached to Acad. of Sciences of the Czech Republic; research in physical chemistry, electrochemistry and chemical physics; library of 18,000 vols, 200 current periodical titles; Dir Prof. Dr ZDENĚK SAMEC; publs *J. Am. Chem. Soc., J. Chem. Phys, J. Phys. Chem.*

Ústav fyziky atmosféry AV ČR, v.v.i. (Institute of Atmospheric Physics AS CR, v.v.i.): 4, Boční II/1401, 141 31 Prague; tel. 272016011; fax 272763745; e-mail iap@ufa .cas.cz; internet www.ufa.cas.cz; f. 1964; attached to Acad. of Sciences of the Czech Republic; monitors atmospheric pollution; carries out research in meteorology, climatology, and ionospheric and magnetospheric physics, space physics, wind energy; library of 8,210 vols, 39 periodicals; Dir Doc. ZBYNĚK SOKOL; Librarian JANA FIALOVA.

Ústav fyziky materiálů AV ČR (Institute of the Physics of Materials AS CR): Žižkova 22, 616 62 Brno; tel. 541212286; fax 541212301; e-mail secretar@ipm.cz; internet www.ipm.cz; f. 1956; attached to Acad. of Sciences of the Czech Republic; Dir Assoc. Prof. Dr PETR LUKÁŠ; publs *Engineering Mechanics* (6 a year), *Metallic Materials* (6 a year).

Ústav jaderné fyziky AV ČR (Nuclear Physics Institute AS CR): 250 68 Řež; tel. 220941147; fax 220941130; e-mail ujf@ujf.cas.cz; internet www.ujf.cas.cz; f. 1955; attached to Acad. of Sciences of the Czech Republic; operated by Nuclear Research Institute Řež plc; library of 50,000 vols; Dir Dr JAN DOBEŠ; Scientific Sec. JAROSLAV DITTRICH.

Ústav jaderného výzkumu Řež a.s. (Nuclear Research Institute Řež plc): Husinec-Řež 130, 250 68 Řež; tel. 266172000; fax 220940840; e-mail paz@ujv.cz; internet www.ujv.cz; f. 1955; nuclear power and safety; fuel cycle chemistry; radiopharmaceuticals; library of 101,200 vols, 21,000 reports; Chair. FRANTIŠEK PAZDERA; publ. *Nucleon* (4 a year).

Ústav makromolekulární chemie AV ČR (Institute of Macromolecular Chemistry AS CR): Heyrovský nám. 2, 162 06 Prague 6; tel. 296809111; fax 296809410; e-mail office@imc.cas.cz; internet www.imc.cas.cz; f. 1959; attached to Acad. of Sciences of the Czech Republic; Dir FRANTIŠEK RYPÁČEK.

Ústav pro hydrodynamiku AV ČR, v.v.i. (Institute of Hydrodynamics AS CR, v.v.i.): Pod Patankou 30/5, 166 12 Prague 6; tel. 233109011; fax 233324361; e-mail ih@ih.cas.cz; internet www.ih.cas.cz; f. 1953; attached to Acad. of Sciences of the Czech Republic; research in hydromechanics, rheology and hydrology; Dir Dr ZDENEK CHARA; publs *Engineering Mechanics* (6 a year), *Journal of Hydrology and Hydromechanics* (6 a year).

Ústav struktury a mechaniky hornin AV ČR (Institute of Rock Structure and Mechanics AS CR): V Holešovičkách 41, 182 09 Prague 8; tel. 266009111; fax 284680105; e-mail irsm@irsm.cas.cz; internet www.irsm.cas.cz; f. 1958; attached to Acad. of Sciences of the Czech Republic; library of 28,000 vols; Dir Ing. KAREL BALIK; publs *Acta Montana, Series A: Geodynamics* (in English, irregular), *Acta Montana, Series B: Fuel, Carbon, Mineral Processing* (in English, irregular), *Acta Montana, Series AB: Geodynamics, Fuel, Carbon, Mineral Processing* (in English and Czech, irregular).

Ústav termomechaniky AV ČR (Institute of Thermomechanics AS CR): Dolejškova 5, 182 00 Prague 8; tel. 286890383; fax 286584695; e-mail secr@it.cas.cz; internet www.it.cas.cz; f. 1954; attached to Acad. of Sciences of the Czech Republic; library of 12,000 vols; Dir Prof. ZBYNEK JANOUR; publs *Acta Technica CSAV* (4 a year), *Engineering Mechanics* (6 a year).

PHILOSOPHY AND PSYCHOLOGY

Centrum pro teoretická studia Univerzity Karlovy (Centre for Theoretical Study at Charles University): Jilská 1, 110 00 Prague 1; tel. 222220671; fax 222220653; e-mail office@cts.cuni.cz; internet www.cts.cuni.cz; attached to Acad. of Sciences of the Czech Republic; Dir Dr IVAN M. HAVEL.

Filozofický ústav AV ČR (Institute of Philosophy AS CR): Jilská 1, 110 00 Prague; tel. 222220124; fax 222220108; e-mail flusekr@site.cas.cz; internet www.flu.cas.cz; f. 1990; attached to Acad. of Sciences of the Czech Republic; Dir Dr PAVEL BARAN; publs *Acta Comeniana* (irregular), *Filosofický časopis* (Philosophical Review, 6 a year), *Teorie vědy* (4 a year).

Psychologický ústav AV ČR (Institute of Psychology AS CR): Veveří 97, 602 00 Brno; tel. 532290270; e-mail cermak@psu.cas.cz; internet www.psu.cas.cz; f. 1967; attached to Acad. of Sciences of the Czech Republic; Dir Doc. Dr IVO ČERMÁK; publs *Bulletin Psychologického ústavu* (irregular), *Československá psychologie* (6 a year), *Zprávy* (irregular).

RELIGION, SOCIOLOGY AND ANTHROPOLOGY

Etnologický ústav AV ČR, v.v.i. (Institute of Ethnology AS CR, v.v.i.): Na Florenci 3, 110 00 Prague; tel. 222828503; fax 222828503; e-mail office@eu.cas.cz; internet www.eu.cas.cz; f. 1954; attached to Acad. of Sciences of the Czech Republic; library of 80,000 ; Dir Dr ZDENĚK UHEREK; publs *Český lid: Etnologický časopis / Český lid Ethnological* (4 a year), *Hudební věda* (4 a year).

Sociologický ústav AV ČR (Institute of Sociology AS CR): Jilská 1, 110 00 Prague; tel. 222221753; e-mail socmail@soc.cas.cz; internet www.soc.cas.cz; f. 1990; attached to Acad. of Sciences of the Czech Republic; Dir Dr MARIE ČERMÁKOVÁ; publs *Historická demografie* (1 a year), *Sociologický časopis* (Czech Sociological Review, 6 a year).

TECHNOLOGY

Laboratoř anorganických materiálů (Laboratory of Inorganic Materials): Institute of Rock Structure and Mechanics V, Holešovičkách 41, 182 09 Prague 8; tel. 220445191; fax 266009421; e-mail lubomir.nemec@vscht.cz; internet www.vscht.cz/sls; f. 1961; attached to Acad. of Sciences of the Czech Republic and Institute of Chemical Technology; Dir Prof. LUBOMÍR NĚMEC.

SVUSS Praha, s. r. o.: Na Harfě 336/9, 190 00 Prague 9–Vysočany; tel. (2) 66035661; fax (2) 66034712; e-mail suchanek@svuss.cz; internet www.svuss.cz; f. 1998; technical studies in engineering, heat transfer and the power industry; carries out tests and research in the field of thermodynamics; library of 10,000 vols; Dir Ing. MIROSLAV SUCHANEK (acting).

Ústav fotoniky a elektroniky AV ČR (Institute of Photonics and Electronics AS CR): Chaberská 57, 182 51 Prague 8; tel. 284681804; fax 284680222; e-mail ufe@ufe.cz; internet www.ure.cas.cz; f. 1955 as Ústav radiotechniky a elektroniky AV ČR, present name 2007; attached to Acad. of Sciences of the Czech Republic; research and devt in photonics, optoelectronics, and signals and systems; library of 16,500 vols, 390 periodicals; Dir Dr Ing. VLASTIMIL MATĚJEC.

Ústav informatiky AV ČR, v.v.i. (Institute of Computer Science AS CR, v.v.i.): Pod Vodárenskou věží 2, 182 07 Prague 8; tel. 266052083; fax 286585789; e-mail ics@cs.cas.cz; internet www.cs.cas.cz; attached to Acad. of Sciences of the Czech Republic; f. 1975; library of 8,000 vols; Dir Prof. Dr JIRI WIEDERMANN; publ. *Neural Network Word* (int. journal on neural and mass-parallel computing and information systems).

Ústav přístrojové techniky AV ČR, v.v.i. (Institute of Scientific Instruments AS CR, v.v.i.): Královopolská 147, 612 64 Brno; tel. 541514111; fax 541514402; e-mail institute@isibrno.cz; internet www.isibrno.cz; f. 1957; attached to Acad. of Sciences of the Czech Republic; methodology in selected areas of physics, chemistry, technology, main programs: electron optics and microscopy, vacuum technologies, coherence optics, magnetic resonance, bioinformatics; Dir Dr LUDĚK FRANK.

Ústav teoretické a aplikované mechaniky AV ČR (Institute of Theoretical and Applied Mechanics AS CR): Prosecká 76, 190 00 Prague 9; tel. 286882121; fax 286884634; e-mail itam@itam.cas.cz; internet www.itam.cas.cz; attached to Acad. of Sciences of the Czech Republic; Dir Dr MILOŠ DRDÁCKÝ; publ. *Engineering Mechanics* (6 a year).

Ústav teorie informace a automatizace AV ČR (Institute of Information Theory and Automation AS CR): POB 18, 182 08 Prague 8; Pod Vodárenskou věží 4, 182 08 Prague 8; tel. 266053111; fax 286890378; e-mail utia@utia.cas.cz; internet www.utia.cas.cz; f. 1959; attached to Acad. of Sciences of the Czech Republic; Dir Prof. Dr JAN FLUSSER; publ. *Kybernetica* (6 a year).

Ústav termomechaniky AV ČR, v.v.i. (Institute of Thermomechanics AS CR, v.v.i.): Dolejškova 1402/5, 182 00 Praha 8; tel. 266052021; fax 286584695; e-mail secr@it.cas.cz; internet www.it.cas.cz; f. 1953, merged with the Institute of Electrical Engineering in 2006; attached to Acad. of Sciences of the Czech Republic; basic research in fluid dynamics, thermodynamics, dynamics of mechanical systems, solid mechanics, interactions of fluids and solids, environmental aerodynamics, biomechanics, mechatronics, electrophysics, electrical machines, drives and electronics and material diagnostics.; Dir Prof. ZBYNĚK JAŇOUR; Deputy Dir Dr JIŘÍ PLEŠEK; publs *Acta Technica* (4 a year), *Engineering Mechanics* (6 a year).

VÚTS Liberec a.s. (Research Institute for Textile Machines, Liberec Co.): U jezu 4, 461 19 Liberec 4; tel. 485301111; fax 485302402; e-mail vuts@vuts.cz; internet www.vuts.cz; f. 1951; library of 10,000 vols; 154 mems; Gen. Dir Prof. Ing. MIROSLAV VÁCLAVÍK.

Libraries and Archives

Brno

Knihovna Moravské galerie v Brně (Library of the Moravian Gallery in Brno): Husova 18, 662 26 Brno; tel. 532169127; fax 532169180; e-mail knihovna@moravska-galerie.cz; internet www.moravska-galerie.cz; f. 1873; 110,000 vols; Dir Dr HANA KARKANOVÁ.

Moravská zemská knihovna (Moravian Library): Kounicova 65A, 601 87 Brno; tel. 541646111; fax 541646100; e-mail mzk@mzk.cz; internet www.mzk.cz; f. 1808; 3,850,000 vols, 4,300 periodicals; Dir Dr J. KUBÍČEK.

Ústřední knihovna a informační středisko Veterinární a farmaceutické univerzity (Central Library and Information Centre of the University of Veterinary and Pharmaceutical Sciences): Palackého 1–3, 612 42 Brno; tel. 541562080; e-mail gect@vfu.cz; internet sis.vfu.cz; f. 1919; 174,126 vols; Chief Librarian TOMÁŠ GEC; publ. *Acta veterinaria Brno* (4 a year).

České Budějovice

Státní vědecká knihovna (State Research Library): Na Sadech 26-27, Lidická 1, 370 59 České Budějovice; tel. 386111211; fax 386351901; e-mail library@cbvk.cz; internet www.cbvk.cz; f. 1885; 1,500,000 vols; Dir Dr KVETA CEMPIRKOVA.

Hradec Králové

Studijní a vědecká knihovna (Research Library): Pospíšilova 395, POB 7, 500 03 Hradec Králové; tel. 495514871; fax 495511781; e-mail knihovna@svkhk.cz; internet www.svkhk.cz; f. 1949; 1,189,172 vols; Dir Mgr EVA SVOBODOVÁ.

Liberec

Krajská vědecká knihovna v Liberci (Research Library in Liberec): Rumjancevova 1362/1, 460 53 Liberec; tel. 482412111; fax 482412122; e-mail library@kvkli.cz; internet www.kvkli.cz; f. 1945; 760,000 books, 1,600 periodicals, 29,000 vols of standards, 380,000 vols of patents, 27,000 vols of printed music, 9,000 sound recordings, 3,500 vols of maps, 600 CD-ROMs; Dir PAVEL HARVÁNEK; publ.

Světlík (World of the Liberec Region Libraries, 6 a year).

Olomouc

Vědecká knihovna v Olomouci (Research Library in Olomouc): Bezručova 3, 779 11 Olomouc; tel. 585223441; fax 585225774; e-mail info@vkol.cz; internet www.vkol.cz; f. 1566; 2,034,000 vols, 1,448 MSS, 1,800 incunabula, 70,000 old prints; Dir JITKA HOLÁSKOVÁ; publ. *Krok* (4 a year).

Ostrava

Moravskoslezská vědecká knihovna v Ostravě (Moravian-Silesian Research Library in Ostrava): Prokešovo nám. 9, 728 00 Ostrava; tel. 596118881; fax 596138322; e-mail msvk@svkos.cz; internet www.svkos .cz; f. 1951; 1,071,144 vols, 577,855 books, 3,679 newspapers and journals, 8,190 sound documents, 60,132 standards, 283,375 patents; Dir Ing. LEA PRCHALOVÁ.

Ústřední knihovna Vysoké školy báňské-Technické univerzity Ostrava (Central Library of the VSB-Technical University of Ostrava): 17 listopadu 15, 708 33 Ostrava-Poruba; tel. 596991278; fax 596994598; e-mail knihovna@vsb.cz; internet www.knihovna.vsb.cz; f. 1849; 380,000 vols; Dir DANIELA TKAČÍKOVÁ; publ. *Sborník vědeckých prací Vysoké školy báňské—Technické univerzity Ostrava* (Transactions, irregular).

Plzeň

Studijní a vědecká knihovna Plzeňského kraje (Education and Research Library of Pilsener Region): Smetanovy sady 2, 305 48 Plzeň; tel. 377224249; fax 377325478; e-mail svk@svkpl.cz; internet www.svkpl.cz; f. 1950; 791,000 books, 1,700 current periodicals, 793,000 documents; Dir Dr JAROSLAV VYČICHLO; publs *Přírůstky zahraniční literatury* (foreign accessions, 4 a year), *Západní Čechy v tisku* (West Bohemia in Print).

Prague

Archiv AV ČR, vědecký útvar Masarykova ústavu a Archivu AVČR, v.v.i. (Archives AS CR, a scientific division of the Masaryk Institute and Archives ASCR, v.v.i.): Gabčíkova 2362/10, 182 00 Prague 8; tel. 286010110; fax 284680150; e-mail sekretariat@mua.cas.cz; internet www.mua .cas.cz; f. 1953; attached to Acad. of Sciences of the Czech Republic; 60,000 vols; Dir Dr LUCIE KOSTRBOVÁ; publs *Práce z Archivu Akademie věd* (Studies of the Archives of the Acad. of Sciences, 1 a year), *Práce z dějin Akademie věd* (Studies on the History of the Academy of Sciences, 2 a year), *Práce z dějin věd* (Studies on the History of Sciences and the Humanities, 2 a year), *Studia historiae academiae scientiarum—Práce z dějin akademie věd* (Studies on the History of the Academy of Sciences, 1 a year), *Studie o rukopisech* (Codicological Studies, 1 a year).

Knihovna Akademie Věd Česky republiky (Library of the Academy of Sciences of the Czech Republic): Národní 3, 115 22 Prague 1; tel. 224240524; fax 224240611; e-mail infoknav@lib.cas.cz; internet www.lib .cas.cz; f. 1952; 1m. vols, 2,102 periodicals; headquarters of the network of information centres and spec. libraries of academic institutes; Dir IVANA KADLECOVÁ.

Knihovna Archeologického ústavu AV ČR, Praha, v. v. i. (Library of the Archaeological Institute of the Academy of Sciences of the Czech Republic): Letenská 4, 118 01 Prague; tel. (2) 57014318; fax (2) 57532288; e-mail knihovna@arup.cas.cz; internet www .arup.cas.cz; f. 1919; 12,426 vols, colln severely affected by flooding in 2002; Chief Librarian EVA ŠOUFKOVÁ; publs *Archeologické rozhledy* (4 a year), *Castellologica bohemica* (irregular), *Castrum Pragense* (irregular), *Mediaevalia archaeologica* (irregular), *Památky archeologické* (1 a year), *Památky Archeologické–Supplementum* (irregular), *Výzkumy v Čechách* (irregular).

Knihovna České geologické služby (Library of the Czech Geological Survey): Klárov 3, 118 21 Prague 1; tel. 257089411; fax 257320438; e-mail breit@cgu.cz; internet www.geology.cz; f. 1924; archive of 60,000 vols; 168,000 vols; Head of Library RNDr HANA BREITEROVÁ; publs *Geological Bibliography of the Czech Republic* (1 a year), *Library of the Geological Survey* (irregular).

Knihovna Evangelické teologické fakulty Univerzity Karlovy (Library of the Protestant Theological Faculty of the Charles University): Černá 9, 115 55 Prague 1; tel. 221988104; fax 221988215; e-mail library@etf.cuni.cz; internet www.etf.cuni.cz/ ~library; f. 1919; 190,000 vols, 185 current periodicals; Dir BARBORA DROBÍKOVÁ; publs *Communio Viatorum* (3 a year), *Teologická reflexe* (2 a year).

Knihovna Národní galerie (Library of the National Gallery): Národní galerie v Praze, Staroměstské nám. 12, 110 15 Prague; Hradčanské nám. 15, 119 04 Prague 1; tel. 220515458; fax 220513180; e-mail library@ ngprague.cz; internet www.ngprague.cz; f. 1880; 100,000 vols; Dir Dr MARTINA HORÁKOVÁ.

Knihovna Národního muzea (Library of the National Museum): Václavské nám. 68, 115 79 Prague 1; tel. 224497111; fax 224224914; e-mail jarmila_kucerova@nm.cz; internet www.nm.cz; f. 1818; 3.6m. vols; Dir Mgr MARTIN SEKERA; Librarian JARMILA KUCEROVA; publ. *Sborník Národního muzea, řada C–Literární Historie*.

Knihovna Národního technického muzea (Library of the National Technical Museum): Kostelní 42, 170 78 Prague 7; tel. 220399233; fax 220399200; e-mail knihovna@ntm.cz; internet www.ntm.cz; f. 1833; 6 mems; 200,000 vols; Chief Librarian Mgr JANA ČEREŠŇOVÁ.

Knihovna Orientálního ústavu Akademie věd České republiky (Library of the Oriental Institute of the Academy of Sciences of the Czech Republic): Pod vodárenskou věží 2, 182 08 Prague; tel. 266053950; fax 286581835; e-mail jan.luffer@orient.cas.cz; internet www.orient.cas.cz; f. 1929; 210,000 vols; 'Lu Xun' Chinese library of 67,000 vols; Korean library of 3,500 vols; Tibetan colln; Librarian Mgr JAN LUFFER; publs *Archiv orientální* (4 a year), *Nový Orient* (4 a year).

Knihovna Uměleckoprůmyslového musea (Museum of Decorative Arts Library): 17 listopadu 2, 110 01 Prague 1; tel. 251093135; fax 251093296; e-mail knihovna@upm.cz; internet www.knihovna .upm.cz; f. 1885; 175,000 vols; Dir Dr JARMILA OKROUHLÍKOVÁ; publ. *Acta UPM* (irregular).

Městská knihovna v Praze (Municipal Library of Prague): Mariánské nám. 1, 115 72 Prague 1; tel. 222113306; fax 222328230; e-mail knihovna@mlp.cz; internet www.mlp .cz; f. 1891; central library, 42 brs and 2 mobile libraries; 2,334,726 vols, incl. books, journals, maps, CDs, DVDs, MP3s, reproductions; Dir Dr TOMÁŠ ŘEHÁK.

Národní knihovna České republiky (National Library of the Czech Republic): Klementinum 190, 110 00 Prague 1; tel. 221663111; fax 221663277; e-mail sekret .ur@nkp.cz; internet www.nkp.cz; f. 1366; 6,559,069 vols, 18,707 MSS, 3,500 incunabula, 200,000 early printed books; Dir Ing. TOMÁŠ BÖHM; publs *Knihovna-knihovnická revue*, *Miscellanea oddělení rukopisů a starých tisků* (1 a year), *Národní knihovna* (4 a year).

Branch Library:

Slovanská knihovna (Slavonic Library): Klementinum 190, 110 00 Prague; tel. 221663356; fax 221663176; e-mail sluzby .sk@nkp.cz; internet www.nkp.cz/slk; f. 1924; 775,000 vols; Dir Dr LUKÁŠ BABKA.

Národní lékařská knihovna (National Medical Library): Nové Město, Sokolská 54, 121 32 Prague 2; tel. 296335911; fax 296335959; e-mail nml@nlk.cz; internet www.nlk.cz; f. 1949; 335,000 vols, 1,500 current periodicals, 6,000 doctoral theses; WHO documentation centre; oversees translation of MeSH into Czech; operates union catalogue of medical literature; Dir HELENA BOUZKOVA; publs *Bibliographia medica čechoslovaca* (12 a year), *Referátový výběr* (series of 4 abstracts journals, 4 or 6 a year).

Národní pedagogická knihovna Komenského (Comenius National Library of Education): Mikulandská 5, 116 74 Prague 1; tel. 221966402; fax 224930550; e-mail library@npkk.cz; internet www.npkk.cz; f. 1919; 471,000 vols; youth br. (Suk Library) of 58,000 vols (since 1790); Dir ALICE KOŠKOVÁ.

Státní technická knihovna (State Technical Library): Mariánské nám. 5, POB 206, 110 01 Prague 1; tel. 2221663111; fax 222221340; e-mail informace@stk.cz; internet www.stk.cz; f. 1718; 1,501,632 vols, 1,524 periodicals, 31 databases; Dir Ing. MARTIN SVOBODA.

Univerzita Karlova, Pedagogická fakulta, Ústřední knihovna (Charles University Faculty of Education, Central Library): Rettigova 4, 116 39 Prague 1; tel. and fax 296242420; e-mail knihovna@pedf .cuni.cz; internet beta.pedf.cuni.cz; f. 1948; 190,859 vols, 239 periodicals; Dir Mgr JITKA BÍLKOVÁ.

Úřad Průmyslového Vlastnictví (Industrial Property Office): Antonína Čermáka 2A, 160 68 Prague 6-Bubeneč; tel. 220383111; fax 224324718; e-mail objednavky@upv.cz; internet www.upv.cz; 30m. documents; Dir of Patent Information Dept Ing. MIROSLAV PACLÍK.

Ústav dějin Univerzity Karlovy a Archiv Univerzity Karlovy Library (Institute of the History of Charles University and Archive of Charles University): Ovocný trh 5, 116 36 Prague 1; tel. 224491463; fax 224491670; e-mail udauk@ruk.cuni.cz; internet udauk .cuni.cz; focuses on history of education and schooling in Czech lands (spec. focus on Charles University); 47,000 vols, 55 km of archival material; Librarian Dr JIŘINA URBANOVÁ; Archivist Dr MAREK DURČANSKÝ; publ. *Acta Universitatis Carolinae—Historia Universitatis Carolinae Pragensis*.

Ústav vědeckých informací 1. lékařské fakulty, Univerzita Karlova (Institute of Scientific Information, First Medical Faculty, Charles University): U Nemocnice 4, 121 08 Prague 2; tel. 224965600; fax 224965601; e-mail knihovna@lf1.cuni.cz; internet uvi.lf1 .cuni.cz; f. 1949; 450,512 vols, 712 current periodicals; Dir Dr HANA SKÁLOVÁ; Sec. BĚLA ČERNÁ; publs *Acta Universitatis Carolinae Medica, Folia Biologica, Prague Medical Report, Proceedings of the Scientific Conferences, Sborník lékařský*.

Ústav zemědělských a potravinářských informací (Institute of Agricultural and Food Information): Londýnská 55, 120 21 Prague 2; tel. 224256387; fax 224253938; e-mail knihovna@uzpi.cz; internet www .knihovna.uzpi.cz; f. 1993; 1.2m. vols; Dir

Ing. C. PERLÍN; publs *Genetika a šlechtění* (Genetics and Plant Breeding, 4 a year), *Lesnictví* (Forest Science, 12 a year), *Ochrana rostlin* (Plant Protection Science, 4 a year), *Potravinářské vědy* (Food Science, 6 a year), *Rostlinná výroba* (Plant Production, 12 a year), *Veterinární medicina* (Veterinary Medicine, 12 a year), *Zahradnictví* (Horticulture, 4 a year), *Zemědělská ekonomika* (Agricultural Economics, 12 a year), *Zemědělská technika* (Agricultural Engineering, 4 a year), *Živočišná výroba* (Journal of Animal Science, 12 a year).

Ústřední tělovýchovná knihovna (Central Library of Physical Training): José Martího 31, 162 52 Prague 6; tel. 220172158; fax 220172018; e-mail utk@ftvs .cuni.cz; internet www.ftvs.cuni.cz/knihovna; f. 1927; 300,000 vols; Dir Dr JANA BĚLÍKOVÁ; publ. *Acta Universitatis Carolinae Kinanthropologica*.

Ústřední zemědělská knihovna (Central Agricultural Library): Slezská 7, POB 39, 120 56 Prague 2; tel. 227010111; fax 227010114; e-mail uzpi@uzpi.cz; internet www.uzpi.cz; f. 1926; a section of the Institute of Agricultural and Food Information; 1.1m. vols; Dir Dr BAŠEK VÁCLAV; publ. *Seznam časopisů* (List of Periodicals, 1 a year).

Ústí nad Labem

Severočeská vědecká knihovna (North Bohemian Research Library): POB 134, W. Churchilla 3, 401 34 Ústí nad Labem; tel. 475209126; fax 475200045; e-mail library@ svkul.cz; internet www.svkul.cz; f. 1945; inter library loan; 12,000 mems; 776,000 vols; Dir ALEŠ BROŽEK; publ. *Výběr kulturních výročí* (online at www.svkul.cz/knihovna/dokumenty).

Museums and Art Galleries

Brno

Moravská galerie v Brně (Moravian Gallery in Brno): Husova 18, 662 26 Brno; tel. 532169111; fax 532169180; e-mail info@ moravska-galerie.cz; internet www .moravska-galerie.cz; f. 1873; mostly European fine and applied art of all periods; library of 120,000 vols; Dir MAREK POKORNÝ; publ. *Bulletin* (1 a year).

Moravské zemské muzeum (Moravian Provincial Museum): Zelný trh 6, 659 37 Brno; tel. 533435220; fax 533435313; e-mail mzm@mzm.cz; internet www.mzm.cz; f. 1817; history, natural history, geology, arts, anthropology, horticulture; library of 260,000 vols; Dir Dr MARTIN REISSNER; publs *Acta Musei Moraviae–Scientiae Biologicae* (2 a year), *Acta Musei Moraviae–Scientiae Geologicae* (2 a year), *Acta Musei Moraviae– Scientiae Sociales* (2 a year), *Anthropologie* (3 a year), *Folia Ethnografica* (2 a year), *Folia Mendeliana* (2 a year), *Folia Numismatica* (2 a year).

Muzeum města Brna (Brno Municipal Museum): Špilberk 1, 662 24 Brno; tel. 542123611; fax 542123613; e-mail muzeum .brno@spilberk.cz; internet www.spilberk.cz; f. 1904; history of Brno and Špilberk Castle; art gallery; Dir Dr PAVEL CIPRIAN.

Technické muzeum v Brně (Technical Museum in Brno): Purkyňova 105, 612 00 Brno; tel. 541421411; fax 541214418; e-mail info@technicalmuseum.cz; internet www .technicalmuseum.cz; f. 1961; library of 42,000 vols; Dir VLASTIMIL VYKYDAL; publs *Archeologia technica* (1 a year), *Muzejní*

noviny, *Nožířské listy* (1 a year), *Sborník z konzervátorského a restaurátorského semináře* (1 a year).

České Budějovice

Jihočeské muzeum v Českých Budějovicích (South Bohemian Museum in České Budějovice): Dukelská 1, 370 51 České Budějovice; tel. 387929311; fax 386356447; e-mail muzeumcb@muzeumcb.cz; internet www.muzeumcb.cz; f. 1877; history, archaeology, natural history, arts; Dir PAVEL SAFR; publs *Archeologické výzkumy v jižních Čechách* (archaeology, 1 a year), *Jihočeský sborník historický* (history, 1 a year), *Sborník Přírodní vědy* (nature, 1 a year), *Výběr Časopis pro historii a vlastivědu jižních Čech* (regional and cultural history, 4 a year).

Cheb

Krajské muzeum Cheb (Cheb Regional Museum): nám. Krále Jiřího z Poděbrad 493/4, 350 11 Cheb; tel. 354400620; fax 354422292; e-mail sekretariat@muzeumcheb .cz; internet www.muzeumcheb.cz; f. 1874; history, local ceramics; library of 15,000 vols; spec. colln: library of Franciscan order; Dir Dr EVA DITTERTOVÁ; publ. *Sborník chebského muzea* (1 a year).

Chrudim

Muzeum loutkářských kultur (Museum of Puppets): Břetislavova 74, 537 60 Chrudim; tel. 469620310; fax 469620650; e-mail puppets@puppets.cz; internet www.puppets .cz; f. 1972; Dir Mgr ALENA EXNAROVÁ.

Harrachov

Muzeum skla (Glass Museum): Harrachov 95, 512 46 Harrachov; tel. 481528141; fax 481528148; e-mail obchod@sklarnaharrachov .cz; internet www.sklarnaharrachov.cz; f. 1972; Dir K. PIPEK.

Hluboká nad Vltavou

Alšova jihočeská galerie (Aleš South Bohemian Gallery): Zámak è. 144, 373 41 Hluboká nad Vltavou; tel. 387967041; fax 387965436; e-mail ajg@ajg.cz; internet www .ajg.cz; f. 1953; Czech art since 13th century, 16th–18th century European art, Czech and world ceramics since early 20th century; library of 12,950 vols; Dir Dr HYNEK RULÍŠEK.

Hradec Králové

Muzeum východních Čech, Hradec Králové (Museum of East Bohemia, Hradec Králové): Eliščino nábřeží 465, 500 01 Hradec Králové; tel. 495512462; fax 495512899; e-mail info@muzeumhk.cz; internet www .muzeumhk.cz; f. 1879; natural sciences, history, archeology, education; 1866 War Memorial; library of 70,000 vols; Dir Dr NADA MACHKOVA PRAJZOVA; publs *Acta* (irregular), *Fontes* (irregular), *Historická fotografie* (irregular), *Královéhradecko* (irregular), *Zpravodaj muzea v Hradci Králové* (irregular).

Hukvaldy

Památník Leoše Janáčka (Leos Janacek Museum): Smetanova 14, Brno; tel. 541212811; e-mail vvejvodova@mzm.cz; internet www.mzm.cz; f. 1933; renovated original house of Leos Janacek; exhibits life and work of Leos Janacek; audiovisual hall; Dir B. VOLNÝ.

Jablonec nad Nisou

Muzeum skla a bižuterie (Museum of Glass and Jewellery): Muzea 398/4, 466 01 Jablonec nad Nisou; tel. 483369011; fax 483369012; e-mail msbjbc@quick.cz; internet www.msb-jablonec.cz; f. 1961; Bohemian glass, Jablonec jewellery; library of 15,000 vols; Dir Ing. JAROSLAVA SLABÁ.

Karlovy Vary

Galerie umění Karlovy Vary (Karlovy Vary Art Gallery): Goethova stezka 6, 360 01 Karlovy Vary; tel. 353224387; fax 353224388; e-mail info@galeriekvary.cz; internet www.galeriekvary.cz; f. 1953; 20thcentury Czech art; Dir JAN SAMEC.

Karlovarské muzeum (Karlovy Vary Museum): Nová louka 23, 360 01 Karlovy Vary; e-mail sekretariat@kvmuz.cz; internet www.kvmuz.cz; f. 1870; history, natural history, arts; Dir JAN BATÍK.

Zlatý klíč muzeum (Golden Key Museum): Lázeňská 3, 360 01 Karlovy Vary; tel. 353223888; f. 1960; art nouveau paintings; Dir MARIE GULGOVÁ.

Kolín

Regionální muzeum v Kolíně (Kolín Regional Museum): Brandlova 35, 280 02 Kolín; tel. 321723841; fax 321719018; e-mail muzeum@kolin.cz; internet www.kolin.cz/ muzeum; f. 1895; local history; open-air museum at Kouřim; library of 49,500 vols; Dir JARMILA VALENTOVÁ.

Kopřivnice

Technické muzeum Tatra (Tatra Cars Museum): Záhumenní 367/1, 742 21 Kopřivnice; tel. 556871106; fax 556821415; e-mail direktor@tatramuseum.cz; internet www .tatramuseum.cz; f. 1947; Tatra cars, trucks, railway carriages, aircraft, engines and chassis, history of Tatra production; Dir LUMÍR KAVÁLEK.

Kutná Hora

České muzeum stříba (Czech Silver Museum): Hrádek, Barborská 28, 284 01 Kutná Hora; tel. 327512159; fax 327513813; e-mail muzeum@kutnohorsko.cz; internet muzeum.kutnohorsko.cz; f. 1877; medieval castle, medieval silver mine, Gothic town house, town life in 17th–19th centuries; Dir S. HRABÁNKOVÁ.

Liberec

Oblastní galerie v Liberci (Liberec Regional Art Gallery): U Tiskárny 1, 460 01 Liberec 5; tel. 485106325; fax 485106321; e-mail oblgal@ogl.cz; internet www.ogl.cz; f. 1873; 16th to 18th century Dutch and Flemish painting, 19th century French landscapes, 20th century Czech art; Dir Dr VĚRA LAŠTOVKOVÁ.

Severočeské muzeum v Liberci (North Bohemian Museum in Liberec): Masarykova tř. 11, 460 01 Liberec; tel. 485246111; fax 485108319; e-mail muzeumlb@muzeumlb.cz; internet www.muzeumlb.cz; f. 1873; European and Bohemian applied arts, regional history, natural history; collections of glass, ceramics, porcelain, textiles, tapestries, jewellery, metal objects, furniture, posters, archaeological artefacts; library of 35,000 vols; Dir ALOIS CVANČARA; publ. *Sborník Severočeského musea* (one issue each on history and natural history, every 2 years).

Lidice

Památník Lidice (Lidice Memorial Museum): Kladno district, 273 54 Lidice; tel. and fax 312253063; e-mail lidice@ lidice-memorial.cz; internet www .lidice-memorial.cz; f. 1948; attached to Ministry of Culture of the Czech Republic; history of the destruction of the village of Lidice in the Second World War; gallery of painting and sculptures devoted to Lidice; Dir MARIE TELUPILOVA.

Litoměřice

Severočeská galerie výtvarného umění v Litoměřicích (North Bohemian Gallery of Fine Art in Litoměřice): Michalská 7, 412 01

Litoměřice; tel. 416732382; fax 416732383; e-mail reditel@galerie-ltm.cz; internet www .galerie-ltm.cz; f. 1958; European art since the 12th century, spec. collns of naive art, Czech Gothic art, Czech to present time; library of 16,000 vols; Dir Dr Jan Štíbr; Vice-Dir Dr Olga Kubelková.

Mariánské Lázně

Městské muzeum Mariánské Lázně (Mariánské Lázně Municipal Museum): Goethovo nám. 11, 353 01 Mariánské Lázně; tel. 354622740; e-mail muzeum@goethe-haus .cz; f. 1887; history, geology; open-air geological park; Dir Ing. Jaromír Bartoš.

Mladá Boleslav

Škoda Auto Museum (Škoda Auto Museum): Tř. Václava Klementa 294, 293 60 Mladá Boleslav; tel. 326831134; fax 326832039; e-mail museum@skoda-auto.cz; internet www.skoda-auto.com/cze/company/ museum; f. 1974; Dir Margit Černá.

Opava

Slezské zemské muzeum (Silesian Museum): Tyršova 1, 746 01 Opava; tel. and fax 553622999; e-mail szmred@szmo.cz; internet www.szmo.cz; f. 1814; history, natural history, social sciences, arts; arboretum at Nový Dvůr; botanic garden; library of 280,000 vols; Dir Dr Jaromír Kalus; Chief Librarian Mgr Jitka Sterbova; publs Časopis Slezskeho zemskeho muzea (natural sciences and historical sciences series, each 3 a year), Slezsky sborník (3 or 4 a year), Vlastivědné listy Slezska a severní Moravy (2 a year).

Pardubice

Východočeské muzeum v Pardubicich (Museum of Eastern Bohemia): Zámek č. 2, 530 02 Pardubice; tel. 466799240; fax 466513056; e-mail vcm@vcm.cz; internet www.vcm.cz; f. 1880; history, natural history, arts; library of 40,000 vols; Dir Dr Frantisek Šebek; publs Panurus (1 a year), Východočeský sborník historický (1 a year), Východočeský sborník přírodovědný (1 a year).

Plzeň

Západočeská galerie v Plzni (West Bohemian Gallery in Plzeň): Pražská 13, 301 00 Plzeň; tel. 377223759; fax 377322970; e-mail info@zpc-galerie.cz; internet www .zpc-galerie.cz; f. 1954; Czech art from the 14th century to the contemporary period; Dir Dr Jana Potužáková.

Západočeské muzeum v Plzni (West Bohemian Museum in Plzeň): Kopeckého sady 2, 301 00 Plzeň; tel. (378) 370110; fax (378) 370113; e-mail info@zcm.cz; internet www.zcm.cz; f. 1878; history, natural history, arts; Dir Dr Frantíšek Frýda; publs Folia Musei Rerum Naturalium Bohemiae Occidentalis (separate series for zoology, geology and botany, each 2 a year), Sborník (Příroda, 5 a year; Historie, 1 a year).

Prace u Brna

Mohyla míru (Peace Monument): 664 58 Prace u Brna; tel. 544244724; fax 544244724; f. 1910; battle of Slavkov (Austerlitz); Dir Mgr Antonín Reček.

Prague

České muzeum výtvarných umění v Praze (Czech Museum of Fine Arts in Prague): Husova 19/21, 110 00 Prague 1; tel. 222220218; fax 222221190; e-mail muzeum@cmvu.cz; internet www.cmvu.cz; f. 1963; temporary exhibitions of modern and contemporary art; Dir Dr Ivan Neumann.

Galerie hlavního města Prahy (City Gallery Prague): Staroměstské Náměstí 13, 110 00 Prague; tel. and fax (2) 33325330; fax (2) 33323664; e-mail office@ghmp.cz; internet www.ghmp.cz; f. 1963; Pragensia, works by Czech artists since 19th century; library of 2,000 vols; Dir Milan Bufka.

Muzeum hlavního města Prahy (Central Museum of the City of Prague): Na Poříčí 52, 110 00 Prague 1; tel. 224223696; fax 224214306; e-mail muzeum@muzeumprahy .cz; internet www.muzeumprahy.cz; f. 1881; history of Prague, archaeology, fine art; library of 17,000 vols; Dir Zuzana Strnadová; publ. Archeologica pragensia (1 a year).

Národní galerie v Praze (National Gallery in Prague): Staroměstské nám. 12, 110 15 Prague 1; tel. and fax 222329331; e-mail genreditel@ngprague.cz; internet www .ngprague.cz; f. 1796; art of all periods; library of 71,000 vols; Dir Prof. Milan Knížák; publ. Bulletin (irregular).

Národní muzeum (National Museum): Central Bldg, Václavské nám. 68, 115 79 Prague 1; tel. 224497111; fax 224226488; e-mail nm@nm.cz; internet www.nm.cz; f. 1818; expositions, spec. exhibitions, lecturing and teaching, pubs; collns of natural history, prehistory, history of Czech and foreign provenance, especially in the field of anthropology, ancient history of the Near E and Africa, Asian culture, bibliology, botanics, classical archeology, Czech history, entomology, ethnography, geology, history of physical education and sport, history of theatre, hydrobiology, medieval archeology, micology, mineralogy, musicology, non-European ethnography, numismatics, paleontology, prehistory, petrology, zoology; library: see Libraries and Archives; Dir-Gen. Dr Michal Lukeš; publs Časopis Národního muzea (Journal of the National Museum, 2 a year), Museum (2 a year), Numismatické listy (Numismatic Papers, 4 a year), Sborník Národního muzea v Praze (Acta Musei Nationalis Pragae, 2 a year).

Constituent Museums:

České muzeum hudby (Museum of Czech Music): Karmeliská 2, 118 00 Prague 1; tel. 257257757; fax 257322216; e-mail c_muzeum_hudby@nm.cz; internet www.nm.cz; f. 1936; incl. Dvořák (Prague 2, Ke Karlovu 20), Smetana (Prague 1, Novotného lávka 1), musical instruments (Prague 1, Karmeliská 2); library, sound archives; Dir Dr Dagmar Fialová.

Historické muzeum (Historical Museum): Václavské nám. 68, 115 79 Prague 1; tel. 224497276; fax 224497246; e-mail pavel_dousa@nm.cz; internet www .nm.cz; f. 1964; history of Czech Republic, history of money, ethnography of the Czech Republic, sport, Czech theatre; Dir Dr Pavel Douša; publs Časopis Národního muzea. Řada historická (2 a year), Fontes archaeologici Pragenses (irregular), Muzeum: Muzejní a vlastivědná práce (2 a year), Numismatické listy (4 a year), Sborník Národního Muzea v Praze, řada A - Historie (2 a year).

Náprstkovo muzeum asijských, afrických a amerických kultur (Náprstek Museum of Asian, African and American Cultures): Betlémské nám. 1, 110 01 Prague 1; tel. 222221416; fax 222221418; internet www.nm.cz; f. 1862; research into Asian, African, American, Australian and Oceanian cultural heritage; permanent and temporary exhibitions, public lectures and cultural events; library of 250,000 vols; Dir Dr Jana Součková; publ. Annals (1 a year).

Přírodovědecké muzeum (Natural History Museum): Václavské nám. 68, 115 79

Prague; tel. 224497111; fax 224222550; e-mail jiri.litochleb@nm.cz; internet www .nm.cz; f. 1964; Dir Dr Jiří Litochleb; publs Acta Entomologica (irregular), Journal of the National Museum, Natural History Series (1 a year), Lynx (1 a year), Sborník Národního muzea, řada B (Acta Musei Nationalis Pragae, Series B).

Národní technické muzeum (National Technical Museum): Kostelní 42, 170 78 Prague 7; tel. 220399111; fax 2203399200; e-mail info@ntm.cz; internet www.ntm.cz; f. 1908; library: see Libraries and Archives; Dir Karel Ksandr; publs Bibliografie a prameny Národního technického muzea, Rozpravy Národního technického muzea, Sborník Národního technického muzea v Praze.

Národní zemědělské muzeum (National Museum of Agriculture): Kostelní 44, 170 00 Prague 7; tel. 233379025; fax 233372561; e-mail nzm.praha@nzm.cz; internet www .nzm.cz; f. 1891; exhibition of agriculture and food industry located in Kačina Castle near Kutná Hora; exhibition of agricultural machinery located in Čáslav; exhibition of forestry, hunting and fisheries in Ohrada Castle nr České Budějovice; exhibition of horticulture in Valtice near Břeclav; library of 120,000 vols, photographic archive; Dir Mgr Přemsyl Reibl; publs Acta Museorum agriculturae, Prameny a studie (Sources and Studies), Vědecké práce ZM. (Scientific Studies).

Památník národního písemnictví (Museum of Czech Literature): Strahovské nádvoří 1/132, 118 38 Prague 1; tel. 220516695; fax 220517277; e-mail post@ pamatnik-np.cz; internet www .pamatniknarodnihopisemnictvi.cz; f. 1953; literary archives containing 6m. objects; collns showing devt of literature and literary culture in historical Czech lands, incl. documents on life, work, and legacy of important figures of Czech literature and literary culture from 18th century until present and colln of works of visual art; library of 600,000 vols; Dir Mgr Zdeněk Freisleben; publ. Literární archiv (1 a year).

Pedagogické muzeum J. A. Komenského v Praze (Pedagogical Museum of J. A. Comenius in Prague): Valdštejnská 20, 118 00 Prague 1; tel. 257533455; fax 257530661; e-mail pedagog@pmjak.cz; internet www .pmjak.cz; f. 1892; documents illustrating the devt of nat. education and the life and work of Comenius; library of 25,000 vols; Dir Dr Markéta Pánková.

Poštovní muzeum (Postal Museum): Nové mlýny 2, 110 00 Prague 1; tel. 222312006; fax 222311930; internet www.cpost.cz; f. 1918; Dir Dr Pavel Čtvrtník.

Uměleckoprůmyslové museum v Praze (Museum of Decorative Arts): 17 listopadu 2, 110 00 Prague 1; tel. 251093111; fax 251093296; e-mail info@upm.cz; internet www.upm.cz; f. 1885; applied art from ancient times to the present; library of 150,000 vols; Dir Dr Helena Koenigsmarková.

Vojenský historický ústav Prahay/Military History Institute, Prague: U. Památníku 2, 130 05 Prague-Žižkov 3; tel. 973204900; fax 222541308; e-mail museum@army.cz; internet www.vhu.cz; f. 1919; library of 250,000 vols books, magazines, historical maps; Dir Mgr Aleš Knížek.

Constituent Museums:

Armádní muzeum Žižkov (Army Museum): U. Památníku 2, 130 05 Prague 3; tel. 220204924.

Letecké muzeum Kbely (Aviation Museum, Kbely): Kbely, Mladoboleslavská ul., 197 00 Prague 3; tel. 220207513; e-mail info@militarymuseum.cz.

Vojenské technické muzeum (Museum of Military Technology): Krhanice, Prague; tel. 317702130; fax 317702123.

Židovské muzeum v Praze (Jewish Museum in Prague): Staré školy 1, 3, 110 00 Prague 1; tel. 221711511; fax 221711584; e-mail office@jewishmuseum.cz; internet www.jewishmuseum.cz; f. 1906; consists of the Maisel Synagogue, the Spanish Synagogue, the Pinkas Synagogue, the Old Jewish Cemetery, the Klausen Synagogue and the Ceremonial Hall; provides detailed commentary on Judaism and Jewish history, as well as the history of the Jews in Bohemia and Moravia; Dir Dr LEO PAVLÁT; publ. *Judaica Bohemiae* (1 a year).

Rožnov pod Radhoštěm

Valašské muzeum v přírodě (Wallachian Open-Air Museum): Palackého 147, 756 61 Rožnov pod Radhoštěm; tel. 571757111; fax 571654494; e-mail muzeum@vmp.cz; internet www.vmp.cz; f. 1925; open-air museum consisting of a wooden town, Wallachian village and mill valley; methodological centre for open-air museums; library of 15,000 vols; Dir Ing. VÍTĚZSLAV KOUKAL.

Slavkov u Brna

Zámek Slavkov—Austerlitz (Chateau Slavkov—Austerlitz): Palackého nám. 1, 684 01 Slavkov u Brna; tel. 544221204; fax 544227305; e-mail info@zamek-slavkov.cz; internet www.zamek-slavkov.cz; f. 1949; Napoleonic wars (particularly the Battle of Austerlitz), 17th- and 18th-century paintings, chapel of the Holy Cross; library colln on Napoleon; Dir Ing. ALEŠ ŠILHÁNEK.

Tábor

Husitské Muzeum (Hussite Museum): Nám. Mikuláše z Husi 44, 390 01 Tábor; tel. 381252242; fax 381252245; e-mail tabor@husmuzeum.cz; internet www.husmuzeum.cz; f. 1878; Hussite movement; library of 40,000 vols; Dir MILOŠ DRDA; publ. *Husitský Tábor* (1 a year).

Teplice

Regionální muzeum v Teplicích (Teplice Regional Museum): Zámecké nám. 14, 415 01 Teplice; tel. 417537869; fax 417572300; e-mail info@muzeum-teplice.cz; internet www.muzeum-teplice.cz; f. 1897; history, natural history, arts; library of 75,000 vols; Dir Dr DUŠAN ŠPIČKA; publs *Archeologický výzkum* (archaeological research, irregular), *Zprávy a studie* (local history and natural history, every 2 years).

Terezín

Památník Terezín (Terezín Memorial): Principova Alej 304, 411 55 Terezín; tel. 416782225; fax 416782245; e-mail pamatnik@pamatnik-terezin.cz; internet www.pamatnik-terezin.cz; f. 1947; museums of the Small Fortress (resistance and political persecution 1940–45) and the wartime Jewish ghetto of Terezín; Art Exhibition of the Terezín Memorial; Terezín 1780–1939; the Litoměřice concentration camp; library of 11,000 vols; Dir Dr JAN MUNK; publs *Newsletter* (4 a year), *Terezínské listy* (1 a year).

Uherské Hradiště

Slovácké muzeum v Uherském Hradišti (Slovácko Museum in Uherské Hradiště): Smetanovy sady 179, 686 01 Uherské Hradiště; tel. 572556556; fax 572554077; e-mail info@slovackemuzeum.cz; internet www .slovackemuzeum.cz; f. 1914; history, art; library of 30,000 vols; Dir Dr IVO FROLEC; publ. *Slovácko* (1 a year).

Uherský Brod

Muzeum J. A. Komenského v Uherském Brodě (Uherský Brod J. A. Comenius Museum): Ul. Přemysla Otakara II 37, 688 12 Uherský Brod; tel. 572632288; fax 572634078; e-mail muzeum@mjakub.cz; internet www.mjakub.cz; f. 1898; life, work and heritage of Protestant bishop and educational reformer, J. A. Comenius (1592–1670); history and ethnology of the Uherskobrodsko region; library of 40,000 vols; Dir Dr PAVEL POPELKA; publ. *Studia Comeniana et historica* (2 a year).

Zlín

Muzeum jihovýchodní Moravy (Museum of South-Eastern Moravia): Soudní 1, 762 57 Zlín; tel. 577004633; fax 577004632; e-mail info@muzeum.zlin.cz; internet www.muzeum .zlin.cz; f. 1953; social science (archaeology, history, ethnography), natural history (botany, entomology, geology), shoe museum; library of 25,220 vols; Dir Dr ANTONIN SOBEK; publs *Acta Carpathica Occidentalis*, *Acta Musealia*.

Obuvnické muzeum (Footwear Museum): Tř. Tomáše Bati 1970, POB 175, 762 57 Zlín; tel. 577213978; fax 577213978; e-mail m .stybrova@seznam.cz; internet www .muzeum.zlin.cz/obuvmuz.htm; f. 1959; library of 3,000 vols; Dir MIROSLAVA ŠTÝBROVÁ.

Universities

ČESKÉ VYSOKÉ UČENÍ TECHNICKÉ V PRAZE
(Czech Technical University in Prague)

Zikova 4, 166 36 Prague 6
Telephone: 224351111
Fax: 224310783
Internet: www.cvut.cz

Founded 1707; reorganized 1806, 1863, 1920, 1960
State control
Languages of instruction: Czech, English
Academic year: October to June

Rector: Prof. Ing. J. WITZANY
Vice-Rector for Construction: Prof. Ing. A. NAVRÁTIL
Vice-Rector for Devt: Prof. Ing. J. MACHÁČEK
Vice-Rector for Education: Prof. Ing. V. STEJSKAL
Vice-Rector for External Relations: Prof. Ing. F. VEJRAŽKA
Vice-Rector for Int. Relations: Prof. Dr M. VLČEK
Vice-Rector for Science and Research: Prof. Ing. L. MUSÍLEK
Chief Admin. Officer: Doc. Ing. Z. VOSPĚL

Number of teachers: 1,468
Number of students: 21,282

Publications: *Acta Polytechnica* (in English, 6 a year), *Pražská Technika* (in Czech, 6 a year)

DEANS

Faculty of Architecture: Prof. Ing. V. ŠLAPETA
Faculty of Civil Engineering: Prof. Ing. Z. BITTNAR
Faculty of Electrical Engineering: Prof. Ing. VLADIMÍR KUČERA
Faculty of Mechanical Engineering: Prof. Ing. PETR ZUNA
Faculty of Nuclear Science and Physical Engineering: Prof. Ing. MIROSLAV HAVLÍČEK
Faculty of Transportation Sciences: Doc. Ing. JOSEF JÍRA

ATTACHED INSTITUTES

Centre for Radiochemistry and Radiation Chemistry: Dir Doc. Ing. J. JOHN.

Computing and Information Centre: Dir Doc. Ing. L. OHERA.

Institute of Biomedical Engineering: Dir Prof. Ing. M. VRBOVÁ.

Institute of Experimental and Applied Physics: Dir Ing. S. POSPÍŠIL.

Klokner (Building) Institute: Dir Ing. T. KLEČKA.

Masaryk Institute of Advanced Studies: Dir Doc. Ing. J. PETR.

Research Institute for Industrial Heritage: Dir Dr B. FRAGNER.

Technology Innovation Centre: Plzeňská 130/221, 15000 Prague 5; tel. 257199913; fax 257212340; e-mail office@ tic.cvut.cz; internet www.tic.cvut.cz/l=en; Dir Dr MILAN PRESS.

ČESKÁ ZEMĚDĚLSKÁ UNIVERZITA V PRAZE
(Czech University of Life Sciences, Prague)

Kamýcká 129, 165 21 Prague 6–Suchdol
Telephone: 224381111
Internet: www.czu.cz

Founded 1906
State control
Language of instruction: Czech
Academic year: September to August

Rector: Prof. Dr JOSEF KOZÁK
Pro-Rectors: Prof. Dr JIŘÍ BALÍK, Prof. Dr PAVEL KOVÁŘ, Prof. Dr VÁCLAV SLAVÍK, Prof. Dr MIROSLAV SVATOŠ
Registrar: Dr MILOŠ FRÝBORT
Librarian: Dr IVAN HAUZNER

Library of 225,000 vols
Number of teachers: 429
Number of students: 5,000

Publications: *Agricultura tropica et subtropica* (1 or 2 a year), *Scientia Agriculturae Bohemica* (4 a year), *Scientific Papers*

DEANS

Faculty of Agricultural Economics and Management: Prof. Dr JAN HRON
Faculty of Agronomy: Prof. Dr KAREL VOŘÍŠEK
Faculty of Forestry: Prof. Dr JOSEF GROSS
Technical Faculty: Prof. Dr KAREL POKORNÝ
Institute of Applied Ecology: RNDr ZDENĚK LIPSKÝ (Vice-Dean)
Institute of Tropical and Subtropical Agriculture: Prof. Dr BOHUMIL HAVRLAND

UNIVERZITA HRADEC KRÁLOVÉ
(University of Hradec Králové)

Rokitanského 62, 500 03 Hradec Králové
Telephone: 493331111
Fax: 493332544
Internet: www.uhk.cz

Founded 1959, as Institute of Education; univ. status 2000
State control

Rector: Doc. Dr JOSEF HYNEK
Vice-Rector for Int. Affairs and Science: Prof. Dr ANTONÍN SLABÝ
Vice-Rector for Internal Affairs: Dr DANA MUSILOVÁ
Vice-Rector for Strategy and Devt: Dr MONIKA ŽUMÁROVÁ
Librarian: Mgr ZDENKA JEŽKOVÁ

Number of teachers: 658
Number of students: 8,778

DEANS

Faculty of Arts: Mgr Dr PETR GRULICH

Faculty of Education: Doc. Ing. VLADIMÍR JEHLIČKA

Faculty of Informatics and Management: Doc. Ing. VÁCLAV JANEČEK

Faculty of Science: Dr PAVEL TROJOVSKÝ

Institute of Social Work: MIROSLAV MITLÖHNER

UNIVERZITA JANA EVANGELISTY PURKYNĚ V ÚSTÍ NAD LABEM
(Jan Evangelista Purkyně University in Ústí nad Labem)

Hoření 13, 400 96 Ústí nad Labem

Telephone: 475282111

Fax: 472772781

E-mail: rektor@rek.ujep.cz

Internet: www.ujep.cz

Founded as Pedagogical Faculty in Ústí nad Labem; university status 1991

State control

Rector: Dr Dr STANISLAV NOVÁK

Librarian: Dr IVO BROŽEK

Library of 250,000 vols

Number of teachers: 375

Number of students: 6,000

DEANS

Faculty of Art and Design: Dr VLADIMÍR ŠVEC

Faculty of Education: Dr ZDENĚK RADVANOVSKÝ

Faculty of Environmental Studies: Dr Ing. JOSEF SEJÁK

Faculty of Science: Dr Dr STANISLAV NOVÁK

Faculty of Social and Economic Studies: Prof. Ing. PAVLIK

JIHOČESKÁ UNIVERZITA V ČESKÝCH BUDĚJOVICÍCH
(University of South Bohemia in České Budějovice)

Branišovská 31, 370 05 České Budějovice

Telephone: 389031111

Fax: 385310348

E-mail: rektorat@jcu.cz

Internet: www.jcu.cz

Founded 1991

State control

Academic year: September to June

Rector: Prof. Ing. FRANTIŠEK STŘELEČEK

Vice-Rector for Foreign Relations: Doc. Dr MILAN STRAŠKRABA

Vice-Rector for Science: Doc. Ing. MARTIN KŘÍŽEK

Vice-Rector for Study Programmes: Doc. Dr JIŘÍ DIVÍŠEK

Vice-Rector for University Devt: Prof. Ing. VÁCLAV ŘEHOUT

Number of teachers: 418

Number of students: 5,500

Publications: *Memorial Volume of the Faculty of Agriculture–Economics* (2 a year), *Memorial Volume of the Faculty of Agriculture–Phytotechnics* (2 a year), *Memorial Volume of the Faculty of Agriculture–Zootechnics* (2 a year), *Opera historica* (1 a year)

DEANS

Faculty of Agriculture: Prof. Ing. JAN FRELICH

Faculty of Biological Sciences: Doc. Dr ZDENĚK BRANDL

Faculty of Education: Doc. Dr FRANTIŠEK MRÁZ

Faculty of Health and Social Studies: Doc. Dr VLADIMÍR VURM

Faculty of Theology: Prof. Dr KAREL SKALICKÝ

UNIVERZITA KARLOVA
(Charles University)

Ovocný trh 5, 116 36 Prague 1

Telephone: 224491111

Fax: 224210695

E-mail: sekretariat@ruk.cuni.cz

Internet: www.cuni.cz

Founded 1348

State control

Language of instruction: Czech

Academic year: September to June

Rector: Prof. VACLAV HAMPL

Vice-Rector: Doc. MARTIN PRUDKY

Vice-Rector: Prof. MILAN TICHY

Vice-Rector: Doc. Dr MICHAL SOBR

Vice-Rector: Doc. Dr STANISLAV STECH

Vice-Rector: Prof. Dr JAN SKRHA

Vice-Rector: Prof. Dr IVAN JAKUBEC

Vice-Rector: Prof. SYLVIE OPATRNA

Vice-Rector: Prof. PETR VOLF

Quaestor: Ing. JOSEF KUBÍČEK

Chancellor: RNDr TOMÁŠ JELÍNEK

Library: see Libraries and Archives

Number of teachers: 4,048

Number of students: 53,000

Publications: *Acta Universitatis Carolinae—* series: *Mathematica et Physica*, *Biologica* (4 a year), *Environmentalica* (1 a year), *Folia Pharmaceutica Universitatis Carolinae*, *Geographica* (2 a year), *Geologica* (4 a year), *Historia Universitatis Carolinae Pragensis*, *Iuridica* (4 a year), *Kinanthropologica* (2 a year), *Medica* (1 a year), *Novitates Botanicae Universitatis Carolinae* (1 a year), *Oeconomica* (2 a year), *Philologica* (10 a year), *Philosophica et Historica* (10 a year), *Prague Bulletin of Mathematical Linguistics*, *Psychologie v ekonomické praxi* (2 a year), *Sborník lékařský* (4 a year)

DEANS

Faculty of Catholic Theology: Lic. PROKOP BROZ

Faculty of Education: Doc. Dr RADKA WILDOVA

Faculty of Evangelical Theology: Doc. JINDRICH HALAMA

Faculty of Humanities: Doc. Dr LADISLAV BENYOVSZKY

Faculty of Hussite Theology: Prof. JAN B. LASEK

Faculty of Law: Prof. Dr ALES GERLOCH

Faculty of Mathematics and Physics: Prof. ZDENEK NEMECEK

1st Faculty of Medicine: Prof. TOMAS ZIMA

2nd Faculty of Medicine: Prof. ONDREJ HRUSAK

3rd Faculty of Medicine: Prof. MICHAL ANDEL

Faculty of Medicine in Hradec Králové: Prof. MIROSLAV CERVINKA

Faculty of Medicine in Plzeň: Doc. Dr JAROSLAV KOUTENSKÝ

Faculty of Pharmacy in Hradec Králové: Prof. Dr ALEXANDR HRABALEK

Faculty of Philosophy: Doc. Dr MICHAL STEHLIK

Faculty of Physical Education and Sport: Doc. Dr VLADIMIR SÜSS

Faculty of Sciences: Dr BOHUSLAV GAS

Faculty of Social Sciences: Dr JAKUB KONCELIK

PROFESSORS

Faculty of Catholic Theology (6, Thákurova 3, 160 00 Prague; tel. 220181600; fax 220181215; e-mail dekan@kft.cuni.cz; internet www.ktf.cuni.cz):

MATĚJKA, J., Practical Theology

POLC, J., Church History

SLABÝ, A., Pastoral Medicine

SOUSEDÍK, S., History of Philosophy

WOLF, V., Systematic Theology

ZEDNÍČEK, M., Canon Law

Faculty of Education (M. D. Rettigové 4, Prague; tel. 221900111; fax 224947156; e-mail pavel.vasak@pedf.cuni.cz; internet www.pedf.cuni.cz):

BENEŠ, P., Chemistry

BRABCOVÁ, R., Czech Language

ČORNES, P., History

HEJNÝ, M., Mathematics

HELUS, Z., Pedagogical Psychology

HERDEN, J., Music Education

JELÍNEK, S., Russian Language

KOMAN, M., Mathematics

KOTÁSEK, J., Education

PARIZEK, V., Education

PEŠKOVÁ, J., Philosophy

PIŤHA, P., Philosophy

POLEDŇÁK, K., Music Education

VULTERIN, J., Analytical Chemistry

Faculty of Evangelical Theology (1, Černá 9, 115 55 Prague; tel. 221988216; fax 221988200; e-mail filipi@ftf.cuni.cz; internet www.ftf.cuni.cz):

FILIPI, P., Practical Theology

POKORNÝ, P., New Testament

REJCHRTOVÁ, N., Church History

TROJAN, J., Social Ethics

Faculty of Humanities (5, V. Kříže 10, 150 00 Prague; tel. 251080111; e-mail sokol@fhs.cuni.cz; internet www.fhs.cuni.cz):

BENYOVSZKY, L., Philosophy

BOUZEK, J., Archaeology, Classical Philology

BYSTŘICKÝ, J., Philosophy, Media

ČEŠKA, J., Philosophy, Literature

DOHNALOVÁ, M., Economics

GABRIŠKOVÁ, L., Languages

HALBICH, M., Anthropology

HAVELKA, M., Sociology, Social History

HAVELKOVÁ, H., Gender Studies

HAVLÍČEK, M., Anthropology, Ethnology

HAVRDOVÁ, Z., Social Psychology

HORSKÝ, J., History, Historical Anthropology

HOZÁKOVÁ, J., Sociology

HROCH, M., History

KAČÍREK, M., Law

KRUŽÍK, J., Philosophy

MATOUŠEK, V., Anthropology, Archaeology

MORAVCOVÁ, M., Ethnology

MULLER, K., Sociology

NOVÁK, A., Philosophy

PINC, Z., Philosophy

PRUDKÝ, L., Sociology

RYNDA, I., Human Ecology

SELIGOVÁ, M., History

SHANAHAN, D., Languages, Film

ŠKOVAJSA, M., Political Philosophy

ŠKVAŘILOVÁ, B., Anthropology

SOKOL, J., Anthropology, Philosophy

SOUKUPOVÁ, B., Social History

SVATOŇ, O., Sociology

SVOBODA, A., Art, Design

TURKOVÁ, M., Ethnology

VANČÁT, J., Theory of Art

VANČATOVÁ, M., Ethnology

VOPĚNKA, P., Logic, Mathematics

ZIMA, P., Languages, Sociolinguistics

Faculty of Hussite Theology (4, Pacovská 350/4, 140 21 Prague; tel. 241733131; e-mail jligus@htf.cuni.cz; internet www.htf.cuni.cz):

HAŠKOVCOVÁ, H., Medical Ethics

HOLETON, D. R., Liturgics

KUČERA, Z., Systematic Theology

LIGUŠ, J., Philosophy of Communication

SÁZAVA, Z., Biblical Theology

Faculty of Law (1, nám. Curieových 7, 116 40 Prague; tel. 221005111; e-mail dekan@ius.prf.cuni.cz; internet www.prf.cuni.cz):

BAKEŠ, M., Financial Law

BELINA, M., Labour Law

BOGUSZAK, J., Theory of State and Law

CÍSAŘOVÁ, D., Criminal Law

GERLOCH, A., Theory, Philosophy and Sociology of Law
HENDRYCH, D., Administrative Law
KŘIŽ, J., Civil Law
KUČERA, Z., International Law
MALÝ, K., History of State and Law
NOVOTNÝ, O., Criminal Law
PAVLÍČEK, V., Constitutional Law and Civic Sciences
ŠVESTKA, J., Civil Law
TICHÝ, L., European Law
WINTEROVÁ, A., Civil Law
ZOULÍK, FR., Civil Law

Faculty of Mathematics and Physics (2, K. Karlovu 3, 121 16 Prague; tel. 221951111; fax 221911292; e-mail dekan@dekanat.mff.cuni.cz; internet www.mff.cuni.cz):

ANDĚL, J., Mathematics and Statistics
BARVÍK, I., Physics
BEDNÁŘ, J., Physics
BENEŠ, V., Mathematics
BIČÁK, J., Theoretical Physics
BICAN, L., Mathematics
BIEDERMAN, H., Macromolecular Physics
ČÁPEK, V., Theoretical Physics
CIPRA, T., Mathematics
DUPAČOVÁ, J., Mathematics and Statistics
FEISTAUER, M., Mathematics
FORMÁNEK, J., Theoretical Physics
HAJČOVÁ, E., Information Science
HÁLA, J., Physics
HASLINGER, J., Physics
HORÁČEK, J., Theoretical Physics
HOŘEJŠÍ, J., Nuclear Physics
HÖSCHL, P., Physics
HRACH, R., Electronic Physics
HUŠEK, M., Mathematics
HUŠKOVÁ, M., Mathematics
ILAVSKÝ, M., Macromolecular Physics
JUREČKOVÁ, J., Probability and Statistics
KAKGER, A., Mathematics
KEPKA, T., Mathematics
KOWALSKI, O., Mathematics
KVASIL, J., Experimental Physics
LUKEŠ, J., Mathematical Analysis
MARTINEC, Z., Physics and Geophysics
MATOLÍN, V., Electronic Physics
MATOUŠEK, J., Informatics
NEŠETŘIL, J., Mathematics
NETUKA, I., Mathematics
NOVÁK, B., Mathematics
PANEVOVÁ, J., Information Science
PLÁŠIL, F., Informatics
POKORNÝ, J., Informatics
PULTR, A., Mathematics
ROHN, J., Mathematics
SECHOVSKÝ, V., Physics
SIMON, P., Mathematics
SKÁLA, L., Physics
SOUČEK, V., Mathematics
ŠTĚPÁN, J., Mathematics
ŠTĚPÁNEK, P., Mathematics
SVOBODA, E., Theoretical Physics
TICHÝ, M., Physics
TROJANOVÁ, Z., Electronic Physics
VALVODA, V., Physics
VELICKÝ, B., Physics
VIŠŇOVSKÝ, Š., Physics
ZAJÍČEK, L., Mathematics
ZIMMERMANN, K., Information Science

1st Faculty of Medicine (2, Kateřinská 32, 121 08 Prague; tel. 224961111; fax 224915413; e-mail stepan.svacina@lf1.cuni.cz; internet www.lf1.cuni.cz):

ASCHERMANN, M., Internal Medicine
BENCKO, V., Hygiene
BETKA, J., Otorhinolaryngology
BROULÍK, P., Internal Medicine
DVOŘÁČEK, J., Urology
ELIŠKA, O., Anatomy
ELLEDER, M., Pathology
FARGHALL, H. M., Pharmacology
FUČÍKOVÁ, T., Immunology and Allergology
HÁJEK, Z., Gynaecology
HORKÝ, K., Internal Medicine

HYNIE, S., Pharmacology
KLENER, P., Oncology
KRAML, J., Biochemistry
LAŠTOVKA, M., Otorhinolaryngology
MAREČEK, Z., Internal Medicine
MAREK, J., Internal Medicine
MARTÍNEK, J., Histology and Embryology
NEČAS, E., Normal and Pathological Physiology
NEVŠÍMALOVÁ, S., Neurology
PAFKO, P., Surgery
PETROVICKÝ, P., Anatomy
POKORNY, J., Physiology
POVÝŠIL, C., Pathological Anatomy
RABOCH, J., Psychiatry
RACEK, J., Stomatology
RYBKA, V., Orthopaedic Surgery
ŠKRHA, J., Internal Medicine
SOSNA, A., Surgery
ŠTĚPÁN, J., Biochemistry
ŠTÍPEK, S., Biochemistry
STREJC, P., Forensic Medicine
TERŠÍP, K., Surgery
TESAŘ, V., Internal Medicine
TOPINKOVÁ, E., Social Medicine
TROJAN, S., Medical Physiology
VANĚK, J., Surgery
VÍTEK, F., Biophysics
VYMĚTAL, J., Clinical Psychology
ZEMAN, J., Paediatrics
ZEMAN, M., Surgery
ZIMA, T., Medical Chemistry
ŽIVNÝ, J., Gynaecology and Obstetrics

2nd Faculty of Medicine (5, Vúvalu 84, 150 06 Prague; tel. 224431111; fax 224435820; e-mail josef.koutecky@lfmotol.cuni.cz; internet www.lf2.cuni.cz):

BOUŠKA, I., Forensic Medicine
BROŽEK, G., Physiology
DRUGA, R., Anatomy
GOETZ, P., Biology
HERGET, J., Pathological Physiology
HOŘEJŠÍ, J., Gynaecology and Obstetrics
KODET, R., Pathological Anatomy
KONRÁDOVÁ, V., Histology and Embryology
KOUTECKY, J., Oncology
MATOUŠOVIC, K., Internal Medicine
PELOUCH, V., Medical Chemistry and Biochemistry
SEEMANOVÁ, E., Genetics
ŠNAJDAUF, J., Surgery
ŠVIHOVEC, J., Pharmacology
VÍZEK, M., Pathological Physiology
VOJÁČEK, J., Internal Medicine

3rd Faculty of Medicine (10, Ruská 87, 100 00 Prague; tel. 267102111; e-mail michal.andel@lf3.cuni.cz; internet www.lf3.cuni.cz):

ANDĚL, M., Internal Medicine
CIKRT, M., Hygiene
GREGOR, P., Internal Medicine
HORÁK, J., Internal Medicine
HÖSCHL, C., Psychiatry
JELÍNEK, R., Histology and Embryology, Anatomy
KRŠIAK, M., Pharmacology
KUCHYNKA, P., Ophthalmology
LENER, J., Hygiene
MALINA, L., Dermatology
PROVAZNÍK, K., Hygiene
RAŠKA, I., Medical Biology
ROKYTA, R., Pathological Physiology
SCHINDLER, J., Microbiology
STEFAN, J., Forensic Medicine
STINGL, J., Anatomy

Faculty of Medicine in Hradec Králové (Šimkova 870, 500 38 Hradec Králové; tel. 495816111; fax 495513597; e-mail dekan@lfhk.cuni.cz; internet www.lfhk.cuni.cz):

DOMINIK, J., Surgery
FIXA, B., Internal Medicine
HEJZLAR, M., Microbiology
HRNČÍŘ, P., Internal Medicine
HYBÁŠEK, I., Otorhinolaryngology
KRÁL, B., Internal Medicine

KVASNIČKA, J., Internal Medicine
MALÝ, J., Internal Medicine
MARTÍNKOVÁ, J., Pharmacology
NĚMEČEK, S., Histology and Embryology
PIDRMAN, V., Internal Medicine
ROZSÍVAL, P., Ophthalmology
SPAČEK, J., Pathological Anatomy
ŠRB, V., Hygiene
STEINER, I., Pathological Anatomy
STRANSKY, P., Biophysics
VOBOŘIL, Z., Surgery
VODIČKA, I., Biophysics
ZADÁK, Z., Internal Medicine

Faculty of Medicine in Plzeň (Husova 13, 306 05 Plzeň; tel. 377593400; fax 197221460; e-mail dekan@lfp.cuni.cz; internet www.lfp.cuni.cz):

AMBLER, Z., Neurology
FAKAN, F., Pathological Anatomy
MICHAL, M., Pathological Anatomy
OPATRNÝ, K., Internal Medicine
RACEK, J., Biochemistry
RESL, V., Dermatovenereology
SKÁLOVÁ, A., Pathology
TĚŠÍNSKÝ, P., Ophthalmology
TOPOLČAN, O., Internal Medicine
TŘEŠKA, V., Surgery

Faculty of Pharmacy in Hradec Králové (Heyrovskiho tř. 1203, 501 65 Hradec Králové; tel. 495067111; fax 495512656; e-mail dusek@faf.cuni.cz; internet www.faf.cuni.cz):

DRŠATA, J., Biochemistry
FENDRICH, Z., Pharmacology
JAHODÁŘ, L., Pharmacognosy
KARLÍČEK, R., Analytical Chemistry
KYASNIČKOVÁ, E., Biochemistry
LÁZNÍČEK, M., Radiopharmacy
VIŠŇOVSKÝ, P., Pharmacology
WAISSER, K., Organic Chemistry

Faculty of Philosophy (1, nám. J. Palacha 2, 116 38 Prague; tel. 221619111; e-mail dekan@ff.cuni.cz; internet www.ff.cuni.cz):

BLÁHOVÁ, M., Auxiliary Historical Sciences
BOUZEK, J., Classical Archaeology
ČERMÁK, F., Czech Language
DOHALSKÁ, M., Phonetics
HALÍK, T., Sociology
HILSKY, M., English Literature
HLEDÍKOVÁ, Z., Auxiliary Historical Sciences
HORYNA, M., History of Art
KÖNIGOVÁ, M., Information and Librarianship
KROPÁČEK, L., History and Culture of Africa and Asia
KUČERA, K., Czech Language
KUKLÍK, J., Czech History
MACUROVÁ, A., Czech Language
MAUR, E., Czech History
OPATRNÝ, J., General History
PALEK, B., General Linguistics
PALKOVÁ, Z., Phonetics and Phonology
SKŘIVAN, A., General History
SLÁMA, J., Archaeology
SLAVICKÝ, M., Music Studies
STEHLÍKOVÁ, E., History and Theory of Theatre
ULIČNÝ, O., Czech Language
VACEK, J., Sanskrit and Tamil Philosophy
VERNER, M., Egyptology

Faculty of Physical Education and Sport (6, José Martiho 31, 162 52 Prague; tel. 220562459; fax 220172370; e-mail karger@ftvs.cuni.cz; internet www.ftvs.cuni.cz):

BLAHUŠ, P., Kinanthropology
BUNC, V., Kinanthropology
DYLEVSKÝ, I., Anatomy
HOUDEK, V., Theory of Physical Culture
KOVÁŘ, R., Kinanthropology
OTAHAL, S., Biomechanics and Bionics
RYCHTECKÝ, A., Kinanthropology
SLEPIČKA, P., Kinanthropology
SVOBODA, B., Sports Education
TEPLÝ, Z., Human Movement

Faculty of Sciences (2, Albertov 6, 128 43 Prague; tel. 222112111; e-mail stulik@prfdec .natur.cuni.cz; internet www.natur.cuni.cz):

BOUBLÍK, T., Physical and Macromolecular Chemistry
BOUŠKA, V., Geological Mineralogy
BUCHAR, J., Zoology
ČEPEK, P., Geology
ČERNÝ, M., Organic Chemistry
CHLUPÁČ, I., Geology
DROBNÍK, J., Biotechnology
FELTL, L., Analytical Chemistry
GARDAVSKÝ, V., Regional Geography
HAMPL, M., Regional Geography
HŮRKA, K., Zoology
KALVODA, J., Physical Geography
KLINOT, J., Organic Chemistry
KOŘÍNEK, V., Biology
MAREK, F., Geology
MAREŠ, S., Geophysics
MATOLÍN, M., Geophysics
MEJSNAR, J., Biology
NÁTR, M., Plant Physiology
NEUBAUER, Z., Philosophy of Natural Sciences
NOVOTNÝ, I., Biology and Physiology of Animals
PAVLÍK, Z., Demography
PERTOLD, Z., Geology
PEŠEK, J., Geology
PODLAHA, J., Inorganic Chemistry
RIEDER, M., Geology
SMOLÍKOVÁ, L., Physical and Macromolecular Chemistry
ŠTEHLÍK, E., Mathematics
ŠTEMPROK, M., Geology
STRUNECKÁ, A., Biology
ŠTULIK, A., Analytical Chemistry
STYS, P., Entomology
TICHÁ, M., Biochemistry
VÁŇA, J., Botany
VÁVRA, J., Parasitology
ZADRAŽIL, S., Genetics and Microbiology

Faculty of Social Sciences (1, Smetanavo nábřezí 6, 110 00 Prague; tel. 222112111; fax 224235644; e-mail mlcoch@mbox.fsv.cuni .cz; internet www.fsv.cuni.cz):

HLAVÁČEK, Economics
KOUBA, K., Political Economy
KRAUS, J., Mass Communication
KŘEN, J., Czechoslovak History
MESSTŘÍK, M., Economics
MLČOCH, L., Economics
PEŠEK, J., Modern History
PETRUSEK, M., Sociology
POTŮČEK, M., Sociology
REIMAN, M., History and Politics of Russia and Eastern Europe
SOJKA, M., Economic Theory
TURNOVEC, F., Economics
URBAN, L., Political Economy

MASARYKOVA UNIVERZITA V BRNĚ
(Masaryk University in Brno)

Žerotínovo nám. 9, 601 77 Brno

Telephone: 549491011
Fax: 549491070
E-mail: info@muni.cz
Internet: www.muni.cz

Founded 1919
State control
Language of instruction: Czech
Academic year: September to August

Rector: Prof. Dr PETER FIALA
Vice-Rector for Academic Affairs: Prof. Dr ZUZANA BRÁZDOVÁ
Vice-Rector for Research and Devt: Prof. Dr JANA MUSILOVÁ
Vice-Rector for Social Affairs of Students and External Relations: Assoc. Prof. Ing. ANTONÍN SLANÝ

Library of 1,544,000 vols
Number of teachers: 3,072

Number of students: 26,681
Publications: *Archivum mathematicum* (8 a year), *MUNI.CZ* (10 a year), *Scripta Medica* (6 a year), *Universitas* (4 a year)

DEANS

Faculty of Arts: Dr JAN PAVLÍK
Faculty of Economics and Administration: Assoc. Prof. Dr IVAN MALÝ
Faculty of Education: Assoc. Prof. Dr VLADISLAV MUŽÍK
Faculty of Informatics: Prof. Dr JIŘI ZLATUŠKA
Faculty of Law: Assoc. Prof. Dr JAN SVATOŇ
Faculty of Medicine: Assoc. Prof. Dr JAN ŽALOUDÍK
Faculty of Science: Assoc. Prof. Dr MILAN GELNAR
Faculty of Sports Studies: Dr MICHAL CHARVÁT
School of Social Studies: Assoc. Prof. Dr LADISLAV RABUŠIC

PROFESSORS

Faculty of Arts (Arna Nováka 1, 660 80 Brno; tel. 549491511; fax 549491520; e-mail dekan@phil.muni.cz; internet www.phil .muni.cz):

BÁTORA, J., Archaeology
BLAŽEK, V., Comparative Indo-European Linguistics
CEJPEK, J., Library Studies
FIALA, J., Czech Literature
GAJDOŠ, J., Theory and History of Theatre
HORÁK, P., Philosophy
HORYNA, B., Study of Religion
HROCH, J., Philosophy
KARLÍK, P., Czech Language
KRČMOVÁ, M., Czech Language
KROUPA, J., History of Arts
KURFÜRST, P., Musicology
MALÍŘ, J., Czech History
MĚŘÍNSKÝ, Z., Archaeology
MUNZAR, J., German Literature
NECHUTOVÁ, J., Classics
NEKUDA, V., Slavonic Archaeology
OSLZLÝ, P., Theatre and Film Studies
PLESKALOVÁ, J., Czech Language
POSPÍŠIL, I., History of Russian Literature
RUSÍNOVÁ, Z., Czech Language
ŠLAVÍČEK, L., History of Art
ŠMAJS, J., Philosophy
ŠTEHLÍKOVÁ, E., Theatre and Film Studies
ŠTĚDROŇ, M., Musicology
STŘÍTECKÝ, J., Philosophy
SVOBODA, M., Psychology
ZOUHAR, J., Philosophy

Faculty of Economics and Administration (Lipová 41A, 659 79 Brno; tel. 549491710; fax 549491720; e-mail dekan@econ.muni.cz; internet www.econ.muni.cz):

BLAZEK, L., Theory of Management
IVÁNEK, J., Economics
LANČA, J., Economics and Corporate Management
MÁŠA, M., Management
ONDRČKA, P., Finance
ŠEJBAL, J., Finance
ŽÁK, M., Economics

Faculty of Education (Poříčí 7, 603 00 Brno; tel. 549493050; fax 549491620; e-mail dekan@ped.muni.cz; internet www.ped.muni .cz):

CHALUPA, P., Geography
CHVALINA, J., Mathematics
HLADKÝ, J., English Language
HOROVÁ, I., Mathematics
KOŠUT, M., Teaching of Music
MAŇÁK, J., Education
MAREČKOVÁ, M., History
NOVÁK, V., Mathematics
ŠVEC, V., Education
VÍTKOVÁ, M., Special Education

Faculty of Informatics (Botanická 68A, Brno; tel. 549491810; fax 549491820; e-mail dekan@fi.muni.cz; internet www.fi.muni.cz):

BUZEK, V., Informatics
DOKULIL, M., Philosophy
GRUSKA, J., Informatics
HŘEBÍČEK, J., Company Information Systems
MATERNA, P., Logic
NOVOTNÝ, M., Mathematics and Informatics
SERBA, I., Informatics
ZEZULA, P., Informatics
ZLATUŠKA, J., Informatics

Faculty of Law (Veveří 70, 611 80 Brno; tel. 549491211; fax 541213162; e-mail dekan@ law.muni.cz; internet www.law.muni.cz):

BEJČEK, J., Economic Law
FILIP, J., Constitutional Law and Political Science
HAJN, P., Economic Law
HRUŠÁKOVÁ, M., Civil Law
HURDÍK, J., Civil Law
JÍLEK, D., International Public Law
MALENOVSKÝ, J., International Public Law
ROZEHNALOVÁ, N., International Private Law
TELEC, I., Civil Law
VÁGNER, I., Economics
VLČEK, E., History of State and Law

Faculty of Medicine (Komenského nám. 2, 662 43 Brno; tel. 549491111; fax 542213996; e-mail dekan@med.muni.cz; internet www .med.muni.cz):

ADAM, Z., Internal Medicine
BEDNAŘÍK, J., Neurology
BENDA, K., Radiology
BRÁZDOVÁ, Z., Social Medicine
BRHEL, P., Occupational Medicine
BRYCHTA, P., Surgery
BUČEK, J., Pathology
ČECH, S., Histology
ČEŠKOVÁ, E., Psychiatry
DAPECI, A., Stomatology
DÍTĚ, P., Internal Medicine
DRTÍLKOVÁ, I., Psychiatry
DUBOVÝ, P., Anatomy
DVOŘÁK, K., Pathology
FAKAN, F., Anatomy
FIŠER, B., Pathology and Physiology
GÁL, P., Surgery
HADAŠOVÁ, E., Pharmacology
HEP, A., Internal Medicine
HOLČÍK, J., Social Medicine
HONZÍKOVÁ, N., Pathology and Physiology
HORKÝ, D., Histology
HRUBÁ, D., Social Medicine
JANISCH, R., Biology
KADAŇKA, Z., Neurology
KOSTŘICA, R., Otorhynolaryngology
KUBEŠOVÁ, H., Internal Medicine
KUKLETA, M., Medical Physiology
KUKLETOVA, M., Stomatology
LITZMAN, J., Immunology
LOKAJ, J., Immunology
LUKÁŠ, Z., Anatomy
MALÝ, Z., Gynaecology and Obstetrics
MAYER, J., Internal Medicine
MELUZÍN, J., Internal Medicine
MUNZAROVÁ, M., Internal Medicine
PÁČ, L., Anatomy
PAČÍK, D., Surgery
PENKA, M., Internal Medicine
PETŘEK, M., Immunology
ŘEHŮŘEK, J., Ophthalmology
REJTHAR, A., Pathology
REKTOR, I., Neurology
ROZTOČIL, A., Gynaecology and Obstetrics
SEMRÁD, B., Internal Medicine
ŠEMRÁDOVÁ, V., Dermatovenereology
ŠEVČIK, P., Anaesthesiology
SIEGLOVÁ, J., Functional Diagnostics and Rehabilitation
SMRČKA, V., Surgery

ŠPINAR, J., Internal Medicine
ŠULCOVÁ, A., Pharmacology
ŠVESTKA, J., Psychiatry
SVOBODA, A., Biology
TOMAN, J., Internal Medicine
VÁCHA, J., Pathological Physiology
VÁLEK, V., Radiology
VANĚK, J., Stomatology
VAŠKŮ, A., Pathological Physiology
VENTRUBA, P., Gynaecology and Obstetrics
VESELÝ, J., Surgery
VÍTOVEC, J., Internal Medicine
VLKOVÁ, E., Ophthalmology
VOMELA, J., Surgery
VORLÍČEK, J., Internal Medicine
WECHSLER, J., Surgery
WENDSCHE, P., Surgery
ZÁHEJSKÝ, J., Dermatovenereology
ŽALOUDÍK, J., Surgery
ZEMAN, K., Internal Medicine

Faculty of Science (Kotlářská 2, 611 37 Brno; tel. 549491411; fax 541211214; e-mail dekan@sci.muni.cz; internet www.sci.muni.cz):

BARTŮSEK, M., Analytical Chemistry
BRÁZDIL, R., Physical Geography
BRZOBOHATÝ, R., Palaeontology
DOŠKAŘ, J., Molecular Biology and Genetics
DOŠLÁ, Z., Mathematics
DOŠLÝ, O., Mathematical Analysis
GAISLER, J., Zoology
GLOSER, J., Plant Physiology
HÁLA, J., Inorganic Chemistry
HAVEL, J., Analytical Chemistry
HOLÍK, M., Physical Chemistry
HOLOUBEK, I., Environmental Chemistry
HOLÝ, V., Physics of Condensed Materials
HORSKÝ, J., Theoretical Physics
HUMLÍČEK, J., Physics
JANČA, J., Physics
JONAS, J., Organic Chemistry
KANICKÝ, V., Analytical Chemistry
KAPIČKA, V., Physics
KNOZ, J., Biology
KOČA, J., Organic Chemistry
KOLÁŘ, I., Algebra and Geometry
KOMÁREK, A., Analytical Chemistry
KOTYK, A., Biochemistry
KUČERA, I., Biochemistry
LENC, M., General Physics and Mathematical Physics
MALINA, J., Archaeology
MUSILOVÁ, J., Physics
NOVÁK, M., Geology
NOVÁK, V., Mathematics
NOVOTNÝ, J., Physics
OHLÍDAL, I., Quantum Electronics and Optics
POTÁČEK, M., Organic Chemistry
PŘICHYSTAL, A., Geology
PROŠEK, P., Physical Geography
RELICHOVÁ, J., Genetics
ROSICKÝ, J., Mathematics
ROZKOŠNÝ, R., Entomology
SCHMIDT, E., Physics
ŠKLENÁŘ, V., Physical Chemistry
ŠIMEK, M., Animal Physiology
SKULA, L., Mathematics
SLOVÁK, J., Geometry
STANĚK, J., Mineralogy and Petrography
UNGER, J., Anthropology
VAŇHARA, J., Zoology
VELICKÝ, B., Theoretical Physics
VETTERL, J., Physical Electronics
VICHEREK, J., Botany
VŘEŠŤÁL, J., Physical Chemistry
ŽÁK, Z., Inorganic Chemistry
ZIMA, J., Zoology

School of Social Studies (Gorkého 7, 602 00 Brno; tel. 549491911; fax 549491920; e-mail dekan@fss.muni.cz; internet www.fss.muni.cz):

FIALA, P., Politology
KELLER, J., Sociology

LIBROVÁ, H., Sociology
MACEK, P., Social Psychology
MAREŠ, P., Sociology
MOŽNÝ, I., Sociology
RABUŠIC, L., Sociology
SIROVÁTKA, T., Social Policy and Social Work
ŠMAUSOVÁ, G., Sociology
SMÉKAL, V., Psychology
STRMISKA, M., Political Science

MENDELOVA UNIVERZITA V BRNĚ
(Mendel University in Brno)

Zemědělská 1, 613 00 Brno
Telephone: 545131111
Fax: 545211128
E-mail: info@mendelu.cz
Internet: www.mendelu.cz
Founded 1919, by State Law
State control
Languages of instruction: Czech, English
Academic year: September to June (2 semesters)
Rector: J. HLUŠEK
Pro-Rectors: L. GREGA, M. HAVLÍČEK J. NERUDA R. POKLUDA
Chief Admin. Officer: V. SEDLÁŘOVÁ
Chief Librarian: VERA SVOBODOVÁ
Library of 400,000 vols
Number of teachers: 450
Number of students: 11,000 full-time, 1,200 part-time
Publications: Acta Universitatis Agriculturae et Silviculturae Mendelianae Brunensis (6 a year), Folia Universitatis Agriculturae et Silviculturae Mendelianae Brunensis

DEANS

Faculty of Agronomy: L. ZEMAN
Faculty of Business and Economics: J. STÁVKOVÁ
Faculty of Forestry and Wood Technology: P. HORÁČEK
Faculty of Horticulture: ROBERT POKLUDA
Faculty of Regional Devt and Int. Studies: IVA ŽIVĚLOVÁ

OSTRAVSKÁ UNIVERZITA V OSTRAVĚ
(Ostrava University)

Dvořákova 7, 701 03 Ostrava
Telephone: 597091111
Fax: 596118219
Internet: www.osu.cz
Founded 1991
State control
Rector: Dr JIŘÍ MOČKOŘ
Vice-Rector for Devt and Information Management: Dr Ing CYRIL KLIMEŠ
Vice-Rector for Research and External Relations: Mgr IGOR FOJTÍK
Vice-Rector for Study: Dr JARMILA KRKOŠKOVÁ
Library of 230,000 vols
Number of teachers: 583
Number of students: 9,470

DEANS

Faculty of Arts: Dr EVA MRHAČOVÁ
Faculty of Fine Arts: Dr ZBYNĚK JANÁČEK
Faculty of Science: Dr DANA KRIČFALUŠI
Faculty of Social Studies: Dr OLDŘICH CHYTIL
Medico-Social Faculty: Dr ARNOŠT MARTÍNEK
Pedagogical Faculty: Dr JOSEF MALACH

UNIVERZITA PALACKÉHO V OLOMOUCI
(Palacký University)

Křížkovského 8, 771 47 Olomouc
Telephone: 585631001

Fax: 585631012
E-mail: kancler@upol.cz
Internet: www.upol.cz
Founded 1573, reopened 1946
State control
Languages of instruction: Czech, English, German
Academic year: September to July
Rector: Prof. Dr MIROSLAV MAŠLÁŇ
Vice-Rector for Communication and Further Education: Dr MICHAL MALACKA
Vice-Rector for Information Technology: Prof. Dr VIT VOŽENÍLEK
Vice-Rector for Int. Relations: Mgr JAKUB DÜRR
Vice-Rector for Int. Organization: Dr MONIKA HORÁKOVÁ
Vice-Rector for Regional Devt: Prof. Dr LUBOMÍR DVOŘÁK
Vice-Rector for Science and Research: Prof. Dr JITKA ULRICHOVÁ
Vice-Rector for Study: Doc.Mgr VIT ZOUHAR
Registrar: Ing. HENRIETA CRKOŇOVÁ
Librarian: Dr DANA LOŠŤÁKOVÁ
Library of 600,000 vols
Number of teachers: 1,800
Number of students: 23,000
Publication: Acta Universitatis Palackianae (4 a year)

DEANS

Faculty of Education: Prof. LIBUŠE LUDÍKOVÁ
Faculty of Health Sciences: Doc. JANA MAREČKOVÁ
Faculty of Law: Prof. MILANA HRUŠÁKOVÁ
Faculty of Medicine and Dentistry: Prof. ZDERNĚK KOLÁŘ
Faculty of Philosophy: Prof. Doc. JIŘÍ LACH
Faculty of Physical Culture: Doc. ZBYNĚK SVOZIL
Faculty of Science: Prof. JURAJ ŠEVČÍK
Sts Cyril and Methodius Faculty of Theology: Dr IVANAGABRIELA VLKOVÁ

PROFESSORS

Faculty of Education (Žižkovo nám. 5, 771 40 Olomouc; tel. 585635088; fax 585231400; e-mail jelenka.navratilova@upol.cz):

CHRÁSKA, M., Theory of Education
GRECMANOVÁ, H., Education
HANZEL, P., Mathematics
KLAPIL, P., Music Theory
LUDÍKOVÁ, L., Special Needs Education
LUSKA, J., Music Theory
NELEŠOVSKÁ, A., Theory of Elementary Education
ODALOŠ, P., Czech Language and Literature
POTMĚŠIL, M., Special Needs Education
STEINMETZ, K., Music Theory
STOFFOVÁ, V.
VALENTA, M., Special Needs Education

Faculty of Health Sciences (Tř. Svobody 8, 771 11 Olomouc; tel. and fax 585632852; e-mail romana.schneeweissova@upol.cz):

KAMÍNEK, M., Radiology

Faculty of Law (Tř.17 Listopadu 8, 771 11 Olomouc; tel. 585637509; fax 585637506; e-mail dekanat.pf@upol.cz):

DAVID, V., International Law
FIALA, J., Civic Law
HRUŠÁKOVÁ, M., Civic Law
JELÍNEK, J., Criminal Law
MAREČKOVÁ, M., History
MECL, J., Theory of Law
PORADA, V., Criminal Law
SLÁDEČEK, V., Law
TELEC, I., Civic Law
VLČEK, E., Theory of Law

Faculty of Medicine and Dentistry (Tř. Svobody 8, 771 26 Olomouc; tel. 585632009; fax 585632063; e-mail klosova@tunw.upol.cz):

DLOUHÝ, M., Surgery

DUDA, M., Surgery
EBER, M., Stomatology
EHRMANN, J., Internal Diseases
HÁLEK, J., Electronics and Medical Procedures
HEŘMAN, M., Radiology
HOLIBKA, V., General Anatomy
HOUDEK, M., Neurosurgery
INDRÁK, K., Internal Diseases
JANOUT, V., Epidemiology
JAROŠOVÁ, M., Medigal Genetics
JEZDINSKÝ, J., Pharmacology
JIRAVA, E., Stomatology
KAMÍNEK, M., Stomatology
KAŇOVSKÝ, P., Neurology
KLEIN, J., Surgery
KLENER, P., Paediatry
KODOUSEK, R., Pathological Anatomy
KOLÁŘ, M., Microbiology
KOLÁŘ, Z., Pathology
KOLEK, V., Internal Diseases
KOPŘIVA, F., Paediatry
KRÁL, V., Surgery
KRČ, I., Internal Diseases
KUDELA, M., Gynaecology
LATA, J., Microbiology
LICHNOVSKÝ, V., Histology and Embryology
LUKL, J., Internal Diseases
MAČÁKOVÁ, J., Pathological Physiology
MACHÁČEK, J., Radiology
MELICHAR, B., Oncology
MIHÁL, V., Paediatry
MÍŠEK, I., Paediatry
NEKULA, J., Radiology
PAZDERA, J., Stomatology
PEŠÁK, J., Medical Biophysics
PETŘEK, J., Physiology
PETŘEK, M., Immunology
ŘÍHOVÁ, B., Paediatry
ŠEDLÁČEK, R., Paediatry
ŠANTAVÝ, J., Medical Genetics
ŠČUDLA, V., Internal Diseases
ŠEVČÍK, P., Anesteziology
ŠIMÁNEK, V., Medical Chemistry
STÁREK, I., Othorhinolaryngology
ULRICHOVÁ, J., Medical Chemistry and Biochemistry
URBÁNEK, K., Neurology
VAVERKOVÁ, H., Internal Diseases
VESELÝ, J., Pathological Physiology
WEIGL, E., Immunology

Faculty of Philosophy (Křížkovského 10, 771 80 Olomouc; tel. 585631111; fax 585633000; e-mail dekan.ff@upol.cz):
ANDERŠ, J., Slavonic Studies
ASSENZA, G., Political Science
BARTEČEK, I., History
BLECHA, I., Philosophy
BUREŠOVÁ, A., Theory of Music
BUREŠOVÁ, J., History
ČERNÝ, J., Linguistics
DANIEL, L., History of VisualArts
FIALA, J., History of Czech Literature
FIALOVÁ, I., History of German Literature
FLÍDROVÁ, H., Russian Language
FLOSS, P., History of Philosophy
HECHT, L., Jewish Studies
HLOBIL, T., History of Visual Arts
GERŠLOVÁ, J., Economics
JAŘAB, J., American Literature
KOŘENSKÝ, J., Slavonic Studies
LOTKO, E., Czech Language
MACHÁČEK, J., English Studies
MAREK, P., Czech History
NOVOTNÝ, J., History of Visual Arts
PEPRNÍK, J., English Language
PLHÁKOVÁ, A., Psychology
SEHNAL, J., Theory of Music
SOBOTKOVÁ, M., History of Czech Language
SPÁČILOVÁ, L., German Language
SVOBODA, M., Psychology
ŠIMEK, D., Sociology
ŠRÁMEK, J., French Literature
ŠTĚPÁN, J., Philosophy
ŠTĚPÁNEK, P., History of Visual Arts

ŠVÁCHA, R., History of Visual Arts
ŠVORCOVÁ, Z., Japan Studies
TÁRNYIKOVÁ, J., English Studies
TOGNER, M., History of Visual Arts
TRAPL, M., Czech and Slovak History
ULIČNÝ, O., Chech Studies
UNGER, J., History
VÁCLAVEK, L., History of German Literature
VIČAR, J., Theory of Music
ZAHRÁDKA, M., Russian Literature

Faculty of Physical Culture (Tř. Míru 115, 771 11 Olomouc; tel. 585636009; fax 585412899; e-mail dekanat.ftk@upol.cz):
FRÖMEL, K., Kinanthropology
HODAŇ, B., Theory of Physical Culture
JANURA, M., Biomechanics
OPAVSKÝ, J., Neurology
OŠŤÁDAL, O., Internal Diseases
RIEGEROVÁ, J., Kinanthropology
VÁLKOVÁ, H., Kinanthropology
VAVERKA, F., Kinanthropology

Faculty of Science (Tř.17, Listopadu 1192/12, 77146 Olomouc; tel. 585634060; fax 585634002; e-mail dekanat.prf@upol.cz):
ANDRÉS, J., Mathematical Analysis
BAJER, J., Optics and Optoelectronics
BIČÍK, V., Zoology
BĚLOHLÁVEK, R., Informatics
BOUCHAL, Z., Optics and Optoelectronics
BRABEC, V., Physics
BUREŠ, S., Zoology
CHAJDA, I., Algebra and Geometry
DUŠEK, M., Quantum Optics
DVOŘÁK, L., Biophysics
DVOŘÁK, Z., Cell Biology
FRÉBORT, I., Biochemistry
HALAŠ, R., Algebra and geometry
HOBZA, P., Physical chemistry
HRABOVSKÝ, M., Optics
HRADIL, P., Organic chemistry
HRADIL, Z., Optics and Optoelectronics
HUBA, M., Development Studies
KAMENÍČEK, J., Inorganic Chemistry
KOTOUČEK, M., Analytical Chemistry
KRAHULEC, F., Botany
KRUPKOVÁ, O., Mathematical Physics
KUBÁČEK, L., Mathematical Statistics
KULHÁNEK, P., Optics
LASOVSKÝ, J., Physical Chemistry
LEBEDA, A., Botany
LEMR, K., Analytical Chemistry
MAŠLÁŇ, M., Applied Physics
MIKEŠ, J., Geometry and Topology
NAUŠ, J., Biophysics
NAVRÁTIL, M., Biology
NEZVALOVÁ, D., Paedagogy
OPATRNÝ, T., Mathematical Physics
PASTOREK, R., Inorganic Chemistry
PEČ, P., Biochemistry
PEŘINA, J., Optoelectronics
PEŘINOVÁ, V., Mthematical Physics
POSPÍŠIL, J., Experimental Physics
POULÍČKOVÁ, A., Botany
RACHŮNEK, J., Algebra
RACHŮNKOVÁ, I., Mathematical Analysis
ŠARAPATKA, B., Landscape Engineering
SLOUKA, J., Organic Chemistry
STANĚK, S., Mathematical Analysis
STRÁNSKÝ, Z., Analytical Chemistry
ŠTRNAD, M., Plant Physiology
ŠEBELA, M., Biochemistry
ŠEVČÍK, J., Analytical Chemistry
ŠTĚRBA, O., Ecology
TKADLEC, E., Ecology
TRÁVNÍČEK, Z., Inorganic Chemistry
VOŽENÍLEK, V., Geography
ZAPLETAL, J., Geology

Sts Cyril and Methodius Faculty of Theology (Univerzitní 22, 771 11 Olomouc; tel. 585637111; fax 585637005; e-mail dekanat .cmtf@upol.cz):
AMBROS, P., Theology
GÓRECKI, E., Religious Las

HALAS, F., History
KARFÍKOVÁ, L., Evangelical Theory
POJSL, M., History of Christian Arts
TICHÝ, L., Theology
KUNETKA, F., Liturgical Theology
POMPEY, H., Christian Social Work

UNIVERZITA PARDUBICE
(University of Pardubice)

Studentská 95, 532 10 Pardubice
Telephone: 466036111
Fax: 466036361
E-mail: promotion@upce.cz
Internet: www.upce.cz
Founded 1950 as Vysoká Škola Chemicko-Technologická v Pardubicích; present name and status 1994
State control
Languages of instruction: Czech, English
Academic year: September to August
Rector: Prof. Ing. MIROSLAV LUDWIG
Vice-Rectors: Doc. Ing. JIŘÍ CAKL, Doc. Ing. JAROSLAV JANDA, Doc. Ing. JIŘÍ MÁLEK
Bursar: Ing. MILAN BUKAČ
Librarian: IVA PROCHÁSKOVÁ
Library of 180,000 vols
Number of teachers: 381
Number of students: 4,794
Publications: *Scientific Papers* (1 a year), *Zpravodaj Univerzity Pardubice* (4 a year)

DEANS
Faculty of Chemical Technology: Doc. Ing. PETR MIKULÁŠEK
Faculty of Economics and Administration: Doc. Ing. JAN ČAPEK
Faculty of Humanities: Prof. MILENA LENDEROVÁ
Jan Perner Faculty of Transport: Prof. Dr Ing. KAREL ŠOTEK

ATTACHED RESEARCH INSTITUTES
Institute of Health Studies: Průmyslová 395, 530 03 Pardubice; Dir Prof. Dr ARNOŠT PELLANT.
Institute of Informatics: Studenská 95, 532 10 Pardubice; Dir Doc. Ing. SIMEON KARAMAZOV.

SLEZSKÁ UNIVERZITA V OPAVĚ
(Silesian University in Opava)

Na Rybníčku 626/1, 746 01 Opava
Telephone: 553684621
Fax: 553718019
E-mail: rektorat@slu.cz
Internet: www.slu.cz
Founded 1991
State control
Language of instruction: Czech
Academic year: October to September
Rector: Doc. Dr RUDOLF ŽÁČEK
Quaestor: Ing. JAROSLAV KANIA
Library of 77,000 vols, 256 periodicals
Number of teachers: 400
Number of students: 8,900
Publications: *Acta Academia Karviniensia*, *Acta Historica*, *Noviny Slezské Univerzity*

DEANS
Faculty of Business Administration: Dr BOHUMIL FIALA
Faculty of Philosophy and Science: Prof. ZDENĚK STUCHLÍK
Faculty of Public Policies: Doc. Dr DUŠAN JANÁK
Institute of Mathematics: Prof. JAROSLAV SMÍTAL

TECHNICKÁ UNIVERZITA V LIBERCI
(Technical University of Liberec)

Studentská 2, 461 17 Liberec
Telephone: 485351111
Fax: 485105882
E-mail: rektor@tul.cz
Internet: www.tul.cz

Founded 1953
State control
Languages of instruction: Czech, English
Academic year: September to June

Rector: Prof. ZDENĚK KŮS
Vice-Rector: Prof. JIŘÍ KRAFT
Vice-Rector: Assoc. Prof. ONDŘEJ NOVÁK
Vice-Rector: Assoc. Prof. JANA DRAŠAROVÁ
Registrar: VLADIMÍR STACH
Librarian: ADAM KRETSCHMER

Library of 185,000
Number of teachers: 750
Number of students: 9,800

Publications: *Economics and Management* (7 a year), *Sborník vědeckých prací Technické univerzity* (Annals of Scientific Research)

DEANS

Faculty of Arts and Architecture: Prof. BOŘEK ŠIPEK
Faculty of Economics: Assoc. Prof. OLGA HASPROVA
Faculty of Education: Assoc. Prof. MIROSLAV BRZEZINA
Faculty of Mechanical Engineering: Assoc. Prof. MIROSLAV MALÝ
Faculty of Mechatronics and Interdisciplinary Engineering Studies: Prof. JIŘÍ MARYŠKA
Faculty of Textile Engineering: Prof. VÁCLAV LINKA

PROFESSORS

BAKULE, V., Finance and Credit
BENEŠ, S., Construction of Machines and Appliances
BEROUN, S., Transport Machines
CYHELSKÝ, L., Statistics
DUCHOŇ, B., Management Technology in Transport
EHLEMAN, J., Information Management
EXNER, J., Mechanical Engineering Technology
FOUSEK, J., Electromechanical Properties of Dielectrics
HAJNIŠ, K., Physical Education
HANUŠ, B., Control Engineering
HES, L., Textile Valuation
HINDLS, R., Insurance, Statistics
HONCŮ, J., Machine Design
HÝČA, M., Applied Mechanics
IBRAHIM, S., Textile Technology
JANOVEC, V., Electromechanical Properties of Dielectrics
JIRSÁK, O., Textile Technology
KAŇOKOVÁ, J., Statistics
KARGER, A., Mathematics, Economics, Topology
KONOPA, V., Technical Cybernetics
KOPKA, J., Teaching of Mathematics
KOŠEK, M., Technical Cybernetics
KOVÁŘ, R., Textile Technology
KOVÁŘ, Z., Combustion Engines
KRAFT, J., Enterprise Economics, Management
KRATOCHVÍL, P., Materials Engineering
KRYŠTŮFEK, J., Textile Technology
KVAČEK, R., Czech History
LANDOROVÁ, A., Financing
LUKÁŠ, D., Textile Technology
MILITKÝ, J., Textile Technology
NECKÁŘ, B., Structure of Textiles
NOSEK, J., Physics
NOSEK, S., Textile Machines
NOUZA, J., Technical Cybernetics
NOVÁ, I., Engineering Metallurgy
NOVÁK, O., Technical Cybernetics

OLEHLA, J., Machines and Devices Construction
OLEHLA, M., Production Systems and Processes
PŘIVRATSKÁ, J., Physics
SKALLA, J., Servodrivers and Automation
SODOMKA, L., Applied Physics
STIBOR, I., Organic Chemistry
STRAKOŠ, Z., Technical Cybernetics
STŘÍŽ, B., Elasticity and Strength
SUCHOMEL, J., Architecture and Design
ŠKALOUD, M., Mechanics
ŠKLÍBA, J., Applied Mechanics
ŠPATENKA, P., Mechanical Engineering Technology
ULIČNÝ, O., Czech Language
URSÍNY, P., Textile Technology
VÁGNEROVÁ, M., Psychology
VAVERKA, J., Building Engineering
VĚCHET, V., Technical Cybernetics
VOKURKA, K., Applied Physics
VOSTATEK, J., Finance
ZELINKA, B., Mathematical Informatics and Theoretical Cybernetics

UNIVERZITA TOMÁŠE BATI VE ZLÍNĚ
(Tomas Bata University in Zlín)

Náměstí T. G. Masaryka 5555, 760 01 Zlín
Telephone: 576032222
Fax: 576032444
E-mail: rektor@utb.cz
Internet: www.utb.cz

Founded 2001
State control
Languages of instruction: Czech, English
Academic year: September to August

Rector: Prof. PETR SÁHA
Vice-Rector for International Relations: Assoc. Prof. ALEŠ GREGAR
Vice-Rector for Pedagogical Activities: Assoc. Prof. ZDENKA PROKOPOVÁ
Vice-Rector for Research and Development: Assoc. Prof. BERENIKA HAUSNEROVÁ
Vice-Rector for Social Affairs: Assoc. Prof. DAVID TUČEK

Number of teachers: 450
Number of students: 13,500

DEANS

Faculty of Applied Informatics: Prof. VLADIMÍR VAŠEK
Faculty of Humanities: Assoc. Prof. ANEŽKA LENGÁLOVÁ
Faculty of Logistics and Crisis Management: Prof. JOSEF POLÁŠEK
Faculty of Management and Economics: Prof. DRAHOMÍRA PAVELKOVÁ
Faculty of Multimedia Communications: Assoc. Prof. JANA JANÍKOVÁ
Faculty of Technology: Assoc. Prof. PETR HLAVÁČEK

ATTACHED RESEARCH INSTITUTE

University Institute: e-mail ondrackova@uni.utb.cz; internet www.uni.utb.cz; Dir Ing. JINDŘIŠKA ONDRÁČKOVÁ.

VETERINÁRNÍ A FARMACEUTICKÁ UNIVERZITA BRNO
(University of Veterinary and Pharmaceutical Sciences Brno)

Palackého 1–3, 612 42 Brno
Telephone: 541562000
Fax: 549250478
E-mail: rektor@vfu.cz
Internet: www.vfu.cz

Founded 1918
State control
Languages of instruction: Czech, English
Academic year: September to August

Rector: Prof. Dr VLADIMIR VEČEREK

Pro-Rector for Education and Vice-Rector: Prof. Dr IVA STEINHAUSEROVÁ
Pro-Rector for Scientific Research and Foreign Relations: Doc. MILOSLAVA LOPATÁŘOVÁ
Pro-Rector for Univ. Devt: Prof. Dr Ing. PAVEL SUCHÝ
Registrar: Mgr DANIELA NĚMCOVÁ
Librarian: Mgr JANA SLÁMOVÁ

Library: see Libraries and Archives
Number of teachers: 301
Number of students: 2,951

Publication: *Acta Veterinaria Brno* (4 a year)

DEANS

Faculty of Pharmacy: Doc. Dr MILAN ŽEMLIČKA
Faculty of Veterinary Hygiene and Ecology: Doc. Dr LADISLAV STEINHAUSER
Faculty of Veterinary Medicine: Doc. Dr ALOIS NEČAS

PROFESSORS

Faculty of Pharmacy (tel. 541562801; fax 541219751; e-mail dekanfaf@vfu.cz; internet faf.vfu.cz):

CSÖLLEI, J., Pharmaceutical Chemistry
KVĚTINA, J., Pharmacology and Toxicology
SUCHÝ, J., Pharmacognosy
VÍTOVEC, J., Pharmacology and Toxicology

Faculty of Veterinary Hygiene and Ecology (tel. 541562795; fax 549243020; e-mail fvhe@vfu.cz; internet ww.vfu.cz):

BARANYIOVÁ, E., Behaviour Problems in Animals, Methodology of Scientific Work
BEKLOVÁ, M., Ecology
DVORÁK, P., Physics, Veterinary Biophysics, Radiobiology of Food
LITERÁK, I., Biology and Genetics
PAVLÍK, I., Tuberculosis, Paratuberculosis and Mycobacterioses
PIKULA, J., Ecology, Game Animal Diseases
STRAKOVÁ, E., Farm Animal Nutrition
SUCHÝ, P., Animal Nutrition and Dietetics
ŠUCMAN, E., Veterinary Chemistry and Biochemistry
SVOBODOVÁ, Z., Veterinary Toxicology and Ecotoxicology
VÁVROVÁ, M., Chemistry and Technology of Environment Protection
VEČEREK, V. A., Veterinary Public Health
VORLOVÁ, L., Food Chemistry, Hygiene and Technology

Faculty of Veterinary Medicine (tel. 541562440; fax 549248841; e-mail dekanfvl@vfu.cz; internet www.vfu.cz):

ČELER, V., Veterinary Microbiology
ČÍŽEK, A., Veterinary Microbiology
DVOŘÁK, R., Diseases of Farm Animals
HALOUZKA, R., Veterinary Morphology
HANÁK, J., Equine Diseases
HERA, A., Veterinary Pharmacology
HOŘÍN, P., Animal Genetics
KNOTEK, Z., Diseases of Small Animals
KOUDELA, B., Veterinary Parasitology
KOVÁŘŮ, F., Physiology
MÍŠEK, I., Veterinary Morphology
NEČAS, A., Veterinary Surgery and Orthopaedics
POSPÍŠIL, Z., Epizootiology
SMOLA, J., Microbiology
SVOBODA, M., Diseases of Small Animals
SVOBODOVÁ, V., Veterinary Parasitology
TICHÝ, F., Histology and Embryology
TOMAN, M., Veterinary Immunology
TREML, F., Epizootiology

VYSOKÁ ŠKOLA BÁŇSKÁ – TECHNICKÁ UNIVERZITA OSTRAVA
(Technical University of Ostrava)

17 Listopadu 15, 708 33 Ostrava-Poruba
Telephone: 596991111
Fax: 596918507

E-mail: vaclav.roubicek@vsb.cz
Internet: www.vsb.cz

Founded 1716
State control
Academic year: September to August
Rector: Prof. Ing. VÁCLAV ROUBÍČEK
Vice-Rector for Devt: Prof. Ing. PETR WYSLYCH
Vice-Rector for Education: Prof. Ing. JAROMÍR POLÁK
Vice-Rector for Finance and Organization: Prof. Ing. MIROSLAV NEJEZCHLEBA
Vice-Rector for Research and Devt and Int. Affairs: Prof. Ing. TOMÁŠ ČERMÁK
Registrar: Ing. STANISLAV DZIOB
Librarian: Mgr DANIELA TKAČÍKOVÁ

Number of teachers: 812
Number of students: 14,579

Publications: *Akademik* (6 a year), *Sborník vědeckých prací VSB-TU Ostrava* (irregular)

DEANS

Faculty of Civil Engineering: Prof. Ing. JINDŘICH CIGÁNEK
Faculty of Economics: Prof. Ing. JIŘÍ KERN
Faculty of Electrical Engineering and Informatics: Doc. Ing. KAREL CHMELÍK
Faculty of Mechanical Engineering: Prof. Ing. PETR HORYL
Faculty of Metallurgy and Material Engineering: Prof. Ing. LUDOVIT DOBROVSKÝ
Faculty of Mining and Geology: Prof. Ing. JAROSLAV DVOŘÁČEK

PROFESSORS

Faculty of Civil Engineering (tel. 596991316; fax 596991356; e-mail dekan.fast@vsb.cz):

ALDORF, J., Mine Construction and Geotechnics
CIGANEK, J., Mine Construction and Geotechnics

Faculty of Economics (1, Sokolská tř. 33, 701 21 Ostrava; fax 596110026):

HALÁSEK, D., Macroeconomics
JUREČKA, V., General Economics
KALUŽA, J., Informatics in Economics
KERN, J., Macroeconomics
NEJEZCHLEBA, M., Finance
POLÁCH, J., Finance
SMOLÍK, D., Environmental Protection and Reclamation
ŠNAPKA, P., Mining Economics and Management

Faculty of Electrical Engineering and Informatics (tel. 596995252; fax 596919597):

BLAHETA, R., Applied Mathematics
BLUNÁR, K., Communications Technology
BRANDŠTETTER, P., Electrical Machines, Apparatus and Drives
ČERMÁK, T., Electrical Drives
DIVIŠ, Z., Transport and Infrastructure
DOSTÁL, Z., Applied Mathematics
HASLINGER, J., Applied Mathematics
HRADÍLEK, Z., Electrical Power Engineering
LITSCHMANN, J., Engineering Cybernetics
NEVŘIVA, P., Technical Cybernetics
PALEČEK, J., Electrical Power Engineering
POKORNÝ, M., Measurement and Control Technology
RUSEK, S., Electrical Power Engineering
SANTARIUS, Electrical Power Engineering
SOKANSKÝ, K., Electrical Power Engineering
VONDRÁK, I., Computer Science

Faculty of Mechanical Engineering (tel. 597321216; fax 596916490):

ANTONICKÝ, S., Transportation and Technology
BAILOTTI, K., Transportation and Preparation Equipment
DANĚK, A., Transportation and Technology

DANĚK, J., Transportation and Technology
DEJL, Z., Machine Parts and Mechanisms
FUXA, J., Applied Mechanics
GONDEK, H., Mining Machinery
JANALÍK, J., Hydraulic Machines and Mechanisms
KOLAT, P., Thermal and Nuclear Power Engineering
KOUKAL, J., Engineering Technology
LENERT, J., Mechanics
MAKURA, P., Applied Mechanics
NOSKIEVIČ, P., Power Engineering
ONDROUCH, J., Technical Mechanics
PETRUŽELKA, M., Mechanical Technology
POLÁK, J., Transportation and Manipulation Technology
TŮMA, J., Automation of Machines and Technological Processes
VÍTEČEK, A., Automation of Machines and Technological Processes

Faculty of Metallurgy and Material Engineering (tel. 596995374; fax 596918592; e-mail jiri.kliber@vsb.cz):

ADOLF, Z., Steel-making
BAŽAN, J., Steel-making
DOBROVSKÝ, L., Chemical Metallurgy
FILIP, P., Materials Engineering
HAŠEK, P., Thermal Engineering in Industry
HYSPECKÁ, L., Physical Metallurgy
JELÍNEK, P., Casting
JONŠTA, Z., Physical Metallurgy
KALOČ, M., Technology of Fuels
KLIBER, J., Materials Forming
KLIKA, Z., Geochemistry, Mineralogy and Technology
KRAUSOVÁ, E., Economics and Management of Metallurgy
KURSA, M., Metallurgical Technology
LEŠKO, J., Chemical Metallurgy
MICHALEK, K., Metallurgical Technology
NENADÁL, J., Quality Management
OBROUČKA, K., Thermal Engineering
PETŘÍKOVÁ, R., Quality and Safety of Technical Systems
PŘÍHODA, M., Thermal Engineering
ROUBÍČEK, V., Technology of Fuels
SCHINDLER, J., Metallurgical Technology
SOMMER, B., Metal Forming
STRNADEL, B., Materials Engineering
TOŠENOVSKÝ, J., Industrial Process
TVRDÝ, M., Materials Engineering
VROŽINA, M., Automation of Metallurgical Processes
WICHTERLE, K., Chemical Engineering

Faculty of Mining and Geology (tel. 596995456; fax 596918589):

DIRNER, V., Environmental Protection and Reclamation
DVOŘÁČEK, J., Economics of Mining
FIGALA, J., General Ecology, Chronobiology
GRYGÁREK, J., Underground Mining
KRYL, V., Mining
LÁNÍČEK, J., Mathematics
LEMBÁK, M., Geotechnics and Underground Civil Engineering
MÁDR, V., Physics
NOVÁČEK, J., Mineral Processing and Ecotechnology
PALAS, M., Economic Geology
PETROŠ, V., Underground Mining
PIŠTORA, J., Applied Physics
PROKOP, P., Mine Ventilation
SCHEJBAL, C., Economic Geology
SCHENK, J., Geodesy and Mine Surveying
SIVEK, M., Economic Geology
STRAKOŠ, V., Automation in Mining
VAŠÍČEK, Z., Geology
VIDLÁŘ, J., Mineral Processing
WYSLYCH, P., Applied Physics
ZAMARSKÝ, V., Geology and Mineralogy

VYSOKÁ ŠKOLA CHEMICKO-TECHNOLOGICKÁ V PRAZE (Institute of Chemical Technology, Prague)

Technická 5, 166 28 Prague 6

Telephone: 220444144
Fax: 220445018
E-mail: rektorat@vscht.cz
Internet: www.ict-prague.eu

Founded 1807
State control
Language of instruction: Czech
Academic year: September to June
Rector: Assoc. Prof. JOSEF KOUBEK
Vice-Rector for Devt and Building: Assoc. Prof. JAN STANĚK
Vice-Rector for Education: Prof. PAVEL HASAL
Vice-Rector for Research and Devt: Prof. MILAN POSPÍŠIL
Registrar: Ing. IVANA CHVÁLNÁ
Librarian: Dr ANNA SOUČKOVÁ

Library of 225,000 vols
Number of teachers: 470
Number of students: 3,500

DEANS

Faculty of Chemical Engineering: Assoc. Prof. DANIEL TURZÍK
Faculty of Chemical Technology: Assoc. Prof. ALEŠ HELEBRANT
Faculty of Environmental Engineering: Prof. GUSTAV ŠEBOR
Faculty of Food and Biochemical Technology: Assoc. Prof. KAREL MELZOCH

PROFESSORS

BASAŘOVÁ, G., Fermentation Chemistry and Biotechnology
BENDA, V., Biochemistry and Microbiology
BENEŠ, P., Social Sciences
BUBNÍK, Z., Cereal Chemistry and Technology
BURYAN, P., Gas, Coke and Air Protection
ČERVENÝ, L., Organic Technology
ČURDA, D., Food Preservation
DAVÍDEK, J., Food Chemistry and Technology
DEMNEROVÁ, K., Biochemistry and Microbiology
DEYL, Z., Analytical Chemistry
DOHÁNYOS, M., Water Technology and Environmental Engineering
DUCHÁČEK, V., Polymers
ECKERT, E., Chemical Engineering
GROS, Z., Economics and Management of the Chemical Industry
HAJŠLOVÁ, J., Food Chemistry and Analysis
HANIKA, J., Organic Technology
HLAVÁČ, J., Silicate Technology
HORÁK, J., Organic Technology
HUDEC, L., Technology of Materials for Electronics
JANDA, V., Water Technology and Environmental Engineering
JIRKŮ, V., Fermentation Chemistry and Biotechnology
JURSÍK, F., Inorganic Chemistry
KADLEC, P., Sugar Technology
KÁŠ, J., Biochemistry
KLÍČ, A., Mathematics
KODÍČEK, M., Biochemistry and Microbiology
KRÁLOVÁ, B., Biochemistry and Microbiology
KRATOCHVÍL, B., Solid-state Chemistry
KUBÍČEK, M., Mathematics
KURAŠ, M., Environmental Engineering
LABÍK, S., Physical Chemistry
LIŠKA, F., Organic Chemistry
MALIJEVSKÝ, A., Physical Chemistry
MAREK, M., Chemical Engineering
MATĚJKA, Z., Power Engine
MATOUŠEK, J., Silicate Technology
NĚMEC, L., Inorganic Materials Laboratory
NOVÁK, J., Physical Chemistry
NOVÁK, P., Chemical Metallurgy and Corrosion Engineering

PÁCA, J., Fermentation Chemistry and Biotechnology
PALEČEK, J., Organic Chemistry
PALETA, O., Organic Chemistry
PAŠEK, J., Organic Technology
PECKA, K., Petroleum Technology and Petrochemistry
PITTER, P., Water Technology and Environmental Engineering
POKORNÝ, J., Food Chemistry and Technology
PORUBSKÝ, S., Mathematics
PROCHÁZKA, A., Computing and Control Engineering
RAUCH, P., Biochemistry
RODA, J., Polymers
RUML, T., Biochemistry and Microbiology
RŮŽIČKA, V., Physical Chemistry
RYCHTERA, M., Fermentation Chemistry and Biotechnology
SCHMIDT, O., Automated Control Systems
SEBOR, G., Petroleum Technology and Petrochemistry
SLÁDEČKOVÁ, A., Water Technology and Environmental Engineering
STIBOR, I., Organic Chemistry
SUCHANEK, M., Analytical Chemistry
SVOBODA, J., Organic Chemistry
ŠVORČÍK, V., Materials Science
VELÍŠEK, J., Food Chemistry and Technology
VOLKA, K., Analytical Chemistry
WANNER, J., Water Technology and Environmental Engineering
ZÁBRANSKÁ, J., Water Technology and Environmental Engineering

VYSOKÁ ŠKOLA EKONOMICKÁ V PRAZE
(University of Economics, Prague)

Nám. W. Churchilla 4, 130 67 Prague 3
Telephone: 224095799
Fax: 224095695
E-mail: brazdova@vse.cz
Internet: www.vse.cz
Founded 1919
State control
Languages of instruction: Czech, English
Academic year: September to May
Rector: Prof. JAROSLAVA DURČÁKOVÁ
Vice-Rectors: Prof. IGOR ČERMÁK, Prof. BRONISLAVA HOŘEJŠÍ, Prof. VOJTÍCH KREBS, Prof. JIŘÍ PATOČKA, Prof. ZBYNÍK REVENDA
Bursar: JIŘÍ KŘÍŽ
Number of students: 14,000
Publications: *Acta Economica Pragensia* (2 a year), *Politická Ekonomie* (6 a year), *Prague Economic Papers* (4 a year)

DEANS

Business Administration: Prof. JIŘÍ KLEIBL
Economics and Public Administration: Prof. JIŘÍ SCHWARZ
Finance and Accounting: Prof. BOJKA HAMERNÍKOVÁ
Informatics and Statistics: Prof. RICHARD HINDLS
International Relations: Prof. DANA ZADRAŽILOVÁ
Management: Prof. PAVEL PUDIL

VYSOKÉ UČENÍ TECHNICKÉ V BRNĚ
(Brno University of Technology)

Antonínská 1, 601 90 Brno
Telephone: 541145111
Fax: 541211309
E-mail: rektor@ro.vutbr.cz
Internet: www.vutbr.cz
Founded 1899
State control
Language of instruction: Czech
Academic year: September to July
Rector: Prof. Dr Ing. JAN VRBKA

Pro-Rectors: Asst Prof. PETR DUB, Prof. Dr JOSEF JANČÁŘ, Prof. Ing. JIŘÍ KAZELLE, Asst Prof. LADISLAV ŠTĚPÁNEK
Registrar: JAROMÍR PĚNČÍK
Dir of Public Relations and Admin.: Mgr JITKA VANÝSKOVÁ
Librarian: NATAŠA JURSOVÁ
Number of teachers: 1,026
Number of students: 15,090
Publication: *Události na VUT v Brně* (12 a year)

DEANS

Faculty of Architecture: Asst Prof. Ing. JOSEF CHYBÍK
Faculty of Business and Management: Asst Prof. Ing. KAREL RAIS
Faculty of Chemistry: Prof. Ing. MILAN DRDÁK
Faculty of Civil Engineering: Asst Prof. Ing. JAROSLAV PUCHRÍK
Faculty of Electrical Engineering and Communication: Prof. Ing. RADIMÍR VRBA
Faculty of Fine Arts: Prof. Dr JAN SEDLÁK
Faculty of Information Technology: Prof. Ing. TOMÁŠ HRUŠKA
Faculty of Mechanical Engineering: Prof. Ing. JOSEF VAČKÁŘ

PROFESSORS

Faculty of Architecture (Poříčí 5, 639 00 Brno; tel. 541146600; fax 542142125; e-mail chybik@ucit.fa.vutbr.cz; internet www.fa.vutbr.cz):

GŘEGORČÍK, J., Urban Studies
RULLER, I., Public Constructions
VAVERKA, J., Building Construction
ZEMÁNKOVÁ, H., Industrial Architecture

Faculty of Business and Management (Technická 2, 616 69 Brno; tel. 541141111; fax 541142458; e-mail dean@fbm.vutbr.cz; internet www.fbm.vutbr.cz):

DVOŘÁK, J., Economy and Management
KONEČNÝ, M., Economy and Management
MEZNÍK, I., Mathematics
NĚMEČEK, P., Economy and Management

Faculty of Chemistry (Purkyňova 118, 612 00 Brno; tel. 541149111; fax 541211697; e-mail drdak@fch.vutbr.cz; internet www.fch.vutbr.cz):

BRANDŠTETR, J., Chemistry of Materials
DRDÁK, M., Food Science and Biotechnology
FRIEDL, Z., Chemistry and Technology of Environmental Protection
JANČA, J., Chemistry
JANČÁŘ, J., Chemistry of Materials
KUČERA, M., Chemistry of Materials
NEŠPŮREK, S., Chemistry
OMELKA, L., Chemistry
PELIKÁN, P., Chemistry
RYCHTERA, M., Food Science and Biotechnology
SCHAUER, F., Environmental Chemistry and Technology
SOMMER, L., Chemistry and Technology of Environmental Protection
WEIN, O., Chemistry

Faculty of Civil Engineering (Veveří 95, 662 37 Brno; tel. 541147111; fax 5745147; e-mail dekan@fce.vutbr.cz; internet www.fce.vutbr.cz):

ADÁMEK, J., Structural Materials and Testing Methods
DROCHYTKA, R., Technology of Building Materials and Components
FIXEL, J., Geodesy
KOČÍ, J., Building Construction
KOKTAVÝ, B., Physics
MELCHER, J., Metal and Timber Structures
MYSLÍN, J., Building Construction
NEVOSÁD, Z., Geodesy
ŠÁLEK, J., Water Resources Management

STRÁSKÝ, J., Concrete and Masonry Structures

Faculty of Electrical Engineering and Communication (Údolní 53, 602 00 Brno; tel. 541141111; fax 541146100; e-mail dekan@feec.vutbr.cz; internet www.feec.vutbr.cz):

AUTRATA, R., Electrical and Electronic Technology
BIOLEK, D., Telecommunications
BRZOBOHATÝ, J., Microelectronics
CHVALINA, J., Mathematics
DIBLÍK, J., Mathematics
DOSTÁL, T., Radioelectronics
HAVEL, V., Mathematics
HONZÍKOVÁ, N., Biomedical Engineering
HRUŠKA, K., Physics
JAN, J., Biomedical Engineering
KAZELLE, J., Electrical and Electronic Technology
MELKES, F., Mathematics
MUSIL, J., Microelectronics
PIVOŇKA, P., Automation
POSPÍŠIL, J., Radioelectronics
PROCHÁZKA, P., Electrical Engineering
ŘÍČNÝ, V., Radioelectronics
ŠEBESTA, V., Radioelectronics
SIKULA, J., Physics
SKALICKÝ, J., Power Electrical and Electronic Engineering
SMÉKAL, Z., Telecommunications
SVAČINA, J., Radioelectronics
TOMÁNEK, P., Physics
VALSA, J., Electrical Engineering
VAVŘÍN, P., Automation and Measurement Engineering
VOMELA, J., Biomedical Engineering
VRBA, K., Telecommunications
VRBA, R., Microelectronics

Faculty of Fine Arts (Rybářská 13, 603 00 Brno; tel. 543146850; fax 543212670; e-mail dekan@ffa.vutbr.cz; internet www.ffa.vutbr.cz):

NAČERADSKÝ, J., Painting
RONAI, P., Figure Painting
SEDLÁK, J., History of Art

Faculty of Information Technology (Božetěchova 2, 612 66 Brno; tel. 541141139; fax 541141270; e-mail info@fit.vutbr.cz; internet www.fit.vutbr.cz):

ČEŠKA, M., Intelligent Systems
DVOŘÁK, V., Computer Systems
HONZÍK, J., Information Systems
HRUŠKA, T., Information Systems
SERBA, I., Computer Graphics and Multimedia

Faculty of Mechanical Engineering (Technická 2, 616 00 Brno; tel. 541141111; fax 541142222; e-mail dekan@fme.vutbr.cz; internet www.fme.vutbr.cz):

BABINEC, F., Process Engineering
BOHÁČEK, F., Machine Design
BUMBÁLEK, B., Technology
CHMELA, P., Optics and Fine Mechanics
CIHLÁŘ, J., Ceramics
DRUCKMÜLLER, M., Stochastics, Teaching of Mathematics
FILAKOVSKÝ, K., Aircraft Design
FOREJT, M., Snagging Technology
HLAVENKA, B., Production Engineering
JANÍČEK, P., Mechanics of Solids
JÍCHA, M., Heat and Nuclear Power
KAČUR, J., Mathematics
KADRNOŽKA, J., Heat and Nuclear Power
KAVIČKA, F., Heat and Nuclear Power
KOCMAN, K., Production Engineering
KOHOUTEK, J., Process Engineering
KOMRSKÁ, J., Physics
KRATOCHVÍL, O., Mechanics of Solids
KULČÁK, L., Aerospace Engineering
LIŠKA, M., Physics
MATAL, O., Heat and Nuclear Power
MEDEK, J., Process Engineering
NOVÁK, V., Mathematics
PÍŠTĚK, A., Aerospace Engineering

PÍŠTĚK, V., Combustion Engines and Motor Vehicles
POCHYLÝ, F., Heat and Nuclear Power
POKLUDA, J., Physics
PTÁČEK, L., Materials Engineering
RUSÍN, K., Foundry Engineering
SCHNEIDER, P., Process Engineering
SEDLÁČEK, B., Aerospace Engineering
ŠLAPAL, J., Mathematics, Teaching of Mathematics
SLAVÍK, J., Mechanics of Solids
STEHLÍK, P., Process Engineering
ŠTĚPÁNEK, M., Automation and Computer Science
STRÁNSKÝ, K., Materials Engineering
ŠVEJCAR, J., Materials Engineering
VAČKÁŘ, J., Quality and Metrology
VLK, F., Combustion Engines and Motor Vehicles
VRBKA, J., Mechanics of Solids
ŽENÍŠEK, A., Mathematics

ZÁPADOČESKÁ UNIVERZITA
(University of West Bohemia)

Univerzitní 8, 306 14 Plzeň
Telephone: 377631111
Fax: 377631112
E-mail: rektor@rek.zcu.cz
Internet: www.zcu.cz
Founded 1949 as Plzeň Institute of Technology, present name 1991
State control
Language of instruction: Czech
Academic year: September to June
Chancellor: Dr HELENA HEJDOVÁ
Rector: Doc. Ing. JOSEF PRŮŠA
Vice-Rectors: Doc. Dr FRANTIŠEK JEŽEK, Dr EVA PASÁČKOVÁ, Dr Ing. JAN RYCHLÍK, Doc. Ing. JAN HOREJC
Registrar: Ing. ANTONÍN BULÍN
Librarians: Dr MILOSLAVA FAITOVÁ, Mgr ALENA SCHOŘOVSKÁ
Library of 437,342 vols
Number of teachers: 1,218
Number of students: 18,898
Publications: *Stady* (univ. papers, 12 a year), *Trojúhelník* (univ. journal, 4 a year)

DEANS

Faculty of Applied Sciences: Prof. Ing. JIŘÍ KŘEN
Faculty of Economics: Doc. Dr MIROSLAV PLEVNÝ
Faculty of Education: Doc. Dr JANA COUFALOVÁ
Faculty of Electrical Engineering: Doc. Ing. JIŘÍ HAMMERBAUER
Faculty of Health Care Studies: Dr ILONA MAURITZOVÁ
Faculty of Law: Dr JIŘÍ POSPÍŠIL
Faculty of Mechanical Engineering: Doc. Ing. JIŘÍ STANĚK
Faculty of Philosophy and Arts: Doc. Dr PAVEL VAŘEKA

PROFESSORS

Faculty of Applied Sciences (Univerzitní 22, 306 14 Plzeň; tel. 377632000; fax 377632002; internet www.fav.zcu.cz):

DRÁBEK, P., Mathematics
KŘEN, J., Continuum Mechanics, Biomechanics
KUČERA, M., Mathematics
KUFNER, A., Mathematics
KUNEŠ, J., Applied Physics
LAŠ, V., Mechanics
MAREK, P., Mechanics
MATOUŠEK, V., Man–Machine Communication
MÍKA, S., Mathematics
MUSIL, J., Applied Physics
NOVÁK, P., Geodesy
PLÁNIČKA, F., Mechanics

PŘIKRYL, P., Mathematics
PSUTKA, J., Cybernetics
ROSENBERG, J., Mechanics
RYJÁČEK, Z., Mathematics
ŠAFAŘÍK, J., Informatics and Computing
SCHLEGEL, M., Cybernetics
SKALA, V., Computer Graphics
ŠESTÁK, J., Mechanics
ŠIMANDL, M., Cybernetics
ŠŤASTNÝ, M., Mechanics
VLČEK, J., Applied Physics
ZEMAN, V., Mechanics

Faculty of Economics (Husova 11, 306 14 Plzeň; tel. 377633000; fax 377633002; internet www.fek.zcu.cz):

KŘIKAČ, K., Organization and Management of Engineering Production
MACEK, J., Statistics in Economics
MACH, M., Business Economics
SEMENIUK, P., Marketing, Trade and Services

Faculty of Education (Sedláčkova 38, 306 14 Plzeň; tel. 377636000; fax 377636002; internet www.fpe.zcu.cz):

HÖPPNEROVÁ, V., German Language
JÍLEK, T., Teaching of History
KRAITR, M., Teaching of Chemistry
KUMPERA, J., Teaching of History
MEHNERT, E., Teaching of German Language
NOVÁK, J., Teaching of Chemistry
PILOUS, V., Materials Engineering
RYCHTECKÝ, A., Physical Training
SCHUPPENER, G., German Language
VIKTORA, V., Czech Language

Faculty of Electrical Engineering (Univerzitní 26, 306 14 Plzeň; tel. 377634000; fax 377634002; internet www.fel.zcu.cz):

BARTOŠ, V., Electrical Machines and Apparatus
BENEŠOVÁ, Z., Theory of Electrical Engineering
DOLEŽEL, I., Theory of Electrical Engineering
HALLER, R., Electric Power Engineering
JERHOT, J., Electronics and Vacuum Technology
KOŽENÝ, J., Electric Power Engineering
KŮS, V., Electrical Drives and Power Electronics
MAYER, D., Theory of Electrical Engineering
MENTLÍK, V., Electrical Technology
MÜHLBACHER, J., Electric Power Engineering
PINKER, J., Electronic Systems
ŠKORPIL, J., Enigineering Ecology
STORK, M., Analog and Digital Circuitry
VONDRÁŠEK, F., Electrical Drives and Power Electronics
VOSTRACKÝ, Z., Electric Power Engineering

Faculty of Law (Sady Pětatřicátníků 14, 306 14 Plzeň; tel. 377637000; fax 377637002; internet www.fpr.zcu.cz):

ADAMOVÁ, S., History of the State and Law
BALÍK, S., History of the State and Law
ELIÁŠ, K., Commercial Law
GERLOCH, A., Theory of Law
HRDINA, A., History of Law
HRONCOVÁ, J., Social Pathology
KOPAL, V., International Law
KUČERA, Z., International Law
PAUKNEROVÁ, M., International Law
RŮŽIČKA, K., International Law
RYBÁŘ, M., Criminology
ŠÁMAL, P., Criminal Law
VÁLKOVÁ, H., Criminal Law
WOKOUN, R., Public Service

Faculty of Mechanical Engineering (Univerzitní 22, 306 14 Plzeň; tel. 377638000; fax 377638002; internet www.fst.zcu.cz):

BASL, J., Computer Integrated Production Systems

DVOŘÁKOVÁ, L., Financial and Management Accounting
FIALA, J., Physics of Solids
HOSNEDL, S., Machine Design
JANDEČKA, K., Technology of Metal Cutting
KOTT, J., Design of Power Machines and Equipment
LEEDER, E., Computer Integrated Production Systems
LINHART, J., Power System Engineering
MAREŠ, R., Thermomechanics
MAŠEK, B., Materials Science and Metallography
PFROGNER, F., Materials Science and Metallography
ZRNÍK, J., Materials Science and Metallography

Faculty of Philosophy and Arts (Sedláčkova 38, 306 14 Plzeň; tel. 377635000; fax 377635002; internet www.ff.zcu.cz):

BLAŽEK, V., Anthropology
BUDIL, I., Anthropology
DOUBRAVOVÁ, J., Philosophy
FUNDA, O., Philosophy
JEŘÁBEK, H., Sociology
NEÚSTUPNÝ, E., Archaeology
SKŘIVAN, A., History
VOPĚNKA, P., Philosophy

Institute of Art and Design:

BARTA, J., Animation
BERÁNEK, J., Sculpture
GAJDOŠ, J., Drama Theory and Criticism
JIRKŮ, B., Drawing and Art of Painting
MATASOVÁ-TEISINGEROVÁ, A., Intermediary Production
NOVÁK, ., Jewellery Craft
ŠERÁK, V., Ceramic Design
ZIEGLER, Z., Graphic Design

ATTACHED RESEARCH INSTITUTES

Institute of Art and Design: tel. 377636700; fax 377636702; e-mail mistera@uud.zcu.cz; internet www.uud.zcu.cz; Dir Doc., Akad. mal. JOSEF MIŠTERA.

New Technologies Research Centre: tel. 377634700; fax 377634702; e-mail rosen@ntc.zcu.cz; internet www.ntc.zcu.cz; Dir Prof. Ing. JOSEF ROSENBERG.

Schools of Art and Music

Akademie múzických umění v Praze (Prague Academy of Performing Arts): Malostranské nám. 12, 118 00 Prague 1; tel. 234344514; fax 234244515; e-mail info@amu.cz; internet www.amu.cz; f. 1945; languages of instruction: Czech, English; academic year October to June; Rector IVO MATHÉ; Vice-Rectors ZDENĚK KIRSCHNER, MIROSLAV KLÍMA; Registrar TAMARA CUŘÍKOVÁ; library: 161,374 vols; 338 teachers; 1,178 students; publs *Acta Academica Informatorium* (10 a year), *Disk* (4 a year).

Akademie výtvarných umění v Praze (Prague Academy of Fine Arts): U Akademie 4, 170 22 Prague 7; tel. 220408200; fax 233381662; e-mail avu@avu.cz; internet www.avu.cz; f. 1799; languages of instruction: Czech, English; academic year October to July; Rector Prof. JIŘÍ SOPKO; Pro-Rectors Prof. EMIL PŘIKRYL, Doc. JIŘÍ LINDOVSKÝ; Registrar Ing. VLADIMÍR KALUGIN; library: 75,000 vols; 58 teachers; 265 students; publs *Almanach*, *Exhibition Catalogues*.

Janáčkova Akademie Múzických Umění v Brnì (Janáček Academy of Music and Performing Art in Brno): Beethovenova 2, 662 15 Brno; tel. 542591111; fax 542591140; e-mail rektor@jamu.cz; internet www.jamu.cz; f. 1947; languages of instruction: Czech, English; academic year September to June; Rector Prof. VÁCLAV CEJPEK; Vice-Rector

Prof. Dr LEOŠ FALTUS; Vice-Rector Doc. Dr MIROSLAV PLEŠÁK; Registrar Dr LENKA VALOVÁ; library: 100,000 vols; special collns of printed music and records; 118 teachers; 580 students.

Janáčkova konzervatoř a Gymnázium v Ostravě: Českobratrská 40, 702 00 Ostrava-Moravská; tel. 596112007; fax 596111443; e-mail info@jko.cz; internet www.jko.cz; f. 1953; 145 teachers; 376 students; library: 23,000 vols, 7,000 records; Dir MILAN BÁCHOREK.

Konzervatoř, Brno (Conservatoire in Brno): třída Kpt. Jaroše 45, 662 54 Brno; tel. 545215568; e-mail reditel@konzervatorbrno.cz; internet www.konzervatorbrno.eu; f. 1919; music and drama departments; 124 teachers; 360 students; library: 7,000 vols, 29,900 scores, 1,600 records; Dir Mgr E. ZÁMEČNÍK.

Konzervatoř P. J. Vejvanovského, Kroměříž: Pilařova 7, 767 01 Kroměříž; tel. 573339501; fax 573343270; e-mail konzervator@konzkm.cz; internet www.konzkm.cz; f. 1949; 55 teachers; 190 stu-

dents; library: 16,000 vols, 4,600 records; Dir M. ŠIŠKA.

Konzervatoř, Pardubice: Sukova třída 1260, 530 02 Pardubice; tel. 466513503; fax 466513503; e-mail reditelstvi@konzervatorpardubice.cz; internet www.konzervatorpardubice.cz; f. 1978; 79 teachers; 172 students; library: 2,200 books, 7,500 vols of music, 1,100 records; Dir Mgr JAROMÍR HÖNIG.

Konzervatoř, Plzeň: Kopeckého sady 10, 301 00 Plzeň; tel. 377226325; fax 377226387; e-mail sekretariat@konzervatorplzen.cz; internet www.konzervatorplzen.cz; f. 1961; 78 teachers; 158 students; library: 1,500 books, 1,400 records and CDs, 7,000 scores; Dir MIROSLAV BREJCHA.

Konzervatoř, Teplice: Hudba a Zpěv, Českobratrská 15, 415 01 Teplice; tel. 417538425; fax 417532645; e-mail studijni@konzervatorteplice.cz; internet www.konzervatorteplice.cz; f. 1971; 80 teachers; 200 students; library: 10,000 vols, 800 records; Dir Mgr MILAN KUBÍK.

Pražská konzervatoř: Na Rejdišti 1, 110 00 Prague 1; tel. 222319102; fax 222326406; e-mail conserv@prgcons.cz; internet www.prgcons.cz; f. 1808; 254 professors; 600 students; library: 85,000 vols, 19,000 records; Dir Mgr PAVEL TROJAN; Chief of Library (Archives) MILOSLAV RICHTER.

Taneční konzervatoř Praha (Prague Conservatory of Dance): Křižovnická 7, 110 00 Prague 1; tel. 222319145; fax 222324977; e-mail taneckonzpr@volny.cz; internet www.balet.cz/tkpraha; f. 1945; languages of instruction: Czech, English; 60 teachers; 200 students; Dir Mgr JAROSLAV SLAVICKÝ; publ. *Taneční listy* (Dance Review).

Vysoká Škola Uměleckoprůmyslová (Academy of Art, Architecture and Design): nám. Jana Palacha 80, 116 93 Prague 2; tel. 251098111; fax 251098289; e-mail pr@vsup.cz; internet www.vsup.cz; f. 1885; 55 teachers; 400 students; Rector Dr JIŘÍ PELCL; Vice-Rector for International and Public Relations Dr MARTINA PACHMANOVÁ; Vice-Rector for Study Dr PAVLA PEČINKOVÁ; Registrar Ing. LUBOŠ KVAPIL.

DENMARK

The Higher Education System

Københavns Universitet (founded 1479) is the oldest university in Denmark. There are 12 universities and technical universities and many other university-level institutions, such as professional schools and polytechnics, which offer short- and medium-cycle programmes. These university-level institutions are to be merged into supra-institutions under legislation enacted in 1998 and 2001. Short-cycle vocational colleges are being reorganized as erhvervsakademier (vocational academies) and medium-cycle colleges are being merged into Centres for Higher Education. There is also a university in the Faroe Islands, as well as colleges there and in Greenland.

The higher education system is financed by the State; since 2001 the Ministry of Science, Technology and Innovation has been responsible for higher education. (However, the Ministry of Culture oversees arts and cultural education programmes, and the Ministry of Education is responsible for short- and medium-cycle higher education.) The Act on the Universities (1992) extended the traditional academic freedom and autonomy enjoyed by the universities, but the Ministries still dictate regulations on, inter alia, admissions, curricula, quality assurance and appointments of academic staff. Quality assurance in the public universities is overseen by the Danish Evaluation Institute, which incorporated the former Centre for Quality Assurance and Evaluation of Higher Education. Private universities must submit to an accreditation process run by the Danish Educational Support Agency, a body of the Ministry of Education. The quality assurance system was supplemented by the establishment of a national accreditation system for higher education in 2007 and an accreditation body called ACE Denmark (Akkrediteringsinstitutionen).

To attend university, students must possess one of the secondary school leaving certificates (or equivalent qualification), namely studentereksamen (Upper Secondary School Leaving Examination), højere forberedelseseksamen (Higher Preparatory Examination), højere handelseksamen eksamen (Higher Business Examination) or højere teknisk eksamen (Higher Technical Examination). The number of available places each year is stipulated by the Minister of Education. Since the introduction of in legislation of 1993, reform of the higher education system of qualifications has broadly brought Denmark into line with the Bologna Process, and the standard degree system consists of Bachelors, Masters (candidatus) and Doctorate. Since 2003 only European Bologna-style degrees have been offered. The Bachelors undergraduate degree takes three to three-and-a-half years, or longer for professional programmes such as engineering or medicine. The Masters degree (candidatus) requires two years of study following the Bachelors, and a Doctorate is awarded following at least eight years of higher education. In 2006 some 119,013 students were enrolled in universities, with many more in other centres of higher education.

There are 15 short-cycle, professionally orientated programmes (erhvervsakademiuddannelser) offered by the erhvervsakademier (vocational academies), which last two years, and 20 medium-cycle programmes offered by Centres for Higher Education, leading to the award of the title of professionsbachelor (Professional Bachelors). Adult and continuing education was reformed under Act No. 488 (2000), which created three levels of qualifications: Videregående voksenuddannelse (advanced adult education), Diplomuddannelse (Diploma programmes) and Masteruddannelse (Masters programmes). Programmes of study last two years (part-time).

Technical and vocational education consist of erhvervsuddannelser (training programmes), grundlæggende social- og sundhedsuddannelser (basic social and health education) and other programmes in different fields. These courses are offered by tekniske skoler (technical colleges), handelsskoler (business colleges), landbrugsskoler (agricultural colleges) and social- og sundhedsskoler (social and healthcare colleges). There are a total of 85 programmes of vocational education.

Regulatory and Representative Bodies

GOVERNMENT

Ministry of Culture: Nybrogade 2, 1203 Copenhagen K; tel. 33-92-33-70; e-mail kum@kum.dk; internet www.kum.dk; Min. DR PER STIG MØLLER.

Ministry of Education: Frederiksholms Kanal 21, 1220 Copenhagen K; tel. 33-92-50-00; fax 33-92-55-67; e-mail uvm@uvm.dk; internet www.uvm.dk; Min. TROELS LUND POULSON.

Ministry of Science, Technology and Innovation: Bredgade 43, 1260 Copenhagen K; tel. 33-92-97-00; fax 33-32-35-01; e-mail vtu@vtu.dk; internet www.vtu.dk; Min. CHARLOTTE SAHL-MADSEN.

Attached Bodies:

Danmarks Forskningspolitiske Råd (Danish Agency for Science, Technology and Innovation): Bredgade 40, 1260 Copenhagen K; tel. 72-31-82-37; fax 35-44-62-01; e-mail dfr@dfr.dk; internet www.fi.dk/raad-og-udvalg/danmarks-forskningspolitiske-raad; f. 1996; Chair. and Man. Dir CEO CLAUS HVIID CHRISTENSEN; Head of Secretariat KARIN KJÆR MADSEN.

Det Frie Forskningsråd—Samfund og Erhverv (The Danish Council for Independent Research—Social Sciences): c/o The Danish Agency for Science, Technology and Innovation, Bredgade 40, 1260 Copenhagen K; tel. 35-44-62-00; fax 35-44-62-01; e-mail dasti@dasti.dk; internet www.fi.dk; f. 1968; advises public authorities and instns in social sciences; initiates and supports nat. and int. research; awards grants and fellowships for scientific research; Chair. Prof. PETER MUNK CHRISTIANSEN.

Det Frie Forskningsråd—Sundhed og Sygdom (The Danish Research Council for Independent Research—Medical Sciences): c/o The Danish Agency for Science, Technology and Innovation, Bredgade 40, 1260 Copenhagen K; tel. 35-44-62-00; fax 35-44-62-01; e-mail dasti@dasti.dk; internet en.fi.dk/councils-commissions/the-danish-council-for-independent-research/scientific-research-councils/medical-sciences; f. 1968; advises public authorities and instns in medical sciences, incl. odontology and pharmacy; supports research, coordinates research, nat. and int.; awards grants and fellowships for scientific research; Chair. Prof. Dr LARS FUGGER.

Det Strategiske Forskningsråd (Danish Council for Strategic Research): Bred-gade 40, 1260 Copenhagen; tel. 35-44-62-00; fax 35-44-62-01; internet www.fi.dk/raad-og-udvalg/det-strategiske-forsknings-raad; Dir Prof. PETER OLESEN.

Forsknings–og Innovationsstyrelsen (Danish Agency for Science, Technology and Innovation): Bredgade 40, 1260 Copenhagen; tel. 35-44-62-00; fax 35-44-62-01; e-mail fi@fi.dk; internet www.fi.dk; f. 1968; Dir-Gen. INGE MÆRKEDAHL.

ACCREDITATION

ACE Denmark—Akkrediteringsinstitutionen (ACE Denmark—Accreditation Agency): Studiestræde 5, 1455 Copenhagen K; tel. 33-92-69-00; e-mail acedenmark@acedenmark.dk; internet acedenmark.dk; Dir ANETTE DØRGE JESSEN.

Danish Agency for International Education: Bredgade 36, 1260 Copenhagen K; tel. 33-95-70-00; fax 33-95-70-01; e-mail anerkendelse@iu.dk; internet www.en.iu.dk/recognition; attached to Min. of Science, Technology and Innovation; Dir-Gen. ANDERS GEERTSEN.

Danmarks Evalueringsinstitut (EVA) (Danish Evaluation Institute): Østbanegade 55, 3. sal, 2100 Copenhagen; tel. 35-55-01-01; fax 35-55-10-11; e-mail eva@eva.dk; internet www.eva.dk; f. 1992 as Danish Centre for Quality Assurance and Evaluation of Higher

Education, present name and status 1999; Exec. Dir AGI CSONKA.

FUNDING

Styrelsen for Statens Uddannelsesstøtte (Danish Educational Support Agency): Danasvej 30, 1780 Copenhagen V; tel. 33-26-86-00; fax 33-26-86-11; e-mail sustyrelsen@su.dk; internet www .sustyrelsen.dk; attached to Min. of Education; Dir LARS MORTENSEN.

NATIONAL BODIES

Danske Universiteter (Universities Denmark): Fiolstraede 44, 1. th, 1171 Copenhagen K; tel. 33-92-54-05; fax 33-92-50-75; e-mail dkuni@dkuni.dk; internet www .dkuni.dk; f. 1967; Pres. JOHN DUE; Vice-Pres. NILS STRANDBERG PEDERSEN; Sec. SUSANNE BJERREGAARD.

Folkeuniversitetet I Danmark (University Extension Services in Denmark): c/o Syddansk Universitet, Campusvej 55, 5230 Odense M; tel. 65-50-27-27; e-mail sei@fu.dk; internet www.folkeuniversitet.dk; f. 1898; Chair. INGOLF CHRISTENSEN; Rector Dr SØREN EIGAARD.

Learned Societies

GENERAL

Kongelige Danske Videnskabernes Selskab (Royal Danish Academy of Science and Letters): H. C. Andersens Blvd 35, 1553 Copenhagen V; tel. 33-43-53-00; fax 33-43-53-01; e-mail kdvs@royalacademy.dk; internet www.royalacademy.dk; f. 1742; arranges meetings, public lectures, publishes journals, seminars, symposia; 500 mems (250 Danish, 250 foreign); Pres. Prof. Dr KIRSTEN HASTRUP; Sec.-Gen. and Treas. Prof. Dr SØREN-PETER FUCHS OLESEN; Head of Secretariat PIA GRÜNER; Chair. for History and Philosophy CARL HENRIK KOCH; Chair. for Mathematics and Natural Sciences CHRISTIAN BERG; publs *Biologiske Skrifter* (botany, zoology, palaeontology, general biology, irregular), *Historisk-filosofiske Meddelelser* (history, philosophy, philology, archaeology, art history, irregular), *Historisk-filosofiske Skrifter* (history, philosophy, philology, archaeology, art history, irregular), *Matematisk-fysiske Meddelelser* (mathematics, physics, chemistry, astronomy, geology, irregular), *Oversigt/Yearbook* (1 a year).

AGRICULTURE, FISHERIES AND VETERINARY SCIENCE

Dansk Skovforening (Danish Forestry Society): Amalievej 20, 1875 Frederiksberg C; tel. 33-24-42-66; fax 33-24-02-42; e-mail info@skovforeningen.dk; internet www .skovforeningen.dk; f. 1888; promotes the commercial and professional interests of Danish forestry; also supports conservation of natural values of the Danish forests; Chair. NIELS IUEL REVENTLOW; Vice-Chair. JENS KRISTIAN POULSEN; Dir JAN SØNDERGAARD; publs *Dansk Skovbrugs Tidsskrift* (4 a year), *Skoven* (11 a year); publ. *Skoven Nyt* (22 a year).

Dansk Veterinærhistorisk Samfund (Danish Veterinary History Society): Hoejskolelunden 3C, 6630 Roedding; tel. 74-84-24-76; e-mail oldvet@rnet.dk; f. 1934; annual European tour and seminar on the history of veterinary medicine; 320 mems; library of 44 vols; Pres. Dr CARL ANTON HENRIKSEN; publ. *Dansk Veterinærhistorisk Årbog* (every 2 years).

Foreningen af Mejeriledere og Funktionærer (Association of Dairy Managers): Det gamle Mejeri, Landbrugsvej 65, 5260 Odense S; tel. 66-12-40-25; fax 66-14-40-26; e-mail fmf@maelkeritidende.dk; internet www .maelkeritidende.dk; f. 1887; 823 mems; Pres. SØREN STEEN JENSEN; publ. *Maelkeritidende* (26 a year).

Jordbrugsakademikernes Forbund (JA) (Danish Federation of Graduates in Agriculture, Horticulture, Forestry and Landscape Architecture): Emdrupvej 28A, 2100 Copenhagen Ø; tel. 33-21-28-00; fax 38-71-03-22; e-mail post@ja.dk; internet www.ja.dk; f. 1976, present name 2007; 5,500 mems; works for skills and career devt for mems; highlights the academic and policy issues within the members' disciplines; develops networks and peer cohesion among mems; Pres. KIRSTEN HOLST; Dir ANN-MARGARET DUUS JENSEN; publs *Jord og Viden* (17 a year), *moMentum* (4 a year).

Kongelige Danske Landhusholdningsselskab (Royal Danish Agricultural Society): c/o Landbrug and Fødevarer, Axelborg, Axeltorv 3, 1, 1609 København V; tel. 33-39-42-20; fax 33-39-41-51; e-mail 1769@1769.dk; internet www.1769.dk; f. 1769; provides a forum for debate on sustainable use of the open land and its resources for the benefit of agriculture, society and environment; organizes confs; Pres. FREDERIK LÜTTICHAU; Vice-Pres. STEFFEN HUSTED DAMSGAARD; Sec. JETTE LETHBRIDGE; publ. *Tidsskrift for Landøkonomi*.

ARCHITECTURE AND TOWN PLANNING

Akademisk Arkitektforening (Danish Architects' Association): Arkitekternes Hus, Strandgade 27A, 1401 Copenhagen K; tel. 30-85-90-00; fax 32-83-69-01; e-mail mail@arkitektforeningen.dk; internet www .arkitektforeningen.dk; f. 1879; promotes quality of planning and design of Dannish physical environment and improves and develops conditions for the architect's profession; 7,000 mems; Dir JANE SANDBERG; Exec. Sec. ELSE MARIE MANDØE; publs *Arkitekten*, *Arkitektur*.

Dansk Byplanlaboratorium (Danish Town Planning Institute): Nørregade 36, 1 1165 Copenhagen K; tel. 33-13-72-81; fax 33-14-34-35; e-mail db@byplanlab.dk; internet www.byplanlab.dk; f. 1921; puts considerable effort into both ensuring that current town planning issues and questions attract interest; promotes new knowledge and ideas within town planning; library of 6,000 books; Chair. MAY GREEN; Vice-Chair. MAI-BRITT JENSEN; Vice-Chair. THORKILD AERO; Dir (vacant) ELLEN HØJGAARD JENSEN; publ. *Dansk Byplanlaboratorium*.

BIBLIOGRAPHY, LIBRARY SCIENCE AND MUSEOLOGY

Danmarks Biblioteksforening (Danish Library Association): Farvergade 27D, 1463 Copenhagen K; tel. 33-25-09-35; fax 33-25-79-00; e-mail dbf@dbf.dk; internet www.dbf .dk; f. 1905; advances the devt of the public library system; 432 mems; Pres. VAGN YTTE LARSEN; First Vice-Pres. HANNE PIGONSKA; Second Vice-Pres. KIRSTEN BOELT; Dir MICHEL STEEN-HANSEN; publ. *Biblioteksvejviser* (Directory, 1 a year).

Danmarks Forskningsbiblioteksforening (Danish Research Library Association): DF Secretariat, Statsbiblioteket, Tangen 2, 8200 Århus N; tel. 89-46-22-07; fax 89-46-21-72-20; e-mail df@statsbiblioteket.dk; internet www.dfdf.dk; f. 1978; promotes initiatives for benefit of academic and research libraries and collective library system; forum for consideration and discussions of subjects on library issues and library politics; 700 personal, 145 institutional mems; Pres. PER STEEN HANSEN; Chair. MICHAEL COTTA-SCHØNBERG; Deputy Chair. ELI GREVE; Treas. SUSANNE DALSGAARD KRAG; publ. *REVY* (8 a year).

Dansk Biblioteks Center AS: Tempovej 7–11, 2750 Ballerup; tel. 44-86-77-77; fax 44-86-76-93; e-mail dbc@dbc.dk; internet www.dbc .dk; f. 1991; provides Danish libraries with bibliographic data, a union catalogue, databases and online products; Chair. JØRN LEHMANN PETERSEN; Deputy Chair. KIM ØSTRUP; CEO MOGENS BRABAND JENSEN; Sec. ANNI JACOBSEN; publ. *DBC Avisen*.

Organisationen Danske Museer (Association of Danish Museums): Vartov Farvergade 27D, 1463 Copenhagen K; tel. 49-14-39-66; fax 49-14-39-67; e-mail info@dkmuseer .dk; internet www.dkmuseer.dk; f. 2005 by merger of Foreningen af Danske Kunstmuseer and Dansk Kulturhistorisk Museums Forening; promotes Danish Museums and protects their interests through nat. and int. activities; develops museums as active instns in society to influence public debate and to further the museums' interests in relation to public authorities; establishes a cooperative forum for all professional groups affiliated with Danish museums; disseminates information about museum affairs both to museums and public; contributes to further education and training of museum staff and to instigate learning activities at museums; 180 mems; Chair. LENE FLORIS; Pres. RASMUS VESTERGAARD; Vice-Pres. LISE RAEDER KNUDSEN; Exec. Sec. KIRSTEN REX ANDERSEN.

Styrelsen for Bibliotek og Medier (Danish Agency for Libraries and Media): H. C. Andersens Blvd 2, 1553 Copenhagen V; tel. 33-73-33-73; fax 33-73-33-72; e-mail post@ bibliotekogmedier.dk; internet www .bibliotekogmedier.dk; f. 1920, as the State Inspectorate of Public Libraries, merged with The Office of the National Librarian and The Danish Agency for Media, present name and status 2008; attached to Min. of Culture; adviser to Govt on matters concerning academic and spec. libraries, public libraries, and information and documentation problems; admin. of devt pools and grants, and of nat. Electronic Research Library; media section carries out the daily admin. of broadcasting regulation and assists Govt in matters concerning radio and television; Dir JENS THORHAUGE; publ. *Bibliotek og Medier* (4 a year).

ECONOMICS, LAW AND POLITICS

Danmarks Jurist- og Økonomforbund (Danish Association of Lawyers and Economists): Gothersgade 133, POB 2126, 1015 Copenhagen K; tel. 33-95-97-00; fax 33-95-99-99; e-mail djoef@djoef.dk; internet www .djoef.dk; f. 1972; works towards improving the working conditions of students and employees within the fields of law, admin., state governance, research, education, communication, economics, political and social science; 53,577 mems; Fed. Pres. FINN BORCH ANDERSEN; Dir MOGENS KRING RASMUSSEN; publs *DJØF Efteruddannelse* (2 a year), *Juristen* (lawyer, 6 a year), *Samfundsøkonomen* (societal economist, 6 a year).

Dansk Selskab for Europaforskning (Danish Society for European Studies): c/o Centre for European Studies, University of Southern Denmark, Campusvej 55, 5230 Odense M; tel. 65-50-22-17; fax 65-50-22-80; e-mail ecsa-dk@sam.sdu.dk; internet www .ecsa.dk; f. 1976; promotes Danish academic study, research and teaching of the administrative, legal, economic, political and social aspects of European integration by means of seminars and publications; 100 mems; Pres. Prof. SUSANA BORRAS; Vice-Chair. DORTE

MARTINSEN; Sec. RENS VAN MUNSTER; Treas. HENRIK PLASCHKE.

International Law Association—Danish Branch: Kromann Reumert Sundkrogsgade 5, 2100 Copenhagen O; fax 70-11-11-13; e-mail elf@kromannreumert.com; internet www.ila-hq.org; f. 1925; promotes the study, clarification and devt of int. law, both public and private, and furthers int. understanding and respect for int. law; Pres. HENRIK THAL JANTZEN; Sec. and Treas. EVA LE FEVRE.

Nationaløkonomisk Forening (Danish Economic Society): Danmarks Nationalbank, Havnegade 5, 1093 Copenhagen K; tel. 33-63-63-63; fax 33-63-71-15; internet www.econ .ku.dk/nf; f. 1873; organizes lectures, discussions and encourages int. cooperation with similar asscns in the Nordic and other countries to disseminate and debate on economic issues in Denmark; 1,000 mems; Pres. Prof. PEDER ANDERSEN; Sec. JONAS SØRENSEN; Treas. ULRIKKE EKELUND; publ. *Nationaloekonomisk Tidsskrift* (3 a year).

Udenrigspolitiske Selskab (Danish Foreign Policy Society): Amaliegade 40A, 1256 Copenhagen K; tel. 33-14-88-86; fax 33-14-85-20; e-mail udenrigs@udenrigs.dk; internet www.udenrigs.dk; f. 1946; studies, debates, publs and confs on int. affairs; 1,000 individual mems, 200 corporate mems; library of 100 vols; Chair. UFFE ELLEMANN-JENSEN; Dir KLAUS CARSTEN PEDERSEN; Sec. BRITA V. ANDERSEN; publs *Lande i Lommeformat* (country descriptions: 144 booklets covering 200 countries), occasional monographs, *Udenrigs* (4 a year).

EDUCATION

Danmark-Amerika Fondet (Denmark-America Foundation): Nørregade 7A, 1165 Copenhagen K; tel. 35-32-45-45; e-mail advising@daf-fulb.dk; internet www .wemakeithappen.dk; f. 1914; provides scholarships and internship programme funds; advises about the univ. education in the USA; Pres. STEN SCHEIBYE; Vice-Pres. JØRN KILDEGAARD; Treas. PETER HØJLAND; Exec. Dir MARIE MØNSTED.

Mellemfolkeligt Samvirke (MS ActionAid Denmark): Fælledvej 12, 2200 Copenhagen N; tel. 77-31-00-00; fax 77-31-01-01; e-mail ms@ms.dk; internet www.ms.dk; f. 1944; supports long-term devt work, education programmes and campaigns as well as exchange of experience and knowledge between people; 6,300 mems; library of 40,000 vols on third world issues, immigrants and refugees in Denmark, 600 periodicals, 1,300 films; Chair. TRINE PERTOU MACH; Vice-Chair. BERIT ASMUSSEN; Sec.-Gen. LARS UDSHOLT; publs *Etcetera* (8 a year), *FOCUS Kontakt* (6 a year), *Kontakt Globalt Magasin* (6 a year), *ZAPP Jorden Rundt* (6 a year).

FINE AND PERFORMING ARTS

Billedkunstnernes Forbund (Danish Association of Visual Artists): Vingårdstræde 2, 1, 1070 Copenhagen K; tel. 33-12-81-70; e-mail bkf@bkf.dk; internet www.bkf.dk; f. 1969; influences current policies to enhance economical and social security for visual artists; enhances use of, and respect for, visual art; protects artistic freedom; 1,200 mems; Chair. BJARNE W. SØRENSEN; Vice-Chair. OLE TRACK RING; Treas. JO MILLER; publ. *Billedkunstneren* (4 a year).

Dansk Billedhuggersamfund (Danish Sculptors' Society): c/o Mogens Lund 'Sundhuset', Clarasvej 2, 8700 Horsens; tel. 76-28-20-10; fax 75-65-76-60; e-mail mnl@ billedhuggersamfundet.dk; internet www .skulptur.dk; f. 1905; improves sculptors' opportunities to display and then be able to sell their work; outdoor exhibits of particu-

larly larger works; 120 mems; Chair. KIT KJÆRBYE.

Dansk Komponist Forening (Danish Composers' Society): Gråbrødretorv 16, 1, 1154 Copenhagen K; tel. 33-13-54-05; fax 33-14-32-19; e-mail dkf@komponistforeningen.dk; internet www.komponistforeningen.dk; f. 1913; supports composers and sound artists in their efforts to realize their artistic potential; 220 mems; Chair. NIELS ROSING-SCHOW; Sec. KIRSTEN WREM; Sec. TINA SCHELLE; Sec. KATRINE GREGERSEN DAL; publ. *Hulter til Bulter* (2 a year).

Dansk Korforening (Danish Choral Society): Absalonsgade 3, 4180 Sorø; f. 1911; 27 mems; Pres. ASGER LARSEN.

Danske Kunsthåndværkere (Danish Arts and Crafts Association): Bredgade 66, 1260 Copenhagen K; tel. 33-15-29-40; fax 33-15-26-76; e-mail mail@ danskekunsthaandvaerkere.dk; internet www.danskekunsthaandvaerkere.dk; f. 1976; represents Danish craft professionals at political level; arranges exhibitions; professional advice for schools, museums; 5 regional groups of artist-craftsmen; 460 mems; Pres. MARK LAUBERG; Man. Dir NICOLAI GJESSING; publ. *KUNSTUFF–Danish Crafts and Design* (4 a year).

Kunstforeningen GL STRAND (GL STRAND Gallery of Modern and Contemporary Art): Gammel Strand 48, 1202 Copenhagen K; tel. 33-36-02-60; fax 33-36-02-66; e-mail info@glstrand.dk; internet www .glstrand.dk; f. 1825; exhibitions of modern and contemporary art; Dir HELLE BEHRNDT; publ. *Medlemsnyt* (4 a year).

Kunstnerforeningen af 18. November (Artists' Association of the 18th November): Frederiksgade 8, 1265 Copenhagen K; tel. 33-15-96-14; internet www.18nov.dk/18nov .dk/om_kunstnerforeningen.html; f. 1842; workshop, lectures, concerts, exhibitions, art colln; library of 300 vols; 165 mems; Chair. NIELS WAMBERG; Vice-Chair. POUL JENSEN; Sec. MOGENS KISCHINOVSKY; Treas. EVA NEDERGAARD.

Ny Carlsbergfondet (New Carlsberg Foundation): Brolæggerstræde 5, 1211 Copenhagen K; tel. 33-11-37-65; fax 33-14-36-46; e-mail sekretariatet@nycarlsbergfondet.dk; internet www.ny-carlsbergfondet.dk; f. 1902; supports the New Carlsberg Glyptotek (see Museums and Art Galleries, Copenhagen) and other Danish art museums; promotes the study of art and art history and develops and fulfils the appreciation of and need for art in Denmark; annual awards; Chair. HANS EDVARD NØRREGÅRD-NIELSEN; publ. *Årsskrift* (yearbook).

Samfundet til Udgivelse af Dansk Musik (Society for the Publication of Danish Music): Gråbrødrestræde 18, 1156 Copenhagen K; tel. 33-13-54-45; fax 33-93-30-44; e-mail sales@samfundet.dk; internet www .samfundet.dk; f. 1871; preserves musical works, in printed form, which are important in Danish cultural history; Pres. KLAUS IB JØRGENSEN; Vice-Pres. CHRISTINE CANALS-FRAU.

Sammenslutningen af Danske Kunstforeninger (Association of Danish Art Societies): c/o Mogens Christiansen, Cikorievej 1, 4300 Holbæk Copenhagen K; tel. 59-44-19-08; e-mail mc@mckunst.dk; internet www .sdkunst.dk; f. 1942; arranges touring art exhibitions with govt support; 15,000 mems; Pres. FINN MIKKELSEN; Vice-Chair. JØRN MADSEN; Sec. HANS-JØRGEN HØJVÆLDE; Treas. MOGENS CHRISTIANSEN.

HISTORY, GEOGRAPHY AND ARCHAEOLOGY

Arktisk Institut (Danish Arctic Institute): Strandgade 102, 1401 Copenhagen K; tel. 32-31-50-50; fax 32-88-01-51; e-mail arktisk@ arktisk.dk; internet www.arktiskinstitut.dk; f. 1954; information, scientific and historic activities related to the Arctic; library of 35,000 vols, archives of Arctic expeditions, diaries, and more than 50,000 photographs, mainly of Greenland; Chair. PETER AUGUSTINUS; Dir Dr BENT NIELSEN.

Dansk Selskab for Oldtids- og Middelalderforskning (Danish Society for Research of Ancient and Medieval Times): Nationalmuseet, Frederiksholms Kanal 12 1220 Copenhagen K; tel. 33-47-31-36; e-mail else .rasmussen@natmus.dk; f. 1934; 130 mems; Pres. MICHAEL ANDERSEN; Sec. ELSE MATHORNE RASMUSSEN.

Danske Historiske Forening (Danish Historical Association): Univ. of Copenhagen, SAXO-Institute, Njalsgade 80, 2300 Copenhagen S; tel. 35-32-81-41; e-mail histtid@ hum.ku.dk; internet www.historisktidsskrift .dk; f. 1839; promotes historical and art historical studies; 1,500 mems; Chair. Mag. CARSTEN DUE-NIELSEN; Sec. Dr JAN PEDERSEN; Sec. Dr REGIN SCHMIDT; Treas. ANDERS MONRAD MØLLER; publ. *Historisk Tidsskrift* (2 a year).

Jysk Arkaeologisk Selskab Nordjylland (Jutland Archaeological Society North Jutland): Algade 48, POB 1805, 9100 Aalborg; tel. 99-31-74-00; internet www .jysk-arkaeologi.dk; f. 1951 as Aalborg Archaeological Soc., merged with Jutland Archaeological Soc. Moesgaard 2010, present name and status 2010; lectures and publication of primary archaeological and ethnological investigations; 120 mems; Pres. LARS CHRISTIAN NØRBACH; Treas. PETER VAN HAUEN; publs *Handbooks* (irregular), *KUML* (1 a year).

Jysk Selskab for Historie (Jutland Historical Society): Historisk Institut, Århus Universitet, 8000 Århus C; tel. 89-42-20-23; fax 89-42-20-47; internet www.jyskhistorie .dk; f. 1866; promotes interest in and study of historical topics; 500 mems; Pres. HENRIK FODE; Treas. ERIK STRANGE PETERSEN; publs *Historie* (2 a year), *Nyt fra Historien* (2 a year).

Kongelige Danske Geografiske Selskab (Royal Danish Geographical Society): Øster Voldgade 10, 1350 Copenhagen K; tel. 35-32-25-00; fax 35-32-25-01; e-mail rdgs@geo.ku .dk; internet www.rdgs.dk; f. 1876; furthers interest in geographical science; organizes meetings, expeditions and research projects; 450 mems; Protector HM Queen MARGRETHE II; Pres. HRH Crown Prince FREDERIK; Vice-Pres CHAMBERLIN I. S. HASLUND-CHRISTENSEN; Vice-Pres Prof. CHRISTIAN WICHMANN MATTHIESSEN; Man. Dir PETER AUGUSTINUS; Sec. Gen. Assoc. Prof. OLE MERTZ; Treas. Assoc. Prof. BIRGER U. HANSEN; publ. *Geografisk Tidsskrift* (Danish Journal of Geography).

Kongelige Danske Selskab for Fædrelandets Historie (Royal Danish Society for National History): c/o Erik Goebel, Kingosvej 16, 4600 Koge; e-mail bestil@danskeselskab .dk; internet www.danskeselskab.dk; f. 1745; publishes sources related to country's history; contributes to Danish history research promotion; 65 mems, 20 foreign corresps; Chair. NIELS-KNUD LIEBGOTT; Sec. ERIK GOEBEL; Treas. Dr ANDERS MONRAD MØLLER; publ. *Danske Magazin*.

Kongelige Nordiske Oldskriftselskab (Royal Society of Northern Antiquaries): Frederiksholms Kanal 12, 1220 Copenhagen

K; tel. 33-47-31-59; e-mail oldskriftselskabet@natmus.dk; internet www .oldskriftselskabet.dk; f. 1825 as Nordiske Oldskriftselskab; supports and raises awareness of Denmark and other Nordic culture in ancient and medieval times; publishes books and journals; organizes lectures and excursions; 750 mems; library: in the National Museum; Dir NIELS-KNUD LIEBGOTT; Treas. GEORG LETT; Sec. PETER VANG PETERSEN; publs *Aarbøger for Nordisk Oldkyndighed og Historie, Nordiske Fortidsminder*.

Samfundet for Dansk Genealogi og Personalhistorie (Society for Danish Genealogy and Personal History): c/o Brigit Flemming Larsen, Abbey Field 13, 9000 Aalborg; e-mail info@genealogi.dk; internet www.genealogi.dk; f. 1879 as Society for Danish-Norwegian Genealogy and Personal History, present name 1926; generates interest in genealogy; 1,100 mems; Chair. BRIGIT FLEMMING LARSEN; Vice-Chair. MICHAEL BACH; publs *Hvem forsker Hvad* (1 a year), *Personalhistorisk Tidsskrift* (2 a year).

Selskabet for Dansk Kulturhistorie (Society for the History of Danish Culture): Rosenborg Castle, Øster Voldgade 4A, 1350 Copenhagen K; tel. 33-15-32-86; fax 33-15-20-46; e-mail jh@dkks.dk; f. 1936; promotes study of Danish cultural history, especially after 1500; 50 mems; Pres. STEFFEN HEIBERG; Sec. JØRGEN HEIN; publ. *Cultural Monuments*.

LANGUAGE AND LITERATURE

Alliance Française: Christiansholms Tværvej 19, 2930 Klampenborg, Copenhagen; tel. 26-83-04-28; e-mail internet@ prebenhansen.dk; internet www .alliancefrancaise.dk; f. 1884; offers courses and exams in French language and culture and promotes cultural exchange with France; attached offices in Aarhus and Abyhoj; Chair. PETER PREBEN HANSEN; Vice-Chair. ROLF MEURS-GERKEN.

British Council: Gammel Mønt, 12.3, 1117 Copenhagen K; tel. 33-36-94-00; fax 33-36-94-06; e-mail british.council@britishcouncil .dk; internet www.britishcouncil.org/ denmark; no longer runs educational activities, exams or language courses; activities in 3 regional programme strands: climate change, intercultural dialogue and creative cities; Country Man. HANS MEIER ANDERSEN.

Dansk Forfatterforening (Danish Authors' Society): Strandgade 6 st., 1401 Copenhagen K; tel. 32-95-51-00; fax 32-54-01-15; e-mail df@danskforfatterforening.dk; internet www.danskforfatterforening.dk; f. 1894; professional org. representing fiction writers, non-fiction writers, poets, translators, writers and illustrators of books for children and young people; 1,300 mems; Chair. LOTTE GARBERS; Vice-Chair. ELLEN BOEN; Sec. NENA WIINSTEDT; publ. *Forfatteren* (8 a year).

Danske Sprog- og Litteraturselskab (Society for Danish Language and Literature): Christians Brygge 1, 1219 Copenhagen; tel. 33-13-06-60; fax 33-14-06-08; e-mail sekretariat@dsl.dk; internet www.dsl.dk; f. 1911; reissues Danish language and literary works; publishes bibliographies and scientifically-based dictionaries; builds electronic language resources; 90 mems; Dir Prof. JØRN LUND; Pres. FINN HAUBERG MORTENSEN; Sec. MARIA KROGH LANGNER.

Goethe-Institut: Frederiksborggade 1, 1360 Copenhagen K; tel. 33-36-64-64; fax 33-36-64-61; e-mail info@kopenhagen.goethe.org; internet www.goethe.de/ne/kop; offers exams in German language and culture and promotes cultural exchange with Germany; Dir MATTHIAS MÜLLER-WIERFERIG.

MEDICINE

Danmarks Farmaceutiske Selskab (Danish Pharmaceutical Society): Rygårds Allé 1, 2900 Hellerup; tel. 39-46-36-00; fax 39-46-36-39; e-mail pd@pharmadanmark.dk; internet www.farmaceutisk-selskab.dk; f. 1912; encourages scientific and practical devt of Danish pharmacy; organizes meetings, workshops, confs; 765 mems; Pres. Dr SOREN ILSØE-KRISTENSEN; Vice-Chair. Dr KAMILLA ROLSTED; Treas. Dr DITTE MARIA KARPF.

Dansk Farmaceutforening (Association of Danish Pharmacists): Rygårds Alle 1, 2900 Hellerup; tel. 39-46-36-00; fax 39-46-36-39; e-mail pd@pharmadanmark.dk; internet www.pharmadanmark.dk; f. 1873; spreads awareness of the preconditions for growth and devt of pharmaceuticals; library of 16,000 vols; 3,205 mems; Dir ARNE KURDAHL; publ. *Pharma* (12 a year).

Dansk Knoglemedicinsk Selskab (Danish Bone Medical Society): Arhus Sygehus, Tage-Hansens Gade 2, 8000 Arhus C; e-mail p-vest@post4.tele.dk; internet www.dkms.dk; f. originally known as Danish Society for Bone and Dental Research; promotes and coordinates bone and calcium research; organizes scientific meetings and publishes materials about the treatment of bone diseases; Pres. BENTE LANGDAHL; Sec. PETER VESTERGAARD.

Dansk Medicinsk Selskab (Danish Medical Society): Kristianiagade 12, 2100 Copenhagen Ø; tel. 35-44-81-32; fax 35-44-85-03; e-mail dms@dadl.dk; internet www.dms.dk; f. 1919; an asscn of 100 socs and 18,000 individual mems, working in all aspects of medical science; awards the August Krogh Prize to a leading Danish scientist, annually; 18,000 mems; Chair. Prof. Dr J. MICHAEL HASENKAM; Vice-Chair. Prof. Dr NIELS QVIST; Sec. Dr IDA ELISABETH HOLM; publ. *The Danish Medical Bulletin*.

Lægeforeningen (Danish Medical Association): Kristianiagade 12, 2100 Copenhagen Ø; tel. 35-44-85-00; fax 35-44-85-05; e-mail dadl@dadl.dk; internet www.laeger.dk; f. 1857; protects and promotes the interests of the medical profession; serves as the body through which the influence of the medical profession may be exercised; 24,972 mems; Pres. MADS KOCH HANSEN; Vice-Pres. YVES SALES; Man. Dir BENTE HYLDAHL FOGH; publs *Bibliotek for Læger* (history of medicine, 4 a year), *Danish Medical Bulletin* (English, 6 a year), *DMA Directory (Vejviser)*, *Lægeforeningens Medicinfortegnelse (Physicians Desk Reference)* (every 2 years), *Ugeskrift for Læger* (52 a year).

Medicinske Selskab i København (Medical Society of Copenhagen): Kristianiagade 12, 2100 Copenhagen Ø; tel. 35-44-84-01; e-mail kms@dadl.dk; internet www.dmsk.dk; f. 1772; provides financial support for travel medical scientific use and for young researchers, medical projects; recommends on various awards and scholarships; 2,755 mems; Pres. Dr PETER BYTZER; Vice-Pres. JACOB ROSENBERG; Sec. BITTEN DAHLSTORM.

Osteoporoseforeningen (Osteoporosis Society): Park Allé 5, POB 5069, 8000 Arhus C; tel. 86-13-91-11; fax 86-13-64-47; e-mail info@osteoporose-f.dk; internet osteoporose-f .dk; f. 1992; supports research, prevention projects, lectures on the disease; participates in fairs and exhibitions to create awareness; Chair. ULLA KNAPPE; publ. *Apropos* (4 a year).

Tandlægeforeningen (Danish Dental Association): Amaliegade 17, POB 143, 1004 Copenhagen K; tel. 70-25-77-11; fax 70-25-16-37; e-mail info@tandlaegeforeningen.dk; internet www.tandlaegeforeningen.dk; f.

1873; raises awareness among the public about dental profession being a healthcare profession; 6,345 mems; Pres. SUSANNE ANDERSEN; Vice-Pres. INGE MARIE BEHRNDTZ; Vice-Pres. JAN A. FREDERICKS; publ. *Tandlaegebladet* (15 a year).

NATURAL SCIENCES
General

Selskabet for Naturlærens Udbredelse (Society for the Promotion of Natural Science): c/o UNI-C, Vermundsgade 5, 2100 Copenhagen Ø; tel. 35-87-88-04; e-mail snu@naturvidenskab.net; internet www .naturvidenskab.net; f. 1824; 200 mems; Pres. Prof. Dr DORTE OLESEN; Dir OLE MØRK LAURIDSEN; publ. *KVANT / Tidsskrift for Fysik og Astronomi* (4 a year).

Biological Sciences

Danmarks Naturfredningsforening (Danish Society for Nature Conservation): Masnedøgade 20, 2100 Copenhagen Ø; tel. 39-17-40-00; fax 39-17-41-41; e-mail dn@dn .dk; internet www.dn.dk; f. 1911; promotes nature conservation and access to nature; 140,000 mems, 216 local cttees; Pres. ELLA MARIA BISSCHOP-LARSEN; Dir GUNVER BENNEKOU; publ. *Tidsskriftet natur og miljø* (4 a year).

Dansk Botanisk Forening (Danish Botanical Society): Sølvgade 83, 1307 Copenhagen K; tel. 33-14-17-03; e-mail dbf@mail.tele .dk; internet www.botaniskforening.dk; f. 1840; promotes interest in botany, including the exploration and preservation of the Danish flora; 1,400 mems; Pres. HENRIK ÆRENLUND PEDERSEN; Vice-Pres. PAUL MØLLER PEDERSEN; Treas. KARIN RAVN-JONSEN; publ. *URT* (4 a year).

Dansk Naturhistorisk Forening (Danish Natural History Society): Universitetsparken 15, 2100 Copenhagen Ø; tel. 35-32-11-20; fax 35-32-10-10; e-mail dnf@zmuc.ku.dk; internet www.aki.ku.dk/dnf; f. 1833; promotes interest in all aspects of natural history, particularly zoology; conducts meetings, excursions and travel; 525 mems; Pres. Dr JØRGEN OLESEN; Vice-Pres. Assoc. Prof. NADJA MØBJERG; Treas. Dr LARS VILHELMSEN; publs *Arsskrift for Dansk Naturhistorisk Forening* (1 a year), *Danmarks Fauna* (irregular).

Dansk Ornithologisk Forening (Danish Ornithological Society): Vesterbrogade 140, 1620 Copenhagen V; tel. 33-28-38-00; fax 33-31-24-35; e-mail dof@dof.dk; internet www .dof.dk; f. 1906; 13,000 mems; Chair. CHRISTIAN HJORTH; Vice-Chair. EGON ØSTERGAARD; Vice-Chair. NIELS RIIS; Dir JAN EJLSTED; publs *Dansk Ornitologisk Forenings Tidsskrift* (4 a year), *DOF-Nyt* (4 a year), *Fugle i Felten* (4 a year), *Fugle og Natur* (4 a year).

Entomologisk Forening (Entomological Society): Zoological Museum, Universitetsparken 15, 2100, Copenhagen Ø; internet zoologi.snm.ku.dk/english/forskning/entomology; f. 1868; 360 mems; Pres. MICHAEL FIBIGER; Sec. JAN PEDERSEN; publ. *Entomologiske Meddelelser* (4 a year).

Physical Sciences

Astronomisk Selskab (Astronomical Society): Hviddingvej 48, 2610 Rødovre; tel. 36-72-36-34; e-mail mq@astronomisk.dk; internet www.astronomisk.dk; f. 1916; 600 mems; disseminates knowledge and interest in astronomy and astronomical research; organizes lectures and observing events; Chair. MICHAEL QUAADE; Vice-Chair. STEFFEN LINDEMANN; Treas. INGE FREDERIKSEN; publs *Knudepunktet* (3 a year), *Kvant* (jtly with Danish Physical Soc., 4 a year).

Dansk Fysisk Selskab (Danish Physical Society): c/o Ian Bearden, Niels Bohr Institutet Københavns, Universitet Blegdamsvej 17, 2100 Copenhagen Ø; tel. 45-35-32-53-23; e-mail bearden@nbi.dk; internet www.dfs.nbi .dk; f. 1972; promotes Danish research on physics through meetings and lectures; represents the physicists in Denmark to the European Physical Soc.; 700 mems; Pres. IAN BEARDEN; Vice-Chair. JOHN ANDERSON; Treas. HELGE KNUDSEN; publ. *Kvant* (jtly with Astronomical Soc., 4 a year).

Dansk Geologisk Forening (Geological Society of Denmark): c/o Geologisk Musem, Øster Voldgade 5–7, 1350 Copenhagen K; tel. 35-32-23-54; fax 35-32-23-25; e-mail dgfemail@gmail.com; internet www.2dgf.dk; f. 1893; promotes interest in geology and establishes a forum for geologists; lectures, discussions; excursions; administers 2 prizes; 600 mems; Chair. Dr LARS NIELSEN; Deputy Chair. PAUL MARTIN HOLM; Treas. MARTIN SØNDERHOLM; Sec. GUNVER KRARUP PEDERSEN; publs *Bulletin* (2 a year), *Dansk Geologisk Forening Arsskrift* (online), *Geologisk Tidsskrift* (2 a year).

Dansk Matematisk Forening (Danish Mathematical Society): c/o Vagn Lundsgaard Hansen, Dept of Mathematics, Bldg 303S, Technical Univ. of Denmark, 2800 Kongens Lyngby; tel. 45-25-30-39; fax 45-88-13-99; e-mail dmf@mathematics.dk; internet www .dmf.mathematics.dk; f. 1873; Pres. VAGN LUNDSGAARD HANSEN; Sec. and Vice-Pres. POUL HJORTH; Treas. CARSTEN LUNDE PETERSEN; publs *Mathematica Scandinavica*, *Normat*.

Kemisk Forening (Danish Chemical Society): H. C. Ørsted Institutet, Universitetsparken 5, 2100 Copenhagen Ø; tel. 35-32-01-55; fax 35-32-02-12; e-mail secretary@ chemsoc.dk; internet www.chemsoc.dk; f. 1879; promotes the advancement of chemistry in Denmark; 870 mems; Pres. Prof. PETER WESTH; Vice-Pres. Prof. MORTEN J. BJERRUM; Sec. Asst Prof. MICHAEL PITTELKOW; publ. *Dansk Kemi* (12 a year).

PHILOSOPHY AND PSYCHOLOGY

Dansk Psykolog Forening (Danish Psychological Association): Stockholmsgade 27, 2100 Copenhagen Ø; tel. 35-26-99-55; fax 35-26-97-37; e-mail dp@dp.dk; internet www.dp .dk; f. 1947; deals with questions of education and professional matters; works as a trade union to safeguard psychologists' interests; 8,855 mems; Chair. ROAL ULRICHSEN; Vice-Chair. RIE RASMUSSEN; Dir MARIE ZELANDER; Chief Sec. SUSANNE HØRDAM; publ. *Psykolog Nyt* (26 a year).

RELIGION, SOCIOLOGY AND ANTHROPOLOGY

Danske Bibelselskab (Danish Bible Society): Frederiksborggade 50, 1360 Copenhagen K; tel. 33-12-78-35; fax 33-93-21-50; e-mail bibelselskabet@bibelselskabet.dk; internet www.bibelselskabet.dk; f. 1814; editing and distributing Bibles and other biblical scriptures; Pres. PETER SKOV-JAKOBSEN; Chair. CAI FRIMODT-MØLLER; Gen. Sec TAGE KLEINBECK (acting); publs *News* (4 a year), *Bibliana* (2 a year).

Grønlandske Selskab (Greenlandic Society): Kraemer Hus, L. E. Bruunsvej 10, 2920 Charlottenlund; tel. 39-63-57-33; fax 39-63-55-43; e-mail dgs@groenlandselskab.dk; internet www.groenlandselskab.dk; f. 1905; informs about and builds relations with Greenland; strengthens public knowledge about Greenland and its people, the Arctic region as a whole; supports Danish-Greenlandic cooperation; 1,500 mems; Chair. MAR-

TIN APPELT; Vice-Chair. EINAR LUND JENSEN; Sec. JØRN WÜRTZ; publ. *Grønland* (6 a year).

TECHNOLOGY

Akademiet for de Tekniske Videnskaber (Danish Academy of Technical Sciences): Lundtoftevej 266, 2800 Kgs. Lyngby; tel. 45-88-13-11; fax 45-88-13-51; e-mail atvmail@ atv.dk; internet www.atv.dk; f. 1937; 4 divs, covering fundamental and ancillary sciences, chemical science and engineering, mechanical engineering, civil engineering, electrical engineering, information technology, agricultural and food, industrial org. and economics, environmental issues, biology and technical hygiene; thematic professional group on construction and town planning; undertakes professional meetings and projects within these fields; 650 mems; Pres. Prof. KLAUS BOCK; Vice-Pres. BJERNE STEFFEN CLAUSEN; Dir LASSE SKOVBY.

Byggecentrum (Building Centre): Hindsgavl Allé 2, 5500 Middelfart; tel. 70-12-36-00; fax 70-12-38-00; e-mail info@byggecentrum .dk; internet www.byggecentrum.dk; f. 1956; acts as centre for construction information; bookshop, database services, postgraduate training, exhibitions, training centre; Man. Dir JOERN VIBE ANDREASEN; publ. *BYGGEDATA*.

Dansk Husflidsselskab (Danish Society of Domestic Crafts): Gedskovvej 3, 5300 Kerteminde; tel. 63-32-20-96; fax 63-32-20-97; e-mail dansk@husflid.dk; internet www .husflid.dk; f. 1873; promotes domestic craftsmanship; 3,500 individual mems, 140 local orgs; Pres. ELSE MARIE SCHJERNING; Vice-Pres. BODIL NIELSEN; Treas. AGNES STENSGAARD; Sec. BENTE SKOV MACHHOLM; publ. *Husflid* (6 a year).

Højteknologifonden (Danish National Advanced Technology Foundation): Holbergsgade 14 3, 1057 Copenhagen; tel. 33-63-72-80; fax 33-32-97-87; e-mail info@ hoejteknologifonden.dk; internet hoejteknologifonden.dk; f. 2004; offers funds and framework to private companies and univs for developing new technologies; Chair. JØRGEN MADS CLAUSEN; Vice-Chair. KLAUS BOCK; Dir CARSTEN ORTH GAARN-LARSEN; Vice-Dir TRINE AABO ANDERSEN.

Elektroteknisk Forening (Society of Danish Electrotechnicians): Kronprinsensgade 28, 5000 Odense C; tel. 40-56-01-48; e-mail info@dkef.dk; internet www.dkef.dk; f. 1903; divided into 5 sections, organizes visits, lectures and field trips to establish networks across the industry; 1,400 mems; Chair. BENT CRAMER; Sec.-Gen. ANDERS EBBESEN JENSEN; publ. *Elteknik* (10 a year).

Ingeniørforeningen i Danmark (IDA) (Danish Society of Engineers): Kalvebod Brygge 31–33, 1780 Copenhagen V; tel. 33-18-48-48; fax 33-18-48-99; e-mail ida@ida.dk; internet www.ida.dk; f. 1937; divided into 8 geographical regions; brs in Copenhagen, Odense, Arhus and Aalborg; 78,000 mems; Pres. FRIDA FROST; Vice-Pres. LASSE GRØNBECH; publ. *Ingeniøren* (52 a year).

Research Institutes
GENERAL

Carlsberg Laboratory: Gamle Carlsberg Vej 10, 2500 Copenhagen V; tel. 33-27-52-21; e-mail carlslab@crc.dk; internet www.crc.dk; f. 1875; attached to Carlsberg Foundation; research in biochemistry, biotechnology and chemistry; library of 15,000 vols, 300 periodicals; Dir Dr JENS Ø. DUUS; Sec. ANNETTE PETTERSSON; Head of Research Laboratory Dr KLAUS BREDDAM.

Danish Obesity Research Centre: Øster Søgade 18, 1, 1357 Copenhagen K; tel. 33-38-38-80; fax 33-32-24-24; internet www.danorc .dk; f. 2007; investigates effects of the nutritional components: industrial fatty acids, ruminant fatty acids and milk protein on the devt of overweight and obesity—independent of their caloric value; Centre Leader Prof. Dr THORKILD I. A. SØRENSEN; Sr Dir Prof. HENRIK JØRGEN ANDERSEN; Exec. Vice-Pres. Dr HENRIK DALBØGE.

DTU Fødevareinstituttet (National Food Institute): Mørkhøj Bygade 19, 2860 Søborg; tel. 35-88-70-00; fax 35-88-70-01; e-mail food@food.dtu.dk; internet www.food.dtu.dk; f. 2004, present status 2007; attached to Technical Univ. of Denmark; conducts research into the entire food chain, from primary agricultural production and industrial processing to final preparation in the home of the consumer; provides education and gives advice on nutrition, food safety, food technology, environment and health; Dir HENRIK CASPAR WEGENER.

Nationale Forskningscenter for Arbejdsmiljø (National Research Centre for the Working Environment): Lersø Park Allé 105, 2100 Copenhagen Ø; tel. 39-16-52-00; fax 39-16-52-01; e-mail nfa@ arbejdsmiljoforskning.dk; internet www .arbejdsmiljoforskning.dk; f. 2003; attached to Min. of Employment; monitors, analyses and explores conditions in the working environment affecting health, safety and work role functioning; acts as a gateway to working environment knowledge for enterprises through the Working Environment Information Centre; Chair. Prof. KJELD MØLLER PEDERSEN; Dir-Gen. Dr PALLE ØRBÆK; Deputy Dir-Gen. ULLA W. SKJØTH.

Rockwool Fondens Forskningsenhed (Rockwool Foundation Research Unit): Sølvgade 10, 2. tv., 1307 Copenhagen K; tel. 33-34-48-00; fax 33-34-48-99; e-mail forskningsenheden@rff.dk; internet www.rff .dk; f. 1987; attached to The Rockwool Foundation; produces new, empirically based analyses related to current problems of modern society within the areas of labour market conditions (incl. the spread of black work in Denmark and other North European countries) and of the functions, stability and legitimacy of the welfare state; Pres. ELIN SCHMIDT; Chair. TOM KÄHLER; Deputy Chair. LARS NØRBY JOHANSEN; Dir Prof. TORBEN TRANÆS; Sec. MAI-BRITT SEJBERG.

AGRICULTURE, FISHERIES AND VETERINARY SCIENCE

Det Jordbrugsvidenskabelige Fakultet (Faculty of Agricultural Sciences): Blichers Allé 20, POB 50, 8830 Tjele; tel. 89-99-19-00; fax 89-99-19-19; e-mail djf@agrsci.dk; internet www.agrsci.dk; f. 1928; attached to Aarhus Univ.; researches in agriculture and connected subjects; centres in Foulum, Aarslev, Flakkebjerg; 4 experimental stations; Chair. JENS KAMPMANN; Dean JUST JENSEN; Vice-Dean HENRIETTE GIESE.

DTU Veterinærinstituttet (National Veterinary Institute DTU): Bülowsvej 27, 1790 Copenhagen V; tel. 35-88-60-00; fax 35-88-60-01; e-mail vet@vet.dtu.dk; internet www .vet.dtu.dk; f. 1908, present status and name 2007; attached to Technical Univ. of Denmark; conducts research on infectious diseases in livestock and makes diagnoses in diseased animals; advises public authorities and cooperates with them on the Danish veterinary contingency plan; Dir KRISTIAN MOELLER; Deputy Dir KIRSTEN FLAGSTAD; Chief Sec. KAREN DAMGAARD DUUN.

Hedeselskabet (Danish Land Development Service): Klostermarken 12, POB 91, 8800

Viborg; tel. 87-28-11-33; fax 87-28-10-01; e-mail hedeselskabet@hedeselskabet.dk; internet www.hedeselskabet.dk; f. 1866; forestry, forest nurseries, shelter belts, soil improvement, environmental protection, environmental engineering, land reclamation, drainage, irrigation, hydrology and research; specialists carry out practical assignments and research; technical projects designed and administered for farmers, foresters, industry, government authorities in Denmark and abroad; CEO OVE KLOCH; Chief Finance Officer BENT SIMONSEN; Chair. FRANTS COUNT BERNSTORFF-GYLDENSTEEN; Vice-Chair. PETER HØSTGAARD-JENSEN; publ. *Vækst* (6 a year).

ECONOMICS, LAW AND POLITICS

Danmarks Statistik (Statistics Denmark): Sejrøgade 11, 2100 Copenhagen Ø; tel. 39-17-39-17; fax 39-17-39-99; e-mail dst@dst.dk; internet www.dst.dk; f. 1849; central institution for all Danish statistics; library: see Libraries and Archives; Dir-Gen. JAN PLOVSING; publs *Nyt fra Danmarks Statistik* (daily bulletin for media), *Statistisk Arbog* (1 a year), *Statistiske Efterretninger* (daily bulletin for professional users), *Statistisk Månedsoversigt* (12 a year), *Statistisk Tiårsoversigt* (statistical 10-year survey, 1 a year).

Dansk Center for Internationale Studier og Menneskerettigheder (Danish Centre for International Studies and Human Rights): Strandgade 56, 1401 Copenhagen K; tel. 32-69-87-87; fax 32-69-87-00; e-mail dcism@dcism.dk; internet www.dcism.dk; f. 2003; undertakes research and analysis concerning foreign security and devt policy; conflict and genocide and human rights in Denmark and abroad; library of 115,000 books and reports, 1,000 journal and yearbooks; Head of the Board OLE LØNSMANN POULSEN; Treas. HANNE ERBS.

Constituent Institutes:

Dansk Institut for Internationale Studier (DIIS) (Danish Institute for International Studies (DIIS)): Strandgade 56, 1401 Copenhagen K; tel. 32-69-87-87; fax 32-69-87-00; e-mail diis@diis.dk; internet www.diis.dk; f. 2003 by act of Parliament (Act no. 411 as of 6 June 2002); research depts: conflict and security studies, cold war studies, European studies, devt research, globalization and governance research, holocaust and genocide studies; Dir NANNA HVIDT; publ. *Den Ny Verden* (The New World, 4 a year).

Institut for Menneskerettigheder (Institute for Human Rights): Strandgade 56, 1401 Copenhagen K; tel. 32-69-88-88; fax 32-69-88-00; e-mail center@humanrights.dk; internet www.humanrights.dk; f. 2002; programmes incl. access to justice, civil soc. and networking, human rights and business, European Masters programme, reform of law and state institutions, univs and research partnership programme; Dir JONAS CHRISTOFFERSEN; Deputy Dir CHARLOTTE FLINDT PEDERSEN.

HISTORY, GEOGRAPHY AND ARCHAEOLOGY

Danske Komité for Historikernes Internationale Samarbejde (Danish Committee for International Historical Cooperation): Copenhagen Univ., 2300 Copenhagen S; f. 1926; 43 mems; Chair. Prof. NIELS STEENSGARD.

MEDICINE

CCBR's Clinical Research Center: Telegrafvej 4, 1, 2750 Ballerup; tel. 44-52-54-00; fax 44-52-54-54; e-mail ccbr_ballerup@ccbr.dk; internet www.synarc.com/services/clinical-research-centers/clinical-research-centres.html.; f. 1992 as QAC CCBR, present status and name 1998; operates clinical-trial sites; has 17 offices around the world; Chair. CLAUS CHRISTIANSEN; Chief Financial Officer RALPH REYES.

Center for Integrated Molecular Brain Imaging: Rigshospitalet, section 9201, Blegdamsvej 9, 2100 Copenhagen Ø; tel. 35-45-67-12; fax 35-45-67-13; e-mail cimbi@cimbi.dk; internet www.cimbi.dk; f. 2006; researches on the neural bases of personality dimensions that predispose individuals to affective and substance use disorders; Dir Prof. GITTE MOOS KNUDSEN; Man. KARAM SIDAROS.

Center of Functionally Integrative Neuroscience: Aarhus University Hospital — Arhus Sygehus, Nørrebrogade 44, Bldg 10G, 5th Fl., 8000 Arhus C; Bldg 10G, 5th Fl., 8000 Arhus C; tel. 89-49-43-98; fax 89-49-44-00; e-mail mai@cfin.dk; internet www.cfin.au.dk; f. 2000; attached to Danish Nat. Research Foundation; researches to understand the ability of human brain; Head LEIF ØSTERGAARD.

Dansk Center for Aldringsforskning (Danish Ageing Research Center): J.B Winsløwsvej 9B, st. t.v., 5000 Odense C; tel. 65-50-40-88; e-mail uiversen@health.sdu.dk; internet www.sdu.dk/om_sdu/institutter_centre/darc?sc_lang=en; f. 1996; attached to Univ. of Southern Denmark; conducts and promotes research in human ageing processes from different angles by combining ageing research from the molecular level, to the individual and finally to the entire population; Head Prof. Dr KAARE CHRISTENSEN; Sec. ULLA IVERSEN.

Dansk Psykiatrisk Biobank (Danish Psychiatric Biobank): Boserupvej 2, 4000 Roskilde; tel. 46-33-49-68; fax 46-33-43-67; e-mail kontakt@psykiatriskbiobank.dk; internet www.ribp.dk; f. 2001; ensures long lasting and stable scientific devts that could involve running and integrating new and relevant scientific disciplines in basic and clinical psychiatric research; collaboration with 11 European and American research centres; Dir Dr THOMAS WERGELAND; Man. HENRIK LUBLIN.

Finsen Laboratory: Rigshospitalet, Copenhagen Biocenter, Jagtvej 124, 2200 Copenhagen N; Copenhagen Biocenter, Ole Maaloes Vej 5, Bldg 3, 3rd Fl., 2200 Copenhagen N; tel. 35-45-60-22; fax 35-45-37-97; e-mail finsenlab@finsenlab.dk; internet www.finsenlab.dk; f. 1896; cancer research unit; performs basic cancer research; Head of Laboratory NIELS BEHRENDT (acting).

Institute of Cancer Biology: Strandboulevarden 49, 2100 Copenhagen; tel. 35-25-75-00; fax 35-25-77-21; e-mail bio@cancer.dk; internet www.cancer.dk/bio; f. 1949; experimental cancer research; consists of 6 depts and 2 research centres; Scientific Dir Prof. JULIO E. CELIS; Sec. LAILA FISCHER; publ. *Report* (every 2 years, in English).

Kennedy Centret (Kennedy Center): Gl. Landevej 7, 2600 Glostrup; tel. 43-26-01-00; fax 43-43-11-30; e-mail kennedy@kennedy.dk; internet www.kennedy.dk; f. 2004; attached to Min. of Health and Prevention; nat. research and advisory centre for genetics, visual impairment and mental retardation; Pres. BIRGITTE DISSING NAUNTOFTE; Dir Prof. KAREN BRØNDUM-NIELSEN; Vice-Dir INGER MARIE BRUUN-VIERO.

Wilhelm Johannsen Centre for Functional Genome Research: Bldg 24.4, Blegdemsvej 3, 2200 Copenhagen N; tel. 35-32-78-26; fax 35-32-78-45; e-mail wjc@wjc.ku.dk; internet www.wjc.ku.dk; f. 2001; researches in functional characterization of the human genome by identification of novel human disease genes, novel genetic entities and novel genetic mechanisms; Dir Prof. NIELS TOMMERUP; Vice-Dir Assoc. Prof. LARS ALLAN LARSEN.

NATURAL SCIENCES

General

De Økonomiske Råd (Danish Economic Councils): Amaliegade 44, 1256 Copenhagen K; tel. 33-44-58-00; fax 33-32-90-29; e-mail dors@dors.dk; internet www.dors.dk; consists of the Economic Council and the Environmental Economic Council; Chair. HANS JØRGEN WHITTA-JACOBSEN; Chair. MICHAEL ROSHOLM; Chair. CLAUS THUSTRUP KREINER; Chair. EIRIK SCHRØDER AMUNDSEN; Dir LARS HAAGEN PEDERSEN; publ. *Vismandsrapporterne* (2 a year).

Biological Sciences

Arctic Station, University of Copenhagen: Naturvidenskabelige Fakultet, Københavns Univ., Tagensvej 16, 2200 Copenhagen N; tel. 35-32-42-56; fax 35-32-42-20 Arctic Station, POB 504, 3953 Qeqertarsuaq, Greenland; tel. (299) 92-13-84; fax (299) 92-13-85; e-mail as-science@greennet.gl; internet www.arktiskstation.ku.dk; f. 1906, research facility at Univ. of Copenhagen 1953; study of Arctic nature; laboratory; research ship 'Porsild'; library of 3,000 books, colln of journals; Head of Board Prof. REINHARDT MØBJERG KRISTENSEN; Chief Scientist Dr OUTI M. TERVO; Sec. GITTE HENRIKSEN.

Bioinformatik-centret (Bioinformatics Centre): Dept of Biology, Univ. of Copenhagen, Ole Maaloes Vej 5, 2200 Copenhagen N; tel. 35-32-13-17; fax 35-32-12-81; e-mail info@binf.ku.dk; internet www.binf.ku.dk; f. 2002, present status 2006; attached to Univ. of Copenhagen; conducts research in bioinformatics and covers the span of molecular biology from genomes to RNAs to proteins; Head Prof. ANDERS KROGH; Sec. SIANNY BRANDT.

Biologisk Institut (Institute of Biology): Univ. of Southern Denmark, Campusvej 55, 5230 Odense M; tel. 65-50-27-52; fax 65-50-27-86; e-mail mj@biology.sdu.dk; internet www.sdu.dk/om_sdu/institutter_centre/i_biologi?sc_lang=en; f. 1973; attached to Univ. of Southern Denmark; focuses research on ecotoxicology and environmental stress, bioacoustics and behaviour, and aquatic ecology; library of 1,000 vols; Head Assoc. Prof. OLE NÆSBYE LARSEN; Dept Administrator MERETE JØRGENSEN.

DTU Aqua (National Institute of Aquatic Resources): Jægersborg Alle 1, 2920 Charlottenlund; tel. 35-88-33-00; fax 35-88-33-33; e-mail aqua@aqua.dtu.dk; internet www.aqua.dtu.dk; f. 1995 as Danish Institute for Fisheries Research; organized into 8 scientific sections: fisheries, aquaculture, marine, freshwater and seafood research; large specialist library of fisheries and biology texts; Dir FRITZ W. KÖSTER (acting); Vice-Dir ESKILD KIRKEGAARD; Vice-Dir HELGE A. THOMSEN; Sec. MAJKEN BAGER; publ. *Fisk og Hav*.

Statens Seruminstitut (State Serum Institute): Artillerivej 5, 2300 Copenhagen S; tel. and fax 32-68-32-68; e-mail serum@ssi.dk; internet www.ssi.dk; f. 1902; microbiological and immunological research institute and centre for the prevention and control of infectious diseases and congenital disorders; library of 19,000 vols; Pres. and CEO NILS

STRANDBERG PEDERSEN; Dir of Research ERIK JUHL.

Zoologisk Have (Copenhagen Zoo): Roskildevej 38, POB 7, 2000 Frederiksberg; tel. 72-20-02-00; fax 72-20-02-19; e-mail mst@zoo.dk; internet www.zoo.dk; f. 1859; 3,300 animals of 264 species; participation in nature conservation projects, behaviour, genetics, and veterinary issues worldwide; Man. Dir LARS LUNDING ANDERSEN; publ. *Zoo Nyt* (Zoo News, 4 a year).

Physical Sciences

Center for Sun-Climate Research: Juliane Maries Vej 30, 2100 Copenhagen OE; tel. 35-32-57-00; fax 35-36-24-75; e-mail sunclimate@spacecenter.dk; internet www.dsri.dk/sun-climate; f. 2004; investigates link between Earth's climate and solar activity through effects of cosmic rays on Earth's cloud cover; Dir HENRIK SVENSMARK; Sec. SUSSANE KNAPPE.

Danish Hydraulic Institute: Agern Allé 5, 2970 Hørsholm; tel. 45-16-92-00; fax 45-16-92-92; e-mail dhi@dhigroup.com; internet www.dhi.dk; f. 2005,following merger of DHI Water and Environment and Danish Toxicology Centre; 29 offices around the globe; promotes technological devt and competence building within areas of water, environment and health through research; CEO ASGER KEJ; Chief Financial Officer PETER RASMUSSEN; Chief Operating Officer ANTOINE LABROSSE.

Danmarks Meteorologiske Institut (Danish Meteorological Institute): Lyngbyvej 100, 2100 Copenhagen Ø; tel. 39-15-75-00; fax 39-27-10-80; e-mail epost@dmi.dk; internet www.dmi.dk; f. 1872; attached to Min. of Climate and Energy; meteorology and geophysics; meteorological service for Denmark, Faroe Islands and Greenland; library of 40,000 vols; 400 mems; Dir PETER AAKJÆR; publs *Danmarks Klima* (1 a year), *Magnetic Results* (Godhavn and Thule, Greenland).

De Nationale Geologiske Undersøgelser for Danmark og Grønland (Geological Survey of Denmark and Greenland): Ø. Voldgade 10, 1350 Copenhagen K; tel. 38-14-20-00; fax 38-14-20-50; e-mail geus@geus.dk; internet www.geus.dk; f. 1995; library of 14,800 vols, incl. scientific journals, books, geological maps; Man. Dir JOHNNY FREDERICIA; Deputy Dir BJØRN KAARE JENSEN; Deputy Dir FLEMMING GETREUER CHRISTIANSEN; publs *Geological Survey of Denmark and Greenland Bulletin*, *Geological Survey of Denmark and Greenland Map Series*.

Kort & Matrikelstyrelsen (National Survey and Cadastre): Rentemestervej 8, 2400 Copenhagen NV; tel. 72-54-50-00; fax 35-87-50-51; e-mail kms@kms.dk; internet www.kms.dk; f. 1989 by amalgamation of former Geodetic Institute, Danish Cadastral Dept and Hydrographic Div.; responsible for geodetic survey of Denmark, Faroe Islands and Greenland; topographic survey and mapping of those areas, also nautical charting and issue of nautical publs; cadastral survey, registration, and mapping of Denmark; seismographic service in Denmark, Faroe Islands and Greenland; research and devt within geodesy and seismology; devt of digital maps and charts; Dir JESPER JARMBÆK; Deputy Dir REEBERG SOREN NIELSEN; Deputy Dir KARI CLEMMESEN .

Niels Bohr Institutet: Astronomisk Observatorium, Københavns Universitet, Juliane Maries Vej 30, 2100 Copenhagen Ø; tel. 35-32-59-60; e-mail library@astro.ku.dk; internet www.nbi.dk; f. 1642; merger of Astronomical Observatory, Ørsted Laboratory, Geophysical Institute and Niels Bohr Institute 1993; astronomy, physics and geo-

physics; library of 12,000 vols, 100 periodicals; Head of Dept Prof. J. R. HANSEN; Sec. NINA SANDER BECH.

RELIGION, SOCIOLOGY AND ANTHROPOLOGY

Instytut Polsko–Skandynawski/Polsk-Skandinavisk Forskningsinstitut (Polish–Scandinavian Research Institute): POB 2584, 2100 Copenhagen Ø; tel. 39-29-98-26; f. 1985; ind. research institute for Polish–Scandinavian studies; provides support for research in the field of history and biographical science; organizes lectures; 25 mems; library of 1,000 vols; 20 m of archives; Pres. Prof. Dr hab. E. S. KRUSZEWSKI; Dir Prof. Dr hab. BOLESLAW HAJDUK; Dir Prof. Dr BARBARA TÖRNQUIST-PLEWA.

SFI—Det Nationale Forskningscenter for Velfærd (Danish National Centre for Social Research): Herluf Trolles Gade 11, 1052 Copenhagen K; tel. 33-48-08-00; fax 38-48-08-33; e-mail sfi@sfi.dk; internet www.sfi.dk; f. 1958; ind. nat. research centre operating under Min. of Social Welfare; carries out commissioned projects in the area of welfare state policies, and disseminates the results; library of 32,500 vols; Man. Dir JØRGEN SØNDERGAARD; Chair. Prof. PETER NANNESTAD; Deputy Chair. Prof. MARGARETHA BERTILSSON; publ. *Social Forskning* (4 a year).

TECHNOLOGY

Biotech Research & Innovation Centre: Copenhagen Biocenter, 4th Fl., Ole Maaløes Vej 5, 2200 Copenhagen N; tel. 35-32-56-66; fax 35-32-56-69; e-mail bric@bric.dk; internet www.bric.ku.dk; f. 2003; researches as to how and why disease occurs; discovers new disease-related genes; identifies new diagnostic markers; Chair. PETER HØNGAARD ANDERSEN; Vice-Chair. CARSTEN SCHOU; Dir Prof. KRISTIAN HELIN; Head of Admin. KIRSTEN GRAABÆK LANGE.

Danish Center for Scientific Computing: C/o Niels Bohr Institute (NBI), Univ. of Copenhagen, Blegdamsvej 17, 2100 Copenhagen Ø; tel. 35-32-54-53; e-mail belso@dcsc.dk; internet www.dcsc.dk; f. 2001; attached to Min. of Science, Technology and Innovation; provides scientific or high performance computing and grid infrastructure to researchers working with scientific calculations, simulations and modelling; Chair. HENRIK VISSING; Deputy Chair. Prof. JOHN RENNER HANSEN; Dir RENE BELSO.

Risø Nationallaboratoriet for Bæredygtig Energi (Risø National Laboratory for Sustainable Energy): Frederiksborgvej 399, POB 49, 4000 Roskilde; tel. 46-77-46-77; fax 46-77-56-88; e-mail risoe@risoe.dk; internet www.risoe.dtu.dk; f. 1958; attached to Danmarks Tekniske Universitet; research and devt in fields of industrial materials, new functional materials, energy systems analysis, renewable energy, and nuclear safety; Dir ANDERS BJARKLEV (acting); Deputy Dir LARS MARTINY; publ. *Risø Report*.

Libraries and Archives

Ålborg

Aalborg Bibliotekerne (Central Library for the County of North Jutland): Rendsburggade 2, POB 839, 9100 Ålborg; tel. 99-31-43-00; fax 99-31-43-90; e-mail bibliotek@aalborg.dk; internet www.aalborgbibliotekerne.dk; f. 1895; 15 brs and 3 mobile libraries; 730,000 vols, 1,300 current periodicals; Chief Librarian BODIL HAVE.

Aalborg Universitetsbibliotek (Aalborg University Library): Langagervej 2, POB

8200, 9220 Ålborg; tel. 99-40-94-00; fax 98-15-55-31; e-mail aub@aub.aau.dk; internet www.aub.aau.dk; f. 1973; open to the public; 710,000 vols (incl. 27,000 e-journals and 160,000 e-books); Chief Librarian NIELS-HENRIK GYLSTORFF; Asst Dir MAJ ROSENSTAND.

Allerød

Allerød Biblioteker (Allerød Libraries): Skovensvej 4, 3450 Allerød; tel. 48-10-40-10; fax 48-10-40-11; e-mail info@bibliotek.alleroed.dk; internet www.bibliotek.alleroed.dk; 3,667 vols, colln of CDs, DVDs, films; Librarian ANETTE AALUND; Deputy Man. NINA MADSEN.

Århus

Århus Kommunes Biblioteker (Århus Public Library): Møllegade 1, 8000 Århus C; tel. 89-40-92-00; fax 89-40-93-87; e-mail hovedbibliotek@aarhus.dk; internet www.aakb.dk; f. 1934; 1,124,228 vols (incl. audiovisual materials); 18 brs; Chief Librarian ROLF HAPEL.

Erhvervsarkivet Statens Erhvervshistoriske Arkiv (Danish National Business Archives): Vester Allé 12, 8000 Århus C; tel. 86-12-85-33; fax 86-12-85-60; e-mail mailbox@ea.sa.dk; internet www.sa.dk/content/us/about_us/danish_business_archives; f. 1948; keeps registers, documents, etc. from companies and orgs in the business sector; also a research institute for economic and social history; 100,000 vols; Chief Archivist Hon. Dr MICHAEL H. GELTING; publ. *Erhvervshistorisk Arbog* (Business History Yearbook).

Handelshøjskolens Bibliotek (Library of the Arhus School of Business): Fuglesangs Allé 4, 8210 Århus V; tel. 89-48-65-20; fax 86-15-96-27; e-mail bibliotek@asb.dk; internet www.lib.asb.dk; f. 1939; spec. colln: European documentation centre for EU; 177,000 vols, 75,000 e-book titles, 44,000 e-journal titles; Library Dir TOVE BANG.

Statsbiblioteket (State and University Library): Victor Albecks Vej 1, 8000 Århus C; tel. 89-46-20-22; fax 89-46-22-20; e-mail sb@statsbiblioteket.dk; internet www.statsbiblioteket.dk; f. 1902; legal deposit library, nat. newspaper colln, nat. media archive, loan centre for public libraries; 4,850,022 vols; Dir SVEND LARSEN.

Copenhagen

Administrative Bibliotek: Slotsholmsgade 12, 1216 Copenhagen K; tel. 72-26-98-91; fax 72-26-98-99; e-mail dab@dab.dk; internet www.dab.dk; f. 1924 as the Library for the Mins of Labour and Social Affairs, present status 1995; attached to Min. of Science, Technology and Innovation; central library and documentation centre for civil servants in central govt; 160,000 vols, spec. colln: Danish governmental publs; Head of Library NIELS H. JENSENIUS; publ. *Prima Vista* (4 a year).

CBS Bibliotek (CBS Library): Solbjerg Plads 3, 2000 Frederiksberg; tel. 38-15-38-15; fax 38-15-36-63; e-mail quest.lib@cbs.dk; internet uk.cbs.dk/bibliotek; f. 1922; 400,000 vols, 1,000 current print periodicals, 33,000 electronic periodicals; Dir RENÉ STEFFENSEN; Vice-Dir GERT POULSEN.

Danmarks Biblioteksskoles Bibliotek (Library of the Royal School of Library and Information Science): Birketinget 6, 2300 Copenhagen S; tel. 32-34-14-42; fax 32-84-02-01; e-mail dbilaan@iva.dk; internet www.iva.dk/bibliotek; f. 1956; specializes in library and information science material; mem. of NORFRI cooperation; 180,000 vols,

37,000 e-books; Librarian KAREN MARGRETHE ØRNSTRUP.

Danmarks Kunstbibliotek (Royal Danish Academy of Fine Arts Library): Kgs Nytorv 1, POB 1053, 1007 Copenhagen K; tel. 33-74-48-00; fax 33-74-48-88; e-mail dkb@kunstbib .dk; internet www.kunstbib.dk; f. 1754; 280,000 vols on history of art and architecture, 300,000 architectural drawings, 100,000 photographs, 90,000 slides; spec. library for the schools of Danish Academy of Arts, univ. institutes of art history as well as architecture museum; archive and study colln for practising architects, public authorities and Danish and foreign architecture scholars; Dir Dr PATRICK KRAGELUND; Deputy Dir STEEN SØNDERGAARD THOMSEN.

Danmarks Paedagogiske Bibliotek (National Library of Education): Tuborgvej 164, POB 840, 2400 Copenhagen NV; tel. 88-88-93-00; fax 88-88-93-90; e-mail dpb@dpu .dk; internet www.dpb.dpu.dk; f. 1887; 895,000 vols, 3,057 current periodicals, 600,000 microfiches; colln incl. material in the field of education, educational systems, educational psychology, psychology of children and adolescents, children's literature; Head Librarian JENS BENNEDSEN.

Danmarks Statistiks Bibliotek og Information (Statistics Denmark Library and Information): Sejrøgade 11, 2100 Copenhagen Ø; tel. 39-17-30-30; fax 39-17-30-03; e-mail bib@dst.dk; internet www.dst.dk/ biblioteket; f. 1850; attached to Danmarks Statistik (see under Research Institutes: Economics, Law and Politics); 235,000 vols; principal library for descriptive statistics; Head of Div. PER KNUDSEN.

Det Biovidenskabelige Fakultetsbibliotek (Faculty of Life Sciences Library): Dyrlægevej 10, 1870 Frederiksberg C; tel. 35-33-21-45; fax 35-33-22-55; e-mail bvfb@life.ku .dk; internet www.bvfb.life.ku.dk; f. 1783, present name and status 2008; 586,000 vols; research library within the Faculty of Life Sciences at the Univ. of Copenhagen; Chief Librarian FREDE MØRCH; Sec. HELLE BØJE.

Det Farmaceutiske Fakultetsbibliotek, Københavns Universitet (Pharmaceutical Sciences Faculty Library, Copenhagen University): Universitetsparken 4, 2nd FL, 2100 Copenhagen Ø; tel. 35-33-63-19; fax 35-33-60-60; e-mail bibliotek@farma.ku.dk; internet www.farma.ku.dk/bibliotek; f. 1892; supports research and teaching at the Faculty of Pharmaceutical Sciences, Univ. of Copenhagen; 55,000 vols; Faculty Librarian ALICE NØRHEDE.

Frederiksberg Bibliotek (Frederiksberg Public Library): Falkoner Plads 3, 2000 Frederiksberg; tel. 38-21-18-00; fax 38-21-17-99; e-mail biblioteket@frederiksberg.dk; internet www.fkb.dk; f. 1887; 547,634 vols, 1,000 periodicals; 3 brs; also a music library and a spec. genealogy section; Chief Librarian ANNE MOLLER-RASMUSSEN.

Københavns Biblioteker (Copenhagen Libraries): Biblioteksfaglig Afdeling, Krystalgade 15, 1172 Copenhagen K; tel. 33-42-66-80; fax 33-73-60-20; e-mail hovadm@kff .kk.dk; internet www.bibliotek.kk.dk; f. 1885; 2,240,881 vols; Library Dir JENS STEEN ANDERSEN.

Københavns Stadsarkiv (Copenhagen City Archives): Rådhuset, 1599 Copenhagen V; tel. 33-66-23-70; fax 33-66-70-39; e-mail stadsarkiv@kff.kk.dk; internet www.ksa.kk .dk; f. before 1563; 37 linear km of archive material, 150,000 maps, 200,000 cards and drawings; Dir HENRIK GAUTIER; publ. *København. Kultur og Historie* (1 a year).

Kongelige Bibliotek (Royal Library): POB 2149, 1016 Copenhagen K; tel. 33-47-47-47;

fax 33-93-22-18; e-mail kb@kb.dk; internet www.kb.dk; f. 1482 as univ. library, 1648 as the King's Library, merged 1989; acts as the Danish Nat. Library; principal research and univ. library for theology, the humanities, law and the social sciences, the natural and health sciences; nat. archive for MSS and archives of prominent Danes; incl. Danish Museum of Books and Printing, National Museum of Photography, Museum of Danish Cartoon Art; open to the public; 6,050,545 vols, 4,500 incunabula, 172,000 MSS and archives, 18,000,000 graphic documents, 299,000 maps and prints, 289,000 musical items; Dir-Gen. ERLAND KOLDING NIELSEN; publs *Fund og Forskning i Det Kongelige Biblioteks Samlinger* (1 a year), *Magasin fra Det Kongelige Bibliotek* (4 a year).

Forsvarets Bibliotek (Defence Library): Kastellet 46, 2100 Copenhagen Ø; tel. 33-47-95-25; fax 33-47-95-36; e-mail fbib@fak .dk; internet forsvaret.dk/fak/bibliotek; f. 2009,on merger of Royal Garrison Library, Air Force Library and Naval Library; attached to the Defence Academy; central defence research library; organized under the Defence Academy of Sciences of the Military History and Knowledge Dissemination; 40,000 vols, 5,000 e-journals, 20 electronic encyclopedias; Man. SIMON K. B. PAPOUSEK.

Kunstindustrimuseets Bibliotek (National Art and Design Library): Bredgade 68, 1260 Copenhagen K; tel. 33-18-56-50; fax 33-18-56-66; e-mail bib@ kunstindustrimuseet.dk; internet www .kunstindustrimuseet.dk/bibliotek; f. 1890; reference and research library for design; subject areas incl. applied arts and industrial design: furniture, fashion and costume, glass, ceramics, textiles, metalwork and jewellery, book production, graphic design and posters, and traditional art of Asia; 180,000 books and leaflets, 3,000 magazines, 30,000 posters, 50,000 graphics, prints and sketches; Chief Librarian LARS DYBDAHL.

Patent- og Varemærkestyrelsens bibliotek (Library of the Danish Patent and Trademark Office): Helgeshoj Allé 81, 2630 Taastrup; tel. 43-50-82-90; fax 43-50-80-01; e-mail bibliotek@dkpto.dk; internet www .dkpto.dk/soeg-i-online-registre/bibliotek; f. 1894; 28,860 vols; 35m. patent specifications; Head of Library JON FINSEN; Head of Library LIZZI VESTER; publs *Dansk Brugsmodeltidende* (Danish Utility Models Gazette, 26 a year), *Dansk Mønstertidende* (Danish Design Gazette, 26 a year), *Dansk Patenttidende* (Danish Patent Gazette, 52 a year), *Dansk Varemarketidende* (Danish Trademark Gazette, 52 a year).

Statens Arkiver (Danish State Archives): Rigsdagsgården 9, 1218 Copenhagen K; tel. 33-92-33-10; fax 33-15-32-39; e-mail mailbox@ra.sa.dk; internet www.sa.dk; f. 1582; comprises 4 individual archives: Danish Nat. Archives, Danish Business Archives, Danish Data Archives and The Filming Centre; Dir ASBJØRN HELLUM; publs *Arkiv*, *Siden Saxo*.

Esbjerg

Esbjerg Kommunes Biblioteker (Esbjerg Public Library): Nørregade 19, 6700 Esbjerg; tel. 76-16-20-00; fax 76-16-20-01; e-mail biblio@esbjergkommune.dk; internet www .esbbib.dk; f. 1897; 9 brs; offers materials in all major languages incl. languages spoken by the local immigrant communities; 2,394,810 vols, 71,987 other items, incl. electronic resources, CDs; Chief Librarian ANNETTE BRØCHNER LINDGAARD.

Greve

Greve Bibliotek (Greve Library): Portalen 2, 2670 Greve; tel. 43-95-80-00; fax 43-95-80-80; e-mail greve@grevebib.dk; internet www .grevebibliotek.dk; 3 brs; 162,750 vols, CDs and magazines; Librarian MARIANNE OLSEN.

Hellerup

Gentofte Bibliotekerne (Public Library): Ahlmanns Allé 6, 2900 Hellerup; tel. 39-98-58-00; fax 39-98-58-25; e-mail bibliotek@ gentofte.dk; internet www.genbib.dk; f. 1918; 546,808 vols; 5 brs; Chief Librarian PIA HANSEN.

Lyngby

Danmarks Tekniske Informationscenter (Technical Information Centre of Denmark): Bldg 101D, POB 777, Anker Engelunds Vej 1, 2800 Kgs. Lyngby; tel. 45-25-72-50; fax 45-88-30-40; e-mail dtub@dtic.dtu.dk; internet www.dtic.dtu.dk; f. 1942; centre for scientific information and library for the Technical Univ. of Denmark; 700,000 vols, 4,000 current periodicals, 11,000 e-journals; Dir MOGENS SANDFÆR; Deputy Man. GITTE BRUUN JENSEN.

Odense

Landsarkivet for Fyn (Provincial Archives of Funen): Jernbanegade 36A, 5000 Odense C; tel. 66-12-58-85; fax 66-14-70-71; e-mail mailbox@lao.sa.dk; internet www.sa.dk/ content/us/about_us/provincial_archives/provincial_archives_of_funen; f. 1893; incl. records of local admin. of Funen and neighbouring islands, and colln of private papers; The Karen Brahe Library, the only nearly complete private Danish library dating from the 17th century, with about 3,400 printed books and 1,153 MSS, is deposited in the archives; Dir STEEN OUSAGER.

Odense Centralbibliotek (Odense Central Library): Østre Stationsvej 15, 5000 Odense C; tel. 65-51-43-01; fax 66-13-73-37; e-mail adm-bib@odense.dk; internet www.odensebib .dk; f. 1924; 865,000 vols, 145,000 CDs, audiobooks, video cassettes and DVDs; Library Dir KENT SKOV ANDREASEN; Chief Librarian JYTTE CHRISTENSEN; Chief Librarian PETER THOMSEN.

Syddansk Universitetsbibliotek (University Library of Southern Denmark): Campusvej 55, 5230 Odense M; tel. 65-50-26-11; fax 65-15-00-95; e-mail sdub@bib.sdu.dk; internet www.sdu.dk/bibliotek; f. 1999, by merger between the research libraries of Odense Univ., Southern Denmark School of Business, Southern Denmark School of Engineering and South Jutland Univ. Centre; languages, literature, philosophy, religion, history, music, economics, social sciences, natural sciences, medicine, engineering; 1,600,000 vols, 3,100 paper periodicals, 50,000 e-journals; Head Librarian AASE LINDAHL.

Roskilde

Roskilde Universitetsbibliotek (Roskilde University Library): Universitetsvej 1, POB 258, 4000 Roskilde; tel. 46-74-22-07; fax 46-74-30-90; e-mail rub@ruc.dk; internet www .rub.ruc.dk; f. 1971, present location 2001; open to general public; humanities, social sciences and natural sciences; 833,223 vols, 215,000 units of non-book material, 12,500 electronic books, 25,000 video cassettes and audio cassettes; Dir NIELS SENIUS CLAUSEN; Head of Planning CLAUS VESTERAGER PEDERSEN.

Silkeborg

Silkeborg Bibliotek (Silkeborg Library): Hostrupsgade 41A, 8600 Silkeborg; tel. 87-22-19-00; fax 87-22-19-01; e-mail biblioteket@silkeborg.bib.dk; internet silkeborgbib.dk; f. 1900; 216,000 vols, plus 128,000 in the Children's Dept, 50,000 records and cassettes; Chief Librarian LARS BORNÆS.

Vejle

Vejle Bibliotekerne (Vejle Public Libraries): Willy Sørensens Plads 1, 7100 Vejle; tel. 75-82-32-00; fax 75-82-32-13; e-mail vejlebib@vejlebib.dk; internet www.vejlebib .dk; f. 1895; consists of a main library located in Vejle, brs in Børkop, Egtved, Give and Jelling; mobile library; 487,388 vols (incl. audiobooks, CDs and DVDs), 3,922 periodicals; Chief Librarian LONE KNAKKERGAARD.

Viborg

Landsarkivet for Nørrejylland (Provincial Archives of Northern Jutland): Ll. Sct. Hans Gade 5, 8800 Viborg; tel. 86-62-17-88; fax 86-60-10-06; e-mail mailbox@lav.sa.dk; internet www.sa.dk/content/us/about_us/ provincial_archives/provincial_archives_of_- northern_jutland; f. 1891 as an archival repository; comprises material from state and local authorities and institutions, from private individuals, asscns and orgs, and from the landed estates located in Northern Jutland (1389 until the present day); houses the State Archives Filming Centre; 55 km of shelving; Dir C. R. JANSEN.

Museums and Art Galleries

Ålborg

Aalborg Historiske Museum: Algade 48, POB 1805, 9100 Aalborg; tel. 99-31-74-00; fax 98-16-11-31; e-mail historisk_museum@ aalborg.dk; internet www.nordmus.dk; f. 1863; archaeology, history, ethnology, glass, silver, tobacco industry; Dir LARS CHRISTIAN NØRBACH.

Kunsten Museum of Contemporary Art: Kong Christians Allé 50, 9000 Ålborg; tel. 99-82-41-00; fax 98-16-28-20; e-mail kunsten@ aalborg.dk; internet www.kunsten.dk; f. 1877, building inaugurated 1972; exhibits modern and contemporary art; permanent colln of 1,500 paintings, sculptures and mixed media works dating from 1900 to present day; Fine Art Dept: Danish art since 1900 (painting, sculpture, graphics, sculpture park); Anna and Kresten Krestensen Colln: Danish and int. art 1920–1950; Kirsten and Axel P. Nielsen Colln (art of 1960s and 1970s); Erik Veistrup Colln (art 1906–2006); library of 13,000 vols, a reference library; Chair. ANDERS HJULMAND; Vice-Chair. HANS HENRIK HENRIKSEN; Dir GITTE ØRSKOU.

Århus

ARoS Århus Kunstmuseum (Århus Art Museum): Aros Allé 2, 8000 Århus C; tel. 87-30-66-00; fax 87-30-66-01; e-mail info@aros .dk; internet www.aros.dk; f. 1859; Danish art since the 18th century and modern int. art; library of 21,000 vols; Chair. CARSTEN FODE; Dir JENS ERIK SØRENSEN.

Naturhistorisk Museum (Natural History Museum): Universitetsparken, Wilhelm Meyers Allé 210, 8000 Århus C; tel. 86-12-97-77; fax 86-13-08-82; e-mail nm@nathist .dk; internet www.naturhistoriskmuseum .dk; f. 1921; attached to Min. of Culture; Denmark exhibition: natural history of Danish landscapes; Danish Animals exhibition; Animals of the World exhibition; African Savannah exhibition; permanent field laboratory: 'Molslaboratoriet', Femmöller,

8400 Ebeltoft; the museum laboratories are open to scientists, and specialize in terrestrial ecology, limnology, entomology, acarology, mammalogy, ornithology and bioacoustics; library of 15,000 vols; Dir THOMAS SECHER JENSEN; Deputy Dir Dr HENRIK SELL; publs *Natura Jutlandica* (in English), *Natur og Museum* (in Danish).

Auning

Dansk Landbrugsmuseum (Danish Agricultural Museum): Gl. Estrup, 8963 Auning, Jutland; tel. 86-48-34-44; fax 86-48-41-82; e-mail dlm@gl-estrup.dk; internet www .gl-estrup.dk; f. 1889; exhibitions on the history of country life, agricultural technology and beekeeping; Chair. KNUD ERIK JENSEN; Dir PETER BAVNSHØJ; Sec. BODIL JENSEN.

Charlottenlund

Ordrupgaard: Vilvordevej 110, 2920 Charlottenlund; tel. 39-64-11-83; fax 39-64-10-05; e-mail ordrupgaard@ordrupgaard.dk; internet www.ordrupgaard.dk; f. 1918; French and Danish 19th- and early 20th-century paintings, incl. works by Degas, Delacroix, Gauguin, Hammershøi, Manet, Pissarro and Renoir; Danish arts and crafts of the 19th century; Dir ANNE-BIRGITTE FONSMARK; Sec. DORTHE VANGSGAARD NIELSEN.

Copenhagen

Botanisk Have & Museum (Botanic Garden & Museum): Øster Farimagsgade 2B, 1353 Copenhagen K; tel. 35-32-22-22; fax 35-32-22-21; e-mail snm@snm.ku.dk; internet botanik.snm.ku.dk; f. 1874; attached to Natural History Museum of Denmark, Copenhagen Univ.; 25 acres of landscape garden, palm-house and greenhouses; rare trees, plants (13,000 species); colln of living plants and seed and gene bank for plants, dried plants and fungi; library of 50,000 books, 100,000 issues of periodicals; Head FLEMMING LARSEN.

Danske Filminstitut—Museum og Cinematek (Danish Film Institute—Archive and Cinematheque): Gothersgade 55, 1123 Copenhagen K; tel. 33-74-34-00; fax 33-74-34-01; e-mail dfi@dfi.dk; internet www.dfi.dk; f. 1941,on merger of three institutions: Danish Film Institute, Nat. Film Board, Danish Film Museum 1997; collns of films, books, posters, documentation; cinemas with daily screenings; library of 70,000 vols, 13,500 scripts, 250 periodicals; Dir DAN NISSEN; publ. *Kosmorama* (2 a year).

Davids Samling (David Collection): Kronprinsessegade 30, 1306 Copenhagen K; tel. 33-73-49-49; fax 33-73-49-48; e-mail museum@davidmus.dk; internet www .davidmus.dk; f. 1945; attached to C. L. David Foundation and Colln; colln of Islamic art, European 18th-century art, and Danish early modern art; Chair. ERIK HOFFMEYER; Vice-Chair. AAGE SPANG-HANSSEN; Dir Dr KJELD VON FOLSACH; Curator Dr JOACHIM MEYER; publ. *The Journal of the David Collection*.

Geologisk Museum (Geological Museum): University of Copenhagen, Øster Voldgade 5–7, 1350 Copenhagen K; tel. 35-32-23-45; fax 35-32-23-25; e-mail rcp@snm.ku.dk; internet geologi.snm.ku.dk; f. 1772 as Universitetets Nye Naturaltheater; attached to Univ. of Copenhagen; centre for Danish geology; minerals, rocks, meteorites and fossils; geology of Denmark and Greenland; origin of man; plate tectonics; volcanoes; salt in the subsoil; part of Natural History Museum of Denmark; Chair. Prof. MINIK THORLEIF ROSING.

Hirschsprung: Stockholmsgade 20, 2100 Copenhagen O; tel. 35-42-03-36; fax 35-43-

35-10; e-mail dhs@hirschsprung.dk; internet www.hirschsprung.dk; f. 1902; showcases Heinrich Hirschsprung's colln of paintings, drawings and sculptures by Danish artists, incl. Skagen painters, Symbolists and Fynboerne; impressionist art colln providing overview of Danish 19th-century art; Dir MARIANNE SAABYE; Curator JAN GORM MADSEN; Curator ANNA SCHRAM VEJLBY.

Københavns Museum (Museum of Copenhagen): Absalonsgade 3, 1658 Copenhagen V; Vesterbrogade 59, 1620 Copenhagen V; tel. and fax 33-21-07-72; e-mail sekr@bymuseum .dk; internet www.copenhagen.dk; f. 1901; history of Copenhagen, incl. pictures, architecture, models; colln of Kierkegaard relics; Dir JETTE SANDAHL; Chair. PIA ALLERSLEV.

Kunstindustrimuseet (Danish Museum of Art and Design): Bredgade 68, 1260 Copenhagen K; tel. 33-18-56-56; fax 33-18-56-66; e-mail info@kunstindustrimuseet.dk; internet www.kunstindustrimuseet.dk; f. 1890; European applied art from the Middle Ages to modern times, Chinese and Japanese art; library of 63,000 vols on applied art; Dir BODIL BUSK LAURSEN; Sec. HENRIETTE FALKENBERG; Curator ULLA HOUKJAER; Curator CHRISTIAN HOLMSTED OLESEN.

Nationalmuseet (National Museum): Frederiksholms Kanal 12, 1220 Copenhagen K; tel. 33-13-44-11; fax 33-47-33-33; e-mail nationalmuseet@natmus.dk; internet www .natmus.dk; f. 1807 on basis of the older Royal Collns; consists of 5 divs; colln of archaeological discoveries, royal portraits, coins and medals, Egyptian mummies, Greek vases, Etruscan and Roman glass jewellery; library of 200,000 vols; Dir CARSTEN U. LARSEN; Keeper for Classical and Near Eastern Antiquities BODIL BUNDGAARD RASMUSSEN; Keeper for Danish Prehistory POUL OTTO NIELSEN; Keeper for Exhibition of Modern Danish History VIBEKE ANDERSSON MØLLER; Keeper for Ethnographic Colln KARIN TYBJERG; Keeper for Exhibition of Middle Ages and Renaissance MICHAEL ANDERSEN; publs *Nationalmuseets Arbejdsmark* (1 a year), *Nyt fra Nationalmuseet* (4 a year), *Skrifter* (in 3 series), catalogues.

Attached Museums:

Frihedsmuseet (Museum of Danish Resistance): Churchillparken, 1263 Copenhagen K; tel. 33-47-39-21; fax 33-14-03-14; e-mail frihedsmuseet@natmus.dk; f. 1957; chronological devt of Danish resistance during the Nazi occupation 1940–45, colln of documents related to resistance groups; photo archive with colln of 60,000 pictures; Curator and Head ESBEN KJELDBÆK.

Frilandsmuseet (Open-Air Museum): Kongevejen 100, 2800 Lyngby; tel. 33-47-34-81; fax 33-47-33-97; e-mail fogf@natmus .dk; f. 1897; examples of more than 50 farms, mills and houses from 1650 to 1950, representing virtually every region in Denmark and the Faroe Islands as well as the fmr Danish provinces of southern Sweden and northern Germany; displays of rural crafts; incorporates Brede Works factory community with workmen's and foremen's houses, eating house, orphanage and nursery garden; archives of drawings, photographs, measurements and historical records concerning the bldgs; Curator and Head PETER HENNINGSEN.

Musikmuseet—Musikhistorisk Museum og Carl Claudius' Samling (Music Museum—Musical History Museum and Carl Claudius Collection): Åbenrå 30, 1124 Copenhagen K; tel. 33-11-27-26; fax 33-11-60-44; e-mail musik@ natmus.dk; internet www.natmus.dk; f. 1898; exhibition closed until 2013, library and archive remain open and available to the public; extensive colln of musical instruments from all over the world with spec. emphasis on European instruments from the Renaissance onwards; concerts, library, archives; Dir Dr LISBET TORP.

Ny Carlsberg Glyptotek: Dantes Plads 7, 1556 Copenhagen V; tel. 33-41-81-41; fax 33-91-20-58; e-mail info@glyptoteket.dk; internet www.glyptoteket.dk; f. 1888; Danish and French sculpture and painting since 19th century, Egyptian, Greek, Roman and Etruscan art, mainly sculpture; 10,000 works of art; library of 50,000 vols; Chair. HANS EDVARD NORREGAARD-NIELSEN; Dir FLEMMING FRIBORG; Deputy Dir ANNE MARIE NIELSEN; publ. *Meddelelser fra Ny Carlsberg Glyptotek (ny serie)* (1 a year).

Rosenborg Slot (Rosenborg Castle): Øster Voldgade 4A, 1350 Copenhagen K; tel. 33-15-32-86; fax 33-15-20-46; e-mail museum@dkks .dk; internet www.rosenborgslot.dk; f. 1833; contains 'The Chronological Colln of the Danish Kings'; the colln was founded by Frederik III in about 1660, and depicts the history of Danish kings from Frederik II in the mid-16th century to Frederik VII in the 19th century; consists of arms, apparel, jewellery, and furniture from 1470 to 1863; also houses the Royal Regalia and the Crown Jewels; Dir Chamberlain NIELS EILSCHOU HOLM; Museum Dir NIELS-KNUD LIEBGOTT.

Attached Museum:

Amalienborgmuseet (Amalienborg Museum): Christian VIII's Palace, 1257 Copenhagen K; tel. 33-12-21-86; fax 33-93-32-03; e-mail amalienborgmuseet@dkks .dk; internet www.amalienborgmuseet.dk; f. 1994; exhibitions cover the reigns of Danish kings, from 1863 to 1972 (Christian IX, Frederik VIII, Christian X and Frederik IX); Curator BIRGIT JENVOLD; Sec. JACOB MADSEN.

Statens Forsvarshistoriske Museum (Civil Defence Historical Museum): Frederiksholms Kanal 29, 1220 Copenhagen K; tel. 33-11-60-37; fax 33-93-71-52; e-mail thm@ thm.dk; internet www.sfhm.dk; f. 2004 by merger between Royal Arsenal Museum and Royal Naval Museum; attached to Mini. of Culture; collns of weapons, vehicles, uniforms and other military and civilian equipment from the period after c. 1200; naval colln of 300 years of maritime technology; historic weapons colln merged with a number of other subject collns related to special army history; Dir OLE LOUIS FRANTZEN; Deputy Man. SOREN ALMER NIELSEN.

Statens Museum for Kunst (Danish National Gallery): Sølvgade 48–50, 1307 Copenhagen K; tel. 33-74-84-94; fax 33-74-84-04; e-mail smk@smk.dk; internet www .smk.dk; contains the main colln of Danish paintings and sculpture; a number of works by other Scandinavian artists since 19th century; J. Rump colln of modern French art; about 1,000 paintings by old masters of the Italian, Flemish, Dutch and German Schools (chiefly derived from the old royal colln, which was established as an art gallery in the 1760s); The Print Room incl. about 300,000 Danish and foreign prints and drawings; library: about 130,000 vols; Dir KARSTEN OHRT; Exec. Sec. BIRGITTE KANN MØLLER; publ. *Statens Museum for Kunst Journal* (1 a year).

Teatermuseet (Theatre Museum): Christiansborg, Ridebane 10–18, 1218 Copenhagen K; tel. 33-11-51-76; fax 33-12-50-22; e-mail teatermuseet@teatermuseet.dk; internet www.teatermuseet.dk; f. 1912; situated in the old Court theatre, built in 1767; illustrates the devt of the Danish theatre since 18th century; colln of drawings, engravings, paintings, photographs, costumes, set

models describing the history of Danish-language theatre from 1700 to present day; Dir PETER CHRISTENSEN TEILMANN; Curator MIKAEL KRISTIAN HANSEN; Curator IDA POULSEN.

Thorvaldsens Museum: Bertel Thorvaldsens Plads 2, 1213 Copenhagen K; tel. 33-32-15-32; fax 33-32-17-71; e-mail thm@ thorvaldsensmuseum.dk; internet www .thorvaldsensmuseum.dk; f. 1839; sculptures and drawings by the Danish sculptor Bertel Thorvaldsen (1770–1844), his collns of contemporary European paintings, drawings and prints and classical antiquities; and his library, archives relating to Thorvaldsen's studies and the museum's history; letter archive; library of 8,000 vols; Dir STIGG MISS; Curator MARGRETHE FLORYAN; Curator WILLIAM GELIUS; Curator KRISTINE BØGGILD JOHANNSEN.

Zoologisk Museum (Zoological Museum): Universitetsparken 15, 2100 Copenhagen Ø; tel. 35-32-10-00; fax 35-32-10-10; e-mail snm@snm.ku.dk; internet zoologi.snm.ku.dk; f. 1770; attached to Faculty of Science, Univ. of Copenhagen; collns of multicellular animals, which serve as objects for a wide range of int. research projects; research is organized in 3 scientific depts: Vertebrates and Quaternary Zoology; Invertebrates (excl. insects, myriapods and arachnids); and Entomology; public education programmes and school service; library of 15,000 vols, 750 periodicals; Dir THOMAS PAPE; Curator KIM AARIS-SØRENSEN; publ. *Steenstrupia* (2 a year).

Dronningmølle

Rudolph Tegners Museum og Statuepark (Rudolph Tegners Museum and Statue Park): Museumsvej 19, 3120 Dronningmølle; tel. 49-71-91-77; e-mail museum@ rudolphtegner.dk; internet www .rudolphtegner.dk; f. 1938; devoted to the works and collns of the sculptor Rudolph Tegner (1873–1950); 200 works in plaster, clay, bronze and marble; Dir LUISE GOMARD.

Ebeltoft

Glasmuseet Ebeltoft (Glass Museum Ebeltoft): Strandvejen 8, 8400 Ebeltoft; tel. 86-34-17-99; fax 86-34-60-60; e-mail glasmuseet@ glasmuseet.dk; internet www.glasmuseet.dk; f. 1985; exhibits contemporary, int. studio glass; organizes lectures, talks, concerts, guided tours, video presentations, workshops and children's activities; colln of the latest trends in contemporary glass art; Dir EBBE SIMONSEN; Exec. Dir DAGMAR BRENDSTRUP.

Elsinore

Danmarks Tekniske Museum (Danish Museum of Science and Technology): Fabriksvej 25, 3000 Elsinore; tel. 49-22-26-11; fax 49-22-62-11; e-mail info@tekn)skmuseum .dk; internet www.tekniskmuseum.dk; f. 1911; colln of steam engines, electric appliances (incl. Valdemar Poulsen's telegraphone, the forerunner of modern tape recording), bicycles, cars and aircraft; authentic pewter workshop; library of 18,000 vols; Chair. JØRGEN LINDEGAARD; Vice-Chair. KLAUS BONDE LARSEN; Dir KAI FREDERIKSEN; Curator JENS BREINEGAARD; publ. *Arbog* (Yearbook).

Handels- og Søfartsmuseet (Danish Maritime Museum): Kronborg, 3000 Elsinore; tel. 49-21-06-85; fax 49-21-34-40; e-mail info@ maritime-museum.dk; internet maritime-museum.pro.dir.dk; f. 1915; Danish shipping since 1400, incl. the Sound Dues, the Napoleonic Wars, trade with China and the fmr Danish colonies in India, navigation and the Lifeboat Service; maritime objects, model ships, paintings, photographs

and text boards; depiction of the Danish sailor's life since 16th century; regular temporary exhibitions; store rooms containing several thousand paintings and objects; administrative bldg in the castle grounds containing the museum's records; library of 30,000 vols; spec. collns of logbooks and photographs; Chair. ERIK ØSTERGAARD; Dir JØRGEN SELMER; Sec. ULLA-BRITTA HANSEN; Curator KARI LAURING.

Kronborg Castle: Kronborg 2C, 3000 Elsinore; tel. 49-21-30-78; fax 49-21-30-52; e-mail kronborg@ses.dk; internet www.ses.dk/ kronborg; f. 1425; fortified royal castle dating from the late 16th century; contains the Royal Apartments (furniture, tapestry, regalia), banqueting hall, chapel; known as 'Hamlet's castle'; Dir LARS HOLST.

Faaborg

Faaborg Museum: Grønnegade 75, 5600 Faaborg; tel. 62-61-06-45; fax 62-61-06-65; e-mail info@faaborgmuseum.dk; internet www.faaborgmuseum.dk; f. 1910; colln of paintings and sculptures by the circle of Funenite artists; Dir SUSANNE TRUELSEN.

Frederikssund

J. F. Willumsens Museum: Jenriksvej 4, 3600 Frederikssund; tel. 47-31-07-73; fax 47-38-54-73; e-mail jfw@frederikssund.dk; internet www.jfwillumsensmuseum.dk; f. 1957; colln of J. F. Willumsen's works, his old colln and archive containing photographs, books, letters, diaries; J. F. Willumsen's paintings, drawings, pastels, graphics, ceramics, sculpture, photography and architecture; Chair. MICHAEL HARDER; Vice-Chair. LIS OLSEN; Dir ANNETTE JOHANSEN; Curator LISBETH LUND.

Hillerød

Nationalhistoriske Museum paa Frederiksborg Slot (Museum of National History at Frederiksborg Castle): Frederiksborg Slot, 3400 Hillerød; tel. 48-26-04-39; fax 48-24-09-66; e-mail frederiksborgmuseet@ frederiksborgmuseet.dk; internet www .frederiksborgmuseet.dk; f. 1878; castle built in 1560s, extended 1600–20; contains a chronological colln of portraits and paintings illustrating the history of Denmark, each era in a separate room, the furniture and appointments in keeping with the period of the paintings; 10,000 exhibits; picture archive; library of 15,000 vols; Pres. Chamberlain NIELS EILSCHOU HOLM; Dir METTE SKOUGAARD.

Højbjerg

Moesgård Museum: Moesgård Allé 20, 8270 Højbjerg; tel. 89-42-11-00; fax 86-27-23-78; e-mail moesgaard@hum.au.dk; internet www.moesmus.dk; f. 1861, present name 1997; collns of Danish prehistoric antiquities; exhibition of the Grauballe Man (a two-thousand year old bog body) and war sacrifices from Illerup Adal; research org. in environmental, Danish and Oriental archaeology and ethnology; Dir JAN SKAMBY MADSEN; Curator NIELS H. ANDERSEN.

Horsens

Horsens Kunstmuseum: Carolinelundsvej 2, 8700 Horsens; tel. 76-29-23-70; e-mail kunstmuseum@horsens.dk; internet www .horsenskunstmuseum.dk; f. 1906; colln of modern Danish art, paintings and sculptures; works of Verner Sørensen, Knud Knudsen, Bjorn and Kai E. Christiansen; Man. CLAUS HAGEDORN-OLSEN; Curator LONE SCHUBERT.

Hørsholm

Jagt- og Skovbrugsmuseet (Danish Museum of Hunting and Forestry): Folehavevej 15–17, 2970 Hørsholm; tel. 45-86-05-72; fax 45-76-20-02; e-mail museum@jagtskov .dk; internet www.jagtskov.dk; f. 1942; colln of hunters'and poachers' gear, traps, and home-made weapons that tell illustrate of Danish forestry after the Enlightenment Era; colln of specimens of deformities, abnormalities and diseases in animals, decoy colln; organizes workshops and tours; Pres. OLE ROED JACOBSEN; Dir JETTE BAAGØE; Curator HELLE SERUP.

Humlebæk

Louisiana Museum of Modern Art: Gl. Strandvej 13, 3050 Humlebæk; tel. 49-19-07-19; fax 49-19-35-05; e-mail mail@louisiana .dk; internet www.louisiana.dk; f. 1958; neoclassical villa and estate transformed into a modern museum of art; colln of int. art, incl. works by Arp, Francis Bacon, Calder, Dubuffet, Ernst, Sam Francis, Kiefer, Henry Moore, Picasso, Rauschenberg and Warhol; exhibitions of contemporary artists; cinema, concerts, theatre; Chair. LARS HENRIK MUNCH; Vice-Chair. PETER AUGUSTINUS; Exec. Dir POUL ERIK TØJNER; publs *Louisiana Magasin* (2 a year), *Louisiana Revy* (2 a year).

Ishoj

Arken Museum for Moderne Kunst (Arken Museum of Modern Art): Skovvej 100, 2635 Ishøj; tel. 43-54-02-22; fax 43-54-05-22; e-mail reception@arken.dk; internet www.arken.dk; f. 1996; over 300 works of art; colln of Danish, Nordic and int. contemporary art, from 1990 onwards; interactive installations; photographic and graphic idioms; paintings and sculptures; Chair. OLE BJØRSTORP; Dir CHRISTIAN GETHER; Deputy Dir KAREN HAUMANN; Chief Curator STINE HØHOLT; publ. *KLUB ARKEN* (3 a year).

Kolding

Museet på Koldinghus (Museum of Koldinghus): Markdanersgade 11, POB 91, 6000 Kolding; tel. 76-33-81-00; fax 76-33-81-99; e-mail museum@koldinghus.dk; internet www.koldinghus.dk; f. 1992; colln of Danish fine arts, Danish crafts and decorative art from c. 1550 to c. 1940; colln of silverware and jewellery from Renaissance to present day; Pres. GEORGE A. HOUMANN; Dir POUL DEDENROTH-SCHOU.

Trapholt: Æblehaven 23, 6000 Kolding; tel. 76-30-05-30; e-mail kunstmuseum@trapholt .dk; internet www.trapholt.dk; f. 1988; colln of Danish furniture design; Franciska Clausen colln; modern Danish visual art and sculpture; Richard Mortensen exhibition; ceramics, textiles and product design (mainly sets); sculpture park, with works by Danish contemporary artists; Arne Jacobsen's Cubeflex summer cottage; temporary exhibitions of art, design and handicraft; Pres. OLE F. RASMUSSEN; Vice-Pres. MARLENE B. LORENTZEN; Dir KAREN GRØN (acting); Curator KAREN FRIIS HERBSLEB.

Niva

Nivaagaards Malerisamling (Nivaagaard Picture Gallery): Gl. Strandvej 2, 2990 Nivå; tel. 49-14-10-17; fax 49-14-10-57; e-mail museum@nivaagaard.dk; internet www .nivaagaard.dk; f. 1908; colln of artworks from Italian and Northern European Renaissance, Dutch Baroque and the Danish Golden Age in the form of portrait, landscape painting and religious motif; Chair. EBBE SIMONSEN; Dir MICHAEL VON ESSEN.

Odense

Kunsthallen Brandts: Brandts Torv 1, 5000 Odense C; tel. 65-20-70-00; fax 65-20-70-94; e-mail info@brandts.dk; internet www .brandts.dk; f. 1987, fmrly Kunsthallen Brandts Klædefabrik; exhibits contemporary Danish and int. art that incl. visual art, decorative art, performance, design, architecture and video art; Dir LARS GRAMBYE; Curator LENE BURKARD; Curator ANNA KROGH.

Mediemuseum (Media Museum): Brandts Torv 1, 5000 Odense C; tel. 65-20-70-52; fax 62-20-70-97; e-mail info@mediemuseum.dk; internet www.brandts.dk; f. 1954, present status 1989, present name 2010; over 115,000 artefacts, records, photos, movies, graphs, films,covering Danish media history; colln of newspapers and magazines; library of 10,000 vols; Dir ERVIN NIELSEN; Curator FLEMMING STEEN NIELSEN; Curator CHRISTIAN HVIID MORTENSEN; publ. *Petit Grafiana*.

Museet for Fotokunst (Museum of Photo Art): Brandts Torv 1, 5000 Odense C; tel. 65-20-70-00; fax 65-20-70-94; e-mail info@ brandts.dk; internet www.brandts.dk; f. 1987 as part of The Int. Center for Art and Culture, Brandts Klædefabrik; colln of photographic works focusing on photographic art from 1945; archive of artists and of works; individual spec. collns and reference library for int. photography of the past 50 years; Chair. JØRGEN BRANDT; Dir INGRID FISCHER JONGE; Curator CHARLOTTE PRÆSTEGAARD SCHWARTZ; Curator JENS FRIIS.

Odense Bys Museer (Odense City Museums): Overgade 48, 5000 Odense C; tel. 65-51-46-01; fax 65-90-86-00; e-mail museum@odense.dk; internet www.odmus .dk; f. 1860; Dir Dr TORBEN GRØNGAARD JEPPESEN; Chief Curator DONALD MYRTUE; publs *Anderseniana* (1 a year), *Fynske Fortællinger* (1 a year), *Fynske Minder* (1 a year), *Fynske Studier* (1 a year).
Selected Museums:

Carl Nielsen Museet (Carl Nielsen Museum): Claus Bergs Gade 11, 5000 Odense C; tel. 65-51-46-01; fax 65-90-86-00; e-mail museum@odense.dk; internet www.museum.odense.dk/museer/carl-nielsen-museet.aspx; f. 1980; devoted to the composer's life (1865–1931) and work; Curator EJNAR ASKGAARD.

Fyns Kunstmuseum (Funen Art Museum): Jernbanegade 13, 5000 Odense C; tel. 65-51-46-01; e-mail museum@ odense.dk; internet www.museum.odense .dk/museer/fyns-kunstmuseum.aspx; f. 1880 as a smaller version of the Statens Museum for Kunst; art gallery; colln contains works since 1750; Curator ANNE CHRISTIANSEN.

Fynske Landsby (Funen Village): Sejerskovvej 20, 5260 Odense S; tel. 65-51-46-01; fax 65-90-86-00; e-mail museum@odense .dk; internet www.museum.odense.dk/ museer/den-fynske-landsby.aspx; open-air museum recreating the time of the era of Hans Christian Andersen (1805–75); concerts and musical theatre; Curator MYRTUE ANDERS.

Hans Christian Andersens Hus (Hans Christian Andersen Museum): Bangs Boder 29, 5000 Odense C; e-mail museum@odense.dk; internet www .museum.odense.dk/museer/hc-andersens-hus.aspx; f. 1905; devoted to the writer's life (1805–75) and work; Curator EJNAR ASKGAARD.

Odense City Museum—Møntergården: Overgade 48, 5000 Odense C; tel. 65-51-46-01; fax 65-90-86-00; e-mail museum@ odense.dk; internet www.museum.odense

.dk/museer/moentergaarden.aspx; local cultural history, coins and medals, archaeology; Curator KARSTEN KJER MICHAELSEN; Curator ANDERS MYRTUE.

Randers

Randers Kunstmuseum (Museum of Danish Art): Stemannsgade 2, 2. sal, 8900 Randers; tel. 86-42-29-22; fax 86-43-39-54; e-mail info@randerskunstmuseum.dk; internet www.randers-kunstmuseum.dk; f. 1887; colln of paintings, sculptures and graphics; Danish art from 19th and 20th centuries; int. art from second half of 20th century; Dir FINN TERMAN FREDERIKSEN; Curator LISE JEPPESEN; Sec. SUSANNE CHRISTENSEN.

Roskilde

Museet for Samtidskunst (Museum of Contemporary Art): Stændertorvet 3D, 4000 Roskilde; tel. 46-31-65-70; fax 46-31-65-71; e-mail info@samtidskunst.dk; internet samtidskunst.dk; f. 1991; colln consists of sound art, video art, intermedia art, installation art, media art and documentation; Chair. FRANK BIRKEBÆK; Deputy Chair. JENS BISBALLE; Dir SANNE KOFOD OLSEN; Curator TINE SELIGMANN.

Vikingeskibsmuseet i Roskilde (Viking Ship Museum): Vindeboder 12, 4000 Roskilde; tel. 46-30-02-00; fax 46-30-02-01; e-mail museum@vikingeskibsmuseet.dk; internet www.vikingeskibsmuseet.dk; f. 1969; exhibits the 5 Viking ships found at Skuldelev in 1962, and promotes research in ship-building history in general; research on maritime subjects is carried out in cooperation with the Nat. Museum of Denmark and other nat. and int. research instns; Chair. POUL LINDOR NIELSEN; Deputy Chair. LEO BJØRNSKOV; Dir LARS FREDSTED.

Rungsted Kyst

Karen Blixen Museet (Karen Blixen Museum): Rungsted Strandvej 111, 2960 Rungsted Kyst; tel. 45-57-10-57; fax 45-57-10-58; e-mail karen-blixen@blixen.dk; internet www.karen-blixen.dk; f. 1991; documentary exhibition about Karen Blixens life and work; gallery with Karen Blixens drawings and paintings; a small cinema; spec. exhibition room; Dir CATHERINE LEFEBVRE; Curator ANNE SOFIE TIEDEMANN DA; Sec. YVONNE KATZ JUUL.

Silkeborg

KunstCentret Silkeborg Bad (Art Centre Silkeborg Bad): Gjessøvej 40, 8600 Silkeborg; tel. 86-81-63-29; fax 86-81-63-19; e-mail sb@ silkeborgbad.dk; internet www.silkeborgbad .dk; f. 1992; colln of sculptures in the park area; displays contemporary Danish and foreign art; Dir IBEN FROM; publ. *Nyt*.

Skagen

Skagens Museum: Brøndumsvej 4, 9990 Skagen; tel. 98-44-64-44; fax 98-44-18-10; e-mail museum@skagensmuseum.dk; internet www.skagensmuseum.dk; f. 1908; displays works from the end of the 19th century; Chair. VIVIAN FLOOR; Vice-Chair. ERIK SØRENSEN; Dir LISETTE VIND EBBENSEN.

Vejen

Vejen Kunstmuseums (Vejen Art Museum): Østergade 4, 6600 Vejen; tel. 75-36-04-82; fax 75-36-04-81; e-mail museum@ vejenkom.dk; internet www .vejenkunstmuseum.dk; f. 1924; colln of Danish symbolism from the late 19th century; exhibits works of sculptor and ceramist Niels Hansen Jacobsen; Chair. PETER BREDSTEN; Vice-Chair. CLAUS JACOBSEN; Head TERESA NIELSEN.

Vejle

Vejle Kunstmuseums (Vejle Museum of Art): Flegborg 16–18, 7100 Vejle; tel. 75-72-31-35; fax 75-72-31-99; e-mail vkmus@vejle.dk; internet www.vejlekunstmuseum.dk; f. 1901; collns of Danish art from early 20th century to present, from classic modernism and pre-COBRA until today; Dir NINA DAMSGAARD; Curator SIGNE JACOBSEN; Curator MARIANNE SØRENSEN.

Universities and Technical Universities

AALBORG UNIVERSITET
(Aalborg University)

Fredrik Bajers Vej 5, POB 159, 9100 Ålborg
Telephone: 99-40-99-40
Fax: 98-15-22-01
E-mail: aau@aau.dk
Internet: www.aau.dk

Founded 1974, as Aalborg Univ. Centre, present name 1994
State control
Academic year: September to July

Rector: FINN KJÆRSDAM
Vice-Rector: INGER ASKEHAVE
Dir and Admin. Officer: PETER PLENGE
Librarian: NIELS-HENRIK GYLSTORFF

Library of 710,000 vols, 27,000 e-journals
Number of teachers: 2,500
Number of students: 15,000

Publications: *Studieguiden* (1 a year), *Uglen* (7 a year), *Videnskabet* (2 a year)

DEANS

Faculty of Engineering and Science: Prof. ESKILD HOLM NIELSEN
Faculty of Humanities: LONE DIRCKINCK-HOLMFELD
Faculty of Medicine: Prof. EGON TOFT
Faculty of Social Sciences: HANNE KATHRINE KROGSTRUP

AARHUS UNIVERSITET

Nordre Ringgade 1, 8000 Aarhus C
Telephone: 89-42-11-11
Fax: 89-42-11-09
E-mail: au@au.dk
Internet: www.au.dk

Founded 1928
State control
Languages of instruction: Danish, English
Academic year: September to June

Rector: LAURITZ B. HOLM-NIELSEN
Pro-Rector: SØREN E. FRANDSEN
Chair.: JENS BIGUM
Deputy Chair.: SYS ROVSING
Dir: JØRGEN JØRGENSEN
Deputy Dir: OLE OLSEN

Number of teachers: 2,331
Number of students: 35,000

Publications: *AU-gustus* (4 a year), *CAMPUS* (22 a year)

DEANS

Faculty of Health Sciences: ALLAN FLYVBJERG
Faculty of Humanities: METTE THUNØ
Faculty of Science and Technology: BRIAN BECH NIELSEN
Faculty of Theology: CARSTEN RIIS
School of Business and Social Sciences: SVEND HYLLEBERG

PROFESSORS

Faculty of Health Sciences (Vennelyst Boulevard 9, 8000 Aarhus C; tel. 89-42-11-22; fax 86-12-83-16; e-mail sun@au.dk; internet www.au.dk.sun):

AALKJAER, C., General Physiology
ANDERSEN, J. P., Molecular Physiology
ASTRUP, J., Neurosurgery
AUTRUP, H. N., Environment and Occupational Medicine
BEK, T., Ophthalmology
BLACK, F. T., Medicine
BOLUND, L., Clinical Genetics
BONDE, J. P., Clinical Occupational Medicine
BÜNGER, C., Experimental Orthopaedic Surgery
CHRISTENSEN, B., General Medicine
CHRISTENSEN, E. I., Structural Cell Biology
CHRISTIANSEN, G., Medical Molecular Biology
CLAUSEN, T., Physiology
DAHL, R., Lung Diseases and Allergology
DANSCHER, G., Neurobiology
DJURHUUS, J. C., Surgery
EHLERS, N., Ophthalmology
ESMANN, M., Biophysics
FALK, E., Ischaemic Heart Disease
FOLDSPANG, A., Health Service Research
FRØKIER, J., Clinical Psychology and Nuclear Medicine
FUGLSANG-FREDERIKSEN, A., Neurophysiology
GJEDDE, A., Positron Tomography
GLIEMANN, J., Biochemistry
GREGERSEN, H., Gastrointestinal Sensory Motor Function
GREGERSEN, M., Forensic Medicine
GREGERSEN, N., Medical Molecular Biology
GUNDERSEN, H. J., Stereology
GYLDENSTED, C., X-ray Diagnostics
HAMILTON-DUTOIT, S., Pathology
HASENKAM, J. M., Heart Surgery
HOKLAND, P., Experimental Clinical Research
HÖLLSBERG, P., Virology
HVID, I., Experimental Orthopaedics
ISIDOR, F., Prosthetics
JAKOBSEN, J. K., Neurology
JENSEN, P. H., Medical Biochemistry
JENSEN, T. S., Pain Research
JENSENIUS, J. C. T., Immunology
JØRGENSEN, T. M., Urology
KARRING, T., Periodontology
KILIAN, M., Microbiology and Immunology
KIRKEVOLD, M., Clinical Nursing Science
KØLVRAA, S., Clinical Genetics
LAMBERT, J. D. C., Physiology
LARSEN, M. J., Endodontics
LAURBERG, P., Endocrinology
LAURITZEN, T., General Practice
LEDET, T., Biochemical Pathology
MAASE, H. VON DER, Oncology
MAUNSBACH, A., Anatomy
MELSEN, B., Orthodontics
MOESTRUP, S. K., Medical Biochemistry
MOGENSEN, C. E. S., Medicine
MOGENSEN, S. C., Virology and Immunology
MORS, N. P. O., Experimental Clinical Research
MOSEKILDE, L., Bone Diseases
MULVANY, M., Cardiovascular Pharmacology
MUNK-JØRGENSEN, P., Psychiatry
MØLLER, J. V., Biophysics
NEXOE, E., Clinical Biochemistry
NIELSEN, S., Structural Cell Biology and Pathophysiology
NIELSEN, T. T., Cardiology
NYGAARD, H., Biomedical Engineering
OLSEN, J., Social Medicine
ØRNTOFT, T. F., Molecular Cancer Diagnostics
OVERGAARD, J., Experimental Cancer Research
OVESEN, T., Experimental Clinical Research
PAASKE, W., Cardiovascular Surgery
PAKKENBERG, B., Neurostereology
PAULSEN, P. K., Surgery

PEDERSEN, F. S., Molecular Oncology
PEDERSEN, J. C. M., Microbiology and Immunology
POULSEN, S., Paediatric Dentistry
RICHELSEN, B., Clinical Nutrition
ROSENBERG, R., Psychiatry
SABROE, S., Health Sciences
SCHIØTZ, P. O., Paediatrics
SCHMITZ, O., Clinical Pharmacology
SCHØNHEYDER, H., Clinical Microbiology
SIGSGAARD, T., Occupational Medicine
SØBALLE, K., Experimental Orthopaedic Surgery
SØRENSEN, F. B., Pathology
SØRENSEN, H. T., Clinical Epidemiology
STENGARD-PEDERSEN, K., Rheumatology
SVENSSON, P., Oral Physiology
THOMSEN, P. H., Psychiatry for Children and Adolescents
TOENNESEN, E., Anaesthesiology
VESTERBY, C. A., Forensic Medicine
VESTERGAARD, P., Psychiatry
VÆTH, M., Biostatistics
VILSTRUP, H., Hepatology
WEEKE, J., Medical Endocrinology
WENZEL, A., Oral Radiology

Faculty of Humanities (Nordre Ringgade, Bygning 328, 8000 Aarhus C; tel. 89-42-11-11; fax 89-42-12-00; e-mail hum@au.dk; internet www.au.dk/hum):

ANDERSEN, P. B., Media Science
BACH, S., Latin Languages
BOHN, O.-S., English
BRANDT, P. A., Semiotics
DAY, A., English
ENGBERG, J., History
HANNESTAD, N., Classical Archaeology
JUUL JENSEN, U., Philosophy
KYNDRUP, M., Aesthetics and Culture
LANGSTED, J., Drama
LARSEN, S. E., History of Literature
McGREGOR, W. B., Linguistics
MARSCHNER, B., Music
MØLLER, P. U., Slavonic Languages
MORTENSEN, F., Media Science
NØLKE, H., Latin Languages
OTTO, T., Ethnography
PADE, M., Classical Studies
POULSEN, B., History
ROESDAHL, E., Medieval Archaeology
SCHANZ, H.-J., History of Ideas
SØRENSEN, P. E., Scandinavian Studies
TOGEBY, O., Scandinavian Studies
VANDKILDE, H., Prehistoric Archaeology
WAMBERG, N. J., Art History
WEDELL-WEDELLSBORG, A., Chinese

Faculty of Science and Technology (Ny Munkegade, Bygning 520, 8000 Aarhus C; tel. 89-42-31-88; fax 89-42-35-96; e-mail nat@au.dk; internet au.dk/nat):

ANDERSEN, H. H., Mathematics
ANDERSEN, J. U., Experimental Physics
ASMUSSEN, S., Mathematics
BALSLEV, H., Biology
BESENBACHER, F., Experimental Solid State Physics
BOLS, M., Chemistry
BØDKER, S., Computer Science
BØTTIGER, J., Materials Science
CHRISTENSEN, K. R., Biological Oceanography
CHRISTENSEN, N. E., Theoretical Solid State Physics
CHRISTENSEN-DALSGAARD, J., Astronomy
CHRISTIANSEN, F. V. B., Population Biology
CLARK, B., Chemistry
FIELD, D., Experimental Molecular Physics
GRONBAK, K. G., Computer Science
HANSEN, T. I., Sports Medicine
IVERSEN, B., Materials Chemistry
JACOBSEN, H. J., Chemistry
JANTZEN, J. C., Mathematics
JENSEN, J. L., Mathematical Statistics
JENSEN, K., Computer Science
JØRGENSEN, K. A., Organic Chemistry

JØRGENSEN, P., Theoretical Chemistry
KJEMS, J., Molecular Biology
KORSTGÅRD, J. A., Structural Geology and Basin Tectonics
KRAGH, H., History of Science
KRISTENSEN, M., Nanophotonics
LOESCHKE, V., Biology
MACINTOSH, D. J., Biology
MADSEN, I. H., Mathematics
MADSEN, O. L., Computer Science
MØLMER, K., Physics
NIELSEN, J. A., Mathematical Finance
NIELSEN, M., Theoretical Computer Science
NIELSEN, N. C., Solid State NMR
ODGAARD, B. V., Palynology
OGILBY, P. R., Chemistry
PETERSEN, J. S., Chemistry
PIETROWSKI, J., Quaternary Geology
RATTAN, S. I. S., Molecular Biology
REVSBECH, N. P., Microbial Ecology
SKRYDSTRUP, T., Chemistry
STENSGAARD, I., Experimental Solid State Physics
VEDEL, E. B., Mathematical Statistics
WEBER, R. E., Zoophysiology

School of Business and Social Sciences (Bartholins Allé, Bygning 350 Universitetsparken, 8000 Aarhus C; tel. 89-42-11-33; fax 89-42-15-40; e-mail samfundsvidenskab@au.dk; internet www.socialsciences.au.dk):

AGERVOLD, M., Psychology
ANDERSEN, T. M., Economic Planning
BASSE, E. M., Jurisprudence
BLOM-HANSON, J., Political Science
CHRISTENSEN, B. J., Economic Planning
CHRISTENSEN, J. G., Political Science
CHRISTENSEN, J. P., Jurisprudence
DALBERG-LARSEN, J. V., Jurisprudence
DAMGAARD, E., Political Science
DANIELSEN, J. H., Jurisprudence
ELKLIT, A., Psychology
ELKLIT, J., Political Science
EVALD, J., Jurisprudence
GENEFKE, J., Economic Planning
GERMER, P., Jurisprudence
HALDRUP, N., National Economy
HOEGH-OLESEN, H., Psychology
HYLLEBERG, S. A. F., National Economy
IVERSEN, B. O., Jurisprudence
IVERSEN, T., Jurisprudence
JØRGENSEN, P. L., Economics
KRISTENSEN, L. H., Jurisprudence
KVALE, S., Psychology
MADSEN, O. ø., Economic Planning
MADSEN, P. B., Jurisprudence
MAMMEN, J., Psychology
MOLS, N. P., Management
MORTENSEN, P. B., Register-based Research
NANNESTAD, P., Political Science
NIELSEN, G. T., Jurisprudence
NØRGAARD, I. M., Jurisprudence
NØRGAARD, O., Political Science
NYBORG, H., Psychology
OVERGAARD, P. B., Economic Planning
PALDAM, N. M., Economic Planning
PEDERSEN, J., Jurisprudence
PEDERSEN, P. J., Economics
REVSBECH, K., Jurisprudence
RISBJERG THOMSEN, S., Political Science
ROSHOLM, M., National Economy
SOERENSEN, G., Political Science
SOMMER, D., Psychology
SVENDSEN, G. T., Political Science
SVENSSON, P., Political Science
THOMSEN, H. H. B., Jurisprudence
TOGEBY, L., Political Science
VASTRUP, C., Economics
VEDSTED-HANSEN, J., Jurisprudence
ZACHARIAS, B., Psychology

DANMARKS TEKNISKE UNIVERSITET (Technical University of Denmark)

Anker Engelunds Vej 1, Bygning 101A, 2800 Kgs. Lyngby
Telephone: 45-25-25-25
Fax: 45-88-17-99
E-mail: dtu@adm.dtu.dk
Internet: www.dtu.dk
Founded 1829 as College of Advanced Technology, present name 1994
Pres.: Dr LARS PALLESEN
Provost: Prof. ANDERS OVERGAARD BJARKLEV
Univ. Dir: CLAUS NIELSEN
Dir for Public Sector Consultancy: NIELS AXEL NIELSEN
Dean of Graduate Studies and Int. Affairs: Prof. MARTIN P. BENDSØE
Dean of Undergraduate Studies and Student Affairs: Prof. MARTIN VIGILD
Dir: STEN SCHEIBYE
Number of teachers: 4,502
Number of students: 6,270
Publication: DTU in profile (1 a year)

PROFESSORS

ADLER-NISSEN, J. L., Biotechnology
AHRING, B. K., Biotechnology
ALTING, L., Mechanical Engineering
ANDERSEN, M. A. E., Power Electronics
ANDRAESEN, M. M., Product Development
ANDREANI, P., Analogue Integrated Systems
ARVIN, E., Water Supply Engineering
BAY, N., Materials Processing
BENDSØE, M., Applied Functional Analysis
BJARKLEV, A. O., Optical Communication
BJERG, P. L., Environmental Geochemistry
BJERRUM, N., Chemical Engineering
BJØRNER, D., Computer Science
BLANKE, M.
BOHR, H., Biomolecular Structure and Function
BOHR, J., Physics
BOHR, T., Theoretical Physics
BRUNAK, S., Bio-informatics
BRUUN, K. E., Analogue Electronics
BRUUN, P., Industrial Management
BRØNS, M., Mathmematics
BUCHHAVE, P., Optics
CARLSEN, H., Energy Engineering
CHIFFRE, DE, L., Process Technology, Geometrical Metrology
CHORKENDORFF, I., Heterogeneous Catalysis
CHRISTENSEN, C. J. H., Heterogeneous Catalysis
CHRISTENSEN, E. L., Microwave Systems
CHRISTENSEN, TH. H., Environmental Engineering
CHRISTIANSEN, P. L., Non-linear Dynamics
CLAUSEN, J., Mathematic Optimization
CONRADSEN, K., Statistical Image Analysis
DAM-JOHANSEN, K., Combustion and Chemical Reaction Engineering
DAU, T., Hearing Aid Audiology and Acoustics
DITLEVSEN, O. D., Actions on Structures and Structural Reliability
EMMITT, S., Innovation and Management in Building
FANGER, P. O., Heating and Air Conditioning
FOGED, N., Geotechnical Engineering
FREDSØE, J., Marine Hydraulics
GAARSLEV, A., Construction Management
GANI, R., Systems Design
GIMSING, N. J., Structural Engineering
HAMMER, K., Microbiology
HANSEN, E. H., Analytical Chemistry
HANSEN, H. N., Microtechnical Production
HANSEN, L. K., Digital Signal Processing
HANSEN, P. C., Scientific Computing
HANSEN, P. F., Safety Assessment of Marine Systems
HANSEN, V. L., Mathematics
HASSAGER, O.
HEIN, L., Engineering Design Methodology

HENZE, M., Waste-water Engineering
HVAM, J. M., Optoelectronics
HVILSTED, S.
JACOBI, O. I., Geoinformatics and Photogrammetry
JACOBSEN, K. W., Physics
JAUHO, A.-P., Theoretical Nanotechnology
JENSEN, J. A., Biomedical Signal Processing
JENSEN, J. J., Marine Structures
JENSEN, O. M., Building Materials
JENSEN, P. L., Technology and Working Life, Working Environment
JEPPESEN, P., Optical Communication
JOHNSSON, J. E., Chemical Reaction Engineering
JØRGENSEN, S. B., Technical Chemistry
JUSTESEN, J., Error-Correcting Codes, Information Theory
KLEMM, P., Applied Microbiology
KLIT, P., Machine Elements and Lubrication Theory
KNUDSEN, L. R., Cryptology
KNUDSEN, S., Experimental and Computational Gene Expression Analysis
KRENK, S., Structural Mechanics
KRISTENSEN, M., Glass Components
KROZER, V., Microwave Electronics
LARSEN, P. S., Fluid Mechanics
LELEUR, S., Decision Support Systems and Planning
LIND, M., Control Systems
LUNDT, I.
LYNGAAE-JOERGENSEN, J., Polymer Technology
MADSEN, H.
MADSEN, J., Computer Systems
MADSEN, K., Numerical Analysis
MADSEN, O. G., Transport Optimization
MADSEN, P., Hydrodynamics
MADSEN, S. N.
MARKVORSEN, S., Differential Geometry
MENON, A., Microsystems Technology
MOLIN, S., Applied Microbiogenetics
MOLLERUP, J., Chromatography and Thermodynamics
MØLLER, P., Corrosion and Surface Technology
MØLTOFT, J., Reliability Engineering
MØRK, J., Active Semiconductor Components for Optical Communication Systems
MØRUP, S., Physics of Nanostructures
NIELSEN, J. B., Fermentation Physiology
NIELSEN, M. P., Structural Analysis
NIELSEN, O. A., Transport Planning
NIELSON, F., Computer Science
NIELSON, H. R., Programming Language Technology and Secure IT Systems
NILSSON, J. F., Computer Science
NØRSKOV, J. K., Theoretical Physics
OLESEN, B. W., Indoor Environment and Energy
PAUL, J., Refrigeration
PEDERSEN, N. F.
PEDERSEN, P., Structural Mechanics
PEDERSEN, P. T., Strength of Materials
POLACK, J., Acoustics
QVALE, B., Mechanical Engineering
REITZEL, E., Form-finding of Minimal Structures
ROENNE-HANSEN, J., Electric Power Engineering
SKOU, N., Radar and Radiometer Systems
SKOUBY, K. E., Economy and Regulation of Telecommunication
SKRIVER, H. L.
SOMERS, M. A., Physical Metallurgy
SPLIID, H., Applied Statistics: Statistical Practice and Consulting
STENBY, H. E., Applied Thermodynamics and Separation Processes
STUBKJAER, K. E.
SUNDELL, J.
SVENDSEN, SV. AA. HØJGAARD, Energy Technology in Buildings
SVENSSON, B., Food Protein Biochemistry
TANNER, D., Organic Chemistry

TELLEMAN, P., Biochemical Microsystems
THOMASSEN, C., Mathematics
TØNNESEN, O., Experimental High Voltage Technique
TROMBORG, B., Optoelectronics
TVERGAARD, V., Mechanics of Materials
ULSTRUP, J., Inorganic Chemistry
VESTERAGER, J., Product Development
VILLADSEN, J., Biotechnology
VILLUMSEN, A., Geology
WANHEIM, T., Machine Engineering

HANDELSHØJSKOLEN I KØBENHAVN
(Copenhagen Business School)

Solbjerg Plads 3, 2000 Frederiksberg
Telephone: 38-15-38-15
Fax: 38-15-20-15
E-mail: cbs@cbs.dk
Internet: www.cbs.dk

Founded 1917, present status 1965
Private control
Languages of instruction: Danish, English
Academic year: September to July

Chair.: ANDERS KNUTSEN
Deputy Chair.: PETER SCHÜTZE
Pres.: Dr JOHAN ROOS
Univ. Dir: HAKON IVERSEN
Exec. Sec.: HELLE GRUNNET-JEPSEN

Library: see under Libraries and Archives
Number of teachers: 460 (full time) and 700 (part time)
Number of students: 18,000

Publications: *ARK*, *CEBAL*, *SPRINT*, *Yearbook*

DEANS

Faculty of Business Language: SØREN BAR-LEBO RASMUSSEN
Faculty of Economics and Business Administration: OLE STENVINKEL NILSSON
Faculty of Education: JAN MOLIN
Faculty of Research: ALAN IRWIN

KØBENHAVNS UNIVERSITET
(University of Copenhagen)

Nørregade 10, 1165 Copenhagen K
Telephone: 35-32-26-26
Fax: 35-32-26-28
E-mail: ku@ku.dk
Internet: www.ku.dk

Founded 1479
State control
Language of instruction: English
Academic year: September to August (2 terms)

Rector: RALF HEMMINGSEN
Pro-Rector: THOMAS BJØRNHOLM
Univ. Dir: JØRGEN HONORÉ
Univ. Librarian: MICHAEL COTTA-SCHØNBERG

Number of teachers: 4,719 (f.t.e.)
Number of students: 36,891 (incl. 16,174 postgraduates)

DEANS

Faculty of Health Sciences: ULLA WEWER
Faculty of Humanities: KIRSTEN REFSING
Faculty of Law: Prof. Dr HENRIK DAM
Faculty of Life Sciences: PER HOLTEN-ANDER-SEN
Faculty of Pharmaceutical Sciences: Prof. SVEN FRØKJÆR
Faculty of Science: NILS OVERGAARD ANDER-SEN
Faculty of Social Sciences: Assoc. Prof. TROELS ØSTERGAARD SØRENSEN
Faculty of Theology: STEFFEN KJELDGAARD-PEDERSEN

PROFESSORS

Faculty of Health Sciences (3B, Blegdamsvej, 2200 Copenhagen N; tel. 35-32-79-00; fax 35-

32-70-70; e-mail email@sund.ku.dk; internet healthsciences.ku.dk):

ASMUSSEN, E., Dental Materials
BENDIXEN, G., Internal Medicine
BOCK, E. M., Cellular Biology
BOCK, J. E., Obstetrics and Gynaecology
BOLWIG, T. G., Psychiatry
BOYSEN, G., Neurology
BRETLAU, P., Otorhinolaryngology
BUUS, S., Basic Immunology
CHRISTENSEN, N. J., Internal Medicine
CHRISTOFFERSEN, P., Pathological Anatomy
DABELSTEEN, S. E., Oral Diagnosis
DEURS, B. G., Structural Cell Biology
DIRKSEN, A., Internal Medicine
GALBO, H., Physiopathology
GJERRIS, F. O., Neurosurgery
GYNTELBERG, F., Occupational Medicine
HALD, T., Surgery
HAUNSØ, S., Internal Medicine
HEMMINGSEN, R. P., Psychiatry
HENRIKSEN, J. H., Clinical Physiology
HJØRTING-HANSEN, E., Oral and Maxillofacial Surgery
HOLLNAGEL, H., General Practice
HOLMSTRUP, P., Periodontology
HØIBY, N., Microbiology
HOLST, J. J., Medical Physiology
HORNSLET, A., Virology
HULTBORN, H., Neurophysiology
KEHLET, N., Surgery
KEIDING, N., Statistics
KRASILNIKOFF, P. A., Paediatrics
KRASNIK, A., Social Medicine
KREIBORG, S., Paedodontics
LARSEN, J. F., Obstetrics and Gynaecology
LARSEN, S., Pathological Anatomy
LORENZEN, I., Internal Medicine
LUND, B., Surgery
LUND-ANDERSEN, H., Eye Diseases
MELLERGÅRD, M. J., Psychiatry
MENNÉ, T., Dermatology
MICHELSEN, N., Clinical Social Medicine
MOGENSEN, J. V., Anaesthesiology
MORLING, N., Forensic Genetics
NIELSEN, J. O., Epidemic Diseases
NORÉN, O., Biochemistry
OLESEN, J., Neurology
ØLGAARD, K., Internal Medicine
OTTESEN, B., Obstetrics and Gynaecology
ØWALL, B., Prosthodontics
PAULSON, O. B., Neurology
PETERSEN, P. E., Community Dentistry and Postgraduate Education
PETTERSON, G., Thorax Surgery
PHILIP, J., Obstetrics and Gynaecology
POULSEN, H. E., Clinical Pharmacology
PRAUSE, J. U., Eye Diseases
QUISTOR, F. F., Biochemistry
REHFELD, J. F., Clinical Chemistry
REIBEL, J., Oral Pathology and Oral Medicine
RØRTH, M., Clinical Oncology
ROSTGAARD, J., Normal Anatomy
ROVSING, H. C., Radiology
SCHOU, J., Pharmacology
SCHROEDER, T. V., Surgery
SCHROLL, M., Geriatrics
SCHWARTZ, T. W., Molecular Pharmacology
SIGGAARD-ANDERSEN, O., Clinical Chemistry and Laboratory Technique
SIMONSEN, J., Forensic Pathology
SJÖSTRÖM, H., Biochemistry
SKAKKEBÆK, N., Paediatrics
SKINHØJ, P., Epidemic Diseases
SKOUBY, F., Paediatrics
SOLOW, B., Orthodontics
SØRENSEN, T. I. A., Clinical Epidemiology
STADIL, F. W., Surgery
SVEJGAARD, A., Clinical Immunology
THYLSTRUP, A., Cardiology
TOMMERUP, N., Medical Genetics
TOS, M., Otorhinolaryngology
VEJLSGAARD, G., Dermato-venereology
WULF, H. C., Dermato-venereology

WULFF, H. R., Clinical Decision Theory and Ethics

Faculty of Humanities (Njalsgade 80, 2300 Copenhagen S; tel. 35-32-88-11; fax 35-32-80-52; e-mail hum-fak@hum.ku.dk; internet humanities.ku.dk):

BOLVIG, A., History
BONDEBJERG, I., Film Studies
COLLIN, F., Philosophy
DUNCAN, R., American Studies
EKSELL, K., Semitic Philosophy
ELBRO, C., Linguistics
FLOTO, I., History
FORTESQUE, M., Linguistics
GABRIELSEN, V., Ancient History
HARDER, P., English Literature
HJARVARD, S., Film Studies
HØJRUP, T., Ethnology
HOV, L., Theatre
JENSEN, K. B., Media Studies
JØRGENSEN, J. N., Danish Language
LIND, G., History
LUND, N., History
RANDSBORG, K., Archaeology
RUUS, H., Danish Language
SCHWAB, H., Music
VILLAUME, P., History
ZERLANG, M., Comparative Literature

Faculty of Law (Studiestraede 6, 1455 Copenhagen K; tel. 35-32-26-26; fax 35-32-35-86; e-mail jurfak@jur.ku.dk; internet jura.ku.dk):

BALVIG, F., Legal Sociology and Sociology of Law
BLUME, P., Legal Informatics
BONDESON, U., Criminology
BRYDE ANDERSEN, M., Private Law, Computer Law
DUE, O., European Union Law
FOIGEL, I., Law of Taxation
GREVE, V., Criminal Law
KETSCHER, K., Social Law
KOKTVEDGAARD, M., Law of Competition, Intellectual Property Law
KRARUP, O., Public Law
LOOKOFSKY, J., Law of Contracts and Torts, Private International Law
NIELSEN, L., Family Law
RASMUSSEN, H., International Law and European Union Law
RØNSHOLDT, S., Administrative Law
SMITH, E., Legal Procedure
TAKSØE-JENSEN, F., Family Law, Law of Wills and Succession
TAMM, D., History of Law
VON EYBEN, B., Law of Property
ZAHLE, H., Jurisprudence

Faculty of Life Sciences (Bülowsvej 17, 1870 Frederiksberg C; tel. 35-33-28-28; fax 35-28-26-64; e-mail life@life.ku.dk; internet www.life.ku.dk):

AASTED, B., Veterinary Microbiology
ANKER, H., Economics and Natural Resources
ASTRUP, A., Human Nutrition
BAUER, R., Mathematics and Physics
BISGAARD, M., Veterinary Microbiology
BJERRUM, M., Chemistry
BLIXENKRONE-MØLLER, M., Veterinary Microbiology
BOGETOFT, P., Economics and Natural Resources
BORGGÅRD, O., Chemistry
CHRISTENSEN, L. P. G., Animal Sciences and Animal Health
CHWALIBOG, A., Animal Science and Animal Health
COLLINGE, D., Plant Biology
ERIKSEN, E. N., Agricultural Sciences
ESBJERG, P., Ecology and Molecular Biology
FLAGSTAD, A., Clinical Sciences
FLENSTED-JENSEN, M., Mathematics and Physics

FRANDSEN, F., Ecology and Molecular Biology

FREDHOLM, M., Animal Sciences and Animal Health

FRIIS, C., Pharmacology and Pathobiology

GIESE, H., Ecology and Molecular Biology

GREVE, T., Clinical Sciences

HANSEN, A. K., Pharmacology and Pathobiology

HANSEN, H. C. B., Chemistry

HAVE, H., Agricultural Sciences

HELLES, F., Economics and Natural Resources

HOVE, H., Animal Sciences and Animal Health

HYLDGAARD-JENSEN, J., Anatomy and Physiology

HYTTEL, P., Anatomy and Physiology

JACOBSEN, N., Botany and Forest Genetics

JAKOBSEN, M., Agricultural Sciences

JENSEN, A. L., Clinical Sciences

JENSEN, H. E., Agricultural Sciences

KÆRGAARD, N., Economics and Natural Resources

KJELDSEN-KRAGH, S., Economics and Natural Sciences

LADEWIG, J., Animal Sciences and Animal Health

LARSEN, J. B., Economics and Natural Resources

LARSEN, J. L., Veterinary Microbiology

LARSEN, L. E., General and Inorganic Chemistry

LARSSON, L., Anatomy and Physiology

MADSEN, A., Animal Sciences and Animal Health

MARTENS, M., Dairy and Food Science

MØLLER, B. LINDBERG, Plant Biology

MUNCK, L., Dairy and Food Sciences

NIELSEN, J., Chemistry

NIELSEN, J. P., Clinical Sciences

NIELSEN, N. E., Agricultural Sciences

OLESEN, P. O., Agricultural Sciences

OLSEN, I. A., Economics and Natural Resources

OLSEN, J. E., Veterinary Microbiology

PALMGREN, M., Plant Biology

PORTER, J. R., Agricultural Sciences

PRIMDAHL, J., Economics and Natural Resources

QVIST, K. B., Dairy and Food Sciences

RUDEMO, M., Mathematics and Physics

SANDOE, P., Animal Sciences and Animal Health

SANDSTRÖM, B., Human Nutrition

SEBEK, M., Agricultural Sciences

SKADHAUGE, E., Anatomy and Physiology

SKIBSTED, L. H., Dairy and Food Sciences

SKOVGAARD, I. M., Mathematics and Physics

SØRENSEN, J., Ecology and Molecular Biology

STAUN, H., Animal Sciences and Animal Health

STREIBIG, J. C., Agricultural Sciences

SVALASTOGA, E., Clinical Sciences

SVENDSEN, O., Pharmacology and Pathobiology

THAMSBORG, S. M., Veterinary Microbiology

WEINER, J., Ecology and Molecular Biology

Faculty of Science (Tagensvej 16, 2200, Copenhagen N; tel. 35-32-42-00; fax 35-32-80-52; e-mail science@science.ku.dk; internet www.science.ku.dk):

ALS-NIELSEN, J., Experimental Condensed-Matter Physics

AMBJØRN, J., Physics

ANDERSEN, H. H., Physics

ANDERSEN, J. E. B., Human Physiology

ANDERSEN, N. O., Physics

ARCTANDER, P., Zoology

BATES, J. R., Meteorology

BERCHTOLD, M., Molecular Cell Biology

BERG, C., Mathematics

BJØRNHOLM, T., Chemistry

BONDE, H., Human Physiology

BOOMSMA, J., Zoology

BREUNING-MADSEN, H., Geography

CHRISTENSEN, S., Zoology

CHRISTIANSEN, C., Geography, Geomorphology

DAHL-JENSEN, D., Physics

EGEL, R., Genetics

ENGHOFF, H., Zoological Systematics and Zoological Geography

FENCHEL, T. M., Marine Biology

FJELDSÅ, J., Biodiversity

FREI, R. E., Geology

FRIIS, I., Systematic Botany and Plant Geography

GARRETT, R., Biology

GRIMMELIKHUIJZEN CORNELIS, J. P., Zoology

GRUBB, G., Mathematics

HAMANN, O., Botany

HAMMER, C. U., Geophysics

HANSEN, J., Physics

HANSEN, J. R., Physics

HARPER, D. A. T., Geology

HENGLEIN, F., Computer Science

JACKSON, A. O., Theoretical Nuclear Physics

JENSEN, K. H., Geology

JENSEN, K. S., Zoology

JENSEN, M. H., Physics

JOHANSEN, P., Computer Science

JOHANSEN, S., Mathematical Statistics

JONASSON, S. E., Ecological Botany

JONES, N. D., Computer Science

JØRGENSEN, H. E., Astronomy

JUL, E., Computer Science

KIMING, I., Mathematics

KRARUP, J. F., Computer Science

KRISTENSEN, N. P., Systematic Entomology

KRISTENSEN, R. M., Invertebrate Zoology

KROGH, A. S., Bioinformatics

KRÜGER, J., Geography

KÜHL, M., Zoology

LARSEN, E. H., Zoophysiological Laboratory

LARSEN, S. Y., Chemistry

LAURITSEN, F. R., Chemistry

LETH-JØRGENSEN, P., Cell Biology

McGREGOR, P. K., Zoology

MAKOVICKY, E., Geology

MATTHIESSEN, C. W., Geography

MIKKELSEN, K. V., Chemistry

MIKOSCH, T., Mathematics

MOESTRUP, Ø., Spore Plants

MUNDY, J., Plant Physiology

NIELSEN, H. B., Theoretical Physics

NIELSEN, M. S., Freshwater Biology

NIELSEN, O. H., Molecular Biology

NIELSEN, O. J., Chemistry

NOVIKOV, I., Astronomy

ØDUM, N. F., Molecular Biology

OLESEN, P., Physics

PEDERSEN, G. K., Mathematics

PEDERSEN, P. A., Cell Biology

PEJRUP, M., Geography

PFISTER, G. U., Human Physiology

POLZIK, E., Physics

POULSEN, F. M., Molecular Biology

RAHBEK, C., Zoology

RICHTER, E. A., Exercise Physiology, Human Physiology

ROSENDAHL, S., Botany

ROSING, M. T., Geology

SCHMIDLI, H. P., Mathematics

SHAFFER, G., Geophysics

SKELBOE, S., Computer Science

SMITH, H., Physics

SOLOVEJ, J. P., Mathematics

SØRENSEN, M., Mathematics

SURLYK, F., Geology

THYBO, H., Geology

TIND, J., Mathematical Economics

TSCHERNING, C., Geophysics

WILLUMSEN, B. M., Molecular Biology

WINSLØW, C. E. B., Science Education

Faculty of Social Sciences (Øster Farimagsgade 5, Bldg 12, 1st Fl. 1353 Copenhagen K; tel. 35-32-35-46; fax 35-32-35-32; e-mail samf-fak@samf.ku.dk; internet socialsciences.ku.dk):

ANDERSEN, E., Economics

ANDERSEN, E. B., Theoretical Statistics

BERTILSSON, M., Sociology

ESTRUP, H., Economics

GRODAL, B. K., Economics

GØRTZ, E., Social Description

GUNDELACH, P., Sociology

HASTRUP, K., Anthropology

HEURLIN, B., Political Science

HJORTH-ANDERSEN, C., Economics

JØRGENSEN, T. B., Political Science

JUSELIUS, K., Economics

KEIDING, H., Economics

KNUDSEN, T., Political Science

PEDERSEN, O. K., International Politics

PEDERSEN, O. K., Political Science

SCHULTZ, C., Economics

SJØBLOM, B. G., Political Science

SØRENSEN, P. B., Economics

THYGESEN, N. C., Economics

VIND, K., Economic

Faculty of Theology (Købmagergade 44–46, POB 2164, 1150 Copenhagen K; tel. 35-32-39-61; fax 35-32-36-00; e-mail dtf@fak.teol.ku.dk; internet www.teol.ku.dk):

GLEBE-MØLLER, J., Dogmatics

GRANE, L., Church History

GRØN, A., Ethics and Philosophy of Religion

HANSEN, H. B., Church History

HYLDAHL, N. C., New Testament Exegesis

JØRGENSEN, T., Dogmatics

KJELDGAARD-PEDERSEN, S., Church History, History of Dogma

LAUSTEN, M. S., Theology, Danish Church History

LEMCHE, N. P., Old Testament Exegesis

MÜLLER, M., New Testament Exegesis

THOMPSON, T. L., Old Testament Exegesis

ROSKILDE UNIVERSITET

Universitetsvej 1, POB 260, 4000 Roskilde

Telephone: 46-74-20-00

Fax: 46-74-30-00

E-mail: ruc@ruc.dk

Internet: www.ruc.dk

Founded 1972 as Roskilde Univ. Centre, present name 2008

State control

Academic year: September to June (2 semesters)

Rector: Prof. Dr IB POULSEN

Pro-Rector: Prof. Dr HANNE LETH ANDERSEN

Chair.: CHRISTIAN S. NISSEN

Univ. Dir: PETER LAURITZEN

Librarian: NIELS SENIUS CLAUSEN

Library of 840,055 vols, incl. audiovisual media, 9 e-journals

Number of teachers: 500

Number of students: 9,500

PROFESSORS

Humanities:

BRASK, P., Science of Texts, Theory and Methodology of Literary Analysis

BRYLD, C., History

DENCIK, L., Social Psychology

ELLE, B., Educational Psychology

HELTOFT, L., Danish

ILLERIS, K., Educational Research

KAMPMANN, J., Educational Research

KJØRUP, S., Philosophy and Communication

McGUIRE, B. P., History

MORTENSEN, A. T., Philosophy and Communication

NISSEN, G., History

OLESEN, H. S., Educational Psychology

PEDERSEN, S., Philosophy
POULSEN, IB., Danish
POULSEN, J., Journalism
PREISLER, B., English
SCHRØDER, K. CHR., Communication
SIMONSEN, B., Educational Research
WEBER, K., Educational Research
WUCHERPHENNIG, W. P., German

Natural Sciences:

AGGER, P., Environmental Planning
ANDERSEN, O., Environmental Science
BRANDT, J., Geography
DYRE, J. C., Physics
FORBES, V. E., Environmental Biology
GALLAGHER, J. P., Computer Science
HANSEN, P. E., Chemistry
ILLERIS, S., Geography
LØBNER-OLESEN, A., Molecular Biology
NIELSEN, L. K., Transport and Environment
NISS, M., Mathematics
PRÆSTGAARD, E., Chemistry
SCHROLL, H., Environmental Assessment
SIMONSEN, K. F., Geography
SØRENSEN, B. E., Physics
THULSTRUP, E., Chemistry
WESTH-ANDERSEN, P., Chemistry

Social Sciences:

AAGE, H., Political Economy
ANDERSEN, J., Social Sciences
BOGASON, P., Public Administration
BOJE, TH. P., Social Sciences
DAVIS, J. D., Political Economy
FRAMKE, W., Tourism Planning
GREVE, B., Public Administration
JESPERSEN, J., Welfare State Studies
LAURIDSEN, L. S., International Development
MARCUSSEN, H. S., Institutional Aspect of Natural Resource Management
MATTSON, J., Business Administration
NIELSEN, K., Industrial Theory
NIELSEN, K. A., Technological and Organizational Development of Enterprises
OLSEN, O. J., Planning
SCHEUER, S., Social Sciences
SUNDBO, J., Business Administration
TORFING, J., Social Sciences
WHISTON, TH. G., Environmental Regulation

SYDDANSK UNIVERSITET (University of Southern Denmark)

Campusvej 55, 5230 Odense M
Telephone: 65-50-10-00
Fax: 65-50-10-90
E-mail: sdu@sdu.dk
Internet: www.sdu.dk

Founded 1966 as Odense Univ., present name 1998, following merger with Handelshøjskole Syd–Ingeniørhøjskole Syd and several other instns of higher education
State control
Languages of instruction: Danish, English
Academic year: September to June (2 semesters)

Vice-Chancellor: JENS ODDERSHEDE
Pro-Vice-Chancellor: BJARNE G. SØRENSEN
Univ. Dir: PER OVERGAARD NIELSEN
Chief Librarian: AASE LINDAHL

Library: see under Libraries and Archives
Number of teachers: 747
Number of students: 20,000
Publication: *Ny Viden* (12 a year)

DEANS

Faculty of Engineering: PER MICHAEL JOHANSEN
Faculty of Health Sciences: Prof. OLE SKØTT
Faculty of Humanities: Dr FLEMMING G. ANDERSEN
Faculty of Science: Prof. HENRIK PEDERSON

Faculty of Social Sciences: JESPER STRANDSKOV

PROFESSORS

Faculty of Health Sciences (J.B. Winsløws Vej 19, 3, 5000 Odense C; tel. 65-50-30-18; fax 65-91-89-14; e-mail fac@health.sdu.dk; internet www.sdu.dk/om_sdu/fakulteterne/naturvidenskab.aspx):

ANDERSEN, K. E., Dermato-venereology
BAKKETEIG, L., Epidemiology
BARINGTON, T., Clinical Immunology
BECK-NIELSEN, H., Medical Endocrinology
BENDIX, T., Biomechanics
BIE, P., Physiology
BINDSLEV-JENSEN, C., Dermatological Allergology
BRO, F., General Practice
BRØSEN, K., Clinical Pharmacology
CHRISTENSEN, K., Ageing and Longevity
DITZEL, H., Biomedicine
DOBBELSTEIN, M., Biomedicine
FENGER, C., Pathology
FINSEN, B., Biomedicine
GRANDJEAN, P. A., Environmental Medicine
GREEN, A., Clinical Epidemiology
HAGHFELT, T., Cardiology
HALLAS, J., Clinical Pharmacology
HØILUND-CARLSEN, P., Clinical Physiology
HOLMSKOV, U., Biomedicine
HØRDER, M., Clinical Chemistry
HUSBY, S., Paediatrics
JAKOBSON, A., Cancer Therapy
JENSEN, W. A., Biomedicine
JUNKER, P., Rheumatology
KASSEM, M., Biomedicine
KOLMOS, H. J., Microbiology
KRAGH-SØRENSEN, P., Psychiatry
LOUS, J., General Practice
MANNICHE, C., Biomechanics
OWENS, T., Biomedicine
PEDERSEN, C., Infectious Medicine
PETERSEN, S., Asthma and Allergy in Childhood
RASMUSSEN, J. Z., Anatomy
RITSKES-HOITINGA, M., Comparative Medicine and Laboratory Animal Science
SAHLIN, K., Exercise Physiology
SCHAFFALITZKY DE MUCKADELL, O. B., Medical Gastroenterology
SCHRØDER, H. D., Neuropathology and Neuromuscular Biology
SJØLIE, A. K., Ophthalmology
SKØTT, O., Physiology
SØRENSEN, T., Psychiatry
THOMSEN, J., Forensic Medicine
TOFT, P., Anaesthesiology
VACH, W., Medical Statistics
VAUPEL, J. W., Demographic Studies
WALTER, S., Surgery
WESTERGAARD, J. G., Obstetrics

Faculty of Humanities (Campusvej 55, 5230 Odense M; tel. 65-50-20-79; fax 65-50-20-55; e-mail humfak@sdu.dk; internet www.sdu.dk/om_sdu/fakulteterne/humaniora.aspx):

BACHE, C., English Language and Literature
BASBØLL, H., Scandinavian Language
BORGNAKKE, K., General Pedagogy
DROTNER, K., Media Studies and Media Culture
HAMMER, O., Religious Studies and Comparative Religion
HOLM, P., Maritime and Regional History
JAKOBSEN, H. G., Scandinavian Language
JENSEN, B., Slavic Studies
JESPERSEN, K. J. V., History
JOHANSEN, J. D., Comparative Literature
JUST, F., History
KLAWONN, E. G., Philosophy
MAI, A.-M., Danish Literature
MORTENSEN, F. H., Scandinavian Language and Literature
NIELSEN, H. F., Historical and Comparative Germanic Linguistics

NYE, D., American Studies
QVORTRUP, L., Multimedia
ROBERING, K., Humanistic Information Science
SAUERBERG, L. O., English Language and Literature
SINHA, C. G., Language and Cognitive Linguistics

Faculty of Science (Campusvej 55, 5230 Odense M; tel. 65-50-20-99; fax 65-93-38-05; e-mail anc@sdu.dk; internet www.sdu.dk/om_sdu/fakulteterne/naturvidenskab.aspx):

ANGELOV, C. K., Software Engineering
BERNSEN, N. O., Natural Interactive Systems
BJERREGAARD, P., Biology
BUUR, J., User-oriented Product Development
CANFIELD, D., Biology
DOUTHWAITE, S. R., Molecular Biology
DYBKJÆR, L., Natural Interactive Systems
GERDES, K., Molecular Microbiology
HAAGERUP, U., Mathematics
ISSINGER, O., Biochemistry
JENSEN, J. B., Computer Science
JENSEN, O. N., Protein Mass Spectrometry
JØRGENSEN, B., Statistics
KNUDSEN, J., Biochemistry
KORNERUP, P., Computer Science
KRISTENSEN, B. B., Software Engineering
KRISTIANSEN, K., Eukaryotic Molecular Biology
LARSEN, K. S., Computer Science
LUND, H. H., Information Technology
MCKENZIE, C. J., Nanobioscience
MANN, M., Molecular Biology
MICHELSEN, A., Biology
MOURITSEN, O. G., Physics
NIELSEN, H. T., Chemistry
ØSTERGARD, J. E., Physics and Technology
PEDERSEN, H., Mathematics
PERRAM, J. W., Applied Mathematics
PETERSEN, H. G., Applied Mathematics
ROEPSTORFF, P., Molecular Biology
RUBAHN, H.-G., Physics and Technology
RØRDAM, M., Mathematics
SIGMUND, H. P., Physics
TOWN, R. M., Chemistry
VALENTIN-HANSEN, P., Molecular Biology
WENGEL, J., Chemistry
WIIL, U. K., Software Engineering
WILLATZEN, H., Mathematical Modelling

Faculty of Social Sciences (Campusvej 55, 5230 Odense M; tel. 65-50-22-00; fax 65-93-56-92; e-mail office@sam.sdu.dk; internet www.sdu.dk/om_sdu/fakulteterne/samfundsvidenskab.aspx):

ASKEGAARD, S., Business Studies
BAGER, T., Business Studies
BOUCHET, D., Business Studies
CHRISTENSEN, J. A., Business Studies
CHRISTENSEN, L. T., Business Studies
CHRISTENSEN, P. M., Political Sciences
CHRISTENSEN, P. O., Business Studies
CHRISTENSEN, P. R., Business Studies
CHRISTIANSEN, T., Health Economics
CLAUSEN, N. J., Law
DAHLER-LARSEN, P., Political Sciences
ERIKSEN, B., Business Studies
FREYTAG, P. V., Business Studies
FRIMOR, H., Business Studies
GYRD-HANSEN, D., Health Economics
HANSEN, J. D., Business Studies
HANSEN, S. F., Law
JENSEN, S. E. H., National Economics
JØRGENSEN, N., Business Studies
JØRGENSEN, S., Business Studies
KAISER, V., National Economics
KLAUSEN, K. K., Public Organization Theory
KNUDSEN, T., Business Studies
LARSEN, P., Journalism
LAURSEN, F., Political Science
LUND, A., Journalism
MADSEN, T. K., Business Studies

MORTENSEN, B. O., Law
MOURITZEN, P. E., Political Sciences
MUNK, C., Business Studies
OBEL, B., Business Studies
PEDERSEN, K. M., Health Economics
PEDERSEN, M. N., Political Sciences
PETERSEN, H., Law
PETERSEN, J. H., Social Science
PETERSEN, N. C., Business Studies
SKYRUM-NIELSEN, P., Journalism
SLOTH, B., National Economics
SØRENSEN, C. J., National Economics
STEINICKE, M., Law
TETZSCHNER, H., Business Economics
VESTERGAARD, N., Business Economics

University-level Institutions

Arkitektskolen i Århus (Århus School of Architecture): Nørreport 20, 8000 Århus C; tel. 89-36-00-00; fax 86-13-06-45; e-mail a@ aarch.dk; internet www.aarch.dk; f. 1965; under the Min. of Culture; offers courses in architectural design, planning, furniture and industrial design; library: 44,000 vols, 170 journals; 160 teachers; 850 students; Rector TORBEN NIELSEN; Pro-Rector CHARLOTTE BUNDGAARD; publs *Skolehåndbogen* (1 a year), *Virksomhedsregnskab* (1 a year).

Danmarks Biblioteksskole (Royal School of Library and Information Science): Birketinget 6, 2300 Copenhagen S; tel. 32-58-60-66; fax 32-84-02-01; e-mail db@iva.dk; internet www.iva.dk; f. 1956; library: 182,000 vols; 70 teachers; 1,000 students; Rector Prof. Dr PER HASLE; Admin. Dir HANNE FRIIS KAAS.

Attached Institute:

Danmarks Biblioteksskole Aalborg (Royal School of Library and Information Science, Aalborg): Fredrik Bajers Vej 7K, 9220 AalborgØ; tel. 98-15-79-22; fax 98-15-10-42; e-mail dbaa@iva.dk; internet www .iva.dk; f. 1973; Head JESPER W. SCHNEIDER.

Danmarks Designskole (Danish Design School): Strandboulevarden 47, 2100 Copenhagen Ø; tel. 35-27-75-76; fax 35-27-76-00; e-mail mail@dkds.dk; internet www.dkds.dk; f. 1875 as Tegne- og Kunstindustriskolen (School of Drawing and Art Industry), present name 1989, present status 1998; attached to Min. of Culture; part of Danish National Centre for Design Research; offers courses in fashion, furniture, graphic communication and digital design, glass, industrial design, pottery, scenography, space, textiles; library: 14,000 vols, 100 magazines, video cassettes, CD-ROMs and DVDs; 110 teachers; 700 students; Rector ANNE-LOUISE SOMMER; Pres. GØSTA KNUDSEN.

Designskolen Kolding (Kolding Design School): Ågade 10, 6000 Kolding; tel. 76-30-11-00; fax 76-30-11-12; e-mail dk@ designskolenkolding.dk; internet www .designskolenkolding.dk; f. 1967, present name 1998; attached to Min. of Culture; institute for form and theory, fashion and textiles, visual communication, industrial design and interactive media; dept of ceramics; temporary exhibitions; library: 20,000

vols, 60 periodicals; 350 students; Rector ELSEBETH GERNER NIELSEN; Chair. MADS NIPPER LEGO.

Erhvervsakademiet Lillebælt (Lillebaelt Academy of Professional Higher Education): Munke Mose Allé 9, 5000 Odense C; tel. 70-10-58-00; e-mail eal@eal.dk; internet www .eal.dk; f. 2009; campuses in Odense and Vejle; offers courses in Danish business, technology, economics, trade, nutrition and hospitality; 1,200 students; Chair. PETER ZINCK; Vice-Chair. TORBEN MØLGAARD ANDERSEN; Prin. JENS MEJER PEDERSEN.

Ingeniørhøjskolen i Århus (Engineering College of Arhus): Dalgas Ave 2, 8000 Århus C; tel. 87-30-22-00; fax 87-30-27-31; e-mail iha@iha.dk; internet www.iha.dk; f. 1903; library: 18,000 vols; 110 teachers; 2,000 students; Rector OLE POULSEN; Pro-Rector KELD LAURSEN.

Ingeniørhøjskolen i København (Copenhagen University College of Engineering): Lautrupvang 15, 2750 Ballerup; tel. 44-80-50-88; fax 44-80-50-10; e-mail studadm@ihk .dk; internet www.ihk.dk; f. 1879; applied sciences; awards BSc in engineering; library: 32,900 vols; 250 teachers; 2,300 students; Rector FLEMMING KROGH.

Jyske Musikkonservatorium (Royal Academy of Music): Skovgaardsgade 2c, 8000 Århus C; tel. 72-26-74-00; e-mail mail@musikkons.dk; internet www .musikkons.dk; f. 2010,on merger of Northern Acad. of Music (f. 1927) in Aalborg and Royal Acad. of Music (f. 1930) in Aarhus; attached to Min.of Culture; 3 main areas of study: classical music, rhythmic music and electronic music; Prin. THOMAS WINTHER; Vice-Prin. MICHAEL BUNDGAARD; Admin. Dir KIRSTEN PRÆSTEGAARD.

Københavns Tekniske Skole (Copenhagen Technical College): Lygten 16, 2400 Copenhagen NV; tel. 35-86-35-86; fax 35-86-35-87; e-mail kts@kts.dk; internet www.kts .dk; f. 1843, present name 1978; offers courses in chemistry, communication, Danish, foreign languages, information technology, mathematics, physics, social studies, technology; 4,000 students; Chair. HENRY SALE; Dir MOGENS OVE NIELSEN; Vice-Pres. FLEMMING S. BRANDT; Admin. Man. PER NIELSEN; publ. *Indtryk*.

Kongelige Danske Kunstakademi, Konservatorskolen (Royal Danish Academy of Fine Arts, School of Conservation): Esplanaden 34, 1263 Copenhagen K; tel. 33-74-47-00; fax 33-74-47-77; e-mail kons@kons.dk; internet www.kons.dk; f. 1973; attached to Min. of Culture; offers courses in graphic art, object conservation, pictorial art, monumental art, natural history; library: 7,000 vols, 150 periodicals; 20 teachers; 100 students; Rector Assoc. Prof. Dr RENÉ LARSEN.

Kongelige Danske Kunstakademis Arkitektskole (Royal Danish Academy of Fine Arts, School of Architecture): Philip de Langes Allé 10, 1435 Copenhagen K; tel. 32-68-60-00; fax 32-68-61-11; e-mail arkitektskolen@karch.dk; internet www .karch.dk; f. 1754 as The Royal Danish Painting, Sculpture and Building Acad., present status 1960; offers Bachelors and Masters courses in architectural design and restoration, urban and landscape planning,

and industrial, graphic and furniture design; library: see Libraries and Archives; 1,100 students; Rector SVEN FELDING; Pro-Rector Assoc. Prof. JØRGEN HAUBERG.

Kongelige Danske Kunstakademis Billedkunstskoler (School of Visual Arts of the Royal Danish Academy of Fine Arts): Kgs. Nytorv 1, POB 3014, 1050 Copenhagen K; tel. 33-74-46-00; fax 33-74-46-64; e-mail bks@ kunstakademiet.dk; internet www .kunstakademiet.dk; f. 1754; attached to Min. of Culture; library: see Libraries and Archives; Rector MIKKEL BOGH; Pro-Rector KATYA SANDER.

Kongelige Danske Musikkonservatorium (Royal Danish Academy of Music): Rosenørns Allé 22, 1970 Frederiksberg C; tel. 72-26-72-26; fax 72-26-72-72; e-mail dkdm@dkdm.dk; internet www.dkdm.dk; f. 1867, present status 1948; offers courses aimed at performance at the highest level; pedagogical training with a view to professional music teaching; specialized courses in the fields of music teaching, composition, conducting and church music, as well as recording direction; library: 50,000 vols; 170 teachers; 400 students; Prin. BERTEL KRARUP; Vice-Prin. TIM FREDERIKSEN; Admin. Dir CARSTEN RUBY; Librarian MUSSE MAGNUSSEN SVARE.

Rytmisk Musikkonservatorium (Rhythmic Music Conservatory): Leo Mathisens Vej 1, Holmen, 1437 Copenhagen K; tel. 32-68-67-00; fax 32-68-67-66; e-mail rmc@rmc.dk; internet www.rmc.dk; f. 1986; state control; attached to Min. of Culture; music teaching, music and movement, music performance, sound engineering, music management; 30 teachers; 220 students; Prin. HENRIK SVEIDAHL.

Syddansk Musikkonservatorium & Skuespillerskole (The Academy of Music and Dramatic Arts, Southern Denmark): Islandsgade 2, 5000 Odense C; tel. 63-11-99-00; fax 63-11-99-20; e-mail info@smks.dk; internet www.smks.dk; f. 2010,on by merger of Carl Nielsen Academy of Music, Odense, and Academy of Music, Esbjerg; attached to Min. of Culture; Rector AXEL MOMME; Pro-Rector INGER ALLAN.

Velkommen Til Teknologisk Institut (Danish Technological Institute): Gregersensvej 3, 2630 Tåstrup; tel. 72-20-20-00; fax 72-20-20-19; e-mail info@teknologisk.dk; internet www.teknologisk.dk; f. 1906; building technology, energy, environment, industry, industrial and business development; maintains br. in Århus; Pres. SØREN STJERNQVIST.

VIA University College: Skejbyvej 1, 8240 Risskov; tel. 87-55-00-00; fax 87-55-00-01; e-mail viauc@viauc.dk; internet www.viauc .dk; f. 2008,on merger of Alpha Centre for Higher Education, the Mid-West Centre for Higher Education, the Vita Centre for Higher Education, the University College Jutland and Vitus Bering Denmark; faculty of education and social studies, faculty of health sciences, faculty of performing arts, school of technology and business; 2,100 teachers; 16,000 students; Rector HARALD MIKKELSEN; Pro-Rector PETER FRIESE; College Dir ASBJORN CHRISTENSEN.

FAROE ISLANDS

Learned Societies
GENERAL

Føroya Fróðskaparfelag/Societas Scientiarum Faeroensis (Faroese Society of Science and Letters): POB 209, FO110 Tórshavn; tel. and fax 322074; e-mail fff@frodskaparfelag.fo; internet www.frodskaparfelag.fo; f. 1952; procures scientific and scholarly literature and promotes research work; 170 mems; Pres. Dr ANDRAS MORTENSEN; publs *Fróðskaparrit* (Annals), *Supplementa*.

HISTORY, GEOGRAPHY AND ARCHAEOLOGY

Føroya Forngripafelag (Faroese Archaeological Society): POB 1173, FO110 Tórshavn; tel. 312259; f. 1898; attached to Føroya Fornminnissavn (Historical Museum); works in conjunction with the Nat. Museum of Antiquities; Pres. MORTAN WINTHER POULSEN.

LANGUAGE AND LITERATURE

Rithøvundafelag Føroya (Faroese Writers' Association): POB 1124, FO100 Tórshavn; e-mail rit@rit.fo; internet www.rit.fo; f. 1957; promotes the growth of Faroese literature and protects authors' rights; 102 mems; Pres. RAKEL HELMSDAL.

Research Institutes
AGRICULTURE, FISHERIES AND VETERINARY SCIENCE

Havstovan (Faroe Marine Research Institute): Nóatún 1, POB 3051, FO110 Tórshavn; tel. 353900; fax 353901; e-mail hav@hav.fo; internet www.hav.fo; f. 1951; attached to govt of the Faroe Islands; depts of environment, fisheries and technology; Dir EILIF GAARD; publ. *Fiskirannsóknir* (1 or 2 a year).

Heilsufrøðiliga Starvsstovan (Faroese Food and Veterinary Agency): Falkavegur 6, 2 hæddd, FO100 Tórshavn; tel. 556400; fax 556401; e-mail hfs@hfs.fo; internet www.hfs.fo; f. 1975; research, services, quality control and inspection in the fish and food industry and in the environment; govt dept; Dir BARÐUR ENNI.

Libraries and Archives
Tórshavn

Býarbókasavnið (Public Library): Niels Finsens gøta 7, POB 358, FO100 Tórshavn; tel. 302020; fax 302031; e-mail bbs@bbs.fo; internet www.bbs.fo; f. 1969; 73,443 vols; City Librarian ANNA BRIMNES; Librarian HANNE MAGNUSSEN.

Føroya Landsbókasavn (National Library of the Faroe Islands): J. C. Svabosgøtu 16, POB 61, FO110 Tórshavn; tel. 356500; fax 318895; e-mail utlan@flb.fo; internet www.flb.fo; f. 1828; attached to govt of the Faroe Islands; open to the public; responsible for 15 public and 11 school libraries; 168,083 vols (20,000 scientific vols); Exec. Dir ERHARD JACOBSEN; Chief Librarian ANNIKA SMITH; publ. *Føroyskur Bókalisti* (list of Faeroese publs, 1 a year).

Landsskjalasavnið (National Archives of the Faroe Islands): V. U. Hammershaimbs-gøta 24, FO100 Tórshavn; tel. 316677; fax 318677; e-mail fararch@lss.fo; internet www.lss.fo; f. 1932; medieval documents (1298–1599), archives of parliament and central and local admin. (1615–1980); Dir SÁMAL T. F. JOHANSEN; Archivist JOHN KJÆR.

Museums and Art Galleries
Tórshavn

Føroya Fornminnissavn (National Museum of Archaeology and Cultural History): Kúrdalsvegur 2, POB 1155, FO110 Tórshavn; tel. 310700; fax 312259; e-mail fornminni@fornminni.fo; internet www.fornminni.fo; f. 1898, taken over by State 1952; archaeology, ethnology, inspection of ancient monuments; Dir ANDRAS MORTENSEN; Museum Curator ERLAND VIBERG JOENSEN.

Føroya Náttúrugripasavn (Natural History Museum): V. U. Hammershaimbsgøta 13, FO100 Tórshavn; tel. 352300; fax 352301; e-mail ngs@ngs.fo; internet www.ngs.fo; f. 1955; depts of botany, zoology; Dir DORETE BLOCH.

Savnið 1940–45 (Faroe-British Museum): POB 362, FO110 Tórshavn; tel. 312074; f. 1983; military and civilian artefacts from British occupation during Second World War (1939–45).

University

FRÓDSKAPARSETUR FØROYA/ UNIVERSITAS FÆROENSIS (University of the Faroe Islands)

J. C. Svabos gøta 14, POB 272, FO110 Tórshavn

Telephone: 352500
Fax: 352501
E-mail: setur@setur.fo
Internet: www.setur.fo

Founded 1965
Language of instruction: Faroese
Academic year: August to June

Rector: JÓAN PAULI JOENSEN
Vice-Rector: SÚSANNA M. MORTENSEN
Univ. Dir: RÚNA HJELM
Chair.: HERÁLVUR JOENSEN
Sec. Gen.: RÚNA HJELM

Number of teachers: 65
Number of students: 475

DEANS

Faculty of Language and Literature: TURIÐ SIGURÐARDÓTTIR
Faculty of History and Social Sciences: HANS ANDR SOLVARA
Faculty of Natural Sciences and Technology: HANS PAULI JOENSEN
Nursing College: SÚSANNA M. MORTENSEN
Teachers College: JÓANNES HANSEN

PROFESSORS

ANDREASSEN, E., Oral Literature
BLOCH, D., Zoology
BROWN, R. J., Geophysics
HANSEN, B., Oceanography
JOENSEN, J. P., History and Ethnology
MARNERSDÓTTIR, M., Literature
SIGURDARDÓTTIR, T., Literature
SPARRE ANDERSEN, M., Geophysics

GREENLAND

Regulatory Body
GOVERNMENT

Ministry of Education, Research and Nordic Cooperation: Indaleeqqap Aqq. 3, POB 1029, 3900 Nuuk; tel. (299) 345000; fax (299) 322073; e-mail kiiip@nanoq.gl; internet uk.nanoq.gl/emner/government/departments.aspx; Min. PALLE CHRISTIANSEN.

Learned Societies
GENERAL

Grønlandske Selskab (The Greenland Society): see under Denmark.

Nunani Avannarlerni Piorsarsimassut-sikkut Attaveqaat (NAPA)/Nordens Institut i Grønland (The Nordic Institute of Greenland): Imaneq 21, POB 770, 3900 Nuuk; tel. (299) 324733; fax (299) 325733; e-mail napa@napa.gl; internet www.napa.gl; f. 1987; cultural instn: financed by the Nordic Ccl of Mins, 5 Nordic countries and 3 home-rule areas within them; develops, supports and stimulates Greenlandic cultural life, prioritizing youth and children; advances inter-Nordic cultural relations; Dir (vacant);

Chair. VIVIAN MOEN; Deputy Chair. CLAUS NIELSEN; Institute Man. ANDERS BERNDTSSON; Project Man. BOAZ MILLER.

BIBLIOGRAPHY, LIBRARY SCIENCE AND MUSEOLOGY

NUKAKA–Nunatsinni Katersugaasiviit Kattuffiat/Sammenslutningen af museer i Grønland (Association of Museums in Greenland): c/o Nunatta Katersugaasivia Allagaateqarfialu, POB 145, 3900 Nuuk; tel. (299) 322611; fax (299) 642833; e-mail hans .lange@natmus.gl; internet www.nukaka.gl; f. 1993; supports the interests and devt of archives, local and spec. museums; Chair. HANS LANGE; Vice-Chair. TEA DAHL CHRISTENSEN; Treas. OLE G. JENSEN.

FINE AND PERFORMING ARTS

'Simerneq' (Artists' Society): POB 1009, 3900 Nuuk; f. 1979; arranges exhibitions of works of mems and others; Sec. INGER HAUGE.

LANGUAGE AND LITERATURE

Kalaallit Atuakkiortut/Den Grønlandske Forfatterforening (Greenlandic Authors' Society): c/o ICC, Dronning Ingridsvej 1, POB 25, 3900 Nuuk; tel. (299) 323632; fax (299) 323001; e-mail kalatu@greennet.gl; internet forfatternet.katak.gl; f. 1975; copyrights for authors and translators; writing workshops and poetry festivals fostering interest in poetry among the youth; 80 mems; Pres. HANS A. LYNGE; Chair. AQQALUK LYNGE; Secs RIIKKI GRONVOLD, KARL ELIAS OLSEN; Treas ANE MARIE B. PEDERSEN, T. P. POULSEN; publ. *Kalaaleq* (magazine).

Research Institutes

AGRICULTURE, FISHERIES AND VETERINARY SCIENCE

Dansk Polarcenter (Danish Polar Center): Strandgade 102, 1401 Copenhagen K, Denmark; tel. 32-88-01-00; fax 32-88-01-01; e-mail dpc@dpc.dk; internet www.dpc.dk; f. 1989; attached to Danish Agency for Science, Technology and Innovation; supports and coordinates Arctic and Antarctic research in Denmark and Greenland; provides information on polar issues; library of 35,000 vols incl. 26,000 books, 9,000 pamphlets, 3,000 theses, 700 periodicals (300 current); Dir HANNE PETERSEN; Librarian VIBEKE SLOTH JAKOBSEN.

Forsøgsstationen 'Upernaviarsuk' (Upernaviarsuk Agricultural Research Station): POB 152, 3920 Qaqortoq; tel. (299) 649303; e-mail forsupv@greennet.gl; govt instn carrying out experiments in sheep rearing, fodder crops, tree planting and gardening in a polar environment.

MEDICINE

Greenland Institute for Circumpolar Health Research: Peqqissaannermik Ilinniarfik, POB 1499, 3900 Nuuk; e-mail gihr@ peqqik.gl; internet www.pi.gl/content/dk/ greenland_institute_f_circumpolar_health_research; f. 2008; attached to Peqqissaannermik Ilinniarfik; enhances cooperation between researchers from other countries and health professionals in Greenland; develops, exchanges, disseminates and applies scientific knowledge; creates nat. and int. networks; Chair. KARIN LADEFOGED; Vice-Chair. and Sec. GERT MULVAD; Research Dir Prof. PETER BJERREGAARD; Treas. SUZANNE MØLLER.

NATURAL SCIENCES
General

Kommissionen for Videnskabelige Undersøgelser i Grønland (Commission for Scientific Research in Greenland): Forsknings- og Innovationsstyrelsen, Bredgade 40, 1260 Copenhagen K, Denmark; tel. and fax 35-44-63-66; e-mail kec@fi.dk; internet www.kvug.dk; f. 1878; attached to Danish Agency for Science, Technology and Innovation; Greenlandic-Danish comm.; proposes jt strategies for polar research; Chair. Prof. MINIK ROSING; Deputy Chair. DANIEL THORLEIFSEN; Spec. Consultant KIRSTEN CANING; publ. *Grønlandsforskning historie og perspektiver*.

Biological Sciences

Arctic Station, University of Copenhagen: see under Denmark.

Danmarks Miljøundersøgelser, Afdeling for Arktisk Miljø (National Environmental Research Institute): Frederiksborgvej 399, POB 358, 4000 Roskilde, Denmark; tel. 46-30-12-00; fax 46-30-19-14; e-mail dmu@dmu .dk; internet www.dmu.dk; f. 1989; attached to Aarhus Univ.; monitors esp. effects of mineral exploitation, climate-change ecology in the Arctic, contaminants in Arctic ecosystems; marine mammal research and monitoring; coordinates the Greenland Ecosystem Monitoring programme; 3 research sections: applied arctic environmental research, climate effects and systems modelling, marine mammals and toxicology; 420 staff; Research Dir JESPER MADSEN.

Grønlands Naturinstitut/Pinngortitaleriffik (Greenland Institute of Natural Resources): POB 570, 3900 Nuuk; tel. (299) 361200; fax (299) 361212; e-mail info@natur .gl; internet www.natur.gl; applied research in natural resources, environmental protection and biodiversity; depts of birds and mammals, fish and shrimp, marine ecology and climate impact; Dir KLAUS HOYER NYGAARD; Chair. LENE KIELSEN HOLM.

Physical Sciences

Danmarks Meteorologiske Institut (Danish Meteorological Institute): see under Denmark.

Libraries
Nuuk

Groenlandica (Greenlandic National Library): Manutooq 1, POB 1074, 3900 Nuuk; tel. (299) 362380; fax (299) 362381; e-mail groenlandica@katak.gl; internet www .groenlandica.gl; f. 2008; attached to Nunatta Atuagaateqarfia Central and Public Library of Greenland); collects, records and stores all Greenlandic literature and publs; colln of foreign literature and information about Inuit and the Arctic area; nat. colln; spec. collns: Samuel Petrus Kleinschmidts Reference Library and Archive, The Oldendow Colln, Svend Frederiksen's Archive, The Jonathan Petersen Colln, The Frederik Nielsen (Faré) Colln; 50,000 vols in nat. colln, 30,000 in study colln; Head CHARLOTTE D. ANDERSON.

Nunatta Atuagaateqarfia/Grønlandske Landsbibliotek (National Library of Greenland): Imaneq 26, POB 1011, 3900 Nuuk; tel. (299) 321156; fax (299) 348949; e-mail nalib@ katak.gl; internet www.katak.gl; 70,426 vols; Dir ELISA JEREMIASSEN; Librarian KIRSTEN BIRKEFOSS; Librarian KIRSTEN HEILMANN; Librarian SØREN JENSEN; Librarian STEEN JEPPSON; Librarian VIVI MOTZFELDT.

Museums
Ilulissat

Ilulissat Museum: Nuisariannguaq 9, POB 99, 3952 Ilulissat; tel. (299) 943643; e-mail ilumus@ilulissat.gl; internet www.ilumus.gl; f. 1979; local, cultural and natural history; cultural history of the North Greenlandic sledgedog and the Sermermiut settlement; library and archive of photographs and materials on Knud Rasmussen; Curator and Head of Museum Mag. KIRSTEN STRANDGAARD.

Kangilinnguit

Ivittuut Mine- og Mineralmuseum (Ivittuut Mining and Mineral Museum): 3930 Kangilinnguit; tel. (299) 691077; fax (299) 691073; e-mail museum.ivittuut@sermersooq .gl; internet www.ivittuut.dk/museum; f. 2006; minerals and industrial history and the use of Greenland's raw materials; Pres. PER NUKAARAQ HANSEN; Curator HELLE B. PETERSEN.

Nuuk

Nunatta Katersugaasivia Allagaateqarfialu/Grønlands Nationalmuseum og Arkiv (Greenland National Museum and Archive): Hans Egedesvej 8, POB 145, 3900 Nuuk; tel. (299) 322611; fax (299) 322622; e-mail nka@natmus.gl; internet www .natmus.gl; f. 1966; advises the self-rule Govt in matters concerning archaeological excavations and the final deposition of the excavated material; maintains the central files about preserved ruins, graveyards, bldgs, and participates in nature conservation and town planning; collns cover the 4,500 years of history in Greenland; collns: Inuit Archaeological Collns, Norse Collns, Gustav Holm Colln (Ammassalik c. 1880), Inughuit and Polareskimos (c. 1900), kayaks; arts, handicrafts and photographic colln; Dir DANIEL THORLEIFSEN; Deputy Dir PAULINE KNUDSEN; Curator MIKKEL MYRUP.

Nuuk Kunstmuseum/Nuup Katersugaasivii (Nuuk Artmuseum): Kissarneqqortuunnguaq 5, POB 1005, 3900 Nuuk; tel. (299) 327733; e-mail kunstmuseum@ greennet.gl; internet www .nuukkunstmuseum.gl; f. 2005 by Svend and Helen Junge; displays Svend and Helen Junge's 45-year colln of 300 pictures, paintings, drawings and graphics, 400 sculptures made of soapstone, tooth and wood, colln of 150 paintings by Emanuel A. Petersen (1894–1948).

Qaqortoq

Qaqortoq Museum: Torvevej B-29, POB 154, 3920 Qaqortoq; tel. (299) 641080; fax (299) 642833; e-mail geny@qaqortoq.gl; Dir OLE G. JENSEN.

Qasigiannguit

Qasigiannguit Katersugaasiviat/Qasigiannguit lokalmuseum (Qasigiannguit Museum): Poul Egedesvej 24, POB 130, 3951 Qasigiannguit; tel. and fax (299) 911477; e-mail qasmus@qaasuitsup.gl; internet www.museum.gl/qasigiannguit; 5 bldgs with separate exhibitions; displays a permanent exhibition of costumes and fishing equipment, colln of stuffed Arctic birds, unique items from the 4,500-year-old Saqqaq culture (first human settlement in West Greenland); provisions for overnight stay at museum cottage for visitors; Dir LAILA MIKAELSEN.

Upernavik

Upernaviup Katersugaasivia (Upernavik Museum): Niuertup Ottup Aqq. B-12, POB 93, 3962 Upernavik; tel. (299) 961085; e-mail inussuk@greennet.gl; internet www .upernivik.gl; f. c. 1950; colln of photographs, historical objects, items representing Greenland's hunting culture; Upervanik Retreat: artists' residence.

University

ILISIMATUSARFIK/GRØNLANDS UNIVERSITET
(University of Greenland)

Manutooq 1, POB 1061, 3900 Nuuk

Telephone: (299) 362300

Fax: (299) 362301

E-mail: mail@uni.gl

Internet: www.ilisimatusarfik.gl

Founded 1984

Public control

3 Univ. instns: Ilimmarfik Institute (depts of cultural and social history, journalism, language, literature and media, management and economics, social work, theology and religion); institutes of learning (Arctic education and teacher training), nursing and health sciences

Vice-Chancellor (Rector and Pres.): OLE MARQUARDT

Pro-Vice-Chancellor: KAREN LANGGÅRD

Univ. Librarian: BOLETHE OLSEN

Library of 25,000 vols, 125 journals

Number of teachers: 14

Number of students: 150

Publication: *Grønlandsk Kultur- og Samfundsforskning* (1 a year).

Colleges

Eqqumiitsuliornermik Ilinniarfik/ Kunstskolen (School of Arts): c/o KIIIP, POB 286, 3900 Nuuk; tel. (299) 322640; fax (299) 322644; e-mail kunst@greennet.gl; f. 1973; Dir ARNANNGUAQ HØEGH.

Ilinniarfissuaq/Grønlands Seminarium (Greenlands Teacher-Training College): C. E. Jansensvej 2, POB 1026, 3900 Nuuk; tel. (299) 321191; fax (299) 322099; e-mail ilinnia@teachnet.gl; internet www .ilinniarfissuaq.gl; f. 1845; attached to Univ. of Greenland; pedagogical, social and administrative education and in-service training;

25 teachers; 163 students; Rector DORTHE KORNELIUSSEN; Librarian LIDA LORENTZEN.

Niuernermik Ilinniarfik/Grønlands Handelsskole (Greenland Business College): Aqqusinersuaq 18, POB 1038, 3900 Nuuk; tel. (299) 323099; fax (299) 323255; e-mail ninuuk@ninuuk.gl; internet www .ninuuk.gl; f. 1979; courses and in-service training in journalism, interpreting and mercantile matters, also technical mercantile training; library: 8,000 vols, 27 journal titles on finance, IT, management, marketing, personnel and sales; 15 full-time teachers; 250 full-time students; Dir BO NÓRRESLET; Librarian CHRISTIAN KIRKEGAARD.

Peqqissaanermik Ilinniarfik (Centre for Health Studies): Centre for Sundhedsuddannelser, POB 1499, 3900 Nuuk; tel. (299) 349950; fax (299) 323985; e-mail cfspost@ nanoq.gl; internet www.pi.gl; f. 1993; attached to Min. of Education, Research and Nordic Cooperation; nurse training, health care and health education; 40 students; Superintendent LISA EZEKIASSEN; Librarian HANNE KRISTOFFERSEN.

DJIBOUTI

The Higher Education System

Higher education in Djibouti is modelled after the French system. The sole university in Djibouti, the Université de Djibouti, was founded in 2006 to replace the Pôle Universitaire de Djibouti, which was founded in 2000 and had 1,928 students in 2005/06. Higher education is the responsibility of the Ministry of National Education and Professional Training.

The University offers undergraduate and postgraduate courses, and admission is on the basis of secondary school qualifications, including the Baccalauréat de l'Enseignement Secondaire, the Baccalauréat Technologique or the Baccalauréat Professionnel. Higher education degrees are divided into three cycles: the Diplôme d'Études Universitaires Générales (DEUG) or Diplôme Universitaire de Technologie (DUT) is awarded after two years; the Licence requires one further year of study and the Maîtrise two; and finally the Diplôme Universitaire d'Études Approfondies (DEA) is awarded after a further two years of study.

Regulatory Bodies

GOVERNMENT

Ministry of Communication and Culture: BP 32, 1 rue de Moscou, Djibouti; tel. 355672; fax 353957; e-mail mccpt@intnet.dj; internet www.mccpt.dj; Minister ABDI HUSSAIN AHMED.

Ministry of National Education and Professional Training: BP 16, Cité Ministérielle, Djibouti; tel. 350997; fax 354234; e-mail education.gov@intnet.dj; internet www.education.gov.dj; Minister Dr ADAWA HASSAN ALI.

Learned Society

LANGUAGE AND LITERATURE

Alliance Française: BP 56, Djibouti; tel. 353091; fax 355957; e-mail alliance-francaise@intnet.dj; offers courses and examinations in French language and culture and promotes cultural exchange with France.

Research Institute

GENERAL

Institut Supérieur d'Études et de Recherches Scientifiques et Techniques (ISERT): BP 486, Djibouti; tel. 352795; fax 354812; Dir NABIL MOHAMED.

Library

Djibouti

Assemblée Nationale, Service de la Bibliothèque: BP 138, Djibouti; tel. 350172; fax 355503; f. 1977; 2,000 vols; Librarian ILTIREH DJAMA GUIREH.

University

UNIVERSITÉ DE DJIBOUTI

Ave Georges Clemenceau, BP 1904, Djibouti

Telephone: 250459

Fax: 250474

E-mail: ud@univ.edu.dj

Internet: www.univ.edu.dj

Founded 2000 as Pôle Universitaire de Djibouti, present name adopted 2006

Rector: AIDID ADEN GUEDI

Sec.-Gen.: PHILIPPE RIBIERE

Librarian: SAFIA ALI SAID

Number of teachers: 96

Number of students: 1,749

DIRECTORS

Faculty of Languages, Literature and Human Sciences: ABDOULMALIK IBRAHIM ZEID

Faculty of Law, Economics, Management and Tertiary Technological Procedures: Mag. TEEREY IBRAHIM

Faculty of Sciences and Industrial Technological Procedures: IBRAHIM SOULEIMAN GUILLEM

DOMINICA

The Higher Education System

Higher education is provided by a centre of the University of the West Indies, and the Ross University School of Medicine in Dominica (affiliated to the Ross University School of Medicine, NJ, in the USA). There is also a teacher-training college and nursing school. In 1995/96 there were 461 students in higher education.

Admission to higher education is based on the Caribbean Examinations Council Secondary Education Certificate or GCE A-levels and O-levels. Students may also be required to sit an entrance examination. The University of the West Indies offers undergraduate Bachelors and postgraduate Masters degrees.

Regulatory Body

GOVERNMENT

Ministry of Education and Human Resource Development: Kennedy Ave, Roseau; tel. 4482401; fax 4480644; e-mail minedu@cwdom.dm; Minister PETER SAINT JEAN.

Learned Society

LANGUAGE AND LITERATURE

Alliance Française: Elmshall Rd, Bath Estate Bridge, POB 251, Roseau; tel. 4484557; fax 4486008; offers courses and examinations in French language and culture and promotes cultural exchange with France.

Library

Roseau

Library of the House of Assembly: Victoria St, Roseau; tel. 4482401; fax 4498353; f. 1968; 300 vols of parliamentary reports, Proceedings of the House, speeches, ministerial statements, debates, legislation.

Museum

Roseau

Dominica Museum: Bay Front, Roseau; tel. 4488923; exhibits on Dominica's geology, history, archaeology, economy and culture, including its pre-Columbian population and the slave trade.

University

ROSS UNIVERSITY SCHOOL OF MEDICINE IN DOMINICA

POB 266, Portsmouth
Telephone: 4455355
Fax: 4455383
New York office: 460 West 34th St, 12th Floor, New York, NY 10001, USA
Telephone: (212) 279-5500 (New York)
Fax: (212) 629-3147 (New York)
Internet: www.rossmed.edu.dm; attached to Ross University School of Medicine, NJ (USA)
Library of 5,000 books, 190 current journals, 100 audiovisual items, 30 multimedia programmes.

College

University of the West Indies, Dominica Centre: Univ. Centre, POB 82, Roseau; tel. 4483182; fax 4488706; e-mail uwi@cwdom.dm; internet www.cavehill.uwi.edu/bnccde/dominica.

DOMINICAN REPUBLIC

The Higher Education System

The Universidad Autónoma de Santo Domingo, founded by Papal Bull in 1538, claims to be the oldest university in the Americas. Other universities in the Republic were all founded during the 20th century. There are 16 public and private universities under the supervision of the Consejo Nacional de Educación Superior. In 2003/04 there were 293,565 students enrolled in universities. There are also 31 other institutions recognised by the Secretariat of State for Higher Education, Science and Technology. In 2007/08 there were 41,314 students enrolled in vocational studies.

The secondary school qualification (Bachillerato) is the main requirement for admission to higher education. Undergraduate students are awarded the Licenciado or professional title after four years of study, and postgraduate students receive the Maestría after one- to three-years' study following the Licenciado. In some disciplines (law, medicine, dentistry, veterinary medicine) the Doctorado degree may be awarded. Both universities and technological institutes offer technical and vocational education. Courses last for two to three years and students gain the title Técnico.

In 2010 the Government agreed a US $100m. loan with the Inter-American Development Bank for school improvements as part of its 10-year plan for education.

Regulatory and Representative Bodies

GOVERNMENT

Secretaría de Estado de Cultura (Secretariat of State for Culture): Avda George Washington, esq. Pte. Vicini Burgos, 11903 Santo Domingo; tel. 221-4141; fax 555-5555; e-mail contacto@cultura.gov.do; internet www.cultura.gov.do; Sec. of State for Culture JOSÉ RAFAEL LANTIGUA.

Secretariat of State for Education: Secretaría de Estado de Educación, Avda Máximo Gómez 10, esq. Santiago No. 02, Gazcue, 10205 Santo Domingo; tel. 688-9700; fax 689-8688; e-mail libreacceso@see.gov.do; internet www.see.gov.do; Sec. JOSEFINA PIMENTEL.

Secretariat of State for Higher Education, Science and Technology: Secretaría de Estado de Educacíon Superior Ciencia y Tecnologia, Avda Máximo Gómez 31, esq. Pedro Henríquez Ureña, 11903 Santo Domingo, DN; tel. 731-1100; fax 535-4694; e-mail info@seescyt.gov.do; internet www.seescyt.gov.do; Sec. LIGIA AMADA DE MELO.

NATIONAL BODY

Asociación Dominicana de Rectores de Universidades (Dominican Association of University Presidents): Apdo 2465, Santo Domingo, DN; Calle Juan Paradas Bonilla 5, Apto 3, tercer Nivel, Ensanche Naco, 11093 Santo Domingo; tel. 683-0003; fax 565-4933; e-mail adru@verizon.net.do; internet www.adru.org; f. 1980, present status 1981; 18 mem. univs and higher education institutes; Exec. Dir Ing. JOSÉ JORGE GOICO GERMOSÉN.

Learned Societies

GENERAL

Instituto de Cultura Dominicana: Biblioteca Nacional, César Nicolás Penson, 11903 Santo Domingo; f. 1971; promotes cultural tradition of the country, encourages artistic creation and the expression of the spirit of the Dominican people; Pres. ENRIQUE APOLINAR HENRÍQUEZ; Sec. PEDRO GIL ITURBIDES.

BIBLIOGRAPHY, LIBRARY SCIENCE AND MUSEOLOGY

Asociación Dominicana de Bibliotecarios, Inc. (Librarians' Association): c/o Biblioteca Nacional, Plaza de la Cultura, César Nicolás Penson 91, 11903 Santo Domingo; tel. 688-4086; f. 1974; develops library services in the Republic; increases the standing of the profession and encourages the training of its mems; 90 mems; Pres. PRÓSPERO J. MELLA CHAVIER; Sec.-Gen. V. REGÚS; publ. *El Papiro* (4 a year).

Sociedad Dominicana de Bibliófilos: Calle Las Damas 106, 11903 Santo Domingo; internet bibliofilos.org.do; f. 1973; promotes culture and dissemination of works and productions; library of 13,951 vols; Pres. MARIANO MELLA; Sec. OCTAVIO AMIAMA; Treas. TOMÁS W. FERNÁNDEZ.

HISTORY, GEOGRAPHY AND ARCHAEOLOGY

Academia Dominicana de la Historia (Dominican Academy of History): Casa de las Academias, Calle Mercedes 204, Ciudad Colonial, 10210 Santo Domingo; tel. 689-7907; fax 221-8430; e-mail academiahis@codetel.net.do; internet www.academiahistoria.org.do; f. 1931; promotes knowledge and study of the past in gen. and esp. of the Dominican nation; 24 mems, 36 nat. corresp. mems, 210 foreign corresp. mems; Pres. Dr EMILIO CORDERO MICHEL; Admin. Man. VERONICA CASS; Exec. Sec. TESSIE BRENS; publ. *Clio* (2 a year).

LANGUAGE AND LITERATURE

Academia Dominicana de la Lengua (Dominican Academy): Casa de las Academias, Calle Mercedes 204, 11903 Santo Domingo; tel. and fax 687-9197; e-mail info@academia.org.do; internet www.academia.org.do; f. 1927; Corresp. of the Real Academia Española (Madrid); studies and encourages the devt of the culture and language of Dominican people; 24 mems, 32 corresp. mems, 9 partner mems; library of 50,000 vols; Pres. MARIANO LEBRÓN SAVIÑÓN; Dir Dr BRUNO ROSARIO CANDELIER; Sec. MANUEL GOICO CASTRO.

Alliance Française: Horacio Vicioso 103, Centro De los Heroes, 11903 Santo Domingo; tel. 532-2935; fax 535-0533; e-mail alianza.francesa@afsd.net; internet www.afsd.net; f. 1914; offers courses and examinations in French language and culture; promotes cultural exchange with France; attached offices in Higuey, Mao, Monte Cristi, San Francisco de Macoris and Santiago de los Caballeros; Hon. Pres. Pozzo Di Borgo S.E. CÉCILE; Pres. MARIO TOLENTINO DIPP; Vice-Pres. JOSEFINA PIMENTEL BOVES; Treas. SANTIAGO COLLADO CHASTEL.

MEDICINE

Asociación Médica de Santiago (Santiago Medical Association): Apdo 445, Santiago de los Caballeros; f. 1941; library of 1,500 vols; 65 mems; Pres. Dr RAFAEL FERNÁNDEZ LAZALA; Sec. Dr JOSÉ COROMINAS P.; publ. *Boletín Médico* (4 a year).

Asociación Médica Dominicana (Dominican Medical Association): Apdo 1237, 11903 Santo Domingo; f. 1941; 1,551 mems; Pres. Dr ANGEL S. CHAN AQUINO; Sec. Dr CARLOS LAMARCHE REY; publ. *Revista Médica Dominicana*.

Research Institutes

AGRICULTURE, FISHERIES AND VETERINARY SCIENCE

Instituto Azucarero Dominicano (Dominican Sugar Institute): Avda Jiménez Moya, Apdo 667, 11903 Santo Domingo; tel. 532-5571; fax 533-2402; e-mail inst.azucar2@verizon.net.do; internet www.inazucar.gov.do; f. 1965; promotes enhancement and improvement of products derived from the sugar industry; market studies; assists in promotion and removing trade barriers; domestic marketing by setting formalities; supervises policies; Exec. Dir FAUSTINO JIMENEZ.

HISTORY, GEOGRAPHY AND ARCHAEOLOGY

Instituto Cartográfico Militar de las Fuerzas Armadas (Military Cartographic Institute): Base Naval 27 de Febrero, 11903 Santo Domingo; tel. 686-2954; f. 1950; photogrammetry, cartography, geodesy, hydrography, photographic laboratory; sells all kinds of speciality maps of the country; Dir Capt. DOMINGO GÓMEZ.

Libraries and Archives

Baní

Biblioteca 'Padre Billini': Calle Baní 6, 31000 Duarte; f. 1926; 38,000 vols; Dir Lic. FERNANDO HERRERA.

Moca

Biblioteca Municipal 'Gabriel Morillo': Calle Antonio de la Maza esq. Independencia, 83000 Moca; f. 1942; 6,422 vols; Dir Lic. ADRIANO MIGUEL TEJADA.

San Pedro de Macorís

Biblioteca del Ateneo de Macorís (Library of the Athenaeum of Macorís): 21000 San Pedro de Macorís; f. 1890; 6,274 vols; Pres. Lic. JOSÉ A. CHEVALIER.

Santiago de los Caballeros

Biblioteca de la Sociedad Amantes de la Luz: España esq. Avda Central, Santiago de los Caballeros; f. 1874; public library of cultural society; 18,000 vols; Dir Lic. BERENI ESTRELLA DE INOA.

Santo Domingo

Archivo General de la Nación: Calle Modesto Diaz 2, Zona Universitaria, 10103 Santo Domingo; f. 1935, present status 2000; attached to Secretariat of State for Culture; documents dating from the founding of the Republic and others that were inherited from the colonial era; documents of public and private interest; 16,000 vols; Dir-Gen. Dr ROBERTO CASSÁ; Sub-Dir Dr LUÍS MANUEL PUCHEU; publs *Boletín AGN* (4 a year), *Proceedings of Quisqueya* (4 a year).

Cámara de Comercio y Producción de Santo Domingo, Centro de Información y Documentación Comercial (Commercial Information and Documentation Centre of the Chamber of Commerce and Production of Santo Domingo): Arzobispo Nouel 206, Zona Colonial, 10210 Santo Domingo; tel. 682-2688; fax 685-2228; e-mail ccpsd@camarasantodomingo.org.do; internet www.camarasantodomingo.org.do; f. 1848; provides specialized economic, business and trade information; focuses on topics such as trade regulations and Dominican labour, int. economics, nat. and regional trade regulations, foreign trade, economic and fiscal policy and many other related topics; 13,500 vols, incl. books, journals, video cassettes and CD-ROMs; Technician FRANCISCO A. DE LA ROSA; publs *Boletín Digital Camar@cción* (via email), *Camar@cción* (irregular).

Centro Nacional de Conservación de Documentos, Secretaría de Estado de Cultura (Library and Documentation Section): Archivo General de la Nación, Calle Modesto Díaz No.2, Zona, 10210 Universitaria, Santo Domingo; tel. 532-2508; f. 1976, present name 2000; offers services in environmental health; restoration; digital restoration; consultancy; workshops (technical training); Dir Lic. ELIDA JIMÉNEZ.

Biblioteca de la Secretaría de Estado de Relaciones Exteriores (Library of the Secretariat of State for Foreign Affairs): Estancia Ramfis, Santo Domingo; spec. collns relating to int. law; Dir Dr PRÓSPERO J. MELLA CHAVIER.

Biblioteca de la Universidad Autónoma de Santo Domingo (Library of Santo Domingo University): Ciudad Universitaria, Apdo 1355, Santo Domingo; 104,441 vols (Dominicana, historical archives, prints, maps, microfilms, etc.), 782,795 reviews (chiefly foreign, relating to the different faculties), gramophone records; Dir Dra MARTHA MARÍA DE CASTRO COTES; publ. *Boletín de Adquisiciones*.

Biblioteca República Dominicana: Dr Delgado esq. Avda Francia, Santo Domingo; tel. 686-0028; fax 688-2009; e-mail biblioteca_rd@yahoo.com; f. 1989, present bldg a chapel of the Dominican Order dating from 1729; promotes culture; collns of periodicals; also contains a students' reading room, textbooks, maps; over 30,000 vols, of which Dominican authors comprise 700; Dir JOSÉ RIJO.

Biblioteca Municipal de Santo Domingo (Municipal Library of Santo Domingo): Padre Billini 18, Santo Domingo; f. 1922; Librarian LUZ DEL CARMEN RAPOZO.

Biblioteca Nacional Pedro Henríquez Ureña: César Nicolás Penson 91, 20711 Santo Domingo; tel. 688-4086; fax 685-8941; f. 1971; collects government publs; houses Nat. Bibliography; exhibits, confs, research and documentation; 153,955 vols; Dir Lic. ROBERTO DE SOTO.

Museums and Art Galleries

Santo Domingo

Amber World Museum: Arz. Mariño 452, Esq. Restauración, Zona Colonial, 10210 Santo Domingo; tel. 682-3309; fax 688-1142; internet www.ambermuseum.com; f. 1996; historical and scientific data of the creation of amber; exhibitions and workshops; Pres. JORGE CARIDAD.

Galería Nacional de Bellas Artes (National Fine Arts Gallery): Santo Domingo; f. 1943; contains the later paintings and sculptures previously exhibited in the Museo Nacional; controlled by the Dirección Gen. de Bellas Artes (Fine Arts Ccl); Dir Dr JOSÉ DE J. ALVAREZ VALVERDE.

Museo Alcázar de Colón: la Plaza España, Zona Colonial, 10210 Santo Domingo; tel. 682-4750; historical colln of over 800 pieces of furniture, carpets, ceramics, sculptures and paintings dating from the 12th century; research and conservation; Dir VICKY JAQUEZ.

Museo Bellapart: Avda JF Kennedy esq. Dr Lembert Peguero, Edif. Honda 5to Nivel, Santo Domingo; tel. 541-7721; fax 542-5913; e-mail info@museobellapart.com; internet www.museobellapart.com; f. 1999; devoted solely to Dominican art; paintings from the 1890s; covers all styles and artistic movements of the 20th century to the present; incl. paintings, sculptures, prints and drawings; Pres. JUAN JOSE BELLAPART; Dir PAULA GOMEZ JORGE.

Museo Casa de Tostado: Calle Arzobispo Meriño, esq. Padre Billini, Ciudad Colonial, 10210 Santo Domingo; tel. and fax 689-5000; e-mail casadetostado@cultura.gov.do; f. 1973; museum of the Dominican family; preserves information of nat. and foreign history; traditions and customs since mid-19th century; exhibits major colln of decorative arts; Dir EVA CAMILO.

Museo de Arte Moderno (Museum of Modern Art): Avda Pedro Henríquez Ureña, Plaza de la Cultura 'Juan Pablo Duarte' 10204 Santo Domingo; tel. 685-2153; fax 685-8280; e-mail museo_de_arte_moderno@yahoo.com; f. 1976 as Gallery of Modern Art, present name 1992; attached to Secretaria de Estado de Cultura; state controlled; modern art of nat. and foreign artists; permanent and exchange exhibitions; organizes lectures, confs, films and children's workshops; library: art library of 2,047 vols, children's library of 2,050 vols; Dir Lic. MARÍA ELENA DITRÉN; publs *Boletín mensual de actividades* (12 a year), *Revista especializada*.

Larimar Museum: Meriño No. 452, esq. Restauración Zona Colonial, Santo Domingo; tel. 686-5700; fax 688-1142; e-mail info@larimarfactory.com; internet www.larimarmuseum.com; f. 1996; educational unit of Amabar Nacional; facts and scientific explanations about blue pectolite or larimar; Pres. JORGE CARIDAD; Pres. ARELIS DE CARIDAD.

Museo de las Atarazanas Reales: Calle Colón, No. 4, Ciudad Colonial, 10210 Santo Domingo; tel. 682-5834; conserves, exhibits and distributes underwater archaeological heritage on nat. art.

Museo de las Casas Reales (Museum of the Royal Houses): Calle Las Mercedes esq Damas, Ciudad Colonial, Apdo 2664, 10210 Santo Domingo; tel. 682-4202; fax 688-6918; e-mail museodelacasar@verizon.net.do; f. 1511, present status 1973, officially opened 1976; bldgs used to be the headquarters of the colonial government (houses both the Palace of the Governor General and the Royal Court and Accounts); exhibition of items from that period (1492–1821); arms and armour, ceramics and items from shipwrecks; library of 17,700 vols; Dir ANNA YEE; publ. *Casas Reales* (3 a year).

Museo del Hombre Dominicano (Museum of Dominican Man): Plaza de la Cultura Juan Pablo Duarte, Calle Pedro Henríquez Ureña, Santo Domingo; tel. 687-3622; fax 682-9112; e-mail info@museodelhombredominicano.org.do; internet www.museodelhombredominicano.org.do; f. 1973 as Museo Nacional; 19,000 exhibits: *Pre-Columbian* (Indian archaeological, anthropological and ethnographical exhibits; ceramics, wooden objects, idols, amulets, charms, weapons and tools, pots, osseous remains); *Colonial* (weapons and armour, parts of ships, Spanish religious objects, ceramics, bells); educational confs. and workshops; offers specialized courses in social science with emphasis on social research, archaeology and socio-cultural anthropology; library of 4,000 vols; Dir Dr CARLOS HERNÁNDEZ SOTO; publs *Boletín*, *Serie Investigaciones Antropológicas*.

Museo Faro a Colón: Avda Bulv. del Faro, Villa Duarte, 11602 Santo Domingo; tel. 591-1492; dedicated to the memory and houses the remains of Admiral Don Cristobal Colon; researches, exhibits, preserves and disseminates the history and the int. heritage related to the discovery, colonization and evangelization of the Americas.

Museo Nacional de Historia Natural (National Museum of Natural History): Calle César Nicolás Penson, Plaza de la Cultura, 10204 Santo Domingo; tel. 689-0106; fax 689-0100; e-mail c.mir@museohistorianatural.gov.do; internet www.museohistorianatural.gov.do; f. 1974; conserves, researches, exhibits and disseminates nat. natural heritage; geology, palaeontology, zoology; library of 3,000 vols, 10 periodicals; Dir CELESTE MIR; publs *Hispaniolana* (journal, irregular), *Novitates Caribaea* (irregular).

Museo Nacional de Historia y Geografía (National Museum of History and Geography): Calle Pedro Henríquez Ureña, Plaza de la Cultura Juan Pablo Duarte, Santo Domingo; tel. 686-6668; fax 686-4943; e-mail museohistoriard@yahoo.com; f. 1982; history, geographical features and phenomena of the island of Santo Domingo; Dir HECTOR LUIS MARTINEZ; publ. *Revista de Historia y Geografía*.

Oficina de Patrimonio Cultural: Las Atarazanas 2, Santo Domingo; tel. 682-4750; f. 1967; Dir Arq. MANUEL E. DEL MONTE URRACA.

Controls:

Alcázar de Colón (Columbus Palace): Plaza Spain, Ciudad Colonial, 10210 Santo Domingo; tel. 682-4750; f. museum 1957; the castle, built in 1510, was the residence of Don Diego Columbus, son of Christopher

Columbus, and Viceroy of the island; period furniture and objects, paintings, musical instruments, ceramics, and the most important colln of tapestries in the Caribbean.

Casa-Fuerte de Ponce de León (Ponce de León's Fort): San Rafael del, Yuma, Higüey; tel. 551-0118; museum; conservation, exhibition and dissemination of the life of Juan Ponce de Leon,; f. 1972; the residence of Ponce de León, who discovered Florida and Puerto Rico; authentic furniture and household items from a 16th-century house.

Fortaleza de San Felipe (St Philip's Fortress): West End Malecon, 57000 Puerto Plata; tel. 261-6043; museum; disseminates information about military life of the 18th and 19th centuries; f. 1972; 16th-century fort; archaeological objects found during restoration.

Museo de la Familia Dominicana Siglo XIX (Museum of the Dominican Family): Casa de Tostado, Calle Arzobispo Meriño, Santo Domingo; f. 1973, built in 1503; a 16th-century house displaying household items of a noble family of the 19th century.

Sala de Arte Prehispánico: Avda San Martín 279, POB 723, Santo Domingo; tel. 540-7777; fax 541-0201; e-mail saladearte@embodom.com; f. 1973; run by the García Arévalo Foundation; studies and exhibits culture of pre-Hispanic times; library of 6,000 vols on anthropology and the history of Santo Domingo and the Caribbean; Dir MANUEL ANTONIO GARCÍA ARÉVALO; publs *Caney, Salida Semestral*.

Universities

PONTIFICIA UNIVERSIDAD CATÓLICA MADRE Y MAESTRA

Autopista Duarte, Santiago de los Caballeros
Telephone: 580-1962
Fax: 581-7750
E-mail: anunez@pucmmsti.edu.do
Internet: www.pucmmsti.edu.do
Founded 1962, present bldg 1967
Private control
Academic year: August to May (2 semesters) and a session May to July

Rector: Mgr AGRIPINO NÚÑEZ COLLADO
Acad. Vice-Rector: Ing. NELSON GIL
Exec. Vice-Rector: Lic. SONIA GUZMÁN DE HERNÁNDEZ
Registrar: Lic. DULCE RODRÍGUEZ DE GRULLÓN
Librarian: Lic. ALTAGRACIA PEÑA
Number of teachers: 755
Number of students: 9,918

Publications: *Boletín de Noticias, Revista de Ciencias Jurídicas*

DEANS

Faculty of Engineering: Ing. VICTOR COLLADO
Faculty of Health Sciences: Dr RAFAEL FERNANDEZ LAZALA
Faculty of Humanities and Sciences: Lic. DAVID ALVAREZ MARTÍN

Campuses in Santo Domingo, Puerto Plata, Bonao

UNIVERSIDAD ABIERTA PARA ADULTOS

Apdo postal 1238, Avda Hispanoamérica, Urb. Thomén, Santiago de los Caballeros
Telephone: 724-0266
Fax: 724-0329
E-mail: univ.adultos@uniabierta.edu.do
Internet: www.uapa.edu.do

Founded 1991, present status 1995
Academic year: January to December

Rector: Dr ÁNGEL HERNÁNDEZ
Vice-Chancellor for Academics: RAFAEL ESPINAL
Vice-Chancellor for Finance: Dr MIRIAN ACOSTA
Vice-Rector for International Relations: MAGDALENA CRUZ
Pres.: Lic. RUBEN HERNANDEZ
Treas.: CORINA MONTERO
Sec.: FRANCISCO SANTOS

Publications: *Boletin UAPA Informa* (newsletter), *Revista Educación Superior*.

UNIVERSIDAD ADVENTISTA DOMINICANA

Au. Duarte km 74 1/2, Monsignor Nouel, Bonao, Sonador
Telephone: 525-7533
Fax: 525-4048
E-mail: info@unad.edu.do
Internet: www.unad.edu.do
Founded 1947, present bldg 1976
Private control
Faculties of administrative sciences, engineering and technology, humanities, theology.

UNIVERSIDAD APEC

Avda Máximo Gómez 72, El Vergel, Apdo 2867, Santo Domingo
Telephone: 686-0021
Fax: 685-5581
E-mail: univ.apec@codetel.net.do
Internet: www.unapec.edu.do
Founded 1965
Academic year: July to June
Pres.: Dr LUIS HEREDIA BONETTI
Rector: Lic. DENNIS R. SIMÓ
Vice-Rector for Academics: Lic. JUSTO PEDRO CASTELLANOS KHOURI
Vice-Rector for Admin.: Lic. CÉSAR REYNOSO
Vice-Rector for International Affairs: Lic. INMACULADA MADERA
Librarian: Lic. RAMÓN CEDANO
Library of 37,525 vols
Number of teachers: 658
Number of students: 9,000

Publications: *Boletín Trimestral* (4 a year), *Coloquios Jurídicos, Investigación y Ciencia*.

UNIVERSIDAD AUTÓNOMA DE SANTO DOMINGO

Ciudad Universitaria, Apdo 1355, Santo Domingo
Telephone and fax 535-8273
E-mail: info@uasd.edu.do
Internet: www.uasd.edu.do
Founded 1538 by Papal Bull of Paul III, closed 1801–15; reopened as a lay institution in 1815, reorganized in 1914, present status 1961, oldest univ. in the Americas
Academic year: January to December

Rector: Dr JULIO RAVELO ASTACIO
Vice-Rector for Academic Affairs: Lic. RAMÓN CAMACHO JIMÉNEZ
Vice-Rector for Admin. Affairs: Lic. JULIO URBÁEZ
Sec.-Gen.: MARIO SURIEL
Personnel Dir: Lic. JULIO CÉSAR RODRÍGUEZ
Number of teachers: 1,665
Number of students: 26,040

Publications: *Ciencia, Derecho y Política*

DEANS

Faculty of Agronomy and Veterinary Science: Ing. Agr. FRANK M. VALDÉZ

Faculty of Economic and Social Sciences: Dr EDILBERTO CABRAL
Faculty of Engineering and Architecture: Ing. MIGUEL ROSADO MONTES DE OCA
Faculty of Humanities: Lic. ANA DOLORES GUZMÁN DE CAMACHO
Faculty of Law and Politics: Lic. ROBERTO SANTANA
Faculty of Medicine: Dr CÉSAR MELLA MEJÍAS
Faculty of Sciences: Lic. PLÁCIDO CABRERA

UNIVERSIDAD CATÓLICA NORDESTANA

Los Arroyos, Apdo 239, San Francisco de Macorís
Telephone: 588-3505
Fax: 244-1647
E-mail: rectoria@ucne.edu
Internet: www.ucne.edu
Founded 1978
Language of instruction: Spanish
Academic year: January to December (3 semesters)

Rector: Rev. Dr RAMÓN ALFREDO DE LA CRUZ BALDERA
Chancellor: Mgr JESÚS MARÍA DE JESÚS MOYA
Vice-Rector: Dra ZAMIRA ASILIS
Vice-Rector: Dra YANY ALTAGRACIA ALMÁNZAR
Vice-Rector for Academics: ZAMIRA ASILIS ESTÉVEZ
Vice-Pres. for Projects: Dr FREDDY ARTURO MARTINEZ
Admin. Vice-Chancellor-Financial: Dr YANY ALTAGRACIA ALMANZAR
Librarian: Lic. VICTOR BELÉN
Library of 58,000 vols
Number of teachers: 210
Number of students: 4,300

Publications: *Ciencia y Humanismo* (3 a year), *Gaceta Jurídica* (3 a year), *Innovación Académica* (4 a year)

DEANS

Faculty of Architecture: Arq. MANUEL ORTEGA
Faculty of Education: Lic. LUZ ESPERANZA FRANCISCO
Faculty of Engineering: Ing. MARTIN PANTALEON
Faculty of Health Sciences: Dr JOSÉ BONILLA
Faculty of Legal Sciences: Dr MARTIN ORTEGA
Faculty of Modern Languages: Lic. EMELDA RAMOS
Faculty of Social Sciences and Economics: Lic. JUAN CASTILLO
Faculty of Tourism: Lic. CLARA DE LEÓN
School of Computing and Systems: Ing. CRISTOPHER BELLO (Dir)
School of Dentistry: DEYSEI ROMERO (Dir)
School of Medicine: Dr JOSÉ DE PEÑA AÑIL (Dir)

UNIVERSIDAD CATÓLICA SANTO DOMINGO

Calle Santo Domingo No.3, Ens. La Julia, POB 2733, Santo Domingo
Telephone: 544-2812
Fax: 472-0999
Internet: www.ucsd.edu.do
Founded 1982
Private control
Pres.: NICOLÁS DE JESÚS CARDENAL LÓPEZ RODRÍGUEZ
Sec.: Lic. ALLAN RAMOS
Deputy Sec.: Lic. LUÍS GARCÍA DUBUS
Treas.: Sr DON ANTONIO NAJRI
Vice-Treas.: Dr JUAN J. GASSÓ PEREYRA
Rector: Rev. Fr Dr P. RAMÓN ALONSO
Vicer-Rector for Academics: Licda ROSA KRANWINKEL
Vice-Rector for Admin.: Ing. ANGEL MENA

Vice-Rector for Planning: Lic. FRANCISCO CRUZ PASCUAL

Number of teachers: 250
Number of students: 5,000

DEANS

Faculty of Health Sciences: Dr JESÚS ANT. FIALLO
Faculty of Humanities and Education: Licda CARMEN MILDRED LÓPEZ
Faculty of Legal and Political Sciences: Dr MANUEL RAMÓN PEÑA CONCE
Faculty of Science and Technology: Ing. ROBERTO MOREL
Faculty of Religious Science: SOCORRO ALVÁREZ

UNIVERSIDAD CATÓLICA TECNOLÓGICA DEL CIBAO

Avda Universitaria, esq. Pedro A. Rivera, Apdo 401, La Vega

Telephone: 573-1020
Fax: 573-6194
E-mail: uteci@codetel.net.do
Internet: www.ucateci.edu.do

Founded 1983, present name 2002, present status 2006

Academic year: January to December

Rector: Rev. Dr FAUSTO RAMON MEJIA VALLEJO
Pres.: HUGO ALVAREZ VALENCIA
Vice-Pres.: JESUS RUBEN GOMEZ
Sec.: HILDA PEREZ PICHARDO
Treas.: PEDRO ANT RIVERA TORRES

DEANS

Faculty of Health Sciences: Dr JOSE N. PIMENTEL
Faculty of Humanities: JOSE RAFAEL ABREU

UNIVERSIDAD CENTRAL DEL ESTE

Avda Francisco, Alberto Caamaño Deñó, San Pedro de Macorís

Telephone: 529-3562
Fax: 529-5146
E-mail: info@uce.edu.do
Internet: www.uce.edu.do

Founded 1970
Private control

Academic year: January to December (3 semesters)

Pres. and Rector: Dr JOSÉ E. HAZIM FRAPPIER
Exec.Rector: Lic. RICHARD PEGUERO
Vice-Rector for Academics: Lic. ISMENIA JIMÉNEZ ABUD
Vice-Rector for Admin.: Lic. DOLORES MONTALVO
Sec.-Gen.: Lic. PIEDAD L. NOBOA MEJÍA
Registrar: Lic. PIEDAD L. NOBOA MEJÍA
Librarian: Lic. LIXONDER CAÑAS

Library of 150,000 vols
Number of teachers: 677
Number of students: 6,700

Publications: *Anuario Científico*, *Publicaciones Periódicas*, *UCE*

DEANS

Faculty of Administration and Systems: Lic. JESÚS STERLING
Faculty of Engineering and Natural Resources: Ing. MARÍA CRISTINA TEJADA
Faculty of Law: Dr JUANA OZUNA
Faculty of Medicine: Dr JOSÉ GUILLERMO WAZAR
Faculty of Science and Technology: Dr FERMÍN MERCEDES
Faculty of Sciences and Humanities: Lic. LEÓN ALBERTO

UNIVERSIDAD CENTRAL DOMINICANA DE ESTUDIOS PROFESIONALES

Avda Independencia, km 9, Colegio San Gabriel, Apdo Postal 1263, Santo Domingo

Telephone: 508-3279
Fax: 699-2675
E-mail: info@ucdep.edu.do
Internet: 66.98.64.31

Founded 1975
Private control

Rector: Dr DULCÍLIDO VÁSQUEZ
Vice-Rector for Admin.: Lic. XIOMARA PÉREZ
Vice-Rector for Planning and Devt: Lic. CARLOS HERNÁNDEZ
Exec. Vice-Rector: Ing. MARIO BONILLA M.
Sec.-Gen.: Lic. JUDITH J. VÁZQUEZ

DEANS

Faculty of Health Sciences: CHARLOTTE KING
Faculty of Humanities and Social Sciences: FÉLIX SÁNCHEZ
Faculty of Technology and Natural Resources: RAFAEL LEBRON

UNIVERSIDAD DE LA TERCERA EDAD

Calle Camila Henríquez Ureña, esq. Jesús Maestro, Mirador Norte, Santo Domingo

Telephone: 482-7093
Fax: 482-0109
E-mail: tercera.edad@codetel.net.do
Internet: www.ute.edu.do

Founded 1989, present status 1992
State control

Academic year: January to December (2 semesters)

Rector: Dr JOSÉ NICOLÁS ALMÁNZAR GARCÍA
Vice-Rector for Academics: Lic. ALTAGRACIA NÚÑEZ
Vice-Rector for Admin. and Devt: Dra FANNY POLANCO JORGE

SUBJECT COORDINATORS

Design: Lic. ALICIA ARBAJE
Economics and Administration: Lic. RAFAEL OVIEDO JIMÉNEZ
Education: Lic. CARMEN PEÑA
Law: Lic. RHINA DE LOS SANTOS
Psychology: Lic. GERMANIA MORALES
Public Relations and Social Communication: Lic. RAFAEL PARADELL DÍAZ

UNIVERSIDAD DEL CARIBE

Autopista 30 de Mayo km 7½, POB 67-2, Santo Domingo

Telephone: 616-1616
Fax: 535-0489
E-mail: univ.delcaribe@codetel.net.do
Internet: www.unicaribe.edu.do

Founded 1995

Rector: MIGUEL ROSADO
Vice-Rector for Admin.: ARTURO MENDÉZ.

UNIVERSIDAD DOMINICANA O&M

Apdo postal 509, Avda Independencia 200, Santo Domingo

Telephone: 533-7733
Fax: 535-0084
E-mail: info@udoym.edu.do
Internet: www.udoym.edu.do

Founded 1966
Academic year: January to December

Faculties of continuing education, economics and administration, engineering and technology, humanities and social science, and law; campuses in La Romana, Moca, Puerto Plata, San José de Ocoa, and Santiago

Rector: Dr JOSÉ RAFAEL ABINADER

Number of students: 28,000

UNIVERSIDAD EUGENIO MARÍA DE HOSTOS

Apdo Postal 2694, Santo Domingo

Telephone: 532-2495
Fax: 535-4636
Internet: www.uniremhos.edu.do

Founded 1981
Private control

Rector: Lic. CARMEN MARÍA CASTILLO SILVA
Vice-Rector for Academics: Lic. CARMEN ROSA MARTÍNEZ V.
Vice-Rector for Admin.: Rev. RAFAEL MARCIAL SILVA
Gen. Admin.: Dr JORGE DÍAZ VARGAS

DIRECTORS

Faculty of Health Sciences: Dr JOSÉ RODRÍGUEZ SOLDEVILLA
School of Computer Studies: Lic. SANDY SANTOS
School of Law: Lic. CECILIO GÓMEZ PÉREZ
School of Marketing Studies: Lic. PEDRO MELO
School of Medicine: Dr RAÚL ALVAREZ STURLA
School of Nursing: Lic. AMANDA PEÑA DE SANTANA
School of Oral Medicine: Dr CÉSAR LINARES IMBERT
School of Public Health: Dr MANUEL TEJADA BEATO
School of Veterinary Medicine: Dr TULIO S. CASTAÑOS VÉLEZ
Campus in Ozama: Lic. GUILLERMO DÍAZ
Campus in San Cristóbal: Lic. EMILIANO DE LA ROSA

UNIVERSIDAD EXPERIMENTAL 'FELIX ADAM'

Calle Plaza de la Cultura 151, El Millón, Santo Domingo

Telephone: 683-3121
Fax: 683-3425
E-mail: universidadunefa@unefa.edu.do
Internet: www.unefa.edu.do

Founded 1996

Chair.: Dr ANDRÉS MATOS SENA
Rector: Dr BRITO JOSE RAMON HOLGUIN

Number of teachers: 36

UNIVERSIDAD FEDERICO HENRÍQUEZ Y CARVAJAL

Isabel Aguiar No. 100 casi esq. Guarocuya, Herrera, Santo Domingo Oeste

Telephone: 531-1000
Fax: 539-8168
E-mail: info@ufhec.edu.do
Internet: www.ufhec.edu.do

Depts of dentistry, nursing, sciences and humanities.

UNIVERSIDAD IBEROAMERICANA

Apdo Postal 22-333, Avda Francia 129, Gazcue, 10205 Santo Domingo

Telephone: 689-4111
Fax: 687-9384
E-mail: unibe@codetel.net.do
Internet: www.unibe.edu.do

Founded 1982
Academic year: September to August

Rector: Dr JULIO AMADO CASTAÑOS
Academic Dean: NEY ARIAS SCHEKER

Library of 20,000 vols

Publications: *Aretha* (journal of social sciences and economics), *Baka*, *Informa UNIBE*, *Revista UNIBE de Ciencia y Cultura* (3 a year), *Scientia* (science magazine)

DEANS

Faculty of Health Sciences: Dr JULIO CASTA-
ÑOS

Faculty of Law and Politics: Dr GUILLERMO
MORENO

DIRECTORS

Faculty of Economics and Social Sciences:

School of Business Administration: Lic.
MIGUELINA FRANCO
School of Hotel Management and Tourism:
Lic. PILAR CONSTANZO
School of Marketing: Lic. ZAYENKA MAR-
TÍNEZ ROA

Faculty of Health Sciences:

School of Dentistry: Dr JACQUELINE RODRI-
GUEZ RAMIREZ

Faculty of Human Sciences:

School of Advertising and Communication:
Lic. RAFAEL RINCÓN M.
School of Architecture: Arq. VENCIAN BEN
School of Design: SANDRA GÓMEZ
School of Education: LAURA SARTORI
School of Psychology: Lic. FRANCESCA HER-
NÁNDEZ

UNIVERSIDAD INTERAMERICANA

Apdo postal 20687, C/Dr Baez 2 y 4, Gazcue,
10205 Santo Domingo

Telephone: 685-6562

Fax: 689-8581

E-mail: unica@codetel.net.do

Internet: www.unica.edu.do

Founded 1977

Private control

Rector: Lic. GABRIEL READ

Pres.: Dr ZORAIDA HALL VDA. SUNCAR

Vice-Chancellor for Academics: PARMENIO
RAUL DIAZ

Vice-Chancellor of Planning and Devt:
MIGUEL CIPRIAN

Dean of Faculty and Students: NESTOR
MELENCIANO

DEANS

Faculty of Science and Technology: MAX
MENDEZ

Faculty of Social Sciences and Humanities:
MARY FRANCES CARABALLO

DIRECTORS

Experimental College: Licda JUAN CACERES

School of Accountancy and Business Administration: HENRY JEROME

School of Advertising: FEDERICO SANCHEZ

School of Dental Technology: Dr WALTER
SUERO MENDEZ

School of Education: Licda ALTAGRACIA CAB-
RERA

School of Informatics: NARCISO RAMIREZ

School of Law: RODOLFO JIMENEZ

(School of Marketing): RODOLFO JIMENEZ

School of Social Communication and Public
Relations: ADRIANO DE LA CRUZ

UNIVERSIDAD NACIONAL
EVANGÉLICA

San Carlos, Calle Libertador No. 18, esq.
Emilio Prud'Homme, Santo Dominigo

Telephone: 221-6786

Fax: 686-1001

E-mail: rectoria@unev.edu.do

Internet: www.unev-rd.edu.do

Founded 1986

Private control

Pres: Dr PETER GOMEZ

Vice-Pres: Rev. JUAN CARLOS INFANTE, Dr
ANA INES POLANCO

Sec.: PABLO VENTURA

Treas.: HOMER BERG

Rector: Lic. SALUSTIANO BOLIVAR MOJICA RIJO

Vice-Rector for Academics: Lic. FÉLIX MIGUEL
URENA

Vice-Rector for Admin.: Ing. EPIFANIO GONZA-
LEZ MINAYA

DEANS

Faculty of Health Sciences: Dr WILFREDO
MANON ROSSI

Faculty of Humanities: SANTOS GUZMAN

Faculty of Rural Development: Dr CESAR
LOPEZ

UNIVERSIDAD NACIONAL 'PEDRO
HENRÍQUEZ UREÑA'

Avda John F. Kennedy km 6 ½, Santo
Domingo

Telephone: 562-6601

Fax: 540-0425

E-mail: info@unphu.edu.do

Internet: www.unphu.edu.do

Founded 1966, present status 1967

Private control

Languages of instruction: Spanish, English

Academic year: September to August (3
semesters)

Rector: Arq. MICHAEL R FIALLOS

Vice-Rector for Academic Affairs: Lic.
DANIELA FRANCO DE GUZMÁN

Vice-Rector for Admin. Affairs: Lic. JOSE
RAFAEL ESPAILLAT

Vice-Rector for Devt Affairs: Ing. VICTOR
BERAS

Registrar: Dra SARI DUVERGÉ MEJÍA

Librarian: Dra CARMEN IRIS OLIVO

Library of 80,000 vols

Number of teachers: 759

Number of students: 8,000

Publications: *Aula, Biblionotas, Cuadernos
de Filosofía, Cuadernos Jurídicos*

DEANS

Faculty of Agronomy and Veterinary Science:
Dr MIGUEL GONZALEZ

Faculty of Architecture and Arts: Arq. DIANA
LAPAIX

Faculty of Economics and Social Sciences:
Lic. LUIS MARTINEZ SILFA

Faculty of Engineering and Technology: Ing.
CARLOS TRONCOSO

Faculty of Health Science: Dr CARLOS MON-
TERO

Faculty of Humanities: Lic. DIANA FRANCO DE
GUZMAN

Faculty of Law and Politics: Dr MANUEL
BERGÉS CHUPANI

Faculty of Postgraduate Studies: Dr VICTOR
BERAS

Faculty of Science: Ing. CARLOS TRONCOSO

UNIVERSIDAD NACIONAL
TECNOLÓGICA

Calle Dr Delgado 103, Gazcue, 10205

Telephone: 731-3200

Fax: 221-7907

E-mail: info@unnatec.edu.do

Internet: www.insutec.edu.do

Founded 2003

Private control

Academic year: January to December (3
trimesters)

Pres.: CIELO REYNOSO DE REYES

Dir of Business Admin.: MAESTRA YSAMNA M.
MONTERO T.

UNIVERSIDAD ODONTOLÓGICA
DOMINICANA

Avda 27 de Febrero esq. Calle ira. Las
Caobas, 10905 Santo Domingo

Telephone: 338-7461

Fax: 560-7524

Internet: www.uod.edu.do

Founded 1983

Rector: DESCHAMPS VILMA BAEZ.

UNIVERSIDAD PSICOLOGÍA
INDUSTRIAL DOMINICANA

Calle 1era. No. 27 Urb. KG km 6½, Carretera
Sánchez, Linea

Telephone: 533-7141

Fax: 274-7827

E-mail: psicologiadom@codetel.net.do

Internet: www.upid.edu.do

Founded 1976 as Industrial Psychology
Dominicana, present status 2001

Private control

Rector: Lic. MILDRED DÍAZ ÁLVAREZ

Vice-Rector for Academics: Lic. MILDRED DÍAZ
ÁLVAREZ

Vice-Rector for Admin.: Lic. SORAIMA E.
REYES GÓMEZ.

UNIVERSIDAD TECNOLÓGICA DE
SANTIAGO (UTESA)

Avda Estrella Sadhalá, esq. Av. Circunvalación, Apdo 685, Santiago de los Caballeros

Telephone: 582-7156

Fax: 582-7644

E-mail: utesa@codetel.net.do

Internet: www.utesa.edu

Founded 1974

Private control

Academic year: January to December

Faculties of architecture and engineering,
health sciences, sciences and humanities,
secretarial sciences, social and economic sciences

Rector: Dr PRIAMO RODRÍGUEZ CASTILLO

Asst Rector: JOSELINA TAVAREZ

Vice-Rector for Academics: Mag. ARNALDO
PEÑA VENTURA

Vice-Rector for Admin.: MARÍA ESTHER U.

Vice-Rector for Campus Premises: Mag.
RAMÓN ANÍBAL CASTRO

Sec.-Gen.: Mag. JOSEFINA CRUZ

Registrar: Lic. ANDRÉS VIVAS

Librarian: Mag. ILUMINADA DE LA HOZ

Library of 157,976 vols

Number of teachers: 1,027

Number of students: 35,742

Publications: *Ciencias y Tecnología, Revista
Universitas.*

UNIVERSIDAD TECNOLÓGICA DEL
SUR

Avda Enriquillo 1, Mejoramiento Social,
Azua de Compostela

Telephone: 521-3785

Fax: 521-4164

E-mail: info@utesur.edu.do

Internet: www.utesur.edu.do

Founded 1978

Rector: ALTAGRACIA MILAGROS GARRIDO DE
SÁNCHEZ

Pres.: JUAN VALERIO SÁNCHEZ.

Colleges

Barna Business School: Avda John F.
Kennedy 34, Ens. Naco; tel. 683-4461; fax
683-4873; e-mail barna@barna.edu.do;
internet www.barna.edu.do; offers programmes in credit risk management, executive development, financial management,
general management, marketing management; MBA and MBA intensive.

**Centros APEC de Educación a Distan-
cia:** Avda San Martin No. 147, Villa Juana,
10412 Santo Domingo; tel. 472-1155; fax 472-

1189; e-mail cenapec@cenapec.edu.do; internet www.cenapec.edu.do; f. 1972; offers low-cost educational programmes by means of distance education system; 525 teachers; 31,800 students; Pres. LUIS TAVERAS AZAR; Exec. Dir JUAN MIGUEL PEREZ; Admin. Dir Lic BELKIS SANTANA; Academic Dir ANA BELKIS AVILA; Treas. JAIME R. FERNANDEZ; Sec. SONIA VILLANUEVA DE BROUWER.

El Domínico–Americano: Avda Abraham Lincoln 21, Santo Domingo; tel. 535-0665; fax 533-8809; internet www.icda.edu.do; f. 1947; promotes English as a foreign language; broadening relationships between the Dominican Republic and the USA; conducts exchange programmes; library: 13,300 vols; Dir Lic. ELIZABETH DE WINDT; Gen. Academic Dir Lic. THELMA CAMARENA; Pres. ENGRACIA FRANJUL DE ABATE; Sec. ELLEN DUCY DE PÉREZ; Treas. ERNESTO L. BETANCOURT.

Instituto Politécnico Loyola: Calle Padre Angel Arias 1, 91000 San Cristóbal; tel. 528-4010; fax 528-9229; internet www.ipl.edu.do; f. 1966; offers industrial engineering, network and telecommunications engineering, professional devt and training; library: 20,000 vols; Rector P. FRANCISCO ESCOLÁSTICO H.; Vice-Rector for Academics Lic. MARINO BRITO GUILLÉN.

Instituto Superior de Agricultura (Higher Institute of Agriculture): Avda 166, Av. Antonio Guzmán Fdez, km 51/2, La Herradura, 51000 Santiago; tel. 247-2000; fax 247-2626; internet www.isa.edu.do; f. 1962; ind. instn but operates joint pro-gramme in agriculture with the Universidad Católica Madre y Maestra; training in agricultural sciences at high school and undergraduate level; offers courses in admin., agrarian reform, agricultural economics, agricultural engineering, animal production, aquaculture, biotechnology, epidemiology, food technology, forestry, horticulture, irrigation, veterinary medicine and animal husbandry; library: 15,000 vols; Rector BENITO FERREIRAS; Pres. ACHILLES BERMDEZ; Treas. FLIX GARCA.

Instituto Tecnológico de Santo Domingo: Avda de los Próceres, Galá, Apdo 342-9, Santo Domingo; tel. 567-9271; fax 566-3200; e-mail desarrollo@mail.intec.edu.do; internet www.intec.edu.do; f. 1972, present status 1973; depts of basic sciences and environment, business, engineering, health, social sciences and humanities; library: 44,000 books, 1,400 periodicals; 2,300 students; Rector Dr MICHAEL J. SCALE; Acad. Vice-Rector Lic. ALTAGRACIA LÓPEZ; Man. EMIL PELLETIER; Librarian Lic. LUCERO ARBO-LEDA DE ROA; publs *Ciencia y Sociedad* (4 a year), *Documentos Intec* (1 a year), *Índice de Publicaciones de Universidades* (1 a year).

Instituto Tecnológico del Cibao Oriental: Avda Universitaria 100, Sanchez Ramirez, Cotuí; tel. 585-2291; fax 240-0603; e-mail iteco@verizon.net.do; internet www.iteco.edu.do; f. 1982, present status 1983; courses in agricultural engineering, bioanalysis, business, law, civil engineering, education, geology and mines; Rector Lic. ESCLARECIDA NÚÑEZ DE ALMONTE; Pres. Lic. JULIO TEJEDA; Vice-Pres. Dr LUIS GARCÍA SANTOS; Sec. Dr MANUEL DE JESÚS BRITO O.

Schools of Art and Music

Dirección General de Bellas Artes (Fine Arts Council): Máximo Gómez esq. Avda Independencia, Santo Domingo; tel. 687-0504; fax 687-2707; e-mail dgba.do@hotmail.com; internet www.bellasartes.gov.do; f. 1940; Dir-Gen. FRANKLIN DOMINGUEZ.

Controls:

Academias de Música (Academies of Music): Villa Consuelo and Villa Francisca, Santo Domingo; also 19 provincial towns.

Conservatorio Nacional de Música (National Conservatoire of Music): Santo Domingo.

Escuela de Arte Escénico (School of Scenic Art): Santo Domingo.

Escuela de Artes Plásticas (School of Plastic Arts): Santiago.

Escuela de Bellas Artes (School of Fine Arts): San Francisco de Macorís.

Escuela de Bellas Artes (School of Fine Arts): San Juan de la Maguana.

Escuela Nacional de Bellas Artes (National School of Fine Arts): Santo Domingo.

ECUADOR

The Higher Education System

The Universidad Central del Ecuador, founded in 1586 as Universidad de San Fulgencio, is among the oldest universities in the Americas. Several universities were established in the 1860s, but most were founded during the 20th century. In 1990/91 there were 206,500 students in higher education. Higher education is administered by the Consejo Nacional de Educación Superior (National Council for Higher Education), and is governed by the Ley de Educación Superior (number 16 RO/77 of 15 May 2000).

Admission to higher education is on the basis of the Bachillerato, the main secondary school qualification; some universities also set entrance examinations. The main undergraduate degree is the Licenciado, which requires four years of study. (A professional title can also be awarded.) Following the Licenciado, the Masterado/Magister is a postgraduate degree that is awarded after two years of study. Finally, the Doctorado requires two to three years of study following the Licenciado. Not all institutions offer doctorate programmes. The Tecnólogo is the main qualification for technical and vocational education and is awarded after three-year 'short-cycle' courses.

Regulatory and Representative Bodies

GOVERNMENT

Ministry of Culture: Quito; Min. ANTONIO PRECIADO BEDOYA.

Ministry of Education: San Salvador E 6–49 y Eloy Alfaro, Quito; tel. (2) 255-5014; e-mail info@mec.gov.ec; internet www.mec.gov.ec; Min. RAÚL VALLEJO CORRAL.

ACCREDITATION

Consejo Nacional de Educación Superior (CONESUP): Whymper E7–37 y Alpallana, Quito; tel. (2) 222-1147; fax (2) 222-9576; e-mail gvega@conesup.edu.ec; internet www.conesup.net; f. 1982; responsible for coordination, regulation of univs, technological institutes and academic programmes; Pres. Dr GUSTAVO VEGA; Exec. Dir Ing. TONNY GONZÁLEZ; publs *Boletín Bimensual* (6 a year), *Investigación Universitaria* (2 a year), *Planinformativo*.

Learned Societies

GENERAL

Casa de la Cultura Ecuatoriana 'Benjamín Carrión': Apdo 67, Avda 6 de Diciembre 794, Quito; tel. 223-391; fax 223-391; f. 1944; covers all aspects of Ecuadorian culture; attached museums: see Museums and Art Galleries; library: see Libraries and Archives; 673 mems; Pres. Dr STALIN ALVEAR; Sec.-Gen. Dr MARCO PLACENCIA; publs *Letras de Ecuador* (2 a year), *Línea Imaginaria* (1 a year).

UNESCO Office Quito and Regional Bureau for Communication and Information: Juan León Mera y Avda Patria, Edificio CFN 6to piso, Quito; tel. (2) 252-9085; fax (2) 250-4435; e-mail lospina@unesco.org.ec; designated Cluster Office for Bolivia, Colombia, Ecuador, Peru and Venezuela; Dir GUSTAVO LÓPEZ OSPINA.

LANGUAGE AND LITERATURE

Academia Ecuatoriana de la Lengua (Academy of Ecuador): Apdo 17-07-9699, Quito; tel. (2) 543-234; fax (2) 901-518; f. 1875; 20 mems; Corresp. of the Real Academia Española (Madrid); library of 3,000 vols; Dir CARLOS JOAQUÍN CÓRDOVA; Sec. Emb. FILOTEO SAMANIÉGO; publs *Memorias* (1 a year), *Horizonte Cultural* (12 a year).

Alliance Française: Eloy Alfaro 32–468, Casilla 17-11-6275, Quito; tel. (2) 245-2017; fax (2) 244-2293; internet www.afquito.org.ec; offers courses and examinations in French language and culture and promotes cultural exchange with France; attached teaching offices in Cuenca, Guayaquil, Loja and Portoviejo; Dir MARCEL TAILLEFER.

MEDICINE

Academia Ecuatoriana de Medicina (Ecuadorian Academy of Medicine): Abel Gilbert N34-13 y Antonio Flores Jijon, Bellavista, Quito; tel. (2) 244-7356; fax (2) 246-5557; e-mail jmalvear@uio.satnet.net; internet www.sg61.org/profjma.htm; f. 1958; 120 mems; Pres. Prof. Dr JOSÉ MIGUEL ALVEAR.

Federación Médica Ecuatoriana (Medical Federation of Ecuador): Avda Naciones Unidas E2-17 e Iñaquito, Quito; tel. (2) 245-6812; fax (2) 245-2660; f. 1942; 1,435 mems; Pres. Dr EDUARDO CAMACHO; Gen. Sec. Dr JENNY AGUIRRE H.

Sociedad Ecuatoriana de Pediatría (Paediatrics Society of Ecuador): Av. Naciones Unidas E2-17 e Iñaquito, Quito; tel. (2) 226-2881; e-mail secretaria@pediatria.org.ec; f. 1945; scientific extension courses and lectures; Pres. Dr PATRÍCIO PROCEL; Sec. Dr MÓNICA CEVALLOS NOROÑA; publ. *Revista Ecuatoriana de Pediatría*.

Research Institutes

GENERAL

Institut de Recherche pour le Développement (IRD): Apdo 17-12-857, Quito; Whymper 442 y Coruña, Quito; tel. (2) 250-4856; fax (2) 250-4020; internet www.arqueo-ecuatoriana.ec; f. 1974; geology, pedology, hydrology, botany and vegetal biology, agronomy, geography, human sciences, economics; library of 550 vols, 400 periodicals, 80 extracts; Dir FRANCISCO VALDEZ; (see main entry under France).

AGRICULTURE, FISHERIES AND VETERINARY SCIENCE

Instituto Nacional Autónomo de Investigaciones Agropecuarias (Autonomous National Institute of Agricultural Research): Apartado Postal 17-17-1362, Quito; Avda Amazonas y Eloy Alfaro 30–350, Edif. MAG (4° piso), Quito; tel. (2) 252-8650; fax (2) 240-4240; e-mail iniap@iniap-ecuador.gov.ec; internet www.iniap-ecuador.gov.ec; f. 1959;

Gen. Dir JULIO CÉSAR DELGADO ARCE; publ. *Revista* (4 a year).

Instituto Nacional de Pesca (National Fishery Institute): Letamendi 102 y La Ría, Guayaquil; tel. (4) 401-773; fax (4) 401-776; internet www.inp.gov.ec; f. 1960; fishing research and devt; library of 20,000 vols; Gen. Dir Ing. YAHIRA PIEDRAHITA-FALQUEZ; publs *Boletín Científico y Técnico*, *Boletín Informativo*, *Revista Científica de Ciencias Marinas y Limnología*.

ECONOMICS, LAW AND POLITICS

Instituto Latinoamericano de Investigaciones Sociales (ILDIS) (Latin American Social Sciences Research Institute): Casilla 17-03-367, Quito; Avda República 500 y Diego de Almagro, Edif. Pucará, 4to. Piso, Of. 404, Quito; tel. (2) 256-2103; fax (2) 250-4337; e-mail ildis@fes.ec; internet www.fes.ec/public/ildis.do; f. 1974; affiliated to the Friedrich-Ebert Foundation; research in economics, sociology, political science and education; library of 15,000 vols; Dir Dr REINHART WETTMANN.

Instituto Nacional de Estadística y Censos (National Statistics and Census Institute): Juan Larrea N15-36 y José Riofrío, Quito; tel. (2) 255-6124; fax (2) 250-9836; e-mail inec1@ecnet.ec; internet www.inec.gov.ec; f. 1976; library of 6,500 vols; Dir-Gen. Ing. VÍCTOR MANUEL ESCOBAR BENAVIDES; publs *Indice de Precios al Consumidor Urbano* (12 a year), *Indice de Precios de Materiales, Equipo y Maquinaria de la Construcción* (12 a year), *Indice de Precios al Productor* (12 a year).

HISTORY, GEOGRAPHY AND ARCHAEOLOGY

Instituto Geográfico Militar (Military Geographical Institute): Senierges y Gral Paz y Miño, Sector El Dorado, Pichincha, Quito; tel. (2) 397-5100; fax (2) 397-5194; e-mail igm1@igm.mil.ec; internet www.igm.gov.ec; f. 1928; part of Min. of Defence; main activity is preparation of national map series; undertakes projects for public and private organizations; provides cartographic and geographic documentation for national development and security; formulates disaster and land information systems; library of 10,500 vols; Dir Col IVAN F. ACOSTA A.; publs *Indices Toponímicos*, *Revista Geográfica* (2 a year).

MEDICINE

Instituto Nacional de Higiene y Medicina Tropical 'Leopoldo Izquieta Pérez' (National Institute of Hygiene): Julian Coronel 905 y Esmeraldas, Guayaquil; tel. (4) 281-542; fax (4) 394-189; f. 1941; 120 depts and sections; library of 5,600 vols; Dir Dr FRANCISCO HERNÁNDEZ MANRÍQUEZ; publ. *Revista Ecuatoriana de Higiene y Medicina Tropical*.

NATURAL SCIENCES
General

Instituto Oceanográfico de la Armada (Naval Oceanographic Institute): Avda 25 de Julio, Apdo 5940, Guayaquil; tel. (4) 248-4723; fax (4) 248-5166; e-mail inocar@inocar .mil.ec; internet www.inocar.mil.ec; f. 1972 to study oceanography and hydrography; library of 2,500 vols; Dir BYRON SANMIGUEL MARÍN (acting); publ. *Acta Oceanográfica del Pacífico* (1 a year).

Biological Sciences

Charles Darwin Research Station: Casilla 17-01-3891, Quito; Puerto Ayora, Isla Santa Cruz, Galapagos; tel. (5) 252-6147; fax (5) 252-6146; e-mail cdrs@ fcdarwin.org.ec; internet www .darwinfoundation.org; f. 1964 under the auspices of the Ecuadorian Government, UNESCO and the Charles Darwin Foundation; maintains meteorological stations, a herbarium, a zoological museum and a marine laboratory; breeding programme for endangered reptiles; studies and preserves the flora and fauna of the archipelago; library of 4,000 vols, 12,000 separates, 105 current periodicals, slides, aerial photographs, maps; Dir Dr J. GABRIEL LÓPEZ; publ. *Noticias de Galápagos* (2 a year).

Physical Sciences

Instituto Nacional de Meteorología e Hidrología (Hydrometeorological Office): Iñaquito 36–14 y Corea, Quito; tel. (2) 397-1100; fax (2) 224-1874; e-mail cpaez@inamhi .gov.ec; internet www.inamhi.gov.ec; f. 1961; library of 6,500 vols; Exec. Dir Ing. CARLOS PÁEZ PÉREZ; publs *Anuario Hidrológico*, *Anuario Meteorológico*, *Boletín Climatológico* (12 a year).

Observatorio Astronómico de Quito (Quito Astronomical Observatory): Apdo 17-01-165, Quito; Avda Gran Colombia s/n, Interior del parque 'La Alameda', Quito; tel. (2) 2570765; fax (2) 2583451; e-mail observaquito@gmail.com; internet oaq.epn .edu.ec; f. 1873; astronomy, astrophysics, seismology, meteorology and archaeoastronomy; library of 5,000 vols; Dir Dr ERICSON LÓPEZ IZURIETA; publs *Boletín Astronómico* (Series A, B), *Boletín Meteorológico*.

RELIGION, SOCIOLOGY AND ANTHROPOLOGY

Instituto Ecuatoriano de Antropología y Geografía (Ecuadorian Institute of Anthropology and Geography): Apdo 17-01-2258, Quito; Avda Orellana 557 y Coruña, Quito; tel. (2) 506-324; fax (2) 509-436; f. 1950; research in anthropology, folklore, history, social psychology and nat. questions; library of 5,000 vols; Dir Lic. RODRIGO GRANIZO R.; publ. *Llacta* (review, 2 a year).

TECHNOLOGY

Comisión Ecuatoriana de Energía Atómica (Atomic Energy Commission of Ecuador): Juan Larrea N15-36 y Riofrío, Quito; tel. (2) 222-5166; fax (2) 256-3336; e-mail comecen1@comecenat.gov.ec; f. 1958; 40 mems; research in nuclear physics, radioisotopes, radiobiology, chemistry, medicine; library of 5,000 vols; Exec. Dir Dr MARCOS BRAVO SALVADOR; publ. *Noticias Trimestrales*.

Dirección General de Hidrocarburos (General Directorate of Hydrocarbons): Avda 10 de Agosto 321, Quito; f. 1969; supervises enforcement of laws relating to petroleum exploration and devt, and sets standards for mining-petroleum industry; 210 mems; Dir-Gen. GUILLERMO BIXBY; Sec. ERNESTO CORRAL; publs *Estadística Petrolera*, *Indice de Leyes y Decretos de la Industria Petrolera*, *Reporte Geológico de la Costa Ecuatoriana*.

Instituto de Ciencias Nucleares (Institute of Nuclear Science): Escuela Politécnica Nacional, Apdo 17-01-2759, Quito; tel. (2) 250-7126; fax (2) 256-7848; e-mail rmunoz@ server.epn.edu.ec; f. 1957; library with department of microcards and microfilms; equipment for application of radioisotopes to chemistry, agriculture, medicine and radiation control; cobalt-60 pilot irradiator, batch type 40-10 kilocuries, linear electron accelerator 8 MeV with conveyor; 4 departments: Department of Applied Research, Head Prof. RICARDO MUÑOZ BURGOS; Department of Biomedical Applications, Dir RODRIGO FIERRO B.; Department of Industrial Applications, Head Ing. TRAJANO RAMÍREZ; Department of Radiation Control, Dir Ing. FREDDIE ORBE M.; Dir Dr FLORINELLA MUÑOZ BISESTI; publ. *Politécnica* (4 a year).

Libraries and Archives
Cuenca

Biblioteca Panamericana (Pan-American Library): Apdo 57, Cuenca; tel. (7) 826-130; f. 1912; 64,000 vols; Dir LADY LISSETH MONAR CADENA.

Biblioteca Pública Municipal (Public Municipal Library): Apdo 202, Cuenca; f. 1927; 50,000 vols; Dir JUAN TAMA MÁRQUEZ.

Centro de Documentación Regional 'Juan Bautista Vázquez' de la Universidad de Cuenca (Juan Bautista Vázquez Regional Documentation Centre): Avda 12 de Abril y Agustín Cueva, Cuenca; f. 1882; 250,000 vols; Dir MICHURÍN AUGUSTO VÉLEZ VALAREZO.

Guayaquil

Biblioteca 'Angel Andrés García' de la Universidad 'Vicente Rocafuerte': Avenida de las Américas frente al Cuartel Modelo, Apartado Postal 1133, Guayaquil; f. 1847; 13,000 vols; Dir SONIA MORETA; publ. *Revista de la Universidad 'Vicente Rocafuerte'*.

Biblioteca de Autores Nacionales 'Carlos A. Rolando' (Library of Ecuadorian Writers): Apartado 6069, Guayaquil; 10 de Agosto entre Chile y Pedro Carbo Palacio Municipal, Guayaquil; tel. (4) 515-738; f. 1913; 12,000 vols, 15,000 pamphlets, 17,000 leaflets, 3,000 MSS relating to Ecuadorian authors and foreign works about Ecuador; Dir (vacant).

Biblioteca General, Universidad de Guayaquil: Ciudadela Universitaria Salvador Allende, Malecón del Salado entre Avda Fortunato Safadi y Avda Kennedy, Guayaquil; tel. (4) 282-440; f. 1901; 50,000 vols; Dir Lic. LEONOR VILLAO DE SANTANDER; publs *El Universitario*, *Revista*.

Biblioteca Histórica y Archivo Colonial (Historical Library and Colonial Archives): Palacio de la Municipalidad, Apdo 75, Guayaquil; f. 1930; Dir Dr CARLOS A. ROLANDO; Sec. Prof. GUSTAVO MONROY GARAICOA.

Biblioteca Municipal 'Pedro Carbo' (Public Library): Avda 10 de Agosto entre Pedro Carbo y Chile, Guayaquil; tel. (4) 524-100 ext. 2105; fax (4) 524-100 ext. 2140;

e-mail dcpc_bib@hotmail.com; f. 1862; 550,000 vols; Dir NANCY PALACIOS DE MEDINA; (see also under Museums).

Quito

Archivo-Biblioteca de la Función Legislativa: Av. 10 de Agosto y Briceño, Quito; f. 1886; scientific and cultural; 27,000 vols; Dir Lic. RAFAEL A. PIEDRA SOLÍS; publs *Clave de la Legislación Ecuatoriana*, *Diario de Debates de la Legislatura*.

Archivo Nacional de Historia (National Historical Archives): Avda Santa Prisca y Av. 10 de Agosto, Quito; f. 1938; 2,500 vols; colonial documents from the 16th to 19th century; Dir JORGE A. GARCÉS Y GARCÉS; Sec. JUAN R. FREKE-GRANIZO; publ. *Arnahis*.

Biblioteca de la Universidad Central del Ecuador (Central University Library): Avda América s/n, Ciudadela Universitaria, Hall del Teatro Universitario, Quito; tel. (2) 250-5859; e-mail bgeneral@ac.uce.edu.ec; f. 1826; 170,000 vols; Dir ALONSO ALTAMIRANO; publs *Anales*, *Anuario Bibliográfico*, *Bibliografía Ecuatoriana*.

Biblioteca del Banco Central del Ecuador: Avda 10 de Agosto N11-409 y Briceño, Casilla Postal 339, Quito; tel. 568-957; fax 568-973; f. 1938; 100,000 vols, 2,000 periodicals; specializes in economics, administration, banking and finance, social sciences; open to the public; Dir CARLOS LANDAZURI; publ. *Boletín Bibliográfico* (irregular).

Has Attached:

Hemeroteca: Calle Arenas y 10 de Agosto, Apdo 17-15-0029-C, Quito; tel. 561-521; 5,000 periodicals; Dir JULIO OLEAS.

Musicoteca: Calles García Moreno y Sucre, Apdo 339, Quito; tel. 572-784; music and video library; Dir ADRIANA ORTIZ.

Biblioteca Ecuatoriana 'Aurelio Espinosa Pólit': José Nogales y Francisco Arcos, Cotocollao, Apdo 17-01-160, Quito; tel. (2) 249-1157; fax (2) 249-3928; e-mail director@ beaep.org.ec; internet www.beaep.org.ec; f. 1928; Ecuadorian library, archive, Ecuadorian art and history museum; 300,000 vols; Librarian JULIAN G. BRAVO.

Biblioteca Municipal (Municipal Library): García Moreno 882 y Sucre, Quito; tel. (2) 222-8418; e-mail bibmuni@yahoo.com; internet www.centrocultural-quito.com/; f. 1886; 12,500 vols, 300 MSS, 4 incunabula.

Biblioteca Nacional del Ecuador (National Library): 12 de Octubre 555, Apdo 67, Quito; tel. (2) 290-2272; f. 1792; 70,000 vols of which 7,000 date from the 16th to 18th centuries; shares legal deposit with municipal libraries; Dir LAURA DE CRESPO.

Attached Library:

Biblioteca de la Casa de la Cultura Ecuatoriana (Library of Ecuadorian Culture): Apdo 67, Avda Colombia, Quito; tel. (2) 222-3391; e-mail biblioteca@cce.org.ec; f. 1944; 12,000 vols and over 20,000 periodicals; incl. the 'Laura de Crespo' Room of Nat. Authors; Dir LUCY MALDONADO.

Museums and Art Galleries
Guayaquil

Museo Antropológico del Banco Central: Avda de las Américas 1100 y Avda Juan Tanca Marengo, Guayaquil; tel. (4) 285-800; internet www.bce.fin.ec/contenido .php?cnt=arb0000393; f. 1974; archaeology of the Ecuadorian coast; gallery of contemporary Latin American art; research; library of 7,500 vols; Dir Freddy Olmedo R.; publ. *Miscelánea Antropológica Ecuatoriana*.

Museo Municipal (Municipal Museum): Calle Sucre entre Chile y Pedro Carbo, Guayaquil; tel. (4) 259-9100 ext. 7404; e-mail info@mumg.info; internet www .mumg.info; f. 1862; historical, ethnographical, palaeontological, geological exhibits; colonial period and modern paintings and numismatics (see also Libraries).

Quito

Museo Antropológico 'António Santiana': Universidad Central del Ecuador, Quito; f. 1925; sections of anthropology, archaeology, ethnography; library of 2,000 vols; Dir Dr Holguer Jara; publs *Humanitas, Boletín Ecuatoriano de Antropología* (irregular).

Museo de Arte Colonial: Cuenca St and Mejía St, Quito; tel. (2) 221-2297; f. 1914; attached to Casa de la Cultura Ecuatoriana 'Benjamín Carrión'; many examples of art from the Escuela Quiteña of the colonial epoch (17th and 18th centuries); Dir Juan Carlos Fernández-Catalán.

Museo de Artes Visuales e Instrumentos Musicales: Avda 12 de Octubre 555 y Patria, Quito; tel. (2) 222-3392; internet www .cultura.com.ec/martemoderno.htm; attached to Casa de la Cultura Ecuatoriana 'Benjamín Carrión'; art from Ecuador and Latin America since 19th century.

Museo de Ciencias Naturales de la Escuela Militar 'Eloy Alfaro': Avda Orellana y Amazonas, Quito; f. 1937; geological specimens and fauna from the Galapagos Islands; taxidermy and anatomy illustrated, espec. of mammals and birds; Taxidermist Luis Alfredo Pérez Vaca; publ. *Revista Anual del Plantel*.

Museo Jacinto Jijón y Caamaño (Jacinto Jijón y Caamaño Museum): Edificio de la Biblioteca General de la PUCE 3er piso, Avda 12 de Octubre 1076 y Roca, Quito; tel. (2) 299-1242; e-mail jmjaramillo@puce.edu.ec; internet www.puce.edu.ec/index .php?pagina=museojjc; f. 1969; archaeology, art, ethnography; library of 2,000 vols; Dir Ernesto Salazar.

Museo Municipal de Arte e Historia 'Alberto Mena Caamaño' (Civic Museum of Arts and History): Espejo 1147 y Benalcázar, Pichincha, Quito; tel. (2) 214-018; f. 1959; archaeology, colonial art, 19th-century art, items of historical interest; history archive (1583–1980), information library; Dir Alfonso Ortiz Crespo.

Museo Nacional de la Dirección Cultural del Banco Central del Ecuador: Reina Victoria y Jorge Washington (esquina), Edificio Aranjuez, Apdo 339, Quito; tel. (2) 220-547; fax (2) 568-972; e-mail jortiz@uio .bce.fin.ec; f. 1969; prehistoric archaeological exhibits; colonial and modern art (sculpture, paintings, etc.); library of 6,000 vols; Dir Juan Ortiz García.

Universities and Technical Universities

ESCUELA POLITÉCNICA DEL EJERCITO

Campus Politécnico, Avda El Progreso s/n, POB 171-5-231B, Sangolquí
Telephone: (2) 233-4950
Fax: (2) 233-4952
E-mail: espe@espe.edu.ec
Internet: www.espe.edu.ec
Founded 1922, present name 1977

State control
Academic year: March to February (2 semesters)

Rector: Brig. Gen. Rubén Navia Loor
Vice-Rector for Academic: Ing. Col Carlos Rodríguez Arrieta
Vice-Rector for Research: Ing. Lt Col José Aguiar Villagómez
Admin. Man.: Col Fernando Proaño Cadena.

ESCUELA POLITÉCNICA NACIONAL (National Polytechnic School)

Ladrón de Guevara s/n, Apdo 17-01-2759, Quito
Telephone: (2) 250-7144
Fax: (2) 223-6147
E-mail: dri@epn.edu.ec
Internet: www.epn.edu.ec

Founded 1869
Public control
Academic year: September to August

Rector: Ing. Renán Alfonso Espinosa Ramón
Vice-Rector: Ing. Adrian Peña
Sec. Atty: Abog. Xavier Ortíz
Librarian: Germania Merizalde

Number of teachers: 443
Number of students: 9,566
Publication: *Politécnica* (3 a year)

DEANS

Administrative Sciences: Ing. Giovanni D'Ambrosio
Chemical and Agroindustrial Engineering: Ing. Ernesto De la Torre
Civil and Environmental Engineering: Dr Laureano Andrade
Electrical and Electronics Engineering: Ing. Pablo Rivera
Geology and Petroleum Engineering: Ing. Johny Zambrano
Mechanical Engineering: Dr Víctor Cárdenas
Sciences: Dr Eduardo Avalos
Systems Engineering: Ing. Carlos Montenegro

ESCUELA SUPERIOR POLITÉCNICA AGROPECUARIA DE MANABÍ

10 de Agosto 82 y Granda Centeno, Calceta
Telephone: (5) 268-5134
Fax: (5) 268-5156
E-mail: espam@espam.edu.ec
Internet: www.espam.edu.ec
Founded 1999
State control
Academic year: June to May (two semesters)
Rector: Leonardo Félix López
Sec.-Gen.: Lya Villafuerte Vélez
Library of 800 vols

DIRECTORS

Agricultural Industry: Susana Dueñas de la Torre
Agriculture: Kléber Palacios Saltos
Cattle: Kléber Palacios Saltos
Computer Science: Vicente Aveiga de Santana
Environmental Science: Dr Ronaldo Mendoza Vélez

ESCUELA SUPERIOR POLITÉCNICA DE CHIMBORAZO

Panamericana Sur km 1½, Riobamba
Telephone: (3) 299-8200
Internet: www.espoch.edu.ec
Founded 1972
Autonomous control
Language of instruction: Spanish
Rector: Dr Silvio Alvarez Luna

Vice-Rector for Academic Affairs: Edgar Cevallos Acosta
Vice-Rector for Research and Devt: Jorge Gonzalo Bermeo Rodas
Gen.-Sec.: Dr Julio Falconí Mejía
Librarian: Carlos Rodríguez C.
Library of 35,000 vols, 80,000 periodicals
Number of teachers: 264
Number of students: 4,500 (excluding students from the Dept of Languages)
Publication: *GACETA* (4 a year)

DEANS

Faculty of Animal Husbandry: José M. Pazmiño
Faculty of Business Administration: Víctor Cevallos V.
Faculty of Computer and Electronic Engineering: Dr Romeo Rodríguez
Faculty of Mechanical Engineering: Geovanny Guillermo Novillo Andrade
Faculty of Natural Resources: Federico Rosero
Faculty of Public Health: Dr Silvia Veloz M.
Faculty of Sciences: Dr Edmundo Caluña

ESCUELA SUPERIOR POLITÉCNICA DEL LITORAL

Apartado 09-01-5863, Guayaquil
Km 30½ Vía Perimetral, Guayaquil
Telephone: (4) 285-1095
Fax: (4) 285-4629
E-mail: correo@espol.edu.ec
Internet: www.espol.edu.ec

Founded 1958
State control
Language of instruction: Spanish
Academic year: May to February

Rector: Dr Moisés Tacle
Gen. Vice-Rector: Armando Altamirano
Vice-Rector for Welfare and Student Affairs: Miguel Fierro
Sec.-Gen.: Jaime Véliz Litardo
Librarian: Eloísa Patiño Lara

Library of 47,000 vols
Number of teachers: 550
Number of students: 12,005

Publications: *Boletín Informativo Polipesca, Informes de Actividades, Tecnológica*

DIRECTORS

Agriculture School: Haydée Torres
Centre for the Study of Foreign Languages: Dennis Maloney S.
Computer Science School: Alexandra Paladines
Dept of Electrical Engineering and Computer Science: Carlos Villafuerte
Dept of Geology, Mines and Petroleum Engineering: Miguel A. Chávez
Dept of Maritime Engineering: Eduardo Cervantes
Dept of Mechanical Engineering: Eduardo Rivadeneira
Electrical and Electronics School: Camilo Arellano
Fisheries School: Francisco Pacheco
Food Science School: Ma. Fernanda Morales
Furniture and Cabinet School: Víctor Fernández
Graduate School of Business: Moisés Tacle
Institute of Chemistry: Justo Huayamave
Institute of Humanities: Omar Maluk
Institute of Mathematics: Jorge Medina
Institute of Physics: Jaime Vásquez
Mechanics School: Miguel Pisco

UNIVERSIDAD AGRARIA DEL ECUADOR

Apdo 09-01-1248, Avda 25 de Julio y Avda Juan Pio Jaramillo, Via Puerto Maritimo, Guayaquil

Telephone and fax (4) 493-441
E-mail: info@uagraria.edu.ec
Internet: www.uagraria.edu.ec

Founded 1992

Rector: JACOBO BUCARAM ORTÍZ
Vice-Rector: GUILLERMO ROLANDO.

UNIVERSIDAD ANDINA SIMÓN BOLÍVAR ECUADOR

POB 17-12-569, Toledo N22-80 (Plaza Brasilia), Quito

Telephone: (2) 322-8031
Fax: (2) 322-8426
E-mail: uasb@uasb.edu.ec
Internet: www.uasb.edu.ec

Founded 1992
State control

Rector: ENRIQUE AYALA MORA
Sec.-Gen.: VIRGINIA ALTA PERUGACHI
Librarian: ENRIQUE ABAD ROA

Publications: *Comentario Internacional: Revista del Centro Andino de Estudios Internacionales, Foro: Revista de Derecho, Kipus: Revista Andina de Letras, Procesos: Revista Ecuatoriana de Historia*

Campuses in Sucre (Bolivia) and Caracas (Venezuela); offices in Bogotá (Colombia) and La Paz (Bolivia)

DIRECTORS

Arts: FERNANDO BALSECA
Business: ALFONSO TROYA
Communication: JOSÉ LASO
Education: MARIO CIFUENTES
Health Studies: PLUTARCO NARANJO
History: GUILLERMO BUSTOS
Law: JOSÉ VICENTE TROYA
Social and Global Studies: CÉSAR MONTÚFAR

ATTACHED RESEARCH INSTITUTES

Centro Andino de Estudios Internacionales: tel. (4) 256-0945; e-mail dctena@hoy.net; Pres. DIEGO CORDOVEZ.

Programa Andino de Derechos Humanos: tel. (4) 255-6403; e-mail roque@uasb.edu.ec; Regional Coordinator ROQUE ESPINOSA.

UNIVERSIDAD CENTRAL DEL ECUADOR

Avda América y A. Pérez Guerrero, Casilla 1456, Quito

Telephone: (2) 226-080
Fax: (2) 505-860
E-mail: rectorado@ucentral.edu.ec
Internet: www.ucentral.edu.ec

Founded 1586 as Univ. de San Fulgencio, became Real y Pontificia Univ. de San Gregorio in 1622, Univ. de Santo Tomás de Aquino in 1688, then Univ. Central del Sur de la Gran Colombia, present name 1826.
State control
Language of instruction: Spanish
Academic year: September to July

Rector: VICTOR HUGO OLALLA PROAÑO
Vice-Rector: CARLOS ARROYO ALVAREZ
Registrar: Dr LIDA FLORES CHACÓN
Librarian: JANETH CORNEJO

Number of teachers: 2,137
Number of students: 31,663

Publication: *Anales*

DEANS

Faculty of Administrative Sciences: Dr JOSÉ VILLAVICENCIO

Faculty of Agricultural Sciences: MIGUEL ARAQUE
Faculty of Architecture and Urbanism: PATRICIO AGUILAR VEINTIMILLA
Faculty of Arts: Prof. VICTORIA CARRASCO
Faculty of Chemistry: Dr ARTURO BASTIDAS
Faculty of Dentistry: Dr GUSTAVO RON
Faculty of Economics: JOSÉ VILLACÍS PAZ Y MIÑO
Faculty of Engineering, Physics and Mathematics: MARCO AYABACA CAZAR
Faculty of Geology, Mines, Petroleum and Environmental Studies: GUSTAVO PINTO ARTEAGA
Faculty of Law and Political and Social Sciences: Dr HOLGER CÓRDOVA
Faculty of Medical Sciences: Dr RICARDO CARRASCO
Faculty of Philosophy and Education: Mgr GUILLERMO PÉREZ
Faculty of Psychology: Dr OSWALDO MONTENEGRO JIMÉNEZ
Faculty of Social Communication: PATRICIO MONCAYO
Faculty of Veterinary Medicine: Dr OSWALDO ALBORNÓZ

Campus at Riobamba offers courses in education, literature and philosophy

UNIVERSIDAD DE CUENCA

Avda 12 de Abril y Agustín Cueva, Cuenca

Telephone: (7) 831-556
Fax: (7) 835-197
Internet: www.ucuenca.edu.ec

Founded 1867
Academic year: October to July

Rector: Dr JAIME ASTUDILLO ROMERO
Vice-Rector: FABIÁN CARRASCO CASTRO
Sec.-Gen.: Dr WILSON ANDRADE R.
Admin. Dir: MARGARITA GUTIERREZ
Librarian: CELIANO A. VINTIMILLA V.

Number of teachers: 613
Number of students: 8,500

Publications: *Anales de la Universidad de Cuenca, Informe de Coyuntura-Facultad de Ciencias Económicas, IURIS—Revista de la Facultad de Jurisprudencia, Revista de la Facultad de Ciencias Agropecuarias, Revista de la Facultad de Ciencias Médicas, Revista del IDICSA, Revista del IDIS, Revista del IICT*

DEANS

Faculty of Agriculture: Dr MANUEL SORIA PARRA
Faculty of Architecture: ALCIBÍADES VEGA MALO
Faculty of Arts: Dr JULIO MOSQUERA
Faculty of Chemistry: SILVANA LARRIVA GONZÁLEZ
Faculty of Dentistry: Dr OSWALDO VÁSQUEZ CORDERO
Faculty of Economics: MARCO VALENCIA ORELLANA
Faculty of Engineering: BOLÍVAR PEÑAFIEL GONZÁLEZ (acting)
Faculty of Jurisprudence: Dr JORGE MORALES ALVAREZ
Faculty of Medical Sciences: Dr ARTURO QUIZHPE PERALTA
Faculty of Philosophy: MARÍA EUGENIA MALDONADO

DIRECTORS

Institute of Computing and Information Science (ICEI): SALVADOR MONSALVE R.
Institute of Physical Education: JULIO ABAD
Planning Unit: RAFAEL ESTRELLA A.
Research Institute: Dr ALBERTO QUEZADA R.

UNIVERSIDAD DE GUAYAQUIL

Ciudadela Universitaria Salvador Allende, Avda Kennedy y Avda Delta, Guayaquil

Telephone: (4) 229-3598
E-mail: ugrector@ug.edu.ec
Internet: www.ug.edu.ec

Founded 1867
Private control
Language of instruction: Spanish
Academic year: April to February (2 semesters)

Rector: CARLOS CEDENO NAVARRETE
Gen. Vice-Rector: OSWALDO PACHECO GIL
Vice-Rector for Academic Affairs: JOSÉ LIZARDO APOLO PINEDA
Vice-Rector for Admin. Affairs: CÉSAR ROMERO VILLAGRÁN
Librarian: Licda LEONOR V. DE SANTANDER

Number of teachers: 2,222
Number of students: 83,448

Publication: *Revista*

DEANS

Faculty of Administrative Sciences: CARLOS SAN ANDRÉS RIVADENEIRA
Faculty of Agriculture: CÉSAR PACHECO MONROY (acting)
Faculty of Architecture and Town Planning: JORGE CABELLO FARAH
Faculty of Chemical Engineering: FERNANDO QUIROZ PÉREZ
Faculty of Chemistry: Dr CARLOS SILVA HUILCAPI
Faculty of Economics: WASHINGTON AGUIRRE GARCÍA
Faculty of Industrial Engineering: ALFREDO BUCARAM ORTIZ
Faculty of Law, Social Sciences and Politics: ALFREDO RUIZ GUZMÁN
Faculty of Mathematics and Physics: SANTIAGO ABAD MONTERO (acting)
Faculty of Medicine: Dr GONZALO MAITTA MENDOZA
Faculty of Natural Sciences: CARMITA BONIFAZ BALSECA
Faculty of Odontology: Dr WASHINGTON ESCUDERO DOLTZ
Faculty of Philosophy, Literature and Education: Dr FRANCISCO MORÁN MÁRQUEZ
Faculty of Physical Education, Sport and Recreation: ENRIQUE N. GAMBOA ABRIL
Faculty of Psychology: LUIS ALVARADO SANCHEZ
Faculty of Social Communication: HÉCTOR CHÁVEZ VILLAO
Faculty of Veterinary Medicine: MARÍO COBO CEDEÑO (acting)

UNIVERSIDAD DEL AZUAY

Avda 24 de Mayo 7-77 y Hernán Malo, Cuenca, Azuay

Telephone: (7) 288-1333
Fax: (7) 281-5997
E-mail: webmaster@uazuay.edu.ec
Internet: www.uazuay.edu.ec

Founded 1968, present status 1990
Academic year: October to July

Rector: Dr MARIO JARAMILLO PAREDES
Vice-Rector: FRANCISCO SALGADO ARTEGA
Dean (Admin. and Finance): CARLOS CORDERO DÍAZ
Dean (Research): JACINTO GUILLÉN GARCÍA

Library of 40,000 vols

Publication: *Marginalia* (2 a year)

DEANS

Faculty of Administration: MIGUEL MOSCOSO COBOS
Faculty of Design: PATRICIO LEÓN BUSTOS
Faculty of Law: Dr PATRICIO CORDERO ORDOÑEZ

Faculty of Medicine: Dr EDGAR RODAS
ANDRADE
Faculty of Philosophy: JORGE QUINTUÑA
ALVAREZ
Faculty of Science and Technology: MIRIAM
BRIONES GARCÍA
Faculty of Theology: Fr ANTONIO ALONSO
MARTÍNEZ

UNIVERSIDAD ESTATAL DE BOLÍVAR

km 3½ sector Alpachaca, Guaranda
Telephone: (3) 298-0121
Fax: (3) 298-0123
Internet: www.ueb.edu.ec
Founded 1989
State control
Rector: GABRIEL GALARZA LÓPEZ
Vice-Rector for Academic Affairs: PEDRO
PABLO LUCIO GAIBOR
Vice-Rector for Finance: DIÓMEDES NÚÑEZ
MINAYA
Registrar: GONZALO LOPEZ RIVADENEIRA
Librarian: RODRIGO SALTOS CHAVES
Number of teachers: 182
Number of students: 5,801 (3,063 full-time,
2,738 part-time)
Publication: *Enlace Universitario*

DEANS

Faculty of Administrative Sciences, Business
Management and Informatics: ÁNGEL GAR-
CÍA
Faculty of Agriculture, Natural Resources
and the Environment: HUGO VÁZQUEZ
COLOMA
Faculty of Education, Social Sciences, Phil-
osophy and Humanistic Sciences: MARCO
LARA OLALLA
Faculty of Health Sciences and of the Human
Being: CECILIA VILLAVICENCIO
Faculty of Jurisprudence and Politics: CECI-
LIA VILLAVICENCIO

UNIVERSIDAD ESTATAL DE MILAGRO

Km 1½, Vía Milagro Km 26, Los Rios,
Milagro
Telephone: (4) 297-0881
Fax: (4) 297-4319
E-mail: unemi@hotmail.com
Founded 2001
Rector: Dr RÓMULO MINCHALA MURILLO
Sec.-Gen.: AGUSTIN ARELLANO QUIROZ.

UNIVERSIDAD ESTATAL DEL SUR DE MANABÍ

Complejo Universitario, Ciudadela 10 de
Agosto, Vía a Noboa, Jipijapa
Telephone: (5) 260-0229
E-mail: unesum@hotmail.com
Founded 2001
State control
Rector: JORGE CLIMACO CAÑARTE MURILLO.

UNIVERSIDAD ESTATAL PENÍNSULA DE SANTA ELENA

Avda 9 de Octubre 515, Edificio Ching, 2
Piso, La Libertad
Telephone: (4) 278-0018
Fax: (4) 278-5398
E-mail: unipen@interactive.net.ec
Founded 1998
Academic year: September to April
Rector: XAVIER TOMALÁ
Vice-Rector: GEORGE CLEMENTE.

UNIVERSIDAD NACIONAL DE CHIMBORAZO

Avda Eloy Alfaro y 10 de Agosto, Riobamba
Telephone and fax (3) 296-2611
E-mail: rector@unach.edu.ec
Internet: www.unach.edu.ec
Founded 1995
State control
Academic year: October to July (two semes-
ters)
Faculties of education, engineering, human-
ities and technology, physical education and
health sciences, political science and admin-
istration
Rector: EDISON RIERA RODRÍGUEZ
Vice-Rector: ENRIQUE CRESPO.

UNIVERSIDAD NACIONAL DE LOJA

Casilla letra 'S', Loja
Ciudad Universitaria Guillermo Falconí
Espinosa 'La Argelia', Loja
Telephone: (7) 254-7252
Fax: (7) 254-6075
E-mail: rector@unl.edu.ec
Internet: www.unl.edu.ec
Founded 1859 as the Junta Universitaria,
univ. status 1943
State control
Language of instruction: Spanish
Academic year: October to July
Rector: Dr GUSTAVO ENRIQUE VILLACÍS RIVAS
Vice-Rector: Dr ERNESTO RAFAEL GONZÁLEZ
PESANTES
Librarian: Dr ENITH COSTA MUÑOZ
Library of 3,500 vols
Number of teachers: 720
Number of students: 13,280
Publications: *Estudios Universitarios*,
Revista Científica, and various faculty
bulletins

DIRECTORS

Agriculture and Renewable Natural
Resources: Dr EDGAR BENÍTEZ GONZÁLEZ
Education, Art and Communication: Dr
YOVANY SALAZAR ESTRADA
Energy, Industry and Non-Renewable Nat-
ural Resources: JOSÉ OCHOA ALFARO
Health Sciences: Dr AMABLE BERMEO FLORES
Law and Social and Politicalciences: Dr
ROGELIO CASTILLO BERMEO

UNIVERSIDAD TÉCNICA DE AMBATO

Casilla 18-01-334, Ambato
Telephone: (3) 853-905
Fax: (3) 849-164
Internet: www.uta.edu.ec
Founded 1969
Rector: VÍCTOR HUGO JARAMILLO
Vice-Rector: ANÍBAL SALTOS SALTOS
Sec.-Gen.: Dr PATRICIO POAQUIZA
Librarian: ELSA NARANJO
Number of teachers: 332
Number of students: 7,200

DEANS

Centro de Estudios a Distancia: GALO JAR-
AMILLO
Centro de Estudios de Postgrado: FRANCISCO
FERNÁNDEZ B.
Faculty of Accountancy: SANTIAGO BARRIGA
Faculty of Administration: JOSÉ SILVA
Faculty of Agricultural Engineering: NELLY
CHERREZ
Faculty of Civil Engineering: MIGUEL MORA
Faculty of Education: Dr JULIO SALTOS
Faculty of Food Technology: ROMEL RIVERA
Faculty of Systems Engineering: VÍCTOR
GUACHIMBOZA

UNIVERSIDAD TÉCNICA DE BABAHOYO

Apdo 66, Babahoyo, Los Ríos
Vía Flores, Babahoyo, Los Ríos
Telephone: (5) 730-646
Fax: (5) 730-647
E-mail: blupera@utb.edu.ec
Internet: www.utb.edu.ec
Founded 1971
Rector: BOLÍVAR LUPERA YCAZA
Vice-Rector for Academic Affairs: Dr RAFAEL
FALCONI MONTALVAN
Vice-Rector for Admin. Affairs: Dr ZOILA
SÁNCHEZ ANCHUNDIA
Sec.-Gen.: ALBERTO BRAVO MEDINA
Librarian: MIGUEL BASTIDAS
Number of teachers: 450
Number of students: 5,000

DEANS

Faculty of Administration, Finance and
Informatics: AUSBERTO COLINA GONZALVO
Faculty of Agriculture: OTTO ORDEÑANA
BURNHAN
Faculty of Health Sciences: Dr CÉSAR NOBOA
AQUINO
Faculty of Social Sciences and Education: Dr
JACINTO MUÑOZ MUÑOZ

UNIVERSIDAD TÉCNICA DE COTOPAXI

Campus Universitario, Avda Simón
Rodríguez s/n, Barrio El Ejido, Latacunga,
Cotopaxi
Telephone: (3) 281-0296
Fax: (3) 281-0295
E-mail: webmaster@utc.edu.ec
Internet: www.utc.edu.ec
Founded 1995
Rector: FRANCISCO RAMIRO ULLOA ENRÍQUEZ
Vice-Rector: HERNÁN YÁNEZ
Sec.-Gen.: WILLIAM ESPINOZA
Publication: *Alma Mater*.

UNIVERSIDAD TÉCNICA DE ESMERALDAS 'LUIS VARGAS TORRES'

Avda Kennedy 704 entre Hilda Padilla y
Calle H, Esmeraldas
Telephone: (6) 272-3700
E-mail: utelvt@utelvt.edu.ec
Internet: www.utelvt.edu.ec
Founded 1970
Rector: Dr BENITO REYES PAZMIÑO
Vice-Rector for Academic Affairs: BETTO
VERNAZA CASTILLO
Vice-Rector for Admin. Affairs: LUIS FELIPE
PACHECO
Sec.-Gen.: MARCO REINOSO CAÑOTE
Librarian: SOLANDA GOBEA
Number of teachers: 180
Number of students: 800

DEANS

Faculty of Administration and Economics:
ARMENGOL PINEDA CUERO
Faculty of Education and Health Sciences:
Dr ERMEL TAPIA S.
Faculty of Engineering and Technology:
GUILLERMO MOSQUERA Q.
Faculty of Social Sciences and Development
Studies: Dr GIRARD VERNAZA A.
Faculty of Stockbreeding and Environmental
Science: Dr JEFFERSON QUIÑONEZ B.

UNIVERSIDAD TÉCNICA DE MACHALA

Avda Panamerica Km 5 1/2 via a Pasaje, Machala

Telephone: (72) 992-687
E-mail: utmachala@utmachala.edu.ec
Internet: www.utmachala.edu.ec

Founded 1969
State control
Language of instruction: Spanish
Academic year: March to January

Rector: Víctor Hernán Cabrera Jaramillo
Vice-Rector: Alcides Espinoza Ramirez
Sec.-Gen.: José Antonio Romero Tandazo
Librarian: María Unda Serrana de Barrezueta

Library of 5,000 vols
Number of teachers: 600
Number of students: 9,636

Publication: *Revista de la Facultad de Agronomía y Veterinaria*

DEANS

Faculty of Agronomy and Veterinary Science: Max Iñiguez
Faculty of Business Administration and Accountancy: Danilo Pico
Faculty of Chemical Sciences: Alberto Game
Faculty of Civil Engineering: Luis Ordóñez Jaramillo
Faculty of Sociology: Ramiro Ordoñez
Institute of Languages: Laura León de Astudillo
School of Nursing: Daysi Espinoza de Ramírez

UNIVERSIDAD TÉCNICA DE MANABÍ

Apdo 82, Portoviejo, Manabí
Avenida Universitaria, Portoviejo, Manabí

Telephone: (5) 263-2677
Fax: (5) 265-1569
Internet: www.utm.edu.ec

Founded 1954
State control
Academic year: May to January (two semesters)

Rector: José Félix Véliz Briones
Sec.: Dr Plutarco García Saltos
Librarian: María Angela de Coronel

Number of teachers: 489
Number of students: 8,000

Publication: *Revista*

DEANS

Faculty of Administration and Economics: Guillermo Hinostroza
Faculty of Agricultural Engineering: César Jarre
Faculty of Agronomy: Julio Toro García
Faculty of Arts and Education: José Cobeña
Faculty of Chemistry, Mathematics and Physics: Hernán Nieto
Faculty of Health Sciences: Dr Bosco Barberán
Faculty of Humanistic Sciences: Cloris Cevallos de Ormaza
Faculty of Information Science: Carlos Intriago
Faculty of Veterinary Sciences: Dr Bolívar Ortega
Faculty of Zootechnology: Dr Mario Mata Moreira

UNIVERSIDAD TÉCNICA DEL NORTE

Ciudadela Universitaria 'El Olivo', Avda 17 de Julio, Ibarra

Telephone: (6) 295-3461
Fax: (6) 295-5833
Internet: www.utn.edu.ec

Founded 1986

Faculties of administration, animal husbandry and environment, applied sciences, educational sciences, health sciences

Rector: Dr Marco L. Muñoz Herreria.

UNIVERSIDAD TÉCNICA ESTATAL DE QUEVEDO

Km 1.5 Vía a Quito, Casilla 73, Quevedo, Los Ríos

Telephone: (52) 751-430
Fax: (52) 753-300
E-mail: rector@uteq.edu.ec
Internet: www.uteq.edu.ec

Founded 1984
State control
Language of instruction: Spanish

Rector: Eng. Roque Luis Vivas Moreira
Vice-Rector: Eng. Guadalupe del Pilar Murillo Campuzano
Vice-Rector: Eng. Williams Burbano Montecé
Librarian: Eng. Ariosto Vicuña

Number of teachers: 144
Number of students: 2,900

DEANS

Faculty of Agrarian Science: Segundo Bravo
Faculty of Cattle Science: Délsito Zambrano Gracia
Faculty of Enterprise Science: Mag. Wilson Cerezo Segovia
Faculty of Environmental Science: Antonio Véliz Mendoza
Cooperation Office: Eng. Tito Efraín Cabrera Vicuña

Private Universities

PONTIFICIA UNIVERSIDAD CATÓLICA DEL ECUADOR

Avda 12 de Octubre 1076 y Roca, Apdo 17-01-2184, Quito

Telephone: (2) 299-1700
Fax: (2) 256-7117
E-mail: webmaster@puce.edu.ec
Internet: www.puce.edu.ec

Founded 1946
Private control
Language of instruction: Spanish
Academic year: August to July

Grand Chancellor: Mons. Fausto Trávez Trávez
Vice-Grand Chancellor: Gilberto Freire Yánez S.J.
Rector: Dr Manuel Corrales Pascual S.J.
Vice-Rector: Dr Manuel Corrales Pascual
Librarian: Oswaldo Orbe Cortez

Number of teachers: 1,817
Number of students: 13,200

Publications: *Economía y Humanismo* (4 a year), *Nuestra Ciencia*, *Revista PUCE* (2 a year)

DEANS

Faculty of Accounting and Administrative Sciences: Paulina Cadena Vinueza
Faculty of Architecture, Design and Arts: Alexis Mosquera Rivera
Faculty of Communication, Linguistics and Literature: Dr Lucía Lemos Silva
Faculty of Ecclesiastical Philosophical-Theological Sciences: Mr Fernando Barredo Heinert S.J.
Faculty of Economics: Mónica Mancheno Karolys
Faculty of Education Sciences: Dra Myriam Aguirre Montero
Faculty of Engineering: Diego Andrade Stacey

Faculty of Exact and Natural Sciences: Dr Laura Arcos Terán
Faculty of Human Sciences: Dr Juan Hidalgo Aguilera
Faculty of Jurisprudence: Dr Santiago Guarderas Izquierdo
Faculty of Medicine: Dr Edison Chaves Almeida
Faculty of Nursing: Nelly Sarmiento Sarmiento
Faculty of Psychology: Marie-France Merlyn Sacoto

DIRECTORS

School of Medical Technology: Lucía Ulloa Andrade
School of Social Work: Carmen Galindo Salinas

REGIONAL CAMPUSES

Ambato Campus: Rocafuerte y Lalama (Esq.), Apdo 18-01-662, Ambato; tel. (3) 241-6722; fax (3) 241-1868; e-mail pucesa@puce.edu.ec; internet www.pucesa.edu.ec; courses in computer technology and English; Pro-Rector Dr César González Loor.

Esmeraldas Campus: Calle Espejo y Santa Cruz S/n, Apdo 08-01-0065, Esmeraldas; tel. (6) 272-6613; fax (6) 272-6509 ext. 114; e-mail prorector@pucese.net; internet www.pucese.net; 391 students; courses in education, accountancy, nursing, English; Pro-Rector Aitor Urbina García de Vicuña.

Ibarra Campus: Avda Aurelio Espinosa Pólit, Cdla. 'La Victoria' , Apdo 10-10-34, Ibarra; tel. and fax (2) 264-1786; e-mail prorect@pucei.edu.ec; internet www.pucei.edu.ec; 741 students; courses in administration and accountancy, tourism and hotel management, design, civil engineering; Pro-Rector Dr María José Rubio Gómez.

PUCE—Manabí: Campus Portoviejo, Ciudadela 1° de Mayo, Calle Eudoro Loor s/n y 25 de Diciembre, Portoviejo;Campus Chone, Vía Chone-El Carmen, Km 11, Chone;Campus Bahía de Caráquez, Vía Bahía-Chone, Km 8; tel. and fax (5) 263-7300 (Portoviejo); tel. and fax (5) 295-7269 (Chone); tel. and fax (5) 239-9030 (Bahía de Caráquez); fax (5) 263-7305; e-mail pucemanabi@hotmail.com; Pro-Rector Rev. Homero Fuentes Vera, S.J.

PUCE—Santo Domingo de los Colorados: Vía Chone Km 2 y San Cristóbal, Apdo 17-24-539, Santo Domingo de los Tsáchila; tel. and fax (2) 370-2860; e-mail sprorrectorado@pucesd.edu.ec; Pro-Rector Dr Margalina Font Roig.

UNIVERSIDAD CATÓLICA DE CUENCA

Apdo 01-01-1937, Cuenca

Telephone: (7) 842-606
Fax: (7) 831-040
E-mail: uccsis@etapa.com.ec
Internet: www.ucacue.edu.ec

Founded 1970
Private control
Academic year: October to July (3 semesters)

Rector: Dr César Cordero Moscoso
Assoc. Rector: Dr Carlos Darquea López
Pro-Rector: Dr Marco Vicuña Domínguez
Academic Vice-Rector: Dr Eduardo Coronel Díaz
Administrative Vice-Rector: Dr Enrique Pozo Cabrera
Extension Vice-Rector: Dr Hugo Ortiz Segarra
Academic Dir: Pablo Cisneros Quintanilla
Finance Dir: Patricio Arévalo Vintimilla
Chief Admin. Officer: Dr Enrique Campoverde Cajas
Sec.-Gen.: Dr Rodrigo Cisneros Aguirre
Librarian: Prof. Angel López Vázquez

Library of 8,000 vols
Number of teachers: 850
Number of students: 12,000
Publications: *Diálogo, Estudios, Panoramas, Presencia, Retama*

DEANS

Bilingual Secretarial School: OSCAR CALLE MASACHE
Communications, Radio and Television Channel 2: Ing. JHONNY PERALTA IZQUIERDO
Delegation in Europe: Prof. Dr FRANZ KANEHL (Germany)
Extension Univ. at Azogues: Dr MARCO VICUÑA DOMÍNGUEZ
Extension Univ. at Cañar: Dr BOLÍVAR CABRERA BERREZUETA
Extension Univ. at Macas: JOSÉ MERINO V.
Extension Univ. at Méndez: Dr JORGE CÁRDENAS ESPINOZA
Extension Univ. at San Pablo, Troncal: REMIGIO VÁZQUEZ LÓPEZ
Faculty 'Cardenal Echeverría': PATRICIO BONILLO
Faculty of Agricultural Engineering, Mines and Veterinary Science: Ing. HUMBERTO SALAMEA CARPIO
Faculty of Chemical and Industrial Engineering: Ing. SANTIAGO GÓMEZ LIVISACA
Faculty of Civil Engineering and Architecture: GERARDO AREVALO IDROVO
Faculty of Commercial Engineering: Dra GLADIS LEMARIE CAICEDO
Faculty of Distance Learning: Dr HUGO ORTIZ SEGARRA
Faculty of Ecotourism: JUANA CATALINA JARAMILLO
Faculty of Economics: Dr HUGO ORTIZ SEGARRA
Faculty of Education and Psychology: Dr ENRIQUE CAMPOVERDE CAJAS
Faculty of Electrical Engineering: Dr EDUARDO CORONEL DÍAZ
Faculty of Enterprise Engineering: RAMIRO CARANGUI CÁRDENAS
Faculty of Informatics Systems: Dr EDUARDO CORONEL DIAZ
Faculty of Law and Social Sciences: Dr ENRIQUE POZO CABRERA
Faculty of Medicine and Health Sciences: Dr CARLOS DARQUEA LOPEZ
Faculty of Odontology: Dr CARLOS MORALES VILLAVICENCIO
Institute of Languages: Ing. RAÚL CAMPOVERDE CAJAS
Institute of Nursing: Dra MARÍA FERNANDA ORTIZ HINOJOSA
Postgraduate Cttee: Dr MARCO VICUNA DOMÍNGUEZ
School of Drama and Aerobics: Dr CARLOS EFRAÍN CRESPO
School of Journalism and Communications: Dr IVÁN CULCAY VILLAVICENCIO
School of Physical Education: Dr ROLANDO CORONEL DÍAZ
School of Social Service: LEONOR MASACHE MALDONADO
University Hospital: Dr CARLOS DARQUEA LÓPEZ

UNIVERSIDAD CATÓLICA DE SANTIAGO DE GUAYAQUIL

Avda Carlos Julio Arosemena Km 1½ Vía Daule, Guayaquil
Telephone: (4) 220-6950
Internet: www.ucsg.edu.ec
Founded 1962
Private control
Academic year: May to April
Rector: Dr MICHEL DOUMET ANTÓN
Vice-Rector: MAURO TOSCANINI SEGALE

Vice-Rector for Academic Affairs: ELIZABETH LARREA DE GRANADOS
Librarian: CLEMENCIA MITE DE SANTILLÁN
Library of 32,974 vols
Number of teachers: 612
Number of students: 6,249
Publications: *Revista Cuadernos, Revista Universidad*

DEANS

Faculty of Architecture: ROSA EDITH RADA ALPRECH
Faculty of Arts and Humanities: Dr MARÍA DE LOURDES ESTRADA RUIZ
Faculty of Business: LUIS FERNANDO HIDALGO PROAÑO
Faculty of Economics: KLEBER ALBERTO CORONEL LÓPEZ
Faculty of Engineering: WALTER VICENTE MERA ORTIZ
Faculty of Law: JOSÉ MIGUEL GARCÍA BAQUERIZO
Faculty of Medicine: Dr ALFREDO JOSÉ ESCALA MACCAFERRI
Faculty of Philosophy, Literature and Education: MARÍA CECILIA LOOR DUEÑAS
Faculty of Technical Education for Development: Dr KLEVER GUIDO LÓPEZ PARRALES

UNIVERSIDAD LAICA 'VICENTE ROCAFUERTE' DE GUAYAQUIL

Apartado Postal 1133, Guayaquil
Avda de las Américas frente al Cuartel Modelo, Guayaquil
Telephone: (4) 228-7200
E-mail: laicared@gye.satnet.net
Internet: www.ulaicavr.edu.ec
Founded 1847, univ. status 1966
Private control
Language of instruction: Spanish
Academic year: April to January
Faculties of administration, architecture, civil engineering, economics, education, journalism, jurisprudence and social sciences; Schools of accountancy, child education, design, foreign trade, languages, marketing, publicity, secretarial administration
Rector: Dr ELSA ALARCÓN SOTO
Gen. Vice-Rector: ALFREDO AGUILAR ALAVA
Vice-Rector for Academic Affairs: ALFONSO SÁNCHEZ GUERRERO
Gen.–Sec.: ALFONSO AGUILAR ALAVA
Librarian: CECILIA RODRÍGUEZ GRANDA
Library of 8,000 vols
Number of teachers: 307
Number of students: 9,317
Publications: *Boletín de Información Académica* (1 a year), *Boletín el Contador Laico.*

UNIVERSIDAD TÉCNICA PARTICULAR DE LOJA

Apartado postal 11-01-608, Loja
San Cayetano Alto, Loja
Telephone: (7) 257-0275
Fax: (7) 258-4893
E-mail: utpl_ects@utpl.edu.ec
Internet: www.utpl.edu.ec
Founded 1971
Private control
Language of instruction: Spanish
Academic year: October to August (2 semesters)
Rector-Chancellor: Pe Dr LUIS MIGUEL ROMERO FERNÁNDEZ
Vice-Chancellor: Dr JOSÉ BARBOSA CORBACHO
Sec.-Gen.: Ing. GABRIEL GARCÍA TORRES
Dir of Open and Distance Education: Dra MARÍA JOSÉ RUBIO GÓMEZ
Librarian: Lic. AMADA JARAMILLO LOJÁN

Library of 25,000 vols
Number of teachers: 190 full-time, 121 distance education
Number of students: 2,200 full-time, 7,218 distance education
Publications: *El Reloj* (12 a year), *Universidad* (12 a year), *Universidad Técnica Particular de Loja* (1 a year)

DIRECTORS

Electronics and Telecommunications Programme: JORGE JARAMILLO
Environmental Management Programme: FAUSTO LÓPEZ
School of Accounting and Auditing: Dr LUPE ESPEJO
School of Agricultural Engineering: HERNÁN LUCERO MOSQUERA
School of Agro-Industry Engineering: RUTH MARTÍNEZ ESPINOZA
School of Architecture: KARINA MONTEROS
School of Arts and Design: ELENA MALO
Banking and Financial Administration Programme: RAMIRO ARMIJOS
School of Biochemistry and Pharmacy: Dr PAULA TORRES BAILÓN
School of Biology: ESTEBAN TORRACHI
School of Business Administration: ANDREA LOAIZA
School of Chemical Engineering: Dr OMAR MALAGÓN AVILÉS
School of Civil Engineering: VINICIO SUÁREZ
School of Economics: JUAN MANUEL GARCÍA
School of English: ANNA GATES TAPIA
School of Geology and Mining: JHON SOTO
School of Hotel and Tourism Administration: MARTHA RUIZ RODRÍGUEZ
School of Information Systems and Computing Engineering: NELSON PIEDRA
School of Law: Dr SILVANA ERAZO
School of Management Assistance and Public Relations: MÓNICA ABENDAÑO
School of Medicine: Dr JUAN VALDIVIESO ARIAS
School of Psychology: SILVIA VACA
School of Social Communication: ABEL SUING RUIZ

College

Centro Internacional de Estudios Superiores de Comunicación para América Latina (International Centre for Advanced Studies in Communications for Latin America): Diego de Almagro N32-113 y Andrade Marín, Apdo 17-01-584, Quito; tel. (2) 544-624; fax (2) 502-487; e-mail ejaramillo@ciespal.net; internet www.ciespal .net; f. 1959 with UNESCO aid; training, documentation and research in fields of information science, radio and television; library: 2,000 vols, 20,700 documents; Dir-Gen. EDGAR JARAMILLO SALAS; publ. *Chasqui* (4 a year).

Schools of Art and Music

Conservatorio de Música 'José María Rodríguez': Cuenca; f. 1938; Dir Prof. RAFAEL SOJOS JARAMILLO.

Conservatorio Superior Nacional de Música: Casilla 17-01-3358, Quito; Cochapata E12-56 y Manuel Abascal, Quito; tel. (2) 248-666; fax (2) 248-666 ext. 128; e-mail conamusidireccion@uio.satnet.net; internet www.conservatorionacional.com.ec; f. 1900; library: 14,000 vols; 120 teachers; 800 students; Dir LUCIANO CARRERA GALARZA; publ. *Conservatorio.*

EGYPT

The Higher Education System

The higher education system in Egypt consists of Islamic and secular sectors. The Islamic sector is based upon Al-Azhar University in Cairo, founded in AD 970 as an adjunct to Al-Azhar mosque. Cairo University, the first secular university, was founded in 1908, and in 1925 it became a public institution. The Ministry of Higher Education and Scientific Research governs secular higher education through the aegis of the Supreme Council of Universities, while the Central Administration of Al-Azhar Institutes, a department of the Supreme Council of Al-Azhar Institutes, controls Islamic higher education. The Government is constitutionally required to provide free higher education to all, but students also pay enrolment fees. In 2004/05 there were an estimated 2,594,186 students enrolled in higher education. By 2009 there were 17 public universities, 51 public non-university institutions, 16 private universities and 89 private higher institutions. Out of the 51 non-university institutions, 47 were two-year middle technical institutes and four were four- to five-year higher technical institutes.

Students intending to attend university must hold the General Secondary School Certificate (or the Technical Secondary School Certificate); exact entry requirements vary between institutions. Islamic or Al-Azhar higher education requires the student to successfully complete Al-Azhar secondary school, otherwise applicants must take one year of Arabic and Koranic studies. The American University in Cairo, founded in 1919, is independent of the Egyptian higher education system but its degrees are recognized as equivalent to those awarded by Egyptian universities.

The main undergraduate degree is the Bachelors, which is usually awarded after four years, but in some disciplines may take five (architecture, dentistry, engineering, pharmacy, veterinary medicine) or six years (medicine). Instruction is in Arabic, except in dentistry, engineering, medicine, pharmacy, science and veterinary medicine, for which it is in English. The first postgraduate degree is the Diploma, which lasts for one year and leads to the award of the Diploma in Higher Studies, Diploma of Graduate Studies or simply the Diploma. The next postgraduate degree, the Masters, requires two years of study. Finally, the Doctor of Philosophy (PhD) is a three- to four-year course, based entirely on research.

Technical and vocational training is available at intermediate vocational institutes, higher technical institutes and as non-formal education. Intermediate technical institutes specialize in post-secondary, two-year diploma courses in the fields of commerce, health and industry; higher technical institutes focus on advanced courses in technical education across a wide range of subjects, leading to either the Diploma (two years) or Bachelors degree (four to five years). Non-formal education consists of refresher courses, evening classes and on-the-job training.

In 2007 a National Authority for Quality Assurance and Accreditation of Education (NAQAAE) was established to oversee the 50,000 educational institutes and prepare them for accreditation. It is the accrediting body for all Egyptian educational society (higher education, pre-university and Al-Azhar education).

Regulatory and Representative Bodies

GOVERNMENT

Ministry of Culture: 2 Sharia Shagaret el-Dor, Cairo (Zamalek); tel. (2) 37486957; fax (2) 33461417; e-mail mculture@idsc.gov.eg; Min. FAROUK ABD AL-AZIZ HOSNI.

Ministry of Education: 12 Sharia el-Falaky, Cairo; tel. (2) 27959939; fax (2) 27942700; e-mail info@mail.emoe.org; internet www.emoe.org; Minister Dr YOUSRI SABER HUSSEIN EL-GAMAL.

Ministry of Higher Education and Scientific Research: 101 Sharia Qasr el-Eini, Cairo; tel. (2) 27924189; fax (2) 27941005; e-mail info@egy-mhe.gov.eg; internet www.egy-mhe.gov.eg; Minister Dr HANY MAHFOUZ HELAL.

ACCREDITATION

National Authority for Quality Assurance and Accreditation of Education (NAQAAE): Building of the Telecom Institute, 5 Mahmoud Elmeligy St, 6th District, Nasr City; tel. (2) 22630672; fax (2) 22636802; e-mail nagdy@naqaae.org; internet www.naqaae.org; f. 2007; board of 15 mems; Chair. Dr MAGDY KASSEM.

NATIONAL BODY

Supreme Council of Universities: 96 Ahmed Orabi, Mohandsen, Giza; tel. (2) 33029271; e-mail scu@mailer.eun.eg; internet www.scu.eun.eg; f. 1950; delineates gen. policy of univ. education and scientific research in order to attain nat. objectives in social, economic, cultural and scientific devt plans; determines admission numbers, fields of specialization and equivalences; the Egyptian Universities Network links univ. computer centres and research institutes throughout Egypt, and is the Egyptian gateway to the internet, and provides information services and online learning facilities; 33 mem. univs and private institutes; library of 3,300 vols (English and Arabic); Pres. THE MINISTER OF HIGHER EDUCATION AND MINISTER OF STATE FOR SCIENTIFIC RESEARCH; Sec.-Gen. Prof. SALWA EL-GHARIB.

Learned Societies

GENERAL

Academy of the Arabic Language: 15 Aziz Abaza St, Zamalek, Cairo; tel. (2) 27362002; fax (2) 27362002; e-mail acc@idsc.net.eg; internet www.arabicacademy.org.eg; f. 1932; 40 Egyptian active mems, also corresp. mems, hon. mems and foreign active mems; library of 60,000 vols; Pres. Prof. AHMED SHAWKY DHEIF; Sec.-Gen. IBRAHIM ABDEL MEGEED; publ. *Review* (2 a year).

African Society: 5 Ahmed Hishmat St, Zamalik, Cairo; f. 1972 to promote knowledge about Africa and nat. liberation movements in the Afro-Arab world and encourage research on Africa; organizes lectures, debates, seminars, symposia and conferences; participates in celebration of African nat. occasions; arranges cultural and scientific exchange with similar African societies; publishes bulletins and books in Arabic and English; 500 mems; library of 1,500 vols in Arabic; library of 2,000 vols in other languages; Sec.-Gen. M. FOUAD EL BIDEWY; publs *Africa Newsletter* (in Arabic), *African Studies* (irregular).

Institut d'Égypte (Egyptian Institute): 13 Sharia Sheikh Rihane, Cairo; f. 1798 by Napoleon Bonaparte; literature, arts and science relating to Egypt and neighbouring countries; 60 mems; 50 assoc. mems; 50 corresp. mems; library of 160,000 vols; Pres. Dr SILEMAN HAZIEN; Sec.-Gen. P. GHALIOUN-GUI; publs *Bulletin* (1 a year), *Mémoires*.

AGRICULTURE, FISHERIES AND VETERINARY SCIENCE

Egyptian Society of Dairy Science: 1 Ouziris St, Garden City, Cairo; f. 1972; Pres. Dr ISMAEL YOUSRY; publ. *Egyptian Journal of Dairy Science*.

BIBLIOGRAPHY, LIBRARY SCIENCE AND MUSEOLOGY

Egyptian Association for Library and Information Science: c/o Dept of Archives, Librarianship and Information Science, Faculty of Arts, Univ. of Cairo, Cairo; tel. (2) 35676365; fax (2) 35729659; f. 1956; 4,000 mems; Pres. Dr S. KHALIFA; Sec. M. HOSAN EL DIN.

Supreme Council of Antiquities: 3 Al-Adel Abou Bakr St, Zamalek, Cairo; tel. (2) 27365645; fax (2) 27357239; e-mail hawass@sca.gov.eg; internet www.sca.gov.eg; f. 1859 to oversee the preservation of Egyptian cultural heritage; attached to Ministry of Culture of Egypt; Dir Dr GABBALLAH ALI GABBALLAH; Sec.-Gen. Dr ZAHI HAWASS.

ECONOMICS, LAW AND POLITICS

Egyptian Society of International Law: 16 Sharia Ramses, Cairo; tel. and fax (2) 25743162; f. 1945; to promote the study of int. law and to work for the establishment of int. relations, based on law and justice; lectures; Pres. Dr MOUFEED CHEHAB; Sec.-Gen. Dr SALAH AMER; Admin. Dir A. EL MAHROUKY; 800 mems; library of 4,100 books, 120 periodicals, 100,000 documents; publ. *Revue Egyptienne de Droit International* (1 a year).

Egyptian Society of Political Economy, Statistics and Legislation: 16 Sharia Ramses, BP 732, Cairo; tel. (2) 25750797; fax (2) 25743491; e-mail espesl@hotmail.com; internet www.espesl.org.eg; f. 1909; 3,018 mems; library of 45,000 vols; Pres. Prof. AHMAD FATHI SOROOR; Gen.-Sec. Dr MUSTAFA EL SAID; publ. *L'Egypte Contemporaine* (in Arabic, English and French, 4 a year).

FINE AND PERFORMING ARTS

Armenian Artistic Union: 3 Sharia Soliman, el-Halaby, BP 1060, Cairo; tel. (2) 25742282; f. 1920; promotion of Armenian and Arabic culture; 120 mems; Pres. VAHAG DEPOYAN.

L'Atelier: 6 Victor Bassili St, al Pharaana, Azarita, Alexandria; tel. and fax (3) 24860526; e-mail info@atelieralex.com; internet www.atelieralex.com; f. 1935; soc. of artists and writers; 350 mems; library of 5,500 vols; Pres. Dr MOHAMED RAFIK KHALI; Vice-Pres. Dr MOHAMED SALEM; publ. *Bulletin*.

High Council of Arts and Literature: 9 Sharia Hassan Sabri, Zamalek, Cairo; f. 1956; publishes books on literature, arts and social sciences.

Institute of Arab Music: 22 Sharia Ramses, Cairo; tel. (2) 22750702; f. 1924; promotion and teaching of Arab music; libraries of records, tapes and scores of Arab music; Chair. of Board HASSAN TAKER MOK; Sec.-Gen. FARZY RASHAD.

HISTORY, GEOGRAPHY AND ARCHAEOLOGY

Egyptian Geographical Society: 109 Qasr Al-Aini St, BP 422 Mohamed Farid, Cairo; tel. (2) 27945450; fax (2) 27956771; e-mail geoegypt@hotmail.com; internet www-egs-online.com; f. 1875, reorganized 1917; cartography section incl. 15,000 maps; 1,500 mems; library of 50,000 vols; Pres. Prof. M. S. ABULEZZ; Sec.-Gen. Prof. S. AL-HOSEINY; Library Dir H. LOTFY; publs *Al-Majallah Al-Jugrafiyah Al-'Arabiyah* (2 a year), *Bulletin of the Egyptian Geographical Society (Bulletin de la Soeiété de Géographie d'Egypte)* (1 a year), *Geographical research series* (24 occasional issues), proceedings of symposia, conferences workshops dealing with current geographical issues.

Hellenic Society of Ptolemaic Egypt: 20 Sharia Fouad I, Alexandria; f. 1908; Pres. Dr G. PARTHENIADIS; Sec. COSTA A. SANDI.

Société Archéologique d'Alexandrie: 6 Mahmoud, Moukhtar St, BP 815, Alexandria 21111; tel. and fax (3) 24820650; e-mail asalex@yahoo.col; f. 1893; 248 mems; Pres. Prof. M. EL ABBADI; Sec.-Gen. Prof. M HAGGAG.

Society for Coptic Archaeology: 222 Sharia Ramses, Cairo; tel. (2) 24824252; e-mail bgwassif@yahoo.com; f. 1934; studies Coptic archaeology, linguistics, papyrology, church history, liturgy and art; organizes symposia and confs; 360 mems; library of 16,000 vols; Pres. WASSIF BOUTROS-GHALI; Vice-Pres. Dr PETER GROSSMANN; Librarian Dr AWAD WADI; publ. *Bulletin de la Société Copte d'Archéologie (BSAC)* (1 a year).

LANGUAGE AND LITERATURE

Alliance Française: 4 Aboul Feda St, Port Saïd; tel. and fax (66) 3227431; fax (66) 3227431; e-mail allianceportsaid@suezcanal.net; offers courses and examinations in French language and culture and promotes cultural exchange with France; library of 4,000 vols; Dir BERNARD CHAUMONT-GAILLAIRD.

British Council: 192 el Nil St, Agouza, Cairo; tel. (2) 33031514; fax (2) 33443076; e-mail information@britishcouncil.org.eg; internet www.britishcouncil.org/egypt; teaching centre; offers courses and examinations in English language and British culture and promotes cultural exchange with the UK; attached offices in Alexandria and Heliopolis (teaching centre); Dir Dr JOHN GROTE; Dir, English Language Services STEVEN MURRELL.

Goethe-Institut: 5 Sharia el-Bustan, Cairo 11518; tel. (2) 25759877; fax (2) 25771140; e-mail info@cairo.goethe.org; internet www.goethe.de/ins/eg/kai; offers courses and examinations in German language and culture and promotes cultural exchange with Germany; attached centre in Alexandria; Dir and Regional Man. HEIKO SIEVERS.

Instituto Cervantes: 20 Boulos Hann St, Dokki, Cairo; tel. (2) 37601746; fax (2) 37601743; e-mail cencai@cervantes.es; internet elcairo.cervantes.es; offers courses and examinations in Spanish language and culture and promotes cultural exchange with Spain and Spanish-speaking Latin and Central America; library of 18,500 vols; Dir LUIS JAVIER RUIZ SIERRA.

MEDICINE

Alexandria Medical Association: 4 G. Carducci St, Alexandria; f. 1921; 1,200 mems; Pres. Prof. H. S. EL BADAWI; Sec.-Gen. Prof. TOUSSOUN ABOUL AZI; publ. *Alexandria Medical Journal* (English, French and Arabic, 4 a year).

Egyptian Dental Association: 84A Mat'haf el-Manial St, el-Manial, Cairo; tel. (2) 23658568; fax (2) 25319143; internet www.eda-egypt.org; f. 1937; 1960 separated from Egyptian Medical Asscn; Pres. Prof. HATEM ABDEL RAHMAN; Gen. Sec. Dr AHMED FARID SHEHAB; publ. *Egyptian Dental Journal* (4 a year).

Egyptian Medical Association: 42 Sharia Kasr el-Aini, Cairo; tel. (2) 33543406; f. 1919; 2,142 mems; Pres. Prof. A. EL KATEB; Sec.-Gen. Prof. A. H. SHAABAN; Vice-Pres. Prof. M. IBRAHIM; publ. *Journal* (in Arabic and English, 1 a year).

Egyptian Medical Association for the Study of Obesity: 14 el Khalil St, el Mohandessin, Giza, Cairo; tel. (2) 33023642; fax (2) 33027672; e-mail info@emaso-eg.org; internet www.emaso-eg.org; f. 2003; Pres. SHERIF HAFEZ; Gen. Sec. MOHAMED ABOULGHATE.

Egyptian Orthopaedic Association: 16 Sharia Houda Shaarawi, Cairo 11111; tel. (2) 23930013; fax (2) 23930054; e-mail eoa@eoa.org.eg; internet www.eoa.org.eg; f. 1948; scientific and social activities in the field of orthopaedic surgery and traumatology; holds bi-annual scientific meetings, monthly clinical meetings; 1,700 mems; Pres. Prof. KHAMIS H. EL DEEB; Sec.-Gen. Prof. ABDEL MOHSEN ARAFA; publ. *Egyptian Orthopaedic Journal* (4 a year).

Ophthalmological Society of Egypt: Dar el Hekma, 42 Sharia Kasr el-Aini, Cairo; e-mail eos@eyegypt.com; f. 1902; Pres. Prof. KHALIL ABOU SHOUSA EL SAID; Hon. Sec. Dr AHMAD EZ EL DIN NAIM; 480 mems.

NATURAL SCIENCES

Biological Sciences

Egyptian Botanical Society: 1 Ozoris St, Tager Bldg, Garden City, Cairo; f. 1956 to encourage students of botany and links between workers in botany; organizes confs, seminars, lectures, and field trips for collecting, preserving and identifying plants; 230 mems; Pres. Prof. A. M. SALAMA; Sec. Dr MOHAMED FAWZY; publ. *Egyptian Journal of Botany* (3 a year).

Egyptian Entomological Society: 14 Sharia Ramses, BP 430, Cairo; tel. (2) 25750979; fax (2) 25766683; e-mail ees@ees.eg.net; internet www.ees.eg.net; f. 1907; 502 mems; library: publishes bulletins and economic series, library of 28,000 vols; Pres. Prof. MAHMOUD HAFEZ; Vice-Pres. Prof. MOHAMMAD ALI MOHAMMAD; Sec.-Gen. Prof. IBRAHIM MOHAMED.

Egyptian Society of Parasitology: 1 Ozoris St, Tager Bldg, Garden City, Cairo; fax (2) 24036497; f. 1967; holds scientific meetings, annual conf.; covers subjects in the fields of helminthology, medical entomology, protozoology, molluscs, insect control, immuno-diagnosis of parasitic diseases, treatment, etc.; 350 mems; Pres. Prof. MAHMOUD HAFEZ; Sec.-Gen. Prof. TOSSON A. MORSY; publ. *Journal* (2 a year).

Zoological Society of Egypt: Giza Zoo, Giza; f. 1927; aims to promote zoological studies and to foster good relations between zoologists in Egypt and abroad; field courses, lectures, etc.; library of 2,500 vols; 260 mems; Pres. Dr HASSAN A. HAFEZ; Sec. MOHAMED H. AMER; publ. *Bulletin*.

PHILOSOPHY AND PSYCHOLOGY

Egyptian Association for Mental Health: 1 Sharia Ilhami, Qasr al-Doubara, Cairo; internet www.arabpsynet.com/associations/eamh.ass.htm; f. 1948; 630 mems; Pres. Dr JAMEL ABOU ELAZAYEM.

Egyptian Association for Psychological Studies: 1 Osiris St, Tager Bldg, Garden City, Cairo; tel. (2) 33541857; internet www.arabpsynet.com/homepage/psy-ass.htm; f. 1948; 1,200 mems; Pres. Dr ATEF KAMEL; publ. *Yearbook of Psychology*.

RELIGION, SOCIOLOGY AND ANTHROPOLOGY

Institut Dominicain d'Etudes Orientales: Priory of the Dominican Fathers, 1 Sharia Masna al-Tarabish, BP 18, Abbassiah, Cairo 11381; tel. (2) 24825509; fax (2) 26820682; e-mail ideo@link.com.eg; internet www.ideo-cairo.org; f. 1952; library of 100,000 vols; Dir Fr R. MORELON; publ. *Mélanges* (every 2 years).

Social Sciences Association of Egypt: Cairo; f. 1957; 1,234 mems.

TECHNOLOGY

Egyptian Materials Research Society: 33 Abdel-Khalik Tharwat St, Cairo; tel. (2) 23925997; e-mail contact@egmrs.org; internet www.egmrs.org; f. 1978 as Egyptian Soc. of Solid State Science and Applications (ESSA); present name 2003; 500 mems; Chair Prof. KAMEL ABD EL-HADY; publ. *Egyptian Journal of Solids*.

Egyptian Society of Engineers: 28 Sharia Ramses, Cairo; e-mail ese@rusys.eg.net; internet www.ese.eg.net; f. 1920; Pres. Prof. IBRAHIM ADHAM EL DEMIRDASH; Sec. Dr MOHAMED M. EL HASHIMY.

Research Institutes

GENERAL

Academy of Scientific Research and Technology: 101 Kasr el-Eini St, Cairo 11516; tel. (2) 27921267; fax (2) 27921270; e-mail info@asrt.sci.eg; internet www.asrt.sci .eg; f. 1972; nat. body responsible for science and technology; promotes the creation of an integrated system of scientific research; encourages female and youth participation in scientific leadership; affiliated instns: Central Metallurgical Research and Devt Institute, Egyptian Nat. Scientific and Technological Information Network, Gen. Directorate of Statistics on Science and Technology, Institute of Astronomy and Geophysics, Institute of Oceanography and Fisheries, Nat. Information and Documentation Centre, Nat. Institute for Standards, Nat. Network for Technology and Devt (UNTD), Nat. Research Centre, Petroleum Research Institute, Remote Sensing Centre, Scientific Instruments Centre, Science Museum; library of 34,000 vols, 50,000 periodicals; Pres. Prof. MOHAMMAD TAREK HUSSEIN.

National Research Centre: Al-Tahrir St, Dokki, Cairo; tel. (2) 33337615; fax (2) 33370931; e-mail info@nrc.sci.eg; internet www.nrc.sci.eg; f. 1956; began functioning in 1947 and laboratory work started in 1956; fosters and carries out research in both pure and applied sciences; the 54 laboratories are divided into 13 sections: Textile Industries, Food Industries and Nutrition, Pharmaceutical Industries, Chemical Industries, Engineering, Agriculture and Biology, Medical, Applied Organic and Inorganic Chemistry, Physics, Basic Sciences, Environment, Genetic Engineering and Biotechnology; library of 12,000 vols; Pres. Dr HANY EL NAZER; publs *Bulletin*, *NRC News*.

AGRICULTURE, FISHERIES AND VETERINARY SCIENCE

Agricultural Research Centre, Ministry of Agriculture: 9 Gamaa St, Giza; tel. (2) 35720944; fax (2) 35722069; e-mail abouhadid@arc.sci.eg; internet www.arc.sci .eg; Pres. Prof. AYMAN FARID ABOU HADID; Vice-Pres. Prof. MOHAMMED MOSTAFA EL GHARY.

Attached Research Institutes:

Agricultural Economics Research Institute: 7 Nadi El Said St, Dokki, Giza; tel. (2) 33354549; fax (2) 37607651; e-mail aeri84@hotmail.com; f. 1973; Dir Prof. FAUZY ABD ELAZIZ EL SHAZLY; publ. *Classification of the Agricultural Land Resources according to the Yield of the Most Important Field Crops* (every 5 years).

Agricultural Engineering Research Institute: Nadi El Said St, Dokki, Giza; tel. (2) 37487212; fax (2) 33356867; e-mail aenri@aenri.org; internet www.aenri.org; Dir Prof. GAMAL HASSAN EL SAYED; publs *Egyptian Journal of Agricultural Research* (4 a year), *Misr Journal of Agricultural Engineering* (4 a year).

Agricultural Extension and Rural Development Research Institute:tel. (2) 25716301; fax (2) 25716303; e-mail aerdri@hotmail.com; f. 1977; Dir Prof. A. G. EL DEIN SAYED MAHMOUD WAHBA.

Agricultural Genetic Engineering Research Institute:e-mail taymourm@ ageri.sci.eg; Dir Prof. TAYMOUR MOHAMED NASR EL DIN IBRAHIM.

Animal Health Research Institute: Nadi El Said St, Dokki; tel. (2) 33374856; fax (2) 33350030; e-mail ahriegypt@gawab .com; internet www.ahri.gov.eg; f. 1928; Nat. Veterinary Laboratory of the Egyptian Veterinary Services; animal health and safety of food from animal origin; centre of excellence and the point of reference in animal disease diagnosis; Dir Prof. MONA MEHREZ ALY.

Animal Production Research Institute: Nadi El Said St, Dokki, Cairo; tel. and fax (2) 33372934; e-mail apri_arc@ hotmail.com; internet apri.arc.sci.eg; f. 1938; Dir Prof. Dr FATEN FAHMY MOHAMED ABOU-AMMO.

Animal Reproduction Research Institute: 5 Hadek el Ahram, Giza; tel. (2) 33764325; fax (2) 33770822; e-mail arri2002@arabia.com; Dir Prof. ATEF ABEELMONSEF AHMED.

Cotton Research Institute:tel. and fax (2) 35725035; e-mail cri_egypt@yahoo.com; internet arc.claes.sci.eg; f. 1919; Dir Prof. MOHAMED ABD EL MAGEED ABD EL AZIZ.

Field Crops Research Institute: Cairo University St, Giza; tel. and fax (2) 35738425; internet www.fcri-egypt.com; f. 1971; Dir Prof. MOHAMED ABOU ZEID EL NAHRAWY.

Food Technology Research Institute:tel. (2) 35735090; fax (2) 35684669; e-mail nlftri@ie-eg.com; f. 1991; Dir Prof. Dr SAEB ABDEL-MONEIM HAFEZ.

Horticultural Research Institute: 9 Cairo University St, Giza; tel. (2) 35720617; fax (2) 35721628; e-mail hortinst@yahoo.com; f. 1948; produces new high-yielding early-maturing horticulture crop cultivars; maintains horticulture crop genetic resources; introduces new cultivars and germplasm of certain promising horticulture species; conducts research for optimizing the best cultural practices; implements extension and training programmes to transfer new technologies to farmers nationwide; 695 mems; Dir. Prof. SALAMA EID SALEM SHREIF; publ. *Egyptian Journal of Horticulture* (2 a year).

Plant Pathology Research Institute:tel. (2) 35724893; fax (2) 35723146; e-mail nagiabouzeid@link.net; f. 1919; research in various aspects of disease survey: ecology, biology, epidemiology and control measures; 170 research staff; library of 1,098 vols; Dir Prof. NAGI MOHAMED ABOU ZEID; publs *Agricultural Research Review*, *Egyptian Phytopathology*, *Journal of Applied Microbiology*.

Plant Protection Research Institute: 7 Nadi El Said St, Dokki, Giza 12311; tel. (2) 37486163; fax (2) 33372193; e-mail ppri@ arc.sci.eg; f. 1912; Dir Prof. NAGI MOHAMED ABOU ZEID.

Soil, Water and Environment Research Institute: Cairo University St, Giza; tel. and fax (2) 35720608; e-mail swerisweri@hotmail.com; f. 1969; Dir Prof. HAMDY EL HOUSSANY KHALIFA.

Sugar Crops Research Institute: 9 Cairo University St, Giza; tel. (2) 35735699; fax (2) 35697052; e-mail scriare@yahoo.com; Dir Prof. SAMIA SAAD EL SAYED EL MAGHRABY.

Veterinary Serum and Vaccine Research Institute: Abbasia, Cairo; tel. (2) 23421009; fax (2) 23428321; e-mail svri@idsc.gov.eg; internet www.vsvri-eg .com; Dir Prof. FEKRIA ABD ELHAFEZ EL BORDENY.

Institute of Freshwater Fishery Biology: 10 Hassan Sabry St (Fish Garden), BP Zamalik, Cairo; f. 1954; undertakes research in fish biology and culture; 7 scientists; Dir Prof. A. R. EL BOLOCK.

Institute of Oceanography and Fisheries: 101 Kasr El-Aini St, Cairo; tel. (2) 27921342; fax (2) 27921339; e-mail soliman@niof.sci.eg; internet www.niof.sci .eg; f. 1931 in connection with the Faculty of Science, Cairo; undertakes oceanographical, environmental and fisheries research at Alexandria, the Red Sea, the Aqaba and Suez Gulfs at Attaka, inland waters and at Kanater (aquaculture); attached to the Academy of Scientific Research; Dir Prof. SOLIMAN HAMED; publ. *Journal of Aquatic Research*.

Attached Institute:

National Oceanographic Data Center:e-mail ahmedmoustafaelnemr@ yahoo.com; internet www.nodc-egypt.org; Dir Dr AHMAD EL NEMR.

ARCHITECTURE AND TOWN PLANNING

Housing and Building National Research Centre: BP 1770, Cairo 12311; tel. (2) 33356853; fax (2) 33351564; e-mail hbrc@hbrc.edu.eg; internet www.hbrc.edu .eg; attached to the Min. of Housing, Utilities and Urban Devt; carries out basic and applied research work on building materials and means of construction; also provides technical information and acts as consultant to the different authorities concerned with bldg and construction materials; 8 specialized laboratories; Chair. Prof. MOSTAFA EL DEMERDASH.

ECONOMICS, LAW AND POLITICS

Centre d'Etudes et de Documentation Economique, Juridique et Sociale: 2 Sikkat al-Fadl, BP 392, Muhammad Farid, Cairo; tel. (2) 23928711; fax (2) 23928791; e-mail cedej@cedej.org.eg; internet www .cedej.org.eg; f. 1969; attached to Sous-direction des Sciences Sociales et Humaines (MAE) and Centre National de la Recherche Scientifique (CNRS), Paris; cooperation, documentation and research on an exchange basis between Egypt and France; research on Egypt (19th and 20th century) and the Arab world; univ. exchanges in cooperation with Egyptian Govt; library of 30,000 vols, 8 documentalists scan and classify 40 Egyptian periodicals; Dir MARC LAVERGNE; publs *Egypte—Monde Arabe* (2 a year), *Mutun* (in Arabic, 2 a year).

Institute of Arab Research and Studies: BP 229, 1 Tolombat St, Garden City, Cairo; tel. (2) 33551648; fax (2) 33562543; f. 1953; affiliated to the Arab League Educational, Cultural and Scientific Organization (ALECSO); library of 77,000 vols, 1,068 periodicals; studies in contemporary Arab affairs, economics, sociology, history, geography, law, literature, linguistics; Dir Prof. AHMED YOUSSEF AHMED; publ. *Bulletin of Arab Research and Studies* (1 a year).

Institute of National Planning: Salah Salem St, Nasr City, Cairo; tel. (2) 22629225; fax (2) 22621151; e-mail inplanning@idsc.net.eg; internet www .inplanning.gov.eg; f. 1960; research, training, documentation and information; organized in 11 scientific and technical centres; library of 70,000 vols; Dir Dr OLA SULEIMAN KHALIL YUSUF AL HAKIM; publs *Egyptian Review of Development and Planning, Issues in Planning and Development* (irregular).

EDUCATION

National Centre for Educational Research: Central Ministry of Education, 33 Sharia Falaky, Cairo; f. 1972; coordinates current educational policy with that of the National Specialized Councils; exchanges information with like instns throughout the world; provides local and foreign documents on education; Dir Dr YOUSSEF KHALIL YOUSSEF; publs *Contemporary Trends in Education* (2 a year), *Educational Information Bulletin* (12 a year); and various works on education in Egypt and the Arab world.

HISTORY, GEOGRAPHY AND ARCHAEOLOGY

Deutsches Archäologisches Institut (German Archaeological Institute): 31 Sharia Abu El-Feda, Cairo-Zamalek 11211; tel. (2) 27351460; fax (2) 27370770; e-mail sekretariat@kairo.dainst.org; internet www .dainst.org; Dir Prof. Dr STEPHAN J. SEIDLMAYER; Sec. IRENE EL KHORAZATY.

Institut Français d'Archéologie Orientale (French Institute of Oriental Archaeology): 37 rue al Cheikh Ali Youssef, BP 11562 Qasr al-Aïny, Cairo 11441; tel. (2) 27971600; fax (2) 27950869; e-mail direction@ifao.egnet.net; internet www.ifao .egnet.net; f. 1880; excavations, research, seminars and publs intended to widen knowledge of Egyptian history from the Pharaohs to the Islamic period; library of 82,000 books; Dir BÉATRIX MIDANT-REYNES; publs *Annales Islamologiques* (1 a year), *Bulletin Critique des Annales Islamologiques, Bulletin de l'Institut Français d'Archéologie Orientale* (1 a year), *Cahiers des Annales Islamologiques, Cahiers de la Céramique Égyptienne.*

MEDICINE

Central Health Laboratories: Ministry of Health, 19 Sheikh Rehan, Cairo; f. 1885; Dir-Gen. Dr ABDEL MONEIM EL BEHAIRY; Bacteriology: Dr GUERGIS EL MALEEH; Clinical Pathology: Dr NADIR MOHARRAM; Sanitary Chemistry: MOUNIR AYAD; Toxicology: DALAL ABDEL REHIM; Food Microbiology: Dr MAGDA RAKHA; library of 2,000 vols; publs *Bacteriology, Virology, Sera and Vaccines Production.*

National Hepatology and Tropical Medicine Research Institute: 10 Sharia Kasr el-Aini, Cairo; tel. (2) 23642494; fax (2) 23683723; e-mail info@nhtmri.org; internet www.nhtmri.org; f. 1932; depts of Biochemistry, Clinical Pharmacy, Dermatology and Andrology, Haematology, Microbiology, Paediatrics, Parasitology, Pathology, Public Health Epidemiology, Radiology, Tropical and Liver Surgery, Tropical Medicine; library of 4,000 vols; Dir-Gen. Prof. Dr WAHEED DOSS.

Memorial Institute for Ophthalmic Research: Sharia Al-Ahram, Giza, Cairo; f. 1925; library of 2,800 vols; Dir Dr ABDEL MEGID ABDEL RAHMAN.

National Nutrition Institute: Min. of Health, 16 Kasr El-Aini St, Cairo; tel. (2) 23646413; fax (2) 23647476; e-mail admin@ nni.org.eg; internet www.nni.org.eg; f. 1955; research, analysis, training and education in nutrition science; 469 staff; Dir Dr AZZA GOHAR; publ. *Bulletin.*

National Organization for Drug Control and Research: 6 Abou Hazem St, Giza; tel. (2) 27480472; fax (2) 27480478; f. 1976; 300 staff; Chair. Dr ALI HIGAZI.

VACSERA Holding Company for Biological Products and Vaccines: 51 Sharia Wezarat El-Zeraa, Agouza, Giza 22311; tel. (2) 37611111; fax (2) 37609177; e-mail ceo@ vacsera.com; internet www.vacsera.com; Chair. Dr MOHAMED RABIE.

Theodor Bilharz Research Institute: Warak el Hadar, Embaba, BP 30, Giza 12411; tel. (2) 35401019; fax (2) 35408125; e-mail info@tbri.sci.eg; internet www.tbri.sci .eg; f. 1979; for the control, diagnosis and treatment of endemic diseases, especially urinary and hepatic schistosomiasis; Dir Prof. JEHAN G. EL FENDI; publs *Egyptian Journal of Shistosomiasis, TBRI Biomedical Bulletin, TBRI Today.*

NATURAL SCIENCES
General

UNESCO Office Cairo and Regional Bureau for Science and Technology in the Arab States: 8 Abdel Rahman Fahmy St, Garden City, Cairo 11511; tel. (2) 27945599; fax (2) 27945296; e-mail info@unesco.org; internet www.unesco.org/en/cairo; f. 1947; designated Cluster Office for Egypt, Sudan and Yemen; Dir TAREK SHAWKI.

Physical Sciences

Egyptian Mineral Resources Authority: BP 11511 Ataba, Cairo; fax (2) 24820128; e-mail info@egsma.gov.eg; internet www .egsma.gov.eg; f. 1896; regional geological mapping, mineral prospecting, evaluation of mineral deposits, and granting mineral exploration and exploitation rights; cartography laboratory; 763 research workers; library of 82,000 vols; Chair. HUSSEIN HAMOUDA.

National Authority for Remote Sensing and Space Sciences: BP 1564, Alf Maskan, Cairo; tel. (2) 26225801; fax (2) 26225800; e-mail info@narss.sci.eg; internet www.narss .sci.eg; f. 1972; covers geology, mineral and energy resources, hydrogeology, agriculture, soils, geophysics, photogrammetry, engineering, physics and environment; operates advanced digital data processing facility for satellite and aircraft data, also Beechcraft King-Air aeroplane with most advanced remote sensing equipment; design and implementation of nat. space scientific and technical activities; library of 2,500 books; Chair. Prof. AYMAN EL DESSOUKI IBRAHIM; publ. *Journal* (1 a year).

National Research Institute of Astronomy and Geophysics: BP 11421, Helwan, Cairo; tel. (2) 25549780; fax (2) 25548020; e-mail astro@nriag.sci.eg; internet www .nriag.sci.eg; f. 1903; comprises the Helwan Observatory, the Kottamyia Observatory, the Misallat geomagnetic observatory, seismic stations at Helwan, Aswan, Matrouh, and satellite tracking stations at Helwan and Abu Simbel; attached to the Academy of Scientific Research and Technology; library of 10,594 vols; Pres. Prof. ANAS MOHAMED IBRAHIM OSMAN; publs *Journal of Astronomy and Astrophysics, Journal of Geophysics.*

RELIGION, SOCIOLOGY AND ANTHROPOLOGY

Ibn Khaldun Centre for Development Studies: BP 13, Mokatim, Cairo; tel. (2) 25081617; fax (2) 26670973; e-mail info@ eicds.org; internet www.eicds.org; f. 1988; advancement of applied social sciences with special emphasis on Egypt and the Arab and Third Worlds; the Centre is an associated centre of the Arab Social Science Research network of the Arab Institute for Studies and Communication (ASSR–AISC); Dir Dr SAAD EDDIN IBRAHIM; publ. *Civil Society* (12 a year).

TECHNOLOGY

Central Metallurgical Research and Development Institute: 1 Elfelezat St, Helwan, Cairo 11421; tel. (2) 25010642; fax (2) 25010639; e-mail rucmrdi@rusys.eg.net; internet www.cmrdi.sci.eg; f. 1972; attached to the Ministry of Scientific Research; extractive metallurgy, ore dressing, technical services, metal-forming and working, welding research; library of 4,000 vols; Chair. Prof. Dr BAHAA ZAGHLOUL.

Egyptian Atomic Energy Authority: 8 Ahmad Elzomor St, Nasr City, Children Village BP, Cairo 11787; tel. (2) 22876033; fax (2) 22876031; e-mail hisham_f@frcu.eun .eg; internet www.eaea.org.eg; f. 1957; maintains 22-MW open pool multipurpose reactor at the Inshas site for production of radioisotopes for industrial and medical applications, research on neutron physics and personnel training; employs 850 academic scientists supported by 650 technical staff; Pres. Prof. ALY ISLAM METWALLY ALY.

Attached Research Centres:

National Centre for Radiation Research and Technology (NCRRT): tel. (2) 22746791; fax (2) 22749298; internet www.eaea.org.eg/ncrrt .html; f. 1972; main facilities incl. a 400,000 Ci, Co-60 unit and an electron accelerator (under construction); organized in 3 divs: radiation research, industrial irradiation, biotechnology; Chair. Prof. AMIN EL BAHY.

Nuclear Research Centre (NRC): BP 13975, Abu Zabal; tel. (4) 620810; fax (4) 620812; internet www.eaea.org.eg/nrc .html; main facilities incl. a 2-MW ET-RR-1 research reactor, a 2.5 Van de Graaff accelerator, a radioisotope production laboratory, nuclear fuel research and devt laboratory, laboratories for application of radioisotopes, electronic instrumentation laboratory and radiation protection laboratory; organized in 4 divs: basic nuclear sciences, reactors, material and nuclear industry, radioisotope applications; Chair. Prof. NASF CAMSAN.

The Hot Laboratories and Waste Management Centre (HLWMC): BP 13975, Abu Zabal; tel. (2) 44620784; fax (2) 44620806; internet www.eaea.org.eg/ hlwmc.html; f. 1980; main facilities incl. low and intermediate level liquid waste station, radioisotope production laboratories, radwaste disposal site; organized in 3 divs: radioisotopes, fuel treatment, radwaste treatment.

The National Centre for Nuclear Safety and Radiation Control (NCNSRC): tel. (2) 22728793; fax (2) 22740308; internet www.eaea.org.eg/ ncnsrc.html; f. 1982; organized in 3 divs: nuclear regulations and emergencies, radiation control, safety of nuclear installations.

Egyptian Petroleum Research Institute: 1 Ahmed el Zomor St, Nasr City, Cairo 11727; tel. (2) 22747847; fax (2) 22747433; e-mail research@epri.sci.eg; internet www .epri.sci.eg; f. 1976; organ of the Min. for Scientific Research; joint Board with Egyptian Gen. Petroleum Corporation; 7 research sections, dealing with all aspects of petroleum and energy-related problems; contract research and commercial services to local oil companies; library of over 5,000 books and periodicals; 850 staff; Dir Prof. AHMED MOHAMMAD AHMED AL SABAGH; publ. *Egyptian Journal of Petroleum.*

Hydraulics Research Institute: POB 13621, Police Station St, Delta Barrage, Cairo; tel. (2) 42188268; fax (2) 42189539; e-mail info@hri-egypt.org; internet www .hri-egypt.org; f. 1949; depts of Calibration and Instrumentation, Numerical Modelling, Physical Modelling, Sedimentation and Field Measurements; Dir Prof. FATTHY SAAD HASANAIN AL-GAMAL.

National Institute for Standards: Tersa St, el-Matbaa, el Haram, POB 136, Giza 12211; fax (2) 33867451; internet www.nis .sci.eg; f. 1963; attached to the Min. of Higher Education and Scientific Research; 197 staff; responsible for maintenance of nat. standards for physical units and their use for purposes of calibration; research on scientific metrology, to develop new techniques for measurements, calibrations, and devt of new standards; constituent laboratories: electricity, photometry, frequency, thermometry, radiation, acoustics, mass, length metrology, engineering metrology, testing of materials, safety tests and textile testing, ultrasonics, polymer testing, and reference materials; Dir Prof. ALI ABUELEZZ; publ. *Egyptian Journal of Measurement Science and Technology.*

Textile Consolidation Fund: 7 el-Taher St, Abdin, Cairo; tel. (2) 23925521; fax (2) 23928013; e-mail tcf_textiles@tcfegypt.org .eg; internet www.tcfegypt.org.eg; f. 1953; incl. textiles quality control centre and textiles devt centre; library of 5,000 vols; Gen. Man. MAGDI EL AREF.

Libraries and Archives
Alexandria
Alexandria Municipal Library: 18 Sharia Menasha Moharrem Bey, BP 138 el Shatby, Alexandria 21526; tel. (3) 24839999; fax (3) 24820461; e-mail secretariat@bibalex.org; f. 1892; under control of the Bibliotheca Alexandrina; 22,390 Arabic vols, 35,399 European vols, 4,086 MSS; Chief Librarian BESHIR BESHIR EL SHINDI.

Alexandria University Central Library: 136 Horiyah Rd, Shatby, Alexandria; tel. (3) 24282928; fax (3) 24282927; e-mail auclib@ auclib.edu.eg; f. 1942; 45,000 books, 1m. microfiches and roll films, 1,200 periodicals, 2,500 MSS, 17,500 dissertations; Supervisor Prof. SHAWKY SALEM.

Bibliotheca Alexandrina: El Shatby, BP 138, Alexandria 21526; tel. (3) 24839999; fax (3) 24820460; e-mail infobib@bibalex.org; internet www.bibalex.org; f. 2001; built as successor to ancient Alexandria library; 1,500,000 vols, 100,000 MSS, 50,000 maps, 250,000 audio and audiovisual items; incl. collns from the Sidi Mursi Abul Abbas Mosque and the Al Azhar Religious Institute in Smouha; deposit library for UNESCO, WTO, Red Cross and Council of Europe; Dir-Gen. Dr ISMAIL SERAGELDIN.

Library of the Greek Orthodox Patriarchate of Alexandria: BP 2006, Alexandria; tel. (3) 24868595; fax (3) 24875684; e-mail patriarchate@ greekorthodox-alexandria.org; internet www .greekorthodox-alexandria.org; f. AD 43; 41,000 vols, 542 MSS, contains 2,241 rare editions; Librarian NICOLAS ALEXOPOULOS.

Assiut
Assiut University Library: Assiut; tel. (88) 2412526; e-mail auslibrarynquiries@yahoo .com; internet www.aun.edu.eg/library/index .htm; 250,000 vols; Dir S. M. SAYED.

Cairo
Al-Azhar University Library: Nasr City, Cairo; 80,000 vols, including 20,000 MSS; Librarian M. E. A. HADY.

American University in Cairo Library: AUC Ave, POB 74, New Cairo 11835; tel. (2) 6153648; fax (2) 27974903; e-mail library@ aucegypt.edu; internet library.aucegypt.edu; f. 1919; 403,722 vols; Dean of Libraries and Learning Technologies SHAHIRA EL-SAWY.

Arab League Information Centre (Library): Midan al-Tahir, Cairo 11642; tel. (2) 25750511; fax (2) 25740331; f. 1945; Sec.-Gen. Dr SAUD ABD AL AZIZ EL ZABIDI; 30,000 vols, 250 periodicals.

Cairo University Library: Orman, Giza; tel. (2) 37759743; fax (2) 35726747; e-mail sherifshn@cu.edu.eg; internet www.cl.cu.edu .eg; f. 1932; 1,407,000 vols, 10,000 periodicals; Gen. Dir Dr SHERIF SHAHEEN.

Centre of Documentation and Studies on Ancient Egypt: 3 Sharia el-Adel Abou Bakr, Zamalek, Cairo; f. 1956; scientific and documentary reference centre for all Egyptian Pharaonic monuments; 4,500 vols, 33,000 photographs; Dir-Gen. Dr MAHMOUD MAHER TAHA.

Egypt National Agricultural Library: 7 Nadi el Said St, Dokki, Giza; tel. (2) 33351313; fax (2) 33351302; e-mail magdy@ nile.enal.sci.eg; internet nile.enal.sci.eg; f. 1920; 25,000 vols; Dir Dr MAGDY ABD EL RAHMAN; publ. *Egyptian Journal of Agricultural Research.*

Egyptian National Library and Archives: Sharia Corniche el-Nil, Bulaq, Cairo; internet www.darelkotob.gov.eg; f. 1870; 1,500,000 vols (400,000 European); 11 brs with 250,000 vols, incl. fine arts library; deposit library; Dir Gen. ALI ABDUL MOHSEN.

Egyptian Library: Abdin Palace, Cairo; over 20,000 vols; Dir ABDEL HAMID HOSNI.

Library of the Central Bank of Egypt: 153 Mohamed Farid St, Cairo; tel. (2) 23905427; fax (2) 23904232; e-mail info@cbe .org.eg; f. 1961; 15,430 vols; publ. *Economic Review* (4 a year).

Library of the Ministry of Education: 16 Sharia el-Falaki, Cairo; tel. (2) 38544805; f. 1927; 55,966 vols (European and Arabic); Dir HASSAN ABDEL SHAFI.

Library of the Ministry of Health: Sharia Magles el Shaab, Cairo 11467; fax (2) 27953966; over 27,000 vols.

Library of the Ministry of Justice: Midan Lazoghli, Cairo; f. 1929; over 90,000 vols and periodicals in Arabic, French and English (law and social science); private library for the use of judges and members of the Parquet (public prosecution and criminal investigation authority); a centre attached to the library contains the latest texts of local and comparative legislature on Personal Status; Dir F. ABOU EL KHEIR.

Library of the Ministry of Supply and Internal Trade: 99 Sharia Kasr el-Aini, Cairo; internet msht.tripod.com; over 20,000 vols.

Library of the Ministry of Waqfs: Sharia Sabri Alu Alam, Ean el-Luk, Cairo; f. 1942; 20,219 vols.

Library of the Monastery of St Catherine: 18 Midan El Daher, Cairo; f. 6th century; over 4,000 Greek, Oriental and Slavonic MSS; contains the Codex Sinaiticus Syriacus; Librarians Monk DANIEL, Monk SYMEON.

Library of the National Research Institute of Astronomy and Geophysics: Helwan, Cairo; internet www.nriag.sci.eg; f. 1903; 11,000 vols; Dir Prof. R. M. KEBEASY.

National Assembly Library: Palace of the National Assembly, Cairo; internet www .parliament.gov.eg/english/publicsec/library; f. 1924; over 61,000 vols; Dir ANTOUN MATTA.

National Research Centre: El Buhoth St, Dokki Cairo; tel. (2) 33371362; fax (2) 33370931; e-mail info@nrc.sci.eg; internet www.nrc.sci.eg; f. 1955; accumulates and disseminates information in all languages and in all branches of science and technology; 35,600 vols, 2,500 periodicals, UNESCO and WHO special collns; Dir WAGLAA MAHMOUD FAHMY.

Damanhour
Damanhour Municipal Library: Damanhour; 13,431 vols.

Mansoura
Mansoura Municipal Library: Mansoura; contains 17,984 vols (Arabic 13,036, European 4,948).

Zagazig
Sharkia Provincial Council Library: Zagazig; contains 12,238 vols (Arabic 7,861, European 4,377).

Museums and Art Galleries
Alexandria
Greco-Roman Museum: Museum St, Alexandria; tel. (3) 24865820; fax (3) 24876434; internet www.grm.gov.eg; f. 1892; exhibits from the Greek, Roman and Byzantine eras; library of 15,500 vols, Omar Tousson colln of 4,000 vols; Dir DOREYA SAID; publs *Annuaire du Musée Gréco-Romain, Guide to the Alexandrian Monuments.*

National Maritime Museum: Alexandria; Dir Dr MEHREZ EL HUSSEINI.

Aswan
Nubia Museum: el Fanadek St, Aswan; tel. (97) 319333; fax (97) 317998; e-mail nubiamuseum@numibia.net; internet www .numibia.net/nubia; f. 1997; history of Nubia since prehistoric times; Dir OSSAMA A. W. ABDEL MAGUID.

Cairo
Agricultural Museum: Al Sawra St, Dokki, Cairo; tel. (2) 33608682; f. 1938; exhibits of ancient and modern Egyptian agriculture and rural life, horticulture, irrigation; botanical and zoological sections; library of 8,885 vols; Dir SAMIR M. SULTAN.

Al-Gawhara Palace Museum: The Citadel, Cairo; tel. (2) 25116187; f. 1954, refurnished 1956; built in 1811 in the Ottoman style, the Palace retains much of its original interior; contains Oriental and French furniture, including gilded throne, Turkish paintings, exhibitions of clocks, glass, 19th-century costumes.

Cairo Geological Museum: BP Dawawin, Cairo 11521; Cornish el-Nil, Maadi Rd, Cairo; tel. (2) 23187056; fax (2) 33820128; e-mail info@egsma.gov.eg; internet www .egsma.gov.eg/default2.htm; a general dept of the Egyptian Geological Survey; f. 1904; 50,000 specimens, mostly Egyptian; depts: vertebrates, invertebrates, rocks and minerals; library of 4,200 vols and 6,000 periodicals; Dir-Gen. MOHAMMED AHMED EL BEDAWI.

Cairo Museum of Hygiene: Midan-el-Sakakini, Daher, Cairo; Dir Dr FAWZI SWEHA.

Coptic Museum: Fakhry Abd el Nour St, Abbassia, Cairo; tel. (2) 23639742; f. 1910; sculpture and frescoes, MSS, textiles, icons, ivory and bone, carved wood, metalwork, pottery and glass; library of 6,587 vols; Dir Dr MAHAR SALIB.

Cotton Museum: Gezira, Cairo; tel. (2) 33608682; f. 1923; established by the Egyptian Agricultural Society; all aspects of cotton growing, diseases, pests, and methods of spinning and weaving are shown; Dir M. EL BAHTIMI.

Egyptian (National) Museum: Midan-el-Tahrir, Cairo; tel. (2) 25796948; fax (2) 25794596; e-mail egymu1@idsc.net.eg; f. 1902; exhibits from prehistoric times until the 3rd century AD; excludes Coptic and

Islamic periods; established by decree in 1835 to conserve antiquities; the Antiquities Dept administers the archaeological museums and controls excavations; library of 40,000 vols; Dir MAMDOUH MOHAMED ELDAMATY; publ. *Annals of the Antiquities Service of Egypt*.

Egyptian National Railways Museum: Cairo Station Bldgs, Ramses Sq., Cairo 11669; tel. (2) 25763793; fax (2) 25740000; f. 1933; contains models of foreign and Egyptian railways, and technical information and statistics on the evolution and devt of the Egyptian railway services; library of 5,595 vols (Arabic 2,694, European 2,901); Curator IBRAHIM SALEH ALY.

Gayer-Anderson Museum: Beit el-Kretlia, Cairo; f. 1936; private collns of Oriental art objects bequeathed to Egypt by R. G. Gayer-Anderson Pasha in 1936; Curator YOUNES MAHRAN.

Museum of Islamic Art: Ahmed Maher Sq., Bab al-Khalq, Cairo 11638; tel. (2) 23901520; e-mail islam_mus_director@hotmail.com; internet www.islamicmuseum.gov.eg; f. 1881; colln of 86,000 items representing the evolution of Islamic art from the first quarter of the 7th century to 1900; library of 15,000 vols; Dir-Gen. Dr NIMAT M. ABU-BAKR; publs *Islamic Archaeological Studies* (1 a year), catalogues on Islamic decorative arts.

Museum of Modern Art: 4 Sharia Kasr el-Nil, Cairo; internet www.modernartmuseum.gov.eg; f. 1920; Chair. AHMED NAWAR.

War Museum: The Citadel, Cairo; library of 6,000 vols.

Universities

AIN SHAMS UNIVERSITY

Elkhalifa Elmaamoon St, Abbassia, Cairo 11566

Telephone: (2) 26831231
Fax: (2) 26847824
E-mail: pres@asunet.shams.edu.eg
Internet: net.shams.edu.eg

Founded 1950
Languages of instruction: Arabic, English, French
Academic year: October to June

Pres.: Prof. MAGED MOHAMMED ALI KHALIL EL-DEEB
Vice-Pres. for Community and Environment: Prof. GAMAL SAMY ALI MAHMOUD
Vice-Pres. for Education and Student Affairs: Prof. ATEF MOHAMMED AWAD EL AWAM
Vice-Pres. for Postgraduate Studies and Research: Prof. MOHAMMED SAID SALAMA ALI
Sec.-Gen.: Prof. HASSAN ABD EL AZEEZ AMMAR
Chief Librarian: SOHAIR HASSAN SOMIDA

Library of 15,786 vols (3,318 Arabic, 12,468 English), 63 periodicals, 133,000 theses (30,000 Arabic, 103,000 English)
Number of teachers: 7,297
Number of students: 185,000

DEANS

Faculty of Agriculture: Prof. ESAM OSMAN FAYED
Faculty of Al-Alsun: Prof. ABDEL KADER ATTIA MOHAMMED ABO EL-ANIN
Faculty of Arts: Prof. MAMDOUH MOHAMMED GAD EL-DMATY
Faculty of Commerce: Prof. HUSSEIN MOHAMMED AHMED EID
Faculty of Computer and Information Sciences: Prof. MOHAMED ESAAM KHALIFA
Faculty of Dentistry: Prof. TAREK SALAH EL-DIN HUSSEIN

Faculty of Education: Prof. SUZAN MOHAMMED SALAH EL-DIN FOUAD
Faculty of Engineering: Prof. HADIA MOHAMMED SAID EL-HANAWY
Faculty of Law: Prof. EL SAID EID NAIL
Faculty of Medicine: Prof. AHMED IBRAHIM NASAR
Faculty of Nursing: Prof. SABAH SAAD EL SAID EL SHARKAWY
Faculty of Pharmacy: Prof. NAHED DAWOOD MORTADA
Faculty of Science: Prof. ADEL RAMDAN MOSTFA EL SAYED AHMED
Faculty of Specific Education: Prof. NADIA EL SAYED EL HOSENY
Faculty of Women: Prof. WAFAA MOHAMMED AHMED IBRAHIM
Institute of Environmental Studies and Research: Prof. AHMED MUSTAFA HUSSIEN EL ATIK
Institute of Childhood Studies: Prof. KHALID HUSSEIN MOSTAFA TAMAN

ALEXANDRIA UNIVERSITY

22 el Geish Ave, el Shatby, Alexandria

Telephone: (3) 5960720
Fax: (3) 5960720
E-mail: info@alexeng.edu.eg
Internet: www.alex.edu.eg

Founded 1942
State control

Languages of instruction: Arabic, English, French
Academic year: October to June

Pres.: Prof. HASSAN NADIR KHAIRALLAH
Vice-Pres. for Community Services and Environmental Affairs: Prof. EZAT KHAMES AMIN MOSTAFA
Vice-Pres. for Damanhour Br.: Prof. MOHAMED AHMED BAUOMY
Vice-Pres. for Postgraduate Studies and Research: Prof. GOAD GOAD HAMADA
Vice-Pres. for Undergraduate Studies: Prof. OKASHA MOHAMED ABDEL AAL
Sec.-Gen.: MOHAMED ROSHDY ABDEL GHANI
Chief Librarian: SOHER GAMAL

Library: see Libraries and Archives
Number of teachers: 3,979
Number of students: 144,707

DEANS

Faculty of Agriculture: Prof. TAREK MAHMOUD ELKIEY
Faculty of Agriculture (in Damanhour): Prof. ABDEL SALAM HELMY MOHAMED BELAL
Faculty of Agriculture (in Saba Basha): Prof. ALY IBRAHIM ALY EBEDA
Faculty of Arts: Prof. FATHY ABDEL AZIZ ABORADY
Faculty of Arts (in Damanhour): Prof. MOHAMED ALY BAHGAT EL FADLY
Faculty of Commerce: Prof. MOHAMED ELFAUOMY MOHAMED IBRAHIM
Faculty of Commerce (in Damanhour): Prof. KAMAL ELDIN MOSTAFA ELDAHRAWY
Faculty of Dentistry: Prof. MOSTAFA MOHAMED EL DEBANY
Faculty of Education (in Damanhour): Prof. ANTAR LOTFY
Faculty of Education (in Marsa Matrouh): Prof. SHEBL BADRAN MOHAMED EL GHAREEB
Faculty of Engineering: Prof. ABDEL LOTFY MOHAMADEEN
Faculty of Fine Arts: Prof. MAGDY MOHAMED MOUSSA
Faculty of Kindergartens: Prof. ELHAM MOSTAFA MOHAMED EBED
Faculty of Law: Prof. Dr MAGDY MAHMOUD MOHAMED SHEHAB
Faculty of Medicine: Prof. ABDEL AZIZ BELAL
Faculty of Nursing: Prof. NADIA TAHA MOHAMED AHMED

Faculty of Pharmacy: Prof. NABIL AHMED MOHAMED ABDEL SALAM
Faculty of Physical Education (Females): Prof. SADIA ABDEL GOAD MOHAMED SHEHA
Faculty of Physical Education (Males): Prof. ABDEL MONIEM BADEER ELKOSIER
Faculty of Science: Prof. MOSTAFA HUSSIEN FAHMY
Faculty of Specific Education: Prof. ABDEL RAZEK MOHAMED ELSAYED
Faculty of Tourism and Hotels: Prof. MAHER ABDEL KADER MOHAMED ALY
Faculty of Veterinary Medicine: Prof. Dr MOHAMED ALY EKELA TORKY
Higher Institute of Public Health: Prof. HASSAN KAMEL BASSOUNY MOHAMED (see also under Colleges)
Institute of Medical Research: Prof. AASSER ABDEL HAMIED HAFEZ (Dir)
Institute of Postgraduate Studies and Research: Prof. MOHAMED EZZ ELDIN ELRAIE

AL AZHAR UNIVERSITY

Cairo 11751

Telephone: (2) 22623278
Fax: (2) 22623284
E-mail: azhar@azhar.eun.eg
Internet: www.azhar.edu.eg

Founded AD 970; modernized and expanded 1961
Academic year: September to June

Rector: AHMAD AL TAYIB
Vice-Rectors: Prof. SAMA GAD, Prof. TAHA ABU KREISHA

Library: see Libraries and Archives
Number of teachers: 9,000
Number of students: 185,000 (on several campuses)

DEANS

Faculty of Agriculture: Prof. AMIN YOUSSEF
Faculty of Arabic and Islamic Studies: Prof. MAHMOUD EL SAIED SHAIKHOON
Faculty of Arabic Studies: Prof. ABDULLAH HELLAL
Faculty of Commerce: Prof. ABDEL-HAMID RABEE
Faculty of Education: MUHAMMAD ABDEL SAMEE OTHMAN
Faculty of Engineering: Prof. ABDEL-WAHID AHMAD
Faculty of Islamic Jurisprudence and Law: Prof. MOHAMMAD RAFAT OTHMAN
Faculty of Islamic Theology: Prof. ABDEL-MOUTI MOHAMMAD BAYOMI
Faculty of Language and Translation: Prof. AHMAD BASEM ABDEL-GHAFFAR
Faculty of Medicine: Prof. ISMAEEL KHALAF
Faculty of Science: Prof. ABDEL-WAHAB AL SHARKAWI
Islamic Women's College: Prof. KAWTHAR KAMEL

AMERICAN UNIVERSITY IN CAIRO

Tahrir Sq. Campus, BP 2511, 113 Sharia Kasr el Aini, Cairo 11511
New Cairo Campus, BP 74, Cairo 11835
American Office: 3rd Fl., 420 Fifth Ave, New York, NY 10018-2729, USA

Telephone: (2) 27942964
Fax: (2) 27957565
Internet: www.aucegypt.edu

Founded 1919
Private control
Language of instruction: English
Academic year: September to June

Pres.: DAVID A. ARNOLD
Provost: LISA ANDERSON
Vice-Provost: ALI HADI
Vice-Pres. and Exec. Sec. of Board of Trustees: MARY CORRARINO

Vice-Pres. for Continuing Education: EDWARD SIMPSON

Vice-Pres. for Finance: ANDREW SNAITH

Vice-Pres. for Institutional Advancement: JAMES L. BULLOCK

Vice-Pres. for Planning and Admin.: PAUL DONOGHUE

Vice-Pres. for Student Affairs: ASHRAF EL FIQI

Dean of Libraries: SHAHIRA EL SAWY

Library: see Libraries and Archives

Number of teachers: 303

Number of students: 5,577

Publications: *Alif* (English and Arabic poetry), *Cairo Papers in Social Science*

DEANS

School of Business, Economics and Communications: D. O'CONNOR

School of Humanities and Social Sciences: A. M. LESCH

School of Sciences and Engineering: M. HAROUN

ATTACHED UNITS

Centre for Adult and Continuing Education: non-credit study programme for 30,000 students a year; offers courses and post-secondary and postgraduate career programmes in Arabic/English, Arabic/French translation, English language, business and secretarial skills, and computing; Dean Dr HARRY MILLER.

Desert Development Centre: research to improve the social and economic well-being of new desert settlers, integrating agriculture, renewable energy and community research; Dir Dr RICHARD TUTWILER.

Social Research Centre: current research projects on demography and human resettlement; Dir Dr HODA RASHAD.

ASSIUT UNIVERSITY

Assiut Governorate, Assiut Univ. POB, Assiut 71515

Telephone: (88) 2357007

Fax: (88) 2354130

E-mail: info@aun.eun.eg

Internet: www.aun.edu.eg

Founded 1957

Languages of instruction: Arabic, English

Academic year: September to June

State

Rector: Prof. MOSTAFA MOHAMAD KAMAL

Deputy-Rector for Community Services and Environmental Devt: Prof. MOHAMED AHMED SHANAWANY

Deputy-Rector for Postgraduate Studies and Research Affairs: Prof. MOHAMED RAGAB BAYOUMI

Deputy-Rector for Student Affairs and Education: Prof. SAID AHMED IBRAHIM

Sec.-Gen.: MOHAMED MAHMOUD OMAR

Chief Librarian: SAMIA ALI ISMAIL

Accredited by the Nat. Authority of Education Accreditation and Quality Assurance, Min. of Higher Education

Library of 40,000 vols, abstracts covering all educational and research fields, 35,000 full text periodicals, 28,000 e-books; 28 br. libraries

Number of teachers: 3,975

Number of students: 79,140

Publications: *Assiut Journal of Agricultural Sciences, Assiut Medical Journal, Assiut University Bulletin for Environmental Researches, Assiut University Journal of Computer Science, Assiut University Journal of Geology, Assiut University Journal of Mathematics, Assiut University Journal of Zoology, Assiut Veterinary Medical Journal, Bulletin of Faculty of Physical Education, Bulletin of Pharmaceutical Sci-* ences, *Egyptian Sugar Journal, Journal of Engineering Sciences, Journal of Faculty of Education, Journal of Law Studies* (Arabic)

DEANS

Faculty of Agriculture: Prof. MOHAMED ABD EL WAHAB ABO NOHOUL

Faculty of Arts: Prof. NASEEF SHAKER SAYED

Faculty of Commerce: Prof. ADEL RAYAN MOHAMED RAYAN

Faculty of Education: Prof. SALAH EL DEEN HUSSIEN EL SHARIEF

Faculty of Education (New Valley Branch): Prof. AHMED SAYED MOHAMED IBRAHIM

Faculty of Engineering: Prof. IBRAHIM M. ISMAIL SALEH

Faculty of Information and Computer and Information Sciences: Prof. HOSSNI MOHAMED IBRAHIM (acting)

Faculty of Law: Prof. ESSAM MOHAMED AHMED ZANNATI

Faculty of Medicine: Prof. MAHER ABDEL SALAM EL ASSAL

Faculty of Nursing: Prof. IKRAM ALI HASHIM SOLIMAN

Faculty of Pharmacy: Prof. GAMAL AHMED S. ABD-ELAAL

Faculty of Physical Education: Prof. TAREQ MOHAMED MOHAMED ABDEL AZIZ

Faculty of Science: Prof. AHMED YEHYA ABDEL-MALEK

Faculty of Social Service: Prof. NABIEL IBRAHIM AHMED

Faculty of Specific Education: Prof. MOHAMED SALAH EL-DIN YOUSSEF (acting)

Faculty of Veterinary Medicine: Prof. MOSTAFA KHALIL MOSTAFA

ATTACHED RESEARCH INSTITUTES

South Egypt Cancer Institute: El-Methaq St, Mansheit El-Omara Sq., POB 171516, Assiut; tel. (88) 2337670; fax (88) 2348609; e-mail seci@seci.info; f. 1997 as part of the Faculty of Medicine, present status 1999; depts of Surgical Oncology, Anesthesia, ICU and Pain Relief, Radiology, Radiotherapy and Nuclear Medicine, Medical Oncology, Pediatric Oncology, Clinical Pathology, Cancer Biology, Biostatistics and Cancer Epidemiology; Dean Prof. MAHMOUD MOHAMED MOSTAFA.

Sugar Technology Research Institute: Assiut Univ. Old Bldg; tel. (88) 2313713; fax (88) 2313713; e-mail sugar@acc.aun.edu.eg; internet www.aun.edu.eg/suger/general .html; language of instruction: English; teaching, training, devt and research in the Egyptian sugar industry; offers postgraduate diplomas; depts of sugar industry, industrial engineering and management, chemical and pharmaceutical industries, materials and applications, advanced agricultural technology, environmental sciences and pollution treatment; Dean Prof. ABDEL AZIZ AHMED SAID.

There are 46 attached university centres and special units

CAIRO UNIVERSITY

BP 12611, Orman, Giza, Cairo

Telephone: (2) 35729584

Fax: (2) 35688884

E-mail: info@main-scc.cairo.edu.eg

Internet: www.cu.edu.eg

Founded 1908

State control

Languages of instruction: Arabic, English and French

Academic year: October to June

Pres.: Prof. HOSSAM KAMEL

Vice-Pres. for Beni-Suef Br.: Prof. MOHAMED ANAS KASEM GAFAR

Vice-Pres. for Community Services and Environmental Affairs: Prof. ABDALLA ABDEL FATTAH ELTATAWY

Vice-Pres. for Fayoum Branch: Prof. GALAL MOSTAFA SAEED

Vice-Pres. for Postgraduate Studies and Research: Prof. MOTAZ MOHAMED HOSNY KHORSHED

Vice-Pres. for Undergraduate Studies: Prof. HAMED TAHER HASSANEEN FOAD

Sec.-Gen.: FAYZA MEGAHED

Librarian: AHMED SHOAB

Library: see Libraries and Archives

Number of teachers: 7,066

Number of students: 202,167

DEANS

Faculty of Agriculture: Prof. SALWA BAYOUMY MOHAMED EL MAGHOULY

Faculty of Agriculture (in Fayoum): Prof. ABDALLA MOHAMED ABDEL RAHMAN MOUSA

Faculty of Arabic and Islamic Studies (in Fayoum): Prof. MOHAMED SALAH EL DEEN MOSTAFA

Faculty of Archaeology: Prof. OLA MOHAMED ABD EL AZIZ ELAGEZY

Faculty of Archaeology (in Fayoum): Prof. MOHAMED ABDEL HALIM NOUR ELDIN (acting)

Faculty of Arts: Prof. AHMED MAGDY HEGAZY

Faculty of Arts (in Beni-Suef): Prof. MOHAMED MAHRAN RASHWAN (acting)

Faculty of Commerce: Prof. AHMED FARGHALY MOHAMED HASSAN

Faculty of Commerce (in Beni-Suef): Prof. KAWSSAR ABDEL FATTAH MAHAMED AL-ABAGY

Faculty of Computer and Information Science: Prof. Dr ALY ALY MOHAMED FAHMY

Faculty of Dar el Oloum: Prof. AHMED MOHAMED ABD EL AZIZ KESHK

Faculty of Dar el Olum (in Fayoum): Prof. IBRAHIM MOHAMED IBRAHIM SAKR

Faculty of Dentistry: Prof. MAHMOUD IBRAHIM FAHMY EL REFAAY

Faculty of Economics and Political Science: Prof. KAMAL MAHMOUD EL MENOUFY

Faculty of Education (in Beni-Suef): Prof. MOSTAFA HASSAN MOHAMED EL NASHAR

Faculty of Education (in Fayoum): Prof. MOHAMED ABD EL RAHMAN EL SHARNOBY

Faculty of Engineering: ALY ABDEL RAHMAN YOUSEF

Faculty of Engineering (in Fayoum): Prof. SAMY EL BADAWY YEHYA

Faculty of Kindergartens: Prof. MONA MOHAMED ALY GAD

Faculty of Law: Prof. AHMED ELSAYED SAWY

Faculty of Law (in Beni-Suef): Prof. Dr REDA IBRAHIM EBEID

Faculty of Mass Communication: Prof. MAGY EL HALAWANY

Faculty of Medicine: Prof. MADIHA MOAHMOUD KHATAB

Faculty of Medicine (in Beni-Suef): Prof. MOHAMED ELSAYED EL BATANOUNY

Faculty of Medicine (in Fayoum): Prof. KAMAL ELBASYOUNY

Faculty of Nursing: Prof. BASAMAT OMAR AHMED

Faculty of Pharmacy: Prof. AHMED ATTEIA MOHAMED SEADA

Faculty of Pharmacy (in Beni-Suef): Prof. AHMED ABDEL BARY ABDEL RAHMAN

Faculty of Physiotherapy: Prof. KAMAL EL SAYED MOHAMED SHOKRY

Faculty of Science: Prof. HAMDY MAHMOUD HASSANEN ELSAYED

Faculty of Science (in Beni-Suef): Prof. AHMED HAFEZ HUSSEIN EL GHANDOUR

Faculty of Science (in Fayoum): Prof. KAMAL AHMED MOHAMED HASSAN DEEB

Faculty of Social Service (in Fayoum): Prof. AHMED MAGDY HEGAZY MAHMOUD (acting)

Faculty of Specific Education: Prof. ALY MOHAMED ALY ELMELEGY

Faculty of Specific Education (in Fayoum): Prof. AHMED GALAL EWIES ELAWA

Faculty of Tourism and Hotels (in Fayoum): Prof. AWAD ABBAS RAGAB

Faculty of Urban Planning: Prof. MAHER MOHEB ISTENO AFANDY

Faculty of Veterinary Medicine: Prof. MOHAMED IBRAHIM MOHAMED DESOUKY

Faculty of Veterinary Medicine (in Beni-Suef): Prof. SHAWKY SOLIMAN IBRAHIM SOLIMAN

Institute of African Studies and Research: Prof. EL SAYED ALY FLEEFEL

Institute of Educational Studies and Research: Prof. MOSTAFA ABDEL SAMIAA

Institute of Statistical Studies and Research: Prof. ABDEL GHANI MOHAMED ABDEL GHANI IBRAHIM

National Institute of Laser Science: Prof. HUSSIEN MOSTAFA MUSA KHALED

National Institute of Tumours: Prof. MOHAMED ABDEL HARETH MOHAMED ABDEL-RAHMAN

HELWAN UNIVERSITY

Ain Helwan, Helwan, Cairo

Telephone: (2) 25590000

Fax: (2) 25555023

E-mail: info@helwan.edu.eg

Internet: www.helwan.edu.eg

Founded 1975, incorporating existing institutes of higher education

State control

Languages of instruction: Arabic, English

Academic year: September to June

Pres.: Prof. ABD ALLAH BARAKAT

Vice-Pres. for Community Service and Environmental Devt: ABLA HANAFY

Vice-Pres. for Postgraduate Studies and Research: Prof. AHMAD ABD EL KAREEM SALAMA

Vice-Pres. for Undergraduate Studies and Student Affairs: MOHAMMAD HAZEM FATHALLAH

Sec.-Gen.: SEKINA HANAFY MAHMOUD MOHAMED

Librarian: MAHMOUD QATR

Library of 34,795 vols, 425 journals, 9,379 theses

Number of teachers: 2,179

Number of students: 95,567

Publications: *Journal of Economic and Legal Studies* (2 a year), *Journal of Educational and Social Studies*, *Journal of Engineering Research* (6 a year), *Journal of the Faculty of Arts* (2 a year), *Journal of Research on Art Education* (3 a year), *Journal of the Science and Art of Sport* (2 a year), *Journal of Studies on Social Work and Humanities*, *Science and Art of Music* (2 a year), *Scientific Journal of Commercial Studies and Research* (4 a year), *Scientific Journal of Physical Studies* (4 a year)

DEANS

Faculty of Applied Arts: Prof. ADEL HEFNAWY

Faculty of Art Education: Prof. MOHAMMAD LABEEB NADA

Faculty of Arts: Prof. MOHAMED YEHIA MOHAMED

Faculty of Commerce and Business Administration: Prof. MOHAMED AMIN ABDALLA AMIN KAED

Faculty of Education: Prof. ABD EL EL-MOTTELEB AL KORETY

Faculty of Engineering (Mataria): Prof. TAHANY YOUSSEF

Faculty of Engineering and Technology (Helwan): Prof. OMAR HANAFY

Faculty of Fine Arts: Prof. MOHAMMAD TAWFEEK

Faculty of Home Economics: Prof. ABD EL RAHMAN ATIA

Faculty of Information and Computer Sciences: Prof. YEHIA KAMAL HELMY

Faculty of Law: Prof. MOHAMED ELSHAHAT ELGENDY

Faculty of Music Education: Prof. AMERA FARAG

Faculty of Pharmacy: Prof. MOHAMED MOHY ELDIN ELMAZAR

Faculty of Physical Education (Men): Prof. SOBHY HASANEIN

Faculty of Physical Education (Women): Prof. HANAN ROSHDY

Faculty of Science: Prof. MOHAMMAD EL SAYYED

Faculty of Social Work: Prof. MOHAMED REFAAT KASSEM ABDEL RAHMAN

Faculty of Tourism and Hotel Management: Prof. DOHA MOUSTAFA

MANSOURA UNIVERSITY

60 Elgomhoria St, Mansoura

Telephone and fax (50) 347900

E-mail: info@mans.edu.eg

Internet: www.mans.eun.eg

Founded 1973 from the Mansoura br. of Cairo Univ.

State control

Languages of instruction: Arabic, English

Academic year: October to June

Pres.: Prof. AHMED GAMAL ELDIN ABDEL FATTAH MOUSA

Vice-Pres. for Community Services and Environmental Affairs: Prof. MOHAMED AHMED GABALLA YOSSEF

Vice-Pres. for Postgraduate Studies and Research: Prof. MAGDY MOHAMED ABOU RAYAAN

Vice-Pres. for Undergraduate Studies: Prof. MOHAMED SUIELM MOHAMED ELBASUONY

Sec.-Gen.: MAGDY AHMED MAHMOUD SALEH

Chief Librarian: ABDALLA HUSSIEN

Number of teachers: 2,230

Number of students: 107,022

Publications: *Egyptian Journal for Commercial Studies* (4 a year), *Journal of the Faculty of Arts* (2 a year), *Journal of Veterinary Medical Research* (1 a year), *Mansoura Dental Journal* (4 a year), *Mansoura Engineering Journal* (4 a year), *Mansoura Faculty of Education Journal* (3 a year), *Mansoura Journal of Forensic Medicine and Clinical Toxicology* (2 a year), *Mansoura Journal of Pharmaceutical Sciences* (2 a year), *Mansoura Medical Journal* (2 a year), *Mansoura Science Bulletin* (2 a year), *Mansoura University Journal of Agriculture* (12 a year), *Revue des Recherches Juridiques et Economiques* (2 a year)

DEANS

Faculty of Agriculture: Prof. HESHAM NAGY ABDEL MAGEED

Faculty of Commerce: Prof. NABIL AL HUSSINI AL NAGGAR

Faculty of Computer and Information Science: FATMA ABOU-CHADI

Faculty of Medicine: Prof. AMR SARHAN

Faculty of Nursing: Prof. FARDOS RAMADAN

Faculty of Science: Prof. TAHA ZAKI NABAWY SOKKAR

Faculty of Science (in Damiatta): Prof. MOHAMED R. MOSTAFA

Faculty of Veterinary Medicine: Prof. MOHAMED MOHAMED FOUDA

MENIA UNIVERSITY

Menia Governorate, Menia

Telephone: (86) 361443

Fax: (86) 342601

E-mail: info@minia.edu.eg

Internet: www.minia.edu.eg

Founded 1976, incorporating existing faculties of Assiut Univ.

Languages of instruction: Arabic, English

Academic year: October to June

Pres.: Prof. ABD EL MONIEM ABD EL HAMID EL BASSIOUNY

Vice-Pres. for Community Services and Environmental Affairs: Prof. ABD EL GHAFAR FARIED ABD EL GHAFAR

Vice-Pres. for Postgraduate Studies and Research: Prof. MOHAMED SAIED MOHAMED ALY

Vice-Pres. for Undergraduate Studies: Prof. MAHER GABER MOHAMED AHMED

Sec.-Gen.: LAILA AHMED IBRAHIM SOROOR

Chief Librarian: NABELA EL SAWY

Number of teachers: 1,288

Number of students: 36,906

DEANS

Faculty of Agriculture: Prof. MOHAMED ATEF FAHMY AHMED KESHK

Faculty of al Alsun (Languages): Prof. AMAL MOSTAFA KAMAL MOHAMED

Faculty of Arts: Prof. MOHAMED NAGEEB AHMED MOHAMED

Faculty of Computer and Information Science: (vacant)

Faculty of Dar al Olum: Prof. MOHY ELDIN OTHMAN RASHDAN

Faculty of Dentistry: Prof. HANY HUSSIEN MOHAMED AMIN

Faculty of Education: Prof. ATTA TAHA ZEDAN SHEHATA

Faculty of Engineering: Prof. MOHAMED MONESS ALY AHMED

Faculty of Fine Arts: Prof. WAFAA OMAR ABD ELHALEEM

Faculty of Medicine: Prof. MOHAMED IBRAHIM BASUONY

Faculty of Nursing: Prof. GALAL MOHAMED SHAWKY HAMED

Faculty of Pharmacy: Prof. MOHAMED MONTASER ABD ELHAKIM

Faculty of Physical Education (Female): (vacant)

Faculty of Physical Education (Male): Prof. BAHY ELDIN IBRAHIM SALAMA

Faculty of Science: Prof. ABD ELRAHMAN ABD ELAZIZ AHMED

Faculty of Specific Education: Prof. ABD ELAZEEM ABD ELSALAM ELFERGANY

Faculty of Tourism and Hotel Management: Prof. ABD ELBARY AHMED ALY DAWOOD

MINUFIYA UNIVERSITY

Gamal Abd el Nasser St, BP 32511, Shebeen el Kam

Telephone: (48) 222170

Fax: (2) 5752777

E-mail: menofia@menofia.edu.eg

Internet: www.menofia.edu.eg

Founded 1976

State control

Languages of instruction: Arabic, English

Academic year: September to July

Pres.: Prof. MOHAMED A. IZZULARAB

Vice-Pres. for Community and Environmental Devt: Prof. ABD EL ALEEM MOHAMMED ABD EL KHALIK EL DERAEE

Vice-Pres. for Graduate Studies and Research: Prof. THABET ABD EL RAHAMAN EDRESE

Vice-Pres. for Undergraduate Education: Prof. MOSTAFA ABD EL RAHMAN

Vice-Pres. for Sadat Br.: Prof. AHMED HAMED ZAGHLOL

Sec.-Gen.: MOSTAFA SADAK KHALIL

Librarian: HAMDY EL SHAMY

Number of teachers: 2,928

Number of students: 71,225

Publications: *Minoufiya Journal of Electronic Engineering Research* (2 a year), *Minoufiya Medical Journal* (2 a year), *Scientific Journal of the Faculty of Science* (1 a year)

DEANS

Faculty of Agriculture: Prof. ALI IBRAHIM FARAG
Faculty of Arts: Prof. AHMED ABD EL KADER EL SHATHLY
Faculty of Commerce: Prof. GAMAL EL DIN MOHAMED EL MORSEY
Faculty of Commerce (Sadat Br.): Prof. HASANIEN SAYED TAHA
Faculty of Computers and Information: Prof. MOHIEY MOHAMED HADHOUD
Faculty of Education: Prof. ALI MOHAMED SHUAIB
Faculty of Education (Sadat Br.): Prof. ABD EL AAL AGWA
Faculty of Electroni Engineering: Prof. ATEF EL SAYED ABOU EL AZM
Faculty of Engineering: Prof. ADEL ALI ABOU EL ALA
Faculty of Home Economics: Prof. FATMA EL ZAHRAA EL SHERIEF
Faculty of Hotels and Tourism: (vacant)
Faculty of Law: Prof. MOHAMED SAMY EL SHAWA
Faculty of Law (Sadat Br.): Prof. ABD EL HADEY MOHAMED EL ASHREY
Faculty of Medicine: Prof. SAID SHALABY IBRAHIM
Faculty of Science: Prof. GAMALAT YOUSEF OSMAN
Faculty of Special Education: Prof. ALI BADAWI MAHROUS
Faculty of Physical Education: Prof. ESAM EL DIN METWALY ALI
Faculty of Veterinary Medicine: Prof. SALAH EL SAYED IBRAHIM
Institute of Desert Environment Research: Prof. MUBARAK HASSANY ALI
Genetic Engineering and Biotechnology Research Institute: (vacant)
Faculty of Nursing: Prof. MAGDA MOAWAD
National Liver Research Institute: Prof. EMAM ABD EL LATIEF EMAM

MISR UNIVERSITY FOR SCIENCE AND TECHNOLOGY (MUST)

BP 77, Sixth of October City
Telephone: (2) 38354686
E-mail: must@must.edu
Internet: www.must.edu
Founded 1996
Private control
Language of instruction: English
Academic year: October to July
Chancellor: KHALED M. EL-TOUKHY
Pres.: Prof. MOHAMED RAAFAT MAHMOUD
Vice-Pres. for Community Service: Prof. FAROUK ABU-ZAID
Vice-Pres. for Int. Cooperation and Quality Assurance: Prof. MOSTAFA M. KAMEL
Registrar: ASHRAF ABDULLAH
Librarian: Prof. KAMAL ARAFAT
Library of 70,000 vols
Number of teachers: 533
Number of students: 12,348

DEANS

College of Applied Medical Sciences: FATIMA AL-SHARQAWI
College of Archaeology and Tourist Guidance: MOHAMMED IBRAHIM BAKR
College of Biotechnology: Prof. ALI Z. ABDUL-SALAM
College of Business: Prof. MOHAMMED H. AZZAZI
College of Dental Medicine: Prof. TAREK M. AL-SHARKAWI

College of Engineering: Prof. MOHAMMED K. BEDEEWI
College of Foreign Languages and Translation: Prof. MOHSEN ABU-SEDA
College of Information Technology: MOHAMMED S. ABDUL-WAHHAB
College of Mass Media: Prof. FAROUK ABU-ZIED
College of Medicine: Prof. MAJED GAMAL ZAYED
College of Pharmacy: Prof. MOHAMMED F. AL-MELEEGI
College of Physical Therapy: Prof. BASEM AL-NAHHAS

SOUTH VALLEY UNIVERSITY

Qena Governorate, Qena
Telephone: (96) 5211277
Fax: (96) 5211279
E-mail: info@svu.edu.eg
Internet: www.svu.edu.eg
Founded 1995
State control
Languages of instruction: Arabic, English
Academic year: September to June

Campuses in Luxor, Hurghada, Aswan

Pres.: Prof. ABBAS MOHAMED MOHAMED MANSOUR
Vice-Pres. for Aswan Campus: Prof. FAWI MOHAMED ASSUGHAYER
Vice-Pres. for Community Services and Environmental Affairs: Prof. MAHMOUD KHODARI MA'LA
Vice-Pres. for Undergraduate Studies: Prof. MOHAMED THARWAT ABDLRAHMAN
Vice-Pres. for Post-Graduate Studies and Research: Prof. ABDEL-FATAH M. HASHEM
Chief Librarian: AWATEF YASSIEN ALQADI
Number of teachers: 795 assts, 691 PhDs
Number of students: 43,201

DEANS

Faculty of Agriculture: Prof. MOHAMMAD ALI
Faculty of Archaeology: Prof. ABDULLAH K. MOUSA
Faculty of Arts: Prof. ABUELFADL M. M. BADRAN
Faculty of Commerce: Prof. JAMAL IBRAHIM
Faculty of Education: Prof. SAMEH A. M. JAFAR
Faculty of Education (Hurghada): Prof. KAREEMA KHATAAB
Faculty of Engineering: Prof. AREF M. SULAIMAN
Faculty of Fine Arts (Luxor): Prof. MOHAMED ORABY
Faculty of Hotel and Tourism: Prof. SALEH ABDELMUTI
Faculty of Law: Prof. THARWAT M. ABDEL-'AAL
Faculty of Medicine: Prof. MANSOUR KABBASH
Faculty of Nursing: Prof. SAYED TAHA
Faculty of Physical Education: Prof. EMAD ABU-ELQASEM
Faculty of Science: Prof. SAYED O. AL-KHATEEB
Faculty of Social Work: Prof. ALI A. DANDARAWI
Faculty of Specific Education: Prof. HIFNI ISMAIEL
Faculty of Veterinary Medicine: Prof. ABDEL-LATIF S. SHAKER

DEANS (ASWAN CAMPUS)

Faculty of Arts: Prof. AHAMD SUKRANO ABDEL-HAFEZ (acting)
Faculty of Education: Prof. NADY K. AZIZ
Faculty of Engineering: Prof. ABD-ALLAH IBRAHIM
Faculty of Science: Prof. ALI K. KHALAF-ALLAH
High Institute of Energy: Prof. JABER SHABIB

SUEZ CANAL UNIVERSITY

el Shikh Zayed, Ismailia
Telephone: (64) 3297020
Fax: (64) 325208
E-mail: info@suez.edu.eg
Internet: scuegypt.edu.eg
Founded 1976
State control
Languages of instruction: Arabic, English
Academic year: October to June
Pres.: Prof. FAROUK MAHMOUD ABD EL KADER
Vice-Pres. for Community Services and Environmental Affairs: Prof. ALY IBRAHIM ELSAYED IBRAHIM BADR
Vice-Pres. for Port Said: MOHAMED ELSAYED ALY RAHEEM
Vice-Pres. for Postgraduate Studies and Research: Prof. MOSTAFA KAMEL MOHAMED MOSBAH
Vice-Pres. for Undergraduate Studies: Prof. IBRAHIM ASHOUR IBRAHIM BADR
Sec.-Gen.: NAINAA MOHAMED MOHAMED KHALIFA
Librarian: KAMILIA ALHOSARY
Number of teachers: 1,466
Number of students: 47,488

DEANS

El Arish:

Faculty of Agricultural and Environmental Sciences: Prof. MOHAMED RAGAB ABDO HUMOS
Faculty of Education: Prof. NASSEF BEDEER IBRAHIM ELAASY

Ismailia:

Faculty of Agriculture: Prof. MOHAMED SAMIR MOHAMED ATTEYA ELSHAZLY
Faculty of Commerce: Prof. MOSTAFA ALY MAHMOUD ELBAZ
Faculty of Computers and Information Science: Prof. MOHAMED HELMY MAHRAN
Faculty of Dentistry: Prof. MOHAMED ELHUSSEINY MOHAMED MEKY
Faculty of Education: Prof. MAHMOUD ABBASS MAHMOUD ABDEIN
Faculty of Medicine: Prof. SOLIMAN HAMED SOLIMAN ELKAMASH
Faculty of Pharmacy: Prof. SALAH ELDIN MOHAMED ABDALLA
Faculty of Science: Prof. ELSAYED HUSSEIN MOSTAFA ELTAMNY
Faculty of Tourism and Hotels: Prof. ABD EL RAHMAN ABD EL FATTAH MOHAMED
Faculty of Veterinary Medicine: Prof. MOHAMED ELSAYED ANANY

Port Said:

Faculty of Commerce: Prof. MOHAMED ABD EL RAHMAN ELAADY
Faculty of Education: FAKRY IBRAHIM KHALIL KHALAF
Faculty of Engineering: Prof. AHMAD KAMAL ABD-EL KHALEK
Faculty of Nursing: Prof. HODA WADEEA TAWFEK
Faculty of Physical Education (Male): Prof. SAYED ABDEL GAWAD ELSAYED AHMED
Faculty of Specific Education: Prof. MOHAMED SAYED AHMED SALEH

Suez:

Faculty of Commerce: Prof. MAHMOUD SAYED AHMED SALEM
Faculty of Education: Prof. BELAL AHMED SOLIMAN AHMED
Faculty of Industrial Education: Prof. AHMED ESSA GAMEA ELNEKHILY
Faculty of Petroleum and Mining Engineering: Prof. SHUHDY EL MAGHRABY ELALFY SHALABY

TANTA UNIVERSITY

El Geish St, Tanta
Telephone: (40) 3317928
Fax: (40) 3302785
E-mail: president@tainta.edu.eg
Internet: www.tanta.edu.eg
Founded 1972
State control
Languages of instruction: Arabic, English
Academic year: October to June

Pres.: Prof. ABDELFATTAH A. SADAKAH
Vice-Pres. for Community Service and Environment Devt: Prof. MOHAMED MOSAAD NASSAR
Vice-Pres. for Graduate Studies and Research: Prof. MOHAMED ADEL KHALIFAA
Vice-Pres. for Education and Student Affairs: Prof. AZIZ MAHFOUZ KAFAFY
Sec.-Gen.: RAWIA SOLIMAN GAD
Chief Librarian: ADEL YASSIEN

Number of teachers: 2,042
Number of students: 109,037

DEANS

Faculty of Agriculture: Prof. HELMY ALI ANBAR
Faculty of Arts: Prof. ZAIN EL DEIN MOSTAFA
Faculty of Commerce: Prof. SAID LEBDA
Faculty of Dentistry: Prof. SHWKRIA MOHAMMED ESMAIL
Faculty of Education: Prof. MOHAMMED AMIN ATWA
Faculty of Engineering: Prof. ABDEL-WAHED ASAR
Faculty of Law: Prof. HUSIEN MOHAMMED FATHY
Faculty of Medicine: Prof. SHAWKI ABD-ELAZIZ EL ABD
Faculty of Nursing: Prof. Dr HELMY HAMAD AHMED SHALABY
Faculty of Pharmacy: Prof. MOKHTAR MOHAMMED MABROUK
Faculty of Physical Education: Prof. REYAD ZAKRIA EL MENSHAWY
Faculty of Science: Prof. EBRAHIM KAMEL EL SHORBAGY
Faculty of Specific Education: Prof. HUSIEN MOHAMMED FATHY (acting)

ZAGAZIG UNIVERSITY

Sharkia Governorate, Zagazig
Telephone and fax (55) 238470
E-mail: info@zu.edu.eg
Internet: www.zu.edu.eg
Founded 1974, incorporating existing faculties of Ain-Shams Univ.
State control
Languages of instruction: Arabic, English
Academic year: October to June

Pres.: Prof. MAHER MOHAMED ALI EL DOMIATY
Vice-Pres. for Education and Student Affairs: Prof. AHMED ELREFAAY BAHGAT EL AZIZY
Vice-Pres. for Environmental Affairs: Prof. TAREK YOUSSEF GAAFAR
Vice-Pres. for Postgraduate Studies: Prof. MOHAMED BAHGAT AWAD
Sec.-Gen.: MOHAMMED MOHAMMED HASHEM
Chief Librarian: RAMADAN ALY OTHMAN

Number of teachers: 4,250
Number of students: 151,091

DEANS

Faculty of Agriculture: Prof. MOHAMMED BASSEM ASHOUR
Faculty of Arts: Prof. HASSAN MOHAMMED HAMMAD
Faculty of Commerce: Prof. IBRAHIM MOUSSA ABD ELFATAH
Faculty of Computer and Information Science: Prof. D MOHAMMED ABBAS SHOUMAN
Faculty of Education: Prof. HAMDY HASSAN ELMAHROUKY

Faculty of Engineering: Prof. ASHRAF MOHAMMED ELSHEIHY
Faculty of Law: Prof. ATEF HASSAN MAHMOUD ELNOKALY
Faculty of Medicine: Prof. SAAD SABRY ELOSH
Faculty of Nursing: Prof. NAGWA AHMED ELSHAFEEY
Faculty of Pharmacy: Prof. MOHAMMED NAGUIB MOHAMMED ZAKARIA
Faculty of Physical Education (Female): Prof. NABILA ABDALLA MOHAMED OMRAN
Faculty of Physical Education (Male): Prof. ABD ELAZEEM ABD ELHAMID ELSAYED
Faculty of Science: Prof. MOHAMMED GAMAL HELMY ABD ELWAHED
Faculty of Specific Education: Prof. ADEL EBRAHIM ELBAZ
Faculty of Veterinary Medicine: Prof. ALAA ELDEEN MOHAMMED MORSHEDY
Higher Institute of Ancient Near East Civilizations: Prof. MAHMOUD OMAR MOHAMED
Higher Institute of Asian Research and Studies: Prof. BAYOUMI AWAD ALLAH TARTOUR
Higher Institute of Productive Efficiency: Prof. MOHAMMED NAGY ELGAAFRY

University-Level Institute

BENHA HIGHER INSTITUTE OF TECHNOLOGY

New Benha, el Kaludia, Benha City 13512
Telephone: (13) 3229263
Fax: (13) 3230297
E-mail: ahuzayyin@gmx.net
Internet: www.bhit-buni.edu.eg
Founded 1988
State control

Dean: AHMED SOLIMAN HUZAYYIN
Vice-Dean for Postgraduates: ADEL ALAM EL DIN
Vice-Dean for Students: MAHMOUD FATHY M. HASSAN

Library of 8,100 vols
Number of teachers: 275
Number of students: 1,530

Depts of basic sciences, civil engineering, electrical engineering and mechanical engineering.

Colleges

Arab Academy for Science and Technology and Maritime Transport: Gamal Abdel Naser St, BP 1029, Miami, Alexandria; tel. (3) 5622366; fax (3) 5622525; internet www.aast.edu; f. 1972; Colleges of Engineering and Technology, Management and Technology and Maritime Transport; library: 36,000 vols, 350 periodicals; 490 teachers; 4,000 students; Pres. Dr GAMAL MOKHTAR.

Cairo Polytechnic Institute: 108 Shoubra St, Shoubra, Cairo; f. 1961; Engineering, Agriculture, Commerce; Dir H. H. MOHAMED.

Higher Industrial Institute: Aswan; f. 1962; State control; courses in mechanical, electrical and chemical engineering, mining and natural sciences.

Higher Institute of Public Health: 165 el Horreya Ave, el Hadra, Alexandria; tel. (3) 4285575; fax (3) 4288436; e-mail hiph.adv@gmail.com; internet www.hiph-egypt.net; an autonomous unit of the Univ. of Alexandria; f. 1956; undertakes fundamental teaching and applied public health research; 81 staff mems and 50 instructors; depts of public health administration, biostatistics, nutrition, epidemiology, tropical health, microbiology, occupational and environmental health,

family health; library: 10,000 vols; Dean Prof. MOUSRAFA I. MOURAD; Vice-Dean for Postgraduate Studies and Research Prof. NIHAD I. DABBOUS; Vice-Dean for Community Service and Environmental Affairs Prof. MOHAMED A. EL BARRAWY.

Mansoura Polytechnic Institute: Mit-Khamis St, Mansoura; f. 1957; 147 teachers; 2,290 students; library: 21,400 vols; Dir Dr ESAYED SELIM ELMOLLA.

Regional Centre for Adult Education (ASFEC): Sirs el Layyan, Menoufia; tel. (48) 351596; f. 1952 by UNESCO; training of specialists in fields of literacy, adult education and education for rural devt; production of prototype educational material, research in community devt problems; advisory service; Chair. F. A. GHONEIM; Dir SALAH SHARAKAM.

Sadat Academy for Management Sciences: Kernish el Nile el Maadi, BP 2222, Cairo; tel. (2) 23787628; fax (2) 27530043; e-mail info@sadatacademy.edu.eg; internet www.sadatacademy.edu.eg; f. 1981; prin. governmental org. for management devt in Egypt; activities carried out through 10 academic depts: business admin., public admin., economics, production, admin. law, personnel and organizational behaviour, accountancy, insurance and quantitative analysis, computer and information systems, languages; also consists of 4 professional centres: Training, Consultation, Research and Local Administration; and Faculty of Management (undergraduate) and Nat. Institute of Management Devt (postgraduate); library: 32,000 vols, 250 periodicals; 124 teachers; 4,948 students; Pres. Prof. AHMED MAHMOUD YOUSSEF; Vice-Pres. for Education and Research Prof. SHERIEF HASSAN; Vice-Pres. for Training and Consultation Prof. ABDELHAMED MOSTAFA ABO NAAM; Vice-Pres. for Postgraduate Studies and Research Prof. MOHAMED ZAKY EID; publ. *Magalet Al-Behouth Al Edaria* (Administrative Research Review, 4 a year, in Arabic and English).

Branches:

Alexandria Branch: 59 Menshya Moharram Bak St, Alexandria; tel. (3) 3931515; fax (3) 3935887; e-mail alex-sams@sadatacademy.edu.eg; Dir Dr BADEAA ELDIN RESHO.

Assyot Branch: Mogamaa al Masaleh, Assyot; tel. and fax (88) 2310499; e-mail asiut-sams@sadatacademy.edu.eg; Dir Dr ABDEL MOHAMMED.

Dekkernes Branch: Korneish el Bahr St, Dekernes; tel. (50) 7472521; fax (50) 7472520; e-mail dekernes-sams@sadatacademy.edu.eg; Dir SALAH ABD EL HAY.

Port Said Branch: Abdel-Salam Arif St, Port Said; tel. (66) 3351396; fax (66) 3352396; e-mail portsaid-sams@sadatacademy.edu.eg; Dir Prof. SAFWAT ALI HMEDA.

Ramsis Branch (Faculty of Management): 14 Ramsis St, Cairo; tel. (2) 225764337; fax (2) 225753350; e-mail ramsis-sams@sadatacademy.edu.eg; Dir MOHAMMED MOUSSA.

Tanta Branch: Sedkee St, Tanta; tel. (40) 3302083; fax (40) 3302017; e-mail tanta-sams@sadatacademy.edu.eg; Dir Prof. SAYED ABD EL MOULA.

Schools of Art and Music

Academy of Arts: el Afghany St, off Alharam Ave, Giza; tel. (2) 35850727; fax (2) 35611230; e-mail aoarts@idsc.gov.eg; f.

1959; comprises 8 institutes of univ. status; Pres. Prof. FAWZY FAHMY AHMED; Dir of Public Relations AWAD KAMEL FAHMI; publ. *Alfann Almuasir* (4 a year).

Constituent Institutes:

Higher Institute of Arab Music: Cairo; tel. (2) 24851561; f. 1967; depts of instrumentation, singing, theory of composition; Postgraduate Studies; library of 11,000 vols; 125 teachers; 280 students; Dean Dr SAID HAIKUL.

Higher Institute of Art Criticism: Cairo; library of 2,500 vols; 8 teachers; 90 students; Dean Dr NAHIL RACHAB.

Higher Institute of Ballet: Cairo; tel. (2) 35853999; f. 1958; 2 brs in Alexandria and Ismailia; depts of classical ballet, choreography, postgraduate studies; library of 3,500 vols; 21 teachers; 21 students; Dean Dr MAGDA EZZ.

Higher Institute of Child Arts: Cairo; tel. (2) 35850727; f. 1990; postgraduate studies.

Higher Institute of Cinema: Cairo; tel. (2) 35850291; f. 1959; depts of scriptwriting, directing, editing, photography and camerawork, scenery design, sound production, animation, cartoons; postgraduate studies; library of 5,000 vols; 90 teachers; 450 students; Dean Dr SHAWKY ALY MOHAMED.

Higher Institute of Folklore: Cairo; tel. (2) 35851230; f. 1981; dept of postgraduate studies; library of 6,000 vols; 25 teachers; 60 students; Dean Dr ALYAA SHOUKRY.

Higher Institute of Music (Conservatoire): Cairo; tel. (2) 35853451; f. 1959; depts of composition and theory, piano, string instruments, wind instruments, percussion, singing, solfa and music education, musicology; postgraduate studies; library of 24,000 vols, 3,000 records; 90 teachers; 78 students; Dean Prof. NIBAL MOUNIB.

Higher Institute of Theatre Arts: Cairo; tel. (2) 35853233; f. 1944; depts of acting and directing, drama and criticism, scenic and stage design; postgraduate studies; library of 15,500 vols; 90 teachers; 330 students; Dean Dr SANAA SHAFIE.

EL SALVADOR

The Higher Education System

The state-controlled Universidad de El Salvador, founded in 1841, was the only university until the mid-1960s, since when several private universities have been established. The Ministry of Education oversees higher education. Other institutions of higher education include colleges and technical institutes. In 2006/07 there were 132,200 students enrolled in tertiary education.

Entrance to higher education is achieved on the basis of obtaining the main secondary school qualification, the Bachillerato, and success in an entrance examination. The first undergraduate degree is the Diplomado, awarded after two to three years' study. Following this, the Licenciado can last from four to seven years and may also lead to a professional title. The Maestría is awarded after a further two years, and the Doctorado is available in some subjects.

Both universities and non-university institutions (colleges and technical institutes) offer technical and vocational qualifications. Courses last for two to three years, and qualifications include Técnico (two years), Perito, Auxiliar and Técnico Superior (three-and-a-half years).

Regulatory and Representative Bodies

GOVERNMENT

Ministry of Education: Edif. A, Centro de Gobierno, Alameda Juan Pablo II y Calle Guadalupe, San Salvador; tel. 2281-0044; fax 2281-0077; e-mail educacion@mined.gob.sv; internet www.mined.gob.sv; Min. SALVADOR SÁNCHEZ CERÉN.

ACCREDITATION

Comisión de Acreditación de la Calidad de la Educación Superior (Commission for the Accreditation of Quality in Higher Education): Alameda Juan Pablo II y Calle Guadalupe, Plan Maestro, Centro de Gobierno, Edificio A2, San Salvador; tel. 2281-0282; e-mail cda_dnes@mined.gob.sv; internet www.mined.gob.sv/cda; autonomous body attached to the Min. of Education; awards accredited status to univs and other higher education instns proving their commitment to continuing improvement in academic standards; 7 mems; Pres. Dr HÉCTOR LINDO FUENTES; Exec. Dir Lic. MARÍA DE LOS ÁNGELES DE SALGUERO.

Learned Societies

GENERAL

Academia Salvadoreña (El Salvador Academy): Casa de las Academias, 9A Avda Norte y Alameda Juan Pablo II, San Salvador; fax 2222-9721; e-mail denysfuentesmyk@hotmail.com; f. 1876; corresp. of the Real Academia Española (Madrid); 22 mems; Dir ALFREDO MARTÍNEZ MORENO; Sec. RENÉ FORTÍN MAGAÑA.

HISTORY, GEOGRAPHY AND ARCHAEOLOGY

Academia Salvadoreña de la Historia (El Salvador Academy of History): Km 10 Planes de Renderoz, Col. Los Angeles, Villa Lilia 13, San Salvador; f. 1925; Corresp. of the Real Academia de la Historia (Madrid); 18 mems; library of 9,000 vols; Dir JORGE LARDÉ Y LARÍN; Sec. PEDRO ESCALANTE MENA; publ. *Boletín* (irregular).

LANGUAGE AND LITERATURE

Alliance Française: 51 Avda Norte 152, Col. Escalon, Apdo 0175, San Salvador; tel. 2260-5807; fax 2260-5762; e-mail alliafrance@navegante.com.sv; offers courses and examinations in French language and culture, and promotes cultural exchange with France.

MEDICINE

Colegio Médico de El Salvador: Final Pasaje 10, Col. Miramonte, San Salvador; tel. 2260-1111; fax 2260-0324; f. 1943; 1,710 mems; promotes medical research and cooperation; Pres. Dr J. ASCENCIÓN MARINERO CÁCERES; publs *Archivos* (3 a year), *Revista Lealo* (6 a year).

Sociedad de Ginecología y Obstetricia de El Salvador: Colegio Médico de El Salvador, Final Pasaje 10, Col. Miramonte, San Salvador; tel. 2235-3432; fax 2235-3432; f. 1947; 150 mems; library of 2,000 vols; Pres. Dr JORGE CRUZ GONZALEZ; Sec. Dr HENRY AGREDA RODRIGUEZ.

Research Institutes

AGRICULTURE, FISHERIES AND VETERINARY SCIENCE

Centro Nacional de Tecnología Agropecuaria y Forestal: Km 33½, Carretera a Santa Ana, La Libertad; tel. 2302-0200; e-mail info@centa.gob.sv; internet www.centa.gob.sv; f. 1942; research and devt of seeds; library of 11,000 vols, 134 current periodicals; Exec. Dir ERNESTO DAGLIO VAN SEVEREN; publs *Agricultura en El Salvador* (irregular), *Boletín Técnico* (irregular), *Circular* (irregular).

Instituto Salvadoreño de Investigaciones del Café: Ministerio de Agricultura y Ganadería, 23 Avda Norte No. 114, San Salvador; f. 1956; administered by the Min. of Agriculture and Livestock; publs monographs, *Boletín Informativo* (6 a year).

ECONOMICS, LAW AND POLITICS

Dirección General de Estadística y Censos (Statistical Office): Avda Juan Bertis 79, Ciudad Delgado, Apdo Postal 2670, San Salvador; tel. 2276-5900; fax 2286-2505; f. 1881; Dir-Gen. SALVADOR ARMANDO MELGAR; publs *Anuario Estadístico* (1 a year), *Encuesta de Hogares de Propósitos Múltiples* (1 a year), *Encuesta Económica* (1 a year), *IPC* (12 a year).

NATURAL SCIENCES

Physical Sciences

Centro de Investigaciones Geotécnicas: Apdo 109, San Salvador; tel. 2293-1442; fax 2293-1462; reorganized 1964; departments of seismology, soil mechanics, building materials, geological surveys; 250 mems; library of 1,000 vols; Dir DOUGLAS HERNANDEZ; publs *Investigaciones Geológicas*, reports.

Servicio Meteorológico Nacional: Kilómetro 5½ Carretera a Nueva San Salvador, Calle las Mercedes frente a Círculo Militar y contiguo a Parque de Pelota, San Salvador; tel. 2223-7797; fax 2283-2269; internet www.snet.gob.sv; f. 1889; library of 2,000 vols; Dir LUIS GARCÍA GUIROLA; publs *Almanaque Marino Costero*, *Almanaque Climatológico*, *Boletines Agroclimáticos* (online), *Boletines Climatológicos* (online), *Boletines El Niño* (online), *Weather Forecast, 24 hrs, 48 hrs, 7 days* (online).

TECHNOLOGY

Comisión Salvadoreña de Energía Nuclear (COSEN): c/o Ministerio de Economía, 1A Calle Poniente y 73 Avda Norte, San Salvador; f. 1961; to consider the applications in medicine, agriculture and industry of radioisotopes and nuclear energy.

Libraries and Archives

San Salvador

Archivo General de la Nación: Palacio Nacional, San Salvador; tel. 2222-9418; f. 1948; 2,000 vols; Dir ALBERTO ATILIO SALAZAR; publ. *Repositorio*.

Biblioteca del Ministerio de Relaciones Exteriores (Library of the Ministry of Foreign Affairs): Carretera a Santa Tecla, San Salvador; 10,000 vols; Librarian MANUEL ANTONIO LÓPEZ.

Biblioteca Nacional (National Library): 4ta Calle Oriente y Avda Mons. Oscar A. Romero # 124, San Salvador; tel. 2221-2099; fax 2221-8847; internet www.binaes.gob.sv; f. 1870; 150,000 vols; special collections: old books, titles on int. organizations, Braille room; Dir Dr H. C. MANLIO ARGUETA.

Sistema Bibliotecario de la Universidad de El Salvador: Final 25 Avda Norte, Ciudad Universitaria, Apdo 2923, San Salvador; tel. and fax 2225-0278; e-mail sb@biblio.ues.edu.sv; internet www.ues.edu.sv/biblio.html; f. 1847; 44,000 vols; Dir CARLOS R. COLINDRES.

Museums and Art Galleries

San Salvador

Museo de Historia Natural de El Salvador: Final Calle Los Viveros, Col. Nicaragua, San Salvador; tel. 2270-9228; fax 2221-4419; f. 1976; Dir DANIEL AGUILAR.

Museo Nacional 'David J. Guzmán' (National Museum): Avda la Revolución, Col. San Benito, San Salvador; f. 1883; specializes in history, archaeology, ethnology, library science and restoration; travelling exhibits programme; Dir MANUEL R. LÓPEZ; publs *Anales*, *Colección Antropología e Historia*, *El Xipe*, *La Cofradía*.

Attached Museums:

    Museo de Sitio San Andrés: Parque Arqueológico San Andrés, Km 32, Carretera Panamericana, Ciudad Arce, Dpto de La Libertad; tel. and fax 2221-4419; e-mail direcciondepatrimonio@concultura.gob.sv; internet www.cultura.gob.sv; f. 1996; museum at major archaeological site of San Andrés, occupation of which spans c. 2,000 years; its apogee was during the Late Classic period (AD 600–900), when it became the capital of a Mayan realm; Head of Cultural Heritage Dr SONIA BAIRES.

    Museo Tazumal: Chalchuapa, Dpto de Santa Ana; f. 1951; archaeological site museum.

Parque Zoológico Nacional: Final Calle Modelo, San Salvador; tel. 270-0828; fax 2274-3950; f. 1953; recreation, environmental education and research, conservation; library of 1,800 vols; Dir Arq. ELIZABETH DE QUANT.

Universities

UNIVERSIDAD CATÓLICA DE OCCIDENTE

25 Calle Oriente y 25 Avda Sur, Santa Ana
Telephone: 2447-8785
Fax: 2441-2655
E-mail: catolica@unico.edu.sv
Internet: www.unico.edu.sv

Founded 1983
Private control
Language of instruction: Spanish
Academic year: February to December

Rector: ROMEO TOVAR ASTORGA
Vice-Rector: MOISÉS ANTONIO MARTINÉZ ZALDIVÁR LACALLE
Sec.-Gen.: CÁSTULO AFRANIO HERNÁNDEZ ROBLES
Dir of Admin.: ROBERTO CHACÓN
Dir of Communications: KAREN MÉNDEZ
Dir of Library: MAURICIO EDGARDO MENENDÉZ LEMUS
Dir of Public Relations: JOSÉ JAIME DELEÓN
Dir of Univ. Welfare: Lic JOSÉ ARÍSTIDES MÉNDEZ

Number of teachers: 200
Number of students: 3,200

DEANS

Faculty of Economic Sciences: JOSÉ RICARDO RIVAS
Faculty of Engineering and Architecture: JULIO ENRIQUE NÁJERA
Faculty of Law and Social Sciences: ROBERTO ANTONIO SAYES
Faculty of Science and Humanities: JAIME OSMÍN TRIGUEROS FLORES

DIRECTORS

Department of Languages: JUAN FRANCISCO LINARES LINARES
Research Unit: NERY FRANCISCO HERRERA

ATTACHED INSTITUTES

Departamento de Educación a Distancia: promotes teacher training courses.

Instituto de Desarrollo Rural: promotes extra-curricular activities in the rural sphere, projects on agricultural devt, training courses for the rural population, technical analysis for agricultural cooperatives and environmental health and hygiene projects.

Instituto de Promoción Humana: promotes courses in administration, administration for rural cooperatives, nutrition, administration for small businesses.

UNIVERSIDAD CENTROAMERICANA 'JOSÉ SIMEÓN CAÑAS'

Apdo 01-168, San Salvador
Blvd Los Próceres, San Salvador
Telephone: 2210-6600
Fax: 2210-6655
E-mail: correo@www.uca.edu.sv
Internet: www.uca.edu.sv

Founded 1965
Private control (Soc. of Jesus)
Language of instruction: Spanish
Academic year: March to December

Rector: Ing. ANDREU OLIVA DE LA ESPERANZA
Vice-Rector for Academics: Ing. CELINA PÉREZ RIVERA
Vice-Rector for Finance: Ing. AXEL SÖDERBERG
Gen.-Sec.: Lic. RENÉ ALBERTO ZELAYA
Librarian: JACQUELINE MORALES DE COLOCHO

Library of 347,450 vols
Number of teachers: 544
Number of students: 9,650
Publications: *Boletín Economía Hoy* (12 a year), *Comunica* (online, 15 a year), *De Legibus* (2 a year), *El Salvador en la Mira* (online, 24 a year), *En Plural* (2 a year), *Estudios Centroamericanos ECA* (2 or 3 a year), *La Casa de Todos: Revista de Arquitectura y Urbanismo* (3 a year), *Realidad: Revista de Ciencias Sociales y Humanidades* (4 a year), *Revista Carta a las Iglesias* (12 a year), *Revista Contabilidad y Empresa* (3 a year), *Revista de Administración y Empresas* (2 a year), *Revista Latinoamericana de Teología* (3 a year)

DEANS

Faculty of Economics: JOSÉ MEJÍA HERRERA
Faculty of Engineering: CARLOS CAÑAS
Faculty of Human And Natural Sciences: Dr SILVIA AZUCENA DE FERNÁNDEZ
Faculty of Post-grade: LIDIA SALAMANCA

UNIVERSIDAD DE EL SALVADOR

Final 25 Avda, Ciudad Universitaria, Apdo 3110, San Salvador
Telephone: 2225-8826
Fax: 2225-8826
E-mail: mirsalva@navegante.com.sv
Internet: www.ues.edu.sv

Founded 1841
State control
Academic year: February to December
Brs in the Western, Eastern and Paracentral regions of El Salvador

Rector: Dr MARÍA ISABEL RODRÍGUEZ
Vice-Rector for Academics: JOAQUÍN ORLANDO MACHUCA
Vice-Rector for Admin.: Dr CARMEN RODRÍGUEZ DE RIVAS

Registrar: ALICIA MARGARITA RIVAS
Library Dir: JOSEFINA ROQUE
Number of teachers: 1,877
Number of students: 28,306
Publications: *Aquí Odontología* (odontology, 12 a year), *Boletín Informativo de la Facultad de Ciencias Económicas* (12 a year), *Búho Dilecto* (science and humanities, 6 a year), *Contacto Universitario* (bulletin of the Secretariat for National and International Relations, 12 a year), *El Quehacer Científico* (natural sciences and mathematics, 1 a year), *El Salvador: Coyuntura Económica* (economics, 4 a year), *El Universitario* (academic review, 4 a year), *Enfoque Tecnológico* (nuclear research, 2 a year), *Revista Electrónica de la Facultad de Medicina* (2 a year), *Ventana Informativa* (bulletin of the Multidisciplinary Faculty of the Western Region, 12 a year)

DEANS

Faculty of Agriculture: JORGE ALBERTO ULLOA
Faculty of Chemistry and Pharmacy: SALVADOR CASTILLO ARÉVALO
Faculty of Dentistry: Dr OSCAR RUBÉN COTO DIMAS
Faculty of Economics: EMILIO RECINOS FUENTES
Faculty of Engineering and Architecture: Ing. MARIO ROBERTO NIETO
Faculty of Humanities: ANA MARÍA GLOWER DE ALVARADO
Faculty of Jurisprudence and Social Sciences: MORENA ELIZABETH NOCHEZ DE ALDANA
Faculty of Medicine: Dr ANA LETICIA ZAVALETA DE AMAYA
Faculty of Natural and Mathematical Sciences: LETICIA NOEMÍ PÁUL DE FLORES
Multidisciplinary Faculty of the Eastern Region: JUAN FRANCISCO MÁRMOL CANJURA
Multidisciplinary Faculty of the Paracentral Region: JOSÉ NOEL ARGUETA
Multidisciplinary Faculty of the Western Region: JORGE MAURICIO RIVERA

UNIVERSIDAD 'DR JOSÉ MATÍAS DELGADO'

Km 8$\frac{1}{2}$ carretera a Santa Tecla, Ciudad Merliot
Telephone: 2212-9400
Fax: 2289-5314
E-mail: informacion@umjd.edu.sv
Internet: www.ujmd.edu.sv

Founded 1977
Private control
Language of instruction: Spanish
Academic year: January to June, July to December

Rector: Dr DAVID ESCOBAR GALINDO
Vice-Rector: CARLOS QUINTANILLA SCHMIDT
Academic Vice-Rector: Dr FERNANDO BASILIO CASTELLANOS
Registrar: Dr FERNANDO BASILIO CASTELLANOS
Library Dir: SARA ESCOBAR DE GONZÁLEZ

Library of 25,000 vols
Number of teachers: 380
Number of students: 4,000

DEANS AND DIRECTORS

Faculty of Agriculture and Agricultural Research: MARÍA GEORGIA GÓMEZ DE REYES
Faculty of Economics: ROBERTO ALEJANDRO SORTO FLETES
Faculty of Health Sciences: Dr JUAN JOSÉ FERNÁNDEZ
Faculty of Jurisprudence and Social Sciences: Dr HUMBERTO GUILLERMO CUESTAS
Faculty of Sciences and Arts: LUIS SALAZAR RETANA

School of Applied Arts: LUIS SALAZAR RETANA
School of Architecture: LUIS SALAZAR RETANA
School of Business Administration and Marketing: PATRICIA LINARES DE HERNÁNDEZ
School of Communications: RICARDO CHACÓN
School of Industrial Engineering: SILVIA BARRIOS DE FERREIRO
School of Psychology: ROXANA VIDES

UNIVERSIDAD DE ORIENTE

4A Calle Poniente 705, San Miguel
Telephone: 2661-1180
Fax: 2660-0879
E-mail: info@univo.edu.sv
Internet: www.univo.edu.sv
Founded 1981
Private control
Rector: Dr JOAQUÍN APARICIO ZELAYA
Pres.: Prof. GREGORIO BALMORE IRAHETA
Sec.-Gen.: ROGELIO CISNEROZ LAZO

DEANS

Faculty of Agriculture: ALVARO ARMANDO HERRERA COELLO
Faculty of Economics: LUIS ALONSO SILVA
Faculty of Engineering and Architecture: DAVID ARNOLDO FLORES GARAY
Faculty of Law: Dr GODOFREDO LAHUD
Faculty of Science and Humanities: JOSÉ DAVID DÍAZ REYES

UNIVERSIDAD PANAMERICANA DE EL SALVADOR

Calle El Progreso 214, a 60m de Avda Bernal Colonia Miramonte Poniente, San Salvador
Telephone: 2260-1906
Fax: 2260-1859
E-mail: upaninfo@upan.edu.sv
Internet: www.upan.edu.sv
Founded 1989
Private control
Rector: OSCAR ARMANDO MORÁN FOLGAR
Vice-Rector: NUBIA ADALILA MENDOZA FIGUEROA
Sec.-Gen.: CELINA DEL CARMEN LÓPEZ URÍAS
Registrar: ALMA ARACELY POZAS DE IBARRA
Librarian: RAQUEL HERNÁNDEZ

DEANS

Faculty of Economics: JOSUÉ ELÍAS MONTOYA

Faculty of Jurisprudence: ALEJANDRO GARCÍA GARAY
Faculty of Science and Humanities: NUBIA ADAILILA MENDOZA FIGUEROA

DIRECTORS

Institute of Research, Guidance and Assessment: VIRGINIA QUINTANA ESTRADA
School of Legal Sciences: MARGORI CAROLINA JUSTO
School of Library Science and Information Science: CARLOS FERRER

UNIVERSIDAD SALVADOREÑA ALBERTO MASFERRER

19 Avda Norte, entre 3A Calle Poniente y Alameda Juan Pablo II, Apdo 2053, San Salvador
Telephone: 2221-1136
Fax: 2222-8006
E-mail: informacion@mail.usam.edu.sv
Internet: www.usam.edu.sv
Founded 1979
State control
Language of instruction: Spanish
Academic year: January to December
Rector: Dr CÉSAR AUGUSTO CALDERÓN
ViceRector: Dr MIGUEL ANTONIO BARRIOS
Sec.-Gen.: DAYSI C. M. DE GOMEZ
Registrar: ANA LORENA DE MELÉNDEZ
Librarian: XIMENA TIZNADO
Number of teachers: 283
Number of students: 2,000
Publication: Revista Somos (4 a year)

DEANS

Faculty of Dentistry: Dr ARMANDO RAFAEL MARTÍNEZ
Faculty of Law and Social Sciences: DELMER EDMUNDO CRUZ RODRÍGUEZ
Faculty of Medicine: Dra CARMEN J. CABEZAS DE SÁNCHEZ
Faculty of Pharmacy: SOCORRO VALDEZ
Faculty of Veterinary Medicine: Dr ANA EUGENIA VÉZQUEZ LIÉVANO

UNIVERSIDAD TECNOLÓGICA DE EL SALVADOR

Calle Arce 1120, San Salvador
Telephone: 2275-8888
Fax: 2275-8813
E-mail: infoutec@utec.edu.sv

Internet: www.utec.edu.sv
Founded 1981
Private control
Academic year: January to December
Pres. and Rector: JOSÉ MAURICIO LOUCEL
Asst Rector: CARLOS REYNALDO LÓPEZ NUILA
Vice-Rector for Academic Affairs and Strategic Devt: NELSON ZÁRATE SÁNCHEZ
Vice-Rector for Admin.: DANILO DÍAZ
Vice-Rector for Finance: MARÍA DE LOS ANGELES LOUCEL
Vice-Rector for Research and Extramural Studies: RAFAEL RODRÍGUEZ LOUCEL
Registrar: Dr JOSÉ ENRIQUE BURGOS
Librarian: MARÍA ELSA LÉMUS FLORES
Library of 16,000 vols
Number of teachers: 349
Number of students: 14,618
Publications: Boletín Comunica, Revista de Aniversario, Revista Entorno, Revista Redes

DIRECTORS

School of Architecture and Design: (vacant)
School of Art and Culture: Dr RAMÓN RIVAS
School of Business: VILMA FLORES DE AVILA
School of Communications: (vacant)
School of Languages: (vacant)
School of Law: RENE ALFREDO PORTILLO CUADRA
School of Oceanography: SUSAN LYN DE GUZMÁN
School of Science and Technology: RICARDO NAVARRETE

Colleges

Central American Technical Institute: Apdo 133, Santa Tecla, La Libertad; tel. 2228-0845; fax 2228-1277; f. 1969; courses in agricultural, civil and construction engineering, architecture, electronics, mechanical engineering; library: 6,000 vols; Dir ROLANDO MARÍN COTO.

Escuela Nacional de Agricultura 'Roberto Quiñónez': Km 33½ Carr. a Sta Ana, Apdo 2139, San Salvador; tel. 2228-2735; f. 1956; 350 students; 60 teachers; library: 7,000 vols; Dir Ing. MAURICIO ARÉVALO.

EQUATORIAL GUINEA

The Higher Education System

Equatorial Guinea has been independent for just over three decades, of which two were dominated by a brutal dictatorship. Its intellectual and cultural traditions were determined by colonial values rather than by its own cultural values, although it is slowly redressing this situation. The condition of general education (Equatorial Guinea has very limited resources) has an adverse affect on higher education, with students arriving having had very little access to books, and with an education based almost entirely on recitation. This naturally limits the level and type of coursework that may be offered. That the language of instruction is mainly Spanish while the majority of good jobs require English also presents difficulties. Many students elect to study abroad; this is supported by scholarships from foreign countries or agencies, administered by the Government. Equatorial Guinea has no national programme of scholarship for foreign study. In 1999/2000 there were 1,003 pupils in higher education. Since 1979 assistance in the development of the educational system has been provided by Spain. The Universidad Nacional de Guinea Ecuatorial (UNGE), founded in 1995, is Equatorial Guinea's only university. Two higher education centres, at Bata and Malabo, are administered by the Spanish Universidad Nacional de Educación a Distancia.

Regulatory Bodies

GOVERNMENT

Ministry of Education, Science and Sports: Malabo; Min. CRISTOBAL MEÑANA ELA.

Ministry of Information, Culture and Tourism: Malabo; Min. SANTIAGO NSOBEYA EFUMAN NCHAMA.

Learned Societies

LANGUAGE AND LITERATURE

Centro Cultural Hispano-Guineano: Malabo; f. 1982; maintains library; organizes cultural events; publs *Africa 2000* (3 a year), *Ediciones del Centro Cultural Hispano-Guineano* (series dedicated to Ecuatoguinean writers).

Institut Culturel d'Expression Française (ICEF): BP 936, Malabo; tel. 92660; fax 92985; internet www.chez.com/icefmalabo; f. 1984; offers courses and examinations in French language and culture and promotes cultural exchange with France; Dir VINCENT BRACK.

Research Institute

NATURAL SCIENCES

Biological Sciences

Bioko Biodiversity Protection Program: c/o Universidad Nacional de Guinea Ecuatorial, Carretera Luba s/n, Malabo; tel. 286768; e-mail butynski@bioko.org; internet www.bioko.org; part of academic partnership between Arcadia University (USA, *q.v.*) and Universidad Nacional de Guinea Ecuatorial (*q.v.*); conservation of Bioko Island's biodiversity, especially its critically endangered primates and nesting sea turtles, through devt of economically sustainable educational programmes, research programmes and conservation activities; maintains wildlife research centre at Moka; Co-Dirs GAIL HEARN, WAYNE MORRA; Project Dir JOSE MANUEL ESARA ECHUBE; Research Dir CLAUDIO POSA BOHOME.

Universities

UNIVERSIDAD NACIONAL DE EDUCACIÓN A DISTANCIA (UNED), EQUATORIAL GUINEA BRANCH

Edificio Poveda, C/o Amanecer de África s/n, Barrio de Ela Nguema, Malabo

Telephone: 92911
Fax: 92932

E-mail: unedmalabo@yahoo.es
Founded 1993
Language of instruction: Spanish
Part of Universidad Nacional de Educación a Distancia (Spain); br. in Bata (tel. 82277)

Dir: PILAR MONTES PALOMINO
Dir of Studies: Dr ANDRÉS ESONO ONDÓ
Library of 10,000 vols.

UNIVERSIDAD NACIONAL DE GUINEA ECUATORIAL (UNGE)

Carretera Luba s/n, Malabo
Telephone: 91644
Fax: 94361
Founded 1995
State control
Languages of instruction: Spanish, French, English

Rector: CARLOS NSE NSUGA

Library of 7,500 vols
Number of teachers: 100
Number of students: 1,200

Schools of administration (Malabo), agriculture, arts and social science (Malabo), engineering and technology (Bata), fisheries and forestry, medicine (Bata), nursing (Bata) teacher training (Malabo, with br. in Bata).

ERITREA

The Higher Education System

From 1962 to 1993 Eritrea was a *de facto* province of Ethiopia. Independence was achieved in 1993 following a 33-year war of secession. Since independence Eritrea has begun to rebuild its infrastructure, economy and government. The University of Asmara (the only university) was founded by the Camboni Sisters Missionary Institute in 1958 and was originally known as the Holy Family University Institute. In 1960 the Institute was accredited by the Superior Council of the Institute of Italian Universities and in 1968 it achieved university status under its current name; an English section was opened in the same year. In 2004/05 there were some 5,500 students enrolled on Bachelors degree courses at the University of Asmara, which was under the control of the Ministry of Education. Masters degrees were offered from autumn 2004.

The University of Asmara closed in September 2006. Higher education was then provided by six newly established technical institutes, each associated with a relevant Government ministry. The institutes provide education in the fields of science, technology, business and economics, social sciences, agriculture and marine training. The university administration remains on the site and it is thought that the university will start again with postgraduate and research programmes.

Regulatory Body
GOVERNMENT

Ministry of Education: POB 5610, Asmara; tel. (1) 113044; fax (1) 113866; internet www.erimoe.gov.er; Min. SEMERE RUSOM.

Learned Societies
LANGUAGE AND LITERATURE

Alliance Française: POB 209, Asmara; tel. (1) 126599; fax (1) 121036; internet www.afasmara.org.er; offers courses and examinations in French language and culture and promotes cultural exchange with France.

British Council: 175-11, St No. 23, POB 997, Asmara; tel. (1) 123415; fax (1) 127230; e-mail information@britishcouncil.org.er; internet www.britishcouncil.org/africa; f. 1971; offers courses and examinations in English language and British culture and promotes cultural exchange with the UK; library of 7,000 vols; 1,500 mems; Information and Knowledge Centre Man. MICHAEL TEKIE.

Libraries and Archives
Asmara

Asmara Public Library: 82 Felket Ave 173, Asmara; tel. (1) 127044; f. 1959; 32,400 vols; branch library with 11,000 vols in north Asmara; Dir EFREM MATHEWOS KAHSAY.

Massawa

Massawa Municipal Library: POB 17, Massawa; tel. (1) 552407; fax (1) 552249; f. 1997; 10,000 vols; Chief Librarian MUHAMMED NUR SAID.

Museum
Asmara

National Museum of Eritrea: St Mariam Ghimbi H., Asmara; tel. and fax (1) 122389; e-mail yozuky@gmail.com; internet www.mrieka.com; f. 1992; archaeology, ethnography, medieval period, natural history and militaria, paleontology; oversees excavations and preservation of the national archaeological heritage; Dir-Gen. Dr YOSIEF LIBSEQAL.

ESTONIA

The Higher Education System

From 1940 until 1991 Estonia was a Soviet Socialist Republic within the USSR. Higher education was based on the Soviet system, but following independence the Estonian Education Act of 1992 identified the development of Estonian language and culture as one of the main aims of education. Estonia implemented the Bologna Process at undergraduate level in 2002 and at postgraduate level in 2005; this has led to the establishment of a two-tier Bachelors and Masters degree system (with exceptions in certain subjects). Institutions of higher education are either universities or applied higher education institutes. Universities provide academic education and applied higher education institutes provide vocational education. In 2007/08 there were 34 higher education institutions, including the University of Tartu (founded in 1632) and Tallinn University, with a total of 68,399 students enrolled. The Ministry of Education and Research is responsible for higher education, and up to 2008 several organizations were also involved in administrative and academic oversight; these included the Higher Education Advisory Chamber (HEAC), the Research and Development Council, the Estonian Science Council, the Estonian Innovation Fund and the Higher Education Quality Assessment Council QAC). In January 2009 the Higher Education Quality Agency (HEQA) took over from the HEAC and QAC as an autonomous and independent quality assessment agency. From 2009 to 2011 all higher education institutions will be required to go through the external quality assessment organized by the HEQA. By 2012 no institute will be able to operate without being accredited by the HEQA.

The Ministry of Education and Research sets requirements for admission to higher education, which generally consists of the Secondary Education Leaving Certificate (Gümnaasiumi lõputunnistus) and performance in national entrance examinations (Riigieksamitunnistus). Public university admissions are determined by the State, which sets enrolment quotas, although universities may take additional paying students once the quotas have been met. Specialist institutions may also set specific admissions criteria. Under the Bologna Process, higher education qualifications consist of Bachelors, Masters and Doctoral degrees. The Bakalaureusekraad (Bachelors) is the main undergraduate degree, consisting of three years of study. However, some degrees leading to professional qualifications require five years of study; this is particularly the case in medicine, veterinary medicine, pharmacy, architecture, engineering and teacher training. The first postgraduate degree is the Magistrikaad (Masters), which lasts two years and is dependent on attainment of the Bakalaureusekraad. The second level of postgraduate qualification (and final university degree) is the Doktorikraad; studies at this level last four years. Both the Magistrikaad and Doktorikraad may be either academic or professional qualifications. Since their introduction in 1999, the main institutions of post-secondary vocational and technical education are the rakenduskõrgkool (applied higher education institutes), which offer three- to four-year Diplom degrees.

Regulatory and Representative Bodies

GOVERNMENT

Ministry of Culture: Suur Karja 23, Tallinn 15076; tel. 628-22-22; fax 628-22-00; e-mail min@kul.ee; internet www.kul.ee; Min. LAINE JÄNES.

Ministry of Education and Research: Munga 18, Tartu 50088; tel. 735-02-22; fax 730-10-80; e-mail hm@hm.ee; internet www .hm.ee; Min. TÕNIS LUKAS.

ACCREDITATION

ENIC/NARIC Estonia: Academic Recognition Information Centre, Foundation 'Archimedes', L. Koidula 13A, 10125 Tallinn; tel. 696-24-15; fax 696-24-19; e-mail enic-naric@ archimedes.ee; internet www.archimedes.ee/ enic; Head GUNNAR VAHT.

Sihtasutus Archimedes, Eesti Kõrghariduse Kvaliteediagentuur (Archimedes Foundation, Estonian Higher Education Quality Agency): Toompuiestee 30, 10149 Tallinn; tel. 640-04-55; fax 696-24-27; e-mail ekka@archimedes.ee; internet www.ekka .archimedes.ee; f. 2009; conducts institutional accreditation and quality assessment of study programme groups in Estonian higher education instns and develops principles and procedures for such assessments; represents Estonia in issues concerning quality of higher and vocational education; 8 mems; Dir HELI MATTISEN.

NATIONAL BODY

Rektorite Nõukogu (Estonian Rectors' Conference): Ülikooli 18, 50090 Tartu; tel. and fax 736-68-67; e-mail mart.laidmets@ern .ee; internet www.ern.ee; f. 2000; 6 public univs as mems; Chair. Prof. ALAR KARIS; Sec. Gen. MART LAIDMETS.

Learned Societies

GENERAL

Estonian Academy of Sciences: Kohtu 6, 10130 Tallinn; tel. 644-21-29; fax 645-18-05; e-mail foreign@akadeemia.ee; internet www .akadeemia.ee; f. 1938 to advance scientific research and represent Estonian science nationally and internationally; promotes the adaptation of new knowledge for economic growth and improvement of the quality of life in Estonia; promotes the public appreciation of science and scientific methods of thought; encourages research co-operation at nat. and int. levels; divs of astronomy and physics (Head P. SAARI), biology, geology and chemistry (Head I. KOPPEL), humanities and social sciences (Head P. TULVISTE), informatics and technical Sciences (Head R. KÜTTNER); 75 mems (60 ordinary, 15 foreign); Pres. Prof. Dr RICHARD VILLEMS; Sec.-Gen. Prof. Dr LEO MÕTUS; publs *Acta Historica Tallinnensia*, *Linguistica Uralica*, *Oil Shale*, *Toimetised* (Proceedings: physics and mathematics, engineering, chemistry, Estonian Journal of Earth Sciences; biology/ecology), *Trames*.

HISTORY, GEOGRAPHY AND ARCHAEOLOGY

Estonian Geographical Society: Kohtu 6, 10130 Tallinn; Pres. JAAN-MATI PUNNING; Scientific Sec. LAINE MERIKALJU.

LANGUAGE AND LITERATURE

Alliance Française: Liivaluite 5, 11214 Tallinn; tel. 672-20-13; fax 672-11-98; e-mail hellemichelson@hot.ee; offers courses and examinations in French language and culture and promotes cultural exchange with France.

British Council: Vana-Posti 7, 10146 Tallinn; tel. 625-77-88; fax 625-77-99; e-mail british.council@britishcouncil.ee; internet www.britishcouncil.org/estonia; offers examinations in English; introduces British culture and promotes cultural exchange with the UK; library of 6,000 vols; Dir KYLLIKE TOHVER.

Estonian Mother Tongue Society: Roosikrantsi 6, 10119 Tallinn; tel. 644-93-31; e-mail es@eki.ee; internet www .emakeeleselts.ee; f. 1920; promotes and maintains interest in the Estonian language; coordinates language research and development; systematic research into Estonian dialects; language-planning and modern literary language research; arranges language days outside Estonia; also focuses on the modern literary language, loan-words in Estonian and the Estonian dialectal landscape; 360 mems (350 ordinary, 10 hon.); library of 6,125 vols; Chair. Prof. HELLE METSLANG; Academic Sec. ANNIKA HUSSAR; publs *Emakeele Seltsi aastaraamat* (1 a year), *Oma Keel* (2 a year).

Goethe-Institut: Suurtüki 4B, 10133 Tallinn; tel. 627-69-60; fax 627-69-62; e-mail goethe@goethe.ee; internet www.goethe.de/ ne/tal/deindex.htm; offers courses and examinations in German language and culture, and promotes cultural exchange with Germany; library of 9,000 vols, 25 periodicals; Dir MIKKO FRITZE.

NATURAL SCIENCES
General
Estonian Union of the History and Philosophy of Science: Ülikooli 18, 50090 Tartu; tel. 742-15-14; f. 1967; attached to Estonian Acad. of Sciences; 93 mems; Chair. JAAK AAVIKSOO; Scientific Sec. ERKI TAMMIKSAAR.

Biological Sciences
Estonian Naturalists' Society: Struve 2, 51003 Tartu; tel. 734-19-35; fax 742-70-11; e-mail elus@elus.ee; internet www.elus.ee; f. 1853; 21 scientific and environmental sections; library of 160,056 vols; 763 mems; Pres. Dr TÕNU VIIK; Sec. SILJA KANA; publs *Folia Cryptogamica Estonica*, *Schola Biotheoretica*, *Yearbook*.

Research Institutes
GENERAL
Institute for Islands Development: Lossipargi 1, 93811 Kuressaare; tel. and fax 453-91-45; e-mail kaia@si.edu.ee; attached to Tallinn Univ. of Technology; f. 1991; socioeconomic and technological devt of the Estonian islands; Dir MARET PANK.

AGRICULTURE, FISHERIES AND VETERINARY SCIENCE
EAU Plant Biotechnological Research Centre EVIKA: Harjumaa, Teaduse 6A, 75501 Saku; tel. 604-14-84; fax 604-11-36; e-mail hilja.pihl@mail.ee; attached to Min. of Education and Research, and Estonian Univ. of Life Sciences; Dir KATRIN KOTKAS.

Estonian Agrobiocentre: Rõõmu tee 10, 51013 Tartu; tel. and fax 733-97-17; attached to Min. of Agriculture; veterinary research; Dir JÜRI KUMAR.

Estonian Institute of Agricultural Engineering: Harjumaa, Teaduse 13, 76609 Saku; tel. 272-18-54; fax 272-19-61; e-mail ergo@peak.edu.ee; attached to Min. of Agriculture; Dir ARVI KALLAS.

Estonian Research Institute of Agriculture: Teaduse 13, 75501 Saku; tel. 671-15-42; fax 671-15-40; e-mail info@eria.ee; internet www.eria.ee; Dir HINDREK OLDER.

Jõgeva Plant Breeding Institute: Aamisepa 1, 48309 Jõgeva; tel. and fax 776-01-26; e-mail jogeva@jpbi.ee; attached to Min. of Agriculture; f. 1920; Dir MATI KOPPELL.

ARCHITECTURE AND TOWN PLANNING
OÜ ETUI BetonTEST—Ehitusinstituut (ETUI BetonTEST Ltd—Building Institute): Estonia pst. 7, 10143 Tallinn; tel. 645-41-58; fax 644-23-25; e-mail etui@betontest.ee; internet www.betontest.ee; Dir OLAV SAMMAL.

ECONOMICS, LAW AND POLITICS
Estonian Institute for Futures Studies: Lai 34, 10133 Tallinn; tel. 641-11-65; fax 641-17-59; future scenarios for the development of Estonia and its neighbouring areas; Dir ERIK TERK.

Estonian Institute of Economic Research: Rävala puiestee 6, 19080 Tallinn; tel. 681-46-50; fax 667-83-99; e-mail eki@ki.ee; internet www.ki.ee; f. 1934; Dir MARJE JOSING; publs *Economic Indicators of Estonia* (10 a year), *Economic Survey of Baltic States* (4 a year), *Konjunktuur* (4 a year), *Baltic Facts* (1 a year).

Estonian Institute of Economics at Tallinn University of Technology: Estonia tee 7, 10143 Tallinn; tel. 644-45-70; fax 699-88-51; e-mail mail@tami.ee; internet www.tami.ee; f. 1947; attached to Tallinn University of Technology; 19 mems; Dir TIIA PÜSS; Research Dir ÜLO ENNUSTE.

HISTORY, GEOGRAPHY AND ARCHAEOLOGY
Institute of History: Rüütli 6, 10130 Tallinn; tel. 644-65-94; fax 644-37-14; e-mail ai@teleport.ee; f. 1947; Dir PRIIT RAUDKIVI; publs *Acta Historica Tallinnensia* (1 a year), *Eesti Arheoloogia Ajakiri* (1 a year).

LANGUAGE AND LITERATURE
Institute of the Estonian Language: Roosikrantsi 6, 10119 Tallinn; tel. and fax 641-14-43; e-mail eki@eki.ee; internet www.eki.ee; f. 1947; Dir Dr URMAS SUTROP; publ. *Eesti Keele Instituudi Toimetised* (irregular).

Under and Tuglas Literature Centre: Roosikrantsi 6, 10119 Tallinn; tel. 644-31-47; fax 644-01-77; e-mail utkk@utkk.ee; internet www.utkk.ee; f. 1993; attached to Estonian Acad. of Sciences; Dir Dr JAAN UNDUSK.

MEDICINE
Cardiology Centre: Ravi 18, 10138 Tallinn; tel. 620-72-50; fax 620-70-02; e-mail jyri.kaik@mail.ee; f. 1984 as Estonian Institute of Cardiology; present name 2007; attached to Tallinn Univ. of Technology; research areas incl. cardiac arrhythmias, electrophysiology, clinical and preventative cardiology; Dir JÜRI KAIK.

National Institute for Health Development: Hiiu 42, 11619 Tallinn; tel. 659-39-00; fax 659-39-01; e-mail tai@tai.ee; internet www.tai.ee; f. 1947 as Estonian Institute of Experimental and Clinical Medicine; attached to Min. of Social Affairs; Dir MAARIKE HARRO.

Pärnu Institute of Health Resort Treatment and Medical Rehabilitation: Kuuse 4, 40012 Pärnu; tel. 442-59-00; Dir ENDEL VEINPALU.

NATURAL SCIENCES
General
Estonian Marine Institute: Mäealuse 14, 12618 Tallinn; tel. 671-89-01; fax 671-89-00; e-mail meri@sea.ee; internet www.sea.ee; f. 1992; biology and ecology of freshwater and marine fish, population and community dynamics; long-term dynamics of Baltic Sea ecosystem and basic mechanisms behind it; effect of temporal and spatial variability of coastal processes on the biological and functional diversity; optics and remote sensing of coastal and inland waters; investigations on dynamics and regularities of devt of ecological subsystems in the NE Baltic, Gulfs of Finland and Rīga; modelling of the Baltic Sea and Estonian large lakes ecosystems and composing of the operational forecasting models; effect of aquatic invasive species on ecosystems; effect of human induced eutrophication processes on coastal ecosystems of the Baltic Sea; Dir Prof. TOOMAS SAAT; publ. *Estonian Marine Institute Report Series* (irregular).

Biological Sciences
Estonian Biocentre: Riia 23B, 51010 Tartu; tel. 737-50-64; fax 742-01-94; e-mail rvillems@ebc.ee; Dir RICHARD VILLEMS.

Institute of Ecology: Kevade 2, 10137 Tallinn; tel. 662-18-53; fax 662-22-83; e-mail eco@eco.edu.ee; internet www.eco.edu.ee; f. 1992; Dir J.-M. PUNNING.

Institute of Experimental Biology: Instituudi tee 11, 76902 Harku; tel. 656-06-05; fax 650-60-91; e-mail ebi@ebi.ee; f. 1957; attached to Estonian Univ. of Life Sciences; Dir. Prof. A. AAVIKSAAR.

Institute of Zoology and Botany: Riia 181, 51014 Tartu; tel. 742-80-21; fax 738-30-13; internet www.zbi.ee; f. 1947; Dir URMAS TARTES.

International Centre for Environmental Biology: Mustamäe tee 4, 10621 Tallinn; tel. 611-58-04; fax 611-58-05; Dir JÜRI MARTIN.

Physical Sciences
Estonian Meteorological and Hydrological Institute: Rävala puiestee 8, 10143 Tallinn; tel. 646-15-63; e-mail jaan.saar@emhi.ee; internet www.emhi.ee; weather forecasts; environmental protection; collation, treatment and storage of results of meteorological and hydrological measurements; climatological survey of Estonia; attached to Min. of the Environment; Dir-Gen. JAAN SAAR.

Geological Survey of Estonia: Kadaka tee 80–82, 12618 Tallinn; tel. 672-00-94; fax 672-00-91; e-mail egk@egk.ee; internet www.egk.ee; attached to Min. of the Environment; Dir. VELLO KLEIN.

Institute of Geology: Ehitajate tee 5, 19086 Tallinn; tel. 620-30-10; fax 620-30-11; e-mail inst@gi.ee; internet www.gi.ee; f. 1947; attached to Tallinn Univ. of Technology; Dir Dr ALVAR SOESOO; Sec. HELLE POHL-RAIDLA; publ. *Proceedings* (4 a year).

Institute of Physics: Riia 142, 51014 Tartu; tel. 737-46-02; fax 738-30-33; e-mail dir@fi.tartu.ee; internet www.fi.ut.ee; f. 1973; attached to Univ. of Tartu; research and higher education in physics, materials science and nanotechnology; library of 30,000 vols, 50 periodicals; Dir Dr MARCO KIRM.

National Institute of Chemical Physics and Biophysics: Akadeemia tee 23, 12618 Tallinn; tel. 639-83-00; fax 670-36-62; e-mail kbfi@kbfi.ee; internet www.kbfi.ee; f. 1979; Dir AGO SAMOSON.

Oil Shale Research Institute: Järveküla tee 12, 30328 Kohtla-Järve; tel. 334-45-50; fax 334-47-82; f. 1958; library of 100,000 vols; Dir RICHARD JOONAS.

Tartu Observatory: Tõravere, 61602 Tartu Maakond; tel. 741-02-65; fax 741-02-05; e-mail aai@aai.ee; internet www.aai.ee; f. 1808 present status 1947; research in astrophysics and cosmology, atmospheric physics and remote sensing of the earth; library of 100,000 vols; Dir LAURITS LEEDJÄRV; publ. *Tartu Tähetorni Kalender* (1 a year, in Estonian).

RELIGION, SOCIOLOGY AND ANTHROPOLOGY
Estonian Interuniversity Population Research Centre: POB 3012, 10504 Tallinn; tel. 645-41-25; fax 660-41-98; e-mail asta@ekdk.estnet.ee; Dir KALEV KATUS; publ. *EKDK RY* (series A, B, C and D, all irregular).

Institute of International and Social Studies: Estonia puiestee 7, 10143 Tallinn; tel. and fax 645-49-27; e-mail rasi@iiss.ee; internet www.iiss.ee; f. 1988; 25 mems; Dir RAIVO VETIK (acting).

TECHNOLOGY
Estonian Energy Research Institute: Paldiski maantee 1, 10137 Tallinn; tel. 662-20-28; fax 661-36-55; e-mail eeri@eeri.ee; internet www.eeri.ee; Dir ÜLO RUDI.

Institute of Cybernetics: Akadeemia tee 21, 12618 Tallinn; tel. 620-41-50; fax 620-41-51; e-mail dir@ioc.ee; internet www.ioc.ee; f. 1960; attached to Tallinn Univ. of Technology; library of 8,000 vols; Dir ANDRUS SALUPERE.

Libraries and Archives

Tallinn

Academic Library of Tallinn University: Rävala Ave 10, 15042 Tallinn; tel. 665-94-01; fax 665-94-00; e-mail tlulib@tlulib.ee; internet www.tlulib.ee; f. 1946; 2,445,165 vols, incunabula; Dir ANDRES KOLLIST.

Eesti Rahvusraamatukogu (National Library of Estonia): Tõnismägi 2, 15189 Tallinn; tel. 630-76-11; fax 631-14-10; e-mail nlib@nlib.ee; internet www.nlib.ee; f. 1918, nat. library status 1988, parliamentary library 1989; nat. and parliamentary library with public access; nat. ISBN, ISSN and ISMN agency; research library for the humanities and social sciences; professional devt centre; cultural centre for book and art exhibitions, concerts, confs; 34m. vols; Dir-Gen. JANNE ANDRESOO; publs *Eesti Rahvusraamatukogu Toimetised* (Acta Bibliothecae Nationalis Estoniae), *Raamatukogu* (The Library, 6 a year).

Tartu

Tartu University Library: W. Struve 1, 50091 Tartu; tel. 737-57-02; fax 737-57-01; e-mail library@utlib.ee; internet www.utlib.ee; f. 1802; 4,050,000 vols, 505,000 theses, 28,000 MSS; Dir MALLE ERMEL (acting); Sec. KERSTI KUUSEMÄE.

Museums and Art Galleries

Tallinn

Art Museum of Estonia: Weizenbergi 34, Valge 1, 10127 Tallinn; tel. 602-60-01; fax 602-60-02; e-mail muuseum@ekm.ee; internet www.ekm.ee; f. 1919; colln of fine and applied art; art exhibitions; 55,135 items; Dir SIRJE HELME.

Estonian History Museum: Pirita tee 56, 10127 Tallinn; tel. 641-16-30; fax 644-34-46; e-mail post@eam.ee; internet www.eam.ee; f. 1842; archeology, medieval and near history, numismatics and cultural history; research work of the museum is based mostly on rich museum collns comprising 282,669 artefacts; temporary exhibits, concerts, lectures, publs; library of 11,000 vols; Dir SIRJE KARIS.

Estonian Open Air Museum: Vabaõhumuuseumi tee 12, 13521 Tallinn; tel. 654-91-17; fax 654-91-27; e-mail evm@evm.ee; internet www.evm.ee; f. 1957; architectural and ethnographical objects from 18th–20th centuries; Dir M. LANG.

Estonian Theatre and Music Museum: Müürivahe 12, 10146 Tallinn; tel. 644-21-32; fax 641-81-66; e-mail info@tmm.ee; internet www.tmm.ee; f. 1924; library of 50,000 vols; Dir ÜLLE REIMETS; publ. *AegiKiri* (1 a year).

Tallinn City Museum: Vene 17, 10123 Tallinn; tel. 644-18-29; fax 644-15-74; e-mail info@linnamuuseum.ee; internet www.linnamuuseum.ee; f. 1937; library of 6,300 vols; Dir MARUTA VARRAK.

Tartu

Estonian Literary Museum: Vanemuise 42, POB 368, 50002 Tartu; tel. 737-77-00; fax 737-77-06; e-mail kirmus@kirmus.ee; internet www.kirmus.ee; f. 1909; comprises Archival Library (incl. bibliography dept), Estonian Folklore Archives, Estonian Cultural History Archives, folklore dept and ethnomusicology dept; Dir Mag. JANIKA

KRONBERG; publs *Folklore/Electronic Journal of Folklore* (print and electronic, 4 a year), *Maetagused* (print and electronic, 4 a year), *Paar sammukest* (Some Small Steps, 1 a year), *Pro Folkloristika: Estonian Folklore Archives* (1 a year).

Estonian National Museum: Veski 32, 51014 Tartu; tel. 735-04-00; fax 742-22-54; e-mail erm@erm.ee; internet www.erm.ee; f. 1909; ethnology and culture of the Estonian and Finno-Ugric people; 100 mems; library of 34,482 vols; Dir KRISTA ARU; publs *Eesti Rahva Muuseumi Aastaraamat* (1 a year), *Journal of Ethnology and Folkloristics* (2 a year), *Eesti Rahva Muuseumi Sari* (1 a year).

Tartu Art Museum: Vallikraavi 14, 51003 Tartu; tel. and fax 734-10-50; e-mail tartmus@tartmus.ee; internet www.tartmus.ee; f. 1940; Estonian and European art since 19th century; library of 20,000 vols; Dir REET MARK.

University of Tartu Art Museum: Ülikooli 18, 50090 Tartu; tel. 737-53-84; fax 737-54-40; e-mail kmm@ut.ee; internet www.ut.ee/artmuseum; f. 1803; mainly plaster casts of ancient sculpture, gems and coins, graphic art from 15th–19th centuries, Russian icons, applied art, Greek and Roman antiquities; Dir INGE KUKK.

Universities

EESTI MAAÜLIKOOL
(Estonian University of Life Sciences)

Kreutzwaldi 1A, 51014 Tartu

Telephone: 731-30-01
Fax: 731-30-63
E-mail: info@emu.ee
Internet: www.emu.ee

Founded 1951 as Estonian Agricultural Univ., present name 2005
Public control
Languages of instruction: Estonian, English
Academic year: September to June

Rector: Prof. MAIT KLAASSEN
Vice-Rector for Research: Prof. ANNE LUIK
Vice-Rector for Students: Dr JÜRI LEHTSAAR

Number of teachers: 380
Number of students: 4,700

Library of 600,000 vols

Publication: *Eesti Maaülikooli Teaduslike Tööde Kogumik*

DEANS

Institute of Agricultural and Environmental Sciences: ARET VOOREMÄE
Institute of Economics and Social Sciences: RANDO VÄRNIK
Institute of Forestry and Rural Engineering: PAAVO KAIMRE
Institute of Technology: MARGUS ARAK
Institute of Veterinary Medicine: TOOMAS TIIRATS

TALLINN UNIVERSITY OF TECHNOLOGY

Ehitajate tee 5, 19086 Tallinn

Telephone: 620-20-02
Fax: 620-20-20
E-mail: ttu@ttu.ee
Internet: www.ttu.ee

Founded 1918
Public control
Languages of instruction: Estonian, Russian, English
Academic year: September to June

Rector: Prof. ANDRES KEEVALLIK
Vice-Rector for Academic Affairs: Prof. JAKOB KÜBARSEPP

Vice-Rector for Devt: ANDRES KEEVALIK
Vice-Rector for Research: Prof. ERKKI TRUVE
Academic Sec.: KAI AVIKSOO
Librarian: JÜRI JÄRS
Library of 750,000 vols, 730 periodicals
Number of teachers: 1,600 (incl. affiliated institutions)
Number of students: 14,000
Publication: *Mente et Manu* (newsletter, 52 a year)

DEANS

Faculty of Chemistry and Materials Technology: Prof. ANDRES ÖPIK
Faculty of Civil Engineering: Prof. ROODE LIIAS
School of Economics and Business Admin.: Prof. ÜLLAS EHRLICH
Faculty of Social Sciences: Prof. SULEV MÄELTSEMEES
Faculty of Information Technology: Prof. ENNU RÜSTERN
Faculty of Mechanical Engineering: Prof. TAUNO OTTO
Faculty of Power Engineering: Prof. TÕNU LEHTLA
Faculty of Science: Prof. TÕNIS KANGER

PROFESSORS

Faculty of Chemistry and Materials Technology (tel. 620-27-96; fax 620-27-96; e-mail k@ttu.ee):

CHRISTJANSON, P., Polymer Technology
KALLAVUS, U., Materials Research
KAPS, T., Woodworking
MELLIKOV, E., Semiconductor Materials Technology
MUNTER, R., Environmental Technology
OJA, V., Chemical Engineering
ÖPIK, A., Physical Chemistry
PAALME, T., Food Science and Technology
SOONE, J., Environmental Technology
TRIKKEL, A., Physical Chemistry
VIIKNA, A., Textile Technology
VOKK, R., Food Science

Faculty of Civil Engineering (tel. 620-25-00; e-mail e@ttu.ee):

AAVIK, A., Road Construction
ENGELBRECHT, J., Applied Mechanics
IDNURM, S., Steel Structures
KLAUSON, A., Structural Mechanics
KÕIV, T. A., Heating and Ventilation
KOPPEL, T., Hydrodynamics
LAVING, J., Traffic and Transportation Engineering
LIIAS, R., Construction Economics and Management
LILL, I., Building Technology
RAADO, L.-M., Building Materials
RANDLEPP, A., Geodesy
SALUPERE, A., Solid Mechanics
SOOMERE, T., Hydrodynamics
SUTT, J., Construction Economics and Management

School of Economics and Business Administration (Kopli tn. 101, 11712 Tallinn; tel. 620-41-11; fax 620-39-46; e-mail t@ttu.ee):

AASMA, A., Economic Mathematics
ALVER, J., Accounting
ALVER, L., Financial Accounting
KEREM, K., Economic Theory
KILVITS, K., Economic Policy
KOLBRE, E., Management Economics
KUKRUS, A., Economic Law and Regulation
LEIMANN, J., Organization and Management
LISTRA, E., Finance and Banking
SAAT, M., Business Administration
TEDER, J., Small Businesses
TINT, P., Working Environment and Safety

Faculty of Humanities (tel. and fax 646-71-48; e-mail h@ttu.ee):

DRECHSLER, W., Governance

KAEVATS, Ü., Philosophy
KATTEL, R., Public Administration and European Studies
MÄELTSEMEES, S., Regional Policy
RAJANGU, V., Educational Policy
TEICHMANN, M., Psychology

Faculty of Information Technology (Raja tn. 15, 12618 Tallinn; tel. 620-22-51; fax 620-22-46; e-mail i@ttu.ee):

BULDAS, A., Information Security
KALJA, A., Systems Programming
KUKK, V., Circuit and Systems Theory
KUUSIK, R., Informatics
LOSSMANN, E., Telecommunications
MIN, M., Electronic Measurement
MÕTUS, L., Real Time Systems
ÕUNAPUU, E., IT Systems
PENJAM, J., Theoretical Computer Science
RANG, T., Electronics Design
RÜSTERN, E., Automatic Control and Systems Analysis
TAKLAJA, A., Microwave Engineering
TAMMET, T., Network Software
TEPANDI, J., Applied Artificial Intelligence
UBAR, R.-J., Computer Engineering and Diagnostics
VAIN, J., Formal Methods

Faculty of Mechanical Engineering (tel. 620-33-50; fax 620-31-96; e-mail m@ttu.ee):

AJAOTS, M., Fine Mechanics
EERME, M., Computer-aided Design and Manufacturing
KIITAM, A., Quality Engineering
KULU, P., Materials Science
KÜTTNER, R., Computer-aided Design and Manufacturing
LAANEOTS, R., Metrology and Measurement Techniques
LAVRENTJEV, J., Automotive Engineering
MELLIKOV, E., Semiconductor Materials Technology
PAIST, A., Thermal Power Engineering
PAPPEL, T., Machine Mechanics
PAPSTEL, J., Production Engineering
ROOSIMÖLDER, L., Product Development
SIIRDE, A., Thermal Power Equipment
TAMRE, M., Mechatronics

Faculty of Power Engineering (Ehitajate tee 5, 19086 Tallinn; tel. 620-35-48; fax 620-36-96; e-mail a@ttu.ee):

JARVIK, J., Electrical Machines
LAUGIS, J., Electrical Drives and Electricity Supply
LEHTLA, T., Robotics
MELDORF, M., Transfer in Power Systems
TAMMOJA, H., Electrical Power Engineering
VALGMA, I., Rock Engineering

Faculty of Science (tel. 620-29-95; fax 620-26-45; e-mail y@ttu.ee):

ELKEN, J., Oceanography
JÄRVEKÜLG, L., Molecular Diagnostics
KALJURAND, M., Analytical Chemistry
KARELSON, M., Molecular Technology
KRUSTOK, J., Applied Physics
LIPPING, T., Radiophysics
LOPP, M., Organic Chemistry
MEIGAS, K., Biomedical Technology
PAAL, E., Algebra and Geometry
PALUMAA, P., Genomics and Proteomics
PUUSEMP, P., Algebra and Geometry
SAMEL, N., Bio-organic and Natural Products Chemistry
TAMM, T., Inorganic and Gen. Chemistry
TAMMERAID, L., Mathematical Analysis
TIMMUSK, T., Molecular Biology
TRUVE, E., Gene Technology
VILU, R., Biochemistry

TALLINN UNIVERSITY

Narva mnt 25, 10120 Tallinn
Telephone: 640-91-01

Fax: 640-91-16
E-mail: tlu@tlu.ee
Internet: www.tlu.ee

Founded 2005, merger of Tallinn Pedagogical Univ., Estonian Academic Library, Estonian Institute of Humanities and Institute of History
Language of instruction: Estonian
Rector: MATI HEIDMETS
Vice-Rector for Academic Affairs: HELI MATTISEN
Vice-Rector for Open Univ.: MADIS LEPIK
Vice-Rector for Research and Devt: PEETER NORMAK
Number of teachers: 844
Number of students: 7,421

DEANS

Faculty of Educational Sciences: Assoc. Prof. PRIIT REISKA
Faculty of Fine Arts: Prof. EHA RÜÜTEL
Faculty of Mathematics and Natural Sciences: Prof. ANDI KIVINUKK
Faculty of Philology: Prof. SULIKO LIIV
Faculty of Physical Education: Assoc. Prof. KRISTJAN PORT
Faculty of Social Sciences: Prof. ALEKSANDER PULVER

UNIVERSITY OF TARTU

Ülikooli 18, 50090 Tartu
Telephone: 737-51-00
Fax: 737-54-40
E-mail: info@ut.ee
Internet: www.ut.ee

Founded 1632
State control
Language of instruction: Estonian
Academic year: September to June

Rector: ALAR KARIS (acting)
Pro-Rector for Academic Affairs: MARTIN HALLIK
Pro-Rector for Research: Prof. KRISTJAN HALLER
Acad. Sec.: IVAR-IGOR SAARNIIT
Library Dir: MALLE ERMEL

Library: see Libraries and Archives
Number of teachers: 925
Number of students: 18,136

Publications: *Acta et Commentationes Universitatis Tartuensis* (44 series), *Universitas Tartuensis* (12 a year)

DEANS

Faculty of Economics and Business Administration: Prof. TOOMAS HALDMA
Faculty of Law: Prof. JAAN GINTER
Faculty of Mathematics and Computer Science: Prof MATI KILP
Faculty of Medicine: Prof. JOEL STARKOPF
Faculty of Philosophy: Prof. VALTER LANG
Faculty of Physical Education and Sports Sciences: Prof. MATI PÄÄSUKE
Faculty of Physics and Chemistry: Prof. J. JÄRV
Faculty of Science and Technology: PEETER BURK
Faculty of Social Sciences and Education: Prof. JAANUS HARRO
Faculty of Theology: Prof. RIHO ALTNURME

PROFESSORS

Faculty of Theology:

ALTNURME, R., Church History
KULL, A., Systematic Theology
KULMAR, T., Comparative Religion
KÄMMERER, T., Ancient Near-Eastern Languages
LEHTSAAR, T., Psychology of Religion

Faculty of Law:

BACHMANN, T., Cognitive Psychology and Psychology of Law

GINTER, J., Criminology
KULL, I., Civil Law
LUTS-SOOTAK, M., Legal History
MERUSK, K., Constitutional and Administrative Law
NARITS, R., Comparative Jurisprudence
PISUKE, H., Intellectual Property Law
SAAR, J., Criminology
SOOTAK, J., Criminal Law
TRUUVÄLI, E., Theory of Law
VARUL, P., Civil Law

Faculty of Medicine:

ALTRAJA, A., Pulmonology
AREND, A., Histology and Embryology
ASSER, T., Neurosurgery
EHA, J., Cardiology
EVERAUS, H., Haematology and Oncology
KAASIK, A., Molecular Toxicology
KARRO, H., Obstetrics and Gynaecology
KIIVET, R., Health Care Management
KÕKS, S., Ship of Physiological Genomics
LEMBER, M., Propaedeutics of Internal Medicine
LUTSAR, I., Medical Microbiology and Virology
MAAROOS, H., Polyclinic and Family Medicine
MAAROOS, J., Sports Medicine and Rehabilitation
MIKELSAAR, A., Human Biology and Genetics
MIKELSAAR, M., Medical Biotechnology
PEETSALU, A., Surgical Diseases
SEPPET, E., Pathological Physiology
SILM, H., Dermatology and Venerology
STARKOPF, J., Anaesthesiology and Intensive Care
ZILMER, M., Medical Biochemistry
ŽARKOVSKI, A., Pharmacology and Toxicology
TAMM, A., Laboratory Medicine
TEESALU, P., Ophthalmology
TILLMANN, V., Paediatrics
UIBO, R., Immunology
UUSKÜLA, A., Epidemiology
VASAR, E., Physiology
VASAR, V., Psychiatry
VESKI, P., Pharmaceutical Technology and Biopharmaceutics
VÄLI, M., Forensic Medicine

Faculty of Philosophy:

COHNITZ, D., Theoretical Philosophy
DULITŠENKO, A., Slavic Languages and Literature
EHALA, M., Didactics of Estonian and Applied Linguistics
ELKEN, J., Painting
HUUMO, T., Finnish Language and Culture
KIRSS, T., Estonian Literature
KISSELJOVA, L., Russian Literature
KRIISKA, A., Laboratory Archaeology
KULL, K., Biosemiotics
KUUTMA, K., Cultural Research
KÜLMOJA, I., Russian Language
LANG, V., Archaeology
LAUR, M., Modern History
LEETE, A., Ethnology
LILL, A., Classical Philology
MAISTE, J., Art History
MATJUS, Ü., History of Estonian Philosophy
MEDIJAINEN, E., Contemporary History
METSLANG, H., Modern Estonian
MUST, A., Archival Studies
PAJUSALU, K., History and Dialects of Estonian Language
PAJUSALU, R., General Linguistics
ROSENBERG, T., Estonian History
SUTROP, M., Practical Philosophy
SUTROP, U., Anthropological and Ethnolinguistics
TALVET, J., Comparative Literature
TOROP, P., Semiotics of Culture
VALK, Ü., Estonian and Comparative Folklore

VALLIKIVI, A., Liberal Arts
VIHALEMM, R., the Philosophy of Science
VOGELBERG, K., English Language and Literature

Faculty of Education:

KIKAS, E., Initial and Primary Education
KRULL, E., General Paedagogy
TOOMELA, A.

Faculty of Exercise and Sport Sciences:

JÜRIMÄE, J., Coaching
JÜRIMÄE, T., Sport Pedagogy
PÄÄSUKE, M., Kinesiology and Biomechanics
RAUDSEPP, L., Sport Psychology
ÖÖPIK, V., Exercise Physiology

Faculty of Science and Technology:

AABLOO, A., the Technology of Polymeric Materials
AHAS, R., Human Geography
BURK, P., Chemical Physics
FREIBERG, A., Biophysics and Plant Physiology
HEINARU, A., Genetics
HÕRAK, P., Animal Physiological Ecology
JAAGUS, J., Climatology
JÄRV, J., Organic Chemistry
KALM, V., Applied Geology
KARELSON, M., Molecular Technology
KÄRNER, J., General Zoology
KIKAS, J., Disordered Systems Physics
KIRSIMÄE, K., Geology and Mineralogy
KIVISAAR, M., Bacterial/microbial genetics
KURG, A., Molecular Biotechnology
KÕLJALG, U., Mycology
LAAN, M., Biotechnology
LANGEL, Ü., Molecular Biotechnology
LEITO, I., Analytical Chemistry
LUST, E., Physical Chemistry
LUŠTŠIK, A., Solid State Physics
LÕHMUS, K., Applied Ecology
MAIMETS, T., Cell Biology
MANDER, Ü., Physical Geography and Landscape Ecology
MEIDLA, T., Palaeontology and Stratigraphy
MERISTE, M., the Technology of Proactive Systems
MERITS, A., Applied Virology
METSPALU, A., Biotechnology
MÄND, R., Animal Ecology
NOOLANDI, J., Polymer Physics
OJA, T., Geoinformatics and Cartography
PAAL, J., Plant Ecology
POOGA, M., Chemical Biology
PÄRTEL, M., Botany
RANNIKMÄE, M., Science Education
REMM, M., Bioinformatics

REMME, J., Molecular Biology
RINKEN, A., Bio-organic Chemistry
RÕÕM, R., Meteorology
SAARI, P., Wave Optics
SAMMELSELG, V., Inorganic Chemistry
SARAPUU, T., Educational Technology in Science
SEDMAN, J., General and Microbial Biochemistry
TAMMARU, T., Integrative Zoology
TAMMELO, R., Field Theory
TENSON, T., the Technology of Anti-microscopic Substances
USTAV, M., Biomedical Technology
VILLEMS, R., Archaegenetics
ZOBEL, K., Ecological Plant Ecology
ZOBEL, M., Plant Ecology

Faculty of Economics and Business Administration:

EAMETS, R., Macroeconomics
HALDMA, T., Accounting
KALDARU, H., Microeconomics
METS, T., Entrepreneurship
PAAS, T., Econometrics
RAJU, O., Economic Theory
REILJAN, J., International Economics
SEPP, J., Economic Policy
VADI, M., Management
VARBLANE, U., International Business

Faculty of Mathematics and Computer Science:

ABEL, M., Geometry and Topology
BULDAS, A., Cryptography
DUMAS MENJIVAR, M., Software Equipment
KAARLI, K., Universal Algebra
KILP, M., Algebra
KOIT, M., Speech Technology
KOLLO, T., Mathematical Statistics
LEIGER, T., Mathematical Analysis
LELLEP, J., Theoretical Mechanics
OJA, E., Functional Analysis
PEDAS, A., Differential and Integral Equations
PÄRNA, K., Probability Theory
VAINIKKO, E., Distributed Systems
VENE, V., Programming Languages Semantics
VILO, J., Bioinformatics

Faculty of Social Sciences:

ALLIK, J., Experimental Psychology
BERG, E., International Relations Theory
HARRO, J., Psychophysiology
KASEKAMP, A., Baltic Politics
LAUK, E., Journalism
LAURISTIN, M., Social Communication
NÄÄTÄNEN, R., Cognitive Neuroscience
PETTAI, V., Comparative Politics

TULVISTE, P., Cultural Psychology
TULVISTE, T., Developmental Psychology
VIHALEMM, P., Media Studies

Viljandi Culture Academy:

AGAN, A.
KOMISSAROV, K., Dramatic Arts
NOORMETS, M.
PEDASTSAAR, T.
RATTUS, K.
VESKI, V.

ATTACHED RESEARCH INSTITUTES

Centre of Excellence in Chemical Biology: Nooruse St 1, Tartu 50411; tel. 737-48-44; e-mail tanel.tenson@ut.ee; Head Prof. TANEL TENSON.

Centre of Excellence in Cultural Theory: tel. 737-56-54; e-mail monika.tasa@ut.ee.

Centre of Excellence for Translational Medicine: Ravila 19, Tartu 50411; tel. 737-53-25; e-mail eero.vasar@ut.ee; Head Prof. EERO VASAR.

Frontiers in Biodiversity Research (FIBIR): Centre of Excellence Lai 40, Tartu 51005; tel. 737-62-23; e-mail martin.zobel@ut.ee; Head Prof. MARTIN ZOBEL.

Other Higher Educational Institutes

Estonian Academy of Arts: Tartu Maantee 1, 10145 Tallinn; tel. 626-73-09; fax 626-73-50; e-mail public@artun.ee; internet www.artun.ee; f. 1914; faculties of fine arts (painting, stage design, sculpture, graphics), applied art (textiles, fashion design, leather work, ceramics, glass and metal work), architecture (interior design, architecture), design (product design, graphic design), art history; 160 teachers; 523 students; library: 54,427 vols; Rector Prof. SIGNE KIVI.

Estonian Academy of Music: Rävala pst. 16, 10143 Tallinn; tel. 667-57-00; fax 667-58-00; e-mail ema@ema.edu.ee; internet www.ema.edu; f. 1919; departments: piano, strings, brass and woodwind, vocal, chamber music, conducting, composition, musicology; institute of music education; institute of teaching training in vocal and instrumental music; higher school of drama; 120 teachers; 560 students; library: 245,000 vols; Rector P. LASSMANN; publ. *Scripta Musicalia* (4 a year).

ETHIOPIA

The Higher Education System

Addis Ababa University is the oldest university in the country. It was originally founded in 1950 as University College of Addis Ababa, became known as Haile Selassie University in 1961 and adopted its current name in 1975. There have been efforts to establish higher education institutions in outlying areas of Ethiopia; however, most institutions are located in the central, north and north-western parts of the country (mostly Addis Ababa, Bahir Dar, Mekelle, Alemaya, Awassa and Jimma). A total of 91,655 students were enrolled in higher education in 2004/05, according to government statistics. By 2007 there were 15,000 students enrolled in Addis Ababa university alone. The private higher education sector in Ethiopia has grown at an impressive rate. From practically zero in 1998, enrolment in privately owned higher education institutions had grown to 39,691 in 2005/06. In 2008/09 there were 20 universities, all state-controlled.

Higher education is financed by the Government, and the budget of each university is supervised by its Board. The University Senate is the managerial body of a University; the Academic Commission is the main academic body. The Academic Commission controls all aspects regarding the structure of degree programmes, certification and student issues. Heads of Department chair Department Councils, which are subordinate to the Academic Commission, and which make recommendations on matters of study, research, staff recruitment, pedagogy and examinations. The Ministry of Education appoints senior university officers, such as the President and Vice-Presidents. Heads of Department are either appointed by Deans of Faculty or elected by Department Councils.

The Ethiopian School Leaving Certificate Examination is the main requirement for admission to higher education. The primary undergraduate degree is the Bachelors, which takes four years, although some subjects require longer (five years for engineering, law and pharmacy; six years for medicine and veterinary medicine). The first postgraduate degree is the Masters, which lasts for two to three years, and the second postgraduate degree is the Doctor of Philosophy, which is awarded three years after the Masters.

A formal system of qualifications for technical and vocational education is still evolving, with the aim of creating a uniform structure based on courses of one to three years. Certificates are awarded following completion of Levels I (one year) and II (two years), and a Diploma is awarded after completion of Level III (three years).

In an effort to improve the quality of higher education in Ethiopia a new bill was approved in June 2009 that built upon the 2003 Higher Education proclamation to oversee both state run and private higher educational institutions. The Higher Education Proclamation 351 (Ethiopian Federal Ministry of Education, 2003) made provision for the creation of the Higher Education Relevance and Quality Agency and this was established in 2003 with the aim of safeguarding and enhancing the quality and relevance of higher education. Its mission includes ensuring that accredited higher education institutions are of an appropriate standard and establishing that programmes of study offered are of appropriate quality and relevance to employment and the development needs of the country.

Regulatory Bodies

GOVERNMENT

Ministry of Culture and Tourism: POB 2183, Addis Ababa; tel. (11) 5512310; fax (11) 5512889; e-mail tourismethiopia@ethionet.et; internet www.tourismethiopia.org; Minister MAHMUD DIRIR.

Ministry of Education: POB 1367, Addis Ababa; tel. (11) 1553133; fax (11) 1550877; e-mail heardmoe@telecom.net.et; Minister Dr SINTAVEHU WOLDEMIKAEL.

Learned Societies

GENERAL

UNESCO Office Addis Ababa: POB 1177, Addis Ababa; ECA Bldg, Menelik Ave, POB 1177, Addis Ababa; tel. (11) 5513953; fax (11) 5511414; e-mail addis@unesco.org; designated Cluster Office for Djibouti, Eritrea and Ethiopia; Dir NURELDIN SATTI.

AGRICULTURE, FISHERIES AND VETERINARY SCIENCE

Association for the Advancement of Agricultural Sciences in Africa: POB 30087, Addis Ababa; tel. (11) 5443536; f. 1968; aims to promote the devt and application of agricultural sciences and the exchange of ideas, to encourage Africans to enter training, and to hold seminars annually in different African countries; crop production and protection, animal health and production, soil and water management, agricultural mechanization, agricultural eco-nomics, agricultural education, extension and rural sociology, food science and technology; 1,200 mems (individual and institutional); library of 5,000 items; Admin. Sec.-Gen. Prof. M. EL-FOULY (acting); publs *African Journal of Agricultural Sciences, Conferences, Proceedings of workshops*.

BIBLIOGRAPHY, LIBRARY SCIENCE AND MUSEOLOGY

Ethiopian Library and Information Association: POB 30530, Addis Ababa; tel. (11) 5518020; f. 1961; to promote the interests of libraries, archives, documentation centres, etc., and to serve those working in them; 200 mems; Pres. TAMIRAT MOTA; Sec. ZINABIE MEKONNEN; publs *Bulletin* (2 a year), *Directory of Ethiopian Libraries, Newsletter* (2 a year).

LANGUAGE AND LITERATURE

Alliance Française: Wavel St, POB 1733, Addis Ababa; tel. (11) 1550213; fax (11) 1553681; e-mail aef@allianceaddis.org; internet www.allianceaddis.org; offers courses and examinations in French language and culture and promotes cultural exchange with France; attached teaching centre in Dire Dawa.

British Council: POB 1043, Comoros St, Addis Ababa; tel. (11) 6620388; fax (11) 6623315; e-mail information@et.britishcouncil.org; internet www.britishcouncil.org/africa; offers courses and examinations in English language and British culture and promotes cultural exchange with the UK; library of 25,000 vols; Dir BARBARA WICKHAM.

Goethe-Institut: POB 1193, Addis Ababa; tel. (11) 1552888; fax (11) 1551299; e-mail vl@telecom.net.et; internet www.goethe.de/af/add/enindex.htm; offers courses and examinations in German language and culture and promotes cultural exchange with Germany; library of 1,500 vols, 24 periodicals; Dir Dr DIETER WERNER KLUCKE.

MEDICINE

Ethiopian Medical Association: POB 2179, Addis Ababa; tel. (11) 5533742; e-mail ema.emj@telecom.net.et; f. 1961; Pres. Dr TELAHUM TEKA; publ. *Ethiopian Medical Journal* (4 a year).

Ethiopian Public Health Association: Dembel City Centre, POB 7117 Addis Ababa; tel. (11) 5540391; fax (11) 5514870; e-mail epha@ethionet.et; internet www.epha.org.et; f. 1989; promotes public health, prevention of diseases, timely treatment of the sick and rehabilitation of the disabled; Pres. Dr DAMEN HAILEMARIAM; Exec. Sec. Dr GETNET MITIKE; publ. *Ethiopian Journal of Health Development*.

NATURAL SCIENCES

Physical Sciences

Geophysical Observatory: Faculty of Science, Addis Ababa University, POB 1176, Addis Ababa; tel. (11) 1239477; fax (11) 1551863; internet www.sc.aau.edu.et/geophysical; f. 1958; research in seismology, gravity, tectonics, crustal deformation, geomagnetic observation and geodesy; library of 100 vols and 10 periodicals; Sec. Assoc. Prof. LAIKE M. ASFAW; publ. *Seismological Bulletin* (2 a year).

Research Institutes

AGRICULTURE, FISHERIES AND VETERINARY SCIENCE

Awasa Agriculture Research Centre: c/o Awasa Agricultural College, POB 6, Awasa; tel. (46) 2200224; fax (46) 2204521; e-mail arc@padis.gn.apc.org; f. 1967; soil and water management, crop protection, horticulture, field crops, agronomy and crop physiology, agricultural economics and farming systems, livestock, forestry; library of 2,300 vols, 28 journals; Man. DANIEL DAURO.

Ethiopian Institute of Agricultural Research: POB 2003, Addis Ababa; tel. (11) 6460137; fax (11) 6461294; e-mail infocom@eiar.gov.et; internet www.eiar.gov.et; f. 1966; agronomy and crop physiology, crop protection, animal production, animal feeds and nutrition, animal health, agricultural mechanization, horticulture, soil and water management, field crops, forestry, post-harvest technologies, biotechnology; financial aid provided by the Ethiopian govt and other sources; 50 research centres and stations nationally; 2,915 mems; library of 150,000 vols; Deputy Dir-Gen. Dr SOLOMON ASEFA; publs *Ethiopian Journal of Agricultural Economics*, *Ethiopian Journal of Agricultural Science*, *Ethiopian Journal of Animal Production*, *Pest Management Journal of Ethiopia*.

HISTORY, GEOGRAPHY AND ARCHAEOLOGY

Archaeological Institute: POB 76, Addis Ababa; Dir Dr BERHANOU ABBÉBÉ; publ. *Annales d'Ethiopie*.

Ethiopian Mapping Agency: POB 597, Addis Ababa; tel. (11) 5518445; fax (11) 5515189; e-mail ema@ethionet.net.et; internet www.ema.gov.net; f. 1955; under Min. of Economic Development and Co-operation; conducts land surveying, mapping, remote sensing and geographical research; 350 mems; library of 3,000 vols; Dir-Gen. SULTAN MOHAMMED; publ. *Geo-Information Bulletin of Ethiopia* (2 a year).

NATURAL SCIENCES

Biological Sciences

Desert Locust Control Organization for Eastern Africa (DLCO EA): POB 4255, Addis Ababa; tel. (11) 6461477; fax (11) 6460296; e-mail dlc@telecom.net.et; f. 1962; mems: Djibouti, Eritrea, Ethiopia, Kenya, Somalia, Sudan, Tanzania, Uganda; research into and control of desert locust and other pests, incl. armyworm, quelea, tsetse fly and mosquito; library of 2,000 vols; Dir PETER ONYANGO ODIYO.

Institute of Biodiversity Conservation and Research: POB 30726, Addis Ababa; tel. (11) 6612244; fax (11) 6613722; e-mail bioresearch@telecom.net.et; internet www.telecom.net.et/~ibcr; f. 1998; promotes and carries out research into the devt and sustainable use of the country's biodiversity; Gen. Man. Dr ABEBE DEMISSIE.

National Herbarium: Biology Dept, Addis Ababa University, POB 3434, Addis Ababa; tel. (11) 1236760; fax (11) 1236769; e-mail info@bio.aau.edu.et; f. 1959; Keeper Prof. SEBSEBE DEMISSEW; Curator Dr ENSERMU KELBESSA; publ. *Flora of Ethiopia and Eritrea* (10 a year).

Physical Sciences

Geological Survey of Ethiopia: POB 2302, Addis Ababa; tel. (11) 6464482; fax (11) 6463326; internet www.geology.gov.et; f. 1968 as a Department within the Ministry of Mines; as Ethiopian Institute of Geological Surveys 1984; 778 mems; library of 66,877 vols; Gen. Man. KETEMA TADESSE; Chief Geologist AMENTI ABRAHAM; Head of Geoscience Information Centre SISAY TESFAY.

RELIGION, SOCIOLOGY AND ANTHROPOLOGY

Institute of Ethiopian Studies: Addis Ababa University, POB 1176, Addis Ababa; tel. (11) 1119469; fax (11) 1552688; e-mail ies.aau@ttelecom.net.et; internet www.ies-ethiopia.org; f. 1963; conducts, promotes and coordinates research and publication on Ethiopian Studies with special emphasis on the humanities and cultural studies; operates an advanced study and documentation centre and an ethnological-historical museum: see Museums and Art Galleries; library: see Libraries and Archives; Dir ELIZABETH W. GIORGIS (acting); publs *IES Bulletin* (4 a year), *Journal of Ethiopian Studies* (2 a year).

Libraries and Archives

Addis Ababa

Addis Ababa University Libraries: POB 1176, Addis Ababa; tel. (11) 1239720; e-mail infolib@lib.aau.edu.et; internet www.aau.edu.et/libraries; f. 1950; 500,000 vols, 632 microfiches, 3,000 serial titles and an electronic journals database, colln incl. 90000 vols on Ethiopia; consists of the main University library and six branch libraries: the Science Library, Technology North Library (Amist Kilo campus), Technology South Library (Lideta Campus), Faculty of Business and Economics Library, Central Medical Library and Law Library; Librarian Dr TAYE TADESSE.

British Council Knowledge and Learning Services: POB 1043, Artistic Bldg, Adwa Ave, Addis Ababa; tel. (11) 1550022; fax (11) 1552544; e-mail kls@et.britishcouncil.org; f. 1959; 51,000 vols, 137 periodicals; Librarian Ato MULUGETA HUNDE.

Ethiopia National Archives and Library Agency: POB 717, Addis Ababa; tel. (11) 5516532; fax (11) 5526411; e-mail nale@ethionet.et; internet www.nale.gov.et; f. 1944; 164,000 vols; consists of: Reference, Documentation and Periodical Division; Legal Deposit and Copyright Registration; Archives Repository and Research; Microfilm and Microfiche Library; Ethiopian Studies and MSS Division; Dir-Gen. ATIKILT ASSEFA.

Institute of Ethiopian Studies Library: Addis Ababa University, POB 1176, Addis Ababa; tel. (11) 1550844; fax (11) 1123456; e-mail girmajem@ies.aau.edu.et; internet www.ies-ethiopia.org/indexf.htm; f. 1963; colln of printed and non-printed materials on Ethiopia, Somalia, Djibouti, Red Sea, Indian Ocean, Sudan; also materials on Middle East; 110,000 vols, 9,000 MSS; Librarian GIRMA JEMANEH.

Museums and Art Galleries

Addis Ababa

Museum of the Institute of Ethiopian Studies: University of Addis Ababa, POB 1176, Addis Ababa; tel. (11) 1550844; fax (11) 1552688; e-mail ies.aau@telecom.net.et; internet www.ies-ethiopia.org; f. 1963; sections: exhibit of Haile Selassie's bedroom, material culture (household artefacts, clothing, handicrafts, etc.); ethno-musicology (all types of Ethiopian musical instruments, religious music and poetry, record archive of oral tradition and folklore); traditional art (church paintings and furnishings, icons, etc., Islamic calligraphy); stamps, coins and banknotes of Ethiopia; Curator AHMED ZEKARIA.

National Museum of Ethiopia: POB 76, Addis Ababa; tel. (11) 1119113; fax (11) 1553188; collns of early hominid fossils, incl. 'Lucy', a nearly complete skeleton of *Australopithecus afarensis*; Dir MAMITU YILMA.

Universities

ADDIS ABABA UNIVERSITY

POB 1176, Addis Ababa

Telephone: (11) 1239800

Internet: www.aau.edu.et

Founded 1950 as Univ. College of Addis Ababa; became Haile Selassie Univ. 1961; present name 1975

State control

Language of instruction: English

Academic year: September to July

Pres.: Prof. ANDREAS ESHETÉ
Vice-Pres. for Business and Devt: Ato MOHAMMED HABIB
Assoc. Vice-Pres. for Academic Affairs and External Relations Officer: Dr BUTTE GOTU
Assoc. Vice-Pres. for Continuing and Distance Education Programmes: Dr MEKONEN DISASA
Assoc. Vice-Pres. for Research and Graduate Programmes: Prof. ENDASHAW BEKELE
Registrar: Dr ZEMEDE ASFAW
Librarian: Dr TAYE TADESSE

Library of 493,000 vols
Number of teachers: 948
Number of students: 15,364

Publications: *Ethiopian Journal of Development Research*, *Ethiopian Journal of Education*, *Register of Current Research on Ethiopia and the Horn of Africa*, *SINET: An Ethiopian Journal of Science*

DEANS

Faculty of Business and Economics: Dr MULAT DEMEKE
Faculty of Education: Ato AKALU GETANEH
Faculty of Informatics: Ato GETACHEW JEMANEH
Faculty of Law: Ato GETACHEW ABERA
Faculty of Medicine: Dr ZUFAN LAKEW
Faculty of Science: Prof. GEZAHEGN YIRGU
Faculty of Technology: Dr ABEBE DINKU
Faculty of Veterinary Medicine: Dr MERGA BEKANA
College of Social Sciences: Dr BEKELE GUTEMA
School of Pharmacy: Dr TSIGE GEBREMARIAM
Institute of Language Studies: Dr GEREMEW LEMU

DIRECTORS

School of Fine Arts and Design: Dr MELAKU AYELE
School of Music: AKILU ZEWDIE
Institute of Development Research: Asst Prof. MULUGETA FISSEHA
Institute of Education: Ato DANIEL DESTA
Institute of Ethiopian Studies: ELIZABETH GEBREGIORGIS
Institute of Pathobiology: Prof. MOGESSIE ASHENAFI

BAHIR DAR UNIVERSITY

POB 79, Bahir Dar

Telephone: (58) 2200137

Fax: (58) 2202025

E-mail: infobdu@gmail.com

Internet: www.bdu.edu.et
Founded 2000 by merger of Bahir Dar Teachers' College and Bahir Dar Polytechnic Institute
Public control
Language of instruction: English
Academic year: September to June
Pres.: Assoc. Prof. BAYLIE DAMTIE
Vice-Pres. for Academic Affairs: Asst Prof. FIREW TEGEGNE
Vice-Pres. for Business and Devt: Assoc. Prof. G. EGZIABHER KAHSAY
Vice-Pres. for Information and Strategic Communication: Asst Prof. FANTAHUN AYELE
Number of teachers: 1,314
Number of students: 34,972
Publications: *Journal of Law*, *Journal of Social Science*, *The Ethiopian Journal of Science and Technology*

DEANS

College of Agriculture and Environmental Science: Assoc. Prof. ZELEKE MEKURIAW
College of Business and Economics: TESFAYE MELAKU
College of Medical and Health Science: Asst Prof. WORKU BELAY
College of Science: Asst Prof. ASSEFA SERGAWE

HARAMAYA UNIVERSITY

POB 138, Dire Dawa
Telephone: (25) 5530319
Fax: (25) 5530325
E-mail: talamirew@haramaya.edu.et
Internet: www.haramaya.edu.et
Founded 1952; university status 1985
State control
Language of instruction: English
Academic year: September to June
Pres.: Prof. BELAY KASSA
Vice-Pres. for Academic Affairs: Dr TENA ALAMIREW
Vice-Pres. for Admin. and Student Affairs: Dr BELAINEH LEGESSE
Vice-Pres. for Research: Dr NIGUSSIE DECHASA
Registrar: Dr DESSALEGNE CHEMEDA
Librarian: YARED MAMO
Number of teachers: 960
Number of students: 31,419 (13,548 full-time, 17,571 evening, distance-education, summer in-service)
Publications: *Alemaya Annual Research Report*, *East African Journal of sciences*, *HU Newsletter*, *The Alemayan*

DEANS

College of Agriculture and Environmental Sciences: Dr KINDIE TESFAYE
College of Computing and Informatics: ADEM KEDIR
College of Continuing and Distance Education: Dr TEGEGN SINISHAW
College of Economics and Business: MULUGETA DEMIE
College of Education and Behavioural Sciences: Dr BEHAVIOURAL SCIENCES

College of Health Sciences: BIFTU GEDA
College of Law: GIZACHEW ADMASU
College of Medical Sciences: TEKABE ABDOSH
College of Natural and Computational Sciences: Dr ABI TADESSE
College of Social Sciences and Humanities: JEYLAN WOLIYE
College of Veterinary Medicine: Dr DESTA BEYENE
Institute of Technology: Dr SOLOMON WORKU
School of Graduate Studies: Dr YOSEF MEKASHA

HAWASSA UNIVERSITY

POB 5, Hawassa
Telephone: (46) 2200221
Fax: (46) 2205421
E-mail: info@hu.edu.et
Internet: hu.edu.et
Founded 2000 as Debub Univ. by merger of Hawassa College of Agriculture, Dilla College of Teachers' Education and Health Science and Wondo Genet College of Forestry; present name 2006
State control
Pres.: Dr ADMASU TSEGAYE
Library of 200,000 vols
Number of teachers: 963
Number of students: 20,000

Faculties of Business and Economics, Hotel Management and Tourism, Law, Medicine, Natural Sciences, Public Health, Social Sciences, Technology, Veterinary Medicine; Colleges of Agriculture, Forestry, Health Sciences, Teachers' Education.

JIMMA UNIVERSITY

POB 378, Jimma
Telephone: (47) 1112202
Fax: (47) 1111450
Internet: www.ju.edu.et
Founded 1999 through merger of Jimma College of Agriculture (f. 1952) and Jimma Institute of Health Sciences (f. 1983)
Pres.: Asst Prof. DAMTEW MARIAM
Vice-Pres. for Academics and Research: Asst Prof. SOLOMON MOGUS
Vice-Pres. for Admin. and Devt: KORA TUSHUNE
Vice-Pres. for Training and Health Services: ABRAHAM AMLAK
Registrar: Dr SOLOMON GENET
Dean of Students: EWNETU SEID
Head of External Relations Office: Assoc. Prof. CHALLI JIRA
Head of Library and Documentation Service: GETACHEW BAYISA
Number of teachers: 370
Number of students: 16,279

DEANS

Faculty of Business: Asst Prof. SOLOMON ALEMU
Faculty of Education: ZELALEM TESHOME
Faculty of Medical Sciences: Asst Prof. MINAS TSADIK
Faculty of Public Health: Asst Prof. KIFLE MIKAEL

Faculty of Science and Liberal Arts: TAREKEGN BIRHANU
Faculty of Technology: ADMASSU SHIMELES
College of Agriculture, Ambo: EYLACHEW ZEWDIE
College of Agriculture, Jimma: BERHANU BELAY
School of Graduate Studies: Prof. MEKONNEN ASSEFA

UNIVERSITY OF MEKELLE

POB 231, Mekelle, Tigray Region
Telephone: (34) 4407500
Fax: (34) 4409304
E-mail: mekelle.university@telecom.net.et
Internet: www.mu.edu.et*Adi-Haqi Campus*: POB 451, Mekelle, Tigray Region
Telephone: (34) 4407600
Fax: (34) 4407610
Aider Campus: POB 1871 Mekelle, Tigray Region
Telephone: (34) 4416690
Fax: (34) 4416681
E-mail: mbc@telecom.net.et
State control
Founded 2000
Library of 200,000 vols, 18 periodical titles
Number of teachers: 1,119
Number of students: 16,470
Pres.: Prof. MITUKU HAILE
Vice-Pres. for Academics: Dr KINDEYA GEBREHIWOT
Vice-Pres. for Research and Community Service: Dr ABDELKADIR KEDIR
Vice-Pres. for Support Services: Dr YASIN IBRAHIM
Librarian: Dr HAGOS
Faculties of agriculture, business and commerce, engineering
Publications: *Journal of Drylands* (2 a year), *Momona Ethiopian Journal of Science* (2 a year)

DEANS

College of Business and Economics: Dr ZAID NEGASH
College of Dry Land Agriculture and Natural Resources: Dr GIRMAY TESFAY
College of Engineering: Dr GEBREMESKEL KAHSAY
College of Law and Governance: FANA HAGOS
College of Medicine: Dr ABDELKADIR M.SEID
College of Natural and Computational Sciences: Dr ALEM ABREHA
College of Social Science and Languages: Dr ASSEFA ABEGAZ
College of Veterinary Science: Dr GEBREHIWOT TADESSE

College

Yared Music School: POB 30097, Addis Ababa; tel. (11) 1550166; f. 1967; attached to Addis Ababa University; 130 students; Head TEKLE YOHANES ZIKE.

FIJI

The Higher Education System

The supra-national University of the South Pacific maintains one of its 12 campuses in Fiji. In 2004 there were 16,444 students at the University and its extension centres, of whom 200 held scholarships from the Fijian Government. Other institutes include the Fiji School of Medicine, the Fiji Institute of Technology, both based in Suva, and the Teachers College based in Lautoka on the western side of Viti Levu. In 2008 there were 66 vocational and technical institutions (with 3,162 enrolled students). In the same year Fiji had four teacher-training colleges (with 824 students).

The Fiji School Leaving Certificate and Form Seven Examination are the main criteria for admission to higher education. The undergraduate Bachelors degree lasts for three years, the postgraduate Masters degree for one to two years and the Doctorate for two years following award of the Masters. Post-secondary vocational and technical training is offered by the University and colleges and institutes of professional training and vocational education. The main qualifications are the Certificate and Diploma.

In August 2007 plans were agreed to establish a Higher Education Advisory Commission to develop the higher education sector, which would be referred to as the Higher Education Advisory Board. In 2008 the Higher Education Promulgation law came into effect, which meant that all higher education institutions providing post-secondary education had to register with the Higher Education Commission at the start of the new year. After January 2010 any new institution must apply to the Commission for approval.

Regulatory Body

GOVERNMENT

Ministry of Education: Marela House, Thurston St, PMB, Suva; tel. 3314477; fax 3303511; internet www.education.gov.fj; Min. FILIPE BOLE.

Learned Societies

ECONOMICS, LAW AND POLITICS

Fiji Law Society: 100 Gordon St, POB 2389, Govt Bldgs, Suva; tel. 3315690; fax 3314334; e-mail vanita@fls.org.fj; internet www.fls.org.fj; f. 1956; Pres. DORSAMI NAIDU; Sec. and CEO VANITA SINGH (acting).

LANGUAGE AND LITERATURE

Alliance Française: 14 MacGregor Rd, POB 14548, Suva; tel. 3313802; fax 3313803; e-mail allifra@is.com.fj; offers courses and exams in French language and culture and promotes cultural exchange with France.

MEDICINE

Fiji Medical Association: Ellery St, POB 1116, Suva; tel. and fax 3315388; e-mail fijimedassoc@connect.com.fj; f. 1953; 215 mems; Pres. Dr MARY SCHRAMM; publ. *Fiji Medical Journal* (4 a year).

Libraries and Archives

Lautoka

Western Regional Library: POB 150, Lautoka; tel. 6660091; f. 1964; books, periodicals, audio visual cassette tapes.

Suva

Library Service of Fiji: Ministry of Education, POB 2526, Govt Bldgs, Suva; tel. 3315344; fax 3314994; f. 1964; public spec. and school library service; 12 e-Community Learning Centres, 1 mobile library, 28 school media centres, 40 govt dept libraries; 1.5m. vols; Prin. Librarian SOKOVETI TUIMOALA; publ. *Fiji National Bibliography* (publ. suspended until 2009).

National Archives of Fiji: POB 2125, Govt Bldgs, Suva; 25 Carnarvon St, Suva; tel. 3304144; fax 3307006; e-mail salesia .ikaniwai@govnet.gov.fj; f. 1954 as the Central Archives of Fiji and the Western Pacific High Comm.; govt records since 1871, Anglican and Methodist church records since 1835; 15,000 vols of monographs on the South Pacific, files on local newspapers since 1869, Fiji official publs since 1874, 3,800 reels of microfilm; Prin. Archivist SETAREKI TALE; Librarian SALESIA IKANIWAI.

Suva City Library: POB 176, Suva; tel. 3313433; fax 3302158; f. 1909, known as Carnegie Library, until 1953; public lending library; 77,000 vols (48,000 in children's library, 29,000 in adults' library), 25 periodicals; special collection: Fiji and the Pacific; mobile library service for schools; Chief Librarian HUMESH PRASAD.

Museums and Art Galleries

Suva

Fiji Museum: POB 2023, Government Buildings, Suva; tel. 3315944; fax 3305143; e-mail information@fijimuseum.org.fj; internet www.fijimuseum.org.fj; f. 1904; contains archaeological, ethnological and historical collections relating to Fiji; archives of Fijian oral traditions; photographic archives; Dir SAGALE BUADROMO; publs *Bulletin* (irregular), *Domodomo* (2 a year).

University

FIJI NATIONAL UNIVERSITY

POB 7222, Nasinu
Telephone: 3393245
Fax: 3370915
E-mail: vc@fnu.ac.fj
Internet: www.fnu.ac.fj
Founded 2009
State control
Language of instruction: English
Academic year: January to December
Vice-Chancellor: Dr GANESH CHAND

DEANS
College of Agriculture, Fisheries and Forestry: Prof. PARAS NATH
College of Engineering, Science and Technology: Dr SURENDRA B. PRASAD
College of Humanities and Education: Dr ECI NABALARUA
College of Medicine, Nursing and Health Sciences: Prof. IAN ROUSE

UNIVERSITY OF THE SOUTH PACIFIC

Private Mail Bag, Suva
Telephone: 3313900
Fax: 3301305
Internet: www.usp.ac.fj
Founded 1968
State control; regional univ. with 12 island state mems
Language of instruction: English
Academic year: February to November (two semesters)

Extension centres in the Cook Islands, Fiji, Kiribati, Marshall Islands, Nauru, Niue, Samoa, Solomon Islands, Tonga, Tuvalu, Vanuatu; link arrangements with Tokelau; the university's second campus is in Alafua, Samoa; third campus is in Vanuatu

Chancellor: FIAME NAOMI MATA'AFA
Vice-Chancellor: (vacant)
Deputy Vice-Chancellor: Dr KONAIHOLEVA THAMAN (acting)
Pro-Vice Chancellors: Prof. ALBERT EBENEBE, Prof. JOHN LYNCH MERE PULEA
Registrar: WALTER FRASER
Librarian: ESTHER WININAMAORI WILLIAMS

Library of 830,000 vols
Number of teachers: 1,159
Number of students: 6,204 on campus, 9,109 extension students

Publications: *Alafua Agricultural Bulletin, Journal of Pacific Studies, Pacific Islands Communications Journal, South Pacific Agricultural News* (26 a year), *SSED Review* (4 a year)

HEADS OF SCHOOLS

School of Agriculture: Prof. ALBERT EBENEBE (acting)
School of Humanities: Dr AKINISI KEDRAYATE
School of Law: Prof. ROBERT HUGHES
School of Pure and Applied Sciences: Dr ANJEELA JOKHAN

School of Social and Economic Development:
Dr ROPATE QALO

PROFESSORS

BHASKARA, R., Economics
CAMPBELL, I., History and Politics
GASKELL, I., Literature and Language
HASSALL, G., Governance
HUGHES, R., Law
MEAKINS, R., Biology
NUNN, P., Oceanic Geoscience
OMLIN, C., Computer Science
ONWOBOLU, G., Engineering
PATHAK, R., Management
PETERSON, R., Banking
SHARMA, M. D., Banking
SOTHEESWARAN, S., Organic Chemistry
SUBRAMANI, Literature and Language
THAMAN, R., Pacific Island Biogeography
WHITE, M., Accounting and Financial Management
ZANN, L., Marine Studies

Colleges

Fiji College of Agriculture: POB 1544, Koronivia, Nausori; tel. 3479200; fax 3400275; e-mail elenibai@is.com.fj; f. 1954, reorganized 1962; 3-year diploma course in tropical agriculture; library: 9,000 books, 450 periodicals; 10 teachers; 150 students; Prin. FIUWAKI WAQALALA; publs *Annual Research Report*, *Fiji Agricultural Journal* (2 a year), *Fiji Farmer*, *MAFF Technical Bulletin* (12 a year).

Fiji Institute of Technology: POB 3722, Samabula, Suva; tel. 3381044; fax 3370375; e-mail webmaster@fit.ac.fj; internet www.fit.ac.fj; f. 1964 as Derrick Technical Institute; offers courses in building and civil engineering, business studies, electrical and electronic engineering, mechanical engineering, aeronautical engineering, maritime studies, printing, graphic design, hospitality and tourism, automobile engineering, applied computing, applied science, secretarial studies, agricultural engineering, environmental science, occupational health and safety, general studies; 210 full-time teachers; 6,000 students; library: 50,000 vols; Dir GANESH CHAND.

Fiji School of Medicine: Private Mail Bag, Hoodless House, CWM Hospital Campus, Suva; tel. 3311700; fax 3303469; internet www.fsm.ac.fj; f. 1885 as Suva Medical School, reorganized as Central Medical School 1928; present name 1961; courses in medicine, dentistry, physiotherapy, environmental health, radiography, medical laboratory technology, dietetics and nutrition and pharmacy; 780 students; library: 16,000 vols; Dean Dr WAME BARAVILALA.

FINLAND

The Higher Education System

The higher education system consists of two parallel systems, universities and polytechnics: universities focus on academic teaching and research while polytechnics specialize in professional and vocational training. The structure of the degree system is the same in both sectors. There are 20 universities and 31 polytechnics. The oldest university is the Kuvataideakatemia (Academy of Fine Arts), which was founded in 1848. In 2007 student enrolments were as follows: Vocational and professional institutions 266,479; Polytechnics 133,284; Universities 176,304.

All universities are state-owned and are administered by the Ministry of Education's Department for Education and Science Policy. University-level education is currently free but students may be required to pay extraneous services, such as health care and compulsory membership of the Student's Union. Under the Universities Act, universities are obliged to promote free research and provide free education. However, the Organisation for Economic Cooperation and Development suggested in 2010 that students be charged to study as part of a number of reforms to help Finland out of recession. This might encourage them to finish their degrees more quickly. Other suggestions include replacing grants with repayable loans and speeding up the admissions system by standardizing university entrance requirements. Universities have enjoyed relative autonomy in decision-making, based on three-year performance agreements with the Ministry of Education. Government funding used to account for about 64% of university budgets, with the rest coming from the Academy of Finland, the Technology Development Centre Tekes, business enterprises, the European Union and other public bodies. The new Universities Bill of June 2009 further extended the autonomy of universities by giving them an independent legal personality, either as a public corporation or as a foundation under private law, with university staff no longer being employed by the State. The Government continued to provide core funding with the universities responsible for acquiring additional finance.

The current polytechnic system emerged during the 1990s and was in place by 2000. Like the universities, the polytechnics are controlled by the Department for Education and Science Policy within the Ministry of Education. The polytechnics are a mix of municipal and private ownership. Funding of public polytechnics is shared between central government and local government. Polytechnics follow performance agreements made with the Ministry of Education.

Admission to both universities and polytechnics is on the basis of completed secondary education and entrance examinations. University admissions are subjected to the Universities Decree (115/1998), and admission to polytechnics is governed by the Polytechnic Studies Act (351/2003). In 2005 a two-tier Bachelors and Masters degree system was implemented in both universities and polytechnics, in accordance with the Bologna Process. The award of degrees is based on a US-style academic 'credit' system. The university Bachelors degree lasts for three years and students must accrue 120 credits; the university Masters degree is a two-year course requiring 40–60 credits. The polytechnic Bachelors requires 120–160 credits over three-and-a-half to four years, and the polytechnic Masters 40–60 credits in one-and-a-half years. (Admission to the polytechnic Masters requires a polytechnic Bachelors and three years' professional experience.)

In some subject areas the old-style degree system remains in place. For dentistry, medicine and veterinary medicine, the first degree is the Lisensiaatti or Licentiate, which requires 200–250 credits and takes five to six years. The Lisensiaatti/Licentiate is a doctoral-level degree. Students who have received the Masters may take the Tohtori or Doctorate, which lasts four years. In addition to the technical and vocational education offered by polytechnics there is also an apprenticeship scheme combining workplace and classroom learning.

Regulatory and Representative Bodies

GOVERNMENT

Ministry of Education: POB 29, 00023 Helsinki; Meritullinkatu 10, 00171 Helsinki; tel. (9) 16004; fax (9) 1359335; e-mail opmkirjaamo@minedu.fi; internet www.minedu.fi; Min. HENNA VIRKKUNEN.

Opetusministeriö Koulutus-ja tiedepolitiikan osasto (Ministry of Education, Department for Education and Science Policy): POB 29, 00023 Helsinki; tel. (9) 16077415; fax (9) 16077150; e-mail miia.maffeo@minedu.fi; internet www.minedu.fi; f. 1809; prepares and implements legislation relating to basic education, upper secondary education and basic education in the arts, vocational education and training, adult education and training, polytechnics and univs, student financial aid, scientific research, and examination boards for tests in Finnish and Swedish; Dir-Gen. Dr SAKARI KARJALAINEN.

Tutkimus ja Innovaationeuvosto (Research and Innovation Council): POB 29 00023 Helsinki; Meritullinkatu 10, 00171 Helsinki; tel. (9) 16077362; fax (9) 16077136; e-mail tin@minedu.fi; f. 2009; Chair. THE PRIME MINISTER OF FINLAND; Sec. ILKKA TURUNEN.

ACCREDITATION

ENIC/NARIC Finland: Opetushallitus/Utbildningsstyrelsen, Finnish Nat. Board of Education, Hakaniemenranta 6, POB 380, 00531 Helsinki; tel. (40) 3487555; fax (40) 3487865; e-mail recognition@oph.fi; internet www.oph.fi/recognition; Counsellor of Education, Head of Unit Dr CARITA BLOMQVIST.

FUNDING

Tekes/Teknologian ja Innovaatioiden Kehittämiskeskus (Finnish Funding Agency for Technology and Innovation): POB 69, Kyllikinportti 2, 00101 Helsinki; tel. (10) 6055000; fax (9) 6949196; e-mail tekes@tekes.fi; internet www.tekes.fi; f. 1983; funding org. for research and devt projects run by private enterprise, research institutes and univs; encourages cooperation between differing fields of technology; assists companies in research; not for profit, does not claim intellectual proprietary rights; has technology devt depts at 14 regional Employment and Economic Devt Centres (known as the T&E Centres); maintains offices in Beijing, Brussels, Tokyo, Silicon Valley, Shanghai and Washington, DC; Dir-Gen. Dr VELI-PEKKA SAARNIVAARA.

NATIONAL BODIES

Arene ry/Ammattikorkeoulujen rehtorineuvosto (Finnish Conference of Polytechnic Rectors): Pohjoinen Makasiinikatu 7 A 2, 00130 Helsinki; tel. and fax (9) 61299230; e-mail timo.luopajarvi@arene.fi; internet www.arene.fi; Sec.-Gen. Dr TIMO LUOPAJÄRVI.

CIMO Kansainvälisen liikkuvuuden ja yhteistyön keskus (Centre for International Mobility): POB 343 (Hakaniemenranta 6), 00531 Helsinki; tel. (9) 207868500; fax (9) 207868601; e-mail cimoinfo@cimo.fi; internet www.cimo.fi; f. 1991; attached to Min. of Education; administers scholarship and exchange programmes; responsible for implementing EU education, training, culture and youth programmes in Finland; offers training, information, advisory services and publs; promotes and organizes int. trainee exchanges; Dir PASI SAHLBERG.

Korkeakoulujen arviointineuvosto (KKA) (Finnish Higher Education Evaluation Council): POB 133, Meritullinkatu 1, 00171 Helsinki; tel. (9) 16076913; fax (9) 16077608; e-mail finheec@minedu.fi; internet www.finheec.fi; f. 1995; ind. body assisting higher education instns and the Min. of Education in evaluation; carries out audits of higher education systems of higher education instns and other evaluations; Sec.-Gen. Dr HELKA KEKÄLÄINEN.

Opetushallitus (Finnish National Board of Education): POB 380, 00531 Helsinki; tel. (40) 3487555; fax (40) 3487865; e-mail opetushallitus@oph.fi; internet www.oph.fi; f. 1991; is the agency responsible for the devt of education in Finland; draws up core curricula for basic and upper secondary education, and the framework for vocational qualifications and competence-based qualifications; evaluates learning results and improves the efficiency of training; Dir-Gen. TIMO LANKINEN.

Suomen yliopistot UNIFI ry (Universities Finland UNIFI): Pohjoinen Makasiinikatu 7 A 2, 00130 Helsinki; tel. (50) 5229421; e-mail rectors-council@helsinki.fi; internet www .rectors-council.helsinki.fi; f. 1969 as Finnish Council of University Rectors, present name 2010; promotes cooperation between univs and helps them to achieve their common strategic goals; works with political decision-makers, nat. authorities, ministries and central interest groups to advance research and higher education; strengthens role of univs as key partners in social and political discussion; promotes int. cooperation between univs, esp. in the Nordic countries, Europe and Asia; 17 mems; Sec.-Gen. Dr LIISA SAVUNEN.

Learned Societies

GENERAL

Elintarviketieteiden Seura (Finnish Society of Food Science and Technology): POB 115, (Pasilankatu 2), 00241 Helsinki; tel. (9) 5474700; fax (9) 5474700; e-mail sihteeri@ets .fi; internet www.ets.fi; f. 1947; promotes and develops scientific and technological research and education on the food chain; 1,100 mems; Chair. HEIKKI MANNER; Vice-Chair. EILA JÄRVENPÄÄ; Sec. ANNA KOJO; publ. *Kehittyvä Elintarvike* (6 a year).

Finska Vetenskaps-Societeten/Suomen Tiedeseura (Finnish Society of Sciences and Letters): Ritarihuone, Hallituskatu 2, 00170 Helsinki; tel. (9) 633005; fax (9) 661065; e-mail societas@scientiarum.fi; internet www.scientiarum.fi; f. 1838; promotes science and the humanities by arranging public lectures, seminars and symposia; publishing scientific literature; awarding grants and prizes; promoting contacts within the scientific community; offering mems possibilities for interdisciplinary contacts; 357 mems; Chair. Prof. PEKKA PYYKKÖ; Permanent Sec. Prof. CARL G. GAHMBERG; publs *Commentationes Humanarum Litterarum*, *Commentationes Scientiarum Socialium*, *Sphinx-Arsbok-Vuosikirja* (1 a year).

Liikuntatieteellinen Seura (Finnish Society of Sport Sciences): Olympiastadion, Eteläkaarre, 00250 Helsinki; tel. (9) 7786600; fax (9) 7786619; e-mail toimisto@lts.fi; internet www.lts.fi; f. 1933; promotes Finnish sports, health and wellbeing through physical sciences; disseminates information pertaining to sport; holds seminars and discussion events; carries out surveys and

compiles summaries; 903 individual mems, 15 institutional mems; Chair. ANTTI UUTELA; Vice-Pres. Prof. TARU LINTUNEN; Sec. KARI L. KESKINEN; publ. *Motion-Sport in Finland* (2 a year).

Suomen Aktuaariyhdistys ry (The Actuarial Society of Finland): Porkkalankatu 1, 00018 Ilmarinen; e-mail secretary@actuary .fi; internet www.actuary.fi; f. 1922; promotes insurance sciences and actuarial mathematics; 300 mems; Chair. MARKKU MIETTINEN; Sec. BARBARA D'AMBROGI-OLA.

Suomen Arkkitehtiliiton (Finnish Association of Architects): Runeberginkatu 5, 00100 Helsinki; tel. (9) 584448; fax (9) 58444222; e-mail safa@safa.fi; internet www .safa.fi; f. 1892; non-profit org.; supervises professional standards; works to influence architectural legislation; 3,074 mems; Chair. RAINER MAHLAMÄKI; Sec. PAULA HUOTELIN; publs *ark – Finnish Architectural Review* (6 a year), *SAFA yearbook* (1 a year).

Suomen Kaupunkitutkimuksen Seuran (Finnish Society for Urban Studies): Tieteiden talo, Kirkkokatu 6, 00170 Helsinki; e-mail skts@kaupunkitutkimuksenseura.fi; internet www.kaupunkitutkimuksenseura .fi; f. 1999; promotes interdisciplinary urban research; functions as an academic forum for scholars; increases appreciation of urban studies; organizes symposia, conferences and public discussions; cooperation with foreign univs. and clubs; 85 mems; Chair. ANJA KERVANTO NEVANLINNA; Vice-Pres. MARJAANA NIEMI; Sec. MATTI HANNIKAINEN.

Suomen Naistutkimuksen Seura (Association for Women's Studies in Finland): POB 111, 80101 Joensuu; e-mail maiju .parviainen@uef.fi; internet www.nt-suns .org; f. 1988; promotes women's studies; 600 mems; Chair. KAIJA HEIKKINEN; Sec. MAIJU PARVIAINEN; publ. *Naistutkimus—Kvinnoforskning* (4 a year, in Finnish and Swedish).

Suomen Rakennusinsinöörien Liitto (Finnish Association of Civil Engineers): Töölönkatu 4, 1st Fl., 00100 Helsinki; tel. (20) 7120600; fax (20) 7120619; e-mail ril@ril .fi; internet www.ril.fi; f. 1934; org. for civil engineering with MSc and univ. students of civil engineering; 5,700 mems; Chair. RALF LINDBERG; Vice-Pres. HARRI KAILASALO; Vice-Pres. TAPIO JALO; publs *Building magazine* (52 a year), *Rakennustekniikka* (4 a year).

Suomen Tähtitieteilijäseura ry (Finnish Astronomical Society): Univ. of Helsinki, POB 64, (Gustaf Hällströminkatu 2A), 00014 Helsinki; tel. (9) 19150600; fax (9) 19150610; e-mail stt.seura@gmail.com; internet www.gastro.physics.helsinki.fi/ tt-seura; f. 1969; organizes scientific meetings and consultations; maintains contacts with foreign astronomers, int. orgs; liaises with govt; 100 mems; Pres. ELIZAVETA RASTORGUEVA; Vice-Pres. MIKA JUVELA.

Suomalainen Tiedeakatemia (Finnish Academy of Science and Letters): Mariankatu 5, 00170 Helsinki; tel. (9) 636800; fax (9) 660117; e-mail acadsci@acadsci.fi; internet www.acadsci.fi; f. 1908; 642 ordinary mems, 195 foreign mems; Pres. SIRPA JALKANEN; Sec.-Gen. OLLI MARTIO; publs *Annales Academiae Scientiarum Fennicae* (Mathematica, Geologica-Geographica and Humaniora), *Folklore Fellows' Communications*, *Yearbook*.

Tiedotusopillinen yhdistys (Finnish Association for Mass Communication Research): TOY ry, Mikko Hautakangas, Department of Journalism and Mass Communication, Vuolteenkatu 20, 33014 Univ. of Tampere; tel. (40) 1901692; e-mail mikko.hautakangas@ uta.fi; internet www.uta.fi/laitokset/tiedotus/ tiedotustutkimus/toy; 500 mems; Pres. JUHA

KOIVISTO; Sec. MIKKO HAUTAKANGAS; publ. *Media & viestintä* (4 a year).

Tieteellisten seurain valtuuskunta/ Vetenskapliga samfundens delegation (Federation of Finnish Learned Societies): Mariankatu 5, 00170 Helsinki; tel. (9) 228691; fax (9) 22869291; e-mail tsv@tsv.fi; internet www.tsv.fi; f. 1899; promotes scholarly publishing, scientific information, scientific cooperation and science policy; houses the Exchange Centre for Scientific Literature and a meeting and conf. centre; 251 mem. socs; Pres. Prof. ILKKA NIINILUOTO; Exec. Dir Prof AURA KORPPI-TOMMOLA; publs *Catalogue* (every 5 years), *Tieteessä tapahtuu* (journal, 8 a year).

Vapaan Sivistystyön Yhteisjärjestö (Finnish Adult Education Association): Annankatu 12 A 15, 00120 Helsinki; tel. (9) 6120370; fax (9) 646504; e-mail toimisto@ vsy.fi; internet www.vsy.fi; f. 1969; NGO; umbrella org. for non-formal adult education; 11 mem. orgs; Sec.-Gen. AARO HARJU; Sec. PIA ADIBE.

AGRICULTURE, FISHERIES AND VETERINARY SCIENCE

Meijeritieteellinen Seura ry (Finnish Society for Dairy Science): Dept of Food Technology, POB 30, 00039 Valio; e-mail emmi.martikainen@valio.fi; f. 1938; promotes research work and cooperation in the field of dairy science; 200 mems; Chair. Prof. TAPANI ALATOSSAVA; Sec. EMMI MARTIKAINEN; publ. *Meijeritieteellinen Aikakauskirja* (Finnish Journal of Dairy Science).

Suomen Eläinlääkäriliitto (Finnish Veterinary Association): Aleksis Kiven katu 52–54, 00510 Helsinki; tel. (9) 77454810; fax (9) 77454818; internet www.sell.fi; f. 1892; promotes veterinary science and the practice of veterinary medicine; 2,200 mems; Chair. KIRSI SARIO; Chief Exec. MIKA LEPPINEN; Sec EIJA PIETILÄ; publ. *Suomen Eläinlääkärilehti* (Finnish Veterinary Journal, 10 a year).

Suomen Maataloustieteellinen Seura r.y. (Scientific Agricultural Society of Finland): c/o MTT Agrifood Research Finland, Myllytie 1, 31600 Jokioinen; tel. (3) 41883689; e-mail tiedotus@smts.fi; internet www.smts.fi; f. 1909; 504 mems; Chair. Prof. MARKKU OLLIKAINEN; Vice-Pres. LAURA ALA-KUKKU; Sec. ARI RAJALA; publ. *Agricultural and Food Science* (4–6 a year).

Suomen Metsätieteellinen Seura (Finnish Society of Forestry Science): POB 18, 01301 Vantaa; tel. (10) 2112144; fax (10) 2112103; e-mail sms@helsinki.fi; internet www.metsatieteellinenseura.fi; f. 1909; encourages forest research and wood science in Finland; colln of vols held within the Viikki Science Library (see Libraries and Archives); organizes seminars, workshops, excursions and distributes grants; 500 mems; Chair. Prof. ANNIKA KANGAS; Vice-Pres. ANSSI NISKANEN; Sec.-Gen. Dr RIITTA VÄÄNÄNEN; publs *Dissertationes Forestales* (irregular), *Metsätieteen aikakauskirja* (www.metla.fi/aikakauskirja), *Silva Fennica* (www.metla.fi/silvafennica).

Suoseura ry (Finnish Peatland Society): Vapaudenkatu 12, 40100 Jyväskylä; tel. (14) 3385420; fax (14) 3385410; e-mail birgit .hyyrylainen@turveteollisuusliitto.fi; internet www.suoseura.fi; f. 1949; encourages study and research of peat and peatlands and their sustainable and socio-economic use; organises meetings and excursions; takes part in nat. and int. working groups; operates International Peat Society and Finnish National Committee; 450 mems; Chair. RIITTA KORHONEN; Vice-Chair. OLLI REINIKAINEN; Sec. LEILA KORPELA; Treas.

HARRI VASANDER; publ. *SUO (Mires and peat)* (4 a year).

Suomen Vesiyhdistys (Water Association Finland): POB 721, 00101 Helsinki; tel. (40) 0351883; internet www.vesiyhdistys.fi; f. 1969, as Water Association; disseminates information on hydrology, limnology, aquatic ecology, fisheries, water supply, civil engineering, water conservation, water management and water areas of law; organizes professional seminars, study tours and publishing; 500 mems, incl. 20 institutional mems; Pres. TAPIO KOVANEN; Vice-Pres. PERTTI SEUNA; Sec. JARI KOSKIAHO.

BIBLIOGRAPHY, LIBRARY SCIENCE AND MUSEOLOGY

Suomen Kirjastoseura/Finlands biblioteksförening (Finnish Library Association): Runeberginkatu 15 A 23, 00100 Helsinki; tel. (44) 5222941; e-mail fla@fla.fi; internet kirjastoseura.kaapeli.fi; f. 1910; 2,000 mems; Pres. JUKKA RELANDER; Sec.-Gen. SINIKKA SIPILÄ; publ. *Kirjastolehti* (Bulletin, 4 a year).

Suomen museoliitto/Finlands museiförbund (Finnish Museums Association): Annankatu 16 B 50, 00120 Helsinki; tel. (9) 58411700; fax (9) 58411750; e-mail museoliitto@museoliitto.fi; internet www .museoliitto.fi; f. 1923; devt of museum sector; dissemination of information on museums; training and spec. information for mems; library of 2,000 vols; 200 mem. museums; Chair. PIRJO ALA-KAPEE; Sec.-Gen. ANJA-TUULIKKI HUOVINEN; publ. *Museo* (4 a year).

Suomen Tieteellinen Kirjastoseura (Finnish Research Library Association): POB 217, Kirkkokatu 6 (Tieteiden talo), 00171 Helsinki; tel. (9) 61299240; fax (9) 61299230; e-mail meri.kuula-bruun@finlit.fi; internet pro.tsv.fi/stks; f. 1929; 700 mems; Chair. KIMMO TUOMINEN; Sec. VEERA RISTIKARTANO; publ. *Signum* (journal, 6 a year).

ECONOMICS, LAW AND POLITICS

Ekonomiska Samfundet i Finland (Economic Society of Finland): Swedish School of Economics and Business Admin., POB 479, 00101 Helsinki; tel. (9) 431331; fax (9) 43133333; internet www .ekonomiskasamfundet.fi; f. 1894; 806 mems; Pres. HENRIK WINBERG; Chair. EDVARD JOHANSSON; Vice-Pres. ANNIKA SANDSTRÖM; Sec. JOHAN WIKSTRÖM (acting); publ. *Ekonomiska Samfundets Tidskrift* (Journal, 3 a year).

Finnish Legal Society: Advokatbyrå Borenius & Kemppinen Ab, Georgsgatan 13A, 00120 Helsinki; tel. (9) 61533489; fax (9) 61533499; f. 1862; 794 mems; Pres. GUSTAF MÖLLER; Sec. JOHAN ROMAN; publ. *Tidskrift utgiven av Juridiska Föreningen i Finland.*

Hallinnon Tutkimuksen Seura ry/Sällskapet för Förvaltningsforskning (Finnish Association for Administrative Studies): Dept of Political Science, POB 54, 00014 Univ. of Helsinki; tel. (9) 19124826; e-mail anna-liisa.heusala@helsinki.fi; internet pro .tsv.fi/hts; f. 1981; aims to function as a common link for depts and researchers studying admin. questions, to coordinate planning and surveillance of training in admin. sciences, to hold lectures and discussions, to take part in int. scientific cooperation; a mem. of the European Group of Public Admin.; 660 individual mems, 4 organizational mems; Pres. Dr ANTTI SYVÄ-JÄRVI; Vice-Pres. Dr PERTTI AHONEN; Sec. JAANA LEINONEN; publ. *Hallinnon Tutkimus* (4 a year).

International Law Association, Finnish Branch: Relinsgatan 12 A 2, 20810 Abo; fax

(20) 5066100; e-mail finnish-ila@helsinki.fi; internet www.ila-hq.org; f. 1946; 105 mems; Pres. Judge. GUSTAF MOLLER; Treas. UWE UUSITALO; Sec. JUHO VUORI.

Ius Gentium (Finnish Society of International Law): POB 208, 00171 Helsinki; tel. (9) 19122468; fax (9) 19123076; e-mail iusgentium@iusgentium.fi; internet www .iusgentium.fi; f. 1983; research on int. law and legal theory; organizes seminars and lectures on topics relating to int. law and legal theory; 100 mems; Chair. TARU KUOS-MANEN; publs *Acta Societatis Fennicae Iuris Gentium, Finnish Yearbook of International Law, Kansainoikeus/Ius Gentium*, A, B and C series.

Kansantaloudellinen Yhdistys (Finnish Economic Association): c/o Merja Kauhanen, Labour Institute for Economic Research, Pitkänsillanreta 3A, 00530 Helsinki; tel. (9) 25357345; e-mail yhdistys@ktyhdistys.net; internet www.ktyhdistys.net; f. 1884; 1,012 mems; Pres. JUHA TARKKA; Sec. and Treas. MERJA KAUHANEN; publs *Kansantaloudellinen Aikakauskirja* (Finnish Economic Journal), *Kansantaloudellisia Tutkimuksia* (Economic Studies).

Suomalainen Lakimiesyhdistys ry (Finnish Lawyers' Society): Kasarmikatu 23A 17, 00130 Helsinki; tel. (9) 6120300; fax (9) 604668; e-mail toimisto@lakimiesyhdistys.fi; internet www.lakimiesyhdistys.fi; f. 1898; 2,700 mems; Pres. TATU LEPPÄNEN; publs *Lakimies-aikakauskirja* (8 a year), *Oikeustiede-Jurisprudentia* (1 a year), *Suomalaisen Lakimiesyhdistyksen Julkaisuja* (series A, B, C, D and E).

Suomen Kriminalistiyhdistys (Finnish Association of Criminologists): c/o Sakari Melander, POB 4, 00014 University of Helsinki; tel. (1) 9121781; fax (1) 9123090; e-mail etunimi.sukunimi@helsinki.fi; internet www .kriminalistiyhdistys.fi; f. 1934; promotes research, organizes debates on topical criminological policy subjects; 260 mems; Chair. Prof. KIMMO NUOTIO; Vice-Chair. ESA VESTERBACKA; Sec. SAKARI MELANDER; Treas. MIKKO VIRKAMÄKI; publ. *Nordisk Tidskrift for Kriminalividenskab* (4 a year).

Suomen Taloushistoriallinen Yhdistys/Ekonomisk-Historiska föreningen i Finland (Finnish Economic History Association): Dept of History and Ethnology, POB 35 (H), 40014 Univ. of Jyväskylä; tel. (14) 2601284; fax (14) 2601231; e-mail juhamart@jyu.fi; internet groups.jyu.fi/taloushistoria/en .shtml; f. 1952; studies economic and social history; 100 mems; Chair. Prof. Dr ILKKA NUMMELA; Sec. Prof. JARI OJALA; Exec. Dir JUUSO MARTTILA; publs *Scandinavian Economic History Review* (in cooperation with other Scandinavian socs for the advancement of the study of economic history), *Suomen talouselämän vaikuttajat* (in cooperation with Finnish Literature Soc.).

Suomen Tilastoseura/Statistiska Samfundet i Finland (Finnish Statistical Society): c/o Statistics Finland, POB 5V, 00022; tel. (9) 173412628; e-mail sihteeri@ tilastoseura.fi; internet www.tilastoseura.fi; f. 1920; not for profit; aims to promote the development of theoretical and applied statistics, to unite statisticians working in various fields, to promote statistical education and research; 400 mems; Pres. TIMO ALANKO; Vice-Pres. KIMMO VEHKALAHTI; Sec. ARTO KOKKINEN; publ. *Scandinavian Journal of Statistics* (4 a year, published with other Nordic statistical associations).

Suomen Väestötieteen Yhdistys (Finnish Demographic Society): Dept of Social Research, POB 18 (Unioninkatu 35), 00014 Univ. of Helsinki; tel. (9) 19123885; fax (9) 19123967; internet blogit.helsinki.fi/svy; f.

1973; fosters research and promotes interaction between scholars in the field of population studies; 101 mems; Chair. Prof. PEKKA MARTIKAINEN; Sec. HANNA REMES; publ. *Finnish Yearbook of Population Research* (published in collaboration with The Population Research Institute).

Suomen Ympäristöoikeustieteen Seura/Miljörättsliga Sällskapet i Finland (Finnish Society of Environmental Law): POB 1225, 00101 Helsinki; tel. (9) 27091890; fax (9) 6222293; e-mail sys@pro.tsv.fi; internet pro.tsv.fi/sys; f. 1980; supports and promotes legal and admin. research of environmental problems, and promotes cooperation between researchers and authorities; 350 mems; Chair. Prof. ERKKI J. HOLLO; Vice-Pres. TIMO KOTKASAARI; Sec. ROBERT UTTER; publ. *Ympäristöjuridiikka-Miljöjuridik* (Journal of Environmental Law, 4 a year).

Taloustieteellinen Yhdistys (Economic Science Association): Suomen Pankki, POB 160, Helsinki 00101; tel. (40) 7542781; e-mail sihteeri@taloustieteellinenyhdistys.fi; internet www.taloustieteellinenyhdistys.fi; f. 1936; scientific society to support economic research and promotion of economic and political debate; 845 mems; Pres. IIKKA KORHONEN; Sec. HELINÄ LAAKKONE; publs *Finnish Economic Papers* (2 a year), *Kansantaloudellinen aikakauskirja* (4 a year).

Valtiotieteellinen Yhdistys (Finnish Political Science Association): Department of Political Science, c/o Swedish School of Social Sciences, POB 16, 00014, University of Helsinki; tel. (9) 19124919; e-mail marjukka .weide@helsinki.fi; internet www.helsinki.fi/jarj/vty; f. 1935; promotes political science in Finland; 590 mems; Chair. HANNA WASS; Sec. MARJUKKA WEIDE; publ. *Politiikka* (4 a year).

FINE AND PERFORMING ARTS

Suomen Etnomusikologinen Seura ry (Finnish Society for Ethnomusicology): POB 35, (Vironkatu 1), 00014 Univ. of Helsinki; tel. 19124777; fax 19124755; e-mail liisa .tuomi@helsinki.fi; internet www .etnomusikologia.fi; f. 1974; promotes ethnomusicology research and disseminates information on world music cultures; culturally sensitive attitude of music study; organizes seminars, lectures, concerts; 151 mems; Pres. Dr PIRKKO MOISALA; Sec. LIISA TUOMI; publs *Musiikin suunta* (4 a year), *Yearbook of Ethnomusicology.*

Suomen Musiikkitieteellinen Seura ry/Musikvetenskapliga Sällskapet i Finland rf (Finnish Musicological Society): Musikin laitos, PL 35, 00014 Univ. of Helsinki; tel. (14) 2601397; fax (9) 19124755; e-mail jokavuos@campus.jyu.fi; internet www.musiikilehti.fi; f. 1911; aims to encourage musicological research, develop int. exchanges, and to function for the good of Finnish musical life by broadening knowledge of music and musical culture; 200 mems; Chair. Dr TUOMAS EEROLA; Sec.-Gen. Prof. JONNY VUOSKOSKI; publs *Acta Musicologica Fennica, Musiikki* (4 a year).

Suomen Näytelmäkirjailijalitto (Finnish Dramatists' Union): Meritullinkatu 33G, 00170 Helsinki; tel. (9) 1356796; fax (9) 1356171; e-mail info@sunklo.fi; internet www.sunklo.fi; f. 1921; Chair. SATU RASILA; Vice-Chair. JUKKA ASIKAINEN; Sec. MARKUS PYHÄLTÖ.

Suomen Säveltäjät ry/Finlands Tonsättare rf (Society of Finnish Composers): Runeberginkatu 15A 11, 00100 Helsinki; tel. (9) 445589; fax (9) 440181; e-mail saveltajat@ composers.fi; internet www.composers.fi; f. 1945; 176 mems; Pres. TAPIO TUOMELA; Vice Pres. RIIKKA TALVITIE; Exec. Dir ANNU MIK-KONEN.

Suomen Taideyhdistys (Finnish Art Society): Helsingin Taidehalli, Nervanderinkatu 3, 00100 Helsinki; tel. 4577314315; fax (9) 45420610; e-mail info@suomentaideyhdistys.fi; internet www.suomentaideyhdistys.fi; f. 1846; arranges exhibitions, presents awards and scholarships; 1,700 mems; Pres. VEIKKO KASURINEN; Vice-Pres. RIITTA VALORINTA; Sec. ANNA KINNUNEN.

Suomen Taiteilijaseura/Konstnärsgillet i Finland (Artists' Association of Finland): Iso Roobertinkatu 3–5 A 22, 00120 Helsinki; tel. (9) 61292120; fax (9) 61292160; e-mail aaf@artists.fi; internet www.artists.fi; f. 1864; 2,800 mems; mem. socs consist of the Finnish Painters' Union, the Asscn of Finnish Sculptors, the Artists Asscn MUU ry, the Assocn of Finnish Printmakers, the Union of Artist Photographers and the Union of Finnish Art Asscns; promotes professional interests of artists and holds an annual exhibition; Chair. HANNA OJAMO; Exec. Dir. PETRA HAVU; publs *Taide* (Art), *Taiteilijalenti* (4 a year).

Taidehistorian seura/Föreningen för konsthistoria ry (Society for Art History in Finland): PL 3, 00014 Univ. of Helsinki; fax (9) 19122961; e-mail pinja.metsaranta@helsinki.fi; internet www.taidehistorianseura.fi; f. 1974; promotes research in art history in Finland; 483 mems; Chair. JOHANNA VAKKARI; Vice-Chair. HANNA PIRINEN; publ. *Taidehistoriallisia tutkimuksia/Konsthistoriska studier (Studies in Art History)*.

Turun Soitannollinen Seura (Musical Society of Turku): Sibelius Museum, Piispankatu 17, 20500 Turku; tel. (2) 2313789; fax (2) 518528; internet www.musisoi.net; f. 1790; 655 mems; Chair. EMILIE GARDBERG; Vice-Pres. ALARIC REPO; Sec. INKA-MARIA PULKKINEN.

HISTORY, GEOGRAPHY AND ARCHAEOLOGY

Ethnos—Suomen Kansatieteilijöiden Yhdistys (Ethnos—The Association of Finnish Ethnologists): c/o Tieteiden talo, Kirkkokatu 6, 00170 Helsinki; tel. (40) 5120061; fax (2) 2154845; e-mail sihteeri@ethnosry.org; internet www.ethnosry.org; f. 1972; seminars, trips, book clubs, publs to raise awareness on ethnology research; Pres. KATRIINA SIIVONEN; Sec. AURA KIVILAAKSO; publ. *Ethnologia Fennica* (English and German).

Historian Ystäväin Liitto (Society of the Friends of History): Tieteiden talo, Kirkkokatu 6, 00170 Helsinki; tel. (9) 22869351; e-mail shs@histseura.fi; internet pro.tsv.fi/hyl; f. 1926; 1,500 mems; Sec. JULIA BURMAN; publs *Historiallinen Aikakauskirja* (Finnish Historical Review, 4 a year), *Historiallinen Kirjasto* (irregular), *Historian Aitta* (irregular).

Metsähistorian Seura (Finnish Forest History Society): c/o Lusto, Suomen Metsämuseo, 58450 Punkaharju; tel. (50) 3669552; fax (15) 3451050; e-mail metsahistorian.seura@lusto.fi; internet www.lusto.fi; f. 1994; research, documentation and public attention of forest history and tradition; arranges meetings, seminars and study tours; 294 mems; Chair. MARKKU RAUHALAHTI; Sec. LEENA PAASKOSKI.

Suomen Arkeologinen Seura ry (The Archaeological Society of Finland): c/o The House of Sciences and Letters, Kirkkokatu 6, 00170 Helsinki; e-mail wesa.perttola@helsinki.fi; internet www.sarks.fi; f. 1982; maintains contacts among archaeologists in various capacities; Chair. TUIJA RANKAMA; Sec. MIIKKA TALLAVAARA; publs *Fennoscandia*

archaeologica (1 a year), *Muinaistutkija* (4 a year).

Suomen Historiallinen Seura/Finska Historiska Samfundet (Finnish Historical Society): Tieteiden talo, Kirkkokatu 6, 00170 Helsinki; tel. (9) 22869351; e-mail shs@histseura.fi; internet www.histseura.fi; f. 1875; 900 mems; Chair. Dr MARJAANA NIEMI; Exec. Dir JULIA BURMAN; publs *Bibliotheca Historica* (historical studies in Finnish, English and German), *Historiallinen Arkisto* (Historical Archives), *Historiallisia Tutkimuksia* (Historical Researches), *Suomen historian lähteitä* (Sources of the History of Finland), *Studia Fennica: Historica*, *Studia Historica* (historical studies in German, French and English).

Suomen Kartografinen Seura (Cartographic Society of Finland): c/o Ulla-Maarit Saarinen, 00022 Tilastokeskus; tel. (9) 17343544; e-mail sihteeri@kartogra.fi; internet www.kartogra.fi; f. 1957; meetings, lectures, exhibitions and visits to mapping orgs; 140 mems; Pres. ANTTI JAKOBSSON; Sec. ULLA-MAARIT SAARINEN.

Suomen Kirkkohistoriallinen Seura/Finska Kyrkohistoriska Samfundet (Finnish Society of Church History): Finnish Church History Society, POB 33 (Aleksanterinkatu 7, Fifth Fl.), 00014 Univ. of Helsinki; tel. (9) 400941723; fax (9) 19123033; e-mail juha.merilainen@helsinki.fi; internet www.skhs.fi; f. 1891; 660 mems; Chair. MIKKO KETOLA; Vice-Pres. MARKUS HIEKKANEN; Sec. Dr JUHA MERILÄINEN; Treas. TIMO VALTONEN; publs *Toimituksia-Handlingar* (research mongraphs, 3–6 a year), *Vuosikirja-Arsskrift* (1 a year).

Suomen Maantieteellinen Seura/Geografiska Sällskapet i Finland (Geographical Society of Finland): Geographical Soc. of Finland, POB 64 (Gustaf Hällströmin k. 2), 00014 Univ. of Helsinki; tel. (9) 19150765; fax (9) 19150760; e-mail olli.ruth@helsinki.fi; internet www.helsinki.fi/maantiede/geofi; f. 1888; 1,300 mems; library of 56,000 vols; Pres. Dr PIRJO HELLEMAA; Vice-Pres. Dr. SANNA MÄKI; Sec. OLLI RUTH; publs *Fennia* (2 a year), *Terra* (4 a year).

Suomen Muinaismuistoyhdistys/Finska Fornminnesföreningen (Finnish Antiquarian Society): POB 913, 00101 Helsinki; tel. (9) 40509287; fax (9) 40509400; e-mail mikko.terasvirta@nba.fi; internet www.muinaismuistoyhdistys.fi; f. 1870; 600 mems; Pres. HELENA EDGREN; Vice-Pres. PAULA PURHONEN; Sec. MIKKO TERÄSVIRTA; publs *Suomen Museo ja Finskt Museum*, *Iskos*, *Kansatieteellinen Arkisto*, *Suomen Muinaismuistoyhdistyksen Aikakauskirja—Finska Fornminnesföreningens Tidskrift*.

Suomen Sukututkimusseura/Genealogiska Samfundet i Finland (Genealogical Society of Finland): Liisankatu 16A, 00170 Helsinki; tel. (10) 3877901; e-mail seura@genealogia.fi; internet www.genealogia.fi; f. 1917; 5,800 mems; library of 45,000 vols; Chair. LARS HOLM; Vice-Chair. ROY SJÖBLOM; Sec. P. T. KUUSILUOMA; publs *Genos* (4 a year), *Sukutieto* (4 a year), *Vuosikirja—Arsskrift* (1 a year).

LANGUAGE AND LITERATURE

Kirjallisuudentutkijain Seura (Finnish Literary Research Society): Domestic Literature, Finnish Language and Literature Department, POB 3 (Fabianinkatu 33), 00014 Univ. of Helsinki; e-mail kts@uta.fi; internet www.helsinki.fi/jarj/skts; f. 1927; advances the study of literature and promotes general interest in literary research; organises annual research seminar; 170 mems; Chair. TIINA KÄKELÄ-PUUMALA; Sec.

MATTI KANGASKOSKI; publ. *Avain–Finnish Review of Literary Studies* (4 a year).

British Council: Urho Kekkosen katu 2C, 00100 Helsinki; tel. (9) 7743330; fax (9) 7018725; e-mail info@britishcouncil.fi; internet www.britishcouncil.fi; promotes cultural exchange with the UK; Country Man. MARJO SOMARI; Dir TUIJA TALVITIE.

Finlands svenska författareförening (Society of Swedish Authors in Finland): Urho Kekkonens gata 8 B 14, 00100 Helsinki; tel. (9) 446266; e-mail forfattarna@kaapeli.fi; internet www.forfattarna.fi; f. 1919; 195 mems; Pres. MIKAELA STRÖMBERG; Sec.-Gen. MERETE JENSEN.

Goethe-Institut: Mannerheimintie 20A, 00100 Helsinki; tel. (9) 6803550; fax (9) 604377; e-mail info@helsinki.goethe.org; internet www.goethe.de/ne/hel/deindex.htm; offers courses and examinations in German language and culture and promotes cultural exchange with Germany; library of 2,800 vols, 30 periodicals; Dir MIKKO FRITZE.

Klassillis-filologinen yhdistys (Society for Classical Philology): c/o World Cultures Dept of Classical Philology, POB 24, 00014 Univ. of Helsinki; fax (9) 19122161; internet www.helsinki.fi/hum/kla/kfy; f. 1879; promotes the study of classical philology and classical antiquity in gen.; 91 mems; Pres. Prof. OLLI SALOMIES; Vice-Pres. ANTERO TAMMISTO; Sec. LAURA BUCHHOLZ; publ. *Arctos: Acta Philologica Fennica* (1 a year).

Kotikielen Seura (Society for the Study of Finnish): POB 3, 00014 Univ. of Helsinki; fax (9) 19123329; e-mail seura@kotikielenseura.fi; internet www.kotikielenseura.fi; f. 1876; Finnish linguistics; 792 mems; Pres. Dr MARJA-LEENA SORJONEN; Sec. RIITTA JUVONEN; publ. *Virittäjä* (4 a year).

Suomalais-Ugrilainen Seura (Finno-Ugrian Society): POB 320, Mariankatu 7, 00171 Helsinki; tel. (9) 662149; fax (9) 6988249; internet www.sgr.fi; f. 1883; Northern Eurasian linguistics and ethnography; 800 mems; Pres. Prof. Dr ULLA-MAIJA FORSBERG; Sec. PAULA KOKKONEN; publs *Finnisch-Ugrische Forschungen* (every 2 years), *Journal de la Société Finno-Ougrienne* (every 2 years), *Mémoires de la Société Finno-Ougrienne* (2–5 a year), *Uralica Helsingiensia*.

Suomalaisen Kirjallisuuden Seura/Finska Litteratursällskapet (Finnish Literature Society): Hallituskatu 1, POB 259, 00171 Helsinki; tel. (20) 1131231; fax (9) 13123220; e-mail sks@finlit.fi; internet www.finlit.fi; f. 1831 to promote study of folklore, ethnology, literature and Finnish language; 4,132 mems; Chair. Prof. AILI NENOLA; Dir-Gen. and Sec. TUOMAS LEHTONEN; library: see Libraries and Archives; publs *Studia Fennica: Ethnologica*, *Studia Fennica: Folkloristica*, *Studia Fennica: Historica*, *Studia Fennica: Linguistica* (1 a year), *Studia Fennica: Litteraria*.

Suomen englanninopettajat ry (Association of Teachers of English in Finland): Rautatieläisenkatu 6A, 00520 Helsinki; tel. (9) 145414; fax (9) 2788100; e-mail english@suomenenglanninopettajat.fi; internet www.suomenenglanninopettajat.fi; f. 1948; 3,000 mems; Pres. KATI VENEMIES; publ. *Tempus* (8 a year).

Suomen Kirjailijaliitto (The Union of Finnish Writers): Runeberginkatu 32, C 2 8, 00100 Helsinki; tel. (9) 445392; fax (9) 492278; e-mail info@suomenkirjailijaliitto.fi; internet www.suomenkirjailijaliitto.fi; f. 1897; allied to the Scandinavian Authors' Council and European Writers' Congress; 600 mems; Pres. TUULA-LIINA VARIS; Sec. SUVI OINONEN; publs *Suomalaiset kertojat*, *Suomen Runotar*.

Svenska litteratursällskapet i Finland (Society of Swedish Literature in Finland): Riddareg. 5, 00170 Helsinki; tel. (9) 618777; e-mail info@sls.fi; internet www.sls.fi; f. 1885; preserves, develops and mediates Swedish cultural heritage in Finland; 1,000 mems; library: see Libraries and Archives; Pres. Prof. MAX ENGMAN; Sec. Prof. MARIKA TANDEFELT; publ. *Skrifter* (15–20 a year).

Uusfilologinen Yhdistys (Modern Language Society): POB 24 (Unioninkatu 40), 00014 Univ. of Helsinki; tel. (9) 19123502; fax (9) 19122384; e-mail marianna.hintikka@helsinki.fi; internet www.helsinki.fi/jarj/ufy; f. 1887; 244 mems; Pres. Prof. JUHANI HÄRMÄ; Hon. Sec. MARIANNA HINTIKKA; publs *Mémoires de la Société Néophilologique* (irregular), *Neuphilologische Mitteilungen* (Bulletin, 4 a year).

MEDICINE

Brain Research Society of Finland: POB 63 (Hartmaninkatu 8), 00290 Helsinki; e-mail tiina-kaisa.kukko-lukjanov@utu.fi; internet www.brsf.org; f. 1973; organizes lectures and courses for scientists; works to improve brain research opportunities; 220 mems; Chair. IRMA HOLOPAINEN; Sec. TIINA-KAISA KUKKO-LUKJANOV.

Cancer Society of Finland: Pieni Roobertinkatu 9, 00130 Helsinki; tel. (9) 135331; fax (9) 1351093; e-mail society@cancer.fi; internet www.cancer.fi; f. 1936; 140,000 mems; Chair. Prof. SEPPO PYRHÖNEN; Sec.-Gen. Dr HARRI VERTIO; publs *Focus Oncologie* (1 a year), *Syöpä— Cancer* (6 a year).

Finska Läkaresällskapet (Medical Society of Finland): Johannesbergsvägen 8, POB 82, 00251 Helsinki; tel. (9) 47768090; fax (9) 4362055; e-mail kansliet@fls.fi; internet www.fls.fi; f. 1835; 1,000 mems; library of 35,000 vols; Pres. ULF-HÅKAN STENMAN; Sec. ULLA WIKLUND; publ. *Finska Läkaresällskapets Handlingar*.

Lääketieteellinen Radioisotooppiyhdistys (Finnish Society of Nuclear Medicine): Helsingin Diakonissalaitos, Isotooppilaboratorio, Alppikatu 2, 00530 Helsinki; tel. (9) 77507218; fax (9) 7534025; e-mail eeva.boman@kuh.fi; internet www.fsnm.org; f. 1959; promotes devt and application of nuclear medicine; acts as a link between field practitioners and the public sector; organizes meetings, lectures and training sessions; maintains relationships with int. socs. of nuclear medicine, ind. laboratories in Finland; supplies equipment and radiopharmaceuticals; 300 mems; Chair. Dr JARI HEIKKINEN; Vice-Chair. MARKO SEPPÄNEN; Sec. EEVA BOMAN; Treas. Prof. JYRI TOIKKA.

Sosiaalilääketieteen Yhdistys ry (Society for Social Medicine): c/o Reetta Lehto, Folkhälsan Research Centre, Paasikivenkatu 4, 00250 Helsinki; tel. (9) 7886296; e-mail sihteeri@socialmedicine.fi; internet www.socialmedicine.fi; f. 1968; promotes factors contributing to social medical research; organizes seminars, lectures, presentations, courses, symposia; publishes, supports research in the field; gives opinions on matters of social medicine and maintains relations with foreign sector orgs; 700 mems; Chair. Dr AINI OSTAMO; Vice-Chair. PIA SOLIN; Sec. REETTA LEHTO; publ. *Sosiaalilääketieteellinen Aikakauslehti* (4 a year).

Suomalainen Lääkäriseura Duodecim (Finnish Medical Society Duodecim): Kalevankatu 11A, POB 713, 00100 Helsinki; tel. (9) 618851; fax (9) 61885200; internet www.duodecim.fi; f. 1881; 20,000 mems; library of 22,500 vols; Pres. Dr MARKKU HEIKINHEIMO; Sec. Dr MATTI RAUTALAHTI; publ. *Duodecim* (26 a year).

Suomen Farmakologiyhdistys (Finnish Pharmacological Society): University of Tampere, Medical School, Medisiinarinkatu 3, 33014 Tampere; tel. (3) 5516554; e-mail riku.korhonen@uta.fi; internet www.sfy.fi; f. 1948; supports the development of Finnish Pharmacology; organizes nat. and int. scientific meetings; 450 mems; Pres. Prof. EEVA MOILANEN; Vice-Pres. Dr EWEN MACDONALD; Sec. RIKU KORHONEN.

Suomen Farmaseuttinen Yhdistys/ Farmaceutiska Föreningen i Finland (Finnish Pharmaceutical Society): Fredrikinkatu 61, 2. kerros, 00100 Helsinki; tel. (9) 19159159; internet pro.tsv.fi/finpharmsociety; f. 1887; 300 mems; Pres. Dr TOM WIKBERG; Sec. Dr LEENA PELTONEN.

Suomen Hammaslääkäriseura Apollonia (Finnish Dental Society Apollonia): Bulevardi 30 B 5, 00120 Helsinki; tel. (9) 6803120; fax (9) 646263; e-mail toimisto@apollonia.fi; internet www.apollonia.fi; f. 1892; 6,400 mems; Pres. Dr PEKKA LAINE; Gen. Sec. Dr VESA POHJOLA.

Suomen Kardiologinen Seura (Finnish Cardiac Society): Isokatu 47, 90100 Oulu; tel. (10) 5481000; fax (8) 335551; e-mail fcs@fincardio.fi; internet www.fincardio.fi; f. 1967; supports cardiac research; awards yearly grants for research; 760 mems, 38 industrial mems; Pres. PEKKA RAATIKAINEN; Sec. KARI YLITALO; publ. *Sydänääni* (5 a year).

Suomen Sairaanhoitajaliitto ry (Finnish Nurses Association): Asemamiehenkatu 2, 00520 Helsinki; tel. (9) 2290020; fax (9) 22900240; e-mail info@sairaanhoitajaliitto.fi; internet www.sairaanhoitajaliitto.fi; f. 1925; offers learning and networking opportunities to nurses; 50,000 mems; Pres. KATRIINA LAAKSONEN; Vice-Pres. MARIANNE SIPILÄ; publs *Sairaanhoitaja* (12 a year), *Premissi* (6 a year), *Tutkiva Hoitotyö* (4 a year).

Suomen Toksikologiyhdistys (Finnish Society of Toxicology): c/o Juha Laakso, Elintarviketurvallisuusvirasto, Evira/Riskinarviointiyksikkö, Mustialankatu 3, 00790 Helsinki; e-mail tarja.kohila@helsinki.fi; internet www.toksikologit.fi; f. 1979; organizes annual scientific meetings and promotes cooperation in toxicology with nat. and int. socs; 300 mems; Chair. KIRSI VÄHÄKANGAS; Sec. JUHA LAAKSO; Treas. KIRSI MYÖHÄNEN.

NATURAL SCIENCES
Biological Sciences

Birdlife Finland: Annankatu 29A 16, 00101 Helsinki; tel. (9) 41353300; fax (9) 41353322; e-mail office@birdlife.fi; internet www.birdlife.fi; f. 1973; protection of birds, promotes biodiversity conservation and sustainable development; 30 nat. assoc. orgs; affiliated to BirdLife International; 10,000 mems; Chair. AKI ARKIOMAA; Dir MATTI RIIHIMÄKI; publs *Linnut* (Birds, 4 a year), *Linnut-vuosikirja* (1 a year), *Ornis Fennica* (4 a year), *Tiira-lehti* (4 a year).

Kasvinsuojeluseura ry (Plant Protection Society): Raitamaantie 8A (Kannelmäki), 00420 Helsinki; tel. (10) 4394770; fax (9) 47707920; e-mail pertti.rajala@forestum.fi; internet www.kasvinsuojeluseura.fi; f. 1931; research on, and protection from, diseases, pests and weeds; arranges meetings and excursions, awards grants to researchers; 1,500 mems; Chair. PAAVO AHVENNIEMI; Sec. KATIE LINDFORS; publ. *Kasvinsuojelulehti*.

Societas Amicorum Naturae Ouluensis/ Oulun Luonnonystäväin Yhdistys ry (Natural History Society of Oulu): Dept of Biology (Botany), 90570 Univ. Oulu; tel. (8) 5531546; fax (8) 5531500; f. 1925; 436 mems; Pres. Prof. P. LAHDESMAKI; Chair. JAAKKO LUMME; Sec. S. KONTUNEN-SOPPELA; publs *Aquilo ser. botanica* (1 a year), *Aquilo ser. zoologica* (1 a year).

Societas Biochemica, Biophysica et Microbiologica Fenniae (Biochemical, Biophysical and Microbiological Society of Finland): Folkhälsan Research Centre, POB 63, 00014 Univ. of Helsinki; tel. (9) 19125618; e-mail mervi.kuronen@helsinki.fi; internet www.biobio.org; f. 1945; 900 mems; Pres. Dr MARC BAUMANN; Sec. MERVI KURONEN.

Societas Biologica Fennica Vanamo/ Suomen Biologian Seura Vanamo: POB 7, Latokartanonkaari 7, 00014 Univ. of Helsinki; Department of Biosciences, POB 65 (Viikinkaari 1), 00014 Univ. of Helsinki; internet www.vanamo.fi; f. 1896; Pres. JOUKO RIKKINEN; Sec. SARI SIIPOLA; publs *Atlas Florae Europaeae*, *Luonnon Tutkija* (The Naturalist, 5 a year).

Societas Entomologica Fennica/Suomen Hyönteistieteellinen Seura (Entomological Society of Finland): Finnish Museum of Natural History, 00014 Univ. of Helsinki; tel. (9) 19158662; fax (9) 19158663; internet www.suomenhyonteistieteellinenseura.org; f. 1935; library; Pres. Dr ILKKA TERÄS; Sec. Dr NINA LAURENNE; publ. *Entomologica Fennica* (4 a year).

Societas pro Fauna et Flora Fennica: c/o F. Högnabba, Finnish Museum of Natural History, Mycology Division, POB 7, Unionsgatan 44, 00014 Univ. of Helsinki; tel. (9) 19124495; fax (9) 19124456; e-mail filip.hognabba@helsinki.fi; internet www.societasfff.fi; f. 1821; discussion and research on all aspects of animals and plants in Finland; 1,041 mems; library of 44,000 vols; Pres. Prof. CARL-ADAM HÆGGSTRÖM; Hon. Sec. Dr FILIP HÖGNABBA; publ. *Memoranda Societatis pro Fauna et Flora Fennica* (3 a year).

Physical Sciences

Geofysiikan Seura/Geofysiska Sällskapet (Geophysical Society of Finland): c/o Hanna Tietäväinen, Finnish Meteorological Institute, POB 503, 00101 Helsinki; tel. (9) 19293512; fax (9) 19293146; internet pro.tsv.fi/geofysiikanseura; f. 1926; aims to promote geophysical research and provide links between researchers; 230 mems; Chair. Dr HEIKKI VIRTANEN; Sec. HANNA TIETÄVÄINEN; publ. *Geophysica* (2 a year).

Suomen Geologinen Seura r y/Geologiska Sällskapet i Finland (Geological Society of Finland): Geological Survey of Finland, POB 96, 02151 Espoo; tel. (20) 205502414; e-mail sihteeri@geologinenseura.fi; internet www.geologinenseura.fi; f. 1886; 1,200 mems; Pres. Dr AARNO KOTILAINEN; Sec. MARI TUUSJÄRVI; Treas. LARS KAISLANIEMI; publs *Bulletin* (2 a year), *Geologi* (6 a year).

Suomen Kemian Seura/Kemiska Sällskapet i Finland (Association of Finnish Chemical Societies): Urho Kekkosen katu 8C 31, 00100 Helsinki; tel. (10) 4256300; fax (10) 4256309; e-mail toimisto@kemianseura.fi; internet www.kemianseura.fi; f. 1970; organizes annual Finnish Chemical Congress; acts as link between the three mem. socs, promotes research in chemistry, chemical education, chemical industry; library of 800 vols; Chair. HILKKA VAHERVUORI; publs *Acta Chemica Scandinavica*, *Kemia-Kemi* (8 a year).

Constituent Societies:

Finska Kemistsamfundet/Suomen Kemistiseura (Finnish Society of Chemistry): Urho Kekkonen gata 8 C 31, 00100 Helsinki; tel. (9) 4542040; fax (9)

45420440; e-mail toimisto@kemianseura.fi; f. 1891; 564 mems; Pres. Triin Gyllen-berg; Sec. Maria Wikström.

Kemiallisteknillinen Yhdistys/ Kemisktekniska Forening ry (Finnish Society of Chemical Engineers): Urho Kekkosen katu 8 C 31, 00100 Helsinki; tel. (50) 3518303; fax (9) 45420440; e-mail kty@kty.fi; internet www.kty.fi; f. 1970; 816 mems; Pres. Tiina Piira; Sec. Helena Laavi.

Suomalaisten Kemistien Seura (Finnish Chemical Society): Urho Kekkosen katu 8 C 31, 00100 Helsinki; tel. (10) 4256302; e-mail heleena.karrus@kemianseura.fi; f. 1919; 3,480 mems; Pres. Dr Jussi Kivikoski; Sec. Heleena Karrus.

Suomen Limnologinen yhdistys (Finnish Limnological Society): Pyhäjärvi-Instituutti, Ruukinpuisto, Sepäntie 7, 27500 Kauttua; tel. (50) 9194909; internet www.suomenlimnologinenyhdistys.fi; f. 1950; preservation and management of aquatic systems; fosters Finnish limnological research; provides information and a discussion forum for experts in this field; 180 mems; Chair. Jukka Horppila; Vice-Pres. Prof. Lauri Arvola; Sec. Anna Paloheimo; publ. *Boreal Environment Research* (6 a year).

Suomen luonnonsuojeluliitto (Finnish Association for Nature Conservation): Kotkankatu 9, 00510 Helsinki; tel. (9) 228081; fax (9) 22808200; e-mail toimisto@sll.fi; internet www.sll.fi; f. 1938; largest NGO in Finland for environmental protection and nature conservation; 30,000 mems; Pres. Risto Sulkava; Exec. Dir Eero Yrjö-Koski-nen; publs *Suomen Luonto* (10 a year), *Luonnonsuojelija* (6 a year).

Suomen Matemaattinen Yhdistys (Finnish Mathematical Society): Department of Mathematics and Statistics, POB 68 (Garfield Place katu 2B), 00014 Univ. of Helsinki; tel. (9) 19151495; fax (9) 1915140; e-mail tadeas.priklopil@helsinki.fi; internet www.math.helsinki.fi/~smy; f. 1868; supports research and education in mathematics; improves awareness about mathematics in general; organizes int. visitor programme, annual Mathematics Day event; 308 mems; Pres. Prof. Mats Gyllenberg; Sec. Tadeas Priklopil; publ. *Arkhimedes*.

Suomen Sammalseura ry (Finnish Bryological Society): POB 7 (Unioninkatu 44), 00014 Univ. of Helsinki; tel. (9) 1912442; fax (9) 19124456; e-mail xhe@mappi.helsinki.fi; internet pro.tsv.fi/sammalseura; f. 1987; promotes bryological research; supports cooperation of bryologists; 78 mems; Chair. Sinikka Piippo; Sec. Xiolan He-Nygrén; publ. *Bryobrothera* (irregular).

Suomen Sukututkimusseura (Genealogical Society of Finland): Liisankatu 16A, 00170 Helsinki; tel. (9) 3877901; e-mail samfundet@genealogia.fi; internet www.genealogia.fi; f. 1917; promotes genealogical and biographical research; 5,950 mems; library of 45,000 vols; Chair. Anu Lahtinen; Deputy Chair. Roy Sjöblom; Exec. Dir P. T. Kuusiluoma; publs *Genealogical Society of Finland Year Book*, *Genosta* (4 a year), *Sukutieto* (4 a year).

Ympäristötieteellinen Seura (Finnish Society for Environmental Sciences): Åbo Akademi, Organisk kemi Biskopsgatan 8, 20500 Turku; tel. (2) 2154805; e-mail jenny-maria.brozinski@abo.fi; internet www.fses.fi; f. 1987; encourages environment science research and spread information about protection of environment; organizes seminars, workshops, conference; 200 mems; Chair. Prof. Dr Leif Kronberg; Sec. and Treas. Jenny-Maria Brozinski.

PHILOSOPHY AND PSYCHOLOGY

Suomen Estetiikan Seura ry (Finnish Society for Aesthetics): POB 3, 00014 Univ. of Helsinki; tel. (9) 19121665; e-mail kalle.puolakka@helsinki.fi; internet www.estetiikka.fi; f. 1972; promotes research in aesthetics; creates contacts between arts and sciences; encourages discussions on aesthetic values; organizes annual seminars; 100 mems; Chair. Prof. Arto Haapala; Sec. Kalle Puolakka; publ. *Synteesi* (1 a year).

Suomen Filosofinen Yhdistys (Philosophical Society of Finland): Dept of Philosophy, POB 24 (Unioninkatu 40A), 00014 Univ. of Helsinki; tel. (9) 77488232; fax (9) 19128060; e-mail risto.vilkko@helsinki.fi; internet www.helsinki.fi/jarj/sfy; f. 1873; promotes the study of philosophy and related disciplines in Finland; 417 mems; Pres. Prof. Ilkka Niiniluoto; Sec. Dr Risto Vilkko; publs *Acta Philosophica Fennica* (1–3 a year), *Ajatus* (1 a year).

Suomen Psykiatriyhdistys (Finnish Psychiatric Association): Fredrikinkatu 71 A 4, 00100 Helsinki; tel. (9) 4770660; fax (9) 47706611; e-mail psy@psy.fi; internet www.psy.fi; f. 1913; promotes scientific psychiatry and occupational functioning, and mental health work; organizes meetings training; participates in int. activities; 1,400 mems; Pres. Prof. Jyrki Korkeila; Vice-Pres. Parta-nen Anneli; Treas. Assoc. Prof. Eronen Markku; Sec. Gen. Asst Prof. Minna Valk-onen-Korhonen.

Suomen Psykologinen Seura ry (Finnish Psychological Society): Liisankatu 16A, 00170 Helsinki; tel. (9) 2782122; fax (9) 2781300; e-mail psykologia@genealogia.fi; internet www.psykologienkustannus.fi/sps; f. 1952; 1,600 mems; small library; Pres. Prof. Jarkko Hautamäki; Sec.-Gen. Taina Schakir; publs *Acta Psychologica Fennica* (series A, irregular, and series B, irregular), *Psykologia* (6 a year).

RELIGION, SOCIOLOGY AND ANTHROPOLOGY

Suomalainen Teologinen Kirjallisuus-seura (Finnish Theological Literature Society): POB 33 (Aleksanterinkatu 7, 5. krs), 00014 Univ. of Helsinki; tel. (45) 1390879; fax (9) 19123033; e-mail stksj@pro.tsv.fi; internet pro.tsv.fi/stksj; f. 1891; 850 mems; Chair. Prof. Risto Saarinen; Secs Virve Saarinen, Joona Salminen.

Suomen Antropologinen Seura/Antro-pologiska Sällskapet i Finland (Finnish Anthropological Society): POB 59, 00014 Univ. of Helsinki; tel. (9) 19123094; fax (9) 19123006; e-mail info@suomenantropologinenseura.fi; internet www.antropologinenseura.fi; f. 1975; promotes research in the fields of anthropology and related disciplines; organizes meetings, lectures, public events, seminars and confs; 400 mems; Pres. Dr Minna Ruckenstein; Sec. Anna Autio; publ. *Suomen Antropologi/Antropologi i Finland* (Journal of the Finnish Anthropological Society, 4 a year).

Suomen Itämainen Seura (Finnish Oriental Society): c/o Asian and African Languages and Cultures Department, POB 59 (Unioninkatu 38B), 00014 Univ. of Helsinki; tel. (9) 19122224; fax (9) 19122094; e-mail riikka.tuori@helsinki.fi; internet www.suomenitamainenseura.org; f. 1917; 192 mems; Pres. Prof. Tapani Harviainen; Sec. Riikka Tuori; publ. *Studia Orientalia*.

Suomen Kansantietouden Tutkijain Seura ry (Finnish Folklore Society): c/o The Research Tradition, Univ. of Joensuu, POB 111, 80101 Joensuu; tel. 251 4058; e-mail kari.korolainen@uef.fi; internet cc.joensuu.fi/~loristi/skts; f. 1937; promotes knowledge of the disciplines of folklore and research; organises seminars, meetings, tours and photographic competition; 145 mems; Chair. Tuulikki Kurki; Sec. Kari Korolainen; publ. *Elore* (2 a year).

Suomen Kirkkohistoriallinen Seura (Finnish Society of Church History): POB 33, 00014 Univ. of Helsinki; fax (9) 19123033; e-mail info@skhs.fi; internet www.skhs.fi; f. 1887; colln of the sources of nat. church history; publishes monograhs, other work related to church; organizes excursions to historically interesting places; Chair. Mikko Ketola; Vice-Chair. Markus Hiekkanen; Sec. and Treas. Dr Juha Meriläinen; publ. *Yearbook*.

TECHNOLOGY

Akustinen Seura ry (Acoustical Society of Finland): c/o Aalto University Institute of Technology, Signal Processing and Acoustics, POB 13000, 00076 Aalto; tel. (9) 47022457; fax (9) 460224; e-mail akustinen.seura@hut.fi; internet www.acoustics.hut.fi/asf; f. 1943; ties together acousticians and people interested in acoustics; research and publishing; 220 mems; 20 supporting cos; Chair. Tapio Lokki; Sec. Marko Hiipakka.

Ilmansuojeluyhdistys ry (Finnish Air Pollution Prevention Society): POB 136, 00251 Helsinki; tel. (45) 1335989; e-mail sihteeri@isy.fi; internet www.isy.fi; f. 1976; air and climate protection; research and development; 400 mems; Pres. Jari Viinanen; Sec. Kerttu Kotakorpi; publ. *Ilmansuojelu* (4 a year).

Maanmittaustieteiden seura ry (Finnish Society of Surveying Sciences): POB 60, 00520 Helsinki; tel. (9) 1481900; fax (9) 1483580; e-mail sihteeri@maanmittaustieteidenseura.fi; internet mts.fgi.fi; f. 1926; 710 mems; Pres. Katri Kois-tinen; Sec. Juhana Hiironen; publ. *Nordic Journal of Surveying and Real Estate Research* (2 a year).

Rakenteiden Mekaniikan Seura (Finnish Association for Structural Mechanics): Rakentajanaukio 4A, POB 12100, 00076 Aalto; tel. (9) 47022264; fax (9) 47022267; e-mail juha.paavola@hut.fi; internet rmseura.tkk.fi; f. 1970 for promoting research and exchange of knowledge on engineering materials, structural mechanics and design; 222 individual mems, 10 collective mems; Chair. Jouni Freund; Sec. Sami Pajunen; publ. *Rakenteiden Mekaniikka* (Journal of Structural Mechanics, 4 a year).

Suomen Aerosolitutkimusseura ry (Finnish Association for Aerosol Research): Department of Physics, POB 64 (Gustaf Hällströmin katu 2), 00014 Univ. of Helsinki; tel. (40) 5684487; fax (9) 19150860; e-mail katrianne.lehtipalo@helsinki.fi; internet www.atm.helsinki.fi/faar; f. 1983; acts as a link between researchers in various institutes and univs; 180 mems; Chair. Kaarle Hämeri; Sec. Katrianne Lehtipalo; publ. *Report Series in Aerosol Science*.

Suomen Atomiteknillinen Seura/Atom-tekniska Sällskapet i Finland (Finnish Nuclear Society): Finnish nuclear society, POB 78, 02151 Espoo; tel. (40) 0236898; fax (20) 7225000; e-mail sihteeri@ats-fns.fi; internet www.ats-fns.fi; f. 1966; promotes knowledge and devt of nuclear technology in Finland, exchange information on an int. level; 617 mems, 18 corporate mems; Chair. Eija-Karita Puska; Sec. Silja Holopainen; publ. *ATS Ydintekniikka* (4 a year).

Suomen Automaatioseura ry (Finnish Society of Automation): Asemapäällikönkatu 12B, 00520 Helsinki; tel. (20) 1981220; fax

(20) 1981227; e-mail office@atu.fi; internet www.automaatioseura.fi; f. 1966; promotes the automation technology, theory and applications; operates a process, factory and building automation industry; organizes exhibition, conference, meeting, course, provides publications in the field; formulate opinions, makes suggestions and proposals; Chair. JEAN-PETER YLÉN; Vice-Chair. YRJÖ MAJANNE; Treas. KIMMO SIMOMAA; Sec. MIKKO LEHTO; publ. *Automaatioväylä-lehti* (7 a year).

Suomen Operaatiotutkimusseura (Finnish Operations Research Society): POB 702, 00101 Helsinki; e-mail fors@hse.fi; internet www.operaatiotutkimus.fi; f. 1973; promote and advances operations research; organizes seminars, excursions, training courses, and conferences; 180 mems; Chair. Prof. AHTI SALO; Sec. JUSSI KANGASPUNTA.

Suomen Tekoälyseura (Finnish Artificial Intelligence Society): Kuusitie 4 B 66, 00270 Helsinki; tel. (40) 5665832; e-mail toimisto@stes.fi; internet www.stes.fi; f. 1986; promotes public knowledge about artificial intelligence; offers channel for discussion; 200 mems; Chair. JUKKA KORTELA.

Suomen Tribologiayhdistys ry (Finnish Society for Tribology): c/o Pekka Salonen, STADIA, Tekniikka ja liikenne, POB 4201, 00099 Helsinki; e-mail pekka_salonen@kolumbus.fi; internet www.tribologysociety.fi; f. 1977; supports the research, technical devt and education of tribology; maintains int. cooperation to foreign tribology socs; 111 mems; Chair. PEKKA SALONEN; Vice-Pres. PEKKA SALONEN; Sec. JUSSI LEHTIÖ; publ. *Tribologia* (4 a year).

Svenska Tekniska Vetenskapsakademien i Finland (Swedish Academy of Engineering Sciences in Finland): Norra esplanaden 33A, 00100 Helsinki; tel. (40) 7225711; fax (9) 6818095; e-mail stv@stvif.fi; internet www.stvif.fi; f. 1921; promotes research in engineering sciences; 175 mems; Pres. HENRIK WOLFF; Sec. ÅSA LINDBERG; publ. *Förhandlingar* (Proceedings).

Tekniikan Akateemisten Liitto TEK ry (Academic Engineers and Architects in Finland—TEK): Ratavartijankatu 2, 00520 Helsinki; tel. (9) 229121; fax (9) 22912911; e-mail webmaster@tek.fi; internet www.tek.fi; f. 1896; negotiates and concludes collective agreements regarding salaries and work conditions for mems, serves as link between engineers and architects, regional offices in Espoo, Tampere, Oulu, Lappeenranta and Turku; 73,500 mems; Exec. Dir HEIKKI KAUPPI; publ. *TEK Member Magazine* (9 a year).

Tekniikan edistämissäätiö (Technological Foundation): c/o Työ ja elinkeinoministeriö, POB 32 (Aleksanterinkatu 4), 00023 Helsinki; tel. (10) 6064917; fax (9) 16062161; internet www.kolumbus.fi/tes; f. 1949; provides yearly fellowships for the advancement of technology; Pres. YRJÖ NEUVO; Sec.-Gen. KARI MÄKINEN.

Teknillisten Tieteiden Akatemia/Akademin för Tekniska Vetenskaper ry (Finnish Academy of Technology): Teknillisten Tieteiden Akatemia, Pohjoisesplanadi 33A, 00100 Helsinki; tel. (9) 6818090; fax (9) 68180955; e-mail facte@facte.com; internet www.ttatv.fi; f. 1957; promotes technical-scientific research; 440 mems; Pres. ASKO SAARELA; Gen. Sec. ARI MUHONEN.

Tekniska Föreningen i Finland (Engineering Society in Finland): Banvaktsg. 2A, 00520 Helsinki; tel. (9) 7184767; fax (9) 47677333; e-mail helpdesk@tfif.fi; internet www.tfif.fi; f. 1880; 4,300 mems; Chair. MIKAELA RUNEBERG; Man. Dir LARS ENGSTRÖM; publ. *Forum för ekonomi och teknik*.

Tietojenkäsittelytieteen Seura ry (Finnish Society for Computer Science): c/o Hannakaisa Isomäki, Univ. of Jyväskylä, Information Technology Research Institute, POB 35, 40014 Jyväskylä; tel. (14) 2603021; e-mail chairman@tkts.fi; internet www.tkts.fi; f. 1982; forum for researchers in the area of computer science; promotes computer science research, applications and the publ. of research results; arranges discussions and courses; nat. and int. cooperation; organizes annual computer science event; 420 mems; Chair. TARJA COURS; Vice-Pres. BARBRO BACK; Sec. HANNAKAISA ISOMÄKI; Treas. VILLE LEPPÄNEN; publ. *Tietojenkäsittelytiede*.

Research Institutes

GENERAL

Kuluttajatutkimuskeskus (National Consumer Research Centre): POB 5 (Kaikukatu 3), 00531 Helsinki; tel. (10) 6059000; fax (9) 8764374; internet www.kuluttajatutkimuskeskus.fi; f. 1990; investigates change and risk factors in consumer behaviours; Dir EILA KILPIÖ.

Suomen Akatemia (Academy of Finland): Vilhonvuorenkatu 6, POB 99, 00501 Helsinki; tel. (9)774881; fax (9)77488299; e-mail keskus@aka.fi; internet www.aka.fi; f. 1969; promotes and provides funding for research in Finland; 37 acad. professorships; library of 30,000 vols; Pres. MARKKU MATTILA; Dir of Admin. OSSI MALMBERG; Dir of Research RIITTA MUSTONEN.

AGRICULTURE, FISHERIES AND VETERINARY SCIENCE

Elintarviketurvallisuusvirsato—Evira (Finnish Food Safety Authority—Evira): Mustialankatu 3, 00790 Helsinki; tel. (20) 690999; fax (20) 7724350; e-mail info@evira.fi; internet www.evira.fi; food control supervision and guidance, laboratory operations, risk assessments and scientific research; Dir Gen. JAANA HUSU-KALLIO.

Maa-ja elintarviketalouden tutkimuskeskus (MTT Agrifood Research Finland): 31600 Jokioinen; tel. (3) 41881; fax (3) 41882222; internet www.mtt.fi; f. 1898; consists of 4 research units, 2 research programmes; Dir-Gen. Prof. ERKKI KEMPPAINEN; publs *Agricultural and Food Science* (Journal), *Finnish Agriculture and Rural Industries* (1 a year).

Research Units:

Kasvintuotannon tutkimus (Plant Production Research): 31600 Jokioinen; tel. (3) 41881; fax (3) 41882437; Dir Prof. AARNE KURPPA.

Kotieläintuotannon tutkimus (Animal Production Research): 31600 Jokioinen; tel. (3) 41881; fax (3) 41883661; Dir Dr TUOMO VARVIKKO.

Maatalousteknologian tutkimus (Agricultural Engineering Research): Vakolantie 55, 03400 Vihti; tel. (9) 224251; fax (9) 2246210; Dir Prof. HANNU HAAPALA.

MTT Biotekniikka-ja elintarviketutkimus (MTT Agrifood Research Finland, Biotechnology and Food Research): 31600 Jokioinen; tel. (3) 41881; fax (3) 41883244; Dir Dr EEVA-LIISA RYHÄNEN.

Taloustutkimus (Economic Research): Latokartanonkaari 9, 00790 Helsinki; tel. (20) 772004; fax (20) 772040; Dir Dr PASI RIKKONEN.

Ympäristöntutkimus (Environmental Research): Humppilantie 14, 31600 Jokioinen; tel. (3) 41881; fax (3) 41882222; Dir Prof. JYRKI AAKKULA.

Metsäntutkimuslaitos (Metla) (Finnish Forest Research Institute): Jokiniemenkuja 1, POB 18, 01301 Vantaa; tel. (10) 2111; fax (10) 2112103; e-mail kirjaamo@metla.fi; internet www.metla.fi; f. 1917; maintains 9 research units; library of 45,000 vols; Dir-Gen. HANNU RAITIO; publs *Finnish Forest Sector Economic Outlook* (1 a year), *Metla Bulletin* (online), *Metsätieteellinen aikakauskirja* (4 a year), *Metsätieteen aikakauskirja*, *Silva Fennica* (4 a year), *Working Papers of Metla* (online).

Riista ja Kalatalouden Tutkimuslaitos (Finnish Game and Fisheries Research Institute): Viikinkaari 4, POB 2, 00791 Helsinki; tel. (20) 57511; fax (20) 5751201; e-mail julkaisumyynti@rktl.fi; internet www.rktl.fi; f. 1971; assesses, forecasts and compiles statistics on fish and game resources; Dir-Gen. EERO HELLE.

Riista ja Kalatalouden Tutkimuslaitos (Finnish Game and Fisheries Research Institute): Viikinkaari 4, POB 2, 00791 Helsinki; tel. (20) 57511; fax (20) 5751201; e-mail julkaisumyynti@rktl.fi; internet www.rktl.fi; f. 1971; assesses, forecasts and compiles statistics on fish and game resources; Dir-Gen. EERO HELLE.

BIBLIOGRAPHY, LIBRARY SCIENCE AND MUSEOLOGY

Museovirasto (National Board of Antiquities): Nervanderinkatu 13, POB 913, 00101 Helsinki; tel. (9) 40501; fax (9) 40509300; internet www.nba.fi; f. 1884; directs and supervises Finland's admin. of antiquities; researches cultural heritage, preserves artefacts, buildings and sites of cultural and historical value; maintains the National Museum and other museums; closed for relocation; library of 180,000 vols with the Finnish Antiquarian Soc.; Dir-Gen. JUHANI KOSTET; Chief Librarian TUIJA SIIMES.

ECONOMICS, LAW AND POLITICS

Elinkeinoelämän Tutkimuslaitos (ETLA) (Research Institute of the Finnish Economy): Lönnrotinkatu 4B, 00120 Helsinki; tel. (9) 609900; fax (9) 601753; e-mail info@etla.fi; internet www.etla.fi; f. 1946; research in economics, business economics and social policy; 3 research units, 1 forecasting unit; Man. Dir Dr SIXTEN KORKMAN.

Tilastokeskus (Statistics Finland): 00022 Statistics Finland; tel. (9) 17341; fax (9) 17342750; e-mail kirjaamo@stat.fi; internet www.stat.fi; f. 1865; library: see Libraries and Archives; Dir-Gen. HELI JESKANEN-SUNDSTRÖM; publs *Bulletin of Statistics* (4 a year), *Official Statistics of Finland* (statistical publs on 26 subjects), *Statistical Yearbook of Finland* (1 a year).

Ulkopoliittinen Instituutti (The Finnish Institute of International Affairs): POB 400, 00161 Helsinki; Kruunuvuorenkatu 4, 00160 Helsinki; tel. (20) 6111700; fax (20) 6111799; e-mail kirjaamo@upi-fiia.fi; internet www.upi-fiia.fi; f. 1961; conducts research, organizes seminars, publishes reports on international relations and the EU; library of 21,300 vols, 250 periodicals; Dir RAIMO VÄYRYNEN; publ. *Ulkopolitiikka* (4 a year).

Valtion Taloudellinen Tutkimuskeskus (Government Institute for Economic Research): POB 1279, 00101 Helsinki; Arkadiankatu 7, 00101 Helsinki; tel. (40) 3045500; fax (9) 47802929; e-mail tietopalvelu@vatt.fi; internet www.vatt.fi; analyses public finances and evaluates economic reforms; Dir-Gen. SEIJA ILMAKUNNAS;

publ. *Finnish Economy—Structural Indicators* (1 in 2 years).

EDUCATION

Suomen Kasvatustieteellinen Seura/Samfundet för Pedagogisk Forskning (Finnish Educational Research Association): POB 35, 40014 Univ. of Jyväskylä; e-mail mailis.salo@jyu.fi; internet www.kasvatus .net; f. 1967; Chair. MARJATTA LAIRIO; Sec. JUHANI TÄHTINEN; publ. *Kasvatus* (5 a year).

MEDICINE

Minerva Foundation Institute for Medical Research: Biomedicum Helsinki 2U, Tukholmankatu 8, 00290 Helsinki; tel. (9) 19125700; fax (9) 19125701; e-mail dan .lindholm@helsinki.fi; internet www.helsinki .fi/minerva; f. 1959; non-profit org. owned by Minerva Foundation; basic and experimental biomedical, genetic and nutritional research; library of 4,000 vols; Chair. PER-HENRIK GROOP; Head of Inst. Prof. DAN LINDHOLM.

Terveyden ja Hyvinvoinnin Laitos (National Institute for Health and Welfare): POB 30, 00271 Helsinki; Mannerheimintie 166, 00271 Helsinki; tel. (20) 6106000; e-mail info@thl.fi; internet www.thl.fi; f. 2009 by merger of National Research and Development Centre for Welfare and Health and National Public Health Institute; statutory statistical authority in health and welfare; library of 35,000 vols, 300 journals, 7000 e-journals; Dir Gen. PEKKA PUSKA; Sec. AINO LEHIKOINEN; publs *Dialogi* (6 to 8 a year in Finnish; 1 a year in English), *Nordisk alkohol- & narkotikatidskrift* (Nordic Studies on Alcohol and Drugs), *Yhteiskuntapolitiikka*.

NATURAL SCIENCES

Physical Sciences

Geodeettinen Laitos/Geodetiska Institutet (Finnish Geodetic Institute): Geodeetinrinne 2, POB 15, 02431 Masala; tel. (9) 295550; fax (9) 29555200; e-mail kirjasto@fgi.fi; internet www.fgi.fi; f. 1918; 45 mems; library of 23,000 vols; Dir-Gen. Prof. Dr RISTO KUITTINEN; publs *Suomen geodeettisen laitoksen julkaisuja* (Publications of the Finnish Geodetic Institute), *Suomen geodeettisen laitoksen tiedonantoja* (Reports of the Finnish Geodetic Institute), *Tiedote*.

Geologian Tutkimuskeskus/Geologiska Forskningscentralen (Geological Survey of Finland): POB 96, Betonimiehenkuja 4, 02151 Espoo; tel. (20) 55011; fax (20) 55012; e-mail gtk@gtk.fi; internet www.gtk.fi; f. 1885; library of 152,000 vols; Dir-Gen. Dr ELIAS EKDAHL.

Ilmatieteen Laitos/Meteorologiska Institutet (Finnish Meteorological Institute): POB 503, Erik Palménin aukio 1, 00101 Helsinki; tel. (9) 19291; fax (9) 179581; internet www.fmi.fi; f. 1838; 10,000 offprints; library of 37,000 vols; Dir-Gen. Dr PETTERI TAALAS; Dir MIKKO ALESTALO; publ. *Suomen meteorologinen vuosikirja* (Meteorological Yearbook of Finland, in Finnish and English).

Merentutkimuslaitos (Finnish Institute of Marine Research): Lyypekinkuja 3A, POB 33, 00931 Helsinki; tel. (9) 613941; fax (9) 61394494; e-mail info@fimr.fi; internet www .fimr.fi; f. 1918; physical, chemical and biological oceanography, polar studies, Baltic Sea research; library of 55,000 vols; Dir-Gen. Prof. EEVA-LIISA POUTANEN (acting); publs *Contributions* (dissertations), *Meri* (report series).

Mittatekniikan Keskus (Centre for Metrology and Accreditation): Tekniikantie 1 POB 9, 02151 Espoo; tel. (10) 6054000; fax (10) 6054299; internet www.mikes.fi; SI system measurement units, metrological research, developing measuring applications; Dir-Gen. TIMO HIRVI.

Säteilyturvakeskus (STUK)/Strålsäkerhetscentralen (Radiation and Nuclear Safety Authority): Laippatie 4, POB 14, 00881 Helsinki; tel. (9) 759881; fax (9) 75988500; e-mail palaute@stuk.fi; internet www.stuk.fi; f. 1958; govt authority for radiation protection and nuclear safety, incl. inspection and research in the field; library of 30,000 vols; Dir-Gen. Prof. JUKKA LAAKSONEN; publs *Alara* (4 a year), *STUK-A Reports* (irregular).

Suomen Ympäristökeskus (Finnish Environment Institute): POB 140, 00251 Helsinki; Mechelininkatu 34A, Töölö, 00251 Helsinki; tel. (20) 610123; fax (9) 54902190; e-mail kirjaamo.syke@ymparisto.fi; internet www .environment.fi/syke; f. 1995; library of 60,000 vols, 14,000 electronic journals, 800 journals; Dir Gen. LEA KAUPPI; publ. *Ympäristö-lehti* (8 a year).

RELIGION, SOCIOLOGY AND ANTHROPOLOGY

Donnerska institutet för religionshistorisk och kulturhistoriskforskning/Steinerbiblioteket (Donner Institute for Research in Religious and Cultural History/Steiner Memorial Library): POB 70, 20501 Turku; tel. (20) 7861451; fax (2) 2311290; e-mail donner.institute@abo.fi; internet www .abo.fi/instut/di; f. 1959; promotes research in religious and cultural history; organizes Nordic conference on comparative religion every 3 years; library of 70,000 vols, 600 journals; Chair. Prof. ULRIKA WOLF-KNUTS; Sec. Dr TORE AHLBÄCK; publ. *Scripta Instituti Donneriani Aboensis* (conference papers, 5 a year).

Kotimaisten Kielten Tutkimuskeskus (Research Institute for the Languages of Finland): Vuorikatu 24, 00100 Helsinki; tel. (20) 7813200; fax (20) 7813219; internet www .kotus.fi; national research centre and expert institution for linguistic studies; library of 110,000 vols; 700 periodicals; Dir PIRKKO NUOLIJÄRVI; publs *Kielikello* (4 a year), *Språkbruk* (in Swedish).

TECHNOLOGY

VTT Technical Research Centre of Finland: Vuorimiehentie 5, POB 1000, 02044 VTT; tel. (20) 722111; fax (20) 7227001; e-mail info@vtt.fi; internet www.vtt.fi; f. 1942; largest multi-technological applied research org. in N Europe; provides research, development, testing and information services to the public sector, companies and int. orgs; technological focus areas are applied materials, biotechnology and chemistry processes, energy, information and communication technologies, industrial systems management, microtechnologies and electronics, and technology in the community; Chair. (vacant) ERKKI K. M. LEPPÄVUORI; Sec. ANNELI KARTTUNEN; publs *VTT Review, VTT Symposium, VTT Tiedotteita—Research Notes* (technology magazine), *VTT Impulse* (technology magazine).

Libraries and Archives

Aalto

Aalto-yliopiston Kirjasto (Aalto University Library): Otaniementie 9, POB 17000, 00076 Aalto; tel. (9) 47024111; fax (9) 47024132; e-mail infolib@aalto.fi; internet lib.tkk.fi/en/news/aalto; f. 1849; nat. resource library for technology; fmr Helsinki Univ. of Technology Library, now one of its units; libraries of Helsinki School of Economics, Univ.; of Art and Design and Helsinki Univ.; of Technology merged into its 3 campus libraries; 1m. vols, 5,000 periodicals on engineering and allied sciences, mathematics, environmental sciences, architecture, urban planning and industrial economy; online databases: index to Finnish technical periodical articles, Masters' theses in engineering and architecture, TKK Research Register, TKK Publs Register, TKK Expert Register; Chief Librarian Lic. Tech. ARI MUHONEN.

Åbo

Åbo Akademis Bibliotek (Åbo Akademi University Library): Tuomiokirkonkatu 2–4, 20500 Turku; tel. (2) 2154180; fax (2) 215479; e-mail biblioteket@abo.fi; internet www.abo .fi/library; f. 1919; 2m. vols (excluding pamphlets and MSS); Chief Librarian Dr PIA SÖDERGÅRD; publ. *Skrifter utgivna av Åbo Akademis bibliotek.*

Espoo

Espoon Kaupunginkirjasto/maakuntakirjasto (Espoo City Library/Regional Central Library): Kamreerintie 3C, POB 36, 02070 Espoo; tel. (9) 8165011; fax (9) 81657660; f. 1869; 1m. vols; spec. collns Uusimaa-Nylandica (provincial colln), Norwegian colln; 14 br. libraries, 2 in hospitals and instns, 2 mobile units; Chief Librarian ULLA PACKALÉN.

Helsinki

Celia: POB 20, 00030 IIRIS; Marjaniementie 74 (Iiris Centre), 2nd Fl., Helsinki; tel. (9) 229521; fax (9) 22952295; e-mail info@celialib .fi; internet www.celia.fi; f. 1890; state-owned specialist library; provides books for print-disabled people; 25,000 vols of talking books.

Deutsche Bibliothek (German Library): Pohjoinen Makasiinikatu 7, 00130 Helsinki; tel. (9) 669363; fax (9) 654010; e-mail deutsche.bibliothek@kolumbus.fi; internet www.deutsche-bibliothek.org; f. 1881; 36,000 vols; spec collns incl. Fennica colln; publ. *Jahrbuch für Englisch-deutsche Literaturbeziehungen* (1 a year).

Eduskunnan kirjasto (Library of Parliament): Aurorankatu 6, 00102 Helsinki; tel. (9) 4323432; fax (9) 4323495; e-mail library@parliament.fi; internet www.parliament.fi/library; f. 1872; 500,000 vols on parliamentary information, legal information, social and political information, admin.; the library is open to the public; reference and archival services, information service, interlibrary loans service, e-services, electronic resources, the Finnish parliamentary glossary, archive of parliament, parliamentary photographic archive, information management training; Dir SARI PAJULA; publs *Bibliographia Iuridica Fennica 1982–1993, Eduskunnan kirjaston tutkimuksia ja selvityksiä* (Library of Parliament Studies and Reports), *Valtion virallisjulkaisut* (Govt Publs in Finland, 1961–1996).

Helsingin Kaupunginkirjasto (Helsinki City Library): POB 4100, 0099 Helsinki; Rautatieläisenkatu 8, 00520 Helsinki; tel. (9) 3108511; fax (9) 31085517; e-mail city .library@hel.fi; internet www.lib.hel.fi; f. 1860; 36 br. libraries, 2 mobile libraries; total 1.9m. vols (1.3m. Finnish, 157,397 Swedish, 191,416 foreign), 208,961 sound recordings, 1,035 newspaper and journal titles; Dir MAIJA BERNDTSON; Chief Librarian KARI VANTE.

Helsingin Yliopiston Kirjasto (Helsinki University Library): POB 53 (Fabianinkatu 32), 00014 Univ. of Helsinki; tel. (9) 19123955; fax (9) 19122700; e-mail library@

helsinki.fi; internet www.helsinki.fi/library; 4 brs: City Centre campus, Kumpula campus, Viikki campus, Meilahti campus Library Terkko; became independent institute of Univ. in 2010; 2.3m. vols, 17,000 e-journals, 81 shelf kms, 260,000 e-books; Library Dir KAISA SINIKARA.

Helsingin Yliopiston Kirjasto, Slaavilainen Kirjasto (Helsinki University Library, Slavonic Library): POB 15 (Unioninkatu 36), 00014 Univ. of Helsinki; tel. (9) 19124066; fax (9) 19124067; e-mail kk-slav@helsinki.fi; internet www.lib.helsinki.fi/hyk/hul; the library held a legal deposit right to all publications printed in Russia from 1828–1917; now acquires available literature in arts and humanities in Slavonic languages; 450,000 vols; Librarian JARMO SUONSYRJÄ.

Kansallisarkisto (National Archives of Finland): Rauhankatu 17, POB 258, 00171 Helsinki; tel. (9) 228521; fax (9) 176302; e-mail kansallisarkisto@narc.fi; internet www.arkisto.fi; f. 1869; central office for public archives; controls seven Provincial Archives at Turku, Hämeenlinna, Mikkeli, Vaasa, Oulu, Jyväskylä and Joensuu; holds historical documents and archives of the Govt, Supreme Court and other court records, and private papers of statesmen and politicians; the Provincial Archives contain documents relating to regional and local admin; 88,070 vols, 100,913 m of shelvable archival material, 1,000,025 cartographical items; Dir-Gen. Dr JUSSI PEKKA NUORTEVA.

Attached Archive:

Helsingin Kaupunginarkisto (Helsinki City Archives): 53 Eläintarhantie, 3rd Fl., POB 5510, 00099 Helsinki; tel. (9) 31043571; fax (9) 31043814; e-mail kaupunginarkisto@hel.fi; internet www.hel2.fi/tietokeskus; f. 1945; central archive repository for City Admin.; private archives; Dir EEVA MIETTINEN.

Kansalliskirjasto (National Library of Finland): POB 15 (Unioninkatu 36), 00014 Univ. of Helsinki; tel. (9) 19123196; fax (9) 19122719; e-mail kk-palvelu@helsinki.fi; internet www.nationallibrary.fi; f. 1640 in Turku (Åbo), moved to Helsinki 1828; nat. library of Finland and research library of arts and humanities; comprehensive colln of books printed in Finland, large foreign colln, incl. the Slavonic library and the American resource center; Nordenskiöld colln (cartography), Finnish historical newspaper library, spec. collns; web archive, nat. electronic library; 3m. vols, 670,000 MSS, and 410 incunabula, 108,000 m of shelving; Dir Prof. KAI EKHOLM; publ. *The National Library of Finland Bulletin*.

Sibelius-Akatemian Kirjasto/Sibelius-Akademins bibliotek (Sibelius Academy Library): POB 86, 00251 Helsinki; Töölönkatu 28, 00260 Helsinki; tel. (40) 7104223; fax (20) 7539662; e-mail sibakirjasto@siba.fi; internet lib.siba.fi/eng; f. 1885; 72,000 items of sheet music, 34,000 audio recordings, 17,000 books, 800 video cassettes, collected works and anthologies; Head Librarian IRMELI KOSKIMIES.

Suomalaisen Kirjallisuuden Seuran Kirjasto (Library of the Finnish Literature Society): Hallituskatu 1, POB 259, 00171 Helsinki; tel. (20) 1131272; fax (9) 13123220; e-mail kirjasto@finlit.fi; internet www.finlit.fi; f. 1831; 235,000 vols on folklore, ethnology, cultural anthropology and Finnish literature; Chief Librarian Dr Phil. CECILIA AF FORSELLES.

Attached Libraries:

Suomalaisen Kirjallisuuden Seuran Kansanrunousarkisto (Folklore Archives of the Finnish Literature Society): Hallituskatu 1, POB 259, 00171 Helsinki; fax (9) 13123220; e-mail kansanrunousarkisto@finlit.fi; internet www.finlit.fi; f. 1934; 600 shelf m of MSS, audio recordings, video cassettes and photographs on Finnish folklore and oral history; Dir LAURI HARVILAHTI.

Suomalaisen Kirjallisuuden Seuran Kirjallisuusarkisto (Literary Archives of the Finnish Literature Society): Hallituskatu 1, POB 259, 00171 Helsinki; tel. (20) 1131260; fax (9) 13123268; e-mail kirjallisuusarkisto@finlit.fi; internet www.finlit.fi; f. 1831; 1,300 shelf m of MSS, correspondence, recordings and photographs on Finnish literature, history and language; Chief Archivist ULLA-MAIJA PELTONEN.

Hanken Svenska Handelshögskolans Bibliotek (Library of the Swedish School of Economics): Arkadiagatan 22, POB 479, 00101 Helsinki; tel. (40) 3521265; fax (9) 43133425; e-mail lanedisk@hanken.fi; internet www.hanken.fi/library; f. 1909; 100,000 vols; Library Dir TUA HINDERSSON-SÖDERHOLM.

Svenska litteratursällskapet i Finland, arkiv och bibliotek (Archives and library): Riddaregatan 5, 00170 Helsinki; tel. (9) 61877119; fax (9) 61877477; e-mail info@sls.fi; internet www.sls.fi; f. 1885; 2,200 collns, 300,000 photographs; Librarian MARTIN GINSTRÖM; publs *Folklivsstudier, Källan, Meddelanden från Folkkultursarkivet*.

Tilastokirjasto (Library of Statistics): POB 2B, Statistics Finland, Helsinki; Työpajankatu 13B, 2nd Fl., 00022 Helsinki; tel. (9) 17342220; fax (9) 17342279; e-mail library@stat.fi; internet www.stat.fi/library; f. 1865; service centre for Finnish and int. statistics; 330,000 vols, 2,509 periodicals, 35,000 microfiches, 1,064 electronic publs; Dir for Information Service HELI MIKKELÄ, SARI PALÉN; Sec. MINNA LEINONEN.

Joensuu

Joensuun seutukirjasto–Pohjois-Karjalan maakuntakirjasto (Joensuu Regional Library–Central Library of North Karelia): POB 114, Koskikatu 25, 80101 Joensuu; tel. (13) 2677111; fax (13) 267 6210; e-mail kirjasto@jns.fi; internet seutukirjasto.jns.fi; f. 1862; spec. colln of N Karelia; 500,000 vols; Dir of Libraries REBEKKA PILPPULA.

Joensuun yliopiston kirjasto (Joensuu University Library): Yliopistokatu 4, POB 107, 80100 Joensuu; tel. (13) 2512690; fax (13) 2512691; e-mail joyk@joensuu.fi; internet www.joensuu.fi/library/english; f. 1970 to become the Univ. of E Finland Library in 2010 by merger of Joensuu Campus Library, Kuopio Campus Library, Savonlinna Campus Library; deposit library; European Documentation Centre; 400,000 vols, 9,000 electronic journals; spec. colln on Kalevala; Library Dir HELENA HÄMYNEN.

Jokioinen

MTT (Maa ja elintarviketalouden tutkimuskeskus) kirjasto (MTT Agrifood Research Finland Library): M-Building, 2nd Fl., Data Path, 31600 Jokioinen; tel. (3) 41881; fax (3) 41882339; e-mail kirjasto@mtt.fi; internet www.mtt.fi; f. 1935; 80,000 vols, 600 periodicals; Information Specialists SIRPA SUONPÄÄ, NINA-MARI SALMINEN.

Jyväskylä

Jyväskylän Yliopiston Kirjasto (Jyväskylä University Library): POB 35 (Seminaarinkatu 15, Building B), 40014 Univ. of Jyväskylä; tel. (14) 2601211; fax (14) 2603371; e-mail jyk@library.jyu.fi; internet kirjasto.jyu.fi; f. 1912; depository library for Finnish prints and audiovisual material; European Documentation Centre for EU resources; nat. resource library for education, physical education and psychology; 1.7m. vols; 7,500 journals, 10,000 e-journals; Dir KIMMO TUOMINEN; publs *Jyväskylä Studies in Biological and Environmental Science, Jyväskylä Studies in Business and Economics, Jyväskylä Studies in Computing, Jyväskylä Studies in Education, Psychology and Social Research, Jyväskylä Studies in Humanities, Studies in Sport, Physical Education and Health*.

Kuopio

Kuopion kaupunginkirjasto–Pohjois-Savon maakuntakirjasto (Kuopio City Library—Northern Savo Regional Library): Maaherrankatu 12, POB 157, 70101 Kuopio; tel. (17) 182111; fax (17) 182340; e-mail kirjasto.kut@kuopio.fi; internet www.kuopio.fi/kirjasto; f. 1967; 700,000 vols; collns: letters of the author Minna Canth, Kuopio Lyceum colln, Iceland colln, North Saivo region colln; Library Dir. MARJA-TIITTANEN SAVOLAINEN; Chief Librarian HILKKA KOTILAINEN.

Itä-Suomen yliopiston kirjasto (University of Eastern Finland Library): Snellmania Yliopistonranta 1E, POB 1627, 70211 Kuopio; tel. (20) 7872001; fax (17) 163410; e-mail library@uef.fi; internet www.uef.fi/kirjasto/etusivu; f. 2010, merged with Joensuu and Kuopio University Libraries; 1,000,000 vols, 33 000 e-books, 600 printed journals, 19,250 e-journals; focused on health sciences, pharmacy, biosciences, environmental sciences, information technology, business, social sciences; 3 campus libraries in Joensuu, Kuopio and Savonlinna; Dir Dr JARMO SAARTI; Deputy Dir HELENA HÄMYNEN.

Varastokirjasto (National Repository Library): Päivärannantie 10, POB 1710, 70421 Kuopio; tel. (17) 2646000; fax (17) 3645050; e-mail varkirja@nrl.fi; internet www.varastokirjasto.fi; f. 1989; repository to be shared by all libraries in Finland; 1,300,000 vols, 80,000 periodicals, 500,000 dissertations; Dir PENTTI VATTULAINEN.

Oulu

Oulun yliopiston kirjasto (Oulu University Library): POB 7500, 90014 Univ. of Oulu; tel. (8) 5531011; fax (8) 5533572; e-mail kirjasto@oulu.fi; internet www.kirjasto.oulu.fi; f. 1959; depository library; European Documentation Centre; spec. collns incl. material concerning N and Arctic research; 1.7m. vols; Library Dir PÄIVI KYTÖMÄKI; publ. *Acta Universitatis Ouluensis*.

Pori

Porin kaupunginkirjasto–Satakunnan maakuntakirjasto (Pori City Library–Satakunta County Library): Gallen-Kallelankatu 12, POB 200, 28101 Pori; tel. (2) 6215800; fax (2) 6332582; e-mail kirjasto@pori.fi; internet www.pori.fi/kirjasto; f. 1858; centre of Hungarian literature; 506,339 vols; Librarian ASKO HURSTI.

Tampere

Tampereen kaupunginkirjasto–Pirkanmaan maakuntakirjasto (Tampere City Library–Pirkanmaa Regional Library): Pirkankatu 2, POB 152, 33101 Tampere; tel. (3) 565611; fax (3) 31464100; e-mail tampereen.kaupunginkirjasto@tt.tampere.fi; internet www.tampere.fi/kirjasto; f. 1861; spec. collns: Poland, Pirkanmaa region; 1.1m. vols, 300 newspapers, 2,700 periodicals, 120,000 items of audiovisual material, 20,000 microfilms; Dir of Libraries TUULA HAAVISTO.

Tampereen teknillisen yliopiston kirjasto (Tampere University of Technology

Library): Korkeakoulunkatu 10, POB 537, 33101 Tampere; tel. (3) 311511; fax (3) 31152907; e-mail kirjasto@tut.fi; internet www.tut.fi/library; f. 1956; 210,000 vols, 500 printed periodicals, 15,500 electronic journals, 122,000 e-books; Library Dir ARJA-RIITTA HAARALA.

Tampereen yliopistollisen sairaalan lääketieteellinen kirjasto (Medical Library of Tampere University Hospital): Box 2000, 33521 Tampere; fax (3) 2474364; e-mail kirjasto@pshp.fi; internet www.pshp.fi/kirjasto; f. 1962; 70,000 vols, 900 periodicals, 3,000 electronic journals; Librarian MERVI AHOLA.

Tampereen yliopiston kirjasto (Tampere University Library): Kalevantie 5, POB 617, 33014 Univ. of Tampere; tel. (40) 1909696; fax (3) 35517493; e-mail yliopiston.kirjasto@uta.fi; internet www.uta.fi/laitokset/kirjasto; f. 1925; 552,178 vols, 347,794 e-books, 31,012 e-journals; Chief Librarian Dr MIRJA IIVONEN; publ. *Bulletiini*.

Turku

Turun kauppakorkeakoulun kirjastotietopalvelu (Turku School of Economics, Library and Information Services): Rehtorinpellonkatu 3, 20500 Turku; tel. (2) 3339161; fax (2) 3338900; e-mail lainaus@tse.fi; internet www.tse.fi/kirjasto; f. 1950; 110,000 vols; Dir ULLA NYGRÉN.

Turun yliopiston kirjasto (Turku University Library): 20014 Univ. of Turku; tel. (2) 3336177; fax (2) 3335050; e-mail library@utu.fi; internet kirjasto.utu.fi; f. 1921; large colln of old Finnish literature; first European Documentation Centre of Finland; 2.8m. vols; Chief Librarian ULLA NYGRÉN; publ. *Annales Universitatis Turkuensis*.

Museums and Art Galleries

Helsinki

Amos Andersonin taidemuseo (Amos Anderson Art Museum): POB 14, 00101 Helsinki; Yrjönkatu 27, 00100 Helsinki; tel. (9) 6844460; fax (9) 68444622; e-mail museum@amosanderson.fi; internet www.amosanderson.fi; f. 1965; largest private art museum in Finland; collection of modern art; Dir KAI KARTIO.

Ateneumin Taidemuseo (Ateneum Art Museum): Kaivokatu 2, 00100 Helsinki; tel. (9) 173361; fax (9) 17336403; e-mail ainfo@ateneum.fi; internet www.ateneum.fi; f. 1888; Finnish art from mid-18th century to 1950s; international art; Dir MAIJA TANNINEN-MATTILA.

Designmuseo/Designmuseet (Design Museum): Korkeavuorenkatu 23, 00130 Helsinki; tel. (9) 6220540; fax (9) 62205455; e-mail info@designmuseum.fi; internet www.designmuseum.fi; f. 1873; specialist museum; exhibits of industrial design and handicrafts; library of 10,000 vols; Dir MARIANNE AAV.

Didrichsen Taidemuseo (Didrichsen Art Museum): Kuusilahdenkuja 1, 00340 Helsinki; tel. (9) 4778 330; fax (9) 489167; e-mail office@didrichsenmuseum.fi; internet www.didrichsenmuseum.fi; f. 1965; Finnish art from the 20th century; modern international art; oriental art and Finland's only pre-Columbian art colln; Dir PETER DIDRICHSEN.

Helsingin Kaupunginmuseoon/Helsingfors Stadsmuseum (Helsinki City Museum): Sofiankatu 4, POB 4300, 00099 Helsinki; tel. (9) 31036630; fax (9) 31036664; e-mail kaupunginmuseo@hel.fi; internet www.hel.fi/hki/museo/en/etusivu; f. 1911; cultural history museum; main exhibition on the history of Helsinki; spec. exhibitions to highlight various features of the city's past; colln of 200,000 objects; documentation and inventory pertaining to different eras; photographic archive with photographs from 1860s to the present; Helsinki landscape paintings and graphics; library of 15,000 vols; Dir TIINA MERISALO; publs *Memoria*, *Narinkka*, *Sofia* (2 a year).

Kiasma–Museum of Contemporary Art: Mannerheiminaukio 2, 00100 Helsinki; tel. (9) 173361; fax (9) 17336503; e-mail info@kiasma.fi; internet www.kiasma.fi; f. 1998; contemporary art; Dir PIRKKO SIITARI; publ. *Kiasma magazine*.

Luonnontieteellinen Keskusmuseo/Naturhistoriska Centralmuseet (Finnish Museum of Natural History): Pohjoinen, Rautatiekatu 13, POB 17, 00014 Univ. of Helsinki; tel. and fax (9) 1911; e-mail luonnontieteellinenmuseo@helsinki.fi; internet www.luomus.fi; f. 1925; Dir J. LOKKI; publs *Delectus Seminum* (every 2 years), *Lutukka* (4 a year), *Norrlinia*, *Sahlbergia* (2 a year).

Constituent Museums:

Eläinmuseo/Zoologiska Museet (Zoological Museum): P. Rautatiekatu 13, POB 17, 00014 Univ. of Helsinki; tel. (9) 19150034; fax (9) 19128888; e-mail luonnontieteellinenmuseo@helsinki.fi; Dir LEIF SCHULMAN.

Geologian Museo/Geologiska Museet (Geological Museum): Arkadiankatu 7, POB 11, 00014 Univ. of Helsinki; tel. (9) 19128745; fax (9) 19122925; e-mail luonnontieteellinenmuseo@helsinki.fi; Dir MARTTI LEHTINEN; Sr Curator Dr ARTO LUTTINEN.

Kasvimuseo/Botaniska Museet (Botanical Museum): Unioninkatu 44, POB 7, 00014 Univ. of Helsinki; tel. (9) 19124456; fax (9) 19124456; e-mail luonnontieteellinenmuseo@helsinki.fi; Dir PERTTI UOTILA.

Mannerheim-museo/Mannerheimmuseet (Mannerheim Museum): Kalliolinnantie 14, 00140 Helsinki; tel. (9) 635443; fax (9) 636736; e-mail info@mannerheim-museo.fi; internet www.mannerheim-museo.fi; f. 1951; fmr home of Baron G. Mannerheim (1867–1951), Marshal of Finland and Pres. of the Republic (1944–46): exhibitions relating to his life and to the history of Finland; Dir VERA VON FERSEN.

Postimuseo (Post Museum): POB 167, 00101 Helsinki; General Post Office, Asema-aukio 5H, 00101 Helsinki; tel. (40) 7556267; e-mail postimuseo@posti.fi; internet www.posti.fi/postimuseo; 6,000 artefacts, 30,000 photographs, 350,000 negatives and slides, 2,100 posters, 28,000 postcards, 1,500 video films; library of 27,000 vols; Dir PETTERI TAKKULA; publ. *Tabellarius* (1 a year).

Sinebrychoffin Taidemuseo (Sinebrychoff Art Museum): Bul. 40, 00120 Helsinki; tel. (9) 173361; fax (9) 17336476; e-mail leena.hannula@fng.fi; internet www.sinebrychoffintaidemuseo.fi; f. 1921; foreign art; 20 private collns; Dir ULLA HUHTAMÄKI.

Sotamuseo (Military Museum): Maurinkatu 1, POB 266, 00170 Helsinki; tel. (29) 9530241; fax (29) 9530262; e-mail sotamuseo@mil.fi; internet www.puolustusvoimat.fi; f. 1929; central museum of defence forces; over 200,000 artefacts and 200,000 photographs; Dir HARRI HUUSKO.

Suomen Kansallismuseo/Finlands Nationalmuseum (National Museum of Finland): POB 913, 00101 Helsinki; Mannerheimintie 34, 00100 Helsinki; tel. (9) 40509544; fax (9) 40509400; e-mail kansallismuseo@nba.fi; internet www.nba.fi/fi/skm; f. 1893; archaeology, history, ethnography, ethnology, numismatics; open-air museum at Seurasaari; Cygnaeus Gallery at Kaivopuisto, and several historical bldgs throughout Finland; Dir-Gen. Dr HELENA EDGREN.

Suomen Rakennustaiteen Museo (Museum of Finnish Architecture): Kasarmikatu 24, 00130 Helsinki; tel. (9) 85675100; fax (9) 85675101; e-mail mfa@mfa.fi; internet www.mfa.fi; f. 1956; nat. specialist museum; 500,000 drawings, 85,000 photographs, 30,000 pictures; library of 33,000 vols; Fennica colln 9,000 vols, 100 periodicals; Dir JUULIA KAUSTE.

Suomen Valokuvataiteen Museo (Finnish Museum of Photography): Tallberginkatu 1C 85, 00180 Helsinki; The Cable Factory, Tallberginkatu 1G, 00180 Helsinki; tel. (9) 6866360; fax (9) 68663630; e-mail fmp@fmp.fi; internet www.valokuvataiteenmuseo.fi; f. 1969; nat. specialist museum; 3.7m. prints and negatives; Dir ELINA HEIKKA.

Valtion Taidemuseo/Statens Konstmuseum (Finnish National Gallery): Kaivokatu 2, 00100 Helsinki; tel. (9) 173361; fax (9) 17336248; e-mail info@fng.fi; internet www.fng.fi; f. 1887 as the Ateneum, re-organized as the Finnish National Gallery in 1990; comprises Ateneum Art Museum, Museum of Contemporary Art Kiasma, Sinebrychoff Art Museum, Central Art Archives; library of 50,000 vols; Dir-Gen. RISTO RUOHONEN; Dir for Ateneum Art Museum MAIJA TANNINEN-MATTILA; Dir for Central Art Archives ULLA VIHANTA; Dir for Kiasma Museum of Contemporary Art PIRKKO SIITARI; Dir for Sinebrychoff Art Museum ULLA HUHTAMÄKI; Librarian IRMELI ISOMÄKI.

Hyvinkaa

Hyvinkää Taidemuseo (Hyvinkää Art Museum): Hämeenkatu 3D, 05800 Hyvinkää; tel. (40) 4801644; fax (19) 455930; e-mail taidemuseo@hyvinkaa.fi; internet www.hyvinkaantaidemuseo.fi; f. 1982; domestic and foreign contemporary art and art history; Dir RAISA LAURILA-HAKULINEN.

Suomen Rautatiemuseo (Finnish Railway Museum): Hyvinkäänkatu 9, 05800 Hyvinkää; tel. (30) 725241; fax (30) 725240; e-mail info@rautatie.org; internet www.rautatie.org; f. 1898; nat. specialist museum; 20,000 items, 150,000 photographs; library of 16,000 vols.

Jyvaskyla

Alvar Aalto Museo (Alvar Aalto Museum): POB 461, 40101 Jyväskylä; Alvar Aallon katu 7, 40600 Jyväskylä; tel. (14) 2667113; fax (14) 619009; e-mail museum@alvaraalto.fi; internet www.alvaraalto.fi; f. 1966; 1,600 objects; 120,000 drawings and sketches; 20,000 letters; 20,000 photographs; library of 3,000 vols; Dir SUSANNA PETTERSSON.

Jyväskylän Yliopiston Museo (Jyväskylä University Museum): POB 35, 40014 Jyväskylä; Seminaarinkatu 15 (C, Päärakennus), 40014 Jyväskylä; tel. (14) 2601211; fax (14) 2601021; internet www.jyu.fi/erillis/museo; f. 1900; collects, preserves, researches and exhibits material related to univ. history; Dir JANNE VILKUNA.

Kuopio

Kuopion Taidemuseo (Kuopio Art Museum): Kauppakatu 35, 70100 Kuopio; tel. (17) 182633; fax (17) 182642; e-mail taidemuseo.kut@kuopio.fi; internet www.taidemuseo.kuopio.fi; f. 1980; Finnish art from end of 19th century; emphasis on local painters; theme is nature and environment; Dir AIJA JAATINEN.

Oulu

Pohjois-Pohjanmaan Museo (Northern Ostrobothnia Museum): Ainolan Puisto, POB 26, 90015 Oulu; tel. (8) 55847161; fax (8) 55847199; e-mail ppm@ouka.fi; internet www.ouka.fi/ppm; f. 1896; specializes in historical-ethnological research on northern Ostrobothnia; Dir PASI KOVALAINEN.

Parola

Pansasarimuseo (Tank Museum): POB 31, 13721 Parola; Hattulantie 334, 13720 Parola; tel. (40) 5681186; fax (3) 18144522; e-mail toimisto@panssarimuseo.fi; internet www .panssarimuseo.fi; f. 1961; military historical museum; Dir TIMO TERÄSVALLI; publ. *Armour Magazine*.

Pori

Porin Taidemuseo (Pori Art Museum): Eteläranta, 28100 Pori; tel. (2) 6211080; fax (2) 6211091; e-mail taidemuseo@pori.fi; internet www.poriartmuseum.fi; f. 1981; 2,800 works of Finnish art and int. contemporary art; library of 2,711 vols, 6,166 exhibition catalogues; Dir ESKO NUMMELIN.

Satakunta Museo (Satakunta Museum): Hallituskatu 11, 28100 Pori; tel. (2) 6211078; fax (2) 6211061; e-mail satakunnanmuseo@pori.fi; internet www .pori.fi/smu; f. 1888; 80,000 archaeological and historical exhibits; 300,000 photographs relating to the history of Satakunta province; library of 13,115 vols in reference library and 9,228 old books; Dir JUHANI RUOHONEN; publ. *Sarka* (1 a year).

Pietarsaari

Nanoq-museon (Arctic Museum Nanoq): Pörkenäsintie 60, 68620 Pietarsaari; tel. (6) 7293679; fax (6) 7293679; e-mail info@nanoq .fi; internet www.nanoq.fi; f. 1991; Arctic people and cultures; Dir PENTTI KRONQVIST.

Rauma

Lönnströmin Taidemuseo (Lönnström Art Museum): Valtakatu 7, 26100 Rauma; tel. (2) 83874700; fax (2) 83874742; internet www .lonnstromintaidemuseo.fi; f. 1993; contemporary and traditional art; Dir SELMA GREEN.

Riihimaki

Riihimäen Taidemuseo (Riihimäki Art Museum): Temppelikatu 8, 11100 Riihimäki; tel. (19) 7584124; fax (19) 7584126; e-mail riihimaen.taidemuseo@riihimaki.fi; internet www.riihimaki.fi/riihimaki/taidemuseo; f. 1994; Finnish art; foreign art; antiquities; Curator SOILE HAAPALA.

Tampere

Sara Hildénin Taidemuseo (Sara Hildén Art Museum): Laiturikatu 13, Särkänniemi, 33230 Tampere; tel. (3) 56543500; e-mail sara.hilden@tampere.fi; internet www .tampere.fi/sarahilden; f. 1979; exhibition centre for the works of the Sara Hildén Foundation collection (f. 1962 when Sara Hildén donated all her art works to it); 4,500 collns, modern art, with emphasis on Finnish and foreign art of the 1960s and 1970s; library of 9,000 vols; Dir RIITTA VALORINTA.

Tampereen Museot (Tampere Museums): POB 487, 33101 Tampere; tel. (3) 56566966; fax (3) 56566808; e-mail vapriikki@tampere .fi; internet www.tampere.fi/vapriikki; Dir TOIMI JAATINEN.

Component Museums:

Amurin Työläismuseokortteli (Amuri Museum of Workers' Housing): Satakunnankatu 49, 33210 Tampere; f. 1974; the devt of workers' housing 1880–1970, with authentic buildings; Dir TOIMI JAATINEN.

Hämeen Museo (Häme Museum): POB 487, 33101 Tampere; tel. (3) 31465306; f. 1904; prehistory and folk art of the cultural district of Tampere and the old Häme province; closed for renovation during 2010.

Tampereen Taidemuseo (Tampere Art Museum): Puutarhakatu 34, POB 487, 33101 Tampere; tel. (3) 56566577; fax (3) 56566584; e-mail tamu@tampere.fi; internet www.tampere.fi/taidemuseo; f. 1931; 7,000 works; Finnish art since early 19th century; Dir TAINA MYLLYHARJU.

Attached Museum:

Moominvalley of the Tampere Art Museum: Hämeenpuisto 20, POB 487, 33101 Tampere; tel. (3) 56566578; fax (3) 56566567; e-mail muumi@tampere.fi; internet www.inter9.tampere.fi/ muumilaakso; f. 1987; based on the Moomin books by Tove Jansson; 2,000 works.

Turku

Aboa Vetus & Ars Nova Museum: Itäinen Rantakatu 4–6, 20700 Turku; tel. (20) 7181640; e-mail info@aboavetusarsnova.fi; internet www.aboavetusarsnova.fi; f. 1991; private museum; focuses on Finnish middle ages and contemporary art; Dir JOHANNA LEHTO-VAHTERA; publ. *Aboa Vetus & Ars Nova Magazine*.

Sibeliusmuseum/Sibelius-museo (Sibelius Museum): Biskopsgatan 17, 20500 Turku; tel. (2) 2154494; fax 3(2) 2518528; e-mail sibeliusmuseum@abo.fi; internet www .sibeliusmuseum.abo.fi; f. 1926; archive and library, instrument colln and an exhibition section; archives and library contain material related to Jean Sibelius and Finnish music; instrument colln includes 1,800 musical instruments; associated with the musicological research department of Åbo Akademi Univ.; Dir and Curator Dr INGER JAKOBSSON-WÄRN.

Turun Maakuntamuseo/Åbo Landskapsmuseum (Turku Provincial Museum): POB 286, 20101 Turku; tel. (2) 330000; fax (2) 2620444; e-mail museokeskus@turku.fi; internet www.turku.fi/museo; f. 1881; consists of the Castle of Turku with the collns of Turku Historical Museum, Luostarinmäki Handicrafts Museum, Pharmacy Museum and the Qwensel House, Kylämäki Village of living history, Turku Biological Museum, furniture, paintings, costumes, textiles, porcelain, glass, silver, copper, firearms, uniforms, weapons, coins and medals, etc.; Dir IMMONEN OLLI; publs *Aboa* (yearbook), *Raportteja* (Studies).

Turun Taidemuseo/Åbo Konstmuseum (Turku Art Museum): Aurakatu 26, 20100 Turku; tel. (2) 2627100; fax (2) 2627090; e-mail info@turuntaidemuseo.fi; internet www.turuntaidemuseo.fi; f. 1891; 6,000 works of art; paintings, sculpture, prints and drawings, mainly of Finnish and Scandinavian art since early 19th century; Pres. ROGER BROO; Dir KARI IMMONEN.

Wäinö Aaltosen Museo (Wäinö Aaltonen Museum of Art): Itäinen Rantakatu 38, 20810 Turku; tel. (2) 2620850; fax (2) 2620862; e-mail wam@turku.fi; internet www.wam.fi; f. 1967; Waino Aalto's work; recent focus on sculpture; library of 8,000 works collected by Waino Aalto; Dir OLLI IMMONEN.

Universities

AALTO-YLIOPISTO
(Aalto University)

POB 11000, 00076 Aalto

Telephone: (9) 47001
E-mail: viestinta@aalto.fi
Internet: www.aalto.fi

Founded 2010 by merger of Helsingin kauppakorkeakoulu (f. 1911), Teknillinen korkeakoulu (f. 1908), Taideteollinen korkeakoulu (f. 1871)

Languages of instruction: Finnish, Swedish, English

Academic year: September to May

Pres.: TUULA TEERI
Vice-Pres.: HANNU SERISTÖ
Vice-Pres.: HEIKKI MANNILA
Vice-Pres.: JORMA KYYRÄ
Vice-Pres.: MARTTI RAEVAARA
Librarian: ARI MUHONEN

Number of teachers: 932
Number of students: 19,743

DEANS

School of Art and Design: HELENA HYVÖNEN
School of Economics: EERO KASANEN
School of Science and Technology: MATTI PURSULA

PROFESSORS

School of Art and Design:

CEDERSTRÖM, E., Motion Picture, Documentary
DEAN, P., New Media
DIAZ-KOMMONEN, L., New Media, Design for Systems of Representations
GRÖNDAHL, L., Scenography, Stage Design
HAKURI, M., Environmental Art
HEIKKILÄ, S., Furniture Design
HEINÄNEN, T., Motion Picture, Filming
HIRVONEN, P., Fashion Design
HYVÖNEN, H., Textile Design
ITKONEN-TOMASZEWSKI, L., Graphic Design
JACUCCI, G., Industrial Design
JULIN-ARO, J., Functional Materials and Design
KÄÄRIÄINEN, P., Textile Design
KAREOJA, P., Spatial Design
KEINONEN, T., Industrial and Strategic Design
KELLY, P., International Design and Production
KORVENMAA, P., Design and Culture
KOSKINEN, I., Industrial and Strategic Design
KUPIAINEN, R., Visual Culture, Theory
LAAKSO, H., Visual Culture
LAKANEN, A., Motion Picture, Editing
LAMPELA, J., Motion Picture, Directing
LEINONEN, T., New Media
LEVANTO, I., Art History
McGRORY, P., Industrial and Strategic Design
MÄENPÄÄ, M., Media Production
MAJA, A., Scenography, Film and Television
MÄKI, T., Fine Arts
MIETTINEN, E., Industrial Design
NIEMINEN, E., Design, Material Research
NIKKANEN, R., Industrial Design
PARANTAINEN, J., Photography
POHJAKALLIO-KOSKINEN, P., Art Pedagogy
PRIHA, P., Textile Design
RAEVAARA, M., Art Education, Visual Knowledge Building
RITALAHTI, R., Motion Picture, Production
RYYNÄNEN, M., Visual Culture, Theory
SALLI, T., Product Design
SALO, M., Photography
SEDERHOLM, M., Art Education
SONVILLA-WEISS, S., e-Pedagogy Design, Visual Knowledge Building
SOTAMAA, Y., Design and Innovation

SUOMINEN, J., Mass Customization in Design

TÖYRY, M., Journalism

VAPAASALO, T., Graphic Design and Communication

VARTO, J., Art Education, Research

VIENO, J., Motion Picture, Screenwriting

VIHMA, S., Design Semiotics

VON BAGH, P., Motion Picture, History and Theory

YLI-VIIKARI, T., Ceramics Design

School of Economics:

AHTOLA, O., Marketing

ANTTILA, M., Marketing

DEB, K., Quantitative Methods in Economics and Management Science

HAAPARANTA, P., Economics

HALME, M., Management Science

HALME, M., Organization and Management

HOPPU, K., Business Law

IKÄHEIMO, S., Accounting

ILMAKUNNAS, P., Economics

KAKKURI-KNUUTTILA, M., Organization and Management

KALLIO, M., Management Science

KASANEN, E., Finance

KELOHARJU, M., Finance

KEMPPAINEN, K., Logistics

KINNUNEN, J., Accounting

KIVIJÄRVI, H., Information Systems Science

KORHONEN, P., Quantitative Methods in Economics and Management Science

KUOSMANEN, T., Quantitative Methods in Economics and Management Science

KUULA, M., Logistics

KYRÖ, P., Entrepreneurship

LAHTI, A., Entrepreneurship

LILJA, K., Organization and Management

LINDBLOM, A., Marketing

LISKI, M., Economics

LOVIO, R., Organization and Management

MALMI, T., Accounting

MOISANDER, J., Communications

MÖLLER, K., Marketing

NISKAKANGAS, H., Business Law

PARVINEN, P., Marketing

PIEKKARI, R., International Business

POHJOLA, M., Economics

PUTTONEN, V., Finance

RÄSÄNEN, K., Organization and Management

ROSSI, M., Information Systems Science

RUDANKO, M., Business Law

SAARINEN, T., Information Systems Science

SALMI, A., International Business

SUOMINEN, M., Finance

TAINIO, R., Organization and Management

TERVIÖ, M., Economics

TIKKANEN, H., Marketing

TORSTILA, S., Finance

TROBERG, P., Accounting

TUUNAINEN, V., Information Systems Science

VAIVIO, J., Accounting

VÄLIKANGAS, L., Organization and Management

VÄLIMÄKI, J., Economics

VEPSÄLÄINEN, A., Logistics

WALLENIUS, J., Management Science

School of Science and Technology

Faculty of Chemistry and Materials Sciences:

ALOPAEUS, V., Chemical Engineering and Plant Design

DAHL, O., Chemical Pulping and Environmental Technology

FORSEN, O., Laboratory of Corrosion and Material Chemistry

FRANSSILA, S., Materials science

GANE, P., Paper Technology

GASIK, M., Materials Processing and Powder Metallurgy

HANNULA, S., Processing and Heat Treatment of Materials

HEISKANEN, K., Mechanical Process and Recycling Technology

HUGHHES, M., Wood Technology

HURME, M., Chemical Engineering and Plant Design

JÄMSÄ-JOUNELA, S., Laboratory of Process Control and Automation

JOKELA, R., Laboratory of Organic Chemistry

KAIRI, M., Wood Technology

KARPPINEN, M., Laboratory of Inorganic and Analytical Chemistry

KIVIVUORI, S., Processing and Heat Treatment of Materials

KONTTURI, K., Laboratory of Physical Chemistry

KORHONEN, A., Department of Materials Science and Engineering

KOSKINEN, A., Laboratory of Organic Chemistry

KOSKINEN, J., Department of Materials Science and Engineering

KRAUSE, O., Laboratory of Industrial Chemistry

KULMALA, S., Laboratory of Inorganic and Analytical Chemistry

LAAKSO, S., Laboratory of Biochemistry

LAINE, J., Forest Products Chemistry

LEISOLA, M., Laboratory of Bioprocess engineering

MALONEY, T., Paper Technology

NORDSTRÖM, K., Laboratory of Biochemistry and Microbiology

PALTAKARI, J., Wood Technology

PAULAPURO, H., Paper Technology

ROJAS, O.

SEPPÄLÄ, J., Laboratory of Polymer Technology

SIXTA, H., Chemical Pulping and Wood Refinery

TASKINEN, P., Department of Materials Science and Engineering

VAN HEININGEN, A., Forest Products Chemistry

VIITANIEMI, P., Wood Technology

VUORINEN, T., Forest Products Chemistry

WINTER, S.

YAMAUCHI, H.

Faculty of Electronics, Communications and Automation:

AALTO, S., Teletraffic Theory

ALKU, P., Acoustics and Audio Signal Processing

ARKKIO, A., Electromechanics

ARO, M., Power Systems and High Voltage Engineering

ESKELINEN, P., Radio Science and Engineering

HAARLA, L., Electromechanics

HÄGGMAN, S., Communications and Networking

HALLIKAINEN, M., Space Technology

HALME, A., Automation Technology

HALONEN, K., Electronic Circuit Design

HALONEN, L., Lighting Technology

HÄMMÄINEN, H., Communications and Networking

HONKANEN, S., Photonics, Micro and Nano sciences

IKONEN, E., Metrology Research Institute

KANTOLA, R., Communications and Networking

KARJALAINEN, M., Acoustics and Audio Signal Processing

KOIVO, H., Systems Technology

KOIVUNEN, V., Signal Processing

KUIVALAINEN, P., Electron Physics

KYYRÄ, J., Power Systems and High Voltage Engineering

LAINE, U., Acoustics and Audio Signal Processing

LEHTONEN, M., Power Systems and High Voltage

LIPSANEN, H., Nanotechnology

LUOMI, J., Electromagnetic

NIKOSKINEN, K., Electromagnetics

ÖSTERGÅRD, P., Information Theory, Discrete Mathematics and Algorithms

OVASKA, S., Power Electronics

PAKANEN, J., Lighting Technology

PAULASTO-KRÖCKEL, M., Electronics

RÄISÄNEN, A., Radio Science and Engineering

RICHTER, A., Signal processing

RYYNÄNEN, J., Electronic Circuit Design

SEPPONEN, R., Applied Electronics

SIHVOLA, A., Electromagnetic

SIMOVSKI, C., Radio Science and Engineering

SKYTTÄ, J., Signal Processing

TIRKKONEN, O., Communications and Networking

TITTONEN, I., Metrology Research Institute

TRETYAKOV, S., Radio Science

VAINIKAINEN, P., Radio Science

VÄLIMÄKI, V., Acoustics and Audio Signal Processing

VALTONEN, M., Circuit Theory

WICHMAN, R., Signal Processing

Faculty of Engineering and Architecture:

AALTO, J., Structural Mechanics

AALTONEN, K., Production Engineering

ACHE, P., Urban and Regional Planning

AHTILA, P., Energy Economics and Power Plant Engineering

AIRILA, M., Machine Design

EKMAN, K., Machine Design

EKROOS, A., Law

ERNVALL, T., Transportation Engineering

FOGELHOLM, C., Energy Engineering and Environmental Protection

HAGGREN, H., Photogrammetry and Remote Sensing

HÄKKINEN, P., Ship Laboratory

HÄNNINEN, H., Engineering Materials

HARRIS, T., Urban Design

HEDMAN, M., Architecture

HEIKKINEN, P., Wood Program

HUOVINEN, S., Structural Engineering and Building Physics

JOLMA, A., Cartography and Geoinformatics

JUHALA, M., Automotive Engineering

JUTILA, A., Bridge Engineering

KAILA, J., Waste Management Technology

KANKAINEN, J., Construction Economics and Management

KARVONEN, T., Water Resources

KIIRAS, J., Construction Economics and Management

KOMONEN, M., Public Building Design

KUOSMANEN, P., Machine Design

LAMPINEN, M., Applied Thermodynamics

LAPINTIE, K., Urban and regional planning

LARMI, M., Internal Combustion Engine Laboratory

LEVÄINEN, K., Real Estate Studies

LOUKOLA-RUSKEENIEMI, K., Rock Engineering

LUTTINEN, T., Transportation Engineering

MÄKELÄINEN, P., Steel Structures

MATUSIAK, J., Ship Laboratory

NISKANEN, A., History of Architecture

NYKÄNEN, P., Industrial History

ORKAS, J., Foundry Engineering

PAAVILAINEN, S., Basics and Theory of Architecture

PAAVOLA, J., Structural mechanics

PELLINEN, T., Highway Engineering

PELTONIEMI, M., Rock Engineering

PENTTALA, V., Building Materials Technology

PIETOLA, M., Machine Design

PIRILÄ, P., Energy Economics and Power Plant Engineering

PURSULA, M., Transportation Engineering

PUTTONEN, J.

RAUTAMÄKI, M., Landscape Planning

RAVASKA, O., Soil Mechanics and Foundation Engineering

SAARELA, O., Aeronautical Engineering
SÄRKKÄ, P., Rock Engineering
SEPPÄNEN, O., Heating Ventilating and Air-Conditioning
SIIKALA, A., Building Technology
SIIKONEN, T., Applied Thermodynamics
SIITONEN, T., Housing design
SIREN, K., Heating Ventilating and Air-Conditioning
SOINNE, E., Aeronautical Engineering
TALVITIE, A.
TUHKURI, J., Mechanics of Materials
VAHALA, R., Water and Wastewater Engineering
VAKKILAINEN, P., Water Resources Engineering
VARSTA, P., Ship Laboratory
VEPSÄLÄINEN, P., Soil Mechanics and Foundation Engineering
VERMEER, M., Geodesy
VIITANEN, K., Real Estate Studies
VILJANEN, M., Structural Engineering and Building Physics
VIRRANTAUS, K., Cartography and Geoinformatics
VITIKAINEN, A., Real Estate Studies
WECK, T., Building Structures

Faculty of Information and Natural Sciences:
ALA-NISSILÄ, T., Physics
ALAVA, M., Physics
ARTTO, K., Industrial Management
AURA, T., Media Technology
AURELL, E., Information and Computer Science
AUTERE, J., Software Business
EHTAMO, H., System Analysis
EIROLA, T., Mathematics
ELORANTA, E., Industrial Management
FRIBERG, A., Optical Physics
GRIPENBERG, G., Mathematics
HÄMÄLÄINEN, M., Computer and Information Science
HÄMÄLÄINEN, R., Applied Mathematics
HELJANKO, K., Information and Computer Science
HOLMSTRÖM, J., Industrial Management
HYVÖNEN, E., Media Technology
IKKALA, O., Applied Physics
ILMONIEMI, R., Applied Physics
JÄÄSKELÄINEN, I., Cognitive Systems
JAATINEN, M., Business Processes and Services in Digital Networks
JÄRVENPÄÄ, E., Work Psychology and Leadership
JÄRVENPÄÄ, S., Networked Business Processes and Business Models
JAUHO, A., Applied Physics
KAIVOLA, M., Applied Physics
KARHUNEN, J., Information and Computer Science
KASKI, K., Computational Engineering
KASKI, S., Information and Computer Science
KAUPPINEN, E., Physics
KAUPPINEN, M., Software Business
KAURANEN, I., Development and Management in Industry
KEIL, T., Strategic Management
KERTÉSZ, J., Computational Complex Systems
KINNUNEN, J., Mathematics
KOSKELAINEN, A., Applied Physics
LAAMANEN, T., Strategic Management
LÄHDESMÄKI, H., Information and Computer Science
LAINE, J., Software Business
LAMBERG, J., Strategic Management
LAMPINEN, J., Computational Engineering
LASSENIUS, C., Computer Science
LILLRANK, P., Quality Management
LIPPONEN, J., Work Psychology and Leadership
LUND, P., Applied Physics
MALMI, L., Information Processing Science

MANNILA, H., Information and Computer Science
MÄNNISTÖ, T., Software Business
MÄNTYLÄ, M., Computer and Information Science
MAULA, M., Venture Capital
MERILÄINEN, P., Applied Physics
NEVANLINNA, O., Mathematics
NIEMELÄ, I., Information and Computer Science
NIEMINEN, M., Software Business and Engineering
NIEMINEN, R., Physics
NYBERG, K., Information and Computer Science
OITTINEN, P., Media Technology
OJA, E., Information and Computer Science
ORPONEN, P., Information and Computer Science
PITKÄRANTA, J., Mathematics
PUOLAMÄKI, K., Virtual Techniques
PUSKA, M., Physics
RAUSCHECKER, J., Systems Neuroscience
RUOKOLAINEN, J., Applied Physics
SAARINEN, E., System Analysis
SAIKKONEN, H., Computer Science and Engineering
SALO, A., System Analysis
SALOMAA, R., Applied Physics
SAMS, M., Cognitive Systems
SAVIOJA, L., Media Technology
SIMULA, O., Information and Computer Science
SMEDS, R., Business and Service Processes in Digital Networks
SOISALON-SOININEN, E., Software Technology
STENBERG, R., Mechanics
SULONEN, R., Software Business and Engineering
TAKALA, T., Telecommunication Software and Multimedia
TANSKANEN, K., Logistics
TARHIO, J., Information Processing Science
TÖRMÄ, P., Applied Physics
TULKKI, J., Computational Science
VALKEILA, E., Mathematics
VAN DIJKEN, S., Physics
VARTIAINEN, M., Work Psychology and Leadership
VUORIMAA, P., Multimedia Technology
WALLENIUS, H., Economics
YLÄ-JÄÄSKI, A., Telecommunications Software and Multimedia

ÅBO AKADEMI
(Åbo Akademi University)

Tuomiokirkontori 3, 20500 Turku
Telephone: (2) 21531
Fax: (2) 2517553
Internet: www.abo.fi

Founded 1918
Language of instruction: Swedish
State control
Academic year: September to May
Chancellor: JARL-THURE ERIKSSON
Rector: JORMA MATTINEN
Vice-Rector: CHRISTINA NYGREN-LANDGÄRDS
Second Vice-Rector: KAISA SERE
Third Vice-Rector: MALIN BRÄNNBACK
Head of Admin.: ULLA ACHRÉN
Chief Librarian: PIA SÖDERGÅRD

Number of teachers: 360
Number of students: 7,000
Publications: *Årsberättelse* (Annual Review), *Acta Academiae Aboensis*

DEANS

Faculty of Arts: Prof. ULRIKA WOLF-KNUTS
Faculty of Chemical Engineering: Prof. TAPIO SALMI

Faculty of Education: Prof. ANNA-LENA ØSTERN
Faculty of Theology: Prof. I. DAHLBACKA
School of Business and Economics: Prof. JAN-ÅKE TÖRNROOS

PROFESSORS

Department of Biosciences:
BONSDORFF, E., Marine Ecology
ERIKSSON, J., Cell Biology
JOHNSON, M., Biochemistry
LINDSTRÖM, K., Ecology and Environmental Biology
SISTONEN, L., Cell and Molecular Biology
SLOTTE, J. P., Biochemistry
TÖRNQUIST, K., Biology
VUORELA, P., Pharmacy

Department of Chemical Engineering:
FARDIM, P., Fibre and Cellulose Technology
FAGERVIK, K., Chemical Engineering
HUPA, M., Inorganic Chemistry
IVASKA, A., Analytical Chemistry
LEWENSTAM, A., Analytical Chemistry
MIKKOLA, J-P., Industrial Chemistry and Reaction Engineering
MURZIN, D., Industrial Chemistry and Reaction Engineering
PELTONEN, J., Paper Coating and Converting
SALMI, T., Industrial Chemistry and Reaction Engineering
SAXÉN, H., Thermal and Flow Engineering
TOIVAKKA, M., Paper Coating and Converting
WÄRNÅ, J., Industrial Chemistry and Reaction Engineering
WESTERLUND, T., Process Design and Systems Engineering
WIKSTRÖM, K., Industrial Management
WILÉN, C.-E., Polymer Technology
WILLFÖR, S., Wood and Paper Chemistry
ZEVENHOVEN, R., Thermal and Flow Engineering

Department of Information Technologies:
BACK, B., Information Systems
BACK, R.-J., Computer Science
CARLSSON, C., Information Systems
LILIUS, J., Computer Engineering
PETRE, I., Computer Science
PORRES PALTOR, I., Computer Engineering
SERE, K., Computer Science
TOIVONEN, H., Computer Engineering
WALDEN, P., Information Systems
WESTERHOLM, J., Computer Engineering

Department of Natural Sciences:
CORANDER, J., Mathematics and Statistics
EHLERS, C., Geology and Mineralogy
HÖGNÄS, G., Mathematics
HOTOKKA, M., Physical Chemistry
LEINO, R., Organic Chemistry
LINDBERG, M., Physics
SALMINEN, P., Mathematics
SJÖHOLM, R., Organic Chemistry
STAFFANS, O., Mathematics
ÖSTERBACKA, R., Physics

Department of Law:
HONKA, H., Commercial Law
PIRJATANNIEMI, E., Public International Law
SUKSI, M., Public Law
WETTERSTEIN, P., Private Law

Department of Political Science:
ANCKAR, C., Political Science
DJUPSUND, G., Political Science
JOAS, M., Public Administration
KARVONEN, L., Political Science

Department of Psychology and Logopedics:
LAINE, M., Psychology
SANDNABBA, K., Psychology
SANTTILA, P., Psychology
TUOMAINEN, J., Logopedics

Department of Social Sciences:
BJÖRKQVIST, K., Developmental Psychology
EKLUND, E., Rural Studies
ERIKSSON, K., Caring Science
FINNÄS, F., Demograhy
HURME, H., Developmental Psychology
JAKOBSSON, G., Social Policy
LINDSTRÖM, U., Caring Science
LAGERSPETZ, M., Sociology
SILIUS, H., Women's Studies
SUNDBACK, P., Sociology

Faculty of Arts:
AHLUND, C., Comparative Literature
ANDERSSON, E., Swedish Language
ÅSTROM, A.-M., Nordic Ethnology
BERGGREN, L., Art History
BRUSILA, J., Musicology
GUSTAFSSON, M., Philosophy
HAAPAMÄKI, S., Swedish Language
LARJAVAARA, M., French Language and
  Literature
LÖNNQVIST, B., Russian Language and Lit-
  erature
NIKANNE, U., Finnish Language and Lit-
  erature
NEUENDORFF, D., German Language
NYNÄS, P., Comparative Religion
RINGBOM, A., Art History
SELL, R., English Language and Literature
VILLSTRAND, N. E., Nordic History
VIRTANEN-ULFHIELM, T., English Language
WOLF-KNUTS, U., Nordic Folklore

Faculty of Education:
BJÖRKQVIST, O., Didactics of Mathematics
  and Sciences
GRÖNHOLM, M., Didactics of Languages and
  the Humanities
ITKONEN, T., Special Education
LINDAHL, M., Early Childhood Education
NYGREN-LANDGÅRDS, C., Pedagogics in
  Sloyd Education
SALO, P., Adult Education
SJÖHOLM, K., Didactics of Languages and
  the Humanities
ULJENS, N., General Education

Faculty of Theology:
AF HÄLLSTRÖM, G., Dogmatics
DAHLBACKA, I., Church History
KURTÉN, T., Theological Ethics
LAATO, A., Old Testament Exegesis and
  Jewish Studies
SUNDKVIST, B., Practical Theology
SYREENI, K., New Testament Exegetics

School of Business and Economics:
BRÄNNBACK, M., International Marketing
HASSEL, L., Accounting
JÄNTTI, M., Economics
KRISTENSSON UGGLA, B., Organization and
  Management
ÖSTERMARK, R., Accounting
REHN, A., Business Administration
TÖRNROOS, J.-Å., Management Science
WIDÉN, G., Information Studies
WILLNER, J., Economics

**HELSINGIN YLIOPISTO/
HELSINGFORS UNIVERSITET
(University of Helsinki)**

POB 33 (Yliopistonkatu 4), 00014 Univ. of
Helsinki
Telephone: (9) 1911
Fax: (9) 19123008
E-mail: collegium-office@helsinki.fi
Internet: www.helsinki.fi/university
Founded 1640 Turku (Åbo), 1828 Helsinki
Languages of instruction: Finnish, Swedish
State control
Academic year: September to May (2 terms)
Chancellor: Prof. ILKKA NIINILUOTO
Rector: Prof. THOMAS WILHELMSSON

Vice-Rector for Academic Quality Assurance
  and Int. Affairs: Prof. ULLA-MAIJA FORS-
  BERG
Vice-Rector for Education and Lifelong
  Learning: Prof. JUKKA KOLA
Vice-Rector for Research and Innovation:
  Prof. JOHANNA BJÖRKROTH
Vice-Rector for Social Interaction and Fund-
  raising: Prof. KIMMO KONTULA
Dir of Admin.: KARI SUOKKO
Librarian: KAISA SINIKARA
Number of teachers: 1,694
Number of students: 35,258

DEANS

Faculty of Agriculture and Forestry: Prof.
  JUKKA KOLA
Faculty of Arts: Prof. ANNA MAURANEN
Faculty of Behavioural Sciences: Prof. PATRIK
  SCHEININ
Faculty of Biological and Environmental
  Sciences: Prof. JARI NIEMELÄ
Faculty of Law: Prof. KIMMO NUOTIO
Faculty of Medicine: Prof. RISTO RENKONEN
Faculty of Pharmacy: Prof. JOUNI HIRVONEN
Faculty of Science: Prof. KEIJO HÄMÄLÄINEN
Faculty of Social Sciences: Prof. LIISA LAAKSO
Faculty of Theology: Prof. AILA LAUHA
Faculty of Veterinary Medicine: Prof. ANTTI
  SUKURA

PROFESSORS

Faculty of Agriculture and Forestry (POB 62
(Viikinkaari 11), 00014 Univ. of Helsinki; tel.
(9) 19158247; fax (9) 19158575; e-mail
mmtdk-international@helsinki.fi; internet
www.mm.helsinki.fi):

AHOKAS, J. M., Agricultural Engineering
ALATOSSAVA, J. T., Dairy Technology
DAHLIN, S. B., Logistics
HARI, P. K. J., Forest Ecology
HARTIKAINEN, H. H., Soil and Environment
  Chemistry
HATAKKA, A., Environmental Biotechnol-
  ogy
HEINONEN, I. M., Functional Food
HELENIUS, J. P., Agroecology
HELIÖVAARA, K. T., Forest Zoology
HOKKANEN, H. M. T., Agricultural Zoology
HYVÖNEN, L. E. T., Food Technology
HYVÖNEN, S. M., Marketing
JAAKKOLA, A. O., Agricultural Chemistry
  and Physics
JUSLIN, H. J., Forest Products Marketing
KANGAS, A., Forest Mensuration and Man-
  agement
KOLA, J. T. S., Agricultural Politics
KOSKELA, M. O., Food Economics
KUULUVAINEN, J. T. M., Social Economics of
  Forestry
LAASASENAHO, J. E., Forest Mensuration
  and Management
LUUKKANEN, M. O., Silviculture in Devel-
  oping Countries
MAKAROW, M. T., Applied Biochemistry
MÄKELÄ, P. S. A., Crop Production
MÄKINEN, V.-P. J., Agricultural Entrepre-
  neurship
MIKKONEN, E. U. A., Logging and Utiliza-
  tion of Forest Products
MUTANEN, M. L., Nutrition Physiology
NÄSI, J. M., Animal Nutrition
OJALA, M. J., Animal Breeding
OLLIKAINEN, M. M. O., Environmental Eco-
  nomics
PEHKONEN, A. I., Agricultural Engineering
PIIRONEN, V. I., Food Chemistry
PUOLANNE, T. E. J., Meat Technology
PUTTONEN, P. K., Silviculture
RÄSÄNEN, L. K., Nutrition
SALKINOSA-SALONEN, M. S., Microbiology
SALOVAARA, H. O., Cereal Technology
SARIS, P.-E. J., Food Microbiology
SIPI, M. H., Forest Technology

SJÖBERG, A.-M. K., Technology of House-
  holds and Institutions
SUMELIUS, J. H., Agricultural Economics
TEERI, T. H., Plant Production
TENKANEN, T. M., Chemistry of Bioproduc-
  tion
TERVO, M. J., Forest Product Marketing
TOKOLA, T. E., Geoinformatics
TUORILA, H. M., Food Technology
VALKONEN, P. T., Plant Pathology
VALSTA, L., Business Economics of Forestry
VANHATALO, A. O., Animal Science
WESTERMARCK, H. E., Extension Education
WESTMAN, C. J. V., Forest Soil Science
YLÄTALO, E. M. O., Agricultural Economics

Faculty of Arts (POB 3 (Fabianinkatu 33,
2nd Fl.), 00014 Univ. of Helsinki; fax (9)
19123100; e-mail hum-info@helsinki.fi;
internet www.hum.helsinki.fi):

APO, S.-K., Folklore
BACON, G. H. A., Film and Television
  Research
BREUER, U. M., German Philology
CARLSON, L. H., Language Theory and
  Translation
CHESTERMAN, A. P. C., Multilingual Com-
  munication
CLARK, P. A., Urban History
GOTHONI, R. R., Study of Religions
HAAPALA, A. K., Aesthetics
HAKULINEN, A. T., Finnish Language
HÄMEEN-ANTTILA, J. M., Arabic Language
  and Islamic Research
HÄRMÄ, J., Romance Philology
HARVIAINEN, J. M. T., Semitic Languages
HELKKULA, M., French Language
HENRIKSSON, M. J., American Studies
HIETARANTA, P. S., English Language
HURSKAINEN, A. J., African Languages and
  Cultures
HYVÄRINEN, I. K., German Philology
JANHUNEN, J.-A., East Asian Languages
  and Cultures
KALLIOKOSKI, J. T., Finnish Language
KARLSSON, F. G., General Linguistics
KONTTINEN, K. P. R., Art History
KORHONEN, J. A., German Philology
KOSKENNIEMI, K. M., Computer Linguistics
KOSKI, P. K. M., Theatre Science and
  Drama Literature
KOURI, E. I., General History
KULONEN, U.-M., Finno-Ugrian Philology
LAITINEN, L. M., Finnish Language
LARJAVAARA, M. E. T., Finnish Philology
LAVENTO, M. T., Archaeology
LEHTINEN, A. T., Finnish Philology
LEHTONEN, J. U. E., Finno-Ugrian Ethnol-
  ogy
LEINO, P. A., Finnish Language
LINDSTEDT, J. S., Slavonic Philology
LYYTIKÄINEN, P. R., Finnish Literature
MAZZARELLA, S. M., Scandinavian Litera-
  ture
MEINANDER, C. H., History
MUSTAJOKI, A. S., Russian Language and
  Literature
NENOLA, A. A., Women's Studies
NEVALAINEN, T. T. A., English Philology
NIINILUOTO, I. M. O., Theoretical Philoso-
  phy
NIKULA, R. K., Arts History
NUMMI, J. T., Finnish Literature
ÖSTMAN, J.-O. I., English Philology
PARPOLA, S. K. A., Assyriology
PEKKILÄ, E. O., Musicology
PESONEN, P. J., Russian Literature
PETTERSSON, B. J. O., American Literature
PYRHÖNEN, H. M., General Literature and
  Aesthetics
RAUD, R., Japanese Languages and Cul-
  ture
RHO, T. T., Iberian Languages and Roma-
  nian
RIIKONEN, H. K., General Literature
SAARI, M. H., Scandinavian Languages

SAARINEN, H. K., General History
SALOMIES, O. I., Latin Language and Roman Literature
SANDU, N.-G., Theoretical Philosophy
SIIKALA, A. A.-L., Folklore
SILTALA, J. H., Finnish History
SUOMELA-HÄRMÄ, M. E., Italian Philology
TAAVITSAINEN, I. A. J., English Philology
TARASTI, E. A. P., Musicology
VEHMAS-LEHTO, R. L. I., Russian Language
VENTOLA, E. M., English Philology
VIHAVAINEN, T. J., Russian Studies
VON PLATO, J., Philosophy

Faculty of Behavioural Sciences (POB 9 (Siltavuorenpenger 5A), 00014 Univ. of Helsinki; tel. (9) 19120509; fax (9) 19120520; e-mail kaytt-tdk@helsinki.fi; internet www .helsinki.fi/behav):

ÅHLBERG, M. K., Biology Pedagogics
ALHO, K. A., Psychology
BUCHBERGER, A.-I. V., Pedagogics of Mother Tongue Teaching
ENGESTRÖM, Y. H. M., Adult Education
HAUTAMÄKI, J. J., Special Pedagogics
HYTÖNEN, J. M. K., Pedagogics
IIVONEN, A. K., Phonetics
KALLIONIEMI, A. J. V., Theological Pedagogy
KAUKINEN, L. K., Crafts
KELTIKANGAS-JÄRVINEN, A.-L., Applied Psychology
KLIPPI, A. M. K., Logopaedics
KRAUSE, M. C., Cognitive Science
KROKFORS, L. M., Pedagogics
LAVONEN, J. M. J., Pedagogy of Physics and Chemistry
NIEMI, H. M., Pedagogics
NYMAN, G. S., Psychology
OJALA, M. O., Pre-school and Early Childhood Education
PEHKONEN, E. K., Pedagogy of Mathematics and Computer Science
SCHEININ, P. M., Pedagogics
SIMOLA, H. J., Pedagogics
SUMMALA, K. H. I., Psychology
TANI, S. H., Pedagogy of Geography and the Environment
TELLA, S. K., Pedagogics
TUOMI-GRÖHN, T. T., Home Economics
TURKKI, K. M., Home Economics
UUSIKYLÄ, K. T., Pedagogics
VIRKKUNEN, R. J. T., Developmental Work Research
VIRSU, V. V. E., Neuropsychology
VUORINEN, R. H. E., Applied Psychology

Faculty of Biological and Environmental sciences (POB 56 (Viikinkaari 9), 00014 Univ. of Helsinki; tel. (9) 1911; fax (9) 19157561; e-mail bio-sci@helsinki.fi; internet www.helsinki.fi/bio):

BAMFORD, D. H., General Microbiology
DONNER, K. K., Zoology
ELORANTA, P. V., Limnology
GAHMBERG, C.-G., Biochemistry
HÄNNINEN, H. J. P., Zoology
HANSKI, I. A., Morphology and Ecology
HOLM, L. U. T., Bioinformatics
HYVÖNEN, J. T., Botany
KAILA, K. K., Physiological Zoology
KAIRESALO, T. A., Freshwater Ecology
KANGASJÄRVI, J. S., Plant Biology
KAUPPI, P. E., Environmental Protection
KEINÄNEN, K. P., Molecular Biology
KOKKO, H. M., Veterinary Ecology
KORHOLA, A. A., Arctic Global Change
KORHONEN, T. K., General Microbiology
KUIKKA, O. S., Fisheries Biology
KUOSA, H. J., Baltic Sea Research
KUPARINEN, J. S., Marine Biology
LEHTONEN, H. V. T., Fisheries Science
MERILÄ, J. K. K., Population Biology
NIEMELÄ, J. K., Urban Ecology
PALVA, E. T., Genetics
RANTA, E. J., Zoology
RIKKINEN, J. K., Zoology

ROMANTSCHUK, M. L., Environmental Biotechnology
SCHRÖDER, J. P., Genetics
STRÖMMER, R. H., Soil Ecology
SUNDSTRÖM, L. B., Evolution Biology
VIHKO, P., Biochemistry
VOIPIO, J. T. I., Electrophysiology

Faculty of Law (POB 4 (Yliopistonkatu 5), 00014 Univ. of Helsinki; tel. (9) 1911; fax (9) 19122152; internet www.helsinki.fi/oik/tdk):

AUREJÄRVI, E. I., Civil Law
FRÄNDE, D. G., Criminal Law and Judicial Procedure
HALILA, H. J., Sports Law
HAVANSI, E. E. T., Judicial Procedure
HEIMONEN, M. O., Economics
HEMMO, M. A., Insurance and Tort Law
HOLLO, E. J., Environmental Law
KALIMA, K.-E. K., Financial Law
KANGAS, U. P. A., Civil Law
KEKKONEN, J. T., Judicial History and Roman Law
KONSTARI, T. T., Administrative Law
KOSKENNIEMI, M. A., International Law
KOSKINEN, P. T., Criminal Law
LAHTI, R. O. K., Criminal Law
LAPPALAINEN, J. A., Judicial Procedure
MAJAMAA, V. V., Environmental Law
MÄENPÄÄ, O. I., Administrative Law
MAJANEN, M. I., Criminal Law
MIKKOLA, M. L. A., Labour Law
RISSANEN, K. K., Commercial Law
RYYNÄNEN, O. J., Public Law
SISULA-TULOKAS, L. M., Civil Law
TEPORA, J. K., Civil Law
TIITINEN, K.-P., Labour Law
TIKKA, K. S., Financial Law
TUORI, K. H., Administrative Law
WILHELMSSON, T. K. J., Private and Commercial Law

Faculty of Medicine (POB 20 (Tukholmankatu 8), 00014 Univ. of Helsinki; tel. (9) 1911; fax (9) 19126629; e-mail med-studentaffairs@ helsinki.fi; internet www.med.helsinki.fi):

ALALUUSUA, A. S. K., Dentistry
ALMQVIST, S. F., Child Psychiatry
ANDERSSON, L. C. L., Pathological Anatomy
BROMMELS, M. H., Health Care Administration
HAAHTELA, T. M. K., Clinical Allergology
HARJULA, A. L. J., Surgery
HÄYRY, P. J., Transplantation Surgery and Immunology
HERNESNIEMI, J. A., Neurosurgery
HIETANEN, J. H. P., Dentistry
HÖCKERSTEDT, K. A. V., Surgery
HOLMBERG, P. E., Physics
HUUSKONEN, M. S., Occupational Health
IKONEN, E. M., Cell and Tissue Biology
JÄNNE, O. A., Physiology
JOENSUU, H. T., Radiotherapy and Oncology
KALIMO, H. O., Applied Neuropathology
KALSO, E. A., Internal Medicine
KAPRIO, J. A., Public Health Service
KARLSSON, H. E., Psychiatry
KARMA, P. H., Otorhinolaryngology
KARPPANEN, H. O., Pharmacology
KARVONEN, J. M., Applied Dermatology and Venereology
KASTE, K. A. M., Neurology
KEKKI, P. V., General Practice and Primary Health Care
KESKI-OJA, J. K., Cell Biology
KINNULA, V. L., Pulmonary Medicine
KINNUNEN, P. K. J., Chemistry
KIVILAAKSO, E. O., Surgery
KIVISAARI, M. L., Diagnostic Radiology
KLOCKARS, M. L. G., General Practice
KNIP, J. M., Paediatrics
KÖNÖNEN, M. H. O., Stomatognatic Physiology and Prosthetic Dentistry
KONTTINEN, Y. T., Oral Medicine
KONTULA, K. K., Molecular Medicine
KORPI, E. R., Pharmacology

KORTTILA, K. T., Anaesthesiology and Intensive Care
LAHELMA, E. T., Public Health Science
LAITINEN, L. A. I., Tuberculosis and Pulmonary Medicine
LEHTO, V. P., Pathological Anatomy
LEIRISALO-REPO, T. K. M., Rheumatology
LEPÄNTALO, M. J. A., Vascular Surgery
LINDQVIST, J. C., Oral and Maxillofacial Surgery
LÖNNQVIST, J. K., Psychiatry
MÄKELÄ, T. P., Biochemistry and Cell Biology
MAURY, C. P. J., Internal Medicine
MERI, S. K., Immunology
MEURMAN, J. H., Dentistry
MURTOMAA, H. T., Oral Public Health
NEUVONEN, P. J., Clinical Pharmacology
NIEMINEN, M. S., Cardiology
NILSSON, C.-G. D., Obstetrics and Gynaecology
PAAKKARI, A. T. I., Pharmacology
PAAVONEN, J. A., Obstetrics and Gynaecology
PANULA, P. A. J., Biomedicine
PELTOLA, H. O., Infectious Diseases
PELTOMÄKI, P. T., Medical Genetics
PELTONEN-PALOTIE, L. P. M., Medical Genetics
PERTOVAARA, A. Y., Physiology
RANKI, P. A., Dermatology and Venereology
REPO, H., Internal Medicine
RINTALA, R. J., Child Surgery
ROSENBERG, P. H., Anaesthesiology
RUUTU, M. L., Urology
SAJANTILA, A. J., Genetic Forensic Medicine
SALASPURO, M. P. J., Alcohol and Narcotics Medicine
SANTAVIRTA, S. S., Orthopaedics and Traumatology
SARNA, S. J., Biometry
SIIMES, M. A., Paediatrics
SINTONEN, H. P., Health Economics
SKURNIK, M., Bacteriology
SOVIJÄRVI, A. R. A., Clinical Physiology
STENMAN, U.-H. E., Clinical Chemistry
TASKINEN, M.-R., Internal Medicine
TERVO, T. M. T., Applied Ophthalmology
TIKKANEN, M. J., Internal Medicine
TILVIS, R. S., Geriatrics
TUOMILEHTO, J. O. J., Public Health Science
UITTO, V. V.-J., Oral Biology
VIRKKUNEN, M. E., Forensic Psychiatry
VIRTANEN, I. T., Anatomy
VON WENDT, L. O. W., Child Neurology
VUORI, E. O., Forensic Chemistry
WAHLBECK, K. L. R., Psychiatry
YKI-JÄRVINEN, H., Internal Medicine
YLIKORKALA, R. O., Obstetrics and Gynaecology

Faculty of Pharmacy (POB 56 (Viikinkaari 9), 00014 Univ. of Helsinki; tel. (9) 1911; fax (9) 19159138; e-mail ftdk-hallinto@helsinki .fi; internet www.helsinki.fi/farmasia):

AIRAKSINEN, M. S. A., Social Pharmacy
ELO, H. O., Pharmacological Chemistry
HILTUNEN, R. V. K., Pharmacognosy
HIRVONEN, J. T., Pharmaceutical Technology
KOSTIAINEN, R. K., Pharmaceutical Chemistry
MÄNNISTÖ, P. T., Pharmacology and Drug Development
MARVOLA, M. L. A., Biopharmacy
TASKINEN, J. A. A., Pharmaceutical Chemistry
TUOMINEN, R. K., Pharmacology and Toxicology
VUORELA, H. J., Pharmacognosy
YLIRUUSI, J. K., Pharmaceutical Technology

Faculty of Science (POB 44 (Jyrängöntie 2), 00014 Univ. of Helsinki; tel. (9) 19150058;

fax (9) 19150039; e-mail sci-info@helsinki.fi; internet www.helsinki.fi/facultyofscience):

AHLGREN, T. J., Physics
AHONEN-MYKA, A. H., Computer Science
ANNILA, A. J., Biophysics
ARJAS, E., Biometry
ASTALA, K. O., Mathematics
BECKMANN, A. H.-T., Geophysics
CHAICHIAN, M., High Energy Physics
ENQVIST, K.-P., Cosmogony
ERONEN, M. J., Geology and Palaeontology
FORTELIUS, H. L. M., Evolution Palaeontology
GYLLENBERG, M. A. G., Applied Mathematics
HALONEN, L. O., Physical Chemistry
HÄMERI, K. J., Aerosol Physics
HÄMÄLÄINEN, K. J., Physics
HOYER, P. G., Elementary Particle Physics
ILLMAN, S. A., Mathematics
KAJANTIE, K. O., Theoretical Physics
KARHU, J. A., Geology and Mineralogy
KASKI, S. J. I., Computer Science
KEINONEN, J., Applied Physics
KILPELÄINEN, I. A., Organic Chemistry
KIVINEN, J. T., Computer Science
KOSKINEN, H. E. J., Space Physics
KOSONEN, M. E., Planning Geography
KOTIAHO, A. A. T., Environmental Chemistry and Analytics
KULMALA, M. T., Physics
KUPIAINEN, A. J., Mathematics
LAHTINEN, O. A., Applied Mathematics
LEPPÄRANTA, M. J., Geophysics
LESKELÄ, M. A., Inorganic Chemistry
LÖYTÖNEN, M. K., Cultural Geography
LUMME, K. A., Astronomy
MARTIO, O. T., Mathematics
MATTILA, P. E. J., Mathematics
MATTILA, V. A. K., Astronomy
MAUNU, S.-L., Polymer Chemistry
MICHELSSON, J. A., Mathematics
NORDLUND, K. H., Aerosol Physics
NUMMELIN, E., Applied Mathematics
OIVANEN, M. T., Organic Chemistry
ORAVA, R. O., Experimental Particle Physics
PAAKKI, J. P., Computer Science
PÄIVÄRINTA, L. J., Applied Mathematics
PELLIKKA, P. K. E., Geoinformatics
PESONEN, L. J., Geophysics
PYYKKÖ, V. P., Chemistry
RAATIKAINEN, K. E. E., Computer Science
RÄISÄNEN, J. A., Physics
RÄMÖ, O. T., Geology and Mineralogy
RÄSÄNEN, M. O., Physical Chemistry
RIEKKOLA, M.-L., Analytical Chemistry
RISKA, D.-O. W., Physics
RITALA, M. K., Inorganic Chemistry
SAARIKKO, H. M. T., Physics
SAARINEN, H. S. S., Chemistry
SALONEN, V.-P., Environmental Geology
SAVIJÄRVI, H. I., Meteorology
SEPPÄLÄ, M. K., Computer-applied Mathematics
SEPPÄLÄ, M. K., Geography
SERIMAA, R. E., Physics
SIPPU, S. S., Computer Science
SUOMINEN, J. K., Mathematics
TALMAN, P. K., Geography
TENHU, H. J., Polymer Chemistry
TIKKANEN, M. J., Geography
TIRRI, H. R., Computer Science
TOIVONEN, H. T. T., Computer Science
TOPPILA, O. S., Mathematics
TÖRNROOS, R. F., Geology and Mineralogy
TUKIA, P. P., Mathematics
UKKONEN, E. J., Computer Science
VÄÄNÄNEN, J. A., Mathematics
VERKAMO, A. I., Software Engineering
VESALA, T. V., Meteorology
VIITALA, P. J., Planning Geography
WESTERHOLM, J. O., Geography
WÄHÄLÄ-HASE, K., Organic Chemistry

Faculty of Social Sciences (POB 54 (Unioninkatu 37), 00014 Univ. of Helsinki; tel. (9) 1911; fax (9) 19124835; e-mail soc-sci@helsinki.fi; internet www.helsinki.fi/socialsciences):

ÅBERG, L. E. G., Communication
AIRAKSINEN, T., Practical Philosophy
ALAPURO, R. S., Sociology
ARMSTRONG, K. V., Cultural Anthropology
AULA, P. S., Communication
BLOMBERG-KROLL, H. K., Social Policy
ERÄSAARI, R. O., Social Policy
GYLLING, H. A., Applied Ethics
HAILA, A.-K. E., Social Policy
HAUTAMÄKI, A. A., Social Psychology and Psychology
HÄYRINEN-ALESTALO, M. G., Science and Technology and Research
HELKAMA, K. E., Social Psychology
HENTILÄ, S. J., Political History
HJERPPE, R. T., Economic History
HONKAPOHJA, S. M. S., Economics
HUOTARI, K. H., Social Work
JALLINOJA, R. I., Family Sociology
KANNIAINEN, V. L., Economics
KARISTO, A. O., Social Policy
KARVINEN-NIINIKOSKI, S. M. E., Social Policy
KETTUNEN, P. T., Political History
KIVIKURU, U., Journalism
KOPONEN, M. J., Development Studies
KOSKELA, E. A., Economics
KULTTI, K. K., Economics
LIEBKIND-ORMALA, K. R., Social Psychology
MASSA, J. K., Environmental Politics
MORING, T. A., Communication
NIEMI, H. O., Statistics
NYLUND, M., Social Work
PALOKANGAS, T. K., Economics
PATOMÄKI, H. O., Political Science
PEKONEN, K. J., Political Science
PELTONEN, M. T., Social History
PERÄKYLÄ, A. M., Sociology
PIRTTILÄ-BACKMAN, A.-M., Social Psychology
RISKA, E. K., Sociology
ROOS, J. P., Social Policy
SAIKKONEN, P. J., Statistics
SASSI, S. S., Communication
SATKA, M. E. A., Social Policy
SIIKALA, J. J. T., Sociology
SJÖBLOM, S. M., Municipal Administration
SULKUNEN, P. J., Sociology
SUNDBERG, J. H., Political Science
TARKKONEN, L. J., Statistics
TÖRRÖNEN, L. M., Social Work
TUOMELA, R. H., Practical Philosophy
VÄLIVERRONEN, E. T., Mass Communication
VALKONEN, Y. T., Sociology
VARTIA, Y. O., Economics
VIRTANEN, T. I., Political Science

Faculty of Theology (POB 33 (Aleksanterinkatu 7), 00014 Univ. of Helsinki; tel. (09) 1911; fax (9) 19122106; internet www.helsinki.fi/teol):

AEJMELAEUS, L. J. T., Exegetics
HALLAMAA, J. I., Social Ethics
HEIKKILÄ, M. K. J., Practical Theology
HEININEN, S. K. M., General Church History
HELANDER, E. M., Church Sociology
KNUUTTILA, S. J. I., Theological Ethics and Philosophy of Religion
KOTILA, H. T., Practical Theology
LAUHA, A. M., Church History
PENTIKÄINEN, J. Y., Study of Religions
RÄISÄNEN, H. M., New Testament Exegetics
RUOKANEN, M. M., Doctrinal Theology
SAARINEN, R. J., Ecumenics
SOLLAMO, R. T., Biblical Languages
TIRRI, K. A. H., Theological Pedagogy
TYÖRINOJA, R. J., Systematic Theology
VEIJOLA, T. K., Old Testament Exegetics

Faculty of Veterinary Medicine (POB 66 (Agnes Sjöbergin katu 2), 00014 Univ. of Helsinki; tel. (9) 1911; fax (9) 19157161; internet www.vetmed.helsinki.fi):

ANDERSSON, C. M., Animal Breeding
BJÖRKROTH, K. J., Food Hygiene
HÄNNINEN, M. L., Veterinary Environmental Hygiene
JÄRVINEN, A.-K., Pet Diseases
KATILA, M. T. H., Animal Breeding
KORKEALA, H. J., Food Hygiene
LINDBERG, L.-A., Anatomy
PALVA, A., Veterinary Microbiology
POHJANVIRTA, R. K., Toxicology
PÖSÖ, A. R., Veterinary Physiology
PYÖRÄLÄ, S. H. K., Veterinary Medicine
SALONIEMI, H., Animal Hygiene
SNELLMAN, P. M., Diagnostic Radiology
SPILLMANN, T., Veterinary Internal Medicine
SUKUNA, A. K. K., Veterinary Pathology
TULAMO, R.-M., Veterinary Surgery
VAINIO-KIVINEN, O. M., Pharmacology
VAPAATALO, O. P., Virology

ITÄ-SUOMEN YLIOPISTO
(University of Eastern Finland)

Joensuu Campus: POB 111, 80101 Joensuu
Telephone: (13) 251111
Fax: (13) 2512050
Kuopio Campus: POB 1627, 70211 Kuopio
Telephone: (20) 7872211
Fax: (17) 162131
Internet: www.uef.fi

Founded 2010, merger of Univ. of Joensuu and the Univ. of Kuopio
Languages of instruction: Finnish, some courses in English
Academic year: August to June
Public control

Rector: PERTTU VARTIAINEN
Rector for Academics: KALERVO VÄÄNÄNEN
Dir for Admin.: MATTI PAAVONSALO
Library Dir: JARMO SAARTI
Number of teachers: 3,000
Number of students: 14,000

DEANS

Faculty of Health Sciences: Prof. JUKKA MÖNKKÖNEN
Faculty of Philosophy: Prof. MARKKU FILPPULA
Faculty of Science and Forestry: Prof. TIMO JÄÄSKELÄINEN
Faculty of Social Sciences and Business Studies: Prof. JUHA KINNUNEN

PROFESSORS

Faculty of Health Sciences:

AHONEN, R., Pharmacy Practice
AIRENNE, K., Molecular Medicine
ALAFUZOFF, I., Kuopio, Neuropathology
ALHONEN, L., Kuopio, Animal Biotechnology
AURIOLA, S., Mass Spectrometry
AUVINEN, P., Radiotherapy and Oncology
AZHAYEV, A., Bio-organic Chemistry
COURTNEY, M., Cell Signalling
DUNKEL, L., Paediatrics
ENLUND, K., Kuopio, Social Pharmacy
ESKELINEN, M., Kuopio, Surgery
FORSBERG, M., Pharmacology
GINIATULLIN, R., Cell Biology
GRÖHN, O., Biomedical NMR
GYLLING, H., Kuopio, Nutrition
HÄMEEN-ANTTILA, K., Social Pharmacy
HANNONEN, P., Rheumatology
HARTIKAINEN, S., Geriatric Medical Treatment
HARTIKAINEN, J., Cardiology
HARTIKAINEN, P., Neurology
HARVIMA, I., Kuopio, Dermatology and Allergology

HEINONEN, S., Obstetrics and Gynaecology
HINKKANEN, A., Gene Transfer Technology
HINTIKKA, J., Kuopio, Psychology
HONKAKOSKI, P., Kuopio, Biopharmacy
HOVATTA, O., Stem Cell Biology
ILONEN, J., Kuopio, Clinical Microbiology
JÄÄSKELÄINEN, J., Neurosurgery
JÄKÄLÄ, P., Kuopio, Neurodegenerative Diseases and Rehabilitation
JÄRVINEN, P., Kuopio, Pharmaceutical Technology
JOHANSSON, R., Radiotherapy and Oncology
KAARNIRANTA, K., Ophthalmology
KÄLVIÄINEN, R., Kuopio, Clinical Epileptology
KARHU, J., Physiology
KAUHANEN, J., Kuopio, Public Health
KERÄNEN, T., Clinical Pharmacology and Medical Treatment
KETOLAINEN, J., Pharmaceutical Technology
KOISTINAHO, J., Molecular Brain Research
KOKKI, H., Anaesthesiology
KOPONEN, H., Psychiatry
KOSMA, V., Pathology
KRÖGER, H., Surgery
KUMPULAINEN, K., Child Psychiatry
KUMPUSALO, E., General Practice
LAAKKONEN, P., Novel Target Molecules and Gene Therapy
LAAKSO, M., Internal Medicine
LAITINEN, T., Kuopio, Clinical Physiology and Nuclear Medicine
LAKKA, T., Kuopio, Medical Physiology
LAPINJOKI, S., Pharmaceutical Chemistry
LAUKKANEN, E., Kuopio, Adolescent Psychiatry
LÖPPÖNEN, H., Otorhinolaryngology
LOUHEVAARA, V., Ergonomics
MANNINEN, H., Kuopio, Interventional Radiology
MERVAALA, E., Clinical Neurophysiology
MÖNKKÖNEN, J., Biopharmacy
MYKKÄNEN, H., Kuopio, Nutrition
NEVALAINEN, T., Kuopio, Laboratory Animalscience
NISKANEN, L., Internal Medicine
NUUTINEN, J., Otorhinolaryngology
PAAJANEN, H., Orthopaedics and Traumatology
PALVIMO, J., Medical Biochemistry
PASANEN, M., Medicinal Toxicology
PEKKANEN, J., Environmental Health Care
PELKONEN, J., Clinical Microbiology
PIETILÄ, A., Nursing Science
PITKÄNEN, A., Neurobiology
POSO, A., Kuopio, Pharmaceutical Chemistry
PULKKI, K., Clinical Chemistry
RÄSÄNEN, K., Occupational Health Care
RAUNIO, H., Kuopio, Pharmacology
RAUNIO, H., Pharmacology
RAUTIO, J., Pharmaceutical Chemistry
RUOKONEN, E., Intensive Care
RYYNÄNEN, O., General Practice
SOINI, Y., Pathology
SOININEN, H., Neurology
SULKAVA, R., Geriatrics
TAMMI, M., Anatomy
TAMMI, R., Kuopio, Anatomy
TANILA, H., Molecular Neurobiology
TIIHONEN, J., Forensic Psychiatry
TOSSAVAINEN, K., Nursing Science
TUKIAINEN, H., Pulmonary Diseases
TUOMAINEN, T., Public Health
TUPPURAINEN, M., Obstetrics and Gynaecology
TURUNEN, H., Nursing Science
UUSITUPA, M., Kuopio, Nutritional Genomics Andnutrigenetics
VÄHÄKANGAS, K., Toxicology
VANHALA, M., General Practice
VANNINEN, R., Radiology
VASKILAMPI, T., Health Sociology
VEHVILÄINEN-JULKUNEN, K., Nursing Science

VIINAMÄKI, H., Psychiatry
VOUTILAINEN, R., Paediatrics
WONG, G., Bioinformatics
YLÄ-HERTTUALA, S., Molecular Medicine

Faculty of Science and Forestry:
AHONEN, J., Computer Science
ALHO, J., Statistics
AULASKARI, R., Mathematics
CARLBERG, C., Biochemistry
EEROLA, A., Computer Science
ERKAMA, T., Applied Mathematics
FRÄNTI, P., Computer Science
FRIBERG, A., Finland Distinguished Professor Programme
HAUKKA, M., Inorganic Chemistry
HILTUNEN, Y., Environmental Technology
HIRVONEN, M., Environmental Toxicology
HOLOPAINEN, J., Applied Ecology
HOLOPAINEN, T., Ecological Environmental Science
HYNYNEN, K., Medical Physics
HÄMÄLÄINEN, J., Industrial Physics
JÄÄSKELÄINEN, T., Physics
JÄNIS, J., Chemistry
JOKINIEMI, J., Fine Particle Technology
JULKUNEN-TIITTO, R., Plant Ecology
JURVELIN, J., Medical Physics
JUUTILAINEN, J., Radiation Biology and Epidemiology
KAIPIO, J., Physics
KALLIOKOSKI, P., Environmental Hygiene
KARJALAINEN, P., Signal and Image Processing
KELLOMÄKI, S., Silviculture
KILPELÄINEN, P., Computer Science
KOLEHMAINEN, M., Environmental Informatics
KOLEHMAINEN, O., Statistics
KORHONEN, R., Mathematics
KORTET, R., Biology
KOUKI, J., Forest Ecology
KUITTINEN, M., Physics
KUKKONEN, J., Biology
KÄRENLAMPI, P., Forest Products Technology
KÄRENLAMPI, S., Biotechnology
LAAKSONEN, A., Environmental Physics
LAATIKAINEN, R., Chemistry
LAMMI, M., Biochemistry
LAPPALAINEN, R., Biomaterials Technology
LEHTINEN, K., Atmospheric Physics and Chemistry
LEHTO, T., Forest Soil Science
LEHTO, V., Industrial Physics
MALTAMO, M., Forest Mensuration Science
MARTIKAINEN, P., Environmental Microbiology
MONONEN, J., Zoology
NIHTILÄ, M., Mathematics
NYKÄNEN, M., Computer Science
OKSANEN, E., Botany
OLKKONEN, H., Physics
PAKKANEN, T., Chemistry
PALANDER, T., Forest Engineering
PAPPINEN, A., Forest Protection
PARKKINEN, J., Computer Science
PASANEN, P., Environmental Science
PEIPONEN, K., Physics
PELKONEN, P., Energy Wood and Peat Production
PENTTONEN, M., Computer Science
PUKKALA, T., Forestry Planning
ROININEN, H., Animal Ecology
ROUVINEN, J., Organic Chemistry
RUUSKANEN, J., Environmental Science
SAASTAMOINEN, O., Forest Economics
SAJANIEMI, J., Computer Science
SIKANEN, L., Energy Pellet Research
SILLANPÄÄ, M., Applied Environmental Chemistry
SMITH, J., Climate Change Research
SUTINEN, E., Computer Science
SVIRKO, Y., Physics
SYVÄOJA, J., Biochemistry
TOIVANEN, P., Computer Science

TOKOLA, T., Forest Information Systems
TUKIAINEN, M., Computer Science
TUOMELA, J., Applied Mathematics
TURUNEN, J., Physics
TÖYRÄS, J., Medical Physics and Engineering
VAHIMAA, P., Theoretical Optics
VAUHKONEN, M., Industrial Mathematics and Physics
VEPSÄLÄINEN, J., Chemistry
VON, W., Food and Nutrition Biotechnology
VORNANEN, M., Animal Physiology
WANG, K., Finland Distinguished Professor Programme

Faculty of Social Sciences and Business Studies:
AHPONEN, P., Social and Public Policy
ARAJÄRVI, P., Social Law
COLPAERT, A., Geography
ERIKSSON, P., Management
ESKELINEN, H., Regional Studies
HÄMÄLÄINEN, J., Social Work
HÄMYNEN, T., Finnish History
HÄNNINEN, V., Social Psychology
HUSA, J., Constitutional Law and General Jurisprudence
JOKINEN, E., Social and Studies
JOKINEN, P., Natural Resources Policy
JUNTTO, A., Housing
KANTANEN, J., Marketing
KATAJALA, K., Finnish History
KATILA, S., Kuopio, Innovation Cultures and Diversity Management
KEINÄNEN, A., Legislative Studies and Empirical Forensics
KINNUNEN, J., Kuopio, Health Management Science
KOMPPULA, R., Tourism Business
KORPELA, J., General History
KORTELAINEN, J., Human Geography
KOSKI, L., Sociology
KUOKKANEN, T., International Environmental Law
LÄHTEENMÄKI, M., Finnish History
LAMMINTAKANEN, J., Health Management Science
LAUKKANEN, T., Marketing
LAURINKARI, J., Social Policy
LEHTINEN, A., Geography
LIIKANEN, I., Border and Russian Studies
LINDEN, M., Economics
LITTUNEN, H., Kuopio, Business Economics
MÄÄTTÄ, K., Law and Economics
MÄÄTTÄ, T., Environmental Law
MIETTINEN, T., Administrative Law
MYRSKY, M., Tax Law
NIEMELÄ, P., Kuopio, Social Policy
NIIRANEN, V., Social Work
NISKANEN, J., Financial Administration and Financing
NISKANEN, M., Financing
NYSTÉN-HAARALA, S., Civil Law
PASO, M., European Law
POHJOLA, K., Kuopio, Social Pedagogy
PÖLKKI, P., Child Welfare
PÖLÖNEN, I., Environmental Law
RANNIKKO, P., Environmental Policy
RISSANEN, S., Hele, Kuopio, Social Work
SAARI, J., Sociology
SABOUR, M., Sociology
SAIRINEN, R., Social Environmental Research
SAJAMA, S., Philosophy
SARANTO, K., Kuopio, Health and Human Services Informatics
SAVOLAINEN, T., Business Administration
SCOTT, J., Border and Regional Studies
SIISKONEN, H., General History
SUUTARI, P., Cultural Studies
TOLONEN, Y., Economics
TOLVANEN, M., Criminal Law and Judicial Procedure
TÖTTÖ, P., Methods of Social Research, Teaching in Quantitative and Qualitative Methods

TURTIAINEN, M., Financial Markets and Financial Market Services
TYKKYLÄINEN, M., Rural Studies
VALTONEN, H., Kuopio, Health Economics
VARTIAINEN, P., Human Geography
VOHLONEN, I., Kuopio, Health Policy
VORNANEN, R., Social Work, Kuopio
VUORI, J., Health Management Science

FACULTY OF PHILOSOPHY:

ATJONEN, P., Education
BASCHMAKOFF, N., Russian Language
DILLON, P., Education
FILPPULA, M., English Language
FORSBERG, H., Finnish Language
HAAPASALO, L., Education
HALL, C., German Language
HÄRKÖNEN, U., Education
HEIKKINEN, K., Women's Studies
HOLOPAINEN, L., Special Education
JÄÄSKELÄINEN, R., English Language (Translation and Interpreting)
JÄRVILUOMA-MÄKELÄ, H., Cultural Research
KALASNIEMI, M., Russian Language
KANTELINEN, R., Education
KÄRNÄ, E., Special Education
KEINONEN, T., Education
KETTUNEN, P., Practical Theology
KNUUTTILA, S., Folklore Studies
KOMULAINEN, K., Psychology
KOSONEN, A., Home Economics
KOTIRANTA, M., Church History
KUJAMÄKI, P., German Language (Translation and Interpreting)
LEIMAN, M., Psychology
MÄKISALO, J., Translation Studies
MANNINEN, J., Adult Education
MUIKKU-WERNER, P., Finnish Language
MUSTAKALLIO, H., Church History
NIEMI, J., General Linguistics
NIEMI, S., Swedish Language
NUUTINEN, P., Education
NYMAN, J., English Language
PAATELA-NIEMINEN, M., Education
PALANDER, M., Finnish Language
PERHO, H., Psychology
PIIROINEN, P., Practical Theology
PÖLLÄNEN, S., Education
RÄSÄNEN, A., Pedagogy of Religious Education
RÄTY, H., Psychology
RAUNIO, A., Systematic Theology
SAVOLAINEN, H., Special Education
SEPÄNMAA, Y., Environmental Aesthetics
SEPPÄLÄ, H., Church Music
SEPPÄLÄ, S., Systematic Theology and Patristics
SEVÄNEN, E., Literature
SIILIN, L., Russian Language
SKINNARI, S., Education
THURÉN, L., Biblical Studies
TURUNEN, R., Literature
VÄISÄNEN, P., Education
VANHALAKKA-RUOHO, M., Educational Psychology
WATSON, G., English Language
ZAYKOV, P., Karelian Language and Culture

JYVÄSKYLÄN YLIOPISTO
(University of Jyväskylä)

POB 35, 40014 Univ. of Jyväskylä
Telephone: (14) 2601211
Fax: (14) 2601021
E-mail: tiedotus@jyu.fi
Internet: www.jyu.fi

Founded as Teacher Training School 1863, became College of Education 1934, and Univ. 1966
Languages of instruction: Finnish, English
State control
Academic year: September to July (3 terms)

Rector: Prof. AINO SALLINEN
Vice-Rector: Prof. JAAKKO PEHKONEN
Vice-Rector: Prof. MATTI MANNINEN
Vice-Rector: Prof. HELENA RASKU-PUTTONEN
Admin. Dir: KIRSI MOISANDER
Library Dir: KIMMO TUOMINEN

Number of teachers: 900
Number of students: 15,500

Publications: *Jyväskylä Studies in the Arts, Jyväskylä Studies in Biological and Environmental Science, Jyväskylä Studies in Business and Economics, Jyväskylä Studies in Communication, Jyväskylä Studies in Computing, Jyväskylä Studies in Education, Psychology and Social Research, Jyväskylä Studies in Humanities, Jyväskylä Studies in Languages, Jyväskylä Studies in Sport, Physical Education and Health, Kasvatus* (Finnish Journal of Education), *Studia Historica Jyväskyläensia, Studia Philologica Jyväskyläensia*

DEANS

Faculty of Education (incl. Dept of Teacher Training): Prof. MARJATTA LAIRIO
Faculty of Humanities: Prof. PETRI KARONEN
Faculty of Information Technology: Dr PEKKA NEITTAANMÄKI
Faculty of Mathematics and Science: Prof. HENRIK KUNTTU
Faculty of Social Sciences: Prof. TIMO AHONEN
Faculty of Sport and Health Sciences: Prof. LASSE KANNAS
School of Business and Economics: Prof. JUKKA PELLINEN

PROFESSORS

Faculty of Education (POB 35 (Educa/D), 40014 Univ. of Jyväskylä; tel. (14) 2601600; fax (14) 2601601; e-mail ktk.tdk@edu.jyu.fi; internet www.jyu.fi/tdk/kastdk):

ALANEN, L., Early Childhood Education
HAKALA, J., Education
HÄNNIKÄINEN, M., Early Childhood Education
KAIKKONEN, P., Foreign Language Education
KAUPPINEN, A., Finnish Language Education
KORPINEN, E., Education
LAURINEN, L., Education
MÄÄTTÄ, P., Special Education
POIKKEUS, A.-M., Early Childhood Education
PUOLIMATKA, T., Education
RASKU-PUTTONEN, H., Educational Psychology
SALOVIITA, T., Special Education
VIIRI, J., Pedagogy of Mathematics and Science

Faculty of Humanities (POB 35 (A), 40014 Univ. of Jyväskylä; tel. (14) 2601200; fax (14) 2601201; e-mail humtdk@campus.jyu.fi; internet www.jyu.fi/hum):

ERKKILÄ, J., Music Therapy
HANKA, H., Art History
KALAJA, P., English Language
KARONEN, P., History
KIRSTINÄ, L., Literature
KOSKIMAA, R., Digital Culture
KUNNAS, T., Literature
LAHDELMA, T., Hungarology
LEPPÄNEN, S., English Language
LOUHIVUORI, J., Musicology
LUUKKA, M.-R., Finnish Language
MARTIN, M., Finnish Language
MERISALO, O., Romance Philology
MIELIKÄINEN, A., Finnish Language
MUITTARI, V., Scandinavian Philology
NUMMELA, I., History
PIIRAINEN-MARSH, A., English Philology
RAHKONEN, M., Scandinavian Philology
SALLINEN, A., Speech Communication
SALOKANGAS, R., Journalism
SALO-LEE, L., Intercultural Communication

SIHVOLA, J., History
STARK, L., Ethnology
TOIVIAINEN, P., Musicology
VAINIO, M., Musicology
VALO, M., Speech Communication
VANHALA-ANISZEWSKI, M., Russian Language and Literature
VESTERINEN, I., Cultural Anthropology
VON BONSDORFF, P., Art Education
WAENERBERG, A., Art History
ZETTERBERG, S., History

Faculty of Information Technology (POB 35 (Agora), 40014 Univ. of Jyväskylä; tel. (14) 2601211; fax (14) 2602209; internet www.infotech.jyu.fi):

HÄMÄLÄINEN, T., Information Technology: Telecommunications
HEIKKILÄ, J., Information Systems and Electronic Business
JOUTSENSALO, J., Information Technology: Telecommunications
KÄRKKÄINEN, T., Software Engineering
LYYTINEN, K., Information Systems
MÄKINEN, R. A. E., Applied Mathematics
NEITTAANMÄKI, P., Mathematical Information Technology
PUURONEN, S., Information Systems
ROSSI, T., Software Technology
SAARILUOMA, P., Cognitive Science
SAKKINEN, M., Software Production
SALMINEN, A., Information Technology
TIIHONEN, T., Mathematical Information Technology
TYRVÄINEN, P., Digital Media
VEIJALAINEN, J., Software Production

Faculty of Mathematics and Science (POB 35 (MaD), 40014 Univ. of Jyväskylä; fax (14) 2602201; e-mail pylvanai@jyu.fi; internet www.jyu.fi/science):

AHLSKOG, M., Physics
ALATALO, R., Ecology
ALÉN, R., Applied Chemistry
ÄYSTÖ, J., Physics
BAMFORD, J., Molecular Biology
GEISS, S., Stochastics
HOIKKALA, A., Evolutionary Genetics
JÄRVENPÄÄ, E., Mathematics
JONES, R. I., Limnology
JULIN, R., Physics
KARJALAINEN, J., Fish Biology and Fisheries
KATAJA, M., Physics
KILPELÄINEN, T., Mathematics
KNUUTINEN, J., Applied Chemistry
KOLEHMAINEN, E., Organic Chemistry
KORPPI-TOMMOLA, J., Chemistry
KOSKELA, P., Mathematics
KUITUNEN, M., Environmental Sciences
KUNTTU, H., Physical Chemistry
KUUSALO, T., Mathematics
LEINO, M., Physics
LESKINEN, E., Statistics
MAALAMPI, J., Physics
MANNINEN, M., Physics
MAPPES, J., Ecology and Environmental Management
MÖNKKÖNEN, M., Applied Ecology
NÄKKI, R., Mathematics
NYBLOM, J., Statistics
OIKARI, A., Environmental Sciences
OKER-BLOM, C., Biotechnology
PENTTINEN, A., Statistics
RINTALA, J., Environmental Sciences
RISSANEN, K., Chemistry
SAKSMAN, E., Mathematics
SILLANPÄÄ, R., Chemistry
TIMONEN, J., Applied Physics
TÖRMÄ, P., Physics
VALKONEN, J., Chemistry
VIRTANEN, J., Nanoscience
VUENTO, M., Biochemistry
WHITLOW, H., Physics
YLÄNNE, J., Cell Biology

Faculty of Social Sciences (POB 35, 40014
Univ. of Jyväskylä; tel. (14) 2602800; fax (14)
2602801; internet www.jyu.fi/ytk):

AHONEN, T., Psychology
HEISKALA, R., Social Policy
JÄRVELÄ, M., Social Policy
JYRKÄMÄ, J., Social Gerontology
KANGAS, A., Cultural Policy
KORHONEN, T., Psychology
LYYTINEN, H., Developmental Neuropsychology
MÄNTYSAARI, M., Social Work
NURMI, J.-E., Psychology
PALONEN, K., Political Science
PULKKINEN, T., Political Science and
Women's Studies
SIISIÄINEN, M., Sociology
WAHLSTRÖM, J., Psychology

Faculty of Sport and Health Sciences (POB
35 (L), 40014 Univ. of Jyväskylä; tel. (14)
2602000; fax (14) 2602001; internet www.jyu
.fi/liikunta):

HÄKKINEN, K., Sport Coaching and Fitness
Testing
HEIKINARO-JOHANSSON, P., Physical Education
HEINONEN, A., Physiotherapy
ITKONEN, H., Sport Sociology
KAINULAINEN, H., Sport Physiology
KANNAS, L., Health Education
KUJALA, U., Sport Medicine
LAAKSO, L., Physical Education
LINTUNEN, T., Sports Psychology
MÄLKIÄ, E., Physiotherapy
RANTANEN, T., Gerontology and Public
Health
RINTALA, P., Applied Physical Education
SILVENNOINEN, M., Physical Education
SUOMINEN, H., Sports Gerontology

School of Business and Economics (POB 35
(MaE), 40014 Univ. of Jyväskylä; tel. (14)
2602977; fax (14) 2603331; e-mail taltdk@
econ.jyu.fi; internet www.jyu.fi/jsbe):

AALTIO, J., Management and Leadership
KOIRANEN, M., Entrepreneurship
NIITTYKANGAS, H., Entrepreneurship
PEHKONEN, J., Economics
PELLINEN, J., Accounting
PESONEN, H.-L., Corporate Environmental
Management
TAKALA, T., Management and Leadership
TERVO, H., Economics
UUISTALO, O., Marketing
VIRTANEN, A., Accounting

KUVATAIDEAKATEMIA
(Academy of Fine Arts)

Kaikukatu 4, 00530 Helsinki
Telephone: (9) 6803320
Fax: (9) 68033260
E-mail: kanslia@kuva.fi
Internet: www.kuva.fi
Founded 1848
Rector: MARKUS KONTTINEN
Number of teachers: 50
Number of students: 270

Degree courses in painting, sculpture, graphics, time and space arts (incl. moving image,
photography, site and situation specific arts).

LAPIN YLIOPISTO
(University of Lapland)

POB 122, 96101 Rovaniemi
Telephone: (16) 341341
Fax: (16) 362936
E-mail: tiedotus@ulapland.fi
Internet: www.ulapland.fi
Founded 1979
Languages of instruction: Finnish, English
Public control
Academic year: August to July

Rector: Prof. MAURI YLÄ-KOTOLA
Vice-Rector: Prof. JUKKA MÄKELÄ
Vice-Rector: Dr KAARINA MÄÄTTÄ
Vice-Rector: Prof. SUVI RONKAINEN
Dir of Administration and Legal Affairs:
MARKUS AARTO
Dir of Int. Relations: OUTI SNELLMAN
Dir of Planning and Finance: TARJA SÄRKKÄ
Dir of Human Resources: MIRJA VÄYRYNEN
Library Dir: SUSANNA PARIKKA
Library of 410,000 vols, 1,740 periodicals,
342,960 electronic books, 37,231 electronic
periodicals
Number of teachers: 325
Number of students: 4,840

DEANS

Faculty of Art and Design: Prof. TIMO JOKELA
Faculty of Education: Prof. Dr KYÖSTI KURTAKKO
Faculty of Law: Prof. Dr MATTI NIEMIVUO
Faculty of Social Sciences: Prof. Dr JUHA
PERTTULA

PROFESSORS

Faculty of Art and Design (POB 122, 96101
Rovaniemi; tel. (40) 7396034; fax (16) 341
2361):

BRUSILA-RÄSÄNEN, R., Media Communication
GRANÖ, P., Art Education
HAUTALA-HIRVIOJA, T., Art History
HEIKKILÄ-RASTAS, M., Fashion and Textile
Design
HÄNNINEN, K., Textile Design
JOKELA, T., Art Education
KETTUNEN, I., Industrial Design
TUOMINEN, J., Fine Art
UOTILA, M., Design Research
YLÄ-KOTOLA, M., Media Studies

Faculty of Education (POB 122, 96101 Rovaniemi; tel. (16) 3412420; fax (16) 3412401):

KURTAKKO, K., Adult Education, Continuing Education
LAURIALA, A., Teacher Education
MÄÄTTÄ, K., Educational Psychology
NASKALI, P., Women's Studies
POIKELA, E., Education
RAJALA, R., Education
RUOKAMO, H., Media Education

Faculty of Law (POB 122, 96101 Rovaniemi;
tel. (16) 341341; fax (16) 3412500):

HALTTUNEN, R., Legal Systems and Legal
History, Legal Theory
JUANTO, J., Tax Law
KARHU, J., Civil Law, Law of Obligations
KOKKO, K., Environmental Law
KORHONEN, R, Legal Informatics
KOSKINEN, S., Labour and Social Welfare
Law
KUUSIKKO, K., Administrative Law
MIKKOLA, T., Private International Law
and Comparative Law
NIEMIVUO, M., Administrative Law
SAARENPÄÄ, A., Family and Inheritance
Law, Privacy Law
TAMMI-SALMINEN, E., Property Law
UTRIAINEN, T., Criminal Law
VIIKARI, L, Public International Law
VIROLAINEN, J., Procedural Law
VIRTANEN, P., Commercial Law

Faculty of Social Sciences (POB 122, 96101
Rovaniemi; tel. (16) 3412620; fax (16)
3412600):

HAAHTI, A., Tourism Studies
JÄRVIKOSKI, A., Rehabilitation Science
KINNUNEN, M., Sociology
MERILÄINEN, S., Management
PERTTULA, J., Psychology
POHJOLA, A., Social Work
STENVALL, J., Public Admin.
SUIKKANEN, A., Sociology
TUOMINEN, M., Cultural History
TYRVÄINEN, L., Nature-based Tourism

VEIJOLA, S., Cultural Studies of Tourism
VIERU, M., Accounting
Arctic Centre Research:
FORBES, B., Global Change
KOIVUROVA, T., Environmental and Minority Law
MOORE, J., Climate Change
TENNBERG, M., Sustainable Development

ATTACHED RESEARCH INSTITUTES

Arctic Centre: POB 122, 96101 Rovaniemi;
tel. (16) 341341; fax (16) 362934; internet
www.arcticcentre.org; Dir Prof. Dr PAULA
KANKAANPÄÄ.

Centre for Continuing Education: Chair.
Dr HELKA URPONEN; Dir KAUKO HÄMÄLÄINEN.

Language Centre: Dir VILLE JAKKULA.

Teacher Training School: POB 122, 96101
Rovaniemi; tel. (16) 341341; Principal Dr
EIJA VALANNE.

Lapland University Consortium: Jokiväylä 11c, 96300 Rovaniemi; Dir Lic.
MARKKU TARVAINEN.

LAPPEENRANNAN TEKNILLINEN
KORKEAKOULU
(Lappeenranta University of
Technology)

POB 20, 53851 Lappeenranta
Telephone: (5) 62111
Fax: (5) 6212350
E-mail: info@lut.fi
Internet: www.lut.fi
Founded 1969
Languages of instruction: Finnish, English
State control
Academic year: August to July (2 terms)
Rector: Prof. ILKKA PÖYHÖNEN
Vice-Rector for Research: Prof. VELI-MATTI
VIROLAINEN
Vice-Rector for Education: Prof. HANNU RANTANEN
Dir for Admin.: JUHA-MATTI SAKSA
Librarian: ANJA UKKOLA
Library of 145,000 vols, 600 journals
Number of teachers: 930
Number of students: 5,500

DEANS

Faculty of Technology: ESA MARTTILA
Faculty of Technology Management: MARKKU
TUOMINEN
School of Business: JAANA SANDSTRÖM

PROFESSORS

AALTIO, I., Management and Organization
HANDROOS, H., Machine Automation
KÄLVIÄINEN, H., Information Processing
KÄSSI, T., Industrial Economics
KERTTULA, E., Telematics
KOSKELAINEN, L., Power Plant Engineering
KYLÄHEIKO, K., Economics
LARJOLA, J., Heat Transfer and Fluid Dynamics
LEHTOMAA, A., Entrepreneurship in Technology
LINDSTRÖM, M., Physical Chemistry
LIUHTO, K., International Operations
LUKKA, A., Logistics (esp. Transport), Inventories, Purchasing
LUKKA, M., Applied Mathematics
LUUKKO, A., Physics
MANNER, H., Paper Technology
MARQUIS, G., Steel Structures
MARTIKAINEN, J., Welding Technology
MARTIKKA, H., Design of Machine Elements
MARTTILA, E., Environmental Engineering
MIKKOLA, A., Virtual Engineering
MINKKINEN, P., Inorganic and Analytical
Chemistry
NAOUMOV, V., Data Communications
NIEMI, M., Civil Law

NYSTRÖM, L., Process Technology
NYSTRÖM, M., Membrane Technology
PAATERO, E., Chemical Technology
PARTANEN, J., Electrical Systems
PIRTTILÄ, T., Industrial Engineering and Management (esp. Logistics)
PITKÄNEN, S., Engineering and Technology Management
PORRAS, J., Data Communications
PÖYHÖNEN, I., Wood Technology
PYRHÖNEN, J., Electrical Machines and Drives
PYRHÖNEN, O., Control Engineering
RANTANEN, H., Industrial Engineering
SARKOMAA, P., Technical Thermodynamics
TARJANNE, R., Energy Management and Economics
TIUSANEN, T., International Operations of Industrial Firms
TOIVANEN, P., Information Processing
TUOMINEN, M., Industrial Engineering and Management
TURUNEN, I., Process Systems Engineering
VERHO, A., Structural Design of Machinery
VORACEK, J., Information Processing
ZAMANKHAN, P., Computational Heat and Fluid Dynamics

OULUN YLIOPISTO
(University of Oulu)

Pentti Kaiteran Katu 1, POB 8000, 90014 Univ. of Oulu

Telephone: (8) 5531011
Fax: (8) 5534112
E-mail: kirjaamo@oulu.fi
Internet: www.oulu.fi

Founded 1958
Language of instruction: Finnish
State control
Academic year: September to May (2 terms)

Rector: Prof. LAURI LAJUNEN
Vice-Rector for Research: Dr TAINA PIHLAJA-NIEMI
Vice-Rector for Education: OLLI SILVÉN
Admin. Dir: HANNU PIETILÄ
Librarian: PÄIVI KYTÖMÄKI

Number of teachers: 236
Number of students: 15,661

DEANS

Faculty of Economics and Business Administration: Prof. KIMMO ALAJOUTSIJÄRVI
Faculty of Education: Prof. RIITTA-LIISA KORKEAMÄKI
Faculty of Humanities: Prof. TIMO LAUTTAMUS
Faculty of Medicine: Prof. KARI MAJAMAA
Faculty of Science: Prof. JOUNI PURSIAINEN
Faculty of Technology: Prof. KAUKO LEIVISKÄ

PROFESSORS

Faculty of Economics and Business Administration (POB 4600, 90014 Univ. of Oulu; tel. (8) 5532905; fax (8) 5532906; e-mail international.tatk@oulu.fi; internet www.taloustieteet.oulu.fi):

ALAJOUTSIJÄRVI, K., Marketing
JUGA, J., Logistics
KALLUNKI, J. P., Accounting
KOIVUMÄKI, T., Electronic Commerce
PELTONEN, T., Management and Organization
PERTTUNEN, J., Finance
PUHAKKA, M., Economics
RAHIALA, M., Econometrics
SVENTO, R., Economics

Faculty of Education (POB 2000, 90014 Univ. of Oulu; tel. (8) 5531011; fax (8) 5533600; e-mail studentaffairs.ktk@oulu.fi; internet www.edu.oulu.fi):

FREDRIKSON, M., Music Education
HAKKARAINEN, P., Early Childhood Education

JÄRVELÄ, S., Education
JÄRVIKOSKI, T., Social Science
JÄRVILEHTO, T., Psychology
KALAOJA, E., Didactics
KERANTO, T., Mathematics and Science Education
KORKEAMÄKI, R.-L., Education
LUUKKONEN, J., Education
MÄKINEN, K., Didactics of Foreign Languages
RUISMÄKI, H., Music Education
SILJANDER, P., Education
SOINI, H., Educational Psychology
SUORTTI, J., Education
SYRJÄLÄ, L., Education
VARIS, M., Didactics of Finnish Language and Literature
YLI-LUOMA, P., Education

Faculty of Humanities (POB 1000, 90014 Univ. of Oulu; tel. (8) 5533221; fax (8) 5533230; internet www.oulu.fi/hutk):

BLUHM, L., German Language and Literature
FÄLT, O. K., History
HUHTALA, L., Literature
JOHNSON, A., English
KORPILAHTI, P., Logopaedics
LAUTTAMUS, T., English
LEHTIHALMES, M., Logopaedics
LEHTOLA, V.-P., Saami Culture
MANNINEN, J., History of Science and Ideas
MANTILA, H., Finnish
NUÑES GARCES, M., Archaeology
PENNANEN, J., Cultural Anthropology
ROSSI, P., Scandinavian Languages
SAMMALLAHTI, P., Saami (Lapp) Language and Culture
SORVALI, I., Scandinavian Languages
SULKALA, H., Finnish
SUOMI, K., Phonetics
VAHTOLA, J., Finnish and Scandinavian History

Faculty of Medicine (POB 5000, 90014 Univ. of Oulu; tel. (8) 5375011; fax (8) 5375111; internet www.medicine.oulu.fi):

AIRAKSINEN, P. J., Ophthalmology
ALAHUHTA, S., Anaesthesiology
ALA-KOKKO, L., Medical Biochemistry
HALLMAN, M., Paediatrics
HAUSEN, H., Dentistry
HILLBOM, M., Neurology
HUIKURI, H., Internal Medicine
ISOHANNI, M., Psychiatry
ISOLA, A., Nursing Science
JAAKKOLA, M., Pulmonary Disease
JALOVAARA, P., Surgery
JÄMSÄ, T., Medical Technology
JANHONEN, S., Nursing Didactics
JÄRVELIN, M.-R., Public Health Science
JOUKAMAA, M., Psychiatry
JUVONEN, T., Surgery
KAPRIO, J., Public Health Science
KEINÄNEN-KIUKAANNIEMI, S., General Practice
KESÄNIEMI, A., Internal Medicine
KNUUTTILA, M., Dentistry
KOIVUKANGAS, J., Neurosurgery
KOPONEN, H., Psychiatry
KORTELAINEN, M., Forensic Medicine
LARMAS, M., Dentistry
MÄKELÄ, J., Gastroenterological Surgery
MOILANEN, I., Child Psychiatry
MYLLYLÄ, V., Neurology
NIKKILÄ, J., Health Administration
OIKARINEN, A., Dermatology and Venereology
OIKARINEN, K., Dentistry
PAAVONEN, T., Pathological Anatomy
PELKONEN, O., Pharmacology
PELTONEN, J., Anatomy
PIHLAJANIEMI, T., Medical Biochemistry
PYHTINEN, J., Diagnostic Radiology
RAJANIEMI, H., Anatomy
RÄSÄNEN, P., Psychiatry
RAUSTIA, A., Dentistry

RISTELI, J., Clinical Chemistry
RUOKONEN, A., Clinical Chemistry
RUSKOAHO, H., Molecular Pharmacology
RYYNÄNEN, M., Obstetrics and Gynaecology
SALO, T., Oral Pathology
SAVOLAINEN, M., Internal Medicine
SORRI, M., Otorhinolaryngology
STENBÄCK, F., Pathology
SURAMO, I., Diagnostic Radiology
TAPANAINEN, J., Obstetrics and Gynaecology
TUULONEN, A., Ophthalmology
UHARI, M., Paediatrics
VAINIO, O., Clinical Microbiology
VAINIO, S., Developmental Biochemistry
VIROKANNAS, H., Occupational Health
VUOLTEENAHO, O., Physiology

Faculty of Science (POB 3000, 90014 Univ. of Oulu; tel. (8) 5531011; fax (8) 5531060; internet www.science.oulu.fi):

AKSELA, H., Physics
AKSELA, S., Physics
ALAPIETI, T., Geology and Mineralogy
HÄGGMAN, H., Plant Physiology
HANSKI, E., Geochemistry
HEIKKINEN, O., Geography
HEISKANEN, A., Information Processing Science
HILTUNEN, K., Biochemistry
HOHTOLA, A., Plant Physiology
HOHTOLA, E., Zoology
HOLMSTRÖM, L., Applied Mathematics
HORMI, O., Chemistry
HUTTUNEN, S., Botany
IIVARI, J., Information Processing Science
JÄRVILEHTO, M., Animal Physiology
JAUHIAINEN, J., Applied Geography and Regional Planning
JOKISAARI, J., Physics
KAIKKONEN, P., Geophysics
KAITALA, A., Zoology
KARJALAINEN, P. T., Geography
KINNUNEN, J., Mathematics
KUUTTI, K., Information Processing Science
LAAJOKI, K., Geology and Mineralogy
LÄÄRÄ, E., Statistics
LAASONEN, K., Chemistry
LAITINEN, R., Chemistry
LAJUNEN, L., Inorganic Chemistry
LUNKKA, J. P., Surficial Geology
MUOTKA, T., Zoology
MURSULA, K., Physics
MUSTONEN, V., Mathematics
MYLLYLÄ, R., Biochemistry
NORDSTRÖM, K., Statistics
NYGRÉN, T., Physics
OINAS-KUKKONEN, H., Information Processing Science
OIVO, M., Information Processing Science
OKSANEN, J., Plant Ecology
ORELL, M., Zoology
PAASI, A., Geography
PAMILO, P., Genetics
PERÄMÄKI, P., Inorganic Chemistry
PEURANIEMI, V., Surficial Geology
POUTANEN, J., Astronomy
PULLI, P., Information Processing Science
PURSIAINEN, J., Chemistry
RAHIALA, M., Econometrics
RUDDOCK, L., Protein Science
RUMMUKAINEN, K., Theoretical Physics
RUSANEN, J., Geoinformatics
SAARINEN, J., Geography
SARANEN, J., Applied Mathematics
SAUKKONEN, S., Information Processing Science
SAVOLAINEN, O., Genetics
SEPPÄNEN, V., Information Processing Science
SIMILÄ, J., Information Processing Science
TERVONEN, I., Information Processing Science
THUNEBERG, E., Theoretical Physics
TUOMI, J., Botany
VÄÄNÄNEN, K., Mathematics

WECKSTRÖM, M., Biophysics
WIERENGA, R., Biochemistry

Faculty of Technology (POB 4000, 90014 Univ. of Oulu; tel. (8) 5532001; fax (8) 5532006; e-mail international.ttk@oulu.fi; internet www.ttk.oulu.fi):

BRONER-BAUER, K., Architecture
GLISIC, S., Telecommunication
HAAPASALO, H., Industrial Engineering and Management
HÄRKKI, J., Metallurgy
HENTILÄ, H., Planning and Urban Design
HEUSALA, H., Electronics
IINATTI, J., Telecommunications
JUNTTI, M., Telecommunications
KARHU, S., Radio Technology
KARHUNEN, J., Machine Design
KARJALAINEN, J., Production Engineering
KARJALAINEN, P., Physical Metallurgy
KEISKI, R., Mass and Heat Transfer Processes
KESS, P., Industrial Engineering and Management
KLØVE, B., Water Management
KOISO-KANTTILA, J., Architecture
KORTELA, U., Control and Systems Engineering
KOSTAMOVAARA, J., Electronics
LAHDELMA, S., Machine Condition Diagnostics
LAKSO, E., Environment Engineering
LANTTO, V., Material Physics
LAPPALAINEN, K., Production Engineering
LATVA-AHO, M., Telecommunications
LEIVISKÄ, K., Process Engineering
LEPPÄNEN, P., Telecommunications
MÄÄTTÄ, K., Electronics
MAHLAMÄKI, R., Architecture
MÄNTYLÄ, P., Mechanical Metallurgy
MYLLYLÄ, R., Optoelectronics and Electronic Measurement Technology
NEUBAUER, P., Bioprocess Engineering
NEVALA, K., Mechatronics
NIINIMÄKI, J., Mechanical Process Engineering
NISKANEN, J., Machine Construction
OJALA, T., Computer Engineering
PIETIKÄINEN, M., Computer Technics
PRAMILA, A., Technical Mechanics
RAHKONEN, T., Electronics
RIEKKI, J., Software Architecture for Embedded Systems
RÖNING, J., Embedded Systems
RUOTSALAINEN, K., Mathematics
SALONEN, E., Radio Technology
SAUVOLA, J., Multimedia Systems
SEIKKALA, S., Applied Mathematics
SEPPÄNEN, T., Biomedical Technology
SILVÉN, O., Signal Processing
SJÖLIND, S., Engineering Mechanics
TARUMAA, A., Planning and Urban Design
TASA, J., Architecture
TUPPURAINEN, Y., Architecture
VÄHÄKANGAS, J., Electronics Production Technology
VÄYRYNEN, S., Work Science

ATTACHED INSTITUTES

Institute for Electron Microscopy: POB 7100, 90014 Univ. of Oulu; Dir JANNE REMES.
Kajaani University Consortium: Seminaarinkatu 2, POB 51, 87100 Kajaani; Dir JUHANI SUORTTI.
Laboratory Animal Centre: Keks 5, POB 5000, 90014 Univ. of Oulu; Dir H.-M. VOIPIO.
Language Centre: POB 7200, 90014 Univ. of Oulu; Dir HARRY. ANTTILA.
Learning and Research Services: POB 7910, 90014 Univ. of Oulu; Dir ANNA-MAIJA YLIMAULA.
Meri-Lappi Institute: 94600 Kemi; Dir A. TIILIKAINEN.

Sodankylä Geophysical Observatory: Tähteläntie 62, 99600 Sodankylä; Dir TAUNO TURUNEN.

Thule Institute: POB 7300, 90014 Univ. of Oulu; Dir KARI LAINE.

SIBELIUS-AKATEMIA
(Sibelius Academy)

POB 86, 00251 Helsinki
Telephone: (20) 75390
Fax: (20) 7539600
E-mail: info@siba.fi
Internet: www.siba.fi
Founded 1882
Languages of instruction: Finnish, Swedish
State control
Academic year: September to May
Univ. status
Rector: GUSTAV DJUPSJÖBACKA
Vice-Rector: JARI PERKIÖMÄKI, KARI KURKELA
Admin. Dir: SEPPO SUIHKO
Library: see Libraries and Archives
Number of teachers: 480
Number of students: 1,700

DEANS

Church Music: PETER PEITSALO
Church Music (in Kuopio): OLAVI HAUTSALO
Composition and Music Theory: RIITTA VALKEILA
Folk Music: HEIKKI LAITINEN
Jazz Music: JARI PERKIÖMÄKI
Music Education: SOILI PERKIÖ
Music Technology: ROBERT DE GODZINSKY
Orchestral Instruments: MERIT PALAS
Piano Music: HUI-YING TAWASTSTJERNA
Vocal Music: OUTI KÄHKÖNEN

PROFESSORS

CANTELL, T., Arts Management
CASTRÉN, M., Music Research
GOTHONI, R., Chamber Music
HELASVUO, M., Wind Instrument Music
JOKINEN, E., Composition
JUSSILA, K., Organ Music
KURKELA, K., Music Performance and Research
KURKELA, V., Popular Music
LAITINEN, H., Folk Music
LAITINEN, M., Music Education
LEE, M.-K., Violin
LEHTINEN, M., Operatic Training
MURTOMÄKI, V., History of Music
NORAS, A., Cello Music
ORAMO, I., Music Theory
PORTHAN, O., Organ Music
PUUMALA, V.-M., Composition
RAEKALLIO, M., Piano Music
ROUSI, M., Cello Music
RUOHONEN, S., Opera
SAARIKETTU, K., Violin Music
SALOMAA, P., Vocal Music
SEGERSTAM, L., Orchestral Conducting
SIVUOJA-GUNARATNAM, A., Music Performance and Research
SUURPÄÄ, L., Music Theory
SZILVAY, R., Violin Music
TAITTO, I., Church Music
TAWASTSTJERNA, E. T., Piano Music
TUPPURAINEN, E., Church Music
UOTILA, J., Jazz Music
WESTERLUND, H., Music Education

SVENSKA HANDELSHÖGSKOLAN
(Hanken School of Economics)

Helsinki Campus, POB 479, Arkadiagatan 22 00101 Helsinki
Telephone: (9) 431331
Fax: (9) 43133333
Vasa Branch Campus, POB 287, Handelsesplanaden 2, 65101 Vasa
Telephone: (6) 3533700

Fax: (6) 3533703
E-mail: info@hanken.fi
Internet: www.hanken.fi
Founded 1909
Languages of instruction: Swedish, English
Semi-state control
Academic year: September to May
Founded 1909
Rector: EVA LILJEBLOM
Vice-Rector: EERO VAARA
Vice-Rector: SÖREN KOCK
Admin. Dir: M. LINDROOS
Librarian: TUA HINDERSSON-SÖDERHOLM
Library of 97,900 vols, 55,000 books, 187 periodicals, 20,200 e-journals
Number of teachers: 120
Number of students: 2,147 , 169 doctoral

PROFESSORS

Accounting:
EKHOLM, B.
TALLBERG, A.
VIITANEN, J.
WALLIN, J.
VEST, T.

Commercial Law:
BRUUN, N.
KUKKONEN, M.
MÄNTYSAARI, P.
NORRGÅRD, M.

Economics and Statistics:
BERGLUND, T.
BLOMQVIST, H. C.
ROSENQVIST, G., Statistics
STENBACKA, R.
TERÄSVIRTA T., Statistics

Finance:
HANSSON, M.
HÖGHOLM, K.
KNIF, J.
KORKEAMÄKI, T.
LÖFLUND, A.

Management and Organization:
BJÖRKMAN, I.
FURU P.
HEARN, J.
MANTERE, S.
SVEIBY, K.
VAARA, E.

Informatics:
BJÖRK, B.

Entrepreneurship, Management and Organisation:
KOCK, S.
LINDELL, M.

Supply Chain Management and Corporate Geography:
SPENS, K.

Marketing:
BJÖRK, P.
GRÖNROOS, C.
HOLMLUND-RYTKÖNEN, M.
LILJANDER, V.
LINDQVIST, L.
STORBACKA, K.
STRANDVIK, T.

Swedish:
TANDEFELT, M.

TAMPEREEN TEKNILLINEN
YLIOPISTO
(Tampere University of Technology)

POB 527, 33101 Tampere
Telephone: (3) 311511
Fax: (3) 3652170
Internet: www.tut.fi
Founded 1965
Language of instruction: Finnish

State control
Academic year: September to May
Rector: Prof. MARKKU KIVIKOSKI
Vice-Rectors: Prof. PAUL H. ANDERSSON, Prof. MATTI PENTTI
Dir of Admin.: TIINA ÄIJÄLÄ
Librarian: ARJA-RIITTA HAARALA
Number of teachers: 1,906
Number of students: 12,000

DEANS

Faculty of Automation, Mechanical and Material Engineering: TOIVO LEPISTÖ
Faculty of Built Environment: TERTTU PAKARINEN
Faculty of Business and Technology Management: MIKA HANNULA
Faculty of Computing and Electrical Engineering: ULLA RUOTSALAINEN
Faculty of Science and Environmental Engineering: MARTTI KAURANEN

PROFESSORS

AITTOMÄKI, A., Refrigeration Technology
ASTOLA, J., Digital Signals Processing
AUMALA, O., Metrology
ERIKSSON, J.-T., Electrodynamics and Magnetism
GABBOUJ, M., Information Technology
HAIKALA, I., Computer Science
HARJU, J., Telecommunications
HARTIKAINEN, J., Soil Mechanics and Foundation Engineering
JAAKKOLA, H., Information Technology
JALLINOJA, R., Architectural Theory
JARSKE, P., Telecommunications
KALLBERG, H., Transport
KALLI, S., Information Technology
KÄRNÄ, J., Electrical Power Engineering
KARVINEN, R., Fluid Dynamics and Heat Transfer
KATAINEN, J., Architectural Design
KAUNONEN, A., Control Engineering
KIVIKOSKI, M., Industrial Electronics
KORPINEN, L., Electrical Power Engineering
KOSKI, J., Structural Mechanics
KURKI-SUONIO, R., Computer Science and Engineering
LAKSO, T., Production Engineering
LAUTALA, P., Control Engineering
LEMMITYINEN, H., Chemistry
LEPISTÖ, T., Mathematics
LINDBERG, R., Structural Engineering
MÄKILÄ, P., Automation Technology
MALMIVUO, J., Bioelectronics
MATTILA, M., Occupational Safety Engineering
MAULA, J., Urban Planning
NOUSIAINEN, P., Textile Technology
NYBERG, T., Paper Machine Automation
OTALA, M., Industrial Management
PESSA, M., Semiconductor Technology
PUHALKA, J., Environmental Biotechnology
RENFORS, M., Telecommunications Engineering
RIIHELÄ, S., Construction Economics and Management
RIITAHUHTA, A., Machine Design
RISTALAINEN, E., Electronics
SAARIKORPI, J., Industrial Management and Engineering
SAARINEN, J., Signal Processing Laboratory
SARAMAKI, T., Signal Processing
SAVOLAINEN, J., Process Engineering
SIEKKINEN, V., Maintenance Technology
SIIKANEN, U., Architectural Construction
TALLQVIST, T., History of Architecture
TIANEN, T., Materials Engineering
TOMBERG, J., Information Technology
TÖRMÄLÄ, P., Plastics Technology
TORVINEN, S., Production Automation
TUHKANEN, T., Environmental Engineering
TUOKKO, R., Automation Technology
TUOMALA, M., Structural Mechanics

UUSI-RAUVA, E., Industrial Management and Engineering
VANHARANTA, H., Industrial Management and Engineering
VILENIUS, M., Hydraulic Machines

TAMPEREEN YLIOPISTO
(University of Tampere)

Kalevantie 4, 33014 Univ. of Tampere
Telephone: (3) 355111
Fax: (3) 2134473
E-mail: kirjaamo@uta.fi
Internet: www.uta.fi
Founded 1925
Languages of instruction: Finnish, English
State control
Academic year: September to May
Chancellor: Dr KRISTA. VARANTOLA
Rector: Prof. KAIJA HOLLI
Vice-Rector: Prof. HARRI MELIN
Vice-Rector: Prof. PERTTI HAAPALA
Admin. Dir: PETRI LINTUNEN
Librarian: MIRJA IIVONEN
Number of teachers: 694
Number of students: 15,643
Publication: *Acta Universitatis Tamperensis*

DEANS

Institute of Biomedical Technology: Prof. HANNU HANHIJÄRVI
School of Communication, Media and Theatre: HEIKKI HELLMAN
School of Education: Prof. JUHA SUORANTA
School of Health Sciences: Prof. PEKKA RISSANEN
School of Information Sciences: Prof. KARI-JOUKO RÄIHÄ
School of Language, Translation, and Literary Studies: Prof. JUKKA HAVU
School of Management: Prof. MARKKU SOTARAUTA
School of Medicine: Prof. MATTI LEHTO
School of Social Sciences and Humanities: Prof. RISTO KUNELIUS

TEATTRIKORKEAKOULU
(Theatre Academy Helsinki)

POB 163, 00531 Helsinki
Haapaniemenkatu 6, 00530 Helsinki
Telephone: (9) 431361
Fax: (9) 43136200
E-mail: international@teak.fi
Internet: www.teak.fi
Founded 1979
State control
Languages of instruction: Finnish, Swedish
Rector: PAULA TUOVINEN
Vice-Rector: ESA KIRKKOPELTO
Head of Admin.: ESA HAMALAINEN
Librarian: PIRKKO-LIISA NURMINEN
Library of 40,000 vols, 200 periodicals
Number of teachers: 41
Number of students: 380

PROFESSORS

ARLANDER, A., Performance and Theory
KIRKKOPELTO, E., Artistic Research
LIIMATAINEN, J., Sound Design
MONNI, K., Choreography
OUTINEN, K., Acting (Finnish)
RUIKKA, M., Directing
RUOHONEN, L., Dramaturgy
SÖDERBLOM, E., Acting (Swedish)
TENHULA, N., Contemporary Dance
UIMONEN, M., Lighting Design
VIERIKKO, V., Acting (Finnish)

TURUN YLIOPISTO
(University of Turku)

20014 Univ. of Turku
Telephone: (2) 33351
Fax: (2) 3336363
E-mail: international@utu.fi
Internet: www.utu.fi
Founded 1920
State control
Languages of instruction: Finnish, English
Academic year: August to July (2 semesters)
Chancellor: Prof. PEKKA PUSKA
Rector: Prof. KEIJO VIRTANEN
Vice-Rector: Prof. HARRI LÖNNBERG
Vice-Rector: Prof. TAPIO REPONEN
Vice-Rector: Prof. PIRJO NUUTILA
Chief Operating Officer: PÄIVI MIKKOLA
Chief Librarian: ULLA NYGRÉN
Library: 2.8m. vols
Number of teachers: 810
Number of students: 17,925
Publication: *Annales Universitatis Turkuensis*

DEANS

Faculty of Education: Prof. MARJA VAURAS
Faculty of Humanities: Prof. RISTO HILTUNEN
Faculty of Law: Prof. JUKKA MÄHÖNEN
Faculty of Mathematics and Natural Sciences: Prof. REIJO LAHTI
Faculty of Medicine: Prof. TAPANI RÖNNEMAA
Faculty of Social Sciences: Prof. VELI-MATTI RITAKALLIO

PROFESSORS

Faculty of Education (tel. (2) 3338803; fax (2) 3338500; e-mail education@utu.fi; internet www.edu.utu.fi):

HELENIUS, A., Early Education
KESKINEN, S., Education
KIVIRAUMA, J., Education
KOSKENSALO, A., Teaching of Foreign Languages
LAINE, K., Early Education
LEHTINEN, E., Teacher Training
LEHTONEN, K., Open Univ. Education
NIEMI, P., Education
NIINISTÖ, K., Education (Teacher Training)
NUPPONEN, H., Physical Education
OLKINUORA, E., Education
PELTONEN, J., Education (Teaching of Handicrafts)
RINNE, R., Adult Education
SARMAVUORI, K., Teaching of Mother Tongue
SOININEN, M., Didactics
VAURAS, M., Education (Learning and Teaching)
VIRTA, A., Teaching of History and Social Sciences

Faculty of Humanities (tel. (2) 3335201; fax (2) 3335200; e-mail hum-info@utu.fi; internet www.hum.utu.fi):

AHOKAS, P., Comparative Literature
ANTTONEN, V., Comparative Religion
CARCEDO, A., Spanish Language, Culture and Translation
DE ANNA, L., Italian Language, Culture and Translation
GAMBIER, Y., French Translation Studies
GRANÖ, P., Cultural Production and Landscape Studies
HAKAMIES, P., Folkloristics
HÄKKINEN, K., Finnish Language
HÄYRYNEN, M., Landscape Studies
HELASVUO, M.-L., Finnish Language
HILTUNEN, R., Finnish Language
HIRVONEN, I., Scandinavian Philology
HOVI, K., General History
HUUMO, T., Cultural History
IMMONEN, K., French Language and Culture
ITÄLÄ, M.-L., German Translation Studies

ITKONEN, E., General Linguistics
JOHANSSON, M., Art History
KEINÄSTÖ, K., Finnish Literature
KORPILAHTI, P., Logopaedics
KOSTIAINEN, A., Ethnology
KUUSAMO, A., Art History
LAPPALAINEN, P., German Language
LEIMU, P., Russian Language and Culture
LILJESTRÖM, M., Women's Studies
MOISALA, P., Musicology
MYLLYNTAUS, T., Finnish History
MYLLYNTAUS, T., Media Studies
NIKULA, H., Finnish Literature
PIETILÄ, P., English
PYYKKÖ, R., Comparative Literature and Drama
RIDELL, S., Media Studies
ROJOLA, L., Finnish Literature
SAARILUOMA, L., English Philology
SAARINEN, S., Scandinavian Philology
SIHVONEN, J., French Language
SUNDMAN, M., English Translation Studies
SUOMELA-SALMI, E., French Language and Culture
TAAVITSAINEN, J.-P., Archaeology
TOMMOLA, J., English Translation Studies
VAAHTERA, J., Classical Languages and Culture
VIRTANEN, K., Cultural History

Faculty of Law (tel. (2) 3336307; fax (2) 3336570; e-mail tls@utu.fi; internet www.law.utu.fi):

ÄMMÄLÄ, T., Procedural Law
BACKMAN, E. V., Criminal Law
BJÖRNE, L., Roman, Law and Legal History
HANNIKAINEN, L., Int. Law
HELIN, M., Private Law
JOKELA, A. T., Procedural Law
KAIRINEN, M., Labour Law
KULLA, H., Admin. Law
LAITINEN, A., Criminology and Sociology of Law
MÄHÖNEN, J., Civil Law
OJANEN, T., European Law
OSSA, J., Financial Law
SAARNILEHTO, A., Civil Law
TALA, J., Legislative Studies
TOMMOLA, J., International Commercial Law
TUOMISTO, J., Civil Law
VILJANEN, P., Criminal and Procedural Law
WIKSTRÖM, K., Financial Law

Faculty of Mathematics and Natural Sciences (tel. (2) 3336576; fax (2) 3336575; e-mail intsci@utu.fi; internet www.sci.utu.fi):

ANDERSSON, H., Human Geography
ARO, E.-M., Plant Physiology
ÄYRÄS, P., Organic Chemistry
EKLUND, O., Geology and Mineralology
GLOOS, K., Physics
HAAPAKKA, K., Analytical Chemistry
HARJU, T., Mathematics
HEINO, J., Biochemistry
HIETARINTA, J., Theoretical Physics
HÖLSÄ, J., Inorganic Chemistry
HONKALA, I., Mathematics
HUOPALAHTI, R., Food Chemistry
ISOAHO, J., Electronics and Information Technology
JORMALAINEN, V., Ecology
KALLIO, H., Food Chemistry
KANKARE, J., Analytical Chemistry
KARHUMÄKI, J., Mathematics
KARI, J., Mathematics
KARSTÉN, E., Information Systems Science
KÄYHKÖ, J., Geography
KNUUTILA, T., Computer Science
KORPIMÄKI, E., Ecology
KUKK, E., Physics
LAHDELMA, R., Information Systems Science
LAHTI, R., Biochemistry
LAIHO, R., Physics
LEIPÄLÄ, T., Applied Mathematics

LÖNNBERG, H., Organic Chemistry
LÖVGREN, T., Biotechnology
LUKKARI, J., Physical Chemistry
MÄKELÄ, M., Applied Mathematics
NEVALAINEN, O., Computer Science
NIKINMAA, M., Animal Physiology
NORRDAHL, K., Ecology
NURMINEN, M., Information Systems Science
OKSANEN, LAURI, Plant Ecology
PAASIO, A., Microelectronics
PETTERSSON, K., Biotechnology
PIHLAJA, K., Physical Chemistry
PRIMMER, C., Genetics
RÄSÄNEN, M., Quaternary Geology
RINTAMÄKI, E., Genetics
SAARINEN, T., Geology and Mineralogy
SALAKOSKI, T., Computer Science
SALMINEN, S., Food Devt
SALO, J., Biodiversity Research
SARVALA, J., Ecology
SAVILAHTI, H., Genetics
SOLIN, O., Radiochemistry
SUNDBLAD, K., Geology and Mineralogy
SUOMINEN, K.-A., Physics
TAPANINEN, U., Logistic Systems of Maritime Transport
TENHUNEN, H., Nanoelectronics
TORSTI, J., Space Research
TUOMINEN, A., Electronics
VALTAOJA, E., Astronomy
VALTONEN, M., Astronomy
VÄYRYNEN, J., Physics
YLI-JOKIPII, P., Human Geography
YLINEN, K., Mathematics

Faculty of Medicine (tel. (2) 33351; fax (2) 3338413; e-mail intmedi@utu.fi; internet www.med.utu.fi):

ARO, H., Orthopaedics and Traumatology
ARONEN, P., Diagnostic Radiology
CARPÉN, O., Pathology
DEAN, P., Diagnostic Radiology
ELENIUS, K., Medical Biochemistry
GRÉNMAN, R., Otorhinolaryngology
HÄNNINEN, P., Medical Physics
HAPPONEN, R.-P., Oral Surgery
HARTIALA, J., Clinical Physiology and Nuclear Medicine
HIETALA, J., Psychiatry
HUUPPONEN, R., Pharmacology
ISOLAURI, E., Paediatrics
JALKANEN, S., Immunology
JALONEN, J., Anaesthesiology
KÄHÄRI, V.-M., Dermatology and Venereal Diseases
KANERVA, L., Synthetic Drug Chemistry
KEMPPAINEN, P., Stomatognathic Physiology
KIVELÄ, S.-L., General Practice
KÖNÖNEN, E., Dentistry
KOTILAINEN, P., Infectious Diseases
KOULU, M., Drug Devt
LAUNIS, V., Medical Ethics
LEINO-KILPI, H., Nursing Science
MÄKELA, S., Drug Devt
MÄKINEN, J., Obstetrics and Gynaecology
MÖTTÖNEN, T., Rheumatology
NÄRHI, T., Dental Prosthetics
NUUTILA, P., Internal Medicine
OLKKOLA, K., Anaesthesiology
PELLINIEMI, L., Electron Microscopy
PELTONEN, J., Anatomy
PIHA, J., Child Psychiatry
PUOLAKKAINEN, P., Surgery
PYRHÖNEN, S., Oncology and Radiotherapy
RÖNNEMAA, T., Internal Medicine
ROBERTS, P. J., Surgery
SALOKANGAS, R., Psychiatry
SAUKKO, P., Forensic Medicine
SCHEININ, M., Biomaterial Technology
SCHEININ, M., Clinical Pharmacology
SIMELL, O. G., Paediatrics
SYRJÄNEN, S., Oral Pathology and Radiology

TENOVUO, J. O., CardiologyTOPPARI, J., Physiology
TUOMINEN, R., Public Health
VÄÄNÄNEN, K., Cell Biology
VÄLIMÄKI, M., Nursing Science
VALLITTU, P., Prosthetic Dentistry and Biomaterials Science
VARRELA, J., Oral Devt and Orthodontics
VIIKARI, J., Internal Medicine
VIITANEN, M., Geriatrics

Faculty of Social Sciences (tel. (2) 3335362; fax (2) 3336270; e-mail webyht@utu.fi; internet www.soc.utu.fi):

AINAMO, A., Innovation, Technology and Science Policy
FORSSÉN, K., Social Work
HAKOVIRTA, H., Political Science, International Politics
HÄMÄLÄINEN, H., Psychology
KESKINEN, E., Psychology
KIVINEN, O., Sociology of Education
KOISTINEN, O., Theoretical Philosophy
LAGERSPETZ, E., Practical Philosophy
MELIN, H., Sociology
NIEMI, P., Psychology
NURMI, H., Political Science
PÖNTINEN, S., Sociology
RÄIHÄ, H., Psychology
RENTOLA, K., Contemporary History
RITAKALLIO, V.-M., Social Policy
SALMIVALLI, C., Psychology
SALONEN, H., Economics
SOIKKANEN, T., Contemporary History
UUSIPAIKKA, E., Statistics
VIRÉN, M., Economics
WIBERG, M., Political Science

Turku School of Economics:

ALVAREZ, L., Quantitative Methods in Management
GRANLUND, M., Management Accounting
HALINEN-KAILA, A., Marketing
IMMONEN, R., Business Law
KAUPPI, H., Economics
KOVALAINEN, A., Women's Studies
LÄHTEENMÄKI, S., Management and Organisation
LAURILA, J., Management and Organisation
LIUHTO, K., Marketing International Business, Pan-European Institute
LUKKA, K., Management Accounting
MARJANEN, H., Economic Geography
NUMMELA, N., International Business
OJALA, L., Logistics
OLKKONEN, R., Marketing
PAASIO, A., Business and Innovation Development, Business
PAASIO, A., Business and Innovation Development, Microelectronics
RÄSÄNEN, P., Economic Sociology
REPONEN, T., Information Systems Science
SALONEN, H., Economics
SCHADEWITZ, H., Accounting and Finance
SILLANPÄÄ, M., Commercial Law
STENBERG, E., International Marketing
SUOMI, R., Information Systems Science
VARTIAINEN, H., Public Economics
VIRÉN, N., Economics

VAASAN YLIOPISTO
(University of Vaasa)

Wolffintie 34, POB 700, 65101 Vaasa

Telephone: (6) 3248111
Fax: (6) 3248208
E-mail: kirjaamo@uwasa.fi
Internet: www.uwasa.fi

Founded 1966
Languages of instruction: Finnish, Swedish, English
State control
Academic year: September to May

Rector: MATTI JAKOBSSON
Vice-Rector: TAUNO KEKÄLE

Vice-Rector: JUKKA VESALAINEN
Admin. Dir: ANITA NIEMI-IILAHTI
Librarian: VUOKKO PALONEN

Library of 120,000 vols
Number of teachers: 270
Number of students: 4,800
Publication: *Acta Wasaensia*

DEANS

Faculty of Business Studies: Prof. VESA SUUTARI
Faculty of Philosophy: Prof. MERJA KOSKELA
Faculty of Technology: Prof. ERKKI ANTILA

PROFESSORS

Faculty of Business Studies (tel. (6) 3248111; fax (6) 3248171; internet www.uwasa.fi/kauppatieteet):

ÄIJÖ, J., Accounting and Business finance AnnolA, V., Business Law
GABRIELSSON, P., Management and Organization
GAHMBERG, H., Marketing
LAAKSONEN, P., Marketing
LAITINEN, E. K., Accounting and Business Finance
LAITINEN, T., Accounting and Business Finance
LARIMO, J., Int. Marketing
LEHTONEN, A., Law
LINDMAN, M., Marketing
LUOMALA, H., Marketing
NIKKINEN, J., Accounting and Business Finance
PIEKKOLA, H., Economics
ROTHOVIUS, T., Accounting and Business Finance
ROUTAMAA, V., Management and Organization
SALMI, T., Accounting and Business Finance
SUUTARI, V., Management and Organization
VATAJA, J., Economics
VESALAINEN, J., Management and Organization
VIITALA, R., Management and Organization

Faculty of Humanities (tel. (6) 3248111; fax (6) 3248131; internet www.uwasa.fi/hmanistien):

AALTONEN, S., English Language, Literature and Culture
BJÖRKLUND, S., Language Immersion
KOSKELA, M., Applied Linguistics
LAURÉN, CH., Swedish
LEHTINEN, E., Modern Finnish
NORDMAN, M., Swedish
PIEKKOLA, H., Economics

Faculty of Philosophy (tel. (6) 3248111; fax (6) 3248465; internet www.uwasa.fi/filosofinen):

AALTONEN, S., English Language, Literature and Culture
BJÖRKLUND, S., Language Immersion
LEHTINEN, E., Modern Finnish
MALMBERG, T., Communications
MÅRD-MIETTINEN, K., Swedish Language
NUOPPONEN, A., Applied Linguistics
PARRY, C., German Language
PORTER, G., English Language
SALMINEN, A., Public Admin.
SKOG-SÖDERSVED, M., German Language
VIRKKALA, S., Regional Studies

Faculty of Public Administration (tel. (6) 3248111; fax (6) 3248465; internet www.uwasa.fi/hallintotieteet):

HYYRYLÄINEN, E., Public Admin
KATAJAMÄKI, H., Regional Studies
SALMINEN, A., Public Admin.
VARTIAINEN, P., Public Admin.

Faculty of Technology (tel. (6) 32481111; fax (6) 3248344; internet www.uwasa.fi/trkniikka):

ALANDER, J., Production Automation
ELMUSRATI, M., Telecommunication Engineering
HASSI, S., Mathematics
HELO, P., Logistics
KAUHANIEMI, K., Electrical Engineering
PYNNÖNEN, S., Statistics
SOTTINEN, T., Business Mathematics
TAKALA, J., Production Economics
VEKARA, T., Electrical Engineering
WANNE, M., Information Technology

Polytechnics

Diakonia-ammattikorkeakoulu (Diaconia University of Applied Sciences): Sturenkatu 2, 00510 Helsinki; tel. (20) 690431; fax (9) 47800794; e-mail international.office@diak.fi; internet www.diak.fi; f. 1996; education, nursing, social welfare, sign language interpretation and media; library: 150,000 vols, periodicals and audiovisual items; 3,000 students; Rector Dr JORMA NIEMALÄ.

Etelä-Karjalan ammattikorkeakoulu (South Karelia Polytechnic): Pohjolankatu 23, POB 303, 53100 Lappeenranta; tel. (20) 4966411; fax (20) 4966505; e-mail info@scp.fi; internet www.scp.fi; faculties of business administration, fine arts and design, health care and social services, technology and tourism and hospitality; 260 teachers; 2,700 students; Rector ANNELI PIRTTILÄ.

HAAGA-HELIA Ammattikorkeakoulu (HAAGA-HELIA University of Applied Sciences): Ratapihantie 13, 00520 Helsinki; tel. (9) 229611; fax (9) 147063; e-mail hakutoimisto@haaga-helia.fi; internet www.haaga-helia.fi; Bachelors programmes in business administration, hospitality management, journalism, sport and leisure; campuses in Haaga, Malmi, Pasila, Provoo (two), Villila, Vierumäki; 600 teachers; 10,000 students; Rector RITVA LAAKSO-MANNINEN.

Hämeen Ammattikorkeakoulu (Häme Polytechnic): POB 230, 13100 Hämeenlinna; tel. (3) 6461; fax (3) 6464200; e-mail hamk@hamk.fi; internet www.hamk.fi; f. 1996; culture, natural resources and the environment, natural sciences, social sciences, business and administration, social services, health and sports technology, communication and transport tourism, catering and domestic services and vocational teacher education; library: 120,000 vols, 450 periodicals in Finnish, 350 in other languages; 349 teachers; 7,000 students; Rector VEIJO HINTSANEN.

Helsinki Metropolia University of Applied Sciences: POB 4000, Blvd 31, 00079 Metropolia; tel. (20) 7835000; fax (20) 7835500; e-mail viestinta@metropolia.fi; internet www.metropolia.fi; f. 2008 by merger of EVTEK University of Applied Sciences and Helsinki Polytechnic Stadia; courses in culture, business, healthcare, social services and technology; 14,000 students; Pres. RIITTA KONKOLA.

HUMAK (Hakutoimistoon) (Humanities Polytechnic): Ilkantie 4, 95410 Helsinki; tel. (20) 7621320; fax (20) 7621321; e-mail helsinki@humak.fi; internet www.humak.fi; f. 1998; programmes in civic activities and youth work, cultural management and production, and sign language interpreting; 120 teachers; 1,300 students; Pres. EEVA-LIISA ANTIKAINEN.

Jyväskylän Ammattikorkeakoulu (Jyväskylä Polytechnic): Rajakatu 35, 40200 Jyväskylä; tel. (20) 7438100; fax (14) 4499694; internet www.jamk.fi; incl. School of Business and Services Management, School of Health and Social Studies, School of Technology and Teacher Education College; 600 teachers; 8,000 students; Rector JUSSI HALTTUNEN.

Kajaanin Ammattikorkeakoulu (Kajaani Polytechnic): POB 52, Ketunpolku 3, 87101 Kajaani; tel. (8) 618991; fax (8) 61899603; e-mail kajaanin.amk@kajak.fi; internet www.kajak.fi; f. 1992; business and administration, tourism and hospitality management, health and sports and engineering; library: 27,000 vols, 350 periodicals; 80 teachers; 1,500 students; Pres. TURO KILPELÄINEN.

Kemi-Tornion Ammattikorkeakoulu (Kemi-Tornio Polytechnic): POB 505, 94101 Kemi; tel. (10) 38350; fax (16) 251120; internet www.tokem.fi; f. 1992; business administration, business and data-processing, cultural and media arts, health care, social services, technology; library: 100,000 vols, 6,300 e-journals, 37,000 e-books; 260 teachers; 2,600 students; Rector REIJO TOLPPI.

Kymenlaakso Ammattikorkeakoulu (Kymenlaakso Polytechnic): POB 9, 48401 Kotka; tel. (44) 7028888; fax (5) 2302430; e-mail kirjaamo@kyamk.fi; internet www.kyamk.fi; f. 1992; courses in technology and transport, natural resources and the environment, social sciences, business and administration, natural sciences, culture, and social, health and physical education; library: 100,000 vols, 500 periodicals; 220 teachers; 4,500 students; Rector RAGNAR LUNDQVIST.

Lahden Ammattikorkeakoulu (Lahti Polytechnic): Paasikivenkatu 7A, POB 214, 15101 Lahti; tel. (3) 82818; fax (3) 882064; e-mail lamk@lamk.fi; internet www.lamk.fi; f. 1991; courses in business studies, design, fine arts, music, hospitality management, social and health care, sports, technology and engineering, and visual communication; 200 teachers; 5,000 students; Dr RISTO ILOMÄKI.

Laurea Ammattikorkeakoulu (Laurea Polytechnic): Ratatie 22, 01300 Vantaa; tel. (9) 88687293; fax (9) 88687298; internet www.laurea.fi; courses in culture, natural resources and the environment, natural sciences, social sciences, business and administration, social services, health and sports, tourism, catering and domestic services, hotel and restaurant studies, and correctional services; library: 115,300 vols, 10,000 e-journals; 8,000 students; Rector PENTTI RAUHALA.

Mikkelin Ammattikorkeakoulu (Mikkeli Polytechnic): Tarkkampujankuja 1, POB 181, 50101 Mikkeli; tel. (15) 35561; fax (15) 3556464; e-mail mamk@mamk.fi; internet www.mamk.fi; Business School, School of Engineering, School of Social Work and Health Care, School of Culture and Youth Work, School of Hospitality Management, School of Forestry (Pieksämäki), School of Health Care, Tourism and Culture (Savonlinna); 200 teachers; 4,500 students; Rector ERKKI KARPPANEN.

Novia Yrkeshögskolan (Novia Polytechnic): Tehtaankatu 1, 65100 Vaasa; tel. (6) 3285000; fax (6) 3285110; e-mail admissions@novia.fi; internet www.novia.fi; f. 2008 by merger of Svenska Yrkeshögskolan and Yrkeshögskolan Sydväst; language of instruction: Swedish; courses in culture, healthcare, social welfare, technology, and communications; 4,000 students; Rector ÖRJAN ANDERSSON.

Österbottens Yrkeshögskola (Central Ostrobothnia Polytechnic): Talonpojankatu 4, 67100 Kokkola; tel. (6) 8250000; fax (6) 8252000; internet www.cop.fi; f. 1998; languages of instruction: Finnish, Swedish,

English; technology, communication and transport, social sciences, business and administration, social services, health and sports, natural sciences, culture, humanities and education, tourism, catering and domestic services; post graduate programmes in business administration and technology; 246 teachers; 3,300 students; Rector MARJA-LIISA TENHUNEN.

Oulun Seudun Ammattikorkeakoulu (Oulu Polytechnic): POB 222, 90101 Oulu; tel. (10) 2721030; fax (10) 2721371; e-mail international@oamk.fi; internet www.oamk .fi; f. 1992; courses in culture, natural resources and the environment, natural sciences, social sciences, business and administration, social services, health and sports, and technology, communication and transport; 800 teachers; 9,000 students; Rector JOUKO PAASO.

Pohjois-Karjalan Ammattikorkeakoulu (North Karelia Polytechnic): Tikkarinne 9, 80200 Joensuu; tel. (13) 2606404; fax (13) 2606401; e-mail info@pkamk.fi; internet www.ncp.fi; f. 1992; courses in culture, social sciences, business and administration, natural sciences, natural resources and the environment, tourism, catering and domestic services, social services, health and sports, technology, communication and transport; adult education; 450 teachers; 4,000 students; Pres. VESA SAARIKOSKI.

Rovaniemen Ammattikorkeakoulu (Rovaniemi Polytechnic): Jokiväylä 11C, 96300 Rovaniemi; tel. (20) 7984000; fax (20) 7985499; e-mail polytechnic@ramk.fi; internet www.ramk.fi; f. 1996; courses in business and administration, forestry and rural industries, health care and social services, sports and leisure, technology, tourism and hospitality management; 3,000 students; Pres. MARTTI LAMPELA.

Saimaan Ammattikorkeakoulu (Saimaa University of Applied Sciences): Pohjolan-katu 23, 53100 Lappeenranta; tel. (20) 4966411; fax (20) 4966505; e-mail info@saimia.fi; internet www.saimia.fi; 20 degree programmes in technology, health care and social services, business and culture, tourism and hospitality, fine arts; 260 teachers; 2,700 students; Rector ANNELI PIRTTILÄ; publ. *Puhuri*.

Satakunnan Ammattikorkeakoulu (Satakunta Polytechnic): Tiedepuisto 3, 28600 Pori; tel. (2) 6203000; fax (2) 6203030; e-mail info@samk.fi; internet www.samk.fi; f. 1997; courses in business, fine art and media studies, social services and healthcare, technology, and maritime management and tourism; 530 teachers; 6,500 students; Pres. SEPPO PYNNÄ.

Savonia Ammattikorkeakoulu (Savonia Polytechnic): POB 1028, 70111 Kuopio; tel. (17) 2555044; e-mail admissions@savonia.fi; internet www.savonia-amk.fi; f. 1992; courses in social sciences, business and administration, culture, natural resources and the environment, tourism, catering and domestic services, social services, health and sports technology, communication and transport, and natural sciences; 350 teachers; 7,000 students.

Seinäjoen Ammattikorkeakoulu (Seinäjoki Polytechnic): Keskuskatu 34, POB 412, 60101 Seinäjoki; tel. (20) 1245000; fax (20) 1245001; e-mail seamk@seamk.fi; internet www.seamk.fi; f. 1996; courses in natural resources and the environment, natural sciences, social sciences, business and administration, technology, communication and transport, tourism, catering and domestic services and culture; 220 teachers; 4,700 students; Rector TAPIO VARMOLA.

Tampereen Ammattikorkeakoulu (Tampere University of Applied Sciences): Kuntokatu 3, 33520 Tampere; tel. (3) 2452111; fax (3) 2452222; e-mail international.office@tamk.fi; internet www.tamk.fi; f. 1996, merged with PIRAMK University of Applied Sciences 2010; languages of instruction: Finnish, English; Bachelors-level degrees in art and media, business economics and technology, international business, environmental engineering; teacher education centre; 400 full-time teachers, 700 part-time; 10,000 students; Rector MARKKU LAHTINEN.

Turun Ammattikorkeakoulu (Turku Polytechnic): Joukahaisenkatu 3A, 20520 Turku; tel. (10) 55350; fax (10) 5535791; e-mail ammattikorkeakoulu@turkuamk.fi; internet www.turkuamk.fi; f. 1992; courses in arts and media, healthcare, sports, social services, natural resources, environment, natural sciences, social sciences, business and administration, technology, communication, transport, tourism, catering and hospitality management; library: 130,000 vols, 1,500 journals, 7,000 e-journals; 750 teachers; 9,000 students; Rector JUHA KETTUNEN.

Vaasan Ammattikorkeakoulu (Vaasa Polytechnic): Wolffintie 30, 65200 Vaasa; tel. (20) 7663300; fax (6) 3263002; e-mail info@puv.fi; internet www.puv.fi; f. 1996; languages of instruction: Finnish, Swedish, English; faculties of business economics, tourism, health care and social services, technology and communication; 250 teachers; 3,500 students; Rector TAUNO KEKÄLE.

Yrkeshögskolan Arcada (Arcada Polytechnic): Jan-Magnus Janssons plats 1, 00550 Helsinki; tel. (20) 7699699; fax (20) 7699622; e-mail information@arcada.fi; internet www.arcada.fi; f. 1996; offers education in sports, health care, social services, business administration, media and technology; library: 22,169 vols, 45,000 e-books, 263 journals, 8,757 e-journals; 170 teachers; 2,700 students; Rector HENRIK WOLFF.

ÅLAND ISLANDS

Learned Societies

LANGUAGE AND LITERATURE

Nordens Institut på Åland (Nordic Institute on Åland): Köpmansgatan 4, AX- 22100 Mariehamn; tel. (18) 25000; fax (18) 13301; e-mail asa.juslin@nipa.ax; internet www .nipa.ax; f. 1985; attached to Nordic Council of Ministers; cultural institution; strengthens cultural life through contacts with other Nordic countries; Dir ÅSA JUSLIN; Sec. HARRIET LUNDELL.

RELIGION, SOCIOLOGY AND ANTHROPOLOGY

Ålands Kulturstiftelse r.s. (Åland Cultural Foundation): POB 172, AX-22101 Mariehamn; tel. (18) 19535; internet www.kultur .aland.fi/kulturstiftelsen; f. 1950; promotes scientific research of Åland history and cultural life in the islands; engages and supports publishing; Pres. and Chair. HENRIK GUSTAFSSON; Vice-Pres. PETER WAHLBERG; Sec. THÉRÈSE KÄHRE; Treas. BEN-ERIK ALM; publs *Det åländska folkets historia* (The History of the Åland People), *Internationella avtal och dokument rörande Åland, läs dem direkt på internet*, *Meddelanden från Ålands kulturstiftelse* (Communications), *Skrifter utgivna av Ålands kulturstiftelse* (Papers), *Urkundssamlingen* (The Tract Collection).

MEDICINE

Ålands Cancerförening (Ålands Cancer Association): Nyfahlers, Skarpansvägen 30, AX- 22100 Mariehamn; tel. (18) 22419; fax (18) 22409; e-mail forening@cancer.ax; internet www.cancer.ax; f. 1986; organizes support groups and rehabilitation courses for cancer patients and their families; Dir HELKA ANDERSSON.

Ålands Hälso–och Sjukvård (Ålands Health): POB 1091, AX-22111 Mariehamn; Doktorsvägen 1, AX-22100 Mariehamn; tel. (18) 5355; fax (18) 538661; e-mail info@ahs .ax; internet www.ahs.ax; health services; provides safe working environment for health professionals; Pres. TORBJÖRN BJÖRKMAN; Vice-Pres. JAN SALMÉN.

Research Institutes

ECONOMICS, LAW AND POLITICS

Ålands Emigrantinstitut (Åland Islands' Emigrant Institute): Norra Esplanadgatan 5, AX- 22100 Mariehamn; tel. (18) 13325; e-mail emi.inst@aland.net; internet www .eminst.net; f. 1996, admin. by the Åland Islands Emigrant Institute Society; promotes research into Ålandic emigration; collects, catalogues and distributes material connected with Ålandic emigration; Chair. ERIK LINDHOLM; Vice-Chair. BERTIL LINDQVIST; Treas. MAJVOR SÖDERBERG.

Ålands Fredsinstitut (Ålands Islands Peace Institute): Hamngatan 4, POB 85 AX-22101 Mariehamn; tel. (18) 15570; fax (18) 21026; e-mail peace@peace.ax; internet www .peace.ax; f. 1992; conducts projects and research into peace and conflict issues with regard to Ålands and spec. status of Ålands under int. law; library: holds material on peace and conflict issues, minorities, autonomy and human rights; Dir SIA SPILIOPOULOU

ÅKERMARK; Head, Library and Archive JOHN KNIGHT.

Libraries and Archives
Mariehamn
Ålands Landskapsarkiv (Provincial Archives of Åland): Självstyrelsegården, Strandgatan, POB 1060 AX- 22100 Mariehamn; tel. (18) 25344; fax (18) 12908; e-mail arkivet@regeringen.ax; internet www.arkivet.ax; f. 1978; archives incl. older documents from parishes and rural districts, documents from asscns, businesses, foundations, individuals, farms and village communities; archives belonging to the State of Finland pertaining to Åland Islands.

Mariehamns Stadsbibliotek–Central-Bibliotek för Åland (Mariehamn City Library–Central Library of Åland): POB 76, Strandgatan 29, AX-22101 Mariehamn; tel. (18) 531411; fax (18) 531419; e-mail biblioteket@mariehamn.ax; internet www.bibliotek.ax; f. 1890 as Åland lending library, present bldg 1989, present name 1987; Alandica colln (works relating to the islands); 120,008 vols, incl. 99,175 books, 7,819 CDs and cassettes, 1,820 DVDs and video cassettes, 259 magazine subscriptions and 19 newspapers; Chief Librarian EVA GUSTAFSSON-LINDVALL; Cultural Dir TOM ECKERMAN.

Sund
Sunds Bibliotek: Sundsvägen 1158, Finby, AX- 22530 Sund; tel. and fax (18) 45978; e-mail sundsbibliotek@aland.net; internet www.sund.ax/bibliotek.pbs; Librarian SONJA BERGLUND.

Museums and Art Galleries
Kastelholm
Ålands Fotografiska Museum i Kastelholm (Åland's Camera Museum in Kastelholm): Källbacksvägen 19, AX- 22520 Kastelholm; tel. and fax (18) 43964; e-mail alands.fotografiska.museum@aland.net; internet www.aland.com/se/fotografiskamuseum; colln of cameras, accessories and photographic equipment; spec. exhibitions.

Lappo
Skärgårdsmuseet (Archipelago Museum): AX- 22840 Lappo; tel. (400) 529462; e-mail erik.h.ohlson@gmail.com; internet www.lappo.net; f. 1982; traditional island and fishing culture; blacksmith's workshop with colln of old utensils; colln of 10 traditional rural boats; photographic exhibition; short films of life in the Finnish archipelago.

Mariehamn
Ålands Konstmuseum (Åland Art Museum): Storagatan 1, 22100 Mariehamn; tel. (18) 25426; fax (18) 17440; e-mail konst.info@regeringen.ax; internet www.museum.ax/museum/konstmuseum.pbs; f. 1963; attached to Museibyrån; local artists since 19th century; promotes artistic activity and disseminates knowledge about art; Curator SUSANNE PROCOPÉ ILMONEN.

Ålands Museum: POB 1060, AX- 22111 Mariehamn; tel. (18) 25000; fax (18) 17440; e-mail museum.info@regeringen.ax; internet www.museum.ax; f. 1934; attached to Museibyrån; prehistoric, historic and ethnological material; permanent exhibition of cultural history; spec. exhibitions; free entry October–April; library of 11,000 vols; Curator ANNIKA DAHLBLOM; publs *Åländsk odling* (1 a year), *Sevärt* (series).

Ålands Sjöfartsmuseum (Åland Maritime Museum): Hamngatan 2, POB 98, AX-22101 Mariehamn; tel. (18) 19930; fax (18) 19936; e-mail info@sjofartsmuseum.ax; internet www.sjofartsmuseum.ax; f. 1935, opened to public 1954; collns and exhibitions focusing on Alands's maritime heritage; ships' documents, model ships and figureheads; closed for renovation 2010–11; library: collns of Alandica nautical literature, archives incl. muster rolls, log books, colln of clippings, photographs, drawings and charts; Pres. JAN LIMNELL; Dir Dr HANNA HAGMARK-COOPER; publ. *Sjöhistorisk Årsskrift för Åland* (1 a year).

Museibyrån (Åland Board of Antiquities): POB 1060, AX- 22111 Mariehamn; tel. (18) 25000; fax (18) 17440; e-mail museum.info@regeringen.ax; internet www.museum.ax; administers Åland's antiquities, researches its cultural heritage, preserves artefacts, bldgs and sites of cultural and historical value; maintains Ålands museum and Konstmuseum; responsible for other museums located on the islands; library of 11,000 vols; Dir and Curator VIVEKA LÖNDAHL; publs *Åländsk odling* (1 a year), *Sevärt* (series).

University
HÖGSKOLAN PÅ ÅLAND
(Åland University of Applied Sciences)
POB 1010, AX- 22111 Mariehamn
Telephone: (18) 537000
Fax: (18) 16913
E-mail: info@ha.ax
Internet: www.ha.ax

Founded 1997, fmrly Åland Polytechnic, present name 2003 after merger with Åland Open Univ.
Public control
Language of instruction: Swedish

Rector: AGNETA ERIKSSON-GRANSKOG
Vice-Rector: HENRIK KARLSSON

Number of teachers: 32
Number of students: 400

Faculties of business administration, electrical engineering, health and caring sciences, hospitality management, information technology, marine engineering, navigation.

FRANCE

The Higher Education System

The French higher education system was restructured following the student-led unrest of 1968. The Loi de l'Orientation d'Education was enacted (it was reconfirmed 1989) and greater autonomy was granted to institutions. However, ultimate responsibility for determining the curricula and teaching methods remains with the Ministries of Education. France and the French Overseas Posssessions are divided into 35 educational districts, called Académies, each responsible for the administration of education, from primary to higher levels, in its area. There are 91 universities (a term that includes instituts universitaires de technologie—university institutes of technology) under the Ministries of Education, including universities in French Overseas Possessions; these institutions are: Université des Antilles et de la Guyane (French Guiana, Guadeloupe, Martinique), Université de la Polynésie Française (French Polynesia), Université de Nouvelle Calédonie (New Caledonia) and Université de la Réunion (Réunion).

Students must have achieved the baccalauréat, the main secondary school qualification, to gain admission to higher education. Some institutions may set additional entrance examinations, and the grandes écoles require students to undertake two to three years' additional study at a lycée. Since 2002 France has gradually implemented the Bologna Process and established a two-tier Bachelors and Masters degree system, completed by Doctoral studies. Some institutions may still offer professional qualifications or non-standard degrees. The standard undergraduate degree is now the three-year Licence (equivalent to Bachelors). Following the Licence, students may take the Masters, which is awarded after two years and replaces the range of pre-Bologna five-year degrees. There are two Masters tracks, Research or Professional. The Research Masters is required for entry to Doctoral studies, and the Doctorate is awarded after three years of study. Alternatively, medical students are required to study for a total of seven years for the Doctoral degree of Diplôme d'état de Docteur en Médecine.

In addition to universities and instituts universitaires de technologie, other public institutions offering higher education include instituts universitaires professionnalisés, grandes écoles and écoles normales supérieures. There are also professional schools for engineering, business and management, political sciences and veterinary sciences. Instituts universitaires de technologie were first established in 1966 and offer specialist two-year programmes leading to the award of Diplôme Universitaire de Technologie. Instituts universitaires professionnalisés have been established since 1992 and train senior executives for engineering, business and management, general administration, information and communication. Courses last for six years, including a six-month work placement, and culminate in the award of the Maîtrise degree. Grandes écoles are regarded as the most prestigious establishments for graduates wishing to enter high public service or business. The most prominent grandes écoles are the écoles normales supérieures; courses last for four years and students are awarded the Diplôme d'Études Appronfondies. In 2006/07 2,254,400 students were enrolled in higher education, including universities and university institutes of technology and schools of engineering.

Technical and vocational education is broken down into five levels, Niveau V to Niveau I, and is offered by secondary and post-secondary institutions. Broadly speaking, Niveaux III–I cover the post-secondary level, and lead to the award of a title such as Brevet de Technicien Supérieur, Diplôme d'Etat de Technicien, or Diplôme Universitaire de Technologie.

In August 2007 under the new Nicolas Sarkozy administration the Higher Education Minister, Valérie Pécresse, proposed a law concerning the 'freedom and responsibilities of the universities'. Under the law universities were to be reformed within a year, and were all to become fully autonomous by 2012. University Presidents, elected by an Administrative Council including representatives of industry, were to have more control over how research staff divided their time between research and teaching, and how students were recruited. Publication quotas were to be imposed on researchers and faculties were to become more competitive and productive in terms of the professional market, and were to be free to gain funding by working more closely with industry. The intention was for universities to function much like successful commercial enterprises.

However, the reform project met with considerable resistance amongst the student and researcher populations who saw it as an attack on the traditional republican value of freedom to education, and as undermining fundamental research in favour of applied research. A growing social movement of protest within the academic world began at the end of 2008 and was still in evidence in summer 2009. Strikes at a number of universities that year endangered the end of year examinations and the government eventually sent in security forces to evict students. However, by 2010 51 universities were autonomous as were six higher education schools. By 2012 another 19 universities and six engineering schools are expected to be autonomous.

Regulatory and Representative Bodies

GOVERNMENT

Ministry of Culture and Communication: 3 rue de Valois, 75001 Paris; tel. 1-40-15-80-00; fax 1-40-15-81-72; e-mail point .culture@culture.fr; internet www.culture .gouv.fr; Minister CHRISTINE ALBANEL.

Ministry of Higher Education and Research: 1 rue Descartes, 75231 Paris Cedex 05; tel. 1-55-55-90-90; e-mail secretariat-communication@recherche.gouv .fr; internet www .enseignementsup-recherche.gouv.fr; Minister VALÉRIE PÉCRESSE.

Ministry of National Education: 110 rue de Grenelle, 75357 Paris Cedex 07; tel. 1-55-55-10-10; fax 1-45-51-53-63; internet www .education.gouv.fr; Minister XAVIER DARCOS.

ACCREDITATION

Comité national d'évaluation (CNE): 43 rue de la Procession, 75015 Paris; tel. 1-55-55-60-97; fax 1-55-55-63-94; e-mail sgcne@ cne-evaluation.fr; internet www .cne-evaluation.fr; f. 1984; govt org. with authority over all instns of higher education in France; evaluation of quality of main 'missions of public service' of each such instn; First Vice-Pres. MICHEL HOFFERT.

Commission des Titres d'Ingénieur (CTI): Greffe de la CTI, Direction Générale de l'Enseignement Supérieur, 110 rue de Grenelle, 75357 Paris 07 SP; tel. 1-55-55-67-25; e-mail greffe-cti@education.gouv.fr; internet www.cti-commission.fr; f. 1934; quality assurance and accreditation for engineers; Pres. BERNARD REMAUD.

ENIC/NARIC France: Centre international d'études pédagogiques (CIEP), 1 rue Descartes, 75231 Paris Cedex 05; tel. (1) 55-55-04-28; fax (1) 55-55-00-39; e-mail enic-naric@ ciep.fr; internet www.ciep.fr/enic-naricfr; Dir FRANÇOISE PROFIT.

NATIONAL BODIES

Conférence des Directeurs des Ecoles Françaises d'Ingénieurs (CDEFI): 151 blvd de l'Hôpital, 75013 Paris; tel. 1-44-24-64-49; fax 1-44-24-64-51; e-mail cdefi@cdefi .fr; internet www.cdefi.fr; f. 1976; Exec. Dir ALEXANDRE RIGAL.

Conférence des Présidents d'Université: 103 blvd Saint-Michel, 75005 Paris; tel. 1-44-32-90-00; fax 1-44-32-91-02; e-mail contact@cpu.fr; internet www.cpu.fr; f. 1971; consultative body at the disposition of the Min. of Nat. Education; also studies questions of interest to all univs and co-ordinates the activities of various commissions on all aspects of education; mems: 103 pres of univs and state instns; 109 mems; Pres. LIONEL COLLET.

Conférence des Recteurs Français (French Rectors' Conference): Chancellerie des universités de Paris, 47 rue des Ecoles, 75005 Paris; f. 1987; establishes personal and permanent links between mems; encourages the discussion of professional problems; establishes relations with nat. and int. bodies concerned with education, science and culture; the Rectors are Chancellors of the state univs in their admin. area; Pres. Rector MICHEL LEROY (Acad. de Nancy-Metz); Sec.-Gen./Treas. Rector WILLIAM MAROIS (Acad. de Bordeaux).

Fédération Interuniversitaire de l'Enseignement à Distance (FIED): Université de Provence, 29 ave Robert Schuman, 13621 Aix-en-Provence Cedex 1; tel. 4-42-95-34-80; fax 4-42-95-31-41; e-mail info@fied-univ.fr; internet www.fied-univ.fr; f. 1987; promotes distance learning by encouraging co-operation between French and int. univs and instns; 35 mems; Pres. Prof. JACQUES CARPENTIER; Sec. Dr BERNAR DE GIORGI; Treas. Dr ANTOINE RAUZY.

Office national d'information sur les enseignements et les professions (ONISEP) (National Office for Information on Study and the Professions): 12 mail Barthélémy Thimonnier, 77437 Marne la Vallée Cedex 2; tel. 1-64-80-35-00; internet www.onisep.fr; attached to Min. of Nat. Education; produces careers information for schools, colleges and careers centres; website helps students to search for a course by field, level of study and instn; Dir HERVÉ DE MONTS DE SAVASSE.

Union des Établissements d'Enseignement Supérieur Catholique (UDESCA) (Union of Catholic Higher Education Establishments): 21 rue d'Assas, 75720 Paris Cedex 06; tel. 1-44-39-52-02; comprises the 5 Catholic institutes and univs at Angers, Lille, Lyon, Paris and Toulouse, and represents them in dealings with state instns; Pres. Prof. MICHEL QUESNEL.

Union des Professeurs de Spéciales (Mathématiques et Sciences Physiques): 3 rue de l'École Polytechnique, 75005 Paris; tel. and fax 1-43-26-97-92; fax 9-79-94-36-97; e-mail ups@prepas.org; internet www.prepas.org/ups; f. 1927; 2,500 mems; Pres. BRUNO JEAUFFROY; Sec. ERIC MERLE; publ. *Bulletin* (4 a year).

Learned Societies

GENERAL

Académie des Jeux Floraux: Hotel d'Assézat, 31000 Toulouse; tel. 5-61-21-22-85; e-mail jeux.floraux@free.fr; internet jeux.floraux.free.fr; f. 1323; human sciences; composed of 40 'mainteneurs' and 25 'Maîtres ès Jeux Floraux'; Permanent Sec. JEAN NAYRAL DE PUYBUSQUE; publ. *Recueil* (1 a year).

Académie des Sciences, Agriculture, Arts et Belles-Lettres d'Aix: 2A rue du 4 Septembre, 13100 Aix-en-Provence; tel. 4-42-38-38-95; e-mail musee.arbaud@dbmail.com; f. 1829; collns of ceramics, paintings, sculptures; library of 60,000 journals and plates, 10,000 books, 5,000 biographical MSS, 2,000 MSS related to local history, 1,200 portraits and 60 paintings of the Aix-en-Provence region; 40 fellows, 50 assoc. mems; Pres. ROGER BOOT; Perm. Sec. JEAN LUC KIEFFER; publ. *Bulletin*.

Académie des Sciences, Arts et Belles-Lettres de Dijon: 5 rue de l'Ecole-de-Droit, 21000 Dijon; tel. 3-80-54-22-93; e-mail acascia@orange.fr; internet www.acascia-dijon.fr; f. 1740; library, symposiums, communications; 550 mems; Pres. PIERRE BODINEAU; Sec. MARTINE CHAUNEY-BOUILLOT; publs *Mémoires de l'Académie* (every 2 years), *Mémoires de la Commission des Antiquités de la Côte d'Or* (every 2 years).

Académie des Sciences, Belles-Lettres et Arts de Lyon: Palais Saint-Jean, 4 ave Adolphe Max, 69005 Lyons; tel. 4-78-38-26-54; fax 4-72-77-90-56; e-mail secretariat@academie-sbla-lyon.fr; internet www.academie-sbla-lyon.fr; f. 1700; weekly meetings, annual grant for researchers in nuclear physics, medicine (oncology), literature, poetry; 52 elected mems; library of 60,000 vols; Pres. Prof. GÉRARD PAJONK; Chancellor Prof. JACQUES R. FAYETTE; publ. *Mémoires* (1 a year).

Académie des Sciences d'Outre-mer: 15 rue Lapérouse, 75116 Paris; tel. 1-47-20-87-93; fax 1-47-20-89-72; e-mail chefdecab@academiedoutremer.fr; internet www.academiedoutremer.fr; f. 1922; sections on economics and sociology, education, geography, law, politics and administration, science and medicine; 275 mems (incl. 100 corresp., 50 assoc., 25 free mems); library of 80,000 vols and 3,000 periodicals; Permanent Sec. PIERRE GENY; publ. *Mondes et Cultures* (1 a year).

Académie Goncourt: Société de Gens de Lettres, c/o Drouant, Place Gaillon, 75002 Paris; internet www.academie-goncourt.fr; f. 1896 by Edmond de Goncourt; comprises 10 writers in the French language; each year they compile a shortlist of the most noteworthy fiction written in French and award 'le prix Goncourt' to the author of the work judged the best; Pres. FRANÇOIS NOURISSIER; Sec.-Gen. DIDIER DECOIN.

Agence de la Francophonie: 28 rue de Bourgogne, 75007 Paris; tel. 1-44-11-12-50; fax 1-44-11-12-76; e-mail oif@francophonie.org; internet www.francophonie.org; f. 1970; an intergovernmental organization of French-speaking countries for co-operation in the fields of education, culture, science, technology, and in any other ways to bring the peoples of those countries closer together; 47 mems; Dir CHRISTIAN VALANTIN.

Alliance Française de Paris: 101 blvd Raspail, 75270 Paris Cedex 06; tel. 1-42-84-90-00; fax 1-42-84-90-91; e-mail info@alliancefr.org; internet www.alliancefr.org; f. 1883; French language school for foreigners; independent institution; 20,000 students; Pres. JACQUES VIOT; Sec.-Gen. JEAN HARZIC; Dir of the School ANNIE MONNERIE-GOARIN.

Comité des Travaux Historiques et Scientifiques: 110 rue de Grenelle, 75357 Paris Cedex 7; tel. 1-55-95-89-10; fax 1-55-95-89-60; e-mail catherine.gros@cths.fr; internet www.cths.fr; f. 1834; attached to Min. of Higher Education and Research; research and publs in the fields of history, archaeology, geography, human sciences, natural sciences, life sciences; organizes annual nat. congress of learned socs; 255 mems; Pres. Prof. M. CLAUDE MORDANT; Vice-Pres. M. J.-R. GABORIT; Gen.-Sec. CATHERINE GROS; publ. *Actes du Congrès national des Sociétés savantes*.

Euskaltzaindia/Académie de la Langue Basque: Plaza Barria 15, 48005 Bilbao; tel. 9-44-155-81-55; fax 9-44-15-81-44; e-mail webmaster@euskaltzaindia.net; internet www.euskaltzaindia.net; See also Spain chapter, Learned Societies.

Institut de France: 23 quai de Conti, 75270 Paris Cedex 06; tel. 1-44-41-44-41; fax 1-44-41-43-41; e-mail com@institut-de-france.fr; internet www.institut-de-france.fr; f. 1795; 623 mems; Chancellor PIERRE MESSMER; Dir of Services ERIC PEUCHOT.

Constituent Academies:

Académie des Beaux-Arts: 23 quai Conti, 75270 Paris Cedex 06; tel. 1-44-41-43-20; fax 1-44-41-44-99; internet academie-des-beaux-arts.fr; f. 1648; sections of painting, sculpture, architecture, engraving, musical composition, free members, artistic creation (cinema and audiovisual arts); 126 mems (55 ordinary, 55 corresp., 16 foreign assocs); Pres. JEAN PRODROMIDRÈS; Permanent Sec. ARNAUD D'HAUTERIVES; publ. *La Lettre de l'Académie des Beaux-Arts* (4 a year).

Académie des Inscriptions et Belles-Lettres: 23 quai Conti, 75270 Paris Cedex 06; tel. 1-44-41-43-10; fax 1-44-41-43-11; e-mail secretaireperpetuel@aibl.fr; internet www.aibl.fr; f. 1663; 195 mems (55 academicians, 40 foreign assocs, 50 French and 50 foreign corresp.); Pres. MICHEL ZINK; Permanent Sec. JEAN LECLANT; Gen. Sec. HERVÉ DANESI; publs *Comptes Rendus des Séances* (4 a year), *Journal des Savants* (2 a year), *Monuments et Mémoires de la Fondation Eugène Piot* (1 a year).

Académie des Sciences: 23 quai Conti, 75270 Paris Cedex 06; tel. 1-44-41-44-41; fax 1-44-41-43-63; internet www.academie-sciences.fr; f. 1666; sections of the first div.: mathematics, mechanical engineering and informatics, physics, sciences of the universe; sections of the second div.: chemistry, genomics, human biology and medical sciences, integrative biology, molecular and cellular biology; inter-section; 250 mems, at most 150 foreign assocs and 143 corresp. mems; Pres. JULES HOFFMANN; Vice-Pres. JEAN SALENÇON; Permanent Secs JEAN DERCOURT (Sciences of the Universe and their Applications), JEAN-FRANÇOIS BACH (Chemical, Biological and Medical Sciences and their Applications); publs *Comptes Rendus Mathématique* (24 a year), *Comptes Rendus Mécanique* (12 a year), *Comptes Rendus Physique* (10 a year), *Comptes Rendus Geoscience* (16 a year), *Comptes Rendus Palevol* (palaeontology and evolution, 8 a year), *Comptes Rendus Chimie* (12 a year), *Comptes Rendus Biologies* (12 a year).

Académie des Technologies: Grand Palais des Champs Elysées, Porté C, ave Franklin D. Roosevelt, 75008 Paris; tel. 1-53-85-44-44; fax 1-53-85-44-45; e-mail secretariat@academie-technologies.fr; internet www.academie-technologies.fr; f. 2000; analyses and publicizes academic studies on technology and its impact on society; ensures that society benefits from technological progress; 218 mems; Pres. BRUNO REVELLIN-FALCOZ; Dir SYLVIE GOUGON.

Académie des Sciences Morales et Politiques: 23 quai Conti, 75270 Paris Cedex 06; tel. 1-44-41-43-26; fax 1-44-41-43-27; e-mail kerbrat@asmp.fr; internet www.asmp.fr; f. 1795; sections of philosophy, moral and sociological sciences, legislation, public law and jurisprudence, political economy, statistics and finance, history and geography, general interest; 122 mems (50 ordinary, 60 corresp., 12 foreign assocs); Pres. JEAN MESNARD; Permanent Sec. MICHEL ALBERT; publs *Notices biographiques et bibliographiques, Cahiers des sciences morales et politiques*.

Académie Française: 23 quai Conti, 75270 Paris Cedex 06; tel. 1-44-41-43-00; fax 1-43-29-47-45; e-mail contact@academie-francaise.fr; internet www.academie-francaise.fr; f. 1635; 40 mems; Permanent Sec. HÉLÈNE CARRÈRE D'ENCAUSSE.

AGRICULTURE, FISHERIES AND VETERINARY SCIENCE

Académie d'Agriculture de France: 18 rue de Bellechasse, 75007 Paris; tel. 1-47-05-10-37; fax 1-45-55-09-78; e-mail aaf@paris.inra.fr; internet www.academie-agriculture.fr; f. 1761; 120 mems; 60 foreign mems; 180 corresp. mems; 60 foreign corresp. mems; Pres. ANDRÉ FROUIN; Perm. Sec. GEORGES PÉDRO; library of 80,000 vols, 500 periodicals; publ. *Comptes rendus* (4 a year).

Académie Vétérinaire de France: 34 rue Bréguet, 75011 Paris; tel. 1-53-36-16-19; e-mail academie@veterinaire.fr; internet www.academie-veterinaire-france.fr; f. 1844; 44 mems; Pres. PIERRE LARVOR; Sec.-Gen. CLAUDE MILHAUD.

Association Centrale des Vétérinaires: 10 place Léon Blum, 75011 Paris; tel. 1-43-56-21-02; fax 1-64-46-54-42; e-mail acveto@orange.fr; internet asso-acv.veterinaire.fr; f. 1889; 1,700 mems; Pres. Dr B. WILMET.

Association Française pour l'Etude du Sol: INRA, CS40001, 2163 ave de la Pomme de Pin, Ardon 45075 Orléans Cedex 2; tel. 2-38-41-48-23; fax 2-38-41-78-69; e-mail afretsol@orleans.inra.fr; internet www.afes.fr; f. 1934; pedology, agronomy; 800 mems; Pres. Dr JEAN-PAUL LEGROS; publ. *Etude et Gestion des Sols* (4 a year).

Société Française d'Economie Rurale: 19 Av. du Maine, 75732 Paris Cedex 15; tel. 1-45-49-88-40; fax 1-45-49-88-41; e-mail sfer@engref.fr; internet www.sfer.asso.fr/sfer; f. 1949; 2 study sessions a year; 400 mems; Pres. LUCIEN BOURGEOIS; Sec.-Gen. DENIS HAIRY; publ. *Economie Rurale* (6 a year).

Société Nationale d'Horticulture de France (SNHF): 84 rue de Grenelle, 75007 Paris; tel. 1-44-39-78-78; fax 1-45-44-76-57; e-mail info@snhf.org; internet www.snhf.asso.fr; f. 1827; 8,000 mems, 120,000 affiliated mems; library of 16,000 vols; Pres. JEAN PUECH; Gen. Sec. (vacant); publ. *Jardins de France* (10 a year).

Société Vétérinaire Pratique de France: 10 Pl. Léon Blum, 75011 Paris; tel. 6-36-19-64-57; e-mail veterinaire-pratique@club-internet.fr; internet www.svpf.fr; f. 1879; 750 mems; Pres. PATRICK PERRIN; Sec.-Gen. MICHEL BERNADAC; publ. *Bulletin* (4 a year).

ARCHITECTURE AND TOWN PLANNING

Académie d'Architecture: 9 place des Vosges, 75004 Paris; tel. 1-48-87-83-10; internet www.archi.fr/aa; f. 1840 as Société Centrale des Architectes, name changed 1953; 100 elected mems; Pres. AYMERIC ZUBLENA; Gen. Sec. JEAN-MARIE VALENTIN.

Association Nationale pour la Protection des Villes d'Art: 39 ave de La Motte-Picquet, 75007 Paris; tel. 1-47-05-37-71; e-mail florence.rouxcourtois@orange.fr; f. 1963; an association of local societies in 40 cities for the protection and restoration of historic and artistic buildings; Pres. PAULE ALBRECHT.

Cité de l'Architecture et du Patrimoine: Palais de Chaillot, 1 pl. du Trocadéro, 75116 Paris; tel. 1-58-51-52-00; fax 1-58-51-52-50;

e-mail info@citechaillot.org; internet www.citechaillot.org; f. 1980; funded by Min. of Culture and Communication; contemporary French architecture and architectural heritage; library of 10,000 vols, 70 periodicals; Pres. FRANÇOIS DE MAZIÈRES; publs *Archiscopie* (12 a year), *Colonnes* (2 a year).

Compagnie des Experts-Architectes près la Cour d'Appel de Paris: 24 rue Bezout, 75014 Paris; tel. 1-43-27-59-69; fax 1-43-20-47-96; e-mail info@ceacap.org; internet www.ceacap.org; f. 1928; 125 mems; Pres. MICHEL AUSTRY; Gen. Sec. ROBERT LEGRAS.

Conseil National de l'Ordre des Architectes: Tour Maine Montparnasse, 33 ave du Maine, BP 154, 75755 Paris Cedex 15; tel. 1-56-58-67-00; fax 1-56-58-67-01; e-mail info@cnoa.com; internet www.architectes.org; f. 1977; official regulating body for the architectural profession; Pres. of Conseil LIONEL CARLI; Vice-Pres. FRÉDÉRIC DENISART; Vice-Pres. BÉRENGÈRE PY-RODRIGUES DE SA; publ. *d'Architectures* (12 a year).

Office Général du Bâtiment et des Travaux Publics: 55 ave Kléber, 75784 Paris Cedex 16; tel. 1-40-69-51-00; internet www.ogbtp.com; f. 1918; combines the majority of societies, unions and federations of architects and contractors; Pres. YVES TOULET.

Société Française des Architectes: 247 rue St Jacques, 75005 Paris; tel. 1-56-81-10-25; fax 1-56-81-10-26; e-mail contact@sfarchi.org; internet www.sfarchi.org; f. 1877; cultural association; 1,000 mems; Pres. LAURENT SALOMON; publs *Tribune d'Histoire et d'Actualité de l'Architecture* (20 a year), *Le Visiteur* (2 a year).

Société pour la Protection des Paysages et de l'Esthétique de la France: 39 ave de la Motte-Picquet, 75007 Paris; e-mail sppef@wanadoo.fr; internet sppef.free.fr; f. 1901; protection and promotion of towns and landscapes; 4,000 mems; Pres. P. ALBRECHT; publ. *Sites et Monuments* (4 a year).

BIBLIOGRAPHY, LIBRARY SCIENCE AND MUSEOLOGY

Association des Archivistes Français: 9 rue Montcalm, 75018 Paris Cedex 03; tel. 1-46-06-39-44; fax 1-46-06-39-52; e-mail secretariat@archivistes.org; internet www.archivistes.org; f. 1904; 700 mems; Pres. HENRI ZUBER; Sec. AGNÈS DEJOB; publ. *La Gazette des Archives* (4 a year).

Association des Bibliothécaires Français: 31 rue de Chabrol, 75010 Paris; tel. 1-55-33-10-30; fax 1-55-33-10-31; e-mail abf@abf.asso.fr; internet www.abf.asso.fr; f. 1906; 2,500 mems; Pres. GILLES EBOLI; Gen. Sec. DANIEL LE GOFF; publ. *ABF Bulletin d'Informations* (4 a year).

Association des Professionnels de l'Information et de la Documentation (ADBS): 25 rue Claude Tillier, 75012 Paris; tel. 1-43-72-25-25; fax 1-43-72-30-41; e-mail adbs@adbs.fr; internet www.adbs.fr; f. 1963; 5,000 mems; organizes annual congress with Groupement français de l'industrie de l'information; Pres. CAROLINE WIEGANDT; publ. *Documentaliste—sciences de l'information* (6 a year).

Association Générale des Conservateurs des Collections Publiques de France: 6 ave du Mahatma Gandhi, 75116 Paris; tel. 1-44-17-60-00; fax 1-44-17-60-60; internet www.agccpf.com; f. 1922; promotes and improve museums and museums' curatorship; 1,000 mems; Pres. JACQUES MAIGRET; publ. *Musées et Collections Publiques de France* (4 a year).

Centre d'Archives et de Documentation Politiques et Sociales: 86 blvd Haussmann, 75008 Paris; f. 1949; Dir Dr G.

ALBERTINI; publs *Est et Ouest* (12 a year), *Informations Politiques et Sociales* (52 a year in France, Africa and Asia), *Le Monde des Conflits* (12 a year).

ECONOMICS, LAW AND POLITICS

Association d'Etudes et d'Informations Politiques Internationales: 86 blvd Haussmann, 75008 Paris; f. 1949; Dir G. ALBERTINI; publs *Documenti sul Comunismo* (Rome), *Est & Ouest* (Paris, 26 a year), *Este y Oeste* (Caracas).

Fondation Nationale des Sciences Politiques: 27 rue Saint Guillaume, 75337 Paris Cedex 07; tel. 1-45-49-50-50; fax 1-42-22-31-26; internet www.sciences-po.fr; f. 1945; administers the Institut d'Etudes Politiques de Paris (*q.v.*); promotes research centres and social science studies, documentation service; library of 620,000 vols; Pres. RENÉ RÉMOND; Admin. R. DESCOINGS; publs *Critique Internationale, Mots* (4 a year), *Revue de l'OFCE* (4 a year), *Revue Economique* (6 a year), *Revue Française de Science Politique* (6 a year), *Vingtième Siècle*.

Institut des Actuaires Français: 4 rue Chauveau-Lagarde, 75008 Paris; tel. 1-44-51-72-72; fax 1-44-51-72-73; e-mail info@actuaires-paris.com; internet www.institutdesactuaires.com; f. 1890; 600 mems; library of 5,000 vols; Pres. DANIEL BLANCHARD; publ. *Bulletin* (4 a year).

Institut d'Histoire Sociale: 4 ave Benoît-Frachon, 92023 Nanterre Cedex; tel. 1-46-14-09-29; fax 1-46-14-09-25; e-mail bibliotheque@souvarine.fr; internet www.souvarine.fr; f. 1935; study of Communist and Soviet activities; library of 40,000 vols specializing in political sciences and history of workers' movements since beginning of 19th century, trade union periodicals and political reviews; Pres. EMMANUEL LE ROY LADURIE; Librarian VIRGINIE HÉBRARD; publ. *Histoire & Liberté* (4 a year).

Institut Français des Relations Internationales: 27 rue de la Procession, 75740 Paris Cedex 15; tel. 1-40-61-60-00; fax 1-40-61-60-60; e-mail ifri@ifri.org; internet www.ifri.org; f. 1979; studies foreign policy, economy, defence and strategy; 560 mems; library of 32,000 vols; Dir-Gen. THIERRY DE MONTBRIAL; Sec.-Gen. VALÉRINE GENIN; publs *Cahiers d'Asie, Etudes de l'Ifri, Notes du Cerfa* (12 a year), *Notes du CFE, Notes de l'IFRI, Nouvelles de Chine* (12 a year), *Policy Papers, Politique Etrangère* (4 a year), *RAMSES (Rapport Annuel sur le Système Economique et les Stratégies)* (1 a year), *Travaux et Recherches*.

Société d'Economie et de Science Sociales: 20 rue Notre-Dame-de-Nazareth, 75003 Paris; tel. 1-40-29-96-29; e-mail socsciencesociale@free.fr; internet www.science-sociale.org; f. 1856; concerned with social reforms and sociology; 300 mems; library of 3,000 vols, including collection 'La Réforme Sociale'; Pres. EDOUARD SECRETAN; Sec. Prof. ANTOINE SAVOYE; publ. *Les Etudes Sociales*.

Société de Législation Comparée: 28 rue St Guillaume, 75007 Paris; tel. 1-44-39-86-23; fax 1-44-39-86-28; e-mail slc@legiscompare.com; internet www.legiscompare.com; f. 1869; comparative law; publishes books on comparative and foreign law; library of 100,000 vols; 600 mems (400 French, 200 overseas); Pres. EMMANUEL PIWNICA; Gen. Sec. BÉNÉDICTE FAUVARQUE-COSSON; publ. *Revue Internationale de Droit Comparé* (4 a year).

Société d'Etudes Jaurésiennes: 21 blvd Lefebvre, 75015 Paris; tel. 1-48-28-25-89; fax 1-48-28-25-89; internet www.jaures.info/

welcome/index.php; f. 1959; promotes all aspects of the life and works of Jean Jaurès; promotes the publication or re-edition of his speeches and writings; 500 mems; Pres. MADELEINE REBERIOUX; Sec.-Gen. GILLES HEURÉ; publs *Cahiers Jean Jaurès* (4 a year), *Cahiers Trimestriels* (4 a year).

Société d'Histoire du Droit: Université de Paris II, 12 place du Panthéon, 75005 Paris; f. 1913; 550 mems; Pres. Prof. OLIVIER GUILLOT; Sec. A. LEFEBVRE.

Société Française de Statistique: c/o Institut Henri Poincaré, 11 rue Pierre et Marie Curie, 75231 Paris Cedex 05; tel. 1-44-27-66-60; fax 1-44-07-04-74; e-mail sfds@ihp .jussieu.fr; internet www.sfds.asso.fr; f. 1997; 1,100 mems; library of 60,000 vols; Pres. AVNER BAR-HEN; Gen.-Sec. JEAN-MICHEL MARIN; publs *Journal de la Société Française de Statistique* (4 a year), *Revue de Statistique Appliquée* (4 a year).

EDUCATION

Association Francophone d'Education Comparée (AFEC): c/o Abdel-Rahamane Baba-Moussa, Université de Caen Basse-Normandie, Esplanade de la Paix, 14032 Caen Cedex; e-mail afec-bureau@hotmail.fr; internet www.afec-info.org; f. 1973; promotes comparative education among francophone teachers and educationalists; organizes one seminar a year and participates in meetings of the Comparative Education Soc. in Europe and the World Ccl of Comparative Educational Socs; 100 mems; Pres. Dr ABDEL RAHAMANE BABA-MOUSSA; Vice-Pres. MOUSSA DAFF; Sec.-Gen. EVE COMANDÉ; publs *Bulletin de liaison et d'information* (3 a year), *Education comparée—nouvelle série* (2 a year).

Centre Culturel Calouste Gulbenkian: 51 ave d'Iéna, 75116 Paris; tel. 1-53-23-93-93; fax 1-53-23-93-99; e-mail calouste@ gulbenkian-paris.org; internet www .gulbenkian-paris.org; f. 1965; attached to Calouste Gulbenkian Foundation in Lisbon (Portugal); non-profit-making; exhibitions, lectures, seminars, concerts; awards grants in the fields of education, art, science and charity; library of 70,000 vols; Dir JOÃO PEIRO GARCIA.

Fondation Biermans-Lapôtre: 9A blvd Jourdan, 75014 Paris Cedex 14; tel. 1-40-78-72-00; fax 1-45-89-00-03; e-mail admin@ fbl-paris.org; internet www.ciup.fr/ biermans-lapotre.htm; f. 1924; attached to Fondation Universitaire (see Belgium chapter); house for Belgian and Luxembourg students; promotes academic and scientific exchanges between France and Belgium; offers grants; Dir JOS AELVOET; Dir Adjunct CLAUDE GONFROID.

Office National d'Information sur les Enseignements et les Professions: 12 mail B. Thimonnier, BP 86 Lognes, 77423 Marne la Vallée, Cedex 02; tel. 1-64-80-35-00; fax 1-64-80-35-01; internet www.onisep.fr; f. 1970; Dir MICHEL VALDIGUIÉ; publs *Avenirs*, *Bulletin d'Information* (12 a year), *Les Cahiers de l'ONISEP, ONISEP Communiqué* (6 a year), *Réadaptation* (12 a year).

FINE AND PERFORMING ARTS

Association Française d'Action Artistique: 1 bis, ave de Villars, 75007 Paris; tel. 1-53-69-83-00; fax 1-53-69-33-00; e-mail info@ afaa.asso.fr; internet www.afaa.asso.fr; f. 1922; offers international cultural exchanges; assists in the development of the performing arts, visual arts, architecture, heritage and cultural projects in France; Pres. ROBERT LION.

Association du Salon d'Automne: Grand Palais, Porte H, 75008 Paris; tel. 1-43-59-46-07; fax 1-53-76-00-60; e-mail contact@ salon-automne-paris.com; internet www .salon-automne-paris.com; f. 1903; sections: painting, engraving, mural and decorative art, sculpture, photography; Pres. JEAN-FRANÇOIS LARRIEU.

Jeunesses Musicales de France: 20 rue Geoffroy l'Asnier, 75004 Paris; tel. 1-44-61-86-86; fax 1-44-61-86-88; e-mail info@lesjmf .org; internet www.lesjmf.org; f. 1944; encourages young audiences, promotes concerts, festivals; 320 delegates in 450 towns; Pres. J. L. TOURNIER; Dir BRUNO BOUTLEUX.

Société de l'Histoire de l'Art Français: 2 rue Vivienne, 75084 Paris Cedex 02; tel. 1-40-20-50-77; fax 1-40-20-51-17; f. 1873; 1,000 mems; Pres. DANIEL ALCOUFFE; Gen.-Sec. ELIZABETH FOUCART-WALTER; publs *Annuels*, *Archives de l'Art Français*, *Bulletin*.

Société des Amis du Louvre: Palais du Louvre, 75058 Paris Cedex 01; tel. 1-40-20-53-34; fax 1-40-20-53-44; e-mail contact@ amis-du-louvre.org; internet www .amis-du-louvre.org; f. 1897; 70,000 mems; Pres. MARC FUMAROLI; Sec.-Gen. SERGE-ANTOINE TCHEKHOFF; publs *Bulletin Trimestriel* (4 a year), *Chronique*.

Société des Artistes Décorateurs (SAD): Grand Palais, Porte C, ave Franklin D. Roosevelt, 75008 Paris; tel. 1-43-59-66-10; fax 1-49-53-07-89; e-mail info@sad-expo.com; internet www.sad-expo.com; f. 1901 to promote modern art; 400 mems; Pres. CLAUDE MOLLARD.

Société des Artistes Français: Grand Palais, Porte C, ave Franklin Roosevelt, 75008 Paris; tel. 1-43-59-52-49; fax 1-45-62-85-97; internet www.lesalon-artistesfrancais .com; f. 1882; 5,000 members; organizes the annual Salon des Artistes Français (open to French and foreign artists); Pres. CHRISTIAN BILLET; publ. *Bulletin*.

Société des Artistes Indépendants: Grand Palais, Porte C, ave Franklin D. Roosevelt, 75008 Paris; tel. 1-45-63-39-15; fax 1-43-59-50-89; e-mail indep@ club-internet.fr; internet www .artistes-independants.fr; f. 1884; 2,500 members; supports modern artists; annual exhibition of paintings, sculpture, tapestry; Salon des Artistes Indépendants since 1884; Pres. ALAIN COLLIARD; Sec.-Gen. FRANÇOISE LE GOFF.

Société des Auteurs, Compositeurs et Editeurs de Musique: 225 ave Charles-de-Gaulle, 92528 Neuilly sur Seine Cedex; tel. 1-47-15-47-15; fax 1-47-45-45-72; e-mail communication@sacem.fr; internet www .sacem.fr/eptic; f. 1851; 120,000 mems; deals with colln and distribution of performing rights; Pres. LAURENT PETITGIRARD; Chair. BERNARD MIYET.

Société d'Histoire du Théâtre: BnF, 58 rue de Richelieu, 75084 Paris Cedex 02; tel. 1-42-60-27-05; fax 1-42-60-27-65; e-mail info@sht.asso.fr; internet www.sht.asso.fr; f. 1933; performing arts library; 650 mems; library of 15,000 books; Dir ROMAIN MARYLINE; Sec.-Gen. ROSE MARIE MOUDOUÈS; publ. *Revue d'Histoire du Théâtre* (4 a year).

Société Française de Musicologie: 2 rue Louvois, 75002 Paris; tel. 1-53-79-88-45; e-mail sfmusico@club-internet.fr; internet www.sfm.culture.fr; f. 1917; 650 mems; Pres. DENIS HERLIN; Sec.-Gen. ANNE-SYLVIE BARTHEL-CALVET; publ. *Revue de Musicologie* (2 a year).

Société Française de Photographie: 71 rue de Richelieu, 75002 Paris; tel. 1-42-60-05-98; fax 1-47-03-75-39; internet www.sfp .photographie.com; f. 1854; 430 mems; library of 10,000 vols, and 25,000 old photo-graphs; Pres. MICHEL POIVERT; publs *Bulletin* (4 a year), *Etudes photographiques* (2 a year).

Société Nationale des Beaux-Arts: 11 rue Berryer, 75008 Paris; tel. 1-43-59-47-07; fax 1-43-59-47-07; e-mail snba.berryer@ libertysurf.fr; f. 1890; organizes art exhibitions; 900 mems; Pres. ETIENNE AUDFRAY; Gen. Sec. GUY PERRON.

HISTORY, GEOGRAPHY AND ARCHAEOLOGY

Association de Géographes Français: 191 rue Saint-Jacques, 75005 Paris; tel. 1-44-32-14-00; fax 1-45-29-13-40; e-mail assogeo@wanadoo.fr; internet www .association-de-geographes-francais.fr; f. 1920; 200 mems; Pres. R. POURTIER; Sec. Y. BOQUET; publs *Bulletin de l'Association de Géographes Français* (4 a year), *Bibliographie géographique annuelle* (1 a year).

Association des Amis de la Revue de Géographie de Lyon: 18 rue Chevreul, 69362 Lyons Cedex 07; tel. 4-78-78-75-44; fax 4-78-78-71-58; e-mail buisson@univ-lyon3 .fr; internet www.geocarrefour.org; f. 1923; Pres. NICOLE COMMERÇON; publ. *Revue de Géographie de Lyon* (4 a year).

Centre International d'Etudes Romanes: 7 pl. des Arts, 71700 Tournus; tel. 3-85-32-54-45; fax 3-85-32-18-98; internet www.art-roman.org; f. 1952; 400 mems; Hon. Pres. HUBERT BLANC; Vice-Pres. and Sec.-Gen. MARGUÉRITE THIBERT; publ. *Bulletin* (every 2 or 3 years).

Comité National Français de Géographie: 191 rue Saint-Jacques, 75005 Paris; internet cnfg.univ-paris1.fr; co-ordinates French geographical activity and participates in the work of the International Geographical Union; 400 mems; Pres. ALAIN MIOSSEC; Sec.-Gen. P. ARNOULD; publ. *Bibliographie Géographique Internationale* (published jointly with the International Geographical Union).

Comité Scientifique du Club Alpin Français: 24 ave de Laumière, 75019 Paris; tel. 1-53-72-87-13; fax 1-42-03-55-60; internet www .clubalpin.com; f. 1874; 90,000 mems; Dir J. MALBOS.

Demeure Historique: Hôtel de Nesmond, 57 quai de la Tournelle, 75005 Paris; tel. 1-55-42-60-00; fax 1-43-29-36-44; internet www .demeure-historique.org; f. 1924; study, research and conservation of historic bldgs, châteaux, etc.; 3,000 mems; Pres. JEAN DE LAMBERTYE; publ. *La Demeure Historique* (4 a year).

Fédération Française de Spéléologie: 28 rue Delandine, 75011 Paris; tel. 4-72-56-09-63; fax 4-78-42-15-98; e-mail secretariat@ ffspeleo.fr; internet ffspeleo.fr; f. 1963; speleology; 12,000 mems; library of 2,000 vols, 600 periodicals; Pres. LAURENCE TANGUILLE; Sec.-Gen. HENRY VAUMORON; publs *Bulletin Bibliographique Spéléologique*, *Karstologia* (2 a year), *Karstologia Mémoires*, *Spelunca* (4 a year), *Spelunca Mémoires*.

Institut Français d'Etudes Byzantines: 21 rue d'Assas, 75006 Paris; tel. 1-44-39-52-24; fax 1-44-39-52-36; e-mail bibliotheque .vernon.ifeb@icp.fr; internet www.icp.fr; f. 1897; Byzantine research, particularly on sources of ecclesiastical history; library of 50,000 vols; publ. *Revue des Etudes Byzantines* (1 a year).

Institut Français d'Histoire Sociale: Centre de documentation et de recherche, Archives Nationales, 60 rue des Francs-Bourgeois, 75141 Paris Cedex 03; tel. 1-40-27-64-49; f. 1948; 57 mems; library of 11,000 vols, 50,000 pamphlets, large collection of periodicals, manuscripts and illustrated documents; Pres. JEAN-PIERRE CHALINE.

Société de Biogéographie: 57 rue Cuvier, 75231 Paris Cedex 05; f. 1924; 350 mems; Pres. C. SASTRE; Sec.-Gen. M. SALOMON; publs *Biogeographica, Mémoires hors série.*

Société de Géographie: 184 blvd St-Germain, 75006 Paris; tel. 1-45-48-54-62; fax 1-42-22-40-93; e-mail socgeo@socgeo.org; internet www.socgeo.org; f. 1821; 850 mems; library of 40,000 vols, 120,000 photographs at Bibliothèque Nationale de France, 58 rue de Richelieu, 75084 Paris Cedex 02 (Librarian JEAN-YVES SARAZIN); Pres. Prof. JEAN-ROBERT PITTE; Sec.-Gen. MICHEL DAGNAUD; publs *Bulletin de liaison des membres de la Société de Géographie, La Géographie* (4 a year).

Société de Géographie Humaine de Paris: 8 rue Roquépine, 75008 Paris; f. 1873; Pres. JACQUES AUGARDE; library of 2,000 vols; publ. *Revue Economique Française* (4 a year).

Société de l'Histoire de France: 60 rue des Francs-Bourgeois, 75003 Paris; fax 1-55-42-75-09; internet www.shfrance.org; f. 1834; publishes a series of French historical texts and documents; gives public lectures on French history; 250 mems; Pres. Prof. CLAUDE GAUVARD; Sec. Prof. MARC H. SMITH; publ. *Annuaire-Bulletin* (1 a year).

Société d'Emulation du Bourbonnais: 93 rue de Paris, 03000 Moulins; tel. and fax 4-70-34-08-13; e-mail emulation.bourbonnais@orange.fr; internet www.societedemulationdubourbonnais.com; f. 1845; 400 mems; activities in the fields of history, science, arts and literature; library of 30,000 vols; Pres. SYLVIE VILATTE; publ. *Bulletin* (4 a year).

Société des Océanistes: Musée du Quai Branly, 222 rue de l'Université, 75343 Paris Cedex 7; tel. 1-56-61-71-16; e-mail sdo@projetmuse.net; internet www.oceanistes.org/oceanie; f. 1945; 560 mems; Pres. MAURICE GODLIER; Sec.-Gen. PHILIPPE PELTIER; publs *Journal* (2 a year), *Publications.*

Société d'Ethnographie de Paris: 6 rue Champfleury, 75007 Paris; f. 1859; 400 mems; Dirs A.-M. D'ANS, R. LACOMBE; publ. *L'Ethnographie* (2 a year).

Société d'Ethnologie Française: 6 ave du Mahatma Gandhi, 75116 Paris; tel. 1-44-17-60-00; 500 mems; holds annual nat. conf. and study sessions; Pres. F. LAUTMAN; Sec.-Gen. F. MAGUET; publ. *Ethnologie Française* (4 a year).

Société d'Etude du XVIIe Siècle: c/o Université de Paris-Sorbonne, Occident Moderne, 1 rue Victor-Cousin, 75230 Paris Cedex 05; f. 1948; 1,250 mems; Pres. JEAN-ROBERT ARMOGATHE; Sec. JEAN-LOUIS QUANTIN; publ. *XVIIe Siècle* (4 a year).

Société d'Histoire Générale et d'Histoire Diplomatique: 13 rue Soufflot, 75005 Paris; tel. 1-43-54-05-97; fax 1-46-34-07-60; f. 1887; history and diplomatic relations; 400 mems; publ. *Revue d'Histoire Diplomatique.*

Société d'Histoire Moderne et Contemporaine: Bureau 114, 56 rue Jacob, 75006 Paris; tel. 1-45-45-11-11; fax 1-58-71-71-96; e-mail rhmc@ens.fr; f. 1901; early modern and modern French and foreign history; European and world history; 600 mems; Pres. Prof. PIERRE MILZA; Pres. Prof. DANIEL ROCHE; Sec.-Gen. Prof. PHILIPPE MINARD; publ. *Bulletin-Revue d'Histoire Moderne et Contemporaine* (4 a year, and a supplementary Bulletin 1 a year).

Société Française d'Archéologie: Musée National des Monuments Français, Palais de Chaillot, 1 place du Trocadéro, 75116 Paris; tel. 1-42-73-08-07; fax 1-42-73-09-66; e-mail sfa.sfa@wanadoo.fr; internet www.sf-archeologie.net; f. 1834; mem. of CSSF;

1,500 mems; Pres. CHRISTIAN PATTYN; publs *Bulletin Monumental* (4 a year), *Congrès Archéologiques de France* (1 a year).

Société Française d'Egyptologie: Collège de France, pl. Marcelin-Berthelot, 75231 Paris Cedex 05; tel. 1-40-46-94-31; fax 1-40-46-94-31; e-mail s.f.e@orange.fr; internet www.egypt.edu; f. 1923; 850 mems; Pres. D. VALBELLE; Sec. MARIE-CLAIRE CUVILLIER; publs *Bulletin* (3 a year), *Revue d'Egyptologie* (1 a year).

Société Française de Numismatique: Bibliothèque Nationale de France, Département des Monnaies, Médailles et Antiques, 58 rue de Richelieu, 75002 Paris; tel. 1-53-79-86-26; fax 1-53-79-86-26; e-mail secretariat@sfnum.asso.fr; internet www.sfnum.asso.fr; f. 1865; 700 mems; Pres. GEORGES GAUTIER; Gen. Sec. ANDRÉ RONDE; publs *Bulletin de la S. F. N.* (12 a year), *Revue Numismatique* (1 a year).

Société Française d'Histoire d'Outre-Mer: 15 rue Catulienne, 93200 Saint Denis; tel. 6-07-30-04-22; fax 1-45-82-62-99; e-mail sfhom4@yahoo.fr; internet www.sfhom.com; f. 1913; 420 mems; Pres. HÉLÈNE D'ALMEIDA-TOPOR; Sec.-Gen. JOSETTE RIVALLAIN; publ. *Outre-Mers* (history, 2 a year).

Société Historique, Archéologique et Littéraire de Lyon: Archives Municipales de Lyon, 1 place des Archives, 69002 Lyon; e-mail shallyon@cegetel.net; f. 1807; 78 mems; Pres. PHILIPPE DUFIEUX; Sec. PAUL CHOPELIN; publ. *Bulletin* (1 a year).

Société Nationale des Antiquaires de France: Palais du Louvre, Pavillon Mollien, 75058 Paris Cedex 01; f. 1804; history, philology and archaeology of Antiquity, Middle Ages and Renaissance; 434 mems, 10 hon. mems, 10 hon. foreign corresps, 45 resident mems; Pres. HERVÉ PINOTEAU; Vice-Pres. JANIC DURAND; Vice-Pres. MICHEL AMANDRY; Sec.-Gen. Prof. FRANÇOIS DOLBEAU; publs *Bulletin de la Société nationale des Antiquaires de France* (1 a year), *Mémoires de la Société nationale des Antiquaires de France* (irregular).

Vieilles Maisons Françaises: 93 rue de l'Université, 75007 Paris; tel. 1-40-62-61-71; fax 1-45-51-12-26; internet www.vmf.net; f. 1958; the society seeks to bring together all those who own buildings of historical interest and those who help to preserve them; 16,000 mems; Pres. PHILIPPE TOUSSAINT; publ. *Vieilles Maisons Françaises.*

LANGUAGE AND LITERATURE

Association des Ecrivains de Langue Française (ADELF) (French Language Writers Association): 14 rue Broussais, 75014 Paris; tel. 1-43-21-95-99; e-mail adelf.paris@yahoo.fr; f. 1926 as 'Société des romanciers et auteurs coloniaux français' to bring together writers of all nationalities whose works are published in French; awards 10 literary prizes; 1,200 mems in 79 countries; library of 2,500 vols; Pres. JACQUES CHEVRIER; Sec.-Gen. SIMONE DREYFUS; publs *Collection des Colloques, Lettres et Cultures de langue française* (2 a year).

Association Française des Professeurs de Langues Vivantes: 19 rue de la Glacière, 75013 Paris; f. 1902; 3,000 mems; Pres. SYLVESTRE VANUXEM; Gen. Sec. JEAN-YVES PETITGIRARD; publs *Le Polyglotte* (4 a year), *Les Langues Modernes.*

Association Guillaume Budé: 95 blvd Raspail, 75006 Paris; e-mail info@bude.asso.fr; internet www.bude.asso.fr; f. 1917; 3,000 mems; publishes ancient Greek, Latin and Byzantine texts, classical texts with French translations and studies on history, philology and archaeology, which are published by the

Société d'éditions 'Les Belles Lettres' at the same address; Pres. JACQUES JOUANNA; Vice-Pres. BERNARD DEFORGE, ALAIN MICHEL; publ. *Bulletin* (2 a year).

British Council: 9 rue de Constantine, 75340 Paris Cedex 07; tel. 1-49-55-73-00; fax 1-47-05-77-02; e-mail projects@britishcouncil.fr; internet www.britishcouncil.fr; teaching centre; offers courses and exams in English language and British culture and promotes cultural exchange with the UK; Dir JOHN TOD.

Centre National du Livre: 53 rue de Verneuil, 75343 Paris Cedex 07; tel. 1-49-54-68-68; fax 1-45-49-10-21; internet www.centrenationaldulivre.fr; f. 1946, present name 1993, to uphold and encourage the work of French writers; to give financial help to writers, editors and public libraries; to promote translation into French; Pres. BENOIT YVERT; Sec.-Gen. MARC-ANDRE WAGNER; publ. *Lettres.*

Espéranto-Jeunes (JEFO): 4 bis rue de la Cerisaie, 75004 Paris; tel. 1-42-78-68-86; fax 1-42-78-08-47; internet esperanto-jeunes.org; f. 1969; promotes Esperanto among young people; 145 mems; Pres. BERTRAND HUGON; publs *JEFO informas* (4 a year), *Koncize* (4 a year).

Fondation Saint-John Perse: Cité du Livre, 10 rue des Allumettes, 13098 Aix-en-Provence Cedex 2; tel. 4-42-91-98-85; fax 4-42-27-11-86; e-mail fondation.saint.john.perse@wanadoo.fr; internet www.up.univ-mrs.fr/~wperse; f. 1975; collection of 16,000 documents comprising all MSS, books, correspondence, private library and personal belongings of Saint-John Perse (Nobel Prize for literature 1960); organizes annual exhibition and symposium; 500 mems; Pres. YVES-ANDRÉ ISTEL; Dir BEATRICE COIGNET; publs *Cahiers Saint-John Perse* (irregular), *Souffle de Perse* (irregular).

Goethe-Institut: 17 Ave d'Iéna, 75116 Paris; tel. 1-44-43-92-30; fax 1-44-43-92-40; e-mail kallies@paris.goethe.org; internet www.goethe.de/fr/par/deindex.htm; offers courses and exams in German language and culture and promotes cultural exchange with Germany; attached centres in Bordeaux, Lille, Lyons, Nice and Toulouse; library of 25,000 vols; Dir MARION HAASE.

Instituto Cervantes: 7 rue Quentin Bauchart, 75008 Paris; tel. 1-40-70-92-92; fax 1-47-20-27-49; e-mail cenpar@cervantes.es; internet paris.cervantes.es; offers courses and exams in Spanish language and culture and promotes cultural exchange with Spain and Spanish-speaking South and Central America; attached centres in Bordeaux and Lyon; library of 42,000 vols, 100 periodicals; Dir AUGUSTÍN VERA LUJÁN.

La France Latine: Université de Rennes II, 1 Place du Recteur le Moal, C524307, 35043 Rennes Cedex; e-mail philippe.blanchet@univ-rennes2.fr; internet www.prefics.org/credilif/la_france.html; f. 1957; studies romance culture and civilization in southern France in all its forms; maintains regional traditions and the 'Langues d'Oc' (Occitan); library of 150 vols; Scientific Dir Prof. PHILIPPE BLANCHET; Scientific Dir Prof. SUZANNE THIOLIER-MÉJEAN; publ. *Revue* (2 a year).

Maison de Poésie (Fondation Emile Blémont): 11 bis rue Ballu, 75009 Paris; tel. 1-40-23-45-99; f. 1928; library of 16,000 vols; annual prizes: Grand Prix de la Maison de Poésie, Prix Paul Verlaine, Prix Edgar Poe, Prix Louis Maudin, Prix Emile Verhaeren, Prix Philippe Chahaneix, Prix Arthur Rimbaud; Pres. JACQUES CHARPENTREAU; Sec. BERNARD PLIN; publ. *Le Coin de Table* (4 a year).

PEN International (Centre français): 6 rue François-Miron, 75004 Paris; tel. 1-42-77-37-87; fax 1-42-78-64-87; e-mail penfrancais@aol.com; internet www.penclub .fr; f. 1921; 550 mems; Pres. SYLVESTRE CLANCIER; Sec.-Gen. PHILIPPE PUJAS; publ. *La Lettre du PEN Club français* (6 a year).

Société de Linguistique de Paris: Ecole Pratique des Hautes Etudes, 4e section, Sorbonne, 47 rue des Ecoles, 75005 Paris; internet www.slp-paris.com; f. 1864; 800 mems; Pres. A. BORILLO; Sec. M. A. LEMARECHAL; publs *Bulletin, Collection Linguistique, Mémoires* (1 a year).

Société des Anciens Textes Français: 19 rue de la Sorbonne, 75005 Paris; f. 1875; 125 mems; Pres. Prof. G. BIANCIOTTO; Dir Prof. G. HASENOHR; Gen. Sec. R. TRACHSLER.

Société des Auteurs et Compositeurs Dramatiques: 11 bis rue Ballu, 75442 Paris Cedex 09; tel. 1-40-23-44-44; fax 1-45-26-74-28; e-mail infosacd@sacd.fr; internet www .sacd.fr; f. 1777; protects the rights of authors of theatre, radio, cinema, television and multimedia; Pres. CHRISTINE MILLER; publ. *La Revue de la SACD.*

Société des Etudes Latines: 1 rue Victor-Cousin, 75230 Paris Cedex 05; e-mail societe-etudes-latines@paris-sorbonne.fr; internet www.societedesetudeslatines.com; f. 1923; Admin. Prof. JACQUELINE CHAMPEAUX; publ. *Revue des Etudes Latines* (1 a year).

Société des Gens de Lettres: Hôtel de Massa, 38 rue du Faubourg St Jacques, 75014 Paris; tel. 1-53-10-12-00; fax 1-53-10-12-12; e-mail sgdl@sgdl.org; internet www .sgdl.org; f. 1838; defends the moral and social rights of authors and writers; Pres. ALAIN ABSIRE; Gen. Sec. DOMINIQUE LE BRUN; publ. *Lettre.*

Société d'Histoire Littéraire de la France: 112 rue Monge, 75005 Paris; tel. 1-45-87-23-30; fax 1-45-87-23-30; f. 1894; 400 mems; Pres. M. FUMAROLI; Dir S. MENANT; publ. *Revue d'Histoire Littéraire de la France* (6 a year).

MEDICINE

Académie Nationale de Chirurgie: 'Les Cordeliers', 15 rue de l'Ecole de Médecine, 75006 Paris; tel. 1-43-54-02-32; fax 1-43-29-34-44; e-mail ac.chirurgie@bhdc.jussieu.fr; internet www.bium.univ-paris5.fr/ acad-chirurgie; f. 1731; 500 mems; library of 5,000 vols; Pres. Prof. HENRI BISMUTH; Vice-Pres. Prof. JACQUES BAULIEUX; Sec.-Gen. Dr HENRI JUDET; publs *Académie de Chirurgie Magazine* (4 a year), *e-Memoires* (online, 4 a year).

Académie Nationale de Médecine: 16 rue Bonaparte, 75272 Paris Cedex 06; tel. 1-42-34-57-70; fax 1-40-46-87-55; internet www .academie-medecine.fr; f. 1820 by Louis XVIII; library of 400,000 vols; 130 mems attached to sections on medicine, surgery, hygiene, biological sciences, social sciences, veterinary medicine, pharmacy; Pres. CLAUDE BOUDÈNE; Perm. Sec. JACQUES-LOUIS BINET; publ. *Bulletin de l'Académie nationale de médecine* (9 a year).

Académie Nationale de Pharmacie: 4 ave de l'Observatoire, 75006 Paris; tel. 1-43-25-54-49; fax 1-43-29-45-85; e-mail info@ acadpharm.org; internet www.acadpharm .org; f. 1803; 440 mems; Pres. FRANÇOIS CHAST; Gen. Sec. J.-P. CHIRON; publ. *Annales Pharmaceutiques Françaises.*

Association des Morphologistes: BP 184, 54505 Vandoeuvre-lès-Nancy; f. 1899; 1,005 mems; Chief Editor Prof. G. GRIGNON; publ. *Morphologie* (4 a year).

Association Française d'Urologie: Colloquium, 12 rue de la Croix Faubin, 75577 Paris Cedex 11; tel. 1-44-64-15-15; fax 1-44-64-15-16; e-mail contact@urofrance.org; internet www.urofrance.org; f. 1896; 1,027 mems; Pres. PASCAL RISCHMANN; Sec.-Gen. Dr PATRICK COLOBY; publ. *Progrès en Urologie* (6 a year).

Association Générale des Médecins de France: 34 blvd de Courcelles, 75809 Paris Cedex 17; tel. 1-40-54-54-54; fax 1-40-54-54-40; Pres. P. BAUDOUIN; Sec. Dr TOUCHARD; publ. *Bulletin.*

Association Scientifique des Médecins Acupuncteurs de France (ASMAF): 2 rue du Général de Larminat, 75015 Paris; tel. 1-42-73-37-26; f. 1945 as Société d'Acupuncture; 1,500 mems; Pres. Dr GEORGES CANTONI; Sec.-Gen. Dr H. OLIVO; publ. *Méridiens* (4 a year).

Centre d'Etude de l'Expression: Centre hospitalier Sainte-Anne, 100 rue de la Santé, 75014 Paris; tel. 1-45-89-21-51; e-mail cee75@orange.fr; internet www .centre-etude-expression.fr; f. 1973; exhibitions of artworks from Sainte-Anne's colln and contemporary artists; develops psychological studies of various forms of expression: plastic, verbal, mimic, dance-movement, musical, theatrical; Pres. JEAN-PIERRE LIMOUSIN; Sec.-Gen. Dr ANNE-MARIE DUBOIS.

Comité National contre les Maladies Respiratoires: 66 blvd Saint-Michel, 75006 Paris; tel. 1-46-34-58-80; fax 1-43-29-06-26; e-mail contact@lesouffle.org; internet www .lesouffle.org; f. 1916; research, information, health education, assistance for the handicapped; Pres. GERARD HUCHON; publ. *La Lettre du Souffle* (4 a year).

Confédération des Syndicats Médicaux Français: 79 rue de Tocqueville, 75017 Paris; tel. 1-43-18-88-00; fax 1-43-18-88-20; e-mail csmf@csmf.org; internet www.csmf .org; f. 1930; 16,000 mems; Pres. Dr MICHEL CHASSANG; Sec.-Gen. Dr WANNEPAIN.

Fédération des Gynécologues et Obstétriciens de Langue Française: Hôpital St-Antoine, 184 rue du Fg St-Antoine, 75012 Paris; tel. 1-49-28-28-76; fax 1-49-28-27-57; f. 1950; 600 mems; Pres. Prof. ULYSSE GASPARD (Liège); Sec.-Gen. Prof. JACQUES MILLIEZ (Paris); publ. *Journal de Gynécologie Obstétrique et Biologie de la Reproduction* (8 a year).

Fédération Nationale des Médecins Radiologues: 62 blvd de Latour Maubourg, 75007 Paris Cedex 07; tel. 1-53-59-34-00; fax 1-45-51-83-15; e-mail fnmr@fnmr.org; internet www.fnmr.org; f. 1907; 4,800 mems; Pres. Dr DENIS AUCANT; Secs-Gen. Dr JACQUES NINEY, Dr LAURENT VERZAUX.

Société de Médecine de Strasbourg: Faculté de Médecine, 4 rue Kirschleger, 67085 Strasbourg Cedex; tel. 3-88-11-62-59; f. 1919; 450 mems; organizes medical confs; Pres. Prof. E. QUOIX; Sec.-Gen. Prof. E. ANDRÈS; publ. *Journal de Médecine de Strasbourg* (12 a year).

Société de Médecine Légale et de Criminologie de France: 2 place Mazas, 75012 Paris; tel. 1-43-43-42-54; e-mail dgosset@adm .univ-lille2.fr; internet www.smlc.asso.fr; f. 1868; Pres. Prof. MICHEL PENNEAU; Sec. DIDIER GOSSET; publ. *Médecine légale-droit médical.*

Société de Neurophysiologie Clinique de Langue Française: Hôpital Sainte Anne, 1 rue Cabanis, 75674 Paris Cedex 14; tel. 1-40-48-82-03; f. 1948; 520 mems; Pres. Dr LUIS GARCIA-LARREA; Sec.-Gen. Dr S. S. LEFAUCHER; publ. *Neurophysiologie Clinique* (6 a year).

Société de Pathologie Exotique: 25 rue du Docteur-Roux, 75724 Paris Cedex 15; tel. 1-45-66-88-69; fax 1-45-66-44-85; e-mail socpatex@pasteur.fr; internet www.pasteur .fr/socpatex; f. 1908; 637 mems; library of 2,000 vols, 125 periodicals; Pres. P. SALIOU; Sec.-Gen. Y. BUISSON; publ. *Bulletin* (5 a year).

Société de Pneumologie de Langue Française: 66 blvd Saint-Michel, 75006 Paris; tel. 1-46-34-03-87; fax 1-46-34-58-27; e-mail splf@splf.org; internet www.splf.org; Pres. M. FOURNIER; Secs-Gen. J. F. CORDIER, J. P. GRIGNET, B. HOUSSET, E. LEMARIÉ; publ. *Revue des Maladies Respiratoires.*

Société d'Histoire de la Pharmacie: 4 ave de l'Observatoire, 75270 Paris Cedex 06; tel. and fax 1-53-73-97-37; f. 1913; 1,000 mems; Pres. Prof. OLIVIER LAFONT; Sec. B. BONNEMAIN; publ. *Revue d'Histoire de la Pharmacie* (4 a year).

Société d'Ophtalmologie de Paris: 108 rue du Bac, 75007 Paris; f. 1888; Sec.-Gen. Dr JEAN-PAUL BOISSIN; publ. *Bulletin* (12 a year).

Société Française d'Allergologie et d'Immunologie Clinique: Institut Pasteur, 28 rue du Dr Roux, 75724 Paris Cedex 15; tel. 1-45-68-82-41; fax 1-40-61-31-60; internet www.sfaic.com; f. 1947; 860 mems; Pres. Prof. D. VERVLOET; publ. *Revue Française d'Allergologie et d'Immunologie clinique* (5 a year).

Société Française d'Anesthésie et de Réanimation: 74 rue Raynouard, 75016 Paris; tel. 1-45-25-82-25; fax 1-40-50-35-22; e-mail contact@sfar.org; internet www.sfar .org; f. 1934; 4,298 mems; Pres. LAURENT JOUFFROY; Sec.-Gen. DAN BENHAMOU; publ. *Annales françaises d'Anesthésie et de Réanimation* (12 a year).

Société Française d'Angéiologie: 153 ave Berthelot, 69007 Lyons; tel. 4-78-72-38-98; internet www.sfa-online.com; f. 1947; 450 mems; Pres. Dr FRANÇOIS ANDRÉ ALLAERT; Sec.-Gen. Dr MICHÈLE CAZAUBON; publ. *La revue Angéiologie* (4 a year).

Société Française de Biologie Clinique: 194 Ave de Strasbourg, 54000 Nancy Cedex; tel. 3-83-35-36-25; fax 3-83-32-75-13; e-mail sfbc@orange.fr; internet www.sfbc.asso.fr; Pres. ALAIN LEGRAND; Sec.-Gen. NELLY JACOB.

Société Française de Chirurgie Orthopédique et Traumatologique: Secrétariat: 56 rue Boissonade, 75014 Paris; tel. 1-43-22-47-54; fax 1-43-22-46-70; e-mail sofcot@sofcot .com.fr; internet www.sofcot.com.fr; f. 1918; 1,950 mems; Pres. J. M. THOMINE; publs *Revue de Chirurgie Orthopédique, Bulletin des Orthopédistes Francophones* (2 a year).

Société Française de Chirurgie Pédiatrique: 149 rue de Sèvres, 75015 Paris; tel. 4-91-38-66-82; fax 4-91-38-47-14; e-mail webmaster-sfcp@chirpediatric.fr; internet www.chirpediatric.fr; f. 1959; 350 mems; Pres. Prof. PAUL MITROFANOFF; Sec.-Gen. Prof. J. L. CLAVERT; publ. *European Journal of Paediatric Surgery* (6 a year).

Société Française de Chirurgie Plastique, Reconstructive et Esthétique: 26 rue de Belfort, 92400 Courbevoie; tel. 1-46-67-74-85; fax 1-46-67-74-89; e-mail sofcpre@ wanadoo.fr; internet www.plasticiens.fr; f. 1953; 621 mems; Pres. Dr J. L. FOYATIER; Sec.-Gen. Dr M. REVOL; publ. *Annales de Chirurgie Plastique et Esthétique* (6 a year).

Société Française de Chirurgie Thoracique et Cardio-vasculaire: 56 Blvd Vincent Auriol, 75013 Paris; tel. 1-42-16-42-10; fax 1-42-16-42-09; e-mail sfctcv@sfctcv.net; internet www.fstcvs.org; f. 1948; 643 mems; studies problems linked with thoracic and cardiovascular surgery; Pres. Prof. ALAIN PAVIE; Sec.-Gen. Dr R. NOTTIN; publ. *Journal de Chirurgie Thoracique et Cardiovasculaire* (4 a year).

Société Française de Gynécologie: 36 rue de Toqueville, 75017 Paris; tel. 1-42-27-95-59; e-mail jean.belaisch@wanadoo.fr; internet www.sfgynecologie.org; 582 mems; Pres. J. P. WOLFF; Sec.-Gen. ANDRÉ GORINS; publ. *Gynécologie* (6 a year).

Société Française de Médecine Aérospatiale: Laboratoire de Médecine Aérospatiale du Centre d'Essais en Vol, 91228 Brétigny sur Orge Cedex; tel. 1-69-88-23-80; fax 1-69-88-27-25; internet www.soframas.asso.fr; f. 1960; publishes papers on experimental and clinical studies; 1,100 mems; Pres. Dr M.-P. CHARETTEUR; Sec.-Gen. Prof. G. SOLIGNAC; publ. *Médecine Aérospatiale* (4 a year).

Société Française de Mycologie Médicale: 191 rue de Vaugirard, 75015 Paris; tel. 1-43-06-68-72; fax 1-42-73-61-10; e-mail sfmm1@orange.fr; internet pagesperso-orange.fr/sfmm; f. 1956; 250 mems; Pres. CLAUDE GUIGUEN; Sec.-Gen. Dr PATRICIA ROUX; publ. *Journal de Mycologie Médicale* (4 a year).

Société Française de Neurologie: Service de Neurologie 1, Clinique Paul Castaigne, Hôpital de la Salpêtrière, 47 blvd de l'Hôpital, 75651 Paris Cedex 13; tel. 1-42-16-18-28; fax 1-44-24-52-47; internet www.sf-neuro .org; f. 1899; 550 mems; library of 22,000 vols; Sec.-Gen. Prof. C. PIERROT-DESEILLIGNY; publ. *Revue Neurologique* (12 a year).

Société Française de Pédiatrie: Hôpital Trousseau, 26 ave du Dr Arnold Netter, 75571 Paris Cedex 12; tel. 1-49-28-92-96; e-mail sfpediatrie@orange.fr; internet www .sfpediatrie.com; f. 1929; 1,500 mems; Pres. Prof. ALAIN CHANTEPIE; Sec.-Gen. Prof. PACTRICK TOUNIAN; publ. *Archives de Pédiatrie* (12 a year).

Société Française de Phlébologie: 46 rue Saint-Lambert, 75015 Paris; tel. 1-45-33-02-71; fax 1-42-50-75-18; e-mail sfphlebo@club-internet.fr; internet www.sf-phlebologie .org; f. 1947; 2,000 mems; Pres. M. PERRIN; Sec.-Gen. F. VIN; publ. *Phlébologie—Annales Vasculaires* (4 a year).

Société Française de Phytiatrie et de Phytopharmacie: CNRA, Route de Saint Cyr, 78000 Versailles; tel. 1-49-50-75-22; f. 1951; 1,000 mems.

Société Française de Radiologie: 20 ave Rapp, 75007 Paris; tel. 1-53-59-59-69; fax 1-53-59-59-60; e-mail sfr@sfradiologie.org; internet www.sfrnet.org; f. 1909; 6,785 mems; Pres. GÉRARD MORVAN; Gen. Sec. PHILIPE GRENIER; publ. *Journal de Radiology* (12 a year).

Société Française de Santé Publique: BP 7, 2 rue Doyen Jacques-Parisot, 54501 Vandoeuvre lès Nancy Cedex; tel. 3-83-44-39-17; fax 3-83-44-37-76; internet www.sfsp.fr; f. 1877; 750 mems; Pres. Dr FRANÇOIS BOURDILLON; publ. *Santé publique* (6 a year).

Société Française d'Endocrinologie: c/o Sylvia Delplanque, 88 rue de la Roquette, 75011 Paris; tel. (1) 40-24-02-72; fax (1) 40-24-02-71; e-mail sfesecret@wanadoo.fr; internet www.sf-endocrino.net; f. 1939; 850 mems; Pres. Prof. VINCENT ROHMER; Sec.-Gen. Prof. HERVÉ LEFEBVRE; Treas. Prof. LAURENCE LEENHARDT; publ. *Annales d'Endocrinologie* (6 a year).

Société Française d'Histoire de la Médecine: c/o Dr Jean-Jacques Ferrandis, 6 rue des Impressionnistes, 91210 Draveil; tel. 6-18-46-72-49; e-mail jj.ferrandis@orange.fr; internet www.bium.univ-paris5.fr/sfhm; f. 1902; 700 mems; library; Pres. Prof. GUY PALLARDY; Gen. Sec. Dr JEAN-JACQUES FERRANDIS; publ. *Histoire des Sciences médicales* (4 a year).

Société Française d'Hydrologie et de Climatologie Médicales: 15 ave Charles de Gaulle, 73100 Aix-les-Bains; tel. 4-79-35-14-87; internet www.soc-hydrologie.org; f. 1853; 320 mems; Pres. Prof. MICHEL BOULANGÉ; Sec.-Gen. Dr ROMAIN FORESTIER; publ. *La Presse Thermale et Climatique* (1 a year).

Société Française d'Ophtalmologie: Maison de l'Ophtalmologie, 17 Villa d'Alésia, 75014 Paris; tel. 1-44-12-60-50; fax 1-44-12-23-00; internet www.sfo.asso.fr; f. 1883; annual conference; 7,200 mems; Pres. Dr J. L. ARNÉ; Sec.-Gen. Dr J. P. RENARD; publ. *Journal Français d'Ophtalmologie* (10 a year).

Société Française d'Oto-Rhino-Laryngologie et de Pathologie Cervico-Faciale: 9 rue Villebois-Mareuil, 75017 Paris; internet orl-france.org; f. 1880; 1,500 mems; Pres. Dr R. BATISSE; Sec. Prof. CHARLES FRECHE; publ. *Comptes Rendus and Rapports Discutés au Congrès.*

Société Française du Cancer: 14 rue Corvisart, 75013 Paris; tel. 1-45-87-27-62; fax 1-46-33-20-09; e-mail info@sfc.asso.fr; internet www.sfc.asso.fr; f. 1906; 440 mems; offers grants to doctors from abroad or French doctors for work abroad; quarterly meetings, annual symposium; Pres. JACQUES POUYSSEGUR; Sec.-Gen. FRANÇOIS LAVELLE; publ. *Bulletin du Cancer* (12 a year).

Société Médicale des Hôpitaux de Paris: Hôpital Hôtel-Dieu, 1, place du Parvis Notre-Dame, 75181 Paris Cedex 04; e-mail smhp@wanadoo.fr; internet www.smhp.fr; f. 1849; Sec. Prof. CLAIRE LE JEUNNE; publ. *Annales de Médecine Interne.*

Société Médico-Psychologique: 14/16 ave Robert Schuman, 92100 Boulogne; f. 1852; 675 mems; Pres. Prof. JEAN-FRANÇOIS ALLILAIRE; Sec.-Gen. Dr CHRISTINE NIRABEL SARRON; publ. *Annales médico-psychologiques* (10 a year).

Société Nationale Française de Gastro-Entérologie: CHU Reims, rue Serge Kochman, 51092 Reims Cedex; tel. 3-26-35-94-31; fax 3-26-35-95-91; e-mail secretariat.reims@snfge.org; internet www.snfge.org; f. 1947; 1,800 mems; Pres. Dr ALEX PARIENTE; Sec.-Gen. Prof. GUILLAUME CADIOT; publs *Gastroentérologie Clinique et Biologique*, *Hepato-Gastro et Oncologie Digestive.*

Société Odontologique de Paris: 6 rue Jean Hugues, 75116 Paris; tel. 1-42-09-29-13; fax 1-42-09-29-08; internet www.sop.asso.fr; 2,500 mems; Pres. PHILIP SAFAR; Man. PHILIPPE CHALANSET; publs *Journal de la Société Odontologique de Paris*, *Revue d'Odonto-Stomatologie* (4 a year).

Société Scientifique d'Hygiène Alimentaire: 16A rue de l'Estrapade, 75005 Paris; tel. 1-43-25-11-85; fax 1-46-34-07-45; e-mail isa@ssha.asso.fr; internet www.ssha.asso.fr; f. 1904; 1,182 mems; Pres. Dr GUY EBRARD.

NATURAL SCIENCES
General

Comité National Français des Recherches Arctiques et Antarctiques: c/o Expéditions Polaires Françaises, 47 ave du Maréchal Fayolle, 75016 Paris; tel. 1-40-79-37-56; fax 1-40-79-37-71; f. 1958; Pres. J.-C. HUREAU.

Fédération Française des Sociétés de Sciences Naturelles: 57 rue Cuvier, 75231 Paris Cedex 05; tel. 1-40-79-34-95; fax 1-40-79-34-88; f. 1919; natural sciences and nature conservation; groups 175 socs; Pres. J. LESCURE; Gen. Sec. J. FRETEY; publ. *Revue de la FFSSN* (1 a year).

Biological Sciences

Les Naturalistes Parisiens: 45 rue de Buffon, 75005 Paris; f. 1904; undertakes research in natural history and deepens the scientific knowledge of its mems; 600 mems; Pres. C. DUPUIS; publs *Bulletin* (4 a year), *Cahiers des Naturalistes.*

Société Botanique de France: rue J. B. Clément, 92296 Châtenay-Malabry Cedex; tel. 1-46-83-55-20; fax 1-46-83-13-03; internet www.bium.univ-paris5.fr/sbf; f. 1854; 800 mems; President ANDRÉ CHARPIN; Sec. ELISABETH DODINET; publs *Acta Botanica Gallica* (6 or 7 a year), *Le Journal de Botanique* (4 a year).

Société de Biologie: Université Pierre et Marie Curie, CP 2A, 7 quai St Bernard, 75252 Paris Cedex 05; tel. 1-44-27-35-50; e-mail societe.biologie@snv.jussieu.fr; internet www.societedebiologie.com; f. 1848; organizes meetings about innovative biological research; 140 hon. mems; 120 elected mems; Pres. Dr FRANÇOISE DIETERLEN; Sec.-Gen. Dr CLAUDE JACQUEMIN; publ. *Biologie Aujourd'hui* (4 a year, online at www.biologie-journal.org).

Société d'Etudes Ornithologiques de France: Muséum National d'Histoire Naturelle, 55 rue Buffon, CP 51, 75231 Paris Cedex 05; tel. 1-40-79-38-34; fax 1-40-79-30-63; e-mail seof@mnhn.fr; internet www.mnhn .fr/assoc/seof; f. 1993; scientific study of wild birds and their protection; publishes monographs, national and regional ornithological lists, atlases, CDs; 800 mems; library of 23,500 vols; Pres. P. NICOLAU-GUILLAUMET; Sec.-Gen. J. PH. SIBLET; Librarian E. BREMOND-HOSLET; publ. *Alauda* (4 a year).

Société Entomologique de France: 45 rue Buffon, 75005 Paris; tel. 1-40-79-33-84; fax 1-40-79-36-99; e-mail secretaire-general@lasef .org; internet www.lasef.org; f. 1832; 650 mems; library of 12,000 vols, 80 periodicals; Gen. Sec. H. PIGUET; publs *Annales* (4 a year), *Bulletin* (5 a year), *L'Entomologiste* (6 a year).

Société Française de Biologie Végétale: 4 place Jussieu, 75252 Paris Cedex 05; tel. 1-44-27-59-18; fax 1-44-27-61-51; e-mail marie-france.laforge@snv.jussieu.fr; internet www.sfbv.org; f. 1955; 600 mems; Pres. P. MOREAU; Sec.-Gen. A. ZACHOWSKI; publ. *Plant Physiology and Biochemistry* (12 a year).

Société Française d'Ichtyologie: 43 rue Cuvier, 75231 Paris Cedex 05; tel. 1-40-79-37-49; fax 1-40-79-37-71; e-mail keith@mnhn .fr; internet www.mnhn.fr/sfi; f. 1976; fish culture, biology and systematics of fish, sea and freshwater fisheries; 320 mems; library of 5,000 vols, 800 periodicals; Pres. M. GAYET; Sec. P. KEITH; publ. *Cybium* (4 a year).

Société Mycologique de France: 20 rue Rottembourg, 75012 Paris; tel. and fax 1-44-67-96-90; e-mail smf@mycofrance.org; internet mycofrance.org; f. 1884; 1,800 mems; Pres. M. BUYCK; Sec.-Gen. M. CHALANGE; publ. *Bulletin Trimestriel.*

Société Nationale de Protection de la Nature: 9 rue Cels, 75014 Paris; tel. 1-43-20-15-39; fax 1-43-20-15-71; e-mail snpn@wanadoo.fr; internet www.snpn.com; f. 1854; 4,000 mems; Pres. FRANÇOIS RAMADE; Gen. Sec. MICHEL ECHAUBARD; publs *La Terre et la Vie* (4 a year), *Le Courrier de la Nature* (7 a year), *Zones Humides Infos* (4 a year).

Société Zoologique de France: 195 rue St Jacques, 75005 Paris; tel. 1-40-79-31-10; fax 1-40-79-57-35; e-mail dhondt@mnhn.fr; internet www.snv.jussieu.fr/zoologie; f. 1876; zoology, evolution; 600 mems; Pres. Prof. J. DAGUZAN; Gen. Sec. Dr J. L. D'HONDT; publs *Bulletin* (4 a year), *Mémoires* (irregular).

Mathematical Sciences
Comité National Français de Mathématiciens: c/o S. Ferenczi, Institut de Mathé-

matiques de Luminy, 163 ave de Luminy, Case 907, 13288 Marseilles Cedex 9; fax 4-91-26-96-55; e-mail ferenczi@iml.univ-mrs.fr; f. 1951; Pres. P. ARNOUX; Sec. S. FERENCZI.

Société Mathématique de France: Institut Henri Poincaré, 11 rue Pierre et Marie Curie, 75231 Paris Cedex 05; tel. 1-44-27-67-96; fax 1-40-46-90-96; e-mail smf@dma.ens.fr; internet smf.emath.fr; f. 1872; 2,000 mems; Pres. BERNARD HELFFER; Gen.-Sec. CLAIRE ROPARTZ; publs *Annales Scientifiques de l'Ecole Normale Supériure* (6 a year), *Astérisque* (12 a year), *Bulletin* (4 a year), *Cours Spécialisés* (2 a year), *Gazette des Mathématiciens* (4 a year), *Mémoires* (4 a year), *Panoramas et Synthèses* (2 a year), *Revue d'Histoire des Mathématiques* (2 a year).

Physical Sciences

Association Française d'Observateurs d'Etoiles Variables: Observatoire Astronomique, 11 rue de l'Université, 67000 Strasbourg; tel. 3-85-89-09-78; e-mail afoev@astro.u-strasbg.fr; internet www.astro.u-strasbg.fr/afoev; f. 1921; observations (visual, photographic, PEP, CCD) of variable stars; 110 mems; Pres. M. VERDENET; Sec.-Gen. J. GUNTHER; Sec.-Gen. D. PROUST; publ. *Bulletin de l'AFOEV* (4 a year).

Association Française pour l'Etude du Quaternaire: Maison de la Géologie, 79 rue Claude Bernard, 75005 Paris; e-mail pierre.antoine@cnrs-bellevue.fr; internet www.afeq.cnrs-bellevue.fr; f. 1962 to prepare scientific publications and exchange information on the Quaternary; 600 mems; Pres. Dr D. LEFÈVRE; Sec. Dr C. FERRIER; publ. *Quaternaire* (4 a year).

Association Scientifique et Technique pour l'Exploitation des Océans: Immeuble Ile de France, La Défense 9, 4 place de la Pyramide, 92070 Paris La Défense Cedex 33; tel. 1-47-67-25-32; f. 1967; oil technology and allied activities, pollution control, polymetallic nodules, sand and gravel workings, fishing technology and fish farming; 80 mem. industries; Chair. PIERRE JACQUARD; Man. Dir B. E. DIMONT; publ. *Annuaire Technique et Industriel*.

Fédération Française pour les Sciences de la Chimie: 28 rue Saint-Dominique, 75007 Paris; tel. 1-53-59-02-10; fax 1-45-55-40-33; e-mail pascale.bridou@wanadoo.fr; internet www.ffc-asso.fr; f. 2005; 4,000 mems.

Société Astronomique de France: 3 rue Beethoven, 75016 Paris; tel. 1-42-24-13-74; fax 1-42-30-75-47; e-mail ste.astro.france@wanadoo.fr; internet www.saf-lastronomie.com; f. 1887; 2,200 mems; Pres. PHILIPPE MOREL; Sec.-Gen. FRANCIS OGER; publs *L'Astronomie* (12 a year), *Les Éphémérides* (1 a year), *Observations et Travaux* (3 a year).

Société des Experts-Chimistes de France: 23 rue Saint-Dominique, 75007 Paris; tel. 1-53-59-02-16; fax 1-45-55-40-33; e-mail contact@chimie-experts.org; internet www.chimie-experts.org; f. 1912; 300 mems; Pres. JEAN-PIERRE DAL PONT; Sec.-Gen. THÉRÈSE GIBERT; publ. *Annales des Falsifications de l'Expertise Chimique et Toxicologique*.

Société Française de Biochimie et Biologie Moléculaire: 45 Rue des Saints-Pères, 75270 Paris Cedex 06; tel. 1-42-86-33-77; fax 1-42-86-33-73; e-mail sfbbm@cep.u-psud.fr; internet coli.polytechnique.fr/sfbbm; f. 1914; 1,320 mems; Pres. E. WESTHOF; Gen. Sec. P. DESSEN; publs *Biochimie*, *Regard sur la Biochimie*.

Société Française de Chimie: 250 rue St Jacques, 75005 Paris; tel. 1-40-46-71-60; fax 1-40-46-71-61; e-mail sfc@sfc.fr; internet www.sfc.fr; f. 1857; 4,600 mems; Pres. ARMAND LATTES; Sec.-Gen. JEAN-CLAUDE BRUNIE; publs *Analusis* (10 a year), *Journal de Chimie physique* (10 a year), *L'Actualité chimique* (12 a year).

Société Française de Minéralogie et de Cristallographie: 4 place Jussieu, casier 83, 75252 Paris Cedex 05; tel. 1-44-27-60-24; fax 1-44-27-60-24; e-mail sfmc@ccr.jussieu.fr; internet www.sfmc-fr.org; f. 1878; 600 mems; Pres. JEAN-ROBERT KIENAST; Gen.-Sec. DANIEL NEUVILLE; publs *Bulletin de Liaison*, *European Journal of Mineralogy*.

Société Française de Physique: 33 rue Croulebarbe, 75013 Paris; tel. 1-44-08-67-10; fax 1-44-08-67-19; e-mail sfp@sfpnet.org; internet sfp.in2p3.fr; f. 1873; 2,500 mems; Pres. EDOUARD BREZIN; Gen. Sec. JEAN VANNIMENUS; publs *Annales de Physique*, *Bulletin*, *Catalogue de l'Exposition de Physique*, *Colloques*, *Journal de Physique*.

Société Géologique de France: 77 rue Claude-Bernard, 75005 Paris; tel. 1-43-31-77-35; fax 1-45-35-79-10; e-mail accueil@sgfr.org; internet www.sgfr.org; f. 1830; 1,100 mems; library of 65,000 vols, 500 periodicals; Pres. ISABELLE COJAN; Vice-Pres. PIERRE BARBEY; Exec. Dir FRANÇOISE PEIFFER-RANGIN; Sec. NICOLAS BELLAHSEN; Sec. PIERRE-YVES COLLIN; publs *Bulletin* (6 a year), *Géochronique* (co-edited with BRGM, 4 a year), *Géologie de la France* (co-edited with BRGM, online), *Mémoires* (irregular), *Terra Nova* (co-edited with EUG and Sociétés Géologiques Européennes).

Union des Professeurs de Physique et de Chimie: 42 rue Saint Jacques, 75005 Paris Cedex 06; tel. 1-40-46-83-80; fax 1-46-34-76-61; e-mail secretariat.national@udppc.asso.fr; internet www.udppc.asso.fr; f. 1906; 4,000 mems; Pres MICHELINE IZBICKI; publ. *Le Bup physique-chimie* (12 a year).

PHILOSOPHY AND PSYCHOLOGY

Association pour la Diffusion de la Pensée Français: 6 rue Ferrus, 75683 Paris Cedex 14; tel. 1-43-13-11-00; fax 1-43-13-11-25; f. 1946; aims to promote the French language and Francophone culture worldwide; 600 overseas mems; Pres. JACQUES BLOT.

Société Française de Philosophie: c/o 45 rue d'Ulm, 75320 Paris Cedex 005; f. 1901; 180 mems; Pres. DIDIER DELEULE; Sec.-Gen. CHRISTIANE MENASSEYRE; publs *Bulletin*, *Revue de Métaphysique et de Morale* (4 a year).

Société Française de Psychologie: 71 ave Edouard-Vaillant, 92774 Boulogne Cedex; tel. 1-55-20-58-32; fax 1-55-20-58-34; e-mail sfp@psycho.univ-paris5.fr; internet www.sfpsy.org; f. 1901; 1,000 mems; Pres. JACQUES PY; Sec.-Gen. ALAIN PAINEAU; publs *La Lettre de SFP*, *Pratiques Psychologiques*, *Psychologie Française*.

RELIGION, SOCIOLOGY AND ANTHROPOLOGY

Association Française des Arabisants: Collège de France, 52 rue du Cardinal Lemoine, 75005 Paris; e-mail afda@afda.asso.fr; internet www.afda.asso.fr; f. 1973; promotes Arabic studies; studies questions of doctrine and practice relative to teaching and research in Arabic; keeps its members informed of ideas and activities of interest to teachers, researchers and students of Arabic; 450 mems; Pres. JEAN-YVES L'HOPITAL; Sec. ABDELLATIF IDRISSI; publs *Actes des journées d'études arabes* (irregular), *Annuaire des Arabisants* (every 2 years), *L'Arabisant* (every 2 years), *Lettre d'Information* (2 a year).

Société Asiatique: Palais de l'Institut, 23 quai de Conti, 75006 Paris; tel. 1-44-41-43-14; fax 1-44-41-43-14; internet www.aibl.fr/fr/asie/home.html; f. 1822; library of 90,000 vols; 725 mems; Pres. JEAN-PIERRE MAHÉ; publs *Cahiers*, *Journal Asiatique* (2 a year).

Société d'Anthropologie de Paris: Musée de l'Homme, 17 place du Trocadéro, 75116 Paris; tel. 1-45-59-53-31; fax 1-45-59-53-31; e-mail secretairegeneral@sapweb.fr; internet www.sapweb.fr; f. 1859; biological anthropology; 310 mems; Pres. OLIVIER DUTOUR; Sec.-Gen. ALAIN FROMENT; publ. *Bulletins et Mémoires* (4 a year).

Société de l'Histoire du Protestantisme Français: 54 rue des Saints-Pères, 75007 Paris; tel. 1-45-48-62-07; fax 1-45-44-94-87; e-mail shpf@libertysurf.fr; f. 1852; library of 150,000 vols, 12,000 MSS, 2,000 periodical titles; Pres. THERRY DU PASQUIER; Sec.-Gen. JEAN-HUGUES CARBONNIER; publs *Bulletin*, *Cahiers de Généalogie Protestante* (4 a year).

Société de Mythologie Française: 3 rue St-Laurent, 75010 Paris; tel. 1-42-05-30-57; e-mail phparrain@mythofrancaise.asso.fr; internet www.mythofrancaise.asso.fr; f. 1950; 200 mems; Pres. BERNARD SERGENT; publ. *Mythologie Française* (4 a year).

Société des Africanistes: Musée de l'Homme, 17 Place du Trocadéro, 75116 Paris; tel. 1-47-27-72-55; fax 1-47-04-63-40; e-mail africanistes@wanadoo.fr; internet www.mae.u-paris10.fr/africanistes; f. 1931; 400 mems; Pres. PHILIPPE LABURTHE-TOLRA; Sec. FRANÇOIS GAULME; publ. *Journal des Africanistes* (2 a year).

Société des Américanistes: Maison René Ginouvès, 21 allée de l'Université, 92023 Nanterre Cedex; tel. 1-46-69-26-34; e-mail jsa@mae.u-paris10.fr; f. 1895; 500 mems; Pres. PHILIPPE DESCOLA; Gen. Sec. DOMINIQUE MICHELET; publ. *Journal* (2 a year).

Société d'Histoire Religieuse de la France: 26 rue d'Assas, 75006 Paris; internet www.enc.sorbonne.fr/shrf; f. 1910; 560 mems; Pres. BERNARD BARBICHE; Sec.-Gen. OLIVIER PONCET; publ. *Revue d'Histoire de l'Eglise de France* (2 a year).

Société Française de Sociologie: 59/61 rue Pouchet, 75849 Paris Cedex 17; tel. 1-40-25-12-63; fax 1-42-28-95-44; e-mail afs@iresco.fr; internet www.iresco.fr/societes/afs; f. 1962; Pres. DANIEL BERTAUX; Sec. MICHÈLE VINAUGER.

TECHNOLOGY

Académie de marine: CC 11, 75398 Paris Cedex 08; 21 pl. Joffre, 75007 Paris; tel. 1-44-42-82-02; fax 1-44-42-82-04; e-mail academiedemarine@wanadoo.fr; internet www.academiedemarine.com; f. 1752; sections on history, literature and arts, law and economics, mercantile marine, military affairs, naval equipment, navigation and oceanic sciences, yachting and fishing; 109 mems; Pres. Prof. JEAN-PIERRE QUÉNEUDEC; Vice-Pres. ANDRÉ RAVIER; Sec.-Gen. VERONIQUE DE LONGEVIALLE; publ. *Communications et Mémoires* (3 a year).

Association Aéronautique et Astronautique de France (AAAF): 61 Ave du Château, 78480 Verneuil-sur-Seine; tel. 1-39-79-75-15; fax 1-39-79-75-27; internet www.aaafasso.fr; f. 1972; 1,800 mems; formed by merger of Asscn Française des Ingénieurs de l'Aéronautique et de l'Espace and Société Française d'Astronautique; Pres. MICHEL SCHELLER; Sec.-Gen. ROBERT DUBOST; publ. *La Nouvelle Revue d'Aéronautique et d'Astronautique* (4 a year).

Association des Anciens Elèves de l'Ecole Nationale Supérieure des Industries Agricoles et Alimentaires: 9–11 ave

Franklin D. Roosevelt, 75008 Paris; tel. 1-42-25-92-48; fax 1-45-62-77-13; internet www.uniagro.fr/gene/main.php?base=1141&url_assoc=y; 1,500 mems; Pres. JEAN-LOUIS TIXIER; Sec.-Gen. MICHEL MERY; publ. *Industries Alimentaires et Agricoles* (12 a year).

Association Française des Sciences et Technologies de l'Information: 4 place Jussieu, 75252 Paris Cedex 05; tel. 3-83-59-20-51; e-mail asti.asso@lri.fr; internet www.asti.asso.fr; f. 1998; 25 mem. orgs; Pres. JEAN-PAUL HATON; Sec.-Gen. CLAUDE GIRAULT; publ. *Hebdo*.

Association Française du Froid: 17 rue Guillaume Apollinaire, 75006 Paris; tel. 1-45-44-52-52; fax 1-42-22-00-42; e-mail a.f.f@wanadoo.fr; internet www.aff.asso.fr; f. 1908; 1,000 mems; Pres. LOUIS LUCAS; Sec.-Gen. JEAN LETEINTURIER-LAPRISE; publs *Bulletin: Kryos, Revue Générale du Froid* (10 a year).

Association Nationale de la Recherche Technique: 41 Blvd des Capucines, 75002 Paris; tel. 1-55-35-25-50; fax 1-55-35-25-55; internet www.anrt.asso.fr; f. 1953 to promote technical research and organizations, and to foster contact with technical research institutions abroad; Pres. JEAN-FRANÇOIS DEHECQ; publ. *La lettre Européenne du Progrès Technique* (10 a year).

Conseil National des Ingénieurs et des Scientifiques de France: 7 rue Lamennais, 75008 Paris; tel. 1-44-13-66-88; fax 1-42-89-82-50; internet www.cnisf.org; f. 1848; Pres. NOËL CLAVELLOUX; Sec. MONIQUE MONIN; publ. *I.D.*

Société de l'Electricité, de l'Electronique, et des Technologies de l'Information (SEE): 17 rue de l'Amiral Hamelin, 75783 Paris Cedex 16; tel. 1-56-90-37-00; fax 1-56-90-37-19; e-mail see@see.asso.fr; internet www.see.asso.fr; f. 1883; Pres. ALAIN BRAVO; Sec. PATRICK MORO; publs *e-STA—Revue des Sciences et Technologies de l'Automatique* (online), *Revue de l'Electricité et de l'Electronique* (10 a year), *3EI—Enseigner l'Electrotechnique et l'Electronique Industriel* (4 a year).

Société d'Encouragement pour l'Industrie Nationale: 4 place Saint-Germain-des-Prés, 75006 Paris; e-mail adm@industrienationale.fr; internet www.industrienationale.fr; f. 1801; Dir BERNARD MOUSSON; publ. *L'Industrie Nationale*.

Société Française de Métallurgie et de Matériaux (SF2M): 250 rue Saint Jacques, 75005 Paris; tel. 1-46-33-08-00; fax 1-46-33-08-80; internet www.sf2m.asso.fr; f. 1945; 1,200 mems; Pres. ANNICK PERCHERON-GUEGAN; Sec. PAUL V. RIBOUD.

Société Française de Photogrammétrie et de Télédétection: 2 ave Pasteur, 94165 St Mandé Cedex; tel. 1-64-15-32-86; fax 1-64-15-32-85; e-mail sfpt@ensg.ign.fr; internet www.ign.fr/sfpt; f. 1959; photogrammetry and remote sensing; 615 mems; Pres. G. BEGNI; Sec.-Gen. I. VEILLET; publ. *Bulletin* (4 a year).

Société Française des Microscopies: Case 243, Université Pierre et Marie Curie, 4 pl. Jussieu, 75252 Paris Cedex 05; tel. 1-44-27-26-21; fax 1-44-27-26-22; e-mail sfmu@sfmu.fr; internet www.sfmu.fr; f. 1959; all types of microscopy, electronic optics and electronic diffraction, optics, spectroscopy, microprobe, x-ray; physics, chemistry, biology; 470 mems; Pres. VIRGINIE SERIN; publs *Biology of the Cell* (9 a year), *European Physical Journal: Applied Physics* (6 a year).

Société Hydrotechnique de France: 25 rue des Favorites, 75015 Paris; tel. 1-42-50-91-03; fax 1-42-50-59-83; e-mail shf@shf.asso.fr; internet www.shf.asso.fr; f. 1912; fluid mechanics, applied hydraulics, geophysical hydraulics and water conservation; 600 mems; Pres. DANIEL LOUDIERE; Pres. for Scientific Cttee PIERRE-LOUIS VIOLLET; Gen. Dir JEAN-GEORGES PHILIPPS; publs *La Houille Blanche—Revue Internationale de l'Eau* (6 a year), *Proceedings, Journées de l'Hydraulique* (1 a year), guides on hydroelectricity and flood forecasts, research documents.

Research Institutes

GENERAL

Centre National de la Recherche Scientifique (CNRS): 3 rue Michel-Ange, 75794 Paris Cedex 16; tel. 1-44-96-40-00; fax 1-44-96-53-90; internet www.cnrs.fr; f. 1939; coordinates and promotes scientific research, and proposes to the Govt means of doing research and how to allocate funds; makes grants-in-aid to scientific bodies and to individuals to enable them to carry out research work; subsidizes or sets up laboratories for scientific research; is split into 40 sections, covering all scientific fields; funds 11,600 researchers, 14,400 engineers and 4,000 technicians and admin. staff; depts of chemistry (Scientific Dir GILBERT CHAMBAUD), engineering (Scientific Dir PIERRE GUILLON), environment and sustainable development (Scientific Dir BERNARD DELAY), human and social sciences (Scientific Dir MARIE-FRANÇOISE COUREL), life sciences (Scientific Dir MICHEL VAN DER REST), mathematics, physics, planet and universe (Scientific Dir MICHEL LANOO),; Pres. CATHÉRINE BRÉCHIGNAC; Dir-Gen. ARNOLD MIGUS; Sec.-Gen. JACQUES BERNARD.

AGRICULTURE, FISHERIES AND VETERINARY SCIENCE

Centre de Co-opération Internationale en Recherche Agronomique pour le Développement (CIRAD): 42 rue Scheffer, 75116 Paris; tel. 1-53-70-20-00; fax 1-47-55-15-30; internet www.cirad.fr; (laboratories: BP 5035, 34032 Montpellier Cedex 1; tel. 4-67-61-58-00); f. 1970, present name 1986; state-owned; research and devt within the framework of French scientific and technical cooperation with developing countries; stations in over 50 countries; library of 134,000 vols, 3,300 scientific periodicals; Dir-Gen. GÉRARD MATHERON; Sec.-Gen. HERVÉ DEPERROIS.

Research Departments:

Département d'Amélioration des Méthodes pour l'Innovation Scientifique (CIRAD-AMIS): 2477 ave Agropolis, TA 40/02, 34398 Montpellier Cedex 5; tel. 4-67-61-58-00; fax 4-67-61-44-55; e-mail amis@cirad.fr; plant modelling, food production, agronomy, crop protection, biotechnology and plant genetic research, economics, policy and marketing; Dir JACQUES MEUNIER; publ. *Sésame bulletin*.

Département d'Élevage et de Médecine Vétérinaire (CIRAD-EMVT): Campus international de Baillarguet, BP 5035, 34398 Montpellier Cedex 5; tel. 4-67-59-37-10; fax 4-67-59-37-95; e-mail valo.emvt@cirad.fr; f. 1948; research and missions to countries of Africa, Asia and South America; Dir EMMANUEL CAMUS; publ. *Revue d'Elevage et de Médecine Vétérinaire des Pays Tropicaux* (4 a year).

Département des Cultures Annuelles (CIRAD-CA): 2477 ave Agropolis, BP 5035, 34398 Montpellier Cedex 5; tel. 4-67-61-58-00; fax 4-67-61-59-88; e-mail dirpersyst@cirad.fr; f. 1992; experts stationed in Benin, Brazil, Burkina Faso, Burundi, Cameroon, Central African Republic, Chad, Colombia, Costa Rica, Côte d'Ivoire, Dominica, Gabon, Ghana, Guinea, Honduras, Laos, Madagascar, Mali, Niger, Paraguay, Philippines, Senegal, Thailand, Togo, Turkey, Viet Nam; Dir MARCO WOPEREIS; publ. *Agriculture et développement* (4 a year, abstracts in French, English and Spanish).

Département des Cultures Pérennes (CIRAD-CP): Boulevard de la Lirondem, TA 80/PS3, 34398 Montpellier Cedex 5; tel. 4-67-61-58-00; fax 4-67-61-56-59; e-mail dircp@cirad.fr; f. 1992; research and technical assistance relating to cocoa, coconuts, coffee, oil palm and rubber; Dir DOMINIQUE BERRY; publ. *Plantations, recherche, développement* (in French and English or Spanish).

Département des Territoires, Environnement et Acteurs (CIRAD-TERA): 73 rue Jean-François Breton, TA 60/15, 34398 Montpellier Cedex 5; tel. 4-67-61-58-00; fax 4-67-61-12-23; e-mail tera@cirad.fr; smallholder farming, land and resources, savannah and irrigated systems, humid tropics; Dir ROLLAND GUIS.

Département Forestier (CIRAD-Forêt): Campus international de Baillarguet, BP 5035, 34398 Montpellier Cedex 5; tel. 4-67-59-37-10; fax 4-67-59-37-55; e-mail forets@cirad.fr; forestry; Dir BERNARD MALLET; publ. *Bois et forêts des tropiques*.

Centre de Recherches de Jouy: Domaine de Vilvert, 78352 Jouy-en-Josas Cedex; tel. 1-34-65-21-21; fax 1-34-65-20-51; e-mail communication@jouy.inra.fr; internet www.jouy.inra.fr; f. 1950; linked to Institut National de la Recherche Agronomique (*q.v.*); scientific research on livestock production and health, human nutrition, animal biology, microbiology, applied mathematics and bioinformatics, animal models for human and animal health; library of 6,000 vols, 2,200 periodicals; Pres. Dr EMMANUEL JOLIVET.

Institut d'Immunologie Animale et Comparée: Ecole Nationale Vétérinaire d'Alfort, 7 ave du Général de Gaulle, 94704 Maisons-Alfort Cedex; tel. 1-43-68-98-82; f. 1981; organizes courses; research in immunostimulation, clinical immunology, immunopathology; Dir Prof. CH. PILET.

Institut National de la Recherche Agronomique (INRA): 147 rue de l'Université, 75338 Paris Cedex 07; tel. 1-42-75-90-00; fax 1-47-05-99-66; internet www.inra.fr; f. 1946; agricultural research, incl. agricultural and food industries, rural economics and sociology, plant and animal production and forestry; administers and subsidizes a large number of centres, laboratories and experimental farms in France; Pres. and Dir-Gen. MARION GUILLOU; publs *Agronomy for Sustainable Development* (10 a year), *Animal Research* (6 a year), *Annales des Sciences Forestières* (6 a year), *Apidologie* (6 a year), *Archorales: Les Métiers de la Recherche* (online), *Bulletin des Technologies* (1 a year), *Cahiers d'Economie et Sociologie rurales* (4 a year), *Courrier de l'Environnement* (online), *Genetics Selection Evolution* (6 a year), *INRA Sciences Sociales* (6 a year), *Le Lait* (6 a year), *Production Animales* (3 a year), *Reproduction Nutrition Development* (6 a year), *Veterinary Research* (6 a year).

Laboratoire Central de Recherches Vétérinaires: BP 67, 22 rue Pierre Curie, 94703 Maisons-Alfort Cedex; tel. 1-49-77-13-00; fax 1-43-68-97-62; f. 1901; 140 mems; study of contagious diseases in domestic and wild animals; supervises sanitary regulations for import and export of livestock; Dir Dr ERIC PLATEAU.

ECONOMICS, LAW AND POLITICS

Centre d'Etudes de l'Emploi: Le Descartes I, 29 promenade Michel Simon, 93166 Noisy-le-Grand Cedex; tel. 1-45-92-68-00; fax 1-49-31-02-44; internet www.cee-recherche.fr; attached to Min. of Employment and Min. of Education; for the study and research of changes in the field of employment; research units: age and work, employment and social security, employment markets and instns, workers and orgs; Dir PIERRE RALLE; publs *CEE.INFO* (3 a year), *Connaisance de l'Emploi* (12 a year).

Centre d'Etudes Prospectives et d'Informations Internationales: 113 rue de Grenelle, 75007 Paris; tel. 1-53-68-55-00; fax 1-53-68-55-03; e-mail cepiiweb@cepii.fr; internet www.cepii.fr; f. 1978 by the Govt, under the aegis of Centre d'analyse strategique; aids public and private decision-makers in the int. economic field by conducting synthetic studies of the global economic environment in the mid-term (5–10 years), constructing economic models and databases, and by providing a coherent statistical information system of the world economy and its major participants; 50 mems; library of 30,000 vols, 500 periodicals; Dir AGNÈS BÉNASSY-QUÉRÉ; publs *CEPII Working Papers* (12 a year), *CHELEM Data Bank: bilingual DVD and internet* (1 a year), *Economie Internationale* (4 a year), *La Lettre du CEPII* (11 a year), *L'Economie mondiale* (1 a year), *Modelling International Relationships in Applied General Equilibrium: MIRAGE.*

Institut de Recherches Economiques et Sociales: 16 blvd du Mont d'Est, 93192 Noisy-Le-Grand Cedex; tel. (1) 48-15-18-93; fax (1) 48-15-19-18; e-mail contact@ires-fr.org; internet www.ires-fr.org; f. 1982 by the main French trade unions in association with the French Govt to meet the economic and social research needs of trade unions; central research areas: employment patterns, industrial relations, wage patterns, work patterns; Pres. PIERRETTE CROSEMARIE; Dir JACKY FAYOLLE; publs *La Chronique Internationale* (6 a year), *La Lettre de l'IRES* (4 a year), *La Revue de L'IRES* (3 a year).

Institut de Sciences Mathématiques et Economiques Appliquées: 1 rue Maurice Arnoux, 92120 Montrouge; tel. 1-55-48-90-70; fax 1-55-48-90-71; e-mail perroux@univ-mlv.fr; internet www.ismea.org; f. 1944; int. cooperation and links with Third World univs; library of 14,500 vols; Chair. Prof. G. DESTANNE DE BERNIS; publs *Economie Appliquée* (4 a year), *Economies et Sociétés* (12 a year).

Institut National de la Statistique et des Etudes Economiques: 18 blvd Adolphe Pinard, 75675 Paris Cedex 14; tel. 1-41-17-50-50; fax 1-41-17-66-66; e-mail insee-contact@insee.fr; internet www.insee.fr; f. 1946; statistical research: population census, economic indices and forecasts, economic and social studies; library: see Libraries; Dir-Gen. JEAN-PHILIPPE COTIS; publs *Annuaire Statistique de la France* (1 a year, free online), *Bulletin Statistique* (online), *Economie et Statistique* (12 a year, free online), *Insee Méthodes, Insee Première* (60 a year), *Informations Rapides* (370 a year), *Insee Résultats, La Commerce en France (Collection Références), La France des Services (Collection Références), La France et ses Régions, Les salaires en France (Collection Références), L'industrie en France (Collection Références), Note de Conjoncture* (4 a year), *Tableaux de l'économie Française* (1 a year).

Institut National d'Etudes Démographiques: 133 Blvd Davout, 75980 Paris Cedex 20; tel. 1-56-06-20-00; fax 1-56-06-21-99; internet www.ined.fr; f. 1945; library of 40,000 vols; Dir FRANÇOIS HÉRAN; publs *Classiques de l'Économie et de la Population* (2 or 3 a year), *Les Cahiers de l'INED* (4–6 a year), *Population* (4 a year), *Population et Sociétés* (12 a year).

EDUCATION

Centre International d'Etudes Pédagogiques de Sèvres: 1 ave Léon Journault, BP 75, 92318 Sèvres Cedex; tel. 1-45-07-60-00; fax 1-45-07-60-01; internet www.ciep.fr; f. 1945; research and studies in comparative education; training overseas teachers in French as a foreign language; 170 mems; Dir M. LÉOUTRE; publ. *Revue Internationale d'Education.*

Institut National de Recherche Pédagogique: 19 Mail de Fontenay, BP 17424, 69347 Lyons Cedex 07; tel. 4-72-76-61-71; fax 4-72-76-61-42; e-mail contact@inrp.fr; internet www.inrp.fr; f. 1879; develops and promotes research into teaching and education; 280 staff, 1652 assoc. mems; library: see Libraries and Archives; Dir EMMANUEL FRAISSE; publs *Aster* (2 a year), *Didaskalia* (2 a year), *Etapes de la Recherche, Histoire de l'Education* (4 a year), *Perspectives Documentaires* (3 a year), *Recherche et Formation* (3 a year), *Repères* (2 a year), *Revue Française de Pédagogie* (4 a year).

FINE AND PERFORMING ARTS

Institut de Recherche et Co-ordination Acoustique et de la Musique: Centre National d'Art et de Culture Georges-Pompidou, 1 pl. Igor-Stravinsky, 75004 Paris Cedex 04; tel. 1-44-78-48-43; fax 1-44-78-15-40; internet www.ircam.fr; attached to Centre National d'Art et de Culture Georges-Pompidou; interdisciplinary research centre for musicians and scientists; data processing, electroacoustics, instrumental and vocal research; Dir FRANK MADLENER.

Institut National d'Histoire de l'Art (INHA): 2 rue Vivienne, 75002 Paris; tel. 1-47-03-86-04; fax 1-47-03-86-36; e-mail inha@inha.fr; internet www.inha.fr; f. 2001; library: Bibliothèque d'art et d'archéologie Jacques Doucet; Dir-Gen. ANTOINETTE LE NORMAND-ROMAIN.

HISTORY, GEOGRAPHY AND ARCHAEOLOGY

Centre de Recherches Historiques: Ecole des Hautes Etudes en Sciences Sociales, UMR 8558, 54 blvd Raspail, 75006 Paris; tel. 1-49-54-24-42; fax 1-49-54-23-99; e-mail crh@msh-paris.fr; internet www.ehess.fr; f. 1950; joint research in economic, social, cultural and political history; 126 mems; Dir GÉRARD BÉAUR; Dir PAUL-ANDRÉ ROSENTAL; Dir JUDITH LYON-CAEN; publs *Annales* (history, social sciences, 6 a year), *Cahiers* (2 a year), *Entreprises et Histoire* (4 a year), *Histoire et Mesure* (4 a year), *1900* (1 a year).

Centre d'Études Supérieures de la Renaissance: 59 rue Néricault-Destouches, BP 11328, 37013 Tours Cedex 1; tel. 2-47-36-77-60; fax 2-47-36-77-62; e-mail cesr@univ-tours.fr; internet www.cesr.univ-tours.fr; f. 1956; library of 45,000 vols; Dir Prof. G. CHAIX; Sec. M. ANCELIN.

Fondation et Institut Charles de Gaulle: 5 rue de Solférino, 75007 Paris; tel. 1-44-18-66-77; fax 1-44-18-66-99; e-mail contact@charles-de-gaulle.org; internet www.charles-de-gaulle.org; f. Institute 1971, Foundation f. 1992; assembles material related to the life and work of Charles de Gaulle for the purpose of scholarship; library of 4,500 vols, periodicals, documents, cuttings, 4,000 photographs, recorded interviews, audiovisual material; Pres. YVES GUÉNA.

Institut Géographique National: 73 avenue de Paris, 94165 Saint-Mandé; tel. 1-43-98-80-00; fax 1-43-98-84-00; internet www.ign.fr; f. 1940; satellite-image, aerial and ground surveys, map printing; nat. map and aerial photograph library, scientific library; administers Ecole Nat. des Sciences Géographiques (q.v.); Pres. MICHEL FRANC; Dir-Gen. JEAN POULIT; publ. *Bulletin d'Information* (4 a year).

Sous-Direction de l'Archéologie: 4 rue d'Aboukir, 75002 Paris; tel. 1-40-15-77-81; fax 1-40-15-77-00; e-mail jean-francois.texier@culture.gouv.fr; f. 1964; library of 4,500 vols, 47 periodicals; Dir JEAN-FRANÇOIS TEXIER.

MEDICINE

Institut Alfred-Fournier: 25 blvd Saint-Jacques, 75014 Paris; internet www.institutfournier.org; research into sexually transmitted diseases; f. 1923; Dir Dr P. BARBIER.

Institut Arthur-Vernes: 36 rue d'Assas, 75006 Paris; tel. 1-44-39-53-00; fax 1-42-84-26-09; internet www.institut-vernes.fr; f. 1981; Pres. J. C. SERVAN-SCHREIBER; Gen. Man. CATHERINE RAUCHE.

Institut Gustave-Roussy: 39 rue Camille Desmoulins, 94805 Villejuif Cedex; tel. 1-42-11-42-11; fax 1-42-11-53-00; e-mail roussy@igr.fr; internet www.igr.fr; f. 1921; diagnosis and treatment of cancer, research, and training in oncology (affiliated with Univ. Paris-Sud for teaching purposes); library of 11,000 vols, with spec. colln on cancerology; Dir Prof. GILBERT LENOIR.

Institut National de la Santé et de la Recherche Médicale (INSERM): 101 rue de Tolbiac, 75654 Paris Cedex 13; tel. 1-44-23-60-00; fax 1-44-23-60-99; internet www.inserm.fr; f. 1941 as Institut National d'Hygiène, renamed 1964; assisted by scientific commissions and the Scientific Council; 270 research units throughout France; Pres. MONIQUE CAPRON; Dir-Gen. Prof. CHRISTIAN BRÉCHOT; publs *Annuaire des laboratoires, rapport d'activité, INSERM Actualités,* Collections, etc.

Institut Pasteur: 25–28 rue du Dr Roux, 75015 Paris; tel. 1-45-68-80-00; e-mail info@pasteur.fr; internet www.pasteur.fr; f. 1887; Pres. ALICE DAUTRY; Sec. AGNÈS LABIGNE; publs *Annales: Actualités, Annales Research in Virology, Bulletin* (4 a year), *Immunology and Microbiology* (16 a year).

NATURAL SCIENCES

General

Institut de Recherche pour le Développement (IRD): 44 blvd de Dunkerque, 13002 Marseille; tel. 4-91-99-92-00; e-mail dic@ird.fr; internet www.ird.fr; f. 1944; public corpn charged to aid developing countries by means of research, both fundamental and applied, in the non-temperate regions, with spec. application to human environment problems, food production and tropical diseases; 35 centres in Africa, Asia, the Pacific, South America and French overseas territories; library and documentation centre; Pres. DICHEL LAURENT; publ. *Sciences au Sud* (5 a year).

Maintains the Following Services:

Antenne IRD de Bouaké: BP 1434, Bouaké, Côte d'Ivoire; tel. 31-63-95-43; fax 31-63-27-38; e-mail bouake@ird.ci;

internet www.ird.ci/ird/bouake.html; f. 1976; jt research project with l'Institut des Savanes; studies of dams for agricultural irrigation, social mobility and sexually transmitted diseases, production and distribution of foodstuffs in the central region of Côte d'Ivoire.

Centre IRD de Bondy: 32 ave Henri Varagnat, 93143 Bondy Cedex; tel. 1-48-02-55-00; fax 1-48-47-30-88; e-mail bondy@ird.fr; internet www.bondy.ird.fr; f. 1945; geophysics, geodynamics, social sciences, entomology, applied computer science, scientific information (cartography, documentation, audiovisual); Dir GEORGES DE NONI.

Centre IRD de Bretagne: BP 70, 29280 Plouzané Cedex; tel. 2-98-22-45-01; fax 2-98-22-45-14; e-mail brest@ird.fr; internet www.brest.ird.fr; f. 1975; oceanography; Dir CLAUDE ROY.

Centre IRD de Montpellier: BP 64501, 34394 Montpellier Cedex 5; tel. 4-67-41-61-00; fax 4-67-41-63-30; e-mail montpellier@ird.fr; internet www.mpl.ird.fr; hydrology, hydrobiology and oceanography, soil biology, agrarian research, phytopathology, phytovirology, applied zoology, medical entomology, nutrition, geology, genetics; Dir YVES DUVAL.

Centre IRD d'Orléans: Technoparc, 5 rue du Carbone, 45072 Orléans Cedex 2; tel. 2-38-49-95-00; fax 2-38-49-95-10; e-mail orleans@ird.fr; internet www.orleans.ird.fr; human adaptation to tropical environments, environmental dynamics between forests, agriculture and biodiversity, valorization of vegetal biodiversity; Dir YVELINE PONCET.

Centre IRD de Sète: CRHMT, Ave Jean Monnet, BP 171, 34203 Sète Cedex; tel. 4-99-57-32-34; fax 4-99-57-32-95; e-mail philippe.cury@ird.fr; Dir Gen. MICHEL LAURENT.

Institut Français de l'Environnement: 5 route d'Olivet, BP 16105, 45061 Orléans Cedex 2; tel. 2-38-79-78-78; fax 2-38-79-78-70; e-mail cgdd-soes-orleans@developpement-durable.gouv.fr; internet www.ifen.fr; f. 1991; attached to Min. of Town and Country Planning and the Environment; collects and disseminates statistical information about the environment; focal point in France for European Environment Agency.

Biological Sciences

Institut de Biologie Physico-chimique: 13 rue Pierre et Marie Curie, 75005 Paris; tel. 1-58-41-50-00; fax 1-58-41-50-20; e-mail ifr550@ibpc.fr; internet www.ibpc.fr; f. 1927; Dir Dr J.-P. HENRY; Dirs of Laboratories R. LAVERY (Theoretical Biochemistry), J.-L. POPOT (Molecular Physical Chemistry of Biological Membranes), M. SPRINGER (Regulation of Microbial Gene Expression), J.-P. HENRY (Molecular and Cell Biology of Secretion), F.-A. WOLLMAN (Molecular and Membrane Physiology of the Chloroplast).

Institut de Biologie Structurale (IBS): 41 rue Jules Horowitz, 38027 Grenoble Cedex 1; tel. 4-38-78-95-50; fax 4-38-78-54-94; internet www.ibs.fr; jointly financed by the Commissariat à l'Energie Atomique (CEA) and the Centre National de la Recherche Scientifique (CNRS); Dir Prof. EVA PEBAY-PEYROULA.

Station Biologique de Roscoff: Place Georges-Teissier, BP 74, 29682 Roscoff Cedex; tel. 2-98-29-23-23; fax 2-98-29-23-24; e-mail guyard@sb-roscoff.fr; internet www.sb-roscoff.fr; f. 1872; attached to Univ. Paris VI and CNRS; chemical and biological oceanography, plankton research, microbiology, biology of hydrothermal vent fauna, cell cycle and developmental biology, cell and molecu-lar biology on macroalgae, population genetics, marine genomics; library of 5,000 vols, 1,000 periodicals; Dir Prof. BERNARD KLOAREG; Librarian GUYARD NICOLE; publs *CBM-Cahiers de Biologie marine* (4 a year), *Travaux* (1 a year).

Physical Sciences

Association Nationale pour l'Etude de la Neige et des Avalanches (ANENA): 15 rue Ernest Calvat, 38000 Grenoble; tel. 4-76-51-39-39; fax 4-76-42-81-66; internet www.anena.org; f. 1971; promotes knowledge and give advice about avalanches and safety in snowy, mountainous terrain; 700 mems; library of 2,000 vols; publ. *Neige et Avalanches* (4 a year).

Bureau de Recherches Géologiques et Minières (BRGM): 3 ave Claude Guillemin, BP 6009, 45060 Orléans Cedex 2; tel. 2-38-64-34-34; fax 2-38-64-35-18; internet www.brgm.fr; f. 1959; publicly owned industrial and trading org.; study and devt of underground resources in France and abroad; library of 22,000 vols, 4,000 scientific journals, 55,000 maps; Dir-Gen. Y. LE BARS; publs *Chronique de la Recherche minière* (4 a year), *Géochronique* (published with Société géologique de France, 4 a year), *Géologie de la France* (4 a year), *Hydrogéologie* (4 a year), geological maps, bibliographies, SDI and retrospective searches.

Bureau des Longitudes: Palais de l'Institut, 3 Quai de Conti, 75006 Paris; tel. 1-43-26-59-02; fax 1-43-26-80-90; e-mail contact@bureau-des-longitudes.fr; internet www.bureau-des-longitudes.fr; f. 1795 by Convention Nationale; 50 mems and corresp.; Pres. NICOLE CAPITAINE; Vice-Pres. PIERRE BAÜER; Sec. PASCAL WILLIS; publs *Ephémérides Astronomiques*, *Connaissance des Temps*, *Ephémérides Nautiques*, *Cahier des Sciences de l'Univers*, and supplements to *Connaissance des Temps* (1 a year).

Centre de Recherches Atmosphériques: 8 route de Lannemezan, 65300 Campistrous; tel. 5-62-40-61-00; fax 5-62-40-61-01; e-mail campistrous@free.fr; internet campistrous.free.fr; f. 1960; cloud physics, atmospheric chemistry, planetary boundary layer; library of 2,000 vols; Dir R. DELMAS; publ. *Atmospheric Research* (4 a year).

Centre d'Etudes Marines Avancées: c/o Equipe Cousteau, 7 rue Amiral d'Estaing, 75116 Paris; tel. 1-53-67-77-77; fax 1-53-67-77-71; f. 1953; underwater exploration, study and research; Pres. (vacant); Sec.-Gen. HENRI JACQUIER; publ. *Calypso Log* (12 a year).

Centre International pour la Formation et les Echanges en Géosciences (CIFEG): 3 ave Claude Guillemin, BP 36517, 45065 Orléans Cedex 2; tel. 2-38-64-33-67; fax 2-38-64-34-72; e-mail m.laval@cifeg.org; internet www.cifeg.org; f. 1981; geoscientific information networking; documentation centre on earth sciences of Africa and South-East Asia; exchanges between developed and developing countries; library of 3,500 vols, 65 periodicals, 400 maps; Pres. J. GIRI; Dir M. LAVAL; publ. *PANGEA* (2 a year).

Centre National de Recherches Météorologiques: 42 ave G. Coriolis, 31057 Toulouse Cedex; tel. 5-61-07-93-70; fax 5-61-07-96-00; internet www.cnrm.meteo.fr; f. 1946; meteorological research; 250 staff; Dir ERIC BRUN.

Commissariat à l'Energie Atomique (CEA): Centre d'Etudes de Saclay, 91191 Gif sur Yvette Cedex 15; tel. 1-64-50-10-00; internet www.cea.fr; f. 1945; basic and applied nuclear research, energy generator studies; 5 affiliated civil research centres; Pres. of Atomic Energy Cttee the Prime Minister; library; Man. Dir YANNICK D'ESCATHA; publs *CEA-Technologies*, *Clefs CEA*, *Les Défis du CEA*.

Attached Research Centres:

Centre CEA de Cadarache (Bouches-du-Rhone): 13108 St-Paul-lez-Durance Cedex; tel. 4-42-25-70-00; fax 4-42-25-45-45; e-mail wwwcad@dircad.cea.fr; internet www-cadarache.cea.fr; f. 1960; nuclear reactor devt (fission and fusion); research and development on new energies: biofuels, hydrogen or solar, nuclear safety and environmental protection; fundamental research; industrial innovation; Dir SERGE DURAND.

Centre CEA de Fontenay-aux-Roses (Hauts-de-Seine): BP 6, 92265 Fontenay-aux-Roses Cedex; tel. 1-46-54-70-80; fax 1-42-53-98-51; f. 1945; first French reactor; Zoé natural uranium, heavy water moderated; work in life sciences; research in: radiobiology, environmental toxicology, neurovirology and emerging diseases; research and development in biomedical imaging and health technologies; cognitics, robotics for nuclear, industrial and medical needs; Dir MALGORYATA TKATCHENKO.

Centre CEA de Grenoble (Isère): 17 rue des Martyrs, 38054 Grenoble Cedex 9; tel. 4-76-78-44-00; fax 4-76-88-34-32; f. 1957; applied nuclear research on heat transfer studies and on behaviour of nuclear fuels; fundamental research on physics, chemistry, biology, materials science; advanced technologies: microelectronics, optronics, instrumentation, materials, heat exchangers, life sciences and tracer studies; library of 31,000 vols; Dir GEORGES CAROLA.

Centre CEA de Saclay (Essonne): 91191 Gif-sur-Yvette Cedex; tel. 1-69-08-90-32; e-mail internet.saclay@cea.fr; internet www-centre-saclay.cea.fr; f. 1949; equipped with 2 high-flux experimental reactors, 6 particle accelerators and special laboratories: spent fuel study facility, isotope and labelled molecule production laboratories, activation analysis centre, ionizing radiations applications centre; laboratories specializing in research on reactors, nuclear metallurgy and chemistry, elementary particle physics, nuclear physics, astrophysics, condensed-matter physics, earth sciences, biology, radioactivity measurement and electronics; library of 48,000 vols, 400,000 reports; Dir ELIANE LOQUET.

Centre CEA de la Marcoule (Gard): BP 171, 30207 Bagnols-sur-Cèze Cedex; tel. 4-66-79-60-00; fax 4-66-90-14-35; internet www-marcoule.cea.fr; f. 1982; fuel cycle research and devt: uranium isotopic enrichment, spent fuel processing, waste conditioning, dismantling; fast reactors; Dir JEAN-YVES GUILLAMOT.

Centre CEA de Valduc: 21120 Is-sur-Tille; tel. 3-80-23-40-00; e-mail webdam@cea.fr; internet www-dam.cea.fr; f. 1996; nuclear materials used in arms production.

Centre CEA/Cesta (Gironde): BP 2, 33114 Le Barp; tel. 5-57-04-40-00; internet www-dam.cea.fr; production of nuclear arms.

Centre CEA/DAM Ile de France (Essonne): Bruyères-le-Châtel, 91297 Arpajon Cedex; tel. 1-69-26-40-00; internet www-dam.cea.fr; computerized research into nuclear explosions; monitoring of global seismic activity.

Institut Curie: 26 rue d'Ulm, 75248 Paris Cedex 05; tel. 1-44-32-40-00; fax 1-43-29-02-03; internet www.curie.fr; f. 1978 (fmrly Fondation Curie—Inst. du Radium); treatment, research and teaching in cancer; library of 7,000 vols; two sections: Research

(Dir M. BORNENS), Medicine (Dir P. BEY); Pres. CLAUDE HURIET; Dir PHILIPPE KOUR-ILSKY.

Institut Français de Recherche pour l'Exploitation de la Mer (IFREMER): 155 rue J. Jacques Rousseau, 92138 Issy-les-Moulineaux Cedex; tel. 1-46-48-21-00; fax 1-46-48-21-21; internet www.ifremer.fr; f. 1984; research in all fields of oceanography and ocean technology; Pres./Dir-Gen. JEAN-FRANÇOIS MINSTER; publs *Aquatic Living Resources* (6 a year), *Oceanologica Acta* (6 a year).

Attached Institutes:

Centre IFREMER de Brest: BP 70, 29280 Plouzane; tel. 2-98-22-40-40; fax 2-98-22-45-45; e-mail egiordma@ifremer.fr; internet www.ifremer.fr/brest; f. 1968; Dir FRANÇOIS LE VERGE.

Centre IFREMER de Nantes: BP 21105, 44311 Nantes Cedex 03; tel. 2-40-37-40-43; fax 2-40-37-40-01; internet www.ifremer.fr/nantes; Dir ROBERT POGGI.

Centre IFREMER de Toulon: BP 330, 83507 La Seyne sur Mer; tel. 4-94-30-48-00; internet www.ifremer.fr/toulon; Dir GUY HERROUIN.

Centre IFREMER Océanologique du Pacifique: BP 7004, 98719 Taravao, Tahiti French Polynesia; tel. 54-60-00; fax 54-60-99; internet www.ifremer.fr/cop/tahiti.htm; f. 1972; development of ocean resources: minerals, fishing and aquaculture in French South Pacific territories; 70 staff; library of 200 vols; Dir DOMINIQUE BUESTEL.

Institut Polaire Français Paul Emile Victor: Technopôle Brest-Iroise, BP 75, 29280 Plouzané; tel. 2-98-05-65-00; fax 2-98-05-65-55; e-mail infoipev@ipev.fr; internet www.ipev.fr; f. 1992, by merger of Mission de Recherche des Terres Australes et Antarctiques Françaises and Expéditions Polaires Françaises; Dir GÉRARD JUGIE.

Laboratoire d'Astronomie de Lille 1: 1 impasse de l'Observatoire, 59000 Lille; tel. 3-20-52-44-24; internet lal.univ-lille1.fr; f. 1934; astronomy, celestial mechanics; Dir ALAIN VIENNE.

Météo-France: 1 quai Branly, 75340 Paris Cedex 07; tel. 1-45-56-71-71; fax 1-45-56-70-05; internet www.meteofrance.com; f. 1945; Dir JEAN-PIERRE BEYSSON; publs *Atmospheriques* (3 a year), *Bibliographies*, *Bulletin Climatique* (12 a year), *Cours et Manuels* (irregular), *Données et Statistiques*, *La Météorologie* (3 a year), *METEO-HEBDO* (52 a year), *Met Mar* (3 a year), *Monographies*, *Notes techniques*, *Phénomènes Remarquables* (irregular).

Observatoire de Bordeaux: Université de Bordeaux I, CNRS, 2 rue de l'Observatoire, BP 89, 33270 Floirac; tel. 5-57-77-61-00; fax 5-57-77-61-10; internet www.obs.u-bordeaux1.fr; f. 1879; astrometry, astrodynamics, solar physics, radioastronomy, helioseismology, planetary atmosphere, radio aeronomy; library of 3,700 vols; Dir A. CASTETS.

Observatoire de la Côte d'Azur: Boulevard de l'Observatoire, BP 4229, 06304 Nice Cedex 4; tel. 4-92-00-30-11; fax 4-92-00-30-33; internet www.oca.eu; f. 1881; earth science, astronomy and astrophysics; library of 20,000 vols, 250 periodicals; Dir FARROKH VAKILI.

Observatoire de Lyon: 9 ave Charles-André, 69561 Saint-Genis-Laval Cedex; tel. 4-78-86-85-34; fax 4-78-86-83-86; e-mail accueil@obs.univ-lyon1.fr; internet www-obs.univ-lyon1.fr; f. 1880; specializes in two-dimensional photometry and infra-red

imagery; library of 20,000 vols; Dir BRUNO GUIDERDONI.

Observatoire Astronomique de Marseille–Provence: 38 rue Frédéric Joliot-Curie, 13388 Marseilles Cedex 13; tel. 4-95-04-41-00; fax 4-91-62-11-90; e-mail oampdirection@oamp.fr; internet www.oamp.fr; library of 5,000 vols; Dir OLIVIER LE FÈVRE.

Observatoire de Paris: 61 ave de l'Observatoire, 75014 Paris; tel. 1-40-51-22-21; fax 1-43-54-18-04; internet www.obspm.fr; f. 1667; library of 60,000 vols; Pres. D. EGRET.

Attached Stations:

Observatoire de Paris, Site de Meudon: 5 place Jules Janssen, 92195 Meudon Principal Cedex; tel. 1-45-07-75-30; fax 1-45-07-74-69; administered by the Observatoire de Paris; f. 1875; astrophysics; Dir M. COMBES.

Station de Radioastronomie de Nançay: 18330 Nançay; tel. 2-48-51-82-41; fax 2-48-51-83-18; administered by the Observatoire de Paris; f. 1953; study of the sun, comets, planets and radio sources; radio telescopes; Dir M. COMBES.

Observatoire de Physique du Globe de Clermont-Ferrand: 24 ave des Landais, 63171 Aubière Cedex; tel. 4-73-40-73-80; fax 4-73-40-73-82; e-mail p.bachelery@opgc.univ-bpclermont.fr; internet www.obs.univ-bpclermont.fr; f. 1871; atmospheric physics, cloud systems, earth sciences, and geophysical surveillance; Dir Prof. PATRICK BACHELERY.

Observatoire Astronomique de Strasbourg: 11 rue de l'Université, 67000 Strasbourg; tel. 3-90-24-24-10; fax 90-24-24-32; internet astro.u-strasbg.fr; f. 1882; specializes in astronomical data and information, galactic evolution, cosmology, high-energy astrophysics; houses the Strasbourg Astronomical Data Centre (CDS); library of 16,000 vols; Dir JEAN-MARIE HAMEURY; publ. *Publications de l'Observatoire* (irregular).

Observatoire des Sciences de l'Univers de Besançon: BP 1615, 41 bis ave de l'Observatoire, 25010 Besançon Cedex; tel. 3-81-66-69-00; fax 3-81-66-69-44; e-mail direction@obs-besancon.fr; internet www.obs-besancon.fr; f. 1882; a research unit of the Université de Franche-Comté; library of 15,000 vols; Dir Prof. FRANÇOIS VERNOTTE.

Observatoire Midi-Pyrénées: Headquarters: 14 ave E. Belin, 31400 Toulouse; tel. 5-61-33-29-29; fax 5-61-33-28-88; internet www.omp.obs-mip.fr; library of 50,000 vols; solar, planetary, stellar, galactic and extragalactic astrophysics, atmospheric physics and chemistry, physical oceanography, surface sciences, earth sciences; Dir DOMINIQUE LE QUEAU.

RELIGION, SOCIOLOGY AND ANTHROPOLOGY

Centre Européen de Recherches sur les Congrégations et Ordres Religieux (CERCOR): 35 rue du 11 Novembre, Bâtiment M, 42023 Saint-Etienne Cedex 2; tel. 4-77-42-16-70; fax 4-77-42-16-84; e-mail cercor@univ-st-etienne.fr; internet cercor.univ-st-etienne.fr; f. 1982; a research group of CNRS (q.v.); studies the history of the monastic and religious institutions in Western and Eastern Christianity of Christian antiquity to the 20th century; coordinates and promotes research (conferences, etc.), runs a specialized documentation service, publishes texts; 1,400 researchers in 35 countries; library of 6,500 vols; Dir DANIEL-ODON HUREL; publ. *Bulletin du CERCOR* (1 a year).

Fondation Maison des Sciences de l'Homme: 54 blvd Raspail, 75270 Paris Cedex 06; tel. 1-49-54-20-00; fax 1-49-54-21-33; internet www.msh-paris.fr; f. 1963; supports research and int. cooperation in the social sciences; library of 155,000 vols, 2,000 current periodicals; Administrator ALAINE D'IRIBARNE; publ. *Lettre d'informations* (4 a year).

Institut d'Ethnologie du Muséum National d'Histoire Naturelle: Musée de l'Homme, Palais de Chaillot, Place du Trocadéro, 75116 Paris; tel. 1-44-05-73-45; fax 1-44-05-73-44; f. 1925; social anthropology, archaeology, linguistics; Dir M. PANOFF; publs *Collections Travaux et Mémoires*, *Mémoires*.

Institut d'Etudes Augustiniennes: 3 rue de l'Abbaye, 75006 Paris; tel. 1-43-54-80-25; fax 1-43-54-39-55; e-mail iea@wanadoo.fr; f. 1943; research into life, thought and times of St Augustine; library of 53,000 vols, 2,000 early printed books, 19 incunabula; Dir J.-C. FREDOUILLE; publs *Recherches Augustiniennes* (irregular), *Revue des Etudes Augustiniennes* (2 a year).

Institut du Monde Arabe: 1 rue des Fossés Saint Bernard, Place Mohammed-V, 75236 Paris Cedex 05; tel. 1-40-51-38-38; fax 1-43-54-76-45; e-mail ahull@imarabe.org; internet www.imarabe.org; f. 1980 by France and 21 Arab countries to promote knowledge of Arab culture and civilization; aims to encourage cultural exchanges, communication and co-operation between France and the Arab world, particularly in the fields of science and technology; international library and documentation centre of 60,000 vols, 1,200 periodicals; museum of Arab-Islamic civilization from 7th–19th century; exhibitions of Arab contemporary art; audio visual centre; Pres. YVES GUÉNA; Dir MOKHTAR TALEB-BENDIAB; publs *Qantara* (4 a year), *Al-Moukhtarat*.

Institut International d'Anthropologie: 1 place d'Iéna, 75116 Paris; tel. 1-47-93-09-73; fax 1-47-93-09-73; internet www.multimania.com/anthropa; f. 1920; 400 mems; affiliated to Ecole d'Anthropologie (q.v.); incorporates intercultural documentation centre; Pres. Dr A. PAJAULT; Sec.-Gen. Dr B. HUET; publ. *Nouvelle Revue Anthropologique* (irregular).

Institut Kurde de Paris (Kurdish Institute): 106 rue La Fayette, 75010 Paris; tel. 1-48-24-64-64; fax 1-48-24-64-66; internet www.institutkurde.org; f. 1983; research into Kurdish language, culture and history; Kurdish language teaching and publication of textbooks, maps, music cassettes, video films in Kurdish; library of 10,000 vols (accessible to the public); Pres. KENDAL NEZAN; publs *Etudes Kurdes* (2 a year), *Information Bulletin* (12 a year), *Kurmancî* (2 a year).

Maison Rhône-Alpes de Sciences de l'Homme (MRASH): 14 ave Berthelot, 69363 Lyons Cedex 07; tel. 4-72-72-64-64; fax 4-72-80-00-08; f. 1988; supports research in the social sciences; Dir ALAIN BONNAFOUS.

TECHNOLOGY

Association Française pour la Protection des Eaux: 67 rue de Seine, 94140 Alfortville; tel. 1-43-75-84-84; fax 1-45-18-92-90; e-mail president@anpertos.org; internet www.anpertos.org; f. 1960; brings to public notice the necessity of protecting and preserving the quality and quantity of water-supplies, studies problems of water pollution and its prevention; 800 mems; Pres. P. L. TENAILLON; publ. *TOS*.

Centre National d'Etudes Spatiales (CNES): 2 place Maurice Quentin, 75001 Paris; internet www.cnes.fr; f. 1961; prepares national programmes of space research, provides information, promotes international co-operation; Pres. YANNICK D'ESCATHA; Dir-Gen. MICHEL LEFÈVRE.

France Telecom R & D: 38–40 rue du Général Leclerc, 92131 Issy les Moulineaux; tel. 1-45-29-44-44; internet www.rd.francetelecom.com; f. 1944; engaged in the devt of future communications systems; responsible for according official approval for telecommunications equipment; 3,700 staff; library of 2,500 vols, 1,000 periodicals; CEO THIERRY BRETON; publs *Annales des Télécommunications* (6 a year), *Bulletin Signalétique des Télécommunications* (12 a year), *Innovation Telecom* (12 a year), *L'Echo des Recherches* (4 a year), *Networks*.

Institut d'Hydrologie et de Climatologie: Faculté de Médecine, Pitié-Salpêtrière, 91 blvd de l'Hôpital, 75013 Paris; tel. 1-45-83-69-92; 5 main laboratories in Paris, and further laboratories at the principal spas; Gen. Sec. Prof. G. OLIVE.

Institut Français du Pétrole: 1 et 4 ave de Bois-Préau, 92852 Rueil-Malmaison Cedex; tel. 1-47-52-60-00; fax 1-47-52-70-00; internet www.ifp.fr; f. 1945; scientific and technical organization for the purpose of research, development and industrialization, training specialists at the Ecole Nationale Supérieure du Pétrole et des Moteurs, information and documentation, international technical assistance in the different fields of the oil, gas and automotive engineering industries; library of 275,000 vols; Chair. and CEO O. APPERT; publ. *Oil and Gas Science and Technology*.

Institut Laue-Langevin (ILL): BP 156, 38042 Grenoble Cedex 9; tel. 4-76-20-71-11; fax 4-76-48-39-06; e-mail welcome@ill.fr; internet www.ill.fr; f. 1967 by France and Fed. Repub. of Germany, UK became third equal partner in 1973; associated scientific members are Spain (1987), Switzerland (1988), Austria (1990), Russia (1996), Italy (1997) and Czech Republic (1999); research on fundamental and nuclear physics, solid state physics, metallurgy, chemistry and biology by using reactor neutrons; receives 1,500 guest scientists a year and carries out experiments on 25 ILL-funded instruments and several instruments funded by collaborating research groups; central facility is high flux beam reactor producing maximum flux of $1.5 \times 10^{15} \text{n/cm}^2/\text{s}$; library of 11,000 vols, 250 periodicals; Dir Dr C. CARLILE.

Institut National de l'Audiovisuel: 4 ave de l'Europe, 94366 Bry-sur-Marne Cedex; tel. 1-49-83-23-67; fax 1-49-83-21-23; internet www.ina.fr; f. 1975; two research depts: *Recherche Prospective* (research combining telecommunications, computer science and audiovisual science); *Groupe de Recherches Musicales* (numerical development of synthesis and treatment of sound psychoacoustics and musical perception, technology of electroacoustical instruments); library of 3,000 vols; Pres. EMMANUEL HOOG; publ. *Dossiers Audiovisuels* (6 a year).

Institut National de l'Environnement Industriel et des Risques (INERIS) (National Institute for Environmental Technology and Hazards): Parc Technologique ALATA, BP 2, 60550 Verneuil-en-Halatte; tel. 3-44-55-66-77; fax 3-44-55-66-99; e-mail ineris@ineris.fr; internet www.ineris.fr; f. 1990; library of 28,000 vols; Dir-Gen. GEORGES LABROYE; publ. *INERIS Magazine* (5 a year).

Institut National de Recherche en Informatique et en Automatique (INRIA): Domaine de Voluceau, Rocquencourt, BP 105, 78153 Le Chesnay Cedex; tel. 1-39-63-55-11; fax 1-39-63-53-30; e-mail communication@inria.fr; internet www.inria.fr; f. 1967; eight research units; library of 45,000 vols; Pres. and Dir-Gen. MICHEL COSNARD; publs *ERCIM News*, *Les conférences et supports de cours INRIA*, *Rapports d'activités scientifiques*, *Rapports de recherche et thèses*.

Institut National des Sciences et Techniques Nucléaires (INSTN) (National Institute of Nuclear Science and Technology): CEA-Saclay, 91191 Gif-sur-Yvette Cedex; internet www-instn.cea.fr; f. 1956; provides courses in nuclear engineering, robotics and computer-integrated manufacturing (CIM) and, in co-operation with the univs, postgraduate courses in reactor physics, dynamics of structures, analytical chemistry, radiochemistry, metallurgy, data processing, robotics, radiobiology, energy management, the use of radioisotopes in medicine and pharmacy; Dir JEAN-PIERRE LE ROUX; Pres. BERNARD BIGOT.

Laboratoire de Biotechnologie de l'Environnement: Ave des Etangs, 11100 Narbonne; tel. 4-68-42-51-51; fax 4-68-42-51-60; internet www.montpellier.inra.fr/narbonne; f. 1895; attached to INRA; research in microbiological wastewater treatment; library of 5,000 vols; Dir JEAN-PHILIPPE DELGENÈS; publ. *Water Research*.

Office International de l'Eau (International Office for Water—IOW): 21 rue de Madrid, 75008 Paris; tel. 1-44-90-88-60; fax 1-40-08-01-45; e-mail cnide@oieau.fr; internet www.oieau.fr; f. 1991; documentation centre on water problems and management; library of 37,000 vols and 180,000 articles; Pres. M. ROUSSEL; Dir D. PREUX; publs *AquaVeille* (52 a year, e-newsletter), *Information Eaux* (24 a year).

Office National d'Etudes et de Recherches Aérospatiales (ONERA): 29 ave de la Division-Leclerc, 92322 Châtillon; tel. 1-46-73-40-40; fax 1-46-73-41-41; internet www.onera.fr; f. 1946 to develop, direct, and coordinate scientific and technical research in the field of aeronautics and space; library of 40,000 vols, 150,000 reports, 11,000 microfiches, 850 periodicals; Pres. MICHEL DE GLINIASTY; publ. *Aerospace Science and Technology* (English, 8 a year).

Libraries and Archives

Abbeville

Bibliothèque Municipale: Hôtel d'Emonville, place Clemenceau, BP 20010, 80101 Abbeville Cedex; tel. 3-22-24-95-16; fax 3-22-19-16-93; internet www.ville-abbeville.fr/equipculturels.htm; f. 1643; 140,000 vols; Librarian P. HAZEBROUCK.

Aix-en-Provence

Bibliothèque Méjanes: 8–10 rue des Allumettes, 13090 Aix-en-Provence; tel. 4-42-91-98-88; fax 4-42-91-98-64; internet www.citedulivre-aix.com; f. 1810; 590,000 vols; Dir GILLES EBOLI.

Bibliothèque de l'Université d'Aix-Marseille III: 3 ave Robert-Schuman, 13626 Aix-en-Provence Cedex 1; tel. 4-42-17-24-40; fax 4-42-17-24-67; internet infobu.u-3mrs.fr; 156,000 vols, 273,000 periodicals, 86,000 theses; Librarian J. C. RODA.

Albi

Mediathèque Pierre Amalric: Ave Charles de Gaulle, 81000 Albi; tel. 5-63-38-56-10; fax 5-63-38-56-15; e-mail mediatheque@albi.fr; internet www.mediatheque-albi.fr; f. during the French Revolution; 300,000 vols of monographs and 500 MSS; Librarian MATTHIEU DESACHY.

Amiens

Bibliothèque d'Amiens Métropole: 50 rue de la République, BP 542, 80005 Amiens Cedex 1; tel. 3-22-97-10-10; fax 3-22-97-10-70; internet www.bm-amiens.fr; f. 1826; 800,000 vols, 2,500 MSS, 300 incunabula; Chief Librarian SÉVERINE MONTIGNY.

Bibliothèque de l'Université de Picardie Jules Verne: 15 placette Lafleur, BP 446, 80004 Amiens Cedex 01; tel. 3-22-82-71-65; fax 3-22-82-71-66; internet www.bu.u-picardie.fr; f. 1966; 330,000 vols, 3,900 periodicals; Dirs F. MONTBRUN, B. LOCHER.

Angers

Bibliothèque Municipale: 49 rue Toussaint, 49100 Angers; tel. 2-41-24-25-50; fax 2-41-81-05-72; internet www.bm.angers.fr; f. during the French Revolution; 400,000 vols, 2,120 MSS, 111 incunabula; Librarian CLAUDINE BELAYCHE.

Bibliothèque Universitaire d'Angers: 5 rue Le Nôtre, 49045 Angers Cedex; tel. 2-41-22-64-00; fax 2-41-22-64-05; e-mail bu@univ-angers.fr; internet bu.univ-angers.fr; f. 1970; Dir OLIVIER TACHEAU.

Avignon

Bibliothèque Universitaire: 74 rue Louis Pasteur, 84018 Avignon Cedex 1; tel. 4-90-16-27-60; fax 4-90-16-27-70; e-mail bu@univ-avignon.fr; internet www.bu.univ-avignon.fr; f. 1968; 100,000 books, 1,200 periodicals, 3,000 electronic periodicals; Dir FRANÇOISE FEBVRE.

Médiathèque Ceccano: 2 bis rue Laboureur, BP 349, 84025 Avignon Cedex 1; tel. 4-90-85-15-59; fax 4-90-82-82-01; e-mail bibliotheque.ceccano@mairi-avignon.com; internet www.avignon.fr/fr/pratique/biblio/ceccano.php; f. 1810; 300,000 vols, 7,000 MSS, 700 incunabula, 2,700 musical scores, 40,000 engravings and maps, 30,000 coins; Chief Librarian CÉCILE FRANC.

Besançon

Bibliothèques Municipales: 1 rue de la Bibliothèque, BP 09, 25012 Besançon Cedex; tel. 3-81-87-81-40; fax 3-81-61-98-77; internet www.besancon.com/biblio/francais/bm1.htm; f. 1694; 350,000 vols, 3,800 MSS, 1,000 incunabula; Dir HENRY FERREIRA-LOPES.

Bibliothèque de l'Université de Franche-Comté: 32 rue Mégevand, BP 1057, 25001 Besançon Cedex; tel. 3-81-66-53-50; fax 3-81-66-53-00; internet scd.univ-fcomte.fr; f. 1880; Dir SOPHIE DESSEIGNE.

Bordeaux

Bibliothèque Municipale: 85 cours du Maréchal Juin, 33075 Bordeaux Cedex; tel. 5-56-10-30-00; fax 5-56-10-30-90; e-mail bibli@mairie-bordeaux.fr; internet www.mairie-bordeaux.fr/bibliotheque/bibintro.htm; f. 1736; 900,000 vols, 4,200 MSS, 333 incunbula, 1,000 current periodicals; Chief Librarian PIERRE BOTINEAU.

Service Interétablissements de Co-opération Documentaire des Universités de Bordeaux: 4 ave des Arts, 33607 Pessac Cedex; tel. 5-56-84-86-86; fax 5-56-84-86-96; e-mail sicod@bu.u-bordeaux.fr; internet www.montesquieu.u-bordeaux.fr/presentation/sicod.html; 3.2m. vols; Dir GÉRARD BRIAND.

Brest

Service Commun de Documentation:; tel. 2-98-01-64-04; fax 2-98-47-75-25; e-mail scd@univ-brest.fr; internet www.univ-brest .fr; f. 1968; Dir ALAIN SAINSOT.

Caen

Bibliothèque de Caen: Place Louis-Guil-louard, 14053 Caen Cedex; tel. 2-31-30-47-00; fax 2-31-30-47-01; e-mail bibliotheque.caen@ agglo-caen.fr; internet www.caenlamer.fr/ bibliothequecaen; f. 1809; 693,000 vols, 6,055 periodicals, 12,000 pre-1800 printed items, 6,000 slides, 5,700 video cassettes, 70,000 CDs, 7,500 talking books for the visually impaired, 1,900 software disks for micro-computer and CD-ROMs; spec. Normandy colln; Librarian NOËLLA DU PLESSIS.

Bibliothèque de l'Université de Caen: Esplanade de la Paix, 14032 Caen Cedex; tel. 2-31-56-58-70; fax 2-31-56-56-13; e-mail bibliotheque@unicaen.fr; internet scd .unicaen.fr; f. 1955; Dir BERNARD VOUILLOT.

Cambrai

Bibliothèque Municipale Classée: 37 rue St Georges, BP 179, 59403 Cambrai Cedex; tel. 3-27-82-93-93; fax 3-27-82-93-94; e-mail admin@media-cambrai.com; f. 1791; 130,000 vols, 1,400 MSS, 600 incunabula; Librarian BÉNÉDICTE TÉROUANNE.

Carpentras

Bibliothèque Inguimbertine et Musées de Carpentras: 234 blvd Albin-Durand, 84200 Carpentras; tel. 4-90-63-04-92; fax 4-90-63-19-11; e-mail jf.delmas@carpentras.fr; f. 1745; 265,000 vols, 3,126 MSS; Librarian JEAN-FRANÇOIS DELMAS.

Châlons-sur-Marne

Bibliothèque Municipale à Vocation Régionale Georges Pompidou: 68 rue Léon-Bourgeois, 51038 Châlons-en-Cham-pagne Cedex; tel. 3-26-26-94-30; fax 3-26-26-94-32; e-mail bibliotheque.mairie@ chalons-en-champagne.net; internet www .chalons-en-champagne.net/bmvr; f. 1803; 330,000 vols, 2,000 MSS, 120 incunabula; Librarian RÉGIS DUTRÉMÉE.

Chambéry

Bibliothèque de l'Université de Savoie (SCD, Service commun de la documen-tation): Direction et Service centraux, Domaine universitaire de Jacob-Bellecomb-ette, Bât. 15, BP 1104, 73011 Chambéry Cedex; tel. 4-79-75-91-13; fax 4-79-75-84-90; e-mail contact-scd@univ-savoie.fr; internet www.scd.univ-savoie.fr; f. 1962; 199,861 vols, 2,032 periodicals, 37,931 e-periodicals; Dir ALAIN CARACO.

Clermont-Ferrand

Bibliothèque Municipale et Interuniver-sitaire: 1 blvd Lafayette, BP 27, 63001 Clermont-Ferrand Cedex 01; tel. 4-73-40-62-40; fax 4-73-40-62-19; e-mail bmiu@ univ-bpclermont.fr; internet bmiu .univ-bpclermont.fr; f. 1902; 682,437 vols, 2,587 current periodicals; Dir LIVIA RAPATEL.

Colmar

Bibliothèque de la Ville de Colmar: 1 place des Martyrs de la Résistance, BP 509, 68021 Colmar Cedex; tel. 3-89-24-48-18; fax 3-89-23-33-80; e-mail bibliotheque@ ville-colmar.com; f. 1803; 400,000 vols, 1,300 MSS, 2,500 incunabula; Chief Librarian FRANCIS GUETH.

Dijon

Bibliothèque Municipale: 3–7 rue de l'Ecole-de-Droit, 21000 Dijon; tel. 3-80-44-94-14; fax 3-80-44-94-34; e-mail bmdijon@ ville-dijon.fr; internet bm-dijon.fr; f. 1701; 460,000 vols; Chief Librarian ANDRÉ-PIERRE SYREN.

Bibliothèque de l'Université de Bour-gogne: 7 blvd du Docteur Petitjean, 21078 Dijon; tel. 3-80-39-64-63; e-mail emmanuelle .ashta@u-bourgogne.fr; internet scd .u-bourgogne.fr; Dir F. HAGENE.

Douai

Bibliothèque Municipale: rue de la Fond-erie, 59500 Douai; tel. 3-27-97-88-51; fax 3-27-99-71-80; e-mail bibliotheque@biblio .ville-douai.fr; internet www.ville-douai.fr/ culture/bibliot/accueil.htm; f. 1770; 250,000 vols, 2,000 MSS, 300 incunabula, 200 peri-odicals; Librarian MICHELE DEMARCY.

Grenoble

Bibliothèque Municipale d'Etude et d'Information: 12 blvd Maréchal Lyautey, BP 1095, 38021 Grenoble Cedex 1; tel. 4-76-86-21-00; fax 4-76-86-21-19; e-mail info@ bm-grenoble.fr; internet www.bm-grenoble .fr; f. 1772; 600,000 vols, 654 incunabula, 20,980 MSS, 81,000 prints, 2,575 maps; special collection: local history; Dir CATHE-RINE POUYET.

Service de Co-opération Documentaire Sciences-Médecine: BP 66, 38402 St Mar-tin d'Hères; tel. 4-76-51-42-84; fax 4-76-51-98-51; internet www.ujf-grenoble.fr/bus; linked with university science and medical libraries; Dir MARIE-FRANCE ROCHARD.

Service Interétablissements de Co-opér-ation Documentaire: Domaine universi-taire BP 85, 38402 St Martin d'Hères Cedex; tel. 4-76-82-61-61; fax 4-76-82-61-68; e-mail sicd2admin@upmf-grenoble.fr; internet odyssee.upmf-grenoble.fr; f. 1880; Dir MARIE-NOËLLE ICARDO.

Haguenau

Musée Historique et Archives Munici-pales: 9 rue du Maréchal Foch, BP 40 261, 67504 Haguenau Cedex; tel. 3-88-90-29-39; fax 3-88-90-29-49; e-mail musees-archives@ ville-haguenau.fr; f. 1899; 8,000 vols; Dir PIA WENDLING; publ. *Etudes Haguenoviennes* (1 a year).

La Rochelle

Médiathèque Michel Crépeau: Commu-nauté de Villes, Ave Marillac, 17042 La Rochelle Cedex 1; tel. 5-46-45-71-71; fax 5-46-45-03-22; e-mail mediatheque@ agglo-larochelle.fr; f. 1750; 360,000 vols; Librarian BRUNO CARBONE.

Le Havre

Bibliothèque Municipale: 17 rue Jules Lecesne, 76600 Le Havre; tel. 2-32-74-07-40; fax 2-32-74-07-50; e-mail biblio@ville-lehavre .fr; internet www.ville-lehavre.fr/quotidien/ culture/bibliotheque/cadre.htm; f. 1796; pub-lic borrowing, reference, record library; 389,237 vols, 1,449 periodicals, 1,020 MSS; Librarian PATRICIA DOULERS.

Le Mans

Bibliothèque de l'Université du Maine: Avenue Olivier Messiaen, 72085 Le Mans Cedex 09; tel. 2-43-83-30-48; fax 2-43-83-35-37; e-mail bu@univ-lemans.fr; internet scd .univ-lemans.fr; 140,000 vols, 800 period-icals; Dir C. MENIL.

Lille

Bibliothèque Municipale: 32–34 rue Edouard Delesalle, 59043 Lille Cedex; tel. 3-20-15-97-20; fax 3-20-63-94-59; e-mail bmlille@mairie-lille.fr; internet www.bm-lille .fr; f. 1726; 650,000 vols; Librarian ISABELLE DUQUENNE; Librarian LAURE DELRUE-VAN-DENBULCKE.

Bibliothèque de l'Université des Sci-ences et Technologies de Lille: Service commun de la documentation de Lille I: Ave Henri Poincaré, BP 155, 59653 Ville-neuve d'Ascq Cedex; tel. 3-20-43-44-10; fax 3-20-33-71-04; e-mail jean-bernard.marino@ univ-lille1.fr/ internet www.univ-lille1.fr/ bustl; 160,000 books, 60,000 theses; econom-ics, humanities, technology, science; Chief Librarian JEAN-BERNARD MARINO.

Service Commun de la Documentation de Lille II: (Secteur Médecine/Pharmacie and Secteur Droit/Gestion): 1 place Déliot, BP 179, 59017 Lille Cedex; tel. 3-20-90-76-50; fax 3-20-90-76-54; internet www.scd .univ-lille2.fr; f. 1993; Chief Librarian BRI-GITTE MULETTE.

Service Commun de la Documentation de l'Université de Lille III – Charles de Gaulle: Domaine universitaire du Pont-de-bois, BP 99, 59652 Villeneuve d'Ascq Cedex; tel. 3-20-41-70-00; fax 3-20-91-46-50; internet www.univ-lille3.fr/portail/index.php?pa-ge=scd; Dir JEAN-PAUL CHADOURNE.

Limoges

Bibliothèque Francophone Multimédia: 2 pl. Aimé Césaire, 87032 Limoges Cedex; tel. 5-55-45-96-00; fax 5-55-45-96-96; e-mail francophonie@bm-limoges.fr; internet www .bm-limoges.fr; f. 1804; spec. collns incl. enamels, ceramics, porcelain; 530,000 vols, 900 periodicals, 14,000 video cassettes, 32,000 records; Librarian FRANÇOISE DIET-ESCARFAIL; Librarian CHANTAL DE GRANDPRÉ.

Bibliothèque de l'Université de Limoges: 39C rue Camille-Guérin, 87031 Limoges Cedex; tel. 5-55-43-57-00; fax 5-55-43-57-01; internet www-scd.unilim.fr; f. 1965; 100,000 vols; Dir ODILE ROHOU.

Lyons

Bibliothèque Interuniversitaire de Let-tres et Sciences Humaines: 5 parvis René-Descartes, BP 7000, 69342 Lyon; tel. 4-37-37-65-00; internet biu.ens-lsh.fr/biu; Dir CHARLES MICOL.

Bibliothèque Municipale: 30 blvd Vivier-Merle, 69431 Lyon Cedex 03; tel. 4-78-62-18-00; fax 4-78-62-19-49; e-mail bm@bm-lyon.fr; internet www.bm-lyon.fr; f. 1565; 2.4m. vols, 12,449 MSS, 1,157 incunabula, 130,000 prints, 12,399 periodicals, 172,000 records, 59,883 photographs; Dir PATRICK BAZIN.

Marseilles

Bibliothèque et Archives, Chambre de Commerce et d'Industrie Marseille-Provence: La Canebière, Palais de la Bourse, BP 21856, 13221 Marseilles; tel. 4-91-39-33-21; fax 4-91-39-56-15; e-mail sylvie .drago@ccimp.com; internet www .marseille-provence.cci.fr; f. 1872; economics, law, business, industry, commerce, agricul-ture, marine, Provence, overseas, history, geography; online information service; 60,000 vols, 60,000 brochures, 3,000 period-icals; Dir PATRICK BOULANGER; Librarian SYLVIE DRAGO.

Bibliothèque Municipale: 23 rue de la providence, 13001 Marseilles; tel. 4-91-55-90-00; fax 4-91-55-23-44; internet www.bmvr .mairie-marseille.fr; f. 1800; 750,000 vols; Dir FRANÇOIS LARBRE.

Bibliothèque de l'Université de la Méd-iterranée (Aix-Marseille II): Campus Timone, 27 blvd Jean Moulin, 13385 Mar-seille Cedex 05; tel. 4-91-32-45-37; fax 4-91-25-60-22; e-mail anne.dujol@univmed.fr; internet bu.univmed; f. 1987; 7 academic libraries in Marseilles, Aix en Provence and Gap; medicine, pharmacy, dental sciences, sports economics; rare books on medicine; Dir ANNE DUJOL.

Metz

Bibliothèque Municipale: 1 cour Elie Fleur, 57000 Metz; tel. 3-87-55-53-33; fax 3-87-30-42-88; internet bm.mairie-metz.fr/metz; f. 1811; 400,000 vols, 1,195 MSS, 5,000 engravings, 463 incunabula; video cassettes, slides; Chief Librarian Pierre Louis.

Service Commun de Documentation de l'Université Paul Verlaine–Metz: Ile du Saulcy, 57045 Metz Cedex 1; tel. 3-87-31-50-80; fax 3-87-33-22-90; e-mail colinmaire@scd .univ-metz.fr; internet www.scd.univ-metz .fr; f. 1972; 250,000 vols, 1,100 periodicals; Dir Hervé Colinmaire.

Montpellier

Bibliothèque Interuniversitaire: Administration: 60 rue des Etats généraux, 34965 Montpellier Cedex 2; tel. 4-67-13-43-50; fax 4-67-13-43-51; internet www.biu .univ-montp1.fr; f. 1890; Chief Librarian Pierre Gaillard.

Médiathèque Centrale d'Agglomération Emile Zola: 240 rue de l'Acropole, 34000 Montpellier; tel. 4-67-34-87-10; fax 4-67-34-87-01; e-mail accueil.mca@montpellier-agglo .com; internet services.mediathequed .montpellier-agglo.com; f. during the French Revolution; 720,000 vols; Dir M. G. Gudin de Vallerin.

Mulhouse

Bibliothèque de l'Université et de la Société Industrielle de Mulhouse (Section Histoire des Sciences): 12 rue de la Bourse, 68100 Mulhouse; tel. 3-89-56-12-74; fax 3-89-33-63-79; e-mail f.pascal@uha.fr; internet www.scd.uha.fr; f. 1826; 30,000 vols, 700 (and 150 current) periodicals; Dir Philippe Russell.

Université de Haute Alsace, Service Commun de Documentation: 8 rue des Frères Lumière, 68093 Mulhouse; tel. 3-89-33-63-60; fax 3-89-33-63-79; e-mail scdmulhouse@uha.fr; internet www.scd.uha .fr; f. 1977; Dir Philippe Russell.

Nancy

Bibliothèque Municipale: 43 rue Stanislas, CS 64230, 54042 Nancy Cedex; tel. 3-83-37-38-83; fax 3-83-37-91-82; e-mail bmnancy@mairie-nancy.fr; f. 1750; 500,000 vols; Chief Librarian André Markiewicz.

Service Commun de Documentation: 30 rue Lionnois, 54000 Nancy; tel. 3-83-68-22-00; fax 3-83-68-22-03; internet scd.uhp-nancy .fr; 356,000 vols, 4,100 periodicals; Chief Librarian Sebastien Bogaert.

Nantes

Bibliothèque Municipale: 15 rue de l'Heronnière, BP 44113, 44041 Nantes Cedex 01; tel. 2-40-41-95-95; fax 2-40-41-42-00; e-mail bm@mairie-nantes.fr; internet www.bm .nantes.fr; f. 1753; 900,000 vols; Chief Librarian Agnès Marcetteau.

Bibliothèque Universitaire de Nantes: Chemin de la Censive du Tertre, BP 32211, 44322 Nantes Cedex 03; tel. 2-40-14-12-30; internet www.bu.univ-nantes.fr; f. 1962; 260,000 vols, 5,000 periodicals; Chief Librarian Michelle Guiot.

Nice

Bibliothèque Municipale à Vocation Régionale de Nice: 1 ave Saint-Jean-Baptiste, 06364 Nice Cedex 4; tel. 4-97-13-48-00; fax 4-97-13-48-05; internet www.bmvr-nice .com.fr; f. 1802; network of 15 br. libraries; spec. colln on Michel Butor; 1m. vols, 208,700 compact discs, records and cassettes, 17,002 video cassettes, 519 CD-ROMs; Chief Librarian Françoise Michelizza.

Bibliothèque de l'Université de Nice–Sophia Antipolis: Parc Valrose, BP 2053, 06101 Nice Cedex 02; tel. 4-92-07-60-00; fax 4-92-07-60-10; internet www.unice.fr/bu; f. 1963; 260,000 vols, 4,400 periodicals; Dir Louis Klee.

Nîmes

Carré d'Art Bibliothèques: Mairie, Place de l'Hôtel de Ville, 30033 Nîmes Cedex 9; tel. 4-66-76-70-01; e-mail webmaster@ ville-nimes.fr; internet bibliotheque.nimes.fr; f. 1803; 323,000 vols, 590 periodicals, 800 MSS, 40,000 ancient books, 19,000 CDs; Chief Librarian J.-M. Massadau; publ. *Journal Carré d'Art* (3 a year).

Orléans

Médiathèque d'Orléans: 1 place Gambetta, 45043 Orléans Cedex 1; tel. 2-38-65-45-45; fax 2-38-65-45-40; e-mail bibliotheques@ville-orleans.fr; internet www .bm-orleans.fr; f. 1714; 420,000 vols, 2,550 MSS; Librarian Agnès Chevalier.

Service Commun de la Documentation de l'Université d'Orléans: Domaine de la Source, 6 rue de Tours, 45072 Orléans Cedex 02; tel. 2-38-41-71-84; fax 2-38-41-71-87; e-mail secretariat.scd@univ-orleans.fr; internet scd.univ-orleans.fr; f. 1965; 290,301 vols and theses, 3,300 periodicals; Dir Catherine Moreau.

Paris

American Library in Paris: 10 rue du Général Camou, 75007 Paris; tel. 1-53-59-12-60; fax 1-45-50-25-83; e-mail alparis@ americanlibraryinparis.org; internet americanlibraryinparis.org; f. 1920; private English-language lending and reference library open to all nationalities (subject to payment of fees); organizes lectures, talks, book signings, exhibits, concerts and performances; 113,000 vols, 250 periodicals, 2,500 online periodicals; Chair. William Torchiana; Dir Charles Trueheart.

Archives de France: 56 rue des Francs-Bourgeois, 75141 Paris Cedex 03; tel. 1-40-27-60-00; fax 1-40-27-66-06; internet www .archivesdefrance.culture.gouv.fr; f. 1790; 480 km documents; Dir Herve Lemoine.

Attached Units:

> **Archives Nationales du Monde du Travail:** 78 blvd du Général Leclerc, BP 405, 59057 Roubaix Cedex 1; tel. 3-20-65-38-00; fax 3-20-65-38-01; f. 1993; Chief Curator Françoise Bosman.
>
> **Centre des Archives Contemporaines:** 2 rue des Archives, 77300 Fontainebleau; tel. 1-64-31-73-00; fax 1-64-31-73-03; Chief Curator Christine Petillat.
>
> **Centre des Archives d'Outre-Mer:** 29 chemin du Moulin-Detesta, 13090 Aix-en-Provence; tel. 4-42-93-38-50; fax 4-42-93-38-89; f. 1962; Chief Curator Martine Cornede.
>
> **Centre Historique des Archives Nationales:** 60 rue des Francs-Bourgeois, 75003 Paris; Chief Curator Gérard Ermisse.
>
> **Centre National du Microfilm:** Domaine d'Espeyran, 30800 St-Gilles-du-Gard; tel. 4-66-87-30-09; fax 4-66-87-03-44; Chief Curator Anne Debant.

Bibliothèque Administrative de la Ville de Paris: Hôtel de Ville, 75196 Paris Cedex 04; tel. 1-42-76-48-87; fax 1-42-76-63-78; e-mail bavp@paris.frr; f. 1872; 550,000 vols (reports, studies, statistics, official texts, budgets, etc.); 3,200 periodicals, 8,000 photographs, 2,700 MSS, 12,000 architectural designs, 40,000 microfiches, 2,000 microfilms covering areas of French and foreign local admin., French legislation, economic, polit-

ical and social history, ex-French colonies and gen. biography; Chief Librarian Pierre Casselle.

Bibliothèque Centrale et Archives des Musées Nationaux: 6 rue des Pyramides, 75041 Paris Cedex 01; tel. 1-40-20-52-66; fax 1-40-20-51-69; e-mail sbadg.dmf@culture .gouv.fr; internet www.inha.fr/bibliotheque/ bcmn.html; f. 1871; 180,000 vols, 1,800 periodicals; books and MSS connected with the Louvre and the National Museums (Egyptology colln, Oriental antiquities, Graeco-Roman antiquities, drawings, paintings and sculptures); open only to curators and authorized persons; Conservateur Général and Librarian Françoise Petitou.

Bibliothèque Centrale de l'Ecole Polytechnique: Plateau de Saclay, 91128 Palaiseau Cedex; tel. 1-69-33-40-76; fax 1-69-33-28-33; internet www.bibliotheque .polytechnique.fr; f. 1794; 300,000 vols, 1,700 periodicals; Chief Librarian Madeleine de Fuentes.

Bibliothèque Centrale du Muséum National d'Histoire Naturelle: 38 rue Geoffroy-Saint-Hilaire, 75005 Paris; tel. 1-40-79-36-27; fax 1-40-79-36-56; e-mail milenoir@mnhn.fr; internet mussi.mnhn.fr; f. 1635; 405,000 books, 7,050 MSS, 12,000 periodicals; Chief Librarian Michelle Lenoir.

Bibliothèque de Documentation Internationale Contemporaine: Centre Universitaire, 6 allée de l'Université, 92001 Nanterre Cedex; tel. 1-40-97-79-00; fax 1-40-97-79-40; e-mail courrier@bdic.fr; internet www.bdic.fr; f. 1914; over 1m. vols, 90,000 series of periodicals, history of the two World Wars and int. relations since beginning of 20th century, social and revolutionary movements, political emigrations; Dir Geneviève Dreyfus-Armand; publs *Journal* (irregular), *Matériaux pour l'Histoire de Notre Temps* (3 a year).

Bibliothèque de Géographie—Sorbonne: 191 rue Saint-Jacques, 75005 Paris; tel. 1-44-32-14-63; fax 1-44-32-14-67; e-mail bibgeo@univ-paris1.fr; internet www .univ-paris1.fr; f. 1927; geography; 92,000 vols, 4,600 periodicals, 100,000 maps, 40,000 photographs, 500 other media; Librarian Rachel Creppy.

Bibliothèque de la Cour des Comptes: 13 rue Cambon, 75100 Paris Cedex; tel. 1-42-98-97-12; fax 1-42-60-01-59; f. 1807 by Napoleon I; 50,000 vols on finance, law and economy; Librarian (vacant).

Bibliothèque de l'Institut National de la Statistique et des Etudes Economiques: 18 blvd Adolphe Pinard, 75675 Paris Cedex 14; tel. 1-41-17-67-18; fax 1-41-17-50-69; e-mail dg75-bibliotheque-service-public@ insee.fr; internet www.insee.fr/fr/ insee-statistique-publique/default.asp?page=bibliotheque/bibliotheque.htm; f. 1946; 100,000 vols, 5,000 periodicals; current and historical publs on french statistics and economics; regional publs; official publs on int. statistics and economics and publs of statistical offices around the world; Chief Librarian Pierre-Yves Renard; Head of Documentation Bernard Lancelot.

Bibliothèque de la Sorbonne: 13 rue de la Sorbonne, 75257 Paris Cedex 05; tel. 1-40-46-30-27; fax 1-40-46-30-44; e-mail info@biu .sorbonne.fr; internet www.bibliotheque .sorbonne.fr/biu; f. 1762; over 22m. vols, 13,000 periodicals; Chief Librarian Philippe Marcerou; publ. *Mélanges de la Bibliothèque de la Sorbonne.*

Bibliothèque de l'Académie Nationale de Médecine: 16 rue Bonaparte, 75272 Paris Cedex 06; tel. 1-46-34-60-70; fax 1-43-

25-84-14; e-mail bibliotheque@academie-medecine.fr; internet www.academie-medecine.fr; f. 1820; 450,000 vols, 113 incunabula, 4,000 periodicals (500 current); 7,000 biographical dossiers; Archives of the Académie Royale de Chirurgie (1731–93), Société Royale de Médecine (1776–93), Société de l'Ecole de Médecine (1800–21), Comité Central de Vaccine (1803–23) and Académie de Médecine (since 1820); also portraits, medals and sculptures; Librarian LAURENCE CAMOUS; publ. *Bulletin de l'Académie nationale de Médecine* (9 a year).

Bibliothèque de l'Arsenal: 1 rue de Sully, 75004 Paris; tel. 1-42-77-44-21; fax 1-42-77-01-63; internet www.bnf.fr/fr/la_bnf/anx_autres_sites/a.arsenal_salle_lecture.html; f. 1756, by the Marquess of Paulmy, public library in 1797; inc. Bibliothèque Nat. 1934; open to scholars; houses performing arts colln of the Bibliothèque Nationale (2.5m. vols and other items); incl. archives of the Bastille; 1m. vols, 15,000 MSS, autographs, 100,000 prints, 18th-century maps; Dir BRUNO BLASSELLE; Deputy Dir EVE NETCHINE.

Service de la Bibliothèque et des archives de l'Assemblée Nationale: Palais Bourbon, 126 rue de l'Université, 75007 Paris; tel. 1-40-63-64-74 (library); 1-40-63-85-77 (archives); fax 1-40-63-52-53; e-mail archives@assemblee-nationale.fr; internet www.assemblee-nationale.fr; f. 1796; open to deputies, staff members, secretaries of political groups, civil servants of the Assembly; 700,000 vols, 1,870 MSS, and 80 incunabula, 3,000 periodicals, 50,000 microfiches, 2,500 microfilms, mainly on history, political science, law, economy; Dir ELIANE FIGHIERA; publs *Sélection d'articles de périodiques*, *Sélection d'ouvrages récemment acquis* (8 a year).

Bibliothèque de l'Ecole Nationale Supérieure des Mines: 60 blvd Saint-Michel, 75272 Paris Cedex 06; tel. 1-40-51-90-56; fax 1-43-25-53-58; e-mail bib@bib.ensmp.fr; internet bib.ensmp.fr; f. 1783; 300,000 vols, 3,820 periodicals, 30,000 maps; Chief Librarian Mme F. MASSON.

Bibliothèque de l'Ecole Normale Supérieure: 45 rue d'Ulm, 75230 Paris Cedex 05; internet halley.ens.fr; f. 1810; 500,000 vols; Chief Librarian LAURE LÉVEILLÉ.

Bibliothèque de l'Institut de France: 23 quai Conti, 75006 Paris; tel. 1-44-41-44-10; fax 1-44-41-44-11; e-mail mireille.pastoureau@bif.univ-paris5.fr; internet www.bibliotheque-institutdefrance.fr; f. 1795; comprises five acads: Académie française, Académie des Inscriptions et Belles-Lettres, Académie des Sciences, Académie des Beaux-Arts, Académie des Sciences morales et politiques; 1m. vols, 8,000 periodicals, 10,000 MSS; Chief Curator Dr MIREILLE PASTOUREAU.

Bibliothéque de l'Institut National de Recherche Pédagogique: 5 parvis René Descartes, 69342 Lyons Cedex 07; tel. 1-37-37-66-10; fax 1-37-37-66-06; e-mail soula@inrp.fr; internet www.inrp.fr; f. 1879; 550,000 vols, 5,000 periodicals, 100,000 textbooks; educational research; Chief Librarian MARIE-LOUISE SOULA.

Bibliothèque de l'Institut National d'Histoire de l'Art—Collections Jacques Doucet: 2 rue Vivienne, 75002 Paris; 58 rue de Richelieu, 75083 Paris Cedex 02; tel. 1-47-03-76-23; fax 1-47-03-76-30; e-mail bibliotheque@inha.fr; internet www.inha.fr; f. 1918; 450,000 vols, 6,674 periodicals; Chief Librarian MARTINE POULAIN.

Bibliothèque des Avocats à la Cour d'Appel: Palais de Justice, 75001 Paris; f. 1708; confiscated during the Revolution, but refounded in 1810; 160,000 vols; not open to the public; Librarian MICHEL BRICHARD.

Bibliothèque Centrale du Conservatoire National des Arts et Métiers: 292 rue St-Martin, 75141 Paris Cedex 03; tel. 1-40-27-27-03; fax 1-40-27-29-87; e-mail mireille.le_van_ho@cnam.fr; internet bibliotheque.cnam.fr; f. 1794; 150,000 vols, 3,600 periodicals on science, technology, political economy; spec. collns: exhibition catalogues, Bartholdi, Organum; Dir MIREILLE LE VAN HO.

Bibliothèque du Ministère des Affaires Etrangères: 3 rue Suzanne Masson, La Courneuve, 93126 Paris; tel. 1-43-17-42-61; fax 1-43-17-51-48; e-mail biblio.archives@diplomatie.gouv.fr; internet www.diplomatie.gouv.fr; f. 1680; 500,000 vols; Head Librarian ISABELLE LEFORT; Librarian LIONEL CHENÉDÉ.

Bibliothèque du Sénat: Palais du Luxembourg, 15 rue de Vaugirard, 75291 Paris Cedex 06; tel. 1-42-34-35-39; fax 1-42-34-27-05; f. 1818; 450,000 vols, chiefly on history and law, 1,343 MSS and 45,000 prints; open to members of Parliament; Dir PHILIPPE MARTIAL.

Bibliothèque du Service Historique de la Marine: Château de Vincennes, BP 122, 00481 Armées; tel. 1-43-28-81-50; fax 1-43-28-31-60; e-mail contact@servicehistorique.marine.defense.gouv.fr; internet www.servicehistorique.marine.defense.gouv.fr; f. 1919; 300,000 vols on naval history; Chief Curator ALAIN MORGAT.

Bibliothèque du Service Historique de l'Armée de Terre: Château de Vincennes, BP 107, 00481 Armées; tel. 1-41-93-34-62; f. c.1800; over 600,000 vols; 16th- to 20th-century science and military history, French history, cartography; Librarian RAPHAËL MASSON.

Bibliothèque et Archives du Conseil d'Etat: Place du Palais-Royal, 75100 Paris 01 SP; tel. 1-40-20-81-31; fax 1-42-61-69-95; internet www.conseil-etat.fr; f. 1871; 100,000 vols on jurisprudence, administrative science, political science and legislation; Librarian SERGE BOUFFANGE.

Bibliothèque Forney: 1 rue du Figuier, 75004 Paris; tel. 1-42-78-14-60; fax 1-42-78-22-59; e-mail bibliotheque.forney@paris.fr; f. 1886; art library; reference library; wallpapers, posters, ephemera; 250,000 vols, 20,000 periodicals (chiefly on arts and crafts), 38,000 posters, 5,000 wallpapers, 1.5m. postcards; Librarian Conservateur Gen. FRÉDÉRIC CASIOT.

Bibliothèque Georges-Duhamel: 44 ave de Paris, 95290 L'Isle-Adam; tel. 1-34-69-41-99; f. 1797; encyclopaedic library; 88,882 vols; record library: 6,400 records, 1,500 compact discs; permanent exhibitions in Georges Duhamel picture gallery; Dir PAUL JOLAS; publ. *Rencontres Artistiques et Littéraires.*

Bibliothèque Gustav Mahler: 11 bis rue Vézelay, 75008 Paris; tel. 1-53-89-09-10; fax 1-43-59-70-22; internet www.bgm.org; f. 1986; reference colln for musicians, students, researchers; 30,000 vols, 35,000 musical scores, 6,000 reviews, 70,000 records; archives: MSS, letters, photos, etc. on Mahler's life and works; also 16,000 dossiers on contemporary composers, autographs and MSS of 19th- and 20th-century musicians; Pres. PIERRE BERGÉ; Librarian ALAIN GALLIARI; publ. *Bulletin d'information de la BMGM* (1 a year).

Bibliothèque Historique de la Ville de Paris: 24 rue Pavée, 75004 Paris; tel. 1-44-59-29-40; fax 1-42-74-03-16; f. 1871; 650,000 vols, 15,000 MSS on history of Paris; Curator JEAN DERENS.

Bibliothèque Interuniversitaire Cujas de Droit et Sciences Économiques: 2 rue Cujas, 75005 Paris; tel. 1-44-07-79-87; fax 1-44-07-78-32; e-mail cujasdr@univ-paris1.fr; internet www-cujas.univ-paris1.fr; f. 1876; 1m. vols; Chief Librarian DOMINIQUE ROCHE.

Bibliothèque Interuniversitaire de Médecine: 12 rue de l'Ecole-de-Médecine, 75270 Paris Cedex 06; tel. 1-40-46-19-51; fax 1-44-41-10-20; e-mail bium@bium.univ-paris5.fr; internet www.bium.univ-paris5.fr; f. 1733; 1m. vols, 30,000 pre-1800 books and theses, 109 incunabula, 20,000 periodicals (2,300 current); Chief Librarian GUY COBOLET.

Bibliothèque Interuniversitaire de Santé: 4 ave de l'Observatoire, 75270 Paris Cedex 06; tel. 1-53-73-95-23; fax 1-53-73-95-05; internet www.biup.parisdescartes.fr; f. 1570; centre for the acquisition and dispersion of scientific and technical information (CADIST) on beauty care; 280,000 vols, 945 periodicals, archives of Parisian apothecaries; Dir GUY COBOLET.

Bibliothèque Mazarine: 23 quai de Conti, 75006 Paris; tel. 1-44-41-44-06; fax 1-44-41-44-07; e-mail webmaster@bibliotheque-mazarine.fr; internet www.bibliotheque-mazarine.fr; f. 1643 by Cardinal Mazarin, present status 1945; attached to Institut de France; 600,000 vols, 4,642 MSS, 2,370 incunabula; Dir CHRISTIAN PÉLIGRY.

Bibliothèque-Musée de l'Opéra: 8 rue Scribe, 75009 Paris; tel. 1-53-79-37-40; fax 1-53-79-39-59; internet www.bnf.fr; f. 1875; a service of Bibliothèque Nationale, music dept; 200,000 vols, 30,000 scores, 80,000 libretti, 100,000 drawings, 40,000 lithographs, 100,000 photographs, 2,000 periodicals; Dir ODILE DUPONT; Curator ROMAIN FEIST.

Bibliothèque Nationale de France: quai François Mauriac, 75013 Paris; tel. 1-53-79-53-79; internet www.bnf.fr; f. 14th century; specialized depts: printed books (11m. vols), periodicals (350,000 titles), maps and plans (890,000), prints and photographs (11m.), MSS (350,000 bound vols), coins, medals and antiques (580,000 items), music (incl. Bibliothèque-Musée de l'Opéra (q.v.)), sound archive and audiovisual aids (1m. discs and tape recordings, 20,000 films, 40,000 video materials), performing arts (3m. items), Bibliothèque de l'Arsenal (q.v.); Pres. JEAN-NOËL JEANNENEY; Dir-Gen. AGNÈS SAAL; publs *Bibliographie nationale Française* (52 a year), *Chronique de la Bibliothèque Nationale de France* (6 a year).

Bibliothèque Polonaise de Paris (Polish Library in Paris): 6 quai d'Orléans, 75004 Paris; tel. 1-55-42-83-83; fax 1-46-33-36-31; e-mail b.skrzypek@bplp.fr; internet www.bibliotheque-polonaise-paris-shlp.fr; f. 1854; resources centre specializes in 19th- and 20th-century history, literature and art; organizes cultural meetings, confs and colloquia, musical events, temporary exhibitions; administered by the Polish Historical and Literary Society (Société Historique et Littéraire Polonaise); 200,000 vols, 3,000 MSS (archives of 19th- and 20th-century Polish emigration to France), 1,000 magazines, 90,000 brochures, 1,000 posters, 1,420 paintings, 25,000 drawings and engravings, 350 sculptures, 600 medals and coins, 4,000 maps (16th to 20th centuries), 5,000 old photographs; Pres. C. PIERRE ZALESKI; Dir DANUTA DUBOIS.

Bibliothèque Publique d'Information: Centre Georges-Pompidou, 75197 Paris Cedex 04; tel. 1-44-78-12-33; fax 1-44-78-12-15; e-mail bpi-info@bpi.fr; internet www.bpi

.fr; f. 1977; 400,000 books, 2,722 periodicals, 2,425 films, 10,000 music records; Dir PATRICK BAZIN.

Bibliothèque Sainte-Geneviève: 10 pl. du Panthéon, 75005 Paris; tel. 1-44-41-97-97; fax 1-44-41-97-96; e-mail bsgmail@ univ-paris1.fr; internet www-bsg.univ-paris1 .fr; f. 1624 by Cardinal F. de La Rochefoucauld as library of the Abbaye Sainte-Geneviève; collns on computer science, information, general works, philosophy and psychology, religion, social sciences, languages, science and mathematics, technology and applied science, arts and recreation, literature, history and geography; interlibrary loan; guided tours; online databases; 45,000 mems; 1.3m. vols, 14,000 periodicals, 120,000 early printed books, 1,500 incunabula and 4,200 MSS, 50,000 prints; encyclopaedic library; spec. colln: Bibliothèque Nordique (160,000 vols, 3,500 periodicals), Estonian colln (1,000 vols), 3,800 current serial titles; Dir YVES PEYRÉ.

Bibliothèque Thiers: 27 pl. Saint-Georges, 75009 Paris; tel. 1-48-78-14-33; fax 1-48-78-92-92; e-mail bibliotheque.thiers@free.fr; internet www.institut-de-france.fr; f. 1906; attached to Institut de France; 150,000 vols, 3,000 MSS and 30,000 engravings on 19th century-history; Dir SYLVIE BIET.

Bibliothèque Universitaire des Langues et Civilisations: 4 rue de Lille, 75007 Paris; tel. 1-44-77-87-20; fax 1-44-77-87-30; e-mail webmaster@bulac.sorbonne.fr; internet www .bulac.fr; f. 1868; languages and cultures of countries in Asia, Africa, Central and Eastern Europe, and Middle Eastern, Oceanian and Amerindian languages; 660,000 vols, 8,695 periodicals; Dir MARIE-LISE TSAGOURIA.

Bibliothèques de l'Institut Catholique de Paris: c/o Bibliothèque de Fels, 21 rue d'Assas, 75270 Paris Cedex 06; tel. 1-44-39-52-30; fax 1-44-39-52-98; e-mail bibliotheque .de.fels@icp.fr; internet www.icp.fr; f. 1875; philosophy, theology, history, literature, psychology, pedagogy; 600,000 vols, incl. 450,000 books, 623 current periodicals, 6,000 other periodicals; Dir of Libraries ODILE DUPONT.

Attached Library:

> **Bibliothèque Jean de Vernon:** 21 rue d'Assas, 75006 Paris; tel. 44-39-52-32; e-mail bibliotheque.de.vernon@icp.fr; internet ipac.icp.fr; 100,000 vols, 400 periodicals; biblical exegesis, archaeology and languages of the ancient Near E, Orthodox Church instns, history of the Byzantine Empire; Dir. of Library MARIE-FRANÇOISE PAPE.

CÉDIAS—Musée Social: 5 rue Las-Cases, 75007 Paris; tel. 1-45-51-66-10; fax 1-44-18-01-81; e-mail bibliotheque@cedias.org; internet www.cedias.org; f. 1894; social information and documentation; public library; 100,000 vols; Dir JEAN-YVES BARREYRE; publ. *Vie Sociale* (4 a year).

Centre de Documentation Economique de la Chambre de Commerce et d'Industrie de Paris: 16 rue de Châteaubriand, 75008 Paris; tel. 1-55-65-72-72; fax 1-55-65-72-86; f. 1821; economics, business information, management, market surveys, companies; 300,000 vols, 750 periodicals; economic data bank (DELPHES); Dir GÉRARD FALCO.

Centre de Documentation et d'Information Scientifique pour le Développement (CEDID): 209 rue La Fayette, 75010 Paris; tel. 1-48-03-75-95; fax 1-48-03-08-29; f. 1985 by ORSTOM; 70,000 documents on development and North-South co-operation, world environment, tropical agriculture, health, evolving societies, and women in third world countries; 200 general and scientific reviews, press cuttings, database, etc.; open to the public.

Direction des Services d'Archives de Paris: 18 blvd Sérurier, 75019 Paris; tel. 1-53-72-41-23; fax 1-53-72-41-34; f. 1872; collns of various kinds of documents relating to the history of Paris, urbanization and architecture; 34,000 vols specializing in history of Paris and admin. publs, 1,200 periodicals; Dir AGNÈS MASSON.

Institut François-Mitterrand: 10 rue Charlot, 75003 Paris; tel. 1-44-54-53-93; fax 1-44-54-53-99; e-mail ifm@mitterrand.org; internet www.mitterrand.org; f. 1996; archives documents relevant to the history of the second half of the 20th century.

Service Documentaire de l'Ecole Ponts et ParisTech: 6 et 8 ave Blaise Pascal, Cité Descartes, Champs sur Marne, 77455 Marne-la-Vallée Cedex 2; tel. 1-64-15-36-90; fax 1-64-15-34-79; e-mail bibliotheque@enpc.fr; internet www.enpc.fr; f. 1747; over 200,000 vols on bldg, civil engineering, urban and regional planning, and transport, 3,200 MSS, 3,000 maps, 10,000 photographs 1850–1900, 10 libraries; Dir ISABELLE GAUTHERON.

UNESCO Library: UNESCO, 7 pl. de Fontenoy, 75007 Paris; tel. 1-45-68-03-56; fax 1-45-68-56-98; e-mail library@unesco.org; internet www.unesco.org/library; f. 1946; reference and information services, incl. online searches, for the org. as a whole, as well as for the gen. public with an interest in UNESCO's fields of competence; manages multilingual UNESCO Thesaurus; 150,000 vols, 800 periodicals; Chief Librarian JOHN MILLER; Reference Librarian PETRA VAN DEN BORN.

Pau

Bibliothèque Square Paul Lafond: Rue Mathieu Lalanne, 64000 Pau; tel. 5-59-27-15-72; fax 5-59-83-94-47; e-mail accueil.bipp@ agglo-pau.fr; internet mediatheques .agglo-pau.fr; f. 1803; 350,000 vols; includes municipal archives; spec. collns on Henri IV and Béarn; Librarian OLIVIER CAUDRON.

Bibliothèque de l'Université de Pau et des Pays de l'Adour: Campus universitaire, 64000 Pau; tel. 5-59-92-33-60; fax 5-59-92-33-62; internet www.univ-pau.fr/scd; f. 1962; 142,000 vols, 2,067 periodicals; Dir SYLVAINE FREULON.

Périgueux

Bibliothèque Municipale: 12 ave Georges Pompidou, 24000 Périgueux; tel. 5-53-45-65-45; fax 5-53-45-65-49; e-mail bibliotheque@ perigueux.fr; f. 1809; 170,000 vols; Librarian J. L. GLÉNISSON.

Perpignan

Bibliothèque Universitaire: BP 59939, Moulin à Vent, 52 ave Paul Alduy, 66962 Perpignan Cedex 9; tel. 4-68-66-22-99; fax 4-68-50-37-72; internet www.univ-perp.fr/ scms/bu/buweb.htm; f. 1962; 155,000 vols and 100,000 theses; spec. collns: Catalan, Mexican studies, history of Languedoc-Roussillon, renewable energy, materials science, geology of North Africa; Dir JOËL MARTRES.

Poitiers

Bibliothèque Universitaire de Poitiers: BP 605, 86022 Poitiers Cedex; tel. 5-49-45-33-11; fax 5-49-45-33-56; e-mail bu@ univ-poitiers.fr; internet www.scd .univ-poitiers.fr; f. 1879; 452,000 vols, 5,830 periodicals; spec. collns: 30,000 early printed vols, Fonds Dubois (16th–19th centuries, economics, politics, social history), Argenson family archives; Dir STÉPHANE BASSINET.

Médiathèque François-Mitterrand: 4 rue de l'Université, BP 619, 86022 Poitiers Cedex; tel. 5-49-52-31-51; fax 5-49-52-31-60; e-mail mediatheque@mairie-poitiers.fr; internet www.bm-poitiers.fr; f. 1803; 750,000 vols, 550 current periodicals; Dir AGNES MACQUIN; publ. *Programme* (5 a year).

Reims

Bibliothèque Municipale: 2 rue des Fuseliers, 51095 Reims Cedex; tel. 3-26-35-68-00; fax 3-26-35-68-34; e-mail cathedrale@ bm-reims.fr; internet www.bm-reims.fr; f. 1809; 800,000 vols, 3,000 MSS; Librarian DELPHINE QUÉREUX-SBAÏ; publ. *Ouvrez les guillemets* (12 a year).

Bibliothèque de l'Université de Reims: Ave François Mauriac, 51095 Reims Cedex; tel. 3-26-91-39-28; fax 3-26-91-39-30; e-mail carine.elbekri@univ-reims.fr; internet www .univ-reims.fr/bu; f. 1970; 400,000 vols, 4,278 periodicals; Dir CARINE EL BEKRI.

Rennes

Bibliothèque Municipale: 1 rue de La Borderie, 35042 Rennes Cedex; tel. 2-23-62-26-42; fax 2-23-62-26-45; e-mail bm@ bm-rennes.fr; internet www.bm-rennes.fr; f. 1803; 650,000 vols; Chief Librarian MARINE BEDEL.

Bibliothèque de l'Université de Rennes I:; tel. 2-23-23-34-18; fax 2-23-23-34-19; internet www.scd.univ-rennes1.fr; f. 1855; 550,000 vols; Dir GHYSLAINE DUONG-VINH.

Bibliothèque de l'Université de Rennes II: Place du Recteur Henri Le Moal, 35043 Rennes Cedex; tel. 2-99-14-12-55; fax 2-99-14-12-85; internet www.uhb.fr/scd; Librarian E. LEMAU.

Rouen

Bibliothèque Municipale: 3 rue Jacques-Villon, 76043 Rouen Cedex 1; tel. 2-35-71-28-82; fax 2-35-70-01-56; e-mail bibliotheque@ rouen.fr; f. 1791; 500,000 vols incl. 600 incunabula, 6,000 MSS; Chief Librarian F. LEGENDRE.

Bibliothèque de l'Université de Rouen: Anneau central, rue Lavoisier, 76821 Mont-Saint-Aignan Cedex; tel. 2-35-14-81-75; fax 2-35-76-93-77; internet www.univ-rouen.fr; 400,000 vols; Dir YANNICK VALIN.

St-Etienne

Bibliothèque de l'Université Jean-Monnet: 1 rue Tréfilerie, 42023 St-Etienne Cedex 2; tel. 4-77-42-16-99; fax 4-77-42-16-20; e-mail achard@univ-st-etienne.fr; internet www.univ-st-etienne.fr/scdoc; Dir MARIE-CLAUDE ACHARD.

Strasbourg

Bibliothèque Nationale et Universitaire: 5 rue du Maréchal Joffre, BP 51029, 67070 Strasbourg Cedex; tel. 3-88-25-28-00; fax 3-88-25-28-03; e-mail contact@bnu.fr; internet www.bnu.fr; f. 1871; 3.5m. vols; books, newspapers, reviews, MSS; Admin. ALBERT POIROT.

Toulon

Bibliothèque de l'Université de Toulon et du Var: BP 10122, 83957 La Garde Cedex; tel. 4-94-14-23-26; fax 4-94-14-21-38; e-mail scd@univ-tln.fr; internet bu.univ-tln.fr; f. 1971; general library; Dir J. KERIGUY.

Toulouse

Bibliothèque de Toulouse: 1 rue de Périgord, BP 7092, 31070 Toulouse Cedex 7; tel. 5-61-22-21-78; fax 5-61-22-34-30; internet www.bibliothequedetoulouse.fr; f. 1782; 20 brs; 914,000 vols, 3,700 periodicals; Chief Librarian PIERRE JULLIEN (acting).

Bibliothèque Universitaire de l'Arsenal (Toulouse 1): 11 rue des Puits-Creusés, BP 7093, 31070 Toulouse Cedex 7; tel. 5-34-45-61-11; fax 5-34-45-61-30; internet www.univ-tlse1.fr/scd; f. 1879; 900,000 vols; spec. collns: Fonds Pifteau (books printed in Toulouse, books on regional history and geography), Fonds Chabaneau (18th-century books), Fonds Liguge (Spanish history), Fonds Claude Perroud (French Revolution), Fonds Montauban (History of Protestantism); Dir MARCEL MARTY; Chief Librarian M. VAN DOOREN.

Tours

Bibliothèque Municipale: 2 bis ave André Malraux, 37042 Tours Cedex; tel. 2-47-05-47-33; fax 2-47-31-07-33; e-mail contact@bm-tours.fr; internet www.bm-tours.fr; f. 1791; original library destroyed in 1940; 142 mems; 552,000 vols, 3,400 periodicals, 1,632 MSS; Dir RÉGIS RECH.

Service Commun de la Documentation de l'Université de Tours: 5 rue des Tanneurs, 37041 Tours Cedex (Letters); tel. 2-47-36-64-86; fax 2-47-36-67-99 Parc de Grandmont, 37200 Tours (Sciences and Pharmacy); 2 bis blvd Tonnellé, 37032 Tours Cedex (Medicine); 50 ave Portalis, 37206 Tours Cedex 3 (Law); tel. 2-47-36-11-24 6 place Jean-Jaurès, 41000 Blois (Blois section); internet www.scd.univ-tours.fr; Dir GIL-FRANÇOIS EUVRARD.

Troyes

Médiathèque de l'Agglomération Troyenne: 7 rue des Filles-Dieu, BP 602, 10088 Troyes Cedex; tel. 3-25-43-56-20; fax 3-25-43-56-21; e-mail contact@mediatheque-agglo-troyes.fr; internet www.mediatheque-agglo-troyes.fr; f. 1651; 400,000 vols; Librarian THIERRY DELCOURT.

Valence

Médiathèque Publique et Universitaire: Place Charles Huguenel, 26000 Valence; tel. 4-75-79-23-70; fax 4-75-79-23-82; e-mail medieval@wanadoo.fr; internet sicd2.upmf-grenoble.fr/bu/valence; f. 1775; 100,000 vols, 650 periodicals; Librarian JOHANN BERTI.

Valenciennes

Bibliothèque Municipale: 2–6 rue Ferrand, BP 282, 59300 Valenciennes Cedex; tel. 3-27-22-57-00; fax 3-27-22-57-01; e-mail mpdion@ville-valenciennes.fr; internet www.bibliotheque.valenciennes.fr; f. 1598; 400,000 vols, also incl. 80,000 prints, photographs, maps; Dir MARIE-PIERRE DION.

Vandoeuvre-lès-Nancy

Institut de l'Information Scientifique et Technique (INIST-CNRS): 2 allée du Parc de Brabois, 54514 Vandoeuvre-lès-Nancy Cedex; tel. 3-83-50-46-00; fax 3-83-50-46-50; e-mail infoclient@inist.fr; internet www.inist.fr; f. 1988; collects, processes and distributes international research findings; produces two databases: PASCAL (Sciences, Technology, Medicine) and FRANCIS (Humanities, Social Sciences, Economics); 10,000 vols, 26,000 serial titles, 60,000 scientific reports, 62,000 conference proceedings, 110,000 doctoral theses; Dir-Gen. RAYMOND DUVAL.

Versailles

Bibliothèque Municipale: 5 rue de l'Indépendance Américaine, 78000 Versailles; tel. 1-39-07-13-20; fax 1-39-07-13-22; e-mail bibliotheque@versailles.fr; internet www.bibliotheques.versailles.fr/statique; f. 1803; 800,000 vols, 900 periodicals; Chief Librarian SOPHIE DANIS.

Museums and Art Galleries

Agen

Musée des Beaux-Arts: Place du Docteur Esquirol, 47916 Agen Cedex 9; tel. 5-53-69-47-23; fax 5-53-69-47-77; e-mail musee@ville-agen.fr; internet www.ville-agen.fr/musee; f. 1876; local, Roman and medieval archaeology; paintings by Corneille de Lyon, de Troy, Drouais, Nattier, Goya, the Impressionists, Roger Bissière and François-Xavier Lalanne; ceramics; Chinese art; Curator MARIE-DOMINIQUE NIVIÈRE.

Aix-en-Provence

Musée Granet: Place Saint Jean de Malte, 13100 Aix-en-Provence; tel. 4-42-52-88-32; fax 4-42-26-84-55; internet www.museegranet-aixenprovence.fr; f. 1765; Egyptian, Greek, Celto-Ligurian, Roman and Gallo-Roman archaeology; pictures of Cézanne and the French Schools, with special emphasis on Provence; Italian, Spanish, Flemish, Dutch and German Schools; modern painting; sculpture; furniture of 16th, 17th and 18th centuries; Curator DENIS COUTAGNE.

Alençon

Musée des Beaux-Arts et de la Dentelle: Cour Carrée de la Dentelle, 61000 Alençon; tel. 2-33-32-40-07; fax 2-33-26-51-66; e-mail musee@mairie-calais.fr; internet www.musee.calais.fr; f. 1857; French, Dutch and Flemish paintings from 17th–19th centuries; French, Italian and Dutch drawings from 16th–19th centuries; French, Flemish, Italian and Eastern European lace since 16th century; French and British prints from 16th–19th centuries; ethnological items from Cambodia; Curator AUDE PESSEY-LUX.

Amboise

Musée de l'Hôtel de Ville: rue François I, BP 247, 37402 Amboise; tel. 2-47-23-47-42; fax 2-47-23-19-80; e-mail a.guenand@ville-amboise.fr; internet www.ville-amboise.fr; f. 1970; colln incl. tapestries, statues and paintings relating to the history of Amboise; Curator AGATHE GUENAND.

Amiens

Musée de Picardie: 48 rue de la République, 80000 Amiens; tel. 3-22-97-14-00; fax 3-22-97-14-26; e-mail musees-amiens@amiens-metropole.com; internet w2.amiens.com/museedepicardie; f. 1854; fine colln of paintings of Northern and French Schools; murals by Puvis de Chavannes and Sol Le Witt; Egyptian, Greek and Roman antiquities; prehistoric, Iron and Bronze age collns; objets d'art of Middle Ages and Renaissance; 19th-century sculpture; 20th-century paintings; Chief Curator SABINE CAZENAVE.

Angers

Musée des Beaux-Arts: 14 rue du Musée, 49100 Angers; tel. 2-41-05-38-00; fax 2-41-86-06-38; e-mail musees@ville.angers.fr; internet www.angers.fr/mba; f. 1797; housed in 15th-century 'logis Barrault'; paintings of 18th-century French School and 17th-century Dutch and Flemish Schools; sculpture, including busts by Houdon; Dir PATRICK LE NOUÈNE.

Affiliated Museums:

Galerie David d'Angers: 33 bis rue Toussaint, 49100 Angers; tel. 2-41-05-38-90; fax 2-41-05-38-09; e-mail musees@ville.angers.fr; internet www.angers.fr/musees; f. 1984; sited in restored gothic church; almost all the sculptor's work; Dir and Curator PATRICK LE NOUÈNE.

Musée Jean Lurçat et de la Tapisserie Contemporaine: 4 blvd Arago, 49100 Angers; tel. 2-41-24-18-45 (Musée Jean Lurçat); tel. 2-41-24-18-48 (Musée de la Tapisserie Contemporaine); fax 2-41-86-06-38; occupies 12th-century Hôpital Saint-Jean; paintings of Jean Lurçat and tapestry.

Musée Pincé: 32 bis rue Lenepveu, 49100 Angers; tel. 2-41-88-94-27; fax 2-41-86-06-38; f. 1889; Greek, Roman, Etruscan and Egyptian antiquities; Chinese and Japanese art.

Antibes

Musée Picasso: Château Grimaldi, 06600 Antibes; tel. 4-92-90-54-20; fax 4-92-90-54-21; e-mail musee.picasso@ville-antibes.fr; internet www.antibes-juanlespins.com/fr/culture; f. 1948; 230 works by Picasso; collection of modern and contemporary art: Atlan, Miró, Calder, Richier, Ernst, Hartung and others; Nicolas de Staël room with works from Antibes period; sculpture garden; Dir MAURICE FRÉCHURET; publ. catalogues.

Arras

Musée des Beaux-Arts d'Arras: Ancienne Abbaye Saint-Vaast, 22 rue Paul Doumer, 62000 Arras; tel. 3-21-71-26-43; fax 3-21-23-19-26; e-mail musee.arras@ville-arras.fr; internet www.musenor.com/gm/gmarras.htm; f. 1825; medieval sculpture, 17th- and 19th-century paintings, porcelain, Gallo-Roman archaeology; Chief Curator STEPHANIE DESCHAMPS.

Arromanches

Exposition Permanente du Débarquement (Permanent Exhibition of the Landings): Place du 6 Juin, 14117 Arromanches; tel. 2-31-22-34-31; fax 2-31-92-68-83; e-mail info.arromanches@normandy1944.com; internet www.normandy1944.com; f. 1954; exhibition of the Normandy landings of D-Day, 6th June 1944; comprises artificial harbour and museum of relief maps, working models, photographs, diorama and films.

Avignon

Musée Calvet: 65 rue Joseph Vernet, 84000 Avignon; tel. 4-90-86-33-84; fax 4-90-14-62-45; e-mail musee.calvet@wanadoo.fr; internet www.musee-calvet-avignon.com; f. 1810; fine art since 16th century; Dir SYLVAIN BOYER; Curator for Archaeology ODILE CAVALIER.

Musée Lapidaire: 27 rue de la République, 84000 Avignon; tel. 4-90-85-75-38; internet www.avignon.fr/fr/culture/musees/lapidaire.php; f. 1933; ancient Egyptian, Greek and Gallo-Roman sculpture; Curator ODILE CAVALIER.

Musée du Petit Palais: Place du Palais des Papes, 84000 Avignon; tel. 4-90-86-44-58; fax 4-90-82-18-72; internet www.avignon.fr/fr/culture/musees/petipal.php; f. 1976; in the old archbishop's palace (14th–15th century); medieval and Renaissance paintings of the Avignon and Italian Schools, medieval sculpture from Avignon; Curator DOMINIQUE VINGTAIN.

Bayonne

Musée Basque et de l'histoire Bayonne: 37 quai des Corsaires, 64100 Bayonne; tel. 5-59-59-08-98; fax 5-59-25-73-38; internet www.musee-basque.com; f. 1922; 4 sections covering the history and folklore of the town of Bayonne, the French Basque country, the Spanish Basque country, and the Basques in the New World; library of 30,000 vols; Dir RAFAEL ZULAIKA; Curator OLIVIER RIBETON; publ. *Bulletin* (2 a year).

Besançon

Musée des Beaux-Arts et d'Archéologie: 1 place de la Révolution–place du Marché, 25000 Besançon; tel. 3-81-87-80-49; fax 3-81-80-06-53; e-mail musee-beaux-arts-archeologie@besancon.fr; internet www.musee-arts-besancon.org; f. 1694, moved to present bldgs 1843; Danish (pre- and protohistoric), Egyptian, Greek, Etruscan and Roman antiquities; regional (pre- and protohistoric, Gallo-Roman, early medieval) antiquities; medieval objets d'art; 15th- to 20th-century European paintings (especially French 18th–19th century), sculpture, ceramics and objets d'art; 15th- to 20th-century drawings in temporary exhibitions; Curators F. SOULIER-FRANÇOIS, P. LAGRANGE, F. THOMAS-MAURIN.

Biot

Musée National Fernand Léger: Chemin du Val de Pome, 06410 Biot; tel. 4-92-91-50-30; fax 4-92-91-50-31; internet www.musee-fernandleger.fr; permanent exhibition of paintings, drawings, ceramics.

Blérancourt

Musée National de la Coopération Franco-Américaine: Château de Blérancourt, 33 place du Général Leclerc, 02300 Blérancourt; tel. 3-23-39-60-16; fax 3-23-39-62-85; e-mail musee.blerancourt@culture.gouv.fr; internet www.museefrancoamericain.fr; f. 1924 to contain collections presented to the State by Mrs Anna Murray Dike, Miss Anne Morgan, and other French and American benefactors, relating to the history of Franco-American relations; the castle, formerly the ancestral home of the Ducs de Gesvres, is classed as an historical monument; library of 3,500 vols; Curator PHILIPPE GRUNCHEC.

Bordeaux

Musée d'Aquitaine: 20 cours Pasteur, 33000 Bordeaux; tel. 5-56-01-51-00; fax 5-56-44-24-36; e-mail musaq@mairie-bordeaux.fr; internet www.mairie-bordeaux.fr; f. 1987; regional prehistory, history and ethnology; ethnographical collection of pieces from Africa and Oceania; library of 20,000 vols; Curator HÉLÈNE LAFONT-COUTURIER.

CAPC Musée d'Art Contemporain de Bordeaux: Entrepôt Lainé, 7 rue Ferrère, 33000 Bordeaux; tel. 5-56-00-81-50; fax 5-56-44-12-07; e-mail capc@mairie-bordeaux.fr; internet www.capc-bordeaux.fr; f. 1984, by 'Capc' asscn (f. 1974); temporary exhibitions; permanent collns; education dept for children; library of 60,000 vols, mostly catalogues; Dir Dr CHARLOTTE LAUBARD; publs *Cultural Programme* (4 a year), *Exhibition Catalogue* (4 a year), *RosaB* (online, 2 a year).

Musée des Beaux-Arts: Jardin de la Mairie, 20 cours d'Albret, 33000 Bordeaux; tel. 5-56-10-20-56; fax 5-56-10-25-13; e-mail musbxa@mairie-bordeaux.fr; internet www.culture.fr/culture/bordeaux; f. 1801; permanent colln of 2,300 paintings, 504 sculptures, 2,370 drawings; archive; library of 25,000 vols, not open to public; Curator GUILLAUME AMBROISE.

Caen

Musée de Normandie: Château de Caen, 14000 Caen; tel. 2-31-30-47-60; fax 2-31-30-47-69; e-mail mdn@ville-caen.fr; internet www.musee-de-normandie.caen.fr; f. 1946; history, archaeology and ethnology of Normandy; Dir J.-Y. MARIN; publs *Annales de Normandie* (4 a year), *Publications* (irregular).

Carnac

Musée de Préhistoire: 10 pl. de la Chapelle, 56340 Carnac; tel. 2-97-52-22-04; fax 2-97-52-64-04; e-mail contact@museedecarnac.fr; internet www.museedecarnac.com; municipal museum; f. 1881; local prehistory and archaeology; most important museum in the world for collns from megalithic period; research library; photographic archive (3,000 items); Dir ANNE-ELISABETH RISKINE.

Chantilly

Musée et Château de Chantilly (Musée Condé): Château de Chantilly, 60500 Chantilly; tel. 3-44-27-31-80; fax 3-44-54-90-73; e-mail daniele.clergeot@fondationdechantilly.org; internet www.chateaudechantilly.com; f. 1898; paintings, miniatures, furniture, drawings, 70,000 books, 3,000 MSS, etc.; Curator OLIVIER BOSC; publ. *Le Musée Condé* (1 a year).

Compiègne

Musée National du Château de Compiègne: 60200 Compiègne; tel. 3-44-38-47-02; fax 3-44-38-47-01; e-mail chateau.compiegne@culture.gouv.fr; internet www.musee-chateau-compiegne.fr; royal palace of the first kings of France, reconstructed under Louis XV and Louis XVI and partly redecorated under the 1st Empire; furniture of 18th and 19th centuries, mostly 1st Empire period; tapestries of 18th century; collns from the 2nd Empire period; souvenirs of the Empress Eugénie; Chief Curator EMMANUEL STARCKY.

Affiliated Museum:

> **Musée National de la Voiture et du Tourisme:** Château de Compiègne, 60200 Compiègne; tel. 3-44-38-47-00; fax 3-44-38-47-01; e-mail chateau.compiegne@culture.gouv.fr; internet www.musee-chateau-compiegne.fr; f. 1927 with the cooperation of the Touring Club de France; old carriages, sedan chairs, survey of devt of the bicycle and the automobile; 180 vehicles; Chief Curator JACQUES PEROT.

Dijon

Musée des Beaux-Arts: Palais des Etats, Cour de Bar, 21000 Dijon; tel. 3-80-74-52-70; fax 3-80-74-53-44; e-mail museedesbeauxarts@ville-dijon.fr; internet www.ville-dijon.fr; f. 1787 and housed in the Palace of the Dukes of Burgundy and the Palace of the States of Burgundy; Swiss primitives; paintings of Franco-Flemish School of 15th century and of other French and foreign schools; prints and drawings; sculptures from tombs of the Dukes of Burgundy; marble, ivory, armour; modern art; Granville colln; Chief Curator EMMANUEL STARCKY.

Musée Magnin: 4 rue des Bons-Enfants, 21000 Dijon; tel. 3-80-67-11-10; fax 3-80-66-43-75; internet www.musee-magnin.fr; Italian and French paintings from 16th–19th centuries; Curator RÉMI CARIEL.

Fontainebleau

Musée National du Château de Fontainebleau: 77300 Château de Fontainebleau; tel. 1-60-71-50-70; fax 1-60-71-50-71; e-mail contact.chateau-de-fontainebleau@culture.fr; internet www.musee-chateau-fontainebleau.fr; bldgs from 12th–19th centuries; paintings, interior decoration and furniture of the Renaissance, 17th and 18th centuries, 1st and 2nd Empires and 19th century; Dir BERNARD NOTARI.

Giverny

Claude Monet Foundation: 84 rue Claude Monet, 27620 Giverny; tel. 2-32-51-28-21; fax 2-32-51-54-18; e-mail contact@fondation-monet.com; internet www.fondation-monet.com; f. 1980 after restoration; consists of Monet's house and garden where he lived from 1883 to 1926; it was left by his son in 1966 to the Académie des Beaux-Arts; the house contains Monet's collection of Japanese engravings; Curator GERALD VAN DER KEMP; Sec.-Gen. Mme C. LINDSEY.

Grenoble

Musée de Grenoble: 5 pl. Lavalette, BP 326, 38010 Grenoble Cedex 01; tel. 4-76-63-44-44; fax 4-76-63-44-10; internet www.museedegrenoble.fr; f. 1796; art and antiquities; library of 50,000 vols; Dir GUY TOSATTO.

Langeais

Château de Langeais: 37130 Langeais; tel. 2-47-96-72-60; fax 2-47-96-54-44; e-mail contact@chateau-de-langeais.com; internet www.chateau-de-langeais.com; built in 15th century by Louis XI, given to the Institut de France in 1904; furniture and tapestries from the 13th–15th centuries and 15th-century architecture; Admin. SANDRINE DURAND.

Le Havre

Musée des Beaux-Arts 'André Malraux': Blvd J. F. Kennedy, 76600 Le Havre; tel. 2-35-19-62-62; fax 2-35-19-93-01; internet www.ville-lehavre.fr; f. 1845; permanent colln from 14th to 20th century (Boudin, Impressionists, Dufy); Dir ANNETTE HAUDIQUET.

Affiliated Museums:

> **Espace Maritime et Portuaire du Havre:** Quai Frissard, 76600 Le Havre; tel. 2-35-24-51-00; fax 2-35-26-76-69; e-mail musees.histoire@ville-lehavre.fr; internet www.ville-lehavre.fr; Le Havre maritime and port history since 1830; Dir C. MAUBANT.

> **Musée de l'Hôtel Dubocage de Bléville:** Rue Jérôme Bellarmato, 76600 Le Havre; tel. 2-35-42-27-90; fax 2-35-26-76-69; e-mail musees.histoire@ville-lehavre.fr; internet www.musees-haute-normandie.fr; f. 2010; fmrly Musée de l'Ancien Havre; drawings and documents on the history of Le Havre from 1517 to the present; reserves colln; Dir ELISABETH LEPRÊTRE.

> **Musée du Prieuré de Graville:** Rue Elisée Reclus, 76600 Le Havre; tel. 2-35-24-51-00; fax 2-35-26-76-69; e-mail musees.histoire@ville-lehavre.fr; internet www.ville-lehavre.fr; f. 1926; sculpture from the 12th to 18th century; models of old houses; Dir ELIZABETH LEPRÊTRE.

Le Mans

Musée Automobile de la Sarthe: Circuit des 24 Heures du Mans, BP 29254, 72009 Le Mans Cedex 1; tel. 2-43-72-72-24; fax 2-43-85-38-96; e-mail musee.automobile.lemans@wanadoo.fr; internet www.sarthe.com/sport/museeauto.htm; f. 1961; cars, cycles and motorcycles; Dir FRANCIS PIQUERA.

Musée de la Reine Bérengère: 9–13 rue de la Reine Bérengère, 72000 Le Mans; tel. 2-43-47-38-51; fax 2-43-47-49-93; e-mail musees@ville-lemans.fr; 16th-century architecture, folklore, ceramics, local history; Curator FRANÇOISE CHASERANT.

Musée de Tessé: 2 ave de Paderborn, 72000 Le Mans; tel. 2-43-47-38-51; fax 2-43-47-49-93; fine arts, paintings and sculpture, archaeology, Egyptology; Curator FRANÇOISE CHASERANT.

Les Eyzies de Tayac

Musée National de Préhistoire: 1 rue du Musee, BP 7, 24620 Les Eyzies de Tayac; tel. (5) 53-06-45-45; fax (5) 53-06-45-55; e-mail reservation.prehistoire@culture.gouv.fr; internet www.musee-prehistoire-eyzies.fr; f. 2004; 18,000 exhibited objects, incl. prehistoric carvings; permanent exhibitions on human evolution and the prehistoric people of the Périgord region; Dir JEAN-JACQUES CLEYET-MERLE.

Lille

Palais des Beaux-Arts de Lille (Museum of Fine Arts of Lille): 18 bis rue de Valmy, 59000 Lille; tel. 3-20-06-78-00; fax 3-20-06-78-15; e-mail cvilliers@mairie-lille.fr; internet www.pba-lille.fr; f. 1801, closed for renovation in 2006; paintings of Flemish, Italian, Spanish, German, French and Dutch Schools; exceptional colln of drawings; sculpture, ceramics and archaeological exhibits; colln of over 4,000 Art Brut pieces; Chief Curator ALAIN TAPIÉ.

Limoges

Musée Municipal de l'Evêché: Place de la Cathédrale, 87000 Limoges; tel. 5-55-45-98-10; fax 5-55-34-44-14; e-mail museveche@ville-limoges.fr; internet www.ville-limoges.fr; f. 1912; paintings, drawings, engravings, sculptures, Limoges enamels, metalwork; Egyptian colln; archaeological and lapidary colln; enamels research centre; library of 7,000 vols; Curator VÉRONIQUE NOTIN.

Musée National Adrien Dubouché: Place Winston Churchill, 87000 Limoges; tel. 5-55-33-08-50; fax 5-55-33-08-55; e-mail contact.musee-adriendubouche@culture.gouv.fr; internet www.musee-adriendubouche.fr; f. 1900; ceramics and glass; Curator CHANTAL MESLIN-PERRIER.

Lyons

Musée des Beaux-Arts: 20 place des Terreaux, 69001 Lyons; tel. 4-72-10-17-40; fax 4-78-28-12-45; internet www.mba-lyon.fr; f. 1801 and housed in the former Benedictine Abbey of the Dames de Saint-Pierre, built in 1659; the important collection contains paintings of French, Flemish, Dutch, Italian and Spanish Schools, and sections devoted to local painters, modern art, and murals by Puvis de Chavannes; ancient, medieval and modern sculpture; French, Italian, Oriental and Hispano-Moorish ceramics; drawings, prints, furniture, numismatic collection; Egyptian, Greek, Roman and Near and Middle Eastern antiquities; library of 50,000 vols; Chief Curator SYLVIE RAMOND; publs *Cahiers du Musée des Beaux-Arts de Lyon* (1 a year), illustrated guides.

Magny-les-Hameaux

Musée National de Port-Royal des Champs: Route des Granges, 78114 Magny-les-Hameaux; tel. 1-39-30-72-72; fax 1-30-64-79-55; e-mail musee.port-royal@culture.gouv.fr; internet www.port-royal-des-champs.eu; f. 1952; history of Port-Royal and Jansenism; ruins of the Abbey of Port-Royale; presented in the house of 'Petites Ecoles' where Racine studied; Curator PHILIPPE LUEZ.

Maisons-Laffitte

Château de Maisons-Laffitte: 78600 Maisons-Laffitte; tel. 1-39-62-01-49; fax 1-39-12-34-37; internet www.maisonslaffitte.net; château dates from 1642; contains paintings, sculptures, tapestries; Curator FLORENCE DE LA RONCIÈRE.

Marseilles

Musée d'Archéologie Méditerranéenne: 2 rue de la Charité, 13002 Marseilles; tel. 4-91-14-58-80; fax 4-91-14-58-81; internet www.mairie-marseille.fr/vivre/culture/musees/archeo.htm; f. 1863; Egyptian, Greek, Cypriot, Celto-Ligurian, Etruscan, Roman and Gallo-Roman antiquities; library of 4,500 vols; Curators ANNIE PHILIPPON, BRIGITTE LESCURE.

Affiliated Museum:

Musée des Docks Romains: 28 place Vivaux, 13002 Marseilles; tel. 4-91-91-24-62; internet www.culture.gouv.fr/culture/archeosm/fr/fr-act-mus4.htm; f. 1963; ancient commerce; exhibits include amphorae, ingots and marine archaeology; Curator AGNÈS DURAND.

Musée des Beaux-Arts: Palais Longchamp, Aile Gauche, 7 rue Edouard Stephan, 13004 Marseilles; tel. 4-91-14-59-30; fax 4-91-14-59-31; e-mail dgac-musee-beauxarts@mairie-marseille.fr; internet www.mairie-marseille.fr/vivre/culture/musees/boart.htm; f. 1802; paintings (French, Italian, Flemish and German schools); murals by French artists, including Courbet, Corot, Daubigny, Millet, Daumier and Puvis de Chavannes; collection of paintings and sculptures by Puget; sculptures by Daumier and Rodin; Curator MARIE-PAULE VIAL.

Musée Cantini: 19 rue Grignan, 13006 Marseilles; tel. 4-91-54-77-75; fax 4-91-55-03-61; internet www.mairie-marseille.fr/vivre/culture/musees/cantini.htm; f. 1936; modern art (1900–60); library of 20,000 vols on 20th-century art; Curators NICOLAS CENDO, OLIVIER COUSINOU.

Musée de la Marine et de l'Economie de Marseille: Chambre de Commerce et d'Industrie Marseille-Provence, Palais de la Bourse, La Canebière, BP 21856, 13221 Marseilles Cedex 1; tel. 4-91-39-33-21; fax 4-91-39-56-15; e-mail patrick.boulanger@ccimp.com; internet www.ccimp.com/patrimoine; f. 1932; history of Marseilles and Mediterranean shipping; models of ships, paintings, drawings, plans; 25,000 tape recordings; Nossof, Cantelar and Grimard collns (history of steam ships); Archivist, Chief of Cultural Heritage Dept PATRICK BOULANGER.

Metz

Metz, Musées de La Cour d'Or: 2 rue du Haut Poirier, 57000 Metz; tel. 3-87-68-25-00; fax 3-87-36-51-14; e-mail musees@ca2m.com; internet www.mairie-metz.fr:8080; f. 1839; prehistory, protohistory, arts and popular traditions of northern Lorraine, and natural history collections (not open to public); architecture; fine arts (since 15th century); archaeology and history; military collns (not open to public); library of 5,000 vols, 100 periodicals; Dir CLAUDE VALENTIN.

Montpellier

Musée Atger: Faculté de Médecine, 2 rue de l'Ecole de Médecine, 34000 Montpellier; tel. 4-67-41-76-30; fax 4-67-41-76-39; internet www.biu-montpe1lier.fr; f. 1813; drawings and paintings of French, Italian and Flemish schools, 16th–18th centuries (Fragonard, Natoire, Tiepolo); Curator H. LORBLANCHET.

Musée Fabre: 13 rue Montpelliéret, 34000 Montpellier; tel. 4-67-14-83-00; fax 4-67-66-09-20; e-mail musee.fabre@montpellier-agglo.com; internet museefabre.montpellier-agglo.com; f. 1825 by the painter François-Xavier Fabre; paintings of French (Greuze, Delacroix, Courbet, Bazille, Géricault), Italian, Spanish, Dutch and Flemish Schools; drawings, sculpture (Houdon), furniture, tapestries, porcelain, silver; Dir MICHEL HILAIRE.

Mulhouse

Cité de l'Automobile—Musée National, Collection Schlumpf: 192 ave de Colmar, BP 1096, 68051 Mulhouse; tel. 3-89-33-23-23; fax 3-89-32-08-09; internet www.collection-schlumpf.com/schlumpf; f. 1982; history of the motor car since 1878; 424 vehicles on display, incl. an important colln of Bugattis; library of 4,500 vols; Dir EMANUEL BACQUET.

Musée de l'Impression sur Etoffes: 14 rue Jean-Jacques Henner, BP 1468, 68072 Mulhouse; tel. 3-89-46-83-00; fax 3-89-46-83-10; e-mail accueil@musee-impression.com; internet www.musee-impression.com; f. 1955; 18th–20th century printed textiles; Curator JAQUELINE JACQUÉ; publ. *L'Imprimé* (2 a year).

Nancray

Musée de Plein Air des Maisons Comtoises: 25360 Nancray; tel. 3-81-55-29-77; fax 3-81-55-23-97; e-mail musee@maisons-comtoises.org; internet www.maisons-comtoises.org; f. 1984; folklore of Franche-Comté; 60,000 illustrations of rural architecture; Dir CATHERINE LOUVRIER; publs *Barbizier*, *Revue Régionale d'Ethnologie Comtoise* (1 a year).

Nancy

Musée des Beaux-Arts: Place Stanislas, 54000 Nancy; tel. 3-83-85-30-72; fax 3-83-85-30-76; e-mail mbanancy@mairie-nancy.fr; internet www.mairie-nancy.fr; f. 1793; paintings, sculpture, drawings, prints and glass from 15th–20th century; temporary exhibitions; Curator BLANDINE CHAVANNE.

Nantes

Musée des Beaux-Arts: 10 rue Georges-Clemenceau, 44000 Nantes; tel. 2-51-17-45-00; fax 2-51-17-45-16; e-mail contact@nantes.fr; internet www.nantes.fr/culture/musees-nantais/musee-des-beaux-arts.html; f. 1800; 2,200 paintings; library of 10,000 vols; Curator JEAN AUBERT.

Nice

Direction des Musées de Nice: Palais Masséna, 65 rue de France, 06050 Nice Cedex 1; tel. 4-93-88-11-34; fax 4-93-82-39-79; f. 1935; Dir JEAN FRANÇOIS MOZZICONACCI.

Comprises:

Galerie de la Marine: 59 quai des Etats-Unis, 06300 Nice; tel. 4-93-62-37-11; Curator ANNE-MARIE VILLERI.

Galerie des Ponchettes: 77 quai des Etats-Unis, 06300 Nice; tel. 4-93-62-31-24; Curator ANNE-MARIE VILLERI.

Musée d'Archéologie: 160 Ave des Arènes de Cimiez, 06000 Nice; tel. 4-93-81-59-57; fax 4-93-81-08-00; f. 1989; Curator Mlle D. MOUCHOT.

Musée d'Art et d'Histoire: Palais Masséna, 65 rue de France, 06050 Nice Cedex 1; tel. 4-93-88-11-34; fax 4-93-88-11-34; f. 1921; art and history; Dir LUC THEVENON.

Musée d'Art Moderne et d'Art Contemporain: Promenade des Arts, 06300 Nice; tel. 4-93-62-61-62; fax 4-93-13-09-01; e-mail mamac@ville-nice.fr; internet www.mamac-nice.org; f. 1990; colln 'Nice à partir des années 60'; nouveaux réalistes, pop art, fluxus, colour field painting; Dir GILBERT PERLEIN.

Musée des Beaux-Arts: 33 ave des Baumettes, 06000 Nice; tel. 4-93-44-50-72; fax 4-93-97-67-07; internet www.musee-beaux-arts-nice.org; f. 1928; 18th- and 19th-century painting and sculpture, (Impressionists, Van Dongen); works of Jules Chéret; Dir BÉATRICE DEBRABANDÈRE-DESCAMPS.

Muséum d'Histoire Naturelle: 60 bis blvd Risso, 06300 Nice; tel. 4-97-13-46-80;

fax 4-97-13-46-85; f. 1823; Curator ALAIN BIDAR.

Musée International d'Art Naïf Anatole Jakovsky: Château Ste Hélène, ave Val-Marie, 06200 Nice; tel. 4-93-71-78-33; fax 4-93-72-34-10; f. 1982; Dir ANNE DEVROYE-STILZ.

Musée Matisse: 164 ave des Arènes de Cimiez, 06000 Nice; tel. 4-93-81-08-08; fax 4-93-53-00-22; e-mail matisse@ nice-coteazur.org; internet www .musee-matisse-nice.org; f. 1963; collns of paintings and sculptures by Henri Matisse; Curator MARIE-THÉRÈSE PULVÉNIS DE SELIGNY.

Musée Naval: Tour Bellanda, Colline du Château, 06300 Nice; tel. 4-93-80-47-61; Curator JEAN WURSTHORN.

Musée de Paléontologie–Terra Amata: 25 blvd Carnot, 06300 Nice; tel. 4-93-55-59-93; fax 4-93-89-91-31; f. 1976; Curator Mme M. GOUDET.

Musée du Vieux-Logis: 59 ave Saint Barthélémy, 06100 Nice; tel. 4-93-84-44-74; f. 1937; medieval furniture and sculpture; Curator LUC THEVENON.

Palais Lascaris: 15 rue Droite, 06300 Nice; tel. 4-93-62-72-40; fax 4-93-92-04-19; f. 1970; 17th- and 18th-century frescoes, furniture and art; Curator CH. ASTRO.

Musée National Message Biblique Marc Chagall: Ave du Dr Ménard, 06000 Nice; tel. 4-93-53-87-20; fax 4-93-53-87-39; e-mail museecie@rmn.fr; internet www .musee-chagall.fr; f. 1973; permanent collection of the artist's biblical works; temporary exhibitions; library of 3,000 vols; Curator JEAN LACAMBRE.

Nîmes

Musée Archéologique: 13 blvd Amiral-Courbet, 30000 Nîmes; tel. 4-66-76-74-80; fax 4-66-76-74-94; internet musees.nimes.fr; f. 1823; protohistoric and Gallic and Roman archaeology; library of 6,000 vols; Curator DOMINIQUE DARDE.

Carré d'Art–Musée d'Art Contemporain: pl. de la Maison Carrée, 30000 Nîmes Cedex 1; tel. 4-66-76-35-70; fax 4-66-76-35-85; e-mail info@carreartmusee.com; internet carreartmusee.nimes.fr; f. 1993; Dir FRANÇOISE COHEN.

Musée d'Histoire Naturelle: 13 blvd Amiral-Courbet, 30033 Nîmes Cedex 9; tel. 4-66-76-73-45; fax 4-66-76-73-46; e-mail museum@ville-nimes.fr; internet musees .nimes.fr; f. 1892; library of 3,000 vols; Dir LUC GOMEL.

Musée du Vieux Nîmes: Place aux Herbes, 30000 Nîmes Cedex; tel. 4-66-76-73-70; fax 4-66-76-73-71; e-mail musee.vieux-nimes@ ville-nimes.fr; internet musees.nimes.fr; f. 1921; local history, folklore and traditional crafts; Curator MARTINE NOUGARÈDE.

Orléans

Musée des Beaux-Arts: 1 rue Fernand Rabier, 45000 Orléans; tel. 2-38-79-21-55; fax 2-38-79-20-08; e-mail vgalliot-rateau@ ville-orleans.fr; internet www.ville-orleans .fr; f. 1823; sculpture since 16th century; French, Flemish, Italian, Dutch, German and Spanish paintings and pastels (esp. of 18th century); Max Jacob and Gaudier-Brzeska room; library of 30,000 vols; Curator and Dir ISABELLE KLINKA-BALLESTEROS.

Attached Museum:

Musée Historique et Archéologique de l'Orléanais: Hôtel Cabu, Place Abbé Desnoyers, 45000 Orléans; tel. (2) 38-79-21-55; fax (2) 38-79-20-08; e-mail vgalliot-rateau@ ville-orleans.fr; internet www.ville-orleans .fr; f. 1855; Gallo-Roman bronzes from

Neuvy-en-Sullias; 17th- to 19th-century Orléans arts and crafts; the old port and river traffic; glassware and ceramics; Renaissance sculpture; room devoted to Joan of Arc; Curator ISABELLE KLINKA-BALLESTEROS; Muséum Asst CATHERINE GORGET.

Paris

Centre des Monuments Nationaux (Monum): Hôtel Béthune-Sully, 62 rue Saint-Antoine, 75004 Paris; tel. 1-44-61-21-54; fax 1-44-61-20-36; e-mail courrier@ monuments-nat.fr; internet www.monum.fr; Dir CHRISTOPHE VALLET.

Cité des Sciences et de l'Industrie: 30 ave Corentin Cariou, 75930 Paris Cedex 19; tel. 1-40-05-70-00; fax 1-40-05-73-44; internet www.cite-sciences.fr; f. 1986; located in La Villette complex; permanent exhibitions: the universe, the earth, the environment, space, life, communication, etc.; multimedia public library (300,000 vols, 2,700 periodicals, 4,000 films, 1,300 educational software discs), history of science multimedia library, the Louis Braille room for the visually handicapped, Science Newsroom; Pres. GÉRARD THÉRY.

Galerie Nationale du Jeu de Paume: 1 place de la Concorde, 75008 Paris; tel. 1-47-03-12-50; fax 1-47-03-12-51; internet www .jeudepaume.org; re-f. 1991; devoted to temporary exhibitions of contemporary art; Dir DANIEL ABADIE.

Galeries Nationales du Panthéon Bouddhique: 19 ave d'Iéna, 75116 Paris; tel. 1-40-73-88-00; Chinese and Japanese art; Curator JEAN-FRANÇOIS JARRIGE.

Les Arts Décoratifs: 107 rue de Rivoli, 75001 Paris; tel. 1-44-55-57-50; fax 1-44-55-57-84; e-mail webmaster@lesartsdecoratifs .fr; internet www.lesartsdecoratifs.fr; f. 1864; library of 120,000 vols, 2,000 periodicals, 40,000 sale catalogues since 18th century; Pres. HÉLÈNE DAVID-WEILL; Gen. Man. SOPHIE DURRLEMAN; Dir of Museums BÉATRICE SALMON.

Affiliated Museums:

Musée des Arts Décoratifs: Les Arts Décoratifs, 107 rue de Rivoli, 75001 Paris; tel. 1-44-55-57-50; fax 1-44-55-57-84; e-mail webmaster@lesartsdecoratifs.fr; internet www.lesartsdecoratifs.fr; f. 1883; colln from Middle Ages to the present: woodwork, sculpture, tapestries, textiles, jewels, ceramics, furniture, painting, gold and silver work, glass; library of 100,000 vols, 1,500 periodicals; Dir BÉATRICE SALMON.

Musée de la Mode et du Textile: Les Arts Décoratifs, 107 rue de Rivoli, 75001 Paris; tel. 1-44-55-57-50; fax 1-44-55-57-84; e-mail webmaster@lesartsdecoratifs.fr; internet www.lesartsdecoratifs.fr; f. 1985; fashion, textiles and accessories; Dir BÉATRICE SALMON.

Musée Nissim de Camondo: Les Arts Décoratifs, 63 rue de Monceau, 75008 Paris; tel. 1-53-89-06-40; fax 1-53-89-06-42; e-mail webmaster@lesartsdecoratifs.fr; internet www.lesartsdecoratifs.fr; bequeathed by Count Moïse de Camondo, who collected unique 18th-century objects in his Hôtel Parc Monceau; Dir BÉATRICE SALMON; Chief Curator SYLVIE LEGRAND-ROSSI.

Musée de la Publicité: Les Arts Décoratifs, 107 rue de Rivoli, 75001 Paris; tel. 1-44-55-57-50; fax 1-44-55-57-84; e-mail webmaster@lesartsdecoratifs.fr; internet www.lesartsdecoratifs.fr; non-permanent exhibitions of posters, television, film and radio commercials; interactive multimedia library; Dir BÉATRICE SALMON.

Maison de Balzac: 47 rue Raynouard, 75016 Paris; tel. 1-55-74-41-80; fax 1-45-25-19-22; internet www.balzac.paris.fr; f. 1960; museum and library of 15,000 books and periodicals; documents relating to life and work of Honoré de Balzac; first edns and autographed letters; comprehensive range of work from the romantic period; Curator YVES GAGNEUX.

Maison de Victor Hugo: 6 place des Vosges, 75004 Paris; tel. 1-42-72-10-16; fax 1-42-72-06-64; e-mail maisonsvictorhugo@ paris.fr; internet www.musee.hugo.paris.fr; f. 1903; personal belongings, correspondence, first editions, drawings by Victor Hugo; library of 10,000 vols, 6,000 pamphlets; Curator DANIELLE MOLINARI.

Musée Astronomique de l'Observatoire de Paris: 61 ave de l'Observatoire, 75014 Paris; f. 1667; astronomical instruments of the 16th, 17th, 18th and 19th centuries; statues and pictures of celebrated astronomers.

Musée Carnavalet—Histoire de Paris: 23 rue de Sévigné, 75003 Paris; tel. 1-44-59-58-58; fax 1-44-59-58-11; internet www .carnavalet.paris.fr; f. 1880; Paris and its history from prehistoric times; depts of archaeology, graphic arts, furniture, numismatics, painting, architectural models, sculpture; Chief Curator JEAN-MARC LÉRI.

Musée Cernuschi: 7 ave Vélasquez, 75008 Paris; tel. 1-53-96-21-50; fax 1-53-96-21-96; internet www.paris.fr/musees/cernuschi; f. 1896; Chinese art; Dir CHRISTINE SHIMIZU.

Musée Cognacq-Jay: 8 rue Elzévir, 75003 Paris; tel. 1-40-27-07-21; fax 1-40-27-89-44; internet www.paris.fr/musees/cognacq_jay; f. 1929; 18th-century works of art, French and English paintings, pastels, sculptures, porcelain, furniture, etc.; Curator JOSE DE LOS LLANOS.

Musée d'Art Moderne de la Ville de Paris: 9 rue Gaston de Saint-Paul, 75116 Paris; located at: 11 ave du Président Wilson, 75116 Paris; tel. 1-53-67-40-00; fax 1-47-23-35-98; internet www.mam.paris.fr; f. 1961; modern and contemporary art; Curator FABRICE HERGOTT.

Musée d'Ennery: 59 ave Foch, 75116 Paris; tel. 1-45-53-57-96; fax 1-45-05-02-66; f. 1903; 17th- to 19th-century Far East decorative arts; closed for renovation; Curator JEAN-FRANÇOIS JARRIGE.

Musée d'Histoire Contemporaine: Hôtel National des Invalides, 129 rue de Grenelle, 75007 Paris; tel. 1-44-42-42-44; fax 1-44-18-93-84; e-mail mhc@bdic.fr; internet www .bdic.fr/page.php?id_page=125; f. 1914; attached to Bibliothèque de Documentation Internationale Contemporaine (q.v.); 400,000 documents (paintings, engravings, posters, cartoons, etc.); 800,000 photographs and postcards; Curator LAURENT GERVEREAU.

Musée d'Orsay: 62 rue de Lille, 75343 Paris; tel. 1-40-49-48-00; fax 1-45-44-63-82; internet www.musee-orsay.fr; f. 1986; works from the second half of the 19th century and early 20th century: paintings and pastels, sculptures, art objects, photographs, also plans, sketches, etc.; audiovisual information, database, cultural service, exhibitions and dossier-exhibitions, cinema, lectures, concerts; Pres. SERGE LEMOINE.

Musée de l'Air et de l'Espace: BP 173, Aéroport du Bourget, 4 93352 Le Bourget Cedex; tel. 1-49-92-71-99; fax 1-49-92-70-95; internet www.mae.org; f. 1919; aeronautics, representative colln of aircraft; library of 40,000 vols; Dir-Gen. GERARD FELDZER; publ. *Pégase* (4 a year).

Musée de l'Armée: Hôtel des Invalides, 129 rue de Grenelle, 75007 Paris; tel. 1-44-42-38-

77; fax 1-44-42-38-44; e-mail accueil-ma@
invalides.org; internet www.invalides.org; f.
1905; collections of artillery, arms, armour,
uniforms, flags; history of French Army from
its origin to present day; Napoleon's tomb;
Second World War; library of 50,000 vols,
60,000 prints, 74,400 photographs; Dir B.
DEVAUX; publ. *Revue de la Société des Amis
du Musée de l'Armée* (2 a year).

Musée de l'Histoire de France: Centre
historique des Archives nationales, 60 rue
des Francs-Bourgeois, 75141 Paris Cedex 03;
tel. 1-40-27-60-96; fax 1-40-27-66-45; e-mail
infomusee.archivesnationales@culture.gouv
.fr; f. 1867; frequent exhibitions showing
original documents from the Nat. Archives
tracing the principal events in the history of
France; also historical objects and iconography; Dir ISABELLE NEUSCHWANDER; Curator
PIERRE FOURNIÉ.

Musée de l'Homme: Palais de Chaillot,
place du Trocadéro, 75116 Paris; tel. 1-44-
05-72-03; fax 1-44-05-72-12; e-mail bmhweb@
mnhn.fr; internet www.mnhn.fr/mnhn/bmh;
f. 1878; library of 400,000 vols, 5,000 periodicals, 1,000 microfiches; ethnography,
anthropology, prehistory; attached to the
Muséum National d'Histoire Naturelle
(*q.v.*); also a research and education centre;
Profs BERNARD DUPAIGNE, ANDRÉ LANGANEY,
HENRY DE LUMLEY.

Musée de l'Orangerie: Jardin des Tui-
leries, 75001 Paris; tel. 1-44-50-43-00; fax 1-
44-50-43-30; e-mail musee.orangerie@culture
.gouv.fr; internet www.musee-orangerie.fr; f.
1927; permanent exhibition of the 'Nym-
phéas' (Water Lilies) murals by Claude
Monet, and Jean Walter et Paul Guillaume
colln (Cézanne, Renoir, Rousseau, Picasso,
Matisse, Derain, Modigliani, Soutine,
Utrillo); Dir EMMANUEL BRÉON.

Musée de la Marine: Palais de Chaillot, 17
place du Trocadéro, 75116 Paris; tel. 1-53-65-
69-69 ext. 120; fax 1-53-65-69-42; internet
www.musee-marine.fr; f. 1827; colln of
models and paintings of the navy; oceanographic research; library: 50,000 documents,
190,000 photographs; Dir Rear-Adm.
GEORGES PRUD'HOMME; publs *Neptunia* (4 a
year), catalogues.

Musée de la Monnaie: Monnaie de Paris,
11 quai de Conti, 75270 Paris Cedex 06; tel.
1-40-46-55-60-10; fax 1-40-46-57-09; e-mail
musee@monnaiedeparis.fr; internet www
.monnaiedeparis.fr; f. 1771; closed since July
2010; visits to manufacturers' workshops
closed; colls of coins, medals, drawings,
paintings, old machines, engravings and
stained glass windows; Dir BENOIT MONTAR-
IOL.

Musée de la Poste: 34 blvd de Vaugirard,
75015 Paris; tel. 1-42-79-24-24; fax 1-42-79-
24-00; e-mail reservation.dnmp @laposte.fr;
internet www.ladressemuseedelaposte.fr; f.
1971; colln incl. material on historic postal
services and transport; Curator CHAPPE.

Musée des Arts et Métiers: 60 rue Réau-
mur, 75003 Paris; 292 rue St Martin, 75141
Paris Cedex 03; tel. 1-53-01-82-00; fax 1-53-
01-82-01; e-mail musee@cnam.fr; internet
www.arts-et-metiers.net; f. 1794; evolution of
industrial technology from 16th century to
the present; Dir DANIEL THOULOUZE.

Musée des Monuments Français: Palais
de Chaillot, 1 place du Trocadéro, 75116
Paris; tel. 1-44-05-39-10; fax 1-47-55-40-13;
internet www.citechaillot.fr/musee.php; f.
1882; casts of portions of monuments and
sculptures from beginning of Christianity to
20th century; architectural models; library of
10,000 works on history of art, 200,000
photographs, colln of scale reproductions of
murals of the Middle Ages and materials

connected with building and decoration; Dir
GUY COGEVAL; publ. *Guides.*

Musée des Plans-Reliefs: Hôtel National
des Invalides, 75007 Paris; tel. 1-45-51-95-05;
fax 1-47-05-11-07; internet
.museedesplansreliefs.culture.fr; f. 1668; Dir
MAX POLONOVSKI.

Musée du Louvre: 75058 Paris Cedex 01;
tel. 1-40-20-50-50; fax 1-40-20-54-42; e-mail
info@louvre.fr; internet www.louvre.fr; f.
1793; Gen.-Dir HENRI LOYRETTE; depts and
curators: Oriental antiquities (ANNIE CAU-
BET), Egyptian antiquities (CHRISTIANE ZIEG-
LER), Greek, Etruscan and Roman antiquities
(ALAIN PASQUIER), Islamic art (FRANÇIS
RICHARD), sculpture (JEAN-RENÉ GABORIT),
objets d'art (DANIEL ALCOUFFE), paintings
(VINCENT POMAREDE), drawings and prints
(FRANÇOISE VIATTE).

Musée du Luxembourg: 19 rue de Vaugirard, 75006 Paris; tel. 1-43-54-87-71; fax 1-43-
25-20-33; e-mail info@museeduluxembourg
.fr; internet www.museeduluxembourg.fr; f.
1750; hosts temporary exhibitions, according
to a programme decided by the Min. of
Culture and Communications and the Senate; Pres. of Senate CHRISTIAN PONCELET.

Musée du Petit Palais: 5 ave Dutuit, 75008
Paris; Ave Winston Churchill, 75008 Paris;
tel. 1-53-43-40-00; fax 1-53-43-40-52; internet
petitpalais.paris.fr; f. 1902; paintings, sculptures and works of art from antiquity to
1925; organizes visits, concerts, lectures,
literary events, screenings, shows; Dir
GILLES CHAZAL.

**Musée Galliera Musée de la Mode de la
Ville de Paris:** 10 ave Pierre Ier de Serbie,
75116 Paris; tel. 1-56-52-86-46; fax 1-47-23-
38-37; e-mail bibliodoc.galliera@paris.fr;
internet www.galliera.paris.fr; f. 1977; temporary exhibitions of French costumes and
accessories from 1725 to the present day;
library of 9,000 vols; Dir OLIVIER SAILLARD;
Librarian DOMINIQUE REVELLINO.

Musée Gustave Moreau: 14 rue de la
Rochefoucauld, 75009 Paris; tel. 1-48-74-38-
50; fax 1-48-74-18-71; e-mail info@
musee-moreau.fr; internet www
.musee-moreau.fr; f. 1903 from a bequest by
the painter Gustave Moreau of his house and
contents, including paintings, watercolours,
sketches, wax sculptures and designs; Curator GENEVIÈVE LACAMBRE.

Musée Jacquemart-André: 158 blvd
Haussmann, 75008 Paris; tel. 1-45-62-11-59;
fax 1-45-62-16-36; e-mail message@
musee-jacquemart-andre.com; internet www
.musee-jacquemart-andre.com; f. 1912; painting, sculpture, ceramics, tapestry and furniture from Renaissance to 18th century; Dir
ALAIN SCHIÉDÉ.

Musée Marmottan: 2 rue Louis Boilly,
75016 Paris; tel. 1-44-96-50-33; fax 1-40-50-
65-84; e-mail marmottan@marmottan.com;
internet www.marmottan.com; f. 1932;
Primitives, Renaissance, Empire and
Impressionist; Wildenstein Colln of medieval miniatures; permanent exhibition
'Monet et ses Amis'; affiliated to the Académie des Beaux-Arts-Fondation Rouart; Dir
JEAN-MARIE GRANIER.

Musée National d'Art Moderne: 75191
Paris Cedex 04; tel. 1-44-78-12-33; internet
www.centrepompidou.fr; attached to Centre
National d'Art et de Culture Georges-Pompidou; painting since beginning of 20th century, sculpture, architecture, design, new
media, drawings, photographs, art films;
Dir ALFRED PACQUEMENT.

**Musée National de la Légion d'Honneur
et des Ordres de Chevalerie:** Hôtel de
Salm, 2 rue de la Légion d'Honneur, 75007
Paris; tel. 1-40-62-84-25; e-mail musee.gclh@

free.fr; internet www.legiondhonneur.fr; f.
1925; contains histories of National Orders
from the Middle Ages until the present and
Awards of all countries: unique collection of
decorations, costumes, arms, documents,
etc.; also collection and documents relating
to Napoleon I; Centre de Documentation
International de l'Histoire des Ordres et des
Décorations; Dir-Curator ANNE DE CHEFDE-
BIEN.

**Musée National des Arts Asiatiques
Guimet:** 6 place d'Iéna, 75116 Paris; tel. 1-
56-52-53-00; fax 1-56-52-53-54; internet www
.guimet.fr; f. 1889; Asiatic Dept of Nat.
Museums; library of 100,000 vols; art,
archaeology, religions, history and music of
India, Central Asia, Tibet, Afghanistan,
China, Korea and Japan, Cambodia, Thai-
land and Indonesia; Chief Curator JACQUES
GIES; Librarian FRANCIS MACOUIN; publs
Annales, Arts Asiatiques.

**Musée National des Arts d'Afrique et
d'Océanie:** 293 ave Daumesnil, 75012 Paris;
tel. 1-44-74-84-80; f. 1931 as Musée des
Colonies, 1935 Musée de la France d'Outre-
Mer, present name 1960; exhibits from
Maghreb, Africa and the Pacific Islands;
tropical aquarium; temporary exhibitions;
library: c. 5,000 vols, 160 periodicals; Dir
GERMAIN VIATTE.

**Musée National des Arts et Traditions
Populaires:** 6 ave du Mahatma Gandhi,
75116 Paris; tel. 1-44-17-60-00; fax 1-44-17-
60-60; f. 1937; 142,000 objects; library:
90,000 books, 2,000 periodicals; 281,000
photographic documents, 70,000 tape
records; Curator MICHEL COLARDELLE; publs
*Architecture rurale française, Mobilier tradi-
tionnel français, Récits et contes populaires,
Archives d'Ethnologie Française, Guides Ethnologiques, Catalogues des Expositions, Ethnologie française* (4 a year).

**Musée National du Moyen Âge/Musée de
Cluny:** 6 pl. Paul Painlevé, 75005 Paris; tel.
1-53-73-78-00; fax 1-43-25-85-27; e-mail
contact.musee-moyenage@culture.gouv.fr;
internet www.musee-moyenage.fr; f. 1843;
everyday life and fine and decorative arts of
the Middle Ages; medieval art; sculptures,
illuminated MSS, stained-glass panels, goldsmith work, furniture and tapestries; Lady
and the Unicorn tapestries set; Dir ELISA-
BETH DELAHAYE.

Musée Picasso: 5 rue de Thorigny, 75003
Paris; tel. 1-42-71-25-21; fax 1-48-04-75-46;
internet www.musee-picasso.fr; f. 1985 from
a colln begun in 1979; traces the evolution of
Picasso's art; 251 paintings, 160 sculptures,
107 ceramics, 1,500 drawings and engravings; library: c. 2,000 vols on Picasso and his
world; Dir ANNE BALDASSARI; Chief Curator
GÉRARD RÉGNIER; publs catalogues, guides.

Musée Rodin: Hôtel Biron, 79 rue de
Varenne, 75007 Paris; tel. 1-44-18-61-10;
fax 1-44-51-17-52; internet www
.musee-rodin.fr; f. 1919; sculpture and drawings by Rodin and objects from his collns;
annexe in Meudon; Dir DOMINIQUE VIÉVILLE.

Muséum National d'Histoire Naturelle:
see under State Colleges and Institutes.

Palais de la Découverte: ave Franklin D.
Roosevelt, 75008 Paris; tel. 1-56-43-20-21;
fax 1-56-43-20-29; internet www
.palais-decouverte.fr; f. 1937 as a scientific
centre for the popularization of science;
experiments explained to the public; depts
of mathematics, astronomy, physics, chemistry, biology, medicine, earth sciences; also
includes a Planetarium and cinema; library
of 7,000 vols; Dir JACK GUICHARD; publs
Revue, Monographies.

Palais du Cinéma: Palais de Tokyo, 24 rue
Hamelin, 75116 Paris; tel. 1-45-53-74-74; fax

1-45-53-74-76; exhibitions concerning motion pictures; motion picture theatres; library and film archive; Dir XAVIER NORTH.

Pavillon de l'Arsenal: 21 blvd Morland, 75004 Paris; tel. 1-42-76-33-97; fax 1-42-76-26-32; internet www.pavillon-arsenal.com; f. 1988; information and documentation centre on urban planning and architecture; permanent exhibition on Paris; temporary exhibitions, photo library, educational facilities, etc.; Dir Mme DOMINIQUE ALBA; publ. catalogues.

Pavillon des Arts: Les Halles—Porte Rambuteau—Terrasse Lautréamont, 101 rue Rambuteau, 75001 Paris; tel. 1-42-33-82-50; fax 1-40-28-93-22; f. 1983; municipal art gallery for temporary exhibitions; Dir BÉATRICE RIOTTOT EL-HABIB.

Pau

Musée Bernadotte: 8 rue Tran, 64000 Pau; tel. 5-59-27-48-42; internet musee.ville-pau .fr/infospratiques/liens/bernadotte; f. 1935; pictures and documents tracing the career of Jean Baptiste Bernadotte, Marshal under Napoleon, later King of Sweden; Swedish pictures; Curator PH. COMTE; publ. *Bulletin* (1 a year).

Musée des Beaux-Arts: rue Mathieu Lalanne, 64000 Pau; tel. 5-59-27-33-02; fax 5-59-98-70-10; e-mail museedesbeauxarts .pau@laposte.net; internet musee.ville-pau .fr; f. 1864; pictures from French, Flemish, Dutch, English, Italian and Spanish schools; contemporary artists; sculptures, engravings and drawings; numismatic collections; Curator GUILLAUME AMBROISE.

Musée National du Château de Pau: 64000 Pau; tel. 5-59-82-38-02; fax 5-59-82-38-18; e-mail olivier.pouvreau@culture.gouv .fr; internet www.musee-chateau-pau.fr; f. 1927; 16th- and 17th-century colln of tapestries; state apartments of Louis-Philippe I and Napoleon III; exhibition on the reign of King Henry IV; engravings, drawings; library and research facility (Centre Jacques de Laprade) for students of history, literature and history of art; Curator PAUL MIRONNEAU; publ. *Bulletin* (4 a year).

Musée Régional Béarnais: 64000 Pau; tel. 5-59-27-07-36; a colln relating to the Bearnese country.

Perpignan

Casa Pairal, Musée Catalan des Arts et Traditions Populaires: Mairie de Perpignan, BP 931, 66931 Perpignan Cedex; located at: Le Castillet, Place de Verdun, 66000 Perpignan; tel. 4-68-35-42-05; fax 4-68-66-32-80; internet www.mairie-perpignan .fr; f. 1963; ethnography, folklore and anthropology of the Catalan region; Curator JACQUES-GASPARD DELONCLE.

Poitiers

Conservation des Musées de Poitiers: 3 bis rue Jean-Jaurès, 86000 Poitiers; tel. 5-49-41-07-53; fax 5-49-88-61-63; e-mail musees .poitiers@alienor.org; internet www .musees-poitiers.org; f. 1794; library of 10,000 vols, 50 periodicals; Curators MICHEL REROLLE, MARIE-CHRISTINE PLANCHARD, MARYSE REDIEN, PHILIPPE BATA.

Attached Museums:

Baptistère Saint-Jean: rue Jean-Jaurès, 86000 Poitiers; c/o Office de Tourisme de Poitiers, 45 pl. Charles De Gaulle, 86009 Poitiers; tel. 5-49-41-21-24; e-mail accueil@ ot-poitiers.fr; internet www.ot-poitiers.fr; f. 1836; Merovingian archaeology.

Hypogée des Dunes: 101 rue du Père de la Croix, 86000 Poitiers; f. 1909; 7th–8th-century Merovingian archaeology.

Musée Rupert de Chièvres: 9 rue Victor Hugo, 86000 Poitiers; tel. 5-49-41-07-53; f. 1887; reconstruction of a 19th-century collector's private house; pre-1800 paintings, furniture, objets d'art.

Musée Sainte-Croix: 3 bis rue Jean-Jaurès, 86000 Poitiers; tel. 5-49-41-07-53; f. 1974; fine arts, history of Poitou (archaeological, ethnographical collections, sculpture and paintings post 1800).

Reims

Musée des Beaux-Arts: 8 rue Chanzy, 51100 Reims; tel. 3-26-35-36-00; fax 3-26-86-87-75; e-mail sylvie.leibel@mairie-reims .fr; internet www.ville-reims.fr/fr/culture/ a-visiter/musee-des-beaux-arts; f. 1795; paintings (especially French School, 17th-century Le Nain, and 19th-century Corot–Delacroix), and Cranach drawings; 15th- and 16th-century 'Toiles Peintes'; colln of ceramics; Curator DAVID LIOT.

Musée Saint-Remi: 53 rue Simon, 51100 Reims; tel. 3-26-35-36-30; fax 3-26-82-07-99; internet www.ville-reims.fr/fr/culture/ a-visiter/musee-saint-remi; the old Abbey of St Remi (12th to 18th centuries); Prehistoric, Celtic, Gallo-Roman, Romanesque and Gothic antiquities and sculptures; tapestries of St-Remi life (1530); old weapons; Chief Curator MARC BOUXIN.

Rennes

Musée des Beaux-Arts: 20 quai Emile Zola, 35000 Rennes; tel. 2-99-28-55-85; fax 2-99-28-55-99; e-mail museebeauxarts@ ville-rennes.fr; internet www.mbar.org; f. 1799; paintings, drawings, engravings, sculpture of French and foreign Schools from the 15th century; archaeology; library of 35,000 vols; Curator FRANCIS RIBEMONT.

Musée de Bretagne: 46 blvd Magenta, CS 51138, 35011 Rennes Cedex; tel. 2-23-40-66-70; fax 2-23-40-66-94; internet www .musee-bretagne.fr; f. 1960; geology, prehistory, Armorica at the Roman period, medieval art, historical documents, popular art, furniture, 19th-century costumes, contemporary regional art and history; Dir PASCAL AUMASSON.

Rouen

Musées de la Ville de Rouen: 1 pl. Restout, 76000 Rouen; tel. 2-35-71-28-40; fax 2-35-15-43-23; internet www.rouen-musees.com.

Attached Museums:

Musée des Beaux-Arts: Esplanade Marcel Duchamp, 76000 Rouen; tel. 2-35-71-28-40; fax 2-35-15-43-23; f. 1801; paintings, drawings, sculpture, decorative art; Dir LAURENT SALOMÉ.

Musée de la Céramique: 1 rue Faucon, 76000 Rouen; tel. 2-35-07-31-74; fax 2-35-15-43-23; f. 1983; 16th–19th–century ceramics.

Musée de la Ferronnerie: rue Jacques Villon, 76000 Rouen; tel. 2-35-88-42-92; fax 2-35-15-43-23; f. 1922; 3rd to 19th-century ironwork; Curator MARIE PESSIOT.

Rueil-Malmaison

Musée National des Châteaux de Malmaison et de Bois-Préau: 92500 Rueil-Malmaison; tel. 1-41-29-05-55; fax 1-41-29-05-56; internet www.chateau-malmaison.fr; f. 1906; historical colln of Napoleon I and Joséphine; Dir AMAURY LEFEBURE.

St-Denis

Musée d'art et d'histoire: 22 bis rue Gabriel Péri, 93200 St-Denis; tel. 1-42-43-05-10; fax 1-48-20-07-60; e-mail musee@ ville-saint-denis.fr; internet www .musee-saint-denis.fr; f. 1901; located in a

disused 17th-century Carmelite monastery; collns: medieval archaeology and ceramics; history and memorabilia from the monastery and Madame Louise; the Paris Commune; paintings by Albert André; Paul Eluard and Francis Jourdain collns; remains of the old hospital; documentation room for researchers and students; Curator SYLVIE GONZALEZ.

St-Etienne

Musée d'Art et d'Industrie: place Louis Comte, 42000 St-Etienne; tel. 4-77-49-73-00; fax 4-77-49-73-05; e-mail museemai@ mairie-st-etienne.fr; internet www .mairie-st-etienne.fr; f. 1833, at Palais des Arts since 1850; armaments, fabrics, bicycles; Curator NADINE BESSE.

Attached Museums:

Musée d'Art Moderne de Saint-Etienne Métropole: La Terrasse, BP 80241 42006 St-Etienne, Cedex 1; tel. 4-77-79-52-52; fax 4-77-79-52-50; e-mail mam@ agglo-st-etienne.fr; internet www .mam-st-etienne.fr; f. 1987; colln of modern and contemporary art; temporary exhibitions; library of 40,000 vols; Gen. Dir Dr LORAND HEGYI.

Musée de la Mine: 3 blvd Franchet d'Esperey, 42000 St-Etienne; tel. 4-77-43-83-23; fax 4-77-43-83-29; e-mail museemin@mairie-st-etienne.fr; mining and industrial museum on the site of a former working mine.

St-Germain-en-Laye

Musée des Antiquités Nationales: Château, BP 3030, 78103 St-Germain-en-Laye Cedex; tel. 1-39-10-13-00; fax 1-34-51-73-93; internet www.musee-antiquitesnationales.fr; f. 1862; prehistoric, Bronze Age, Celtic, Gallo-Roman and Merovingian antiquities, comparative archaeology; library of 25,000 vols; Dir PATRICK PÉRIN; publ. *Antiquités nationales* (1 a year).

St-Malo

Musée de St-Malo: Château de St-Malo, 35400 St-Malo; tel. 2-99-40-71-57; fax 2-99-40-71-56; e-mail musee@ville-saint-malo.fr; f. 1950; history of Saint-Malo and temporary exhibitions; Curator PH. PETOUT.

Attached Museum:

Musée International du Long Cours Cap-Hornier: Tour Solidor, St-Servan, 35400 St-Malo; tel. 2-99-40-71-58; e-mail musee@ville-saint-malo.fr; f. 1969; int. history of sailing around the world since 16th century; Curator PH. PETOUT.

St-Paul-de-Vence

Fondation Maeght: 06570 St-Paul-de-Vence; tel. 4-93-32-81-63; fax 4-93-32-53-22; e-mail contact@fondation-maeght.com; internet www.fondation-maeght.com; f. 1964; modern paintings and sculpture incl. Bonnard, Braque, Giacometti, Miró and Calder; work by contemporary artists; library of 40,000 vols on modern arts and daily films on art and artists; Dir ISABELLE MAEGHT.

St-Tropez

Annonciade, Musée de St-Tropez: place Georges Grammont, 83990 St-Tropez; tel. 4-94-17-84-10; fax 4-94-97-87-24; e-mail annonciade@ville-sainttropez.fr; internet www.saint-tropez.fr; f. 1955; French paintings 1890–1950; Curator JEAN-PAUL MONERY.

Saumur

Château Musée: Hôtel de Ville, 49408 Saumur Cedex; tel. 2-41-40-24-40; fax 2-41-40-24-49; e-mail chateau.musee@ ville-saumur.fr; internet www.ville-saumur

.fr; f. 1829, and reorganized 1960; local archaeology, the Comte Charles Lair colln of decorative arts, incl. tapestries, furniture, wood carvings, liturgical ornaments; fine porcelain of 16th–18th centuries; Curator JACQUELINE MONGELLAZ.

Sceaux

Parc et musée de l'Ile de France: Château de Sceaux, Domaine de Sceaux, 92330 Sceaux; tel. 1-41-87-29-50; fax 1-41-87-29-51; e-mail museeidf@cg92.fr; internet www .chateau-sceaux.fr; f. 1935; old and modern paintings, sculpture, engravings, furniture, decorative art, tapestries, history and drawings of the environs of Paris; documentation centre on the Paris region; educational services; multimedia centre; annexes: Orangerie and Pavillon de l'Aurore, les Ecuries (Parc de Sceaux); Dir DOMINQUE BREME.

Sèvres

Musée National de Céramique: place de la Manufacture, 92310 Sèvres; tel. 1-41-14-04-20; fax 1-45-34-67-88; e-mail musee .sevres@culture.gouv.fr; f. 1824; ancient and modern ceramic art; Curator ANTOINETTE HALLÉ; publ. *Revue de la Société des Amis du Musée National de Céramique* (1 a year).

Soissons

Musée Municipal: 2 rue de la Congrégation, 02200 Soissons; tel. 3-23-93-30-50; fax 3-23-93-30-51; e-mail musee@ville-soissons .fr; internet www.musee-soissons.org; f. 1857; antiquities, medieval sculpture, paintings since 17th century, local history and protohistory; archaeology of the Aisne Valley from Neolithic to Middle Ages; Curator DOMINIQUE ROUSSEL.

Attached Museum:

Musée Arsenal: Site de l'abbaye Saint-Jean-des-Vignes, rue Saint Jean, 02200 Soissons; tel. 3-23-53-42-40; fax 3-23-93-30-51; e-mail musee@ville-soissons.fr; internet www.musee-soissons.org; temporary exhibition space in the Arsenal; Dir DOMINIQUE ROUSSEL.

Strasbourg

Palais Rohan: 2 place du Château, 67076 Strasbourg Cedex; tel. 3-88-52-50-00; fax 3-88-52-50-09; internet www .musees-strasbourg.org..

Attached Museums:

Musée Archéologique: c/o Palais Rohan, 2 place du Château, 67000 Strasbourg; tel. 3-88-52-50-00; fax 3-88-52-50-09; f. 1856; prehistoric, Celtic, Gallo-Roman and Merovingian collns; results of excavations in Alsace; Curator BERNADETTE SCHNITZLER.

Musée des Arts Décoratifs et Appartements Historiques: c/o Palais Rohan, 2 place du Château, 67076 Strasbourg Cedex; tel. 3-88-52-50-00; fax 3-88-52-50-46; f. 1883; furniture from 18th and 19th centuries; French paintings; ceramics; silver objects; musical instruments; wrought-iron and tin; Curator ETIENNE MARTIN.

Musée des Beaux-Arts: c/o Palais Rohan, 2 place du Château, 67000 Strasbourg; tel. 3-88-52-50-00; fax 3-88-52-50-09; f. 1801; French and foreign paintings: Old Masters, art from 14th–19th centuries, Italian, Spanish, Flemish, Dutch and French schools; Chief Curator DOMINIQUE JACQUOT.

Toulouse

Musée des Augustins: 21 rue de Metz, 31000 Toulouse; tel. 5-61-22-21-82; fax 5-61-22-34-69; e-mail augustins@mairie-toulouse .fr; internet www.augustins.org; f. 1793 and housed in the former Augustine Convent, of

which parts date from the 14th and 15th centuries; Roman and Gothic sculptures, 16th–19th-century local and foreign paintings; Curator ALAIN DAGUERRE DE HUREAUX.

Tours

Musée des Beaux-Arts: 18 place François-Sicard, 37000 Tours; tel. 2-47-05-68-73; fax 2-47-05-38-91; e-mail musee-beauxarts@ ville-tours.fr; internet www.musees .regioncentre.fr; f. 1793 and moved in 1910 to the fmr Archbishop's palace; paintings by Mantegna, Rembrandt, Rubens, Vignon, Lancret, Boucher, Delacroix, Degas, Debré; sculpture by Le Moyne, Houdon, Bourdelle, Davidson, Calder; furniture, tapestries and objets d'art; library of 15,000 vols; Curator PHILIPPE LE LEYZOUR..

Affiliated Museums:

Château d'Azay-le-Ferron: 36290 Azay-le-Ferron; tel. 2-54-39-20-06; bldgs, objets d'art and furniture of the 15th to 19th centuries; Curator PHILIPPE LE LEYZOUR.

Musée Saint-Martin: 3 rue Rapin, 37000 Tours; tel. 2-47-64-48-87; fax 2-47-05-38-91; f. 1990; contains collection of souvenirs of St Martin; Curator PHILIPPE LE LEYZOUR.

Musée du Compagnonnage: 8 rue Nationale, 37000 Tours; tel. 2-47-61-07-93; fax 2-47-21-68-90; e-mail museecompagnonnage@ ville-tours.fr; f. 1968; archives and historical masterpieces; Curator LAURENT BASTARD.

Musée de la Société Archéologique de Touraine: Hôtel Gouin, 25 rue du Commerce, 37000 Tours; tel. 2-47-66-22-32; Gallic and Roman archaeology, medieval and 16th century sculptures, prehistoric artefacts; iconography of Tours, 18th–19th century pottery; closed for renovation until 2012.

Musée des Vins de Touraine: 16 rue Nationale (parvis Saint-Julien), 37000 Tours; tel. 2-47-61-07-93; fax 2-47-21-68-90; f. 1975; Curator LAURENT BASTARD.

Ungersheim

Ecomusée d'Alsace: BP 71, 68190 Ungersheim; tel. 3-89-74-44-74; fax 3-89-74-44-65; e-mail contact@ecoparcs.com; internet www .ecomusee-alsace.com; f. 1984 by the Asscn Maisons Paysannes d'Alsace to safeguard the rural architecture of Alsace; an open-air museum comprising a reconstituted village of 70 cottages, showing life in olden days with a baker, an oil-mill, a blacksmith, a clog-maker, and a sawmill working on site; nature walks, seminars; library of 950 vols, 4,000 drawings and reliefs, 25,000 photographs, video cassettes; Pres. MARC GRODWOHL.

Vaison-la-Romaine

Musée Archéologique Théo Desplans: Colline de Puymin, 84110 Vaison-la-Romaine; tel. 4-90-36-50-48; fax 4-90-35-66-17; e-mail reservegroupe@vaison-la-romaine .com; internet www.vaison-la-romaine.com; f. 1920, present site 1975; archaeological colln from excavations at Vaison; Curator CHRISTINE BEZIN.

Valenciennes

Musée des Beaux-Arts: blvd Watteau, 59300 Valenciennes; tel. 3-27-22-57-20; fax 3-27-22-57-22; e-mail mba@ ville-valenciennes.fr; internet www .valenciennes.fr; painting, sculpture, archaeology, etc.; Dir P. RAMADE.

Vallauris

Musée National Picasso 'La Guerre et la Paix': place de la Libération, 06220 Vallauris; tel. 4-93-64-71-83; fax 4-93-64-50-32; internet www.musee-picasso-vallauris.fr; f. 1959; works by Picasso incl. *La Guerre et la

Paix in 12th-century chapel; Curator JEAN-MICHEL FORAY.

Verdun

Centre Mondial de la Paix, des Libertés et des Droits de l'Homme: Palais Épiscopal, BP 183, 55100 Verdun; tel. 3-29-86-55-00; fax 3-29-86-15-14; e-mail cmpaix@ wanadoo.fr; f. 1994; exhibition on the First World War; and 'From War to Peace', an interactive exhibition, which depicts the origins of war in Europe, attempts at peace-keeping and punishment of war crimes, the history of European cooperation and the EU, the UN, and the nature and application of human rights; meetings, confs and roleplay situations for students; Dir JEAN-LUC DEMANDRE.

Versailles

Musée et Domaine National du Château de Versailles: Château de Versailles, place d'Armes, RP 834, 78000 Versailles; tel. 1-30-83-78-00; e-mail direction.public@ chateauversailles.fr; internet www .chateauversailles.fr; f. 1623 by Louis XIII; historical painting and sculpture, furniture of the 17th to 19th centuries; Grand Trianon, Petit Trianon châteaux, Hameau de la Reine, park; Pres. JEAN-JACQUES AILLAGON.

Vizille

Musée de la Révolution Française: Château de Vizille, 38220 Vizille; tel. 4-76-68-07-35; fax 4-76-68-08-53; e-mail musee .revolution@cg38.fr; internet www .musee-revolution-francaise.fr; f. 1984; relics, art and library connected with the French Revolution of 1789; library of 20,000 vols, 25,000 microfiches; Dir ALAIN CHEVALIER.

State Universities

CENTRE UNIVERSITAIRE DE FORMATION ET DE RECHERCHE JEAN-FRANÇOIS CHAMPOLLION

pl. de Verdun, 81012 Albi Cedex 9
Telephone: 5-63-48-17-17
Fax: 5-63-48-17-19
E-mail: contact.albi@univ-jfc.fr
Internet: www.univ-jfc.fr

Pres.: JEAN-LOUIS DARRERON
Vice-Pres: MICHEL ROUSTAN (Ccl of Admin.), PIERRE LAGARRIGUE (Science and Education Ccl)
Dir: HERVÉ PINGAUD
Sec.-Gen.: PASCAL GUERRIN
Librarian: FLORENCE LUNARDI

Number of teachers: 80
Number of students: 2,600

Areas of study: computer science, law, economics, management, sport, arts, literature, languages, social science, humanities, science.

INSTITUT NATIONAL POLYTECHNIQUE DE GRENOBLE

46 ave Félix Viallet, 38031 Grenoble Cedex 1
Telephone: 4-76-57-45-00
Fax: 4-76-57-45-01
E-mail: contact@grenoble-inp.fr
Internet: www.grenoble-inp.fr

Founded 1907

29 Research laboratories, 6 constituent schools

Pres.: PAUL JACQUET
Vice-Pres. for Admin. Ccl: DIDIER GEORGES
Vice-Pres. for Studies and Univ. Life: NADINE GUILLEMOT
Vice-Pres. for Scientific Ccl: FRANÇOIS WEISS

Vice-Pres. for Int. Relations: JEAN-LUC KON-
ING
Vice-Pres. for Industry Partnership: CHRIS-
TIAN VOILLOT
Sec.-Gen.: JEAN-FRANÇOIS PICQ
Number of teachers: 350
Number of students: 5,076
Publication: *Ingénieurs INPG* (52 a year).

CONSTITUENT SCHOOLS

**Ecole Nationale Supérieure d'Ingé-
nieurs pour l'Energie, l'Eau et l'Environnement (ENSE3):** rue de la Houille
Blanche, BP 46, 38402 Saint Martin d'Hères
Cedex; tel. 4-76-82-62-00; e-mail direction
.ense3@grenoble-inp.fr; internet ense3
.grenoble-inp.fr; f. 2008 by merger of Ecole
Nationale Supérieure d'Ingénieurs Electri-
ciens de Grenoble (ENSIEG) and Ecole
Nationale Supérieure d'Hydraulique et de
Mécanique de Grenoble (ENSHMG).

**Ecole Nationale Supérieure d'Informa-
tique, de Mathématiques Appliquées et
de Télécommunications (ENSIMAG):** 681
rue de la Passerelle, BP 72, 38402 Saint
Martin d'Hères Cedex; tel. 4-76-82-72-00;
internet ensimag.grenoble-inp.fr; f. 2008 by
merger of Ecole Nationale Supérieure
d'Informatique et de Mathématiques Appliquées de Grenoble (ENSIMAG) and INP
Grenoble TELECOM; Dir BRIGITTE PLATEAU.

**Ecole Nationale Supérieure des Sys-
tèmes Avancés et Réseaux (ESISAR):** 50
rue Barthélémy de Laffemas, BP 54, 26902
Valence Cedex 9; tel. 4-75-75-94-00; fax 4-75-
43-56-42; e-mail direction@esisar
.grenoble-inp.fr; internet esisar.grenoble-inp
.fr; Dir Prof. CHANTAL ROBACH.

**Ecole Internationale du Papier de la
Communication Imprimée et des Bioma-
tériaux (PAGORA):** 461 rue de la Papeterie, BP 65, 38402 Saint Martin d'Hères
Cedex; tel. 4-76-82-69-00; fax 4-76-82-69-33;
e-mail contact.pagora@grenoble-inp.fr;
internet pagora.grenoble-inp.fr; f. 2008,
fmrly l'Ecole Française de Papeterie et des
Industries Graphiques (EFPG); Dir BERNARD
PINEAUX.

**Ecole Nationale Supérieure de Phys-
ique, Electronique, Matériaux
(PHELMA):** 3 Parvis Louis Néel, BP 257,
38016 Grenoble Cedex 1; tel. 4-56-52-91-00;
fax 4-56-52-91-03; internet phelma
.grenoble-inp.fr; f. 2008 by merger of Ecole
Nationale Supérieure de Physique de Grenoble (ENSPG), Ecole Nationale Supérieure
d'Electricité et de Radioelectricité (ENSERG)
and Ecole Nationale Supérieure d'Electro-
chimie et d'Electrométallurgie de Grenoble
(ENSEEG); Dir PIERRE BENECH.

Génie Industriel: 46 ave Félix Viallet,
38031 Grenoble Cedex 1; tel. 4-76-57-46-01;
fax 4-76-57-47-93; e-mail corinne.mairot@
grenoble-inp.fr; internet genie-industriel
.grenoble-inp.fr; f. 2008 by merger of Ecole
Nationale Supérieure de Génie Industriel
(ENSGI) and part of the Ecole Nationale
Supérieure d'Hydraulique et de Mécanique
de Grenoble (ENSHMG); Dir JEANNE DUVAL-
LET.

INSTITUT NATIONAL
POLYTECHNIQUE DE LORRAINE

2 ave de la Forêt de Haye, BP 3, 54501
Vandoeuvre
Telephone: 3-83-59-59-59
Fax: 3-83-59-59-55
E-mail: inpl@inpl-nancy.fr
Internet: www.inpl-nancy.fr
Founded 1970
Language of instruction: French

28 Research laboratories, 7 constituent
schools
Pres.: FRANÇOIS LAURENT
Vice-Pres: CHRISTINE ROIZARD (Ccl of Admin.),
PIERRE ARCHAMBAULT (Scientific Ccl),
DOMINIQUE PETITJEAN (Studies and Univ.
Life)
Sec.-Gen.: JEAN-YVES RIVIÈRE
Number of teachers: 560
Number of students: 4,000.

CONSTITUENT SCHOOLS

**Ecole Européenne d'Ingénieurs en
Génie des Matériaux (EEIGM):** 6 rue
Bastien Lepage, BP 630, 54010 Nancy Cedex;
tel. 3-83-36-83-00; fax 3-83-36-83-36; e-mail
eeigm@eeigm.inpl-nancy.fr; internet www
.eeigm.inpl-nancy.fr; f. 1991; 191 students;
Dir ISABELLE HENROT.

**Ecole Nationale Supérieure d'Agrono-
mie et des Industries Alimentaires
(ENSAIA):** 2 ave de la Forêt de Haye, BP
172, 54505 Vandoeuvre Cedex; tel. 3-83-59-
59-59; fax 3-83-59-58-04; e-mail ensaia@
ensaia.inpl-nancy.fr; internet www.ensaia
.inpl-nancy.fr; f. 1970; 58 teachers; 436 students; library of 7,500 vols; Dir MICHEL FICK;
publ. *Bulletin Scientifique* (1 a year).

**Ecole Nationale Supérieure d'Electri-
cité et de Mécanique (ENSEM):** 2 ave de
la Forêt de Haye, 54516 Vandoeuvre; tel. 3-
83-59-55-43; fax 3-83-44-07-63; e-mail
ensem@ensem.inpl-nancy.fr; internet www
.ensem.inpl-nancy.fr; f. 1990; 50 teachers;
379 students; Dir YVES GRANJON.

**Ecole Nationale Supérieure en Génie
des Systèmes Industriels (ENSGSI):** 8
rue Bastien Lepage, BP 90647, 54010 Nancy
Cedex; tel. 3-83-19-32-32; fax 3-83-19-32-00;
e-mail ensgsi@ensgsi.inpl-nancy.fr; internet
www.ensgsi.inpl-nancy.fr; f. 1993; 24 teachers; 315 students; Dir PASCAL LHOSTE.

**Ecole Nationale Supérieure de Géologie
(ENSG):** rue du Doyen Marcel Roubault, BP
40, 54501 Vandoeuvre lès Nancy; tel. 3-83-
59-64-02; fax 3-83-59-64-87; e-mail
direction@ensg.inpl-nancy.fr; internet www
.ensg.inpl-nancy.fr; f. 1908; 36 teachers; 300
students; Dir JEAN-MARC MONTEL.

**Ecole Nationale Supérieure des Indus-
tries Chimiques (ENSIC):** 1 rue Grand-
ville, 54001 Nancy; tel. 3-83-17-50-00; fax 3-
83-35-08-11; e-mail ensic@ensic.inpl-nancy
.fr; internet www.ensic.inpl-nancy.fr; f.
1887; 63 teachers; 420 students; Dir MICHAEL
MATLOSZ.

**Ecole Nationale Supérieure des Mines
de Nancy (ENSMN):** Parc de Saurupt, CS
14234, 54042 Nancy Cedex; tel. 3-83-58-42-
32; fax 3-83-58-43-44; e-mail ensmn@mines
.inpl-nancy.fr; internet www.mines
.inpl-nancy.fr; f. 1919; 803 students; library
of 37,500 vols, 180 periodicals; Dir MICHEL
JAUZEIN.

INSTITUT NATIONAL
POLYTECHNIQUE DE TOULOUSE

6 allée Emile Monso, BP 34038, 31029
Toulouse Cedex 4
Telephone: 5-34-32-30-00
Fax: 5-34-32-31-00
E-mail: inp@inp-toulouse.fr
Internet: www.inp-toulouse.fr
Founded 1970

4 Constituent schools and 17 research labora-
tories
Pres., Ccl of Admin.: GILBERT CASAMATTA
Vice-Pres: OLIVIER SIMONIN (Scientific Ccl),
GRÉGORY DECHAP-GUILLAUME (Studies and
Univ. Life)
Sec.-Gen.: GILLES BOUCHER
Librarian: SANDRINE MALOTAUX.

CONSTITUENT SCHOOLS

**Ecole Nationale Supérieure Agronomi-
que de Toulouse (ENSAT):** ave de l'Agro-
biopole, BP 32607, Auzeville-Tolosane, 31326
Castanet-Tolosan Cedex; tel. 5-34-32-39-00;
fax 5-34-32-39-01; e-mail sandrine.audran@
ensat.fr; internet www.ensat.fr; f. 1909 as
Institut Agricole de Toulouse; Dir GRÉGORY
DECHAP-GUILLAUME.

**Ecole Nationale Supérieure d'Electro-
technique, d'Electronique, d'Informatique et d'Hydraulique et des
Télécommunications (ENSEEIHT):** 2
rue Charles Camichel, BP 7122, 31071
Toulouse Cedex 7; tel. 5-34-32-20-00; fax 5-
34-32-21-20; e-mail ric@enseeiht.fr; internet
www.enseeiht.fr; Dir ALAIN AYACHE.

**Ecole Nationale Supérieure des Arts
Chimiques et Technologiques (ENSIA-
CET):** 4 allée Emile Monso, BP 44362, 31030
Toulouse Cedex 4; tel. 5-34-32-33-00; fax 5-
34-32-33-99; e-mail directeur@ensiacet.fr;
internet www.ensiacet.fr; f. 2001; Dir JEAN-
MARC LE LANN; 105 teachers; 750 students.

**Ecole Nationale d'Ingénieurs de Tarbes
(ENIT):** 47 ave d'Azereix, BP 1629, 65016
Tarbes Cedex; tel. 5-62-44-27-00; fax 5-62-44-
27-27; e-mail directeur@enit.fr; internet
www.enit.fr; f. 1963; Dir TALAL MASRI.

UNIVERSITÉ DE PROVENCE—AIX-
MARSEILLE I

3 pl. Victor Hugo, 13331 Marseilles Cedex 03
Telephone: 4-13-55-00-00
Fax: 4-13-55-03-72
E-mail: presidence@univ-provence.fr
Internet: www.univ-provence.fr
Founded 1970; attached to PRES Aix-Mar-
seille Université

University restructured in 2009 into 9
research units, an engineering school, an
institute of technology, and a Masters insti-
tute based on campuses in Aix, Marseille,
Aubagne, Lambesc, Salon de Provence, Arles,
Digne, and Avignon
Pres.: JEAN-PAUL CAVERNI
Vice-Pres: JEAN-CLAUDE LORAUD (Ccl of
Admin.), DENIS BERTIN (Scientific Ccl),
CATHERINE VIRLOUVET (Studies and Univ.
Life)
Sec.-Gen.: FATHIE BOUBERTEKH
Librarian: Mme GACHON
Library: see Libraries
Number of teachers: 1,087
Number of students: 22,334.

TEACHING AND RESEARCH UNITS

**Centre de Formation des Musiciens
Intervenants (CFMI):** 29 ave Robert Schuman, 13621 Aix-en-Provence Cedex 01; tel. 4-
42-95-32-40; fax 4-42-65-32-60; e-mail cfmi@
univ-provence.fr; Dir PHILIPPE BOIVIN.

**Centre Interuniversitaire de Mécanique
(UNIMECA):** 60 rue Joliot-Curie, 13453
Marseilles Cedex 13; tel. 4-91-11-38-00; fax
4-91-11-38-19; internet artemmis.univ-mrs
.fr/im2; Dir PATRICK VIGLIANO.

**Département Environnement Technolo-
gie et Société (DENTES):** 3 pl. Victor
Hugo, Case 75, 13331 Marseilles Cedex 03;
tel. 4-91-10-63-28; fax 4-91-10-62-85; Dir
RÉMI CHAPPAZ.

**Département Métiers de l'Image et du
Son (SATIS):** 9 blvd Lakanal, 13400
Aubagne; tel. 4-13-55-18-88; fax 4-13-55-18-
90; e-mail satis@univ-provence.fr; internet
sites.univ-provence.fr/satis; Dir JACQUES
SAPIEGA.

**École Polytechnique Universitaire de
Marseille:** 60 rue Joliot-Curie, 13453 Marseilles Cedex 13; tel. 4-91-11-26-56; fax 4-91-

11-38-54; e-mail direction@polytech
.univ-mrs.fr; internet www
.polytech-marseille.com; Dir DAVID E. ZEI-
TOUN.

Institut de la Francophonie: tel. 4-42-95-
35-53; internet sites.univ-provence.fr/
francophonie; Dir ROBERT CHAUDENSON.

**Institut Universitaire de Formation des
Maîtres (IUFM) de l'Académie d'Aix-
Marseille:** 33 rue Eugène Cas, 13248 Mar-
seilles Cedex 04; tel. 4-91-10-75-75; fax 4-91-
08-40-67; internet www.aix-mrs.iufm.fr; Dir
JACQUES GINESTIÉ.

IUT de Provence (Arles): rue Raoul Foller-
eau, BP 90178, 13637 Arles Cedex; tel. 4-90-
52-24-10; fax 4-90-52-24-15; e-mail iut-arles@
up.univ-mrs.fr; Dir ROBERT PUJADE.

IUT de Provence (Digne-les-Bains): 19
blvd Saint-Jean Chrysostome, 04000 Digne-
les-Bains; tel. 4-92-30-23-70; fax 4-92-30-23-
71; internet sites.univ-provence.fr/iutdigne;
Dir YVES ALPE.

**Maison Méditerranéenne des Sciences
de l'Homme (MMSH):** 5 rue du Château de
l'Horloge, BP 647, 13094 Aix-en-Provence
Cedex 02; tel. 4-42-52-40-00; internet www
.mmsh.univ-aix.fr; Dir BERNARD MOREL.

**Observatoire Astronomique de Mar-
seille-Provence (OAMP):** see Research
Institutes.

UFR Civilisations et Humanités: 29 ave
Robert Schuman, 13621 Aix-en-Provence
Cedex 01; tel. 4-42-95-32-90; fax 4-42-52-43-
91; e-mail elisabeth.malamut@univ-provence
.fr; Dir XAVIER LAFON.

**UFR de Psychologie, Sciences de l'Édu-
cation:** 29 ave Robert Schuman, 13621 Aix-
en-Provence Cedex 01; tel. 4-42-95-37-09;
e-mail thierry.ripoll@univ-provence.fr;
internet sites.univ-provence.fr/wpse; Dir
THIERRY RIPOLL.

**UFR Études Romanes, Latino-améri-
caines, Orientales et Slaves (ERLAOS):**
29 ave Robert Schuman, 13621 Aix-en-Provence Cedex 01; tel. 4-42-95-34-46; internet
www.univ-provence.fr/erlaos; Dir PASCAL
GANDOULPHE.

**UFR Langue Anglo-saxonnes et Germa-
niques–Langues Etrangères Appliquées
(LAG–LEA):** 29 ave Robert Schuman, 13621
Aix-en-Provence Cedex 01; tel. 4-42-95-36-42;
fax 4-42-95-35-68; Dir DOMINIQUE BATOUX.

**UFR Lettres, Arts, Communications et
Sciences du langage (LACS):** 29 ave
Robert Schuman, 13621 Aix-en-Provence
Cedex 01; internet sites.univ-provence.fr/
lacs; Dir HENRIETTE STOFFEL.

**UFR Mathématiques, Informatique,
Mécanique (MIM):** 39 rue Joliot-Curie,
13453 Marseilles Cedex 13; tel. 4-13-55-11-
11; fax 4-91-11-35-02; e-mail denis.lugiez@
univ-provence.fr; internet gsite
.univ-provence.fr; Dir DENIS LUGIEZ.

UFR Sciences de la Matière (SM): ave
Escadrille-Normandie-Niemen, service 411,
entrée BJ4, 13397 Marseilles Cedex 20; tel.
4-91-28-90-40; fax 4-91-28-90-48; e-mail
ufrsm@up.univ-mrs.fr; internet sites
.univ-provence.fr/~ufrsm; Dir ANDRÉ THE-
VAND.

**UFR Sciences de la Vie, de la Terre et de
l'Environnement (SVTE):** 3 pl. Victor
Hugo, Case 82, 13331 Marseilles Cedex 03;
tel. 4-13-55-11-25; fax 4-91-10-63-03; Dir
JACQUES MARVALDI.

**UFR Sciences Géographiques et de
l'Aménagement:** 29 ave Robert Schuman,
13621 Aix-en-Provence Cedex 01; tel. 4-42-
95-38-44; fax 4-42-95-38-80; internet sites
.univ-provence.fr/wgeo; Dir JEAN-LUC BONNE-
FOY.

UNIVERSITÉ DE LA MÉDITERRANÉE—AIX-MARSEILLE II

58 blvd Charles Livon, 13284 Marseilles
Cedex 07

Telephone: 4-91-39-65-00
Fax: 4-91-31-31-36
E-mail: service-communication@univmed.fr
Internet: www.univmed.fr

Founded 1973
Language of instruction: French
Academic year: October to June

Univs of Aix-en-Provence consist of three
univs in Aix-en-Provence; economic science
and information technology are the principal
subjects of instruction here

Pres.: Prof. YVON BERLAND
Vice-Pres. for Admin. Council: DIDIER LAUS-
SEL
Vice-Pres. for Science Council: PIERRE CHIAP-
PETTA
Vice-Pres. for Education and Student Life:
THIERRY PAUL
Vice-Pres. for Communication: PATRICE
VANELLE
Vice-Pres. for Int. Relations: PIERRE FUENTES
Sec.-Gen.: DAMIEN VERHAEGHE

Number of teachers: 1,500
Number of students: 22,000

TEACHING AND RESEARCH UNITS

Faculté de Médecine: 27 blvd Jean Moulin,
13385 Marseilles Cedex 5; tel. 4-91-32-43-00;
fax 4-91-32-44-96; internet www.timone
.univ-mrs.fr/medecine; Dean GEORGES LEO-
NETTI.

Faculté d'Odontologie: 27 blvd Jean Moulin, 13385 Marseilles Cedex 5; tel. 4-86-13-
68-68; fax 4-86-13-68-69; internet www
.univmed.fr/odontologie; Dean JACQUES
DEJOU.

Faculté de Pharmacie: 27 blvd Jean
Moulin, 13385 Marseilles Cedex 5; tel. 4-91-
83-55-00; fax 4-91-80-26-12; internet www
.pharmacie.univ-mrs.fr; Dean PATRICE
VANELLE.

Faculté des Sciences (Luminy): 163 ave
de Luminy, 13288 Marseilles Cedex 09; tel. 4-
91-82-90-00; fax 4-91-26-92-00; internet www
.sciences.univmed.fr; Dean CHENG-CAI
ZHANG.

**Faculté des Sciences Economiques et de
Gestion:** 14 ave Jules Ferry, 13621 Marseilles; tel. 4-42-91-48-00; fax 4-42-91-48-07;
e-mail webscol@sceco.univmed.fr; internet
sceco.univ-aix.fr; Dean PIERRE GRANIER.

Faculté des Sciences du Sport: 163 ave de
Luminy, Case 910, 13288 Marseilles Cedex 9;
tel. 4-91-17-04-12; fax 4-91-17-04-10; internet
www.staps.univ-mrs.fr; Dean ERIC BERTON.

**Ecole de Journalisme et de Communi-
cation de Marseille:** 21 rue Virgile Marron,
13392 Marseilles Cedex 05; tel. 4-91-24-32-
00; fax 4-91-24-32-07; e-mail ejcm@ejcm
.univmed.fr; internet www.ejcm.univ-mrs.fr;
Dir LIONEL FLEURY.

**Ecole Supérieure d'Ingénieurs de
Luminy (ESIL):** 163 ave de Luminy, Case
925, 13288 Marseilles Cedex 9; tel. 4-91-82-
85-00; fax 4-91-82-85-91; e-mail contact@esil
.univmed.fr; internet www.esil.univmed.fr;
Dir HENRI KANOUI.

**Ecole Universitaire de Maïeutique Mar-
seille Mediterranée (EU3M):** Site de la
Faculté de Médecine Nord, blvd Pierre
Dramard, 13344 Marseilles Cedex 15; tel. 4-
91-24-32-00; fax 4-91-24-32-07; Dir ANNE
DEMEESTER.

ATTACHED INSTITUTES

**Centre International de Formation et de
Recherche en Didactique (CIFORD):**
Faculté des Sciences de Luminy, 163 ave de

Luminy, 13288 Marseilles Cedex 9; tel. 4-91-
26-90-30; fax 4-91-26-93-55; Dir PAUL
ALLARD.

Centre d'Océanologie de Marseille: Campus de Luminy, 163 ave de Luminy, 13288
Marseilles Cedex 9; tel. 4-91-82-93-00; fax 4-
91-82-93-03; internet www.com.univ-mrs.fr;
Dean M. IVAN DEKEYSER.

**Centre de Recherche pour l'Enseigne-
ment des Mathématiques (IREM):**
Faculté des Sciences de Luminy, 163 ave de
Luminy, 13288 Marseilles Cedex 9; tel. 4-91-
26-90-91; fax 4-91-26-93-43; research into the
teaching of mathematics; Dir ROBERT ROLL-
AND.

**Centre Universitaire Régional d'Etudes
Municipales (CURET):** 191 rue Breteuil,
13006 Marseilles; tel. 4-91-37-61-62; fax 4-
91-37-61-63; courses in local government
administration; Dir M. FOUCHET.

Institut de Mécanique de Marseille: 60
rue Joliot Curie, 13453 Marseilles; tel. 4-91-
11-38-02; fax 4-91-11-38-38; internet
artemmis.univ-mrs.fr/unimecafr; Dir
PATRICK VIGLIANO.

Institut Régional du Travail: 12 traverse
St Pierre, 13100 Aix-en-Provence; tel. 4-42-
17-43-11; fax 4-42-21-20-12; e-mail irt@
univmed.fr; internet irt.univmed.fr; Dir
MARIO CORREIA.

**Institut Universitaire Professionnalisé
(IUP) Affaires et Finances:** Faculté des
Sciences Economiques, 14 ave Jules Ferry,
13621 Aix-en-Provence Cedex; tel. 4-42-33-
48-70; fax 4-42-33-48-72; course on business
and finance.

**Institut Universitaire de Technologie
d'Aix-en-Provence:** 413 ave Gaston Berger,
13625 Aix en Provence Cedex 1; tel. 4-42-93-
90-00; fax 4-42-93-90-90; internet www.iut
.univ-aix.fr; Dir CLAUDE FIORE.

UNIVERSITÉ PAUL CEZANNE—AIX-MARSEILLE III

3 ave Robert Schuman, 13628 Aix-en-Provence Cedex 1

Telephone: 4-42-17-28-00
Internet: www.univ-cezanne.fr

Founded 1973 as Univ. d'Aix-Marseille III
(Univ. de Droit, d'Economie et des Sci-
ences)
Academic year: September to June

Univs of Aix-en-Provence consist of 3 univs
in Aix-en-Provence; law, economics and foundation science are the principal subjects of
instruction here

Pres.: MARC PENA
Vice-Pres: BRUNO HAMELIN (Ccl of Admin.),
PIERRE MULLER (Scientific Ccl), DOMINIQUE
VIRIOT-BARRIAL (Studies and Univ. Life)
Sec.-Gen.: THÉRÈSE CHETAIL
Librarian: DOMINIQUE JACOBI

Number of teachers: 1,133
Number of students: 22,800

Publications: *Interface* (12 a year), *L'Inter
Cours* (12 a year), annual research reports.

TEACHING AND RESEARCH UNITS

Faculté de Droit et de Science Politique:
3 ave Robert Schuman, 13628 Aix-en-Provence; tel. 4-42-17-28-05; fax 4-42-20-46-51;
e-mail secretariat.sridroit@univ-cezanne.fr;
internet www.facdedroit.univ-cezanne.fr;
Dean GILBERT ORSONI.

Faculté d'Economie Appliquée: 3 ave
Robert Schuman, 13628 Aix-en-Provence;
tel. 4-42-17-29-85; fax 4-42-17-29-98;
internet www.fea-upcam.fr; Dean JEAN-
PIERRE CENTI.

Faculté des Sciences et Techniques: ave
Escadrille Normandie-Niemen, 13397 Mar-

seilles Cedex 20; tel. 4-91-28-84-46; fax 4-91-28-89-46; e-mail sec-doyen.fst@univ-cezanne.fr; internet www.fst.univ-cezanne.fr; Dean JEAN-MARC PONS.

Institut d'Administration des Entreprises: chemin de la Quille, Puyricard, CS 30063, 13089 Aix-en-Provence Cedex 2; tel. 4-42-28-08-08; fax 4-42-28-08-00; internet www.iae-aix.com; Dir PATRICK ROUSSEAU.

Institut d'Etudes Françaises pour Etudiants Etrangers: 23 rue Gaston de Saporta, 13100 Aix-en-Provence; tel. 4-42-21-70-90; fax 4-42-23-02-64; internet www.iefee.com; Dir CARINE FERRADOU.

Institut d'Etudes Politiques: 25 rue Gaston de Saporta, 13625 Aix-en-Provence; tel. 4-42-17-01-60; fax 4-42-96-36-99; e-mail directeur@sciencespo-aix.fr; internet www.sciencespo-aix.fr; Dir CHRISTIAN DUVAL.

Institut de Management Public et Gouvernance Territoriale: 21 rue Gaston de Saporta, 13625 Aix-en-Provence Cedex 1; tel. 4-42-17-05-54; fax 4-42-17-05-56; internet www.managementpublic.univ-cezanne.fr; Dir ROBERT FOUCHET.

Institut Universitaire de Technologie: 142 Traverse Charles Susini, 13013 Marseilles Cedex 13; tel. 4-91-28-93-00; fax 4-91-28-94-94; internet iutmrs.univ-cezanne.fr; Dir MICHEL GAUCH.

UNIVERSITÉ D'ANGERS

40 rue de Rennes, BP 73532, 49035 Angers Cedex

Telephone: 2-41-96-23-23
Fax: 2-41-96-23-00
E-mail: presidence@univ-angers.fr
Internet: www.univ-angers.fr

Founded 1971; fmrly Centre Universitaire d'Angers

President: DANIEL MARTINA
Vice-President: GÉRARD MOGUEDET
Sec.-Gen.: HENRI-MARC PAPAVOINE
Librarian: OLIVIER TACHEAU

Number of teachers: 959
Number of students: 18,514

Publications: *Plantes médicinales et phytothérapie, Journal of the Short Story in English, Publications du Centre de Recherche en Littérature et Linguistique de l'Anjou et des Bocages*

DEANS

Faculty of Law, Economic Sciences and Business Sciences: MICHÈL FAVREAU,
Faculty of Letters and Human Sciences: DIDIER LE GALL
Faculty of Medicine: JEAN-PAUL SAINT-ANDRE
Faculty of Pharmacy: OLIVIER DUVAL
Faculty of Science: DANIEL SCHAUB

ATTACHED INSTITUTES

Etudes Supérieures de Tourisme et Hôtellerie d'Angers (ESTHUA): 7 allée François Mitterrand, BP 40455, 49004 Angers; tel. 2-41-96-21-99; fax 2-41-96-22-00; Dir M. BONNEAU.

Institut des Sciences et Techniques de l'Ingénieur d'Angers (ISTIA): 62 ave Notre-Dame du Lac, 49000 Angers; tel. 2-41-22-65-00; fax 2-41-22-65-01; Dir C. ROBLEDO.

Institut Universitaire de Technologie (IUT): 4 blvd Lavoisier, BP 42018, 49016 Angers Cedex; tel. 2-41-73-52-52; fax 2-41-73-53-30; Dir Y. MEIGNEN.

UNIVERSITÉ D'ARTOIS

9 rue du Temple, BP 10665, 62030 Arras Cedex

Telephone: 3-21-60-37-00

Fax: 3-21-60-37-37
E-mail: sio-arras@univ-artois.fr
Internet: www.univ-artois.fr

Founded 1991

Pres.: CHRISTIAN MORZEWSKI (acting)
Sec.-Gen.: MARIE-PAULE DEJONGHE
First Vice-Pres.: ROMÉO CECCHELLI
Librarians: CORINNE LEBLOND (Arras), CHANTAL DUBOIS (Béthune), FRÉDÉRIC WATRELOT (Douai), VIRGINIE JUSTIN-LABONNE (Lens), GHISLAINE HEYER (Liévin)

Number of teachers: 850
Number of students: 14,500

Publication: *Interpôles Artois* (8 a year).

TEACHING AND RESEARCH UNITS

Faculté de Droit Alexis de Tocqueville: rue d'Esquerchin, 59500 Douai; tel. 3-27-94-50-50; fax 3-27-94-50-55; e-mail nathalie.sammartino@univ-artois.fr; Dean TANGUY LE MARC'HADOUR.

Faculté d'Économie, Gestion, Administration et Sciences Sociales: 9 rue du Temple, BP 10665, 62030 Arras Cedex; tel. 3-21-60-37-62; fax 3-21-60-38-64; e-mail fegass@univ-artois.fr; Dir NICOLAS BLONDEL.

Faculté d'Histoire et Géographie: 9 rue du Temple, BP 10665, 62030 Arras Cedex; e-mail richard.chapelet@univ-artois.fr; Dir STÉPHANE CURVEILLER.

Faculté de Langues et Civilisations Étrangères: 9 rue du Temple, BP 10665, 62030 Arras Cedex; tel. 3-21-60-37-45; fax 3-21-60-37-47; e-mail langues@univ-artois.fr; Dir AHMED EL KALADI.

Faculté de Lettres et Arts: 9 rue du Temple, BP 10665, 62030 Arras Cedex; tel. 3-21-60-49-54; fax 3-21-60-37-29; e-mail lettres@univ-artois.fr; Dir JEAN-MARC VERCRUYSSE.

Faculté des Sciences Jean Perrin: rue Jean Souvraz, SP 18, 62307 Lens Cedex; tel. 3-21-79-17-00; fax 3-21-79-17-17; e-mail aurore.atmania@univ-artois.fr; Dir PASQUALE MAMMONE.

Faculté des Sciences Appliquées: Technoparc Futura, 62400 Béthune Cedex; tel. 3-21-64-71-23; fax 3-21-64-71-26; e-mail patrick.bonnel@univ-artois.fr; Dir HERVÉ ROISSE.

Faculté des Sports et de l'Education Physique: Chemin du Marquage, 62800 Béthune Cedex; tel. 3-21-45-85-00; fax 3-21-45-85-01; e-mail facdessports@univ-artois.fr; Dir NICOLAS BLONDEL.

Institut Universitaire de Formation des Maîtres: 365 bis rue Jules Guesde, BP 50458, 59658 Villeneuve d'Ascq Cedex; tel. 3-20-79-86-00; fax 3-20-79-86-01; e-mail webmaster@lille.iufm.fr; internet www.lille.iufm.fr; Dir DOMINIQUE-GUY BRASSART.

ATTACHED RESEARCH INSTITUTES

Institute Universitaire de Technologie de Béthune: 1230 rue de l'Université, BP 819, 62408 Béthune Cedex; tel. 3-21-63-23-00; fax 3-21-68-49-57; Dir PATRICK MARTIN.

Institute Universitaire de Technologie de Lens: rue de l'université, SP 16, 62307 Lens Cedex; tel. 3-21-79-32-32; fax 3-21-79-32-40; e-mail contact@iut-lens.univ-artois.fr; Dir NATASHA LACROIX.

UNIVERSITÉ D'AUVERGNE (CLERMONT-FERRAND I)

49 blvd F. Mitterrand, BP 32, 63001 Clermont-Ferrand Cedex

Telephone: 4-73-17-79-79
Fax: 4-73-17-72-01
Internet: www.u-clermont1.fr

Founded 1976; present status 1985

Pres.: PHILIPPE DULBECCO
Vice-Pres.: MICHEL MADESCLAIRE
Sec.-Gen.: MARTINE HENAULT
Librarian: Mlle SART

Number of teachers: 650
Number of students: 15,000.

TEACHING AND RESEARCH UNITS

Medicine: 28 place Henri Dunant, BP 38, 63001 Clermont-Ferrand; tel. 4-73-17-79-00; fax 4-73-17-79-13; e-mail doyen.medecine@u-clermont1.fr; internet medecine.u-clermont1.fr; Dean Prof. PATRICE DETEIX.

Pharmacy: 28 place Henri Dunant, BP 38, 63001 Clermont-Ferrand; tel. 4-73-17-79-00; fax 4-73-17-79-39; Dean Prof. JOSEPH FIALIP.

Law and Politics: 41 blvd F. Mitterrand, BP 38, 63002 Clermont-Ferrand; tel. 4-73-17-75-74; fax 4-73-17-75-75; e-mail ufr-droit@droit.u-clermont1.fr; internet www-droit.u-clermont1.fr; Dean Prof. JEAN-PIERRE JARNEVIC.

Economic and Social Sciences: 41 blvd F. Mitterrand, BP 54, 63002 Clermont-Ferrand; tel. 4-73-43-42-00; fax 4-73-17-75-75; internet www.ecogestion.u-clermont1.fr; Dir Prof. MARY-FRANÇOISE RENARD.

University Institute of Technology (Clermont-Ferrand): Ensemble universitaire des Cézeaux, BP 86, 63172 Aubière; tel. 4-73-17-70-01; fax 4-73-17-70-20; internet iutweb.u-clermont1.fr; Dir Prof. JEAN-MARC LAVEST.

Dentistry: 11 blvd Charles de Gaulle, 63000 Clermont-Ferrand Cedex; tel. 4-73-17-73-00; fax 4-73-17-73-09; internet webodonto.u-clermont1.fr; Dean Prof. THIERRY ORLIAGUET.

University Professional Institute of Business Management: Pôle Tertiaire et Technologique, 26 ave Léon-Blum, 63000 Clermont-Ferrand; tel. 4-73-17-77-00; fax 4-73-17-77-01; internet iup-management.net; Dir Prof. MAURICE CHENEVOY.

IPAG: 26 ave Léon-Blum, 63000 Clermont-Ferrand; tel. 4-73-17-77-50; fax 4-73-17-77-55; internet www.u-clermont1.fr/institut-de-preparation-a-l-administration--generale; Dir FRANÇOIS CHOUVEL.

UNIVERSITÉ D'AVIGNON ET DES PAYS DE VAUCLUSE

74 rue Louis Pasteur, 84029 Avignon Cedex 1

Telephone: 4-90-16-25-00
Fax: 4-90-16-25-20
E-mail: presidence@univ-avignon.fr
Internet: www.univ-avignon.fr

Founded 1303; closed in 1793 after French revolution; reopened in 1963; univ. status since 1984
State control
Language of instruction: French
Academic year: September to June

Pres.: Prof. EMMANUEL ETHIS
Dir. Gen.: LUÇAY SAUTRON
Librarian: ISABELLE DIMONDO

Library of 155,600 vols, 73 online databases, 8,311 periodical titles
Number of teachers: 357
Number of students: 7,125

Publications: *Culture et Musée, Etudes Vauclusiennes, Ecologia Mediterranea*.

TEACHING AND RESEARCH UNITS

Faculté des Arts, Lettres et Langues: 74 rue Louis Pasteur, 84029 Avignon Cedex 1; tel. 4-90-16-26-64; fax 4-90-16-27-02; e-mail secretariat-pedagogique-lettres@univ-avignon.fr; Dir ALAIN SERVEL.

Faculté de Droit, Economie et Gestion: 74 rue Louis Pasteur, 84029 Avignon Cedex

1; tel. 4-90-16-27-41; fax 4-90-16-27-44; e-mail dir-droit@univ-avignon.fr; Dean PIERRE FRESSOZ.

Faculté des Sciences Humaines et Sociales: 74 rue Louis Pasteur, 84029 Avignon Cedex 1; tel. 4-90-16-27-18; fax 4-90-16-27-19; e-mail sla@univ-avignon.fr; Dir PIERRE-LOUIS SUET.

Faculté des Sciences et Technologies: 33 rue Louis Pasteur, 84000 Avignon Cedex 1; tel. 4-90-14-40-00; fax 4-90-14-40-09; e-mail sciences@univ-avignon.fr; Dir PASCAL LAURENT.

ATTACHED RESEARCH INSTITUTES

Centre d'Enseignement et de Recherche en Informatique (CERI): 339 Chemin des Meinajaries, 84911 Avignon Cedex 9; tel. 4-90-84-35-00; fax 4-90-84-35-01; e-mail ceri-info@univ-avignon.fr; Dir MARC EL-BÈZE.

Institut Universitaire de Technologie (IUT): 337 Chemin des Meinajaries, BP 1207, 84911 Avignon Cedex 9; tel. 4-90-84-14-00; fax 4-90-84-38-62; e-mail info-sg-iut@univ-avignon.fr; internet www.iut.univ-avignon.fr; Dir HÉLÈNE DOMINGUEZ.

UNIVERSITÉ BLAISE PASCAL

34 ave Carnot, BP 185, 63006 Clermont-Ferrand Cedex 1

Telephone: 4-73-40-63-63
Fax: 4-73-40-64-31
E-mail: president@univ-bpclermont.fr
Internet: www.univ-bpclermont.fr
Founded 1810, present status 1984 as Université de Clermont-Ferrand II—Université Blaise Pascal

Pres.: NADINE LAVIGNOTTE
Vice-Pres: BETTINA ABOAB, MARIE-JOSEPH BIACHE, PASCALE DUCHÉ
Sec.-Gen.: HERVÉ COMBAZ
Librarian: L. RAPATEL

Number of teachers: 970
Number of students: 14,400

Publication: *Journal de l'Université Blaise-Pascal* (3 a year).

TEACHING AND RESEARCH UNITS

Ecole Nationale Supérieure de Chimie de Clermont-Ferrand (ENSCCF—National Higher School of Chemistry): Campus des Cézeaux, 24 ave des Landais, BP 10187, 63174 Aubière Cedex; tel. 4-73-40-71-45; fax 4-73-40-70-95; e-mail scolarite@ensccf.fr; internet ensccf.univ-bpclermont.fr; Dir SOPHIE COMMEREUC.

Institut Supérieur d'Informatique de Modélisation et de leurs Applications (ISIMA—Graduate Engineering School focused on Computing): Campus des Cézeaux, BP 10125, 63173 Aubière Cedex; tel. 4-73-40-50-00; fax 4-73-40-50-01; e-mail secretariat@isima.fr; internet www.isima.fr; Head ALAIN QUILLIOT.

Institut Universitaire de Formation des Maîtres d'Auvergne (IUFM—University Institute for Teacher Training): 36 ave Jean Jaurès, CS 20001, 63407 Chamalières Cedex; tel. 4-73-31-71-50; fax 4-73-36-56-48; e-mail elsa.graive@univ-bpclermont.fr; internet www.auvergne.iufm.fr; Dir DIDIER JOURDAN.

Institut Universitaire de Technologie d'Allier de Montluçon (MONIUT—University Institute of Technology): ave Aristide Briand, BP 2235, 03107 Montluçon Cedex; tel. 4-70-02-20-00; fax 4-70-02-20-78; e-mail secretariat.geii@moniut.univ-bpclermont.fr; internet www.moniut.univ-bpclermont.fr; Dir CÉCILE CHARASSE.

Langues appliquées, Commerce et Communication (LACC—Applied Language, Business and Communication): 34 ave Carnot, 63037 Clermont-Ferrand Cedex; tel. 4-73-40-64-05; fax 4-73-40-64-24; e-mail eric.agbessi@univ-bpclermont.fr; internet www.lacc.univ-bpclermont.fr; Dir ERIC AGBESSI.

Lettres, Langues et Sciences Humaines (Literature, Languages and Human Sciences): 29 blvd Gergovia, 63037 Clermont-Ferrand Cedex; tel. 4-73-34-65-04; fax 4-73-34-65-44; e-mail secretariat.lettres@univ-bpclermont.fr; internet www.lettres.univ-bpclermont.fr; Dir MATHIAS BERNARD.

Observatoire de Physique du Globe de Clermont-Ferrand (OPGC): Campus des Cézeaux, 24 ave des Landais, BP 80026, 63177 Aubière Cedex; tel. 4-73-40-73-80; fax 4-73-40-73-82; e-mail g.delcampo@opgc.univ-bpclermont.fr; internet www.opgc.univ-bpclermont.fr; Dir PATRICK BACHÈLERY.

Polytech Clermont-Ferrand: 24 ave des Landais, BP 20206, 63174 Aubière Cedex; tel. 4-73-40-75-00; fax 4-73-40-75-10; e-mail claude-gilles.dussap@polytech.univ-bpclermont.fr; internet www.cust.univ-bpclermont.fr; Dir CLAUDE-GILLES DUSSAP.

Psychologie, Sciences sociales, Sciences de l'éducation (Psychology, Social Sciences and Educational Science): 34 ave Carnot, 63037 Clermont-Ferrand Cedex; tel. 4-73-40-64-63; fax 4-73-40-64-82; e-mail scolarite.psycho@univ-bpclermont.fr; internet www.psycho.univ-bpclermont.fr; Dir DELPHINE MARTINOT.

Sciences et Techniques des Activités Physiques et Sportives (STAPS—Science and Engineering in Physical Education and Sport): Campus des Cézeaux, 24 ave des Landais, BP 104, 63172 Aubière Cedex; tel. 4-73-40-75-35; fax 4-73-40-74-46; e-mail secretariat.staps@univ-bpclermont.fr; internet www.staps.univ-bpclermont.fr; Dir ÉRIC DORÉ.

Sciences et Technologies (Science and Technology): 24 ave des Landais, BP 80026, 63171 Aubière Cedex; tel. 4-73-40-70-02; fax 4-73-40-70-12; e-mail secretariat.sciences@univ-bpclermont.fr; internet www.sciences.univ-bpclermont.fr; Dir GILLES BOURDIER.

UNIVERSITÉ DE BORDEAUX I

351 cours de la Libération, 33405 Talence Cedex

Telephone: 5-40-00-60-00
Fax: 5-56-80-08-37
E-mail: communication@u-bordeaux1.fr
Internet: www.u-bordeaux1.fr

Pres.: ALAIN BOUDOU
Vice-Pres: JEAN-BAPTISTE VERLHAC (Admin.), ACHILLE BRAQUELAIRE (Curriculum and Univ. Life), DEAN LEWIS (Science), JEAN-MICHEL BAUDERON (Int. Relations)
Sec.-Gen.: ERIC DUTIL

Number of teachers: 1,000
Number of students: 11,150

TEACHING AND RESEARCH UNITS

Faculté de Chimie: 351 cours de la Libération, 33405 Talence Cedex; tel. 5-40-00-61-45; fax 5-40-00-60-43; e-mail sec-ufrchimie@adm.u-bordeaux1.fr; Dir ALAIN FRITSCH.

Faculté de Mathématiques et Informatique: 351 cours de la Libération, 33405 Talence Cedex; tel. 5-40-00-64-21; fax 5-40-00-69-55; e-mail direction@ufr-mi.u-bordeaux1.fr; internet www.u-bordeaux1.fr/ufr/math-info; Dir CHARLES-HENRI BRUNEAU.

Faculté de Physique: 351 cours de la Libération, 33405 Talence Cedex; tel. 5-40-00-62-17; e-mail sec@crphy.u-bordeaux1.fr; internet www.ufr-physique.u-bordeaux1.fr; Dir GENEVIÈVE DUCHAMP.

Faculté des Sciences Biologiques: ave des Facultés, 33405 Talence Cedex; tel. 5-40-00-87-00; e-mail ufr-biologie@adm.u-bordeaux1.fr; internet www.u-bordeaux1.fr/biologie; Dir JEAN-PIERRE RENAUDIN.

Faculté des Sciences de la Terre et de la Mer: ave des Facultés, 33405 Talence Cedex; tel. 5-40-00-88-79; e-mail ufr-termer@adm.u-bordeaux1.fr; internet www.u-bordeaux1.fr/terre_mer; Dir PASCAL LECROART.

UNIVERSITY PROFESSIONAL INSTITUTES

University Professional Institute of Computer-Assisted Management: tel. 5-40-00-89-49; internet miage.u-bordeaux.fr; Dir NICOLE BIDOIT.

University Professional Institute of Electrical Engineering and Industrial Informatics: tel. 5-40-00-28-30; internet www.creea.u-bordeaux.fr; Dir YVES DANTO.

University Professional Institute of Industrial Systems Engineering—Aircraft Maintenance: tel. 5-56-13-31-58; internet www.u-bordeaux1.fr/ima; Dir CHRISTIAN BOUILLE.

University Professional Institute of Mechanical Engineering: tel. 5-40-00-65-15; internet www.u-bordeaux1.fr/iup_gm; Dir MICHEL NOUILLANT.

ATTACHED INSTITUTES

École Nationale Supérieure de Chimie et de Physique de Bordeaux (ENSCPB): 16 ave Pey Berland, 33607 Pessac Cedex; tel. 5-40-00-65-65; fax 5-40-00-66-33; e-mail admin@enscpb.fr; internet www.enscpb.fr; Dir BERNARD CLIN.

École Nationale Supérieure d'Électronique et de Radiocommunication de Bordeaux (ENSERB): 1 ave du Dr Albert Schweitzer, 33402 Talence Cedex; tel. 5-56-84-65-00; fax 5-56-37-20-23; internet www.enserb.u-bordeaux.fr; Dir PHILIPPE MARCHEGAY.

Institut de Chimie de la Matière Condensée de Bordeaux (ICMCB): tel. 5-40-00-62-96; fax 5-40-00-66-34; internet www.icmcb-bordeaux.cnrs.fr; Dir CLAUDE DELMAS.

Institut Européen de Chimie et Biologie (IECB): tel. 5-40-00-22-16; internet www.iecb-polytechnique.u-bordeaux.fr; Dir JEAN-JACQUES TOULME.

Institut de Mathématiques de Bordeaux (IMCB): tel. 5-40-00-60-70; fax 5-40-00-21-23; e-mail institut@math.u-bordeaux1.fr; internet www.math.u-bordeaux.fr/maths; Dir PHILIPPE CASSOU-NOGUES.

Institut de Physique Fondamentale (IPF): tel. 5-40-00-83-13; internet www.u-bordeaux1.fr/ipf; Dir ERIC FREYS.

Institut du Pin (IP): tel. 5-40-00-64-20; fax 5-40-00-64-22; e-mail ipin@ipin.u-bordeaux1.fr; internet www.u-bordeaux1.fr/ipin; Dir JEAN BARANGER.

Institut de Recherche pour l'Enseignement des Mathématiques (IREM): tel. 5-40-00-89-74; Dir PIERRE DAMEY.

Institut des Sciences et Techniques d'Alimentation de Bordeaux (ISTAB): tel. 5-40-00-87-53; fax 5-56-37-03-36; e-mail scolarite@istab.u-bordeaux1.fr; internet www.u-bordeaux1.fr/istab; Dir FRANÇOIS RIBOULET.

Institut Universitaire de Technologie: Domaine Universitaire, 33405 Talence Cedex; tel. 5-56-84-57-02; internet www.iut.u-bordeaux1.fr; Dir PIERRE LAFON.

Observatoire: 2 rue de l'Observatoire, 33270 Floirac; tel. 5-57-77-61-63; fax 5-57-

77-61-10; internet www.obs.u-bordeaux1.fr;
Dir THIERRY JACQ.

UNIVERSITÉ BORDEAUX II (VICTOR SEGALEN)

146 rue Léo-Saignat, 33076 Bordeaux Cedex
Telephone: 5-57-57-10-10
Fax: 5-56-99-03-80
E-mail: info@u-bordeaux2.fr
Internet: www.u-bordeaux2.fr
Founded 1970
Academic year: September to July
Pres.: MANUEL TUNON DE LARA
Vice-Pres: Prof. ANTOINE DE DARUVAR (Ccl of Admin.), Prof. ALAIN BLANCHARD (Scientific Ccl), Prof. NICOLE RASCLE (Studies and Univ. Life), Prof. VINCENT DOUSSET (Int. Relations)
Sec.-Gen.: CORINNE DUFFAU
Librarian: ANNE-MARIE BERNARD
Number of teachers: 1,000
Number of students: 19,000

Publication: *Anima* (4 a year).

TEACHING AND RESEARCH UNITS

Faculté d'Odontologie: tel. 5-57-57-30-01; fax 5-57-57-30-10; e-mail admin.odonto@u-bordeaux2.fr; Dir Dr JEAN-FRANÇOIS PÉLI.

Faculté d'Oenologie: tel. 5-57-57-58-58; fax 5-57-57-58-13; internet www.oenologie.u-bordeaux2.fr; Dir Prof. BERNARD DONÈCHE.

Faculté des Sciences de l'Homme: tel. 5-57-57-18-06; fax 5-56-91-32-90; e-mail fsh@u-bordeaux2.fr; Dir Prof. JACK DORON.

Faculté des Sciences Médicales: tel. 5-57-57-13-13; fax 5-57-57-15-89; e-mail jacqueline.hubert@u-bordeaux2.fr; Dean Prof. JEAN-LUC PELLEGRIN.

Faculté de Sciences et Modélisation: tel. 5-57-57-31-18; fax 5-57-57-31-44; e-mail elise.keou@u-bordeaux2.fr; internet www.sm.u-bordeaux2.fr; Dir MICHEL LANGLAIS.

Faculté des Sciences Pharmaceutiques: tel. 5-57-57-12-00; fax 5-56-93-88-82; e-mail doyen.pharmacie@u-bordeaux2.fr; internet www.pharmacie.u-bordeaux2.fr; Dir Prof. BERNARD MULLER.

Faculté des Sciences et Techniques des Activités Physiques et Sportives: tel. 5-56-84-52-00; fax 5-56-84-94-89; e-mail fac.sci-sport@u-bordeaux2.fr; internet www.staps.u-bordeaux2.fr; Dir MARIANO CID.

Faculté des Sciences de la Vie: tel. 5-57-57-10-91; fax 5-56-24-99-78; e-mail ufrsdv@u-bordeaux2.fr; internet www.ufrsdv.u-bordeaux2.fr; Dir NADINE THÉZÉ.

UNIVERSITÉ BORDEAUX III (MICHEL DE MONTAIGNE)

Domaine Universitaire, 33607 Pessac Cedex
Telephone: 5-57-12-44-44
Fax: 5-57-12-44-90
E-mail: accueil@u-bordeaux3.fr
Internet: www.u-bordeaux3.fr; attached to PRES Université de Bordeaux
Pres.: PATRICE BRUN
Vice-Pres: JEAN-PAUL JOURDAN (Ccl of Admin.), JEAN-YVES COQUELIN (Studies and Univ. Life), PATRICK BAUDRY (Scientific Ccl)
Sec.-Gen.: THOMAS RAMBAUD
Librarian: ANITA LARGOUET
Number of teachers: 646
Number of students: 15,200

Publications: *Annales du Midi, Aquitania, Bulletin hispanique, Cahier d'outre-mer, Communication et organisation, Revue des études anciennes, Sud-Ouest européen.*

TEACHING AND RESEARCH UNITS

Faculté des Humanités: Maison des Pays Ibériques, Domaine Universitaire, 33607 Pessac Cedex; tel. 5-57-12-46-38; fax 5-57-12-45-29; e-mail accueil-ufr-humanites@u-bordeaux3.fr; Dir MARIE-BERNADETTE DUFOURCET-HAKIM.

Faculté des Langues et Civilisations: Bâtiment A, 1er étage, Domaine Universitaire, 33607 Pessac Cedex; tel. 5-57-12-44-71; fax 5-57-12-46-01; e-mail accueil-ufr-langues@u-bordeaux3.fr; Dir STEPHAN MARTENS.

Faculté des Sciences des Territoires et de la Communication: Domaine Universitaire, 33607 Pessac Cedex; tel. 5-57-12-62-80; fax 5-57-12-45-33; e-mail accueil-ufr-stc@u-bordeaux3.fr; Dir HÉLÈNE VELASCO-GRACIET.

Institut Environnement, Géo-ingénierie et Développement (EGID): 1 allée Daguin, 33607 Pessac Cedex; tel. 5-57-12-10-10; fax 5-57-12-10-01; e-mail administration@egid.u-bordeaux.fr; Dir JEAN-MARIE MALEZIEUX.

Institut de Journalisme Bordeaux Aquitaine (IJBA): 1 rue Jacques Ellul, 33080 Bordeaux Cedex; tel. 5-57-12-20-20; fax 5-57-12-20-81; e-mail journalisme@ijba.u-bordeaux3.fr; Dir MARIA SANTOS-SAINZ.

Institut Universitaire de Technologie: Quartier Sainte Croix, 1 rue Jacques Ellul, 33080 Bordeaux Cedex; tel. 5-57-12-20-44; fax 5-57-12-20-09; e-mail direction@iut.u-bordeaux3.fr; internet www.iut.u-bordeaux3.fr; Dir CLOTILDE DE MONTGOLFIER

PROFESSORS

ABECASSIS, A., Philosophy
AGOSTINO, M., Contemporary History
AGUILA, Y., Spanish
AUGUSTIN, J.-P., Geography
BARAT, J.-C., English
BART, F., Geography
BAUDRY, P., Sociology
BECHTEL, F., Physics applied to Archaeology
BERIAC, F., Medieval History
BERTIN-MAGHIT, J.-P., Cinema
BESSE, M. G., Portuguese Literature
BOHLER, D., Medieval Languages and Literature
BOST, J.-P., Ancient History
BOUCARUT, M., Petrography
BRAVO, F., Spanish
BRESSON, A., Medieval History
CABANES, J.-L., Contemporary French Literature
CAMBRONNE, P., Latin
CHAMPEAU, G., Spanish
CHARRIE, J.-P., Geography
COCULA, A.-M., Modern History
COCULA, B., French Language
CORZANI, J., Contemporary French Literature
COSTE, D., Comparative Literature
DEBORD, P., Ancient History
DE CARVALHO, P., Latin
DECOUDRAS, P. M., Land and Society in Tropical Environments
DEPRETTO, C., Russian
DESCAT, R., Greek History
DESCHAMPS, L., Latin
DES COURTILS, J., History of Art
DESVOIS, J.-M., Spanish
DI MÉO, G., Geography
DOTTIN ORSINI, M., Comparative Literature
DUBOIS, C., French
DUCASSE, R., Information Science
DURRUTY, S., English
DUTHEIL, F., Italian
DUVAL, G., English
FONDIN, H., Information and Communication Science
FOURTINA, H., English

FRANCHET D'ESPEREY, H., Latin
GARMENDIA, V., Spanish
GAUTHIER, M., American English
GILBERT, B., English
GORCEIX, P., German
GOZE, M., Urban Planning
GRANDJEAT, Y., North American Civilization
GUILLAUME, P., Modern History
GUILLAUME, S., Modern History
HOTIER, H., Information and Communication Science
HUMBERT, L., Geology
JARASSE, D., History of Modern Art
JOLY, M., Image Analysis
JOUVE, M., English
LACHAISE, B., Modern History
LACOSTE, J., History of Art
LAMORE, J., Spanish
LANGHADE, J., Arabic
LARRERE, C., Philosophy
LAVAUD, C., Philosophy
LAVEAU, P., German
LEBIGRE, J.-M., Physical Geography, Biogeography
LEPRUN-PIÉTON, S., Art, Plastic Arts
LERAT, C., English
LOPEZ, F., Spanish
LOUISE, G., Medieval History
LOUPES, P., History
LY, A., Spanish
MAILLARD, J.-C., Geography
MALEZIEUX, J.-M., Geology
MALLET, D., Arabic
MANTION, J.-R., 18th-century French Literature
MARIEU, J., Urban Planning and Projects
MARQUETTE, J.-B., History
MARTIN, D., French Language and Literature
MATHIEU, M., Contemporary Francophone Literature
MAZOUER, C., Contemporary French Literature
MONDOT, J., German
MORIN, S., Tropical Geography
MOULINE, L., Theatre
MULLER, C., General Linguistics
NAVARRI, R., French Language and Literature
NOTZ, M.-F., Medieval Language and Literature
OLLIER, N., English
ORPUSTAN, J.-B., Basque
PAILHE, J., Geography
PELLETIER, N., German
PERRIN-NAFFAKH, A.-M., Contemporary Language and Literature
PERROT, M., Information and Communications Science
PEYLET, G., Contemporary Language and Literature
PICCIONE, M.-L., Contemporary Language and Literature
PONCEAU, J.-P., Medieval Language and Literature
PONTET, J., Modern History
PORTINE, H., Teaching French as a Foreign Language
POUCHAN, P., Geology
RABATE, D., Contemporary French Literature
RAMOND, C., Philosophy
REYNIER-GIRARDIN, C., English
RIBEIRO, M., Portuguese
RICARD, M., Tropical Pacific Phytoplankton
RIGAL-CELLARD, B., English
RITZ, R., English
ROCHER, A., Japanese
RODDAZ, J.-M., Ancient History
ROSSI, G., Geography
ROUCH, M., Italian
ROUDIE, P., Geography
ROUYER, M.-C., English
ROUYER, P., Plastic Art
RUIZ, A., German
SALOMON, J.-N., Geography

SCHVOERER, M., Physics applied to Archae-ology
SENTAURENS, J., Spanish
SEVESTRE, N., Music and History of Music
SHEN, J., Applied Mathematics
SHUSTERMAN, R., English
SINGARAVELOU, Geography
TAILLARD, C., History of Modern Art
TERREL, J., Philosophy
VADE, Y., Contemporary Language and Literature
VAGNE-LEBAS, M., Social Communication
VIGNE, M.-P., English
VITALIS, A., Information and Communication Science
VLES, V., Urban Planning
ZAVIALOFF, N., Russian

UNIVERSITÉ BORDEAUX IV (MONTESQUIEU)

ave Léon-Duguit, 33608 Pessac Cedex
Telephone: 5-56-84-85-86
Fax: 5-56-37-00-25
E-mail: umb4@montesquieu.u-bordeaux.fr
Internet: www.u-bordeaux4.fr
Founded 1995 from units fmrly within the Univ. of Bordeaux I
State control; attached to PRES Université de Bordeaux

7 Establishments at Bordeaux, Agen and Périgeux; 3 doctoral schools, 12 research units, 2 technology institutes, 1 business management institute, 1 political science institute

Pres.: YANNICK LUNG
Vice-Pres. for Admin. and Finance: CLAUDE DUPUY
Vice-Pres. for Education: GÉRARD BORDENAVE
Vice-Pres. for Research: DANIEL BOURMAUD
Sec.-Gen.: MARLÈNE BARBOTIN
Librarian: DOMINIQUE MONTBRUN-ISRAËL

Number of teachers: 690 incl. researchers
Number of students: 18,700.

TEACHING AND RESEARCH UNITS

Faculté de Droit et Science Politique: Dean JEAN-FRANÇOIS BRISSON.

Faculté d'Économie, Gestion et AES: Dir BERTRAND BLANCHETON.

Institut d'Administration des Entre-prises (IAE): 35 ave Abadie, 33100 Bor-deaux Cedex; tel. 5-56-00-45-67; fax 5-56-00-45-66; internet www.iae-bordeaux.fr; Dir SERGE EVRAERT.

Institut Universitaire de Formation des Maîtres d'Aquitaine (IUFM): 160 ave de Verdun, BP 90152, 33705 Mérignac; tel. 5-56-12-67-00; fax 5-56-12-67-99; internet iufm .u-bordeaux4.fr; f. 1991; in 2008 became Univ. School; Dir PHILIPPE GIRARD.

Institut Universitaire de Technologie Bordeaux Montesquieu: 35 ave Abadie, 33072 Bordeaux Cedex; tel. 5-56-00-96-05; e-mail directeur-iutbxm@u-bordeaux4.fr; internet www.iut.u-bordeaux4.fr; Dir ANNIE LESPINASSE.

Institut Universitaire de Technologie Périgueux Bordeaux IV: 39 rue Paul Mazy, 24019 Périgueux Cedex; tel. 5-53-02-58-58; fax 5-53-02-58-71; e-mail iutpxbx4@ u-bordeaux4.fr; internet www.perigueux .u-bordeaux4.fr; Pres. PATRICK MONTFORT.

ATTACHED INSTITUTE

Institut d'Etudes Politiques: 11 allée Ausone, 33607 Pessac Cedex; tel. 5-56-84-42-52; fax 5-56-84-44-00; e-mail direction@ sciencespobordeaux.fr; internet www .sciencespobordeaux.fr; Dir VINCENT HOFF-MANN-MARTINOT.

UNIVERSITÉ DE BOURGOGNE

Maison de l'Université, Esplanade Erasme, BP 27877, 21078 Dijon Cedex
Telephone: 3-80-39-50-00
Fax: 3-80-39-50-69
E-mail: presidente@u-bourgogne.fr
Internet: www.u-bourgogne.fr
Founded 1722 as Dijon Faculty of Law

Pres.: SOPHIE BÉJEAN
Vice-Pres.: ALAIN BONNIN
Sec.-Gen.: JEAN NARVAEZ
Librarian: NATALIE CÊTRE

Number of teachers: 1,500
Number of students: 27,400

Publications: *Journal d'Information*, *Livret de la recherche*, *Publications de l'Univer-sité* (irregular series of monographs).

TEACHING AND RESEARCH UNITS

Faculté de Droit et de Science Politique: tel. and fax 3-80-39-54-26; e-mail estelle .mielle@u-bourgogne.fr; internet ufr-juridique.u-bourgogne.fr; Dean LAUR-ENCE RAVILLON.

Faculté de Langues et Communication: 2 blvd Gabriel, 21000 Dijon; tel. 3-80-39-55-00; fax 3-80-39-56-19; Dir MME. GERRER.

Faculté de Lettres et Philosophie: 2 blvd Gabriel, 21000 Dijon; tel. 3-80-39-56-01; e-mail seclphi@u-bourgogne.fr; internet ufr-lettres-philosophie.u-bourgogne.fr; Dean PHILIPPE MONNERET.

Faculté de Médecine: 7 blvd Jeanne d'Arc, BP 87900, 21079 Dijon; tel. 3-80-39-32-00; fax 3-80-39-33-00; internet medecine .u-bourgogne.fr; Dean FRÉDÉRIC HUET.

Faculté de Science Economique et Ges-tion: 7 blvd Jeanne d'Arc, BP 87900, 21079 Dijon; tel. 3-80-39-54-00; fax 3-80-39-54-07; e-mail edlisit@u-bourgogne.fr; internet ufr-economique.u-bourgogne.fr; Dean STÉ-PHANE TIZIO.

Faculté des Sciences de la Vie, de la Terre et de l'Environnement: Batiment Gabriel, 6 blvd Gabriel, 21079 Dijon; tel. 3-80-39-50-30; e-mail direction-ufrsvte@ u-bourgogne.fr; internet ufr-svte .u-bourgogne.fr; Dir MICHEL NARCE.

Faculté des Sciences du Sport: Campus Universitaire Montmuzard, BP 27 877, 21078 Dijon; tel. 3-80-39-67-01; fax 3-80-39-67-02; e-mail tania.carnet@u-bourgogne.fr; Dir JEAN-PIERRE REY.

Faculté des Sciences et Techniques: Bâtiment Mirande, 9 ave Alain Savary, BP 47870, 21078 Dijon; tel. 3-80-39-67-01; fax 3-80-39-67-02; e-mail thierry.grison@ u-bourgogne.fr; internet sciences-techniques .u-bourgogne.fr; Dir THIERRY GRISSON.

Faculté des Sciences Humaines: 2 blvd Gabriel, 21000 Dijon; e-mail carine .lausseur@u-bourgogne.fr; internet sciences-humaines.u-bourgogne.fr; Dir DANIEL DURNEY.

Faculté des Sciences Pharmaceutiques et Biologiques: 7 blvd Jeanne d'Arc, BP 87900, 21079 Dijon; tel. 3-80-39-33-00; e-mail secretariat.doyen.pharmacie@u-bourgogne .fr; internet pharmacie.u-bourgogne.fr; Dir Prof. EVELYNE KOHLI

PROFESSORS

Arts Faculties:
ABDI, Psychology
ALI BOUACHA, French Linguistics
BASTIT, Philosophy
BAVOUX, Geography
BENONY, Psychology
Mme BERCOT, Modern Literature
CHAPUIS, Geography
CHARRIER, Geography

CHARUE, German
Mme CHARUE, German
CHEVIGNARD, American English
CHIFFRE, Geography
COMANZO, English
Mme COURTOIS, Comparative Literature
Mme DOBIAS, Classical Literature
DUCHENE, History
Mme DUCOS, Classical Literature
DURIX, English
Mme DURU, Education
Mme FAYARD, Modern History
FAYOL, Psychology
FERRARI, Philosophy
FOYARD, French Philology
GARNOT, Modern History
Mme HAAS, French Linguistics
IMBERTY, Italian
JACOBI, Information and Communication Science
Mlle JOLY, Latin
LAMARRE, Geography
LARRAZ, Romance Languages
Mme LAVAUD, Spanish
LAVAUD, Spanish
McCARTHY, English
MORDANT, Protohistory
NOUHAUD, Spanish
Mlle PELLAN, English
Mme PERARD, Geography
Mme PERROT, Philosophy
Mme PIROELLE, English
PITAVY, English
Mme PITAVY, English
Mme POURKIER, Greek
QUILLIOT, Philosophy
RATIE, English
REFFET, German
RONSIN, Modern History
Mme SADRIN, English
SADRIN, French Literature
SAINT-DENIS, Medieval History
SAURON, Audiology
SOUILLER, Comparative Literature
SOUTET, Linguistics, Phonetics
TABBAGH, Medieval Archaeology
TAVERDET, French Philology
TUROWSLI, History of Art
Mme VINTER, Psychology
WOLIKOW, History and Civilization
WUNENBURGER, Philosophy
ZAGAR, Psychology

Faculties of Law and Economic Science:
BALESTRA, Economic Sciences
BART, Law, Roman Law
Mme BAUMONT, Economics
BODINEAU, History of Law
BOLARD, Private Law
BROUSSOLLE, Public Law
CASIMIR, Management
CHADEFAUX, Management
CHAPPEZ, Public Law
CHARREAUX, Management
CLERE, History of Law
COURVOISIER, Political Sciences
DE MESNARD, Economics
DESBRIÈRES, Economics
DOCKES, Private Law
DUBOIS, Public Law
FILSER, Management Sciences
Mme FORTUNET, History of Law
FRITZ, Political Sciences
Mme GADREAU, Economics
HURIOT, Economic Sciences
JACQUEMONT, Management
JOBERT, History of Law
KORNPROBST, Public Law
LOQUIN, Private Law
Mme MARTIN-SERF, Private Law
MATHIEU, Public Law
MICHELOT, Economics, Mathematics
PAUL, Economics of Education
PERREUR, Economic Sciences
PICHERY, M. C., Economics
PIERI, History of Law

Mme PIERI, Private Law
PIZZIO, Private Law
ROUGET, Economics
SALMON, Political Economy
SIMON, Public Law

Faculties of Medicine and Pharmacy:
ARTUR, Physical Biochemistry
AUTISSIER, Anatomy
Mme AUTISSIER, Physical Chemistry
BEDENNE, Gastroenterology
BELON, Pharmacology
BESANCENOT, Internal Medicine
BINNERT, Radiology
BLETTERY, Resuscitation
BONNIN, Parasitology
BRALET, Physiology
BRENOT, Vascular Surgery
BRON, Ophthalmology
BROSSIER, Physical Chemistry
BRUN, Endocrinology
BRUNOTTE, Biophysics
CAMUS, Pneumology
Mme CARLI, Haematology
CASILLAS, Rehabilitation
CHAILLOT, Pharmacy
CHAVANET, Infectious Diseases
COUGARD, Surgery
CUISENIER, Surgery
DAVID, Thoracic and Cardiac Surgery
DELCOURT, Pharmacy
DIDIER, Rehabilitation
Mme DUBOIS-LACAILLE, Pharmacognosy
DUMAS, Neurology
Mme DUMAS, Pharmacology
DUSSERRE, Biostatistics
ESCOUSSE, Clinical Pharmacology
FAIVRE, Gastroenterology
FANTINO, Physiology
FAVRE, General Surgery
FELDMAN, Gynaecology and Obstetrics
FREYSZ, Anaesthesiology
GAMBERT, Biochemistry
GIRARD, Anaesthesiology
GIROUD, Neurology
GISSELMANN, Epidemiology
GOUYON, Paediatrics
GRAMMONT, Orthopaedic Surgery and Traumatology
GUERRIN, Oncology
HILLON, Hepatology, Gastroenterology
HORIOT, Radiotheraphy
Mme HUICHARD, Pharmaceutical Law
JEANNIN, Pneumology
Mlle JUSTRABO, Pathological Anatomy
KAZMIERCZAK, Bacteriology, Virology
KRAUSE, Radiology
LAMBERT, Dermatology
LORCERIE, Internal Medicine
LOUIS, Cardiology
MABILLE, S. P., Radiology
MACK, Biochemistry
MALKA, Stomatology and Maxillofacial Surgery
MARTIN, F., Immunology
MOURIER, Neurosurgery
NEEL, Biochemistry
NIVELON, Paediatrics
PADIEU, Biological Chemistry
PFITZEMEYER, Internal Medicine
Mme PIARD, Pathological Anatomy
PORTIER, Infectious and Tropical Diseases
POTHIER, Bacteriology
Mme POURCELOT, Pharmacy
RAT, General Surgery
RIFLE, Nephrology
Mme ROCHAT, Pharmacy
ROCHETTE, Pharmacy
ROMANET, Otorhinolaryngology
ROUSSET, Bacteriology
SAGOT, Gynaecology
SAUTREAUX, Neurosurgery
SCHREIBER, Pharmacy
SMOLIK, Occupational Medicine
SOLARY, Haematology
TAVERNIER, Rheumatology

TEYSSIER, Cytogenetic Histology
THEVENIN, Pharmacy
THIERRY, Neurosurgery
TRAPET, Adult Psychiatry
TROUILLOUD, Orthopaedic Surgery and Anatomy
VERGES, Endocrinology of Metabolic Diseases
WEILLER, Radiology
WILKENING, Anaesthesiology
WOLF, Cardiology
ZAHND, Embryology

Higher Institute of Transport and the Car:
AIVAZZADEH, S., Mechanics
LESUEUR, Mechanics
VERCHERY, Mechanics

Higher National School of Applied Biology:
BELIN, Alimentary Biotermology
BESNARD, Physiology of Nutrition
DIVIES, Microbiology
GERVAIS, Process Engineering
LE MESTE, Physical Chemistry of Food
L'HUGUENOT, Biochemistry
MOLIN, Mathematics
TAINTURIER, Organic Chemistry
Mme VOILLEY, Biology, Biochemistry

Physical Education and Sport:
MORLON, B., Biophysics
VANHOECKE, J., Physical Education and Sport

Science Faculties:
ANDREUX, Geochemistry
BELLEVILLE, J., Animal Physiology
BERGER, Physics
BERTRAND, Chemistry
BESANÇON, Chemistry
BOBIN, Physics
BONNARD, Mathematics
BOQUILLON, Physics
CAMPY, Geology
CEZILLY, Ecology
CHABRIER, Computer Sciences
CHAMPION, Physics
CLOUET, Animal Physiology
COLSON, Chemistry
CONNAT, Animal Biology
COQUET, Physics
CORTET, Mathematics
DEMARQUOY, Animal Physiology
DEREUX, Physics
DOLECKI, Mathematics
DORMOND, Chemistry
DULIEU, Animal Physiology
FANG, Mathematics
FLATO, Mathematics
FRANGE, Chemistry
FROCHOT, B., Ecology
GAUTHERON, B., Chemistry
GOUDONNET, Physics
GUILARD, R., Mathematics
GUIRAUD, Geology
JANNIN, Physics
JANNOT, Physics
JAUSLIN, Physics
JOUBERT, Mathematics
KUBICKI, Chemistry
LALLEMANT, Chemistry
LANG, J., Geology
LANGEVIN, Mathematics
LARPIN, Physical Chemistry
LASSALE, Mathematics
LATRUFFE, Biochemistry
LAURIN, Geology
LENOIR-ROUSSEAU, Zoology
LINES, Mathematics
LOETE, Physics
LOREAU, Geology
MARCUARD, Statistical Probability
MARNIER, Physics
MARTY, Plant Biology
MATVEEV, Mathematics
MAUME, B., Biochemistry
MEUNIER, Chemistry
Mme MICHELOT, Physics

MICHON, Mathematics
MILAN, Electronics
MILLOT, Physics
MOÏSE, C., Chemistry
MOUSSU, Mathematics
MUGNIER, Chemistry
NIEPCE, J.-CL., Chemistry
PAINDAVOINE, Automatics
PALLO, Informatics
PAUL, Plant Biology
PAUTY, Physics
PERRON, Mathematics
PIERRE, Physics
PINCZON, Mathematics
PRIBETICH, Electronics
PUGIN, Biochemistry
RACLIN, Mechanics
REMOISSENET, Physics
ROUSSARIE, Mathematics
SCHMITT, Mathematics
SEMENOV, Mathematics
SIEROFF, Neurophysiology
SIMON, Mathematics
STEINBRUNN, Chemistry
THIERRY, Geology
Mme TOURNEFIER, Biology
VALLADE, Plant Biology
WABNITZ, Physics
YETONGNON, Informatics

University Institute of Technology:
BELEY, Biology, Applied Biochemistry
BERLIÈRE, Contemporary History
BERNARD, Physiology and Nutrition
BESSIS, Botany
BIZOUARD, M., Thermodynamics
BUGAUT, Biochemistry
CHANUSSOT, Physics
DIOU, Industrial Computer Science
GORRIA, Computer Engineering
GREVEY, Materials
POISSON, Biochemistry
SACILOTTI, Physics
TRUCHETET, Computer Engineering

University Professional Institute of Management in Education, Training and Culture:
JAROUSSE, J.-P., Education
PATRIAT, C., Informatics and Communication
SOLAUX, A., Education

Viticulture and Oenology Experimental Centre:
CHARPENTIER, O., Oenology
FEUILLAT, M., Oenology

UNIVERSITÉ DE BRETAGNE OCCIDENTALE

Site 1–3, rue des Archives, BP 808, 29285 Brest Cedex

Telephone: 2-98-01-60-03
Fax: 2-98-01-73-40
E-mail: secretariat.general@univ-brest.fr
Internet: www.univ-brest.fr

Pres.: PASCAL OLIVARD
Vice-Pres.: GEORGES TYMEN
Sec.-Gen.: STÉPHANE CHARPENTIER
Librarian: ALAIN SAINSOT

Number of teaching staff: 820
Number of students: 20,000.

TEACHING AND RESEARCH INSTITUTES

Faculté de Droit, Économie et Gestion: 12 rue de Kergoat, CS 93837, 29238 Brest Cedex 3; tel. 2-98-01-60-23; fax 2-98-01-65-30; e-mail directeur.deg@univ-brest.fr; internet www.univ-brest.fr/ufr-droit-economie; Dean BÉATRICE THOMAS-TUAL.

Faculté de Lettres et Sciences Humaines: 20 rue Duquesne, CS 93837, 29238 Brest Cedex 3; tel. 2-98-01-67-98; fax 2-98-01-63-90; e-mail scolarite.lettres@univ-brest.fr; internet www

.faculte-lettres-shs-brest.fr; Dir MARIE-ARMELLE BARBIER.

Faculté de Médecine et Sciences de la Santé: 22 rue Camille Desmoulins, CS 93837, 29238 Brest Cedex 3; tel. 2-98-01-64-73; fax 2-98-01-64-74; e-mail doyen .medecine@univ-brest.fr; internet www .faculte-medecine-brest.fr; Dean Prof. MARC DE BRAEKELEER.

Faculté d'Odontologie: 22 rue Camille Desmoulins, CS 93837, 29238 Brest Cedex 3; tel. 2-98-01-64-89; fax 2-98-01-69-32; e-mail alain.zerilli@univ-brest.fr; Dean ALAIN ZERILLI.

Faculté des Sciences et Techniques: 6 ave Victor Le Gorgeu, CS 93837, 29238 Brest Cedex 3; tel. 2-98-01-61-22; fax 2-98-01-61-31; e-mail directeur.sciences@univ-brest.fr; internet www.faculte-sciences-brest.fr; Dir CORINNE TARITS.

Faculté de Sport et Éducation Physique: 6 ave Victor Le Gorgeu, CS 93837, 29238 Brest Cedex 3; tel. 2-98-01-71-47; fax 2-98-01-79-46; e-mail secretaps@univ-brest.fr; internet www.univ-brest.fr/ufr-sport; Dir GILLES KERMARREC.

ATTACHED RESEARCH INSTITUTES

École Supérieure de Microbiologie et Sécurité Alimentaire de Brest (ESMI-SAB): Technopôle Brest-Iroise, 29280 Plouzané; tel. 2-98-05-61-00; fax 2-98-05-61-01; e-mail esmisab@univ-brest.fr; internet www .univ-brest.fr/esmisab; Dir YVES TIRILLY.

Institut de Recherche sur l'Enseignement des Mathématiques (IREM): 6 Ave Victor Le Gorgeu, 29238 Brest Cedex 3; tel. 2-98-01-65-44; fax 2-98-01-64-41; e-mail irem@univ-brest.fr; Dir (vacant).

Institut des Sciences Agro-alimentaires et du Monde Rural: 2 rue de l'université, 29334 Quimper Cedex; tel. 2-98-90-85-48; Dir ADRIEN BINET.

Institut de Synergie des Sciences de la Santé: Site CHU Morvan, 29609 Brest Cedex; tel. 2-98-01-81-30; fax 2-98-01-81-24; internet www.univ-brest.fr/i3s; Dir CLAUDE FEREC.

Institut Universitaire Européen de la Mer (IUEM): place Nicolas Copernic, 29280 Plouzané; tel. 2-98-49-86-00; fax 2-98-49-86-09; e-mail direction.iuem@univ-brest.fr; internet www.univ-brest.fr/iuem; Dir PAUL TREGUER.

UNIVERSITÉ DE BRETAGNE-SUD

BP 92116, 56321 Lorient Cedex
Telephone: 2-97-01-70-89
Fax: 2-97-01-70-98
Internet: www.univ-ubs.fr
Founded 1995
Pres.: OLIVIER SIRE
Vice-Pres: IOANA GALLERON (Ccl of Admin.), PIERRE-FRANÇOIS MARTEAU (Scientific Ccl), GILBERT LE BOUAR (Studies and Univ. Life), GEOFFREY WILLIAMS (Int. Relations)
Sec.-Gen.: CHRISTIAN BILY
Librarian: ANNIE COISY
Number of teachers: 427
Number of students: 8,576.

TEACHING AND RESEARCH UNITS

École Nationale Supérieure d'Ingénieurs de Bretagne Sud: 2 rue le Coat Saint-Haouen, BP 92116, 56321 Lorient Cedex; tel. 2-97-88-05-59; fax 2-97-88-05-51; e-mail ensibs.scol@listes.univ-ubs.fr; internet www-ensibs.univ-ubs.fr; Dir JEAN-LUC PHILIPPE.

Faculté de Droit, des Sciences Economiques et de Gestion: 1 rue de la Loi,

56000 Vannes; tel. 2-97-01-26-00; e-mail dseg@univ-ubs.fr; Dir PATRICK LE MESTRE.

Faculté de Lettres Langues Sciences Humaines et Sociales: 4 rue Jean Zay, BP 92116, 56321 Lorient Cedex; tel. 2-97-87-29-67; fax 2-97-87-29-70; e-mail helene .tanguy@univ-ubs.fr; Dir ERIC LIMOUSIN.

Faculté des Sciences et Sciences de l'Ingénieur: 2 rue Coat Saint-Haouen, BP 92116, 56321 Lorient Cedex; tel. 2-97-88-05-50; e-mail helene.tanguy@univ-ubs.fr; Dir VIRGINIE DUPONT.

Institut Universitaire et Technologique de Lorient: 10 rue Jean Zay, 56325 Lorient Cedex; tel. 2-97-87-28-03; fax 2-97-87-28-08; e-mail iutlo.dir@listes.univ-ubs.fr; internet www-iutlorient.univ-ubs.fr; Dir JEAN VERGER.

Institut Universitaire et Technologique de Vannes: 8 rue Montaigne, BP 561, 56017 Vannes Cedex; tel. 2-97-62-64-64; fax 2-97-63-47-22; e-mail iutva.com@listes.univ-ubs .fr; internet www.iu-vannes.fr; Dir PATRICE KERMORVANT.

UNIVERSITÉ DE CAEN BASSE-NORMANDIE

Esplanade de la Paix, BP 5186, 14032 Caen Cedex 5
Telephone: 2-31-56-55-00
Fax: 2-31-56-56-00
E-mail: presidence@unicaen.fr
Internet: www.unicaen.fr
Founded 1432; reorganized 1985
Pres.: JOSETTE TRAVERT
Vice-Pres: RÉGIS CARIN, DOMINIQUE KERVADEC
Sec.-Gen.: HÉLÈNE BROCHET-TOUTIRI
Librarian: BERNARD VOUILLOT
Number of teachers: 1,364
Number of students: 24,244.

TEACHING AND RESEARCH UNITS

Faculté de Droit et Sciences Politiques: Esplanade de la paix, BP 5186, 14032 Caen Cedex 5; e-mail droit.direction@unicaen.fr; internet www.unicaen.fr/droit; Dean Prof. JEAN-FRANÇOIS AKANDJI-KOMBE.

Faculté de Géographie: Esplanade de la paix, BP 5186, 14032 Caen Cedex 5; tel. 2-31-56-54-64; fax 2-31-56-55-80; e-mail geographie.direction@unicaen.fr; internet www.unicaen.fr/geographie; Dir STÉPHANE COSTA.

Faculté d'Histoire: Esplanade de la paix, BP 5186, 14032 Caen Cedex 5; tel. 2-31-56-58-30; fax 2-31-56-65-80; e-mail histoire .secretariat@unicaen.fr; internet www .unicaen.fr/ufr/histoire; Dir JEAN QUELLIEN.

Faculté des Langues Vivantes Etrangères: Esplanade de la paix, BP 5186, 14032 Caen Cedex 5; tel. 2-31-56-57-77; fax 2-31-56-54-96; e-mail lve.secretariat@ unicaen.fr; internet www.unicaen.fr/lve; Dir ERIC GILBERT.

Faculté de Médecine: ave de la Côte de Nacre, 14000 Caen Cedex 5; tel. 2-31-56-57-77; fax 2-31-56-54-96; internet www.unicaen .fr/medecine; Dean Prof. JEAN-LOUIS GERARD.

Faculté de Psychologie: Esplanade de la paix, BP 5186, 14032 Caen Cedex 5; tel. 2-31-56-57-61; fax 2-31-56-59-60; e-mail dominique.bour@unicaen.fr; internet www .unicaen.fr/psychologie; Dir JOËLLE LEBREUILLY.

Faculté de Sciences: blvd Maréchal Juin, 14032 Caen Cedex; tel. 2-31-56-73-10; fax 2-31-56-73-00; e-mail sciences@unicaen.fr; internet www.unicaen.fr/sciences; Dir MARC LEVALOIS.

Faculté des Sciences Economiques et de Gestion: 19 rue Claude Bloch, BP 1586,

14000 Caen Cedex; tel. 2-31-56-55-27; e-mail sciences.economiques.scolarite@unicaen.fr; internet www.unicaen.fr/sc-eco; Dir BONIFACE MBIH.

Faculté des Sciences de l'Homme: Esplanade de la paix, BP 5186, 14032 Caen Cedex 5; tel. 2-31-56-54-51; e-mail sciences .homme@unicaen.fr; internet www.unicaen .fr/sc-homme; Dir YINSU VIZCARRA.

Faculté des Sciences Pharmaceutiques: blvd Becquerel, 14032 Caen Cedex; tel. 2-31-56-60-00; fax 2-31-56-60-20; e-mail pharmacie.administration@unicaen.fr; internet www.unicaen.fr/pharmacie; Dean JEAN-MARIE GAZENGEL.

Faculté des Sciences et Techniques des Activités Physiques et Sportives: blvd Maréchal Juin, 14032 Caen Cedex; tel. 2-31-56-60-00; fax 2-31-56-60-20; e-mail catherine .garncarzyk@unicaen.fr; internet www .unicaen.fr/staps; Dir CATHERINE GARNCARZYK.

ATTACHED INSTITUTES

Ecole Nationale Supérieure d'Ingénieurs de Caen: 6 Blvd Maréchal Juin, 14050 Caen Cedex; tel. 2-31-45-27-50; fax 2-31-45-27-60; internet www.ensicaen.fr; Dir D. GUERREAU.

Institut Universitaire de Formation des Maîtres: 186 rue de la Délivrande, 14053 Caen Cedex 04; tel. 2-31-46-70-80; fax 2-31-93-31-27; internet www.caen.iufm.fr; Dir JEAN MARC GUEGUENIAT.

UNIVERSITÉ DE CERGY-PONTOISE

33 blvd du Port, 95011 Cergy-Pontoise Cedex
Telephone: 1-34-25-60-00
Fax: 1-34-25-49-04
Internet: www.u-cergy.fr
Founded 1991
Pres.: FRANÇOISE MOULIN CIVIL
Vice-Pres.: ANNE-SOPHIE BARTHEZ
Sec.-Gen.: BERNARD FRADIN
Number of teachers: 833
Number of students: 17,000

UNIVERSITÉ DE CORSE PASQUALE PAOLI/UNIVERSITÀ DI CORSICA

BP 52, 7 ave Jean-Nicoli, 20250 Corti
Telephone: 4-95-45-00-00
Internet: www.univ-corse.fr
Founded 1976; opened 1981
Language of instruction: French
Pres.: ANTOINE AIELLO
Sec.-Gen.: FABIENNE PALMARO
Chief Librarian: PEREZ MARIE-PAULE
Library of 80,000 vols
Number of students: 4,400

DEANS

Faculty of Law, Economics and Management: JEAN-YVES COPPOLANI
Faculty of Literature, Languages, Arts and Human Sciences: JEAN-MARIE COMITI
Faculty of Sciences and Techniques: VANINA PASQUALINI
University Institute of Technology: CHRISTIAN CRISTOFARI
University Trainees Training Centre: CHRISTOPHE STORAI

ATTACHED RESEARCH INSTITUTES

Centre de Recherche Corse Méditerranée (CRCM): tel. 4-95-45-00-77; Dir PHILIPPE PESTEIL.

Institut de Développement des Iles Méditerranéennes (IDIM): tel. 4-95-45-00-18; Dir JEAN YVES COPPOLANI.

Institut d'Études Scientifiques de Carg-èse: 20130 Cargèse; fax 4-95-26-80-45; internet cargese.univ-corse.fr; Dir ÉLISABETH DUBOIS-VIOLETTE.

'Lieux, Identités, eSpaces et Acitvités': tel. 4-95-45-01-78; fax 4-95-45-01-66; Dir MARIE-ANTOINETTE MAUPERTUIS.

'Sciences pour l'environnement': SPE UMA 6134, Quartier Grossetti, BP 52, 20250 Corte; tel. 4-95-45-01-65; fax 4-95-45-01-62; e-mail spe@univ-corse.fr; internet spe .univ-corse.fr; Dir PAUL BISGAMBIGLIA.

UNIVERSITÉ D'ÉVRY-VAL D'ESSONNE

blvd F. Mitterrand, 91025 Évry Cedex

Telephone: 1-69-47-70-00
Fax: 1-64-97-27-34
E-mail: olivier.emery@univ-evry.fr
Internet: www.univ-evry.fr

Pres.: RICHARD MESSINA
First Vice-Pres.: ALIAN ZOZIME
Second Vice-Pres.: GÉRARD PORCHER
Sec.-Gen.: HAKIM KHELLAF

Number of teachers: 473
Number of students: 10,000.

TEACHING AND RESEARCH UNITS

Faculté de Droit: 335 Bâtiment Ile-de-France, 91025 Évry Cedex; tel. 1-69-47-70-97; e-mail nadine.bonnet@univ-evry.fr; Dir FRANÇOIS COLLY.

Faculté de Langues, Arts et Musique: B104 bis Bâtiment 1° cycles, 1° étage, 91025 Évry Cedex; tel. 1-69-47-74-44; e-mail secretariat.art@univ-evry.fr; Dir BRIGITTE GAUTHIER.

Faculté des Sciences Fondamentales et Appliquées: Bâtiment Maupertuis, rue du Père André Jarlan, 91025 Évry Cedex; tel. 1-69-47-74-44; e-mail ufrsfa@univ-evry.fr; Dir ANNIE CHAUSSE.

Faculté des Sciences Sociales et Ges-tion: 2 rue du Facteur Cheval, 91025 Évry Cedex; tel. 1-69-47-78-90; e-mail corinne .garault@univ-evry.fr; Dir EMMANUEL QUENSON.

Faculté des Sciences et Technologie: 40 rue du Pelvoux, 91020 Évry Cedex; tel. 1-69-47-75-24; e-mail ufrst@univ-evry.fr; Dir GÉRARD PORCHER.

ATTACHED RESEARCH INSTITUTE

Institut Universitaire de Technologie (IUT): 22 allée Jean Rostand, 91025 Évry Cedex; tel. 1-69-47-72-00; e-mail f .quemener@iut.univ-evry.fr; internet www .iut.univ-evry.fr; Dir PAUL DEMAREZ.

UNIVERSITÉ DE FRANCHE-COMTÉ

1 rue Claude Goudimel, 25030 Besançon Cedex

Telephone: 3-81-66-66-66
Fax: 3-81-66-50-36
E-mail: dri@univ-fcomte.fr
Internet: www.univ-fcomte.fr

Founded 1423 at Dôle, 1691 at Besançon

Pres.: CLAUDE CONDÉ
Vice-Pres.: DANIEL SECHTER, JACQUES BAHI, OUSSAMA BARAKATT
Sec.-Gen.: LOUIS BÉRION

Library: see Libraries
Number of teachers: 1,400
Number of students: 19,519

Publications: *En Direct*, *Tout l'U*.

TEACHING AND RESEARCH INSTITUTES

Faculté des Sciences Juridiques, Econ-omiques, Politiques et de Gestion: 45D ave de l'Observatoire, 25030 Besançon

Cedex; tel. 3-63-08-25-47; e-mail catherine .tirvaudey@univ-fcomte.fr; internet sjepg .univ-fcomte.fr; Dir CATHERINE TIRVAUDEY.

Faculté des Sciences du Langage, de l'Homme et de la Société: 30 rue Még-vand, 25030 Besançon Cedex; tel. 3-81-66-53-10; fax 3-81-66-53-00; internet slhs .univ-fcomte.fr; Dir ANDRÉ MARIAGE.

Faculté des Sciences Médicales et Phar-maceutiques: place Saint-Jacques, 25030 Besançon Cedex; tel. 3-81-66-55-05; fax 3-81-66-55-29; internet medecine-pharmacie .univ-fcomte.fr; Dir Prof. EMMANUEL SAMAIN.

Faculté des Sciences et Techniques: 16 route de Gray, 25030 Besançon Cedex; tel. 3-81-66-69-51; fax 3-81-66-63-70; e-mail webst@univ-fcomte.fr; internet sciences .univ-fcomte.fr; Dir ABDERRAZZAK KADMIRI.

Faculté des Sciences, Techniques et Gestion de l'Industrie: Campus Universi-taire, 4 place Tharradin, BP 71427, 25211 Montbéliard Cedex; tel. 3-81-99-46-62; fax 3-81-99-46-61; e-mail ufr-stgi@univ-fcomte.fr; internet stgi.univ-fcomte.fr; Dir ABDERRAZ-ZAK KADMIRI.

Unité de Promotion, de Formation et de Recherche des Sports: 31 chemin de l'Épitaphe, 25000 Besançon Cedex; tel. 3-81-66-67-90; fax 3-81-53-73-38; internet ufrstaps .univ-fcomte.fr; Dir ERIC PREDINE.

UNIVERSITÉ DE GRENOBLE I (UNIVERSITÉ JOSEPH FOURIER)

BP 53, 38041 Grenoble Cedex 9

Telephone: 4-76-51-46-00
Fax: 4-76-51-48-48
E-mail: service.communication@ujf-grenoble .fr
Internet: www.ujf-grenoble.fr

Founded 1339
Academic year: September to June

Pres.: FARID OUABDESSELAM
Vice-Pres: ARTHUR SOUCEMARIANADIN, ROMAIN LAJARGE, ANNICK VILLET, HENRI PARIS, JEAN-GABRIEL VALAY, LAURENT DAUDEVILLE, MICHAEL KLASEN, PIERRE BACONNIER, BER-NARD SELE ERIC BEAUGNON CATHERINE BERRUT
Sec.-Gen.: JEAN-LUC ARGENTIER

Number of teachers: 1,500
Number of students: 18,900

Publications: *La Pie* (12 a year), *Papyrus* (2 a year), *Visioncrasées* (3 a year)

TEACHING AND RESEARCH UNITS

Applied Mathematics and Computer Sci-ences: Dir: JEAN-CLAUDE FERNANDEZ
Biology: Dir: STÉFAN NONCHEV
Chemistry: Dir: YANNICK VALLÉE
Geography: Dir: JOHN TUPPEN
Mathematics: Dir: EMMANUEL PEYRE
Mechanical Engineering: Dir: HENRI PARIS
Medicine: Dir: BERNARD SÈLE
Pharmacy: Dir: RENÉE GRILLOT
Physical Education and Sport: Dir: ISABELLE OLIVIER
Physics: Dir: KONSTANTIN PROTASSOV

ATTACHED INSTITUTES

Centre Scientifique Joseph Fourier Drôme-Ardèche: BP 2, 26901 Valence Cedex 9; tel. 4-56-52-11-11; fax 4-75-56-16-20; e-mail contact.valence@ujf-grenoble.fr; internet www-valence.ujf-grenoble.fr; Dir ISABELLE COLOMB.

Collège des Ecoles Doctorales: tel. 4-76-51-45-08; fax 4-76-51-44-22; Dir PATRICK WITOMSKI.

Département Licence Sciences et Tech-nologies: 480 ave centrale, 38400 St Martin d'Hères; tel. 4-76-51-45-63; fax 4-76-51-42-

68; internet dlst.ujf-grenoble.fr; Dir BERNARD YCART.

Ecole de Physique des Houches: La Côte des Chavants, 74310 Les Houches; tel. 4-50-54-40-69; fax 4-50-55-53-25; e-mail secretariat.houches@ujf-grenoble.fr; internet houches.ujf-grenoble.fr; Dir LETICIA CUGLIAN-DOLO.

Ecole Polytechnique—Polytech'Greno-ble: 28 ave Benoît Frachon, 38400 St Martin d'Hères; tel. 4-76-82-79-02; fax 4-76-82-79-01; e-mail polytech@ujf-grenoble.fr; internet www.polytech-grenoble.fr; Dir RENÉ-LOUIS INGLEBERT.

Floralis–Filiale de la Valorisation de la Recherche de l'UJF: 6 allée de Bethléem, 38610 Gières; tel. 4-76-00-70-30; fax 4-76-00-70-28; e-mail contact@floralis.fr; internet www.floralis.fr; Dir ERIC LARREY.

Formation Continue: 2 ave de Vignate, 38610 Gières; tel. 4-56-52-03-29; fax 4-56-52-03-32; e-mail formation-continue@ ujf-grenoble.fr; Dir JEAN-GABRIEL VALAY.

Institut Universitaire de Formation des Maîtres: 30 ave Marcelin Berthelot, 38100 Grenoble; tel. 4-56-52-07-00; fax 4-76-87-19-47; internet iufm.ujf-grenoble.fr; Dir PATRICK MENDELSON.

Institut Universitaire de Technologie: 151 rue de la Papeterie, 38402 St Martin d'Hères; tel. 4-76-82-53-00; fax 4-76-82-53-26; e-mail administration.iut@ujf-grenoble .fr; internet www-iut.ujf-grenoble.fr; Dir JEAN-MICHEL TERRIEZ.

Observatoire des Sciences de l'Univers Grenoble: 414 rue de la Piscine, 38400 St Martin d'Hères; tel. 4-76-51-49-81; fax 4-76-63-55-35; e-mail obs-dir@ujf-grenoble.fr; internet www.obs.ujf-grenoble.fr/osug; Dir HENRI-CLAUDE NATAF.

Service Commun des Enseignements Transversaux: Dir JEAN-PIERRE HENRY.

UNIVERSITÉ DE GRENOBLE II (UNIVERSITÉ PIERRE MENDÈS-FRANCE)

BP 47X, 38040 Grenoble Cedex

Telephone: 4-76-82-54-00
Fax: 4-76-82-56-54
E-mail: presidence@upmf-grenoble.fr
Internet: www.upmf-grenoble.fr

Founded 1970
Academic year: September to June

Pres.: ALAIN SPALANZANI
Vice-Pres.: THÉOPHILE OHLMANN (Intervar-sity), MARCEL-RENÉ TERCINET (Ccl of Admin.), ALAIN FERNEX (Curriculum and University Life), RENÉ FAVIER (Scientific Ccl), CLAUDE BENOIT (Finance and Capital), LIONEL FILIPPI (Continuing Education and Educational ICT), JACQUES FONTANEL (Int. Relations), THIERRY MENISSIER (Develop-ment), DOMINIQUE RIEU (Information Sys-tem), SOUHAIL MANAI (Student Body)
Sec.-Gen.: FRANCK LENOIR

Library: see Libraries
Number of teachers: 718
Number of students: 19,531

Publication: *Intercours*.

TEACHING AND RESEARCH UNITS

Faculté de Droit: BP 47, 38040 Grenoble Cedex 9; tel. 4-76-82-55-01; fax 4-76-82-56-69; e-mail chantal.fayen@upmf-grenoble.fr; internet www.facdroit-grenoble.org; Dean SÉBASTIEN BERNARD.

Faculté de l'Economie de Grenoble: 1241 rue des Résidences, Domaine Universitaire, BP 47, 38040 Grenoble Cedex 9; tel. 4-76-82-55-01; fax 4-76-82-56-69; e-mail accueil.ese@

upmf-grenoble.fr; internet ese.upmf-grenoble
.fr; Dir MICHEL ROCCA.

**Faculté des Sciences de l'Homme et de la
Société:** 1251 ave Centrale, Domaine Universitaire, BP 47, 38040 Grenoble Cedex 9;
tel. 4-76-82-59-00; fax 4-76-82-56-65; e-mail
sonia.rocton@upmf-grenoble.fr; internet shs
.upmf-grenoble.fr; Dir RÉMI KOUABENAN.

Faculté des Sciences Humaines: 1281 ave
Centrale, Domaine Universitaire, BP 47,
38040 Grenoble Cedex 9; tel. 4-76-82-73-50;
fax 4-76-82-73-56; e-mail philippe.saltel@
upmf-grenoble.fr; internet sh.upmf-grenoble
.fr; Dir PHILIPPE SALTEL

PROFESSORS

ALBOUY, M., Management
ANTONIADIS, A., Mathematics
ARNAUD, P., Sociology
BAILLE, J., Education
BARREYRE, P.-Y., Management
BELLISSANT, C., Computer Science
BERNARD, J.-P., Political Science
BIAYS, J. P., Political Science
BILLAUDOT, B., Economics
BORRELLY, R., Economics
BOUTOT, A., Philosophy
BRECHON, P., Political Science
CHATELUS, M., Economics
CHIANEA, G., History of Law
COURTIN, J., Informatics
COVIAUX, C., Private Law
CROISAT, M., Political Science
D'ARCY, F., Political Science
DESTANNE DE BERNIS, G., Economics
DIDIER, P., History of Law
DROUET D'AUBIGNY, G., Mathematics
EUZEBY, A., Economics and Management
EUZEBY, C., Economics
FOUCHARD, A., History
FRANCILLON, J., Private Law
GIROD, P., Management
GLEIZAL, J.-J., Public Law
GOUTAL, J.-L., Private Law
GRANGE, D., History
GRELLIERE, V., Law
GROC, B., Computer Science
GUILHAUDIS, M., Public Law
HOLLARD, M., Economics
JOLIBERT, A., Management
LARGUIER, J., Private Law
LESCA, H., Management
LE STANC, C., Law
MAISONNEUVE, B., Mathematics
MARIGNY, J., History
MARTIN, C., Management
N'GUYEN XUAN DANG, M.
OHLMANN, T., Psychology
PAGE, A., Management
PARAVY, P., History
PASCAL, G., Philosophy
PATUREL, R., Management
PECCOUD, F., Computer Science
PETIT, B., Private Law
PIETRA, R., Philosophy
POUSSIN, G., Psychology
POUYET, B., Public Law
RENARD, D., Political Science
RICHARD, A., Economics
ROMIER, G., Applied Mathematics
ROUSSET, M., Public Law
SALVAGE, PASCALE, Law
SALVAGE, PHILIPPE, Law
SCHNEIDER, C., Public Law
SEGRESTIN, D., Industrial Engineering
SIRONNEAU, J.-P., Sociology
SOLE, J., History
SOULAGE, B., Political Science
TERCINET, M., Public Law
TESTON, G.
TIBERGHIEN, G., Psychology
TRAHAND, J., Management
VALETTE-FLORENCE, P.
VERNANT, D., Philosophy

ATTACHED INSTITUTE

Institut d'Études Politiques: 1030 ave
Centrale, Domaine Universitaire, 38400
Saint-Martin-d'Hères; tel. 4-76-82-60-00; fax
4-76-82-60-70; e-mail accueil@iep-grenoble
.fr; internet www-sciences-po.upmf-grenoble
.fr; Dir OLIVIER IHL.

UNIVERSITÉ DE GRENOBLE III
(UNIVERSITÉ STENDHAL)

BP 25, 38040 Grenoble Cedex 9
1180 ave Centrale, 38400

Telephone: 4-76-82-43-00
Fax: 4-76-82-41-85
E-mail: presidence@u-grenoble3.fr
Internet: www.u-grenoble3.fr

Founded 1970

Pres.: LISE DUMASY
Vice-Pres.: FRANCIS GROSSMANN, ISABELLE
    PAILLIART, LAURENCE GARINO-ABEL, ELISA-
    BETH LAVAULT-OLLÉON, FRANÇOIS MANGE-
    NOT
Sec.-Gen.: MARTINE PEVET

Number of teachers: 330
Number of students: 12,000.

TEACHING AND RESEARCH INSTITUTES

Faculté d'Etudes Anglophones: Bâtiment
C, 1180 ave Centrale, 38400 Grenoble Cedex
9; tel. 4-76-82-41-93; fax 4-76-82-41-21;
e-mail christine.morenas@u-grenoble3.fr;
Dir DONNA ANDRÉOLLE.

**Faculté de Langues, Littératures et Civ-
ilisations Etrangères:** Bâtiment G, 1381
rue des résidences, 38400 Grenoble Cedex 9;
tel. 4-76-82-43-54; fax 4-76-82-43-51; e-mail
jacques.rambert@u-grenoble3.fr; Dir ALMU-
DENA DELAGADO-LARIOS.

Faculté des Lettres et Arts: Bâtiment B,
1180 ave Centrale, 38400 Grenoble Cedex 9;
tel. 4-76-82-43-15; fax 4-76-82-41-24; e-mail
gisele.nesta@u-grenoble3.fr; Dir BRIGITTE
COMBE.

**Faculté des Sciences de la Communica-
tion:** Institut de la Communication et des
Médias, 11 ave du 8 mai 1945, BP 337, 38434
Grenoble Cedex 9; tel. 4-56-52-87-17; Dir
FABIENNE MARTIN-JUCHAT.

Faculté des Sciences du Langage: Bâtiment B, 1180 ave Centrale, 38400 Grenoble
Cedex 9; tel. 4-76-82-43-19; fax 4-76-82-41-
34; e-mail solange.puret@u-grenoble3.fr; Dir
JEAN-PIERRE CHEVROT

DIRECTORS OF DEPARTMENTS

Languages, Literature and Foreign Civilizations:

    Applied Foreign Languages: (vacant)
    German and Dutch Studies: JEAN-FRAN-
        ÇOIS MARILLIER
    Iberian and Spanish-American Studies:
        ANNE CAYUELA
    Italian and Romanian Studies: ENZO NEPPI
    Oriental Studies: RITA MAZEN
    Russian and Slav Studies: ISABELLE
        DESPRES
    Trilingual Law and Economics: SUZAN
        BERTHIER
Modern and Classical Literature:

    Classical Studies: BENOÎT GOIN
    Comparative Literature: FLORENCE GOYET
    Languages, Literatures and French Civili-
        zation: BRIGITTE COMBE
Sciences of Language:

    French as a Foreign Language: VIOLAINE
    DE NUCHÈZE, JEAN EMMANUEL LE BRAY

UNIVERSITÉ DE HAUTE-ALSACE

2 rue des Frères Lumière, 68093 Mulhouse
Cedex

Telephone: 3-89-33-63-00
Fax: 3-89-33-63-19
E-mail: presidence@uha.fr
Internet: www.uha.fr

Founded 1975
Languages of instruction: English, French
Academic year: September to June

Pres.: Prof. Dr ALAIN BRILLARD
Sec.-Gen.: ALAIN COLLANGE
Librarian: ANNE-MARIE SCHALLER

Library of 150,000 vols
Number of teachers: 580
Number of students: 7,861

DEANS

Faculty of Arts, Languages and Humanities:
    Dr YANN KERDILÈS
Faculty of Economics, Social Sciences and
    Law: Dr GÉRALD COHEN
Faculty of Science and Technology: Dr CHRIS-
    TOPHE KREMBEL

UNIVERSITÉ DU HAVRE

25 rue Philippe Lebon, BP 1123, 76063 Le
Havre Cedex

Telephone: 2-32-74-40-00
Fax: 2-35-21-49-59
E-mail: presidence@univ-lehavre.fr
Internet: www.univ-lehavre.fr

Founded 1984
State control
Academic year: September to July

Pres.: CAMILLE GALAP
Vice-Pres: PASCAL REGHEM (Ccl of Admin.),
    ELAINE TALBOT (Studies and Univ. Life),
    MOULAY AZIZ ALAOUI (Scientific Ccl)
Sec.-Gen.: JEAN CLARISSE
Librarian: PIERRE-YVES CACHARD

Number of teachers: 399
Number of students: 7,040.

TEACHING AND RESEARCH UNITS

Centre de Formation des Apprentis: 25
rue Philippe Lebon, BP 1123, 76063 Le
Havre Cedex; tel. 2-32-74-44-67; fax 2-32-
74-44-70; e-mail cfa@univ-lehavre.fr; Dir
STÉPHANE LAUWICK.

Faculté des Affaires Internationales: 25
rue Philippe Lebon, BP 420, 76057 Le Havre
Cedex; tel. 2-32-74-41-00; fax 2-32-74-40-86.

**Faculté des Lettres et Sciences
Humaines:** 25 rue Philippe Lebon, 76086
Le Havre Cedex; tel. 2-32-74-42-00; fax 2-32-
74-42-04; e-mail lsh@univ-lehavre.fr; Dir
ELISABETH ROBERT-BARZMAN.

Faculté des Sciences et Techniques: 25
rue Philippe Lebon, BP 540, 76058 Le Havre
Cedex; tel. 2-32-74-43-00; fax 2-32-74-43-14;
e-mail ufr-st@univ-lehavre.fr.

Institut Universitaire de Technologie:
pl. Robert Schuman, BP 4006, 76610 Le
Havre Cedex; tel. 2-32-74-46-63; fax 2-32-
74-46-71; e-mail christian.delaruelle@
univ-lehavre.fr; internet www-iut
.univ-lehavre.fr; Dir CHRISTIAN DELARUELLE.

Institut Supérieur d'Etudes Logistiques:
Ecole d'Ingénieurs, Quai Frissard, BP 1137,
76063 Le Havre Cedex; tel. 2-32-74-49-00;
fax 2-32-74-49-11; e-mail isel@univ-lehavre
.fractiver; internet www.isel-logistique.fr;
Dir EDOUARD REPPERT.

Service Formation Continue: tel. 2-32-74-
44-50; e-mail formation.continue@
univ-lehavre.fr; Dir STÉPHANE LAUWICK.

UNIVERSITÉ DE LILLE I (UNIVERSITÉ DES SCIENCES ET TECHNOLOGIES DE LILLE)

Cité Scientifique, 59655 Villeneuve d'Ascq Cedex

Telephone: 3-20-43-43-43
Fax: 3-20-43-49-95
E-mail: presidence@univ-lille1.fr
Internet: www.univ-lille1.fr

Founded 1855 as Faculty of Sciences, present status 1971

Pres.: PHILIPPE ROLLET
Vice-Pres: FRANCIS MEILLIEZ, SALAH MAOUCHE, ISAM SHAHROUR, FRANÇOIS BUYLE-BODIN, JEAN-PHILIPPE CASSAR, NABI EL HAGGAR, JAMAL EL KHATTABI, NINA HAUTEKEETE, MICHÈLE HOCHEDEZ, JACKY LESAGE, PHILIPPE MATHIEU, WALID OURAHMA
Sec.-Gen.: PATRICE SERNICLAY
Number of teachers: 1,500
Number of students: 18,000

TEACHING AND RESEARCH UNITS

Biology: Dir: FRANÇOIS FONTAINE
Chemistry: Dir: ALAIN RIVES
Computer Science, Electronics; Electrical Engineering and Automation: Dir: NOUR-EDDINE OUSSOUS
Earth Sciences: Dir: JEAN-LUC POTDEVIN
Economics and Social Sciences: Dir: FARIDAH DJELLAL
Geography and Spatial Development: Dir: HELGA-JANE SCARWELL
Higher National School of Chemistry in Lille: Dir: JEAN GRIMBLOT
Institute of Business Studies: Dir: PIERRE LOUART
Marine Station at Wimereux: Dir: SÉBASTIEN LEFEBVRE
Pure and Applied Mathematics: Dir: CHARLES SUQUET
Physics: Dir: MICHEL FOULON
Polytech'Lille: Dir: JEAN-CHRISTOPHE CAMART
Telecom Lille: Dir: BERTRAND BONTE
University Centre for the Economics of Permanent Education: Dir: JEAN-LOUIS COGEZ
University Institute of Technology (Lille): Dir: MOULAY-DRISS BENCHIBOUN

PROFESSORS

BOILLY, B., Biology
BONNELLE, J.-P., Chemistry
BREZINSKI, C., Computer Sciences
BRUYELLE, P., Geography
CHAMLEY, H., Geotechnics
CONSTANT, E., Electronics
CORDONNIER, V., Calculus and Information Science
DAUCHET, M., Theoretical Computing
DEBOURSE, J.-P., Management Science
DEBRABANT, P., Engineering
DEGAUQUE, P., Electronics
DHAINAUT, A., Biology
DORMARD, S., Economics
DOUKHAN, J.-C., Engineering
DUPOUY, J.-P., Biology
DYMENT, A., Mathematics
ESCAIG, B., Solid State Physics
FOCT, J., Chemistry
FOURET, R., Physics
FRONTIER, S., Biology
GLORIEUX, P., Physics
GOSSELIN, G., Sociology
GOUDMAND, P., Energy Generation
GRUSON, L., Pure and Applied Mathematics
GUILBAULT, Biology
LABLACHE-COMBIER, A., Organic Chemistry
LAVEINE, J.-P., Palaeobotany
LEHMANN, D., Geometry
Mme LENOBLE, Atmospheric Optics
LOMBARD, J., Sociology
LOUCHEUX, C., Macromolecular Chemistry
MACKE, B., Physics

MAILLET, P., Economic and Social Sciences
MICHEAUX, P., Mechanical Engineering
PAQUET, J., Applied Geology
PORCHET, M., Biology
PROUVOST, J., Mineralogy
RACZY, L., Computer Sciences
SALMER, G., Electronics
SCHAMPS, J., Physics
SEGUIER, G., Electro-Technology
SIMON, M., Economic and Social Sciences
SLIWA, H., Chemistry
SPIK, G., Biology
STANKIEWICZ, F., Economic Sciences
TOULOTTE, J.-M., Computer Sciences
TURREL, G., Chemistry
VERNET, P., Biology of Populations and Eco-systems
VIDAL, P., Automation
ZEYTOUNIAN, R., Mechanics

UNIVERSITÉ DE LILLE II (DROIT ET SANTÉ)

42 rue Paul Duez, 59000 Lille

Telephone: 3-20-96-43-43
Fax: 3-20-88-24-32
E-mail: sg@univ-lille2.fr
Internet: www.univ-lille2.fr

Founded 1969
State control
Language of instruction: French
Academic year: October to June

Pres.: Prof. CHRISTIAN SERGHERAERT
Vice-Pres: Prof. VÉRONIQUE DEMARS, Prof. RÉGIS MATRAN, Prof. MARIE-HÉLÈNE FOSSE-GOMEZ, Prof. SALEM KACET, CLAIRE DAVAL, IRÈNE LAUTIER, Prof. XAVIER VAN-DENDRIESSCHE, PATRICK PELAYO, LARBI AIT HENNANI, RÉMY PAMART
Sec.-Gen.: GUY BAILLIEUL
Number of teachers: 1,198
Number of students: 28,330

DEANS

Faculty of Biological and Pharmaceutical Sciences: Prof. LUC DUBREUIL
Faculty of Dentistry: Prof. PIERRE HUBERT DUPAS
Faculty of Finance, Banking and Accountancy: Dir: PASCAL GRANDIN
Faculty of Legal, Political and Social Sciences: Prof. BERNARD BOSSU
Faculty of Medical Engineering and Management: Dir: Prof. ALAIN DUROCHER
Faculty of Medical Sciences: Prof. DIDIER GOSSET
Faculty of Physical Education and Sport: Dir: Prof. PATRICK PELAYO

ATTACHED INSTITUTE

Institut d'Études Politiques: 84 rue de Trévise, 59000 Lille; tel. 3-20-90-48-40; fax 3-20-90-48-60; e-mail directeur@iep.univ-lille2.fr; internet www.sciencespo-lille.eu; Dir PIERRE MATHIOT.

UNIVERSITÉ DE LILLE III, CHARLES DE GAULLE (SCIENCES HUMAINES, LETTRES ET ARTS)

Domaine Universitaire du Pont de Bois, BP 60149, 59653 Villeneuve d'Ascq Cedex

Telephone: 3-20-41-60-00
Fax: 3-20-91-91-71
E-mail: valerie.souilleux@univ-lille3.fr
Internet: www.univ-lille3.fr

Founded 1560, present status 1985

Pres.: JEAN-CLAUDE DUPAS
Sec.-Gen.: EMMANUEL PARISIS
Librarian: JEAN-PAUL CHADOURNE
Number of teachers: 830
Number of students: 18,500

Publications: Bien dire, bien apprendre, Cahiers de Recherches de l'institut de Papyrologie et d'Egyptologie, Etudes Irlandaises (2 a year), Germanica (1 or 2 a year), Graphé, Lexique (1 a year), Revue des Sciences Humaines (4 a year), Revue du Nord (history, 5 a year), Roman 20–50 (2 a year), Uranie

TEACHING AND RESEARCH UNITS

Applied Foreign Languages: Dir: HEROGUEL ARMAND
Arts and Culture: (vacant)
Classical Languages and Culture: Dir: ALAIN DEREMETZ
Education: Dir: CORA COHEN-AZRIA
English Language, Literature and Civilization: Dir: JEAN-LUC SWITALSKI
German and Scandinavian Studies: Dir: DOMINIQUE HERBET
History, Art and Politics: Dir: LAURIANNE SÈVE
INFOCOM: Dir: BERNARD DELFORCE
Information, Documentation and Scientific and Technical Information: Dir: JOACHIM SCHOPFEL
IUP–Artistic and Cultural Professions: Dir: PIERRE DELCAMBRE
IUP–Information Communication: Dir: OLIVIER CHANTRAINE
Mathematics, Economics and Social Sciences: Dir: LAURENCE BROZE
Modern Literature: Dir: THIERRY CHARNAY
Romance, Slav and Oriental Studies: Dir: CONSTANTIN BOBAS
Philosophy: Dir: PHILIPPE SABOT
Psychology: Dir: Mme S. DE BOSSCHER
Training Centre for Accompanying Musicians: Dir: PASCAL HAMEAUX
University Institute of Technology B: Dir: BRUNO TRINEL (acting)

PROFESSORS (1ST CLASS AND EXCEPTIONAL)

Classics:

BOULOGNE, J., Greek Language and Literature
DUMONT, J.-CHR., Social History of the Roman Republic

English Studies:

BECQUEMONT, D., History of Ideas, Phonetics and Phonology
DUPAS, J. C., Anglo-Saxon Language and Literature
DURAND, R., North American Literature and Civilization
ESCARBELT, B., Anglo-Saxon Language and Literature
GOURNAY, J.-F., 19th-century Literature and Civilization
SYS, J., British Civilization, History of Ideas

French Linguistics and Literature:

ALLUIN, B., Modern and Contemporary Language and Literature
BONNEFIS, PH., 19th-century Literature
BRASSEUR, A., Medieval Language and Literature
BUISIRE, A., French Language and Literature
CORBIN, D., French Language
GARY-PRIEUR, M. N., French Language
GUILLERM, J.-P., 19th-century Literature
GUILLERM-CURUTCHET, L., French Language and Literature
HORVILLE, R., 17th-century Literature
LESTRINGANT, FR., 16th-century Literature
MALANDAIN, P., Modern and Contemporary Language and Literature

German Studies:

COLONGE, P., 19th- and 20th-century Literature and Civilization
ROUSSEAU, A., Dutch Linguistics
VAN DE LOUW, G., Dutch
VAYDAT, P., Anglo-German Relations: 1870–1914

History, Art and Politics:

CHADEAU, E., Contemporary History
DELMAIRE, B., Medieval History
DELMAIRE, R., Ancient Roman History
GUIGNET, PH., Modern History
ROSSELLE, D., Modern Economic and Social History
VALBELLE, D., Egyptology

Mathematics, Economics, Social Sciences:

CELEYRETTE, J., Mathematics

Philosophy:

KINTZLER, C., General Philosophy and Aesthetics
KIRSCHER, G., Modern and Contemporary Philosophy
MACHEREY, P., Aesthetics and History of Philosophy

Psychology:

LECONTE, P., Experimental Psychology
VERQUERRE, R., Psychology

Romance, Slav, Semitic and Hungarian Studies:

ALLAIN, A., Russian

Other Professors:

LOSFELD, G., Information Science
REUTER, Y., Teaching of French

UNIVERSITÉ DE LIMOGES

33 rue François Mitterrand, BP 23204, 87032 Limoges Cedex 01
Telephone: 5-55-14-91-00
Fax: 5-55-14-91-01
Internet: www.unilim.fr
Founded 1968
Academic year: September to June
Pres.: JACQUES FONTANILLE
Sec.-Gen.: DANIEL POUMÉROULY
Librarian: JOËLLE CARTIGNY
Library: see Libraries
Number of teachers: 1,050
Number of students: 14,109

DEANS

Faculty of Arts and Humanities: PHILIPPE ALLÉE
Faculty of Law and Economic Sciences: PASCALE TORRE
Faculty of Medicine: DENIS VALLEIX
Faculty of Pharmacy: JEAN-LUC DUROUX
Faculty of Science and Technology: ANNE-MERCEDES BELLIDO

PROFESSORS

Faculty of Arts and Humanities (39E rue Camille Guérin, 87036 Limoges Cedex; tel. 5-55-43-56-00; fax 5-55-43-56-03; e-mail jacques.migozzi@unilim.fr; internet www.flsh.unilim.fr):

BALABANIAN, O., Geography and Development
BARRIÈRE, B., Medieval Archaeological History
BEDON, R., Ancient Language and Literature
BEHAR, P., Germanic and Scandinavian Language and Literature
CAPDEBOSCQ, A. M., Romance Language and Literature
CARON, P., Modern and Contemporary French Language and Literature
CHANDES, G., Middle Age to Renaissance French Language and Literature
DUMONT, J., Ancient World Archaeological History
EL GAMMAL, J. M., World Medieval Archaeological History
FILTEAU, C., Modern and Contemporary French Language and Literature
FONTANILLE, J., Language Sciences
GENDREAU-MASSALOUX, Romance Language and Literature

GRASSIN, J.-M., Comparative Literature
GRASSIN, M., Anglo-Saxon English Language and Literature
LECLANCHE, J.-L., Middle Age to Renaissance French Language and Literature
LEMOINE, B., Anglo-Saxon English Language and Literature
LEVET, J.-P., Ancient Language and Literature
MOREAU, J.-P., Anglo-Saxon English Language and Literature
NOUHAUD, M., Ancient Language and Literature
RAMBAUX, C., Ancient Language and Literature
VALADAS, B., Economic and Regional Geography
VERDON, J., World Medieval Archaeological History

Faculty of Law and Economic Sciences (5 rue Félix Eboué, BP 3127, 87031 Limoges Cedex 1; tel. 5-55-34-97-03; fax 5-55-34-97-11; e-mail helene.pauliat@unilim.fr; internet www.fdse.unilim.fr):

ALAPHILIPPE, F., Private Law and Criminology
ARCHER, R., Economics
CAVAGNAC, M., Economics
DARREAU, P., Economics
FLANDIN-BLETY, P., Legal and Institutional History
KARAQUILLO, J.-P., Private Law and Criminology
LENCLOS, J.-L., Public Law
MARGUENAUD, J.-P., Private Law
MOULY, J., Private Law
PAULIAT, H., Public Law
PRIEUR, M., Public Law
SAUVIAT, A., Economics
TARAZI, A., Economics
TEXIER, P., Legal and Institutional History
VAREILLE, B., Private Law

Faculty of Medicine (2 rue du docteur Marcland, 87025 Limoges Cedex; tel. 5-55-43-58-00; fax 5-55-43-58-01; e-mail doyen .medecine@unilim.fr; internet www.unilim .fr/medecine):

ADENIS, J.-P., Ophthalmology
ALAIN, L., Infantile Surgery
ALDIGIER, J.-C., Cardiology
ARCHAMBEAUD, F., Clinical Medicine
ARNAUD, J. P., Orthopaedics, Traumatology, Plastic Surgery
BARTHE, D., Histology, Embryology
BAUDET, J., Obstetrics and Gynaecology
BENSAID, J., Clinical Cardiology
BERTIN, P., Therapeutics
BESSEDE, J.-P., Otorhinolaryngology
BONNAUD, F., Pneumo-Phthisiology
BONNETBLANC, J.-M., Dermatology, Venereology
BOULESTEIX, J., Paediatrics and Medical Genetics
BOUQUIER, J.-J., Clinical Paediatrics
BOUTROS, T. F., Epidemiology
BRETON, J.-C., Biochemistry
CATANZANO, G., Pathological Anatomy
COLOMBEAU, P., Urology
CUBERTAFOND, P., Digestive Surgery
DARDE, M. L., Parasitology
DE LUMLEY-WOODYEAR, L., Paediatrics
DENIS, F., Bacteriology, Virology
DENIZOT, N., Anaesthesiology
DESCOTTES, B., Anatomy
DUDOGNON, P., Occupational Therapy
DUMAS, J. PH., Urology
DUMAS, M., Neurology
DUMONT, D., Occupational Medicines
DUPUY, J.-P., Radiology
FEISS, P., Anaesthesiology
GAINANT, A., Digestive Surgery
GAROUX, R., Child Psychiatry
GASTINNE, H., Resuscitation
HUGON, J., Histology, Embryology
LABROUSSE, C., Occupational Therapy

LASKAR, M., Thoracic and Cardiovascular Surgery
LAUBIE, B., Endocrinology, Metabolism, Nutrition
LEGER, J.-M., Adult Psychiatry
LEROUX-ROBERT, C., Nephrology
MENIER, R., Physiology
MERLE, L., Pharmacology
MOREAU, J.-J., Neurosurgery
MOULIES, D., Infantile Surgery
PECOUT, C., Orthopaedics, Traumatology, Plastic Surgery
PICHON BOURDESSOULE, D., Haematology
PILLEGAND, B., Hepatogastroenterology
PIVA, C., Forensic Medicine and Toxicology
PRA LORAN, V., Haematology
RAVON, R., Neurosurgery
RIGAUD, M., Biochemistry
ROUSSEAU, J., Radiology
SAUVAGE, J.-P., Otorhinolaryngology
TABASTE, J.-L., Gynaecology, Obstetrics
TREVES, R., Rheumatology
VALLAT, J.-M., Neurology
VALLEIX, D., Anatomy
VANDROUX, J.-C., Biophysics
WEINBRECK, P., Tropical Medicine

Faculty of Pharmacy (2 rue du docteur Marcland, 87025 Limoges Cedex; tel. 5-55-43-58-00; fax 5-55-43-58-01; e-mail doyen .pharmacie@unilim.fr; internet www .facpharmacie.unilim.fr):

BERNARD, M., Physical Chemistry and Pharmaceutical Technology
BOSGIRAUD, C., Biology
BROSSARD, C., Physical Chemistry and Pharmaceutical Technology
BUXERAUD, J., Pharmacology
CARDOT, PH., Physical Chemistry and Pharmaceutical Technology
CHULIA, A., Pharmacology
CLEMENT-CHULIA, D., Physical Chemistry and Pharmaceutical Technology
DELAGE, C., Physical and Mineral Chemistry
GHESTEM, A., Botany
HABRIOUX, G., Biochemistry
OUDART, N., Pharmacology

Faculty of Science and Technology (123 ave Albert Thomas, 87060 Limoges Cedex; tel. 5-55-45-72-00; fax 5-55-45-72-01; e-mail directeur.sciences@unilim.fr; internet www .sciences.unilim.fr):

BARONNET, J.-M., Energetics
BERLAND, R., Electronics, Electrotechnology and Automatics
BESSON, J.-L., Dense Media and Materials
CAPERAA, S., Civil Engineering
CARON, A., Information Processing
CATHERINOT, A., Energetics
COLOMBEAU, B., Optics
COUDERT, J. F., Methodology, Plasma and Automation
DECOSSAS, J. L., Electronics, Electrotechnology and Automatics
DESCHAUX, P., Physiology
DESMAISON, J., Mineral Chemistry
DUVAL, D., Mathematics
FAUCHAIS, P., Energetics
FRAY, C., Electronics, Electrotechnology and Automatics
FRIT, B., Mineral Chemistry
GAUDREAU, B., Mineral Chemistry
GLANDUS, J.-C., Mechanics, Mechanical Engineering and Civil Engineering
GOURSAT, P., Mineral Chemistry
GUILLON, P., Electronics, Electrotechnology and Automatics
JECKO, B., Electronics, Electrotechnology and Automatics
JECKO, F., Electronics, Electrotechnology and Automatics
JULIEN, R., Biochemistry
KRAUSZ, P., Organic, Analytical and Industrial Chemistry
LABBE, J.-C., Chemistry of Materials

LAUBIE, F., Mathematics
MALAISE, M., Mechanics, Mechanical Engineering and Civil Engineering
MARCOU, J., Electronics, Electrotechnology and Automatics
MARTIN, C., Energetics
MAZET, M., Organic, Analytical and Industrial Chemistry
MERCURIO, D., Mineral Chemistry
MERCURIO, J.-P., Mineral Chemistry
MOLITON, A., Optics
MOLITON, J. P., Electronics, Electrotechnology and Automatics
MORVAN, H., Biology
NARDOU, F., Physical Chemistry
OBREGON, J., Electronics, Electrotechnology and Automatics
PLATON, F., Mechanics, Mechanical Engineering and Civil Engineering
QUERE, R., Electronics, Electrotechnology and Automatics
QUINTARD, P., Dense Media and Materials
RATINAUD, M. M., Biochemistry and Biology
SABOURDY, G., Geology
THERA, M., Mathematics

AFFILIATED INSTITUTES

ENSIL (Limoges Engineering School): 16, Rue d'Atlantis, parc ESTER, 87068 Limoges Cedex; tel. 5-55-42-36-70; fax 5-55-42-36-80; e-mail direction@ensil.unilim.fr; internet www.ensil.unilim.fr; Dir PATRICK LEPRAT.

GEIST Institute ('Genetics, Environment, Immunity, Health and Therapy'): Faculty of Medecine, 2 rue du Docteur Marcland, 87000 Limoges; tel. 5-55-43-58-48; e-mail michel.cogne@unilim.fr; Dir MICHEL COGNÉ.

Higher National School of Industrial Ceramics: 47–73 ave Albert Thomas, 87065 Limoges Cedex; tel. 5-55-45-22-22; fax 5-55-79-09-98; e-mail directin@ensci.fr; internet www.ensci.fr; Dir CHRISTIAN GAULT.

IAE (Institute of Business Administration): 3 rue François Mitterrand, 87031 Limoges; tel. 5-55-14-90-32; e-mail alain .rivet@unilim.fr; internet www.iae.unilim.fr; Dir ALAIN RIVET.

Institute of Life and Health Sciences: 123 ave Albert Thomas, 87060 Limoges Cedex; tel. 5-55-45-76-76; fax 5-55-45-72-01; Dir RAYMOND JULIEN.

Institute of the Environment and Water: 123 ave Albert Thomas, 87060 Limoges Cedex; tel. 5-55-45-74-69; fax 5-55-45-74-59; Dir JEAN-CLAUDE BOLLINGER.

IPAG (Institute of Preparation for General Administration/Institut de Préparation à l'Administration Générale): 32 rue Turgot, 87000 Limoges; tel. 5-55-34-97-44; e-mail ipag@unilim.fr; internet www.ipag .unilim.fr; Dir CHRISTIAN MOULINARD.

IPAM 'Processes Applied to Materials' Research Institute: Faculty of Sciences and Technology, 123 ave Albert Thomas, 87060 Limoges Cedex; tel. 5-55-45-76-70; fax 5-55-45-72-70; e-mail armelle.vardelle@ unilim.fr; Dir ARMELLE VARDELLE.

IUFM (Institute for Teacher Training): 209 boulevard de Vanteaux, 87000 Limoges; tel. 5-55-01-76-86; fax 5-55-01-76-99; internet www.limousin.iufm.fr; Dir VALÉRIE LEGROS.

IUT (University Institute of Technology (Limousin)): Allée Andrés Maurois, 87065 Limoges Cedex; tel. 5-55-43-43-55; fax 5-55-43-43-56; e-mail dir.iut@unilim.fr; internet www.iut.unilim.fr; Dir GILLES BROUSSAUD.

Science, Technology, Health: 13 Rue de Genève, 87065 Limoges Cedex; tel. 5-55-45-76-74; fax 5-55-45-76-73; e-mail ed-sts@ unilim.fr; internet www.unilim.fr/edsts; Dir ABBAS CHAZAD MOVAHHEDI.

SHS Institute of Human and Social Sciences: Faculty of Law and Economics, 5 rue Félix Eboué, BP 3127, 87031 Limoges Cedex; tel. 5-55-14-92-10; e-mail alain.sauviat@ unilim.fr; Dir ALAIN SAUVIAT.

University Professional Institute: 2 Rue du Docteur Marcland, 87025 Limoges Cedex; tel. 5-55-43-59-15; fax 5-55-43-59-36; e-mail iup@unilim.fr; Dir JEAN-FRANÇOIS NYS.

XLIM Mixed Research Unit: Faculty of Sciences and Technology, 123 ave Albert Thomas, 87060 Limoges Cedex; tel. 5-55-45-72-50; fax 5-55-45-72-01; e-mail dominique .cros@unilim.fr; internet www.xlim.fr; Dir DOMINIQUE CROS.

UNIVERSITÉ DU LITTORAL CÔTE D'OPALE

Services Centraux, 1 pl. de l'Yser, BP 1022, Général-De-Gaulle, 59375 Dunkerque Cedex 1

Telephone: 3-28-23-73-73
Fax: 3-28-23-73-95
E-mail: web-ulco@univ-littoral.fr
Internet: www.univ-littoral.fr

Founded 1991

Campuses in Boulogne, Calais, Dunkerque and St-Omer

Pres.: ROGER DURAND
Sec.-Gen.: CATHERINE SION
Vice-Pres: FAUSTIN AISSI (Ccl of Admin.), ROBIN BOQUET (Scientific Ccl), SABINE DUHAMEL (Studies and Univ. Life)
Librarian: MIREILLE CHAZAL

Library of 100,000 vols, 900 periodical subscriptions; CD-ROM databases; spec. colln: Centre de Documentation Européenne, Relais INSEE (statistics), science fiction, cartoons, theses

Number of students: 11,000

Areas of study: law, economics, management, literature, languages, fine and performing arts, humanities, social sciences, natural sciences, technology, sport.

UNIVERSITÉ DE LYON

Caserne Sergent Blandan, 37 rue du Repos, 69361 Lyon

Telephone: 4-37-37-26-70
Fax: 4-37-37-26-71
E-mail: contact@universite-lyon.fr
Internet: www.universite-lyon.fr

Founded 2007 by merger of 9 founding mems and 11 assoc. mems

State control

Pres.: MICHEL LUSSAULT

Number of teachers: 11,500
Number of students: 120,000.

FOUNDING MEMBER INSTITUTIONS

Université Lyon I (Université Claude-Bernard)

43 blvd du 11 Novembre 1918, 69622 Villeurbanne Cedex

Telephone: 4-72-44-80-00
Fax: 4-72-43-10-20
E-mail: secretariat.presidence@univ-lyon1.fr
Internet: www.univ-lyon1.fr

Founded 1970
State control
Language of instruction: French
Academic year: October to June

Pres.: ALAIN BONMARTIN
Vice-Pres: GUY ANNAT (Administration), JEAN-FRANÇOIS MORNEX (Research), DANIEL SIMON (Studies)
Sec.-Gen.: GILLES GAY

Number of teachers: 2,630
Number of students: 36,000

Publications: *Annuaire sur la Recherche* (1 a year), *Lettre FLASH/INFO* (4 a year), *Livret de l'Etudiant* (1 a year).

TEACHING AND RESEARCH UNITS

Faculté de Médecine Lyon Est: 8 ave Rockefeller, 69373 Lyon Cedex 08; tel. 4-78-77-70-00; Dean Prof. JÉRÔME ETIENNE.

Faculté de Médecine et de Maïeutique Lyon Sud—Charles Mérieux: 165 chemin du Petit Revoyet, BP 12, 69921 Oullins Cedex 08; tel. 4-26-23-59-05; fax 4-26-23-59-01; Dean Prof. FRANÇOIS-NOËL GILLY.

Faculté d'Odontologie: 11 rue Guillaume Paradin, 69372 Lyon Cedex 08; tel. 4-78-77-86-00; fax 4-78-77-86-96; Dean Prof. DENIS BOURGEOIS.

Université Lyon 2 (Université Louis Lumière)

86 rue Pasteur, 69635 Lyon Cedex 07

Telephone: 4-78-69-70-00
Fax: 4-78-69-56-01
Internet: www.univ-lyon2.fr

Pres.: ANDRÉ TIRAN
First Vice-Pres. for Ccl of Admin.: MARIE ANAUT
Vice-Pres. for Studies and Univ. Life: JACQUES BONNIEL
Vice-Pres. for Scientific Ccl: NATHALIE FOURNIER
Vice-Pres. for Culture and Student Life: JACQUES GERSTENKORN
Vice-Pres. for Human Resources: MICHEL GUILLOT
Vice-Pres. for Finance and Capital: GÉRARD KLOTZ
Vice-Pres. for Int. Relations: CHRISTIAN MONTÈS
Sec.-Gen.: BERNARD FRADIN

Number of teachers: 976
Number of students: 28,322

Publication: *Le Rayon Vert* (10 a year)

DEANS

Faculty of Anthropology and Sociology: ALI CHEIBAN
Faculty of Economics and Business Studies: LUC BAUMSTARK
Faculty of Geography, History, History of Art and Tourism: JEAN-LUC LAMBOLEY
Faculty of Law and Political Science: MARIE-ODILE NICOUD
Faculty of Literature, Science of Language and Arts: PIERRE SABY
Faculty of Modern Languages: JOSIANE PACCAUD-HUGUET

DIRECTORS

Institute of Communication: ALAIN GIROD
Institute of Labour: PATRICK ROZENBLATT
Institute of Political Studies: GILLES POLLET
Institute of Psychology: ISABELLE TAPIERO
Institute of Teacher Training: ALAIN KERLAN
Institute of Trade Union Training: JEAN-FRANÇOIS PAULIN
Institut Universitaire de Technologie Lumière: MICHEL LE NIR

Université Lyon 3 (Université Jean Moulin)

1 rue de l'Université, BP 0638, 69239 Lyon Cedex 02

Telephone: 4-78-78-77-78
Fax: 4-78-78-79-79
E-mail: webmaster@univ-lyon3.fr
Internet: www.univ-lyon3.fr

Founded 1973

President: HUGUES FULCHIRON

Vice-Pres: PIERRE SERVET (Ccl of Admin.), CYRIL NOURISSAT (Scientific Ccl), SABINE DANA-DEMARET (Studies and Univ. Life), LAÏD BOUZIDI (Information Systems and New Technologies), JACQUES COMBY (Research)
Sec.-Gen.: BERNARD PASCAL
Number of teachers: 650
Number of students: 23,137
Publication: *Lyon 3 Infos* (12 a year)

DEANS

Faculty of Languages: DENIS JAMET
Faculty of Law: LOUIS-AUGUSTIN BARRIERE
Faculty of Letters and Civilizations: NICOLE GONTHIER
Faculty of Philosophy: DENIS FOREST
School of Management: JÉRÔME RIVE
Institut Universitaire de Technologie: SYLVAIN CORNIC

Université Jean Monnet de Saint-Etienne

10 rue Tréfilerie, CS 82301, 42023 Saint-Etienne Cedex 2
Telephone: 4-77-42-17-00
Fax: 4-77-42-17-99
Internet: www.univ-st-etienne.fr
Founded 1969 as Université de Saint-Étienne; present name 1991
State control
Language of instruction: French
Academic year: October to June
Pres.: KHALED BOUABDALLAH
Vice-Pres: JEAN-YVES COTTIN (Scientific Ccl), MARIE-HÉLÈNE LAFAGE-PROUST (Ccl of Admin.), AGNÈS MORINI (Studies and Univ. Life)
Sec.-Gen.: EVELYNE SARMEJEANNE
Librarian: BRIGITTE RENOUF
Number of teachers: 592
Number of students: 13,684
Publications: *L'Université communique* (52 a year), and various institute bulletins

DEANS

Arts, Letters and Languages: Dir: YVES CLAVARON (acting)
Humanities and Social Sciences: Dir: JEAN FRANÇOIS BRUN
Law: Dean: NATACHA VIGNE
Medicine: Dean: Prof. FABRICE ZENI
Sciences: Dir: ALAIN TROUILLET
University Institute of Technology: Dir: J. MAZERAN
Institut d'Administration des Entreprises: Dir: BERNARD BOUREILLE
Institut du Travail: Pres.: DOMINIQUE TERRAT
Télécom Saint-Etienne: Dir: LAURENT CARRARO

Ecole Centrale de Lyon

36 ave Guy de Collongue, 69134 Ecully Cedex
Telephone: 4-72-18-60-00
Fax: 4-78-43-39-62
Internet: www.ec-lyon.fr
Pres.: CHRISTIAN MARI
Vice-Pres.: FRANÇOIS VIDAL
Dir: PATRICK BOURGIN
Deputy Dir: PIERRE DREUX
Dir of Studies: MARIE-ANNICK GALLAND
Dir of Research: JEAN-PIERRE BERTOGLIO
Sec.-Gen.: PHILIPPE WISLER

DIRECTORS

Communication, Languages, Business and Sport: Dir: JACQUELINE VACHERAND-REVEL
Electronics: Dir: FRANÇOIS BURET
Mathematics and Computer Science: Dir: LIMING CHEN
Fluid Mechanics, Acoustics and Energy: Dir: GILLES ROBERT

Solid Mechanics and Mechanical and Civil Engineering: Dir: FABRICE THOUVEREZ
Surface Science and Materials: Dir: YVES ROBACH

Institut National des Sciences Appliquées de Lyon

20 ave Albert Einstein, 69621 Villeurbanne Cedex
Telephone: 4-72-43-83-83
Fax: 4-72-43-85-00
E-mail: accueil@insa-lyon.fr
Internet: www.insa-lyon.fr
Founded 1957
Library of 80,000 vols
Biochemistry, computer science, civil, electrical, energetics, production and mechanical engineering, material science
Dir: Prof. ALAIN STORCK
Number of teachers: 500
Number of students: 5,400

DIRECTORS

Business Relations: Dir: Prof. JEAN-MARIE PINON
Human Resources: Dir: CLAUDE GUÉDAT
Information Systems: Dir: YVES CONDEMINE
Internal Relations: Dir: CORINNE SUBAÏ
Int. Relations: Dir: MARIE-PIERRE FAVRE
Research: Dir: Prof. JEAN-MARIE REYNOUARD
Training: Dir: Prof. CHRISTOPHE ODET
Fondation Partenariale de l'INSA de Lyon: Dir: ALEXIS MÉTÉNIER

Ecole Nationale des Mines de Saint-Etienne

158 cours Fauriel, 42023 Saint-Étienne Cedex 2
Telephone: 4-77-42-01-23
Fax: 4-77-42-00-00
E-mail: inform@emse.fr
Internet: www.emse.fr
Founded 1816
Dir: PHILIPPE JAMET
Sec.-Gen.: RACHEL VITANI
Number of students: 1,550

DIRECTORS

Engineering and Health: Dir: STÉPHANE AVRIL
Industrial and Natural Processes: Dir: CHRISTOPHE PIJOLAT
Material and Structural Science: Dir: DAVID DELAFOSSE
Microelectronics (Provence): Dir: PHILIPPE COLLOT
Institut Henri Fayol: Dir: XAVIER OLAGNE

UNIVERSITÉ DU MAINE

ave Olivier Messiaen, 72085 Le Mans Cedex 9
Telephone: 2-43-83-30-00
Fax: 2-43-83-30-77
E-mail: webmaster@univ-lemans.fr
Internet: www.univ-lemans.fr
Founded 1977
Pres.: YVES GUILLOTIN
Vice-Pres: RACHID EL GUERJOUMA (Ccl of Admin.), JEAN-YVES BUZARÉ (Scientific Ccl), DANIEL LUZZATI (Studies and Univ. Life)
Sec.-Gen.: ANNE-MARIE RIOU
Librarian: MICHÈLE NARDI
Number of teachers: 628
Number of students: 10,308

DEANS

Faculty of Law, Economic Science and Management: LAURENT PUJOL
Faculty of Letters, Languages and Human Sciences: DOMINIQUE AMIARD

Faculty of Sciences and Technology: MICHEL PEZERIL

ATTACHED INSTITUTES

Higher National School of Engineering: Rue Aristote, 72085 Le Mans Cedex 09; tel. 2-43-83-35-93; fax 2-43-83-37-94; e-mail ensim@univ-lemans.fr; internet ensim.univ-lemans.fr.
University Institute of Technology (Laval): 52 rue des docteurs Calmette et Guérin, BP 2045, 53000 Laval Cedex 09; tel. 2-43-59-49-05; fax 2-43-59-49-08; internet www.iut-laval.univ-lemans.fr.
University Institute of Technology (Le Mans): Ave Olivier Messiaen, 72085 Le Mans Cedex 09; tel. 2-43-83-34-01; fax 2-43-83-30-88; internet iut.univ-lemans.fr.

UNIVERSITÉ DE MARNE-LA-VALLÉE

5 blvd Descartes, Champs/Marne, 77454 Marne-la-Vallée Cedex 2
Telephone: 1-60-95-75-00
Fax: 1-60-95-75-75
E-mail: com@univ-mlv.fr
Internet: www.univ-mlv.fr
Founded 1991
Pres.: FRANCIS GODARD
Sec.-Gen.: SOPHIE JULIEN
Librarian: CHRISTELLE OTIN
Number of teachers: 400
Number of students: 11,000

TEACHING AND RESEARCH UNITS

Economic Sciences and Management: MURIEL JOUGLEUX
Engineering: DOMINIQUE REVUZ
Francilien Institute of Applied Sciences: MICHEL MADON
Francilien Institute of Engineering Services: CHRISTIAN BOURRET
French Institute of Town Planning: CHRISTIAN LEFEVRE
Gaspard Monge Institute of Electronics and Computing: JEAN-MARC LAHEURTE
Humanities and Social Sciences: FREDÉRIC MORET
Languages and Civilization: CLAUDIE TERRASSON
Letters, Arts, Communication and Technology: PASCALE ALEXANDRE
Mathematics: DANIEL LAMBERTON
Sports Science: ERIC LEVET-LABRY
University Institute of Technology: JACQUES DESARMENIEN

UNIVERSITÉ MONTPELLIER I

Service Communication, 5 blvd Henri IV, CS 19044, 34967 Montpellier Cedex 2
Telephone: 4-67-41-74-00
Fax: 4-67-41-02-46
E-mail: presidence@univ-montp1.fr
Internet: www.univ-montp1.fr
Founded 1970
State control
Language of instruction: French
Academic year: September to June
Pres.: PHILIPPE AUGÉ
Vice-Pres: JEAN MARTINEZ (Ccl of Admin.), JACQUES MERCIER (Scientific Ccl), CHANTAL MARION (Studies and Univ. Life)
Gen. Sec.: PASCAL BEAUREGARD
Librarian: HÉLÈNE LORBLANCHET
Number of teachers: 829
Number of students: 18,538
Publications: *Cadran, Journal de Médecine, L'Economie Méridionale, Le Ligament, Revue de la Société d'Histoire du Droit.*

TEACHING AND RESEARCH UNITS

Faculté d'Administration Économique et Sociale: ave Raymond Dugrand, CS 59640, 34960 Montpellier Cedex 2; tel. 4-67-15-84-60; Dir PATRICE N'DIAYE.

Faculté de l'Economie: ave de la Mer, CS 79606, 34960 Montpellier Cedex 2; tel. 4-67-15-84-50; fax 4-67-15-84-86; Dir CHRISTIAN LAGARDE.

Faculté du Droit et Science Politique: 39 rue de l'Université, 34960 Montpellier Cedex 2; tel. 4-67-61-54-00; fax 4-67-60-42-31; Dir MARIE ELISABETH ANDRÉ.

Faculté de Médecine: 2 rue Ecole de Médecine, CS 59001, 34960 Montpellier Cedex 2; tel. 4-67-60-10-00; fax 4-67-66-17-57; Dir JACQUES BRINGER.

Faculté d'Odontologie: 545 ave du Prof. J. L. Viala, 34193 Montpellier Cedex 2; tel. 4-67-10-44-70; fax 4-67-10-45-82; Dir JEAN VALCARCEL.

Faculté de Pharmacie: 15 ave Charles Flahault, BP 14491, 34093 Montpellier Cedex 2; tel. 4-67-54-80-00; fax 4-67-54-80-39; Dir LAURENCE VIAN.

Faculté des Sciences du Sport: 700 ave du Pic Saint-Loup, 34090 Montpellier Cedex 2; tel. 4-67-41-57-00; fax 4-67-41-57-08; Dir DENIS DELIGNIÈRES.

Institut de Préparation à l'Administration Générale: Espace Richter, rue Vendémiaire, Bâtiment B, CS 19519, 34960 Montpellier Cedex 2; tel. 4-67-15-85-46; fax 4-67-15-85-47; Dir ETIENNE DOUAT.

Institut des Sciences de L'Entreprise et du Management: Espace Richter, rue Vendémiaire, Bâtiment B, CS 19519, 34960 Montpellier Cedex 2; tel. 4-67-13-02-00; fax 4-67-13-02-10; Dir MONIQUE LACROIX.

UNIVERSITÉ DE MONTPELLIER II (SCIENCES ET TECHNIQUES DU LANGUEDOC)

pl. Eugène Bataillon, 34095 Montpellier Cedex 5

Telephone: 4-67-14-30-30
Fax: 4-67-14-30-31
E-mail: presidence@univ-montp2.fr
Internet: www.univ-montp2.fr

Pres.: DANIÈLE HÉRIN
Vice-Pres. for Ccl of Admin.: ERIC BUFFENOIR
Vice-Pres. for Ccl of Studies and Univ. Life: CHRISTOPHE IUNG
Vice-Pres. for Scientific Ccl: CHRISTIAN PERIGAUD
Sec.-Gen.: PHILIPPE PAILLET
Librarian: MIREILLE GALCERAN

Number of teachers: 797
Number of students: 15,878

Publications: *Cahiers de Mathématiques, Naturalia Monspelianesia, Paléobiologie Continentale—Paléovertebrata.*

TEACHING AND RESEARCH UNITS

Faculté des Sciences: pl. Eugène Bataillon, 34095 Montpellier Cedex 5; tel. 4-67-14-30-34; fax 4-67-14-47-00; e-mail facsciences@univ-montp2.fr; internet www.ufr.univ-montp2.fr; Dir GILLES HALBOUT.

Institut d'Administration des Entreprises: pl. Eugène Bataillon, 34095 Montpellier Cedex 5; tel. 4-67-14-38-65; fax 4-67-14-42-42; e-mail secretariat.direction.iae@univ-montp2.fr; internet www.iae.univ-montp2.fr; Dir ERIC STEPHANY.

Institut Universitaire de Formation des Maîtres: 2 pl. Marcel Godechot, 34092 Montpellier Cedex 5; tel. 4-67-61-83-00; fax 4-67-61-83-10; e-mail iufm-direction@univ-montp2.fr; internet www.montpellier.iufm.fr; Dir PATRICK DEMOUGIN.

Institut Universitaire de Technologie de Béziers: 17 Quai Port Neuf, 34500 Béziers Cedex; tel. 4-67-11-18-00; fax 4-67-11-18-01; e-mail iut-beziers-direction@univ-montp2.fr; internet www.iutbeziers.univ-montp2.fr; Dir YVES MOREAU.

Institut Universitaire de Technologie de Montpellier: 99 ave d'Occitanie, 34296 Montpellier Cedex 5; tel. 4-99-58-50-40; fax 4-99-58-50-41; e-mail iut-montpellier-direction@univ-montp2.fr; internet www.iutmontp.univ-montp2.fr; Dir PHILIPPE PEIRROT.

Institut Universitaire de Technologie de Nîmes: 8 rue Jules-Raimu, 30907 Nîmes Cedex; tel. 4-66-62-85-00; fax 4-66-62-85-01; e-mail ut-nimes-direction@univ-montp2.fr; internet www.iut-nimes.fr; Dir SALAM CHARAR.

Observatoire de Recherche Méditerranéen de l'Environnement (OSI—OREME): Bâtiment 22, CC 060, pl. Eugène Bataillon, 34095 Montpellier Cedex 5; tel. 4-67-14-40-85; fax 4-67-14-40-30; e-mail oreme@univ-montp2.fr; internet www.oreme.univ-montp2.fr; Dir NICOLAS ARNAUD.

Polytech' Montpellier: pl. Eugène Bataillon, 34095 Montpellier Cedex 5; tel. 4-67-14-31-60; fax 4-67-14-45-14; e-mail polytech-direction@univ-montp2.fr; internet www.polytech.univ-montp2.fr; Dir SERGE PRAVOSSOUDOVITCH.

UNIVERSITÉ DE MONTPELLIER III (UNIVERSITÉ PAUL VALÉRY)

route de Mende, BP 5043, 34199 Montpellier Cedex 5

Telephone: 4-67-14-20-00
Fax: 4-67-14-20-52
E-mail: communication@univ-montp3.fr
Internet: www.univ-montp3.fr

Founded 1970
State control
Language of instruction: French
Academic year: September to July

Pres.: ANNE FRAÏSSE
Vice-Pres. for Ccl of Admin.: YANN BISIOU
Vice-Pres. for Int. Relations: BURGHART SCHMIDT
Vice-Pres. for Scientific Ccl: PATRICK GILLI
Vice-Pres. for Studies and Univ. Life: CÉCILE POUSSARD
Sec.-Gen.: YVES CHAIMBAULT
Librarian: JEAN-FRANCOIS FOUCAUD

Number of teachers: 486
Number of students: 15,117

Publication: 68 research periodicals

TEACHING AND RESEARCH UNITS

Letters, Arts, Philosophy and Psychoanalysis: Dir: CHRISTIAN BELIN
Languages and Foreign and Regional Cultures: Dir: MARIE-PAULE MASSON
Human and Environmental Sciences: Dir: Prof. DAVID LEFÈVRE
Economic, Mathematical and Social Sciences: Dir: PATRICE SÉÉBOLD
Science of Society: Dir: RENÉ PRY

UNIVERSITÉ DE NANCY I (HENRI POINCARÉ)

24–30 rue Lionnois, BP 60120, 54003 Nancy Cedex

Telephone: 3-83-68-20-00
Fax: 3-83-68-21-00
E-mail: info@uhp-nancy.fr
Internet: www.uhp-nancy.fr

Founded 1970

Pres.: JEAN-PIERRE FINANCE
Vice-Pres. of the Ccl of Admin.: BRUNO LEHEUP

Vice-Pres. of the Scientific Ccl: PIERRE MUTZENHARDT
Vice-Pres. of Studies and Univ. Life: CHRISTINE ATKINSON
Sec.-Gen.: LUC ZIEGLER
Librarian: ANNE-PASCALE PARRET

Number of teachers: 1,703
Number of students: 17,928

Publication: *Transversales* (3 a year)

TEACHING AND RESEARCH UNITS

Dental Surgery: Dean: PIERRE BRAVETTI
Higher School of Computing and its Applications: Dir: ANDRÉ SCHAFF
Higher School of the Science and Technology of Engineering: Dir: ARNAUD DELEBARRE
Higher School of the Science and Technology of the Wood Industry: Dir: JEAN-MICHEL LEBAN
Medicine: Dean: HENRY COUDANE
Pharmacy: Dean: FRANCINE PAULUS
Science and Technology: Dir: PIERRE STEINMETZ
Sport: Dean: ALAIN PIZZINATO
University Institute of Teacher Training (Lorraine): Dir: FABIEN SCHNEIDER
University Institute of Technology (Longwy): Dir: ANTOINE DI SANO
University Institute of Technology (Nancy-Brabois): Dir: EDDY BAJIC
University Institute of Technology (Saint Dié): Dir: PATRICE NUS

UNIVERSITÉ DE NANCY II

25 rue Baron Louis, BP 454, 54001 Nancy Cedex

Telephone: 3-83-34-46-00
Fax: 3-83-30-05-65
Internet: www.univ-nancy2.fr

Founded 1970
State control
Language of instruction: French
Academic year: October to May

Pres.: MARTIAL DELIGNON
Vice-Pres. of Ccl of Admin.: PASCALE FADE
Vice-Pres. of Scientific Ccl: MATTIEU PETRISSANS
Vice-Pres. of Studies and Univ. Life: CHICOT ÉBOUÉ
Sec.-Gen.: FRANÇOIS NOËL
Librarian: FLORENCE BOUCHET

Library: see Libraries
Number of teachers: 531
Number of students: 22,000

Publications: *Les Annales de l'Est, Verbum, Revue Géographique de l'Est, Autrement dire, Etudes d'archéologie classique, La Revue française d'études américaines*

TEACHING AND RESEARCH UNITS

Arts: Dir: MARCEL PAUL-CAVALLIER
History, Geography and Musicology: Dir: EMMANUEL CHIFFRE
Human Sciences: Dir: CHRISTINE BOCEREAN
Languages and Foreign Culture: Dir: ELSA CHAARANI
Science of Languages: Dir: RICHARD DUDA

UNIVERSITÉ DE NANTES

1 quai de Tourville, BP 13522, 44035 Nantes Cedex 1

Telephone: 2-40-99-83-83
Fax: 2-40-93-83-00
E-mail: president@president.univ-nantes.fr
Internet: www.univ-nantes.fr

Founded 1962
State control

Pres.: Prof. YVES LECOINTE
Vice-Pres: GWENAËLLE LE DREFF (Ccl of Admin.), VINCENT LANG (Studies and Univ. Life), JACQUES GIRARDEAU (Scientific

Ccl), FRANÇOISE LEJEUNE (Int. Relations), JEAN-CHARLES CADIOU (Business Relations), DANIELLE PAILLER (Culture and Initiatives), MARC JOYAU (Capital)
Librarian: HÉLÈNE GROGNET
Number of teachers: 1,569
Number of students: 33,182
Publication: *Prisme* (6 a year)

TEACHING AND RESEARCH UNITS
Arts and Languages: FRÉDÉRIC LE BLAY
Dentistry: Dean: OLIVIER LABOUX
History, Art History and Archaeology: JEAN-NOËL GUYODO
Institute of Economy and Management (Nantes): BERNARD FIOLEAU
Institute of Geography and Planning: PAUL FATTAL
Institute of Preparatory Administrative Studies: THIBAUT DE BERRANGER
Institute for Research and Training in French as a Foreign Language: LOIC FRAVALO
Institute of Technology (Nantes): JEAN-PIERRE CITEAU
Institute of Technology (Roche-sur-Yon): THIERRY GUINET
Institute of Technology (St-Nazaire): Prof. RONALD GUILLÉN
International Language Centre: HERVÉ QUINTIN
Law and Political Sciences: GILLES DUMONT
Medicine: JEAN-MICHEL ROGEZ
Observatory of the Sciences of the Universe: PATRICK LAUNEAU
Pharmacology and Biology: ALAIN PINEAU
Polytech'Nantes: l'Ecole d'ingénieurs de l'Université: RENÉ LE GALL
Psychology: MOHAMMED BERNOUSSI
Science and Technology: MICHEL EVAIN
Sociology: RÉMY LE SAOUT
Sports Science: BRUNO PAPIN
Teacher Training: MICHEL HEICHETTE

UNIVERSITÉ DE NICE SOPHIA ANTIPOLIS
Grand Château, 28 ave Valrose, BP 2135, 06103 Nice Cedex 2
Telephone: 4-92-07-60-60
Fax: 4-92-07-66-00
E-mail: presidence@unice.fr
Internet: www.unice.fr
Founded 1965
State control
Language of instruction: French
Pres.: ALBERT MAROUANI
First Vice-Pres.: PIERRE COULLET
Vice-Pres: JEAN-MARC LARDEAUX ELIANE KOTLER, LUDOVIC ARNAULT
Sec.-Gen.: ALAIN MIAOULIS
Librarian: LOUIS KLEE
Number of teachers: 1,311
Number of students: 26,196.

TEACHING AND RESEARCH UNITS
École Polytech'Nice-Sophia: 930 route des Colles, BP 145, 06303 Sophia Antipolis Cedex; internet www.polytech.unice.fr; Dir PHILIPPE GOURBESVILLE.

Faculté de Chirurgie Dentaire: 24 ave des Diables Bleus, 06357 Nice Cedex 4; tel. 4-92-00-11-11; fax 4-92-00-12-63; e-mail doyen-odonto@unice.fr; internet odontologie.unice.fr; Dean Prof. MARC BOLLA.

Faculté de Droit et Science Politique: ave Doyen L. Trotabas, 06050 Nice Cedex 1; tel. 4-92-15-70-00; fax 4-92-15-70-18; internet droit.unice.fr; Dean CHRISTIAN VALLAR.

Faculté Espaces et Cultures: 98 blvd Edouard Herriot, BP 3209, 06204 Nice Cedex 3; tel. 4-93-37-53-59; fax 4-93-37-54-87; internet unice.fr/gaed; Dir HLIMI TOURIA.

Faculté des Lettres, Arts et Sciences Humaines: 98 blvd Edouard Herriot, BP 3209, 06204 Nice Cedex 3; tel. 4-93-37-53-53; internet lettres.unice.fr; Dean JEAN-YVES BOURSIER.

Faculté de Médecine: 28 ave de Valombrose, 06107 Nice Cedex 2; tel. 4-93-37-76-02; e-mail sfaure@unice.fr; internet medecine.unice.fr; Dean Prof. DANIEL BENCHIMOL.

Faculté des Sciences: 28 ave Valrose, 06108 Nice Cedex 2; tel. 4-92-07-69-96; fax 4-92-07-69-76; e-mail direction-sciences@unice.fr; internet sciences.unice.fr; Dir FRÉDÉRIQUE VIDAL.

Faculté des Sciences du Sport: 261 route de Grenoble, 06205 Nice Cedex 3; tel. 4-92-29-65-00; fax 4-92-29-65-49; e-mail dir-staps@unice.fr; internet staps.unice.fr; Dir JEAN-MARIE GARBARINO.

Institut d'Administration des Entreprises: 24 ave des Diables Bleus, 06357 Nice Cedex 4; tel. 4-92-00-11-39; fax 4-92-00-11-43; e-mail sylvie.thiery@unice.fr; internet www.iae-nice.fr; Dir JACQUES SPINDLER.

Institut du Droit de la Paix et du Développement (IDPD): ave Doyen L. Trotabas, 06050 Nice Cedex 1; tel. 4-92-15-71-94; fax 4-92-15-71-97; e-mail cammarer@unice.fr; internet idpd.unice.fr; Dean ALAIN PIQUEMAL.

Institut Supérieur d'Economie et de Management: 24 ave des Diables Bleus, 06300 Nice Cedex; tel. 4-92-00-12-22; e-mail isem@unice.fr; internet unice.fr/isem; Dir (vacant).

Institut Universitaire de Formation des Maîtres (IUFM): 89 ave George V, 06046 Nice Cedex 1; tel. 4-93-53-75-28; e-mail mohamed.najmi@unice.fr; internet www.iufm.unice.fr; Dir MOHAMED NAJMI.

Institut Universitaire des Langues: 98 blvd Edouard Herriot, BP 3209, 06204 Nice Cedex 3; tel. 4-93-37-54-10; fax 4-93-37-56-96; e-mail iul@unice.fr; internet www.unice.fr/iul; Dir DOMINIQUE BOSQUELLE.

Institut Universitaire de Technologie: 41 blvd Napoléon III, 06206 Nice Cedex 3; tel. 4-97-25-82-34; fax 4-97-25-83-29; internet iut.unice.fr; Dir HENRI ALEXIS.

UNIVERSITÉ DE NÎMES
rue du Docteur Georges Salan, 30021 Nîmes Cedex 1
Internet: www.unimes.fr
Pres.: JACQUES MARIGNAN
Vice-Pres: CATHERINE BERNIÉ-BOISSARD (Research), EMMANUEL ROUX (Admin. and Finance), ERIC AUZIOL (Support, Training and Student Life)
Sec.-Gen.: STÉPHANIE MENSAH
Librarian: VALÉRIE TRAVIER
Number of teachers: 85
Number of students: 3,618

UNIVERSITÉ D'ORLÉANS
Château de la Source, ave du Parc Floral, BP 6749, 45067 Orléans Cedex 2
Telephone: 2-38-41-71-71
Fax: 2-38-41-70-69
Internet: www.univ-orleans.fr
Founded 1961
Language of instruction: French
Academic year: September to June
Pres.: YOUSSOUFI TOURÉ
Vice-Pres: PIERRE ALLORANT, ANNE LAVIGNE, PHILIPPE FAURE, ISABELLE RANNOU, FLORIAN BOITEUX
Sec.-Gen.: ANDRÉ PILLOT
Librarian: Mme DESBORDES

Number of teachers: 1,106
Number of students: 16,001
Publications: *Plaquette en direction des entreprises* (1 a year), research catalogue.

TEACHING AND RESEARCH UNITS
Ecole Polytechnique: 12 rue de Blois, BP 6744, 45067 Orléans Cedex 2; tel. 2-38-41-70-50; e-mail concours.polytech@univ-orleans.fr; internet www.univ-orleans.fr/polytech; Pres. RICHARD ROZIECKI.

Faculté de Droit, d'Economie et de Gestion: rue de Blois, BP 6739, 45067 Orléans Cedex; tel. 2-38-41-70-31; fax 2-38-41-73-60; e-mail rsa.deg@univ-orleans.fr; Dean STÉPHANE ONNÉE.

Faculté des Lettres, Langues et Sciences Humaines: 10 rue de Tours, BP 46527, 45065 Orléans Cedex 2; tel. 2-38-49-25-00; fax 2-38-41-73-25; Dir ALAIN DAVESNE.

Faculté des Sciences: 1 rue de Chartres, BP 6759, 45067 Orléans Cedex 2; tel. 2-38-41-71-71; e-mail directeur.sciences@univ-orleans.fr; Dir NIRINA ANDRIANARIVELO.

Faculté des Sciences et Techniques des Activités Physiques et Sportives: allée du château, BP 6237, 45062 Orléans Cedex 2; tel. 2-38-41-71-78; fax 2-38-41-72-60; e-mail infos.staps@univ-orleans.fr; Dir RÉGIS DE REYKE.

Institut Universitaire de Formation des Maîtres (Centre Val de Loire): 72 rue du Faubourg de Bourgogne, 45044 Orléans Cedex 2; tel. 2-38-49-26-00; fax 2-38-42-04-60; e-mail directeur.iufm@univ-orleans.fr; Dir JEAN-MARIE GINESTA.

ATTACHED RESEARCH INSTITUTES
Institut Universitaire de Technologie de Bourges: 63 ave de Lattre de Tassigny, 18020 Bourges Cedex; tel. 2-48-23-80-80; fax 2-48-23-80-23; e-mail irection@bourges.univ-orleans.fr; internet www.bourges.univ-orleans.fr/iut; Dir GÉRARD POISSON.

Institut Universitaire de Technologie de Chartres: 1 place Roger Joly, 28000 Chartres; tel. 2-37-91-83-00; fax 2-37-91-83-01; e-mail monique.guerin@univ-orleans.fr; internet www.univ-orleans.fr/iut-chartres/iut.

Institut Universitaire de Technologie de l'Indre: 2 ave F. Mitterrand, 36000 Chateauroux; tel. 2-54-08-25-50; fax 2-54-07-78-00; e-mail gerard.guillaume@univ-orleans.fr; internet www.univ-orleans.fr/composantes/iut-indre/iut-indre-new; Dir JEAN-CHRISTOPHE BARDET.

Institut Universitaire de Technologie d'Orléans: 16 rue d'Issoudun, BP 16729, 45067 Orléans Cedex 2; tel. 2-38-49-44-00; fax 2-38-49-44-01; e-mail scolarite.iut45@univ-orleans.fr.

Observatoire des Sciences de l'Univers en région Centre (OSUC): Campus Géosciences, 1A rue de la Férolerie, 45071 Orléans Cedex 2; tel. 2-38-49-49-45; e-mail dir-osuc@univ-orleans.fr; Dir ELISABETH VERGÈS.

UNIVERSITÉ PARIS I (PANTHÉON-SORBONNE)
12 pl. du Panthéon, 75231 Paris Cedex 05
Telephone: 1-44-07-77-04
Fax: 1-46-34-20-56
E-mail: cabpresi@univ-paris1.fr
Internet: www.univ-paris1.fr
Founded 1971
State control
Language of instruction: French
Academic year: September to June
Pres.: JEAN-CLAUDE COLLIARD

Vice-Pres: JEAN DA SILVA (Ccl of Admin.),
YVONNE FLOUR (Scientific Ccl), GRÉGOIRE
LOISEAU (Studies and Univ. Life)
Sec.-Gen.: FRANÇOIS RIOU
Librarian: ANNE MAGNAUDET
Number of teachers: 1,603
Number of students: 39,234

TEACHING AND RESEARCH UNITS

Business Law: Dir: Prof. JEAN-JACQUES DAI-
GRE (acting)
Economic and Social Administration, Labour
and Social Studies: Dir: SABINE MONNIER
Economics: Dir: JEAN-CLAUDE BERTHÉLEMY
Business Management and Economics: Dir:
PIERRE MEDAN
Geography: Dir: Prof. BERNARD TALLET (act-
ing)
History: Dir: Prof. JEAN-MARIE BERTRAND
(acting)
History of Art and Archaeology: Dir: Prof.
MICHEL POIVERT
International and European Studies: Dir:
Prof. PIERRE MICHEL EISEMANN
Legal Studies: Dir: Prof. EMMANUEL JEULAND
(acting)
Mathematics and Computer Science: Dir:
PASCAL GOURDEL (acting)
Philosophy: Dir: JACQUES DUBUCS
Plastic Arts and Science of Art: Dir: JOSÉ
MOURE (acting)
Political Science: Dir: Prof. FRANÇOIS BASTIEN
(acting)
Public Administration and Public Law: Dir:
Prof. GÉRALDINE CHAVRIER (acting)

INSTITUTES

French Institute of Communication: Pres.:
MATHIEU GALLET
Institute of Business Administration: Dir:
PIERRE-LOUIS DUBOIS
Institute of Demography: Dir: MARLÈNE LAMY
(acting)
Institute of Economic and Social Develop-
ment Studies: Dir: Prof. ANFRÉ GUICHAOUA
(acting)
Institute of Insurance: Dirs: VINCENT HEUZE,
JÉRÔME KULLMANN
Institute of Labour Social Sciences: Dir:
JEAN-MARIE MONNIER
Institute of Legal Studies: Dir: FRANÇOIS-
XAVIER LUCAS
Institute of Tourism Research and Higher
Study: (vacant)

DEPARTMENTS

Applied Modern Languages, Economics and
Law: Dir: L. THOMPSON (acting)
Applied Modern Languages, Humanities:
Dir: A. HAKKAK (acting)
Social Sciences: Dir: Mme YOTTE

PROFESSORS

Applied Modern Languages, Economics and
Law (12 place du Panthéon, 75005 Paris; tel.
1-44-07-78-33; fax 1-44-07-78-33; e-mail
seglas@univ-paris1.fr):

BULLIER, A.-J., Legal English Studies
KERSAUDY, F., English for Economists

Business Law (tel. 1-44-07-77-35; fax 1-44-
07-75-11; e-mail ufr05@univ-paris1.fr):

AYNES, L., Private and Civil Law
BOULOC, B., Criminal Law
CADIET, L., Civil Procedure
CHAPUT, Y., Commercial Law—Insolvency
DAIGRE, J. J., Business Law
DAVID, C., Tax Law
DELEBECQUE, P., Civil Law
FLOUR, Y., Civil Law
GAUDU, F., Labour Law
GIUDICELLI, G., Criminal Law
GUTMANN, D., Insurance Law
HEUZE, V., Insurance Law
JOURDAIN, P., Civil Law
LABRUSSE, C., Civil Law

LE CANNU, P., Business Law
LE NABASQUE, H., Business Law
LIBCHABER, R., Civil Law
LUCAS DE LEYSSAC, C., Commercial Law
MENJUCQ, M., International Corporate Law
MUIR-WATT, H., Civil Law and Inter-
national Civil Law
PARLEANI, G., Business Law
POLLAUD-DULIAN, F., Artistic and Literary
Copyright Law
THIREAU, J. L., History of Law
VINEY, G., Civil Law

Business Management and Economics (17
rue de la Sorbonne, 75005 Paris Cedex 05;
tel. 1-40-46-27-77; fax 1-40-46-31-77; e-mail
ufr06@univ-paris1.fr):

AMADIEU, J. F., Human Resources Man-
agement
BAETCHE, A., Scientific Methods Applied to
Marketing
CHIROLEU-ASSOULINE, M., Macroeconomics
COT, A., Economics
COURET, A., Business Law
DE LA BRUSLERIE, H., Finance
DESAIGUES, B., Environmental Economics
GOFFIN, R., Finance
GREGORY, P., Marketing
IPSOMER, I., Marketing
LAURENT, P., Business Law
MUCHIELLI, J.-L., Industrial Economics
PEYRARD, M., International and European
Business
PONCET, P., Finance
RAIMBOURG, P., Finance
RAY, J.-E., Labour Law
ROJOT, J., Organization Theory and
Human Resources Management
ROLLAND, C., Computer Science
ROURE, F., Finance
STEYER, A., Speculative Methods in Mar-
keting

Economics (Centre P.M.F., 90 rue de Tolbiac,
75634 Paris Cedex 13; tel. 1-44-07-88-88; fax
1-44-07-86-14; e-mail ufr02@univ-paris1.fr):

ANDREFF, W., Economy of the Transition
ARCHAMBAULT, E., Accountancy and Social
Economics
BERTHELEMY, J. C., International Econom-
ics
BORDES, C., Money and Macroeconomics
CHAUVEAU, TH., Money and Finance
DE BOISSIEU, C., Monetary Economics
ENCAOUA, D., Industrial Economics
FARDEAU, M., Health Economics, Social
Economics
FAU, J., Economic Analysis
FONTAGNE, L., International Economics
GARDES, F., Econometrics
GREFFE, X., Political Economy
HAIRAULT, J. O., Macroeconomics
HENIN, P., Macroeconomics
KEMPF, H., Macroeconomics
KOPP, P., Microeconomics
LAFAY, J. D., Public Economy
LAFFARGUE, J. P., International Economics
LANTNER, R., Economics and Industrial
Politics
LAPIDUS, A., History of Economic Thought
LEVY-GARBOUA, L., Microeconomics
MASSON-D'AUTUME, A., Macroeconomics
MEIDINGER, C., Microeconomics
MENARD, C., Theory of Organization
PRADEL, J., Statistics
SCHUBERT, K., Macroeconomics
SOFER, C., Microeconomics
SOLLOGOUB, M., Microeconomics
VERNIÈRES, M., Economic Analysis
WIGNIOLLE, B., Macroeconomics
ZAGAME, P., Macroeconomics

Economic and Social Administration, Labour
and Social Studies (1 rue d'Ulm, Bureau 14,
75005 Paris; tel. 1-44-07-79-28; fax 1-44-07-
79-08; e-mail dirufr12@univ-paris1.fr):

CHAPOULIE, Sociology

COUTURIER, G., Labour Law
GAZIER, B., Labour Economy
LENOIR, R., Sociology
PIGENET, Sociology
RODIÈRE, P., Labour Law
TSIKOUNAS, History

Economic and Social Development (Centre de
Nogent-sur-Marne, 45 bis ave de la Belle-
Gabrielle, 94736 Nogent-sur-Marne Cedex;
tel. 1-43-94-72-15; fax 1-43-94-72-44; e-mail
iedes@univ.-paris1.fr):

GRELLET, G., Economic Development
HAUBERT, M., Social Development
LAUTIER, B., Economic and Social Develop-
ment

International and European Studies (12 pl.
du Panthéon, Bureau 304, 75005 Paris; tel. 1-
44-07-77-33; fax 1-44-07-75-12; e-mail ufr07@
univ-paris1.fr):

BARAV, A., European Community Law
BERLIN, D., European Community Law
BURDEAU, G., International Public Law
CARREAU, D., Economic Public Law
DAUDET, Y., International Public Law
DELMAS-MARTY, M., Penal Law
EISEMAN, P. M., International Public Law
HUDAULT, J., History of Law
IDOT, L., European Community Law
JUILLARD, P., International Economic Law
LAGARDE, P., International Private Law
LEGRAND, P., Comparative Law
LE ROY, E., Legal Anthropology
LOVISI, C., History of Law
MANIN, P., European Community Law
MASCLET, J. C., European Community Law
MAYER, P., International Private Law
RENOUX-ZAGAMÉ, M. F., History of Law
RUIZ FABRI, H., Constitutional Law
SIRINELLI, P., Private Law
SOREL, J. M., International Public Law
STERN, B., International Public Law

Geography (191 rue St Jacques, 75231 Paris
Cedex 05; tel. 1-44-32-14-00; fax 1-44-32-14-
54; e-mail geo1@univ-paris1.fr):

BECKOUCHE, P., Economic Geography
BOUINOT, J., Planning and Economic Geog-
raphy
BRUN, J., Social Geography
CAZES, G., Geography of Tourism
CHALÉARD, J. L., Geography of Developing
Countries
FRUIT, J. P., Rural Geography
KAISER, B., Geomorphology
LE COEUR, C., Natural Resources, Geomor-
phology
MALEZIEUX, J., Regional Geography, Land
Use
MERLIN, P., Urban Geography
PECH, P., Environment
POURTIER, R., Tropical Geography
PREVELAKIS, G., Geopolitics
PUMAIN, D., Urban Geography
SAINT-JULIEN, TH., Human Geography,
Statistics
SOPPELSA, J., Geopolitics
TABEAUD, M., Climatology

History (17 rue de la Sorbonne, 75005 Paris
Cedex 05; tel. 1-40-46-27-88; fax 1-40-46-31-
80; e-mail hist1@univ-paris1.fr):

BALARD, M., Mediterranean Medieval His-
tory
BENOÎT, P., Modern History
BERTRAND, J. M., Ancient History
BOULÈGUE, J.-M., History of Black Africa
BOURIN, M., Medieval History
CABANTOUS, A., Modern History
CHARLE, C., Contemporary History
CHARPIN, D., Near Eastern History
CHRISTOL, M., Roman History
CORBIN, A., Contemporary History
CORSI, P., Modern History
D'ALMEIDA-TOPOR, H., Contemporary His-
tory
DAVID, J. M., Ancient History

FRANK, R., Contemporary History
GAUVARD, C., Medieval History
GENET, J. P., Medieval History
GUERRA, F., History of Latin America
KAPLAN, M., Byzantine Medieval History
KASPI, A., History of North America
LEMAITRE, N., Modern History
MARSEILLE, J., Economic and Social History
MARTIN, J. C., Modern History
MICHAUD, C., Modern History
MICHEAU, F., Medieval History
MICHEL, B., History of Eastern Europe
ORY, P., Contemporary History
PARISSE, M., Medieval History
REY, M. P., Contemporary History
RIVET, D., Contemporary History
ROBERT, J. L., Contemporary History
SCHMITT, P., Ancient History
WORONOFF, D., Economic and Social History
ZYLBERBERG, M., Modern History

History of Art and Archaeology (3 rue Michelet, 75006 Paris Cedex 06; tel. 1-53-73-71-11; fax 1-53-73-71-13; e-mail ufr03sec@univ-paris1.fr):

BURNOUF, J., Medieval Archaeology
CROISSANT, F., Greek Archaeology
DAGEN, P., Contemporary Art
DARRAGON, E., Contemporary Art
DEMOULE, J.-P., Protohistory
DENTZER, J. M., Oriental Archaeology
DUMASY, F., Classical Archaeology
GILI, J., Cinema
HUOT, J. L., Oriental Archaeology
LICHARDUS, M., Protohistory
MONNIER, G., History of Contemporary Art
MOREL, P., Modern Art
PIGEOT, N., Archaeology and Protohistory
POLET, J., African Art and Archaeology
PRESSOUYRE, L., Medieval Art and Archaeology
PRIGENT, C., Medieval Art
RABREAU, D., Modern Art
SCHNAPP, A., Greek Archaeology
SODINI, J. P., Byzantine Archaeology
TALADOIRE, E., Meso-American Archaeology
TREUIL, R. A., Archaeology and Protohistory
VANCI, M., Contemporary Art
VAN DER LEEUW, S., Archaeology and Protohistory
VOLFOVSKY, C., Preservation of Cultural Heritage

Institute of Business Administration (21 rue Broca, 75240 Paris Cedex 05; tel. 1-53-55-27-47; fax 1-53-55-27-01; e-mail iae@univ-paris1.fr; internet www.iae-paris.com):

ALLOUCHE, J., Human Resources Management
GIARD, V., Operations Management
HELFER, J.-P., Marketing and Strategy
HOARAU, C., Finance and Control
LE FLOCH, P., Business Law
MAILLET, P., Finance
PAUCELLE, J. L., Information Systems
TRIOLAIRE, G., Management

Institute of Demography (i DUP, Centre PMF, 90 rue de Tolbiac, 75013 Paris Cedex 13; tel. 1-44-07-86-46; fax 1-44-07-86-47; e-mail idup@univ-paris1.fr):

DITTGEN, A., Socio-Demography
GROSSAT, B., Socio-Demography
LAMY-FESTY, M., Social Demography
NORVEZ, A., Socio-Demography

Institute of Social Sciences (tel. 1-45-36-16-40; fax 1-46-65-70-80; e-mail patrick.diez@univ-paris1.fr):

FREYSSINET, J., Economics
OFFERLE, M., Political Science
PAULRE, B., Economics
PIOTEL, F., Sociology

Mathematics and Computer Science (Centre Pierre Mendès-France, 14ème étage, Bureau C 14-03, 90 rue de Tolbiac, 75013 Paris; tel. 1-44-07-89-84):

ABDOU, J., Game Theory
AUSLENDER, A., Optimization
BALASKO, Y., Mathematical Economics
BONNISSEAU, J.-M., Mathematics and Economics
CORNET, B., Mathematics and Economics
COTTRELL, M., Probability, Statistics and Neural Networks
GIRE, F., Computer Science
GUYON, X., Probability and Statistics
HADDAD, G., Differential Equations and Functional Analysis
JOUINI, E., Mathematics and Economics

Philosophy (90 rue de Tolbiac, 75013 Paris; tel. 1-44-07-88-32; e-mail philo1@univ-paris1.fr):

BLONDEL, E., Moral and Political Philosophy
BONARDEL, F., Philosophy of Religion
BRAGUE, R., History of Philosophy
CHAUVIRÉ, C., American Philosophy and Anthropology
CHEDIN, O., History of Philosophy
GRAS, A., Social Philosophy
KAMBOUCHNER, D., History of Philosophy
KERVEGAN, J. F., Philosophy of Law
MICHAUD, Y., Political Philosophy
MOEGLIN-DELCROIX, A., Aesthetics
MOSCONI, J., Philosophy of Mathematics
PINTO, E., Aesthetics
POLITIS, H., History of Philosophy
RIVENC, F., Philosophy of Logic
SALEM, J., History of Philosophy

Plastic Arts and Science of Art (Centre Saint Charles, 47 rue des Bergers, 75015 Paris; tel. 1-44-07-84-40; fax 1-44-07-84-72; e-mail raufr04@univ-paris1.fr):

BAQUE, P., Visual Arts
CHATEAU, D., Aesthetics
CHIRON, E., Visual Arts
CLANCY, G., Aesthetics
CONTE, R., Visual Arts
DARRAS, B., Culture and Communication
DUGUET, A. N., Video and Media
FRENAULT-DERUELLE, P., Semiotics
HUYGHE, P. D., Visual Arts and Aesthetics
JIMENEZ, M., Aesthetics
LANCRI, J., Visual Arts
LEBENSZTEJN, J. C., History of Art
MIEREANU, C., Musicology
NOGUEZ, D., Cinema and Audiovisual Arts
SERCEAU, D., Cinema and Audiovisual Arts
SICARD, N., Visual Arts

Political Science (17 rue Cujas, 75005 Paris; tel. 1-40-46-28-04; fax 1-40-46-31-65; e-mail raufr11@univ-paris1.fr):

BIRNBAUM, P., Political Sociology
BRAUD, P., Political Sociology
COLLIARD, J. C., Comparative Government
COTTERET, J.-M., Political Communication
FRANÇOIS, B., Constitutional Law
GAXIE, D., Political Sociology
GRESLE, F., Sociology
KLEIN, J., International Relations
LAGROYE, J., Political Ideology
LESAGE, M., Theory of Organizations
SFEZ, L., Communication
ZORGBIBE, C., International Relations

Public Administration and Public Internal Law (12 pl. du Panthéon, 75005 Paris; tel. 1-44-07-77-38; fax 1-44-07-75-09; e-mail ufr01@univ-paris1.fr):

BRECHON-MOULÈNES, C., Public Economic Law
CASTAGNEDE, B., Public Finance
DURUPTY, M., Public Law
FATOME, E., Administrative Law
FRIER, P., Public Law
GICQUEL, J., Public Law

JEGOUZO, Y., Administrative Law
LE MIRE, P., Public Law
MAISL, H., Administrative Law
MARCOU, G., Administrative Law
MATHIEU, B., Constitutional Law
MODERNE, F., Administrative Law
MORABITO, M., History of Law
MORAND-DEVILLER, J., Administrative Law
PFERS MANN, O., Comparative Public Law
PICARD, E., Administrative Law
RICHER, L., Administrative Law
TIMSIT, G., Public Law

UNIVERSITÉ DE PARIS II (UNIVERSITÉ PANTHÉON-ASSAS)

12 place du Panthéon, 75005 Paris Cedex 05

Telephone: 1-44-41-55-01
Fax: 1-44-41-55-13
E-mail: presidence@u-paris2.fr
Internet: www.u-paris2.fr

Founded 1970

Pres.: LOUIS VOGEL
Vice-Pres: Prof. JEAN-DIDIER LECAILLON (Ccl of Admin.), JEAN COMBACAU (Scientific Ccl), CHRISTA VALTCHEVA (Studies and Univ. Life)
Sec.-Gen.: SYLVIE TORAILLE
Librarian: GENEVIÈVE SONNEVILLE

Number of teachers: 1,547
Number of students: 17,900

TEACHING AND RESEARCH UNITS

Centre for Human Resources Training: Dir: F. BOURNOIS
Centre for Studies and Research in Construction and Housing: Dir: Prof. P. MALINVAUD
Law (First cycle): Dir: PIERRE CROCQ
Law (Second cycle) and Political Science: Dir: M. COMBACAU
Law (Third cycle) and Political Science: Dir: LAURENT LEVENEUR
Economics: ANTOINE BILLOT
Economic and Social Administration (First and Second cycles): Dir: MARTINE PELE
Higher Institute for Defence Studies: Dir: Prof. YVES CARO
Information Sciences (French Press Institute): Dir: Prof. NADINE TOUSSAINT-DESMOULINS
Image and Communication Institute: Dir: Prof. C. TUAL
Institute for Administration Training: Dir: JEAN-MICHEL DE FORGES
Institute of Advanced International Studies: Dirs: C. LEBEN, P.-MARIE DUPUY
Institute of Business Law: Dir: Prof. MICHEL GERMAIN
Institute of Comparative Law: Dir: Prof. LOUIS VOGEL
Institute of Criminology: Dir: Prof. JACQUES-HENRI ROBERT
Institute of Judicial Studies: Dir: Prof. S. GUINCHARD
IUP–Management: Dir: Prof. RAYMOND TRÉMOLIÈRES

PROFESSORS

ALLAND, D., Public Law
ALPHANDERY, E., Economic Sciences
AMSELEK, P., Public Law
ANCEL, D., Private Law
AUBY, J. B., Public Law
AUDIT, B., Private Law
AVRIL, P., Political Science
BALLE, F., Political Science
BALLOT, G., Economic Sciences
BARRAT, J., Information Sciences
BÉAUD, O., Public Law
BENZONI, L., Economic Sciences
BERNARD, M., Education Sciences
BETBEZE, J.-P., Economic Sciences
BETTATI, M., Public Law
BIENVENU, J. J., Public Law

BILLOT, A., Economic Sciences
BLAISE, J.-B., Private Law
BLUMANN, C., Public Law
BOISIVON, J.-P., Management Science
BONET, G., Private Law
BONNEAU, T., Private Law
BOURNOIS, F., Management Science
BRESSON, G., Economic Sciences
BURDEAU, F., History of Law
BUREAU, D., Private Law
CARBASSE, J. M., History of Law
CARO, J.-Y., Economic Sciences
CARTIER, M.-E., Private Law
CASTALDO, A., History of Law
Mme CATALA, N., Private Law
CAZENAVE, P., Economic Sciences
CHAGNOLLAUD, D., Political Science
CHAMPENOIS, G., Private Law
CHARPIN, F., Economic Sciences
CHEVALLIER, J., Public Law
CHRISTIN, Y., Economic Sciences
COCATRE-ZILGIEN, P., History of Law
COHEN-JONATHAN, G., Public Law
COMBACAU, J., Public Law
CROCQ, P., Private Law
DECOCQ, A., Private Law
DELVOLVE, P., Public Law
DERIEUX, E., Information Sciences
DESNEUF, P., Economic Sciences
DESPLAS, M., Economic Sciences
DIBOUT, P., Public Law
DIDIER, P., Private Law
DISCHAMPS, J. C., Management Science
DONIO, J., Computing
DRAGO, G., Public Law
DUBOIS, P.-M., Public Law
DUPUY, G., Public Law
DURRY, G., Private Law
DUTHEIL DE LA ROCHÈRE, J., Public Law
FACCARELLO, G., Economic Sciences
FEYEL, G., History
FOUCHARD, P., Private Law
FOYER, J., Private Law
GAUDEMET, Y., Public Law
GAUDEMET-TALLON, H., Private Law
GAUTIER, P. Y., Private Law
GERMAIN, M., Private Law
GHOZI, A., Private Law
GJIDARA, M., Public Law
GOYARD, C., Public Law
GRIMALDI, M., Private Law
GUINCHARD, S., Private Law
HAROUEL, J.-L., History of Law
HUET, J., Private Law
HUMBERT, M., History of Law
JAHEL, S., Private Law
JARROSON, C., Private Law
JAUFFRET-SPINOSI, C., Private Law
JAVILLIER, J.-C., Private Law
JOUET, J., Information Sciences
LABROUSSE, C., Economic Sciences
LAFAY, G., Economic Sciences
LAINGUI, A., History of Law
LAMARQUE, J., Public Law
LARROUMET, C., Private Law
LEBEN, C., Public Law
LEFEBVRE-TEILLARD, A., History of Law
LE GALL, J.-P., Private Law
LEMENNICIER-BUCQUET, B., Economic Sciences
LEMOYNE DE FORGES, J. M., Public Law
LEQUETTE, Y., Private Law
LEVENEUR, L., Private Law
LOMBARD, M., Public Law
LOMBOIS, C., Private Law
LUBOCHINSKY, C., Economic Sciences
MALINVAUD, P., Private Law
MARTINEZ, J. C., Public Law
MAYAUD, Y., Private Law
MAZEAU, D., Private Law
MERLE, P., Private Law
MOLFESSIS, N., Private Law
MONCONDUIT, F., Political Science
MORANGE, J., Public Law
MOREAU, J., Public Law
Mme MOURGUES, M. DE, Economic Sciences

Mme NÈME, C., Economic Sciences
OLIVIER, J. M., Private Law
OTTAYJ, L., Private Law
PELÉ, M., Management Science
PERINET-MARQUET, H., Private Law
PONDAVEN, C., Economic Sciences
PORTELLI, H., Political Science
QUENET, M., History of Law
RAYNAUD, P., Political Science
REDSLOB, A., Economic Sciences
RIALS, S., Public Law
RIEFFEL, R., Information Sciences
RIGAUDIERE, A., History of Law
ROBERT, J.-H., Private Law
ROUGEMONT, M. DE, Computing
SCANNAVINO, A., Economic Sciences
SCHWARTZENBERG, R. G., Public Law
SUR, S., Public Law
SYNVET, H., Private Law
TERRÉ, F., Private Law
TEYSSIÉ, B., Private Law
THERY, P., Private Law
TOUSSAINT-DESMOULINS, N., Information Sciences
TREMOLIÈRES, R., Management Science
TRUCHET, D., Public Law
TUAL, C., English
VEDEL, C., Economic Sciences
VERPEAUX, M., Public Law
VITRY, D., Economic Sciences
VOGEL, L., Private Law
ZOLLER, E., Public Law

UNIVERSITÉ DE PARIS III (SORBONNE-NOUVELLE)

17 rue de la Sorbonne, 75230 Paris Cedex 05
Telephone: 1-40-46-28-84
Fax: 1-43-46-29-36
E-mail: presidence@univ-paris3.fr
Internet: www.univ-paris3.fr
Founded 1970
State control
Language of instruction: French
Academic year: October to June
Pres.: Prof. MARIE-CHRISTINE LEMARDELEY
Vice-Pres.: CARLE BONAFOUS-MURAT (Ccl of Admin.), PIERRE CIVIL (Scientific Ccl), ANNE SALAZAR ORVIG (Studies and Univ. Life)
Sec.-Gen.: VINCENT GAILLOT
Number of teachers: 680
Number of students: 18,307

TEACHING AND RESEARCH UNITS

Arts and Media: Dir: BRUNO PÉQUIGNOT (acting)
Languages, Literature, Culture and Foreign Societies: Dir: JEAN-PATRICK GUILLAUME (acting)
Literature, Linguistics and Language Instruction: Dir: JEAN-LOUIS CHISS
Higher School of Interpreters and Translators: Dir: CLARE DONOVAN
Institute for the Advanced Study of Latin America: Dir: GEORGES COUFFIGNAL

UNIVERSITÉ DE PARIS IV (PARIS-SORBONNE)

1 rue Victor-Cousin, 75230 Paris Cedex 05
Telephone: 1-40-46-22-11
Fax: 1-40-46-25-88
E-mail: president@paris-sorbonne.fr
Internet: www.paris-sorbonne.fr
Founded 1970
State control
Language of instruction: French
Academic year: October to June
Pres.: GEORGES MOLINIÉ
Vice-Pres: DENIS LABOURET (Ccl of Admin.), ARIANE BUISSON (Studies and Univ. Life), BARTHÉLÉMY JOBERT (Scientific Ccl)
Sec.-Gen.: SYLVIE N'GUYEN

Librarian: JOËLLE CLAUD
Number of teachers: 1,300
Number of students: 23,271

TEACHING AND RESEARCH UNITS

Applied Foreign Languages: Dir: Prof. LILIANE GALLET-BLANCHARD
English: Dir: Prof. PIERRE COTTE
French and Comparative Literature: Dir: Prof. DIDIER ALEXANDRE
French Language: Dir: Prof. OLIVIER SOUTET
Geography and Planning: Dir: Prof. GUY CHEMLA
Germanic Studies: Dir: Prof. MARTINE DALMAS
Greek: Dir: Prof. ALAIN BILAUT
History: Dir: Prof. A. TALLON
History of Art and Archaeology: Dir: Prof. THIBAUT WOLVESPERGES
Iberian and Latin-American Studies: Dir: Prof. SADI LAKHDARI
Institute for the Research of the Civilisations of the Modern Western World: Dir: Prof. DENIS CROUZET
Italian and Romanian: Dir: Prof. ANDREA FABIANO
Latin Language and Literature: Dir: Prof. GÉRARD CAPDEVILLE
Music and Musicology: Dir: Prof. FRÉDÉRIC BILLIET
Philosophy and Sociology: Dir: Prof. STÉPHANE CHAVIER
Slavonic Studies: Dir: Prof. LAURE TROUBETZKOY
Institute of Applied Humanities: Dir: Prof. CLAUDE MONTACIÉ

DIRECTORS OF GRADUATE SCHOOLS

Ancient and Medieval Worlds: Prof. PAUL DEMONT
Civilization, Cultures, Literature and Societies: GÉRARD RAULET
Concepts and Languages: Prof. JEAN-PIERRE BARTOLI
French and Comparative Literatures: Prof. BERTRAND MARCHAL
Graduate School of Geography, Paris: space, society and planning: Prof. CHRISTIAN GRATALOUP
History of Art and Archaeology: Prof. MARIANNE GRIVEL
Modern and Contemporary History: Prof. JACQUES-OLIVIER BOUDON

UNIVERSITÉ PARIS V (DESCARTES)

12 rue de l'École de Médecine, 75270 Paris Cedex 06
Telephone: 1-40-46-16-16
Fax: 1-40-46-16-15
E-mail: secretaire.general@parisdescartes.fr
Internet: www.parisdescartes.fr
Founded 1970
Academic year: October to July
Pres.: AXEL KAHN
Vice-Pres: ARNAUD DUCRUIX (Ccl of Admin.), BRUNO VARET (Scientific Ccl), MARIE-HÉLÈNE JEANMERET-CRETTEZ (Studies and Univ. Life)
Sec.-Gen.: FRANÇOIS PAQUIS
Librarian: JÉRÔME KALFON
Number of teachers: 2,177
Number of students: 38,000

Publication: *Diologues de Descartes* (4 a year).

TEACHING AND RESEARCH UNITS

Faculté Biomédicale: 45 rue des Saints-Pères, 75006 Paris Cedex 06; tel. 1-42-86-22-33; e-mail responsable-administratif@biomedicale.univ-paris5.fr; Dir DANIEL JORE.
Faculté de Chirurgie Dentaire: 1 rue Maurice Arnoux, 92120 Montrouge; tel. 1-

58-07-67-00; fax 1-58-07-68-99; e-mail gerard .levy@parisdescartes.fr; Dean GÉRARD LÉVY.

Faculté de Droit: 10 ave Pierre Larousse, 92240 Malakoff; tel. 1-41-17-30-00; fax 1-46-56-05-29; internet www.droit.univ-paris5.fr; Dean JEAN-PIERRE MACHELON.

Faculté de Mathématique et Informatique: 45 rue des Saints-Pères, 75006 Paris; tel. 1-42-86-40-41; e-mail scolarite@mi .parisdescartes.fr; Dir CHRISTINE GRAFFIGNE.

Faculté de Médecine: 15 rue de l'école de médecine, 75270 Paris Cedex 06; tel. 1-53-10-46-00; e-mail scolarite@mi.parisdescartes.fr; Dir PATRICK BERCHE.

Faculté des Sciences Humaines et Sociales: rue des Saints-Pères, 75270 Paris Cedex 06; tel. 1-53-10-50-60; e-mail accueil@ shs.parisdescartes.fr; Dean SYLVETTE MAURY.

Faculté des Sciences Pharmaceutiques et Biologiques: 4 ave de l'Observatoire, 75006 Paris; tel. 1-53-73-95-95; fax 1-43-29-05-92; e-mail martine.aiach@parisdescartes .fr; Dean MARTINE AIACH.

Faculté des Sciences et Techniques des Activités Physiques et Sportives: 1 rue Lacretelle, 75015 Paris; tel. 1-56-56-12-00; fax 1-56-56-12-24; e-mail bertrand.during@ parisdescartes.fr; Dir BERTRAND DURING.

Institut de Psychologie: Centre Henri Piéron, 71 ave Edouard Vaillant, 92774 Boulogne-Billancourt Cedex; tel. 1-55-20-58-58; fax 1-55-20-57-45; e-mail communication@psychologie.parisdescartes .fr.

Institut Universitaire de Technologie: 143 ave de Versailles, 75016 Paris; tel. 1-42-86-47-00; fax 1-42-24-18-50; e-mail iut@iut .univ-paris5.fr; Dir GUILLAUME BORDRY.

UNIVERSITÉ DE PARIS VI (PIERRE ET MARIE CURIE)

4 place Jussieu, 75005 Paris
Telephone: 1-44-27-44-27
Fax: 1-44-27-38-29
E-mail: dag@upmc.fr
Internet: www.upmc.fr
Founded 1971
Pres.: JEAN-CHARLES POMEROL
Vice-Pres. for Resources and Means: MAURICE RENARD
Vice-Pres. for Research: JEAN CHAMBAZ
Vice-Pres. for Training and Professional Integration: PATRICK PORCHERON
Vice-Pres. for Medicine: BRUNO RIOU
Vice-Pres. for Int. Relations: SERGE FDIDA
Sec.-Gen.: CLAUDE RONCERAY

Number of teachers: 3,250
Number of students: 29,570

TEACHING AND RESEARCH UNITS

Biology: DANIEL VERGÉ
Chemistry: DIDIER DEVILLIERS
Earth Sciences, Environment and Biodiversity: LUC ABBADIE
Engineering: JEAN DEVARS
Mathematics: HERVÉ LE DRET (Dean)
Medicine: SERGE UZAN (Dean)
Physics: PATRICK BOISSÉ
Apprenticeship Training Centre (CFA): DENIS POULAIN
Henri Poincaré Institute: CÉDRIC VILLANI
Polytech'Paris-UPMC: JEAN-MARIE CHESNEAUX
Institute of Astrophysics, Paris (IAP): LAURENT VIGROUX
Institute of Doctoral Training (IFD): PHILIPPE DENOULET
Institute of Statistics (ISUP): MICHEL DELECROIX
Oceanological Observatory, Banyuls: PHILIPPE LEBARON

Oceanological Observatory, Roscoff: BERNARD KLOAREG
Oceanological Observatory, Villefranche-sur-Mer: FAUZI MANTOURA

UNIVERSITÉ DE PARIS VII (DENIS DIDEROT)

2 place Jussieu, 75251 Paris Cedex 05
Telephone: 1-44-27-44-27
Fax: 1-44-27-69-64
E-mail: mmtx@sigu7.jussieu.fr
Internet: www.diderotp7.jussieu.fr
Founded 1970
Pres.: VINCENT BERGER
Vice-Pres: LAURE ELIE (Ccl of Admin.), RICHARD LAGANIER (Scientific Ccl), JEAN-LOUIS COLLIN (Studies and Univ. Life), FRÉDÉRIC OGEE (Int. Relations), FRANÇOIS MONTARRAS (Projects and Building Planning), BERNADETTE BRICOUT (Cultural Life and Univ. Integration)
Sec.-Gen.: DENIS GUILLAUMIN

Number of teachers: 1,400
Number of students: 26,000

TEACHING AND RESEARCH UNITS

Anthropology, Ethnology and Religious Studies: Dir: P. DESHAYES
Biochemistry: Dir: PATRICK VICART
Biology and Natural Sciences: Dir: CLAUDE LAMOUR-ISNARD
Chemistry: Dir: JEAN AUBARD
Clinical Human Sciences: Dir: PAUL-LAURENT ASSOUN
Computer Studies: Dir: GUY COUSINEAU
Dental Surgery: Dir: MARIE-LAURE BOY-LEFEVRE
Earth and Physical Sciences: Dir: YVES GAUDEMER
Eastern Asian Languages and Literature: Dir: CÉCILE SAKAI
Film, Communication and Information Studies: Dir: BAUDOIN JURDANT
Geography, History and Social Sciences: Dir: JEAN-PIERRE VALLAT
Institute of English: Dir: PHILIPPE JAWORSKI
Institute of Haematology: Dir: FRANÇOIS SIGAUX
Intercultural Studies in Applied Languages: Dir: JOHN HUMBLEY
Linguistic Research: Dir: ALAIN ROUVERET
Mathematics: Dir: PIERRE VOGEL
Medicine (Lariboisière-Saint-Louis): Dir: ALAIN LE DUC
Medicine (Xavier-Bichat): Dir: J. M. DESMONTS
Physics: Dir: LUC VALENTIN
Sciences of Texts and Documents: Dir: PIERRE CHARTIER
Social Sciences: Dir: ETIENNE TASSIN
University Institute of Technology: Dir: ALAIN JUNGMAN

UNIVERSITÉ DE PARIS VIII— VINCENNES À ST-DENIS

2 rue de la Liberté, 93526 St Denis Cedex 02
Telephone: 1-49-40-67-89
Fax: 1-48-21-04-46
E-mail: presidence@univ-paris8.fr
Internet: www.univ-paris8.fr
Founded 1969
State control
Language of instruction: French
Pres.: PASCAL BINCZAK
Vice-Pres: CHRISTINE BOUISSOU (Ccl of Admin.), ELISABETH BAUTIER (Scientific Ccl), JEAN-MARC MEUNIER (Studies and Univ. Life)
Sec.-Gen.: BERNARD FRADIN
Librarian: CAROLE LETROUIT

Number of teachers: 1,047
Number of students: 21,815

Publications: *Extrême-Orient / Extrême-Occident, Marges, Médiévales, Recherches linguistiques de Vincennes, Théorie, Littérature, Epistémologie*

TEACHING AND RESEARCH UNITS

Arts, Philosophy and Aesthetics: Dir: ERIC LECERF
Culture and Communication: Dir: MARTINE POUPON-BOUFFIERE
Economy and Management: Dir: PATRICK BOULOGNE
Educational Science, Psychoanalysis and French as a Foreign Language: Dir: JEAN-LOUIS LEGRAND
French Institute of Geopolitics: Dir: BARBARA LOYER
Institute of Distance Learning: Dir: GILLES BERNARD
Institute of European Studies: Dir: MIRELLE AZZOUG
Languages and Foreign Cultures: Dir: ANNICK ALLAIGRE
Law: Dir: JEAN-YVES ROCHEX
Mathematics, Computer Studies, Technology and ICT: Dir: ARAB BEN ALI CHÉRIF
Psychology: Dir: MARIE CARMEN CASTILLO
Science of Language: Dir: ANNE ZRIBI HERTZ
Territory, Environment and Societies: Dir: ANTOINE DA LAGE
Texts and Society: Dir: MARTINE CREACH
University Institute of Technology (Montreuil): Dir: ANDRÉ-MAX BOULANGER
University Institute of Technology (Tremblay): Dir: GORGUI SEYE

UNIVERSITÉ DE PARIS IX (PARIS-DAUPHINE)/UNIVERSITÉ PARIS DAUPHINE

place du Maréchal de Lattre de Tassigny, 75775 Paris Cedex 16
Telephone: 1-44-05-44-05
Fax: 1-44-05-49-49
E-mail: service.communicationping@ dauphinepong.fr
Internet: www.dauphine.fr
Founded 1968
State control
Language of instruction: French
Pres.: LAURENT BATSCH
Vice-Pres: ARNAUD RAYNOUARD (International Relations), ELYÈS JOUINI (Scientific Ccl), DOMINIQUE DAMAMME (Studies and Univ. Life)
Head of Secretariat: MAGALI ALZRAA
Library: General library of 170,000 vols, 9,000 current periodicals
Number of teachers: 400
Number of students: 8,867

DIRECTORS

Teaching and Research Units:

Analysis and Systems Modelling for Decision Mathematics (LAMSADE): VANGÉLIS PASCHOS
Cultural Identity and Speciality Languages (CICLaS: MARTINE PIQUET
Decision Mathematics (CEREMADE): (vacant): ERIC SÉRÉ
Economics (LEDa): PATRICE GEOFFRON
Law (L2D): JOËL MONÉGER
Management (DRM): ISABELLE HUAULT
Social Sciences (IRISSO): DOMINIQUE DAMAMME

University Professional Institutes:

Institute of Finance (IFD): ELYÈS JOUINI
Institute for the Management of Research and Innovation (IMRI): MICHEL POIX

PROFESSORS

ALTER, N., Sociology
ARNOLD, V., Mathematics
AUBIN, J.-P., Mathematics

BENSOUSSAN, A., Applied Mathematics
BERLIOZ-HOUIN, B., Business Law
BERTHET, CH., Computer Studies
BIENAYME, A., Industrial Economics
BLONDEL, D., Economics
BOUQUIN, H., Finance
BRUNET, A., Civil Law
CAREY-ABRIOUX, C.
CAZES, P., Statistics
CHAITIN-CHATELIN, F., Mathematics
CHAVENT, G., Mathematics
CHEDIN, G., English Language
CHEVALIER, J.-M., Economics
CLAASSEN, E., Economics
COHEN, E., Finance
COLASSE, B., Finance
COTTA, A., Business Organization
COUSOT, P., Computer Studies
DANA, R.
DE MONTMORILLON, B., Finance
DESMET, P.
DIDAY, E., Computer Studies
DOSS, H., Mathematics
EKELAND, I., Mathematics
ETNER, F., Economics
FLORENS, D., Mathematics
FRISON-ROCHE, M. A., Civil Law
GAUVIN, C., English Language
GEMAN, H., Finance
GHOZI, A., Civil Law
GIOVANNANGELI, J.-L., English Language and
    Literature
GOURIEROUX, C., Mathematics
GRELON, B., Civil Law
GUILLAUME, M., Economics
GUILLOCHON, B., Economics
HADDAD, S., Computer Studies
HAMON, J., Finance
HESS, C., Mathematics
JOMIER, G., Computer Studies
LARNAC, P.-M., Economics
LENA, H., Public Law
LE PEN, C., Economics
LE TALLEC, P., Mathematics
LEVY, E., Economics
LEVY, G., Computer Studies
LIONS, P.-L., Mathematics
LIU, M., Sociology
LOMBARD, M., Public Law
LORENZI, J.-H., Economics
MAILLES, D., Computer Studies
MANIN, A., Public Law
MARIET, F., Education
MATHIS, J., Finance
METAIS, J., Economics
MEYER, Y., Mathematics
MICHALET, C., Economics
MOREL, J.-M., Mathematics
NUSSENBAUM, M., Finance
PALMADE, J., Sociology
PARLY, J.-M., Economics
PASCHOS, V., Computer Studies
PIGANIOL, B., Management
PILISI, D., Economics
PINSON, S., Computer Studies
PIQUET, M., English Language and Litera-
    ture
PRAS, B., Finance
RICHARD, J., Finance
RIGAL, J.-L., Computer Studies
RIVES-LANGE, J. L., Civil Law
ROMELAER, P., Finance
ROUX, D., Business Economics
ROY, B., Scientific Methods of Management
SALIN, P., Monetary Economics
SCHMIDT, C., Sociology
SIMON, Y., Finance
SIROEN, J.-M., Economics
SULZER, J.-R., Finance
TERNY, G., Public Economics
THIETART, R., Finance
TOLLA, P., Computer Studies
TRINH-HEBREARD, S., Sociology
VALLEE, C., Public Law

UNIVERSITÉ DE PARIS X (PARIS-NANTERRE)

200 ave de la République, 92001 Nanterre Cedex

Telephone: 1-40-97-72-00
Fax: 1-40-97-75-71
E-mail: service.communication@u-paris10.fr
Internet: www.u-paris10.fr

Pres.: BERNADETTE MADEUF
Vice-Pres: CORNELIUS CROWLEY (Studies and
    Univ. Life), PHILIPPE GUTTINGER (Ccl of
    Admin. and Training), DANIELLE LEEMAN
    (Int. Devt and the Foreign Language Pol-
    icy), SÉBASTIEN KOTT (Resources and the
    Steering Committee), BERNARD LAKS (Sci-
    entific Ccl), COLETTE VALLAT (Capital)
Sec.-Gen.: DIDIER RAMOND
Librarian: EVELYNE DIECKHOFF

Number of teachers: 1,500
Number of students: 36,500

TEACHING AND RESEARCH UNITS

Economic Sciences, Management, Maths and
    Computer Science: Dir: FRANÇOISE LABRE
Industrial Systems and Communication
    Technology: Dir: ALAIN PRIOU
Institute of Technology (Ville d'Avray): Dir:
    JACKY BARRAUD
Languages and Foreign Cultures: Dir: SYL-
    VAINE HUGHES
Law and Political Science: Dir: MATTHIEU
    CONAN
Literature, Languages and Philosophy: Dir:
    JEAN-FRANÇOIS BALAUDE
Psychology and Education Sciences: Dir:
    PASCAL MALLET
Science and Techniques of Physical and
    Sporting Activities: Dir: TARAK DRISS
Social Science and Administration: Dir: BER-
    NARD BAZIN

UNIVERSITÉ DE PARIS XI (PARIS-SUD)

15 rue G. Clémenceau, 91405 Orsay Cedex

Telephone: 1-69-41-67-50
Fax: 1-69-41-61-35
E-mail: secretariat@presidence.u-psud.fr
Internet: www.u-psud.fr

Founded 1970
State control
Language of instruction: French
Academic year: September to June

Pres.: GUY COUARRAZE
Vice-Pres: JEAN-JACQUES GIRERD (Ccl of
    Admin.), JACQUES BITTOUN (Scientific Ccl),
    COLETTE VOISIN (Studies and Univ. Life)
Sec.-Gen.: CHRISTINE ARNULF-KOECHLIN
Librarian: FRANÇOISE MEIGNIEN

Number of teachers: 1,800
Number of students: 30,000

Publications: Aspects de la recherche (1 a
    year), Plein-Sud (6 a year).

TEACHING AND RESEARCH UNITS

Faculté de Droit, Economie et Gestion
(Sceaux): 54 blvd Desgranges, 92331 Sceaux
Cedex; tel. 1-40-91-17-00; fax 1-46-60-18-03;
Dean JÉRÔME FROMAGEAU.

Faculté de Médecine (Kremlin-Bicêtre):
63 rue Gabriel Péri, 94276 Le Kremlin-
Bicêtre Cedex; tel. 1-49-59-67-67; fax 1-49-
59-67-00; Dean SERGE BOBIN.

Faculté de Pharmacie (Châtenay-
Malabry): 5 rue Jean-Baptiste Clément,
92296 Châtenay-Malabry Cedex; tel. 1-46-
83-57-89; fax 1-46-83-57-35; Dean DOMINIQUE
PORQUET.

Faculté des Sciences (Orsay): 15 rue
Georges Clémenceau, 91405 Orsay Cedex;
tel. 1-69-15-74-08; fax 1-69-15-63-64; Dir
PHILIPPE MASSON.

Faculté des Sciences et Techniques des
Activités Physiques et Sportives
(Orsay): Bâtiment 335, 91405 Orsay Cedex;
tel. 1-69-15-61-57; fax 1-69-15-62-37; e-mail
christine.le-scanff@u-psud.fr; Dir CHRISTINE
LE SCANFF.

UNIVERSITY INSTITUTES

Instituts Universitaires de Technologie
de Génie Électrique, Informatique
Industrielle, Génie Mécanique et Productique (Cachan): 9 ave de la Division
Leclerc, 94234 Cachan Cedex; tel. 1-41-24-
11-00; fax 1-46-24-11-99; Dir SOUHIL
MEGHERBI.

Instituts Universitaires de Technologie
d'Informatique, Mesures Physiques et
Chimie (Orsay): Plateau du Moulon, BP
127, 91400 Orsay Cedex; tel. 1-69-33-60-00;
fax 1-60-19-33-18; Dir NELLY BENSIMON.

Instituts Universitaires de Technologie
de Gestion et Commerce (Sceaux): 8 ave
Cauchy, 92330 Sceaux Cedex; tel. 1-40-91-24-
99; fax 1-46-60-64-79; Dir JEAN-GILLES
MBIANGA.

Polytech'Paris-Sud: Bâtiment 620, 91405
Orsay Cedex; tel. 1-69-33-86-13; fax 1-69-41-
99-57; Dir FRANÇOIS AGUILLON.

UNIVERSITÉ DE PARIS XII (PARIS-VAL-DE-MARNE)

61 ave du Général de Gaulle, 94010 Créteil
Cedex

Telephone: 1-45-17-10-00
Fax: 1-42-07-70-12
E-mail: sgp12@u-pec.fr
Internet: www.univ-paris12.fr

Founded 1970
Academic year: October to July

Pres.: SIMONE BONNAFOUS
Vice-Pres: SUZANNE PONTIER (Ccl of Admin.),
    CHRISTIAN REGNAUT (Studies and Univ.
    Life), LUC HITTINGER (Scientific Ccl),
    JEAN-FRANÇOIS DUFEU (Institutional Rela-
    tions), DIDIER NICOLLE (Information Sys-
    tems)
Sec.-Gen.: PASCALE SAINT-CYR
Librarian: SOPHIE MAZENS

Number of teachers: 1,200
Number of students: 32,000.

TEACHING AND RESEARCH UNITS

Faculté d'Administration et Echanges
Internationaux: tel. 1-45-17-18-79; e-mail
marie.berrous@u-pec.fr; Dean JOSIANE
ATTUEL.

Faculté de Droit: 83–85 ave du Général de
Gaulle, 94000 Créteil Cedex; tel. 1-56-72-60-
02; e-mail secdoyen-droit@u-pec.fr; Dean
Prof. JEAN-JACQUES ISRAEL.

Faculté des Lettres, Langues et Sciences
Humaines: tel. 1-45-17-11-92; e-mail
com-llsh@u-pec.fr; Dean JEANNE-MARIE BOI-
VIN.

Faculté de Médecine: tel. 1-49-81-36-20;
e-mail conseilmed@u-pec.fr; Dir Prof. JEAN-
LUC DUBOIS-RANDÉ.

Faculté de Sciences Économiques et de
Gestion: tel. 1-41-78-46-34; e-mail sophie
.pointereau@u-pec.fr; Dean PHILIPPE ADAIR.

Faculté de Sciences de l'Education, Sciences Sociales et STAPS: SESS, Immeuble
Pyramide, 80 ave du Général de Gaulle,
94009 Créteil Cedex;STAPS, Centre Duvau-
chelle, 27 rue Magellan, 94000 Créteil Cedex.

Faculté des Sciences et Technologie: tel.
1-45-17-13-35; fax 1-45-17-13-34; e-mail
doyen.sciences@u-pec.fr; Dean MARIE-
CLAUDE MILLOT.

UNIVERSITÉ DE PARIS XIII (PARIS-NORD)

99 ave Jean-Baptiste Clément, 93430 Ville-taneuse
Telephone: 1-49-40-30-00
Fax: 1-49-40-33-33
E-mail: cab-pres@upn.univ-paris13.fr
Internet: www.univ-paris13.fr
Founded 1970
Academic year: September to June
Pres.: JEAN-LOUP SALZMANN
Vice-Pres: ARIANE DESPORTE (Ccl of Admin.), CHARLES DESFRANÇOIS (Scientific Ccl), ANDRÉ TARDIEU (Studies and Univ. Life)
Sec.-Gen.: RÉMY GICQUEL
Librarian: DOMINIQUE BAUDIN

Number of teachers: 1,181
Number of students: 22,000

Publications: *Psychologie clinique, Annales du CESER, Cahiers de Linguistique Hispanique Médiévale.*

TEACHING AND RESEARCH UNITS

Faculté de Droit et des Sciences Politiques et Sociales: 99 ave Jean-Baptiste Clément, 93430 Villetaneuse; tel. 1-49-40-32-97; fax 1-49-40-33-47; e-mail sec-ufrd@univ-paris13.fr/dsps; Dir ROBERT ETIEN.

Faculté des Lettres, Sciences de l'Homme et des Sociétés: 99 ave Jean-Baptiste Clément, 93430 Villetaneuse; tel. 1-49-40-32-11; e-mail sec-ufrl@univ-paris13.fr; internet www.univ-paris13.fr/lshs; Dir ELISABETH BELMAS.

Faculté de Santé, Médecine et Biologie Humaine: 74 rue Marcel Cachin, 93017 Bobigny Cedex; tel. 1-48-38-73-18; fax 1-48-38-77-77; e-mail f.boullay_rollin@smbh.univ-paris13.fr; internet www.smbh.univ-paris13.fr; Dir JEAN-LUC DUMAS.

Faculté des Sciences de la Communication: 99 ave Jean-Baptiste Clément, 93430 Villetaneuse; tel. 1-49-40-44-78; fax 1-49-40-44-79; e-mail sec-ufrc@univ-paris13.fr; internet www.univ-paris13.fr/communication; Dir VINCENT BRULOIS.

Faculté des Sciences Économiques et de Gestion: 99 ave Jean-Baptiste Clément, 93430 Villetaneuse; tel. 1-49-40-35-38; fax 1-49-40-33-34; e-mail arbia.kefi@univ-paris13.fr; internet www.univ-paris13.fr/ecogestion; Dir PHILIPPE BARBET.

Institut Galilée: 99 ave Jean-Baptiste Clément, 93430 Villetaneuse; tel. 1-49-40-36-65; fax 1-49-40-33-66; e-mail secretariat1.direction.galilee@univ-paris13.fr; internet www.galilee.univ-paris13.fr; Dir JEAN-PIERRE ASTRUC.

Institut Universitaire de Technologie (Bobigny): L'Illustration, 1 rue de Chablis, 93017 Bobigny Cedex; tel. 1-48-38-88-36; fax 1-48-38-88-39; e-mail diriut@iutb.univ-paris13.fr; internet www.iut-bobigny.univ-paris13.fr; Dir DANIEL VERBA.

Institut Universitaire de Technologie (Saint-Denis): place du 8 Mai 1945, 93206 Saint-Denis Cedex; tel. 1-49-40-61-00; e-mail diriut@iutb.univ-paris13.fr; internet www.iutsd.univ-paris13.fr; Dir JEAN-MARIE GOURDON.

Institut Universitaire de Technologie (Villetaneuse): 99 ave Jean-Baptiste Clément, 93430 Villetaneuse; tel. 1-49-40-30-28; fax 1-49-40-20-21; e-mail secrdir@iutv.univ-paris13.fr; internet www.iutv.univ-paris13.fr; Dir PASCAL COUPEY.

UNIVERSITÉ DE PAU ET DES PAYS DE L'ADOUR

ave de l'Université, BP 576, 64012 Pau Cedex
Telephone: 5-59-40-70-00
Fax: 5-59-40-70-01
E-mail: communication@univ-pau.fr
Internet: www.univ-pau.fr
Founded 1970
State control
Pres.: JEAN-LOUIS GOUT
Vice-Pres: JEAN GOURDOU (Ccl of Admin.), MOHAMED AMARA (Scientific Ccl), MICHEL BRAUD (Studies and Univ. Life), ALAIN GRACIAA (Property), VINCENT VLES (Relations with the Territorial Collectivities), DAVID BESSIÈRES (Int. Relations), DAVID CARASSUS (Resources and Budget), MICHEL MAGOT (Development and Technological Tranfer)
Sec.-Gen.: JEAN-LOUIS FOURCAUD
Librarian: MARIE-ANNICK CAZAUX

Number of teachers: 693
Number of students: 11,401

TEACHING AND RESEARCH UNITS

Faculty of Law, Economics and Management: Dean: JEAN-JACQUES LEMOULAND
Faculty of Letters, Languages and Human Sciences: Dean: JEAN-PIERRE BARRAQUÉ
Faculty of Science and Technical Studies (la Côte Basque): Dean: CLAUDE MOUCHÈS
Faculty of Science and Technical Studies (Pau): Dean: VÉRONIQUE LAZZERI-PORDOY
Multidisciplinary Faculty (Bayonne Anglet Biarritz): Dean: PHILIPPE ZAVOLI

UNIVERSITÉ PAUL VERLAINE—METZ

Ile du Saulcy, BP 80794, 57012 Metz Cedex 1
Telephone: 3-87-31-50-50
Fax: 3-87-31-50-55
E-mail: com@univ-metz.fr
Internet: www.univ-metz.fr
Founded 1970
Pres.: LUC JOHANN
Vice-Pres: ANDRÉ PETITJEAN (Ccl of Admin.), GÉRARD MICHAUX (Studies and Univ. Life), PHILIPPE BURG (Scientific Ccl)
Sec.-Gen.: HÉLÈNE TIXIER
Librarian: SYLVIE DEVILLE

Number of teachers: 786
Number of students: 14,231.

TEACHING AND RESEARCH UNITS

Faculté de Droit, Economie et Administration: Ile du Saulcy, 57045 Metz Cedex 1; tel. 3-87-31-50-51; e-mail mangematin@univ-metz.fr; Dir YAHN MANGEMATIN.

Faculté des Etudes Supérieures de Management: 1 rue Augustin Fresnel BP 15100, 57073 Metz Cedex 1; tel. 3-87-37-84-80; fax 3-87-37-84-81; e-mail accueil@esm.univ-metz.fr; Dir GUY SOLLE.

Faculté de Lettres et Langues: Ile du Saulcy, 57045 Metz Cedex 1; tel. 3-87-31-52-53; e-mail clerc@univ-metz.fr; Dir KATHIE BIRAT.

Faculté de Mathématiques, Informatique et Mécanique: Ile du Saulcy, 57045 Metz Cedex 1; tel. 3-87-31-53-54; e-mail rollin@univ-metz.fr; Dir NIDHAL REZG.

Faculté des Sciences Fondamentales et Appliquées: Rue du Général Delestraint, 57070 Metz Cedex 1; tel. 3-87-37-86-00; e-mail gasser@univ-metz.fr; Dir JEAN-GEORGES GASSER.

Faculté de Sciences Humaines et Arts: tel. 3-87-54-72-03; e-mail lanfranchi@univ-metz.fr; Dir JEAN-BAPTISTE LANFRANCHI.

UNIVERSITÉ DE PERPIGNAN

52 ave Paul Alduy, 66860 Perpignan Cedex
Telephone: 4-68-66-20-00
Fax: 4-68-66-20-19
E-mail: webmaster@univ-perp.fr
Internet: www.univ-perp.fr
Founded 1971
Pres.: JEAN BENKHELIL
Vice-Pres: MARTIN GALINIER (Ccl of Admin.), OLIVIER PANAUD (Scientific Ccl), FABRICE LORENTE (Studies and Univ. Life)
Sec.-Gen.: PAUL TAVERNER
Librarian: JOËL MARTRES

Number of teachers: 450
Number of students: 10,500

TEACHING AND RESEARCH UNITS

Comparative Law and Francophone States: Dir: D. BAISSET
Exact and Experimental Sciences: Dir: L. ASPART
Legal and Economic Science: Dir: Y. PICOD
Letters and Humanities: Dir: N. MARTY
Sports, Tourism and the International Hotel Industry: Dir: J. M. HOERNER

PROFESSORS

Exact and Experimental Sciences:
AMOUROUX, M., Applied Physics and Computer Science
BAILLY, J. R., Biochemistry
BERÇOT, P., Applied Organic Synthesis
BLAISE, P., Chemistry
BODIOT, D., Mineral Chemistry and Thermochemistry
BOMBRE, F., Solid State Physics
BONNARD, M., Algebraic Topology
BOURGAT, R., General Biology
BRUNET, S., Applied Physics and Computer Science
BRUSLE, J., Marine Biology
CAUVET, A. M., Plant Biology and Physiology
CHOU, C. C., Functional Analysis
CODOMIER, L., Biology and Chemistry of Marine Plants (Research)
COMBES, C., Animal Biology
CROZAT, G., Physics
DAGUENET, M., Thermodynamics and Energetics
DUPOUY, J., General Biology
EL JAÏ, A., Computer Science
FABRE, B., Thermology
FOUGERES, A., Mathematics
GIRESSE, P., Marine Sedimentology Research Centre
GONZALEZ, E., Organic Chemistry
GOT, H., Sedimentology and Marine Geochemistry
HENRI-ROUSSEAU, O., Theoretical Chemistry
HILLEL, R., Chemistry
HORVATH, C., Mathematics
HUYNH, V. C., Atomic and Molecular Physics
JUPIN, H., Plant Biology
MARTY, R., Mathematics applied to Human Sciences
MEYNADIER, CHR., Thermodynamics and Energetics
PENON, P., Plant Physiology
SOULIER, J., Organic Chemistry
SOURNIA, A., Atomic and Molecular Physics
SPINNER, B., Mineral Chemistry and Thermochemistry
VIALLET, P., Physical Chemistry

Humanities, Legal, Economic and Social Sciences

Humanities:
ANDIOC, R., Romance Languages and Literature
AUBAILLY, J.-C., French

BELOT, A., Romance Languages and Literature
BROC, N., Geography
DAUGE, Y., Classics
DELEDALLE, G., Philosophy
DENJEAN, A., English Language and Anglo-Saxon Literature
HOLZ, J. M., Geography
HUGUET, L., Germanic and Scandinavian Languages and Literature
ISSOREL, J., Spanish
LEBLON, B., Romance Languages and Literature
MEYER, J., Contemporary History
RETHORE, J., Literature
SAGNES, J., History

Law and Economics:
BLANC, F. P., History of Law
BREJON DE LAVERGNEE, N., Economic Dynamics
CONSTANS, L., Public Law
Mme DONAT, J., Private Law and Criminology
DOUCHEZ, M.-H., Administrative Law
HUNTZINGER, J., International Law
PEROCHON, F., Law
RUDLOFF, M., Economics
SAINT-JOURS, Y., Private Law and Criminology
SERRA, Y., Private Law

University Institute of Technology:
AZE, D., Mathematics
BARRIOL, R., Mechanical Engineering
BARUSSEAU, J. P., Marine Sedimentology
COMBAUT, G., Marine Chemistry
COSTE, C., Industrial Chemistry
FARINES, M., Organic Chemistry
GRELLET, P., Biochemistry, Applied Biology
MASSE, J., Organic Chemistry
MASSON, PH., Animal Husbandry

UNIVERSITÉ DE PICARDIE JULES VERNE

chemin du Thil, 80025 Amiens Cedex 01
Telephone: 3-22-82-72-72
Fax: 3-22-82-75-00
Internet: www.u-picardie.fr
Founded 1965
Academic year: October to June
Pres.: GEORGES FAURÉ
Vice-Pres: JEANNINE RICHARD-ZAPPELLA (Ccl of Admin.), SAID KAMEL (Scientific Ccl), GÉRARD BRÛLÉ (Studies and Univ. Life)
Sec.-Gen.: LAURENT ANNE
Librarian: DESSAIVRE LOUISE
Number of teachers: 800
Number of students: 23,000.

TEACHING AND RESEARCH UNITS

Faculté des Arts: 30 rue des Teinturiers, 80000 Amiens Cedex 01; tel. 3-22-22-43-43; fax 3-22-22-43-49; Dir Prof. SERGE BISMUTH.

Faculté de Droit et de Science Politique: 10 placette Lafleur, BP 2716, 80027 Amiens Cedex 01; tel. 3-22-82-71-52; fax 3-22-82-71-51; Dir BENOIT MERCUZOT.

Faculté d'Economie et de Gestion: 10 placette Lafleur, BP 2716, 80027 Amiens Cedex 01; tel. 3-22-82-71-28; fax 3-22-82-71-27; Dir Prof. JEAN-PIERRE GIRARD.

Faculté d'Histoire et de Géographie: chemin du Thil, 80025 Amiens Cedex 01; tel. 3-22-82-73-29; fax 3-22-82-73-32; Dir Prof. PHILIPPE NIVET.

Faculté de Langues et Cultures Etrangères: chemin du Thil, 80025 Amiens Cedex 01; tel. 3-22-82-73-73; Dir Prof. WOLFGANG SABLER.

Faculté des Lettres: chemin du Thil, 80025 Amiens Cedex 01; tel. 3-22-82-73-85; Dir MARIE FRANCOISE MONTAUBIN.

Faculté de Médecine: 3 rue des Louvels, 80036 Amiens Cedex 01; tel. 3-22-82-77-45; Dir Prof. DANIEL LE GARS.

Faculté de Pharmacie: 1 rue des Louvels, 80037 Amiens Cedex 01; tel. 3-22-82-77-54; Dir GILLES DUVERLIE.

Faculté de Philosophie et Sciences Humaines et Sociales: Bâtiment E, chemin du Thil, 80025 Amiens Cedex 01; tel. 3-22-82-74-04; fax 3-22-82-74-08; Dir Prof. PHILIPPE MONCHAUX.

Faculté des Sciences: 33 rue Saint-Leu, 80039 Amiens Cedex 01; tel. 3-22-82-75-22; fax 3-22-82-75-83; Dir Prof. F. ROPEZ.

Faculté des Sciences du Sport: allée Paul Grousset, 80025 Amiens Cedex 01; tel. 3-22-82-73-74; Dir Prof. ARNAUD JAILLET.

University Campus at Beauvais: 52 blvd Saint-André, 60000 Beauvais Cedex; tel. 3-44-06-88-00; fax 3-44-06-88-50; Administrator LAURENT SEGUIN.

UNIVERSITÉ DE POITIERS

15 rue de l'Hôtel Dieu, 86034 Poitiers Cedex
Telephone: 5-49-45-30-00
Fax: 5-49-45-30-50
E-mail: webmaster@univ-poitiers.fr
Internet: www.univ-poitiers.fr
Founded 1431
Pres.: JEAN-PIERRE GESSON
Sec.-Gen.: BERNARD CONTAL
Librarian: MYRIAM MARCIL
Number of teachers: 870
Number of students: 24,000
Publications: *Les Cahiers de Civilisation Médiévale, Les Cahiers Forell, La Licorne, Migrinter, Revue Norois.*

TEACHING AND RESEARCH INSTITUTES

Faculté des Sciences du Sport: Bâtiment C6, 8 allée Jean Monnet, 86000 Poitiers; tel. 5-49-45-33-43; fax 5-49-45-33-96; e-mail ufr .scsport@univ-poitiers.fr; internet scsport .univ-poitiers.fr; Dir LAURENT BOSQUET.

Faculté de Droit et Sciences Sociales: Bâtiment A1, 2 rue Jean Carbonnier, 86022 Poitiers; tel. 5-49-45-31-43; fax 5-49-45-40-37; e-mail ufr.droit@univ-poitiers.fr; internet droit.univ-poitiers.fr; Dean JOËL MONNET.

Faculté de Lettres et Langues: Bâtiment A3, 1 rue Raymond Cantel, BP 613, 86022 Poitiers; tel. 5-49-45-32-71; fax 5-49-45-32-90; e-mail ufr.ll@univ-poitiers.fr; internet ll .univ-poitiers.fr; Dir JEAN-LOUIS DUCHET.

Faculté de Médecine et Pharmacie: Bâtiment D1, 6 rue de la Miletrie, BP 199, 86034 Poitiers; tel. 5-49-45-43-43; fax 5-49-45-43-05; e-mail faculte.medecine@univ-poitiers.fr; internet medphar.univ-poitiers.fr; Dean MICHEL MORICHAU BEAUCHANT.

Faculté des Sciences Économiques: Bâtiment A1, 2 rue Jean Carbonnier, 86022 Poitiers; tel. 5-49-45-31-35; fax 5-49-45-33-19; e-mail ufr.sceco@univ-poitiers.fr; internet sceco.univ-poitiers.fr; Dean CHRISTIAN AUBIN.

Faculté des Sciences Fondamentales et Appliquées: Bâtiment B5, 9 rue C. C. Chenou, BP 633, 86022 Poitiers; tel. 5-49-45-30-00; fax 5-49-45-36-00; e-mail ufr.sfa@ univ-poitiers.fr; internet sfa.univ-poitiers.fr; Dean YVES BERTRAND.

Faculté des Sciences Humaines et Arts: 8 rue René Descartes, 86022 Poitiers; tel. 5-49-45-45-45; fax 5-49-45-45-79; e-mail ufr .sha@univ-poitiers.fr; internet sha .univ-poitiers.fr; Dir YVES JEAN.

UNIVERSITÉ DE REIMS CHAMPAGNE-ARDENNE

9 blvd de la Paix, 51097 Reims Cedex
Telephone: 3-26-05-30-00
Fax: 3-26-05-30-98
E-mail: presidence@univ-reims.fr
Internet: www.univ-reims.fr
Founded 1548
Pres.: RICHARD VISTELLE
Vice-Pres: COLLETTE PADET (Ccl of Admin.), YANNICK REMION (Scientific Ccl), GUILLAUME GELLE (Studies and Univ. Life)
Sec.-Gen.: ISABELLE TERRAIL
Library: see Libraries
Number of teachers: 1,106
Number of students: 22,163
Publications: *Cahiers de l'Institut du Territoire et de l'Environnement de l'Université de Reims* (1 a year), *Cahiers du Centre de Recherches sur la Décentralisation Territoriale* (1 a year), *Etudes Champenoises* (1 a year), *Imaginaires, Jurisprudence Cour d'appel* (4 a year).

TEACHING AND RESEARCH UNITS

Faculté de Droit et de Science Politique: 57 rue Pierre Taittinger, 51096 Reims Cedex; tel. 3-26-91-38-44; fax 3-26-91-83-63; e-mail aurelien.patit@univ-reims.fr; Dean OLIVIER DUPERON.

Faculté de Lettres et Sciences Humaines: 57 rue Pierre Taittinger, 51096 Reims Cedex; tel. 3-26-91-36-38; fax 3-26-91-36-40; Dean M. BOULANGER.

Faculté de Médecine: 51 rue Cognacq Jay, 51095 Reims Cedex; tel. 3-26-91-81-83; fax 3-26-91-35-63; e-mail scolmed@univ-reims.fr; Dean JACQUES MOTTE.

Faculté d'Odontologie: 2 rue du Général Koenig, 51100 Reims Cedex; tel. 3-26-91-34-55; e-mail nathalie.antoni@univ-reims.fr; Dean LOUIS-FRÉDÉRIC JACQUELIN.

Faculté de Pharmacie: 51 rue Cognacq Jay, 51095 Reims Cedex; tel. 3-26-91-81-82; fax 3-26-91-35-52; e-mail scol.pharmacie@ univ-reims.fr; Dean MATTHIEU KALTENBACH.

Faculté des Sciences Economiques, Sociales et de Gestion: e-mail info.seg@ univ-reims.fr; Dir MARTINE GUILLEMIN.

Faculté des Sciences Exactes et Naturelles: e-mail scolarite.sciences@univ-reims .fr.

Faculté des Sciences et Techniques des Activités Physiques et Sportives: chemin des Rouliers, 51682 Reims Cedex; Dir PASCAL LEGRAIN.

UNIVERSITÉ DE RENNES I

2 rue du Thabor, CS 46510, 35065 Rennes Cedex
Telephone: 2-23-23-35-35
Fax: 2-23-23-36-00
E-mail: sai@listes.univ-rennes1.fr
Internet: www.univ-rennes1.fr
Academic year: September to May
Pres.: GUY CATHELINEAU
Vice-Pres: DAVID ALIS (Ccl of Admin.), CLAUDE LABIT (Scientific Ccl), NATHALIE PAYELLE (Studies and Univ. Life)
Sec.-Gen.: MARTINE RUOUD
Number of teachers: 1,601
Number of students: 23,884.

TEACHING AND RESEARCH UNITS

Faculté de Droit et Science Politique: 9 rue Jean Macé, CS 54203, 35042 Rennes Cedex; tel. 2-23-23-76-76; fax 2-23-23-76-55; Dean Prof. EDOUARD VERNY.

Faculté de Médecine: 2 rue du Professeur Léon Bernard, CS 34317, 35043 Rennes

Cedex; tel. 2-23-51-13-96; Dean Prof. PHI-LIPPE DELAVAL.

Faculté d'Odontologie: 2 rue du Professeur Léon Bernard, CS 34317 Rennes Cedex; tel. 2-23-23-43-41; fax 2-23-23-43-93; Dean Dr ANNE DAUTEL-MORAZIN.

Faculté des Sciences Economiques: 7 place Hoche, CS 86514, 35065 Rennes Cedex; tel. 2-23-23-35-45; fax 2-99-38-80-84; e-mail eco-scol@univ-rennes1.fr; Dean Prof. ISA-BELLE CADORET.

Faculté de Pharmacie: 2 rue du Professeur Léon Bernard, CS 34317, 35043 Rennes Cedex; tel. 2-23-23-44-30; fax 2-23-23-49-75; internet www.pharma.univ-rennes1.fr; Dean Prof. JEAN DEUFF.

UFR Sciences de la Vie et de l'Environnement: Bât. 13, Campus Scientifique de Beaulieu, 263 rue du Général Leclerc, 35042 Rennes Cedex; tel. 2-23-23-61-12; fax 2-23-23-67-69; Dir Prof. HUBERT LERIVRAY.

UFR Mathématiques: 263 rue du Général Leclerc, CS 74205, 35042 Rennes Cedex; tel. 2-23-23-59-51; fax 2-23-23-54-64; e-mail andre.rebour@univ-rennes1.fr; Dir BERNARD DELYON.

UFR Philosophie: 263 rue du Général Leclerc, CS 74205, 35042 Rennes Cedex; tel. 2-23-23-63-02; fax 2-23-23-51-51; e-mail sophie.rabaux@univ-rennes1.fr; Dir PIERRE JORAY.

UFR Sciences et Propriétés de la Matière: 263 rue du Général Leclerc, CS 74205 Rennes Cedex; tel. 2-23-23-62-44; fax 2-23-23-69-85; e-mail spm-administration@listes.univ-rennes1.fr; Dir PATRICIA BÉNARD-ROCHERULLÉ.

Ecole Nationale Supérieure des Sciences Appliquées et de Technologie: 6 rue de Kérampont, BP 80518, 22305 Lannion Cedex; tel. 2-96-46-90-00; fax 2-96-37-01-99; e-mail accueil@enssat.fr; internet www.enssat.fr; Dir JEAN-CHRISTOPHE PETTIER.

Ecole Supérieure d'Ingénieur de Rennes: e-mail gwenaelle.merel@univ-rennes1.fr; internet www.esir.univ-rennes1.fr; Dir CHRISTOPHE WOLINSKI.

Institut de Formation Supérieure en Informatique et Communication: Campus de Beaulieu, 35042 Rennes Cedex; tel. 2-99-84-74-02; fax 2-99-84-71-71; Dir GILLES LESVENTES.

Institut de Gestion de Rennes: 11 rue Jean Macé, CS 70803, 35708 Rennes Cedex 7; tel. 2-23-23-77-77; fax 2-23-23-78-00; e-mail igriae@univ-rennes1.fr; internet www.igr.univ-rennes1.fr; Dir LAURENT BIRONNEAU.

Institut de Préparation à l'Administration Générale: 106 blvd de la Duchesse Anne, 35700 Rennes Cedex; tel. 2-23-23-78-93; fax 2-23-23-78-92; e-mail ipag@univ-rennes1.fr; internet www.ipag.univ-rennes1.fr; Dir GILLES GUIHEUX.

Institut Universitaire de Technologie de Lannion: rue Edouard Branly, BP 30219, 22302 Lannion Cedex; tel. 2-96-46-93-00; fax 2-96-48-13-20; e-mail scol.iutlan@univ-rennes1.fr; internet www.iut-lannion.fr; Dir DIDIEU DEMIGNY.

Institut Universitaire de Technologie de Rennes: 3 rue du Clos-Courtel, BP 90422, 35704 Rennes Cedex 7; tel. 2-23-23-40-00; fax 2-23-23-40-01; e-mail iutren-contact@listes.univ-rennes1.fr; internet www.iutren.univ-rennes1.fr; Dir JACQUES MIRIEL.

Institut Universitaire de Technologie de St Brieuc: 18 rue Henri Wallon, BP 406, 22004 St Brieuc Cedex 1; tel. 2-96-60-96-60; fax 2-96-60-96-12; e-mail iut-st-brieuc@univ-rennes1.fr; internet www.iutsb.univ-rennes1.fr; Dir JACQUES BERTHOUX.

Institut Universitaire de Technologie de St-Malo: rue de la Croix Desilles, CS 51713, 35417 St-Malo Cedex 1; tel. 2-99-21-95-00; fax 2-99-21-95-01; e-mail iutsm-scolarite@univ-rennes1.fr; internet www.iutsm.univ-rennes1.fr; Dir Prof. JEAN-JACQUES MONTOIS.

Observatoire des Sciences de l'Univers de Rennes: Campus de Beaulieu, Bâtiment 15 303-2, 263 ave du Général Leclerc, 35042 Rennes Cedex; tel. 2-23-23-52-22; internet osur.univ-rennes1.fr; Dir P. DAVY.

ATTACHED INSTITUTE

Institut d'Études Politiques: 104 blvd de la Duchesse-Anne, 35700 Rennes; tel. 2-99-84-39-39; fax 2-99-84-39-00; e-mail scolarite@sciencespo-rennes.fr; internet www.sciencespo-rennes.fr; Dir PATRICK LE FLOCH.

UNIVERSITÉ RENNES II—HAUTE BRETAGNE

pl. du Recteur Henri Le Moal, CS 24307, 35044 Rennes Cedex

Telephone: 2-99-14-10-00
Fax: 2-99-14-10-17
E-mail: martine.autret@univ-rennes2.fr
Internet: www.uhb.fr

Founded 1969
Pres.: JEAN EMILE GOMBERT
First Vice-Pres.: RAYMONDE SECHET (Scientific Ccl)
Second Vice-Pres.: ALAIN ABELHAUSER (Studies and Univ. Life)
Third Vice-Pres.: DANIELLE CHARLES-LE BIHAN (Ccl of Admin.)
Sec.-Gen.: AMINE AMAR
Librarian: ELISABETH LEMAU

Number of teachers: 643
Number of students: 17,004.

TEACHING AND RESEARCH UNITS

Faculté des Activités Physiques et Sportives: tel. 2-99-14-17-65; e-mail evelyne.delanoe@univ-rennes2.fr; Dir PAUL DELA-MARCHE.

Faculté des Arts, Lettres et Communication: tel. 2-99-14-15-01; e-mail francois-xavier.rouxel@univ-rennes2.fr; Dir YVES HELIAS.

Faculté des Langues: tel. 2-99-14-16-01; e-mail dominique.colin@univ-rennes2.fr; Dir FRANÇOISE DUBOSQUET.

Faculté des Sciences Humaines: tel. 2-99-14-19-02; e-mail elisabeth.garnier@univ-rennes2.fr; Dir LOÏC BRÉMAUD.

Faculté des Sciences Sociales: tel. 2-99-14-17-82; e-mail pierrette.mauger@univ-rennes2.fr; Dir JACQUELINE SAINCLIVIER.

UNIVERSITÉ DE LA ROCHELLE

Technoforum, 23 ave Albert Einstein, 17071 La Rochelle Cedex 9

Telephone: 5-46-45-91-14
Fax: 5-46-44-93-76
Internet: www.univ-larochelle.fr

Founded 1993
Pres.: GÉRARD BLANCHARD
Vice-Pres: MATHIAS TRANCHANT (Ccl of Admin.), PIERRE COURTELLEMONT (Studies and Univ. Life), FRANCIS ALLARD (Scientific Ccl)
Sec.-Gen.: PHILIPPE BÉZAGU
Librarian: OLIVIER CAUDRON

Number of teachers: 471
Number of students: 7,444.

TEACHING AND RESEARCH UNITS

Faculté de Droit, Science politique et Gestion: 45 rue François de Vaux de Foletier, 17024 La Rochelle Cedex 1; tel. 5-46-45-85-20; fax 5-46-45-85-33; e-mail contact_droit@univ-lr.fr; Dir ANDRÉ GIUDI-CELLI.

Faculté des Lettres, Langues, Arts et Sciences Humaines: 1 Parvis Fernand Braudel, 17042 La Rochelle Cedex 1; tel. 5-46-45-68-00; fax 5-46-50-59-95; e-mail contact_flash@univ-lr.fr; Dir CHARLES ILLOUZ.

Faculté des Sciences Fondamentales et Sciences pour l'Ingénieur: ave Michel Crepeau, 17042 La Rochelle Cedex 1; tel. 5-46-45-82-59; fax 5-46-45-82-91; e-mail sci_direction@univ-lr.fr; Dir CHRISTIAN INARD.

Institut Universitaire de Technologie: 15 rue François de Vaux de Foletier, 17026 La Rochelle Cedex 1; tel. 5-46-51-39-00; fax 5-46-51-39-39; e-mail kaszewski@univ-lr.fr; Dir PATRICE JOUBERT.

UNIVERSITÉ DE ROUEN

1 rue Thomas Becket, Secrétariat-Général, 76821 Mont-Saint-Aignan Cedex

Telephone: 2-35-14-60-00
Fax: 2-35-14-63-48
Internet: www.univ-rouen.fr

Founded 1966
Academic year: September to June
Pres.: CAFER ÖZKUL
First Vice-Pres.: JOËL ALEXANDRE (Ccl of Admin.)
Vice-Pres: DANIÈLE CARRICABURU (Ccl of Admin.), NICOLE ORANGE, LAURENCE VILLARD (Scientific Ccl), SABINE MÉNAGER, LAURENT YON (Studies and Univ. Life)
Sec.-Gen.: (vacant)
Librarian: LAURENCE BOITARD

Number of teachers: 1,371
Number of students: 24,044.

TEACHING AND RESEARCH UNITS

Faculté de Droit, Sciences Economiques et Gestion: 3 avenue Pasteur, 76186 Rouen Cedex; tel. 2-32-76-98-98; Dean GUY QUITAINE.

Faculté de Lettres et Sciences Humaines: rue Lavoisier, 76821 Mont-Saint-Aignan Cedex; tel. 2-35-14-64-00; Dir J. MAURICE.

Faculté de Médecine et Pharmacie: 22 blvd Gambetta, 76183 Rouen Cedex; tel. 2-35-14-85-55; Dean PIERRE FREGER.

Faculté des Sciences de l'Homme et de la Société: rue Lavoisier, 76821 Mont-Saint-Aignan Cedex; Dir R. WEIL.

Faculté des Sciences du Sport et Education Physique: blvd Siegfried, 76821 Mont-Saint-Aignan Cedex; Dean ALAIN LORET.

Faculté des Sciences et Techniques: pl. Emile Blondel, 76821 Mont-Saint-Aignan Cedex; Dean JEAN-PAUL DUPONT.

Institut d'Administration des Entreprises: 3 ave Pasteur, 76100 Rouen Cedex 1; tel. 2-32-76-95-84; fax 2-32-76-95-80; e-mail iae@univ-rouen.fr; Dir CHRISTIAN HURSON.

Institut de Préparation à l'Administration Générale: 3 ave Pasteur, 76186 Rouen Cedex 1; tel. 2-32-76-98-46; fax 2-32-76-98-33; e-mail ipag76@univ-rouen.fr; Dir CECILE-ANNE SIBOUT.

Institut Universitaire de Formation des Maîtres: 2 rue du Tronquet, BP 18, 76131 Mont-Saint-Aignan Cedex; tel. 2-32-82-30-40; fax 2-35-74-11-52; internet www.rouen.iufm.fr; Dir BRUNO MAHEU.

Institut Universitaire de Technologie (Evreux): 55 rue Saint Germain, 27000 Evreux Cedex; tel. 2-32-19-15-00; fax 2-32-

19-15-06; e-mail direction.iutevreux@
univ-rouen.fr; Dir BRUNO QUERRÉ.

**Institut Universitaire de Technologie
(Rouen):** rue Lavoisier, 76821 Mont-Saint-
Aignan Cedex; tel. 2-35-14-62-03; fax 2-35-
14-00-50; e-mail iut.rouen@univ-rouen.fr;
internet www.univ-rouen.fr/iutrouen; Dir
MOULAY ABDELGHANI IDRISSI

PROFESSORS

Behavioural and Educational Sciences:

ABALLERA, F., Sociology
ASTOLFI, J. P., Educational Sciences
DURAND, J., Sociology
GATEAUX, J., Educational Sciences
HOUSSAYE, J., Educational Sciences
KOKOSOWSKI, A., Educational Sciences
LEMOINE, CL., Psychology
MALANDAIN, CL., Psychology
MARBEAUX-CLEIRENS, B., Psychology
MELLIER, D., Psychology

Law and Economics:

BADEVANT, B., Law
BRAS, J. P., Public Law
CAYLA, O., Public Law
CHRÉTIEN, P., Public Law
COURBE, P., Private Law
DAMMAME, D., Political Science
EPAULARD, A., Economics
GOY, R., Public Law
KULLMANN, J., Private Law
LEHMANN, P., Economics
MONNIER, L., Economics
PORTIER, F., Economics
RENOUX, M. F., Law
SASSIER, Y., Law
TAVERNIER, P., Public Law
TEBOUL, G., Public Law
TONNEL, M., Economics
VATTEVILLE, E., Administration and Man-
agement
VESPERINI, J.-P., Economics

Letters and Humanities:

ARNAUD, J. C., Geography
BALAN, B., Epistemology
BENAY, J., German
BERGER, PH., Spanish
CAITUCOLI, C., Linguistics
CAPET, A., English
COIT, K., English
CORTES, J., Linguistics
CYMERMAN, C., Spanish
DELAMOTTE, R., Linguistics
GARDIN, B., Linguistics
GRANIER, J., Philosophy
GUERMOND, Y., Geography
HUSSON, G., Greek
LE BOHEC, S., Ancient History
LECLAIRE, J., English
LECLERC, Y., French
LEGUAY, J.-P., Medieval History
LEMARCHAND, G., Modern History
LESOURD, M., Geography
MAQUERLOT, J. P., English
MAURICE, J., French
MAZAURIC, C., Modern History
MERVAUD, C., French
MERVAUD, M., Russian
MILHOU, A., Spanish
MORTIER, D., Comparative Literature
NIDERST, A., French
NOISETTE DE CRAUZAT, CL., Musical History
PASTRE, J. M., German
PHILONENKO, A., Philosophy
PICHARDIE, J. P., English
PIERROT, J., Modern French Literature
and Language
PIGENET, M., Contemporary History
POINSOTE, J. L., Classics
PUEL, M., English
RAVY, G., German
RETAILLE, B., Geography
ROUDAUT, F., French
SALAZAR, B., Spanish

SOHNA, R., Modern History
THELAMON, F., Ancient History
TREDE, M., Classics
VAN DER LYNDEN, A. M., Spanish
WALLE, M., German
WILLEMS, M., English
ZYLBERBER, G. M., Modern History

Medicine and Pharmacy:

ANDRIEU-GUTTRANCOURT, J., Otorhinolar-
yngology
AUGUSTIN, P., Neurology
BACHY, B., Infantile Surgery
BENOZIO, E., Radiology
BERCOFF, E., Internal Medicine
BESANÇON, P., Chemistry
BESSOU, J. P., Surgery
BEURET, F., Rehabilitation
BIGA, N., Orthopaedics
BLANQUART, F., Rehabilitation
BONMARCHAND, G., Resuscitation
BONNET, J. J., Pharmacology
BRASSEUR, G., Ophthalmology
BRASSEUR, P. H., Bacteriology
CAILLARD, J.-F., Industrial Medicine
CAPRON, R., Biophysics
COLIN, R., Gastroenterology
COLONNA, L., Psychiatry
COMOY, D., Biochemistry
COSTENTIN, J., Pharmacology
COURTOIS, H., Internal Medicine
CRIBIER, A., Cardiology
CZERNICHOW, P., Epidemiology
DEHESDIN, D., Otorhinolaryngology
DENIS, P., Physiology
DUCROTTE, P., Hepatology
DUVAL, C., Clinical Obstetrics
FESSARD, C., Paediatrics
FILLASTRE, J. P., Nephrology
FREGER, P., Anatomy
GARNIER, J., Botany and Cryptogamy
GODIN, M., Nephrology
GRISE, PH., Urology
HECKETSWEILER, P., Hepatology
HEMET, J., Pathological Anatomy
HUMBERT, G., Tropical and Infectious
Diseases
JANVRESSE, C., Hygiene
JOLY, P., Dermatology
JOUANY, M., Toxicology
KUHN, J. M., Endocrinology
LAFONT, O., Organic Chemistry
LAURET, P., Dermatology
LAVOINNE, D., Biochemistry
LECHEVALLIER, J., Infantile Surgery
LEDOSSEUR, P., Radiology
LEFUR, R., Cancerology
LELOET, X., Rheumatology
LEMELAND, J. F., Hygiene
LEMOINE, J. P., Gynaecology
LEREBOURS, E., Nutrition
LEROY, J., Therapeutics
LETAC, B., Cardiology
MACE, B., Histology
MAITROT, B., Biochemistry
MALLET, E., Biology
MARCHAND, J., Chemical Pharmacology
MATRAY, F., Medical Biochemistry
METAYER, J., Anatomy
MICHOT, F., Digestive Tract Surgery
MIHOUT, B., Neurology
MITROFANOFF, P., Infantile Surgery
MONCONDUIT, M., Haematology
MUIR, J. F., Pneumology
NOUVET, G., Pneumology
ORECCHIONI, A.-M., Pharmacology
PASQUIS, P., Physiology
PEILLON, C., Orthopaedic and Traumato-
logical Surgery
PERON, J. M., Stomatology
PETIT, M., Psychiatry
PIGUET, H., Immuno-haematology
PROTAIS, P., Physiology
PROUST, B., Forensic Medicine
SAOUDI, N., Cardiology
SORIA, C., Pharmaceutical Biochemistry

SOYER, R., Thoracic Surgery
TADIE, M., Neurosurgery
TENIÈRE, P., General Surgery
TESTART, J., Clinical Surgery
THIEBOT, J., Radiology
THOMINE, M., Orthopaedic and Traumato-
logical Surgery
THUILLIEZ, C., Therapeutics
TILLY, H., Haematology
TRON, F., Immunology
TRON, P., Paediatrics
VANNIER, J. P., Paediatrics
WATELET, J., General Surgery
WINCKLER, C., Anaesthesiology
WOLF, L., Therapeutic Internal Medicine

Sciences and Technology:

ANTHORE, R., Physics
ATTIAS, J., Biochemistry
AUGER, P., Physics
BALANGE, P., Biochemistry
BANEGE, A., Physics
BARBEY, G., Chemistry
BLANCHARD, D., Mechanics
BLAVETTE, D., Physics
BOISARD, J., Vegetal Biology
BORGHI, R., Mechanics
BOUAZIZ, R., Chemistry
BRISSET, J. L., Chemistry
CAGNON, M., Physics
CALBRIX, J., Mathematics
CARLES, D., Electronics
CARPENTIER, J. M., Chemistry
CASTON, J., Biology
CAZIN, L., Biology
CHAMPRANAUD, J. M., Computer Sciences
CHARPENTIER, J., Physiology
CHERON, B., Thermodynamics
COMBRET, C., Chemistry
COTTEREAU, M. J., Thermodynamics
DAVOUST, D., Chemistry
DEBRUCQ, D., Electronics
DERRIDJ, M., Mathematics
DE SAM LAZARO, J., Mathematics
DESBENE, A., Chemistry
DESBENE, P., Chemistry
DONATO, P., Mathematics
DOSS, H., Mathematics
DUHAMEL, P., Chemistry
DUVAL, J.-P., Computer Sciences
DUVAL, P., Physics
FOUCHER, B., Biochemistry
FRILEUX, P. N., Biology
GALLOT, J., Physics
GAYOSO, J., Chemistry
GORALCIK, P., Computer Sciences
GRENET, J., Physics
GUESPIN, J., Microbiology
HANNOYER, B., Physics
HANSEL, G., Mathematics
HUSSON, A., Biology
LAMBOY, M., Geology
LANERY, E., Mathematics
LANGE, C., Chemistry
LECOURTIER, Y., Electronics
LEDOUX, M., Thermodynamics
LENGLET, M., Chemistry
LOPITAUX, J., Chemistry
MAHEU, B., Thermodynamics
MENAND, A., Physics
METAYER, M., Chemistry
MEYER, R., Geology
MICHON, J. F., Computer Sciences
OZKUL, C., Physics
PAULMIER, C., Chemistry
PEREZ, G., Chemistry
PETIPAS, C., Physics
POIRIER, J. M., Chemistry
QUEGUINNER, G., Chemistry
RIPOLL, C., Biochemistry
SELEGNY, E., Chemistry
STRELCYN, J. M., Mathematics
SURIN, A., Mathematics
TEILLET, J., Physics
UNANUE, A., Chemistry
VAILLANT, R., Animal Physiology

VAUTIER, C., Physics
VERCHERE, J. F., Chemistry
VIGER, C., Electronics
VIGIER, P., Physics
WEILL, M., Thermodynamics

UNIVERSITÉ DE SAVOIE (CHAMBÉRY)

BP 1104, 73011 Chambéry Cedex
27 rue Marcoz, 73000 Chambéry

Telephone: 4-79-75-85-85
Fax: 4-79-75-91-05
E-mail: guide@univ-savoie.fr
Internet: www.univ-savoie.fr

Founded 1970
Academic year: October to July

Pres.: GILBERT ANGÉNIEUX
Vice-Pres: DENIS VARASCHIN (Ccl of Admin.), LUC FRAPPAT (Scientific Ccl), PASCAL MOUILLE (Studies and Univ. Life), ERIC BRUNAT (Int. Relations)
Sec.-Gen.: GILLES STOLL
Dir of Libraries: ALAIN CARACO

Number of teachers: 412
Number of students: 11,500

Publications: *Annales* (1 a year), *Présences* (12 a year)

TEACHING AND RESEARCH UNITS

Centre Interdisciplinaire Scientifique de la Montagne: Bâtiment Belledonne, Campus scientifique, 73376 Le Bourget du Lac Cedex; tel. 4-79-75-81-29; fax 4-79-75-87-77; e-mail secretariat.montagne@univ-savoie .fr; internet www.cism.univ-savoie.fr; Dir THIERRY VILLEMIN.

Faculté de Droit et d'Economie: BP 1104, 73011 Chambéry Cedex; tel. 4-79-75-84-30; e-mail secretariat.fde@univ-savoie.fr; internet www.fde.univ-savoie.fr; Dir MICHEL JULIEN.

Faculté des Lettres, Langues et Sciences Humaines: route du Sergent Revel, 73000 Jacob-Bellecombette Cedex; tel. 4-79-75-84-79; fax 4-79-75-85-93; internet www.llsh .univ-savoie.fr; Dir OLIVIER DESRICHARD.

Faculté des Sciences Fondamentales et Appliquées: Campus scientifique, 73376, Le Bourget du Lac Cedex; tel. 4-79-75-87-01; fax 4-79-75-81-21; e-mail sfa-contact@ univ-savoie.fr; internet www.sfa.univ-savoie .fr; Dir PATRICE ORRO.

ATTACHED INSTITUTES

Annecy National College of Engineering: BP 806, 74016 Annecy Cedex;5 chemin de Bellevue, 74016 Annecy-Le-Vieux; tel. 4-50-09-66-00; fax 4-50-09-66-49; e-mail etudes@esia.univ-savoie.fr; internet www .esia.univ-savoie.fr; Dir LAURENT FOULLOY.

Chambéry National College of Engineering: 73376 Le Bourget du Lac Cedex; tel. 4-79-75-88-06; fax 4-79-75-87-72; internet www.esigec.univ-savoie.fr; Dir PIERRE BATTISTI.

Institute of Technology Annecy: 9 rue de l'Arc-en-ciel, BP 240, 74942 Annecy-Le-Vieux; tel. 4-50-09-22-22; fax 4-79-75-87-72; internet www.iut.univ-savoie.fr; Dir GILLES HEIDSIECK.

Institute of Technology Chambéry: Savoie Technolac, 73376 Le-Bourget-du-Lac Cedex; tel. 4-79-75-81-75; fax 4-79-75-81-64; internet src-serveur2.univ-savoie.fr; Dir NICOLE ALBEROLA.

UNIVERSITÉ DE STRASBOURG

4 rue Blaise Pascal, CS 90032, 67081 Strasbourg Cedex

Telephone: 3-68-85-00-00
E-mail: president@unistra.fr

Internet: www.unistra.fr

Founded 2009 by merger of Universités de Strasbourg I (Université Louis Pasteur), II (Université Marc Bloch, Sciences Humaines) and III (Université Robert Schuman)
State control

Pres.: ALAIN BERETZ
First Vice-Pres.: MICHEL DENEKEN
Vice-Pres. for Basic and Continuing Education: FRÉDÉRIQUE GRANET
Vice-Pres. for Research and Doctoral Studies: ERIC WESTHOF
Vice-Pres. for Univ. Life: CLEMENT RAUSCHER
Vice-Pres. for Social Sciences: BERNARD ANCORI
Vice-Pres. for Human Resources and Social Policy: HUGUES DREYSSÉ
Vice-Pres. for Business Partnerships: JEAN-MARC JELTSCH
Vice-Pres. for Int. Relations: ANNE KLEBES-PÉLISSIER
Vice-Pres. for Heritage: YVES LARMET
Vice-Pres. for Digital Policy and Information Systems: CATHERINE MONGENET

Library: 1.2m.vols
Number of teachers: 2,676
Number of students: 42,448.

TEACHING AND RESEARCH UNITS

Centre d'Etudes Internationales de la Propriété Intellectuelle: 11 rue du Maréchal Juin, BP 68, 67046 Strasbourg Cedex; tel. 3-68-85-88-00; fax 3-68-85-85-66; e-mail ceipi@ceipi.edu; Dir CHRISTOPHE GEIGER.

Centre Universitaire d'Enseignement du Journalisme: 11 rue du Maréchal Juin, CS 10068, 67046 Strasbourg Cedex; tel. 3-68-85-83-00; fax 3-68-85-85-74; e-mail nicole .gauthier@cuej.unistra.fr; Dir NICOLE GAUTHIER.

Ecole Européenne de Chimie, Polymères et Matériaux: 25 rue Becquerel, 67087 Strasbourg Cedex 2; tel. 3-68-85-26-00; e-mail daniel.guillon@unistra.fr; Dir DANIEL GUILLON.

Ecole de Management Strasbourg: 61 ave de la Forêt Noire, 67085 Strasbourg Cedex; tel. 3-68-85-80-00; fax 3-68-85-85-93; e-mail contact@em-strasbourg.eu; Dir MICHEL KALIKA.

Ecole Nationale Supérieure de Physique: Parc d'Innovation, blvd Sébastien Brant, BP 10413, 67412 Illkirch Cedex; tel. 3-68-85-43-32; e-mail eric.fogarassy@unistra .fr; Dir ERIC FOGARASSY.

Ecole et Observatoire des Sciences de la Terre: 5 rue René Descartes, 67084 Strasbourg Cedex; tel. 3-68-85-00-29; fax 3-68-85-01-25; e-mail michel.granet@eost.u-strasbg .fr; Dir MICHEL GRANET.

Ecole Supérieure de Biotechnologie: Parc d'Innovation, blvd Sébastien Brant, BP 10413, 67412 Illkirch Cedex; tel. 3-68-85-43-32; e-mail claude.kedinger@unistra.fr; Dir CLAUDE KEDINGER.

Faculté des Arts: Bâtiment Le Portique, 14 rue René Descartes, BP 80010, 67084 Strasbourg Cedex; tel. 3-68-85-63-46; fax 3-68-85-63-81; e-mail arts@unistra.fr; Dir FRANCIS GAST.

Faculté de Chimie: 1 rue Blaise Pascal, 67008 Strasbourg Cedex; tel. 3-68-85-16-60; e-mail planeix@unistra.fr; Dir JEAN-MARC PLANEIX.

Faculté de Chirurgie Dentaire: 1 pl. de l'Hôpital, 67000 Strasbourg Cedex; tel. 3-88-85-39-01; e-mail dentaire@unistra.fr; Dean Prof. YOUSSEF HAIKEL.

Faculté de Droit, de Sciences Politiques et de Gestion: 1 pl. d'Athènes, BP 66, 67045 Strasbourg Cedex; tel. 3-68-85-81-00; fax 3-68-61-73-51; e-mail j.poughon@unistra.fr; Dean JEAN-MICHEL POUGHON.

Faculté de Géographie et d'Aménagement: 3 rue de l'Argonne, 67083 Strasbourg Cedex; tel. 3-68-85-08-91; e-mail geographie@unistra.fr; Dean JOËL HUMBERT.

Faculté des Langues et Sciences Humaines Appliquées: Bâtiment Le Patio, 22 rue René Descartes, 67084 Strasbourg Cedex; tel. 3-68-85-67-51; e-mail lsha@ unistra.fr; Dir NATHALIE HILLENWECK.

Faculté des Langues Vivantes: Bâtiment Le Patio, 22 rue René Descartes, 67084 Strasbourg Cedex; tel. 3-68-85-65-72; e-mail languesvivantes@unistra.fr; Dean BERNARD GENTON.

Faculté des Lettres: Bâtiment Le Portique, 14 rue René Descartes, BP 80010, 67081 Strasbourg Cedex; tel. 3-68-85-64-03; e-mail revol@unistra.fr; Dean THIERRY REVOL.

Faculté de Mathématique et d'Informatique: 7 rue René Descartes, 67084 Strasbourg Cedex; tel. 3-88-85-02-03; e-mail noot@ unistra.fr; Dir RUTGER NOOT.

Faculté de Médecine: 4 rue Kirschleger, 67085 Strasbourg Cedex; tel. 3-88-85-35-20; fax 3-88-85-35-18; e-mail medecine@unistra .fr; Dean BERTRAND LUDES.

Faculté de Pharmacie: 74 route du Rhin, BP 60024, 67401 Illkirch Cedex; tel. 3-88-85-42-87; fax 3-88-85-42-86; e-mail doyen .pharma@unistra.fr; Dean JEAN-YVES PABST.

Faculté de Philosophie: Bâtiment Le Portique, côté Campus, 14 rue René Descartes, BP 80010, 67084 Strasbourg Cedex; e-mail jchiroll@unistra.fr; Dir JEAN-CLAUDE CHIROLLET.

Faculté de Physique et Ingénierie: 3–5 rue de l'Université, 67084 Strasbourg Cedex; tel. 3-88-85-06-72; fax 3-88-85-06-69; e-mail phi-contact@unistra.fr; Dir ABDELMJID NOUR-REDDINE.

Faculté de Psychologie: 12 rue Goethe, 67000 Strasbourg Cedex; tel. 3-68-85-19-45; e-mail kelche@unistra.fr; Dean CHRISTIAN KELCHE.

Faculté des Sciences Economiques et de Gestion: Pôle européen de gestion et d'économie, 61 ave de la Forêt Noire, 67085 Strasbourg Cedex; tel. 3-68-85-20-58; e-mail heraud@unistra.fr; Dean JEAN-ALAIN HÉRAUD.

Faculté des Sciences de l'Education: 7 rue de l'Université, 67000 Strasbourg Cedex; tel. 3-68-85-06-18; e-mail pascal.marquet@ unistra.fr; Dean PASCAL MARQUET.

Faculté des Sciences Historiques: Palais Universitaire, 9 pl. de l'Université, 67084 Strasbourg Cedex; tel. 3-68-85-68-61; e-mail jeanmarie.husser@unistra.fr; Dir JEAN MARIE HUSSER.

Faculté des Sciences Sociales, Pratiques Sociales et Développement: Bâtiment Le Patio, 22 rue René Descartes, 67084 Strasbourg Cedex; tel. 3-68-85-60-26; e-mail sciencessociales@unistra.fr; Dir JACQUELINE IGERSHEIM.

Faculté des Sciences du Sport: Bâtiment Le Portique, 14 rue René Descartes, BP 80010, 67084 Strasbourg Cedex; tel. 3-68-85-64-41; e-mail staps@unistra.fr; Dir GILLES ERB.

Faculté des Sciences de la Vie: 28 rue Goethe, 67083 Strasbourg Cedex; tel. 3-68-85-66-88; e-mail gauer@unistra.fr; Dean FRANÇOIS GAUER.

Faculté de Théologie Catholique: Palais Universitaire, 9 pl. de l'Université, BP 90020, 67084 Strasbourg Cedex; tel. 3-68-85-68-22; e-mail theo-catho@unistra.fr; Dean JEAN-PIERRE WAGNER.

Faculté de Théologie Protestante: Palais Universitaire, 9 pl. de l'Université, BP 90020, 67084 Strasbourg Cedex; tel. 3-68-85-68-34; e-mail theoprot@unistra.fr; Dean REMI GOUNELLE.

Institut d'Etudes Politiques: 47 ave de la Forêt Noire, 67082 Strasbourg Cedex; tel. 3-68-85-84-00; fax 3-68-85-86-15; e-mail scolarite.iep@unistra.fr; internet www-iep.u-strasbg.fr; Dir SYLVAIN SCHIRMANN.

Institut des Hautes Etudes Européennes: 10 rue Schiller, 67081 Strasbourg Cedex; tel. 3-68-85-82-00; fax 3-68-85-85-90; e-mail ihee@unistra.fr; Dir ERIC MAULIN.

Institut de Préparation à l'Administration Générale: 47 ave de la Forêt Noire, 67082 Strasbourg Cedex; tel. 3-68-85-85-00; fax 3-68-85-86-13; e-mail ipag@unistra.fr; Dir FRANCESCO DE PALMA.

Institut du Travail: 39 ave de la Forêt Noire, 67000 Strasbourg Cedex; tel. 3-68-85-87-00; fax 3-68-85-85-94; e-mail institut.travail@unistra.fr; Dir FABIENNE MULLER.

Institut Universitaire de Formation des Maîtres: 141 ave de Colmar, 67100 Strasbourg Cedex; tel. 3-88-43-82-07; e-mail jean-claude.bove@iufm.unistra.fr; internet www.alsace.iufm.fr; Dir FRANÇOIS WERCKMEISTER.

Institut Universitaire de Technologie (Haguenau): 30 rue du Maire André Traband, 67500 Haguenau Cedex; tel. 3-88-05-34-00; fax 3-88-05-34-10; e-mail iuthag-contact@unistra.fr; Dir FRANCIS BRAUN.

Institut Universitaire de Technologie (Louis Pasteur): 1 allée d'Athènes, 67300 Schiltigheim Cedex; tel. 3-88-85-25-26; fax 3-88-85-25-01; e-mail violaine.delarchand@unistra.fr; Dir PASCALE BERGMANN.

Institut Universitaire de Technologie (Robert Schuman): 72 route du Rhin, BP 10315, 67411 Illkirch Cedex; tel. 3-88-85-89-00; fax 3-88-85-86-05; e-mail iutrs@unistra.fr; Dir BERNARD LICKEL.

Observatoire Astronomique: 11 rue de l'Université, 67000 Strasbourg Cedex; tel. 3-88-85-24-45; e-mail herve.wozniak@astro.unistra.fr; Dir HERVÉ WOZNIAK.

UNIVERSITÉ DU SUD TOULON VAR

ave de l'Université, BP 20132, 83957 La Garde Cedex
Telephone: 4-94-14-20-00
Fax: 4-94-14-21-57
E-mail: inscriptions@univ-tln.fr
Internet: www.univ-tln.fr
Founded 1970
Academic year: September to July
Pres.: PHILIPPE TCHAMITCHIAN
Vice-Pres.: (vacant)
Sec.-Gen.: FRANÇOISE VILLEVAL
Librarian: DANIEL EYMARD
Number of teachers: 380
Number of students: 10,700

TEACHING AND RESEARCH UNITS

Business Administration: PIERRE GENSSE
Economic Sciences and Management: PHILIPPE GILLES
Letters and Humanities: GILLES LEYDIER
Law: JEAN JACQUES PARDINI
Sciences and Technology: SERGE DESPIAU
Sports: PIERRE FONTANARI
School of Engineering: OLIVIER LE CALVÉ
Media and Information Technology Institute: FRANCK RENUCCI
University Institute of Technology: ROBERT CHANU

UNIVERSITÉ DE TECHNOLOGIE DE BELFORT-MONTBÉLIARD

90010 Belfort Cedex
Telephone: 3-84-58-30-00
Fax: 3-84-58-30-30
E-mail: contact@utbm.fr
Internet: www.utbm.fr
Founded 1999 as a result of merger of Ecole Nationale d'Ingénieurs de Belfort and Institut Polytechnique de Sévenans
State control
Dir: CHRISTIAN LERMINIAUX.

UNIVERSITÉ DE TECHNOLOGIE DE COMPIÈGNE

Centre Pierre Guillaumat BP 60319, 60203 Compiègne Cedex
Telephone: 3-44-23-44-23
Fax: 3-44-23-43-00
E-mail: accueil@utc.fr
Internet: www.utc.fr
Founded 1972
Public control
Language of instruction: French
Academic year: September to August (2 semesters)
Pres.: Dr PIERRE CHARREYRON
Gen. Sec.: SOLANGE BONNEAUD
Librarian: ANNIE BERTRAND
Number of teachers: 450
Number of students: 4,450
Publication: *Interactions* (6 a year)

DIRECTORS

Dept of Biological Engineering: CÉCILE LEGALLAIS
Dept of Chemical Engineering: PIERRE GUIGON
Dept of Computer Science: AZIZ MOUKRIM
Dept of Mechanical Engineering: MICHÈLE GUIGON
Department of Mechanical Engineering Systems: BENOÎT EYNARD
Dept of Technology and Human Sciences: FRANÇOIS SEBBAH
Dept of Urban Engineering Systems: JEAN-PASCAL FOUCAULT

UNIVERSITÉ DE TECHNOLOGIE DE TROYES

12 rue Marie Curie, BP 2060, 10010 Troyes Cedex
Telephone: 3-25-71-76-00
Fax: 3-25-71-76-76
E-mail: infos@utt.fr
Internet: www.utt.fr
Founded 1994
State control
Academic year: September to June
Pres.: Prof. CHRISTIAN LERMINIAUX
Vice-Pres: PHILIPPE ADNOT, BRUNO GUELORGET
Librarian: GILLES-FRANÇOIS EUVRARD
Library of 10,000 vols
Number of teachers: 165
Number of students: 2,500 (of which 180 are postgraduate)

UNIVERSITÉ DE TOULOUSE I (SCIENCES SOCIALES)

2 rue du Doyen-Gabriel-Marty, 31042 Toulouse Cedex 9
Telephone: 5-61-63-35-00
Fax: 5-61-63-37-98
Internet: www.univ-tlse1.fr
Founded 1229
State control
Pres.: BRUNO SIRE

Vice-Pres: CHRISTIAN LAVIALLE (Ccl of Admin.), GÉRARD JAZOTTES (Studies and Univ. Life), HUGUES KENFACK (Scientific Ccl)
Sec.-Gen.: CÉCILE CHICOYE
Librarians: BRUNO VAN DOOREN
Number of teachers: 554
Number of students: 18,267
Publications: *Annales*, *Livre de la Recherche*

TEACHING AND RESEARCH UNITS

Administration and Communication: Dir: FRANCIS BESTION
Economics: Dir: MARIE-FRANÇOISE CALMETTE
Information Science: Dir: CHANTAL SOULE-DUPUY
Law: Dir: BERNARD BEIGNIER

ATTACHED INSTITUTES

Centre Universitaire d'Albi: 2 ave Franchet d'Espérey, 81011 Albi Cedex 09; tel. 5-63-48-19-79; fax 5-63-48-19-71; Dir O. DEVAUX.

Centre Universitaire de Montauban: 116 blvd Montauriol, 82017 Montauban Cedex; tel. 5-63-63-32-71; fax 5-63-66-34-07; Dir B. MARIZ.

Ecole Supérieure Universitaire de Gestion: 2 rue Albert Lautmann, 31042 Toulouse Cedex; tel. 5-61-21-55-18; fax 5-61-23-84-33; Dir P. SPITERI.

Institut d'Etudes Politiques: 2 ter rue des Puits-creusés, BP 88562, 31685 Toulouse Cedex 6; tel. 5-61-11-02-60; fax 5-61-22-94-80; e-mail contact@sciencespo-toulouse.fr; internet www.sciencespo-toulouse.fr; Dir PHILIPPE RAIMBAULT.

Institut Universitaire Technologique de Rodez: 33 ave du 8 mai 1945, 12000 Rodez; tel. 5-65-77-10-80; fax 5-65-77-10-81; Dir B. ALLAUX.

UNIVERSITÉ DE TOULOUSE II (LE MIRAIL)

5 allées Antonio Machado, 31058 Toulouse Cedex 9
Telephone: 5-61-50-42-50
Fax: 5-61-50-42-09
Internet: www.univ-tlse2.fr
Pres.: DANIEL FILATRE
Vice-Pres.: PIERRE-YVES BOISSAU (Ccl of Admin.)
Vice-Pres.: MARIE CHRISTINE JAILLET (Scientific Ccl)
Vice-Pres.: MARIE-HÉLÈNE GARELLI (Studies and Univ. Life)
Number of teachers: 1,095
Number of students: 23,117
Publications: *Anglophonia* (2 a year), *Caravelle* (2 a year), *Cinémas d'Amérique Latine* (1 a year), *Clio* (2 a year), *Criticón* (3 a year), *Homo* (1 a year), *Kairos* (2 a year), *Littératures* (2 a year), *Pallas* (2 a year), *Science de la Société* (3 a year), *Sud/Ouest Européen*.

TEACHING AND RESEARCH UNITS

Faculté d'Histoire, Arts et Archéologie: tel. 5-61-50-41-98; fax 5-61-50-43-11; Dir JEAN-MICHEL MINOVEZ.

Faculté de Langues, Littératures et Civilisations Étrangères: tel. 5-61-50-38-20; fax 5-61-50-37-92; e-mail uflrlangu@univ-tlse2.fr; Dir ALAIN COZIC.

Faculté de Langues, Littératures et Civilisations Etrangères: tel. 5-61-50-37-91; fax 5-61-50-48-52; e-mail uflrlettr@univ-tlse2.fr; Dir VALÉRIE VISA-ONDARCHUHU.

Faculté de Psychologie: tel. 5-61-50-49-50; fax 5-61-50-43-90; e-mail accueil.psycho@

univ-tlse2.fr; internet ufr-psycho.univ-tlse2
.fr; Dir PIERRE LARGY.

Faculté des Sciences, Espaces, Sociétés:
tel. 5-61-50-38-44; fax 5-61-50-38-50; e-mail
ufrses@univ-tlse2.fr; Dir RÉGIS GUILLAUME.

UNIVERSITÉ TOULOUSE III (PAUL SABATIER)

118 route de Narbonne, 31062 Toulouse
Cedex 9

Telephone: 5-61-55-66-11
Fax: 5-61-55-64-70
E-mail: contactweb@cict.fr
Internet: www.ups-tlse.fr
Founded 1969
State control
Academic year: September to June
Number of teachers and researchers: 1,650
Pres.: GILLES FOURTANIER
Vice-Pres: MARC REVERSAT (Ccl of Admin.),
ALAIN MILON (Scientific Ccl), Prof. JEAN-
LUC ROLS (Council of Studies and Univ.
Life)
Sec.-Gen.: Mme A. VERDAGUER
Librarian: Mme HEUSSE
Number of teachers: 2,784
Number of students: 28,451.

TEACHING AND RESEARCH UNITS

Faculté de Chirurgie Dentaire: 3 chemin
des Maraîchers, 31062 Toulouse Cedex 9; tel.
5-62-17-29-30; e-mail resdenta@adm.ups-tlse
.fr; internet dentaire.ups-tlse.fr; Dir Prof.
MICHEL SIXOU.

Faculté des Langues Vivantes: 118 route
de Narbonne, 31062 Toulouse Cedex 9; tel. 5-
61-55-83-60; e-mail reslv@adm.ups-tlse.fr;
internet langues.ups-tlse.fr; Dir JEAN-BER-
NARD HISLEN.

**Faculté de Mathématiques, Informa-
tique et Gestion:** 118 route de Narbonne,
31062 Toulouse Cedex 9; tel. 5-61-55-67-73;
e-mail secmig@adm.ups-tlse.fr; internet
www.ufr-mig.ups-tlse.fr/index; Dir JEAN-
PAUL BAHSOUN.

Faculté de Médecine Purpan: 37 allées
Jules Guesde, 31062 Toulouse Cedex 9; tel. 5-
61-14-59-07; e-mail respurpa@adm.ups-tlse
.fr; internet www.medecine.ups-tlse.fr; Dir
Prof. JEAN-PIERRE VINEL.

Faculté de Médecine Rangueil: 33 route
de Narbonne, 31062 Toulouse Cedex 9; tel. 5-
62-88-90-05; e-mail resrangu@adm.ups-tlse
.fr; internet www.medecine.ups-tlse.fr; Dir
Prof. DANIEL ROUGÉ.

**Faculté de Physique et Chimie Automa-
tique:** 118 route de Narbonne, 31062 Toulouse Cedex 9; tel. 5-61-55-68-28; e-mail
dirpca@adm.ups-tlse.fr; internet pca3w
.ups-tlse.fr/inter/index; Dir Prof. JEAN-MARC
BROTO.

Faculté des Sciences Pharmaceutiques:
35 chemin des Maraîchers, 31062 Toulouse
Cedex 9; tel. 5-62-25-68-04; e-mail
respharm@adm.ups-tlse.fr; internet www
.pharmacie.ups-tlse.fr; Dir Prof. RAYMOND
BASTIDE.

**Faculté des Sciences et Techniques des
Activités Physiques et Sportives:** 118
route de Narbonne, 31062 Toulouse Cedex
9; tel. 5-61-55-66-34; e-mail resstaps@adm
.ups-tlse.fr; internet www.ufrstaps.ups-tlse
.fr; Dir Prof. GÉRARD AUNEAU.

**Faculté des Sciences de la Vie et de la
Terre:** 118 route de Narbonne, 31062 Toulouse Cedex 9; tel. 5-61-55-69-30; e-mail
dirsvt@adm.ups-tlse.fr; internet ufrsvt
.ups-tlse.fr; Dir Prof. BERNARD KNIBIEHLER.

UNIVERSITÉ DE TOURS (UNIVERSITÉ FRANÇOIS-RABELAIS)

3 rue des Tanneurs, BP 4103, 37041 Tours
Cedex 01

Telephone: 2-47-36-66-00
Fax: 2-47-36-64-10
E-mail: suio@univ-tours.fr
Internet: www.univ-tours.fr
Founded 1970
State control
Languages of instruction: English, French
Academic year: September to June
Pres.: LOÏC VAILLANT
Vice-Pres: ALAIN RONCINI (Ccl of Admin.),
MICHEL ISINGRINI (Scientific Ccl), NADINE
IMBAULT (Studies and Univ. Life), ARNAUD
GIACOMETTI (Int. Relations)
Sec.-Gen.: PIERRE GABETTE
Librarian: CORINNE TOUCHELAY
Library of 600,000 vols, 5,600 periodical
titles
Number of teachers: 1,300
Number of students: 22,000.

TEACHING AND RESEARCH UNITS

**Centre d'Etudes Supérieures de la
Renaissance:** 59 rue Néricault-Destouches,
BP 11328, 37013 Tours Cedex 01; tel. 2-47-
36-77-60; fax 2-47-36-77-62; e-mail cesr@
univ-tours.fr; internet cesr.univ-tours.fr; Dir
VENDRIX PHILIPPE.

Ecole d'ingénieurs Polytechnique: 64
ave Jean Portalis, 37200 Tours Cedex 01;
tel. 2-47-36-14-14; fax 2-47-36-14-22; e-mail
polytech@univ-tours.fr; internet polytech
.univ-tours.fr; Dir CHRISTIAN PROUST.

Faculté des Arts et Sciences Humaines:
3 rue des Tanneurs, 37041 Tours Cedex 01;
tel. 2-47-36-68-36; fax 2-47-36-66-72; e-mail
secrtash@univ-tours.fr; internet ash
.univ-tours.fr; Dir BERNARD BURON.

**Faculté de Droit, d'Economie et des
Sciences Sociales:** 50 ave Jean Portalis,
BP 0607, 37206 Tours Cedex 03; tel. 2-47-36-
10-92; fax 2-47-36-10-90; e-mail fac-droit@
univ-tours.fr; internet droit.univ-tours.fr;
Dean Prof. CLAUDE OPHELE.

Faculté de Lettres et Langues: 3 rue des
Tanneurs, 37041 Tours Cedex 01; tel. 2-47-
36-68-35; fax 2-47-36-68-31; e-mail
jean-michel.fournier@univ-tours.fr; internet
lettres.univ-tours.fr; Dir JEAN-MICHEL FOUR-
NIER.

Faculté de Médecine: 10 Bd Tonnellé, BP
3223, 37032 Tours Cedex 01; tel. 2-47-36-60-
04; fax 2-47-36-60-99; e-mail dominique
.perrotin@univ-tours.fr; internet med
.univ-tours.fr; Dean DOMINIQUE PERROTIN.

Faculté de Pharmacie: 31 ave Monge,
37200 Tours Cedex 01; tel. 2-47-36-71-42;
fax 2-47-36-71-44; e-mail ufrpharmacie@
univ-tours.fr; internet pharma.univ-tours.fr;
Dir ALAIN GUEIFFIER.

Faculté des Sciences: Parc Grandmont,
37200 Tours Cedex 01; tel. 2-47-36-70-30; fax
2-47-36-70-40; e-mail scosciences@univ-tours
.fr; internet sciences.univ-tours.fr; Dir ALAIN
VERGER.

**Institut Universitaire de Technologie
(Blois):** 15 rue de la Chocolaterie, CS 2903,
41000 Tours Cedex 02; tel. 2-54-55-21-33; fax
2-54-55-21-09; e-mail isabelle.laffez@
univ-tours.fr; internet iut-blois.univ-tours.fr;
Dir ISABELLE LAFEZ.

UNIVERSITÉ DE VALENCIENNES ET DU HAINAUT-CAMBRESIS

Le Mont Houy, BP 311, 59304 Valenciennes
Cedex

Telephone: 3-27-14-12-34
Fax: 3-27-14-11-00

E-mail: uvhc@univ-valenciennes.fr
Internet: www.univ-valenciennes.fr
Founded 1964
State control
Language of instruction: French
Academic year: September to June
Pres.: MOHAMED OURAK
Vice-Pres: J. M. FLAMME (Ccl of Admin.), A.
ARTIBA (Scientific Ccl), A. KABILA (Studies
and Univ. Life)
Sec.-Gen.: P. CHABASSE
Librarian: FRANÇOISE TRUFFERT
Library of 180,000 vols
Number of teachers: 650
Number of students: 10,300

TEACHING AND RESEARCH UNITS

Higher Industrial Institute: Dir: FRANÇOIS
VERHEYDE
Higher National School of Engineering and
Computer Science: Dir: DANIEL COUTELLIER
Institute of Business Administration: Dir:
PATRICK LELEU
Institute of General of Administrative Stud-
ies: Dir: EMMANUEL CHERRIER
Institute of Science and Technology: Dir:
CLAUDINE FOLLET
Institute of Technology: Dir: JEAN-PIERRE
ROUZÉ
Law, Economics and Management: Dean:
ALEXANDRE BONDUELLE
Letters, Languages, Arts and Humanities:
Dir: SERGE GOUAZÉ
School of Continuing Education and Social
and Economic Promotion: Dir: D. WILLAEYS
Sport Science: Dir: FRANCK BARBIER

UNIVERSITÉ DE VERSAILLES SAINT-QUENTIN-EN-YVELINES

55 ave de Paris, 78035 Versailles Cedex

Telephone: 1-39-25-78-00
Fax: 1-39-25-78-01
E-mail: secretariat@ilei.uvsq.fr
Internet: www2.uvsq.fr
Founded 1991
Pres.: SYLVIE FAUCHEUX
Vice-Pres: JEAN-LUC VAYSSIÈRE (Ccl of
Admin.), GÉRARD CAUDAL (Scientific Ccl),
SONJA DENOT-LEDUNOIS (Studies and Univ.
Life)
Sec.-Gen.: NICOLAS MIGNAN
Librarian: CHRISTOPHE PÉRALES
Number of teachers: 1,360
Number of students: 18,000.

TEACHING AND RESEARCH UNITS

Faculté de Droit et de Science Politique:
43 rue de la Division Leclerc, 78280 Guyancourt Cedex; tel. 1-39-25-53-13; fax 1-39-25-
53-89; e-mail doyen@droit.uvsq.fr; Dir THO-
MAS CLAY.

Faculté des Sciences: 45 ave des Etats-
Unis, 78035 Versailles; tel. 1-39-25-41-12; fax
1-39-25-43-03; e-mail dominique.barth@uvsq
.fr; Dir DOMINIQUE BARTH.

Fafculté des Sciences de la Santé: Bâtiment François Rabelais, 9 blvd d'Alembert,
78280 Guyancourt; tel. 1-39-25-57-40; fax 1-
39-25-57-41; e-mail djillali.annane@uvsq.fr;
Dean DJILLALI ANNANE.

Faculté des Sciences Sociales: 47 blvd
Vauban, 48047 Guyancourt Cedex; tel. 1-39-
25-51-01; fax 1-39-25-53-55; e-mail direction
.ufr-scs@uvsq.fr; Dir MARYSE BRESSON.

Institut d'Etudes Culturelles: Bâtiment
Vauban, 47 blvd Vauban, 78047 Guyancourt
Cedex; tel. 1-39-25-50-02; e-mail christian
.delporte@uvsq.fr; Dir CHRISTIAN DELPORTE.

**Institut des Langues et des Etudes
Internationales:** Bâtiment Vauban, 47
blvd Vauban, 78280 Guyancourt Cedex; tel.

1-39-25-52-70; e-mail secretariat@ilei.uvsq
.fr; Dir LAURENT BAZIN.

**Institut des Sciences et Techniques des
Yvelines:** 10–12 ave de l'Europe, 78140
Vélizy; tel. 1-39-25-38-50; fax 1-39-25-38-51;
e-mail directeur@isty.uvsq.fr; Dir PIERRE
BLAZEVIC.

Institut Supérieur de Management: Bâtiment Vauban, 47 blvd Vauban, 78047
Guyancourt Cedex; tel. 1-39-25-55-34;
e-mail secretariat.ism@uvsq.fr; Dir PHILIPPE
HERMEL.

**Institut Universitaire de Technologie
(Mantes-en-Yvelines):** 7 rue Jean Hoët,
78200 Mantes-la-Jolie; tel. 1-30-98-13-62;
fax 1-30-98-16-96; e-mail directeur@
iut-mantes.uvsq.fr; Dir SAMIR ALLAL.

**Institut Universitaire de Technologie
(Vélizy):** 7 rue Jean Hoët, 78200 Mantes-
la-Jolie; tel. 1-39-25-48-33; fax 1-30-98-48-13;
e-mail iut@iut-velizy.uvsq.fr; Dir STÉPHANE
DELAPLACE.

State Colleges and Institutes

GENERAL

Collège de France: 11 pl. Marcelin Berthelot, 75231 Paris Cedex 05; tel. 1-44-27-12-11;
fax 1-44-27-12-61; e-mail message@
college-de-france.fr; internet www
.college-de-france.fr; f. 1530 by François I;
library: 85,000 vols; 54 professors; Administ-
trator PIERRE CORVOL.

**Ecole des Hautes Etudes en Sciences
Sociales:** 190–198 ave de France, 75244
Paris Cedex 13; tel. 1-49-54-25-25; fax 1-45-
44-93-11; internet www.ehess.fr; f. 1947; 300
teachers; 3,000 students; Pres. FRANÇOIS
WEIL.

Ecole Pratique des Hautes Etudes: 46
rue de Lille, 75007 Paris; tel. 1-53-63-61-20;
fax 1-53-63-61-94; e-mail nicole.daire@ephe
.sorbonne.fr; internet www.ephe.sorbonne.fr;
f. 1868; library: 50,000 vols; 300 teachers;
4,000 students; Pres. JEAN-CLAUDE WAQUET;
Sec.-Gen. NICOLE DAIRÉ.

Divisions:

Department of History and Philology:
190 ave de France, 75013 Paris; tel. 1-49-
54-83-59; e-mail danielle.jacquart@ephe
.sorbonne.fr; f. 1868; Dean DANIELLE JAC-
QUART; publ. *Annuaire.*

Department of Life and Earth Science:
46 rue de Lille, 75007 Paris; tel. 1-53-63-
61-95; e-mail michel.veuille@mnhn.fr; f.
1868; Dean MICHEL VEUILLE; publ.
Annuaire.

Department of Religious Studies: 46,
rue de Lille, 75007 Paris; tel. 153-63-61-96;
e-mail hubert.bost@ephe.sorbonne.fr; f.
1886; Dean HUBERT BOST; publ. *Annuaire.*

Attached Institutes:

**Institut Européen en Sciences des
Religions:** 14 rue Ernest Cresson, 75014
Paris; tel. 1-40-52-10-00; fax 1-40-52-10-01;
e-mail iesr@ephe.sorbonne.fr; internet
www.iesr.fr; Dir ISABELLE SAINT-MARTIN.

**Institut Transdisciplinaire d'Etude du
Vieillissement:** Université Montpellier II,
Batiment 24, pl. Eugène Bataillon, CC 105,
34095 Montpellier Cedex 5; tel. 6-70-53-84-
05; e-mail verdier@univ-montp2.fr; Dir
JEAN-MICHEL VERDIER.

Pôle Universitaire Léonard de Vinci:
92916 Paris La Défense Cedex; located at:
12 ave Léonard de Vinci, 92400 Courbevoie,
Hauts-de-Seine; tel. 1-41-16-70-00; fax 1-41-
16-70-99; e-mail contact@devinci.fr; internet
www.devinci.fr; f. 1995 by the Gen. Ccl of the
Hauts-de-Seine Département; depts: economics and social sciences, languages, gen. culture, personal devt, sport; library: 80,000
books, reports, memoirs, market research
reports, 400 journals, 1,000 CD-ROM and
DVD titles, 20 online databases; 6,418 students; Pres. CHARLES PASQUA.

ADMINISTRATION

Ecole Nationale d'Administration: 2 ave
de l'Observatoire, 75272 Paris Cedex 06; tel.
1-44-41-85-00; fax 1-44-41-86-49; internet
www.ena.fr; f. 1945 to provide training for
the higher ranks of the civil service; 600
teachers; 2,050 students; library: 25,000 vols;
Dir BERNARD BOUCAULT.

Groupe ESC Clermont: 4 blvd Trudaine,
63037 Clermont-Ferrand Cedex 01; tel. 4-73-
98-24-24; fax 4-73-98-24-49; e-mail info@
esc-clermont.fr; internet www.esc-clermont
.fr; f. 1919; dependent on the Direction de
l'Enseignement Supérieur du Ministre de
l'Education; 200 teachers; 600 students;
library: 9,000 vols, Chamber of Commerce
library of 12,000 vols; Dir DAVID MARKER;
publs *Développements* (3 a year), *Point Zéro*
(6 a year).

AGRICULTURE, FORESTRY, VETERINARY SCIENCE

AgroParisTech: 16 rue Claude Bernard,
75231 Paris Cedex 05; tel. 1-44-08-168-50;
fax 1-44-08-16-00; e-mail marie-pierre
.quessette@agroparistech.fr; internet www
.agroparistech.fr; f. 2007 by a merger of Ecole
Nationale Supérieure des Industries Agricoles et Alimentaires, f. 1893, the Institut
National Agronomique Paris-Grignon, f.
1971, and Ecole Nationale du Génie Rural,
des Eaux et des Forêts, f. 1965.; 230 teachers;
2,000 students; library: 50,000 vols and 1,700
periodicals; Dir-Gen. REMI TOUSSAIN.

Attached Institute:

**AgroParisTech—Grignon Energie
Positive:** Ferme expérimentale AgroParisTech, 78850 Thiverval-Grignon; tel. 1-30-
54-57-40; fax 1-30-54-53-26; e-mail
grignonenergiepositive@agroparistech.fr;
internet www.agroparistech.fr/
energiepositive; f. 1979; library: c. 1,000
vols; Dir OLIVIER LAPIERRE; publ. *Sols* (3 or
4 a year).

Ecole Nationale Supérieure du Paysage:
10 rue du Maréchal-Joffre, 78000 Versailles;
tel. 1-39-24-62-00; fax 1-39-24-62-01; e-mail b
.welcomme@versailles.ecole-paysage.fr;
internet www.ecole-paysage.fr; f. 1975; rural
development, ecology, humanities, plastic
arts, architecture, landscaping, town planning; library: 6,000 vols, 75 periodicals; Dir
M. BERNARD; publ. *Les Carnets du Paysage* (4
a year).

Ecole Nationale Vétérinaire d'Alfort: 7
ave Général de Gaulle, 94704 Maisons Alfort;
tel. 1-43-96-71-00; fax 1-43-96-71-25; e-mail
web-direction@vet-alfort.fr; internet www
.vet-alfort.fr; f. 1765; 80 teachers; 700 students; library: 150,000 vols; Dean Prof. JEAN-
PAUL MIALOT; publ. *Le Recueil de Médecine
Vétérinaire.*

Ecole Nationale Vétérinaire de Nantes:
Atlanpole-La Chantrerie, BP 40706, 44307
Nantes Cedex 03; tel. 2-40-68-77-77; fax 2-40-
68-77-78; e-mail direction@vet-nantes.fr;

internet www.oniris-nantes.fr; f. 1979; 73
teachers; 634 students; Dir-Gen. PIERRE SAÏ.

**Ecole Nationale Vétérinaire de Tou-
louse:** 23 chemin des Capelles, BP 87614,
31076 Toulouse Cedex 3; tel. 5-61-19-38-00;
fax 5-61-19-39-93; e-mail direction@envt.fr;
internet www.envt.fr; f. 1828; library: 50,000
vols; 75 teachers; 570 students; Dir Prof.
ALAIN MILON; Sec.-Gen. JEAN-CLAUDE
BRETHES; Librarian Prof. GAËLLE JAN; publ.
Revue de Médecine Vétérinaire (12 a year).

**Institut Supérieur des Sciences Agrono-
miques, Agroalimentaires, Horticoles et
du Paysage:** 65 rue de Saint-Brieuc, CS
84215, 35042 Rennes Cedex; tel. 2-23-48-50-
00; fax 2-41-73-15-57; e-mail dircom@
agrocampus-ouest.fr; internet www
.agrocampus-ouest.fr; f. 2008 by the merger
of the Institut National d'Enseignement
Supérieur et de Recherche Agronomique et
Agro-alimentaire in Rennes and the Institut
National d'Horticulture et de Paysage in
Angers, f. 1874.; library: 19,000 vols; Campuses in Angers, Beg-Meil and Rennes.; 135
teachers; 1,880 students; Dir-Gen. Prof.
GRÉGOIRE THOMAS.

**Montpellier SupAgro/Centre Inter-
national d'Etudes Supérieures en Sciences Agronomiques:** 2 pl.Viala, 34060
Montpellier Cedex 2; tel. 4-99-61-22-00; fax
4-99-61-29-00; e-mail contact@supagro.inra
.fr; internet www.supagro.fr; f. 2007 by the
merger of Ecole Nationale Supérieure Agronomique de Montpellier, f. 1872, the Centre
National d'Etudes Agronomiques des
Régions Chaudes, f. 1902, the Département
Industries Agroalimentaires Régions
Chaudes de l'Ecole Nationale Supérieure
des Industries Agricoles et Alimentaires, f.
1893, and the Centre d'Expérimentations
Pédagogiques de Florac, f. 1970; 100 teachers; 1,250 students; library: 100,000 vols,
1,400 periodicals; Dir-Gen. ÉTIENNE LANDAIS;
Sec.-Gen. PHILIPPE DE CORNELISSEN.

Attached Institutes:

**Centre d'Expérimentations Pédagogi-
ques de Florac:** 9 rue Célestin Freinet,
BP 35, 48400 Florac; tel. 4-66-65-65-65; fax
4-66-65-65-50; e-mail admin.cep@educagri
.fr; internet www.cep.educagri.fr; Dir
PATRICK AUMASSON.

**Institut des Hautes Etudes de la Vigne
et du Vin:** e-mail ihev@supagro.inra.fr;
Dir HERVÉ HANNIN.

Institut des Régions Chaudes: 1101 ave
Agropolis, BP 5098, 34093 Montpellier; tel.
4-67-61-70-00; fax 4-67-41-02-32; e-mail
fabrice.dreyfus@supagro.inra.fr; internet
www.supagro.fr/irc; Dir FABRICE DREYFUS.

**VetAgro Sup (Institut d'Enseignement
Supérieur et de Recherche en Alimentation, Santé Animale, Sciences Agronomiques et d'Environnement):** 1 ave
Bourgelat, BP 83, 69280 Marcy L'Etoile; tel.
4-78-87-25-25; fax 4-78-87-26-59; internet
www.vet-lyon.fr; f. 2010 by the merger of
Ecole Nationale Vétérinaire de Lyon, f. 1762,
Ecole Nationale d'Ingénieurs des Travaux
Agricoles de Clermont-Ferrand, f. 1984, and
Ecole Nationale des Services Vétérinaires, f.
1973; library: 10,000 vols; 120 teachers;
1,200 students.

Attached Institute:

**Ecole Nationale des Services
Vétérinaires:** tel. 4-78-87-25-45; fax 4-
78-87-25-48; e-mail ensv@ensv.vetagro-sup
.fr; internet blanc.vet-lyon.fr; Dir Dr OLI-
VIER FAUGÈRE.

ARCHITECTURE

**Ecole d'Architecture de Lille et des
Régions Nord:** 2 rue Verte, quartier de

l'Hôtel de Ville, 59650 Villeneuve d'Ascq; tel. 3-20-61-95-50; fax 3-20-61-95-51; internet www.lille.archi.fr; f. 1755 as Ecole d'Architecture, reorganized 1968; library: 15,000 vols; 127 teachers; 700 students; Dir JEAN MARC ZURETTI.

Ecole Nationale Supérieure d'Architecture de Paris-La Villette: 144 ave de Flandre, 75019 Paris; tel. 1-44-65-23-00; fax 1-44-65-23-01; e-mail directeur@paris-lavillette.archi.fr; internet www.paris-lavillette.archi.fr; f. 1969, present name 1982; attached to Min. of Culture and Communications; 80 teachers; 2,300 students; library: 25,000 vols; Dir GILLES ENRIQUEZ.

Ecole Spéciale d'Architecture: 254 blvd Raspail, 75014 Paris; tel. 1-40-47-40-47; fax 1-43-22-81-16; e-mail info@esa-paris.fr; internet www.esa-paris.fr; f. 1865; library: 7,000 vols; 80 teachers; 675 students; Pres. FRANÇOIS BORDRY.

ECONOMICS, LAW AND POLITICS

Centre Français de Droit Comparé: 28 rue Saint-Guillaume, 75007 Paris; tel. 1-44-39-86-23; fax 1-44-39-86-28; e-mail cfdc@legiscompare.com; internet www.centrefdc.org; f. 1951; library: 100,000 vols; Pres. JACQUES ROBERT; Sec.-Gen. DIDIER LAMÈTHE; publ. *Revue Internationale de Droit Comparé* (4 a year).

Ecole Nationale de la Magistrature: 10 rue des Frères Bonie, 33080 Bordeaux Cedex; tel. 5-56-00-10-10; fax 5-56-00-10-99; e-mail initiale@enm_magistrature.fr; internet www.enm.justice.fr; f. 1958; 450 students; library: 50,000 vols; Dir JEAN-FRANÇOIS THONY; publ. *Les Cahiers de la Justice* (2 a year).

Ecole Nationale de la Statistique et de l'Administration Economique (ENSAE): 3 ave Pierre Larousse, 92245 Malakoff Cedex; tel. 1-41-17-65-25; fax 1-41-17-38-52; e-mail info@ensae-paristech.fr; internet www.ensae.fr; f. 1942; attached to the Institut National de la Statistique et des Etudes Economiques (see Research Institutes); economics, statistics, finance; 344 students; Dir SYLVIANE GASTALDO.

Ecole Nationale de la Statistique et de l'Analyse de l'Information (ENSAI): Campus de Ker Lann, rue Blaise Pascal, 35170 Bruz; tel. 2-99-05-32-32; fax 2-99-05-32-05; e-mail communication@ensai.fr; internet www.ensai.com; f. 1942; attached to the Institut National de la Statistique et des Etudes Economiques (see Research Institutes); statistics and information processing at Masters level; 21 teachers; 335 students; Dir LAURENT DI CARLO (acting).

Institut d'Etudes Politiques de Paris: 27 rue Saint-Guillaume, 75337 Paris Cedex 07; tel. 1-45-49-50-50; fax 1-42-22-31-26; internet www.sciences-po.fr; f. 1945 as successor to l'Ecole Libre des Sciences Politiques; attached to Fondation Nationale des Sciences Politiques; seven campuses in France: Dijon, Le Havre, Menton, Nancy, Paris, Poitiers and Reims; library: 700,000 vols; 10,000 students; Dir RICHARD DESCOINGS.

EDUCATION

Ecole Normale Supérieure: 45 rue d'Ulm, 75230 Paris Cedex 05; tel. 1-44-32-30-00; fax 1-44-32-20-99; e-mail communication@ens.fr; internet www.ens.fr; f. 1794 by the National Convention; library: see Libraries; 800 teachers; 2,300 students; graduate and postgraduate studies in humanities, social sciences and science; Dir MONIQUE CANTO-SPERBER; Sec.-Gen. CORALIE WALUGA; Librarian PIERRE

PETITMENGIN; publ. *Annales Scientifiques de l'Ecole Normale Supérieure.*

Ecole Normale Supérieure de Cachan: 61 ave du Président Wilson, 94235 Cachan Cedex; tel. 1-47-40-20-00; fax 1-47-40-20-74; e-mail webmaster@ens-cachan.fr; internet www.ens-cachan.fr; f. 1912 as Ecole Normale de l'Enseignement Technique; became Ecole Normale Supérieure in 1985; library: 55,000 vols; 145 teachers; 1,150 students; Dir YANN BARBAUX.

Ecole Normale Supérieure de Lyon: 15 parvis René Descartes, BP 7000, 69342 Lyon Cedex 07; tel. 4-37-37-60-00; e-mail webmaster@ens-lyon.fr; internet www.ens-lyon.fr; f. 2010 by the merger of Ecole Normale Supérieure Lettres et Sciences Humaines, fmrly Ecole Normale Supérieure de Fontenay/Saint-Cloud, and Ecole Normale Supérieure de Lyon.; Pres. JACQUES SAMARUT; Dir-Gen. OLIVIER FARON; Sec.-Gen. YVES QUINTEAU; Librarian CHRISTINE ANDRÉ; library: 1,200,000 vols; 230 teachers; 2,000 students; publ. 1,000 annually.

GEOGRAPHY

Ecole Nationale des Sciences Géographiques: 6 et 8 ave Blaise Pascal, Cité Descartes, Champs-sur-Marne, 77455 Marne-la-Vallée Cedex 2; tel. 1-64-15-30-01; fax 1-64-15-31-07; e-mail info@ensg.ign.fr; internet www.ensg.ign.fr; f. 1941; administered by Institut Géographique National; library: specialized library of 36,000 books, 950,000 maps, 1.1m. aerial photographs; 30 teachers; 300 students, 2,000 trainees; Dir MICHEL KASSER.

HISTORY

Ecole Nationale des Chartes: 19 rue de la Sorbonne, 75005 Paris; tel. 1-55-42-75-00; fax 1-55-42-75-09; e-mail secretariat@enc.sorbonne.fr; internet www.enc.sorbonne.fr; f. 1821, reorganized 1846; library: 150,000 vols; 170 students; Dir JACQUES BERLIOZ; Librarian ISABELLE DIU; publs *Etudes et Rencontres, Matériaux pour l'Histoire, Mémoires et Documents, Positions des thèses* (1 a year).

Institut National du Patrimoine: Galerie Colbert, 2 rue Vivienne, 75002 Paris; tel. 1-44-41-16-41; fax 1-44-41-16-76; e-mail webmaster@inp.fr; internet www.inp.fr; f. 1990; trains curators of museums, archives and historical monuments; Dir ERIC GROSS; Sec.-Gen. SOPHIE SEYER.

LANGUAGE AND LITERATURE

Institut National des Langues et Civilisations Orientales (INALCO): 2 rue de Lille, 75343 Paris Cedex 07; tel. 1-49-23-26-00; fax 1-49-23-26-99; e-mail secretariat.general@inalco.fr; internet www.inalco.fr; f. 1669; 228 teachers; 10,500 students; Pres. JACQUES LEGRAND; Sec.-Gen. JEAN BAYLE.

Research Centres:

Centre d'Etudes Japonaises: 49 bis ave de la Belle Gabrielle, 75012 Paris; tel. 1-80-51-95-00; fax 1-80-51-95-49; e-mail anne.bayard-sakai@inalco.fr; internet inalcocej.free.fr; Dir ANNE BAYARD-SAKAI.

Centre d'Etudes et de Recherche sur les Littératures et les Oralités du Monde: 49 bis ave de la Belle Gabrielle, 75012 Paris; tel. 1-80-51-95-00; fax 1-80-51-95-49; e-mail gilles.delouche@inalco.fr; internet www.cerlom.fr; Dir GILLES DELOUCHE.

Centre de Recherches Europes-Eurasie: 49 bis ave de la Belle Gabrielle, 75012 Paris; tel. 1-80-51-95-00; fax 1-80-51-95-49;

e-mail marie.vrinat-nikolov@inalco.fr; internet inalcocej.free.fr; Dir MARIE VRINAT NIKOLOV; Comprises Centre d'Etudes Balkaniques, Centre d'Etude de l'Europe Médiane and Centre de Recherches Russes et Euro-Asiatique.

Centre de Recherches Linguistiques sur l'Asie Orientale: c/o EHESS, 54 blvd Raspail, 75006 Paris; tel. 1-80-51-95-00; fax 1-80-51-95-49; e-mail djamouri@ehess.fr; internet crlao.ehess.fr; Dir REDOUANE DJAMOURI.

Centre de Recherche Moyen-Orient et Méditerranée: 49 bis ave de la Belle Gabrielle, 75012 Paris; tel. 1-80-51-95-00; fax 1-80-51-95-49; e-mail cermom@gmail.com; Dir MASHA ITZHAKI.

Equipe Asies: 49 bis ave de la Belle Gabrielle, 75012 Paris; tel. 1-80-51-95-00; fax 1-80-51-95-49; e-mail isabelle.rabut@inalco.fr; Dir ISABELLE RABUT; Comprises Centre d'Etudes Chinoises, Centre d'Etudes Coréennes, Centre de Recherche sur l'Océan Indien Occidental et le Monde Austronésien, Centre Asie du Sud et du Sud-Est and Littérature et société : Tibet, Népal, Mongolie.

Equipe de Recherche en Textes, Informatique, Multilinguisme: 49 bis ave de la Belle Gabrielle, 75012 Paris; tel. 1-80-51-95-00; fax 1-80-51-95-49; e-mail crim@inalco.fr; internet www.crim.fr; Dir VALETTE MATHIEU.

Histoire Sociétés et Territoires du Monde: 49 bis ave de la Belle Gabrielle, 75012 Paris; tel. 1-80-51-95-00; fax 1-80-51-95-49; e-mail robert.ziavoula@inalco.fr; Dir ROBERT ZIAVOULA.

Langues et Cultures du Nord de l'Afrique et Diasporas: 49 bis ave de la Belle Gabrielle, 75012 Paris; tel. 1-80-51-95-00; fax 1-80-51-95-49; e-mail abounf@inalco.fr; Dir ABDELLAH BOUNFOUR; Comprises Centre de Recherche Berbère, Centre de Recherche et Etudes en Arabe Maghrébin and Langues et Cultures Juives du Maghreb et de la Méditerranée Occidentale.

Langages, Langues et Cultures d'Afrique Noire: UMR 8135 du CNRS, 7 rue Guy Môquet, BP 8, 94801 Villejuif; tel. 1-49-58-38-46; fax 1-49-58-38-00; e-mail llacan@vjf.cnrs.fr; internet llacan.vjf.cnrs.fr; Dir MARTINE VANHOVE.

Mondes Iranien et Indien: 27 rue Paul Bert, 94204 Ivry-sur-Seine; tel. 1-49-60-40-05; fax 1-45-21-94-19; e-mail iran-inde@ivry.cnrs.fr; internet www.iran-inde.cnrs.fr; Dir POLLET SAMVELIAN.

Pluralité des Langues et des Idendités en Didactique: Acquisition, Médiations: 49 bis ave de la Belle Gabrielle, 75012 Paris; tel. 1-80-51-95-00; fax 1-80-51-95-49; e-mail gzarate@inalco.fr; internet www.plidam.fr; Dir GENEVIÈVE ZARATE.

LIBRARIANSHIP

Ecole Nationale Supérieure des Sciences de l'Information et des Bibliothèques (ENSSIB): 17–21 blvd du 11 Novembre 1918, 69623 Villeurbanne Cedex; tel. 4-72-44-43-43; fax 4-72-44-43-44; e-mail enssib@enssib.fr; internet www.enssib.fr; f. 1963 as Ecole Nationale Supérieure de Bibliothécaires; 12 teachers; 300 students; library: 17,000 vols and 585 periodicals, also audiovisual items; Dir ANNE-MARIE BERTRAND; publ. *Bulletin des Bibliothèques de France* (6 a year).

MEDICINE

Ecole des Hautes Etudes en Santé Publique (EHESP): ave du Professeur Léon-Bernard, CS 74312, 35043 Rennes Cedex; tel. 2-99-02-22-00; fax 2-99-02-26-25; internet www.ehesp.fr; f. 1945; post-university courses; 60 full-time teachers; 500 full-time students; 4,000 part-time students; library: 15,000 vols; Dir Prof. ANTOINE FLAHAULT.

Ecole du Val-de-Grâce: 1 pl. Alphonse Laveran, 75230 Paris Cedex 05; tel. 1-40-51-69-69; fax 1-40-51-47-74; internet www.ecole-valdegrace.sante.defense.gouv.fr; f. 1850 as Ecole d'Application du Service de Santé des Armées (name changed as above in 2005); mainly two-year graduate courses; library: 40,000 vols and 2,067 periodicals; Dir MGI DE SAINT-JULIEN; publ. *Médecine et Armées*.

SCIENCES

Ecole Nationale de la Météorologie: 42 ave Gaspard Coriolis, 31057 Toulouse Cedex 1; tel. 5-61-07-94-19; fax 5-61-07-96-30; e-mail enm.fr@meteo.fr; internet www.enm.meteo.fr; f. 1948; attached to attached to INP de Toulouse; library: 4,000 vols; 35 teachers; 230 students; Dir FRANÇOIS LALAURETTE.

Institut National des Sciences Appliquées de Lyon (INSA Lyon): 20 ave Albert Einstein, 69621 Villeurbanne Cedex; tel. 4-72-43-83-83; e-mail accueil@insa-lyon.fr; internet www.insa-lyon.fr; f. 1957; Dir Prof. ALAIN STORCK.

Institut National des Sciences Appliquées de Rennes (INSA Rennes): 20 ave des Buttes de Coësmes, CS 70839, 35708 Rennes Cedex 7; tel. 2-23-23-82-00; fax 2-23-23-83-96; internet www.insa-rennes.fr; f. 1961; physical and materials science, electronic engineering, civil engineering and town planning, computer science, communications systems, mechanical engineering and control; 150 teachers; 1,700 students; Dir M'HAMED DRISSI.

Institut National des Sciences Appliquées de Rouen (INSA Rouen): ave de l'Université, 76801 Saint-Étienne-du-Rouvray Cedex; tel. 2-32-95-97-00; fax 2-32-95-98-60; e-mail insa@insa-rouen.fr; internet www.insa-rouen.fr; f. 1985; chemistry, mathematics, energy, mechanical engineering, technology and applied sciences; 141 teachers; 1,546 students; library: 15,000 vols, 200 periodicals; Dir Prof. JEAN-LOUIS BILLOËT.

Institut National des Sciences Appliquées de Strasbourg (INSA Strasbourg): 24 blvd de la Victoire, 67084 Strasbourg Cedex; tel. 3-88-14-47-00; fax 3-88-24-14-90; e-mail secretariat.direction@insa-strasbourg.fr; internet www.insa-strasbourg.fr; f. 1875 and rejoined the INSA group in 2003; 1,300 students; Dir MARC RENNER.

Institut National des Sciences Appliquées de Toulouse (INSA Toulouse): 135 ave de Rangueil, 31077 Toulouse Cedex 4; tel. 5-61-55-95-13; fax 5-61-55-95-00; e-mail webmaster@insa-toulouse.fr; internet www.insa-toulouse.fr; 10,000 students; Dir DIDIER MARQUIS.

Muséum National d'Histoire Naturelle: Jardin des Plantes, 57 rue Cuvier, 75005 Paris Cedex 05; tel. 1-40-79-56-01; fax 1-40-79-54-48; e-mail webaccueil@mnhn.fr; internet www.mnhn.fr; f. 1635 as the Jardin Royal des Plantes Médicinales (current organization adopted in 1793); teaching and research in natural history; administers the Zoological Garden, the Musée de l'Homme and several other natural history depts and

institutions; Dir Prof. BERTRAND-PIERRE GALEY; Librarian MONIQUE DUCREUX.

TECHNOLOGY

Conservatoire National des Arts et Métiers: 292 rue St-Martin, 75141 Paris Cedex 03; tel. 1-40-27-20-00; internet www.cnam.fr; f. 1794; 55 regional centres, diploma and doctorate courses; library: see Libraries and Archives; 470 teachers; 100,000 students (full- and part-time); Pres. GÉRARD MESTRALLET.

Ecole Centrale des Arts et Manufactures/Ecole centrale Paris: Grande Voie des Vignes, 92295 Châtenay-Malabry Cedex; tel. 1-41-13-10-00; fax 1-41-13-10-10; e-mail direction@ecp.fr; internet www.ecp.fr; f. 1829; higher degrees in multiple disciplines of engineering; library: 60,000 vols and 340 periodicals; 224 teachers (full-time); 1,589 students; Dir HERVÉ BIAUSSER; publ. *Centraliens* (12 a year).

Ecole Centrale de Lille: Cité Scientifique, BP 48, 59651 Villeneuve d'Ascq Cedex; tel. 3-20-33-53-53; fax 3-20-33-54-99; e-mail renseignements@ec-lille.fr; internet www.ec-lille.fr; f. 1872; 6 research laboratories; library: 10,000 vols; 100 teachers; 1,400 students; Dir Prof. ETIENNE CRAYE.

Ecole Nationale de l'Aviation Civile: 7 ave Edouard-Belin, BP 54005, 31055 Toulouse Cedex 4; tel. 5-62-17-40-00; fax 5-62-17-40-23; internet www.enac.fr; f. 1948; training of civil aviation personnel; advanced studies in engineering; library: 30,000 vols; 400 teachers and researchers; 2,000 students; Dir M. HOUALLA.

Ecole Nationale du Génie de l'Eau et de l'Environnement de Strasbourg: 1 quai Koch, BP 61039, 67000 Strasbourg Cedex; tel. 3-88-24-82-82; fax 3-88-37-04-97; e-mail engees@engees.u-strasbg.fr; internet www-engees.u-strasbg.fr; f. 1960; 450 students; Dir CLAUDE BERNHARD.

Ecole Nationale de la Photographie: 16 rue des Arènes, BP 149, 13200 Arles Cedex; tel. 4-90-99-33-33; fax 4-90-99-33-59; e-mail communication@enp-arles.com; internet www.enp-arles.com; f. 1982; under auspices of Ministry of Culture and Communications; 3-year course; 7 teachers; 75 students; library: 10,000 vols; Dir RÉMY FENZY.

Ecole Nationale Supérieure des Arts et Industries Textiles (ENSAIT): 2 allée Louise et Victor Champier, BP 30329, 59056 Roubaix Cedex 01; tel. 3-20-25-64-64; fax 3-20-24-84-06; e-mail xavier.flambard@ensait.fr; internet www.ensait.fr; f. 1883; library: 3,844 vols; 50 teachers; 210 students; Dir XAVIER FLAMBARD.

Ecole Nationale Supérieure d'Arts et Métiers ParisTech: 151 blvd de l'Hôpital, 75013 Paris; tel. 1-44-24-62-99; fax 1-45-85-87-04; e-mail alex.remy@ensam.eu; internet www.ensam.eu; comprises 11 Centres d'Enseignement et de Recherche in Aix-en-Provence, Angers, Bastia, Bordeaux-Talence, Châlon-en-Champagne, Châlon-sur-Saône, Chambéry, Cluny, Lille, Metz and Paris; f. 1871 as Ecole Nationale des Arts et Métiers (current structure adopted in 2007)

DIRECTORS

PIERRE-JEAN BARRE (Aix-en-Provence)
LAURENT GUILLAUMAT (Angers)
DIDIER LIBERT (Bastia (acting))
FRANÇOIS ROUTABOUL (Bordeaux-Talence)
GIOVANNI RADILLA (Châlon-en-Champagne (acting))
JEAN-LUC MARTINEZ (Châlon-sur- Saône)
ALAIN CORNIER (Chambéry)
ALAIN DOVILLAIRE (Cluny)
ERIC DUMETZ (Lille)

JEAN CHRÉTIEN (Metz)
ALEX RÉMY (Paris)

Ecole Nationale Supérieure de Céramique Industrielle: 12 rue Atlantis, 87068 Limoges Cedex; tel. 5-87-50-23-00; fax 5-87-50-23-01; e-mail direction@ensci.fr; internet www.ensci.fr; f. 1893; library: 4,000 vols; 23 teachers; 190 students; Dir AGNES SMITH; publ. *Annuaire*.

Ecole Nationale Supérieure de l'Electronique et de ses Applications (ENSEA): 6 ave du Ponceau, 95014 Cergy-Pontoise Cedex; tel. 1-30-73-66-66; fax 1-30-73-66-67; e-mail directeur@ensea.fr; internet www.ensea.fr; f. 1952; postgraduate courses in electrical engineering, computing and telecommunications; library: 6,000 vols, 150 periodicals; 90 teachers and researchers; 700 students; Dir PIERRE POUVIL.

Ecole Nationale Supérieure de Mécanique: see under University of Nantes.

Ecole Nationale Supérieure du Pétrole et des Moteurs: 228–232 ave Napoléon Bonaparte, 92852 Rueil-Malmaison Cedex; tel. 1-47-52-64-57; fax 1-47-52-67-65; e-mail info-ifpschool@ifp.fr; internet www.ifp-school.com; f. 1954 by the merger of Ecole Nationale Supérieure du Pétrole et des Combustibles Liquides and Ecole Nationale des Moteurs à Combustion et à Explosion; successor to the Institut Français du Pétrole, f. 1944; 400 students; five centres: geological or geophysical exploration; petroleum engineering and project management; refining, petrochemicals, gas; internal combustion engines; economics and management; Dir JEAN-LUC KARNIK.

Ecole Nationale Supérieure de Techniques Avancées (ENSTA ParisTech): 32 blvd Victor, 75739 Paris; tel. 1-45-52-54-01; fax 1-45-52-55-87; e-mail secretariat-general@ensta.fr; internet www.ensta-paristech.fr; f. 1741, refounded 1970; systems engineering, naval architecture, oceanology, mechanics, nuclear techniques, chemical engineering, electronics, information technology; 3-year curriculum; 180 permanent teachers, 650 visiting; 480 students (not incl. doctoral candidates); undergraduate and postgraduate studies; library: 10,000 vols; Dir YVES DEMAY.

Ecole Nationale des Travaux Publics de l'Etat: 3 rue Maurice Audin, 69518 Vaulx en Velin Cedex; tel. 4-72-04-70-70; fax 4-72-04-62-54; e-mail webmaster@entpe.fr; internet www.entpe.fr; f. 1953 in Paris, moved 1975; 689 teachers (full-time and part-time); 614 students; library: 14,000 vols; Dir JEAN-BAPTISTE LESORT.

Ecole Polytechnique: 91128 Palaiseau Cedex; tel. 1-69-33-33-33; internet www.polytechnique.fr; f. 1794; 660 teachers; 2,700 students; library: 300,000 vols; Dir-Gen. XAVIER MICHEL.

Ecole des Ponts ParisTech: 6–8 ave Blaise Pascal, Cité Descartes, Champs-sur-Marne, 77455 Marne-la-Vallée Cedex 2; tel. 1-64-15-30-30; e-mail brigitte.millard@enpc.fr; internet www.enpc.fr; f. 1747; civil and mechanical engineering, town and country planning, transport; library: 85,000 vols, 2,500 periodicals, 37,000 18th-century MSS, 900 maps, 30,000 photographs; 1,700 students; Dir PHILIPPE COURTIER.

Ecole Supérieure de Physique et de Chimie Industrielles de la Ville de Paris (ParisTech): 10 rue Vauquelin, 75231 Paris Cedex 5; tel. 1-40-79-44-00; fax 1-40-35-14-74; e-mail direction.@espci.fr; internet www.espci.fr; f. 1882; training of research engineers; 20 research laboratories; library: 5,000 vols; 67 teachers; 75 to 80 students per year; Pres. JEAN-LOUIS MISSIKA.

ENILIA-ENSMIC, Lycée de l'Alimentation: ave François Mitterrand, BP 49, 17700 Surgères; tel. 5-46-27-69-00; fax 5-46-07-31-49; e-mail epl.surgeres@educagri.fr; internet www.enilia-ensmic.fr; f. 2010 by the merger of Ecole Nationale d'Industrie Laitière et des Industries Agroalimentaires (f. 1906 as Ecole Professionnelle de Laiterie) and Ecole Nationale Supérieure de Meunerie et des Industries Céréalières (f. 1924 as Ecole Française de Meunerie); 230 students; Dir CHRISTIANE MAZEL; publ. *Industries des Céréales* (6 a year).

Groupe des Ecoles des Mines: 60 blvd St-Michel, 75272 Paris Cedex 06; e-mail jcontact@gemtech.fr; internet www.gemtech.fr; f. 1783; library: 200,000 vols, 350 periodicals; 1,000 teachers; 6,200 students.

Campuses:

Ecole des Mines d'Albi-Carmaux: Campus Jarlard, 81013 Albi Cedex 09; tel. 5-63-49-30-00; fax 5-63-49-30-99; e-mail ecole@enstimac.fr; internet www.enstimac.fr; Dir BRUNO VERLON.

Ecole des Mines d'Alès: internet www.mines-ales.fr; Dir ALAIN DORISON.

Ecole des Mines de Douai: 91 rue Charles Bourseul, BP 838, 59508 Douai Cedex; e-mail jean-claude.duriez@mines-douai.fr; internet www2.mines-douai.fr; Dir JEAN-CLAUDE DURIEZ.

Ecole des Mines de Nancy: Parc De Saurupt, CS 14234, 54042 Nancy Cedex; tel. 3-83-58-42-32; e-mail ensmn@mines.inpl-nancy.fr; internet www.mines.inpl-nancy.fr; Dir MICHEL JAUZEIN.

Ecole des Mines de Nantes: La Chantrerie 4, rue Alfred Kastler, BP 20722, 44307 Nantes Cedex 03; tel. 2-51-85-81-00; e-mail stephane.cassereau@emn.fr; internet www.mines-nantes.fr; Dir STÉPHANE CASSEREAU.

Ecole des Mines de Saint-Etienne: 158 cours Fauriel, 42023 Saint-Etienne Cedex 02; tel. 4-77-42-01-23; fax 4-77-42-00-00; e-mail webmaster@emse.fr; internet www.emse.fr; Dir PHILIPPE JAMET.

Mines ParisTech: 60 blvd St-Michel, 75272 Paris Cedex 06; tel. 1-40-51-90-00; e-mail benoit.legait@mines-paristech.fr; internet www.mines-paristech.fr; Dir BENOÎT LEGAIT.

Groupe ENI (Ecoles Nationales d'Ingénieurs): 1 route d'Ars Laquenexy, CS 65820, 57078 Metz Cedex 3; tel. 3-87-34-42-61; fax 3-87-34-66-66; internet www.ingenieur-eni.fr; comprises five schools in Brest, Metz, Saint-Etienne, Tarbes and Val de Loire.

Schools:

Ecole Nationale d'Ingénieurs de Brest (ENIB): Site de la pointe du Diable, Technopôle Brest-Iroise, 29280 Plouzané; tel. 2-98-05-66-00; fax 2-98-05-66-10; e-mail secretariat@enib.fr; internet www.enib.fr; Dir JACQUES TISSEAU.

Ecole Nationale d'Ingénieurs de Metz (ENIM): 1 route d'Ars Laquenexy, CS 65820, 57078 Metz Cedex 3; tel. 3-87-34-69-03; fax 3-87-34-69-00; e-mail enim@enim.fr; internet www.enim.fr; Dir PIERRE PADILLA.

Ecole Nationale d'Ingénieurs de Saint-Etienne (ENISE): 58 rue Jean Parot, 42100 St-Etienne; tel. 4-77-43-84-84; fax 0-477-43-84-75; e-mail secretariat.etudes@enise.fr; internet www.enise.fr; Dir ROLAND FORTUNIER.

Ecole Nationale d'Ingénieurs de Tarbes (ENIT): 47 ave d'Azereix, BP 1629, 65016 Tarbes Cedex; tel. 5-62-44-27-00; fax 5-62-44-27-27; e-mail directeur@enit.fr; internet www.enit.fr; 60 teachers;

850 students; library of 4,000 vols; Dir TALAL MASRI.

Ecole Nationale d'Ingénieurs de Val de Loire (ENIVL): rue de la Chocolaterie, BP 3410, 41034 Blois Cedex; tel. 2-54-55-84-00; fax 2-54-55-84-35; e-mail scolarite@enivl.fr; internet www.enivl.fr; Dir ROMUALD BONÉ.

Institut des Hautes Etudes Scientifiques: Le Bois-Marie, 35 route de Chartres, 91440 Bures-sur-Yvette; tel. 1-60-92-66-00; fax 1-60-92-66-69; internet www.ihes.fr; f. 1958; advanced research in mathematics, theoretical physics; library: 4,000 vols, 125 periodicals; Dir JEAN PIERRE BOURGUIGNON; publ. *Publications Mathématiques* (2 a year).

Institut Polytechnique de Bordeaux: 1 ave du Dr Albert Schweitzer, BP 99, 33402 Talence Cedex; tel. 5-40-00-37-26; fax 5-56-37-20-23; e-mail direction@ipb.fr; internet www.ipb.fr; f. 2009; comprises five schools; Dir-Gen. FRANÇOIS CANSELL.

Schools:

Ecole Nationale Supérieure de Chimie, de Biologie et de Physique: 16 ave Pey-Berland, 33607 Pessac Cedex; tel. 5-40-00-65-65; internet www.enscpb.fr; 60 teachers; 550 students; Dir JEAN-MARC HEINTZ.

Ecole Nationale Supérieure de Cognitique: 146 rue Léo Saignat, Case 40, 33076 Bordeaux Cedex; tel. 5-57-57-17-00; internet www.ensc.fr; Dir BERNARD CLAVERIE.

Ecole Nationale Supérieure d'Electronique, Informatique, Télécommunications, Mathématiques et Mécanique de Bordeaux: 1 ave du Dr Albert Schweitzer, BP 99, 33402 Talence Cedex; tel. 5-56-84-65-00; e-mail direction@enseirb-matmeca.fr; internet www.enseirb-matmeca.fr; f. 2009 by the merger of Ecole Nationale Supérieure d'Electronique et de Radioélectricité de Bordeaux and Ecole d'Ingénieurs en Modélisation Mathématique et Mécanique; Dir MARC PHALIPPOU.

Ecole Nationale Supérieure en Environnement, Géoressources et Ingénierie du Développement Durable: 1 allée F. Daguin, 33607 Pessac Cedex; tel. 5-57-12-10-00; fax 5-57-12-10-01; e-mail direction@ensegid.fr; internet www.ensegid.fr; f. 2011; Dir J. M. MALÉZIEUX.

Ecole Nationale Supérieure de Technologie des Biomolécules de Bordeaux: 146 rue Léo Saignat, 33076 Bordeaux Cedex; tel. 5-57-57-10-44; fax 5-57-57-17-11; e-mail enstbb@ipb.fr; internet www.enstbb.ipb.fr; Dir MARC BONNEU.

Institut Supérieur de l'Aéronautique et de l'Espace (ISAE): 10 ave Edouard Belin, BP 54032, 31055 Toulouse Cedex 4; tel. 5-61-33-80-80; fax 5-61-33-83-30; e-mail communication@isae.fr; internet www.isae.fr; f. 2007 by the merger of Ecole Nationale Supérieure de l'Aéronautique et de l'Espace (f. 1909) and Ecole Nationale Supérieure d'Ingénieurs de Constructions Aéronautiques (f. 1945); aeronautics and space; library: 10,000 vols; 106 teachers; 4,277 students; Dir-Gen. OLIVIER FOURURE.

Supméca Paris—Institut Supérieur de Mécanique de Paris: 3 rue Fernand Hainaut, 93407 St-Ouen Cedex; tel. 1-49-45-29-00; fax 1-49-45-29-91; e-mail informations@supmeca.fr; internet www.supmeca.fr; f. 1948; 400 students; library: 3,000 vols; Dir ALAIN RIVIÈRE; publ. *La Lettre de l'ISMCM-CESTI* (2 a year).

Supméca Toulon—Institut Supérieur de Mécanique de Toulon: Maison des Tech-

nologies, pl. Georges Pompidou, Quartier Mayol, 83000 Toulon; tel. 4-94-03-88-00; fax 4-94-03-88-04; e-mail informations@toulon.supmeca.fr; internet www.supmeca.fr; f. 1994; training of engineers, applied research in automation and industrial engineering; 30 teachers; 150 students; Dir PASCALE AZOU-BRIARD.

Télécom Bretagne—Ecole Nationale Supérieure des Télécommunications de Bretagne: Technopôle Brest-Iroise, CS 83818, 29238 Brest Cedex 3; tel. 2-29-00-11-11; fax 2-29-00-10-00; internet www.enst-bretagne.fr; f. 1977; attached to Min. of Technology, Information and Posts; 108 full-time teachers; 1,217 students; Dir PAUL FRIEDEL.

Télécom SudParis—Télécom Ecole de Management: 9 rue Charles Fourier, 91011 Evry Cedex; tel. 1-60-76-40-40; fax 1-60-76-43-25; e-mail webmaster@it-sudparis.eu; internet www.it-sudparis.eu; f. 1979; attached to Min. of Finance, Industry and the Economy; mem. of Conférence des Grandes Ecoles; engineering and business schools; 150 full-time teachers; 1,000 students; Dir SÉBASTIEN CAUWET.

TELECOM ParisTech – Ecole Nationale Supérieure des Télécommunications: 46 rue Barrault, 75634 Paris Cedex 13; tel. 1-45-81-77-77; fax 1-45-89-79-06; e-mail communication@telecom-paristech.fr; internet www.telecom-paristech.fr; f. 1878; attached to France Télécom; Dir YVES POLLANE.

Catholic Colleges and Institutes

INSTITUT CATHOLIQUE DE PARIS

21 rue d'Assas, 75270 Paris Cedex 06

Telephone: 1-44-39-52-00

Fax: 1-45-44-27-14

E-mail: contact@icp.fr

Internet: www.icp.fr

Founded 1875

Academic year: October to June

Chancellor: Mgr ANDRÉ VINGT-TROIS

Rector: JOSEPH MAÏLA

Vice-Rector: Sr GENEVIÈVE MEDEVIELLE

Gen. Sec.: FRANÇOIS ARDONCEAU

Dir of Communication: FRANÇOISE GARDERE-CREAC'H

Librarian: ODILE DUPONT

Library: see Libraries

Number of teaching staff: 847, including 96 professors

Number of students: 15,000 (excluding affiliated schools)

Publications: *Guide des Études* (1 a year), *Transversalités: Revue de l'Institut Catholique de Paris* (4 a year)

DEANS AND DIRECTORS

Faculty of Canon Law: Père JEAN-PAUL DURAND

Faculty of Letters: NATHALIE NABERT

Faculty of Philosophy: Abbé P. CAPELLE

Faculty of Theology: Abbé HENRI-JÉRÔME GAGEY

Higher Institute of Ecumenical Studies: Abbé YVES-MARIE BLANCHARD

Higher Institute of Liturgy: Frère PATRICK PRÉTOT

Higher Institute of Pastoral Catechetics and University Extension: DENIS VILLEPELET

Higher Institute of Pedagogy: FRANÇOISE CHEBAUX

Institute for French Language and Culture and University Summer School: MURIEL CORDIER
Institute of Music and Liturgical Music: E. BELLANGER
Institute of Sacred Art: GENEVIÈVE HEBERT
Institute of Science and Theology of Religions: R. P. PAUL COULON
Institute of Social Sciences and Economics: JOSEPH MAÏLA
Biblical and Systematic Theology: Abbé JESUS ASURMENDI
Doctoral Studies: P. HERVÉ LEGRAND
School of Ancient Oriental Languages: FLORENCE MALBRAN-LABAT
University for Retired People: Dir: J. MENU

AFFILIATED SCHOOLS AND INSTITUTES

Centre de Formation Pédagogique Emmanuel Mounier: 78A rue de Sèvres, 75341 Paris Cedex 07; Dir R. MOREAU.

Ecole de Bibliothécaires-Documentalistes: Paris; Dir D. VIGNAUD.

Ecole de Formation Psycho-Pédagogique: Paris; Dir M. C. DAVID.

Ecole de Psychologues-Praticiens: Paris; Dir J. P. CHARTIER.

Ecole Supérieure de Chimie Organique et Minérale: 95000 Cergy; Dir G. SANTINI.

Ecole Supérieure des Sciences Economiques et Commerciales: 95000 Cergy; Dir P. TAPIE.

Institut Géologique Albert-de-Lapparent: 95000 Cergy; Dir C. CHOMAT.

Institut Libre d'Education Physique Supérieure: 95000 Cergy; Dir F. HELAINE.

Institut Polytechnique Saint-Louis: 95000 Cergy.

Constituent Schools:

Ecole de Biologie Industrielle: 95000 Cergy; Dir F. DUFOUR.

Ecole d'Electricité, de Production et des Méthodes Industrielles: 95000 Cergy; Dir M. DARCHERIF.

Institut d'Agro-Développement International: 95000 Cergy; Dir S. LAMY.

Institut Supérieur Agricole de Beauvais: Rue Pierre Waguet, 60000 Beauvais and 95000 Cergy; f. 1855; Dir M. P. CHOQUET.

Institut Supérieur d'Electronique de Paris: Dir M. CIAZYNSKI.

Institut Supérieur d'Interprétation et de Traduction: Paris; Dir M. MERIAUD.

INSTITUT CATHOLIQUE DE TOULOUSE

31 rue de la Fonderie, BP 7012, 31068 Toulouse Cedex 7
Telephone: 5-61-36-81-00
Fax: 5-61-36-81-08
E-mail: documentation@ict-toulouse.asso.fr
Internet: www.ict-toulouse.asso.fr
Founded 1877 and administered by a Ccl of Bishops of the region
Academic year: October to June
Chancellor: HE Mgr ROBERT LE GALL (Archbishop of Toulouse)
Rector: Père PIERRE DEBERGÉ
Registrar: MONIQUE DELCROIX
Librarian: MAGALI HURTREL-PIZARRO (acting)
Library of 250,000
Number of teachers: 238
Number of students: 6,334
Publications: *Bulletin de Littérature ecclésiastique* (4 a year), *Revue Purpan* (4 a year)

DEANS

Faculty of Canon Law: B. DU PUY-MONTBRUN
Faculty of Law: A. MASSART

Faculty of Letters: B. BILLEREY
Faculty of Philosophy: B. HUBERT
Faculty of Theology: P. MOLAC

INSTITUT DE SCIENCES ET THÉOLOGIE DES RELIGIONS

11 Impasse Flammarion, 13001 Marseilles
Telephone: 4-91-50-35-50
Fax: 4-91-50-35-55
E-mail: istr@cathomed.cef.fr
Internet: cathomed.cef.fr
Founded 1991 by the Diocese of Marseilles
Rector: CHRISTIAN SALENSON
Library of 500 vols
Number of teachers: 30
Number of students: 250
Publication: *Chemins de Dialogue* (every 2 years).

UNIVERSITÉ CATHOLIQUE DE LILLE

60 blvd Vauban, BP 109, 59016 Lille Cedex
Telephone: 3-20-13-40-00
Fax: 3-20-13-40-01
E-mail: saio@icl-lille.fr
Internet: www.univ-catholille.fr
Founded 1875 as Faculty of Law, became univ. instn in 1877
Private (Roman Catholic) control
Rector: Mme TH. LEBRUN
Vice-Rectors: Père B. CAZIN, O. TRANCHANT, J. C. CAILLIEZ
Admin. Officer: B. MAELFAIT
Librarian: D. PENEZ
Library: nearly 500,000 vols
Number of teachers: 3,284
Number of students: 20,186
Publications: *Catho Actualités, Encyclopédie Catholicisme, La Lettre de la Catho, Mélanges de Science Religieuse* (3 a year), *Mémoires et Travaux, Repères, Vie et Foi, Vues d'ensemble*

DEANS

Faculty of Economic Sciences: D. VANPETEGHEM
Faculty of Law: A. MASSART
Faculty of Letters and Human Sciences: J. HEUCLIN
Faculty of Medicine: G. FORZY
Faculty of Science: J. C. CAILLIEZ
Faculty of Theology: J. Y. BAZIOU

FEDERATED INSTITUTES

Centre de Recherches Economiques, Sociologiques et de Gestion (CRESGE): Rue du Port, 59000 Lille; tel. 3-20-54-58-92; f. 1964; Dir L. AUBREE.

Ecole de Hautes Etudes Commerciales du Nord (EDHEC): 58 rue du Port, 59046 Lille Cedex; tel. 3-20-15-45-00; f. 1920; 1,886 students; Dirs-Gen. O. OGER, J.-L. TURRIÈRE.

Branch:

EDHEC Nice: 393 Promenade des Anglais, BP 116, 06202 Nice Cedex; tel. 4-93-18-99-66; 736 students; EDHEC Paris; 131 students.

Ecole des Hautes Etudes Industrielles (HEI): 13 rue de Toul, 59046 Lille Cedex; tel. 3-28-38-48-58; f. 1885; civil engineering, chemistry and electrical engineering; 1,676 students; Dir J. M. IDOUX.

Ecole de Sages-Femmes (ESF): Campus Saint Raphaël, 59000 Lille; tel. 3-20-13-47-36; f. 1882; 109 students; Dir CHRISTIANE ROUX.

Ecole Supérieure de Traducteurs, Interprètes, et de Cadres du Commerce Extérieur (ESTICE): 83 blvd Vauban, BP 109, 59016 Lille Cedex; tel. 3-20-54-90-90; f. 1961; 113 students; Dir O. TRANCHANT.

Ecole Supérieure de Management et l'Entreprise (ESPEME): 23 rue Delphin Petit, 59046 Lille Cedex; tel. 3-20-15-45-00; f. 1988; 912 students; Dir A. F. MALVACHE.

Branch:

ESPEME Nice: 393 Promenade des Anglais, BP 116, 06202 Nice Cedex; tel. 4-93-18-99-66; 912 students; Dir BERNARD BOTTERO.

Ecole Supérieure Privée d'Application des Sciences (ESPAS): 83 blvd Vauban, 59800 Lille; tel. 3-20-57-58-71; f. 1988; 88 students; Dir O. TRANCHANT.

IFsanté (Ecole d'aides soignants IFAS + école de puéricultrices ECPUER + école de formation aux soins infirmiers IFSI): Campus Saint Raphaël, 59000 Lille; tel. 3-28-36-10-10; f. 1927; 499 students; Dir BERNADETTE MIROUX.

Institut Catholique d'Arts et Métiers (ICAM): 6 rue Auber, 59046 Lille Cedex; tel. 3-20-22-61-61; f. 1898; 850 students; Dir-Gen. G. CARPIER; Dir PH. CARPENTIER.

Institut de Communication Médicale: 83 blvd Vauban, 59000 Lille Cedex; tel. 3-20-57-58-71; f. 1988; 20 students; Dir MARC DENEUCHE.

Institut d'Economie Scientifique et de Gestion (IESEG): 3 rue de la Digue, 59800 Lille; tel. 3-20-54-58-92; f. 1964; 1,702 students; Dir J. P. AMMEUX.

Institut de Formation d'Animateurs de Catéchèse pour Adultes (IFAC): 60 blvd Vauban, 59016 Lille Cedex; tel. 3-20-57-69-33; f. 1980; 113 students; Dir J.M. BEAURENT.

Institut de Formation en Kinésithérapie, Pédicurie et Podologie: 10 rue J. B. de la Salle, 59000 Lille; tel. 3-20-92-06-99; f. 1964; 798 students; Dirs M. PAPAREMBORDE, D. VENNIN.

Institut de Formation Pedagogique (IFP): 236 rue du Fg de Roubaix, 59041 Lille Cedex; tel. 3-20-13-41-20; f. 1962; 584 students; Dir E. THEVENIN.

Institut des Stratégies et Techniques de Communication (ISTC): 83 blvd Vauban, 59800 Lille; tel. 3-20-54-32-32; f. 1991; 262 students; Dir CLAUDE DOGNIN.

Institut Social Lille (ISL): 83 blvd Vauban, BP 12, 59004 Lille Cedex; tel. 3-20-21-93-93; f. 1932; 527 students; Dir E. PRIEUR.

Institut Supérieur d'Agriculture (ISA): Blvd Vauban, , 59046 Lille Cedex; tel. 3-28-38-48-48; f. 1963; agricultural, agro-engineering; five-year course; 952 students; Dir P. CODRON.

Institut Supérieur d'Electronique du Nord (ISEN): 41 blvd Vauban, 59046 Lille Cedex; tel. 3-20-30-40-50; f. 1956; electronics engineering; 107 teachers; 614 students; Dir-Gen. PAUL ASTIER; Dir P. GIORGINI.

Institution Saint Jude: 18/22 rue Larmartine, 59820 Cambria; tel. 3-20-77-10-49; 82 students; Dir N. CARLIER.

Lycée privé commercial 'De la Salle': 2 rue Jean Le Vasseur, 59046 Lille Cedex; tel. 3-20-93-50-11; 267 students; Dir GUY MICHEL MAHIEU.

Lycée privé La Sagesse: 7 rue du temple, 59400 Cambria; tel. 3-27-82-28-28; 188 students; Dir B. DUMORTIER.

Lycée privé Notre-Dame de Grâce: Quai des Nerviens, BP 127, 59602 Maubeuge Cedex; tel. 3-27-53-00-66; 82 students; Dir JEAN-PIERRE LAMQUET.

Lycée privé Saint-Joseph: 26 route de Calais, 62200 Saint-Martin-lez-Boulogne; tel. 3-21-99-06-99; 274 students; Dir MICHEL DUFAY.

Lycée privé Saint Paul: 25bis rue Colbert, 59000 Lille Cedex; tel. 3-20-55-10-20; 168 students; Dir JEAN-CLAUDE PONTHIER.

Lycée Technologique OZANAM: 50 rue Saint Gabriel, 59000 Lille; tel. 3-20-21-96-50; 384 students; Dir R. PRIESTER.

UNIVERSITÉ CATHOLIQUE DE L'OUEST

3 place André Leroy, BP 808, 49008 Angers Cedex 01

Telephone: 2-41-81-67-55
Fax: 2-41-81-66-45
E-mail: relint@uco.fr
Internet: www.uco.fr

Founded 1875, under the patronage of the Bishops of the western region of France

Academic year: September to June

Rector: Dr ROBERT ROUDDEAU
Vice-Rectors: LUC PASQUIER PATRICK GILLET
Sec.-Gen.: BERNARD FLOURIOT
Librarian: Y. LE GALL

Library of 200,000 vols and periodicals
Number of students: 12,500

Publications: *Annuaire*, *Impacts* (4 a year)

DEANS

Applied Ecology Institute: P. GILLET
Applied Mathematics Institute: J. M. MARION
Basic and Applied Research Institute: J. P. BOUTINET
Education and Communication Institute: CATHERINE NAFTI-MALHERBE
Faculty of Theology: LOUIS MICHEL RENIER
Institute of Applied Psychology and Sociology: PATRICK MARTIN
International Centre for French Studies (for Foreign Students): MARC RELIN
Literature and History Institute: B. HAM
Modern Languages Institute: D. STAQUET
Teacher Training Institute: R. MARTIN

AFFILIATED SCHOOLS

Ecole Supérieure d'Electronique de l'Ouest: 4 rue Merlet de la Boulaye, 49000 Angers; f. 1956; Dir M. V. HAMON.

Ecole Supérieure des Sciences Commerciales d'Angers: 1 rue Lakanal, 49000 Angers; Dir M. POTE.

Ecole Technique Supérieure de Chimie de l'Ouest: 50 rue Michelet, 49000 Angers; Dir B. DAVID.

Institut de Formation et de Recherche pour les Acteurs du Développement et de l'Entreprise: 1 place A. Leroy, 49008 Angers Cedex 01; Dir FASICURE LEBLOND.

Institut Supérieur d'Action Internationale et de Production: 18 rue du 8 Mai 1945, 49124 St Barthélemy; Dir J. Y. BIGNONET.

Institut Supérieur des Métiers: 91 rue Haute Follio, 53000 Laval; Dir EMMANUEL ROUSSEAU.

Maison de L'Initiative: Campus de la Tour, d'Auvergne, 37 rue du Maréchal Foch, 22204 Guingamp Cedex; Dir C. NAFTI-MALHERBE.

Université Catholique de l'Ouest Bretagne Nord: Campus de la Tour, d'Auvergne, 37 rue du Maréchal Foch, 22204 Guingamp Cedex; Dir MICHEL DORVEAUX.

Université Catholique de l'Ouest Bretagne Sud: Le Vincin, BP 17, 56610 Arradon; Dir SYLVIE MURZEAU.

UNIVERSITÉ CATHOLIQUE DE LYON

25 rue du Plat, 69288 Lyons Cedex 02

Telephone: 4-72-32-50-12
Fax: 4-72-32-50-19
Internet: www.univ-catholyon.fr

Founded 1875
Rector: MICHEL QUESNEL
Vice-Rector: DENISE LE LOUP
Sec.-Gen.: PATRICK BORDET
Librarian: Mlle BEHR

Library of 240,000 vols
Number of teachers: 300
Number of students: 7,422

Publications: *Bulletin*, *Cahiers*

DEANS

Faculty of Law: PASCALE BOUCAUD
Faculty of Letters: HENRI BRENDERS
Faculty of Philosophy: PIERRE GIRE
Faculty of Science: J. M. EXBRAYAT
Faculty of Theology: JEAN-PIERRE LEMONON

Independent Institutes
GENERAL

American University of Paris: 31 ave Bosquet, 75007 Paris; tel. 1-40-62-06-00; fax 1-47-05-34-32; e-mail admissions@aup.edu; internet www.aup.edu; f. 1962; language of instruction: English; mem. of Middle States Asscn of Colleges and Schools; 4-year arts and sciences undergraduate courses; two summer sessions; adult education programmes; large computer science laboratory; technical writing programme; library: over 100,000 vols; 100 teachers; 800 students; Pres. Dr MICHAEL K. SIMPSON.

Groupe IPAC:; e-mail info@ipac-france.com; internet www.ipac-france.com; private control; accredited by the state for studies up to Masters level; courses in management, consulting, design, health, social and environmental studies, business; attached institute IFALPES offers French as a foreign language for adults; Pres. JEAN-MICHEL DELAPLAGNE.

Campuses:

IPAC Albertville: 542 rue Louis Armand Za du Chiriac, 73200 Albertville; tel. 4-79-37-14-01; fax 4-79-37-17-29; Dir JÉRÔME BAPTENDIER.

IPAC Annecy: 42 chemin de la Prairie, 74000 Annecy; tel. 4-50-45-13-91; fax 4-50-45-84-81; Dir PAUL TARDIVEL.

IPAC Chambéry: L'Axiome, 44 rue Charles Montreuil, 73000 Chambéry; tel. 4-79-69-65-91; fax 4-79-62-94-79; Dir ISABELLE DELIÈGE.

IPAC Geneva: 58 Rue du Grand pré, 1201 Geneva, Switzerland; tel. 22-340-42-00; fax 22-344-62-36.

IPAC Genvois–Léman: 15 rue Montréal, 74100 Ville la Grand; tel. 4-50-37-14-32; fax 4-50-87-22-93; Dir GÉRARD PONT.

IPAC Thonon: 5F ave du Général de Gaulle, Centre commercial de l'Etoile, 74200 Thonon les Bains; tel. 4-50-70-72-43; fax 4-50-70-68-78.

IPAC Vallée de l'Arve: Espace Scionzier, Bâtiment 3, 360 ave des Lacs, 74950 Scionzier; tel. 4-50-96-13-00; fax 4-50-96-14-50; Dir RÉGIS DUVAL.

Schiller International University—France: (For general information, see entry for Schiller International University in Germany chapter).

Campuses:

Schiller International University—Paris Campus: 32 blvd de Vaugirard, 75015 Paris; tel. 1-45-38-56-01; fax 1-45-38-54-30; e-mail info-schiller@schillerparis.com; internet www.paris-schiller.com; Dir SOUHA AKIKI.

Schiller International University—Strasbourg Campus: Château du Pourtalès, 161 rue Mélanie, 67000 Strasbourg; tel. 3-88-45-84-64; fax 3-88-45-84-60; e-mail blasiush@aol.com; internet www.schillerstrasbourg.com.

AGRICULTURE

Ecole Supérieure d'Agriculture de Purpan: 75 voie du Toec, 31076 Toulouse Cedex 3; tel. 5-61-15-30-30; fax 5-61-15-30-00; e-mail malummer@esa_purpan.fr; internet www.esa_purpan.fr; f. 1919; 5-year diploma course; Masters degrees in agriculture, management and technology in the food industry, agricultural economics and management, environment and regional devt; library: 20,000 vols, 1,100 periodicals; 100 teachers (37 full-time); 700 students; Dir MICHEL ROUX; publ. *Purpan* (4 a year).

Esitpa – Ecole d'Ingénieurs en Agriculture: 3 rue du Tronquet, BP 40118, 76134 Mont-Saint-Aignan Cedex; tel. 2-32-82-92-00; fax 2-35-05-27-40; e-mail webmaster@esitpa.org; internet www.esitpa.org; f. 1919; 5-year diploma courses for agricultural engineers; Dir P. DENIEUL.

Groupe ESA – Ecole Supérieure d'Agriculture d'Angers: 55 rue Rabelais, BP 30748, 49007 Angers Cedex 01; tel. 2-41-23-55-55; fax 2-41-23-55-00; e-mail webmaster@groupe-esa.com; internet www.groupe-esa.com; f. 1898; library: 45,000 vols, 520 periodicals; 600 students; Dir AYMARD HONORÉ; publs *Bibliographie Agricole et Rurale* (5 a year), *Cahiers Agriscope* (3 a year).

COMMERCE, BUSINESS ADMINISTRATION AND STATISTICS

Audencia Nantes Ecole de Management: 8 route de la Jonelière, BP 31222, 44312 Nantes Cedex 3; tel. 2-40-37-34-34; fax 2-40-37-34-07; internet www.audencia.com; f. 1900; library: 13,000 vols, 450 periodicals; 343 teachers (43 full-time, 300 part-time); 1,200 students; Pres. JEAN-FRANÇOIS MOULIN; Dir-Gen. and Dean AÏSSA DERMOUCHE.

Centre Européen d'Education Permanente (CEDEP) (European Centre for Executive Development): Blvd de Constance, 77305 Fontainebleau Cedex; f. 1971; management development courses in business administration for member companies (6 French, 2 Danish, 3 British, 1 Swedish, 2 Belgian, 1 Indian, 2 Dutch, 5 European); associated with the Institut Européen d'Administration des Affaires; Gen. Dir MITCHELL KOZA.

CERAM Business School: Rue Dostoïevski, BP 085, 06902 Sophia Antipolis Cedex; tel. 4-89-88-98-24; fax 4-93-65-45-24; e-mail info@ceram.fr; internet www.ceram.edu; f. 1978 by Nice Chamber of Commerce; library: 16,000 vols; 100 full-time; 120 part-time teachers; 750 students, plus 100 on Masters course; Dir MAXIME CRENER.

Ecole de Management de Normandie: 30 rue de Richelieu, 76087 Le Havre Cedex; tel. 2-32-92-59-99; e-mail info@ecole-management-normandie.fr; internet www.ecole-management-normandie.fr; f. 1871; campuses in Caen, Cherbourg and Deauville; courses in business administration, tourism and leisure management; library: 37,050 vols, 39 databases; 37 teachers; 1,302 students; Dir-Gen. JEAN GUY BERNARD.

Ecole du Chef d'Entreprise (ECE): 24–26 rue Hamelin, 75116 Paris; f. 1944; business administration; 50 teachers; Pres. M. Y. CHOTARD; Dir C. GOURDAIN; Sec.-Gen. Mlle M. JANNOR.

Ecole Nouvelle d'Organisation Economique et Sociale – Groupe ENOES: 62 rue de Miromesnil, 75008 Paris; internet www.enoes.com; f. 1937; courses in transport and logistics, business administration and accountancy; Pres. GILLES DE COURCEL; Gen. Sec. MICHEL OHAYON.

Ecole Supérieure de Commerce de Montpellier: 2300 ave des Moulins, 34185 Montpellier Cedex 4; tel. 4-67-10-25-00; fax 4-67-45-13-56; e-mail info@supco-montpellier.fr; internet www.supdeco-montpellier.com; f. 1897; 250 teachers; 1,750 students; three-year courses in business administration and management sciences; Dir Dr DIDIER JOURDAN.

Ecole Supérieure des Sciences Economiques et Commerciales (ESSEC Business School – Paris): Ave Bernard Hirsch, BP 50105, 95021 Cergy-Pontoise Cedex; tel. 1-34-43-30-00; fax 1-34-43-30-01; e-mail indigo@essec.fr; internet www.essec.com; f. 1907; 4-year, 3-year, 2-year and 1-year degree courses; Masters degree in business administration and management; MSc in marketing, finance, logistics, information and decision systems, international law and management, agribusiness management, international supply management, urban management, and strategy and management of international business; MBA programmes in hospitality, luxury-brand management; Exec. MBA and other executive education courses; doctoral and BBA programmes; library: 49,000 vols, 1,500 periodicals; 370 teachers (100 full-time, 270 part-time); 3,700 students; Pres. PIERRE TAPIE.

EDHEC Business School: 58 rue du Port, 59046 Lille Cedex; tel. 3-20-15-45-00; fax 3-20-15-45-01; internet www.edhec.com; f. 1906; MBA programmes; Dir-Gen. OLIVIER OGER.

EMLYON Business School: 23 ave Guy de Collongue, 69134 Ecully Cedex; tel. 4-78-33-78-00; fax 4-78-33-61-69; e-mail info@ em-lyon.com; internet www.em-lyon.com; f. 1872; library: 12,927 vols; 80 teachers; 1,250 students; Dir-Gen. PATRICK MOLLE.

ESC Bretagne Brest: 2 ave de Provence, CS23812, 29238 Brest Cedex 3; tel. 2-98-34-44-44; fax 2-98-34-44-69; e-mail info@ esc-bretagne-brest.com; internet www .esc-brest.fr; f. 1962; library: 5,000 vols, 150 periodicals; 110 teachers; 533 students; Dir C. MONIQUE.

ESC Pau – Groupe Ecole Supérieure de Commerce de Pau: 3 rue Saint John Perse, Campus Universitaire BP 7512, 64075 Pau Cedex; tel. 5-59-92-64-64; fax 5-59-92-64-55; e-mail info@esc-pau.fr; internet www.esc-pau .fr; f. 1970 by the Chamber of Commerce; library: 5,000 vols; 16 full-time; 120 part-time teachers; 500 students; Dir LAURENT HUA.

ESCP-EAP European School of Management: 79 ave de la République, 75543 Paris Cedex 11; tel. 1-49-23-20-00; fax 1-49-23-22-12; e-mail info@escp-eap.net; internet www .escp-eap.net; f. 1999 by merger of Groupe ESCP and Ecole Européenne des Affaires (EAP); 120 teachers in five countries; 3,000 students in five countries; campuses in Paris (France), London (UK), Berlin (Germany), Madrid (Spain) and Turin (Italy); postgraduate degree programmes, executive education; 5 research centres; Dean JEAN-LOUIS SCARINGELLA.

Groupe CPA – Centre de Perfectionnement aux Affaires: 14 ave de la Porte de Champerret, 75017 Paris; tel. 1-44-09-34-00; fax 1-44-09-34-99; f. 1930 by the Paris Chamber of Commerce and Industry; gen. management courses for top executives; establishing close links with Groupe HEC

(Hautes Etudes Commerciales); Dir JEAN-LOUIS SCARINGELLA.

Branches; see entry for HEC School of Management for details of branch institutions:

CPA Paris.

CPA Lyon.

CPA Nord.

CPA Grand Sud-Ouest.

CPA Méditerranée.

CPA Madrid.

ESC Bordeaux: 680 cours de la Libération, 33405 Talence Cedex; tel. 5-56-84-55-55; fax 5-56-84-55-00; e-mail info@bem.edu; internet www.bem.edu; f. 1874 by Chamber of Commerce; library: 17,000 vols; 74 teachers; 1,800 students; Dir GEORGES VIALA.

ESCEM – Groupe Ecole Supérieure de Commerce et de Management: 1 rue Léo Delibes, BP 0535, 37205 Tours Cedex 3; tel. 2-47-71-71-71; fax 2-47-71-72-10; e-mail com@escem.fr; internet www.escem.fr; f. 1961; graduate management degree programme, Masters and int. MBA degree programmes, continuing education and distance learning in management; courses in economics, marketing, finance, accountancy, management information systems, international business; Masters degrees in business admin. and information systems; 405 teachers (55 full-time, 350 part-time); 1,600 students; library: 13,000 vols; Dir GUY LE BOUCHER; publ. *Les Cahiers de Recherche de l'ESCEM* (2 a year).

Branch campus:

Groupe ESCEM Campus Poitiers: 11 rue de l'Ancienne Comédie, BP 5, 86001 Poitiers Cedex; tel. 5-49-60-58-00; fax 5-49-60-58-30; internet www.escem.fr.

ESIDEC – Ecole Supérieure Internationale de Commerce de Metz: 3 place Edouard Branly, BP 95090, 57073 Metz Cedex 3; tel. 3-87-56-37-37; fax 3-87-56-37-99; e-mail gregory.marongio@icn-groupe.fr; internet www.esidec.fr; f. 1988; run by the Moselle Chamber of Commerce and Industry; courses in management, logistics, marketing, finance, law, trade, purchasing; 40 teachers; 210 students; Dir THIERRY JEAN.

Groupe ESC Lille – Ecole Supérieure de Commerce de Lille: Ave Willy Brandt, 59777 Euralille; tel. 3-20-21-59-62; fax 3-20-21-59-59; internet www.esc-lille.fr; f. 1892; library: 3,700 vols, 270 periodicals; 1,000 students; Dir JEAN-PIERRE DEBOURSE.

Groupe EAC – Ecole Supérieure d'Economie, d'Art et de Communication: 33 rue de La Boétie, 75008 Paris; tel. 1-47-70-23-83; fax 1-47-70-17-83; e-mail paris@groupeeac .com; internet www.groupeeac.com; f. 1987; library: 500 vols; 70 teachers; 350 students; Dir CLAUDE VIVIER.

HEC School of Management: 78351 Jouy-en-Josas Cedex; tel. 1-39-67-70-00; fax 1-39-67-74-40; e-mail hecinfo@hec.fr; internet www.hec.edu; f. 1881; sponsored by the Paris Chamber of Commerce and Industry; incorporates CPA (Centre de Perfectionnement aux Affaires) degree courses in fields of management; executive development programmes; library: 60,000 vols; 589 teachers (104 full-time, 450 part-time, 35 visiting); 2,500 students; Dean BERNARD RAMANANTSOA; Dir of CPA JEAN-MARC DE LEERSNYDER.

CPA Sites:

CPA Grand Sud-Ouest: 20 blvd Lascrosses, 31000 Toulouse; tel. 5-61-29-49-91; fax 5-61-13-98-31; Dir ALAIN MAINGUY.

CPA Lyon: 93 chemin des Mouilles, 69130 Ecully Cedex; tel. 4-78-33-52-12; fax 4-78-33-37-06; Dir CHARLES AB-DER-HALDEN.

CPA Madrid: Calle Serrano 208, 28012 Madrid, Spain; tel. 91-538-37-59; fax 91-538-37-58; Dir TEODORO AGUADO DE LOS RÍOS.

CPA Méditerranée: c/o CERAM II, 60 rue Dostoïevski, 06902 Sophia Antipolis; tel. 4-92-96-96-95; fax 4-93-95-44-21; Dir ADRIEN CORBIÈRE-MÉDECIN.

CPA Nord: 551 rue Albert Bailly, 59700 Marcq-en-Baroeul; tel. 3-20-25-97-53; fax 3-20-27-12-94; Dir JEAN-CLAUDE VACHER.

CPA Paris: 14 ave de la Porte de Champerret, 75017 Paris; tel. 1-44-09-34-00; fax 1-44-09-34-99.

INSEAD: Blvd de Constance, 77305 Fontainebleau; tel. 1-60-72-40-00; fax 1-60-74-55-00; internet www.insead.fr; f. 1958; postgraduate MBA programme; PhD programme; executive development programmes; 100 professors; library: 40,000 vols; Chair. Board of Govs CLAUDE JANSSEN; Dean Prof. GABRIEL HAWAWINI.

Reims Management School: 59 rue Pierre-Taittinger, 51100 Reims Cedex; tel. 3-26-77-47-47; fax 3-26-04-69-63; e-mail service.com@ reims-ms.fr; internet www.reims-ms.fr; f. 1928; schools and subject areas: Sup de Co (new economy), Cesem (International School of Management), Tema (management school with emphasis on technology), Sup TG (sales and administration), MBA (part- and full-time); 62 full-time teachers; 2,600 students; Dir DOMINIQUE WAQUET.

LAW AND POLITICAL SCIENCE

American Graduate School of International Relations and Diplomacy: 6 rue de Lubeck, 75116 Paris; tel. 1-47-20-00-94; fax 1-47-20-81-89; e-mail info@agsird .edu; internet www.agsird.fu; f. 1994; MA and PhD programmes; 11 teachers; 90 students (50 full-time, 40 part-time); Dir Dr MARCIA A. GRANT.

Ecole des Hautes Etudes Internationales: 107 rue de Tolbiac, 75013 Paris; tel. 1-45-70-73-37; fax 1-45-70-99-33; e-mail contact@hep-hei-esj.net; internet www .hep-hei-esj.net; f. 1904; Pres. M. SCHUMANN; Dir P. CHAIGNEAU.

Ecole de Notariat d'Amiens: 44 square des 4 Chênes, 80000 Amiens; tel. 3-22-92-61-26; fax 3-22-92-90-84; e-mail ecolenotariat-amiens@wanadoo.fr; internet www.cr-picardie.notaires.fr/front/actualites/ ecolenotariat.asp; f. 1942; Dir ALAIN DORÉ.

Ecole de Notariat de Paris: 9 rue Villaret-de-Joyeuse, 75017 Paris; tel. 1-43-80-87-62; fax 1-46-22-01-46; f. 1896; Dir M. P. MATHIEU.

Ecole Supérieure de Journalisme: 107 rue Tolbiac, 75013 Paris; tel. 1-45-70-73-37; fax 1-45-70-99-33; e-mail contact@hep-hei-esj .net; internet www.hep-hei-esj.net; f. 1899; Pres. M. CAZENEUVE; Dir P. CHAIGNEAU.

Institut International des Droits de l'Homme (International Institute of Human Rights): 2 Allée René Cassin, 67000 Strasbourg; tel. 3-88-45-84-45; fax 3-88-45-84-50; e-mail administration@iidh.org; internet www.iidh.org; f. 1969 by René Cassin; postgraduate teaching in international and comparative law of human rights; annual study session during July; annual two-week course in June on refugee law, organized in collaboration with the United Nations High Commissioner for Refugees (in French); 50 teachers; 350 students; Pres. GÉRARD COHEN-JONATHAN; Sec.-Gen. JEAN-FRANÇOIS FLAUSS.

Attached Centre:

International Centre for University Human Rights Teaching: Strasbourg; f. 1973 at the request of UNESCO; two-week courses for university teachers; 2 teachers; 40 students; Sec.-Gen. Prof. JEAN-FRANÇOIS FLAUSS.

MEDICINE

Ecole Dentaire Française: 1 bis 3 rue de l'Est, 75020 Paris; tel. 1-47-97-77-81; fax 1-47-97-46-64; e-mail edf@lesmetiersdelasante .com; internet www.ecole-dentaire.fr; f. 1886; Dir R. J. CACHIA.

Institut et Centre d'Optométrie: 134 route de Chartres, 91440 Bures-sur-Yvette; tel. 1-64-86-12-13; fax 1-69-28-49-99; e-mail ico.direction@wanadoo.fr; internet www .ecole-optometrie.fr; f. 1917; 40 teachers; 350 students; Dir JEAN-PAUL ROOSEN.

RELIGION

Faculté Libre de Théologie Protestante de Paris: 83 blvd Arago, 75014 Paris; tel. 1-43-31-61-64; fax 1-43-31-62-67; e-mail secretariat@iptheologie.fr; internet www .iptheologie.fr; f. 1877; religious history, Old and New Testament, ecclesiastical history, systematic theology, philosophy, practical theology, Hebrew, Greek, German, English; library: 60,000 vols; 12 professors, 180 students; Dean JACQUES-NOËL PÉRÈS.

Institut de Théologie Orthodoxe Saint-Serge: 93 rue de Crimée, 75019 Paris; tel. 1-42-01-96-10; fax 1-42-08-00-09; e-mail ito@ saint-serge.net; internet www.saint-serge .net; f. 1925; 15 professors and 50 students; library: 30,000 vols; Dean Rev. Fr BORIS BOBRINSKOY; publ. *Pensée Orthodoxe* (every 2 years).

Institut Européen des Sciences Humaines: Centre de Bouteloin, 58120 Saint-Léger-de-Fougeret; tel. 3-86-79-40-62; fax 3-86-85-01-19; internet www.iesh.org; f. 1990; Muslim theology; library: 5,000 vols; 8 teachers; capacity for 200 students; Dir ZUHAIR MAHMOOD.

Institut Orthodoxe Français de Paris Saint-Denys: 96 blvd Auguste-Blanqui, 75013 Paris; tel. 6-89-32-25-38; e-mail institut.saintdenys@club-internet.fr; internet institutdetheologie.free.fr; f. 1944; 20 professors and 125 students; library: 5,000 vols; faculties of theology and philosophy; Rector BERTRAND-HARDY (Bishop Germain of Saint Denis); publ. *Présence Orthodoxe*.

Séminaire Israélite de France (Ecole Rabbinique): 9 rue Vauquelin, 75005 Paris; tel. 1-47-07-21-22; fax 1-43-37-75-92; f. 1829; Talmud, Bible, Jewish history and philosophy, Hebrew language and literature studies, rabbinical law; 6 teachers; 15 students; library: 60,000 vols; Dir Chief Rabbi MICHEL GUGENHEIM.

SCIENCES

Ecole d'Anthropologie: 1 place d'Iéna, 75116 Paris; tel. 1-47-93-09-73; fax 1-47-93-09-73; e-mail institutanthropologie@hotmail .fr; internet www.multimania.com/anthropa; f. 1876 by Prof. Broca; prehistory, physical anthropology, ethnology, biology, genetics, immunology, ethnography, demography, third-world problems, psychology, criminology, anthropotechnics, biometeorology; Dir Prof. BERNARD J. HUET; publ. *Nouvelle revue anthropologique* (irregular).

Institut de Paléontologie Humaine: 1 rue René Panhard, 75013 Paris; tel. 1-43-31-62-91; fax 1-43-31-22-79; e-mail iph@mnhn.fr; f. 1910 by Prince Albert I of Monaco; vertebrate palaeontology, palynology, palaeo-anthropology, prehistory, quaternary geology, sedimentology, geochronology; library: 25,000 vols; 107 students; Dir HENRY DE LUMLEY; publs *Archives*, *L'Anthropologie*, *Etudes Quaternaires*.

Institut Edouard Toulouse: 1 rue Cabanis, 75014 Paris; tel. 1-45-65-81-36; f. 1983; teaching, training and research in psychiatry, seminars on psychoanalysis; Pres. Dr JEAN AYME; Sec. Dr MARCEL CZERMAK; publ. *Cahiers de l'Hôpital Henri Rousselle*.

Institut Océanographique: 195 rue Saint Jacques, 75005 Paris; tel. 1-44-32-10-70; fax 1-40-51-73-16; e-mail institut@oceano.org; internet www.oceano.org; education, scientific research, museology, publishing; f. 1906 by Prince Albert I of Monaco; library: 30,000 vols; Pres. JEAN CHAPON; Dir LUCIEN LAUBIEN; Sec. C. BEAUVERGER; publ. *Oceanis* (4 a year).

Attached Museum:

Musée Océanographique: see under Monaco.

SOCIAL AND ECONOMIC SCIENCES

Collège Libre des Sciences Sociales et Economiques: 184 blvd Saint-Germain, 75006 Paris; f. 1895; composed of six sections: social, economic, international and public relations; evening and correspondence courses; diplomas conferred after two or three years' study, and submission of theses on some aspect of applied economics; Pres. J. RUEFF; Dir L. DE SAINTE-LORETTE.

Ecole de Hautes Etudes Sociales: 107 rue Tolbiac, 75013 Paris; tel. 1-45-70-73-37; fax 1-45-70-99-33; e-mail contact@hep-hei-esj .net; internet www.hep-hei-esj.net; f. 1899; Pres. M. SCHUMANN; Dir P. CHAIGNEAU.

Faculté des Lettres et Sciences Sociales: BP 800, 29200 Brest; tel. 2-98-80-19-87; f. 1960; library: 18,000 vols; 105 teachers; 2,752 students; President and Dean Prof. MICHEL QUESNEL.

IFG-CNOF: 37 quai de Grenelle, 75015 Paris; tel. 1-40-59-30-30; internet www .ifgcnof.com; f. 1926; provides executive, managerial and administrative training.

Institut Européen des Hautes Etudes Internationales (IEHEI): 10 ave des Fleurs, 06000 Nice; tel. 4-93-97-93-70; fax 4-93-97-93-71; e-mail iehei@wanadoo.fr; internet www.iehei.org; f. 1964; library: 4,000 vols; 20 teachers; 35 students; Pres. VLAD CONSTANTINESCO; Dir CLAUDE NIGOUL.

TECHNOLOGY

Ecole Catholique d'Arts et Métiers (ECAM): 40 montée Saint-Barthélemy, 69321 Lyons Cedex 05; tel. 4-72-77-06-00; fax 4-72-77-06-11; e-mail info@ecam.fr; internet www.ecam.fr; f. 1900; courses in mechanical engineering, materials science, electrical and electronic engineering, automation, information technology, production engineering; library: 5,000 vols; 525 students; Dir BERNARD PINATEL; publ. *Bulletin* (4 a year).

Ecole de Thermique: 3 rue Henri Heine, 75016 Paris; tel. 1-44-30-41-00; fax 1-40-50-07-54; teaching centre for the Institut Français de l'Energie (IFE); Dir (vacant).

Ecole Généraliste d'Ingénieurs de Marseille (EGIM): Technopôle de Château-Gombert, 38 rue Joliot Curie, 13451 Marseilles Cedex 20; tel. and fax 4-91-05-45-45; e-mail sdei@egim-mrs.fr; internet www .egim-mrs.fr; f. 1891; specialist courses in information and communications technology, mechatronics, systems engineering, marine engineering, thermal systems engineering, mechanical and materials engineering, microelectronics design, civil engineering; 70 teachers; 778 students; Dir JEAN-PAUL FABRE.

Ecole Spéciale des Travaux Publics, du Bâtiment et de l'Industrie: 57 blvd Saint-Germain, 75005 Paris; tel. 1-44-41-11-18; fax 1-44-41-11-12; e-mail information@adm.estp .fr; internet www.estp.fr; f. 1891; civil engineering training programmes at undergraduate and graduate levels; continuing education courses; 700 teachers; 2,000 students; library: 10,000 vols; Dir S. EYROLLES.

Ecole Supérieure d'Optique et Institut d'Optique: Centre Scientifique d'Orsay, Bât. 503, 91403 Orsay Cedex; tel. 1-69-35-88-88; fax 1-69-35-87-00; e-mail international@iota .u-psud.fr; internet www.institutoptique.fr; attached to Univ. Paris XI; f. 1920; optical engineering, optics and photonics at postgraduate level; 60 teachers (20 full-time, 40 assoc.); 240 students; Dir Prof. ANDRÉ DUCASSE.

Ecole Supérieure de Fonderie et de Forge: 44 ave de la division Leclerc, 92310 Sèvres; tel. 1-55-64-04-40; fax 1-55-64-04-45; e-mail contact@esff.fr; internet www.esff.fr; f. 1923; library: 2,150 vols; Dir G. CHAPPUIS.

Ecole Supérieure des Industries du Vêtement: 73 blvd Saint-Marcel, 75013 Paris; tel. 1-40-79-92-60; fax 1-40-79-92-91; e-mail info@esiv.fr; internet www.esiv.fr; f. 1946; 14 teachers; 70 students; Dir ANNE STEFANINI.

Ecole Supérieure des Industries Textiles d'Epinal: 85 rue d'Alsace, 88025 Epinal Cedex; tel. 3-29-35-50-52; fax 3-29-35-39-21; e-mail esite@wanadoo.fr; f. 1905; training of industrial textile engineers; library: 1,500 vols; Dir J. TIERCET.

Ecole Supérieure des Techniques Aéronautiques et de Construction Automobile: 34 rue Victor Hugo, 92300 Levallois-Perret; tel. 1-41-27-37-00; fax 1-47-37-50-83; e-mail infos@estaca.fr; internet www.estaca .fr; f. 1925; private school offering 5-year courses in aeronautical, automotive, railway and space engineering; Masters course in safety of transportation systems (taught in English); EUROMIND, European Masters in design and technology of advanced vehicle systems (taught in English); 1,000 students; Dir ERIC PARLEBAS.

Ecole Supérieure du Bois: rue Christian Pauc, BP 10605, 44306 Nantes Cedex 3; tel. 2-40-18-12-12; fax 2-40-18-12-00; e-mail contact@ecolesuperieuredubois.com; internet www.ecolesuperieuredubois.com; f. 1934; training of engineers and management for wood industry; 13 full-time, 20 external; 250 students; Dir X. MARTIN.

Ecole Supérieure du Soudage et de ses Applications (Advanced Postgraduate Welding Engineering School): BP 50362, 95942 Roissy CDG Cedex; tel. 1-49-90-36-27; fax 1-49-90-36-50; e-mail m.d.jols@ institutdesoudure.com; internet www .institutdesoudure.com; f. 1930; 55 teachers; 30 students; Dir MICHEL DIJOLS.

Ecole Technique Supérieure du Laboratoire: 95 rue du Dessous-des-Berges, 75013 Paris; tel. 1-45-83-76-34; fax 1-45-83-58-85; e-mail mail@etsl.fr; internet www.etsl.fr; f. 1934; Pres. J. CHOMIENNE; Dir. F. LAISSUS.

EFREI – Ecole Française d'Electronique et d'Informatique: 30–32 ave de la République, 94815 Villejuif; tel. 1-46-77-64-67; fax 1-46-77-65-77; e-mail admission@efrei.fr; internet www.efrei.fr; f. 1936; courses in telecommunications, electronic engineering and computer science; 50 teachers; 1,170 students; Dir ERIC PARLEBAS.

ESIEE Paris: Cité Descartes, BP 99, 93162 Noisy-le-Grand Cedex; tel. 1-45-92-65-00; fax 1-45-92-66-99; e-mail admissions@esiee.fr; internet www.esiee.fr; f. 1962; computer science, automation, telecommunications, signal processing, microelectronics; 100 teachers; 1,000 students; library: 18,000 vols; Dir ALAIN CADIX.

ESME Sudria: 38 rue Molière, 94200 Ivry-sur-Seine; 51 blvd de Brandenbourg, 94200 Ivry-sur-Seine; tel. 1-56-20-62-00; fax 1-56-20-62-62; e-mail contact@esme.fr; internet www.esme.fr; f. 1905; training in electrical engineering, electronics, telecommunications and computer engineering; Dir-Gen. HERVÉ LABORNE.

EPF – Ecole d'Ingénieurs: 3 bis rue Lakanal, 92330 Sceaux; tel. 1-41-13-01-51; fax 1-46-60-39-94; internet www.epf.fr; f. 1925; engineering training; Pres. Dr ALAIN JENEVEAU.

European Institute of Technology: 8 rue Saint Florentin, 75001 Paris; tel. 1-40-15-05-69; fax 1-49-27-98-11; f. 1988 to strengthen industrial research and development, and to increase the contribution of technological innovation to economic growth in Europe; Sec.-Gen. JOHN M. MARCUM.

IFOCA – Institut National de Formation et d'Enseignement Professionnel du Caoutchouc: 60 rue Auber, 94408 Vitry-sur-Seine Cedex; tel. 1-49-60-57-57; fax 1-49-60-70-66; e-mail info@ifoca.com; internet www.ifoca.com; f. 1941; 8 teachers; 35 students; Dir GÉRARD GALLAS.

Institut Français Textile–Habillement: Ave Guy de Collongue, 69134 Ecully Cedex; tel. 4-72-86-16-00; fax 4-72-86-16-50; e-mail information@ifth.org; internet www.ifth.org; f. 1946; library: 255 vols and documents; Dir M. BEDEAU.

Institut Textile et Chimique de Lyon (ITECH): 87 chemin des Mouilles, 69134 Ecully Cedex; tel. 4-72-18-04-80; fax 4-72-18-95-45; e-mail info@itech.fr; internet www.itech.fr; f. 1899; diploma courses in leather technology, painting and adhesives technology; plastics, textiles; 120 teachers; 360 students; Dir JEAN-PIERRE GALLET; Dean CHRISTIANE BASSET.

International Space University: Parc d'Innovation, 1 rue Jean Dominique Cassini, 67400 Illkirch-Graffenstaden; tel. 3-88-65-54-30; fax 3-88-65-54-47; e-mail info@isu.isunet.edu; internet www.isunet.edu; f. 1987; offers Master of Space Studies and Master of Space Management degree pro-

grammes, introductory space course and a summer session programme; 6 full-time, 6 part-time and 100 visiting teachers; 150 students; Pres. Dr MICHAEL SIMPSON.

Supélec – Ecole Supérieure d'Electricité: Plateau du Moulon, 3 rue Joliot-Curie, 91192 Gif-sur-Yvette Cedex; tel. 1-69-85-12-12; fax 1-69-85-12-34; internet www.supelec.fr; campuses at Gif, Metz and Rennes; f. 1894; two- or three-year courses in electrical engineering, radio engineering, information science, electronics and computer science; 120 permanent teachers; 1,200 students; attached to Univ. Paris XI; Dir-Gen. J. J. DUBY; Dir of Studies F. MESA; Gen.-Sec. A. POTONNIER.

SUPINFO – Ecole Supérieure d'Informatique: 23 rue du Château Landon, 75010 Paris; tel. 1-53-35-97-00; e-mail paris@supinfo.com; internet www.supinfo.com; f. 1965; 90 teachers; 1,000 students; Dir LEO ROZENTALIS; publ. *Dossiers de l'Association pour la Promotion de l'Ecole Supérieure d'Informatique.*

Schools of Art and Music

Conservatoire National de Région de Musique et de Danse de Lyon: 4 montée Cardinal Decourtray, 69321 Lyons; tel. 4-78-25-91-39; fax 4-78-15-09-60; e-mail communication@conservatoire-lyon.fr; internet www.conservatoire-lyon.fr; f. 1872; 190 teachers; 2,900 students; library: 2,600 vols, 40,000 scores, 4,500 records, 2,000 orchestral scores; Dir ALAIN JACQUON.

Conservatoire à Rayonnement Régional de Boulogne-Billancourt—Centre Georges-Gorse: 22 rue de la Belle-Feuille, 92100 Boulogne-Billancourt; tel. 1-55-18-45-85; fax 1-55-18-45-86; internet www.bb-cnr.com; f. 1959 as Conservatoire de Boulogne-Billancourt; achieved national school status as Conservatoire National de Région de Musique et de Danse de Boulogne-Billancourt in 1979; present name and status 2007; library: 7,000 books, 40 periodicals, 20,000 scores, 6,000 records, 600 audiovisual and multimedia items; 90 teachers; 1,650 students; Dir ALAIN LOUVIER.

Conservatoire National Supérieur d'Art Dramatique: 2 bis rue du Conservatoire, 75009 Paris; tel. 1-42-46-12-91; fax 1-48-00-94-02; e-mail communication@cnsad.fr; internet www.cnsad.fr; f. 1786; 55 teachers; 100 students; library: 23,500 vols; Dir DANIEL MESGUICH.

Conservatoire National Supérieur de Musique et de Danse de Paris: 209 ave

Jean Jaurès, 75019 Paris; tel. 1-40-40-45-45; fax 1-40-40-45-00; e-mail cnsmdp@cnsmdp.fr; internet www.cnsmdp.fr; f. 1795; 386 teachers; 1,413 students; Dir ALAIN POIRIER.

Conservatoire National Supérieur Musique et Danse de Lyon: 3 quai Chauveau, CP 120, 69266 Lyons Cedex 09; tel. 4-72-19-26-26; fax 4-72-19-26-00; e-mail cnsmd@cnsmd-lyon.fr; internet www.cnsmd-lyon.fr; f. 1980; library: 42,000 vols; 170 teachers; 550 students; Dir HENRY FOURÈS.

Ecole supérieure des beaux-arts de Marseille: 184 ave de Luminy, 13288 Marseilles Cedex 9; tel. 4-91-82-83-10; fax 4-91-82-83-11; e-mail fballongue@mairie-marseille.fr; internet www.esbam.fr; f. 1710; 420 students; library: 15,000 vols; Dir NORBERT DUFFORT; publs *Verba Volant* (2 a year), *Recherche et Création Artistiques* (monographs, 5 a year).

Ecole du Louvre: Palais du Louvre, Porte Jaujard, Place du Carrousel, 75038 Paris Cedex 01; tel. 1-55-35-18-00; fax 1-42-60-40-36; internet www.ecoledulouvre.fr; f. 1882; library: 40,000 vols; 1,700 students; Principal PH. DUREY; Sec.-Gen. M. C. DEVEVEY.

Ecole Nationale Supérieure des Arts Décoratifs (ENSAD): 31 rue d'Ulm, 75240 Paris Cedex 05; tel. 1-42-34-97-00; fax 1-42-34-97-85; e-mail info@ensad.fr; internet www.ensad.fr; f. 1766; visual arts and design; library: 15,000 vols and spec. colln; 164 teachers; 600 students; Dirs ELIZABETH FLEURY PATRICK RAYNAUD; publs *Catalogue des Projets de Fin d'Etudes* (2 a year), *Journal des Arts-Déco* (3 a year).

Ecole Nationale Supérieure des Beaux-Arts: 14 rue Bonaparte, 75272 Paris Cedex 06; tel. 1-47-03-50-00; fax 1-47-03-50-80; f. 1648 as Académie Royale de Peinture et de Sculpture, and in 1671 as Académie Royale d'Architecture; library: 120,000 vols; 75 teachers; 650 students; Dir (vacant); publs *Beaux-Arts Histoire, Ecrits d'Artistes, Espaces de l'art.*

Ecole Supérieure d'Art Clermont Communauté: 142 ave Jean Mermoz, 63100 Clermont-Ferrand; tel. 4-73-91-43-86; fax 4-73-90-27-80; e-mail erba@ville-clermont-ferrand.fr; internet www.ecoledart.ville-clermont-ferrand.fr; f. 1882; library: 7,000 vols and spec. colln; 17 teachers; 130 students; Dir SYLVAIN LIZON.

Schola Cantorum: 269 rue St Jacques, 75005 Paris; tel. 1-43-54-15-39; fax 1-43-29-78-70; e-mail info@schola-cantorum.com; internet www.schola-cantorum.com; f. 1896 by Vincent d'Indy; music, dance and dramatic art; Dir MICHEL DENIS.

FRENCH GUIANA

Regulatory Bodies
GOVERNMENT

Commission for Culture, Sport, Associations, Urban Policy and Environment: 66 ave du Général de Gaulle, 97300 Cayenne; tel. 5-94-25-66-84; fax 5-94-37-94-24; e-mail ccee@cr-guyane.fr; internet www.cr-guyane

.fr; Pres. MYRIAM KEREL; Vice-Pres. ODILE PRINCE-TONY.

Commission for Higher Education, Research, Science and Technology of Information and Communication: 66 ave du Général de Gaulle, 97300 Cayenne; tel. 5-94-25-66-84; fax 5-94-37-94-24; e-mail ccee@cr-guyane.fr; internet www.cr-guyane

.fr; Pres. JOSEPHINE EGALGI; Vice-Pres. LYDIA CARISTAN.

Research Institutes
GENERAL

Institut de Recherche pour le Dévelop-

pement: 0,275 km route de Montabo, BP 165, 97323 Cayenne Cedex; tel. 5-94-29-92-92; fax 5-94-31-98-55; e-mail guyane@ird.fr; internet www.cayenne.ird.fr; f. 1949; teledetection, pedology, hydrology, sedimentology, botany and vegetal biology, medical and agricultural entomology, ornithology, phytopharmacology, oceanography, sociology; library of 7,000 vols; Rep. JEAN-MARIE FOTSING; publ. *L'Homme et la Nature en Guyane*; (see main entry under France).

ECONOMICS, LAW AND POLITICS

Institut d'Etudes Judiciaires (Institute of Judicial Studies): Cayenne; tel. 5-96-72-73-80; fax 5-96-72-73-73; internet www.univ-ag.fr/fr/institution/instituts/iej.html; attached to Univ. des Antilles et de la Guyane; offers programmes for training of legal professionals; organizes seminars, conferences and courses.

EDUCATION

Institut d'Enseignement Supérieur de la Guyane (Institute of Higher Education of Guyana): Campus Saint-Denis, ave d'Estrés; tel. 5-94-29-62-00; fax 5-94-29-62-10; internet www.univ-ag.fr/fr/institution/instituts/iesg.html; f. 1991; attached to Univ. des Antilles et de la Guyane; depts of arts, languages and humanities, legal science and economics, science, technology and health; 1,500 students.

Institut de Recherche sur l'Enseignement en Mathématiques (Institute for Research in Mathematics Education): Cayenne; tel. 5-90-48-30-43; e-mail irem.antilles-guyana@univ-ag.fr; internet www.univ-ag.fr/fr/institution/instituts/irem.html; research in mathematics education; training; Dir ALEX MERIL.

MEDICINE

Institut Pasteur de la Guyane: 23 ave Pasteur, BP 6010, 97306 Cayenne Cedex; tel. 5-94-29-26-00; fax 5-94-30-94-16; e-mail reseau@pasteur.fr; internet www .pasteur-cayenne.fr; f. 1940, fmrly Institute of Hygiene and Prophylaxis; medical and biological research; Dir Dr ANDRÉ SPIEGEL.

TECHNOLOGY

Institut Universitaire de Technologie (University Institute of Technology): ave Bois Chaudat, BP 725, Cayenne; tel. 5-94-32-80-00; fax 5-94-32-22-63; internet www .univ-ag.fr/fr/institution/instituts/iut.html; f. 1986, opened 1988; attached to Univ. des Antilles et de la Guyane; depts of biological engineering, business management and administration, electrical engineering and computer industrial, health safety and environment, logistics and transport management, marketing techniques, networking and telecommunications; 200 students.

Libraries and Archives
Cayenne

Archives Départementales: Pl. Léopold Héder, BP 5021, 97397 Cayenne Cedex; tel. 5-94-29-52-70; fax 5-94-29-52-89; internet www.cg973.fr/archives-departementales; f. 1796, present status 1983; history of French Guiana; classification; storage; research; Dir FRANÇOISE LEMAIRE-THABOUILLOT.

Bibliothèque Alexandre Franconie: 1 ave du Général de Gaulle, 97300 Cayenne; tel. 5-94-29-59-16; fax 5-94-29-59-12; e-mail bibliotheque.franconie@cg973.fr; internet biblioweb.cg973.fr; f. 1885; attached to Bibliothèques du Conseil Général de la Guyane (Library of the Gen. Council of Guiana); gen. lending library; 35,000 vols; Dir MARIE-ANNICK ATTICOT.

Service Commun de la Documentation (Bibliothèques de la Guyane): Campus St-Denis, BP 1179, 97346 Cayenne Cedex; tel. 5-94-29-40-46; fax 5-94-29-40-17; e-mail nicole.clementmartin@guyane.univ-ag.fr; internet www.univ-ag.fr/fr/documentation .html; f. 1984; attached to Université des Antilles et de la Guyane; 36,000 vols, 240 periodicals; Dir of French Guiana Branch NICOLE CLÉMENT-MARTIN.

Museums
Cayenne

Musée Départemental: 1 ave du Général de Gaulle, 97300 Cayenne; tel. 5-94-29-59-13; fax 5-94-29-59-11; e-mail musee@cg973.fr; internet www.cg973.fr/-musee-franconie; f. 1901; flora and fauna of Guiana; historical documents; Dir JEAN-PASCAL STERVINOU.

Museum of Guianese Cultures: 78 rue Mme Payé, 97300 Cayenne; tel. 5-94-31-41-72; fax 5-94-35-48-45; e-mail mcg87@ wanadoo.fr; exhibitions and documentation centre on social history and culture of French Guiana; housed in a typical Guianese house built over 100 years ago; incl. an indoor garden with aromatic and medicinal plants.

University
UNIVERSITÉ DES ANTILLES ET DE LA GUYANE

Campus de Saint-Denis, BP 1179, 97346 Cayenne Cedex

Telephone: 5-94-29-40-16
Fax: 5-94-29-40-17
E-mail: charge.communication@guyane .univ-ag.fr
Internet: www.univ-ag.fr
Founded 1880, present status 1982
State control
(See also under Guadeloupe and Martinique)
Pres.: PASCAL SAFFACHE
Vice-Pres. (French Guiana): ANTOINE PRIMEROSE
Library: see Libraries and Archives
Number of students: 1,692

FRENCH POLYNESIA

Regulatory Bodies
GOVERNMENT

Ministry of Culture and Handicrafts: tel. 47-22-80; fax 47-22-90; e-mail ambroise .colombani@presidence.pf; internet www .culture.gov.pf; Min. MITA TERIIPAIA.

Ministry of Education, Higher Education and Research: Pirae, Près Ecole Tuterai Tane; tel. 54-49-00; fax 54-49-10; Min. MOANA GREIG.

Learned Societies
GENERAL

Te Fare Tauhiti Nui–Maison de la Culture: 646 Blvd Pomaré, BP 1709, 98713 Papeete; tel. 54-45-44; fax 42-85-69; e-mail secretariat@maisondelaculture.pf; internet www.maisondelaculture.pf; f. 1971 as Maison des Jeunes–Maison de la Culture, change in admin. 1980, present name and status 1998; promotes culture locally and abroad; sponsors many public and private cultural events; library of 13,000 vols, children's library of 7,000 vols; Dir HEREMOANA MAAMAATUAIATAPU (acting); Sec. CHRISTIANE BROTHERSON BALDERANIS.

NATURAL SCIENCES
General

Société des Etudes Océaniennes: BP 110, 98713 Papeete Tahiti; tel. 41-96-03; fax 41-96-04; e-mail seo@archives.gov.pf; internet www.seo.pf; f. 1917; study of archeology, anthropology, ethnography, natural sciences, philosophy, history, customs and traditions of Polynesia; attached library; 450 mems; library of 7,000 vols; Pres. SIMONE GRAND; Vice-Pres. FASAN CHONG DIT JEAN KAPE; Sec. MICHEL BAILLEUL; Treas. YVES BABIN; publ. *Bulletin de la Société des Etudes Océaniennes* (4 a year).

Research Institutes
GENERAL

Institut de Recherche pour le Développement (IRD) Centre de Tahiti: BP 529, 98713 Papeete Tahiti; tel. 50-62-00; fax 42-95-55; e-mail dirpapet@ird.pf; f. 1963; medical entomology, anthropology, oceanography; library of 7,000 vols; Rep. JACQUES ILTIS; (see main entry under France).

AGRICULTURE, FISHERIES AND VETERINARY SCIENCE

Centre Océanologique du Pacifique: BP 7004, 98719 Taravao Tahiti; tel. 54-60-00; fax

54-60-99; e-mail communication@ifremer.fr; internet www.ifremer.fr/cop; f. 1972; part of IFREMER (*q.v.*); research in aquaculture (crustacea, fish, shellfish); spec. library; 49 mems; Dir MARC TAQUET.

FINE AND PERFORMING ARTS

Institut de la Communication Audiovisuelle: BP 4469, 98713 Papeete Tahiti; tel. 50-67-50; fax 50-67-57; internet www.ica.pf; attached to Min. of Culture and Handicrafts; collects, preserves and restores audiovisual heritage of Polynesia; produces television programmes and documentaries; collns incl. video recordings, local television broadcasts and feature films; colln of images and sounds on the archipelagos of French Polynesia (Australes, Tuamotu, Gambier, Marquises, Société); library of 34,000 vols in reference colln.

MEDICINE

Institut Louis Malardé: BP 30, 98713 Papeete Tahiti; tel. 41-64-65; fax 43-15-90; internet www.ilm.pf; f. 1947, present bldg 1950, present name and status 2001; parasitology (particularly lymphatic filariasis), virology (dengue), microbiology, immunology, serology, biochemistry, pharmacotoxicology, bio-ecology and marine biochemistry, medical entomology; library of 1,000 vols, 9,185 periodicals; Dir Dr PATRICK HOWELL; Exec. Sec. MARIE-CLAUDE RENARD.

RELIGION, SOCIOLOGY AND ANTHROPOLOGY

Département des Traditions Orales, du Centre Polynésien des Sciences Humaines 'Te Anavaharau': Pk 15, Pointe de Pêcheurs, Punaauia Tahiti; tel. 58-34-76; fax 58-43-00; study of Polynesian oral tradition.

Archive

Papeete

Service des Archives Territoriales: BP 9063, 98715 Papeete Tahiti; tel. 41-96-01; fax 41-96-04; e-mail service.archives@archives .gov.pf; Head of Service PIERRE MORILLON.

Museums and Art Galleries

Papeari

Musée Paul Gauguin: BP 7029, 98727 Papeari Tahiti; tel. 57-10-58; fax 57-10-42; e-mail museegauguin@mail.pf; f. 1964; 1,000 documents on the life and work of the artist Paul Gauguin (1848–1903), who spent the last part of his life in Tahiti and other parts of the South Pacific; library of unpublished documents; colln of paintings by Buffet, R. Delaunay, S. Delaunay and others; 20 original works by Gauguin (paintings, sculptures, watercolours); Curator G. ARTUR.

Papeete

Pearl Museum: Vaima Centre, Rue Jeanne d'Arc, Papeete; tel. 45-21-22; e-mail iweber@ tahitiperles.pf; cultured pearls, spec. Tahitian Black Pearl.

Tamanu

Te Fare Manaha–Musée de Tahiti et des Iles: Pointe des Pêcheurs 'Nu'uroa, Punaauia, BP 380 354, 98718 Tamanu; tel. 58-34-76; fax 58-43-00; e-mail secretariat@ museetahiti.pf; internet www.museetahiti .pf; f. 1974, fmrly as Musée de Tahiti et des Iles–Te Fare Iamanaha, present name 2005; collects, conserves and appreciates Polynesian cultural heritage; Dir HIRIATA MILLAUD.

University

UNIVERSITÉ DE LA POLYNÉSIE FRANÇAISE (University of French Polynesia)

BP 6570, 98702 Faa'a Tahiti

Telephone: 80-38-94

Fax: 80-38-04

E-mail: courrier@upf.pf

Internet: www.upf.pf

Founded 1999 from the French Polynesia centre of the fmr Université Française du Pacifique (f. 1987)

State control

Academic year: September to June

Library of 50,000 books, 260 periodicals, 700 audiovisual items

Number of teachers: 95

Number of students: 3,211

Pres.: Prof. LOUISE PELTZER

Depts of arts and humanities, law, economics and management, physical activities and sport, and science, medicine and technology.

College

Conservatoire artistique de Polynésie française 'Te Fare Upa Rau': BP 463, 98713 Papeete Tahiti; tel. 50-14-14; fax 43-71-29; e-mail conserv.artist@mail.pf; internet www.conservatoire.pf; f. 1979; attached to Min. of Culture and Handicrafts; conserves and promotes Polynesian culture; provides theoretical and practical training in fine and performing arts; 1,693 students; Dir FABIEN DINARD.

GUADELOUPE

Research Institutes

AGRICULTURE, FISHERIES AND VETERINARY SCIENCE

CIRAD Guadeloupe: Station de Neufchâteau, Sainte-Marie, 97130 Capesterre-Belle-Eau; tel. 5-90-86-30-21; fax 5-90-86-80-77; e-mail cecile.gaume@cirad.fr; internet www .cirad.fr/guadeloupe; cultivation of bananas and other fruits, sugar cane, flowers; animal parasitology and control; biodiversity management; 31 research staff; Regional Dir PHILIPPE GODON; Head of Caribbean Regional Cooperation DOMINIQUE POLTI; (see main entry under France).

INRA Antilles-Guyane: Domaine Duclos, Prise d'Eau, 97170 Petit Bourg; tel. 5-90-25-59-00; fax 5-90-25-59-98; e-mail xande@ antilles.inra.fr; internet www.antilles.inra .fr; f. 1949 as Centre de Recherches des Antilles et de la Guyane; attached to Min. of Higher Education and Research and Min. of Agriculture, Food, Fisheries, Rural Affairs and Planning; (see main entry under France); soil science, animal science, forestry, plant science, rural economy and sociology, zoology and biological control,

technology transfer; controls 5 research units, 3 experimental farms and a documentation service; Pres. DANIELLE CÉLESTINE-MYRTIL-MARLIN.

MEDICINE

Institut Pasteur de la Guadeloupe: BP 484, 97183 Abymes Cedex; tel. 5-90-89-69-40; fax 5-90-89-69-41; internet www .pasteur-guadeloupe.fr; f. 1948; medical and microbiological analysis laboratories; int. vaccination centre; Public Health Dept certified laboratories for water and food analysis (chemical and microbiological); mycobacteria research centre; small library; Dir Dr ANTOINE TALARMIN; Exec. Sec. Dr HENRIETTA DESIREE; publ. *Archives* (1 a year).

Libraries and Archives

Basse-Terre

Département de la Guadeloupe Archives Départementales: BP 74, 97102 Basse-Terre Cedex; tel. 5-90-81-13-02; fax 5-90-81-97-15; e-mail info@cg971.fr; internet

www.cg971.fr/archives; f. 1951; holds records that date back to 1661; 10,000 vols; Dir ANNE LEBEL; publ. *Bulletin de la Société d'Histoire de la Guadeloupe* (3 a year).

Pointe-à-Pitre

Bibliothèque Universitaire Antilles-Guyane: Campus de Fouillole, BP 32, 97159 Pointe-à-Pitre Cedex; tel. 5-96-48-90-01; fax 5-96-48-90-89; e-mail jacques.faule@ univ-ag.fr; internet www.univ-ag.fr/buag; f. 1972; 65,000 vols, 750 periodicals, 2,200 electronic journals; Dir, Guadeloupe Br. JACQUES FAULE.

Museums and Art Galleries

Basse-Terre

Historical Museum of Guadeloupe: Fort Delgrès, 97100 Basse-Terre; tel. 5-90-81-37-48.

Pointe-à-Pitre

Musée Municipal Saint John Perse: 9 rue Noziéres, 97110 Pointe-à-Pitre; tel. 5-90-90-01-92; fax 5-90-83-98-31; e-mail musee.st-john-perse@wanadoo.fr; f. 1987; 2-storey 19th-century colonial house: colln of accounts from life of poet St John Perse; exhibits incl. MSS and personal items; attached library and videotheque.

Musée Victor Schoelcher: 24 rue Peynier, 97110 Pointe-à-Pitre; tel. 5-90-82-08-04; fax 5-90-83-78-39; e-mail musee.schoelcher@cg971.fr; internet www.cg971.fr/musees/schoelcher/index_schoecher.htm; f. 1883; colln assembled by Victor Schoelcher (1804–1893), local politician and campaigner against slavery; pictures of European monuments and historic sites, reproductions of antique sculptures from the Musée du Louvre, Paris; Egyptian antiquities, Senegalese ritual bell, Aztec and Greek pottery fragments; writing on travel and slavery by Schoelcher; Dir H. PETITJEAN ROGET.

Affiliated Museums:

Musée Edgar Clerc: La Rosette, 97160 Le Moule; tel. 5-90-23-57-57; fax 5-90-23-57-43; internet www.cg971.fr/musees/clerc/index_edgar.htm; f. 1984; archaeological museum; library of 800 vols.

Ecomusée de Marie-Galante: Habitation Murat, 97112 Grand Bourg, Marie Galante; tel. 5-90-97-94-41; internet www.cg971.fr/musees/ecomuse/index_ecomuse.htm; f. 1980; local arts, history and traditions and history of sugar cane; medicinal herb garden in the fmr animal enclosure; library of 400 vols; Dir C. MOMBRUN.

Musée Fort Fleur d'Epée: Bas du Fort, 97190 Gosier; tel. 5-90-90-94-61; internet www.cg971.fr/musees/fleurdepee/index_e-pee.htm; f. 1759; military history; art gallery; coin colln.

Parc Archéologique des Roches Gravées: Bord de mer, 97114 Trois-Rivières; tel. 5-90-92-91-88; internet www.cg971.fr/musees/parc/index_roche.htm; f. 1970; 1 ha, containing tropical vegetation, volcanic rocks and stones bearing marks made by Arawak Indians, the original inhabitants of the island.

Vieux-Habitants

Musée du Café: Le Bouchu, 97119 Vieux-Habitants; tel. 5-90-98-54-96; fax 5-90-98-54-59; e-mail cafe.chaulet@wanadoo.fr; internet www.in-west-indies.com/site-museums-musee-du-cafe-cafe-chaulet-909.htm; history of coffee from 1721 to present-day Guadeloupe; production and processing techniques of picking, roasting and converting coffee beans into a beverage.

University

UNIVERSITÉ DES ANTILLES ET DE LA GUYANE

Fouillole, BP 250, 97157 Pointe-à-Pitre Cedex

Telephone: 5-90-48-30-30
Fax: 5-90-91-06-57
Internet: www.univ-ag.fr

Founded 1982
Public control

Pres.: PASCAL SAFFACHE
Vice-Pres. for Guadeloupe: EUSTADE JANKY
Vice-Pres. for Martinique: PHILIPPE SAINT-CYR
Vice-Pres. for Guyana: ANTOINE PRIMEROSE
Librarian: SYLVAIN HOUDEBERT

Library: see under Libraries and Archives
Number of teachers: 233
Number of students: 5,728

TEACHING AND RESEARCH UNITS

Arts and Humanities: Dean: CORINNE MENCE-CASTER
Exact and Natural Sciences: Dean: HUBERT TREFLE
Law and Economics: Dir: EMMANUEL JOS
Medicine: Dir: Prof. PASCAL BLANCHET
Sports: Dir: CLAUDE HERTOGH

MARTINIQUE

Learned Society

AGRICULTURE, FISHERIES AND VETERINARY SCIENCE

Martinique Billfish Association: Chevalier de Ste-Marthe, 97200 Fort-de-France; tel. 5-96-55-26-73; fax 5-96-63-94-48; e-mail referencement@pixellweb.com; internet www.martinique-billfish.org; f. 1993; devt and practice of fishing; study of ecosystems, wildlife and underwater biological balance; Pres. JOSÉ ZÉCLER.

Research Institutes

AGRICULTURE, FISHERIES AND VETERINARY SCIENCE

Institut de Recherche pour le Développement (IRD) – Centre IRD Martinique-Caraïbe: BP 8006, 97259 Fort de France Cedex; tel. 5-96-39-77-39; fax 5-96-50-32-61; e-mail martinique@ird.fr; internet www.mq.ird.fr; f. 1958, fmrly ORSTOM; soil science, nematology; library of 1,700 vols; Dir and Rep. MARC MORELL; (see main entry under France).

Martinique Agricultural Research Pole: BP 214, 97285 Le Lementin; tel. 5-90-42-30-00; fax 5-90-42-31-00; e-mail dir-reg.martinique@cirad.fr; internet www.cirad.fr; attached to CIRAD Agricultural Research for Devt; cultivation of bananas, pineapples, fruit-producing trees and intensive farming; Rep. CHRISTIAN CHABRIER.

MEDICINE

Laboratoire Départemental d'Analyses: 35 blvd Pasteur, BP 628, 97261 Fort de France Cedex; tel. 5-96-71-34-52; fax 5-96-70-61-23; e-mail lda@cg972.fr; internet lda97.com; f. 1977; attached to Le Conseil Général de la Martinique; hygiene research and analysis of human blood and food and water; entomology; immunology of parasitic diseases; Pres. of Gen. Ccl CLAUDE LISE; Dir Dr J. M. P. LAFAYE.

Libraries and Archives

Fort-de-France

Archives Départementales de la Martinique: 19 ave Saint-John-Perse, BP 649, 97263 Fort-de-France Cedex; tel. 5-96-63-88-46; fax 5-96-70-04-50; e-mail archives@cg972.fr; f. 1949; 12,000 vols; Dir DOMINIQUE TAFFIN.

Bibliothèque Schoelcher: 1 rue de la Liberté, BP 640, 97264 Fort-de-France Cedex; tel. 5-96-70-26-67; fax 5-96-72-45-55; e-mail bibliotheque.schoelcher@cg972.fr; internet www.cg972.fr/biblio_schoelcher/html/default.htm; f. 1883; attached to Le Conseil Général de la Martinique; promotes study and research in heritage and modernity, literary and scientific culture of the city; 226,000 vols; Dir ANIQUE SYLVESTRE; Adjoint Dir LUCIEN PAVILLA.

Schoelcher

Bibliothèque Universitaire Antilles Guyane, Service Commun de la Docu-mentation: BP 7210, 97275 Schoelcher Cedex; tel. 5-96-72-75-30; fax 5-96-72-75-27; e-mail sylvain.houdebert@univ-ag.fr; internet www.univ-ag.fr/buag/main.php; f. 1972; admin. HQ for the 3 brs of the univ. library (see also French Guiana and Guadeloupe); 100,000 vols, 738 periodicals; Dir of SCDUAG SYLVAIN HOUDEBER; Dir of Martinique Br. MARIE-FRANCE GROUVEL.

Museums and Art Galleries

Anse-Turin

Gauguin Art Centre and Museum: Anse-Turin; tel. 5-96-78-22-66; historical site; art and history museum; art of famous painter Gaugin.

Fort-de-France

Musée Départemental d'Archéologie Précolombienne et de Préhistoire de la Martinique: 9 rue de la Liberté, 97200 Fort-de-France; tel. 5-96-71-57-05; fax 5-96-73-03-80; e-mail musarc@cg972.fr; f. 1971; prehistory of Martinique; archaeological colls; Dir CÉCILE CELMA.

Musée Régional d'Histoire et d'Ethnographie: 10 blvd du Général de Gaulle, 97200 Fort-de-France; tel. 5-96-72-81-87; fax 5-96-63-74-11; e-mail cr.972.musees@wanadoo.fr; internet www.cr-martinique.fr; f. 1999; attached to Conseil Régional Martinique; displays furnishings, antiques, a gallery of traditional costumes and jewellery, as well as numerous paintings and engravings (18th and 19th centuries) retracing briefly the historical milestones of the island and the history of Saint-Pierre and Fort-de-France; attached library specializing in works on slavery; Curator LYNE-ROSE BEUZE.

Riviere-Pilote

L'Ecomusée (The Living Museum): Anse Figuier, 97211 Riviere-Pilote; tel. 5-96-62-79-14; fax 5-96-62-73-77; internet www.cr-martinique.fr; f. 1993 by Asscn Martiniquaise de Promotion et de Protection des Arts et Traditions Populaires; attached to Conseil Régional Martinique; displays prehistory to present-day Native America; beginnings of French colonialism; economy-oriented cultures of cotton, tobacco and indigo; slave-period crops of sugar cane, coffee, and cocoa; central factories; advent of the banana economy; Conservateur LYNE-ROSE BEUZE.

Trois-Ilets

La Savane des Esclaves: Quartier La Ferme, 97229 Trois-Ilets; tel. 5-96-68-33-91; e-mail lasavanedesesclaves@wanadoo.fr; restored habitat that displays the way of life of slaves who fled the plantations to seek refuge in nature.

Maison De La Canne (House of Cane): Quartier Valable, 97229 Trois-Ilets; tel. 5-96-68-31-68; fax 5-96-68-42-69; internet www.cr-martinique.fr; f. 1987; attached to Conseil Régional Martinique; history and devt of sugar cane products; Conservator LYNE-ROSE BEUZE; Documentalist MARIE-JOSÉ SYLVESTRE.

University

UNIVERSITÉ DES ANTILLES ET DE LA GUYANE

Campus de Shoelcher, BP 7209, 97275 Schoelcher Cedex
Telephone: 5-90-48-91-98
Fax: 5-90-48-92-78
E-mail: vp-cur-gpe@univ-ag.fr
Internet: www.univ-ag.fr
Public control

(See also under French Guiana and Guadeloupe)

Pres.: PASCAL SAFFACHE
Vice-Pres. for Martinique: PHILIPPE SAINT CYR

Library: see Libraries and Archives
Number of teachers: 158
Number of students: 5,607

TEACHING AND RESEARCH UNITS

Arts and Humanities: Dean: CORINNE MENCE-CASTER
Law and Economics: Dean: JUSTIN DANIEL

NEW CALEDONIA

Regulatory Bodies

GOVERNMENT

Department of Cultural and Customary Affairs: 8 rue de Sébastopol, BP T5, 98852 Nouméa; tel. 26-97-66; fax 26-97-67; e-mail secretariat.dacc@gouv.nc; internet www.gouv.nc/portal/page/portal/gouv/annuaire_administration/administration/daccnc; Min. EPÉRI 'DÉWÉ GORODEY; Dir RÉGIS VENDEGOU.

Department of Education: 19 ave du Maréchal Foch, Immeuble Foch, BP 8244, 98807 Nouméa; tel. 23-96-00; fax 27-29-21; e-mail denc@gouv.nc; internet www.denc.gouv.nc; Dir JACQUES BRIAND; Sec. SANDRA SERCAN.

Department of Vocational Training: 19 ave du Maréchal Foch, BP 110, 98845 Nouméa; tel. 24-66-22; fax 28-16-61; e-mail dfpc@gouv.nc; internet www.dfpc.gouv.nc; Min. PIERRE NGAIHONI.

Learned Societies

GENERAL

Groupe de Recherche en Histoire Océanienne Contemporaine (GRHOC) (Research Group for the Modern History of Oceania): BP R4, 98845 Nouméa; tel. 26-58-58; e-mail angleviel@univ-nc.nc; f. 1996; historical and anthropological research; devt of regional research; 10 mems; Pres. (vacant); publs *101 Mots pour Comprendre* (1 a year), *Annales d'Histoire Calédonienne* (1 a year).

HISTORY, GEOGRAPHY AND ARCHAEOLOGY

Société d'Etudes Historiques de la Nouvelle-Calédonie (New Caledonia Society for Historical Studies): BP 63, 98845 Nouméa; tel. 76-71-55; e-mail seh_nc@lagoon.nc; f. 1968; research and study of the past; heritage conservation; publishes books and periodicals on history, prehistory, Melanesian society; close contact with the univs of the Pacific area; archives; 200 mems; Pres. GABRIEL VALET; Vice-Pres. MAXWELL SHEKELTON; publ. *Bulletin* (4 a year).

LANGUAGE AND LITERATURE

Association des Ecrivains de Nouvelle-Calédonie (Writers' Association of New Caledonia): 8 rue Paul Monchovet, Pointe Brunelet, BP 712, 98800 Nouméa; e-mail contact@ecrivains-nc.net; internet www.ecrivains-nc.net; f. 1996; exchanges ideas and promotes writing in all its forms; 27 mems; Pres. JEAN VANMAI; Vice-Pres. NICOLAS KURTOVITCH; Treas. MARC BOUAN; Sec. CLAUDE MAILLAUD.

Research Institutes

GENERAL

Institut de Recherche pour le Développement (IRD) (Institute of Research for Development): Centre de Nouméa, 101 Promenade Roger Laroque, Anse Vata, BP A5, 98848 Nouméa Cedex; tel. 26-10-00; fax 26-43-26; internet www.ird.nc; f. 1946; agropedology, archaeology, botany and plant ecology, geology, geophysics, hydrology, microbiology, pharmacology, phytopathology and applied zoology, physical and biological oceanography; library of 12,500 vols, 150 periodicals; Dir FABRICE COLIN; Commr and Dir of the Centre for South Pacific CATHERINE HARTMANN (acting); Asst Dir ANNE-SOPHIE IHOPU; publs *Earth Sciences*, *Life Sciences*, *Sea Sciences*, *Social Sciences*; (see main entry under France).

EDUCATION

Centre de documentation pédagogique de Nouvelle-Calédonie (New Caledonia Centre for Pedagogic Documentation): Immeuble Flize, 6 rue Carcopino, BP 215, 98845 Nouméa Cedex; tel. 24-28-34; fax 28-31-13; e-mail librairie@cdp.nc; internet www.cdp.nc; f. 1978 fmrly Centre Territorial de Recherche et de Documentation Pédagogiques de Nouvelle-Calédonie; research in education; library of 12,000 vols, 800 video tapes, 2,200 slide serials; Pres. IVES MELET; Dir CHRISTIAN LUCIEN; Sec.-Gen. HENRI TOURNACHE.

MEDICINE

Institut Pasteur de Nouvelle Calédonie (Pasteur Institute of New Caledonia): 9–11 ave Paul Doumer, BP 61, 98845 Nouméa Cedex; tel. 27-26-66; fax 27-33-90; e-mail direction@pasteur.nc; internet www.institutpasteur.nc; f. 1913 as Institut de Microbiologie de Nouvelle-Calédonie, name changed to Institut Pasteur de Nouméa 1954, present name 1990; medical analysis laboratory; research laboratory: dengue fever, leptospirosis, tuberculosis; library of 1,080 vols; Dir Prof. SUZANNE CHANTEAU; Exec. Sec. SIDAVY SABOT; publ. *Rapport technique* (1 a year).

RELIGION, SOCIOLOGY AND ANTHROPOLOGY

Coordination pour l'Océanie des Recherches sur les Arts, les Idées et les Littératures (CORAIL): BP 2448, 98846 Nouméa Cedex; fax 25-95-27; f. 1987; studies francophone and anglophone literatures and civilizations of the South Pacific; annual themed conference; Pres. VÉRONIQUE FILLIOL; Sec. JACQUES VERNAUDON; publ. *Actes du Colloque* (1 a year).

Libraries and Archives

Nouméa

Bibliothèque Bernheim (Bernheim Library): BP G1, 98848 Nouméa Cedex; tel. 24-20-90; fax 27-65-88; e-mail contact@bernheim.nc; internet www.bernheim.nc; f. 1901; public library (adults and children); record library; historical, ethnological collns of 2,500 vols dealing with New Caledonia and the Pacific Islands; associated with the Bibliotheque Nationale de France for the colln of legal deposit; 141,000 vols, 28,500 vols of children's books, 85 periodicals; Librarian J. F. CARREZ-CORRAL.

Secretariat of the Pacific Community Library: 95 Promenade Roger Laroque, Anse Vata, BP D5, 98848 Nouméa Cedex; tel. 26-20-00; fax 26-38-18; e-mail library@spc.int; internet www.spc.int/library; f. 1947; SPC Nouméa reference library: collns on health, women, youth, statistics, demography, cultural policy, agriculture, forestry, fisheries, and economic and social devt in the Pacific Islands; br. library in Suva, Fiji: holds 6 collns serving the forestry regional office, maritime programme, community education centre, regional media centre, agriculture and adolescent reproductive health; 40,000 regional and int. publs in French, English and other Pacific languages; Librarian ELEANOR KLEIBER; Archivist ROBERT APPEL; publs *New Additions to the Library* (4 a year), *Select List of Publications* (1 a year).

Service des Archives de Nouvelle Calédonie (New Caledonia Archive Service): 3 rue Félix Raoul Thomas, Nouville, BP 525, 98845 Nouméa Cedex; tel. 26-60-20; fax 27-12-92; e-mail archives@gouv.nc; internet www.archives.gouv.nc; f. 1987; manages the historical and administrative archives of the territory; 7,000 vols, 5,196 linear m of archives; Dir JACQUES ANCEY (acting).

Museums

Nouméa

Musée de l'Histoire Maritime (Museum of Maritime History): 11 ave James Cook, BP 1755, 98845 Nouméa Cedex; tel. 26-34-43; fax 28-68-21; e-mail mdhm@canl.nc; internet www.patrimoine-maritime.asso.nc; f. 1999; attached to Patrimoine Maritime de Nouvelle Calédonie; preserves and displays collns from archaeological underwater excavations carried out by the Fortunes de Mer Calédoniennes and Assn Salomon.

Musée de Nouvelle-Calédonie (Museum of New Caledonia): BP 2393, 98846 Nouméa Cedex; 45 ave du Maréchal Foch, Nouméa; tel. 27-23-42; fax 28-41-43; e-mail smp@gouv.nc; f. 1971; colln of 4,500 items; emblematic wooden sculptures, masks, ritual dance costumes, jewellery, pottery and other objects reflecting cultural practices and religious beliefs; Dir MARIE-SOLANGE NEAOUTYINE.

University

UNIVERSITÉ DE LA NOUVELLE-CALÉDONIE
(University of New Caledonia)

BP R4, 98851 Nouméa Cedex

Telephone: 29-02-90

Fax: 25-48-29

E-mail: president@univ-nc.nc

Internet: www.univ-nc.nc

Founded 1999 from the New Caledonia centre of the fmr Université Française du Pacifique

State control

Academic year: February to November

Pres.: JEAN-MARC BOYER

Vice-Pres.: YANNICK LERRANT (Ccl of Admin.)

Vice-Pres.: MICHEL ALLENBACH (Scientific Ccl)

Sec.-Gen.: ODILE BOYER

Registrar: CHRISTIAN CABOTTE

Library Dir: PHILIPPE BESNIÉ

Library of 34,000 books, 350 periodicals

Number of teachers: 100

Number of students: 3,000

Publication: *UNC-Info* (12 a year)

Depts of arts, economics and management, languages and humanities, law, science and technology.

Colleges

Conservatoire National des Arts et Métiers (National Conservatory of the Arts and Crafts): 15 rue de Verdun, Immeuble CCI, 2ième étage, BP 3562, 98846 Nouméa Cedex; tel. 28-37-07; fax 27-79-96; e-mail noucnam@offratel.nc; internet cnam.nc; f. 1794; attached to the Conservatoire National des Arts et Métiers in Paris; higher technical education; 12 staff; 500 students; Pres. JEAN BEGAUD; Dir BERNARD SCHALL; Dir-Gen. CHRISTIAN FOREST; Dir for Teaching HENRI CHARLES.

Institut de Formation des Maîtres de Nouvelle-Calédonie (Institute of Teacher Training of New Caledonia): 14 rue Pierre Sauvan, BP 8036, 98807 Nouméa; tel. 26-45-41; fax 26-28-50; e-mail cp@ifmnc.nc; internet www.ifmnc.nc; f. 1990, present status 2001; continuing education for teachers; Dir CHANTAL MANDAOUÉ; Sec.-Gen. MICHEL PIOT.

RÉUNION

Learned Societies

GENERAL

Académie de la Réunion: 24 ave Georges Brassens, Le Moufia, 97702 St-Denis Messag. Cedex 9; tel. 2-62-48-10-10; fax 2-62-48-69-48; e-mail communication.secretariat@ac-reunion.fr; internet www.ac-reunion.fr; f. 1913; 25 mems; Rector MOSTAFA FOURAR; Deputy Rector BERNARD ZIER; Sec.-Gen. EUGÈNE KRANTZ; publ. *Bulletin*.

HISTORY, GEOGRAPHY AND ARCHAEOLOGY

Association Historique Internationale de l'Océan Indien: c/o Archives Départementales de la Réunion, 4 rue Marcel Regnol, 97490 St-Denis; f. 1960; 86 mems; Pres. CL. WANQUET; Sec.-Gen. B. JULLIEN; publ. *Bulletin de Liaison et d'Information* (2 a year).

NATURAL SCIENCES

Association Réunionnaise de Développement de l'Aquaculture: Z. I. Les Sables, BP 16, 97427 Etang-Salé; tel. 2-62-26-50-82; fax 2-62-26-50-01; e-mail arda.reunion@wanadoo.fr; internet www.arda.fr; f. 1991 by the Conseil Régional de La Réunion; inland and marine aquaculture; study and devt of aquatic environments.

Research Institutes

AGRICULTURE, FISHERIES AND VETERINARY SCIENCE

CIRAD la Réunion: Station de la Bretagne, BP 20, 97408 St-Denis Messag. Cedex 9; tel. 2-62-52-80-00; fax 2-62-52-80-01; e-mail dir-reg.reunion@cirad.fr; internet www.cirad.fr/reunion; f. 1962; attached to CIRAD Agricultural Research for Devt (France); agronomic research, mainly on sugar cane, fruit, vegetables, maize and fodder crops; water management and prevention of soil erosion; 181 staff, 55 researchers; 6 research stations; 1,180 publs; library of 5,000 vols; Regional Dir GILLES MANDRET; Dir for Environmental Risk, Agriculture and Integrated Management of Resources PAUL FALLAVIER; Dir for Plant Protection BERNARD REYNAUD; Dir for Quality of Agricultural and Tropical Food Productions ERIC CARDINALE.

ECONOMICS, LAW AND POLITICS

Institut National de la Statistique et des Études Économiques–Direction Régionale de la Réunion (National Institute of Statistics and Economic Studies–Regional Directorate of Réunion): 10 rue Demarne, BP 13, 97408 St-Denis Cedex 9; tel. 2-62-48-89-63; fax 2-62-48-89-89; internet www.insee.fr/fr/insee_regions/reunion/home/home_page.asp; f. 1966; attached to INSEE, Paris (see main entry in chapter on France); produces statistical data, economic studies; database with 10,000 bibliographical references on the region, data bank with 2,000 chronological series; Dir PASCAL CHEVALIER; publs *L'Economie de la Réunion* (4 a year), *Tableau Economique de la Réunion* (1 a year).

HISTORY, GEOGRAPHY AND ARCHAEOLOGY

CRESOI Centre d'Histoire de l'Université de la Réunion Histoire, Politique et Patrimoine (CRESOI Centre of History

University of Reunion Island History, Politics and Heritage): Univ. of Reunion, Rue René Cassin, 97400 St-Denis; e-mail cresoi@centre-histoire-ocean-indien.fr; internet www.centre-histoire-ocean-indien.fr; f. 2001; attached to Univ. de La Réunion; researches colonization, decolonization, heritage, history of slavery, industrial tourism, political and cultural history, tourism; Dir Prof. YVAN COMBEAU; publ. *Revue Historique de l'Océan Indien.*

Libraries and Archives
St-Denis

Bibliothèque Centrale de Prêt de la Réunion: 1 pl. Joffre, 97400 St-Denis; tel. 2-62-21-03-24; fax 2-62-21-41-30; e-mail bdp@cg974.fr; f. 1956; 100,000 vols; Dir ELISABETH DÉGON.

Bibliothèque Départementale de la Réunion: 52 rue Roland Garros, 97400 St-Denis; tel. 2-62-21-13-96; fax 2-62-21-54-63; e-mail bdr@cg974.fr; f. 1855; 95,000 vols; Dir ALAIN VAUTHIER.

Service Commun de la Documentation (Bibliothèque Universitaire): Université de la Réunion, 15 ave René Cassin, BP 7152, 97715 St-Denis Cedex 9; tel. 2-62-93-83-79; fax 2-62-93-83-64; e-mail scd@univ-reunion.fr; internet bu.univ-reunion.fr; f. 1971; attached to Univ. de la Réunion; arts, economics, human sciences, law, management, medicine, politics, social sciences, science; 171,252 vols, 1,495 current periodicals, 3,000 online periodicals; special collns on the Indian Ocean islands; Library Dir ANNE-MARIE BLANC.

St-Pierre

Mediathèque Raphaël Barquissau: Rue du Collège Arthur, BP 396, 97458 St-Pierre Cedex; tel. 2-62-96-71-96; fax 2-62-25-74-10; e-mail ksl@mediatheque-saintpierre.fr; internet www.mediatheque-saintpierre.fr; f. 1967; 130,000 vols, 190 periodicals, more than 530 ancient books, 12,000 CDs, 2,500 videotapes; Dir and Chief Librarian LINDA KOO SEEN LIN.

Ste-Clotilde

Archives Départementales de La Réunion: 4 rue Marcel Pagnol, Champ-Fleuri, 97490 St-Clotilde; tel. 2-62-94-04-14; fax 2-62-94-04-21; f. 1946; public and private sources of history on Bourbon Island and Réunion French dept; some Mauritius island archives on microfilms from French period; 5,000 vols, 163,000 items in public and private archives; Dir NADINE ROUAYROUX.

Museums and Art Galleries
St-Denis

Muséum d'Histoire Naturelle: Jardin de l'Etat, 97400 St-Denis; tel. 2-62-20-02-19; fax 2-62-21-33-93; e-mail museum@cg974.fr; internet www.cg974.fr; f. 1855, fmrly the Legislative Palace built by the East India Co; zoology and mineralogy; permanent colln of rocks, minerals, wildlife from the Indian Ocean region; library of 7,000 vols; Dir S. RIBES.

Musée Léon-Dierx: 28 rue de Paris, 97400 St-Denis; tel. 2-62-20-24-82; fax 2-62-21-82-87; e-mail musee.dierx@cg974.fr; internet www.cg974.fr/culture; f. 1911, old bldg destroyed 1963, museum reopened to the public 1965, colln and reserves reinstated 1970; fine arts; colln of contemporary art, installations and videos; library: literature on featured artists, history of art, catalogues, monographs, essays and articles; Curator LAURENCE LECIEUX.

St-Gilles-les-Hauts

Musée Historique de Villèle:; e-mail valerie.sinama@cg974.fr Domaine Panon-Desbassyns, 97435 St-Gilles-les-Hauts; tel. 2-62-55-64-10; fax 2-62-55-51-91; e-mail musee.villele@cg974.fr; internet www.cg974.fr/index.php/culture-et-sport/les-musees/musee-historique-de-villele.html; f. 1974; 18th-century plantation house and adjoining properties; French East India Co furniture and china, prints, models, weapons, documents; Curator JEAN BARBIER.

St-Lue

Musée Stella Matutina: 6 allée des Flamboyants, 97424 St Leu; tel. 2-62-34-16-24; e-mail com.seml@wanadoo.fr; f. 1991 as museum, fmr sugar cane factory built 1855, closed 1978, bought and restored by Réunion Island dept 1986; dedicated to sugar cane production and other agricultural products like coffee, spices and vanilla; a laboratory that teaches the art of smelling and creating fragrances.

University
UNIVERSITÉ DE LA RÉUNION

15 ave René Cassin, BP 7151, 97715 St-Denis Messag. Cedex 9
Telephone: 2-62-93-80-80
Fax: 2-62-93-80-13
E-mail: contact@univ-reunion.fr
Internet: www.univ-reunion.fr

Founded 1970, present status 1982

Pres.: Prof. MOHAMED ROCHDI
Vice-Pres. for Ccl of Admin.: Prof. HARRY BOYER
Vice-Pres. for Int. Relations: Prof. LAURENT SERMET
Vice-Pres. for External Relations and Professional Integration: Dr FRÉDÉRIC MIRANVILLE
Vice-Pres. for Scientific Ccl: Prof. DOMINIQUE STRASBERG
Vice-Pres. for Students: NICAISE GONTHIER
Vice-Pres. for Studies and Univ. Life: Dr FABRICE LEMAIRE
Librarian: JEAN-CLAUDE MIRÉ
Library: see Service Commun de la Documentation, Réunion
Number of teachers: 1,301
Number of students: 12,000

DEANS

Faculty of Arts and Humanities: Prof. GUY FONTAINE
Faculty of Health: Prof. PASCAL GUIRAUD
Faculty of Human and Environmental Science: PIERRE LEROYER
Faculty of Law and Economics: Prof. PASCAL PUIG
Faculty of Science and Technology: Prof. JEAN-PIERRE CHABRIAT

Colleges

Ecole Supérieure d'Ingénieurs Réunion Océan Indien: ESIROI-IDAI, Parc Technologique Universitaire, 2 rue Joseph Wetzell, 97490 St Clotilde; tel. 2-62-48-33-44; fax 2-62-48-33-48 ESIROI-CODE, 117 rue du Général Ailleret, 97430 Le Tampon; tel. 2-62-57-91-60; fax 2-62-57-95-51 ESIROI-STIM, 15, ave René Cassin, BP 7151, 97715 St-Denis Messag. Cedex 9; tel. 2-62-52-89-06; fax 2-62-52-89-05; e-mail secretariat.stim@univ-reunion.fr; internet esiroi.univ-reunion.fr; attached to Univ. de la Réunion; depts of integrated agri-food innovation and development (IDAI), sustainable construction and environment (CODE), telecommunications services, computer and multimedia (STIM); Dir for Integrated Agri-Food Innovation and Development (ESIROI-IDAI) Dr MIREILLE FOUILLAUD.

Institut d'Administration des Entreprises de La Réunion: 24–26 ave de la victoire, BP 7151, 97715 St-Denis Messag. Cedex 9; tel. 2-62-21-16-26; fax 2-62-21-48-56; e-mail iae@univ-reunion.fr; internet www.iae-reunion.fr; f. 1998; attached to Univ. de la Réunion; industry research; devt of science and management techniques; Dir Prof. MICHEL BOYER; Exec. Sec. VERONIQUE ROCHE.

Institut Universitaire de Technologie: 40 ave de Soweto, Terre Ste, BP 373, 97410 St-Pierre; tel. 2-62-96-28-70; fax 2-62-96-28-79; e-mail iut.contact@univ-reunion.fr; internet www.univ-reunion.fr/universite/composantes/iut.html; attached to Univ. de la Réunion; depts of biological engineering, business management and administration, civil engineering, network telecommunications; Dir FRANCK LUCAS.

GABON

The Higher Education System

Gabon gained its independence from France in 1960, and the higher education system still reflects its French heritage; many students also go to France to attend university or receive technical training. The first institutions of higher education were a polytechnic institute and law school associated with the Central African Higher Education Foundation, created in 1961 by the heads of state of the former French Equatorial Africa. Université Omar Bongo, the first university, was founded in 1970 and adopted its current name in 1978. The other two universities are Université des Sciences et Techniques de Masuku (founded 1986) and Université des Sciences de la Santé (founded 2002). Higher education is highly centralized and controlled mostly by the State, which subsidizes each student for about 95% of the cost of education and provides financial aid equivalent to 40% of the total budget allocation for higher education. Student fees represent only 3% of income. In 1998/99 there were some 7,473 students enrolled in tertiary education.

Admission to higher education is dependent upon award of the Baccalauréat, the main secondary-school qualification. University-level degrees are divided into three cycles. The first cycle lasts for two years and leads to the award of Diplôme Universitaire d'Études Littéraires, Diplôme Universitaire d'Études Scientifiques, Diplôme Universitaire d'Études Juridiques, or Diplôme Universitaire d'Études Économiques. A further year of study (three in total) leads to the award of the Licence; alternatively, a further two years (four in total) leads to the Maîtrise; these degrees comprise the second cycle. Some professional titles, such as Diplôme d'Ingénieur and the Doctorat en Médecine, are awarded after five to six years of study. Finally, the third cycle consists of diploma programmes offered by professional institutions, admission to which is conditional on the Maîtrise. Higher vocational education is offered by professional schools and institutes.

Higher education has contributed significantly to Gabon's development. Graduates operate effectively at all levels of public and private administration. However, the recent increase in student numbers and the lack of sufficient funds are likely to have an adverse affect on the quality of both teaching and research. Despite this, higher education is still viewed as an investment that benefits all levels of society.

Regulatory Bodies

GOVERNMENT

Ministry of National Education, Higher Education, Scientific Research and Innovation and Culture: BP 6, Libreville; tel. (1) 72-44-61; fax (1) 72-19-74; Min. Séraphin Moundounga.

Learned Societies

GENERAL

UNESCO Office Libreville: BP 2183, Libreville; Cité de la Démocratie, Bâtiment 6, Libreville; tel. (1) 762879; fax (1) 762814; designated Cluster Office for Republic of Congo, Democratic Republic of Congo, Equatorial Guinea, Gabon, São Tomé e Príncipe; Dir Makhily Gassama.

LANGUAGE AND LITERATURE

Alliance Française: BP 1371, Port Gentil; tel. and fax (2) 565941; offers courses and exams in French language and culture and promotes cultural exchange with France.

Research Institutes

GENERAL

Centre National de la Recherche Scientifique et Technologique (CENAREST): BP 13354, Libreville; tel. (1) 732578; internet www.cenarest.org; f. 1976; principal research body; designs and operates research programmes into human sciences, tropical ecology, agronomy, medicinal plants and plant biotechnology; consists of 5 research institutes: l'Institut de Pharmacopée et de Médecine Traditionnelles; l'Institut de Recherches Agronomiques et Forestières; l'Institut de Recherches en Ecologie Tropicale; l'Institut de Recherches en Sciences Humaines; and l'Institut des Recherches Technologiques; Dir Samuel Mbadiga.

AGRICULTURE, FISHERIES AND VETERINARY SCIENCE

Centre Technique Forestier Tropical, Section Gabon: BP 149, Libreville; f. 1958; silviculture, technology, genetic improvement; library of 500 vols; Dir J. Leroy Deval.

Institut de Recherches Agronomiques et Forestières (IRAF): BP 2246, Libreville; tel. (1) 732375; fax (1) 732378; e-mail angoye@assala.com; internet www.cenarest .org/instituts/iraf; f. 1977; attached to Centre National de la Recherche Scientifique et Technologique (CENAREST); research into agronomy, silviculture and forestry; Dir Alfred Ngoye.

MEDICINE

Centre International de Recherches Médicales de Franceville: BP 769, Franceville; tel. (2) 677096; fax (2) 677295; e-mail faxcirmf@cirmf.sci.ga; f. 1979; undertakes basic and applied research in medical parasitology (e.g. malaria, filariosis, trypanosomiasis) and viral diseases (incl. HIV/AIDS, Ebola); library of 1,800 vols, 72 periodicals, 20,000 microfiches; Dir-Gen. Prof. Philippe Blot.

Institut de Pharmacopée et de Médecine Traditionnelle (IPHAMETRA): BP 1935, Libreville; tel. (1) 734786; fax (1) 732578; internet www.cenarest.org/instituts/ iphametra; f. 1976; attached to Centre National de la Recherche Scientifique et Technologique (CENAREST); Dir Dr Henri Paul Bourobou.

NATURAL SCIENCES

Biological Sciences

Institut de Recherche en Ecologie Tropicale (IRET): BP 13354, Makokou; tel. (1) 443319; internet www.cenarest.org/instituts/ iret; f. 1979; attached to Centre National de la Recherche Scientifique et Technologique (CENAREST); Dir Paul Posso.

RELIGION, SOCIOLOGY AND ANTHROPOLOGY

Institut de Recherches en Sciences Humaines (IRSH): BP 846, Libreville; tel. (1) 734719; internet www.cenarest.org/ instituts/irsh; f. 1976; attached to Centre National de la Recherche Scientifique et Technologique (CENAREST); Dir Dr Magloire Moungangai.

TECHNOLOGY

Bureau de Recherches Géologiques et Minières (BRGM): BP 175, Libreville; f. 1960; Dir M. Bertucat; (See main entry under France).

Institut de Recherches Technologiques (IRT): BP 14070, Libreville; tel. (1) 733089; internet www.cenarest.org/instituts/irt; f. 1976; attached to Centre National de la Recherche Scientifique et Technologique (CENAREST); Dir Dr Jean Daniel Mbegai.

Libraries and Archives

Libreville

Bibliothèque du Centre d'Information: BP 750, Libreville; f. 1960; 6,000 vols; 80 current periodicals.

Direction Générale des Archives Nationales, de la Bibliothèque Nationale et de la Documentation Gabonaise (DGABD): BP 1188, Libreville; tel. (1) 736310 (Archives Nationales); tel. (1) 730972 (Bibliothèque Nationale); tel. (1) 737247 (Documentation Gabonaise); f. 1969 (Nat. Archives and Nat. Library), 1980 (Gabonese Documentation); 36 mems; 29,000 vols, 2,000 periodical titles; 2 linear km archives, 639 microfilms, 666 maps and plans, 1,712 archive photographs; Archives Dir Jérôme Angoume-Ngoghe; Nat. Library Dir Jean Michel Noudodo; Documentation Dir Jean Paul Mifouna; Dir-Gen. René Georges Sonnet-Azize.

Museum

Libreville

Musée National des Arts et Traditions du Gabon: BP 4018, Libreville; tel. (1) 761456; national museum; thematic exhibition on Gabonese masks; public library on arts from Gabon; Dir Prof. PAUL ABA'A NDONG.

Universities

UNIVERSITÉ OMAR BONGO

BP 13 131, blvd Léon M'Ba, Libreville

Telephone: (1) 732045

E-mail: uob@internetgabon.com

Internet: www.uob.ga

Founded 1970, renamed 1978

State control

Language of instruction: French

Academic year: October to July

Rector: JEAN-ÉMILE MBOT

Vice-Rector for Academic Affairs and Research: JÉRÔME KWENZI-MAKALA

Vice-Rector for Admin. and Inter-university Cooperation: JÉRÔME NDZOUNGOU

Sec.-Gen.: GUY ROSSATANGA-RIGNAULT

Librarian: FERDINAND NGOUNGOULOU

Library of 12,000 vols

Number of teachers: 300

Number of students: 4,800

Publications: *Cahiers Gabonais d'Anthropologie, Cahiers d'Histoire et d'Archéologie, Exchorésis, Gabonica, Kilombo, Psychologie et Culture, Revue Gabonaise des Sciences de l'Homme, Revue Gabonaise des Sciences du Langage, Waves*

DEANS

Faculty of Law and Economics: Prof. JEAN JACQUES EKOMIE

Faculty of Letters and Sciences: GUY SERGE BIGNOUMBA

ATTACHED RESEARCH INSTITUTES

Centre d'Études en Littérature Gabonaise: Dir HÉMERY-HERVAIS SIMA EYI.

Centre d'Études et de Recherches d'Histoire Économique, Administrative et Financière (CERHEAF): Dir Prof. PIERRE NDOMBI.

Centre d'Études et de Recherches du Monde Anglophone (CERMA): Dir DANIEL RENÉ AKENDENGUE.

Centre d'Études et de Recherches Philosophiques (CERP): Dir GILBERT ZUE NGUEMA.

Centre de Recherches Afro-Hispaniques (CRAHI): Dir GISÈLE AVOME MBA.

Centre de Recherches et d'Études en Psychologie (CREP): Dir THÉODORE KOUMBA.

Groupe de Recherches en Langues et Cultures Orales (GRELACO): Dir Prof. JAMES DUPLESSIS EMEJULU.

Institut Cheikh Anta Diop (ICAD): Dir GRÉGOIRE BIYOGO NANG.

Laboratoire d'Analyse Spatiale et des Environnements Tropicaux (LANASPET): Dir GALLEY YAWO.

Laboratoire de Graphique et de Cartographie (LAGRAC): Dir Dr JULES DJEKI.

Laboratoire National d'Archéologie (LANA): Dir MICHEL ATHANASE LOCKO.

Laboratoire Universitaire de la Tradition Orale (LUTO): Dir Prof. FABIEN OKOUE-METOGO.

Politiques et Développement des Espaces et Sociétés de l'Afrique Subsaharienne (CERGEP): Dir MARC LOUIS ROPIVIA.

UNIVERSITÉ DES SCIENCES DE LA SANTÉ

BP 18231, Owendo, Libreville

Telephone: (1) 702028

Fax: (1) 702919

E-mail: rectorat@uss-univ.com

Founded 2002

State control

Courses in health sciences

Rector: ANDRÉ MOUSSAVOU-MOUYAMA.

UNIVERSITÉ DES SCIENCES ET TECHNIQUES DE MASUKU

BP 901, Franceville

Telephone: (2) 677449

Fax: (2) 677520

Founded 1986

State control

Language of instruction: French

Rector: JACQUES LEBIBI

Vice-Rector for Academic Affairs and Research: BERTRAND M'BATCHI

Vice-Rector for Admin. Affairs and Inter-university Cooperation: Prof. AMBROISE EDOU MINKO

Sec.-Gen.: Dr GEORGES AZZIBROUCK

Librarian: YVES NTOUTOUME

Library of 11,000 vols

Number of teachers and researchers: 110

Number of students: 800

DEAN

Faculty of Sciences: Dr LÉON NGADI

Colleges

École Interprovinciale de Santé: BP 530, Mouila; tel. (2) 861177; f. 1981; 18 teachers; 76 students; Dir PIERRE FRANKLIN NGUEMA ONDO.

Institut Africain d'Informatique: BP 2263, Libreville; tel. (1) 720005; fax (1) 720011; e-mail info@iai.ga; internet www.iai.ga; f. 1971 by member states of OCAM to train computer programmers, computer science engineers and analysts; small library; 8 permanent teachers; 281 students; Dir FABIEN MBALLA.

GAMBIA

The Higher Education System

Higher education, in the sense of an institution offering Bachelors, Masters and Doctorate degrees, did not exist in Gambia until 1995. Prior to this, Gambians wishing to pursue higher education could either study abroad or enrol at a post-secondary institution, the main such institutions being the Gambia College and the Gambia Technical Training Institute. A University Extension Programme was established in 1995 as a collaborative effort between the Government and the Nova Scotia Gambia Association (NSGA), a Canadian NGO, and Saint Mary's University (located in Halifax, Nova Scotia). The first university, the University of The Gambia, was opened in 1999, with the assistance of Saint Mary's University. The higher education sector in Gambia is administered and funded by the Government. Some 1,591 students were enrolled at tertiary establishments in 1994/95, but by 2007 the number had risen to 8,373. In addition to the tertiary institutions, there are about 103 registered Skills Training Centres providing courses towards local and external certificates and diplomas in a variety of professional fields. These are mainly privately operated centres.

Admission to university is on the basis of the West African Secondary School Certificate or equivalent qualification. The University of The Gambia offers Bachelors degrees, which are awarded following four years. Until recently, there were no postgraduate degree courses, but in 2007 a Master of Arts degree programme in history was introduced. Technical and vocation education is offered by the Gambia Technical Training Institute and Gambia College. The main qualifications are the Diploma and Certificate.

A higher education policy is being developed following the establishment of a Ministry of Higher Education, Research and Science in early 2007. In the interim, the tertiary and higher education component of the Education Policy 2004–2015, prepared by the Ministry of Basic and Secondary Education, is being used to guide the activities of the new Minstry.

Regulatory Bodies

GOVERNMENT

Ministry of Basic and Secondary Education: Willy Thorpe Bldg, Banjul; tel. 4227236; fax 4224180; internet www .edugambia.gm; Min. FATOU L. FAYE.

Ministry of Higher Education, Research and Science: Banjul; tel. 4466752; fax 4465408; e-mail mendyag@yahoo.com; internet www.moherst.gov.gm; Minister Dr MARIAMA SARR-CESAY.

Ministry of Tourism and Culture: New Administrative Bldg, The Quadrangle, Banjul; tel. 4229844; fax 4227753; e-mail masterplan@gamtel.gm; internet mote.gov .gm; Min. FATOU MASS JOBE-NJIE.

Learned Society

LANGUAGE AND LITERATURE

Alliance Franco-Gambienne: Kairaba Ave, Kanifing, POB 2930, Serrekunda, Banjul; tel. 4375418; fax 4374172; e-mail alliancefg@hotmail.com; internet www .alliancefranco.gm; offers courses and exams in French language and culture and promotes cultural exchange with France.

Research Institutes

MEDICINE

Medical Research Council: POB 273, Banjul; Atlantic Blvd, Fajara; tel. 4496715; fax 4494154; e-mail aoffong@mrc.gm; internet www.mrc.gm; f. 1947; laboratory research, field research and clinical studies aimed at reducing illness and death from tropical infectious diseases; research on viral diseases, bacterial diseases and malaria; a nutrition research group is based at the MRC Keneba Field Site; Unit Dir and Chair. Prof. TUMANI CORRAH.

Medical Research Council Dunn Nutrition Unit, Keneba: Keneba, West Kiang; f. 1974; field station of the Dunn Nutrition Unit laboratory in Cambridge, UK; research on maternal undernutrition, including work on paediatric gastroenterology and nutrition, and the physiological adaptation of mothers to pregnancy and lactation; maternal vitamin and mineral requirements; research into long-term effects of antenatal and early postnatal nutrition; research on growth deficiency and the role of economic status on malnutrition; calorimetry research on comparisons of energy expenditure between Gambians and Europeans; Supervisor Dr ELIZABETH POSKITT.

Library

Banjul

Gambia National Library: Department Mail Bag, Reg Pye Lane, Banjul; tel. 4228312; fax 4223776; f. 1946 by British Ccl, taken over by Govt 1962, autonomous 1985; serves as a public and nat. library; nat. deposit library; 115,400 vols, 85 periodicals; spec. colln of Gambiana; Dir ABDOU WALLY MBYE; publs *National Bibliography*, *Wax Taani Xalel Yi* (children's magazine).

Museum

Banjul

Gambia National Museum: PMB 151, Independence Drive, Banjul; tel. 4226244; fax 4227461; e-mail musmon@qanet.gm; library of 645 vols; f. 1982; Curator HASSOUM CESSAY.

University

UNIVERSITY OF THE GAMBIA

Administration Bldg, Kanifing, POB 3530, Serrekunda

Telephone: 4372213
Fax: 4395064
E-mail: unigambia@qanet.gm
Internet: www.unigambia.gm
Founded 1999
State control
Academic year: October to July (two semesters)
Vice-Chancellor: Prof. DONALD E. U. EKONG
Registrar: E. J. AKPAN
Student Affairs: LAMIN S. JAITEH
Senate: LANG SAJO MUSTAPHA JADAMA
Council: MOMODOU LAMIN TARRO

Number of teachers: 99 (78 full-time, 21 part-time)
Number of students: 1,356

DEANS

Faculty of Economics and Management Sciences: SULAYMAN M. B. FYE
Faculty of Humanities and Social Sciences: Prof. EDRIS MAKWARD
Faculty of Medicine and Allied Health Sciences: Prof. ETIM M. ESSIEN
Faculty of Science and Agriculture: Prof. FELIXTINA JONSYN-ELLIS (acting)

College

Gambia College: Brikama Campus, POB 144, Banjul; tel. 4484812; fax 4483224; e-mail gcollege@qanet.gm; f. 1978; library: 23,000 vols; 57 teachers; 400 students; Pres. A. B. SENGHORE; Registrar N. S. MANNEH

HEADS OF SCHOOLS

Agriculture: EBRIMA CHAM (acting)
Education: W. A. COLE
Nursing and Midwifery: F. SARR
Public Health: B. A. PHALL

GEORGIA

The Higher Education System

Georgia was formerly a constituent republic of the USSR, from which it gained its independence in 1999. Most institutions were founded during the Soviet period and consequently reflected Soviet practices, but since independence there have been numerous reforms and ongoing projects. The Law of Education (2004) laid out further plans for the reform of secondary and higher education, including implementation of the Bologna Process. In addition to state institutions, many private institutions of higher education were opened after 1991; there were 109 in 2008/09. In 2008/09 there were 93,637 students enrolled at institutions of higher education (including universities). Higher education is administered by the Ministry of Education and Science.

Higher education admissions are determined on the basis of performance in the Unified National University Entry Examinations, administered by the National Assessment and Examinations Centre. Students take a range of compulsory and voluntary subjects relevant to their intended path of study. In May 2005 Georgia signed up to the Bologna Process. It was intended that Georgia would have a new degree structure in place by 2007/08, consisting of Bachelors, Masters and Doctorate degrees, and that the European Credit Transfer System (ECTS) would be adopted to facilitate student transfers. The Bakalavris Diplomi (Bachelors) is the main undergraduate degree and is awarded after three to fours years' study. The older, Soviet-style Certified Specialist degree is still awarded in some (mainly) professional fields. A Masters degree is awarded after the Bachelors following two years of study. A new doctoral degree is being developed to replace the old-style Candidate of Science and Doctor of Science degrees.

Since 2004 the accreditation of institutes of higher education has been the responsibility of the State Accreditation Service (SAS). Full institutional accreditation is only granted when institutions have completed a full self-evaluation and have satisfied the standards of the SAS with regard to the quality of their programmes, their teaching and their physical environment.

Regulatory and Representative Bodies

GOVERNMENT

Ministry of Culture and the Protection of Monuments: 0108 Tbilisi, Pr. Rustaveli 37; tel. (32) 93-22-55; fax (32) 99-90-37; e-mail info@mcs.gov.ge; internet www.mcs.gov.ge; Min. NIKOLOZ RURUA.

Ministry of Education and Science: 0102 Tbilisi, D. Uznadze 52; tel. (32) 95-70-10; fax (32) 91-04-47; e-mail pr@mes.gov.ge; internet www.mes.gov.ge; Min. DIMITRI SHASHKIN.

ACCREDITATION

ENIC/NARIC Georgia: Div. of Academic Recognition and Mobility, Min. of Education and Science, 0102 Tbilisi, D. Uznadze 52; tel. (32) 95-75-23; fax (32) 96-98-21; e-mail mobility_division@yahoo.com; Head Dr IRAKLI MACHABELI.

Learned Societies

GENERAL

Georgian Academy of Sciences: 0108 Tbilisi, Pr. Rustaveli 52; tel. (32) 99-88-91; fax (32) 99-88-23; e-mail academy@science.org.ge; internet www.science.org.ge; f. 1941; depts of agricultural science problems (Academician-Sec. O. G. NATISHVILI), applied mechanics, machine building and control processes (Academician-Sec. M. E. SALUKVADZE), biology (Academician-Sec. G. KVESITADZE), chemistry and chemical technology (Academician-Sec. G. TSINTSADZE), earth sciences (Academician-Sec. E. P. GAMKRELIDZE), linguistics and literature (Academician-Sec. G. KVARATSKHELIA), mathematics and physics (Academician-Sec. J. LOMINADZE), physiology and experimental medicine (Academician-Sec. T. N. ONIANI), social sciences (Academician-Sec. R. METREVELI); 117 mems (45 academicians, 72 corresp.); library: see Libraries and Archives; Pres. Acad. Prof. Dr THOMAS V. GAMKRELIDZE; publs Academy of Sciences (3 a year, in Georgian and English), Metsnierba da Technika (12 a year), Metsnierba da Technologiebi (12 a year).

HISTORY, GEOGRAPHY AND ARCHAEOLOGY

Georgian Geographical Society: 0107 Tbilisi, Ketskhoveli 11; attached to Georgian Acad. of Sciences; Chair. V. SH. DZHAOSHVILI.

Georgian History Society: 0108 Tbilisi, Pr. Rustaveli 52; attached to Georgian Acad. of Sciences; Vice-Chair. A. M. APAKIDZE.

LANGUAGE AND LITERATURE

Amateur Society of Basque Language and Culture: 0108 Tbilisi, Pr. Rustaveli 52; attached to Georgian Acad. of Sciences; Chair. SH. V. DZIDZIGURI.

British Council: 0108 Tbilisi, Pr. Rustaveli 34; tel. (32) 25-04-07; fax (32) 98-95-91; e-mail office@ge.britishcouncil.org; internet www.britishcouncil.org.ge; offers courses and examinations in English language and British culture and promotes cultural exchange with the UK; Dir JO BAKOWSKI; Librarian TAMUNA KVACHADZE.

Goethe-Institut: 0108 Tbilisi, ul. Sandukeli 16; tel. (32) 93-89-45; fax (32) 93-45-68; internet www.goethe.de/ins/ge/tif/deindex.htm; offers courses and examinations in German language and culture and promotes cultural exchange with Germany; library of 3,500 vols; Dir UWE RIEKEN.

MEDICINE

Georgian Bio-Medico-Technical Society: 0103 Tbilisi, Telavi 51; attached to Georgian Acad. of Sciences; Chair. K. SH. NADAREISHVILI.

Georgian Neuroscience Association: c/o Beritashvili Institute of Physiology, 0160 Tbilisi, Gotua St 14; tel. (32) 37-21-50; fax (32) 37-12-31; e-mail nodmit@biphysiol.ge; internet www.itic.org.ge/gena; f. 1996; 105 mems; Pres. Prof. SIMON KHECHINASHVILI; Exec. Sec. Prof. Dr NODAR MITAGVARIA.

Georgian Society of Patho-Anatomists: 0103 Tbilisi, V. Pshavela 27B; attached to Georgian Acad. of Sciences; Chair. T. I. DEKANOSIDZE.

NATURAL SCIENCES

Biological Sciences

Georgian Botanical Society: 0107 Tbilisi, Kodzhorskoe shosse; attached to Georgian Acad. of Sciences; Chair. G. SH. NAKHUTSRISHVILI.

Georgian Society of Biochemists: 0177 Tbilisi, Universitetis 2; tel. (32) 30-39-97; fax (32) 22-11-03; f. 1958; attached to Georgian Acad. of Sciences; 850 mems; Pres. Prof. NOUGZAR ALEKSIDZE; Sec. NANA ABASHIDZE.

Georgian Society of Geneticists and Selectionists: 0160 Tbilisi, ul. L. Gotua 3; tel. (32) 37-42-27; attached to Georgian Acad. of Sciences; Chair. T. G. CHANISHVILI.

Georgian Society of Parasitologists: 0179 Tbilisi, Pr. Chavchavadze 31; tel. (32) 22-33-53; fax (32) 22-01-64; attached to Georgian Acad. of Sciences; f. 1958; 83 mems; Pres. Prof. B. E. KURASHVILI; Sec. K. G. NIKOLAISHVILI; publ. Actual Problems of Parasitology in Georgia.

Physical Sciences

Georgian Geological Society: 0108 Tbilisi, Pr. Rustaveli 52; tel. (32) 99-64-45; fax (32) 99-88-23; f. 1933; attached to Georgian Acad. of Sciences; 500 mems; Chair. IRAKLI P. GAMKRELIDZE.

Georgian National Speleological Society: 0193 Tbilisi, M. Aleksidze (Bl. 8); tel. (32) 33-74-49; fax (32) 33-14-17; f. 1980; attached to Georgian Acad. of Sciences; 75 mems; Chair. Z. K. TATASHIDZE; publ. Caves of Georgia (irregular).

PHILOSOPHY AND PSYCHOLOGY

Georgian Philosophy Society: 0108 Tbilisi, Pr. Rustaveli 29; attached to Georgian Acad. of Sciences; Chair. N. Z. CHAVCHAVADZE.

Georgian Society of Psychologists: 0179 Tbilisi, Janashvili 22; attached to Georgian Acad. of Sciences; Chair. N. Z. NADIRASHVILI.

Research Institutes

GENERAL

Kutaisi Scientific Centre: 4600 Kutaisi, Abashidze 22; tel. (331) 7-77-77; attached to Georgian Acad. of Sciences; Dir R. ADAMAI.

AGRICULTURE, FISHERIES AND VETERINARY SCIENCE

Gulisashvili, V. Z., Institute of Mountain Forestry: 0186 Tbilisi, E. Mindeli 9; tel. (32) 30-34-66; e-mail postmaster@forest.acnet.ge; f. 1945; attached to Georgian Acad. of Sciences; Dir G. N. GIGAURI.

Institute of Water Management and Engineering Ecology: 0162 Tbilisi, Pr. Chavchavadze 60; tel. (32) 22-72-00; fax (32) 22-74-01; e-mail tsotnem@rambler.ru; f. 1929; attached to Georgian Acad. of Sciences; Dir T. MIRTSHOULAVA; publs *Proceedings*, *Recent Problems of Water Management*, *Transactions of International Conferences*.

Scientific Research Centre of the Biological Basis of Cattle-Breeding: 0162 Tbilisi, Paliashvili 87; tel. (32) 29-40-03; f. 1991; attached to Georgian Acad. of Sciences; Dir A. DOLMAZASHVILI.

ARCHITECTURE AND TOWN PLANNING

Kiriak Zavriev Institute of Structural Mechanics and Earthquake Engineering: 0193 Tbilisi, M. Aleksidze 8; tel. (32) 33-59-28; fax (32) 33-27-52; e-mail info@ismee .ge; internet ismee.ge; f. 1947; attached to Georgian Acad. of Sciences; Dir Prof. P. REKVAVA.

BIBLIOGRAPHY, LIBRARY SCIENCE AND MUSEOLOGY

Kekelidze, K. S., Institute of Manuscripts: 0193 Tbilisi, Merab Aleksidze St, Korp. 3; tel. (32) 36-24-54; fax (32) 94-25-18; e-mail manuscript@iatp.org.ge; internet www.acnet.ge/manuscr.htm; f. 1958; attached to Georgian Acad. of Sciences; Dir Z. ALEKSIDZE; publ. *Mravaltavi* (philology and history, 1 a year).

ECONOMICS, LAW AND POLITICS

Gugushvili, P. V., Institute of Economics: 0105 Tbilisi, ul. Kikodze 22; tel. (32) 99-68-53; fax (32) 99-83-89; e-mail root@econom .acnet.ge; f. 1944; attached to Georgian Acad. of Sciences; Dir G. TSERETELI.

Institute of Political Science: 0162 Tbilisi, Paliashvili 87; tel. (32) 22-41-04; e-mail politic@gw.acnet.ge; f. 2000; attached to Georgian Acad. of Sciences; Dir V. KESHELAVA.

Institute of State and Law: 0105 Tbilisi, ul. Kikodze 14; tel. (32) 98-32-45; e-mail root@stlow.acnet.ge; f. 1957; attached to Georgian Acad. of Sciences; Dir (vacant).

FINE AND PERFORMING ARTS

Chubinashvili, G. N., Institute of History of Georgian Art: 0108 Tbilisi, Pr. Rustaveli 52; tel. (32) 99-05-88; f. 1941; attached to Georgian Acad. of Sciences; Dir T. SAKVARELIDZE; publ. *Ars Georgica*.

HISTORY, GEOGRAPHY AND ARCHAEOLOGY

Ivane Javakhishvili Institute of History and Ethnology: 0179 Tbilisi, ul. Melikishvili 10; tel. (32) 99-06-82; e-mail histend55@ yahoo.com; f. 1941; attached to Iv. Javakhishvili Tbilisi State Univ.; scientific researches in ancient and modern history; confs, seminars; library of 55,000 vols; Dir Prof. Dr VAZHA I. KIKNADZE; Vice-Dir GURAM NIKOLASHVILI; publ. *Proceedings of the Institute of History and Ethnology* (1 a year).

Lordkipanidze Centre for Archaeological Studies: 0102 Tbilisi, D. Uznadze 14; tel. (32) 95-97-65; attached to Georgian Acad. of Sciences.

Mtskheta Institute of Archaeology: 3300 Mtskheta; f. 1994; attached to Georgian Acad. of Sciences; Dir A. APAKIDZE; publ. *Mtskheta*.

Vakhushti Bagrationi Institute of Geography: 0193 Tbilisi, M. Aleksidze 1 (Bl. 8); tel. (32) 33-74-49; fax (32) 33-14-07; e-mail geograf@gw.acnet.ge; f. 1933; attached to Georgian Acad. of Sciences; library of 68,000 vols; Dir ZURAB TATASHISZE; publ. *Caves of Georgia* (irregular).

LANGUAGE AND LITERATURE

Chikobava, A. S., Institute of Linguistics: 380002 Tbilisi, P. Ingorokva St 8; tel. (32) 93-29-21; internet www.acnet.ge/ike .htm; e-mail root@ike.acnet.ge; f. 1941; attached to Georgian Acad. of Sciences; Dir G. KVARATSKHELIA; publs *Dialectological Studies*, *Etymological Studies*, *Iberian-Caucasian Linguistics*, *Problems of Georgian Language Structure*, *Problems of Georgian Literary Norms*, *Problems of Modern General Linguistics*.

Shota Rustaveli Institute of Georgian Literature: 0108 Tbilisi, Kostava St 5; tel. (32) 99-53-00; fax (32) 99-53-00; e-mail litinst@litinstituti.ge; internet www .litinstituti.ge; f. 1932; attached to Georgian Acad. of Sciences; Georgian literature; literature theory and folklore; Dir Prof. IRMA RATIANI; Deputy Dir Prof. MAKA ELBAKIDZE; publs *Literary Researches* (1 a year), *Litinfo* (electronic), *Sjani* (peer-reveiwed int. journal of literary theory and comparative literature, 1 a year).

Tsereteli, G. V., Institute of Oriental Studies: 0103 Tbilisi, ul. G. Tsereteli 3; tel. (32) 23-23-72; fax (32) 23-30-08; e-mail root@ orient.acnet.ge; f. 1960; attached to Georgian Acad. of Sciences; Dir T. GAMKRELIDZE.

MEDICINE

Beritashvili Institute of Physiology: 0160 Tbilisi, ul. Gotua 14; tel. (32) 37-12-31; fax (32) 37-34-11; e-mail info@biphysiol.ge; internet www.biphysiol.ge; f. 1935 as Academic Research Institute; attached to Min. of Education and Science; library of 48,000 vols; Dir Dr M. G. TSAGARELI; Sec. N. EMUKHVARI.

Eliyava Institute of Bacteriophage, Microbiology and Virology: 0160 Tbilisi, ul. L. Gotua 3; tel. (32) 37-42-27; fax (32) 99-91-53; e-mail chanish@kheta.ge; f. 1923; attached to Georgian Acad. of Sciences; Dir T. CHANISHVILI.

Georgian Scientific Research Institute of Industrial Hygiene and Occupational Diseases: 0102 Tbilisi, D. Agmashenebeli 60; tel. (32) 95-65-94; f. 1927; library of 24,000 vols; Dir RUSUDAN DJAVAKHADZE; publ. periodicals on occupational hygiene and industrial diseases.

Institute of Medical Biotechnology: 0159 Tbilisi, Chiaureli 2; tel. and fax (32) 54-07-25; e-mail imb_admin@caucasus.net; internet www.imb.org.ge; f. 1991; attached to Min. of Education and Science; Dir TEIMURAZ TOPURIA; Head of Scientific Board Assoc. Prof. IA PANTSULAIA.

Institute of Pharmaceutical Chemistry: 0159 Tbilisi, P. Sarajishvili 36; tel. (32) 52-98-50; fax (32) 25-00-26; e-mail root@ pharmac.acnet.ge; f. 1932; attached to Georgian Acad. of Sciences; library of 3,500 vols, 40 periodicals; Dir Prof. ETHER P. KEMERTELIDZE; publ. *Transactions*.

Natishvili, A. N., Institute of Experimental Morphology: 0159 Tbilisi, Chiaureli 2; tel. (32) 52-09-06; f. 1946; attached to Georgian Acad. of Sciences; Dir N. A. JAVAKHISHVILI; publ. *Proceedings*.

Research and Teaching Clinical and Experimental Centre of Traumatology and Orthopaedics: 0102 Tbilisi, ul. Kalinina 51; tel. (32) 95-53-81; Dir B. TSERETELI.

Research Institute of Clinical Medicine: 0112 Tbilisi, 13, Tevdore Mgvdeli St; tel. (32) 94-02-89; fax (32) 34-49-23; f. 1991; Dir Prof. FRIDON TODUA; publ. *Georgian Journal of Radiology* (4 a year).

Research Institute of Psychiatry: 0177 Tbilisi, ul. M. Asatiani 10; tel. (32) 39-47-65; fax (32) 94-36-73; f. 1925; library of 8,000 vols, 7,000 periodicals.

Research Institute of Skin and Venereal Diseases: 0112 Tbilisi, ul. Ninoshvili 55; tel. (32) 95-35-64; fax (32) 96-48-02; f. 1935; library of 23,800 vols; Dir Dr BADZI CHLAIDZE; publ. *Trudy* (Proceedings, 1 a year).

Scientific Research Centre for Radiobiology and Radiation Ecology: 0103 Tbilisi, Telavi 51; tel. (32) 94-20-17; fax (32) 93-61-26; e-mail kiazo@gw.acnet.ge; internet www.acnet.ge/radiobio; f. 1990; attached to Georgian Acad. of Sciences; Dir K. SH. NADAREISHVILI; publs *Biomedical Techniques* (2 a year), *Problems of Ecology* (2 a year), *Radiation Studies* (2 a year).

Virsaladze Institute of Medical Parasitology and Tropical Medicine: 0112 Tbilisi, D. Agmashenebeli 139; tel. (32) 95-92-26; e-mail medpari@yahoo.com; internet geoparasitology.dsl.ge; f. 1924; parasitic and tropical diseases; Dir GIA CHUBABRIA; Deputy Dir NINO IASHVILI.

Zhordania Institute of Human Reproduction: 0109 Tbilisi, Kostava 43; tel. (32) 99-61-97; fax (32) 99-81-08; e-mail archil@list .ru; Dir Prof A. KHOMASSURIDZE.

NATURAL SCIENCES

Biological Sciences

Batumi Botanical Gardens: 6400 Makhinjauri; f. 1912; attached to Georgian Acad. of Sciences; Dir V. PAPUNIDZE; publ. *Bulletin*.

Central Botanical Gardens: 0105 Tbilisi, Botanikuri 1; tel. and fax (32) 72-34-09; f. 1636; attached to Georgian Acad. of Sciences; Dir J. KERESELIDZE; publ. *Proceedings*.

Davitashvili, L. Sh., Institute of Palaeobiology: 0108 Tbilisi, Niagvris 4; tel. (32) 93-12-82; e-mail guram@paleobi.acnet.ge; f. 1957; attached to Georgian Acad. of Sciences; Dir G. A. MCHEDLIDZE.

Durmishidze Institute of Plant Biochemistry: 0102 Tbilisi, D. Agmashenebeli 10; tel. (32) 95-81-45; fax (32) 25-06-04; e-mail postmaster@biochem.acnet.ge; f. 1971; attached to Georgian Acad. of Sciences; library of 72,000 vols; Dir Prof. Dr G. I. KVESITADZE.

Institute of Molecular Biology and Biological Physics: 0160 Tbilisi, ul. L. Gotua 14; tel. (32) 37-17-33; fax (32) 93-91-57; e-mail admin@biophys.org.ge; f. 1986; attached to Georgian Acad. of Sciences; Dir Dr M. M. ZAALISHVILI.

Institute of Zoology: 0179 Tbilisi, Pr. Chavchavadze 31; tel. (32) 22-01-64; f. 1941; attached to Georgian Acad. of Sciences; Dir I. ELIYAVA.

Ketskhoveli, N., Institute of Botany: 0105 Tbilisi, Kojori 1; tel. (32) 99-74-48; fax (32) 00-10-77; e-mail nakhutsrishvili@yahoo .com; f. 1933; attached to Georgian Acad. of Sciences; Dir G. NAKHUTSRISHVILI.

Mathematical Sciences

A. Razmadze Mathematical Institute: 0186 Tbilisi, 2 Universitry St; tel. (32) 30-40-78; fax (32) 36-40-86; e-mail ninopa@rmi .ge; internet www.rmi.ge; f. 1935; attached to I. Javakhishvili Tbilisi State Univ.; 70 mems; library of 95,690 vols; Dir Prof. NINO PARTSVANIA; publs *Georgian Mathematical Journal* (in English, 4 a year), *Memoirs on Differential Equations and Mathematical Physics* (in English, 3 a year), *Proceedings* (in English, 3 a year).

Muskhelishvili Institute of Computational Mathematics: 0171 Tbilisi, Akuri 8; tel. (32) 33-24-38; e-mail root@compmath .acnet.ge; f. 1956; attached to Georgian Acad. of Sciences; Dir Prof. N. VAKHANIYA; publs *Computational Mathematics and Programming, Mathematical and Technical Cybernetics.*

Physical Sciences

Abastumani Astrophysical Observatory: 0301 Abastumani, Kanobili Mountain; tel. (32) 95-53-67 0179 Tbilisi, ul. Kazbegi 2A; tel. (32) 37-63-03; e-mail roki@gw.acnet.ge; f. 1941; attached to Georgian Acad. of Sciences; Dir R. KILADZE; publ. *Bulletin.*

Andronikashvili Institute of Physics: 0162 Tbilisi, ul. Tamarashvili 6; f. 1950; attached to Georgian Acad. of Sciences; Dir G. A. KHARADZE.

Dzanelidze, A. I., Geological Institute: 0193 Tbilisi, M. Aleksidze 1 Bldg 9; tel. (32) 29-39-41; e-mail geolog@gw.acnet.ge; f. 1925; attached to Georgian Acad. of Sciences; incorporates Scientific and Technical Centre of Physical Crystallography; Dir Prof. MIRIAN TOPCHISHVILI; publ. *Proceedings* (irregular).

Ferdinand Tavadze Institute of Metallurgy and Materials Science: 1060 Tbilisi, Al. Kazbegi Ave 15; tel. (32) 37-02-67; fax (32) 37-02-67; e-mail info@mmi.ge; internet mmi .ge; f. 1945; attached to Georgian Acad. of Sciences; main fields of research: metallurgical processes, new materials and technologies, materials science and powder metallurgy; 136 mems; library of 152,953 vols; Dir Prof. Dr GIORGI F. TAVADZE.

Institute of Hydrometeorology: 0112 Tbilisi, D. Agmashenebeli 150A; tel. (32) 95-10-47; fax (32) 95-11-60; e-mail root@hydmet .acnet.ge; f. 1953; attached to Georgian Acad. of Sciences; Dir G. G. SVANIDZE; publ. *Transactions.*

Institute of Inorganic Chemistry and Electrochemistry: 0186 Tbilisi, Mindeli 11; tel. (32) 54-15-59; fax (32) 30-14-30; e-mail iice@caucasus.net; internet www .iice-eng.myweb.ge; f. 1956 to explore research opportunities in hydrogen and solar power generation, corrosion-resistant coatings and using uranium filters for water purification; attached to Georgian Acad. of Sciences; main fields of research: electrochemistry, inorganic chemistry, physical chemistry, chemical physics; Dir GRIGOR TATISHVILI.

Ferdinand Tavadze Institute of Metallurgy and Materials Science: 1060 Tbilisi, Al. Kazbegi Ave 15; tel. (32) 37-02-67; fax (32) 37-02-67; e-mail info@mmi.ge; internet mmi .ge; f. 1945; attached to Georgian Acad. of Sciences; main fields of research: metallurgical processes, new materials and technologies, materials science and powder metallurgy; 136 mems; library of 152,953 vols; Dir Prof. Dr GIORGI F. TAVADZE.

M. Nodia Institute of Geophysics: 0171 Tbilisi, M. Alexidze 1; tel. (32) 36-37-93; fax (32) 33-28-67; e-mail tamaz.chelidze@gmail .com; internet www.ig-geophysics.ge; f. 1933; attached to I. Tbilisi 'Javakhishvili'

State Univ.; incorporates National Service of Seismic Defence; library of 40,000 vols; Dir Dr NUGZAR GHLONTI; publ. *Journal of Georgian Geophysical Society* (Series A: Solid Earth Physics,Series B: Physics of Atmosphere, Ocean and Space Plasma, 1 a year).

Melikishvili, P. G., Institute of Physical and Organic Chemistry: 0186 Tbilisi, V. Jikia 5; tel. (32) 99-88-23; f. 1929; attached to Georgian Acad. of Sciences; Dir T. ANDRONIKASHVILI.

Transcaucasian Hydrometeorological Research Institute: 0112 Tbilisi, D. Agmashenebeli 150A; tel. (32) 63-74-01; fax (32) 23-22-93.

PHILOSOPHY AND PSYCHOLOGY

Tsereteli Institute of Philosophy: 0108 Tbilisi, Pr. Rustaveli 29; tel. (32) 99-52-62; e-mail root@philos.acnet.ge; attached to Georgian Acad. of Sciences; f. 1946; Dir T. BUACHIDZE.

Uznadze, D. N., Institute of Psychology: 0105 Tbilisi, ul. Iashvili 22; tel. (32) 93-24-54; e-mail root@psycho.acnet.ge; f. 1943; attached to Georgian Acad. of Sciences; Dir SH. NADIRASHVILI.

RELIGION, SOCIOLOGY AND ANTHROPOLOGY

Abuserisdze Tbeli Batumi Scientific Research Institute: 6016 Batumi, Ninoshvili 20; tel. (222) 3-29-01; fax (222) 7-58-17; e-mail isac@batumi.net; f. 1958; attached to Georgian Acad. of Sciences; Dir Dr IURI BIBILEISHVILI; publs *Culture and Life in South-Western Georgia* (1 a year), *Economic Problems in South-Western Georgia* (1 a year), *Folklore of South-Western Georgia* (1 a year), *Monuments of South-Western Georgia* (1 a year).

Institute of Demography and Sociological Studies: 0105 Tbilisi, ul. Pushkina 5; tel. (32) 93-36-93; fax (32) 98-65-88; internet www.acnet.ge/demograph; f. 1990; attached to Georgian Acad. of Sciences; Dir Dr L. L. CHIKAVA; publ. *Demography* (4 a year).

TECHNOLOGY

Eliashvili Institute of Control Systems: 0160 Tbilisi, K. Gamsakhurdia 34; tel. (32) 37-20-44; e-mail postmaster@contsys.acnet .ge; f. 1956; attached to Georgian Acad. of Sciences; library of 10,000 vols; Dir M. SALUKVADZE; publs *Language Processors and Speech Recognition* (1 a year), *Theory and Devices of Automatic Control* (1 a year).

G.Tsulukidze Mining Institute: 0186 Tbilisi, Mindelli 7; tel. (32) 32-47-16; fax (32) 32-59-90; e-mail im_mod@mining.org.ge; internet www.mining.org.ge; f. 1957; attached to Min. of Defence; underground structures construction and underground mining; open-cast operations and blast technologies; rock properties and in-massif physical processes research; special transport, reliability and diagnostics; mineral dressing, high-tech materials and mining wastes processing; Dir Dr NIKOLOZ CHIKHRADZE.

Institute of Cybernetics: 0186 Tbilisi, ul. S. Euli 5; tel. (32) 30-30-49; e-mail inst@ cybern.acnet.ge; f. 1960; attached to Georgian Acad. of Sciences; Dir G. KHARATISHVILI.

Institute of Hydrogeology and Engineering Geology: 0188 Tbilisi, Rustaveli Ave 31; tel. (32) 52-72-19; fax (32) 00-11-53; e-mail bguram@gw.acnet.ge; internet www .acnet.ge/hydrogeology_eng.htm; f. 1958; attached to Georgian Acad. of Sciences; Dir G. BUACHIDZE; publ. *Problems of Hydrogeology and Engineering Geology.*

Institute of Machine Mechanics: 0186 Tbilisi, Mindeli 10; tel. (32) 32-11-65; fax (32) 32-39-56; e-mail rdimmg@yahoo.com; internet www.imm.ge; f. 1953; attached to Georgian Acad. of Sciences; Dir TAMAZ NATRIASHVILI.

Sukhumi I. N. Vekua Institute of Physics and Technology: 0108 Tbilisi, Pr. Rustaveli 52; tel. and fax (32) 99-69-13; e-mail sipt@myoffice.ge; internet www.sipt .org.ge; f. 1945; attached to Georgian Acad. of Sciences; relocated from Sukhumi due to conflict in Abkhazia; Dir V. KASHIA.

Tbilisi Scientific-Industrial Institute 'Analizkhelsatsko': 0190 Tbilisi, Georgia Kakheti 36; tel. and fax (32) 77-68-22; e-mail ninodzagania@yahoo.com; f. 1956; attached to Georgian Acad. of Sciences; Dir-Gen. TAMAZ DZAGANIA.

Libraries and Archives

Tbilisi

Central Library of the Georgian Academy of Sciences: 0193 Tbilisi, M. Aleksidze 1–4; tel. (32) 36-34-13; fax (32) 33-01-35; e-mail acadlibrary@gw.acnet.ge; f. 1941; 3,200,000 vols; Dir M. ZAALISHVILI.

I. 'Javakhishvili' Tbilisi State University Library: 0128 Tbilisi, Pr. Chavchavadze 1; tel. (32) 22-10-32; internet www .tsu.edu.ge; f. 1918; 3,000,000 vols; Dir S. APAKIDZE.

Mikeladze, G. S., Scientific and Technical Library of Georgia: 0100 Tbilisi, ul. Dzneladze 27; 10,100,000 vols (without patents); Dir R. D. GORGILADZE.

National Library of Georgia: 0107 Tbilisi, Gulisashvili 5; tel. and fax (32) 99-80-95; f. 1846; 6,000,000 vols, 24,000 periodicals; Dir LEVAN BERDZENISHVILI.

Museums and Art Galleries

Kutaisi

Berdzenishvili, N. A., Kutaisi State Museum of History and Ethnography: 4600 Kutaisi, ul. Tbilisi 1; tel. (331) 5-56-76; f. 1912; attached to Georgian Acad. of Sciences; library of 25,000 vols; Dir Dr M. V. NIKOLEISHVILI.

Sokhumi

Sokhumi Botanical Garden: 6600 Sokhumi, ul. Chavchavadze 20; tel. (122) 2-44-58; attached to Georgian Acad. of Sciences; Dir (vacant).

State Museum of the Abkhazian Autonomous Republic: 6600 Sokhumi, ul. Lenina 22; f. 1915; history of the Abkhazian people; Dir A. A. ARGUN.

Tbilisi

Georgian National Museum: 0105 Tbilisi, 3 Rustaveli Ave; tel. (32) 99-80-22; fax (32) 98-21-33; e-mail info@museum.ge; internet www.museum.ge; f. 1852; history, natural history; attached to Georgian Acad. of Sciences; library of 250,000 vols; Gen. Dir Acad. DAVID LORDKIPANIDZE.

Georgian National Museum—National Gallery of Art: 0108 Tbilisi, Rustaveli Ave 11; tel. (32) 98-48-14; fax (32) 98 21 33; e-mail lanakaraia@yahoo.com; internet www .museum.ge; f. 1920; merged with Georgian National Museum in 2007; collns of modern Georgian art (painting, drawing, sculpture, applied art); Dir-Gen. DAVID LORDKIPANIDZE; Admin. Man. LANA KARAIA.

Georgian State Art Museum: 0107 Tbilisi, Ul. Gulisashvili 1; tel. (32) 99-66-35; f. 1920; Dir NODAR LOMOURI.

Georgian State Museum of Oriental Art: 0100 Tbilisi, ul. Azizbekova 3; Georgian fine and applied art; Dir G. M. GVISHIANI.

State Museum of Georgian Literature: 0108 Tbilisi, Giorgi Chanturia 10; tel. (32) 99-86-67; f. 1930; Georgian literature since 19th century; library of 11,893 vols; Dir I. A. ORDZHONIKIDZE; publ. *Literary Chronicle*.

Tbilisi State Museum of Anthropology and Ethnography: 0100 Tbilisi, Pr. Komsomolskii 11; history and ethnography of Georgia; library of 150,000 vols; Dir A. V. TKESHELASHVILI.

Universities

ABKHAZIAN 'A. M. GORKII' STATE UNIVERSITY

6600 Sokhumi, ul. Tsereteli 9
Telephone: (122) 2-25-98
Founded 1985
State control
Number of students: 3,800

Faculties of biology and geography, economics, history and law, philology, physics and mathematics, teacher training.

AKAKI TSERETELI STATE UNIVERSITY

4600 Kutaisi, Tamar Mepe St 59
Telephone: (331) 4-57-84
Fax: (331) 4-38-33
E-mail: atsu@atsu.edu.ge
Internet: atsu.edu.ge
Founded 1933
State control

Rector: GIORGI ONIANI
Number of teachers: 437
Number of students: 5,987

DEANS

Faculty of Arts: Prof. NINO CHIKHLADZE
Faculty of Exact and Natural Sciences: Assoc. Prof. EREKLE JAPARIDZE
Faculty of Maritime Transport: Prof. ZURAB ARKANIA
Faculty of Medicine: Prof. BORIS CHAKVETADZE
Faculty of Pedagogics: Prof. GOGI BERDZULISHVILI
Faculty of Social Science: Assoc. Prof. GODERDZI VACHRIDZE
Faculty of Technical Engineering: Prof. AVTANDIL TVALCHRELIDZE
Faculty of Technological Engineering: Prof. MERAB SHALAMBERIDZE

BATUMI 'M. ABASHIDZE' STATE INSTITUTE OF CULTURE

6000 Batumi, Tamaris Dasaheba
Telephone: (222) 5-02-64
Founded 1992
State control

Rector: GAIOZ JORDANIA (acting)
Vice-Rector for Academic Affairs: NODAR VARSHANIDZE

Faculties of art research, ballet, cinema, drama, fine arts, musical disciplines, television and radio journalism.

BATUMI 'RUSTAVELI' STATE UNIVERSITY

6010 Batumi, Ninoshvili 35
Telephone: (222) 7-17-80
Fax: (222) 7-17-86
E-mail: info@bsu.edu.ge
Internet: bsu.edu.ge
Founded 1935
State control

Rector: NUGZAR MGELADZE

Faculties of biology, economics, education, foreign languages, geography, history, initial military education and physical culture, medicine, philology, physics and mathematics.

GEORGIAN ACADEMY OF PHYSICAL EDUCATION

0179 Tbilisi, Pr. Chavchadze 49
Telephone: (32) 22-31-60
Fax: (32) 29-37-59
Founded 1938
State control

Rector: OMAR GOGIASHVILI.

GEORGIAN STATE ACADEMY OF ANIMAL HUSBANDRY AND VETERINARY MEDICINE

0114 Tbilisi, Krtsanisi
Telephone: (32) 72-04-49
Fax: (32) 99-50-91
Founded 1932
State control

Rector: JEMAL GUGUSHVILI
Vice-Rector: ROMAN TSAGAREISHVILI.

GEORGIAN TECHNICAL UNIVERSITY

0171 Tbilisi, ul. M. Kostava 77
Telephone: (32) 44-11-66
Fax: (32) 44-11-66
E-mail: intrelgu@yahoo.com
Internet: www.gtu.edu.ge
Founded 1990 (1922 as Georgia Polytechnic Institute)
State control
Languages of instruction: Georgian, Russian, English
Academic year: September to June

Rector: Prof. R. KHURODZE
Vice-Rector: Prof. ARCHIE PRANGISHVILI
Head of Foreign Affairs: TARIEL TAKTAKISHVILI
Head of Teaching and Methodology: O. ZUMBURIDZE
Librarian: V. PAPASKIRI
Number of teachers: 2,050
Number of students: 28,000
Publication: *Agmshenebeli* (newspaper)

DEANS

Faculty of Architecture: G. MIKIASHVILI
Faculty of Aviation: S. TEPNADZE
Faculty of Basic Sciences: T. DADIANI
Faculty of Chemical Engineering: N. KUTSLAVA
Faculty of Civil Engineering: C. LAGUNDARIDZE
Faculty of Communication: A. ROBITACHVILI
Faculty of Humanities: K. KOKRASHVILI
Faculty of Hydraulic Engineering: L. GOGELIANI
Faculty of Information Technology: Z. TSVERAIDZE
Faculty of Mechanics and Machine-building: A. TAVKHELIDZE
Faculty of Metallurgy: N. TSERETELI
Faculty of Mining and Geology: A. ABSHILAVA
Faculty of Power Engineering: G. ARABIDZE
Faculty of Transport: O. GEBASHVILI

GORI STATE UNIVERSITY

1400 Gori, Chavchavadze 53
Telephone: (370) 7-29-97
Fax: (370) 7-32-13
E-mail: gori@ip.osgf.ge
Founded 1935
State control

Depts of auditing, accountancy and statistics, business and management, correspondence learning, finance and commerce, foreign languages, history and law, international economic relations, nature and philology, pedagogics and medicine

Rector: GEDEVAN KHELAIA
Vice-Rector for Admin.: JEMALI DZIDZIGURI
Library of 200,000 vols.

I. TBILISI 'JAVAKHISHVILI' STATE UNIVERSITY

0179 Tbilisi, Pr. Chavchavadze 1
Telephone and fax (32) 22-56-79
E-mail: international@tsu.ge
Internet: www.tsu.edu.ge
Founded 1918
State control
Language of instruction: Georgian
Academic year: September to June

Chancellor: ROMAN KHARBEDIA
Rector: Prof. GIORGI KHUBUA
Vice-Rector: Dr IRINE DARCHIA
Head of the Scientific Library: TAMAR NEMSITSVERIDZE

Library: see Libraries and Archives
Number of teachers: 1,340
Number of students: 18,000
Publications: *Proceedings* (4 a year, in 2 series), *Tbilisi University* (52 a year)

DEANS

Faculty Economics and Business: ELENE KHARABADZE
Faculty of Exact and Natural Sciences: RAMAZ BOTCHORISHVILI
Faculty of Humanities: GOCHA JAPARIDZE
Faculty of Law: IRAKLI BURDULI
Faculty of Medicine: ALEXANDER TSISKARIDZE
Faculty of Social and Political Sciences: NODAR BELKANIA

'ILIA CHAVCHAVADZE' STATE UNIVERSITY

0179 Tbilisi, Pr. I. Chavchavadze 32
Telephone: (32) 29-41-97
Fax: (32) 22-00-09
E-mail: uni@iliauni.edu.ge
Internet: www.iliauni.edu.ge
Founded 2006 by merger of Tbilisi 'Ilia Chavchavadze' State Univ. of Language and Culture and Tbilisi 'Sulkhan-Saba Orbeliani' State Pedagogical Univ.
State control

Rector: Prof. GIGI TEVZADZE
Admin. Dir: SERGO RATIANI

DEANS

Faculty of Education: IVANE KALADZE
Faculty of Humanities and Cultural Studies: SHUKIA APRIDONIDZE
Faculty of Life Sciences: GIORGI NAKHUTSRISHVILI
Faculty of Philology of Foreign Languages: MZIA BAKRADZE
Faculty of Philosophy and Social Sciences: Prof. GIGI TEVZADZE
Faculty of Physics and Mathematics: JUANSHER CHKAREULI

PROFESSORS

Faculty of Education (depts of correctional pedagogy and pre-school pedagogy, education economics and management, education psychology, general pedagogy, specific methods):

IMEDADZE, NATELA
KALADZE, IVANE
KORINTELI, REVAZ
MALAZONIA, DAVID
MAQASHVILI, KETEVAN
SHAVERDASHVILI, EKATERINE

Faculty of Humanities and Cultural Studies (depts of culture, history, linguistics, literary studies):

APRIDONIDZE, SHUKIA
GHAGHANIDZE, MERAB
KOBALAVA, IZABELA
KOCHLAMAZASHVILI, TAMAZ
LADARIA, NODAR
PITSKHELAURI, KONSTANTINE

Faculty of Life Sciences (dept of biology):

BADRIDZE, IASON, Ecology of Behaviour
GEGELASHVILI, GIORGI, Molecular and Cellular Biochemistry
KOPALIANI, NATIA, Zoology, Conservative Biology
NAKHUTSRISHVILI, GIORGI, Botany, Ecology
SHATIRISHVILI, AIVENGO, Genetics, Evolutionary Biology
SOLOMONIA, REVAZ, Biochemistry, Physiology
TARKHNISHVILI, DAVID, Ecology, Evolutionary Biology

Faculty of Philology of Foreign Languages (depts of American/English studies, comparative literary studies, Germanic studies, linguoculturology, Oriental studies, Romance studies, Slavic studies):

BAKRADZE, MZIA
DOKHTURISHVILI, MZAGHO
GAJIEV, VALEKH
GOGOLADZE, TEIMURAZ
GVENTSADZE, MZIA
JASHI, KETEVAN
LEBANIDZE, GURAM VAKHTANG
MARSAGISHVILI, REZO
MIKADZE, MZIA
PIRTSKHALAVA, NINO

Faculty of Philosophy and Social Sciences (depts of economics, international relations and security studies, journalism, philosophy, politology, psychology, sociology and demography):

BERIASHVILI, MAMUKA
DARCHIASHVILI, DAVID
IMEDADZE, IRAKLI
NODIA, GIORGI
SURGULADZE, REVAZ
TEVZADZE, GIGI
TEVZADZE, GURAM
TSULADZE, GIOGI

Faculty of Physics and Mathematics (depts of mathematics, physics):

CHKAREULI, JUANSHER
JANGVELADZE, TEMUR
KHARAZISHVILI, ALEXANDRE
KHIMSHIASHVILI, GIORGI
MURUSIDZE, IVANE
SVANADZE, MERAB
TSIBAKHASHVILI, NELI

TBILISI STATE INSTITUTE OF CULTURE

0102 Tbilisi, D. Agmashenebeli 40
Telephone: (32) 95-10-50
Fax: (32) 94-37-28

Founded 1992
State control

Rector: TEMUR ZHGENTI
Vice-Rector: VLADIMER KIRVALISHVILI

Faculties of choreography, fine and applied arts, humanities and musicology.

TBILISI STATE MEDICAL UNIVERSITY

0177 Tbilisi, Vazha-Pshavela 33
Telephone: (32) 54-24-50
Fax: (32) 54-24-51
E-mail: iad@tsmu.edu
Internet: www.tsmu.edu

Founded 1918
State control
Languages of instruction: English, Georgian
Academic year: September to June

Rector: Prof. ZURAB VADACHKORIA

Library of 500,000 vols
Number of teachers: 700
Number of students: 5,000

Publications: *Annals of Biomedical Research and Education* (4 a year), *Georgian Medical News* (12 a year), *Research* (1 a year)

DEANS

Faculty of Medicine: Prof. TINATIN CHIKOVANI
Faculty of Pharmacy: Prof. DALI BERASHVILI
Faculty of Physical Medicine and Rehabilitation: Prof. KAKHA CHELIDZE
Faculty of Public Health: Prof. BIDZINA ZURASHVILI
Faculty of Stomatology: Prof. SAMSON MGEBRISHVILI

TBILISI STATE UNIVERSITY OF ECONOMIC RELATIONS

0144 Tbilisi, Ketevan Tsamebuli 55
Telephone: (32) 94-28-83
Fax: (32) 94-31-60
E-mail: rectori@internet.ge

Founded 1992
State control

Rector: AVTANDIL CHUTLASVILI
Vice-Rector: GURAM TAVARTKILADZE

Library of 29,000
Number of students: 1,811

DEANS

Business Administration: Prof. GELA ALADASHVILI
Law: Prof. VENEDI BENIDZE

TELAVI 'I. GOGEBASHVILI' STATE UNIVERSITY

2200 Telavi, Universitetis 1
Telephone: (350) 7-15-33
Fax: (350) 7-32-64
E-mail: office_teasu@grena.ge
Internet: www.tesau.edu.ge

Founded 1939
State control
Academic year: September to June

Rector: GEORGE GOTSIRIDZE
Head of Admin.: HAMLET RAZMADZE
Head of Quality Assurance Office: TINATIN ZURABISHVILI
Head of Library: NANA KARAULASHVILI

Library of 148,000 vols; 3 periodical titles
Number of teachers: 212
Number of students: 1,652

DEANS

Faculty of Actuarial and Natural Sciences: TEA MCHEDLURI
Faculty of Agriculture and Food Processing: NIKO SULKHANISHVILI
Faculty of Humanities: MALKHAZ TCIRIKIDZE
Faculty of Medicine: LALI MEKOKISHVILI
Faculty of Pedagogical Sciences: NINO NAKHUTSRISHVILI
Faculty of Social Sciences, Business and Law: IRMA SHIOSHVILI

PROFESSORS

BERTLANI, A., Russian Philology
BOKHASHVILI, I., Law
BURDULI, M., Medicine
CHACHANIDZE, G., Informatics
CHANTURIA, E., Law
CHIBURDANIDZE, L., Economics
CHICHIASHVILI, E., Foreign Languages
CHIKADZE, R., Georgian Philology
CHKHARTISHVILI, N., Viti Culture
DOGONADZE, N., Pedagogical Sciences
ELANIDZE, V., History of Georgia
ELIZBARASHVILI, E., Geography
FARSADANISHVILI, A., History of Diplomacy
GELDIASHVILI, N., Georgian Philology
GIGASHVILI, K., Georgian Philology
GIORGADZE, G., Law
GOGOCHURI, N., Georgian Philology
GOTSIRIDZE, G., World History
IANVARASHVILI, L., Philosophy and Social Sciences
JACHVADZE, E., World History
JANASHIA, L., Pedagogical Sciences
JANGULASHVILI, E., Pedagogical Sciences
JAVAKHISHVILI, A., Economics
JAVAKHISHVILI, G., Georgian Philology
JAVAKHISHVILI, M., Chemistry and Technology
KATSITADZE, N., Physical Culture
KHOSITASHVILI, M., Wine Making
KOKILASHVILI, V., Physics and Mathematics
KURATASHVILI, A., Economics
KVASHILAVA, A., Law
MALATSIDZE, V., Medicine
MAMUKELASHVILI, E., Political Studies
MCHEDLISHVILI, D., Physics and Mathematics
MIKELADZE, M., Georgian Philology
MODEBADZE, N., Physics and Mathematics
NADIRADZE, T., Biology and Ecology
NANOBASHVILI, K., Informatics
RAINAULI, Z., Medicine
RCHEULISHVILI, G., History of Georgia
ROSTOMASHVILI, N., Physics and Mathematics
SHALVASHVILI, L., Georgian Philology
SHIOSHVILI, I., Philosophy and Social Sciences
VAKHTANGISHVILI, T., History of Georgia
ZURABISHVILI, T., Philosophy and Social Sciences
ZUROSHVILI, L., Biology and Ecology

TSKHINVALI PEDAGOGICAL INSTITUTE–GEORGIAN SECTOR

Shida Qartli, 1400 Gori, Chavchavadze 57
Telephone: (370) 2-19-35

Founded 1932
State control

Rector: VAHTANG AHALAIA
Vice-Rector: V. BURCHULADZE

Faculties of biology, chemistry and physical training, education, teaching and methods, foreign languages, Georgian language and literature, history and philology, mathematics and physics, natural sciences.

Other Higher Educational Institutes

Georgian 'S. Rustaveli' State Institute of Theatre and Cinematography: 0108 Tbilisi, Pr. Rustaveli 17; tel. (32) 99-94-11; fax (32) 98-30-97; e-mail eliso@geo.net.ge; f. 1939; drama, film, television, stage management, archive management, art history; library: 50,000 vols; 150 teachers; 800 students; Rector Prof. GIGA LORDKIPHANIDZE.

Georgian State Agrarian University: 0131 Tbilisi, D. Agmashenebeli 13-km, Dighomi; tel. (32) 95-71-47; fax (32) 52-00-47; e-mail agrdig@geointer.net.ge; f. 1929 as Georgian Agricultural Institute; present name and status 1991; faculties of agricultural electrification and automation, agricultural mechanization, agronomy, economics and humanities, forestry, hydromelioration and engineering ecology, technology and viticulture; library: 747,600 vols; 583 teachers; 7,500 students; Rector Prof. Dr NAPOLEON KARKASHADZE.

Georgian State Institute of Subtropical Agriculture: 4600 Kutaisi, Pr. Chavchavadze 13; tel. (331) 7-06-14; e-mail ssmsi@sanet.net.ge; faculties of agri-business, agricultural engineering, agriculture and food technology, economics; library: 90,000 vols; Rector GURAM KILASONIA.

Kutaisi 'N. I. Muskhelishvili' Technical University: 4614 Kutaisi, Akhalgazrdobis Gamziri 98; tel. and fax (331) 2-06-90; e-mail vg@posta.ge; f. 1973; institutes of automobile and transport, cybernetics, electrical engineering, food and chemical industry, humanities and economics, mechanical engineering, technology and design; library: 250,000 vols; 300 periodicals; 360 teachers; 5,600 students; Rector AMIRAN HVADAGIANI.

Tbilisi State Academy of Arts: 0108 Tbilisi, ul. Griboedova 2; tel. and fax (32) 93-69-59; e-mail nanniashuili@posta.ge; f. 1922; faculties of architecture, art history and theory, design, fine arts; library: 42,000 vols; 355 teachers; 1,600 students; Rector Prof. IOSEB KOIAVA; publ. *Works* (1 a year).

Tbilisi 'V. Saradzhishvili' State Conservatoire: 0108 Tbilisi, ul. Griboedova 8; tel. and fax (32) 99-91-44; e-mail tbil_conservatory@hotmail.com; f. 1917; courses in choral conducting, composition, musicology, orchestral instruments, piano, singing; library: 100,000 vols; 205 teachers; 700 students; Rector Prof. MANANA DOLJASHVILI.

GERMANY

The Higher Education System

During 1949–90 Germany was divided between the sovereign states of the Federal Republic of Germany (FRG) and the German Democratic Republic (GDR). Both states developed their own higher education systems. In the FRG, the Grundgesetz (Basic Law) of 1949 stated that the majority of aspects of the administration and legislation of the education system were the responsibility of the Länder (States). Following reunification in 1990, the former GDR was incorporated into the Federal structure, and adopted the higher education standards already implemented in the former FRG. Higher education thus remains the responsibility of the 16 Länder, and is overseen by the national Kultusministerkonferenz (Standing Conference of the Ministers of Education and Cultural Affairs of the Länder). Higher education is divided between Hochschulen and Fachhochschulen. Hochschulen encompass classical universities (Universität), technical universities (Technische Hochschulen/Universität), combined Hochschulen-Fachhochschulen (Universität-Gesamthochschulen), teacher-training institutes (Pädagogische Hochschulen), theological universities (Theologische Hochschulen), art universities (Kunsthochschulen) and music universities (Musikhochschulen). Fachhochschulen are universities of applied science specializing in technical vocation education and training. In 2005/06 335,961 students were enrolled in higher education (non-university) institutions and 1,953,504 were enrolled in universities and equivalent institutions.

Admission to Hochschulen is based on performance in Zeugnis der Allgemeinen Hochschulreife or Fachgebundene Hochschulreife, and admission to Fachhochschulen depends on Fachhochschulreife, Zeugnis der Allgemeinen Hochschulreife or Fachgebundene Hochschulreife. Germany has implemented the Bologna Process and introduced a two-tier Bachelors and Masters degree system to replace the traditional German degrees in Hochschulen. The Bachelors lasts three to four years and the Masters a further one to two years. Doctoral studies follow the Masters. In Fachhochschulen, the traditional Fachhochschuldiplom (four years) has been retained as, unlike the Bachelors, it involves a large element of practical training; however, both the Bachelors and Masters degrees have been introduced in Fachhochschulen.

Mixed academic and vocational training is also offered by Berufsakademien or Studienakademien, which were first established in Baden-Württemberg in 1974; they are not present in every Land. Students are awarded the Berufsakademien Diplom after a three-year course. Technical and vocational education is offered by different types of institution in addition to the degree-level programmes offered by the Fachhochschulen. An estimated two-thirds of German students of the relevant age attend Berufsschulen, which combine classroom-based instruction and practical experience in a three-year course. Berufsfachschulen specialize in two- to three-year occupational training courses, leading to the award of the titles Facharbeiterbrief (Skilled Worker Certificate), Kaufmannsgehilfenbrief (Clerical Assistant Certificate) and Gesellenbrief (Craftsman Certificate). Berufsoberschulen are only available in some Länder and allow those who have completed secondary education and have acquired at least five years of professional experience to study for the Fachgebundende Hochschulreife, which confers eligibility to enter Hochschulen and Fachhochschulen. Fachschulen provide one- to three-year courses for those who already have previous vocational education and professional experience.

Regulatory and Representative Bodies

GOVERNMENT

Federal Ministry of Education and Research: Hannoversche Str. 28–30, 10115 Berlin; tel. (30) 18570; fax (30) 185783601; e-mail information@bmbf.bund.de; internet www.bmbf.de; Federal Min. ANNETTE SCHAVAN.

Gemeinsame Wissenschaftskonferenz (Joint Science Conference): Friedrich-Ebert-Allee 38, 53113 Bonn; tel. (228) 54020; fax (228) 5402150; e-mail gwk@gwk-bonn.de; internet www.gwk-bonn.de; f. 1970 as Bund-Länder Commission for Educational Planning (Bund-Länder-Kommission für Bildungsplanung) by agreement between the Federal and Länder govts; granted additional functions in 1975 by the Skeleton Agreement on Research Promotion; present name and status 2008; intergovernmental commission; permanent forum for discussion of all questions of education and research promotion that are of common interest to the Fed. and Länder govts; makes recommendations to the Heads of the Fed. and Länder govts on educational planning and research promotion; cooperates closely with the various Conferences of Länder Ministers; Chair. Prof. Dr E. JÜRGEN ZÖLLNER; Deputy Chair. Prof. Dr ANNETTE SCHAVAN; Sec.-Gen. Dr HANS-GERHARD HUSUNG.

Kultusministerkonferenz/Die Ständige Konferenz der Kultusminister der Länder in der Bundesrepublik Deutschland (Standing Conference of the Ministers of Education and Cultural Affairs of the Länder): POB 2240, 53012 Bonn; Graurheindorfer Str. 157, 53117 Bonn; tel. (228) 5010; fax (228) 501777; e-mail poststelle@kmk.org; internet www.kmk.org; f. 1948; conference of ministers and senators of the 16 Länder whose portfolios encompass culture, education, research and training; maintains offices in Berlin; Pres. Dr BERND ALTHUSMANN; Vice-Pres. Prof. Dr BIRGITTA WOLFF; Vice-Pres. Dr HERLIND GUNDELACH; Vice-Pres. Dr LUDWIG SPAENLE; Gen. Sec. Prof. Dr ERICH THIES.

ACCREDITATION

Akkreditierungs-, Certifizierungs- und Qualitätssicherungs-Instituts (ACQUIN) (Accreditation, Certification and Quality Assurance Institute): Brandenburger Str. 2, 95448 Bayreuth; tel. (921) 53039050; fax (921) 53039051; e-mail sekr@acquin.org; internet www.acquin.org; f. 2001 as a consequence of the Bologna process and the need for assuring the quality of newly introduced undergraduate and postgraduate degrees in Germany; member-based, non-profit org.; licensed by the Akkreditierungsrat (q.v.) to award its quality seal to study programmes that have successfully undergone accreditation; accreditation of German Bachelors and Masters study programmes in all subject fields based on the expertise of Standing Expert Cttee mems; evaluation and accreditation of selected int. study programmes; int. cooperation and networking; organizes projects and workshops with nat. and int. partners; develops new quality assurance methods; pilot project: 'Process Quality in Teaching and Learning'; Chair. Prof. Dr Ing. GERD ZIMMERMAN; Dir THOMAS REIL; Sec. URSULA HAMMON.

Akkreditierungsagentur für Studiengänge der Ingenieurwissenschaften, der Informatik, der Naturwissenschaften und der Mathematik—ASIIN eV (Accreditation Agency for Degree Programmes in Engineering, Informatics, Natural Sciences and Mathematics): c/o VDI, POB 10 11 39, 40002 Düsseldorf; Robert-Stolz-Str. 5, 40470 Düsseldorf; tel. (211) 9009770; fax (211) 90097799; e-mail info@asiin.de; internet www.asiin.de; f. 1999 as ASII, merged with Akkreditierungsagentur für die Studiengänge Chemie, Biochemie und Chemieingenieurwesen an Universitäten und Fachhochschulen (A-CBC) and adopted present name in 2002; accredited by Akkreditierungsrat since 2002, full member of ENQA since 2007, accepted into EQAR since 2009; not-for-profit branch of ASIIN, official accreditation in Germany since 2002; the only German accreditation agency to be explicitly specialized in accrediting degree programmes in engineering, informatics, natural sciences and mathematics; non-profit, registered asscn; accredited by Akkreditierungsrat (q.v.); represents competence in mechanical engineering, process engineering, civil engineering, surveying, architecture, city and spatial planning, physical technologies, materials and processes, agronomy, nutritional science, landscape architecture, life sciences, physics, electrical engineering, IT, informatics, computer science, business informatics, information systems, industrial engineering, chemistry, geosciences, mathematics as well as in quality management and quality assurance in higher education; also incl. system accreditation and institutional reviews/accreditation; 40 mems; Chair. Dr Ing. HANS-HEINZ ZIMMER; Deputy Chair. Prof. Dr Ing. JÖRG STEINBACH; Man. Dir Dr IRING WASSER; Vice-Man. Dir BIRGIT HANNY; Sec. KARIN BERG.

Akkreditierungsagentur für Studiengänge im Bereich Gesundheit und Soziale (AHPGS) (Accreditation Agency for Study Programmes in Health and Social Sciences): Sedanstr. 22, 79098 Freiburg; tel. (761) 20853309; e-mail ahpgs@ahpgs.de; internet www.ahpgs.de; promotes quality and transparency of German univ. study courses for health and social professionals; works to guarantee uniform and internationally comparable quality standards in the new Bachelors and Masters degrees through accreditation procedures; operates continual information exchange with other nat. and int. accreditation agencies as well as univ. representatives, practitioners' orgs and asscns; mems incl. the dean conference nursing science (33 univs), the assemblies of the depts of social work (73 univs) and remedial education (8 univs) as well as the German Coordinating Agency for Public Health; accredited by the Akkreditierungsrat (q.v.); Chair. Prof. Dr JÜRGEN VON TROSCHKE; CEO GEORG RESCHAUER; Sec. GABRIELE KRAUSE.

Akkreditierungsrat (Accreditation Council): Adenauerallee 73, 53113 Bonn; tel. (228) 3383060; fax (228) 33830679; e-mail akr@akkreditierungsrat.de; internet www.akkreditierungsrat.de; f. 1999 by Kultusministerkonferenz (q.v.) and Hochschulrektorenkonferenz (q.v.); attached to Stiftung zur Akkreditierung von Studiengängen in Deutschland (Foundation for the Accreditation of Study Programmes in Germany); acts on behalf of Länder to accredit accreditation agencies and degree programmes leading to Bakkalaureus/Bachelors and Magister/Masters degrees; financed by Stifterverband für die Deutsche Wissenschaft (q.v.); Chair. Prof. Dr REINHOLD R. GRIMM; Man. Dir Dr ACHIM HOPBACH; Sec. Prof. Dr THOMAS DEUFEL.

AQAS eV/Agentur für Qualitätssicherung durch Akkreditierung von Studiengängen: In der Sürst 1, 53111 Bonn; tel. (228) 9096010; fax (228) 9096019; e-mail info@aqas.de; internet www.aqas.de; f. 2002; accredited by Akkreditierungsrat (q.v.); 71 univs, 2 scientific asscns; Chair. Prof. Dr HOLGER BURCKHART; Deputy Chair. Prof. INGEBORG HENZLER; Man. Dir Dr VERENA KLOETERS; Dir for Strategy, Process, Int. Affairs DORIS HERRMANN.

ENIC/NARIC Germany: Central Office for Foreign Education, Secretariat of the Standing Conference of the Ministers of Education and Cultural Affairs, POB 2240, 53012 Bonn; Graurheindorfer Str. 157, 53117 Bonn; tel. (228) 501264; fax (228) 501229; e-mail zab@kmk.org; internet www.kmk.org/zab; f. 1905; attached to Kultusministerkonferenz (q.v.); Head of Dept BARBARA BUCHAL-HÖVER.

Foundation for International Business Administration Accreditation (FIBAA): Berliner Freiheit 20–24, 53111 Bonn; tel. (228) 2803560; fax (228) 28035620; e-mail brackmann@fibaa.org; internet www.fibaa.org; f. 1995; accredits Bachelors, Masters and Diploma courses in fields such as eco-

nomics, business computing, engineering and business admin., business psychology, business law, etc., in Germany, Austria and Switzerland; provides information and advice on Bachelors and Masters courses to univs, students and private enterprises; maintains offices in Zürich (Switzerland); Man. Dir DAISUKE MOTOKI; Man. Dir HANS-JÜRGEN BRACKMANN.

FUNDING

Deutscher Akademischer Austausch Dienst eV (DAAD) (German Academic Exchange Service): POB 20 04 04, 53134 Bonn; Kennedyallee 50, 53175 Bonn; tel. (228) 8820; fax (228) 882444; e-mail postmaster@daad.de; internet www.daad.de; f. 1925 as Academic Exchange Service, present name 1931; br. office in Berlin; foreign brs in Beijing, Brussels, Cairo, Hanoi, Jakarta, London, Mexico City, Moscow, Nairobi, New Delhi, New York, Paris, Rio de Janeiro, Tokyo, Warsaw; awards scholarships and grants, largely funded from Federal budget, to promote academic and cultural exchange between German and foreign students and thereby encourage closer relations between Germany and other countries; exchange of professors, lecturers in German for foreign universities, IAESTE—student-trainees, scholarships for German and foreign students and graduates; 234 mem. univs, 124 students; Pres. Prof. Dr SABINE KUNST; Vice-Pres. Prof. Dr MAX G. HUBER; Sec.-Gen. Dr DOROTHEA RÜLAND; publ. Change by Exchange (image brochure and flyers).

NATIONAL BODIES

Deutsche Hochschulverband (DHV) (German Association of University Professors and Lecturers): Rheinallee 18, 53173 Bonn; tel. (228) 9026666; fax (228) 9026680; e-mail dhv@hochschulverband.de; internet www.hochschulverband.de/cms1; f. 1920 as German Association of Universities, dissolved in 1936, refounded 1950; 24,000 mems; Pres. Prof. Dr BERNHARD KEMPEN; Vice-Pres. Prof. Dr BERND HELMIG; Vice-Pres. Prof. Dr DANIELA WAWRA; Vice-Pres. Prof. Dr Ing. ILONA ROLFES; Vice-Pres. Prof. Dr JOHANNA HEY; Vice-Pres. Prof. Dr JOSEF PFEILSCHIFTER; Vice-Pres. Prof. Dr ULRICH SCHOLLWÖCK; Man. Dir Dr MICHAEL HARTMERE; Deputy Man. Dir Dr HUBERT DETMER.

Deutscher Volkshochschul-Verband eV (German Adult Education Association): Obere Wilhelmstr. 32, 53225 Bonn; tel. (228) 9756920; fax (228) 9756930; e-mail info@dvv-vhs.de; internet www.dvv-vhs.de; f. 1953; 16 regional asscns of 1,000 Volkshochschulen with 4,000 brs; Pres. Prof. Dr RITA SÜSSMUTH; Chair. Dr ERNST-DIETER ROSSMANN; Dir ULRICH AENGENVOORT; Deputy Dir GUNDULA FRIELING; publs Adult Education and Development (2 a year, in English, French and Spanish), DVV magazin dis.kurs (4 a year).

Hochschulrektorenkonferenz (HRK) (German Rectors' Conference): Ahrstr. 39, 53175 Bonn; tel. (228) 8870; fax (228) 887110; e-mail post@hrk.de; internet www.hrk.de; f. 1949; central voluntary body representing the univs and higher education instns; 258 mem instns; Pres. Prof. Dr MARGRET WINTERMANTEL; Sec.-Gen. Dr Ing. THOMAS KATHÖFER.

Katholischer Akademischer Ausländer-Dienst: Hausdorffstr. 151, 53129 Bonn; tel. (228) 917580; fax (228) 9175858; e-mail zentrale@kaad.de; internet www.kaad.de; f. 1954; coordinates activities of Catholic orgs concerned with foreign students in Germany and grants scholarships; Pres.

Prof. Dr JOSEF REITER; Gen. Sec. Dr HERMANN WEBER; publ. Jahresakademie (1 a year).

Learned Societies

GENERAL

Akademie der Künste (Academy of Arts): POB 210250, 10502 Berlin; Pariser Pl. 4, 10117 Berlin; tel. (30) 200570; fax (30) 200571702; e-mail info@adk.de; internet www.adk.de; f. 1696; sections of fine art, architecture, music, literature, performing arts, film and media arts; 398 mems; Pres. Prof. KLAUS STAECK; Vice-Pres. NELE HERTLING; publ. Sinn und Form (6 a year).

Akademie der Wissenschaften zu Göttingen (Göttingen Academy of Sciences and Humanities): Theaterstr. 7, 37073 Göttingen; tel. (551) 395362; fax (551) 395365; e-mail adw@gwdg.de; internet www.adw-goe.de; f. 1751; attached to Univ. of Göttingen; sections of philology and history, mathematics and physics; 381 mems and corresp. mems; Pres. Prof. Dr CHRISTIAN STARCK; Vice-Pres. Prof. Dr NORBERT ELSNER; Vice-Pres. Prof. Dr WERNER LEHFELDT; publs Abhandlungen, Neue Folge, Göttingische Gelehrte Anzeigen, Jahrbuch.

Akademie der Wissenschaften und der Literatur Mainz (Mainz Academy of Sciences, Humanities and Literature): Geschwister Scholl-Str. 2, 55131 Mainz; tel. (6131) 5770; fax (6131) 577206; e-mail generalsekretariat@adwmainz.de; internet www.adwmainz.de; f. 1949; 250 mems; Pres. Prof. Dr ELKE LÜTJEN-DRECOLL; Sec.-Gen. Prof. Dr CLAUDIUS GEISLER; Vice-Pres. for Literature Prof. Dr NORBERT MILLER; Vice-Pres. for Mathematics and Natural Sciences Prof. Dr GERHARD WEGNER; Vice-Pres. for Philosophy and Social Sciences Prof. Dr GERNOT WILHELM; publs Abhandlungen, Forschungsreihen.

Bayerische Akademie der Wissenschaften (Bavarian Academy of Sciences and Humanities): Alfons-Goppel-Str. 11, 80539 Munich; tel. (89) 230310; fax (89) 230311100; e-mail info@badw.de; internet www.badw.de; f. 1759; sections of mathematics and natural sciences (Secs Prof. Dr GOTTFRIED SACHS, Prof. Dr HORST KESSLER) and philosophy and history (Secs Prof. Dr ARNOLD PICOT, Prof. Dr THOMAS O. HÖLLMANN); 172 mems; Pres. Prof. Dr KARL-HEINZ HOFFMANN; Gen. Sec. BIANCA MARZOCCA.

Berlin-Brandenburgische Akademie der Wissenschaften (Berlin-Brandenburg Academy of Sciences and Humanities): Jaegerstr. 22/23, 10117 Berlin; tel. (30) 203700; fax (30) 20370600; e-mail bbaw@bbaw.de; internet www.bbaw.de; f. 1700, refounded 1992/93; sections of humanities, of social sciences, of mathematics and natural sciences, of biological and medical sciences, of engineering sciences; 307 mems (166 ordinary, 69 extraordinary, 70 emeriti, 2 hon.); Pres. Prof. Dr GÜNTER STOCK; Vice-Pres. Prof. Dr JÜRGEN KOCKA; Vice-Pres. Prof. Dr KLAUS LUCAS; publs Berichte und Abhandlungen (irregular), Gegenworte—Zeitschrift für den Disput über Wissen, Jahrbuch (1 a year).

Leopoldina—Nationale Akademie der Wissenschaften (German Academy of Sciences Leopoldina): POB 110543, 06019 Halle (Saale); Emil-Abderhalden-Str. 37, 06108 Halle (Saale); tel. (345) 472390; fax (345) 4723919; e-mail leopoldina@leopoldina.org; internet www.leopoldina.org; f. 1652, present status 2008; attached to Nationale Akademie der Wissenschaften; br. in Berlin; advises govt, parliament, public on socially relevant scientific issues; represents German scientists in int. acad. circles and maintains links with scientific instns in other European and non-European countries; supports training of junior scientists; promotes cooperation among researchers by organizing meetings, symposia, biennial conferences, assemblies, monthly lectures, seminars on history of science; 1,300 mems; library: see Libraries and Archives; Pres. Prof. Dr JÖRG HACKER; Sec.-Gen. Prof. Dr JUTTA SCHNITZER-UNGE-FUG; Sec., Medicine Prof. Dr INGO HANSMANN; publs *Acta Historica Leopoldina*, *Jahrbuch* (1 a year), *Nova Acta Leopoldina*.

Goethe-Gesellschaft in Weimar eV: Burgpl. 4 99423 Weimar; POB 2251, 99403 Weimar; tel. (3643) 202050; fax (3643) 202061; e-mail info@goethe-gesellschaft.de; internet www.goethe-gesellschaft.de; f. 1885; literature, art and history of Goethe's time; 3,000 mems; Pres. Dr Hab. JOCHEN GOLZ; Dir Dr PETRA OBERHAUSER; publs *Goethe-Jahrbuch*, *Schriften der Goethe-Gesellschaft* (irregular).

Goethe-Institut: Dachauer Str. 122, 80637 Munich; tel. (89) 159210; fax (89) 15921450; e-mail info@goethe.de; internet www.goethe .de; f. 1951; 147 institutes globally, 13 in Germany; promotes German language and fosters cultural cooperation with other countries; sets internationally recognized standards in the teaching and learning of German as a foreign language; Pres. Prof. Dr KLAUS-DIETER LEHMANN; Sec.-Gen. Dr HANS-GEORG KNOPP; Business Dir JÜRGEN MAIER; publs *Fikrun wa fann* (in Arabian, English, Persian; 2 a year), *Goethe-Institut aktuell* (4 a year), *Humboldt* (in Brazilian, Portuguese, Spanish; 2 a year), *Willkommen*, *Yearbook* (1 a year).

Heidelberger Akademie der Wissenschaften (Heidelberg Academy of Sciences and Humanities): Karlstr. 4, 69117 Heidelberg; tel. (6221) 543265; fax (6221) 543355; e-mail haw@adw.uni-heidelberg.de; internet www.haw.uni-heidelberg.de; f. 1909; sections of mathematics and natural sciences (Sec. Prof. Dr WOLFGANG SCHLEICH), philosophy and history (Sec. Prof. Dr SILKE LEO-POLD); Pres. Prof. Dr HERMANN H. HAHN; Man. Dir GUNTHER JOST.

Institut für Auslandsbeziehungen (IFA) (Institute for Foreign Cultural Relations): POB 102463, 70020 Stuttgart; Charlottenpl. 17, 70173 Stuttgart; tel. (711) 22250; fax (711) 2264346; e-mail info@ifa.de; internet www.ifa.de; f. 1917; promotes artistic exchange and dialogue between civil societies; provides information about foreign cultural policy; library of 450,000 vols; Pres. URSULA SEILER-ALBRING; Gen. Sec. RONALD GRÄTZ; Librarian GUDRUN CZEKALLA; publs *Ifa//dokumente*, *Ifa///literaturrecherchen*, *Kulturaustausch*, *Reihe Dokumentation*.

Nordrhein-Westfälische Akademie der Wissenschaften und der Künste (Northrhine-Westphalia Academy of Sciences and Humanities): Palmenstr. 16, 40217 Düsseldorf; tel. (211) 617340; fax (211) 341475; e-mail awk@awk.nrw.de; internet www .akdw.nrw.de; f. 1950, present status 1970, present name 1993; sections of natural, engineering and economic sciences, philosophy; 356 mems (225 full, 131 corresp.); Pres. Prof. Dr Hab. HANNS HATT; Vice-Pres. Prof. Dr Ing. Hab. HELMUT ERMERT; Vice-Pres. Prof. Dr PETER M. LYNEN; Vice-Pres. Prof. Dr WOLFGANG DIETER LEBEK; publs *Abhandlungen*, *Jahrbuch* (Yearbook), *Sitzungsberichte*.

Prinz-Albert-Gesellschaft eV (Prince Albert Society): Seidmannsdorfer Str. 5, 96450 Coburg; tel. (921) 554190; fax (921) 55844188; e-mail prinz-albert-gesellschaft@ uni-bayreuth.de; internet www

.prinz-albert-gesellschaft.uni-bayreuth.de; f. 1981; encourages research into Anglo-German relations in spheres of scholarship, culture and politics; Chair. Prof. Dr DIETER WEISS; Exec. Chair. MICHAEL ECKSTEIN; Sec. SILVIA BÖCKING; publs *Prinz Albert Forschungen* (Prince Albert Research, Series), *Prinz-Albert-Studien* (Prince Albert Studies, Series).

Sächsische Akademie der Wissenschaften zu Leipzig (Saxony Academy of Sciences in Leipzig): POB 100440, 04004 Leipzig; Karl-Tauchnitz Str. 1, 04107 Leipzig; tel. (341) 7115350; fax (341) 7115344; e-mail sekretariat@saw-leipzig.de; internet www.saw-leipzig.de; f. 1846; about 30 research projects; 221 mems (142 ordinary, 79 corresp.); Pres. Prof. Dr PIRMIN STEKELER-WEITHOFER; Vice-Pres. Prof. Dr HEINER KADEN; Sec.-Gen. Dr UTE ECKER; Head of Mathematics and Natural Sciences Section Prof. Dr DIETER MICHEL; Head of Philology and History Section Prof. Dr HEINER LÜCK; Head of Technical Sciences Section Prof. Dr HARTMUT WORCH; publs *Abhandlungen*, *Denkströme* (www.denkstroeme.de), *Jahrbuch* (every 2 years), *Sitzungsberichte*.

Union der Deutschen Akademien der Wissenschaften (Union of the German Academies of Sciences and Humanities): Geschwister-Scholl-Str. 2, 55131 Mainz; tel. (6131) 2185280; fax (6131) 21852811; e-mail info@akademienunion.de; internet www .akademienunion.de; f. 1973; consists of academies of sciences and humanities in Berlin, Düsseldorf, Göttingen, Heidelberg, Leipzig, Mainz and Munich; deals with research projects common to the academies and coordinates the work of their mems; Pres. Prof. Dr GÜNTER STOCK; Vice-Pres. Prof. Dr ELKE LÜTJEN-DRECOLL; Gen. Sec. Dr DIETER HERRMANN.

AGRICULTURE, FISHERIES AND VETERINARY SCIENCE

Agrarsoziale Gesellschaft eV (ASG): POB 1144, 37001 Göttingen; Kurze Geismarstr. 33, 37073 Göttingen; tel. (551) 497090; fax (551) 4970916; e-mail info@asg-goe.de; internet www.asg-goe.de; f. 1947; works for improvement of living conditions in rural areas; 330 mems, plus 130 corporate mems; library of 6,000 vols; Chair. Dr MARTIN WILLE; Man. Dir. Dr DIETER CZECH; Sec. KARIN SCHÄFER; publs *Arbeitsbericht der ASG*, *Kleine Reihe der ASG*, *Ländlicher Raum* (4 a year), *Materialsammlung der ASG*, *Schriftenreihe für ländliche Sozialfragen*.

Dachverband Wissenschaftlicher Gesellschaften der Agrar-, Forst-, Ernährungs-, Veterinär- und Umweltforschung eV: Eschbormer Landstr. 122, 60489 Frankfurt am Main; tel. (69) 24788321; fax (69) 24788114; e-mail a .schaffner@dlg.org; internet www .agrarforschung.de; f. 1973; advancement and coordination of research; information; contacts; representation; 34 mem instns; Pres. Prof. Dr OLAF CHRISTEN; Man. Dir Dr ACHIM SCHAFFNER.

Deutsche Landwirtschafts-Gesellschaft eV (German Agricultural Society): Eschborner Landstr. 122, 60489 Frankfurt; tel. (69) 247880; fax (69) 24788110; e-mail info@dlg .de; internet www.dlg.org; f. originally 1885, refounded 1947; 22,000 mems; Pres. CARL-ALBRECHT BARTMER; Dir Dr REINHARD GRANDKE; publs *Agrifuture* (for European farmers, in English, 4 a year), *Entwicklung und ländlicher Raum* (in German, English and French, 12 a year), *Journal of International Agriculture* (4 a year), *Mitteilungen*

(1 a year), *Zeitschrift für Agrargeschichte und Agrarsoziologie* (4 a year).

Deutsche Veterinärmedizinische Gesellschaft (German Veterinary Medical Society): Friedrichstr. 17, 35392 Gießen; tel. (641) 24466; fax (641) 25375; e-mail info@dvg .net; internet www.dvg.net; f. 1949; 5,000 mems; Chair. Prof. Dr VOLKER MOENNIG; Man. Dir. Dr SUSANNE ALLDINGER; publ. *Kongressbericht* (every 2 years).

Deutscher Forstwirtschaftsrat (German Forestry Council): Claire-Waldoff-Str. 7, 10117 Berlin; tel. (30) 31904560; fax (30) 31904564; e-mail info@dfwr.de; internet www.dfwr.de; f. 1950; promotes forestry; 67 mems; Pres. GEORG SCHIRMBECK; Vice-Pres. NORBERT LEBEN; Man. Dir DIRK ALFTER.

Verband Deutscher Landwirtschaftlicher Untersuchungs- und Forschungsanstalten eV (VDLUFA) (Association of German Agricultural, Analytical and Research Institutes): c/o LUFA Speyer, Obere Langgasse 40, 67346 Speyer; tel. (6232) 136121; fax (6232) 136122; e-mail info@vdlufa.de; internet www.vdlufa.de; f. 1888; devt of methods and quality assurance in agricultural analytical sector; provides bases for a standardized evaluation of test results; initiates and advances applied agricultural research; 550 mems; Pres. Prof. Dr FRANZ WIESLER; Vice-Pres. for Animals Prof. Dr HANS SWALVE; Vice-Pres. for Plants Prof. Dr THOMAS EBERTSEDER; Exec. Sec. Dr HANS-GEORG BROD; publs *Handbuch der landwirtschaftlichen Versuchs- und Untersuchungsmethodik* (*VDLUFA-Methodenbuch*), *VDLUFA-Mitteilungen*, *VDLUFA-Schriftenreihe*.

ARCHITECTURE AND TOWN PLANNING

DAI–Verband Deutscher Architekten- und Ingenieurvereine eV: Keithstr. 2–4, 10787 Berlin; tel. (30) 21473174; fax (30) 21473182; e-mail dai@architekt.de; internet www.architekt.de; f. 1871; 5,500 mems; Chair. Prof. Dr-Ing. JÜRGEN FISSLER; publ. *DAI-Verbandszeitschrift BAUKULTUR*.

Deutscher Verband für Wohnungswesen, Städtebau und Raumordnung eV (German Federation for Housing and Planning): Littenstr. 10, 10179 Berlin; tel. (30) 20613250; fax (30) 20613251; e-mail info@ deutscher-verband.org; internet www .deutscher-verband.org; f. 1946; independent research in housing; urban and country planning; 700 mems; Pres. GERNOT MITTLER; Vice-Pres. HELMUT RAUSCH; Vice-Pres. Dr JOSEF MEYER; Sec.-Gen. CHRISTIAN HUTTEN-LOHER.

Stiftung Bauhaus Dessau (Bauhaus Dessau Foundation): Gropiusallee 38, 06846 Dessau; tel. (340) 6508-0; fax (340) 6508-226; e-mail service@bauhaus-dessau.de; internet www.bauhaus-dessau.de; f. 1994; preserves and conveys the historic heritage of Bauhaus and contributes ideas and solutions to the problems of design in the contemporary environment; library: public research and reference library with particular reference to urban design, architecture and living; archive of 25,000 items from collections and legacies of Bauhaus teachers and students; Dir Prof. PHILIPP OSWALT.

Attached College:

Bauhaus Kolleg: Gropiusallee 38, 06846 Dessau; tel. (340) 6508403; fax (340) 6508404; e-mail goegel@bauhaus-dessau .de; f. 1999; 1-year postgraduate programme; language of instruction: English; Man. INA GOEGEL.

BIBLIOGRAPHY, LIBRARY SCIENCE AND MUSEOLOGY

Arbeitsgemeinschaft der Spezialbibliotheken eV: Geschaeftsstelle, c/o Ms Jadwiga Warmbrunn, Herder Institut eV Forschungbibliothek, Gisonenweg 5–7, 35037 Marburg; tel. (6421) 184150; fax (6421) 184139; e-mail geschaeftsstelle@aspb .de; internet www.aspb.de; f. 1946; asscn of specialized libraries in the German-speaking countries; organizes conferences; acts as Section 5 (Spec. Libraries) of the German Libraries Asscn; 560 mems; Pres. Dr JÜRGEN WARMBRUNN; Deputy Pres. HENNING FRANKENBERGER; Treas. MICHAEL NORMANN; publ. *Conference proceedings (Tagungsband der Arbeits- und Fortbildungstagung)* (every 2 years).

Berufsverband Information Bibliothek eV (Association of Information and Library Professionals): POB 13 24, Gartenstr. 18, 72703 Reutlingen; tel. (7121) 34910; fax (7121) 300433; e-mail mail@bib-info.de; internet www.bib-info.de; f. 1949 as Verein der Bibliothekare und Assistentenen, present name 2000; represents the interests of librarians; maintains professional standards; stresses the importance of professional training and salaries that correspond to the level of training; increases public awareness of the social and educational importance of libraries and professional standards; 6,300 mems; Pres. SUSANNE RIEDEL; Sec. MICHAEL REISSER; publ *BuB (Buch und Bibliothek)—Forum Bibliothek und Information* (10 a year), *OPL-Checklisten*.

Deutsche Gesellschaft für Informationswissenschaft und Informationspraxis eV: C/O Leiterin Nadja Strein, Windmühlstr. 3, 60329 Frankfurt am Main; tel. (69) 430313; fax (69) 4909096; e-mail mail@ dgi-info.de; internet www.dgi-info.de; f. 1948 as Deutsche Gesellschaft für Dokumentation, present name 1999; promotion of information and documentation, information science and practice; 1,100 mems; Pres. Prof. Dr STEFAN GRADMANN; Vice-Pres. ANNE BEIN; Vice-Pres. Dr LUZIAN WEISEL; publs *Information–Wissenschaft & Praxis-IWP* (8 a year), *Nachrichten für Dokumentation* (6 a year), *Proceedings DGI-Online-Conference/DGI-Connference* (1 a year), *Proceedings Oberhofer Kolloquium* (every 2 years).

Deutscher Museumsbund eV (German Museums Association): In der Halde 1, 14195 Berlin; tel. (30) 84109517; fax (30) 84109519; e-mail office@museumsbund.de; internet www.museumsbund.de; f. 1917 to promote museums, their development and museology; 2,000 mems; Pres. Dr VOLKER RODEKAMP; Dir ANJA SCHALUSCHKE; Deputy Dir VERA NEUKIRCHEN; publs *Bulletin* (4 a year), *Das MuseumsMagazin, Einkaufsführer für Museen* (1 a year), *Museumskunde* (2 a year).

Internationale Vereinigung der Musikbibliotheken, Musikarchive und Musikdokumentationszentren (IVMB) Gruppe Deutschland eV (International Association of Music Libraries, Archives and Documentation Centres—IAML): c/o Universitäts- und Landesbibliothek, 64283 Darmstadt; tel. (6151) 165807; fax (3212) 1011715; e-mail sekretaerin@aibm.info; internet www .aibm.info; f. 1951; 210 mems; Pres. Dr BARBARA WIERMANN; Vice-Pres. Dr ANDREAS ODENKIRCHEN; Sec. Dr SILVIA UHLEMANN; Treas. PETRA WAGENKNECHT; publs *Fontes Artis Musicae* (4 a year), *Forum Musikbibliothek* (4 a year).

Verein Deutscher Bibliothekare eV (Association of German Academic Librarians): Universitätsbibliothek Augsburg, Universitätsstr 22, 86159 Augsburg; tel. (821) 5985300; fax (821) 5985354; e-mail ulrich .hohoff@bibliothek.uni-augsburg.de; internet www.vdb-online.org; f. 1900, refounded 1948; annual librarians' congress, workshops, seminars; 1,700 mems; Pres. Dr ULRICH HOHOFF; Sec. Dr THOMAS STÖBER; publs *Jahrbuch der Deutschen Bibliotheken* (every 2 years), *VDB-Mitteilungen* (2 a year).

Württembergische Bibliotheksgesellschaft (Society of Friends of the Württemberg State Library): POB 105441, 70047 Stuttgart; tel. (711) 2124428; fax (711) 2124422; e-mail wbg@wlb-stuttgart.de; internet www.wlb-stuttgart.de/die-wlb/ freunde-der-bibliothek; f. 1946; supports the reconstruction of the Württemberg State Library, holds lectures, meetings, exhibitions, etc.; 400 mems; Pres. (vacant); Chair. Prof. Dr WULF D. VON LUCIUS; Sec. CHRISTINE DEMMLER.

ECONOMICS, LAW AND POLITICS

AFW Wirtschaftsakademie Bad Harzburg GmbH (Academy for Distance Study of Economics in Bad Harzburg): An den Weiden 15, 38667 Bad Harzburg; tel. (5322) 90200; fax (5322) 902040; e-mail bildung@ afwbadharzburg.de; internet www .afwbadharzburg.de; f. as Akademie für Fernstudium (AfF), present name and status 1999; Man. Dr FRANK EDELKRAUT.

Deutsche Aktuarvereinigung eV: Hohenstaufenring 47–51, 50674 Cologne; tel. (221) 9125540; fax (221) 91255444; e-mail info@ aktuar.de; internet www.aktuar.de; f. 1948; society for promotion of actuarial theory in collaboration with the univs; 3,400 mems; Chair. Dr MICHAEL RENZ; Deputy Chair. Dr JOHANNES LÖRPER; publs *Aktuar aktuell* (3 a year), *Blätter der DGVFM* (2 a year), *Der Aktuar* (4 a year).

Deutsche Gesellschaft für Auswärtige Politik eV (German Council on Foreign Relations): Rauchstr. 17–18, 10787 Berlin; tel. (30) 2542310; fax (30) 25423116; e-mail info@dgap.org; internet www.dgap.org; f. 1955; discusses and promotes research on problems of int. politics; operates one of the oldest specialized libraries on German foreign policy (open to the public); library of 85,000 vols, 270 periodicals; 3,200 mems; Pres. Dr AREND OETKER; Exec. Vice-Pres. PAUL VON MALTZAHN; Otto Wolff-Dir of the Research Institute EBERHARD SANDSCHNEIDER; Deputy Librarian HEIKE ZANZIG; publs *Die Internationale Politik* (1 a year), *Internationale Politik* (6 a year, supplement 'Global Edition').

Deutsche Gesellschaft für Osteuropakunde eV (German Association for East European Studies): Schaperstr. 30, 10719 Berlin; tel. (30) 21478412; fax (30) 21478414; e-mail info@dgo-online.org; internet www.dgo-online.org; f. 1913; 850 mems; Pres. Prof. Dr RITA SÜSSMUTH; Exec. Dir Dr GABRIELE FREITAG; publs *Osteuropa* (12 a year), *Osteuropa-Recht* (6 a year), *Osteuropa-Wirtschaft* (4 a year).

Deutsche Statistische Gesellschaft: 22039 Hamburg; Holstenhofweg 85, 22043 Hamburg; tel. (40) 65412779; fax (40) 65412565; e-mail post@dstatg.de; internet www.dstatg.de; f. 1911; 800 mems; Pres. Prof. Dr WILFRIED SEIDEL; Vice-Pres. Prof. Dr KARL MOSLER; Vice-Pres. JÜRGEN CHLUMSKY; Man. Dir Dr THOMAS SCHUELER; publs *AStA–Advances in Statistical Analysis* (4 a year), *AStA–Wirtschafts- und Sozialstatistisches Archiv*.

Deutsche Vereinigung für Politische Wissenschaft (German Political Science Association): c/o Osnabrück University, FB1-Sozialwissenschaften, 49069 Osnabrück; Seminarstr. 33, 49074 Osnabrück; tel. (541) 9696264; fax (541) 9696266; e-mail dvpw@dvpw.de; internet www.dvpw.de; f. 1951; 1,700 mems; Pres. Prof. Dr HUBERTUS BUCHSTEIN; Vice-Pres. Prof. Dr ANDREA LENSCHOW; Vice-Pres. Prof. Dr FRANK NULLMEIER; Dir FELIX W. WURM; publ. *Politische Vierteljahresschrift* (4 a year).

Deutscher Juristentag eV: POB 1169, 53001 Bonn; Sterntorhaus, Oxfordstr. 21, 53111 Bonn; tel. (228) 9839185; fax (228) 9839140; e-mail info@djt.de; internet www .djt.de; f. 1860; furthers discussion among jurists; 7,000 mems; Pres. Prof. Dr MARTIN HENSSLER; Gen.-Sec. Dr ANDREAS NADLER.

Gesellschaft für Öffentliche Wirtschaft (Society for Public Economy): Sponholzstr. 11, 12159 Berlin; tel. (30) 8521045; fax (30) 8525111; e-mail goew.dsceep@t-online.de; f. 1951; 70 mems; research and information service and providers of public services; Pres. MICHAEL SCHÖNEICH; Dir WOLF LEETZ; publ. *Zeitschrift für öffentliche und gemeinwirtschaftliche Unternehmen* (4 a year).

Gesellschaft für Rechtsvergleichung eV (Society for Comparative Law eV): Belfortstr. 16, 79098 Freiburg; tel. (761) 2032126; fax (761) 2032127; e-mail gfr@uni-freiburg.de; internet www.gfr.jura.uos.de; f. 1894; 1,000 mems; Chair. Prof. Dr JÜRGEN SCHWARZE; Sec.-Gen. Prof. Dr MARTIN SCHMIDT-KESSEL; publs *Ausländische Aktiengesetze, Rechtsvergleichung und Rechtsvereinheitlichung*.

Gesellschaft für Sozial- und Wirtschaftsgeschichte (Society for Social and Economic History): Friedrich-Wilhelms-Universität Bonn, Konviktstr. 11, 53113 Bonn; tel. (228) 735172; fax (228) 735171; e-mail gswg@ uni-bonn.de; internet www.gswg.net; f. 1961; 219 mems; Pres. Prof. Dr GÜNTHER SCHULZ; Vice-Pres. Prof. Dr GERHARD FOUQUET; Sec. Prof. Dr RAINER METZ.

Kommission für Geschichte des Parlamentarismus und der Politischen Parteien eV (Commission for History of Parliamentarianism and Political Parties): Schiffbauerdamm 17, 10117 Berlin; tel. (30) 22792572; e-mail info@kgparl.de; internet www.kgparl.de; f. 1952, present location 2006; 27 mems; Pres. Prof. Dr ANDREAS WIRSCHING; Vice-Pres. Prof. Dr HANS-WERNER HAHN; Man. Prof. Dr ANDREAS SCHULZ; Sec. JUTTA GRAF; publs *Beiträge zur Geschichte des Parlamentarismus und der politischen Parteien, Quellen zur Geschichte des Parlamentarismus und der politischen Parteien.*

EDUCATION

Humboldt Gesellschaft für Wissenschaft, Kunst und Bildung eV (Humboldt Society for Science, Art and Education): Kronberg 6, 35582 Wetzlar; tel. (641) 21424; fax (2054) 2827; e-mail erwin.kuntz@puscher .com; internet www.humboldt-gesellschaft .org; f. 1962; 650 mems; Pres. Prof. Dr ERWIN KUNTZ; Vice-Pres. Dr ERICH BAMMEL; Vice-Pres. Dr WOLFGANG SIEGFRIED; Sec. Dr HORST REDLOF; publs *Abhandlungen* (every 2 years), *Mitteilungen* (every 2 years).

FINE AND PERFORMING ARTS

Bayerische Akademie der Schönen Künste (Bavarian Academy of Fine Arts): Max-Joseph-Pl. 3, 80539 Munich; tel. (89) 2900770; fax (89) 29007723; e-mail info@ badsk.de; internet www.badsk.de; f. 1948; 242 mems; Pres. Prof. Dr DIETER BORCHMEYER; Gen. Sec. Dr KATJA SCHAEFER; publ. *Jahrbuch.*

Deutsche Gesellschaft für Photographie eV (German Society for Photography): Rheingasse 8–12, 50676 Cologne; tel. (221) 9232069; fax (221) 9232070; e-mail dgph@ dgph.de; internet www.dgph.de; f. 1951; photography, visual media; 1,000 mems; Chair. DITMAR SCHÄDEL; Vice-Chair. Dr CHRISTIANE STAHL; publ. *DGPh-Intern* (4 a year).

Deutsche Mozart-Gesellschaft eV (German Mozart Society): Frauentorstr. 30, 86152 Augsburg; tel. (821) 518588; fax (821) 157228; e-mail deutsche-mozart-gesellschaft@t-online.de; internet www.deutsche-mozart-gesellschaft .de; f. 1951; 3,000 mems; Pres. Dr DIRK HEWIG; publ. *Acta Mozartiana* (1 a year).

Deutscher Komponistenverband eV (German Composers' Association): Kadettenweg 80B, 12205 Berlin; tel. (30) 84310580; fax (30) 84310582; e-mail info@ komponistenverband.org; internet www .komponistenverband.de; f. 1954; promotes professional interests of German composers; 1,200 mems; Pres. JÖRG EVERS; Vice-Pres. Prof. LOTHAR VOIGTLÄNDER; Man. SABINE BEGEMANN.

Deutscher Verein für Kunstwissenschaft eV (German Society for Studies in Art History): Jebensstr. 2, 10623 Berlin; tel. (30) 3139932; fax (30) 75632108; e-mail dvfk@aol.com; internet www.dvfk-berlin.de; f. 1908; support, promotion and publication of research in German art history; 1,000 mems; Chair. Prof. Dr RAINER KAHSNITZ; Sec. Dr JOSEF RIEDMAIER; publ. *Zeitschrift des Deutschen Vereins für Kunstwissenschaft.*

Kestnergesellschaft: Goseriede 11, 30159 Hanover; tel. (511) 701200; fax (511) 7012020; e-mail kestner@kestner.org; internet www.kestner.org; f. 1916, refounded 1948; activities concerned with the promotion of modern art; 4,300 mems; Pres. UWE REUTER; Dir Dr VEIT GÖRNER; Man. Dir MAIRI KROLL.

Stiftung Preussischer Kulturbesitz (Prussian Cultural Foundation): Von-der-Heydt-Str. 16–18, 10785 Berlin; tel. (30) 266412888; fax (30) 266412821; e-mail info@ hv.spk-berlin.de; internet www .preussischer-kulturbesitz.de; f. 1961 to preserve, augment and reunite the Prussian cultural heritage; comprises 16 State Museums, the State Library, the State Privy Archives, the Iberian-American Institute and the State Institute for Research in Music with the Museum for Musical Instruments; Pres. Prof. Dr HERMANN PARZINGER; Vice-Pres. NORBERT ZIMMERMANN; publ. *Jahrbuch* (1 a year).

Verband Deutscher Kunsthistoriker eV (Association of German Art Historians): Haus der Kultur, Weberstr. 59A, 53113 Bonn; tel. (228) 18034182; fax (228) 18034209; e-mail info@kunsthistoriker.org; internet www.kunsthistoriker.org; f. 1948; 2,500 mems; Pres. Prof. Dr GEORG SATZINGER; Dir. Dr KATHARINA CORSEPIUS; publ. *Kunstchronik* (11 a year).

HISTORY, GEOGRAPHY AND ARCHAEOLOGY

Arbeitsgemeinschaft Historischer Kommissionen und Landesgeschichtlicher Institute (Association of Historic Councils and Regional History Institutes): Schückingstr. 36, 35037 Marburg; tel. (6421) 1840; f. 1898; controls 51 societies and institutes; Pres. Prof. Dr RODERICH SCHMIDT; Man. Dir Dr WINFRIED IRGANG.

Deutsche Akademie für Landeskunde eV (German Academy for Regional Geography of Germany): c/o Institut für Länderkunde, Schongauerstr. 9, 04329 Leipzig; tel. (341) 60055110; fax (341) 60055198; internet www.deutsche-landeskunde.de; f. 1882, refounded 1946; study of regional geography of Germany and German-speaking Central Europe; 66 mems; Chair.

(Bochum) Prof. Dr HARALD ZEPP; Chair. (Bonn) Prof. Dr WINFRIED SCHENK; publs *Berichte zur deutschen Landeskunde* (4 a year), *Forschungen zur deutschen Landeskunde* (series, 1 or 2 a year).

Deutsche Gesellschaft für Geographie eV (German Geographical Society): c/o Universität Kiel, Ökologie-Zentrum, Olshausenstr. 75, 24118 Kiel; tel. (431) 8803953; internet www.geographie.de; promotes scientific and practical cartography; 25,000 mems; Pres. Prof. Dr HANS-RUDOLF BORK; Vice-Pres. Prof. Dr DIETER BÖHN; Vice-Pres. Dr RUDOLF JUCHELKA; Gen. Sec. Dr ARNO BEYER.

Deutsche Gesellschaft für Kartographie eV (German Cartographic Society): c/o Dr Peter Aschenberner, Bergkammst 13, 30453 Hannover; tel. (511) 4505136; fax (511) 4505140; e-mail sekretaer@dgfk.net; internet www.dgfk.net; f. 1951; promotes scientific and practical cartography; 2,000 mems; Pres. Dr PETER ASCHENBERNER; Vice-Pres. Prof. Dr MANFRED BUCHROITHNER; Vice-Pres. Prof. Dr Ing. MANFRED WEISENSEE; Sec. STEFFEN HILD; publs *Bibliographia Cartographica, Kartographische Nachrichten* (6 a year).

Deutsche Gesellschaft für Ortung und Navigation eV (German Institute of Navigation): Kölnstr. 70, 53111 Bonn; tel. (228) 201970; fax (228) 2019719; e-mail dgon .bonn@t-online.de; internet www.dgon.de; f. 1951 as Ausschuss für Funkortung, present name 1961; promotes research and devt of methods and systems used for navigation; Pres. Prof. Dr HERMANN ROHLING; Man. Dir BERND MARTENS; publ. *European Journal of Navigation* (jt publ. of various European navigation instns, 3 a year).

Deutscher Nautischer Verein von 1868 eV (German Nautical Association of 1868): Striepenweg 31, 21147 Hamburg; tel. (40) 79713401; fax (40) 79713402; e-mail info@ dnvev.de; internet www.dnvev.de; f. 1868; 4,598 mems in 20 local nautical asscns, 47 corporate mems; Pres. REEDER FRANK WESSELS; Vice-Pres. Dr FRITZ FRANTZIOCH; Vice-Pres. and Man. Dir NICOLAI WOELKI; publ. *Kalendar* (1 a year).

Fränkische Geographische Gesellschaft: Kochstr. 4/4, 91054 Erlangen; tel. (9131) 8522633; fax (9131) 8522013; e-mail fgg@geographie.uni-erlangen.de; internet www.fgg.uni-erlangen.de; f. 1954; 830 mems; library of 60,000 vols, 250 current periodicals; Pres. Prof. Dr HORST KOPP; Pres. Ing. HELMUT MAI; Gen. Sec Dr MANFRED SCHNEIDER; Gen. Sec Dr UWE TRETER; Sec. SABINE DONNER; publs *Erlanger Geographische Arbeiten* (1 a year), *Erlanger Geographische Arbeiten, Sonderband* (irregular), *Mitteilungen der Fränkischen Geographischen Gesellschaft* (1 a year).

Gesamtverein der Deutschen Geschichts- und Altertumsvereine eV (Union of German Historical and Archaeological Societies): Institut für bayerische Geschichte, Ludwigstr. 14, 80539 Munich; tel. (89) 286382800; fax (89) 286382506; e-mail wolfgang.schuster@lmu.de; internet www.gesamtverein.de; f. 1852; 238 affiliated asscns; Pres. Prof. Dr HEINZ-GÜNTHER BORCK; Pres. Prof. Dr MANFRED TREML; publ. *Blätter für deutsche Landesgeschichte.*

Gesellschaft für Erdkunde zu Berlin (Geographical Society of Berlin): Arno-Holz-Str. 14, 12165 Berlin; tel. (30) 7900660; fax (30) 79006612; e-mail mail@gfe-berlin.de; internet www.gfe-berlin.de; f. 1828 by Heinrich Berghaus, Carl Ritter and other eminent Prussian scientists of the early 19th century, with the support of Alexander von Humboldt; study of geography, geosciences and related disciplines; lectures, seminars, confs and

excursions; 300 mems; library of 100,000 vols; Pres. Dr HARTMUT ASCHE; Gen. Sec. Dr CHRISTOF ELLGER; publs *DIE ERDE—Zeitschrift der Gesellschaft für Erdkunde zu Berlin (Journal of the Geographical Society of Berlin)* (4 a year), *Verhandlungen der Gesellschaft für Erdkunde zu Berlin* (1 a year).

Monumenta Germaniae Historica: Ludwigstr. 16, Postfach 34 02 23, 80099 Munich; tel. (89) 286382384; fax (89) 281419; e-mail sekretariat@mgh.de; internet www.mgh.de; f. 1819; library of 130,000 vols; Pres. Prof. Dr RUDOLF SCHIEFFER; Sec. Prof. Dr GERHARD SCHMITZ; Exec. Sec. Dr HORST ZIMMERHACKL; Librarian Prof. Dr ARNO MENTZEL-REUTERS; publ. *Deutsches Archiv für Erforschung des Mittelalters.*

Verband der Historiker und Historikerinnen Deutschlands (Union of German Historians): c/o Goethe-Universität (Campus Westend), Grüneburgplatz 1, 60323 Franfurt am Main; tel. (69) 79832571; fax (69) 79832570; e-mail info@historikerverband.de; internet www.historikerverband.de; f. 1893, refounded 1949; 2,300 mems; Pres. Prof. Dr WERNER PLUMPE; Vice-Pres. Prof. Dr HARTMUT LEPPIN; Sec. Prof. Dr SIMONE LÄSSIG; Man. Dir NORA HELMLI.

LANGUAGE AND LITERATURE

British Council: Alexanderpl. 1, 10178 Berlin; tel. (30) 3110990; fax (30) 31109920; e-mail info@britishcouncil.de; internet www .britishcouncil.de; teaching centre; offers courses and exams in English language and British culture and promotes cultural exchange with the UK; attached offices in Düsseldorf, Leipzig and Munich; Dir JOHN WHITEHEAD; IELTS Man. CAROLINE MURDOCH.

Deutsche Gesellschaft für Sprachwissenschaft (German Linguistic Society): c/o Nicole Dehé, Universität Konstanz, FB Sprachwissenschaft, Fach 186 , 78457 Konstanz; tel. (7531) 882928; fax (7531) 884149; e-mail nicole.dehe@uni-konstanz.de; internet dgfs.de; f. 1978; supports advancement of the scientific investigation of language, and the linguists engaged in this; 1,180 mems; Pres. Prof. Dr JÜRGEN LENERZ; Vice-Pres. SILVIA KUTSCHER; Sec. Dr NICOLE DEHÉ; publ. *Zeitschrift für Sprachwissenschaft* (2 a year).

Gesellschaft für deutsche Sprache eV (Society for the German Language): Spiegelgasse 13, 65183 Wiesbaden; tel. (611) 999550; fax (611) 9995530; e-mail sekr@gfds.de; internet www.gfds.de; f. 1947; 3,000 mems; library of 20,000 vols; Chair. Prof. Dr RUDOLF HOBERG; Vice-Chair. Prof. Dr Ing. ALFRED WARNER; Man. Dir Dr ANDREA-EVA EWELS; publs *Der Sprachdienst* (6 a year), *Muttersprache* (4 a year).

Hölderlin-Gesellschaft eV: Bursagasse 6, 72070 Tübingen; tel. (7071) 22040; fax (7071) 22948; e-mail info@hoelderlin-gesellschaft .de; internet www.hoelderlin-gesellschaft .info; f. 1943, reconstituted 1946; 1,300 mems; Pres. Prof. Dr SABINE DOERING; Vice-Pres. Prof. Dr MICHAEL FRANZ; Dir VALÉRIE LAWITSCHKA; publs *Hölderlin-Jahrbuch* (every 2 years), *Lyrik im Hölderlinturm, Schriften der Hölderlin-Gesellschaft* (irregular), *Turm-Vorträge.*

Instituto Cervantes: Rosenstr. 18–19, 10178 Berlin; tel. (30) 2576180; fax (30) 25761819; e-mail berlin@cervantes.de; internet www.cervantes.de; f. 2003; offers courses and exams in Spanish language and culture and promotes cultural exchange with Spain and Spanish-speaking Latin and Central America; attached centres in Bremen and Munich; library of 4,500 vols; Dir GASPAR

CANO PERAL; Head Librarian CRISTINA BARÓN MARTIN.

Mommsen-Gesellschaft eV: Geschäftsstelle Jacob-Burckhardt-Str. 5, 79098 Freiburg i.Br.; internet www .mommsen-gesellschaft.de; f. 1950; 620 mems; asscn of univ. teachers of classics, ancient history and archaeology; named after the classicist Theodor Mommsen (1817–1903); Pres. Prof. Dr WULF RAECK; Second Pres. Prof. Dr CHRISTIANE REITZ; Man. Dir Dr THOMAS GANSCHOW; Sec Dr NADIN BURKHARDT.

PEN Zentrum Deutschland (German PEN Centre): Kasinostr. 3, 64293 Darmstadt; tel. (6151) 23120; fax (6151) 293414; e-mail pen-germany@t-online.de; internet www .pen-deutschland.de; f. 1951; attached to Int. Asscn of Writers; 705 mems; Pres. JOHANO STRASSER; Man. Dir CLAUDIA C. KRAUßE; Sec.-Gen. HERBERT WIESNER.

MEDICINE

Anatomische Gesellschaft (Anatomical Society): Institut für Anatomie LST II, Friedrich–Alexander–Universität, Universitätstr. 19, 91054 Erlangen; tel. (9131) 8522865; fax (9131) 8522862; e-mail friedrich.paulsen@anatomie2.med.uni-erlangen.de; internet www .anatomische-gesellschaft.de; f. 1886; 850 mems; Sec. Prof. Dr FRIEDRICH PAULSEN; publs *Annals of Anatomy* (6 a year), Congress abstracts.

Deutsche Dermatologische Gesellschaft (DDG) (German Dermatologic Society): Robert-Koch-Pl. 7, 10115 Berlin; tel. (30) 2462530; fax (30) 24625329; e-mail ddg@ derma.de; internet www.derma.de; f. 1888; promotes scientific and clinical dermatology, venereology and allergology; disciplines of andrology, phlebology, proctology, dermatologic-oncology, dermatologic radiation therapy, dermatologic microbiology, occupational and environmental dermatology, preventive dermatology/rehabilitation; 3,500 mems; Pres. Prof. Dr THOMAS A. LUGER; Sec.-Gen. Prof. Dr RUDOLF STADLER; Sec.-Gen. Prof. Dr RUDOLF STADLER; publs *Derma News & Views* (4 a year), *Hautarzt* (12 a year), *JDDG (Journal of the German Society of Dermatology)*.

Deutsche Gesellschaft für Anästhesiologie und Intensivmedizin eV: Roritzerstr. 27, 90419 Nuremberg; tel. (911) 933780; fax (911) 3938195; e-mail dgai@dgai-ev.de; internet www.dgai.de; f. 1953; 10,000 mems; Pres. Prof. Dr GABRIELE NÖLDGE-SCHOMBURG; Vice-Pres. Prof. Dr JÜRGEN SCHÜTTLER; Dir HOLGER SORGATZ; Sec.-Gen. Prof. Dr HUGO VAN AKEN; publ. *Anästhesiologie, Intensivmedizin, Notfallmedizin und Schmerztherapie (AINS)*.

Deutsche Gesellschaft für Angewandte Optik eV (German Society for Applied Optics): c/o Elizabeth Nagel, Coburger Str. 11, 91056 Erlangen; tel. (9131) 758587; e-mail dgao-sekretariat@dgao.de; internet www.dgao.de; f. 1923; 570 individual mems, 28 corporate mems; Pres. Prof. Dr MICHAEL PFEFFER; Vice-Pres. Dr RAINER SCHUHMANN; Sec. Prof. Dr HARTMUT BARTELT; publs *DGaO-Proceedings* (online), *Optik* (12 a year), *Photonik*.

Deutsche Gesellschaft für Chirurgie (German Surgical Society): Luisenstr. 58/59, 10117 Berlin; tel. (30) 28876290; fax (30) 28876299; e-mail dgchirurgie@t-online.de; internet www.dgch.de; f. 1872; promotes scientific and practical aspects of surgery; 6,500 mems; Pres. Prof. Dr AXEL HAVERICH; Sec.-Gen. HARTWIG BAUER; publ. *Langenbecks Archiv für Chirurgie*.

Deutsche Gesellschaft für Endokrinologie: c/o EndoScience, Endokrinologie Service GmbH, Mozartstr. 23, 93128 Regenstauf; tel. (9402) 9481112; fax (9402) 9481119; e-mail dge@endokrinologie.net; internet www .endokrinologie.net; f. 1953; 1,500 mems; Pres. Prof. Dr ANDREAS PFEIFFER; Vice-Pres. Prof. Dr DAGMAR FÜHRER; Vice-Pres. Dr JÖRG GROMOLL; Sec. Prof. Dr MARTIN GRUßENDORF; publ. *Endokrinologie-Informationen* (6 a year).

Deutsche Gesellschaft für Gynäkologie und Geburtshilfe eV (German Society for Gynaecology and Birth Support): Robert-Koch-Pl. 7, 10115 Berlin; tel. (30) 514883340; fax (30) 51488344; e-mail info@ dggg.de; internet www.dggg.de; f. 1885; Pres. Prof. Dr KLAUS FRIESE; Vice-Pres. Prof. Dr ROLF KREIENBERG; Vice-Pres. Prof. Dr THOMAS DIMPFL; Sec. Dr CHRISTIAN DANNECKER; Sec. Prof. Dr DIETHELM WALLWIENER.

Deutsche Gesellschaft für Hals-Nasen-Ohren-Heilkunde, Kopf- und Hals-Chirurgie eV (German Society for Otorhinolaryngology, Head and Neck Surgery): c/o Ulrike Fischer, Friedrich-Wilhelm-Str. 2, 53113 Bonn; tel. (228) 9239220; fax (228) 92392210; e-mail info@hno.org; internet www.hno.org; f. 1921 by merger of German Association of Otorhinolaryngologists and the German Otological Society, present name 1968; 10 European archives of Otorhinolaryngology; 4,200 mems; Pres. Prof. Dr ROLAND LASZIG; Vice-Pres. Prof. Dr NORBERT STASCHE; Sec.-Gen. Prof. Dr FRIEDRICH BOOTZ; publs *European Archives of Oto-Rhino-Laryngology and Head & Neck* (in English, 12 a year), *HNO* (in German, 12 a year), *Laryngo-Rhino-Otologie* (in German, 12 a year), *ORL–Journal for Oto-Rhino-Laryngology and its Related Specialties* (6 a year).

Deutsche Gesellschaft für Hygiene und Mikrobiologie eV: c/o Medizinische Hochschule Hannover, Institut für Medizinische Mikrobiologie und Krankenhaushygiene, Carl-Neuberg-Str. 1, 30625 Hannover; tel. (511) 5324655; fax (511) 5324355; e-mail dghm@mh-hannover.de; internet www.dghm .org; f. 1906; 1,900 mems; Pres. Prof. Dr SEBASTIAN SUERBAUM; Vice-Pres. Prof. Dr HELGE KARCH; Vice-Pres. Prof. Dr STEFFEN STENGER; Sec. Prof. Dr JAN BUER; Man. Dir Dr NICOLE FREIFRAU VON MALTZAHN.

Deutsche Gesellschaft für Innere Medizin (German Society for Internal Medicine): Irenenstr. 1, 65189 Wiesbaden; tel. (611) 20580400; fax (611) 205804046; e-mail info@ dgim.de; internet www.dgim.de; f. 1882; 21,000 mems; Chair. Prof. Dr HENDRIK LEHNERT; Gen. Sec. Prof. Dr HANS-PETER SCHUSTER; Man. Dir MAXIMILIAN GUIDO GUIDO BROGLIE; publ. *Supplementum of Abstracts* (1 a year).

Deutsche Gesellschaft für Kinder- und Jugendmedizin eV (German Society of Pediatrics and Adolescent Medicine): Chausseestr. 128/129, 10115 Berlin; tel. (30) 30877790; fax (30) 308777999; e-mail info@ dgkj.de; internet www.dgkj.de; f. 1883; 14,000 mems; Pres. Prof. Dr FRED ZEPP; Vice-Pres. Prof. Dr NORBERT WAGNER; Dir Dr GABRIELE OLBRISCH; Sec. SABINE KÜHNE; publ. *Monatsschrift Kinderheilkunde* (12 a year).

Deutsche Gesellschaft für Neurochirurgie: c/o Porstmann Kongresse GmbH, Alte Jakobstr. 77, 10179 Berlin; tel. (30) 28449922; fax (30) 28449911; e-mail gs@ dgnc.de; internet www.dgnc.de; f. 1950; promotes science, research and practical work in the field of neurosurgery; 244 mems; Chair. Prof. Dr JÜRGEN MEIXENSBERGER; Chair. Prof. Dr GABRIELE SCHACKERT; Sec. Prof. Dr VEIT

BRAUN; publ. *Zentralblatt für Neurochirurgie* (4 a year).

Deutsche Gesellschaft für Orthopädie und Orthopädische Chirurgie eV: Langenbeck-Virchow-Haus, Luisenstr. 58/59, 10117 Berlin; tel. (30) 84712131; fax (30) 84712132; e-mail info@dgooc.de; internet www.dgooc.de; f. 1901; Pres. Prof. Dr DIETER KOHN; Vice-Pres. Dr DANIEL FRANK; Vice-Pres. Prof. Dr Hab. WOLFRAM MITTELMEIER; Gen. Sec. Prof. Dr FRITZ UWE NIETHARD; publs *Der Orthopäde* (12 a year), *Der Unfallchirurg* (12 a year), *Orthopädie Mitteilungen* (6 a year), *Zeitschrift für Orthopädie und Unfallchirurgie* (6 a year).

Deutsche Gesellschaft für Physikalische Medizin und Rehabilitation: Budapester Str. 31, 01069 Dresden; tel. (351) 8975932; fax (351) 8975939; e-mail info@dgpmr.de; internet www.dgpmr.de; f. 1886; physical medicine and rehabilitation; 400 mems; Pres. Prof. Dr MICHAEL N. BERLINER; Dir HELFRIED BÖHME; publs *Kurortmedizin* (6 a year), *Physikalische Medizin, Rehabilitationsmedizin*.

Deutsche Gesellschaft für Plastische und Wiederherstellungschirurgie eV (German Society for Plastic and Reconstructive Surgery): Beethoven Str. 12, 04107 Leipzig; tel. (341) 12457114; fax (341) 12457110; e-mail geschaeftstelle@dgpw.de; internet www.dgpw.de; f. 1962; 30 hon. mems, 20 corresp. mems; Gen. Sec. Prof. Dr R. GAHR; publs *German Medical Science e-journal* (online), *Journal* (2 a year).

Deutsche Gesellschaft für Psychiatrie, Psychotherapie und Nervenheilkunde (German Association for Psychiatry and Psychotherapy): Reinhardtstr. 14, 10117 Berlin; tel. (30) 240477212; fax (30) 240477229; e-mail sekretariat@dgppn.de; internet www .dgppn.de; f. 1842; scientific asscn of doctors and scientists working in the field of psychiatry, psychotherapy and psychosomatics in Germany; 5,500 mems; Pres. Prof. Dr PETER FALKAI; Man. Dir Dr THOMAS NESSELER; Sec. Dr OLIVER GRUBER; publs *Nervenarzt, Spektrum*.

Deutsche Gesellschaft für Psychoanalyse, Psychotherapie, Psychosomatik und Tiefenpsychologie (DGPT) eV: Johannisbollwerk 20, 20459 Hamburg; tel. (40) 75664990; fax (40) 756649929; e-mail psa@dgpt.de; internet www.dgpt.de; f. 1949; 3,400 mems; Pres. ANNE SPRINGER.

Deutsche Gesellschaft für Rechtsmedizin (German Society of Legal Medicine): Albertstr. 9, 79104 Freiburg; tel. (761) 2036854; fax (761) 2036858; e-mail legalmed@uniklinik-freiburg.de; internet www.dgrm.de; Pres. Prof. Dr STEFAN POLLAK.

Deutsche Gesellschaft für Sozialmedizin und Prävention (German Society for Social Medicine and Prevention): c/o Institut für Sozialmedizin und Gesundheitsökonomie, Leipziger Str. 44, 39120 Magdeburg; tel. (391) 6724300; fax (391) 6724310; internet www.dgsmp.de; f. 1964; 510 mems; Pres. Dr GERT V. MITTELSTAEDT; publ. *Das Gesundheitswesen* (12 a year).

Deutsche Gesellschaft für Tropenmedizin und Internationale Gesundheit eV: Bernhard-Nocht-Str. 74, 20359 Hamburg; tel. (40) 42818478; fax (40) 42818512; e-mail dtg@bni-hamburg.de; internet www.dtg.org; f. 1907; 870 mems; Pres. Prof. T. LOESCHER; Sec. Dr H. SUDECK.

Deutsche Gesellschaft für Zahn-, Mund- und Kieferheilkunde (German Society for Dental, Oral and Craniomandibular Sciences): Liesegangstr. 17A, 40211 Düsseldorf; tel. (211) 6101980; fax (211) 61019811; e-mail dgzmk@dgzmk.de; internet www.dgzmk.de;

f. 1859; 10,500 mems; Pres. Prof. Dr HENNING SCHLIEPHAKE; Sec. Dr ULRICH GAA; publs *APW DVD Journal*, *Clinical Oral Investigations*, *Deutsche Zahnärtztliche Zeitung* (12 a year), *Oralprophylaxe*, *Zeitschrift für Zahnärztliche Implantologie*.

Deutsche Ophthalmologische Gesellschaft eV: Platenstr. 1, 80336 Munich; tel. (89) 55057680; fax (89) 550576811; e-mail geschaeftsstelle@dog.org; internet www.dog.org; f. 1857; 5,800 mems; Pres. Prof. Dr THOMAS REINHARD; Sec. Prof. Dr ANSELM KAMPIK; publs *Der Ophthalmologe* (12 a year), *Graefe's Archive for Clinical Research* (12 a year), *Klinische Monatsblätter für Augenheilkunde* (12 a year).

Deutsche Physiologische Gesellschaft eV (German Society of Physiology): Institut für Physiologie, Universität Rostock, Gertrudenstr. 9, 18057 Rostock; tel. (381) 4948001; fax (381) 4948002; e-mail dpg.sekr@uni-rostock.de; internet www.physiologische-gesellschaft.de; f. 1904; 890 mems; Pres. Prof. Dr ARMIN KURTZ; Pres. Prof. Dr ANDREAS DEUßEN; Sec. Prof. Dr RÜDIGER KÖHLING; publ. *Zeitschrift: Physiologie* (2 a year).

Deutsche Psychoanalytische Gesellschaft: Goerzallee 5, 12207 Berlin; tel. (30) 84316152; fax (30) 84316153; e-mail geschaeftsstelle@dpg-psa.de; internet www.dpg-psa.de; f. 1910; psychoanalytic training, education and research; 500 mems; Pres. Prof. Dr FRANZ WELLENDORF; Pres. Dr JOCHEN HAUSTEIN; Man. Dir Dr THILO EITH; Sec. ERIKA LÜCK; publs *Forum der Psychoanalyse*, *Praxis der Kinderpsychologie und Kinderpsychiatrie*, *Zeitschrift für Psychosomatische Medizin und Psychoanalyse*.

Deutsche Psychoanalytische Vereinigung eV: Körnerstr. 11, 10785 Berlin; tel. (30) 26552504; fax (30) 26552505; e-mail geschaeftsstelle@dpv-psa.de; internet www.dpv-psa.de; f. 1950; br. of the International Psychoanalytical Association; Pres. Prof. Dr MARTIN TEISING; Vice-Pres. Dr CHRISTOPH E. WALKER; Vice-Pres. Dr GERHARD SCHNEIDER; Sec. DANIELA DUTSCHKE.

NATURAL SCIENCES

General

Georg-Agricola Gesellschaft zur Förderung der Geschichte der Naturwissenschaften und der Technik eV: c/o SAXONIA Standortentwicklungs- und -verwaltungsgesellschaft mbH Halsbrücker Str. 34, 09599 Freiberg; tel. (3731) 395040; fax (3731) 395042; e-mail tina.zaenssler@saxonia-freiberg.de; internet www.georg-agricola-gesellschaft.de; f. 1926, present location 2007; promotes study of the history of science and technology; organizes annual meetings; 190 mems; 23 mem. asscns; Pres. Prof. REINHARD SCHMIDT; Vice-Pres. ERICH FRITZ; Man. Dir Dr NORMAN POHL; Chair. of the Scientific Bd Prof. Dr HANS-JOACHIM BRAUN; publ. *Die Technikgechichte als Vorbild moderner Technik*.

Gesellschaft Deutscher Naturforscher und Ärzte eV (Association of German Natural Scientists and Physicians): Hauptstr. 5, 53604 Bad Honnef; tel. (2224) 980713; fax (2224) 980789; e-mail info@gdnae.de; internet www.gdnae.de; f. 1822; 4,000 mems; Pres. Prof. Dr LUDWIG SCHULTZ; Vice-Pres. Prof. Dr HANS-PETER ZENNER; Vice-Pres. Prof. Dr KLAUS MÜLLEN; Gen. Sec. Prof. Dr JÖRG STETTER; publ. *Verhandlungen der GDNAe* (every 2 years).

Görres-Gesellschaft zur Pflege der Wissenschaft: Adenauerallee 19, 53111 Bonn; tel. (228) 2674371; fax (228) 2674379; e-mail verwaltung@goerres-gesellschaft.de; inter-net www.goerres-gesellschaft.de; f. 1876; 3,290 mems; Pres. Prof. Dr WOLFGANG BERGSDORF; Vice-Pres. Prof. Dr OTTO DEPENHEUER; Man. H. REINARTZ; Gen. Sec. Prof. Dr RUDOLF SCHIEFFER; publs *Historisches Jahrbuch* (1 a year), *Jahrbuch für Volkskunde* (1 a year), *Kirchenmusikalisches Jahrbuch* (1 a year), *Literaturwissenschaftliches Jahrbuch* (1 a year), *Oriens Christianus*, *Philosophisches Jahrbuch* (1 a year), *Portugiesische Forschungen*, *Römische Quartalschrift*, *Spanische Forschungen*, *Vierteljahrsschrift für wissenschaftliche Pädagogik*, *Zeitschrift für medizinische Ethik*.

Joachim Jungius-Gesellschaft der Wissenschaften: Edmund-Siemers-Allee 1, 20146 Hamburg; tel. (40) 417444; fax (40) 4480752; e-mail jungiusges@uni-hamburg.de; internet www.jungius-gesellschaft.de; f. 1947; 145 mems (107 ordinary, 38 corresp.); Pres. Dr K. PAWLIK; Vice-Pres. Prof. Dr JÖRN HENNING WOLF; publs *Berichte aus den Sitzungen* (4 a year), *Veröffentlichungen* (1 a year).

Naturwissenschaftlicher Verein für Bielefeld und Umgegend eV (Natural History Society for Bielefeld and the Region): c/o Namu, Adenauerpl. 2, 33602 Bielefeld; tel. (521) 172434; fax (521) 5218810; e-mail info@nwv-bielefeld.de; internet www.nwv-bielefeld.de; f. 1908; 14 working groups, incl. astronomy, entomology and experimental archaeology; 600 mems; Chair. Prof. Dr PETER FINKE; Vice-Chair. Dr MICHAEL VON TSCHIRNHAUS; Pres. CLAUDIA QUIRINI-JÜRGENS; Pres. Dr MARTIN BÜCHNER; Pres. MATHIAS WENNEMANN; publ. *ILEX* (2 a year).

Wissenschaftsrat (German Council of Science and Humanities): Brohler Str. 11, 50968 Cologne; tel. (221) 37760; fax (221) 388440; e-mail post@wissenschaftsrat.de; internet www.wissenschaftsrat.de; f. 1957 through cooperation of Länder and Federal Governments; advisory and coordinating body for science policy; makes recommendations on the structural and curricular development of the universities and on the organization and promotion of science and research; 54 nominated mems in two commissions (Scientific and Administrative); Chair. Prof. Dr Ing. WOLFGANG MARQUARDT; Sec.-Gen. THOMAS MAY; publ. *Empfehlungen und Stellungnahmen* (1 a year).

Biological Sciences

Bayerische Botanische Gesellschaft eV (Bavarian Botanical Society): Menzinger Str. 67, 80638 Munich; tel. (89) 17861267; fax (89) 172638; e-mail bbg@lrz.uni-muenchen.de; internet www.bbgev.de; f. 1890; research into the flora of Bavaria and adjacent countries; preservation of species and plant communities; 874 mems; library of 20,000 vols; Pres. Prof. Dr SUSANNE RENNER; Pres. Dr PETER DÖBBELER; Sec. Dr EVA FACHER; publ. *Berichte der Bayerischen Botanischen Gesellschaft*.

Botanischer Informationsknoten Bayern (BIB) (Botanical Information Agency of Bavaria): Am Galgenberg 7, 93109 Wiesent; tel. (9482) 90494; e-mail wolfgang.ahlmer@biologie.uni-regensburg.de; internet www.bayernflora.de; collects information and data on flora from regional research institutes; Pres. WOLFGANG AHLMER.

Deutsche Botanische Gesellschaft eV (German Botanical Society): c/o Prof. Dr Rudolf Ehwald, Institut für Biologie, Humboldt-Universität zu Berlin, Invalidenstr. 42, 10115 Berlin; tel. (30) 20938816; fax (30) 20938445; e-mail info@deutsche-botanische-gesellschaft.de; internet www.deutsche-botanische-gesellschaft.de; f. 1882; advances scientific botany nationally and internationally; 1,050 mems; Pres. Prof. Dr ULF-INGO FLÜGGE; Gen. Sec. Prof. Dr VOLKER WISSEMANN; publs *Actualia* (3 a year), *Plant Biology* (6 a year).

Deutsche Gesellschaft für Allgemeine und Angewandte Entomologie eV (German Society for General and Applied Entomology): c/o Senckenberg Deutsches Entomologisches Institut, Eberswalder Str. 90, 15374 Müncheberg; tel. (333432) 736983777; fax (333432) 736983706; e-mail dgaae@dgaae.de; internet www.dgaae.de; f. 1976; 870 mems; Pres. Prof. Dr GERALD BERND MORITZ; Man. ORTRUD TAEGER; Sec.-Gen. Dr PETER LÖSEL; publs *DGaaE Nachrichten* (3–4 a year), *Journal of Applied Entomology*, *Mitteilungen* (every 2 years).

Deutsche Gesellschaft für Züchtungskunde eV (DGfZ) (German Society for Animal Production): Adenauerallee 174, 53113 Bonn; tel. (228) 9144761; fax (228) 9144766; e-mail info@dgfz-bonn.de; internet www.dgfz-bonn.de; f. 1905; livestock breeding, animal housing, reproduction, hygiene, nutrition; 650 mems; Pres. Dr OTTO-WERNER MARQUARDT; Vice-Pres. Prof. Dr GEORG ERHARDT; Vice-Pres. Prof. Dr HARALD SIEME; Man. Dir Dr BETTINA BONGARTZ; publ. *Züchtungskunde* (6 a year).

Deutsche Malakozoologische Gesellschaft: Senckenberganlage 25, 60325 Frankfurt am Main; internet www.hausdernatur.de; f. 1868; study of Mollusca; 270 mems; library of 30,000 vols; Pres. Dr VOLLRATH WIESE; publs *Archiv für Molluskenkunde* (2 a year), *Mitteilungen* (1–2 a year).

Deutsche Ornithologen-Gesellschaft eV: c/o Institut f. Vogelforschung, An der Vogelwarte 21, 26386 Wilhelmshaven; tel. (4421) 96890; fax (4421) 968955; e-mail geschaeftsstelle@do-g.de; internet www.do-g.de; f. 1850; 2,200 mems; Pres. Prof. Dr FRANZ BAIRLEIN; publs *Journal of Ornithology* (4 a year), *Vogelwarte* (4 a year).

Deutsche Phytomedizinische Gesellschaft eV (German Phytomedical Society): Messeweg 11/12, 38104 Brunswick; tel. (531) 2993213; fax (531) 2993019; e-mail geschaeftsstelle@dpg.phytomedizin.org; internet www.phytomedizin.org; f. 1949; 1,200 mems; Pres. Prof. Dr ANDREAS VON TIEDEMANN; Pres. Dr BERND HOLTSCHULTE; Pres. Dr KLAUS STENZEL; Man. Dir Dr FALKO FELDMANN.

Deutsche Zoologische Gesellschaft eV (German Zoological Society): Corneliusstr. 12, 80469 München; tel. (89) 54806960; fax (89) 26024574; e-mail dzg@zi.biologie.uni-muenchen.de; internet www.dzg-ev.de; f. 1890; represents zoological sciences in Germany, Austria and Switzerland; promotes zoology as a modern, multi-disciplinary and integrating science and enables the exchange of recent scientific findings; 1,700 mems; Pres. Prof. Dr HERMANN WAGNER (Aachen); Sec. Dr THOMAS KEIL (München); publs *Frontiers in Zoology* (online only), *Zoologie—Mitteilungen der Deutschen Zoologischen Gesellschaft*.

Gesellschaft für Biochemie und Molekularbiologie (Society for Biochemistry and Molecular Biology): Mörfelder Landstr. 125, 60598 Frankfurt; tel. (69) 6605670; fax (69) 66056722; e-mail info@gbm-online.de; internet www.gbm-online.de; f. 1947; research in molecular life sciences in all its forms, such as biochemistry, molecular biology, molecular medicine; 5,500 mems; Chair. Prof. Dr NIKOLAUS PFANNER; Vice-Pres. Prof. Dr ALFRED WITTINGHOFER; Vice-Pres. Prof. Dr IRMGARD SINNING; Sec. Prof. Dr ULRICH BRANDT; publs *Biological Chemistry* (12 a year), *BIOspektrum* (7 a year).

Gesellschaft für Naturkunde in Württemberg: Rosenstein 1, 70191 Stuttgart; tel. (711) 8936-201; fax (711) 8936-100; internet www.ges-naturkde-wuertt.de; f. 1844; 668 mems; Pres. Prof. Dr HANS-DIETER GÖRTZ; publ. *Jahreshefte.*

Münchner Entomologische Gesellschaft eV (Munich Entomological Society): c/o J. Schuberth, Zoologische Staatssammlung, Münchhausenstr. 21, 81247 Munich; tel. (89) 81070; fax (89) 8107300; e-mail megmail@zsm.mwn.de; internet www.zsm .mwn.de/meg; f. 1904; 550 mems; library of 13,406 vols, 383 running journals, 6,800 separata; attached to library of the Zoological State Collection; Pres. Prof. Dr ERNST-GERHARD BURMEISTER; Vice-Pres. HANS MÜHLE; Man. Dir ERICH DILLER; Chief Librarian Dr JULIANE DILLER; Sec. Dr JOHANNES SCHUBERTH; publs *Mitteilungen* (1 a year), *Nachrichtenblatt der Bayerischen Entomologen* (2 a year).

Naturhistorische Gesellschaft Hannover (Hanover Society of Natural History): Willy-Brandt-Allee 5, 30169 Hanover; Fössestr. 99, 30453 Hanover; tel. (511) 9807871; fax (511) 9807844; e-mail info@n-g-h.org; internet www.n-g-h.org; f. 1797; 501 mems; Pres. Dr DIETER SCHULZ; Pres. Prof. Dr HANSJÖRG KÜSTER; publs *Beihefte, Berichte, Naturhistorica – Berichte der NGH* (1 a year).

Naturkundeverein Schwäbisch Gmünd eV (Natural History Society of Schwäbisch Gmünd): Münsterpl. 15, 73525 Schwäbisch Gmünd; tel. (7171) 6034130; e-mail vorstand@nkv-gd.de; internet www.nkv-gd .de; f. 1890; works to promote public awareness of and protection of the natural environment; oversees protected sites; Pres. Prof. Dr FRIEDER BAY; Vice-Pres. UDO GEDACK; Sec. MANFRED BONI; publ. *Unicornis.*

Naturwissenschaftlicher und Historischer Verein für das Land Lippe eV (Natural History and Historical Society for the Lippe Region): Willi-Hofmann-Str. 2, 32756 Detmold; tel. (5231) 3033233; fax (5231) 766114; e-mail info@nhv-lippe.de; internet www.nhv-lippe.de; f. 1835; 4 groups in Detmold, Bad Salzuflen, Lage and Lemgo; research into natural sciences, prehistory and local folk and art history; 800 mems; Pres. Dr CHRISTIAN REINICKE; Vice-Pres. Prof. Dr JÜRGEN DÖHL; Vice-Pres. Prof. Dr STEFAN BAUMEIER; Sec. Dr RALF FABER; publs *Lippische Mitteilungen aus Geschichte und Landeskunde* (1 a year), *Lippischen Geschichtsquellen.*

Naturwissenschaftlicher Verein der Niederlausitz eV (Natural History Society of Lower Lusatia): POB 101005, 03010 Cottbus; e-mail info@nvn-cottbus.de; internet www.nvn-cottbus.de; f. 1990; research into local natural sciences and protection of nature and the environment; 90 mems; Pres. URSULA STRIEGLER; Pres. CAROLA BUDE.

Naturwissenschaftlicher Verein in Hamburg (Natural History Society of Hamburg): c/o Biozentrum Grindel und Zoologisches Museum, Martin-Luther-King-Pl. 3, 20146 Hamburg; tel. (40) 428385635; fax (40) 428383937; e-mail nwv.zoologie@ uni-hamburg.de; internet www.biologie .uni-hamburg.de/zim/nwv; f. 1837; 460 mems; Chair. Prof. Dr HARALD SCHLIEMANN.

Naturwissenschaftlicher Verein zu Bremen (Bremen Natural Science Association): c/o Übersee-Museum, Bahnhofspl. 13, 28195 Bremen; tel. (421) 16038153; fax (421) 1603899; e-mail info@nwv-bremen.de; internet www.nwv-bremen.de; f. 1864; 400 mems; Chair. Dr HANS-KONRAD NETTMANN; Vice-Chair. Dr JENS LEHMANN; Vice-Chair.

Dr MONIKA STEINHOF; publ. *Abhandlungen* (1 a year).

Verein Naturschutzpark eV (Nature Reserves Federation): Niederhaverbeck 7, 29646 Bispingen; tel. (5198) 987030; fax (5198) 987039; e-mail vnp-info@t-online.de; internet www.verein-naturschutzpark.de; f. 1909; 4,500 mems; Dir Dr MATHIAS ZIMMERMANN; publ. *Naturschutz- und Naturparke.*

Vereinigung für Angewandte Botanik eV (Association for Applied Botany): Ohnhorststr. 18, 22609 Hamburg; tel. (40) 42816324; fax (40) 42816565; e-mail hans .weigel@vti.bund.de; internet www .angewandtebotanik.de; f. 1902; 150 mems; Pres. Prof. Dr HANS-JOACHIM WEIGEL; publ. *Angewandte Botanik* (Journal of Applied Botany and Food Quality, 2 a year).

Mathematical Sciences

Berliner Mathematische Gesellschaft eV (Berlin Mathematical Society): c/o Freie Universität Berlin, Institut für Mathematik, Arnimallee 3, 14195 Berlin; tel. (30) 8544602; e-mail bmg@berlin.de; internet www .berlmathges.de; f. 1901; Pres. Prof. Dr GERHARD PREUß; Vice-Pres. Prof. Dr RUDOLF BAIERL; Sec. Prof. Dr WOLFGANG VOLK; publ. *Sitzungsberichte.*

Deutsche Mathematiker Vereinigung eV (German Mathematical Society): c/o WIAS, Mohrenstr. 39, 10117 Berlin; tel. (30) 20372306; fax (30) 20372307; e-mail dmv@ wias-berlin.de; internet dmv.mathematik.de; f. 1890; 4,000 mems; Pres. Prof. Dr CHRISTIAN BÄR; Sec. Prof. Dr GÜNTER TÖRNER.

Gesellschaft für Angewandte Mathematik und Mechanik (International Association of Applied Mathematics and Mechanics): c/o Prof. Dr Ing. Hab. Michael Kaliske, Institut für Statik und Dynamik der Tragwerke, Fakultät Bauingenieurwesen, 01062 Dresden; tel. (351) 46333448; fax (351) 46337086; e-mail gamm@mailbox .tu-dresden.de; internet www.gamm-ev.de; f. 1922; advancement of scientific work and int. cooperation in applied mathematics, mechanics and physics; 2,300 mems; Pres. Prof. V. MEHRMANN; Vice-Pres. Prof. P. WRIGGERS; Sec. Prof. Dr Ing. Hab. MICHAEL KALISKE.

Gesellschaft für Operations Research eV (GOR) (German Society for Operations Research): Joseph-Sommer-Str. 34, 41812 Erkelenz; tel. (2431) 9026710; fax (2431) 9026711; e-mail info@gor-ev.de; internet gor .uni-paderborn.de; f. 1998 by merger of Deutsche Gesellschaft für Operations Research and Gesellschaft für Mathematik, Ökonometrie und Operations Research; promotes devt of operations research and encourages coordination of theoretical and practical advances in the area; 1,200 mems; Pres. Prof. Dr BRIGITTE WERNERS; Man. Dir CHRISTIANE PIENTKA; publs *Mathematical Methods of Operations Research* (6 a year), *OR News* (3 a year), *OR Spectrum* (4 a year).

Physical Sciences

Astronomische Gesellschaft eV: c/o Regina von Berlepsch, Astrophysical Institute Potsdam, An der Sternwarte 16, 14482 Potsdam; tel. (331) 7499-348; fax (331) 7499-216; e-mail info@astronomische-gesellschaft .de; internet www .astronomische-gesellschaft.org; f. 1863, present status 1995; 800 mems; Pres. Prof. Dr RALF-JUERGEN DETTMAR; Vice-Pres. Prof. Dr ANDREAS BURKERT; Sec. REGINA VON BERLEPSCH; publs *Mitteilungen der Astronomischen Gesellschaft* (1 a year), *Reviews in Modern Astronomy* (1 a year).

Deutsche Bunsen-Gesellschaft für Physikalische Chemie eV (German Bunsen Society for Physical Chemistry): POB 150104, 60061 Frankfurt; Theodor-Heuss Allee 25, 60486 Frankfurt; tel. (69) 7564621; fax (69) 7564622; e-mail woehler@ bunsen.de; internet www.bunsen.de; f. 1894, present name 1902; promotes research and technical advances in the area of physical chemistry; 1,500 mems; Chair. Prof. Dr MARTIN QUACK; Vice-Chair. Prof. Dr WOLFGANG VON RYBINSKI; Dir Dr FLORIAN AUSFELDER; Sec. ERIKA WÖHLER; publs *Bunsen-Magazin* (6 a year), *Physical Chemistry Chemical Physics* (jtly with other learned socs, 52 a year).

Deutsche Geophysikalische Gesellschaft eV (German Geophysical Society): c/o Birger-G, Lühr Helmholtz-Zentrum Potsdam, Deutsches GeoforschungsZentrum, Telegrafenberg E 453, 14473 Potsdam; tel. (331) 2881206; fax (331) 2881204; e-mail ase@gfz-potsdam.de; internet www .dgg-online.de; f. 1922; 1,050 mems; supports cttees, working groups and student activities; Pres. Prof. Dr EIKO RÄKERS; Vice-Pres. Prof. Dr UGUR YARAMANCI; Exec. Man. Dr BIRGER-G. LÜHR; publs *DGG Mitteilungen (Red Pages)* (3 or 4 a year), *Geophysical Journal International* (12 a year), *GMIT* (2 a year).

Deutsche Gesellschaft für Biophysik eV: c/o Prof. Dr Ulrike Alexiev, Fachbereich Physik, Freie Universität Berlin, Arnimallee 14, 14195 Berlin; tel. (30) 83855157; fax (30) 83856510; e-mail ulrike.alexiev@physik .fu-berlin.de; internet www.dgfb.org; f. 1943; 450 mems; Chair. Prof. Dr GERD H. J. GALLA; Vice-Pres. Prof. Dr ULI NIENHAUS; Vice-Pres. Prof. Dr CLAUDIA STEINEM; Sec. Dr ULRIKE ALEXIEV.

Deutsche Gesellschaft für experimentelle und klinische Pharmakologie und Toxikologie: Achenbachstr. 43, 40237 Düsseldorf; tel. (211) 60069277; fax (211) 60069278; e-mail mitglieder@dgpt-online.de; internet www.dgpt-online.de; f. 1920; 2,500 mems; Pres. Prof. Dr U. GUNDERT-REMY; Man. Dir Dr J. KNOLLMEYER.

Deutsche Gesellschaft für Geowissenschaften (DGG) (German Geological Society): Stilleweg 2, 30655 Hanover; tel. (511) 6432507; fax (511) 6432695; e-mail dgg@bgr.de; internet www.dgg.de; f. 1848; scientific and technical congresses, confs and meetings, several spec. sections (Fachsektionen); 3,000 mems; library of 130,000 vols; Chair. Prof. Dr STEFAN WOHNLICH; Sec. KARIN SENNHOLZ; Librarian ANDREAS NIKOLAUS KÜPPERS; publs *Exkursionsführer & Tagungspublikationen (EDGG)* (irregular), *Geowissenschaftliche Mitteilungen* (4 a year), *Schriftenreihe der Deutschen Gesellschaft für Geowissenschaften (SDGG)* (irregular), *Zeitschrift der Deutschen Gesellschaft für Geowissenschaften (ZDGG)* (4 a year).

Deutsche Meteorologische Gesellschaft (German Meteorological Society): c/o Institut für Meteorologie, Freie Universität Berlin, Carl-Heinrich-Becker-Weg 6-10, 12165 Berlin; tel. (30) 79708324; fax (30) 7919002; e-mail sekretariat@dmg-ev.de; internet www .dmg-ev.de; f. 1883; 1,750 mems; Pres. Prof. Dr HELMUT MAYER; Prof. Dr HERBERT FISCHER; Sec. Dr DIRK SCHINDLER; publs *Meteorologische Zeitschrift* (6 a year), *Mitteilungen DMG* (4 a year).

Deutsche Mineralogische Gesellschaft (German Mineralogical Society): Institut für Mineralogie und Lagerstättenlehre, RWTH Aachen, 52056 Aachen; tel. (241) 8095774; fax (7071) 8092153; e-mail info@dmg-home .de; internet www.dmg-home.de; f. 1908; crystallography, petrology, geochemistry, ore minerals, applied mineralogy; 1,300 mems; Pres. Prof. Dr RAINER ALTHERR; Vice-

Pres. Prof. Dr Falko Langenhorst; Sec. Prof. Dr F. Michael Meyer; publs *Beihefte* (1 a year), *European Journal of Mineralogy (EJM)* (6 a year), *GMit*.

Deutsche Physikalische Gesellschaft eV: Hauptstr. 5, 53604 Bad Honnef; tel. (2224) 92320; fax (2224) 923250; e-mail dpg@dpg-physik.de; internet www.dpg-physik.de; f. 1845; 59,485 mems; Pres. Prof. Dr Wolfgang Sandner; Vice-Pres. Prof. Dr Gerd Litfin; Sec. Dr Bernhard Nunner; publs *Physik Journal* (12 a year), *Verhandlungen der DPG* (3 or 6 a year).

Deutscher Zentralausschuss für Chemie: c/o Gesellschaft Deutscher Chemiker, POB 90 04 40, 60444 Frankfurt am Main; Carl Bosch-Haus, Varrentrappstr. 40–42, 60486 Frankfurt am Main; tel. (69) 7917323; fax (69) 7917307; e-mail b.koehler@gdch.de; internet www.gdch.de/gdch/koop/iupac.htm; f. 1952; 7 mems; Pres. Prof. Dr Lutz Friedjan Tietze; Man. Dir Prof. Dr Wolfram Koch; publ. *Chemistry International* (6 a year).

Deutsches Atomforum eV (German Forum on Nuclear Energy): Robert-Koch-Pl. 4, 10115 Berlin; tel. (30) 4985550; fax (30) 49855519; internet www.kernenergie.de; f. 1959; promotes the peaceful uses of atomic energy; Pres. Dr Ralf Güldner; Dir Dieter H. Marx.

Geologische Vereinigung e.V. (Geological Association): Vulkanstr. 23, 56743 Mendig; tel. (2652) 989360; fax (2652) 989361; e-mail info@g-v.de; internet www.g-v.de; f. 1910; 1,700 mems; Chair. Prof. Dr Ralf Littke; Sec. Rita Spitzlei; publ. *Geologische Rundschau* (International Journal of Earth Sciences, 8 a year).

Gesellschaft Deutscher Chemiker (German Chemical Society): POB 90 04 40, 60444 Frankfurt am Main; Varrentrappstr. 40–42, 60486 Frankfurt am Main; tel. (69) 79170; fax (69) 7917232; e-mail gdch@gdch.de; internet www.gdch.de; f. 1946; 29,000 mems; Pres. Prof. Dr Michael Dröscher; Vice-Pres. Prof. Dr Barbara Albert; Vice-Pres. Prof. Dr François Diederich; Exec. Dir Prof. Dr Wolfram Koch; publs *Analytical and Bioanalytical Chemistry* (24 a year), *Angewandte Chemie* (int. edn in English, 52 a year), *ChemBioChem* (12 a year), *Chemie-Ingenieur-Technik* (12 a year), *Chemie in unserer Zeit* (6 a year), *Chemischer Informationsdienst* (52 a year), *Chemistry—A European Journal* (24 a year), *ChemPhysChem* (12 a year), *European Journal of Inorganic Chemistry* (24 a year), *European Journal of Organic Chemistry* (24 a year), *Nachrichten aus der Chemie* (12 a year).

Paläontologische Gesellschaft (Palaeontological Society): Weismüllerstr. 45, 60314 Frankfurt am Main; tel. (69) 400301971; fax (69) 400301974; e-mail geschaeftsstelle@palges.de; internet www.palges.de; f. 1912; 1,065 mems; Pres. Dr Michael Wuttke; Vice-Pres. Prof. Dr Rainer Springhorn; Vice-Pres. Prof. Dr Thomas Martin; Vice-Pres. Dr Thomas Mörs; publ. *Paläontologische Zeitschrift* (4 a year).

PHILOSOPHY AND PSYCHOLOGY

Deutsche Gesellschaft für Philosophie eV: c/o Prof. Dr Michael Quante, Philosophisches Seminar, Univ. zu Köln, Albertus-Magnus-Pl., 50923 Cologne; tel. (221) 4706360; fax (221) 4705006; e-mail dgphil-sekretariat@uni-koeln.de; internet www.dgphil.de; f. 1948 as Allgemeine Gesellschaft für Philosophie in Deutschland eV; 1,370 mems; Pres. Prof. Dr Julian Nida-Rumelin; Dir Prof. Dr Michael Quante.

Deutsche Gesellschaft für Psychologie eV (German Psychological Society): POB 42 01 43, 48068 Münster; tel. (2533) 2811520; fax (2533) 281144; e-mail geschaeftsstelle@dgps.de; internet www.dgps.de; f. 1904; promotes and disseminates scientific psychology; 2,800 mems; Pres. Prof. Dr Ursula M. Staudinger; Vice-Pres. Dr Peter Frensch; Vice-Pres. Prof. Dr Reinhard Pietrowsky; Sec. Prof. Dr Christoph Steinebach; publ. *Psychologische Rundschau* (4 a year).

Gesellschaft für antike Philosophie eV: c/o Prof. Dr Christoph Horn, Institut für Philosophie, Universität Bonn, Am Hof 1, 53113 Bonn; e-mail philosophie.lfb2@uni-bonn.de; internet www.ganph.de; f. 1999; promotes research into ancient philosophy; Pres. Prof. Dr Thomas Buchheim; Vice-Pres. Prof. Dr Christian Brockmann; Man. Dir Prof. Dr Christoph Horn.

Gesellschaft für Geistesgeschichte (Society for the History of Ideas): Am Neuen Markt 8, 14467 Potsdam; tel. (331) 2809417; fax (331) 2809450; e-mail aludewig@uni-potsdam.de; internet www.geistesgeschichte.net; f. 1958; 80 mems; Pres. Prof. Dr Julius H. Schoeps; Man. Dir Dr Anna-Dorothea Ludewig; publ. *Zeitschrift für Religions- und Geistesgeschichte*.

Gesellschaft für Wissenschaftliche Gerichts- und Rechtpsychologie (Society for Forensic and Legal Science): Rablstr. 45, 81669 Munich; tel. (89) 4481282; fax (89) 44718018; e-mail info@gwg.info; internet www.gwg-institut.com; f. 1982; community of psychologists and doctors specializing in forensics; Dir Dr Joseph Salzgeber.

Gottfried-Wilhelm-Leibniz-Gesellschaft: c/o Gottfried Wilhelm Leibniz Bibliothek, Niedersächsische Landesbibliothek, Waterloostr. 8, 30169 Hanover; tel. (511) 1267331; fax (511) 1267202; e-mail info@leibnizgesellschaft.de; internet www.gottfried-wilhelm-leibniz-gesellschaft.de; f. 1966; 400 mems; Pres. Prof. Rolf Wernstedt; Vice-Pres. Prof. Dr Hans Poser; Vice-Pres. Prof. Dr Michel Fichant; Gen. Sec. Dr Wolfgang Dittrich; publs *Studia Leibnitiana, Studia Leibnitiana Supplementa / Sonderhefte, Supplementa*.

RELIGION, SOCIOLOGY AND ANTHROPOLOGY

Albertus-Magnus-Institut: Adenauerallee 17, 53111 Bonn; tel. (228) 201460; fax (228) 2014630; e-mail ami@albertus-magnus-institut.de; internet www.albertus-magnus-institut.de; f. 1931; critical publishing of the works of Albertus Magnus; 8 mems; library of 5,000 vols; Dir Prof. Dr Ludger Honnefelder; Deputy Dir Dr Hannes Möhle; Sec. Monika Geyer; publs *Editio Coloniensis, Lectio Albertina, Subsidia Albertina*.

Berliner Gesellschaft für Anthropologie, Ethnologie und Urgeschichte (Berlin Society for Anthropology, Ethnology and Prehistory): c/o Alix Hänsel, Museum für Vor- und Frühgeschichte, Schloss Charlottenburg-Langhansbau, Spandauer Damm 22, 14059 Berlin; tel. (30) 32674817; fax (30) 32674812; internet www.bgaeu.de; f. 1869; 350 mems; Pres. Prof. Dr Carsten Niemitz; Vice-Pres. Dr Markus Schindlbeck; Vice-Pres. Prof. Dr Wolfram Schier; Sec. Dr Peter Bolz; publ. *Mitteilungen*.

Deutsche Gesellschaft für Asienkunde eV (German Association for Asian Studies): Rothenbaumchaussee 32, 20148 Hamburg; tel. (40) 445891; fax (40) 4107945; e-mail post@asienkunde.de; internet www.asienkunde.de; f. 1967; promotes and coordinates contemporary Asian research;

800 mems; Pres. Dr Peter Christian Hauswedell; Exec. Sec. M. Fölster; publ. *ASIEN—The German Journal on Contemporary Asia* (4 a year).

Deutsche Gesellschaft für Soziologie (German Sociological Association): c/o Kulturwissenschaftliches Institut, Goethestr. 31, 45128 Essen; tel. (351) 46337404; fax (351) 46337405; e-mail dgs@mailbox.tu-dresden.de; internet www.soziologie.de; f. 1909; 1,600 mems; Pres. Prof. Dr Hans-Georg Soeffner; Man. Dana Giesecke; publ. *Soziologie–Forum der DGS*.

Deutsche Gesellschaft für Volkskunde (German Society for European Ethnology): Ludwig-Uhland-Institut für Empirische Kulturwissenschaft, Burgsteige 11, 72070 Tübingen; tel. (7071) 2974047; fax (7071) 295330; e-mail geschaeftsstelle@d-g-v.de; internet www.d-g-v.de; f. 1904, present status 1963; 1,200 mems; Pres. Prof. Dr Reinhard Johler; Vice-Pres. Dr Monika Kania-Schütz; Vice-Pres. Dr Sabine Hess; Man. Dir Christian Marchetti; Sec. Sebastian Mohr; publs *Internationale Volkskundliche Bibliographie* (1 a year), *Mitteilungen der Deutschen Gesellschaft für Volkskunde* (4 a year), *Zeitschrift für Volkskunde* (2 a year).

Deutsche Morgenländische Gesellschaft (German Oriental Society): c/o Prof. Dr. Walter Slaje, Seminar für Indologie, Martin-Luther-Universität Halle-Wittenberg, 06099 Halle; tel. (345) 5523650; fax (345) 5527139; e-mail walter.slaje@indologie.uni-halle.de; internet www.dmg-web.de; f. 1845; 698 mems; attached research institutes (Orient-Institut) in Beirut and Istanbul: see chapters on Lebanon and Turkey; library of 50,000 vols; Pres. Prof. Dr Jens Peter Laut; Man. Prof. Dr Walter Slaje; Sec. Prof. Dr Leslie Tramontini; publs *Abhandlungen für die Kunde des Morgenlandes, Beiruter Texte und Studien, Bibliotheca Islamica, Journal of the Nepal Research Centre, Verzeichnis der orientalischen Handschriften in Deutschland, Wörterbuch der klassischen arabischen Sprache, Zeitschrift der Deutschen Morgenländischen Gesellschaft*.

Deutsche Orient-Gesellschaft (German Oriental Society): c/o Institut für Altorientalistik, Hüttenweg 7, 14195 Berlin; tel. (30) 844147925; fax (30) 83853600; e-mail dogva@mail.zedat.fu-berlin.de; internet www.orient-gesellschaft.de; f. 1898; 976 mems; Pres. Prof. Dr Markus Hilgert; Vice-Pres. Prof. Dr Hans Neumann; Sec. Prof. Dr Felix Blocher; publs *Abhandlungen, Alter Orient aktuell* (1 a year), *Mitteilungen der DOG* (1 a year), *Wissenschaftliche Veröffentlichungen*.

Gesellschaft für Anthropologie (Society for Anthropology): c/o Dr Christiane Scheffler, Institut für Biochemie und Biologie der Universität Potsdam, FG Humanbiologie, Maulbeerallee 1, 14469 Potsdam; tel. (331) 9771917; e-mail scheffle@rz.uni-potsdam.de; internet www.gfanet.de; f. 1992 by merger of Deutsche Anthropologische Gesellschaft and Gesellschaft für Anthropologie und Humangenetik; Chair. Prof. Dr Frank J. Rühli; Sec. Dr Albert Zink; publ. *Anthropologischer Anzeiger* (4 a year).

Gesellschaft für Evangelische Theologie: Universität Bamberg, Evangelische Theologie, Markuspl. 3, 96045 Bamberg; tel. (951) 8631844; fax (951) 8634844; e-mail heinrich.bedford-strohm@ppp.uni-bamberg.de; internet www.gevth.de; f. 1940; c. 800 mems; Pres. Prof. Dr Heinrich Bedford-Strohm; publ. *Verkündigung und Forschung* (2 a year).

GIGA German Institute of Global and Area Studies/Leibniz-Institut für Globale und Regionale Studien: Neuer Jungfernstieg 21, 20354 Hamburg; tel. (40)

42825593; fax (40) 42825547; e-mail info@ giga-hamburg.de; internet www .giga-hamburg.de; f. 1964, fmrly German Overseas Institute, present name and status 2006; research on political, economic and social devts in Africa, Asia, Latin America, North Africa and the Middle East; 125 mems; library of 170,000 vols, 850 current journals; Pres. Prof. Dr ROBERT KAPPEL; Vice-Pres. Prof. Dr DETLEF NOLTE; publs *Africa Spectrum* (online), *GIGA Focus*, *GIGA Working Papers* (online), *Journal of Current Chinese Affairs—China aktuell* (4 a year), *Journal of Current Southeast Asian Affairs* (4 a year), *Journal of Politics in Latin America* (online), *Korea Yearbook—Politics, Economy and Society* (1 a year).

Rheinische Vereinigung für Volkskunde: Am Hofgarten 22, 53113 Bonn; tel. (228) 737618; fax (228) 739440; e-mail d .haverkamp@uni-bonn.de; internet www .rvvb.uni-bonn.de; f. 1947; regional ethnology of the Rhineland; 300 mems; Pres. HEINRICH LEONARD COX; Pres. Prof. Dr HELMUT FISCHER; publs *Bonner kleine Reihe zur Alltagskultur, Rheinisches Jahrbuch für Volkskunde.*

Wissenschaftliche Gesellschaft für Theologie eV: Paulsenstr. 55-56, 12163 Berlin; tel. (30) 82097223; fax (30) 82097105; e-mail wgth.berlin@gmx.de; internet www.wgth.de; f. 1973; mems in Germany, Switzerland, Austria, UK, Netherlands, Romania, Czech Republic, Hungary and Scandinavia; 6 sections: Old Testament, New Testament, Church History, Systematic Theology, Practical Theology, Missions and Religion; 700 mems; Pres. Prof. Dr CHRISTOPH SCHWÖBEL; Vice-Pres. Prof. Dr ALBRECHT BEUTEL; Sec. Prof. Dr MICHAEL MEYER-BLANCK; publ. *Veröffentlichungen der Wissenschaftlichen Gesellschaft für Theologie.*

TECHNOLOGY

DECHEMA Gesellschaft für Chemische Technik und Biotechnologie eV (Society for Chemical Engineering and Biotechnology): POB 150104, 60061 Frankfurt am Main; Theodor-Heuss-Allee 25, 60486 Frankfurt am Main; tel. (69) 75640; fax (69) 7564201; e-mail info@dechema.de; internet www.dechema.de; f. 1926; promotes and supports research and technological progress in chemical technology and biotechnology; an interface between science, economy, state and public; organizes ACHEMA summit for chemical technology, environmental protection and biotechnology; 5,500 mems; library of 25,000 vols; Chair. Dr HANS JÜRGEN WERNICKE; Deputy Chair. Prof. Dr FERDI SCHÜTH; Deputy Chair. Dr ALDO BELLONI; Exec. Dir Dr KURT WAGEMANN; publs *Chemie — Ingenieur — Technik* (12 a year), *Materialwissenschaft und Werkstofftechnik* (12 a year), *Materials and Corrosion* (1 a year).

Deutsche Gemmologische Gesellschaft eV (German Gemmological Association): Prof. Schlossmacher Str. 1, 55743 Idar-Oberstein; tel. (6781) 50840; fax (6781) 508419; e-mail info@dgemg.com; internet www.dgemg.com; f. 1932; administers the German Gemmological Training Centre; 1,500 mems; library of 2,500 vols; Dir Dr ULRICH HENN; publ. *Gemmologie* (4 a year, currently as 2 double issues).

Deutsche Gesellschaft für Bauingenieurwesen eV (German Society for Constructional Engineering): Barbarossaplatz 2, 76137 Karlsruhe; f. 1946; 490 mems; Pres. Prof. Dr WILHELM STRICKLER; Sec. Ing. GERHART BOCHMANN.

Deutsche Gesellschaft für Luft- und Raumfahrt—Lilienthal-Oberth eV (DGLR) (German Society for Aeronautics and Astronautics): Godesberger Allee 70, 53175 Bonn; tel. (228) 308050; fax (228) 3080524; e-mail info@dglr.de; internet www .dglr.de; f. 1912; support of aeronautics and astronautics for all scientific and technical purposes; 3,000 mems; Pres. Dr Ing. DETLEF MÜLLER-WIESNER; Vice-Pres Dipl.-Ing. CLAUDIA KESSLER; Vice-Pres Prof. Ing. ROLF HENKE; Sec.-Gen. PETER BRANDT; publs *Aerospace Science and Technology* (1 a year), *DGLR–Mitteilungen* (6 a year), *Luft- und Raumfahrt* (6 a year).

Deutsche Gesellschaft für Materialkunde eV (Materials Science and Engineering): Senckenberganlage 10, 60325 Frankfurt am Main; tel. (69) 75306750; fax (69) 75306733; e-mail dgm@dgm.de; internet www.dgm.de; f. 1919; 2,198 mems; Pres. Dr ULRICH HARTMANN; Vice-Pres. Prof. Dr WOLFGANG KAYSSER; Man. Dir Dr Ing. FRANK O. R. FISCHER; publs *Advanced Engineering Materials* (12 a year), *Materialwissenschaft und Werkstofftechnik* (in German, 12 a year), *Praktische Metallographie* (Practical Metallography), *Zeitschrift für Metallkunde–International Journal for Materials Research.*

Deutsche Gesellschaft für Photogrammetrie, Fernerkundung und Geoinformation eV (DGPF) (German Society for Photogrammetry, Remote Sensing and Geoinformation): c/o EFTAS GmbH, Oststr. 2–18, 48145 Münster; tel. (251) 133070; fax (251) 1330733; e-mail sekretaer@dgpf.de; internet www.dgpf.de; f. 1909, present name 2002; 850 mems; Pres. Prof. Dr CORNELIA GLÄSSER; Vice-Pres. Prof. Dr THOMAS H. KOLBE; Sec. Dr Ing. MANFRED WIGGENHAGEN; publ. *Photogrammetrie-Fernerkundung-Geoinformation* (6 a year).

Deutsche Gesellschaft für Zerstörungsfreie Prüfung eV (DGZfP) (German Society for Non-Destructive Testing): Max-Planck-Str. 6, 12489 Berlin; tel. (30) 678070; fax (30) 67807109; e-mail mail@ dgzfp.de; internet www.dgzfp.de; f. 1933; conferences, training courses and personnel certification; 1,500 mems; Pres. Dr Ing. FRANZISKA AHRENS; CEO MATTHIAS PURSCHKE; publ. *ZfP-Zeitung* (12 a year).

Deutsche Glastechnische Gesellschaft eV (German Society of Glass Technology):; tel. (69) 9758610; fax (69) 97586199; e-mail info@hvg-dgg.de; internet www.hvg-dgg.de; f. 1922; 1,200 mems; deals with different glass technology problems; promotes knowledge of devts in the field of glass and develops contacts amongst members; library of 21,500 vols; Pres. Prof. Dr Ing HANSJÜRGEN BARKLAGE-HILGEFORT; Dir Dr Ing. ULRICH ROGER; publ. *dgg journal* (for mems).

Deutsche Keramische Gesellschaft eV (German Ceramic Society): Am Grott 7, 51147 Cologne; tel. (2203) 966480; fax (2203) 69301; e-mail info@dkg.de; internet www.dkg.de; f. 1919; promotes ceramics in technical, scientific and artistic point of view; 1,229 mems; Chair. Prof. Dr RAINER TELLE; Deputy Chair. Dr BÄRBEL VOIGTSBERGER; Dir Dr MARKUS BLUMENBERG; publ. *cfi-ceramic forum international / Berichte der DKG* (12 a year).

Deutsche Lichttechnische Gesellschaft eV (German Technical-Scientific Society for Light and Lighting): Burggrafenstr. 6, 10787 Berlin; tel. (30) 26012439; fax (30) 26011255; e-mail info@litg.de; internet www.litg.de; f. 1912 as Deutsche Beleuchtungstechnische Gesellschaft; 2,300 mems; Pres. HENNING V. WELTZIEN; Vice-Pres. Prof. Dr Ing. STEPHAN VÖLKER; Man. Dir Dr Ing. MICHAEL L. SEIDL; Sec. REGINA VOIGT; publ. *Licht* (12 a year).

Deutscher Beton- und Bautechnik-Verein eV (German Concrete Association): POB 11 05 12, 10835 Berlin; Kurfürstenstr. 129, 10785 Berlin; tel. (30) 2360960; fax (30) 23609623; e-mail info@betonverein.de; internet www.betonverein.de; f. 1898; quality control, research, standardization and construction advice; 750 mems; Pres. Prof. DrIng. MANFRED NUSSBAUMER; Vice-Pres. Dipl. Ing. DIETER STRAUB; Vice-Pres. Dipl. Ing. HENNER MAHLSTEDT; Man. Dir Dr Ing. LARS MEYER; publs *Bemessungsbeispiele, Beton-Handbuch, Vorträge Betontag.*

Deutscher Kälte- und Klimatechnischer Verein eV (DKV) (German Refrigeration Association): POB 0420, 30004 Hanover; Striehlstr. 11, 30159 Hanover; tel. (511) 8970814; fax (511) 8970815; e-mail info@ dkv.org; internet www.dkv.org; f. 1909; 5 sections for production and industrial application of refrigeration, food science and technology, storage, transport and air conditioning; 1,300 mems; Pres. Prof. Dr-Ing. MICHAEL ARNEMANN; Gen. Man. CARMEN STADTLÄNDER; Vice-Pres. Dr Ing. JOSEF OSTHUES; publs *DKV-Aktuell* (4 a year), *DKV Arbeitsblätter* and *kältemaschinenregeln, DKV-Forschungsberichte* (irregular), *DKV-Statusberichte* (irregular), *DKV-Tagungsbericht* (1 a year).

Deutscher Markscheider Verein eV (German Association of Mining Surveyors): Shamrockring 1, 44623 Herne; tel. (2323) 154660; fax (2323) 154611; e-mail geschaeftsstelle@dmv-ev.de; internet www .dmv-ev.de; assists devt of mining and geotechnical engineering; mountain economy and mining law; participates in education and training in mine surveying; promotes science, research and practice in mine surveying; Pres. Dr Ing. PETER GOERKE-MALLET; Vice-Pres. CARSTEN WEDEKIND; Sec. Prof. Dr Ing. AXEL PREUSSE.

Deutscher Verband für Materialforschung und -prüfung eV (DVM) (German Association for Materials Research and Testing): Unter den Eichen 87, 12205 Berlin; tel. (30) 8113066; fax (30) 8119359; e-mail office@dvm-berlin.de; internet www .dvm-berlin.de; f. 1896; organizes conferences, seminars and workshops; 350 mems; Pres. Dr Ing. MANFRED BACHER-HÖCHST; Vice-Pres. Dipl. Ing. LOTHAR KRÜGER; Man. Dir KATHRIN LEERS; publs *DVM-Nachrichten* (news, 3–4 a year), *Materialprüfung* (12 a year).

Deutscher Verband für Schweissen und verwandte Verfahren eV (DVS) (German Welding Society): POB 10 19 65, 40010 Düsseldorf; Aachener Str. 172, 40223 Düsseldorf; tel. (0211) 15910; fax (0211) 1591200; e-mail verwaltung@dvs-hg.de; internet www .die-verbindungs-spezialisten.de; f. 1947; welding and allied processes; 20,000 mems; Pres. Prof. Dr. H. FLEGEL; Vice-Pres. Dipl. Ing. P. BOYE; Vice-Pres. Dipl. Ing. O. RECKENHOFER; Man. Dir Dr Ing K. MIDDELDORF; publs *Aufbau und Verbindungstechnik in der Elektronic* (also English edn), *Der Praktiker, Die Schweisstechnische Praxis, DVS-Berichte, DVS-Merkblätter, DVS-Richtlinien, DVS-Videos, Fachbibliographie Schweisstechnik, Fachbuchreihe Schweisstechnik, Fachwörterbücher, Forschungsberichte Humanisierung des Arbeitslebens der Schweisser, Referateorgan Schweissen und verwandte Verfahren, Schweissen und Schneiden* (also English edn), *Schweisstechnische Forschungsberichte, Schweisstechnische Software.*

Deutscher Verband Technisch-wissenschaftlicher Vereine (Federation of Technical and Scientific Associations): Steinpl. 1, 10623 Berlin; tel. (30)

310078386; fax (30) 310078216; e-mail info@dvt-net.de; internet www.dvt-net.de; f. 1916; natural science and technology and represents the interests of engineers in relation to science, economics, society, politics and administration; comprises 45 technical and scientific asscns; 45 mems; Chair. Prof. Dr Ing. BRUNO O. BRAUN; Vice-Chair. Dr Ing. WALTER THIELEN; Dir JÖRG MAAS.

Deutscher Verein des Gas- und Wasserfaches eV (DVGW) (German Technical and Scientific Association for Gas and Water): Josef-Wirmer Str. 1–3, 53123 Bonn; tel. (228) 91885; fax (228) 9188990; e-mail info@dvgw.de; internet www.dvgw.de; f. 1859 as Association of German Gas Experts and Agents of German Gas Works; present name and status 2000; specifications and standardization, testing and certification, research and devt, training, providing consultancy services and information; 12,734 mems; Pres. Dr Ing. BERNHARD HÖRSGEN; Man. Dir Dr Ing. WALTER THIELEN; publs *DVGW—Informationen, DVGW—Nachrichten, DVGW—Regelwerk, DVGW—Schriftenreihen, Gas/Erdgas* (Gas/Natural Gas), *GWF–Das Gas- und Wasserfach* (GWF–the Gas and Water Industry), *Wasser/Abwasser* (Water/Wastewater).

DIN Deutsches Institut für Normung eV (German Institute for Standardization): Burggrafenstr. 6, 10787 Berlin; tel. (4930) 26010; fax (4930) 26011231; e-mail info@din.de; internet www.din.de; f. 1917 as Standards Association of German Industry; 1,796 mems; Pres. Prof. Dr-Ing. KLAUS HOMANN; Dir Dr-Ing. TORSTEN BAHKE; publs *DIN-Catalogue* (1 a year), *DIN Management Letter* (6 a year), *DIN-Mitteilungen* (12 a year).

Fachgebiet Wasserwirtschaft und Hydrosystemmodellierung (Chair of Water Resources Management and Modeling of Hydrosystems): Institut für Bauingenieurwesen, Fakultät VI Planen Bauen, Umwelt, Sekr. TIB1-B14, Gustav-Meyer-Allee 25, 13355 Berlin; tel. (30) 31472308; fax (30) 31472430; e-mail reinhard.hinkelmann@wahyd.tu-berlin.de; internet www.wahyd.tu-berlin.de; f. 1891, fmrly Deutscher Verband für Wasserwirtschaft und Kulturbau; hydromechanics, hydrology, hydraulic engineering, hydrosystems, modelling, water resources management; 118 mems; Dir Prof. Dr-Ing. REINHARD HINKELMANN; Sec. MATA KRISHNA.

Gesellschaft für Informatik eV: Wissenschaftszentrum, Ahrstr. 45, 53175 Bonn; tel. (228) 302145; fax (228) 302167; e-mail gs@gi-ev.de; internet www.gi-ev.de; f. 1969; promotes informatics in research, education, applications; 24,500 mems; Pres. Prof. Dr STEFAN JAEHNICHEN; Man. Dir Dr PETER FEDERER; Exec. Dir CORNELIA WINTER; publs *Informatik Spektrum, Künstliche Intelligenz, Wirtschaftsinformatik*.

Informationstechnische Gesellschaft im VDE (ITG) (Information Technology Society within VDE): Stresemannallee 15, 60596 Frankfurt am Main; tel. (69) 6308284; fax (69) 96315215; e-mail presse@vde.com; internet www.vde.com; f. 1954; 35,000 mems; Pres. Dipl. Ing ALF HENRYK WULF; Vice-Pres. Dr Ing. JOACHIM SCHNEIDER; CEO Dr-Ing. HANS HEINZ ZIMMER; Deputy CEO Prof. Dr Ing. HELMUT KLAUSING; publs *AEU International Journal of Electronics, Nachrichtentechnische Zeitschrift (NTZ)* (12 a year).

IWL—Institut für gewerbliche Wasserwirtschaft und Luftreinhaltung Dienstleistung und Consulting GmbH (Institute for Commercial Water Supply and the Prevention of Air Pollution): Hauptstr. 73, 50996 Cologne; tel. (221) 9354623; fax (2233) 9354833; e-mail schopka-iwl@t-online.de; internet www.iwl-koeln.de; Man. Dir Dr SVERRIR SCHOPKA.

RKW Rationalisierungs- und Innovationszentrum der Deutschen Wirtschaft eV (German Centre for Productivity and Innovation): Kompetenzzentrum, Düsseldorfer Str. 40, 65760 Eschborn; tel. (6196) 4950; fax (6196) 4954801; e-mail heitzer@rkw.de; internet www.rkw.de; f. 1921; 4,000 mems; Man. Dir W. AXEL ZEHRFELD; Deputy Dir Dr INGRID VOIGT; publ. *RKW-Magazin* (4 a year).

Stahl–Zentrum: Sohnstr. 65, 40237 Düsseldorf; tel. (211) 6707870; fax (211) 6707-310; e-mail martin.kunkel@stahl-zentrum.de; internet www.stahl-online.de; f. 1998; umbrella org. for Steel Institute VDEh, German Steel Federation, and other orgs and institutes of steel industry; 9,000 mems; library of 120,000 vols; publs *Literaturschau Stahl und Eisen* (26 a year), *MPT Metallurgical Plant and Technology International* (6 a year), *Stahl* (6 a year), *Stahl und Eisen* (12 a year), *Stahlmarkt* (12 a year), *Steel Research (Archiv für das Eisenhüttenwesen)* (12 a year).

VDE Verband der Elektrotechnik Elektronik Informationstechnik eV (VDE Association for Electrical, Electronic & Information Technologies): Stresemannallee 15, 60596 Frankfurt am Main; tel. (69) 63080; fax (69) 6312925; e-mail service@vde.com; internet www.vde.com; f. 1893; 35,000 mems; Pres. Dipl. Ing ALF HENRYK WULF; Vice-Pres. Dr Ing. JOACHIM SCHNEIDER; CEO Dr Ing. HANS HEINZ ZIMMER; Deputy CEO Prof. Dr Ing. HELMUT KLAUSING; publs *Dialog VDE-Mitglieder-Information, Elektrotechnische Zeitschrift, Nachrichtentechnische Zeitschrift, VDE-Buchreihe, VDE-Fachberichte, VDE-Schriftenreihe, VDE-Vorschriften*.

Verein der Zellstoff- und Papier-Chemiker und -Ingenieure eV (ZELLCHEMING) (Association of Pulp and Paper Chemists and Engineers): Emilestrasse 21, 64293 Darmstadt; tel. (6151) 33264; fax (6151) 311076; e-mail info@zellcheming.de; internet www.zellcheming.com; f. 1905; 2,050 mems; Chair. Dipl. Ing. CLAUS M. PALM; Vice-Chair. Dipl. Ing. THOMAS REIBELT; Exec. Dir Dr Ing. WILHELM BUSSE; publ. *ipw—Das Papier*.

Verein Deutscher Giessereifachleute eV (VDG) (German Foundrymen's Association): POB 10 51 44, 40042 Düsseldorf; Sohnstr. 70, 40237 Düsseldorf; tel. (211) 68710; fax (211) 6871364; e-mail info@vdg.de; internet www.vdg.de; f. 1909; 2,600 mems; library of 35,000 vols; Chair. Dr Ing. GOTTHARD WOLF; Sec. GABRIELA BEDERKE; publs *Casting Plant Technology International* (4 a year), *Giesserei* (12 a year), *Giessereiforschung* (4 a year), *Giesserei Jahrbuch, VDG aktuell*.

Verein Deutscher Ingeenieure eV (VDI) (Association of German Engineers): POB 101139, 40002 Düsseldorf; VDI-Pl. 1, 40468 Düsseldorf; tel. (211) 62140; fax (211) 6214169; e-mail kundencenter@vdi.de; internet www.vdi.de; f. 1856; technical and scientific cooperation in 21 engineering sections concerning all fields of technology; training courses for professional engineers; documentation in various branches of engineering and prevention of air pollution and noise; 140,000 mems; Pres. Prof. BRUNO O. BRAUN; Dir Dr WILLI FUCHS; publs *VDI-Verlag: Program: VDI-Nachrichten* (weekly newspaper), technical journals, books, etc.

Research Institutes
GENERAL

Max-Planck-Gesellschaft zur Förderung der Wissenschaften eV (Max Planck Society for the Advancement of Science): POB 101062, 80084 Munich; tel. (89) 21080; fax (89) 21081111; e-mail webmaster@gv.mpg.de; internet www.mpg.de; f. 1948; Pres. Prof. Dr PETER GRUSS; Sec.-Gen. Dr BARBARA BLUDAU; publ. *MaxPlanckResearch* (4 a year).

Attached Research Institutes:

Bibliotheca Hertziana–Max-Planck-Institut für Kunstgeschichte (Bibliotheca Hertziana—Max Planck Institute for Art History): See Italy Chapter.

Friedrich-Miescher-Laboratorium für Biologische Arbeitsgruppen in der Max-Planck-Gesellschaft (Friedrich Miescher Laboratory of the Max Planck Society): POB 2109, 72011 Tübingen; Spemannstr. 39, 72076 Tübingen; tel. (7071) 601800; fax (7071) 601801; e-mail herta.soffel@tuebingen.mpg.de; internet www.fml.tuebingen.mpg.de; f. 1969; Man. Dir Dr CHRISTIANE NÜSSLEIN-VOLHARD.

Fritz-Haber-Institut der Max-Planck-Gesellschaft: Faradayweg 4–6, 14195 Berlin; tel. (30) 841330; fax (30) 84133155; e-mail fhi@fhi-berlin.mpg.de; internet www.fhi-berlin.mpg.de; f. 1911; physical chemistry; Chair. Prof. GERARD MEIJER; Vice-Chair. Prof. MARTIN WOLF.

Kunsthistorisches Institut in Florenz–Max-Planck-Institut (Art History Institute in Florence—Max Planck Institute): Via Giuseppe Guisti 44, 50121 Florence, Italy; tel. 055-249111; fax 055-2491155; e-mail khi-presse@khi.fi.it; internet www.khi.fi.it; f. 1897, present status 2002; library of 310,000 vols, 2,600 periodicals, 600,000 reproductions, spec. collns incl. art in Italy; Dir Prof. Dr GERHARD WOLF; Man. Dir Prof. Dr ALESSANDRO NOVA; Dir Prof. Dr MAX SEIDEL; publs *Italienische Forschungen, Kleine Schriftenreihe des KHI, Mitteilungen des KHI, Studi e ricerche*.

Max-Planck-Arbeitsgruppen für strukturelle Molekularbiologie (Max Planck Working Group for Structural Molecular Biology): c/o DESY, Notkestr. 85, Geb. 25B, 22607 Hamburg; tel. (40) 89982801; fax (40) 89716810; e-mail office@mpasmb.desy.de; internet www.mpasmb-hamburg.mpg.de; f. 1985; Head Prof. Dr ADA YONATH; Head Prof. Dr ECKHARD MANDELKOW; Head Dr HANS-DIETER BARTUNIK.

Max-Planck-Forschungsstelle für Enzymologie der Proteinfaltung (Max Planck Research Unit for Enzymology of Protein Folding): Weinbergweg 22, 06120 Halle (Saale); tel. (345) 5522801; fax (345) 5511972; e-mail user@enzyme-halle.mpg.de; internet www.enzyme-halle.mpg.de; f. 1996; Man. Dir Prof. Dr GUNTER S. FISCHER; Admin. Man. ANGELICA NIEPHAGEN.

Max-Planck-Institut für Ornithologie (Max Planck Research Institute for Ornithology): Schlossallee 2, 78315 Radolfzell; tel. (7732) 1501740; fax (7732) 1501069; e-mail apitz@orn.mpg.de; internet orn.mpg.de; f. 1998; library of 11,000 journals, 6,000 monographs; Man. Dir Prof. Dr MARTIN WIKELSKI.

Max-Planck-Institut für Astronomie (Max Planck Institute for Astronomy): Königstuhl 17, 69117 Heidelberg; tel. (6221) 5280; fax (6221) 528246; e-mail sekretariat@mpia.de; internet www.mpia .de; f. 1967; Man. Dir Prof. Dr THOMAS HENNING; publ. *Sterne und Weltraum* (12 a year).

Max-Planck-Institut für Astrophysik (Max Planck Institute for Astrophysics): POB 1317, 85741 Garching; Karl-Schwarzschild-Str. 1, 85741 Garching; tel. (89) 300000; fax (89) 300002235; e-mail info@mpa-garching.mpg.de; internet www .mpa-garching.mpg.de; f. 1958; Man. Dir Prof. Dr WOLFGANG HILLEBRANDT.

Max-Planck-Institut für Ausländisches und Internationales Privatrecht (Max Planck Institute for Comparative and International Private Law): Mittelweg 187, 20148 Hamburg; tel. (40) 419000; fax (40) 41900288; e-mail info@mpicc.de; internet www.mpipriv.de; f. 1926; library of 460,000 vols; Dir Prof. Dr HOLGER FLEISCHER; Dir Prof. Dr JÜRGEN BASEDOW; publ. *Rabels Zeitschrift für ausländisches und internationales Privatrecht – The Rabel Journal of Comparative and International Private Law (RabelsZ)* (4 a year).

Max-Planck-Institut für Ausländisches und Internationales Sozialrecht (Max Planck Institute for Foreign and International Social Law): Amalienstr. 33, 80799 Munich; tel. (89) 386020; fax (89) 38602490; e-mail beckersek@mpisoc.mpg .de; internet www.mpisoc.mpg.de; f. 1980; Chair. Prof. Dr FRANZ RULAND; Man. Dir Prof. Dr ULRICH BECKER; publ. *Zeitschrift für ausländisches und internationales Arbeits- und Sozialrecht* (4 a year).

Max-Planck-Institut für Ausländisches und Internationales Strafrecht (Max Planck Institute for Foreign and International Criminal Law): Günterstalstr. 73, 79100 Freiburg im Breisgau; tel. (761) 70810; fax (761) 7081294; e-mail info@mpicc.de; internet www.mpicc.de; f. 1938; library of 400,000 vols, 1,500 journals and periodicals; Dir Prof. Dr HANS-JÖRG ALBRECHT; Dir Prof. Dr ULRICH SIEBER; publs *Auslandsrundschau der Zeitschrift für die gesamte Strafrechtswissenschaft, European Journal of Crime, Criminal Law and Criminal Justice* (4 a year).

Max-Planck-Institut für Ausländisches Öffentliches Recht und Völkerrecht (Max Planck Institute for Comparative Public Law and International Law): Im Neuenheimer Feld 535, 69120 Heidelberg; tel. (6221) 4821; fax (6221) 482288; e-mail information@mpil.de; internet www.mpil.de; f. 1924; library of 602,000 vols, 2,680 periodicals; Man. Dir Prof. Dr ARMIN VON BOGDANDY; Dir Prof. Dr RÜDIGER WOLFRUM; publ. *Zeitschrift für ausländisches öffentliches Recht und Völkerrecht*.

Max-Planck-Institut für Bildungsforschung (Max Planck Institute for Human Development): Lentzeallee 94, 14195 Berlin; tel. (30) 824060; fax (30) 8249939; e-mail info@mpib-berlin.mpg.de; internet www.mpib-berlin.mpg.de; f. 1963; library of 206,000 vols, 530 print journals; Man. Dir Prof. Dr GERD GIGERENZER.

Max-Planck-Institut für Bioanorganische Chemie (Max Planck Institute for Bioinorganic Chemistry): POB 10 13 65, 45413 Mülheim/Ruhr; Stiftstr. 34–36, 45470 Mülheim/Ruhr; tel. (208) 3064; fax (208) 3063951; e-mail mpibac@ mpi-muelheim.mpg.de; internet ewww

.mpi-muelheim.mpg.de/bac; f. 1958, fmrly Institute for Radiation Chemistry; Man. Dir Prof. Dr WOLFGANG LUBITZ; Dir Prof. Dr KARL WIEGHARDT.

Max-Planck-Institut für Biochemie (Max Planck Institute for Biochemistry): Am Klopferspitz 18, 82152 Martinsried; tel. (89) 85780; fax (89) 85783777; e-mail konschak@biochem.mpg.de; internet www .biochem.mpg.de; f. 1973; Man. Dir Dr RALF TATZEL.

Max-Planck-Institut für Biogeochemie (Max Planck Institute for Biogeochemistry): Hans-Knöll-Str. 10, 07745 Jena; tel. (3641) 5760; fax (3641) 5770; e-mail info@bgc-jena.mpg.de; internet www.bgc-jena.mpg.de; f. 1997; Man. Dir Prof. Dr SUSAN TRUMBORE.

Max-Planck-Institut für Biologische Kybernetik (Max Planck Institute for Biological Cybernetics): Spemannstr. 38, 72076 Tübingen; tel. (7071) 601510; fax (7071) 601520; e-mail info.kyb@tuebingen .mpg.de; internet www.kyb.tuebingen.mpg .de; f. 1968; works in the elucidation of cognitive processes; 350 mems; Man. Dir Prof. Dr NIKOS K. LOGOTHETIS.

Max-Planck-Institut für Biophysik (Max Planck Institute for Biophysics): Max-von-Laue-Str. 3, 60438 Frankfurt am Main; tel. (69) 63030; fax (69) 63034502; e-mail info@biophys.mpg.de; internet www .biophys.mpg.de; f. 1937; Man. Dir Prof. Dr WERNER KÜHLBRANDT.

Max-Planck-Institut für Biophysikalische Chemie (Karl-Friedrich-Bonhoeffer-Institut) (Max Planck Institute for Biophysical Chemistry): Am Fassberg 11, 37077 Göttingen; tel. (551) 2011211; fax (551) 2011222; e-mail pr@mpibpc.mpg .de; internet www.mpibpc.gwdg.de; f. 1971; Man. Dir Prof. Dr GREGOR EICHELE; publ. *MPIbpc News*.

Max-Planck-Institut für Chemie (Otto-Hahn-Institut) (Max Planck Institute for Chemistry): POB 30 60, 55020 Mainz; Joh.-Joachim-Becher-Weg 27, 55128 Mainz; tel. (6131) 3050; fax (6131) 305388; e-mail gfd@ mpic.de; internet www.mpch-mainz.mpg .de; f. 1912, present status 1949; Man. Dir Prof. Dr JOS LELIEVELD.

Max-Planck-Institut für Chemische Ökologie (Max Planck Institute for Chemical Ecology): Hans-Knoell-Str. 8, 07745 Jena; tel. (3641) 570; fax (3641) 571002; e-mail info@ice.mpg.de; internet www.ice .mpg.de; f. 1996; Chair. Prof. JOHN A. PICKETT; Man. Dir Prof. Dr BILL S. HANSSON.

Max-Planck-Institut für Chemische Physik fester Stoffe (Max Planck Institute for Chemical Physics of Solids): Nöthnitzer Str. 40, 01187 Dresden; tel. (351) 46460; fax (351) 464610; e-mail cpfs@cpfs .mpg.de; internet www.cpfs.mpg.de; f. 1995; Dir Prof. Dr FRANK STEGLICH; Dir Prof. JURI GRIN; Dir Prof. Dr LIU HAO TJENG; Dir Prof. Dr RÜDIGER KNIEP.

Max-Planck-Institut für Demografische Forschung (Max Planck Institute for Demographic Research): Konrad-Zuse-Str. 1, 18057 Rostock; tel. (381) 20810; fax (381) 2081202; e-mail info@demogr.mpg .de; internet www.demogr.mpg.de; f. 1996; Exec. Dir Prof. JOSHUA R. GOLDSTEIN; Dir Prof. Dr JAMES W. VAUPEL.

Max-Planck-Institut für Dynamik Komplexer Technischer Systeme (Max Planck Institute for Dynamics of Complex Technical Systems): Sandtorstr. 1, 39106 Magdeburg; tel. (391) 61100; fax (391) 6110500; e-mail info@mpi-magdeburg.mpg

.de; internet www.mpi-magdeburg.mpg.de; f. 1996; Man. Dir Prof. Dr Ing. UDO REICHL.

Max-Planck-Institut für Dynamik und Selbstorganisation (Max Planck Institute for Dynamics and Self-Organization): POB 28 53, 37018 Göttingen; Bunsenstr. 10, 37073 Göttingen; tel. (551) 51760; fax (551) 5176702; e-mail stephan .herminghaus@ds.mpg.de; internet www .mpisf.mpg.de; f. 1925 as Kaiser Wilhelm Institute for Fluid Dynamics, present name 2004; Man. Dir Prof. Dr STEPHAN HERMINGHAUS.

Max-Planck-Institut für Eisenforschung GmbH (Max Planck Institute for Iron Research): POB 140444, 40074 Düsseldorf; Max-Planck-Str. 1, 40237 Düsseldorf; tel. (211) 67920; fax (211) 6792440; e-mail info@mpie.de; internet www.mpie .de; f. 1917; CEO Prof. Dr DIERK RAABE; Vice-CEO Prof. Dr MARTIN STRATMANN.

Max-Planck-Institut für Entwicklungsbiologie (Max Planck Institute for Developmental Biology): Spemannstr. 35, 72076 Tübingen; tel. (7071) 601350; fax (7071) 601300; e-mail mpi .entwicklungsbiologie@tuebingen.mpg.de; internet www.eb.tuebingen.mpg.de; f. 1937; Man. Dir Prof. Dr ELISA IZAURRALDE.

Max-Planck-Institut für Ethnologische Forschung (Max Planck Institute for Social Anthropology): POB 11 03 51, 06017 Halle (Saale); Advokatenweg 36, 06114 Halle (Saale); tel. (345) 29270; fax (345) 2927502; e-mail hann@eth.mpg.de; internet www.eth.mpg.de; f. 1998; library of 30,200 monographs, 540 videos, 177 subscribed journals, 3,300 journal vols; Man. Dir Prof. Dr CHRIS HANN; Dir Prof. Dr GÜNTHER SCHLEE.

Max-Planck-Institut für Europäische Rechtsgeschichte (Max Planck Institute for European Legal History): POB 930227, 60457 Frankfurt am Main; Hausener Weg 120, 60489 Frankfurt am Main; tel. (69) 789780; fax (69) 78978169; e-mail duve@rg .mpg.de; internet www.rg.mpg.de; f. 1964; library of 320,000 vols; Man. Dir Prof. Dr THOMAS DUVE; publ. *Jus Commune*.

Max-Planck-Institut für Evolutionäre Anthropologie (Max Planck Institute for Evolutionary Anthropology): Deutscher Pl. 6, 04103 Leipzig; tel. (341) 35500; fax (341) 3550119; e-mail info@eva.mpg.de; internet www.eva.mpg.de; f. 1997; Man. Dir Prof. Dr BERNARD COMRIE.

Max Planck-Institut für Evolutionsbiologie (Max Planck Institute for Evolutionary Biology): POB 165, 24302 Plön; August-Thienemann-Str. 2, 24306 Plön; tel. (4522) 7630; fax (4522) 763310; e-mail tautz@evolbio.mpg.de; internet www .evolbio.mpg.de; f. 1891 as Biologische Station zu Plön, present name 2007; library of 12,000 vols; Man. Dir Prof. Dr DIETHARD TAUTZ; Librarian BRIGITTE LECHNER.

Max-Planck-Institut für Experimentelle Endokrinologie (Max Planck Institute for Experimental Endocrinology): Feodor-Lynen-Str. 7, 30625 Hanover; tel. (511) 53590; fax (511) 5359148; e-mail gottschalk@vw.endo.mpg.de; internet www.endo.mpg.de; f. 1979; Man. Dir Prof. Dr GREGOR EICHELE.

Max-Planck-Institut für Experimentelle Medizin (Max Planck Institute for Experimental Medicine): Hermann-Rein-Str. 3, 37075 Göttingen; tel. (551) 38990; fax (551) 3899201; e-mail kraemer@em .mpg.de; internet www.em.mpg.de; f. 1947; molecular biology, neurosciences; library of

80,000 vols; Man. Dir Prof. Dr NILS BROSE; Librarian INGEBORG KRAEMER.

Max-Planck-Institut für Extraterrestrische Physik (Max Planck Institute for Extraterrestrial Physics): POB 1312, 85741 Garching; Giessenbachstr., 85748 Garching; tel. (89) 300000; fax (89) 300003569; e-mail mpe@mpe.mpg.de; internet www.mpe.mpg.de; f. 1963, present status 1991; Man. Dir Prof. Dr RALF BENDER (acting).

Max-Planck-Institut für Festkörperforschung (Max Planck Institute for Solid State Research): Heisenbergstr. 1, 70569 Stuttgart; tel. (711) 6890; fax (711) 6891010; e-mail www@fkf.mpg.de; internet www.fkf.mpg.de; f. 1969; Man. Dir Prof. Dr KLAUS KERN; Man. Dr MICHAEL EPPARD.

Max-Planck-Institut für Immaterialgüter- und Wettbewerbsrecht (Max Planck Institute for Intellectual Property and Competition Law): Marstallpl. 1, 80539 Munich; tel. (89) 242460; fax (89) 24246501; e-mail institut@ip.mpg.de; internet www.ip.mpg.de; f. 1966; Dir Prof. Dr JOSEF DREXL; Dir Prof. Dr RETO M. HILTY.

Max-Planck-Institut für Gesellschaftsforschung (Max Planck Institute for the Study of Societies): Paulstr. 3, 50676 Cologne; tel. (221) 2767-0; fax (221) 2767-555; e-mail info@mpifg.de; internet www .mpifg.de; f. 1984; library of 57,000 vols, 280,000 items in catalogue incl. articles from journals and edited vols; researches on sociology of markets, institutional change in contemporary capitalism, European liberalization policies, institution building across borders, economic patriotism, science, technology and innovation, governance of global structures, theories and methods; runs the Int. Max Planck Research School on Social and Political Constitution of the Economy (IMPRS-SPCE), a doctoral programme, with Univ. of Cologne; Man. Dir Prof. Dr JENS BECKERT; Man. Dir Prof. Dr WOLFGANG STREECK; publs *MPIfG Discussion Papers, MPIfG Journal Articles, MPIfG Working Papers*.

Max-Planck-Institut für Gravitationsphysik (Albert-Einstein-Institut) (Max Planck Institute for Gravitational Physics): Am Mühlenberg 1, 14476 Golm; tel. (331) 56770; fax (331) 5677298; e-mail office@aei.mpg.de; internet www.aei.mpg .de; f. 1995; experimental br. in Hanover; library of 7,800 monographs, 140 scientific journals; Man. Dir Prof. Dr GERHARD HUISKEN; Vice-Man. Dir Prof. KARSTEN DANZMANN.

Max-Planck-Institut für Herz- und Lungenforschung (W. G. Kerckhoff-Institut) (Max Planck Institute for Heart and Lung Research): Ludwigstr. 43, 61231 Bad Nauheim; tel. (6032) 7050; fax (6032) 7051104; e-mail info@mpi-bn.mpg.de; internet www.mpi-hlr.de; f. 1931, present status 1972; Man. Dir Prof. Dr THOMAS BRAUN.

Max-Planck-Institut für Hirnforschung (Max Planck Institute for Brain Research): POB 71 06 62, 60496 Frankfurt; Deutschordenstr. 46, 60528 Frankfurt am Main; tel. (69) 967690; fax (69) 96769440; e-mail maja.fricke@vw .mpih-frankfurt.mpg.de; internet www .mpih-frankfurt.mpg.de; f. 1914 as Kaiser Wilhelm Institute for Brain Research, present name and status 1948; Man. Dir Prof. Dr GILLES LAURENT.

Max-Planck-Institut für Immunbiologie und Epigenetik (Max Planck Institute for Immunobiology and Epigenetics):

Stübeweg 51, 79108 Freiburg; tel. (761) 51080; fax (761) 5108220; e-mail presse@ immunbio.mpg.de; internet www3 .immunbio.mpg.de; f. 1961; Man. Dir Prof. Dr RUDOLF GROSSCHEDL.

Max-Planck-Institut für Infektionsbiologie (Max Planck Institute for Infection Biology): Charitéplatz 1, Campus Charite Mitte, 10117 Berlin; tel. (30) 284600; fax (30) 28460141; e-mail sek@ mpiib-berlin.mpg.de; internet www .mpiib-berlin.mpg.de; f. 1993; Man. Dir Prof. Dr THOMAS F. MEYER.

Max-Planck-Institut für Informatik (Max Planck Institute for Informatics): Campus E1 4, 66123 Saarbrücken; tel. (681) 9325700; fax (681) 9325719; e-mail info@mpi-inf.mpg.de; internet www.mpi-inf .mpg.de; f. 1988; Man. Dir Prof. Dr KURT MEHLHORN.

Max-Planck-Institut für Kernphysik (Max Planck Institute for Nuclear Physics): POB 103980, 69029 Heidelberg; Saupfercheckweg 1, 69117 Heidelberg; tel. (6221) 5160; fax (6221) 516601; e-mail info@mpi-hd.mpg.de; internet www .mpi-hd.mpg.de; f. 1958; Man. Dir Prof. Dr MANFRED LINDNER.

Max-Planck-Institut für Kognitions- und Neurowissenschaften (Max Planck Institute for Human Cognitive and Brain Sciences): POB 500355, 04303 Leipzig; Stephanstr. 1A, 04103 Leipzig; tel. (341) 994000; fax (341) 9940104; e-mail info@cbs .mpg.de; internet www.cbs.mpg.de; f. 2004 by merger of Leipzig Max Planck Institute of Cognitive NeuroScience and Munich Max Planck Institute for Psychological Research; Man. Dir Prof. ARNO VILLRINGER; publ. *MPI Series in Human Cognitive and Brain Sciences.*

Max-Planck-Institut für Kohlenforschung (Max Planck Institute for Coal Research): Kaiser-Wilhelm-Pl. 1, 45470 Mülheim an der Ruhr; tel. (208) 3061; fax (208) 3062980; e-mail contact@ mpi-muelheim.mpg.de; internet www.kofo .mpg.de; f. 1912 as Kaiser Wilhelm Institut für Kohlenforschung, present name 1949; library of 17,000 vols; research in the catalytic transformation of compounds and materials with the highest degree of chemo-, regio- and stereoselectivity under mild conditions and with an economical use of energy and resources in the following five areas: synthetic organic chemistry, homogeneous catalysis, heterogeneous catalysis, organometallic chemistry and theory; Man. Dir Prof. Dr ALOIS FÜRSTNER.

Max-Planck-Institut für Kolloid- und Grenzflächenforschung (Max Planck Institute for and Interface Research): Am Mühlenberg 1, OT Golm, 14476 Potsdam; tel. (331) 5677814; fax (331) 5677875; e-mail andreas.stockhaus@mpikg.mpg.de; internet www.mpikg.mpg.de; f. 1992; research concerned with structures at nano- and micrometer level; Man. Dir Prof. Dr MARKUS ANTONIETTI; Admin. Man. ANDREAS STOCKHAUS.

Max-Planck-Institut für Marine Mikrobiologie (Max Planck Institute for Marine Microbiology): Celsiusstr. 1, 28359 Bremen; tel. (421) 202850; fax (421) 2028580; e-mail contact@mpi-bremen.de; internet www.mpi-bremen.de; f. 1992; Dir Prof. Dr RUDOLF AMANN; Sec. ULRIKE TIETJEN.

Max-Planck-Institut für Mathematik (Max Planck Institute for Mathematics): POB 7280, 53072 Bonn; Vivatsgasse 7, 53111 Bonn; tel. (228) 4020; fax (228) 402277; e-mail admin@mpim-bonn.mpg .de; internet www.mpim-bonn.mpg.de; f.

1981; Man. Dir Prof. Dr DON ZAGIER; Sec. ANDREA KOHLHUBER.

Max-Planck-Institut für Mathematik in den Naturwissenschaften (Max Planck Institute for Mathematics in the Natural Sciences): Inselstr. 22, 04103 Leipzig; tel. (341) 995950; fax (341) 9959658; e-mail avanden@mis.mpg.de; internet www.mis.mpg.de; f. 1996; Dir Prof. Dr FELIX OTTO; Dir Prof. Dr JÜRGEN JOST (acting); Dir Prof. Dr WOLFGANG HACKBUSCH.

Max-Planck-Institut für Medizinische Forschung (Max Planck Institute for Medical Research): POB 10 38 20, 69028 Heidelberg; Jahnstr. 29, 69120 Heidelberg; tel. (6221) 4860; fax (6221) 486351; e-mail sekr@mpimf-heidelberg.mpg.de; internet www.mpimf-heidelberg.mpg.de; f. 1930 as Kaiser Wilhelm Institute for Medical Research, present name and status 1948; Chair. Dr WINFRIED DENK.

Max-Planck-Institut für Metallforschung (Max Planck Institute for Metals Research): Heisenbergstr. 3, 70569 Stuttgart; tel. (711) 6890; fax (711) 6891010; e-mail info@mf.mpg.de; internet www.mf.mpg.de; f. 1920; condensed matter science fluctuations, self org. and structure formation in nanoconfinement synchrotron radiation, neutrons, microscopy nano-oxidation, solid–liquid interfaces; Dir Prof. Dr JOACHIM P. SPATZ (acting); publ. *Focus on Materials*.

Max-Planck-Institut für Meteorologie (Max Planck Institute for Meteorology): Bundesstr. 53, 20146 Hamburg; tel. (40) 411730; fax (40) 41173298; e-mail annette .kirk@zmaw.de; internet www.mpimet .mpg.de; f. 1975; Man. Dir Prof. Dr JOCHEM MAROTZKE.

Max-Planck-Institut für Mikrostrukturphysik (Max Planck Institute for Microstructure Physics): Weinberg 2, 06120 Halle; tel. (345) 558250; fax (345) 5511223; e-mail hoehl@mpi-halle.de; internet www.mpi-halle.mpg.de; f. 1992; Man. Dir Prof. Dr JÜRGEN KIRSCHNER.

Max-Planck-Institut für Molekulare Biomedizin (Max Planck Institute for Molecular Biomedicine): Röntgenstr. 20, 48149 Münster; tel. (251) 703650; fax (251) 70365199; e-mail presse@ mpi-muenster.mpg.de; internet www .mpi-muenster.mpg.de; f. 2001; Man. Dir Prof. Dr RALF HEINRICH ADAMS.

Max-Planck-Institut für Molekulare Genetik (Max Planck Institute for Molecular Genetics): Ihnestr. 63–73, 14195 Berlin; tel. (30) 84130; fax (30) 84131388; e-mail info@molgen.mpg.de; internet www.molgen.mpg.de; f. 1964; analysis of human genes, their function and evolution; bioinformatics, devt and implementation of new methods for functional genome analysis; library of 50,000 vols; Man. Dir Prof. Dr MARTIN VINGRON.

Max-Planck-Institut für Molekulare Pflanzenphysiologie (Max Planck Institute for Molecular Plant Physiology): Am Mühlenberg 1, 14476 Potsdam- Golm; tel. (331) 56780; fax (331) 5678408; e-mail contact@mpimp-golm.mpg.de; internet www.mpimp-golm.mpg.de; f. 1994; Man. Dir Prof. Dr MARK STITT.

Max-Planck-Institut für Molekulare Physiologie (Max Planck Institute for Molecular Physiology): POB 50 02 47, 44202 Dortmund; Otto-Hahn-Str. 11, 44227 Dortmund; tel. (231) 1330; fax (231) 1332699; e-mail roger.goody@ mpi-dortmund.mpg.de; internet www .mpi-dortmund.mpg.de; f. present status

1948, present name 1993; Man. Dir Prof. Dr ROGER S. GOODY; Gen. Man. Dr PETER HERTER.

Max-Planck-Institut für Molekulare Zellbiologie und Genetik (Max Planck Institute for Molecular Cell Biology and Genetics): Pfotenhauerstr. 108, 01307 Dresden; tel. (351) 2100; fax (351) 2102000; e-mail info@mpi-cbg.de; internet www.mpi-cbg.de; f. 1998; Man. Dir Prof. Dr MARINO ZERIAL.

Max-Planck-Institut für Neurobiologie (Max Planck Institute for Neurobiology): Am Klopferspitz 18, 82152 Martinsried; tel. (89) 85781; fax (89) 85783541; e-mail merker@neuro.mpg.de; internet www.neuro.mpg.de; f. 1917, present name 1998; research on the devt, functions and diseases of the nervous system; molecular developmental biology, cellular and systems studies of neural plasticity, pathology and immunology of the central and peripheral nervous system, information processing in the invertebrate visual system; incl. four depts and several independent research groups; Man. Dir Prof. Dr HARTMUT WEKERLE; Public Relations Officer Dr STEFANIE MERKER.

Max-Planck-Institut für Neurologische Forschung (Max Planck Institute for Neurological Research): POB 41 06 29, 50866 Cologne; Gleueler Str. 50, 50931 Cologne; tel. (221) 47260; fax (221) 4726203; e-mail info@nf.mpg.de; internet www.nf.mpg.de; f. 1982; library of 5,200 monographs, 4,800 journals; Dir Prof. Dr U. BENJAMIN KAUPP; Deputy Dir Prof. Dr RUDOLF GRAF.

Max-Planck-Institut für Ökonomik (Max Planck Institute for Economics): Kahlaische Str. 10, 07745 Jena; tel. (3641) 6865; fax (3641) 686990; e-mail mader@econ.mpg.de; internet www.econ .mpg.de; f. 1993; library of 25,000 vols, 190 current journals; Exec. Dir Prof. Dr WERNER GÜTH.

Max-Planck-Institut für Pflanzenzüchtungsforschung (Max Planck Institute for Plant Breeding Research): Carl-von-Linné-Weg 10, 50829 Cologne; tel. (221) 50620; fax (221) 5062674; e-mail prag@mpipz.mpg.de; internet www .mpiz-koeln.mpg.de; f. 1928; Man. Dir Prof. Dr PAUL SCHULZE-LEFERT.

Max-Planck-Institut für Physik (Werner-Heisenberg-Institut) (Max Planck Institute for Physics): Föhringer Ring 6, 80805 Munich; tel. (89) 323540; fax (89) 3226704; e-mail hollik@mpp.mpg.de; internet www.mpp.mpg.de; f. 1917 as Kaiser-Wilhelm-Institut für Physik, present name and status 1948; Man. Dir Prof. Dr WOLFGANG HOLLIK.

Max-Planck-Institut für Physik komplexer Systeme (Max Planck Institute for Physics of Complex Systems): Nöthnitzer Str. 38, 01187 Dresden; tel. (351) 8710; fax (351) 8711999; e-mail info@ mpipks-dresden.mpg.de; internet www .mpipks-dresden.mpg.de; f. 1992; Dir Prof. Dr RODERICH MOESSNER.

Max-Planck-Institut für Plasmaphysik (Max Planck Institute for Plasma Physics): Boltzmannstr. 2, 85748 Garching; tel. (89) 329901; e-mail info@ipp.mpg .de; internet www.ipp.mpg.de; f. 1960; Scientific Dir Prof. Dr SIBYLLE GÜNTER.

Max-Planck-Institut für Polymerforschung (Max Planck Institute for Polymer Research): POB 3148, 55021 Mainz; Ackermannweg 10, 55128 Mainz; tel. (6131) 3790; fax (06131) 379100; e-mail info@mpip-mainz.mpg.de; internet www

.mpip-mainz.mpg.de; f. 1983; Man. Dir Prof. Dr KLAUS MÜLLEN.

Max-Planck-Institut für Psychiatrie (Deutsche Forschungsanstalt für Psychiatrie) (Max Planck Institute for Psychiatry): Kraepelinstr. 2–10, 80804 Munich; tel. (89) 306221; fax (89) 30622605; e-mail holsboer@mpipsykl.mpg.de; internet www .mpipsykl.mpg.de; f. 1917; basic and clinical research, clinical services in psychiatry and neurology; main topics incl. depression, anxiety disorders, multiple sclerosis; Man. Dir Prof. Dr FLORIAN HOLSBOER.

Max-Planck-Institut für Psycholinguistik (Max Planck Institute for Psycholinguistics): See Netherlands chapter.

Max-Planck-Institut für Psychologische Forschung (Max Planck Institute for Psychological Research): POB 340 121, 80098 Munich; Amalienstr. 33, 80799 Munich; tel. (89) 386020; fax (89) 38602199; f. 1981; Man. Dir Prof. Dr WOLFGANG PRINZ.

Max-Planck-Institut für Quantenoptik (Max Planck Institute of Quantum Optics): Hans-Kopfermann-Str. 1, 85748 Garching; tel. (89) 32 9050; fax (89) 32905200; e-mail gerhard.rempe@mpq .mpg.de; internet www.mpq.mpg.de; f. 1981; Man. Dir Prof. Dr GERHARD REMPE.

Max-Planck-Institut für Radioastronomie (Max Planck Institute for Radio Astronomy): POB 20 24, 53010 Bonn; Auf dem Hügel 69, 53121 Bonn; tel. (228) 5250; fax (228) 525229; e-mail postmaster@ mpifr-bonn.mpg.de; internet www .mpifr-bonn.mpg.de; f. 1966; Man. Dir Dr KARL M. MENTEN.

Max-Planck-Institut für Sonnensystemforschung (Max Planck Institute for Solar System Research): Max-Planck-Str. 2, 37191 Katlenburg-Lindau; tel. (5556) 9790; fax (5556) 979240; e-mail presseinfo@mps.mpg.de; internet www .mps.mpg.de; f. 1957 AS Max Planck Institute for Aeronomy, present name 2004; Man. Dir Prof. Dr ULRICH R. CHRISTENSEN.

Max-Planck-Institut für Terrestrische Mikrobiologie (Max Planck Institute for Terrestrial Microbiology): Karl-von-Frisch-Str. 10, 35043 Marburg; tel. (6421) 1780; fax (6421) 178999; e-mail office@ mpi-marburg.mpg.de; internet www .mpi-marburg.mpg.de; f. 1991; Man. Dir Prof. Dr REGINE KAHMANN.

Max-Planck-Institut für Wissenschaftsgeschichte (Max Planck Institute for History of Science): Boltzmannstr. 22, 14195 Berlin; tel. (30) 226670; fax (30) 22667238; e-mail public@mpiwg-berlin .mpg.de; internet www.mpiwg-berlin.mpg .de; f. 1994; library of 65,000 vols; Exec. Dir Prof. Dr JÜRGEN RENN; Dir Prof. Dr HANS-JÖRG RHEINBERGER; Dir Prof. Dr LORRAINE DASTON.

Max Planck-Institut zur Erforschung Multireligiöser und Multiethnischer Gesellschaften (Max Planck Institute for the Study of Religious and Ethnic Diversity): POB 28 33, 37018 Göttingen; Hermann-Föge-Weg 11, 37073 Göttingen; tel. (551) 49560; fax (551) 4956170; e-mail info@mmg.mpg.de; internet www.mmg .mpg.de; f. 2007, fmrly Max-Planck-Institut für Geschichte; multi-disciplinary study of diversity in historical and contemporary societies particularly concerning ethnic and religious forms and dynamics;

library of 121,000 vols; Man. Dir Prof. Dr STEVE VERTOVEC; Head Librarian Dr KRISTIN FUTTERLIEB.

Max-Planck-Institut zur Erforschung von Gemeinschaftsgütern (Max Planck Institute for Research on Collective Goods): Kurt-Schumacher-Str. 10, 53113 Bonn; tel. (228) 914160; fax (228) 9141655; e-mail info@coll.mpg.de; internet www.coll .mpg.de; f. 2003; library of 40,000 vols; Dir Prof. Dr CHRISTOPH ENGEL; Dir Prof. Dr MARTIN HELLWIG; Head Librarian REGINA GOLDSCHMITT.

AGRICULTURE, FISHERIES AND VETERINARY SCIENCE

Deutsche Gesellschaft für Holzforschung eV (German Society for Wood Research): Bayerstr. 57–59, 5 Stock, 80335 Munich; tel. (89) 5161700; fax (89) 531657; e-mail mail@dgfh.de; internet www.dgfh.de; f. 1942; Pres. Dipl.-Ing. X. HAAS; Man. Dipl.-Ing. AXEL YEUTSCH; publ. DGfH aktuell (3 a year).

Gesellschaft für Hopfenforschung eV (Society of Hops Research): Hüll 5 1/3, 85283 Wolnzach; tel. (8442) 3597; fax (8442) 2871; e-mail gfh@hopfenforschung.de; internet www.hopfenforschung.de; f. 1926; Chair. Dr MICHAEL MÖLLER; Vice-Chair. Dr BERND SCHMIDT.

Johänn Heinrich von Thünen Institute/ Federal Research Institute for Rural Areas, Forestry and Fisheries: Bundesalle 50, 38116 Braunschweig; tel. (531) 5961003; fax (531) 5961099; e-mail info@vti .bund.de; internet www.vti.bund.de; f. 2008, by merger of Federal Research Centre for Fisheries (f. 1948), the Federal Research Centre for Forestry and Forestry Products and divs of the Federal Agricultural Research Centre; library of 68,500 vols; Pres. Prof. Dr FOLKHARD ISERMEYER; publs Information on Fishery Research (1 a year), Landbauforschung (4 a year), Silvae Genetica (1 a year), Wissenschaft erleben (2 a year).

Attached Research Institutes:

Institut für Fischereiökologie (Institute of Fisheries Ecology): Palmaille 9, 22767 Hamburg; tel. (40) 38905290; fax (40) 38905261; e-mail foe@vti.bund.de; f. 1885, present name 1993; investigates marine ecological system and the German fresh waters; Dir Dr REINHOLD HANEL; Deputy Dir Dr THOMAS LANG; Sec ANNE EBERT.

Institut für Ostseefischerei (Institute for Baltic Sea Fisheries): Alter Hafen Süd 2, 18069 Rostock; tel. (381) 8116102; fax (381) 8116199; e-mail osf@vti.bund.de; f. 1991; in charge of fed. tasks of sea research in the Baltic Sea for the Min. of Nutrition, Agriculture and Consumer Protection; conducts research to establish scientific basis for advising in political decision in fisheries; Dir Prof. Dr Hab. CORNELIUS HAMMER; Deputy Dir Dr CHRISTOPHER ZIMMERMAN; Sec. WALTRAUD KLEINFELDT.

Institut für Seefischerei (Institute of Sea Fisheries): Palmaille 9, 22767 Hamburg; tel. (40) 38905178; fax (40) 38905263; e-mail sf@vti.bund.de; research on ecological and economic principles underlying sustainable exploitation of natural marine resources; Dir Dr GERD KRAUS; Deputy Dir Dr CHRISTOPH STRANSKY; Sec. KONSTANZE VON SCHUDNAT.

ARCHITECTURE AND TOWN PLANNING

Akademie für Raumforschung und Landesplanung (Academy for Spatial Research and Planning): Hohenzollernstr.

11, 30161 Hanover; tel. (511) 348420; fax (511) 3484241; e-mail arl@arl-net.de; internet www.arl-net.de; f. 1946; 189 mems; library of 20,000 vols; Pres. Ing. Dr BERN-HARD HEINRICHS; Gen. Sec. Prof. Dr-Ing. DIETMAR SCHOLICH; publ. *Raumforschung und Raumordnung* (Spatial Research and Planning, 6 a year, in German with summaries in English).

Deutsche Akademie für Städtebau und Landesplanung (German Academy for Urban and Regional Spatial Planning): Stresemannstr. 90, 10963 Berlin; tel. (30) 23082231; fax (30) 23082232; e-mail info@dasl.de; internet www.dasl.de; f. 1922 as Free Academy of Town Planning; spatial and regional planning, town planning, landscape and open-space planning, transport policy, urban economic devt, protection of built heritage and social policy; 600 mems; library of 5,000 vols; Pres. Prof. Dr-Ing. CHRISTIANE THALGOTT; Vice-Pres. Prof. Dr MICHAEL KRAUTZBERGER; Sec. Prof. Ing. JULIAN WÉKEL; publs *Almanach* (1 a year), *Vorbereitende Bericht* (1 or 2 a year).

IKT-Institut für Unterirdische Infrastruktur GmbH (IKT-Institute for Underground Infrastructure): Exterbruch 1, 45886 Gelsenkirchen; tel. (209) 178060; fax (209) 1780688; e-mail info@ikt.de; internet www.ikt.de; research related to construction of underground pipes and networks for gas, water and waste-water; Man. Dir Dr-Ing. ROLAND W. WANIEK; Scientific Dir Dr Ing. BERT BOSSELER; publ. *IKT-LinerReports*.

ILS—Institut für Landes- und Stadtwicklungsforschung GmbH (ILS—Research Institute for Regional and Urban Development): Brüderweg 22–24, 44135 Dortmund; tel. (231) 90510; fax (231) 9051155; e-mail poststelle@ils-research.de; internet www.ils-forschung.de; spatial sciences; analyses causes and consequences of new urbanization processes and urban future; library of 44,000 vols, 150 current journals; Dir Prof. Dr RAINER DANIELZYK; publs *ILS-Journal* (3 a year), *ILS-Trends* (3 a year).

Institut für Wohnungswesen, Immobilienwirtschaft, Stadt- und Regionalentwicklung GmbH (InWIS) (Institute of Housing, Real Estate, Urban and Regional Development Ltd): Springorumallee 20, 44795 Bochum; tel. (234) 890340; fax (234) 8903449; e-mail info@inwis.de; internet www.inwis.de; attached to Ruhr Univ.; interdisciplinary basic and applied research of housing, real estate, urban and regional science topics; library of 13,000 vols, 85 periodicals; Chair. KLAUS LEUCHTMANN; Dir MICHAEL NEITZEL.

BIBLIOGRAPHY, LIBRARY SCIENCE AND MUSEOLOGY

Internationale Gutenberg-Gesellschaft (International Gutenberg Society): Liebfrauenpl. 5, 55116 Mainz; tel. (6131) 226420; fax (6131) 233530; e-mail info@gutenberg-gesellschaft.de; internet www.gutenberg-gesellschaft.de; f. 1901; promotes research into the history of printing and of the book; 1,300 mems; Pres. THE MAYOR OF THE CITY OF MAINZ; Gen. Sec. CHRISTINA SCHMITZ; publ. *Gutenberg-Jahrbuch* (1 a year).

ECONOMICS, LAW AND POLITICS

Arbeitsgemeinschaft Deutscher Wirtschaftswissenschaftlicher Forschungsinstitut eV (Association of German Economic Science Research Institutes): c/o DIW Berlin, 10108 Berlin; Mohrenstr. 58, 10117 Berlin; tel. (30) 89789211; fax (30) 89789100; e-mail arge@diw.de; f. 1949; 29

mem. colleges and institutes; coordinates programmes of the institutes and provides a permanent base for research exchange and cooperation; Chair. Prof. Dr KLAUS F. ZIMMERMANN; Sec.-Gen. RALF MESSER; publ. *Gemeinschaftsdiagnose* (2 a year).

Member Institutes:

Abteilung Wirtschaftswissenschaft im Osteuropa Institut an der Freien Universität Berlin (Economics Department of the East European Institute at the Free University, Berlin): Garystr. 55, 14195 Berlin; tel. (30) 83854008; fax (30) 83852072; e-mail schrettl@wiwiss.fu-berlin.de; internet www.oei.fu-berlin.de/wirtschaft; f. 1950; economic research on East European countries; 10 mems; library of 85,000 vols and 95 periodicals; Dir Prof. Dr WOLFRAM SCHRETTL; publs *Berichte des Osteuropa Instituts/Reihe Wirtschaft und Recht, Wirtschaftswissenschaftliche Veröffentlichungen*.

BAW Institut für Wirtschaftsforschung GmbH (BAW Economic Research Institute Ltd): Wilhelm-Herbst-Str. 5, 28359 Bremen; tel. (421) 206990; fax (421) 2069999; e-mail n.lutzky@baw-bremen.de; f. 1947; library of 20,000 vols; Dir Dr NIKOLAI LUTZKY; publs *BAW-Monatsbericht* (12 a year), *Regionalwirtschaftliche Studien* (irregular).

CESifo Group: Poschingerstr. 5, 81679 Munich; tel. (89) 92241410; fax (89) 92241409; e-mail office@cesifo.de; internet www.cesifo-group.de; f. 1999; consists of Centre for Economic Studies (CES), Ifo Institute for Economic Research and CESifo GmbH (Munich Society for the Promotion of Economic Research); empirical economic research; library of 90,000 vols; Pres. Dr HANS-WERNER SINN; publs *CESifo DICE* (in English, 4 a year), *CESifo Economic Studies* (in English), *CESifo Forum* (in English, 4 a year), *ifo Dresden berichtet* (6 a year), *ifo Schnelldienst* (36 a year), *ifo Wirtschaftskonjunktur* (12 a year).

Deutsches Institut für Wirtschaftsforschung (German Institute for Economic Research): 10108 Berlin; Mohrenstr. 58, 10117 Berlin; tel. (30) 897890; fax (30) 89789200; e-mail presse@diw.de; internet www.diw.de; f. 1925; application-oriented economic research and policy advice; Pres. Prof. Dr GERT G. WAGNER; Man. Dir Dr CORNELIUS RICHTER; Vice-Pres. Prof. Dr GEORG WEIZSÄCKER; publs *Economic Bulletin* (12 a year), *Vierteljahrshefte zur Wirtschaftsforschung* (4 a year), *Wochenbericht* (52 a year).

Energiewirtschaftliches Institut an der Universität zu Köln: Alte Wagenfabrik, Vogelsanger Str. 321, 50827 Cologne; tel. (221) 27729100; fax (221) 27729400; internet www.ewi.uni-koeln.de; f. 1943; energy economics, environmental economics; library of 12,000 vols, 90 periodicals; Dir Prof. Dr MARC O. BETTZÜGE; publ. *Zeitschrift für Energiewirtschaft* (4 a year).

Forschunginstitut für Wirtschaftspolitik an der Universität Mainz: see under Johannes Gutenberg-Universität.

Forschungsstelle für Allgemeine und Textile Marktwirtschaft an der Universität Münster (Research Institute for General and Textile Economics): Fliednerstr. 21, 48149 Münster; tel. (251) 22939; fax (251) 8331438; e-mail 22fatm@wiwi.uni-muenster.de; internet www.wiwi.uni-muenster.de; f. 1941; library of 15,000 vols; Dir Prof. Dr DIETER AHLERT.

Friedrich-Ebert-Stiftung eV: Godesberger Allee 149, 53175 Bonn; tel. (228) 8830; fax (228) 8839207; e-mail presse@fes.de; internet www.fes.de; f. 1925; int. cooperation, social democracy, political education, research and consulting; library of 855,000 vols; Chair. Dr PETER STRUCK; Man. Dir Dr ROLAND SCHMIDT.

GfK Verein (GfK Association): Nordwestring 101, 90319 Nuremberg; tel. (911) 3952231; fax (911) 3952715; e-mail info@gfk-verein.org; internet www.gfk-verein.de; f. 1934; promotion of market research; carries out research and maintains close cooperation with scientific instns, particularly Friedrich-Alexander Univ. at Erlangen-Nuremberg; supports the education of market researchers, the ongoing training of leadership personnel and participation in commercial ventures; Pres. PETER ZÜHLSDORFF; Vice-Pres. Prof. HUBERT WEILER; Vice-Pres. RALF KLEIN-BÖLTING; Vice-Pres. Prof. Dr NICOLE KOSCHATE; Vice-Pres. Dr RAIMUND WILDNER; publ. *Yearbook of Marketing and Consumer Research*.

Hamburgisches WeltWirtschafts Institut GmbH: Heimhuder Str. 71, 20148 Hamburg; tel. (40) 3405760; fax (40) 340576776; e-mail straubhaar@hwwi.org; internet www.hwwi.org; f. 2005; Dir Prof. Dr THOMAS STRAUBHAAR; publ. *HWWI Insights* (in German, 1 a year).

Institut der Deutschen Wirtschaft Köln: POB 101863, 50458 Cologne; Konrad-Adenauer-Ufer 21, 50668 Cologne; tel. (221) 49811; fax (221) 4981533; e-mail welcome@iwkoeln.de; internet www.iwkoeln.de; f. 1951; education and labour market; economic and social policy; library of 200,000 vols; Pres. Dr HANS-DIETRICH WINKHAUS; Dir Prof. Dr MICHAEL HÜTHER; publ. *iw-trends* (4 a year).

Institut für Angewandte Wirtschaftsforschung eV (Institute for Applied Economic Research): Ob dem Himmelreich 1, 72074 Tübingen; tel. (7071) 98960; fax (7071) 989699; e-mail iaw@iaw.edu; internet www.iaw.edu; f. 1957; int. integration and regional development, labour markets and social security, public finance and environmental economics; library of 1,250 vols; Chair. Prof. Dr WILHELM RALL; Dir Prof. Dr CLAUDIA M. BUCH; publ. *IAW-News* (4 a year).

Institut für Arbeitsmarkt- und Berufsforschung der Bundesanstur für Arbeit (Institute for Employment Research): Regensburger Str. 104, 90478 Nürnberg; tel. (911) 1790; fax (911) 1793258; e-mail info@iab.de; internet www.iab.de; f. 1967; researches the labour market to advise policy-makers at all levels; library of 70,000 vols; Dir Prof. Dr JOACHIM MÖLLER; publ. *Zeitschrift für ArbeitsmarktForschung (ZAF)* (4 a year).

Institut für Handelsforschung GmbH: Dürener Str. 401B, 50858 Cologne; tel. (221) 9436070; fax (221) 94360799; e-mail info@ifhkoeln.de; internet www.ifhkoeln.de; Dir Dr KAI HUDETZ; Dir BORIS HEDDE.

Institut für Marktanalyse und Agrarhandelspolitik des Johann Heinrich von Thünen-Institut (vTI) (Institute for Market Analysis and Agricultural Trade Policy): Bundesallee 50, 38116 Brunswick; tel. (531) 5965301; fax (531) 5965399; e-mail ma@fal.de; internet www.ma.fal.de; f. 1948; Dir Dr MARTIN BANSE (acting); publ. *Agrarwirtschaft* (11 a year).

Institut für Mittelstandsforschung: Maximilianstr. 20, 53111 Bonn; tel. (228) 729970; fax (228) 7299734; e-mail post@ifm-bonn.org; internet www.ifm-bonn.org; f. 1957; Pres. Dr JOHANN EEKHOFF; Deputy

Dir Dr OLIVER ARENTZ; publ. *Jahrbuchs zur Mittelstandsforschung* (yearbook).

Institut für Ökologische Wirtschaftsforschung (IÖW) (Institute for Ecological Economy Research): Potsdamer Str. 105, 10785 Berlin; tel. (30) 8845940; fax (30) 8825439; e-mail mailbox@ioew.de; internet www.ioew.de; f. 1985; research for sustainable management; Scientific Dir THOMAS KORBUN; Financial Dir MARION WIEGAND; publ. *Ökologisches Wirtschaften* (Ecological Economy, 24 a year).

Institut für Seeverkehrswirtschaft und Logistik (Institute of Shipping Economics and Logistics): Universitätsallee 11–13, 28359 Bremen; tel. (421) 220960; fax (421) 2209655; e-mail info@isl.org; internet www.isl.org; f. 1954; applied research and devt projects in logistics systems, maritime economics and transport, information logistics/planning and simulation systems; library of 125,000 vols, 230 periodicals and newspapers; Exec. Dir Prof. Dr HANS-DIETRICH HAASIS; publs *ISL Book Series, ISL Lectures, Contributions and Presentations, Shipping Statistics and Market Review* (figures of shipping, shipbuilding, sea ports and seaborne trade, 10 a year and online at www.infoline.de), *Shipping Statistics Yearbook* (and online at www.infoline.de).

Institut für Weltwirtschaft an der Universität Kiel: see under Christian-Albrechts Universität.

Institut für Wirtschaftsforschung Halle (IWH) (Halle Institute for Economic Research): POB 11 03 61, 06017 Halle; Kleine Märkerstr. 8, 06108 Halle; tel. (345) 775360; fax (345) 7753820; f. 1992; research in macroeconomics, structural change, urban economics; library of 55,000 vols; Pres. Prof. Dr ULRICH BLUM; CEO FROWIN GENSCH; publ. *Wirtschaft im Wandel* (12 a year).

Institut für Wirtschaftspolitik an der Universität zu Köln (Institute for Economic Policy at University of Cologne): Pohligstr. 1, 50969 Cologne; tel. (221) 4705347; fax (221) 4705350; e-mail iwp@wiso.uni-koeln.de; internet www.iwp.uni-koeln.de; f. 1950; economic policy, foreign trade policy, EU research; library of 70,000 vols; Dir Prof. Dr JOHANN EEKHOFF; Dir Prof. Dr JÜRGEN B. DONGES; publs *Untersuchungen zur Wirtschaftspolitik, Zeitschrift für Wirtschaftspolitik* (3 a year).

Institut zur Zukunft der Arbeit (Institute for the Study of Labour): Schaumburg-Lippe-Str. 5–9, 53113 Bonn; tel. (228) 38940; fax (228) 3894180; e-mail iza@iza.org; internet www.iza.org; f. 1998; Pres. Dr KLAUS ZUMWINKEL; Dir Prof. Dr KLAUS F. ZIMMERMANN; Dir for Admin. MARTIN T. CLEMENS; Dir for Labour Policy Dr HILMAR SCHNEIDER; Dir for Research Dr MARCO CALIENDO.

Internationale Wissenschaftliche Vereinigung Weltwirtschaft und Weltpolitik eV (IWVWW): Waltersdorfer Str. 51, 12526 Berlin; tel. (30) 6763387; fax (30) 6763387; e-mail iwvww@t-online.de; f. 1989; Pres. Prof. Dr Hab. KARL HEINZ DOMDEY; Man. Dir Prof. Dr H. ENGELSTÄDTER.

Niedersächsische Institut für Wirtschaftsforschung (NIW): Königstr. 53, 30175 Hanover; tel. (511) 12331630; fax (511) 12331655; e-mail niw@niw.de; internet www.niw.de; f. 1981; Chair. Prof. Dr JAVIER REVILLA DIEZ; Dir Dr RAINER ERTEL.

Osteuropa-Institut Regensburg (Institute for East European Studies): Land-shuter Str. 4, 93047 Regensburg; tel. (941) 9435410; fax (941) 9435427; e-mail oei@osteuropa-institut.de; internet www.osteuropa-institut.de; f. 1952; research into the history and economics of Eastern Europe and fmr USSR; library of 174,000 vols; Pres. Prof. Dr WOLFRAM SCHRETTL; Dir Prof. Dr JÜRGEN JERGER; Man. Dir Dr RICHARD FRENSCH (acting); publs *Economic Systems* (4 a year), *Jahrbücher für Geschichte Osteuropas* (4 a year).

Rheinisch-Westfälisches Institut für Wirtschaftsforschung eV (Rhine-Westphalia Institute for Economic Research): Hohenzollernstr. 1–3, 45128 Essen; tel. (201) 81490; fax (201) 8149200; e-mail rwi@rwi-essen.de; internet www.rwi-essen.de; f. 1926; study of the structure and devt of the German (and int.) economy; spec. research facilities, advice on admin. and economics for firms and students; 80 mems; library of 110,000 vols; Pres. Prof. Dr CHRISTOPH M. SCHMIDT; Vice-Pres. Prof. Dr THOMAS K. BAUER; Dir Prof. Dr WIM KÖSTERS; publs *Konjunkturberichte* (Economic Report, 2 a year), *Materialien* (surveys and extensive articles, irregular), *Ruhr Economic Papers* (irregular), *Schriften* (articles on aspects of economic policy, irregular).

Statistisches Bundesamt (Federal Statistical Office): Gustav-Stresemann-Ring 11, 65189 Wiesbaden; tel. (611) 751; fax (611) 724000; e-mail poststelle@destatis.de; internet www.destatis.de; f. 1950; library of 500,000 vols; Pres. RODERICH EGELER; publs *Datenreport* (2 a year), *Die Bundesländer: Strukturen und Entwicklungen* (2 a year), *Glossar statistischer Fachbegriffe* (irregular), *Kreiszahlen* (1 a year), *Statistik lokal—Daten für die Gemeinden, kreisfreien Städte und Kreise Deutschlands* (1 a year), *Statistik regional—Daten für die Kreise und kreisfreien Städte Deutschlands* (database, published in English as *Regional Statistics*, 1 a year), *Statistisches Jahrbuch für das Ausland* (Statistical Yearbook for Foreign Countries, 1 a year), *Statistisches Jahrbuch für die Bundesrepublik Deutschland* (Statistical Yearbook for the Federal Republic of Germany, 1 a year), *STATmagazin, Wirtschaft und Statistik* (12 a year), *Zahlenkompass—Statistisches Taschenbuch für Deutschland* (published in English as *Key Data on Germany*, 1 a year).

Stiftung Marktwirtschaft (Market Economy Foundation): Charlottenstr. 60, 10117 Berlin; tel. (30) 2060570; fax (30) 20605757; e-mail info@stiftung-marktwirtschaft.de; internet www.stiftung-marktwirtschaft.com; f. 1982; Dir Prof. Dr BERND RAFFELHÜSCHEN; Dir Prof. Dr MICHAEL EILFORT; publ. *Blickpunkt Marktwirtschaft* (Focus Market Economy, 2 a year).

vTI Johann Heinrich von Thünen-Institut: Bundesallee 50, 38116 Braunschweig; tel. (531) 5961003; fax (531) 5961099; e-mail info@vti.bund.de; internet www.vti.bund.de; f. 2008; research areas incl. agriculture and food economy, forestry and wood economy, fisheries and aquaculture; Pres. Prof. Dr FOLKHARD ISERMEYER.

Walter Eucken Institut: Goethestr. 10, 79100 Freiburg im Breisgau; tel. (761) 790970; fax (761) 7909797; e-mail wei-freiburg@walter-eucken-institut.de; internet www.walter-eucken-institut.de; f. 1954; centre for regulatory and constitutional economic research; Dir Prof. Dr LARS P. FELD.

Wirtschafts- und Sozialwissenschaftliches Institut in der Hans-Böckler-Stiftung (Economic Research Institute of the Hans Böckler Foundation): Hans-Böckler-Str. 39, 40476 Düsseldorf; tel. (211) 77780; fax (211) 7778120; e-mail zentrale@boeckler.de; internet www.boeckler.de; Dir Prof. Dr HEIDE PFARR; publ. *Mitteilungen* (12 a year).

Arnold Bergstraesser Institut für kulturwissenschaftliche Forschung (ABI): Windausstr. 16, 79110 Freiburg im Breisgau; tel. (761) 888780; fax (761) 8887878; e-mail abifr@arnold-bergstraesser.de; internet www.arnold-bergstraesser.de; f. 1960; socio-political research particularly on education, admin., political devt and ethnic conflicts in Africa, Asia, Middle East and Latin America; depts of overseas education and overseas admin.; 4 regional depts: Africa, Asia, Latin America, Middle East/North Africa; 20 mems; library of 72,000 vols; Dir Prof. Dr HERIBERT WEILAND; publ. *International Quarterly for Asian Studies* (2 a year).

Frobenius-Institut an der Johann Wolfgang Goethe-Universität: Grüneburgpl. 1, 60323 Frankfurt am Main; tel. (69) 79833050; fax (69) 79833101; internet www.frobenius-institut.de; f. 1898; African, Indonesian and Melanesian cultures and history; library of 114,000 vols; Dir Prof. Dr KARL-HEINZ KOHL; Deputy Dir Prof. Dr MAMADOU DIAWARA; publs *Afrika Archiv, Paideuma* (1 a year), *Religionsethnologische Studien, Studien zur Kulturkunde.*

Gesellschaft für Deutschlandforschung eV (Society for Research on Germany): c/o Prof. Dr. Tilman Mayer, Institut für Politische Wissenschaft und Soziologie, Lennéstr. 25, 53113 Bonn; tel. (228) 735870; fax (228) 735296; e-mail info@gfd-berlin.de; internet www.gfd-berlin.de; f. 1978; contemporary research on Germany; seminars and conferences; Pres. Prof. Dr TILMAN MAYER; Vice-Pres. Prof. Dr HANS-JÖRG BÜCKING.

Herder-Institut eV: Gisonenweg 5–7, 35037 Marburg; tel. (6421) 1840; fax (6421) 184139; e-mail mail@herder-institut.de; internet www.herder-institut.de; f. 1950; historical research on countries and peoples of Eastern Central Europe; library: see Libraries and Archives; Dir Prof. Dr PETER HASLINGER; publ. *Zeitschrift für Ostmitteleuropa-Forschung* (4 a year).

Institut Finanzen und Steuern eV (Finance and Taxation Institute): Gertraudenstr. 20, 10178 Berlin; tel. (30) 20616774; fax (30) 20282475; e-mail info@ifst.de; internet www.ifst.de; f. 1949; Dir Prof. Dr JOHANNA HEY.

Leibniz Institut für Globale und Regionale Studien (German Institute of Global and Area Studies (GIGA)): Neuer Jungfernstieg 21, 20354 Hamburg; tel. (40) 42825593; fax (40) 42825547; e-mail info@giga-hamburg.de; internet www.giga-hamburg.de; f. 1964; basic and applied research on political, economic and social devts in Africa, Asia, Latin America, and the Near and Middle East; policy advice to political instns, business community and media; networking within the area studies and comparative area studies community; 4 constituent orgs: Institute of African Affairs (IAA), Institute of Asian Studies (IAS), Institute of Latin American Studies (ILAS), Institute of Middle East Studies (IMES); library of 100,000 vols and 400 periodicals; Dir Prof. Dr ROBERT KAPPEL; publs *GIGA Focus, GIGA Journal Family, NORD-SÜD aktuell* (4 a year).

Stiftung Wissenschaft und Politik (SWP) (German Institute for International and Security Affairs): Ludwigkirchpl. 3–4, 10719 Berlin; tel. (30) 880070; fax (30) 88007100; e-mail swp@swp-berlin.org; internet www.swp-berlin.org; f. 1962; interdisciplinary research in int. affairs and security, computerized information system for fields of int. relations and area studies (660,000 references), publicly available database 'World Affairs On-line'; library of 94,000 vols, 360 periodicals; Pres. Prof. Dr Ing HANS-PETER KEITEL; Dir Prof. Dr VOLKER PERTHES; Dir for Studies Dr BARBARA LIPPERT; Deputy Dir Prof. Dr GÜNTHER MAIHOLD; publs *SWP Comments*, *SWP Research Papers*.

Wissenschaftszentrum Berlin für Sozialforschung (Social Science Research Centre): Reichpietschufer 50, 10785 Berlin; tel. (30) 254910; fax (30) 25491684; e-mail wzb@wzb .eu; internet www.wzb.eu; f. 1969; a non-profit org.; conducts int. and interdisciplinary, empirical social science research on 4 research areas: education, work and life chances, markets and politics, society and economic dynamics, civil society, conflicts and democracy; library of 150,000 vols, 450 periodicals (printed), 10,000 periodicals (online access), 80 databases; Pres. Prof. Dr JUTTA ALLMENDINGER; Man. Dir HEINRICH BAßLER; publs *WZB-Bericht* (1 a year), *WZBrief Arbeit*, *WZBrief Bildung*, *WZBrief Zivilengagement*, *WZB-Mitteilungen* (4 a year).

EDUCATION

Deutsches Institut für Internationale Pädagogische Forschung (German Institute for International Educational Research): Schloss-Str. 29, 60486 Frankfurt am Main; tel. (69) 247080; fax (69) 24708444; e-mail dipf@dipf.de; internet www.dipf.de; f. 1951; educational information and research; library of 920,000 vols; libraries in Berlin and Frankfurt; Chair. Dr CHRISTINE HOHMANN-DENNHARDT; Deputy Chair. Dr SUSANNE EICKEMEIER; Dir Prof. Dr MARC RITTBERGER; Deputy Dir Prof. Dr MARCUS HASSELHORN; Man. Dir SUSANNE BOOMKAMP-DAHMEN; publ. *DIPF informiert* (2 a year).

Gesellschaft für Pädagogik und Information eV: Allee der Kosmonauten 28, 12681 Berlin; tel. (30) 51069333; fax (30) 51652786; e-mail mikuszeit@gpi-online.de; internet www.gpi-online.de; f. 1964; promotes research and devt in the field of educational technology and information science; 400 mems; Chair. Prof. Dr GERHARD E. ORTNER; Chair. Dr JOACHIM THOMA; Dir Dr BERND MIKUSZEIT; publs *Pädagogik und Information*, *Schul Praxis—Wirtschaft und Weiterbildung*.

Gesellschaft zur Förderung Pädagogischer Forschung eV (Society for the Promotion of Educational Research): POB 900270, 60442 Frankfurt am Main; Schloss-Str. 29, 60486 Frankfurt am Main; tel. (69) 24708313; fax (69) 24708444; e-mail merz@ dipf.de; internet www2.dipf.de/gfpf; f. 1950; dissemination of research results, org. of communication processes between educational research and school practice; 300 mems; Pres. BERND FROMMELT; Vice-Pres. Prof. Dr ECKHARD KLIEME; Man. Dr PETER DÖBRICH; publ. *Materialen zur Bildungsforschung* (book series, 2–3 a year).

FINE AND PERFORMING ARTS

Gesellschaft für Musikforschung: c/o Barbara Schumann, Heinrich-Schütz-Allee 35, 34131 Kassel-Wilhelmshöhe; tel. (561) 3105255; fax (561) 3105254; e-mail g.f .musikforschung@t-online.de; internet www .musikforschung.de; f. 1946; promotes musicological research in respect with other disciplines; history of music, ethnomusicology and systematic musicology; 1,800 mems; Pres. Prof. Dr WOLFGANG AUHAGEN; Vice-Pres. Prof. Dr DÖRTE SCHMIDT; publ. *Die Musikforschung* (4 a year).

Staatliches Institut für Musikforschung: Tiergartenstr. 1, 10785 Berlin; tel. (30) 254810; fax (30) 25481172; e-mail sim@sim.spk-berlin.de; internet www .sim-berlin.de; f. 1888 as Königliche akademische Hochschule, present name and status 1945; attached to Prussian Cultural Heritage Foundation; collects musicological material, instruments, records, phonograms and tape recordings; conducts research into the devt and history of musicology, incl. acoustics, musical instruments and the style and practice of executing music of the past; archival and documentary research and comparative musicological research; open to the public; lectures, concerts and exhibitions; library of 67,000 vols; Dir Dr THOMAS ERTELT; publs *Bibliographie des Musikschrifttums* (1 a year, online), *BMS online* (digital successor of the printed Bibliography), *Briefwechsel der Wiener Schule*, *Geschichte der Musiktheorie*, *Jahrbuch* (1 a year), *Klang und Begriff: Perspektiven musikalischer Theorie und Praxis*, *Studien zur Geschichte der Musiktheorie*.

Zentralinstitut für Kunstgeschichte (History of Art): Katharina-von-Bora-Str. 10, 80333 Munich; tel. (89) 28927556; fax (89) 28927607; e-mail direktion@zikg.eu; internet www.zikg.eu; f. 1947; library of 480,000 vols; 800,000 photographs in image colln; Dir Prof. Dr WOLF TEGETHOFF; Deputy Dir Prof. Dr WOLFGANG AUGUSTYN; publs *Kunstchronik* (12 a year), *Reallexikon zur Deutschen Kunstgeschichte*, *RIHA Journal*.

HISTORY, GEOGRAPHY AND ARCHAEOLOGY

Deutsches Archäologisches Institut (German Archaeological Institute): Podbielskiallee 69–71, 14195 Berlin; tel. (1888) 7711-0; fax (1888) 7711-191; e-mail info@dainst.de; internet www.dainst.org; f. 1829; brs in Rome (Prof. Dr DIETER MERTENS), Athens (Prof. Dr WOLF-DIETRICH NIEMEIER), Cairo (Prof. Dr GÜNTER DREYER), Istanbul (Prof. Dr ADOLF HOFFMANN), Madrid (Prof. Dr DIRCE MARZOLI), Middle East (Prof. Dr RICARDO EICHMANN), Sana'a (Dr IRIS GERLACH), Damascus (Dr KARIN BARTL), Eurasia (Prof. Dr SVEND HANSEN) and Tehran; also Römisch-Germanische Kommission, Frankfurt am Main (Prof. Dr SIEGMAR FREIHERR VON SCHNURBEIN), Kommission für Alte Geschichte und Epigraphik, München (Prof. Dr CHRISTOF SCHULER) and Kommission für Allgemeine und Vergleichende Archäologie, Bonn (Dr BURKHARDT VOGT); Pres. Prof. Dr FRIEDERIKE FLESS; Sec.-Gen. Prof. Dr ORTWIN DALLY; publs *Archäologischer Anzeiger*, *Archäologische Berichte aus dem Yemen*, *Athenische Mitteilungen*, *Baghdader Mitteilungen*, *Berichte der Römisch-Germanischen Kommission*, *Chiron*, *Damaszener Mitteilungen*, *Germania*, *Istanbuler Mitteilungen*, *Jahrbuch*, *Madrider Mitteilungen*, *Mitteilungen des DAI Kairo*, *Römische Mitteilungen*, *Teheraner Mitteilungen*, *Zeitschrift für Orient-Archäologie*, *Zeitschrift für Archäologie Außereuropäischer Kulturen*.

Institut für Europäische Geschichte (Institute of European History): Alte Universitätsstr. 19, 55116 Mainz; tel. (6131) 3939360; fax (6131) 3930154; e-mail ieg1@ ieg-mainz.de; internet www.ieg-mainz.de; f. 1950; conducts and promotes research on the historical foundations of Europe; cross-cultural projects on European communication and transfer processes; projects on concepts and perceptions of Europe since 1450; research fellowship programme (research, training and int. networking); library of 220,000 vols; Dir for History of Religion Prof. Dr IRENE DINGEL; Dir for Universal History Prof. Dr HEINZ DUCHHARDT; Research

Coordinator Dr JOACHIM BERGER; publs *Archiv für Reformationsgeschichte–Literaturbericht* (1 a year), *IEG-MAPS* (online), *Jahrbuch für Europäische Geschichte* (1 a year), *Veröffentlichungen des Instituts für Europäische Geschichte* (monographs and conf. documentation), *Veröffentlichungen des Instituts für Europäische Geschichte, Beihefte online* (conf. documentation, online).

Institut für Zeitgeschichte München–Berlin (Institute of Contemporary History Munich and Berlin): Leonrodstr. 46B, 80636 Munich; tel. (89) 126880; fax (89) 12688191; e-mail ifz@ifz-muenchen.de; internet www .ifz-muenchen.de; f. 1949; German and European history research since 1918, particularly Weimar Republic, National Socialism and post-1945 history; library of 200,500 vols; Dir Prof. Dr Dr h.c. HORST MOELLER; Deputy Dir Prof. Dr UDO WENGST; publs *Biographische Quellen zur Zeitgeschichte*, *Quellen und Darstellungen zur Zeitgeschichte*, *Schriftenreihe der Vierteljahrshefte für Zeitgeschichte* (2 a year), *Studien zur Zeitgeschichte*, *Texte und Materialien zur Zeitgeschichte*, *Vierteljahrshefte für Zeitgeschichte* (4 a year), *Zeitgeschichte im Gespräch*.

Vereinigung zur Erforschung der Neueren Geschichte eV (Modern History Research Association): Argelanderstr. 59, 53115 Bonn; tel. (228) 216205; fax (228) 2426044; e-mail apw@uni-bonn.de; internet www.pax-westphalica.de; f. 1957; history from 17th century to present day; library of 8,000 vols; Dir Prof. Dr MAXIMILIAN LANZINNER; Vice-Dir Prof. Dr KONRAD REPGEN; Sec. Prof. Dr CHRISTOPH KAMPMANN; publ. *Acta Pacis Westphalicae* (Sources of the Westphalian Peace Conf.).

LANGUAGE AND LITERATURE

Arbeitsstelle für Österreichische Literatur und Kultur Robert-Musil-Forschung: Universität des Saarlandes, Campus 53/3 or, OG/323, 66123 Saarbrücken; tel. (681) 3023334; fax (681) 3023034; e-mail fzoelk@mx.uni-saarland.de; internet www.uni-saarland.de/fak4/fr41/ afoelk; f. 1970; archives; study programmes, publs, symposia, bibliography; library of 12,000 vols; Dir Prof. Dr MARIE-LOUISE ROTH; Dir Prof. Dr PIERRE BÉHAR.

Institut für Deutsche Sprache: POB 10 16 21, 68016 Mannheim; R5 6–13, 68161 Mannheim; tel. (621) 15810; fax (621) 1581200; e-mail trabold@ids-mannheim.de; internet www.ids-mannheim.de; f. 1964; scientific study of present-day and historical German; library of 80,000 vols, 500 journals; Dir Prof. Dr LUDWIG M. EICHINGER; publs *Amades-Arbeitspapiere und Materialien zur deutschen Sprache*, *Deutsch im Kontrast*, *Deutsche Sprache* (4 a year), *Jahrbuch*, *Phonai*, *Schriften*, *Sprachreport* (4 a year), *Studienbibliographien Sprachwissenschaft*, *Studien zur deutschen Sprache*.

MEDICINE

Bernhard-Nocht-Institut für Tropenmedizin (Bernhard-Nocht-Institute for Tropical Medicine): POB 30 41 20, 20324 Hamburg; Bernhard-Nocht-Str. 74, 20359 Hamburg; tel. (40) 428180; fax (40) 42818400; e-mail bni@bni-hamburg.de; internet www .bni-hamburg.de; f. 1900 as Institute for Maritime and Tropical Diseases; tropical medicine and parasitology; Nat. Reference Centre for Tropical Infections; library of 43,000 vols and 48,000 reprints, 160 journals; Chair. Prof. Dr ROLF HORSTMANN; Vice-Chair. Prof. Dr BERNHARD FLEISCHER; Admin. Man. UDO GAWENDA; publ. *Scientific Report* (1 a year).

C. & O. Vogt-Institut für Hirnforschung, Universität Düsseldorf (Brain Research): POB 101007, 40001 Düsseldorf; Universitätsstr. 1, 40225 Düsseldorf; tel. (211) 8112777; fax (211) 8112336; e-mail zilles@hirn.uni-duesseldorf.de; internet www.uniklinik-duesseldorf.de/hirnforschung; f. 1937; morphometry, neuroanatomy, immunohistochemistry, psychopharmacology; neurochemistry; Dir Prof. Dr KARL ZILLES.

Chemotherapeutisches Forschungsinstitut Georg-Speyer-Haus (Institute for Biomedical Research Georg-Speyer-Haus): Paul-Ehrlich-Str. 42–44, 60596 Frankfurt am Main; tel. (69) 633950; fax (69) 63395297; e-mail kost@em.uni-frankfurt.de; internet www.georg-speyer-haus.de; f. 1906; research into HIV/AIDS, tumours and allergies; library of 27,664 vols; Dir Prof. Dr BERND GRONER.

Deutsche Gesellschaft für Kardiologie, Herz- und Kreislaufforschung eV (German Cardiac Society): Achenbachstr. 43, 40237 Düsseldorf; tel. (211) 6006920; fax (211) 60069210; e-mail info@dgk.org; internet www.dgk.org; f. 1927; 5,140 mems; Dir KONSTANTINOS PAPOUTSIS; publs *Basic Research in Cardiology* (6 a year), *Clinical Research in Cardiology, Herzschrittmachertherapie und Elektrophysiologie, Intensiv- und Notfallmedizin.*

Deutsche Gesellschaft für Sexualforschung eV (German Association for Research on Sexuality): Universitätsklinikum Hamburg-Eppendorf, Zentrum für Psychosoziale Medizin, Institut und Poliklinik für Sexualforschung und Forensische Psychiatrie, Martinistr. 52, 20246 Hamburg; tel. (40) 428032225; fax (40) 428036406; e-mail briken@uke.uni-hamburg.de; internet www.dgfs.info; f. 1950; 300 mems; Chair. Prof. Dr PEER BRIKEN; Chair. Prof. Dr HERTHA RICHTER-APPELT; Dir ARNE DEKKER; publ. *Zeitschrift für Sexualforschung.*

Deutsche Krebsgesellschaft eV (German Cancer Society): Tiergarten Tower, Str. des 17, Juni 106–108, 10623 Berlin; tel. (30) 32293290; fax (30) 322932966; e-mail service@krebsgesellschaft.de; internet www.deutsche-krebsgesellschaft.de; f. 1900; promoting research, treatment and prevention of cancer; Pres. Prof. Dr WERNER HOHENBERGER; Man. Dir Dr DANIELA M. CHRISTMANN; Sec.-Gen. Dr JOHANNES BRUNS; publs *Der Onkologe, Forum* (German Cancer Society news, 6 a year), *Journal of Cancer Research and Clinical Oncology* (6 a year).

Geomedizinische Forschungsstelle der Heidelberger Akademie der Wissenschaften (Geomedical Research Office of the Heidelberg Academy of Sciences): Karlstr. 4, 69117 Heidelberg; tel. (6221) 543265; fax (6221) 543355; e-mail haw@urz.uni-heidelberg.de; f. 1952; epidemiology of atherosclerotic diseases in Europe and Asia; 50 mems; library of 3,000 vols; Dir Prof. Dr G. SCHETTLER; publs *Geomedical Monographs Series* (6 vols), *World Atlas of Epidemic Diseases* (3 vols 1952–1961), *World Maps of Climatology,* geomedical studies.

Helmholtz Zentrum München-Deutsches Forschungszentrum für Gesundheit und Umwelt (German Research Center for Environmental Health): Ingolstädter Landstr. 1, 85764 Neuherberg; tel. (89) 31870; e-mail info@helmholtz-muenchen.de; internet www.helmholtz-muenchen.de; f. 1964; controls 31 institutes; 1,700 mems; library: central library of 120,000 vols, 350 journals; Scientific and Technical Dir Prof. Dr G. WESS; Admin. Dir Dr N. BLUM.

Herz- und Diabeteszentrum NRW (Heart and Diabetes Center NRW): Georgstr. 11, 32545 Bad Oeynhausen; tel. (5731) 970; fax (5731) 972300; e-mail info@hdz-nrw.de; internet www.hdz-nrw.de; f. 1984; cardiology, thoracic and cardiovascular surgery, paediatric cardiology, diabetology, gastroenterology, nuclear medicine, anaesthesiology, radiology, molecular biophysics, radiopharmacy, laboratory and transfusion medicine; library of 3,000 vols and 180 periodicals; CEO WILHELM HECKER; Vice-CEO GÜNTHER WYPPLER; Medical Dir Prof. Dr DIETHELM TSCHÖPE.

Hygiene-Instituts des Ruhrgebiets—Institut für Umwelthygiene und Umweltmedizin (Institute of Environmental Hygiene and Medicine): POB 10 12 55, 45812 Gelsenkirchen; Rotthauser str. 21, 45879 Gelsenkirchen; tel. (209) 92420; fax (209) 9242105; e-mail info@hyg.de; internet www.hyg.de; f. 1902; attached to Ruhr Univ.; Chair. HENRIETTE REKER; Dir Prof. Dr LOTHAR DUNEMANN.

Institut für Prävention und Arbeitsmedizin der Deutschen Gesetzlichen Unfallversicherung (IPA) (Institute for Prevention and Occupational Medicine of the German Social Accident Insurance): Bürkle-de-la-Camp-Pl. 1, 44789 Bochum; tel. (234) 3024501; fax (234) 3024505; e-mail ipa@ipa-dguv.de; internet www.ipa.ruhr-uni-bochum.de; attached to Ruhr Univ.; research areas incl. allergology/immunology, epidemiology, medicine molecular medicine; library of 53,000 vols, 15,000 monographs; Dir Prof. Dr T. BRÜNING.

Institut für Wasserchemie und Chemische Balneologie der Technischen Universität München (Institute for Hydrochemistry and Chemical Balneology at the Technical University of Munich): Marchioninistr. 17, 81377 Munich; tel. (89) 218078231; fax (89) 218078255; e-mail cornelia.popp@ch.tum.de; internet www.ws.chemie.tu-muenchen.de; f. 1951; analytical methods and measurement techniques for biology, chemical engineering, chemistry, geology, physics; Dir Prof. Dr REINHARD NIESSNER.

Leibniz–Institut für Umweltmedizinische Forschung an der Heinrich-Heine-Universität Düsseldorf (Leibniz Research Institute for Environmental Medicine): POB 10 30 45, 40021 Düsseldorf; Auf'm Hennekamp 50, 40225 Düsseldorf; tel. (211) 33890; fax (211) 3190910; e-mail krutmann@uni-duesseldorf.de; internet www.iuf.uni-duesseldorf.de; f. 2001; molecular preventive medical research in the field of environmental health; evaluation of risks to human health that result from environmental factors, in order to develop preventive and therapeutic strategies; 110 mems; library of 15,000 vols; Dir Prof. Dr JEAN KRUTMANN.

Max von Pettenkofer-Institut für Hygiene und Medizinische Mikrobiologie (Max von Pettenkofer Institute of Hygiene and Medical Microbiology): Pettenkoferstr. 9A, 80336 Munich; tel. (89) 51605201; fax (89) 51605202; e-mail sekretariat@mvp.uni-muenchen.de; internet www.mvp.uni-muenchen.de; Chair. for Bacteriology Prof. Dr JÜRGEN HEESEMANN; Chair. for Virology Prof. Dr ULRICH KOSZINOWSKI.

Paul-Ehrlich-Institut, Bundesamt für Impfstoffe und biomedizinische Arzneimittel: Paul-Ehrlich-Str. 51–59, 63225 Langen; tel. (6103) 77-0; fax (6103) 77-1234; e-mail pei@pei.de; internet www.pei.de; f. 1896, as Institute for Serum Testing and Serum Research; German and European medicinal product legislation; approval of clinical trials; marketing authorization of biological medicinal products, vaccines for humans and animals, medicinal products containing antibodies, allergens for therapy and diagnostics, blood and blood products, tissue and medicinal products for gene therapy, somatic cell therapy and xenogenic cell therapy; research in the field of life sciences; depts of bacteriology, virology, immunology, veterinary medicine, allergology, medicinal biotechnology, haematology and transfusion medicine; research into safety of medicinal products and devices; c. 770 mems; library of 55,000 vols; Pres. Prof. Dr KLAUS CICHUTEK; Vice-Pres. STEFAN VIETHS; publ. *Arbeiten aus dem Paul-Ehrlich-Institut.*

Verein für Wasser-, Boden- und Lufthygiene eV (Society for Water, Soil and Air Purity): POB 10 12 55, 45812 Gelsenkirchen; Rotthauser Str. 19, 45879 Gelsenkirchen; tel. (209) 9242190; fax (209) 9242199; e-mail verein@wabolu.de; internet www.wabolu.de; f. 1902; researches and subsidizes int. studies into environmental water and air issues; Chair. Prof. Dr VOLKER HINGST; Vice-Chair. Dr ANDREAS SCHIRMER; Vice-Chair. Dr DIETMAR PETERSOHN; Dir Prof. Dr LOTHAR DUNEMANN.

NATURAL SCIENCES
General

Senckenberg Gesellschaft für Naturforschung (Senckenberg Research Institute and Natural History Museum): Senckenberganlage 25, 60325 Frankfurt; tel. (69) 75420; fax (69) 746238; e-mail soeren.duerr@senckenberg.de; internet www.senckenberg.de; f. 1817; systematics, anatomy, distribution, ecology, evolution in zoology, botany, palaeozoology, palaeobotany, marine biology and geology, palaeoanthropology; 4,600 mems; Pres. DIETMAR SCHMID; Dir Prof. Dr VOLKER MOSBRUGGER; publs *Abhandlungen der Senckenbergischen Naturforschenden Gesellschaft, Archiv für Molluskenkunde, Arthropod Systematics & Phylogeny* (3 a year), *Beiträge zur Entomologie – Contributions to Entomology* (2 a year), *Courier Forschungsinstitut Senckenberg, Marine Biodiversity, Natur und Museum* (6 a year), *Palaeobiodiversity and Palaeoenvironments, Senckenbergiana biologica, Soil Organisms* (in English), *Vertebrate Zoology.*

Biological Sciences

Alfred-Wegener-Institut für Polar- und Meeresforschung (Alfred Wegener Institute for Polar and Marine Research): POB 120161, 27515 Bremerhaven; tel. (471) 48310; fax (471) 48311149; e-mail info@awi.de; internet www.awi.de; f. 1980; conducts research in the Arctic, Antarctic and oceans of high and mid-latitudes; coordinates polar research in Germany; provides major infrastructure to int. scientific community, such as the research icebreaker Polarstern and stations in the Arctic and Antarctica; Dir Prof. Dr KARIN LOCHTE; Admin. Dir Dr HEIKE WOLKE; Deputy Dir Prof. Dr HEINRICH MILLER; Sec. J. MARTIN; publ. *Berichte zur Polar- und Meeresforschung* (Reports of Polar and Marine Research, irregular).

Constituent Research Units:

Biologische Anstalt Helgoland (Biological Institute Helgoland): POB 180, 27483 Helgoland; Kurpromenade 201, 27498 Helgoland; tel. (4725) 8190; fax (4725) 8193283; e-mail karen.wiltshire@awi.de; internet www.awi.de; f. 1892; research in marine ecology, esp. in the North Sea; library of 63,000 vols; Dir Prof. Dr KAREN WILTSHIRE; publ. *Helgoländer Meeresuntersuchungen* (Heligoland Marine Research, 4 a year).

Forschungsstelle Potsdam des Alfred-Wegener-Instituts für Polar und Meeresforschung (Potsdam Research Unit of the Alfred Wegener Institute for Polar and

Marine Research): POB 60 01 49, 14401 Potsdam; Telegrafenberg A 43, 14473 Potsdam; tel. (331) 2882100; fax (331) 2882137; e-mail gabriela.schlaffer@awi.de; internet www.awi.de; f. 1992; terrestrial geoscientific research in the periglacial regions; research into atmospheric processes; Head Prof. Dr HANS-WOLFGANG HUBBERTEN.

Wadden Sea Station Sylt: Hafenstr. 43, 25992 List/Sylt; tel. (4651) 9560; fax (4651) 956200; e-mail ragnhild.asmus@awi.de; internet www.awi.de; f. 1924; studies of coastal biological processes and ecosystems and monitoring of coastal changes and their long-term impact; Dir Prof. Dr KAREN WILTSHIRE; Head Dr RAGNHILD ASMUS.

Biozentrum Klein Flottbek: Ohnhorststr. 18, 22609 Hamburg; tel. (40) 428160; fax (40) 42816248; e-mail sekretariat@botanik .uni-hamburg.de; internet www.biologie .uni-hamburg.de/bzf; f. 1821; research in plant physiology, cell biology, plant systematics, genetics and microbiology, applied plant molecular biology; botanical garden and herbarium comprising 800,000 specimens; 250 mems; library of 45,000 vols and 49,000 reprints; Man. Dir Prof. Dr WOLFGANG STREIT; Man. Dir Prof. Dr DIETER HANELT; publs *Institut für Allgemeine Botanik Hamburg, Mitteilungen*.

Deutsche Gesellschaft für Moor- und Torfkunde (German Peat Society): Stilleweg 2, 30655 Hanover; tel. (511) 6433612; fax (511) 643533612; e-mail gerfried.caspers@ lbeg.niedersachsen.de; internet www.dgmtev .de; f. 1970; 350 mems; Pres. Dr G. CASPERS; publ. *TELMA* (1 a year).

Forschungszentrum Borstel Leibniz-Zentrum für Medizin und Biowissenschaften (Borstel Research Centre for Medicine and Biological Sciences): Parkallee 1–40, 23845 Borstel; tel. (4537) 1880; fax (4537) 188721; internet www.fz-borstel.de; f. 1947; research in fields of pneumology, infection biology, allergology and inflammation medicine; library of 50,000 vols; Dirs Prof. Dr SILVIA BULFONE-PAUS, Prof. Dr PETER ZABEL, Prof. Dr ULRICH SCHAIBLE; Admin. Man. SUSANN SCHRADER.

Institut für Angewandte Botanik (Institute of Applied Botany at Hamburg University): Biozentrum Klein Flottbek und Botanischer Garten der Universität Hamburg, Ohnhorststr. 18, 22609 Hamburg; tel. (40) 428160; fax (40) 42816248; e-mail secretariat@botanik.uni-hamburg.de; internet www.biologie.uni-hamburg.de/bzf; f. 1885; library of 130,000 vols; 140 mems; research on plant products, agriculture and horticulture; Man. Dir Prof. Dr WOLFGANG STREIT; Deputy Man. Dir Prof. Dr DIETER HANELT.

Institut für Gerontologie: Evinger Pl. 13, 44339 Dortmund; tel. (231) 7284880; fax (231) 72848855; e-mail ffg@post .uni-dortmund.de; internet www.ffg .uni-dortmund.de; attached to Technische Univ.; Dir Prof. Dr GERHARD NAEGELE.

Institut für Vogelforschung 'Vogelwarte Helgoland' (Institute of Avian Research 'Vogelwarte Helgoland'): An der Vogelwarte 21, 26386 Wilhelmshaven; tel. (4421) 96890; fax (4421) 968955; e-mail ifv@ifv-vogelwarte .de; internet www.vogelwarte-helgoland.de; f. 1910; research in the fields of bird migration, bird population dynamics, climate change and applied aspects; Dir Prof. Dr FRANZ BAIRLEIN; publ. *Vogelwarte* (4 a year).

Naturforschende Gesellschaft Bamberg eV: Hertzstr. 31, 96050 Bamberg; e-mail nfg@bnv-bamberg.de; internet www .bnv-bamberg.de/home/ba6296; f. 1834; 250

mems; library of 18,000 vols; Dir Dr DIETER BÖSCHE; publ. *Berichte*.

Naturforschende Gesellschaft zu Freiburg im Breisgau: Albertstr. 23B, 79104 Freiburg im Breisgau; tel. (761) 2036484; fax (761) 2036483; e-mail naturforschende@ geologie.uni-freiburg.de; internet www .naturforschende-gesellschaft.uni-freiburg .de; f. 1821; 300 mems; Chair. Prof. Dr WERNER KONOLD; Vice-Chair. THOMAS UHLENDAHL; Sec. Prof. Dr ALBERT REIF.

Mathematical Sciences

Mathematisches Forschungsinstitut Oberwolfach GmbH (Mathematical Research Institute): Schwarzwaldstr. 9–11, 77709 Oberwolfach-Walke; tel. (7834) 9790; fax (7834) 97938; e-mail admin@mfo.de; internet www.mfo.de; f. 1944; library of 75,000 vols; Dir Prof. Dr GERT-MARTIN GREUEL; Vice-Dir Prof. Dr HORST KNÖRRER; Librarian VERENA FRANKE; publs *Oberwolfach Preprints*, *Oberwolfach Reports* (4 a year), *Oberwolfach Seminars*.

Physical Sciences

Astronomisches Rechen-Institut (Astronomical Institute): Mönchhofstr. 12–14, 69120 Heidelberg; tel. (6221) 541845; fax (6221) 541888; e-mail direktor@ari .uni-heidelberg.de; internet www.ari .uni-heidelberg.de; f. 1700; attached to Zentrum für Astronomie der Universität Heidelberg; theoretical astronomy; 50 mems; library of 30,000 vols, 102 journals; Dir Prof. Dr EVA GREBEL; Dir Prof. Dr JOACHIM WAMBSGANß; publs *Apparent Places of Fundamental Stars*, *Astronomische Grundlagen für den Kalender*, *Veröffentlichungen*.

Astrophysikalisches Institut und Universitäts-Sternwarte: Schillergässchen 2–3, 07745 Jena; tel. (3641) 947501; fax (3641) 947502; e-mail moni@astro.uni-jena.de; internet www.astro.uni-jena.de; f. 1813; Dir Prof. Dr RALPH NEUHÄUSER.

Bundesamt für Seeschiffahrt und Hydrographie (Federal Maritime and Hydrographic Agency): POB 30 12 20, 20305 Hamburg; Bernhard-Nocht-Str. 78, 20359 Hamburg; tel. (40) 31900; fax (40) 30195000; e-mail posteingang@bsh.de; internet www.bsh.de; f. 1945; under the Fed. Min. of Transport; oceanography, tides and currents, geomagnetism, gravimetry, nautical technics, navigating methods, tonnage measurement, hydrographic surveying and nautical geodesy, bathymetry, seabed geology, pollution control, ice information service, nautical charts and publs; library of 170,000 vols; hydrographic information service; 900 mems; Pres. MONIKA BREUCH-MORITZ; Vice-Pres. CHRISTOPH BROCKMANN; publs *Deutsche Hydrographische Zeitschrift* (4 a year), *Nachrichten für Seefahrer* (52 a year).

Bundesanstalt für Geowissenschaften und Rohstoffe (BGR) (Federal Institute for Geosciences and Natural Resources): Stilleweg 2, 30655 Hanover; tel. (511) 6430; fax (511) 6432304; e-mail poststelle@bgr.de; internet www.bgr.bund.de; f. 1958; geoscientific investigation, evaluation of mineral resources, environmental protection, geotechnology, seismology, marine and polar research; library of 296,000 vols; Pres. Prof. Dr HANS-JOACHIM KÜMPEL; Vice-Pres. JÖRG HAMMANN; publs *Geologisches Jahrbuch*, *Zeitschrift für angewandte Geologie*.

Deutscher Wetterdienst (German Meteorological Service): POB 10 04 65, 63004 Offenbach am Main; Frankfurter Str. 135, 63067 Offenbach am Main; tel. (69) 80620; fax (69) 80624484; e-mail info@dwd .de; internet www.dwd.de; f. 1952; central office for the Fed. Republic; library of 178,000

vols; Pres. Prof. Dr GERHARD ADRIAN; Vice-Pres. Dr PAUL BECKER; Chief Librarian BRITTA BOLZMANN; publs *Annalen der Meteorologie*, *Berichte des Deutschen Wetterdienstes*, *Deutsches Meteorologisches Jahrbuch* (1 a year), *Die Grosswetterlagen Europas* (12 a year, online), *Europäischer Wetterbericht* (online), *Geschichte der Meteorologie*, *Klimastatusbericht* (1 a year), *promet-Meteorologische Fortbildung* (4 a year), *Witterungsreport*.

Dr Remeis-Sternwarte Bamberg (Astronomical Institute of the University of Erlangen-Nuremberg): Sternwartstr. 7, 96049 Bamberg; tel. (951) 952220; fax (951) 9522222; internet www.sternwarte .uni-erlangen.de; f. 1889; stellar astrophysics; library of 2,000 vols; Chair. Prof. Dr JÖRN WILMS; Chair. Prof. Dr ULRICH HEBER.

Forschungszentrum Jülich GmbH (Jülich Research Centre): 52425 Jülich; Wilhelm-Johnen-Str., 52428 Jülich; tel. (2461) 610; fax (2461) 618100; e-mail info@fz-juelich .de; internet www.fz-juelich.de; f. 1956; operated jtly by German fed. Govt (90%) and state of North Rhine-Westphalia (10%); research in information technology and physical basic research, energy (materials and technology), environmental life sciences; library of 600,000 vols, 250,000 microforms, 2,000 journal titles; Pres. Dr KARL EUGEN HUTHMACHER; Chair. Prof. Dr ACHIM BACHEM.

Fraunhofer-Gesellschaft zur Förderung der Angewandten: POB 20 07 33, 80007 Munich; Hansastr. 27C, 80686 Munich; tel. (89) 12050; fax (89) 12057531; e-mail info@ fraunhofer.de; internet www.fraunhofer.de; f. 1968; inc. GMD–Forschungszentrum Informationstechnik GmbH; research and devt in the fields of engineering science and information technology; 80 research units, incl. 58 Fraunhofer Institutes, at more than 40 locations throughout Germany; 12,500 staff; library of 110,000 vols; Pres. Prof. Dr HANS-JÖRG BULLINGER; publ. *Fraunhofer Magazine*.

Fraunhofer-Institut für Bauphysik (Fraunhofer Institute for Building Physics): POB 80 04 69, 70504 Stuttgart; POB 800469, Nobelstr. 12, 70504 Stuttgart; tel. (711) 97000; fax (711) 9703395; e-mail info@ibp .fraunhofer.de; internet www2.ibp .fraunhofer.de; f. 1929; research, devt, testing, demonstration and consulting in the field of building physics; noise control, sound insulation, optimization of audibility conditions in lecture halls, measures for energy conservation, lighting technology, new building materials, indoor climate, weathering protection, hygrothermics; Pres. Prof. Dr HANS-JÖRG BULLINGER; Dir Prof. Dr GERD HAUSER; Dir Prof. Dr KLAUS SEDLBAUER; publ. *IBP Report* (building physics research results).

Geologisch-Paläontologisches Institut und Museum, Universität Hamburg (Geological and Palaeontological Institute and Museum): Bundesstr. 55, 20146 Hamburg; tel. (40) 428384999; fax (40) 428385007; e-mail christian.betzler@uni-hamburg.de; internet www.uni-hamburg.de/geol_pal; f. 1907; 12 scientific mems; library of 80,000 vols; Man. Dir Prof. Dr CHRISTIAN BETZLER; Deputy Dir Prof. Dr CLAUS-DIETER REUTHER; publ. *Mitteilungen aus dem Geologisch-Paläontologischen Institut der Universität Hamburg* (1 a year).

Hamburger Sternwarte (Hamburg Observatory): Gojenbergsweg 112, 21029 Hamburg; tel. (40) 428388512; fax (40) 428388598; e-mail sternwarte@hs .uni-hamburg.de; internet www.hs .uni-hamburg.de; f. 1833; cosmology, exoplanets, stellar physics, model atmospheres; library of 65,000 vols; Dir Prof. P.H. HANSCHILDT.

Helmholtz-Zentrum Berlin für Materialien und Energie GmbH: Hahn-Meitner-Pl. 1, 14109 Berlin; tel. (30) 80620; fax (30) 80622181; e-mail info@helmholtz-berlin.de; internet www.helmholtz-berlin.de; f. 1959 as Hahn-Meitner-Institut Berlin GmbH, merged with BESSY GmbH in 2008; solid state physics, atomic and molecular structures, solar energy (photovoltaic); library of 61,000 vols, 420,000 reports; Chair. Prof. Dr J. TREUSCH; Dir Prof. Dr ANKE KAYSSER-PYZALLA; Dir Dr ULRICH BREUER; Dir Prof. Dr WOLFGANG EBERHARDT; Librarian Dr WOLFGANG FRITSCH.

Institut für Astronomie und Astrophysik Tübingen: Sand 1, 72076 Tübingen; tel. (7071) 2972486; fax (7071) 293458; internet www.uni-tuebingen.de; f. 1949; attached to Dept of Mathematics and Physics of Eberhard-Karls Univ. of Tübingen; UV- and X-ray astronomy, optical astronomy, stellar atmospheres; library of 14,112 vols; Head Prof. KLAUS WERNER; Sec. and Librarian HEIDRUN OBERNDÖRFFER.

Institut für Astrophysik Göttingen (Institute of Astrophysics, Göttingen): Friedrich-Hund-Pl. 1, 37077 Göttingen; tel. (551) 395053; fax (551) 395043; e-mail sekr@astro .physik.uni-goettingen.de; internet www .uni-sw.gwdg.de; f. 1750; attached to Georg-August-Univ.; galactic and extragalactic astrophysics, high-energy astrophysics, solar physics, stellar spectroscopy and theoretical astrophysics; houses a modern Cassegrain reflecting telescope with 50 cm mirror diameter and 5 m focal length; Dir Prof. Dr W. KOLLATSCHNY (acting).

Institut für Gefährstoff-Forschung (IGF) (Institute for Research into Dangerous Substances): Waldring 97, 44789 Bochum; tel. (234) 306359; fax (234) 306353; e-mail igf@bgrci.de; internet www.igf-bbg.de; attached to Ruhr Univ.; Dir Dr DIRK DAHMANN.

Institut für Umwelt- und Zukunftsforschung (IUZ) an der Sternwarte Bochum: Blankensteiner Str. 200A, 44797 Bochum; tel. (234) 47711; fax (234) 5798958; e-mail info@iuz-bochum.de; internet www .sternwarte-bochum.de; devt and testing of electronic equipment for tracking and reception of satellite data; devt of display and reproduction systems for satellite imagery; photo-interpretation of satellite imagery for geo-scientific and environmental studies; remote sensing; Dir THILO ELSNER.

Karlsruhe Institute of Technology: Kaiserstr. 12, 76131 Eggenstein-Leopoldshafen; tel. (721) 6080; fax (721) 6084290; e-mail info@kit.edu; internet www.kit.edu; f. 2009; energy, nano, micro science and technology, elementary particle and astro-particle physics, climate and environment, computation, mobility systems, optics and photonics, humans and technology, new and applied materials; 8,500 mems; library of 500,000 vols, 1,600 periodical titles, 587,000 reports; Pres. Prof. Dr EBERHARD UMBACH; Pres. Prof. Dr HORST HIPPLER; publs clicKIT (online), FZKA-Berichte, KIT dialog, KIT Members Magazine, KIT Public Magazine.

Kiepenheuer-Institut für Sonnenphysik: Schöneckstr. 6, 79104 Freiburg im Breisgau; tel. (761) 31980; fax (761) 3198111; e-mail secr@kis.uni-freiburg.de; internet www.kis.uni-freiburg.de; f. 1942; optical investigation of the solar atmosphere, observatory at Tenerife (Canary Islands); 57 mems; Dir Prof. Dr OSKAR VON DER LÜHE; Deputy Dir Prof. Dr SVETLANA BERDYUGINA.

Landessternwarte Königstuhl: Königstuhl 12, 69117 Heidelberg; tel. (6221) 541700; fax (6221) 541702; e-mail postmaster@lsw.uni-heidelberg.de; internet www.lsw.uni-heidelberg.de; f. 1897, present status 2005; attached to Zentrum für Astronomie of Heidelberg Univ.; astronomical scientific research; 50 mems; library of 25,000 vols; Dir Prof. Dr ANDREAS QUIRRENBACH.

Lehrstuhl für Astronomie, Universität Würzburg: Am Hubland, 97074 Würzburg; tel. (931) 8885031; fax (931) 8884603; e-mail mannheim@astro.uni-wuerzburg.de; internet www.astro.uni-wuerzburg.de; f. 1967; astronomy, theoretical astrophysics; library of 5,000 vols, 50 journals; Dir Prof. Dr KARL MANNHEIM.

Leibniz-Institut für Analytische Wissenschaften—ISAS—eV (Institute for Analytical Sciences): Bunsen-Kirchhoff-Str. 11, 44139 Dortmund; tel. (231) 13920; fax (231) 1392120; e-mail info@isas.de; internet www .isas.de; f. 1952 as Institute of Spectrochemistry and Applied Spectroscopy; focuses on analytical and spectroscopical methods in material sciences and life sciences; Dir Prof. Dr ALBERT SICKMANN; Dir Prof. Dr NORBERT ESSER.

Leibniz-Institut für Arbeitsforschung (IfADo) (Leibniz Research Centre for Working Environment and Human Factors): Ardeystr. 67, 44139 Dortmund; tel. (231) 10840; fax (231) 1084308; e-mail gude@ifado .de; f. 1969; attached to Technische Univ.; investigates potentials and risks of modern work on basis of behavioural and life sciences; Dir Prof. Dr JAN G. HENGSTLER; Head Librarian SUSANNE LINDEMANN.

Universitäts-Sternwarte–Institut für Astronomie und Astrophysik und Observatorium Wendelstein: Scheinerstr. 1, 81679 Munich; tel. (89) 21806001; fax (89) 21806003; internet www.usm.uni-muenchen .de; f. 1816; extragalactic astronomy, plasma astrophysics, stellar atmospheres, stellar evolution, cosmochemistry; library of 18,000 vols; Dir Prof. Dr MANFRED HIRT.

UWG Gesellschaft für Umwelt- und Wirtschaftsgeologie GmbH: Wolfener 36, Aufg. K, 12681 Berlin; tel. (30) 23144684; fax (30) 23144700; geoscientific and environmental library (books, data, photographs (remote sensing), maps); Dir Dr KLAUS ERLER.

PHILOSOPHY AND PSYCHOLOGY

Institut für Forensische Psychiatrie: Charité–Universitätsmedizin Berlin, Oranienburger Str. 285, 13437 Berlin; tel. (30) 84451411; fax (30) 84451440; e-mail info@ forensik-berlin.de; internet www .forensik-berlin.de; f. 1970; studies and research in forensic psychiatry and psychology; weekly interdisciplinary colloquium; annual forensic science conference; library of 21,257 vols, 61 current periodicals, 1,476 special prints, 104 video cassettes; Dir Prof. Dr HANS-LUDWIG KRÖBER.

Institut für Gerichtspsychologie (IfG) (Institute for Forensic Psychology): Gilsingstr. 5, 44789 Bochum; tel. (234) 34091; internet www.gerichtspsychologie-bochum .de; f. 1951; carries out reports on behalf of the courts and solicitors; 41 mems; Dir Dr FRIEDRICH ARNTZEN.

Institut für Philosophie (Institute of Philosophy): Unter den Linden 6, 10099 Berlin; tel. (30) 20932204; fax (30) 20932419; e-mail schaume@philosophie.hu-berlin.de; internet www.philosophie.hu-berlin.de; attached to Humboldt Univ.; offers open lectures; Kant archive; Dir Prof. Dr THOMAS SCHMIDT; Sec. ELKE SCHAUM.

Institut für Philosophie Universität Leipzig (Institute of Philosophy at Leipzig University): POB 920, 04009 Leipzig; Beethovenstr. 15, 04107 Leipzig; tel. (341) 9735820; fax (341) 9735849; e-mail busch@uni-leipzig .de; internet www.uni-leipzig.de/~philos; attached to Leipzig Univ.; organizes conferences and weekly colloquia; Dir Prof. Dr ANDREA KERN; Sec. FRANZISKA RÖDER; publ. Leipziger Schriften zur Philosophie.

Institut für Rechtspsychologie Halle (Saale) (Institute for Forensic Psychology, Halle): Kleine Marktstr. 5, 06108 Halle/Salle; tel. (345) 6140680; fax (345) 61406820; e-mail institut@rechtspsychologie-halle.de; internet www.rechtspsychologie-halle.de; f. 1997; carries out studies in forensic psychology for law courts; Man. BÄRBEL GOLDHAMMER.

RELIGION, SOCIOLOGY AND ANTHROPOLOGY

Arbeitsgemeinschaft Sozialwissenschaftlicher Institute eV (Association of Social Science Institutes): Dreizehnmorgenweg 42, 53175 Bonn; tel. (228) 2281574; fax (228) 2281550; e-mail asi@asi-ev.org; internet www.asi-ev.org; f. 1949; promotes research in social sciences; 100 mems; Pres. Prof. Dr FRANK FAULBAUM; Man. Dir MATTHIAS STAHL; publs ASI-Schriftenreihe, Soziale Welt (4 a year).

Bundesinstitut für Bevölkerungsforschung (Federal Institute for Population Research): POB 5528, 65180 Wiesbaden; Friedrich-Ebert-Allee 4, 65185 Wiesbaden; tel. (0611) 752235; fax (0611) 753960; e-mail bib@destatis.de; internet www .bib-demografie.de; f. 1973; attached to Statistisches Bundesamt; promotes all fields of demographic research and coordinates research work undertaken by demographers, incl. those in foreign countries; Dir Prof. Dr NORBERT F. SCHNEIDER; publs Beiträge zur Bevölkerungswissenschaft – Schriftenreihe des BiB (2–3 a year), Bevölkerungsforschung Aktuell (6 a year), Comparative Population Studies—CPoS, Demographie: Zeitschrift für Bevölkerungswissenschaft (4 a year).

Forschungsgruppe für Anthropologie und Religionsgeschichte eV (Research Group for Anthropology and History of Religion): Droste-Hülshoff-Str. 9B, 48341 Altenberge; tel. and fax (2505) 1347; e-mail ugarit@uni-muenster.de; internet www .ugarit-verlag.de; f. 1970; research and documentation refer to all fields of religion including interconnections with anthropology, psychology, culture and environment; methodology of research; int. cooperation and exchange; Pres. Prof. Dr M. L. G. DIETRICH; Pres. Prof. Dr R. SCHMITT; publs Forschungen zur Anthropologie und Religionsgeschichte (3 a year), Mitteilungen für Anthropologie und Religionsgeschichte (1 a year).

GESIS-Leibniz-Institut für Sozialwissenschaften (GESIS-Leibniz-Institute for the Social Sciences): POB 12 21 55, 68072 Mannheim; B2, 1, 68159 Mannheim; tel. (621) 12460; fax (621) 1246100; e-mail info@ gesis.org; internet www.gesis.org; f. 2007, by merger of Social Science Information Centre (IZ) in Bonn, Central Archive for Empirical Social Research in Cologne (ZA), and Centre for Survey Research and Methodology (ZUMA) in Mannheim; infrastructural services on numerical data, information bases and research methods for social scientists; library of 114,000 vols, 750 journals; Chair. Prof. STEFAN HORNBOSTEL; Pres. Prof. Dr YORK SURE; publs CEWS-publications (irregular), GESIS Recherche Spezial (irregular), GESIS Series (irregular), GESIS Technical Reports (irregular), HSR Historical Social Research (4 a year), Informationsdienst Soziale Indikatoren (2 a year), Methods, Data, Analysis MDA (2 a year), ZA Information (2 a year).

Institut für Diaspora- und Genozidforschung (Institute of Diaspora and Genocide Studies): Universitätsstr. 150, 44801 Bochum; tel. (234) 3229700; fax (234) 3214770; e-mail idg@ruhr-uni-bochum.de; attached to Ruhr Univ.; Dir Prof. Dr MIHRAN DABAG.

Sozialforschungsstelle Dortmund: Evinger Pl. 17, 44339 Dortmund; tel. (231) 85960; fax (231) 8596100; e-mail pr@sfs-dortmund.de; internet www.sfs-dortmund.de; f. 1946; research in social sciences; attached to Technische Univ.; Dir Prof. Dr JÜRGEN HOWALDT; Deputy Dir ELLEN HILF.

TECHNOLOGY

Arbeitsgemeinschaft Industrieller Forschungsvereinigungen 'Otto von Guericke' eV (AiF) (AiF—German Federation of Industrial Research Associations): Bayenthalgürtel 23, 50968 Cologne; tel. (221) 376800; fax (221) 3768027; e-mail info@aif.de; internet www.aif.de; f. 1954; promotes cooperative research for small and medium-sized industry; mems incl. 101 industrial research asscns; Pres. Dr JOHANN THOMAS GRAEBENER; CEO Prof. Dr STEFANIE HEIDEN; publs AiF aktuell (3–4 a year), Innovationen (3–4 a year).

Bundesanstalt für Materialforschung und -prüfung (Federal Institute for Materials Research and Testing): Unter den Eichen 87, 12205 Berlin; tel. (30) 81040; fax (30) 8112029; e-mail info@bam.de; internet www.bam.de; f. 1871; analytical chemistry; reference materials, chemical safety engineering, containment systems for dangerous goods, materials and the environment, materials engineering, materials protection and surface technologies, safety of structures, nondestructive testing, accreditation, quality in testing; library of 80,000 vols; Chair. JÜRGEN MEYER; Pres. Prof. Dr MANFRED HENNECKE; Vice-Pres. Prof. Dr Ing. THOMAS BÖLLINGHAUS; publ. Amtsblatt (4 a year).

Clausthaler Umwelttechnik-Institut GmbH (Clausthal Institute of Environmental Technology): Leibnizstr. 21–23, 38678 Clausthal-Zellerfeld; tel. (5323) 9330; fax (5323) 933100; e-mail cutec@cutec.de; internet www.cutec.de; f. 1990; wholly owned by state of Lower Saxony; research into waste avoidance, recycling and disposal; Chair. Dr HANS SCHROEDER; Man. Dir Prof. Dr Ing. OTTO CARLOWITZ.

Deutsche Forschungsanstalt für Lebensmittelchemie (German Research Institute for Food Chemistry): Lise-Meitner Str. 34, 85354 Freising; tel. (8161) 712932; fax (8161) 712970; e-mail dfa@lrz.tum.de; internet dfa.leb.chemie.tu-muenchen.de; f. 1918; library of 3,000 vols; Dir Prof. Dr PETER SCHIEBERLE; Deputy Dir Prof. Dr PETER KÖHLER.

Deutsche Montan Technologie GmbH (DMT): Am Technologiepark 1, 45307 Essen; tel. (201) 17201; fax (201) 1721462; e-mail dmt-info@dmt.de; internet www.dmt.de; f. 1990; specialists in mining; Chair. HEINZ-GERD KÖRNER.

Deutsche Zentrum für Luft- und Raumfahrt eV (DLR) (German Aerospace Centre): Linder Höhe, 51147 Cologne; tel. (2203) 6010; fax (2203) 67310; e-mail redaktion@dlr.de; internet www.dlr.de; f. 1969; flight mechanics, guidance and control, fluid mechanics, structures and materials, space flight, telecommunication technology and remote sensing, energetics; library of 400,000 vols; Chair. JOHANN-DIETRICH WÖRNER; Vice-Chair. KLAUS HAMACHER; publs DLR-Forschungsberichte (irregular), DLR-Mitteilungen (irregular), DLR-Nachrichten (4 a year).

Deutsches Textilforschungszentrum Nord-West eV: Öffentliche Prüfstelle (ÖP), Adlerstr. 1, 47798 Krefeld; tel. (2151) 8430; fax (2151) 843143; e-mail info@dtnw.de; internet www2.dtnw.de; f. 1990; research groups incl. biotechnology and katalysis, colloid chemistry and nanotechnology, physical technology and measurement technique, supramolecular and polymer chemistry; 100 mems; Man. Dir Prof. Dr JOCHEN GUTMANN; Deputy Dir Prof. Dr MATHIAS ULBRICHT.

Forschungsinstitut Edelmetalle & Metallchemie (fem) (Research Institute of Precious Metals and Metals Chemistry): Katharinenstr. 17, 73525 Schwäbisch Gmünd; tel. (7171) 10060; fax (7171) 100654; e-mail fem@fem-online.de; internet www.fem-online.de; f. 1922; basic and applied research into precious metals science and technology, electrochemical deposition, corrosion, light metals surface technology, plasma surface technology, physical metallurgy, environmental technology and analyses; Dir Dr A. ZIELONKA.

Forschungsinstitut für Wärmeschutz eV München (Thermal Insulation, Testing, Research): Lochhamer Schlag 4, 82166 Gräfelfing; tel. (89) 858000; fax (89) 8580040; e-mail info@fiw-muenchen.de; internet www.fiw-muenchen.de; f. 1918; 140 mems; Scientific Dir Dr Ing. MARTIN SPITZNER; Scientific Dir Dr Ing. MARTIN ZEITLER; Scientific Dir Dr ROLAND GELLERT; publ. Mitteilungen aus dem FIW München (irregular).

Fraunhofer-Institut für Verfahrenstechnik und Verpackung (Fraunhofer Institute for Process Engineering and Packaging): Giggenhauser Str. 35, 85354 Freising; tel. (8161) 4910; fax (8161) 491491; e-mail info@ivv.fraunhofer.de; internet www.ivv.fraunhofer.de; f. 1942; food processing, environmental technology, preservation and packaging, gen. packaging; library of 6,000 vols; Dir Prof. Dr HORST-CHRISTIAN LANGOWSKI; Deputy Dir Dr CLAUDIA SCHÖNWEITZ.

Fraunhofer Institut für Materialfluss und Logistik: Joseph-von-Fraunhofer-Str. 2–4, 44227 Dortmund; tel. (231) 97430; e-mail info@iml.fraunhofer.de; internet www.iml.fraunhofer.de; f. 1981; attached to Technische Univ.; Head Prof. Dr AXEL KUHN; Head Prof. Dr MICHAEL TEN HOMPEL; Head Prof. Dr UWE CLAUSEN.

Fraunhofer Institut für Software- und Systemtechnik (ISST) (Fraunhofer Institute for Software and Systems Engineering (ISST)): Emil-Figge-Str. 91, 44227 Dortmund; tel. (231) 976770; fax (231) 97677199; e-mail info@isst.fraunhofer.de; internet www.isst.fraunhofer.de; f. 1992; attached to Technische Univ.; br. in Berlin; Dir Prof. Dr JAKOB REHOF; Man. Dir Dr VOLKER ZURWEHN.

GSI Helmholtzzentrum für Schwerionenforschung GmbH (GSI Helmholtz Centre for Heavy Ion Research GmbH): Planckstr. 1, 64291 Darmstadt; tel. (6159) 710; fax (6159) 712785; e-mail info@gsi.de; internet www.gsi.de; f. 1969; carries out basic research with heavy ions in nuclear physics and chemistry, solid state and atomic physics, radiation biology, tumour therapy with ion beams, etc.; heavy ion linear accelerator, synchrotron, storage ring and laboratory; library of 3,000 vols; Chair. Dr BEATRIX VIERKORN-RUDOLPH; Scientific Dir Prof. Dr HORST STÖCKER; publ. GSI-Scientific Report (1 a year).

Institut für Angewandte Innovationsforschung eV (Institute for Applied Innovation Research): Buscheypl. 13, 44801 Bochum; tel. (234) 971170; fax (234) 9711720; e-mail info@iai-bochum.de; internet www.iai-bochum.de; attached to

Ruhr Univ.; applied innovation research; Chair. Prof. Dr BERND KRIEGESMANN; Man. Dr HORST KUNHENN; publs Berichte aus der angewandten Innovationsforschung (series), Innovation: Forschung und Management (series).

Institut für Bauforschung eV (Institute for Building Research): An der Markuskirche 1, 30163 Hanover; tel. (511) 965160; fax (511) 9651626; e-mail office@bauforschung.de; internet www.bauforschung.de; f. 1946; research in areas of planning in construction, building materials, construction types, construction and building damage and their causes; Dir Dipl. Ing. HEIKE BÖHMER.

Institut für Erdöl- und Erdgasforschung (Institute for Petroleum Research): Agricolastr. 10, 38678 Clausthal-Zellerfeld; tel. (5323) 722239; fax (5323) 723146; e-mail bibliothek@ite.tu-clausthal.de; internet www.ite.tu-clausthal.de; f. 1943; attached to Technische Universität Clausthal; drilling and production technology, gas supply systems, oil and gas recovery, reservoir engineering, refinery technology, research in petroleum products, hydrocarbons and environment; 53 mems; library of 5,000 vols.

Institut für Roboterforschung (Robotics Research Institute): 44221, Dortmund; Otto-Hahn-Str. 8, 44227, Dortmund; tel. (231) 7552634; fax (231) 7553251; e-mail uwe.schwiegelshohn@tu-dortmund.de; internet www.irf.tu-dortmund.de; attached to Technische Univ.; Head Prof. Dr Ing. UWE SCHWIEGELSHOHN.

Institut für Textil- und Verfahrenstechnik Denkendorf (Institute for Textile Technology and Process Engineering Denkendorf): Körschtalstr. 26, 73770 Denkendorf; tel. (711) 93400; fax (711) 9340297; e-mail itv@itv-denkendorf.de; internet www.itv-denkendorf.de; f. 1921; library of 2,500 vols; Dir Prof. Dr-Ing. HEINRICH PLANK; Deputy Dir Dr MICHAEL DOSER.

Landesamt für Natur, Umwelt und Verbraucherschutz Nordrhein-Westfalen (North Rhine-Westphalia State Agency for Nature, Environment and Consumer Protection): Leibnizstr. 10, 45659 Recklinghausen; tel. (2361) 3050; fax (2361) 3053215; e-mail poststelle@lanuv.nrw.de; internet www.lanuv.nrw.de; f. 2007; research and advice in the fields of air pollution and noise control; prevention of accidental releases; water, wastewater, groundwater and waste management; engineering, circular economy, veterinary issues, food safety and agricultural commodity market; Pres. Dr HEINRICH BOTTERMANN.

Lehr- und Forschungsgebiet Internationale Wirtschaftsbeziehungen (Chair of International Economics): Templergraben 64, 52056 Aachen; tel. and fax (241) 8093931; fax (241) 80693931; internet www.iw.rwth-aachen.de; f. 2004; 6 mems; library of 100,000 vols; Dir Prof. Dr OLIVER LORZ; Sec. SUSANNE MOHAMMAD ZADEH; publs Canadian Journal of Economics, Economics Letters, Journal of Economic Behavior and Organization, Journal of Urban Economics, Public Choice.

Leibniz-Institut für Analytische Wissenschaften — ISAS – eV: Bunsen-Kirchhoff-Str. 11, 44139 Dortmund; tel. (231) 13920; fax (231) 1392120; e-mail info@isas.de; internet www.isas.de; f. 1952, present name 2009; promotes research in analytical sciences; attached to Technische Univ.; Dir Prof. Dr NORBERT ESSER; Dir Prof. Dr ALBERT SICKMANN.

Max Rubner-Institut, Bundesforschungsinstitut für Ernährung und Lebensmittel (Max Rubner Institute, Federal Research Institute for Nutrition and Food): Haid-und-

Neustr. 9, 76131 Karlsruhe; tel. (721) 66250; fax (721) 6625111; e-mail kontakt@mri.bund .de; internet www.mri.bund.de; f. 2008; research instn of the Fed. Min. of Food, Agriculture and Consumer Protection; focuses on health and consumer protection in the food sector, incl. determination and nutritional assessment of food ingredients, investigation of processing procedures, quality assurance of vegetable and animal food, investigation of the motivation of nutritional behaviour, and improvement of nutritional information; library of 300,000 vols; 470 mems; Pres. Prof. Dr GERHARD RECHKEMMER.

Physikalisch-Technische Bundesanstalt (National Metrology Institute): Bundesallee 100, 38116 Brunswick; tel. (531) 5923006; fax (531) 5923008; e-mail presse@ptb.de; internet www.ptb.de; f. 1887; divs for mechanics and acoustics, electricity, thermodynamics and explosion protection, optics, precision engineering, ionizing radiation, temperature and synchrotron radiation, and medical physics and information technology; library of 125,000 vols; Pres. Prof. Dr ERNST OTTO GÖBEL; Vice-Pres. Prof. Dr MANFRED PETERS; publs Maßstäbe (1 a year), PTB-Mitteilungen (4 a year), PTB news (3 a year).

Technologie Zentrum Dortmund GmbH: Emil-Figge-Str. 76–80, 44227 Dortmund; tel. (231) 9742100; fax (231) 9742395; e-mail technobox@tzdo.de; internet www.tzdo.de; attached to Technische Univ.; Chair. ERNST PRÜSSE; Man. Dir GUIDO BARANOWSKI; Man. Dir STEFAN SCHREIBER; Man. Dir UDO MAGER.

Zentrum für Konstruktionswerkstoffe, Staatliche Materialprüfungsanstalt Darmstadt–Fachgebiet und Institut für Werkstoffkunde (Centre for Construction Materials, State Material-Testing Foundation-Faculty and Institute of Material Science): Grafenstr. 2, 64283 Darmstadt; tel. (6151) 162351; fax (6151) 166118; e-mail oechsner@mpa-ifw.tu-darmstadt.de; internet www.mpa-ifw.tu-darmstadt.de; f. 1927; attached to Technical Univ. of Darmstadt; Dir Prof. Dr Ing. CHRISTINA BERGER; Dir Prof. Dr Ing MATTHIAS OECHSNER.

Libraries and Archives

Aachen

Hochschulbibliothek der RWTH Aachen: Templergraben 61, 52056 Aachen; tel. (241) 8094445; fax (241) 8092273; e-mail bth@bth.rwth-aachen.de; internet www.bth .rwth-aachen.de; f. 1870; 2,100,000 vols; Dir Dr ULRIKE EICH.

Stadtbibliothek Aachen (Aachen Public Library): Couvenstr. 15, 52058 Aachen; tel. (241) 47910; fax (241) 408007; e-mail bibliothek@mail.aachen.de; internet stadtbibliothek-aachen.de; f. 1831; gen. information about Aachen and the region, regional history; 511,000 vols, spec. collns incl. folklore, ethnology, archaeology, organ literature; Dir MANFRED SAWALLICH.

Amberg

Staatsarchiv Amberg: Archivstr. 3, 92224 Amberg; tel. (9621) 307270; fax (9621) 307288; e-mail poststelle@staam.bayern.de; f. 1437, became state archive in 1921; 2.9m. items in archives; 34,000 vols; Co-Dir Dr MARIA RITA SAGSTETTER; Co-Dir R. FRITSCH.

Augsburg

Staats- und Stadtbibliothek: Stadt Augsburg, 86143 Augsburg; Schaezlerstr. 25, 86152 Augsburg; tel. (821) 3242739; fax (821) 3242732; e-mail bibliothek.stadt@ augsburg.de; internet www.sustb.augsburg .de; f. 1537; 529,444 vols, 3,662 MSS, 2,798

incunabula, 16,250 drawings and engravings; Dir Dr HELMUT GIER; Librarian EDELTRAUD PRESTEL.

Staatsarchiv Augsburg: Salomon-Idler-Str. 2, 86159 Augsburg; tel. (821) 5996330; fax (821) 59963333; e-mail poststelle@staau .bayern.de; internet www.gda.bayern.de/ augsburg; f. 1830 in Neuburg; 3.05m. items; Dir Dr THOMAS ENGELKE.

Universitätsbibliothek: Universitätsstr. 22, 86159 Augsburg; tel. (821) 5985300; fax (821) 5985354; e-mail dir@bibliothek .uni-augsburg.de; internet www.bibliothek .uni-augsburg.de; f. 1970; 2,053,854 vols, 77,395 theses, 59,270 maps, 397,393 items of audiovisual material and microforms, 1,267 incunabula, 1,544 MSS, 2,295 music MSS; Dir Dr ULRICH HOHOFF.

Aurich

Niedersächsisches Staatsarchiv Aurich: Oldersumer Str. 50, 26603 Aurich; tel. (4941) 176660; fax (4941) 176673; e-mail aurich@nla .niedersachsen.de; internet www .staatsarchiv-aurich.niedersachsen.de; f. 1872; 20,000 vols; Dir Dr BERNHARD PARISIUS.

Bamberg

Staatsarchiv Bamberg: Hainstr. 39, 96047 Bamberg; tel. (951) 986220; fax (951) 9862250; e-mail poststelle@staba.bayern.de; internet www.gda.bayern.de/archive/ bamberg; f. 13th century, became Bavarian state archive in 1803; 2.3m vols; special collns: Frankish history, maps, plans, MSS, documents; Dir Dr STEFAN NÖTH.

Staatsbibliothek Bamberg (Bamberg State Library): Neue Residenz, Dompl. 8, 96049 Bamberg; tel. (951) 955030; fax (951) 95503145; e-mail info@ staatsbibliothek-bamberg.de; internet www .staatsbibliothek-bamberg.de; f. 1803; 502,793 vols, spec. colln of 6,148 MSS, 3,520 incunabula and 80,000 prints and drawings; Dir Prof. Dr WERNER TAEGERT; Deputy Dir Dr STEFAN KNOCH.

Universitätsbibliothek: POB 2705, 96018 Bamberg; Feldkirchenstr. 21, 96052 Bamberg; tel. (951) 8631501; fax (951) 8631565; e-mail universitaetsbibliothek@uni-bamberg .de; internet www.uni-bamberg.de/ub; f. 1973; 1,625,000 vols; Dir Dr FABIAN FRANKE; publ. Schriften der Universitätsbibliothek Bamberg.

Bayreuth

Universitätsbibliothek Bayreuth: Universität Bayreuth, 95440 Bayreuth; Universitätsstr. 30, 95447 Bayreuth; tel. (921) 553420; fax (921) 553442; e-mail info@ub .uni-bayreuth.de; internet www.ub .uni-bayreuth.de; f. 1973; 1,743,000 vols, 3,500 current periodicals; Dir Dr RALF BRUGBAUER.

Berlin

Akademiebibliothek der Berlin-Brandenburgischen Akademie der Wissenschaften: Jägerstr. 22–23, 10117 Berlin; tel. (30) 20370487; fax (30) 20370476; e-mail bib.benutzung@bbaw.de; internet bibliothek.bbaw.de; f. 1700; spec. colln of the publs of academies and learned socs; 650,000 vols, 730 periodicals; Dir Dr STEFAN WIEDERKEHR; Sec. ANDREA M'BATCHI.

Auswärtiges Amt, Referat 116, Bibliothek und Informationsvermittlung: Werderscher Markt 1, 10117 Berlin; tel. (30) 18172208; fax (30) 181752208; e-mail 116-information@auswaertiges-amt.de; 320,000 vols, 1,100 periodicals; Dir Dr GUNDULA FELTEN; Librarian ANNETT JUHRIG.

Bibliothek des Deutschen Bundestages: Pl. der Republik 1, 11011 Berlin; tel. (30)

22733073; fax (30) 22736087; e-mail bibliothek@bundestag.de; internet www .bundestag.de/htdocs_e/documents/library; f. 1949; 1,400,000 vols, 7,500 periodicals; spec. collns of German and foreign official publs and parliamentary papers; depository library of 10 int. orgs; Dir URSULA FREYSCHMIDT; Librarian ELISABETH MÄRZ; publs Literaturtipps (on topical economic and political subjects), Neue Bücher und Aufsätze in der Bibliothek, Schnellinformationen.

Bibliothek für Bildungsgeschichtliche Forschung: POB 171138, 10203 Berlin; Warschauer Str. 34–38, 10243 Berlin; tel. (30) 2933600; fax (30) 29336025; e-mail bbf@ dipf.de; internet www.bbf.dipf.de; f. 1876; holds conferences and exhibitions; 719,000 vols; Dir Dr CHRISTIAN RITZI; publs Bestandsverzeichnisse zur Bildungsgeschichte (directory of publications on the history of education, series), Jahrbuch für Historische Bildungsforschung (yearbook of education research history, 1 a year), Neuerwerbungsverzeichnis (list of new acquisitions, 12 a year), Quellen und Dokumente zur Alltagsgeschichte der Erziehung (sources and documents on the everyday history of education, series), Tagungsbände (conf. papers).

Geheimes Staatsarchiv Preussischer Kulturbesitz (Secret Central Archives of the Prussian Cultural Possession): Dahlem, Archivstr. 12–14, 14195 Berlin; tel. (30) 266447500; fax (30) 266443126; e-mail gsta .pk@gsta.spk-berlin.de; internet www.gsta .spk-berlin.de; f. 1598; material and research on history of Prussia and the former Prussian territories since 12th century; 185,000 vols, 2,000 periodicals, 650,000 records and files, 120,000 maps; Dir Prof. Dr JÜRGEN KLOOSTERHUIS; publ. Veröffentlichungen (2–3 a year).

Ibero-Amerikanisches Institut Preussischer Kulturbesitz: Potsdamer Str. 37, 10785 Berlin; tel. (30) 266451500; fax (30) 266351550; e-mail iai@iai.spk-berlin.de; internet www.iai.spk-berlin.de; f. 1930; research institute and library dedicated to Latin America, Spain and Portugal; 1,200,000 vols, 4,700 current periodicals; Dir Dr BARBARA GÖBEL; publs Bibliotheca Ibero-Americana, Biblioteca Luso-Brasileira, Iberoamericana, Indiana, Revista Internacional de Linguistica Iberoamericana.

Kunstbibliothek Staatliche Museen zu Berlin: Matthäikirchpl. 6, 10785 Berlin; tel. (30) 266424141; fax (30) 266422290; e-mail auskunft.kb@smb.spk-berlin.de; internet www.smb.museum/kb; f. 1867; 480,000 vols; spec. collns: ornamental and architectural books, Lipperheidesche Kostumbibliothek, artists' books, posters, photographs, graphic design, drawings; Dir Dr MORITZ WULLEN; Deputy Dir Dr JOACHIM BRAND.

Landesarchiv Berlin (Berlin Regional Archive): Eichborndamm 115–121, 13403 Berlin; tel. (30) 902640; fax (30) 90264250; e-mail info@landesarchiv-berlin.de; internet www.landesarchiv-berlin.de; f. 1948; legal documents, etc. for the Berlin area, and important material on the history of Berlin; 76,000 vols and 5,200 film rolls; Dir Prof. Dr UWE SCHAPER; publs Berlin in Geschichte und Gegenwart, Jahrbuch des Landesarchivs Berlin.

Politisches Archiv des Auswärtigen Amts (Political Archive of the Foreign Office): Kurstr. 33, 10117 Berlin; tel. (30) 18172159; fax (30) 18173948; e-mail 117-r@ diplo.de; internet www.auswaertiges-amt.de; f. 1920; Foreign Office archives; documents since 1867; archives of fmr Foreign Min. of the German Democratic Republic; Dir L. BIEWER; publs Akten zur auswärtigen Politik der Bundesrepublik Deutschland (series),

Akten zur deutschen auswärtigen Politik 1918–1945 (series), *Biographisches Handbuch des deutschen Auswärtigen Dienstes 1871–1945* (series).

Staatsbibliothek zu Berlin–Preußischer Kulturbesitz: Unter den Linden 8, 10117 Berlin; also: Potsdamer Str. 33 (Tiergarten), 10785 Berlin; tel. (30) 2660; fax (30) 266331301; e-mail katja.duehlmeyer@sbb .spk-berlin.de; internet www .staatsbibliothek-berlin.de; f. 1661; 10,900,000 vols, 25,000 current periodicals and newspapers, 18,400 occidental MSS, 66,500 musical MSS, 462,300 music prints, 1m. maps, 4,442 incunabula, 321,080 autographs, 17,500,000 pictures, 2m. microforms; Mendelssohn archive; Gen. Dir BARBARA SCHNEIDER-KEMPF.

Universitätsbibliothek der Freien Universität Berlin: Garystr. 39, 14195 Berlin; tel. 83851111; fax 83853738; e-mail auskunft@ub.fu-berlin.de; internet www.ub .fu-berlin.de; f. 1952; 2,100,000 vols, 1,800 periodicals, 38,500 e-journals, 362,000 theses, 7.6m. vols in departmental libraries; Dir Prof. Dr ULRICH NAUMANN; publ. *Universitätsbibliographie.*

Universitätsbibliothek der Humboldt-Universität zu Berlin (University Library of Humboldt University in Berlin): Unter den Linden, 10099 Berlin; Geschwister-Scholl-Str. 1–3, 10117 Berlin; tel. (30) 209399300; fax (30) 209399311; e-mail info@ub.hu-berlin .de; internet www.hu-berlin.de; f. 1831; 6.5m vols, 10,000 current periodicals; Dir Dr MILAN BULATY; Deputy Dir IMMA HENDRIX; publ. *Schriftenreihe.*

Universitätsbibliothek der Technische Universität Berlin: Universitätsbibliothek, Fasanenstr. 88, (im Volkswagen-Haus), 10623 Berlin; tel. (30) 31476101; fax (30) 31476104; e-mail info@ub.tu-berlin.de; internet www.ub.tu-berlin.de; f. 1884; 2,286,726 vols, 2,564 periodicals, 14,850 e-journals, 128,325 architectural drawings and prints, complete German standards; Dir Dr W. ZICK.

Zentral- und Landesbibliothek Berlin (Berlin Central and Provincial Library): Breite Str. 30–36, 10178 Berlin; tel. (30) 90226401; fax (30) 90226163; e-mail info@zlb .de; internet www.zlb.de; f. 1901; central public library of Berlin; 3.3m vols, in print and online; Gen. Dir Prof. Dr CLAUDIA LUX; Man. Dir HANS JOACHIM RIESEBERG.

Bochum

Stadtbücherei Bochum: Gustav-Heinemann Pl. 2–6 (BVZ), 44777 Bochum; tel. (234) 910-2496; fax (234) 9101703; e-mail stadtbue@bochum.de; internet www.bochum .de/stadtbuecherei; f. 1905; 406,000 vols; Dir HEINZ ALBRECHT.

Universitätsbibliothek (University Library of Bochum): 44780 Bochum; Universitaetsstr. 150, 44801 Bochum; tel. (234) 3222788; fax (234) 3214736; e-mail ub-information@ruhr-uni-bochum.de; internet www.ub.ruhr-uni-bochum.de; f. 1962; attached to Ruhr-Univ., 2,015,000 vols, 2,000 periodicals, 371,000 theses; Univ. Librarian Dr ERDMUTE LAPP; Deputy Librarian GEORG SANDER.

Bonn

Archiv der sozialen Demokratie (Friedrich-Ebert-Stiftung) (Archive of Social Democracy—Friedrich Ebert Foundation): 53170 Bonn; Godesberger Allee 149, 53175 Bonn; tel. (228) 8839046; fax (228) 8839209; e-mail archiv.auskunft@fes.de; internet www .fes.de; f. 1969; contains material relating to the Sozialdemokratische Partei Deutschlands (SPD) and the German trade unions;

history of German and int. social movement, labour movement, labour problems; 600,000 vols, 3,000 periodicals; Dir for the Archive of Social Democracy Dr ANJA KRUKE; Dir for the Library of the Friedrich-Ebert-Foundation Dr RÜDIGER ZIMMERMANN.

Bibliothek der Hochschulrektorenkonferenz (Library of the University Rectors' Conference): Ahrstr. 39, 53175 Bonn; tel. (228) 887159; fax (228) 887110; e-mail bibliothek@hrk.de; internet www.hrk.de/ bibliothek; f. 1954 (Westdeutsche Rektorenkonferenz); 68,000 vols, 800 periodicals, 68,000 monographs, 95,000 records and acts; Head Dr ULRICH MEYER-DOERPINGHAUS; Librarian THOMAS LAMPE.

Bundesamts für Bauwesen und Raumordnung, Wissenschaftliche Bibliothek: POB 210150, 53156 Bonn; tel. (1888) 4012281; fax (1888) 4012249; e-mail karin.goebel@bbr.bund.de; internet www.bbr .bund.de; f. 1941; 150,000 vols, 450 periodicals; Dir Dr phil. KLAUS SCHLIEBE; publs *Forschungen* (series, irregular), *Informationen zur Raumentwicklung* (12 a year), *Raumforschung und Raumordnung* (5 or 6 issues a year), *Werkstatt: Praxis* (series, irregular).

Stadtarchiv und Stadthistorische Bibliothek Bonn (Bonn City Archive and Historical Library): Berliner Platz 2, 53103 Bonn; tel. (228) 772530; fax (228) 774301; e-mail stadtarchiv@bonn.de; f. 1899; 140,000 vols; Head Archivist and Librarian Dr NORBERT SCHLOSSMACHER; publs *Bonner Geschichtsblätter* (1 a year), *Studien zur Heimatgeschichte des Stadtbezirkes Bonn-Beuel, Veröffentlichungen des Stadtarchivs Bonn.*

Universitäts- und Landesbibliothek: POB 2460, 53014 Bonn; Adenauerallee 39–41, 53113 Bonn; tel. (228) 737350; fax (228) 737546; e-mail ulb@ulb.uni-bonn.de; internet www.ulb.uni-bonn.de; f. 1818; 2,090,000 vols, 6,100 periodicals, 13,500 electronic periodicals, 1,300 incunabula, 880 MSS; Dir Dr RENATE VOGT.

Bremen

Bibliothek/Informationszentrum des Instituts für Seeverkehrswirtschaft und Logistik (ISL) (ISL Information Centre/Library): Universitätsallee GW1 Block A, 28359 Bremen; tel. (421) 21869699; fax (421) 2209655; e-mail library@isl.org; internet www.isl.org; f. 1954; centre for maritime information and documentation offering professional services about industries, markets and companies within the areas of maritime industries, transport and logistics; 125,000 vols; Head of Information Centre BRIGITTE OGIOLDA; Head of Library ANGELA FEGBEITEL.

Staats- und Universitätsbibliothek: POB 330160, 28331 Bremen; Bibliothekstr. 28359 Bremen; tel. (421) 2182615; fax (421) 2182614; e-mail suub@suub.uni-bremen.de; internet www.suub.uni-bremen.de; f. 1660; 3,297,785 vols, 8,257 current print periodicals, 21,003 online periodicals; Dir MARIA ELISABETH MÜLLER; publ. *Jahresbibliographie Massenkommunikation.*

Staatsarchiv: Am Staatsarchiv 1, 28203 Bremen; tel. (421) 3616221; fax (421) 36110247; e-mail office@staatsarchiv .bremen.de; internet www .staatsarchiv-bremen.de; f. 1727; Dir Prof. Dr KONRAD ELMSHÄUSER (acting); publs *Bremisches Jahrbuch, Kleine Schriften des Staatsarchivs Bremen, Veröffentlichungen aus dem Staatsarchiv der Freien Hansestadt Bremen.*

Brunswick

Bundesforschungsinstitut für Kulturpflanzen Informationszentrum und Bibliothek (Federal Research Centre for Cultivated Plants Information Centre and Library): Messeweg 11/12, 38104 Braunschweig; tel. (531) 2993397; fax (531) 2993018; e-mail julia.schollbach@jki.bund.de; internet www.jki.bund.de; f. 1950; attached to Julius Kühn-Institut; plant protection and related fields; 370,000 vols, 1,200 periodicals, 44,000 reprints, 2,200 microfilms; Head Dr OLAF HERING; publs *Amtliche Pflanzenschutzbestimmungen* (irregular), *Berichte aus der Biologischen Bundesanstalt für Land- und Forstwirtschaft, Nachrichtenblatt des Deutschen Pflanzenschutzdienstes* (12 a year), *Pflanzenschutzmittel-Verzeichnis* (1 a year).

Stadtarchiv (City Archive): Schlosspl. 1, 38100 Braunschweig; tel. (531) 4704711; fax (531) 4704725; e-mail stadtarchiv@ braunschweig.de; internet www .braunschweig.de/stadtarchiv; f. 1860; 125,000 documents since 1031, municipal records, charters, maps and plans since 1228, spec. collns on the history of the town; spec. historical archive on prominent Brunswick women; Head Dr HENNING STEINFÜHRER.

Stadtbibliothek: POB 3309, 38023 Braunschweig; Schlosspl. 2, 38100 Braunschweig; tel. (531) 4706801; fax (531) 4706899; e-mail stadtbibliothek@braunschweig.de; internet www.braunschweig.de/ stadtbibliothek; f. 1861; spec. colln on the history of the town; 604,603 vols, medieval MSS, 426 incunabula, 2,500 maps and plans up to 1850; Dir Dr ANETTE HAUCAP-NASS; publs *Braunschweiger Werkstücke, Kleine Schriften* (irregular).

Universitätsbibliothek Braunschweig: Pockelsstr. 13, 38106 Braunschweig; tel. (531) 3915018; fax (531) 3915002; e-mail ub@tu-bs.de; internet www.biblio.tu-bs.de; f. 1748; exhibitions; various lectures; Digitale Bibliothek Braunschweig with nearly 7,000 documents; archive of the Technische Universität Braunschweig; 21,687 mems; 1,414,708 vols, 2,420 periodicals, 40,500 online journals, about 120,000 standards, 175,000 printed dissertations; 51,000 microfiches; areas of specialization incl. pharmacy (virtual library), DFG-Sondersammelgebiet, 15th–19th century technology and natural history, children's books since 16th century, archive library of 6 publishing houses; Dir Prof. Dr DIETMAR BRANDES; Deputy Dir Dr BEATE NAGEL.

Bückeburg

Niedersächsisches Landesarchiv, Staatsarchiv Bückeburg: Schlosspl. 2, 31675 Bückeburg; tel. (5722) 967730; fax (5722) 1289; e-mail bueckeburg@nla.niedersachsen .de; internet www.nla.niedersachsen.de; f. 1961; archives of old county, later principality, of Schaumburg-Lippe and district of Schaumburg; central workshops for restoration and security filming for Lower Saxony; 40,000 vols, 4,100 documents, 35,000 maps; Dir Dr STEFAN BRÜDERMANN; publs *Inventare und kleinere Schriften des Staatsarchivs Bückeburg, Schaumburger Studien.*

Chemnitz

Stadtbibliothek (City Library): Moritzstr. 20, 09111 Chemnitz; tel. (371) 4884222; fax (371) 4884299; e-mail information@ stadtbibliothek-chemnitz.de; internet www .stadtbibliothek-chemnitz.de; f. 1869; 500,000 vols; spec. colln of literature on local govt; Dir ELKE BEER.

Universitätsbibliothek: 09107 Chemnitz; Str. der Nationen 62, 09111 Chemnitz; tel. (371) 53113100; fax (371) 53113109; e-mail sekretariat@bibliothek.tu-chemnitz.de; internet www.bibliothek.tu-chemnitz.de; f. 1836; attached to Chemnitz Univ. of Technology; 1,188,540 vols, 98,000 theses, 1,668 periodicals, 15,282,500 patents; Dir ANGELA MALZ.

Clausthal-Zellerfeld

Universitätsbibliothek der Technischen Universität Clausthal (Library of the Technical University of Clausthal): Leibnizstr. 2, 38678 Clausthal-Zellerfeld; tel. (5323) 722301; fax (5323) 723639; e-mail ubclz@tu-clausthal.de; internet www.bibliothek.tu-clausthal.de; f. 1810; 490,000 vols, 660 current journals, 805 periodicals, 5,000 geological maps; Dir Dr J. SCHÜLING.

Coburg

Landesbibliothek (State Library): Schlosspl. 1, 96450 Coburg; tel. (9561) 85380; fax (9561) 8538201; e-mail geschaeftsstelle@landesbibliothek-coburg.de; internet www.landesbibliothek-coburg.de; f. c. 1550, fmr ducal library of the duchy of Saxe-Coburg (until 1918); 410,000 vols, 600 periodicals; Dir Dr SILVIA PFISTER.

Staatsarchiv Coburg (State Archive of Coburg): Herrngasse 11, 96450 Coburg; tel. (9561) 427070; fax (9561) 4270720; e-mail poststelle@staco.bayern.de; internet www .gda.bayern.de/archive/coburg/; f. 13th century; present title 1939; archives of the duchy and republic of Saxe-Coburg, since 1920 county of Coburg; 380,000 documents; 8,000 vols; Dir HORST GEHRINGER.

Cologne

Deutsche Zentralbibliothek für Medizin (German National Library of Medicine): Gleueler Str. 60, 50931 Cologne; tel. (221) 4785600; fax (221) 4785697; e-mail info@ zbmed.de; internet www.zbmed.de; f. 1908; 1,250,000 vols and microforms, 7,300 current periodicals; virtual library of medicine (www.medpilot.de), virtual library of nutrition, environment and agriculture (www.greenpilot.de), open access journals in medicine (www.egms.de); offers document delivery by post, fax and e-mail; Dir ULRICH KORWITZ; publ. *German Medical Science.*

Erzbischöfliche Diözesan- und Dombibliothek mit Bibliothek St Albertus Magnus (Archbishop's Diocesean and Cathedral Library incl. Library St Albertus Magnus): POB 10 11 45, 50451 Cologne; Kardinal-Frings-Str. 1–3, 50668 Cologne; tel. (221) 16423781; fax (221) 16423783; e-mail dombibliothek@erzbistum-koeln.de; internet www.dombibliothek-koeln.de; f. 1738; 700,000 vols; Dir Prof. Dr HEINZ FINGER; Dir Prof. Dr SIEGFRIED SCHMIDT; publ. *Analecta Coloniensia, Libelli Rhenani.*

Historisches Archiv der Stadt Köln: Heumarkt 14, 50667 Cologne; tel. (221) 22122327; fax (221) 22122480; e-mail historischesarchiv@stadt-koeln.de; internet www.stadt-koeln.de/historisches-archiv/; f. 1322; records since AD 875; 140,000 vols; Dir Dr BETTINA SCHMIDT-CZAIA; publ. *Mitteilungen.*

Kunst- und Museumsbibliothek mit Rheinischem Bildarchiv (Art and Museum Library of the City of Cologne): Kattenbug 18–24, 50667 Cologne; tel. (221) 22122438; fax (221) 22122210; e-mail kmb@ stadt-koeln.de; internet www.museenkoeln .de/kmb; f. 1957; 420,000 vols, 792 current journals; Dir Dr ELKE PURPUS.

LVR- Archivberatungs-und Fortbildungszentrum, Abteilung Archivbera-

tung (Archive and Museums Office of the Rheinland, Department of Archive Services): POB 2140, 50250 Pulheim; Ehrenfriedstr. 19, 50259 Pulheim; tel. (2234) 98540; fax (2234) 9854285; e-mail afz@lvr.de; internet www .rafo.lvr.de; f. 1929; archive of the Landschaftsverband Rheinland with sources of the last 200 years; collns relating to local history; 16,500 vols; Dir Dr ARIE NABRINGS; Sec. SANDRA KASCHUBA; publs *Archivhefte* (archival science in Rheinland), *Inventare nichtstaatlicher Archive* (inventories of non-state archives in Rheinland), *Rheinprovinz* (regional history of Rheinland).

Stiftung Rheinisch-Westfälisches Wirtschaftsarchiv zu Köln: Unter Sachsenhausen 10–26, 50667 Cologne; tel. (221) 1640800; fax (221) 1640829; f. 1906; economic records of the region; research and publication of research results; lending and reference library of business documents; 35,000 vols; Dir Dr ULRICH S. SOÉNIUS; publ. *Schriften zur rheinisch-westfälischen Wirtschaftsgeschichte.*

Universitäts- und Stadtbibliothek Köln (University and City Library of Cologne): Universitätsstr. 33, 50931 Cologne; tel. (221) 4702374; fax (221) 4705166; e-mail eauskunft@ub.uni-koeln.de; internet www .ub.uni-koeln.de; f. 1920; 3.6m vols, 8,500 periodicals; Dir Prof. Dr W. SCHMITZ; Deputy Dir Dr R. THIELE.

Darmstadt

Hessisches Staatsarchiv Darmstadt (State Archive of Hesse): Karolinenpl. 3, 64289 Darmstadt; tel. (6151) 165900; fax (6151) 165901; e-mail poststelle@stad .hessen.de; internet www .staatsarchiv-darmstadt.hessen.de; f. 1567; Dir Prof. Dr FRIEDRICH BATTENBERG; publs *Darmstädter Archivdokumente für den Unterricht, Darmstädter Archivenschriften, Geschichte im Archiv.*

Universitäts- und Landesbibliothek Darmstadt: Schloss, 64283 Darmstadt; tel. (6151) 165850; fax (6151) 165897; e-mail info@ulb.tu-darmstadt.de; internet www.ulb .tu-darmstadt.de; f. 1560; 3,800,000 vols, 4,090 MSS, 2,050 incunabula, 15,000 musicalia, 28,000 maps, 4,600,000 German and European patent documents, 400,000 digital documents, 21,500 e-journals; Dir Dr HANS-GEORG NOLTE-FISCHER.

Dessau

Anhaltische Landesbücherei Dessau (Anhalt Library of Dessau): Zerbster Str. 10/35, 06844 Dessau; tel. (340) 2042648; fax (340) 2042948; e-mail bibliothek@ dessau-rosslau.de; internet www.bibliothek .dessau.de; f. 1898; 285,195 vols, 133 incunabula, 599 MSS, 342 current periodicals; Dir GABRIELE SCHNEIDER.

Detmold

Landesarchiv Nordrhein-Westfalen-Staats- und Personenstandarchiv Detmold: Willi-Hofmann-Str. 2, 32756 Detmold; tel. (5231) 7660; fax (5231) 766114; e-mail stadt@lav.nrw.de; internet www.archive.nrw .de; f. 1957 (fmrly Lippisches Landesarchiv, f. 16th century); archives of fmr regions of Lippe (12th century to 1947) and Minden (1815–1947), Dominion of Vianen (Netherlands), Detmold (since 1947); spec. collns: genealogy, French Citizens' Registers, Parish Registers, Jewish and Dissenters' Registers of Westphalia (1808–1874); copies of registers of births, deaths and marriages (1874–1938); 72,000 vols; Dir Dr JUTTA PRIEUR-POHL.

Lippische Landesbibliothek Detmold: Hornsche Str. 41, 32756 Detmold; tel. (5231) 926600; fax (5231) 9266055; e-mail

llbmail@llb-detmold.de; internet www .llb-detmold.de; f. 1614; 550,000 vols, 10,000 MSS; Dir DETLEV HELLFAIER.

Dortmund

Stadt- und Landesbibliothek Dortmund: Königswall 18, 44137 Dortmund; tel. (231) 5023209; fax (231) 5023199; e-mail stlb@ stadtdo.de; internet www.bibliothek .dortmund.de; f. 1907; 1,200,000 vols; spec. colln of MSS and autographs and material on Westphalia; music dept; Dir ULRICH MOESKE; publs *Autographenausstellungen* (irregular), *Mitteilungen* (irregular), *Mitteilungen aus dem Literaturarchiv Kulturpreis der Stadt Dortmund* (every 2 years).

Stiftung Westfälisches Wirtschaftsarchiv (WWA) (Foundation of the Westphalian Economic Archive): Märkische Str. 120, 44141 Dortmund; tel. (231) 5417296; fax (231) 5417117; e-mail wwado@dortmund.ihk .de; internet www.archive.nrw.de; f. 1941; records of the economic, social and industrial history of Westphalia and the Ruhr; research; 4,000 shelf-metres of records; 50,000 vols; Dir Dr KARL-PETER ELLER ʙ ROCK.

Universitätsbibliothek Dortmund: 44222 Dortmund; Vogelpothsweg 76, 44227 Dortmund; tel. (231) 7554001; fax (231) 7554032; e-mail information@ub.tu-dortmund.de; internet www.ub.tu-dortmund.de; f. 1965; 1.76m. vols, 7,500,000 patents; Dir Dr JOACHIM KREISCHE.

Dresden

Sächsische Landesbibliothek–Staats- und Universitätsbibliothek Dresden (SLUB) (Saxony State and University Library Dresden): 01054 Dresden; Zellescher Weg 18, 01069 Dresden; tel. (351) 4677420; fax (351) 4677111; e-mail generaldirektion@ slub-dresden.de; internet www.slub-dresden .de; f. 1996; 4,989,600 vols, 147,000 theses, 131,000 maps, 178,000 tapes and records, 2,000,000 photographs, 131,000 standards, 16,953 current periodicals; Dir-Gen. Prof. Dr THOMAS BÜRGER; Deputy Dir-Gen. Dr ACHIM BONTE; Deputy Dir-Gen. MICHAEL GOLSCH; publs *Bibliographie Geschichte der Technik* (1 a year), *BIS:Das Magazin der Bibliotheken in Sachsen* (4 a year), *Sächsische Bibliographie* (1 a year), *SLUB-Kurier* (4 a year).

Sächsisches Staatsarchiv—Hauptstaatsarchiv Dresden: POB 100 444, 01074 Dresden; Wilhelm-Buck-Str. 4, 01097 Dresden; tel. (351) 5643740; fax (351) 5643739; e-mail poststelle@sta.smi.sachsen.de; internet www.archiv.sachsen.de; f. 1834; 71,000 vols; Dir Dr JÜRGEN RAINER WOLF; publs *Einzelveröffentlichungen, Schriftenreihe des Sächsischen Hauptstaatsarchivs* (13 vols).

Städtische Bibliotheken Dresden (Dresden Public Libraries): Freibergerstr. 35, 01067 Dresden; tel. (351) 8648101; fax (351) 8648102; e-mail mail@bibo-dresden.de; internet www.bibo-dresden.de; f. 1910; 751,490 vols; Man. Dr AREND FLEMMING; Deputy Man. ROMAN RABE.

Duisburg

Stadtarchiv Duisburg (City Archives of Duisburg): Karmelpl. 5 (Am Innenhafen), 47049 Duisburg; tel. (203) 2832154; fax (203) 2834330; e-mail stadtarchiv@ stadt-duisburg.de; internet www.archive .nrw.de; f. 12th century; admin., research into local and city history; reference library on local history and customs of Duisburg and Lower Rhine; 60,000 vols; Dir Dr HANS GEORG KRAUME; publs *Duisburger Forschungen, Duisburger Geschichtsquellen.*

Stadtbibliothek Duisburg (City Library): Düsseldorfer Str. 5–7, 47049 Duisburg; tel.

(203) 2834218; fax (203) 2834294; e-mail stadtbibliothek@stadt-duisburg.de; internet www.duisburg.de/micro/stadtbibliothek; f. 1901; 700,000 vols, 1,177 periodicals; Dir Dr JAN-PIETER BARBIAN; publs *Blickpunkt Bibliothek* (26 a year), *Literary Catalogues* (Amerikanische Literatur, Schiller, Heine, Brecht, Böll, Kafka).

Düsseldorf

Bibliotek und Archiv des Heinrich-Heine-Instituts (Heinrich Heine Institute Library and Archives): Bilker Str. 12–14, 40213 Düsseldorf; tel. (211) 8995574; fax (211) 8929044; e-mail elena.camaiani@ duesseldorf.de; internet www.duesseldorf.de/ heineinstitut; f. 1970; exhibitions, readings, lectures; 55,000 vols, literature by/on Heinrich Heine, documents regarding the revolutionary 'Vormärz' era and the Rhineland as well as music and arts in Düsseldorf; MSS collns from 1600 to the present, more than 130 literary, musical and artistic estates, among them the largest colln of autographs by Heinrich Heine, spec. collns of autographs by Clara and Robert Schumann as well as the Düsseldorf School of Painting; Dir Dr SABINE BRENNER-WILCZEK; Librarian ELENA CAMAIANI; publs *Archiv–Bibliothek–Museum* (irregular), *Heine-Jahrbuch* (1 a year), *Heine-Studien* (irregular).

Landesarchiv Nordrhein-Westfalen: Graf-Adolf-Str. 67, 40210 Düsseldorf; tel. (211) 1592380; fax (211) 159238111; e-mail poststelle@lav.nrw.de; internet www.lav.nrw .de; f. 2004; consists of Zentrale Dienste, Fachbereich Grundsätze, Abteilung Rheinland (f. 1832), Abteilung Westfalen (f. 1829), Abteilung Ostwestfalen-Lippe (f. 1955); Pres. Prof. Dr WILFRIED REININGSHAUS; publ. *Archivar. Zeitschrift für Archivwesen* (4 a year).

Universitäts- und Landesbibliothek Düsseldorf (University and State Library of Düsseldorf): Universitätsstr. 1, 40225 Düsseldorf; tel. (211) 8112030; fax (211) 8113054; e-mail sekretariat@ub .uni-duesseldorf.de; internet www.ub .uni-duesseldorf.de; f. 1970; 2,409,305 vols, 13,892 electronic periodicals, 3,744 in print; Dir Dr IRMGARD SIEBERT.

Eichstätt

Universitätsbibliothek Eichstaett-Ingolstadt (University Library of Eichstätt-Ingolstadt): Universitätsallee 1, 85072 Eichstätt; tel. (8421) 931330; fax (8421) 931791; e-mail ub-direktion@ku-eichstaett.de; internet www .ku-eichstaett.de/bibliothek; f. 16th century; developed from fmr Library of Diocesan Seminary and State Library; spec. collns: theology, archives of Asscn of German Catholic Press and of Asscn of Catholic publishers and booksellers, Schlecht music library and MSS, Glossner Oriental and Judaistic library, archives and library of the Inklings Society; 1,846,548 vols, 433,987 units of nonbook materials, 2,844 MSS, 3,001 musical MSS, 1,247 incunabula, 3,280 periodicals; Dir Dr ANGELIKA REICH; publs *Aus den Beständen der Universitätsbibliothek Eichstätt*, *Bibliographien der Universitätsbibliothek Eichstätt*, *Kataloge der Universitätsbibliothek Eichstätt*, *Schriften der Universitätsbibliothek Eichstätt*.

Erfurt

Stadt- und Regionalbibliothek Erfurt: 40.03, 99111 Erfurt; Dompl. 1, 99084 Erfurt; tel. (361) 6551590; fax (361) 6551599; e-mail bibliothek@erfurt.de; internet bibliothek .erfurt.de; f. 1897; 526,712 vols (237,312 vols in scientific spec. collns), 500 periodicals; Dir Dr EBERHARD KUSBER.

Erlangen

Universitätsbibliothek Erlangen-Nürnberg (University Library of Erlangen-Nuremberg): 91051 Erlangen; Universitätsstr. 4, 91054 Erlangen; tel. (9131) 8523950; fax (9131) 8529309; e-mail hb.info@bib .uni-erlangen.de; internet www.ub .uni-erlangen.de; f. 1743; spec. collns on education, science and philosophy; 5,400,000 vols, 890,000 theses, 2,432 MSS, 140 papyri, 2,136 incunabula; Dir KONSTANZE SÖLLNER.

Frankfurt am Main

Bibliothek des Freies Deutschen Hochstifts (Library of the Free German Literature Institute): Frankfurter Goethe-Haus, Grosser Hirschgraben 23–25, 60311 Frankfurt am Main; tel. (69) 13880262; fax (69) 13880222; e-mail jseng@ goethehaus-frankfurt.de; internet www .goethehaus-frankfurt.de; f. 1859; 130,000 vols, 40,000 MSS and handwritten letters, 500 paintings and 16,000 prints on public display in the graphic art colln; Dir Dr JOACHIM SENG; Librarian NORA SCHWARZ.

Deutsche Nationalbibliothek (German National Library): Adickesallee 1, 60322 Frankfurt am Main; tel. (69) 15250; fax (69) 15251010; e-mail info-f@dnb.de; internet www.dnb.de; f. 1912; present name and status 2006; central archival library and nat. bibliographic centre; collects, permanently archives, documents, records and makes available to public all German and German-language publs from 1913 onwards; spec. collns incl. Reichsbibliothek 1848, German exile literature 1933–1945, Anne-Frank-Shoah-Bibliothek; 25.4m. vols; Dir UTE SCHWENS; publ. *Deutsche Nationalbibliografie* (48 a year, 12 a year and 4 a year, online).

Constituent Libraries:

Deutsche Nationalbibliothek Deutsches Musikarchiv: Deutscher Pl. 1, 04103 Leipzig; tel. (341) 22710; fax (341) 2271444; e-mail info-b@d-nb.de; internet www.d-nb.de; f. 1970; 1,200,000 vols; Head of Dept Dr INGO KOLASA.

Deutsche Nationalbibliothek Leipzig: Deutscher Pl. 1, 04103 Leipzig; tel. (341) 22710; fax (341) 2271444; e-mail info-l@ dnb.de; internet www.dnb.de; f. 1912; 26,160,516 vols; Dir-Gen. Dr ELISABETH NIGGEMANN.

Institut für Stadtgeschichte (Stadtarchiv) (Institute for Urban History (City Archives)): Münzgasse 9, 60311 Frankfurt am Main; tel. (69) 21230142; fax (69) 21230753; e-mail michael.fleiter@ stadt-frankfurt.de; internet www .stadtgeschichte-ffm.de; f. 1436, fmrly Historical City Archives; municipal records; documents since 9th century, registers since 13th century, deeds since 14th century; records on Frankfurt from other archives; historical records in writings, pictures and sound; 50,000 vols, 750 current periodicals; Dir Dr EVELYN BROCKHOFF.

Universitätsbibliothek Johann Christian Senckenberg: Bockenheimer Landstr. 134–138, 60325 Frankfurt am Main; tel. (69) 79839205; fax (69) 79839380; e-mail auskunft@ub.uni-frankfurt.de; internet www .ub.uni-frankfurt.de; f. 1484; present name 2005 following merger of Stadt- und Universitätsbibliothek Frankfurt am Main (StUB) and the Senckenbergische Bibliothek (SeB) 2005; 6,600,000 vols; Dir BERNDT DUGALL; Deputy Dir Dr WILHELM R. SCHMIDT.

Freiberg im Sachsen

Technische Universität Bergakademie Freiberg Universitätsbibliothek 'Geor-

gius Agricola': Agricolastr. 10, 09599 Freiberg in Sachsen; tel. (3731) 392959; fax (3731) 393289; e-mail unibib@ub.tu-freiberg .de; internet tu-freiberg.de/ze/ub; f. 1765; 717,200 vols, 2,820 autographs, 26,000 standards, 4,470 cards, 71,300 univ. publs; spec. collns: mining and metallurgy, geosciences; Dir KATRIN STUMP; Deputy Dir SABINE ALBANI; publ. *Veröffentlichungen der Bibliothek 'Georgius Agricola' der TU Bergakademie Freiberg* (irregular).

Freiburg im Breisgau

Deutsches Volksliedarchiv, Institut für internationale Popularliedforschung (German Folksong Archive, Research Centre for Song and Popular Culture): Silberbachstr. 13, 79100 Freiburg in Breisgau; tel. (761) 705030; fax (761) 7050328; e-mail info@ dva.uni-freiburg.de; internet www.dva .uni-freiburg.de; f. 1914; 70,000 vols; Head Dr NILS GROSCH (acting); publs *Deutsche Volkslieder mit ihren Melodien, Historisch-kritisches Liederlexikon 2005ff* (1 a year), *Jahrbuch für Volksliedforschung, Populäre Kultur und Musik. 2010ff, Volksliedstudien 2001ff.*

Stadtarchiv Freiburg im Breisgau (City Archive of Freiburg im Breisgau): Grünwälderstr. 15, 79098 Freiburg im Breisgau; tel. (761) 2012701; fax (761) 2012799; e-mail stadtarchiv@stadt.freiburg.de; internet www .freiburg.de; f. 1840; 5 km of records from 12th century to present day; 75,000 vols; Dir Dr ULRICH P. ECKER; publs *Neue Reihe, Schau-ins-Land, Veröffentlichungen aus dem Archiv der Stadt Freiburg.*

Universitätsbibliothek: POB 1629, 79016 Freiburg im Breisgau; Schwarzwaldstr. 80, 79016 Freiburg im Breisgau; Rempartstr. 10–16, 79016 Freiburg im Breisgau; tel. (761) 2033918; fax (761) 2033987; e-mail info@ub.uni-freiburg.de; internet www.ub .uni-freiburg.de; f. 1457; 4m. vols, incl. dissertations; Dir Dr ANTJE KELLERSOHN.

Fulda

Hochschul- und Landesbibliothek: Heinrich-von-Bibra-Pl. 12, 36037 Fulda; tel. (661) 9640970; fax (661) 9640954; e-mail hlb@hlb .hs-fulda.de; internet www.hs-fulda.de/hlb; f. 1778; 700,000 vols, 3,916 MSS and 431 incunabula; Dir Dr MARIANNE RIETHMÜLLER; Deputy Librarian BERTHOLD WEISS.

Giessen

Universitätsbibliothek Giessen: Otto-Behaghel-Str. 8, 35394 Giessen; tel. (641) 9914032; fax (641) 9914009; e-mail auskunft@bibsys.uni-giessen.de; internet www.ub.uni-giessen.de; f. 1612; 3,887,035 vols, 400,197 dissertations, 2,721 MSS, 877 incunabula, 2,841 papyri; Dir Dr PETER REUTER; Librarian CORINA THOMÄ.

Görlitz

Oberlausitzische Bibliothek der Wissenschaften Görlitz (Upper Lusatian Library of Science in Görlitz): Neiss Str. 30, POB 300131, 02826 Görlitz; tel. (3581) 671350; fax (3581) 671375; e-mail olb@ goerlitz.de; internet olb.goerlitz.de; f. 1950 (original library 1779); scientific, historical and gen. library incl. rare book colln; 140,000 vols; Librarian MATTHIAS WENZEL.

Gotha

Universitäts- und Forschungsbibliothek Erfurt/Gotha (University and Research Library of Erfurt/Gotha): POB 90 02 22, 99105 Erfurt; Nordhäuser Str. 63, 99089 Erfurt; tel. (361) 7375800; fax (361) 7375509; e-mail information.ub@uni-erfurt .de POB 10 01 30, 99851 Gotha; Schloss Friedenstein, 99867 Gotha; tel. (361)

7375530; fax (361) 7375539; e-mail bibliothek .gotha@uni-erfurt.de; internet www .uni-erfurt.de/bibliothek; f. 1994 at Erfurt; 1,080,506 vols, 1,950 MSS, 639 incunabula; f. 1647 at Gotha: 690,215 vols, 11,371 handwritings 1,062 incunabula; Dir CHRISTIANE SCHMIEDEKNECHT.

Göttingen

Niedersächsische Staats- und Universitätsbibliothek Göttingen: Platz der Göttinger Sieben 1, 37073 Göttingen; tel. (551) 395212; fax (551) 395222; e-mail sekretariat@sub.uni-goettingen.de; internet www.sub.uni-goettingen.de; f. 1734; 4,275,494 vols, 51,830 electronic publs, 11,695 print periodicals, 27,741 electronic periodicals, 13,680 MSS, 3,109 incunabula, 313,166 map sheets, 1,522,058 microforms; Dir and Head Librarian Prof. Dr NORBERT LOSSAU.

Greifswald

Universitätsbibliothek (University Library): Felix-Hausdorff-Str. 10, 17489 Greifswald; tel. (3834) 861515; fax (3834) 861501; e-mail ub@uni-greifswald.de; internet www.ub.uni-greifswald.de; f. 1604; attached to Ernst Moritz Arndt Univ. of Greifswald; 3.2m. vols; Dir Dr PETER WOLFF; Librarian PETRA ZEPERNICK.

Halle am Saale

Bibliothek der Deutschen Akademie der Naturforscher Leopoldina: POB 110543, 06019 Halle/Saale; August-Bebel-Str. 50A, 06108 Halle/Saale; tel. (345) 4723947; fax (345) 4723949; e-mail biblio@leopoldina.org; internet www.leopoldina.org; f. 1731; 268,000 vols; Dir JOCHEN THAMM.

Universitäts- und Landesbibliothek Sachsen-Anhalt: August-Bebel-Str. 13/50, 06108 Halle/Saale; tel. (345) 5522000; fax (345) 5527140; e-mail direktion@bibliothek .uni-halle.de; internet bibliothek.uni-halle .de; f. 1696; 5.5m. vols, 15,500 periodicals, 8,600 online journals, 115,200 MSS and autographs; spec. collns incl. Middle East and North Africa, regional studies and history of Saxony-Anhalt; Ponikau's library; Library of the Deutsche Morgenländische Gesellschaft; 20 br. libraries; Dir Dr HEINER SCHNELLING; publs *Hercynia, Regionalbibliographie Sachsen-Anhalt* (online), *Schlechtendalia*.

Hamburg

Bibliothek des Max-Planck-Institut für Ausländisches und Internationales Privatrecht (Max-Planck Institute Library for Foreign and International Private Law): Mittelweg 187, 20148 Hamburg; tel. (40) 419000; fax (40) 41900288; e-mail knudsen@ mpipriv.de; internet www.mpipriv.mpg.de; f. 1926; 460,000 vols, 4,000 periodicals; Dir Prof. Dr HOLGER KNUDSEN.

Commerzbibliothek der Handelskammer Hamburg: Adolphspl. 1, 20457 Hamburg; tel. (40) 36138138; fax (40) 36138437; e-mail info@commerzbibliothek.de; internet www.commerzbibliothek.de; f. 1735 by the Commerzdeputation, later Hamburg Chamber of Commerce; historical map series; Hamburg newspapers 1721–1915; 180,000 vols on law, economics and social science; Head DAGMAR GROOTHUIS.

Deutsches Bibel-Archiv (German Bible Archive): Von Melle Park 6, 20146 Hamburg; tel. (40) 428384781; fax (40) 428384785; internet www.slm.uni-hamburg.de/ berichte97_00/bibel.html; f. 1931; biblical traditions in German literature and art; Bible translations; 8,000 vols; Dir Prof. Dr HEIMO REINITZER; publs *Abhandlungen und*

Vorträge, Bibel und deutsche Kultur, Naturalis historia bibliae, Vestigia bibliae.

Staats- und Universitätsbibliothek Hamburg 'Carl von Ossietzky': Von-Melle-Park 3, 20146 Hamburg; tel. (40) 428382233; fax (40) 428383352; e-mail auskunft@sub.uni-hamburg.de; internet www.sub.uni-hamburg.de; f. 1479; deposit library for literature published in Hamburg; spec. collns: political science, admin. science, literature on American Indians and Eskimos, sea and coastal fishing, literature on Portugal and Spain; 3,407,000 vols, 20,344 MSS (incl. 990 papyri); Dir Prof. Dr GABRIELE BEGER; publs *Kataloge der Handschriften, F. G. Klopstock: Werke und Briefe, Publikationen der Staats-und Universitätsbibliothek Hamburg.*

Staatsarchiv der Freien und Hansestadt Hamburg (State Archive of the Free and Hanseatic City of Hamburg): Kattunbleiche 19, 22041 Hamburg; tel. (40) 428313200; fax (40) 428313201; e-mail poststelle@ staatsarchiv.hamburg.de; internet www .hamburg.de/staatsarchiv/; f. 13th century; history of Hamburg; 150,000 books; Dir Dr UDO SCHÄFER; publs *Hamburgisches Urkundenbuch, Veröffentlichungen.*

Hanover

Gottfried Wilhelm Leibniz Bibliothek— Niedersächsische Landesbibliothek (Gottfried Wilhelm Leibniz Library): Waterloostr. 8, 30169 Hanover; tel. (511) 12670; fax (511) 1267202; e-mail information@gwlb.de; internet www.gwlb.de; f. 1665; colln of coats of arms and seals; Leibniz archive; 1,600,000 vols, 5,113 periodicals, 4,424 MSS, 80,000 autographs, 395 incunabula, several thousand maps, etchings, woodcuts; Dir Dr GEORG RUPPELT; Deputy Dir PETER MARMEIN.

Niedersächsisches Landesarchiv (Regional Archive of Lower Saxony): Am Archiv 1, 30169 Hanover; tel. (511) 1206601; fax (511) 1206639; e-mail poststelle@nla.niedersachsen.de; internet www.nla.niedersachsen.de; fmrly Hauptstaatsarchiv Hannover, 32,000 m shelfspace; Dir Dr BERND KAPPELHOFF.

Stadtbibliothek (City Library): Hildesheimer Str. 12, 30169 Hanover; tel. (511) 16842169; fax (511) 16846410; e-mail stadtbibliothek-hannover@hannover-stadt .de; internet www.stadtbibliothek-hannover .de; f. 1440; gen. information about the city and region; 17 br. libraries; 680,000 vols, 2,000 periodicals; Dir Dr CAROLA SCHELLE-WOLFF; Divisional Dir UWE NIETIEDT.

Technische Informationsbibliothek und Universitätsbibliothek Hannover (TIB/ UB) (German National Library of Science and Technology and University Library Hanover): POB 60 80, 30060 Hanover; Welfengarten 1B, 30167 Hanover; tel. (511) 7622268; fax (511) 7624076; e-mail auskunft@tib .uni-hannover.de; internet www.tib .uni-hannover.de; f. 1831; German research reports, patent specifications, standards; conf. proceedings; doctoral dissertations and American reports (microforms); spec. emphasis on technical and scientific literature in Eastern and E Asian languages; acts as German Nat. Library of Science and Technology; 8,900,000 vols, 21,000 current periodicals; Dir UWE ROSEMANN.

Heidelberg

Bibliothek des Max-Planck-Instituts für Ausländisches Öffentliches Recht und Völkerrecht (Library of the Max Planck Institute for Comparative Public Law and International Law): Im Neuenheimer Feld 535, 69120 Heidelberg; tel. (6221) 4821; fax (6221) 482288; e-mail library@mpil.de;

internet www.mpil.de/ww/de/pub/bibliothek .cfm; f. 1924; 601,000 vols, 2,680 periodicals; Dir Dr HARALD MÜLLER; Deputy Dir RUTH FUGGER.

Universitätsbibliothek (University Library): Plöck 107–109, 69117 Heidelberg; tel. (6221) 542380; fax (6221) 542623; e-mail ub@uni-hd.de; internet www.ub .uni-heidelberg.de; f. 1386; 3,000,000 vols, 6,600 MSS, 1,800 incunabula; Dir Dr VEIT PROBST; publs *Schriften der Universitätsbibliothek, Theke* (online).

Jena

Thüringer Universitäts- und Landesbibliothek Jena: POB, 07737 Jena; Bibliothekspl. 2, 07743 Jena; tel. (3641) 940000; fax (3641) 940002; e-mail thulb_auskunft@thulb.uni-jena.de; internet www.thulb.uni-jena.de; f. 1558; 171 mems; Dir Dr SABINE WEFERS; Deputy Dir GABOR KUHLES; Deputy Dir MICHAEL LÖRZER; publ. *Thüringen-Bibliographie* (online).

Karlsruhe

Badische Landesbibliothek: POB 1429, 76003 Karlsruhe; Erbprinzenstr. 15, 76133 Karlsruhe; tel. (721) 1752222; fax (721) 1752333; e-mail informationszentrum@ blb-karlsruhe.de; internet www .blb-karlsruhe.de; f. 1500; 2,394,352 vols, 18,258 current periodicals; 1,363 incunabula; Dir Dr JULIA DAME HILLER GAERTRINGEN; Deputy Dir Dr VOLKER WITTENAUER.

Bibliothek des Bundesgerichtshofs (Library of the Federal Court): Herrenstr. 45A, 76133 Karlsruhe; tel. (721) 1595000; fax (721) 1595612; e-mail bibliothek@bgh.bund .de; internet www.bundesgerichtshof.de; f. 1950; law library; 439,000 vols; Deputy Dir Dr MARCUS OBERT.

KIT-Bibliothek: POB 6920, 76049 Karlsruhe; tel. (721) 60843101; fax (721) 60844886; e-mail infodesk@bibliothek.kit .edu; internet www.bibliothek.kit.edu; f. 1840; 2,030,134 vols, 28,000 periodicals; Dir FRANK SCHOLZE; Librarian SABINE BENZ.

Landesarchiv Baden-Württemberg—Generallandesarchiv Karlsruhe: Nördliche Hildapromenade 2, 76133 Karlsruhe; tel. (721) 9262206; fax (721) 9262231; e-mail glakarlsruhe@la-bw.de; internet www .landesarchiv-bw.de/glak; f. 1803; 79,000 vols on Baden history, 130,000 documents, 42,000 MSS, 3.5m. report files; Dir Dr WOLFGANG ZIMMERMANN; Archivist Dr RAINER BRÜNING; publ. *Zeitschrift für die Geschichte des Oberrheins* (1 a year).

Kassel

Documenta Archiv: Untere Karlsstr. 4, 34117 Kassel; tel. (561) 7874022; fax (561) 7874028; e-mail documentaarchiv@ stadt-kassel.de; internet www .documentaarchiv.de; f. 1961; also a research institute; administers the Arnold Bode Estate and the Harry Kramer Estate; 30,000 monographs, 60,000 exhibition catalogues, 150 journals and magazines, 2,000 new acquisitions annually, 2,000 file archives, 250,000 newspaper clippings, 150,000 invitations, 25,000 slides, 3,000 video titles, 450 DVDs, 10,000 photographs, 1,000 Ektachromes, 2,000 artist portraits; Librarian PETRA HINCK; Librarian SABINE FRANKE.

Universitätsbibliothek Kassel–Landesbibliothek und Murhardsche Bibliothek der Stadt Kassel: 34111 Kassel; Diagonale 10, 34127 Kassel; tel. (561) 8042117; fax (561) 8042125; e-mail direktion@bibliothek .uni-kassel.de; internet www.ub.uni-kassel .de; f. 1580; 1,883,890 vols, 30,234 MSS, 26,228 musical scores, 17,936 maps, 20,047 autographs, 4,162 print and 21,299 electronic periodicals; 10 departmental libraries; Head Librarian Dr AXEL HALLE; Deputy Librarian Dr HELGE STEENWEG.

Kiel

Deutschen Zentralbibliothek für Wirtschaftswissenschaften (ZBW) (German National Library of Economics): Düsternbrooker Weg 120, 24105 Kiel; tel. (431) 8814555; fax (431) 8814520; e-mail info@zbw .eu; internet www.zbw.eu; f. 1919; attached to Leibniz Information Centre for Economics; 4,200,000 vols; Dir Prof. Dr KLAUS TOCHTERMANN; publs *Intereconomics—Review of European Economic Policy* (6 a year), *Wirtschaftsdienst—Journal for Economic Policy* (12 a year).

Schleswig-Holsteinische Landesbibliothek: Wall 47–51, 24103 Kiel; tel. (431) 6967733; fax (431) 6967711; e-mail landesbibliothek@shlb.de; internet www.shlb .de; f. 1895; culture, civilization, literature, musical scores and pictorial representations of topics concerning Schleswig-Holstein, editors of Schleswig-Holstein Bibliography and Dictionary of Schleswig-Holstein biography; spec. colln on chess; 280,000 vols and literary bequests of about 100 authors and scholars; Dir Dr JENS AHLERS.

Universitätsbibliothek Kiel (Kiel University Library): Leibnizstr. 9, 24118 Kiel; tel. (431) 8804701; fax (431) 1596; e-mail auskunft@ub.uni-kiel.de; internet www.ub .uni-kiel.de; f. 1665; 3 depts and 49 specialist libraries; spec. colln on Scandinavian languages, history and literature; 4,672,000 vols, 7,550 periodicals; Dir Dr ELSE MARIA WISCHERMANN.

Koblenz

Bundesarchiv (Federal Archives): POB 56064 Koblenz; Potsdamer Str. 1, 56075 Koblenz; tel. (261) 5050; fax (261) 505226; e-mail koblenz@bundesarchiv.de; internet www.bundesarchiv.de; f. 1952; central archives of the Fed. Republic; 2,157,426 vols; 306,518 m of records of Reich, Federal and GDR Govts, agencies, political parties, private asscns; colln of private papers; 1.0m. documentaries and newsreels (incl. 146,000 feature films), 12.4m. photographs; 87,370 posters, 1.2m. maps and technical drawings, 42,722 audio recordings, 9.3m. files of machine-readable data held at various sites throughout Germany; Pres. Prof. Dr HARTMUT WEBER.

Landesbibliothekszentrum Rheinland-Pfalz/Rheinische Landesbibliothek: Bahnhofpl. 14, 56068 Koblenz; tel. (261) 91500101; fax (261) 91500102; e-mail info@ lbz-rlp.de; internet www.lbz-rlp.de; f. 1987, became part of Landesbibliothekszentrum Rheinland-Pfalz 2004; 598,821 vols, 3,039 periodicals, vols on all subjects, with spec. references to N part of Rhineland-Palatinate; Central Educational Library of Rhineland-Palatinate; Dir Dr HELMUT FRÜHAUF; Deputy Dir GÜNTER PFLAUM.

Landeshauptarchiv Koblenz (Central State Archive): POB 20 10 47, 56010 Koblenz; tel. (261) 91290; fax (261) 9129112; e-mail post@landeshauptarchiv.de; internet www.landeshauptarchiv.de; f. 1832; attached to Rheinland-Pfälzischen Landesarchive; 48,260 vols, 47,900 linear m of archives; history of Rhineland Palatinate and fmr territories; Dir Dr ELSBETH ANDRE; publs *Blätter für deutsche Landesgeschichte* (1 a year), *Jahrbuch für westdeutsche Landesgeschichte* (1 a year).

Konstanz

Bibliothek der Universität Konstanz (University of Konstanz Library): Universitätsstr. 10, 78464 Konstanz; tel. (7531) 882871; fax (7531) 883082; e-mail information.ub@uni-konstanz.de; internet www.ub.uni-konstanz.de; f. 1965; 2,000,000 vols, 110,000 theses; Dir PETRA HAETSCHER; Vice-Dir OLIVER KOHL-FREY.

Landshut

Staatsarchiv Landshut: Burg Trausnitz, 84036 Landshut; tel. (871) 923280; fax (871) 92328-8; e-mail poststelle@stala.bayern.de; internet www.gda.bayern.de; f. 1753; 34,000 vols; Dir Dr M. RÜTH.

Leipzig

Leibniz-Institut für Länderkunde eV Geographische Zentralbibliothek und Archiv für Geographie (Central Library and Archive of the Leibniz Institute for Regional Geography): Schongauer Str. 9, 04328 Leipzig; tel. (341) 60055129; fax (341) 60055198; e-mail bibliothek@ifl-leipzig.de; internet www.ifl-leipzig.de; f. 1896; central geographical library containing 220,000 vols, spec. colln of maps and atlases of the 16th–18th centuries, geography archives; Dir Prof. Dr SEBASTIAN LENTZ; Librarian DOROTHEE ZICKWOLFF; publs *Beiträge zur Regionalen Geographie* (2 a year), *Berichte zur Deutschen Landeskunde* (4 a year), *Daten, Fakten, Literatur zur Geographie Europas* (1 a year), *Europa regional* (4 a year), *Forum IfL*.

Leipziger Städtische Bibliotheken: POB 100927, 04009 Leipzig; Nonnenstr. 44, 04229 Leipzig; tel. (341) 1235343; fax (341) 1235305; e-mail stadtbib@leipzig.de; internet www.leipzig.de/stadtbib; f. 1677; 1,065,182 vols; Head Dr ARNE ACKERMANN.

Stadtarchiv: 04092 Leipzig; Torgauer Str. 74, 04318 Leipzig; tel. (341) 24290; fax (341) 2429121; e-mail stadtarchiv@leipzig.de; internet www.leipzig.de/stadtarchiv; f. c. 1100; Dir Dr BEATE BERGER.

Universitätsbibliothek Leipzig (University Library): Beethovenstr. 6, 04107 Leipzig; tel. (341) 9730577; fax (341) 9730596; e-mail auskunft@ub.uni-leipzig.de; internet www .ub.uni-leipzig.de; f. 1543; Hirzel colln contains books and material by and about Johann Wolfgang von Goethe (1749–1832); 23 brs; 5.4m. vols, 7,200 periodicals; Dir Prof. Dr ULRICH JOHANNES SCHNEIDER; Deputy Dir CHARLOTTE BAUER.

Lübeck

Archiv der Hansestadt Lübeck: Mühlendamm 1–3, 23552 Lübeck; tel. (451) 1224152; fax (451) 1221517; e-mail archiv@luebeck.de; internet archiv.luebeck.de; f. 1298; municipal archives and documents of the churches, recognized public bodies, instns and private persons; 40,000 vols; Dir Dr JAN LOKERS; Deputy Dir Prof. Dr ROLF HAMMEL-KIESOW.

Bibliothek der Hansestadt Lübeck (Library of the Hanseatic City of Lübeck): Hundestr. 5–17, 23552 Lübeck; tel. (451) 1224114; fax (451) 1224112; e-mail stadtbibliothek@luebeck.de; internet www .stadtbibliothek.luebeck.de; f. 1616; 1.1m. vols, 3,676 maps, 45,391 vols of printed music, 11,922 MSS; 18,279 mems; Dir B. HATSCHER.

Ludwigsburg

Landesarchiv Baden-Württemberg—Staatsarchiv Ludwigsburg: Arsenalpl. 3, 71638 Ludwigsburg; tel. (7141) 186310; fax (7141) 186311; e-mail staludwigsburg@la-bw .de; internet www.landesarchiv-bw.de/stal; f. 1868; archives for the admin. dist. of Stuttgart (Nordwürttemberg); 36,000 m of deeds; 500,000 files from the time of the Third Reich and the time after the Second World War; 43,000 vols; Pres. Prof. Dr ROBERT KRETZSCHMAR; Dir Dr PETER MÜLLER; Deputy Dir Prof. Dr STEPHAN MOLITOR.

Magdeburg

Landeshauptarchiv Sachsen-Anhalt (State Archive of Saxony-Anhalt): POB 4023, 39105 Magdeburg; Hegelstr. 25, 39104 Magdeburg; tel. (391) 598060; fax (391) 59806600; e-mail poststelle@lha.mi .sachsen-anhalt.de; internet www .sachsen-anhalt.de; f. 1823; 103,000 vols; 48,000 m of records, 158,000 maps; archives of state public record offices; Dir Dr ULRIKE HÖROLDT.

Stadtbibliothek Magdeburg: Breiter Weg 109, 39104 Magdeburg; tel. (391) 5404880; fax (391) 5404803; e-mail stadtbibliothek@ magdeburg.de; internet www.magdeburg.de; f. 1525; 404,000 vols; Dir PETER PETSCH.

Mainz

Universitätsbibliothek Mainz (University Library of Mainz): Jakob-Welder-Weg 6, 55128 Mainz; tel. (6131) 3922633; fax (6131) 3923822; e-mail info@ub.uni-mainz.de; internet www.ub.uni-mainz.de; f. 1946; 4,000,000 vols, 814 MSS; Dir Dr A. BRANDTNER; Librarian MARCEL LILL.

Wissenschaftliche Stadtbibliothek: Rheinallee 3B, 55116 Mainz; tel. (6131) 122649; fax (6131) 123570; e-mail stb.direktion@stadt .mainz.de; internet www.bibliothek.mainz .de; f. 1477, as University Library, taken over by the City of Mainz in 1805; 646,680 vols, 2,364 incunabula, 1,332 MSS; Dir Dr STEPHAN FLIEDNER (acting); publs *Beiträge zur Geschichte der Stadt Mainz*, *Mainzer Zeitschrift*, *Veröffentlichungen der Bibliotheken der Stadt Mainz*.

Mannheim

Universitätsbibliothek Mannheim (Mannheim University Library): Schloss Schneckenhof West, 68131 Mannheim; tel. (621) 1812948; fax (621) 1812939; e-mail zbinfo@ bib.uni-mannheim.de; internet www.bib .uni-mannheim.de; 2.2m. vols; Dir CHRISTIAN BENZ; Deputy Librarian PER KNUDSEN.

Marbach am Neckar

Deutsches Literatur Archiv Marbach: Schillerhöhe 8–10, 71672 Marbach; tel. (7144) 8480; fax (7144) 848299; e-mail info@ dla-marbach.de; internet www.dla-marbach .de; f. 1895; German literature since 1750; 800,000 vols, large colln of autographs and documents, 1,100 legacies; Man. Dir Prof. Dr ULRICH RAULFF; publs *Jahrbuch der Deutschen Schillergesellschaft* (1 a year), *Marbacher Bibliothek* (1 a year), *Marbacher Katalog* (1 a year), *Marbacher Magazin* (4 a year).

Marburg

Deutsches Adelsarchiv (Germany Archive of the Nobility): Schwanallee 21, 35037 Marburg; tel. (6421) 26162; fax (6421) 27529; e-mail info@adelsarchiv.de; internet www.vdda.org; f. 1945; genealogy of German nobility; 20,000 vols; Dir Dr CHRISTOPH FRANKE; publ. *Genealogisches Handbuch des Adels*.

Forschungsbibliothek des Herder-Instituts: Gisonenweg 5–7, 35037 Marburg; tel. (6421) 184150; fax (6421) 184139; e-mail bibliothek@herder-institut.de; internet www .herder-institut.de; f. 1950; research library specializing in the history and culture of East Central Europe (Poland, Czech Republic, Slovakia, Estonia, Latvia, and Lithuania); 420,000 vols; Chief Librarian Dr JÜRGEN WARMBRUNN; Deputy Librarian Dr JAN LIPINSKY.

Hessisches Staatsarchiv Marburg: Friedrichspl. 15, 35037 Marburg; tel. (6421)

92500; fax (6421) 161125; e-mail postelle@stama.hessen.de; internet www .staatsarchiv-marburg.hessen.de; f. 1870; 150,097 books, 130,120 charts, 330,004 maps and plans, 66 km of records of the Electorate of Hesse-Kassel, the abbeys of Fulda, Hersfeld, the principality of Waldeck; Dir Dr ANDREAS HEDWIG; publs *Repertorien*, *Schriften*.

Universitätsbibliothek: POB 1920, 35008 Marburg; Wilhelm-Röpke-Str. 4, 35039 Marburg; tel. (6421) 2821319; fax (6421) 2826506; e-mail verwaltung@ub.uni-marburg.de; internet www.uni-marburg.de/bis; f. 1527; 2,057,493 vols, 716,860 theses, 3,020 MSS; Dir Dr H. NEUHAUSEN; Librarian ANDREAS SEIBEL.

Mönchengladbach

Bibliothek Wissenschaft und Weisheit (Library of Theology and Philosophy): Franziskanerstr. 30, 41063 Mönchengladbach; tel. (2161) 899135; fax (2161) 899171; e-mail herbert.schneider.ofm@gmx.de; f. 1929; attached to Zentralbibliothek der Kölnischen Franziskanerprovinz (fmrly Hochsculbibliothek); 70,000 vols; Dir Dr P. HERBERT SCHNEIDER.

Stadtbibliothek (City Library): Blücherstr. 6, 41061 Mönchengladbach; tel. (2161) 256345; fax (2161) 256369; e-mail stadtbibliothek@moenchengladbach.de; internet www.stadtbibliothek-mg.de; f. 1904; 440,443 vols; special colln on social and political questions, library of the 'Volksverein für das katholische Deutschland 1890–1933'; Head BRIGITTE BEHRENDT; Head GUIDO WEYER.

Munich

Bayerische Staatsbibliothek: 80328 Munich; Ludwigstr. 16, 80539 Munich; tel. (89) 286380; fax (89) 286382200; e-mail direktion@bsb-muenchen.de; internet www .bsb-muenchen.de; f. 1558; deposit library for Bavaria; 9,530,000 vols, 1.2m. microforms, 93,000 MSS, 55,000 current periodicals, 400,000 maps, 360,000 scores, 88,000 audiovisual items, 2.2m. single sheets and photographs; Dir-Gen. Dr ROLF GRIEBEL; Deputy Dir Dr KLAUS CEYNOWA; publs *Bibliotheksforum Bayern* (4 a year), *Bibliotheksmagazin* (3 a year).

Bayerisches Hauptstaatsarchiv (Bavarian State Archives): POB 22 11 52, 80501 Munich; Schönfeldstr. 5–11, 80539 Munich; tel. (89) 286382596; fax (89) 286382954; e-mail poststelle@bayhsta.bayern.de; internet www.gda.bayern.de; f. 13th century, reorganized 1978; comprises 5 departments: (1) Ältere Bestände: 268,500 charters, 589,900 documents and vols, 24,000 maps and plans; (2) Neuere Bestände (since 19th century): 4,100 charters, 1,010,700 documents, 174,900 maps and plans; (3) Geheimes Hausarchiv: 10,500 charters, 27,300 documents and vols, 9,900 pictures; (4) Kriegsarchiv: 477,900 documents and vols, 130,300 maps and plans, 99,700 pictures; (5) Nachlässe und Sammlungen: collections of private papers, publications, posters, pictures, etc.; Dir Dr GERHARD HETZER; publs *Archivalische Zeitschrift*, *Archive in Bayern*, *Bayerische Archivinventare*, *Nachrichten aus den Staatlichen Archiven Bayerns*.

Bibliothek des Deutschen Museums: Museumsinsel 1, 80538 Munich; tel. (89) 2179224; fax (89) 2179262; e-mail bibliothek@deutsches-museum.de; internet www.deutsches-museum.de/bibliothek; f. 1903; research library for history of science and technology; 900,000 vols; Dir Dr HELMUT HILZ.

Deutsches Bucharchiv München (Institut für Buchwissenschaften): Bibliothek und Dokumentationsstelle, Literaturhaus München, Salvatorpl. 1, 80333 Munich; tel. (89) 2919510; fax (89) 29195195; e-mail kontakt@bucharchiv.de; internet www .bucharchiv.de; f. 1948; documentation, scientific and technical information about books and periodicals; special library for book research; 30,000 vols, 180 periodicals; Dir Prof. Dr LUDWIG DELP.

Deutsches Patent- und Markenamt (German Patent and Trademark Office): Abt. Informationsdienste (Bibliothek), 80297 Munich; Zweibrückenstr. 12, 80331 Munich; tel. (89) 21950; fax (89) 21952221; e-mail info@dpma.de; internet www.dpma.de; f. 1877; industrial property protection; 1,116,000 vols, 37m. patent specifications; Pres. CORNELIA RUDLOFF-SCHÄFFER; Vice-Pres. GÜNTHER SCHMITZ.

Evangelischer Presseverband für Bayern eV (Evangelical Press Society of Bavaria): Birkerstr. 22, 80636 Munich; tel. (89) 121720; fax (89) 12172138; e-mail redaktion@epv.de; internet www.epv.de; f. 1963; Pres. Dr ROLAND GERTZ.

Münchner Stadtbibliothek (City Library of Munich): Rosenheimer Str. 5, 81667 Munich; tel. (89) 480983313; fax (89) 480983233; e-mail stb.zentraledienste .sekretariat.kult@muenchen.de; internet www.muenchner-stadtbibliothek.de; f. 1843; 3m. vols; Dir Dr WERNER SCHNEIDER.

Staatsarchiv (State Archive): Schönfeldstr. 3, 80539 Munich; tel. (89) 286382525; fax (89) 286382526; e-mail poststelle@stam.bayern .de; internet www.gda.bayern.de; f. 1814; 11,295,125 files (records), 9,157 documents (charts), 30,455 maps and plans, 25,000 vols (library); Dir Dr PETER FLEISCHMANN.

Stadtarchiv (City Archives): Winzererstr. 68, 80797 Munich; tel. (89) 2330308; fax (89) 23330830; e-mail stadtarchiv@muenchen.de; internet www.muenchen.de/stadtarchiv; f. 1520; 65,000 vols, 78,000 documents, 16m. deeds, 22,000 maps and plans, 1,200,000 photos and postcards, 3,050 soundtracks, 1,500 films, 26,629 posters; Dir Dr MICHAEL STEPHAN; Deputy Dir HANS-JOACHIM HECKER.

Universitätsbibliothek: Geschwister-Scholl-Pl. 1, 80539 Munich; tel. (89) 21802428; e-mail direktion@ub .uni-muenchen.de; internet www.ub .uni-muenchen.de; f. 1473; 6,800,000 vols, 3,300 MSS, incl. 650 from the Middle Ages, 179 estates, containing about 55,000 autographs, 475,000 old books published before 1900, rare book colln with around 13,000 vols, ex libris colln, broadsheet and handbill collns; Dir Dr KLAUS-RAINER BRINTZINGER.

Universitätsbibliothek der Technischen Universität (Technical University Library): Arcisstr. 21, 80333 Munich; tel. (89) 28928601; fax (89) 28928622; e-mail infocenter@ub.tum.de; internet www.ub.tum .de; f. 1868; 1,859,075 vols; Dir Dr REINER KALLENBORN.

Münster

Landesarchiv Nordrhein-Westfalen Abteilung Westfalen: Bohlweg 2, 48147 Münster; tel. (251) 48850; fax (251) 4885100; e-mail westfalen@lav.nrw.de; internet www.archive.nrw.de; f. 1829 as Provinzialarchiv for Westphalia, present title since 2008; 30,000 m of documents and 100,000 charters, from 9th century to the present; 180,000 vols; Pres. Prof. Dr WILFRIED REININGHAUS; Dir Dr MECHTHILD BLACK-VELTRUP.

LWL-Archivamt für Westfalen Landschaftsverband Westfalen-Lippe: Jahnstr. 26, 48133 Münster; tel. (251) 5913890; fax (251) 591269; e-mail lwl-archivamt@lwl.org; internet www .lwl-archivamt.de; f. 1927; non-state archives; training of archivists; 30,000 vols; Dir Dr MARCUS STUMPF; publs *Inventare der nichtstaatlichen Archive Westfalens*, *Westfälische Quellen und Archivpublikationen*, *Archivpflege in Westfalen-Lippe* (Journal, 2 a year), *Texte und Untersuchungen zur Archivpflege*.

Universitäts- und Landesbibliothek: POB 8029, 48043 Münster; Krummer Timpen 3, 48143 Münster; tel. (251) 8324021; fax (251) 8328398; e-mail sekretariat.ulb@ uni-muenster.de; internet www.ulb .uni-muenster.de; f. 1588, refounded 1902; attached to Univ. of Münster; 2,334,800 vols incl. 305,660 theses, 821 incunabula, 1,406 MSS, 10,000 current periodicals, 3,214 e-journals; Dir Dr BEATE TRÖGER.

Nuremberg

Bibliothek des Germanischen Nationalmuseum: POB 119580, 90105 Nuremberg; Kornmarkt 1, 90402 Nuremberg; tel. (911) 1331151; fax (911) 1331351; e-mail bibliothek@gnm.de; internet www.gnm.de; f. 1852; arts, history of civilization, German-speaking regions; special colln of art-history works since AD 800; 650,000 vols, 3,380 MSS, 3,000 16th-century prints, 1,708 current periodicals; Dir Dr EBERHARD SLENCZKA; Librarian Dr JOHANNES POMMERANZ; publs *Anzeiger des Germanischen Nationalmuseums* (1 a year), *Schrifttum zur Deutschen Kunst* (1 a year).

Landeskirchliches Archiv der Evangelisch-Lutherischen Kirche in Bayern: Veilhofstr. 28, 90489 Nuremberg; tel. (911) 588690; fax (911) 5886969; e-mail elkb@ elkb.de; internet www.archiv-elkb.de; f. 1931; 170,000 vol, 12,000 m of documents; 23,000 microfiches; Dir Dr ANDREA SCHWARZ; Archivrat Dr JÜRGEN KÖNIG.

Staatsarchiv (State Archive): Archivstr. 17, 90408 Nuremberg; tel. (911) 935190; fax (911) 9351999; e-mail poststelle@stanu .bayern.de; f. 1806; archives of middle Franconia since the Middle Ages; incl. Nuremberg trial documents; 49,000 vols; Dir Dr RECHTER.

Stadtarchiv Nürnberg: Marientorgraben 8, 90402 Nuremberg; tel. (911) 2312770; fax (911) 2314091; e-mail stadtarchiv@stadt .nuernberg.de; internet www.stadtarchiv .nuernberg.de; f. 1865; reference library of 45,000 vols; Dir Dr MICHAEL DIEFENBACHER; Librarian WALTER GEBHARDT; publs *Ausstellungskataloge*, *Nürnberger Werkstücke zur Stadt- und Landesgeschichte*, *Quellen und Forschungen zur Geschichte und Kultur der Stadt Nürnberg*.

Stadtbibliothek im Bildungscampus Nürnberg: Egidienpl. 23, 90403 Nürnberg; tel. (911) 2312790; fax (911) 2315476; e-mail stadtbibliothek-nuernberg@stadt.nuernberg .de; internet www.stadtbibliothek.nuernberg .de; f. 1370; 90,000 vols, 3,132 MSS, 2,140 incunabula; Dir ELISABETH STRÄTER.

Universitätsbibliothek Erlangen-Nürnberg, Wirtschafts- und Sozialwissenschaftliche Zweigbibliothek (University Library of Erlangen-Nuremberg, Economics and Social Studies Branch): Lange Gasse 20, 90403 Nuremberg; tel. (911) 5302830; fax (911) 5302852; e-mail bibliothek@wiso.uni-erlangen.de; internet www.ub.uni-erlangen.de; f. 1919; 243,000 vols, 1,390 current periodicals; Dir JOACHIM HENNECKE.

Offenbach am Main

Deutscher Wetterdienst Deutsche Meteorologische Bibliothek (German

Meteorological Service National Meteorological Library): POB 100465, Frankfurter Str. 135, 63067 Offenbach am Main; tel. (69) 80624276; fax (69) 80624123; e-mail bibliothek@dwd.de; internet www.dwd.de/bibliothek; f. 1847; nat. library for meteorology and climatology, inter-library loans; 180,000 vols, 20 incunabula, 14,000 pre-1900, 1000 current periodicals; Chief Librarian BRITTA BOLZMANN.

Oldenburg

Landesbibliothek: Pferdemarkt 15, POB 3480, 26024 Oldenburg; tel. (441) 7992800; fax (441) 7992865; e-mail lbo@lb-oldenburg.de; internet www.lb-oldenburg.de; f. 1792; regional library; 818,676 vols, 94,916 microforms, 1,121 MSS; Dir C. ROEDER; Librarian Dr K.-P. MÜLLER; Librarian M. KLINKOW; Librarian Dr R. FIETZ; publ. *Schriften.*

Niedersächsisches Staatsarchiv in Oldenburg (Archive of Lower Saxony in Oldenburg): Damm 43, 26135 Oldenburg; tel. (441) 9244100; fax (441) 9244292; e-mail oldenburg@nla.niedersachsen.de; internet www.staatsarchive.niedersachsen.de; f. before 1615; public record office for the fmr dist. of Oldenburg; record repository with 13,000 m of files; contributes to *Veröffentlichungen der Niedersächsischen Archivverwaltung;* 66,000 vols; Dir Prof. Dr GERD STEINWASCHER; Librarian HANNELORE KLÖCKER.

Osnabrück

Niedersächsisches Landesarchiv—Staatsarchiv Osnabrück (State Archive of Lower Saxony): Schloßstr. 29, 49074 Osnabrück; tel. (541) 331620; fax (541) 3316262; e-mail osnabrueck@nla.niedersachsen.de; internet www.staatsarchive.niedersachsen.de; f. 1869; 82,000 vols; Dir Dr BIRGIT KEHNE.

Passau

Staatliche Bibliothek: Michaeligasse 11, 94032 Passau; tel. (851) 7564400; fax (851) 75644027; e-mail sbp_info@staatliche-bibliothek-passau.de; internet www.staatliche-bibliothek-passau.de; f. 1612 as Jesuit library, refounded 1803 as nat. library; spec. collns: philosophy, theology, regional history and literature, emblematic, Jesuitica; 326,000 vols, 151 MSS, 322 incunabula; Dir Dr MARKUS WENNERHOLD.

Universitätsbibliothek (University Library): 94030 Passau; Innstr. 29, 94032 Passau; tel. (851) 5091630; fax (851) 5091602; e-mail ubinfo@uni-passau.de; internet www.ub.uni-passau.de; f. 1976; attached to Universität Passau; 2m. vols, 88,000 theses; Dir Dr STEFFEN WAWRA.

Potsdam

Brandenburgisches Landeshauptarchiv in Potsdam (Brandenburg State Central Archive): POB 60 04 49, 14404 Potsdam; Zum Windmühlenberg, 14469 Potsdam; tel. (331) 56740; fax (331) 5674212; e-mail poststelle@blha.brandenburg.de; internet www.blha.de; f. 1949; brs at Lübben (Spreewald) and Frankfurt an der Oder; 109,000 vols, 46,000 linear m of files; Dir Dr KLAUS NEITMANN; publs *Brandenburgische Archive* (1 a year), *Quellen, Findbücher und Inventare des Brandenburgischen Landeshauptarchivs, Veröffentlichungen des Brandenburgischen Landeshauptarchivs.*

Stadt- und Landesbibliothek Potsdam: Am Kanal 47, 14467 Potsdam; tel. (331) 2896600; fax (331) 2896402; e-mail slb@bibliothek.potsdam.de; internet www.bibliothek.potsdam.de; f. 1969; Brandenburg colln, Gottfried Benn colln; presently located at Friedrich-Ebert-Str. 4 due to renovation at

main site; 585,000 vols; Dir MARION MATTEKAT.

Regensburg

Bischöfliche Zentralbibliothek (Central Library of the Diocese of Regensburg): St Petersweg 11–13, 93047 Regensburg; tel. (941) 5972513; fax (941) 5972521; e-mail bibliothek@bistum-regensburg.de; internet www.bistum-regensburg.de; f. 1972; incl. the library of St Jacob's Irish monastery and Proske's music library; 309,578 vols, 419 journals, with spec. collns on ascetics and sacred music; Dir PAUL MAI; Librarian WEINBERGER ROSEMARIE.

Staatliche Bibliothek Regensburg: Gesandtenstr. 13, 93047 Regensburg; tel. (941) 6308060; fax (941) 63080628; e-mail info@staatliche-bibliothek-regensburg.de; internet www.staatliche-bibliothek-regensburg.de; f. 1816; spec. colln of regional history; 350,000 vols, 13,264 maps, 16,302 microforms; Dir Dr BERNHARD LUEBBERS.

Universitätsbibliothek Regensburg (University Library of Regensburg): 93042 Regensburg; Universitätsstr. 31, 93053 Regensburg; tel. (941) 9433901; fax (941) 9433285; e-mail rafael.ball@bibliothek.uni-regensburg.de; internet www.bibliothek.uni-regensburg.de; f. 1964; 3,600,000 vols, 6,824 print periodicals, 21,847 electronic journals, 376 databases; all fields of science except technology and agriculture; spec. holdings: Library of the Regensburg Botanical Soc., Prince Thurn and Taxis Court Library and Central Archive, Regensburg Portrait Gallery, Archive of Historical Radio Commercials; Dir Dr RAFAEL BALL.

Rostock

Universitätsbibliothek: 18051 Rostock; Albert-Einstein-Str. 6, 18059 Rostock; tel. (381) 4988601; fax (381) 4988602; e-mail direktion.ub@uni-rostock.de; internet www.uni-rostock.de/ub; f. 1569; attached to Univ. of Rostock; 2,300,000 vols, 330,000 theses, 1,729 print periodicals, 24,039 e-periodicals, 3,350 MSS, 6,085,000 patents, 49,500 standards, 337 databases; Dir RENATE BÄHKER (acting).

Saarbrücken

Landesarchiv Saarbrücken (State Archive of Saarbrücken): Dudweilerstr. 1, 66133 Saarbrücken; tel. (681) 50100; fax (681) 5011933; e-mail landesarchiv@landesarchiv.saarland.de; internet www.landesarchiv.saarland.de; f. 1948; 14,000 m of archives concerning the Saar, 25,000 vols; Dir Dr LUDWIG LINSMAYER; 170 official publs.

Saarländische Universitäts- und Landesbibliothek (University and State Library of the Saarland): POB 15 11 41, 66041 Saarbrücken; tel. (681) 3022070; fax (681) 3022796; e-mail sulb@sulb.uni-saarland.de; internet www.sulb.uni-saarland.de; Medical Library in Homburg, Saar; f. 1950; 1,705,000 vols incl. 375,000 theses; Dir Dr BERND HAGENAU; Librarian CHRISTEL BAUER-LANGGUTH.

Schleswig

Landesarchiv Schleswig-Holstein: Prinzenpalais, 24837 Schleswig; tel. (4621) 861800; fax (4621) 861801; e-mail landesarchiv@la.landsh.de; internet www.schleswig-holstein.de/la; f. 1870; 35,000 m of documents since 1059; 450,000 m of documentary film on Schleswig-Holstein; 137,000 vols; Dir Prof. Dr RAINER HERING.

Schwerin im Meckl

Landesbibliothek Mecklenburg-Vorpommern: Johannes-Stelling-Str. 29,

19053 Schwerin; tel. (385) 58879210; fax (385) 58879224; e-mail lb@lbmv.de; internet www.lbmv.de; f. 1779; 650,000 vols; Dir Dr FRANK PILLE.

Sigmaringen

Landesarchiv Baden-Württemberg–Abteilung Staatsarchiv Sigmaringen: POB 1638, 72486 Sigmaringen; Karlstr. 1–3, 72488 Sigmaringen; tel. (7571) 101551; fax (7571) 101552; e-mail stasigmaringen@la-bw.de; internet www.landesarchiv-bw.de/stas; f. 1865; archives of Regierungsbezirk Tübingen and Sigmaringen municipal archive; family archives of the princes of Hohenzollern, barons of Stauffenberg, etc.; 19,500 m of archives since 11th century; 66,000 vols; Co-Dir Dr FRANZ-JOSEF ZIWES; Co-Dir Dr VOLKER TRUGENBERGER.

Speyer

Landesarchiv: Otto-Mayer-Str. 9, 67346 Speyer; tel. (6232) 91920; fax (6232) 9192100; e-mail bibliothek@landesarchiv-speyer.de; internet www.landeshauptarchiv.de/speyer; f. 1817; historical archives of the Palatinate (878–1798), of the French admin. until 1815 and the Bavarian admin. until 1945; current accessions of admins in the Palatinate and Rheinhesse; colln of maps; 59,173 vols; Dir Dr WALTER RUMMEL; Librarian SCHMIDT.

Landesbibliothekszentrum/Pfälzische Landesbibliothek (Regional Library of Palatinate): Otto-Mayer-Str. 9, 67343 Speyer; tel. (6232) 9006224; fax (6232) 9006200; e-mail info.plb@lbz-rlp.de; internet www.lbz-rlp.de; f. 1921, part of the Landesbibliothekszentrum Rheinland-Pfalz 2004; 1,053,975 vols on all subjects, with spec. reference to the Palatinate and the Saar, 4,177 periodicals, incl. library of the Historischer Verein der Pfalz; Dir Dr HELMUT FRÜHAUF; Man. UTE BAHRS.

Stuttgart

Bibliothek der Staatlichen Hochschule für Musik und Darstellende Kunst: Urbanstr. 25, 70182 Stuttgart; tel. (711) 2124664; fax (711) 2124663; e-mail bibliothek@mh-stuttgart.de; internet www.mh-stuttgart.de; f. 1857; 21,373 vols, 88,475 musical scores, 3,623 records, 9,802 CDs, 576 DVDs; Chief Librarian CLAUDIA NIEBEL.

Bibliothek des Instituts für Auslandsbeziehungen (Institute for Foreign Relations, Library): POB 10 24 63, 70020 Stuttgart; Charlottenpl. 17, 70173 Stuttgart; tel. (711) 2225147; fax (711) 2225131; e-mail bibliothek@ifa.de; internet cms.ifa.de/info/bibliothek; f. 1917; 415,000 vols, 2,300 current periodicals, 11,000 microfilms; Head GUDRUN CZEKALLA; publ. *KulturAustausch* (online).

Bibliothek für Zeitgeschichte in der Württembergischen Landesbibliothek: Konrad Adenauer Str. 8, 70173 Stuttgart; tel. (711) 2124516; fax (711) 2124517; e-mail bfz@wlb-stuttgart.de; internet www.wlb-stuttgart.de/sammlungen/bibliothek--fuer-zeitgeschichte; f. 1915; contemporary history, political sciences, military sciences, esp. concerning First and Second World Wars, and other conflicts since the beginning of 20th century; 380,000 vols, 450 current periodicals, and special collns (photographs, maps, leaflets, posters, microfiches, etc.); Dir Prof. Dr GERHARD HIRSCHFELD; Vice-Dir Dr HANS-CHRISTIAN PUST; publs *Schriften der Bibliothek für Zeitgeschichte–Neue Folge, Stuttgarter Vorträge zur Zeitgeschichte.*

Fraunhofer-Informationszentrum Raum und Bau (IRB) (Fraunhofer Information Centre for Planning and Building): POB 80 04 69, 70504 Stuttgart; Nobelstr. 12,

70569 Stuttgart; tel. (711) 9702500; fax (711) 9702508; internet www.irb.fraunhofer.de; f. 1941; information centre for architecture and town and regional planning in Germany; 117,200 vols and 5,600 research reports, standards, test certificates and licences; Dir THOMAS H. MORSZECK; publs *ARCONIS Wissen zum Planen und Bauen und zum Baumarkt* (4 a year), *Kurzberichte aus der Bauforschung* (6 a year).

Hauptstaatsarchiv Stuttgart: Konrad-Adenauer-Str. 4, 70173 Stuttgart; tel. (711) 2124335; fax (711) 2124360; e-mail hstastuttgart@la-bw.de; internet www .landesarchiv-bw.de/hstas; history and regional studies of SW Germany, with particular reference to Württemberg and Baden-Württemberg since 9th century; archives of 107,000 charters, 18,000 m of files and vols, 40,000 maps and plans, 100,000 seals and arms; Dir Dr NICOLE BICKHOFF; Deputy Dir Dr ALBRECHT ERNST.

Rathausbücherei der Landeshauptstadt Stuttgart (Town Hall Library of the State Capital of Stuttgart): Marktpl. 1, 70173 Stuttgart; tel. (711) 2163301; fax (711) 2163506; internet www.stuttgart.de/ stadtbuecherei/rathausbuecherei; f. archives 1730; history of Stuttgart and Württemberg, legal history, public admin.; 128,483 vols; spec. collns incl. first editions published in Stuttgart during 18th–19th centuries; Dir GABY VOLLMER.

Universitätsbibliothek (University Library): POB 104941, 70043 Stuttgart; Holzgartenstr. 16, 70174 Stuttgart; tel. (711) 68582222; fax (711) 68583502; e-mail sekretariat@ub.uni-stuttgart.de; internet www.ub.uni-stuttgart.de; f. 1829; attached to Univ. of Stuttgart; 1,276,849 books, incl. 215,000 theses, 2,017 print and 25,757 electronic periodicals, 190,000 standards and 110,000 micromaterials, 301,368 electronic documents; Dir WERNER STEPHAN; publs *Dissertationen und Hochschulschriften der Universität Stuttgart* (2 a year), *Reden und Aufsätze der Universität Stuttgart* (irregular).

Universitätsbibliothek Hohenheim: Garbenstr. 15, 70599 Stuttgart; tel. (711) 45922096; fax (711) 45923262; e-mail ubmail@uni-hohenheim.de; internet ub .uni-hohenheim.de; f. 1818; 500,000 vols; agriculture, sciences, economics; Dir KARL-WILHELM HORSTMANN; Asst Dir Dr CHRISTINE BORKOWSKI.

Württembergische Landesbibliothek (State Library of Württemberg): POB 10 54 41, 70047 Stuttgart; Konrad Adenauerstr. 8, 70173 Stuttgart; tel. (711) 2124454; fax (711) 2124422; e-mail direktion@wlb-stuttgart.de; internet www.wlb-stuttgart.de; f. 1765; 5,581,971 vols, 7,084 incunabula; large colln of old Bibles; 15,407 MSS; Hölderlin archive and Stefan George archive; music and ballet colln; Dir Dr HANNSJÖRG KOWARK; Deputy Dir MARTINA LÜLL.

Trier

Bibliothek des Priesterseminars Trier: POB 1330, 54203 Trier; Jesuitenstr. 13, 54290 Trier; tel. (651) 9484141; fax (651) 9484181; e-mail bibliothek@bps-trier.de; internet www.bps-trier.de; f. 1805; 470,582 vols on philosophy and theology, 543 theological MSS, and 122 incunabula; Librarian REINHOLD BOHLEN; Librarian PATRICK TRAUTMANN.

Stadtbibliothek und Stadtarchiv Trier (Municipal Library and Archives of Trier): Weberbach 25, 54290 Trier; tel. (651) 7181429 (library); tel. (651) 7184420 (archives); fax (651) 7181428 (library); fax 7184428 (archives); e-mail stadtbibliothek@ trier.de (library); e-mail stadtarchiv@trier.de (archives); internet cms.trier.de/weberbach; f. Library 1804; Library: developed from the fmr Jesuit Library (f. 1560) and Univ. Library (f. 1722); contains considerable parts of the libraries of the dissolved religious instns of the region of Trier (since 1802); contains 2,800 MSS and about 3,000 incunabula; 422,000 younger media; scientific library; colln incl. a Gutenberg Bible, and a page of the *Codex Egberti*; UNESCO world heritage site; f. Archive 1894; Archives: inc. into the library; contains royal and papal charters since the 8th century for the above named religious instns and (since 1149) for the town, 5 km of younger archive material (originating from the town, the religious instns and from the Counts of Kesselstatt); collns: portraits, maps, photographs; Chief Librarian Prof. Dr MICHAEL EMBACH; Chief Archivist Dr REINER NOLDEN; publs *Ausstellungskataloge Trierer Bibliotheken, Kurtrierisches Jahrbuch, Landeskundliche Vierteljahrsblätter, Ortschroniken des Trierer Landes, Rheinland-pfälzische Bibliographie*.

Universitätsbibliothek: Universitätsring 15, 54296 Trier; tel. (651) 2012420; fax (651) 2013977; e-mail auskunft@uni-trier .de; internet www.ub.uni-trier.de; f. 1970; attached to Univ. of Trier; open to the public; colln of 699 papyri, colln of Chinese and Japanese woodcuts.; 2,031,804 vols; Dir Dr HILDEGARD MÜLLER.

Tübingen

Universitätsbibliothek Tübingen: POB 2620, 72016 Tübingen; Wilhelmstr 32, 72074 Tübingen; tel. (7071) 2972846; fax (7071) 293123; e-mail sekretariat@ub .uni-tuebingen.de; internet www.ub .uni-tuebingen.de; f. in the last quarter of 15th century; central library of Tübingen Univ.; archive and lending library; platforms and support for e-Learning and online publs for mems of the univ.; 3,672,271 vols, journals, microfilms and microfiches, 2,800,000 vols and journals in faculty libraries, 2,148 incunabula, 8,863 MSS; Dir Dr MARIANNE DÖRR; Deputy Dir Dr EBERHARD PIETZSCH; publ. *Index theologicus (Ixtheo) Zeitschrifteninhaltsdienst Theologie*.

Ulm

Stadtbibliothek Ulm (City Library of Ulm): POB, 89070 Ulm; Vestgasse 1, 89073 Ulm; tel. (731) 1614140; fax (731) 1614103; e-mail stadtbibliothek@ulm.de; internet www .stadtbibliothek.ulm.de; f. 1516; 559,208 vols, 518 current periodicals; spec. collns: the arts, regional history; Dir JÜRGEN LANGE; Deputy Dir ALEXANDER ROSENSTOCK.

Weimar

Herzogin Anna Amalia Bibliothek: Pl. der Demokratie 1, 99423 Weimar; tel. (3643) 545200; fax (3643) 545220; e-mail haab@ klassik-stiftung.de; internet www .klassik-stiftung.de/einrichtungen/herzogin-anna-amalia-bibliothek; f. 1691; history of literature, art and music; special collns: German literature of the Classical Period (1750–1850), Faust, Liszt, Nietzsche, Shakespeare; 50,000 vols destroyed by fire September 2004; reopened in 2007; 62,000 destroyed books to be restored by 2015; 1,000,000 vols; Dir Dr MICHAEL KNOCHE; publ. *Internationale Bibliographie zur deutschen Klassik* (online).

Thüringisches Hauptstaatsarchiv Weimar (Central State Archive of Thuringia in Weimar): POB 2726, 99408 Weimar; Marstallstr. 2, 99423 Weimar; tel. (3643) 8700; fax (3643) 870100; e-mail weimar@ staatsarchive.thueringen.de; internet www .thueringen.de/de/staatsarchive; f. 1547; Dir Dr BERNHARD POST.

Wiesbaden

Bibliothek des Statistischen Bundesamtes (Library of the Federal Statistical Office): 65180 Wiesbaden; Gustav-Stresemann-Ring 11, 65180 Wiesbaden; tel. (611) 754573; fax (611) 754433; e-mail bibliothek@ destatis.de; internet www.destatis.de; f. 1948; colln of statistical records, esp. on the economic and demographic devt of all countries; 500,000 vols, 1,000 journals; Head of Library HARTMUT RAHM; Librarian GÜNTER HINKES.

Hessisches Hauptstaatsarchiv Wiesbaden (Hesse Main State Archive): Mosbacher Str. 55, 65187 Wiesbaden; tel. (611) 8810; fax (611) 881145; e-mail poststelle@hhstaw .hessen.de; internet www.hauptstaatsarchiv .hessen.de; f. 1963; regional documents since 10th century; Dir Dr KLAUS EILER; publ. *Nassauische Annalen* (1 a year).

Hochschul- und Landesbibliothek RheinMain Landesbibliothek Wiesbaden (State Library of Hesse in Wiesbaden): Rheinstr. 55–57, 65185 Wiesbaden; tel. (611) 94951820; fax (611) 94951809; e-mail information-landesbibliothek@hs-rm.de; internet www.hlb-wiesbaden.de; f. 1813; 850,000 vols, 4,500 current periodicals, 300 MSS and 400 incunabula; Dir (vacant).

Wolfenbüttel

Herzog August Bibliothek: POB 1364, 38299 Wolfenbüttel; Lessingplatz 1, 38304 Wolfenbüttel; tel. (5331) 8080; fax (5331) 808173; e-mail auskunft@hab.de; internet www.hab.de; f. 1572; cultural history from the Middle Ages to the Enlightenment; 902,711 vols, 12,296 manuscripts, 3,500 incunabula, 3,600 artists' books; Dir Prof. Dr HELWIG SCHMIDT-GLINTZER; publs *Ausstellungskataloge, Kleine Schriften, Repertorien zur Erforschung der frühen Neuzeit, Wolfenbütteler Abhandlungen zur Renaissance-Forschung, Wolfenbütteler Arbeiten zur Barockforschung, Wolfenbütteler Barocknachrichten, Wolfenbütteler Beiträge, Wolfenbütteler Bibliotheks-Informationen, Wolfenbütteler Forschungen, Wolfenbütteler Hefte, Wolfenbütteler Mittelalter-Studien, Wolfenbütteler Notizen zur Buchgeschichte, Wolfenbütteler Renaissance-Mitteilungen, Wolfenbütteler Schriften zur Geschichte des Buchwesens*.

Niedersächsisches Staatsarchiv (State Archive of Lower Saxony): Forstweg 2, 38302 Wolfenbüttel; tel. (5331) 9350; fax (5331) 935211; e-mail wolfenbuettel@nla .niedersachsen.de; internet www .staatsarchive.niedersachsen.de; f. 16th century; contains documents and records of the province of Brunswick; 60,000 vols; Dir Dr HORST-RÜDIGER JARCK; Dir Dr BRAGE BEI DER WIEDEN.

Worms

Stadtarchiv im Raschi Haus: Hintere Judengasse 6, 67547 Worms; tel. (6241) 8534700; fax (6241) 8534799; e-mail stadtarchiv@worms.de; internet www .stadtarchiv.worms.de; Judaic museum; colln of records, documents and maps; Head Archivist Dr GEROLD BOENNEN.

Stadtbibliothek (City Library): Marktpl. 10, 67547 Worms; tel. (6241) 8534209; fax (6241) 8534299; e-mail stadtbibliothek@ worms.de; internet www .stadtbibliothek-worms.de; f. 1881; 324,000 vols, 165 incunabula; spec. collns on Luther, Kant and the Nibelungenlied; Dir Dr BUSSO DIEKAMP; publ. *Der Wormsgau*.

Wuppertal

Stadtbibliothek (City Library): Kolpingstr. 8, 42103 Wuppertal; tel. (202) 5632373; fax (202) 5638489; e-mail stadtbibliothek@stadt.wuppertal.de; internet www.wuppertal.de/stadtbib; f. 1852; central library and 9 brs; spec. collns: theology, early socialism; Else Lasker-Schüler-Archiv, Armin T. Wegner-Archiv; 750,000 vols; Dir UTE SCHARMANN.

Würzburg

Staatsarchiv Würzburg (State Archive of Würzburg): Residenz-Nordflügel, 97070 Würzburg; tel. (931) 355290; fax (931) 3552970; e-mail poststelle@stawu.bayern.de; internet www.gda.bayern.de/staarin.htm; f. in Middle Ages; 36,000 vols, 6,850,000 documents; archives of Lower Franconia since Middle Ages; Dir Dr WERNER WAGENHÖFER.

Universitätsbibliothek: Am Hubland, 97074 Würzburg; tel. (931) 3185943; fax (931) 3185970; e-mail direktion@bibliothek.uni-wuerzburg.de; internet www.bibliothek.uni-wuerzburg.de; f. 1619; 3,324,306 vols, 225,063 theses, 2,949 incunabula, 2,258 manuscripts, 73 papyri; spec. Franconian colln; Dir Dr KARL SUEDEKUM.

Zweibrücken

Landesbibliothekszentrum/Bibliotheca Bipontina: Bleicherstr. 3, 66482 Zweibrücken; tel. (6332) 16403; fax (6332) 18418; e-mail bipontina@lbz-rlp.de; internet www.lbz-rlp.de; f. 1817, 2004 became part of the Landesbibliothekszentrum Rheinland-Pfalz; 115,948 vols, 128 periodicals, 12,000 vols from 16th–18th centuries, incl. libraries of Historischer Verein Zweibrücken, Pollichia Zweibrücken, Naturwissenschaftlicher Verein Zweibrücken and Verein Deutscher Rosenfreunde; Dir Dr HELMUT FRÜHAUF; Man. Dr SIGRID HUBERT-REICHLING.

Museums and Art Galleries

Aachen

Couven-Museum: Hühnermarkt 17, 52062 Aachen; tel. (241) 4324421; fax (241) 4324959; e-mail infor@couven-museum.de; internet www.couven-museum.de; f. 1958 in a house built in 1662; 20 rooms showing history of interior design during 18th–19th centuries, featuring the rococo, Louis XVI, Napoleon Empire and Biedermeier periods; incl. reconstructed 'Adler-Apotheke', where chocolate was made for the first time in the city; collns of porcelain and silverware; Dir DAGMAR PREISING.

Internationales Zeitungsmuseum der Stadt Aachen (International Newspaper Museum): Pontstr. 13, 52062 Aachen; tel. (241) 4324910; fax (241) 4090656; e-mail izm@mail.aachen.de; internet www.izm.de; f. 1886; 200,000 newspapers; spec. library for press history; Dir ANDREAS DÜSPOHL.

Ludwig Forum für Internationale Kunst (Ludwig Forum for International Art): Jülicher Str. 97–109, 52070 Aachen; tel. (241) 1807104; fax (241) 1807101; e-mail info@ludwigforum.de; internet www.ludwigforum.de; f. 1969; modern art since 1960s; spec. collns of graffiti, light sculptures, American pop art and video art; library: Modern art library of 45,000 vols, periodicals and video cassettes; Dir BRIGITTE FRANZEN.

Museum Burg Frankenberg (Burg Museum of Frankenberg): Bismarckstr. 68, 52066 Aachen; tel. (241) 479800; fax (241) 37075; e-mail info@suermondt-ludwig-museum.de; internet www.burgfrankenberg.de; f. 1961, castle dates from 13th century; history of the city from Karl the Great to present; collns of coins, local art; Dir Dr ADAM C. OELLERS.

Suermondt-Ludwig-Museum: Wilhelmstr. 18, 52070 Aachen; tel. (241) 479800; fax (241) 37075; e-mail info@suermondt-ludwig-museum.de; internet www.suermondt-ludwig-museum.de; f. 1882; Gothic art and sculptures; 17th-century paintings (Dutch and Flemish Schools in particular); 10,000 sketches and watercolours, incl. some by Dürer, Rembrandt and Goya; local art since 19th century; library: history of art library of 55,000 vols; Dir ADAM C. OELLERS.

Zollmuseum Friedrichs (Customs Museum): Horbacher Str. 497, 52072 Aachen; tel. (241) 99706015; internet www.zollmuseum-friedrichs.de; 20 rooms and 3,000 exhibits documenting customs practice and history; collns of confiscated materials and smugglers' devices; Dir KURT CREMER.

Baden-Baden

Museum Frieder Burda: Lichtentaler Allee 8B, 76530 Baden-Baden; tel. (7221) 398980; fax (7221) 3989830; e-mail office@museum-frieder-burda.de; internet www.museum-frieder-burda.de; f. 2004; colln of 850 works of modern art with focus on German expressionism, German contemporary art, American abstract expressionism and later works by Picasso; colln is shown in alternation with spec. exhibitions of modern art; Dir Prof. Dr LUDGER HÜNNEKENS; Man. Dir ANNETTE SMETANIG.

Staatliche Kunsthalle Baden-Baden (State Art Exhibition Hall): Lichtentaler Allee 8A, 76530 Baden-Baden; tel. (7221) 300763; fax (7221) 30076500; e-mail info@kunsthalle-baden-baden.de; internet www.kunsthalle-baden-baden.de; f. 1909; int. exhibitions of classical and contemporary art; Dir KAROLA KRAUS (acting); Admin. Dir URSULA EBERHARDT.

Bayreuth

Deutsches Freimaurer Museum in Bayreuth (German Freemasons' Museum in Bayreuth): Im Hofgarten 1, 95444 Bayreuth; tel. (921) 69824; fax (921) 512850; e-mail museum.bayreuth@freimaurer.org; internet museum.freimaurer.org; f. 1902; freemasonry history and practice; library of 25,000 membership records since 1933; incl. sections on Rosicrucians, Illuminati, Templars; Dir THAD PETERSON.

Historisches Museum Bayreuth (Historical Museum of Bayreuth): Habichtweg 11, 95445 Bayreuth; tel. (921) 764010; fax (921) 7640123; e-mail museum@historischesmuseum-bayreuth.de; internet www.historischesmuseum-bayreuth.de; f. 1996; covers 1,200 sq. m, 34 exhibition rooms recording history of Bayreuth since 15th century; Dir Dr SYLVIA HABERMANN; Deputy Dir WILFRIED ENGELBRECHT.

Kunst Museum Bayreuth (Art Museum of Bayreuth): Altes Rathaus, Maximilianstr. 33, 95444 Bayreuth; tel. (921) 7645312; fax (921) 7645320; e-mail info@kunstmuseum-bayreuth.de; internet www.kunstmuseum-bayreuth.de; f. 1999; art since beginning of 20th century; collns include Dr Helmut und Constanze Meyer Kunststiftung, fantastic realism of Caspar Walter Rauh, British-American Tobacco colln on history of the tobacco industry; Dir Dr MARINA VON ASSEL.

Richard-Wagner-Museum mit Nationalarchiv und Forschungsstätte der Richard-Wagner-Stiftung Bayreuth (Richard Wagner Museum with National Archive and Richard Wagner Foundation Research Centre): Richard-Wagner-Str. 48, 95444 Bayreuth; tel. (921) 757280; fax (921) 7572822; e-mail info@wagnermuseum.de; internet www.wagnermuseum.de; f. 1976; closed for renovation until early 2013; archives and admin., accessible; museum and archive of life and works of Richard Wagner (1813–1883) and of history of Bayreuth festival (early 1870s to present); Dir Dr SVEN FRIEDRICH; Librarian KRISTINA UNGER.

Berlin

Berlinische Galerie: Alte Jakobstr. 124–28, 10969 Berlin; tel. (30) 78902600; fax (30) 78902700; e-mail bg@berlinischegalerie.de; internet www.berlinischegalerie.de; f. 1975; permanent colln of works since beginning of 20th century: paintings and drawings (incl. works by Dix, Grosz and Kirchner), photographs, architectural drawings and models; temporary exhibitions of modern art; library of 65,000 vols, mainly on art since beginning of 20th century; Dir Dr THOMAS KÖHLER; Librarian SABINE SCHARDT.

Botanischer Garten und Botanisches Museum Berlin-Dahlem (Botanic Garden and Botanical Museum Berlin-Dahlem): Königin-Luise-Str. 6–8, 14195 Berlin; tel. (30) 83850100; fax (30) 83850186; e-mail zebgbm@bgbm.org; internet www.bgbm.org; f. 1679, Herbarium (f. 1815), Museum (f. 1879); attached to Freie Universität Berlin; plant taxonomy and phytogeography; library of 200,000 vols, 1,300 periodicals, 3.5m. specimens; Dir Prof. Dr T. BORSCH; publs Englera (irregular), Willdenowia (2 a year).

Brücke-Museum: Bussardsteig 9, 14195 Berlin; tel. (30) 8312029; fax (30) 8315961; e-mail bruecke-museum@t-online.de; internet www.bruecke-museum.de; f. 1967; German expressionism, paintings, sculptures and graphic art of the Brücke group; Dir Prof. Dr MAGDALENA MOELLER; publ. Brücke Archiv (1 a year).

Deutsches Historisches Museum (German Historical Museum): Unter den Linden 2, 10117 Berlin; tel. (30) 203040; fax (30) 20304444; e-mail info@dhm.de; internet www.dhm.de; f. 1987; German and modern European history; library of 216,000 vols; Pres. Prof. Dr ALEXANDER KOCH.

Haus der Wannsee-Konferenz, Gedenk- und Bildungsstätte (House of the Wannsee Conference, Memorial and Educational Site): Am Grossen Wannsee 56–58, 14109 Berlin; tel. (30) 8050010; fax (30) 80500127; e-mail info@ghwk.de; internet www.ghwk.de; f. 1992; memorial and educational site, with permanent exhibition documenting persecution and murder of Jews in Europe 1933–1945; educational dept; offers multilingual seminars and study days; library of 30,000 vols, 120 journals; Dir Dr NORBERT KAMPE; Vice-Dir Dr WOLF KAISER.

Käthe-Kollwitz-Museum Berlin: Fasanenstr. 24, 10719 Berlin; tel. (30) 8825210; fax (30) 8811901; e-mail info@kaethe-kollwitz.de; internet www.kaethe-kollwitz.de; f. 1986; private museum (colln of Prof. Hans Pels-Leusden); permanent exhibition of Käthe Kollwitz's work; temporary exhibitions of artists influenced by Käthe Kollwitz; Dir MARTIN FRITSCH.

Museum für Asiatische Kunst (Asian Art Museum): Lansstr. 8 14195 Berlin-Dahlem; tel. (30) 8301382; fax (30) 8301501; e-mail aku@smb.spk-berlin.de; internet www.smb.museum/aku; f. 2006 from merger of Museum of Indian Art (Museum für Indische Kunst) and the Museum of East Asian Art (Museum für Ostasiatische Kunst); art from China (religious bronzes and ceramics), Korea (celadon objects of the 10th- to 14th-century Koryo dynasty) and Japan (Buddhist painting and wood sculpture, Japanese screen painting); art from the Indo-Asian cultural area of 4 millennium BC to present, stone sculptures and reliefs, bronze and terracotta figurines from Hinduism, Buddhism and Jainism, metal, ceramics, wood carvings, ivory and jade and precious textiles from Islamic rule in India, Nepal and Tibet represented through fabric painting (thangka), wood sculptures and bronzes; Dir. Prof. Dr KLAAS RUITENBEEK.

Museum für Naturkunde der Humboldt-Universität zu Berlin (Natural History Museum): Invalidenstr. 43, 10115 Berlin; tel. (30) 20938591; fax (30) 20938561; e-mail info@mfn-berlin.de; internet www .naturkundemuseum-berlin.de; f. 1889, east wing of building destroyed 1945 and reopened 2010, present status 2006, present name 2009; attached to Leibniz Institute for Research on Evolution and Biodiversity, Humboldt Univ.; scientific collns incl. mineralogical, geological, palaeontological, zoological specimens; library of 850 vols; Dir Dr FERDINAND DAMASCHUN; publs *Deutsche Entomologische Zeitschrift, Fossil Record, Zoosystematics and Evolution.*

Staatliche Museen zu Berlin—Preussischer Kulturbesitz: Stauffenbergstr. 41, 10785 Berlin; tel. (30) 2662610; fax (30) 2662992; internet www.smb.museum; f. 1957; supervises museums and collns at the following sites in Berlin: Berlin–Mitte (Museumsinsel), Tiergarten (Kulturforum), Dahlem, Charlottenburg, Köpenick; Gen. Dir Prof. Dr STEFAN WEBER.

Museums:

Ägyptisches Museum und Papyrussammlung (Egyptian Museum and Papyrus Collection): Bodestr. 1–3, 10178 Berlin; tel. (30) 20905101; fax (30) 20905102; e-mail aemp@smb.spk-berlin .de; internet www.smb.museum/aemp; f. 1828 as a section of the fmr Royal Art Collection, collns united 1991; Dir Dr FRIEDERIKE SEYFRIED.

Alte Nationalgalerie (Old National Gallery): Bodestr. 1–3, 10178 Berlin; tel. (30) 20905801; fax (30) 20905802; e-mail ang@smb.spk-berlin.de; internet www.smb .museum; f. 1861; 19th-century sculpture and painting; Dir UDO KITTELMANN.

Antikensammlung, Pergamonmuseum und Altes Museum (Collection of Classical Antiquities at the Pergamon Museum and the Old Museum): Bodestr. 1–3, 10178 Berlin; tel. (30) 20905201; fax (30) 20905202; e-mail ant@smb.spk-berlin.de; internet www.smb.museum/ant; f. 1830; colln also presented in Neues Museum; displays Egyptian and prehistoric objects; Dir Prof. Dr ANDREAS SCHOLL; Deputy Dir Dr MARTIN MAISCHBERGER.

Berggruen Museum (Berggruen Museum): Schlossstr. 1, 14059 Berlin–Charlottenburg; tel. (30) 32695815; fax (30) 32695819; e-mail museum-berggruen@smb.spk-berlin.de; internet www.smb.museum/mb; f. 1996 by the art dealer and collector Heinz Berggruen; colln focusing on Picasso and his contemporaries, incl. Braque, Matisse, Klee, Laurens, Giacometti; Curator Dr KYLLIKKI ZACHARIAS.

Ethnologisches Museum (Ethnological Museum): Arnimallee 27, 14195 Berlin; tel. (30) 8301438; fax (30) 8301500; e-mail md@smb.spk-berlin.de; internet www.smb .museum/em; f. 1829 as the Ethnographic Colln, museum f. 1873; Dir Prof. Dr VIOLA KÖNIG.

Friedrich Christian Flick Collection: Invalidenstr. 50/51, 10557 Berlin; tel. and fax (30) 39783412; e-mail hbf@smb .spk-berlin.de; internet www.smb .museum; 2,000 works, mainly since 1990.

Friedrichswerdersche Kirche (Friedrichswerder Church): Werderscher Markt, Berlin; tel. (30) 2081323; e-mail nng@smb.spk-berlin.de; internet www.smb .museum/fwk; early 19th-century sculpture; Dir UDO KITTELMANN.

Gemäldegalerie (Old Masters' Gallery): Stauffenbergstr. 40, 10785 Berlin; tel. (30) 266424001; fax (30) 266424003; e-mail gg@smb.spk-berlin.de; internet www.smb .museum/gg; f. 1830 from collns of The Great Elector (1620–1688) and Frederick the Great (1712–1786); Dir Prof. Dr BERND LINDEMANN.

Gipsformerei: Sophie-Charlotten-Str. 17–18, 14059 Berlin; tel. (30) 32676911; fax (30) 32676912; e-mail gf@smb .spk-berlin.de; internet www.smb .museum/gf; f. 1819; replicas of 6,500 sculptures, from Germany and other European museums; Dir MIGUEL HELFRICH.

Hamburger Bahnhof—Museum für Gegenwart—Berlin (Museum of the Present): Invalidenstr. 50–51, Berlin; tel. (30) 39783411; fax (30) 39783413; e-mail hbf@smb.spk-berlin.de; internet www .hamburgerbahnhof.de; f. 1996; art since 1950; Head Dr EUGEN BLUME.

Helmut Newton Stiftung (Helmut Newton Foundation): Jebensstr. 2, 10623 Berlin; tel. (30) 31864856; fax (30) 31864855; e-mail info@helmut-newton-stiftung.org; internet www.helmutnewton.com; f. 2003 by the photographer Helmut Newton (1920–2004); preserves and displays Newton's works and those of his wife, June (Alice Springs); temporary exhibitions of work by other photographers; Head Dr MATTHIAS HARDER.

Kunstbibliothek: see under Libraries and Archives.

Kunstgewerbemuseum (Museum of Decorative Arts): Tiergartenstr. 6, 10785 Berlin; tel. (30) 266424336; fax (30) 266424311; e-mail kgm@smb.spk-berlin .de; internet www.smb.museum; f. 1867; Dir Dr SABINE THÜMMLER.

Kupferstichkabinett–Sammlung der Zeichnungen und Druckgraphik (Museum of Prints and Drawings): Matthäikirchpl. 8, 10785 Berlin; tel. (30) 266424201; fax (30) 266424214; e-mail kk@smb.spk-berlin.de; internet www .kupferstichkabinett.de; f. 1831; colln covers Europe from the Middle Ages to the present and incl. more recent items from the USA; 111,000 drawings, 550,000 prints, illuminated MSS, printed illustrated books, etc.; works by Botticelli, Dürer, Bruegel the Elder, Rembrandt, Schinkel, Menzel, Kirchner, Picasso, Warhol, Hirst; Dir Prof. Dr HEIN-TH. SCHULZE ALTCAPPENBERG; Curator Dr DAGMAR KORBACHER.

Münzkabinett der Staatlichen Museen zu Berlin, Stiftung Preussischer Kulturbesitz (Numismatic Collection): Bodestr. 1–3, 10178 Berlin; tel. (30) 20905701; fax (30) 20905702; e-mail mk@smb .spk-berlin.de; internet www.smb .museum/mk; f. 1868, fmrly Kunstkammer of Prussian Electors (f. 1649); more than 500,000 coins, medals, paper money, seals, models, dies, minting tools: Greek, Roman, Middle Ages to present European, Oriental and Islamic; 4 permanent and 1 additional temporary exhibition gallery in Bode-Museum, additional permanent exhibits

at Pergamonmuseum (antiquity), Altes Museum (antiquity) and Neues Museum (antiquity and Middle Ages); Dir Prof. Dr BERND KLUGE.

Museum Europäischer Kulturen (Museum of European Culture): Im Winkel 6–8, 14195 Berlin; tel. (30) 266426802; fax (30) 266426804; e-mail mek@smb .spk-berlin.de; internet www.smb .museum/mek; f. 1999 following merger of the Museum für Volkskunde (Museum of Folklore) and European holdings from the Museum für Völkerkunde (Museum of Ethnology); Dir Prof. Dr KONRAD VANJA.

Museum für Asiatische Kunst (Museum of Asian Art): Takustr. 40, 14195 Berlin; tel. (30) 8301382; fax (30) 8301501; e-mail oak@smb.spk-berlin.de; internet www.smb .museum/aku; f. 2006 by merger of Museum of East Asian Art and Museum of Indian Art; Dir Prof. Dr KLAAS RUITENBEEK.

Museum für Fotografie (Museum of Photography): Jebensstr. 2, Berlin; tel. (30) 266424242; e-mail mv@smb .spk-berlin.de; internet www.smb .museum; f. 1829 as the Ethnographic Colln, museum f. 1873; Head Dr MATTHIAS HARDER.

Museum für Islamische Kunst (Museum of Islamic Art): Bodestr. 1–3, 10178 Berlin; tel. (30) 20905401; fax (30) 20905402; e-mail isl@smb.spk-berlin.de; internet www.smb.museum/isl; f. 1904 as dept of Kaiser Friedrich Museum (now Bodemuseum); Dir Prof. Dr STEFAN WEBER.

Museum für Vor- und Frügeschichte (Museum of Pre- and Early History): Bodestr. 1–3, 10178 Berlin; tel. (30) 32674840; fax (30) 32674812; e-mail mvf@smb.spk-berlin.de; internet www .neues-museum.de/mvf; f. 1931, colln made independent from the Museum for Ethnology; Dir Prof. Dr MATTHIAS WEMHOFF.

Neue Nationalgalerie (New National Gallery): Potsdamer Str. 50, Berlin; tel. (30) 266424500; fax (30) 266424545; e-mail nng@smb.spk-berlin.de; internet www.smb .museum/nng; f. 1968 following merger of collns from the Alte Nationalgalerie and the Gallery of 20th Century Art; painting and sculpture since early 20th century; Dir Dr JOACHIM JÄGER.

Skulpturensammlung und Museum für Byzantinische Kunst (Sculpture Collection and Museum of Byzantine Art): Bodestr. 1–3, 10178 Berlin; tel. (30) 20905601; fax (30) 20905602; e-mail sbm@smb.spk-berlin.de; internet www.smb .museum; f. 2000, by merger of Sculpture Colln and Museum of Byzantine Art; Dir Prof. Dr BERND LINDEMANN; Head Dr JULIEN CHAPUIS.

Vorderasiatisches Museum (Museum of Ancient Near East): Bodestr. 1–3, 10178 Berlin; tel. (30) 20905301; fax (30) 20905302; e-mail vam@smb.spk-berlin.de; internet www.smb.museum; f. 1899 as Dept of Ancient Near East; Dir Prof. Dr BEATE SALJE; Deputy Dir Dr RALF-B. WARTKE.

Stiftung Stadtmuseum Berlin, Landesmuseum für Kultur und Geschichte Berlins: Poststr. 13–14, 10178 Berlin; tel. (30) 24002150; fax (30) 24002187; e-mail info@stadtmuseum.de; internet www .stadtmuseum.de; f. 1874 as Märkisches Museum; illustrates history of Berlin, its culture and its art; library of 102,000 vols; Dir-Gen. Dr FRANZISKA NENTWIG.

Verwaltung der Staatlichen Schlösser und Gärten, West-Berlin (Administration of State Castles and Gardens): Charlottenburg Luisenpl., 10585 Berlin, Schloss; tel. (30) 320911; f. 1927; the admin. controls Charlottenburg Castle, Grunewald Hunting Castle (with colln of paintings), Glienicke Castle and Peacock Island (Castle and Park); library of 5,000 vols; Chief Officer Prof. Dr HELMUT BÖRSCH-SUPAN; Chief Officer Prof. Dr JÜRGEN JULIER; Chief Officer Prof. Dr WINFRIED BAER.

Bonn

Beethoven-Haus: Bonngasse 18–26, 53111 Bonn; tel. (228) 981750; fax (228) 9817531; e-mail info@beethoven-haus-bonn.de; internet www.beethoven-haus-bonn.de; f. 1889; birthplace of Ludwig van Beethoven (1770–1827); museum and research centre with library; library of 57,000 vols, 125 periodicals, 25,000 music scores (6,000 by Beethoven); Dir Dr MANFRED HARNISCHFE-GER; Head of Museums and Curator Dr MICHAEL LADENBURGER.

Kunstmuseum Bonn: Friedrich-Ebert-Allee 2, 53113 Bonn; tel. (228) 776260; fax (228) 776220; e-mail kunstmuseum@bonn.de; internet www.kunstmuseum-bonn.de; f. 1882, restored 1948, new building 1992; colln of 20th-century art; German expressionist painting, with important August Macke colln; contemporary int. graphic art, contemporary German art, photos and video cassettes; library of 47,000 vols; Dir Prof. Dr STEPHAN BERG; Deputy Dir Dr CHRISTOPH SCHREIER.

LVR—LandesMuseum Bonn (LVR State Museum Bonn): Colmantstr. 14–16, 53115 Bonn; tel. (228) 20700; fax (228) 2070299; e-mail info.landesmuseum-bonn@lvr.de; internet www.landesmuseum-bonn.lvr.de; f. 1820; prehistoric, Roman and Frankish antiquities of the Rhineland; Rhenish sculpture, painting and applied arts up to the 20th century; Dutch paintings; library of 180,000 vols; Dir Dr GABRIELE UELSBERG; publs Bonner Jahrbücher des Rheinischen Landesmuseums und des Vereins von Altertumsfreunden im Rheinlande (1 a year), Das Rheinische Landesmuseum Bonn (4 a year).

Zoologisches Forschungsmuseum 'Alexander Koenig' (Zoological Research Museum 'Alexander Koenig'): Adenauerallee 160, 53113 Bonn; tel. (228) 91220; fax (228) 9122212; e-mail info.zfmk@uni-bonn.de; internet www.museumkoenig.de; f. 1912; zoology—vertebrates and insects; library of 150,000 vols; Dir Prof. Dr J. W. WÄGELE; publs Bonner zoologische Beiträge (4 a year), Myotis: Mitteilungsblatt für Fledermauskundler (1 a year).

Bremen

Focke-Museum (District Museum for Art and Culture): Schwachhauser Heerstr. 240, 28213 Bremen; tel. (421) 6996000; fax (421) 69960066; e-mail post@focke-museum.de; internet www.focke-museum.de; f. 1900; exhibits from Stone Age to 20th century; library of 40,000 vols, 200 periodicals; Dir Dr FRAUKE VON DER HAAR.

Kunsthalle Bremen – Der Kunstverein in Bremen (Bremen Art Museum): Am Wall 207, 28195 Bremen; tel. (421) 329080; fax (421) 32908470; e-mail office@kunsthalle-bremen.de; internet www.kunsthalle-bremen.de; f. 1823; European paintings since 14th century, prints and drawings; sculpture since 16th century; Japanese drawings and books; 7,000 mems; library of 100,000 vols; Dir Prof. Dr WULF HERZOGENRATH.

Übersee-Museum Bremen (Museum of Overseas Culture, Bremen): Bahnhofspl. 13, 28195 Bremen; tel. (421) 16038101; fax (421) 1603899; e-mail office@uebersee-museum.de;

internet www.uebersee-museum.de; f. 1896; ethnology, history of commerce, natural history; library of 70,000 vols; Dir Dr WIEBKE AHRNDT; publ. TenDenZen (1 a year).

Brunswick

Herzog Anton Ulrich-Museum: Museumstr. 1, 38100 Brunswick; tel. (531) 12250; fax (531) 12252408; e-mail info@haum.niedersachsen.de; internet www.haum.niedersachsen.de; f. 1754; colln incl. old pictures, prints and drawings, medieval art, ceramics, 16th-century French enamels, carvings in ivory, bronzes, colln of lace, old clocks, etc.; library: art library of 60,000 vols; Dir Prof. Dr JOCHEN LUCKHARDT.

Städtisches Museum (City Museum): Steintorwall 14 (Am Löwenwall), 38100 Brunswick; tel. (531) 4704505; fax (531) 4704555; e-mail staedtisches.museum@braunschweig.de; internet www.braunschweig.de/staedtisches_museum; f. 1861; collns illustrate topography, history and culture of the town; paintings since 19th century; coins and medals (all periods and territories, with about 80,000 pieces); ethnographical collns; closed until 2012; Dir Dr CECILIE HOLLBERG; publs Arbeitsberichte, Braunschweiger Werkstücke, Miszellen.

Branch Museum:

Zweigmuseum Altstadtrathaus: Altstadtmarkt 7, 38100 Brunswick; tel. (531) 4704551; fax (531) 4704544; e-mail staedtisches.museum@braunschweig.de; f. 1991; bldg dates from late 13th century; history of the city since 9th century.

Cologne

Kölnisches Stadtmuseum: Zeughausstr. 1–3, 50667 Cologne; tel. (221) 22125789; fax (221) 22124154; e-mail ksm@museenkoeln.de; internet www.museenkoeln.de; f. 1888; history of Cologne from the Middle Ages to the present day; collns illustrate local culture, economy and everyday life, political history, craftsmen's and merchants' guilds, devotional objects, Judaica, transport, inventions made in the city, paintings by the Berckheyde brothers and Geldorp Gortzius, crafts, early globes, puppet theatre, Eau de Cologne; library of 30,000 vols; Dir Dr MARIO KRAMP (acting); Curator for Graph Dept RITA WAGNER; Curator for Middle Ages Dr BETTINA MOSLER.

Museum für Angewandte Kunst (Museum of Applied Art): An der Rechtschule, 50667 Cologne; tel. (221) 22123860; fax (221) 22123885; e-mail makk@stadt-koeln.de; internet www.museenkoeln.de; f. 1888; library: see under Libraries and Archives; applied art since Middle Ages; design colln since 1900; Dir Dr PETRA HESSE.

Museum Ludwig: Heinrich-Böll-Pl., 50667 Cologne; tel. (221) 22126165; fax (221) 22124114; e-mail info@museum-ludwig.de; internet www.museum-ludwig.de; f. 1976; paintings, modern sculpture, prints, photos, video cassettes; library; largest colln of Pop Art outside the USA; Russian avant-garde art; several hundred works by Picasso; collns Agfa Foto–Historma: photographs, caricatures and documents; colln of cameras returned to Agfa and Gevaert in Belgium; Dir Prof. KASPER KÖNIG; Deputy Dir KATIA BAUDIN.

Museum Schnütgen: Leonhard-Tietz-Str. 10, 50676 Cologne; Cäcilienstr. 29–33, 50667 Cologne; tel. (221) 22123620; fax (221) 22128489; e-mail museum.schnutgen@stadt-koeln.de; internet www.museenkoeln.de; f. 1906; library of 20,000 vols; 13,000 works of medieval art; houses 11th-century

wooden crucifix; Dir Dr DAGMAR TÄUBE (acting).

Rautenstrauch-Joest-Museum: Leonhard-Tietz-Str. 10, 50676 Cologne; Cäcilienstr. 29–33, 50667 Cologne; tel. (221) 22123620; fax (221) 22131333; e-mail rjm@stadt-koeln.de; internet www.museenkoeln.de/rautenstrauch-joest-museum; f. 1901; ethnological museum; library of 44,300 vols; Dir Prof. Dr KLAUS SCHNEIDER; Deputy Dir Dr JUTTA ENGELHARD; publ. Ethnologica.

Römisch-Germanisches Museum: Roncallipl. 4, 50667 Cologne; tel. (221) 22124438; fax (221) 22124030; e-mail roemisch-germanisches-museum@stadt--koeln.de; internet www.museenkoeln.de/roemisch-germanisches-museum; f. 1946; library of 14,000 vols; Dir Dr MARCUS TRIER (acting); publs Kölner Forschungen, Kölner Jahrbuch (prehistory and early history, 1 a year).

Wallraf-Richartz-Museum & Fondation Corboud: Obenmarspforten (Am Kölner Rathaus), 50667 Cologne; tel. (221) 22121119; fax (221) 22122629; e-mail wallraf@museenkoeln.de; internet www.wallraf.museum; f. 1824; paintings, sculpture, prints, drawings dating from the Middle Ages, Baroque period, and 18th and 19th centuries; library: see under Libraries and Archives; Dir Dr ANDREAS BLÜHM; Deputy Dir Dr ROLAND KRISCHEL; publs Jahrbuch für Kunstgeschichte, Wallraf-Richartz-Jahrbuch.

Darmstadt

Grossherzoglich-Hessische Porzellansammlung (Grand-Ducal Porcelain Collection): Schlossgartenstr. 10, Prinz-Georg-Palaïs, 64289 Darmstadt; tel. (6151) 713233; e-mail info@porzellanmuseum-darmstadt.de; internet www.schlossmuseum-darmstadt.de; f. 1908; colln consists of a variety of products manufactured by the European porcelain and faience artists of the 18th and 19th centuries; Head ALEXA-BEATRICE CHRIST (acting).

Hessisches Landesmuseum Darmstadt (State Museum of Hesse in Darmstadt): Friedenspl. 1, 64283 Darmstadt; tel. (6151) 165703; fax (6151) 28942; e-mail info@hlmd.de; internet www.hlmd.de; f. 1820; archaeology, prehistory, zoology, geology, palaeontology, mineralogy; art collns and cultural history since 9th century, incl. crafts, prints and drawings, stained glass, sculptures, paintings, European art since 1945; library of 55,000 vols; Dir Dr INA BUSCH; Dir Dr THEO JÜLICH; publs Kaupia–Darmstädter Beiträge zur Naturgeschichte (2 a year), Kunst in Hessen und am Mittelrhein (1 a yearl).

Museum Jagdschloss Kranichstein: Kranichsteiner Str. 261, 64289 Darmstadt; tel. (6151) 9711180; fax (6151) 97111818; e-mail museum@schloss-huntingkranichstein.de; internet www.jagdschloss-kranichstein.de; f. 1918; pictures, hunting trophies and weapons, furnished rooms; owned by Stiftung Hessischer Jägerhof; Dir NADINE KRÄMER.

Schlossmuseum (Castle Museum): Residenzschloss, Marktpl. 15, 64283 Darmstadt; tel. (6151) 24035; fax (6151) 997457; e-mail info@schlossmuseum-darmstadt.de; internet www.schlossmuseum-darmstadt.de; f. 1924; furnished rooms with paintings, porcelain, glass, etc.; military colln, ceremonial carriages and harness; Head ALEXA-BEATRICE CHRIST (acting).

Dortmund

Museum für Kunst und Kulturgeschichte Dortmund (Dortmund Museum of Art and Cultural History): Hansastr. 3, 44137 Dortmund; tel. (231) 5025522; fax (231) 5025511; internet www .museendortmund.de/mkk; f. 1883; collns incl. medieval art and sculpture, furniture since 15th century, design, *objets d'art*, paintings, archaeology; library of 18,000 vols; Dir WOLFGANG E. WEICK.

Dresden

Landesamt für Archäologie mit Landesmuseum für Vorgeschichte (State Office of Archaeology and Museum of Prehistory): Japanisches Palais, Zur Wetterwarte 7, 01109 Dresden; tel. (351) 8926603; fax (351) 8926604; e-mail archsax .smwk.sachsen.de; f. 1993; preservation of ancient monuments, archaeological research and exhibitions; library of 40,000 vols specializing in prehistory; Dir Dr J. OEXLE; publs *Arbeits- und Forschungsberichte* (1 a year), *Archäologie aktuell im Freistaat Sachsen* (1 a year).

Mathematisch-Physikalischer Salon: Zwinger, 01067 Dresden; tel. (351) 49140; fax (351) 4914666; e-mail besucherservice@ skd.museum; internet www.skd.museum; f. 1560; historical watches and clocks, globes, scientific instruments, etc.; library of 7,000 vols; Dir Dr PETER PLABMEYER.

Militärhistorisches Museum der Bundeswehr (Military-Historical Museum of the Federal Army): Olbrichtpl. 2, 01099 Dresden; tel. (351) 8232803; fax (351) 8232805; e-mail milhistmuseumbweingang@ bundeswehr.org; internet www .militaerhistorisches-museum.bundeswehr .de; f. 1990; German military history from the late Middle Ages to the present; exhibits include weapons, equipment, documents, uniforms and combat vehicles; cannons and caissons; also a mid-19th-century submarine, models, dioramas, paintings and sculptures; exhibition closed until late 2011; library of 31,000 vols; Dir Lt Col Dr DOGG.

Museum für Tierkunde Dresden (Dresden Museum of Zoology): Königsbrücker Landstr. 159, 01109 Dresden; tel. (351) 7958414326; fax (351) 7958414327; e-mail birgit.walker@senckenberg.de; internet www .senckenberg.de; f. 1728; more than 6m. animal specimens; library of 60,000 vols; Dir UWE FRITZ; publs *Entomologische Abhandlungen, Faunistische Abhandlungen, Malakologische Abhandlungen, Reichenbachia Zeitschrift für entomolog. Taxonomie* (1 a year), *Zoologische Abhandlungen*.

Museum Schloss Moritzburg (Museum of Moritzburg Castle): Schloss Moritzburg, 01468 Moritzburg bei Dresden; tel. (35207) 8730; fax (35207) 87311; e-mail moritzburg@ schloesserland-sachsen.de; internet www .schloss-moritzburg.de; f. 1947; leather hangings, furniture, paintings, statues, porcelain, glasswork, principally of the 18th century; Dir INGRID MÖBIUS.

Staatliche Ethnographische Sammlungen Sachsen: see Staatliche Ethnographische Sammlungen Sachsen, Leipzig.

Staatliche Kunstsammlungen Dresden: POB 12 05 51, 01006 Dresden; Residenzschloss, Taschenberg 2, 01067 Dresden; tel. (351) 491420; fax (351) 4914616; e-mail besucherservice@skd.museum; internet www .skd.museum; f. 1560; library of 130,000 vols, housed in the Residenzschloss; Gen. Dir Prof. Dr MARTIN ROTH; publs *Dresdener Kunstblätter* (6 a year), *Jahrbuch* (1 a year).

Constituent Institutions:

Gemäldegalerie Alte Meister (Old Masters Picture Gallery): Semperbau am Zwinger, Theaterpl. 1, 01067 Dresden; tel. (351) 49146679; fax (351) 49146694; e-mail gam@skd.museum; internet www.skd

.museum; f. 16th century; Italian Renaissance artists Raffael, Giorgione and Titian; 17th-century Flemish art, Rembrandt, Vermeer, Rubens; old German and Dutch, Jan van Eyck, Dürer, Cranach, Holbein; Spanish and French 17th-century artists Ribera, Murillo, Poussin, Lorrain; Dir Prof. Dr BERNHARD MAAZ.

Gemäldegalerie Neue Meister (New Masters Gallery): Albertinum, Brühlsche Terrasse, 01067 Dresden; tel. (351) 49149731; fax (351) 49149732; e-mail gnm@skd.museum; internet www.skd .museum; f. 1960; art since 19th century; collns of German Impressionism and Expressionism; Dir Prof. Dr ULRICH BISCHOFF.

Grünes Gewölbe (Green Vault): Residenzschloss, Taschenberg 2, 01067 Dresden; tel. (351) 4914-0; e-mail besucherservice@skd.museum; internet www.skd.museum; Renaissance and Baroque artefacts; f. 1723; Dir Prof. Dr DIRK SYNDRAM.

Kunstgewerbemuseum (Museum of Decorative Arts): Schloss Pillnitz, August-Böckstiegel-Str. 2, 01326 Dresden; tel. (351) 26130; fax (351) 2613222; e-mail besucherservice@skd.museum; internet www.skd.museum; f. 1876; courtly items incl. textiles and ceramics; Dir Dr PETER PLABMEYER (acting); Sec. NADJA WENZEL.

Kupferstich-Kabinett (Cabinet of Prints and Drawings): POB 12 05 51, 01006 Dresden; Taschenberg 2, 01067 Dresden; tel. (351) 49143211; fax (351) 49143222; e-mail kk@skd.museum; internet www.skd .museum; f. 1720; 50,000 paper works by 11,000 artists since 12th century; Dir Prof. Dr BERNHARD MAAZ.

Münzkabinett (Coin Cabinet): POB 12 05 51, 01006 Dresden; Taschenberg 2, 01067 Dresden; tel. (351) 49143231; fax (351) 49143233; e-mail mk@skd.museum; internet www.skd.museum; f. early 16th century; library of 30,000 specialist vols; 300,000 objects, incl. coins, medals, banknotes; Dir Dr RAINER GRUND (acting).

Museum für Sächsische Volkskunst mit Puppentheatersammlung (Museum of Saxon Folk Art with Puppet Theatre Collection): Jägerhof, Köpckestr. 1, 01097 Dresden; tel. (351) 49144502; fax (351) 49144500; e-mail elke.wengerek@skd .museum; internet www.skd.museum; f. 1897; items of folk history; costumes; puppet colln; Dir Dr IGOR A. JENZEN.

Porzellansammlung (Porcelain Collection): Zwinger, Glockenspielpavillon, 01067 Dresden; tel. (351) 49146612; fax (351) 49146629; e-mail ps@skd.museum; internet www.skd.museum; f. 1717; 20,000 pieces of Meissner, Japanese and Chinese porcelain; Dir Dr ULRICH PIETSCH.

Rüstkammer (Armoury): Semperbau am Zwinger, Theaterpl. 1, 01067 Dresden; tel. (351) 49148591; fax (351) 4918599; e-mail gg@skd.museum; internet www.skd .museum; f. 1567; 10,000 chivalric objects, weapons and costumes; Dir Prof. Dr DIRK SYNDRAM.

Skulpturensammlung (Sculpture Collection): Albertinum, Brühlsche Terrasse, 01067 Dresden; tel. (351) 49149741; fax (351) 49149350; e-mail skd@skd.museum; internet www.skd.museum; sculptures since 3,000 BC; Dir Dr MORITZ WOELK.

Staatliches Museum für Mineralogie und Geologie (State Museum of Mineralogy and Geology): Königsbrücker Landstr. 159, 01109 Dresden; tel. (351) 7958414403; fax (351) 7958414404; e-mail ulrike.kloss@ senckenberg.de; internet www.senckenberg

.de; f. 1728; library of 35,000 vols; 400,000 minerals and fossils; Dir Dr ULF LINNEMANN; Sec. ULRIKE KLOSS; publs *Geologica Saxonica–Abhandlungen* (1 a year), *Schriften* (1–2 a year).

Stadtmuseum Dresden (Dresden City Museum): Wilsdruffer Str. 2, 01067 Dresden; tel. (351) 4887301; fax (351) 4887303; e-mail sekretariat@museen-dresden.de; internet www.stmd.de; f. 1891; Dresden history and culture; library of 7,500 vols, 22,500 pictures, 55,000 photographs; Dir Dr ERIKA ESCHEBACH.

Attached Museums:

Kraszewski-Museum: Nordstr. 28, 01099 Dresden; tel. (351) 8044450; fax (351) 5633476; e-mail joanna.magacz@ museen-dresden.de; internet www.stmd .de; exhibition on Polish history, in particular Józef Ignacy Kraszewski (1812–1887), who fought for Polish independence in the 19th century; exhibits in German and Polish; Dir JOANNA MAGACZ.

Kügelgenhaus–Museum der Dresdner Romantik (Museum of German Romanticism): Hauptstr. 13, 01097 Dresden; tel. and fax (351) 8044760; e-mail michaela .hausding@museen-dresden.de; internet www.stmd.de; f. 1981; home to the Museum der Dresdner Romantik; Dir MICHAELA HAUSDING.

Schillerhäuschen (The Schiller House): Schillerstr. 19, 01326 Dresden; tel. (351) 4887372; e-mail joachim.vocke@ museen-dresden.de; internet www.stmd .de; dedicated to the poet Friedrich Schiller (1759–1805).

Weber-Museum: Dresdner Str. 44, 01326 Dresden; tel. and fax (351) 2618234; e-mail dorothea.renz@museen-dresden.de; internet www.stmd.de; dedicated to the works of composer Carl Maria von Weber (1786–1826); concert venue; Dir DOROTHEA RENZ.

Verkehrsmuseum Dresden (Transport Museum Dresden): Augustusstr. 1, 01067 Dresden; tel. (351) 86440; fax (351) 8644110; e-mail info@ verkehrsmuseum-dresden.de; internet verkehrsmuseum-dresden.de; f. 1952; colln of automobiles, motorcycles, bicycles, streetcars, aircraft, model ships and railways; library of 59,000 vols (14,156 vols in spec. colln); Dir JOACHIM BREUNINGER.

Düsseldorf

Aquazoo Löbbecke Museum: Kaiserswertherstr. 380, 40200 Düsseldorf; tel. (211) 8996198; fax (211) 8994493; internet www .dusseldorf.de/aquazoo; f. 1904 (museum), 1876 (zoo); zoo and natural science museum; library of 600 vols; Dir Dr W. W. GETTMANN; publs *Aquarius* (2 a year), *Westdeutscher Entomologentag Düsseldorf*.

Kunsthalle Düsseldorf: Grabbepl. 4, 40213 Düsseldorf; tel. (211) 8996243; fax (211) 8929168; e-mail mail@ kunsthalle-duesseldorf.de; internet www .kunsthalle-duesseldorf.de; f. 1967; contemporary art; Chair. DIRK ELBERS; Man. Dir ARIANE BERGER; Man. Dir Dr GREGOR JANSEN; Man. Dir Dr VANESSA JOAN MÜLLER.

Kunstsammlung Nordrhein-Westfalen (North Rhine-Westphalia Art Collection): Grabbepl. 5, 40213 Düsseldorf; tel. (211) 8381204; fax (211) 8381209; e-mail info@ kunstsammlung.de; internet www .kunstsammlung.de; f. 1961; painting and sculpture since beginning of 20th century; Dir Dr MARION ACKERMANN; publs *K20K21 Programmbroschüre* (4 a year), *Quartalsprogramm* (4 a year), *20_21* (2 a year).

Museum Kunst Palast (mit Sammlung Kunstakademie and Glasmuseum Hen-

trich) (Art Palace Museum (incorporating the Art Academy Collection and Hentrich Glass Museum)): Ehrenhof 4–5, 40479 Düsseldorf; tel. (211) 8990200; fax (211) 8992460; e-mail info@smkp.de; internet www .museum-kunst-palast.de; f. 1913; European art and applied art from the Middle Ages to 1800; colln of 19th-century German painting; early Iranian bronzes and ceramics; 6,500 textiles from late antiquity to the 19th century; glass colln, mainly Art Nouveau, Jugendstil and Art Deco; colln of prints and drawings, incl. extensive colln of Italian Baroque drawings; contemporary art; design; museum for young visitors; library of 80,000 vols; Dir BEAT WISMER.

Essen

Museum Folkwang: Goethestr. 41, 45128 Essen; tel. and fax (201) 8845444; e-mail info@museum-folkwang.essen.de; internet www.museum-folkwang.de; f. 1902; art since 19th century, incl. drawings, prints, posters and photographs; incl. German Poster Museum (Deutsches Plakat Museum) with 340,000 posters; library of 100,000 vols; Dir Dr HARTWIG FISCHER; Deputy Dir Prof. UTE ESKILDSEN.

Flensburg

Museumsberg Flensburg: Museumsberg 1, 24937 Flensburg; tel. (461) 852956; fax (461) 852993; e-mail museumsberg@ flensburg.de; internet www.museumsberg .flensburg.de; f. 1876; contains about 26,000 exhibits, mainly arts and crafts, peasant art, and prehistory of Schleswig; library of 12,000 vols; Dir Dr MICHAEL FUHR; publs Beiträge zur Kunst- und Kulturgeschichte, Nordelbingen.

Frankfurt am Main

Archäologisches Museum (Archaeological Museum): Karmelitergasse 1, 60311 Frankfurt am Main; tel. (69) 21235896; fax (69) 21230700; e-mail info.archaeolmus@ stadt-frankfurt.de; internet www .archaeologisches-museum.frankfurt.de; f. 1937; prehistoric, Roman and early medieval objects from the Frankfurt area; Mediterranean and oriental archaeology; Dir Prof. Dr EGON WAMERS.

Deutsches Architekturmuseum (German Architecture Museum): Schaumainkai 43, 60596 Frankfurt am Main; tel. (69) 21238844; fax (69) 21236386; e-mail info .dam@stadt-frankfurt.de; internet www .dam-online.de; f. 1979, opened 1984; int. colln of plans, sketches, paintings and models primarily of modern architecture; changing exhibitions, lectures, symposia; library and archive; library of 20,000 vols, 60 current periodicals and yearbooks; Dir Ing. PETER CACHOLA SCHMAL; Deputy Dir Dr Ing. WOLFGANG VOIGT; publs German Architecture (1 a year), Jahrbuch Architektur.

Deutsches Filmmuseum (German Film Museum): Schaumainkai 41, 60596 Frankfurt am Main; tel. (69) 9612200; fax (69) 961220999; e-mail info@ deutsches-filmmuseum.de; internet www .deutschesfilmmuseum.de; f. 1984; exhibits relating to the German and int. film industry; library: see library and archives of the Deutsches Filminstitut; Dir CLAUDIA DILLMANN.

Freies Deutsches Hochstift, Frankfurter Goethe-Haus Museum (Free German Literature Institute, Frankfurt Goethe-Museum (Goethe House)): Gr. Hirschgraben 23–25, 60311 Frankfurt am Main; tel. (69) 138800; fax (69) 13880222; e-mail info@ goethehaus-frankfurt.de; internet www .goethehaus-frankfurt.de; f. 1859; birthplace of Johann Wolfgang von Goethe (1749–1832);

German literature of the Romantic period and of Goethe's time; selected works since 19th century; 30,000 MSS of German poetry principally from Goethe's time; 400 paintings, 16,000 etchings; library: see Libraries and Archives; Dir Dr PETRA MAISAK; publs Jahrbuch, Reihe der Schriften.

Historisches Museum Frankfurt: Saalgasse 19, 60311 Frankfurt am Main; tel. (69) 21235599; fax (69) 21230702; e-mail info .historisches-museum@stadt-frankfurt.de; internet www.historisches-museum .frankfurt.de; f. 1878; history of Frankfurt to the present; spec. colln: documents relating to elections of emperors 1562–1792, to the Assembly of Paulskirche 1848/49, and to trade fairs in the 16th–18th centuries; Hoechst Porcelain 1746–1796; comic art and caricature; coin colln; children's museum; library of 50,000 vols; Dir Dr JAN GERCHOW; Deputy Dir Dr WOLFGANG CILLEßEN.

Museum für Angewandte Kunst Frankfurt (Museum of Applied Art Frankfurt): Schaumainkai 17, 60594 Frankfurt am Main; tel. (69) 21234037; fax (69) 21230703; e-mail info.angewandte-kunst@stadt-frankfurt.de; internet www.angewandtekunst-frankfurt .de; f. 1877; European art craft of 12th to 21st century, design, book art and graphics, Islamic and East Asian art and int. product design; 65,000 exhibits; library of 65,000 vols, 170 current periodicals and yearbooks; Dir Prof. Dr ULRICH SCHNEIDER.

Museum für Kommunikation: Schaumainkai 53, 60596 Frankfurt am Main; tel. (49) 6960600; fax (49) 696060666; e-mail mfk-frankfurt@mspt.de; internet www .mfk-frankfurt.de; f. 1872; items on history of post and telecommunications; library of 35,000 vols; Dir Dr HELMUT GOLD.

Museum für Moderne Kunst (Museum of Contemporary Art): Domstr. 10, 60311 Frankfurt am Main; tel. (69) 21230447; fax (69) 21237882; e-mail mmk@stadt-frankfurt .de; internet www.mmk-frankfurt.de; f. 1991; art since the 1960s; library of 40,000 vols; Dir SUSANNE GAENSHEIMER; Deputy Dir PETER GORSCHLÜTER.

Städel Museum: Dürerstr. 2, 60596 Frankfurt am Main; Schaumainkai 63, 60596 Frankfurt am Main; tel. (69) 6050980; fax (69) 605098111; e-mail info@staedelmuseum .de; internet www.staedelmuseum.de; f. 1816; 2,700 paintings, 100,000 drawings and prints, 600 sculptures spanning 700 years; library of 50,000 vols; Chair. Prof. Dr NIKOLAUS SCHWEICKART; Dir MAX HOLLEIN.

Weltkulturen Museum: Schaumainkai 29–37, 60594 Frankfurt am Main; tel. (69) 21235391; fax (69) 21230704; e-mail museum.weltkulturen@stadt-frankfurt.de; internet www.weltkulturenmuseum.de; f. 1904; collns of art and ethnography from all continents, esp. Oceania, South-East Asia, Africa, North and South America; spec. colln of contemporary art; library of 43,000 vols, 90 periodicals; Dir Dr CLÉMENTINE DELISS; publ. Journal-Ethnologie (online, www.journal-ethnologie.de).

Freiburg im Breisgau

Adelhausermuseum: Gerberau 32, 79098 Freiburg im Breisgau; tel. (761) 2012566; fax (761) 2012563; e-mail adelhausermuseum@ stadt.freiburg.de; internet www.museen .freiburg.de; f. 1895; native and exotic fauna; herb collection, mineralogy, precious stones, wood types, beekeeping, traditional arts and crafts from Africa, America, Asia and Oceania; social and cultural anthropology; library: ethnology: 4,700 vols, natural history: 5,000 vols; Dir Dr EVA GERHARDS.

Archäologisches Museum Colombischlössle: Rotteckring 5, 79098 Freiburg im

Breisgau; tel. (761) 2012574; fax (761) 2012579; e-mail arco-museum@stadt .freiburg.de; internet www.freiburg.de/ museen; f. 1936; regional archaeology; library of 5,000 vols; Dir Dr HELENA PASTOR BORGOÑÓN.

Augustinermuseum: Augustinerpl., 79098 Freiburg im Breisgau; tel. (761) 2012521; fax (761) 2012597; e-mail augustinermuseum@ stadt.freiburg.de; internet www.freiburg.de/ museen; f. 1923; art and culture of Upper Rhine area from Middle Ages to the 20th century; library of 50,000 vols; Dir Dr TILMANN VON STOCKHAUSEN; Deputy Dir Dr DETLEF ZINKE.

Museum für Neue Kunst (Museum of Modern Art): Marienstr. 10A, 79098 Freiburg im Breisgau; tel. (761) 2012583; fax (761) 2012589; e-mail mnk@stadt.freiburg.de; internet www.museen.freiburg.de; f. 1985; German art since 1910; Dir Dr JOCHEN LUDWIG.

Museum für Stadtgeschichte (Museum of City History): Münsterpl. 30, 79098 Freiburg im Breisgau; tel. (761) 2012515; fax (761) 2012598; e-mail msg@stadt.freiburg.de; internet www.museen.freiburg.de; city history since 1100; Dir PETER KALCHTHALER.

Giessen

Liebig Museum: Liebigstr. 12, 35390 Giessen; tel. (641) 76392; fax (641) 2502599; internet www.liebig-museum.de; exhibition of the life and work of Liebig through documents and pictures; pharmaceutical laboratory and display of chemical analysis since 19th century; Chair. WOLFGANG BERGENTHUM.

Oberhessisches Museum und Gailsche Sammlungen der Stadt Gießen: Brandpl. 2, 35390 Giessen; tel. (641) 3062477; fax (641) 3012005; e-mail museum@giessen.de; internet www.giessen.de; f. 1879; palaeolithic colln, first Middle European flint tools; archaeological collns and treasures of Roman-German and Hessian Franconian culture; oil paintings, watercolours and modern copperplate engravings; Dir Dr FRIEDHELM HÄRING.

Comprises:

Altes Schloss: Abteilung Gemäldegalerie und Kunsthandwerk, Brandpl. 2 35390 Giessen; tel. (641) 9609730; fax (641) 96097317; e-mail museum@giessen.de; internet www.giessen.de; houses furniture and art in 14th-century bldg; collns of Gothic, Baroque, Renaissance, artefacts since 19th century.

Leib'sches Haus: Abteilung für Stradtgeschichte und Volkskunde, Georg-Schlosser-Str. 2, 35390 Giessen; tel. (641) 3012448; f. 1978; originally the seat of the Junkers of Rodenhausen; now museum of local history and culture; exhibits of material culture of Gießen and surrounding area; portraits, pictures, maps, engravings, textile manufacture and handicraft; furniture, farm implements, costumes, pottery; spec. exhibitions on the political thinkers Georg Büchner and Wilhelm Liebknecht (founder of the German Social Democratic Party).

Wallenfels'sches Haus: Abteilung für Vor- und Frühgeschichte, Archäologie und Völkerkunde mit der Sammlung Heinz Beer, Kirchenpl. 6, 35390 Giessen; tel. (641) 3012037; ethnological museum with artefacts dating from prehistoric times; examples from India, China, Japan, Sri Lanka, Java, East and West Africa, Egypt, New Guinea and Australia.

Gotha

Kommunale Galerien am Hauptmarkt: Hauptmarkt 44, 99867 Gotha; tel. (3621) 401101; fax (3621) 52669; Dir MARLIES MIKOLAJCZAK.

Münzkabinett (Coin Cabinet): POB 10 03 19, 99867 Gotha; Schloss Friedenstein, 99867 Gotha; tel. (3621) 82340; fax (3621) 823457; e-mail wallenstein@stiftungfriedenstein.de; 130,000 numismatic objects; Dir UTA WALLENSTEIN.

Museum der Natur: POB 10 03 19, 99853 Gotha; Parkallee 15, 99867 Gotha; tel. (3621) 82340; fax (3621) 823457; e-mail mng@stiftungfriedenstein.de; internet www.stiftungfriedenstein.de; f. 1843; animal and fossil exhibitions, insects, local natural history; Dir RAINER SAMIETZ; publ. *Abhandlungen und Berichte*.

Museum für Kartographie (Museum of Cartography): Schloss Friedenstein, 99867 Gotha; tel. (3621) 854016; e-mail vorstand@stiftungfriedenstein.de; maps, atlases and globes; original copper engraving; Curator JUTTA SIEGERT.

Museum für Regionalgeschichte und Volkskunde (Museum of Regional History and Folklore): Schloss Friedenstein, 99867 Gotha; tel. (3621) 82340; fax (3621) 823457; e-mail mrv@stiftungfriedenstein.de; internet www.stiftungfriedenstein.de; f. 1928; exhibition of local history, with *Ekhof-Theater* (baroque theatre); Dir THOMAS HUCK; publ. *Gothaisches Museumsjahrbuch* (1 a year).

Schlossmuseum (Castle Museum): Schloss Friedenstein, 99867 Gotha; tel. (3621) 82340; fax (3621) 823457; e-mail schlossmuseum@stiftungfriedenstein.de; internet www.stiftungfriedenstein.de; art collections, historical rooms, coin collns, Egyptological exhibition; Dir Dr KATHARINA BECHLER.

Göttingen

Städtisches Museum (Municipal Museum): Ritterplan 7/8, 37073 Göttingen; tel. (551) 4002843; fax (551) 4002059; e-mail museum@goettingen.de; internet www.museum.goettingen.de; f. 1889; prehistory and early history, ecclesiastical art, history of Göttingen and the Univ., arts and crafts, etc.; library of 30,000 vols; Dir Dr ERNST BÖHME.

Halle am Saale

Landesamt für Denkmalpflege und Archäologie Sachsen-Anhalt (Landesmuseum für Vorgeschichte) (State Office for Heritage Management and Archaeology—State Museum of Prehistory): Richard-Wagner-Str. 9, 06114 Halle Saale; tel. (345) 5247580; fax (345) 5247351; e-mail poststelle@lda.mk.sachsen-anhalt.de; internet www.lda-lsa.de; f. 1882; pre- and medieval history; library of 121,000 vols; Dir Dr HARALD MELLER; publs *Archäologie in Sachsen-Anhalt* (1 a year), *Jahresschrift für mitteldeutsche Vorgeschichte* (1 a year), *Veröffentlichungen* (1 a year).

Hamburg

Altonaer Museum für Kunst und Kulturgeschichte (Altona Museum in Hamburg/North German Regional Museum): POB 50 01 25, 22701 Hamburg; Museumstr. 23, 22765 Hamburg; tel. (40) 42813582; fax (40) 42812122; e-mail info@altonaermuseum.de; internet www.altonaer-museum.de; f. 1863; collns on art and cultural history, folk art, shipping and fishing; library of 70,000 vols; Chair. Prof. Dr KIRSTEN BAUMANN; Dir Prof. Dr TORKILD HINRICHSEN; Man. Dir HELMUT SANDER; publs *Altonaer Museum in Hamburg, Jahrbuch* (Yearbook), catalogues of collections and exhibitions.

Hamburger Kunsthalle: Glockengiesserwall, 20095 Hamburg; tel. (40) 428131200; fax (40) 428543409; e-mail info@hamburger-kunsthalle.de; internet www.hamburger-kunsthalle.de; f. 1869; paintings since 14th century, sculpture since 19th century, drawings and engravings since 14th century, Greek and Roman coins, medals since 14th century; library of 167,377 vols; Dir Prof. HUBERTUS GASSNER.

Museum für Hamburgische Geschichte: Holstenwall 24, 20355 Hamburg; tel. (40) 4281322380; fax (40) 4281323103; e-mail info@hamburgmuseum.de; internet www.hamburgmuseum.de; f. 1839; attached to Stiftung Historische Museen Hamburg; political history of Hamburg, library, coins, handicrafts, models, paintings, history of music, etc.; Chair. Prof. Dr KIRSTEN BAUMANN; Dir Prof. Dr LISA KOSOK; publs *Beiträge zur deutschen Volks- und Altertumskunde, Hamburger Beiträge zur Numismatik, Numismatische Studien*.

Museum für Kunst und Gewerbe Hamburg (Hamburg Museum of Art and Industry): Steintorpl. 1, 20099 Hamburg; tel. (40) 428134880; fax (40) 428134999; e-mail service@mkg-hamburg.de; internet www.mkg-hamburg.de; f. 1877; European sculpture and art since the Middle Ages, ancient art, art of the Near and Far East, European popular art, graphic, photographic and textile collns, contemporary design, historical keyboard instruments; library of 160,000 vols, 450 current periodicals; Dir Prof. Dr SABINE SCHULZE.

Museum für Völkerkunde Hamburg: Rothenbaumchaussee 64, 20148 Hamburg; tel. (40) 428879-0; fax (40) 428879-242; e-mail marketing@voelkerkundemuseum.com; internet www.voelkerkundemuseum.com; f. 1879; ethnological collns from Africa, America, Australia, Indonesia and the South Seas; library of 130,000 vols; Dir Prof. Dr W. KÖPKE; publs *Beiträge zur Mittelamerikanischen Wegweiser zur Völkerkunde* (irregular), *Mitteilungen aus dem Museum für Völkerkunde, N.F.* (1 a year).

Hanover

Historisches Museum Hannover (Historical Museum Hanover): Pferdestr. 6, 30159 Hanover; tel. (511) 16843052; fax (511) 16845003; e-mail historisches.museum@hannover-stadt.de; internet www.hannover-museum.de; f. 1903 as Vaterländisches Museum, 1937–50 as Niedersächsisches Volkstumsmuseum, 1950–66 as Niedersächsisches Heimatmuseum; three sections: Lower Saxon Folklore, History of the City of Hanover, History of the Kingdom of Hanover up to 1866; library of 20,000 vols; Dir Dr T. SCHWARK.

Museum August Kestner: Trammpl. 3, 30159 Hanover; tel. (511) 16842730; fax (511) 16846530; e-mail museum-august-kestner@hannover-stadt.de; internet www.hannover.de/kestner; f. 1889; Egyptian, Greek, Etruscan and Roman art; illuminated MSS, incunabula, applied art and design since the Middle Ages; ancient, medieval and modern coins, medals; library of 40,000 vols, 200 current periodicals; Dir Dr WOLFGANG SCHEPERS; Curator for Classical Archaelogy Dr ANNE VIOLA SIEBERT; Curator for Egyptology Dr CHRISTIAN E. LOEBEN; Curator for Numismatics Dr SIMONE VOGT.

Niedersächsisches Landesmuseum Hannover (Hanover State Museum): Willy-Brandt-Allee 5, 30169 Hanover; tel. (511) 9807686; fax (511) 9807684; e-mail info@nlm-h.niedersachsen.de; internet www.landesmuseum-hannover.de; f. 1852; art dating from the Middle Ages to the early 20th century; natural archaeology and ethnology sections; libraries attached to each section; Dir MARTIN SCHMIDT (acting); Dir (Ethnology) Dr ANNA SCHMID; Dir (Landesgalerie) Dr THOMAS ANDRATSCHKE; Dir (Natural History) ANDREA SPAUTZ; Dir (Prehistory) Prof. Dr DAGMAR-BEATRICE GAEDTKE-ECKARDT (acting); Operational Dir STEFFEN FÄRBER.

Heidelberg

Kurpfälzisches Museum der Stadt Heidelberg: Hauptstr. 97, 69117 Heidelberg; tel. (6221) 5834020; fax (6221) 5834900; e-mail kurpfaelzischesmuseum@heidelberg.de; internet www.museum-heidelberg.de; f. 1879; Dir Prof. Dr FRIEDER HEPP.

Hildesheim

Roemer- und Pelizaeus Museum: Am Steine 1–2, 31134 Hildesheim; tel. (5121) 93690; fax (5121) 35283; e-mail info@rpmuseum.de; internet www.rpmuseum.de; f. 1844; natural history, applied art, prehistory, ethnography, Egyptian art; library of 35,000 vols; Dir Dr KATJA LEMBKE.

Jena

Goethe-Gedenkstätte (im Inspektorhaus des Botanischen Gartens): Friedrich Schiller Universität Jena, Fürstengraben 26, 07743 Jena; tel. (3641) 931188; fax (3641) 949009; f. 1921; Curator Dr MICHAEL PLATEN.

Optisches Museum der Ernst-Abbe-Stiftung Jena (Optical Museum at the Ernst Abbe Foundation): Carl-Zeiss-Pl. 12, 07743 Jena; tel. (3641) 443165; fax (3641) 443224; e-mail info@optischesmuseum.de; internet www.optischesmuseum.de; f. 1922; history and devt of optical instruments; vision aids and glasses, cameras and magic lanterns, stereoscopes and magic lantern images, historic workshop of Carl Zeiss; library of 4,000 vols.

Romantikerhaus—Museum der Deutschen Frühromantik (Romantikerhaus—Museum of Early German Romanticism): Unterm Markt 12A, 07743 Jena; tel. (3641) 498249; fax (3641) 498245; e-mail romantikerhaus@jena.de; internet www.romantikerhaus.jena.de; f. 1981; Dir KLAUS SCHWARZ.

Stadtmuseum (City Museum): Markt 7, 07743 Jena; tel. (3641) 498261; fax (3641) 498255; e-mail stadtmuseum@jena.de; internet www.museen.jena.de; f. 1903; library of 30,000 vols; regional historical literature; art colln and town historical colln; Dir Dr MATIAS MIETH.

Karlsruhe

Badisches Landesmuseum Karlsruhe: Schloss, 76131 Karlsruhe; tel. (721) 9266514; fax (721) 9266537; e-mail info@landesmuseum.de; internet www.landesmuseum.de; f. 1919; colln incl. prehistoric, Egyptian, Greek and Roman antiquities, medieval, renaissance and baroque sculpture, works of art from the Middle Ages to the 20th century, weapons, folklore and coins, colln of Turkish trophies; library of 75,000 vols; Dir Prof. Dr HARALD SIEBENMORGEN.

Museum für Literatur am Oberrhein: Prinz-Max-Palais, Karlstr. 10, 76133 Karlsruhe; tel. and fax (721) 1334087; e-mail info@literaturmuseum.de; internet www.literaturmuseum.de; f. 1965; exhibition of the works, MSS and pictures of various authors; library of 8,000 vols; Pres. Prof. Dr HANSGEORG SCHMIDT-BERGMANN; Sec. MONIKA RIHM; publs *Jahresgabe, Mitteilungen*.

Staatliche Kunsthalle: POB 11 12 53, 76062 Karlsruhe; Hans-Thoma-Str. 2–6, 76133 Karlsruhe; tel. (721) 9263359; fax (721) 9266788; e-mail info@ kunsthalle-karlsruhe.de; internet www .kunsthalle-karlsruhe.de; f. 1846; German, Dutch, Flemish, French paintings and sculpture from the 14th–20th centuries; print room; 90,000 prints and drawings; education service; library of 150,000 vols; Dir Dr PIA MÜLLER-TAMM.

Staatliches Museum für Naturkunde Karlsruhe (State Museum of Natural History, Karlsruhe): Erbprinzenstr. 13, 76133 Karlsruhe; tel. (721) 1752111; fax (721) 1752110; e-mail museum@naturkundeka-bw .de; internet www .naturkundemuseum-karlsruhe.de; f. 1785; research and exhibitions in botany, zoology, mineralogy, geology, entomology, palaeontology, vivarium; library of 50,000 vols; Dir Prof. Dr NORBERT LENZ; publs *Andrias*, *Carolinea*, *Exhibition Catalogues* (irregular).

Kassel

Brüder Grimm-Museum Kassel: Brüder Grimm-Pl. 4, 34117 Kassel; tel. (561) 103235; fax (561) 713299; e-mail grimm-museum@ t-online.de; internet www.grimms.de; f. 1960; preservation of works of Jacob, Wilhelm and Ludwig Emil Grimm; colln of works by the brothers; original paintings, autographs, letters, drawings, etchings; Dir Dr BERNHARD LAUER.

Museumslandschaft Hessen Kassel (State Art Museums): POB 41 04 20, 34066 Kassel; Schloss Wilhelmshöhe, 34131 Kassel; tel. (561) 316800; fax (561) 31680111; e-mail info@museum-kassel.de; internet www .museum-kassel.de; f. 18th century; Dir Prof. Dr BERND KÜSTER.

Constituent Museums:

Astronomisch-Physikalisches Kabinett: Karlsaue 20c, Kassel; tel. (561) 31680500; fax (561) 31680555; e-mail info@museum-kassel.de; internet www .museum-kassel.de; f. 1992; astronomy and physics colln with history of technology section; planetarium; Dir Dr KARSTEN GAULKE.

Museum Schloss Friedrichstein: Schlossstr., Bad Wildungen; tel. (5621) 6577; fax (5621) 3650700; e-mail a .scherner@museum-kassel.de; internet www.museum-kassel.de; f. 1980; military and hunting exhibits from 15th–19th centuries; Curator Dr ANTJE SCHERNER.

Museum Schloss Wilhelmshöhe: Schlosspark 1, 34131 Kassel; tel. (561) 316800; fax (561) 31680111; e-mail info@ museum-kassel.de; internet www .museum-kassel.de; f. 1800; department of classical antiquities, gallery of old master paintings from 15th–18th centuries, collection of drawings and engravings; library of 105,000 vols, 600 journals; Dir Dr MICHAEL EISSENHAUER.

Neue Galerie: Schöne Aussicht 1, Kassel; tel. (561) 316800; fax (561) 31680444; e-mail info@museum-kassel.de; internet www.museum-kassel.de; f. 1976; paintings and sculpture from 1750 to present; closed for renovation; Dir Dr MICHAEL EISSENHAUER.

Konstanz

Archäologisches Landesmuseum (Regional Archaeological Museum): Benediktinerpl. 5, 78467 Konstanz; tel. (7531) 98040; fax (7531) 68452; e-mail info@konstanz .alm-bw.de; internet www.konstanz.alm-bw .de; f. 1990; local archaeological artefacts; Dir Dr JÖRG HEILIGMANN.

Bodensee-Naturmuseum (Lake Constance Natural History Museum): Hafenstr. 9, 78462 Konstanz; tel. (7531) 900915; fax (7531) 900608; e-mail krothm@stadt .konstanz.de; internet www.konstanz.de/ naturmuseum; f. 1967; geology, palaeontology, zoology and botany of Lake Constance; Dir MARTINA KROTH.

Hus-Museum: Hussenstr. 64, 78462 Konstanz; tel. (7531) 29042; e-mail hus-museum@t-online.de; internet www .konstanz.de/tourismus; f. 1965; house of religious thinker, philosopher and reformer, Jan Hus (c. 1369–1415); display by Czech and Slovak artists depicting Hus's life, Council of Constance and the Hussite wars; Dir Dr LIBUSE RÖSCH.

Rosgarten Museum: Rosgartenstr. 3–5, 78462 Konstanz; tel. (7531) 900277; internet www.konstanz.de/rosgartenmuseum; f. 1870; central museum for Lake Constance area; prehistoric, early historic colln; arts and crafts from the Middle Ages to 19th century; library of 6,000 vols; Dir Dr TOBIAS ENGELRING.

Leipzig

Deutsches Buch- und Schriftmuseum der Deutschen Nationalbibliothek Leipzig (German Book Museum): Deutscher Pl. 1, 04103 Leipzig; tel. (341) 2271324; fax (341) 2271440; e-mail dbsm@dnb.de; internet www .dnb.de; f. 1884; exhibits relate to history of books, writing and paper; closed for refurbishment, scheduled to reopen in 2012; library of 172,519 vols, 1,156 incunabula and MSS, 43,127 items of graphic art, 406,597 watermarks, 82,749 printed books since 1501; Dir Dr STEPHANIE JACOBS.

Museum der Bildenden Künste Leipzig (Leipzig Museum of Fine Arts): Katharinenstr. 10, 04109 Leipzig; tel. (341) 2169990; fax (341) 21699999; e-mail mdbk@ leipzig.de; internet www.mdbk.de; f. 1837; 3,000 paintings; collns of drawings and sculptures; Dir Dr HANS-WERNER SCHMIDT.

Museum für Kunsthandwerk Leipzig, Grassi-Museum (Museum of Applied Arts): Neumarkt 20, 04109 Leipzig; tel. (341) 2133719; fax (341) 2133715; e-mail grassimuseum@leipzig.de; internet www .grassimuseum.de; f. 1874; textiles, ceramics, glass, wood, and metal objects; prints and patterns relating to design; Dir Dr EVA M. HOYER.

Staatliche Ethnographische Sammlungen Sachsen, Staatlichen Kunstsammlungen Dresden (State Ethnographical Collection of Saxony): POB 10 09 55, 04009 Leipzig; Museum für Völkerkunde zu Leipzig/Grassimuseum, Johannispl. 5–11, 04103 Leipzig; tel. (341) 9731900; fax (341) 9731909; e-mail mvl-grassimuseum@ses .museum; internet www.mvl-grassimuseum .de; f. 2003 by the merger of Museum für Völkerkunde zu Leipzig, Museum für Völkerkunde Dresden and Völkerkundemuseum Herrnhut; Dir Dr CLAUS DEIMEL.

Constituent Museums:

Museum für Völkerkunde Dresden (Ethnographical Museum Dresden): Königsbrücker Landstr. 159, 01109 Dresden; tel. (351) 8926202; fax (351) 8926203; e-mail voelkerkunde.dresden@ses .museum; internet www .voelkerkunde-dresden.de; f. 1875; ethnography, physical anthropology; library of 350,000 vols; Dir Dr CLAUS DEIMEL; publs *Abhandlungen und Berichte* (Essays and Records), *Bibliographien Africa 1–3, Oceania 1–3* (irregular), *Dresdner Tagungsberichte* (irregular), *Kleine Beiträge* (irregular).

Museum für Völkerkunde zu Leipzig (Ethnographical Museum in Leipzig): POB 10 09 55, 04009 Leipzig; GRASSI Museum für Völkerkunde zu Leipzig, Johannispl. 5–11, 04103 Leipzig; tel. (341) 9731900; fax (341) 9731909; e-mail mvl-grassimuseum@ ses.museum; internet www .mvl-grassimuseum.de; f. 1869; ethnographical collns from Asia, Australia, Pacific Islands, Africa, America, Europe; library of 275,000 vols; Dir Dr CLAUS DEIMEL; publs *Abhandlungen und Berichte, Jahrbuch* (1 a year).

Völkerkundemuseum Herrnhut (Ethnographical Museum Herrnhut): Goethestr. 1, 02747 Herrnhut; tel. and fax (35873) 2403; e-mail voelkerkunde .herrnhut@ses.museum; internet www .voelkerkunde-herrnhut.de; f. 1878; ethnography; contains collns made by Moravian Church missionaries; library of 6,000 vols; Curator STEPHAN AUGUSTIN.

Stadtgeschichtliches Museum Leipzig: Böttchergäßchen 3, 04109 Leipzig; tel. (341) 965130; fax (341) 9651352; e-mail stadtmuseum@leipzig.de; internet www .stadtgeschichtliches-museum-leipzig.de; f. 1909; library of 160,000 items; Dir Dr VOLKER RODEKAMP.

Lübeck

Museen für Kunst und Kulturgeschichte (Museums for Art and Cultural History): Düvekenstr. 21, 23552 Lübeck; tel. (451) 1224134; fax (451) 1224183; e-mail mkk@ luebeck.de; internet www.museen.luebeck .de; library of 30,000 vols; Dir Dr THORSTEN RODIEK; publs *Katalog des Behnhauses*, *Kataloge des St Annen-Museums*.

Branch Museums:

Katharinenkirche: Königstr. 27, 23552 Lübeck; tel. (451) 1224143; fax (451) 1224183; e-mail mkk@luebeck.de; 14th-century bldgs; fmrly Franciscan monasteries church; Dir Dr THORSTEN RODIEK.

Museum Behnhaus Drägerhaus: Königstr. 9–11, 23552 Lübeck; tel. (451) 1224148; fax (451) 1224149; e-mail behnhaus@luebeck.de; internet www .die-luebecker-museen.de; f. 1921; museum of 19th-century art located in late 18th-century patrician house; art from Overbeck to Munch; Dir Dr ALEXANDER BASTEK.

Museum Holstentor: Holstentorpl., 23552 Lübeck; tel. (451) 1224129; fax (451) 1224183; e-mail mkk@luebeck.de; internet www.die-luebecker-museen.de; built 1464–1478; history of the city and the merchant of Lübeck; Dir Dr THORSTEN RODIEK.

St Annen-Museum und Kunsthalle St Annen (St Annen Museum and Art Gallery): St Annenstr. 15, 23552 Lübeck; tel. (451) 1224137; fax (451) 1224183; e-mail mkk@luebeck.de; internet www .die-luebecker-museen.de; f. 1915 (Museum), 2003 (Art Gallery); Late Gothic convent, built 1502–1515; medieval ecclesiastical art from Lübeck; domestic art from Lübeck, from Middle Ages to 18th century; modern and contemporary art; Dir Dr HILDEGARD VOGELER.

Völkerkundesammlung (Ethnographic Collection): Grosser Bauhof 14, 23522 Lübeck; Parade 10, 23552 Lübeck; tel. (451) 1224342; fax (451) 1224348; e-mail vks@ luebeck.de; internet www.vkhl.de; f. 1893; Dir BRIGITTE TEMPLIN.

Magdeburg

Magdeburger Museen: Otto-von-Guericke-Str. 68–73, 39104 Magdeburg; tel. (391) 5403501; fax (391) 5403510; e-mail museen@magdeburg.de; internet www

.magdeburgermuseen.de; f. 1906; local history colln, art gallery, sculptures, handicrafts, graphics, bibliophilia, costumes, sociology, natural history and prehistory colln; Kulturhistorisches Museum, Kunstmuseum Kloster Unser Lieben Frauen, Museum für Naturkunde, Technikmuseum; library of 50,000 vols; Dir Prof. Dr MATTHIAS PUHLE; publs *Abhandlungen und Berichte Naturkunde und Vorgeschichte*, *Magdeburger Museumshefte* (irregular), *Magdeburger Museumsschriften* (irregular).

Mainz

Gutenberg-Museum: Liebfrauenpl. 5, 55116 Mainz; tel. (6131) 122640; fax (6131) 123488; e-mail gutenberg-museum@stadt .mainz.de; internet www.gutenberg-museum .de; f. 1900; world museum of typography; library of 90,000 vols; Dir Dr ANNETTE LUDWIG.

Landesmuseum Mainz (Mainz State Museum): Grosse Bleiche 49–51, 55116 Mainz; tel. (6131) 28570; fax (6131) 2857288; e-mail landesmuseum-mainz@ gdke.rlp.de; internet www .landesmuseum-mainz.de; f. 1803; cultural history and art; Dir Dr ANDREA STOCKHAMMER; Deputy Dir Dr NORBERT SUHR.

Münzsammlung (Coin Collection): Stadtarchiv Mainz, Rheinallee 3B, 55116 Mainz; tel. (6131) 122178; fax (6131) 123569; e-mail stadtarchiv@stadt.mainz.de; internet www .stadtarchiv.mainz.de; f. 1784; Dir Dr WOLFGANG DOBRAS.

Naturhistorisches Museum Mainz (Natural History Museum): Reichklarastr. 1, 55116 Mainz; tel. (6131) 122646; fax (6131) 122975; e-mail naturhistorisches.museum@ stadt.mainz.de; internet www.mainz.de/ nhm; f. 1834 (collns; museum f. 1910); mineralogy, geology, palaeontology, zoology and botany of Rheinland-Pfalz and Rwanda; library of 40,000 vols, 60,000 pamphlets; Dir Dr MICHAEL SCHMITZ; Deputy Dir Dr HERBERT LUTZ; publs *Mainzer Naturwissenschaftliches Archiv* (1 a year), *Mainzer Naturwissenschaftliches Archiv, Beihefte*, *Mitteilungen der Rheinischen Naturforschenden Gesellschaft* (1 a year).

Römisch-Germanisches Zentralmuseum–Forschungsinstitut für Vor- und Frühgeschichte (Central Roman-German Museum–Research Museum for Prehistory and Early History): Ernst-Ludwig-Pl. 2, 55116 Mainz; tel. (6131) 9124113; fax (6131) 9124199; e-mail info@rgzm.de; internet web .rgzm.de; f. 1852; studies in Old World archaeology and prehistory, conservation of prehistoric, Roman and early medieval antiquities; library of 120,000 vols; Gen. Dir Prof. Dr FALKO DAIM; publs *Arbeitsblätter für Restauratoren*, *Archäologisches Korrespondenzblatt*, *Ausstellungskataloge*, *Corpus Signorum Imperii Romani*, *Führer durch die Ausstellungen*, *Jahrbuch*, *Kataloge*, *Restaurierung und Archäologie*, *Studien zu den Anfängen der Metallurgie*, *Vulkanpark-Forschungen*.

Mannheim

Kunsthalle Mannheim: Moltkestr. 9, 68165 Mannheim; Friedrichspl. 4, 68165 Mannheim; tel. (621) 2936452; fax (621) 2936412; e-mail kunsthalle@mannheim.de; internet www.kunsthalle-mannheim.eu; f. 1909; 33,000 drawings, water colours and graphics, 1,700 paintings and 600 sculptures; Dir Dr ULRIKE LORENZ; Deputy Dir Dr INGE HEROLD.

Reiss-Engelhorn-Museen Mannheim: POB 10 30 51, 68030 Mannheim; Museum Weltkulturen D5, 68159; tel. (621) 2933150; fax (621) 2939539; e-mail reiss-engelhorn-museen@mannheim.de; internet www.rem-mannheim.de; f. 1957 as Reiss-Museum; museum of art, crafts and decorative arts, local theatre history, archaeology and prehistory, ethnology, local history and natural history; colln of historical European musical instruments; Forum Internationale Photgraphie (FIP); library of 120,000 vols; Dir-Gen. Prof. Dr ALFRIED WIECZOREK.

Marburg

Museum für Kunst und Kulturgeschichte: Biegenstr. 11, 35037 Marburg; tel. (6421) 2822355; fax (6421) 2822166; e-mail museum@verwaltung.uni-marburg .de; internet www.uni-marburg.de/ uni-museum; f. 1927; attached to Philipps-Univ.; comprises Museum für Bildende Kunst and Museum für Kulturgeschichte; cultural history and fine art; Dir Dr AGNES TIEZE; Sec. MARIA KATZ.

Mettmann

Neanderthal-Museum: Talstr. 300, 40822 Mettmann; tel. (2104) 97970; fax (2104) 979796; e-mail museum@neanderthal.de; internet www.neanderthal.de; f. 1996; human evolution since earliest times; library of 4,000 vols; Dir Prof. Dr GERD-C. WENIGER.

Munich

Archäologische Staatssammlung München (Bavarian State Archaeological Collection): Lerchenfeldstr. 2, 80538 Munich; tel. (89) 2112402; fax (89)21124401; e-mail archaeologische.staatssammlung@extern .lrz-muenchen.de; internet www .archaeologie-bayern.de; f. 1885; prehistoric, Roman and early medieval antiquities from Southern Germany, prehistoric archaeology of Mediterranean and Near East; Dir Prof. Dr Hab. RUPERT GEBHARD; Deputy Dir Dr BERND STEIDL; publ. *Kataloge* (irregular).

Bayerische Staatsgemäldesammlungen (Bavarian State Painting Collections): Barerstr. 29, 80799 Munich; tel. (89) 238050; fax (89) 23805251; e-mail info@ pinakothek.de; internet www.pinakothek.de; medieval to modern art, painting and sculpture; Gen. Dir Prof. Dr KLAUS SCHRENK.

Bayerisches Nationalmuseum (National Bavarian Museum): Prinzregentenstr. 3, 80538 Munich; tel. (89) 2112401; fax (89) 21124201; e-mail bay.nationalmuseum@bnm .mwn.de; internet www .bayerisches-nationalmuseum.de; f. 1855; European fine arts, especially sculpture, decorative art and folk art; library of 75,000 vols; Dir Dr RENATE EIKELMANN; publs *Bayerische Blätter für Volkskunde*, *Bildführer*, *Forschungshefte*, *Kataloge*.

Deutsches Museum von Meisterwerken der Naturwissenschaft und Technik (German Museum of Scientific and Technological Masterpieces): 80306 Munich; Museumsinsel 1, 80538 Munich; tel. (89) 2179213; fax (89) 2179262; e-mail information@deutsches-museum.de; internet www.deutsches-museum.de; f. 1903; history of science and technology from its origins to the present day; spec. colln of MSS and autographs, trade literature, plans, pictorial art, films, commemorative medals; research institute for the history of science and technology; 'Kerschensteiner Kolleg' for teacher in-service training; library of 920,000 vols, 3,500 current periodicals; Dir-Gen. Prof. Dr WOLFGANG M. HECKL; publ. *Kultur und Technik* (4 a year).

Affiliated Museums:

Deutsches Museum Bonn (German Museum in Bonn): Ahrstr. 45, 53175 Bonn; tel. (228) 302255; fax (228) 302254; e-mail info@deutsches-museum-bonn.de; internet www.deutsches-museum-bonn .de; f. 1995; science and technology in Germany since 1945; Dir Dr ANDREA NIEHAUS.

Deutsches Museum Flugwerft Schleissheim (German Museum in Flugwerft Schleissheim): Effnerstr. 18, 85764 Oberschleissheim; tel. (89) 3157140; fax (89) 31571450; e-mail fws@deutsches-museum .de; f. 1992; aeronautical colln; Dir-Gen. Prof. Dr WOLFGANG M. HECKL.

Deutsches Museum Verkehrszentrum (German Museum—Transport Centre): Theresienhöhe 14A, 80339 Munich; tel. (89) 500806762; fax (89) 500806501; e-mail verkehrszentrum@ deutsches-museum.de; internet www .deutsches-museum.de/verkehrszentrum; f. 2003; traffic museum; Dir Gen. Prof. Dr WOLFGANG M. HECKL.

Neue Sammlung–Staatliches Museum für Angewandte Kunst (State Museum for Applied Arts): POB 34 01 34, 80098 Munich; Türkenstr. 15 (Pinakothek der Moderne), 80333 Munich; tel. (89) 2727250; fax (89) 272725561; e-mail info@ die-neue-sammlung.de; internet www .die-neue-sammlung.de; f. 1925; modern industrial arts and crafts, architecture, urban planning; industrial and graphic design; Dir Prof. Dr FLORIAN HUFNAGL.

Staatliche Antikensammlungen und Glyptothek (State Antique Collections): Königspl. 1, 80333 Munich; tel. (89) 286100; fax (89) 28927516; e-mail info@ antike-am-koenigsplatz.mwn.de; internet www.antike-am-koenigsplatz.mwn.de; Greek and Etruscan vases and bronzes, Greek and Roman sculpture, terracottas and bronzes, glass, jewellery; Conservator Dr MATTHIAS STEINHART; Conservator Dr CHRISTIAN GLIWITZKY; Conservator Dr FLORIAN KNAUSS.

Staatliche Graphische Sammlung München: Katharina-von-Bora-Str. 10, 80333 Munich; tel. (89) 28927650; fax (89) 28927653; e-mail info@sgsm.eu; internet www.sgsm.eu; f. 1758; German, Dutch, French and Italian prints and drawings since 15th century; Dir Dr MICHAEL SEMFF.

Staatliche Münzsammlung (State Coin Collection): Residenzstr. 1, 80333 Munich; tel. (89) 227221; fax (89) 299859; e-mail info@ staatliche-muenzsammlung.de; internet www.staatliche-muenzsammlung.de; f. 16th century; coins from different countries and centuries; spec. collns: Greek, Roman and Byzantine coins, German and Italian Renaissance medals, Bavarian coins, precious stones from antiquity, Middle Ages and Renaissance, Japanese lacquer cabinets; library of 26,000 vols; Dir Dr DIETRICH KLOSE.

Staatliche Naturwissenschaftliche Sammlungen Bayerns, München (Bavarian Natural History Collections): Menzingerstr. 71, 80638 Munich; tel. (89) 17999240; fax (89) 17999255; e-mail generaldirektion@snsb.de; internet www .naturwissenschaftlichesammlungenbayerns .de; f. 1827; scientific colln of c. 30m. specimens; Gen. Dir Prof. Dr GERHARD HASZPRUNAR.

Subordinate Institutions:

Bayerische Staatssammlung für Paläontologie und Geologie: Richard-Wagner-Str. 10, 80333 Munich; tel. (89) 21806630; fax (89) 21806601; e-mail pal .sammlung@lrz.uni-muenchen.de; internet www.palmuc.de/bspg; f. 1759; colln and preservation of fossils and rock materials; library of 120,000 vols; Dir Prof. Dr GERT WÖRHEIDE; publ. *Zitteliana*.

Botanische Staatssammlung: Menzinger-Str. 67, 80638 Munich; tel. (89) 17861265; fax (89) 17861193; e-mail office@bsm.mwn.de; internet www .botanischestaatssammlung.de; f. 1813; natural history colln; library of 30,000 vols; Dir Prof. Dr SUSANNE RENNER; publ. *Arnoldia*.

Botanischer Garten München–Nymphenburg: Menzinger Str. 65, 80638 Munich; tel. (89) 17861316; fax (89) 17861340; e-mail info@botmuc.de; internet www.botmuc.de; f. 1914; Dir Prof. Dr SUSANNE RENNER.

Jura-Museum: Willibaldsburg, 85072 Eichstätt; tel. (8421) 2956; fax (8421) 89609; e-mail sekretariat@jura-museum .de; internet www.altmuehlnet.de/ ~jura-museum; f. 1976; natural history; Dir Dr MARTINA KÖLBL-EBERT; publ. *Archaeopteryx*.

Mineralogische Staatssammlung (Mineralogical State Collection Munich): Theresienstr. 41, 80333 Munich; tel. (89) 21804312; fax (89) 21804334; e-mail mineralogische.staatssammlung@lrz .uni-muenchen.de; internet www.lrz.de/ ~mineralogische.staatssammlung; f. 1823; Dir Prof. Dr WOLFGANG SCHMAHL.

Museum Mensch und Natur (Museum of Man and Nature): Schloss Nymphenburg, 80638 Munich; tel. (89) 1795890; fax (89) 179589100; e-mail museum@musmn .de; internet www.musmn.de; f. 1990; modern natural history with interactive exhibition design; permanent exhibitions cover range of subjects from geology and mineralogy to neurobiology, genetics, ecology; temporary exhibitions; Dir MICHAEL APEL; Deputy Dir Dr SIMON GILLA.

Naturkunde-Museum   Bamberg: Fleischstr. 2, 96047 Bamberg; tel. (951) 8631249; fax (951) 8631250; e-mail info@ naturkundemuseum-bamberg.de; internet www.naturkundemuseum-bamberg.de; f. 1790; colln of 200,000 objects from the fields of geology, mineralogy, palaeontology, zoology and botany; Man. Dr MATTHIAS MÄUSER.

Rieskrater-Museum   Nördlingen: Eugene-Shoemaker-Pl. 1, 86720 Nördlingen; tel. (9081) 2738220; fax (9081) 27382220; e-mail rieskratermuseum@ noerdlingen.de; internet www .riescrater-museum.de; f. 1990; natural history; Man. Dr MICHAEL SCHIEBER.

Staatssammlung für Anthropologie und Paläoanatomie: Karolinenpl. 2A, 80333 Munich; tel. (89) 54884380; fax (89) 548843817; e-mail asm.boulesnam@extern .lrz-muenchen.de; internet www .naturwissenschaftlichesammlungen-bayerns.de/anthropologie/anthro.html; f. 1886; Dir Prof. Dr GISELA GRUPE; Dir Prof. Dr JORIS PETERS.

Urwelt-Museum Oberfranken: Kanzleistr. 1, 95444 Bayreuth; tel. (921) 511211; fax (921) 511212; e-mail verwaltung@urwelt-museum.de; internet www.urwelt-museum.de; f. 1997; natural history; Man. Dr JOACHIM MARTIN RABOLD.

Zoologische   Staatssammlung München: Münchhausenstr. 21, 81247 Munich; tel. (89) 81070; fax (89) 8107300; e-mail zsm@zsm.mwn.de; internet www .zsm.mwn.de; f. 1807; more than 20m. zoological objects; library of 92,664 vols (books and serials), 823 running journals, 129,020 separata; Dir Prof. Dr GERHARD HASZPRUNAR; publs *Journal of Zoology*, *Spixiana*, *Spixiana Supplements*.

Staatliches Museum Ägyptischer Kunst (State Museum of Egyptian Art): Katharina-von-Bora-Str. 10, 80333 Munich; Hofgartenstr., Munich; tel. (89) 28927630; fax (89) 28927638;   e-mail   info@ aegyptisches-museum-muenchen.com; internet www.aegyptisches-museum-muenchen .de; f. 1966; library: small specialized library; Dir Dr SYLVIA SCHOSKE.

Staatliches Museum für Völkerkunde München (State Museum of Ethnology Munich): Maximilianstr. 42, 80538 Munich; tel. (89) 210136100; fax (89) 210136247; e-mail museum.voelkerkunde@mfv.bayern .de;   internet   www .voelkerkundemuseum-muenchen.de;   f. 1868; collns on Asia, America, Africa and the Pacific Islands; library of 50,000 vols, 75 current periodicals; Dir Dr CHRISTINE STELZIG.

Städtische Galerie im Lenbachhaus: Nymphenburger Str. 84, 80636 Munich; Luisenstr. 33, 80333 Munich; tel. (89) 23332000; fax (89) 23332003; e-mail lenbachhaus@muenchen.de; internet www .lenbachhaus.de; f. 1929; Munich artists including paintings by Kandinsky, Klee and the Blaue Reiter group; int. contemporary art; exhibitions, lectures, performances; library of 65,000 vols; Dir Prof. Dr HELMUT FRIEDEL; Man. KURT LAUBE.

Münster

Landesmuseum für Kunst und Kulturgeschichte (Westphalian Museum of Art and Cultural History): Dompl. 10, 48143 Münster; tel. (251) 590701; fax (251) 5907210; e-mail landesmuseum@lwl.org; internet www.lwl-landesmuseum-muenster .de; f. 1908; sculpture, painting, graphic art, goldsmith work since 9th century; engraved portraits, history, numismatics; library of 128,000 vols; Dir Dr WOLFGANG KIRSCH.

Nuremberg

Albrecht-Dürer-Haus: Albrecht-Dürer-Str. 39, 90403 Nuremberg; tel. (911) 2312271; fax (911) 2314971; e-mail museen@stadt .nuernberg.de; internet www.museen .nuernberg.de; f. 1828; life and work of the engraver Albrecht Dürer (1471–1528) presented in his home (inhabited 1509–28); Dir Dr THOMAS SCHAUERTE.

Germanisches Nationalmuseum: Kartäusergasse 1, 90402 Nuremberg; tel. (911) 13310; fax (911) 1331200; e-mail info@gnm .de; internet www.gnm.de; f. 1852; German art and culture from prehistoric times to the present, fine art galleries, folk art, public library, archives, print room, musical instruments, arms, toys, etc.; library of 548,000 vols, 1,600 current periodicals; Chief Dir Prof. Dr G. ULRICH GROSSMANN.

Kunsthalle Nürnberg im KunstKultur-Quartier (Nuremberg Art Museum): 90317 Nuremberg; Lorenzer Str. 32, 90402 Nuremberg; tel. (911) 2312853; fax (911) 2313721; e-mail kunsthalle@stadt.nuernberg.de; internet www.kunsthalle.nuernberg.de; f. 1967; changing exhibitions of int. contemporary art; Dir ELLEN SEIFERMANN.

Stadtmuseum Fembohaus: Burgstr. 11, 90403 Nuremberg; tel. (911) 2315418; fax (911) 2315422; internet www.museen .nuernberg.de; f. 1958; art and cultural history of Nuremberg; Dir RUDOLF KÄS.

Offenbach am Main

Klingspor-Museum Offenbach: Herrnstr. 80, 63061 Offenbach am Main; tel. (69) 80652954; fax (69) 80652669; e-mail klingspormuseum@offenbach.de; internet www.offenbach.de/klingspor-museum; f. 1953; colln and exhibition of calligraphy, typography, bookbinding, modern book art and private presses; spec. colln of 20th-century calligraphy; library of 73,000 vols; Dir Dr STEFAN SOLTEK; Librarian MARTINA WEISS; Librarian STEPHANIE EHRET.

Pforzheim

Schmuckmuseum Pforzheim im Reuchlinhaus: Jahnstr. 42, 75173 Pforzheim; tel. (7231) 392126; fax (7231) 391441; e-mail schmuckmuseum@stadt-pforzheim.de; internet www.schmuckmuseum.de; f. 1938; permanent and temporary exhibitions about jewellery and its history, displaying past 5,000 years; Dir CORNELIE HOLZACH.

Potsdam

Brandenburgisches Landesmuseum für Ur- und Frühgeschichte (Pre- and Early History): Forstweg 1, 14656 Brieselang; tel. (332) 3236940; f. 1953; Dir Prof. Dr J. KUNOW; publs *Forschungen zur Archäologie im Land Brandenburg* (1 a year), *Veröffentlichungen des Brandenburgischen Landesmuseums für Ur- und Frühgeschichte* (1 a year).

Stiftung Preussische Schlösser und Gärten Berlin-Brandenburg (Prussian Palaces and Gardens Foundation of Berlin-Brandenburg): POB 60 14 62, 14414 Potsdam; Allee nach Sanssouci 5, 14471 Potsdam; tel. (331) 9694200; fax (331) 9694107; e-mail info@spsg.de; internet www.spsg.de; f. 1995; administers gardens and 150 palaces and other historic bldgs in and around Berlin and Potsdam; Dir-Gen. Prof. Dr HARTMUT DORGERLOH; Admin. Dir Dr HEINZ BERG.

Recklinghausen

Museen der Stadt Recklinghausen (Recklinghausen City Museums): Grosse-Perdekamp-Str. 25–27, 45657 Recklinghausen; tel. (2361) 501935; fax (2361) 501932; e-mail info@kunst-re.de; internet www .kunst-re.de; f. 1950; Dir Dr FERDINAND ULLRICH.

Attached Museums:

Ikonen-Museum   (Icon   Museum): Kirchpl. 2A, 45657 Recklinghausen; tel. (2361) 501941; fax (2361) 501942; e-mail ikonen@kunst-re.de;   internet   www .kunst-re.de; f. 1956; Russian, Byzantine, Greek and Balkan icons, miniatures, metal work, Coptic art and textiles; Dirs Prof. Dr FERDINAND ULLRICH; Curator Dr EVA HAUSTEIN-BARTSCH.

Städtische Kunsthalle (City Art Gallery): Recklinghausen; tel. (2361) 501935; fax (2361) 501932; e-mail info@kunst-re .de; internet www.kunst-re.de; f. 1950; paintings, drawings, prints and sculptures by contemporary artists; Dir Dr FERDINAND ULLRICH; Dir Dr HANS-JUERGEN SCHWALM.

Vestisches   Museum: Hohenzollernstr. 12, 45659 Recklinghausen; tel. (2361) 501946; fax (2361) 501932; e-mail info@ kunst-re.de; internet www.kunst-re.de; f. 1987; Westphalian arts and crafts, local history, native art; Dir Dr FERDINAND ULLRICH; Dir Dr HANS-JUERGEN SCHWALM.

Schleswig

Stiftung Schleswig-Holsteinische Landesmuseen Schloss Gottorf (Foundation of State Museums in Schleswig-Holstein in Schloss Gottorf): Schloss Gottorf, 24837 Schleswig; tel. (4621) 813222; fax (4621) 813555; e-mail info@schloss-gottorf.de; internet www.schloss-gottorf.de; f. 1835; houses archaeological and art and culture museums and the Centre for Baltic and Scandinavian Archaeology; library of 40,000 vols; Dir Prof. Dr CLAUS VON CARNAP-BORNHEIM; Dir Dr JÜRGEN FITSCHEN; publs *Ausgrabungen in Haithabu* (irregular), *Ausgrabungen in Schleswig* (irregular), *Ber-*

ichte über die Ausgrabungen in Haithabu (irregular), *Die Funde der älteren Bronzezeit des nordischen Kreises* (irregular), *Offa* (1 a year), *Offa Bücher* (irregular), *Untersuchungen und Materialien zur Steinzeit in Schleswig-Holstein* (irregular).

Affiliated Museums:

Archäologisches Landesmuseum (Provincial Museum of Archaeology): Schloss Gottorf, 24837 Schleswig; tel. (4621) 813222; internet www.schloss-gottorf.de/alm; f. 1835; archaeological and ethnological exhibits.

Eisenkunstgussmuseum Büdelsdorf (Ironwork Museum): Glück-Auf-Allee 4, 24782 Büdelsdorf; internet www.schloss-gottorf.de/ekg; f. 1981; history of ironwork.

Jüdisches Museum Rendsburg (Jewish Museum): Prinzessinstr. 7–8, 24768 Rendsburg; tel. (4331) 25262; fax (4331) 24714; e-mail info@jmrd.de; internet www.schloss-gottorf.de/jm; f. 1988.

Landesmuseum für Kunst und Kulturgeschichte (Museum of Art and Culture): Schloss Gottorf, 24837 Schleswig; tel. (4621) 813222; internet www.schloss-gottorf.de/lmkk; artefacts from Middle Ages onwards; colln of 19th-century paintings.

Volkskunde Museum Schleswig (Folklore Museum in Schleswig): Schloss Gottorf, 24837 Schleswig; Suadicanistr. 46–54, 24837 Schleswig; tel. (4621) 96760; fax (4621) 967634; e-mail volkskunde@schloss-gottorf.de; internet www.schloss-gottorf.de/vkm; f. 1993; history of local arts and crafts; Dir GUNTRAM TURKOWSKI.

Wikinger Museum Haithabu–Stiftung Schleswig-Holsteinische Landesmuseen Schloss Gottorf (Museum of the Viking—Age settlement Haithabu): Schloss Gottorf, 24837 Schleswig; tel. (4621) 813222; fax (4621) 813555; e-mail info@schloss-gottorf.de; internet www.schloss-gottorf.de/wmh; history of the archaeological dig; restored longship on port.

Schwerin

Archäologisches Landesmuseum und Landesamt für Bodendenkmalpflege Mecklenburg-Vorpommern: Domhof 4/5, 19055 Schwerin; tel. (385) 52140; fax (385) 5214198; e-mail poststelle@kulturerbe-mv.de; internet www.kulturerbe-mv.de; f. 1953; library of 44,000 vols; Dir Dr FRIEDRICH LÜTH; publs *Archäologie in Mecklenburg-Vorpommern*, *Archäologische Berichte aus Mecklenburg-Vorpommern*, *Beiträge zur Ur- und Frühgeschichte Mecklenburg-Vorpommerns*, *Bodendenkmalpflege in Mecklenburg-Vorpommern Jahrbuch*, *Materialhefte*, *Museumskataloge*.

Speyer

Historisches Museum der Pfalz Speyer (Historical Museum of the Palatinate): Dompl. 4, 67346 Speyer; tel. (6232) 13250; fax (6232) 132540; e-mail info@museum.speyer.de; internet www.museum.speyer.de; f. 1869; art and cultural history of the Palatinate, includes wine museum and diocesan museum; library of 20,000 vols; Dir Dr ALEXANDER KOCH; publs *Mitteilungen des Historischen Vereins* (1 a year), *Pfälzer Heimat* (4 a year).

Stralsund

Kulturhistorisches Museum der Hansestadt Stralsund (Cultural and Historical Museum of Stralsund): Mönchstr. 25–27, 18439 Stralsund; tel. (3831) 28790; fax (3831) 25253600; e-mail kulturhistorisches-museum@stralsund.de; internet www.stralsund.de; f. 1858; prehistory, ecclesiastical art, folklore, local history, furniture, history of navigation and navy, modern art, handicrafts, 18th-century products; Dir Dr ANDREAS GRÜGER.

Stuttgart

Kunstmuseum Stuttgart (Stuttgart Art Museum): Kleiner Schlosspl. 1, 70173 Stuttgart; tel. (711) 2162188; fax (711) 216-7824; e-mail info@kunstmuseum-stuttgart.de; internet www.kunstmuseum-stuttgart.de; f. 1924; paintings, drawings, graphics and sculptures by artists since 19th century; Otto Dix colln, Adolf Hölzel colln, Willi Baumeister archive; Dir Dr ULRIKE GROOS; Curator Dr DANIEL SPANKE; Curator Dr SIMONE SCHIMPF.

Landesmuseum Württemberg: Altes Schloss, 70173 Stuttgart; tel. (711) 89535111; fax (711) 89535444; e-mail info@landesmuseum-stuttgart.de; internet www.landesmuseum-stuttgart.de; f. 1862; archaeology, art history and cultural history from prehistoric to medieval times; 4,000 years of glass-making, Swabian sculpture, Renaissance clocks, musical instruments, Württemberg crown jewels; Roman lapidarium; museum for children; Dir Prof. Dr CORNELIA EWIGLEBEN; Chief Curator THOMAS BRUNE.

Linden-Museum Stuttgart, Staatliches Museum für Völkerkunde (Linden Museum Stuttgart, State Museum for Ethnography): Hegelpl. 1, 70174 Stuttgart; tel. (711) 2022456; fax (711) 2022590; e-mail sekretariat@lindenmuseum.de; internet www.lindenmuseum.de; f. 1882; ethnographical museum, exhibitions; library of 50,000 vols, 270 current periodicals; Dir Prof. Dr INÈS DE CASTRO; Librarian GÜNTER DARCIS; publ. *Tribus* (1 a year).

Staatliches Museum für Naturkunde Stuttgart: Rosenstein 1, 70191 Stuttgart; tel. (711) 89360; fax (711) 8936100; e-mail museum@smns-bw.de; internet www.naturkundemuseum-bw.de; f. 1791; colln and research in botany, palaeontology, zoology; exhibition (permanent and spec.), education; library of 75,000 vols; Dir Prof. Dr JOHANNA EDER; publs *Stuttgarter Beiträge zur Naturkunde, Serie A: Biologie* (irregular—up to 25 a year), *Stuttgarter Beiträge zur Naturkunde, Serie B: Geologie/Paläontologie* (irregular—up to 25 a year), *Stuttgarter Beiträge zur Naturkunde, Serie C: Wissen für Alle* (2 a year).

Staatsgalerie Stuttgart: POB 10 43 42, 70038 Stuttgart; Konrad-Adenauerstr. 30–32, 70173 Stuttgart; tel. (711) 470400; fax (711) 2369983; e-mail info@staatsgalerie.de; internet www.staatsgalerie.de; f. 1843; art since the Middle Ages; colln of prints, drawings and photographs; Oskar Schlemmer Archive, Will Grohmann Archive, Sohm Archive, Adolf Hölzel's art-theoretical writings; library of 120,000 vols; Dir SEAN RAINBIRD.

Trier

Rheinisches Landesmuseum Trier (Museum of the Rheinland in Trier): Weimarer Allee 1, 54290 Trier; tel. (651) 97740; fax (651) 9774222; e-mail landesmuseum-trier@gdke.rlp.de; internet www.landesmuseum-trier.de; f. 1877; Roman and early medieval exhibits excavated in Trier and the local area; art history from the Middle Ages to the 19th century; numismatic colln; restoration workshops; dendro-chronological and archeobotanical analyses; municipal and regional archaeological research; library of 100,000 vols, 3,000 journals; Dir Dr ECKART KÖHNE; publs *Funde und Ausgrabungen im Bezirk Trier* (1 a year), *Schriftenreihe des Rheinischen Landesmuseums Trier* (irregular), *Trierer Grabungen und Forschungen* (irregular), *Trierer Zeitschrift für Geschichte und Kunst* (1 a year).

Ulm

Ulmer Museum (Ulm Museum): Marktpl. 9, 89070 Ulm; tel. (731) 1614300; fax (731) 1611626; e-mail info.ulmer-museum@ulm.de; internet www.museum.ulm.de; f. 1924; collns of Ulm and Swabian art from 14th–19th centuries, international art since beginning of 20th century, archaeological collns, archives of the fmr Ulm School of Design (Hochschule für Gestaltung); Dir (vacant).

Weimar

Klassik Stiftung Weimar: Burgpl. 4, 99423 Weimar; tel. (3643) 545400; fax (3643) 419816; e-mail info@klassik-stiftung.de; internet www.klassik-stiftung.de; f. 1953; preserves and researches Weimar's artistic and cultural sites and collns, primarily the classical period in Weimar and modern art in Weimar; administers the Goethe-National Museum (comprises 23 museums and houses connected with Goethe and Schiller, and other bldgs, incl. Liszt's house); also the Nietzsche-Archiv, the Schlossmuseum, the Bauhaus Museum, the Neues Museum, the Goethe- und Schiller-Archiv (800,000 MSS of German writers, artists, composers and scientists) and the Duchess Anna Amalia Bibliothek (850,000 vols); Pres. HELLMUT SEEMANN; Admin. Dir (vacant).

Thüringisches Landesamt für Denkmalpflege und Archäologie (Thuringian Regional Office for the Preservation of Monuments and Archaeology): Humboldtstr. 11, 99423 Weimar; tel. (3643) 818300; fax (3643) 818390; e-mail post.weimar@tlda.thueringen.de; internet www.thueringen.de/denkmalpflege; f. 1888; library of 28,000 vols; Pres. Dr Hab. SVEN OSTRITZ; publs *Ausgrabungen und Funde im Freistaat Thüringen*, *Jahresschrift 'Alt-Thüringen'*, *Restaurierung und Museumstechnik*, *Weimarer Monographien zur Ur- und Frühgeschichte*.

Attached Museums:

Museum für Ur- und Frühgeschichte Thüringens (Thuringian Museum for Pre- and Early History): Humboldtstr. 11, 99423 Weimar; tel. (3643) 818331; fax (3643) 818390; e-mail museum@tlda.thueringen.de; local history since 400,000 BC.

Steinsburgmuseum: Waldhaussiedlung 8, 98631 Römhild; tel. (36948) 20561; fax (36948) 82853; Celtic site and artefacts; Dir Dr M. SIEDEL.

Wittenberg

Lutherhaus, Reformationsgeschichtliches Museum (Museum of the History of the Reformation): Collegienstr. 54, 06886 Lutherstadt Wittenberg; tel. (3491) 4203118; fax (3491) 4203270; e-mail lutherhaus@martinluther.de; internet www.martinluther.de; f. 1883; portraits, MSS, pictures, woodcuts, copperplates, medallions and original works on the history of the Reformation; library of 60,000 vols; Dir Dr STEFAN RHEIN.

Worms

Museum der Stadt Worms im Andreasstift (Worms City Museum): Weckerlingpl. 7, 67547 Worms; tel. (6241) 946390; fax (6241) 24068; e-mail museum@worms.de; internet www.museum.worms.de; f. 1881; archaeology, town history of Worms, spec. colln of glassware, Luther Room (diet of 1521); Dir for Admin. Dr GERALD BOENNEN; publs *Der Wormsgau* (1 a year, with supplements),

Zeitschrift der Stadt Worms und des Altertumsvereins Worms.

Museum Heylshof: Stephansgasse 9, 67547 Worms; tel. (6241) 22000; fax (6241) 309485; e-mail museum@heylshof.de; internet www .heylshof.de; f. 1923; paintings, sculptures, pottery, porcelains and glass from 15th–19th centuries; Curator CORNELIUS ADALBERT; Curator F. V. HEYL.

Universities

ALBERT-LUDWIGS-UNIVERSITÄT FREIBURG

Fahnenbergpl., 79085 Freiburg im Breisgau
Telephone: (761) 2030
Fax: (761) 2034369
E-mail: info@verwaltung.uni-freiburg.de
Internet: www.uni-freiburg.de
Founded 1457
Academic year: October to July
Rector: Prof. Dr HANS-JOCHEN SCHIEWER
Vice-Rector for Academic Affairs: Prof. Dr HEINER SCHANZ
Vice-Rector for Internationalization and Technology Transfer: Prof. Dr JÜRGEN RÜHE
Vice-Rector for Medicine: Prof. Dr CHARLOTTE NIEMEYER
Vice-Rector for Research: Prof. Dr HERMANN SCHWENGEL
Chancellor: Dr MATTHIAS SCHENEK
Library Dir: ANTJE KELLERSOHN
Library: see Libraries and Archives
Number of teachers: 5,000
Number of students: 21,622

DEANS

Faculty of Biology: Prof. Dr GUNTHER NEUHAUS
Faculty of Chemistry, Pharmacy and Earth Sciences: Prof. Dr HARALD HILLEBRECHT
Faculty of Economics and Behavioural Sciences: Prof. Dr DIETER K. TSCHEULIN
Faculty of Engineering: Prof. Dr BERND BECKER
Faculty of Forestry and Environmental Sciences: Prof. Dr JÜRGEN BAUHUS
Faculty of Humanities: Prof. Dr HANS-HELMUTH GANDER
Faculty of Law: Prof. Dr SEBASTIAN KREBBER
Faculty of Mathematics and Physics: Prof. Dr KAY KÖNIGSMANN
Faculty of Medicine: Prof. Dr HUBERT ERICH BLUM
Faculty of Philology: Prof. Dr BERND KORTMANN
Faculty of Theology: Prof. Dr KLAUS BAUMANN

PROFESSORS

Faculty of Applied Sciences:

ALBERS, S., Parallel and Distributed Computing
BASIN, D., Informatics
BECKER, B., Informatics
BERGARD, W., Autonomous Intelligent Systems
BURKHARDT, H., Informatics
HAUSSELT, J., Microsystems Technology
KORVINK, J. G., Microsystems Technology
KUNTZ, Information Technology
LAUSEN, G., Informatics
LEUE, S., Computer Networks
MANOLI, Information Technology
MENZ, W., Microsystems Technology
NEBEL, B., Informatics
OTTMANN, TH., Informatics
PAUL, Information Technology
RAEDT, L. DE, Machine Learning
RÜHE, Information Technology

SCHMIDT-THIEME, L., Computer-Based New Media
SCHNEIDER, G., Communication Systems
SCHOLL, C., Operating Systems
THIEMANN, P., Programming Languages
URBAN, G. A., Microsystems Technology
WILDE, Information Technology
WOIAS, Information Technology
ZAPPE, Information Technology
ZENGERLE, Information Technology

Faculty of Biology:

AERTSEN, A., Neurobiology
BAUER, G., Evolutionary Biology
BAUMEISTER, R., Neurogenetics
BECK, C., Biology
BEYER, P., Cell Biology
BOGENRIEDER, A., Geobotany
DEIL, U., Geobotany
DRIEVER, W., Neurobiology
FISCHBACH, K. F., Biology
FUCHS, G., Microbiology
FUKSHANSKY, L., Botany
GÜNTHER, K., Neurobiology
HAEHNEL, W., Biochemistry
HARTMANN, R., Neurobiology
HERTEL, R., Biology
KLEINIG, H., Cell Biology
MÜLLER, J., Chemical Ecology
NEUBÜSER, A., Neurobiology
NEUHAUS, G., Cell Biology
OELZE, J., Microbiology
PESCHKE, K., Zoology
RESKI, R., Biotechnology
RETH, M., Molecular Immunology
ROSSEL, S., Neurobiology
SCHÄFER, E., Botany
SCHRÖDER, J., Biochemistry
VOGT, K., Neurobiology
WAGNER, E., Botany
WECKESSER, J., Microbiology
WELLMANN, E., Botany

Faculty of Business and Behavioural Sciences:

BLÜMLE, G., Mathematical Economics
FRANCKE, H. H., Financial Economics
FUCHS, R., Sport Science
GEHRIG, T., Economic Development
GIEß-STÜBER, P., Sport Science
GOLLHOFER, A., Sport Science
HAUSER, S., Imperial Economics
HILKE, W., Commercial Economics
KESSLER, W., Business Economics
KNIEPS, G., Political Economy
LANDMANN, O., Economic Theory
RAFFELHÜSCHEN, Financial Economics
REHKUGLER, H., Commercial Economics
SCHAUENBERG, B., Management Economics
SCHOBER, F., Computer Science
SCHULTZ, G., Socio-Political Economics
STRUBE, G., Cognition Science
TSCHEULIN, D., Health Service Economics
VANBERG, V., Political Economics

Faculty of Chemistry, Pharmacology and Geosciences:

BANNWARTH, W., Organic Chemistry
BECHTHOLD, A., Pharmaceutical Biology
BEHRMANN, J., Geology
BREIT, B., Organic Chemistry
BRÜCKNER, R., Organic Chemistry
BUCHER, K., Mineralogy
EBERBACH, W., Biochemistry
FINKELMANN, H., Molecular Chemistry
FRIEDRICH, K., Organic Chemistry
GLAWION, R., Geography
GOSSMANN, H., Geography
GRAPES, R., Geosciences
GRONSKI, W., Macromolecular Chemistry
HENK, A., Geology
HILLEBRECHT, H., Inorganic Chemistry
JANIAK, CH., Inorganic Chemistry
KELLER, J., Mineralogy
KRAMER, V., Crystallography
LEIBUNDGUT, CH., Hydrology
MÄCKEL, R., Geography

MAYER, H., Meteorology
MERFORT, I., Pharmaceutical Biology
MÜHLHAUPT, R., Macromolecular Chemistry
OTTO, H. H., Pharmaceutical Technology
PLATTNER, D., Organic Chemistry
PRINZBACH, H., Organic Chemistry
RÖHR, C., Inorganic Chemistry
RÜCHARDT, C., Organic Chemistry
SCHULZ, G. E., Biochemistry
SCHWESINGER, R., Organic Chemistry
SEITZ, S., Ethnology
STADELBAUER, J., Geography
TIPPER, J. C., Geology
VAHRENKAMP, H., Inorganic Chemistry
WIMMENAUER, W., Geosciences

Faculty of Forestry and Environmental Sciences:

ABETZ, P., Forest Growth
BAUHAUS, J., Silviculture
BECKER, G., Forest Utilization and Work Science
BECKER, M., Forest Policy
BOPPRÉ, M., Forest Zoology
EISFELD, D., Forest Zoology
ESSMANN, H., Environmental Policy
FINK, S., Forest Botany
HILDEBRAND, E. E., Soil Sciences and Forest Nutrition
JAEGER, L., Meteorology
KOCH, B., Land Information Systems
KONOLD, W., Land Use Planning
KRINGS, T., Cultural Geography
LEWARK, S., Forest Utilization and Work Science
MAYER, H., Meteorology
MEIDINGER, E., Forest Management
MITSCHERLICH, G., Forest Growth
OESTEN, G., Forest Management
PELZ, D. R., Biometrics
REIF, A., Silviculture
RENNENBERG, H., Tree Science
ROEDER, A., Forest Management
SCHMIDT, U., Environmental Policy
SCHRÖDER, E.-J., Cultural Geography
SPIECKER, H., Forest Production
VOLZ, K., Forest Policy

Faculty of Law:

BLAUROCK, U., Economic Law
BLOY, R., Penal Law
ESER, A., Penal Law
FRISCH, W., Penal Law
HAEDICKE, M., Civil Law
HAGER, G., International Civil Law
HOHLOCH, G., International Civil Law
HOLLERBACH, A., History of Law, Church Law, Philosophy of Law
KÖBL, U., Social Insurance Law
LEIPOLD, D., Civil, Labour and Procedural Law
LIEBS, D., History of Modern Law
LÖWISCH, M., Civil, Labour, Social Insurance and Commercial Law
MERKT, H., International Civil Law
MURSWIEK, D., State Law
NEHLSEN-VON STRYCK, K., History of Law
PERRON, W., Penal Law
SCHOCH, F., Public Law
SCHWARZE, J., European and International Law
STÜRNER, R., Civil Law
TIEDEMANN, K., Criminal Law and Procedure
VOßKUHLE, A., History of Law, Philosophy of Law
WAHL, R., Administrative Law
WÜRTENBERGER, T., State Law

Faculty of Mathematics and Physics:

BAMBERGER, A., Experimental Physics
BANGERT, V., Mathematics
BLUMEN, A., Theoretical Physics
BRENN, R., Experimental Physics
BRIGGS, J. ST., Theoretical Physics
DZIUK, G., Applied Mathematics

EBBINGHAUS, H.-D., Mathematical Logic
EBERLEIN, E., Stochastics
FLUM, J., Mathematical Logic
GRABERT, H., Theoretical Physics
GROHE, M., Logic
HABERLAND, H., Experimental Physics
HEINZEL, T., Physics
HELM, H., Experimental Physics
HERMES, H., Logic
HERTEN, G., Physics
HONERKAMP, J., Theoretical Physics
JAKOBS, K., Physics
KLAR, H., Physics
KÖNIGSMANN, K., Physics
KRÖNER, D., Applied Mathematics
KUWERT, E., Analysis
LANDGRAF, U., Physics
LUDWIG, J., Physics
POHLMEYER, K., Theoretical Physics
RÖMER, H., Theoretical Physics
RÖPKE, H., Experimental Physics
RÜSCHENDORF, L., Stochastics
RUZICKA, M., Applied Mathematics
SCHMIDT, V., Physics
SCHMITT, H., Experimental Physics
SCHNEIDER, R., Mathematics
SIEBERT, B., Geometry
SOERGEL, W., Algebra
SPILKER, J., Actuarial Mathematics
STROBL, G., Experimental Physics
VAN DER BIJ, J., Theoretical Physics
WAGNER, F., Logic
WEIDEMÜLLER, M., Physics
WITTING, H., Applied Mathematics
WOLKE, D., Mathematics
ZIEGLER, M., Mathematical Logic

Faculty of Medicine:

AKTORIES, K., Pharmacology and Toxicology
BEHRENDS, J., Physiology
BESSLER, W., Immunology
BEYERSDORF, F., Cardiovascular Surgery
BIRNESSER, H., Sports Traumatology
BLUM, H., Gastroenterology
BODE, C., Cardiology
BOGDAN, CH., Microbiology
BORNER, C., Stem Cell Research
BRAND-SABERI, B., Anatomy and Cell Biology
BRANDIS, M., Paediatrics
BRANDSCH, R., Biochemistry
CHRIST, B., Anatomy
DASCHNER, F., Environmental Medicine
DECKER, K., Biochemistry
DICKHUT, H.-H., Rehabilitation and Sports Medicine
FAKLER, Physiology
FROMMHOLD, H., Radiology
FROTSCHER, M., Anatomy
FUNK, J., Eye Hospital
GEIGER, K., Anaesthesiology
GITSCH, G., Gynaecology
GOEPPERT, S., Medical Psychology
GUTTMAN, J., Anaesthesiology
HASSE, J., Surgery
HELLWIG, E., Dentistry
HOFFMAN, H.-D., Anatomy
HOPT, U., General and Visceral Surgery
HUANG, R., Anatomy
JACKISCH, R., Pharmacology and Toxicology
JONAS, Physiology
JONAS, J., Dentistry
KECECIOGLU, D., Paediatric Cardiology
KIST, M., Microbiology
KLAR, R., Medicine Informatics
KORINTHENBERG, R., Neurology and Muscular Diseases
KURZ, H., Anatomy
LANGER, M., Radiology
LASZIG, R., Otorhinolaryngology
LEVEN, K.-H., History of Medicine
MERTELSMANN, R., Internal Medicine
MEYER, D. K., Pharmacology and Toxicology

MOSER, E., Radiology
MÜLLER-QUERNHEIM, J., Pneumology
NIERNEYER, C., Paediatric Haemotology and Oncology
NIKKHAH, G., Neurosurgery
OSTERTAG, C., Neurosurgery
PAHL, H., Anaesthesiology
PANNEN, B., Anaesthesiology
PETER, H. H., Rheumatology
PETERS, C., Molecular Medicine
PFANNER, N., Biochemistry
PIRCHER, H., Immunology
POLLAK, S., Forensic Medicine
REICHELT, A., Orthopaedics
ROSPERT, S., Biochemistry
SCHEMPP, W., Cytogenetics
SCHMELZEISEN, R., Oral and Maxillofacial Surgery
SCHÖPF, E., Dermatology
SCHUMACHER, M., Medical Statistics
SIEBERT, F., Biophysics
STARK, B., Plastic and Hand Surgery
STARKE, K., Pharmacology and Toxicology
STRUB, J., Dentistry
SÜDKAMP, N. P., Traumatology
SZABO, B., Pharmacology and Toxicology
TRÖHLER, U., History of Medicine
TROPSCHUG, M., Biochemistry
VOLK, B., Neuropathology
VON TROSCHKE, J., Medical Sociology
VOOS, W., Biochemistry
WALZ, G., Nephrology
WERNER, M., Pathology
WETTERAUER, U., Urology
WOLF, U., Human Genetics and Anthropology
ZENTNER, J. F., General Neurosurgery

Faculty of Philology:

ADAMS, J., American Literature
ANZ, H., Scandinavian Studies
ARNHAMMER, A., German Philology
AUER, P., German Philology
BANNERT, R., Scandinavian Studies
BERG, W. B., Literature
BLANK, W., German Philology
BÖNING, T., German Philology
CHEURÉ, E., Slavonics
DANGEL-PELLOQUIN, E., German Philology
DITTMANN, J., German Philology
DREWS, P., Slavonics
FLUDERNIK, M., English Philology
GÜNTHER, H.-C.
HAHN, U., German Philology
HALFORD, B., Oral Language
HAUSMANN, R., Romance Philology
HERRMANN, H.-P., German Philology
HESS, R., Romance Philology
HOCHBRUCK, W., Literature
JURT, J., Literature
KAISER, G., German Philology
KÄSTNER, H.-J., German Philology
KILIAN, E., Literature
KNOOP, U., German Philology
KOCHENDÖRFER, G., German Philology
KOHL, N., English Literature
KORTE, B., Literature
KORTMANN, B., English Philology
KÜHNE, U., German Philology
KUNZE, K., German Philology
LEFÈVRE, E., Classical Philology
LÖNKER, F., German Philology
MAIR, C., Caribbean Language and Literature
MATTHEWS, R., Linguistics
MAUSER, W., German Philology
MICHEL, W., German Philology
MÜRB, F., German Philology
PIETZCKER, C., German Philology
PILCH, H., English Philology
PÖRKSEN, U., German Philology
PÜTZ, M., English Philology
RAIBLE, W., Romance Philology
RENNER, F., German Philology
RIX, H., Indogermanic Languages
SASSE, G., German Philology

SCHÄFER, E., Latin Philology
SCHMIDT, J., German Philology
SCHOLZ, R., German Philology
SCHWAN, W., German Philology
SIEGERT, R., German Philology
THOMAS, C., German Philology
TICHY, E., Indogermanic Languages
TRISTRAM, H., German Philology
WEIHER, E., Slavonics
ZIMMERMAN, B., German Philology
ZUTT, H., German Philology

Faculty of Philosophy:

ASCHE, R., Modern History
BERGER, C., Music
BRÜGGEMEIER, F.-J., Economic and Social History
DEGELE, N., Sociology
ESSBACH, W., Sociology
FIGAL, G., Philosophy
GEHRKE, H.-J., Ancient History
GREINER, P., Sinology
HINÜBER, O., Indology
JÄGER, W., Political Science
JANHSEN, A., History of Art
KUNTZ, A., Ethnology
KÜSTER, K., Music
LAUT, J.-P., Islamic History
MARTIN, J., Ancient History
MATTER, M., Ethnology
MERTENS, D., Medieval History
MEZGER, W., Ethnology
MORDEK, H., Medieval History
NEUTATZ, D., Modern and East European History
NUBER, H. U., Roman Provincial Archaeology
PALETSCHEK, S., Modern History
PRATER, A., History of Art
REBSTOCK, U., Islamic History
RIESCHER, G., Political History
RÜLAND, J., Political History
SCHLEHE, J., Ethnology
SCHLINK, W., History of Art
SCHMIDT, G., Medieval Latin Philology
SCHNITZLER, G., Modern German Literature and Music
SCHWENGEL, H., Sociology
SEITZ, S., Ethnology
SENGER, H., Sinology
STEIBLE, H., Oriental Philology
STEUER, H., Prehistory
STRAHM, C., Prehistory
STROCKA, V., Classical Archaeology
TRÖHLER, U., History of Medicine
WARLAND, R., Christian Archaeology and Byzantine Art
WINDLER, C., Modern History
WINTERLING, A., Ancient History
ZOTZ, T., Medieval History

Faculty of Theology:

ALBUS, M., Pedagogics and Catechism
ENDERS, M., Philosophy
FRANK, S., Old Church History
GLATZEL, N., Christian Society
HOPING, H., Dogmatics and Liturgical History
IRSIGLER, H., Old Testament
NOTHELLE-WILDFEUER, U., Pastoral Theology
OBERLINNER, L., New Testament Literature
POMPEY, H., Caritas Science and Social Work
RAFFELT, A., Dogmatics
SCHOCKENHOFF, E., Moral Theology
SMOLINSKY, H., New Church History
TZSCHEETZSCH, W., Pedagogics and Catechism
UHDE, B., History
VERWEYEN, H. J., Fundamental Theology
WALTER, P., Dogmatics
WARLAND, R., Christian Archaeology and Art History
WINDISCH, H., Pastoral Theology
ZAPP, H., Church Law

BAUHAUS-UNIVERSITÄT WEIMAR

Geschwister-Scholl-Str. 8, 99421 Weimar
Telephone: (3643) 580
Fax: (3643) 581120
E-mail: international-office@uni-weimar.de
Internet: www.uni-weimar.de
Founded 1860
Academic year: October to June

Rector: Prof. Dr Ing. KARL BEUCKE
Vice-Rector for Academic Affairs: Prof. Dr
  ANDREA DREYER
Vice-Rector for Research: Prof. Dr Hab.
  HANS-RUDOLF MEIER
Chancellor: Dr-Ing. HEIKO SCHULTZ
Librarian: Dr FRANK SIMON-RITZ

Number of teachers: 83
Number of students: 5,000

Publications: *Der Bogen* (9 a year), *Philosophische Diskurse* (1 a year), *Schriften der Bauhaus-Universität* (2 a year), *Thesis* (6 a year), *VERSO-Architekturtheorie* (1 a year)

DEANS

Faculty of Architecture: Prof. Dipl. Ing.
  BERND RUDOLF
Faculty of Art and Design: Prof. Dr SIEGFRIED
  GRONERT
Faculty of Civil Engineering: Prof. Dr Ing.
  HANS-JOACHIM BARGSTÄDT
Faculty of Media: Prof. Dr ANDREAS ZIEMANN

PROFESSORS

Faculty of Architecture (tel. (3643) 583113; fax (3643) 583114; e-mail lars-christian .uhlig@archit.uni-weimar.de; internet www .uni-weimar.de/cms/?297):

  BARZ-MALFATTI, H., Design and Settlement Planning I
  BÜTTNER-HYMAN, H., Principles of Design
  CHRIST, W., Design and Town Planning I
  DONATH, D., Information Technology in the Architectural Planning Process
  GLEITER, J. H., Design and Architectural Theory
  GLÜCKLICH, D., Principles of Ecological Construction
  GRASHORN, B., Design and Building Construction
  GUMPP, R., Design and Structural Engineering
  HASSENPFLUG, D., Sociology and Social History of Towns
  KÄSTNER, A., Technology of Building Design
  KIEßL, K., Building Ecology and Air-Conditioning
  KLEIN, B., Design and Town Planning II
  KOPPÁNDY, J., Landscape Architecture
  LOUDON, M., Design and Industrial Buildings
  NENTWIG, B., Building Industry and Building Management
  RIEß, H., Design and Building Construction I
  RUDOLF, B., Theory of Building Construction
  RUTH, J., Structural Engineering
  SCHIRMBECK, E., Design and Interior Design
  SCHMITZ, K.-H., Design and Building Construction II
  SCHULZ, M., Construction Technology
  STAMM-TESKE, W., Design and House-Building
  WELCH GUERRA, M., Space Research, Development and Land Planning

Faculty of Arts (tel. (3643) 583206; fax (3643) 583230; e-mail christa.billing@gestaltung .uni-weimar.de; internet www.uni-weimar .de/gestaltung):

  BABTIST, G., Product Design
  BACHHUBER, L., Free Art
  BARTELS, H., Product Design
  BOCK, W., Art Science
  FRÖHLICH, E., Free Art
  GRONERT, S., Art Science
  HINTERBERGER, N. W., Free Art
  HOLZWARTH, W., Visual Communication
  NEMITZ, B., Free Art
  PREIß, A., Art Science
  RUTHERFORD, J., Visual Communication
  SATTLER, W., Product Design
  SCHAWELKA, K., Art Science
  STAMM, H., Visual Communication
  WEBER, O., Art Science
  WENTSCHER, H., Visual Communication

Faculty of Construction Engineering (tel. (3643) 584415; fax (3643) 584413; e-mail elke.lindner@bauing.uni-weimar.de; internet www.uni-weimar.de/bauing):

  ALFEN, Construction Management
  BARGSTÄDT, Construction Site Management
  BECKMANN, Waste Management
  BERGMANN, Experimental Analysis of Materials and Structures
  BEUCKE, Informatics in Construction
  BIDLINGMAIER, Waste Management
  BRANNOLTE, General Building Materials
  BUCHER, Construction Engineering
  FREUNDT, Applied Mathematics
  GÜRLEBECK, Applied Mathematics
  HACK, Preparation of Materials and Recycling
  HÜBLER, Information Processing
  KAPS, Chemistry for Building
  KÖNKE, Building Statistics
  KORNADT, Physics of Building
  KRANAWETTREISER, Electrical Engineering
  LONDONG, Urban Water Management
  MÜLLER, Preparation of Materials and Recycling
  RAUE, Solid Buildings I
  RAUTENSTRAUCH, Wood and Stone Construction
  RUTH, Solid Buildings II
  SCHANZ, Soil Mechanics
  SCHWARZ, Earthquake Centre
  SCHWARZ, Surveying
  STARK, General Building Materials
  TRABERT, Construction Engineering Planning
  WERNER, Steel Construction
  WITT, Foundation Engineering

Faculty of Media (tel. (3643) 583703; fax (3643) 583701; e-mail medien@uni-weimar .de; internet www.uni-weimar.de/medien):

  ENGELL, L., Media Philosophy
  FRÖHLICH, B., Virtual Reality Systems
  GEELHAAR, J., Interface Design
  GROSS, T., Computer Supported Cooperative Work
  HENNIG-THURAU, T., Marketing and Media
  KISSEL, W., Media Events
  LEEKER, M., History and Theory of Artificial Worlds
  MAIER, M. (acting), Media Management
  MINARD, R., Electronic Sound Production
  SIEGERT, B., History and Theory of Cultural Technologies
  STEIN, B., Content Management and Web Technology
  WÜTHRICH, C., Graphical Data Processing

BERGISCHE UNIVERSITÄT WUPPERTAL

42097 Wuppertal
Gaussstr. 20, 42119 Wuppertal
Telephone: (202) 4390
Fax: (202) 4392901
E-mail: kanzler@uni-wuppertal.de
Internet: www.uni-wuppertal.de
Founded 1972
State control
Language of instruction: German

Academic year: October to September

Rector: Prof. Dr LAMBERT T. KOCH
Vice-Rector for Academic Affairs: Prof. Dr
  ANDREAS FROMMER
Vice-Rector for Finance, Corporate Planing
  and Information: Prof. Dr HEINZ-REINER
  TREICHEL
Vice-Rector for Research, External Funding
  and Advanced Scientific Training: Prof. Dr
  MICHAEL SCHEFFEL
Vice-Rector for Transfer and Int. Relations:
  Prof. Dr Ing. PETRA WINZER
Chancellor: Dr ROLAND KISCHKEL
Librarian: UWE STADLER

Number of teachers: 298
Number of students: 14,000

DEANS

Faculty of Architecture, Civil, Mechanical
  and Safety Engineering: Prof. Dr Ing.
  DIETRICH HOEBORN
Faculty of Art and Design: Prof. Dr ULRICH
  HEINEN
Faculty of Educational and Social Science:
  Prof. Dr ANDREAS SCHAARSCHUCH
Faculty of Electrical, Information and Media
  Engineering: Prof. Dr Ing. ANTON KUM-
  MERT
Faculty of Humanities: Prof. Dr GERRIT
  WALTHER
Faculty of Mathematics and Natural Sci-
  ences: Prof. Dr PETER WIESEN
School of Education: Prof. Dr CORNELIA
  GRÄSEL
Schumpeter School of Business and Econom-
  ics: Prof. Dr MICHAEL J. FALLGATTER

BRANDENBURGISCHE TECHNISCHE UNIVERSITÄT COTTBUS

POB 10 13 44, 03013 Cottbus
Konrad-Wachsmann-Allee 1, 03046 Cottbus
Telephone: (355) 690
Fax: (355) 692108
E-mail: intoff@tu-cottbus.de
Internet: www.tu-cottbus.de
Founded 1991
State control
Academic year: October to July

Chancellor: WOLFGANG SCHRÖDER
Pres.: Prof. Dr Hab WALTHER CH. ZIMMERLI
Vice-Pres.: MATTHIAS KOZIOL
Vice-Pres.: Prof. Dr Hab. DIETER SCHMEIßER
Librarian: MAGDALENE FREWER-SAUVIGNY

Library of 577,000 vols, 2,000 periodicals,
  80,000 technical standards
Number of teachers: 651
Number of students: 6,400

Publications: *Bodenschutz* (4 a year), *Bodenschutz und Rekultivierung* (10–12 a year), *Energie, Forum der Forschung, Wissenschaftsmagazin der BTU Cottbus* (1 a year), *Lehrstuhl Industriesoziologie* (2 a year)

DEANS

Faculty of Architecture, Civil Engineering
  and Urban Planning: Prof. Dipl.-Ing.
  HEINZ NAGLER
Faculty of Environmental Sciences and Pro-
  cess Engineering: Prof. Dr GERHARD WIE-
  GLEB
Faculty of Mathematics, Natural Sciences
  and Computer Science: Prof. Dr WOLFGANG
  FREUDENBERG
Faculty of Mechanical, Electrical and Indus-
  trial Engineering: Prof. Dr Ing. BERND
  VIEHWEGER

CARL VON OSSIETZKY UNIVERSITÄT OLDENBURG

POB 2503, 26111 Oldenburg
Ammerländer Heerstr. 114–118, 26129 Oldenburg
Telephone: (441) 7980
Fax: (441) 7983000
E-mail: praesidium@uni-oldenburg.de
Internet: www.uni-oldenburg.de
Founded 1973
Academic year: October to September (two terms)
Pres.: Prof. Dr BABETTE SIMON
Vice-Pres. for Academic Affairs: Prof. Dr GUNILLA BUDDE
Vice-Pres. for Admin. and Finance: Dr HEIDE AHRENS
Vice-Pres. for Research: Prof. Dr KATHARINA AL-SHAMERY
Vice-Pres. for Young Scientists and Quality Management: Prof. Dr BERND SIEBENHÜNER
Library Dir: HANS-JOACHIM WÄTJEN
Library of 1,333,870 vols
Number of teachers: 181
Number of students: 10,688
Publications: *Data Work* (computer sciences, 3 a year), *Einblicke* (research at the University, 2 a year), *Monoculus* (biology, 2 a year)

DEANS

Faculty 1 (School of Educational and Social Sciences): Prof. Dr MANFRED WITTROCK
Faculty 2 (School of Computer Science, Business Admin., Economics and Law): Prof. Dr THORSTEN RAABE
Faculty 3 (School of Linguistics and Cultural Studies): Prof. Dr KAREN ELLWANGER
Faculty 4 (School of Humanities and Social Sciences): Prof. Dr JOHANN KREUZER
Faculty 5 (School of Mathematics and Natural Science): Prof. Dr MARTIN HOLTHAUS

PROFESSORS

Faculty 1 (School of Educational and Social Sciences) (Ammerländer Heerstr. 114–118, 26129 Oldenburg; tel. (441) 7982002; fax (441) 7982924; e-mail dekanat.fk1@uni-oldenburg.de; internet www.uni-oldenburg.de/fk1):

Department of Education:

HANFT, A., Adult Education and Continuing Vocational Education
KAISER, A., Elementary Science, Elementary Social Studies
KIPER, H., Theory and Practice in Secondary Education
MEYER, H., General Education, School Teaching
MOSCHNER, B., Teaching and Learning Research
NITSCH, W., Theory of Knowledge
SCHMIDTKE, H.-P., Intercultural Education

Department of Special Needs Education:

ORTMANN, M., Education for the Physically Handicapped
SCHULZE, G. C., Special Education Needs
WITTROCK, M., Education for People with Disturbed Behaviour

Faculty 2 (School of Computer Science, Business Administration, Economics and Law) (Ammerländer Heerstr. 114–118, 26129 Oldenburg; tel. (441) 7984140; fax (441) 7984199; internet www.uni-oldenburg.de/fk2):

Business Administration and Education:

BREISIG, T., Organization and Human Resources
LACHNIT, L., Financial and Management Accounting
MOHE, X., Business Consultancy

MÜLLER, M., Production and Environmental Management
PFRIEM, R., General and Environmental Management
RAABE, T., Marketing
REBMANN, K., Vocational and Business Education
SIEBENHÜNER, Ecological Economics

Computer Science:

APPELRATH, H.-J., Information Systems and Databases
BEST, E., Parallel Systems
DAMM, W., Safety Critical Embedded Systems
FATIKOW, S., Microrobotics, Control Engineering
FRÄNZLE, M., Hybrid Systems
HABEL, A., Formal Languages
HASSELBRING, W., Software Engineering
HEIN, A., Automation and Measurement Engineering
JENSCH, P., Image Processing and Process Control
KOWALK, W., Computer Networks and Telecommunications
MÖBUS, C., Learning Environments and Knowledge-Based Systems
NEBEL, W., Embedded Hardware/Software Systems Design
OLDEROG, E.-R., Correct System Design
SONNENSCHEIN, M., Environmental Informatics
STIEGE, G., Graphs and Networks
THEEL, O., System Software and Distributed Systems

Economics:

EBERT, U., Public Finance
LITZ, H.-P., Economic Statistics
SCHEELE, Economic Policy
SCHÜLER, K. W., Econometrics
TRAUTWEIN, H. M., International Economics
WELSCH, H., Economic Theory

Law:

BLANKE, T., Labour Law
FRANK, G., Public Economic Law
SCHIEK, D., European Economic Law
TAEGER, J., Private Law, Business and Economic Law, Legal Informatics

Teaching of Economics and of Technology:

HENSELER, K., Teaching of Technology
KAMINSKI, H., Teaching of Economics
LEWALD, A., Home Economics
REICH, G., Teaching of Technology

Faculty 3 (School of Linguistics and Cultural Studies) (Ammerländer Heerstr. 114–118, 26129 Oldenburg; tel. (441) 7982347; fax (441) 7982115; e-mail fk3@uni-oldenburg.de; internet www.uni-oldenburg.de/fk3):

Dutch Studies:

GRÜTTEMEIER, R., Dutch Literature

English Studies:

GELUYKENS, R., Pragmatics, Discourse Analysis, Social Variation
HAMANN, C., Acquisition of First and Second Languages, Bilingualism, Formal Syntax and Semantics
KOEHRING, K., American Literature and Culture

Fine Arts and Visual Communication:

HOFFMANN, D., History of Fine Arts
SPRINGER, P., Theory and History of Art
THIELE, J., Fine Arts and Visual Communication
WENK, S., History of Art, Gender Studies

German Studies:

BRANDES, H., Literature
DOERING, S., Literature
EICHLER, W., Didactics and Linguistics
GLOY, J., Linguistics
KYORA, S., Literature

MEVES, U., Medieval German Literature and Language
STÖLTING, W., German as a Second or Foreign Language

Music:

DINESCU, V., Applied Composition
HOFFMANN, F., Music Education
SCHLEUNING, P., History of Music, Music Teaching
STROH, W. M., Theory of Music and Music Pedagogics

Slavonic Studies:

GRÜBEL, R., Slavonic Literature
HENTSCHEL, G., Linguistics and Slavonic Languages

Visual and Material Culture:

ELLWANGER, K., History of Culture
MÖRSCH, C., Teaching of Material Culture

Faculty 4 (School of Humanities and Social Sciences) (Ammerländer Heerstr. 114–118, 26129 Oldenburg; tel. (441) 7982634; fax (441) 7982624; e-mail dekanat.fk4@uni-oldenburg.de; internet www.uni-oldenburg.de/fk4):

Geography:

HAGEN, D., Cartography and Physical Geography

History:

BUDDE, G., 19th- and 20th-century German and European History
ETZEMÜLLER, T., Contemporary History
FREIST, D., Early Modern History
GÜNTHER-ARNDT, H., Teaching of History
HAHN, H.-H., Modern and East European History (esp. History of Poland)
HOLBACH, R., Medieval History
REEKEN, D. VON, Teaching of History
SCHEER, T., Ancient History

Philosophy:

GERHARD, M., Philosophy of Nature and of Science, Continental Philosophy
KREUZER, J., Philosophy and History of Philosophy
MÖBUSS, S., Philosophy and Jewish Philosophy
PUSTER, E., Epistemology, Philosophy of Language, Ethics
RUSCHIG, U., Philosophy
SCHULZ, R., Philosophy and History of Science
SUKALE, M., Philosophy and Philosophy of Science

Psychology:

BELSCHNER, W., Psychology
COLONIUS, H., Psychological Methods
HELLMAN, A., Psychological Methods
HÖGE, H., Environmental Psychology and Empirical Aesthetics
LAUCKEN, U., Social Psychology
MEES, U., General Psychology
NACHREINER, F., Applied Psychology
SCHICK, A., Psychological Acoustics and Environmental Psychology
SZAGUN, D., Developmental Psychology
VIEBAHN, P., Educational Psychology
WALCHER, K.-P., Psychology of Personality, Environmental Psychology

Social Sciences:

FLAAKE, K., Women's Studies
GRUNENBERG, A., Political Theory and Political Culture
KRAIKER, G., Social and Political Theory
LOEBER, H.-D., Sociology of Labour and Education
MÜLLER-DOOHM, S., Sociology of the Mass Media
NASSMACHER, K.-H., Comparative Politics
WEISMANN, A., Sociology, Methods of Social Research

Sports Science:

ALKEMEYER, T., Sociology and Philosophy of Sport
LIPPENS, V., Motor Control and Learning
SCHIERZ, M., Sports Science
SCHMÜCKER, B., Sports Science and Sports Medicine

Theology:

GOLKA, F., Jewish Studies, Old Testament
HEUMANN, J., Religious Education
LINK-WIECZOREK, U., Systematic Theology and Religious Education
WEISS, W., New Testament

Faculty 5 (School of Mathematics and Natural Science) (Ammerländer Heerstr. 114–118, 26129 Oldenburg; tel. (441) 7983442; fax (441) 7985601; e-mail fk5@uni-oldenburg.de; internet www.uni-oldenburg.de/fk5):

Biology, Earth and Environmental Sciences:

BRUMSACK, H.-J., Geomicrobiochemistry
CYPIONKA, H., Palaeomicrobiology
EBER, W., Botany, Morphology
GIANI, L., Soil Sciences
HAESELER, V., Terrestrial Ecology
HAGEN, D., Cartography and Physical Geography
HOESSLE, C., Biology, School Teaching
JANIESCH, P., Botany, Physiological Ecology
KLEYER, M., Landscape Ecology
KLUMP, G. M., Zoophysiology
KOCH, K.-W., Biochemistry
KRETZBERG, J.
KUMMERER, K., Regional Planning and Development
RICHTER-LANDSBERG, C., Molecular Neurobiology, Neurochemistry
RINKWITZ, S., Neurogenetics
SCHMINKE, H. K., Zoology, Zoosystematics and Morphology
SIMON, U., Biology of Geological Processes
STABENAU, H., Plant Physiology
VARESCHI, E., Aquatic Ecology
WACKERNAGEL, W., Genetics
WEILER, R., Zoology, Neurobiology
WINDELBERG, J., Infrastructure and Environmental Planning

Chemistry:

AL-SHAMERY, K., Physical Chemistry
BECKHAUS, R., Inorganic Chemistry
GMEHLING, J., Industrial Chemistry
KLEINER, T., Physical Chemistry
KÖLL, P., Organic Chemistry
MARTENS, J., Organic Chemistry
METZGER, J. O., Organic Chemistry
POWCHMANN, J., Chemistry, Theory and Practice of School Teaching
RÖSSNER, F., Industrial Chemistry
WICKLEDER, M., Inorganic Chemistry
WITTSTOCK, G., Physical Chemistry

Mathematics:

DEFANT, A., Mathematics, Functional Analysis
HERZBERGER, J., Applied Mathematics, Instrumental Mathematics
KNAUER, U., Mathematics, Algebraic Methods
LEISSNER, W., Mathematics, Geometry
MÜLLER, CH., Mathematics, Stochastics
PFLUG, P., Mathematics, Complex Variables
PIEPER-SEIER, I., Mathematics, Algebra
QUEBBEMANN, H.-G., Mathematics, Number Theory
SCHMALE, W., Mathematics, Dynamic Systems
SCHMIEDER, G., Mathematics, Complex Analysis
SPÄTH, H., Applied Mathematics
VETTER, U., Mathematics, Commutative Algebra

Physics:

BAUER, G. H., Experimental Physics

ENGEL, A., Theoretical Physics
HINSCH, K., Experimental Physics
HOLTHAUS, M., Theoretical Physics
KOLLMEIER, B., Applied Physics
KOLNY, J., Applied Physics
KUNZ-DROLSHAGEN, J., Theoretical Physics, Field Theory
MAIER, K. H., Experimental Physics
MELLERT, V., Applied Physics
MERTINS, A., Applied Physics
PARISI, J., Experimental Physics
PEINKE, J., Experimental Physics
RIESS, F., Teaching of Physics
VERHEY, J., Applied Physics

CHRISTIAN-ALBRECHTS UNIVERSITÄT ZU KIEL

24098 Kiel
Christian-Albrechts-Pl. 4, 24118 Kiel
Telephone: (431) 88000
Fax: (431) 8802072
E-mail: mail@uni-kiel.de
Internet: www.uni-kiel.de

Founded 1665
State control
Academic year: October to July (two terms)
Pres.: Prof. Dr GERHARD FOUQUET
Vice-Pres.: Prof. Dr FRANK KEMPKEN
Vice-Pres.: Prof. Dr THOMAS BOSCH
Chancellor: FRANK EISOLDT, Prof. Dr. SIEGFRIED WOLFFRAM
Librarian: Dr ELSE M. WISCHERMANN

Number of teachers: 1,700
Number of students: 23,000

Publications: *Christiana Albertina* (2 a year), *Unizeit* (6 a year)

DEANS

Faculty of Agricultural and Nutritional Sciences: Prof. Dr KARIN SCHWARZ
Faculty of Economics and Social Sciences: Prof. Dr BIRGIT FRIEDL
Faculty of Engineering: Prof. Dr REINHARD KNÖCHEL
Faculty of Law: Prof. Dr jur. ALEXANDER TRUNK
Faculty of Mathematics and Natural Sciences: Prof. Dr LUTZ KIPP
Faculty of Medicine: Prof. Dr STEFAN SCHREIBER
Faculty of Philosophy: Prof. Dr MARKUS HUNDT
Faculty of Theology: Prof. Dr HARTMUT ROSENAU

PROFESSORS

Faculty of Agricultural and Nutritional Sciences (Hermann-Rodewald-Str. 4, 24098 Kiel; tel. (431) 8802591; fax (431) 8807334; e-mail dekanat@agrar.uni-kiel.de; internet www.agrar.uni-kiel.de):

ABDULAI, A., Food Economics and Food Policy
BRUHN, M., Agricultural Marketing
FOHRER, N., Hydrology and Water Resources Management
HENNING, C., Agricultural Policy
HORN, R., Soil Science
JUNG, C., Plant Breeding and Genetics
KAGE, H., Crop Science
KALM, E., Animal Breeding and Genetics
KRIETER, J., Animal Husbandry, Quality of Products
LATACZ-LOHMANN, U., Farm Management and Production Economics
LOY, J.-P., Agricultural Market Theory
MÜLLER, M. J., Internal Medicine, Human Nutrition
MÜLLER, R. A. E., Agricultural Economics, Information, Innovation
RIMBACH, G., Food Science
ROOSEN, J., Health Economics
ROWECK, H., Landscape Ecology

SATTELMACHER, B., Plant Nutrition
SCHALLENBERGER, E., Animal Husbandry, Hygienics
SCHWARZ, K., Food Technology
SUSENBETH, A., Animal Nutrition
TAUBE, F., Grass and Forage Science, Organic Farming
VERREET, J.-A., Phytopathology, Plant Diseases
WOLFFRAM, S., Animal Nutrition and Nutritional Physiology
WYSS, U., Phytopathology, Biotechnology

Faculty of Economics and Social Sciences (Wilhelm-Seelig-Platz 1, 24098 Kiel; (431) 8802140; fax (431) 8801691; e-mail dekanat@bwl.uni-kiel.de; internet www.bwl.uni-kiel.de):

ALBERS, S., Innovation, New Media and Marketing
BRÖCKER, J., Regional Science
DREXL, A., Production Management and Logistics
FRIEDL, B., Controlling
HERWARTZ, H., Econometrics
KLAPPER, D., Marketing
KRAUSE, J., Politics
KRUBER, K.-P., Political and Economic Education
LIESENFELD, R., Statistics and Empirical Economics
LUX, T., Monetary Economics and International Financial Markets
NIPPEL, P., Financial Management
RAFF, H., Industrial Economics
REQUATE, T., Economics of Innovation, Competition and Institutions
SEIDL, C., Public Finance and Choice Theory
SNOWER, D., Economics
VEIT, K.-R., Accounting
WALTER, A., Entrepreneurship and Innovation Management
WOHLTMANN, H.-W., Macroeconomics
WOLF, J., Organization

Faculty of Engineering (Kaiserstr. 2, 24143 Kiel; tel. (431) 8806001; fax (431) 8806003; e-mail dekanat@tf.uni-kiel.de; internet www.tf.uni-kiel.de):

BERGHAMMER, R., Computer-Aided Program Development
BROCKS, W., Material Mechanics
DIRKS, H., Electromagnetic Field Theory
FAUPEL, F., Multicomponent Materials
FÖLL, H., General Materials Science
FUCHS, F. W., Power Electronics and Electrical Devices
HACKBUSCH, W., Practical Mathematics
HANUS, M., Programming Languages and Compiler Construction
HANXLEDEN, R. VON, Real-Time and Embedded Systems
HEUBERGER, A., Semiconductor Technology
HEUTE, U., Circuits and System Theory
HÖHER, P., Information and Coding Theory Laboratory
JÄGER, W., Centre for Microanalysis
JANSEN, K., Theory of Parallelism
KLINKENBUSCH, I., Computational Electromagnetics Group
KNÖCHEL, R., Microwave Group
KOCH, R., Multimedia Information Processing
LUTTENBERGER, N., Communication Systems
RÖCK, H., Automation and Control Engineering
ROEVER, W. P. DE, Software Technology
ROSENKRANZ, W., Communications
SCHIMMLER, M., Computer Engineering
SCHNEIDER, R., Scientific Computing
SEEGEBRECHT, P., Semiconductor Electronics
SOMMER, G., Cognitive Systems
SRIVASTAV, A., Discrete Optimization

THALHEIM, B., Information Systems Engineering

WEPPNER, W., Sensors and Solid State Ionics

WILKE, T., Theoretical Computer Science

Faculty of Law (Leibnizstr. 4, 24098 Kiel; tel. (431) 8802125; fax (431) 8801689; e-mail dekanat@law.uni-kiel.de; internet www.uni-kiel.de/fakultas/jura):

ALEXY, R., Public Law and Legal Philosophy

ECKERT, J., History of German and European Civil Law, Commercial Law

EINSELE, D., Civil Law, Commercial Law, Private International Law, Comparative Law

FISCHER, M., Civil, Commercial and Economic Tax Law

FROMMEL, M., Criminology and Criminal Law

HOYER, A., Penal Law and Procedure

IGL, G., Public Law, Social Law

JICKELI, J., Civil Law, Commercial Law

KRACK, R., Penal Law and Procedure

MEYER-PRITZL, R., Civil Law, Roman Law, History of Law in Modern Times, Comparative Law

MUTIUS, A. VON, Public Law and Administration

REUTER, D., Civil, Commercial and Economic Law

SCHACK, H., International Civil Law, Private and Civil Trial Law, Copyright Law

SCHMIDT-JORTZIG, E., Public Law

SMID, S., Civil Law and Procedure

TRUNK, A., Civil and Civil Trial Law, International Private Law and Comparative Law

ZIMMERMANN, A., German and Foreign Public, International, and European Law, and General Theory of the State

Faculty of Mathematics and Natural Sciences (Christian-Albrechts-Platz 4, 24098 Kiel; tel. (431) 8802128; fax (431) 8802320; e-mail dekanat@mnf.uni-kiel.de; internet www.uni-kiel.de/fakultas/mathnat):

ALBAN, S., Pharmaceutical Biology

BÄHR, J., Geography

BAUER, T., Ecology

BAYRHUBER, H., Teaching Methods of Biology

BENDER, H., Mathematics

BENSCH, W., Inorganic Chemistry

BERGWEILER, W., Mathematics

BERNDT, R., Solid-State Physics

BETTEN, D., Mathematics

BILGER, W., Ecology

BISCHOF, K., Marine Biology

BLASCHEK, W., Pharmaceutical Biology

BODENDIEK, R., Mathematics

BÖNING, C., Theoretical Oceanography

BONITZ, M., Theoretical Physics

BORK, H.-R., Ecology System Research

BOSCH, T., General Zoology

BRENDELBERGER, H., Zoology and Limnology

CEMIČ, L., Mineralogy and Petrology

CLEMENT, B., Pharmaceutical Chemistry

COLIJN, F., Coastal Ecology

CORVES, C., Geography

DAHMKE, A., Applied Geology

DEMUTH, R., Teaching of Chemistry

DEPMEIER, W., Mineralogy and Crystallography

DEVEY, C., Geology

DIERSSEN, K., Botany

DOMMENGET, D., Meteorology

DULLO, W. C., Palaeo-Oceanography

DUTTMANN, R., Geography

EISENHAUER, A., Marine Ecogeology

EULER, M., Teaching of Physics

FRANK, M., Geology

GÖTZE, H.-J., Geophysics

GROOTES, P., Experimental Physics, Isotope Research

GROTEMEYER, J., Physical Chemistry

HACKNEY, R., Geophysics

HAMMANN, M., Teaching Methods of Biology

HANEL, R., Fishery Biology

HÄNSEL, W., Pharmaceutical Chemistry

HARTKE, B., Theoretical Chemistry

HARTL, G. B., Zoology

HASSENPFLUG, W., Geography

HEBER, J., Mathematics

HELBIG, V., Physics

HERGES, R., Organic Chemistry

HERZIG, P., Marine Science

HOERNLE, K., Vulcanology, Magmatic Petrology

HOPPE, H. G., Microbiology

IMHOFF, J., Marine Microbiology

IRLE, A., Probability Theory and Mathematical Statistics

KEMPKEN, F., Botany

KIPP, L., Experimental Physics

KOESTER, D., Astronomy and Astrophysics, Theoretical Physics

KÖNIG, H., Mathematics

KÖRTZINGER, A., Organic Marine Chemistry

KRUPINSKA, K., Cell Biology

KUHNT, W., Geology and Palaeontology

KUNZE, T., Pharmaceutical Chemistry

LATIF, M., Meterology

LEIPPE, M., Zoology

LINDHORST, T., Organic Chemistry

LOCHTE, K., Plankton

LÜNING, U., Organic Chemistry

MACKE, A., Meteorology

MÄDER, H., Physical Chemistry

MAGNUSSEN, O. M., Experimental Physics

MAYERLE, R., Applied Coastal Geology

MIKELSKIS-SEIFERT, S., Teaching Methods of Physics

MÜLLER, B., Pharmaceutical Technology

MÜLLER, D., Mathematics

MÜLLER, M., Physics

NELLE, O. A., Ecology

NERDEL, C., Teaching Methods of Chemistry

NEWIG, J., Geography

PEHLKE, E., Theoretical Physics

PIEL, A., Experimental Physics

PRECHTL, H., Teaching Methods of Biology

RABBEL, W., Geophysics

REISE, K., Biological Oceanography

RESTON, T. J., Marine Geophysics

REVILLA DIEZ, J., Economy of Geography

RIEBESELL, U., Marine Biology

ROEDER, T., Zoology

ROHR, G. VON, Geography

RÖSLER, U., Stochastics

RUPRECHT, E., Meteorology

SAUTER, M., Botany

SCHÄFER, P., Geology

SCHANZE, S., Teaching Methods of Chemistry

SCHENK, V., Petrology and Mineralogy

SCHMIDT, R., Mathematics

SCHMITZ-STREIT, R. A., Microbiology

SCHNACK, D., Ichthyology

SCHNEIDER, R., Geology

SCHÖNHEIT, P., Microbiology

SCHREMPP, B., Theoretical Physics

SCHULZ-FRIEDRICH, R., Botany

SCHUSTER, H. G., Theoretical Physics

SEND, U., Physical Oceanography

SOMMER, U., Sea-Floor Ecology

SPENGLER, U., Teaching Methods of Mathematics

SPINAS, O., Logic

SPINDLER, M., Polar Ecology

STATTEGGER, K., Geology and Palaeontology

STELLMACHER, B., Mathematics

STERR, H., Physical Geography

STOCK, N., Inorganic Chemistry

STOFFERS, P., Geology

SUESS, E., Marine Environmental Geology

TEMPS, F., Physical Chemistry

TUCZEK, F., Inorganic Chemistry

UHLARZ, H., Botany

VISBECK, M., Physical Oceanography

VON KLITZING, R., Physical Chemistry

WAHL, M., Marine Biology and Zoology

WALLACE, D., Marine Chemistry

WALTHER, G., Teaching of Mathematics

WILLBRAND, J., Oceanography

WIMMER-SCHWEINGRUBER, R., Experimental Physics

Faculty of Medicine (Christian-Albrechts-Platz 4, 24098 Kiel; tel. (431) 8802126; fax (431) 8802129; e-mail dekanat@med.uni-kiel.de; internet www.uni-kiel.de/fak/med/med.html):

ALBERS, H.-K., Dentistry

ALDENHOFF, J., Psychiatry, Psychotherapy

ALZHEIMER, C., Psychology

AMBROSCH, P., Otorhinolaryngology

BARON, R., Neurology

BLEICH, M., Physiology

CREMER, J., Surgery

DEUSCHL, G., Neurology and Neurophysiology

FICKENSCHER, H., Medical Microbiology

FISCHER-BRANDIES, H., Dentistry

FÖLSCH, U. R., Internal Medicine

GERBER, W.-D., Clinical Psychology

GIESELER, F., Internal Medicine

GLÜER, C., Medicinal Physics

GROTE, W., Human Genetics

HASSENPFLUG, J., Orthopaedics

HELLER, M., Radiological Diagnosis

HENZE, E., Nuclear Medicine

HERDEGEN, T., Physiology, Molecular Pharmacology

ILLERT, M., Physiology

JANSEN, O., Neuroradiology

JONAT, W., Gynaecology and Obstetrics

JÜNEMANN, K.-P., Urology

JUST, U., Biochemistry

KAATSCH, H.-J., Legal Medicine

KABELITZ, D., Medical Microbiology and Immunology

KALTHOFF, H., Immunology and Cell Biochemistry

KERN, M., Dentistry

KIMMIG, B. N., Clinical Radiology

KLÖPPEL, G., Pathology and Pathological Anatomy

KNEBA, M., Internal Medicine

KOVACS, G., Clinical Radiology

KRAMER, H.-H., Child Medicine, Child Cardiology

KRAWCZAK, M., Human Genetics

KREMER, B., Surgery

KUNZENDORF, U., Internal Medicine, Nephrology

LUCIUS, R., Anatomy

LÜLLMANN-RAUCH, R., Anatomy

MASER, E., Toxicology

MEHDORN, H., Neurosurgery

METTLER, L., Gynaecology

OEHMICHEN, M., Legal Medicine

PARWARESCH, R., Haematopathology

PLAGMANN, H.-CH., Dentistry

PROKSCH, E., Dermatology and Venereology

ROIDER, J., Opthalmology

ROSE-JOHN, S., Biochemistry

SAFTIG, P., Biochemistry

SCHÖCKLMANN, H., Nephrology, Internal Medicine

SCHOLZ, J., Anaesthesiology

SCHRAPPE, M., Paediatrics

SCHREIBER, S., Internal Medicine and Gastroenterology

SCHRÖDER, J. M., Experimental Dermatology

SCHÜNKE, M., Anatomy

SCHÜTZE, G., Child Psychiatry

SCHWARTZ, T., Dermatology

SIEVERS, J., Anatomy

SIMON, R., Cardiology

STEPHANI, U., Paediatrics, Neuropaediatrics
STICK, C., Physiology
TONNER, P., Anaesthesiology
WEILER, M., Anaesthesiology
WILTFANG, J., Dental Surgery

Faculty of Philosophy (Christian-Albrechts-Pl. 4, 24098 Kiel; tel. (431) 8803055; fax (431) 8807301; e-mail dekan@philfak.uni-kiel.de; internet www.uni-kiel.de/fakultas/philosophie):
BILLER, K.-H., Pedagogics
BLIESENER, T., Medieval and Modern History
BRINKHAUS, H., Indology
BRINKMANN, W., Pedagogics
CARNAP-BORNHEIM, C. VON, Prehistory and Early History
CONZELMANN, A., Sports Psychology
CORNELISSEN, C., Modern and Contemporary History
DORMEIER, H., Medieval and Modern History
ENGEL, A., Slavic Philology
FERSTL, R., Clinical Psychology
FLEISCHMANN, B., English Philology
FOUQUET, G., Economic and Social History
GÓMEZ-MONTERO, J., Romance Philology
GÖTTSCH-ELTEN, S., Folklore
GROSS, K., English Philology
HAAS, R., English Language and Literature
HAMEYER, U., Pedagogics
HANISCH, M., Teaching of History
HARRINGTON, J., Phonetics
HELDMANN, K., Classical Philology
HOEKSTRA, J., Friesian Philology
HOINKES, U., Romance Philology
HORATSCHEK, A. M., English Philology
JAWORSKI, R., East European History
JOBST, C., Art History
JONGEBLOED, H. C., Pedagogics
KAPP, V., Romance Philology
KÄPPEL, L., Classical Philology
KERSTING, W., Philosophy
KLEIN, D., Old German Literature
KÖHNKEN, G., Diagnostic and Differential Psychology
KONERSMANN, R., Teaching of Philosophy
KONRADT, U., Industrial, Marketing and Organizational Psychology
KROPE, P., Pedagogics
KUDER, U., Art History
KÜHNE, U., Ancient History, Medieval Linguistics
LINCK, G., Sinology
MAROLD, E., Old Norse Philology
MAUSFELD, R., Psychology
MEIER, A., History of Modern German Literature
MEYER, M., English Philology
MIETHLING, W.-D., Sports Pedagogics
MOERKE, O., Early Modern and Modern History
MÖLLER, J., Psychology
MOSEL, U., Linguistics
MÜLLER, J., Prehistory and Early History
MÜLLER, W.-U., Prehistory and Early History
NÜBLER, N., Slavic Philology
OECHSLE, S., Music
PALLASCH, W., Pedagogics
PETERSEN, J., Pedagogics
PISTOR-HATAM, A., Oriental Philology
POHL, K.-H., Teaching of History
PRAHL, H.-W., Pedagogics
PRENZEL, M., Pedagogics
RADICKE, J., Classical Philology
REBAS, H., Northern History
RIIS, T., History of Schleswig-Holstein
RÜHLING, L., Modern Scandinavian Literature
SCHMALTZ, B., Classical Archaeology
SCHMIDT, A., Folklore
SIELERT, U., Pedagogics

SIMON, B., Psychology
SOMMER, M., Philosophy
SPONHEUER, B., Music
STEINDORFF, L., East European History
THUN, H., Romance Philology
TUCHOLSKI-DÄKE, B.-C., Art
ULRICH, W., German Philology, Teaching of German Language
WEISS, P., Ancient History
WEISSER, B., Sports Medicine
WIESEHÖFER, J., Ancient History
WULFF, H. J., Theatre and Film Studies
WÜNSCH, M., History of Modern German Literature

Faculty of Theology (Leibnitzstr. 4, 24118 Kiel; tel. (431) 8802124; fax (431) 8801735; e-mail dekanattheo@email.uni-kiel.de; internet www.uni-kiel.de/fak/theol):
BARTELMUS, R., Old Testament Studies, Biblical and Middle Eastern Languages
BOBERT, S., Practical Theology
HÜBNER, U., Old Testament Studies and Biblical Archaeology
MECKENSTOCK, G., Systematic Theology
PREUL, R., Practical Theology
ROSENAU, H., Systematic Theology
SÄNGER, D., New Testament Studies
SCHILLING, J., Church History
VON BENDEMANN, R., New Testament Studies

ATTACHED INSTITUTES

Institut für Sicherheitspolitik an der Universität Kiel (ISUK) (Institute for Security Policy at Kiel University): Olshausenstr. 40, 24098 Kiel; Dir Prof. Dr J. KRAUSE.

Institut für Weltwirtschaft an der Universität Kiel (Institute for World Economics at Kiel University): Düsternbrooker Weg 120, 24105 Kiel; Pres. Prof. D. SNOWER.

Leibniz-Institut für Meereswissenschaften (IFM-GEOMAR) (Leibniz Institute of Marine Sciences): Wischhofstr. 1–3, 24148 Kiel; Dir Prof. Dr P. HERZIG.

Leibniz-Institut für die Pädagogik der Naturwissenschaften an der Universität Kiel (Leibniz Institute for Science Education at Kiel University): Olshausenstr. 62, 24098 Kiel; Dir Prof. Dr M. PRENZEL.

Lorenz-von-Stein-Institut für Verwaltungswissenschaften an der Universität Kiel (Lorenz von Stein Institute for Management Sciences at Kiel University): Olshausenstr. 40, 24098 Kiel; Dir Prof. Dr JOACHIM JICKELI.

Schleswig-Holsteinisches Institut für Friedenswissenschaften (Schleswig Holstein Institute for Peace Studies): Kaiserstr. 2, 24143 Kiel; Dir Prof. Dr K. POTTHOFF.

DEUTSCHE HOCHSCHULE FÜR VERWALTUNGSWISSENSCHAFTEN SPEYER

Freiherr-vom-Stein-Str. 2, 67346 Speyer
Telephone: (6232) 6540
Fax: (6232) 654208
E-mail: dhv@dhv-speyer.de
Internet: www.dhv-speyer.de

Founded 1947
State control
Languages of instruction: German, English
Academic year: May to January

Rector: Prof. Dr STEFAN FISCH
Vice-Rector: Prof. Dr JOACHIM WIELAND
Admin. Officer: CHRISTIANE MÜLLER
Librarian: (vacant)

Library of 302,000 vols
Number of teachers: 90 (incl. 72 part-time)
Number of students: 500

PROFESSORS
BOHNE, E., Public Administration
FÄRBER, G., Public Finance and Economics
FISCH, R., Empirical Social Sciences
FISCH, S., Modern History
HILL, H., Public Administration, Public Law
JANSEN, D., Sociology of Organizations
KNORR, A., International Economics
KÖNIG, T., Political Science
MAGIERA, S., Public Law, European Law and Public International Law
MERTEN, D., Public Law, Social Law
MÜHLENKEMP, H., Public Finance
PITSCHAS, R., Public Administration, Development Policy and Public Law
REINERMANN, H., Public Administration, Information Technology
SIEDENTOPF, H., Public Administration, Public Law
SOMMERMANN, K.-P., Public Law, Constitutional Law, Comparative Law
WIRTZ, B., Information and Communication Management
ZIEKOW, J., Public Law and Administrative Law

ATTACHED INSTITUTE
Forschungsinstitut für Öffentliche Verwaltung (Research Institute for Public Administration): Dir Prof. Dr JAN ZIEKOW.

DEUTSCHE SPORTHOCHSCHULE KÖLN
(German Sport University Cologne)

Am Sportpark, Müngersdorf 6, 50933 Cologne
Telephone: (221) 49820
Fax: (221) 49828330
Internet: www.dshs-koeln.de

Founded 1920 in Berlin, reopened in Cologne 1947
State control
Academic year: October to March,April to September

Rector: Prof. Dr WALTER TOKARSKI
Chancellor: Dr JOHANNES HORST
Vice-Rector: Prof. Dr HEIKO STRÜDER
Vice-Rector: Prof. Dr WILHELM KLEINE
Librarian: Dr HEIKE SCHIFFER

Number of teachers: 230
Number of students: 5,381

EBERHARD-KARLS-UNIVERSITÄT TÜBINGEN

Geschwister-Scholl-Pl., 72074 Tübingen
Telephone: (7071) 290
Fax: (7071) 295990
E-mail: info@uni-tuebingen.de
Internet: www.uni-tuebingen.de

Founded 1477
Academic year: October to September

Rector: Prof. Dr BERND ENGLER
Pro-Rector for Research: Prof. Dr HERBERT MÜTHER
Pro-Rector for Structure and Int. Affairs: Prof. Dr HEINZ-DIETER ASSMANN
Pro-Rector for Students, Teaching and Learning: Prof. Dr STEFANIE GROPPER
Chancellor: Dr ANDREAS ROTHFUß
Librarian: Dr MARIANNE DÖRR

Number of teachers: 2,000
Number of students: 24,400

Publications: *attempto! Forum der Universität Tübingen* (2 a year), *Jahresbericht des Rektors* (1 a year), *Uni Tübingen aktuell* (8 a year)

DEANS
Faculty of Biology: Prof. Dr VOLKER DREHSEN
Faculty of Catholic Theology: Prof. Dr ALBERT BIESINGER

Faculty of Chemistry and Pharmacy: Prof. Dr BARBARA REMMERT
Faculty of Cultural Sciences: Prof. Dr INGO B. AUTENRIETH
Faculty of Economics: Prof. Dr JÜRGEN LEONHARDT
Faculty of Geosciences: Prof. Dr JOSEF SCHMID
Faculty of Science: Prof. Dr WOLFGANG ROSENSTIEL
Faculty of Law: Prof. Dr HERMANN REICHOLD
Faculty of Mathematics and Physics: Prof. Dr WOLFGANG KNAPP
Faculty of Medicine: Prof. Dr INGO B. AUTENRIETH
Faculty of Modern Languages: Prof. Dr JOHANNES KABATEK
Faculty of Philosophy and History: Prof. Dr GEORG SCHILD
Faculty of Protestant Theology: Prof. Dr FRIEDRICH SCHWEITZER

PROFESSORS

Faculty of Biology (Auf der Morgenstelle 28, 72076 Tübingen; tel. (7071) 2976853; fax (7071) 295134; e-mail dek-bi@uni-tuebingen.de; internet www.mikrobio.uni-tuebingen.de):

BRAUN, V., Microbiology
ENGELS, E.-M., Development Physiology
GÖTZ, F., Microbiological Genetics
HAMPP, R., Botany
HARTER, K., Plant Physiology
JÜRGENS, G., Development Genetics
MAIER, W., Zoology
MALLOT, H., Cognitive Neurosciences
MICHIELS, N., Evolution Ecology of Animals
NORDHEIM, A., Molecular Biology
OBERWINKLER, F., Botany
SCHNITZLER, H.-U., Zoophysiology
SCHÖFFL, F., Genetics
WOHLLEBEN, W., Microbiology, Biotechnology

Faculty of Catholic Theology (Liebermeisterstr. 18, 72076 Tübingen; tel. (7071) 2972544; fax (7071) 295407; e-mail u02-info@uni-tuebingen.de; internet www.uni-tuebingen.de/kath-theologie):

BIESINGER, A., Educational Religion
ECKERT, M., Fundamental Theology
FREYER, T., Dogmatic Theology
FUCHS, O., Practical Theology
GROSS, W., Old Testament
HILBERATH, B. J., Systematics
HOLZEM, A., Medieval and Modern Church History
MIETH, D., Moral Theology and Social Sciences
PUZA, R., Church Law
SEELIGER, H.-R., Ancient Church History, Patrology, Christian Archaeology
THEOBALD, M., New Testament

Faculty of Chemistry and Pharmacy (Auf der Morgenstelle 8, 72076 Tübingen; tel. (7071) 2972920; fax (7071) 295198; e-mail dekanat-chem-pharm@uni-tuebingen.de; internet www.uni-tuebingen.de/chemie):

HAMPRECHT, B., Biochemistry
HEIDE, L., Pharmacology
LAUFER, S., Pharmacology
MAIER, M., Organic Chemistry
MEIXNER, A., Physical Chemistry
NÜRNBERGER, T., Organic Biochemistry
OBERHAMMER, H., Physical Chemistry
RUTH, P., Pharmacology
STEHLE, T., Biochemistry
STRÄHLE, J., Inorganic Chemistry
WESEMANN, L., Inorganic Chemistry
ZIEGLER, T., Organic Chemistry

Faculty of Cultural Sciences (Hölderlinstr. 19, 72074 Tübingen; tel. (7071) 2976858; fax (7071) 551567; e-mail a11-info@uni-tuebingen.de; internet www.uni-tuebingen.de/kultur-dekanatl):

ANTONI, K., Japanology
BUTZENBERGER, K., Indology, Comparative Religion
EGGERT, M., Pre- and Ancient History
GERÖ, ST., Oriental Christian Philology and Culture
HOFMANN, H., Classical Philology
KLEIN, P., Art History
LEITZ, C., Egyptology
LEONHARDT, J., Latin Philology
PERNICKA, E., Archaeometry, Archaeometallurgy
RICHTER-BERNBURG, L., Oriental Studies
SCHAEFER, T., Classical Archaeology
SCHMID, M. H., Music
SCHUBERT, G., Sinology
STELLRECHT, I., Ethnography
SZLEZÁK, TH., Greek Philology
VOGEL, H.-U., Sinology
VOLK, K., Oriental History

Faculty of Economics (Nauklerstr. 47, 72074 Tübingen; tel. (7071) 2972563; fax (7071) 295179; e-mail w04.dekanat@uni-tuebingen.de; internet www.uni-tuebingen.de/uni/w04):

BATEN, J., Economic History
BERNDT, R., Commerce
BUCH, C.-M., Economics
CANSIER, D., Economics
GRAMMIG, J., Economics and Statistics
HECKER, R., Commerce
HOFMANN, C., Commerce
JAHNKE, B., Commerce
KOHLER, W., Economics
NEUS, W., Commerce
PULL, K., Commerce
SCHAICH, E., Economics and Statistics
SCHÖBEL, R., Commerce
STADLER, M., Economics
STARBATTY, J., Economics
WAGNER, F. W., Commerce

Faculty of Geosciences (Sigwartstr. 17, 72076 Tübingen; tel. (7071) 2976861; fax (7071) 550744; e-mail e16-info@uni-tuebingen.de; internet www.uni-tuebingen.de/geo):

CONARD, N., Palaeohistory and Protohistory
EBERLE, D., Geography
FÖRSTER, H., Geography
FRISCH, W., Geology
HADERLEIN, S., Environmental Mineralogy
KUCERA, M., Micropalaeontology
MOSBRUGGER, V., Palaeontology
SATIR, M., Geological Chemistry

Faculty of Information Science and Computer Science (Sand 13, 72076 Tübingen; tel. (7071) 2977046; fax (7071) 295919; e-mail dekanat@informatik.uni-tuebingen.de; internet www.informatik.uni-tuebingen.de):

CARLE, G., Computer Science
DIEHL, M., Psychology
HAUCK, P., Computer Science
HAUTZINGER, M., Psychology
HESSE, F., Psychology
HUSON, D., Computer Science
KLAEREN, H., Computer Science
KOHLBACHER, O., Computer Science
LANGE, K.-J., Computer Science
ROSENSTIEL, W., Computer Science
SCHWAN, S., Psychology
STAPF, K.-H., Psychology
STRASSER, W., Computer Science
ULRICH, R., Psychology
ZELL, A., Computer Science

Faculty of Law (tel. (7071) 2972545; fax (7071) 295178; e-mail dekanat@jura.uni-tuebingen.de; internet www.jura.uni-tuebingen.de):

ASSMANN, H.-D., Civil Law, Trade and Commercial Law
GÜNTHER, H.-L., Penal Law
HAFT, F., Penal Law and Procedural Law
KÄSTNER, K.-H., Civil Law, State Church Law

KERNER, H.-J., Criminology
KIRCHHOF, F., Public Law
KÜHL, K., Penal Law and Procedural Law
MAROTZKE, W., Civil Law and Procedural Law
MÖSCHEL, W., Civil, Trade and Commercial Law
NETTESHEIM, M., Public Law, European Law, Civil Law
PICKER, E., Civil Law, Labour and Trade Law
REICHOLD, H., Public Law, Trade and Commercial Law, Labour Law
REMMERT, B., Public Law, European Law and Constitution History
RONELLENFITSCH, M., Public Law
SCHIEMANN, G., Civil Law
SCHRÖDER, J., Penal and Private Law, History of German Law
VITZTHUM, W. GRAF, Public Law
VOGEL, J., Penal Law, Procedural Law
WEBER, U., Penal Law, Procedural Law
WESTERMANN, H. P., Civil, Trade and Commercial Law

Faculty of Mathematics and Physics (Auf der Morgenstelle 4, 72076 Tübingen; tel. (7071) 2972567; fax (7071) 295400; e-mail dekanat.physik@uni-tuebingen.de; internet www.physik.uni-tuebingen.de/dekanat):

BATYREV, V., Algebra
FÄSSLER, A., Theoretical Physics
HERING, N., Geometry
JOCHUM, J., Experimental Physics
KAUP, W., Complex Analysis
KERN, D., Basic Physical Computer Science
KLEY, W., Computational Physics
LUBICH, C., Numerical Analysis
PLIES, E., Applied Physics
REINHARDT, H., Theoretical Physics
RUDER, H., Theoretical Astrophysics
SANTANGELO, A., Astronomy, Astrophysics
SCHÄTZLE, R., Analysis
SCHOPOHL, N., Theoretical Physics
SCHREIBER, F., Biophysical Structures
TEUFEL, S., Mathematical Methods in Natural Sciences
WERNER, K., Astronomy and Astrophysics
YSERENTANT, H., Numerical Analysis
ZERNER, M., Stochastics
ZIMMERMANN, C., Experimental Physics

Faculty of Medicine (Geissweg 5, 72076 Tübingen; tel. (7071) 2972566; fax (7071) 295188; e-mail judith.jovanovic@med.uni-tuebingen.de; internet www.medizin.uni-tuebingen.de/pages/med_fakultaet):

AUTENRIETH, I. B., Medical Microbiology
BAMBERG, M., Radiography
BARES, R., Nuclear Medicine
BARTZ-SCHMIDT, K.-U., Ophthalmology
BECKER, H. D., Surgery
BIRBAUMER, N., Psychology
BUCHKREMER, G., Psychiatry
BÜLTMANN, B., Pathology
CLAUSSEN, C., Radiography
DICHGANS, H., Neurology
DIETZ, K., Medical Biometrics
DREWS, U., Anatomy
FUCHS, J., Child Surgery
GAWAZ, M., Internal Medicine
GOSSER, T., Neurology
GÖZ, G., Dentistry
GREGOR, M., Internal Medicine
HÄRING, H.-U., Internal Medicine
HOFBECK, M., Paediatrics
JAHN, G., Medical Virology
JUCKER, M., Neurology
KANDOLF, R., Molecular Pathology
KANZ, L., Internal Medicine
KLOSINSKI, G., Child and Youth Psychiatry
KNOBLOCH, J., Tropical Medicine
KÖNIGSRAINER, A., Surgery
KRÄGELOH-MANN, J., Paediatrics
LANG, F., Physiology
LÖST, C., Dentistry
MEYERMANN, R., Neuropathology

NIESS, A., Sports Medicine
OSSWALD, H., Pharmacology
POETS, C. F., Paediatrics
RAMMENSEE, H.-G., Immunology
REINERT, S., Maxillofacial Surgery
RIESS, O., Clinical Genetics
RÖCKEN, M., Dermatology
SCHALLER, H.-E., Plastic, Hand and Burns Surgery
SCHWEIZER, P., Child Surgery
SELBMANN, H.-K., Medical Statistics and Data Processing
STENZL, A., Urology
TATAGIBA, M., Neurosurgery
THIER, H. P., Neurology
UNERTL, K., Anaesthesiology
VOIGT, K., Neuroradiology
WAGNER, H.-J., Anatomy
WALLWIENER, D., Gynaecology
WEBER, H., Dentistry
WEHNER, H.-D., Forensic Medicine
WEISE, K., Traumatology
WIESING, U., Medical Ethics
WULKER, N., Orthopaedics
ZENNER, H.-P., Otorhinolaryngology
ZIEMER, G., Thoracic and Cardiovascular Surgery
ZIPFEL, S., Psychosomatic Medicine, Psychotherapy
ZRENNER, E., Ophthalmology

Faculty of Modern Languages (Wilhelmstr. 50, 72074 Tübingen; tel. (7071) 2972952; fax (7071) 294253; e-mail dek-nphil@uni-tuebingen.de; internet www .uni-tuebingen.de/neuphil-dekanat):

BAUER, M., English Philology
BERGER, T., Slavonic Philology
BRAUNGART, G., German Philology
ENGLER, B., English Philology
FICHTE, J., English Philology
HINRICHS, E., Computing Science of Linguistics
HOTZ-DAVIES, I., English Philology
HUBER, CH., Medieval German Literature
KEMPER, H.-G., German Philology
KILCHER, A., German Philology
KLUGE, R.-D., Slavonic Philology
KOBATEK, J., Romance Philology
KOCH, P., German Philology
KOHN, K., English Philology
MATZAT, W., Romance Philology
MOOG-GRÜNEWALD, M., Romance Philology
REINFANDT, C., English Philology
REIS, M., German Philology
RIDDER, K., Medieval German Literature
SCHAHADAT, S., Slavonic Philology
STECHOW, A. VON, Theoretical Linguistics
UEDING, G., Rhetorics
WERTHEIMER, J., German Philology

Faculty of Philosophy and History (*Philosophy Section*, Bursagasse 1, 72070 Tübingen; tel. (7071) 2976852; fax (7071) 295295; e-mail dekanat@philosophie.uni-tuebingen.de; internet www.uni-tuebingen.de/ philosophie*History Section*, Sigwartstr. 17, 72076 Tübingen; tel. (7071) 29-72568; fax (7071) 29-252897; e-mail stefan.zaunder@ uni-tuebingen.de; internet www .uni-tuebingen.de/dekanat-geschichte):

BEYRAU, D., East European History
DOERING-MANTEUFFEL, A., Modern and Contemporary History
FRANK, M., Philosophy
HARTMANN, W., Medieval and Modern History
HEIDELBERGER, M., Philosophy
HÖFFE, O., Philosophy
KOCH, A. F., Philosophy
KOLB, F., Ancient History
LANGEWIESCHE, D., Medieval and Modern History
LORENZ, S., Medieval and Modern History
SCHINDLING, A., Medieval and Modern History

Faculty of Protestant Theology (Liebermeisterstr. 12, 72076 Tübingen; tel. (7071) 2972538; fax (7071) 293318; e-mail ev .theologie@uni-tuebingen.de; internet www .uni-tuebingen.de/ev-theologie):

BAYER, O., Systematic Theology
BLUM, E., Old Testament
DRECOLL, V., Church History
DREHSEN, V., Practical Theology
ECKSTEIN, H.-J., New Testament
HENNIG, G., Practical Theology
HERMS, E., Systematic Theology
HOFIUS, O., New Testament
JANOWSKI, B., Old Testament
KÖPF, U., Church History
LICHTENBERGER, H., New Testament and Ancient Jewish Culture
SCHWEITZER, F., Practical Theology
SCHWÖBEL, C., Systematic Theology

Faculty of Social and Behavioural Sciences and Pedagogics (Wächterstr. 67, 72074 Tübingen; tel. (7071) 2976857; fax (7071) 295115; e-mail s08info@uni-tuebingen.de; internet www.uni-tuebingen.de/faksozver):

BOECKH, A., Political Studies
DEUTSCHMANN, CH., Sociology
DIGEL, H., Theory of Physical Education
GILDEMEISTER, R., Sociology
HORN, K.-P., Pedagogics
HRBEK, R., Political Studies
HUBER, G., Pedagogics
JOHLER, R., Cultural Studies
MÜLLER, S., Social Pedagogics
RITTBERGER, V., Political Studies
SCHRADER, J., Pedagogics
THIEL, A., Theory of Physical Education
TREPTOW, R., Pedagogics
WANK, V., Theory of Physical Education

ATTACHED INSTITUTES

Goethe-Wörterbuch: Frischlinstr. 7, 72074 Tübingen; Dir of Commission Prof. Dr W. KÜHLMANN.

Institut für Wissensmedien (Media Institute): Konrad-Adenauer-Str. 40, 72072 Tübingen; Dir Prof. Dr FRIEDRICH W. HESSE.

EBS UNIVERSITÄT FÜR WIRTSCHAFT UND RECHT

Gustav-Stresemann-Ring 3, 65189 Wiesbaden

Telephone: (611) 710200
Fax: (611) 71021999
E-mail: info@ebs.edu
Internet: www.ebs.edu

Founded 1971 as European Business School, present name and status 2010
Pres. and CEO: Prof. CHRISTOPHER JAHNS
Vice-Pres.: Prof. Dr GERRICK FREIHERR V. HOYNINGEN-HUENE
Vice-Pres.: Prof. Dr ROLF TILMES
Chancellor: Dr GEORG NIKOLAUS GARLICHS
Head Librarian: SILVA SCHELLHAS
Library of 32,000 vols
Number of teachers: 85

ERNST-MORITZ-ARNDT-UNIVERSITÄT GREIFSWALD

Domstr. 11, 17487 Greifswald

Telephone: (3834) 860
Fax: (3834) 861151
E-mail: rektor@uni-greifswald.de
Internet: www.uni-greifswald.de

Founded 1456
Academic year: October to September
Chancellor: Dr WOLFGANG FLIEGER
Rector: Prof. Dr RAINER WESTERMANN
Pro-Rectors: Prof. Dr MICHAEL HERBST, Prof. Dr FRIEDER DÜNKEL

Number of teachers: 235
Number of students: 12,000

Publications: *Greifswalder Universitätsreden* (irregular), *Wissenschaftliche Beiträge* (irregular)

DEANS

Faculty of Law and Economics: Prof. Dr WALTER RIED
Faculty of Mathematics and Natural Sciences: Prof. Dr KLAUS FESSER
Faculty of Medicine: Prof. Dr HEYO K. KROEMER
Faculty of Philosophy: Prof. Dr ALEXANDER WÖLL
Faculty of Theology: Prof. Dr HEINRICH ASSEL

EUROPA-UNIVERSITÄT VIADRINA (Viadrina European University)

Grosse Scharrnstr. 59, 15230 Frankfurt an der Oder

Telephone: (335) 55340
Fax: (335) 5534305
E-mail: study@euv-frankfurt-o.de
Internet: www.euv-ffo.de

Founded 1991
Languages of instruction: German, English, Polish
Academic year: October to July
Pres.: Dr GUNTER PLEUGER
Chancellor: CHRISTIAN ZENS
Registrar: BEATRIX ECKERT
Int. Office: PETRA WEBER
Librarian: Dr HANS-GERD HAPPEL
Library of 525,000 vols
Number of teachers: 190
Number of students: 6,200

DEANS

Faculty of Cultural and Social Studies: Prof. Dr KONSTANZE JUNGBLUTH
Faculty of Economics: Prof. Dr SVEN HUSMANN
Faculty of Law: Prof. Dr MATTIAS PECHSTEIN

ATTACHED COLLEGE

Collegium Polonicum: (situated in Slubice in Poland, and managed jointly by the Europa-Universität Viadrina and the Adam Mickiewicz University in Poznań).

FERNUNIVERSITÄT IN HAGEN (Distance-Learning University in Hagen)

58084 Hagen
Universitätsstr. 11, 58097 Hagen

Telephone: (2331) 9872444
Fax: (2331) 987316
E-mail: info@fernuni-hagen.de
Internet: www.fernuni-hagen.de

Founded 1974
54 Study centres within Germany, Austria, Switzerland, Hungary and Russia
State control
Language of instruction: German
Academic year: October to September
Rector: Prof. Dr Ing. HELMUT HOYER
Vice-Rector: Prof. Dr RAINER OLBRICH
Vice-Rector: Prof. Dr RAINER OLBRICH
CEO and Chancellor: REGINA ZDEBEL
Librarian: KARIN MICHALKE (acting)
Library of 800,000 vols, 2000 print journals, 36,000 e-journals
Number of teachers: 942
Number of students: 74,223

Publications: *Anleitung zur Belegung, FernUni Perspektive* (newspaper of the univ.), *Forschungsbericht, Informationen zum Studium, Schriftenreihen* (scientific publ.)

DEANS

Faculty of Business Administration and Economics: Prof. Dr Hab. THOMAS HERING

Faculty of Culture and Social Sciences: Prof. Dr THEO BASTIAENS

Faculty of Law: Prof. Dr ANDREAS HARATSCH

Faculty of Mathematics and Computer Science: Prof. Dr RUTGER VERBEEK

FREIE UNIVERSITÄT BERLIN

Kaiserswerther Str. 16–18, 14195 Berlin

Telephone: (30) 8381

Fax: (30) 83873217

E-mail: praesident@fu-berlin.de

Internet: www.fu-berlin.de

Founded 1948

Academic year: October to July

Pres.: Prof. Dr PETER-ANDRÉ ALT

Exec. Vice-Pres.: Prof. Dr MONIKA SCHÄFER-KORTING

Vice-Pres.: Prof. Dr WERNER VÄTH

Vice-Pres.: Prof. Dr MICHAEL BONGARDT

Vice-Pres.: Prof. Dr-Ing. BRIGITTA SCHÜTT

Dir of Admin. and Finance: PETER LANGE

Librarian: Prof. Dr ULRICH NAUMANN

Library: see Libraries and Archives

Number of teachers: 2,800

Number of students: 32,000

DEANS

Dept of Biology, Chemistry and Pharmacy: Prof. Dr HARTMUT H. HILGER

Dept of Economics: Prof. Dr RONNIE SCHÖB

Dept of Earth Sciences: Prof. Dr ULRICH CUBASCH

Dept of Education and Psychology: Prof. Dr HARM KUPER

Dept of History and Cultural Studies: Prof. Dr VERENA BLECHINGER-TALCOTT

Dept of Law: Prof. Dr MARTIN SCHWAB

Dept of Mathematics and Computer Science: Prof. Dr RUPERT KLEIN

Dept of Philosophy and Humanities: Prof. Dr JOACHIM KÜPPER

Dept of Physics: ROBERT BITTL

Dept of Political and Social Sciences: Prof. Dr KLAUS BECK

Dept of Veterinary Medicine: Prof. Dr LEO BRUNNBERG

Medical School—Charité: Prof. Dr ANNETTE GRÜTERS-KIESLICH

CENTRAL ATTACHED INSTITUTES

John F. Kennedy-Institut für Nordamerikastudien (J. F. K. Institute of North American Studies): Lanstr. 7, 14195 Berlin; tel. (30) 83852703; fax (30) 83852882; e-mail jfki@zedat.fu-berlin.de; internet web.fu-berlin.de/jfki; Chair. DETLEF BROSE.

Lateinamerika-Institut (Institute of Latin American Studies): Rüdesheimer Str. 54-56, 14197 Berlin; tel. (30) 83853073; fax (30) 83855464; e-mail ai@zedat.fu-berlin.de; internet web.fu-berlin.de/lai; Chair. Prof. Dr MARIANNE BRAIG.

Osteuropa-Institut (Institute of East European Studies): Garystr. 55, 14195 Berlin; tel. (30) 83853380; fax (30) 83853788; e-mail oei@zedat.fu-berlin.de; internet www.oei.fu-berlin.de; Chair. DETLEF BROSE.

FRIEDRICH-ALEXANDER-UNIVERSITÄT ERLANGEN-NÜRNBERG

POB 35 20, 91023 Erlangen

Schlosspl. 4, 91054 Erlangen

Telephone: (9131) 850

Fax: (9131) 8522131

E-mail: praesident@uni-erlangen.de

Internet: www.uni-erlangen.de

Founded 1743, merged with Univ. Altdorf 1809

State control

Pres.: Prof. Dr KARL-DIETER GRÜSKE

Vice-Pres.: Prof. Dr CHRISTOPH KORBMACHER

Vice-Pres.: Prof. Dr HANS-PETER STEINRÜCK

Vice-Pres.: Prof. JOHANNA HABERER

Chancellor: THOMAS A. H. SCHÖCK

Librarian: Dr KONSTANZE SÖLLNER

Library: see Libraries and Archives

Number of teachers: 590

Number of students: 28,677

Publications: *Erlanger Bausteine zur fränkischen Heimatforschung, Erlanger Forschungen, Geologische Blätter für Nordost-Bayern und angrenzende Gebiete, Jahrbuch für fränkische Landesforschung, Jahresbericht, Jahresbibliographie und Forschungsbericht, Unikurier, Unikurier aktuell*

DEANS

Faculty of Engineering: Prof. Dr GÜNTER ILGENFRITZ

Faculty of Humanities, Social Sciences and Theology: Prof. Dr HEIDRUN STEIN-KECKS

Faculty of Law, Business and Economics: Prof. Dr MICHAEL AMBERG

Faculty of Sciences: Prof. Dr FRANK DUZAAR

Faculty of Medicine: Prof. Dr JÜRGEN SCHÜTTLER

FRIEDRICH-SCHILLER-UNIVERSITÄT JENA
(Friedrich Schiller University of Jena)

07737 Jena

Telephone: (3641) 9300

Fax: (3641) 931682

E-mail: rektor@uni-jena.de

Internet: www.uni-jena.de

Founded 1558

State control

Rector: Prof. Dr KLAUS DICKE

Vice-Rector for Research: Prof. HERBERT WITTE

Vice-Rector for Graduate Academy: Prof. Dr AMÉLIE MUMMENDEY

Vice-Rector for Teaching and Structure: Prof. Dr KURT-DIETER KOSCHMIEDER

Chancellor: Dr KLAUS BARTHOLMÉ

Library: see under Libraries and Archives

Number of teachers: 2,360

Number of students: 25,000

DEANS

Faculty of Biology and Pharmacy: Prof. Dr THORSTEN HEINZEL

Faculty of Chemical and Earth Sciences: Prof. Dr REINHARD GAUPP

Faculty of Economics and Business Admin.: Prof. Dr JOHANNES RUHLAND

Faculty of Law: Prof. Dr EBERHARD EICHENHOFER

Faculty of Mathematics and Computer Science: Prof. Dr HANS-JÜRGEN SCHMEIßER

Faculty of Philosophy: Prof. Dr HERMANN FUNK

Faculty of Physics and Astronomy: Prof. Dr BERND BRÜGMANN

Faculty of Social and Behavioural Sciences: Prof. Dr STEPHAN LESSENICH

Faculty of Theology: Prof. Dr MICHAEL WERMKE

School of Medicine: Prof. Dr KLAUS BENNDORF

GEORG-AUGUST-UNIVERSITÄT GÖTTINGEN

Wilhelmspl. 1, 37073 Göttingen

Telephone: (551) 390

Fax: (551) 394135

E-mail: poststelle@uni-goettingen.de

Internet: www.uni-goettingen.de

Founded 1737

Academic year: October to July

Pres.: Prof. Dr ULRIKE BEISIEGEL

Vice-Pres: Prof. Dr HILTRAUD CASPER-HEHNE

Vice-Pres: Prof. Dr JOACHIM MÜNCH

Vice-Pres: Dipl.-Kfm. MARKUS HOPPE

Vice-Pres: Prof. Dr WOLFGANG LÜCKE

Librarian: Dr NORBERT LOSSAU

Number of teachers: 800

Number of students: 24,380

Publications: *Georgia-Augusta* (2 a year), *Jahresforschungsbericht* (every 2 years), *Spektrum* (4 a year)

DEANS

Faculty of Agricultural Sciences: Prof. Dr ACHIM SPILLER

Faculty of Biology: Prof. Dr RALF FICNER

Faculty of Chemistry: Prof. Dr CLAUDIA STEINEM

Faculty of Economic Sciences: Prof. Dr OLAF KORN

Faculty of Forest Sciences and Forest Ecology: Prof. Dr CHRISTOPH KLEINN

Faculty of Geoscience and Geography: Prof. Dr SHARON WEBB

Faculty of Humanities: Prof. Dr UDO FRIEDRICH

Faculty of Law: Prof. Dr ANDREAS SPICKHOFF

Faculty of Mathematics and Computer Science: Prof. Dr DIETER HOGREFE

Faculty of Medicine: Prof. Dr CORNELIUS FRÖMMEL

Faculty of Physics: Prof. Dr HANS CHRISTIAN HOFSÄSS

Faculty of Social Sciences: Prof. Dr GABRIELE ROSENTHAL

Faculty of Theology: Prof. Dr CHRISTINE AXT-PISCALAR

GOETHE-UNIVERSITÄT FRANKFURT AM MAIN

POB 11 19 32, 60054 Frankfurt am Main

Senckenberganlage 31, 60325 Frankfurt am Main

Telephone: (69) 7980

Fax: (69) 79828383

E-mail: presse@uni-frankfurt.de

Internet: www.goethe-universitaet.de

Founded 1914

Academic year: October to September (2 semesters)

Pres.: Prof. Dr WERNER MÜLLER-ESTERL

Vice-Pres.: Prof. Dr MANFRED SCHUBERT-ZSILAVECZ

Vice-Pres.: Prof. Dr MARIA ROSER VALENTI

Vice-Pres.: Prof. Dr MATTHIAS LUTZ-BACHMANN

Vice-Pres.: Prof. Dr RAINER KLUMP

Chancellor: HANS GEORG MOCKEL

Library Dir: BERNDT DUGALL

Number of teachers: 2,656

Number of students: 36,625

Publications: *Forschung Frankfurt* (4 a year), *Forschungsbericht* (1 a year), *Uni-Report* (6 or 7 a year)

DEANS

Department of Biochemistry, Chemistry and Pharmaceutical Sciences: Prof. Dr DIETER STEINHILBER

Department of Biological Sciences: Prof. Dr A. STARZINSKI-POWITZ

Department of Computer Science and Mathematics: Prof. Dr TOBIAS WETH

Department of Economics and Business Administration: Prof. Dr ALFONS WEICHENRIEDER

Department of Educational Sciences: Prof. Dr BARBARA FRIEBERTSHÄUSER

Department of Geosciences and Geography: Prof. Dr ROBERT PÜTZ

Department of Law: Prof. Dr MANFRED WANDT

Department of Linguistic, Cultural and Civilization Studies, Art Studies: Prof. Dr RÜDIGER KRAUSE

Department of Medical Science: Prof. Dr JOSEF M. PFEILSCHIFTER

Department of Modern Languages: Prof. Dr SUSANNE OPFERMANN

Department of Philosophy and History: Prof. Dr ANDRÉ FUHRMANN

Department of Physics: Prof. Dr MICHAEL HUTH

Department of Protestant Theology: Prof. Dr HANS-GÜNTER HEIMBROCK

Department of Psychology and Sports Sciences: Prof. Dr HELFRIED MOOSBRUGGER

Department of Roman Catholic Theology: Prof. Dr THOMAS SCHMELLER

Department of Social Sciences: Prof. Dr UTA RUPPERT

PROFESSORS

Department of Biochemistry, Chemistry and Pharmaceutical Sciences (Max-von-Laue-Str. 9, 60438 Frankfurt am Main; tel. (69) 79829545; fax (69) 79829546; e-mail dekanatfb14@uni-frankfurt.de):

AUNER, N., Inorganic Chemistry
BADER, H.-J., Chemistry Teaching
BAMBERG, E., Biophysical Chemistry
BRUTSCHY, B., Physical Chemistry
DINGERMANN, TH., Pharmaceutical Biology
DRESSMAN, J. B., Pharmaceutical Technology
EGERT, E., Organic Chemistry
ENGELS, J., Organic Chemistry
GÖBEL, M., Organic Chemistry
KARAS, M., Analytical Chemistry
KOLBESEN, B., Inorganic Chemistry
KREUTER, J., Pharmaceutical Technology
LAMBRECHT, G., Pharmacology for Natural Scientists
LUDWIG, B., Biochemistry
MARSCHALEK, R., Pharmaceutical Biology
MOSANDL, A., Food Chemistry
MÜLLER, W. E., Pharmacology and Toxicology
PRISNER, TH. F., Physical Chemistry
REHM, D., Physical and Organic Chemistry
RÜTERJANS, H., Physical Biochemistry
SCHUBERT-ZSILAVECZ, M., Pharmaceutical Chemistry
STARK, H., Pharmaceutical Chemistry
STEINHILBER, D., Pharmaceutical Chemistry
STOCK, G., Theoretical Chemistry
WACHTVEITL, J., Physical Chemistry
WAGNER, M., Inorganic Chemistry

Department of Biological Sciences (Max-von-Laue-Str. 9, 60438 Frankfurt am Main; tel. (69) 79846471; fax (69) 79846470; e-mail dekanat15@bio.uni-frankfurt.de):

BEREITER-HAHN, J., Cell Research
BRÄNDLE, K., Zoology
BRENDEL, M., Biology for Doctors
BRÜGGEMANN, W., Botany
DROBNIK, O., Architecture and Business Systems
ENTIAN, K.-D., Microbiology
FEIERABEND, F., Botany
FLEISSNER, G., Zoology
GEIHS, K., Practical Informatics
GNATZY, W., Zoology
HAGERUP, T., Theoretical Informatics
KAHL, G., Botany
KEMP, R., Applied Informatics
KOENIGER, N., Apiculture
KROEGER, A., Microbiology
KRÖMKER, D., Graphical Data Processing
KUNZ, W., Drafting Methods
LANGE-BERTALOT, H., Botany
MASCHWITZ, U., Zoology
NOVER, L., Botany
OSIEWACZ, H., Botany
PONS, F., Microbiology
PRINZINGER, R., Zoology
PROTSCH VON ZIETEN, R., Anthropology
SANDMANN, G., Botany

SCHMIDT-SCHAUSS, M., Artificial Intelligence
SCHNITGER, G., Theoretical Informatics
STARZINSKI-POWITZ, A., Human Genetics
STEIGER, H., Microbiology
STREIT, B., Zoology
TROMMER, G., Biology Teaching
WALDSCHMIDT, K., Applied Informatics
WILTSCHKO, W., Zoology
WITTIG, R., Botany
WOTSCHKE, D., Computer Languages
ZICARI, R., Databases
ZIMMERMANN, H., Zoology
ZIZKA, G., Botany

Department of Computer Science and Mathematics (Robert-Mayer-Str. 10, 60054 Frankfurt am Main; tel. (69) 79824602; fax (69) 79824619; e-mail dekan@fb12.uni-frankfurt.de):

BAUMEISTER, J. B., Optimum and Convex Functions
BEHR, H., Pure Mathematics
BIERI, R., Pure Mathematics
BLIEDTNER, J., Pure Mathematics
CONSTANTINESCU, F., Mathematics
DINGES, H., Probability Theory and Statistics
FÜHRER, L., Mathematics Teaching
GROOTE, H. DE, Applied Mathematics
KERSTING, G., Stochastics
KLOEDEN, P. E., Applied Mathematics
KRUMMHEUER, G., Mathematics Teaching
LUCKHARDT, H., Fundamental Mathematics
METZLER, W., Mathematics
MÜLLER, K. H., Applied Mathematics
REICHERT-HAHN, M., Mathematics
SCHNORR, C., Applied Mathematics
SCHWARZ, W., Mathematics
SIEVEKING, M., Applied Mathematics
WAKOLBINGER, A., Probability Theory
WEIDMANN, J., Mathematics
WOLFART, J., Mathematics

Department of Economics and Business Administration (Grüneburgpl. 1, 60323 Frankfurt am Main; tel. (69) 79834601; fax (69) 79835000; e-mail dekanat02@wiwi.uni-frankfurt.de):

BARTELS, H. G., Business Administration, Operational Research
BAUER, T., Economic Systems and Transition
BINDER, M., Macroeconomics
BLONSKI, M., Microeconomics
BÖCKING, H.-J., Corporate Governance
EWERT, R., Controlling and Auditing
FITZENBERGER, B., Labour Economics
GEBHARDT, G., Economic Management
GOMBER, P., e-Finance
HALIASSOS, M., Macroeconomics and Financial Markets
HASSLER, U., Statistics
HOLTEN, R., Business Information Systems
HOMMEL, M., Auditing and Invoicing
HORLEBEIN, M., Economic Pedagogics
HUJER, R., Statistics and Econometrics
ISERMANN, H., Business Administration
KAAS, K. P., Industrial Economics
KLAPPER, D., Marketing
KLUMP, R., Business Development
KÖNIG, W., Economic Management
KRAHNEN, J. P., Financial Management
KRÜGER, D., Macroeconomy
LAUX, H., Theory of Organization
MATHES, H. D., Production Planning
MAURER, R., Investment
MELLWIG, W., Industrial Economics
NATTER, M., Trade
NAUTZ, D., Empirical Macroeconomy
RANNENBERG, K., Business Computing
ROMMELFANGER, H., Mathematics for Economists
SCHEFOLD, B., Political Economics
SCHLAG, CH., Financial Economics
SCHMIDT, R., Economic Management

SKIERA, B., Electronic Commerce
VELTHUIS, L., Organization and Management
WAHRENBURG, M., Business Administration (Banking)
WALZ, U., Industry Economics
WEICHENRIEDER, A., Financial Economics
WIELAND, V., Money Theory and Policy

Department of Educational Sciences (POB 109, Senckenberganlage 15, 60054 Frankfurt am Main; tel. (69) 79828729; fax (69) 79828760; e-mail dekanatfb4@em.uni-frankfurt.de):

BRAKEMEIER-LISOP, I., Economic Pedagogics
BRUMLIK, M., Pedagogics
CREMER-SCHÄFER, H., Pedagogics and Social Pedagogics
DEPPE-WOLFINGER, H., Special Education
DUDEK, P., Pedagogics
FAUST-SIEHL, G., Primary Education
GRUSCHKA, A., Teacher Training
HESS, H., Social Pedagogics
HOFMANN-MÜLLER, C. H., Pedagogics
JACOBS, K., Special and Remedial Education
KADE, J., Theory and Practice of Adult Education
KALLERT, H., Social Pedagogics
KAMINSKI, W., Pedagogics
KATZENBACH, D., Pedagogics
MARKERT, W., Economic Pedagogics
MEIER, R., Primary Teacher Training
NITTEL, D., Social Pedagogics and Adult Education
NYSSEN, F., Teacher Training
OVERBECK, A., Special Education
RADTKE, F.-O., Pedagogics
RANG, B., History and Pedagogics of Women's Studies
SCHLÖMERKEMPER, J., Pedagogics
SCHOLZ, G., Primary Education
ZANDER, H., Social Pedagogics
ZENZ, G., Social Pedagogics

Department of Geosciences and Geography (Altenhöferallee 1, 60438 Frankfurt am Main; tel. (69) 79840208; fax (69) 79840210; e-mail dekanat-geowiss@em.uni-frankfurt.de):

ALBRECHT, V., Teaching of Geography
ANDRES, W., Physical Geography
BATHELT, H., Economic Geography
BREY, G., Mineralogy
BRINKMANN, W. L. F., Hydrology
HASSE, J., Teaching of Geography
HERBERT, F., Theoretical Meteorology
HUESSNER, H., Geology and Palaeontology
JUNGE, A., Geophysics
KLEINSCHMIDT, G., Geology
KOWALCZYK, G., Regional Geology
MÜLLER, G., Mathematical Geophysics
OSCHMANN, W., Palaeontology
PÜTTMANN, W., Environmental Analysis
RUNGE, J., Physical Geography
SCHAMP, E., Economic Geography
SCHICKHOFF, I., Human Geography
SCHMELING, H., Solid Earth Physics
SCHMIDT, U., Atmospheric Physics
SCHÖNWIESE, C., Meteorological Environmental Research
SCHROEDER, R., Palaeontology
STEIN, N., Physical Geography
STEININGER, F. F., Palaeontology and Historical Geology
THARUN, E., Cultural Geography
THIEMAYER, H., Hydrology
WOLF, K., Cultural Geography

Department of Law (Grüneburgpl. 1, 60323 Frankfurt am Main; tel. (69) 798-23956; ; tel. (69) 79834206; fax (69) 79834530; e-mail ddekanatfb1@rz.uni-frankfurt.de):

ALBRECHT, P., Criminology and Criminal Law

BAUMS, TH., Business Law (Banking and Media)
CAHN, A., Law and Finance
CORDES, A., European History of Law
EBSEN, I., Constitutional, Administrative and Social Law
FABRICIUS, D., Criminal Law, Criminology and Psychology of Law
FRANKENBERG, G., Public Law
GILLES, P., Legal Procedure, Civil and Comparative Law
GÜNTHER, K., Theory of Law, Penal Law and Law of Criminal Procedure
HAAR, BRIGITTE, Civil Law
HASSEMER, W., Theory of Law, Social and Criminal Law
HERMES, G., Public Law
HOFMANN, R., Civil Law
KADELBACH, S., Public Law, European Law
KARGL, W., Theory of Law, Philosophy of Law and Criminal Law
KOHL, H., Civil Law
NEUMANN, U., Social, Criminal, and Criminal Adjective Law and Philosophy of Law
OGOREK, R., Roman Law, Civil Law
OSTERLOH, L., Public Law, Tax Law
PRITTWITZ, C., Criminal Law
REHBINDER, E., Business, Environmental and Comparative Law
RÜCKERT, J., History of Law
SACKSOFSKY, U., Public Law and Comparative Law
SIEKMANN, H., Money and Bank Law
SIRKS, B., History of Law and Civil Law
STOLLEIS, M., Public Law, History of Law
TEUBNER, G., Civic Rights, Commercial Law
VESTING, T., Public Law, Media Law
WANDT, M., German and International Civil Law, Commercial and Insurance Law
WEISS, M., Labour Law and Civic Rights
WELLENHOFER, M., Civil and Process Law
WIELAND, J., Public Law, Financial Law and Tax Law
ZEKOLL, J., Civil Law

Department of Linguistic, Cultural and Civilization Studies, Art Studies (Mertonstr. 17–21, 60054 Frankfurt am Main; tel. (69) 79825023; fax (69) 79828474; e-mail dekanat-fb09@em.uni-frankfurt.de):

BASTIAN, H. G., Teaching of Music
BÜCHSEL, M., History of European Art
DAIBER, Oriental Studies
ERDAL, M., Turkish Studies
FASSLER, M., European Ethnology
FISCHER, J., Art Teaching
FREIDHOF, G., Slavonic Studies
GIPPERT, J., Comparative Linguistics
HERDING, K., Art History
LANGER, G., Slavonic Studies
MEYER, J.-W., Archaeology
NEU, T., Art Teaching
NEUMEISTER, C., Classical Philology
NOTHOFER, B., Southeast Asian Studies
NOVA, A., Art History
NOWAK, A., Musicology
RAECK, W., Classical Archaeology
RICHARD, B., Art Teaching
SCHLÜTER, M., Jewish Studies
SCHMITZ, TH., Greek Philology
SIEVERT, A., Art Teaching
VOSSEN, R., African Languages
WELZ, G., European Ethnology

Department of Medicinal Science (Theodor-Stern-Kai 7, 60590 Frankfurt am Main; tel. (69) 63016010; fax (69) 63015922; e-mail dekan@kgu.de):

AUBURGER, G., Applied Neurology
BITTER, K., Maxillofacial Surgery
BÖHLES, H. J., Paediatrics
BÖTTCHER, H. D., Radiation Therapy
BRAAK, H., Anatomy
BRADE, V., Hygiene, Microbiology

BRANDT, U., Biochemistry
BRATZKE, H., Forensic Medicine
BRETTEL, H.-F., Forensic Medicine
BUSSE, R., Physiology
CASPARY, W., Internal Medicine and Gastroenterology
CHANDRA, P., Therapeutic Biochemistry
DELLER, T., Anatomy
DEPPE, H.-U., Medical Sociology
DOERR, H. W., Medical Virology
DUDZIAK, R., Anaesthesiology
ELSNER, G., Industrial Medicine
ENCKE, A., General and Abdominal Surgery
FELLBAUM, CH., Pathology and Pathological Anatomy
FIEGUTH, H.-B., Thoracic Surgery
FÖRSTER, H., Applied Biochemistry
GALL, V., Child Audiology
GEIGER, H., Internal Medicine
GEISSLINGER, G., Clinical Pharmacology
GIERE, W., Documentation and Data Processing
GRONER, B., Molecular Infection and Tumour Biology
GROSS, W., Physiological Chemistry
GRÜNWALD, F., Nuclear Medicine
GSTÖTTNER, W., Ear, Nose and Throat Surgery
HANSMANN, M.-L., Pathology
HEIDEMANN, D., Dental and Maxillofacial Medicine
HELLER, K., Surgery
HOELZER, D., Haematology
HOFMANN, D., Child Health
HOFSTETTER, R., Child Cardiology
HOHMANN, W., Materials in Dentistry
JONAS, D., Urology
JORK, K., General Medicine
KAUERT, G., Forensic Toxicology
KAUFMANN, M., Gynaecology
KAUFMANN, R., Dermatology and Venereology
KERSCHBAUMER, F., Orthopaedics and Orthopaedic Surgery
KLINGEBIEL, T., Child Health
KLINKE, R., Physiology
KOCH, F.-H., Ophthalmology
KORF, H.-W., Anatomy
KUHL, H., Experimental Endocrinology
LANGENBECK, U., Human Genetics
LAUER, H.-CHR., Dentistry
LEUSCHNER, U., Gastroenterology
MAURER, K., Psychiatry
MELCHNER VON DYDIOWA, H., Clinical Molecular Biology
MOELLER, M., Medical Psychology
MORITZ, A., Thoracic, Heart and Vessel Surgery
MÜLLER-ESTERL, W., Biological Chemistry
MÜLSCH, A., Physiology
NENTWIG, G.-H., Dental and Maxillofacial Medicine
NÜRNBERGER, F., Anatomy, Neurobiology
OHRLOFF, CH., Ophthalmology and Experimental Ophthalmology
OVERBECK, G., Psychosomatics
PFEILSCHIFTER, J. M., Pharmacology and Toxicology
PFLUG, B., Psychiatry
POUSTKA, F., Child and Adolescent Psychiatry
RÄTZKE, P., Dental and Maxillofacial Medicine
SCHMIDT, H., Paediatric Radiology
SCHMITZ-RIXEN, TH., Vascular Surgery
SCHOPF, P., Maxillofacial Surgery
SCHUBERT, R., Hygiene
SEIFERT, V., Neurosurgery
SIEFERT, H., History of Medicine
SIGUSCH, V., Sexology
STEIN, J., Gastroenterology and Clinical Nutrition
STEINMETZ, H., Neurology
STÜRZEBECHER, E., Medical Acoustics
USADEL, K.-H., Internal Medicine

VOGL, TH., Radiological Diagnosis
VON JAGOW, G., Psychological Chemistry
VON LOEWENICH, V., Child Health
WAGNER, TH., Internal Medicine and Allergistics
WINCKLER, J., Anatomy
ZANELLA, F., Neuroradiology
ZEIHER, A. M., Internal Medicine
ZICHNER, L., Orthopaedics

Department of Modern Languages (Grüneburgpl. 1, 60629 Frankfurt am Main; tel. (69) 79832742; fax (69) 79832743; e-mail dekanat10@lingua.uni-frankfurt.de):

BOHN, V., Modern German Philology
BROGGINI, G., German Philology
BUSCHENDORF, C., American Studies
ERFURT, J., Romance Philology
EWERS, H., German Philology and Literature (Children's Literature)
FREY, W., German
GARSCHA, K., Romance Philology
GREWENDORF, G., German Linguistics
HAMACHER, W., Modern German Philology
HANSEN, O., American Studies
HELLINGER, M., English Studies
HERRMANN, W., Teaching of German Language and Literature
KELLER, U., English
KLEIN, H. G., Romance Philology
KÜHNEL, W., English and American Studies
LAUERBACH, G., English Studies
LEHMANN, H.-T., Theatre Studies
LEUNINGER, H., German Linguistics
LINDNER, B., German Language and Literature Teaching
LOBSIEN, E., English
METZNER, E., German
MITTENZWEI, I., Modern German
OPFERMANN, S., American Studies
OSSNER, J., Language Science of Modern German
QUETZ, J., English Teaching
RAITZ, W., History of German Literature
REICHERT, K., English/American Language
ROSEBROCK, C., Teaching of Literary Appreciation
RÜTTEN, R., French Language and Literature
SCHARLAU, B., Romance Philology
SCHEIBLE, H., German Language and Literature
SCHLOSSER, H. D., German
SCHLÜPMANN, H., Film Science
SCHNEIDER, G., Romance Philology
SCHRADER, H., Teaching of French
SEITZ, D., German
SOLMECKE, G., Teaching of English Language
STEGMANN, T., Romance Languages and Literature
WEISE, W.-D., English Teaching
WIETHÖLTER, W., Modern German Literature
WOLFZETTEL, F., Romance Philology
ZIMMERMANN, TH., Semantics

Department of Philosophy and History (Grüneburgpl. 1, 60323 Frankfurt am Main; tel. (69) 79832758; fax (69) 79832759; e-mail dekanat08@em.uni-frankfurt.de):

BREUNIG, P., Archaeology
CLAUSS, M., Ancient History
DETEL, W., Philosophy
ESSLER, W. K., Philosophy, Logic and Educational Theory
FEEST, CHR., Ethnology
FRIED, J., Ancient History
GALL, L., Medieval and Modern History
GREFE, E.-H., Teaching of History
HENNING, J., Prehistory
HONNETH, A., Social Philosophy
KOHL, K.-H., Ethnology
KULENKAMPFF, A., Philosophy
LENTZ, C., Ethnology
LÜNING, J., Prehistory

LUTZ-BACHMANN, M., Medieval Philosophy
MERKER, B., Philosophy
MUHLACK, U., General History
MÜLLER, H., Medieval Philosophy
PLUMPE, W., Economic and Social History
RECKER, M.-L., Recent History
SCHORN-SCHÜTTE, L., The Renaissance
VON KAENEL, H. M., Greek and Roman History

Department of Physics (Max-von-Laue-Str.1, 60438 Frankfurt am Main; tel. (69) 79847202; fax (69) 79847205; e-mail dekanat@physik.uni-frankfurt.de):

ASSMUS, W., Experimental Physics
BECKER, R., Applied Physics
DREIZLER, R., Theoretical Physics
ELZE, T., Nuclear Physics
GÖRNITZ, T., Physics Teaching
GREINER, W., Theoretical Physics
HAUG, H., Theoretical Physics
HENNING, W., Experimental Nuclear Physics
JELITTO, R., Theoretical Physics
KEGEL, W., Theoretical Physics
KING, D. A., History of Natural Sciences
KOPIETZ, P., Theoretical Solid State Physics
LACROIX, A., Applied Physics
LANG, M., Experimental Physics
LYNEN, U., Nuclear Physics
MÄNTELE, W., Biophysics
MARUHN, J., Theoretical Physics
MESTER, R., Applied Physics
MOHLER, E., Applied Physics
RATZINGER, U., Applied Physics
RISCHKE, D.-H., Theoretical Heavy Ion Physics
ROSKOS, H., Experimental Physics
SALTZER, W., History of Science
SCHMIDT-BÖCKING, H., Experimental Atomic Physics
SCHUBERT, D., Physics for Doctors
SIEMSEN, F., Physics Teaching
STOCK, R., Experimental Nuclear Physics
STÖCKER, H., Theoretical Physics
STRÖBELE, H., Experimental Nuclear Physics

Department of Protestant Theology (Grüneburgpl. 1, 60629 Frankfurt am Main; tel. (69) 79833344; fax (69) 79833358; e-mail dekanat.evtheol@em.uni-frankfurt.de):

DEUSER, H., Protestant Theology
FAILING, W.-E., Protestant Theology
HEIMBROCK, H. G., Protestant Theology
WEBER, E., Protestant Theology

Department of Psychology and Sports Science (Kettenhofweg 128, 60054 Frankfurt am Main; tel. (69) 79823267; fax (69) 79824956; e-mail dekanat@psych.uni-frankfurt.de):

BALLREICH, A., Training Science
BANZER, W., Prevention and Rehabilitation
BAUER, W., General Psychology
DEGENHARDT-EWERT, A., Diagnostic Psychology
ECKENSBERGER, L. H., Psychology
EMRICH, E., Sport Science
GIESEN, H., Educational Psychology
GOLD, A., Pedagogical Psychology
HAASE, H., Psychology and Sociology of Sport
HODAPP, V., Diagnostic Psychology
KNOPF, M., Psychology
LANGFELDT, H.-P., Pedagogical Psychology
LAUTERBACH, W., Clinical Psychology
MOOSBRUGGER, H., Psychological Methodology, Statistics
PREISER, S., Educational Psychology
PROHL, R., Sports
ROHDE-DACHSER, CH., Psychoanalysis
SARRIS, V., Psychology
SCHMIDTBLEICHER, D., Training Science
SCHWANENBERG, E., Social Psychology
SIRETEANU, R., Physiological Psychology
ZAPF, D., Psychology

Department of Roman Catholic Theology (Grüneburgplatz 1, 60323 Frankfurt am Main; tel. (69) 79833346; fax (69) 79833354; e-mail dekanat07@uni-frankfurt.de):

DENINGER-POLZER, G., Catholic Theology
HAINZ, J., Exegesis of the New Testament
HOFFMANN, J., Moral Theology, Social Ethics
KESSLER, H., Systematic Theology
RASKE, M., Practical Theology
SCHREIJÄCK, T., Catholic Theology
WIEDENHOFER, S., Systematic Theology

Department of Social Sciences (Robert-Mayer-Str. 5, 60054 Frankfurt am Main; tel. (69) 79822521; fax 79828465; e-mail dekanat.fb03@soz.uni-frankfurt.de):

ALLERBECK, K., Sociology
ALLERT, T., Sociology and Social Psychology
APITZSCH, U., Sociology
BOSSE, H., Theory of Socialization
BROCK, L., International Politics
CLEMENZ, M., Sociology of Education
ESSER, J., Study of Politics, Sociology
GERHARD, U., Sociology
GLATZER, W., Social Structures
GRESS, F., Political Science
HELLMANN, G., Foreign Policy
HIRSCH, J., Political Science
HOFMANN, G., Methods of Social Research, Statistics
HONDRICH, K. O., Sociology
KAHSNITZ, D., Polytechnic and Technical Instruction Course
KELLNER, H.-F., Sociology
KRELL, G., Political Science
MANS, D., Methods of Social Research
MAUS, I., History of Political Ideas
MÜLLER, H., Political Science
NEUMANN-BRAUN, K., Sociology
NONNENMACHER, F., Teaching of Social Sciences
OEVERMANN, U., Sociology, Social Psychology
PROKOP, D., Mass Communications Research
PUHLE, H.-J., Political Science
RODENSTEIN, M., Sociology
ROPOHL, G., Polytechnic and Technical Instruction Course
ROTTLEUTHNER-LUTTER, M., Methodology
SCHMID, A., Polytechnic and Technical Instruction Course
SCHUMM, W., Sociology
SIEGEL, T., Sociology of Industrialized Societies
STEINERT, H., Sociology
TATUR, M., Political Science and Political Sociology

HAFENCITY UNIVERSITÄT/ UNIVERSITÄT FÜR BAUKUNST UND METROPOLENENTWICKLUNG (HafenCity University Hamburg — University Of The Built Environment And Metropolitan Development)

Hebebrandstr. 1, 22297 Hamburg
Lohsepl. 1A, 20457 Hamburg(40) 428275354
Fax: (40) 428272728
E-mail: info@hcu-hamburg.de
Internet: www.hcu-hamburg.de
Founded 2006
Public control
Pres.: Dr Ing. WALTER PELKA
Vice-Pres. for Research: Prof. Dr JÖRG KNIELING
Vice-Pres. for Teaching and Studies: Prof. Dr HARALD STERNBERG
Chancellor: NIELS HELLE-MEYER

DEANS

School of Architecture: Prof. REINOLD JOHRENDT

School of Civil Engineering: Prof. Dr HOLGER HAMFLER
School of Geomatics: Prof. Dr THOMAS SCHRAMM
School of Management: Prof. Dr JÖRG KNIELING
School of Metropolitan Culture: Prof. Dr ANGELUS EISINGER, Prof. Dr GESA ZIEMER
School of Urban Planning: Prof. Dr MARTIN WICKEL

HEINRICH-HEINE-UNIVERSITÄT DÜSSELDORF

Universitätsstrasse 1, 40225 Düsseldorf
Telephone: (211) 8100
Fax: (211) 342229
E-mail: planung@zuv.uni-duesseldorf.de
Internet: www.uni-duesseldorf.de
Founded 1965; fmrly Medizinische Akademie, f. 1907
State control
Language of instruction: German
Academic year: October to September
Rector: Prof. Dr MICHAEL PIPER
Chancellor: ULF PALLME KÖNIG
Vice-Rector for Excellence in Teaching: Prof. Dr ULRICH VON ALEMANN
Vice-Rector for Research an Innovation: Prof. Dr LUTZ SCHMITT
Vice-Rector for Structural Devt: Prof. Dr KLAUS PFEFFER
Vice-Rector for Univ. Management and Internationalization: Prof. Dr AXEL BUCHNER
Librarian: Dr IRMGARD SIEBERT
Library: see Libraries and Archives
Number of teachers: 2,016
Number of students: 17,000

DEANS

Faculty of Arts: Prof. Dr HANS T. SIEPE
Faculty of Business Administration and Economics: Prof. Dr BERND GÜNTER
Faculty of Law: Prof. Dr JAN BUSCHE
Faculty of Mathematics and Natural Sciences: Prof. Dr ULRICH RUETHER
Faculty of Medicine: Prof. Dr JOACHIM WINDOLF
Faculty of Philosophy: Prof. Dr BRUNO BLECKMANN

PROFESSORS

Faculty of Business Administration and Economics (Universitätsstr. 1, Bld. 24.31 40225 Düsseldorf; tel. (211) 8113620; fax (211) 8115353; e-mail wiwi.fakultaet@uni-duesseldorf.de; internet www.wiwi.uni-duesseldorf.de):

BORNER, C., Business Administration and Finance
DEGEN, H., Statistics and Econometrics
FRANZ, K. P., Control and Taxation
GÜNTER, B., Business Administration and Marketing
HAMEL, W., Management and Business Administration
SCHIRMEISTER, R., Business Administration and Finance
SMEETS, H.-D., Economics
THIEME, H. J., Economics
WAGNER, G. R., Business Administration, Production Management and Environmental Economics

Faculty of Law (Universitätsstr. 1, Gebäude 24.91 U1 R65, 40225 Düsseldorf; tel. (211) 8111414; fax (211) 8111431; e-mail dekanat.jura@uni-duesseldorf.de; internet www.jura.uni-duesseldorf.de):

ALTENHAIN, K., Criminal Law
BUSCHE, J., Civil Law
DIETLEIN, J., Public Law
FEUERBORN, A., Civil Law, Industrial Law and International Civil Law

FRISTER, H., Criminal Law and Law of Criminal Procedure
HEY, J., Entrepreneurial Tax Law
JANSEN, N., German and International Private Law
LOOSSCHELDERS, D., Civil Law and International Law
LORZ, R. A., German and International Public Law
MICHAEL, L., Public Law
MORFOCK, M., Public Law, Sociology of Law and Economic Law
NOACK, U., Civil Law and Commercial Law
OLZEN, D., Civil Law and Law of Civil Procedure
POHLMAN, P., Civil Law and International Commercial Law
PREUSS, N., Civil Law, Int. Economic Law, Commercial Law
SCHLEHOFER, H., Criminal Law and Law of Criminal Procedure

Faculty of Mathematics and Natural Sciences (Universitätsstr. 1, Bld. 25.32 40225 Düsseldorf; tel. (211) 8112193; fax (211) 8115191; e-mail schmitzu@mail.math-nat-fak.uni-duesseldorf.de; internet www.math-nat-fak.uni-duesseldorf.de):

ALFERMANN, A.-W., Botany
AURICH, V., Informatics
BOTT, M., Biochemistry
BRAUN, M., Organic Chemistry
BUCHNER, A., Psychology
BUELDT, G., Biological Structural Research
CONRAD, S., Informatics
DHONT, J.-K., Physics
EGGER, R., Theoretical Physics
ERNST, J. F., Microbiology
FISCHER, G., Mathematics
FRANK, W., Inorganic and Structural Chemistry
GANTER, CH., Inorganic and Structural Chemistry
GETZLAFF, M., Applied Physics
GÖRLITZ, A., Physics
GREVEN, H., Zoology
GRIESHABER, M., Zoophysiology
GRUNEWALD, F., Mathematics
HEGEMANN, J., Microbiology
HEHL, F.-J., Psychology
HEIL, M., Psychology
HEINZEL, T., Experimental Physics
HOCHBRUCK, M., Applied Mathematics
HOLLENBERG, C., Microbiology
HÖLTJE, H.-D., Pharmacy
HUSTON, J. P., Psychology
JAEGER, K.-E., Molecular Enzyme Technology
JAHNS, H. M., Botany
JANSSEN, A., Statistics and Documentation
JANSSEN, K., Mathematics
JARRE, F., Mathematics
JORDAN, E., Physical Geography
KERNER, O., Mathematics
KIRSCHBAUM, C., Psychology
KISKER, E., Applied Physics
KLÄUI, W., Inorganic Chemistry
KLEINEBUDDE, P., Pharmaceutical Technology
KLEINERMANNS, K., Physical Chemistry
KLÜNERS, J., Mathematics
KNUST, E., Genetics
KÖHLER, K., Mathematics
KÖHNEN, W., Teaching of Mathematics
KORNYSHEV, A., Physics
KOWALLIK, K. V., Botany
KRAUTH, J., Psychology
KUCKLÄNDER, U., Pharmaceutical Chemistry
KUNZ, W., Genetics
LÄER, S., Clinical Pharmacy
LEUSCHEL, M., Informatics
LI, SHU-MING, Pharmaceutical Biology and Biotechnology
LIKOS, CH., Theoretical Physics
LÖSCH, R., Botany

LÖWEN, H., Theoretical Physics
LUNAU, K., Neurobiology
MARIAN, CH., Theoretical Chemistry
MARTIN, W., Botany
MAURE, M., Informatics
MEHLHORN, H., Zoology
MEISE, R., Mathematics
MEWIS, A., Inorganic and Structural Chemistry
MÜLLER, T., Organic Chemistry
MUSCH, J., Psychology
NÄGELE, G., Physics
OLBRICH, S., Informatics
PAUSE, B., Psychology
PIETROWSKY, R., Psychology
PIETRUSZKA, J., Bio-organic Chemistry
PRETZLER, G., Experimental Physics
PROKSCH, P., Pharmaceutical Biology
PUKHOV, A., Theoretical Physics
RATSCHEK, H., Mathematics
REITER, D., Laser and Plasma Physics
RIESNER, D., Physical Biology
RITTER, H., Organic Chemistry
ROSE, C. R., Neurobiology
ROTHE, J., Informatics
RUETHER, U., Zoophysiology
SAHM, H., Biotechnology
SAMM, U., Plasma Physics
SCHIERBAUM, K., Raw Materials Science
SCHILLER, S., Experimental Physics
SCHLUE, W.-R., Neurobiology
SCHMITT, L., Biochemistry
SCHÖTTNER, M., Informatics
SCHRÖER, S., Mathematics
SCHURR, U., Botany
SEIDEL, C., Physical Chemistry
SIMON, R., Genetics
SINGHOF, W., Mathematics
SPATSCHEK, K.-H., Theoretical Physics
STANDT-BICKEL, C., Organic Chemistry
STAUDT, C., Organic Chemistry
STEFFEN, K., Mathematics
STOERIG, P., Psychology
STREHBLOW, H.-H., Physical Chemistry
VOLLMER, G., Teaching of Chemistry
VON HAESELER, A., Bioinformatics
WAGNER, R., Physical Biology
WANKE, E., Informatics
WEBER, H., Pharmacy
WEIN, N., Teaching Geography
WEINKAUF, R., Physical Chemistry
WEISS, H., Biochemistry
WENZENS, G., Geography
WESTHOFF, P., Botany
WILLBOLD, D., Physical Biology
WILLI, O., Experimental Physics
WISBAUER, R., Mathematics
WITSCH, K., Mathematics
WUNDERLICH, F., Parasitology

Faculty of Medicine (Universitätsstr. 1, Bld. 11.72, Moorenstr. 5, 40225 Düsseldorf; tel. (211) 8104602; fax (211) 8104612; e-mail med.dekanat@uni-duesseldorf.de; internet medfak.uniklinikum-duesseldorf.de):

ABHOLZ, H.-H., General Medicine
ACKERMANN, R., Urology
ALBERTI, L., Psychosocial Disturbances
ANGERSTEIN, W., Phoniatry and Audiology
BARZ, J., Forensic Medicine
BAYER, R., Physiology
BECKER, J., Dentistry
BENDER, H. G., Obstetrics and Gynaecology
BÖCKING, A., General Pathology and Pathological Anatomy
BOEGE, F., Clinical Chemistry and Laboratory Diagnostics
BOJAR, H., Physiological Chemistry
BORNSTEIN, ST., Internal Medicine
BORSCH-GALETKE, E., Industrial Medicine
BUDACH, W., Radiology
DAHL, ST. VOM, Industrial Medicine
DALDRUP, T., Forensic Toxicology
DALL, P., Obstetrics and Gynaecology
DRESCHER, D., Dentistry

FISCHER, J. H., Pharmacology and Toxicology
FÖRSTER, I., Molecular Immunology
FRANZ, M., Psychiatry, Clinical Psychology
FRITZEMEIER, C. U., Dentistry
FÜRST, G., Radiology
GABBERT, H. E., Pathology
GAEBEL, W., Psychiatry
GAMS, E., Cardiological Surgery
GANZER, U., Otorhinolaryngology
GERAEDTS, M., Health Sciences and Social Medicine
GERHARZ, C.-D., Pathology
GIANI, G., Diabetes Research, Biometry
GÖBEL, U., Paediatrics
GÖDECKER, A., Physiology
GOTTMAN, K., Neurophysiology
GRABENSEE, B., Internal Medicine
HAAS, H., Neurophysiology
HAAS, R., Internal Medicine
HÄUSSINGER, D., Internal Medicine
HARTUNG, H.-P., Neurology
HARTWIG, H.-G., Anatomy
HEINZ, H.-P., Medical Microbiology
HENGEL, H., Virology
HERFORTH, A., Dentistry
HERING, P., Laser Medicine
HERNER, B., Neurology
HEUCK, C. C., Clinical Chemistry and Biochemistry
HEUGGE, U., Dermatology
HOHLFELD, T., Experimental Pharmacology
HOMEY, B., Dermatology
IDEL, H., Hygiene
JANSSEN, A., Opthalmology
KAHL, R., Toxicology
KELM, M., Internal Medicine
KNOEFEL, W., Internal Surgery
KRAUSPE, R., Orthopaedics
KRUTMANN, J., Dermatology and Venereology
KÜBLER, N., Dentistry and Plastic Surgery
LABISCH, A., History of Medicine
LINS, E. J. F., Neuroradiology
LUDWIG, A., Molecular Medicine
MAI, J. K., Neuroanatomy
MANNHOLD, R., Investigation of Molecular Active Substances
MAU, J., Statistics and Biomathematics in Medicine
MAYATEPEK, E., General Paediatrics
MEYER, U., Dentistry
MÖDDER, U., Clinical Radiology
MORGENSTERN, J., Applied Biomedicine
MSCHEN, M., Immunology
MUELLER, H. W., Neurobiology
MUELLER, H. W., Nuclear Medicine
MÜLLER-WIELAND, D., Clinical Biochemistry
NANENBERG, H., Paediatrics
NOVOTNY, G. E. K., Anatomy
NÜRNBERG, B., Physiological Chemistry
PFEFFER, K. D., Medical Microbiology
POREMBA, C., Pathology
RAAB, W., Dentistry
REHKAEMPER, G., Brain Research
REIFFENBERGER, G., Neuropathology
RITZ-TIMME, S., Forensic Medicine
ROSS, H.-G., Physiology
ROYER-POKORA, B., Human Genetics
RUZICKA, T., Dermatology and Venereology
SANDMANN, W., Surgery
SCHARF, R., Haematology
SCHERBAUM, W. A., Internal Medicine
SCHMIDT, K. G., Paediatrics
SCHMITT, G., Radio-oncology
SCHNEIDER, F., Psychiatry
SCHNEIDER, M., Internal Medicine
SCHNITZLER, A., Neurology
SCHRADER, J., Physiology
SCHRÖR, K., Pharmacology and Toxicology
SCHULZE-OSTHOFF, K., Molecular Medicine
SEITZ, R., Neurology
SIEGRIST, J., Medical Sociology
SIES, H., Physiological Chemistry
STAHL, W. J., Physiological Chemistry

STEIGER, H.-J., Neurology
STEINGRÜBER, H.-J., Medical Psychology
STRAUER, B.-E., Internal Medicine
STÜTTGEN, U., Dentistry
SUNDMACHER, R., Ophthalmology
TARNOW, J., Anaesthesiology
THÄMER, V., Physiology
TRESS, W., Psychiatry
WEHLING, P., Molecular Orthopaedics
WENDEL, U., Paediatrics
WINDOLF, J., Internal Surgery
WINTERER, G., Neurology, Psychiatry
ZILLES, K., Anatomy

Faculty of Philosophy (Universitätsstr. 1, Bld. 23.21 Ebene 00 Raum 63—Dekanats büro, 40225 Düsseldorf; tel. (211) 8112936; fax (211) 8112244; e-mail dobbeler@phil-fak .uni-duesseldorf.de; internet www.phil-fak .uni-duesseldorf.de):

APTROOT, M., Yiddish Culture, Language and Literature
BARZ, H., Education
BAURMANN, M., Sociology
BEEH, V., Germanic Philology
BIRNBACHER, D., Philosophy
BLECKMANN, B., Ancient History
BÖHME-DÜRR, K., Media Sciences
BÖRNER-KLEIN, D., Yiddish Studies
BORSÒ, V., Romance Languages and Literature
BRANDES, D., Culture and History of Germans in Eastern Europe
BROCKE, M., Yiddish Studies
BÜHLER, A., Philosophy
BUSSE, D., Germanic Philosophy
BUSSE, W., English
DIETZ, S., Philosophy
FRIEDL, H., English
GEISLER, H., Romance Languages and Literature
GLOGER-TIPPELT, G., Developmental and Educational Psychology
GOMILLE, M., English
GÖRLING, R., Media and Cultural Sciences
GÖTZ VON OLENHUSEN, I., Modern History
HARTMANN, P., Sociology
HECKER, H., East European History
HERWIG, H., Germanic Philology
HÜLSEN-ESCH, A., Art History
HUMMEL, H., Politics
KANN, C., Philosophy
KELLER, R., Germanic Philology
KILBURY, J., Computer Linguistics
KÖRNER, H., Art History
KOUTEVA, T., English
KROPP, S., Politics
KRUMEICH, G., Modern History
KÜPPERS, J., Classical Philology
LABISCH, A., History of Medicine
LAHIRI, A., Linguistics
LAUDAGE, J., Medieval History
MAE, M., Modern Japan
MATUSSEK, P., Modern German
MILLER-KIPP, G., Education
MOLITOR, H., Modern History
NOUN, CH., Modern History
POTT, H.-G., Modern German
REICHEL, M., Classical Philology
RETTIG, W., Romance Philology
REUBAND, K. H., Sociology
ROHRBACHER, S., Yiddish Studies
SCHAFROTH, E., Romance Languages and Literature
SCHURZ, G., Philosophy
SCHWARZER, C., Education
SEIDEL, T., English
SHIMADA, SHINGO, Modern Japan
SIEPE, H., Romance Philology
STEIN, D., English
STEIN, M., Classical Philology/Latin Sciences
STIERSTORFER, K., English
STOCK, W. G., English
TIEGEL, G., Sport

VON ALEMANN, U., Politics
VOWE, G., Communication and Media Sciences
WEBER, CH., Modern History
WEISS, R., Communication and Media Sciences
WITTE, B., Modern German
WUNDERLI, P., Romance Philology

ATTACHED INSTITUTES

Arbeitsgemeinschaft Elektrochemischer Forschungsinstitutionen AGEF eV: Universitatsstr. 1, 40225 Düsseldorf; Chair. Prof. Dr J. W. SCHULTZE.

Deutsches Diabetes-Forschungsinstitut an der Heinrich-Heine-Universität Düsseldorf: Auf'm Hennekamp 65, 40225 Düsseldorf; Dir Prof. Dr D. MÜLLER-WIELAND.

Deutsches Krankenhausinstitut: Tersteegenstr. 3, 40474 Düsseldorf; Dir UDO MÜLLER.

Düsseldorfer Institut für Dienstleistungs-Management: Dir Prof. Dr W. HAMEL.

Eichendorff-Institut—Literaturwissenschaftliches Institut der Stiftung Haus Oberschlesien: 6-Hösel, Bahnhofstr. 71, 40883 Ratingen; Dir Prof. Dr B. WITTE.

Institut für Biologische Informationsverarbeitung, Forschungszentrum Jülich GmbH: Dir Prof. Dr G. BÜLDT.

Institut für Biotechnologie, Forschungszentrum Jülich GmbH: 52428 Jülich; Dir Prof. Dr H. SAHM.

Institut für Chemie und Dynamik der Geosphäre: 52428 Jülich; Dir Prof. Dr U. SCHURR.

Institut für die Kultur und Geschichte der Deutschen im ostlichen Europa: Dir Prof. Dr DETLEF BRANDES.

Institut für Internationale Kommunikation: Hildebrandtstr. 4, 40215 Düsseldorf; Man. Dir Dr M. JUNG.

Institut für Medizin, Forschungszentrum Jülich GmbH: 52428 Jülich; Dir Prof. Dr K. ZILLES.

Institut für Umweltmedizinische Forschung an der Heinrich-Heine-Universität Düsseldorf: see under Research Institutes

Institut 'Moderne im Rheinland': Dir Prof. Dr CEPL-KAUFMANN.

Neurologisches Therapiezentrum (NTC) an der Heinrich-Heine-Universität Düsseldorf: Hohensandweg 37, 40591 Düsseldorf; Dir Prof. Dr V. HÖMBERG.

Ostasien-Institut: Dir Prof. Dr MICHIKO MAE.

Technische Akademie Wuppertal eV: Postfach 100409, 42004 Wuppertal; Man. Dir Dipl. oec. ERICH GIESE.

HELMUT SCHMIDT UNIVERSITÄT/ UNIVERSITÄT DER BUNDESWEHR HAMBURG
(University of the Federal Armed Forces, Hamburg)

POB 70 08 22, 22008 Hamburg
Holstenhofweg 85, 22043 Hamburg

Telephone: (40) 65411
Fax: (40) 65412869
Internet: www.hsu-hh.de

Founded 1972
State control
Languages of instruction: German, English
Academic year: October to September

Chancellor: VOLKER STEMPEL
Pres.: Prof. Dr WILFRIED SEIDEL
Vice-Pres.: Prof. Dr KLAUS BECKMANN
Vice-Pres.: Prof. Dr.-Ing. JENS WULFSBERG

Librarian: N. N.
Library of 800,000 vols
Number of teachers: 100
Number of students: 2,800
Publications: *Uniforum* (1 a year), *Uniforschung* (1 a year)

DEANS

Dept of Economics and Social Sciences: Prof. Dr MICHAEL STAACK
Dept of Educational Science: Prof. Dr CHRISTINE ZEUNER
Dept of Electrical Engineering: Prof. Dr-Ing. JOACHIM HORN
Dept of Mechanical Engineering: Prof. Dr-Ing. ALEXANDER FAY

HOCHSCHULE FÜR FILM UND FERNSEHEN 'KONRAD WOLF' POTSDAM-BABELSBERG
(Konrad Wolf Potsdam-Babelsberg Film and Television University)

Marlene-Dietrich-Allee 11, 14482 Potsdam

Telephone: (331) 62020
Fax: (331) 6202549
E-mail: info@hff-potsdam.de
Internet: www.hff-potsdam.de

Founded 1954
Pres.: Prof. Dr DIETER WIEDEMANN
Vice-Pres.: Prof. MARTIN STEYER
Librarian: LYDIA WIEHRING VON WENDRIN
Library of 100,000 vols
Number of teachers: 100
Number of students: 500

Publication: *BFF (Beiträge zur Film- und Fernsehwissenschaft)* (irregular).

HOCHSCHULE WISMAR

Philipp-Müller-Str., POB 1210, 23952 Wismar

Telephone: (3841) 7530
Fax: (3841) 753383
E-mail: postmaster@hs-wismar.de
Internet: www.hs-wismar.de

Founded 1908 as Ingenieurhochschule Wismar, renamed 1939, 1969, 1988; present name 1992
State control
Academic year: September to August

Rector: Prof. Dr NORBERT GRÜNWALD
Vice-Rector for Education: Prof. Dr KAI NEUMANN
Vice-Rector for Research: Prof. MARTIN WOLLENSAK
Head of Admin.: Dr WOLFGANG GREINER
Librarian: UTE KINDLER
Library of 65,000 vols
Number of teachers: 223
Number of students: 6,208

DEANS

Architecture and Design: Prof. GEORG GIEBELER
Economics: Prof. Dr JOACHIM WINKLER
Engineering: Prof. Dr Ing. INGO MÜLLER

HUMBOLDT-UNIVERSITÄT ZU BERLIN

Unter den Linden 6, 10099 Berlin

Telephone: (30) 20932946
Fax: (30) 20932107
E-mail: pr@hu-berlin.de
Internet: www.hu-berlin.de

Founded 1810
State control
Academic year: October to September

Pres.: Prof. Dr JAN-HENDRIK OLBERTZ

Vice-Pres. for Academic and Int. Affairs: Prof. Dr MICHAEL KÄMPER-VAN DEN BOOGAART
Vice-Pres. for Finance/Personnel and Technical Matters: Dr FRANK EVESLAGE
Vice-Pres. for Research: Prof. Dr PETER A. FRENSCH
Librarian: Dr M. BULATY
Library: see Libraries and Archives
Number of teachers: 2,167 (incl. 411 professorships, no FTEs)
Number of students: 36,636
Publications: *Humboldt-Spektrum* (4 a year), *Humboldt-Zeitung* (12 a year during each semester)

DEANS

Charité—Berlin University Medicine: Prof. Dr KARL MAX EINHÄUPL (Chair. of Exec. Board)
Faculty of Agriculture and Horticulture: Prof. Dr FRANK ELLMER
Faculty of Arts and Humanities I: Prof. MICHAEL SEADLE
Faculty of Arts and Humanities II: Prof. Dr HELGA SCHWALM
Faculty of Arts and Humanities III: Prof. Dr BERND WEGENER
Faculty of Arts and Humanities IV: Prof. Dr ERNST VON KARDOFF
Faculty of Law: Prof. Dr BERND HEINRICH
Faculty of Mathematics and Natural Sciences I: Prof. Dr ANDREAS HERRMANN
Faculty of Mathematics and Natural Sciences II: Prof. Dr ELMAR KULKE
Faculty of Theology: Prof. Dr DOROTHEA WENDEBOURG
School of Business and Economics: Prof. Dr OLIVER GÜNTHER

INTERNATIONAL SCHOOL OF MANAGEMENT

Otto-Hahn-Str. 19, 44227 Dortmund
Telephone: (231) 9751390
Fax: (231) 97513939
E-mail: ism.dortmund@ism.de
Internet: www.ism.de
Founded 1990 as IDB-Wirtschaftsakademie, present name 1992
Private control
Pres.: Prof. Dr BERT RÜRUP
Vice-Pres.: Prof. Dr INGO BÖCKENHOLT
Man. Dir: WOLFGANG DITTMANN
Number of students: 800

JACOBS UNIVERSITY BREMEN GMBH

Campus Ring 1, 28759 Bremen
Telephone: (421) 20040
Fax: (421) 200-4113
E-mail: info@jacobs-university.de
Internet: www.jacobs-university.de
Founded 1999
Private control
Language of instruction: English
Academic year: September to May
Pres.: Prof. Dr JOACHIM TREUSCH
Chair.: Prof. Dr KARIN LOCHTE
Dir for Academic Affairs: ANTONIA GOHR
Dir for Admissions: JON IKRAM
Dir for Campus Activities and College Coordination: MARITA HARTNACK
Dir for Corporate Communications and Media Relations: PETER WIEGAND
Dir for Information Resources and Multimedia (IRC): HANS ROES
Dir for Resource Devt: ULF HANSEN
Dir for Student Marketing: CHRISTINE SOUDERS
Dir for Studies: MANDY BOEHNKE
Vice-Pres. for Science Park and Business Devt: Dr ALEXANDER ZIEGLER-JOENS

Librarian: HANS ROES
Library of 45,000 vols, 14,500 e-books, 100 journals, 35,000 e-journals
Number of teachers: 385
Number of students: 1,245

DEANS

Jacobs Centre for Lifelong Learning and Institutional Development: Prof. Dr URSULA M. STAUDINGER
School of Engineering and Science: Prof. Dr BERNHARD KRAMER
School of Humanities and Social Sciences: Prof. Dr HENDRIK BIRUS

JOHANNES GUTENBERG UNIVERSITY MAINZ

55099 Mainz
Saarstr. 21, 55128 Mainz
Telephone: (6131) 390
E-mail: presse@uni-mainz.de
Internet: www.uni-mainz.de
Founded 1477, closed 1816; reopened 1946
Public control
Pres.: Prof. Dr GEORG KRAUSCH
Chancellor: GOETZ SCHOLZ
Vice-Pres. for Study and Teaching: Prof. Dr MECHTHILD DREYER
Vice-Pres. for Research: Prof. Dr ULRICH FÖRSTERMANN
Librarian: Dr ANDREAS BRANDTNER
Library: see Libraries and Archives
Number of teachers: 2,800
Number of students: 36,000
Publications: *Forschungsbericht*, *Forschungsmagazin*

DEANS

Faculty of Applied Linguistic and Cultural Studies: KARL-HEINZ STOLL
Faculty of Biology: Prof. Dr HARALD PAULSEN
Faculty of Catholic and Evangelical Theology: Prof. Dr LEONHARD HELL
Faculty of Chemistry, Pharmacy and Earth Sciences: Prof. Dr PETER LANGGUTH
Faculty of Evangelical Theology: Prof. Dr FRIEDRICH-WILHELM HORN
Faculty of History and Cultural Studies: Prof. JAN KUSBER
Faculty of Law and Economics: Dr ROLAND EULER
Faculty of Medicine: Prof. Dr med. Dr rer. nat. R. URBAN
Faculty of Philosophy and Pedagogics: Prof. Dr STEPHAN FÜSSEL
Faculty of Physics, Mathematics and Computing: Prof. Dr DIETRICH VON HARRACH
Music College and Academy of Art: Prof. Dr phil. JÜRGEN BLUME

PROFESSORS

Faculty of Applied Linguistic and Cultural Studies (06) (An der Hochschule 2, 76711 Germersheim; tel. (7274) 5080; fax (7274) 50835429; e-mail dekan06@uni-mainz.de; internet www.fask.uni-mainz.de):
FORSTNER, M.
GIPPER, A.
HUBER, D.
KELLETAT, A.
KLENGEL, S.
KUPFER, P.
LOENHOFF, J.
MENZEL, B.
MÜLLER, K. P.
PERL, M.
SCHREIBER, M.
STOLL, K.-H.
VON BARDELEBEN, R.
WORBS, E.

Faculty of Biology (10) (Gresemundweg 2, 55128 Mainz; tel. (6131) 3922548; fax (6131)

3923500; internet www.uni-mainz.de/fb/biologie/biologie.html):
ALT, K. W.
BÖHNING-GAESE, K.
CLAßEN-BOCKHOFF, R.
DECKER, H.
EISENBEIS, G.
HANKELN, T.
HENKE, H.
KADEREIT, J. W.
KAMP, G.
KÖNIG, H.
MARKL, J.
MARTENS, J.
NEUMEYER, C.
PAULSEN, H.
PFLUGFELDER, G.
ROTHE, G.
SCHMIDT, E. R.
SEITZ, A.
STÖCKER, W.
TECHNAU, G.
TROTTER, J.
UNDEN, G.
WEGENER, G.
WERNICKE, W.
WOLFRUM, U.
ZISCHLER, H.

Faculty of Catholic and Evangelical Theology (01) (Forum 6, 55099 Mainz; tel. (6131) 3922215; fax (6131) 3923501; e-mail kath-dekanat@uni-mainz.de; internet www.theologie.uni-mainz.de):
BAUMEISTER, T.
DIETZ, W.
DINGEL, I.
FECHTNER, K.
FRANZ, A.
HELL, L.
HORN, F. W.
LANDMESSER, C.
LEHNARDT, A.
MEIER, J.
REISER, M.
REITER, J.
RIEDEL-SPANGENBERGER, I.
SIEVERNICH, M.
SIMON, W.
SLENCZKA, N
WEYER-MENKHOFF, S.
WIßMANN, H.
ZWICKEL, W.

Faculty of Chemistry, Pharmacy and Earth Sciences (09) (Becherweg 14, 55128 Mainz; tel. (6131) 3922273; fax (6131) 3923521; e-mail dekan19@uni-mainz.de; internet www.uni-mainz.de/fb/chemie/fbhome):
BANHART, F.
BASCHÉ, T.
DANNHARDT, G.
DOMRÖS, M.
EPE, B.
ESCHER, A.
FAHRENHOLZ, F.
FELSER, C.
FOLEY, S. F.
FREY, H.
GAUß, J.
GRUNERT, J.
HOFFMANN, T.
JANSHOFF, A.
KERSTEN, M.
KLINKHAMMER, K.
KOCH-BRANDT, C.
KRATZ, J. V.
KRÖNER, A.
KUNZ, H.
LANGGUTH, P.
LÖWE, H.
MEIER, H.
MEYER, G.
NUBBEMEYER, U.
PASSCHIER, C. W.
PINDUR, U.

PREUß, J.
RATTER, B. M. W.
REGENAUER-LIEB, K.
REICH, T.
RENTSCHLER, E.
RÖSCH, F.
SCHENK, D.
SCHMIDT, M.
SIROCKO, F.
STÖCKIGT, J.
TREMEL, W.
WILCKE, W.
WILKEN, R.
WITULSKI, B.
ZENTEL, R.

Faculty of History and Cultural Studies (07)
(Jakob-Welder-Weg 18, 55128 Mainz; tel.
(6131) 3923346; fax (6131) 3924619):

ALTHOFF, J.
BEER, A.
BIERSCHENK, T.
BLÜMER, WI.
BRAUN, E. A.
FELTEN, F. J.
GAUDZINSKI-WINDHEUSER, S.
KASTENHOLZ, R.
KIßENER, M.
KREIKENBOM, D.
KUSBER, J.
LENTZ, C.
MATHEUS, M.
MÜLLER, M.
OY-MARRA, E.
PARE, C. F. E.
PESCHLOW, U.
PRECHEL, D.
PRINZING, G.
RÖDDER, A.
SCHUMACHER, L.
VERHOEVEN-VAN ELSBERGEN, U.
WALDE, C.
WIESEND, R.

Faculty of Law and Economics (03) (Jakob-
Welder-Weg 9, 55128 Mainz; tel. (6131) 39-
22225; fax (6131) 39-23529; e-mail
dekanat-fb03@uni-mainz.de; internet www
.uni-mainz.de/fachbereiche/1754.php):

BECK, K.
BELLMANN, K.
BOCK, M.
BREUER, K.
BRONNER, R.
DÖRR, D.
DREHER, M.
ERB, V.
EULER, R.
FINK, U.
FRIEDL, G.
GOERKE, L.
GRÖSCHLER, P.
GURLIT, E.
HAAS, U.
HABERSACK, M.
HAIN, K.-E.
HEIL, O. P.
HENTSCHEL, V.
HEPTING, R.
HERGENRÖDER, C. W.
HETTINGER, M.
HUBER, F.
HUBER, P.
HUFEN, F.
KAISER, D.
KOLMAR, M.
KUBE, H.
LEISEN, D.
MÜLBERT, P. O.
OECHSLER, J.
PEFFEKOVEN, R.
RAMMERT, S.
ROTH, A.
RUTHIG, J.
SAUERNHEIMER, K
SCHULZE, P. M.
TRAUTMANN, S.

VOLKMANN, U.
WEDER, B.
ZOPFS, J.

Faculty of Medicine (04) (Obere Zahlbacher
Str. 63, 55131 Mainz; tel. (6131) 39-33180;
internet dekanat.medizin.uni-mainz.de):

BARTENSTEIN, P.
BEHL, C.
BEHNEKE, N.
BEUTEL, M. E.
BHAKDI, S.
BIRKLEIN, F.
BLETTNER, M.
BORK, K.
BRISENO, B.
BROCKERHOFF, P.
BUHL, R.
D'HOEDT, B.
DICK, B.
DIETERICH, M.
DÜBER, C.
DUSCHNER, H.
FISCHER, T.
FÖRSTERMANN, U.
GALLE, P. R.
HAAF, T.
HEINE, J.
HEINEMANN, M.
HEINRICHS, W.
HIEMKE, C.
HOMMEL, G.
HUBER, C.
JAGE, J.
JANSEN, B.
JUNGINGER, T.
KAINA, B.
KEMPSKI, O.
KIRKPATRICK, C. J.
KLEINERT, H.
KNOP, J.
KÖLBL, H.
KONERDING, M. A.
KRAFT, J.
KÜMMEL, W. F.
LACKNER, K. J.
LETZEL, S.
LEUBE, R.
LOOS, M.
LÜDDENS, H.
LUHMANN, H.
LUTZ, B.
MAEURER, M.
MANN, W.
MICHAELIS, J.
MÜLLER, W. E. G.
MÜLLER-KLIESER, W.
MÜNTEFERING, H.
MÜNZEL, T.
MUSHOLT, T.
NEURATH, M.
NIX, W.
OESCH, F.
OTTO, G.
PAUL, N. W.
PERNECZKY, A.
PFEIFFER, N.
PIETRZIK, C.
PLACHTER, B.
POHLENZ, J.
POLLOW, K.
POMMERENING, K.
REDDEHASE, M. J.
REITTER, B.
RESKE-KUNZ, A. B.
ROMMENS, P. M.
SAHIN, U.
SCHELLER, H.
SCHIER, F.
SCHILD, H.
SCHMIDBERGER, H.
SCHMITT, H. J.
SCHRECKENBERGER, M.
SCHREIBER, W.
SCHULTE, E.
SCHUMACHER, R.

SOMMER, C.
STOETER, P.
STOFFT, E.
STOPFKUCHEN, H.
STREECK, R. E.
THEOBALD, M.
THÜROFF, J. W.
TREEDE, R.-D.
VAUPEL, P.
VON BAUMGARTEN, R.
WAGNER, W.
WEBER, M. M.
WEHRBEIN, H.
WEILEMANN, L. S.
WERNER, C.
WILLERSHAUSEN, B.
WOJNOWSKI, L.
WÖLFEL, T.
ZABEL, B.
ZANDER, R.
ZEPP, F.
ZÖLLNER, E. J.

Faculty of Philosophy and Pedagogics (05)
(Jakob-Welder-Weg 18, 55128 Mainz; tel.
(6131) 3920005; fax (6131) 3920085; e-mail
fsb05@uni-mainz.de):

BISANG, W.
BOESCHOTEN, H.
BRENDEL, E.
BREUER, U.
DREYER, M.
ECKEL, W.
EICHLER, K.-D.
ERLEBACH, P.
FISCHER, E.
FÜSSEL, S.
GEISLER, E.
GIRKE, W.
GÖBLER, F.
GRÄTZEL, S.
HORNUNG, A.
KREUDER, F.
KROPP, M.
LAMPING, D.
LEY, K.
MARTIN, A.
MEIBAUER, J.
MEISIG, K.
METZINGER, T.
MÜLLER-WOOD, A.
NÜBLING, D.
PORRA, V.
REITZ, B.
SARHIMAA, A.
SCHEIDING, O.
SCHULTZE, B.
SEELBACH, D.
SIMON, M.
SOLBACH, A.
SPIES, B.
STAIB, B.
STÖRMER-CAYSA, U.
VEITH, W. H.
VON HOFF, D.
WEHR, B.

**Faculty of Physics, Mathematics and Com-
puting (08)** (Staudingerweg 9, 55128 Mainz;
tel. (6131) 3922267; fax (6131) 3922994;
e-mail info@phmi.uni-mainz.de; internet
www.phmi.uni-mainz.de):

ADRIAN, H.
ARENDS, H.-J.
BACH, V.
BINDER, K.
BLOCH, I.
BORRMANN, S.
BROCKMANN, R.
DE JONG, T.
DOLL, T.
ELMERS, H.-J.
GÖTTLER, H.
GRAMSCH, B.
HANKE-BOURGEOIS, M.
HEIL, W.
HÖPFNER, R.

HUBER, G.
JAENICKE, R.
JÜNGEL, A.
KLEINKNECHT, K.
KLENKE, A.
KÖPKE, L.
LEHN, M.
MÜLLER-STACH, S.
OSTRICK, M.
PALBERG, T.
PAPADOPOULOS, N.
PERL, J.
POCHODZALLA, J.
REUTER, M.
ROWE, D. E.
SANDER, H.-G.
SCHILCHER, K.
SCHILLING, R.
SCHLEINKOFER, G.
SCHÖMER, E.
SCHÖNHENSE, G.
SCHUH, H.-J.
TAPPROGGE, S
VAN DONGEN, P. J.
VAN STRATEN, D.
VON HARRACH, D.
WALZ, J.
WERNLI, H.
WIRTH, V.
WITTIG, H.
ZUO, K.

**Faculty of Social Sciences, Media and Sport
(02)** (Colonel-Kleinmann-Weg 2, 55128
Mainz; tel. (6131) 3922247; fax (6131)
3923347; e-mail fritsche@mail.uni-mainz.de):

AUFENANGER, S.
AUGUSTIN, D.
BÜRMANN, J.
DITTGEN, H.
DORMANN, C.
DRUWE, U.
FALTER, J. W.
GARZ, D.
GROB, N.
HAMBURGER, F.
HECHT, H.
HEINEMANN, E.
HILLER, W.
HRADIL, S.
HUFNAGEL, E.
JUNG, K.
KEPPLINGER, H. M.
KOEBNER, T.
KOLBE, F.-U.
KROHNE, H. W.
KUNCZIK, M.
KUNZ, V.
MEINHARDT, G.
MESSING, M.
MÜLLER, N.
NIENSTEDT, H.-W.
OCHSMANN, R.
PREISENDÖRFER, P.
RENNER, K.N.
RICKER, R.
ROLLER, E.
SCHELLE, C.
SCHNEIDER, N. F.
SCHWEPPE, C.
SEIFFGE-KRENKE, I.
VON FELDEN, H.
WILKE, J.
WOLFF, V.
ZIMMERLING, R.

Music College and Academy of Art (11)
(Binger Str. 26, 55122 Mainz; tel. (6131)
3935538; fax (6131) 3930146; e-mail wenkel@
mail.uni-mainz.de; internet www.musik
.uni-mainz.de):

BERNING, A., Academy of Art
BLUME, J., Theory of Music
DAUS, J., College of Music
DELNON, G., Stage Theory
DEUTSCH, N., Oboe
DEWALD, T., Singing

DOBNER, M., Double Bass
DREYER, L., Music Theory
EDER, C., Singing
FRANK, B., Piano
GAVRIC, D., Chamber Music
GERMER, K., Piano
GMEINDER, J., Clarinet
GNANN, G., Church Music
HAHN, G., Academy of Art
HELLMANN, U., Academy of Art
KAISER, H.-J., Church Music
KIEFER, P., Modern Music
KIESSLING, D., Academy of Art
KNOCHE-WENDEL, E., Academy of Art
MARX, K., Chamber Music
REICHERT, M., Modern Music
SHIH, A., Violin
SPACEK, V., Academy of Art
STRIEGEL, L., Music Theory
VETRE, O., Piano
VIRNICH, W., Academy of Art
VOGELGESANG, K., Academy of Art
WALLFISCH, R., Violoncello
ZARBOCK, H., Piano
ZIMMERMANN, J., Academy of Art

ATTACHED INSTITUTES

**Forschungsinstitut für Wirtschaftspoli-
tik** (Institute for Economic Research): Uni-
versität, Jakob-Welder-Weg 4, 55099 Mainz;
Dirs Prof. Dr HARTWIG BARTLING, Prof. Dr
HELMUT DIEDERICH, Prof. Dr WALTER HAMM,
Prof. Dr WERNER ZOHLNHÖFER.

Forschungsinstitut Lesen und Medien
(Institute for Media Research): Fischtorpl.
23, 55116 Mainz; Dir Prof. Dr STEPHAN
FÜSSEL.

Institut für Europäische Geschichte
(Institute for European History): see under
Research Institutes.

**Institut für Geschichtliche Landes-
kunde** (Institute for Historical Regional
Studies of Rhineland-Palatinate): Universität, Johann-Friedrich-von-Pfeiffer-Weg 3,
55099 Mainz; Dirs Prof. Dr A. HAVERKAMP,
Prof. Dr W. KLEIBER, Prof. Dr M. MATHEUS.

**Institut für Internationales Recht des
Spar-, Giro- und Kreditwesens** (Institute
for International Law of Banking): Universi-
tät, Saarstrasse 21, Haus Recht und
Wirtschaft, 55122 Mainz; Dirs Prof. Dr W.
HADDING, Prof. Dr U. H. SCHNEIDER.

Institut für Mikrotechnik GmbH (Institute for Microtechnology): Postfach 421364,
55071 Mainz;Carl-Zeiss-Str. 18–20, 55129
Mainz; Dir Prof. Dr W. EHRFELD.

Tumorzentrum Rheinland-Pfalz eV
(Tumour Centre Rhineland-Palatinate): Am
Pulverturm 13, 55101 Mainz; Dir Prof. Dr C.
HUBER.

JULIUS-MAXIMILIANS-UNIVERSITÄT WÜRZBURG

Sanderring 2, 97070 Würzburg

Telephone: (931) 310
Fax: (931) 312600
E-mail: universitaet@zv.uni-wuerzburg.de
Internet: www.uni-wuerzburg.de

Founded 1582
State control
Academic year: October to September

Pres.: Prof. Dr A. FORCHEL
Vice-Pres.: Prof. Dr E. PACHE
Vice-Pres.: Prof. Dr M. GOTZ
Vice-Pres.: Prof. Dr M. LOHSE
Vice-Pres.: Prof. Dr W. RIEDEL
Dir of Finance and Admin.: E. KRUSE
Chief Librarian: Dr KARL SÜDEKUM

Library of 3,000,000 vols
Number of teachers: 900
Number of students: 22,500
Publications: *RückBlick* (2 a year), *UniZeit*

DEANS

Faculty of Biology: Prof. Dr THOMAS DANDE-
KAR
Faculty of Catholic Theology: Prof. Dr ERICH
GARHAMMER
Faculty of Chemistry and Pharmacy: Prof.
Dr ULRIKE HOLZGRABE
Faculty of Economics: Prof. Dr CHRISTIAN
GRUND
Faculty of Law: Prof. Dr ERIC HILGENDORF
Faculty of Mathematics and Computer Sci-
ence: Prof. Dr UWE HELMKE
Faculty of Medicine: Prof. Dr MATTHIAS
FROSCH
Faculty of Philosophy I (Historical, Philo-
logical, Culture and Geographical Sci-
ences): Prof. Dr ULRICH KONRAD
Faculty of Philosophy II (Philosophy, Educa-
tion Sciences and Social Sciences): Prof. Dr
WOLFGANG SCHNEIDER
Faculty of Physics and Astronomy: Prof. Dr
THOMAS TREFZGER

PROFESSORS

Faculty of Biology (Am Hubland, Biozentrum, 97074 Würzburg; tel. (931) 3184440;
e-mail i-tbi@biozentrum.uni-wuerzburg.de):

DANDEKAR, TH., Bioinformatics
GOEBEL, W., Microbiology
HEDRICH, R., Botany
HEISENBERG, M., Genetics
LINSENMAIR, K. E., Zoology
MÜLLER, M., Pharmaceutical Biology
RIEDERER, M., Botany
SCHEER, U., Zoology
ZIMMERMANN, U., Biotechnology

Faculty of Catholic Theology (Sanderring 2,
97070 Würzburg; tel. (931) 3182252; fax
(931) 3182673; e-mail thde001@mail
.uni-wuerzburg.de):

DROESSER, G., Christian Sociology
DÜNZL, F., Church History
ERNST, S., Moral Theology
GARHAMMER, E., Pastoral Theology
HALLERMANN, H., Theological Law
HEININGER, B., New Testament Exegesis
KLAUSNITZER, W., Basic Theology and Com-
parative Religion
MEUFFELS, O., Dogmatics
SEIDL, TH., Old Testament Exegesis and
Biblical Oriental Languages
WEISS, W., History of the Frankish Church
ZIEBERTZ, H.-G., Religious Instruction

Faculty of Chemistry and Pharmacy (Am
Hubland, 97074 Würzburg; tel. (931)
8885364; fax (931) 8884607; e-mail hopf
.dekanat@uni-wuerzburg.de):

BRAUNSCHWEIG, H., Inorganic Chemistry
BRINGMANN, G., Organic Chemistry
FISCHER, U., Biochemistry
HOLZGRABE, U., Pharmaceutical Chemistry
TACKE, R., Inorganic Chemistry
WÜRTHNER, F., Organic Chemistry
ZIMMERMANN, I., Pharmaceutical Technol-
ogy

Faculty of Economics (Sanderring 2, 97070
Würzburg; tel. (931) 312901; fax (931)
312101; e-mail f-wifak@wifak
.uni-wuerzburg.de):

BERTHOLD, N., Political Economy
BOFINGER, P., Political Economy
BOGASCHEWSKY, R., Industrial Manage-
ment
FEHR, J., Economics
FREERICKS, W., Business Management Tax-
ation
KUKUK, M., Econometrics
LENZ, H., Accounting and Consultancy
MEYER, M., Marketing
SCHULZ, N., Political Economy
THOME, R., Economics and Computer Sci-
ence
WÄLDE, K., Political Economy
WENGER, E., Banking

Faculty of Law (Domerschulstr. 16, 97070 Würzburg; tel. (931) 3182389; fax (931) 3182477; e-mail dekanat@jura .uni-wuerzburg.de):

DREIER, H., Philosophy of Law, Political and Administrative Law
HARKE, J., Civil Law, Roman Law and Historical Comparative Law
HILGENDORF, E., Criminal Law, Criminal Procedural Law
KIENINGER, E.-M., German and European Civil Law, International Civil Law
LAUBENTHAL, K., Criminology and Penal Law
PACHE, E., State Law, International Law, International Economic Law, Economic Administrative Law
REMIEN, O., Civil Law and European Economic Law
SCHERER, I., Civil Law
SCHULZE-FIELITZ, H., Public Law, Environmental Law and Administrative Science
SOSNITZA, O., Civil Law
SUERBAUM, J., Public and Administrative Law
WEBER, C., Civil Law and Labour Law
WEITZEL, J., Civil Law, History of European Law and Procedural Law
ZIESCHANG, F., Criminal Law, Criminal Procedural Law

Faculty of Mathematics and Computer Science (Am Hubland, 97074 Würzburg; tel. (931) 8885021; fax (931) 8884614; e-mail dekan@mathinfo.uni-wuerzburg.de):

ALBERT, J., Computer Science
DOBROWOLSKI, M., Applied Mathematics
FALK, M., Mathematical Statistics
GRUNDHÖFER, TH., Mathematics
HELMKE, U., Mathematics
KANZOW, CH., Applied Mathematics
KOLLA, R., Computer Science
MÜLLER, P., Mathematics and Algebra
NOLTEMEIER, H., Computer Science
PUPPE, F., Computer Science
RUSCHEWEYH, S., Mathematics
SCHILLING, K., Technical Computer Science
TRAN-GIA, P., Computer Science
WAGNER, K. W., Computer Science
WEIGAND, H.-G., Teaching of Mathematics

Faculty of Medicine (Josef-Schneider-Str. 2, Klinikum (Haus D7), 97080 Würzburg; tel. (931) 20155458; fax (931) 20153860; e-mail f-medizin@uni-wuerzburg.de):

BECKMANN, H., Psychiatry
BRÖCKER, E.-B., Dermatology, Venerology and Allergology
DIETL, J., Obstetrics and Gynaecology
DRENCKHAHN, D., Anatomy
EINSELE, H., Internal Medicine
ELERT, O., Thoracic and Cardiovascular Surgery
ERTL, G., Internal Medicine
EULERT, J., Orthopaedics
FLENTJE, M., Radiology
FROSCH, M., Hygiene and Microbiology
GREHN, F., Ophthalmology
HACKER, J., Molecular Biology of Infections
HAGEN, R., Molecular Biology of Infections
HAHN, D., Radiodiagnostics
HELMS, J., Otorhinolaryngology
HÖHN, H., Human Genetics
HÜNIG, T., Virology
KARSCHIN, A., Neurophysiology
KLAIBER, B., Dentistry
KOEPSELL, H., Anatomy
KUHN, M., Physiology
LOHSE, M., Pharmacology
LUTZ, W., Toxicology
MÜLLER-HERMELINK, H. K., Pathology
PATZELT, D., Forensic and Social Medicine
RAPP, U., Medical Radiology
REINERS, CH., Medical Radiology
RETHWILM, A., Virology

REUTHER, J., Dentistry, Maxillofacial Surgery
RICHTER, E.-J., Dental and Facial Medicine
RIEDMILLER, H., Urology
ROEWER, N., Anaesthesiology
ROOSEN, K., Neurosurgery
SCHARTL, M., Physiological Chemistry
SEBALD, W., Physiological Chemistry
SENDTNER, M., Clinical Neurobiology
SPEER, C., Paediatrics
STELLZIG-EISENHAUER, A., Dental and Facial Orthopaedics
STOLBERG, M., History of Medicine
TOYKA, K. V., Neurology
WALTER, U., Clinical Biochemistry and Pathobiochemistry
WARNKE, A., Child Psychiatry

Faculty of Philosophy I and Institute of Geosciences (Residenzpl. 2, 97070 Würzburg; tel. (931) 312879; fax (931) 8887050; e-mail f-philfak1@uni-wuerzburg.de):

BRÜCKNER, H., Indology
BRUSNIAK, F., Music Education, Teaching of Music
ERLER, M., Classical Philology
HANNICK, CH., Slavic Philology
HETTRICH, H., Comparative Linguistics
KONRAD, U., Musicology
KUHN, D., Oriental Philology
SCHIER, W., Prehistoric Archaeology
SCHOLZ, U. W., Classical Philology
SCHÖNBEIN, M., Japanology
SINN, U., Classical Archaeology
WILHELM, G., Oriental Philology

Faculty of Philosophy II (Am Hubland, 97074 Würzburg; tel. (931) 8885221; fax (931) 8884601; e-mail f-philfak2@mail .uni-wuerzburg.de):

ACHILLES, J., American Studies
ALT, P.-A., History of Modern German Literature
ALTGELD, W., Modern and Contemporary History
BRUNNER, H., German Philology
BURGSCHMIDT, E., English Linguistics
DAXELMÜLLER, C., European Ethnology
DIETZ, K., Early History
FLACHENECKER, H., Frankish History
FUCHS, F., Medieval History
KOHL, ST. M., English Literature and British Cultural Studies
KUMMER, S., History of Art
NEUGEBAUER, W., Modern History
PENZKOFER, G., Romance Philology
PFOTENHAUER, H., History of Modern German Literature
PÖTTERS, W., Romance Philology
WOLF, N. R., German Linguistics

Faculty of Physics and Astronomy (Am Hubland, 97074 Würzburg; tel. (931) 8885720; fax (931) 8885508; e-mail f-physik@physik .uni-wuerzburg.de):

CLAESSEN, R., Experimental Physics
DYAKONOV, V., Experimental Physics, Energy Research
FORCHEL, A., Semiconductor Technology and Physics
GERBER, G., Experimental Physics
HANKE, W., Theoretical Physics
HEUER, D., Physics Teaching
JAKOB, P., Biophysics
KINZEL, W., Computational Physics
MANNHEIM, K., Astronomy
MOLENKAMP, L., Experimental Physics
RÜCKL, R., Theoretical Physics
UMBACH, E., Experimental Physics

JUSTUS-LIEBIG-UNIVERSITÄT GIEßEN

Ludwigstr. 23, 35390 Gießen
Telephone: (641) 990
Fax: (641) 9912259
Internet: www.uni-giessen.de

Founded 1607
Public control
Languages of instruction: English, German
Academic year: October to September (two terms)
Pres.: Prof. Dr JOYBRATO MUKHERJEE
Vice-Pres: Prof. Dr EVA BURWITZ-MELZER, Prof. Dr KATJA BECKER
Head of Admin.: Dr MICHAEL BREITBACH
Librarian: Dr PETER REUTER
Library of 3,600,000 vols, 5,500 periodicals, 21,000 electronic periodicals
Number of teachers: 1,700 incl. 300 Profs
Number of students: 24,000
Publication: *Spiegel der Forschung* (1 a year)

DEANS

Department of Agrarian Sciences, Nutritional Sciences, Environmental Management: Prof. Dr UTE LEONHÄUSER
Department of Biology, Chemistry and Geosciences: Prof. Dr VOLKMAR WOLTERS
Department of Economics: Prof. Dr JÜRGEN MECKL
Department of History and Cultural Studies: Prof. Dr PETER VON MÖLLENDORF
Department of Human Medicine: Prof. Dr TRINAD CHAKRABORTY
Department of Language, Literature and Culture: Prof. Dr CORA DIETL
Department of Law: Prof. Dr JENS ADOLPH-SEN
Department of Mathematics and Information Studies, Physics, Geography: Prof. CHRISTIAN DILLER
Department of Psychology and Sport: Prof. Dr MARKUS KNAUFF
Department of Social and Cultural Studies: Prof. Dr JUTTA ECARIUS
Department of Veterinary Medicine: Prof. Dr MARTIN KRAMER

PROFESSORS

Department of Agrarian Sciences, Nutritional Sciences, Environmental Management (Bismarckstr. 24, 35390 Gießen; tel. (641) 9937001; fax (641) 9937009):

BAUER, S., Project and Regional Planning
BECKER-BRANDENBURG, K., Nutritional Biochemistry
BOLAND, H., Agricultural Extension and Communication
BRÄUNIG, D., Management of Services for Persons
BRÜCKNER, H.-O., Food Science
DZAPO, V., Genetics, Breeding and Husbandry of Pigs and Small Animals
ERHARDT, G., Animal Breeding and Genetics
EVERS, A., Comparative Health and Social Policy
FELIX-HENNINGSEN, P., Soil Science and Soil Conservation
FREDE, H.-G., Resources Management
FRIEDT, W., Plant Breeding
GÄTH, S., Waste Management and Environmental Research
HERRMANN, R., Agricultural and Food Market Analysis
HOFFMANN, I., Nutritional Ecology
HONERMEIER, B., Crop Science
HOY, S., Farm Animal Housing and Biology
HUMMEL, H. E., Biological and Biotechnical Plant Protection
KÄMPFER, P., Recycling Microbiology
KOGEL, K.-H., Molecular Plant Pathology
KÖHLER, W., Biometry and Population Genetics
KRAWINKEL, M., Human Nutrition, International Nutrition
KÜHL, R. W., Food Economics and Marketing Management
KUHLMANN, F., Farm Management

KUNZ, C., Human Nutrition, Evaluation of Food
LEITHOLD, G., Organic Farming
LEONHÄUSER, I.-U., Nutrition Education and Consumer Behaviour
MEIER, U., Economics of Private Households and Family Sciences
MÜHLING, K.-H., Biochemical Aspects of Plant Nutrition
NEUHÄUSER-BERTHOLD, M., Human Nutrition
NUPPENAU, E. A., Agricultural and Environmental Policy
OPITZ VON BOBERFELD, W., Grassland Management and Forage Growing
OTTE, A., Landscape Ecology and Landscape Planning
PALLAUF, J., Animal Nutrition
SCHLICH, E., Home Engineering
SCHMITZ, P. M., Agricultural and Development Economics and Policy Analysis
SCHNELL, S., General and Soil Microbiology
SCHNIEDER, B., Housing and Human Ecology
SCHUBERT, S., Plant Nutrition
SEUFERT, H., Agricultural Engineering
VILCINSKAS, A., Applied Entomology

Department of Biology, Chemistry and Geosciences (Heinrich-Buff-Ring 58, 35392 Gießen; tel. (641) 9935001; fax (641) 9935009):

ASKANI, R., Organic Chemistry
BINDEREIF, A., Biochemistry
CLAUß, W., Animal Physiology
DORRESTEIJN, A. W. CH., Zoology
EHRENHOFER-MURRAY, A. E., Cosmetics
EMMERMANN, R., Mineralogy
ESSER, G., Plant Ecology
FORCHHAMMER, K., Microbiology
FRANKE, W., Geology
FRÖBA, M., Inorganic Chemistry
GEBELEIN, H., Chemistry Teaching
HAACK, U., Mineralogy
HUGHES, J., Plant Physiology
IPAKTSCHI, J., Organic Chemistry
JÄGER, H.-J., Experimental Plant Ecology
JANEK, J., Physical Chemistry
KLEE, R., Biology Teaching
KLUG, G., Microbiology
KUNTER, M., Anthropology
KUNZE, C., Botany
LAKES-HARLAN, R., Sensory Physiology
MARTIN, M., Immunology
MAYER, J., Teaching of Biology
OVER, H., Physical Chemistry
PINGOUD, A., Biochemistry
RENKAWITZ, R., Genetics
SCHINDLER, S., Inorganic Chemistry
SCHREINER, P., Organic Chemistry
SCHULTE, E., Zoology
SPENGLER, B., Analytical Chemistry
TRENCZEK, M., Zoology
VAN BEL, A. J. E., Organic Botany
VOLAND, E., Philosophy
WAGNER, G., Botany
WIEKE, T., Zoology and Biodiversity
WOLTERS, V., Animal Ecology

Department of Economics (Licher Str. 74, 35394 Gießen; tel. (641) 9922001; fax (641) 9922009; e-mail dekanat@wirtschaft .uni-giessen.de):

ABERLE, G., General Economics, Price Theory, Industrial Organization and Competition Policy, Transport Economics
ALEXANDER, V., General Economics, Money, Credit and Currency
BESSLER, W., General Business Administration, Finance and Banking
ESCH, F.-R., General Business Administration, Marketing
GLAUM, M., Business Administration, International Management, Accounting and Auditing
HEMMER, H.-R., General Economics, Development Economics

KABST, R., General Business Administration, Human Resource Management
KRÜGER, W., General Business Management, Organization, Leadership
MECKL, H., General Economics, International Economics
MORLOCK, M., General Business Management, Risk Management and Insurance
MÜLLER, H., General Economics, Economics for Subsidiary Students, Environmental Economics
RINNE, H., Statistics and Econometrics
SCHERF, W., General Economics, Public Finance
SCHWICKERT, A., General Business Administration, Computer Science in Business
SPENGEL, C., General Business Administration, Company Taxation
WEIßENBERGER, B., Business Administration, Management of Industrial Corporations, Controlling

Department of History and Cultural Studies (Otto-Behaghel-Str. 10, Haus G, 35394 Gießen; tel. (641) 9928000; fax (641) 9928009; e-mail dekanat@fb04.uni-giessen .de):

BÄUMER, F.-J., Religious Education Studies and Teaching of Religion
BAUMGARTNER, M., History of Art
CARL, H., Medieval and Modern History
EISEN, U., Bible Studies, Old Testament and New Testament
GOSEPATH, S., Practical Philosophy
GRÄB-SCHMIDT, E., Systematic Theology
HARTMANN, A., Islamic Studies
HAUSER, L., Systematic Theology
KIRCHNER, M., Turcology
KRASSER, H., Classical Philology
KURZ, W., Religion Lessons
LENGER, F., Medieval and Modern History
LEXUTT, A., History of the Church
MARTINI, W., Classical Archaeology
OSWALT, V., History Teaching
PROSTMEIER, F., Bible Studies, New Testament
QUANDT, S., History Teaching
REINELE, C., German Regional History
REULECKE, J., Modern History
RÖSENER, W., Medieval and Modern History
SPEITKAMP, W., Modern History
SPICKERNAGEL, E., History of Art
TAMMEN, S., History of Art
VON MÖLLENDORFF, P., Greek Philology

Department of Human Medicine (Rudolf-Buchheim-Str. 6, 35392 Gießen; tel. (641) 9948001; fax (641) 9948009):

ALZEN, G., Paediatric Radiology
BAUER, R., Nuclear Medicine
BAUMGART-VOGT, E., Anatomy and Cellular Biology
BECK, E., Molecular Biology
BECKMANN, D., Medical Psychology
BEIN, G., Clinical Immunology and Transfusion Medicine
BOHLE, R., Pathology
BÖKER, D.-K., Neurosurgery
BRETZEL, R., Internal Medicine
CHAKRABORTY, T., Medical Microbiology
DREYER, F., Pharmacology and Toxicology
EIKMANN, T., Hygiene
ENGELHART-CABILLIC, R., Radiology
FERGER, D., Dentistry
FLEISCHER, G., Auditory Research
FRIEDRICH, R., Molecular Genetics and Virology
GALLHOFER, B., Psychiatry
GERLICH, W., Medical Virology
GEYER, R., Biochemistry
GIELER, U., Psychosomatics and Psychotherapy
GLANZ, H., Otorhinolaryngology
GRIMMINGER, F., Internal Medicine, Pneumology

HEMPELMANN, G., Anaesthesiology and Operative Intensive Medicine
HOWALDT, H.-P., Surgery of the Mouth, Jaws and Face
KAPS, M., Neurology
KATZ, N., Clinical Chemistry
KAUFMANN, H., Ophthalmology
KIESSLING, J., Audiology
KLIMEK, J., Dentistry
KOCKAPAN, C., Endodontics
KRAWINKEL, M., Paediatrics, Nutritional Science
KREUDER, J., Paediatrics
KUMMER, W., Anatomy and Cellular Biology
LINDEMANN, H., Paediatrics
LOHMEYER, J., Internal Medicine
MEINHARDT, A., Anatomy and Cellular Biology
MERSCH-SUNDERMANN, V., Indoor-Air Toxicology and Environmental Toxicology
MEYLE, J., Paradontology
MIDDENDORFF, R., Anatomy and Cellular Biology
MÜLLER, U., Human Genetics
NEUBAUER, B., Paediatrics
PADBERG, W., Visceral, Thoracic and Transplantation Surgery
PANCHERZ, H. J., Dental Orthopaedics
PIPER, H. M., Physiology
PRALLE, H., Internal Medicine
PREISSNER, K., Biochemistry
RAU, W. S., Radiological Diagnostics
REIMER, C., Clinical Psychosomatics and Psychotherapy
REITER, A., Paediatric Haematology and Oncology
ROELCKE, V., History of Medicine
SAUER, H., Physiology
SCHACHENMAYR, W., Neuropathology
SCHÄFFER, R., Cytopathology
SCHILL, W.-B., Dermatology and Andrology
SCHLÜTER, K.-D., Physiology
SCHNETTLER, R., Accident Surgery
SCHRANZ, D., Paediatric Cardiology
SCHULZ, A., Pathology
SEEGER, W., Internal Medicine, Pneumology
SKRANDIES, W., Physiology
STÜRZ, H., Orthopaedics
TILLMANNS, H., Internal Medicine, Cardiology
TINNEBERG, H.-R., Gynaecology
TRAUPE, H., Neuroradiology
VOGT, P., Cardiology, Vascular Surgery
WEIDNER, W., Urology
WEILER, G., Forensic Medicine
WETZEL, W.-E., Paediatric Dentistry
WÖSTMANN, B., Gerodontology and Clinical Aspects of Dental Materials

Department of Language, Literature and Culture (Otto-Behaghel-Str. 10, Haus G, 35394 Gießen; tel. (641) 9931001; fax (641) 9931009):

BERSCHIN, H., Romance Linguistics
BORGMEIER, R., Modern English and American Literature
EHLER, S., Teaching of German Language and Literature
EHRISMANN, O., German Language, Historical Linguistics
FEIEKE, H., German Linguistics and Teaching of German Language
FINTER, H., Applied Theatre Studies
FLOECK, W., Spanish Literature
FRITZ, G., German Philology
GANSEL, C., Teaching of German Language and Literature
GAST, W., Teaching of German Language and Literature
GOEBBELS, H., Applied Theatre Studies
GRAF, A., Slavonic Literatures
HORSTMANN, U., Modern English and American Literature

KURZ, G., History of Modern German Literature
LEGUTKE, M., Teaching of English Language
LEIBFRIED, E., General Literature and History of Literature
LOBIN, H., Applied Linguistics and Computer Linguistics
MEISSNER, F.-J., Teaching of Romance Languages and Literature
MUKHERJEE, J., English Language
NÜNNING, A., English and American Literature and Cultural Studies
OESTERLE, G., Modern German Literature
PRINZ, M., Teaching of Romance Languages and Literature
RAMGE, H., German Linguistics
RIEGER, D., Romance Literature
RÖSLER, D., German as a Foreign Language
SEEL, M., Philosophy
STENZEL, H., Romance Literature and Cultural Studies
WINGENDER, M., Slavonic Linguistics
WINKELMANN, O., Romance Linguistics

Department of Law (Licher Str. 72, 35394 Gießen; tel. (641) 9921000; fax (641) 9921109; e-mail dekanat@fb01.uni-giessen .de):

BEHNICKE, C., Civil Law, Commercial Law, Comparative Law, International Civil Law
BRITZ, G., Public Law, European Law
BRYDE, B.-O., Public Law
EKKENGA, J., Civil Law, Commercial Law
GIESEN, R., Civil Law, Labour and Social Law
GROPP, W., Criminal Law, Criminal Procedural Law
GROSS, T., Public Law, Administrative Science
HAMMEN, H., Civil Law, Commercial Law
HECKER, B., Criminal Law, Criminal Procedural Law
KREUZER, A., Criminology, Juvenile Criminal Law
LANGE, K., Public Law, Administration Teaching
LIPP, M., German Legal History and Civil Law
MARAUHN, T., Public Law, International Public Law, European Law
SCHAPP, J., Civil Law and Philosophy of Law
WALKER, W.-D., Civil Law, Labour Law, Civil Procedural Law
WOLFSLAST, G., Criminal Law, Criminal Procedural Law

Department of Mathematics and Information Studies, Physics, Geography (Heinrich-Buff-Ring 16, 35392 Gießen; tel. (641) 9933000; fax (641) 9933009):

BARTSCH, T., Analysis
BAUMANN, B., Mathematics, Algebra
BEUTELSPACHER, A., Mathematics, Geometry
BUHMANN, M., Numerical Mathematics
BUNDE, A., Theoretical Physics
CASSING, W., Theoretical Physics
DÜREN, M., Experimental Physics
FELIX-HENNINGSEN, P., Soil Science, Land Conservation
FENSKE, C., Mathematics
FRANKE, M., Teaching of Mathematics
GIESE, E., Economic Geography
HÄUSLER, E. K., Stochastics
HAVERSATH, J. B., Teaching of Geography
HERMANN, G., Experimental Physics
KANITSCHEIDER, B., Philosophy of Natural Sciences
KING, L., Geography
KOHL, C.-D., Applied Physics
KÜHN, W., Experimental Physics
METAG, V., Experimental Physics
METSCH, K., Mathematics, Geometry

MEYER, B., Experimental Physics
MOSEL, U., Theoretical Physics
MÜLLER, A., Experimental Physics
OVERBECK, L., Mathematics
PROFKE, L., Didactics of Mathematics
SALZBORN, E., Nuclear Physics
SAUER, T., Numerical Mathematics
SCHEID, W., Theoretical Physics
SCHLETTWEIN, D., Applied Physics
SCHOLZ, U., Geography
SCHWARZ, G., Teaching of Physics
SEIFERT, V., Geography
STUTE, W., Mathematical Statistics
TIMMESFELD, F. G., Mathematics, Algebra
WALTHER, H.-O., Mathematics, Analysis
WERLE, O., Didactics of Geography

Department of Psychology and Sport (Otto-Behaghel-Str. 10, Haus F1, 35394 Gießen; tel. (641) 9926000; fax (641) 9926009; e-mail dekanat@fb06.uni-giessen.de):

BORG, I., Applied Psychological Methods
BRUNNSTEIN, J., Educational Psychology
ENNEMOSER, M., Special Educational Psychology
FRESE, M., Work and Organizational Psychology
GEGENFURTNER, K., General and Experimental Psychology
GLOWALLA, U., Educational Psychology
HALDER-SINN, P., Psychological Diagnosis
HENNIG, J., Differential Psychology
MUNZERT, J., Sports Psychology
NEUMANN, H., Sport and Training
PROBST, H., Special Educational Psychology
SCHUSTER, C., Psychological Methodology
SCHWARZER, G., Developmental Psychology
SCHWIER, J., Sport and Teaching of Sport
SPORER, S., Social Psychology
STIENSMEIER-PELSTER, J., Educational Psychology

Department of Social and Cultural Studies (Karl-Glöckner-Str. 21, Haus E/B, 35394 Gießen; tel. (641) 9923001; fax (641) 9923009; e-mail dekan@fb03.uni-giessen.de; internet www.uni-giessen.de/fb03):

BIRCKENBACH-WELLMANN, H.-M., Political Science, European Studies
BULLERJAHN, C., Political Science, European Studies
CLAUS-BACHMANN, M., Music
DUBIEL, H., Sociology
DUNCKER, L., Educational Science
EBERS, A., Comparative Health and Social Policy
ECARIUS, J., Educational Science
FORNECK, H., Educational Science
FRITZSCHE, K., Political Science
GRONEMEYER, R., Sociology
HOFMANN, C., Educational Science
HOLLAND-CUNZ, B., Political Science, Gender Studies
KREBS, D., Empirical Research in Social Sciences
LEGGEWIE, C., Political Science
LIPPITZ, W., Philosophy of Education, Comparative Studies of Education
MOSER, V., Educational Science
NECKEL, S., Sociology
NITSCHE, P., Music
PHLEPS, T., Music
REIMANN, B., Sociology
RICHTER-REICHENBACH, K.-S., Teaching of Art
SANDER, W., Teaching of Social Sciences
SCHMIDT, P., Empirical Social Research
SCHWANDER, M., Educational Science
SEIDELMANN, R., Political Science, International Relations
SPICKERNAGEL, E., History of Art
STACHOWIAK, F., Educational Science
STANICZEK, J., Art Practice
STÖPPLER, R., Educational Science
WILLEMS, H., Microsociology and Qualitative Methods

WISSINGER, J., Educational Science

Department of Veterinary Medicine (Frankfurter Str. 74, 35392 Gießen; tel. (641) 9938001; fax (641) 9938009; e-mail dekanat@vetmed.uni-giessen.de):

BALJER, G., Infectious Diseases and Hygiene
BAUERFEIND, R., Control of Epidemics
BERGMANN, M., Veterinary Anatomy, Histology and Embryology
BOSTEDT, H., Physiology and Pathology of Reproduction
BÜLTE, M., Veterinary Nutrition
CLAUß, W., Animal Physiology
DIENER, M., Veterinary Physiology
DOLL, K., Diseases of Ruminants
EISGRUBER, H., Hygiene of Food of Animal Origin and Consumer Protection
ERHARDT, G., Animal Breeding and Genetics of Domestic Animals
GERSTBERGER, R., Veterinary Physiology
HOFFMANN, B., Physiology and Pathology of Reproduction
KALETA, E., Diseases and Hygiene of Poultry
KÖLLE, S., Veterinary Anatomy, Histology and Embryology
KRAMER, M., Small Animal Surgery
KRESSIN, M., Veterinary Anatomy, Histology and Embryology
LEISER, R., Veterinary Anatomy, Histology and Embryology
LITZKE, L.-F., Equine Surgery
MORITZ, A., Internal Medicine
NEIGER, R., Small Animal Internal Medicine
PETZINGER, E. D., Pharmacology and Toxicology
REINACHER, M., Pathology
REINER, G., Department of Swine Diseases (Internal Medicine and Surgery)
RÜMENAPF, T., Clinical Virology
THIEL, H.-J., Virology
USLEBER, E., Milk Science
WENGLER, G., Virology and Cellular Biology
WÜRBEL, H., Animal Welfare and Ethology
ZAHNER, H., Parasitology

KARLSRUHER INSTITUTS FÜR TECHNOLOGIE

Kaiserstr. 12, 76131 Karlsruhe

Telephone: (721) 6080
Fax: (721) 60844290
E-mail: info@kit.edu
Internet: www.kit.edu

Founded 2009 by merger of Forschungszentrum Karlsruhe and Universität Karlsruhe (f. 1825)
State control
Academic year: October to September

Library: 1.5m.

Pres.: Prof. Dr HORST HIPPLER
Pres.: Prof. Dr EBERHARD UMBACH
Vice-Pres. for Finance and Business Affairs: Dr ALEXANDER KURZ
Vice-Pres. for Human Resources and Law: ELKE-LUISE BARNSTEDT
Vice-Pres. for Research and Information: Prof. Dr DETLEF LÖHE
Vice-Pres. for Research and Innovation: Dr PETER FRITZ
Chief Admin. Officer: (vacant)
Librarian: Dipl. Ing. CHRISTOPH-HUBERT SCHÜTTE

Number of teachers: 1,200
Number of students: 21,000

Publications: ClicKIT (online), Fridericiana (2 a year), LooKIT (online)

DEANS

Faculty of Architecture: Prof. Dipl.-Ing. MARKUS NEPPL

Faculty of Chemical and Process Engineering: Prof. Dr-Ing. HERRMANN NIRSCHL

Faculty of Chemistry and Biosciences: Prof. Dr STEFAN BRÄSE

Faculty of Civil, Geo- and Environmental Sciences: Prof. Dr-Ing. BERNHARD HECK

Faculty of Computer Science: Prof. Dr HEINZ WÖRN

Faculty of Economics and Business Engineering: Prof. Dr CLEMENS PUPPE

Faculty of Electrical Engineering and Information Technology: Prof. Dr GERT F. TROMMER

Faculty of Humanities and Social Sciences: Prof. Dr KLAUS BÖS

Faculty of Mathematics: Prof. Dr FRANK HERRLICH

Faculty of Mechanical Engineering: Prof. Dr-Ing. MARTIN GABI

Faculty of Physics: Prof. Dr HEINZ KALT

PROFESSORS

Faculty of Architecture:

BAVA, H.
BÖKER, H. J.
CRAIG, S.
GOTHE, K.
JANSON, A.
NÄGELI, W.
NEPPL, M.
PFEIFFER, M.
RICHTER, P.
SCHNEIDER, N.
SCHULZE, U.
SEWING, W.
VON BOTH, P.
WAGNER, A.
WALL, A.

Faculty of Chemical and Process Engineering:

BOCKHORN, H.
FRIMMEL, F. H.
HUBBUCH, I.
KASPER, G.
KIND, M.
KOLB, T.
KRAUSHAAR-CZERNETSKI, B.
NIRSCHL, H.
OELLRICH, L.
OLIVEROS, E.
POSTEN, C.
REIMERT, R.
SCHABEL, W.
SCHABER, K.
SCHAUB, G.
SCHUCHMANN, H.
SYLDATK, C.
WETZEL, T.
WILLENBACHER, N.
ZARZALIS, N.

Faculty of Chemistry and Biosciences:

AHLRICHS, R.
BARNER-KOWOLLIK, C.
BASTMEYER, M.
BOCKHORN, H.
BRÄSE, S.
DEUTSCHMANN, O.
FELDMANN, C.
FISCHER, R.
GECKEIS, H.
HIPPLER, H.
KÄMPER, J.
KAPPES, M.
KLOPPER, W.
LAMPARTER, T.
MARKO, D.
METZLER, M.
NICK, P.
OLZMANN, M.
PODLECH, J.
POWELL, A.
PUCHTA, H.
RICHERT, C.
ROESKY, P.

SCHUSTER, R.
SCHWARZ, U.
TARASCHEWSKI, H.
ULRICH, A.
WEDLICH, D.
WILHELM, M.

Faculty of Civil, Geo- and Environmental Sciences:

BLAß, H. J.
BURGER, D.
GEHBAUER, F.
GENTES, S.
GREILING, R.
HECK, B.
HENNES, M.
HINZ, S.
HOHNECKER, E.
JIRKA, G.
KRAMER, C.
LENNERTS, K.
MEURER, M.
MÜLLER, H.
NESTMANN, F.
ROOS, R.
RUCK, B.
SCHILLING, F.
SCHMITT, G.
SCHWEIZERHOF, K.
STEMPNIEWSKI, L.
STOSCH, H.-G.
STÜBERN, D.
TRIANTATYLLIDIS, T.
UHLMANN, M.
UMMENHAFER, T.
VOGT, J.
WAGNER, W.
WINTER, J.
ZUMKELLER, D.

Faculty of Electrical Engineering and Information Technology:

BECKER, J.
BOLZ, A.
BRAUN, M.
DÖSSEL, O.
DOSTERT, K.
FREUDE, W.
IVERS-TIFFÉE, E.
JONDRAL, F.
KREBS, V.
LEIBFRIED, T.
LEMMER, U.
LEUTHOLD, J.
MOREIRA, A.
MÜLLER-GLASER, K.-D.
NOE, M.
PUENTE, F.
SIEGEL, M.
TROMMER, G.
TUUMM, M.
ZWICK, T.

Faculty of Humanities and Social Sciences:

BÖHN, A.
BÖS, K.
FISCHER, M.
FRIES, S.
GIDION, G.
GLEITSMANN-TOPP, R.-J.
GRUNWALD, A.
GUTMANN, M.
JAPP, U.
NOLLMANN, G.
PFADENHAUER, M.
REKUS, J.
SCHÜTT, H.-P.
SCHWAMEDER, H.

Faculty of Mathematics:

ALEFELD, G.
AUMANN, G.
BÄUERLE, N.
DÖRFLER, W.
HENZE, N.
HERRLICH, F.
HEUVELINE, V.
JANNHE, T.

KAUCHER, E.
KIRSCH, A.
LAST, G.
LEUZINGER, E.
PLUM, M.
REICHEL, W.
RIEDER, A.
SCHMIDT, C.-G.
VERAANT, L.
WEIL, W.
WEIß, J.-P.
WEIS, L.
WIENERS, N.

Faculty of Mechanical Engineering:

ALBERS, A.
BAUER, H.-J.
BÖHLKE, T.
BRETTHAUER, G.
CACCUCI, D.
ELSHER, P.
FLEISCHER, J.
FURMANS, K.
GABI, M.
GAUTERIN, F.
GEIMER, M.
GRATZFELD, P.
GUMBSCH, P.
HENNING, F.
HOFFMANN, M. J.
KRAFT, O.
LANZA, G.
LÖHE, D.
MAAS, U.
OERTEL, H.
OVTCHAROVA, J.
PROPPE, C.
SAILE, W.
SEEMANN, W.
SPICHER, U.
STILLER, C.
WANNER, A.
ZÜLCH, G.
ZUM GAHR, K.-H.

Faculty of Physics:

BAUMBACH, T.
BEHENG, K. D.
BLÜMER, H.
BUSCH, K.
DE BOER, W.
DREXLIN, G.
FEINDT, M.
GERTHSEN, D.
GUAST, G.
JONES, S.
KALT, H.
KLINGSHIRN, C.
KOHMEIER, C.
KÜHN, J.
MÜLLER, TH.
NIERSTE, U.
SCHIMMERL, T.
SCHÖN, G.
SHNIRMAN, A.
STEINHAUSER, M.
USTINOV, A.
VON LÖHNEYSEN, H.
WEGENER, M.
WEIß, G.
WENZEL, F.
WÖLFLE, P.
WULFHEKEL, W.
ZEPPENFELD, D.

KATHOLISCHE UNIVERSITÄT EICHSTÄTT-INGOLSTADT

Ostenstrasse 26–28, 85072 Eichstätt

Telephone: (8421) 930
Fax: (8421) 931796
E-mail: info@ku-eichstaett.de
Internet: www.ku-eichstaett.de

Founded 1972, reviving a foundation of 1564
Academic year: April to February

Pres.: Prof. Dr ANDREAS LOB-HÜDEPOHL

Vice-Pres.: Prof. Dr MICHAEL BECHT
Vice-Pres.: Prof. Dr GABRIELE GIEN
CEO: CLAUDIA UHRMANN
Librarian: Dr ANGELIKA REICH

Library of 1,600,000 vols
Number of teachers: 460
Number of students: 4,500

Publications: *Agora* (2 a year), *Eichstätter Beiträge* (2 a year), *Eichstätter Materialen* (2 a year), *Eichstätter Studien* (3 a year)

DEANS

Faculty of Economic Sciences: Prof. Dr HEINRICH KUHN
Faculty of History and Social Sciences: Prof. Dr LEONID LUKS
Faculty of Languages and Literature: Prof. Dr THOMAS PITTROF
Faculty of Mathematics and Geography: Prof. Dr WOLFGANG BISCHOFF
Faculty of Philosophy and Education: Prof. Dr WOLFGANG SCHÖNIG
Faculty of Religious Education: Prof. Dr MARKUS EHAM
Faculty of Social Studies: Prof. Dr STEFAN SCHIEREN
Faculty of Theology: Prof. Dr KONSTANTIN MAIER

PROFESSORS

Faculty of Economic Sciences (Auf den Schanz 49, 85049 Eichstätt; tel. (8421) 9371801; fax (8421) 9371950; e-mail elisabeth.batz@ku-eichstaett.de; internet www.ku-eichstaett.de/fakultaeten/wwf):

BURGER, A., General Business Management
BÜSCHKEN, J., Business Administration and Marketing
DJANANI, C., General Business Management
FISCHER, H., Economics
FISCHER, T. M., General Business Management Controlling
FUCHS, M., Law for Economists
GENOSKO, J., Economic and Social Policy
KUHN, H., Business Administration, Production and Operations Management
KÜSTERS, U., Statistics
KUTSCHKER, M., General Business Management, International Management
LUTTERMANN, C., Law for Economists
RINGLSTETTER, M., General Business Management
SCHNEIDER, J., Economics
STAUSS, B., Business Administration and Services Management
WILDE, K., General Business Management and Economic Information Technology
WILKENS, M., General Business Management, Financing

Faculty of History and Social Sciences (Universitätsallee 1, 85072 Eichstätt; tel. (8421) 931286; fax (8421) 931798; e-mail gertraud.reinwald@ku-eichstaett.de; internet www.ku-eichstaett.de/fakultaeten/ggf):

DETJEN, J., Political Science
DICKERHOF, H., Medieval History
GRECA, R., Sociology
KÖNIG, H.-J., Latin American History
LAMNEK, S., Sociology
LUKS, L., Contemporary Eastern European History
MALITZ, J., Ancient History
MÜLLER, R. A., Early Modern History
RUPPERT, K., Modern and Contemporary History
SCHREIBER, W., Theory and Teaching of History
SCHUBERT, K., Political Science
SCHWINN, T., Sociology
TREIBER, A., Folklore
ZSCHALER, F., History of Economics and Social Development

Faculty of Languages and Literature (Universitätsallee 1, 85072 Eichstätt; tel. (8421) 931517; fax (8421) 931797; e-mail monika.bittl@ku-eichstaett.de; internet www.ku-eichstaett.de/fakultaeten/slf):

BAMMESBERGER, A., English Linguistics
DICKE, G., German Literature
GSELL, O., Romance Linguistics
HÖMBERG, W., Journalism
KLÖDEN, H., Romance Linguistics
KRAFFT, P., Classical Philology
MARTIN, F.-P., Teaching of French Language
MUELLER, K., German as a Foreign Language
NATE, R., English Literature
NEUMANN, M., Modern German Literature
PITTROF, T., New German Literature
RENK, H. E., Teaching of German Language and Literature
RONNEBERGER-SIBOLD, E., Historic German Linguistics
SCHNACKERTZ, H.-J., American Literature
TONNEMACHER, J., Journalism
TSCHIEDEL, H.-J., Classical Philology
WEHLE, W., Romance Literature
WEIGAND, R. U., Medieval German Literature
ZIMMER, G., Classical Archaeology

Faculty of Mathematics and Geography (Ostenstr. 28, 85072 Eichstätt; tel. (8421) 931456; fax (8421) 931789; e-mail claudia.banzer@ku-eichstaett.de; internet www.ku-eichstaett.de/fakultaeten/mgf):

BECHT, M., Physical Geography
BISCHOFF, W., Mathematics
BLATT, H.-P., Mathematics
DESEL, J., Informatics
DIEHL, S., Informatics
FELIX, R., Mathematics
FISCHER, H., Mathematics
HEMMER, I., Teaching of Geography
HOPFINGER, H., Geography
KUTSCH, H., Physical Geography
PECHLANER, H., Tourism
RESSEL, P., Mathematics
RICKER, W., Mathematics
ROHLFS, J., Mathematics
SOMMER, M., Mathematics
STEINBACH, J., Geography

Faculty of Philosophy and Education (Ostenstr. 26, 85072 Eichstätt; tel. (8421) 931298; fax (8421) 931799; e-mail dekanat.ppf@ku-eichstaett.de; internet www.ku-eichstaett.de/fakultaeten/ppf):

BRÜNGER, P., Music Education
FELL, M., Adult Education
FETZ, R., Philosophy
GEISER, G., Pedagogics of Work
GRABOWSKI, F., Psychology
HABISCH, A., Central Institute for Marriage and Family in Society
HELLBRÜCK, J., Psychology
JENDROWIAK, H.-W., General Pedagogics
KALS, E., Psychology
KERKHOFF, G., Psychology
KÖCK, M., Pedagogics of Work
KONRAD, F.-M., Historical and Comparative Pedagogy
KÖPPEL, G., Art
LÄMMERMANN, G., Protestant Theology
LOVEN, C., Musicology
LUTTER, K., Sports
SCHMIDT, H.-L., Social Pedagogics
SCHÖNIG, W., Pedagogics of School
SCHULTHEIS, K., Elementary Education
THOMAS, F., Psychology
ZIMMERMANN, M., Art History

Faculty of Religious Education (vocational courses) (Pater-Philipp-Jeningen-Platz 6, 85072 Eichstätt; tel. (8421) 931275; fax (8421) 931784; e-mail dekanat.rpf@ku-eichstaett.de; internet www.ku-eichstaett.de/fakultaeten/rpf):

EHAM, M., Music and Voice Training
KURTEN, P., Dogmatics
MEIER, U., Religious Education
OBERRÖDER, W., Theory and Practice of Church Work
SCHUSTER, B., Psychology
SILL, B., Moral Theology and Social Ethics
STAUCHIGL, B., Pedagogics
TAGLIACARNE, P., Old Testament
TRAUTMANN, M., New Testament
WILLERS, U., Fundamental Theology and Philosophy

Faculty of Social Studies (vocational courses) (Ostenstr. 26, 85072 Eichstätt; tel. (8421) 931246; fax (8421) 931773; e-mail dekanat.fsw@ku-eichstaett.de; internet www.ku-eichstaett.de/fakultaeten/swf):

BARTOSCH, U., Pedagogics
BECK, C., Social Work
ERATH, P., Social Work
GÖPPNER, H.-J., Psychology
KLUG, W., Social Work
OXENKNECHT-WITZSCH, R., Law
SCHIEREN, S., Political Science

Faculty of Theology (P.-Philipp-Jeningen-Platz 6, 8507 Eichstätt; tel. (8421) 931437; fax (8421) 931779; e-mail karin.lepschy@ku-eichstaett.de; internet www.ku-eichstaett.de/fakultaeten/thf):

BÄRSCH, F., Liturgy
BÖTTIGHEIMER, C., Fundamental Theology
FISCHER, N., Philosophy and Basic Questions of Theology
GERWING, M., Dogmatics
GROSS, E., Religious Teaching and Teaching of Catholic Religion
HOFMANN, J., Old Church History and Patrology
MAIER, K., Middle and New Church History
MAYER, B., New Testament
MÖDE, E., Homiletics
MÜLLER, S. E., Moral Theology
SCHIFFERLE, A., Pastoral Theology
WEISS, A., Canon Law/History of Church Law
ZAPFF, B., Old Testament

LEIBNIZ UNIVERSITÄT HANNOVER

POB 6009, 30060 Hanover
Welfengarten 1, 30167 Hanover
Telephone: (511) 7620
Fax: (511) 7623456
E-mail: info@pressestelle.uni-hannover.de
Internet: www.uni-hannover.de

Founded 1831

Pres.: Prof. Dr Ing. ERICH BARKE
Vice-Pres. for Finance and Admin.: GÜNTER SCHOLZ
Vice-Pres. for Research: Prof. Dr KLAUS HULEK
Vice-Pres. for Teaching, Academic Programmes and Continuing Education: Prof. Dr GABRIELE DIEWALD
Library Dir: UWE ROSEMANN

Library: see Libraries and Archives
Number of teachers: 1,272
Number of students: 35,000

DEANS

Faculty of Architecture and Landscape: Prof. MARGITTA BUCHERT
Faculty of Civil Engineering and Geodetic Science: Prof. CHRISTIAN HEIPKE
Faculty of Economics and Management: Prof. ANDREAS WAGENER
Faculty of Electrical Engineering and Computer Science: Prof. BERNARDO WAGNER
Faculty of Humanities: Prof. ROLF WERNING
Faculty of Law: Prof. HENNING RADTKE
Faculty of Mathematics and Physics: Prof. ROLF HAUG

Faculty of Mechanical Engineering: Prof.
JÖRG SEUME
Faculty of Natural Sciences: Prof. MARKUS
KALESSE
Quest Leibniz Research School: Prof. Dr
WOLFGANG ERTMER

PROFESSORS

Department of Architecture and Landscape
(Schlosswender Str. 1, 30159 Hanover; tel.
(511) 7624276; fax (511) 7622115; e-mail
hobert@dek-arch.uni-hannover.de):

BARTH, H. G., Regional Planning
BRAUM, M., Town Planning
BUCHERT, M., History of Art and Construction
DWORSKY, A., Rural Design
ECKERLE, E., Fine Arts
EHRMANN, W., Work Methods and Processing of Wood and Artificial Materials
FRIEDRICH, J., Design and Building Construction
FURCHE, A., Structural Design and Research
FÜRST, D., Regional Planning
GABRIEL, I., Construction and Design
GANZERT, J., History of Art and Construction
GENENGER, H.-G., Architecture
GERKEN, H., Planning Technology
HAAREN, CHR. V., Conservation
HACKER, E., Conservation
KAPPELER, D., Painting and Graphic Arts
KAUP, P., Construction and Design
KENNEDY, M., Resource-Saving in Building
LÉON, H., Building Typology and Design Section
LITTMAN, K., Work Methods and Processing of Wood and Artificial Materials
LÖSKEN, G., Open Space Planning and Garden Architecture
OPPERMANN, B., Open Space Planning
PARAVICINI, U., Theory of Architecture
POHL, W.-H., Building Materials Technology
REICH, M., Plant Ecology
SCHMID-KIRSCH, A., Drawing and Computer-Assisted Design
SCHOMERS, M., Design
SCHULTE, K., Industrial Design
SLAWIK, H., Construction and Design
TESSIN, W., Planning-Related Sociology
TROJAN, K., Town Planning
TURKALI, Z., Construction and Design
VON SEGGERN, H., Open Space Planning
WEILACHER, U., Landscape Architecture
WÖBSE, H. H., Landscape Aesthetics and Design
WOLSCHKE-BULMAHN, J., Open Space Planning and Garden Architecture
ZIBELL, B., Theory of Architecture

Department of Civil Engineering (Callinstr.
34, Hanover; tel. (511) 7622447; fax (511)
7624783; e-mail dekanat@fb-bauing
.uni-hannover.de; internet www.fb-bauing
.uni-hannover.de):

ACHMUS, M., Foundations, Dams
BILLIB, M., Hydrology
BLÜMEL, W., Foundations, Dams
DAMRATH, R., Applied Informatics
DOEDENS, H., Water Supply
FRIEDRICH, B., Traffic Economics, Highway System, Town Planning
GRÜNBERG, J., Concrete Construction
HOFFMANN, B., Hydrology
HOTHAN, J., Traffic Economics, Highway Systems, Town Planning
IWAN, G., Construction Management
KONECNY, G., Photogrammetry and Engineering Surveying
KUNST, S., Water Supply
LECHER, K., Hydrology
LIERSE, J., Building Construction
LOHAUS, L., Building Materials Science
MARKOFSKY, M., Flow Mechanics

MULL, R., Hydrology
MÜLLER, U., Graduate Centre for Environmentally Relevant Fluxes in Water and Soil
MÜLLER-KIRCHENBAUER, H., Foundations, Dams
NACKENHORST, U., Mechanics and Computational Mechanics
PELZER, H., General Surveying
ROKAHR, R., Statics and Geomechanics
ROSEMEIER, G., Flow Mechanics
ROSENWINKEL, K.-H., Water Supply
ROTHERT, H., Statics
SCHAUMANN, P., Steel Construction
SCHELLING, W., Building Technology
SEEBER, G., Geodesy
SESTER, M., Cartography
SIEFERT, T., Railways and Roads
SIEKER, F., Hydrology
VERWORN, H.-R., Hydrology
WRIGGERS, P., Mechanics and Computational Mechanics
ZIELKE, W., Flow Mechanics
ZIMMERMANN, C., Hydroengineering

Department of Economics (Königsworther
Platz 1, 30167 Hanover; tel. (511) 7625350;
fax (511) 7625665; e-mail heer@mbox.vul
.uni-hannover.de; internet www.wiwi
.uni-hannover.de):

BREITNER, M. H., Computer Science
FÖRSTER, G., Business Taxation
GEIGANT, F., Money, Credit, Currency
GERLACH, K., Political Economy and Labour Economics
HANSEN, U., Marketing
HASLINGER, F., Economics
HEINEMANN, H.-J., International Economic Relations
HOFMANN, CH., Controlling
HOMBURG, S., Public Economics
HÜBL, L., Economic Policy
HÜBLER, O., Econometrics
JÖHNK, M.-D., Econometrics and Statistics
KIRSCH, H.-J., Economics
LÖFFLER, A., Economics
MENKHOFF, L., Money, Credit, Currency
MEYER, W., Economic Policy
MÜLLER, U., Economic Systems, Anti-Trust Policy and Stabilization
RIDDER, H.-G., Personnel Management
SCHMIDT, U., Economics
SCHULENBURG, J.-M. GRAF VON DER, Insurance
SCHWARZE, J., Computer Science
STEINLE, C., Management Economics
WAIBEL, H., Horticultural Economics
WIEDMANN, K.-P., Marketing

Department of Electrical Engineering and
Information Technology (Appelstr. 9A, 30167
Hanover; tel. (511) 76219645; fax (511)
76219646; e-mail fbbuero@et.uni-hannover
.de; internet www.et.uni-hannover.de):

BARKE, E., Microelectronic Systems
EUL, H., High Frequency Technology
GARBE, H., Basic Electrical Engineering
GERTH, W., Control Technology
GOCKENBACH, E., High Voltage
GRABINSKI, H., Theoretical Electrical Engineering
GRAUL, J., Semiconductor Technology and Materials of Electrical Engineering
HAASE, H., Electrical Engineering
HOFMANN, K., Semiconductor Technology and Materials of Electrical Engineering
JOBMANN, K., General Communications Technology
KUCHENBECKER, H.-P., General Communications Technology
LIEDTKE, C.-E., Theoretical Communications Technology
MARQUARDT, J., High Frequency Technology
MATHIS, W., Theoretical Electrical Engineering

MUCHA, J., Theoretical Electrical Engineering
MÜLLER-SCHLOER, C., Computing Sciences
MUSMANN, H.-G., Theoretical Communications Technology
NACKE, B., Electrical Process Technology
NEJDL, W., Knowledge-Based Systems
NESTLER, J., Power Electronics
OSTEN, J., Technology and Materials of Electrical Engineering
OSWALD, B. R., Electricity Supply
PIRSCH, P., Microelectronical Engineering
PONICK, B., Electrical Machines and Drives
SEINSCH, H. O., Electrical Machines and Drives
STÖLTING, H.-D., Electrical Machines and Drives
WAGNER, B., Electrical Systems and Teaching of Electrical Engineering

Department of Law (Königsworther Platz 1,
30167 Hanover; tel. (511) 7628104; fax (511)
7628107; e-mail dekanat@jura.rw
.uni-hannover.de; internet www.jura
.uni-hannover.de):

ABELTSHAUSER, T., Civil Law
BUCK, P., Civil Law
BUTZER, H., Public Law
CALLIESS, R.-P., Criminal Law
DORNDORF, E., Civil Law
EPPING, V., Public Law
FABER, H., Public Law
FENGE, H., Civil Law
FOLZ, H.-E., Public Law
FORGÓ, N., Civil Law
FRANK, J., Economics
HESSE, H. A., Teaching of Law, Sociology of Law
KILIAN, W., Civil Law
KÜHNE, J.-D., Public Law
MAGOULAS, G., Economics
MASSING, O., Politics
MEDER, S., Civil Law, History of Law
MEIER, B.-D., Criminal Law
NAHAMOWITZ, P., Theory of Organization and Planning
NOCKE, M., Teaching of Law
OPPERMANN, B., Civil Law
PFEIFFER, C., Criminology
RÜPING, H., Criminal Law
SALJE, P., Civil Law
SCHNEIDER, H.-P., Public Law
SCHWARZE, R., Civil Law
SCHWERDTFEGER, G., Public Law
TREIBER, H., Theory of Organization and Planning
WAECHTER, K., Public Law
WALTHER, M., Teaching of Law and Philosophy
WENDELING-SCHRÖDER, U., Civil Law
WOLF, CH., Civil Law
ZIELINSKI, D., Criminal Law

Department of Mathematics and Physics (tel.
(511) 7624466; fax (511) 7625819; e-mail
dekanat@math.uni-hannover.de):

BARINGHAUS, L., Mathematical Stochastics
BARKE, E., Microelectronic Systems
BÄUERLE, N., Mathematical Stochastics
BESSENRODT, CH., Mathematics
BOTHMER, H.-CH. V., Mathematics
BREHM, B., Atomic Processes
DANZMANN, K., Experimental Physics
DEMMIG, F., Plasma Physics
DRAGON, N., Theoretical Physics
EBELING, W., Mathematics
ERNÉ, M., Mathematics
ERTMER, W., Experimental Physics
ESCHER, J., Applied Mathematics
ETLING, D., Theoretical Meteorology
EVERTS, H.-U., Theoretical Physics
FORSTER, P., Applied Mathematics
GROSS, G., Meteorology
GROSSER, J., Atomic Processes
GRÜBEL, R., Probability Theory and Statistics
HAUF, T., Meteorology

HAUG, R., Experimental Physics
HEINE, J., Applied Mathematics
HENZLER, M., Experimental Physics
HOTJE, H., Mathematics
HULEK, K., Mathematics
KOCK, M., Plasma Physics
LECHTENFELD, O., Theoretical Physics
LEWENSTEIN, M., Theoretical Physics
LIPECK, U., Computer Science
MIKESKA, H. J., Theoretical Physics
MÜHLBACH, G., Approximation Theory and Numerical Analysis
MÜLLER, D., Computer Science
NEJDL, W., Computer Science
OESTREICH, M., Experimental Physics
PARCHMANN, R., Computer Science
PFNÜR, H., Experimental Physics
PIRSCH, P., Microelectronic Systems
PRALLE, H., Head of Regional Computer Centre, Lower Saxony
REINEKE, J., Mathematics
SAUER, P. U., Theoretical Physics
SCHMIDT-WESTPHAL, U., Mathematics
SCHNOEGE, K. J., Applied Mathematics
SCHULZ, E., Plasma Physics
SCHULZ, H., Theoretical Physics
SECKMEYER, G., Meteorology
STARKE, G., Applied Mathematics
STEFFENS, K., Mathematics
STEPHAN, E., Applied Mathematics
SZCZERBICKA, H., Systems Engineering
TIEMANN, E., Experimental Physics
VOLLMER, H., Computer Science
WAGNER, B., Systems Engineering
WELLEGEHAUSEN, B., Applied Physics
WOLTER, F.-E., Applied Systems
ZAWISCHA, D., Theoretical Physics

Department of Mechanical Engineering (Im Moore 11B, 30167 Hannover; tel. (511) 7622779; fax (511) 7622763; e-mail dekan@maschinenbau.uni-hannover.de; internet www.maschinenbau.uni-hannover.de):

BACH, F.-W., Materials
BESDO, D., Mechanics
BRAUNE, R., Mechanisms and Machine Elements
DEKENA, B., Production Engineering and Machine Tools
DOEGE, E., Metal Forming and Machines
GATZEN, H.-H., Microtechnology
GERTH, W., Machine Dynamics
GIETZELT, M., Steam and Fuel Engineering
HAFERKAMP, H. D., Materials
HALLENSLEBEN, M. L., Macromolecular Chemistry
HEIMANN, B., Machine Dynamics
KABELAC, S., Thermodynamics
LOUIS, H., Material Testing
MEIER, G. E. A., Fluid Mechanics
MERKER, G. P., Internal Combustion Engine
MEWES, D., Chemical Engineering
NYHUIS, P., Factory Building and Logistics
OVERMEYER, L., Conveying Technology and Mining Machinery
POLL, G., Construction Science
POPP, K., Mechanics
RAUTENBERG, M., Radial Compressors
REDEKER, G., Factory Building
REHFELDT, D., Welding Technology
REITHMEIER, E., Measurement and Control Technology
RIESS, W., Turbo Machinery
ROSEMANN, H., Construction Science
SCHULZE, L., Department Planning, Control of Warehouse and Transport Systems
SCHWERES, M., Labour Science, Ergonomics
SENME, J., Turbo Machinery
STEGEMANN, D., Nuclear Technology
VOSS, G., Railway Machines
WIENDAHL, H.-P., Plant Engineering and Production Control

Department of Natural Sciences (Schneiderbeg 50, 30167 Hanover; tel. (511) 7623318; fax (511) 7625874; internet www.unics.uni-hannover.de/geo/index.html):

ANDERS, A., Biophysics
ARNOLD, A., Human Geography
AULING, G., Microbiology
BECKER, J. A., Physical Chemistry
BEHRENS, P., Inorganic Chemistry
BELLGARDT, K.-H., Technical Chemistry
BERGER, R. G., Applied Chemistry
BINNEWIES, M., Inorganic Chemistry
BÖTTCHER, J., Soil Science
BRAKHAGE, A., Microbiology
BUCHHOLZ, H. J., Human Geography
BUHL, J.-CH., Mineralogy
BUTENSCHÖN, H., Organic Chemistry
CARO, J., Physical Chemistry
DUDDECK, H., Organic Chemistry
FENDRIK, I., Biophysics
FISCHER, R., Palaeontology
FISCHER, W. R., Soil Science
HAHN, A., Domestic Technology
HALLENSLEBEN, M. L., Macromolecular Chemistry
HAU, B., Phytopathology
HEITJANS, P., Physical Chemistry
HESSE, D., Technical Chemistry
HITZMANN, B., Technical Chemistry
HOFFMANN, H. M. R., Organic Chemistry
HOLTZ, F., Mineralogy
HÖRMANN, D., Gardening Management
HORST, W., Plant Nutrition
HOTHORN, L., Biology Informatics
HUCHZERMEYER, B., Botany
HÜPPE, J., Palaeoecology
IMBIHL, R., Physical Chemistry
JACOBSEN, H.-J., Molecular Biology
JUG, K., Theoretical Chemistry
KIRSHNING, A., Organic Chemistry
KLOPPSTECH, K., Botany
KOLB, A., Biophysics
KRETZMER, G., Technical Chemistry
KUHLMANN, H., Plant Nutrition
KUHNT, G., Physical Geography
KUSTER, H., Palaeoecology
LIEFNER, I., Economic Geography
MAISS, E., Phytopathology
MARTEN, I., Biophysics
MEYER, H. H., Organic Chemistry
MOSIMANN, T., Physical Geography
NAUMANN, I., Domestic Technology
NIEMEYER, R., Botany
POTT, R., Botany
RATH, T., Horticulture
ROTZOLL, G., Technical Chemistry
SCHÄTZL, L., Economic Geography
SCHENK, E.-W., Gardening Management and Accountancy
SCHENK, M., Plant Nutrition
SCHEPER, T., Technical Chemistry
SCHERER, G., Crop Physiology
SCHMIDT, A., Botany
SCHMIDT, E., Horticultural Economics
SCHMITZ, U. K., Applied Genetics
SCHÖNHERR, J., Fruit Science
SCHÜLKE, I., Geology
SCHÜNGERL, K., Technical Chemistry
SEREK, M., Gardening Management and Accountancy
SPETHMANN, W., Nursery Gardening
STÜTZEL, Vegetable Science
TANTAU, H.-J., Horticultural Engineering
TATLIOGLU, T., Applied Genetics
URLAND, W., Inorganic Chemistry
VAN DER PLOEG, R., Soil Science
VOGT, C., Inorganic Chemistry
VON BLANCKENBURG, F., Mineralogy
WAIBEL, H., Horticultural Economics
WATKINSON, B. M., Food Science
WINSEMANN, J., Geology
WINTERFELDT, E., Organic Chemistry
WÜNSCH, G., Inorganic Chemistry
ZIMMER, K., Ornamental Plants

Department of Philosophy (Königsworther Platz 1, 30167 Hanover; tel. (511) 7624556; fax (511) 7628243; e-mail dekanat@fbls.uni-hannover.de; internet www.fbls.uni-hannover.de):

ACHINGER, G., Sociology
AHLERS, I., Human Geography
ANTES, P., Study of Religions
ASCHOFF, H.-G., Modern History and Ecclesiastical History
AVERKORN, R., Medieval History
BARMEYER-HARTLIEB, H., Modern History
BAUSENHART, G., Roman Catholic Religious Education
BAYER, K., German
BECKER-SCHMIDT, R., Psychology
BERG, D., Medieval History
BEUTLER, K., Education
BEZZEL, CH., German Language
BICKES, H., German Language
BILLMANN-MAHECHA, H., Psychology
BINDEL, W.-R., Special Education
BIRKNER, G., English Philology
BLANKE, B., Political Science
BLELL, G., Teaching of English
BLEY, H., Modern History
BOLSCHO, D., Pedagogy
BÖNSCH, M., School Pedagogy
BRODTMANN, D., Sports
BROKMEIER, P., Political Science
BRÜGGEMANN, H., Modern German Literature
BUCKMILLER, M., Political Science
BULTHAUP, P., Philosophy
CALLIES, H., Ancient History
CLAUSSEN, D., Sociology
DAIBER, K.-F., Study of Religions
DIEWALD, G., Modern German Literature
DISCHNER-VOGEL, G., Modern German Literature
DITTRICH, J.-H., Technology of Clothing and Textiles
DORDEL, H. J., Sports
DUDEN, B., Sociology
EBINGHAUS, H., Physics
EGGERT, D., Psychology
EGGS, E., Romance Philology and Language
EHRHARDT, J., Education
EHRHARDT, M. L., German
FELDMANN, K., Sociology
FISCHER, H., German Literature
FRACKMANN, M., Social Education
FRANZKE, R., Social Education
FÜLLBERG-STOLLBERG, O., Modern History
GHOLAMASAD, D., Sociology
GIPSER, D., Special Education
GLAGE, L., English Literature
GLITHO, S., Modern German Literature
GÖRTZ, H.-J., Roman Catholic Religious Education
HAENSCH, D., Political Science
HASEMANN, K., Mathematics
HAUPTMEYER, C.-H., Early Medieval History
HEINEMANN, M., Education
HERWIG, J., Music
HIEBER, L., Sociology
HOECKER, B., Political Science
HOEGES, D., Romance Philology and Literature
HÖLKER, K., Romance Philology and Literature
HORSTER, D., Education
ILIEN, A., Education
JANSSEN, B., School Pedagogy
JETTER, K., Therapy
JOHANNSEN, F., Evangelical Religious Education
JUNGK, D., Vocational Education
KENTLER, H., Social Education
KIESELBACH, T., Psychology
KNAPP, G.-A., Psychology
KOETHEN, E., Art and Visual Media, Teaching of Art and Visual Media

KÖPCKE, K. M., German
KORFF, F.-W., Philosophy
KREUTZER, L., Modern German Literature
KRIWET, I., Education of Mentally Handicapped People
KROVOZA, A., Psychology
KRUIP, G., Roman Catholic Religious Education
KÜHNE, A., Psychology
KUNTZ, K. M., Education
KUPETZ, R., Teaching of English, Applied Linguistics
LAGA, G., Sociology
LEMKE, C., Political Science
LENK, E., German Literature
LOHRER-PAPE, Arts
LUDWIG, O., German Language
MANZ, W., Vocational Education
MAYER, R., English Literature
MENSCHING, G., Philosophy
MESCHKAT, K., Sociology
MICKLER, O., Sociology
MÜHLHAUSEN, K., Education
MÜLLER, R.-W., Political Science
NARR, R., School Pedagogy
NAUMANN, G., Home Technology
NAUMANN, H., German
NEGT, O., Sociology
NOLL, A.-H., Social Studies
NOLTE, H.-H., Medieval History
NOORMANN, J., Teaching of Evangelical Relations
OELSCHLÄGER, H., Educational Planning and Reform
PAEFGEN, E., German
PEIFFER, L., Sports
PERELS, J., Political Science
PETERS, J., Modern German Literature
RAUFUSS, D., Education
RECTOR, M., Modern German Literature
REHKÄMPER, K., Modern German Literature
REISER, H., Special Education
REUMANN, R.-D., Technology of Clothing and Textiles
RIEDEL, M., Modern History
RIEMEN, F., Music
RIES, W., Philosophy
ROHLOFF, H., English Philosophy
RUNTE, A., Modern German Literature
RUST, H., Sociology
RÜTTERS, K., Vocational Education
SANDERS, H., Romance Philology and Literature
SAUER, W., German Language
SCHÄFER, G., Political Science
SCHAEFFNER, L., Adult Education
SCHLOBINSKI, P., German Language
SCHMAUDERER, E., Food Science
SCHMID, H.-D., History and History Teaching
SCHMIDT, M., Adult Education
SCHMITZ, K., Education
SCHÖNBERGER, F., Special Education
SCHREIBER, G., Technology of Clothing and Textile
SCHUCHARDT, E., Education
SCHULZE, R., English Language and Linguistics
SCHWARZ, B., Medieval History
SIEBERT, H., Adult Education
STIMPFLE, A., Roman Catholic Religious Education
SWIENTEK, CH., Special Education
TIEDEMANN, J., Psychology
TILCH, H., Social Education
TREBELS, A. H., Sports
TROCHOLEPCZY, B., Roman Catholic Religious Education
URBAN, A., Psychology
VASSEN, F., Modern German Literature
VESTER, M., Political Science
VON SALDERN, A., Modern History
WACKER, A., Psychology
WAGNER-HASEL, B., Ancient History
WATKINSON, B. M., Food Science

WEBER, H., English Philology
WELLENDORF, F., Psychology
WELZER, H., Psychology
WENZEL, F., Scientific and Technical Russian
WERNER, W., Roman Catholic Religious Education
WERNING, R., Education of Mentally Handicapped People
WILHARM, I., History and History Teaching
WILKEN, E., Special Education
WIPPERMANN, H., Mathematics
WÜNDERICH, V., Latin American History
WÜNDERICH, V., Sociology
ZIEHE, T., Education

LEUPHANA UNIVERSITÄT LÜNEBURG

Scharnhorststr. 1, 21335 Lüneburg
Telephone: (4131) 6770
Fax: (4131) 6771090
E-mail: praesidium@leuphana.de
Internet: www.leuphana.de
Founded 1946
State control
Pres.: Prof. Dr SASCHA SPOUN
Vice-Pres: Prof. Dr BURKHARDT FUNK
Vice-Pres: Prof. Dr FERDINAND MÜLLER-ROMMEL
Vice-Pres: HOLM KELLER
Vice-Pres: Prof. Dr NILS OLE OERMANN
Librarian: TORSTEN AHRENS
Library of 664,000 vols, 1,255 print journals, 23,296 e-journals
Number of teachers: 443
Number of students: 7,541
Publication: *Forschungsberichte* (every 3 years)

DEANS

Faculty of Cultural Studies: Prof. Dr PETER PEZ
Faculty of Economics: Prof. Dr THOMAS WEIN
Faculty of Education: Prof. Dr SILKE RUWISCH
Faculty of Sustainability: Prof. Dr Ing. WOLFGANG K. L. RUCK

PROFESSORS

Faculty of Business Administration, Behavioural Sciences and Law (tel. (4131) 6772001; fax (4131) 782009; e-mail hackbarth@uni.leuphana.de; internet www.leuphana.de/fakultaet2):
BAXMANN, U., Banking, Finance and Accounting
HEINEMANN, M., Economics
LOHMANN, M., Experimental Industrial Psychology (LüneLab)
MARTIN, A., Small- and Medium-Sized Enterprises
MERZ, J., Research Institute on Professions
REMDISCH, S., Small- and Medium-Sized Enterprises
WEINRICH, G., Analytical Management
WEISENFELD, U., Corporate Development
ZENZ, E., Business Law
Faculty of Education, Cultural and Social Sciences (tel. (4131) 6771601; fax (4131) 6771608; e-mail sartisohn@uni.leuphana.de; internet www.leuphana.de/fakultaet1):
BURKART, G., Sociology
CZERWENKA, K., School and Higher Education Research
FAULSTICH, W., Applied Media Research
GUDER, K., Mathematics and Mathematics Education
KARSTEN, M., Social Work and Social Pedagogy
KIRCHBERG, V., Cultural Research and Arts
KIRSCHNER, U., Urban and Cultural Area Research
MASET, P., Studies in Arts, Music and Mediation

MÜLLER-ROMMEL, F., Political Science
NEIDHARDT, E., Psychology
O SULLIVAN, E., English Studies
ROOSE, H., Theology and Pedagogy of Religion
RÖSER, J., Communications and Media Culture
RUWISCH, S., Mathematics and Mathematics Education
STANGE, W., Social Work and Social Pedagogy
STOLTENBERG, U., Integrative Studies
UHLE, R., Educational Science
WEINHOLD, S., German Language and Literature Education
WÖHLER, K., Leisure Science, Play and Physical Education
Faculty of Environmental Sciences and Information Technology (tel. (4131) 6772801; fax (4131) 6772803; e-mail dembeck@uni-lueneburg.de; internet www.uni-lueneburg.de/fakultaet3/):
AßMANN, TH., Ecology and Environmental Chemistry
BAUMGÄRTNER, S., Sustainability Management
BONIN, H., Computer Science
GROß, M., Electronic Business Management
HOFMEISTER, S., Environmental Strategy
MICHELSEN, G., Environmental and Sustainability Communication
RUCK, W., Ecology and Environmental Chemistry
SCHALTEGGER, S., Sustainability Management
SCHLEICH, H., Production Technologies
SCHOMERUS, T., Environmental Strategy
WEINRICH, G., Analytical Management
WELGE, R., Distributed Autonomic Systems and Technologies

LUDWIG-MAXIMILIANS-UNIVERSITÄT MÜNCHEN

Geschwister-Scholl-Pl. 1, 80539 Munich
Telephone: (89) 21800
Fax: (89) 21802322
E-mail: praesidium@lmu.de
Internet: www.lmu.de
Founded 1472
Academic year: October to July
Pres.: Prof. Dr BERND HUBER
Vice-Pres.: Prof. Dr BEATE KELLNER
Vice-Pres.: Prof. Dr CHRISTOPH MÜLKE
Vice-Pres.: Prof. Dr MARTIN WIRSING
Vice-Pres.: Dr SIGMUND STIUTZING
Vice-Pres.: Prof. Dr ULRICH POHL
Dir of Library: Dr KLAUS-RAINER BRINTZINGER
Library: see Libraries and Archives
Number of teachers: 3,576
Number of students: 46,723
Publications: *'Einsichten'* (1 a year), *LMU at a glance* (every 2 years), *MUM* (4 a year), *Veranstaltungskalender* (12 a year), *Vorlesungsverzeichnis* (2 a year)

DEANS

Faculty of Biology: Prof. Dr BENEDIKT GROTHE
Faculty of Business Admin.: Prof. Dr THOMAS HESS
Faculty of Catholic Theology: Prof. Dr KONRAD HILPERT
Faculty of Chemistry and Pharmacy: Prof. Dr MARTIN BEIL
Faculty of Cultural Studies: Prof. Dr KLAUS VOLLMER
Faculty of Economics: Prof. Dr ANDREAS HAUFLER
Faculty of Geosciences: Prof. Dr WOLFRAM MAUSER
Faculty of History and the Arts: Prof. Dr MARIE-JANINE CALIC

Faculty of Languages and Literatures: Prof.
Dr ULRICH SCHWEIER
Faculty of Law: Prof. Dr ALFONS BÜRGE
Faculty of Mathematics, Computer Science
and Statistics: Prof. Dr HEINRICH HUSS-
MANN
Faculty of Medicine: Prof. Dr MAXMILIAN
REISER
Faculty of Philosophy, Philosophy of Science
and the Study of Religion: Prof. Dr JULIAN
NIDA-RUEMELIN
Faculty of Physics: Prof. Dr AXEL SCHENZLE
Faculty of Protestant Theology: Prof. Dr
CHRISTOPH LEVIN
Faculty of Psychology and Educational Sci-
ences: Prof. Dr JOACHIM KAHLERT
Faculty of Social Sciences: Prof. Dr HANS-
BERND BROSIUS
Faculty of Veterinary Medicine: Prof. Dr
JOACHIM BRAUN

MARTIN LUTHER-UNIVERSITÄT HALLE-WITTENBERG

06099 Halle (Saale)
Universitätspl. 10, 06108 Halle
Telephone: (345) 5520
Fax: (345) 5527077
E-mail: rektor@uni-halle.de
Internet: www.uni-halle.de
Founded 1502 (Wittenberg), 1694 (Halle),
1817 (Halle-Wittenberg)
Academic year: October to September
Rector: Prof. Dr UDO STRÄTER
Vice-Rector: Prof. Dr CHRISTOPH WEISER
Vice-Rector: Prof. BIRGIT DRÄGER
Vice-Rector: Prof. Dr GESINE FOLJANTY-JOST
Chancellor: Dr MARTIN HECHT
Number of teachers: 340
Number of students: 17,500

Publication: *Scientia halensis* (4 a year)

DEANS

Faculty of Law, Economics and Business:
Prof. Dr CHRISTIAN TIETJE
Faculty of Medicine: Prof. Dr MICHAEL GEKLE
Faculty of Natural Sciences I: Prof. Dr
REINHARD NEUBERT
Faculty of Natural Sciences II: Prof. Dr WOLF
WIDDRA
Faculty of Natural Sciences III: Prof. Dr
PETER WYCISK
Faculty of Philosophy I: Prof. Dr BURKHARD
SCHNEPEL
Faculty of Philosophy II: Prof. Dr GERD
ANTOS
Faculty of Philosophy III: Prof. Dr HARALD
SCHWILLUS
Faculty of Theology: Prof. Dr MICHAEL DOMS-
GEN

MEDIZINISCHE HOCHSCHULE HANNOVER
(Hanover Medical School)

Carl-Neuberg-Str. 1, 30625 Hanover
Telephone: (511) 5320
Fax: (511) 5325550
E-mail: pressestelle@mh-hannover.de
Internet: www.mh-hannover.de
Founded 1965
Pres.: Prof. Dr DIETER BITTER-SUERMANN
Vice-Pres: Dr ANDREAS TECKLENBURG
Vice-Pres: HOLGER BAUMANN
Librarian: Dr ANNAMARIE FELSCH-KLOTZ
Library of 280,000 vols
Number of teachers: 614
Number of students: 3,197

DEANS

Biology: Prof. Dr G. GROS
Dentistry: Prof. Dr H. TSCHERNITSCHEK
Medicine: Prof. Dr HERMANN HALLER

PROFESSORS

Anatomy:
GROTE, C., Neuroanatomy
GRUBE, D., Microscopic Anatomy
PABST, R., Functional and Applied Anat-
omy
UNGEWICKELL, E., Anatomy
Biochemistry:
GAESTEL, M., Physiological Chemistry
GERARDY-SCHAHN, R., Cellular Chemistry
LENZEN, S., Biochemistry
MANSTEIN, D., Biophysical Chemistry
Laboratory Medicine:
BLASCZYK, R., Transfusion Medicine
FÖRSTER, R., Immunology
GOSSLER, A., Molecular Biology
HEDRICH, H.-J., Animal Research
SCHULZ, T., Laboratory Medicine
SUERBAUM, S., Microbiology and Hospital
Hygiene
Medical Technologies:
HECKER, H., Biometry
MATTHIES, H., Medical Computing
Pathology, Genetics and Forensic Medicine:
KREIPE, H.-H., Pathology
SCHLEGELBERGER, B., Pathology, Genetics
and Forensic Medicine
SCHMIDTKE, J., Human Genetics
TRÖGER, H.-D., Medical Law
Pharmacology and Toxicology:
JUST, I., Toxicology
RESCH, K., Pharmacology
STICHTENOTH, O., Clinical Pharmacology
WRBITZKY, R., Occupational Medicine
Physiology:
BRENNER, B., Molecular and Cell Physi-
ology
FAHLKE, C., Neurophysiology
GROS, G., Vegetative Physiology
MAASEEN, N., Sports Physiology/Sports
Medicine
Public Health Care:
GEYER, S., Medical Sociology
HUMMERS-PRADIER, E., General Medicine
LANGE, K., Medical Psychology
LOHFF, B., History, Ethics and Philosophy
of Medicine
SCHWARTZ, F. W., Epidemiology, Social
Medicine and Health Systems Research

OTTO-FRIEDRICH-UNIVERSITÄT BAMBERG

Kapuzinerstr. 16, 96045 Bamberg
Telephone: (951) 8630
Fax: (951) 8631005
E-mail: post@uni-bamberg.de
Internet: www.uni-bamberg.de
Founded 1647
State control
Academic year: October to September (2
semesters)
Pres.: Prof. Dr Hab. GODEHARD RUPPERT
Vice-Pres. for Research: Prof. Dr ANNA
STEINWEG
Vice-Pres. for Teaching: Prof. Dr SEBASTIAN
KEMPGEN
Chancellor: Dr DAGMAR STEUER-FLIESER
Librarian: Dr FABIAN FRANKE
Library: see Libraries and Archives
Number of teachers: 138
Number of students: 10,409

Publications: *Bamberger Beiträge zur Eng-
lischen Sprachwissenschaft* (1 a year),
*Bamberger Editionen. Hg. v. H. Unger
und H. Wentzlaff-Eggebert*, *Bamberger
Geographische Schriften* (1–2 a year),
Bamberger Universitätszeitung "uni.doc"
(7 a year), *Bericht des Rektors*, *Gratia:
Bamberger Schriften zur Renaissance-*

forschung (2 a year), *Forschungsforum* (1
a year), *Informationen* (irregular), *Per-
sonal- und Vorlesungsverzeichnis* (1 a
term), *Pressemitteilungen, Uni.kat, uni.-
vers* (2 a year)

DEANS

Faculty of Human Sciences and Education:
Prof. Dr SIBYLLE RAHM
Faculty of Humanities: Prof. Dr KLAUS VAN
EICKELS
Faculty of Information Systems and Applied
Computer Science: Prof. Dr CHRISTOPH
SCHLIEDER
Faculty of Social Sciences, Economics and
Business Administration: Prof. Dr THOMAS
GEHRING

PROFESSORS

Faculty of Human Sciences and Education:
ARTELT, C., Educational Research
BEDFORD-STROHM, H., Protestant Theology/
Systematic Theology and Contemporary
Theological Issues
BENDER, W., Andragogy
CARBON, C., General Psychology and Meth-
odology
CARSTENSEN, C., Psychology (Empirical
Educational Research)
FAUST, G., Primary School Education
HERAN-DÖRR, E., Primary School Educa-
tion (Science Education)
HOCK, M., Educational Psychology
HÖRMANN, G., Pedagogics
HÖRMANN, S., Music Pedagogy and Music
Didactics
LAUTENBACHER, S., Physiological Psych-
ology
LAUX, L., Psychology
RAHM, S., School Education
REINECKER, H., Clinical Psychology and
Psychotherapy
RITTER, W., Protestant Theology/Religious
Pedagogy and Didactics
ROßBACH, H., Early Childhood Education
RÜSSELER, J., General Psychology
SCHAAL, S., Science Education
SCHÄFER, CH., Philosophy I
SCHRÖDTER, M., Social Pedagogy
STEINWEG, A., Mathematics Education and
Computer Science Education
WEINERT, S., Developmental Psychology
WOLSTEIN, J., Pathopsychology
Faculty of Humanities:
ABRAHAM, U., German Language and Lit-
erature Instruction
ALBRECHT, S., Art History (Medieval Art
History)
ALZHEIMER, H., European Ethnology
BARTL, A., Modern German Literature
BECKER, T., German Linguistics
BEHMER, M., Media Studies (Journalism
Research)
BEHZADI, L., Arabic Studies
BENNEWITZ, I., Medieval German Philology
BIEBERSTEIN, K., Old Testament
BRANDT, H., Ancient History
BRASSAT, W., History of Art (Early Modern
and Modern Art)
BREITLING, S., Building Research
BRUNS, P., Church History and Patrology
DE RENTIIS, D., Romance Philology
DIX, A., Historical Geography
DORNHEIM, A., Modern and Contemporary
History
DREWELLO, R., Building Preservation Sci-
ences
ECKER, H., Diffusion Processes of Litera-
ture
ENZENSBERGER, H., History (Diplomatics
and Palaeography)
ERICSSON, I., Medieval and Post Medieval
Archaeology
FÖLLINGER, S., Greek Studies
FRANKE, P., Islamic Studies

FREYBERGER, B., History Instruction
GIER, A., Romance Literature
GLÜCK, H., German Linguistics and German as a Foreign Language
GÖLER, D., Human Geography I (Social and Population Geography)
HAASE, M., Romance Philology
HÄBERLEIN, M., Early Modern History
HEIMBACH-STEINS, M., Christian Social Theory
HERZOG, C., Turkish Studies
HOFFMANN, B., Iranian Studies
HOUSWITSCHKA, C., English Literature
HUBEL, A., Monument Preservation and Restoration
ILLIES, C., Philosophy II
ILYASOV, D., Islamic Art and Archaeology
JANSOHN, C., British Culture
JÜNKE, C., Spanish and Latin American Literature
KEMPGEN, S., Slavic Linguistics
KONRAD, M., Archaeology of the Roman Provinces
KORN, L., Islamic Art and Archaeology
KRUG, M., English Linguistics
KÜGLER, J., New Testament Sciences
MARX, F., Modern German Literature
MÜLLER, M., English and American Studies (American Literatures)
NOEL, P., German Linguistics
RAEV, A., Slavic Art and Cultural History
RAHNER, J., Systematic Theology
SAALFELD, T., Comparative Politics
SCHÄFER, A., Prehistoric Archaelogy
SCHAMBECK, M., Religious Education
SCHELLMANN, G., Geography II (Physical Geography and Landscape History)
SCHINDLER, A., Medieval German Philology
SCHÖTTLER, H., Pastoral Theology
STÖBER, R., Communication Studies
TALABARDON, S., Jewish Studies
THEIS-BERGLMAIR, A., Communication Theory and Journalism
ULRICH, M., Romance Linguistics
VAN EICKELS, K., Medieval History incl. Regional History of the Middle Ages
VON ERDMANN, E., Slavic Literatures
WAGNER-BRAUN, M., Economic and Innovation History

Faculty of Information Systems and Applied Computer Science:
FERSTL, O., Information Systems (Industrial Application Systems)
HEINRICH, A., Media Informatics
KRIEGER, U., Computer Networks Group
LÜTTGEN, G., Software Engineering and Programming Languages
MENDLER, M., Foundation of Computer Science
SCHLIEDER, C., Computing in the Cultural Sciences
SCHMID, U., Applied Informatics (Cognitive Systems)
SINZ, E. J., Information Systems (Systems Engineering)
WEITZEL, T., Information Systems and Services
WIRTZ, G., Practical Computer Science, Distributed and Mobile Systems

Faculty of Social Sciences, Economics and Business Administration (Feldkirchenstr. 21, 96052 Bamberg; tel. (951) 8632501; fax (951) 8631200; e-mail dekanat@sowi.uni-bamberg.de; internet www.uni-bamberg.de/sowi):
ANDRESEN, M., Human Resource Management
BECKER, W., Business Administration
BIRK, U.-A., Social Security
BLIEN, U., Sociology (Labour Market and Area Studies)
BLOSSFELD, H., Sociology
BRÜCKER, H., Economics (European Markets)
DERLIEN, H., Public Administration
ECKEL, C., International Economics

EGNER, T., Business Administration and Taxation
EIERLE, B., International Accounting and Auditing
ENGELHARD, J., Business Administration (International Management)
ENGELHARDT-WÖLFLER, H., Population Studies
GEHRING, T., International Policy
IVENS, B., Marketing
MUCK, M., Financial Control
MÜNCH, R., Sociology
OEHLER, A., Finance, Management, and Business Administration
PIEPER, R., Town and Social Planning
RÄSSLER, S., Statistics and Econometrics
RIEGER, E., Sociology of Transnational and Global Processes
SCHNEIDER, T., Sociology (Educational Inequality in the Life-Course)
SCHOEN, H., Political Sociology
SCHWARZE, J., Social Policy
SEMBILL, D., Business and Human Resource Education
STOCKÉ, V., Sociology (Longitudinal Educational Research)
STRUCK, O., Ergonomics and Sociology of Work
SUCKY, E., Operations Management and Business Logistics
WALZL, M., Economics (Industrial Economics)
WENZEL, H., Public Economics
WESTERHOFF, F., Economics (Economic Policy)
ZINTL, R., Political Science
ZOHLNHÖFER, R., Comparative Public Policy

OTTO-VON-GUERICKE-UNIVERSITÄT MAGDEBURG

POB 4120, 39016 Magdeburg
Universitätspl. 2, 39106 Magdeburg
Telephone: (391) 6701
Fax: (391) 6711156
E-mail: akaa@uni-magdeburg.de
Internet: www.uni-magdeburg.de
Founded 1953, present status 1993
State control
Academic year: October to September (two semesters)
Rector: Prof. Dr KLAUS ERICH POLLMANN
Vice-Rector for Planning and Devt: Prof. Dr HELMUT WEISS
Vice-Rector for Research: Prof. Dr VOLKMAR LESSMANN
Vice-Rector for Study: Prof. Dr JENS STRACK-ELJAN
Chancellor: VOLKER ZEHLE (acting)
Librarian: Dr-Ing. ECKHARD BLUME
Library of 1,208,500 vols, 2,124 print journals, 22,680 e-journals
Number of teachers: 1,698
Number of students: 13,625 incl. 1,410 int. students
Publications: *Research-Journal* (1 a year), *Science Journal* (2 a year), *Uni-Report* (6 a year)

DEANS

Faculty of Computer Sciences: Prof. Dr GRAHAM HORTON
Faculty of Economics and Management: Prof. Dr KARL-HEINZ PAQUÉ
Faculty of Electrical and Information Engineering: Prof. Dr ANDREAS LINDEMANN
Faculty of Humanities, Social Sciences and Education: Prof. Dr MARTIN DREHER
Faculty of Mathematics: Prof. Dr WOLFGANG WILLEMS
Faculty of Mechanical Engineering: Prof. Dr KARL-HEINRICH GROTE

Faculty of Medicine: Prof. Dr HERRMANN-JOSEF ROTHKOETTER
Faculty of Natural Sciences: Prof. Dr JÜRGEN CHRISTEN
Faculty of Process and Systems Engineering: Prof. Dr Hab. JUERGEN TOMAS

PROFESSORS

Faculty of Computer Sciences (Universitätspl. 2, Bldg 29, 39106 Magdeburg; tel. (391) 67-18853):
DACHSELT, R., User Interface and Software Engineering
DASSOW, J., Theoretical Informatics
DITTMANN, J., Applied Informatics and Multimedia and Security
DUMKE,, R., Software Engineering
HORTON, G., Simulation and Graphics
KAISER, J., Information System
KRUSE, R., Neural and Fuzzy Systems
NETT, E., Distributive Systems
NUERNBERGER, A., Advanced Topics in Machine Learning
PREIM, B., Computervisualistics
ROESNER, D., Knowledge-Based Systems and Documents Processing
SAAKE, G., Technical Information Systems
SCHIRRA, S., Algorithmics
SCHULZE, T., IT-Skills
SPILIOPOULOU, M., Business Informatics
THEISEL, H., Visual Computing
TOENNIS, K., Computer Graphics

Faculty of Economics and Management (Universitätspl. 2, Bldg 22, 39106 Magdeburg; tel. (391) 67-18585):
BURGARD, U., Law and Economics
CHWOLKA, A., Accounting
ERICHSON, B., Marketing
GISCHER, H., Finance and Credit
GÓMEZ ANSÓN, S., Management
GUNKEL, M., Management
INDERFURTH, K., Logistics
JACOB, M., Management and Economics
KELLE, P., Management
KIRSTEIN, R., Economics of Business and Law
KNABE, A., Business Theory
LUKAS, E., Finance
PAQUÉ, K., International Business
PUPPIN DE OLIVEIRA, J., Management
RAITH, M., Finance and Banking
REBEIZ, K., Management
REICHLING, P., Finance and Banking
REIMANN, M., Marketing
RUNKEL, M., Economics and Policy Consulting
SADRIEH, A., Business
SCHANZ, S., Fiscal Theory
SCHOENDUBE-PIRCHEGGER, B., Financial Accounting
SPENGLER, T., Management and Organization
THOMSEN, S., Job Market Economics
VOGT, B., Business Research
WAESCHER, G., Management Science
WEIMANN, J., Political Economy III

Faculty of Electrical and Information Engineering (Universitätspl. 2, Bldg 09, 39106 Magdeburg; tel. (391) 67-18635):
DIEDRICH, C., Industrial Engineering
FINDEISEN, R., System Technique and Engineering Cybernetics
KIENLE, A., Automation Engineering
KLEINE, U., Electronics Circuits
KORN, U., Control Engineering
LINDEMANN, A., Power Electronics
MICHAELIS, B., Technical Computer Science
NITSCH, J., Theory of Electrical Engineering
OMAR, A., Microwave and Communications Engineering
PALIS, F., Power Electronics
RAISCH, J., System Theory
ROSE, G., Medical Systems Engineering

SCHMIDT, B., Measurement Technology and Microsystems
STYCZYNSKI, Z., Electrical Power Networks and Renewable Energy Resourses
VICK, R., Electro-Techniques
WENDEMUTH, A., Cognitive Systems
WOLLENBERG, G., Theoretical and General Electrical Engineering

Faculty of Humanities, Social Sciences and Education (Zschokkestr. 32, Bldg 40, 39104 Magdeburg; tel. (391) 67-16541):

BERGIEN, A., English Linguistics
BLASER, P., Administrative Sciences
BRUCHHAEUSER, H., Administrative Management and New Media
BURKHARDT, A., Germanistics
DIPPELHOFER-STIEM, B., Methology Social Research
DITTRICH, E., Macrosociology
DREHER, M., Ancient History
EDELMANN-NUSSER, J., Computer Science in Sport
FREUND, S., History
FRITZSCHE, K., Comparative Political Systems
FROMME, J., Media Education and Adult Education
FUHRER, U., Developmental ad Educational Psychology
GIRMES, R., General Didatics and Theory of Education
GOES, G., Culture Science
HOEKELMANN, A., Basics of Movement Science
JENEWEIN, K., Didactics Technical Subject Areas
JOBST, S., Education Science
KAISER, F., Psychology
KERSTEN, H., English esp. American Studies
LABOUVIE, E., Contemporary History and Sexual Research
LEHMANN, W., Psychology
LOHMANN, G., Practical Philosophy
LYRE, H., Philosophy
MAROTZKI, W., General Education
NAGEL, U., Sociology
PETERS, S., Work Based Education
RENZSCH, W., Political System and Sociology of the Federal Republic
SCHILLING, M., Older German Literature and Linguistics
SCHLICHTE, K., Politic Science
SCHRADER, H., Sociology
SUEß, H., Psychology
TULLNER, M., History
WITTE, K., Research

Faculty of Mathematics (Universitätspl. 2, Bldg 03, 39106 Magdeburg; tel. (391) 67-18322):

BENNER, P., Analysis and Numerics
BLEY, A., Linear Optimization
BURKSCHAT, M., Biological Statistics
CHRISTOPH, G., Mathematical Stochastics
DECKELNICK, K., Analysis
GAFFKE, N., Mathematical Stochastics
GIRLICH, E., Mathematics Optimization
GRUNAU, H., Analysis
HENK, M., Geometry
HENNING, H., Algebra and Geometry
JUHNKE, F., Mathematics Optimization
KAIBEL, V., Mathematics Optimization
POTT, A., Discrete Mathematics
SCHWABE, R., Mathematics Stochastics
SIMON, M., Analysis and Numerics
TOBISKA, L., Numerical Analysis
WARNECKE, G., Numerical Mathematics
WILLEMS, W., Mathematics

Faculty of Mechanical Engineering (Universitätspl. 2, Bldg 10, 39106 Magdeburg; tel. (391) 67-18519):

BERTRAM, A., Strength of Materials
DEML, B., Ergonomics and Work Design

DETERS, L., Machine Elements and Tribology
GABBERT, U., Numerical Mechanics
GATZKY, T., Industry Design
GROTE, K., Product Devt and Engineering Design
HEYN, A., Anti-Corrosion Protection
KARPUSCHEWSKI, B., Metal Cutting and Remove Technology
KASPER, R., Mechatronics
KATTERFELD, A., Constant Advancement
KUEHNLE, H., Factory Operation and Manufacturing Systems
MARTINEK, I., Connecting Techniques
MOLITOR, M., Manufacturing Measurement Technology and Quality Management
MOOK, G., Materials Testing Techniques
SCHEFFLER, M., Material Techniques
SCHENK, M., Logistic Systems
SINAPIUS, M., Adaptive Lightweight Construction
STRACKELJAN, J., Technical Dynamics
VAJNA, S., Computer Applications in Mechanical Engineering
VLASENKO, D., Computer Science in Mechanical Engineering
WENDT, U., Materials Technique and Non-Metal Materials
WISWEH, L., Production Engineering and Quality Management
ZADEK, H., Logistics

Faculty of Medicine (Leipzigerstr. 44, 39120 Magdeburg; tel. (391) 67-15750):

BEHRENS-BAUMANN, W., Ophthalmology
BERNARDING, J., Biometry and Medical Computer Science
BODE-BOEGER, S., Clinical Pharmacology
BOECKELMANN, I., Occupational Medicine
BOGERTS, B., Psychiatric Medicine
BRAUN-DULLAEW, G., Internal Medicine
BRINKSCHULTE, E., History, Ethnic and Theory of Medicine
COSTA, S., Gynaecology
DUEZEL, E., Clinic Neurology
FIRSCHING, R., Neurosurgery
FISCHER, K., Biological Chemistry
FISCHER, T., Oncology
FLECHTNER, H., Psychiatry for Kids and Adolescents
FROMMER, J., Psychotherapy
GADEMANN, G., Radiotherapy
GEGINAT, G., Microbiology
GERLACH, K., Oral and Maxillofacial Surgery
GOLLNICK, H., Dermatology and Venereology
GREKSCH, G., Pharmacology and Toxicology
GUNZER, M., Immunology
HACHENBERG, T., Anaesthesiology and Intensive Therapy
HALANGK, W., Operative Medicine
HEIM, M., Transfusion Medicine
HEINZE, H., Neurophysiology
HERMANN, M., General Medicine
HOELLT, V., Pharmacology and Toxicology
HOFFMANN, W., Molecularbiology and Medical Chemistry
HUTH, C., Cardiothoracic Surgery
ISERMANN, B., Clinical Chemistry
JORCH, G., Paediatrics and Neonatology
KEILHOFF, G., Biology
KLEINSTEIN, J., Urogynaecology
KRAUSE, H., Law Medicine
KROPF, S., Biometrics and Medical Computer Science
LEßMANN, V., Physiology Internship
LIEHR, U., Orology
LINKE, R., Clinical Anatomy
LIPPERT, H., General Surgery
LOHMANN, C., Orthopaedic Pathology
MALFERTHEINER, P., Gastroenterology and Hepatology
MAWRIN, C., Forensic Medicine
MERTENS, P., Internal Medicine

NAUMANN, M., Experimental Internal Medicine
REINHOLD, D., Immunphysiology
REISER, G., Neuro-Biochemistry
RICKE, J., Radiology
ROBRA, B., Social Medicine and Health Economic
ROESSNER, A., Pathology
ROSKODEN, T., Microscopic Anatomy
ROTHKOETTER, H., Anatomy
SABEL, B., Medical Psychology
SCHLUETER, D., Medical Microbiology
SCHOENFELD, P., Biological Chemistry
SCHRAVEN, B., Immunology
SCHWEGLER, H., Anatomy
SKALEJ, M., Diagnostic Radiology
VOGES, J., Neurosurgery
WINKLER, S., Accident Surgery
ZENKER, M., Human Genetics

Faculty of Natural Sciences (Universitätspl. 2, Bldg 16, 39106 Magdeburg; tel. (391) 67-18678):

BRAUN, A., Biology and Zoology
CHRISTEN, J., Experimental Physics
FUHRER, U., Psychology
HAUSER, M., Biophysics
KASSNER, K., Computational Physics
KROST, A., Experimental Physics
MARWAN, W., Regulations Biology
NOESSELT, T., Psychology
POLLMANN, S., General Psychology
RICHTER, J., Theoretical Physics
STANNARIUS, R., Experimental Physics and Nonlinear Phenomena
WIERSIG, J., Theoretical Physics

Faculty of Process and Systems Engineering (Universitätspl. 2, Bldg 10, 39106 Magdeburg; tel. (391) 67-11190):

HAAK, E., Inorganic Chemistry
KOESER, H., Apparatus Environmental and Technical Engineering
KRAUSE, U., Apparatus Environmental and Technical Engineering
MOERL, L., Chemical Apparatus Construction
REICHL, U., Biochemical Engineering
SCHEFFLER, F., Engineering Chemistry
SCHINZER, D., Organic Chemistry
SCHMIDT, J., Thermodynamics
SEIDEL-MORGENSTERN, A., Chemical Reaction Engineering
SPECHT, E., Technical Thermodynamics and Combustion
SUNDMACHER, K., Process System Engineering
THÉVENIN, D., Fluid Dynamics
TOMAS, J., Mechanical Process Engineering
TSOTSAS, E., Thermal Process Engineering
WEIß, H., Chemical Engineering

PÄDAGOGISCHE HOCHSCHULE FREIBURG
(Freiburg University of Education)

Kunzenweg 21, 79117 Freiburg

Telephone: (761) 6820

Fax: (761) 682402

E-mail: epp@ph-freiburg.de

Internet: www.ph-freiburg.de

Founded 1962

Public control

Rector: Prof. Dr ULRICH DRUWE
Vice-Rector for Academic Affairs: Prof. Dr HANS-WERNER HUNEKE
Vice-Rector for Research: Prof. Dr TIMO LEUDERS
Chancellor: HENDRIK BÜGGELN
Number of students: 4,432

DEANS

Faculty of Cultural Studies and Social Sciences: Prof. Dr MECHTILD FUCHS
Faculty of Education: Prof. Dr ELMAR STAHL

Faculty of Mathematics, Science and Technology: Prof. Dr ULRIKE SPÖRHASE

PÄDAGOGISCHE HOCHSCHULE HEIDELBERG
(Heidelberg University of Education)

Keplerstr. 87, 69120 Heidelberg

Telephone: (6221) 4770
Fax: (6221) 477432
E-mail: info@ph-heidelberg.de
Internet: www.ph-heidelberg.de
Public control

Rector: Prof. Dr ANNELIESE WELLENSIEK
Pro-Rector: Prof. Dr GERHARD HÄRLE
Pro-Rector: Prof. Dr ANNE SLIWKA
Chancellor: CHRISTOPH GLASER

Number of teachers: 180
Number of students: 4,200

DEANS

Faculty of Cultural Studies and Humanities: Prof. Dr GEORG ZENKERT
Faculty of Education and Social Sciences: Prof. Dr KLAUS SARIMSKI
Faculty of Natural, Human and Social Sciences: Prof. Dr BETTINA ALAVI

PÄDAGOGISCHE HOCHSCHULE KARLSRUHE
(Karlsruhe University of Education)

POB 11 10 62, 76060 Karlsruhe
Bismarckstr. 10, 76133 Karlsruhe

Telephone: (721) 9253
Fax: (721) 9254000
E-mail: studium@ph-karlsruhe.de
Internet: www.ph-karlsruhe.de
Founded 1962
Public control

Rector: Prof. Dr LIESEL HERMES
Vice-Rector for Academic Affairs: Prof. Dr SABINE LIEBIG
Vice-Rector for Research and Professional Devt: Prof. Dr GABRIELE WEIGAND
Chancellor: Dr WOLFGANG TZSCHASCHEL

Number of teachers: 180
Number of students: 3,000

DEANS

Faculty I: Prof. Dr KLAUS PETER RIPPE
Faculty II: Prof. Dr HEIDI RÖSCH
Faculty III: Prof. Dr WALTRAUD RUSCH

PÄDAGOGISCHE HOCHSCHULE LUDWIGSBURG
(Ludwigsburg University of Education)

POB 220, 71602 Ludwigsburg
Reuteallee 46, 71634 Ludwigsburg

Telephone: (7141) 1400
Fax: (7141) 140434
E-mail: rektorat@vw.ph-ludwigsburg.de
Internet: www.ph-ludwigsburg.de
Founded 1962
Public control

Rector: Prof. Dr MARTIN FIX
Vice-Rector for Academic and Int. Affairs: Prof. Dr KERSTIN MERZ-ATALIK
Vice-Rector for Research and Professional Devt: Prof. Dr CHRISTINE BESCHERER
Chancellor: VERA BRÜGGEMANN

Number of teachers: 380
Number of students: 4,900

DEANS

Faculty of Cultural Studies and Science: Prof. Dr JÖRG-U. KEßLER
Faculty of Education and Social Science: Prof. Dr GERHARD DREES
Faculty of Special Education: Prof. Dr RAINER TROST

PÄDAGOGISCHE HOCHSCHULE SCHWÄBISCH GMÜND
(Schwäbisch Gmünd University of Education)

Oberbettringer Str. 200, 73525 Schwäbisch Gmünd

Telephone: (7171) 9830
Fax: (7171) 983212
E-mail: info@ph-gmuend.de
Internet: www.ph-gmuend.de
Founded 1825
Public control

Rector: Prof. Dr Hab. ASTRID BECKMANN
Vice-Rector for Academic Affairs: Prof. Dr Hab. ANDREAS BENK
Vice-Rector for Research, Devt and Int. Relations: Prof. Dr THORSTEN PISKE
Chancellor: EDGAR BUHL

Library of 300,000 vols, 670 current periodicals
Number of students: 2,570

DEANS

Faculty I: Prof. Dr MARITA KAMPSHOFF
Faculty II: Prof. Dr ERIKA BRINKMANN

PÄDAGOGISCHE HOCHSCHULE WEINGARTEN
(Weingarten University of Education)

Kirch Pl. 2, 88250 Weingarten

Telephone: (751) 5010
Fax: (751) 5018200
E-mail: poststelle@ph-weingarten.de
Internet: www.ph-weingarten.de
Founded 1947
Public control

Rector: Dr MARGRET RUEP
Vice-Rector for Academic Affairs: Prof. Dr WERNER KNAPP
Vice-Rector for Research and Devt: Prof. Dr Hab. JOACHIM ROTTMANN
Chancellor: ULRICH KLEINER

Library of 290,000 vols
Number of teachers: 140
Number of students: 2,400

DEANS

Faculty I: Dr Hab. URSULA PFEIFFER
Faculty II: Dr PETRA BURMEISTER

PHILIPPS-UNIVERSITÄT MARBURG

Biegenstr. 10–12, 35032 Marburg

Telephone: (6421) 2820
Fax: (6421) 2822500
E-mail: pressestelle@verwaltung.uni-marburg.de
Internet: www.uni-marburg.de
Founded 1527
State control
Academic year: October to July (2 terms)

Pres.: Prof. Dr KATHARINA KRAUSE
Vice-Pres.: Prof. Dr FRANK BREMMER
Vice-Pres.: Prof. Dr HARALD LACHNIT
Vice-Pres.: Prof. Dr JOACHIM SCHACHTNER
Chancellor: Dr FRIEDHELM NONNE
Library Dir: Dr H. NEUHAUSEN

Library: see Libraries and Archives
Number of teachers: 2,144
Number of students: 21,000
Publication: *Journal* (2 a year)

DEANS

Faculty of Biology: Prof. Dr PAUL GALLAND
Faculty of Business Admin. and Economics: Prof. Dr PAUL ALPAR
Faculty of Chemistry: Prof. Dr STEFANIE DEHNEN
Faculty of Education: Prof. Dr WOLFGANG SEITTER

Faculty of Foreign Languages and Cultures: Prof. Dr SONJA FIELITZ
Faculty of Geography: Prof. Dr MARKUS HASSLER
Faculty of German Studies and History of the Arts: Prof. Dr JOACHIM HERRGEN
Faculty of History and Cultural Studies: Prof. Dr VERENA POSTEL
Faculty of Law: Prof. Dr GILBERT GORNIG
Faculty of Mathematics and Computer Science: Prof. Dr MANFRED SOMMER
Faculty of Medicine: Prof. Dr MATTHIAS ROTHMUND
Faculty of Pharmacy: Prof. Dr MICHAEL KEUSGEN
Faculty of Physics: Prof. Dr WOLFRAM HEIMBRODT
Faculty of Protestant Theology: Prof. Dr WOLF-FRIEDRICH SCHÄUFELE
Faculty of Psychology: Prof. Dr RAINER K. SCHWARTING
Faculty of Social Science and Philosophy: Prof. Dr CHRISTOPH DEMMERLING

PROFESSORS

Department of Biology (Karl-von-Frisch-Str., 35032 Marburg; tel. (6421) 2822047; fax (6421) 2822057; e-mail pega@mailer.uni-marburg.de):

BATSCHAUER, A., Plant Physiology, Photobiology
BÖLKER, M., Genetics
BRANDL, R., Animal Ecology
BREMER, E., Microbiology
BUCKEL, W., Microbiology
GALLAND, P., Plant Physiology, Photobiology
HASSEL, M., Morphology
HELDMAIER, G., Zoology
HOMBERG, U., Animal Physiology
KAHMANN, R., Genetics
KIRCHNER, C., Zoology
KLEIN, A., Molecular Genetics
KOST, G., Botany, Mycology
LINGELBACH, U., Zoology, Parasitology
MAIER, U., Cell Biology and Botany
MATTHIES, D., Plant Ecology
PLACHTER, H., Nature Conservancy Studies
RENKAWITZ-POHL, R., Molecular Genetics
THAUER, R., Microbiology
WEBER, H. C., Botany
ZIEGENHAGEN, B., Nature Conservancy Biology

Department of Chemistry (Hans-Meerwin-Str., 35032 Marburg; tel. (6421) 2825543; fax (6421) 2828917; e-mail dekanat@chemie.uni-marburg.de):

BRÖRING, M., Inorganic Chemistry
ELSCHENBROICH, CHR., Inorganic Chemistry
ENSINGER, W., Analytical and Nuclear Chemistry
ESSEN, L.-O., Biochemistry
FRENKING, G., Chemistry-Related Computer Studies
GERMANO, G., Physical Chemistry
GREINER, A., Macromolecular Chemistry
HAMPP, N., Physical Chemistry
HARBRECHT, B., Inorganic Chemistry
HILT, G., Organic Chemistry
KOERT, W., Organic Chemistry
MARAHIEL, M., Biochemistry
MÜLLER, U., Inorganic Chemistry
SCHRADER, T., Organic Chemistry
SEUBERT, A., Analytical Chemistry
STUDER, A., Organic Chemistry
SUNDERMEYER, J., Metal-Organic Chemistry
UHL, W., Inorganic Chemistry
WEITZEL, K.-M., Physical Chemistry
WENDORFF, J., Physical Chemistry

Department of Economics (Universitätsstr. 25, 35032 Marburg; tel. (6421) 2821722; fax (6421) 2824858; e-mail dekanat@wiwi.uni-marburg.de):

ALPAR, P., Economics, Computer Science
FEHL, U., Economic Theory
FELD, L., Financial Science
FLEISCHER, K., Statistics
GERUM, E., Commerce
GÖPFERT, I., Commerce, Logistics
HASENKAMP, U., Business Management and Economic Information Studies
KERBER, W., Political Economy
KIRK, M., Development Policy, Agricultural Economics and Cooperative Science
KRAG, J., Commerce
LINGENFELDER, M., Marketing
PRIEWASSER, E., Banking
RÖPKE, J., Economic Theory
SCHIMENZ, B., Business Economics
SCHÜLLER, A., Economic Theory
STORZ, C., Japanese Economics
WEHRHEIM, M., Commerce

Department of Education (Wilhelm-Röpke-Str. 6B, 35032 Marburg; tel. (6421) 2824770; fax (6421) 2828946; e-mail dekan21@mailer.uni-marburg.de):

ACKERMANN, H., General Teaching
BECKER, P., Sociology of Sports
BÜCHNER, P., Sociology of Education
HAFENEGER, B., Extracurricular Education
KÖNIGS, F., General Teaching, Applied Linguistics
KUCKARTZ, U., Education
LAGING, R., Sports Science
LERSCH, R., School Education
NUISSL VON REIN, E., Adult Education
PROKOP, U., Socialization Theory
ROHR, E., Education
ROHRMANN, E., Education
SCHNOOR, H., Pedagogics
SEEWALD, J., Educational Kinesiology
SEITTER, W., Education
SOMMER, H.-M., Sports Medicine

Department of Foreign Languages and Philology (Wilhelm-Röpke-Str. 6D, 35032 Marburg; tel. (6421) 2824764; fax (6421) 2824715; e-mail kissling@mailer.uni-marburg.de):

BISCHOFF, V., American Literature
HAHN, M., Indology
HANDKE, J., English Linguistics
HOFER, H., Romance Philology
IBLER, R., Slavic Philology
KÖNSGEN, E., Latin Philology of the Middle and Modern Ages
KUESTER, M., English Studies
LEONHARDT, J., Classic Philology
POPPE, E., General Language and Celtology
RIEKEN, E., Comparative Language
SCHALLER, H., Slavic Philology
SCHMITT, A., Classic Philology
SOMMERFELD, W., Ancient Oriental Studies
STILLERS, R., Romance Philology
UHLIG, C., English and American Philology
WENINGER, S., Semitistics
ZIMMERMANN, R., English Linguistics
ZOLLNA, J., Romance Philology

Department of Geography (Deutschhausstr. 10, 35032 Marburg; tel. (6421) 2825916; fax (6421) 2828950; e-mail jansen@mailer.uni-marburg.de):

BARTHELT, H., Cultural Geography
BENDIX, J., Climatic Geography and Geoecology
BRÜCKNER, H., Morphology and Geoecology
MIEHE, G., Geography of Asia and East Africa
OPP, CH., Physical Geography
PAAL, M., Cultural Geography
PLETSCH, A., Cultural Geography and Geography of North America
STRAMBACH, S., Cultural Geography

Department of Geosciences (Hans-Meerwein-Str., 35032 Marburg; tel. (6421) 2823000; fax (6421) 2828919; e-mail napieral@mailer.uni-marburg.de):

BUCK, P., Crystallography

HOFFER, E., Petrology
PRINZ-GRIMM, P., Historical and Regional Geology
SCHMIDT-EFFING, R., Geology
VOGLER, ST., Structural Geology

Department of German Studies and Art (Wilhelm-Röpke-Str. 6A, 35032 Marburg; tel. (6421) 2824542; fax (6421) 2827056; e-mail dekan09@mailer.uni-marburg.de):

ALBERT, R., German Language
ANZ, TH., Modern German Literature
BERTELSMEIER-KIERST, C., German Philology
DEDNER, B., Modern German Literature
DOHM, B., Modern German Literature
HEINZLE, J., German Philology
HELLER, H.-B., Modern German Literature
HENZE-DÖHRING, G., Music
HERKLOTZ, I., History of Art
HERRGEN, J., German Linguistics
HEUSINGER, L., Informatics in History of Art
KRAUSE, K., History of Art
KREMERS, E., Graphics and Painting
KÜNZEL, H., Phonetics
MIX, Y.-G., Modern German Literature
OSINSKI, J., Modern German Literature
PRÜMM, K., Media Teaching
SCHLESEWSKY, M., Neurolinguistics
SCHMIDT, J., Dialect and Linguistics
SCHÜTTE, W., History of Art
WIESE, R., German Linguistics

Department of History and Cultural Sciences (Wilhelm-Röpke-Str. 6C, 35032 Marburg; tel. (6421) 2824518; fax (6421) 2826948; e-mail dekan06@mailer.uni-marburg.de):

BÖHME, H. W., Prehistory
BORSCHEID, P., Social and Economic History
CONZE, E., Modern History
DREXHAGE, H.-J., Ancient History
ERRINGTON, R. M., Ancient History
FRONING, H., Classical Archaeology
HARDACH, G., Social and Economic History
KAMPMANN, C., Modern History
KRIEGER, W., Modern History
LAUTER, H., Classical Archaeology
MEYER, A., Medieval History
MÜLLER-KARPE, A., Prehistory
PAUER, E., Japanese Studies
PLAGGENBORG, S., East European History
POSTEL, V., Medieval History
ÜBELHÖR, M., Sinology
WINTERHAGER, W. E., Modern History

Department of Law (Universitätsstr. 6, 35032 Marburg; tel. (6421) 2823101; fax (6421) 2823181; e-mail dekanat01@mailer.uni-marburg.de):

BACKHAUS, R., Roman and Civil Law
BÖHM, M., Public Law
BUCHHOLZ, ST., German Legal History and Civil Law
DETTERBECK, S., Public Law
FREUND, G., Criminal and Procedural Law, Philosophy of Law
FROTSCHER, W., Public Law
GORNIG, G.-H., Public Law
GOUNALAKIS, G., Civil and Comparative Law
HORN, H.-D., Public Law
LANGENBÜCHER, K., Civil Law
LANGER, W., Criminal and Procedural Law
MENKHAUS, H., Japanese Law
MUMMENHOFF, W., Civil and Labour Law
RADTKE, H., Criminal Law, Procedural Law
RÖSSNER, D., Criminal Law, Procedural Law
RUPPRECHT, H.-A., Papyrology
SCHANZE, E., Civil Law
VOIT, W., Civil Law
WERTENBRUCH, J., Civil Law

Department of Mathematics (Hans-Meerwein-Str., 35032 Marburg; tel. (6421)

2825463; fax (6421) 2825466; e-mail dekan@mathematik.uni-marburg.de):

BAUER, T., Geometrical Algebra
DAHLKE, S., Numerics
FREISLEBEN, B., Practical Informatics
GROMES, W., Analysis
GUMM, H.-P., Theoretical Informatics
HESSE, W., Software Engineering
HÜLLERMEIER, E., Informatics
KNÖLLER, F. W., Topology and Geometry
LOOGEN, R., Functional Programmes
MAMMITZSCH, V., Probability Theory and Mathematical Statistics
PORTENIER, C., Analysis
SCHLICKEWEI, H. P., Algebra
SCHUMACHER, G., Topology and Geometry
SCHWENTICK, T., Theoretical Informatics
SEEGER, B., Databases
SOMMER, M., Practical Informatics
ULTSCH, A., Neuroinformatics
UPMEIER, H., Analysis
WELKER, V., Combinatorics

Department of Medicine (Baldingerstr., 35032 Marburg; tel. (6421) 2866201; fax (6421) 2861548; e-mail dekanat@post.med.uni-marburg.de):

ARNOLD, R., Internal Medicine
AUMÜLLER, G., Anatomy
AUSTERMANN, K.-H., Maxillofacial Surgery
BACK, T., Neurology
BASLER, H.-D., Psychology
BAUER, W., Molecular Biology
BAUM, E., General Medicine
BEHR, T., Nuclear Medicine
BERGER, R., Otorhinolaryngology
BERTALANFFY, H., Neurosurgery
BESEDOVSKY, H., Physiology
BIEN, S., Neurosurgery
CETIN, Y., Anatomy
CZUBAYKO, F., Pharmacology
DAUT, J., Physiology
DIBBETS, J., Dentistry
DONNER-BANZHOFF, N., General Medicine
EILERS, M., Molecular Biology
ENGENHART-CABILLIC, R., Radiotherapy
FEHRENBACH, H.-G., Pneumology
FLORES DE JACOBY, L., Paradontology
GARTEN, W., Virology
GÖKE, R., Internal Medicine
GOTZEN, L., Surgery
GRISS, P., Orthopaedics
GRZESCHIK, K.-H., Human Genetics
GUDERMANN, T., Pharmacology and Toxicology
HAPPLE, R., Dermatology
HASILIK, A., Physiological Chemistry
HEBEBRAND, J., Child Psychiatry
HEEG, K., Microbiology
HOFMANN, R., Urology
JONES, D., Orthopaedics
KANN, P., Internal Medicine
KLENK, H.-D., Virology
KLINGMÜLLER, V., Nuclear Diagnosis
KLOSE, K., Radiology
KRAUSE, W., Andrology
KRETSCHMER, V., Transfusion Medicine
KRIEG, J. C., Psychology
KROLL, P., Ophthalmology
KUHN, K., Medical Informatics
LANG, R. E., Experimental Nuclear Medicine
LILL, R., Cytobiology
LISS, B., Physiology
LOHOFF, M., Microbiology
LOTZMANN, K.-U., Dentistry
MAIER, R., Neonatology
MAISCH, B., Cardiology
MAX, M., Anaesthesiology and Intensive Therapy
MOLL, R., Pathology
MOOSDORF, R., Cardiac Surgery
MUELLER, U., Medical Sociology
MÜLLER, R., Molecular Biology
NEUBAUER, A., Internal Medicine
OERTEL, W., Neurology

PIEPER, K., Dentistry for Children
RADSAK, K., General Medicine
REMSCHMIDT, H., Child Psychology
RENZ, H., Interdisciplinary Medical Centre
RÖPER, J., Physiology
ROSENOW, F., Neurology
ROTHMUND, M., Surgery
RUPP, H., Cardiology
SCHÄFER, H., Medical Biometry
SCHMIDT, S., Obstetrics
SCHWARZ, R., Parasitology
SEITZ, J., Anatomy
SEYBERTH, H. W., Child Medicine, Clinical and Theoretical Pharmacology
SOMMER, N., Neurology (Neuroimmunology)
STACHNISS, V., Dentistry
STEINIGER, B., Anatomy
STREMPEL, J., Ophthalmology
VOGELMEIER, C., Pneumology
VOIGT, K.-H., Physiology
WAGNER, H.-J., Radiology
WAGNER, W., Obstetrics
WEIHE, E., Anatomy
WERNER, J., Otolaryngology, Head and Neck Surgery
WULF, H., Anaesthesiology and Intensive Therapy

Department of Pharmacy (Wilhelm-Roser-Str. 2, 35032 Marburg; tel. (6421) 2825890; fax (6421) 2825815; e-mail dekanat .pharmazie@mailer.uni-marburg.de):

FRIEDRICH, C., History of Pharmacy
HANEFELD, W., Pharmaceutical Chemistry
HARTMANN, R., Pharmaceutical Chemistry
KEUSGEN, M., Pharmaceutical Chemistry
KISSEL, T., Pharmaceutical Technology and Biopharmacy
KLEBE, G., Pharmaceutical Chemistry
KRIEGLSTEIN, J., Pharmacology and Toxicology
KUSCHINSKY, K., Pharmacology and Toxicology
LINK, A., Pharmaceutical Chemistry
MATERN, U., Pharmaceutical Biology
MATUSCH, R., Pharmaceutical Chemistry
PETERSEN, M., Pharmaceutical Biology

Department of Physics (Renthof 6, 35032 Marburg; tel. (6421) 2821314; fax (6421) 2821309; e-mail dekanat@physik .uni-marburg.de):

BREMMER, F., Applied Physics
ECKHARDT, B., Theoretical Physics
ECKHORN, R., Applied Physics
GEBHARD, F., Theoretical Physics
HEIMBRODT, W., Experimental Physics
HÖFER, U., Experimental Physics
JAKOB, P., Experimental Physics
KIRA, M., Theoretical Physics
KOCH, S., Theoretical Physics
LENZ, P., Theoretical Physics
NEUMANN, H., Theoretical Physics
PÜHLHOFER, F., Experimental Physics
RIES, H., Experimental Physics
RÜHLE, W., Experimental Physics
STÖCKMANN, H.-J., Experimental Physics
THOMAS, P., Theoretical Physics
WEISER, G., Experimental Physics

Department of Psychology (Gutenbergstr. 18, 35032 Marburg; tel. (6421) 2823674; fax (6421) 2826949; e-mail dekanpsy@mailer .uni-marburg.de):

LACHNIT, H., General Psychology
LIEBHART, E., Educational Psychology
LOHAUS, A., Developmental Psychology
RIEF, W., Clinical Psychology
RÖHRLE, B., Clinical Psychology
RÖSLER, F., Cognitive Psychology, Neuroscience
ROST, D., Educational Psychology
SCHEIBLECHNER, H., Psychological Methodology
SCHMIDT-ATZERT, L., Psychological Diagnostics

SCHULZE, H.-H., Psychological Methodology
SCHWARTING, R., General and Physiological Psychology
SOMMER, G., Clinical Psychology
STELZL, I., Psychological Methodology and Diagnostics
STEMMLER, G., Psychological Diagnostics
WAGNER, U., Social Psychology

Department of Social Science and Philosophy (Wilhelm-Röpke-Str. 6B, 35032 Marburg; tel. (6421) 2824726; fax (6421) 2825467; e-mail ciok@mailer.uni-marburg.de):

BERG-SCHLOSSER, D., Political Science
BIELING, H.-J., Political Science
BORIS, H.-D., Sociology
BRANN, K., European Ethnology
BREDOW, W. VON, Political Science
DEPPE, F., Political Science
FÜLBERTH-SPERLING, G., Political Science
FUNDER, M., Sociology
GUTMANN, M., Philosophy
JANICH, P., Philosophy
KÄSLER, D., Sociology
KISSLER, L., Sociology
KURZ-SCHERF, I., Political Science
LÜDTKE, H., Sociology
MERKEL, I., Ethnology
MÜNZEL, M., Ethnology
NOETZEL, T., Political Science
PYE, M., General Religious Science
RUPP, H.-K., Political Science
SCHILLER, TH., Political Science
ZIMMERMANN, H.-P., European Ethnology

Department of Theology (Alte Universität, Lahntor 3, 35032 Marburg; tel. (6421) 2822441; fax (6421) 2828968; e-mail dekan05@mailer.uni-marburg.de):

AVEMARIE, F., New Testament
BARTH, H.-M., Systematic Theology
BIENERT, W., Church History
DABROCK, P., Social Ethics
DRESSLER, B., Practical Theology
ELSAS, C., Religious History
JEREMIAS, J., Old Testament
KAISER, J.-C., Church History
KESSLER, R., Old Testament
KOCH, G., Christian Archaeology
KORSCH, D., Systematic Theology
MARTIN, G. M., Practical Theology
NETHÖFEL, W., Social Ethics
PINGGERA, K., Church History
SCHNEIDER, H., Church History
SCHWEBEL, H., Religious Communication
STANDHARTINGER, A., New Testament
WAGNER-RAU, H., Practical Theology

PHILOSOPHISCH-THEOLOGISCHE HOCHSCHULE—THEOLOGISCHE FAKULTÄT, ST AUGUSTIN

Arnold-Janssen-Str. 30, 53754 St Augustin
Telephone: (2241) 237222
E-mail: pth.rektor@steyler.de
Internet: www.philtheol-augustin.de
Founded 1965
State control
Chancellor: Dr ANTONIO PERNIA
Vice-Chancellor: Dr BERND WERLE
Rector: Prof. Dr JOACHIM G. PIEPKE
Vice-Rector: Prof. Dr PETER RAMERS
Librarian: GUIDO HACKELBUSCH
Number of students: 172

PHILOSOPHISCH-THEOLOGISCHE HOCHSCHULE DER SALESIANER DON BOSCOS BENEDIKTBEUERN

Don-Bosco-Str. 1, 83671 Benediktbeuern
Telephone: (57) 88201
Fax: (57) 88249
E-mail: info@pth-bb.de
Internet: www.pth-bb.de
Founded 1931

Private control
Chancellor: Dr PASCUAL CHÁVEZ
Rector: Prof. Dr LOTHAR BILY
Vice-Rector: Prof. Dr NORBERT WOLFF
Head Librarian: Dr PHILIPP GAHN
Number of students: 600

PHILOSOPHISCH-THEOLOGISCHE HOCHSCHULE VALLENDAR GMBH

Pallottistr. 3, 56179 Vallendar
Telephone: (261) 64020
Fax: (261) 6402300
E-mail: sfein@thv.de
Internet: www.pthv.de
Founded 1896
Private control
Chancellor: JACOB NAMPUDAKAM
Rector: Prof. Dr PAUL RHEINBAY
Vice-Rector: Prof. Dr FRANK WEIDNER
Vice-Rector: Prof. Dr JOACHIM SCHMIEDL
Library of 135,000 vols, 228 current periodicals, 18 incunabula

DEANS
Faculty of Theology: Prof. Dr JOACHIM SCHMIEDL
Faculty of Nursing Science: Prof. Dr FRANK WEIDNER

RHEINISCH-WESTFÄLISCHE TECHNISCHE HOCHSCHULE AACHEN

Templergraben 55, 52056 Aachen
Telephone: (241) 801
Fax: (241) 8092312
E-mail: international@zhv.rwth-aachen.de
Internet: www.rwth-aachen.de
Founded 1870 as Polytechnikum, attained univ. status 1880
Academic year: October to September
Rector: Prof. Dr.-Ing. ERNST M. SCHMACHTENBERG
Vice-Rector for Education: Prof. Dr.rer.nat. ALOYS KRIEG
Vice-Rector for Human Resources: Prof. HEATHER HOFMEISTER
Vice-Rector for Industry and Business Relations: Prof. Dr.-Ing. Dipl.-Wirt. Ing. GÜNTHER SCHUH
Vice-Rector for Research: Prof. Dr. med. ROLF ROSSAINT
Chancellor: MANFRED NETTEKOVEN
Head of Int. Office: Dr HEIDE NADERER
Head of Public Relations Office: TONI WIMMER
Head of Technology Transfer and Research Funding: Dr REGINA OERTEL
Librarian: Dr ULRIKE EICH
Library: see under Libraries and Archives
Number of teachers: 4,248
Number of students: 33,000

DEANS
Faculty of Architecture: Prof. PETER J. RUSSELL
Faculty of Arts and Humanities: Prof. Dr PAUL HILL
Faculty of Civil Engineering: Prof. Dr EKKEHARD WENDLER
Faculty of Business and Economics: Prof. Dr MICHAEL BASTIAN
Faculty of Electrical Engineering and Information Technology: Prof. Dr. MICHAEL VORLÄNDER
Faculty of Georesources and Materials Engineering: Prof. Dr KARL BERNHARD FRIEDRICH
Faculty of Mathematics, Computer Science and Natural Sciences: Prof. Dr SIMON
Faculty of Mechanical Engineering: Prof. Dr KLAUS HENNING
Faculty of Medicine: Prof. Dr JOHANNES NOTH

PROFESSORS

Faculty of Architecture (Schinkelstr. 1, 52056 Aachen; tel. (241) 8095000809; fax (241) 8092237; e-mail dekan@architektur .rwth-aachen.de; internet arch.rwth-aachen .de):

BAUM, M., Design Construction
BRUCHHAUS, G., District Planning and Design
COERSMEIER, U., Interior Design
HOFFMANN, H., Visual Form
HUMBLÉ, F., Building Planning and Design
JANSEN, M., History of Urban Devt
KADA, K., Building Design and Function
KRAUSE, C., Landscape Ecology and Landscape Design
LAUENSTEIN, H., Open Space and Landscape Planning
MARKSCHIES, A., History of Art
NICOLIC, V., Building Construction and Design
PIEPER, J., History of Architecture and Conservation
RUOFF, J., Environment, Services and Design
RUSSELL, P., Computer-Aided Design
SCHMIDT, H., Conservation
SCHNEIDER, H. N., Building Construction and Design
SCHULZE, M., Sculpture
SELLE, K., Planning Theory and Town Planning
TRAUTZ, M., Building Construction (Structural Design)
VAN DEN BERGH, W., Housing and Residential Devt
VINKEN, G., Theory of Architecture
WACHTEN, K., Urban Design and Country Planning

Faculty of Arts and Humanities (Kármánstr. 17–19, 52056 Aachen; tel. (241) 8096002; fax (241) 8092334; e-mail adrian.leipold@fb7 .rwth-aachen.de; internet www.rwth-aachen .de/fb7):

BEIER, R., Applied Linguistics
BEIN, T., Medieval German Language and Literature
DERINGER, L., English and American Language and Literature
ERTLER, K., Romance Languages and Literatures
ESSER, A., Philosophy
FICK, M., German Literature
GELLHAUS, A., German Literature
GILLMAYR-BUCHER, S., Biblical Studies
HAMMERICH, K., Sociology
HEINEN, A., Modern and Contemporary History
HILL, P. B., Sociology
HORCH, H.-O., German and Jewish Literature
HÖRNING, K.-H., Sociology
HORNKE, L., Psychology
JÄGER, L., Linguistics and Media Theory
JAKOBS, E.-M., Communication Science
KEIL, G., Theoretical Philosophy
KELLERWESSEL, W., Philosophy
KERNER, M., Medieval and Modern History
KÖNIG, H., Political Science
LEWATER, D., Education Science
LIEDTKE, F., German Language
LUEKE, U., Theology
MEY, H., Sociology
MEYER, G., Theology
MEYER, P. G., English Linguistics (Synchronic)
MICHELSEN, U. A., Education
MOESSNER, L., English Linguistics and Medieval Studies
MÜSSELER, J., Work Psychology and Cognition
NEUSCHAEFER, A., Romance Languages and Literatures
NIEHR, T., German Language
PANGRITZ, A., Theology

RICHTER, E., Political Science
ROTTE, R., Political Science
SCHERBERICH, K., History
SCHMITZ, S., German Language
SPIJKERS, W., Psychology
STETTER, C., Germanic Linguistics
VON HAEHLING, R., History
WENZEL, P., English Literature

Faculty of Civil Engineering (Mies-van-der-Rohe-Str. 1, 52074 Aachen; tel. (241) 8025075; fax (241) 8022201; e-mail dekanat@fb3.rwth-aachen.de; internet www .rwth-aachen.de/fb3):

BECKMANN, K. J., Urban and Transport Planning
BENNING, W., Geodesy
BRAMERSHUBER, W., Building Materials Research
BRUNK, M. F., Construction Management and Building Services
DOETSCH, P., Waste Management
FELDMANN, M., Steel and Light-Metal Construction
GÜLDENPFENNING, J., Mechanics and Building Construction
HEGGER, J., Structural Concrete
KÖNGETER, J., Hydraulic Engineering and Water Resources Management
MESKOURIS, K., Structural Statistics and Dynamics
NACKEN, H., Engineering Hydrology
OSEBOLD, R., Construction Management—Project Management
PINNEKAMP, J., Sanitary and Waste Engineering
RAUPACH, M., Building Materials Research
REICHMUTH, J., Airport and Air-Transportation Research
STEINAUER, B., Road Engineering, Earth Works and Tunnelling
WENDLER, E., Transport Economics, Railway Engineering and Railway Operations
ZIEGLER, M., Geotechnics in Civil Engineering

Faculty of Economics (Kármánstr. 17–19, 52056 Aachen; tel. (241) 8096000; fax (241) 8092166; e-mail dekanat-fb8@rwth-aachen .de; internet www.wiwi.rwth-aachen.de):

BASTIAN, M., Business Information Systems and Operations
BRETTEL, M., Business Admin. and Sciences for Engineers and Scientists (Centre for Entrepreneurship)
BREUER, W., Business Administration (Finance)
DYCKHOFF, H., Business Theory, Environmental Management and Industrial Controlling
FEESS, E., Economics (Microeconomics)
HARMS, P., Macroeconomics
HÖMBURG, R., Business Taxation and Auditing
HUBER, C., Civil Law, Business and Labour Law
LORZ, O., Int. Economics
MÖLLER, H. P., Business Admin., Accounting and Finance
REIMERS, K., Business Information Systems (Electronic Business)
SCHRÖDER, H.-H., Technology and Innovation Management
SEBASTIAN, H.-J., Optimization of Distribution Networks
STEFFENHAGEN, H., Corporate Policy and Marketing
THOMES, P., Economic and Social History
VON NITZSCH, R., Business Management
WOYWODE, M., Int. Management

Faculty of Electrical Engineering and Information Technology (Muffeter Weg 3, 52074 Aachen; tel. (241) 8027572; fax (241) 8022343; e-mail dekanat@fb6.rwth-aachen .de; internet www.fb6.rwth-aachen.de):

AACH, T., Image Processing
ASCHEID, G., Integrated Signal Processing Systems
BEMMERL, T., Operation Systems and Scalable Computing
DE DONCKER, R., Power Electronic and Electrical Drives
HAMEYER, K., Electrical Mechanics
HAUBRICH, H.-J., Power Systems and Power Economics
HEINEN, S., Integrated Analogue Circuits
JANSEN, R., Electromagnetic Theory
KAISER, W., History of Engineering and Technology
KRAISS, K.-F., Technical Informatics and Computer Science
KURZ, H., Semiconductor Technology
LEONHARDT, K. S., Medical Information Technology
LEUPERS, R., Software for Systems on Silicon
MAEHOENEN, P. H., Wireless Networks
MATHAR, R., Information Theory
MEYR, H., Integrated Signal Processing Systems
MOKWA, W., Materials in Electrical Engineering
NOLL, T. G., Electrical Engineering and Computer Systems
OHM, J.-R., Communications Engineering
SAUER, U., Electrochemical Energy Conversion
SCHNETTLER, A., High Voltage Technology
VARY, P., Communication Systems and Data Processing
VESCAN, A., GaN Device Technology
VORLÄNDER, M., Technical Acoustics
WALKE, B., Communications Networks
WASER, R., Materials in Electrical Materials

Faculty of Geo-Resources and Materials Engineering (Intzestr. 1, 52056 Aachen; tel. (241) 8095665; fax (241) 8092370; e-mail dekanat-fb5@rwth-aachen.de; internet www .rwth-aachen.de):

Section of Geoscience:

AZZAM, R., Engineering Geology and Hydrogeology
BREUER, H., Geography, Economic and Applied Geography
CLAUSER, C., Applied Geophysics
FLAJS, G., Geology and Palaeontology
GRÄF, P., Geography, Physical Geography and Climatology
HAVLIK, G., Geography, Physical Geography and Climatology
HEGER, G., Crystallography
KRAMM, U., Mineralogy and Geochemistry
KUKLA, P., Geology and Palaeontology
LEHMKUHL, F., Geography, Physical Geography and Geoecology
LITTKE, R., Geology and Geochemistry of Petroleum and Coal
MEYER, M., Mineralogy and Economic Geology
ROTH, G., Applied Crystallography and Mineralogy
STANJEK, H., Clay Mineralogy
URAI, J. L., Structural Geology, Tectonics and Geomechanics

Section of Metallurgy and Materials Technology:

BLECK, W., Materials Science of Steels
BUERIG-POLACZ, A., Foundry Technology
CONRADT, R., Glass and Ceramic Composites
EMMERICH, H., Computational Materials Engineering
EPPLE, U., Process Control Engineering
FRIEDRICH, B., Process Metallurgy and Metal Recycling
GOTTSTEIN, G., Physical Metallurgy and Metal Physics

KAYSSER, W. A., Materials Science of Non-ferrous Metals
KÖHNE, H., Heat and Mass Transfer
KOPP, R., Metal Forming
ODOJ, R., Materials Chemistry
PFEIFER, H., High Temperature Engineering
SCHNEIDER, J., Materials Chemistry
SENK, D. G., Metallurgy of Iron and Steel
TELLE, R., Ceramics and Refractories

Section of Mining Engineering:

FRENZ, W., Mining and Environment
HEIL, J., Coking, Briquetting and Thermal Waste Treatment
MARTENS, P. N., Mining Engineering
NIEHAUS, K., Excavation and Mining Equipment
NIEMANN-DELIUS, C., Surface Mining and Drilling
PRETZ, T., Processing and Recycling of Solid Waste Materials
PREUSSE, A., Mine Surveying, Mining Subsidence Engineering and Geophysics in Mining
SEELIGER, A., Mining and Metallurgical Machine Engineering
WOTRUBA, H., Mineral Processing

Faculty of Mathematics, Computer Science and Natural Sciences (Templergraben 64, 52064 Aachen; tel. (241) 8094500; fax (241) 8092124; e-mail dekan@fb1.rwth-aachen.de; internet www.fb1.rwth-aachen.de):

ALBRECHT, M., Organic Chemistry
BALLMANN, J., Mechanics
BAUMANN, H., Chemistry
BEGINN, U., Macromolecular and Supramolecular Chemistry
BEMELMANS, V., Mathematics
BENEKE, M., Theoretical Physics
BERGER, C., Experimental Physics
BERLAGE, T., Computer Science (Life Science Informatics)
BERNREUTNER, W., Theoretical Physics
BISCHOF, C., Computer Science (Scientific Computing)
BLUEMICH, B., Macromolecular Chemistry/NMR
BLÜGEL, S., Theoretical Physics
BOCK, H. H., Applied Statistics
BOEHM, A., Experimental Physics
BOHRMANN, J., Zoology and Human Biology
BOLM, C., Chemistry
BORCHERS, J., Computer Science (Media Computing)
BRAEUNIG, P.-M., Developmental Biology and Morphology of Animals
BRUECKEL, T., Experimental Physics
CAPELLMANN, H., Theoretical Physics
CONRATH, U., Plant Biochemistry
CRAMER, E., Applied Statistics
DAHMEN, W., Mathematics
DEDERICHS, P. H., Theoretical Physics
DOHM, V., Theoretical Physics
DRONSKOWSKI, R., Theoretical and Synthetic Solid-State Chemistry
ELLING, L., Biomaterial Sciences
ENDERS, D., Organic Chemistry
ENGLERT, U., Inorganic Chemistry
ENSS, V., Mathematics
ESSER, K.-H., Applied Mathematics
FELD, L., Experimental Physics
FISCHER, R., Molecular Biotechnology
FLEISCHHAUER, J., Theoretical Chemistry
FLÜGGE, G., Experimental Physics
FRENTZEN, M., Botany
GAIS, H.-J., Organic Chemistry
GÄRTNER, F., Computer Science (Dependable Systems)
GIESL, J., Computer Science
GRAEDEL, E., Mathematical Foundations of Computer Science
GÜNTHERODT, G., Experimental Physics
HARTMEIER, W., Biotechnology
HEINKE, H., Experimental Physics
HERMANN, P., Mathematics

HISS, G., Mathematics
HÖLDERICH, W., Fuel Chemistry
HROMKOVIC, J., Computer Science (Algorithms and Complexity)
IBACH, H., Experimental Physics
INDERMARK, K., Computer Science (Programming Languages)
JANK, G., Engineering Mathematics
JARKE, M., Computer Science (Information Systems)
JONGEN, H. TH., Mathematics
KAMPS, U., Statistics
KLEE, D., Biomaterials
KLEMRADT, U., Experimental Physics
KLINNER, U., Applied Microbiology
KOBBELT, L., Computer Science (Computer Graphics and Multimedia)
KÖLLE, U., Organometallic and Coordination Chemistry of the Transition Metals
KOWALEWSKI, S., Computer Science (Embedded Systems)
KREIBIG, U., Experimental Physics
KREUZALER, F., Botany/Molecular Genetics
KRIEG, A., Mathematics
KULL, H.-J., Theoretical Physics
LAKEMEYER, G., Computer Science (Knowledge-Based Systems)
LEITNER, W., Technical Chemistry and Petrochemistry
LENGELER, B., Experimental Physics
LIAUW, M., Technical Chemistry and Reaction Engineering
LICHTER, H., Computer Science (Software Construction)
LÜCHOW, A., Theoretical and Computational Chemistry
LUEKEN, H., Inorganic Chemistry
LUKSCH, P., Computer Science
LÜTH, H., Experimental Physics
MAIER-PAAPE, S., Mathematics
MARTIN, M., Physical Chemistry
MERKE, I., Physical Chemistry
MÖLLER, M., Macromolecular Chemistry
MÜLLER-KRUMBHAAR, H., Theoretical Physics
NAGEL, M., Computer Science (Software Engineering)
NEY, H., Computer Science (Pattern Recognition)
NOELLE, S., Mathematics
OKUDA, J., Organometallic Chemistry
PAHLINGS, H., Mathematics
PLESKEN GEN. WIGGER, W., Mathematics
PRIEFER, U., Biology (Soil Ecology)
PRINZ, W., Computer Science (Cooperation Systems)
RAABE, G., Theoretical Chemistry
RAUHUT, B., Statistics and Mathematics of Economics
RICHTERING, W., Physical Chemistry
ROSSMANITH, P., Computer Science (Theoretical Computer Science)
SALZER, A., Organometallic Chemistry
SCHAEL, S., Experimental Physics
SCHÄFFER, A., Environmental Biology and Chemodynamics
SCHMITZ, D., Experimental Physics
SCHOELLER, H., Theoretical Physics
SCHOLLWOECK, U., Theoretical Physics
SCHROEDER, U., Computer Science (Computer-Based Learning)
SCHUPHAN, I., Biology (Ecology, Ecotoxicology, Ecochemistry)
SCHWEIGERT, CH., Theoretical Physics
SEIDEL, T., Computer Science (Data Mining)
SELKE, W., Theoretical Physics
SIELING, D., Physics
SIMON, U., Inorganic Chemistry and Nanomaterials
SLUSARENKO, A., Plant Physiology
SPANIOL, O., Computer Science (Communication Systems)
STAHL, W., Physical Chemistry
STAPF, S., Macromolecular Chemistry

THOMAS, W., Computer Science (Logic and Discrete Systems)
TRIESCH, E., Mathematics
URBAN, K., Experimental Physics
VON DER MOSEL, H., Mathematics
VON PLESSEN, G., Experimental Physics
WAGNER, H., Biology
WALCHER, S., Mathematics
WEINHOLD, E., Bio-Organic Chemistry
WENZL, H., Experimental Physics
WIEGNER, M., Mathematics
WOLF, K., Microbiology
WUTTIG, M., Experimental Physics
ZEIDLER, M., Physical Chemistry

Faculty of Mechanical Engineering (Eilfschornsteinstr. 18, 52062 Aachen; tel. (241) 8095305; fax (241) 8092144; e-mail dekanat-fb4@rwth-aachen.de; internet www.fb4.rwth-aachen.de):

ABEL, D., Automatic Control
ALLES, W., Flight Dynamics
BEHR, M. A., Computational Analysis of Technical Systems
BEISS, P., Materials Technology
BOBZIN, K., Surface Technology, Materials Science
BOHN, D., Steam and Gas Turbines
BRECHER, C., Machine Tools
BÜCHS, Z., Bioprocess Engineering
CORVES, B., Mechanism Theory and Dynamics of Machines
DELLMANN, T., Rail Vehicles and Materials-Handling Technology
DILTHEY, U., Welding Technology
EL-MAGD, E. A., Engineering Materials
FELDHUSEN, J., Engineering Design
GOLD, P. W., Machine Elements and Design
GRIES, T., Textile Engineering
GRUENEFELD, G., Laser Technology
HABERSTROH, E., Synthetic Rubber Technology
HENNING, K., Methods of Cybernetics in Engineering Sciences
ITSKOV, M., Continuum Machines
KLOCKE, F., Manufacturing Technology
KNEER, R., Heat and Mass Transfer
KUGELER, K., Reactor Safety and Reactor Technology
LOOSEN, P., Technology of Optical Systems
LUCAS, K., Technical Thermodynamics
MAIER, H.-R., Ceramic Components in Mechanical Engineering
MARQUARDT, W., Process Systems Engineering
MELIN, T., Chemical Engineering
MICHAELI, W., Plastics Processing
MODIGELL, M., Mechanical Unit Operations
MURRENHOFF, H., Fluid Power Drives and Control
NIEHUIS, R., Jet Propulsion and Turbo Machinery
OLIVIER, H., High-Temperature Gas Dynamics
PETERS, N., Technical Mechanics
PFENNING, A., Thermal Unit Operations
PISCHINGER, S., Internal Combustion Engines
PITZ-PAAL, R., Solar Technology
POPRAWE, R., Laser Technology
REIMERDES, H.-G., Aerospace and Lightweight Structures
SCHLICK, C., Industrial Engineering and Ergonomics
SCHMACHTENBERG, E., Plastics Materials Technology
SCHMITT, R., Metrology and Quality Management
SCHOMBURG, W. K., Construction and Devt of Microsystems
SCHROEDER, W., Fluid Dynamics
SCHUH, G., Production Engineering
SCHULZ, W., Laser Production Processes
SINGHEISER, L., Materials for Energy Technology

STOLTEN, D., Fuel Cells

WALLENTOWITZ, H., Automotive Engineering

WEICHERT, D., General Mechanics

Faculty of Medicine (Pauwelstr. 30, 52074 Aachen; tel. (241) 8089167; e-mail dekanat@ukaachen.de; internet www.ukaachen.de):

AMUNTS, K., Structural-Functional Brain Mapping

AUTSCHBACH, R., Thoracic and Cardiovascular Surgery

BEIER, H., Anatomy and Reproductive Biology

BERNHAGEN, J., Biochemistry

BÜLL, U., Nuclear Medicine

CONRADS, G., Medical Microbiology

DIEDRICH, P., Orthodontics

DOTT, W., Hygienics and Environmental Medicine

EBLE, M. J., Radiotherapy

ELLING, I., Biomaterial Science

ELLRICH, J., Neurosurgery

FAHLKE, C., Physiology

FINK, G., Cognitive Neurology

FLOEGE, J., Internal Medicine

GAUGGEL, G., Medical Psychology and Medical Sociology

GERZER, R., Aerospace Medicine

GILSBACH, J., Neurosurgery

GRESSNER, A. M., Clinical Chemistry and Pathobiochemistry

GREVEN, J., Pharmacology and Toxicology

GRÜNDER, G., Experimental Neuropsychiatry

GÜNTHER, R., Diagnostic Radiology

HANRATH, P., Internal Medicine

HEIMANN, G., Paediatrics

HEINRICH, P., Biochemistry

HERPERTZ-DAHLMANN, B., Child and Adolescent Psychiatry and Psychotherapy

HILGERS, R.-D., Medical Statistics

HÖRNCHEN, H., Paediatrics

HUBER, W., Neurolinguistics

JAHNEN-DECHENT, W., Cell and Molecular Biology at Interfaces

JAKSE, G., Urology

KAUFMANN, P., Anatomy

KNÜCHEL-CLARKE, C., Pathology

KORR, H., Anatomy

KRAUS, T., Occupational Medicine

KUHLEN, H., Anaesthesiology

KÜPPER, W., Laboratory Animal Science

LAMPERT, F., Conservative Dentistry, Periodontics and Preventive Dentistry

LENDLEIN, A., Technology and Devt of Medical Products

LEONHARDT, S., Medical Informatics Technology

LUECKHOFF, A., Physiology

LUESCHER, B., Biochemistry and Molecular Biology

LUETTICKEN, R., Medical Microbiology

MARX, R., Dental Materials

MATERN, H., Internal Medicine

MATHIAK, K., Behavioural Psychobiology

MERK, H. F., Dermatology

MURKEN, A. H., History of Medicine and Hospitals

NEULEN, J., Gynaecological Endocrinology and Reproductive Medicine

NEUSCHAEFER-RUBE, C., Phoniatrics and Pedaudiology

NIENDORF, T., Experimental MR-Imaging

NIETHARD, F. U., Orthopaedics

NOTH, J., Neurology

OSIEKA, R., Internal Medicine

PAAR, O., Surgery

PALLUA, N., Plastic Surgery, Hand and Reconstructive Surgery

RATH, W., Gynaecology

RIEDIGER, D., Oral, Maxillofacial and Plastic Facial Surgery

RINK, L., Immunology

RITTER, K., Virology

ROSSAINT, R., Anaesthesiology

SCHMALZIG, G., Pharmacology and Toxicology

SCHMITZ-RODE, T., Diagnostic Radiology

SCHNEIDER, F., Psychiatrics and Psychotherapy

SCHUMPELICK, V., Surgery

SEGHAYE, M.-C., Paediatric Cardiology

SPIEKERMANN, H., Prosthodontics

SPITZER, K., Medical Informatics

THRON, A., Neuroradiology

VÁSQUEZ-JIMÉNEZ, J., Paediatric Heart Surgery

WALTER, P., Opthalmology

WEBER, C., Cardiovascular Molecular Biology

WEIS, J., Neuropathology

WELLMANN, A., Pathology (Cytology)

WESTHOFEN, M., Otorhinolaryngology

WILLMES-VON HINCKELDEY, K., Neuropsychology

ZENKE, M., Biomedical Engineering and Cell Biology

ZERRES, K., Human Genetics

AFFILIATED INSTITUTIONS

Aachen Global Academy GmbH: Kármánstr. 17, 52056 Aachen; Dir Dr CHRISTOPH K. HEINEN.

Aachener Demonstrationslabor für integrierte Produktionstechnik GmbH: Seilbachstr. 25, 52062 Aachen; Dir Dr WERNER FISCHER.

ACCES eV—Materials + Processes: Intzestr. 5, 52072 Aachen; Dir ROBERT GUNTLIN.

Deutsches Wollforschungsinstitut eV (German Wool Research Institute): Veltmanplatz 8, 52062 Aachen; Dir Prof. Dr MARTIN MÖLLER.

Forschungsinstitut für Rationalisierung (Institute for Research in Rationalization): Pontdriesch 14–16, 52062 Aachen; Dir Prof. Dr HOLGER LUCZAK.

Forschungsinstitut für Wasser- und Abfallwirtschaft (Research Institute for Water and Waste Management): Mies-van-der-Rohe-Str. 17, 52062 Aachen; Dir FRIEDRICH-WILHELM BOLLE.

Forschungsstelle Technisch-Wirtschaftliche Unternehmensstrukturen der Stahlindustrie (Research Department for Technical and Economic Corporate Structures in the Steel Industry): Intzestr. 1, 52072 Aachen; Dir Prof. Dr WINFRIED DAHL.

Fraunhofer-Institut für Produktionstechnologie (Fraunhofer Institute for Production Technology): Steinbachstr. 17, 52074 Aachen; Dir Prof. Dr G. SCHUH.

Freunde und Förderer der RWTH Aachen: Wüllnerstr. 9, 52062 Aachen; em. Prof. ROLAND WALTER.

Institut für Kunststoffverarbeitung in Industrie und Handwerk (Institute for Plastics Technology): Ponstr. 49–55, 52062 Aachen; Dir Prof. Dr WALTER MICHAELI.

Institut für Prozess- und Anwendungstechnik Keramik (Institute for Process and Application Technology in Ceramics): Dir Prof. Dr HORST R. MAIER.

Prüf- und Entwicklungsinstitut für Abwassertechik: Mies-van-der-Rohe-Str. 1, 52074 Aachen; Dir Dr ELMAR DORGELOH.

Technische Akademie, Wuppertal eV: Hubertusallee 18, 42117 Wuppertal; Dir Dr MARTIN STACHOWSKE.

WZLfoum an der RWTH Aachen: Steinbachstr. 53, 52074 Wuppertal; Dir Dr TORSTEN KURR.

RHEINISCHE FRIEDRICH-WILHELMS-UNIVERSITÄT BONN

53012 Bonn

Regina-Pacis-Weg 3, 53113 Bonn

Telephone: (228) 2870

Fax: (228) 737722

E-mail: presse@uni-bonn.de

Internet: www3.uni-bonn.de

Founded 1786, refounded 1818

State control

Academic year: October to September

Rector: Prof. Dr JÜRGEN FOHRMANN

Chancellor: Dr REINHARDT LUTZ

Deputy Rector for Finances: Prof. Dr ARMIN B. CREMERS

Deputy Rector for Public and International Relations: Prof. Dr CHRISTIANE K. KUHL

Deputy Rector for Research and Academic Staff Development: Prof. Dr JÜRGEN VON HAGEN

Deputy Rector for Teaching, Studies, and Studies Reform: Prof. Dr VOLKMAR GIESELMANN

Library Dir: Dr RENATE VOGT

Library: see under Libraries and Archives

Number of teachers: 4,030

Number of students: 31,200

Publications: *Academica Bonnensia, Alma Mater, Bonner Akademische Reden, Bonner Universitäts-Nachrichten "Forsch"* (4 a year), *Bonn University News International* (in English, 1 a year), *Politeia, Studium Universale*

DEANS

Faculty of Agriculture: Prof. Dr KARL SCHELLANDER

Faculty of Arts: Prof. Dr GÜNTHER SCHULZ

Faculty of Catholic Theology: Prof. Dr CLAUDE OZANKOM

Faculty of Law and Economics: Prof. Dr KLAUS SANDMANN

Faculty of Mathematics and Natural Sciences: Prof. Dr ULF-G. MEIßNER

Faculty of Medicine: Prof. Dr THOMAS KLOCKGETHER

Faculty of Protestant Theology: Prof. Dr GÜNTER RÖHSER

PROFESSORS

Faculty of Agriculture (Meckenheimer Allee 174, 59115 Bonn; tel. (228) 732866; fax (228) 732140; e-mail landwirtschaftliche .fakultaet@uni-bonn.de; internet www.lwf .uni-bonn.de):

BERG, E., Agricultural Economics

DEHNE, H., Phytopathology

FÖRSTNER, W., Photogrammetry

GALENSA, R., Food Science and Food Chemistry

GOLDBACH, H., Plant Nutrition

HELFRICH, H.-P., Practical Mathematics

ILK, K. H., Satellite-Assisted Physical Geodesy

KÖPKE, U., Ecological Agriculture

KÜHBAUCH, W., Plant Breeding

KUNZ, B., Food Technology and Food Biotechnology

KUTSCH, TH., Agricultural and Domestic Sociology

LÉON, J., Plant Production and Breeding

NOGA, G., Fruit and Vegetable Production

SCHELLANDER, K., Animal Breeding

SCHIEFER, G., Agricultural Economy

SCHNABL, H., Botany

STEHLE, P., Nutrition

WEIß, E., House and Town Planning

WITTMANN, D., Agricultural Zoology and Ecology

Faculty of Arts (Am Hof 1, 53113 Bonn; tel. (228) 737295; fax (228) 735986; internet www .philfak.uni-bonn.de):

BONNET, A.-M., History of Art

BREDENKAMP, J., Psychology
BRÜGGEN, E., Germanic Studies
COX, H. L., Folklore
DAHLMANN, D., East European History
DUMKE, D., Psychology
EHLERS, E., Social and Economic Geography
FEHN, K., Historical Geography
FISCHER, E., Musicology
FOHRMANN, J., Germanic Studies
GALSTERER, H., Ancient History
GROTZ, R., Geography
HESS, W., Communication and Phonetics
HILDEBRAND, K., Medieval and Modern History
HILGENHEGER, N., Education
HIRDT, W., Romance Philology
HOGREBE, W., Philosophy
HONNEFELDER, L., Philosophy
HÖNNIGHAUSEN, L., English Philology
KAISER, K., Political Science
KARSTEN, D., Political Science
KEIPERT, H., Slavonic Studies
KELZ, H., Phonetics
KLAUER, K. C., Psychology
KLEIN, TH., Germanic Studies
KLIMKEIT, H.-J., Comparative Religion
KOHRT, M., Germanic Studies
KÖLZER, T., Medieval and Modern History, Archival Science
KREINER, J., Japanology
KUBIN, W., Sinology
KUHN, A., History
KÜHNHARDT, L., Political Science
LADENTHIN, V., Education
LANGE, W. D., Romance Philology
LAUREYS, M., Philology
MECHLING, H., Sports
MIELSCH, H., Archaeology
NEUBAUER, W., Psychology
OEHLER, D., Comparative Science of Literature
PANTZER, P., Japanology
POHL, H., Constitutional History, Economics, Social History
POTTHOFF, W., Slavonic Studies
PREM, H. J., Ethnology
REICHL, K., English Philology
RÖßLER, U., Egyptology
ROSEN, K., Ancient History
SCHALLER, H.-J., Sports
SCHMITT, C., Roman Philology
SCHNEIDER, H., Germanic Studies
SCHOLZ, O. B., Psychology
SCHWARZ, H.-P., Political Science
SIMEK, R., Germanic Studies
STUHLMANN-LAEISZ, R., Logic and Foundations
WEEDE, E., Sociology
WILD, S., Semitic Philology
WINIGER, M., Geography
WOLF, H. J., Romance Philology
ZIMMER, ST., Linguistics
ZWIERLEIN, O., Classical Philology

Faculty of Catholic Theology (An der Schlosskirche 2–4, Bonn; tel. (228) 737344; fax (228) 735985):

FABRY, H. J., Old Testament
FINDEIS, H.-J., New Testament
FÜRST, W., Pastoral Theology
GERHARDS, A., Liturgy
HOPPE, R., New Testament Science
HOSSFELD, F.-L., Old Testament Science
HÖVER, G., Moral Theology
LÜDECKE, N., Canon Law
MENKE, K.-H., Dogmatics, Theological Propaedeutics
MUSCHIOL, G., Church History
SCHÖLLGEN, G., Ancient Church History and Patrology
SCHULZ, M., Dogmatics
SONNEMANS, H., Fundamental Theology

Faculty of Law and Economics (Adenauerallee 24–42, 53113 Bonn; tel. (228) 739101; fax (228) 739100; e-mail dekanat@jura .uni-bonn.de; internet www.jura.uni-bonn .de):

BÖSE, D., Political Economy
BREITUNG, J., Economics
BREUER, R., Public Law
DI FABIO, U., Public Law
DOLZER, R., German and International Public Law
FLEISCHER, H., Civil Law
HERDEGEN, M., Public Law
HILLGRUBER, CHR., Public Law
KINDHÄUSER, U., Criminal Law
KNÜTEL, R., Roman and Civil Law
KÖNDGEN, J., Civil Law
KORTE, B., Operational Research
KRÄKEL, M., Business Administration
LÖWER, W., Public Law
MOLDOVANU, B., Economic Theory, Mathematical Theory of Economics
NEUMANN, M., Economic Policy
PAEFFGEN, H.-U., Criminal Law
PIETZCKER, J., Public Law
ROTH, W.-H., Civil Law, International Private Law, and Comparative Law
SANDMANN, K., Economic Policy
SCHILKEN, E., Civil Law
SCHMIDT-PREUß, M., Public Law
SCHWEIZER, U., Economic Policy
SHAKED, A., Economic Policy
THEISSEN, E., Business Administration
VERREL, T., Criminology
VON HAGEN, J., Economics
WAGNER, G., Civil Law
WALTERMANN, R., Civil Law
ZACZYK, R., Criminal Law, Philosophy of Law
ZIMMER, D., Commercial Law
ZIMMERMANN, K., Economic Policy

Faculty of Mathematics and Natural Sciences (Wegelerstr. 10, 53113 Bonn; tel. (228) 732233; fax (228) 733892; e-mail dekan@iam .uni-bonn.de; internet www .math-nat-fakultaet.uni-bonn.de):

ALBEVERIO, S., Mathematics
ALT, H. W., Mathematics
AUMANN, D., Chemistry
BALLMANN, W., Mathematics
BARGON, J., Physical Chemistry
BARTHLOTT, W., Botanics
BLECKMANN, H., Zoology
BRIESKORN, E., Mathematics
CREMERS, A. B., Informatics
DE BOER, K., Astronomy
DIETZ, K., Theoretical Physics
DIKAU, R., Geography
DÖTZ, K. H., Organic Chemistry
ECKMILLER, R., Informatics
EHLERS, E., Social and Economic Geography
FREHSE, J., Applied Mathematics
GLOMBITZA, K.-W., Pharmaceutical Biology
GRIEBEL, M., Scientific Computing
GROTZ, R., Geography
HAMENSTÄDT, U., Mathematics
HARDER, G., Mathematics
HERZOG, V., Cell Biology
HILDEBRANDT, S., Mathematics
HILGER, E., Experimental Physics
HUBER, M. G., Theoretical Atomic Physics
KARPINSKI, M., Informatics
KELLER, R., Zoology
KILIAN, K., Experimental Atomic Physics
KIRFEL, A., Mineralogy
KLEIN, F., Experimental Physics
KLEMPT, E., Experimental Physics
LEISTNER, E., Pharmaceutical Biology
LIEB, I., Mathematics
MADER, W., Inorganic Chemistry
MAIER, K., Experimental Physics
MASCHUW, R., Atomic Physics
MEBOLD, U., Radio Astronomy
MENZ, G., Geography
MENZEL, D., Botany
MESCHEDE, D., Experimental Physics

MONIEN, H., Theoretical Physics
MÜLLER, W., Mathematics
NAHM, W., Mathematical Physics
NEUGEBAUER, H., Geophysics
NICKEL, P., Pharmaceutical Chemistry
NIECKE, E., Inorganic and Analytical Chemistry
NILLES, H. P., Theoretical Physics
PEYERIMHOFF, S., Theoretical Chemistry
RAITH, M., Geology and Petrology
SANDHAS, W., Theoretical Physics
SANDHOFF, K., Biochemistry
SAUER, K. P., Zoology and Ecological Studies
SCHOCH, B., Physics
SCHÖNHAGE, A., Informatics
SIMMER, C., Meteorology
SPETH, J., Theoretical Physics
STEFFENS, K. J., Pharmaceutical Technology
THEIN, J., Geology
TRÜPER, H. G., Microbiology
VÖGTLE, F., Chemistry
VON KOENIGSWALD, W., Palaeontology
WANDELT, K., Physical Chemistry
WANDREY, CH., Biotechnology
WERMES, N., Experimental Physics
WILLECKE, K., Genetics
WINIGER, M., Geography

Faculty of Medicine (Sigmund-Freud-Str. 25, Haus 23, 53105 Bonn-Venusberg; tel. (228) 28719200; fax (228) 28719211; e-mail med-deha@ukb.uni-bonn.de; internet www .med.uni-bonn.de):

BAUR, M. P., Medical Statistics
BIDLINGMAIER, F., Clinical Biochemistry
BIEBER, TH., Dermatology and Venereology
BIERSACK, H.-J., Nuclear Medicine
ELGER, C. E., Epileptology
EXNER, M., Hygiene
FRANZ, TH., Anatomy
GÖTHERT, M., Pharmacology, Toxicology
GROTE, J., Physiology
HANFLAND, P., Experimental Haematology
HANSIS, M. L., Clinical Quality Management
HERBERHOLD, C., Otorhinolaryngology
HIRNER, A., Surgery
HOEFT, A., Anaesthesiology
JÄGER, A., Dentistry
KOECK, B., Dentistry
LENTZE, M. J., Paediatrics
LIEDTKE, R., Psychosomatic Medicine and Psychotherapy
LÜDERITZ, B., Internal Medicine, Cardiology
MADEA, B., Forensic Medicine
MAIER, W., Psychiatry
MÜLLER, ST., Urology
NOLDEN, R., Dentistry
PFEIFER, U., Pathology, Pathological Anatomy
PROPPING, P., Human Genetics
REICH, R., Oral and Maxillofacial Surgery
SAUERBRUCH, T., Internal Medicine
SCHAAL, K. P., Medical Microbiology
SCHILD, H. H., Radiology
SCHILLING, K., Anatomy
SCHMITT, O., Orthopaedics
SCHOTT, H., History of Medicine
SCHRAMM, J., Neurosurgery
SEITZ, H. M., Medical Parasitology
SPITZNAS, M., Ophthalmology
VETTER, H., Internal Medicine
WAHL, G., Oral Surgery
WIESTLER, O., Neuropathology

Faculty of Protestant Theology (Am Hof 1, 53113 Bonn; tel. (228) 737366; fax (228) 735981):

BADER, G., Systematic Theology
HAUSCHILDT, E., Practical Theology
KINZIG, W., Church History
KREß, H., Systematic Theology, Social Ethics
MEYER-BLANCK, M., Theology Education

PANGRITZ, A., Systematic Theology
RÖHSER, G., New Testament
RÜTERSWÖRDEN, U., Old Testament
SCHMIDT-ROST, R., Practical Theology
STOCK, K., Systematic Theology
WOLTER, M., New Testament

RUHR-UNIVERSITÄT BOCHUM

POB 10 21 48, 44721 Bochum
Universitätsstr. 150, 44801 Bochum
Telephone: (234) 32201
Fax: (234) 3214201
E-mail: monika.sprung@uv.ruhr-uni-bochum
.de
Internet: www.ruhr-uni-bochum.de
Founded 1965
State control
Languages of instruction: German, English
Academic year: October to July
Chair.: JÜRGEN SCHLEGEL
Rector: Prof. Dr ELMAR W. WEILER
Chancellor: GERHARD MÖLLER
Vice-Rector for Research and Structure: Prof.
Dr ULF EYSEL
Vice-Rector for Teaching, Continuing Educa-
tion and Media: Prof. Dr UTA WILKENS
Vice-Rector for Young Scientists and Inter-
national Matters: Prof. Dr NILS METZLER-
NOLTE
Librarian: Dr ERDMUTE LAPP

Library of 2,000,000 vols
Number of teachers: 2,973
Number of students: 34,024

DEANS

Faculty of Biology and Biotechnology: Prof.
Dr F. NARBERHAUS
Faculty of Catholic Theology: Prof. Dr JOA-
CHIM WIEMEYER
Faculty of Chemistry and Biochemistry: Prof.
Dr DOMINIK MARX
Faculty of Civil and Environmental Engin-
eering: Prof. Dr Ing MARKUS THEWES
Faculty of East Asian Studies: Prof. Dr
REGINE MATHIAS
Faculty of Economics: Prof. Dr HELMUT KARL
Faculty of Electrical Engineering and Infor-
mation Technology: Prof. Dr GEORG
SCHMITZ
Faculty of Geosciences: Prof. Dr UTA HOHN
Faculty of History: Prof. Dr RICHARD HOPPE-
SAILER
Faculty of Law: Prof. Dr ADELHEID PUTTLER
Faculty of Mathematics: Prof. Dr GERHARD
KNIEPER
Faculty of Mechanical Engineering: Prof. Dr
Ing WERNER THEISEN
Faculty of Medicine: Prof. Dr KLAUS ÜBERLA
Faculty of Philology: Prof. Dr EVA WARTH
Faculty of Philosophy and Education: Prof.
Dr JOACHIM WIRTH
Faculty of Physics and Astronomy: Prof. Dr
UWE CZARNETZKI
Faculty of Protestant Theology: Prof. Dr
ISOLDE KARLE
Faculty of Psychology: Prof. Dr HEINRICH
WOTTAWA
Faculty of Social Sciences: Prof. Dr JÖRG
BOGUMIL
Faculty of Sports Science: Prof. Dr AUGUST
NEUMAIER

PROFESSORS

Faculty of Biology (tel. (234) 322-4573; fax
(234) 321-4237; internet www.biologie
.ruhr-uni-bochum.de):

BENNERT, W., Plant Taxonomy
DENHARDT, G., General Zoology and Neurobiology
DISTLER, C., General Zoology and Neurobiology
FAISSNER, A., Cell Morphology and Molecular Neurobiology

GERWERT, K., Biophysics
HAEUPLER, H., Geobotany
HAPPE, T., Plant Biochemistry, Photobio-
technology
HATT, H., Cell Physiology
HOFFMANN, K.-P., General Zoology and
Neurobiology
HOFMANN, E., Protein Crystallography,
Biophysics
JANCKE, D., Cognitive Neurobiology, Gen-
eral Zoology and Neurobiology
KIRCHNER, W. H., Behavioural Biology and
Teaching of Biology
KÜCK, U., General and Molecular Botany
LINK, G., Plant Cell Physiology and
Molecular Biology, Plant Physiology
LÜBBEN, M., Biophysics
LÜBBERT, H., Animal Physiology
NARBERHAUS, F., Biology of Micro-Organ-
isms
NECKER, R., Animal Physiology
NICKELSEN, J., Biology of Micro-Organisms
ÖTTMAYER, W., Plant Biochemistry
PÖGGELER, S., General and Molecular Bot-
any
RAETHER, W., Special Zoology
RÖGNER, M., Plant Biochemistry
SCHAUB, G., Animal Taxonomy, Parasitol-
ogy
SCHLITTER, J., Biophysics
SCHMIDT, M., General Zoology and Neuro-
biology
SCHÜNEMANN, O., General and Molecular
Botany
SCHWENN, J.-D., Plant Biochemistry
STÖRTKUHL, K., Cell Physiology, Sensory
Physiology
STÜTZEL, T., Plant Taxonomy, Spermato-
phytes
WAHLE, P., Developmental Neurobiology,
General Zoology and Neurobiology
WEILER, E., Plant Physiology
WETZEL, C., Cell Physiology

Faculty of Catholic Theology (tel. (234) 32-
22619; fax (234) 3214-410; e-mail
kath-theol-fak@ruhr-uni-bochum.de):

DAMBERG, W., Medieval and Modern
Church History
DSCHULNIGG, P., New Testament
FREVEL, C., Old Testament Exegesis and
Theology
GEERLINGS, W., Church History, Patrology
GÖLLNER, R., Practical Theology
KNAPP, M., Fundamental Theology
KNOCH, W., Dogmatics
REINHARDT, H. J. F., Canon Law
WIEMEYER, J., Christian Social Ethics
ZELINKA, U., Moral Theology

Faculty of Chemistry (tel. (234) 32-24732; fax
(234) 32-14108; e-mail chemie-dekanat@
ruhr-uni-bochum.de; internet www
.ruhr-uni-bochum.de/chemie):

BENNECKE, G., Receptor Biochemistry
DYKER, G., Organic Chemistry
FEIGEL, M., Organic Chemistry
FISCHER, R., Inorganic Chemistry
GRÜNERT, W., Technical Chemistry
HAVENITH-NEWEN, M., Physical Chemistry
HERMANN, C., Physical Chemistry
HEUMANN, R., Molecular Neurobiochemis-
try
HOLLMANN, M., Receptor Biochemistry
HOVEMANN, B., Molecular Cell Biochemis-
try
MARX, D., Theoretical Chemistry
MUHLER, M., Technical Chemistry
MÜLLER, S., Organic Chemistry
SANDER, W., Organic Chemistry
SCHUHMANN, W., Analytical Chemistry
SHELDRICK, W. S., Analytical Chemistry
SOMMER, K., Didactics of Chemistry
STAEMMLER, V., Theoretical Chemistry
VON KIEDROWSKI, G., Organic Chemistry
WEINGÄRTNER, H., Physical Chemistry
WÖLL, C., Physical Chemistry

Faculty of Civil Engineering (tel. (234) 322-
6124; fax (234) 3214-147; e-mail dekanat-bi@
ruhr-uni-bochum.de; internet www
.ruhr-uni-bochum.de/fbi):

BREITENBÜCHER, R., Building Materials
BRILON, W., Traffic Engineering
BRUHNS, O. T., Mechanics
HACKL, K., Mechanics
HARTMANN, D., Applied Computer Science
HÖFFER, R., Aerodynamics and Fluid
Mechanics
KINDMANN, R., Steel and Composite Con-
structions
MESCHKE, G., Structural Mechanics
ORTH, H., Environmental Engineering
REESE, S., Computational Mechanics and
Simulation
SCHERER, M., Surveying and Geodesy
SCHMID, G., Structural Mechanics and
Computer Simulation
SCHUMANN, A., Hydrology, Water
Resources Management and Environ-
mental Engineering
STANGENBERG, F., Reinforced and Pre-
stressed Concrete Structures
STOLPE, H., Environmental Technology
and Ecology
TRIANTAFYLLIDIS, TH., Soil Mechanics
WILLEMS, W., Structural Design and Build-
ing Physics

Faculty of East Asian Studies (tel. (234) 322-
6189; e-mail anne.mueller@ruhr-uni-bochum
.de; internet www.ruhr-uni-bochum.de/oaw):

EGGERT, M., Korean Studies
FINDEISEN, R., Chinese Language and Lit-
erature
GU, X., East Asian Politics
KLENNER, W., East Asian Economics
MATHIAS, R., Japanese History
RICKMEYER, J., Japanese Language and
Literature
ROETZ, H., Chinese History and Philosophy

Faculty of Economics (tel. (234) 32-22884; fax
(234) 32-14140; e-mail wiwi-dekanat@
ruhr-uni-bochum.de; internet www.wiwi
.ruhr-uni-bochum.de):

BAUER, T., Empirical Economics
BENDER, D., Int. Economic Relations
DIRRIGL, H., Controlling
FOLKERS, C., Public Finance
GABRIEL, R., Business Informatics
HAMMANN, P., Management and Marketing
HAUCUP, J., Economic Policy
KARL, H., Economic Policy
KÖSTERS, W., Monetary Economics
LÖSCH, M., Statistics and Econometrics
MAG, W., Theoretical Industrial Economics
MANN, T., Law Concerning the Economy
NIENHAUS, V., Economic Policy
PAUL, S., Banking and Finance
PELLENS, B., Int. Accounting
SCHIMMELPFENNIG, J., Theoretical and
Applied Microeconomics
SMOLNY, W., Applied Economics
STEVEN, M., Production and Operations
STREIM, H., Financial Accounting and
Auditing
VOIGT, S., Economic Policy
WERNERS, B., Operations Research and
Accounting

Faculty of Electrical Engineering (tel. (234)
32-25666; fax (234) 3214-444; e-mail
dekanat-ei@ruhr-uni-bochum.de; internet
www.et.ruhr-uni-bochum.de):

AWAKOWICZ, P., General Electrical Engin-
eering/Plasma Technology
BALZERT, H., Software Engineering
BRINKMANN, R. P., Theoretical Electrical
Engineering/Plasma Technology
ERMERT, H., High-Frequency Engineering
FISCHER, H. D., Communications Engin-
eering
GÖCKLER, H., Digital Signal Processing
HAUSNER, J., Integrated Systems

HOFMANN, M., Optoelectronic Devices and Materials
HUDDE, H., Sound and Vibration
KUNZE, U., Electronic Materials and Nanoelectronics
LANGMANN, U., Integrated Circuits
LUNZE, J., Automation
MARTIN, R., Information Technology and Communication Acoustics
MELBERT, J., Electronic Circuits and Measurement Techniques
OEHM, J., Circuit Design
PAAR, CH., Communication Security
SADIGHI, A.-R., Applied Data Security
SCHMILZ, G., Medical Engineering
SCHWENK, J., Network and Data Security
SOURKOUNIS, C., Power System Technology
STEIMEL, A., Power Engineering
TÜCHELMANN, Y., Integrated Information Systems

Faculty of Geosciences (tel. (234) 32-23505; fax (234) 3214-535; e-mail geodekanat@ruhr-uni-bochum.de; internet www.ruhr-uni-bochum.de/exogeol/geowiss.html):

ALBER, M., Engineering Geology
BUTZIN, B., Geography
CHAKRABORTY, S., Mineralogy and Petrology
FLEER, H., Climatology and Hydrogeology
FRIEDRICH, W., Geophysics
GIES, H., Mineralogy and Crystallography
HOHN, U., Economic and Social Geography
JÜRGENS, C., Geo-Remote Sensing
LÖTSCHER, L., Geography and Cultural Geography
MARESCH, W. V., Mineralogy
MÜLLER, J.-C., Cartography
MUTTERLOSE, J., Palaeontology and Geology
OTTO, K.-H., Didactics of Geography
RENNER, J., Seismology
SCHMITT, TH., Geography
STÖCKHERT, B., Geology
WOHNLICH, ST., Applied Geology
ZEPP, H., Physical Geography

Faculty of History (tel. (234) 32-22525; fax (234) 32-14240; e-mail dekan-gw@ruhr-uni-bochum.de; internet www.ruhr-uni-bochum.de/geschichtswissenschaft):

ADANIR, F., Southeast European History
BERGEMANN, J., Archaeology
BLEEK, W., Sociology, Political Science
BONWETSCH, B., East European History
BÜSING, H., Archaeology
EBEL-ZEPEZAUER, W., Pre- and Proto-History
EDER, W., Ancient History
ERBEN, D., History of Art
GÜNTHER, L.-M., Ancient History
HÖLSCHER, L., Theory of History
HOPPE-SAILER, R., History of Art
MATHIAS, R., East Asian Studies
OBERWEIS, M., Auxiliary Sciences (Diplomacy, Palaeography, Numismatics)
SCHULTE, R., Modern and Contemporary History, Gender Studies
SÖNTGEN, B., History of Art
STEINHAUSER, M., History of Art
TENFELDE, K., Social History and Social Movement
VON GRAEVE, V., Archaeology
WALA, M., History of North America
WALZ, R., Early Modern History
WEBER, W., Economic and Technical History
ZIEGLER, D., Economic and Business History

Faculty of Law (tel. (234) 32-26566; fax (234) 3214-530; e-mail denise.sablotny@jura.ruhr-uni-bochum.de; internet www.ruhr-uni-bochum.de/jura):

BERNSMANN, K., Criminal Law, Criminal Procedural Law

BORGES, G., Civil Law, Media Law and Law of Information Technology
BURGI, M., Public Law
FELTES, TH., Criminology
GREMER, W., Public Law, European Law
HÖRNLE, T., Criminal Law, Criminal Procedural Law
HUSTER, S., Public Law
KINDLER, P., Civil Law, Commercial Law, Int. Civil Law and Comparative Law
KRAMPE, CHR., Civil Law, Ancient Law and Roman Law
MUSCHELER, K., History of German Law, Civil Law, Church Law
POSCHER, R., Public Law, Sociology of Law
PUTTLER, A., Public Law
SCHILDT, B., History of Law, Civil Law
SCHREIBER, K., Procedural Law, Civil and Labour Law
SEER, R., Tax Law and Administrative Law
SIEKMANN, H., Public Law
WANK, R., Civil Law, Commercial and Labour Law
WINDEL, A., Procedural Law, Civil Law
WOLF, P., Public Law
WOLTERS, G., Criminal Law, Criminal Procedural Law

Faculty of Mathematics (tel. (234) 322-3476; fax (234) 3214-103; e-mail ffm@ruhr-uni-bochum.de; internet www.ruhr-uni-bochum.de/ffm):

ABRESCH, U., Mathematics
AVANZI, R., Mathematics
BARTENWERFER, W., Mathematics
BERTSCH, E., Computer Science
DEHLING, H., Mathematics
DETTE, H., Mathematics
DOBBERTIN, H., Mathematics, Cryptology
EICHELSBACHER, P., Mathematics
FLENNER, H., Mathematics
GERRITZEN, L., Mathematics
HEINZNER, P., Mathematics
HUCKLEBERRY, A. T., Mathematics
KIRSCH, W., Mathematical Physics
KNIEPER, G., Mathematics
KRIECHERBAUER, T., Mathematics
LAURES, G., Mathematics
MATTHIES, G., Mathematics
SIMON, H., Mathematics, Computer Science
STORCH, U., Mathematics
VERFÜRTH, R., Mathematics
WASSERMANN, G., Differential Topology

Faculty of Mechanical Engineering (tel. (234) 32-26191; fax (234) 32-14291; e-mail dekanmb@itm.ruhr-uni-bochum.de; internet www.ruhr-uni-bochum.de/maschinenbau):

ABRAMOVICI, M., Computer Science
EGGELER, G., Materials Science
MEIER, Production Systems
PAPENFUSS, H.-D., Applied Fluid Mechanics
POHL, M., Materials Testing
PREDKI, W., Mechanical Components—Industrial and Automotive Power Transmission
REINIG, G., Control Systems Engineering
ROGG, B., Fluid Mechanics
RÖHM, H.-J., Chemical and Environmental Engineering
SCHERER, V., Energy Plant Technology
SCHWEIGER, G., Applied Laser Technology and Measuring Systems
STOFF, H., Fluid Flow Machines
STÖVER, D. H. H., Materials Processing
STRATMANN, M., Materials Surfaces and Interfaces
SVEJDA, P., Thermodynamics of Mixtures
THEISEN, W., Materials Technology
WAGNER, G., Mechanical Components and Materials Handling
WAGNER, H.-J., Energy Systems and Energy Economics
WAGNER, W., Thermodynamics
WEIDNER, E., Process Engineering

WELP, E. G., Mechanical Components and Methodical Design

Faculty of Medicine (tel. (234) 32-24960; fax (234) 3214-190; e-mail medizin@rub.de; internet www.ruhr-uni-bochum.de/medizin):

ADAMIETZ, J. A., Radiology
ALTMEYER, P., Dermatology and Venereology
BRÜNING, TH., Industrial Medicine
BUFE, A., Paediatrics
BURCHERT, W., Radiology
DAZERT, S., Otorhinolaryngology
DERMIETZEL, R., Anatomy
ENGERT, J., Paediatric Surgery
EPPLEN, J., Genetics
ERDMANN, R., Biochemistry
EYSEL, U., Physiology
GATERMANN, S., Medical Microbiology
GOODY, R., Physiological Chemistry
GRONEMEYER, U., Ophthalmology
GUZMAN Y ROTAECHE, J., Pathology
HARDERS, A. G., Neurosurgery
HASENBRING, M., Medical Psychology
HERPERTZ, S., Psychosomatic Medicine and Psychotherapy
HEUSER, L., Radiology
HOHLBACH, G.-R., Surgery
HORSTKOTTE, D., Internal Medicine
INOUE, K., Anaesthesiology
JENSEN, A. W. O., Gynaecology and Obstetrics
KLEESIEK, K., Clinical Chemistry and Pathobiochemistry
KLEIN, H. H., Internal Medicine
KOESLING, D., Pharmacology and Toxicology
KÖRFER, R., Thoracic and Cardiovascular Surgery
KÖSTER, O., Radiology
KRÄMER, J., Orthopaedics
KRIEG, M., Clinical Chemistry
LACZKOVICS, A., Surgery, Thoracic and Cardiovascular Surgery
LAUBENTHAL, H., Anaesthesiology
LIERMANN, D., Radiology
MALIN, J.-P., Neurology
MANNHERZ, H. G., Anatomy and Cell Biology
MAYER, H., Paediatric Cardiology
MELLER, K., Experimental Cytology
MORGENROTH, K., Pathology
MÜGGE, A., Internal Medicine
MUHR, G., Surgery
MÜLLER, I., History of Medicine
MÜLLER, K.-M., Pathology
NICOLAS, V., Radiology
NOLDUS, J., Urology
PESKAR, B., Clinical Experimental Medicine
PIENTKA, L., Geriatrics
POTT, L., Cellular Physiology
PRZUNTEK, H., Neurology
PUCHSTEIN, CH., Anaesthesiology
REUSCH, P., Pharmacology and Toxicology
RIEGER, CH., Paediatrics
RUMP, L. C., Nephrology
RUSCHE, H. H., General Medicine
SCHLEGEL, U., Neurology
SCHMIDT, W. E. W., Internal Medicine
SCHMIEGEL, W.-H., Internal Medicine
SCHULTZE-WERNINGHAUS, G., Internal Medicine
STEINAU, H.-U., Surgery
TRAMPISCH, H. J., Medical Informatics and Biomathematics
TRAPPE, H.-J., Internal Medicine
TSCHÖPE, D., Internal Medicine
ÜBERLA, K. T., Virology
UHE, W., Surgery
VIEBAHN, R., Surgery
VON DÜRING, M., Anatomy
WERNER, J., Biomedical Engineering
WILHELM, M., Hygiene
WOLFF, K.-D., Maxillofacial Surgery
ZENZ, M., Anaesthesiology

Faculty of Philology (tel. (234) 32-22623; fax (234) 32-14324; internet www.dekphil .ruhr-uni-bochum.de):

BASTERT, B., German Philology
BAUSCH, K.-R., Romance Philology
BEHRENS, R., Romance Philology
BEILENHOFF, W., Cinematography and Television Studies
BERNHARD, G., Romance Philology
BEYER, M., English Philology
BOETTCHER, W., Teaching of German Language and Literature
BOLLACHER, M., Modern German Literature
DEUBER-MANKOWSKI, A., Media Studies
EBEL, E., Scandinavian Studies
EFFE, B., Classical Philology
EIKELMANN, M., German Philology
ENDRESS, G., Arabic and Islamic Studies
FLUCK, H.-R., German Linguistics
FREITAG, K., American Studies
GLEI, R., Classical Philology/Latin
HASS, U., Theatre Studies
HEDIGER, V., Media Studies
HIMMELMANN, N., General Linguistics
HISS, G., Theatre Studies
HOUWEN, L., English Philology
KISS, T., General Linguistics
KLABUNDE, R., General Linguistics
KLODT, C., Classical Philology/Latin
KNAUTH, K. A., Romance Philology
KRENN, H., Romance Philology
LEBSANFT, F., Romance Philology
MENGE, H., German Linguistics
NIEDERHOFF, B., English
PITTNER, K., German Linguistics
PLUMPE, G., Modern German Literature
REICHMUTH, S., Islamic Studies
RUPP, G., Didactics of German Philology
SAPPOK, C., Slavonic Studies
SCHMID, U., Slavonic Studies
SCHMITZ-EMANS, M., General and Comparative Literature
SCHNEIDER, M., Modern German Literature
SCHÖNEFELD, D., English Philology
SIMONIS, L., General and Comparative Literature
SPANGENBERG, P., Media Sciences
STEINBRÜGGE, L., Romance Philology
THOMAS, B., Media Studies
TIETZ, M., Romance Philology
UHLENBRUCH, B., Russian and Soviet Culture
WARTH, E.-M., Cinematography and Television Studies
WEBER, I., English Philology
WEGERA, K.-P., History of German Language
WIEHL, P., Germanic Philology
ZELLE, C., Modern German Literature

Faculty of Philosophy, Pedagogy and Journalism (tel. (234) 32-22712; fax (234) 32-14505; e-mail reinhild.topp@ ruhr-uni-bochum.de):

ADICK, C., Comparative Education
BELLENBERG, G., Educational Research Focus on Schools
DRIESCHNER, M., Natural Philosophy
HAARDT, A., Philosophy
HARNEY, K., Vocational Education and Lifelong Learning, Methods of Educational Research
HERZIG, B., Learning and Teaching Research
JAESCHKE, W., Classic German Philosophy
KEINER, E., History of Education
LESSING, H.-U., Philosophical Anthropology and Theory of the Humanities
MEYER-DRAWE, K., General Education
MOJSISCH, B., History of Philosophy
PARDEY, Logic and Philosophy of Language
PULTE, H., History and Philosophy of Science
ROSEMANN, B., Educational Psychology

SCHMIDT, K., Classic German Philosophy, Symbolic and Mathematical Logic
SCHOLTZ, G., History and Theory of the Humanities
SCHWEIDLER, Practical Philosophy
STEIGLEDER, K., Ethics in Medicine and Biosciences
WITTPOTH, J., Adult Education

Faculty of Physics and Astronomy (tel. (234) 322-3445; fax (234) 3214-447; e-mail dekanat@physik.ruhr-uni-bochum.de; internet physik.ruhr-uni-bochum.de):

CHINI, R., Astrophysics
CZARNETZKI, U., Experimental Physics
DETTMAR, R.-J., Astronomy
EFETOV, K., Theoretical Physics
FEUERBACHER, B., Experimental Physics
GERWERT, K., Biophysics
GOEKE, K., Theoretical Physics
GRAUER, R., Theoretical Physics
HERLACH, D., Experimental Physics
KOCH, H., Experimental Physics
KÖHLER, U., Experimental Physics
KÖNIG, J., Theoretical Physics
MEYER, W., Experimental Physics
PELZL, J., Experimental Physics
POLYAKOV, U., Theoretical Physics
RITMAN, J., Experimental Physics
ROLFS, C., Experimental Physics
RUHL, H., Theoretical Physics
SCHLICKEISER, R., Theoretical Physics
SCHÖNER, G., Neuroinformatics
SOLTWISCH, H., Experimental Physics
VON DER MALSBURG, C., Neuroinformatics
VON KEUDELL, A., Experimental Physics
WIECK, A., Experimental Physics
WINTER, J., Experimental Physics
WOLF, R., Experimental Physics
ZABEL, H., Experimental Physics

Faculty of Protestant Theology (tel. (234) 32-2250; fax (234) 3214-722; e-mail ulrike .burgner@ruhr-uni-bochum.de; internet www.ruhr-uni-bochum.de/ev-theol):

BEYER, F.-H., Practical Theology
EBACH, J., Old Testament
GELDBACH, E., Ecumenical and Denominational Studies
JÄHNICHEN, T., Christian Social Science
KARLE, J., Practical Theology
KRECH, V., Religious Science
STROHM, C., Church History (Reformation and Modern)
THIEL, W., Old Testament
THOMAS, G., Systematic Theology
WENGST, K., New Testament Exegesis and Theology
WICK, P., New Testament
WYRWA, D., Church History

Faculty of Psychology (tel. (234) 322-4606; fax (234) 3214-588; e-mail psy-dekanat@ ruhr-uni-bochum.de; internet www .ruhr-uni-bochum.de/psy-dekanat):

BIERHOFF, H.-W., Social Psychology
BOCK, M., Psychology of Language and Communication
DAUM, I., Neuropsychology
GÜNTÜRKÜN, O., Biopsychology
GUSKI, R., Cognitive and Environmental Psychology
HASENBRING, M., Medical Psychology
REULECKE, W., Sport Psychology
ROSEMANN, B., Educational Psychology
SCHÖLMERICH, A., Development Psychology
SCHULTE, D., Clinical Psychology and Psychiatry
WOTTAWA, H., Methodology, Diagnostic and Evaluation
ZIMOLONG, B., Industrial and Organizational Psychology

Faculty of Social Sciences (tel. (234) 322-22967; fax (234) 3214-507; e-mail christel .maleszka@ruhr-uni-bochum.de; internet www.ruhr-uni-bochum.de/sowi):

ALTHAMMER, J., Social Politics

ANDERSEN, U., Political Science
BLEEK, W., Political Science
HEINZE, R. G., Sociology
LEHNER, F., Political Science
LENZ, I., Sociology
MINSSEN, H., Labour Organization
NOLTE, H., Social Psychology
OTT, N., Social Politics
PETZINA, D., Social and Economic History
PRIES, L., Participation and Organization
ROHWER, G., Methodology of Social Science and Social Statistics
SCHMIDT, G., Political Science
STROHMEIER, K. P., Sociology
TIEDE, M., Mathematical and Empirical Procedure in Social Sciences
VOSS, W., Mathematical and Empirical Procedure in Social Sciences
WIDMAIER, Political Science
WOLFF, J., Sociology of Developing Countries

Faculty of Sport Science (Gebäude UHW, Stiepelerstr. 129, 44801 Bochum; tel. (234) 322-7793; fax (234) 3214-246; e-mail sportwiss-dekanat@ruhr-uni-bochum.de; internet www.ruhr-uni-bochum.de/spowiss):

BECKERS, E., Pedagogy of Sport
FERRANTI, A., Applied Training Science
HECK, H. J., Medicine in Sport
KELLMANN, M., Sports Psychology
KLEIN, M. L., Sociology of Sport, Sports Management
NEUMAIER, A., Theory of Movement, Biomechanics

Centre for Further Education (Geb. LOTA, 44780 Bochum; tel. (234) 322-6466; fax (234) 321-4255; e-mail wbz@ruhr-uni-bochum.de; internet www.ruhr-uni-bochum.de/wbz):

MUHLER, M.

Institute for Development Research and Development Policy (tel. (234) 322-2418; fax (234) 321-4294; e-mail ieeoffice@ ruhr-uni-bochum.de; internet www .ruhr-uni-bochum.de/iee):

ANDERSEN, U., Society, Politics, Public Admin.
BENDER, D., Int. Economic Relations
DÜRR, H., Social and Economic Geography
NIENHAUS, V., Economic Policy
VOSS, W., Statistics and Econometrics
WOLF, J., Int. Law
WOLFF, J. H., Society, Politics, Public Admin.

Institute for Energy and Natural Resources Law (tel. (234) 322-7333; fax (234) 321-4292; e-mail tbe@ruhr-uni-bochum.de; internet www.ruhr-uni-bochum.de/ibe):

DRESEN, L., Seismology
HÜFFER, U., Civil Law, Commercial Law
IPSEN, K., Public Law
STEIN, D., Pipe Construction and Maintenance
TETTINGER, P. J., Public Law
UNGER, H., Nuclear and Modern Energy Systems
VON DANWITZ, T., Public Law, European Law

Institute for German Cultural Studies (tel. (234) 322-7863; fax (234) 321-4587; e-mail idf@ruhr-uni-bochum.de; internet www .ruhr-uni-bochum.de/deutschlandforschung):

ANDERSEN, U., Political Science
ANWEILER, D., Educational Research, Comparative Educational Research
BLEEK, W., Political Science
FAULENBACH, B., Modern History
KLUSSMANN, P. G., Modern German Literature
KROSS, E., Didactics of Geography
VOSS, W., Mathematical and Empirical Procedure in Social Sciences

Institute for Industrial Engineering (tel. (234) 322-7730; internet www.iaw .ruhr-uni-bochum.de/iaw):

MINNSSEN, H. (Dir)

Institute for Industrial Science (tel. (234) 322-3293; fax (234) 321-4118; internet www .iaw.ruhr-uni-bochum.de):

KAILER, N., Personnel and Qualifications
MINNSSEN, H., Organization of Work
SCHNAUBER, H., Working Systems Design
STAUDT, E., Economics of Work

Institute for International Law of Peace and Human Rights (tel. (234) 322-7366; fax (234) 321-4208; internet www.ruhr-uni-bochum .de/ifhv):

WOLF, J., Int. Law

Institute for Neuro-Computing (tel. (234) 322-7965; fax (234) 321-4209; e-mail institut@neuroinformatik.ruhr-uni-bochum .de; internet www.neuroinformatik .ruhr-uni-bochum.de):

SCHÖNER, G., Theoretical Biology
VON DER MALSBURG, CH., Systems Biophysics

Institute for Social Movements (44789 Bochum, Clemensstr. 17–19; tel. (234) 322-4687; fax (234) 321-4249; internet www .ruhr-uni-bochum.de/isb):

TENFELDE, K., Social History and Social Movements

Institute for Teacher Training (tel. (234) 321-1942; fax (234) 321-4647; e-mail zfl-kontakt@ ruhr-uni-bochum.de; internet www .ruhr-uni-bochum.de/zfl):

BAUSCH, K. R., Romance Philology
BELLENBERG, G., Educational Science
KAMMERTÖNS, A., Didactics of Social Sciences
OTT, N., Social Politics
TIETZ, M., Romance Philology
WIECK, A., Experimental Physics

UNIVERSITÄT HEIDELBERG

POB 10 57 60, 69047 Heidelberg
Grabengasse 1, 69117 Heidelberg
Telephone: (6221) 540
Fax: (6221) 542618
E-mail: rektor@rektorat.uni-heidelberg.de
Internet: www.uni-heidelberg.de
Founded 1386
Academic year: October to September
Rector: Prof. Dr BERNHARD EITEL
Vice-Rector for Education: Prof. Dr FRIEDERIKE NÜSSEL
Vice-Rector for Int. Affairs: Prof. Dr THOMAS PFEIFFER
Vice-Rector for Quality Devt: Prof. Dr KARL-HEINZ SONNTAG
Vice-Rector for Research and Structure: Prof. Dr THOMAS RAUSCH
Chancellor: Dr MARINA FROST
Librarian: Dr VEIT PROBST
Library: see Libraries and Archives
Number of teachers: 4,259
Number of students: 28,266
Publications: *Alumni Revue* (2 a year), *Heidelberger Jahrbücher*, *Personalia* (12 a year), *Ruperto Carola* (3 a year), *Uni-spiegel* (5 a year)

DEANS

Faculty of Behavioural and Cultural Studies: Prof. Dr ANDREAS KRUSE
Faculty of Biosciences: Prof. Dr THOMAS HOLSTEIN
Faculty of Chemistry and Earth Sciences: Prof. Dr A. STEPHEN K. HASHMI
Faculty of Economics and Social Sciences: Prof. Dr JÜRGEN EICHBERGER
Faculty of Law: Prof. Dr HERBERT KRONKE

Faculty of Mathematics and Computer Sciences: Prof. Dr R. RANNACHER
Faculty of Medicine (Heidelberg): Prof. Dr CLAUS R. BARTRAM
Faculty of Medicine (Mannheim): Prof. Dr KLAUS VAN ACKERN
Faculty of Modern Languages: Prof. Dr CHRISTIANE VON STUTTERHEIM
Faculty of Philosophy and History: Prof. Dr HEINZ-DIETRICH LÖWE
Faculty of Physics and Astronomy: Prof. Dr MANFRED SALMHOFER
Faculty of Theology: Prof. Dr WINRICH LÖHR

PROFESSORS (INSTITUTE DIRECTORS)

Faculty of Behavioural and Cultural Sciences (Voßstr. 2, Gebäude 37, I. OG, 69115 Heidelberg; tel. (6221) 542894; fax (6221) 543650; e-mail dekanat@verkult.uni-heidelberg.de):

BOENICKE, R., Education
HAGEMANN, D., Psychology
KRUSE, A., Ethnology
KRUSE, A., Gerontology
ROTH, K., Sports

Faculty of Biology (Im Neuenheimer Feld 234, 69120 Heidelberg; tel. (6221) 545648; fax (6221) 544953; e-mail dekanat-bio@urz .uni-heidelberg.de):

BADING, H., Neurobiology
HELL, R., Heidelberg Plant and Fungal Biology Graduate School
HOLSTEIN, T., Zoology
JÄSCHKE, A., Pharmacy and Molecular Biotechnology

Faculty of Chemistry and Earth Sciences (Im Neuenheimer Feld 234, 69120 Heidelberg; tel. (6221) 544844; fax (6221) 544589; e-mail dcg@urz.uni-heidelberg.de):

BUBENZER, O., Geography
CEDERBAUM, L., Physical Chemistry
HASHMI, S., Organic Chemistry
HIMMEL, H.-J., Inorganic Chemistry
SCHÖLER, F., Earth Sciences

Faculty of Clinical Medicine (Mannheim) (Theodor-Kutzer-Ufer 1-3, 68167 Mannheim; tel. (621) 3839770; fax (621) 3839769; e-mail dekan@medma.uni-heidelberg.de):

FISCHER, J., Public Health
GOERDT, S., Dermatology and Venereal Disease
GRODEN, C., Neuroradiology
HOF, H., Medicine Microbiology and Hygiene
HÖRMANN, K., Oto–Rhino–Laryngology
JONAS, J., Ophthalmology
KLÜTER, H., Transfusions Medicine and Immunology
MARX, A., Pathology
MEYER-LINDENBERG, A., Mental Health
MICHEL, M., Urology
NEUMAIER, M., Clinical Chemistry
POST, S., Surgery
SCHAD, L., Computer-Assisted Clinical Medicine
SCHARF, H., Orthopaedics
SCHMIEDER, K., Neurological Surgery
SCHÖNBERG, S., Clinical Radiology
SCHROTEN, A., Paediatrics
SÜTTERLIN, M., Women's Hospital
VAN ACKERN, K., Anaesthesiology
WEIß, C., Medical Statistics, Biomathematics and Information
WENZ, F., Experimental Radiation Oncology
WESSEL, L., Children's Surgery
WIELAND, T., Pharmacology and Toxicology

Faculty of Economics and Social Sciences (Bergheimer Str. 58, 69115 Heidelberg; tel. (6221) 543445; fax (6221) 543496; e-mail wiso-dekanat@urz.uni-heidelberg.de):

CROISSANT, A., Political Science
GOESCHL, T., Interdisciplinary Institute for Environmental Economics

IRMEN, A., Economics
SCHWINN, T., Sociology

Faculty of Law (Friedrich-Ebert-Anlage 6–10, 69117 Heidelberg; tel. (6221) 547631; fax (6221) 547654; e-mail dekanat@jurs .uni-heidelberg.de):

BALDUS, C., Historical Law
DÖLLING, D., Criminal Law
EBKE, W., German and European Company and Business Law
HESS, B., Foreign and International Private and Business Law
KIRCHHOF, P., Fiscal and Tax Law
MÜLLER-GRAFF, P., Civil, Commercial, Corporate and Commercial Law, European Law and Comparative Law
VON HOYNINGEN-HUENE, G., Civil Law, Labour Law and Insolvency

Faculty of Mathematics and Computer Sciences (Im Neuenheimer Feld 288, 69120 Heidelberg; tel. (6221) 545758; fax (6221) 548312; e-mail dekanat@mathi .uni-heidelberg.de):

DAHLHAUS, R., Applied Mathematics
GERTZ, M., Computer Sciences
WINGBERG, K., Mathematics

Faculty of Medicine (Heidelberg) (Im Neuenheimer Feld 672, 69120 Heidelberg; e-mail dekanat@med.uni-heidelberg.de):

AUFFARTH, G., Ophthalmology
BARTRAM, C., Human Genetics
BÜCHLER, M., Surgery
ECKART, W., History of Medicine
ENK, A., Dermatology
EWERBECK, V., Orthopaedics
GERNER, H., Orthopaedics
HACKE, W., Neurology
HECKER, M., Physiology and Pathophysiology
HERZOG, W., Internal Medicine
HOFFMANN, G., Paediatrics
HOHENFELLNER, M., Urology
KAUCZOR, H., Radiology
KIESER, M., Medical Biometrics and Computer Science in Medicine
KIRSCH, J., Anatomy
KRÄUSSLICH, H., Hygiene
MARTIN, E., Anaesthesiology
MATTERN, R., Forensic Medicine
MEUER, S., Immunology
MÜHLING, J., Dentistry
MUNDT, C., Psychiatry
PLINKERT, P., Oto–Rhino–Laryngology
SCHIRMACHER, P., Pathology
SOHN, C., Women's Hospital
TRIEBIG, G., Social and Industrial Medicine
UNTERBERG, A., Neurosurgery

Faculty of Modern Languages (Voßstr. 2, Gebäude 37, 69115 Heidelberg; tel. (6221) 542891; fax (6221) 543625; e-mail neuphil-fak@uni-hd.de):

WEIAND, C., Romance Philology
FRANK, A., Computer Linguistics
GLAUSER, B., English Philology
GVOZDANOVIC, J., Slavic Philology
HUBER, C., Translating and Interpreting
LICHT, T., Philology of the Middle Ages
RIECKE, J., German Philology
RIECKE, J., Language Laboratory
ROESCH, G., German as a Foreign Language Philology

Faculty of Philosophy and History (Voßstr. 2, Bldg 4370, 69115 Heidelberg; tel. (6221) 542329; fax (6221) 543635; e-mail philosophische-fakultaet@uni-hd.de):

AHN, G., Religious Studies
ENDERWITZ, S., Languages and Cultures of the Near East
HERREN-OESCH, M., History
HESSE, M., European Art History
JÖRDENS, A., Papyrology
KLOSS, G., Classical Studies
LEDDEROSE, L., East Asian Art History

LEOPOLD, S., Musicology
LÖWE, H., History of Eastern Europe
MCLAUGHLIN, P., Philosophy
MARAN, J., Prehistory and Protohistory and Middle Eastern Archaeology
MITTLER, B., Sinology
PANAGIOTOPOULOS, D., Classical Archaeology
QUACK, J., Egyptology
SCHNEIDMÜLLER, B., History of Franconia and the Palatinate
SEIFERT, W., Japanese Studies
STEPHAN-KAISSIS, C., Byzantine Archaeology and Art History
TRAMPEDACH, K., Ancient History and Epigraphics
WEINFURTER, S., History of Franconia and the Palatinate

Faculty of Physics and Astronomy (Albert-Ueberle-Str. 3–5 2OG Ost, 69120 Heidelberg; tel. (6221) 549298; fax (6221) 549347; e-mail dekanat@physik.uni-heidelberg.de):

GREBEL, E., Astronomical Computing Institute
KLESSEN, R., Theoretical Astrophysics
MEIER, K., Kirchhoff-Institute for Physics
PLATT, U., Environmental Physics
QUIRRENBACH, A., National Observatory King Chair
WAMBSGANß, J., Astronomical Computing Institute
WEIDEMÜLLER, M., Physics
WETTERICH, C., Theoretical Physics

Faculty of Theology (Hauptstr. 231, 1 OG, 69117 Heidelberg; tel. (6221) 543334; fax (6221) 543372; e-mail dekanat@theologie.uni-heidelberg.de):

EURICH, J., Study of Christian Social Service
LIENHARD, F., Practical-Theological Seminary
LÖHR, W., Scientific-Theological Seminary
NÜSSEL, F., Ecumenical Institute

ATTACHED INSTITUTES

Biochemie-Zentrum Heidelberg (Heidelberg University Biochemistry Centre): Im Neuenheimer Feld 328, 69129 Heidelberg; Dir Prof. Dr M. BRUNNER.

BioQuant: Im Neuenheimer Feld 267, Raum 741, 69120 Heidelberg; Dir Prof. Dr HANS-GEORG KRÄUSSLICH; Dir Prof. Dr JÜRGEN WOLFRUM; Dir Prof. Dr ROLAND EILS.

Forschungszentrum für Internationale und Interdisziplinäre Theologie (Research Centre for International and Interdisciplinary Theology): Hauptstr. 240, 69117 Heidelberg; Dir Prof. Dr ANDREAS KRUSE; Dir Prof. MICHAEL WELKER; Dir Prof. Dr PETER LAMPE.

Heidelberg Center for American Studies (HCA): Curt und Heidemarie Engelhorn Palais, Hauptstr. 120, 69117 Heidelberg; Dir Prof. Dr DETLEF JUNKER.

Institut für Technische Informatik als zentrale Einrichtung der Universität Heidelberg: B6, 26, Bauteil B, 8131 Mannheim; Dir Prof. Dr K.-H. BRENNER.

Interdisziplinäres Zentrum für Neurowissenschaften (Interdisciplinary Centre for Neuroscience): Im Neuenheimer Feld 307, 69120 Heidelberg; Dir Prof. Dr HILMAR BADING.

Interdisziplinäres Zentrum für Wissenschaftliches Rechnen (Interdisciplinary Centre for Scientific Computing): Im Neuenheimer Feld 368, 69120 Heidelberg; Dir Prof. Dr HANS GEORG BOCK.

Südasien-Institut (South Asia Institute): Im Neuenheimer Feld 330, 69120 Heidelberg; Dir Prof. Dr MARCUS NÜSSER.

Zentrum für Astronomie (Centre for Astronomy of Heidelberg University): Mön-chhofstr. 12–14, 69120 Heidelberg; Dir Prof. Dr JOACHIM WAMBSGANß.

Zentrum für Molekulare Biologie der Universität Heidelberg (Centre for Molecular Biology of Heidelberg University): Im Neuenheimer Feld 282, 69120 Heidelberg; Dir Prof. Dr BERND BUKAU.

Zentrum für Soziale Investitionen und Innovationen (Centre for Social Investment): Adenauerpl. 1, 69115 Heidelberg; Dir Prof. Dr HELMUT K. ANHEIER.

STEINBEIS-HOCHSCHULE BERLIN
(Steinbeis University Berlin)

Gürtelstr. 29A/30, 10247 Berlin
Telephone: (30) 2933090
Fax: (30) 29330920
E-mail: shb@stw.de
Internet: www.steinbeis-hochschule.de
Founded 1998
Private control
Pres. and Man. Dir: Prof. Dr JOHANN LÖHN
Number of students: 4,000

STIFTUNG TIERÄRZTLICHE HOCHSCHULE HANNOVER
(University of Veterinary Medicine Hanover, Foundation)

POB 71 11 80, 30559 Hanover
Bünteweg 2, 30559 Hanover
Telephone: (511) 95360
Fax: (511) 9538050
E-mail: info@tiho-hannover.de
Internet: www.tiho-hannover.de
Founded 1778
Pres.: Dr GERHARD GREIF
Vice-Pres. for Academic Affairs: Prof. Dr ANDREA TIPOLD
Vice-Pres. for Research: Prof. Dr BURKHARD MEINECKE
Number of teachers: 58
Number of students: 2,360

TECHNISCHE UNIVERSITÄT BERGAKADEMIE FREIBERG

Akademiestr. 6, 09599 Freiberg
Telephone: (3731) 390
Fax: (3731) 22195
E-mail: rektorat@zuv.tu-freiberg.de
Internet: tu-freiberg.de
Founded 1765
State control
Academic year: October to August
Rector: Prof. Dr BERND MEYER
Vice-Rector for Education: Prof. Dr DIRK MEYER
Vice-Research for Research: Prof. Dr MICHAEL STELTER
Chancellor: Dr ANDREAS HANDSCHUH
Number of teachers: 383
Number of students: 5,458
Publications: *Fakultät Mathematik und Informatik Preprints*, *Freiberger Forschungshefte*, *Wissenschaftliche Mitteilungen des Instituts für Geologie*

DEANS

Faculty of Chemistry and Physics: Prof. Dr Hab. WOLFGANG VOIGT
Faculty of Economics and Business Administration: Prof. Dr BRUNO SCHÖNFELDER
Faculty of Geosciences, Geoengineering and Mining: Prof. Dr JÖRG MATSCHULLAT
Faculty of Materials Science and Technology: Prof. Dr Hab. PJOTR R. SCHELLER
Faculty of Mathematics and Computer Science: Prof. Dr Hab. STEPHAN DEMPE
Faculty of Mechanical, Process and Energy Engineering: Prof. Dr Hab. GEORG HÄRTEL

TECHNISCHE UNIVERSITÄT BERLIN

Str. des 17 Juni 135, 10623 Berlin
Telephone: (30) 3140
Fax: (30) 31423222
E-mail: pressestelle@tu-berlin.de
Internet: www.tu-berlin.de
The Bauakademie (Building Academy) of Berlin (f. 1799) and the Gewerbeakademie (f. 1821) were merged in 1879 as the Technische Hochschule Berlin, which was opened under its present name in 1946
Pres.: Prof. Dr Ing. JÖRG STEINBACH
Vice-Pres.: Prof. Dr GABRIELE WENDORF
Vice-Pres.: Prof. Dr ULRIKE WOGGON
Vice-Pres.: Prof. Dr Ing. WOLFGANG HUHNT
Chancellor: Dr ULRIKE GUTHEIL
Librarian: Dr WOLFGANG ZICK
Library: see Libraries and Archives
Number of teachers: 3,184
Number of students: 29,510
Publications: *Mitteilungsblatt der TUB* (26 a year), *TU intern* (9 a year), *TU International* (4 a year), *Universitätsführer* (every two years), *Vorlesungsverzeichnis* (2 a year)

DEANS

Economics and Management: Prof. Dr JÜRGEN ENSTHALER
Electrical Engineering and Computer Sciences: Prof. ANJA FELDMANN
Humanities: Prof. Dr ADRIAN VON BUTTLAR
Mathematics and Natural Sciences: Prof. Dr CHRISTIAN THOMSEN
Mechanical Engineering and Transport Systems: Prof. Dr Ing. UTZ VON WAGNER
Planning, Building, Environment: Prof. Dr JOHANN KÖPPEL
Process Sciences: Prof. Dr LOTHAR KROH

TECHNISCHE UNIVERSITÄT CAROLO WILHELMINA ZU BRAUNSCHWEIG

Pockelsstr. 14, 38106 Braunschweig
Telephone: (531) 3910
Fax: (531) 3914577
E-mail: president@tu-bs.de
Internet: www.tu-braunschweig.de
Founded 1745 as Collegium Carolinum; became Herzogliche Polytechnische Schule 1862 and Technische Hochschule 1877; present name 1968
State control
Academic year: October to September (two terms)
Pres.: Prof. Dr-Ing. JÜRGEN HESSELBACH
Vice-Pres.: Prof. Dr HEIKE FASSBENDER
Vice-Pres.: Prof. Dr MARTIN KORTE
Vice-Pres.: DIETMAR SMYREK
Vice-Pres.: Prof. Dr THOMAS SPENGLER
Head of Int. Office: Dr ASTRID SEBASTIAN
Library Dir: Prof. Dr Hab. DIETMAR BRANDES
Library: see Libraries and Archives
Number of teachers: 230 full-time professors
Number of students: 13,500
Publications: *Forschungsbericht* (every 5 years), *Mitteilungen der Carolo-Wilhelmina* (1 or 2 a year), *Personal- und Vorlesungsverzeichnis* (1 a year), *TU-aktuell* (6 a year), *Veröffentlichung der Technischen Universität Braunschweig* (1 a year)

DEANS

Carl-Friedrich-Gauß Faculty: Prof. Dr DIRK C. MATTFELD
Faculty of Architecture, Civil Engineering and Environmental Sciences: Prof. Dr OTTO RICHTER
Faculty of Electrical Engineering, Information Technology, Physics: Prof. Dr JOCHEN LITTERST

Faculty of Humanities and Pedagogics: Prof.
Dr GOTTFRIED ORTH

Faculty of Life Sciences: Prof. Dr DIETER
JAHN

Faculty of Mechanical Engineering: Prof. Dr-
Ing. PETER HECKER

TECHNISCHE UNIVERSITÄT CHEMNITZ
(Chemnitz University of Technology)

09107 Chemnitz
Telephone: (371) 5310
Fax: (371) 5311684
E-mail: pressestelle@tu-chemnitz.de
Internet: www.tu-chemnitz.de

Founded 1836 as a royal trade school of
Chemnitz; became Technische Universtät
Chemnitz-Zwickau 1986; present name
1997

State control

Academic year: October to September

Pres.: Prof. Dr KLAUS-JÜRGEN MATTHES
Vice-Pres. for Marketing and International
Affairs: Prof. Dr CORNELIA ZANGER
Vice-Pres. for Research: Prof. Dr DIETRICH R.
T. ZAHN
Vice-Pres. for Teaching and Learning: Prof.
Dr ALBRECHT HUMMEL
Chancellor: Dr EBERHARD ALLES
Library Dir: ANGELA MALZ

Library: see Libraries and Archives
Number of teachers: 163
Number of students: 10,382

Publication: Spectrum (4 a year)

DEANS

Faculty of Behavioural and Social Sciences:
Prof. Dr ASTRID SCHÜTZ
Faculty of Computer Science: Prof. Dr WOL-
FRAM HARDT
Faculty of Economics and Business Admin-
istration: Prof. Dr LUDWIG GRAMLICH
Faculty of Electrical Engineering and Infor-
mation Technology: Prof. Dr MADHUKAR
CHANDRA
Faculty of Engineering: Prof. Dr BERNHARD
WIELAGE
Faculty of Mathematics: Prof. Dr DIETER
HAPPEL
Faculty of Mechanical Engineering: KLAUS
NENDEL
Faculty of Natural Sciences: Prof. Dr KARL
HEINZ HOFFMANN
School of Philosophy: Prof. Dr CHRISTOPH
FASBENDER

TECHNISCHE UNIVERSITÄT CLAUSTHAL

Adolph-Roemer-Str. 2A, 38678 Clausthal-
Zellerfeld
Telephone: (5323) 720
Fax: (5323) 723500
E-mail: info@tu-clausthal.de
Internet: www.tu-clausthal.de

Founded 1775 as Bergakademie Clausthal,
attained univ. status 1968

State control

Academic year: April to March

Pres.: Prof. Dr. THOMAS HANSCHKE
Vice-Pres.: Dr Ing. INES SCHWARZ
Vice-Pres. for Teaching and Academic Pro-
grammes: Prof. Dr Ing OLIVER LANGEFELD
Vice-Pres. for Research and Technology
Transfer: Prof. Dr Ing VOLKER WESLING
Vice-Pres. for Information Management and
Infrastructure: Prof. Dr ANDREAS RAUSCH
Librarian: Dr HELMUT CYNTHA

Number of teachers: 180 , incl. 90 ordinary
profs
Number of students: 3,569

Publications: Lösestunde, Mitteilungsblatt,
Vorlesungsverzeichnis (1 a year)

DEANS

Faculty of Energy and Environment: Prof. Dr
Ing. NORBERT MEYER
Faculty of Mathematics/Computing and
Engineering: Prof. Dr JÜRGEN DIX
Faculty of Natural and Material Sciences:
Prof. Dr ALBRECHT WOLTER

TECHNISCHE UNIVERSITÄT DARMSTADT

64277 Darmstadt
Karolinenpl. 5, 64289 Darmstadt
Telephone: (6151) 1601
Fax: (6151) 165489
E-mail: praesident@pvw.tu-darmstadt.de
Internet: www.tu-darmstadt.de

Founded 1836 as Höhere Gewerbeschule,
acquired univ. status in 1877

Public control

Pres.: Prof. Dr HANS JÜRGEN PRÖMEL
Chancellor: Dr MANFRED EFINGER
Vice-Pres.: Prof. Dr Ing. CHRISTOPH MOTZKO
Vice-Pres.: Prof. Dr Ing. MARTIN HEILMAIER
Vice-Pres.: Prof. Dr PETRA GEHRING
Vice-Pres.: Prof. Dr REINER ANDERL

Library: see Libraries and Archives
Number of teachers: 270
Number of students: 23,100

Publications: Forschen – the science magazine (2 a year), Hoch³ (7 a year)

DEANS

Architecture: Dipl.-Ing. MARKUS GASSER
Biology: Prof. FELICITAS PFEIFER
Chemistry: Prof. Dr GERD BUNTKOWSKY
Civil Engineering and Geodesy: Prof. Dr Ing
HANS-JOACHIM LINKE
Computational Engineering: Prof. Dr Ing.
UWE RÜPPEL
Computer Science: Prof. Dr OSKAR VON STRYK
Electrical Engineering and Information
Technology: Prof. Dr Ing. HELMUT F.
SCHLAAK
History and Social Sciences: Prof. Dr
MICHÈLE KNODT
Humanities: Prof. Dr WOLFGANG ELLERMEIER
Law and Economics: Prof. Dr DIRK SCHIERECK
Material and Earth Sciences: Prof. Dr Hab.
RALF RIEDEL
Mathematics: Prof. Dr JAN HENDRIK BRUINIER
Mechanical Engineering: Prof. Dr Ing. UWE
KLINGAUF
Mechanics: Prof. Dr Ing. MARTIN OBERLACK
Physics: Prof. Dr BARBARA DROSSEL

PROFESSORS

ABELE, E., Mechanical Engineering
ABROMEIT, H., History and Social Sciences
ADAMY, J. H., Electrical Engineering and
Information Technology
ALBE, K., Material Sciences and Geoscience
ALBER, G., Physics
ALBER, H. D., Mathematics
ALBERT, B., Chemistry
ALEXA, M., Computing
ALFF, L., Material Sciences and Geoscience
ANDERL, R., Mechanical Engineering
ARICH-GERZ, B., History and Social Sciences
ARSLAN, U., Construction Engineering and
Geodesy
BÄCHMANN, K., Chemistry
BALD, S., Construction Engineering and
Geodesy
BALZER, G., Electrical Engineering and Infor-
mation Technology
BARENS, I., Law and Economic Science
BAYREUTHER, F., Law and Economic Science
BECKER, M., Construction Engineering and
Geodesy
BECKER, W., Mathematics

BERGER, C., Mechanical Engineering
BERGES, J., Physics
BERKING, H., History and Social Sciences
BETSCH, O., Law and Economic Science
BETTE, K. H., Human Sciences: Developmen-
tal Sciences, Psychology and Sport Science
BIBEL, W., Computing
BINDER, A., Electrical Engineering and Infor-
mation Technology
BIRKHOFER, H., Mechanical Engineering
BIRKL, G., Physics
BÖHM, H. R., Construction Engineering and
Geodesy
BOKOWSKI, J., Mathematics
BOLTZE, M., Construction Engineering and
Geodesy
BORCHERDING, K., Human Sciences: Develop-
mental Sciences, Psychology and Sport
Science
BRAUN-MUNZINGER, P., Physics
BREUER, B. J., Mechanical Engineering
BRICKMANN, J., Chemistry
BRUDER, R., Mathematics
BRUDER, R., Mechanical Engineering
BUCHLER, J. W., Chemistry
BUCHMANN, A., Computing
BUCHMANN, J., Computing
BURMEISTER, P., Mathematics
BUSCH, M., Chemistry
BUSCHINGER, A., Biology
BUXMANN, P., Law and Economic Science
CASPARI, V., Law and Economic Science
CLAUS, P., Chemistry
CORNEL, P., Construction Engineering and
Geodesy
CREUTZIG, J., Mathematics
DENCHER, N., Chemistry
DENINGER-POLZER, G., History and Social
Sciences
DINSE, K. P., Chemistry
DIPPER, C., History and Social Sciences
DOMSCHKE, W., Law and Economic Science
DÖRSAM, E., Mechanical Engineering
DROSSEL, B., Physics
DÜR, M., Mathematics
ECKERT, C., Computing
ECKERT, J., Material Sciences and Geoscience
EGLOFF, G., History and Social Sciences
ELLERMEIER, W., Mathematics
ELSÄßER, W., Physics
ENCARNACAO, J., Computing
ENDERS, J., Physics
ENSINGER, W., Material Sciences and
Geoscience
ENTORF, H., Law and Economic Science
EPPLE, B., Mechanical Engineering
EULER, P., Human Sciences: Developmental
Sciences, Psychology and Sport Science
EVEKING, H., Electrical Engineering and
Information Technology
EXNER, H. E., Material Sciences and
Geoscience
FARWIG, R., Mathematics
FÄSSLER, T. F., Chemistry
FEILE, R., Physics
FERREIRO MÄHLMANN, R., Material Sciences
and Geoscience
FESSNER, W.-D., Chemistry
FRIEDL, P., Chemistry
FRYDE-STROMER V. REICHENBACH, N., History
and Social Sciences
FUEß, H., Material Sciences and Geoscience
FUJARA, F., Physics
FÜRNKRANZ, J., Computing
GALUSKE, R., Biology
GAMM, G., History and Social Sciences
GATERMANN, D., Architecture
GEHRING, P., History and Social Sciences
GERSHMAN, A., Electrical Engineering and
Information Technology
GERSTENECKER, C., Construction Engineering
and Geodesy
GIERSCH, C., Biology
GIVSAN, H., History and Social Sciences
GLESNER, M., Electrical Engineering and
Information Technology

GÖPFERT, W., Construction Engineering and Geodesy
GÖRINGER, U., Biology
GÖTTSCHING, L., Mechanical Engineering
GRAUBNER, C.-A., Construction Engineering and Geodesy
GREWE, N., Physics
GRIEM, J., History and Social Sciences
GROCHE, P., Mechanical Engineering
GROSS, D., Mathematics
GROSSE-BRAUCKMANN, K., Mathematics
GRUBER, E., Chemistry
GRÜBL, P., Construction Engineering and Geodesy
GRUTTMANN, F., Construction Engineering and Geodesy
HAASE, W., Chemistry
HAGEDORN, P., Mathematics
HAHN, H., Material Sciences and Geoscience
HAMPE, M., Mechanical Engineering
HÄNSEL, F., Human Sciences: Developmental Sciences, Psychology and Sport Science
HANSELKA, H., Mechanical Engineering
HÄNSLER, E., Electrical Engineering and Information Technology
HARD, M., History and Social Sciences
HARTKOPF, T., Electrical Engineering and Information Technology
HARTMANN, E., Mathematics
HARTMANN, H., Human Sciences: Developmental Sciences, Psychology and Sport Science
HARTMANN, M. L., History and Social Sciences
HARTNAGEL, H. L., Electrical Engineering and Information Technology
HASSLER, U., Law and Economic Science
HAUSCHILD, M., Architecture
HEGGER, M., Architecture
HEIDER, J., Biology
HEIL, E., Mathematics
HEINELT, H., History and Social Sciences
HELM, C., Law and Economic Science
HERRMANN, C., Mathematics
HIEBER, M., Mathematics
HIMSTEDT, W., Biology
HINDERER, M., Material Sciences and Geoscience
HINRICHSEN, V., Electrical Engineering and Information Technology
HOFFMANN, D. H. H., Physics
HOFFMANN, H. J., Computing
HOFFMANN, R., Computing
HOFMANN, K. H., Mathematics
HOFMANN, T., Computing
HOHENBERG, G., Mechanical Engineering
HOLSTEIN, T. W., Biology
HOPPE, A., Material Sciences and Geoscience
HUSS, S., Computing
HÜTT, M.-T., Biology
IHRINGER, T., Mathematics
ISERMANN, R., Electrical Engineering and Information Technology
JAEGERMANN, W., Material Sciences and Geoscience
JAGER, J., Construction Engineering and Geodesy
JAKOBY, R., Electrical Engineering and Information Technology
JANICH, N., History and Social Sciences
JANICKA, J., Mechanical Engineering
JANNIDIS, F., History and Social Sciences
JOSWIG, M., Mathematics
KAISER, F., Physics
KAISER, W., Biology
KALDENHOFF, R., Biology
KAMMERER, P., Computing
KANGASHARJU, J., Computing
KANKELEIT, E., Physics
KAST, W., Mechanical Engineering
KATZENBACH, R. H., Construction Engineering and Geodesy
KEIMEL, K., Mathematics
KEMPE, S., Material Sciences and Geoscience
KIEHL, M., Mathematics
KINDLER, J., Mathematics

KLEEBE, H.-J., Material Sciences and Geoscience
KLEIN, A., Electrical Engineering and Information Technology
KLEIN, H.-F., Chemistry
KLINGAUF, U., Mechanical Engineering
KNODT, M., History and Social Sciences
KOCH, A., Computing
KOHLENBACH, U., Mathematics
KOLMAR, H., Chemistry
KÖNIG, H. D., Electrical Engineering and Information Technology
KONIGORSKI, U., Electrical Engineering and Information Technology
KOOB, M., Architecture
KÖRDING, A., Physics
KOSTKA, A., Electrical Engineering and Information Technology
KRAIS, B., History and Social Sciences
KRAMER, L., Mathematics
KÜBLER, J., Physics
KÜHNE, T., Computing
KÜMMERER, B., Mathematics
LANDAU, K., Mechanical Engineering
LANG, J., Mathematics
LANGANKE, K., Physics
LANGE, J., Construction Engineering and Geodesy
LANGHEINRICH, W., Electrical Engineering and Information Technology
LANGNER, G., Biology
LAYER, PAUL G., Biology
LEHN, J., Mathematics
LEICHNER, R., Human Sciences: Developmental Sciences, Psychology and Sport Science
LICHTENTHALER, F., Chemistry
LIEBENWEIN, W., Architecture
LINKE, H.-J., Construction Engineering and Geodesy
LORCH, W., Architecture
LOTH, R., Mechanical Engineering
LÖW, M., History and Social Sciences
LUFT, G., Chemistry
LUSERKE, M., History and Social Sciences
LÜTTGE, U., Biology
MARKERT, R., Mathematics
MARLY, J., Law and Economic Science
MARTIN, A., Mathematics
MATHÉY, G. K., Architecture
MÄURER, H., Mathematics
MAY, A., Mathematics
MAY, H. D., Material Sciences and Geoscience
MEIßNER, P., Electrical Engineering and Information Technology
MEZINI, M., Computing
MOLEK, H., Material Sciences and Geoscience
MOTZKO, C., Construction Engineering and Geodesy
MÜHLHÄUSER, M. E., Computing
MÜLLER, R., Mathematics
MÜLLER, W. F., Material Sciences and Geoscience
MÜLLER-PLATHE, F., Chemistry
MULSER, P., Physics
MÜNK, H. D., Human Sciences: Developmental Sciences, Psychology and Sport Science
MUTSCHLER, P., Electrical Engineering and Information Technology
NEEB, K.-H., Mathematics
NESTLE, N., Physics
NEUHOLD, E., Computing
NEUNHOEFFER, H., Chemistry
NICKEL, E., Law and Economic Science
NOLTE, W., Mathematics
NORDMANN, A., History and Social Sciences
NORDMANN, R., Mechanical Engineering
OBERLACK, M., Mathematics
ORTNER, E., Law and Economic Science
ORTNER, H., Material Sciences and Geoscience
OSTERMANN, K., Computing
OSTROWSKI, M., Construction Engineering and Geodesy
OTTO, M., Mathematics
PAHL, G., Mechanical Engineering

PAULINYI, A., History and Social Sciences
PAUL-KOHLHOFF, A., Human Sciences: Developmental Sciences, Psychology and Sport Science
PAVLIDIS, D., Electrical Engineering and Information Technology
PETZINKA, K.-H., Architecture
PFEIFER, F., Biology
PFEIFER, G., Architecture
PFEIFFER, W., Electrical Engineering and Information Technology
PFLÜGER, M., Law and Economic Science
PFNÜR, A., Law and Economic Science
PFOHL, H.-C., Law and Economic Science
PINNAU, R., Mathematics
PLENIO, H. H., Chemistry
PONGRATZ, L., Human Sciences: Developmental Sciences, Psychology and Sport Science
PORTO, M., Physics
PUHANI, P., Law and Economic Science
QUICK, R., Law and Economic Science
RAUH, H., Material Sciences and Geoscience
REGGELIN, M., Chemistry
REHAHN, M., Chemistry
REIF, U., Mathematics
REISTER, D., Construction Engineering and Geodesy
RETZKO, H. G., Construction Engineering and Geodesy
RICHTER, A., Physics
RIEDEL, R., Material Sciences and Geoscience
RITTER, K., Mathematics
RÖDEL, J., Material Sciences and Geoscience
ROESNER, K., Mathematics
ROSE, H., Physics
ROTH, R., Physics
RÜPPEL, U., Construction Engineering and Geodesy
RÜRUP, H.-A., Law and Economic Science
RÜTZEL, J., Human Sciences: Developmental Sciences, Psychology and Sport Science
SASS, I., Material Sciences and Geoscience
SCHABEL, S., Mechanical Engineering
SCHÄFER, M., Mechanical Engineering
SCHÄFER, R., Chemistry
SCHÄFER, S. M., Construction Engineering and Geodesy
SCHAPPACHER, N., Mathematics
SCHEBEK, L., Construction Engineering and Geodesy
SCHEFFOLD, E., Mathematics
SCHEU, S., Biology
SCHIELE, B., Computing
SCHIFFER, H.-P., Mechanical Engineering
SCHLAAK, H., Electrical Engineering and Information Technology
SCHLEMMER, H., Construction Engineering and Geodesy
SCHMALZ-BRUNS, R., History and Social Sciences
SCHMID, V., Law and Economic Science
SCHMIDT, B., Chemistry
SCHMIDT, R., Human Sciences: Developmental Sciences, Psychology and Sport Science
SCHMIDT-CLAUSEN, H.-J., Electrical Engineering and Information Technology
SCHMIEDE, R., History and Social Sciences
SCHMITZ, B., Human Sciences: Developmental Sciences, Psychology and Sport Science
SCHNEIDER, J., Chemistry
SCHNEIDER, U. H., Law and Economic Science
SCHNEIDER, W. C., History and Social Sciences
SCHNELLENBACH-HELD, M., Construction Engineering and Geodesy
SCHOTT, D., History and Social Sciences
SCHUBERT, E., Construction Engineering and Geodesy
SCHULZ, H., Mechanical Engineering
SCHÜRMANN, H., Mechanical Engineering
SCHÜRR, A., Electrical Engineering and Information Technology
SCHUSTER, R., Chemistry
SCHÜTH, C., Material Sciences and Geoscience
SCHWABE-KRATOCHWIL, A., Biology

SCHWALKE, U., Electrical Engineering and Information Technology
SEELIG, W., Physics
SEILER, T. B., Human Sciences: Developmental Sciences, Psychology and Sport Science
SESINK, W., Human Sciences: Developmental Sciences, Psychology and Sport Science
SESSELMEIER, W., Law and Economic Science
SESSLER, G., Electrical Engineering and Information Technology
SIEKER, S., Law and Economic Science
SORGATZ, H., Human Sciences: Developmental Sciences, Psychology and Sport Science
SPECHT, G., Law and Economic Science
SPELLUCCI, P., Mathematics
STADTLER, H., Law and Economic Science
STAHL, M., History and Social Sciences
STEINMETZ, R., Electrical Engineering and Information Technology
STENZEL, J., Electrical Engineering and Information Technology
STEPHAN, P. C., Mechanical Engineering
STOFFEL, B., Mechanical Engineering
STREICHER, T., Mathematics
STÜHN, B., Physics
SURI, N., Computing
TEICH, E., History and Social Sciences
THIEL, G., Biology
TREBELS, W., Mathematics
TROPEA, C., Mechanical Engineering
TSAKMAKIS, C., Mathematics
TSCHUDI, T., Physics
ULLRICH-EBERIUS, C., Biology
URBAN, W., Construction Engineering and Geodesy
VIADA, E., Mathematics
VOGEL, H., Chemistry
VOGT, M., History and Social Sciences
VON NEUMANN-COSEL, P., Physics
VON SEGGERN, H., Material Sciences and Geoscience
VON STRYK, O., Computing
VORMWALD, M., Construction Engineering and Geodesy
VOß, H.-G., Human Sciences: Developmental Sciences, Psychology and Sport Science
WALDSCHMIDT, H., Computing
WALTER, H., Computing
WALTHER, C., Computing
WALTHER, T., Physics
WAMBACH, J., Physics
WEGMANN, H., Mathematics
WEIHE, K., Computing
WEILAND, T., Electrical Engineering and Information Technology
WEINBRUCH, S., Material Sciences and Geoscience
WEISCHEDE, D., Architecture
WEIßMANTEL, H., Electrical Engineering and Information Technology
WÉKÉL, J., Architecture
WERTHSCHÜTZKY, R., Electrical Engineering and Information Technology
WIEMEYER, J., Human Sciences: Developmental Sciences, Psychology and Sport Science
WILHELM, M., Mechanical Engineering
WILLE, R., Mathematics
WINNER, H., Mechanical Engineering
WIPF, H., Physics
WIRTH, A. E. H., Law and Economic Science
WOLF, K.-D., History and Social Sciences
WÖLFEL, H., Mechanical Engineering
WOLLENWEBER, E., Biology
WROBEL, B., Construction Engineering and Geodesy
WURL, H.-J., Law and Economic Science
ZANKE, U., Construction Engineering and Geodesy
ZILGES, A., Physics
ZOUBIR, A. M. D. E., Electrical Engineering and Information Technology

TECHNISCHE UNIVERSITÄT DORTMUND

44221 Dortmund
August-Schmidt-Str. 4, 44227 Dortmund
Telephone: (231) 75511
Fax: (231) 7555145
E-mail: huesing@verwaltung.tu-dortmund.de
Internet: www.tu-dortmund.de
Founded 1968
State control
Languages of instruction: German, English
Academic year: April to February

Rector: Prof. Dr URSULA GATHER
Vice-Rector: Prof. Dr. BARBARA WELZEL
Vice-Rector: Prof. Dr ANDREJ GÓRAK
Vice-Rector for Academic Affairs: Prof. Dr WALTER GRÜNZWEIG
Vice-Rector for Research: Prof. Dr METIN TOLAN
Vice-Rector for Finance: Prof. Dr UWE SCHWIEGELSHOHN
Chancellor: ALBRECHT EHLERS
Dir: Dr JOACHIM KREISCHE

Library: see under Libraries and Archives
Number of students: 24,000

Publications: *Mundo* (2 a year), *Unizet* (10 a year)

DEANS

Architecture and Civil Engineering: Prof. Ing. WALTER A. NOEBEL
Art and Sport: Prof. Dr GÜNTHER RÖTTER
Biochemical and Chemical Engineering: Prof. Dr Ing. ANDRZEJ GÓRAK
Chemistry: Prof. Dr HEINZ REHAGE
Computer Science: Ing. HANS DECKER
Culture Studies: Prof. Dr HORST PÖTTKER
Economics and Social Sciences: Prof. Dr WOLFGANG B. SCHÜNEMANN
Education and Sociology: Prof. Dr THOMAS GOLL
Electrical Engineering and Information Technology: Prof. Dr Ing. CHRISTIAN WIETFELD
Human Sciences and Theology: Prof. Dr ERNSTPETER MAURER
Mathematics: Prof. Dr STEFAN TUREK
Mechanical Engineering: Prof. Dr Ing. DIRK BIERMANN
Physics: Prof. Dr BERNHARD SPAAN
Rehabilitation Sciences: Prof. Dr ELISABETH WACKER
Spatial Planning: Prof. CHRISTA REICHER
Statistics: Prof. Dr CLAUS WEIHS

PROFESSORS

Faculty of Architecture and Civil Engineering (tel. (231) 7552074; fax (231) 7555279; e-mail dekanat@busch.bauwesen.tu-dortmund.de; internet www.bauwesen.tu-dortmund.de):

BARTHOLD, F.-J., Numerical Methods and Information Processing
BLECKEN, U., Construction Management and Machines
BOFINGER, H., Design and Building Theory
HASSLER, U., Conservation and Building Research
HETTLER, A., Soil Mechanics and Foundation Engineering
MÄCKLER, C., Urban Design
MAURER, R., Concrete Engineering
MÜLLER, H., Environmental Architecture
NALBACH, G., Design, Spatial Design and the Fundamentals of Presentation
NEISECKE, J., Building Materials
NOEBEL, W., Design and Industrial Building
OBRECHT, H., Structural and Computational Mechanics
ÖTES, A., Structural Design
SCHIFFERS, K.-H., Organization of Building Planning and Site Management (OPS)

STANDKE, G. R., Design and Building Construction
UNGERMANN, D., Steel Construction

Faculty of Cultural Studies (tel. (231) 7552919; fax (231) 7552894; e-mail zimmerma@mail.fb15.tu-dortmund.de; internet www.fb15.tu-dortmund.de):

Institute of English and American Studies:

BIMBERG, C.
GRÜNZWEIG, W.
KRAMER, J.
NOLD, G.
PETERS, H.

Institute of German Language and Literature:

BRÜNNER, G.
CONRADY, P.
DENNELER, I.
GERHARD, U.
HOFFMANN, L.
KÜHN, R.
LINK, J.
PARR, R.
QUASTHOFF, U.
RIEMENSCHNEIDER, H.
RISHOLM, E.
STORRER, A.

Institute of History:

HÖMIG, H.
SOLLBACH, G.
ZETTLER, A.

Institute of Journalism:

BOHRMANN, H.
BRANAHL, U.
EURICH, C.
HEINRICH, J.
KOPPER, G.
MACHILL, M.
PÄTZOLD, U.
PÖTTKER, H.
RAGER, G.

Faculty of Economics and Social Sciences (tel. (231) 7553182; fax (231) 7554375; e-mail elke.klika@wiso.tu-dortmund.de; internet www.wiso.tu-dortmund.de):

HIRSCH-KREINSEN, H., Technology and Society
HOLLÄNDER, H., Macroeconomic Theory
HOLZMÜLLER, H., Marketing
JEHLE, E., Operations Management and Logistics
KRAFT, K., Economics (Economic Policy)
LACKES, R., Business Information and Management Information Systems
LEININGER, W., Microeconomic Theory
LIENING, A., Teaching of Economics
NEUENDORFF, H., Sociology
RECHT, P., Operations Research and Economic Informatics
REICHMANN, T., Management Accounting
RICHTER, W., Public Economics
SCHÜNEMANN, W., Private Law
TEICHMANN, U., Money and Credit
WAHL, J., Investments and Finance
WELGE, M., Management
WEYER, J., Sociology

Faculty of Electrical Engineering and Information Technology (tel. (231) 7552123; fax (231) 7552051; e-mail info@dekanat.e-technik.tu-dortmund.de; internet www.e-technik.tu-dortmund.de):

FIEDLER, H., Integrated Systems
GÖTZE, J., Information Processing
HANDSCHIN, E., Electric Power Supply
KAYS, R., Communication Technology
KULIG, S., Electric Machines, Drive and Power Electronics
NEYER, A., Microstructure Technology
PEIER, D., High Voltage Engineering
SCHERRER, R., Electronic Systems and Switching
SCHRÖDER, H., Circuits and Systems

SCHUMACHER, K., Microelectronics
SCHWIEGELSHOHN, U., Computer Engineering
VOGES, E., High Frequency Technology

Faculty of Human Sciences and Theology
(tel. (231) 7552886; fax (231) 7555452; e-mail leschner@fb14.tu-dortmund.de; internet www.fb14.tu-dortmund.de):

Catholic Theology:

DORMEYER, D.
METTE, N.
MÖLLE, H.
RUSTER, T

Home Economics:

EISSING, G.

Organizational Psychology:

KASTNER, M.
KLEINBECK, U.

Philosophy:

FALKENBERG, B.
POST, W.
WINGERT, L.

Politics:

MEYER, T.

Protestant Theology:

BÜTTNER, G.
GREWEL, H.
MAURER, E.
MUNZEL, F.
POLA, T.
RIESNER, R.

Psychology:

GASCH, B.
KASTNER, M.
KLEINBECK, U.
LASOGGA, F.
METZ-GÖCKEL, H.
NEUMANN, R.
ROEDER, B.
ZIMMERMANN, P.

Faculty of Mechanical Engineering (tel. (231) 7552723; fax (231) 7552706; e-mail dekan@mb.tu-dortmund.de; internet www.mb.tu-dortmund.de):

CLAUSEN, U., Transport Systems and Logistics
CROSTACK, H.-A., Quality Control
DEUSE, J., Work and Production Systems
HOMPELTEN, M., Transportation and Storage
JANSEN, R., Logistics
KAUDER, K., Fluid Energy Machines
KLEINER, M., Forming Technology and Lightweight Construction
KREIS, W., Machine Elements, Design and Handling Techniques
KUHN, A., Plant Organization
KÜNNE, B., Machine Elements
OTT, B., Technical Didactics
SVENDSEN, B., Mechanics
THERMANN, K., Machine Dynamics
TILLMANN, W., Materials Technology
UHLE, M., Measurement Technology
WEINERT, K., Machining Technology

Faculty of Rehabilitation Sciences (Emil-Figge-Str. 50, 44227 Dortmund; tel. (231) 7554541; fax (231) 7554503; e-mail dekanat.fb13@tu-dortmund.de; internet www.tu-dortmund.de/fb13):

Adapted Physical Activity and Movement Therapy:

HÖLTER, G.

Art Education and Art Therapy:

JÁDI, F.

Education for Individuals with Mental Disabilities:

DÖNHOFF, K.
HAVEMAN, M.
MEYER, H.

Gender Research in Special Needs Education:

SCHILDMANN, U.

Music Education and Music Therapy:

MERKT, I.

Rehabilitation for Individuals with Blindness and Visual Impairments:

CSOCSÁN, E.
WALTHES, R.

Rehabilitation for Individuals with Communication Disorders:

DUPUIS, G.
KATZ-BERNSTEIN, N.

Rehabilitation and Education for Individuals with Disabilities:

DEDERICH, M.

Rehabilitation for Individuals with Emotional and Behavioural Disorders:

PETERMANN, U.

Rehabilitation for Individuals with Learning Difficulties:

SCHMETZ, D.
WEMBER, F.

Rehabilitation for Individuals with Physical Disabilities:

LEYENDECKER, C.

Rehabilitation Psychology:

FRANKE, A.
FRÖSTER, H.

Rehabilitation Technology:

BÜHLER, C.

Sociology in Rehabilitation:

WACKER, E.

Vocational Education and Training:

BIERMANN, H.

Faculty of Spatial Planning (August-Schmidt-Str. 10, 44221 Dortmund; tel. (231) 7552284; fax (231) 7552620; e-mail dekanat.rp@tu-dortmund.de; internet www.raumplanung.tu-dortmund.de):

BADE, F.-J., Regional Economics
BAUMGART, S., Urban and Regional Planning
BECKER, R., Women's Studies and Housing in Spatial Planning
BLOTEVOGEL, H.-H., Regional and Federal Planning
DAVID, C.-H., Law and Spatial Planning
DAVY, B., Land Policy and Management
FINKE, L., Ecology and Landscape Planning
HENNINGS, G., Industrial and Commercial Development Planning
HOLZ-RAU, C., Transport Planning
KRAUSE, K.-J., Urban and Landscape Design
KREIBICH, V., Spring Centre, Urban and Regional Geography
KROES, G., Spring Centre, Urban and Regional Geography
KUNZMANN, K., Spatial Planning in Europe
REICHER, C., Urban Design and Land Use Planning
RÖDDING, W., Systems Theory and Systems Engineering
SCHMALS, K. M., Sociology and Spatial Planning
TIETZ, H.-P., Supply and Disposal Systems in Spatial Planning
VELSINGER, P., Political Economics, Regional Economics

Department of Arts and Sports Studies (tel. (231) 7554153; fax (231) 7554506; e-mail dek16ri@pop.tu-dortmund.de; internet www.tu-dortmund.de/fb16):

Institute of Art and Education:

BERTRAM-MÖBIUS, U.
BUSSE, K.-P.
VAN HAAREN, B.

WELZEL, B.

Institute of Geography and Education:

NUTZ, M.
SCHMIDT-KALLERT, E.

Institute of Music and Education:

ABEGG, W.
HOUBEN, E.
RÖTTER, G.
STEGEMANN, M.
VON SCHOENEBECK, M.

Institute of Sport and Education:

BRÄUTIGAM, M.
STARISCHKA, S.
THIELE, J.

Institute of Textile Design and Education/ Comparative Textile Sciences:

MENTGES, G.

Department of Biochemical and Chemical Engineering (tel. (231) 7552362; fax (231) 7552361; e-mail dekanat@ct.tu-dortmund.de; internet www.chemietechnik.tu-dortmund.de):

AGAR, D., Technical Chemistry
BEHR, A., Technical Chemistry
ENGELL, S., Plant Control Technology
FAHLENKAMP, H., Environmental Technology
FRIEDRICH, C., Technical Microbiology
GÓRAK, A., Fluid Separation Processes
KÖSTER, U., Materials Science
SADOWSKI, G., Thermodynamics
SCHMID, A., Chemical Biotechnology
SCHMIDT-TRAUB, H., Plant Technology
STRAUß, K., Energy Processing and Fluid Mechanics
WALZEL, P., Mechanical Process Engineering
WEIß, E., Chemical Plant Technology
WICHMANN, R., Biological Engineering

Department of Chemistry (tel. (231) 7553720; fax (231) 7553771; e-mail dekan-chemie@chemie.tu-dortmund.de; internet www.chemie.tu-dortmund.de):

EILBRACHT, P., Organic Chemistry
GEIGER, A., Physical Chemistry
GRAF, D., Biology
HAAG, R., Organic Chemistry
JURKSCHAT, K., Inorganic Chemistry
KELLER, H.-L., Inorganic Chemistry
KRAUSE, N., Organic Chemistry
LIPPERT, B., Inorganic Chemistry
MELLE, I., Chemistry Teaching
MINKWITZ, R., Inorganic Chemistry
MITCHELL, T. N., Organic Chemistry
NIEMEYER, C. M., Biological and Chemical Microstructure Technology
REHAGE, H., Physical Chemistry
SANDMANN, A., Biology
SCHMUTZLER, R.-W., Physical Chemistry
VERBEEK, B., Biology
WALDMANN, H., Organic Chemistry
WINTER, R., Physical Chemistry

Department of Computer Science (tel. (231) 7552121; fax (231) 7552130; e-mail kossmann@dekanat.cs.tu-dortmund.de; internet www.informatik.tu-dortmund.de):

BISKUP, J., Information Systems
BUCHHOLZ, P., Modelling and Simulation
DITTRICH, G., Automata and Systems Theory
DOBERKAT, E.-E., Software Technology
KERN-ISBERNER, G., Information Engineering
KRUMM, H., Computer Networks and Distributed Systems
LINDEMANN, C., Computing Systems and Performance Analysis
MARWEDEL, P., Technical Computer Science, Embedded Systems
MORIK, K., Artificial Intelligence
MÜLLER, H., Computer Graphics
MÜTZEL, P., Algorithm Engineering

PADAWITZ, P., Compiler Construction
REUSCH, B., Automata and Sequential Logic Systems Theory
SCHWEFEL, H.-P., Systems Analysis
STEFFEN, B., Programming Systems
WEDDE, H., Operating Systems/Computer Architecture
WEGENER, I., Efficient Algorithms and Complexity Theory

Department of Education and Sociology (tel. (231) 755-2194; fax (231) 7555285; e-mail dekanat@fb12.tu-dortmund.de; internet www.fb12.tu-dortmund.de):

Institute of General and Vocational Education:

PÄTZOLD, G.
VOGEL, P.
WIGGER, L.

Institute of School Development Research:

BOS, W.
HOLTAPPELS, H.
SCHULZ-ZANDER, R.

Institute of Social and Elementary Education:

BIERFLEITER, C.
FRIED, L.
NOLDA, S.
UHLENDORFF, U.

Institute of Teaching Science:

BEUTEL, S.-I.
KOCH-PRIEWE, B.
WIEDERHOLD, K.-A.
WILDT, J.

Sociology:

BÜHRMANN, A. D.
GOLL, T.
HITZLER, R.
HORNBOSTEL, S.
KALBITZ, R.
NAEGELE, G.
REICHERT, M.
STALLBERG, E.

Department of Mathematics (tel. (231) 755-3051; fax (231) 755-3054; e-mail dekan@mathematik.tu-dortmund.de; internet www.mathematik.tu-dortmund.de):

ACHTZIGER, W., Applied Mathematics
BECKER, E., Algebra
BLUM, H., Applied Mathematics
HAZOD, W., Analysis and Stochastics
HENN, H.-W., Mathematics Teaching
KABALLO, W., Analysis
KOCH, H., Analysis
KREUZER, M., Algebra
KUZMIN, D., Applied Mathematics and Numerics
MENKE, K., Function Theory
MÖLLER, M., Approximation Theory
MÜLLER, G., Mathematics Teaching
ROSENBERGER, G., Algebra
SCHARLAU, R., Geometry and Algebra
SCHWACHTHÖFER, L., Differential Geometry
SELTER, C., Mathematics Teaching
SIBURG, F., Function Theory
SKUTELLA, M., Discrete Optimization
STEINMETZ, N., Function Theory
STÖCKLER, J., Approximation Theory
TUREK, S., Applied Mathematics and Numerics
VOIT, M., Analysis and Stochastics
ZAMFIRESCU, T., Geometry and Algebra

Department of Physics (tel. (231) 7553503; fax (231) 7555027; e-mail dekanat@physik.tu-dortmund.de; internet www.physik.tu-dortmund.de):

BAACKE, J., Theoretical Physics
BAYER, M., Experimental Physics
BÖHMER, R., Experimental Physics
GERLACH, B., Theoretical Physics
GÖßLING, C., Experimental Physics
KEITER, H., Theoretical Physics

NIEMAX, K., Plasma and Laser Spectro-chemistry
PASCHOS, E., Theoretical Physics
PFLUG, A., Physics Teaching
REYA, E., Theoretical Physics
RHODE, W., Experimental Physics
SPAAN, B., Experimental Physics
SUTER, D., Experimental Physics
TOLAN, M., Experimental Physics
WEBER, W., Theoretical Physics
WEISS, T., Acceleration Physics
WESTPHAL, C., Experimental Physics
WILLE, K., Accelerator Physics
WOGGON, U., Experimental Teaching

Department of Statistics (Vogelpothsweg 87, 44227 Dortmund; tel. (231) 7553113; fax (231) 7553454; e-mail dekanat@statistik.tu-dortmund.de; internet www.statistik.tu-dortmund.de):

GATHER, U., Mathematical Statistics and Industrial Application
HARTUNG, J., Statistics Applied in Engineering
ICKSTADT, K., Statistics in Biosciences
KRÄMER, W., Economic and Social Statistics
KUNERT, J., Mathematical Statistics and Scientific Application
TRENKLER, G., Statistics and Econometrics
URFER, W., Statistical Methods in Genetics and Ecology
WEIHS, K., Computer-Aided Statistics

TECHNISCHE UNIVERSITÄT DRESDEN

Mommsenstr. 9, 01062 Dresden

Telephone: (351) 4630
Fax: (351) 46337168
E-mail: infostelle@tu-dresden.de
Internet: www.tu-dresden.de

Founded 1828, Univ. status 1961
State control
Academic year: October to September

Rector: Prof. Dr Ing. Hab. HANS MÜLLER-STEINHAGEN
Vice-Rector for Academic and Int. Affairs: Prof. Dr Hab. URSULA SCHAEFER
Vice-Rector for Research: Prof. Dr Hab. GERHARD ROEDEL
Vice-Rector for Structure and Devt: Prof. Dr Hab. KARL LENZ
Chancellor: WOLF-ECKHARD WORMSER
Library: see Libraries and Archives
Number of teachers: 419
Number of students: 36,066 , not incl. Faculty of Medicine

Publication: *Wissenschaftliche Zeitschrift* (6 a year)

DEANS

'Carl Gustav Carus' Faculty of Medicine: Prof. Dr HEINZ REICHMANN
Faculty of Architecture: Prof. Dr Ing. Hab. HANS-GEORG LIPPERT
Faculty of Arts, Humanities and Social Science: Prof. Dr BRUNO KLEIN
Faculty of Business and Economics: Prof. Dr Hab. ALEXANDER KARMANN
Faculty of Civil Engineering: Prof. Dr Ing. RAINER SCHACH
Faculty of Computer Science: Prof. Dr STEFAN GUMHOLD
Faculty of Education: Prof. Dr Hab. GISELA WIESNER
Faculty of Electrical Engineering and Information Technology: Prof. Dr KLAUS JANSCHEK
Faculty of Forestry, Geosciences and Hydrosciences: Prof. Dr Hab. HANS-GERD MAAS
Faculty of Law: Prof. Dr HORST-PETER GÖTTING

Faculty of Linguistics, Literature and Cultural Studies: Prof. Dr Hab. KARLHEINZ JAKOB
Faculty of Mathematics and Natural Sciences: Prof. Dr BERNHARD GANTER
Faculty of Mechanical Engineering: Prof. Dr Ing. Hab. ECKHARD BEYER
'Friedrich List' Faculty of Transportation and Traffic Sciences: Prof. Dr Ing. CHRISTIAN LIPPOLD

TECHNISCHE UNIVERSITÄT HAMBURG-HARBURG

Schwarzenbergstr. 95, 21073, Hamburg

Telephone: (40) 428780
Fax: (40) 428782288
E-mail: pressestelle@tu-harburg.de
Internet: www.tu-harburg.de

Founded 1978
Academic year: October to September

Pres.: Prof. Dr EDWIN KREUZER
Vice-Pres. for Education: Prof. Dr GARABED ANTRANIKIAN
Vice-Pres. for Research: Prof. Dr HERMANN ROHLING
Chancellor: KLAUS-JOACHIM SCHEUNERT
Librarian: INKEN FELDSIEN-SUDHAUS

Library of 480,000 vols, 700 print journals, 6,000 e-journals
Number of teachers: 710
Number of students: 5,700

DEANS

Civil Engineering: Prof. Dr Ing. JÜRGEN GRABE
Electrical Engineering and Information Technology: Prof. Dr Ing. ARNE JACOB
Management Sciences and Technology: Prof. Dr CHRISTIAN LÜTHJE
Mechanical Engineering: Prof. Dr NORBERT HOFFMANN
Process and Chemical Engineering: Prof. Dr Ing. STEFAN HEINRICH
Vocational Subject Education: Prof. Dr Ing. CLAUS EMMELMANN

TECHNISCHE UNIVERSITÄT ILMENAU

POB 10 05 65, 98684 Ilmenau
Ehrenbergstr. 29, 98693 Ilmenau

Telephone: (3677) 690
Fax: (3677) 691701
E-mail: rektor@tu-ilmenau.de
Internet: www.tu-ilmenau.de

Founded 1953 as Hochschule für Elektrotechnik, present name and status 1992
State control
Academic year: October to September

Rector: Prof. Dr Hab. PETER SCHARFF
Vice-Rector for Science: Prof. Dr Ing. KLAUS AUGSBURG
Vice-Rector for Teaching: Prof. Dr Ing. JÜRGEN PETZOLDT
Chancellor: Dr MARGOT BOCK
Librarian: GERHARD VOGT

Number of teachers: 714
Number of students: 8,010

Publications: *'Information/Dokumentation'* (proceedings, every 2 years), *Tagungsberichte des Internationalen Kolloquiums* (1 a year), *Wissenschaftliches Magazin*

DEANS

Faculty of Computer Science and Automation: Prof. Dr Ing. Hab. JENS HAUEISEN
Faculty of Economics: Prof. Dr Hab. RAINER SOUREN
Faculty of Electrical Engineering and Information Technology: Prof. Dr Ing. Hab. FRANK BERGER
Faculty of Mathematics and Natural Sciences: Prof. Dr Hab. NICOLA DÖRING

Faculty of Mechanical Engineering: Prof. Dr Ing. Hab. PETER KURTZ

TECHNISCHE UNIVERSITÄT KAISERSLAUTERN

POB 3049, 67653 Kaiserslautern
Gottlieb-Daimler-Str., 67663 Kaiserslautern

Telephone: (631) 2050
Fax: (631) 2053200
E-mail: internationales@uni-kl.de
Internet: www.uni-kl.de

Founded 1970 as Universität Trier Kaiserslautern, separated 1975
State control
Languages of instruction: English, German
Academic year: October to September

Pres.: Prof. Dr HELMUT J. SCHMIDT
Vice-Pres. for Research and Technology: Prof. Dr BURKARD HILLEBRANDS
Vice-Pres. for Student and Academic Affairs: Prof. Dr Ing. LOTHAR LITZ
Chancellor: STEFAN LORENZ
Head Librarian: JOAN FERSCHINGER

Library of 435,000 vols
Number of teachers: 767
Number of students: 12,510

DEANS

Faculty of Architecture: Prof. BERND MEYERS-PEER
Faculty of Biology: Prof. Dr JOHANNES HERRMANN
Faculty of Business Studies and Economics: Prof. Dr STEFAN ROTH
Faculty of Chemistry: Prof. Dr JENS HARTUNG
Faculty of Civil Engineering: Prof. Dr Ing. WOLFGANG KURZ
Faculty of Computer Science: Prof. Dr ARND POETZSCH-HEFFTER
Faculty of Electrical and Computer Engineering: Prof. Dr Ing. NORBERT WEHN
Faculty of Mathematics: Prof. Dr RENE PINNAU
Faculty of Mechanical and Process Engineering: Prof. Dr Ing. BERND SAUER
Faculty of Physics: Prof. Dr MICHAEL FLEISCHHAUER
Faculty of Regional Planning: Prof. Dr Ing. GERHARD STEINEBACH
Faculty of Social Sciences: Prof. Dr THOMAS SCHMIDT

PROFESSORS

Faculty of Architecture, Regional Planning and Civil Engineering:

BAYER, D., Digital and Methodical Modelling
BECKMANN, R., Ecological Planning and Environmental Compatibility
BÖHM, W., Theory of Buildings and Design
CASTORPH, M., Component-Orientated Planning Processes
DENNHARDT, H., Regional Planning
FILIBECK, R., Construction Management
GÖPFERT, N., Statics of Rising Structures
GOTZ, M., Urban Construction and Planning
HEINRICH, B., Building Physics and Equipment
HOFRICHTER, H., Architecture, History of Town Planning
KAHLFED, P., Industrial Construction III and Design
KLEINE-KRANEBURG, H., Industrial Construction II and Design
KLOPF, H., Load-bearing Structure Design
KOEHLER, G., Civil Engineering
MECHTCHERINE, V., Construction Material Technology
MEDINA-WARMBURG, H., Construction History
MERX, L., Representation and Composition

MEYERSPEER, B., Industrial Construction I and Design
NADLER, M., Building Development
SCHMITT, T. G., Water Management in Residential Areas
SCHNELL, J., Concrete and Building Construction
SEITZ, E., Room Design
SPANNOWSKY, W., Public Law
SPELLENBERG, A., Urban Sociology
STEITZBACH, G., Urban Planning
STREICH, B., Computer-Assisted Design and Construction
TOBIAS, K., Ecological Planning and Environmental Compatibility
TOPP, H. H., Traffic Management
TROEGER-WEIß, A., Regional Development and Planning
TRUMPKE, K., Surveying
VRETTOS, C., Soil Mechanics and Foundation Engineering
WASSERMANN, K., Civil Engineering
WITTEK, U., Civil Engineering
WÜST, H.-S., Landscaping

Faculty of Biology:

ANKER, T., Biotechnology
BRÜNE, A., Cell Biology
BÜDEL, D., Systematic Botany
CULLUM, J. A., Genetics
DEITMER, J. W., Zoology
FRIAUF, A., Animal Physiology
HAHN, A., Phytopathology
HAKENBECK, R., Microbiology
LAKATOS, A., Ecology
LEITZ, A., Animal Development
NEUHAUS, A., Physiology of Plants
SCHMIDT, H., Physiological Ecology
ZANKL, H., Human Biology and Genetics

Faculty of Chemistry:

EISENBRAND, G., Food Chemistry and Toxicology
ERNST, S., Technical Chemistry
HARTMANN, M., Chemical Technology
HARTUNG, J., Organic Chemistry
HIMBERT, G., Organic Chemistry
KIETZTMANN, T., Biochemistry
KREITER, C., Inorganic Chemistry
KRÜGER, H. J., Inorganic Chemistry
KUBALL, H.-G., Physical Chemistry
KUBIK, S., Organic Chemistry
MARKO, D., Food Chemistry and Toxicology
MEMMER, R., Physical and Theoretical Chemistry
MEYER, W., Physical and Theoretical Chemistry
NIEDER-SCHATTEBURG, A., Physical and Theoretical Chemistry
REGITZ, M., Organic Chemistry
SCHERER, O. J., Inorganic Chemistry
SCHRENK, D., Food Chemistry and Toxicology
SITZMANN, H., Inorganic Chemistry
THIEL, W., Inorganic Chemistry
TROMMER, W., Organic Chemistry, Biochemistry

Faculty of Computer Science:

BERNS, K., Robotic Systems
BREUEL, T., Pattern Recognition
DENGEL, A., Knowledge-Based Systems
DEßLOCK, S., Heterogenous Information Systems
EBERT, A., Visualization
GOTZHEIN, R., Networked Systems
HAGEN, H., Graphic Data Processing, Computer Geometry
HÄRDNER, T., Data Management Systems
HEINRICH, S., Numerical Algorithms in Computer Science
LIGGESMEYER, P., Software Engineering Dependability
MADLENER, K., Principles of Computer Science
MAYER, O., Principles of Programming and Computer Languages

MER, P., Shared Algorithms
MÜLLER, P., Integrated Communication Systems
NEHMER, J., Software Technology
POETZSCH-HEFFTER, A., Software Technology
RAUSCH, A., Software Technology
ROMBACH, D., Software Engineering
SCHMITT, J., Shared Systems (DISCO)
SCHNEIDER, K., Reactive Systems
SCHÜRMANN, B., Modelling of Embedded Systems
UMLAUF, G., Algorithms
WIEHAGEN, R., Algorithmic Learning (Theory)

Faculty of Electrical Engineering:

BAIER, P. W., Radio Frequency Communication
BEISTER, J., Circuits
FREY, A., Agent-Based Automation
HAUCK, A., Power Electronics (Teaching)
HUTH, H., Mechatronics and Electrical Drives
KOENIG, A., Integrated Sensor Systems
KUNZ, A., Electronic Design Automation
LITZ, L., Automatic Control
LIU, A., Control Systems
POTCHINKOV, M., Digital Signal Processing
TIELERT, R., Principles of Microelectronics
TUTTAS, A., Power Systems Transmission and Power Plants (Teaching)
URBANSKY, R., Public Telecommunications Engineering
WEHN, N., Microelectronics
WEISS, P., High-Voltage Engineering, Principles of Electrical Engineering
ZENGERLE, R., Theory of Electrical and Electronic Engineering, Optical Communications

Faculty of Mathematics:

BECKER, H., Mathematics
BRAKHAGE, H., Applied Mathematics
DEMPWOLFF, U., Mathematics
FRANKE, J., Stochastics
FREEDEN, W., Mathematics
GREUEL, G.-M., Topology
HAMACHER, H., Econometrics
LÜNEBURG, H., Mathematics
NEUNZERT, H., Mathematics
PFISTER, G., Computer Algebra
PRÄTZEL-WOLTERS, D., Mathematics
RADBRUCH, K., Mathematics, Teaching of Mathematics
SCHOCK, E., Applied Mathematics
SCHWEIGERT, D., Mathematics
TRAUTMANN, G., Pure Mathematics
VON WEIZÄCKER, H., Analysis

Faculty of Mechanical Engineering:

AURICH, J. C., Institute of Manufacturing Engineering and Production Management
BART, H.-J., Chemical Engineering
EIFLER, D., Materials Science
EIGNER, M., Product Development
FLIERL, R., Workgroup for Combustion Engines
HABERLAND, R., Precision Engineering
HELLMANN, D., Fluid Mechanics
MAURER, G., Thermodynamics
RENZ, R., Recyclability in Product Design and Disassembly
RIPPERGER, S., Institute for Particle Technology
SAUER, B., Machine Components
SCHINDLER, C., Institute of Design Engineering
ZÜLKE, D., Production Automation

Faculty of Physics:

AESCHLIMANN, M., Experimental Physics
BEIGANG, R., Experimental Physics
BERGMANN, K., Experimental Physics
DILL, R., Experimental Physics
EGGERT, S., Theoretical Physics
FLEISCHHAUER, M., Theoretical Physics

FOUCKHARDT, H., Experimental Physics
HILLEBRANDS, B., Experimental Physics
HOTOP, H., Experimental Physics
HÜBNER, W., Theoretical Physics
JODL, H.-G., Teaching of Physics, Experimental Physics
KORSCH, J., Theoretical Physics
KRÜGER, H., Theoretical Physics
KUPSCH, J., Theoretical Physics
OESTERSCHULZE, E., Experimental Physics
SCHMORANZER, H., Experimental and Applied Physics
SCHNEIDER, H. C., Theoretical Physics
SCHÜNEMANN, V., Experimental Physics
URBASSEK, H. M., Applied Physics
ZIEGELER, C., Technical Physics

Faculty of Social and Economic Sciences:

ARNOLD, R., Education
BLIEMEL, F., Marketing
CORSTEN, H., Production Management
DUTKE, S., Psychology
ENSTHALER, J., Civil and Economic Law
FESER, H.-D., Economics and Economic Policy I
GESMANN-NUISSL, D., Business Law
HÖLSCHER, R., Finance and Investment
JAINTER, T., Sports
LINGNAU, H.V., Management Accounting and Management Control Systems
NEUSER, W., Philosophy
PÄTZOLD, H., Education
RITTBERGER, B., Politics
VON HAUFF, M., Economics and Economic Policy
WENDT, O., Information Systems and Operations Research
WILZEWSKI, J., Politics
ZINK, K. J., Business Management

AFFILIATED INSTITUTES

Deutsches Forschungszentrum für Künstliche Intelligenz GmbH (DFKI) (Research Centre for Artificial Intelligence): Erwin-Schrödinger-Str. (Gebäude 57), Postfach 2080, 67663 Kaiserslautern; Dir (vacant).

Institut für Oberflächen- und Schichtanalytik GmbH (Institute for Surface and Coating Analysis): Erwin-Schrödinger-Str. (Gebäude 56), 67663 Kaiserslautern; Dir Prof. Dr HANS OECHSNER.

Institut für Verbundwerkstoffe GmbH (IVW) (Institute for Composite Materials): Erwin-Schrödinger-Str., 67663 Kaiserslautern; Dir Prof. Dr Ing. MANFRED NEITZEL.

TECHNISCHE UNIVERSITÄT MÜNCHEN

Arcisstr. 21, 80333 Munich
Telephone: (89) 28901
Fax: (89) 28922000
E-mail: praesident@tu-muenchen.de
Internet: www.tum.de
Founded 1868
State control
Academic year: October to September
Pres.: Prof. Dr WOLFGANG A. HERRMANN
Vice-Pres: Dr Ing. KAI WÜLBERN
Vice-Pres: Prof. Dr Ing MENG LIQIU
Vice-Pres: Prof. Dr PETER GRITZMANN
Vice-Pres: Prof. Dr THOMAS HOFMANN
Chancellor: ALBERT BERGER
Librarian: Dr REINER KALLENBORN
Library: see Libraries and Archives
Number of teachers: 6,025
Number of students: 26,302
Publication: *Jahrbuch* (1 a year)

DEANS

Centre of Life and Food Sciences Weihenstephan: Prof. Dr ALFONS GIERL

Faculty of Architecture: Prof. Dipl.-Ing. REGINE KELLER
Faculty of Chemistry: Prof. Dr ULRICH HEIZ
Faculty of Civil Engineering and Geodesy: Prof. Dr-Ing. GERHARD MÜLLER
Faculty of Electrical Engineering and Information Technology: Prof. Dr-Ing. ULF SCHLICHTMANN
Faculty of Informatics: Prof. Dr HELMUT KRCMAR
Faculty of Mathematics: Prof. Dr GREGOR KEMPER
Faculty of Mechanical Engineering: Prof. Dr-Ing. HANS-PETER KAU
Faculty of Medicine: Prof. PETER HENNINGSEN
Faculty of Physics: Prof. Dr MARTIN STUTZMANN
Faculty of Sports: Prof. Dr JÜRGEN BECKMANN
School of Education: Prof. Dr MANFRED PRENZEL
School of Management: Prof. GUNTHER FRIEDL

PROFESSORS

Faculty of Architecture (tel. (89) 28922351; fax (89) 28928442; e-mail marga.cervinka@lrz.tu-muenchen.de; internet www.arch.tu-muenchen.de):

BARTHEL, R., Structural Engineering
BOCK, T., Building Implementation and Information Technology
COTELO LÓPEZ, V., Design and the Conservation of Historical Buildings
DEUBZER, H., Design, Spatial Art and Lighting Design
EBNER, P., Housing and Housing Economics
EMMERLING, E., Restoration, Art Technology and Conservation
FINK, D., Integrated Construction
HAUSLADEN, G., Indoor Climate and Mechanical Services
HERZOG, T., Building Technology
HORDEN, R., Architecture and Product Development
HUGUES, T., Building Construction and Materials
HUSE, N., History of Art
KIESSLER, U., Integrated Buildings
KOENIGS, W., History of Building and Building Research
KRAU, I., Town Planning and Urban Development
LATZ, P., Landscape Architecture and Planning
MUSSO, F., Design, Building Construction and Materials Science
OSTERTAG, D., House Technology
REICHENBACH-KLINKE, M., Planning and Construction in Rural Areas
STRACKE, F., Urban Development and Regional Planning
THIERSTEIN, A., Territorial and Spatial Development
WIENANDS, R., Principles of Design and Representation
WITTENBORN, R., Visual Design
WOLFRUM, S., Urban and Regional Planning
ZBINDEN, U., Building Construction and Design Methodology

Faculty of Chemistry (Lichtenbergstr. 4, 85748 Garching; tel. (89) 2893001; fax (89) 2894386; e-mail dekanat@ch.tum.de; internet www.chemie.tu-muenchen.de):

BACH, T., Organic Chemistry I
BACHER, A., Organic Chemistry and Biochemistry
BONDYBEY, V. E., Physical Chemistry
BUCHNER, J., Biotechnology
DOMCKE, W., Theoretical Chemistry
FÄSSLER, T., Inorganic Chemistry
HEIZ, U., Physical Chemistry I
HERRMANN, W., Inorganic Chemistry
HINRICHSEN, O., Chemical Technology I

KESSLER, H., Organic Chemistry II
KETTRUP, A., Ecological Chemistry and Environmental Analytics
LANGOSCH, D., Bipolymer Chemistry
LERCHER, J., Chemical Technology II
LIMBERG, C., Inorganic Chemistry
NEUMEIER, D., Clinical Chemistry and Pathobiochemistry
NIESSNER, R., Hydrogeology, Hydrochemistry and Environmental Analytical Chemistry
NITSCH, W., Chemical Engineering
NUYKEN, O., Macromolecular Substances
PLANK, J., Construction Chemistry
SCHIEBERLE, P., Food Chemistry
SCHIEMANN, O., Physical Chemistry II
SCHMIDBAUR, H., Inorganic and Analytical Chemistry
SKERRA, A., Biological Chemistry
TÜRLER, A., Radiochemistry
VEPREK, S., Chemistry of Inorganic Materials

Faculty of Civil Engineering and Geodesy (tel. (89) 28922400; fax (89) 28923841; e-mail dekanat@bv.tum.de; internet www.bv.tum.de):

ALBRECHT, G., Steel-Girder Construction
BLETZINGER, K., Structural Analysis
BÖSCH, H.-J., Tunnel Construction, Building Management
BUSCH, F., Traffic Engineering and Control
EBNER, H., Photogrammetry
FAULSTICH, M., Water Quality Control and Waste Management
GRUNDMANN, H., Building Mechanics
HAUSER, G., Building Physics
KIRCHHOFF, P., Transport and Town Planning
LEYKAUF, G., Road, Railway and Airfield Construction
MAGEL, H., Ground Preparation and Land Development
MENG, L., Cartography
MÜLLER, G., Building Mechanics
RANK, E., Building Informatics
RUMMEL, R., Astronomical and Physical Geodesy
SCHIESS, R., Building Materials and Materials Testing
SCHIESSL, P., Building Materials and Materials Testing
SCHIKORA, K., Analysis of Civil Engineering Structures
SCHUNCK, E., Building Construction
SPAUN, G., Geology
STROBL, TH., Hydraulic and Water Resources Engineering
THURO, K., Geology
VALENTIN, F., Hydraulics and Hydrography
VOGT, N., Foundations, Soil Mechanics and Rock Mechanics
WILDERER, P., Water Quality and Waste Management
WINTER, S., Building Construction
WUNDERLICH, T., Geodesy
ZILCH, K., Concrete Structures
ZIMMERMANN, J., Building Process Management

Faculty of Economics and Social Sciences (tel. (89) 28925066; fax (89) 28925070; e-mail dekanat@wi.tum.de; internet www.wi.tu-muenchen.de):

ACHLEITNER, A., KfW Entrepreneurial Finance
ANN, C., Corporate Law and Intellectual Property
BÄUMLER, G., Physical Education (Psychology)
BELZ, F., Brewing and Food Industry
BLÜMELHUBER, C., Marketing and Distribution
BÜSSING, A., Psychology
ENNEKING, U., Agribusiness and Food Industry
GRANDE, E., Political Science

GROSSER, M., Science of Movement and Training
HACKER, W., Psychology
HEINRITZ, G., Geography
HEISSENHUBER, A., Agricultural Economics and Farm Management
HENKEL, J., Technology and Innovation Management
HOFMANN, W., Political Science
HOLZHEU, F., Economics
KARG, G., Consumer Economics
KASERER, C., Financial Management and Capital Markets
KOLISCH, R., Technical Services and Operational Management
LEIST, K.-H., Physical Education Teaching
LÜCK, W., Business Management, Accounting, Auditing and Consulting
MOOG, M., Forest Management
REICHWALD, R., Information, Organization and Management
SALHOFER, K., Environmental Economics and Agricultural Policy
SCHELTEN, A., Pedagogics
STEINMÜLLER, H., Social Policy and Insurance
SUDA, M., Forest Policy and Forest History
TRINCZEK, R., Sociology
VON WEIZSÄCKER, R. FRHR., Economics
WEINDLMAIER, J., Dairy and Food Industry Management
WENGENROTH, U., History of Engineering
WILDEMANN, H., Management, Logistics and Production
WITT, D., Service Management
ZACHMANN, K., History of Technology

Faculty of Electrical Engineering and Information Technology (tel. (89) 28928378; fax (89) 28922559; e-mail dekanat@ei.tum.de; internet www.e-technik.tu-muenchen.de):

AMANN, M., Semiconductor Technology
ANTREICH, K., Computer-Aided Design
BIRKHOFER, A., Reactor Dynamics and Reactor Safety
BOECK, W., High Voltage Engineering and Power Plants
BUSS, M., Automatic Control Engineering
DIEPOLD, K., Data Processing
EBERSPÄCHER, J., Communication Networks
FÄRBER, G., Real-Time Computer Systems
GÜNTHER, C., Communication and Navigation
HAGENAUER, J., Communications Engineering
HEKERSDORF, A., Integrated Systems
KINDERSBERGER, J., High Voltage Engineering and Electric Power Transmission
KOCH, A., Measurement Systems and Sensor Technology
LANG, M., Man–Machine Communication
LUGLI, P., Nanoelectronics
NOSSEK, J., Circuit Theory and Signal Processing
RIGOLL, G., Man–Machine Communication
RUGE, I., Integrated Circuits
RUSSER, P., High Frequency Engineering
SCHLICHTMANN, U., Electronic Design Automation
SCHMIDT, G., Control Engineering
SCHMITT-LANDSIEDEL, D., Technical Electronics
SCHRÖDER, D., Electrical Drives
SWOBODA, J., Data Processing
WACHUTKA, G., Physics of Electrotechnology
WAGNER, U., Energy Economy and Application Technology
WOLF, B., Medical Electronics

Faculty of Informatics (Boltzmannstr. 3, 85748 Garching; tel. (89) 28917590; fax (89) 28917591; e-mail gemkow@in.tum.de; internet www.informatik.tu-muenchen.de):

BAYER, R., Computer Science

BICHLER, M., Internet-Based Information Systems
BODE, A., Computer Organization, Parallel Computer Architecture
BRAUER, W., Theoretical Computer Science and Foundations of Artificial Intelligence
BROY, M., Software and Systems Engineering
BRÜGGE, B., Applied Software Engineering
BUNGARTZ, H.-J., Computer Science in Engineering, Numerical Programming
EICKEL, J., Computer Science
FELDMANN, A., Network Architecture
GRUST, T., Database Systems
HEGERING, H.-G., Technical Informatics— Computer Networks
HUBWIESER, P., Didactics of Informatics
JESSEN, E., Computer Science
KNOLL, A., Robotics and Embedded Systems
KRAMER, S., Bioinformatics
KRCMAR, H., Information Systems
MATTHES, F., Software Engineering for Business Applications
MAYR, E. W., Efficient Algorithms
NAVAB, N., Computer-Aided Medical Procedures
RADIG, B., Image Understanding and Knowledge-Based Systems
SCHLICHTER, J., Applied Informatics/Collaborative Systems
SEIDL, H., Formal Languages, Compiler Construction, Software Construction
SPIES, P., System Architecture
WESTERMANN, R., Computer Graphics and Visualization
ZENGER, C., Computer Science

Faculty of Life Science (Alte Akademie 8, 85354 Freising; tel. (8161) 713258; fax (8161) 713900; e-mail dekanat@wzw.tum.de; internet www.wzw.tu-muenchen.de):

AUERNHAMMER, H., Agricultural Engineering
BACK, W., Brewing Technology I
BAUER, J., Animal Hygiene
DANIEL, H., Physiology of Nutrition
DELGADO, A., Fluid Mechanics and Process Automation
ENGEL, K.-H., Food and Nutrition
FAULSTICH, M., Technology of Biogenic Products
FORKMANN, G., Floriculture
FRIEDRICH, J., Physics
FRIES, H.-R., Animal Breeding
GIERL, A., Genetics
GRILL, E., Botany
HABE, W., Landscape Ecology
HAUNER, H., Nutritional Medicine
HOCK, B., Cell Biology
HRABÉ DE ANGELIS, M., Experimental Genetics
KETTRUP, A., Ecological Chemistry and Environmental Analytics
KÖGEL-KNABNER, I., Soil Science
KULOZIK, U., Food Process Engineering
LANGOSCH, D., Biopolymer Chemistry
LANGOWSKI, H.-C., Brewery Installations and Food Packaging Technology
LATZ, P., Landscape Architecture and Planning
MANLEY, G. A., Zoology
MATYSSEK, R., Ecophysiology of Plants
MENZEL, A., Ecoclimatology
MEWES, H.-W., Genome-Orientated Bioinformatics
MEYER, H., Physiology
MEYER-PITTROFF, R., Energy and Environmental Technologies of the Food Industry
MOOG, M., Forestry
MOSANDL, R., Silviculture and Forest Planning
PARLAR, H., Chemical-Technical Analysis and Chemical Food Technology

PFADENHAUER, J., Vegetation Ecology
PRETZSCH, H., Forest Yield Science
QUEDNAU, H.-D., Work Science and Applied Computer Science
RECHKEMMER, G., Biofunctionality of Food
ROTHENBURGER, W., Horticultural Economics
SCHEMANN, M., Human Biology
SCHLEIFER, K.-H., Microbiology
SCHMIDHALTER, U., Plant Nutrition
SCHNITZLER, W. H., Vegetable Science
SCHNYDER, H., Grassland
SCHÖN, J., Land Engineering
SCHOPF, R., Animal Ecology
SKERRA, A., Biological Chemistry
SOMMER, K., Machinery and Apparatus
SUDA, M., Politics and History of Forestry
VALENTIEN, C., Landscape Architecture and Design
VOGEL, R., Industrial Microbiology
WARKOTSCH, W., Forest Industry and Applied Computer Science
WEGENER, G., Wood Science and Wood Engineering
WEISSER, H., Brewery Construction and Food Packaging Technology
WENZEL, G., Plant Cultivation
WOLF, P. F. J., Phytopathology
WOLFRAM, G., Human Nutrition
WURST, W., Developmental Genetics
ZANDER, J., Land Use Planning and Nature Conservation

Faculty of Mathematics (Boltzmannstr. 3, 85747 Garching; tel. (89) 28916806; fax (89) 28917584; e-mail dekanat@ma.tum.de; internet www.ma.tum.de):

BORNEMANN, F., Scientific Computing
BROKATE, M., Mathematical Modelling
BULIRSCH, R., Numerical Analysis
FRIESEKE, G., Global Analysis
GRITZMANN, P., Combinatorial Geometry
HOFFMAN, K.-H., Mathematical Modelling
KEMPER, G., Algorithmic Algebra
KLÜPPELBERG, C., Statistics
LASSER, R., Biomathematics
LOSS, M., Global Analysis
RENTROP, P., Numerical Analysis
RICHTER-GEBERT, J., Geometry and Visualization
RITTER, K., Optimization
SCHEURLE, J., Dynamic Systems
SPOHN, H., Mathematical Physics
ZAGST, R., Mathematical Finance

Faculty of Mechanical Engineering (Boltzmannstr. 15, 85748 Garching; tel. (89) 2895020; fax (89) 2895024; e-mail wagner@mw.tum.de; internet www.mw.tu-muenchen.de):

ADAMS, N., Aerodynamics
BAIER, H., Lightweight Structures
BENDER, K., Information Technology
BUBB, H., Ergonomics and Human Factors
GREGORY, J. K., Materials
GÜNTHER, A., Material Flow and Logistics
GÜNTHNER, W., Production Technology
HEIN, D., Thermal Power Plants
HEINZL, J., Precision Mechanics and Microengineering
HEISSING, B., Automotive Engineering
HOFFMANN, H., Metal Forming and Casting
HÖHN, R., Machine Elements
KAU, H. P., Flight Propulsion
LASCHKA, B., Fluid Mechanics
LINDEMANN, U., Product Development
LOHMANN, B., Automatic Control
PEUKERT, W., Chemical Process Engineering
PEUKERT, W., Solid Fuel Process Engineering
REINHART, G., Assembly Systems and Factories
RENIUS, K. T., Agricultural Machinery
SACHS, G., Flight Mechanics and Control
SATTELMAYER, T., Thermodynamics
SCHILLING, R., Fluid Mechanics

SCHMITT, D., Aeronautical Engineering
STICHLMAIR, J., Process Engineering
STROHMEIER, K., Apparatus and Plant Construction
ULBRICH, H., Applied Mechanics
WACHTMEISTER, G., Internal Combustion Engines
WALL, W., Computational Mechanics
WALTER, U., Astronautics
WERNER, E., Materials Science and Mechanics
WEUSTER-BOTZ, D., Biochemical Engineering
WINTERMANTEL, E., Medical Engineering
ZÄH, M., Machine Tools and Industrial Management

Faculty of Medicine (Ismaninger Str. 48, 81675 Munich; tel. (89) 41402121; fax (89) 41404870; e-mail huebener@nt1.chir.med .tu-muenchen.de; internet www.med .tu-muenchen.de):

ARNOLD, W., Otorhinolaryngology
BURDACH, S., Paediatrics
CLASSEN, M., Internal Medicine
CONRAD, B., Neurology
EISENMENGER, W., Forensic Medicine
EMMRICH, P., Paediatrics
ERFLE, V., Virology
FÖRSTL, H., Psychiatry and Psychotherapy
GÄNSBACHER, B., Experimental Oncology and Therapy Research
GÖTTLICHER, M., Clinic for Industrial and Environmental Medicine
GRADINGER, R., Orthopaedics and Sport Orthopaedics
GREIM, H., Toxicology and Environmental Hygiene
HALLE, M., Preventive and Rehabilitative Sports Medicine
HARTUNG, R., Urology
HAUNER, H., Nutritional Medicine
HESS, J., Paediatric Cardiology
HÖFLER, H., General Pathology and Pathological Anatomy
HOFMANN, F., Molecular Medicine
HOFMANN, F., Pharmacology and Toxicology
HORCH, H.-H., Dentistry
JESCHKE, D., Preventive and Rehabilitative Sports Medicine
KIECHLE, M., Gynaecology
KOCHS, E. F., Anaesthesiology
KUHN, K. A., Medical Statistics and Epidemiology
LANGE, R., Cardiac Surgery
LANZL, I. M., Ophthalmology
MEITINGER, T., Genetics
MERTZ, M., Ophthalmology
MOLLS, M., Radiotherapy and Radiological Oncology
NEISS, A., Medical Statistics and Epidemiology
NEUMEIER, D., Clinical Chemistry and Pathobiochemistry
NOWAK, D., Clinic for Industrial and Environmental Medicine
PESCHEL, C., Internal Medicine III
RING, J., Dermatology and Allergology
RUMMENY, E. J., X-Ray Diagnostics
SCHMID, R., Internal Medicine II
SCHÖMIG, A.-W., Internal Medicine I
SCHWAIGER, M., Nuclear Medicine
SIEWERT, J.-R., Surgery
SPEICHER, M., Genetics
TRAPPE, A. E., Neurosurgery
VON RAD, M., Clinical Psychology and Psychotherapy
WAGNER, H., Clinical Microbiology, Immunology and Hygiene
WILMANNS, J. C., Medical History and Ethics

Faculty of Physics (James Franck Str., 85748 Garching; tel. (89) 28912492; fax (89) 28914474; e-mail dekanat@physik

.tu-muenchen.de; internet www.physik .tu-muenchen.de):

ABSTREITER, G., Experimental Semiconductor Physics I
BÖNI, P., Experimental Physics
BURAS, A. J., Theoretical Physics IV
DIETRICH, K., Theoretical Physics I
FEULNER, P., Physics
FISCHER, S., Theoretical Physics II
FRIEDRICH, H., Theoretical Physics
FRIEDRICH, J., Physics
GROSS, R., Technical Physics
GROß, A., Theoretical Physics
KINDER, H., Experimental Physics
KLEBER, M., Theoretical Physics
KOCH, F., Physics
KRÜCKEN, R., Physics
LAUBEREAU, A., Experimental Physics
LINDNER, M., Theoretical Particle and Astro-Particle Physics
NETZ, R., Theoretical Physics II
PARAK, F. G., Physics and Biophysics
PAUL, S., Physics I
PETRY, W., Experimental Physics
RIEF, M., Physics
RING, P., Theoretical Physics
STIMMING, U., Physics
STUTZMANN, M., Experimental Semiconductor Physics II
VOGL, P., Theoretical Physics III
VAN HEMMEN, J. L., Theoretical Physics
VON FEILITZSCH, F., Experimental Physics and Astro-Particle Physics
WEISE, W., Theoretical Physics
ZWERGER, W., Theoretical Physics V

Faculty of Sports Science (Connollystr. 32, 80809 Munich; tel. (89) 28924601; fax (89) 28924636; e-mail dekanat.sport@sp.tum.de; internet www.sport.tu-muenchen.de):

HACKFORTH, J., Sport, Media and Communication
KELLER, J. A., Sport Psychology
LEIST, K.-H., Sport Pedagogy
MICHNA, H., Sport and Health Promotion
TUSKER, F., Human Movement Science and Training

TIERÄRZTLICHE HOCHSCHULE HANNOVER
(University of Veterinary Medicine Hanover)

POB 71 11 80, 30545 Hanover
Bünteweg 2, 30559 Hanover
Telephone: (511) 95360
Fax: (511) 9538050
E-mail: info@tiho-hannover.de
Internet: www.tiho-hannover.de

Founded 1778 as Königliche Rossarzneischule, attained university status 1887
State control
Academic year: October to September

Pres.: Dr GERHARD GREIF
Vice-Pres. for Teaching: Prof. Dr ANDREA TIPOLD
Vice-Pres. for Research: Prof. Dr ULRICH NEUMANN

Library of 230,000 vols, 1,000 print journals, 3,000 e-journals
Number of teachers: 122
Number of students: 2,360

Publications: *TiHo-Anzeiger* (8 a year), *TiHo Forschung fürs Leben* (1 a year)

HEADS

Centre for Food Toxicology: Prof. Dr HEINZ NAU
Clinic for Cattle: Prof. Dr HEINRICH BOLLWEIN
Clinic for Horses: Prof. Dr KARSTEN FEIGE
Clinic for Pigs, Small Ruminants, Forensic Medicine and Ambulatory Service: Prof. Dr K.-H. WALDMANN
Clinic for Poultry: Prof. Dr SILKE RAUTENSCHLEIN

Clinic for Small Domestic Animals: Prof. Dr INGO NOLTE
Department of Analytical Chemistry and Endocrinology: Prof. Dr H.-O. HOPPEN
Department of Biometry, Epidemiology and Data Processing: Prof. Dr L. KREIENBROCK
Department of Fish Pathology and Fish Farming: Prof. Dr WOLFGANG KÖRTING
Department of General Radiology and Medical Physics: Prof. Dr HERMANN SEIFERT
Department of History of Veterinary Medicine and Domestic Animals: Prof. Dr JOHANN SCHÄFFER
Department of Immunology: Prof. Dr WOLFGANG LEIBOLD
Institute of Anatomy: Prof. Dr CHRISTIANE PFARRER
Institute for Animal Behaviour and Protection: Prof. Dr HANSJOACHIM HACKBARTH
Institute of Animal Breeding and Genetics: Prof. Dr OTTMAR DISTL
Institute for Animal Ecology and Cell Biology: Prof. Dr BERND SCHIERWATER
Institute for Animal Hygiene and Protection: Prof. Dr JÖRG HARTUNG
Institute for Animal Nutrition: Prof. Dr J. KAMPHUES
Institute of Epidemics: Prof. Dr THOMAS BLAHA
Institute for Food Quality and Safety: Prof. Dr G. KLEIN
Institute for Microbiology: Prof. Dr PETER VALENTIN-WEIGAND
Institute for Parasitology: Prof. Dr THOMAS SCHNEIDER
Institute for Pathology: Prof. Dr WOLFGANG BAUMGÄRTNER
Institute for Physiology: Prof. Dr GERHARD BREVES
Institute for Physiological Chemistry: Prof. Dr HASSAN Y. NAIM
Institute for Reproductive Medicine: Prof. Dr EDDA TÖPFER-PETERSEN
Institute for Virology: Prof. Dr VOLKER MOENNIG
Institute for Wildlife Research: Prof. Dr BURKHARD MEINECKE
Institute for Zoology: Prof. Dr ELKE ZIMMERMANN

UKRAINISCHE FREIE UNIVERSITÄT
(Ukrainian Free University)

Barellistr. 9A, 80638 Munich
Telephone: (89) 99738830
Fax: (89) 997388331
E-mail: sekretariat@ufu-muenchen.de
Internet: www.ufu-muenchen.de

Founded 1921
Private, State-approved
Languages of instruction: Ukrainian, English, German
Academic year: October to August (incl. Summer Courses July–August)

Rector: Prof. Dr IVAN MYHUL
Chancellor/Registrar: Prof. Dr NICOLAS SZAFOWAL
Librarian: IWANNA REBET

Number of teachers: 56
Number of students: 110

Publications: *Naukovi Zapysky UVU* (1 a year), *Naukovi Zbirnyky UVU, Specimina dialectorum ucrainorum, Studien zu deutsch–ukrainischen Beziehungen*

DEANS

Faculty of Law and Economics: Prof. Dr JAROSLAW HRYTSAK
Faculty of Philosophy: Prof. Dr FRANK SYSYN
Faculty of Ukrainian Studies: Prof. Dr JAROSLAWA MELNYK

PROFESSORS

Faculty of Govt and Political Economy (tel. (89) 99738842):

FUTEY, B., Law
ISAJIW, V., Sociology
KOSTYCKY, M., Law
MYHUL, I., Political Economics
NAGY, L., Geography
PYNZENYK, V., Political Economics
SUBTELNY, O., History of Political Ideas
SZAFOWAL, N., Political Science

Faculty of Philosophy (Humanities):

ANDRIEWSKY, O., History
DACKO, I., Theology
GUDZIAK, B., Church History
JERABEK, B., Education
KIPA, A., Comparative Literature
KOSYK, W., History
KYSILEWSKA-TKACH, A., Education
LABUNKA, M., Ukrainian History
MAKSYMTSCHUK, W., Comparative Literature
PIETSCH, R., Philosophy
RUDNYTZKY, L., Comparative Literature
STEPOWYK, D., Cultural History
SYSYN, F., History
ZLEPKO, D., History of Eastern Europe
ZUK, L., Ukrainian Music
ZUK, R., History of Architecture

Faculty of Ukrainian Studies:

AVVAKUMOV,, G., Church Slavonic
KOPTILOV, V., Ukrainian Language and Literature
KOZAK, S., Slavonic Literature
MELNYK, Y., Ukrainian Literature
MUSHINKA, M., Ukrainian Ethnology
POHRIBNYJ, A., Ukrainian Language and Literature
PRYSJAZNIJ, M., Journalism
SALYHA, T., History of Ukrainian Literature

UNIVERSITÄT AUGSBURG

Universitätsstr. 2, 86159 Augsburg

Telephone: (821) 5980
Fax: (821) 5985505
E-mail: info@aaa.uni-augsburg.de
Internet: www.uni-augsburg.de

Founded 1970
State control
Language of instruction: German
Academic year: October to July

Pres.: Prof. Dr ALOIS LOIDL (acting)
Vice-Pres.: Prof. Dr ALOIS LOIDL
Vice-Pres.: Prof. Dr ALEX TUMA
Vice-Pres.: Prof. Dr WERNER WIATER
Chancellor: ALOIS ZIMMERMAN
Librarian: Dr ULRICH HOHOFF

Library: see Libraries and Archives
Number of teachers: 458
Number of students: 16,606

Publication: *Mitteilungen Institut fur Europaeische Kulturgeschichte*

DEANS

Faculty of Applied Computer Science: Prof. Dr WOLFGANG REIF
Faculty of Catholic Theology: Prof. Dr GREGOR WURST
Faculty of Economics: Prof. Dr KLAUS TUROWSKI
Faculty of History and Philology: Prof. Dr SABINE DOERING-MANTEUFFEL
Faculty of Law: Prof. Dr ULRICH M. GASSNER
Faculty of Mathematics and Natural Sciences: Prof. Dr ACHIM WIXFORTH
Faculty of Philosophy and Social Sciences: Prof. Dr WERNER SCHNEIDER

PROFESSORS

Faculty of Applied Computing (86135 Augsburg; tel. (821) 5982174; fax (821) 5982175; e-mail reif@informatik.uni-augsburg.de; internet www.uni-augsburg.de/fakultaeten/fai):

ANDRÉ, E., Multimedia Concepts and Applications
BAUER, B., Software and Programming Languages
FRIEDMANN, A., Physical Geography
HAGERUP, T., Theoretical Computing
HILLENBRAND, H., Didactics
HILPERT, M., Human Geography
JACOBEIT, J., Physical Geography
KIESSLING, W., Databases and Information Systems
LIENHART, R., Multimedia Computing
MÖLLER, B., Databases and Information Systems
PEYKE, G., Human Geography
POSCHWATTA, W., Human Geography
REIF, W., Software and Programming Languages
SCHNEIDER, T., Didactics
THIEME, K., Human Geography
UNGERER, T., Information and Communication Systems
VOGLER, W., Software and Programming Languages
WIECZOREK, U., Didactics

Faculty of Catholic Theology (Universitätsstr. 10, 86159 Augsburg; tel. (821) 5985820; fax (821) 5985503; e-mail dekanat@kthf.uni-augsburg.de; internet www.kthf.uni-augsburg.de):

ARNTZ, K., Moral Theology
BALMER, H. P., Philosophy
GÜTHOFF, E., Church Law
HAUSMANNINGER, TH., Christian Ethics
KIENZLER, K., Basic Theology
KÜPPERS, K., Liturgy Science
RIEDL, GERDA, New Testament Exegesis
SCHEULE, R. (acting), Christian Ethics
SEDLMEIER, F. (acting), Old Testament Exegesis
WURST, F., Church History

Faculty of Economics (Universitätsstr. 16, 86159 Augsburg; tel. (821) 5984015; fax (821) 5984212; e-mail dekanat@wiwi.uni-augsburg.de; internet www.wiwi.uni-augsburg.de):

BAMBERG, G., Statistics
BOEHLE, F., Socio-Economics
BUHL, H. U., Business Administration
COENENBERG, A., Business Administration
FLEISCHMANN, B., Business Administration
GIEGLER, H., Sociology
GIERL, H., Business Administration
HANUSCH, H., Economics
HEINHOLD, M., Business Administration
KIFMANN, M., Sociology
KLEIN, R., Sociology
LAU, C., Sociology
LEHMANN, E., Business Management
MAUSSNER, A., Economics
MEIER, M., Economics
MICHAELIS, D., Economics
NEUBERGER, O., Psychology
PFAFF, A., Economics
SCHITTKO, U., Econometrics
STEINER, M., Business Administration
STENGEL, M., Psychology
TUMA, A., Business Administration
TUROWSKI, K., Business Informatics and Systems Engineering
WELZEL, P., Economics

Faculty of History and Philology (Universitätsstr. 10, 86159 Augsburg; tel. (821) 5982764; fax (821) 5985501; e-mail dekan.phil2@phil.uni-augsburg.de; internet www.philhist.uni-augsburg.de):

BICKENDORF, G., Art History
BUBLITZ, W., English Linguistics
BURKHARDT, J., History of Early Modern Times
DOERING-MANTEUFFEL, S., Folklore
ELSPASS, S., German Language

FÄCKE, C., French Didactics
GEPPERT, H. V., German and Comparative Literature
GÖTZ, D., Applied Linguistics
HERINGER, H.-J., German as a Foreign Language, German Philology
JACOB, J., Modern German
KAUFHOLD, M., Medieval History
KIESSLING, R., Bavarian and Swabian History
KOCKEL, V., Classical Archaeology
KRAUSS, H., Romance Literature
LAUSBERG, M., Classical Philology
LÖSER, F., German Language and Medieval History
MAYER, M., English Literature
MIDDEKE, M., English Literature
SCHEERER, T. M., Hispanic Studies
SCHRÖDER, K., Didactics of English
SCHWARZE, S., Romance Languages
TSCHOPP, S. S., History of European Culture
WEBER, G., Ancient History
WERNER, R., Applied Linguistics
WILLIAMS, W., German Language and Medieval Literature
WIRSCHING, A., Modern and Contemporary History
ZAPF, H., American Studies

Faculty of Law (Universitätsstr. 24, 86159 Augsburg; tel. (821) 5984500; fax (821) 5984503; e-mail dekan@jura.uni-augsburg.de; internet www.jura.uni-augsburg.de):

ALBERS, M., Civil Law
APPEL, I. (acting), Constitutional Law
BECKER, C., Civil Law, History of European Law
BEHR, V., Civil Law
BOTTKE, W., Penal Law
BUCHNER, H., Civil Law
GASSNER, U. M., Public Law
GSELL, B., Civil Law
JAKOB, W., Public Law
KORT, M., Civil Law
LEISTNER, M., Civil Law, Trade and Labour Law
MASING, J. (acting), Constitutional and Administrative Law
MÖLLERS, TH., Civil Law, Economic Law, European Law
NEUNER, J., Civil Law, Labour and Trade Law
ROSENAU, H., International Penal Law
ROTSCH, T., Penal Law
VEDDER, CH. (acting), Public Law

Faculty of Mathematics and Natural Sciences (Universitätsstr. 14, 86159 Augsburg; tel. (821) 5982250; fax (821) 5982300; e-mail dekan@mnf.uni-augsburg.de; internet www.uni-augsburg.de/einrichtungen/mnf):

BEHRINGER, K., Experimental Plasma Physics
BRÜTTING, W., Experimental Physics
CLAESSEN, R., Experimental Physics
COLONIUS, F., Applied Mathematics
DORFMEISTER, J., Analysis and Geometry
ECKERN, U. (acting), Theoretical Physics
ESCHENBURG, J., Differential Geometry
GIESL, P., Nonlinear Analysis
HAIDER, F., Experimental Physics
HÄNGGI, P., Theoretical Physics
HARTMANN, L., Chemistry, Physics and Material Sciences
HEINRICH, L., Applied Mathematics
HEINTZE, E., Pure Mathematics
HILSCHER, H., Didactics of Physics
HÖCK, K. H., Theoretical Physics
HOPPE, R. H. W., Applied Mathematics
HORN, S., Experimental Physics
INGOLD, G.-L., Theoretical Physics
JUNGNICKEL, D., Applied Mathematics, Discrete Mathematics, Optimization, Operations Research
KAMPF, A., Theoretical Physics
KIELHÖFER, H.-J., Applied Analysis

KOPP, T., Physics
LOIDL, A., Experimental Physics
MANNHART, J., Experimental Physics
PUKELSHEIM, F., Applied Mathematics
RELLER, A., Solid State Chemistry
RITTER, J., Pure Mathematics
SCHERER, W., Chemistry, Physics and Material Sciences
SCHERTZ, R., Mathematics
SCHNEIDER, E., Didactics
SIEBERT, K. (acting), Applied Analytical Mathematics
STRITZKER, B., Experimental Physics
UNWIN, A., Computer-Oriented Statistics and Data Analysis
VOLLHARDT, D., Theoretical Physics
WIXFORTH, A., Experimental Physics
ZIEGLER, K., Theoretical Physics
ZIMMERMAN, R., Chemistry

Faculty of Philosophy and Social Sciences (Universitätsstr. 10, 86159 Augsburg; tel. (821) 5982605; fax (821) 5985504; e-mail dekan.phil1@phil.uni-augsburg.de; internet www.philso.uni-augsburg.de):

ALTENBERGER, H., Sports Education
ASBACH, O., Protestant Philosophy
ASCHENBRÜCKER, K., Didactics
BOEHLE, F., Sociology
BRUNOLD, A., Social Studies
EILDERS, C., Communications
GIEGLER, H., Sociology and Empirical Social Research
HERWARTZ-EMDEN, L., Pedagogics
HOYER, J., Music
KIRCHNER, C. (acting), Art Education
KRAEMER, R. D., Musical Training
LAEMMERMANN, G., Protestant Theology with Didactics of Religion
LAMES, M., Movement and Training
LAU, C., Sociology
MACHA, H., Pedagogics
MAINZER, K., Philosophy
MATTHES, E., Pedagogics
MÜHLEISEN, H.-O., Political Science
OBENDORFER, B., Protestant Theology
REINMANN, G., Media Education
SCHNEIDER, W., Sociology
SCHRÖER, C., Philosophy
SCHULTZE, R.-O., Political Science
STENGEL, M., Psychology
ULICH, D., Psychology
VON GEMÜNDEN, P., Protestant Theology
WIATER, W., Pedagogics
WÜSTNER, K., Psychology

UNIVERSITÄT BAYREUTH

95440 Bayreuth
Telephone: (921) 550
Fax: (921) 555214
E-mail: kanzler@uvw.uni-bayreuth.de
Internet: www.uni-bayreuth.de
Founded 1972
Academic year: October to September
Pres.: Prof. Dr RÜDIGER BORMANN (acting)
Vice-Pres: Prof. Dr HANS-WARNER SCHMIDT
Vice-Pres: Prof. Dr STEFAN JABLONSKI
Vice-Pres: Prof. Dr STEFAN LEIBLE
Chancellor: Dr MARKUS ZANNER
Librarian: RALF BRUGBAUER
Library: see Libraries and Archives
Number of teachers: 186
Number of students: 9,530

DEANS

Faculty of Applied Natural Sciences: Prof. Dr Ing. DIETER BRÜGGEMANN
Faculty of Biology, Chemistry and Geosciences: Prof. Dr STEPHAN CLEMENS
Faculty of Cultural Studies: Prof. Dr LUDGER KÖRNTGEN
Faculty of Language and Literature: Prof. Dr RAINER OβWALD

Faculty of Law and Economics: Prof. Dr MARKUS MÖSTL
Faculty of Mathematics, Physics and Computer Science: Prof. Dr HANS F. BRAUN

PROFESSORS

Faculty of Applied Natural Sciences (tel. (921) 557101; fax (921) 557106):

AKSEL, N., Applied Mechanics and Fluid Dynamics
ALTSTÄDT, V., Polymerics
BRÜGGEMANN, D., Technical Thermodynamics, Transport Processes
FISCHERAUER, G., Measurement Technology and Control Engineering
FREITAG, R., Bioprocess Technology
GLATZEL, U., Metallic Materials
JESS, A., Chemical Engineering
KRENKEL, W., Ceramic Materials
MOOS, R., Working Materials
RIEG, F., Engineering Design and CAD
STEINHILPER, R., Environmentally Compatible Production Technology
WILLERT-PORADA, M., Materials Processing

Faculty of Biology, Chemistry and Geosciences (tel. (921) 552229; fax (921) 552351):

BACH, L., Urban and Regional Planning
BALLAUFF, M., Physical Chemistry I
BECK, E., Plant Physiology
BEIERKUHNLEIN, C., Biogeography
BITZER, K., Geology
BOGNER, F. X., Didactics of Biology
BREU, J., Inorganic Chemistry I
DETTNER, K., Animal Ecology II
DRAKE, H. L., Soil Microbiology
FOKEN, T., Micrometeorology
FRANK, H., Environmental Pollution
HAUHS, M., Ecological Modelling
HOFFMANN, K. H., Animal Ecology I
HÜSER, K., Geomorphology
HUWE, B., Soil Science
KEMPE, R., Inorganic Chemistry II
KEPPLER, H., Experimental Geophysics
KOMOR, E., Plant Physiology
KRAUSCH, G., Physical Chemistry II
KRAUSS, J., Biochemistry
LEHNER, C., Genetics
LIEDE-SCHUMANN, S., Plant Systematics
LOHNERT, B., Geographical Development Research
MAIER, J., Economic Geography
MATZNER, E., Soil Sciences
MEYER, O., Microbiology
MONHEIM, R., Cultural Geography
MORYS, P., Inorganic Chemistry
MÜLLER, A., Macromolecular Chemistry II
MÜLLER-MAHN, D., Population and Social Geography
OBERMAIER, G., Didactics of Geography
PEIFFER, ST., Hydrology
PLATZ, G., Physical Chemistry I
POPP, H., Urban and Rural Geography
RAMBOLD, G., Plant Systematics
RÖSCH, P., Structure and Chemistry of Biopolymers
RUBIE, D., Structure and Dynamics of Earth Materials
SCHMID, F. X., Biochemistry
SCHMIDT, H.-W., Macromolecular Chemistry I
SCHOBERT, R., Organic Chemistry
SCHUMANN, W., Genetics
SEIFERT, F., Experimental Geosciences
SEIFERT, K., Organic Chemistry I/II
SENKER, J., Organic Chemistry I
SPRINZL, M., Biochemistry
STEUDLE, E., Plant Ecology
TENHUNEN, J., Plant Ecology
ULLMANN, M., Biocomputer Science
UNVERZAGT, C., Bio-Organic Chemistry
VON HOLST, D., Animal Physiology
WESTERMANN, B., Cell Biology
WRACKMEYER, B., Inorganic Chemistry II
ZECH, W., Soil Science and Soil Geography
ZÖLLER, L., Geomorphology

Faculty of Cultural Studies (tel. (921) 554101; fax (921) 55844101):

BARGATZKY, T., Ethnology
BERNER, U., Religious Studies I
BETZWIESER, T., Musicology
BOCHINGER, CH., Religious Studies II
BORMANN, L., Evangelical Theory III
BOSBACH, F., History
BREHM, W., Sport Science and Physical Education
EBNER, R., Catholic Religious Teaching II
HAAG, L., School Education
HEGSELMANN, R., Philosophy I
HIERY, H., History
KLUTE, G., Ethnology (Africa)
KOCH, L., Education
KÜGLER, J., Catholic Theology I
LANGE, D., History (Africa)
LINDGREN, U., History of Science
NEUBERT, D., Developmental Sociology
PUTZ-OSTERLOH, W., Psychology
RITTER, W., Protestant Theology II
SCHEIT, H., Social Philosophy
SCHMIDT, W., Sports Medicine
SCHOBERTH, W., Evangelical Theology I
SCHORCH, G., Elementary School Education
SCHÜSSLER, R., Philosophy II
SPITTLER, G., Ethnology
UNGERER-RÖHRICH, U., Sports
WEISS, D., Bavarian Regional Geology
ZIESCHANG, K., Sport Science and Physical Education
ZINGERLE, A., Sociology
ZÖLLER, M., Sociology II

Faculty of Language and Literature (tel. (921) 553625; fax (921) 553641):

BEGEMANN, C., New German Literature
BENESCH, K., English Literature
BERGER, J., Romance Linguistics
DRESCHER, M., Roman and General Linguistics
HAUSENDORF, H., German Linguistics
IBISZIMOW, D., African Studies II
KHAMIS, S., Literatures in African Languages
KLOTZ, P., German Language and Literature
MIEHE, G., African Linguistics I
MÜLLER, J., Media Studies
MÜLLER-JACQUIER, B., Intercultural German Language and Literature
OSSWALD, R., Islamic Studies
OWENS, J., Arabic Studies
SCHMID, H.-J., English Linguistics
STEPPAT, M., English Literature
VILL, S., Theatre Studies
WOLF, G., Early German Philology

Faculty of Law and Economics (tel. (921) 552894; fax (921) 552985):

BERG, W., Public Law
BÖHLER, H., Economics III
BREHM, W., Civil Law
DANNECKER, G., Criminal Law
EMMERICH, V., Civil Law
EYMANN, T., Economics VIII
GÖRGENS, E., Economics II
GUNDEL, J., Public Law
HEERMANN, P., Civil Law
HERZ, B., Economics I
KAHL, W., Public Law
KLIPPEL, D., Civil Law, History of Law
KÜHLMANN, T., Economics IV
LEPSIUS, O., Public Law
LESCHKE, M., Economics V
LORITZ, K.-G., Civil Law II
MECKL, R., Economics IX
MICHALSKI, L., Civil Law
MÖSTL, M., Public Law and Constitutional History
NAGEL, E., Health Service Management and Health Sciences
OBERENDER, P., Economics IV
OHLY, A., Civil Law
REMER, A., Economics VI

SCHLÜCHTERMANN, J., Economics V
SCHMITZ, R., Criminal Law
SIGLOCH, J., Economics II
SPELLENBERG, U., Civil Law
ULRICH, V., Economics III
WORATSCHEK, H., Economics VIII

Faculty of Mathematics, Physics and Computer Science (tel. (921) 553196; fax (921) 552999):

BAPTIST, P., Mathematics and Didactics
BRAND, H., Theoretical Physics III
BRAUN, D., Experimental Physics V
BÜTTNER, H., Theoretical Physics I
CATANESE, F., Mathematics VIII
ESKA, G., Experimental Physics V
GRÜNE, L., Applied Mathematics
HENRICH, D., Applied Computer Science III
KERBER, A., Mathematics
KÖHLER, J., Experimental Physics IV
KÖHLER, W., Experimental Physics IV
KRAMER, L., Theoretical Physics II
KRÄMER, M., Mathematics
KÜPPERS, J., Experimental Physics III
LAUE, R., Computer Science
LEMPIO, F., Applied Mathematics
MERTENS, F.-G., Theoretical Physics I
MÜLLER, W., Mathematics
OTT, A., Experimental Physics I
PASCHER, H., Experimental Physics I
PESCH, H. J., Engineering Mathematics
PETERNELL, T., Mathematics
RAUBER, T., Applied Computer Science II
REHBERG, I., Experimental Physics V
REIN, G., Applied Mathematics
RIEDER, H., Applied Mathematics
ROESSLER, E., Experimental Physics II
SCHAMEL, H., Theoretical Physics
SCHITTKOWSKI, K., Computer Science
SCHWOERER, M., Experimental Physics II
SEILMEIER, A., Experimental Physics III
SIMADER, C. G., Mathematics
VAN SMAALEN, S., Crystallography
VON WAHL, W., Applied Mathematics
WESTFECHTEL, B., Applied Computer Science
ZIMMERMANN, W., Applied Computer Science

ATTACHED INSTITUTES

Afrikazentrum (IWALENA-Haus) (Africa Centre): Dir Dr T. WENDL.

Bayerisches Forschungsinstitut für Experimentelle Geochemie und Geophysik (Bayerisches Geoinstitut, IBGI) (Bavarian Research Institute for Experimental Geochemistry and Geophysics): Dir Prof. Dr D. RUBIE.

Bayreuther Institut für Europäisches Recht und Rechts Kultur, insbesondere Rechtsvergleichung und Wirtschaftsrecht (Bayreuth Institute for European Law and Legal Culture, Comparative Law and Economic Law): Dir Prof. Dr P. HÄBERLE.

Bayreuther Institut für Makromolekülforschung (BIMF) (Bayreuth Institute for Macromolecular Research): Dir Prof. Dr H.-W. SCHMIDT.

Bayreuther Institut für Terrestrische Ökosystemforschung (BITÖK) (Bayreuth Institute for Terrestrial Ecology Research): Dir Prof. Dr E. MATZNER.

Bayreuther Zentrum für Kolloide und Grenzflächen (BZKG) (Bayreuth Centre for Colloids and Interfaces): Dir Prof. Dr M. BALLAUFF.

Bayreuther Zentrum für Molekulare Biowissenschaften (BZMB) (Bayreuth Centre for Molecular Biosciences): Dir Prof. Dr O. MEYER.

Bayreuther Zentrum für Ökologie und Umweltforschung (Bayreuth Centre for Ecology and Environmental Research): Dir Prof. Dr E. MATZNER.

Forschungsinstitut für Musiktheater (FIMT) (Research Institute for Music Theatre): Dir (vacant).

Institut für Afrikastudien (IAS) (Institute for African Studies): Dir Prof. Dr H. POPP.

Institut für Materialforschung (Institute for Materials Research): Dir Prof. Dr G. ZIEGLER.

Zentrum zur Förderung des Mathematisch- Naturwissenschaftlichen Unterrichts (Centre for Mathematical and Scientific Instruction): Dir Prof. Dr F. X. BOGNER.

UNIVERSITÄT BIELEFELD

POB 10 01 31, 33501 Bielefeld
Universitätsstr. 25, 33615 Bielefeld

Telephone: (521) 10600
Fax: (521) 1065844
E-mail: post@uni-bielefeld.de
Internet: www.uni-bielefeld.de

Founded 1969
State control
Academic year: April to March

Rector: Prof. Dr Ing. GERHARD SAGERER
Vice-Rector for Financial Affairs and Resources: Prof. Dr ROLF KÖNIG
Vice-Rector for Int. Relations and Communications: Prof. Dr SABINE ANDRESEN
Vice-Rector for Quality Devt: Prof. Dr JOHANNES HELLERMANN
Vice-Rector for Research, Young Researchers and Transfer: Prof. Dr MARTIN EGELHAAF
Chancellor: HANS-JÜRGEN SIMM
Librarian: Dr MICHAEL HÖPPNER
Library of 2,200,000 vols
Number of teachers: 4,567
Number of students: 18,935

Publications: *Bielefelder Universitätsgespräche* (irregular), *Bielefelder Universitätszeitung* (4 a year), *Forschungsbericht* (online), *Forschungsmagazin* (2 a year), *Jahresbericht des Rektors und Statistisches Jahrbuch* (1 a year), *Personalverzeichnis/Lehrveranstaltungen* (2 a year), *Pressedienst Forschung* (irregular)

DEANS

Faculty of Biology: Prof. Dr BERND WEISSHAAR
Faculty of Chemistry: Prof. Dr NORBERT SEWALD
Faculty of Economics: Prof. Dr HERBERT DAWID
Faculty of Educational Science: Prof. Dr SUSANNE MILLER
Faculty of Health Sciences: Prof. Dr CLAUDIA HORNBERG
Faculty of History, Philosophy and Theology: Prof. Dr UWE WALTER
Faculty of Law: Prof. Dr MICHAEL KOTULLA
Faculty of Linguistics and Literature: Prof. Dr KAI KAUFFMANN
Faculty of Mathematics: Prof. Dr MICHAEL RÖCKNER
Faculty of Physics: Prof. Dr DOMINIK SCHWARZ
Faculty of Psychology and Sports Science: Prof. Dr FRANK NEUNER
Faculty of Sociology: Prof. Dr VERONIKA TACKE
Faculty of Technology: Prof. Dr JENS STOYE

UNIVERSITÄT BREMEN

POB 33 04 40, 28334 Bremen
Bibliothekstr., 28359 Bremen

Telephone: (421) 2181
Fax: (421) 2184259
E-mail: presse@uni-bremen.de
Internet: www.uni-bremen.de

Founded 1971

State control
Academic year: October to September (two terms)

Rector: Prof. Dr WILFRIED MÜLLER
Chancellor: GERD-RÜDIGER KÜCK
Pro-Rector: Prof. Dr HEIDE SCHWELHOWE
Pro-Rector: Prof. Dr ROLF DRECHSLER
Pro-Rector: Prof. Dr YASEMIN KARAKAŞOĞLU
Librarian: MARIA ELISABETH MÜLLER
Number of teachers: 366
Number of students: 18,000

Publications: *Bremer Uni Schlüssel* (5 a year), *Impulse aus der Forschung* (2 a year), *Highlights* (Research Report, 2 a year)

DEANS

Biology and Chemistry: Prof. Dr SÖRGE KELM
Business Studies and Economics: Prof. Dr JOCHEN ZIMMERMANN
Cultural Studies: Prof. Dr JÜRGEN LOTT
Geosciences: Prof. Dr GERHARD BOHRMANN
Human and Health Sciences: Prof. Dr BIRGIT VOLMERG
Law: Prof. Dr GRALF-PETER CALLIES
Linguistics and Literary Studies: Prof. Dr MATTHIS KEPSER
Mathematics and Computer Science: Prof. Dr JAN PELESKA
Physics and Electrical Engineering: Prof. Dr JENS FALTA
Pedagogy and Education Sciences: Prof. Dr NORBERT RICKEN
Production Engineering-Mechanical Engineering and Process Engineering: Prof. Dr ARNIM VON GLEICH
Social Sciences: Prof. Dr TASSILO SCHMITT

PROFESSORS

Department 1 (Physics; Electrical Engineering)

Electrical Engineering:

ANHEIER, W., Microelectronics, Digital Systems
ARNDT, F., High Frequency Technology
BENECKE, W., Silicon-Micromechanics, Sensors and Actuators
BINDER, J., Micro- and Sensor-Systems, and Space Technology
GRÄSER, A., Automation Engineering
GRONWOLD, D., Electrical Technology
KAMMEYER, K.-D., Communications
LAUR, R., Electronics and Microelectronics
LOHMANN, B., Automatic Control
MARTE, G., Electronics
MEINERZHAGEN, B., Field Theory
MÜLLER, W., Analysis of the Engineering Professions
ORLIK, B., Electrical Drives and Power Electronics
RAUNER, F., Electrical Technology
SILBER, D. H., Power Electronics and Devices

Physics:

AUGSTEIN, E., Meteorology and Physics of the Oceans
BLECK-NEUHAUS, J., Experimental and Environmental Physics
BOSECK, S., Experimental Physics
BURROWS, P., Environmental Physics
CZYCHOLL, G., Theoretical Physics
DIEHL, H., Biophysics
DREYBRODT, W., Experimental Physics, Molecular Spectroscopy
FALTA, J., Surface Science of Semiconductors
GUTOWSKI, J., Semiconductor Optics
HOMMEL, D., Epitaxy of Semiconductors
JÜPTNER, W., Laser Application
KÜNZI, K., Environmental Physics
LANGE, H., Sociology of Labour
NIEDERER, H., Teaching of Physics
NOACK, C. C., Theoretical Physics
OLBERS, D., Theoretical Physics

PAWELZIK, K., Theoretical Biology
RICHTER, P., Theoretical Physics
ROETHER, W., Physical Oceanography in the Polar Regions
RYDER, P., Physics of Metals
SCHMITZ-FEUERHAKE, I., Experimental Physics
SCHWEDES, H., Teaching of Science
SCHWEGLER, H., Theoretical Physics, Theoretical Biophysics
STAUDE, W., Experimental Physics
VON AUFSCHNAITER, S., Teaching of Physics

Department 2 (Biology; Chemistry)

Biology:

ARNTZ, W., Ocean Ecology
BLOHM, D., Biotechology
ENTRICH, H., Theory and Practice of Education in the Natural Sciences
FAHLE, M., Neurobiology and Human Biology
FISCHER, H., Marine Microbiology
FLOHR, H., Biology
GRIMME, L. H., Biology, Biochemistry
HAGEN, W., Marine Zoology
HEYSER, W., Botany
HILDEBRANDT, A., Biology
KIRST, G.-O., Marine Botany
KOENIG, F., Botany
KREITER, A., Neurobiology
MOSSAKOWSKI, D., Evolutionary Biology
POERTNER, H.-O., Marine Biology
REINHOLD-HUREK, B., Microbiology
ROTH, G., Neurobiology
SAINT-PAUL, U., Marine Ecology
SCHLOOT, W., Genetics, Human Genetics
SMETACEK, V., Marine Biology
VALLBRACHT, A., Virology
WITTE, H., Zoology
WOLFF, M., Marine Ecology

Chemistry:

BALZER, W., Marine Chemistry
BEYERSMANN, D., Biochemistry
BREUNIG, H.-J., Inorganic Chemistry
GABEL, D., Organic Chemistry, Biochemistry
JAEGER, N., Physical Chemistry
JASTORFF, B., Organic Chemistry
JUST, E., Teaching of Chemistry
LEIBFRITZ, D., Organic Chemistry
MEWS, R., Inorganic Chemistry
MONTFORTS, F., Organic Chemistry
PLATH, P., Chemistry
RIEKENS, R., Teaching of Chemistry
RÖSCHENTHALER, G., Inorganic Chemistry
SCHREMS, O., Physical Chemistry
SCHROER, W., Physical Chemistry
SCHULZ-EKLOFF, G., Physical Chemistry
STOHRER, W.-D., Chemistry
THIEMANN, W., Physical Chemistry
WANCZEK, K., Inorganic Chemistry
WÖHRLE, D., Chemistry

Department 3 (Mathematics; Computer Science)

Computer Science:

BORMANN, U., Computer Networks
BRUNS, F.-W., Technology Design
FRIEDRICH, J., Computing and Society
GOGOLLA, M., Database Systems
HAEFNER, K., Education Technologies, Social Impacts and Transport Implications
HERZOG, O., Expert Systems and Foundations of Artificial Intelligence
KREOWSKI, H.-J., Theoretical Computer Science
KRIEG-BRÜCKNER, B., Programming Languages, Compilers and Software Engineering
KUBICEK, H., Information Management and Telecommunications
MAASS, S., Women's Studies and Technology
NAKE, F., Graphic Data Processing and Interactive Systems

PELESKA, J., Operating Systems, Distributed Systems
RÖDIGER, K.-H., Software Engineering and Ergonomics
SZCZERBICKA, H., Computer Architecture and Modelling

Mathematics:

ARNOLD, L., Random Dynamic Systems
BAENSCH, E., Numerical Methods for Partial Differential Equations
BECKER, G., Teacher Education
BOEHM, M., Modelling and Partial Differential Equations
BUNSE-GERSTNER, A., Numerical Linear Algebra
DENNEBERG, D., Non-Additive Integration, Risk, Uncertainty and Insurance
DEUTSCH, M., Logic and Foundations of Mathematics
DOMBROWSKI, H.-D., Mathematical Foundations of Physics
FISCHER, H. W., Complex Analysis
GAMST, J., Algorithmic Algebra and Number Theory
HERRLICH, H., Topology, Category Theory
HINRICHSEN, D., Systems and Control Theory
HOFFMANN, R.-E., Topology, Categories and Lattices
HORNEFFER, K., Differential Geometry, Mathematical Foundations of Physics
HUPPERTZ, H., Teacher Education
KRAUSE, U., Positive Dynamic Systems
LINDENAU, V., Teacher Education
MAASS, P., Inverse Problems and Wavelets
MÜNZNER, H.-F., Differential Geometry, Dynamic Systems
OELJEKLAUS, E., Complex Algebraic Geometry
OSIUS, G., Statistics, Biometry
PEITGEN, H.-O., Complex Systems, Computer-Aided Radiology
PORST, H.-E., Categorical Algebra
SCHÄFER, R., Numerical Hydrogeology
WISCHNEWSKY, M., Modelling, Neural Networks, Fuzzy Systems

Department 4 (Production Engineering; Economics for Engineering; Commercial and Technical Science):

BAUCKHAGE, K., Chemical and Process Engineering
BRINKSMEIER, E., Manufacturing Technology
GENTHNER, K., Technical Thermodynamics, Heat and Mass Transfer
GOCH, G., Metrology, Automation and Quality Science
GRATHWOHL, G., Ceramic Materials and Components
HARIG, H., Material Technology and Composites
HEEG, F.-J., Work Science
HENNEMANN, O. D., Bonding Technology and Polymers
HIRSCH, B. E., Production Resources, Logistics, Telematics
HOPPE, M., Vocational Teaching of Metal Engineering
KIENZLER, R., Applied Mechanics and Structural Mechanics
KUNZE, H.-D., Near Net Shape Production Technologies
MAYR, P., Material Science
MÜLLER, D. H., Engineering Design, CAE, CAD
RÄBIGER, N., Environmental Process Engineering
RATH, H. J., Technical Mechanics and Fluid Mechanics
SEPOLD, G., Laser and Plasma Technologies for Materials Processing
VISSER, A., Production Facilities
WITTKOWSKY, A., Design and Development of Technology

Department 5 (Geosciences):

BLEIL, U., Marine Geophysics
BROCKAMP, O., Mineralogy, Petrography, Clay Mineralogy
DEVEY, C., Petrology of the Ocean Crust
FISCHER, R. X., Crystallography
FÜTTERER, D., Geology
HENRICH, R., Sedimentology, Palaeo-Oceanography
HERTERICH, K., Palaeo-Oceanographic Modelling
JÖRGENSEN, B. B., Biogeochemistry
KUSS, H. J., Geology, Stratigraphy, Sedimentology
MILLER, H., Geophysics
OLESCH, M., Geology of the Polar Regions, Petrology
SCHULZ, H., Geochemistry, Hydrogeology
SPIESS, V., Marine Technology, Marine Environmental Geophysics
VILLINGER, H., Marine Technology, Geophysical Sensor Development
WEFER, G., Geology
WILLEMS, H., Historical Geology and Palaeontology

Department 6 (Law):

BÖLLINGER, L., Criminal Law
BRÜGGEMEIER, G., Civil and Economic Law
DAMM, R., Civil Law, Economic Law
DÄUBLER, B., Labour, Commercial and Economic Law
DERLEDER, P., Civil and Banking Law
DUBISCHAR, R., Civil Law
FEEST, J., Criminal Law and Criminology
FRANCKE, R., Legal Didactics
GESSNER, V., Comparative Law and Legal Sociology
HART, D., Economic Law
HINZ, M., Public Law and Political and Legal Sociology
HOFFMANN, R., Public Law, Labour Law and Political Science
JOERGES, C., Civil and Comparative Law
KNIEPER, R., Civil and Economic Law
LICHTENBERG, H., Labour and European Law
REICH, N., Civil and European Law
RINKEN, A., Public Law
RUEHE, U., Public Law
RUST, U., Gender Law
SCHEFOLD, D., Public Law
SCHMIDT, E., Civil Law and Procedure
SCHMINCK-GUSTAVUS, C., History of Law
SCHUMANN, K. F., Criminology
STUBY, G., Public Law and Political Science
THOSS, P., Criminal Law
WASHNER, R., Labour Law
WESSLAU, E., Criminal Law and Procedure
WINTER, G., Public and Environmental Law

Department 7 (Economics):

BAUER, E., Marketing of Research and Management
BIESECKER, A., Economic Theory
BRITSCH, K., Economic Statistics
DWORATSCHEK, S., Project Management
ECKSTEIN, W., Economics of Logistic Systems
ELSNER, W., Economic, Industrial and Regional Policy, Institutional Evolutionary Economics
FRANCKE, R., Economic Theory
GERSTENBERGER, H., Theory of State and Society
GRENZDÖRFFER, K., Economic Statistics, Labour Economics
HAASIS, H.-D., Production Management and Industrial Organization
HEIDE, H., Town and Country Planning
HICKEL, R., Public Finance
HUFFSCHMID, J., Political Economy, Economic Policy
KALMBACH, P., Economics

KOPFER, H., Economics of Logistics Systems
LEITHÄUSER, G., Economic Policy
LEMPER, A., Foreign Trade Theory and Politics
LIONVILLE, J., International Economics
MARX, F. J., Financial Accounting and Business Taxation
PODDIG, TH., Finance
SCHAEFER, H., Theory, Forecasting and Control
SCHMÄHL, W., Economics and Social Policy
SCHWIERING, D., Economics
SELL, A., International Economics
STEIGER, O., General Economic Theory and Monetary Economics
STUCHTEY, R. W., Economics of Marine Transport
VON DER VRING, TH., Political Economy
WOHLMUTH, K., Comparative Economic Systems
ZACHCIAL, M., Transport Science and Transport Planning

Department 8 (Social Sciences)

Cultural History of Eastern Europe:

EICHWEDE, W., History and Politics of Socialist Countries
KRASNODEBSKY, Z., Polish Social and Cultural History
STÄDTKE, K., Cultural History of Eastern Europe

Geography:

BAHRENBERG, G., Social and Economic Geography
SCHRAMKE, W., Geography, Teaching of Geography
TAUBMANN, W., Cultural Geography
TIPPKÖTTER, R., Geography of Soils
VENZKE, J.-F., Physical Geography

History:

BARROW, L., Social and Political History of England
EICHWEDE, W., History and Politics of Socialist Countries
HACHTMANN, R., History of the 19th and 20th Centuries
HÄGERMANN, D., Medieval History
HAHN, M., History of Business, Political Theories
HOEDER, D., Social History of the USA
KLOFT, H., Ancient History
KOPITZSCH, F., History
KRAUSS, M., History of 19th- and 20th-Century Social Economics
RECH, M., Prehistoric and Medieval History
SCHMIDT, J., Curricula in Economic and Social Studies
WAGNER, W., Politics, History of Political Education

Politics:

ALBERS, D., Labour Relations
EICHWEDE, W., History and Politics of Socialist Countries
KOOPMANN, K., Didactics of Social Science Education
LIEBERT, U., Comparative Politics, European Integration
LOTHAR, R., Politics, and Federal and Constitutional Law
PETERS, B., Political Theory and History of Ideas
SCHMIDT, M., Politics, Comparative Social Policies
WAGNER, W., Politics, History of Political Education
WIRTH, M., Parliamentary System of Federal Germany
ZOLL, R., History and Theory of Trade Unions
ZÜRN, M., Politics

Postgraduate Programme Development Policy with Focus on Non-Governmental Organizations:

VON FREYHOLD, M., Development Policy and Sociology of Development

Sociology:

KRÄMER-BADONI, T., Town and Regional Planning
KRAUSE, D., Educational Planning
KRÜGER, M., Social Analysis
LAUTMANN, R., General Sociology and Sociology of Law
LUEDEMANN, CHR., Statistics and Empirical Research
PETER, L., Labour and Industrial Sociology
QUENSEL, S., Resocialization and Rehabilitation
REICHELT, H., Theory of Science and Society
SENGHAAS, D., Peace and Conflict Studies
VON FREYHOLD, M., Social Science
WEYMANN, A., Social Theory, Educational Research

Department 9 (Cultural Sciences)

Art:

BUDDEMEIER, H., Communication, Mass Media
MÜLLER, M., Art History and Cultural Studies
PETERS, M., Art Education
SCHADE-THOLEN, S., Art History, Aesthetics

Cultural Science:

DRÖGE, F., Mass Communication Research
DUERR, H. P., Ethnology and Cultural History
NADIG, M., European Ethnology and Cultural Anthropology
RICHARD, J., Teaching of Drama
RICHTER, D., German Literature

Music:

BRECKOFF, W., Teaching of Music
KLEINEN, G., Teaching of Music, Musicology
RIEGER, E., Musicology

Philosophy:

MOHR, G., Practical Philosophy
SANDKÜHLER, H. J., Theoretical Philosophy
STÖCKLER, M., Philosophy of Natural Sciences

Religious Science:

KIPPENBERG, H.-G., Theory and History of Religions
LOTT, J., Religious Education
SCHULZ, H., Comparative Religion

Sport:

ARTUS, H. G., Teaching of Physical Education
BRAUN, H., History of Sport
FIKUS, M., Psychomotor Behaviour
SCHEELE, K., Sports Medicine

Department 10 (Literature and Language Studies)

Communication:

BACH, G., Teaching of English
BARROW, L., Social and Political History of England
BATEMANN, J. A., Applied Functional Linguistics, Natural Language Processing and Translation Science
DAHLE, W., German Language and Literature
EMMERICH, W., German Literature
FRANZBACH, M., Literature and Social History of Spain and Latin America
GALLAS, H., German Literature
JÄGER, H.-W., History of German Literature
KOCH, H. A., German and Comparative Literature
LIEBE-HARKORT, K., German as a Foreign Language

LIENERT, E., German Literature of the Middle Ages and the Early Modern Period
MENK, A.-K., Linguistics
PASTERNACK, G., Theory of Literature
PAUL, L., Applied Linguistics
SAUTERMEISTER, G., History of German Literature
STOLZ, TH., Linguistics
WAGNER, K.-H., Linguistics
WILDGEN, W., Linguistics
ZIMMERMANN, K., Spanish and Portuguese Linguistics

Department 11 (Health and Human Studies)

Psychology:

BAUMGÄRTL, F., Psychological Diagnosis
BERNDT, J., Physiology
GNIECH, G., Psychology
HEINZ, W.-R., Sociology and Social Psychology
HENNING, H.-J., Psychology
KIESELBACH, TH., Psychology
LEITHÄUSER, T., Developmental Psychology
PETERMANN, F., Clinical Psychology
REINKE, E., Clinical Psychology
STADLER, M., Psychology
VETTER, G., Theory of Learning
VOGT, R., Psychology
VOLMERG, B., Psychology

Public Health:

FRENTZEL-BEYME, R., Occupational and Environmental Epidemiology
GREISER, E., Occupational Health and Social Medicine
MÜLLER, R., Health Policy, Occupational Health and Social Medicine

Social Education:

AMENDT, G., Sub-Cultures
BAUER, R., Social Pedagogy
BLANDOW, J., Social Education
BROCKMANN, A.-D., Town and Regional Planning
HEINSON, G., Social Pedagogy
KEIL, A., General Education
LEIBFRIED, S., Social Planning
MERKEL, J., Pre-School Education

Teacher Training:

GOERRES, ST., Social Gerontology
HYAMS-PETER, H.-U., Social Education
KRÜGER-MÜLLER, H., Sociology
LITTEK, W., Education and Economics
ORTMANN, H., Educational Sciences
VAN MAANEN, H., Nursing Sciences

Work Study:

MÜLLER, R., Health Policy, Occupational Health and Social Medicine
SENGHASS-KNOBLOCH, E., Humanization of Work
SPITZLEY, H., Technology and Society

Department 12 (Social and Educational Sciences)

Education Diploma:

DIETZE, L., Public Law
ROTH, L., Theory of Teaching
SCHÖNWÄLDER, H. G., Educational Planning and Economics
STRAKA, G., Extracurricular Education
ZIECHMANN, J., Psychology of Learning

Educational Science:

BECK, J., Educational Social Sciences
BOEHM, U., Structure and Development of Education
DRECHSEL, R., Education
DRECHSEL, W., Educational Social History
HUISKEN, F., Educational Political Economy
POLZIN, M., Aesthetic Education
PREUSS, O., Sociology of Education
UBBELOHDE, R., Educational Science
VINNAI, G., Analytical Social Psychology
VOIGT, B., Teacher Training

Further Education:

GERL, H., Adult Education
GÖRS, D., Distance Education
HOLZAPPFEL, G., Curricular Planning
KUHLENKAMP, D., Educational Planning
MADER, W., Adult Education
SCHLUTZ, E., Adult Education
WOLLENBERG, J., Adult Education in Political Science

Primary Education:

MILHOFFER, P., Sociology and Political Education
SCHMITT, R., Developmental Psychology
SPITTA, G., Beginning of German Language

Teaching the Handicapped:

DÖHNER, O., Medicine of Mental Illness
FEUSER, G., Education of Mentally Disturbed Children
HOMBURG, G., Educating People with Speech Defects
JANTZEN, W., History of Educating the Handicapped
KRETSCHMANN, R., Training of the Educationally Handicapped
PIXA-KETTNER, U., Educating People with Speech Defects
REINCKE, W., Education for the Mentally Disturbed

Work Experience:

FISCHER, W. C., Consumer Economics
FRÖLEKE, H., Nutrition
HUISKEN, F., Educational Science
SCHRÖDER, A., Textile Technology

UNIVERSITÄT DER BUNDESWEHR MÜNCHEN

Werner-Heisenberg-Weg 39, 85577 Neubiberg

Telephone: (89) 60040
Fax: (89) 60043560
E-mail: info@unibw.de
Internet: www.unibw.de
Founded 1973
Academic year: October to September (3 semesters)
Pres.: Prof. Dr MERITH NIEHUSS
Vice-Pres. for Academics: Prof. Dr UWE M. BORGHOFF
Vice-Pres. for College of Applied Sciences: Prof. Dr Ing. MATTHIAS HEINITZ
Vice-Pres. for Research: Prof. Dr MICHAEL EßIG
Chancellor: SIEGFRIED RAPP
Library Dir: Dr MARIA MANN-KALLENBORN
Library: 1.1m. vols
Number of teachers: 200
Number of students: 3,700
Publications: 'Der Hochschulkurier' (3 a year), Forschungsbericht

DEANS

Faculty of Aeronautics and Astronautics: Prof. Dr Ing. CHRISTIAN MUNDT
Faculty of Civil Engineering and Surveying: Prof. Dr-Ing. MANFRED KEUSER
Faculty of Economics and Organizational Sciences: Prof. Dr STEFAN KOOS
Faculty of Education: Prof. Dr Hab. MANUELA PIETRAß
Faculty of Electrical Engineering and Information Technology: Prof. Dr-Ing. K. HOFFMANN
Faculty of Informatics: Prof. Dr MARK MINAS
Faculty of Political and Social Sciences: Prof. Dr Hab. URSULA MÜNCH

UNIVERSITÄT DER KÜNSTE BERLIN
(Berlin University of the Arts)

POB 12 05 44, 10595 Berlin
Einsteinufer 43–53, 10587 Berlin
Telephone: (30) 31850

Fax: (30) 31852713
E-mail: beratung@udk-berlin.de
Internet: www.udk-berlin.de
Founded 1975 by amalgamation of the Staatliche Hochschule für Bildende Künste (f. 1696) and the Staatliche Hochschule für Musik und Darstellende Kunst (f. 1869)
Pres.: Prof. MARTIN RENNERT
First Vice-Pres.: Prof. Dr Ing. CHRISTOPH GENGNAGEL
Vice-Pres.: Prof. GUNDEL MATTENKLOTT
Chancellor: WOLFGANG ABRAMOWSKI
Library Dir: ANDREA ZEYNS
Library of 650,000 vols
Number of students: 4,300

DEANS

College of Architecture, Media and Design: Prof. Dr MICHAEL BOLLÉ
College of Fine Arts: Prof. Dr TANJA MICHALSKY
College of Music: Prof. Dr WOLFGANG DINGLINGER
College of Performing Arts: Prof. Dr KARL-LUDWIG OTTO

UNIVERSITÄT DES SAARLANDES

POB 15 11 50, 66041 Saarbrücken
Telephone: (681) 3020
Fax: (681) 3022609
E-mail: praesident@uni-saarland.de
Internet: www.uni-saarland.de
Founded 1948
Academic year: October to July
Pres.: Prof. Dr VOLKER LINNEWEBER
Vice-Pres for Admin. and Finance: MARTINA PETERMANN
Vice-Pres for Education: Prof. Dr MANFRED J. SCHMITT
Vice-Pres for European and Cultural Affairs: Prof. Dr PATRICIA OSTER-STIERLE
Vice-Pres for Planning and Strategy: Prof. Dr ALEXANDER BAUMEISTER
Librarian: Dr BERND HAGENAU
Library: see Libraries and Archives
Number of teachers: 1,570
Number of students: 17,600
Publications: Annales Universitatis Saraviensis (4 a year), Campus (irregular), Forschungsbericht (1 a year), Jahresbibliographie (1 a year), Vorlesungsverzeichnis (2 a year)

DEANS

Faculty of Humanities I: Prof. Dr PETER RIEMER
Faculty of Humanities II: Prof. Dr ERICH STEINER
Faculty of Humanities III: Prof. Dr JOCHEN KUBINIOK
Faculty of Law and Economics: Prof. Dr CHRISTIAN SCHOLZ
Faculty of Medicine: Prof. MICHAEL MENGER
Faculty of Natural Sciences and Technology I: Prof. HOLGER HERMANNS
Faculty of Natural Sciences and Technology II: Prof. HELMUT SEIDEL
Faculty of Natural Sciences and Technology III: Prof. Dr WILHELM F. MAIER

PROFESSORS

Faculty of Law and Business (tel. (681) 3022003; fax (681) 3024213; e-mail dekanat@rewi.uni-sb.de; internet www.rewi.uni-sb.de):

ALBERT, M., Economics
AUTEXIER, C., French Public Law
BECKMANN, R., Civil, Commercial, Economic and Labour Law
BIEG, H., Business Economics
CHIUSI, T., Civil Law, Roman Law

FRIEDMANN, R., Statistics
GLASER, H., Business Economics
GRÖPL, C., State and Management Law
GRÖPPEL-KLEIN, A., Business Economics
HERBERGER, M., Civil Law, Theory of Law, Computer Applications in Jurisprudence
JUNG, H., Penal and Procedural Law, Criminal Law, Law of Criminal Procedure, Criminology and Comparative Criminal Jurisprudence
KORIATH, H., Criminal Law, Criminal Procedural Law, Philosophy of Law, Sociology of Law
KUßMAUL, H., Business Economics
KÜTING, K., Business Economics
LOOS, P., Business Economics
MARTINEK, M., Civil, Commercial and Economic Law, International Private Law and Comparative Jurisprudence
MATUSCHE-BECKMANN, A., Civil, Commercial and Economic Law and Labour Law
MENG, W., Public Law, International Law, European Community Law
MOMSEN, C., Penal and Procedural Law
NICKEL, S., Business Economics
PIERZIOCH, C., Economics
RANIERI, F., European Civil Law
RÜSSMANN, H., Civil and Procedural Law, Philosophy of Law
SCHMIDT, G., Business Economics
SCHMIDTCHEN, D., Economics
SCHOLZ, C., Business Economics
STEIN, T., European Law, European Public Law, International Law
STROHMEIER, S., Business Economics
WADLE, E., History of German Law, Civil Law
WASCHBUSCH, G., Business Economics
WENDT, R., Constitutional and Administrative Law, Revenue and Tax Law
WETH, S., German and European Procedural and Industrial Law
WITZ, C., French Public Law
ZENTES, J., Business Economics

Faculty of Medicine (Medizinische Fakultät, Universitätskliniken des Saarlandes, 66421 Homburg; tel. (6841) 1624737; fax (6841) 1626003; e-mail mfdekan@med-rz.uni-sb.de):

ABDUL-KHALIQ, H., Paediatrics
BOCK, R., Anatomy
BOHLE, R., Pathology
BÖHM, M., Internal Medicine
BRUNS, D., Physiology
BUCHTER, A., Occupational Medicine
CAVALIÉ, A., Pharmacology and Toxicology
FALKAI, P., Psychiatry and Psychotherapy
FASSBENDER, K., Psychiatry and Psychotherapy
FEIDEN, W., Neuropathology
FLOCKERZI, V., Pharmacology and Toxicology
FREICHEL, M., Pharmacology and Toxicology
FUHR, G., Medical Technology
GORTNER, L., Paediatrics
GRAF, N., Paediatrics
HANNIG, M., Oral and Maxillofacial Medicine
HERRMANN, E., Mathematical Modelling in Molecular Medicine
HERRMANN, M., Microbiology
HERRMANN, W., Clinical Chemistry
HOTH, M., Physiology
HÜTTERMANN, J., Biophysics
KIENECKER, E.-W., Anatomy
KINDERMANN, W., Sports Medicine
KIRSCH, C.-M., Nuclear Medicine
KÖHLER, H., Internal Medicine
KOHN, D., Orthopaedics
LARSEN, R., Anaesthesiology
LIPP, P., Molecular Cell Biology
LISSON, J., Oral and Maxillofacial Medicine
LÖBRICH, M., Biophysics and Physical Basis of Medicine

MAURER, H. H., Pharmacology and Toxicology
MEESE, E., Human Genetics and Molecular Biology
MENGER, M., Institute for Clinical and Experimental Surgery
MESTRES-VENTURA, P., Anatomy
MEYERHANS, A., Virology
MONTENARH, M., Medical Biochemistry
MÜLLER-LANTZSCH, N., Virology
PFREUNDSCHUH, M., Internal Medicine
POHLEMANN, T., Casualty Surgery
POSPIECH, P., Oral and Maxillofacial Medicine
REITH, W., Diagnostic Radiology
RETTIG, J., Physiology
RÖSLER, M., Psychiatry, Neurology
RÜBE, CH., Radiotherapy
SCHÄFERS, H.-J., Surgery
SCHEIDIG, A., Structural Biology
SCHILLING, M., Surgery
SCHMIDT, W., Gynaecology and Obstetrics
SCHMITZ, F., Neuroanatomy
SCHULZ, I., Physiology
SEITZ, B., Occular Medicine
SPITZER, W. C., Maxillofacial Surgery
STAHL, H., Medical Biochemistry
STEUDEL, W.-I., Neurosurgery
STÖCKLE, M., Urology
SYBRECHT, G. W., Internal Medicine
THIEL, G., Medical Biochemistry
TILGEN, W., Dermatology and Venereology
VON GONTARD, A., Child Psychiatry
WALLDORF, U., Developmental Biology
WANKE, K., Neurology, Psychiatry
WILSKE, J., Forensic Medicine
ZEUZEM, S., Internal Medicine
ZIMMERMANN, R., Physiological Chemistry

Faculty of Natural Sciences and Technology I: Mathematics and Computer Science (tel. (681) 3025070; fax (681) 3025068; e-mail sekr .fakultaet@mx.uni-saarland.de; internet www.uni-saarland.de/fak6):

ALBRECHT, E., Mathematics
BACKES, M., Computer Science
BLÄSER, M., Computer Science
BROSAMLER, G.-A., Mathematics
DECKER, W., Mathematics
ESCHMEIER, J., Mathematics
FUCHS, M., Mathematics
GEKELER, E.-U., Mathematics
HERFET, T., Computer Science
HERMANNS, H., Computer Science
HISCHER, H., Teaching of Mathematics
JOHN, V., Mathematics
KOCH, C., Computer Science
KOHLER, M., Mathematics
LENHOFF, H., Bioinformatics
LOUIS, A. K., Mathematics
PAUL, W., Information Science
RJASANOW, S., Mathematics
SCHEIDIG, H., Informatics
SCHREYER, F.-O., Mathematics
SCHULZE-PILLOT, R., Mathematics
SEIDEL, R., Theoretical Informatics
SIEKMANN, J., Informatics
SLUSALLEK, P., Informatics
SMOLKA, G., Information Science
WAHLSTER, W., Informatics
WEICKERT, J., Mathematics
ZELLER, A., Software Engineering

Faculty of Natural Sciences and Technology II: Physics and Electrical Engineering (tel. (681) 3024943; fax (681) 3024973; e-mail dekan.fak7@mx.uni-saarland.de; internet www.uni-saarland.de/fak7):

BECHER, C., Physical Engineering
BIRRINGER, R., Physical Engineering
DYCZIJ-EDLINGER, R., Electrical Theory
HARTMANN, U., Experimental Physics
JAKOBS, K., Experimental Physics
JANOCHA, H., Process Automation
KLAKOW, D., Speech Processing
KLIEM, H., Electrical Engineering Physics
KNORR, K., Physical Engineering

KÖNIG, K., Microsensor Technology
KRÜGER, J. K., Experimental Physics
KUGI, A., Systems Theory and Control Engineering
LÜCKE, M., Theoretical Physics
MÖLLER, M., Electronics and Circuits
NICOLAY, T., High Frequency Engineering
PELSTER, R. (acting), Experimental Physics
RIEGER, H., Theoretical Physics
SANTEN, L., Theoretical Physics
SCHÜTZE, A., Measurement
SEIDEL, H., Micromechanics
WAGNER, C., Experimental Physics
WICHERT, T., Physical Engineering
XU, CHIHAO, Microelectronics

Faculty of Natural Sciences and Technology III: Chemistry, Pharmacy, Materials Science (tel. (681) 3022400; fax (681) 3023421; e-mail dekan.fak8@mx.uni-saarland.de; internet www.uni-saarland.de/fak8):

BAUER, P., Botany
BECK, H. P., Inorganic and Analytical Chemistry, Radiochemistry
BERNHARDT, I., Biophysics
BERNHARDT, R., Biochemistry
BLEY, H., Production Engineering
BUSCH, R., Metallic Materials
CLASEN, R., Materials Science
DIEBELS, S., Applied Mechanics
GIFFHORN, F., Microbiology
HARTMANN, R. W., Pharmaceutical Chemistry
HEGETSCHWEILER, K., Inorganic Chemistry
HEINZLE, E., Technical Bioengineering
HELMS, V., Computational Biology
HUBER, C., Analytical Chemistry
JAUCH, J., Organic Chemistry
KAZMAIER, U., Organic Chemistry
KIEMER, A. K., Pharmaceutical Biology
KRÖNING, M., Non-Destructive Materials Testing
LEHR, C.-M., Pharmaceutical Technology
MAIER, W., Technical Chemistry
MÜCKLICH, F., Work Materials
MÜLLER, R., Pharmaceutical Biotechnology
MÜLLER, U., Zoology and Physiology
POSSART, W., Polymers and Surfaces
SCHMIDT, H., New Materials
SCHMITT, M., Microbiology
SPRINGBORG, M., Physical Chemistry
VEHOFF, H., Materials Science, Methodology
VEITH, M., Inorganic Chemistry
WALTER, J., Genetics
WEBER, C., Construction Engineering
WENZ, G., Macromolecular Chemistry

Faculty of Philosophy I: History and Cultural Sciences (tel. (681) 3022300; fax (681) 3024234; e-mail u.weisgerber@pfdek.uni-sb .de):

BEHRINGER, W., Early Times
BRANDOLINI, A., Art Education
DE JONG, R., Art Education
DETZLER, B., Art Education
GIRARDET, K. M., Ancient History
GOERTZ, S., Practical Theology and Social Ethics
GRABAS, M., Economic and Social History
GÜTHLEIN, K., History of Art
HAUSIG, D., Art Education
HECKMANN, H., Philosophy
HINSCH, W., Philosophy
HUDEMANN, R., Modern and Contemporary History
HULLMANN, H., Art Education
HÜTTENHOFF, M., Protestant Theology
KASTEN, B., Medieval History
KRAUS, W., New Testament
KUBISCH, C., Art Education
LICHTENSTERN, C., History of Art
MAKSIMOVIC, I., Art Education
NESTLER, W., Art Education
NORTMANN, U., Philosophy
OHLIG, K.-H., Theology
POPP, H., Art Education

REINSBERG, C., Classical Archaeology
RIEMER, P., Classical Philology
ROMPZA, S., Art Education
ROSENBACH, U., Art Education
SACHSSE, R., Art Education
SCHERZBERG, L., Systematic Theology
SCHMITT, R., Comparative Indo-Germanic Languages
SCHNEIDER, H., Medieval History
SCHRÖDER, B., Religious Education
WALICZKY, M., Art Education
WINZEN, A., Art Education
ZIMMERMANN, C., Cultural History and Media History

Faculty of Philosophy II: Language, Literature and Cultural Studies (tel. (681) 3023360; fax (681) 3024535; e-mail g.braun@pfdek .uni-sb.de):

ALBERT, M., Romance Philology
BARRY, W. J., Phonetics, Phonology
BÉHAR, P., German for Francophones
BEM, J., Romance Philology
CROCKER, M., Psycholinguistics
DEMSKE, J., German Linguistics
ENGEL, M., German Language and Literature
GERZYMISCH-ARBOGAST, H., English Translation
GHOSH-SCHELLHORN, M., English Philology
GIL ARROYO, A., Translation Studies, Romance Languages
GÖTZE, L., German as a Foreign Language
HALLER, J., Mechanical Transmission
HAUBRICHS, W., Medieval German Literature
KLEINERT, S., Romance Philology
LOHMEIER, A.-M., Modern German Philology and Literature
LÜSEBRINK, H.-J., Romance Civilization, Intercultural Communication
MARTENS, K., English Philology, American Literature
MARTI, R., Slavonic Philology
NORRICK, N., English Philology, Linguistics
OSTER-STIERLE, P., French Literature
PINKAL, M., Computer Languages
SAUDER, G., Modern German Philology and Literature
SCHMELING, M., General and Comparative Literature
SCHWEICKARD, W., Romance Philology
SPRAUL, H., Russian
STEINER, E., English Linguistics and Translation
USZKOREIT, H., Computer Linguistics

Faculty of Philosophy III: Empirical Humanities (tel. (681) 3023700; fax (681) 3022953; e-mail s.mersdorf@pfdek.uni-sb.de; internet www.uni-saarland.de/fak5):

ASCHERSLEBEN, G., Developmental Psychology
BRÜCHER, W., Geography
BRÜNKEN, R., Education Science
EMRICH, E., Kinesiology and Exercise Science
HERZMANN, P., Education Science
KERKOFF, G., Clinical Neuropsychology
KRAUSE, R., Psychology
KUBINIOK, J., Physical Geography
LÖFFLER, E. W., Physical Geography
MAXEINER, J., Education
SPINATH, F., Differential Psychology and Diagnostics
STARK, R., Personal Development and Education
STOCKMANN, R., Sociology
WASSMUND, H., Political Science
WENTURA, D., General Psychology and Methodology
WINTERHOFF-SPURK, P., Psychology
WINTERMANTEL, M., Social Psychology
WYDRA, G., Sports Education
ZIMMERMANN, H. H., Information Science

UNIVERSITÄT DUISBURG-ESSEN

Campus Duisburg, Forsthausweg 2, 47057 Duisburg

Telephone: (203) 3790

Fax: (203) 3793333*Campus Essen*, Universitätsstr. 2, 45141 Essen

Telephone: (201) 1831

Fax: (201) 1832151

E-mail: rektor@uni-duisburg-essen.de

Internet: www.uni-due.de

Founded 2003 by merger of Gerhard-Mercator-Universität Duisburg (f. 1972) and Universität-Gesamthochschule-Essen (f. 1972)

Academic year: October to September (two semesters)

Rector: Prof. Dr ULRICH RADTKE

Vice-Rector for Diversity Management: Prof. Dr UTE KLAMMER

Vice-Rector for Research, Junior Academic Staff and Knowledge Transfer: Prof. Dr JÖRG SCHROEDER

Vice-Rector for Resource Planning: Dr INGRID LOTZ-AHRENS

Vice-Rector for Teaching and Learning: Prof. Dr FRANZ BOSBACH

Chancellor: Dr RAINER AMBROSY

Librarian: ALBERT BILO (Essen)

Librarian: SIGURD PRAETORIUS (Duisburg)

Library: 2.5m. vols, 4,000 print journals, 17,500 e-journals

Number of teachers: 3,579

Number of students: 31,806

Publications: *Essener Unikate* (2 a year), *Forschungsbericht* (every 2 years), *Forum Forschung* (1 a year), *Results of Mathematics* (4 a year)

DEANS

Faculty of Biology: Prof. Dr BERND SURES

Faculty of Chemistry: Prof. Dr MATTHIAS EPPLE

Faculty of Economics and Business Administration: Prof. Dr MICHAEL GOEDICKE

Faculty of Educational Sciences: Prof. Dr HORST BOSSONG

Faculty of Engineering: Prof. Dr Ing. DIETER SCHRAMM

Faculty of Humanities: Prof. Dr DIRK HARTMANN

Faculty of Mathematics: Prof. Dr WERNER HAUßMANN

Faculty of Medicine: Prof. Dr MICHAEL FORSTING

Faculty of Physics: Prof. Dr MICHAEL SCHRECKENBERG

Faculty of Social Sciences: Prof. Dr GERHARD BÄCKER

Mercator School of Management: Prof. Dr ALF KIMMS

ATTACHED RESEARCH INSTITUTES

Deutsches Textilforschungszentrum Nord-West eV: Dir Prof. Dr ECKHARD SCHOLLMEYER.

Deutsch-Französisches Institut für Automation und Robotik (IAR): Speaker Prof. Dr-Ing. STEVEN X. DING.

Entwicklungszentrum für Schiffstechnik und Transportsysteme eV: Dir Prof. Dr P. ENGELKAMP.

Essener Kolleg für Geschlechterforschung: Dir Prof. Dr DORIS JANSHEN.

Forschungsinstitut für wirtschaftliche Entwicklungen im Pazifikraum eV (FIP): Dir Prof. Dr GÜNTER HEIDUK.

Foundation Centre of Turkish Studies: internet www.zft-online.de; Dir Prof. Dr FARUK SEN.

Institut für Energie- und Umwelttechnik eV (IUTA): internet www.iuta.de; Dir Prof. Dr K. G. SCHMIDT.

Institut für Experimentelle Mathematik (IEM): internet www.exp-math.uni-essen.de; Dir Prof. Dr H. VINCK.

Institut für Mobil- und Satellitenfunktechnik GmbH (IMST GmbH): internet www.imst.de; Dirs Prof. Dr-Ing. INGO WOLFF, Dr-Ing. PETER WALDOW.

Instituts für Niederrheinische Kulturgeschichte und Regionalenwicklung: Dir Prof. Dr DIETER GEUENICH.

Institut für Prävention und Gesundheitsförderung: internet www.ipg-uni-essen.de; Dir Dr ALFONS SCHRÖER.

IWW Rheinisch-Westfälisches Institut für Wasserforschung gemeinnützige GmbH: internet www.iww-online.de; Dirs Dr-Ing. WOLF MERKEL, KLAUS-DIETER NEUMANN.

Rhein-Ruhr-Institut für Sozialforschung und Politikberatung eV (RISP): internet www.risp-duisburg.de; applied regional socio-economic research; promotes communication and co-operation between the academic world and public and private sector institutions in the Ruhrgebiet; Dir Prof Dr HERIBERT SCHATZ.

Salomon Ludwig Steinheim Institut für Deutsch-Jüdische Geschichte eV (StI): internet sti1.uni-duisburg.de; research and adult education on Jewish history in Germany from the Renaissance to the present; Dir Prof. Dr MICHAEL BROCKE.

UNIVERSITÄT ERFURT
(University of Erfurt)

POB 90 02 22, 99105 Erfurt

Nordhäuser Str. 63, 99089 Erfurt

Telephone: (361) 7370

Fax: (361) 7375009

E-mail: praesidiumsbuero@uni-erfurt.de

Internet: www.uni-erfurt.de

Founded 1392, re-founded 1994

Public control

Pres.: Prof. Dr KAI BRODERSEN

Vice-Pres. for Academic Affairs: Prof. Dr ANDREA SCHULTE

Vice-Pres. for Int. Affairs: Prof. Dr MYRIAM WIJLENS

Vice-Pres. for Research and Young Academics: Prof. Dr BETTINA ROCKENBACH

Chancellor: Dr MICHAEL HINZ

Library Dir: CHRISTIANE SCHMIEDEKNECHT

Number of teachers: 108

Number of students: 5,483

DEANS

Faculty of Catholic Theology: Prof. Dr JOSEF FREITAG

Faculty of Education: Prof. Dr MANFRED ECKERT

Faculty of Philosophy: Prof. Dr PATRICK RÖSSLER

Faculty of Political Science: Prof. Dr MANFRED KÖNIGSTEIN

Max Weber College for Cultural and Social Sciences: (vacant)

UNIVERSITÄT FLENSBURG
(University of Flensburg)

Auf dem Campus 1, 24943 Flensburg

Telephone: (461) 80502

Fax: (461) 8052144

E-mail: praesidium@uni-flensburg.de

Internet: www.uni-flensburg.de

Founded 1994

Pres.: Prof. Dr WALTRAUD WENDE

Vice-Pres. for Academic Affairs: Prof. Dr MATTHIAS BAUER

Vice-Pres. for Research and Int. Affairs: Prof. Dr STEPHAN PANTHER

Chancellor: FRANK KUPFER

Head Librarian: Dr ECKHARD EICHLER

Library of 265,000 vols

Number of students: 4,200

UNIVERSITÄT HAMBURG

Edmund-Siemers-Allee 1, 20146 Hamburg

Telephone: (40) 428380

Fax: (40) 428386594

E-mail: praesident@uni-hamburg.de

Internet: www.uni-hamburg.de

Founded 1919

State control

Academic year: October to July

Pres.: Dr Dr DIETER LENZEN

Vice-Pres.: Prof. Dr HOLGER FISCHER

Vice-Pres.: Prof. Dr ROSEMARIE MIELKE

Vice-Pres.: Prof. Dr HANS SIEGFRIED STIEHL

Chancellor: Dr KATRIN VERNAU

State and Univ. Librarian: Prof. Dr GABRIELE BEGER

Library: see Libraries and Archives

Number of teachers: 3,172

Number of students: 40,996

DEANS

Faculty of Education, Psychology and Human Movement: Prof. Dr EVA ARNOLD

Faculty of Humanities: Prof. Dr OLIVER HUCK

Faculty of Law: Prof. Dr TILMAN REPGEN

Faculty of Mathematics, Informatics and Natural Sciences: Prof. Dr HEINRICH GRAENER

Faculty of Medicine: Prof. Dr UWE KOCH-GROMUS

School of Business, Economics and Social Sciences: Prof. Dr GABRIELE LÖSCHPER

PROFESSORS

Department of Biology (Allende-Pl. 2, 20146 Hamburg; tel. (40) 42838-0; fax (40) 42838-7025):

ABRAHAM, R., Entomology

ADAM, G., Phytopathology

BAUCH, J., Timber Biology

BEUSMANN, V., Biotechnics, Society and Environment

BOCK, E., General Microbiology

BÖTTGER, M., General Botany

BRANDT, A., Zoology

BRETTING, H., Zoology

BUCHHOLZ, F.

CHOPRA, V., Anthropology

DREYLING, G., Applied Botany

ECKSTEIN, D., Timber Biology

FLEISCHER, A., Work Science

FORTNAGEL, P., Botany

FRÜHWALD, A., Mechanical Processing of Timber

GANZHORN, J., Zoology

GEWECKE, M., Zoology, Animal Physiology

GIERE, O., Zoology

GRIMM, R., Zoology

HAHN, H., Zoology, Ecology

HARTMANN, H., Systematic Botany

HEINZ, E., Botany

HEUVELDOP, J., International Forest Management

JÜRGENS, N., Biological Systems, Plant Evolution

KAUSCH, H., Hydrobiology

KIES, L., General Botany

KRISTEN, U., General Botany

LIEBEREI, R., Phytopathology

LÖRZ, H., Applied Plant Molecular Biology

MANTAU, U., Economics of Forestry

MERGENHAGEN, D., Cell Biology

MÜHLBACH, H.-P., Molecular Genetics

PARZEFALL, J., Zoology

PATT, R., Chemical Timber Technology

PRATJE, E., General Botany

REISE, K., Heligoland Biological Institute

RENWRANTZ, L., Zoology

RESSEL, J., Wood Physics

RODEWALD, A., Anthropology and Human Genetics
SCHÄFER, W., Biology
SCHURIG, V.
STAHL-BISKUP, E., Pharmaceutical Biology
TEMMING, A., Fisheries Sciences
WEBER, A., General Botany
WIENAND, U., General Botany
WIESE, K., Neurophysiology
WILKENS, H., Zoology
ZEISKE, E., Zoology

Department of Chemistry (Martin-Luther-King-Pl. 6, 20146 Hamburg; tel. (40) 42838-0; fax (40) 42838-2893):

BASLER, W. D.
BEIER, U., Home Economics
BENNDORF, C., Physical Chemistry
BISPING, B., Food Microbiology and Hygiene
BREDEHORST, R., Biochemistry
DEPPERT, W., Molecular Biochemistry
DUCHSTEIN, H.-J., Pharmaceutical Chemistry
FÖRSTER, S., Physical and Macromolecular Chemistry
FRANCKE, W., Organic Chemistry
GEFFKEN, D., Pharmaceutical Chemistry
HECK, J., Inorganic Chemistry
HEISIG, P., Pharmaceutical Biology, Microbiology
KAMINSKY, W., Inorganic Chemistry
KERSCHER, M., Personal Hygiene
KÖNIG, W., Organic Chemistry
KRAMOLOWSKY, R., Inorganic Chemistry
KRICHELDORF, H., Applied Chemistry
KULICKE, W., Technical Chemistry
LECHERT, H., Physical Chemistry
MARGARETHA, P., Organic Chemistry
MEIER, C., Organic Chemistry
MEYER, B., Organic Chemistry
MIELCK, J., Pharmaceutical Technology
MORITZ, H.-U., Technical and Macromolecular Chemistry
MÜHLHAUSER, I., Health
REHDER, D., Inorganic Chemistry
STAHL-BISKUP, E., Pharmaceutical Biology
STEINHART, J., Food Chemistry
THIEM, J., Organic Chemistry
THORN, E., Technical and Macromolecular Chemistry
WELLER, H., Electrochemistry

Department of Computer Science (Vogt-Kölln-Straße 30, 22527 Hamburg; tel. (40) 428830; fax (40) 428382206):

BRUNNSTEIN, K., Computer Applications
DRESCHLER-FISCHER, L., Cognitive Systems
FLOYD, C., Software Technics
FREKSA, C.
HABEL, C., Information and Documentation
JANTZEN, M., Computer Theory
KAISER, K., Computer Applications
KUDLEK, M., Computer Theory
LAMERSDORF, W., Technical Basics of Computer Science
MENZEL, W.
MERTSCHING, B.
MÖLLER, D.
NEUMANN, B., Cognitive Systems
OBERQUELLE, H., Computer Theory
PAGE, B., Computer Applications
ROLF, A., Computer Theory
SCHEFE, P., Computer Applications
STIEHL, H.-S., Cognitive Systems
VALK, R., Computer Theory
VON DER HEIDE, K., Technical Basics of Computer Science
VON HAHN, W., Natural Language Systems
WOLFINGER, B., Computer Organization
ZÜLLIGHOVEN, H.

Department of Cultural History and Cultural Science (Rothenbaumchaussee 67/69, 20148 Hamburg; tel. (40) 428384051; fax (40) 428386530):

ALTENMÜLLER, H., Egyptology
DÖMLING, W., Music
FEHR, B., Classical Archaeology
GREEVE, B., Music
HENGAUTNER, T., Folklore
HIPP, H., History of Art
KEMP, W., Art History
KOKOT, W., Ethnology
KURTH, D., Egyptology
LANG, H., Ethnology
LEHMANN, A., German Archaeology and Folklore
MISCHUNG, B., Ethnology
NIELSEN, I., Classical Archaeology
PETERSEN, P., Musicology
REUDENBACH, B., Art History
ROLLE, R., Prehistory of Europe
RÖSING, H., Systematic Music
SCHNEIDER, A., Systematic Music
SMAILUS, O., Ancient American Languages and Culture
WAGNER, M., Art History
WARNKE, M., History of Art

Department of Earth Sciences (Bundestraße 55, 20146 Hamburg; tel. (40) 428385230; fax (40) 428385270):

BACKHAUS, J., Oceanography
BANDEL, K., Palaeontology and Historical Geology
BETZLER, C., Geology
BISMAYER, U., Mineralogy, Crystallography
BRÜMMER, B., Meteorology
DAHM, T.
FRAEDRICH, K., Meteorology
GAJEWSKI, D., Geophysics
GRASSL, H., Meteorology
GRIMMEL, E., Geography
GUSE, W., Mineralogy
HILLMER, G., Geology and Palaeontology
JASCHKE, D., Geography
LAFRENZ, J., Geography
LEUPOLT, B., Geography
MAKRIS, J., Geophysics
MEINCKE, J., Regional Oceanography
MICHAELIS, W., Organic Geochemistry
MIEHLICH, G., Soil Science
NAGEL, F. N., Geography
OSSENBRÜGGE, J., Geography
POHL, D., Mineralogy
RASCHKE, E., Meteorology
REUTHER, C.-D., Geology
ROSSMANITH, E., Mineralogy
SCHATZMANN, M., Meteorology
SCHLEICHER, H., Mineralogy, Petrography
SCHWARZ, R., Geography
SPAETH, CH., Geology and Palaeontology
SPIELMANN, H.-O., Geography
SÜNDERMANN, J., Oceanography
TARKIAN, M., Mineralogy
THANNHEISER, D., Geography
TIETZ, G. F., Sedimentary Petrography
TOL, R. S., Sustaining the Environment
VINX, R., Mineralogy
WONG, H. K., Geology
ZAHEL, W., Oceanography

Department of Economic Sciences (Von-Melle-Park 5, 20146 Hamburg; tel. (40) 428380; fax (40) 428386322):

ADAMS, M., Economic Law
ALTROGGE, G., Business Administration
ARNOLD, B., National Economy
CZERANOWSKY, G., Business Administration
ENGELHARDT, G., National Economy
FREIDANK, C.-C., Business Administration, Auditing Taxation
FUNKE, M., National Economy
GROTHERR, S., Business Administration
HANSEN, K., Business Administration
HANSMANN, K.-W., Business Administration
HASENKAMP, G., National Economy
HAUTAU, H., National Economy
HESBERG, D.
HOFMANN, H., National Economy

HOLLER, M., National Economy
HUMMELTENBERG, W., Business Administration
KRAUSE-JUNG, G., International Finance
KÜPPER, W., Business Administration
LAYER, M., Business Administration
LORENZEN, G., National Economy
LUCKE, B., National Economy
MAENNIG, W., National Economy
NELL, M., Insurance
PFÄHLER, W., National Economy
PRESSMAR, D., Business Administration
REITSPERGER, W. D., Business Administration
RIETER, H., National Economy
RINGLE, G., Business Administration
SATTLER, H., Business Administration
SCHÄFER, H.-B., National Economy
SCHEER, C., Finance
SCHLITTGEN, R., National Economy, Statistics
SCHMIDT, H., Business Administration
SEELBACH, H., Business Administration
STAHLECKER, H.-P., National Economy, Statistics
STOBER, R., Economic Law
STRAUBHAAR, T.
STREITFERDT, L., Business Administration
TIMMERMANN, V., National Economy
TOL, R. (Endowed Chair, Sustaining the Environment)
VON OEHSEN, J. H., Finance
WEGSCHEIDER, K., National Economy, Statistics

Department of Education (Von-Melle-Park 8, 20146 Hamburg; tel. (40) 428380; fax (40) 428382112):

AUFENANGER, S.
BASTIAN, J.
BECK, I.
BOLLMANN, H.
BOS, W.
BRAND, W.
BRUSCH, W.
BÜRGER, W.
BUTH, M.
CLAUßEN, B.
COMBE, A.
DECKE-CORNILL, H.
DEGENHART, S.
DEHN, M.
DUISMANN, G.
EHNI, H. W.
FAULSTICH, P.
FAULSTICH-WIELAND, H.
FIEDLER, U.
FILIPP, K.
GEBHARD, U.
GOGOLIN, I.
GRAMMES, T.
GRENZ, D.
GUDJONS, H.
GÜNTHER, K.-R.
HARTER-MEYER, R.
HARTMANN, W.
HEMMER, K.
HOFSÄSS, T.
JUNG, H. W.
KAISER, G.
KAISER, H.-J.
KIPP, M.
KLEIN, P.
KOKEMOHR, R.
KOLLER, H.-C.
KRAUTHAUSEN, G.
KRETSCHMER, J.
KÜNNE, W.
LECKE, B.
LEGLER, W.
LOHMANN, I.
MARTENS, E.
MAYER, C.
MEYER, H.
MEYER, M.
MIELKE, R.

MITCHELL, G.
NEUMANN, U.
NEVERS, P.
NOLTE, M.
OPASCHOWSKI, H.
PAZZINI, K.-J.
PETERSEN, J.
RAUER, W.
RENZELBERG, G.
RICHTER, H.
ROTHWEILER, M.
SCARBATH, H.
SCHÄFER, H.-P.
SCHENK, B.
SCHERLER, K.
SCHREIER, H.
SCHUCK, K. D.
SEYD, W.
SPRETH, G.
STRUCK, P.
STRUVE, K.
STÜTZ, G.
TENFELDE, W.
TRAMM, T.
VOLLMER, T.
VON BORRIES, B.
WAGNER, A.
WALLRABENSTEIN, W.
WEICHERT, W.
WEISSE, W.
WELLING, A.
WILLENBERG, H.
WIMMER, K.-M.
WOCKEN, H.
WUDTKE, H.
ZIMPEL, A.

Department of History and Philosophy
(Rothenbaumchaussee 67/69, 20148 Hamburg; tel. (40) 428384049; fax (40)
428386333):

ANGERMANN, N., Medieval and Modern
    History
BARTUSCHAT, W., Philosophy
CLEMENS, G., Modern European History
    (Western European Integration)
DEININGER, J., Ancient History
DIEDERICH, W., Philosophy
DINGEL, J., Classical Philology
EIDENEIER, H., Byzantine and Modern
    Greek Philology
FINZSCH, N., Modern and North American
    History
FREDE, D., Philosophy
GÄHDE, U., Philosophy
GALL, D., Classical Philology
GOETZ, H.-W., Medieval and Modern His-
    tory
GOLCZEWSKI, F., Eastern European History
HALFMANN, H., Ancient History
HARLFINGER, D., Classical Philology
HERGEMÖLLER, B.-U., Medieval History
HERZIG, A., Modern History
KÜNNE, W., Philosophy
MEJCHER, H., Modern History
MOLTHAGEN, J., Ancient History
PIETSCHMANN, H., Modern History
RECKI, B., Philosophy
SARNOWSKY, V., Medieval History
STEINVORTH, U., Philosophy
VOGEL, B., Modern History

Department of Language, Literature and
Media Studies (Rothenbaumchaussee 67/69,
20148 Hamburg; tel. (40) 428380; fax (40)
428385977):

BERG, T., English Linguistics
BLESSIN, S., German Literature, German
    as a Foreign Language
BÖRNER, W., Linguistics
BRAUNMÜLLER, K., Germanic Philology
BRINKER, K., German Linguistics
BUNGARTEN, T., German Linguistics
CORTHALS, J., Comparative Language
    Studies
DAMMANN, G., German Literature

DIEWALD, G., German Linguistics
EDMONDSON, W., Language Instruction
    Research
FISCHER, L., German Literature
FISCHER, R., German Sign Language
FREYTAG, H., German Philology
FREYTAG, W., German Literature
FRIEDL, B., American Studies
GREINER, N., English Literature
GUTJAHR, O., Modern German Literature
GUTKNECHT, C., English Language
HABEL, C., Language Processing
HARTENSTEIN, K., Russian
HASEBRINK, E., Empirical Communications
    Science
HELIMEKI, E., Finno-Ugric Philology
HENKEL, N., German Philology
HENNIG, J., German Linguistics
HICKETHIER, K., German Literature
HILL, P., Slavonic Philology
HODEL, R., Slavonic Philology
HOTTENROTH, P.-M., French and Italian
    Linguistics
HOUSE, J., Language Instruction Research
HÜHN, P., English Philology
IBANEZ, R., Hispanic Linguistics
KÖSTER, U., German Literature
LATOUR, B., German as a Foreign Lan-
    guage
LEHMANN, V., Language Instruction
    Research
LLEO, C., Hispanic Linguistics
MEIER, J., German Linguistics
MEISEL, J. M., Romance Philology
MEYER, W., Romance Philology
MEYER-ALTHOFF, M.
MEYER-MINNEMANN, K., Romance Philology
MÜLLER, H.-H., German Literature
NEUMANN, A., Romance Philology
PANTHER, K.-U., English Linguistics
PÉTURSSON, M., General Applied Phonetics
PRESCH, G., German Linguistics
PRILLWITZ, S., German Linguistics
REHBEIN, J., German Linguistics, German
    as a Foreign Language
REICHARDT, D., Romance Philology
REINITZER, H., German Literature
RODENBURG, H.-P., American Studies
SAGER, S., German Linguistics
SCHLUMBOHM, D., Romance Philology
SCHMID, W., Slavonic Literature
SCHMIDT, J., English Philology
SCHMIDT-KNÄBEL, S., German Linguistics
SCHÖBERL, J., German Literature
SCHÖNERT, J., German Literature
SCHÖPP, J. K., American Studies
SCHULLER, M., German Literature
SCHULMEISTER, R., Higher School Didactics
SCHULTZE, B., English Philology
SEGEBERG, H., German Literature
SETTEKORN, W., French
TERNES, E., Phonetics
TRAPP, F., Modern German Literature
VINKEN, B., Romance Philology
VOIGT, B., Spanish
VON HAHN, W., Natural Language Systems
WERGIN, U., Modern German Literature
WINTER, H.-G., German Literature
WITTSCHIER, H. W., Romance Philology

Department of Law (Rothenbaumchaussee
41, 20148 Hamburg; tel. (40) 428380; fax (40)
428386352):

BEHRENS, P., Civil, Commercial and Inter-
    national Private Law
BORK, R., Civil, Commercial, Economic and
    International Private Law
BRUHA, T., Public, European and Inter-
    national Law
BULL, H. P., Constitutional and Adminis-
    trative Law
FELIX, D., Public and Social Law
FEZER, G., Criminal Law
FROTSCHER, G., International Financial
    and Taxation Law
GIEHRING, H., Criminal Law

HAAG, F., Sociology
HANSEN, U., Criminal Law
HILF, M., Public, European and Inter-
    national Law
HIRTE, H., Public, Commercial and Busi-
    ness Law
HOFFMAN-RIEM, W., Public, Administra-
    tive, Revenue and Tax, and Economic
    Law
JACHMANN, M., Public, Financial and Tax-
    ation Law
JOOST, D., Civil and Labour Law
KARPEN, U., Public Law
KELLER, R., Criminal Law
KOCH, H.-J., Public Law, Philosophy of
    Law
KÖHLER, M., Criminal Law, Philosophy of
    Law
KRIECHBAUM, M., Roman Law
LADEUR, K.-H., Public Law
LAGONI, R., Public, Maritime, International
    and Constitutional Law
LUCHTERHANDT, O., Public and Eastern
    Law
LÜDICKE, J., International Financial and
    Taxation Law
MAGNUS, U., Civil Law
MANKOWSKI, P., Civil, Comparative and
    International Private and Procedural
    Law
MARTENS, K. P., Civil, Labour and Com-
    mercial Law
MERKEL, R., Criminal Law, Philosophy of
    Law
MORITZ, K., Civil and Labour Law, Soci-
    ology of Law
OETER, S., Public, International and Euro-
    pean Law
OTT, C., Sociology of Law, Civil, Commer-
    cial and Company, and Economic Law
PASCHKE, M., Civil, Commercial and Eco-
    nomic Law
PFARR, H., Civil and Labour Law
RAMSAUER, U., Public Law
RANDZIO, R., Civil Law
RITTSTIEG, H., Public Law
SCHÄFER, H.-B., National Economy
SCHEERER, S., Criminology
SCHWABE, J., Public Law
SESSAR, K., Criminology and Juvenile
    Criminal Law
SONNEN, B.-R., Criminal Law
STOBER, R., Economic Law
STRUCK, G., Civil Law
VILLMOW, B., Criminology
WALZ, R., Commercial, Economic, Civil and
    Tax Law
WERBER, M., Civil and Insurance Law

Department of Mathematics (Bundesstr. 55,
20146 Hamburg; tel. (40) 428384106; fax (40)
428384927):

ANDREAE, T.
BANDELT, H.-J.
BÄR, C.
BERNDT, R.
BRÜCKNER, H.
DADUNA, H.
DIESTEL, R.
ECKHARDT, U.
GEIGER, C.
HASS, R.
HOFMANN, W. D.
HÜBNER, G.
HÜNEMÖRDER, C.
KRÄMER, H.
KREMER, E.
KREUZER, A.
LAUTERBACH
MICHALICEK, J.
MÜLLER, H.
NEUHAUS, G.
OBERLE, H. J.
ORTLIEB, C.
REICH, K.
RIEMENSCHNEIDER, O.

SCHRÖDER, E.
SEIER, W.
STRADE, H.
STRUCKMEIER, J.
TAUBERT, K.
WERNER, B.
WOLFSCHMIDT, G.

Department of Medicine (Universitätsklinikum Hamburg-Eppendorf, Martinistr. 52, 20246 Hamburg; tel. (40) 428030; fax (40) 428036752):

ADAM, G., X-Ray Diagnosis
AGARWAL, D., Human Genetics
ALBERTI, W., Radiotherapy
BAISCH, H., Biophysics
BAUR, X., Industrial Medicine
BECK, H., Anaesthesiology
BEIL, F. U., Internal Medicine
BEISIEGEL, U., Biochemistry
BENTELE, K., Paediatrics
BERGER, J., Mathematics and Computer Applications of Medicine
BERGER, M., Child Psychology
BERNER, W., Psychiatry
BÖGER, R., Clinical Pharmacology
BOHUSLAVIZKI, H., Nuclear Medicine
BRAENDLE, L.-W., Gynaecology and Obstetrics
BRAULKE, T., Pathophysiology and Molecular Biological Genetic Health
BRAUMANN, K.-M., Internal-Physiological Sports Medicine
BROMM, B., Physiology
BULLINGER, M., Medical Psychology
BURDELSKI, M., Paediatrics
CLAUSEN, M., Nuclear Medicine
DALLEK, M., Surgery, Accident Surgery
DAVIDOFF, M., Anatomy
DELLING, G., General Pathology and Pathological Anatomy
DENEKE, F.-W., Psychosomatic Medicine
DÖRING, V., Surgery
DRIESCH, P., Dermatology and Venereology
EHMKE, H., Physiology
EIERMANN, T., Transfusion Medicine
ENGELMANN, K., Ophthalmology
FEUCHT, H.-H., Medical Microbiology and Immunology
FIEDLER, W., Internal Medicine
FLEISCHER, B., Immunology, Virology
GAL, A., Medical Genetics
GÖTZE, P., Psychiatry
GRETEN, H., Internal Medicine
HALATA, Z., Anatomy
HAND, I., Psychiatry
HEGEWISCHE-BECKER, S., Internal Medicine
HELLWEGE, H., Paediatrics
HELMCHEN, U., Pathology
HESS, M., Otorhinolaryngology
HÖHNE, K.-H., Information and Data Processing in Medicine
HÖLTJE, W.-J., Maxillary Surgery
HORSTMANN, R., Internal Medicine
HOSSFELD, D., Internal Medicine
HÜBENER, K.-H., Radiology
HULAND, H., Urology
HUNEKE, A., Gynaecology and Obstetrics
IZBICKI, J., Surgery
JÄNICKE, F. K.-H., Gynaecology and Obstetrics
JANKE-SCHAUB, G., Paediatrics
JENTSCH, T., Cell Biology
JÜDE, H. D., Dental Medicine
JUNG, H., Biophysics and Radiobiology
KAHL-NIEKE, B., Orthodontics
KAULFERS, P.-M., Medical Microbiology
KAUPEN-HAAS, H., Medical Sociology
KOCH, U., Otorhinolaryngology
KOCH-GROMUS, U., Medical Psychology
KOHLSCHÜTTER, A., Paediatrics
KOLLEK, R., Biotechnology
KORTH, M., Pharmacology
KRAUSZ, M., Psychiatry
KREYMANN, K. G., Internal Medicine
KRUPPA, J., Physiological Chemistry

KRUSE, H.-P., Internal Medicine
KÜHNL, P., Transfusions, Immuno-Haematology
LAMBRECHT, W., Surgery
LAUFS, R., Medical Microbiology and Immunology
LEICHTWEISS, H.-P., Physiology
LEUWER, R., Otorhinolaryngology
LOCKEMANN, U., Legal Medicine
LÖNING, T., General Pathology, Pathological Anatomy
MACK, D., Medical Microbiology, Infection Epidemiology and Hospital Hygiene
MANGOLD, U., Anatomy
MARQUARDT, H., General Toxicology
MAYR, G. W., Physiological Chemistry
MEINERTZ, T., Cardiology
MESTER, J., Nuclear Medicine
MOLL, I., Dermatology, Venereology
MÜHLHAUSER, I., Health
MÜLLER, D., Neurosurgery
MÜLLER-WIEFEL, D. E., Internal Medicine
MUNZEL, T., Internal Medicine
NABER, D., Psychiatry
NEUBER, K., Dermatology and Venereology
NEUMAIER, M., Clinical Chemistry
NOLDUS, J., Neurology
PANTEL, K., Molecular Genetics in Gynaecological Ontomology
PAUS, R., Dermatology and Venereology
PFEIFFER, E., Hygiene
PFEIFFER, G., Neurology
PFORTE, A., Internal Medicine
PLATZER, U., Dentistry
PONGS, O., Neurology
PÜSCHEL, U., Forensic Medicine
RICHARD, G., Ophthalmology
RICHTER, D., Physiological Chemistry
RICHTER, R., Medical Psychology, Psychosomatics
RIEDESSER, P., Paediatric Psychology
ROGIERS, X., Surgery
ROTHER, U., Radiological Diagnostics in Dental Medicine
RUDAT, T., Radiotherapy
RUEGER, J. M., Accident Surgery
RUMBERGER, E., Physiology
RUTHER, K., Ophthalmology
RUTHER, W., Orthopaedics
SCHACHNER CAMARTIN, M., Neurobiology
SCHÄFER, H., General Pathology and Pathological Anatomy
SCHALLER, C., Neurobiology
SCHIFFNER, U., Dental Medicine
SCHMALE, H., Biochemistry
SCHMELZLE, R., Dental Medicine
SCHMIDT, G., Sexology
SCHMOLDT, A., Forensic Medicine
SCHNEPPENHEIM, R., Paediatric Haematology and Oncology
SCHOLZ, J., Pharmacology and Toxicology
SCHRÖDER, H. J., Physiology
SCHULTE AM ESCH, J., Anaesthesiology
SCHULTE-MARKWORT, M., Child and Youth Psychiatry
SCHULZE, C., Anatomy
SCHULZE, W., Anatomy
SCHUMACHER, U., Anatomy
SCHWARZ, J., Physiology
SCHWORM, H. D., Ophthalmology
SEITZ, H.-J., Physiological Chemistry
SOEHENDRA, N., Surgery
STAHL, R., Internal Medicine
STANDL, T., Anaesthesiology
STAVROU, D., Neuropathology
STEINER, P., Radiology
STRÄTLING, W., Physiological Chemistry
TANNICH, E., Molecular Parasitology
THAISS, F., Internal Medicine
TROJAN, A., Social Medicine
ULLRICH, K. H. O., Paediatrics
UβMULLER, J., Otorhinolaryngology
VAN DEN BUSSCHE, H., Didactics
VONDERLAGE, M., Physiology
WAGENER, C., Clinical Chemistry
WEIL, J., Paediatric Cardiology

WEILLER, C., Neurology
WESTENDORF, J., Toxicology, Pharmacology
WIEDEMANN, K. B., Biological Psychiatry
WIELAND, T., Pharmacology
WILL, H. K., Microbiology
WILLIG, R. P., Paediatrics
WINDLER, E., Internal Medicine
WINTERPACHT, A., Human Genetics
ZANDER, A., Bone Marrow Transplantation
ZEUMER, H., Neuroradiology
ZYWIETE, F., Biophysics, Radiobiology

Department of Oriental Studies and Asia–Africa Institute (Rothenbaumchaussee 67/69, 20148 Hamburg; tel. (40) 428384054; fax (40) 428386530; e-mail aai@uni-hamburg.de):

CARLE, R., Indonesian and South Seas Languages
CONRAD, L., Islamic Sciences
EBERSTEIN, B., Sinology
EMMERICK, R., Iranian Studies
FRIEDRICH, M., Sinology
GERHARDT, L., African Languages and Cultures
JACKSON, D., Tibetology
KAPPERT, P., Turkish Studies
ORANSKAIA, T., Indic Studies
POHL, M., Japanese Politics
REH, M., African Languages and Cultures
ROTTER, G., Islamic Studies
SASSE, W., Chinese
SCHMITHAUSEN, L., Indology
SCHNEIDER, R., Japanese
STUMPFELDT, H., Sinology
TERWIEL, B., Thai Language and Culture
UHLIG, S., African Languages and Cultures
WEZLER, A., Indology

Department of Physical Education (Mollerstr. 10, 20148 Hamburg; tel. (40) 428382474; fax (40) 428385666):

BRAUMANN, K.-M.
EICHLER, G.
FUNKE-WIENEKE, J.
LANGE-AMELSBERG, J.
NIEDLICH, H.-D.
STRIPP, K.
TIEDEMANN, C.
TIWALD, H.
WEINBERG, P.

Department of Physics (Dammtorstr. 12, 2 stock, 20354 Hamburg; tel. (40) 428384056; fax (40) 428386233):

BARTELS, J., Theoretical Physics
BLOBEL, V., Experimental Physics
BÜSSER, F.-W., Experimental Physics
FAY, D., Theoretical Physics
FREDENHAGEN, K., Theoretical Physics
GERAMB, H. V. VON, Theoretical Physics
HANSEN, W., Experimental Physics
HEINZELMANN, G., Experimental Physics
HEITMANN, D., Applied Physics
HEMMERICH, A., Experimental Physics
HEUER, R.-D., Elementary Particle Physics
HEYSZENAU, H., Theoretical Physics
HUBER, G., Experimental Physics
JOHNSON, R., Experimental Physics
KLANNER, R., Experimental Physics
KÖTZLER, J., Applied Physics
KRAMER, B., Theoretical Physics
MACK, G., Theoretical Physics
MERKT, U., Experimental Physics
NAROSKA, B., Experimental Physics
NEUHAUSER, W., Experimental Physics
OEPEN, H. P., Experimental Physics
PFANNKUCHE, D., Theoretical Physics
REIMERS, D., Astronomy
SCHARNBERG, K., Theoretical Physics
SCHMIDT-PARZEFALL, W., Experimental Physics
SCHMITT, J., Astronomy
SCHMÜSER, P., Experimental Physics
SCOBEL, W., Experimental Physics
SENGSTOCK, K., Experimantal Physics
SONNTAG, B., Experimental Physics
SPITZER, H., Fundamental Physics

WAGNER, A., Elementary Particle Physics
WENDKER, H., Astronomy
WICK, K., Experimental Physics
WIESENDANGER, R., Experimental Physics
WURTH, W., Experimental Physics
ZIMMERER, G., Experimental Physics

Department of Protestant Theology (Sedanstr. 19, 20146 Hamburg; tel. (40) 428380; fax (40) 428384013):

AHRENS, T., Missions
DIERKEN, J., Systematic Theology
GRÜNBERG, W., Practical Theology
GUTMANN, H.-M., Practical Theology
KOCH, T., Systematic Theology
LINDNER, W. V., Practical Theology
LOHR, W., Church and Dogmatic History
MAGER, I., Church History and Dogma
MOXTER, M., Systematic Theology
SCHRAMM, T., New Testament
SCHRÖTER, J., New Testament
SCHUMANN, O., Religious and Missionary Science
SELLIN, G., New Testament
STEIGER, J. A., Church and Dogmatic History
TIMM, S., Old Testament
WILLI-PLEIN, I., Old Testament

Department of Psychology (Von-Melle-Park 5, 20146 Hamburg; tel. (40) 428385460; fax (40) 428385492):

BAMBERG, E.
BERBALK, H.
BURISCH, M.
BUSE, L.
DAHME, B.
ECKERT, J.
HEINZE, B.
LANGER, I.
OETTINGEN, G
ORTH, B.
PAWLIK, K.
PROBST, P.
RHENIUS, D.
SCHMIDTCHEN, S.
SCHULZ VON THUN, F.
SCHWAB, R.
TONNIES, S.
VAGT, G.
WITT, H.
WITTE, E.

Department of Social Sciences (Allende-Pl. 1, 20146 Hamburg; tel. (40) 42838-0; fax (40) 42838-4506):

EICHNER, K., Sociology
GOERTZ, H.-J., Social and Economic History
GREVEN, M., Political Science
HEINEMANN, K., Sociology
JAKOBEIT, C., Political Science
KAUPEN-HAAS, H.
KLEINSTEUBER, H. J., Political Science
LANDFRIED, C., Political Science
LÜDE, R. VON, Sociology
MILLER, M., Sociology
NEVERLA, I., Journalism, Communications
PIEPER, M., Sociology
RASCHKE, P., Political Science
RENN, H., Sociology
RUNDE, P., Sociology
SCHEERER, S., Criminology
SEßAR, K., Criminology
TETZLAFF, R., Political Science
TROITZSCH, U., Social Sciences
VILLMOW, B., Criminology
WEISCHENBERG, S., Communications Science, Journalism

UNIVERSITÄT HILDESHEIM

Marienburger Pl. 22, 31141 Hildesheim
Telephone: (5121) 8830
Fax: (5121) 883177
E-mail: studyinfo@uni-hildesheim.de
Internet: www.uni-hildesheim.de

Founded 1978
State control
Academic year: October to September
Pres.: Prof. Dr WOLFGANG-UWE FRIEDRICH
Vice-Pres: Dr CHRISTOPH STRUTZ
Vice-Pres. for Academic Affairs: Prof. Dr TONI THOLEN
Vice-Pres. for Continuing Education: Dr MARGITTA RUDOLPH
Vice-Pres. for Research: Prof. Dr STEPHAN POROMBKA
Library Dir: Dr EWALD BRAHMS
Library of 500,000 vols
Number of teachers: 85
Number of students: 5,325
Publication: *Uni Hildesheim. Das Magazin* (2 a year)

DEANS

Faculty I (Education and Sociology): Prof. Dr MARTIN SCHREINER
Faculty II (Cultural Education): Prof. Dr TILMAN BORSCHE
Faculty III (Information and Communication): Prof. Dr FRIEDRICH LENZ
Faculty IV (Mathematics, Natural Sciences, Economics and Computer Science): Prof. Dr KLAUS AMBROSI

PROFESSORS

Faculty I (Education and Sociology) (tel. (5121) 883401; fax (5121) 883402):

BORSCHE, T., Philosophy
BRÄNDLE, W., Protestant Theology
CLOER, E., General Pedagogy
EBERLE, H.-J., Social Pedagogy
FRIEDRICH, W., Political Science
HELFRICH-HÖLTER, W., Psychology
HOPF, CH., Sociology
JAUMANN-GRAUMANN, O., Education
KECK, R., Education
KÖHNLEIN, W., General Science
KUNERT, H., General Education Studies
MEIER-HILBERT, G., Geography
MÜLLER, B., Social Pedagogy
NICKEL, U., Sport
OVERESCH, M., History
SCHREINER, M., Protestant Theology
SIEBERG, H., Sociology
STRANG, H., Social Education Studies
WALLRAVEN, K., Sociology
WERNER, H., Catholic Theology
WOLFF, ST., Social Education Studies

Faculty II (Cultural Education) (tel. (5121) 883601; fax (5121) 883602):

BERG, J., Media Education
FRÜHSORGE, G., Fine Arts
GIFFHORN, H., Media Education
GORNIK, H., German Literature and Linguistics
GROMES, H., Theatre
GÜNZEL, R., Fine Arts and Visual Communication
HÜGEL, H.-O., Popular Culture
KURZENBERGER, H.-J., Theatre
LÖFFLER, W., Music and Aural Communication
MENZEL, W., German Language and Linguistics
NOLTE, J., Fine Arts and Visual Communication
SCHNEIDER, W., Cultural Politics
TESKE, U., Fine Arts
VIETTA, J., Literature
WEBER, R., Music and Aural Communication

Faculty III (Information and Communication) (tel. (5121) 883801; fax (5121) 883802):

AMBROSI, K., Computer Science
ARNTZ, R., Romance Languages and Linguistics
BENEKE, J., English, Linguistics and Intercultural Communication
BENTZ, H.-J., Mathematics

DIRKS, U., English Studies
FLECHSIG, E., Chemistry
FRANZBECKER, W., Technical Studies
HAUENSCHILD, CH., Computational Linguistics
KAHLE, D., Mathematics
KIERDORF, H., Biology
KOLB, G., General Economics
KREUTZKAMP, TH., Mathematics
SABBAN, A., Romance Languages and Linguistics
SCHWARZER, E., Physics
STURM, H., Biology
WEGNER, N., Technology
WOMSER-HACKER, CH., Information Science

UNIVERSITÄT HOHENHEIM

70593 Stuttgart
Telephone: (711) 4590
Fax: (711) 45923960
E-mail: post@uni-hohenheim.de
Internet: www.uni-hohenheim.de

Founded 1818
Academic year: October to September
Rector: Prof. Dr HANS-PETER LIEBIG
Pro-Rector: Prof. Dr HANS-PETER BURGHOF
Pro-Rector: Prof. Dr KARLHEINZ KÖLLER
Pro-Rector: Prof. Dr MARTIN BLUM
Registrar: ALFRED FUNK
Univ. Librarian: K.-W. HORSTMANN
Number of teachers: 780
Number of students: 8,000

DEANS

Faculty of Agricultural Sciences: Prof. Dr JOACHIM SAUERBORN
Faculty of Business, Economics and Social Sciences: Prof. Dr DIRK HACHMEISTER
Faculty of Natural Sciences: Prof. Dr HEINZ BREER

PROFESSORS

Faculty of Agricultural Sciences:

AMSELGRUBER, W., Anatomy and Physiology of Domestic Animals
BECKER, K., Animal Nutrition in Tropical and Subtropical Areas
BECKER, T., Rural Markets and Rural Marketing
BESSEI, W., Animal Breeding
BLAICH, R., Viticulture
BÖCKER, R., Landscape Ecology
BÖHM, R., Veterinary Hygiene
BUCHENAUER, H., Plant Protection
CLAUPEIN, W., Plant Production
CLAUS, R., Stockbreeding
DABBERT, S., Production Theory in Agriculture
DOLUSCHITZ, R., Farm Management
DOPPLER, W., Farm Management in Tropical and Subtropical Areas
DROCHNER, W., Animal Nutrition
FANGMEIER, A., Plant Ecology and Ecotoxicology
GEIGER, H. H., Genetics
GELDERMANN, H., Stockbreeding
GROSSKOPF, W., Agricultural Politics
HAUSSMANN, A., Stockbreeding
HEIDHUES, F., Agricultural Economics in Tropical and Subtropical Areas
HOFFMANN, V., Agricultural Communication
HURLE, K., Plant Protection
JUNGBLUTH, T., Agricultural Technology
KANDELER, E., Soil Biology
KLEISINGER, S., Agricultural Technology
KÖLLER, K., Agricultural Technology in Developing Countries
KORFF, H.-R., Socioeconomics in the Tropics and Subtropics
KROMKA, F., Agricultural Sociology
KRUSE, M., Seed Technology
KUTZBACH, H.-D., Agricultural Technology

LIEBIG, H.-P., Vegetable Cropping
MELCHINGER, A., Genetics and Plant Breeding
MOSENTHIN, R., Animal Nutrition
MÜHLBAUER, W., Agricultural Technology in Tropical and Subtropical Areas
OPPEN, M. VON, Agricultural Economics in Developing Countries
PIEPHO, H.-P., Bioinformatics
RÖMHELD, V., Plant Nutrition
SAUERBORN, J., Ecology of Tropical and Subtropical Areas
SCHULTZE-KRAFT, R., Biodiversity and Land Rehabilitation in Tropical and Subtropical Areas
STAHR, K., Soil Sciences
STÖSSER, R., Applied Botany
STRECK, T., Biogeophysics
VALLE ZÁRATE, A., Stockbreeding in Tropical and Subtropical Areas
WEBER, G., Special Plant Breeding
VON WIRÉN, N., Plant Nutrition
ZEBITZ, C., Plant Protection
ZEDDIES, J., Agricultural Economics

Faculty of Economics and Social Sciences:

AHLHEIM, M., Environmental Economics
BACKES-HAASE, A., Vocational Training
BAREIS, P., Taxation and Management
BELKE, A., International Economics
BUSS, E., Sociology
CAESAR, R., Financing
DITTMAN, A., Law
ESCHER-WEINGART, C., Law
GERYBADZE, A., International Management
HABENICHT, W., Industrial Economics
HACHMEISTER, B., Accounting and Finance
HAGEMANN, H., Economic Theory
HERDZINA, K., Economics
JUNGKUNZ, D., Vocational Teaching
KIRN, C., Informatics
KUHNLE, H., Business Administration
MACHARZINA, K., Management and Organizational Research
MAST, C., Journalism
MELL, U., Theology and Didactics
MÜHLENKAMP, H., Economics of Social Sciences
MÜLLER, C., Entrepreneurship
PFETSCH, B., Communication Policy
SCHENK, M., Communication and Social Research
SCHRAMM, M, Theology and Didactics
SCHULER, H., Psychology
SCHULZ, W., Environmental Management
SCHWALBE, U., Industrial Economics
SEEL, B., Household Management
SPAHN, P., Economics
STREB, D., Social and Economic History
TROSSMANN, E., Controlling
VOETH, M., Marketing
WAGENHALS, G., Statistics and Econometry

Faculty of Natural Sciences:

BECKER-BENDER, G., Physics
BEIFUSS, U., Bio-Organic Chemistry
BIESALSKI, H. K., Biochemistry and Nutrition
BLUM, M., Zoology
BODE, C., Nutrition
BOSCH, K., Mathematics
BREER, H., Zoophysiology
CARLE, R., Food Technology
DEHNHARDT, W., Informatics
DUFNER, J., Mathematics
EHRENSTEIN, W., Applied Physiology
FISCHER, A., Food Technology
FISCHER, L., Biotechnology
GRAEVE, L., Biochemistry and Nutrition
HAMMES, W., Food Technology
HANKE, W., Zoophysiology
HINRICHS, J., Food Technology
ISENGARD, H.-D., Food Analysis
JETTER, K., Applied Mathematics
KOTTKE, V., Food Process Technology
KUHN, A., Microbiology
KUHN, E., Plant Physiology

KÜPPERS, M., Botany
MACKENSTEDT, U., Zoology
MENZEL, P., Chemistry and Ecology
PFITZNER, A., Virology
PREISS, A., Genetics
RASSOW, J., Microbiology
RÖSNER, H., Zoology
SCHALLER, J., Animal Ecology
SCHWACK, W., Food Chemistry
SPRING, O., Botany
STRASDEIT, H., Bio-Inorganic Chemistry
VETTER, A., Food Technology
WULFMEYER, V., Physics and Meteorology

UNIVERSITÄT KASSEL

Präsidialverwaltung, Mönchebergstr. 19, 34109 Kassel

Telephone: (561) 8040
Fax: (561) 8042330
E-mail: presse@uni-kassel.de
Internet: www.uni-kassel.de

Founded 1971
State control
Language of instruction: German
Academic year: October to July

Pres.: Prof. Dr ROLF-DIETER POSTLEP
Vice-Pres: Prof. Dr ANDREAS HÄNLEIN
Vice-Pres: Prof. Dr CLAUDIA BRINKER-VON DER HEYDE
Vice-Pres: Prof. Dr MARTIN LAWERENZ
Chancellor: Dr ROBERT KUHN
Librarian: Dr AXEL HALLE

Library: see Libraries and Archives
Number of teachers: 1,212
Number of students: 20,643

DEANS

Architecture, Urban Planning, Landscape Planning: Prof. Dr Ing. STEFAN KÖRNER
Business and Economics: Prof. Dr GEORG VON WANGENHEIM
Civil and Environmental Engineering: Prof. Dr Ing. VOLKHARD FRANZ
Educational Science, Humanities and Music: Prof. Dr PAUL-GERHARD KLUMBIES
Electrical Engineering, Computer Science: Prof. Dr Ing. JOSEF BÖRCSÖK
Languages and Literature: Prof. Dr ANDREAS GARDT
Mathematics and Natural Science: Prof. Dr FRIEDRICH W. HERBERG
Mechanical Engineering: Prof. Dr Ing. OLAF WÜNSCH
Social Work, Psychology: Prof. Dr STEPHAN RIXEN
Social Sciences: Prof. Dr BERND OVERWIEN

ATTACHED RESEARCH INSTITUTES

Centre for Environmental Systems Research (CESR): internet www.usf.uni-kassel.de/cesr; Dir Prof. Dr ANDREAS ERNST.

Centre for Nanostructure Science and Technology (CINSaT): Dir Prof. Dr KLAUS MASSELI.

Competence Centre for Climate Change Mitigation and Adaptation (CLIMA): Dir Dr MICHAELA SCHALLER.

International Centre for Development and Decent Work (ICDD): Exec. Dir Prof. Dr CHRISTOPH SCHERRER.

International Centre for Higher Education Research (INCHER-Kassel): Moenchebergstr. 17, 34109 Kassel; tel. (561) 804-2415; fax (561) 804-7415; e-mail mahe@uni-kassel.de; internet www.incher.uni-kassel.de; Dir Prof. Dr BARBARA KEHM.

UNIVERSITÄT KOBLENZ-LANDAU

Campus Koblenz, POB 20 16 02, 56016 Koblenz
Universitätsstr. 1, 56070 Koblenz
Telephone: (261) 2870
Fax: (261) 37524

Campus Landau, Fortstr. 7, 76829 Landau
Telephone: (6341) 2800
Fax: (6341) 28031101
E-mail: service@uni-koblenz-landau.de
Internet: www.uni-koblenz-landau.de

Founded 1990
Public control

Pres.: Prof. Dr ROMAN HEILIGENTHAL
Vice-Pres. for Academic Affairs: Prof. Dr PETER ULLRICH
Vice-Pres. for Research: Prof. Dr ULRICH SARCINELLI
Chancellor: SIMONE MERTEL-SCHERER

Number of teachers: 500
Number of students: 13,000

UNIVERSITÄT KONSTANZ
(University of Konstanz)

78457 Konstanz
Universitätsstr. 10, 78464 Konstanz
Telephone: (7531) 880
Fax: (7531) 883688
E-mail: posteingang@uni-konstanz.de
Internet: www.uni-konstanz.de

Founded 1966
Academic year: October to September

Rector: Prof. Dr ULRICH RÜDIGER
Vice-Rector for Int. Affairs: Prof. Dr KATHARINA HOLZINGER
Vice-Rector for Research: Prof. Dr ANDREAS MARX
Vice-Rector for Study Programmes: Prof. Dr CARSTEN EULITZ
Chancellor: JENS APITZ
Librarian: PETRA HÄTSCHER

Library: see Libraries and Archives
Number of teachers: 177
Number of students: 10,081

Publication: *Uni'kon*

DEANS

Faculty of Humanities: Prof. Dr THOMAS HINZ
Faculty of Law, Economics and Politics: Prof. Dr FRIEDRICH BREYER
Faculty of Sciences: Prof. Dr MARTIN SCHEFFNER

PROFESSORS

Faculty of Humanities

Department of History and Sociology:

GEORG, W., Sociology
GIESEN, B., Sociology
GOTTER, U., History
GÖTZ, T., Empirical Educational Research
HAUSER, S., History
HINZ, T., Sociology
KIRSCH, T., Sociology
KLEEBERG, B., History
KNORR, C., Sociology
OSTERHAMMEL, J., History
PIETROW-ENNKER, B., History
RECKWITZ, A., Sociology
REICHHARDT, S., History
RIEHLE, H., Sports Science
SCHLÖGL, K., History
SIGNORI, G., History
WELTECKE, D., History
WISCHERMANN, C., History
WOLL, A., Sport Science

Department of Linguistics:

BAYER, J.
BRAUN, B.
BREU, W.
BUTT, M.
DEHÉ, N.

EULITZ, C.
GRIJZENHOUT, J.
KABAK, B.
KAISER, G.
PLANKE, F.
REMBERGER, E.-M.
ROMERO, M.

Department of Literature:
ASSMANN, A.
BAUDY, G.
FEICHTINGER, B.
JOAN I TOUS, P.
KOSCHORKE, A.
KÜMMEL-SCHNUR, A.
MATALA DE MAZZA, E.
MERGENTAL, S.
MURASOV, J.
NISCHIK, R.
OCHSNER, B.
OTTO, I.
POLASCHEGG, A.
QUAST, B.
SPRENGER, U.
STIEGLER, B.
THÜRLEMANN, F.
VOGEL, J.
WEITIN, T.
ZIMMERMANN, T.

Department of Philosophy:
ROSEFELDT, T.
SEEBASS, G.
SPOHN, W.
STEMMER, P.
WEBER, M.

Faculty of Law, Economics and Politics
Department of Economics:
ALÓS-FERRER, C.
BREYER, F.
BRÜGGEMANN, R.
BRUTTEL, L.
DEISSINGER, T.
FISCHBACHER, U.
FRANKE, G.
FRIEHE, T.
GENSER, B.
GLASER, M.
GRIEBEN, W.
HERTWECK, M.
HOCHHOLDINGER, S.
JACKWERTH, J.
KAAS, L.
LUKAS, C.
POHLMEIER, W.
SANDER, H.
SCHOLL, A.
SEIFRID, J.
STEFANI, U.
URSPRUNG, H.

School of Law:
ALTHAMMER, C.
ARMGARDT, M.
BOECKEN, W.
EISELE, J.
ENNUSCHAT, J.
FEZER, K.
GLÖCKNER, J.
HAILBRONNER, K.
IBLER, M.
KOCH, J.
RENGIER, R.
RÖHL, H.
SCHÖNBERGER, C.
STADLER, A.
THEILE, H.

Department of Politics and Management:
BEHNKE, N.
BOERNER, S.
FREITAG, M.
HOLZINGER, K.
KELLER, B.
KNILL, C.
SCHNEIDER, G.
SCHNEIDER, V.

SEIBEL, W.
SELB, P.

Faculty of Sciences
Department of Biology:
ADAMSKA, J.
APELL, H.
BÜRKLE, A.
COOK, A.
DEUERLING, E.
DIEDRICHS, K.
DIETRICH, D.
ECKMANN, R.
GALIZIA, G.
GRÖTTRUP, M.
HAUCK, C.
KROTH, P.
KÜPPER, H.
LEIST, M.
MAY, E.
MAYER, T.
MENDGEN, K.
MEYER, A.
OHLSCHLÄGER, P.
PEETERS, F.
ROTHAUPT, K.
SCHEFFNER, M.
SCHINK, B.
STÜRMER, C.
WELTE, W.
WIKELSKI, M.

Department of Chemistry:
EXNER, T.
GROTH, U.
HARTIG, J.
HAUSER, K.
MARX, A.
MECKING, S.
MÖLLER, H.
MÜLLER, G.
POLARZ, S.
PRZYBYLSKI, M.
WITTMANN, V.
ZUMBUSCH, A.

Department of Computer and Information Science:
BERTHOLD, M.
BRANDES, U.
DEUSSEN, O.
KEIM, D.
KOCH, M.
KUHLEN, R.
LEUE, S.
MERHOF, D.
REITERER, H.
SAUPE, D.
SCHOLL, M.
WALDVOGEL, M.

Department of Mathematics and Statistics:
BARTHEL, G.
BERAN, J.
DENK, R.
DREHER, H.
FREISTÜHLER, H.
HOFFMANN, D.
JUNK, M.
KOHLMANN, M.
RACKE, R.
SCHEIDERER, C.
SCHNÜRER, O.
SCHROPP, J.
SCHWEIGHOFER, M.

Department of Physics:
BELZIG, W.
BURKARD, G.
DEKORSY, T.
FUCHS, M.
GANTEFÖR, G.
HAHN, G.
LEIDERER, P.
LEITENSTORFER, A.
MARET, G.
NIELABA, P.
NOWAK, U.

RÜDIGER, U.
SCHEER, E.

Department of Psychology:
ELBERT, T.
GOLLWITZER, P.
HÜBNER, R.
KEMPF, W.
KIßLER, J.
KÜTTNER, C.
RENNER, B.
ROCKSTROH, B.
SCHUPP, H.
SONNENTAG, S.

UNIVERSITÄT LEIPZIG
POB 10 09 20, 04009 Leipzig
Ritterstr. 26, 04109 Leipzig
Telephone: (341) 97108
Fax: (341) 9730099
E-mail: karin.hermann@uni-leipzig.de
Internet: www.uni-leipzig.de
Founded 1409
State control
Academic year: October to September (two semesters)

Rector: Prof. Dr BEATE A. SCHÜCKING
Vice-Rector for Devt and Transfer: Prof. Dr THOMAS LENK
Vice-Rector for Education and Int. Affairs: Prof. Dr CLAUS ALTMAYER
Vice-Rector for Research and Young Academics: Prof. Dr MATTHIAS SCHWARZ
Chancellor: Dr FRANK NOLDEN
Library Dir: Prof. Dr ULRICH JOHANNES SCHNEIDER

Library: see Libraries and Archives
Number of students: 35,000

DEANS

Faculty of Biosciences, Pharmacy and Psychology: Prof. Dr MATTHIAS MÜLLER
Faculty of Chemistry and Mineralogy: Prof. Dr CHRISTOPH SCHNEIDER
Faculty of Economics and Management: Prof. Dr Ing. JOHANNES RINGEL
Faculty of Education: Prof. Dr THOMAS HOFSÄSS
Faculty of History, Art and Oriental Studies: Prof. Dr FRANK ZÖLLNER
Faculty of Law: Prof. Dr CHRISTIAN BERGER
Faculty of Mathematics and Computer Science: Prof. Dr MATTHIAS SCHWARZ
Faculty of Medicine: Prof. Dr JOACHIM THIERY
Faculty of Philology: Prof. Dr WOFGANG LÖRSCHER
Faculty of Physics and Earth Sciences: Prof. Dr JÜRGEN HAASE
Faculty of Social Sciences and Philosophy: Prof. Dr GÜNTER BENTELE
Faculty of Sport Science: Prof. Dr MARTIN BUSSE
Faculty of Theology: Prof. Dr KLAUS FITSCHEN
Faculty of Veterinary Medicine: Prof. Dr UWE TRUYEN

PROFESSORS

Faculty of Biosciences, Pharmacy and Psychology (Brüderstr. 35, 04103 Leipzig; tel. (341) 9736700; fax (341) 9736749; e-mail dekanat.bio@uni-leipzig.de):

BECK-SICKINGER, A. G., Biochemistry
BUSOT, F., Terrestrial Ecology
EGER, K., Pharmaceutical Chemistry
HARMS, H., Environmental Microbiology
HAUSCHILDT, S., Immunobiology
HOFMANN, H.-J., Biophysical Chemistry
JESCHENIAK, D., Cognitive Psychology
MOHR, G., Industrial and Organizational Psychology
MORAWETZ, W., Special Botany
MÖRL, M., Biochemistry and Molecular Biology

MÜLLER, M., Experimental Psychology and Cognitive Neuroscience

NIEBER, K., Pharmacology

PETERMANN, H., Psychology of Personality and Psychological Intervention

POEGGEL, G., Human Biology

RAUWALD, J.-W., Pharmaceutical Biology

REISSER, W., General and Applied Botany

ROBITZKI, A., Molecular Biological-Biochemical Processing Technology

RÜBSAMEN, R., Neurobiology

SASS, H., Genetics

SCHILDBERGER, K.-M., General Zoology and Animal Behaviour Physiology

SCHLEGEL, M., Molecular Evolution and Systematics of Animals

SCHRÖDER, H., Clinical Psychology

SCHRÖGER, E., Cognitive Psychology and Biological Psychology

VON COLLANI, G., Cognitive Social Psychology

WILHELM, CHR., Plant Physiology

WITRUK, E., Educational Rehabilitation Psychology

Faculty of Chemistry and Mineralogy (Johannisallee 29, 04103 Leipzig; tel. (341) 9736000; fax (341) 9736099; e-mail dekanat@ chemie.uni-leipzig.de; internet www .uni-leipzig.de/chemie):

BENTE, K., Mineralogy, Crystallography

BERGER, ST., Analytical Chemistry

BREDE, O., Physical Chemistry

GIANNIS, A., Organic Chemistry

HEY-HAWKINS, E., Inorganic Chemistry

HOFFMANN, R., Bioanalytics

KRAUTSCHEID, H., Inorganic Chemistry

MORGNER, H., Physical Chemistry

PAPP, H., Technological Chemistry

REINHOLD, J., Theoretical Chemistry

SCHNEIDER, C., Organic Chemistry

STRÄTER, N., Structural Analysis of Biopolymers

Faculty of Economics and Management (Marschnerstr. 31, 04109 Leipzig; tel. (341) 9733500; fax (341) 9733509; e-mail dekanat@ wifa.uni-leipzig.de; internet www.uni-leipzig .de/wifa):

BRUHNKE, K.-H., Industrial Engineering and Structural Engineering: Technical and Infrastructural Management

DIEDRICH, R., Business Management: Controlling and Management Accounting

EISENECKER, U., Manager Information Systems: Software Development, Business and Administration

FÖHR, S., Business Management: Personnel Management

FRANCZYK, B., Manager Information Systems: Information Management

GRAW, K.-U., Industrial Engineering and Structural Engineering: Laying of Foundations/Hydraulic Engineering

HASSE, R., Economics: Economic Policy

HEILEMANN, U., Empirical Economics and Econometrics

HOLLÄNDER, R., Environmental Management in Small and Medium Enterprises

KALISKE, M., Industrial Engineering and Structural Engineering: Statics and Dynamics of Structures

LANG, S., Economics, Statistics

LENK, T., Economics: Public Finance Theory

LÖBLER, H., Business Management: Marketing

PAHL, B., Industrial Engineering and Structural Engineering: Drafting/Construction Design

PARASKEWOPOULOS, S., Economics: Macroeconomics

PELZL, W., Business Management: Real Estate Management

POSSELT, T., Business Management: Service Management

RAUTENBERG, H.-G., Business Management: Management Accounting and Corporate Taxation

RINGEL, J., Urban Management

SCHMIDT, H., Business Management: Accounting and Auditing

SCHUHMACHER, F., Business Management: Corporate Finance

SINGER, H. J., Business Management: Banking

TUE, V., Industrial Engineering and Structural Engineering: Solid Construction/ Building Material Technology

VOLLMER, U., Economics and Currency

WAGNER, F., Business Management: Insurance Company Management

WANZEK, T., Industrial Engineering and Structural Engineering: Steel-Girder Construction

WIESE, H., Economics: Microeconomics

Faculty of Education (Karl-Heine-Str. 22B, 04229 Leipzig; tel. (341) 9731400; fax (341) 9731499; e-mail dekanat.fakerz@uni-leipzig .de; internet www.uni-leipzig.de/~erzwiss):

DOBSLAFF, O., Special Education, Language and Speech Pathology

HOFSÄSS, T., Special Education, Learning Disabilities

HOPPE-GRAFF, S., Educational Psychology

HÖRNER, W., Comparative Education

KLAUSER, F., Economics, Business Education and Management Training

KNOLL, J., Adult Education

MARX, H., Psychology in School and Instruction

MELZER, M., School Education

MUTZECK, W., Behaviour Problems and Therapy in Special Education

SCHULZ, D., School Education

TOEPELL, M., Teaching Primary School Mathematics

VON WOLFFERSDORFF-EHLERT, C., Social Education

WOLLERSHEIM, H. W., General Education

Faculty of History, Art and Oriental Studies (Burgstr. 21, 04109 Leipzig; tel. (341) 9737000; fax (341) 9737049; e-mail dekgko@ rz.uni-leipzig.de; internet www.uni-leipzig .de/fak/gesch.htm):

BAUMBACH, G., Drama

BAXMANN, J., Drama (Dance)

BÜNZ, E., History of Saxony

CAIN, H.-U., Classical Archaeology

DENZEL, M. A., Social and Economic History

DINER, D., Jewish History and Culture

EBERHARD, W., East and Middle European History

EBERT, H.-G., Islamic Law

FEURICH, H.-J., Teaching of Music

FISCHER-ELFERT, H.-W., Egyptology

FRANCO, E., Indology

GERTEL, J., Economy and Social Geography of the Middle East

GIRSHAUSEN, TH., Drama

HEEG, G., Drama

HEYDEMANN, G., Modern History

HÖPKEN, W., East and South-East European History

JONES, A., African History

KAPPEL, R., African Politics and Economy

KLOTZ, S., Systematic Musical Science

LANGE, B., History of Art

LOOS, H., Historical Music Science

MAREK, M., History of Art

MORITZ, R., Classical Sinology

PREISSLER, H., History of Middle Eastern Religions

RICHTER, S., Japanology

RIECKHOFF-HESSE, S., Prehistory and Early History

RIEKENBERG, M., Comparative History and Ibero-American History

RUDERSDORF, M., History of the Early Modern Era

SCHUBERT, CH., Classical History

SCHULZ, E., Arabic Linguistic and Translation Science

SCHULZ, F., Teaching of Art

SEIWERT, H., General and Comparative Religion

SÖRENSEN, P. K., Central Asian Studies

STRECK, B., Ethnology

STRECK, M., Ancient Near East

TOPFSTEDT, TH., History of Art

VON FRANZ, R., Modern Sinology

VON HEHL, U., Modern History

WOLFF, E., African Studies

ZÖLLNER, F., History of Art

Faculty of Law (Burgstr. 27, 04109 Leipzig; tel. (341) 9735100; fax (341) 9735299; e-mail simue@rz.uni-leipzig.de; internet www .uni-leipzig.de/~jura):

BECKER-EBERHARD, E., Civil Law and Civil Action Law

BERGER, CHR., Civil and Civil Trial Law, Copyright

BOEMKE, B., Civil and Industrial Law, Social Legislation

DEGENHART, C., Commercial, Environmental and Planning Law

DOLEZALEK, G., Civil Law

DRYGALA, T., Civil Law, Commercial, Social and Business Law

ENDERS, CHR., Public Law

GOERLICH, H., Public, Constitutional and Administrative Law

HÄUSER, F., Civil, Industrial and Banking Law

KAHLO, M., Criminal and Criminal Trial Law, Legal Philosophy

KERN, B.-R., Civil and Medical Law, History of Law

KLESCZEWSKI, D., Criminal Trial Law and European Criminal Law

KÖCK, W., Environmental Law

OLDIGES, M., Public Law

RAUSCHER, TH., Private International Law, Comparative and Civil Law

SCHUMANN, H., Criminal and Commercial Law

STADIE, M.-H., Tax Law and Public Law

WELTER, R., Civil Law, German and International Economic Law

Faculty of Mathematics and Computer Science (Augustuspl. 10–11, 04109 Leipzig; tel. (341) 9732100; fax (341) 9732199; e-mail matinf@mathematik.uni-leipzig.de; internet www.uni-leipzig.de/matinf):

BEYER, K., Applied Mathematics

BORNELEIT, P., Teaching of Mathematics

BREWKA, G., Intelligent Systems

FREY, R., Discrete Mathematics

FRITZSCHE, B., Probability Theory

GIRLICH, H.-J., Stochastics

GRUHN, V., Applied Telematics

GÜNTHER, M., Partial Differential Equations

HERRE, H., Formal Concepts of Computer Science

HERZOG, B., Principles of Mathematics, Logic, Theory of Numbers

HEYER, G., Natural Language Processing

HUBER-KLAWITTER, A., Theoretical Mathematics

IRMSCHER, K., Computer Networks and Split Systems

KEBSCHULL, U., Technical Information Technology

KIRSTEIN, B., Mathematical Statistics

KUNKEL, P., Numerical Mathematics and Scientific Computing

KÜRSTEN, K.-D., Operator Algebra

LUCKHAUS, ST., Mathematical Optimization

MIERSEMANN, E., Calculus of Variations

RADEMACHER, H.-B., Differential Geometry

RAHM, E., Databases

SCHMÜDGEN, K., Functional Analysis

SCHUMANN, R., Analysis

SCHWARZ, M., Mathematics in Science
STADLER, P., Bioinformatics
STÜCKRAD, J., Algebra
WOLLENBERG, M., Mathematical Physics

Faculty of Medicine (Liebigstr. 27, 04103 Leipzig; tel. (341) 9715930; fax (341) 9715939; e-mail teichh@medizin.uni-leipzig .de):

ADAM, H., Anaesthesiology and Intensive Therapy
ALEXANDER, H., Obstetrics and Gynaecology
ALLGAIER, C., Pharmacology and Toxicology
ANGERMEYER, M., Psychiatry
ARENDT, T., Neuroanatomy
ARNOLD, K., Medical Physics and Biophysics
ASMUSSEN, G., Physiology
BADER, A., Cell Biology
BAERWALD, C., Internal Medicine, Rheumatology
BAIER, D., Obstetrics and Gynaecology
BLATZ, R., Medical Microbiology
BÖHME, H.-J., Biochemistry
BRÄHLER, E., Medical Psychology
BÜHRDEL, P., Paediatrics
DANNHAUER, K.-H., Orthodontics
DECKERT, F., Diagnostic Radiology
DIETZ, A., Otorhinolaryngology
DONATH, E., Medical Physics and Biophysics
EICHFELD, U., Thorax Surgery
EILERS, J., Physiology
EMMRICH, P., Pathology
ENGELE, J., Anatomy, Embryology
ENGELMANN, L., Internal Medicine, Intensive Medicine
ESCHRICH, K., Biochemistry
ETTRICH, C., Child and Adolescent Psychiatry, Psychotherapy
FROSTER, U., Genetics
GEBHARDT, R., Biochemistry
GERTZ, H.-J., Psychiatry
GEYER, M., Psychosomatic Medicine and Psychotherapy
GLANDER, H.-J., Andrology
GRÄFE, H.-G., Paediatric Surgery
GRÜNDER, W., Medical Physics and Biophysics
GUMMERT, J. F., Cardiac Surgery
HÄNTZSCHEL, H., Internal Medicine, Rheumatology
HAUSS, J. P., Abdominal, Transplantation and Vascular Surgery
HEMPRICH, A., Maxillofacial Surgery
HENGSTLER, J., Molecular Toxicology
HERBARTH, O., Environmental Medicine
HIRSCH, W., Diagnostic Radiology
HÖCKEL, M., Obstetrics and Gynaecology
HORN, F., Molecular Immunology
HUMMELSHEIM, H., Neurology
ILLES, P., Pharmacology and Toxicology
JAKSTAT, H., Dental Prosthetics and Materials
JANOUSÈK, J., Paediatric Cardiology
JASSOY, C., Molecular Virology
JENTSCH, H., Parodontology
JOSTEN, CH., Traumatology
KAHN, TH., Diagnostic Radiology
KÄSTNER, I., History of Medicine
KELLER, E., Paediatrics
KIESS, W., Paediatrics
KLEEMANN, W. J., Forensic Medicine
KLÖTZER, B., Surgery
KÖNIG, F., Anaesthesiology and Intensive Therapy
KÖNIG, H.-H., Health Economy
KÖRHOLZ, D., Paediatrics, Haematology and Oncology
KORTMANN, R.-D., Radiotherapy
KOSTELKA, M., Paediatrics, Cardiac Surgery
LIEBERT, U. G., Virology

LÖFFLER, M., Medical Informatics, Statistics and Epidemiology
MEIXENSBERGER, J., Neurosurgery
MERKENSCHLAGER, A., Paediatrics
MERTE, K., Restorative Dentistry
METZNER, G., Clinical Immunology, Allergology
MOHR, F.-W., Cardiac Surgery
MÖSSNER, J., Internal Medicine, Gastroenterology
MOTHES, TH., Clinical Chemistry
NIEDERWIESER, D., Internal Medicine, Haematology
NÖRENBERG, W., Pharmacology and Toxicology
OLTHOFF, D., Anaesthesiology and Intensive Therapy
PASCHKE, R., Internal Medicine, Endocrinology
PFÄFFLE, R., Paediatrics, Endocrinology, Gastroenterology
PFEIFFER, D., Internal Medicine, Cardiology
PLÖTTNER, G., Psychosomatic Medicine and Psychotherapy
PREISS, R., Clinical Pharmacology
REIBER, TH., Dental Prosthetics and Materials
REICHENBACH, A., Neurophysiology
RICHTER, V., Clinical Chemistry, Metabolic Disorders
RIEDEL-HELLER, S., Public Health
RIHA, O., History of Medicine
RODLOFF, A., Medical Microbiology
SABRI, O., Nuclear Medicine
SANDHOLZER, H., Internal Medicine
SCHELLENBERGER, W., Biochemistry
SCHMIDT, F., Diagnostic Radiology
SCHOBER, R., Neuropathology
SCHÖNEBERG, T., Biochemistry, Molecular Endocrinology
SCHREINICKE, G., Industrial Medicine
SCHUBERT, ST., Internal Medicine
SCHULER, G., Internal Medicine, Cardiology
SCHUSTER, V., Paediatrics
SCHWARZ, J., Neurology
SCHWARZ, R., Social Medicine
SCHWOKOWSKI, CH., Surgical Oncology
SEIBEL, P., Molecular Cell Therapy
SIMON, J.-C., Dermatology
SPANEL-BOROWSKI, K., Anatomy
STICHERLING, M., Dermatology
STUMWOLL, M., Internal Medicine, Gastroenterology, Hepatology
TANNAPFEL, A., Pathology
THIERY, J., Laboratory Medicine
TILLMANN, H.-L., Internal Medicine, Gastroenterology and Hepatology
TREIDE, A., Child Dentistry
VON CRAMON, Y., Cognitive Neurology
VON SALIS-SOGLIO, G., Orthopaedics
WAGNER, A., Neurology
WIEDEMANN, P., Ophthalmology
WILD, H. A., Paediatric Orthopaedics
WINTER, A., Medical Informatics
WIRTZ, H., Internal Medicine, Pulmology
WITTEKIND, C., Pathology, Immunopathology
ZIMMER, H.-G., Physiology

Faculty of Philology (Beethovenstr. 15, 04107 Leipzig; tel. (341) 9737300; fax (341) 9737349; e-mail dekphilo@uni-leipzig.de; internet www.uni-leipzig.de/~philol):

BARZ, I., Contemporary German Linguistics and Lexicology
BAUMANN, K., Applied Linguistics/LSP Communication (English, Russian, German)
BICKEL, B., Linguistic Typology and Diversity
DE TORO, A., Romance Literature
DEUFERT, M., Classical Philology and Latin Literature
EILERT, H., Modern German Literature

FELTEN, U., French and Italian Literature
FIX, U., Contemporary German Linguistics
GÄRTNER, E., Romance Linguistics
GOTTZMANN, C., Old German Literature
HARRESS, B., Slavic Literature and Cultural History
HINRICHS, U., Southern Slavic Linguistics and Translation Science
HOFFMANN-MAXIS, A., General and Comparative Literature and Literary Theory
KEIL, H., North American Cultural History
KOENEN, A., American Literature
LÖRSCHER, W., English Linguistics
MEIER, B., Teaching of German
MÜLLER, G., General Linguistics
NASSEN, U., Children's Literature and Juvenile Literature
ÖHLSCHLÄGER, G., German Linguistics
PECHMANN, TH., Psycholinguistics
POLLNER, C., English Linguistics
RITZER, M., Modern German Literature
RYTEL-KUC, D., West Slavic Linguistics
SCHENKEL, E., English Literature
SCHMITT, A. P., Linguistics and Translation Studies (English)
SCHWARZ, W., Literature and Cultural History of the Western Slavs
SCHWEND, J., Cultural Studies (Great Britain)
SIER, K., Classical Philology and Greek Literature
STOCKINGER, L., Modern German Literature
TSCHIRNER, E., German as a Foreign Language
UDOLPH, J., Onomastic Science
WERNER, E., Serbian Studies
WIESE, I., Contemporary German Linguistics
WOTJAK, B., German as a Foreign Language, Lexicology of Contemporary German Linguistics
WOTJAK, G., Romance Linguistics and Translation Science (Spanish and French)
ZYBATOW, G., Slavic Linguistics

Faculty of Physics and Earth Science (Linnéstr. 5, 04103 Leipzig; tel. (341) 9732400; fax (341) 9732499; e-mail dekan@physik .uni-leipzig.de):

BUTZ, T., Experimental Physics
EHRMANN, W., Geology
ESQUINAZI, P. D., Experimental Physics
FREUDE, D., Chemical Physics
GLÄSSER, W., Geology, Hydrogeology
GRILL, W., Experimental Physics
GRUNDMANN, M., Experimental Physics
HEINRICH, J., Physical Geography and Landscape-based Environmental Research
HEINTZENBERG, J., Atmospheric Physics
HERRMANN, H., Chemistry of the Atmosphere
IHLE, D., Theoretical Physics
JACOBI, CHR., Meteorology
JACOBS, F., Geophysics
JANKE, W., Theoretical Physics
KÄRGER, J., Experimental Physics
KÄS, J., Experimental Physics
KIRSTEIN, W., Geography and Geoinformatics
KORN, M., Theoretical Geophysics
KREMER, F., Experimental Physics
KROY, K.-D., Theoretical Physics
LENTZ, S., Regional Geography
LÖSCHE, A., Experimental Physics
MELLES, M., Geology
METZ, W., Theoretical Meteorology
OEHME, W., Teaching of Physics
RAUSCHENBACH, B., Applied Physics
RENNER, E., Modelling of Atmospheric Processes
RUDOLPH, G., Theoretical Physics
SALMHOFER, M., Theoretical Physics
SIBOLD, K., Theoretical Physics

TETZLAFF, G., Meteorology
WEILAND, U., Urban Ecology
WIESSNER, R., Anthropogeography, Economic Geography and the Labour Market

Faculty of Social Sciences and Philosophy (Burgstr. 21, 04109 Leipzig; tel. (341) 9735600; fax (341) 9735699; e-mail foerster@rz.uni-leipzig.de):

BARTELBORTH, TH., Philosophy of Science
BENTELE, G., Public Relations
ELSENHANS, H., Political Science and International Politics
FACH, W., Political Theory
FENNER, C., Comparative Politics
FLAM, H., Sociology
FRÜH, W., Empirical Communications and Media Research
GIESEN, K.-G., International Politics
GOTTWALD, S., Logic
HALLER, M., Journalism and Media Science
HUBER, M., International Politics
KALTER, F., Sociology
KÖHNKE, K., Theory and Philosophy of Culture
KUTSCH, A., Historical and Systematic Communication Studies
LÜBBE, W., Philosophy
MACHILL, M., Journalism and Media Science
MEGGLE, G., Philosophy
MEUSCHEL, S., Political Systems
MÜHLER, K., Sociology
SCHORB, B., Teaching of Media Studies, Further Education
SIEGRIST, H., Comparative History of Modern Europe
STEINMETZ, R., Media and Media Culture
STEKELER-WEITHOFER, P., Philosophy
STIEHLER, H.-J., Empirical Communications and Media Research
VOBRUBA, G., Sociology
VOSS, T., Sociology

Faculty of Sports Science (Jahnallee 59, 04109 Leipzig; tel. (341) 9731600; fax (341) 9731699; e-mail spodekan@rz.uni-leipzig.de; internet www.uni-leipzig.de/~sportfak):

ALFERMANN, D., Psychology of Sport
BUSSE, M., Sports Medicine
INNENMOSER, J., Sports Therapy, Sport for Handicapped People
KRUG, J., General Movement and Training Science

Faculty of Theology (Otto-Schill-Str. 2, 04109 Leipzig; tel. (341) 9735400; fax (341) 9735499; e-mail dekanat@theologie.uni-leipzig.de; internet www.uni-leipzig.de/~theolweb):

BERLEJUNG, A., Old Testament
FITSCHEN, K., Church History
HANISCH, H., Religious Education
HERZER, J., New Testament
LUX, R., Old Testament
PETZOLDT, M., Principles of Theology, Hermeneutics
PETZOLDT, M., Systematic Theology
RATZMANN, W., Practical Theology
SCHNEIDER, G., Systematic Theology
SCHRÖTER, J., New Testament
WARTENBERG, G., Church History
WOHLRAB-SAHR, M., Religious and Church Sociology

Faculty of Veterinary Medicine (An den Tierkliniken 19, 04103 Leipzig; tel. (341) 9738000; fax (341) 9738099; e-mail dekanat@vetmed.uni-leipzig.de):

ALBER, G., Immunology
BLESSING, M., Molecular Pathogenesis
BRAUN, R., Milk Hygiene
DAUGSCHIES, A., Parasitology
EDINGER, J., Orthopaedics
EINSPANIER, A., Endocrinology
FEHLHABER, K., Food Hygiene and Consumer Protection

FERGUSON, J., Large-Animal Surgery
FUHRMANN, H., Physiological Chemistry
GÄBEL, G., Physiology
GREVEL, V., Small-Animal Surgery
KRAUTWALD-JUNGHANNS, M.-E., Bird Diseases
KRÜGER, M., Bacteriology and Mycology
LÜCKER, E., Meat Hygiene
MÜLLER, H., Virology
OECHTERING, G., Small-Animal Medicine
SALOMON, F.-V., Anatomy
SCHOON, H.-A., Histopathology and Clinical Pathology
SCHUSSER, G., Large-Animal Medicine
SEEGER, J., Histology and Embryology
SOBIRAJ, A., Obstetrics and Gynaecology
TRUYEN, U., Epidemiology
UNGEMACH, F. R., Pharmacology and Pharmacy

ATTACHED RESEARCH INSTITUTE

Institute of German Literature: Wächterstr. 34, 04107 Leipzig; tel. (341) 9730300; fax (341) 9730319; e-mail kahl@uni-leipzig.de; internet www.uni-leipzig.de/dll

PROFESSORS

HASLINGER, J., Literary Aesthetics
TREICHEL, H.-U., German Literature

UNIVERSITÄT MANNHEIM
(University of Mannheim)

Schloss, 68131 Mannheim
Telephone: (621) 1812222
Fax: (621) 1811050
E-mail: info@uni-mannheim.de
Internet: www.uni-mannheim.de
Founded 1907 as Städtische Handelshochschule, attached to Heidelberg Univ. 1933, reopened as Wirtschaftshochschule 1946, Univ. status 1967
Languages of instruction: German, English
Academic year: April to February
Rector: Prof. Dr HANS-WOLFGANG ARNDT
Pro-Rector: Prof. Dr EVA ECKKRAMMER
Pro-Rector: Prof. Dr HERMANN G. EBNER
Pro-Rector: Prof. Dr MATTHIAS KRAUSE
Chancellor: Dr SUSANN-ANNETTE STORM
Librarian: CHRISTIAN BENZ

Library: see Libraries and Archives
Number of teachers: 140
Number of students: 11,500

DEANS

Business School: Dr JÜRGEN M. SCHNEIDER
School of Humanities: Prof. Dr JOHANNES MÜLLER-LANCÉ
School of Law and Economics: Prof. Dr MARTIN PEITZ
School of Mathematics and Information Sciences: (vacant)
School of Social Sciences: Prof. Dr BERTHOLD RITTBERGER

UNIVERSITÄT OSNABRÜCK

POB 44 69, 49069 Osnabrück
Neuer Graben/Schloss, 49074 Osnabrück
Telephone: (541) 9690
Fax: (541) 96914111
E-mail: info@uni-osnabrueck.de
Internet: www.uni-osnabrueck.de
Founded 1973
Languages of instruction: German, English
Academic year: October to September
Pres.: Prof. Dr CLAUS RAINER ROLLINGER
Vice-Pres. for Budget and Human Resources: Prof. Dr WILFRIED HÖTKER
Vice-Pres. for Research and Graduate Student Devt: Prof. Dr MAY-BRITT KALLENRODE
Vice-Pres. for Study and Teaching: Prof. Dr MARTINA BLASBERG-KUHNKE
Registrar: Dr UWE SIELEMAN

Librarian: FELICITAS HUNDHAUSEN
Number of teachers: 500
Number of students: 10,500
Publication: *Forschungsbericht* (every 2 years)

DEANS

Faculty of Biology/Chemistry: Prof. Dr JACOB PIEHLER
Faculty of Culture and Geography: Prof. Dr BRITTA KLAGGE
Faculty of Economics: Prof. Dr FRANK TEUTEBERG
Faculty of Education and Cultural Studies: Prof. Dr INGRID KUNZE
Faculty of Language and Literature: Prof. Dr ROLF DÜSTERBERG
Faculty of Law: Prof. Dr HANS SCHULTE-NÖLKE
Faculty of Mathematics and Information Science: Prof. Dr HEINZ SPINDLER
Faculty of Physics: Prof. Dr R. BERGER
Faculty of Social Sciences: Prof. Dr WOLFGANG LUDWIG SCHNEIDER

UNIVERSITÄT PADERBORN

Warburger Str. 100, 33098 Paderborn
Telephone: (5251) 600
Fax: (5251) 602519
E-mail: pressestelle@zv.uni-paderborn.de
Internet: www.uni-paderborn.de
Founded 1972
State control
Language of instruction: German
Academic year: October to July
Pres.: Prof. Dr NIKOLAUS RISCH
Vice-Pres.: Prof. Dr BERND FRICK
Vice-Pres.: Prof. Dr DOROTHEE M. MEISTER
Vice-Pres.: Prof. Dr WILHELM SCHÄFER
Chancellor: Dr JÜRGEN PLATO
Library Dir: Dr DIETMAR HAUBFLEISCH
Library of 1,700,000 vols, 1,500 periodicals
Number of teachers: 1,350
Number of students: 14,769

Publications: *Forschungsforum* (1 a year), *Paderborner Universitätsreden* (irregular), *Paderborner Universitätszeitung* (2 a year)

DEANS

Faculty of Arts and Humanities: Prof. Dr VOLKER PECKHAUS
Faculty of Business Administration and Economics: Prof. Dr PETER F. E. SLOANE
Faculty of Computer Science, Electrical Engineering and Mathematics: Prof. Dr FRANZ JOSEF RAMMIG
Faculty of Cultural Studies: Prof. Dr FRANZ GÖTTMANN
Faculty of Mechanical Engineering: Prof. Dr DETMAR ZIMMER
Faculty of Science: Prof. Dr HANS-JOACHIM WARNECKE

PROFESSORS

Faculty of Arts and Humanities:

ALLKEMPER, A.
ARNOLD, R.
AUTSCH, S.
BAUER, G.
BEDER, J.
BRAUERHOCH, A.
BUBLITZ, H.
BURRICHTER, R.
CORTIEL, J.
ECKER, G.
ECKHARDT, J.
EHLAND, C.
EKE, N.
ENGLISCH, B.
FELDBUSCH, E.
FREITAG, C.
GEMBRIS, H.
GÖTTMANN, F.

GROTJAHN, R.
HAGENGRUBER, R.
HERZIG, B.
HOFMANN, M.
HORNÁK, S.
JACKE, C.
KAMP, H.
KEIL, W.
KLENKE, D.
KOELLE, L.
KOLHOFF-KAHL, I.
KRETTENAUER, T.
KUHLMANN, H.
KÜRTZ, A.
LANG, B.
LANGENBACHER-LIEBGOTT, J.
LAUBENTHAL, A.
LEMKE, I.
LEUTZSCH, M.
MARX, N.
MEISTER, D.
MÜLLER, S.
MÜLLER-LIETZKOW, J.
ÖHLSCHLÄGER, C.
PECKHAUS, V.
PIENEMANN, M.
RENDTORFF, B.
RIBBAT, C.
SCHAPER, N.
SCHARLAU, I.
SCHMITZ, S.
SCHROETER-WITTKE, H.
SCHUSTER, B.
SENG, E.
SÖLL, F.
STEINECKE, A.
STRÖTER-BENDER, J.
STROTMANN, A.
STRUBE, M.
SÜßMANN, J.
TÖNNIES, M.
TOPHINKE, D.
VON STOSCH, K.
WILK, N.
WINKLER, H.
ZIELKE, G.

Faculty of Business Administration and Economics:

BARTON, D.
BETZ, S.
BEUTNER, M.
DANGELMAIER, W.
DILLER, M.
EGGERT, A.
EGGERT, W.
FAHR, R.
FENG, Y.
FISCHER, J.
FRICK, B.
GILROY, B.
GRIES, T.
HAAKE, C.
HOGREVE, J.
ISEKE, A.
KLIEWER, N.
KOBERSTEIN, A.
KREMER, H.
KRIEGER, T.
KRIMPHOVE, D.
KUNDISCH, D.
LÖFFLER, A.
MÜLLER, J.
ROSENTHAL, K.
SCHILLER, B.
SCHNEIDER, G.
SCHNEIDER, M.
SLOANE, P.
SUHL, L.
SURETH, C.
WERNER, T.

Faculty of Computer Science, Electrical Engineering and Mathematics:

BELLI, F.
BENDER, P.
BLÖMER, J.

BÖTTCHER, S.
BRINKMANN, A.
BRUNS, M.
BÜRGISSER, P.
DELLNITZ, M.
DIETZ, H.
DOMIK-KIENEGGER, B.
ENGELS, G.
GAUSCH, F.
HÄB-UMBACH, R.
HANSEN, S.
HAUENSCHILD, W.
HENNING, B.
HILLERINGMANN, U.
KASTENS, U.
KEIL, R.
KLEINE, B.
KÖCKLER, N.
MAGENHEIM, J.
MEYER, F.
NOÉ, R.
RAMMIG, F.
RINKENS, H.

Faculty of Mechanical Engineering:

GAUSEMEIER, J.
HOMBERG, W.
KENIG, E.
KOCH, R.
MAHNKEN, R.
MAIER, H.
MORITZER, E.
RICHARD, H.
SCHMID, H.
SCHÖPPNER, V.
SEXTRO, W.
TRÄCHTLER, A.
TRÖSTER, T.
VRABEC, J.
ZIMMER, D.

Faculty of Science:

BECKER, H.
BRANDL-BREDENBECK, H.
BREMSER, W.
FELS, G.
GRUNDMEIER, G.
HENKEL, G.
HESEKER, H.
HUBER, K.
KITZEROW, H.
KUCKLING, D.
LINDNER, J.
LISCHKA, K.
MEIER, C.
MEIER, T.
OLIVIER, N.
REINHOLD, P.
RISCH, N.
SCHINDLMAYR, A.
SCHLEGEL-MATTHIES, K.
SCHMIDT, C.
SCHMIDT, W.
SCHUBERT, V.
SOHLER, W.
WARNECKE, H.
WEIß, M.
ZRENNER, A.

UNIVERSITÄT PASSAU

Innstr. 41, 94032 Passau

Telephone: (851) 5090
Fax: (851) 5091005
E-mail: info@uni-passau.de
Internet: www.uni-passau.de

Founded 1972
State control
Language of instruction: German
Academic year: October to September

Pres.: Prof. Dr WALTER SCHWEITZER
Vice-Pres.: Prof. Dr ERNST STRUCK
Vice-Pres.: Prof. Dr BURKHARD FEITAG
Vice-Pres.: Prof. Dr WOLFGANG HAU
Chancellor: LUDWIG BLOCH
Librarian: Dr STEFFEN WAWRA

Library: see Libraries and Archives
Number of teachers: 237
Number of students: 9,177

DEANS

Faculty of Business Sciences: Prof. Dr FRANZ LEHNER
Faculty of Law: Prof. Dr ULRIKE MÜSSIG
Faculty of Computer Sciences and Mathematics: Prof. Dr HARALD KOSCH
Faculty of Philosophy: Prof. Dr WERNER GAMERITH
Faculty of Theology: Prof. Dr ANTON LANDERSDORFER

PROFESSORS

Faculty of Business Sciences (94030 Passau; tel. (851) 5092400; fax (851) 5092603; e-mail dekanat@wiwi.uni-passau.de; internet www.wiwi.uni-passau.de):

BORCK, R., Economic Policy
BÜHNER, R., Organization and Human Resource Management
FIEDLER, M., Management, People and Information
FISCHER, M, Marketing and Services
JUNGWIRTH, C., Economic Policy
KLEINSCHMIDT, P., Business Computing I
LAMBSDORFF, J. G., Economic Theory
LEHNER, F., Business Computing II
MOOSMÜLLER, G., Statistics
PFLÜGNER, M., Foreign Trade and International Economics
SCHWEITZER, W., Statistics
WAGNER, N., Financial Control
WILHELM, J., Finance
ZIEGLER, H., Production and Logistics

Faculty of Law (94030 Passau; tel. (851) 5092201; fax (851) 5092207; e-mail dekanat.jura@uni-passau.de; internet www.jura.uni-passau.de):

ALTMEPPEN, H., Private Law, Commercial and Business Law I
BAYREUTHER, F., Civil Law and Labour Law
BEULKE, W., Penal Law
BRAUN, J., Civil Law, Civil Procedural Law and Philosophy of Law
DEDERER, H.-G., Constitutional and Administrative Law, Public International Law, European and International Economic Law
ENGLÄNDER, A., Criminal Law and Criminal Procedure
ESSER, R., German, European and International Criminal Law, Criminal Procedure and White-Collar Crime
HAU, W., Private Law, Civil Procedure, Private International Law
HECKMANN, D., Public Law, Security Law and Internet Law
HERRMANN, C., Constitutional and Administrative, European Law, European and International Economic Law
KRAMER, U., Public Law
KUHN, T., Civil Law
MANTHE, U., Civil Law and Roman Law
MÜLLER-TERPITZ, R., State, Administrative, Media and Information Law
MÜSSIG, U., Civil Law, German and European Legal History
PUTZKE, H., Penal Law
SOLOMON, D., Private Law, Private International Law and Comparative Law
WERNSMANN, R., State and Administrative Law, Tax Law

Faculty of Computer Sciences and Mathematics (94030 Passau; tel. (851) 5093001; fax (851) 5093002; e-mail dekanat@fim.uni-passau.de; internet www.fim.uni-passau.de):

BEYER, D., Computer Science, Software Systems

BRANDENBURG, F.-J., Computer Science, Theoretical Computer Science

DE MEER, H., Computer Science, Computer Networks/Computer Communications

DONNER, K., Mathematics, Numerical Mathematics (Analysis)

FREITAG, B., Computer Science, Information Management

GRAF, S., Mathematics, Measure and Integration

KAISER, T., Mathematics

KOSCH, H., Computer Science and Distributed Information Systems

KREUZER, M., Mathematics and Symbolic Computation

LENGAUER, CH., Computer Science and Programming

LUKOWICZ, P., Computer Science and Embedded Systems

MÜLLER-GRONBACH, T., Mathematics, Mathematical Stochastics and its Appliances

POLIAN, I., Computer Science and Computer Engineering

POSEGGA, J., Computer Science and IT Security

SCHWARTZ, N., Mathematics and Algebraic Geometry

Faculty of Philosophy (94030 Passau; tel. (851) 5092600; fax (851) 5092626; e-mail dekanat.phil@uni-passau.de; internet www .phil.uni-passau.de):

ANHUF, D., Physical Geography

BACH, M., Sociology

BARMEYER, C., Ch. Intercultural Communication

BAUER, L., Didadactics of Teaching Mathematics

BAUMGARTNER, I., Science of Christian Society and Charity

BERNERT, W., Didadactics of Teaching Social Studies

ERKENS, F., Medival History

FITZ, K., American Studies

FONK, P., Moral Theology

FRENZ, T., Medieval History and and Historical Science

GAMERITH, W., Regional Geography

GELLNER, W., Political Science II

GLAS, A., Education of Arts

GÖLER, D., European Studies

HARNISCH, R., German Philology

HARTWIG, S., Romanic Literature and Culture

HEINRICH, H., Methods of Empirical Social Research

HIERING, P., Didadactics of Teaching Biology

HINZ, M., Romanic Literature and Applied Geography with Emphasis on Italy

HOHLFELD, R., Media and Communication

KAMM, J., English Literature and Culture

KORFF, R., South-East Asia Studies II

KRAH, H., Modern German Literature

KRAUS, H.-CH., Modern History

LANDERSDORFER, A., Church History

LISKE, M.-TH., Philosophy

MÄGDEFRAU, J., Education and Didactics for Secondary School

MENDL, H., Education of Religion and Didactics of Teaching Religion

MICHLER, A., Didactics of Teaching History

MOGEL, H., Psychology

MÜLLER, K., Didactics of German Language and Literature

NOLTE, T., Medieval German Literature

OBERREUTER, H., Political Science I

POLLAK, G., Science of Education

REUTNER, U., Romanic Linguistics

SCHWANKL, O., Exegesis and Biblical Theology

SEIBERT, N., Science of School Education

STAMPFL, I., Music Education

STINGLHAMMER, H., Dogmatics and History of Dogmata

STOLL, O., Early History

STRUCK, E., Anthropogeography

THIES, C., Philosophy

UFFELMANN, D., Slavic Literature and Culture

WALTER, K., Romanic Literature and Applied Geography with Emphasis on France

WÜNSCH, T., Modern History of Eastern Europe and its Culture

ZECHMEISTER-MACHHART, M., Fundamental Theology

ZEHNPFENNING, B., Political Theory and History

Faculty of Theology (94030 Passau; tel. (851) 5092001; fax (851) 5092003; internet www .ktf.uni-passau.de):

BAUMGARTNER, I., Christian Social Studies and Pastoral Theology

FONK, P., Moral Theology

LANDERSDORFER, A., Church History

LISKE, M.-T., Philosophy

MENDL, J., Religious Education and Teaching Methods

SCHWANKL, O., New Testament Exegesis

SCHWIENHORST-SCHÖNBERGER, L., Old Testament Exegesis and Hebrew

STINGLHAMMER, H., Dogmatics

ZECHMEISTER-MACHHART, Basic Theology

UNIVERSITÄT POTSDAM

POB 60 15 53, 14415 Potsdam
Am Neuen Palais 10, 14469 Potsdam

Telephone: (331) 9770

Fax: (331) 972163

E-mail: presse@uni-potsdam.de

Internet: www.uni-potsdam.de

Founded 1991

Languages of instruction: German, English

Academic year: October to September

Pres.: Dr THOMAS GRÜNEWALD (acting)

Vice-Rector for Int. Affairs and Strategic Devt: Prof. Dr RIA DE BLESER

Vice-Rector for Research and Young Academics: Prof. Dr BERND WALZ

Vice-Rector for Scientific and Technology Transfer and Innovation: Prof. Dr DIETER WAGNER

Vice-Rector for Teaching and Study: Dr THOMAS GRÜNEWALD

Dir for Library: Dr ULRIKE MICHALOWSKY

Library: 1.3m. vols, 2,850 print journals, 8,000 e-journals

Number of teachers: 226 professors, 923 other academic staff

Number of students: 20,000

DEANS

Faculty of Economic and Social Sciences: Prof. Dr KLAUS H. GOETZ

Faculty of Human Sciences: Prof. Dr RIA DE BLESER

Faculty of Law: Prof. Dr HARTMUT BAUER

Faculty of Mathematics and Natural Sciences: Prof. Dr REIMUND GERHARD

Faculty of Philosophy: Prof. Dr JOHANN EV. HAFNER

UNIVERSITÄT REGENSBURG

93040 Regensburg
Universitätsstr. 31, 93053 Regensburg

Telephone: (941) 94301

Fax: (941) 9432305

E-mail: studienberatung@uni-regensburg.de

Internet: www.uni-regensburg.de

Public control

Founded 1962

Languages of instruction: English, German

Academic year: October to September

Rector: Prof. Dr THOMAS STROTHOTTE

Pro-Rector: Prof. Dr HANS GRUBER

Pro-Rector: Prof. Dr INGRID NEUMANN-HOLZSCHUH

Pro-Rector: Prof. Dr OLIVER REISER

Chancellor: Dr CHRISTIAN BLOMEYER

Librarian: Dr RAFAEL BALL

Library: see Libraries and Archives

Number of teachers: 1,590

Number of students: 18,561

Publications: *Blick in die Wissenschaft, Research Report*

DEANS

Faculty of Biology and Pre-Clinical Medicine: Prof. Dr JÜRGEN HEINZE

Faculty of Business, Economics and Management Information Systems: Prof. Dr DIRK MEYER-SCHARENBERG

Faculty of Catholic Theology: Prof. Dr BERNHARD LAUX

Faculty of Chemistry and Pharmacy: Prof. Dr SIGURD ELZ

Faculty of Languages, Literature and Cultural Studies: Prof. Dr EDGAR SCHNEIDER

Faculty of Law: Prof. Dr MICHAEL PAWLIK

Faculty of Mathematics: Prof. Dr FELIX FINSTER

Faculty of Medicine: Prof. Dr BERNHARD WEBER

Faculty of Philosophy, Fine Arts, History and Humanities: Prof. Dr CHRISTOPH MEINEL

Faculty of Physics: Prof. Dr MILENA GRIFONI

Faculty of Psychology, Educational Sciences and Physical Education: Prof. Dr REGINA MULDER

UNIVERSITÄT ROSTOCK

18051 Rostock
Ulmenstr. 69, Bldg 3, 18057 Rostock

Telephone: (381) 4980

Fax: (381) 4981006

E-mail: rektor@uni-rostock.de

Internet: www.uni-rostock.de

Founded 1419

State control

Academic year: October to September

Rector: Prof. Dr WOLFGANG SCHARECK

Vice-Rector for Research and Research Education: Prof. Dr URSULA VAN RIENEN

Vice-Rector for Student Affairs: HEIKO MARSKI

Vice-Rector for Study, Education and Evaluation: Prof. Dr STEFAN GÖBEL

Chancellor: Dr MATHIAS NEUKIRCHEN

Library Dir: RENATE BÄHKER

Library: see Libraries and Archives

Number of teachers: 1,364

Number of students: 15,138

Publications: *Archiv der Freunde der Naturgeschichte in Mecklenburg, Erziehungswissenschaftliche Beiträge, Forschungsbericht der Universität Rostock, Pädagogisches Handeln, Rostocker Agrar- und Umweltwissenschaftliche Beiträge, Rostocker Arbeitspapiere zu Rechnungswesen und Controlling, Rostocker Arbeitspapiere zu Wirtschaftsentwicklung und Human Resource Development, Rostocker Beiträge zur Deutschen und Europäischen Geschichte, Rostocker Beiträge zur Regional- und Strukturforschung, Rostocker Beiträge zur Sprachwissenschaft, Rostocker Beitrage zur Verkehrswissenschaft und Logistik, Rostocker Forum Theologie, Rostocker Informatik-Berichte, Rostocker Informationen zu Politik und Verwaltung, Rostocker Materialen für Landschaftsplanung und Raumentwicklung, Rostocker Mathematisches Kolloquium, Rostocker Medizinische Beiträge, Rostocker Meeresbiologische Beiträge, Rostocker Philosophische Manuskripte, Rostocker Schriften zur Bank und Finanzmarktforschung,*

Rostocker Schriften zum Bankrecht, Rostocker Studien zur Kulturwissenschaft, Schiffbauforschung, Thunen-Reihe Angewandter Volkswirtschftstheorie, and various faculty publs

DEANS

Faculty of Agricultural and Environmental Science: Prof. Dr ELMAR MOHR
Faculty of Computer Science and Electrical Engineering: Prof. Dr Ing. Hab. BERNHARD LAMPE
Faculty of Economic and Social Sciences: Prof. Dr SUSANNE HOMÖLLE
Faculty of Law: Prof. Dr JÖRG BENEDICT
Faculty of Mathematics and Natural Sciences: Prof. Dr CHRISTOPH SCHICK
Faculty of Mechanical Engineering and Marine Technology: Prof. Dr Ing. Hab. EGON HASSEL
Faculty of Medicine: Prof. Dr EMIL CHRISTIAN REISINGER
Faculty of Philosophy: Prof. Dr HANS-JÜRGEN VON WENSIERSKI
Faculty of Theology: Prof. Dr MARTINA KUMLEHN

UNIVERSITÄT SIEGEN

57068 Siegen
Herrengarten 3, 57068 Siegen
Telephone: (271) 7400
Fax: (271) 7404808
E-mail: rektor@uni-siegen.de
Internet: www.uni-siegen.de
Founded 1972
State control
Academic year: October to July (2 semesters)
Rector: Prof. Dr HOLGER BURCKHART
Vice-Rector: Prof. Dr. FRANZ-JOSEF KLEIN
Vice-Rector: Prof. Dr. HANNA SCHRAMM-KLEIN
Vice-Rector: Prof. Dr. PETER HARING BOLIVAR
Vice-Rector: Prof. Dr THOMAS MANNEL
Chancellor: Dr JOHANN PETER SCHÄFER
Librarian: WERNER REINHARDT

Library of 1,234,833 vols
Number of teachers: 882
Number of students: 14,036

Publications: *Diagonal, LiLi—Zeitschrift für Literaturwissenschaft und Linguistik, MuK—Massenmedien und Kommunikation, Navigationen, Reihe Medienwissenschaften, Reihe Siegen*, Research Report, *Siegen: Sozial* (2 a year), *Siegener Hochschulzeitung, Siegener Pädagogische Studien, SPIEL* (2 a year)

DEANS

Faculty of Arts: Prof. Dr PETRA M. VOGEL
Faculty of Business Economics, Business IT and Commercial Law: Prof. Dr VOLKER WULF
Faculty of Education, Architecture, Arts: Prof. Dr-Ing. HILDEGARD SCHRÖTELER-VON BRANDT
Faculty of Science and Technology: Prof. Dr ULLRICH PIETSCH

UNIVERSITÄT STUTTGART
(University of Stuttgart)

POB 10 60 37, 70049 Stuttgart
Telephone: (711) 6850
Fax: (711) 68582271
E-mail: poststelle@uni-stuttgart.de
Internet: www.uni-stuttgart.de
Founded 1829 as Gewerbeschule, univ. status 1967
Public control
Language of instruction: English
Academic year: October to September
Rector: Prof. Dr-Ing. WOLFRAM RESSEL
Vice-Rector for Org.: Prof. Dr-Ing. MANFRED BERROTH

Vice-Rector for Academic Affairs and Continuing Education: Prof. Dr FRANK GIEßELMANN
Vice-Rector for Research and Technology: Prof. Dr SABINE LASCHAT
Registrar: BETTINA BUHLMANN
Chief Librarian: W. STEPHAN
Library: see under Libraries and Archives
Number of teachers: 2,750
Number of students: 20,000

Publications: *alumniNews, Mediendienst Forschung, Themenheft Forschung, Uni-Kurier* (2 a year)

DEANS

Aerospace Engineering and Geodesy: Prof. Dr Ing. ALFRED KLEUSBERG
Architecture and Urban Planning: Prof. Ing. ARNO LEDERER
Chemistry: Prof. Dr HANS-JOACHIM WERNER
Civil and Environmental Engineering: Prof. Dr Ing. ULLRICH MARTIN
Computer Science, Electrical Engineering, and Information Technology: Prof. Dr Ing. JOACHIM SPEIDEL
Energy Technology, Process Engineering and Biological Engineering: Prof. Dr Ing. MICHAEL SCHMIDT
Engineering Design, Production Engineering and Automotive Engineering: Prof. Dr Ing. OLIVER SAWODNY
Humanities: Prof. Dr PETER SCHOLZ
Management, Economics and Social Sciences: Prof. Dr FRANK C. ENGLMANN
Mathematics and Physics: Prof. Dr RICHARD DIPPER

PROFESSORS

Aerospace Engineering and Geodetic Science (Universitätsbereich Vaihingen, Pfaffenwaldring 27, Zi.02, Stuttgart; tel. (711) 6852400; fax (711) 6853617; e-mail dekanat@f06.uni-stuttgart.de; internet www.f06.uni-stuttgart.de):

AUWETER-KURTZ, M., Space Transportation Technology
DRECHSLER, K., Aircraft Construction
FRITSCH, D., Photogrammetry and Land Surveying
GRAFAREND, E. W., Geodetic Science
KELLER, W., Physical Geodetic Science
KLEUSBERG, A., Navigation
KRÄMER, E., Aerodynamics
KRÖPLIN, B.-H., Statics and Dynamics of Aerospace Structures
KÜHN, M., Aerodynamics
MÖHLENBRINK, W., Aviation Telemetry
MUNZ, C.-D., Air and Gas Dynamics
REICHEL, R., Aviation Systems
RÖSER, H.-P., Space Systems
STAUDACHER, S., Turbojet Engines
VOIT-NITSCHMANN, R., Aircraft Construction
VON WOLFERSDORF, J., Aerospace Thermodynamics
WAGNER, S., Air and Gas Dynamics
WEIGAND, B., Aerospace Thermodynamics
WELL, K. H., Guidance and Control of Aerospace Vehicles
WOLF, D., Theory and Modelling of Geodetic Systems

Architecture and City Planning (Universitätsbereich Stadtmitte, Keplerstr. 11, 70714 Stuttgart; tel. (711) 1213223; fax (711) 1212788; e-mail dekanat@f01.uni-stuttgart.de; internet www.architektur.uni-stuttgart.de):

ADAM, J., Design and Construction
BEHLING, S., Building Construction and Design
BOTT, H., City Planning and Urban Design
CHERET, P., Building Construction and Design

DE BRUYN, G., Theory of Architecture and Design
EISENBIEGLER, G., Structures and Constructional Design
ERTEL, H., Building Materials, Building Physics, Mechanical Equipment
HARLANDER, T., Housing and Design
HERRMANN, D., Building Materials, Building Physics, Mechanical Equipment
HÜBNER, P., Building Construction and Design
JESSEN, J., City and Regional Planning
JOCHER, T., Housing and Design
KAULE, G., Landscape Planning and Ecology
KIMPEL, D., History of Architecture
KNIPPERS, J., Structures and Constructional Design
KNOLL, W., Drawing, Drafting and Modelling
MORO, J. L., Planning and Construction of High-Rise Buildings
PESCH, F., City Planning and Urban Design
PODREKA, B., Interior Design and Architectural Design
RIBBECK, E., Planning and Building Development
SCHÖNWANDT, W., Foundations of Planning
SCHÜRMANN, P., Building Materials, Building Physics, Mechanical Equipment
SOBEK, W., Lightweight Structures and Conceptual Design
TRAUB, H., Drawing, Drafting and Modelling
ULLMANN, F., Interior Design and Architectural Design

Biological and Geosciences (Universitätsbereich Vaihingen, Herdweg 51, 70174 Stuttgart; tel. (711) 1211334; fax (711) 2237978; e-mail dekanat@g04.uni-stuttgart.de; internet www.uni-stuttgart.de/geowissenschaft):

BLÜMEL, W. D., Geography
GAEBE, W., Cultural Geography
GHOSH, R., Bioenergetics
GOERTZ, H. D., Zoology
HEYER, A., Botany
JESKE, H., Molecular Biology and Virology of Plants
KELLER, P., Mineralogy and Crystal Chemistry
MASSONNE, H.-J., Mineralogy and Crystal Chemistry
MATTES, R., Industrial Genetics
MUTTI, M., Geology and Palaeontology
NUßBERGER, S., Biophysics
PFIZENMAIER, K., Cell Biology and Immunology
SCHEURICH, P., Molecular Immunology
SCHNEIDER, G., Geophysics
SEUFERT, W., Industrial Genetics
SEYFRIED, H., Geology and Palaeontology
SPRENGER, G., Microbiology
WIELANDT, E., Geophysics
WOLF, D. H., Biochemistry
WOLLNIK, F., Animal Physiology

Chemistry (Universitätsbereich Vaihingen, Pfaffenwaldring 55, 7.OG, Stuttgart; tel. (711) 6854584; e-mail dekanat@f03.uni-stuttgart.de; internet www.uni-stuttgart.de/chemie):

ALDINGER, F., Non-Metallic Inorganic Materials
ARZT, E., Metallurgy
BECKER, G., Inorganic Chemistry
BERTAGNOLLI, H., Physical Chemistry
CHRISTOFFERS, J., Organic Chemistry
EISENBACH, C., Chemical Engineering
GIESSELMANN, F., Physical Chemistry
GUDAT, D., Inorganic Chemistry
HASHMI, S., Organic Chemistry
JÄGER, V., Organic Chemistry
KAIM, W., Inorganic Chemistry
LASCHAT, S., Organic Chemistry
MITTELMEIJER, E., Metallurgy

RODUNER, E., Physical Chemistry
SCHLEID, T., Inorganic Chemistry
SCHMID, R., Technical Biochemistry
WEITKAMP, J., Chemical Engineering
WERNER, H.-J., Theoretical Chemistry
WOLF, D., Biochemistry
ZABEL, F., Physical Chemistry

Civil Engineering and Surveying (Universitätsbereich Vaihingen, Pfaffenwaldring 7, 2.OG, Stuttgart; tel. (711) 6856234; e-mail dekanat@fak2.uni-stuttgart.de; internet www.uni-stuttgart.de/bauingenieur):

BÁRDOSSY, A., Water Management
BERNER, F., Construction Industry
EHLERS, W., Engineering Mechanics
ELIGEHAUSEN, R., Materials Science in Structural Engineering
ENGESSER, K.-H., Biological Cleaning of Used Air
FRIEDRICH, M., Transport Planning and Traffic Control
GERTIS, K., Building Physics
HELMIG, R., Hydromechanics and Hydrosystems Modelling
KRANERT, M., Sanitary Engineering, Waste Water and Solid Waste Management
KUHLMANN, U., Design and Construction
MARTIN, U., Railway and Transportation Engineering
METZGER, J., Hydrochemistry and Hydrobiology, Sanitary Engineering, Waste Water and Solid Waste Management
MIEHE, C., Engineering Mechanics
MÖHLENBRINK, W., Applied Geodesy
MORO, J. L., Planning and Construction of High-Rise Buildings
NOVÁK, B., Large-Scale Construction
PINNEKAMP, J., Waste Water Engineering
RAMM, E., Structural Engineering
REINHARDT, H.-W., Materials Science in Structural Engineering
RESSEL, W., Road and Transport Planning and Engineering
ROTT, U., Water Quality Management, Sanitary Engineering
SEDLBAUER, K., Constructional Physics
SOBEK, W., Interdisciplinary Research, Architecture and Civil Engineering
TREUNER, P., Regional Development Planning
VERMEER, P. A., Geotechnology
WIEPRECHT, S., Water Engineering

Computer Science, Electrical Engineering and Information Technology (Universitätsbereich Vaihingen, Pfaffenwaldring 47, Zi. 4.116, Stuttgart; tel. (711) 6857234; fax (711) 6857236; e-mail dekanat@f-iei.uni-stuttgart.de; internet www.f-iei.uni-stuttgart.de):

BERROTH, M., Communications Engineering
BUNGARTZ, H.-J., Simulation of Large Systems
CLAUS, V., Formal Concepts of Computer Science
DIEKERT, V., Theoretical Computer Science
EGGENBERGER, O., Operating Systems
ERTL, T., Dialogue Systems
ESPARZA, J., Secure and Reliable Software Systems
FRÜHAUF, N., Display Technology
GÖHNER, P., Control Engineering and Process Automation
KASPER, E., Semiconductor Engineering
KÜHN, P. J., Communications Switching and Data Techniques
LAGALLY, K., Operating Systems
LANDSTORFER, F., Radio Frequency Technology
LEHMANN, E., Export Systems
LEVI, P., Computer Vision
LUDEWIG, J., Software Engineering
MITSCHANG, B., User Software
PLÖDEREDER, E., Programming Languages
ROLLER, D., Computer Science Fundamentals

ROTH-STIELOW, J., Power Electronics and Control Engineering
ROTHERMEL, K., Distributed Systems
RUCKER, W., Theory of Electrical Engineering
SCHÄFER, Energy Conversion
SPEIDEL, J., Telecommunications
TENBOHLEN, S., High-Voltage Technology
WERNER, J. H., Physical Electronics
WUNDERLICH, H.-J., Computer Architecture
YANG, B., Network and Systems Theory

Mathematics and Physics (Universitätsbereich Vaihingen, Pfaffenwaldring 57, 70550 Stuttgart; tel. (711) 6852400; fax (711) 6853617; e-mail dekanat@f08.uni-stuttgart.de; internet www.uni-stuttgart.de/mathephysik):

BECHINGER, C., Experimental Physics
BLIND, G., Mathematics
BRÜDERN, J., Mathematics
DENNINGER, G., Physics
DIETRICH, S., Theoretical Physics
DIPPER, R., Mathematics
DOSCH, H., Experimental Physics
DRESSEL, M., Experimental Physics
GEKELER, E., Mathematics
HÄHL, H., Mathematics
HERRMANN, H., Theoretical Physics
HESSE, C., Mathematics
HÖLLIG, K., Mathematics
KÜHNEL, W., Mathematics
LUNK, A., Plasma Research
MAHLER, G., Theoretical Physics
MICHLER, P., Experimental Physics
MIELKE, A., Mathematics
MURAMATSU, A., Theoretical Physics
PFAU, T., Institute of Physics
PÖSCHEL, J., Mathematics
SANTOS, L., Theoretical Physics
SCHWEITZER, D., Experimental Physics
SEIFERT, U., Theoretical Physics
STRAUSS, W., Mathematics
TREBIN, H.-R., Theoretical and Applied Physics
WALK, H., Mathematics
WEIDL, T., Mathematics
WEISS, U., Theoretical Physics
WOHLMUTH, B., Mathematics
WRACHTRUP, J., Experimental Physics
WUNNER, G., Theoretical Physics

Mechanical Engineering (Universitätsbereich Vaihingen, Pfaffenwaldring 9, 5.OG, 70569 Stuttgart; tel. (711) 6856470; fax (711) 6856492; e-mail dekanat@f07.uni-stuttgart.de; internet www.f07.uni-stuttgart.de):

ALLGÖWER, F., Systems Theory in Engineering
BARGENDE, M., Combustion Engines
BERTSCHE, B., Machine Elements (Gear Design, Cab Sealing Technology)
BINZ, H., Machine and Gearing Design
BRUNNER, H., Interface Chemistry
BULLINGER, H.-J., Industrial Science and Technology Management
BUSSE, G., Non-Destructive Testing
CASEY, M., Thermal Turbo-Engines
EBERHARD, P., Mechanics
EIGENBERGER, G., Chemical Process Engineering
EYERER, P., Polymer Testing and Polymer Science
FRIEDRICH, H., Vehicle Concepts
FRITZ, H. G., Polymer Processing
GADOW, R., Manufacturing Technologies of Ceramic Compounds and Composites
GAUL, L., Mechanics
GILLES, E. D., System Dynamics and Control Systems
GÖDE, E., Fluid Machines and Hydraulic Pumps
GRAF, T., Network Engineering
HAASE, H., Technical Thermodynamics
HEIN, K. R. G., Process Engineering and Steam Boiler Technology

HEISEL, U., Machine Tools
KISTNER, A., Engineering Mechanics
KLEMM, P., Control Engineering
KÜCK, H., Time Measuring, Precision Engineering and Microengineering
LAURIEN, E., Nuclear Engineering
LOHNERT, G., Nuclear Engineering and Energy Systems
MAIER, T., Technical Design
MERTEN, C., Chemical Engineering
MÜLLER-STEINHAGEN, H., Thermodynamics and Heat Engineering
NAGEL, J., Biomedical Technology
OSTEN, W., Technical Optics
PIESCHE, M., Mechanical Production Engineering
PLANCK, H., Textile Technology and Process Engineering
PRITSCHOW, G., Control Technology of Machine Tools and Production Systems
REUSS, H.-C., Automobile Mechatronics
REUSS, M., Biochemical Engineering
ROOS, E., Materials Testing, Materials Science and Strength of Materials
SANDMAIER, H., Time Measuring, Precision Engineering and Microengineering
SCHINKÖTHE, W., Design and Production in Precision Engineering
SCHMAUDER, S., Process Development
SCHMIDT, M., Heating and Air-Conditioning Engineering
SEIFERT, H., Thermal Waste Utilization
SIEGERT, K., Metal Forming
SPATH, D., Technology Management
VOSS, A., Energy Economics
WEHKING, K.-H., Conveyer and Transmission Technology, Gear Technology
WEHLAN, H., Process Control Engineering
WESTKÄMPER, E., Industrial Production and Plant
WIEDEMANN, J., Motor Vehicle Engineering
ZEITZ, M., System Dynamics Control

Philosophy and History (Universitätsbereich Stadtmitte, Keplerstr. 17, KII, 3.OG, 70174 Stuttgart; tel. (711) 1213089; fax (711) 1212803; e-mail dekanat@f09.uni-stuttgart.de; internet www.f09.uni-stuttgart.de):

ALEXIADOU, M., Linguistics and English
BAHLKE, J., Early Modern History
BARK, J., Modern German Literature
CZERWINSKI, P., German Philology
DOGIL, G., Computational Linguistics
GÖBEL, W., American Studies and Modern English Literature
HUBIG, C., Theory of Science and Technical Philosophy
KAMP, H., Formal Logic and Philosophy of Language
KRÜGER, R., Roman Studies
MAAG, G., Italian Studies
OLSHAUSEN, E., Ancient History
PAFEL, J., Linguistics and German
PYTA, W., Modern History
QUARTHAL, F., Regional History of Baden-Württemberg
REICHERT, F., History
ROHRER, CH., Computational Linguistics
SEEBER, H. U., Modern English Literature
STEIN, A., Linguistics/Roman Studies
STEINER, R., History of Arts
STÜRNER, W., History
THOMÉ, H., Modern German Literature
VON HEUSINGER, K., Linguistics and German
WYSS, B., History of Arts

Social Sciences and Economics (Universitätsbereich Stadtmitte, Keplerstr. 17, KII, 10 OG, 70174 Stuttgart; tel. (711) 1213046; fax (711) 1212807; e-mail dekanat@wiso.uni-stuttgart.de; internet www.uni-stuttgart.de/wiso):

ACKERMANN, K.-F., Economics
ALT, W., Sports
ARNOLD, U., Economics
BRINKHOFF, K.-P., Sports

ENGLMANN, F., Economics
FRANKE, S. F., Economic Policy and Public Law
FROMM, M., Educational Theory
FUCHS, D., Political Science
GABRIEL, O. W., Political Science
HERZWURM, G., Economics
HORVÁTH, P., Economics
KEMPER, H.-G., Economics
MAJER, H., Economics
NICKOLAUS, R., Vocational and Economic Education
REISS, M., Economics
RENN, O., Sociology of Environment and Technology
SCHÄFER, H., Economics
SCHLICHT, W., Sports
URBAN, D., Sociology
WOECKENER, B., Economics
ZAHN, E., Economics

UNIVERSITÄT TRIER

54286 Trier
Universitätsring 15, 54296 Trier
Telephone: (651) 2010
Fax: (651) 2014299
E-mail: presse@uni-trier.de
Internet: www.uni-trier.de
Founded 1473, reopened 1970
Academic year: October to September
Pres.: Prof. Dr PETER SCHWENKMEZGER
Vice-Pres.: Prof. Dr JOACHIM HILL
Vice-Pres.: Prof. Dr THOMAS RAAB
Chancellor: Dr KLAUS HEMBACH (acting)
Librarian: Dr HILDEGARD MÜLLER
Library: see Libraries and Archives
Number of teachers: 600
Number of students: 14,600
Publications: *Trierer Beiträge* (1 a year), *UNI-Journal* (4 a year)

DEANS

Faculty I: Pedagogy, Philosophy and Psychology: Prof. Dr CONNY H. ANTONI
Faculty II: Language and Literature: Prof. Dr ULRICH PORT
Faculty III: History, Political Science, Classical Archaeology, Egyptology, Art History, Papyrology: Prof. Dr UWE JUN
Faculty IV: Management Economics, Sociology, Political Economy, Applied Mathematics, Computer Science and Ethnology: Prof. Dr RALF MÜNNICH
Faculty V: Law: Prof. Dr JAN VON HEIN
Faculty VI: Geography and Geosciences: Prof. Dr INGO EBERLE
Faculty VII: Theology: Prof. Dr JOACHIM THEIS

PROFESSORS

Faculty I: Pedagogy, Philosophy and Psychology (Fachbereich I, 54286 Trier; tel. (651) 2012015; fax (651) 2013942; e-mail kohrg@uni-trier.de; internet www.psychologie.uni-trier.de/fbi):

ANTON, F., Psychobiology
BECKER, P., Psychology
BRANDTSTÄDTER, J., Psychology
CONNY, A., Psychology
DÖRFLINGER, B., Philosophy
FILIPP, S.-H., Psychology
HELLHAMMER, D., Psychology
HOMFELDT, H.-C., Pedagogy
HONIG, M. S., Pedagogy
KRAMPEN, G., Psychology
MEYER, J., Psychobiology
MULLER, C., Psychobiology
MÜLLER-FOHRBRODT, G., Pedagogy
PRECKEL, F., Psychology
RUSTEMEYER, D., Pedagogy
SCHÄCHINGER, H., Psychobiology
SCHELLER, R., Psychology
SCHWENKMEZGER, P., Psychology

WALTHER, E., Psychology
WENDER, K. F., Psychology

Faculty II: Language and Literature (Fachbereich II, 54286 Trier; tel. (651) 2012210; fax (651) 2013901; e-mail dienhart@uni-trier.de; internet www.uni-trier.de/uni/fb2/dekanat):

ALTHAUS, H. P., German Linguistics, Yiddish Language
BENDER, K.-H., Romance Literature
BREUER, H., English Literature
BUCHER, H.-J., Media Studies
CHIAO, W., Sinology
EIGLER, U., Classical Philology
GÄRTNER, K., German Philology
GELHAUS, H., German Linguistics
GÖSSMANN, H., Japanese Studies
HASLER, J., English and American Literature
HÖLZ, K., Romance Literature
HURM, G., English Literature
KLOOSS, W., English Philology
KÖHLER, H., Romance Literature
KÖHLER, R., Linguistic Data Processing
KÖSTER, J.-P., Applied Linguistics, Phonetics
KRAMER, J., Romance Philology
KREMER, D., Romance Philology
KRÖNER, H. O., Classical Philology
KÜHLWEIN, W., English Philology
KÜHN, P., German as a Foreign Language
LIANG, Y., Sinology
LOIPERDINGER, M., Media Studies
MOULIN, C., Old German Philology
NEUBERG, S., Yiddish Studies
NIEDEREHE, H.-J., Romance Philology
PIKULIK, L., Modern German Literature
PLATZ, N., English Literature
POHL, K. H., Chinese Studies
REINHARDT, H., Modern German Literature
RESSEL, G., Slavistics
RIEGER, B., Linguistic Data Processing, Computer Languages
RÖLL, W., German Philology, Yiddish Language
SCHOLZ-CIONCA, S., Japanese Studies
SCHÖßLER, F., New German Literature
STAHL, H., Slavic Literature
STRAUSS, J., English Philology
STUBBS, M., English Linguistics
THORAU, H.-E., Portuguese Philology
TIMM, E., Yiddish Language
UERLINGS, H., Modern German Literature
WIMMER, R., German Linguistics
WÖHRLE, G., Classical Philology
ZIRKER, H., English Literature

Faculty III: History, Political Science, Classical Archaeology, Egyptology, Art History, Papyrology (Fachbereich III, 54286 Trier; tel. (651) 2012144; fax (651) 2013936; e-mail merz@uni-trier.de; internet www.uni-trier.de/uni/fb3/dekanat/fb3.html):

ANTON, H. H., Medieval History
CLEMENS, L., History
DORN, F., History
EBELING, D., History
FRANZ, G., History
GERHARDT, C., History
GESTRICH, A., Modern History
HAVERKAMP, A., Medieval History
HEINEN, H., Ancient History
HERRMAN-OTTO, E., Ancient History
HOLTMANN, W., History
IRSIGLER, F., Cultural History
KETTENHOFEN, E., History
KÖNIG, I., History
KRAMER, B., Papyrology
MOLT, P., Political Science
RAPHAEL, L., Modern and Recent History
SCHMID, W., History
SCHNABEL-SCHÜLE, H., Modern History
TACKE, A., Art History
VEEN, H. J., Political Science
VLEEMING, S. P., Egyptology
VOLTMER, E., History

WEBER, W., History
WIELING, H., History
WÖHRLE, G., Greek Philology

Faculty IV: Management Economics, Sociology, Political Economy, Applied Mathematics, Computer Science and Ethnology (Fachbereich IV, 54286 Trier; tel. (651) 2012640; fax (651) 2013927; e-mail dekanfb4@uni-trier.de; internet www.uni-trier.de/uni/fb4/dekanat/index.htm):

AMBROSI, C. M., Political Economy
ANTWEILER, C., Ethnology
BAUM, D., Computer Science
BERGMANN, R., Computer Science
BRAUN, H., Sociology
CZAP, H., Computer Science
DICKERTMANN, D., Political Economy
DIEHL, S., Computer Science
ECKERT, R., Sociology
EL-SHAGI, E. S., Political Economy
FILC, W., Political Economy
FEHR, H. J., Accounting
FERNAU, H., Computer Science
GAWRONSKI, W., Mathematics
HAHN, A., Sociology
HAMM, B., Sociology
HARDES, H.-D., Political Economy
HECHELTJEN, P., Political Economy
JÄCKEL, M., Sociology
KLÄS, F., Accounting
KNAPPE, E., Political Economy
LEHMANN, M., Management Economics
LIEBIG, M., Sociology
MILDE, H., Management Economics
MÜNNICH, R., Economics
NÄHER, S., Computer Science
OFFERMANN-CLAS, CH., European Community
RÜCKLE, D., Management Economics
SACHS, E., Mathematics
SADOWSKI, D., Management Economics
SCHERTLER, W., Strategic Management
SCHMIDT, A., Economics
SPEHL, H., Political Economy
STURM, P., Computer Science
SWOBODA, B., Management Economics
WÄCHTER, H., Management Economics
WALTER, B., Computer Science
WEIBER, R., Management Economics

Faculty V: Law (Fachbereich V—Rechtswissenschaft, 54286 Trier; tel. (651) 2012524; fax (651) 2013911; e-mail dekanatfb5@uni-trier.de; internet www.uni-trier.de/uni/fb5/fachbereich/dekanat.htm):

AXER, P., Public Law
BACHMANN, G., Civil Law, Commercial Law
BIRK, R., Private Law, Labour Law, Conflict of Laws
BURMESTER, G., National and International Finance and Tax Law
DORN, F., Private Law, Legal History, Comparative Law
ECKHARDT, D., Civil Law
HENDLER, R., Constitutional and Administrative Law
JÄGER, C., Criminal Law
KREY, V., Criminal Law, Criminal Procedure, Legal Methods
KÜHNE, H.-H., Criminal Law, Criminology, Criminal Procedure
RAAB, T., Public Law, Commercial Law, Labour Law
REIFF, P., Private Law, Commercial Law, Corporation Law, Insurance Law
REINHARDT, M., Constitutional and Administrative Law
ROBBERS, G., Public Law, Ecclesiastical Law, Philosophy of Law
RÜFNER, T., Public Law, German and International Civil Law
SCHRÖDER, M., Public, International and EU Law
VON HOFFMANN, B., Private Law, Conflict of Laws, Comparative Law

Faculty VI: Geography and Geosciences (Fachbereich VI, 54286 Trier; tel. (651) 2014530; fax (651) 2013939; e-mail dekanatfb6@uni-trier.de; internet dekanatfb6.uni-trier.de):

ALEXANDER, J., Physical Geography
BECKER, CHR., Applied Geography and Geography of Tourism
BLÖMEKE, B., Ecotoxicology
BOLLMANN, J., Cartography
CALTEUX, G., Geography of Tourism
DIESTER-HAAß, L., Biogeography
EBERLE, I., Economic and Social Geography
FISCHER, K., Inorganic and Analytical Chemistry
HEINEMANN, G., Climatology
HILL, J., Remote Sensing
HOFFMANN, R., Geography and its Teaching
MONHEIM, H., Applied Geography, Urban and Regional Planning and Development
RIES, J. B., Physical Geography
SAILER, U., Cultural and Regional Geography
SYMADER, W., Hydrology
THOMAS, F., Geobotany
VOGEL, H., Communal Science
WAGNER, J.-F., Geology

Faculty VII: Theology (Universitätsring 19, 54296 Trier; tel. (651) 2013520; fax (651) 2013951; e-mail theofak@uni-trier.de; internet www.uni-trier.de/uni/theo):

BOHLEN, Biblical Studies
BRANDSCHEIDT, Old Testament
ECKERT, New Testament
EULER, Fundamental Theology
FIEDROWICZ, Medieval Church History and Christian Archaeology
GÖBEL, Moral Philosophy
HEINZ, Liturgical Studies
KRÄMER, Church Law
KRIEGER, Philosophy I
OCKENFELS, Medieval Church History
SCHNEIDER, Church History
SCHÜßLER, Philosophy II
THEIS, Religious Instruction
VODERHOLZER, Dogma and History of Dogma
WAHL, Pastoral Theology

UNIVERSITÄT ULM

89069 Ulm
Telephone: (731) 5010
Fax: (731) 5022038
E-mail: praesident@uni-ulm.de
Internet: www.uni-ulm.de

Founded 1967 as Medizinische-Naturwissenschaftliche Hochschule, University charter 1967
State control
Language of instruction: German
Academic year: October to September
Pres.: Prof. Dr KARL JOACHIM EBELING
Vice-Pres. for Academic Affairs: Prof. Dr ULRICH STADTMÜLLER
Vice-Pres. for Medicine: Prof. Dr KLAUS-MICHAEL DEBATIN
Vice-Pres. for Research: Prof. Dr PETER BÄUERLE
Chancellor: DIETER KAUFMANN
Chief Librarian: SIEGFRIED FRANKE
Number of teachers: 480
Number of students: 8,300
Publication: *Uni Ulm Intern* (8 a year)

DEANS

Faculty of Engineering and Computer Science: Prof. Dr Ing. MICHAEL WEBER
Faculty of Mathematics and Economics: Prof. Dr WERNER KRATZ
Faculty of Medicine: Prof. Dr KLAUS-MICHAEL DEBATIN
Faculty of Natural Sciences: Prof. Dr AXEL GROß

UNIVERSITÄT VECHTA
(University of Vechta)

POB 15 53, 49364 Vechta
Driverstr. 22, 49377 Vechta
Telephone: (4441) 150
Fax: (4441) 15444
E-mail: info@uni-vechta.de
Internet: www.uni-vechta.de

Founded 1830, present status 1995, present name 2010
Public control
Pres.: Prof. Dr MARIANNE ASSENMACHER
Vice-Pres. for Research and Young Researchers: Prof. Dr MARTIN WINTER
Vice-Pres. for Teaching and Academic Programmes: Dr MARION RIEKEN
Head Librarian: Dr GUNTER GEDULDIG
Library of 508,000 vols
Number of teachers: 204
Number of students: 3,132

UNIVERSITÄT WITTEN/HERDECKE
(Witten/Herdecke University)

Alfred-Herrhausen-Str. 50, 58448 Witten
Telephone: (2302) 9260
Fax: (2302) 926407
E-mail: public@uni-wh.de
Internet: www.uni-wh.de

Founded 1982
Private control
Languages of instruction: German, English
Academic year: October to July
Chancellor: MICHAEL ANDERS
Librarian: IRIS KOCH
Library of 150,000 books, 500 periodicals
Number of teachers: 295
Number of students: 1,327

DEANS

Faculty of Arts and Cultural Studies: Prof. Dr. HANS-JÜRGEN LANGE
Faculty of Economics: Prof. Dr MONIKA OLIVA
Faculty of Health Sciences: Prof. Dr ECKHART G. HAHN

UNIVERSITÄT ZU KÖLN

Albertus-Magnus-Pl., 50923 Cologne
Telephone: (221) 4700
Fax: (221) 4705151
E-mail: aaa@verw.uni-koeln.de
Internet: www.uni-koeln.de

Founded 1388
Academic year: October to July
Rector and Pres.: Prof. Dr AXEL FREIMUTH
First Vice-Rector: Prof. Dr THOMAS KRIEG
Chancellor: Dr JOHANNES NEYSES
Librarian: Prof. Dr W. SCHMITZ
Library: see Libraries and Archives
Number of teachers: 3,000
Number of students: 42,000
Publications: *Forschung_365* (in English and German), *Kölner Universitätszeitung* (in German)

DEANS

Faculty of Economics, Business Administration and Social Sciences: Prof. Dr FRANK SCHULZ-NIESWANDT
Faculty of Human Sciences: Prof. Dr HANS JOACHIM ROTH
Faculty of Law: Prof. Dr THOMAS WEIOGEND
Faculty of Mathematics and Natural Sciences: Prof. Dr HANS-GÜNTER SCHMALZ
Faculty of Medicine: Prof. Dr med. JOACHIM KLOSTERKÖTRTER
Faculty of Philosophy: Prof. Dr CHRISTIANE BONGARTZ

PROFESSORS

Faculty of Economics, Business Administration and Social Sciences (tel. (221) 4705607; fax (221) 4705179; e-mail dekanat@wiso .uni-koeln.de; internet www.wiso.uni-koeln .de):

ANDEREGG, R. G., Political Economy
BAUM, H., Economics
BEUERMANN, G., Business Administration
DELFMANN, W., Business Administration
DERIGS, U., Information Systems, Operations Research
DONGES, J., Economics
EEKHOFF, J., Economics
EISENFÜHR, F., Business Administration
FELDERER, B., Economics
FELDSIEPER, M., Economics
FISCHER, L., Business Psychology
FRESE, E., Business Administration
FRIEDRICHS, J., Sociology
FUNK, P., Economics
GLÄSSER, E., Economic Geography
HARTMANN-WENDELS, T., Business Administration
HERZIG, N., Business Administration, Taxation
JÄGER, T., Political Science
JAGODZINSKI, W., Sociology
KEMPF, A., Business Administration, Finance
KITTERER, W., Economics
KÖHLER, R., Marketing
KOPPELMANN, U., Business Administration
KUHNER, C., Business Administration
LEIDHOLD, W., Political Science
LINDNER-BRAUN, C., Sociology
LÖBBECKE, C., Electronic Commerce
MELLIS, W., Business Informatics
MEULEMANN, H., Sociology
MOSLER, K., Statistics, Econometrics
MÜLLER-HAGEDORN, L., Business Administration
PIERENKEMPER, T., Economic History
RETTIG, R., Economics
RÖSNER, H. J., Social Politics
SCHELLHAASS, H. M., Economics
SCHMID, F., Statistics
SCHRADIN, H. R., Business Administration, Insurance
SCHULZ-NIESWANDT, F., Social Policy
SEIBT, D., Information Science, Business Administration
STERNBERG, R., Economic Geography
TEMPELMEIER, H., Business Administration
VON WEIZSÄCKER, C. C., Economics
WAGNER, M., Sociology
WESSELS, W., Political Science
WIED-NEBBELING, S., Economics
WISWEDE, G., Business Psychology
ZERCHE, J., Social Policy

Faculty of Education (tel. (221) 4705777; fax (221) 4705073; e-mail dekanat@ew.uni-koeln .de; internet www.uni-koeln.de/ew-fak):

ADOLPHI, K., Biology
ANACKER, U., General Education
AUERNHEIMER, G., Intercultural Education
BANNWARTH, H., Biology
BARTELS, J., Geography
BECKER-MROTZEK, M., German
BOMBEK, M., Textile Design
BREULL, W.-R., Biology and Human Biology
BROSSEDER, J., Catholic Theology
BUKOW, W.-D., Sociology
BURSCHEID, H. J., Mathematics
BUTTERWEGGE, C., Political Science
DONNERSTAG, J., English
GLÜCK, G., General Education and School Education
GRÜNEWALD, B., Philosophy
GÜNTHER, HARTMUT, German Language and Literature
GÜNTHER, HENNING, General Education and School Education
HAIDER-HASEBRINK, H., Psychology

HURRELMANN, B., German Language and Literature
KLEIN, K., Biology
KOCH-PRIEWE, B., General Education and School Education
KOENEN, K., Protestant Theology
KÜNZEL, K., Adult Education
LAMM, H., Psychology
LLARYORA, R., Sociology
MESSELKEN, H., German Language and Literature
MINSEL, W.-R., Psychology
OTT, T., Music
RECH, P., Art
REICH, K., General Education
REINERS, C., Chemistry
SCHÄFER, G., General Education
SCHMIDT, S., Mathematics
SCHNEIDER, R., Music
SCHOLTEN, C., Roman Catholic Theology
SCHÖN, E., German Language and Literature
SCHRÖDER, J., History
SEIBEL, H. D., Sociology
STOCK, A., Theology
STRUVE, H., Mathematics
THIEMANN, F., General Education
THIEME, G., Geography
TIMM, U., Biology
TÖNNIS, G., Art
VOLKENBORN, A., Mathematics
WEGENER-SPÖHRING, G., General Education
WEISER, W., Mathematics
WICHARD, W., Biology
WICKERT, J., Psychology
WIEGERSHAUSEN, H.-W., Art
WILKENDING, G., German Language and Literature
ZILLESSEN, D., Protestant Theology

Faculty of Law (tel. (221) 4702218; fax (221) 4705106; e-mail jura-dekanat@uni-koeln.de; internet www.dekanat.de):

BAUR, J. F., Civil Law, Commercial Law, European Law
BÖCKSTIEGEL, K.-H., International and Constitutional Law, German and International Commercial Law
DAUNER-LIEB, B., Civil Law, Commercial Law, Industrial Law
DEPENHEUER, O., Public Law, Philosophy of Law
GRUNEWALD, B., Civil Law, Commercial Law
HENSSLER, M., Civil Law, Commercial Law, Industrial Law
HOBE, S., Public Law, International Law, European Law
HÖFLING, W., Constitutional Law, Administrative Law, Financial Law
HORN, N., Civil Law, German and International Commercial and Banking Law, Philosophy of Law
HÜBNER, U., Insurance Law, Civil Law, Commercial Law, Foreign and International Private Law
LANG, J., Tax Law, Public Law
MANSEL, H.-P., Civil Law, International Private Law, Comparative Law
MITTENZWEI, I., Civil Law, Civil Process Law, Philosophy of Law
MUCKEL, S., Public Law, Canon Law
NESTLER, C., Criminal Law, Criminal Case Law
PRÜTTING, H., Civil Law, Industrial Law
SCHIEDERMAIR, H., Public Law, International Law, Philosophy of Law
SCHMITT-KAMMLER, A., Constitutional and Administrative Law
SEIER, J., Criminal Law, Criminal Case Law
TETTINGER, P. J., Constitutional and Administrative Law
WALTER, M., Criminology, Criminal Law
WALTHER, S., Criminal Law, Criminal Procedural Law, Comparative Law

WEIGEND, T., Criminal Law, Criminal Procedural Law, Comparative Criminal Law, Criminology

Faculty of Mathematics and Natural Sciences (tel. (221) 4705643; fax (221) 4705108; e-mail math-nat-fakultaet@uni-koeln.de; internet www.uni-koeln.de/math-nat-fak):

ARMBRUST, M., Mathematics
ARNDT, H., Zoology
BACHEM, A., Applied Mathematics and Informatics
BELOW, R., Micropalaeontology and Palaeoecology
BERKESSEL, A., Organic Chemistry
BERKING, S., Zoology
BESLER, H., Geography
BOHATÝ, L., Crystallography
BOTHE, H., Botany
BRUNOTTE, E., Geography
BUNDSCHUH, P., Mathematics
BÜSCHGES, A., Zoology
CAMPOS-ORTEGA, J. A., Developmental Physiology
COENEN, H. H., Nuclear Chemistry
DEITERS, U., Physical Chemistry
DOHMEN, J., Genetics
DOST, M., Physics
ECKART, A., Experimental Physics
EILENBERGER, G., Theoretical Physics
ERMER, O., Organic Chemistry
FAIGLE, U., Applied Mathematics
FLÜGGE, U.-I., Botany
FREIMUTH, A., Experimental Solid State Physics
GOMPPER, G., Theoretical Physics
GRIESBECK, A. G., Organic Chemistry
HAUSEN, K., Zoology
HEHL, F. W., Theoretical Physics
HENKE, W., Mathematics
HERBIG, H.-G., Palaeontology and Historical Geography
HOHLNEICHER, G., Physical Chemistry
HOWARD, J. C., Genetics
HÜLSKAMP, M., Botany
ILGENFRITZ, G., Physical Chemistry
JOLIE, J., Experimental Physics
JÜNGER, M., Informatics
KAUPP, U. B., Biophysical Chemistry
KAWOHL, B., Mathematics
KEMPER, B., Genetics and Genetic Engineering
KERSCHGENS, M., Meteorology
KLEIN, H. W., Biochemistry
KORSCHING, S., Genetics
KRAAS, F., Anthropogeography
KRAMER, R., Biochemistry
KRUMSIEK, K., Geology
KÜPPER, T., Mathematics
LAMOTKE, K., Mathematics
LANGE, H., Mathematics
LANGER, T., Genetics
LEPTIN, M., Genetics
LESCH, M., Mathematics
LEYTHAEUSER, D., Geology
MELKONIAN, M., Botany
MEYER, G., Inorganic Chemistry
MICKLITZ, H., Experimental Physics
MÜHLBERG, M., Crystallography
MÜLLER-HARTMANN, E., Theoretical Physics
NATTERMANN, T., Theoretical Physics
NAUMANN, D., Inorganic and Analytical Chemistry
NEUBAUER, F. M., Geophysics and Meteorology
NEUMANN, M., Applied Mathematics
NEUWIRTH, W., Physics
NIMTZ, G., Physics
NIPPER, J., Geography
PAETZ GEN. SCHIECK, H., Physics
PALME, H., Mineralogy
PLICKERT, G., Zoology
POHLEY, H.-J., Developmental Biology
RADTKE, U., Geography
RAJEWSKY, K., Molecular Genetics

RAMMENSEE, W., Mineralogy
RAPOPORT, M., Mathematics
RECKZIEGEL, H., Mathematics
RICKEN, W., Geology
ROTH, S., Developmental Biology
RUSCHEWITZ, U., Inorganic Chemistry
SCHIEDER, R., Experimental Physics
SCHIERENBERG, E., Zoology
SCHLICHTER, D., Zoology
SCHMALZ, H.-G., Organic Chemistry
SCHMITZ, K., Botany
SCHNEIDER-POETSCH, HJ., Botany
SCHNETZ, K., Genetics
SCHOMBURG, D., Biochemistry
SCHRADER, R., Informatics
SEIDEL, E., Geochemistry
SEYDEL, R., Mathematics
SOYEZ, D., Anthropogeography
SPECKENMEYER, E., Informatics
SPETH, P., Geophysics and Meteorology
STAUFFER, D., Theoretical Physics
STERNER, R., Biochemistry
STREY, R., Physical Chemistry
STRÖHER, H., Experimental Nuclear Physics
STUTZKI, J., Physics
TAUTZ, D., Genetics
TEZKAN, B., Geophysics
THORBERGSSON, G., Mathematics
TIEKE, B., Physical Chemistry
TOPP, W., Zoology
TROTTENBERG, U., Applied Mathematics
WALKOWIAK, W., Zoology
WEISSENBÖCK, G., Botany
WERR, W., Developmental Biology
WESEMANN, L., Inorganic Chemistry
ZIRNBAUER, M., Theoretical Physics
ZITTARTZ, J., Theoretical Physics

Faculty of Medicine (tel. (221) 4780; fax (221) 4784097; e-mail med-dekanat@medizin.uni-koeln.de; internet www.medizin.uni-koeln.de):

ABKEN, H., Onco-Genetics, Cell Biology
ADDICKS, K., Anatomy
BALDAMUS, C., Internal Medicine
BAUMANN, M. A., Dentistry
BERGDOLT, K., History of Medicine, Medical Ethics
BERTHOLD, F., Paediatrics
BÖRNER, U., Anaesthesiology
BRUNKWALL, J. S., Surgery
BUZELLO, W., Anaesthesiology
DECKERT-SCHLÜTER, M., Neuropathology
DE VIVIE, E. R., Thorax- and Cardio-Surgery
DIEHL, V., Internal Medicine
DIENES, H. P., Pathology and Pathological Anatomy
DÖPFNER, M., Psychopathology
ENGELMANN, U., Urology
ERDMANN, E., Internal Medicine
FRICKE, U., Pharmacology and Toxicology
FUHR, U., Pharmacology
GOESER, T., Internal Medicine
HACKENBROCH, M. H., Orthopaedics
HAUPT, G., Urology
HEISS, W.-D., Neurology and Psychiatry
HERHOLZ, K., Neurology
HERZIG, S., Pharmacology and Toxicology
HESCHELER, J., Physiology
HÖLSCHER, A. H., Surgery
HÖPP, H.-W., Internal Medicine
KERSCHBAUM, T., Dentistry
KLAUS, W., Pharmacology and Toxicology
KLOSTERKÖTTER, J., Psychiatry
KLUG, N., Neurosurgery
KOEBKE, J., Anatomy
KÖHLE, K., Psychosomatic Medicine and Psychotherapy
KONEN, W., Ophthalmology
KRIEG, T., Dermatology and Venereology
KRIEGLSTEIN, G. K., Ophthalmology
KRONE, W., Internal Medicine
KRÖNKE, M., Hygiene and Microbiology
LACKNER, K., Clinical Radiology

LAUTERBACH, K. W., Health Economics
LECHLER, E., Internal Medicine
LEHMACHER, W., Medical Statistics, Informatics and Epidemiology
LEHMANN, K., Anaesthesiology
LEHMKUHL, G., Child and Adolescent Psychiatry
MAHRLE, G., Dermatology
MALLMANN, P., Gynaecology and Obstetrics
MICHALK, D., Paediatrics
MÖSGES, R., Medical Informatics
MÜLLER, R.-P., Radiology
MÜLLER-WIELAND, D., Internal Medicine
NEISS, W. F., Anatomy
NIEDERMEIER, W., Dental Prosthetics
NOACK, M. J., Dentistry
NOEGEL, A. A., Biochemistry
PAULSSON, M., Biochemistry
PFAFF, H., Medical Sociology
PFEIFFER, P., Dentistry
PFISTER, H., Virology
PFITZER, G., Physiology
PIEKARSKI, C., Industrial Medicine
REHM, K. E., Surgery and Accident Surgery
ROTH, B., Paediatrics
RÜSSMANN, W., Ophthalmology
SCHEFFNER, M., Biochemistry
SCHICHA, H., Nuclear Medicine
SCHIRMACHER, P., Pathology
SCHRÖDER, H., Anatomy
STENNERT, E., Otorhinolaryngology
STURM, V., Neurosurgery
THIELE, J., Pathology
TROIDL, H., Surgery
TSCHUSCHKE, V., Medical Psychology
WIELCKENS, K., Clinical Chemistry
WIESNER, R. J., Physiology
ZÖLLER, J. E., Dental Surgery

Faculty of Philosophy (tel. (221) 4702212; fax (221) 4705133; e-mail dekan.philfak@ uni-koeln.de; internet www.uni-koeln.de/ phil-fak):

AERTSEN, J., Philosophy
ALEXANDER, M., Modern History
ALLEMANN-GHIONDA, C., Intercultural Education
ANTOR, H., English Philology
ARMBRUSTER, C., Romance Philology
AX, W., Classical Philology
BALD, W.-D., Applied Linguistics
BEHREND-ENGELHARDT, H., African Studies
BENTE, G. M., Psychology
BERRESSEM, H., American Studies
BIEG, L., Modern Chinese Literature
BLAMBERGER, G., Modern German Literature
BLATTMANN, M., Medieval History
BLUMENTHAL, P., Romance Philology
BLUMRÖDER, C. VON, Musicology
BOLLIG, M., Cultural Anthropology
BOS, G., Jewish Studies
BOSCHUNG, D., Classical Archaeology
BOSINSKI, G., Prehistory and Early History
BRENNER, P. J., Modern German Literature
BUCK, E., Theatre, Film and Television Studies
CASIMIR, M., Cultural Anthropology
CLAESGES, U., Philosophy
DÄMMER, H.-W., Prehistory and Early History
DANN, O., Modern History
DIEM, W., Islamic Studies
DIMMENDAAL, G. J., African Studies
DRUX, R., Modern German Literature
DÜLFFER, J., Modern History
DÜSING, K., Philosophy
ECK, W., Ancient History
EHMCKE, F., Japanese Studies
ELEY, L., Philosophy
ENGELS, O., Medieval and Modern History
ERICKSON, J., Applied Linguistics
FISCHER, G., Psychology
FISCHER, T., Classical Archaeology
FRISCH, P., Classical Philology
FROST, U., Education

GARCÍA-RAMÓN, J. L., Linguistics
GAUS, J., History of Art
GEYER, P., Romance Philology
GÖRLACH, M., English Philology
GREIVE, A., Romance Philology
GROEBEN, N., Psychology
GRONEWALD, M., Classical Philology
GÜNTHER, R., Musicology
HEINE, B., African Studies
HEUSER, R., Chinese Law
HÖHN, H.-J., Catholic Theology
HOLKESKAMP, K.-J., Early History
HUSSY, W., Psychology
ISENMANN, E., Medieval History
JÄRVENTAUSTA, M., Finnish Studies
JENAL, G., Medieval History
KABLITZ, A., Romance Philology
KAEHLER, K., Philosophy
KÄMPER, D., Musicology
KAPP, D. B., Indology and Tamil Studies
KINDERMANN, U., Medieval Latin
KLEINSCHMIDT, E., Modern German Literature
KREUTZER, G., Nordic Philology
KUNISCH, J., Medieval and Modern History
KWASMAN, T., Jewish Studies
LEBEK, W. D., Classical Philology
LENERZ, J., German Philology
LIEBRAND, C., Modern German Literature and Gender Studies
MANUWALD, B., Classical Philology
MERTENS, G., Education
NEUHAUS, V., Modern German and Comparative Literature
NEUMEIER, B., English Philology
NITSCH, W., Romance Philology
NUSSBAUM, N., Art History and Urban Conservation
OBST, U., Slavonic Philology
OST, H., Art History
PAPE, W., Modern German Philology
PETERS, U., Medieval German Literature
PLÖGER, W., Education
POTTHAST, B., Latin American History
PRIMUS, B., German Linguistics
ROLSHOVEN, J., Philological and Linguistic Computing
RÜPPELL, H., Education
SALBER, W., Psychology
SASSE, H.-J., Comparative Linguistics
SCHARPING, T., Sinology
SCHMIDT, C., East European History
SCHMIDT-DENTER, U., Psychology
SCHNEIDER, I., Theatre, Film and Television Studies
SCHNEIDER, W., Education
SCHUMACHER, R., Musicology
SEIFERT, U., Musicology
STEPHAN, E., Psychology
STRUVE, T., Medieval History
TAUCHMANN, K., Ethnology
THALLER, M., Informatics in Historical and Cultural Studies
THISSEN, H. J., Egyptology
ULLMANN, H.-P., Modern History
VON GRAEVENITZ, A., Art History
VON HESBERG, H., Classical Archaeology
VON WEIHER, E., Ancient Oriental Philology
WIENBRUCH, U., Philosophy
ZAHRNT, M., Early History
ZELINSKY, B., Slavonic Philology
ZEUSKE, M., Iberian and Latin American History
ZICK, G., Art History
ZIEGELER, H. J., Medieval German Literature
ZIMMERMANN, A., Prehistory and Early History

Faculty of Special Education (tel. (221) 4704640; fax (221) 4705953; internet www .uni-koeln.de/hp-fak):

BUCHKREMER, H., General Therapy and Social Education
CONINX, F., Education of the Deaf and Hard of Hearing

DREHER, W., Education of the Mentally Handicapped
FENGLER, J., Psychology
FISCHER, K., Physical Education
FORNEFELD, B., Education of the Mentally Handicapped
KIRFEL, B., Sociology of the Handicapped
LAUTH, G., Psychology and Psychotherapy
LIST, G., Psychology
MASENDORF, F., Special Education and Rehabilitation of the Educationally Subnormal
OSKAMP, U., Education of the Physically Handicapped
PIEL, W., Music Therapy
SCHLEIFFER, R., Psychiatry and Psychotherapy
SEIFERT, R., Education of the Physically Handicapped
TSCHERNER, K. W. H., Teaching of the Educationally Subnormal
WEINWURM-KRAUSE, E.-M., Psychology and Psychiatry
WICHELHAUS, B., Art Therapy
WILLAND, H., Special Education and Rehabilitation of the Educationally Subnormal
WISOTZKI, K. H., Education of the Deaf and Hard of Hearing
WÖRNER, G., Arts and Crafts

UNIVERSITÄT ZU LÜBECK
(University of Lübeck)

Ratzeburger Allee 160, 23538 Lübeck

Telephone: (451) 5000

Fax: (451) 5003016

E-mail: presse@uni-luebeck.de

Internet: www.uni-luebeck.de

Founded 1973 as Medizinische Universität zu Lübeck, present name and status 2002

State control

Rector: Prof. Dr PETER DOMINIAK
Vice-Pres.: Prof. Dr ENNO HARTMANN
Vice-Pres.: Prof. Dr GABRIELE GILLESSEN-KAESBACH
Vice-Pres.: Prof. Dr THOMAS MARTINETZ
Chancellor: Dr OLIVER GRUNDEI
Librarian: RENA GIESE

Number of teachers: 232

Number of students: 2,500

Publications: *Focus MUL* (4 a year), *Forschungsbericht*

Directors of Institutes

Medicine:

Anaesthesiology: Prof. Dr PETER SCHMUCKER
Anatomy: Prof. Dr JÜRGEN WESTERMANN
Biometry and Statistics: Prof. Dr ANDREAS ZIEGLER
Cardiology: Prof. Dr HANS-HINRICH SIEVERS
Child Psychology: Prof. Dr ULRICH KNÖLKER
Clinical Chemistry: Prof. Dr MICHAEL SEYFARTH
Clinical Rheumatology: Prof. Dr WOLFGANG L. GROSS
Dermatology: Prof. Dr DETLEF ZILLIKENS
Ear, Nose and Throat: Prof. Dr BARBARA WOLLENBERG
Experimental and Clinical Pharmacology and Toxicology: Prof. Dr PETER DOMINIAK
Gynaecology and Childbirth: Prof. Dr KLAUS DIEDRICH
Human Genetics: Prof. Dr GABRIELE GILLESSEN-KAESBACH
Immunology and Transfusion Medicine: Prof. Dr HOLGER KIRCHNER
Jaw and Facial Surgery: Prof. Dr Dr PETER SIEG
Medical Clinic: Prof. Dr WERNER SOLBACH

Medical Clinic I: Prof. Dr HORST LORENZ FEHM

Medical Clinic II: Prof. Dr HERIBERT SCHUNKERT

Medial Clinic III: Prof. Dr PETER ZABEL

Medical Psychology: Prof. Dr Dr FRITZ SCHMIELAU

Molecular Medicine: Prof. Dr GEORG SCZAKIEL

Neuroendocrinology: Prof. Dr JAN BORN

Neurology: Prof. Dr FRITZ HOHAGEN

Neuroradiology: Prof. Dr DIRK PETERSEN

Neurosurgery: Prof. Dr VOLKER TRONNIER

Occupational Medicine: Prof. Dr Dr RICHARD KESSEL

Ophthalmology: Prof. Dr HORST LAQUA

Orthopaedics: Dr MARTIN RUSSLIES

Paediatric Surgery: Prof. Dr LUCAS WESSEL

Paediatrics: Prof. Dr EGBERT HERTING

Pathology: Prof. Dr ALFRED CHRISTIAN FELLER

Physiology: Prof. Dr WOLFGANG JELKMANN

Plastic Surgery: Prof. Dr PETER MAILÄNDER

Psychosomatic Illnesses: Prof. Dr DETLEV-O. NUTZINGER

Radiology and Nuclear Medicine: Prof. Dr THOMAS HELMBERGER

Radiotherapy: Prof. Dr JÜRGEN DUNST

Research Centre Borstel: Prof. Dr Dr SILVIA BULFONE-PAUS

Social Medicine: Prof. Dr Dr HANS-HEINRICH RASPE

Surgery: Prof. Dr HANS-PETER BRUCH

Urology: Prof. Dr DIETER JOCHAM

Science and Technology:

Biochemistry: Prof. Dr ROLF HILGENFELD

Biology: Prof. Dr ENNO HARTMANN

Biomedical Optics: Prof. Dr REGINALD BIRNGRUBER

Chemistry: Prof. Dr THOMAS PETERS

Information Systems: Prof. Dr VOLKER LINNEMANN

International School of New Media: Prof. Dr JOACHIM HASEBROOK

Mathematics: Prof. Dr JÜRGEN PRESTIN

Medical Computing: Prof. Dr SIEGFRIED J. PÖPPL

Molecular Biology: Prof. Dr PETER KARL MÜLLER

Multimedia and Interactive Systems: Prof. Dr MICHAEL HERCZEG

Neuro- and Bioinformatics: Prof. Dr THOMAS MARTINETZ

Physics: Prof. Dr ALFRED X. TRAUTWEIN

Robotics and Cognitive Systems: Prof. Dr ACHIM SCHWEIKARD

Software and Program Languages: Prof. Dr WALTER DOSCH

Technical Informatics: Prof. Dr ERIK MAEHLE

Telematics: Prof. Dr STEFAN FISCHER

Theoretical Computing: Prof. Dr RÜDIGER K. REISCHUK

PROFESSORS

Faculty of Medicine:

ARNOLD, H., Neurosurgery

BRUCH, H.-P., Surgery

DIEDRICH, K., Gynaecology and Obstetrics

DOMARUS, H., Maxillary and Facial Surgery

DOMINIAK, P., Pharmacology, Toxicology and Clinical Pharmacology

FEHM, H. L., Internal Medicine

FELLER, A. C., Pathology

GROSS, W. L., Rheumatology

HALSBAND, H., Paediatric Surgery

HOHAGEN, F., Psychiatry

JELKMANN, W., Physiology

JOCHAM, D., Urology

KATUS, H. A., Internal Medicine

KESSEL, R., Industrial Medicine

KIRCHNER, H., Immunology and Transfusional Medicine

KNÖLKER, U., Child and Adolescent Psychiatry

KÖMPF, D., Neurology

KRUSE, K., Paediatrics

LAQUA, H., Ophthalmology

LÖHR, J., Orthopaedics

OEHMICHEN, M., Forensic Medicine

RASPE, H.-H., Social Medicine

RICHTER, E., Radiotherapy and Nuclear Medicine

SCHMIELAU, F., Medical Psychology

SCHMUCKER, P., Anaesthesiology

SCHWINGER, E., Human Genetics

SCZAKIEL, G., Molecular Medicine

SEYFARTH, M., Clinical Chemistry

SIEVERS, H. H., Cardiac Surgery

SOLBACH, W., Medical Microbiology and Hygiene

WEERDA, H., Otolaryngology

WEISS, H.-D., Radiology

WESTERMANN, J., Anatomy

WOLFF, H. H., Dermatology and Venereology

Faculty of Science and Technology:

AACH, T., Signal Processing and Process Control

DOSCH, W., Software Engineering

DÜMBGEN, L., Mathematics

ENGELHARDT, D., History of Medicine and Science

FISCHER, B., Mathematics

HARTMANN, E., Biology

HERCZEG, M., Multimedia and Interactive Systems

HOGREFE, D., Telematics

KONECNY, E., Medical Technology

LINNEMANN, V., Practical Informatics

MAEHLE, E., Computer Engineering

MARTINETZ, TH., Neuro- and Bioinformatics

MÜLLER, K.-P., Medical Molecular Biology

PETERS, TH., Chemistry

PÖPPL, S., Medical Informatics and Statistics

PRESTIN, J., Mathematics

REISCHUK, K. R., Theoretical Computer Science

RIETSCHEL, E.-TH., Immunochemistry and Biochemical Microbiology

ROELCKE, V., History of Medicine and Science

SCHÄFER, G., Biochemistry

TRAUTWEIN, A., Physics

VOSWINCKEL, P., History of Medicine and Science

ZEUGMANN, TH., Theoretical Computer Science

WESTFÄLISCHE WILHELMS-UNIVERSITÄT MÜNSTER

Schlosspl. 2, 48149 Münster

Telephone: (251) 830

Fax: (251) 8332090

E-mail: verwaltung@uni-muenster.de

Internet: www.uni-muenster.de

Founded 1780, became Acad. in 1818; Univ. status again in 1902

State control

Academic year: October to July (two terms)

Rector: Prof. Dr URSULA NELLES

Vice-Rector for Int. Affairs and Young Researchers: Prof. Dr CORNELIA DENZ

Vice-Rector for Research: Prof. Dr STEPHAN LUDWIG

Vice-Rector for Strategic Planning and Quality Assurance: Prof. Dr JÖRG BECKER

Vice-Rector for Teaching, Reform of Studies and Student Affairs: Dr MARIANNE RAVENSTEIN

Chancellor: Dr STEFAN SCHWARTZE

Library: see Libraries and Archives

Number of teachers: 526

Number of students: 36,027

DEANS

Faculty of Biology: Prof. Dr CHRISTIAN KLÄMBT

Faculty of Business, Economics and Information Systems: Prof. Dr THOMAS APOLTE

Faculty of Catholic Theology: Prof. Dr REINHARD HOEPS

Faculty of Chemistry and Pharmacy: Prof. Dr ANDREAS HENSEL

Faculty of Education and Social Studies: Prof. Dr VOLKER GEHRAU

Faculty of Geosciences: Prof. Dr HANS KERP

Faculty of History/Philosophy: Prof. Dr JÜRGEN HEIDRICH

Faculty of Law: Prof. Dr HANS-MICHAEL WOLFFGANG

Faculty of Mathematics and Computer Sciences: Prof. Dr MATTHIAS LÖWE

Faculty of Medicine: Prof. Dr WILHELM SCHMITZ

Faculty of Philology: Prof. Dr CHRISTOPH STROSETZKI

Faculty of Physics: Prof. Dr TILMANN KUHN

Faculty of Protestant Theology: Prof. Dr KONRAD HAMMANN

Faculty of Psychology and Sport Studies: Prof. Dr MARKUS LAPPE

Faculty of Roman Catholic Theology: Prof. Dr KLAUS MÜLLER

Music School: Prof. MICHAEL KELLER

WHU—OTTO BEISHEIM SCHOOL OF MANAGEMENT

Burgpl. 2, 56179 Vallendar

Telephone: (261) 65090

Fax: (261) 6509509

E-mail: whu@whu.edu

Internet: www.whu.edu

Founded 1984

Private control

Languages of instruction: German, English

Academic year: September to August

Rector: Prof. Dr MICHAEL FRENKEL

Pro-Rector: Prof. Dr MARKUS RUDOLF

Chancellor: Dr PETER STOMBERG

Librarian: HANNELORE PÖTHIG

Library of 40,300 vols, 250 journals

Number of teachers: 125

Number of students: 757

PROFESSORS

BAEDORF, K.

BREXENDORF, T. O.

CZERNY, A.

EHRGOTT, M

EINST, H.

FASSNACHT, M., Marketing and Commerce

FENDEL, R., Monetary Economics

FISCHER, T.

FRENKEL, M., Macroeconomics and Int. Economics

GRICHNIK, D., Entrepreneurship

HACK, A.

HÖFFLER, F., Regulatory Economics

HÖGL, M., Leadership and Human Resource Management

HOZOG, W.

HÜSCHELRATH, K.

HUCHZERMEIER, A., Production Management

HUTZSCHENREUTER, T., Corporate Strategy and Electronic Media Management

JENSEN, O., Business-to-Business Marketing

JOHANNING, L., Empirical Capital Market Research

JOST, P.-J., Organization Theory

KAUFMANN, L., Int. Business and Supply Management

KLEIN, S.

KLEINDIENST, I., Strategy Processes

LAMMERS, C., Corporate Finance

LICHTENTHALER, U.

MAHLENDORF, M.

NÖLDEKE, M., Finance

REHM, S.-V., Business Information Science and Information Management
REIMANN, F.
RUDOLF, F., Organization Theory
RÜLKE, J.-C.
SCHÄFFER, U., Management Accounting and Control
SCHAUZ, D.
SCHUBERT, S.
SCHWEIZER, D.
SELLHORN, T.
SPINLER, S.
WEBER, J., Controlling and Telecommunications
WEIGAND, J., Microeconomics and Industrial Organization

Colleges

GENERAL

ESCP Europe Wirtschaftshochschule Berlin (ESCP Europe Business School Berlin): Heubnerweg 6, 14059 Berlin; tel. (30) 320070; fax (30) 32007111; e-mail info.de@escpeurope.eu; internet www.escpeurope.eu; f. 1985; campuses in France, UK, Germany, Italy, and Spain; masters and doctoral programmes in business admin. and management; 125 teachers; Rector Prof. Dr AYAD AL-ANI; Pro-Rector Prof. Dr ULRICH PAPE; Library Dir REGINA GOLLNICK.

Frankfurt School of Finance and Management: Sonnemannstr. 9–11, 60314 Frankfurt am Main; tel. (69) 1540080; fax (69) 1540084135; e-mail info@frankfurt-school.de; internet www.frankfurt-school.de; f. 1957; bachelors, masters and doctoral programmes in finance and management; 1,800 teachers; 7,800 students; Pres. Prof. Dr UDO STEFFENS; Sec. and Man. Dir INGOLF JUNGMANN; Vice-Pres for Research Prof. Dr HARTMUT KLIEMT; Vice-Pres. for Teaching Prof. Dr MICHAEL H. GROTE.

Handelshochschule Leipzig (HHL) (Leipzig Graduate School of Management): Jahnallee 59, 04109 Leipzig; tel. (341) 985160; fax (341) 9851679; e-mail info@hhl.de; internet www.hhl.de; f. 1898; full-time, part-time masters and doctoral programmes in business and management; Rector Prof. Dr ANDREAS PINKWART; Chancellor Dr AXEL BAISCH; Head Librarian ANDREA LIEB.

Internationales Hochschulinstitut Zittau (IHI) (International Graduate School Zittau): Markt 23, 02763 Zittau; tel. (83) 612700; fax (83) 612734; e-mail info@ihi-zittau.de; internet www.ihi-zittau.de; f. 1993; interdisciplinary and int. masters and doctoral programmes; library: 170,306 vols; 200 students; Rector Prof. Dr Hab. ALBERT LÖHR; Pro-Rector for Research Prof. Dr Hab. MARTIN HOFRICHTER; Chancellor KARIN HOLLSTEIN (acting).

Schiller International University – Germany: Bergstr. 106, 69121 Heidelberg; tel. (6221) 45810; fax (6221) 402703; e-mail campus@siu-heidelberg.de; internet www.siu-heidelberg.de; f. 1964 as independent int. univ.; language of instruction: English (all campuses); campuses in France, Germany, Spain, Switzerland, UK and USA (for which see respective chapters); depts of commercial art, computer studies, engineering management, int. business, int. tourism and hospitality management, int. relations and diplomacy, literature, para-legal studies, pre-medicine; degrees at Florida (USA) campus conferred under charter granted by State of Florida; degrees at all other campuses conferred under charter granted by State of Delaware (USA); library: 10,000 vols (total for all campuses); 25 teachers (Heidelberg campus only); 1,519 students (total for all campuses, of which 210 at Heidelberg campus); Dir THOMAS LEIBRECHT.

Wissenschaftskolleg zu Berlin (Institute for Advanced Study): Wallotstr. 19, 14193 Berlin; tel. (30) 890010; fax (30) 89001300; e-mail wiko@wiko-berlin.de; internet www.wiko-berlin.de; f. 1980; private instn for int. and interdisciplinary post-doctoral research; 40 Fellows; library mainly reference colln; Rector Prof. Dr LUCA GIULIANI; Sec. Dr JOACHIM NETTELBECK; Head Librarian Dr SONJA GRUND; publs *Jahrbuch* (yearbook), *Köpfe und Ideen* (1 a year).

ART, ARCHITECTURE

Akademie der Bildenden Künste (Academy of Fine Arts): Akademiestr. 2–4, 80799 Munich; tel. (89) 38520; fax (89) 3852206; e-mail post@adbk.mhn.de; internet www.adbk.de; f. 1770 (Charter conferred 1808 and 1953); languages of instruction: German, English; library: 122,000 vols, 100 current periodicals; 35 professors; 700 students; Chancellor (vacant); Vice-Chancellor PETER SACHER; Librarian INGE SICKLINGER-SEUß; Librarian SABINE MUSKE.

Akademie der Bildenden Künste in Nürnberg (Academy of Fine Arts in Nuremberg): Bingstr. 60, 90480 Nuremberg; tel. (911) 94040; fax (911) 9404150; e-mail info@adbk-nuernberg.de; internet www.adbk-nuernberg.de; f. 1662; master and postgraduate courses; arts, sculpture, visual arts, painting, artistic concepts, art education, gold- and silversmithing, graphic design, art history; library: 26,200 vols; 27 teachers; 350 students; Pres. Prof. OTTMAR HÖRL; Vice-Pres. Prof. Dr CHRISTIAN DEMAND; Vice-Pres. Prof. HOLGER FELTEN; Chancellor PETER OCHS; Vice-Chancellor UTE GRÖTSCH; Librarian MARTINA KEMMSIES.

Bauhaus Kolleg: see entry for Bauhaus Dessau Foundation.

Deutsche Film- und Fernsehakademie Berlin GmbH (German Film and Television Academy, Berlin GmbH): Potsdamer Str. 2, 10785 Berlin; tel. (30) 257590; fax (30) 25759161; e-mail info@dffb.de; internet www.dffb.de; f. 1966; 40 teachers; 250 students; library: 80,000 vols; Dir Prof. JAN SCHÜTTE.

Hochschule für Bildende Künste Braunschweig (Braunschweig University of Art): Johannes-Selenka-Pl. 1, 38118 Brunswick; tel. (531) 3919122; fax (531) 3919307; e-mail hbk@hbk-bs.de; internet www.hbk-bs.de; f. 1963; depts of art (painting, graphics, sculpture, film, video, performing arts and photography), design (industrial and graphic), art teaching, art history; institute for media and film studies, institute for art history and visual research; languages of instruction: German, English; Pres. Prof. Dr HUBERTUS VON AMELUNXEN; Vice-Pres. GERHARD BALLER; Vice-Pres. RAIMUND KUMMER; Vice-Pres. ULI PLANK; Vice-Pres. ULRIKE BERGERMANN; library: 120,000 vols; 1,200 students; publs *Schriftenreihe* (3–5 a year), *Vorlesungsverzeichnis/Studienführer* (2 a year).

Hochschule für Bildende Künste Dresden: POB 16 01 53, 01287 Dresden; Güntzstr. 34, 01307 Dresden; tel. (351) 492670; fax (351) 4952023; e-mail rektorat@serv1.hfbk-dresden.de; internet www.hfbk-dresden.de; f. 1764; stage and theatre design, costume design, painting, sculpture, graphics, restoration, art therapy; languages of instruction: German, English; library: 55,000 vols, 112 periodicals; 31 teachers; 650 students; Rector Prof. CHRISTIAN SERY; Pro-Rector Prof. ELKE HOPFE; Pro-Rector Prof. JENS BÜTTNER; Chancellor HANS-JÜRGEN SCHÖNEMANN; Head Librarian KARIN HUß; Librarian CHRISTINE POSSEGGA.

Hochschule für Bildende Künste Hamburg: Lerchenfeld 2, 22081 Hamburg; tel. (428) 989264; fax (428) 989271; e-mail presse@hfbk.hamburg.de; internet www.hfbk-hamburg.de; f. 1767, present name and status 1955; depts of design, film, graphic art, typography, photography, painting, drawing, sculpture, stage design, theory and history of art, time-based media; Pres. MARTIN KÖTTERING; Vice-Pres. Dr HANNE LORECK; Vice-Pres. RAIMUND BAUER; Chancellor HORST-VOLKERT THIEL; Head Librarian INES RABE.

Hochschule für Grafik und Buchkunst Leipzig (Academy of Visual Arts, Leipzig): Wächterstr. 11, 04107 Leipzig; tel. (341) 21350; fax (341) 2135-166; e-mail hgb@hgb-leipzig.de; internet www.hgb-leipzig.de; f. 1764 as Zeichnungs-, Mahlerey und Architectur-Akademie, present name 1950; painting, graphic arts, book art, graphic design, photography, media art; 48 teachers; 600 students; library: 40,000 vols, 100 current periodicals; Rector Prof. JOACHIM BROHM; Chancellor MARIA-CORNELIA ZIESCH; Librarian CLAUDIA-MARIA DARMER.

Hochschule für Künste Bremen (University of the Arts Bremen): Am Speicher XI 8, 28217 Bremen; tel. (421) 95951000; fax (421) 95952000; e-mail studsek@hfk-bremen.de; internet www.hfk-bremen.de; f. 1988; library: 40,000 vols; 265 teachers; 900 students; Rector Prof. Dr MANFRED CORDES; Chancellor REGINE OKORO.

Kunstakademie Düsseldorf (Academy of Fine Art, Düsseldorf): Eiskellerstr. 1, 40213 Düsseldorf; tel. (211) 13960; fax (211) 1396225; e-mail postmaster@kunstakademie-duesseldorf.de; internet www.kunstakademie-duesseldorf.de; f. 1773; 50 teachers; 700 students; library: 110,000 vols; Rector Prof. ANTHONY CRAGG; Pro-Rector Prof. Dr SIEGFRIED GOHR; Pro-Rector Prof. GEORG HEROLD; Chancellor DIETRICH KOSKA.

Kunsthochschule Berlin-Weissensee, Hochschule für Gestaltung (Berlin Weissensee School of Art): Bühringstr. 20, 13086 Berlin; tel. (30) 477050; fax (30) 47705290; e-mail rektor@kh-berlin.de; internet www.kh-berlin.de; f. 1946; fine arts, industrial design, ceramics, fashion design, textile design, communication design, architecture, stage design, sculpture; 550 students; 39 teachers; library: 20,000 vols; Rector LEONIE BAUMANN; Pro-Rector Prof. ELSE GABRIEL; Pro-Rector Prof. CAROLA ZWICK; Chancellor SILVIA DURIN.

Staatliche Akademie der Bildenden Künste: POB 6267, 76042 Karlsruhe; Reinhold-Frank-Str. 67, 76133 Karlsruhe; tel. (721) 9265210; fax (721) 9265213; e-mail rektorat@kunstakademie-karlsruhe.de; internet www.kunstakademie-karlsruhe.de; f. 1854; art education, fine arts, drawing, painting, sculpture; library: 40,000 vols; 300 students; Rector Prof. ERWIN GROSS; Chancellor RÜDIGER WEIS; Librarian RENATE WINKLER-WILDE.

Staatliche Akademie der Bildenden Künste (Stuttgart State Academy of Art and Design): Am Weissenhof 1, 70191 Stuttgart; tel. (711) 284400; fax (711) 28440225; e-mail rektorat@abk-stuttgart.de; internet www.abk-stuttgart.de; f. 1761; art, graphics, sculpture, architecture, design, conservation, ceramics, textiles and industrial design; 850 students; Rector PETRA VON OLSCHOWSKI; Pro-Rector Prof. Dr NILS BÜTTNER; Pro-Rector Prof. TOBIAS WALLISSER; Pro-Rector Prof.

VOLKER LEHNERT; Chancellor Dr MATTHIAS KNAPP.

Staatliche Hochschule für Bildende Künste–Städelschule: Dürerstr. 10, 60596 Frankfurt; tel. (69) 6050080; fax (69) 60500827; e-mail rektor@staedelschule.de; internet www.staedelschule.de; f. 1817; art, architecture, film, sculpture, painting, drawing, architecture (conceptual design); 9 profs; 150 students; library: 16,000 vols; Pres. Prof. Dr FELIX SEMMELROTH; Rector Prof. Dr NIKOLAUS HIRSCH; Dir for Admin. ANDREAS LENK; Librarian KAREN LA MACCHIA.

ECONOMICS, POLITICAL AND SOCIAL SCIENCES, PUBLIC ADMINISTRATION

Hochschule für Politik München: Ludwigstr. 8, 80539 Munich; tel. (89) 285018; fax (89) 283705; e-mail hfp-muenchen@hfp.mhn.de; internet www.hfp.mhn.de; f. 1950, present status 1981; theory of politics, law, economics, int. politics and contemporary history; library: 45,000 vols; 150 teachers; 950 students; Rector Prof. Dr RUPERT STETTNER; Pro-Rector Dr HORST MAHR; Librarian Dr BERND MAYERHOFER; publs *Junge Wissenschaft* (irregular), *Schriftenreihe* (irregular), *Zeitschrift für Politik* (4 a year).

Hochschule für Rechtswissenschaft (Bucerius Law School): POB 30 10 30, 20304 Hamburg; Jungiusstr. 6, 20355 Hamburg; tel. (40) 307060; fax (40) 30706145; e-mail info@law-school.de; internet www.law-school.de; f. 2000; doctoral and post-doctoral courses in law; library: 90,000 vols; 23 teachers; 561 students; Pres. Prof. Dr KARSTEN SCHMIDT; Vice-Pres. Prof. Dr FLORIAN FAUST; CEO Dr HARIOLF WENZLER; Library Dir MARTIN VORBERG.

Stuttgart Institute of Management and Technology: Filderhauptstr. 142, 70599 Stuttgart; tel. (711) 4510010; fax (711) 45100145; e-mail information@uni-simt.de; internet www.uni-simt.de; f. 1998; MBA in int. management, finance and investment, management information systems, technology and innovation management; int. exec. MBA; part-time programmes; 68 teachers (8 full-time, 60 part-time); 150 students; CEO Prof. Dr JOHANN LÖHN.

LANGUAGES

Akademie für Fremdsprachen GmbH – private Fachschule (Academy of Foreign Languages — private School): POB 15 01 04, 10663 Berlin; Lietzenburger Str. 102, 10707 Berlin; tel. (30) 88663393; fax 88663394; e-mail post@akafremd.de; internet www.akafremd.de; f. 1971; translators' and interpreters' courses in German, English, French, Spanish, Italian, Russian, and courses in German as a foreign language; 1,600 students; Man. Dir NORBERT ZÄNKER.

MEDICINE

Medizinische Akademie Erfurt: Nordhäuser Str. 74, PSF 595, 99089 Erfurt; tel. (361) 790; fax 23697; f. 1954; 121 teachers; 750 students; library: 140,000 vols; Rector Prof. Dr W. KÜNZEL; Pro-Rector Prof. Dr G. ENDERT; Medical Dir Prof. Dr W. KRAFFT; Librarian Dr B. ADLUNG.

MUSIC AND DRAMA

Filmakademie Baden-Württemberg (Baden-Württemberg Film Academy): Akademiehof 10, 71638 Ludwigsburg; tel. (7141) 9690; fax (7141) 969299; e-mail info@filmakademie.de; internet www.filmakademie.de; f. 1991; full-time programmes in film and media, production,

sound design; 300 teachers; Dir Prof. THOMAS SCHADT.

Hochschule für Musik (University of Music): 79095 Freiburg im Breisgau; Schwarzwaldstr. 141, 79102 Freiburg im Breisgau; tel. (761) 319150; fax (761) 3191542; e-mail info@mh-freiburg.de; internet www.mh-freiburg.de; f. 1946; bachelor, postgraduate and doctoral courses in music; 160 teachers; 540 students; Chair. Dr OTMAR ZWIEBELHOFER; Rector Dr RÜDIGER NOLTE; Vice-Rector Prof. HELMUT LÖRSCHER; Vice-Rector Prof. SCOTT SANDMEIER.

Hochschule für Musik (University of Music Wuerzburg): Hofstallstr. 6–8, 97070 Würzburg; tel. (931) 321870; fax (931) 321872800; e-mail hochschule@hfm-wuerzburg.de; internet www.hfm-wuerzburg.de; f. 1804; bachelor, postgraduate, doctorate, pre-college programmes in music; library: 14,200 vols, 45,400 music scores, 47 current periodicals; 220 teachers; 597 students; library: 14,300 vols; Pres. Prof. HELMUT ERB; Vice-Pres. Prof. Dr THOMAS MÜNCH; Vice-Pres. THEODOR NÜßLEIN; Chancellor Dr EVA STUMPF-WIRTHS; Librarian BARBARA KONRAD.

Hochschule für Musik 'Carl Maria von Weber' Dresden: POB 12 00 39, 01001 Dresden; Wettiner Pl. 13, 01067 Dresden; tel. (351) 4923600; fax (351) 4923657; e-mail rektorat@hfmdd.de; internet www.hfmdd.de; f. 1856; library: 80,000 vols, 7,000 records and CDs, contains Heinrich-Schütz archive; 80 teachers; 631 students; attached institute for musicology (in co-operation with the Heinrich-Schütz Archive), institute for music medicine, studio for voice research, studio for electronic music; Rector EKKEHARD KLEMM; Pro-Rector for Artistic Practice Prof. ANDREAS BAUMANN; Pro-Rector for Education and Studies Prof. ELISABETH HOLMER; publ. *Schriftenreihe der Hochschule für Musik* (irregular).

Hochschule für Musik Detmold: Neustadt 22, 32756 Detmold; tel. (5231) 9755; fax (5231) 975972; e-mail info@hfm-detmold.de; internet www.hfm-detmold.de; f. 1946; library: 157,800 vols; 120 teachers; 580 students; Rector Prof. MARTIN CHRISTIAN VOGEL; Vice-Rector Prof. ANDRÉ STÄRK; Vice-Rector Prof. NORBERT STERTZ; Chancellor HANS BERTELS.

Hochschule für Musik 'Franz Liszt' Weimar (Franz Liszt School of Music Weimar): POB 2552, 99406 Weimar; Pl. der Demokratie 2/3, 99423 Weimar; tel. (3643) 5550; fax (3643) 555188; e-mail study@hfm-weimar.de; internet www.hfm-weimar.de; f. 1872, present name 1956; instruction in: keyboard, string and wind instruments, accordion, guitar, jazz/pop instruments and vocal, composition, conducting, singing and music teaching, church music and musicology; 132 teachers; 950 students; library: 65,000 vols and 45,000 tapes; Pres. Prof. Dr CHRISTOPH STÖLZL; Vice-Pres. for Teaching Prof. Dr HELMUT WELL; Vice-Pres. for Performance Studies Prof. ELMAR FULDA; Chancellor CHRISTINE GURK (acting).

Hochschule für Musik 'Hanns Eisler': Charlottenstr. 55, 10117 Berlin; tel. (30) 90269700; fax (30) 90269701; e-mail rektorat@hfm.in-berlin.de; internet www.hfm-berlin.de; f. 1950 as German Academy of Music, present name 1964; depts of voice, music, stage and theatre direction; strings, harp and guitar; brass, woodwind, percussion and conducting; and piano, accordion and composition/harmony; 433 teachers (113 full-time, 320 part-time); 702 students; Rector Prof. JÖRG-PETER WEIGLE; Pro-Rector Prof. JÖRG MAINKA; Pro-Rector GERT MÜLLER;

Chancellor HANS-JOACHIM VÖLZ; Librarian HILDEGARD KLEEBAUM.

Hochschule für Musik Karlsruhe (University of Music Karlsruhe): POB 6040, 76040 Karlsruhe; Am Schloss Gottesaue 7, 76131 Karlsruhe; tel. (721) 66290; fax (721) 6629266; internet www.hfm-karlsruhe.de; f. 1884; library: 115,000 vols; 200 teachers; 560 students; Rector Prof. HARTMUT HÖLL; Pro-Rector Prof. ANDREA RAABE; Rector Prof. Dr JOHANNES M. WALTER; Pro-Rector Prof. MICHAEL UHDE; Chancellor WOLFRAM SCHERER; Library Dir MARC WEISSER (acting).

Hochschule für Musik Nürnberg: Veilhofstr. 34, 90489 Nuremberg; tel. (911) 2318443; fax (911) 2317697; e-mail hfm-praesidium@hfm-nuernberg.de; internet www.hfm-n-a.de; f. 1873 as Leopold Mozart Konservatorium; present name 1999; int. college of higher education; concerts, productions, International Leopold Mozart Competition for Young Violinists, Studio for Old and New Music; library: 9,000 vols; 98 teachers; 400 students; Pres. Prof. MARTIN ULLRICH; Vice-Pres. Prof. Dr RENATE ULLRICH; Vice-Pres. ALFONS BRANDL; Chancellor HANS-WERNER ITTMANN.

Hochschule für Musik Saar (University of Music Saar): Bismarckstr. 1, 66111 Saarbrücken; tel. (681) 967310; fax (681) 9673130; e-mail presse@hfm.saarland.de; internet www.hfm.saarland.de; f. 1947; 120 teachers; 400 students; library: 82,000 vols; Rector Prof. THOMAS DUIS; Pro-Rector Prof. JÖRG NONNWEILER; Chancellor WOLFGANG BOGLER; Librarian EDGAR COUDRAY.

Hochschule für Musik, Theater und Medien Hannover (University of Music, Drama and Media Hanover): Emmichpl. 1, 30175 Hanover; tel. (511) 31001; fax (511) 3100200; e-mail hmt@hmtm-hannover.de; internet www.hmt-hannover.de; f. 1961; courses of training for musicians, actors, music teachers, musicologists and media scientists; 350 teachers; 1,400 students; library: 203,000 vols; Pres. Prof. Dr SUSANNE RODE-BREYMANN; Vice-Pres. Prof. Dr BEATE SCHNEIDER; Vice-Pres. Prof. GUDRUN SCHRÖFEL; Vice-Pres. JANN BRUNS; Vice-Pres. Prof. MARKUS BECKER; Vice-Pres. Prof. VOLKER JACOBSEN.

Hochschule für Musik und Darstellende Kunst Frankfurt am Main (Frankfurt University of Music and Performing Arts (HfMDK)): Eschersheimer Landstr. 29–39, 60322 Frankfurt am Main; tel. (69) 1540070; fax (69) 154007108; e-mail praesident@hfmdk-frankfurt.de; internet www.hfmdk-frankfurt.info; f. 1878 as Konservatorium, Hochschule since 1938; music, dance, drama; library: 100,000 vols; 385 teachers; 900 students; Pres. Prof. THOMAS RIETSCHEL; Chancellor ANGELIKA GARTNER; Librarian Dr ANDREAS ODENKIRCHEN.

Hochschule für Musik und Darstellende Kunst Mannheim (University of Music and Performing Arts Mannheim): N 7, 18, 68161 Mannheim; tel. (621) 2923503; fax (621) 2922072; e-mail praesidium@muho-mannheim.de; internet www.muho-mannheim.de; f. 1899; orchestral instruments, keyboard instruments, voice concert and opera, conducting orchestra and choir; 200 teachers; 550 students; Pres. Prof. RUDOLF MEISTER; Vice-Pres. Prof. EHRHARD WETZ; Chancellor THILO FISCHER; Librarian KATHRIN WINTER.

Hochschule für Musik und Tanz Köln: Unter Krahnenbäumen 87, 50668 Cologne; tel. (221) 9128180; fax (221) 131204; e-mail kristin.homeier@hfmt-koeln.de; internet www.mhs-koeln.de; f. 1925, reorganized 2009; centres in Cologne, Aachen and Wuppertal; instrumental music and musicology, dance studies; 330 teachers; 1,800 students; library: 136,000 vols, 8,600 records, 400 films; Pres. Prof. REINER SCHUHENN; Vice-Pres. Prof. Dr HEINZ GEUEN; Vice-Pres. Prof. JOACHIM ULLRICH; Chancellor URSULA WIRTZ-KNAPSTEIN; publ. *Journal* (2 a year).

Hochschule für Musik und Theater (Hamburg University of Music and Theatre): Harvestehuder Weg 12, 20148 Hamburg; tel. (40) 428482201; fax (40) 428482666; e-mail info@hfmt.hamburg.de; internet www .hfmt-hamburg.de; f. 1950; music education, music therapy, musicology, cultural and media management, opera, theatre; library: 20,000 vols; 250 teachers; 750 students; Pres. Prof. ELMAR LAMPSON; Vice-Pres. Prof. Dr MICHAEL VON TROSCHKE; Chancellor BERNHARD LANGE; Librarian MAIKE ARNEMANN; Librarian SILKE BROSE.

Hochschule für Musik und Theater 'Felix Mendelssohn Bartholdy' Leipzig (University of Music & Theatre 'Felix Mendelssohn Bartholdy' Leipzig): POB 10 08 09, 04008 Leipzig; Grassistr. 8, 04107 Leipzig; tel. (341) 214455; fax (341) 2144503; e-mail rektor@hmt-leipzig.de; internet www .hmt-leipzig.de; f. 1843; library: 50,000 vols, 150 current periodicals; 900 students; Rector Prof. ROBERT EHRLICH; Vice-Rector Prof. HANNS-MARTIN SCHREIBER; Vice-Rector Prof. MARTIN KÜRSCHNER; Chancellor OLIVER GRIMM.

Hochschule für Musik und Theater München: Arcisstr. 12, 80333 Munich; tel. (89) 28903; fax (89) 28927419; e-mail verwaltung@musikhochschule-muenchen.de; internet website .musikhochschule-muenchen.de; f. 1846; 300 teachers; 900 students; Pres. Prof. Dr SIEGFRIED MAUSER; Chancellor Dr ALEXANDER KRAUSE.

Internationales Musikinstitut Darmstadt (IMD): Nieder-Ramstäder Str. 190, 64285 Darmstadt; tel. (6151) 132416; fax (6151) 132405; e-mail imd@darmstadt.de; internet www.internationales-musikinstitut .de; f. 1946; int. holiday courses on contemporary music (composition, interpretation); int. music lending library (works since beginning of 20th century) of 35,000 scores, 5,000 vols, 4,000 tapes, 1,500 records; Dir THOMAS SCHÄFER; Assoc. Dir JÜRGEN KREBBER.

Musikhochschule Lübeck (University of Music Lübeck): Grosse Petersgrube 21, 23552 Lübeck; tel. (451) 15050; fax (451) 1505300; e-mail info@mh-luebeck.de; internet www.mh-luebeck.de; f. 1933; musical training on all instruments, opera singing and performing, training of music teachers, sacred music (Protestant and Catholic), preparatory training of professional musicians and music teachers; library: 110,000 vols; 130 teachers; 500 students; Rector Prof. INGE-SUSANN RÖMHILD; Vice-Rector Prof. JÖRG LINOWITZKI; Chancellor JÜRGEN R. CLAUßEN; Librarian TORSTEN SENKBEIL.

Robert-Schumann-Hochschule Düsseldorf (Robert Schumann School of Music and Media): Fischerstr. 110, 40476 Düsseldorf; tel. (211) 49180; fax (211) 4911618; e-mail kontakt@rsh-duesseldorf.de; internet www.rsh-duesseldorf.de; f. 1935; audio and video engineering, media, music, music promotion; languages of instruction: German, English; library: 120,000 vols; 195 teachers; 900 students; Rector Prof. RAIMUND WIPPERMANN; Pro-Rector Prof. Dr VOLKER KALISCH; Pro-Rector Prof. THOMAS LEANDER; Chancellor Dr CATHRIN MÜLLER-BROSCH.

Staatliche Hochschule für Musik und Darstellende Kunst (University of Music and Performing Arts Stuttgart): Urbanstr. 25, 70182 Stuttgart; tel. (711) 2124631; fax (711) 2124632; e-mail rektor@mh-stuttgart .de; internet www.mh-stuttgart.de; f. 1857; 200 teachers; 800 students; library: 127,000 vols; Rector Prof. Dr WERNER HEINRICHS; Pro-Rector Prof. MATTHIAS HERMANN; Pro-Rector Prof. SHOSHANA RUDIAKOV; Chancellor ALBRECHT LANG.

PHILOSOPHY, THEOLOGY

Augustana Hochschule: Waldstr. 11, 91564 Neuendettelsau; tel. (9874) 5090; fax (9874) 509555; e-mail hochschule@ augustana.de; internet www.augustana.de; f. 1947; library: 150,000 vols, 350 periodicals; 30 teachers; 200 students; Rector Prof. Dr MARKUS BUNTFUß; Librarian ARMIN STEPHAN.

Hochschule für Jüdische Studien Heidelberg (HfJS): Landfriedstr. 12, 69117 Heidelberg; tel. (21) 5419200; fax (21) 5419209; e-mail info@hfjs.eu; internet www .hfjs.eu; f. 1979; Jewish studies; library: 50,000 vols, 500 periodicals; 8 profs; First Vice-Rector Prof. Dr JOHANNES HEIL; Library Dir MARGARETHA BOOCKMANN; publs *Mussaf*, *Trumah*.

Hochschule für Philosophie (Munich School of Philosophy): Kaulbachstr. 31A, 80539 Munich; tel. (89) 23862300; fax (89) 23862302; e-mail info@hfph.mwn.de; internet www.hfph.mwn.de; f. 1925; library: 199,000 vols; 20 teachers; 500 students; Pres. Prof. Dr MICHAEL BORDT; Chancellor Dr DINA BRANDT; Librarian Dr JOHANNES BAAR; publ. *Theologie und Philosophie* (4 a year).

Kirchliche Hochschule Wuppertal/Bethel: Missionstr. 9A/B, 42285 Wuppertal; tel. (202) 2820100; fax (202) 2820101; e-mail info@kiho-wuppertal-bethel.de; internet www.kiho-wuppertal-bethel.de; f. 2007 by merger of Kirchlichen Hochschule Bethel (f. 1905) and Kirchlichen Hochschule Wuppertal (f. 1935); Protestant; library: 100,000 vols; 15 teachers; 200 students; Rector Prof. Dr SIEGFRIED KREUZER; Pro-Rector Prof. Dr HENNING WROGEMANN.

Lutherische Theologische Hochschule Oberursel: Altkönigstrasse 150, 61440 Oberursel; tel. (6171) 91270; fax (6171) 912770; e-mail verwaltung@lthh-oberursel .de; internet www.lthh-oberursel.de; f. 1947; library: 40,000 vols, 100 periodicals; 8 teachers; 30 students; Rector Prof. Dr ACHIM BEHRENS; Librarian Prof. Dr GILBERTO DA SILVA; publ. *Lutherische Theologie und Kirche* (4 a year).

Philosophisch-Theologische Hochschule Sankt Georgen (St George Graduate School of Philosophy and Theology): Offenbacher Landstr. 224, 60599 Frankfurt am Main; tel. (69) 60610; fax (69) 6061307; e-mail rektorat@sankt-georgen.de; internet www.sankt-georgen.de; f. 1926 (since 1950 combined with Jesuit Theological Faculty, f. 1863); biblical studies, classical and modern languages, historical theology, philosophy, practical theology, systematic theology; languages of instruction: German, English; library: 421,552 vols, 633 current periodicals, 11,497 e-journals; 23 teachers; 460 students; Chancellor Prof. Dr ADOLFO NICOLÁS; Vice-Chancellor Dr STEFAN KIECHLE; Rector Prof. Dr HEINRICH WATZKA; Pro-Rector Prof. Dr KLAUS KIEßLING; Library Dir MARCUS STARK; publs *Frankfurter Theologische Studien* (2–3 a year), *Sankt Georgener Hochschulschriften* (1 a year), *Theologie und Philosophie* (4 a year).

Theologische Fakultät Fulda (Staatlich anerkannte Wissenschaftliche Hochschule) (Fulda Theology Faculty): Eduard-Schick-Pl. 2, 36037 Fulda; tel. (661) 87220; fax (661) 87224; e-mail rektorat@ thf-fulda.de; internet www.thf-fulda.de; f. 1748; languages of instruction: German, English; library: 200,000 vols, 200 print journals; 20 teachers; 44 students; Rector Prof. Dr Hab. CHRISTOPH GREGOR MÜLLER; Library Dir Dr BERTHOLD JÄGER; publs *Fuldaer Hochschulschriften*, *Fuldaer Studien*.

Theologische Fakultät Paderborn (Faculty of Theology in Paderborn): Kamp 6, 33098 Paderborn; tel. (5251) 1216; fax (5251) 121700; e-mail rektorat@theol-fakultaet-pb .de; internet www.theol-fakultaet-pb.de; f. 1615; library: 260,000 vols, 810 incunabula; 26 teachers; 390 students; Rector Prof. Dr BERTHOLD WALD; Pro-Rector Prof. Dr PETER SCHALLENBERG; publ. *Theologie und Glaube* (4 a year).

Theologische Fakultät Trier: Universitätsring 19, 54296 Trier; tel. (651) 2013520; fax (651) 2013951; e-mail theofak@uni-trier .de; internet www.theo.uni-trier.de; f. 1950; library: 400,000 vols; 20 ordinary professors; 315 students; Chancellor Dr REINHARD MARX (Bishop of Trier); Rector Prof. Dr KLAUS PETER DANNECKER; publ. *Trierer Theologische Zeitschrift* (4 a year).

TECHNOLOGY

Burg Giebichenstein Kunsthochschule Halle (Burg Giebichenstein University of Art and Design Halle): POB 20 02 52, 06003 Halle; Neuwerk 7, 06108 Halle; tel. (345) 775150; fax (345) 7751569; e-mail burgpost@halle.de; internet www.burg-halle .de; f. 1915; language of instruction: German; library: 82,000 vols, 140 journals; 90 teachers; 980 students; Rector Prof. AXEL MÜLLER-SCHÖLL; Vice-Rector Prof. ANDREA TINNES; Vice-Rector Prof. KARIN SCHMIDT-RUHLAND; Vice-Rector Prof. Dr NIKE BÄTZNER; Chancellor WOLFGANG STOCKERT.

Attached Research Institutes:

Institut Computer Art & Design: tel. (345) 7751900; fax (345) 7751907; e-mail ca&d@burg-halle.de; internet cad .burg-halle.de; Dir BERND HANISCH.

Institut für Software Consulting und Entwicklung: tel. (345) 7751701; fax (345) 7751719; e-mail isce@burg-halle.de; internet www.burg-halle.de/~isce; Dir Prof. JOSEF WALCH.

Institut idea (Interior Design, Environment and Architecture): tel. and fax (345) 7751868; e-mail idea@burg-halle.de; internet www.burg-halle.de/~idea.

Hochschule Anhalt (FH) (Anhalt University of Applied Sciences): Bernburger Str. 55, 06366 Köthen; tel. (3496) 671000; fax (3496) 671099; e-mail c.knothstk@hs-anhalt.de; internet www.hs-anhalt.de; f. 1891, present status 1992; Köthen: mechanical engineering (plant construction), chemical and environmental engineering, biotechnology and food processing, computer science, electrical engineering; Bernburg: business economics, agriculture, landscape architecture and planning, food and health management; Dessau: architecture, civil engineering, surveying, design; 7,700 students; Pres. Prof. Dr Hab. DIETER ORZESSEK; Vice-Pres. for Information Technology Prof. EINAR KRETZLER; Vice-Pres. for Academic Studies and Teaching Prof. Dr CAROLA GRIEHL; Vice-Pres. for Research and Foreign Relations Prof. Dr RUDOLF LÜCKMANN; Head Librarian BETTINA ELZE.

Hochschule für Technik, Wirtschaft und Kultur Leipzig (Leipzig University of Applied Sciences): POB 30 11 66, 04251 Leipzig; Karl-Liebknecht-Str. 132, 04277 Leipzig; tel. (341) 30760; fax (341) 30766456; e-mail poststelle@htwk-leipzig.de; internet www.htwk-leipzig.de; f. 1992; architecture, civil engineering, electrical engineering, mechanical engineering, printing technology, multimedia technology, publishing, computer science, business mathematics, business administration, social work, library and information science, museology, book trade/publishing, engineering with management (electrical engineering, energy engineering, mechanical engineering, civil engineering), international management; library: 320,000 vols; 180 teachers; 7,000 students; Rector Prof. Dr RENATE LIECKFELDT; Vice-Rector for Education Prof. Dr Hab. SIBYLLE SEYFFERT; Vice-Rector for Scientific Devt and Research Prof. Dr Ing. MICHAEL KUBESSA; Chancellor ULRICH ZIEGLER.

Hochschule Mittweida, University of Applied Sciences: POB 14 57, 09644 Mittweida; Technikumpl 17, 09648 Mittweida; tel. (3727) 580; fax (3727) 581376; e-mail kontakt@hs-mittweida.de; internet www .hs-mittweida.de; f. 1867; electrical engineering, electronics, microelectronics, mechanical engineering, mathematics, physics, economic sciences, social sciences, media technology, media management, microsystems engineer-

ing, precision engineering, steel and metal construction, building engineering, physical engineering, environmental engineering, computer sciences; library: 140,000 vols; 298 teachers; 5,300 students; Rector Prof. Dr Ing. LOTHAR OTTO; Vice-Rector Prof. Dr Ing. Hab. GERHARD THIEM; Vice-Rector Prof. Dr MONIKA HÄUBLER-SCZEPAN; Vice-Rector Prof. Dr Ing. MICHAEL HÖSEL; Chancellor SYLVIA BÄßLER.

Hochschule Zittau/Görlitz–University of Applied Sciences: POB 1454, 02754 Zittau; Theodor-Koerner-Allee 16, 02763 Zittau; tel. (3583) 611400; fax (3583) 611402; e-mail info@hs-zigr.de; internet wwwcms.hs-zigr.de; f. 1992; architecture, civil engineering, business management, chemistry, electrical engineering, process engineering, power and environmental engineering, real estate and housing management, computer science, mechanical engineering, ecology and environmental protection, mechatronics, tourism, translating English and Czech, social work, social education, special needs education, communications psychology, business mathematics, marketing, electrical and electronic engineering, business studies, industrial

engineering; library: 179,254 vols; 130 teachers; 3,800 students; Rector Prof. Dr F. ALBRECHT; Vice-Rector for Research Prof. Dr Ing. ROLAND GIESE; Vice-Rector for Education Prof. Dr TOBIAS ZSCHUNKE; Chancellor KARIN HOLLSTEIN.

Westsächsische Hochschule Zwickau – University of Applied Sciences: Dr-Friedrichs-Ring 2A, 08056 Zwickau; tel. (375) 5360; fax (375) 5361127; e-mail rektorat@ fh-zwickau.de; internet www.fh-zwickau.de; f. 1992; schools of applied arts, applied economics, architecture, electrical engineering, health and healthcare management, languages, mechanical and automotive engineering, physical and computer sciences, textile and leather production engineering; languages of instruction: German, English; library: 198,000 vols; 191 teachers; 4,700 students; Rector Prof. Dr Hab. GUNTER KRAUTHEIM; Vice-Rector Prof. Dr GUNDOLF BAIER; Vice-Rector Prof. Dr Ing. MATTHIAS RICHTER; Vice-Rector Prof. Dr UTE ROSENBAUM; Chancellor Prof. Dr JOACHIM KÖRNER; publs *Campus*[3], *Hochschulforschungsbericht* (1 a year), *Hochschulführer* (1 a year).

GHANA

The Higher Education System

In 1957 the former British dependencies of Togoland and Gold Coast declared the independent state of Ghana, which subsequently became a republic in 1960. The first institution of higher education, Achimota College, was founded in 1924, and the first university-level institution, University College of the Gold Coast, was founded in 1948 in conjunction with the University of London (United Kingdom), and achieved full university status in 1961; it is now known as University of Ghana, and is based in the capital, Accra. Some 82,346 students were enrolled in higher education in 1996/97, with 23,126 students attending the country's five universities. By 1998/99 the number of universities in Ghana had increased to seven. Tertiary institutions also included 38 teacher-training colleges, eight polytechnics and 61 technical colleges. In 2006/07 some 140,000 students were enrolled in tertiary education.

Higher education is administered by the Ministry of Education. The National Council for Tertiary Education is the body that advises the Government on higher education policy. The National Accreditation Board (NAB) classifies institutions of higher education as universities, university colleges, polytechnics, colleges, schools, institutes, academies or tutorial colleges. The NAB is responsible for accrediting private and public institutions of higher education, approving programmes of study, ensuring quality assurance, and determining degree equivalency. Institutions of higher education usually have two-tier systems of governance, consisting of a Council, which oversees administrative issues such as finance and personnel, and either a Senate or Academic Board, which deals with academic issues. The Chancellor is the head of the University.

Admission to university is based on suitable scores in either six subjects at SSSCE (Senior Secondary School Certificate Examinations) level or three subjects at A-level. The main undergraduate degree is the three- to four-year Bachelors, although both University of Ghana and Kwame Nkrumah University of Science and Technology offer two-year Diploma programmes. The Bachelors degree is based on the US-style credit and semester scheme, and students are required to accrue a specified number of credits in major and minor subjects in order to graduate. Only the five state-controlled universities offer postgraduate degrees, which include one- to two-year Masters and Postgraduate Diploma programmes and Doctorate programmes lasting a minimum of three years.

The National Coordinating Committee for Technical and Vocational Education and Training is the government body responsible for technical and vocational education. The leading institutions for technical and vocational education are the polytechnics, which were elevated to higher education-level status in 1993. They offer four main qualifications: Vocational Craft Certificate, Advanced Craft Certificate, Diploma and Higher National Diploma.

Regulatory and Representative Bodies

GOVERNMENT

Ministry of Culture and Chieftaincy: POB 1627 State House, Accra; tel. (30) 2685012; fax (30) 2678361; e-mail chieftancycultur@yahoo.com; Minister ALEXANDER ASUM-AHENSAH.

Ministry of Education: POB M45, Accra; tel. (30) 2666070; fax (30) 2664067; Minister Prof. BETTY MOULD-IDDRISSU.

ACCREDITATION

National Accreditation Board: IPS-Trinity Rd, POB CT 3256, Cantonments, Accra; tel. (30) 2518570; fax (30) 2518629; e-mail nabsec@nab.gov.gh; internet www.nab.gov.gh; f. 1993; attached to Min. of Education; accredits public and private tertiary instns with respect to the content and standard of their programmes; determines the equivalences of diplomas, certificates and other qualifications awarded by instns in Ghana or elsewhere; 15 mems; Chair. Prof. D. A. AKYEAMPONG; Exec. Sec. KWAME DATTEY.

NATIONAL BODY

National Council for Tertiary Education: POB M28, Accra; tel. (30) 2770198; e-mail info@ncteghana.org; f. 1993; attached to Min. of Education, Science and Sports; advises the Minister on the devt of tertiary education instns in Ghana and on their financial needs; recommends nat. standards on staff, costs, accommodation and time utilization, and monitors the implementation of any approved nat. standards by the instns; Exec. Sec. PAUL EFFAH.

Learned Societies

GENERAL

Centre for National Culture: POB 2738, Accra; tel. (30) 2664099; f. 1958; to promote and develop the arts and preserve traditional arts; includes a research section; a regional museum is planned; Chair. NII AYITEY AGBOFU II; Dir M. K. AMOATEY; publ. *DAWURO*.

Ghana Academy of Arts and Sciences: POB M.32, Accra; tel. (30) 2772002; fax (30) 2772032; e-mail gaas@ug.edu.gh; internet www.gaas-gh.org; f. 1959; sections of arts (Chair. Prof. KWAME GYEKYE), sciences (Chair. Prof. IVAN ADDAE MENSAH); 90 Fellows; Pres. Dr S. K. B. ASANTE; Hon. Sec. Prof. KWESI YANKAH; publ. *Proceedings* (1 a year).

UNESCO Accra Cluster Office: POB CT 4949, Accra; 8 Mankralo St, East Cantonments, Accra; tel. (30) 2740840; fax (30) 2765498; e-mail accra@unesco.org; designated Cluster Office for Benin, Côte d'Ivoire, Ghana, Nigeria, Sierra Leone and Togo; Dir ELIZABEH MOUNDO.

ARCHITECTURE AND TOWN PLANNING

Ghana Institute of Architects: POB M.272, Accra; fax (30) 2229464; e-mail giarch@internet.com.gh; internet www.internet.com.gh/gia; f. 1962; 300 mems; Pres. KENNETH AMPRATWUM; Hon. Sec. JOSEPH E. HAYFORD; publs *Bulletin* (12 a year), *Ghana Architect*, *PATO*.

BIBLIOGRAPHY, LIBRARY SCIENCE AND MUSEOLOGY

Ghana Library Association: POB 4105, Accra; tel. (30) 2763523; f. 1962; Pres. HELENA ASAMOAH-HASSAN; Sec. ANGELINA LILY ARMAH; publ. *Ghana Library Journal* (1 a year).

ECONOMICS, LAW AND POLITICS

Economic Society of Ghana: c/o Department of Economics, University of Ghana, POB 57, Legon, Accra; f. 1957; 500 mems; publs *Economic Bulletin of Ghana*, *Social and Economic Affairs* (4 a year).

Ghana Bar Association: POB 4150, Accra; tel. and fax (30) 2226748; 2,500 mems; Nat. Pres. PAUL ADU-GYAMFI; Nat. Sec. BENSON NUTSUKPUI.

EDUCATION

West African Examinations Council: Examination Loop, POB GP 125, Accra; tel. (30) 2248967; fax (30) 2222905; e-mail waechqrs@africaonline.com.gh; internet www.waecheadquartersgh.org; f. 1952 by the 4 W African Commonwealth countries; nat. offices in Lagos, Nigeria; Accra, Ghana; Freetown, Sierra Leone; Banjul, The Gambia; Monrovia, Liberia; conducts the W African Sr School Certificate Examination (WASSCE) for The Gambia, Sierra Leone, Nigeria and Ghana; Basic Education Certificate Examination for The Gambia, Ghana and Sierra Leone; and 9th and 12th grade examinations for Liberia; also selection examinations for entry into secondary schools and similar instns and the public services; entrance and final examinations for teacher-training colleges, commercial and technical examinations at the request of the various Ministries of Education; holds examinations on behalf of the UK examining authorities and the Educational Testing Service, Princeton, NJ, USA; 5 mem. countries; Chair. Prof. JONAS A. S. REDWOOD-SAWYERR; Registrar/Chief Exec. Alhaja MULIKAT AYONI BELLO; publ. *Research Report* (abstracts and findings of research projects conducted by the Ccl).

HISTORY, GEOGRAPHY AND ARCHAEOLOGY

Ghana Geographical Association: University of Ghana; f. 1955; Pres. Prof. E. V. T. ENGMANN; Hon. Sec. Dr L. J. GYAMFI-FENTENG; publ. *Bulletin* (1 a year).

Historical Society of Ghana: POB 12, Legon; f. 1952; formerly Gold Coast and Togoland Historical Soc.; 600 mems; Pres. T. A. OSAE; Sec. R. ADDO-FENING; publ. *Transactions* (1 a year).

LANGUAGE AND LITERATURE

Alliance Française: Liberation Link, Airport Residential Area, POB CT 4904, Accra; tel. (30) 2760278; fax (30) 2760279; e-mail info@alliancefrancaiseghana.org; internet www.alliancefrancaiseghana.org; offers courses and examinations in French language and culture, and promotes cultural exchange with France; attached teaching centres in Cape Coast, Kumasi, Takoradi and Tema.

British Council: Liberia Rd, POB GP 771, Accra; tel. (30) 2683068; fax (30) 2683062; e-mail infoaccra@gh.britishcouncil.org; internet www.britishcouncil.org/ghana; f. 1943; conducts British examinations, supports personal and professional development through physical and electronic resources; projects include school and higher education partnership, leadership training; attached centre in Kumasi; library of 4,000 vols, more than 50 periodicals; 1,500 video cassettes and DVDs, electronic resources; Dir MOSES ANIBABA.

Ghana Association of Writers: POB 4414, Accra; tel. (30) 2776586; f. 1957; aims to bring together all the writers of the country, to protect and champion the interests of Ghanaian writers, to encourage contact with foreign writers, and to foster the development of Ghanaian literature; literary evenings, annual congress, etc.; Pres. ATUKWEI OKAI; Gen. Sec. J. E. ALLOTEY-PAPPOE; publ. *Angla* (anthology, 1 a year).

Goethe-Institut: 30 Kakramadu Rd, Cantonments, Accra; tel. (30) 2776764; fax (30) 2779770; e-mail info@accra.goethe.org; internet www.goethe.de/af/acc/deindex.htm; f. 1961; offers courses and examinations in German language and culture and promotes cultural exchange with Germany; library of 2,603 vols; Dir ELEONORE SYLLA.

MEDICINE

Pharmaceutical Society of Ghana: POB 2133, Accra; tel. (30) 2228341; fax (30) 2239583; f. 1935; aims to advance chemistry and pharmacy and maintain standards of the profession; 8 regional brs; library of 250 vols; 1,200 mems; Pres. ALEXANDER NII OTO DODDO; Executive Sec. DENNIS SENA AWITTY; publ. *The Ghana Pharmaceutical Journal* (4 a year).

NATURAL SCIENCES
General

Ghana Science Association: POB 7, Legon; tel. (21) 500253; f. 1959; Nat. Pres. Dr P. A. KURANCHIE; Nat. Sec. I. J. KWAME ABOH; publ. *The Ghana Journal of Science.*

West African Science Association: c/o Botany Dept, POB 7, University of Ghana, Legon; f. 1953; mems: Ghana, Nigeria, Sierra Leone, Côte d'Ivoire, Senegal, Togo, Niger, Benin; observers: Burkina Faso, Liberia; Pres. Prof. ANDRÉ DOVI KUEVI; Sec. Dr J. K. B. A. ATA; publ. *Journal* (1 a year).

RELIGION, SOCIOLOGY AND ANTHROPOLOGY

Ghana Sociological Association: c/o Dept of Sociology, University of Ghana, Legon; f. 1961; financial aid from the universities and the Academy of Arts and Sciences; academic activities, conferences, etc.; 215 mems; Pres. Prof. J. M. ASSIMENG; Sec. E. H. MENDS; publ. *Ghana Journal of Sociology.*

TECHNOLOGY

Ghana Institution of Engineers: POB 7042, Accra-North; tel. (30) 2772005; e-mail ghie@ncs.com.gh; f. 1968; 1,000 mems; Pres. Ing. K. OFORI-KURAGO; Exec. Sec. Ing. LAURI LAWSON; publ. *The Ghana Engineer* (4 a year).

Research Institutes
GENERAL

Council for Scientific and Industrial Research (CSIR): POB M.32, Accra; tel. (30) 2777651; fax (30) 2777655; internet www.csir.org.gh; f. 1958; functions incl. advice to the Govt, encouragement of scientific and industrial research relevant to nat. devt and commercialization of research results; coordination of research in all its aspects in Ghana, and collation, publ. and dissemination of research results; library: Institute for Scientific and Technological Information: see Libraries and Archives; Dir-Gen. Prof. E. OWUSU-BENNOAH; Sec. E. ODARTEI-LARYEA; publs *CSIR Handbook, Ghana Journal of Agricultural Science, Ghana Journal of Science.*

Attached Research Institutes:

Animal Research Institute: POB AH20, Achimota; tel. (21) 401846; fax (21) 511588; e-mail e-mailari@africaonline.com.gh; f. 1957; Dir Dr K. G. ANING.

Building and Road Research Institute: Univ. POB 40, Knust, Kumasi; tel. (51) 60064; fax (51) 60080; internet www.brri.org; f. 1952; research into bldg and road problems, traffic and transportation, geosciences, material sciences; library of 15,244 vols; Dir EUGENE ATIEMO; publs *Construction Cost Indices* (4 a year), *Journal of Building and Road Research* (2 a year).

Crops Research Institute: POB 3788, Kwadaso, Kumasi; tel. (51) 60389; fax (51) 60396; e-mail cridirector@cropsresearch.org; Dir Rev. Dr J. N. ASAFU-AGYEI.

Food Research Institute: POB M.20, Accra; tel. (30) 2519091; fax (30) 50031115; e-mail director@fri.csir.org.gh; internet www.csir.org.gh; f. 1964; food processing, preservation, storage, analysis, marketing; Dir Dr W. A. PLAHAR; publ. *Bulletin.*

Forestry Research Institute of Ghana: POB 63, Knust, Kumasi; tel. (3220) 60123; fax (3220) 60121; e-mail director@csir-forig.org.gh; Dir Dr VICTOR K. AGYEMAN; publ. *Ghana Journal of Forestry* (every 2 years).

CSIR-Oil Palm Research Institute: POB 74, Kade; tel. (3420) 610257; fax (3420) 610235; e-mail kusi@opri.csir.org.gh; internet www.csir.org.gh; f. 1964; Dir Dr S. K. DERY (acting).

Council for Scientific and Industrial Research-Plant Genetic Resources Research Institute (CSIR-PGRRI): POB 7, Bunso; tel. (28)9525118; e-mail info@pgrri.csir.org.gh; internet www.csir.org.gh; f. 1964; Dir Dr LAWRENCE MISA ABOAGYE.

CSIR-Savanna Agricultural Research Institute: POB TL 52, Tamale; tel. (3720) 91205; e-mail rokowusu@yahoo.com; internet www.csir.org.gh; f. 1947, formerly known as Nyankpala Agricultural Experimental Station; present status since 1996; research in food and fibre crops in 3 northern regions of Ghana; plant breeding, agronomy, plant protection, soil fertility improvement, post-harvest, agricultural economics and rural sociology; library of 5,000 vols; Dir Dr STEPHEN NUTSUGAH.

Science and Technology Policy Research Institute: POB CT 519, Cantonments, Accra; tel. (30) 2773856; fax (30) 2773068; e-mail director@stepri.csir.org.gh; Dir Dr J. O. GOGO.

Soil Research Institute: Academy PO, Kwadaso, Kumasi; tel. (51) 50353; fax (51) 50308; e-mail soil@aol.com.gh; f. 1951; Dir Dr R. D. ASIAMAH.

Water Research Institute: POB AH.38, Achimota; tel. (30) 2775357; fax (30) 2777170; e-mail wri@ghana.com; Dir Dr C. A. BINEY.

AGRICULTURE, FISHERIES AND VETERINARY SCIENCE

Cocoa Research Institute of Ghana: POB 8, New Tafo-Akim; tel. (27) 7609900; fax (27) 7900029; e-mail crig@crig.org; internet www.crig.org; f. 1938; research on cocoa, cola, coffee, shea nuts and cashews; 3 substations; 3 cocoa plantations for research and development of cocoa by-products; library of 17,700 vols, 8,222 pamphlets, 2,054 journals; Exec. Dir Dr F. M. AMOAH; publ. *Technical Bulletin.*

MEDICINE

Health Laboratory Services: Ministry of Health, POB 300, Accra; f. 1920; laboratory services, public health reference laboratory, reference haematology laboratory, training of laboratory technicians; research on public health microbiology, abnormal haemoglobins and allied subjects; library of 8,000 vols combined with that of the Ghana Medical School; Head E. C. MARBELL.

NATURAL SCIENCES
Physical Sciences

Geological Survey of Ghana: POB M.80, Accra; tel. (30) 2228093; fax (30) 2228063; e-mail ghgeosur@ghana.com; f. 1913; geological mapping and geophysical surveying of the country, research and evaluation of mineral resources; library of 30,216 vols; Dir CHARLES EDWARD ODURO.

Ghana Meteorological Agency: POB LG 87, Legon; tel. (30) 27012520; fax (30) 2511981; e-mail meteo@africaonline.com.gh; internet www.meteo.gov.gh; f. 1937 as Ghana Meteorological Services Dept; present name 2004; provision of meteorological information, advice and warnings for the benefit of agriculture, civil and military aviation, surface and marine transport, operational hydrology and management of energy and water resources to mitigate the effects of natural disasters such as floods, storms, and drought on socio-economic devts and projects; Dir ZINEDEME MINIA.

Libraries and Archives
Accra

Accra Central Library: Thorpe Rd, POB 2362, Accra; tel. (30) 2665083; f. 1950; central reference library; central lending library; central children's library; mobile library unit; union catalogues; Regional Librarian SUSANNAH MINYILA.

George Padmore Research Library on African Affairs: POB 663, Accra; tel. (30) 2665083; fax (30) 2662795; e-mail info@ ghanalibraryboard.org; internet www .ghanalibraryboard.org; f. 1961; collection, processing and dissemination of recorded literature related to history, culture, anthropology, economics, law and public administration of all Africa; incl. Ghana National Collection; 52,651 vols, 80 periodicals; Librarian OMARI MENSAH TENKORANG; publs *Ghana National Bibliography* (6 a year and 1 a year), *special subject bibliographies* (irregular).

Ghana Library Board: POB 663, Accra; tel. (30) 2662795; f. 1950; comprises Accra Central Library, regional libraries at Kumasi, Sekondi, Ho, Tamale, Bolgatanga, Cape Coast, Koforidua, Sunyani, Research Library on African Affairs (*q.v.*); 37 br. libraries, mobile libraries, children's libraries; research library 35,029 vols, adults' libraries 1,167,653 vols, children's libraries 1,383,712 vols; Dir of Library Services DAVID CORNELIUS.

Council for Scientific and Industrial Research-Institute for Scientific and Technological Information (INSTI): POB M.32, Accra; tel. (30) 2778808; fax (30) 2777655; e-mail insti@csir.org.gh; internet www.csir.org.gh; f. 1964; attached to Council for Scientific and Industrial Research; 23,473 vols, 60 current periodicals; 70 mems; Dir JOEL SAM; publs *Gains News* (4 a year), *Ghana Journal of Agricultural Science* (2 a year), *Ghana Journal of Science* (2 a year), *Ghana Science Abstracts* (1 a year), *Union List of Agricultural Serials in Ghana, Union List of Scientific and Technological Journals in Ghana*.

Public Records and Archives Administration Department: POB GP. 3056, Accra; tel. (30) 2221234; fax (30) 2220014; e-mail praad@4u.com.gh; internet www.praad.gov .gh; f. 1946 as Nat. Archives of Ghana (legal recognition 1955); preserves Ghana's historical records; regional offices in Kumasi, Cape Coast, Sekondi, Tamale, Sunyani, Koforidua and Ho; 128 staff; provision of Record Centre services for the keeping of semi-current records of Mins, Municipalities, Depts and Agencies of the Govt of Ghana and some other private instns; setting of standards in record management practices for governmental instns; provides search services to the public; certification of archival documents; conservation of archival documents of Ghana; 2,000 documents to provide supplementary services to the searchroom; Dir FELIX NYARKO AMPONG (acting); publs *Brochure, Class Lists of the Holdings of PRAAD*.

Kumasi

Ashanti Regional Library: Bantama Rd, POB 824, Kumasi; tel. (51) 2784; f. 1954; lending, reference and extension services for adults, students and school children; 20,000 vols, incl. local collection on Ghana of 450 vols; Librarian KOFI S. ANTIRI.

Kwame Nkrumah University of Science and Technology Library: University PO, Kumasi; tel. (51) 60133; fax (51) 60358; e-mail library@knust.edu.gh; internet www .knust.edu.gh; f. 1951; 202,810 vols, 340 periodicals, 9,000 e-journals; Librarian H. R. ASAMOAH-HASSAN.

Legon

University of Ghana Library (Balme Library): POB 24, Legon; tel. (302) 512407; fax (302) 502701; e-mail balme@ug.edu.gh; f. 1948; 384,936 vols; comprises Arabic, United Nations, World Bank, Africana, Braille, Volta Basin Research Project collections and Students' Reference libraries; Librarian Prof. EDWIN ELLIS BADU; publ. *Library Bulletin*.

Sekondi

Western Regional Library: Old Axim Rd, POB 174, Sekondi; tel. (31) 46816; f. 1955; 41,480 vols; Librarian S. Y. KWANSA.

Museums and Art Galleries

Accra

Ghana National Museum: Barnes Rd, POB 3343, Accra; tel. (30) 2221633; f. 1957; controlled by the Ghana Museums and Monuments Board; archaeological and ethnological finds from all over Ghana and West Africa; modern works by Ghanaian artists; the preservation and conservation of ancient forts and castles and traditional buildings; the achievement of man in Africa; Dir I. N. DEBRAH (acting).

Museum of Science and Technology: POB 3343, Accra; tel. (30) 2223963; fax (30) 2234843; f. 1965; a temporary exhibition hall with an open-air cinema is used for the display of working models, charts, films and other exhibits on science and technology; collection of exhibits for permanent galleries has begun; temporary exhibitions are taken to the regions, films shown to colleges and schools, and regional and national Science Fairs are organized; Asst Dir K. A. ADDISON.

Cape Coast

Cape Coast Castle Museum: POB 281, Cape Coast; tel. (42) 32701; fax (42) 30264; e-mail ghct@ghana.com; f. 1971; cultural history of Ghana's Central region; Senior Curator ALBERT WUDDAH-MARTEY.

Universities

KWAME NKRUMAH UNIVERSITY OF SCIENCE AND TECHNOLOGY

University PO, Kumasi

Telephone: (51) 60351

Fax: (51) 60137

E-mail: ustlib@ust.gn.apc.org

Internet: www.knust.edu.gh

Founded 1951 as College of Technology, university status 1961

Language of instruction: English

State control

Academic year: October to June (2 semesters)

Chancellor: (vacant)

Vice-Chancellor: Prof. JOHN SEFA KWADWO AYIM

Pro-Vice-Chancellor: Prof. E. Y. SAFO

Registrar: SOPHIA QUASHIE-SAM

Librarian: HELENA ASAMOAH-HASSAN

Number of teachers: 487

Number of students: 11,633

Publication: *Journal of the University of Science and Technology*

DEANS

Faculty of Agriculture: Prof. D. B. OKAI

Faculty of Environmental and Development Studies: Prof. K. K. ADARKWA

Faculty of Pharmacy: Prof. A. K. ABAITEY

Faculty of Science: (vacant)

Faculty of Social Sciences: Prof. A. A. SACKEY

Board of Postgraduate Studies: Prof. ANTHONY A. ADIMADO

College of Art: Dr K. EDUSEI

School of Engineering: Prof. K. A. ANDAM

School of Medical Science: Prof. E. TSIRI AGBENYEGA

DIRECTORS

Bureau of Integrated Rural Development: (vacant)

Centre for Cultural Studies: VESTA ADU-GYAMFI

Distance Education: P. ADOLINAMA

Institute of Land Management and Development: Prof. S. O. ASIAMA

Institute of Mining and Mineral Engineering: Dr E. K. ASIAM

Institute of Renewable Natural Resources: Dr FRIMPONG-MENSAH

Institute of Technical Education: P. ADOLI-NAMA

Technology Consultancy Centre: PETER DON-KOR

Western University College, Tarkwa: Prof. MIREKU-GYIMAH (Provost)

PROFESSORS

ANDAM, K. A., Civil Engineering

BROBBY, G. W., Ear, Eye, Nose and Throat Surgery

KASANGA, K., Land Economy

OSEI, S. A., Animal Science

OWUSU-SARPONG, A. K., Languages

SARPONG, K., Pharmacy

TUAH, A. K., Animal Science

UNIVERSITY FOR DEVELOPMENT STUDIES

POB 1350, Tamale

Telephone: (71) 22078

Fax: (71) 22080

Internet: www.uds.edu.gh

Founded 1992

State control

Accredited by Nat. Accreditation Bd, Ghana Medical and Dental Council, Nurses and Midwives Council of Ghana

Academic year: September to July (three semesters)

Language of instruction: English

Vice-Chancellor: Prof. KAKU SAGARY NOKOE (acting)

Pro-Vice-Chancellor: Prof. DAVID MILLAR

Registrar: S. M. KUUIRE (acting)

Librarian: I. K. ANTWI

Library of 31,906 vols

Number of teachers: 271

Number of students: 10,587

Publications: *Academic Calendar* (every 5 years), *Faculties and Departments at a Glance* (every 2 years), *Ghana Journal of Development Studies* (every 2 years), *Strategic Plan* (every 5 years)

DEANS

Faculty of Agriculture: Dr GABRIEL TEYE

Faculty of Applied Sciences: Dr KENNETH PELIG-BA

Faculty of Integrated Development Studies: Rev. Prof. ABRAHAM BERINYUU

Faculty of Planning and Land Management: Dr FRANCIS BACHO

Faculty of Renewable Natural Resources: Dr THOMAS BAYORBOR

Graduate School: Prof. DAVID MILLAR

School of Medicine and Health Sciences: Dr EBENEZER N. GYADER (acting)

UNIVERSITY OF CAPE COAST

University PO, Cape Coast

Telephone: (42) 32480

Fax: (42) 32485

E-mail: vcucc@yahoo.com

Internet: www.ucc.edu.gh

Founded 1962

Language of instruction: English

State control
Academic year: August to June (2 semesters)
Chancellor: Dr SAM ESSON JONAH
Pro-Chancellor: Dr CHARLES MENSA
Vice-Chancellor: Prof. E. A. OBENG
Pro-Vice-Chancellor: Prof. K. YANKSON
Registrar: S. KOFI OHENE
Librarian: ALFRED K. MARTEY

Number of teachers: 300
Number of students: 11,637

Publications: *ASEMKA* (Faculty of Arts, 2 a year), *Journal of Educational Management* (IEPA, 2 a year), *Journal of the Institute of Education* (IEPA, 2 a year), *Journal of Social Sciences* (Faculty of Social Sciences, 2 a year), *Oguaa Educator* (Faculty of Education, 2 a year), *Primary Teacher* (Dept of Primary Education, 2 a year)

DEANS

Faculty of Arts: Prof. D. D. KUUPOLE
Faculty of Education: Dr J. A. OPARE (acting)
Faculty of Science: Prof. V. P. Y. GADZEKPO
Faculty of Social Sciences: Prof. K. AWUSABO-ASARE
School of Agriculture: Prof. P. K. TURKSON
Graduate Studies: Prof. JANE NAANA OPOKU AGYEMANG

DIRECTORS

Centre for Development Studies: Dr S. B. KENDIE (acting)
Centre for Research on Improving the Quality of Primary Education in Ghana: J. M. DZINYELA
Institute of Education: Dr A. K. AKYEMPONG (acting)
Institute for Educational Planning and Administration: Dr A. L. DARE (acting)

UNIVERSITY OF EDUCATION, WINNEBA

POB 25, Winneba
Telephone and fax (432) 22269
E-mail: info@uew.edu.gh
Internet: www.uew.edu.gh

Founded 1992 as Univ. College of Education of Winneba by merger of 7 colleges: present name and status 2004
Campuses in Winneba, Kumasi, Mampong-Ashanti, and Ajumako; the Ajumako Campus currently hosts the Ghana Education Service Staff Devt Institute (GESDI)
State control; attached to Nat. Accreditation Board, Ghana
Academic year: August to May (2 semesters)
Vice-Chancellor: Prof. AKWASI ASABERE-AMEYAW
Pro-Vice-Chancellor: Prof. MAWUTOR AVOKE
Registrar: CHRISTOPHER Y. AKWAA-MENSAH
Finance Officer: BENJAMIN K. KPODO
Librarian: VALENTINA BANNERMAN

Library of 102,577 vols, 1,427 periodicals, 2,100 online journals, 31 online databases, and over 138 CD-ROMs
Number of teachers: 322
Number of students: 25,024

Publications: *African Journal of Special Needs Education*, *Ghana Educational Media and Technology Association Journal*, *The Social Educator*

DEANS

Faculty of Agriculture Education, Mampong: Prof. K. T. DJANG-FORDJOUR
Faculty of Business Education, Kumasi: GILBERT O. AGYEDU
Faculty of Educational Studies, Winneba: Prof. GRACE Y. GADAGBUI
Faculty of Languages Education, Winneba: Prof. EMMANUEL N. ABAKAH

Faculty of Science Education, Winneba: (vacant)
Faculty of Social Sciences Education, Winneba: Prof. R. H. K. DARKWAH
Faculty of Vocational and Technical Education, Kumasi: Prof. REYNOLDS OKAI
School of Creative Arts, Winneba: Prof. JAMES E. FLOLU
School of Research and Graduate Studies, Winneba: Prof. THOMAS ESSILFIE (acting)

ATTACHED RESEARCH INSTITUTES

Centre for Educational Policy Studies: Winneba; tel. (432) 20337; e-mail aabroni@uew.edu.gh; Dir Rev. Dr Fr ANTHONY AFFUL-BRONI.

Centre for Hearing and Speech Services: Winneba; tel. (246) 782776; e-mail ynyaduoffei@yahoo.com; Coordinator YAW NYADU OFFEI.

Centre for School and Community Science and Technology Studies: Winneba; tel. (432) 22268; e-mail jophusam@gmail.com; Dir Prof. JOPHUS ANAMUAH-MENSAH (acting).

Institute for Educational Development and Extension: Winneba; tel. (432) 22497; e-mail aboagye@yahoo.com; Dir Prof. JOSEPH K. ABOAGYE (acting).

National Centre for Research into Basic Education: Winneba; tel. (432) 20415; e-mail rofori@gmail.com; Dir Dr RICHARD OFORI.

UNIVERSITY OF GHANA

POB 25, Legon, Accra
Telephone: (30) 2501967
Fax: (30) 2502701
E-mail: pad@ug.gn.ape.org
Internet: www.ug.edu.gh

Founded 1948 as University College of Gold Coast; university status 1961
Language of instruction: English
Academic year: September to June
State control
Vice-Chancellor: Prof. CLIFFORD N. B. TAGOE (acting)
Pro-Vice-Chancellor: Prof. KWESI YANKAH (acting)
Director of Finance: J. E. MINLAH
Registrar: A. T. KONU
Librarian: Prof. A. ALEMNA

Number of teachers: 766
Number of students: 27,414

Publications: *Basic Statistics*, *Campus Update*, *Newsfile*, *Universitas*

DEANS

Faculty of Arts: Prof. KWESI YANKAH
Faculty of Law: Prof. NII ASHIE KOTEY
Faculty of Science: Prof. GEORGE ODAMTTEN
Faculty of Social Studies: Prof. ATU AYEE
College of Agriculture: ANNA BARNES
School of Administration: Prof. J. K. A. POKU (acting)
Business School: Prof. KOFI NTI
Dental School: Dr N. O. NARTEY (acting)
Graduate Studies: Prof. JACOB SONGSORE
Medical School: Prof. R. B. BIRITWUM (acting)
International Educational Programmes: Prof. S. SEFA-DEDEH

PROFESSORS

ADDAE, S. K., Physiology
ADDAE-MENSAH, I., Chemistry
ADDO, S. T., Geography and Resource Development
ADU-GYAMFI, Y., Anaesthesia
AHENKORAH, Y., Crop Science
AKYEAMPONG, D. A., Mathematics
ALEMNA, A. A., Information Studies
AMOAH, A. G. B., Medicine and Therapeutics

AMUZU, J. K. A., Physics
ANTESON, R. K., Microbiology
ANYIDOHO, K., English
APT, N. A., Sociology
ARCHAMPONG, E. Q., Surgery
ARDAYFIO-SCHANDORF, E., Geography and Resource Development
ASENSO-OKYERE, K., Institute of Statistical, Social and Economic Research
ASHITEY, G. A., Community Health
ASSIMENG, J. M., Sociology
ASSOKU, R. K. G., Animal Science
AYERTEY, J. N., Crop Science
AYETTEY, A. S., Anatomy
AYETTEY, E., Institute of Statistical, Social and Economic Research
AYISI, N. K., Noguchi Institute for Medical Research
BADOE, E. A., Surgery
BAETA, R. D., Physics
BENNEH, G., Geography and Resource Development
BOADI, L. A., Linguistics
BRITWUM, K., French
CLERK, G. C., Botany
COKER, W. Z., Zoology
DANSO, S. K. A., Soil Science
DOKU, E. V., Crop Science
FYNN, J. K., History
GYASI, E. A., Geography and Resource Development
KROPP DAKUBU, M. E., Sociolinguistics
MINGLE, J. A. A., Microbiology
NEEQUAYE, J. E., Child Health
NKRUMAH, F. K., Paediatrics
NUKUNYA, G. K., Sociology
ODURO, K. A., Anaesthesia
OFORI-AMANKWAH, E. H., Law
OFORI-SARPONG, E., Law
OFOSU-AMAAH, S., School of Public Health
OLIVER-COMMEY, J. O., Child Health
OWUSU, S. K., Medicine and Therapeutics
SEFA-DEDEH, S., Nutrition and Food Science
TAGOE, C. N. B., Anatomy
TETTEH, G. K., Physics
YANKAH, K., Linguistics
YANKSON, P. W. K., Geography and Resource Development
YEBOAH, E. D., Surgery

ATTACHED INSTITUTES

Institute of Adult Education: POB 31, Legon, Accra; Dir R. A. AGGOR.

Institute of African Studies: POB 73, Legon, Accra; Dir Prof. T. MANUH (acting).

Institute of Statistical, Social and Economic Research: POB 74, Legon, Accra; Dir Prof. E. ARYEETEY.

Legon Centre for International Affairs: Legon, Accra; Dir Prof. K. KUMADO (acting).

Noguchi Memorial Institute for Medical Research: POB 25, Legon, Accra; f. 1979; international centre for basic and applied research; Dir Prof. D. OFORI-ADJEI; Provost Rev. Prof. A. S. AYETTEY (acting).

Regional Institute for Population Studies: POB 96, Legon, Accra; f. 1972 with UN aid; Dir Dr S. O. KWANKYE (acting).

Regional Training Centre for Archivists: POB 60, Legon, Accra; Head C. O. KISIEDU.

School of Communication Studies: POB 53, Legon, Accra; Dir Prof. K. ANSU-KYEREMEH.

School of Performing Arts: POB 19, Legon, Accra; Dir Prof. M. OWUSU.

School of Public Health: POB 13, Legon, Accra; Dir Dr I. QUAKYI (acting).

United Nations University Institute for Natural Resources in Africa: Private Mail Bag, Kotoka International Airport, Accra; Dir Dr UZO MOKWUNYE.

Volta Basin Research Project: Legon, Accra; Chair. Prof. S. G. K. ADIKU.

Agricultural Research Station, Accra: POB 38, Legon, Accra; Officer-in-Charge Dr E. A. CANACOO.

Agricultural Research Station, Kade: POB 43, Kade; Officer-in-Charge Dr J. K. OSEI.

Agricultural Research Station, Kpong: POB 9, Kpong; Officer-in-Charge Dr E. O. DARKWA.

Colleges

Accra Polytechnic: POB GP 561, Accra; tel. (30) 2662263; fax (30) 2664797; f. 1949; technical and vocational education with practical research programmes in manufacturing, commerce, science and technology; from technician to higher national diploma level; library: 15,800 vols; 340 teachers; 6,400 students; Principal Prof. RALPH K. ASABERE.

Accra Technical Training Centre: POB M.177, Accra; f. 1966 to train tradesmen for industry and civil service; attached to Ministry of Education; library: 10,500 vols; 350 students; Principal T. K. ADZEI.

Ghana Institute of Management and Public Administration: Greenhill, POB 50, Achimota; tel. (21) 405805; fax (21) 405805; f. 1961; research, consultancy, human resource development, strategic studies and policy analysis and postgraduate studies, diploma, certificate and Masters degree programmes; 30 teachers; library: 50,000 vols; Dir-Gen. Dr STEPHEN ADEI; publs *Administrators' Digest, Ghana Economic Outlook* (2 a year), *GIMPA News* (4 a year), *Greenhill Case Studies Book, Greenhill Journal of Administration* (2 a year).

Ho Polytechnic: POB 217, Ho, Volta Region; tel. (91) 26456; fax (91) 28398; e-mail gafeti@africaonline.com.gh; f. 1968; training of middle-level management personnel and technicians to HND standard; library: 13,000 vols; 100 teachers; 2,500 students; Principal Dr G. M. AFETI; Registrar F. K. DZINEKU.

Koforidua Technical Institute: POB 323, Koforidua; f. 1960; 9 teachers; 206 students; library: 2,000 vols; Principal P. C. NOI.

Kpandu Technical Institute: Technical Division, POB 76, Kpandu, Volta Region; tel. Kpandu 22; f. 1956; 70 teachers; 689 students; library: 4,000 vols; Principal J. Y. VODZI.

National Film and Television Institute (NAFTI): PMB, GPO, Accra; tel. (30) 2777610; fax (30) 2774522; e-mail nafti@ghana.com; f. 1978 by government decree; 4-year Bachelors of Fine Arts degree courses in film and television production with special emphasis on the production of educational programmes, and feature, informative, animation, documentary and industrial films; mem. of CILECT, Int. Asscn of Film and Television Schools; receives financial help from public funds and technical assistance from NGOs and UNESCO; 2-year diploma courses in film and television production; exchange programmes; 68 students; library: specialized library of 51,000 vols; Dir MARTIN LOH; publ. *NAFTI Concept.*

Sunyani Polytechnic: POB 206, Sunyani; tel. (61) 23278; fax (61) 24921; e-mail spolytec@ghana.com.gh; f. 1967 as Technical Institute; present name and status 1997; technical and business education, electrical and electronic engineering, hotel, catering and institutional management, secretaryship and management studies; accredited by International Professional Managers' Association (IPMA—UK) and Charted Institute of Marketing (UK); library: 11,020 vols; 180 teachers; 4,528 students; Principal Dr KWASI NSIAH-GYABAA; Sec. S. A. OBOUR.

Takoradi Polytechnic: POB 256, Takoradi; tel. (31) 22918; fax (31) 25256; f. 1955; 130 teachers; 4,500 students; library: 10,250 vols, 48 periodicals; Principal Dr SAMUEL OBENG APORI; Sec. KOFI MANUKURE-HENAKU.

West Africa Computer Science Institute: POB 1643, Mamprobi, Accra; tel. (30) 2229927; fax (30) 2229575; e-mail wacsi@internetghana.com; f. 1988; independent college providing training in computers, accounting and related fields; 10 teachers; 300 students; Pres. AIKINS BRIGHT KUMI; Principal LAWRENCE NYARKO.

GREECE

The Higher Education System

The country's first universities were established shortly after Greece secured its independence from Ottoman Turkish rule in 1830. Ethniko Metsovio Polytechneio (National Technical University of Athens) was founded in 1836, and both Anotati Scholi Kalon Technon (Athens School of Fine Art) and Ethnikon Kai Kapodistriakon Panepistimion Athinon (National and Capodistrian University of Athens) were founded in 1837. Institutions of higher education are separated into two categories, Anotera Ekpedeftika Idrimata (AEI) and Technologika Ekpedeftika Idrimata (TEI). AEIs are university-level institutions, which encompass universities, polytechneia (technical universities), and the Athens School of Fine Art. TEIs are technological higher education institutions, which were officially upgraded to university status in 2001 but are still regarded as distinct from AEIs. There are 19 AEIs in Greece. Overall responsibility for higher education lies with the Ministry of Education, Lifelong Learning and Religion, and the Constitution stipulates that only public institutions may provide higher education. AEIs and TEIs are autonomous institutions.

Admission to higher education is on the basis of the Apolyterio, the leading secondary school certificate, and Vevaiosi Provasis, a certificate of access to higher education, which is calculated according to scores in the Apolyterio. Although Greece is a signatory to the Bologna Process, it has yet to implement the required reforms; however, the traditional degree system does consist of three stages. In both AEIs and TEIs, the main degree is the Ptychio, which is a four-year programme of study in most subjects, but in some subjects lasts five years (engineering, agriculture, veterinary studies, dentistry and architecture) and in medicine lasts six years. To take postgraduate degrees, students holding the Ptychio must undergo a selection process or sit examinations. The first postgraduate degree is the Metaptychiakon Spoudon, which lasts two years and is broadly equivalent to the Masters. Finally, the Didaktor is a doctoral-level degree awarded following a period of research and submission of a thesis.

The establishment of private institutions of higher education is forbidden by Greek law, and qualifications offered by private institutions are not regarded as equivalent to qualifications from public institutions. However, private institutions may operate as laboratories of liberal science, purely with a view to providing education related to the arts and professional studies.

Technical and vocational education is overseen by different government bodies, notably the Ministry of Education, Lifelong Learning and Religion, the Organization of Vocational Education and the Ministry of Labour and Social Protection. The Organization of Vocational Education runs Institutes of Vocational Training, which offer courses of study leading to the award of diplomas. The Employment and Manpower Organization has a National Council for vocational training, which oversees apprenticeships and on-the-job training.

Figures given for 2005/06 showed that 171,967 students were enrolled in universities (this excludes data from the Medical School of Athens), while 147,715 were enrolled in technical, vocational and ecclesiastical institutions.

Regulatory and Representative Bodies

GOVERNMENT

Ministry of Culture and Tourism: Odos Bouboulinas 42, 106 82 Athens; tel. 210-8894800; fax 210-8894805; e-mail dpse@hch .culture.gr; internet www.culture.gr; Minister PAVLOS GEROULANOS.

Ministry of Education, Lifelong Learning and Religion: Odos Metropoleos 15, 101 85 Athens; tel. 210-3723000; fax 210-3248264; e-mail webmaster@ypepth.gr; internet www.ypepth.gr; Minister ANNA DIAMONTOPOULOU.

ACCREDITATION

ENIC/NARIC Greece: DOATAP, 54, Ag. Konstantinou St, 10437 Athens; tel. (210) 5281000; fax (210) 5239679; e-mail information_dep@doatap.gr; internet www .doatap.gr; Head of Dept of Information BESSY ATHANASOPOULOU.

NATIONAL BODIES

Ethniko Kentro Pistopoiisis (EKEPIS) (National Accreditation Centre for Lifelong Learning Providers): Konstantinoupoleos 49, 118 55 Athens; tel. 210-3403200; e-mail info@ ekepis.gr; internet www.ekepis.gr; f. 1997; attached to Min. of Labour and Social Protection; ensures quality assurance in vocational training; Pres. Dr AGGELOS EFSTRATOGLOU; Dir Prof. M. GEORGIAKODIS.

Syndesmos Ellinidon Epistimonon (SEE) (Hellenic Association of University Women): 44A Voulis St, 105 58 Athens; tel. 210-3234268; e-mail evibatra@central.tee.gr; f. 1924; NGO with particular interest in matters of higher education, environment, family planning, health care, child rearing, and educational support for the advancement of women; aims to fight discrimination against women; helps university women to influence the improvement of working conditions and labour legislation; Pres. PARASKEVI BATRA; Sec.-Gen. FLORA KAMARI.

Synodos Prytaneon Ellinikon Panepistimion (Greek Rectors' Conference): Synodos Prytaneon Ellinikon, Univ. of Athens, Panepistimiou 30, 106 79 Athens; tel. 210-3631813; fax 210-3647337; internet www .crue.org/eurec/member/gr.html; f. 1977; Secs ALKISTIS DAI, LILIANA NIKOLETOPOULOU.

Learned Societies

GENERAL

Akadimia Athinon (Academy of Athens): Odos Panepistimiou 28, 106 79 Athens; tel. 210-3664700; fax 210-3634806; e-mail info@ academyofathens.gr; internet www .academyofathens.gr; f. 1926; sections of literature and fine arts (Pres. SP. LAKOVIDIS), moral and political sciences (Pres. K. DESPOTOPOULOS) and positive sciences (Pres. P. LIGOMENIDIS); 217 mems (43 ordinary, 19 foreign, 149 corresp., 6 hon.); attached research institutes: see Research Institutes; library: see Libraries and Archives; Pres. APOSTOLOS S. GEORGIADES; Sec.-Gen. VASSILIOS CH. PETRAKOS; publ. Praktika (Proceedings, 3 a year).

BIBLIOGRAPHY, LIBRARY SCIENCE AND MUSEOLOGY

Enosi Ellinon Vivliothikonomon kai Epistimon Pliroforisis (EEBEP) (Greek Association of Librarians and Information Scientists): Skoufa 52, 106 72 Athens; tel. 210-3302128; fax 210-3302128; e-mail info@ eebep.gr; internet eebep.gr; f. 1968; 500 mems; Pres. GEORGE YANNAKOPOULOS; Vice-Pres. GEORGIOS GLOSSIOTIS; Gen. Sec. MARIA MARINOPOULOU; publ. Bibliothikes kai Pliroforisi (Libraries and Information).

EDUCATION

Syllogos pros Diadosin ton Hellenikon Grammaton (Society for the Promotion of Greek Education): Odos Pindarou 15 (136), Athens; f. 1869; 9 mems; Pres. PHILIP DRAGOUMIS; Sec.-Gen. ALEXANDRATOS PANAYIOTIS.

FINE AND PERFORMING ARTS

Enosis Hellinon Mousourgon (Union of Greek Composers): Deinokratous 35, 106 76 Athens; tel. and fax 210-7256607; e-mail gcu@otenet.gr; internet www.gcu.org.gr; f. 1931; 200 mems; Pres. THEODORE ANTONIOU; Sec.-Gen. IOSSIF PAPADATOS.

Epimelitirion Ikastikon Technon Ellados (Chamber of Fine Arts): 14 Koletti St, 106 81 Athens; tel. 210-3301206; fax 210-3301408; e-mail chafartg@otenet.gr; f. 1945; promotion of the fine arts, support for artists, organizes exhibitions in Greece and abroad, organizes conferences, etc.; 3,100 mems; library of 2,000 vols; Pres. MICHALIS PAPADAKIS.

HISTORY, GEOGRAPHY AND ARCHAEOLOGY

Archaeologiki Hetairia (Archaeological Society): Odos Panepistimiou 22, 106 72 Athens; tel. 210-3609689; fax 210-3644996; e-mail archetai@otenet.gr; internet www .archetai.gr; f. 1837; 401 mems; library of 118,500 vols; Pres. EPAMINONDAS SPILIOTO-POULOS; Sec.-Gen. BASIL PETRAKOS; publs *Archaeologiki Ephimeris* (1 a year), *Ergon* (1 a year), *O Mentor* (4 a year), *Praktika* (1 a year).

Hellenic Geographical Society: 11 Vou-courestiou St, 106 71 Athens; tel. 210-3631112; f. 1919; 148 mems; Pres. DIMITRIOS DIMITRIADIS; Gen. Sec. GEORGE IVANTCHOS; publ. *Bulletin*.

Historical and Ethnological Society of Greece: Old Parliament, Stadiou St, 105 61 Athens; tel. 210-3237617; fax 210-3213786; internet www.culture.gr; f. 1882; Pres. CONSTANTINOS TSAMADOS; Sec.-Gen. IOANNIS C. MAZARAKIS-AENIAN.

LANGUAGE AND LITERATURE

British Council: 17 Kolonaki Sq., 106 73 Athens; tel. 210-3692333; fax 210-3614658; e-mail customerservices@britishcouncil.gr; internet www.britishcouncil.org/greece; teaching centre; offers courses and exams in English language and British culture and promotes cultural exchange with the UK; attached office in Thessaloniki; f. 1939; Dir DESMOND LAUDER.

Etairia Ellinon Logotechnon (Society of Greek Men of Letters): 8 Gennadiou St and Acadimias, 106 78 Athens; tel. 210-3634559; f. 1934; 700 mems; Pres. PAUL NATHANAIL; Sec. E. ANAGNOSTAKI-TZAVARA.

Etairia Ellinon Theatricon Syngrapheon (Greek Playwrights' Society): Psaromiligkou 24, 10 553 Athens; tel. 210-3232472; e-mail info@eeths.gr; internet www.eeths.gr; f. 1908; 120 mems; Pres. GIORGOS LAZARIDIS; Sec. GIORGOS CHRISTOFI-LAKIS.

Goethe-Institut: Omirou 14–16, POB 30383, 100 33 Athens; tel. 210-3661000; fax 210-3643518; e-mail info@athen.goethe.org; internet www.goethe.de/om/ath/deindex .htm; offers courses and exams in German language and culture and promotes cultural exchange with Germany; attached centre in Thessaloniki; library of 15,000 vols; Dir and Regional Head of Operations HORST DEIN-WALLNER.

Instituto Cervantes: Skoufá 31, 106 73 Athens; tel. 210-3634117; fax 210-3647233; e-mail cenate@cervantes.es; internet atenas .cervantes.es; offers courses and exams in Spanish language and culture and promotes cultural exchange with Spain and Spanish-speaking Latin and Central America; library of 11,000 vols; Dir NATIVIDAD GÁLVEZ GARCÍA.

NATURAL SCIENCES

Mathematical Sciences

Elliniki Mathimatiki Eteria (Greek Mathematical Society): Odos Panepistimiou 34, 106 79 Athens; tel. 210-3616532; fax 210-3641025; e-mail info@hms.gr; internet www .hms.gr; f. 1918; seminars, lectures, summer schools, educational policy; 15,000 mems; library of 2,000 vols; Pres. Prof. NIC ALEXANDRIS; Gen. Sec. JOHN TYRLIS; publs *Astrolavos* (Informatics Review, 2 a year), *Deltion* (Bulletin, 1 a year), *Euclides* (4 a year), *Mathimatiki Epitheorissi* (Review, 2 a year).

Physical Sciences

Enosis Ellinon Chimikon (Association of Greek Chemists): Odos Kanningos 27, 106 82 Athens; tel. 210-3621524; e-mail info@eex.gr; internet www.eex.gr; f. 1924; official adviser to the State on matters relating to chemistry; promotes chemical science in industry, education and research; protects the benefits and the professional rights of chemists; 14,000 mems; library of 5,000 vols, 100 periodicals; Pres. P. HAMAKIOTIS; Gen. Sec. D. PSOMAS; publs *ChemBioChem*, *Chemistry, A European Journal*, *ChemPhysChem*, *European Journal of Inorganic Chemistry*, *European Journal of Organic Chemistry*.

TECHNOLOGY

Elliniki Epitropi Atomikis Energhias (Greek Atomic Energy Commission): POB 60092, 153 10 Aghia Paraskevi, Athens; tel. 210-6506748; fax 210-6533939; internet www .eeae.gr; independent service, supervised by the General Secretariat of Research and Technology (GSRT), under the Ministry of Education, Lifelong Learning and Religion; responsible for nuclear power and technology issues and for the protection of the population, workers and environment from ionization and artificially produced non-ionizing radiation; f. 1954; Pres. Prof. LEONIDAS CAMARINOPOULOS.

Research Institutes

GENERAL

Ethnikon Idryma Erevnon (National Hellenic Research Foundation): 48 Vassileos Constantinou Ave, 116 35 Athens; tel. 210-7273500; fax 210-7246618; internet www.eie .gr; f. 1958; carries out basic and applied research in its own institutes (humanities, natural sciences); library of 2,000 periodicals; Euronet facilities; specialized libraries attached to the humanities institutes; Nat. Documentation Centre: see Libraries and Archives; Dir Prof. DIMITRIOS A. KYRIAKIDIS.

Attached Research Institutes:

Institute of Biological Research and Biotechnology: 48 Vassileos Constantinou Ave, 116 35 Athens; tel. 210-7273740; fax 210-7273677; e-mail skyrt@eie.gr; internet www.eie.gr/nhrf/institutes/ibrb/ index-en.html; f. 1977; research in areas of molecular biology, biomedicine, environmental health, white and industrial biotechnology; Dir Prof. SOTERIOS A. KYRTOPOULOS (acting).

Institute for Byzantine Research: 48 Vassileos Constantinou Ave, 116 35 Athens; tel. (210) 7273619; fax (210) 7273629; e-mail ibe@eie.gr; internet www .eie.gr; f. 1960 as Centre for Byzantine Research; uses archival, literary and archaeological sources for Byzantine cultural history and daily life in the Greek Middle Ages, the relations of Byzantium with the peoples of the Balkans, the E Mediterranean and the W, and the historical geography and historical demography of the Greek world; organizes int. symposia and academic meetings; library of 40,000 books, offprints, journals, maps, audiovisual material; Dir Prof. Dr TAXI-ARCHIS KOLIAS; publ. *Byzantina Symmeikta* (fmrly Symmeikta, 1 a year).

Institute of Greek and Roman Antiquity: 48 Vassileos Constantinou Ave, 116 35 Athens; tel. 210-7273675; fax 210-7234145; e-mail mhatzkop@eie.gr; internet www.eie.gr/nhrf/institutes/igra/ index-en.html; f. 1979; Dir MILTIADES HAT-ZOPOULOS.

Institute for Neohellenic Research: 48 Vassileos Constantinou Ave, 116 35 Athens; tel. 210-7273556; fax 210-7246212; e-mail kne@eie.gr; internet www .eie.gr/nhrf/institutes/inr/index-en.html; f. 1960; Dir Prof. PASCHALIS M. KITROMILIDES; publs *Historical Review* (1 a year), *Tetradia Ergasias* (1 a year).

Institute of Organic and Pharmaceutical Chemistry: 48 Vassileos Constantinou Ave, 116 35 Athens; tel. 210-7273868; fax 210-7273831; e-mail ngo@eie.gr; internet www.eie.gr/nhrf/institutes/iopc/ index-en.html; f. 1979; research in the fields of organic and organometallic chemistry, pharmaceutical chemistry, structural biology and chemistry, computational chemistry and molecular analysis; carries out the rational design, synthesis and evaluation of molecules against major diseases with an emphasis on type 2 diabetes, cancer, inflammation and neurodegeneration; Sec. MARIA KALATZI.

Institute of Theoretical and Physical Chemistry: 48 Vassileos Constantinou Ave, 116 35 Athens; tel. 210-7273792; fax 210-7273794; e-mail eikam@eie.gr; internet www.eie.gr/nhrf/institutes/tpci/ index-en.html; Dir EFSTRATIOS KAMITSOS.

AGRICULTURE, FISHERIES AND VETERINARY SCIENCE

Benaki Phytopathological Institute: St Delta St 8, 145 61 Kifissia, Athens; tel. 210-8079603; fax 210-8077506; e-mail p .panayotounis@bpi.gr; internet www.bpi.gr; f. 1930; phytopathology, entomology, agricultural zoology, pesticides; 21 laboratories; museum of zoological and entomological specimens, including 22,000 species, and culture collns; library of 11,000 vols, 30,000 pamphlets, 1,400 current periodicals; Dir Dr P. PAPAIOANNOU-SOULIOTIS; publ. *Hellenic Plant Protection Journal* (English edition; irregular).

Hellenic Centre for Marine Research: POB 712, 190 13 Anavissos, Attica; tel. 229-1076466; fax 229-1076323; internet www .hcmr.gr; f. 1965 as National Centre for Marine Research (NCMR); merged with Institute of Marine Biology of Crete (IMBC) 2003; marine and freshwater fisheries and biology, marine chemistry, geology and geophysics; operational oceanography, aquaculture, inland waters, marine biology and genetics; operates 2 research vessels, a hydrobiological research station (with aquarium and museum) on Rhodes, and the Thalassocosmos aquarium in Crete; library of 3,000 vols, 541 periodicals; Dir and Pres. Prof. GEORGIOS TH. CHRONIS; publ. *Mediterranean Marine Science* (2 a year).

Attached Research Institutes:

Institute of Aquaculture: Limani Irak-leiou, POB 2214, Heraklion; tel. 2810-346860; fax 2810-241882; Dir Dr PASCAL DIVANACH.

Institute of Inland Waters: POB 712, 190 13 Anavyssos; tel. 22910-76458; fax 22910-76323; Dir Dr ARISTIDIS DIAPOULIS.

Institute of Marine Biological Resources: Agios Kosmas, 166 10 Athens; tel. 210-9821354; fax 210-9811713; Dir Dr K. PAPACONSTANTINOU.

Institute of Marine Biology/Genetics: Gournes Pediados, POB 2214, Heraklion; tel. 2810-337806; fax 2810-337822; Dir Dr A. MAGOULAS.

Institute of Oceanography: POB 17, 190 13 Attica; tel. 22910-76452; fax 22910-76347; Dir Dr EFSTATHIOS BALOPOULOS.

ECONOMICS, LAW AND POLITICS

Centre of International and European Economic Law: POB 14, 55102 Kalamaria, Thessaloniki; tel. 231-0486900; fax 231-

0476366; e-mail kdeod@cieel.gr; internet www.cieel.gr; f. 1977; nat. documentation and research centre, specializing in European Union law, protection of human rights in Europe, int. economic law; European Documentation Centre by decision of the EEC (now EU); library of 55,000 vols, 192 periodicals; Dir and Pres. of Board Prof. WASSILIOS SKOURIS; Dir EVANGELIA KOUTOUPA-REGAKOU; Sec. Prof. GEORGIOS TRANTAS; publs *Hellenic Review of European Law* (4 a year in Greek, 1 a year in English), *Public Procurement and State Aid Law Review* (3 a year).

Centre for Planning and Economic Research: Amerikis 11, 106 72 Athens; tel. 210-3676300; fax 210-3611136; e-mail kepe@kepe.gr; internet www.kepe.gr; f. 1961; scientific study of the economic problems of Greece, the promotion of economic research, and cooperation with other Greek research institutes; library of 30,090 vols, 850 periodical titles, 315 series of statistical bulletins; Chair. and Scientific Dir Prof. PANAGIOTIS G. KORLIRAS; Head Librarian ELEFTHERIA HALVADAKIS; publ. *Economic Perspectives* (3 a year).

Hellenic Centre for European Studies (EKEM): 4 Xenofontos St, 106 80 Athens; tel. 210-3215549; fax 210-3215096; e-mail ekem@ekem.gr; internet www.ekem.gr; f. 1988; non-profit-making independent org. under supervision of the Ministry of Foreign Affairs; advises the Govt, academic bodies and private companies on matters of European policy and integration; organizes conferences and seminars; library: maintains Depository Library of the European Union, with 7,000 vols; Pres. of Admin. Council and Dir Assoc. Prof. KOSTAS IFANTIS.

Hellenic Institute of International and Foreign Law: 1 Vas. Sofias Ave, 106 71 Athens; tel. 210-3681000; internet www.mfa.gr; f. 1939; library of 40,000 vols; Dir Prof. KONSTANTINOS KERAMEUS; publ. *Revue hellénique de droit international* (in English and French, 2 a year).

Institute of International Public Law and International Relations: Vass. Herakliou St, 546 25 Thessaloniki; tel. 2310-552295; fax 2310-566953; e-mail ipilir@otenet.gr; internet web.auth.gr/institute-iplir; f. 1966; research, documentation and education centre; courses run during June to September; library: World Bank and UN depository library; Dir Prof. KALLIOPI K. KOUFA; publ. *Thesaurus Acroasium* (1 a year).

Kentron Ereunes Historias Hellenikou Dikaiou (Centre for Research in the History of Greek Law): Anagnostopoulou 14, 106 73 Athens; tel. 210-3664607; fax 210-3664627; e-mail papariga@academyofathens.gr; internet www.academyofathens.gr; f. 1929; attached to Acad. of Athens; conducts research on legal instns from antiquity, Byzantine and post-Byzantine times; library of 12,000 vols; Pres. Prof. APOSTOLOS GEORGIADIS; Dir Dr LYDIA PAPARRIGA-ARTEMIADI; publs *Epetiris* (1 a year), *Parartima tes Epetiridos* (supplement to *Epetiris*, 1 a year).

FINE AND PERFORMING ARTS

Kentro Erevnas Byzantinis kai Metabyzantinis Technis (Research Centre for Byzantine and Post-Byzantine Art): Odos Anagnostopoulou 14, 106 73 Athens; tel. 210-3664613; fax 210-3664652; e-mail kevmt@academyofathens.gr; internet academyofathens.gr; f. 1994; attached to Akadimia Athinon (Acad. of Athens); research on Byzantine archaeology and wall-paintings in Greece; library of 6,000

vols; Pres. PANAYOTIS L. VOCOTOPOULOS; Dir IOANNA BITHA (acting).

HISTORY, GEOGRAPHY AND ARCHAEOLOGY

Centre for Asia Minor Studies: Kydathineon 11, 105 58 Athens; tel. 210-3239225; fax 210-3229758; e-mail kms@otenet.gr; internet users.otenet.gr/~kms; f. 1930; ind., private, non-profit organization; research into history and civilization of Greek communities in Asia Minor before 1922; library of 15,000 vols, 501 MSS; oral history archive of 150,000 MS pages; photographic archive of 5,000 photographs; folk music archive of 1,000 records, 700 tapes; spec. collns: Karamanli books, and Greek books, newspapers and periodicals printed in Turkey, maps, MSS; Pres. Prof. M. B. SAKELLARIOU; Dir Dr S. TH. ANESTIDIS (acting); publ. *Deltio K. M. S.* (1 a year).

Foundation of the Hellenic World: 38 Poulopoulou St, 118 51 Athens; tel. 212-2543800; fax 212-2543838; e-mail webmaster@fhw.gr; internet www.fhw.gr/fhw/en; f. 1993; uses the latest information and computer technology in pursuit of research, awareness and understanding of Hellenic history and culture; Cultural Centre: Hellenic Cosmos located at 254 Pireos St, 177 78 Athens; Pres. LAZAROS D. EFRAIMOGLOU; Man. Dir DIMITRIS EFRAIMOGLOU.

Institute for Balkan Studies: POB 50932, 540 14, Thessaloniki; Meg. Alexandrou Ave 31A, 546 41 Thessaloniki; tel. 2310-832143; fax 2310-831429; e-mail imxa@imxa.gr; internet www.imxa.gr; f. 1953; research centre concerned with historical, literary, political, economic and social devt of Balkan people since early times; library of 30,000 vols, 260 periodicals; Dir ELEFTHERIA MANTA; Pres. Prof. IOANNIS TSEKOURAS; publs *Balkan Studies* (1 a year), *Valkanika Symmeikta* (1 a year).

International Centre for Classical Research (of the Hellenic Society for Humanistic Studies): 47 Alopekis St, Athens 140; study of and research into ancient Greek culture, scientific research and promotion of popular education through conferences and publications; f. 1959; 700 mems; library of 20,000 vols; Pres. Prof. ARISTOXENOS D. SKIADAS; Sec.-Gen. GEORGE BABINIOTIS; publs *Antiquity and Contemporary Problems, Studies and Research.*

Kentron Erevnis Archaiotitos (Research Centre for Antiquity): Odos Anagnostopoulou 14, 106 73 Athens; tel. 210-3664612; fax 210-3602448; e-mail kea@academyofathens.gr; internet www.academyofathens.gr; f. 1977; attached to Acad. of Athens; Supervisor S. IAKOVIDIS; Dir M. PIPILI.

Kentron Erevnis Messeonikou kai Neou Ellinismou (Research Centre for Medieval and Modern Hellenism): Anagnostopoulou 14, 106 73 Athens; tel. 210-3664611; fax 210-3664637; e-mail kemne@academyofathens.gr; internet www.academyofathens.gr; f. 1930; attached to Acad. of Athens; library of 25,000 vols; Dir R. STAMOULI; publ. *Messeonika kai Nea Ellinika* (1 a year).

Kentron Erevnis Neoterou Ellinismou (Research Centre for the History of Modern Hellenism): Anagnostopoulou St 14, 106 73 Athens; tel. 210-3664603; fax 210-3664661; e-mail keine-academyofathens.gr; internet www.keine-academyofathens.gr; f. 1957; attached to Acad. of Athens; Greek history since 1821; 7 research scholars; library of 15,000 vols, 12,000 microfilms; Head, Supervisory Board MICHAEL SAKELLARIOU; Dir HELEN KATSIADAKIS; publ. *Neoellinika Istorika.*

LANGUAGE AND LITERATURE

Kentron Ereunes Hellenikes kai Latinikes Grammateias (Centre for the Research of Greek and Latin Literature): Anagnostopoulou 14, 106 73 Athens; tel. and fax 210-3664630; e-mail keelg@academyofathens.gr; internet www.academyofathens.gr; f. 1955; attached to Acad. of Athens; Pres. NIKOLAOS KONOMIS; Supervisor ATHANASIOS KAMBYLIS; Librarian ELENI MASTROGEORGIOU.

Research Centre for Modern Greek Dialects-Historical Dictionary: Al. Soutsou 22, 106 71 Athens; tel. 21-12111000; fax 210-3609187; e-mail ksilneg@academyofathens.gr; internet www.academyofathens.gr/ilne; f. 1914; attached to Acad. of Athens; compiles *Historical Dictionary of Modern Greek Dialects and Local Varieties*; maintains modern Greek dialectal archives (1,469 MSS, 3.8m. cards, 300 hours of sound recordings); linguistic research, especially on modern Greek dialects; research on modern Greek onomastics (incl. relevant archives of place names, proper names, etc.); library of 9,300 vols; Pres. Prof. Dr MICHAEL SAKELLARIOU; Dir CHRISTINA BASSEA-BEZANTAKOU; Sec. MARIA PAPPA; publ. *Lexicographikon Deltion (Bulletin lexicographique)* (1 a year).

Research Centre for Scientific Terms and Neologisms: Smolensky 17, 11473 Athens; tel. 210-3664732; fax 210-3626990; e-mail geon@academyofathens.gr; internet www.academyofathens.gr; f. 2003; attached to Acad. of Athens; research studies on neologisms of Greek language; Pres. N. KONOMIS; Dir ANASTASIA CHRISTOFIDOU; publ. *Bulletin of Scientific Terminology and Neologisms.*

MEDICINE

Institut Pasteur Hellénique: 127 Vassilissis Sofias Ave, 115 21 Athens; tel. 210-6478800; fax 210-6423498; internet www.pasteur.gr; f. 1919; study and research of bacteriology, biochemistry, biotechnology, immunology, microbiology, molecular biology, molecular virology, parasitology, virology; library of 3,500 vols and 155 periodicals; Dir A. F. MENTIS.

NATURAL SCIENCES

Physical Sciences

Institouton Geologikon kai Metalleutikon Ereunon (Institute of Geology and Mineral Exploration): 1, Sp. Louis St, Olympic Village, Acharnae, 136 77 Athens; tel. 210-2413000; fax 210-2413015; e-mail dirgen@igme.gr; internet www.igme.gr; f. 1976; operates under the Ministry of the Environment, Energy and Climate Change; consultant to the Government on geoscientific matters and on mine legislation; carries out the geological study of Greece; surveys and evaluates all mineral raw materials, except hydrocarbons, and groundwater resources; 819 mems; library of 9,500 vols, 500 periodicals, 4,000 maps and 6,000 reports; Dir-Gen. ANDREAS N. GEORGAKOPOULOS; publs *Geological and Geophysical Research, Special Research.*

Kentron Erevnis Phissikistis Atmospheras kai Climatologias (Research Centre for Atmospheric Physics and Climatology): Odos Panepistimiou 28, Athens; tel. and fax 210-8832048; e-mail phatmcli@otenet.gr; internet www.academyofathens.gr; f. 1977; attached to Acad. of Athens; Pres. C. ALEXOPOULOS; Dir CHR. REPAPIS.

National Observatory of Athens: POB 20048, 118 10 Athens; tel. 210-3490101; fax 210-3490140; internet www.noa.gr/indexen.html; f. 1842; library of 60,000 vols; Pres.

of the Administration Board Prof. D. P. LALAS; Dir, Institute of Astronomy and Astrophysics Prof. CHRISTOS GOUDIS; Dir, Institute for Astroparticle Physics Prof. LEONIDAS RESVANIS; Dir, Institute for Environmental Research and Sustainable Development Dr PETRAKIS MICHAEL; Dir, Institute of Geodynamics Dr G. STAVRAKAKIS (acting); Dir, Institute for Space Applications and Remote Sensing Dr I. A. DAGLIS; publs *Annals of the National Observatory of Athens, Memoirs, Series I—Astronomy, Series II—Meteorology*, bulletins of the Astronomical, Meteorological, Ionospheric and Geodynamics Institutes.

Research Centre of Pure and Applied Mathematics (RCPAM): Odos Panepistimiou 28, Athens; tel. 210-3664717; fax 210-3664718; e-mail nikartem@academyofathens.gr; internet www.academyofathens.gr; f. 1992; attached to Acad. of Athens; Pres. G. KONTOPOULOS; Supervisor N. K. ARTEMIADIS.

PHILOSOPHY AND PSYCHOLOGY

Kentron Erevnis Ellinikis Philosophias (Centre for Research in Greek Philosophy): Anagnostopoulou St 14, 106 73 Athens; tel. 210-3664626; fax 210-3664624; e-mail emouts@academyofathens.gr; internet www.academyofathens.gr; f. 1971; attached to Acad. of Athens; philosophy research; conferences and monthly seminars on Greek philosophy; bibliographical and consulting services to graduate and postgraduate philosophy students; free use of library for profs, researchers, students; library of 10,000 vols; Pres. Prof. CONSTANTINE DESPOTOPOULOS; Dir Dr MARIA PROTOPAPAS-MARNELI; Supervisor Prof. EVANGHELOS MOUTSOPOULOS (acting); publ. *Philosophia 40* (1 a year).

RELIGION, SOCIOLOGY AND ANTHROPOLOGY

Athens Center of Ekistics: Strat. Syndesmou St 23, 106 73 Athens; tel. 210-3623216; fax 210-3629337; e-mail ekistics@otenet.gr; internet www.ekistics.org; f. 1963; research, education, collaboration and documentation in the devt of human settlements; secretariat of World Soc. for Ekistics; library of 1,000 vols, 100 periodical titles (historic colln of 20,000 vols largely transferred in 2003 to School of Architecture, Nat. Technical Univ. of Athens, *q.v.*); Dir PANAYOTIS C. PSOMOPOULOS; publ. *Ekistics* (6 a year).

Hellenic Folklore Research Centre of the Academy of Athens: Ipitou St 3, 105 57 Athens; tel. 210-3318042; fax 210-3313418; e-mail keel@academyofathens.gr; internet www.kentrolaografias.gr; f. 1918; folklore, anthropology, ethnology (ethnography), folk music, social, spiritual life, archives of folk material, field work, MSS, tapes, video tapes, cassette movies, photos, slides; library of 40,000 vols, 5,055 MSS, 28,000 songs, 17,000 folktales and stories, 200,000 proverbs, customs, etc.; Dir Dr AIK. POLYMEROU-KAMILAKI; publ. *Yearbook*.

Kentron Erevnis Ellinikis Kinonias (Research Centre for Greek Society): 8 Chr. Milioni St, 106 73 Athens; tel. 210-3609990; fax 210-3609960; e-mail keek@academyofathens.gr; internet www.academyofathens.gr; f. 1978; attached to Acad. of Athens; social research into Greek soc., esp. historical devt of the Greek family and the social and economic consequences of migration in Greece; rural reform and consequent sociopathy in rural areas of Greece; library of 5,500 vols; Dir Prof. M.-G. LILY STYLIANOUDI; publ. *Elliniki Koinonia/Greek Society* (Yearbook of the Centre).

National Centre of Social Research (EKKE): 9 Kratinou St and Athinas St, 105

52 Athens; tel. 210-7491678; fax 210-7489130; e-mail president@ekke.gr; internet www.ekke.gr; f. 1959; operates under the Ministry of Health and Social Solidarity; promotes the devt of the social sciences in Greece; organizes and conducts social research and acts as a link between Greek and foreign social scientists; promotes int. cooperation in this field; Dirs THOMAS MALOUTAS, IOANNIS SAKELLIS; Deputy Dir Prof. THOMAS MALOUTAS; publ. *Epitheorissis Koinonikon Erevnon* (Greek Review of Social Research, 4 a year).

Patriarchal Institute for Patristic Studies: 64 Eptapyrgiou St, Moni Vlatadon, 546 34 Thessaloniki; tel. and fax 231-0203620; f. 1968; research centre with depts of patrology, palaeography, history of Byzantine art, history of worship and ecclesiastical history; library of 15,000 vols, 300 periodicals, 115 codex MSS, 450 rare books, 10,000 MSS on microfilm, colour slides of illuminated MSS; Dir Prof. JOHN FOUNTOULIS; publ. *Kleronomia* (2 a year).

TECHNOLOGY

'Demokritos' National Centre for Scientific Research: POB 60228, 153 10 Aghia Paraskevi, Athens; tel. 210-6503285; fax 210-6522965; e-mail info@lib.demokritos.gr; internet www.demokritos.gr; f. 1961; study and research by 8 institutes: biology, informatics and telecommunications, materials science, microelectronics, nuclear physics, nuclear technology and radiation protection, physical chemistry, radioisotopes and radiodiagnostic products; library of 20,000 vols, 300,000 technical reports, 1,500 periodicals; Dir Dr NICK KANELLOPOULOS; Librarian Dr VASSILIOS GEORGIOU; publ. *DEMO Reports*.

Libraries and Archives

Athens

Academy of Athens Library: Anagnostopoulou 14, 106 73 Athens; tel. 210-3664627; fax 210-3364628; e-mail papariga@academyofathens.gr; internet www.academyofathens.gr; f. 1926; collects and publishes Greek historical legal documents, incl. those of the Byzantine and post-Byzantine periods; 10,000 vols; Dir Dr LYDIA PAPARRIGA-ARTEMIADI; Research Staff Dr DIMITRA KARAMBULA, Dr ILIAS ARNAOUTOGLOU, Dr YANNIS HATZAKIS; publs *Epetiris tou Kentrou Ereunes Historias tou Hellenikou Dikaiou* (1 a year), *Supplement (Pazactima) of Epetiris*.

Athens University of Economics and Business Library: 76 Patission St, 104 34 Athens; tel. 210-8203261; fax 210-8221456; e-mail library@aueb.gr; internet www.lib.aueb.gr; f. 1928; 75,000 vols, 700 serial titles (40,000 vols), 30,000 full-text serial titles, 19 databases; 3 documentation centres: European Documentation Center (EDC) f. 1992, Depository Library of OECD f. 1997, and Depository Library of WTO f. 2004; Dirs Prof. E. J. YANNAKOUDIS, GEORGIA THEOPHANOPOULOU.

Eugenides Foundation Library: Syngrou Ave 387, Paleon Phaleron, 175 64 Athens; tel. 210-9469631; fax 210-9469631; e-mail lib@eugenfound.edu.gr; internet www.eugenfound.edu.gr; f. 1966; 60,000 vols, 441 periodicals (science and technology); Head Librarian HARA BRINDESI.

Gennadius Library: Odos Souidias 61, 106 76 Athens; tel. 210-7210536; fax 210-7237767; e-mail gen_recep@ascsa.edu.gr; internet www.ascsa.edu.gr/index.php/gennadius; f. 1926; attached to American

School of Classical Studies; rare book and research library; 118,961 vols, spec. colln on Greece, the Near East, the Balkans and travel accounts; first editions of classics; maps; literary and other archives; Dir Dr MARIA GEORGOPOULOU; Sr Librarian IRINI SOLOMONIDI; publs *Exhibition Catalogues, Gennadeion Monographs, The New Griffon* (1 a year).

Greek Chamber of Deputies Library: Parliament Bldg, 100 21 Athens; tel. 210-3235030; fax 210-3236072; e-mail abadjis@artemis.parl.ariadne-t.gr; f. 1844, damaged by fire 1859, rebuilt 1875; 1.5m. vols; Dir IRENE CON. ELIOPOULOU.

Music Library of Greece 'Lilian Voudouri': Vasilissis Sofias and Kokkali, 115 21 Athens; tel. 210-7282775; fax 210-7259196; e-mail library@megaron.gr; internet www.mmb.org.gr; f. 1994; holds the Greek Music Archives; 130,000 vols, 71 periodicals, 16,000 recordings, microforms, MSS and online databases; Dir STEPHANIA MERAKOU.

National Library of Greece: Odos Panepistimiou 32, 106 79 Athens; tel. 210-3382601; fax 210-3382502; e-mail gzachos@nlg.gr; internet www.nlg.gr; f. 1828; 2.5m. vols; collection of MSS; serves as the national bibliographical centre and as the national centre for ISBN and ISSN; Gen. Dir Dr GEORGE K. ZACHOS.

National Technical University of Athens Central Library: Odos Heroon Polytechniou 9, Zografou Campus, 157 73 Athens; tel. 210-7721570; fax 210-7721565; e-mail library@central.ntua.gr; internet www.lib.ntua.gr; f. 1836; 115,000 vols; Librarian MARIA KALAMPALIKI.

Nordic Library at Athens: Kavalotti 7, 117 42 Athens; tel. 210-9249210; fax 210-9216487; e-mail info@norlib.gr; internet www.norlib.gr; f. 1995; 40,000 vols, 450 periodicals; Greek archaeology and ancient Greek religion and history; jt venture by archaeological institutes of Denmark, Finland, Norway and Sweden; Head Librarian EVI CHARITOUDI.

Technical Chamber of Greece–Documentation and Information Unit: Odos Lekka 23–25, 105 62 Athens; tel. 210-3245180; fax 210-3237525; e-mail tee_lib@tee.gr; internet library.tee.gr; f. 1926; 60,000 vols, 1,400 periodicals, TCG publications; Head of Unit KATERINA TORAKI.

Chios

Koraes Central Public Historical Library of Chios: 2 Korai St, 821 00 Chios; tel. 22710-44246; fax 22710-28251; e-mail bibkor@aegean.gr; internet vivl-chiou.chi.sch.gr; f. 1792; colln of rare and unique Homeric edns; 200,000 vols; Dir ANASTASIOS SARRIS.

Hania

Technical University of Crete Library: 731 00 Hania; tel. 821-037273; fax 821-037576; e-mail maria@library.tuc.gr; internet www.library.tuc.gr; f. 1985; 62,134 vols, 37292 journals, 374 periodicals, maps and dissertations; scientific fields of the institute, arts and history; Library Dir MARIA NTAOUNTAKI.

Patras

University of Patras Library and Information Service: 265 00 Patras; tel. 61-997290; internet www.upatras.gr/services/library/library.php?lang=en; 90,000 vols, 2,400 journals; applied sciences, biology, computer science, economics, education and general reference literature, mathematics, medicine, theatre.

Piraeus

University of Piraeus Library: 80 Dimitriou and Kalaoli Sts, 185 34 Piraeus; internet www.lib.unipi.gr; , business admin., economics, finance, industrial management, and maritime studies; 45,000 vols, 350 periodicals.

Rethymnon

University of Crete Library: Gallos Campus, Knossou Ave, 731 00 Rethymnon; tel. 831-77810; fax 831-77850; e-mail webauthor@lib.uoc.gr; internet www.lib.uoc.gr/english; f. 1978; 3 brs at Heraklion; Dir ELENI DIAMANTAKI.

Thessaloniki

Aristotle University Library: 541 24 Thessaloniki; tel. 231-995378; fax 231-995364; e-mail libraryweb@lib.auth.gr; internet www.lib.auth.gr; f. 1927; attached to Aristotle University of Thessaloniki; 181,500 vols, 122,950 journals, 7,055 dissertations; rare books from the 18th and 19th centuries; Librarians X. AGOROGIANNI, S. ALEXANDRIDOU, EL. KOSEOGLOU.

University of Macedonia, Economic and Social Sciences Library: 156 Egnatia St, 540 06 Thessaloniki; tel. 2310-891752; fax 2310-857794; e-mail maclib@uom.gr; internet www.lib.uom.gr.

Tripolis

Pan Library (Circle of the Friends of Progress): Odos Giorgios 43, Tripolis, Arcadia; vols on all subjects.

Veria

Veria Central Public Library: 8 Ellis St, 591 00 Veria; tel. 2331-24494; fax 2331-24600; e-mail vivlver@libver.gr; internet www.libver.gr; f. 1952; 90,000 vols; Central Library for the Prefecture of Imathia.

Volos

Library of the Three Hierarchs: Demetriados-Ogl, 382 21 Volos; tel. and fax 24210-25641; f. 1907; 23,000 vols; history, literature, philosophy, physical sciences, religion,; Asst Dir ACHILLES K. GLAVATOS.

University of Thessaly Central Library: 2 Metamorforseos St, 383 33 Volos; tel. 24210-74891; fax 24210-74851; e-mail clib@uth.gr; internet www.lib.uth.gr; f. 1988; other brs: veterinary science in Karditsa; medicine in Larisa; physical education and sport in Trikala; humanities, technological sciences and Kitsos Makris Folklore Centre in Volos; 112,000 vols, 75,000 books and 37,000 journals; Library Dir Dr IOANNIS CLAPSOPOULOS.

Museums and Art Galleries

Athens

Acropolis Museum: Dionysiou Arepagitou 15, 117 42 Athens; tel. 210-9000900; fax 210-9000902; e-mail info@theacropolismuseum.gr; internet www.theacropolismuseum.gr; f. 1874; contains the sculptures discovered on the Acropolis; illustrates the origins of Attic art, pedimental compositions, archaic horsemen, Korai, sculptures of the Parthenon, Temple of Niké, Erechtheion; Pres. Prof. DIMITRIOS PANDERMALIS.

Benaki Museum: Odos Koumbari 1, 106 74 Athens; tel. 210-3671000; fax 210-3671063; e-mail benaki@benaki.gr; internet www.benaki.gr; f. 1930; Greek art from Neolithic to late Roman period; Byzantine and post-Byzantine; Greek folk art and costumes; historic memorabilia from the War of Independence in 1821 to 1936; 18th- and 19th-century paintings, engravings and drawings; works of art by N. Hadjikyriakos-Ghikas; Coptic and Islamic art; textiles and embroidery from Far East and Western Europe; Neolithic to modern Chinese porcelain; children's toys and games from antiquity to the mid-20th century; historical and photographic archives (Documentation Centre for Neo-Hellenic Architecture); library of 50,000 vols, 500 MSS; Dir Prof. Dr ANGELOS DELIVORRIAS.

Byzantine and Christian Museum: 22 Vasilissis Sophias Ave, 106 75 Athens; tel. 210-7211027; fax 210-7231883; e-mail documentation@byzantinemuseum.gr; internet www.byzantinemuseum.gr; f. 1914; more than 25,000 objects since 3rd century AD, incl. sculptures, icons and other works of art; wall paintings, ceramics, textiles, MSS, drawings, engravings, incunabula and copies of wall paintings and mosaics of the Byzantine and post-Byzantine eras; Dir Dr EUGENIA HALKIA; Vice-Dir Dr ANASTASIA LAZARIDOU.

National Archaeological Museum: 1 Tositsa St, 106 82 Athens; tel. 210-8217724; fax 210-8213573; e-mail eam@culture.gr; internet www.culture.gr; f. 1889; original Greek sculptures and Roman copies of Greek originals; sculptures of the Archaic, Classical, Hellenistic and Roman periods; Neolithic objects from Thessaly; Bronze Age relics from the mainland and the Aegean Islands; Mycenaean treasures; frescoes and pottery from Thera; rich collns of Greek vases and terracottas; collns of jewels and bronzes; Egyptian antiquities; Dir Dr NIKOLAOS KALTSAS; Head of Bronzes Colln Dr ROZA PROSKYNITOPOULOU; Head of Prehistoric, Egyptian and Anatolian Antiquities Colln Dr ELENI PAPAZOGLOU; Head of Sculpture Colln Dr ELENI KOURINOU; Head of Vases and Minor Art Colln ELISAVET STASINOPOULOU.

National Art Gallery and Alexander Soutzos Museum: 50 Vassileos Konstantinou Ave, 115 28 Athens; tel. 210-7211010; fax 210-7224889; internet www.nationalgallery.gr; f. 1900; Greek paintings since the 17th century, sculptures and prints; European paintings since the 14th century, including El Greco, Caravaggio, Jordaens, Poussin, Tiepolo, Delacroix, Mondrian, Picasso; engravings; drawings; library of 8,000 vols; Dir Prof. MARINA LAMBRAKI-PLAKA.

National Historical Museum of Greece: Old Parliament, Stadiou St, 105 61 Athens; tel. 210-3237617; fax 210-3213786; e-mail info@fhw.gr; internet www.fhw.gr/projects/vouli; f. 1882; chronicles the history of Modern Greece from the 16th to the 20th century; ethnographic colln of traditional regional costumes, jewellery, embroidery and textiles; Dir IOANNIS K. MAZARAKIS-AINIAN.

National Museum of Contemporary Art, Athens (EMST): Vas. Georgiou B'17-19 and Rigillis St, 106 75 Athens; tel. 210-9242111; fax 210-9245200; e-mail protocol@emst.gr; internet www.emst.gr; f. 2000; paintings, installations, photography, video, new media, architecture and industrial design; Dir ANNA KAFETSI.

Stoa of Attalos: 10 555 Athens; tel. 210-3210185; f. as a museum in 1956; the design of the original building (constructed in the 2nd century BC) was exactly reproduced in the reconstruction carried out 1953–56 by the American School of Classical Studies; collections include all material found in the excavations of the Athenian Agora, illustrating 5,000 years of Athenian history; Dir P. KALLIGAS.

Zoological Museum of the University of Athens: Panepistimiopolis, 157 84 Athens; tel. 210-7274609; fax 210-7274619; e-mail zoolmuse@biol.uoa.gr; internet www.biol.uoa.gr/zoolmuseum; f. 1858; permanent and temporary exhibitions on Greek and world fauna: birds, mammals, shells, insects, etc.; research in ecology and zoogeography; Curator Prof. SOTIRIOS MANOLIS.

Canea

Archaeological Museum of Canea: 731 31 Canea; tel. 28210-90334; fax 28210-94487; internet www.culture.gr; f. 1963; housed in the katholikon of the Venetian monastery of St Francis; artefacts of prehistoric and historical times from the dept of Canea; Dir MARIA VLAZAKI.

Maritime Museum of Crete: Akti Koundourioti , 731 36 Canea; tel. 2821-91875; fax 2821-74484; e-mail mar-mus@otenet.gr; internet www.mar-mus-crete.gr; f. 1973; preserves and promotes Cretan maritime tradition; permanent maritime colln and reconstructed Minoan ship; Chair. MANOLIS PETRAKIS.

Corfu

Archaeological Museum: Armeni Vraila 1, 491 00 Corfu; tel. 2661-30680; fax 2661-43452; internet www.greece-museums.com/museum/116; f. 1967; bronze statues from Archaic to Roman era; funeral offerings from the Archaic, Classical and Hellenistic eras; findings from prehistoric era and 7th and 6th centuries BC; Menecrates lion, clay pottery, terracotta statuettes from shrines of Corfu; Gorgon-Medusa pediment from the great temple of Artemis, constructed in 585BC.

Museum of Asian Art: St Michael and St George Palace, 491 00 Corfu; tel. 26610-30443; fax 26610-20193; internet www.greece-museums.com/museum/35; f. 1927; Greek-Buddhistic colln of sculptures from Gadara, Pakistan, dating from the 1st–5th century AD.

Corinth

Archaeological Museum in Corinth: Corinth 200 10; tel. and fax 210-741031207; f. 1932; items from the Geometric to Hellenistic periods, Roman and Byzantine eras, from excavations at the Asklepieion of Corinth; sculptures and inscriptions; Dir ALEXANDROS MANTIS.

Delphi

Archaeological Museum: 330 54 Delphi; tel. 2265-082313; fax 2265-082966; e-mail iepka@culture.gr; internet www.culture.gr; f. 1903; finds from Delphic excavations; library of 5,200 vols; Dir ATHANASIA PSALTI.

Heraklion

Archaeological Museum: 2 Xanthoudidou St, 712 02 Heraklion, Crete; tel. 281-0224630; fax 281-0332610; e-mail protocol@amh.culture.gr; f. 1904; contains rich collection of Minoan art (pottery, sealstones, frescoes, jewellery); traces the development of Cretan art up to the Roman period; Dir RETHEMIOTAKI PANAGIOTA.

Nafplion

Komboloi Museum: 25 Staikopoulou St, 211 00 Nafplion; tel. 2752-21618; e-mail arisevag@otenet.gr; internet www.komboloi.gr; f. 1987; 400 komboloi (prayer beads) from the period 1750–1950; komboloi belonging to Buddhists, Catholics, Hindus, Muslims and Orthodox monks.

Peloponnesian Folklore Foundation: Vas. Alexandrou 1, 211 00 Nafplion; tel. 2752-028379; fax 2752-027960; e-mail pff@otenet.gr; internet www.pli.gr; f. 1974;

research, presentation, study and preservation of the material culture of Greece (costume, music and dance); br. in Stathmos; library of 10,115 vols; Pres. IOANNA PAPANTONIOU; Curator KANELLOS KANELLOPOULOS; publs *Endymatologica*, *Ethnographica*.

Olympia

Archaeological Museum: 270 65 Olympia; tel. and fax 2624-022529; e-mail protocol@zepka.culture.gr; internet www.culture.gr; f. 1970; Greek Geometric and Archaic bronzes; two pediments from Temple of Zeus, Hermes of Praxiteles, Victory of Paionios; finds from Sanctuary of Olympia and Pheidias' workshop; Roman sculpture; Dir GEORGIA CHATZI-SPILIOPOULOU.

Attached Museums:

Museum of the History of Excavations in Ancient Olympia: Olympia; tel. and fax 2624-022529; e-mail zepka@culture.gr; f. 2004; presentation of the history of the 19th-century German excavation and archaeological activity in Ancient Olympia; Dir GEORGIA CHATZI-SPILIOPOULOU.

Museum of the History of the Olympic Games: Olympia; tel. and fax 2624-022529; e-mail protocol@zepka.culture.gr; f. 1888; 463 objects (statues, inscriptions, vases, bronzes, etc.) detailing the history of the Olympic Games from the Mycenean to the Roman periods; Dir GEORGIA CHATZI-SPILIOPOULOU.

Paiania

Vorres Museum of Contemporary Greek Art and Folk Art: 1 Parodos Diad. Konstantinou, 190 02 Paiania, Attica; tel. 210-6642520; fax 210-6645775; e-mail info@vorresmuseum.gr; internet www.vorresmuseum.gr; f. 1983; covers 4,000 years of Greek history; two sections: folk art and architecture (a group of traditional buildings containing artefacts, furniture, etc.) and a museum of contemporary Greek art; Dir IAN VORRES; publ. *Catalogue*.

Rethymnon

Archaeological Museum: 741 00 Rethymnon; tel. 2831-54668; internet www.ellada.net/crete-info/museums/rethymno.php; f. 1991; artefacts from the late Neolithic period, early to late Minoan periods, Geometric and Archaic periods, and Hellenistic and Roman periods.

Historical and Folk Art Museum: 30 M. Vernardou St, 741 00 Rethymnon; tel. 2831-23398; fax 2831-23667; internet www.ellada.net/crete-info/museums/rethymno.php; f. 1998; 5,000 items of folk art; history of textiles; Pres. FALY G. VOYATZAKIS.

Rhodes

Archaeological Museum: Medieval City, 85 100 Rhodes; tel. 2241-365256; fax 2241-030688; e-mail kbepka@culture.gr; f. as Hospital of the Knights, built 1440–89; sculpture, vases and other objects from Rhodes, Ialysos, Kamiros and other sites, from Neolithic to late Roman times, funerary stelae dating from Middle Ages; library of 38,480 vols.

Rhodes Jewish Museum: Dossiadou St, Rhodes; tel. 31047-54779; fax 31047-58144; e-mail info@rhodesjewishmuseum.org; internet www.rhodesjewishmuseum.org; housed in fmr women's prayer rooms at 16th-century Kahal Shalom synagogue; attached to Rhodes Jewish Historical Foundation; Pres. BELLA RESTIS.

Thessaloniki

Archaeological Museum of Thessaloniki: Manolis Andronikos St 6, 546 21 Thessaloniki; tel. 2310-830538; fax 2310-861306; e-mail info.amth@culture.gr; internet www.amth.gr; f. 1912 renovated in 2006; exhibitions on prehistoric Macedonia, the birth of Macedonian cities, Macedonia from the 7th century BC to Late Antiquity, and Thessaloniki; educational activities for children and adults; archaeological and historical lectures; modern theatrical productions of ancient drama; library of 9,000 vols; Dir Dr POLYXENI ADAM-VELENI; publs *Archeologiko Ergo ste Makedonia kai Thrace* (1 a year), *Crater* (1 a year), *Thessaloniki Philippou Vassilissan*.

Macedonian Museum of Contemporary Art of Thessaloniki: 154 Egnatia St, 546 36 Thessaloniki; tel. 2310-240002; fax 2310-281567; e-mail mmcart@mmca.org.gr; internet www.macedonian-heritage.gr/museums; f. 1979; 2,000 works by Greek and foreign artists; library of 2,500 vols; Dir ANTONIS KOURTIS.

State Museum of Contemporary Art at Thessaloniki: Kolokotroni 21, Moni Lazariston, 564 30 Thessaloniki; tel. 2310-589140; fax 2310-600123; internet www.greekstatemuseum.com/contact_en; f. 1997; Costakis colln of 1,275 works of Russian avant-garde art; also houses Museum of Photography and Centre of Contemporary Art; Dir MILTIADES PAPANIKOLAOU.

Thessaloniki Museum of Photography: Warehouse A, Port of Thessaloniki, POB 23, 540 15 Thessaloniki; tel. 2310-566716; fax 2310-566717; e-mail press.thmp@culture.gr; internet www.thmphoto.gr; f. 1997; historical and contemporary Greek and int. photography; collects, preserves and promotes photographic heritage; collns and archives incl. 100,000 photographic objects; library of 17,000 vols; Dir VANGELIS IOAKIMIDIS.

Thessaloniki Olympic Museum: 3rd September & Ag. Dimitriou St, 546 36 Thessaloniki; tel. 2310-968531; fax 2310-968726; e-mail pr@olympicmuseum.org.gr; internet www.olympicmuseum-thessaloniki.org; f. 1998; history of athletics; Dir Arch. KYRIAKI OUDATZI.

Thessaloniki Science Centre & Technology Museum: 6 Km Thessaloniki, Thermi Rd, 57001, Thermi Thessaloniki; tel. 2310-483000; fax 2310-483 020; e-mail info@noesis.edu.gr; internet www.noesis.edu.gr; f. 1978, reorg. 2001; temporary exhibition hall; digital planetarium; cosmotheatre; exhibition related to science and technology; Dir CHRIS G. PAPADAKIS.

Universities

ANOTATI SCHOLI KALON TECHNON
(Athens School of Fine Art)

Odos Patission 42, 106 82 Athens

Telephone: 210-3816930
Fax: 210-3816926
E-mail: info@asfa.gr
Internet: www.asfa.gr

Founded 1837
Rector: YANNIS PAPADAKIS
Library of 29,000 vols
Number of teachers: 38
Number of students: 783

DIRECTORS OF SECTIONS

Painting: Prof. CHR. BOTSOGLOU
Printmaking: Prof. G. MILIOS
Sculpture: Prof. G. LAPPAS
Theoretical Studies: Prof. M. LAMBRAKI

Brs in Delphi, Hydra, Mykonos, Rhodes, Lesbos and Rethymnon.

ARISTOTELEIO PANEPISTIMIO THESSALONIKIS
(Aristotle University of Thessaloniki)

University Campus, 541 24 Thessaloniki

Telephone: 2310-996000
Internet: www.auth.gr

Founded 1925
State univ., with autonomous function
Language of instruction: Greek
Academic year: September to August

Rector: Prof. ANASTASIOS MANTHOS
Vice-Rector for Academic Affairs and Personnel: Prof. ATHANASIA TSATSAKOU
Vice-Rector for Finance and Devt: Assoc. Prof. ANDREAS GIANNAKOUDAKIS
Vice-Rector and Head of the Special Account of Research Funds: Prof. STAVROS PANNAS
Head of International Relations: HELEN KOTSAKI
Librarian: Prof. CHRISTOS BABATZIMOPOULOS
Library: see Libraries and Archives
Number of teachers: 2,287
Number of students: 92,509
Publications: *Panepistimioupoli* (4 a year), catalogue, scientific annals and faculty periodicals

DEANS

Faculty of Agriculture: NIKOLAOS MISOPOLINOS (Chair.)
Faculty of Dentistry: Prof. ATHANASIOS ATHANASIOU (Chair.)
Faculty of Education: Prof. SOFRONIOS CHATZISAVIDIS
Faculty of Engineering: Prof. NIKOLAOS MOUSIOPOULOS
Faculty of Fine Arts: Prof. G. KATSAGELOS
Faculty of Forestry and the Natural Environment: Prof. ANASTASIOS NASTIS (Chair.)
Faculty of Law, Economics and Political Sciences: Prof. GIANNOULA KARYMBALI-TSIPTSIOU
Faculty of Medicine: Prof. IOANNIS BONDIS (Chair.)
Faculty of Philosophy: Prof. PHOEVUS GIKOPOULOS
Faculty of Science: Prof. IOANNIS PAPADOGIANNIS
Faculty of Theology: Prof. IOANNIS KOGOULIS
Faculty of Veterinary Medicine: Prof. DIMITRIOS RAPTOPOULOS (Chair.)

CHAIRMEN OF SCHOOLS

Faculty of Education (tel. 2310-995062; fax 2310-995061):
  School of Early Childhood Education: Prof. GIORGIOS TSIAKALOS
  School of Primary Education: Prof. DEMETRIOS GERMANOS

Faculty of Engineering (tel. 2310-995601; fax 2310-995611):
  School of Architecture: Prof. NIKOLAOS KALOGIROU
  School of Chemical Engineering: Prof. VASSILIOS PAPAGEORGIOU
  School of Civil Engineering: Prof. DIMOSTHENIS ANGELLIDIS
  School of Electrical and Computer Engineering: Prof. NIKOLAOS MARGARIS
  School of Mathematics, Physics and Computational Sciences: Prof. GERASIMOS KOUROUKLIS
  School of Mechanical Engineering: Prof. NIKOLAOS MOUSIOPOULOS
  School of Rural and Survey Engineering: Prof. PETROS PATIAS
  School of Urban Regional Planning and Development (Veroia): Prof. NIKOLAOS RODOLAKIS

Faculty of Fine Arts (tel. 231-995071; fax 231-995073):
  School of Drama: Prof. NIKIFOROS PAPANDREOU

School of Film Studies: Prof. APOSTOLOS-FOKION VETTAS

School of Musical Studies: Prof. DIMITRIOS GIANNOU

School of Visual and Applied Arts: Prof. GEORGIOS GOLFINOS

Faculty of Law, Economics and Political Sciences (tel. 2310-996539; fax 2310-996526):

School of Economics: C. PAPADOPOULOS

School of Law: K. HATZIKONSTANTINOU

Faculty of Philosophy (tel. 2310-995173; fax 2310-997152):

School of English Language and Literature: Prof. ANGELIKI ATHANASIADOU

School of French Language and Literature: Prof. A. NENOPOULOU-DROSOU

School of German Language and Literature: Prof. IOANNA EKONOMOU-AGORASTOU

School of History and Archaeology: Prof. THEOHARIS PAZARAS

School of Italian Language and Literature: Prof. ANTONIOS TSOMPANOGLOU

School of Philology: Prof. ANTONIOS REGAKOS

School of Philosophy and Education: Prof. NIKOLAOS TERZIS

School of Psychology: Prof. G. KIOSEOGLOU

Faculty of Science (tel. 2310-998020; fax 2310-998022):

School of Biology: Prof. Z. SKOURAS

School of Chemistry: Assoc. Prof. ANDREAS GIANNAKOUDAKIS

School of Geology: Prof. GEORGIOS CHRISTOFIDIS

School of Informatics: A. POMBORTZIS

School of Mathematics: Prof. POLYCHRONIS MOISIADES

School of Physics: Prof. STERGIOS LOGOTHETIDIS

Faculty of Theology:

School of Ecclesiastical and Social Theology: Prof. GEORGIOS THEODOROUDIS

School of Theology: Prof. MILTIADES KONSTANTINOU

Independent Schools:

School of Journalism and Mass Media Studies: Prof. THEODOROS KORRES

School of Pharmacy: Prof. ASTERIOS TSIFTSOGLOU

School of Physical Education and Athletics in Serres: Prof. C. KAMPITSIS

School of Physical Education and Athletics in Thessaloniki: Prof. ASTERIOS DELIGIANNIS

DIMOKRITEIO PANEPISTIMIO THRAKIS
('Demokritos' University of Thrace)

Admin. Bldg, University Campus, 691 00 Komotini

Telephone: 2531-039000

Fax: 2531-039081

E-mail: intrela@duth.gr

Internet: www.duth.gr

Founded 1973

State control

Language of instruction: Greek

Academic year: September to August

Rector: A. KARABINIS

Vice-Rectors: K. SIMOPOULOS, ATH. KARABINIS, G. HADJICONSTANTINOU

Administrative Officer: E. TSITSOPOULOS

Library of 236,656 vols, 4,060 periodicals

Number of teachers: 495

Number of students: 18,627

DEANS

Faculty of Educational Sciences: TH. VOUGIOUKLIS

Faculty of Engineering: I. DIAMANTIS

Faculty of Law: K. KALAVROS

Faculty of Medicine: D. HATSERAS

Faculty of the Science of Physical Education and Sport: G. MAVROMMATIS

Department of Agricultural Development: G. VASSILIOU

Department of Architectural Engineering: C. ATHANASSOPOULOS

Department of Civil Engineering: ATH. KARABINIS

Department of Electrical Engineering and Computer Engineering: D. PAPADOPOULOS

Department of Environmental Engineering: VASS. TSICHRINTZIS

Department of Forestry and Management of the Environment and Natural Resources: K. SIDERIS

Department of Greek Literature: A. CHARALAMBAKIS

Department of History and Ethnology: D. SAMSARIS

Department of International Economic Relations and Development: G. HADJICONSTANTINOU

Department of Languages, Literature and Culture of the Black Sea Countries: I. SCHINAS

Department of Molecular Biology and Genetics: G. BOURIKAS

Department of Pre-school Education Sciences: L. BEZE

Department of Production and Management Engineering: ATH. KARABINAS

Department of Social Administration: K. REMELIS

Pedagogical Department of Primary Education: E. TARATORI

PROFESSORS

Faculty of Law (University Campus, New Law School, 691 00 Komotini; tel. 2531-039890; fax 2531-039897):

ALIPRANDIS, N., Labour Law

CHARALAMBAKIS, A., Penal Law

KALAVROS, K., Civil Procedural Law

KONSTANDINIDIS, A., Penal Procedural Law

MANIOTIS, D., Civil Procedural Law

PARARAS, P., Constitutional Law

PITSAKIS, K., History of Law

POULIS, G., Ecclesiastical Law

REMELIS, K., Administrative Law

SCHINAS, J., Commercial Law

Faculty of Medicine (Ioakim Kavyri 6, 681 00 Alexandroupoli; tel. 25510-30921; fax 25510-30922):

BOUGIOUKAS, Cardiac Surgery

BOURIKAS, G., Pathology

BOUROS, D., Pneumonology

CHATSERAS, D., Cardiology

CHOURDAKIS, K., Toxicology, Forensic Medicine

DIMITRIOU, TH., Anatomy

KARTALIS, G., Pathology

KOUSKOUKIS, K., Dermatology, Venereal Diseases

KTENIDOU-KARTALI, S., Microbiology

MALTEZOS, E., Pathology

MANOLAS, K., Surgery

MAROULIS, G., Obstetrics and Gynaecology

MINOPOULOS, G., Surgery

PAPADOPOULOS, E., Urology

PRASSOPOULOS, P., Radiology

SIMOPOULOS, K., Surgery

SIVRIDIS, E., Pathology

VARGEMEZIS, V., Nephrology

Faculty of the Science of Physical Education and Sport (7 km on National Rd, Komotini–Xanthi, 691 00 Komotini; tel. 2531-039621; fax 2531-039623; e-mail tefaa@phyed.duth.gr):

CHARACHOUSOU-KABITSI, Y., Mass Sports

GODOLIAS, G., Sports Medicine

KABITSIS, CH., Classical Athletics

KIOUMOURTZOGLOU, E., Basketball Coaching

LAIOS, ATH., Basketball Coaching

LAPARIDIS, K., Nutrition in Sports

MANDIS, K., Tennis

MAVROMATIS, G., Statistics

SERBEZIS, V., Teaching of Greek Folk Dancing

TAXILDARIS, K., Basketball

TOKMAKIDIS, S., Exercise Physiology

Department of Agricultural Development (Pantazidou 193, 682 00 Orestiada; tel. 2552-041161; fax 2552-041191; e-mail ezelidou@ores.duth.gr):

ABAS, Z., General and Special Animal Husbandry

BEZIRTZOGLOU, E., Microbiology, Microbe Ecology

GALANOPOULOS, K., Agricultural Economy

KOTOULA-SYKA, EL., Pests, Pesticides, Pest Control

KOUTROUMANIDIS, TH., Applied Economic Statistics

KOUTROUMBAS, SP., General and Special Agriculture

SPARTALIS, ST., Algebra

TOKATLIDIS, I., Genetics and Plant Improvement

VASSILIOU, G., Agricultural Pharmacology and Ecotoxicology

Department of Architectural Engineering (Vasilissis Sofias 1, 671 00 Xanthi; tel. 2541-079350; fax 2541-079349; e-mail info@arch.duth.gr):

AMERICANOU, E., Architectural Design

BARKAS, N., Building Construction and Architectural Acoustics

EXARCHOPOULOS, P.-L., Architectural Design and Compositions

KOKKORIS, P., Architectural Design

KOLOKOTRONIS, I., History of Art, European and American Art of the 20th Century

LIANOS, N., Architectural Design

MANTZOU, P., Architectural Design, Building Compositions

MICHAELIDIS, A., Architectural and Construction Sculpture

PATRIKIOS, G., Architectural Design, Spatial Organization and Microenvironment

POLYCHRONOPOULOS, D., Urban Planning

POTAMIANOS, I., History of Architecture

PREPIS, ALK., History of Art

THEONI, X., Architectural Design and Compositions, Creation of Building Units for Professional and Private Use

THOMAS, N., Architectural and Construction Drawing

TSIOUKAS, VASS., Topography

Department of Civil Engineering (Vasilissis Sofias 1, 671 00 Xanthi; tel. 2541-079031; fax 2541-020275; e-mail info@civil.duth.gr):

ATHANASSOPOULOS, CHR., Building Construction

GALOUSSIS, EV., Steel Construction

GDOUTOS, EM., Technical Engineering and Applied Mechanics

KARABINIS, ATH., Reinforced Concrete Structures

KARAGIANNIS, CH., Construction of Reinforced Concrete

KARALIS, TH., Soil Mechanics: Foundations

KOTSOVINOS, N., Hydraulics

LABRINOS, P., Higher Mathematics

LIOLIOS, AST., Higher Mathematics

MATSOUKIS, P.-F., Maritime Engineering

PANAGIOTAKOPOULOS, D., Construction Project Management

PANTAZOPOULOU, ST., Construction of Reinforced Concrete

PAPADOPOULOS, V., General Topology

SIDERIS, K., Building Materials

STEPHANIS, VAS., Transport Engineering, Survey Engineering

Department of Electrical Engineering and Computer Engineering (Vasilissis Sofias 1, 671 00 Xanthi; tel. 2541-079035; fax 2541-079037; e-mail info@ee.duth.gr):

BEKAKOS, M., Computers, Hardware
CHAMZAS, CHR., Signal and Image Processing, Coding, MM Communication Systems, Networks
GEORGOULAS, N., Microelectronic and Optoelectronic Materials and Elements
PAPADOPOULOS, D., Electric Engines
PAPAMARKOS, N., Electric Cicuits, Digital Filters, Digital Image Processing
SARRIS, EM., Electromagnetic Theory
SPARIS, P., Special Mechanical Engineering
THANAILAKIS, A., Electrical and Electronic Materials Technology
TSALIDIS, PH., Computer Science
TSANGAS, N., Nuclear Engineering and Technology

Department of Environmental Engineering (University Campus of Xanthi, Kimmeria, 671 00 Xanthi; tel. 2541-079101; fax 2541-079108; e-mail mlekidou@lib.duth.gr):

AIVAZIDIS, AL., Environmental Technology
OUZOUNIS, K., Environmental Chemistry
RAPSOMANIKIS, SP., Air Pollution, Atmospheric Pollutant Control Technology
TSICHRINTZIS, V., Ecological Engineering Technology
VOUDRIAS, E., Solid Waste Management

Department of Forestry and Management of the Environment and Natural Resources (Pantazidou 193, 682 00 Orestiada; tel. 2552-041171; fax 2552-041192; e-mail impatzio@ores.duth.gr):

AVRAMIDIS, ST., Wood Science
ILIADIS, LAZ., Forestry Informatics
KARANIKOLA, P., Forest Wood Entomology
MANOLAS, EV., Sociology and Environmental Science, Forest Education
MILIOS, IL., Silviculture
PAPAGEORGIOU, AT., Forest Genetics
TSACHALIDIS, E., Game Ecology and Management

Department of Greek Literature (University Campus, 691 00 Komotini; tel. 25310-39900; fax 25310-39901):

IOANNIDOU, CH., Ancient Greek Literature
KAMBAKI-VOUGIOUKLI, P., Applied Linguistics
KONTOGIANNI, VASS., Modern Greek Literature
MANAKIDOU, H., Ancient Greek Literature
MANOS, AND., Ancient Greek Philosophy
PANTELIDIS, N., General Linguistics
TSOURIS, K., Byzantine History and Archaeology
TZIATZI-PAPAGIANNI, M., Byzantine Literature

Department of History and Ethnology (Panaghi Tsaldari 1, 691 00 Komotini; tel. 25310-39462; fax 25310-39462):

CHATZOPOULOS, K., History of Modern Hellenism
GALLIS, K., Prehistoric Archaeology
PAPAZOGLOU, G., History (based on sources such as Codices)
SAMSARIS, D., Roman History
XIROTYRIS, N., Physical Anthropology

Department of International Economic Relations and Development (University Campus, 691 00 Komotini; tel. 2531-039826; fax 2531-039830; e-mail ekostant@ierd.duth.gr; internet www.ierd.duth.gr):

CHATZIKONSTANTINOU, G., Economic Theory
CHIONIS, DION., International (Direct) Investments and Multinationals
KONSTANDINIDIS, E., International Economic Law, International and European Business Law
MOURMOURIS, I., Transportation Economics and Management

Department of Languages, Literature and Culture of the Black Sea Countries (Panaghi Tsaldari 1, 691 00 Komotini; tel. 2531-039413; fax 2531-039421; e-mail ddiamant@kom.duth.gr):

FALANGAS, A., History and Civilization of the Western and Northern Black Sea Area
KEKRIDIS, E., Contemporary and Recent Culture of the Black Sea Peoples
THOMADAKI, EV., Theoretical Linguistics

Department of Molecular Biology and Genetics (Dimitras 19, Old Hospital, 681 00 Alexandroupoli; tel. and fax 25510-30610; e-mail secr@mbg.duth.gr):

CHLICHLIA, AIK., Immunobiology
GRIGORIOU, M., Molecular Biology
KOFFA, M., Cell Biology
PHYLAKTAKIDOU, K., Chemistry
SANDALTZOPOULOS, RAF., Molecular Biology

Department of Pre-school Education Sciences (Nea Chili, 681 00 Alexandroupoli; tel. 25510-39623; fax 25510-39624; e-mail secr@psed.duth.gr; internet www.psed.duth.gr):

BEZE, L., Psychology and Sociology of Education
GOGOU-KRITIKOU, L., Sociology of Education
METAXAKI-KOSIONIDOU, CHR., Informatics Applications in Pre-school Education
PETROGIANNIS, KON., Development Psychology

Department of Production and Management Engineering (University Campus of Xanthi, Kimmeria, 671 00 Xanthi; tel. 2541-079345; fax 2541-079361; e-mail secr@pme.duth.gr):

ANAGNOSTOPOULOS, K., Business Economics and Management with Engineering
CHATZOGLOU, P., Information Systems in Administration
SIMINTIRAS, A., Marketing
TOURASSIS, VASS., Industrial Production

Department of Social Administration (Panaghi Tsaldari 1, 691 00 Komitini; tel. 25310-39409; fax 25310-39442; e-mail dgogou@kom.duth.gr):

CHATZOPOULOS, VASS., EU Law and Policies
KALLINIKAKI-MANGRIOTI, TH., Social Work
KANDYLAKI, AG., Social Work and Local Development in Multicultural Societies
KATROUNGALOS, G., Public Law
PAPASTYLIANOU, A., Social Psychology
PAPATHEODOROU, CH., Social Policy
PETMEZIDOU-TSOULOUVI, M., Social Policy
VENIERIS, D., Social Policy
VIDALI, SOF., Criminology, Anti-crime Policy

Pedagogical Department of Primary Education (Nea Chili, 681 00 Alexandroupoli; tel. 25510-30024; fax 25510-39630; e-mail tsesmel@eled.duth.gr):

DAVAZOGLOU, ANG., Education of Children with Special Needs
KARAKATSANIS, P., Educational Philosophy
KEKKERIS, G., Informatics, Multimedia in Aesthetics Education
KEVREKIDIS, TH., Biology and Ecology
MICHAS, P., Teaching of Natural Sciences
PAPAGEORGIOU, G., Teaching of Chemistry, Environmental Chemistry
PETROPOULOS, I., Ancient Greek Literature
ROKKA, ANG., Earth Sciences, Geology, Geography
SAKONIDIS, CHAR., Teaching of Mathematics
TARATORI, EL., Teaching Methodology
VOUGIOUKLIS, TH., Mathematics

ELLINIKO ANOIKTO PANEPISTIMIO (Hellenic Open University)

18 Parodos Aristotelous St, 26 335 Patra
Telephone: 2610-367300

Fax: 2610-367350
E-mail: info@eap.gr
Internet: www.eap.gr
Founded 1992
State control
Pres.: Prof. HARRY COCCOSSIS
Sec.-Gen.: CHARALAMPOS RODOPOULOS

Number of teachers: 1,565
Number of students: 26,240 (15,541 undergraduate, 10,699 postgraduate)

DEANS

Faculty of Applied Arts: DEMETRIOS ZEVGOLIS
Faculty of Humanities: ALEXIOS KOKKOS
Faculty of Sciences and Technology: ATHANASIOS SKONDRAS
Faculty of Social Sciences: GEORGE AGIOMIRGIANAKIS

ETHNIKON KAI KAPODISTRIAKON PANEPISTIMION ATHINON (National and Capodistrian University of Athens)

Odos Panepistimiou 30, 106 79 Athens
Telephone: 210-3614301
Fax: 210-3602145
Internet: www.uoa.gr
Founded 1837
State control
Language of instruction: Greek
Academic year: September to June

Rector: Prof. D. ASIMAKOPOULOS
Vice-Rector for Academic Affairs and Personnel: Prof. G. KREATSAS
Vice-Rector for Student Affairs, Culture and International Relations: Prof. I. KARAKOSTAS

Number of teachers: 2,200
Number of students: 122,000 (incl. 12,000 postgraduates)

DEANS

School of Health Sciences: KONSTANTINOS DIMOPOULOS
School of Law, Economics and Political Sciences: CHRISTOS ROZAKIS
School of Philosophy: (vacant)
School of Science: HARALAMBOS PAPAGEORGIOU
School of Theology: CONSTANTINE SCOUTERIS

ETHNIKO METSOVIO POLYTECHNEIO (National Technical University of Athens)

Polytechnioupoli, Zografou, 157 80 Athens
Telephone: 210-7722017
Fax: 210-7722028
Internet: www.ntua.gr
Founded 1836
State control
Language of instruction: Greek
Academic year: September to August

Rector: Prof. ANDREAS ANDREOPOULOS
Vice-Rectors: P. KOTTIS, E. DRIS
Chief Admin. Officer: E. RELAKI
Librarian: M. KALABALIKI
Library: see Libraries and Archives
Number of teachers: 700
Number of students: 1,000

Publications: *Pyrphoros* (24 a year), *Scientific Papers*, *Scientific Year Book*

DIRECTORS OF SECTIONS

Applied Mathematics and Physics:
Humanities, Social Science and Law: V. NIKOLAIDOU
Mathematics: K. KYRIAKIS
Physics: P. PISSIS

Architecture:

Architectural Design: AMILIOS KORONAIOS
Design and Technology: ALEKSANDRA MONEMVASITOU
Design, Visual Studies and Communication: IOANNIS TSOUDEROS
Urban and Regional Planning: IOANNIS TERZOGLOU

Chemical Engineering:

Chemical Sciences: A. HARALAMBOUS
Material Science and Engineering: F. ROUBANI-KALANZOPOULOU
Process Analysis and Plant Design: A. BOUDOUVIS
Synthesis and Development of Industrial Processes: A. VLYSSIDIS

Civil Engineering:

Engineering Construction and Management: A. ANAGNOSTOPOULOS
Geotechnical Engineering: (vacant)
Structural Engineering: J. ERMOPOULOS
Transportation Planning and Engineering: J. FRANTSESKAKIS
Water Resources, Hydraulic and Maritime Engineering: A. ADREADAKIS

Electrical and Computing Engineering:

Computer Science: G. STASINOPOULOS
Electrical Power: J. STATHOPOULOS
Electroscience: N. OUZOUNOGLOU

Mechanical Engineering:

Fluid Mechanics Engineering: G. BERGELES
Industrial Management and Operational Research: G. FOKAS-KOSMETATOS
Manufacturing Technology: A. MAMALIS
Mechanical Construction and Automatic Control: P. MAKRIS
Nuclear Engineering: D. LEONIDOU
Thermal Engineering: K. RAKOPOULOS

Mining and Metallurgical Engineering:

Geological Sciences: Prof. Dr E. MPOSKOS
Metallurgy and Materials Technology: Assoc. Prof. K. TSAKALAKIS
Mining Engineering: Prof. ALEXANDROS I. SOFIANOS

PROFESSORS

AFRATI, F., Electrical and Computer Engineering
ANAGNOSTOU, M., Electrical and Computer Engineering
ANASTASSOPOULOU, I., Materials Science and Engineering
ANDREOPOULOS, A., Synthesis and Development of Industrial Processing
ANDROUTSOPOULOS, G., Process Analysis and Plant Design
ANTONOPOULOS, K., Mechanical Engineering
ASSIMAKOPOULO, D., Process Analysis and Plant Design
ASSIMAKOPOULOS, V., Electrical and Computer Engineering
ATHANASOULIS, G., Naval Architecture and Marine Engineering
AVARITSIOTIS, J., Electrical and Computer Engineering
BAFA, G., Process Analysis and Plant Design
BATIS, G., Materials Science and Engineering
BOUDOUVIS, A., Process Analysis and Plant Design
BOURKAS, P., Electrical and Computer Engineering
CAPROS, P., Electrical and Computer Engineering
CAPSALIS, C., Electrical and Computer Engineering
CARAYANNIS, G., Electrical and Computer Engineering
CHRYSSOULAKIS, J., Materials Science and Engineering
CONSTANTINOU, F., Electrical and Computer Engineering
COTTIS, P., Electrical and Computer Engineering

DERVOS, K., Electrical and Computer Engineering
DIALINAS, E., Electrical and Computer Engineering
FRANGOPOULOS, CH., Naval Architecture and Marine Engineering
FRANGOS, P., Electrical and Computer Engineering
FTICOS, CHR., Synthesis and Development of Industrial Processing
GLYTSIS, E., Electrical and Computer Engineering
HATZIARGYRIOU, N., Electrical and Computer Engineering
HIZANIDIS, K., Electrical and Computer Engineering
KAKATSIOS, X., Mechanical Engineering
KAKLIS, P., Naval Architecture and Marine Engineering
KANELLOPOULOS, J., Electrical and Computer Engineering
KASELOURI-RIGOPOULOU, V., Chemical Sciences
KAYAFAS, E., Electrical and Computer Engineering
KOLISIS, FR., Synthesis and Development of Industrial Processing
KOLLIAS, S., Electrical and Computer Engineering
KOUKIOS, E., Synthesis and Development of Industrial Processing
KOULOUMBI, N., Materials Science and Engineering
KOUMANTAKIS, I., Geological Sciences
KOUSSIOURIS, T., Electrical and Computer Engineering
KOUTSOURIS, D., Electrical and Computer Engineering
KRIKELIS, N., Mechanical Engineering
KYRTATOS, N., Naval Architecture and Marine Engineering
LIVADITI, K., Geological Sciences
LOIS, E., Synthesis and Development of Industrial Processing
LOIZIDOU-MALAMIS, M., Chemical Sciences
LOUKAKIS, TH., Naval Architecture and Marine Engineering
MACHIAS, A., Electrical and Computer Engineering
MAGLARIS, V., Electrical and Computer Engineering
MAMALIS, A., Mechanical Engineering
MANIAS, S., Electrical and Computer Engineering
MARAGOS, P., Electrical and Computer Engineering
MARATOS, N., Electrical and Computer Engineering
MARINOS-KOURI, D., Process Analysis and Plant Design
MARKATO, N., Process Analysis and Plant Design
MARKOPOULOU-IGGLESI, O., Chemical Sciences
MAROULI, Z., Process Analysis and Plant Design
MATHIOUDAKIS, K., Mechanical Engineering
MAVRAKOS, S., Naval Architecture and Marine Engineering
MITROU, N., Electrical and Computer Engineering
MOROPOULOU, A., Materials Science and Engineering
MPERGELES, G., Mechanical Engineering
MPOSKOS, E., Geological Sciences
NEOU-SYNGOUNA, P., Metallurgy and Materials Technology
OCHSENKUEHN-PETROPOULOU, M., Chemical Sciences
PANAGIOTOU, G. N., Mining Engineering
PANAGOPOULOS, C., Metallurgy and Materials Technology
PANAGOPOULOS, K. J., Mining Engineering
PAPADIMITRIOU, G., Metallurgy and Materials Technology
PAPAILIOU, K., Mechanical Engineering

PAPAKONSTANTINOU, G., Electrical and Computer Engineering
PAPANIKOLAOU, A., Naval Architecture and Marine Engineering
PAPANTONIS, D., Mechanical Engineering
PAPASPYRIDES, C. D., Synthesis and Development of Industrial Processing
PAPAVASILOPOULOS, G., Electrical and Computer Engineering
PAPAYANNAKI, L., Process Analysis and Plant Design
PAPAYANNAKOS, N., Process Analysis and Plant Design
PAPAZOGLOU, V., Naval Architecture and Marine Engineering
PARASKEVOPOULOS, P., Electrical and Computer Engineering
PASPALIARIS, I., Metallurgy and Materials Technology
PEKMESTZI, K., Electrical and Computer Engineering
PHILIPPOPOULOS, K., Process Analysis and Plant Design
PROTONOTARIOS, E., Electrical and Computer Engineering
PSARAFTIS, CH., Naval Architecture and Marine Engineering
RAKOPOULOS, K., Mechanical Engineering
ROGDAKIS, E., Mechanical Engineering
ROUBANI-KALANZOPOULOU, F., Materials Science and Engineering
ROUMELIOTIS, J., Electrical and Computer Engineering
SAMOUILIDIS, E., Electrical and Computer Engineering
SELLIS, T., Electrical and Computer Engineering
SFANTSIKOPOULOS, M., Mechanical Engineering
SIMITZIS, J., Materials Science and Engineering
SIMOPOULOS, S., Mechanical Engineering
SKORDALAKIS, E., Electrical and Computer Engineering
SPENTZAS, K., Mechanical Engineering
SPYRELLIS, N., Chemical Sciences
STAFYLOPATIS, A. G., Electrical and Computer Engineering
STAMATAKI, S., Mining Engineering
STASSINOPOULOS, G., Electrical and Computer Engineering
STATHOPULOS, I. A., Electrical and Computer Engineering
STOURNAS, S., Synthesis and Development of Industrial Processing
SYKAS, E., Electrical and Computer Engineering
TATSIOPOULOS, I., Mechanical Engineering
THEODOROU, N., Electrical and Computer Engineering
THEODOROU, TH., Materials Science and Engineering
THEOLOGOU, M., Electrical and Computer Engineering
TRIANTAFYLLOU, G., Naval Architecture and Marine Engineering
TSALAMENGAS, J., Electrical and Computer Engineering
TSANAKAS, P., Electrical and Computer Engineering
TSANGARIS, G., Materials Science and Engineering
TSANGARIS, S., Mechanical Engineering
TSEZOS, M., Metallurgy and Materials Technology
TSIMAS, S., Chemical Sciences
TZABIRAS, G., Naval Architecture and Marine Engineering
TZAFESTAS, S., Electrical and Computer Engineering
UZUNOGLOU, N., Electrical and Computer Engineering
VASSILIOU, P., Materials Science and Engineering
VASSILIOU, Y., Electrical and Computer Engineering

VGENOPOULOS, A., Geological Sciences
VLYSSIDIS, A., Synthesis and Development of Industrial Processing
VOMVORIDIS, J., Electrical and Computer Engineering
VOURNAS, C., Electrical and Computer Engineering
XANTHAKIS, J., Electrical and Computer Engineering
YOVA, D., Electrical and Computer Engineering
ZACHOS, S., Electrical and Computer Engineering
ZEVGOLIS, E. N., Metallurgy and Materials Technology

GEOPONIKO PANEPISTIMIO ATHINON
(Athens Agricultural University)

Iera Odos 75, 118 55 Athens
Telephone: 210-5294802
Fax: 210-3460885
E-mail: r@aua.gr
Internet: www.aua.gr

Founded 1920

Rector: Prof. ANDREAS KARAMANOS
Sec.-Gen.: CON. TSAKOUMAKIS

Number of teachers: 177
Number of students: 3,500

Faculties of agricultural biotechnology, animal science, crop science, food science and technology, natural resources management and agricultural engineering, rural economics and development, science.

DIRECTORS

Laboratory of Agribusiness Management: PATSIS PANAGIOTIS
Laboratory of Agricultural Engineering: NICK SIGRIMIS
Laboratory of Agricultural Extension, Agricultural Systems and Rural Sociology: KASIMIS CHARALAMBOS
Laboratory of Agricultural Hydraulics: PETROS G. KERKIDES
Laboratory of Agricultural Zoology and Entomology: NIKOLAOS G. EMMANUEL
Laboratory of Agronomy: ANDREAS KARAMANOS
Laboratory of Anatomy and Physiology of Farm Animals: IOANNIS MENEGATOS
Laboratory of Animal Breeding and Husbandry: ROGDAKIS EMMANUEL
Laboratory of Animal Nutrition: GEORGE ZERVAS
Laboratory of Applied Hydrobiology: SOFRONIOS E. PAPOUTSOGLOU
Laboratory of Botany: GEORGE SARLIS
Laboratory of Dairy Research: IOANNIS KANDARAKIS
Laboratory of Ecology and Environmental Sciences: GERASIMOS ARAPIS
Laboratory of Electron Microscopy: KONSTANTINOS FASSEAS
Laboratory of Enzyme Technology: Y. CLONIS
Laboratory of Floriculture and Landscape Architecture: JOANNIS CHRONOPOULOS
Laboratory of Food Chemistry: M. KOMAITIS
Laboratory of Food Process Engineering, Treatment and Preservation of Agricultural Products: P. RODIS
Laboratory of Food Quality Control and Hygiene: P. ATHANASOPOULOS
Laboratory of General and Agricultural Meteorology: AIKATERINI CHRONOPOULOU-SERELI
Laboratory of General and Agricultural Microbiology: GEORGE AGGELIS
Laboratory of General Chemistry: MOSCHOS POLISSIOU
Laboratory of Genetics: MICHAEL LOUKAS
Laboratory of Informatics: ALEXANDROS SIDERIDIS

Laboratory of Mathematics and Theoretical Mechanics: TAKIS SAKKALIS
Laboratory of Microbiology and Biotechnology of Foods: G. I. NYCHAS
Laboratory of Mineralogy and Geology: GEORGE MIGIROS
Laboratory of Molecular Biology: POLYDEUKIS HATZOPOULOS
Laboratory of Pesticide Science: BASIL ZIOGAS
Laboratory of Physics: ATHANASIOS HOUNTAS
Laboratory of Plant Breeding and Biometry: PANTOUSES J. KALTSIKES
Laboratory of Plant Physiology and Morphology: IOANNIS DROSSOPOULOS
Laboratory of Political Economy and European Integration: MARTINOS NIKOLAOS
Laboratory of Pomology: CONSTANTINE A. PONTIKIS
Laboratory of Rural Economic Development: SOPHIA EFSTRATOGLOU
Laboratory of Rural Policy and Cooperatives: DAMIANOS DIMITRIS
Laboratory of Sericulture and Apiculture: PASCHALIS HARIZANIS
Laboratory of Soil Science and Agricultural Chemistry: KOLLIAS VASSILIKI
Laboratory of Vegetable Crops: CHRISTOS M. OLYMPIOS
Laboratory of Viticulture: MANOLIS N. STAVRAKAKIS

HAROKOPIO PANEPISTIMION
(Harokopio University)

70 El. Venizelou St, 17671 Athens
Telephone: 210-9549100
Fax: 210-9577050
E-mail: haruniv@hua.gr
Internet: www.hua.gr

Founded 1990
State control

Rector: ANDREAS KIRIAKOUSIS
Vice-Rector for Academic Affairs and Staff: KATERINA MARIDAKI-KASSOTAKI
Vice-Rector for Economic Planning and Development: SMARAGDI ANTONOPOULOU

Library of 8,000 vols, 200 journals
Number of teachers: 65
Number of students: 430

IKONOMIKON PANEPISTIMION ATHINON
(Athens University of Economics and Business)

Odos Patission 76, 104 34 Athens
Telephone: 210-8203250
Fax: 210-8228419

47 Evelpidon Str., 113 62 Athens
Telephone: 210-8203640
Fax: 210-8228655
Internet: www.aueb.gr

Founded 1920

Faculties of business administration, computer science, economics, international and European economic studies, management science, marketing and statistics

Rector: Prof. ANDREAS KINTIS
Sec.-Gen.: S. BENOS
Librarian: G. THEOFANOPOULOU

Library of 100,000 vols, 1,000 periodicals: See Libraries and Archives
Number of teachers: 118
Number of students: 11,800

IONIO PANEPISTIMIO
(Ionian University)

Rizospaston Voulefton 7, 491 00 Corfu
Telephone: 2661-044878
Fax: 2661-022549
E-mail: int_rel@ionio.gr
Internet: www.ionio.gr

Founded 1984
State control
Academic year: October to July

Rector: DIMITRIOS TSOUGARAKIS
Vice-Rector for Academic Management and Human Resources: CHARALAMBOS XANTHOUDAKIS
Vice-Rector for Financial Management: VASILIOS CHRISIKOPOULOS

Departments of archives and library science, audio and visual arts, computer science, foreign languages, history, music studies, translation and interpreting.

PANEPISTIMION AEGAEOU
(University of the Aegean)

University Hill, Admin. Bldg 2, 811 00 Mytilene
Telephone: 2251-036000
Fax: 2251-036009
Internet: www.aegean.gr

Founded 1984

Chios campus: depts of business administration, shipping, transport and trade; Mytilene campus: depts of environmental studies, geography, marine sciences, social anthropology, sociology; Rhodes campus: depts of Mediterranean studies, primary education, secondary education; Samos campus: depts of mathematics, information and communication systems

Rector: Prof. SOKRATIS K. KATSIKAS
Librarian: ELLI VLACHOU

Library of 86,674 vols
Number of teachers: 422
Number of students: 11,828 (7,599 undergraduate, 4,229 postgraduate)

PANEPISTIMION IOANNINON
(University of Ioannina)

University Campus, 451 10 Ioannina
Telephone: 2651-097446
Fax: 2651-097200
E-mail: intlrel@cc.uoi.gr
Internet: www.uoi.gr

Founded 1964 as a dept of the Aristotle Univ. of Thessaloniki; ind. univ. 1970
State control
Language of instruction: Greek
Academic year: September to June

Rector: Prof. GEORGIOS DIMOU
Vice-Rectors: Prof. NIKI J. AGNANTIS, Prof. IOANNIS GEROTHANASIS, Prof. CHRISTOS MASSALAS
Registrar: L.-N. PAPALOUKAS
Librarian: GEORGIOS ZACHOS (acting)

Library of 310,000 vols
Number of teachers: 500
Number of students: 13,000

Publications: Eperitis 'Dodoni I' (history and archaeology, 1 a year), Eperitis 'Dodoni II' (philology, 1 a year), Eperitis 'Dodoni III' (philosophy, education and psychology, 1 a year)

DEANS

School of Educational Sciences: Prof. A. PAPAIOANNOU
School of Medicine: Prof. EPAMINONDAS TSIANOS
School of Natural Resources in Agrinio: Prof. GEORGE LEONTARIS (acting)
School of Natural Sciences: Prof. GEORGIOS KARAKOSTAS
School of Philosophy: Prof. ERATOSTHENIS KAPSOMENOS
School of Science and Technology: (vacant)

PROFESSORS

School of Educational Sciences (tel. 2651-097454; fax 2651-097020):

DIMOU, G., Pedagogics and Psychology of Learning Disabilities
KANAVAKIS, M., Pedagogics
KAPSALIS, G.
KARAFYLIS, G., Society Philosophy
KARPOZILOU, M.
KONSTANTINOU, C., School Pedagogics
STAVROU, L., Psychology of Pre-school Education
TZOULIS, CH., Modern Greek Literature
ZAHARIS, D., Evolutionary Psychology in Education

School of Medicine (tel. 2651-097201; fax 2651-097019):

AGNADI-GIRA, N. J., Pathological Anatomy
ANDRONIKOU, S., Neo-natology
ASIMAKOPOULOS, C., Otorhinolaryngology
BERIS, A., Orthopaedics
BOURANTAS, C., Pathology, Haematology
DROSOS, A., Pathology-rheumatology
EFRAIMIDIS, S., Radiology
EVANGELOU, A., Physiology
FOTSIS, TH., Biological Chemistry
GEORGATOS, S., Biology
GEROULANOS, ST., History of Medicine
GLAROS, D., Medical Physics
HATZIS, I., Dermatology
IOANNIDIS, I., Hygiene
KALEF-EZRA, J., Medical Physics
KANAVAROS, P., Anatomy-Histology
KAPPAS, A., Surgery
KIRITSIS, A., Neurology
KONSTANTOPOULOS, S., Pathology and Pneumonology
LOLIS, D., Obstetrics and Gynaecology
MALAMOU-MITSI, V., Pathology
MARSELOS, M.-A., Medical Pharmacology
MAVREAS, V., Psychiatry
PAPADOPOULOS, G., Anaesthiology
PARASKEVAIDIS, C., Organic Peptide Chemistry
PAVLIDIS, N., Oncology
PSILAS, C., Ophthalmology
SEFERIADIS, C., Biological Chemistry
SIAMOPOULOS, K., Pathology and Nephrology
SIAMOPOULOU-MAVRIDOU, A., Paediatrics
SKEVAS, A., Otorhinolaryngology
SOFIKITIS, N., Urology
SOUCACOS, P., Orthopaedics
TSIANOS, E., Oncology
TZAFLIDOU, M., Medical Physics
XENAKIS, T., Orthopaedics

School of Natural Resources in Agrinio:

FOTOPOULOS, CH., Administration of Agricultural Enterprises
MATTHOPOULOS, D., Administration of Environment and Natural Resources

School of Natural Sciences (tel. 2651-097190; fax 2651-097005):

AKRIVIS, G., Computer Science
ALBANIS, T., Environmental Protection
ALISSANDRAKIS, C., Physics of the Sun and Space
ASSIMAKOPOULOS, P., Nuclear Physics and Radio Ecology
BAIKOUSIS, CH., Differential Geometry
BATAKIS, N., Physics
BOLIS, TH., Combinatorial Group Theory
BOLOVINOS, AG., Atomic and Molecular Physics
DOUGIAS, S., Mathematical Analysis
DRAINAS, C., Chemistry
EVANGELOU, SP., Physics, Theory of Condensed Matter
EVMIRIDIS, N., Inorganic Chemistry
FERENTINOS, K., Statistics
FILOS, C., Mathematical Analysis
GALATSANOS, N., Computer Science
GEROTHANASIS, I., Organic Chemistry

GRAMMATIKOPOULOS, M., Differential Equations
HADJILIADIS, N., Inorganic and General Chemistry
HASANIS, T., Differential Geometry
KAMARATOS, E., Physical Chemistry
KAMBANOS, T., Inorganic Chemistry
KARAKOSTAS, G., Mathematical Analysis and Applications
KATSARAS, A., Functional Analysis
KATSOULIS, V., Meteorology and Climatology
KONDOMINAS, M., Chemistry
KOSMAS, M., Chemistry
KOSTARAKIS, P., Physics
KOUFOGIORGOS, TH., Differential Geometry
KOVALA-DEMERTZI, D., Inorganic Chemistry
LAGARIS, I., Computer Science
LEONDARIS, G., Physics, Elemental Multiplets
LOUKAS, S., Statistics
MANESIS, E., Physics, High Energy Theory
MARMARIDIS, N., Algebra
MASSALAS, CH., Continuum Physics and Mechanics
PANTIS, G., Theory of Nuclear Physics
PHILOS, C., Differential Equations
POMONIS, F., Industrial Chemistry
SAKARELLO DAITSO, M., Biochemistry
SAKARELLOS, C., Organic Peptide Chemistry
SDOUKOS, A., Industrial Chemistry
SFIKAS, Y. G., Differential Equations
STAVROULAKIS, I., Differential Equations
TAMVAKIS, K., Elementary Particle Theory and Cosmology
TRIANTIS, F., High-Energy Physics and Related Technological Applications
TSAMATOS, P., Mathematical Analysis
TSANGARIS, J., Inorganic and General Chemistry
VAGIONAKIS, C., Physics
VERGADOS, J., Theoretical Physics

School of Philosophy (tel. 2651-097176):

APOSTOLOPOULOU, G., History, Interpretation and Practice of Philosophy
ATHANASIOU, L., Language Teaching and Evaluation
CHADJIDAKI-BAHARA, T., Byzantine Archaeology
GOTOVOS, A., Pedagogics
HADJIDAKI-BACHARA, T., Byzantine Archaeology
KAPSOMENOS, E., Modern Greek Literature and Literary Theory
KARPOZILOS, A.-D., Medieval Greek Literature
KATSOURIS, A., Ancient Greek Philology
KONDORINI, B., History and Archaeology
KONSTANDINIDIS, C., Ancient and Medieval Greek Literature
KORDOSIS, M., Ancient and Medieval Greek Literature
MARAGOU, E., Classical Archaeology
MAVROMATIS, J., Byzantine Philology and Post-Byzantine Philology
MAVROYIORGOS, Y., Pedagogic Educational Policy
NOUTSOS, CH., History of Education
NOUTSOS, P., Philosophy
PALIOURAS, A., Byzantine Archaeology
PAPACONSTANDINOU, P., Pedagogics
PAPADIMITRIOU, E., Philosophy
PAPADOPOULOS, A., Prehistoric Archaeology
PAPAGEORGIOU, G., Modern History
PAPAPOSTOLOU, J., Classical Archaeology
PERISSINAKIS, J., Ancient Greek Literature
PLOUMIDIS, G., Venetian History and Historical Geography
RAIOS, D., Ancient Greek and Latin Philology
SIOROKAS, G., Modern European History
STASINOS, D., Psychology
SYNODINOU, A., Ancient Greek Philology
TRIANTI, A., Archaeology

TSANGALAS, K., Folklore

School of Science and Technology:

CHARALAMBOPOULOS, A., Material Science
DRAINAS, C., Chemistry
KAXIRAS, E., Material Science
MASSALAS, CH., Continuum Physics and Mechanics
PSARROPOULOU, A., Animal Physiology

Independent Department of Economics:

PALYVOS, TH., Economics

PANEPISTIMIO KRITIS
(University of Crete)

741 00 Rethymnon, Crete
Telephone: 2831-077900
Fax: 2831-077909
E-mail: rectsecr@cc.uoc.gr
Internet: www.uoc.gr
Founded 1973
State control
Language of instruction: Greek
Academic year: September to June

Rector: Prof. CHRISTOS NIKOLAOU
Vice-Rectors: Prof. MICHAEL DAMANAKIS, Prof. AGELOS KRANIDIS
Dir for Int. and Public Relations: Dr STELLA PAPADAKI-TZEDAKI
Librarian: MICHALIS TZEKAKIS

Library of 145,000 vols
Number of teachers: 580
Number of students: 10,628

Publications: *Ariadne* (faculty of letters), *Mandatoforos* (Modern Greek studies).

AFFILIATED INSTITUTION

Foundation for Research and Technology–Hellas: POB 1385, 711 10 Heraklion; tel. 281-391500; fax 281-391555; e-mail central@admin.forth.gr; internet www.forth.gr; f. 1983; 254 research and teaching staff; 374 graduate students; Chair. Prof. E. N. ECONOMOU.

Constituent Institutes:

Institute of Applied and Computational Mathematics: internet www.iacm.forth.gr; Dir Prof. VASSILIOS DOUGALIS.

Institute of Chemical Engineering and High Temperature Chemical Processes: internet www.iceht.forth.gr; Dir Prof. A. C. PAYATAKES.

Institute of Chemical Process Engineering Research: internet www.cperi.forth.gr; Dir Prof. C. KIPARISSIDES.

Institute of Computer Science: internet www.ics.forth.gr; Dir Prof. CONSTANTINE STEPHANIDIS.

Institute of Electronic Structure and Lasers: internet www.iesl.forth.gr; Dir Prof. C. FOTAKIS.

Institute of Mediterranean Studies: internet www.ims.forth.gr; Dir Prof. A. KALPAXIS.

Institute of Molecular Biology and Biotechnology: internet www.imbb.forth.gr; Dir Prof. G. THIREOS.

PANEPISTIMION MAKEDONIAS
(University of Macedonia)

Egnatia 156, POB 1591, 540 06 Thessaloniki
Telephone: 231-0844825
Fax: 231-0844536
E-mail: grad@uom.gr
Internet: www.uom.gr
Founded 1957 as Graduate Industrial School of Thessaloniki
State control
Rector: Prof. KONSTANTINOS VELENZAS

Vice-Rectors: Prof. CONSTANTINOS MARGARITIS, Prof. CONSTANTINOS VELENTZAS
Secretary-General: TSOMOU-FISTA EVAGGELIA
Librarian: ANNA FRANKOU

Number of teachers: 108
Number of students: 8,000

PROFESSORS

ALYGIZAKIS, ANTONIOS, Music Science and Art
BARALEXIS, SPYROS, Accounting and Finance
CHARALAMPOUS, DIMITRIOS, Educational and Social Studies
GEORGANTA, ZOE, Applied Informatics
IOANNIDIS, DIMITRIOS, Economics
KAPSALIS, ACHILEAS, Educational and Social Studies
KARAGIANNI, STELLA, Economics
KARFAKIS, COSTAS, Economics
KATOS, ANASTASIOS, Applied Informatics
KATRANIDIS, STELIOS, Economics
KONSTANTOPOULOU, CHRYSSOULA, Applied Informatics
KOUSKOUVELIS, ILIAS, International, European, Economic and Political Studies
LABRIANIDIS, LOIS, Economics
LAZARIDIS, JOHN, Accounting and Finance
LAZOS, BAIOS, Business Administration
MARGARITIS, KONSTANTINOS, Applied Informatics
MOURMOURAS, IOANNIS, Economics
NOULAS, ATHANASIOS, Accounting and Finance
PALIVOS, THEODORE, Economics
PAPADIMITRIOU, JOHN, Applied Informatics
PAPADOPOULOS, DIMITRIOS, Accounting and Finance
PAPAMATTHEOU MATSCHKE, HANS-UWE, Music Science and Art
PAPARRIZOS, KONSTANTINOS, Applied Informatics
PAULIDIS, GEOGRIOS, Educational and Social Studies
PEKOS, GEORGE, Applied Informatics
PIPEROPOULOS, GEORGE, Business Administration
SKALIDIS, ELEFTHERIOS, Accounting and Finance
TARABANIS, KONSTANTINOS, Business Administration
THEMELI, CHRISANTHI, Accounting and Finance
THEODOSIOU, IOANNIS, Economics
TRIARHOU, LAZAROS, Educational and Social Studies
TSIOTRAS, GEORGE, Business Administration
TSOPELA, VINIA, Music Science and Art
VELENTZAS, KONSTANTINOS, Economics
XIARHOS, STAVROS, Economics
XIROTIRI-KOUFIDOU, STELLA, Business Administration
XOURIS, DIMITRIOS, Business Administration

PANEPISTIMION PATRON
(University of Patras)

Univ. Campus, 265 04 Patras

Telephone: (261) 991822
Fax: (261) 991771
E-mail: rectorate@upatras.gr
Internet: www.upatras.gr

Founded 1964
State control
Language of instruction: Greek
Academic year: September to August

Rector: Prof. GEORGE PANAYIOTAKIS
Vice-Rector for Academic Affairs and Personnel: Prof. ANNA ROUSSOU
Vice-Rector for Financial Planning and Devt: Prof. CHRISTOFOROS KRONTIRAS
Vice-Rector for Strategic Research Planning and Devt: Prof. DIMITRIOS KALPAXIS
Admin. Officer: CHRISTINA KOLOKITHA

Number of teachers: 925
Number of students: 27,586

DEANS

School of Engineering: Prof. NICK ANIFANTIS
School of Health Sciences: Asst Prof. VENETSANA KYRIAZOPOULOU
School of Humanities and Social Sciences: Prof. CHRISTOS TEREZIS
School of Natural Sciences: Prof. CHRISTOS KORDOULIS

PROFESSORS

School of Economics and Management Sciences

Department of Business Administration:
PAVLIDES, G.
SYRIPOULOS, K.
VERNARDAKIS, N.
ZAHARATOS, G.

Department of Economics:
DAOULI-DEMOUSI, I.
DEMOUSSIS, M.
DIMARA, E.
SKOURAS, D.
SYPSAS, P.

School of Engineering

Department of Architecture:
POLYDORIDES, N.

Department of Chemical Engineering:
DASSIOS, G.
KENNOU, ST.
KOUTSOUKOS, P.
KRAVARIS, K.
LADAS, S.
LYBERATOS, G.
NIKOLOPOULOS, P.
PANDIS, S.
PAVLOU, S.
PAYATAKES, A.
RAPAKOULIAS, D.
TSAHALIS, D.
TSAMOPOULOS, J.
TSITSILIANIS, K.
VAYENAS, C.
VERYKIOS, X.

Department of Civil Engineering:
ANAGNOSTOPOULOS, S.
ATHANASOPOULOS, G.
ATMATZIDIS, D.
BESKOS, D.
CHRYSIKOPOULOS, K.
DEMETRACOPOULOS, A.
DRITSOS, ST.
FARDIS, M.
KALERIS, V.
KARABALIS, D.
MAKRIS, N.
PAPAGEORGIOU, A.
STEFANIDIS, G.
THEODORAKOPOULOS, D.
TRIANTAFYLLOU, A.

Department of Computer Engineering and Informatics:
ALEXIOU, G.
BERBERIDIS, K.
BOURAS, CH.
CHRISTODOULAKIS, D.
GALLOPOULOS, E.
KAKLAMANIS, CH.
KIROUSSIS, E.
KOSMADAKIS, S.
LIKOTHANASSIS, S.
NIKOLOS, D.
PAPATHEODOROU, TH.
SPIRAKIS, P.
TRIANTAPHILLOU, P.
TSAKALIDIS, A.
VARVARIGOS, E.
ZAROLIAGKIS, CH.

Department of Electrical and Computer Engineering:
ALEXANDRIDIS, A.
ANTONAKOPOULOS, TH.
AVOURIS, N.

BIRBAS, A.
BITSORIS, G.
FAKOTAKIS, N.
GALATSANOS, N.
GIANNAKOPOULOS, G.
GOUTIS, C.
GROUMPOS, P.
HOUSSOS, E.
KOTSOPOULOS, ST.
KOUBIAS, S.
KOUFOPAVLOU, O.
KOUSSOULAS, N.
MOURTZOPOULOS, I.
MOUSTAKIDES, G.
PIMENIDIS, T.
SAFACAS, A.
SERPANOS, D.
SPYROU, N.
STOURAITIS, A.
TZES, A.
VOVOS, N.

Department of Engineering Science:
HATZIKONSTANTINOU, P.
IOAKIMIDIS, N.
KOUTROUVELIS, I.
LIANOS, P.
MARKELLOS, V.
PAPADAKIS, K.
PERDIOS, E.
POLITIS, C.
SFETSOS, K.
VELGAKIS, M.

Department of Mechanical Engineering and Aeronautics:
AIKATERINARIS, I.
ANIFANTIS, N.
ASPRAGATHOS, N.
CHRYSSOLOURIS, G.
FASSOISS, S.
KALLINTERIS, I.
KARAKAPILIDIS, N.
KOSTOPOULOS, V.
MISSIRLIS, I.
PANTELAKIS, S.
PAPANICOLAOU, G.
POLYZOS, D.
SARAVANOS, D.

School of Health Sciences
Faculty of Medicine:
ALEXANDRIDIS, TH.
ALEXOPOULOS, D.
ANASTASIOU, E.
ANDONOPOULOS, A.
ATHANASIADOU-GIKA, A.
BASSIARIS, H.
BERATI, S.
DIMAKOPOULOS, P.
DIMOPOULOS, J.
DOUGENIS, D.
DRAINAS, D.
FLORDELLIS, CH.
GARTAGANIS, S.
GOGOS, C.
GOUMAS, P.
KALFARENTZOS, F.
KALOFONOS, CH.
KALPAKSIS, D.
KARAVIAS, D.
KOSTOPOULOS, G.
KYRIAZOPOULOU, V.
MANTAGOS, S.
MARAZIOTIS, TH.
MOSXONAS, N.
MOUZAKI, A.
NIKIFORIDIS, G.
NIKOLOPOULOU, V.
PALIOGIANNI, PH.
PALLIKARAKIS, N.
PANAGIOTAKIS, G.
PANAGIOTOPOULOS, I.
PAPANASTASIOU, D.
PAPATHANASOPOULOS, P.
PERIMENIS, P.
SIABLIS, D.

SKOPA, CH.
SPYROPOULOS, K.
SYNETOS, D.
TSAMBAOS, D.
TYLLIANAKIS, M.
TZORAKOELETHERAKIS, E.
VASILAKOS, P.
VLACHOJANNIS, J.
ZOUMBOS, N.

Department of Pharmacy:
CORDOPATIS, P.
TZARTOS, S.

School of Humanities and Social Sciences
Department of Educational Sciences and
Early Childhood Education:
RAVANIS, K.
XIROMERITI, A.
ZOGZA, V.

Department of Philology:
RALLI, A.

Department of Philosophy:
PATELI, I.
TEREZIS, CH.

Department of Primary Education:
BOUZAKIS, J.
DELLIS, I.
GEORGOGIANNIS, P.
KATSILLIS, I.
KOLEZA, E.
KRIVAS, S.
LAMPROPOULOU, V.
PORPODAS, C.
VERGIDIS, D.

Department of Theatre Studies:
STEFANOPOULOS, TH.
XAAS, D.

School of Natural Sciences
Department of Biology:
ALAHIOTIS, ST.
CHRSISTODOULAKIS, D.
DEMOPOULOS, N.
DIMITRIADIS, G.
GEORGIADIS, TH.
GEORGIOU, CH.
ILIOPOULOU, I.
KAMARI-FITOU, G.
KOUTSIKOPOULOS, C.
MANETAS, I.
PSARAS, G.
STEPHANOU, G.
TZANOUDAKIS, D.
YANNOPOULOS, G.
ZACHAROPOULOU, A.
ZAGRIS, N.

Department of Chemistry:
BARLOS, K.
CHRISTOPOULOS, TH.
GLAVAS, S.
IOANNOU, P.
KALLITSIS, I.
KANELLAKI, M.
KARAISKAKIS, G.
KARAMANOS, N.
KLOURAS, N.
KORDOULIS, CH.
KOUTINAS, A.
LYCOURGHIOTIS, A.
MANESI, E.
MAROULIS, G.
MATSOUKAS, J.
MIKROYIANNIDIS, J.
NTALAS, E.
PAPAIOANNOU, D.
PERLEPES, S.
POULOS, C.
TSEGENIDIS, TH.
VYNIOS, D.
ZAFIROPOULOS, TH.

Department of Geology:
CHRISTANIS, K.
CONTOPOULOS, N.

FERENTINOS, G.
FRYDAS, D.
HATZIPANAGIOTOU, K.
KALLERGIS, G.
KATAGAS, C.
KOUKIS, G.
LABRAKIS, N.
PAPAMARINOPOULOS, S.
TSELENTIS, G.
TSOLIS-KATAGAS, P.
VARNAVAS, S.
ZELILIDIS, A.

Department of Material Science:
GALIOTIS, C.
PHOTINOS, D.

Department of Mathematics:
BOUNTIS, A.
COTSIOLIS, A.
DROSSOS, C.
FILIPPOU, A.
KAFOUSSIAS, N.
KONTOLATOU, A.
KOTSIOLIS, A.
KOUROUKLIS, S.
METAKIDES, G.
PAPANTONIOU, V.
PHILIPPOU, A.
PINTELAS, P.
PNEVMATIKOS, S.
SAMARIS, N.
SIAFARIKAS, P.
TSOUBELIS, D.
TZANNES, V.
VRAHATIS, M.
ZAGOURAS, CH.

Department of Physics:
ANASTASOPOULOS, V.
BAKAS, I.
FOTOPOULOS, S.
GEORGAS, A.
GEROGIANNIS, V.
GIANNOULIS, P.
GOUDIS, CHR.
HARITANTIS, I.
KARAHALIOS, G.
KOURIS, ST.
MYTILINEOU, E.
PERSEFONIS, P.
PIZANIAS, M.
SAKKOPOULOS, S.
TOPRAKTSIOGLOU, CH.
YIANOULIS, P.
ZDETSIS, A.
ZIOUTAS, K.

PANEPISTIMIO PELOPONNESOU
(University of the Peloponnese)

28 Erithrou Stayrou and Kariotaki Sts, 221
00 Tripolis
Telephone and fax 2710-230006
E-mail: info@uop.gr
Internet: www.uop.gr
Founded 2002
State control

Chair., Board of Trustees: CONSTANTIN DIMO-
POULOS
Vice-Chair., Board of Trustees: IOANNIS PARA-
SKEVOPOULOS

PROFESSORS

Department of Social and Education Policy
(Damaskinou and Kolokotroni Sts, 201 00
Korinth; tel. 27410-74991; fax 27410-74993;
e-mail sep-secr@uop.gr):
KLADIS, D., Education Policy
KOULAIDIS, V., Design of Educational Pro-
grammes
KOULOURI, C., History of Modern Greek
Education and Society

Department of Telecommunications Science
and Technology (End of Karaiskaki St, 221
00 Tripolis; tel. 2710-372163; fax 2710-
372160; e-mail ntalagan@uop.gr):
BOUCOUVALAS, A. C.
MARAS, A.

PANEPISTIMION PIREOS
(University of Piraeus)

80 Karaoli and Dimitriou St, 185 34 Piraeus
Telephone: 210-4142000
Fax: 210-4142328
E-mail: publ@unipi.gr
Internet: www.unipi.gr
Founded 1938, univ. status 1958

Depts of business administration, digital
systems, economics, statistics and insurance
science, financial management and banking,
industrial management, informatics, maritime studies, and international and European studies

Rector: T. GAMALETSOS
Sec.: A. GOTSIS

Library of 27,000 vols, 200 periodicals
Number of teachers: 90
Number of students: 11,400

Publication: Spoudai (4 a year).

PANEPISTIMIO THESALIAS
(University of Thessaly)

Argonafton and Filellinon, 382 21 Volos
Telephone: 2421-074000
E-mail: webmaster@uth.gr
Internet: www.uth.gr
Founded 1984
State control

Rector: Prof. CONSTANTINOS BAGIATIS
Vice-Rectors: Prof. CONSTANTINOS GOURGOU-
LIANIS, Prof. NAPOLEON MITSIS

Library of 80,000 books, 828 journals

14 Departments in four schools (agricultural
sciences, engineering, health sciences and
humanities), and two independent departments (economic studies and physical education and sport).

PANTEION PANEPESTIMION
IKONOMIKON KAI POLITCON
EPISTIMON
('Panteios' University of Social and
Political Sciences)

Leoforos A. Syngrou 136, 176 71 Athens
Telephone: 210-9220100
Fax: 210-9223690
E-mail: rector@panteion.gr
Internet: www.panteion.gr
Founded 1930

Rector: D. CONSTAS
Gen. Sec.: M. VARELLA
Number of students: 7,500

POLYTECHNION KRITIS
(Technical University of Crete)

Agiou Markou St, 731 32 Chania
Telephone: 2821-037047
Fax: 2821-028418
E-mail: intoffice@isc.tuc.gr
Internet: www.tuc.gr
Founded 1977, first student intake 1984
State control
Academic year: September to June

Rector: Prof. JOAKIM GRISPOLAKIS
Vice-Rector for Academic Affairs and Person-
nel: Prof. MICHALIS PATERAKIS
Vice-Rector for Planning and Devt: Prof.
NIKOS BAROTSIS
Librarian: MARIA NTAOUNTAKI

Library of 30,000 vols
Number of teachers: 212 (incl. 91 full profs)
Number of students: 2,500

DIRECTORS OF LABORATORIES

Air, Water and Solid Wastes Management: ALEXANDER P. ECONOMOPOULOS

Analytical and Environmental Chemistry: NIKOLAOS KALLITHRAKAS-KONTOS

Applied Geology: ZACHARIAS G. AGIOUTANTIS

Applied Geophysics: ANTONIS VAFIDIS

Applied Mathematics and Computers: YIANNIS SARIDAKIS

Applied Mechanics: CONSTAS P. PROVIDAKIS

Applied Mineralogy: GEORGE KOSTAKIS

Applied Socioeconomic Research: GEORGE LIODAKIS

Atmospheric Aerosol: MIHALIS LAZARIDIS

Automation: MICHALIS ZERVAKIS

Biochemical Engineering and Environmental Biotechnology: NIKOS KALOGERAKIS

Ceramics and Glass Technology: ATHINA TSETSEKOU

Chemical Processes and Wastewater Treatment: DIONYSIOS MANTZAVINOS

Computer-aided Design and Robotics: NIKOLAOS BILALIS

Computer-aided Manufacturing: YIANNIS PHILLIS

Data Analysis and Forecasting: CHRISTOS SKIADAS

Decision Support Systems: ATHANASIOS MIGDALAS

Digital Image and Signal Processing: MICHALIS ZERVAKIS

Distributed Multimedia Information Systems and Applications: STAVROS CHRISTODOULAKIS

Drilling Technology and Applied Fluid Mechanics: VASSILIOS KELESSIDIS

Dynamic Systems and Simulation: MARKOS PAPAGEORGIOU

Ecology and Biodiversity: NIKOS KALOGERAKIS

Electric Circuits and Renewable Energy Sources: KOSTAS KALAITZAKIS

Electrical Circuits and Electronics: PAVLOS S. GEORGILAKIS

Electronics: KOSTAS KALAITZAKIS

Environmental Engineering and Management: EVAN DIAMADOPOULOS

Financial Engineering: CONSTANTIN ZOPOUNIDIS

General Geology: EMMANOUEL MANUTSOGLU

Geodesy and Geomatics Enigineering: STELIOS MERTIKAS

Geoenvironmental Engineering: GEORGE KARATZAS

Geostatistics: DIONISSIOS T. HRISTOPOULOS

Hydrogeochemical Engineering and Soil Remediation: NIKOLAOS NIKOLAIDIS

Information and Computer Networks: VASSILIS DIGALAKIS

Inorganic and Organic Geochemistry and Organic Petrography: VASSILIS PERDIKATSIS

Intelligent Systems: EMMANOUEL KOUMBARAKIS

Intelligent Systems and Robotics: NIKOS C. TSOURVELOUDIS

Management Systems: VASSILIS MOUSTAKIS

Materials Structure and Laser Physics: STAVROS MOUSTAIZIS

Microprocessor and Hardware: APOSTOLOS DOLLAS

Mine Design: GEORGE EXADAKTYLOS

Mineral Processing: ELIAS STAMBOLIADIS

Minerals Quality Control – Health and Safety: MICHAEL GALETAKIS

Mining and Metallurgical Waste Management: KOSTAS KOMNITSAS

Petrology and Economic Geology: THEODOROS MARKOPOULOS

Physical Chemistry and Chemical Processes: IOANNIS V. YENTEKAKIS

PVT and Core Analysis: NIKOS VAROTSIS

Robotics: ANASTASIOS POULIEZOS

Rock Mechanics: ZACHARIAS G. AGIOUTANTIS

Safety of Work and Cognitive Ergonomics: TOM KONTOGIANNIS

Software Systems and Network Application: EMMANOUEL KOUMBARAKIS

Solid Fuels Benification and Technology: DESPINA VAMVOUKA

Telecommunications: NIKOS SIDIROPOULOS

Toxic and Hazardous Waste Management: EVANGELOS GIDARAKOS

Transport Phenomena and Applied Thermodynamics: VASSILIS GEKAS

Water Resources Management and Coastal Engineering: IOANNIS K. TSANIS

PROFESSORS

AGIOUTANIS, Z.
ALEVIZOS, G.
AVDELAS, G.
BALAS, K.
BILALIS, N.
CHRISTIDIS, G.
CHRISTODOULAKIS, S.
CHRISTODOULOU, M.
CHRISTOPOULOS, D.
DARRAS, T.
DELLIS, A.
DIAMADOPOULOS, E.
DIGALAKIS, V.
DOLLAS, A.
DOUMPOS, M.
ECONOMOPOULOS, A.
ELLINAS, D.
EXADAKTYLOS, G.
FOSCOLOS, A.
FRAGOMIHELAKIS, M.
GALETAKIS, M.
GEKAS, V.
GEORGILAKIS, P.
GIDARAKOS, E.
GRIGOROUDIS, E.
GRYSPOLAKIS, J.
KALAITZAKIS, K.
KALLITHRAKAS, K. N.
KALOGERAKIS, N.
KANDYLAKIS, D.
KARAKASSIS, I.
KARATZAS, G.
KATSANOS, A.
KAVOURIDIS, K.
KELESIDIS, V.
KOMNITSAS, K.
KONTOGIANNIS, T.
KOSMATOPOULOS, E.
KOSTAKIS, G.
KOUBARAKIS, E.
KOUIKOGLOU, V.
LAZARIDIS, M.
LIODAKIS, G.
MANOUTSOGLOU, E.
MANTZAVINOS, D.
MARIA, E.
MARKOPOULOS, T.
MATHIOUDAKIS, M.
MATSATSINIS, N.
MERTIKAS, S.
MIGDALAS, A.
MONOPOLIS, D.
MOUSTAIZIS, S.
MOUSTAKIS, V.
NIKOLAIDIS, N.
NIKOLOS, I.
PANTINAKIS, A.
PAPADOPOULOU, E.
PAPAGEORGIOU, M.
PASADAKIS, N.
PATELIS, D.
PATERAKIS, M.
PERDIKATSIS, V.
PETRAKIS, E.
PETRAKIS, M.
PHILLIS, Y.
PNEVMATIKATOS, D.
POTAMIANOS, A.
POULIEZOS, A.
PROVIDAKIS, K.

SAMELIS, A.
SAMOLADAS, V.
SARIDAKIS, Y.
SIDIROPOULOS, N.
SINOLAKIS, K.
SKIADAS, C.
STAMPOLIADIS, E.
STAVRAKAKIS, G.
STAVROULAKIS, P.
SYNOLAKIS, C.
TRAFALIS, T.
TSANIS, I.
TSETSEKOU, A.
TSOMPANAKIS, I.
TSOURVELOUDIS, N.
VAFIDIS, A.
VAMVOUKA, D.
VAROTSIS, N.
YENTEKAKIS, Y.
ZERVAKIS, M.
ZOPOUNIDIS, K.

ATTACHED INSTITUTE

Institute of Telecommunications Systems: e-mail tsi@tsinet.gr; internet www.tsinet.gr; Dir Prof. MICHALIS PATERAKIS.

Colleges
ARCHAEOLOGY, GREEK STUDIES

American School of Classical Studies at Athens: Odos Souidias 54, 106 76 Athens; tel. 210-7236313; fax 210-7250584; e-mail ascsa@ascsa.edu.gr; internet www.ascsa.edu.gr; f. 1881; research institute and postgraduate school for students of classical and post-classical literature, history and archaeology; controlled by a committee representing 160 US and Canadian universities; library: Gennadius and Blegen libraries with 195,000 vols; 13 teachers; 60 students; Dir STEPHEN V. TRACY; publ. *Hesperia* (4 a year).

British School at Athens: Odos Souedias 52, 106 76 Athens; tel. 210-7210974; fax 210-7236560 *London office*: Senate House, Malet St, London, WC1E 7HU, United Kingdom; tel. (20) 7862-8732; fax (20) 7862-8733; e-mail admin@bsa.ac.uk; internet www.bsa.gla.ac.uk; f. 1886; archaeology and Hellenic studies; Fitch Laboratory for research and analysis; library: over 60,000 vols (ancient, medieval and post-medieval Greek studies and archaeology of all periods), incl. the Finlay Library (Greek travel and modern Greek studies); Chair. Prof. Lord COLIN RENFREW; Dir Prof CATHERINE MORGAN; London Sec. HELEN FIELDS.

Deutsches Archäologisches Institut, Abteilung Athen (German Archaeological Institute in Athens): Odos Fidiou 1, 106 78 Athens; tel. 210-3307400; fax 210-3814762; e-mail sekretariat@athen.dainst.org; internet www.dainst.de; f. 1874; library: 66,000 vols; Dirs Prof. Dr WOLF-DIETRICH NIEMEIER, Dr REINHARD SENFF; publs *Athenische Mitteilungen* (1 a year), *Beihefte*.

École Française d'Athènes (French Archaeological School): Odos Didotou 6, 106 80 Athens; tel. 210-3679900; fax 210-3632101; e-mail efa@efa.gr; internet www.efa.gr; f. 1846; library: 80,000 vols; Dir D. MULLIEZ; Sec.-Gen. M. BRUNET; publs *Bulletin de correspondance hellénique* (1 a year), *Bulletin des études grecques modernes et contemporaines* (1 a year).

Italian School of Archaeology at Athens/ Scuola Archeologica Italiana di Atene: 14 Parthenonos, 117 42 Athens; tel. 210-9239163; fax 210-9220908; e-mail segretario@scuoladiatene.it; internet www.scuoladiatene.it; f. 1909; postgraduate studies in archaeology, epigraphy and antiquities, ancient architecture; research and excavations in Greece; library: 48,300 vols; Dir Prof. EMANUELE A. GRECO; Library Dir Dr STEFANO GARBIN; publs *Annuario della Scuola Archeologica di Atene e delle Missioni Italiane in Oriente* (1 a year), *Monografie della Scuola Archeologica di Atene e delle Missoni Italiane in Oriente* (irregular), *Notiziario* (2 a year), *Tripodes* (irregular).

Svenska Institutet i Athen (Swedish Institute at Athens): 9 Mitseon St, 117 42 Athens; tel. 210-9232102; fax 210-9220925; e-mail swedinst@sia.gr; internet www.sia.gr; f. 1948; researches into Greek antiquity and archaeology, and cultural exchange between Sweden and Greece; library: 40,000 vols (housed at the Nordic Library, Kavalotti 7, 117 42 Athens); 2 teachers; 15 students; Dir ANNE-LOUISE SCHALLIN; Librarian JENNY WALLENSTEN; publ. *Skrifter utgivna av Svenska Institutet i Athen* (Acta Instituti Atheniensis Regni Sueciae and *Opuscula Atheniensia*).

ARTS, DRAMA, MUSIC

American College of Greece: 6 Gravias St, Aghia Paraskevi, 153 42 Athens; tel. 210-6009800; fax 210-6009811; e-mail acg@acg.edu; internet www.acg.edu; f. 1875; comprises Deree College (BA courses in dance, economics, English, history, history of art, music, philosophy, psychology, sociology, BSc course in business administration, MBA), Junior College (associate degrees in arts and sciences) and Pierce College (high school); library: 150,000 vols; 250 teachers (incl. Junior College division); 5,000 students (incl. Junior College division); Pres. JOHN S. BAILEY; publ. *Library Series*.

Dramatiki Scholi (Drama School): National Theatre, Odos Menandrou 65, Athens; internet www.n-t.gr; f. 1924; open to actors who desire to improve their art and to young people who desire to take up the stage as a career; the staff comprises the director, 11 professors and 2 teachers.

Kratiko Odeio Thessaloniki (State Conservatory of Music): Leondos Sofou Str. 16, 546 25 Thessaloniki; tel. 231-0510551; fax 231-0522158; e-mail odiokrat@otenet.gr; internet www.odiokrat.gr; f. 1914; instrumental, vocal and theoretical studies; 60 teachers; 630 students; library: 17,000 vols, scores, records, slides, compact discs, video cassettes, including collection in Braille; exhibition of musical instruments; Chair. Prof. P. I. RENTZEPERIS.

Attached Conservatory:

Odeion Athenon (Odeon of Athens): Odos Rigillis and Vassileos Georgiou 17–19, Athens; f. 1871; comprises a music section, a drama section, a section for military music, and a section for Byzantine Church music; 53 professors, 40 teachers and 1,200 students; Dir A. GAROUFALIS.

Odeion Ethnikon (National Conservatory): 8 Maizonos and 18 Mayer Sts, Athens 104 38; tel. 210-5233175; fax 210-5245291; e-mail ethnodio@otenet.gr; f. 1926; sections for music and opera; 200 teachers; 5,000 students; Dirs HARA KALOMIRI, PERIKLIS KOUKOS; publ. *Deltio* (1 a year).

GRENADA

The Higher Education System

Before 1968 higher education in Grenada was limited to the provision of sponsorship for study abroad. In that year Grenada acquired the Extra-Mural Department of the University of the West Indies (UWI) and the Grenada Teacher-Training College was founded, its 2-year programme being monitored and certified by the UWI. In 1974 the Government established a number of other colleges relevant to the country's social and economic needs. During 1979–83 the new People's Revolutionary Government enhanced existing teacher-training programmes and increased scholarships offered for university and technical education abroad. The Institute of Higher Education in Grenada, which approximated the idea of a university, was also established during this period. In 1988 the restored, post-colonial Government amalgamated a number of institutions, including the Grenada Teachers' College and the Institute for Further Education, to form the Grenada National College, which was renamed the T. A. Marryshow Community College (TAMCC) in 1996. In the same year the UWI and St George's University expanded their activities. In 1993 there were 651 students in higher education (excluding figures for the Grenada Teachers College). In 2006 there were 2,710 full-time, enrolled students at the TAMCC. Technical Centres have been established in St Patrick's, St David's and St John's, and the Grenada National College, the Mirabeau Agricultural Training School and the Grenada Teachers' College have been incorporated into the Technical and Vocational Institute in St George's.

The Government is responsible for higher education, although both St George's University and the UWI enjoy a greater degree of autonomy than does the TAMCC. The TAMCC is required by law to report directly to the Ministry of Education and Human Resource Development, primarily for financial purposes and for powers of jurisdiction. Higher education is governed by the Grenada Education Act, and the St George's University (School of Medicine) Act, 1976. The Ministry of Education and Human Resource Development is the main source of funding for the TAMCC. It also provides some support for the UWI, although this is largely funded through the collective contributions of the Caribbean countries to the UWI as a whole. St George's University is funded mainly by student fees. The Australian Agency for International Development is providing opportunities through the Australian Leadership Awards Scholarship to study at Masters or Doctorate level in an Australian university commencing in 2011.

Regulatory Bodies

GOVERNMENT

Ministry of Education and Human Resource Development: Min. of Education Bldg, Ministerial Complex, Botanical Gardens, Tanteen, St George's; tel. 440-2737; fax 440-6650; internet www.grenadaedu.com; Min. FRANKA ALEXIS-BERNADINE.

Ministry of National Security, Public Administration, Information, Information Communications Technology, Legal Affairs and Culture: Ministerial Complex, 6th Fl., Botanical Gardens, Tanteen, St George's; tel. 440-2255; fax 440-4116; e-mail pmsec@gov.gd; internet www.pmoffice.gov.gd; Min. TILLMAN THOMAS.

Learned Society

HISTORY, GEOGRAPHY AND ARCHAEOLOGY

Grenada National Trust: Grenada National Museum, Young St, St George's; tel. 440-3725; f. 1967 to preserve evidence of the history and growth of the island, and to support the Grenada National Museum; 240 mems; Pres. GORDON DE LA MOTHE; Sec. KAY SIMON.

Libraries and Archives

St George's

Founders Library, St George's University: POB 7, St George's; tel. 444-1573; fax 444-2884; e-mail library@sgu.edu; internet www.sgu.edu; f. 1979; 13,000 vols, 350 periodicals; Dir JOHN MCGUIRK.

Grenada Public Library: Carenage, St George's; tel. 440-2506; fax 440-6650; e-mail fedon2000@yahoo.com; f. 1853; attached to Min. of Education and Human Resource Devt; 60,000 vols; spec. W Indian and Nat. Archives of Grenada collns; reference, research and lecture facilities; links its activities with other educational agencies; Dir S. LILLIAN SYLVESTER; Librarian DEON DAVID.

Museum

St George's

Grenada National Museum: Young St, St George's; tel. 440-3725; fax 440-9292; f. 1976; history, technology, fauna and flora; Dir JEANNE FISHER; Curator HUGH THOMAS; publs *Art 'y' Facts* (2 a year), *Relics*.

Universities and Colleges

ST GEORGE'S UNIVERSITY

Univ. Centre, POB 7, St George's
Telephone: 444-4175
Fax: 444-4823
E-mail: sguinfo@sgu.edu
Internet: www.sgu.edu
Founded 1977
Private control
Language of instruction: English
Academic year: August to June
Chancellor: CHARLES R. MODICA
Registrar: MARGARET LAMBERT
Librarian: JOHN MCGUIRK

Library: see Libraries and Archives
Number of teachers: 776 (76 full-time, 700 part-time)
Number of students: 2,000

DEANS

Arts and Sciences: T. HOLLIS
Basic Sciences: A. PENSICK
Clinical Studies: STEPHEN WEITZMAN
Veterinary Medicine: R. SIS

T. A. Marryshow Community College (TAMCC): Tanteen, St George's; tel. 440-1389; fax 440-3079; e-mail tamcc@caribsurf.com; internet www.tamcc.edu.gd; f. 1988 by merger of the Grenada Teachers' College, the Grenada Technical and Vocational Institute, the Institute for Further Education, the National Institute of Handicraft, the Mirabeau Agricultural Training School, the Domestic Arts Institute, the Continuing Education Programme and the School of Pharmacy; present name and status 1996; offers full-time and part-time programmes leading to Bachelors and Associate Degrees, Certificates and Diplomas; Prin. Dr JEFFERY BRITTON (acting); Registrar C. NIGEL GRAVESANDE; Dean of Applied Arts and Technology DESMOND LA TOUCHE; Dean of Arts, Sciences and Professional Studies Dr DUNBAR STEELE.

University of the West Indies School of Continuing Studies: Marryshow House, H. A. Blaize St, POB 439, St George's; tel. 440-2451; fax 440-4985; e-mail rtscsuwi@caribsurf.com; internet www.uwichill.edu.bb/bnccde/grenada; f. 1956; first-year univ. courses and gen. courses; library: 10,000 vols; folk theatre, telecommunications distance-teaching centre; 27 teachers; 150 students; Resident Tutor BEVERLEY A. STEELE.

GUATEMALA

The Higher Education System

Under Spanish colonial rule, Guatemala was part of the Viceroyalty of New Spain. Independence was obtained from Spain in 1821, from Mexico in 1824 and from the Federation of Central American States in 1838. The oldest university is the Universidad de San Carlos de Guatemala, which was founded by King Carlos II of Spain in 1676. In total, there are 12 universities, of which 11 are privately run. Figures for 2005/06 showed that some 112,215 students were enrolled in further and higher education.

The main requirement for admission to university is the Bachiller or Bachillerato, the secondary-school qualification. The Licenciado is the undergraduate degree and is awarded after four years, although some subjects (such as medicine) require longer periods of study. In professional fields of study, a professional title is awarded. Following the Licenciado, the first postgraduate degree is the Maestría, which is awarded after two years of study. However, the Doctorado can also be awarded following two years of study after the Licenciado, although some doctoral programmes require a Maestría.

Technical and vocational education is offered by the universities and specialized post-secondary institutions. The Instituto Técnico de Capitación y Productividad provides apprenticeships and courses. The main vocational qualification is the Diplomado, awarded after two-and-a-half to three years of study.

The responsibility for higher education in Guatemala, by constitutional mandate, is shared by the University of San Carlos, which is exclusively in charge of state-owned higher and professional university education, and by the private universities. The first is an autonomous institution, with legal status, which regulates and governs itself, while the latter are authorized and controlled by the Council of Private Higher Education. The University of San Carlos has also undertaken the task of tackling the problems in higher education, including the creation of the Central American Accreditation Council, within the framework of the Central American Higher University Council.

Regulatory and Representative Bodies

GOVERNMENT

Ministry of Culture and Sport: 12 Avda 11-11, Zona 1, Guatemala City; tel. 2253-0543; fax 2253-0540; internet www.mcd.gob.gt; Minister HÉCTOR LEONEL ESCOBEDO AVALA.

Ministry of Education: 6a Calle 1-87, Zona 10, Guatemala City; tel. 2360-0911; fax 2361-0350; e-mail info@mineduc.gob.gt; internet www.mineduc.gob.gt; Minister DENIS ALONZO MAZARIEGOS.

NATIONAL BODIES

Consejo de la Enseñanza Privada Superior (Council of Private Higher Education): Edif. Colegios Profesionales, Segundo Nivel, 0 Calle 15-46 Zona 15, Colonia El Maestro, Guatemala City; tel. 2369-6344; internet www.ceps.edu.gt; f. 1966.

Learned Societies

GENERAL

Academia de Ciencias Médicas, Físicas y Naturales de Guatemala (Academy of Medical, Physical and Natural Sciences): 13 Calle 1-25, Zona 1, Apdo Postal 569, 01001 Guatemala City; tel. (2) 2238-1251; fax (2) 2232-7291; e-mail manuelgonzalez@yahoo.com; f. 1945; 80 mems; library of 4,000 vols; Pres. MANUEL GONZÁLEZ ÁVILA; Sec. Dr CARLOS ROLZ ASTURIAS; publs Annals (irregular), research summaries.

FINE AND PERFORMING ARTS

Sociedad Pro-Arte Musical (Musical Society): 12 Calle 2-09, Zona 3, Apdo 980, Guatemala City; f. 1945; 200 mems; Pres. LULÚ C. DE HERRARTE; Exec. Sec. DORA G. DE MENDIZÁBAL.

HISTORY, GEOGRAPHY AND ARCHAEOLOGY

Academia de Geografía e Historia de Guatemala (Geographical and Historical Academy of Guatemala): 3 Avda 8-35, Zona 1, Guatemala City; tel. 2253-5141; fax 2232-3544; e-mail acgeohis@gmail.com; internet www.academiageohist.org.gt; f. 1923; 45 mems; library of 30,000 vols; Pres. GUILLERMO DÍAZ ROMEU; Sec. BARBARA KNOKE DE ARATHOON; publs Anales (1 a year), Biblioteca Goathemala, Viajeros.

LANGUAGE AND LITERATURE

Academia Guatemalteca de la Lengua (Guatemala Academy of Letters): 12 Calle 6-40, Zona 9, Oficina 403-404, Edificio Plazuela, Guatemala City; tel. 2332-2824; fax 2332-2824; e-mail aglesp@correo.terra.com.gt; f. 1887; corresp. of the Real Academia Española (Madrid, Spain); library of 5,000 vols; Dir MARIO ANTONIO SANDOVAL SAMAYOA; Sec.-Gen. FRANCISCO MORALES SANTOS.

Alliance Française: 5ta Calle 10-55, Zona 13, Finca la Aurora; tel. 2440-2102; e-mail info@alianzafrancesa.org.gt; internet www.alianzafrancesa.org.gt; offers courses and exams in French language and culture, and promotes cultural exchange with France; attached teaching offices in La Antigua and Quetzaltenango.

NATURAL SCIENCES

Biological Sciences

Asociación Guatemalteca de Historia Natural: Jardín Botánico, Universidad de San Carlos, Mariscal Cruz 1-56, Zona 10, Guatemala City; f. 1960; 86 mems; Pres. Dr MARIO DARY RIVERA.

TECHNOLOGY

Colegio de Ingenieros de Guatemala: 7A Avda 39-60, Zona 8, 01008 Guatemala City; tel. 2471-7544; fax 2472-4224; e-mail juntadirectiva@cig.org.gt; internet www.cig.org.gt; f. 1947; 1,965 mems; Pres. Ing. CARLOS GERARDO BRAN GUZMÁN; publ. Revista Ingeniería (4 a year).

Research Institutes

ECONOMICS, LAW AND POLITICS

Centro de Investigaciones Económicas Nacionales (Centre for National Economic Studies): 12 Calle 1-25, Zona 10, Edif. Géminis 10, Torre Norte, Nivel 17, Oficina 1702, Guatemala City; tel. 2335-3415; fax 2335-3416; internet www.cien.org.at; f. 1982; study of economic and social problems; Dir JORGE LAVARREDA; publ. Carta Económica (12 a year).

Instituto Nacional de Estadística (National Statistical Institute): 8A Calle 9-55, Zona 1, Guatemala City; tel. 2232-3188; fax 2232-4790; e-mail fhernandez@ine.gob.gt; internet www.ine.gob.gt; f. 1879 as Sección de Estadística, present name 1985; compiles and publishes nat. statistics; Dir SIEGFRIDO LEE LEIVA; publs Censo Nacional Agropecuario (national agricultural census, online), Censo Nacional de Población y de Habitación (national population and dwellings census, online), Índice de Precios al Consumidor (retail price index; online, 12 a year).

HISTORY, GEOGRAPHY AND ARCHAEOLOGY

Instituto de Antropología e Historia: 12 Avda 11-11, Zona 1, 01001 Guatemala City; tel. 2232-5956; fax 2232-5956; e-mail guatepazidaeh@yahoo.com; f. 1946; research on Middle-American history, Mayan archaeology, ethnology, philology and Spanish colonial history; supervises archaeological sites, monuments and museums; library of 12,000 vols; Dir-Gen. Arq. ARTURO PAZ; publs Revista Anual de Antropología e Historia de Guatemala (1 a year), books and special publs.

Instituto Geográfico Nacional 'Ing. Alfredo Obiols Gómez': Avda Las Américas 5-76, Zona 13, Guatemala City; tel. 2332-2611; fax 2331-3548; e-mail ign@ign.gob.gt; internet www.ign.gob.gt; f. 1945; Dir Ing. FERNANDO AMILCAR BOITON VELÁSQUEZ.

MEDICINE

Instituto de Nutrición de Centro América y Panamá (INCAP) (Institute of Nutrition of Central America and Panama): Calzada Roosevelt 6–25, Zona 11, Apdo Postal 1188-01901, Guatemala City; tel. 2472-3762; fax 2473-6529; internet www.incap.org.gt; f. 1949; mem. countries: Belize, Costa Rica, El Salvador, Guatemala, Honduras, Nicaragua, Panama; administered by Pan American Health Bureau Organization (PAHO)/World Health Organization (WHO); Food and Nutrition Security Program considers food systems, nutrition education and communication, and health and nutrition with an emphasis on mother and child; Masters programme and short training courses; well-documented library publishes scientific articles in Spanish and English, information bulletins, periodic compilations of scientific publs for mem. govts, annual reports, monographs, various other documents; Dir Carolina Siu Bermudez.

NATURAL SCIENCES

Biological Sciences

Centro de Estudios Conservacionistas: Avda La Reforma 0–63, Zona 10, Guatemala City; tel. 2331-0904; fax 2334-7664; e-mail direccioncecon@yahoo.com; internet www.usac.edu.gt/cecon; f. 1981; management and admin. of protected areas; investigation and studies of biodiversity and sustainable management of natural resources; management of nat. botanical garden and nat. biodiversity database; 142 mems; Exec. Dir Jorge Alberto Ruiz Ordoñez.

Physical Sciences

Instituto Nacional de Sismología, Vulcanología, Meteorología e Hidrología (National Institute of Seismology, Vulcanology, Meteorology and Hydrology): 7ta Avda 14–57, Zona 13, Guatemala City; tel. 2331-5944; fax 2331-5005; e-mail direccion@insivumeh.gob.gt; internet www.insivumeh.gob.gt; f. 1976; Dir Eddy Hardie Sánchez; publs Boletín Anual Hidrológico (electronic, hydrology, 1 a year), Boletín de Tsunamis (electronic, catalogue of tsunamis), Boletín Estacional (electronic, quarterly forecast), Boletín Mensual (electronic, monthly forecast), Boletín Meteorológico Diario (electronic, daily weather forecast), Boletín Sismológico (electronic, monthly catalogue of earthquakes), Boletín Sismológico Especial (electronic, catalogue of significant earthquakes), Boletín Vulcanológico Diario (electronic, catalogue of current eruptions), Boletín Vulcanológico Especial (electronic, catalogue of significant eruptions), Mareas Oceánicas (electronic, monthly tidal forecast), Normales Climáticas (electronic, climate statistics), Pronóstico de Fin de Semana (electronic, weekend forecast), Pronóstico de 1 a 3 Dias (electronic, four-day forecast), Tiempo Presente (electronic, current forecast).

TECHNOLOGY

Dirección General de Energía Nuclear: 24 Calle 21–12, Zona 12, Apdo Postal 1421, Guatemala City; tel. 2477-0746; fax 2476-2007; f. 1978; work concerns peaceful application of nuclear energy in medicine, industry, agriculture, etc.; 50 mems; library of 1,200 vols; Dir Ing. Raúl Eduardo Pineda González.

Instituto Centroamericano de Investigación y Tecnología Industrial (ICAITI) (Central American Research Institute for Industry): Apdo Postal 1552-01901, Guatemala City; Avda La Reforma 4–47, Zona 10, Guatemala City; tel. 2331-0631; fax 2331-7470; internet www.icaiti.org.gt; f. 1956; research on marketing, development of new industries and manufacturing techniques, establishment of Central American standards, information services to industry, and professional advice; library of 36,000 vols; Dir Lic. Luis Fidel Cifuentes Echeverria (acting).

Libraries and Archives

Guatemala City

Archivo General de Centro América (National Archives): 4 Avda 7–16, Zona 1, Guatemala City; tel. 2232-3037; f. 1846; comprises two sections: La Colonia, archive with 8,427 files of 99,157 documents relating to Guatemala, Chiapas, El Salvador, Honduras, Nicaragua, Costa Rica; library contains ancient and modern historical volumes; periodicals pertaining to the colonial epoch and the period of independence; microfilm and photocopying service for researchers; Dir Arturo Valdés Oliva; publ. Boletín.

Biblioteca Central de la Universidad de San Carlos de Guatemala: Ciudad Universitaria, Zona 12, Guatemala City; tel. 2476-7217; fax 2476-9652; internet biblioteca.usac.edu.gt; f. 1965; economics, humanities and multidisciplinary collections; thesis collection; newspaper and magazine collection; Guatemalan collection, Carlos Mérida collection; 82,881 vols, 756 periodical titles; Dir Licda Ofelia Aguilar (acting).

Biblioteca del Banco de Guatemala: 7A Avda 22–01, Zona 1, Apdo 365, Guatemala City; tel. 2429-6000; internet www.banguat.gob.gt/biblio; f. 1955; 38,000 vols; Librarian Julio C. Mariscal.

Biblioteca del Congreso Nacional: 9 Avda 9–42, Guatemala City; f. 1823; 7,000 vols; Dir Carlos H. Godoy Z.

Biblioteca del Organismo Judicial: 21 Calle 7–70, Zona 1, Guatemala City; tel. 2248-7000; e-mail biblioteca@oj.gob.gt; f. 1881; 10,000 vols; Dir Dora Cristina Godoy López; publs Informador Bibliotecario (electronic, 52 a year), Informador Bibliotecario Mensual (electronic, 12 a year).

Biblioteca Nacional de Guatemala: 5A Avda 7–26, Zona 1, Guatemala City; tel. 2232-2443; fax 2253-9071; e-mail biblioguatemala@intelnett.com; internet www.biblionet.edu.gt; f. 1879; 350,000 vols; Dir Lic. Victor Castillo López.

Quezaltenango

Biblioteca Pública de Quezaltenango: a/c Casa Cultura Occidente 7A, Calle 11–35, Zona 1, Quezaltenango; reopened 1958; 25,000 vols; Dir Julio César Alvarez.

Museums and Art Galleries

Chichicastenango

Museo Regional de Chichicastenango: 5A Avda 4–47, Zona 1, Chichicastenango; f. 1950; articles of the Maya-Quiché culture; Dir Raúl Pérez Maldonado.

Guatemala City

Museo Nacional de Arqueología y Etnología de Guatemala (Archaeological and Ethnographical Museum): Edif. No. 5, La Aurora, Zona 13, Guatemala City; tel. 2472-0489; fax 2472-0489; f. 1948; collection of some 3,000 archaeological pieces, mainly Mayan art, and 1,000 ethnological exhibits, all from Guatemala; Dir Licda Dora Guerra de González; publ. Revista (2 a year).

Museo Nacional de Arte Moderno: Edif. No. 6, Finca La Aurora, Zona 13, Guatemala City; tel. 2472-0467; fax 2471-1422; f. 1975; paintings, sculpture, engravings, drawings, etc.; Dir J. Oscar Barrientos.

Museo Nacional de Historia (National Museum of History): 9 Calle 9–70, Zona 1, Guatemala City; tel. 2253-6149; fax 2253-6149; f. 1975; 19th- and 20th-century paintings, sculpture, documents, furniture and tools, all from Guatemala; Dir Italo Morales Hidalgo.

Museo Nacional de Historia Natural 'Jorge A. Ibarra': 6A Calle 7–30, Zona 13, Apdo 987, Guatemala City; tel. and fax 2472-0468; f. 1950; colln of geological, botanical and zoological specimens; library of 2,600 vols; Dir and Founder Jorge A. Ibarra.

Universities

UNIVERSIDAD DE SAN CARLOS DE GUATEMALA

Ciudad Universitaria, Zona 12, 01012 Guatemala City
Telephone: 2443-9672
Fax: 2476-7221
E-mail: webmaster@usac.edu.gt
Internet: www.usac.edu.gt

Founded 1676 by King Carlos II, est. in its present form 1927, autonomous status 1944
Private control
Language of instruction: Spanish
Academic year: January to November
Rector: Dr M. V. Luis Alfonso Leal Monterroso
Sec.-Gen.: Dr Carlos Enrique Mazariegos Morales
Dir-Gen. for Admin.: Lic. Carlos Sierra Romero
Dir-Gen. for Planning: Lic. José H. Calderón Díaz
Dir-Gen. for Research: Dr Rodolfo Espinoza Smith
Dir-Gen. for Teaching: Lic. Juan Alberto Martinez
Dir-Gen. for Univ. Devt: Arq. Byron Rabé
Registrar: Ing. Rolando Grajeda
Librarian: Licda Mercedes de Beeck
Library: see Libraries
Number of teachers: 2,600
Number of students: 114,000
Publications: Revista de la Universidad de San Carlos de Guatemala (4 a year), Universidad (12 a year), USAC al Día (26 a year)

DEANS
Faculty of Agronomy: Dr Ariel Abderraman Ortiz
Faculty of Architecture: Arq. Carlos Valladares
Faculty of Chemistry and Pharmacy: Lic. Gerardo Arroyo
Faculty of Dentistry: Dr Carlos Alvarado Cerezo
Faculty of Economics: Lic. Eduardo Velasquez
Faculty of Engineering: Ing. Sydney Samuels
Faculty of Humanities: Lic. Mario Calderon
Faculty of Law and Social Sciences: Lic. Bonerge Mejía Orellana
Faculty of Medicine: Dr Carlos Alvarado Dumas
Faculty of Veterinary Medicine: Dr Mario Llerena

DIRECTORS

School of Communications Science: Lic. GUSTAVO ADOLFO BRACAMONTE CERÓN
School of History: Lic. GABRIEL MORALES
School of Political Science: Lic. FERNANDO MOLINA
School of Psychology: Lic. RIQUELMI GASPARICO
School of Social Work: Lic. RUDY RAMÍREZ
School of Teacher-Training: Ing. FRANCISCO ROSALES CEREZO

UNIVERSIDAD DEL VALLE DE GUATEMALA

Apdo Postal No. 82, 01901 Guatemala City
located at: 18 Avda 11–95, Zona 15, Vista Hermosa III, Guatemala City
Telephone: 2364-0336
Fax: 2364-0212
E-mail: info@uvg.edu.gt
Internet: www.uvg.edu.gt
Founded 1966
Language of instruction: Spanish
Private control
Academic year: February to November
Rector: Lic. ROBERTO MORENO GODOY
Vice-Rector and Dir of Studies: MARÍA LUISA DURANDO DE BOEHM
Registrar: Lda. VICTORIA EUGENIA ROSALES
Librarian: Dra MARÍA EMILIA LÓPEZ
Library of 68,000 vols, 130 current periodicals
Number of teachers: 250
Number of students: 2,000

DEANS

Faculty of Education: JACQUELINE GARCÍA DE DE LEÓN
Faculty of Engineering: Ing. CARLOS PAREDES
Faculty of Science and Humanities: EDUARDO ÁLVAREZ MASSIS
Faculty of Social Sciences: MARÍA DEL PILAR DE RODRÍGUEZ
Research Institute: Ing. CARLOS ROLZ
University College: EDUARDO ÁLVAREZ MASSIS

UNIVERSIDAD FRANCISCO MARROQUIN

6 Calle Final, Zona 10, Guatemala City
Telephone: 2338-7700
Fax: 2334-6896
E-mail: info@ufm.edu.gt
Internet: www.ufm.edu.gt
Founded 1971
Language of instruction: Spanish
Private control
Academic year: January to November
Rector: Ing. GIANCARLO IBÁRGÜEN S.
Sec.-Gen.: Lic. RICARDO CASTILLO
Librarian: Lic. JAQUELINE DE LEÓN
Library of 75,000 vols
Number of teachers: 450
Number of students: 2,579
Publications: Laissez-Faire (2 a year), Revista de la Facultad de Derecho (2 a year)

DEANS

Graduate School of Social Sciences: Dr ARMANDO DE LA TORRE
Graduate School of Economics and Business Administration: Dr HELMUTH CHÁVEZ
Institute of Political Studies and Int. Relations: Lic PEDRO TRUJILLO
School of Architecture: Arq. ROBERTO QUEVEDO
School of Dentistry: Dr RAMIRO ALFARO
School of Economics: Dr FRITZ THOMAS
School of Education: Licda SIANG DE SEIDNER

School of Law: Dr MILTON ARGUETA
School of Medicine: Dr FEDERICO ALFARO
School of Nutrition: Dr JORGE TULIO RODRÍGUEZ
School of Psychology: Dr YETILÚ DE BAESSA

UNIVERSIDAD GALILEO

Calle Dr Eduardo Suger Cofiño (7A Avda Final), Zona 10, 01010 Guatemala City
Telephone: 2423-8000
Fax: 2362-2731
Internet: www.galileo.edu
Founded 2000
Private control
Rector: Dr JOSÉ EDUARDO SUGER COFIÑO
Vice-Rector: Dr JOSÉ CYRANO RUIZ CABARRÚS
Vice-Rector for Academics: Lic. MYRA ROLDAN DE RAMÍREZ
Sec.-Gen.: Lic. JORGE FRANCISCO RETOLAZA

DEANS

Faculty of Education: Dr BERNARDO RENÉ MORALES FIGUEROA
Faculty of Science, Technology and Industry: Ing. JORGE IVÁN ECHEVERRÍA PERMOUT
Faculty of Systems Engineering: Ing. JOSÉ EDUARDO SUGER CASTILLO

DIRECTORS

Institute of Open Education: Ing. STEPHANY OROZCO
School of Graduate Studies: Ing. CARLOS ARNADI-KLEE
School of Professional Development and Training: Lic. LUIS MANUEL ALVAREZ ALVAREZ

UNIVERSIDAD MARIANO GÁLVEZ DE GUATEMALA

Apdo Postal 1811, Guatemala City
Telephone: 2288-7592
Internet: www.umg.edu.gt
Founded 1966
Language of instruction: Spanish
Private control
Academic year: February to November
Rector: Lic. ALVARO R. TORRES MOSS
Vice-Rectors: Lic. HUGO C. MORALES Y MORALES, Dr ALFREDO SAN JOSÉ
Sec.: Licda RUBY SANTIZO DE HERNÁNDEZ
Registrar: Lic. JOSÉ CLODOVEO TORRES MOSS
Librarian: GLORIA MARINA ARROYO
Library of 9,000 vols
Number of teachers: 400
Number of students: 10,000
Publication: Boletín Mensual (12 a year)

DIRECTORS

School of Architecture: Arq. VÍCTOR HUGO HERNÁNDEZ ORDÓÑEZ
School of Business Administration: Lic. CARLOS F. CÁRDENAS C.
School of Civil Engineering: Ing. HANS JOAQUÍN LOTTMANN
Schools of Economics, Public Auditing and Accounting: Lic. OSCAR EUGENIO DUBÓN PALMA
School of Education: Lic. VÍCTOR EGIDIO AGREDA GODÍNEZ
School of Humanities: Lic. VÍCTOR EGIDIO AGREDA GODÍNEZ
School of Information Systems: Ing. JORGE A. ARIAS TOBAR
School of Languages: Dr NEVILLE STILES
School of Law: Lic. RODERIGO SEGURA TRUJILLO
School of Linguistics: Dr DAVID OLTROGGE
School of Nursing: Licda DELIA LUCILA CHANG CHANG

School of Odontology: Dr ROLANDO DÍAZ LOZZA
School of Theology: Lic. ADALBERTO SANTIZO ROMÁN

UNIVERSIDAD RAFAEL LANDÍVAR

Vista Hermosa III, Zona 16, Apdo Postal 39 'C', Guatemala City
Telephone: 2369-2751
Fax: 2369-2756
E-mail: info@url.edu.gt
Internet: www.url.edu.gt
Founded 1961
Language of instruction: Spanish
Private control
Academic year: January to November
Rector: GONZALO DE VILLA
Gen. Vice-Rector: GUILLERMINA HERRERA
Vice-Rectors: RENÉ POITEVIN (Academic), Arq. CARLOS HAUESLER (Administrative)
Gen. Sec.: LUIS QUAN
Librarian: REGINA ROMERO DE LA VEGA
Number of teachers: 1,008
Number of students: 20,000
Publications: Aprapalabra, Boletín de Lingüística (6 a year), Cultura de Guatemala (3 a year), Estudios Sociales (4 a year), Vida Universitaria (12 a year), Revista de Literatura

DEANS

Faculty of Agriculture and Environmental Sciences: Ing. JAIME CARRERA
Faculty of Architecture: Arq. SERGIO TULIO CASTANEDA
Faculty of Economic Sciences: JOSÉ ALEJANDRO AREVADO
Faculty of Engineering: EDWIN ESCOBAR
Faculty of Health Sciences: MIGUEL GARCÉS
Faculty of Humanities: MA. EUGENIA SANDOVAL
Faculty of Political and Social Sciences: RENZO ROSAL
Faculty of Theology: DENIS LEDER

ATTACHED INSTITUTES

Institute of Agriculture, Natural Resources and the Environment: Dir Ing. JUVENTINO GÁLVEZ.
Institute of Dance: Dir Dr SABRINA CASTILLO.
Institute of Economic and Social Research: Dir Dr TOMAS ROSADA.
Institute of Linguistics: Dir Dr LUCIA VERDUGO.
Institute of Musicology: Dir Dr DIETER LEHNHOFF.
Institute of Psychology: Dir Dr FIDELIO SWANA.
Institute of Science and Technology: Dir LYS CIFUENTES.

Schools of Art and Music

Conservatorio Nacional de Música (National Academy of Music): 3A Avda 4–61, Zona 1, 01001 Guatemala City; f. 1875; 40 teachers; 900 students; Dir LUIS A. LIMA Y LIMA.

Escuela Nacional de Artes Plásticas 'Rafael Rodríguez Padilla': 6 Avda 22–00, Zona 1, Guatemala City; f. 1920; library: 2,500 vols; Dir ZIPACNÁ DE LEÓN; publ. Revista de la Escuela Nacional de Artes Plásticas 'Rafael Rodríguez Padilla'.

GUINEA

The Higher Education System

Guinea (formerly French Guinea) was part of French West Africa until it gained its independence in 1958, and the education system is still based on the French system. There are two state-controlled universities, Université Gamal Abdel Nasser de Conakry (founded in 1962) and Université Julius Nyéréré de Kankan (founded in 1963, current name and status since 1987). Additional institutions of higher education include professional institutes and schools attached to the universities. The Ministry of Higher Education and Scientific Research is the main controlling body, under the aegis of the Department for Scientific and Technical Research and the Department for Higher Education, but higher education institutions enjoy significant autonomy. Higher education is wholly financed by the Government (except for private insti-

tutions). In 2005/06 42,700 students were enrolled in further and higher education.

Students must hold the secondary school qualification, Baccalauréat Deuxième Partie, and sit a competitive entrance examination in order to be admitted to university. There are two undergraduate degrees: the Diplôme d'Études Universitaires Générales, which is awarded after two years, and the Licence, which is awarded after four years. Undergraduates may also receive a professional diploma (Diplôme), depending on the subject. After the Licence, the Maîtrise or the Diplôme d'Études Supérieures are the first postgraduate qualifications, both awarded after one year of study. Finally, the third stage of university-level qualifications is the Doctorat, which is a research-based, two-year course leading to submission of a thesis.

Regulatory Bodies

GOVERNMENT

Ministry of Higher Education and Scientific Research: face à la Cathédrale Sainte-Marie, BP 964, Conakry; tel. 30-45-12-17; fax 30-41-20-12; Minister MORIKÉ DAMARO CAMARA.

Ministry of Information and Culture: ave du Port Secrétariat, BP 262, Conakry; tel. 30-41-19-59; fax 30-41-19-26; Minister of Culture and Heritage AHMED TIDIANE CISSÉ.

Learned Society

LANGUAGE AND LITERATURE

PEN Centre de Guinée: BP 107, Labé; tel. 30-44-14-75; f. 1989; 32 mems; library of 92 vols; Sec. ZEINAB KOUMANTHIO DIALLO; publ. *Pour Mémoire.*

Research Institutes

GENERAL

Direction Nationale de la Recherche Scientifique et Technique: Conakry, BP 561; f. 1958; 60 mems; 2 libraries; Dir Dr FODE SOUMAH; publ. *Bulletin.*

AGRICULTURE, FISHERIES AND VETERINARY SCIENCE

Centre de Recherche Agronomique de Foulaya: BP 156, Kindia; tel. 30-61-01-48; e-mail iragdq@irag.org.gn; f. 1946; Dir Dr MAHMOUD CAMARA.

Institut de Recherche Agronomique de Guinée: blvd du Commerce, BP 1523, Conakry; tel. 30-21-19-57; e-mail iragdg@biasy.net.gn.

Institut de Recherche en Animalculture Pastoria: BP 146, Kindia; tel. 30-61-08-11; f. 1923; fmr *Institut Pasteur,* nationalized 1965; research on infectious animal diseases; production of various vaccines; 18 staff; library of 362 vols; Dir Dr ALHASSANE DIALLO.

Libraries and Archives

Conakry

Archives Nationales: BP 1005, Conakry; tel. 30-44-42-97; f. 1960; Dir ALMANY STELL CONTE.

Bibliothèque Nationale: BP 561, Conakry; tel. 30-46-10-10; f. 1958; 40,000 vols, also spec. colln on slavery (500 books, pamphlets and MSS); 225 current periodicals; courses in librarianship; Dir LANSANA SYLLA.

Museum

Conakry

Musée National: BP 139, Conakry; tel. 30-45-10-66; f. 1960; Dir SORY KABA.

Universities

UNIVERSITÉ GAMAL ABDEL NASSER DE CONAKRY

BP 1147, Conakry
Telephone: 30-46-46-89
Fax: 30-46-48-08
E-mail: uganc@mirinet.net.gn
Founded 1962
State control
Rector: OUSMANE SYLLA
Vice-Rector for Academics: JEAN-MARIE TOURÉ
Vice-Rector for Research: Dr M. KODJOUGOU DIALLO
Sec.-Gen.: GALEMA GUILAVOGUI
Dir of Library: MANSA KANTÉ
Library of 4,000 vols
Number of teachers: 824
Number of students: 5,000
Publications: *Guinée Médicale, Horizons*

DEANS

Faculty of Arts and Humanities: GOUDOUSSY DIALLO
Faculty of Law, Economics and Management: HAWA FOFANA
Faculty of Medicine and Pharmacy: (vacant)
Faculty of Science: Dr DJELIMANDJAN CONDÉ
Polytechnic Institute: Prof. NANAMOUDOU MAGASSOUBA (Director-General)

UNIVERSITÉ JULIUS NYÉRÉRÉ DE KANKAN

Ministère de l'Enseignement Supérieur et de la Recherche Scientifique, Conakry
Telephone: 30-71-20-93
Founded 1963; univ. status 1987

State control
Academic year: October to June
Rector: Dr SEYDOUBA CAMARA
Vice-Rector for Academics: Dr MAWIATOU BAH
Vice-Rector for Research: Dr SIDAFA CAMARA
Sec.-Gen.: DOMINIQUE KOLY
Dir of Financial and Administrative Affairs: ELHADJ ALPHA OUSMANE DIALLO
Dir of International Relations and Cooperation: MARTIN KOIVOGUI
Dir of Univ. Publs: ELHADJ NAMANDIAN DOUMBOUYA
Library Dir: JOSEPH KOKOLY DRAMOU
Library of 12,160 vols
Number of teachers: 95
Number of students: 3,012
Publication: *Revue Scientifique de l'Université de Kankan* (2 a year)

DEANS

Faculty of Natural Sciences: Dr BAKARY KAMANO
Faculty of Social Sciences: Dr AMADOU BAÏLO BARRY
École Supérieure des Sciences de l'Information: SIBA BILIVOGUI

Colleges

École Nationale des Arts et Métiers: POB 240, Conakry; tel. 30-46-25-62; fax 30-46-25-62; f. 1962; industrial automation, electro-mechanical engineering, electronics, refrigeration and air-conditioning, diesel mechanics, industrial maintenance; Dir MAHMOUDOU BARRY.

École Nationale de la Santé: Conakry; tel. 30-29-52-49; fax 30-46-50-09; Dir BARRY YAYA.

École Supérieure d'Administration: Conakry; f. 1964.

Institut Supérieur Agronomique et Vétérinaire 'Valéry Giscard d'Estaing' de Faranah: BP 131, Faranah; tel. 30-81-02-15; fax 30-81-08-18; e-mail isav1@mirinet.net.gn; f. 1978; library: 3,629 vols, 207 periodicals; 110 teachers; 2,515 students; faculties of agriculture, agricultural engineering, rural economics, stockbreeding and veterinary medicine, waters and forestry; common-core syllabus; Dir-Gen. Dr YAZORA SOROPO-GUI.

GUINEA-BISSAU

The Higher Education System

Guinea-Bissau was formerly Portuguese Guinea (Guiné), during which time education as a whole was geared to serve a narrow élite, consisting mainly of the colonial rulers' children. The country gained its independence in 1974 following a military coup in Portugal. The first institution of higher education, a school of law, was established in 1979, followed by centres for medicine, education, nursing and sports. In 1999 a government decree placed all these institutions under the authority of the then Ministry of National and Higher Education (formerly Ministry of Education), with a view to establishing a university at the National Institute of Studies and Research.

In 2000/2001 473 students were enrolled in tertiary education. Some 200 students completed their studies in Havana,

Cuba, in 2002, while a further 186 had scholarships to study in Paris, France, and Dakar, Senegal. To counter this trend, in 2003 the Universidade Amílcar Cabral, Guinea-Bissau's first university, was founded. In the same year a private university, the Universidade Colinas de Boé, also opened. In 2004, after three years of a feasibility study, the Universidade Lusófona de Humanidades e Tecnologias based in Lisbon, Portugal, opened its own subsidiary, the Universidade Lusófona de Guiné. By the end of 2008 internal financial problems had caused Amílcar Cabral University to lose its autonomous status and it was subsumed into the Universidade Lusófona de Guiné.

Technical and vocational education is available at two institutions, the Centre of Administrative Training and the Centre of Experimental Training.

Regulatory Bodies

GOVERNMENT

Ministry of National Education, Culture and Science: Rua Areolino Cruz, Bissau; tel. 3202244; Minister ARTUR SILVA.

Research Institutes

GENERAL

Centro de Estudos da Guiné-Bissau (Study Centre of Guinea-Bissau): CP 37, Bissau; f. 1945.

Instituto Nacional de Estudos e Pesquisa (INEP) (National Institute of Studies and Research): CP 112, Bairro Cobornel, Bissau; Complexo Escolar 14 de Novembro, Bissau; tel. 3251867; fax 3251125; f. 1987, damaged during conflict between govt forces and rebels in 1999, restoration, with the support of int. scholars, began in 2000; library of 40,000 vols, incl. archives and museum; also holds periodicals, photographs, plays, press cuttings; fees for using facility and for exhibitions.

Libraries and Archives

Bissau

Biblioteca Nacional da Guiné-Bissau (National Library of Guinea-Bissau): Praça do Impéro, CP 37, Bissau; f. 1970.

Museums and Galleries

Bissau

Museu da Guiné-Bissau (Museum of Guinea Bissau): Praca do Impéro, CP 37, Bissau; f. 1945; library of 14,000 vols; collns of economics, ethnography, history, natural science.

Museu Etnografico Nacional (National Ethnographical Museum): Complexo Escolar 14 de Novembro, CP 338, Bissau; tel. 3215600; fax 3204400; photographic archive depicting former colln of African masks and statues (largely destroyed during military conflict in 1998).

University and Colleges

UNIVERSIDADE AMÍLCAR CABRAL

Endereço Bairro da Ajuda, 2a Fase, CP 659, Bissau

Telephone: 3255970
Fax: 3202244
E-mail: geral@uac.com

Founded 2003

State control

Faculties of agricultural and veterinary science, economics, letters and communications, science, technology; school of physical education and sport

Rector: Prof. Dr TCHERNO DJALÓ.

Faculdade de Direito da Guiné-Bissau: Complexo Escolar 14 de Novembro, CP 595, Bissau Codex; tel. 3252770; fax 3204304; e-mail geral@fdbissau.com; internet www.fdbissau.com; f. 1990; Dir FODÉ ADULAI MANÉ.

Instituto Nacional para o Desenvolvimento da Educação (INDE): Rua Dr Herman Gmeiner, Bairro 7, 2a Fase, CP 132, Bissau; tel. 3204534; fax 3202054; e-mail indebissau@hotmail.com; Pres. ALFREDO GOMES; Dir-Gen. AUGUSTO PEREIRA.

GUYANA

The Higher Education System

Guyana, formerly British Guiana, a colony of the United Kingdom, achieved independence in 1966. The Free Education Act of 1976 guaranteed the right to free education at all levels from pre-school to higher education. The Ministry of Education is the supreme body for higher education. The state-controlled University of Guyana (founded in 1963) is the only university, but higher education is also available at professional schools, technical institutes and colleges. In 1999/200 some 7,496 students were enrolled at the University.

The Caribbean Examinations Council Secondary Education Certificate is the standard requirement for admission to higher education, although GCE O-levels and A-levels are also accepted. The main degrees are the undergraduate Bachelors, which is awarded after four years of study, and the postgraduate Masters, which is awarded after one further year of study. There are also undergraduate and graduate Diploma programmes in mainly professional fields of study. Masters programmes are not offered in all subjects.

The University of Guyana has an Institute of Distance and Continuing Education, which runs extramural courses; the Adult Education Association offers similar programmes. Postsecondary vocational and technical qualifications include the Craft Certificate, Technician Certificate and Technician Diploma.

Regulatory Bodies

GOVERNMENT

Ministry of Culture, Youth and Sport: 71–72 Main St, South Cummingsburg, Georgetown; tel. 227-7860; fax 225-5067; e-mail mincys@guyana.net.gy; Minister Dr FRANK ANTHONY.

Ministry of Education: 21 Brickdam, Stabroek, POB 1014, Georgetown; tel. 223-7900; fax 225-8511; e-mail moegyweb@yahoo.com; internet www.sdnp.org.gy/minedu; Minister SHAIK K. Z. BAKSH.

Learned Societies

BIBLIOGRAPHY, LIBRARY SCIENCE AND MUSEOLOGY

Guyana Library Association: c/o National Library, 76–77 Main St, POB 10240, Georgetown; tel. 226-2690; fax 227-4052; f. 1968; 35 personal mems, 13 institutional mems; Pres. IVOR RODRIGUES; Sec. GWYNETH GEORGE; publ. *Bulletin*.

ECONOMICS, LAW AND POLITICS

Guyana Institute of International Affairs: POB 101176, Georgetown; tel. 227-7768; fax 227-7768; f. 1965; 100 mems; library of 5,000 vols; Pres. DONALD A. B. TROTMAN; publs *Annual Journal of International Affairs*, occasional papers.

EDUCATION

Adult Education Association of Guyana Inc. M.S.: 88 Carmichael St, POB 101111, Georgetown; tel. 225-0758; fax 227-2273; e-mail aea@guyana.net.gy; f. 1957; 1,000 mems; NGO that aims to provide opportunities for Guyanese to improve their skills, raise the level of awareness of their culture, acquire a critical understanding of major contemporary issues; programmes: academic, technical, scientific, creative art, commercial and professional devt; operates remedial school for people who have dropped out of school and slow learners; runs adult literacy classes; Pres. HANSEL BARROW; Exec. Dir PATRICIA DAVID.

LANGUAGE AND LITERATURE

Alliance Française: The Hive, 27/28 Queen St, Kitty, Georgetown; offers courses and exams in French language and culture and promotes cultural exchange with France.

Research Institutes

AGRICULTURE, FISHERIES AND VETERINARY SCIENCE

Inter-American Institute for Cooperation on Agriculture (IICA)– Cooperation Agency in Guyana: Lot 18, Brickdam, Stabroek, POB 10-1089, Georgetown; tel. 226-8347; fax 225-8358; e-mail iica@networksgy.com; internet www.iica.int; f. 1974; Guyana branch of the specialized agency of the OAS for the agricultural sector; promotes food safety and the prosperity of the rural sector in the Americas; library of 1,550 vols, 25 periodicals; Rep. IGNATIUS JEAN; publs *Agriview* (4 a year), *Caribbean News* (4 a year), *COMUNIICA* (4 a year), *Tropical Fruits Newsletter* (4 a year).

MEDICINE

Pan-American Health Organization/ World Health Organization, Guyana Office: Lot 8, Brickdam, Stabroek, POB 10969, Georgetown; tel. 225-5150; fax 226-6654; e-mail hoyteang@guy.paho.org; internet www.new.paho.org/guy; f. 1902; technical cooperation in: family and community health, incl. maternal and child health; non-communicable diseases; communicable diseases; environmental health; disaster risk reduction, preparedness and response; health systems and services, incl. human resources for health; social determinants of health; and programme planning and management for national health devt; library of 3,500 vols; Rep. Dr D. BEVERLEY BARNETT.

Libraries and Archives

Georgetown

Bank of Guyana Library: POB 1003, Georgetown; tel. 226-3261; fax 227-2965; e-mail boglib@guyana.net.gy; internet www.bankofguyana.org.gy; f. 1966; provides support for the information needs of the staff; 15,000 vols, 150 periodicals; special collections: staff publs, conference papers, IMF documents, World Bank publs; Librarian BEVERLY BAKER.

Documentation Centre, Caribbean Community Secretariat: Turkeyen, Greater Georgetown, POB 10827, Georgetown; tel. 222-0001; fax 222-0170; e-mail doccentre@caricom.org; internet www.caricom.org; f. 1980; 18,700 vols, 24,167 books and pamphlets, 18,851 official documents, 16,206 monographic titles, 5,039 microfiches, 229 CD-ROMs, 112 journals, 16 newspapers; collns (documents): CARICOM, UN, UN agencies; Deputy Programme Man. MAUREEN C. NEWTON.

Guyana Medical Science Library: Georgetown Hospital Compound, Georgetown; f. 1966; attached to the Ministry of Health; provides medical information to doctors, nurses and health personnel; 9,914 vols, 300 journals, 1,000 pamphlets; Librarian JENNIFER WILSON; publ. *Bulletin* (4 a year).

National Library: 76–77 Church and Main St, POB 10240, Georgetown; tel. 226-2699; fax 226-4053; internet www.natlib.gov.gy; f. 1909; combines the functions of a nat. library and public library; legal depository for material printed in Guyana; 197,355 vols; special collections: Caribbeana, library science, A. J. Seymour, UNESCO deposit; Chief Librarian GWYNETH BROWMAN (acting); publ. *Guyanese National Bibliography* (4 a year).

University of Guyana Library: POB 101110, Georgetown; fax 225-4885; internet fss.uog.edu.gy/university_library.htm; f. 1963; 200,000 vols, 3,000 periodicals; special collections: UN deposit collection, Caribbean Research Library, Law Collection; Librarian YVONNE LANCASTER; publs *Additions in the Humanities* (6 a year), *Additions in Science and Technology* (6 a year), *Caribbean Additions* (6 a year).

Museums and Art Galleries

Georgetown

Guyana Museum: Company Path, North St, Georgetown; f. 1853 by the Royal Agricultural and Commercial Society; subjects covered incl. industry, art, history, anthropology, zoology; Curator CLAYTON RODNEY; publ. *Journal* (1 a year).

Incorporates:

Guyana Zoological Park, National Parks Commission: Regent & Vlissengen

Rds, Georgetown; tel. 225-8016; e-mail natpark@networksgy.com; f. 1952; specializes in the display, care and management of South American fauna; library of 50 vols; Gen. Man. YOLANDA VASCONCELLOS.

University

UNIVERSITY OF GUYANA

POB 101110, Turkeyen, Greater Georgetown

Telephone: 222-4184

Fax: 222-3596

E-mail: publicrelations@uog.edu.gy

Internet: www.uog.edu.gy

Founded 1963

State control

Language of instruction: English

Academic year: two terms, beginning September and January

Chancellor: Dr COMPTON BOURNE

Vice-Chancellor: Dr LAWRENCE CARRINGTON

Deputy Vice-Chancellor: Dr MARLENE COX

Registrar: Dr VINCENT ALEXANDER

Librarian: GWYNETH GEORGE

Library: See Libraries and Archives

Number of teachers: 248

Number of students: 6,549

Publication: *University of Guyana Bulletin* (1 a year)

DEANS

Faculty of Agriculture and Forestry: LAWRENCE LEWIS

Faculty of Health Sciences: Dr EMANUEL CUMMINGS

Faculty of Natural Sciences: GARY MENDONCA

Faculty of Social Sciences: O'NEIL GREAVES

Faculty of Technology: VERLYN KLASS

School of Earth and Environmental Sciences: Dr PAULETTE BYNOE

School of Education and Humanities: AL CREIGHTON

PROFESSORS

BISHOP, A., Law

BRITTON, P., Law

EVERSELY, C., Law

LONCKE, J., French, Literature and Music

MASSIAH, K., Law

PERSICO, A., Spanish

SAMAD, D., English

TEWARI, B. B., Chemistry

THOMAS, C. Y., Economics and Business Administration

VERMA, V. N., Chemistry

Colleges

American International School of Medicine: Oceanview Campus, POB 101728, Georgetown; e-mail info@aism.edu; internet www.aism.edu; tel. 222-3437; fax 225-1646; f. 1997; library: 2,500 vols; 30 teachers; 50 students; Pres. COLIN A. WILKINSON.

Critchlow Labour College: Woolford Ave, Non Pareil Park, Georgetown; tel. 226-2481; f. 1970; library: 2,000 vols; 40 teachers; 600 students; industrial and social studies; Principal T. ANSON SANCHO.

E. R. Burrowes School of Art: 96 Carmichael St, Georgetown; tel. 226-3649; f. 1975; 4-year diploma course; library: 750 vols; 13 teachers; 52 students; Administrator AGNES JONES.

Government Technical Institute: Woolford Ave, Georgetown; tel. 226-2468; f. 1951; library: 3,500 vols; 37 teachers; 2,000 students; Principal LENNOX B. WILLIAMS.

Guyana Industrial Training Centre: Woolford Ave and Albert St, Non Pareil Park, Georgetown; tel. 226-6196; f. 1966;

library: 1,600 vols; 6 teachers; 120 full-time, 90 part-time students; Dir SYDNEY R. WALTERS.

Guyana School of Agriculture Corporation: Mon Repos, East Coast Demerara; tel. and fax 220-2297; e-mail gsa@sdnp.org.gy; internet www.sdnp.org.gy/minagro/; f. 1963; library: 7,000 vols; Principal LYNETTE P. CUNHA.

Kuru-Kuru Cooperative College: 128 D'Urban St, D'Urban Backlands, Lodge, Georgetown; tel. 225-8433; e-mail kurukuruguy@netscape.net; f. 1973; library: 5,800 vols; 26 teachers; 270 students; Principal AVRIL BACCHUS (acting); Librarian LINDA CALDER.

Linden Technical Institute: Lot 1, New Rd, Constabulary Compound, Mackenzie, Linden; tel. 444-3333; fax 444-6719; internet www.sdnp.org.gy/geap/lti; f. 1958; Guyana technical education examination courses in carpentry and joinery, driver training, electrical installation, internal combustion engines, instrumentation, mechanical fitting, metal machining, motor vehicle work, welding; 10 instructors; 86 full-time students; Principal ISAAC LAMAZON (acting).

New Amsterdam Technical Institute: POB 50, Garrison Rd, Fort Ordnance, New Amsterdam, Berbice; tel. 333-2702; f. 1971; Guyana technical education examination; courses in agricultural mechanics, automotive engineering, electrical trades, fitting, masonry, radio and electronic servicing, plumbing, welding, wood trades; agricultural engineering technician course; architectural and building construction technician course; ordinary technician diploma, mechanical engineering technician course; secretarial and business studies; library: 2,186 vols; 32 teachers; 1,000 students; Principal RONALD L. SIMON.

HAITI

The Higher Education System

Haiti (formerly Saint-Domingue) was under French sovereignty until 1804, when it gained its independence, but later came under US supervision from 1915 until 1934. The traditional education system has strong French influences, though some private institutions follow the American system. French and Creole are the official languages of instruction. The Ministry of Education and Vocational Training has responsibility for education. There are three universities, the state-controlled Université d'État d'Haiti (founded in 1920) and the private Université Quisqueya (founded in 1988) and Université Roi Henri Christophe (founded in 1980). Before the January 2010 earthquake, the Haitian system of higher education comprised at least 159 institutions, divided into disparate public and private sectors. The former consisted of a small network of 14 public, government-run institutions of higher education (Instituts d'enseignement superior, IESs) including the State University of Haiti (Université d'État d'Haiti, or UEH). Besides the UEH, the public university sector also included 13 IESs either affiliated with or independent of the UEH. In contrast, the private higher education sector consisted of a vast array of 145 institutions of varying quality. Of the 145 private universities, 10 provided high-quality, accredited education; of the remaining 135 (often religious-based institutions), 97 did not have permission to operate from the governmental Agency of Higher Education and Scientific Research. In 2007, the Ministry of National Education and Professional Formation reported the university population of Haiti was approximately 40,000 students. Of these 28,000 were in public universities and 12,000 in private ones.

The main secondary school qualification, the Baccalauréat, is the leading requirement for admission to higher education. Undergraduates study for three to four years for the Diplôme d'Etudes Supérieures, Certificat d'Etudes Supérieures or a professional title. The first postgraduate degree is the Maîtrise, received after one year of study following the undergraduate degree. The second postgraduate degree is the Doctorat, but is only available in the fields of ethnology and development sciences.

Many addresses in Port-au-Prince and surrounding areas were destroyed in the earthquake of January 2010. At least 28 of the major universities were completely destroyed and the rest seriously damaged, and 2,599 to 6,000 students may have perished.

Regulatory Bodies

GOVERNMENT

Ministry of Culture: 31 rue Roy, Port-au-Prince; tel. 2223-7357; e-mail dg1@haiticulture.org; likely to have been destroyed in the earthquake of January 2010; Minister DANIEL ELIE.

Ministry of Education and Vocational Training: rue Dr Audain, Port-au-Prince; tel. 2222-1036; fax 2223-7887; likely to have been destroyed in the earthquake of January 2010; Minister GABRIEL BIEN-AIMÉ.

Learned Societies

GENERAL

UNESCO Office Port-au-Prince: 19, Delmas 60, Musseau par Bourdon, Petion Ville, Port-au-Prince; tel. 2511-0460; fax 2244-9366; e-mail unescohaiti@hainet.net; likely to have been destroyed in the earthquake of January 2010; Dir JORGE ESPINAL.

BIBLIOGRAPHY, LIBRARY SCIENCE AND MUSEOLOGY

Le Bibliophile: Cap-Haïtien; f. 1923; promotes knowledge and readership of world literature; 28 mems; Pres. SILVIO FASCHI; Sec. LOUIS TOUSSAINT; publs La Citadelle (52 a year), Stella (12 a year).

LANGUAGE AND LITERATURE

Alliance Française: 99 rue Lamartinière, BP 131, Port-au-Prince; tel. 2244-0016; fax 2244-0017; e-mail dgalliancefr_haiti@yahoo.fr; offers courses and examinations in French language and culture and promotes cultural exchange with France; attached offices in Cap-Haïtien, Gonaïves, Jacmel, Jeremies, Les Cayes, Port-de-Paix; likely to have been destroyed in the earthquake of January 2010.

NATURAL SCIENCES

General

Conseil National des Recherches Scientifiques (National Council for Scientific Research): Département de la Santé Publique et de la Population, Port-au-Prince; f. 1963; to coordinate scientific development and research, particularly in the field of public health; likely to have been destroyed in the earthquake of January 2010; Pres. Prof. VICTOR NOËL; Sec. M. DOUYON.

Research Institute

RELIGION, SOCIOLOGY AND ANTHROPOLOGY

Bureau National d'Ethnologie: Angle rue St Honoré and ave Magloire Ambroise, Place des Héros de l'Indépendance, BP 915, Port-au-Prince; tel. 2222-5232; f. 1941; departments of African and Haitian ethnography, pre-Columbian archaeology; likely to have been destroyed in the earthquake of January 2010; Dir Dr MAX PAUL; publ. Bulletin (2 a year).

Libraries and Archives

Port-au-Prince

Archives Nationales d'Haiti: Angle rues Geffrard et Borgella, BP 1299, Port-au-Prince; tel. 2222-8566; fax 2222-6280; internet www.anhhaiti.org; f. 1860; likely to have been destroyed in the earthquake of January 2010; Dir-Gen. JEAN WILFRID BERTRAND.

Bibliothèque Haitienne des F. I. C.: 180 rue du Centre, BP 1758, Port-au-Prince 6110; tel. 2223-2148; fax 2223-2029; f. 1920; 13,000 vols; Haitian literature, newspapers since the 19th century, history of St Domingue and Haiti, Haitian legislation; likely to have been destroyed in the earthquake of January 2010; Dir ERNEST EVEN.

Bibliothèque Nationale d'Haiti: 193 rue du Centre, Port-au-Prince; tel. 2222-1198; fax 2223-8773; f. 1940; 23,000 vols, 419 periodicals; 12 brs; likely to have been destroyed in the earthquake of January 2010; Dir FRANÇOISE BEAULIEU THYBULLE.

Museums and Art Galleries

Port-au-Prince

Centre d'Art: 58 rue Roy, Port-au-Prince; tel. 2222-2018; f. 1944; arranges representative exhibitions of Haitian art in the Americas and Western Europe; likely to have been destroyed in the earthquake of January 2010; Dir FRANCINE MURAT.

Musée du Panthéon National Haitien: Place des Héros de l'Indépendence, Champ de Mars, Port-au-Prince Ouest; tel. 2222-3167; fax 2221-8838; e-mail mupanah@yahoo.fr; f. 1983; historical artefacts, arts and crafts; likely to have been destroyed in the earthquake of January 2010; Dir-Gen. MARIE-LUCIE VENDRYES.

Universities

UNIVERSITÉ D'ÉTAT D'HAITI

21 rue de Houx, BP 2279, Port-au-Prince
Telephone: 2244-2943
Fax: 2244-2940
E-mail: recteur@ueh.edu.ht
Internet: www.ueh.edu.ht
Founded 1920
State control
Language of instruction: French
Academic year: October to July

Rector: JEAN VERNET HENRY

Vice-Rector for Academic Affairs: MICHEL HECTOR

Vice-Rector for Admin.: MARIE CARMEL AUSTIN

Secretary-General: LESLIE DUCHATELLIER

Librarian: (vacant)

Library of 7,000 vols

Number of teachers: 664

Number of students: 10,446

Likely to have been destroyed in the earthquake of January 2010

DEANS AND COORDINATORS

Faculty of Agronomy and Veterinary Medicine: JEAN VERNET HENRY

Faculty of Applied Linguistics: PIERRE VERNET

Faculty of Ethnology: JEAN YVES BLOT, PATRICIA MICHEL FOUCAULT

Faculty of Humanities: JEAN RENOL ELIE

Faculty of Law and Economics: JUSTIN CASTEL

Faculty of Medicine and Pharmacy: Dr MARIO ALVAREZ

Faculty of Odontology: Dr ALIX CHATEIGNE

Faculty of Science: GUICHARD BEAULIEU (Academic: CHRISTIAN ROUSSEAU (Admin.)

Ecole Normale Supérieure: BERARD CENATUS, ROGER PETIT-FRÈRE

Institut d'Etudes et de Recherches Africaines d'Haiti: ERNST BERNADIN

Institut National d'Administration de Gestion et des Hautes Etudes Internationales (INAGHEI): EDDY CARRÉ

UNIVERSITÉ QUISQUEYA

Angle rue Chareron et boulevard Harry Truman, BP 796, Port-au-Prince

Telephone: 2222-9002

Fax: 2221-4211

E-mail: recteur@uniq.edu

Internet: www.uniq.edu.ht

Founded 1988

Private control

Language of instruction: French

Academic year: September to July

Rector: JACKY LUMARQUE

Vice-Rector for Academic Affairs: EDGARD PRÉVILON

Vice-Rector for Admin.: LIONEL RICHARD

Gen.-Sec.: MARIE GISÈLE PIERRE

Librarian: CARLO DUPUY

Library of 22,000 vols

Number of teachers: 256

Number of students: 2,036

Publication: *Revue Juridique de l'UniQ* (4 a year)

Destroyed in the earthquake of January 2010

DEANS

Faculty of Agriculture and the Environment: EDGARD JEANNITON

Faculty of Economics and Management: NARCISSE FIÈVRE

Faculty of Education: ROLAND MATHIEU

Faculty of Health Sciences: KYSS JEAN-MARY

Faculty of Law: MIRLANDE MANIGAT

Faculty of Science and Engineering: GÉRARD-LUC JEAN-BAPTISTE

UNIVERSITÉ ROI HENRI CHRISTOPHE

BP 98, rues 17–18, H-1, Cap-Haïtien

Telephone: 2262-1316

Fax: 2262-0802

Internet: www.urhchaiti.org

Founded 1980

Private control

Rector: JOSEPH YVON

Administrator: EDGARD BERNARDIN

Librarian: MARIE-MERCIE PREDESTIN

Number of students: 100

DEANS

Faculty of Agriculture: BRUNEL GARÇON

Faculty of Engineering: (vacant)

Faculty of Medicine: Dr GUY DUGUÉ

Colleges

Ecole Nationale des Arts et Métiers: 266 rue Monseigneur Guilloux, Port-au-Prince; tel. 2222-9686; f. 1983; likely to have been destroyed in the earthquake of January 2010; Dirs EMERANTE DE PRADINES MORSE, ROBERT BAU DUY.

Ecole Nationale de Technologie Médicale: Faculty of Medicine and Pharmacy, Université d'État d'Haiti, 89 rue Oswald Durand, POB 2599, Port-au-Prince 6110; tel. 2222-0487; e-mail fmp@ueh.edu.ht; likely to have been destroyed in the earthquake of January 2010; Dir PAULETTE A. CHAMPAGNE.

Institut International d'Etudes Universitaires: c/o Fondation Haitienne de Développement, 106 ave Christophe, Port-au-Prince; likely to have been destroyed in the earthquake of January 2010; Dir Y. ARMAND.

HONDURAS

The Higher Education System

The oldest institution of higher education is the Universidad Nacional Autónoma de Honduras, which was founded in 1847. There are two further state universities and seven private ones. The Ministry of Education is responsible for the provision of higher education. In 2005/06 145,171 students were enrolled in university-level education.

The secondary school qualification Bachillerato (Académico) is the main requirement for admission to higher education. The primary undergraduate degrees are the Licenciado or professional title, awarded after four years of study, and the Bachillerato Universitario, a technological qualification also awarded after four years. Following the Licenciado, the first postgraduate degree is the Maestría, awarded after two to three years of study. The Bachillerato Universitario does not always guarantee admission to postgraduate studies.

Higher technical and vocational education is offered by professional colleges and schools. The leading qualification is the Técnico or Técnico Universitario, which requires one-and-a-half years of study.

Regulatory Bodies

GOVERNMENT

Ministry of Culture, Art and Sports: Avda La Paz, Apdo 328, Tegucigalpa; tel. 236-9643; fax 236-9532; e-mail binah@sdnhon.org.hn; Minister Dr RODOLFO PASTOR FASQUELLE.

Ministry of Education: 1a Avda, 2a y 3a Calle 201, Comayagüela, Tegucigalpa; tel. 222-8571; fax 237-4312; e-mail info@se.gob.hn; internet www.se.gob.hn; Minister of State MARLÓN BREVÉ REYES.

Learned Societies

GENERAL

Academia Hondureña (Honduran Academy): Apdo 4003, Tegucigalpa; located at: Avda Tiburcio Carías Andino 811, Col. Alameda, Tegucigalpa; tel. 232-1322; fax 232-1322; e-mail ahlengua@hotmail.com; f. 1949; corresp. of the Real Academia Española (Madrid); 28 mems; Dir OSCAR ACOSTA; Sec. MARÍA ELBA NIETO SEGOVIA; publ. Boletín.

ARCHITECTURE AND TOWN PLANNING

Colegio de Arquitectos de Honduras (College of Honduran Architects): Apdo 1974, Tegucigalpa; tel. 235-8828; fax 235-7965; e-mail cah1@e-cah.org; internet www.e-cah.org; f. 1979; 727 mems; library; publ. Arquitectura y Contexto (4 a year).

BIBLIOGRAPHY, LIBRARY SCIENCE AND MUSEOLOGY

Asociación de Bibliotecarios y Archivistas de Honduras: 11a Calle, 1a y 2a Avdas No. 105, Comayagüela, Tegucigalpa; f. 1951; 53 mems; library of 3,000 vols; Pres. FRANCISCA DE ESCOTO ESPINOZA; Sec.-Gen. JUAN ANGEL AYES R.; publ. Catálogo de Préstamo (12 a year).

HISTORY, GEOGRAPHY AND ARCHAEOLOGY

Academia Hondureña de Geografía e Historia: Apdo 619, Tegucigalpa; f. 1968; 21 mems; library of 1,535 vols; Pres. Dr RAMÓN E. CRUZ; Sec. PM FERNANDO FERRARI BUSTILLO; publ. Revista.

LANGUAGE AND LITERATURE

Alliance Française: Col. Lomas Del Guijarro, Apdo Postal 3445, Tegucigalpa; tel. 239-6164; fax 239-6163; offers courses and examinations in French language and culture and promotes cultural exchange with France; attached teaching offices in La Ceiba, San Pedro Sula, Tegucigalpa and Tela.

Research Institutes

GENERAL

Instituto Hondureño de Cultura Interamericana (IHCI): Apdo 201, Tegucigalpa; 2da Avda entre 5 y 6, Calle No. 520, Comayagüela; tel. 220-1393; fax 238-0064; f. 1939; courses in English, bilingual secretarial studies; art gallery; library of 8,000 vols (English and Spanish); Dir ROSARIO ELENA CÓRDOVA.

AGRICULTURE, FISHERIES AND VETERINARY SCIENCE

Instituto Hondureño del Café (Honduran Coffee Institute): Apdo Postal 3147, Tegucigalpa; located at: Col. Las Minitas, Edif. El Faro Contiguo a Embajada de Guatemala, Tegucigalpa; tel. 232-2544; fax 232-2768; internet www.cafedehonduras.hn/ihcafe2005/ihcafe/quienessomos.html; f. 1970; CEO JUAN JOSÉ OSORTO.

Instituto Nacional Agrario (National Agrarian Institute): Col. Alameda, Calle Principal, 4a Avda entre 10 y 11 Calle, No. 1009, Tegucigalpa; tel. 232-4893; fax 239-7398; Dir ERASMO PORTILLO.

HISTORY, GEOGRAPHY AND ARCHAEOLOGY

Instituto Geográfico Nacional (IGN) (National Geographic Institute): Apdo Postal 3177, Tegucigalpa; Barrio La Bolsa, Tegucigalpa; tel. 225-2759; fax 225-2753; f. 1946; delineates natural and mineral resources, their evaluation and their exploitation; 130 staff; library of 8,000 vols; Dir-Gen. Ing. ANGEL PORFIRIO SANCHEZ SANCHEZ; publs Boletín de la Dirección General de Cartografía, Boletín de la Dirección General de Cartografía del Ministerio de Obras Públicas, Transporte y Vivienda, Boletín del Instituto Geográfico Nacional.

Instituto Hondureño de Antropología e Historia: Apdo 1518, Villa Roy, Barrio Buenos Aires, Tegucigalpa; tel. 222-3470; fax 222-2552; e-mail ihah2003@yahoo.com; internet www.ihah.hn; f. 1952; library of 12,000 vols; research and conservation of cultural property, archaeology, history, ethnography, linguistics, museology; Dir MARGARITA DURÓN DE GÁLVEZ; publ. Yaxkin (1 a year).

Libraries and Archives

Tegucigalpa

Archivo Nacional de Honduras: Avda Cristóbal Colón, Calle Salvador Mendieta 1117, Tegucigalpa; tel. 222-8338; fax 236-9532; internet www.secad.gob.hn/archi.htm; f. 1880; 700 linear m of documents; 2,700 vols and 100 periodicals; Dir CARLOS WILFREDO MALDONADO.

Biblioteca Nacional de Honduras: Apdo Postal 4563, Tegucigalpa; located at: Ave Cristobal Colón, Calle 'Salvador Mendieta', POB 1117, Tegucigalpa; tel. 228-0241; fax 222-8577; e-mail binah@sdnhon.org.hn; internet www.binah.gob.hn; f. 1880; 70,000 vols; co-ordinates national and international exchange; shares legal deposit with other centres; Dir HECTOR ROBERTO LUNA; publ. Anuario Bibliográfico.

Biblioteca 'Wilson Popenoe': Escuela Agrícola Panamericana, Apdo 93, Tegucigalpa; tel. 776-6140; fax 776-6113; e-mail hgallo@zamorano.edu; internet www.zamorano.edu/biblioteca; f. 1946; tropical agriculture; 19,000 vols, 950 periodicals, 1,200 DVDs; Librarian HUGO ALBERTO GALLO M.; publ. Ceiba (2 a year).

Sistema Bibliotecario Universidad Nacional Autónoma de Honduras: Edif. de Biblioteca, 3er piso, Carretera a Suyapa, Ciudad Universitaria, Tegucigalpa; tel. 232-2204; fax 232-2204; internet www.biblio.unah.hn; f. 1847; 200,000 vols; Librarian ORFYLIA PINEL; publ. Boletín del Sistema Bibliotecario (4 a year).

Museums and Art Galleries

Comayagua

Museo Arqueológico de Comayagua: Frente a Plaza San Francisco, Ciudad de Comayagua; tel. 772-03-86; f. 1946; archaeological collection from the Comayagua Valley; some contemporary items; Dir SALVADOR TURCIOS.

Copán

Museo Regional de Arqueología Maya: Ciudad de Copán; f. 1939; objects relate exclusively to Maya culture; Dir Prof. OSMIN RIVERA.

Cortés

Museo de la Fortaleza de San Fernando de Omoa: Omoa, Cortés; tel. 658-9167;

e-mail ihah2003@yahoo.com; internet www
.ihah.hn; attached to Honduran Institute of
Anthropology and History; f. 1959 in former
prison; colonial and historical items; Dir
GERARDO JOHNSON.

Universities

UNIVERSIDAD NACIONAL AUTÓNOMA DE HONDURAS

POB 3560, Tegucigalpa, DC

Telephone and fax 235-3361

Internet: www.unah.hn

Founded 1847
Autonomous control
Language of instruction: Spanish
Academic year: February to December

Rector: GUILLERMO PÉREZ-CADALSO ARIAS
Vice-Rector: OCTAVIO SÁNCHEZ MIDENCE
Admin.-Sec.: RAÚL FLORES
Gen.-Sec.: AFREDO HAWIT
Librarian: ORFYLIA PINEL

Library: see Libraries and Archives
Number of teachers: 3,486
Number of students: 56,077

Publications: *Catálogo de Estudios, Memoria
Anual, Presencia Universitaria, Revista de
la Universidad, and various faculty publs*

DEANS

Faculty of Chemistry and Pharmacy: GOD-
OFREDO CRUZ
Faculty of Dentistry: RAÚL SANTOS
Faculty of Economics, Business Administra-
tion and Accountancy: GABRIEL ORDOÑEZ
Faculty of Engineering: ADOLFO RACHEL
QUAN
Faculty of Law and Social Sciences: JESÚS
MARTINEZ

Faculty of Medicine and Nursing: GUSTAVO
VALLEJO

DIRECTORS

Atlantic Coast University Centre (La Ceiba):
Ing. JORGE SOTO MONICO
General Studies Centre: RAQUEL ANGULO
Regional Studies Centre: MARTÍN CASTRO
University Centre of the North (San Pedro
Sula): DARIO E. TURCOS

UNIVERSIDAD PEDAGÓGICA NACIONAL 'FRANCISCO MORAZÁN'

POB 3394, Calle El Dorado, Blvd Miraflores,
Tegucigalpa

Telephone: 239-8037

E-mail: webmaster@upnfm.edu.hn

Internet: www.upnfm.edu.hn

Founded 1957 as Escuela Superior del Pro-
fesorado, in cooperation with UNESCO,
present name and status since 1989
State control
Academic year: February to November (two
semesters)

Faculties of humanities, science and technology

Rector: RAMÓN ULISES SALGADO
Vice-Rector for Academic Affairs: LEA AZU-
CENA CRUZ
Vice-Rector for Admin.: DAVID ORLANDO
MARÍN
Vice-Rector for University Centre for Dis-
tance Learning: MARCIO BULNES
Sec.-Gen.: GUSTAVO ZELAYA
Librarian: ADÁN BRITO

Library of 35,000 vols
Number of teachers: 520
Number of students: 9,000

Publications: *Codice* (12 a year), *Revista
Paradigma* (4 a year).

UNIVERSIDAD TECNOLÓGICA DE HONDURAS

Carretera a Armenta, Frente a Rio Blanco,
San Pedro Sula

Telephone: 551-2236

Fax: 551-6108

E-mail: mirna.rivera@uth.hn

Internet: www.uth.hn

Founded 1986 as Instituto Superior Tecноló-
gico; current name and status since 1996
State control

Pres.: Lic. ROGER D. VALLADARES
Rector: RICARDO ANTILLÓN
Vice-Rector: Ing. FERNANDO FERRERA
Academic Dir: Lic. CELESTINO PADILLA
Number of students: 4,100

DIRECTORS

El Progreso Campus: Ing. ROBERTO CÁCERES
La Ceiba Campus: Lic. LUIS RIETTI
Puerto Cortés Campus: Dr MOHAM MERZKANI

College

**Escuela Agrícola Panamericana Zamor-
ano:** Apdo 93, Tegucigalpa; tel. 776-6140; fax
776-6240; e-mail gerencia_mercadeo@
zamorano.edu; internet www.zamorano.edu;
f. 1942; private, non-profit pan-American
instn of higher education; offers 4-year
undergraduate degree, with programmes in
Agricultural Science and Production, Agroin-
dustry, Agribusiness, and Socioeconomic
Development and Environment; 70 teachers;
800 students; library: 14,000 vols, 500 periodicals; Rector Dr KENNETH L. HOADLEY;
publ. *CEIBA* (3 a year).

HUNGARY

The Higher Education System

Higher education in Hungary dates back to the 14th century, with the establishment in 1367 of Pécsi Tudományegyetem (University of Pécs). Other long-established universities include Debreceni Egyetem (University of Debrecen; founded in 1912), Debreceni Református Hittudományi Egyetem (University of Reformed Theology of Debrecen; founded in 1538) and Evangélikus Hittudományi Egyetem (Evangelical–Lutheran Theological University; founded in 1557). In 1999–2000 the system of higher education underwent a major reorganization, as a result of which from 1 January 2000 there were 30 state-run universities and colleges, 26 church universities and colleges and six colleges run by foundations. In 2005 a new Act on Higher Education legislated the creation of a new system of university degrees (see below), and introduced financial and managerial reforms. In 2008/09 the figure for student enrolments in further and higher education was 381,033.

The Ministry of Education and Culture is responsible for establishing and recognizing institutions of higher education, which must gain accreditation from the Hungarian Accreditation Committee and Higher Education and Academic Council. The Act on Higher Education (2005) established an Economic Council to take responsibility for all decisions regarding the financing and management of the higher education sector. Universities and colleges are autonomous institutions and set their own curricula and courses.

Since 2004 admission to higher education has been based purely on results in the Erettsegi or Matura, the main secondary school qualifications. (Previously, admission had been based on a combination of the Erettsegi/Matura and competitive entrance examination.) In September 2006 a Bachelors-Masters-Doctorate degree system was introduced, based on the principles of the Bologna Process. The new courses are based on a 'credit semester' system, with students accruing a specified number of credits each semester in order to graduate. The main undergraduate degree is the Bachelors, which lasts six to eight semesters (three to four years) for which students must accumulate 180–240 credits. Following the Bachelors, the Masters is the first postgraduate degree, lasting two to four semesters (one to two years) during which students must accrue 60–120 credits (teacher training lasts five semesters or two-and-a-half years and requires 150 credits). In total, combined Bachelors and Masters studies must not last less than 10 nor more than 12 semesters. Finally, the Doctoral degree (PhD) is a six-semester programme (three years) requiring 180 credits.

Technical and vocational education has been integrated into the mainstream education system and the old system of apprenticeships has been phased out. Courses are offered by post-secondary vocational schools and last two years. Students are awarded the Technikusi Oklevel qualification and the title of Technikus (Technician).

Regulatory and Representative Bodies

GOVERNMENT

Ministry of Education and Culture: 1055 Budapest, Szalay u. 10-14; tel. (1) 302-0600; fax (1) 302-2002; e-mail info@okm.gov.hu; internet www.okm.gov.hu; Minister ISTVÁN HILLER.

ACCREDITATION

ENIC/NARIC Hungary: Educational Authority, Hungarian Equivalence and Information Centre, 1054 Budapest, Bathory u. 10; tel. (1) 374-2200; fax (1) 374-2492; e-mail ekvivalencia@oh.gov.hu; internet www.naric.hu; Head GABOR MESZAROS.

Magyar Felsőoktatási Akkreditációs Bizottság (Hungarian Accreditation Committee): 1013 Budapest, Krisztina krt. 39/B; tel. (1) 344-0314; fax (1) 344-0313; e-mail titkarsag@mab.hu; internet www.mab.hu; f. 1993; ind. body accrediting higher education instns and study programmes in disciplinary groups, in 5-year cycles; evaluates applications to set up new higher education instns and new study programs (framework requirements on national and program applications on institutional level); 19 mems; Pres. Prof. Dr GYÖRGY BAZSA; Sec.-Gen. TIBOR SZANTO.

NATIONAL BODIES

Felsőoktatási és Tudományos Tanács (Higher Education and Research Council): 1055 Budapest, Szalay u. 10-14, Room 105; tel. (1) 302-8603; fax (1) 269-5559; e-mail ftt@om.hu; internet www.ftt.hu; advisory body assisting the Min. of Education and Culture; reports on plans regarding the devt and modernization of instns and education systems; gives its opinion on preferred professions based on labour-market forecasts and employment statistics; 21 mems; Pres. Prof. Dr GYÖRGY BAZSA; Sec. Dr ANDRÁS VÁRKONYI.

Felsőoktatási Konferenciák Szövetsége (Confederation of Hungarian Conferences on Higher Education): 1146 Budapest, Ajtósi Dürer sor 19-21; tel. (1) 344-0310; fax (1)-251 3003; e-mail bilik@fksz.huninet.hu; Sec. Gen. Dr ISTVÁN BILIK.

Magyar Rektori Konferencia (Hungarian Rectors' Conference): 1064 Bp, Benczúr, u. 43, IV/3; tel. (70) 932-4203; fax (1) 322-9679; e-mail mrk@mail.mrk.hu; internet www.mrk.hu; f. 2006; represents higher education instns and works to protect their interests; mems are 72 heads of higher education instns; Pres. Dr GÁBOR SZABÓ; Co-Pres. Dr ÉVA SÁNDORNÉ KRISZT, Dr IMRE RUDAS.

Learned Societies

GENERAL

Magyar Tudományos Akadémia (Hungarian Academy of Sciences): 1051 Budapest, Roosevelt tér 9; tel. (1) 411-6100; e-mail priroda@office.mta.hu; internet www.mta.hu; f. 1825; sections of 1. Linguistic and Literary Sciences (Chair. MIKLÓS MARÓTH), 2. Philosophy and Historical Sciences (Chair. MIKLÓS SZABÓ), 3. Mathematical Sciences (Chair. DOMOKOS SZÁSZ), 4. Agricultural Sciences (Chair. PÉTER HORN), 5. Medical Sciences (Chair. LÁSZLÓ ROMICS), 6. Technical Sciences (Chair. JÓZSEF GYULAI), 7. Chemical Sciences (Chair. KÁLMÁN MEDZIHRADSZKY), 8. Biological Sciences (Chair. SÁNDOR DAMJANO-VICH), 9. Economics and Law (Chair. ÁDÁM TÖRÖK), 10. Earth Sciences (Chair. JÓZSEF ÁDÁM), 11. Physical Sciences (Chair. ZALÁN HORVÁTH); 707 mems (203 hon., 250 ordinary, 92 corresp., 162 external); attached research institutes: see Research Institutes; library: see Libraries and Archives; Pres. E. SYLVESTER VIZI; Gen. Sec. ATTILA MESKÓ; publs *Acta Agronomica, Acta Alimentaria, Acta Antiqua, Acta Archaeologica, Acta Biologica, Acta Botanica, Acta Chirurgica, Acta Ethnographica, Acta Geodaetica et Geophysica, Acta Historiae Artium, Acta Historica, Acta Juridica, Acta Linguistica, Acta Mathematica, Acta Medica, Acta Microbiologica et Immunologica, Acta Oeconomica, Acta Orientalia, Acta Physica, Acta Physiologica, Acta Phytopathologica, Acta Technica, Acta Veterinaria, Acta Zoologica, Analysis Mathematica, Studia Musicologica, Studia Scientiarium Mathematicarum Hungarica, Studia Slavica,* Bulletins of the Sections of the Academy, in five series.

Müszaki és Természettudományi Egyesületek Szövetsége (Federation of Technical and Scientific Societies): 1055 Budapest, Kossuth L. tér 6–8; tel. (1) 353-2808; fax (1) 353-0317; e-mail mtesz@mtesz.hu; internet www.mtesz.hu; f. 1948; 42 mem. socs; Pres. Dr GÁBOR SZÉLES; Sec.-Gen. ÁGOTA KÓSZ.

Széchenyi Irodalmi és Müvészeti Akadémia (Széchenyi Academy of Letters and Arts): 1051 Budapest, Roosevelt tér 9; tel. (1) 331-4117; fax (1) 331-4117; e-mail szima@office.mta.hu; internet www.mta.hu; f. 1825 as an independent section of Hungarian Acad. of Sciences, ind. 1992; sections of Fine Arts, of Letters, of Music, of Theatre and Film; 98 mems, 86 full mems, 12 hon. mems;

Pres. László Dobszay; Exec. Pres. Győző Ferencz; Exec. Sec. Magda Ferch.

AGRICULTURE, FISHERIES AND VETERINARY SCIENCE

Magyar Agrártudományi Egyesület (Hungarian Society of Agricultural Sciences): 1055 Budapest, Kossuth Lajos tér 6–8; tel. (1) 353-1950; fax (1) 353-0651; f. 1951; 8,500 mems; 17 affiliated socs; Sec.-Gen. Dr Károly Neszmélyi; Pres. Dr Károly Tamás; publ. *Magyar Mezőgazdaság* (Hungarian Agriculture, 12 a year).

Magyar Élelmezésipari Tudományos Egyesület (MÉTE) (Hungarian Scientific Society for Food Industry): 1027 Budapest, Fő u. 68; tel. (1) 214-6691; fax (1) 214-6692; e-mail mail.mete@mtesz.hu; internet www .mete.mtesz.hu; f. 1949; poultry breeding and processing, viticulture, sugar industry, confectionery, grain processing, meat industry, cold storage, canning, paprika, tobacco, oil, soap, cosmetics, brewery, bakery, distillery; 3,800 mems; Pres. Dr Peter Biacs; Exec. Dir Dr László Cserháti; publs *A Hús* (Meat, 4 a year), *Ásványvíz-Üdítőital-Gyümölcslé* (Mineral Water-Softdrink-Juice, 4 a year), *Cukoripar* (Sugar Industry, 4 a year), *Édesipar* (Confectionery Industry, 4 a year), *Élelmezési Ipar* (Food Industry, 12 a year), *Hűtőipar* (Frozen Food Industry, 4 a year), *Konzervújság* (Canning News, 4 a year), *Molnárok Lapja* (Millers' Journal, 6 a year), *Olaj, Szappan, Kozmetika* (Oil, Soap, Cosmetics, 6 a year), *Sütőipar* (Baking Industry, 4 a year), *Szeszipar* (Distilling Industry, 4 a year), *Tejgazdaság* (Dairy Industry, 2 a year).

Országos Erdészeti Egyesület (Hungarian Forestry Association): 1027 Budapest, Fő u. 68; tel. (1) 201-6293; fax (1) 201-7737; e-mail oee@mtesz.hu; internet quercus.emk .nyme.hu/oee; f. 1866; forestry, forest industries, environment protection; 5,000 mems; library of 20,000 vols; Pres. József Káldy; Sec.-Gen. Gábor Barátossy; publ. *Erdészeti Lapok* (Forestry Bulletin).

ARCHITECTURE AND TOWN PLANNING

Építéstudományi Egyesület (Scientific Society for Building): 1027 Budapest, Fő u. 68; tel. and fax (1) 201-8416; e-mail info@ eptud.org; internet www.eptud.org; f. 1949; 3,500 mems; Pres. Dr Celesztin Meszléry; Sec.-Gen. Pál Seenger; publs *Magyar Építőipar* (Hungarian Building Industry), *Magyar Épületgépészet* (Hungarian Sanitary and Installation Engineering).

BIBLIOGRAPHY, LIBRARY SCIENCE AND MUSEOLOGY

Magyar Könyvtárosok Egyesülete (Association of Hungarian Librarians): 1827 Budapest, Budavári Palota F.ép. 439 sz; tel. and fax (1) 311-8634; e-mail mke@oszk.hu; internet www.mke.oszk.hu; f. 1935; decision-making, library education and training; promotes librarianship and information sharing between libraries and librarians; 2,200 mems (incl. institutional mems); Pres. Klára Bakos; Sec.-Gen. Anikó Nagy; Vice-Pres. Prof. Ágnes Hajdu Barát; Vice-Pres. Dr Éva Bartos; Vice-Pres. Gábor Kiss.

Magyar Levéltárosok Egyesülete (Association of Hungarian Archivists): 1014 Budapest, Hess András tér 5; tel. and fax (20) 234-4822; e-mail mle.titkarsag@gmail.com; internet www.leveltaros.hu; f. 1986; 850 mems; Pres. Árpád Tyekvicska; Sec. Anita Kiss.

EDUCATION

Magyar Művelődési Intézet (Hungarian Institute of Culture): 1011 Budapest, Corvin tér 8; tel. (1) 201-5053; fax (1) 201-5764; e-mail mmi@mmi.hu; internet www.mmi.hu; f. 1951; analyses the social impact of cultural values, the changes in the content and organization of community education and the activities of cultural communities; organizes training for professionals in community education; centre for life-long education, folk art, minority cultures, amateur artistic and leisure pursuits, community devt, arts and crafts; 80 mems; library of 60,000 vols; special colln on past and present Hungarian folk high schools; Dir András Földiák; publ. *SZIN* (6 a year).

FINE AND PERFORMING ARTS

Ferenc Liszt Academy of Music: 1391 Budapest, POB 206; 1061 Budapest, Liszt Ferenc tér 8; tel. (1) 462-4600; fax (1) 462-4648; internet www.lisztacademy.hu; f. 1875 to promote the work of the composer Franz Liszt (1811–1886), and to further the interest of audiences in live music; concerts, competitions, annual Liszt Record Grand Prix; establishment of Liszt memorials; 2 attached institutes: Béla Bartók Conservatory of Music and Secondary School, Zoltán Kodály Pedagogical Institute of Music; academic year September to June; 400 mems; library of 500,000 vols; 230 teachers (146 full-time, 84 part-time); 755 students (full-time); Rector Dr András Batta; Vice-Rector János Devich; Librarian Ágnes Gádor.

Magyar Zenei Tanács (Hungarian Music Council): BMC Hungarian Music Information Centre, Lónyay u. 54, 1093 Budapest; tel. (1) 476-1097; fax (1) 210-6908; internet www.bmc.hu; f. 1996, replaced Magyar Zeneművészek Szövetsége; library of 7,400 vols, 13,600 scores, 1,700 CDs, 5,600 records, 800 tapes with 1,400 Hungarian compositions; Dir Adrienne Mankovits; Exec. Sec. Ágnes Páldy; Head of the Music Information Centre Eszter Vida; publs *Magyar Zene* (Hungarian Music, 4 a year), *Polifónia* (irregular).

Magyar Zeneművészeti Társaság (Hungarian Music Society): 1111 Budapest, Bertalan u. 15; tel. (30) 351-8383; e-mail emzete@gmail.com; internet www.mzt008 .hu; f. 1987; 60 mems; fosters cultivation of Hungarian music, promotes interests of musical artists, educates young people's musical taste, preserves Hungarian music past and present and performs only Hungarian contemporary pieces in the concerts of the Mini-Festival, held on the last weekend of every January; Pres. Klára Körmendi; Sec. Eszter Aggházy.

Országos Színháztörténeti Múzeum és Intézet (Hungarian Theatre Museum and Institute): 1013 Budapest, Krisztina-krt. 57; tel. (1) 375-1184; fax (1) 375-1184; e-mail oszmi@szinhaziintezet.hu; internet szinhaziintezet.hu; f. 1952; to research into theatre history and theory, information on Hungarian drama and theatre for abroad and on world drama and theatre for Hungarian professionals; controls the theatrical memorial places, and the Bajor Gizi Actors' Museum; 45 mems; Dir. Dr Piroska Ács; publs *Évkönyv* (Yearbook), *Színháztudományi szemle* (Theatre Studies, 1 a year), *Világszínház* (World Theatre, 6 a year).

HISTORY, GEOGRAPHY AND ARCHAEOLOGY

Magyar Földmérési, Térképészeti és Távérzékelési Társaság (Hungarian Society for Surveying, Mapping and Remote Sensing): 1371 Budapest, POB 433; 1149 Budapest, Bosnyák tér 5; tel. (1) 201-8642;

fax (1) 460-4163; e-mail mfttt@freemail.hu; internet www.mfttt.hu; f. 1956; 1,000 mems; Pres. Dr Szabolcs Mihály; Sec.-Gen. Zoltán Uzsoki; publ. *Geodézia és Kartográfia* (Geodesy and Cartography).

Magyar Irodalomtörténeti Társaság (Society of Hungarian Literary History): 1052 Budapest, Piarista köz 1; tel. (1) 337-7819; f. 1912; Pres. Sándor Iván Kovács; Gen. Sec. Mihály Praznovszky; publ. *Irodalomtörténet* (Literary History, 4 a year).

Magyar Történelmi Társulat (Hungarian Historical Society): 1014 Budapest, Uri u. 53; tel. (1) 375-9011; f. 1867; Pres. Domokos Kosáry; Gen. Sec. Ignác Romsics; publ. *Századok* (6 a year).

LANGUAGE AND LITERATURE

Alliance Française: 6722 Szeged, Petőfi Sandor SGT. 36, POB 1240; tel. and fax (62) 420-427; e-mail szeged@af.org.hu; internet www.af.org.hu; offers courses and examinations in French language and culture and promotes cultural exchange with France; attached offices in Debrecen, Gyor, Miskolc and Pécs; Dir Sümegi István.

British Council: 1068 Budapest, Benczúr u. 26; tel. (1) 478-4700; fax (1) 342-5728; e-mail information@britishcouncil.hu; internet www.britishcouncil.hu; teaching centre; offers courses and examinations in English language and British culture and promotes cultural exchange with the UK; Dir Jim McGrath; Teaching Centre and Examinations Man. John Pare.

Goethe-Institut: 1092 Budapest, Ráday utca 58, Ungarn; tel. (1) 374-4070; fax (1) 374-4080; e-mail info@budapest.goethe.org; internet www.goethe.de/budapest; offers courses and examinations in German language and culture and promotes cultural exchange with Germany; library of 13,000 vols; Dir Dr Brigitte Kaiser-Derenthal.

Hungarian PEN Centre: 1053 Budapest, Károlyi Mihály u. 16; tel. (1) 411-0270; fax (1) 411-0270; e-mail hungary@penclub.t-online .hu; f. 1926; 325 mems; Pres. Gábor Görgey.

Instituto Cervantes: 1064 Budapest, Vörösmarty u. 32; tel. (1) 354-3670; fax (1) 302-2954; e-mail cenbud@cervantes.es; internet budapest.cervantes.es; offers courses and exams in Spanish language and culture and promotes cultural exchange with Spain and Spanish-speaking Latin and Central America; Dir Josep Maria de Sagarra Ángel.

Magyar Írószövetség (Union of Hungarian Writers): 1062 Budapest, Bajza u. 18; tel. (1) 322-8840; fax (1) 321-3419; f. 1945; 1,100 mems; Pres. Márton Kalász.

Magyar Nyelvtudományi Társaság (Hungarian Linguistic Society): 1052 Budapest, Piarista köz 1; tel. (1) 137-6819; f. 1904; 660 mems; Pres. Loránd Benkő; Gen.-Sec. Jenő Kiss; Sec. András Zoltán; publ. *Magyar Nyelv* (The Hungarian Language, 4 a year).

Magyar Ujságírók Országos Szövetsége (National Federation of Hungarian Journalists): 1062 Budapest, Andrássy u. 101; tel. (1) 478-9071; fax (1) 343-4599; e-mail szakoszt@ muosz.hu; internet www.muosz.hu; 5,000 mems; Pres. András Kereszty; Gen. Sec. Gábor Bencsik.

MEDICINE

Magyar Gyógyszerészeti Társaság (Hungarian Pharmaceutical Society): 1085 Budapest, Gyulai Pál u. 16; tel. (1) 266-9395; fax (1) 483-1465; e-mail titkarsag@mgyt.hu; internet www.mgyt.hu; f. 1924; 1,200 mems; Pres. Dr I. Erős; Gen. Sec. L. Botz; publs *Acta Pharmaceutica Hungarica*, *Gyógyszerészet*.

Magyar Orvostársaságok és Egyesületek Szövetsége (MOTESZ) (Association of Hungarian Medical Societies): POB 145, 1443 Budapest; 1051 Budapest, Nádor u. 36; tel. (1) 311-6687; fax (1) 383-7918; e-mail szalma@motesz.hu; internet www.motesz .hu; f. 1966; encourages devt of Hungarian health care; promotes interests of mem. socs; 30,000 mems, 130 mem. socs; Pres. Prof. Dr TIBOR ERTL; Dir-Gen. Dr BÉLA SZALMA; publ. *MOTESZ Magazine* (18 a year).

NATURAL SCIENCES

General

Tudományos Ismeretterjesztő Társulat (Society for the Dissemination of Scientific Knowledge): 1088 Budapest, Bródy Sándor u. 16; tel. (1) 338-2496; fax (1) 338-3320; e-mail eszter@fok.hu; f. 1841; library of 20,000 vols; 17,000 mems; Gen. Dir ESZTER PIRÓTH (acting); publs *Élet és Tudomány* (Life and Science, 52 a year), *Természet Világa* (World of Nature, 12 a year), *Valóság* (Reality, 12 a year).

Biological Sciences

Magyar Biofizikai Társaság (Hungarian Biophysical Society): 1371 Budapest, POB 433;; tel. and fax (1) 202-1216; e-mail mmt@ mtesz.hu; internet www.mbft.hu; f. 1961; medical physics, ultrasound, radiation biophysics, photo-biophysics; 450 mems; Pres. Dr LAJOS KESZTHELYI; Sec.-Gen. Dr SÁNDOR GYÖRGYI; publ. *Magyar Biofizikai Társaság Értesítője* (every 3 years).

Magyar Biokémiai Egyesület (Hungarian Biochemical Society): 1518 Budapest, POB 7; 1113 Budapest, Karolina u. 29; tel. (1) 466-5856; fax (1) 466-5856; e-mail biro@enzim .hu; f. 1949; 1,015 mems; Pres. Dr PETER FRIEDRICH; Sec.-Gen. Dr PETER CSERMELY; publ. *Biokémia*.

Magyar Biológiai Társaság (Hungarian Biological Society): 1027 Budapest, Fő u. 68; tel. (1) 224-1423; fax (1) 201-7456; e-mail mbt@mtesz.hu; internet www.mbt.mtesz.hu; f. 1952; 1,500 mems; Pres. Dr TAMÁS PÓCS; Sec.-Gen. Dr ERNŐ BÁCSY; publs *Allattani Közlemények* (1 a year), *Antropológiai Közlemények* (1 a year), *Botanikai Közlemények* (1 a year), *Természetvédelmi Közlemények* (1 a year).

Magyar Biomassza Társaság (Hungarian Biomass Association): 9400 Sopron, Ady Endre u. 5; tel. (99) 518-188; fax (99) 357-480; e-mail mbmt@asys.hu; internet www .mbmt.hu; f. 1991; Pres. Prof. Dr JENŐ KOVÁCS; Gen. Sec. Prof. Dr BÉLA MAROSVÖLGYI.

Magyar Rovartani Társaság (Hungarian Entomological Society): 1088 Budapest, Baross u. 13; tel. (1) 267-7100; fax (1) 267-3462; internet www.magyarrovartanitarsasag.hu; f. 1910; 400 mems; Pres. Dr K. VIG; Sec. G. PUSKÁS; publ. *Folia Entomologica Hungarica/Rovartani Közlemények* (1 a year).

Mathematical Sciences

Bolyai János Matematikai Társulat (János Bolyai Mathematical Society): 1027 Budapest, Fő u. 68; tel. (1) 225-8410; fax (1) 201-6974; e-mail bjmt@renyi.hu; internet www.bolyai.hu; f. 1891; 2,000 mems; Pres. GYULA KATONA; Gen. Sec. ANDR'AS RECSKI; publs *Abacus* (9 a year), *Alkalmazott Matematikai Lapok* (Gazette for Applied Mathematics, 2 a year), *Combinatorica* (combinatorics and the theory of computing, 6 a year), *Középiskolai Matematikai Lapok* (Mathematical Gazette for Secondary Schools, 9 a year), *Matematikai Lapok* (Mathematical Gazette, 2 a year), *Periodica Mathematica Hungarica* (2 a year).

Physical Sciences

Eötvös Loránd Fizikai Társulat (Roland Eötvös Physical Society): 1027 Budapest, Fő u. 68; tel. (1) 201-8682; fax (1) 201-8682; e-mail mail.elft@mtesz.hu; internet www .kfki.hu/~elfthp; f. 1891; physics and astronomy; 1,800 mems; Pres. JUDIT NÉMETH; Gen. Sec. GÁBOR SZABÓ; publ. *Fizikai Szemle* (Physics Review, 12 a year).

Hungarian Association for Geo-Information (HUNAGI): 1122 Budapest, Pethényi ú. 11B; tel. (30) 415 8276; fax (1) 356-8003; e-mail hunagi@hunagi.hu; internet www.hunagi.hu; f. 1994; non-profit, interdisciplinary umbrella asscn promoting and supporting the devt and use of geo-information and its associated technologies; 88 governmental and non-governmental mem. orgs; Pres. and Chair. ZSOLT BARKÓCZI; Sec.-Gen. Dr GÁBOR REMETEY-FÜLÖPP; publs *Geodézia és Kartográfia, Geomatika*.

Magyar Asztronautikai Társaság (Hungarian Astronautical Society): 1044 Budapest, Ipari park u. 10; tel. (1) 201-8443; e-mail mant@mant.hu; internet www.mant .hu; f. 1956; raises public awareness about space exploration and uses; organizes lectures, conferences, youth forums, summer space camps, issues periodicals, releases media material; 300 mems; Pres. JÁNOS SOLYMOSI; Gen. Sec. LÁSZLÓ BACSÁRDI; publ. *Urtan Evkonyv* (in Hungarian).

Magyar Geofizikusok Egyesülete (Association of Hungarian Geophysicists): 1027 Budapest, Fő u. 68 I/113; tel. and fax (1) 201-9815; e-mail geophysic@mtesz.hu; internet www.elgi.hu/mge; f. 1954; 650 mems; Pres. Dr FERENC ABELE; Sec. ANDRÁS PÁLYI; publ. *Magyar Geofizika* (Hungarian Geophysics, 4 a year).

Magyar Hidrológiai Társaság (Hungarian Hydrological Society): POB 433, 1371 Budapest; tel. (1) 201-7655; fax (1) 202-7244; e-mail mail.mht@mtesz.hu; internet www .mtesz.hu/tagegyesuletek/mht; f. 1917; 5,000 mems; Pres. Dr ÖDÖN STAROSOLSZKY; Sec.-Gen. ZOLTÁN SZÖLLŐSI; publs *Hidrológiai Közlöny* (Hydrological Journal, every 2 months), *Hidrológiai Tájékoztató* (Circular on Hydrology, 1 a year).

Magyar Karszt-és Barlangkutató Társulat (Hungarian Speleological Society): 1025 Budapest, Pusztaszeri u. 35; tel. (1) 346-0494; fax (1) 346-0495; internet www.barlang .hu; f. 1910; 1,000 mems; library of 5,000 vols; Pres. Dr LÁSZLÓ KORPÁS; Sec.-Gen. PÉTER BÖRCSÖK; publ. *Karszt és Barlang* (with summaries in English, 1 a year).

Magyar Kémikusok Egyesülete (Hungarian Chemical Society): 1027 Budapest, Fő u. 68; tel. (1) 201-6883; fax (1) 201-8056; e-mail androsits@mke.org.hu; internet www.mke .org.hu; f. 1907; 6,000 mems; Pres. Dr PÉTER MÁTYUS; Sec.-Gen. Dr ATTILA KOVÁCS; publs *Középiskolai Kémiai Lapok* (Secondary School Chemical Papers, 5 a year), *Magyar Kémiai Folyóirat* (Hungarian Journal of Chemistry, 12 a year), *Magyar Kémikusok Lapja* (Hungarian Chemical Journal, 12 a year).

Magyar Meteorológiai Társaság (Hungarian Meteorological Society): 1371 Budapest, Fő u. 68, POB 433; tel. (1) 201-7525; fax (1) 202-1216; e-mail mmt@mtesz.hu; f. 1925; 360 mems; Pres. Dr PÁL AMBRÓZY; Gen. Sec. Dr GYÖRGY GYURÓ.

Magyarhoni Földtani Társulat (Hungarian Geological Society): 1051 Budapest, Csalogány u. 12. I/1; tel. and fax (1) 201-9129; e-mail mft@mft.t-online.hu; internet www .foldtan.hu; f. 1848; formation and training of geoscientists; organizes meetings, workshops, confs, study tours, itinerary meetings

and congresses; 900 mems; Pres. Dr JÁNOS HAAS; Sec.-Gen. Dr ZOLTÁN UNGER; publ. *Földtani Közlöny* (Bulletin, 4 a year).

Optikai, Akusztikai Film-és Színháztechnikai Tudományos Egyesület (Scientific Society for Optics, Acoustics, Motion Pictures and Theatre Technology): 1027 Budapest, Bartók Béla út 15/A; tel. and fax (1) 783-4781; e-mail info@opakfi.hu; internet www.opakfi.hu; f. 1933; optics, acoustics, noise reduction, fine mechanics, theatre and motion pictures technology, scientific programs, education, research and devt managing; keeping int, connections; organizing nat. and int. scientific congresses; seminars cooperation with Hungarian Acad. of Science, different Hungarian Univs, industrial R+D instns; 1,500 mems; Pres. Dr G. LUPKOVICS; Gen. Sec. Dr F. KVOJKA; publs *Akusztikai Szemle* (Acoustics Journal, 4 a year), *Elektrónikai Technológia-Mikrotechnika* (Electronic Technology-Microtechnics), *Kép és Hangtechnika* (Picture and Audio Techniques).

PHILOSOPHY AND PSYCHOLOGY

Magyar Filozófiai Társaság (Hungarian Philosophical Association): 1364 Budapest, Pf. 107; tel. and fax (1) 266-4195; f. 1987; 400 mems; Pres. KRISTÓF NYÍRI; Gen. Sec. ISTVÁN M. BODNÁR.

Magyar Pszichológiai Társaság (Hungarian Psychological Association): 1132 Budapest, Victor Hugo 18–22; tel. (1) 350-0555; fax (1) 350-0555; f. 1928; 1,293 mems; Pres. MAGDA RITOÓK; Scientific Sec. KATALIN VARGA; publ. *Magyar Pszichológiai Szemle* (Hungarian Psychological Review).

RELIGION, SOCIOLOGY AND ANTHROPOLOGY

Magyar Néprajzi Társaság (Hungarian Ethnographical Society): 1055 Budapest, Kossuth Lajos tér 12; tel. and fax (1) 269-1272; e-mail mnt@neprajz.hu; f. 1889; 1,340 mems; Pres. LÁSZLÓ KÓSA; Sec.-Gen. IMRE GRÁFIK; publ. *Ethnographia* (4 a year).

Magyar Szociológiai Társaság (Hungarian Sociological Association): 1014 Budapest, Országház u. 30; tel. (1) 224-0786; fax (1) 224-0790; e-mail mszt@socio.mta.hu; internet www.szociologia.hu; f. 1978; confs, debates, discussions for domestic and int. researchers in order to facilitate and maintain int. sociological partnerships; follows nat. and int. sociological research and its results; cooperates with the instns of science and education to discuss the training of sociologists; 628 mems; Pres. GYÖRGY CSEPELI; Sec. Gen. VERONIKA PAKSI; publs *Review of Sociology* (2 a year), *Szociológiai Szemle* (3 a year).

TECHNOLOGY

Bőr-, Cipő-, és Bőrfeldolgozóipari Tudományos Egyesület (Scientific Society of the Leather, Shoe and Allied Industries): 1325 Budapest, POB 155; 1047 Budapest, Attila u. 64; tel. (1) 272-0011; fax (1) 369-1058; e-mail bimeo@bimeo.hu; internet www.bimeo.hu/ bor-cipo/bcbte.htm; f. 1930; Pres. Dr TAMÁS KARNITSCHER; publ. *Bőr és Cipőtechnika* (Leather and Shoe News, 6 a year).

Energiagazdálkodási Tudományos Egyesület (Scientific Society of Energy Economics): 1372 Budapest, POB 451; 1055 Budapest, Kossuth Lajos tér 6–8; tel. (1) 153-2751; fax (1) 153-3894; e-mail mail.ete@ mtesz.hu; internet www.ete.mtesz.hu; f. 1949; 3,000 mems; Pres. Dr TAMÁS ZETTNER; Vice-Pres. GYŐZŐ WIEGAND; publ. *Energiagazdálkodás (Energetrics)* (12 a year).

Faipari Tudományos Egyesület (Scientific Society of the Timber Industry): 1027 Budapest, Fő u. 68; tel. (1) 201-9929; e-mail fate.bp@freemail.hu; f. 1950; 1,800 mems; Pres. Dr SÁNDOR MOLNÁR; Sec.-Gen. DEZSŐ LELE; publ. *Faipar* (Timber Industry).

Gépipari Tudományos Egyesület (GTE) (Scientific Society of Mechanical Engineers): 1371 Budapest, Fő u. 68, POB 433; tel. (1) 202-0582; fax (1) 202-0252; e-mail mail.gte@ mtesz.hu; internet www.mtesz.hu/gtagegy/ gte; f. 1949; sciences of mechanical engineering, dissemination of technical culture, assisting the technical and economic development of Hungary; 4,800 mems; library of 1,500 vols; Pres. Prof. Dr JÁNOS TAKÁCS; Sec.-Gen. Dr TAMÁS BÁNKY; publs *Gép* (Machine, 12 a year), *Gépgyártás* (Production Engineering, 12 a year), *Gépipar* (Machinery, 12 a year), *Járművek* (Vehicles, 12 a year), *Műanyag és Gumi* (Plastics and Rubber, 12 a year).

Hírközlési és Informatikai Tudományos Egyesület (Scientific Association for Infocommunication): 1055 Budapest, Pf. 451, Kossuth Lajos tér 6–8; tel. (1) 353-1027; fax (1) 353-0451; e-mail info@hte.hu; internet www.hte.hu; f. 1949; organization of conferences, discussions, seminars, technical exhibitions, postgraduate courses, study trips, expert advice for official organs and enterprises, recommendations for official organs, public discussion and criticism of technical, economic, scientific and educational matters, engineering activities; 2,500 mems; Pres. Prof. Dr GYULA SALLAI; Sec.-Gen. PÁL HORVÁTH; publs *Híradástechnika*, *Hírlevél*.

Közlekedéstudományi Egyesület (Scientific Association for Transport): 1055 Budapest, Kossuth Lajos tér 6–8; tel. (1) 153-2005; fax (1) 153-2005; e-mail info.kte@mtesz.hu; internet www.mtesz.hu/kte; f. 1949; 6,723 mems; Pres. Dr SÁNDOR GYURKOVICS; Sec.-Gen. Dr ANDRÁS KATONA; publs *Közlekedéstudományi Szemle* (Communications Review), *Közúti és Mélyépítési Szemle* (Civil Engineering Review), *Városi Közlekedés* (Urban Transport).

Magyar Elektrotechnikai Egyesület (Hungarian Electrotechnical Association): 1055 Budapest, Kossuth Lajos tér 6–8; tel. (1) 353-0117; fax (1) 353-4069; e-mail mee@ mee.hu; internet www.mee.hu; f. 1900; 6,500 mems; Pres. Dr ISTVÁN KRÓMER; Dir PÉTER LERNYEI; publ. *Electrotechnika* (Electrical Engineering, 12 a year).

Magyar Iparjogvédelmi és Szerzői Jogi Egyesület (Hungarian Association for the Protection of Industrial Property and Copyright): 1055 Budapest, Kossuth Lajos tér 6–8; tel. (1) 153-1661; fax (1) 153-1780; e-mail mie@axelero.hu; internet www.mie.org.hu; f. 1962; 2,250 mems; Pres. Dr BACHER VILMOS; Sec.-Gen. Dr GÖDÖLLE ISTVÁN.

Méréstechnikai és Automatizálási Tudományos Egyesület (Scientific Society for Measurement, Automation and Informatics): 1055 Budapest V, Kossuth tér 6–8; tel. (1) 332-9571; fax (1) 353-1406; e-mail mate@ mtesz.hu; internet www.mate.mtesz.hu; f. 1952; 1,075 mems; Pres. ISTVÁN KOCSIS; Man. Gen. Sec. Dr ZSUZSANNA PINTÉR; publ. *Mérés és Automatika* (Measurement and Automation).

Neumann János Számítógéptudományi Társaság (John von Neumann Computer Society): 1054 Budapest, Báthori u. 16; tel. (1) 472-2730; fax (1) 472-2728; e-mail titkarsag@njszt.hu; internet www.njszt.hu; f. 1968 to promote the study, development and application of computer sciences; 2,400 mems; library of 3,000 vols; Pres. Prof. GÁBOR PÉCELI; Man. Dir ISTVÁN ALFÖLDI.

Országos Magyar Bányászati és Kohászati Egyesület (Hungarian Mining and Metallurgical Society): 1027 Budapest, Fő u. 68; tel. (1) 201-7337; fax (1) 201-7337; e-mail ombke@mtesz.hu; internet www.ombkenet .hu; f. 1892; 4,000 mems; library of 1,500 vols; Pres. Dr LAJOS TOLNAY; Gen. Sec. ÁRPÁD KOVACSICS; publs *Bányászat* (Mining, 6 a year), *Kohászat* (Metallurgy, 6 a year), *Kőolaj és Földgáz* (Oil and Gas, 12 a year).

Papír- és Nyomdaipari Műszaki Egyesület (Technical Association of the Paper and Printing Industry): 1371 Budapest, Pf. 433; 1027 Budapest, Fő u. 68; tel. (1) 457-0633; fax (1) 202-0256; e-mail mail.pnyme@mtesz.hu; internet www.pnyme.hu; f. 1948; 1,800 individual mems, 130 corporate mems; Pres. Dr ZOLTAN SZIKLA; Sec.-Gen. ENDRE FÁBIAN; publs *Magyar Grafika* (Hungarian Printers and Graphic Designers), *Papíripar* (Paper Industry).

Szervezési és Vezetési Tudományos Társaság (Society for Organization and Management Science): 1027 Budapest, Fő u. 68; tel. (1) 202-1083; fax (1) 202-0856; e-mail szvt@szvt.hu; internet www.szvt.hu; f. 1970; 5,000 mems; Pres. Dr FERENC TRETHON; Sec.-Gen. Dr JÁNOS PAKUCS; publ. *Ipar-Gazdaság* (Industrial Economy, 12 a year).

Szilikátipari Tudományos Egyesület (Scientific Society of the Silicate Industry): 1027 Budapest, Fő u. 68; tel. (1) 201-9360; e-mail mail.szte@mtesz.hu; internet www .szte.org.hu; f. 1949; 2,300 mems; library of 2,500 vols; Pres. JENŐ VIG; Sec.-Gen. Dr MÁRTA FODOR; publ. *Építőanyag* (Building Materials).

Textilipari Műszaki és Tudományos Egyesület (Hungarian Society of Textile Technology and Science): 1027 Budapest, Fő u. 68; tel. (1) 201-8782; fax (1) 224-1454; e-mail info@tmte.hu; internet www .tmte.hu; f. 1948; 1,300 mems; Pres. Dr FERENC CSÁSZI; Gen. Sec. Dr KATALIN MÁTHÉ; publs *Magyar Textiltechnika* (Hungarian Textile Engineering), *Textiltisztítás* (Textile Cleaning).

Research Institutes

AGRICULTURE, FISHERIES AND VETERINARY SCIENCE

Állattenyésztési és Takarmányozási Kutatóintézet (Research Institute for Animal Breeding and Nutrition): 2053 Herceghalom, Gesztenyés u. 1; tel. (23) 319-133; fax (23) 319-120; e-mail atk@atk.hu; internet www.atk.hu; research into large animal breeding, nutrition, reproductive biology, genetics, nutrition biology and microbiology; library of 4,800 vols; Gen. Dir Dr JÓZSEF RÁTKY; publ. *Állattenyésztés és Takarmányozás* (Animal Production, 6 a year, with English summaries).

Gabonakutató Nonprofit Közhasznú Kft. (Cereal Research Non-Profit Ltd.): 6701 Szeged, POB 391; tel. (62) 435-235; fax (62) 434-163; e-mail info@gabonakutato.hu; internet www.gabonakutato.hu; f. 1924; research into the cultivation of wheat, barley, oats, maize, triticale, sunflower, linseed, winter rapeseed, red clover, soybean, sorghum, Sudan grass, millet; breeding, agronomy, seed trading, dietetic food; library of 12,000 vols; Dir Dr J. MATUZ; publ. *Cereal Research Communications* (4 a year).

Magyar Tejgazdasági Kisérleti Intézet (Hungarian Dairy Research Institute): 9200 Mosonmagyaróvár, Lucsony u. 24; tel. (96) 215-711; fax (96) 215-789; e-mail mtki@mtki .hu; internet www.mtki.hu; f. 1903; brs in Budapest and Pécs; scientific research of raw materials, technology, engineering, chemistry, microbiology, economics; library of 5,700 vols; Dir Dr ANDRÁS UNGER.

Magyar Tudományos Akadémia Állatorvos-tudományi Kutatóintézete (Veterinary Medical Research Institute, Hungarian Academy of Sciences): 1143 Budapest, Hungária krt. 21; tel. (1) 252-2455; fax (1) 252-1069; e-mail harrach@vmri.hu; internet www.vmri.hu; f. 1949; research in infectious and parasitic diseases of domestic and wild animals (virology, bacteriology, fish parasitology); library of 6,750 vols; Dir Dr TIBOR MAGYAR (acting); Vice-Dir Dr. ISTVAN TOTH; publ. *Acta Veterinaria Hungarica* (4 a year).

Magyar Tudományos Akadémia Mezőgazdasági Kutatóintézete (Agricultural Research Institute of the Hungarian Academy of Sciences): 2462 Martonvásár; tel. (22) 569-500; fax (22) 460-213; internet www .mgki.hu; f. 1949; research in plant genetics, plant physiology, plant breeding and plant cultivation of maize and wheat; library of 16,000 vols; Dir ZOLTÁN BEDŐ; publ. *Martonvásár* (2 a year).

Magyar Tudományos Akadémia Növényvédelmi Kutatóintézete (Plant Protection Institute, Hungarian Academy of Sciences): 1525 Budapest II, Herman Ottó u. 15, Box 102; tel. (1) 487-7500; fax (1) 487-7555; e-mail bbar@nki.hu; internet www.nki .hu; f. 1880, reorganized 1950; research on plant diseases, insect pests, pesticide chemistry and plant biochemistry, biotechnology, virology; 100 mems; library of 20,000 vols; Dir Dr BALÁZS BARNA.

Magyar Tudományos Akadémia Talajtani és Agrokémiai Kutató Intézete (Research Institute for Soil Science and Agricultural Chemistry of the Hungarian Academy of Sciences): 1022 Budapest, Herman Ottó u. 15; tel. and fax (1) 356-4682; e-mail rissac@rissac.hu; internet www.taki .iif.hu; f. 1949; research in soil physics, chemistry, geography and cartography, reclamation of salt-affected and sandy soils, irrigation, conservation, fertilization, soil mineralogy, soil microbiology, soil ecology, recultivation; library of 27,000 vols; Dir Prof. Dr T. NÉMETH; publ. *Agrokémia és Talajtan* (Agrochemistry and Soil Science, 2 a year).

Országos Állategészségügyi Intézet (Central Veterinary Institute): 1149 Budapest, Tábornok u. 2; tel. (1) 252-8444; fax (1) 252-5177; e-mail web@oai.hu; internet sgicenter.oai.hu/oai; f. 1928; diagnostic examinations and research work on the infectious, parasitic and metabolic diseases of animals, also veterinary toxicology and diseases of wild animals; 95 mems; library of 5,966 vols; Dir L. TEKES.

Országos Mezőgazdasági Minősítő Intézet (National Institute for Agricultural Quality Control): 1024 Budapest, Keleti Károly u. 24; tel. (1) 336-9114; fax (1) 336-9011; e-mail novenytermesztesi.ig@ommi.hu; internet www.ommi.hu; f. 1988 by amalgamation of four orgs; 606 mems; library of 20,000 vols; Dir Dr KATALIN ERTSEY; publ. National List of Varieties, Descriptive List of Varieties, List of approved grape and fruit varieties, selections and foreign varieties permitted for propagation (1 a year), *Yearbook* of cattle, pig, sheep, horse, water fowl, fish breeding and beekeeping.

Szőlészeti és Borászati Kutató Intézet (Research Institute for Viticulture and Oenology): 6000 Kecskemét-Miklóstelep, Úrihegy 5/A, POB 25; tel. (76) 494-888; fax (76) 494-924; e-mail titkarsag@szbkik.hu; f. 1898; viticulture, oenology, economy; library of 7,200 vols; Dir Dr ERNŐ PÉTER BOTOS; publ. *Bor és Piac* (12 a year).

VITUKI Környezetvédelmi és Vízgazdálkodási Kutató Intézet nonprofit Kft (VITUKI Environmental and Water Management Research Institute nonprofit Ltd.): 1095 Budapest, Kvassay Jenő u. 1; tel. (1) 215-6140; fax (1) 216-1514; e-mail vituki@vituki.hu; internet www.vituki.hu; f. 1952; basic and applied research associated with hydrological data colln, processing, storage, information; hydrology of groundwater, karst water, regional soil moisture control; hydromechanics of hydraulic structures; pollution and quality control of water; hydrological and hydraulic problems in agricultural water management (drainage, irrigation); air pollution control; odour and noise control; remediation; waste management; library of 13,000 vols; Man. Dir LÁSZLÓ KÓTHAY; publs *Hydrological Yearbook of Hungary* (1 a year), *VITUKI Proceedings* (1 a year).

ECONOMICS, LAW AND POLITICS

Magyar Tudományos Akadémia Jogtudományi Intézete (Institute for Legal Studies of the Hungarian Academy of Sciences): 1014 Budapest, Országház u. 30; tel. (1) 355-7384; fax (1) 375-7858; e-mail lamm@jog.mta .hu; f. 1949; departments of legal theory, international law, constitutional and administrative law, civil law, criminal law, comparative law, human rights; library of 52,000 vols; Dir Prof. Dr VANDA LAMM; publs *Acta Juridica Hungarica* (2 a year), *Állam- és Jogtudomány* (2 a year).

Magyar Tudományos Akadémia Közgazdaságtudományi Intézet (Institute of Economics of the Hungarian Academy of Sciences): 1112 Budapest, Budaörsi u. 45; tel. (1) 309-2651; fax (1) 309-2650; e-mail titkarsag@econ.core.hu; internet econ.core .hu; f. 1954; research in macroeconomics, growth and economic policy, labour economics and human resources, public and institutional economics, microeconomics and sectoral economics, international economics, mathematical economics, history of economic thought, agricultural economics and rural devt, economics of technological change; empirical industrial organization; globalization, EU-integration and convergence; public economics and public policies; economics of education; library of 45,000 vols, 124 periodicals; Deputy Dir for Scientific Issues Prof. LÁSZLÓ HALPERN; Scientific Sec. Dr ZSUZSA BALABÁN; publs *Budapesti Munkagazdaságtani Füzetek* (Budapest Working Papers on the Labour Market, in English and Hungarian, 9 or 10 a year), *Műhelytanulmányok* (Discussion Papers, in English and Hungarian, 9 or 10 a year), *Munkaerőpiaci tükör* (Labour Market Yearbook, with chapters in English), *Munkatudományi Kutatások* (Labour Research Volumes, 1 a year), *Verseny és Szabályozás* (Competition and Regulation, in Hungarian, 2 a year).

Magyar Tudományos Akadémia Politikai Tudományok Intézete (Institute for Political Science of the Hungarian Academy of Sciences): 1014 Budapest, Országház u. 30; tel. (1) 224-6724; fax (1) 224-6727; e-mail ipshas@mtapti.hu; internet www.mtapti.hu; f. 1991; study of political systems, party politics, nat. and local govt, political culture, elections, problems of integration with the EU, migration, security policy and NATO; library of 43,000 vols; Research Dir Dr ANDRÁS KÖRÖSÉNYI; publ. *Hungarian Political Science Review* (in Hungarian, 4 a year).

Magyar Tudományos Akadémia Világgazdasági Kutató Intézete (Institute for World Economics of the Hungarian Academy of Sciences): 1014 Budapest, Országház u. 30; tel. (1) 224-6760; fax (1) 224-6761; e-mail vki@vki3.vki.hu; internet www .vki.hu; f. 1965; research in world economics; library of 102,000 vols; Dir Prof. ANDRÁS INOTAI; publs *Kihívások* (Challenges, irregular), *Műhelytanulmányok* (Workshop Studies, irregular), *Trends in World Economy*, *Working Papers* (in English, irregular).

Teleki László Intézet (László Teleki Institute): 1539 Budapest, POB 615; tel. (1) 224-3832; e-mail telekialapitvany@gmail.com; internet www.telekialapitvany.hu; f. 1999; prepares analytical material and information for foreign policy instns; research on theoretical issues of international relations; organizes round-table conferences, seminars, lectures; reference library; Dir Prof. GYÖRGY GRANASZTÓI; publs *Külügyi Szemec* (foreign policy; in Hungarian 4 a year, in English 2 a year), *Reyio* (minorities, soc., politics; in Hungarian 4 a year, in English 1 a year).

EDUCATION

Felsóoktatási Kutatóintézet (Hungarian Institute for Higher Educational Research): 1146 Budapest, Ajtósi Dürer sor 19–21; tel. (1) 221-0365; fax (1) 208-056; e-mail oktataskutato@ella.hu; internet www.hier.iif .hu; f. 1981; applied social research and postgraduate training in school education, higher education and vocational education; library of 23,000 vols; Dir Dr LISKO ILONA; publs *Educatio* (review, 4 a year), *Kutatás Közben* (Research Papers, 6 a year).

FINE AND PERFORMING ARTS

Magyar Tudományos Akadémia Művészettörténeti Kutatóintézet (Research Institute for Art History of the Hungarian Academy of Sciences): 1014 Budapest, Uri u. 49; tel. (1) 224-6700; fax (1) 375-0493; e-mail arthist@arthist.mta.hu; internet www.arthist.mta.hu; f. 1969; research on Hungarian art since 10th century; library of 40,000 vols; Dir LÁSZLO BEKE; publ. *Ars Hungarica* (2 a year).

Magyar Tudományos Akadémia Zenetudományi Intézet (Institute for Musicology of the Hungarian Academy of Sciences): 1014 Budapest, Táncsics Mihály u. 7; tel. (1) 356 6858; fax (1) 375-9282; e-mail info@zti.hu; internet www.zti.hu; f. 1961; incorporates Bartók Archives, the Museum of Music History, and depts of Folk Dances, Folk Music, History of Early Music, History of Hungarian Music; library of 150,000 vols; 100,000 recorded melodies; Dir Prof. Dr TIBOR TALLIÁN; Deputy Dir PÉTER HALÁSZ; publ. *Studia Musicologica* (4 a year).

HISTORY, GEOGRAPHY AND ARCHAEOLOGY

Magyar Tudományos Akadémia Földrajztudományi Kutatóintézet (Geographical Research Institute, Hungarian Academy of Sciences): 1112 Budapest, Budaörsi u. 45; tel. (1) 309-2600; fax (1) 309-2690; e-mail kocsisk@mtafki.hu; internet www.mtafki.hu; f. 1950, reorg. 1952; research in physical and human geography; library of 71,967 vols; Dir Dr KÁROLY KOCSIS; publs *Földrajzi Értesítő* (Hungarian Geographical Bulletin, 4 a year), *Földrajzi Tanulmányok*, *Geographical Abstracts from Hungary*, *Studies in Geography in Hungary*.

Magyar Tudományos Akadémia Régészeti Intézete (Archaeological Institute of the Hungarian Academy of Sciences): 1250 Budapest, Uri u. 49; tel. (1) 356-4567; fax (1) 224-6719; e-mail konyvtar@archeo .mta.hu; internet www.archeo.mta.hu; f. 1959; research in archaeology and associated sciences; 58 mems; library of 73,911 vols; Dir Prof. CSANÁD BÁLINT; Head of Library JUDIT SOLTI; publs *Antaeus* (yearbook, in German and English), *Magyarország Régészeti Topográfiája* (Archaeological Topography of Hungary), *Varia Archaeologica Hungarica* (in foreign languages, irregular).

Magyar Tudományos Akadémia Regionális Kutatások Központja (Research Centre for Regional Studies of the Hungarian Academy of Sciences): 7621 Pécs, Papnövelde u. 22; tel. (72) 523-800; fax (72) 523-803; e-mail postmaster@rkk.hu; internet www .rkk.hu; f. 1943; research into regional planning, geography, economics, government, sociology, ethnography, and history; 60 mems; library of 40,000 vols; Dir-Gen. Prof. GYULA HORVÁTH; publs *Alföldi Tanulmányok* (irregular), *Tér és Társadalom* (4 a year).

Magyar Tudományos Akadémia Történettudományi Intézete (Institute of Historical Science of the Hungarian Academy of Sciences): 1014 Budapest, Uri u. 53; tel. (1) 224-6755; fax (1) 224-6756; e-mail apok@tti .hu; internet www.tti.hu; f. 1949; five depts of Hungarian history and comparative European history, one dept of documentation and bibliography, historiography; library of 100,000 vols; Dir Prof. FERENC GLATZ; publs *Történelmi Szemle* (4 a year), annual bibliography of historical works published in Hungary.

LANGUAGE AND LITERATURE

Magyar Tudományos Akadémia Irodalomtudományi Intézete (Institute of Literary Studies of the Hungarian Academy of Sciences): 1118 Budapest, Ménesi u. 11–13; tel. (1) 385-8790; fax (1) 185-3876; internet www.iti.mta.hu; f. 1956; research in Hungarian and world literature; library of 170,000 vols; Dir Prof. LÁSZLÓ SZÖRÉNYI; publs *Helikon* (4 a year), *Irodalomtörténeti Füzetek* (studies, irregular), *Irodalomtörténeti Közlemények* (6 a year), *Literatura* (4 a year), *Neohelicon* (2 a year).

Magyar Tudományos Akadémia Nyelvtudományi Intézete (Research Institute of Linguistics of the Hungarian Academy of Sciences): 1399 Budapest, POB 701/518; 1068 Budapest, Benczúr u. 33; tel. (1) 351-0413; fax (1) 322-9297; e-mail kiefer@nytud.hu; internet www.nytud.hu; f. 1949; research in theoretical linguistics, phonetics, neuro- and sociolinguistics, historical linguistics, lexicography, corpus linguistics; library of 40,000 vols; Dir Dr ISTVÁN KENESEI; publs *Magyar Fonetikai Füzetek* (Hungarian Papers in Phonetics, 2 a year), *Műhelymunkák a nyelvészet és társtudományai köréből* (Working Papers on Linguistics and Related Sciences, irregular), *Nyelvtudományi Közlemények* (Linguistic Publications, 2 a year).

MEDICINE

Magyar Tudományos Akadémia Kísérleti Orvostudományi Kutatóintézete (Institute of Experimental Medicine of the Hungarian Academy of Sciences): 1083 Budapest, Szigony u. 43; tel. (1) 210-9400; fax (1) 210-9423; e-mail info@koki.hu; internet www.koki.hu; f. 1952; conducts basic biomedical research, primarily in the field of neuroscience, incl. studies on neurotransmission, learning and memory, behaviour, ischaemic and epileptic brain damage, and the central and peripheral control of hormone secretion; library of 18,500 vols; Dir Prof. Dr TAMAS F. FREUND.

Mozgássérültek Pető András Nevelőképző és Nevelőintézete (András Pető Institute of Conductive Education and Conductor Training College): 1125 Budapest, Kutvölgyi u. 6; tel. (1) 224-1500; fax (1) 224-1531; e-mail info@peto.hu; internet www .peto.hu; f. 1945; library of 35,000 vols; conductive education for 1,200 children and adults with motor disabilities due to damage to the central nervous system; undergraduate conductor training with specialization in preschool or primary school teaching; conductor-helper postgraduate specialist training; higher-level vocational training in youth protection; Rector Dr FRANZ SCHAFFHAUSER; publ. *Conductive Education Occasional Papers* (2 a year).

Országos Epidemiológiai Központ (National Centre for Epidemiology): 1097 Budapest, Gyáli u. 2–6; tel. and fax (1) 476-1369; e-mail konyvtar@oek.antsz.hu; internet www.oek.hu/oek.web; f. 1927; research in epidemiology, microbiology, virology, bacteriology, parasitology, mycology, vaccines; library of 30,000 vols; Dir-Gen. Dr MÁRTA MELLES; publs *EPINFO* (52 a year), *Mikrobiológiai Körlevél (Microbiological Circular)* (4 a year).

Országos Epidemiológiai Központ, Mikrobiológiai Kutatócsoport (Microbiological Research Group of the National Centre for Epidemiology): 1529 Budapest, Pihenő u. 1; tel. (1) 394-5044; fax (1) 394-5409; e-mail mini@microbi.hu; f. 1963; research into oncogenic viruses, virus tumours, HIV/AIDS, interferon, DNA methylation; library of 2,000 vols; Dir Dr JÁNOS MINÁROVITS.

Országos 'Fréderic Joliot-Curie' Sugárbiológiai és Sugáregészségügyi Kutató Intézet (National Research Institute for Radiobiology and Radiohygiene): 1775 Budapest, POB 101; tel. (1) 482-2001; fax (1) 482-2003; e-mail radbiol@hp.osski.hu; f. 1957; under Min. of Health; radiohygiene, including protection of workers from radiation; radiobiology research on effects of external ionizing radiation and incorporated radioisotopes; radiation and radioisotope applications; medical preparedness for response to radio-nuclear emergencies; teaching within the Semmelweis Medical School, Budapest; library of 7,000 vols; Dir Prof. Dr ISTVAN TURAI.

Országos Haematológiai és Immunológiai Intézet (National Institute of Haematology and Immunology): 1519 Budapest, POB 424; 1113 Budapest, Daróczi u. 24; tel. (1) 466-5877; fax (1) 372-4352; internet www.c3.hu/~haemat; f. 1948; research and clinical activities in haematology and immunology, including bone-marrow transplantation; library of 10,000 vols, 91 periodicals; Dir Prof. Dr GYŐZŐ PETRÁNYI; publs *Haematologia* (in English, 4 a year), *Transzfúzió* (in Hungarian, 4 a year).

Országos Onkológiai Intézet (National Institute of Oncology): 1122 Budapest, Ráth György u. 7/9; tel. (1) 224-8600; fax (1) 224-8620; f. 1952; experimental and clinical activities; library of 15,973 vols, 164 periodicals, service for reprints of all publs available; Dir Dr M. KASLER; publ. *Magyar Onkológia* (4 a year).

NATURAL SCIENCES

Biological Sciences

Magyar Tudományos Akadémia Balatoni Limnológiai Kutatóintézete (Balaton Limnological Research Institute of the Hungarian Academy of Sciences): 8237 Tihany, POB 35; tel. (87) 448-244; fax (87) 448-006; e-mail intezet@tres.blki.hu; internet www.blki.hu; f. 1927; research particularly in hydrobiology, and experimental zoology; library of 16,000 vols; Dir Dr SÁNDOR HERODEK; publ. collected reprints, progress report.

Magyar Tudományos Akadémia Ökológiai és Botanikai Kutatóintézete (Institute of Ecology and Botany of the Hungarian Academy of Sciences): 2163 Vácrátót, Alkot-

mány ut. 2–4; tel. (28) 360-122; fax (28) 360-110; e-mail obki@botanika.hu; internet www.obki.hu; f. 1952; theoretical and experimental research in the field of botany, flora, plant, taxonomy, dendrology, aquatic ecology, plant ecology, vegetation and community ecology, functional ecology, forest ecology, landscape ecology, grassland ecology, nature conservation, conservation biology, vegetation mapping, climate change, lichenology, land-use history, botanical gardens, gardening, river restoration, shallow lakes; library of 10,000 vols; Dir Dr KATALIN TÖRÖK.

Magyar Tudományos Akadémia Szegedi Biológiai Kutatóközpont (Biological Research Centre of the Hungarian Academy of Sciences): 6726 Szeged, Temesvári krt. 62, 6701 POB 521; tel. (62) 599-600; fax (62) 432-188; e-mail kulugy@brc.hu; internet www.brc.hu; f. 1971; library of 30,000 vols; Dir-Gen. Prof. PÁL ORMOS.

Attached Institutes:

Biofizikai Intézet (Institute of Biophysics): c/o Magyar Tudományos Akadémia Szegedi Biológiai Kutatóközpontja, 6701 Szeged, Temesvári krt. 62, POB 521; tel. (62) 599-614; f. 1971; Dir PAL ORMOS; Sec. SZILVIA VARGA.

Biokémiai Intézet (Institute of Biochemistry): c/o Magyar Tudományos Akadémia Szegedi Biológiai Központja, 6701 Szeged, Temesvári krt. 62, POB 521; tel. (62) 433-506; f. 1971; Dir LÁSZLÓ VIGH.

Enzimológiai Intézet (Institute of Enzymology): 1113 Budapest, Karolina u. 29; tel. (1) 279-3100; fax (1) 466-5465; f. 1950; Dir PETER ZAVODSKY.

Genetikai Intézet (Institute of Genetics): c/o Magyar Tudományos Akadémia Szegedi Biológiai Kutatóközpont, 6726 Szeged, Temesvári krt. 62; tel. (62) 599-657; fax (62) 433-503; internet www.szbk.u-szeged.hu; f. 1971; Dir Dr MIKLÓS ERDÉLYI; Sec. CSILLA SOLTESZ.

Növénybiológiai Intézet (Institute of Plant Biology): c/o Magyar Tudományos Akadémia Szegedi Biológiai Központja, 6701 Szeged, Temesvári krt. 62, POB 521; tel. (62) 599-714; fax (62) 433-434; e-mail nbititk@brc.hu; internet www.brc.hu; f. 1971; research on molecular background, characterization, structure and function in plants; identification of genes and protein products, which determine stress responses of plants and cyanobacteria; detection of various reactive oxygen species in plant systems, and studies on their role at the molecular and cellular level; Dir Dr IMRE VASS; Sec. MARIANN KAROLYI.

Természetvédelmi Hivatal, Madártani Intézet (Authority for Nature Conservation, Institute for Ornithology): 1121 Budapest, Költő u. 21; tel. (1) 391-1759; e-mail buki@mail.kvvm.hu; internet www.termeszetvedelem.hu; f. 1893; library of 8,000 vols, 1,000 periodicals; Librarian JÓZSEF BÜKI; publ. *Aquila* (1 a year).

Mathematical Sciences

Magyar Tudományos Akadémia Rényi Alfréd Matematikai Kutatóintézet (Alfréd Rényi Institute of Mathematics, Hungarian Academy of Sciences): 1364 Budapest, POB 127; 1053 Budapest, Reáltanoda u. 13–15; tel. (1) 483-8300; fax (1) 483-8333; e-mail math@renyi.hu; internet www.renyi.hu; f. 1950; research in fields of pure and applied mathematics; 80 mems; library of 60,000 vols; Dir G. O. H. KATONA; publ. *Studia Scientiarum Mathematicarum Hungarica*.

Physical Sciences

Magyar Állami Eötvös Loránd Geofizikai Intézet (Eötvös Loránd Geophysical Institute of Hungary): 1145 Budapest, Columbus u. 17–23; tel. (1) 252-4999; fax (1) 363-7256; e-mail elgi@elgi.hu; internet www.elgi.hu; f. 1907; geophysical exploration for hydrocarbons, coal, bauxite, water, ores; engineering geophysics; geophysical research, gravity, magnetics, lithosphere, ionosphere; library of 30,000 vols; Dir Dr TAMÁS FANCSIK; publ. *Geophysical Transactions* (4 a year).

Attached Institute:

Geophysical Observatory: 8237 Tihany; tel. (87) 448-501; fax (87) 538-001; e-mail csontos@elgi.hu; f. 1954; Head LÁSZLÓ HEGYMEGI.

Magyar Tudományos Akadémia Atommagkutató Intézete (Institute of Nuclear Research of the Hungarian Academy of Sciences): 4026 Debrecen, Bem tér 18/C; tel. (52) 509-200; fax (52) 416-181; e-mail fulop@atomki.hu; internet www.atomki.hu; f. 1954; nuclear physics, atomic physics, particle physics, materials science and analysis, earth and cosmic sciences, environmental research, biological and medical research, devt of methods and instruments; 200 mems; library of 55,000 vols; Dir Dr ZSOLT FÜLÖP; Sec. ERZSÉBET LEITER.

Magyar Tudományos Akadémia Csillagászati Kutatóintézete (Konkoly Observatory of the Hungarian Academy of Sciences): 1525 Budapest, POB 67; 1121 Budapest, Konkoly Thege Miklós u. 15–17; tel. (1) 391-9322; fax (1) 275-4668; internet www.konkoly.hu; f. 1871; 52 staff; library of 32,000 vols; Mountain Station: Piszkéstető, Galyatető (f. 1962), with Schmidt telescope, Cassegrain-reflector and 100 cm Ritchey-Chretien telescope; Dir LAJOS G. BALÁZS; publs *Information Bulletin on Variable Stars of Commission 27 of the IAU*, *Mitteilungen der Sternwarte der Ungarischen Akademie der Wissenschaften* (Communications from the Konkoly Observatory of the Hungarian Academy of Sciences).

Magyar Tudományos Akadémia Csillagászati Kutatóintézetének Napfizikai Obszervatóriuma (Heliophysical Observatory of the Hungarian Academy of Sciences): 4010 Debrecen, Egyetem tér 1, POB 30; 4010 Debrecen, Egyetem tér 1; tel. (52) 311-015; internet fenyi.sci.klte.hu; f. 1958; studies of solar activity: sunspots, solar flares, prominences; library of 10,000 vols, 20 periodicals, 5,500 sunspot drawings (1872–1919), 100,000 full-disc solar photographs; Dir B. KÁLMÁN.

Magyar Tudományos Akadémia Geodéziai és Geofizikai Kutató Intézete (Geodetical and Geophysical Research Institute of the Hungarian Academy of Sciences): 9400 Sopron, Csatkai E. u. 6–8; tel. (99) 508-340; fax (99) 508-355; internet www.ggki.hu; f. 1955 as 2 separate laboratories, merged as 1 institute 1972; research in advanced problems of geodesy and geophysics including seismology; library of 34,000 vols; Dir Prof. J. ZAVOTI; publs *Geophysical Observatory Reports* (1 a year), *Publications in Geomatics* (1 a year), *Rapport Microséismique de Hongrie* (1 a year).

Magyar Tudományos Akadémia, Kémiai Kutatóközpont (Chemical Research Centre of the Hungarian Academy of Sciences): 1025 Budapest, Pusztaszeri u. 59-67; tel. (1) 325-7900; fax (1) 325-7554; e-mail palg@chemres.hu; internet www.chemres.hu; f. 1954; fundamental research in organic, medicinal, biomolecular and bio-organic chemistry, surface reactions and heterogeneous catalysis, nanochemistry, kinetics and mechanism of chemical reactions, theoretical chemistry, electrochemistry and corrosion, polymer chemistry and polymer physics, environmental and analytical chemistry, materials chemistry and molecular structure, spectroscopy and diffraction, nuclear and isotope chemistry, photochemistry; library of 60,000 vols; Dir-Gen. Prof. Dr GÁBOR PÁLINKÁS.

Magyar Tudományos Akadémia Kémiai Kutatóközpont Izotóp- és Felületkémiai Intézet (Institute of Isotope and Surface Chemistry Chemical Research Centre of the Hungarian Academy of Sciences): 1525 Budapest, POB 77; 1121 Budapest, Konkoly Thege M. u. 29–33; tel. (1) 392-2222; fax (1) 392-2533; e-mail wojn@alpha0.iki.kfki.hu; internet www.iki.kfki.hu; f. 1959; research in the fields of catalysis, surface chemistry, adsorption, radiation chemistry, photochemistry, molecular spectroscopy, nuclear spectroscopy, nuclear safety, radioactive tracer technique; library of 14,000 vols; Dir Dr LÁSZLÓ WOJNÁROVITS.

Magyar Tudományos Akadémia, KFKI Atomenergia Kutató Intézet (KFKI Atomic Energy Research Institute of the Hungarian Academy of Sciences): 1525 Budapest, POB 49;; tel. (1) 395-9293; fax (1) 392-2222; internet www.kfki.hu/~aekihp; f. 1992; library: shares library of 120,000 vols; Dir JÁNOS GADÓ.

Magyar Tudományos Akadémia, Műszaki Fizikai és Anyagtudományi Kutatóintézet (Research Institute for Technical Physics and Materials Science of the Hungarian Academy of Sciences): 1525 Budapest, POB 49; 1121 Budapest, Konkoly Thege Miklós u. 29–33; tel. (1) 392-2224; fax (1) 392-2226; e-mail info@mfa.kfki.hu; internet www.mfa.kfki.hu; f. 1992; library: shares library of 120,000 vols; Dir Prof. ISTVÁN BÁRSONY.

Műszaki Kémiai Kutató Intézet (Research Institute of Chemical and Process Engineering): 8200 Veszprém, Egyetem u. 10; tel. (88) 624-023; fax (88) 624-025; e-mail ujvari@dcs.vein.hu; f. 1960; attached to University of Veszprem; fundamental and applied research in traditional chemical engineering, bioengineering and systems engineering; library of 8,500 vols; Dir Dr ENDRE NAGY; publ. *Hungarian Journal of Industrial Chemistry*.

Uránia Csillagvizsgáló (Urania Public Observatory): 1016 Budapest, Sánc u. 3B; tel. (1) 186-9233; fax (1) 267-1391; f. 1947; centre of the Hungarian amateur astronomy movement; 8-inch Heyde refractor, 6-inch Zeiss reflector; library of 1,700 vols; Dir OTTO ZOMBORI; publ. *Uránia Füzetek* (Urania Letters, 1 a year).

PHILOSOPHY AND PSYCHOLOGY

Magyar Tudományos Akadémia Filozófiai Kutatóintézete (Research Institute for Philosophy of the Hungarian Academy of Sciences): 1398 Budapest 62, POB 594; tel. and fax (1) 312-0243; internet www.phil-inst.hu; f. 1957 for research into problems of epistemology, philosophy of science, social philosophy, methodological problems of social sciences, philosophy of religion, political philosophy, history of philosophical thought; library: institute library of 26,000 vols; Dir Prof. Dr KRISTÓF NYÍRI.

Magyar Tudományos Akadémia Pszichológiai Kutatóintézet (Institute for Psychology of the Hungarian Academy of Sciences): 1394 Budapest, POB 398; tel. (1) 239-6726; fax (1) 239-6727; e-mail czigler@cogpsyphy.hu; internet www.mtapi.hu; f. 1902; basic research on cognitive psychophysiology and neuropsychology, devtl psychology, social psychology and personality,

research on educational psychology, psychology of decision-making, cross-cultural psychology; library of 20,000 vols; Dir Dr ISTVÁN CZIGLER; publ. *Pszichológia* (4 a year).

RELIGION, SOCIOLOGY AND ANTHROPOLOGY

Magyar Tudományos Akadémia Néprajzi Kutatóintézete (Institute of Ethnology of the Hungarian Academy of Sciences): 1250 Budapest, POB 29; tel. (1) 224-6700; fax (1) 356-8058; e-mail etnologia@etnologia.mta.hu; internet www.etnologia.mta.hu; f. 1967; research in ethnology of the Hungarian people, general anthropology, folklore and traditions, study of gypsies; library of 68,000 vols; Dir Dr BALÁZS BALOGH; Sec. CSILLA KERN; publs *Documentatio Ethnographica*, *Életmód és Tradició*, *Ethnolore*, *Folklór Archivum*, *Folklór és Tradició*, *Magyar Néprajz*, *Népi Kultura—Népi Társadalom*, *Néprajzi tanulmányok*.

Magyar Tudományos Akadémia Szociológiai Kutatóintézet (Institute of Sociology of the Hungarian Academy of Sciences): 1014 Budapest, Uri u. 49; tel. (1) 224-0786; fax (1) 224-0790; e-mail tiborit@socio.mta.hu; internet www.socio.mta.hu; f. 1963; climate change; research of values (European Social Survey); equal opportunities, poverty; environmental policy, sociology; cultures, policies, lifestyle; political cultures, institute systems, European integration; sociology of work and orgs; gender and social minorities; social structure, welfare policy; urban devt policy; knowledge and innovation; ageing; library of 8,000 vols; Dir TIBORI TIMEA; Scientific Sec. VERONIKA PAKSI; publs *INFO—Társadalomtudomány* (INFO—Social Science, 4 a year), *Társadalomkutatás* (Research in the Social Sciences, 4 a year).

TECHNOLOGY

Magyar Tudományos Akadémia Számítástechnikai és Automatizálási Kutató Intézete (Computer and Automation Research Institute of the Hungarian Academy of Sciences): 1518 Budapest, POB 63; tel. (1) 279-6000; fax (1) 466-7503; e-mail pr@sztaki.hu; internet www.sztaki.hu; f. 1964; conducts research in intelligent computing, control and information systems, new computation structures, and computer applications for engineering, production and administration systems; library of 45,600 vols; Dir Dr PÉTER INZELT; publ. *Transactions* (irregular).

Szilikátipari Központi Kutató és Tervező Intézet (Central Research and Design Institute for the Silicate Industry): 1034 Budapest, Bécsi u. 122–124; tel. (1) 188-2360; fax (1) 168-7626; f. 1953; research and technological design in the silicate sciences and building materials industry; library of 25,000 vols, 7,000 periodicals; Dir CSABA ÁRPÁD RÉTI; publs *Transactions* (irregular, in English, German, French, Russian), *Tudományos Közlemények* (irregular, summaries in English, German, French, Russian).

Villamosenergiaipari Kutató Intézet (Institute for Electric Power Research): 1251 Budapest, POB 80; 1016 Budapest, Gellérthegy u. 17; tel. (1) 457-8273; fax (1) 457-8274; e-mail i.kromer@veiki.hu; internet www.veiki.hu; f. 1949; research and development on safety assessment of nuclear power plants, combustion technology and environmental management, mechanical and power engineering technology, equipment of the electricity networks, high voltage and high power laboratory testing, systems of control engineering and telemechanics; library: technical library of 25,000 vols; Gen. Man. Dr ISTVÁN KRÓMER; publ. *VEIKI Publications*

(Hungarian, with abstracts in English, 1 a year).

Libraries and Archives

Budapest

Budapest Főváros Levéltára (Budapest City Archives): 1052 Budapest, Városház u. 9-11; tel. (1) 317-7306; fax (1) 318-3319; e-mail bfl@bparchiv.hu; internet www.bparchiv.hu; f. 1901; 23,000 m of bookshelves; Dir Dr LÁSZLÓ A. VARGA; publ. *Budapesti Negyed* (4 a year).

Budapesti Corvinus Egyetem Entz Ferenc Könyvtár és Levéltár (Corvinus University of Budapest, Entz Ferenc Library and Archives): 1118 Budapest, Villányi u. 29–43; tel. (1) 482-6300; fax (1) 482-6334; internet helix.uni-corvinus.hu; f. 1860; horticulture, floriculture, nursery, medicinal plants, fruitgrowing, landscape and garden architecture, urban planning, environmental protection; food industry, canning technology, food fermentation, processing of animal products, processing of cereals and industrial plants, oenology, brewing; 320,000 vols, 365 current periodicals; Dir Dr ÉVA ZALAI-KOVÁCS; publ. *'Lippay János' Tudományos Ülésszak Előadásai* (every 2 years).

Budapesti Corvinus Egyetem Központi Könyvtár (Corvinus University of Budapest Central Library): 1093 Budapest, Közraktar u. 4–6; tel. (1) 482-7075; fax (1) 482-7072; e-mail konyvtar@uni-corvinus.hu; internet www.lib.uni-corvinus.hu; f. 1850; economic sciences, world economy, management sciences, public admin., business and finance, sociology, political science, social sciences, environment protection, agriculture; 475,848 vols; Dir-Gen. GABRIELLA ALFÖLDI; Dir ZSUZSANNA NAGY.

Budapesti Műszaki és Gazdaságtudományi Egyetem Országos Műszaki Információs Központ és Könyvtár (BME OMIKK) (Budapest University of Technology and Economics National Technical Information Centre and Library): 1502 Budapest, POB 91; 1111 Budapest XI, Muegyetem rkp. 3; tel. (1) 463-2441; fax (1) 463-2440; e-mail ifonyo@omikk.bme.hu; internet www.omikk.bme.hu; f. 1848; 2,084,352 vols, 340,000 periodicals; Dir-Gen. ILONA FONYO; publ. *Tudományos és Műszaki Tajekoztatas* (Scientific and Technical Information, 12 a year).

Egészségügyi Stratégiai Kutatóintézet Egészségpolitikai Szakkönyvtár (National Institute for Strategic Health Research Health Policy Library): 1051 Budapest, Arany János u. 6-8; tel. (1) 354-5377; fax (1) 354-5370; e-mail konyvtar@eski.hu; internet www.eski.hu; f. 1949; library for Ministry of Health staff, health policy makers, health professionals, health care managers, health workers; colln includes Hungarian publications on health policy and related fields, statistics, social and family affairs; selected publs from foreign literature; deposit library of the European regional office of the World Health Org.; 40,000 vols; Dir-Gen. Dr GYORGY SURJAN; Head of Library Dr MARIA PALOTAI; publs *Magyar Orvosi Bibliográfia* (Hungarian Medical Bibliography, 4 a year, online), *Országtanulmányok* (Country Profiles, online).

Eötvös Loránd Tudományegyetem Egyetemi Könyvtára (Eötvös Loránd University Library): 1053 Budapest, Ferenciek tere 6; tel. (1) 411-6738; fax (1) 411-6737; e-mail info@lib.elte.hu; internet www.konyvtar.elte.hu; f. 1635; central library of the Univ. and nat. scientific library for philosophy, psychology, medieval history and history of Christianity; 1,500,000 vols, 1,339 periodicals, 60,000 MSS, 185 codices, 1,150 incunabula, 2,600 old Hungarian printed works (to 1711), 9,600 old and rare books; Dir-Gen. Dr LÁSZLÓ SZÖGI; publ. Egyetemi Könyvtár Évkönyve (University Library Annals, irregular).

Fővárosi Szabó Ervin Könyvtár (Metropolitan Ervin Szabó Library): VIII Szabó Ervin tér 1, Pf. 487, 1371 Budapest; tel. (1) 411-5000; fax (1) 411-5002; e-mail titkar@fszek.hu; internet www.fszek.hu; f. 1904; sociology, humanities, literature, history of Budapest; 3,356,420 vols (1,541,997 vols in central library); 78 brs; Dir PÉTER FODOR; publs Databases (CD-ROM), Yearbook.

Hadtörténeti Könyvtár és Térképtár (Library of Military History and Cartographic Collection): 1014 Budapest, Kapisztrán tér 2; tel. (1) 325-1672; fax (1) 212-0286; e-mail terkeptar@mail.militaria.hu; internet www.hm-him.hu; f. 1920; 190,000 vols, 500,000 maps; Dir LÁSZLÓ VESZPRÉMY; publs Bibliography (1 a year), Hadtörténelmi Közlemények (Review of Military History, 4 a year).

Iparművészeti Múzeum Könyvtára (Library of the Museum of Applied Arts): 1091 Budapest, Üllői u. 33–37; tel. (1) 456-5177; fax (1) 217-5838; e-mail konyvtar@imm .hu; internet www.imm.hu; f. 1874; scientific research library for the decorative arts; 60,000 vols, 20,000 periodicals; Dir ESTHER TISZAVÁRI; publ. Ars Decorativa (1 a year).

Keve András Madártani és Természetvédelmi Szakkönyvtár (Andras Keve Library for Ornithology and Nature Conservation): 1121 Budapest, Költő u. 21; tel. (1) 202-2530; e-mail jozsef.buki@vm.gov.hu; internet aotk.hunteka.ikron.hu/keve; f. 1893; 9,000 vols, 20,000 periodicals, 1,500 scientific reports; Librarian JÓZSEF BÜKI; publ. Aquila (1 a year).

Központi Statisztikai Hivatal Könyvtár (Library of the Central Statistical Office): 1024 Budapest, 1525 Pf. 10, II, Keleti Károly u. 5; tel. (1) 345-6105; fax (1) 345-6112; e-mail kodosz@ksh.hu; internet konyvtar.ksh.hu; f. 1867; 800,000 books, periodicals, maps and electronic documents; nat. and research library of statistics and demography; Dir-Gen. Dr ERZSEBET NEMES; publ. Magyarország Történeti Helységnévtára (Historical Gazetteer of Hungary).

Liszt Ferenc Zeneművészeti Egyetem Könyvtára (Library of the Ferenc Liszt Academy of Music): 1391 Budapest, Liszt Ferenc tér 8, POB 206; tel. (1) 462-4673; fax (1) 462-4672; e-mail agnes.gador@lisztakademia.hu; internet www .zeneakademia.hu; f. 1875; 450,000 musical scores plus 90,000 vols and periodicals, 40,000 records; research library for music history; Dir AGNES GÁDOR.

Magyar Nemzeti Galéria Könyvtára (Library of the Hungarian National Gallery): 1250 Budapest, POB 31; 1014 Budapest, Szent György tér 2; tel. (2) 439-7453; fax (1) 212-7356; e-mail library@mng.hu; internet www.mng.hu; f. 1957; books on art from all over the world, specializing in Hungarian sculpture, wood carvings, panel paintings, Baroque art, art since the 12th century; 80,000 vols, 27,000 catalogues, 8,800 periodicals, 15,000 slides; Dir Mrs FERENC BERÉNYI; Head of Library ANELIA TŰŰ; publ. A Magyar Nemzeti Galéria Évkönyve (Annals).

Magyar Nemzeti Múzeum Központi Könyvtár (Archaeological Library of the Hungarian National Museum): 1088 Budapest, Múzeum-körút 14–16; tel. (1) 113-4400; e-mail konyvtar@hnm.hu; internet www .hnm.hu; f. 1950; 250,000 vols; Dir Dr ENDRE TÓTH; Asst Dir ÉVA HOPPÁL; publs Folia

Archaeologica, Folia Historica, Inventaria Praehistorica Hungariae.

Magyar Országos Levéltár (National Archives of Hungary): 1250 Budapest, POB 3; 1014 Budapest, Bécsi kapu tér 2–4; tel. (1) 225-2800; fax (1) 225-2817; e-mail info@mol .gov.hu; internet www.mol.gov.hu; f. 1756; 80,500 m of shelving; records from the 12th century to 2000; Gen. Dir Dr CSABA T. REISZ; publs Levéltári Közlemények (journal), Levéltári Szemle (journal).

Magyar Tudományos Akadémia Földrajztudományi Kutató Intézet Könyvtára (Library of the Geographical Research Institute of the Hungarian Academy of Sciences): 1388 Budapest, POB 64; 1112 Budapest, Budaörsi u. 45; tel. (1) 319-3119; fax (1) 309-2690; e-mail magyar@sparc.core.hu; internet www.mtafki.hu; f. 1952; 70,580 vols, 17,905 maps, 8,128 MSS, 8,088 periodicals; Librarians ÁRPÁD MAGYAR, GABRIELLA PETZ; publs Elmélet-módszer-gyakorlat (Theory-Methods-Practice), Földrajzi Értesítő, Studies in Geography in Hungary.

Magyar Tudományos Akadémia Könyvtára (Library of the Hungarian Academy of Sciences): 1245 Budapest, Arany János ut. 1, POB 1002; tel. (1) 411-6100; fax (1) 331-6954; e-mail mtak@mtak.hu; internet www.mtak .hu; f. 1826; colln incl. oriental MSS, old prints and incunabula; depository library for Academy's dissertations; Academy's archives; 1,525,785 vols, 362,608 periodicals, 718,450 MSS, 32,588 microfilms, 685 electronic documents, 69 audiovisual titles; Dir-Gen. Prof. GABOR NARAY-SZABO.

Magyar Zsidó Levéltár (Hungarian Jewish Archives): 1075 Budapest, Dohány u. 2; tel. (1) 413-5551; fax (1) 343-6756; e-mail info@milev.hu; internet www.milev.hu; f. 1916; Jewish pieces of archaeology and art history, religious objects; family tree research centre, picture gallery of Hungarian Jewish heritage; Dir ZSUZSANNA TORONYI; publs ISSN 1417-6777, Makor.

Oktatási és Kulturális Minisztérium, Levéltári Osztály (Ministry of Education and Culture, Archives Department): 1055 Budapest, Szalay u. 10–14; tel. (1) 473-7450; fax (1) 473-7018; e-mail radojka .gorjanac@okm.gov.hu; internet www.okm .gov.hu; f. 1950; functions as supervising board of all archives in Hungary; Head RADOJKA GORJANAC.

Országgyűlési Könyvtár (Library of the Hungarian Parliament): 1357 Budapest, Pf. 4, Kossuth Lajos-tér 1–3; tel. (1) 441-4686; fax (1) 441-4853; e-mail ambrusj@ogyk.hu; internet www.ogyk.hu; f. 1870; 820,000 vols; parliamentary papers (Hungarian and foreign), contemporary history, administrative and legal sciences, politics; UN depository library, EU depository library; Librarian JÁNOS AMBRUS; publs Hundok (review on floppy disk and CD-ROM of foreign newspapers and weekly periodicals dealing with Hungarian issues), INFO-Társadalomtudomány (4 a year), Pressdok (review on floppy disk and CD-ROM of Hungarian newspapers and periodicals).

Országos Idegennyelvü Könyvtár (National Library of Foreign Literature): 1056 Budapest, Molnár u. 11; tel. (1) 318-3688; fax (1) 318-0147; e-mail tajekoztato@oik.hu; internet www.oik.hu; f. 1956; fmrly the Gorky State Library; specializing in foreign literature, the theory of literature, linguistics, language teaching materials, musicology, music scores and records, literature concerning national minorities and ethnics; 370,000 vols; Dir IBOLYA MENDER; publs Database of minorities-related articles, Ethnic Minority Bibliography (1 a year),

Literary translations database, New Books for Nationalities (irregular).

Országos Mezőgazdasági Könyvtár és Dokumentációs Központ (National Agricultural Library and Documentation Centre): 1012 Budapest, Attila u. 93; tel. (1) 489-4900; fax (1) 489-4939; e-mail omgkref@omgk.hu; internet www.omgk.hu; f. 1951; 292,820 vols, 443 periodicals; Gen. Dir GABRIELLA LÜKŐ-ŐRSI; publs Agrárkönyvtári Hírvilág (online, 4 a year), Az Európai Unió Agrárgazdasága (12 a year), Magyar Mezőgazdasági Bibliográfia (on disk, 4 a year).

Országos Pedagógiai Könyvtár és Múzeum (National Educational Library and Museum): 1089 Budapest, Könyves Kálmán u. 40; tel. and fax (1) 323-5508; internet www.opkm.hu; f. 1877, reorganized 1958; methodological library for education; pedagogical museum; 550,000 vols; Dir (vacant); publs Könyv és Nevelés (Books and Education, 4 a year), Külföldi Pedagógiai Információ (International Educational Information, on CD-ROM), Magyar Pedagógiai Irodalom (Hungarian Educational Literature, on CD-ROM).

Országos Rabbiképző—Zsidó Egyetem Könyvtára (Library of the Jewish Theological Seminary–University of Jewish Studies): 1428 Budapest, POB 21; 1085 Budapest, Bérkocsis u. 2; tel. (1) 267-5415 ext. 103; fax (1) 318-7049 ext. 150; internet www.rabbi .hu; f. 1877; 100,000 vols; Dir BERTA BIRÓ BÉRI.

Országos Széchényi Könyvtár (National Széchényi Library): 1827 Budapest, Budavári Palota F-épület; tel. (1) 224-3700; fax (1) 202-0804; internet www.oszk.hu; f. 1802; 2,634,000 books and periodicals, 4,750,000 manuscripts, maps, prints, microfilms, etc.; Dir-Gen. ISTVÁN MONOK; publs include Magyar Nemzeti Bibliográfia, Könyvek bibliográfiája (Hungarian National Bibliography, Monographs, 26 a year), Magyar Nemzeti Bibliográfia. Időszaki kiadványok repertóriuma (Hungarian National Bibliography, Repertory of Periodicals, 12 a year), Magyar Nemzeti Bibliográfia, Időszaki kiadványok bibliográfiája (Hungarian National Bibliography, Periodicals, 1 a year), Magyar Nemzeti Bibliográfia (Hungarian National Bibliography, Books and Periodicals CD-ROM, 2 a year); Hungarika Információ(Hungarica Information, 3 current indexes, 1 cumulative index a year), Mikrofilmek cimjegyzéke (lists of microfilms, irregular), Az Országos Széchényi Könyvtár Füzetei (Studies of the National Széchényi Library, irregular), Magyarországi egyházi könyvtárak kéziratkatalógusai (Catalogues of the Manuscript Collections in Hungarian Church Libraries, irregular), Libri de Libris (irregular), National Collection (irregular), Margarithe Bibliothecae Nalis Hungariae (irregular), A Kárpát-medence koraújkori könyvtáraj (Libraries of the Early Modern Age in the Carpathian Basin, irregular).

Affiliated Libraries:

Könyvtártudományi és Módszertani Központ (Centre for Library and Information Science): 1827 Budapest, Budavári Palota F-épület; tel. (1) 224-3788; f. 1959; research and development, promotion of inter-library co-operation, literature propaganda, public relations, training and library documentation services; library science; 107,000 vols; Dir ERZSÉBET GYŐRI (acting); publs Könyvtári Figyelő (Library Review), A Magyar Könyvtári Szakirodalom Bibliográfiája (Bibliography of Hungarian Library Literature), Hungarian Library and Information Science Abstracts (in English), Uj Könyvek (New Books), Uj Periodikumok (New Periodicals), MANCI (database of library science periodical articles with quarterly updates on floppy disk).

Reguly Antal Historic Library: 8420 Zirc, Rákóczi-tér 1; tel. and fax (88) 593-800; f. 1720; 68,618 vols; Librarian KATALIN URBÁN.

Pázmány Péter Katolikus Egyetem, Hittudományi Kar Könyvtára (Library of the Péter Pázmány Catholic University's Faculty of Theology): 1053 Budapest, Veres Pálné u. 24; tel. (1) 318-1643; fax (1) 484-3054; e-mail ppke_htk@ella.hu; internet www.htk.ppke .hu; f. 1635; history, theology and linguistics; 63,500 vols (books from c. 1880, older material kept in the Library of the University); also houses the Collection of the Brothers of St Paul (1775; 12,000 vols; incunabula and MSS from the 15th and 16th centuries), and the Library of the Central Catholic Seminary (Központi Papnevelő Intézet Könyvtára) (f. 1805; 17,300 vols); Dir Dr HUBA RÓZSA.

Politikatörténeti Intézet Könyvtára (Library of the Institute of Political History): 1054 Budapest, Alkotmány u. 2; tel. (1) 301-2024; e-mail konyvtar@phistory.hu; internet www.polhist.hu; f. 1948; 175,000 vols; Chief Librarian ÉVA TÓTH.

Semmelweis Egyetem Egészségtudományi Kar Könyvtár (Semmelweis University Faculty of Health Sciences Library): 1428 Budapest, POB 229; 1088 Budapest, Vas u. 17; tel. (1) 486-5955; fax (1) 486-5951; e-mail lib@se-etk.hu; internet www.se-etk.hu; f. 1975; 50,000 vols; Head IMOLA JEHODA.

Semmelweis Egyetem Központi Könyvtára (Central Library of Semmelweis University): 1085 Budapest, Üllői u. 26; tel. (1) 317-0948; fax (1) 317-1048; e-mail lvasas@lib .sote.hu; internet www.lib.sote.hu; f. 1828; 537,127 vols; Dir Dr LÍVIA VASAS.

Semmelweis Egyetem Testnevelési és Sporttudományi Kar Könyvtára (Library of the Faculty of Physical Education and Sport Sciences, Semmelweis University): 1123 Budapest, Alkotás u. 44; tel. (1) 487-9200 ext. 12-34; fax (1) 356-6337; e-mail linda@mail.hupe.hu; internet www.hupe.hu; f. 1925; collection covers physical education, sport, human kinesiology, management, mental health, recreation and allied domains, also literature by Hungarian and foreign authors; 98,500 vols, 77 domestic and 4 foreign trade papers; Dir FERENC KRASOVEC.

Szent István Egyetem Állatorvostudományi Könyvtár, Levéltár és Múzeum (Veterinary Science Library, Archives and Museum—Szent István University): 1400 Budapest, Pf. 2; 1078 Budapest, István u. 2; tel. (1) 478-4226; fax (1) 478-4227; e-mail library.univet@aotk.szie.hu; internet library .univet.hu; f. 1787; 85,000 vols, 161 current periodicals; spec. collns: ancient veterinary literature, historical archives; museum of veterinary history; distance education for veterinarians; Dir ÉVA ORBÁN; Head of services BEA WINKLER; publs *Bibliography of Hungarian Veterinary Literature* (online), *Noctua* (newsletter, online).

Debrecen

Debreceni Egyetem Egyetemi és Nemzeti Könyvtár (University of Debrecen University and National Library): 4010 Debrecen, Egyetem tér 1, Pf. 39; tel. (52) 410-443; fax (52) 410-443; e-mail marta@lib .unideb.hu; internet www.lib.unideb.hu; f. 1912; 2,178,050 vols and periodicals, 2,618,085 MSS, prints, microfilms, etc.; Dir-Gen. Dr MÁRTA VIRÁGOS; publ. *Könyv és Könyvtár* (1 a year).

Debreceni Egyetem Egyetemi és Nemzeti Könyvtár Kenézy Élettudományi Könyvtára (University of Debrecen, University and National Library, Kenezy Life Sciences Library): 4032 Debrecen, Egyetem tér 1; tel. (52) 518-610; fax (52) 413-847; e-mail kenezy@lib.unideb.hu; internet kenezy.lib.unideb.hu; f. 1947; 201,000 vols; Librarian GYONGYI KARACSONY.

Tiszántúli Református Egyházkerületi és Kollégiumi Nagykönyvtár (Library of the Reformed College and of the Transtibiscan Church District): 4044 Debrecen, Kálvint tér 16, POB 201; tel. (52) 516-856; fax (52) 516-919; e-mail theca@silver.drk.hu; internet silver.drk.hu; f. 1538; 570,000 vols; Dir Dr GÁBORJÁNI SZABÓ BOTOND.

Esztergom

Főszékesegyházi Könyvtár (Library of Esztergom Cathedral): 2500 Esztergom, Pázmány Péter u. 2; tel. (33) 510-130; e-mail bibliotheca@invitel.hu; internet www .bibliothecaesztergom.hu; f. 11th century; 250,000 items, incl. Fugger, Batthyany and Mayer collns; Dir BÉLA CZÉKLI.

Gödöllő

Szent István Egyetem Gödöllői Tudományos Könyvtár (St Stephen's University Gödöllő Campus Library): 2103 Gödöllő, Páter Károly u. 1; tel. (28) 522-004; fax (28) 410-804; f. 1945; 370,000 vols, 535 current periodicals; Dir Dr TIBOR KOLTAY; publ. *Bibliográfia* (every 2 or 3 years).

Keszthely

Veszprémi Egyetem Georgikon Mezőgazdaságtudományi Kar, Keszthely Központi Könyvtár és Levéltár (Georgikon Faculty of Agriculture, University of Veszprém, Keszthely Central Library and Archives): 8360 Keszthely, Deák F. u. 16, POB 66; tel. (83) 312-330; fax (83) 315-105; e-mail lib@georgikon.hu; f. 1797, reorganized 1954; 150,000 vols; Dir CSILLA PÓR; publ. *Georgikon for Agriculture* (2 a year).

Miskolc

Miskolci Egyetem Könyvtár, Levéltár, Múzeum (Library, Archives and Museum of the University of Miskolc): 3515 Miskolc-Egyetemváros; tel. (46) 565-324; fax (46) 563-489; e-mail konzsamb@gold.uni-miskolc.hu; internet www.lib.uni-miskolc.hu; f. 1735; 612,000 vols, 113,000 periodicals; Dir-Gen. Dr LÁSZLÓ ZSÁMBOKI.

Pannonhalma

Főapátsági Könyvtár Pannonhalma (Benedictine Abbey Library): 9090 Pannonhalma, Vár 1; tel. (96) 570-142; fax (96) 470-011; e-mail fokonyvtar@osb.hu; internet www.osb.hu; f. 1802; collection of early records, MSS, codices, source material for the Hungarian language; 350,000 vols; Dir P. MIKSA BÁNHEGYI.

Pécs

Pécsi Tudományegyetem Egyetemi Könyvtára (University Library of Pécs): 7601 Pécs, Pf. 227; 7621 Pécs, Szepesy I. u. 1–3; tel. (72) 501-600; fax (72) 325-552; e-mail webmaster@lib.pte.hu; internet www.lib.pte .hu; f. 1774; 1,165,000 vols; Gen. Dir. Dr ÁGNES FISCHER-DÁRDAI.

Pécsi Tudományegyetem Pekár Mihály Orvosi és Élettudományi Szakkönyvtár (University of Pécs Mihály Pekár Medical and Life Science Library): 7624 Pécs, Szigeti u. 12; tel. (72) 536-000; fax (72) 536-293; e-mail konkozi@aok.pte.hu; internet www .aok.pte.hu; f. 1926; colln covers medicine, health sciences, chemistry, physics and biology; 472,413 vols; Dir Dr TÜNDE GRACZA.

Sárospatak

Sárospataki Református Kollégium Tudományos Gyűjteményei Nagykönyvtára (Scholarly Collection of the Reformed College of Sárospatak): 3950 Sárospatak, Rákóczi u. 1; tel. and fax (47) 311-057; e-mail reftud@iif.hu; internet www .patakarchiv.hu; f. 1531; 404,974 vols; Dir DÉNES DIENES; publ. *Egyháztörténeti Szemle* (www.egyhtortszemle.hu, 4 a year).

Sopron

Nyugat-Magyarországi Egyetem Központi Könyvtár es Leveltar (Central Library and Archives of the University of West Hungary): 9400 Sopron, Bajcsy-Zsilinszky ul. 4; tel. (99) 518-223; fax (99) 518-267; e-mail library@nyme.hu; internet ilex .efe.hu; f. 1735; 306,054 vols; Dir SÁNDOR SARKADY.

Szeged

Somogyi-könyvtár (Somogyi Library): 6720 Szeged, Dóm tér 1–4; tel. (62) 425-525; fax (62) 630-601; e-mail library@sk-szeged .hu; internet www.sk-szeged.hu; f. 1881; 914,000 vols; Dir ZSUZSANNA SEBŐK PALÁNKAI; publs *Csongrád Megyei Könyvtáros* (Librarian of Csongrád County), *Szegedi Műhely* (Workshop of Szeged).

Szegedi Tudományegyetem Egyetemi Könyvtár (University Library of the University of Szeged): 6722 Szeged, Ady tér 10; tel. (62) 546-665; fax (62) 546-665; e-mail mader@bibl.u-szeged.hu; internet www.bibl .u-szeged.hu; f. 1921; 1,500,000 vols; Dir Dr BÉLA MADER; publs *Acta Bibliothecaria, Dissertationes ex Bibliotheca Universitatis de Attila József nominatae*.

Veszprém

Pannon Egyetem, Egyetemi Könyvtár és Levéltár (University of Pannonia, Library and Archive): 8200 Veszprém, Wartha V. u. 1; tel. (88) 624-534; fax (88) 624-531; e-mail hazitibo@almos.uni-pannon.hu; internet library.uni-pannon.hu; f. 1949; 255,516 vols; Dir Dr MÁRTA EGYHÁZY; publs *Hungarian Journal of Industrial Chemistry* (4 a year), *Studia Germanica Universitatis Vesprimensis* (4 a year).

Museums and Art Galleries

Badacsony

Egry József Emlékmúzeum (József Egry Memorial Museum): 8261 Badacsony, Egry József Sétány 12; tel. (87) 431-044; e-mail egry.badacsony@museum.hu; f. 1973; art gallery of works by Lake Balaton landscape painter Egry.

Baja

Türr István Múzeum: 6501 Baja, Deák Ferenc u. 1, POB 55; tel. and fax (79) 324-173; f. 1937; archaeological and ethnographic collections, modern Hungarian painters, local history; library of 10,000 vols; Dir ZSUZSA MERK; publs *Bajai Dolgozatok, Türr István Múzeum Kiadványai*.

Balassagyarmat

Palóc Múzeum: 2660 Balassagyarmat, Palóc liget 1; tel. (35) 300-168; fax (35) 300-168; e-mail pmuzeum@t-online.hu; internet www.nogradi-muzeumok.hu; f. 1891; ethnography, local folk art and shepherds' art; collns of Nógrád costumes, embroidery, folk religion and folk instruments; local history, literary history (Imre Madách & Kálmán

Mikszáth relics); library of 13,000 vols; Dir AGNES LENGYEL.

Békéscsaba

Munkácsy Mihály Múzeum: 5600 Békéscsaba, Széchenyi u. 9; tel. and fax (66) 323-377; e-mail mmm@bmmi.hu; internet www.munkacsy.hu; f. 1899; archaeological, historical and regional ethnographic collns, modern Hungarian paintings, ornithology, natural science; paintings and legacies of the painter Mihály Munkácsy (1844–1900); library of 19,000 vols; Dir Dr IMRE SZATMÁRI.

Budapest

Bartók Béla Emlékház (Béla Bartók Memorial House): 1025 Budapest, Csalán u. 29; tel. (1) 394-2100; fax (1) 394-4472; e-mail bartok-1981@axelero.hu; internet www.bartokmuseum.hu; f. 1981; organizes musical programmes and concerts; Dir JÁNOS SZIRÁNYI.

Budapesti Történeti Múzeum (Budapest History Museum): 1014 Budapest, Szent György tér 2; tel. (1) 487-8801; fax (1) 487-8872; internet www.btm.hu; f. 1887; medieval antiquities, medieval royal castle, Gothic statues; library of 45,700 vols; Dir-Gen. Dr SÁNDOR BODÓ; publs *Budapest Régiségei* (Antiquities of Budapest), *Monumenta Historica Budapestinensia* (irregular), *Tanulmányok Budapest Múltjából* (Studies on the History of Budapest).

Attached Museums:

Aquincum Múzeum: 1033 Budapest, Záhony u. 3; 1033 Budapest, Szentendrei út 139; tel. (1) 430-1081; fax (1) 430-1083; e-mail h7442tot@iif.hu; internet www .aquincum.hu; f. 1894; prehistory and Roman history of Budapest; Dir Dr PAULA ZSIDI; publ. *Aquincumi Füzetek* (excavations and rescue work at the Aquincum Museum).

Fővárosi Képtár (Municipal Picture Gallery): 1037 Budapest, Kiscelli u. 108; tel. (1) 388-8560; fax (1) 368-7917; e-mail fovarosikeptar@mail.btm.hu; internet www.btmfk.iif.hu; fine arts since the 19th century; Dir PÉTER FITZ.

Kiscelli Múzeum: 1037 Budapest, Kiscelli u. 108; tel. (1) 388-7817; fax (1) 368-7917; e-mail fovarosikeptar@mail.btm.hu; internet www.btmfk.iif.hu; f. 1899; history of Budapest since 1686; fine art colln; Dir Dr PÉTER FARBAKY.

Budavári Mátyás-templom Egyházművészeti Gyüjteménye (Matthias Church of Buda Castle Ecclesiastical Art Collection): 1014 Budapest, Szentháromság tér 2; tel. (1) 488-7716; fax (1) 488-7717; e-mail muzeum@ matyas-templom.hu; internet www .matyas-templom.hu; f. 1964; permanent collection of Roman Catholic religious objects in the gallery of Matthias Church; Dir MÁTÉFFY BALÁZS.

HM HIM Hadtörténeti Múzeum és Könyvtár (Military History Museum and Library): located at: Tóth Árpád sétány 40, 1014 Budapest; POB 7, 1250 Budapest; tel. and fax (1) 356-1575; e-mail him.muzeum@ hm-him.hu; internet www.hm-him.hu; f. 1918; Hungarian and Hungarian-related militaria incl. arms, medals, flags, uniforms, art, books, documents, photographs, posters, prints, maps; 39 mems; library of 300,025 vols; Dir Colonel Dr JÓZSEF LUGOSI; publ. *A Hadtörténeti Múzeum Értesítője / Acta Musei Militaris in Hungaria* (Yearbook of the Hungarian Military Museum, with summaries in English and German, 1 a year).

Holocaust Memorial Centre: 1094 Budapest, Páva u. 39; tel. (1) 455-3333; fax (1) 455-3399; e-mail info@hdke.hu; internet www

.hdke.org; f. 2004; Exec. Dir LASZLO HARSANYI.

Iparművészeti Múzeum (Museum of Applied Arts): 1091 Budapest, Üllői u. 33–37; tel. (1) 456-5100; fax (1) 217-5838; internet www.imm.hu; f. 1872; European and Hungarian decorative arts; library: see Libraries; Gen. Dir Dr IMRE TAKÁCS; Deputy Dir PÉTER SIKLÓS; publs catalogues, *Ars Decorativa* (1 a year).

Component Museums:

Hopp Ferenc Kelet-Ázsiai Művészeti Múzeum (Ferenc Hopp Museum of Eastern Asiatic Arts): 1062 Budapest, Andrássy u. 103; tel. (1) 456-5110; fax (1) 218-7257; e-mail info@hoppmuzeum.hu; internet www.hoppmuzeum.hu; f. 1919; collns of Asiatic arts; permanent and periodic exhibitions; research; museum education; publishing. archives; museum library; library of 29,000 vols; Dir Dr GYÖRGYI FAJCSÁK.

Nagytétényi Kastélymúzeum (Castle Museum of Nagytétény): 1225 Budapest, Kastélypark u. 9–11; tel. (1) 207-0005; fax (1) 207-4680; internet www.nagytetenyi .hu; f. 1948; European furniture of the 15th to the 19th centuries; Man. ELUIRA KIRÁLY.

Ráth György Múzeum: 1068 Budapest, Városligeti-fasor 12; tel. (1) 342-3916; f. 1906; Chief Curator Dr GYÖRGYI FAJCSÁK.

Közlekedési Múzeum (Transport Museum): 1146 Budapest, Városligeti krt 11; tel. (1) 273-3840; fax (1) 363-7822; e-mail km@ella.hu; internet www.km.iif.hu; f. 1896; models of railway locomotives and rolling stock, old vehicles, railway, nautical, aeronautic, road and urban transport collns, road- and bridge-building, etc.; 4 br. museums incl. aviation and railway exhibitions with open-air displays; library of 140,000 vols; Dir Dr LÁSZLÓ EPERJESI; publ. *A Közlekedési Múzeum Évkönyve.*

Liszt Ferenc Emlékmúzeum és Kutatóközpont (Ferenc Liszt Memorial Museum and Research Centre): 1064 Budapest VI, Vörösmarty u. 35; tel. (1) 342-7320; fax (1) 413-1526; e-mail lisztmuzeum@ lisztakademia.hu; internet www .lisztmuseum.hu; f. 1986; reconstruction of the composer Franz Liszt's (1811–1886) residence in the bldg of the Old Acad. of Music, with his instruments, furniture, library and other memorabilia; permanent and temporary exhibitions; colln of Liszt's music MSS, letters and other documentation, in collaboration with the Research Library for Music History; Dir Dr ZSUZSANNA DOMOKOS.

Magyar Bélyegmúzeum (Stamp Museum): 1400 Budapest, Pf. 86, 1074 Hársfa u. 47; tel. (1) 341-5526; fax (1) 342-3757; e-mail belyegmuzeum@axelero.hu; f. 1930; collections of 12 million Hungarian and foreign stamps; philatelic history; exhibitions locally and abroad; library of 5,000 vols; Dir ROSALIE SOLYMOSI; publ. *Yearbook.*

Magyar Építészeti Múzeum (Hungarian Museum of Architecture): 1036 Budapest, Mókus u. 20; tel. (1) 388-6170; fax (1) 367-2686; f. 1968; architecture and history of architecture; library of 7,000 vols; Dir KÁROLY BUGAR-MÉSZÁROS; publ. *Pavilon* (1 a year).

Magyar Kereskedelmi és Vendéglátóipari Múzeum (Hungarian Museum of Trade and Tourism): 1051 Budapest, Szent István tér 15; tel. (1) 212-1245; fax (1) 269-5428; e-mail mkvm@iif.hu; internet www .mkvm.hu; f. 1966; catering trade colln f. 1966, covers the subjects of sales and services, particularly in tourism, hotels and hostelry, cuisine, coffee houses, confection-

ery, shop fittings; commerce colln f. 1970, contains shop fittings, samples, storage pots, packing material, measuring instruments and coins; 2 depts also contain documents, photos, posters; library of 21,700 vols; Dir IMPRE KISS.

Magyar Mezőgazdasági Múzeum (Museum of Hungarian Agriculture): 1146 Budapest, Városliget, Vajdahunyadvár; tel. (1) 363-1117; fax (1) 364-0076; e-mail museum@mgm.hu; internet www.mmgm .hu; f. 1896; library of 85,000 vols; collection, preservation and presentation of objects and documents related to the history of agriculture and agro-industries in Hungary; conferences; provincial brs; Dir-Gen. Dr GYÖRGY FEHÉR; publs *Agrártörténeti Szemle* (Agricultural History Review, 2 a year), *Bibliographia Historiae Rerum Rusticarum Internationalis* (International Bibliography of Agrarian History, every 4 years), *Magyar Mezőgazdasági Múzeum Közleményei* (Proceedings, every 2 years).

Magyar Műszaki és Közlekedési Múzeum (Hungarian Museum for Technology and Transport): 1426 Budapest, Pf. 37; 1146 Budapest, Városligeti krt 11; tel. (1) 273-3840; fax (1) 363-7822; e-mail info@ mmkm.hu; internet www.km.iif.hu; f. 2003, merger of Transport museum (f. 1896) and the Nat. Museum for Science and Technology (f. 1973); collection covers inventions and prototypes with reference to natural science and technology, historic exhibits from the early days of industry and its development to the present; colln of locomotives and wagons on a 1:5 scale; railway technology; history of road traffic, the history of sailing and the history of flight and space flight; library of 150,000 vols, 2,889 m of written material; Dir Dr ERZSEBET KOCZIAN-SZENTPETERI; publs *A Közlekedési Múzeum Évkönyve* (Yearbook of the Transport Museum), *Technikatörténeti Szemle* (Review of History of Technology).

Magyar Nemzeti Galéria (Hungarian National Gallery): 1250 Budapest, Budavári Palota, Pf. 31; tel. (1) 375-7533; fax (1) 375-8898; e-mail mng@mng.hu; internet www .mng.hu; f. 1957; collns incl. Hungarian art since the 11th century, paintings, sculptures, drawings, engravings, medals; library of 76,000 vols; Dir Dr LÓRÁND BERECZKY; publ. *A Magyar Nemzeti Galéria Évkönyve* (Annals).

Magyar Nemzeti Múzeum (Hungarian National Museum): 1088 Budapest, Múzeum krt 14–16; tel. (1) 338-2122; fax (1) 317-7806; e-mail info@hnm.hu; internet www.hnm.hu; f. 1802; history, archaeology, numismatics; library of 240,000 vols; Dir-Gen. Dr TIBOR KOVÁCS; publs *A magyar múzeumok kiadványainak bibliográfiája* (Bibliography of the Hungarian Museum's publications), *Bibliotheca Humanitatis Historica, Communicationes Archaeologicae Hungariae* (1 a year), *Folia Archaeologica* (1 a year), *Folia Historica* (1 a year), *Inventaria Praehistorica Hungariae, Múzeumi Műtárgyvédelem* (Protection of Museum Art Objects, 1 a year), *Régészeti Füzetek* (Fasciculi Archaeologici).

Magyar Sportmúzeum (Hungarian Museum of Sport): 1146 Budapest, Dózsa György u. 3; tel. (1) 252-1696; fax (1) 469-5012; internet www.sportmuzeum.hu; f. 1963; documents and photos of history of sport in Hungary and abroad; 7,000 books, 35,000 plaques and medals, 4,000 trophies, etc., 500,000 photos, films; Dir Dr LAJOS SZABÓ.

Magyar Természettudományi Múzeum (Hungarian Natural History Museum): 1088 Budapest, Baross u. 13; tel. (1) 267-7101; fax (1) 317-1669; internet www.nhmus.hu; f. 1802; depts of mineralogy and petrography, geology and palaeontology, botany, zoology, anthropology; library of 250,000 vols; Chief Dir Dr ISTVÁN MATSKÁSI; publs *Acta zoologica Academiae Scientiarum Hungaricae* (4 a year), *Annales Historico-Naturales Musei Nationalis Hungarici* (1 a year), *Folia Entomologica Hungarica* (1 a year), *Fragmenta Palaeontologica Hungarica* (1 a year), *Studia Botanica Hungarica* (1 a year).

Műcsarnok (Palace of Art): 1406 Budapest, POB 35; tel. (1) 460-7000; fax (1) 363-7205; e-mail info@mucsarnok.hu; internet www .mucsarnok.hu; f. 1896; temporary exhibitions of Hungarian and foreign contemporary art; library of 15,000 vols; Dir Dr JULIA FABÉNYI.

Néprajzi Múzeum (Museum of Ethnography): 1055 Budapest, Kossuth Lajos tér 12; tel. (1) 473-2410; fax (1) 473-2411; e-mail info@neprajz.hu; internet www.neprajz.hu; f. 1872; collns and research activities cover peasant and tribal folk cultures; library of 169,000 vols; Ethnographic Archive with 28,000 MSS and 318,000 photographs, 252 films; Folk Music Archive with 62,000 entries; Gen. Dir Dr ZOLTÁN FEJŐS; publs *Fontes Musei Ethnographiae*, *Hungarian Folklore Bibliography* (1 a year), *MaDok-füzetek*, *Néprajzi Ertesitő* (Yearbook), *Tabula* (2 a year).

OMM Elektrotechnikai Múzeuma (Museum of Electrical Engineering): 1075 Budapest, Kazinczy u. 21; tel. and fax (1) 342-5750; e-mail emuzeum@qwertynet.hu; f. 1970; historic colln of electrical engineering; library of 10,000 vols; Dir Dr SÁNDOR JESZENSZKY.

Öntödei Múzeum (Foundry Museum): 1027 Budapest, Bem József u. 20; tel. (1) 201-4370; e-mail ontode@omm.hu; f. 1969; attached to the Hungarian Museum of Science and Technology; used by Abrahám Ganz and others until 1964; original foundry equipment; history of technological devt of foundry trade, old mouldings; library of 1,483 vols; Curator KATALIN LENGYEL-KISS.

Petőfi Irodalmi Múzeum és Kortárs Irodalmi Központ (Petőfi Museum of Hungarian Literature and Centre for Contemporary Literature): 1053 Budapest, Károlyi M. u. 16; tel. (1) 317-3611; fax (1) 317-1722; e-mail muzeuminf@pim.hu; internet www.pim.hu; f. 1954; literature since the 19th century; library of 400,000 vols; archive of 950,000 MSS, 30,000 photographs, 4,900 sound recordings; art colln of 20,000 items; Dir Dr RITA RATZKY.

Postamúzeum (Postal Museum): 1061 Budapest, Andrássy u. 3; tel. (1) 268-1997; fax (1) 268-1958; e-mail info@postamuzeum .hu; internet www.postamuzeum.hu; f. 1955; permanent exhibition of the history of post and telecommunications; library of 11,000 vols; Dir MAKKAI VÁRKONYI ILDIKÓ; publs *Hírközlési Múzeumi Alapítvány*, *Postai és Távközlési Múzeumi Alapítvany Évkönyve* (1 a year).

Semmelweis Orvostörténeti Múzeum, Könyvtár és Levéltár (Semmelweis Museum, Library and Archives of the History of Medicine): 1013 Budapest, Apród. u. 1–3 (Museum); 1023 Budapest, Török u. 12 (Library and Archives); tel. (1) 201-1577 (Museum), (1) 212-5421 (Library and Archives); fax (1) 375-3936; e-mail semmelweis@ museum.hu; internet www.semmelweis .museum.hu; f. 1951 (Library), 1965 (Museum), 1972 (Archives); collects and exhibits items on history of medicine; organizes extra curricula courses for univ. and college students on history of medicine, intellectual history and history of learning; library of 122,000 vols, 20,000 periodicals; Gen. Dir BENEDEK VARGA; Deputy Dir Dr

LASZLO ANDRAS MAGYAR; publ. *Orvostörténeti Közlemények / Communicationes de Historia Artis Medicinae* (1 a year).

Szépművészeti Múzeum (Museum of Fine Arts): 1146 Budapest, Dózsa György u. 41; tel. (1) 469-7100; fax (1) 469-7172; e-mail titkarsag@szepmuveszeti.hu; internet www .szepmuveszeti.hu; f. 1896, opened 1906; collns and galleries incl. Egyptian and Greco-Roman antiquities, foreign paintings, sculptures, drawings and engravings; library of 150,000 vols; Dir-Gen. Dr LÀSZLÓ BAÁN; publs *Bulletin du Musée Hongrois des Beaux-Arts*, *MúzeumCafé* (24 a year).

Attached Museum:

Vasarely Múzeum: 1033 Budapest, Szentlélek tér 1; tel. (1) 388-7551; fax (1) 250-1540; e-mail vasarely.budapest@museum .hr; internet www.muzeum.hu/budapest/ vasarely; Dir LILLA SZABÓ.

Textil és Textilruházati Ipartörténeti Múzeum (Museum of the Textile and Clothing Industry): 1036 Budapest III, Lajos u. 138; tel. (1) 430-1387; fax (1) 367-5910; e-mail vajk.eva@axelero.hu; internet www.museum .hu/budapest/textilmuzeum; f. 1972; exhibits from Hungary and Central Europe; library of 3,690 vols; Dir ÉVA VAJK; publ. *Évkönyv* (Year Book).

Tűzoltó Múzeum (Fire Brigade Museum): 1105 Budapest, Martinovics tér 12; tel. (1) 261-3586; e-mail okf.tuzoltomuzeum@katved .hu; internet www.katasztrofavedelem.hu/ muzeum; f. 1955; includes old fire-fighting equipment, carts, pumps and hoses; universal and Hungarian history of fire protection, its means and organization; library of 15,000 vols; Curator GYULA CSICSMANN; Librarian ESZTER BEREC; publ. *Tűzoltó Múzeum Évkönyve* (Yearbook).

Zenetörténeti Múzeum (Museum of History of Music): H-1014 Budapest, Táncsics M. u. 7; tel. (1) 214-6770; fax (1) 375-9282; e-mail director@zti.hu; internet www.zti.hu; f. 1969; library of 1,200 vols; colln of instruments, MSS, personal objects used by great musicians; Dir Prof. Dr TIBOR TALLIAN.

Cegléd

Kossuth Lajos Múzeum: 2700 Cegléd, Muzeum u. 5; tel. (53) 310-637; fax (53) 310-637; e-mail kossuthmuzeum@pmmi.hu; f. 1917; relics of Lajos Kossuth; ethnography, archaeology, arts, numismatics; library of 14,000 vols; Dir GYULA KOCSIS; publ. *Ceglédi Füzetek* (1 a year).

Debrecen

Déri Múzeum: 4001 Debrecen, Déri tér 1, Pf. 61; tel. (52) 417-577; fax (52) 417-560; e-mail derimuzeum@freemail.hu; internet www.derimuz.hu; f. 1902; archaeological, ethnographic, fine and applied art, natural history, literary and local history collections and exhibitions; library of 50,000 vols, photographic archive of 100,500 negatives and slides; Dir Dr IBOLYA SZATHMÁRI; publs *A Déri Múzeum Évkönyve* (Yearbook), *Múzeumi Kurir* (Review).

Dunaújváros

Fejér Megyei Múzeumok Igazgatósága—Intercisa Múzeum: 2400 Dunaújváros, Városháza tér 4; tel. (25) 408-970; fax (25) 411-315; e-mail intercisamuz@gmail.com; f. 1951; prehistoric, Roman and medieval collns; regional history, archaeology and ethnography; library of 5,900 vols; Curator Dr MÁRTA MATUSSNÉ LENDVAI.

Eger

Dobó István Vármúzeum: 3301 Eger, Vár 1; tel. (36) 312-744; fax (36) 312-450; e-mail varmuzeum@div.iif.hu; f. 1872; originally

archiepiscopal picture gallery and museum; enlarged by Fort Eger excavation material 1949; local remains of archaeology, ethnography, history of literature and of arts; relics of the Turkish occupation; library of 30,000 vols; Dir Dr TIVADAR PETERCSÁK; publs *Agria* (Yearbook), *Studia Agriensia*.

Esztergom

Balassa Bálint Múzeum: 2500 Esztergom, Mindszenty tér 3; tel. (33) 412-185; e-mail balassa.esztergom@museum.hu; f. 1894; history, archaeology, numismatics, applied arts; library of 12,000 vols; Curator Dr ISTVÁN HORVÁTH.

Keresztény Múzeum (Christian Museum): 2501 Esztergom, Mindszenty tér 2; tel. (33) 413-880; fax (33) 413-880; e-mail keresztenymuzeum@vnet.hu; internet www .christianmuseum.hu; f. 1875; Hungarian, Italian, Dutch, Austrian and German late medieval and Renaissance paintings and sculpture; collns of baroque and modern art, decorative arts, prints and drawings; library of 11,000 vols; Dir PÁL CSÉFALVAY.

Magyar Környezetvédelmi és Vízügyi Múzeum (Hungarian Environmental and Water Management Museum): 2500 Esztergom, Kölcsey u. 2; tel. (33) 500-250; fax (33) 500-251; internet www.dunamuzeum.org.hu; f. 1973; history of water management; library of 9,700 vols; Curator IMRE KAJÁN; publ. *Vizgazdálkodás* (Water Management).

Magyar Nemzeti Múzeum Vármúzeuma: 2500 Esztergom, Szent István tér 1; tel. (33) 415-986; fax (33) 500-095; e-mail varmegom@ invitel.hu; internet www.mnmvarmuzeuma .hu; f. 1967; excavated and reconstructed royal palace from the times of the Hungarian House of the Arpáds; municipal history of Esztergom as royal seat in the Middle Ages; Dir GÁBOR REZI KATÓ; Sec. ZOLTÁN VIGH.

Fertőd

Esterházy Castle Museum: 9431 Fertőd, Joseph Haydn u. 2; tel. (99) 537-640; e-mail kastelymuzeum.fertod@museum.hu; f. 1959; historic castle of Esterházy family; local documents, furnishings, applied art, memorabilia of composer Haydn; Dir JOLÁN BAK.

Gyöngyös

Mátra Múzeum (Museum Historico-Naturale Matraense): 3200 Gyöngyös, Kossuth u. 40; tel. (37) 505-530; fax (37) 505-531; internet www.matramuzeum.hu; f. 1957; natural history: palaeontology, zoology and botany of Hungary and Europe; history of hunting; library of 12,000 vols; Curator Dr LEVENTE FÜKÖH; publs *Folia Historico-naturalia Musei Matraensis* (1 a year), *Malacological Newsletter* (1 a year).

Győr

Xántus János Múzeum: 9022 Győr, Széchenyi tér 5; tel. (96) 310-588; fax (96) 310-731; e-mail xantus@gymsmuzeum.hu; f. 1854; archaeological collection containing relics of the ancient town of Arrabona (now Győr); history, art, anthropology, Roman lapidarium; picture gallery; library of 38,000 vols; Dir Dr ESZTER SZŐNYI; publ. *Arrabona* (1 a year).

Gyula

Erkel Ferenc Múzeum (Ferenc Erkel Museum): 5700 Gyula, Kossuth u. 17; tel. (66) 361-236; e-mail erkel.gyula@museum .hu; f. 1868; archaeology, art, local history, musicological and ethnographic collns; library of 9,052 vols; Curator Dr PÉTER HAVASSY.

Hajdúböszörmény

Hajdúsági Múzeum: 4220 Hajdúböszörmény, Kossuth L. u. 1; tel. (52) 371-038; fax (52) 371-038; e-mail hajdusagi .hajduboszormeny@museum.hu; f. 1924; sections: archaeology, ethnography, history and fine arts; library of 15,000 vols; Curator Dr MIKLÓS NYAKAS; publs *Évkönyv* (in Hungarian and German, every 2 years), *Közlemények* (in Hungarian, German, English and Russian, 1 a year).

Herend

Porcelán Múzeum: 8440 Herend, Kossuth u. 140; tel. (88) 523-197; fax (88) 261-801; e-mail porcelanmuveszeti.herend@museum .hu; f. 1964; exhibits from the famous china factory, est. 1826; library of 4,500 vols; Dir MAGDOLNA SIMON.

Hódmezővásárhely

Tornyai János Múzeum és Közművelődési Központ (Tornyai Janos Museum and Cultural Centre): 6800 Hódmezővásárhely, Dr Rapcsák András u. 16–18; tel. (62) 242-224; e-mail tjm@tjm.hu; f. 1905; archaeological, ethnographic and folk-art collns, Tornyai paintings and Medgyessy sculptures; pottery and farm museum; library of 5,500 vols; Dir Dr IMRE NAGY.

Jászberény

Jász Múzeum: 5100 Jászberény, Táncsics-u. 5; tel. (57) 412-753; e-mail jasz .jaszbereny@museum.hu; f. 1873; collns from the late Stone, Copper, Bronze and Iron Ages; ethnography, local history; library of 6,593 vols; Curator JÁNOS TÓTH.

Kalocsa

Viski Károly Múzeum: 6300 Kalocsa, Szent István Király u. 25, POB 82; tel. (78) 462-351; fax (78) 462-351; e-mail viski.kalocsa@ museum.hu; f. 1932; regional museum, folk art; library of 9,000 vols; Dir IMRE ROMSICS.

Kaposvár

Somogy Megyei Múzeumok Igazgatósága (Somogy County Museums Authority): 7400 Kaposvár, Fő u. 10; tel. (82) 314-011; fax (82) 312-822; e-mail titkarsag@smmi.hu; internet www.smmi.hu; f. 1909; archaeological and ethnographic collns, contemporary history, fine arts, natural history; library of 13,000 vols; Dir Dr LÁSZLÓ KÖLTŐ; publs *Múzeumi Tájékoztató*, *Somogyi Múzeumok Füzetei*, *Somogyi Múzeumok Közleményei*.

Karcag

Györffy István Nagykun Múzeum: 5300 Karcag, Kálvin u. 4; tel. (59) 312-087; fax (59) 503-164; e-mail karcagimuzeum@gmail.com; f. 1906; regional museum, ethnography; library of 8,000 vols; Curator MIKLÓS NAGY MOLNÁR.

Kecskemét

Bozsó Collection: 6000 Kecskemét, Klapka u. 34; tel. and fax (76) 324-625; e-mail bozsoal@mail.datanet.hu; internet www .bozso.net; Dir KLÁRA LÓRÁND.

Katona József Memorial House: 6000 Kecskemét, Katona József u. 5; tel. (76) 328-420; fax (76) 328-420; e-mail klio.ilona@ axelero.hu; f. 1894; life and work of 18th-century writer József Katona; library of 16,600 vols; Dir DÁVID MÁRIA KRISKÓNÉ.

Magyar Naiv Művészek Múzeuma (Museum of Hungarian Naive Art): 6000 Kecskemét, Gáspár A. u. 11; tel. (76) 324-767; fax (76) 481-122; e-mail naivmuzeum@ freemail.hu; f. 1976; exhibitions of works of Hungarian primitive painters and sculptors; Dir Dr BÁRT JÁNOS IGAZGATÓ; publ. *Magyar Naiv Művészek Múzeuma*.

Szórakaténusz Játékmúzeum és Műhely (Toy Museum and Workshop): 6000 Kecskemét, Gáspár A. u. 11; tel. and fax (76) 481-469; e-mail muzeumesmuhely@ szorakatenusz.hu; internet www .szorakatenusz.hu; f. 1981; colln of 25,000 items; library of 3,000 vols; Dir ÁGNES KALMÁR; publ. *Studies of the History of Toys*.

Keszthely

Balatoni Múzeum: 8360 Keszthely, Múzeum-u. 2; tel. (83) 312-351; fax (83) 312-351; e-mail info@balatonimuzeum.hu; internet www.balatonimuzeum.hu; f. 1898; prehistoric, historic and ethnographic collns relating to Lake Balaton; library of 29,000 vols; Dir Dr BÁLINT HAVASI.

Helikon Kastélymúzeum (Helikon Castle Museum): 8360 Keszthely, Kastély u. 1; tel. (83) 312-190; fax (83) 315-039; e-mail khelikon@freemail.hu; internet www .helikonkastely.hu; f. 1974; 18th-century castle built by the Festetics family; exhibitions: aristocratic lifestyle, arts of the Islamic world, Helikon library; coach museum, hunting museum and historical model railway exhibit; library of 94,000 vols; Dir Dr LÁSZLÓ CZOMA; Sec. ANNAMARIA BERNATH.

Kiskunfélegyháza

Kiskun Múzeum: 6100 Kiskunfélegyháza, Dr Holló L. u. 9; tel. (76) 461-468; fax (76) 462-542; e-mail kiskun.kiskunfelegyhaza@ museum.hu; f. 1902; ethnography; library of 20,000 vols; Curator Dr ERZSÉBET MOLNÁR.

Kiskunhalas

Thorma János Múzeum: 6400 Kiskunhalas, Köztársaság u. 2; tel. (77) 422-864; fax (77) 422-864; e-mail muzeum@halas.hu; f. 1874; ethnography, archaeology and history; library of 7,000 vols; Curator AURÉL SZAKÁL.

Kőszeg

Városi Múzeum (Municipal Museum): 9730 Kőszeg, Jurisics tér 6; tel. and fax (94) 360-156; e-mail museum.koszeg@axelerod.hu; f. 1932; collection of castle and town history; library of 9,300 vols; Dir Prof. Dr KORNÉL BAKAY.

Mátészalka

Szatmári Múzeum: 4700 Mátészalka, Kossuth-ut. 5; tel. and fax (44) 502-646; e-mail szatmari.mateszalka@museum.hu; internet www.museum.hu/mateszalka/szatmari; f. 1972; local history and ethnographic collections; Dir Dr LÁSZLÓ CSERVENYÁK.

Miskolc

Herman Ottó Múzeum: 3529 Miskolc, Görgey Artúr u. 28; tel. (46) 560-172; fax (46) 555-397; e-mail hermuz@axelero.hu; internet www.hermuz.hu; f. 1899; collections of archaeology, regional ethnography, fine arts and applied arts, natural science, minerals of Hungary, local history, literary history, history of photography; library of 44,000 vols; Dir Dr LÁSZLÓ VERES; publs *A Herman Ottó Múzeum Évkönyve* (Yearbook), *A Miskolci Herman Ottó Múzeum Közleményei* (Communications), *Documentatio Borsodiensis*, *Natura Borsodiensis*, *Néprajzi Kiadványok* (Ethnographical Studies), *Officina Musei*.

Kohászati Múzeum (Foundry Museum): 3517 Miskolc-Felsőhámor, Palota-u. 22; tel. (46) 379-375; e-mail kohmuz@kohmuz .t-online.hu; internet www.kohmuz.t-online .hu; f. 1949; history of the foundry, science and technology; archaeological foundry of the 9th to 12th centuries; technical monument from the 18th century, the Fazola foundry; Dir LÁSZLÓ PORKOLÁB.

Mohács

Kanizsan Dorottya Múzeum: 7700 Mohács, Városház u. 1; tel. (69) 311-536; e-mail kanizsai.mohacs@museum.hu; f. 1923; ethnography of the Serbs, Croats and Slavs; library of 2,300 vols; Curator JAKAB FERKOV.

Mosonmagyaróvár

Hansági Múzeum: 9200 Mosonmagyaróvár, Szent István u. 1; tel. (96) 213-834; fax (96) 212-094; e-mail hansagi.mosonmagyarovar@ museum.hu; f. 1882; regional museum; archaeology, ethnography, lapidarium, local history, paintings by János Szale, Gyurkovits colln; library of 7,216 vols; Dir KÁROLY SZENTKUTI.

Nagycenk

Széchenyi István Emlékmúzeum (Széchenyi Memorial Museum): 9485 Nagycenk, Kiscenki u. 3; tel. (99) 360-023; fax (99) 360-260; e-mail szechenyi.nagycenk@museum .hu; f. 1973; history of the Széchenyi family and life (iconography, bibliography) of 19th-century statesman Count István Széchenyi; library of 5,000 vols; Curator Dr ATTILA KÖRNYEI.

Nagykanizsa

Thury György Múzeum: 8800 Nagykanizsa, Zrínyi u. 62; tel. (93) 317-233; fax (93) 317-233; e-mail tgym@zmmi.hu; f. 1919; archaeological and ethnographical collections, local history displays, numismatics; library of 5,000 vols; Curator Dr LÁSZLÓ HORVÁTH.

Nagykőrös

Arany János Múzeum: 2751 Nagykőrös, Ceglédi-u. 19; tel. (53) 350-810; fax (53) 350-770; e-mail ajmpmi@freemail.hu; f. 1928; regional museum; archaeology, ethnography, local history, literary documents of poet J. Arany; library of 20,019 vols; Dir Dr LÁSZLÓ NOVÁK; publs *Acta Musei*, *Archivum Musei*.

Nyirbátor

Báthory István Múzeum: 4300 Nyirbátor, Károlyi-u. 15; tel. (42) 510-218; fax (42) 510-218; e-mail bathori.nyirbator@museum.hu; f. 1955; archaeology, local history and art; library of 2,900 vols; Curator PILIPKÓ ERZSÉBET.

Nyiregyháza

Jósa András Múzeum: 4400 Nyíregyháza, Benczúr tér 21, Pf. 57; tel. (42) 315-722; fax (42) 315-722; e-mail jam@jam.nyirbone.hu; internet jam.nyirbone.hu; f. 1868; collections of archaeology, ethnography and local history; fine and applied arts, numismatics; library of 20,000 vols; Dir Dr PÉTER NÉMETH; publ. *A nyíregyházi Jósa András Múzeum Évkönyve* (1 a year).

Pannonhalma

Pannonhalmi Főapátság Gyűjteménye (Abbey of Pannonhalma Collection): 9090 Pannonhalma, Vár 1; tel. (96) 570-191; fax (96) 470-011; e-mail foapatsag .pannonhalma@museum.hu; f. 1802; paintings, sculptures, applied arts in an ancient Benedictine Abbey.

Pápa

Gróf Esterházy Károly Kastély- és Tájmúzeum (Count Charles Esterházy Castle and Regional Museum): 8500 Pápa, Fő tér 1, Várkastély; 8501 Pápa, POB 208; tel. (89) 313-584; e-mail kastely.papa@museum.hu; f. 1960; ethnographical, archaeological and industrial collns from the town and environment; library of 10,000 vols; Dir Dr PÉTER LÁSZLÓ; publ. *Acta Musei Papensis* (1 a year).

Pécs

Csontváry Múzeum: 7621 Pécs, Janus Pannonius u. 11; tel. (72) 310-544; fax (72) 315-694; e-mail jpm@jpm.hu; f. 1973; administered by the Baranya County Museums' Directorate; art gallery comprising selected works by the Expressionist painter Tivadar Csontváry Kosztka; Man. GÁBOR TILLAI.

Janus Pannonius Múzeum: 7601 Pécs, POB 158; 7621 Pécs, Káptalan u. 5; tel. (72) 310-172; fax (72) 315-694; e-mail jpm@jpm .hu; f. 1904; natural sciences, archaeology, ethnography, modern Hungarian art, local history; library of 25,000 vols; Dir ZOLTÁN HUSZÁR; publ. *Dunántuli Dolgozatok* (Trans-Danubian Studies).

Modern Magyar Képtár I (Modern Hungarian Gallery I, 1890–1950): 7621 Pécs, Káptalan u. 4; tel. (72) 324-822; e-mail keptar.pecs@museum.hu; f. 1957; administered by the Baranya County Museums' Directorate; examples of the Nagybánya school (Hollósy, Ferenczy), pre-war art (Rippl-Rónai, Gulácsy), the Eight (Pór, Kernstok, Berény, Tihanyi), Activism (Nemes Lampért, Uitz, Mattis-Teutsch), the Avantgarde (Breuer, Molnár, Moholy-Nagy), artists with social sensitivity (Dési Huber, Derkovits, Goldman, Bokros Birman), the school of Rome and artists of Szentendre (Vajda, Ámos, Barcsay, Czóbel, Kmetty), the European school (Korniss, Gyarmathy, Anna Margit).

Modern Magyar Képtár II (Modern Hungarian Gallery II, 1955–2001): 7621 Pécs, Papnövelde u. 5; tel. (72) 324-822; f. 1957; administered by the Baranya County Museums' Directorate; Contemporary Colln: paintings by Barcsay, Bizse, Korniss, Lantos, Orosz.

Vasarely Múzeum: 7621 Pécs, Káptalan-u. 3; tel. (72) 324-822; fax (72) 315-694; e-mail jpm@jpm.hu; f. 1976; administered by the Baranya County Museums' Directorate; art gallery comprising works by Hungarian-born French artist Victor Vasarely; Man. GÁBOR TILLAI.

Rudabánya

Alapítvány Érc- és Ásványbányászati Múzeum (Museum of Mining of Metals and Minerals): 3733 Rudabánya, Petőfi u. 24; tel. (48) 353-151; e-mail eabmuz@axelero.hu; f. 1956; history of the industry, exhibitions; Curator BÉLA SZUROMI.

Salgótarján

Nógrádi Történeti Múzeum (Nógrád Historical Museum): 3100 Salgótarján, Múzeum tér 2, Pf. 3; tel. (32) 314-169; fax (32) 512-335; e-mail nograditmuzeum@nogradi-muzeumok .hu; internet www.museum.hu; f. 1959; social history since the 19th century, history of art, literary history, numismatics, industrial history, esp. mining; library of 16,000 vols; Dir Dr ANNA KOVÁCS; publ. *Yearbook of the Museums of Nógrád County*.

Sárospatak

Rákóczi Múzeum: 3950 Sárospatak, Szent Erzsébet u. 19; tel. (47) 311-083; fax (47) 511-135; internet www.spatak.hu; f. 1950; housed in the Castle of Sárospatak; historical, ethnographic, archaeological and applied art collections; library of 18,000 vols; Curator Dr DANKÓ KATALIN JÓSVAINÉ.

Sárvár

Nádasdy Ferenc Múzeum: 9600 Sárvár, Vár-u. 1; tel. (95) 320-158; e-mail nadasdy .sarvar@museum.hu; f. 1951; late Renaissance and Baroque Hungarian milieu reconstructed in state rooms of 16th-century castle; library of 3,900 vols; Dir ISTVÁN SÖPTEI.

Sopron

Győr-Moson-Sopron Megyei Múzeumok Igazgatósága Soproni Múzeum: 9400 Sopron, Fő tér 8; tel. and fax (99) 311-327; e-mail soproni@gymsmuzeum.hu; internet www.muzeum.sopron.hu; f. 1867; archaeology, folk art, pharmacy, medieval synagogue, local Baroque art and Storno Collns in 11 exhibition halls; library of 25,000 vols; Dir Dr IMRE TÓTH; Librarian BEATA KOLLERITS.

Központi Bányászati Múzeum (Central Mining Museum): 9400 Sopron, Templom u. 2; tel. (99) 312-667; fax (99) 338-902; e-mail info@kbm.hu; internet www.kbm.hu; f. 1957; science and technology; history of mining in the Carpathian basin since prehistoric age; Dir Dr KOVÁCSNÉ BIRCHER ERZSÉBET.

Szarvas

Tessedik Sámuel Múzeum: 5540 Szarvas, Vajda P. u. 1; tel. (66) 312-960; f. 1951; archaeology, ethnography and local history collns; Dir Dr JÓZSEF PALOV.

Szécsény

Kubinyi Ferenc Múzeum: 3170 Szécsény, Ady Endre u. 7; tel. (32) 370-143; e-mail kubinyi.szecseny@museum.hu; f. 1973; archaeology and local history; library of 8,400 vols; Curator Dr KATALIN SIMÁN.

Szeged

Móra Ferenc Múzeum: 6701 Szeged, POB 474; 6720 Szeged, Roosevelt tér 1–3; tel. (62) 549-040; fax (62) 549-061; e-mail info@mfm .u-szeged.hu; internet www.mfm.u-szeged .hu; f. 1883; archaeological, ethnographic and biological collections, history of arts and regional collections; library of 50,000 vols; spec. colln include: Sándor Bálint bequest of 5,500 vols on archaic religions and beliefs, old books of prayers and liturgies, Győző Csongor Bequest of 5,500 vols on local history; Dir Dr GABRIELLA VÖRÖS; publs *Monographia Archaeologica* (1 a year), *Studia Archaeologica* (1 a year), *Studia Ethnographica* (1 a year), *Studia Historiae Literarum et Artium* (1 a year), *Studia Historica* (1 a year), *Studia Naturalia* (1 a year).

Székesfehérvár

Szent István Király Múzeum: 8002 Székesfehérvár, Fő u. 6, P4. 78; tel. (22) 315-583; fax (22) 311-734; e-mail fmmuz@mail.iif.hu; f. 1873; prehistoric, Roman and medieval collections, anthropological collection, regional ethnography, art gallery, musical collection, numismatic collection, stones of the Basilica of King St Stephen; library of 80,000 vols; Dir GYULA FÜLÖP; publs *Alba Regia* (Scientific Almanac), *Bulletin*.

Szekszárd

Wosinsky Mór Megyei Múzeum: 7101 Szekszárd, Szent István tér 26; tel. (74) 316-222; fax (74) 316-222; e-mail wmmm@ terrasoft.hu; f. 1896; collections of folk art, archaeology, history, fine arts and applied arts; library of 11,300 vols; Dir Dr ATTILA GAÁL; publ. *Yearbook*.

Szentendre

Ferenczy Múzeum: 2001 Szentendre, Fő tér 6, pf. 49; tel. (26) 310-244; fax (26) 310-790; e-mail pmmikozmuvelodes@freemail.hu; internet www.pmmi.hu; f. 1951; paintings, drawings, sculptures and Gobelin tapestries; centre for 30 museums in Pest County; library of 24,000 vols, 210 periodicals; Dir Dr LÁSZLÓ SIMON; publ. *Studia Comitatensia* (yearbook of papers published by the Museums of Pest County).

Szabadtéri Néprajzi Múzeum (Hungarian Open-Air Museum): 2001 Szentendre, Sztaravodai u., POB 63; tel. (26) 502-500; fax (26) 502-502; e-mail sznm@sznm.hu; internet www.skanzen.hu; f. 1967; vernacular architecture and furniture; library of 50,000 vols; archive of 110,000 photographs, 20,000 ethnographical, historical, architectural documents, films, maps, drawings, etc.; Dir Dr MIKLÓS CSERI; publs *Ház és Ember* (1 a year), *Téka* (4 a year).

Szentes

Koszta József Múzeum: 6600 Szentes, Szechenyi Liget 1; tel. (63) 313-352; fax (63) 313-352; e-mail muzeum@szentesinfo.hu; f. 1894; archaeological and ethnographical collection and paintings by Koszta; Dir JÁNOS SZABÓ.

Szigetvár

Zrínyi Miklós Vármúzeum: 7900 Szigetvár, Vár u. 1; tel. (73) 311-442; f. 1917; local history colln, relating particularly to the period of Turkish occupation (16th to 17th centuries).

Szolnok

Damjanich János Múzeum: 5000 Szolnok, Templom u. 2; tel. (56) 513-640; fax (56) 341-204; e-mail titkarsag@djm.hu; internet www .djm.hu; f. 1933; archaeology, ethnography, palaeontology, fine arts, applied art and local history collns; library of 50,000 vols; Dir Dr RÓBERT KERTÉSZ; publ. *Tisicum* (1 a year).

Szombathely

Savaria Múzeum: 9701 Szombathely, Kisfaludy Sándor u. 9; tel. (94) 312-554; fax (94) 313-736; e-mail info@savariamuseum.hu; internet www.savariamuseum.hu; f. 1872; natural history, archaeology, local cultural history, ethnography; library of 32,000 vols; Dir Dr SÁNDOR HORVÁTH; publs *Praenorica—Folia Historico-Naturalia* (irregular), *Savaria* (Journal, 1 a year).

Tác

Gorsium Szabadtéri Múzeum (Gorsium Open-Air Museum): 8121 Tác, Fövenypuszta Ady E. u. 56; tel. (22) 362-443; e-mail lak5706@mail.iif.hu; f. 1963; excavations of a Roman city, the ruins showing the original shape; Dir Prof. Dr JENŐ FITZ.

Tata

Kuny Domokos Megyei Múzeum: 2892 Tata, Néppark, Kiskastély, POB 224; tel. (34) 487-888; fax (34) 487-888; e-mail muzeum@ kunymuzeum.hu; internet www .kunymuzeum.hu; f. 1954; history, archaeology, ethnology, art, palaeobotany; library of 27,000 vols; Dir Dr ÉVA MÁRIA FÜLÖP.

Vác

Tragor Ignác Múzeum: 2600 Vác, Zrínyi u. 41A; tel. (27) 500-750; fax (27) 500-758; e-mail muzeum@dunaweb.hu; internet www .muzeum.vac.hu; f. 1895; archaeology, ethnography, local history and fine arts exhibits; library of 10,565 vols, 4,760 periodicals and newsletters; Dir KŐVÁRI KLÁRA; publ. *Váci Könyvek* (Bulletin).

Várpalota

Magyar Vegyészeti Múzeum (Hungarian Chemical Museum): 8100 Várpalota, Szabadság tér 1; tel. (88) 575-670; fax (88) 471-702; e-mail vegymuz@vegyeszetimuzeum.hu; internet www.vegyeszetimuzeum.hu; f. 1963; history of the chemical industry; library of 18,618 vols; Dir ISTVÁN PRÓDER.

Vértesszőllős

Magyar Nemzeti Múzeum Vértesszőllősi Bemutatóhelye: 2837 Vértesszőllős; tel. (1) 327-7744; e-mail hnm@hnm.hu; internet www.hnm.hu; f. 1975; permanent open-air exhibition; dwelling-place and remains of early man; part of Archaeology Dept of Nat. Museum; Curator Dr Viola Dobosi.

Veszprém

Laczkó Dezső Múzeum: 8201 Veszprém, Erzsébet sétány 1; tel. (88) 564-310; fax (88) 426-081; e-mail titkar@vmmuzeum.hu; internet www.c3.hu/~vmmuzeum; f. 1903; ethnographic, archaeological, historical, fine and industrial arts, history of literature, numismatic exhibits from Veszprém County; library of 36,000 vols; Dir Dr Zsuzsa Fodor; publs *Publicationes Museorum Comitatus Vesprimiensis* (Communications of the Museums of Veszprém County), *Veszprém Megyei Múzeumok Közleményei*.

Visegrád

Mátyás Király Múzeum (King Matthias Museum): 2025 Visegrád, Fő u. 23–25; tel. (26) 398-026; fax (26) 398-252; f. 1933; managed by Magyar Nemzeti Múzeum of Budapest; 13th-century upper and lower castle with Roman and medieval archaeological remains; partially restored 15th-century royal palace; library of 10,000 vols; Dir Mátyás Szőke.

Zalaegerszeg

Göcseji Falumúzeum: 8900 Zalaegerszeg, Falumúzeum u. 18., POB 176; tel. (92) 703-295; fax (92) 511-972; e-mail muzeum@zmmi .hu; internet www.zmmi.hu; f. 1968; collections of regional history, archaeology, ethnography, paintings and sculpture; exhibition of sculptures by Zs. Kisfaludi-Strobl; exhibition on the history of County Zala; library of 20,658 vols; Dir Dr László Vándor; publ. *Zalai Múzeum* (1 a year).

Magyar Olajipari Múzeum (Museum of the Hungarian Petroleum Industry): 8900 Zalaegerszeg, Wlassics Gyula. u. 13; tel. (92) 313-632; fax (92) 311-081; e-mail moim@ olajmuzeum.hu; internet www.olajmuzeum .hu; f. 1969; exhibitions of the history of the professional and technical devt of the oil industry; equipment, documents, photographs, etc.; library of 9,000 vols; Dir János Tóth.

Zirc

Bakonyi Természettudományi Múzeum (Bakony Mountains Natural History Museum): 8420 Zirc, Rákóczi tér 3–5; tel. (88) 575-300; fax (88) 575-301; e-mail btmz@ bakonymuseum.koznet.hu; internet www .bakonymuseum.koznet.hu; f. 1972; natural history exhibits from Bakony Mountains, minerals from the Carpathian Basin; library of 25,000 vols, incl. 17,000 journals; Curator Ágota Kasper; publs *A Bakony természettudományi kutatásának eredményei* (Results of Research into the Natural History of Bakony, 1 a year), *Folia Musei Historico-naturalis Bakonyiensis* (A Bakonyi Természettudományi Múzeum Közleményei, Communications of the Bakony Mountains Natural History Museum, 1 a year).

State Universities

BUDAPESTI CORVINUS EGYETEM
(Corvinus University of Budapest)

1093 Budapest, Fövám tér 8
Telephone: (1) 482-5000
Fax: (1) 482-5019

E-mail: intoffice@uni-corvinus.hu
Internet: www.uni-corvinus.hu

Founded 1853
State control
Languages of instruction: Hungarian, English, French, German
Academic year: September to June

Rector: Prof. Dr Tamás Mészáros
Vice-Rector for Educational Policy: Prof. Dr Magdolna
Vice-Rector for Research and Int. Affairs: Prof. Dr Sándor Kerekes
Vice-Rector for Devt and Communication: Prof. Dr Imre Jámbor
Dir-Gen. for Central Library: István György
Dir-Gen. for Finance: Margit Gulyásné Túróczi (acting)
Library of 500,000
Number of teachers: 859
Number of students: 16,815
Publications: *Applied Ecology and Environmental Research* (2 a year), *Társadalom és Gazdaság* (Society and Economy, in Hungarian, 2 a year; in English, 3 a year)

DEANS

Faculty of Business Administration: Prof. Ágnes Hofmeister
Faculty of Economics.: László Trautmann
Faculty of Food Science: Prof. Gyula Vatai
Faculty of Horticultural Science: Prof. Károly Hrotkó
Faculty of Landscape Architecture: Prof. Attila Csemez
Faculty of Public Administration.: Prof. Miklós Imre
Faculty of Social Sciences: Prof. Zsolt Rostoványi

PROFESSORS

Abaffy, J., Computer Science
Abel, I., Macroeconomics
Agh, A., Politics
Angyal, Á., Management and Organization
Balaton, K., Management and Organization
Balázs, P., World Economics
Bánfi, T., Finance
Baricz, R., Accountancy
Bekker, Z., Economic Theory
Berács, J., Marketing
Bernáth, J., Herb and Aroma Products
Biacs, P., Microbiology
Blaho, A., World Economics
Bod, P., Economic Policy
Bradean, N., International Relations
Chikán, A., Logistics
Csaba, L., Comparative Economics
Csáki, C., Agricultural Economics
Csemez, A., Landscape Planning and Development
Cser, L., Computer Science
Csima, P., Landscape Protection
Csizmadia, S., Political Science
Deák, D., Economic Law
Deák, I., Computer Science
Dobák, M., Management and Organization
Egedy, G., Social Theory
Felföldí, J., Physics and Control
Fertő, I., Agricultural Economics
Fodor, P., Applied Chemistry
Forgó, F., Operations Research
Füstös, L., Environmental Economics
Gábor, I., Human Resources
Gál, P., World Economics
Galasi, P., Human Resources
Gálik, M., Media Economics
Gedeon, P., Comparative Economics
Görög, M., Strategy and Project Management
Hadas, M., Sociology
Hajdu, I., Food Economy
Hámori, B., Comparative Economics
Hofmeister, A., Marketing
Horányi, Ö., Communication
Hrotkó, K., Pomology

Ilonszki, G., Political Science
Iványi, A., Strategy and Project Management
Jámbor, I., Landscape Technology and Garden Techniques
Jámborné Benczúr, E., Floriculture and Dendrology
Jenei, G., Public Administration
Kállay, M., Oenology
Kardosné Kaponyi, E., International Relations
Kerekes, S., Environmental Management
Kiss, L., International Relations
Koncz, K., Human Resources
Kosáry, J., Applied Chemistry
Kovács, E., Operations Research
Kuczi, T., Sociology
Ladányi, J., Sociology
Lánczi, A., Political Science
Láng, Z., Technology
Lengyel, G., Sociology
Lőrinc, A., International Relations
Lukács, N., Plant Physiology
Maráz, A., Microbiology
Máthé, O., Jurisprudence
Mészáros, T., Strategy and Project Management
Mezősné Szilágyi, K., Garden and Open Space Design
Miszlivetz, F., Global and European Integration
Móczár, J., Mathematical Economics
Moksony, F., Sociology
Nováky, E., Future Studies
Palkovics, L., Plant Pathology
Pedryc, A., Genetics and Plant Breeding
Rácz, L., Jurisprudence
Radics, L., Ecology and Sustainable Economic Systems
Rimóczi, I., Botanics
Rostoványi, Z., International Relations
Sárközy, T., Business Law
Schmidt, G., Floriculture and Dendrology
Schneller, I., Urban Planning
Stefanovitsné Bányai, É., Applied Chemistry
Surányi, S., Finance
Szabó, K., Comparative Economics
Szabó S., A., Food Chemistry
Szántó, Z., Sociology
Szávai, F., International Relations
Száz, J., Investment and Corporate Finance
Takács, P., Jurisprudence
Tallós, P., Mathematics
Tamás, A., Jurisprudence
Tari, E., Management and Strategy
Temesi, J., Operations Research
Terbe, I., Vegetable and Mushroom growing
Török, G., Private Law
Tóth, M., Pomology
Újvári, M., Sociology
Vastag, G., Computer Science
Vatai, G., Food Engineering
Vecsenyi, J., Development of Enterprises
Végvári, G., Pomology
Virág, M., Corporate Finance
Vita, L., Statistics
Zalai, E., Econometrics
Zámboriné Németh, É., Medicinal and Aromatic Plants
Zsolnai, L., Business Ethics

BUDAPESTI MŰSZAKI ÉS GAZDASÁGTUDOMÁNYI EGYETEM
(Budapest University of Technology and Economics)

1111 Budapest, Műegyetem rkp. 3
Telephone: (1) 463-1111
Fax: (1) 463-1110
E-mail: rektor@mail.bme.hu
Internet: www.bme.hu

Founded 1782 as Institutum Geometricum Hydrotechnicum and reorganized as Hungarian Palatine Joseph Technical Univ. in 1871. Építőipari és Közlekedési Műszaki

Egyetem (Technical Univ. of Building and Transport Engineering) was incorporated with the univ. in 1967. Present name 2000

State control

Languages of instruction: Hungarian, English, German, French, Russian

Academic year: September to June

Rector: Prof. Dr KÁROLY MOLNÁR

Vice-Rectors: Prof. Dr JÁNOS KÖVESI, Dr GYULA SALLAI, Dr MIKLÓS ZRÍNYI

Librarian: ISTVÁNNÉ FONYÓ

Number of teachers: 1,190

Number of students: 22,567

Publication: *A Budapesti Műszaki Egyetem Évkönyve* (1 a year)

DEANS

Faculty of Architecture: Dr GÁBOR BECKER

Faculty of Chemical Technology and Biotechnology: Dr GYÖRGY POKOL

Faculty of Civil Engineering: Dr ANTAL LOVAS

Faculty of Economic and Social Sciences: Dr JÁNOS KÖVESI

Faculty of Electrical Engineering and Informatics: Dr LÁSZLÓ VAJTA

Faculty of Mechanical Engineering: Dr GÁBOR STÉPÁN

Faculty of Natural Sciences: Dr PÉTER MOSON

Faculty of Transportation Engineering: Dr BÉLA KULCSÁR

PROFESSORS

Faculty of Architecture (tel. (1) 463-3521; fax (1) 463-3520; e-mail dekanihivatal@eszk.bme.hu; internet www.epitesz.bme.hu):

BALOGH, B., Design
BITÓ, J., Housing Design
CSÁGOLY, F., Design of Public Buildings
DOMOKOS, G., Structural Mechanics
ISTVÁNFI, GY., History of Architecture
KASZÁS, K., Design of Public Buildings
KLAFSZKY, E., Building Management and Organization
LÁZÁR, A., Industrial and Agricultural Architecture
MAJOROS, A., Sanitary Engineering
MEGGYESI, T., Urban Studies
NAGY, L., Sanitary Engineering
PETRÓ, B., Building Construction
TÖRÖK, F., Design of Public Buildings
VÖRÖS, F., Building Construction
ZÖLD, A., Sanitary Engineering

Faculty of Chemical Technology and Biotechnology (tel. (1) 463-3571; fax (1) 463-3570; e-mail dekan@mail.bme.hu; internet www.ch.bme.hu):

BITTER, I., Organic Chemical Technology
BORSA, J., Plastics and Rubber Industries
FAIGL, F., Organic Chemical Technology
FEKETE, J., General and Analytical Chemistry
FONYÓ, ZS., Chemical Unit Operations
GÁL, S., General and Analytical Chemistry
GROFCSIK, A., Physical Chemistry
HARGITTAI, I., General and Analytical Chemistry
HENCSEI, P., Inorganic Chemistry
HORVAI, GY., Chemical Informatics
KALAUS, GY., Organic Chemistry
KEGLEVICH, GY., Organic Chemical Technology
KEMÉNY, S., Chemical Unit Operations
KUBINYI, M., Physical Chemistry
MIHÁLTZ, P., Chemical Unit Operations
NOVÁK, B., Agricultural Chemical Technology
NOVÁK, L., Organic Chemistry
NYITRAI, J., Organic Chemistry
NYULÁSZI, L., Inorganic Chemistry
ÖRSI, F., Biochemistry and Food Technology

POKOL, GY., General and Analytical Chemistry
PUKÁNSZKY, B., Plastics and Rubber Industries
RÉFFY, J., Inorganic Chemistry
SALGÓ, A., Biochemistry and Food Technology
SEVELLA, B., Agricultural Chemical Technology
SZÉCHY, G., Chemical Technology
SZEPESVÁRI TOTH, K., General and Analytical Chemistry
TŐKE, L., Organic Chemical Technology
TUNGLER, A., Chemical Technology
VESZPRÉMI, T., Inorganic Chemistry
ZRINYI, M., Physical Chemistry

Faculty of Civil Engineering (tel. (1) 463-3531; fax (1) 463-3530; e-mail titkarsag@epito.bme.hu; internet www.epito.bme.hu/hivatal):

ADAM, J., Geodesy and Surveying
BALÁZS, GY., Building Materials and Engineering Geology
BOJTÁR, I., Structural Mechanics
DETREKŐI, Á., Photogrammetry and Geoinformatics
FARKAS, GY., Reinforced Concrete Structures
FARKAS, J., Geotechnics
FÍ, I., Road and Railway Engineering
GÁLOS, M., Building Materials and Engineering Geology
GÁSPÁR, ZS., Structural Mechanics
HEGEDŰS, I., Reinforced Concrete Structures
IJJAS, I., Hydraulic and Water Resources Engineering
IVÁNYI, M., Steel Structures
KISS PAPP, L., Geodesy and Surveying
KURUTZ KOVÁCS, M., Structural Mechanics
MEGYERI, J., Road and Railway Engineering
PATONAI, D., Building Construction
SÁRKÖZY, F., Geodesy and Surveying
SOMLYODY, L., Sanitary and Environmental Engineering
SZALAY, K., Reinforced Concrete Structures
SZÉLL, M., Building Construction
TARNAI, T., Structural Mechanics

Faculty of Economic and Social Sciences (tel. (1) 463-3591; fax (1) 463-3590; e-mail gtk-dekani@gtdh.bme.hu; internet www.gtk.bme.hu):

ANTALOVITS, M., Ergonomics and Psychology
BÁNDI, GY., Environmental Economics and Law
BENEDEK, A., Technical Education
BISZTERSZKY, E., Technical Education
DINYA, L., Industrial Management and Business Economics
FARKAS, J., Sociology
FEHÉR, M., Philosophy and History of Science
HORÁNYI, Ö., Sociology
HRONSZKY, I., Innovation Studies and History of Technology
KERÉKGYÁRTÓ, GY., Economics
KÖVESI, J., Industrial Business and Management
MARGITAY, T., Philosophy and History of Science
PLÉH, CS., Information Management
SÁRKÖZY, T., Law and Business Organization
S. NAGY, K., Sociology
SZLÁVIK, J., Environmental Economics and Technical Law
TÖRÖK, A., Industrial Business and Management
VERESS, J., Economic and Business Policy
VINCZE, P., Physical Education

Faculty of Electrical Engineering and Informatics (1111 Budapest, Egry F. u. 18; tel. (1) 463-3581; fax (1) 463-3580; e-mail vikdhvez@vik-dh.bme.hu; internet www.vik.bme.hu):

ARATÓ, P., Process Control
BENYÓ, Z., Process Control
BERTA, I., High-Voltage Engineering
FRIGYES, I., Microwave Telecommunications
GORDOS, G., Telecommunications and Telematics
GYŐRFI, L., Mathematics
HALÁSZ, S., Electrical Machines
ILLYEFALVI-VITÉZ, ZS., Electronic Technology
KEVICZKY, L., Automation
KÓCZY, T. L., Telecommunications and Telematics
KOLLÁR, I., Measurement and Instrument Engineering
LANTOS, B., Process Control
LEVENDOVSZKY, J., Telecommunications
MOJZES, I., Electronic Technology
PAPP, L., Telecommunications
PÉCELI, G., Measurement and Instrument Engineering
RECSKI, A., Mathematics
RÓNYAI, L., Mathematics
ROSKA, T., Measurement and Instrument Engineering
SALLAI, GY., Telecommunications and Telematics
SCHMIDT, I., Electrical Machines
SELÉNYI, E., Measurement and Instrument Engineering
SZABÓ, CS., Telecommunications
SZÉKELY, V., Electronic Devices
SZIRMAY-KALOS, L., Process Control
TARNAY, K., Electronic Devices
VAJDA, I., Telecommunications
VAJK, I., Automation
VARJU, GY., Electric Power Plants and Networks
VESZELY, GY., Automation
ZOMBORY, L., Microwave Telecommunications

Faculty of Mechanical Engineering (tel. (1) 463-3541; fax (1) 463-3540; e-mail gepeszd@mail.bme.hu; internet www.gepesz.bme.hu):

ARTINGER, I., Mechanical Technology
BÉDA, GY., Technical Mechanics
BÜKI, G., Energetics
CZVIKOVSZKY, T., Polymer Engineering and Textile Technology
GARBAI, L., Sanitary Engineering
GINSZTLER, J., Electrical Materials Technology
HALÁSZ, G., Hydraulic Machines
HALMAI, A., Precision Mechanics—Optics
HORVÁTH, M., Machine Production
JÓRI, J. I., Agricultural Machine Design
KOVÁCS, L., Hydraulic Machines
KOZMA, M., Machine Elements
LAJOS, T., Fluid Mechanics
MEGGYES, A., Heat Engines
MOLNÁR, K., Process Engineering
PARTI, M., Fluid Mechanics
PENNINGER, A., Heat Engines
REMÉNYI, K., Energetics
STÉPÁN, G., Technical Mechanics
VÁRADI, K., Agricultural Machine Design
VARGA, L., Machine Elements
ZIAJA, GY., Mechanical Technology

Faculty of Natural Sciences (tel. (1) 463-3561; fax (1) 463-3560; e-mail ttk-dekani@ttdh.bme.hu; internet www.ttk.bme.hu):

CSISZÁR, I., Stochastics
CSOM, GY., Nuclear Technology
DEÁK, P., Atomic Physics
FRITZ, J., Differential Equations
GYULAI, J., Experimental Physics
JÁNOSSY, A., Experimental Physics
KERTÉSZ, J., Physics

MIHÁLY, GY., Quantum Theory
MOLNÁR, E., Geometry
NAGY, B., Analysis
NOSZTICZIUS, Z., Chemical Physics
PETZ, D., Analysis
RICHTER, P., Atomic Physics
RÓNYAI, L., Algebra
SCHMIDT, T., Algebra
SZÁSZ, D., Stochastics
SZATMÁRY, Z., Nuclear Technology
TÓTH, B., Stochastics
VERHÁS, J., Chemical Physics
VIROSZTEK, A., Quantum Theory
ZAWADOWSKI, A., Physics

Faculty of Transportation Engineering (1111 Budapest, Bertalan L. u. 2; tel. (1) 463-3551; fax (1) 463-3550; e-mail felv@kma.bme.hu; internet www.kozlek.bme.hu):

BOKOR, J., Transport Automatics
ELEÖD, A., Machine Elements
KÖVES GILICZE, É., Transport Operation
KULCSÁR, B., Building and Materials-Handling Machines
MÁRIALIGETI, J., Machine Elements
PALKOVICS, L., Motor Vehicles
ROHÁCS, J., Aircraft and Ships
TAKÁCS, J., Machine Production Technology
TÁNCZOS, LNÉ., Transport Economics
TARNAI, G., Transport Automatics
VÁRLAKI, P., Motor Vehicles
ZOBORY, I., Railway Vehicles

Centre for Learning Innovation and Adult Learning (1111 Budapest, Egry J. u. 1; tel. (1) 463-3866; fax (1) 463-2561; e-mail info@edu-inno.bme.hu; internet www.bme-tk.bme.hu):

SZŰCS, A.

Institute for Continuing Engineering Education (1111 Budapest, Műegyetem rkp. 9; tel. (1) 463-2471; fax (1) 463-2470; e-mail info@mti.bme.hu; internet www.mti.bme.hu):

GINSZTLER, J.

International Education Centre (1111 Budapest, Bertalan L. u. 2; tel. (1) 463-2461; fax (1) 463-2460; e-mail admission@tanok.bme.hu; internet www.tanok.bme.hu):

MÉSZÁROS, P.

DEBRECENI EGYETEM
(University of Debrecen)

4032 Debrecen, Egyetem tér 1,
Telephone: (52) 412-060
Fax: (52) 416-490
E-mail: rector@admin.unideb.hu
Internet: www.unideb.hu

Founded 1538, became Kossuth Lajos Tudományegyetem (Lajos Kossuth Univ.) 1912; present name 2000 upon integration with Debreceni Agrártudományi Egyetem (Debrecen Univ. of Agricultural Sciences), Debreceni Orvostudományi Egyetem (Univ. Medical School of Debrecen) and Wargha István Pedagógiai Főiskola (István Wargha College of Education)

State control
Languages of instruction: Hungarian, English
Academic year: September to June
Rector: Prof. Dr ISTVÁN FÁBIÁN
Vice-Rector for Academic Affairs: Prof. Dr ZSOLT PÁLES
Vice-Rector for Educational Affairs: Prof. Dr ANDRÁS JÁVOR
Vice-Rector for Strategic Affairs: Prof. Dr LAJOS FÜLÖP
Registrar: Dr MÓNIKA RŐFI
Dir of Finance: ZOLTÁN MAG
Dir of Human Resources Management: Dr NOÉMI SIPOSNÉ BÍRÓ
Dir of the Univ. and Nat. Library: Dr MÁRTA VIRÁGOS

Library of 6,000,000 vols
Number of teachers: 1,500
Number of students: 32,000

Publications: *Acta Andragogiae* (1 a year), *Acta Classica* (1 a year), *Acta Debrecina* (1 a year), *Acta geographica ac geologica et meteorologica Debrecina* (1 a year), *Acta Neerlandica* (1 a year), *Acta pericemonologica rerum ambientum Debrecina* (irregular), *Acta Physica et Chimica* (1 a year), *A Debreceni Egyetem évkönyve* (1 a year), *A Debreceni Egyetem Magyar Nyelvtudományi Intézetének kiadványai* (1 a year), *Agrártudományi közlemények* (irregular), *Collectio iuridica Universitatis Debreceniensis* (irregular), *Competitio* (4 a year), *Debreceni szemle* (4 a year), *Ethnica* (irregular), *English Programme Bulletin Dentistry* (1 a year), *English Programme Bulletin Faculty of Medicine* (1 a year), *Ethnographica Folcloristica Carpatica* (1 a year), *Folia Uralica Debreceniensia* (1 a year), *Gond* (4 a year), *Hungarian Journal of English and American Studies* (2 a year), *Italianistica Debreceniensis* (1 a year), *Journal of Agricultural Sciences* (irregular), *Kitaibelia* (2 a year), *Könyv és Könyvtár* (1 a year), *Magyar Nyelvjárások* (1 a year), *Módszerek és eljárások* (1 a year), *Okortudományi Értesítő* (1 a year), *Posztbizánci Közlemények* (every 2 years), *Publ. Mathematicae* (2 a year), *Sprachteorie und Germanistische Linguistik* (2 a year), *Studia Litteraria* (1 a year), *Studia Romanica* (linguistics, 1 a year), *Studies in Linguistics* (1 a year), *Teaching Mathematics and Computer Science* (2 a year), *Történeti Tanulmányok* (irregular)

DEANS

Faculty of Agriculture and Food Sciences and Environmental Sciences: Dr JÁNOS KÁTAI
Faculty of Applied Economics and Rural Development: Dr ANDRÁS NÁBRÁDI
Faculty of Arts: Dr KLÁRA PAPP
Faculty of Child and Adult Education: Dr ÉVA BAKOSI
Faculty of Dentistry: Dr CSABA HEGEDÜS
Faculty of Economics and Business Administration: Dr JÁNOS KORMOS
Faculty of Engineering: Dr EDIT SZŰCS
Faculty of Health: Dr GERGELY FÁBIÁN
Faculty of Informatics: Dr GYÖRGY TERDIK
Faculty of Law: Dr JÓZSEF SZABADFALVI
Faculty of Medicine: Dr LÁSZLÓ CSERNOCH
Faculty of Music: Dr MIHÁLY DUFFEK
Faculty of Pharmacy: Dr MIKLÓS VECSERNYÉS
Faculty of Public Health: Dr RÓZA ÁDÁNY
Faculty of Science and Technology: Dr KORNÉL SAILER

DIRECTORS

Centre for External Relations: GÁBOR TURI (Dir-Gen.)
Div. of Communication: Dr ÁDÁM SZÖŐR (Head)
Electronic Admin. System Management: IBOLYA TŐZSÉRNÉ GÁLL
Mental Health: ANDRÁS BERÉNYI
Office of Academic Affairs: Dr VILMA AGÓCSNÉ ÁDÁM
Scientific Directorate: Dr ZSOLT VARGA
Student Relations: PÉTER PILISHEGYI
Student Union: PÉTER KÖRÖSPARTI
Technology Transfer Office: JUDIT BALOGH

PROFESSORS

Faculty of Agriculture and Food Sciences and Environmental Sciences (4032 Debrecen, POB 36; tel. (52) 508-412; fax (52) 486-292):

BARDÓCZ, Z.
BLASKÓ, L.
CSAPÓ, J.
FÁRI, M.
GONDA, I.

GYŐRI, Z., Food Processing and Quality Control
JÁVOR, A.
KÁTAI, J., Soil Science and Microbiology
KOVÁCS, A.
MIHÓK, S., Animal Husbandry, Breeding and Nutrition
NAGY, J., Land Cultivation
PEPÓ, PÁL, Genetics and Plant Breeding
PEPÓ, PÉTER, Crop Production and Applied Ecology
SINÓROS SZABÓ, B., Land Cultivation
TAMÁS, J.

Faculty of Applied Economics and Rural Development (4015 Debrecen, POB 36; tel. (52) 508-304; fax (52) 413-385; e-mail csapone@helios.date.hu):

ERTSEY, I., Economic Analysis and Statistics
LAZÁNYI, J., Rural Development
NÁBRÁDI, A., Farm Business Management
NAGY, G., Rural Development
NEMESSÁLYI, ZS., Farm Business Management
REKE, B.
SZABÓ, G., Agricultural and General Economics
SZABÓ, Z.

Faculty of Arts (4010 Debrecen, POB 38; tel. (52) 316-210; fax (52) 412-336; e-mail nemesne@tigris.klte.hu):

ABÁDI-NAGY, Z., North American Studies
AGYAGÁSI, K.
BARTA, J., Medieval and Early Modern World History
BARTHA, E., Ethnography
BITSKEY, I., Old Hungarian Literature
CZIEGLER, I., General Psychology
DEBRECZENI, A.
DOBOS, I.
GÖRÖMBEI, A., Modern Hungarian Language
HAJNÁDY, Z.
HUNYADI, L., Applied Linguistics
IMRE, L., 19th-century Hungarian Literature
IMRE, M.
KERTÉSZ, A., German Linguistics
KLEIN, S., Psychology
NÉMETH, GY., Ancient History
NOVÁK RÓZSA, E., History of Philosophy
PAPP, I.
SOLYMOSI, L., History
SZABÓ, L., Ethnography
VARGA, P.
VIRÁGOS, ZS., North American Studies

Faculty of Child and Adult Education (4220 Hajdúböszörmény, Désány I. u. 1–9; tel. (52) 229-433; fax (52) 229-559):

BÁLINT, P.
KOVÁCSNÉ, E. B.
VARGA, G.

Faculty of Dentistry (4012 Debrecen, POB 13; tel. (52) 413-545; fax (52) 342-224; e-mail angyal@fogaszat.dote.hu):

MAJOR, P.
PAP, G.
PETH, A.
STOYAN, G.
SZTRIK, J.
TERDIK, G.
VÉGH, J.
VERTSE, T.

Faculty of Economics and Business Administration (4010 Debrecen, POB 82; tel. (52) 416-580; fax (52) 419-728; e-mail mura@tigris.klte.hu):

CSABA, L., Economics
KORMOS, J.
LOSONCZI, L.
MAKÓ, C.
POLÓNYI, I., Management and Marketing

Faculty of Engineering (4011 Debrecen, POB 40; tel. (52) 417-979; fax (52) 415-155; e-mail kati@infosrv.tech.klte.hu):

CSANÁDY, G.
FERNEZELYI, S.
GULYÁS, L.
HAJDU, M.
HALÁSZ, G.
HORVÁTH, R., Chemical Engineering
JOLÁNKAI, G.
KALMÁR, F.
KOCSIS, I.
KŐSZEGHY, A., Settlement Engineering
KOVÁCS, I.
KULCSÁR, A., Construction Industry
MAJOR, J.
POKRÁDI, L., General Machinery
TELEKES, G.
TIBA, ZS., General Machinery
TÓTH, L.
VARGA, S. E.

Faculty of Health (4400 Nyíregyháza, Sóstói u. 2; tel. (42) 404-403; fax (42) 408-656; e-mail sztunde@creative.doteefk.hu):

CSERI, J.
FÁBIÁN, G.
GÓTH, L., Labour Analysis and Clinical Diagnostics
HAJNAL, B.
KALAPOS, I., Preventive Medicine for District Nurses
LUKÁCSKÓ, ZS., Social Work
PUNYICZKI, M.

Faculty of Informatics (4010 Debrecen, POB 12; tel. (52) 512-900; fax (52) 416-857):

DÖMÖSI, P., Computer Science
PAP, G., Applied Mathematics and Probability Theory
SZTRIK, J., Informatics Systems and Networks
TERDIK, G., Information Technology

Faculty of Law (4010 Debrecen, POB 81; tel. (52) 438-033; fax (52) 446-919; e-mail volosine@delfin.klte.hu; internet www.law.klte.hu):

DÉNES, I. Z., Social Sciences
FARKAS, A.
HORVÁTH M., T.
SZABADFALVI, J., Philosophy and Sociology of Law
SZABÓ, B., History of Law
VÁRNAY, E.

Faculty of Medicine (4012 Debrecen, POB 15; tel. (52) 410-006; fax (52) 410-006; e-mail mfux@jaguar.dote.hu):

ANTAL, M., Anatomy, Histology and Embryology
BAKÓ, GY., Internal Medicine
BALLA, GY., Neonatology
BALLA, J.
BERTA, A., Ophthalmology
BODA, Z., Internal Medicine
BODOLAY, E.
BOGNÁR, L.
BORSOS, A., Obstetrics and Gynaecology
CSERNOCH, L.
CSIBA, L., Neurology
DAMJANOVICH, S., Biophysics and Cell Biology
DOMBRÁDI, V., Medical Chemistry
ÉDES, I., Cardiology
ERDŐDI, F.
FEKETE, I.
FEKETE, K.
FÉSÜS, L., Biochemistry and Molecular Biology
FÜLESDI, B.
GALUSKA, L.
GÁSPÁR, R., Biophysics and Cell Biology
GERGELY, L., Medical Microbiology
GERGELY, P., Medical Chemistry
GÓTH, J.-P.
HERNÁDI, Z., Obstetrics and Gynaecology

HUNYADI, J., Dermatology and Venereology
KAPPELMAYER, J.
KISS, A.
KISS, C.
KOVÁCS, L., Physiology
KOVÁCS, P.
LUKÁCS, G., Surgery
MARÓDI, L., Paediatrics
MATESZ, K., Anatomy, Histology and Embryology
MÁTYUS, L.
MIKÓ, I.
MOLNÁR, P.
MUSZBEK, L., Clinical Biochemistry and Molecular Pathology
NAGY, E.
NAGY, L.
NÁNÁSI, P., Physiology
NEMES, Z., Pathology
OLÁH, E., Paediatrics
PARAGH, GY., Internal Medicine
RAJNAVÖLGYI, S., Immunology
REMENYIK, E.
SÁPY, P., Surgery
SIPKA, S., Internal Medicine
SZABÓ, B.
SZABÓ, G., Biophysics and Cell Biology
SZÁNTÓ, J.
SZEKANECZ, Z.
SZIKLAI, I., Otolaryngology
SZILVÁSSY, Z., Pharmacology
SZÖLLŐSI, J., Biophysics and Cell Biology
SZONDY, Z.
SZŰCS, G., Physiology
TÓTH, CS., Urology
TÓTH, Z., Obstetrics and Gynaecology
TŐZSÉR, J.
TRÓN, L., Positron Emission Tomography Centre
UDVARDY, M., Internal Medicine
VARGA, S., Central Service Laboratory
VIRÁG, L.
ZEHER, M., Internal Medicine

Faculty of Music (4032 Debrecen, Egyetem tér 2; tel. (52) 319-466; fax (52) 411-226):

DUFFEK, M.
KAMMERER, A.
KARASSZON, D.
MATUZ, I.
MOHAY, M.
MOHOS NAGY, E.
NEMES, F.
SZABÓ, J.

Faculty of Pharmacy (4012 Debrecen, Nagyerdei krt. 98; tel. and fax (52) 453-586; e-mail tosaki@king.pharmacol.dote.hu):

BLASKÓ, G.
GUNDA, T.
HALMOS, G.
HERCZEGH, P.
TÓSAKI, A., Pharmacological Effects

Faculty of Public Health (4028 Debrecen, Kassai u. 26/B; tel. (52) 460-194; fax (52) 460-195; e-mail bardos@jaguar.dote.hu):

ÁDÁNY, R., Hygiene and Epidemiology
BALÁZS, M.
ILYÉS, I.
MOLNÁR, P.

Faculty of Science and Technology (4010 Debrecen, POB 18; tel. (52) 316-012; fax (52) 533-677; e-mail labalogh@kltesrv.klte.hu):

ANTUS, S.
BÁNYAI, I.
BATTA, B.
BAZSA, G.
BEKE, D.
ERDŐDINÉ, K.
FÁBIÁN, I.
FARKAS, E.
GAÁL, I.
GÁSPÁR, V.
GYŐRY, K.
JOÓ, F.

JOÓ, P.
KERÉNYI, A.
LÓKI, J.
MAKSA, G.
MOLNÁR, L.
NAGY, A.
NAGY, P.
PÁLES, Z.
PÁLINKÁS, J.
PATONAY, T.
POSTA, J.
RÁBAI, G.
SAILER, K.
SIPICZKI, M.
SOMSÁK, L.
SÓVÁGÓ, I.
SÜLI-ZAKAR, I.
SZÉKELYHIDI, L.
TÓTH, I.
TÓTHMÉRÉSZ, B.
TRÓCSÁNYI, Z.
VARGA, Z.
VIBÓK, A.
ZSUGA, M.

Conservatory (4032 Debrecen, Egyetem tér 2; tel. (52) 411-226; fax (52) 411-226; e-mail adamk@dragon.klte.hu):

ÁDÁM, K., Stringed Instruments
KAMMERER, A., Brass and Percussion
KEDVES, T., Stringed Instruments
KISS, V. P., Stringed Instruments
KÖKÉNYESSY, M., Stringed Instruments
MATÚZ, I., Woodwind
SZESZTAY, ZS., Music Theory, Choir Conducting

Farm and Regional Research Institute (4032 Debrecen, Böszörményi u. 138; tel. (52) 508-334; fax (52) 413-385; e-mail csapone@helios.date.hu):

KONCZ, T., Dir

Hajdúböszörményi College Faculty of Education (4220 Hajdúböszörmény, Désány I u. 1–9; tel. (52) 229-433; fax (52) 229-559; e-mail tit8003@helka.iif.hu):

BAKOSI, É., Children's Education
FRÁTER, K., Children's Education
KÖVÉR, I., Children's Education
VARGA, GY., Social Studies

Institute of Information Technology:

GISPERT, S.
MAJOR, P.
PAP, G.
PETHŐ, A.

EÖTVÖS LORÁND TUDOMÁNYEGYETEM
(Loránd Eötvös University)

1056 Budapest, POB 109
1053 Budapest, Egyetem tér 1–3

Telephone: (1) 411-6500
Fax: (1) 411-6712
Internet: www.elte.hu

Founded 1635
State control
Academic year: September to June (two terms)

Rector: Prof. Dr BARNA MEZEY
Vice-Rector for Strategic Affairs: Prof. Dr ANDRÁS KARÁCSONY
Vice-Rector for Education: Dr CSABA BORSODI
Vice-Rector for Science, Research and Innovation: Prof. Dr ERNŐ KESZEI
Vice-Rector for Int. Affairs: Prof. Dr ZOLTÁN HORVÁTH
Sec.-Gen.: Dr ZOLTÁN RÓNAY
Vice-Rector for Public Affairs and Communication: Dr GYÖRGY FÁBRI
Dir-Gen.: Dr KATALIN JUHÁSZNÉ HUSZTY

Library: see under Libraries and Archives
Number of teachers: 1,090
Number of students: 31,882

Publications: *Acta Facultatis Politico-iuridicae Universitatis Scientiarum Budapestinensis, Annales* (geological, juridical and geological series, 1 a year)

DEANS

Bárczi Gusztáv Faculty of Special Education: Dr Ákosné Szabó
Faculty of Elementary and Nursery Teachers' Training: Dr György Mikonya
Faculty of Humanities: Dr Tamás Dezső
Faculty of Informatics: Dr László Kozma
Faculty of Law and Political Science: Dr Miklós Király
Faculty of Education and Psychology: Prof. Dr Attila Oláh
Faculty of Science: Dr György Michaletzky
Faculty of Social Sciences: Dr Katalin Tausz

PROFESSORS

Faculty of Arts (1088 Budapest, Múzeum körút 4/a):

Adamik, T., Latin Language and Literature
Balázs, G., Linguistics
Balogh, A., Modern World History
Banczerowski, J., Polish Language and Literature
Bárdosi, V., Romance Studies
Bence, Gy., Ethics and Social Philosophy
Bertényi, I., Medieval and Early Modern Hungarian History
Bíró, F., 18th- and 19th-century Hungarian Literature
Dávid, G., Oriental Studies
Domokos, P., Finno-Ugric Linguistics
Erdélyi, A., Philosophy
Fodor, S., Semitic Philology and Arabic Studies
Gaál, E., Egyptology
Géher, I., English
Gergely, A., History
Gergely, J., Modern and Contemporary Hungarian History
Gerő, A., Economic and Social History
Giampaolo, S., Romance Studies
Glatz, F., Historical Auxiliary Sciences
Gósy, M., Linguistics
Granasztói, G., Romance Studies
Gyivicsán, A., Slavonic Studies
Hessky, P., German Linguistics
Horváth, I,, Old Hungarian Literature
Jeremiás, É., Oriental Studies
Kara, Gy., Central Asian Studies
Kardos, J., History
Kardos, J., Historical Auxiliary Sciences
Kelemen, J., Ethics and Social Philosophy
Kélényi, G., History of Art
Kenyeres, Z., Modern Hungarian Literature
Keszler, B., Contemporary Hungarian Linguistics
Kiss, J., Hungarian Historical Linguistics and Dialectology
Klaudy, K., Linguistics
Knipf, E., German
Komoróczy, G., Assyriology and Hebrew Studies
Kósa, L., Cultural History
Kovács, A., Slavonic Studies
Kovács, S. I., Old Hungarian Literature
Kövecses, Z., English
Krausz, T., History
Kulcsár Szabó, E., Comparative Literature
Ludassy, M., Ethics and Social Philosophy
Luft, U., Egyptology
Manherz, K., Germanic Linguistics
Marosi, E., Art History
Masát, A., Scandinavian Languages and Literature
Medgyes, P., English Teacher Training
Miskolczy, A., Romance Studies
Németh, G., History
Nyomárkay, I., Slavic Philology
Orosz, M., German

Paládi-Kovács, A., Ethnography
Palotás, E., East European History
Passuth, K., Art History
Péter, M., Eastern Slavonic and Baltic Philology
Prokopp, M., History of Art
Puskás, I., History
Raczky, P., Archaeology
Radnóti, S., Aesthetics
Romsics, I., Modern and Contemporary Hungarian History
Rónay, L., Modern Hungarian Literature
Sipos, L., Literary History
Solymosi, L., History
Steiger, K., Philosophy
Szabics, I., French Language and Literature
Szabó, K., Medieval World History
Szabó, M., Classical Archaeology
Szávai, J., Comparative and World Literature
Szegedy-Maszák, M., Comparative Literature
Székely, G., History
Szvák, G., History
Tolcsvai, N. G., Linguistics
Tóth, B., Romance Studies
Tverdota, G., Literary History
Varga, L., English
Vargyai, Gy., Historical Auxiliary Sciences
Vásári, I., Turkish Studies
Voigt, V., Folklore
Vörös, I., French Language and Literature

Faculty of Law and Political Science (1053 Budapest, Egyetem tér 1–3):

Bihari, M., Political Science
Böhm, A., Political Science
Burján, L., International Law
Erdei, A., Criminal Procedural Law
Ficzere, L., Public Administration Law
Földesi, T., Philosophy
Földi, A., Roman Law
Gönczöl, K., Criminology
Hamza, G., Roman Law
Harmathy, A., Civil Law
Horváth, P., Universal Legal and Political History
Karácsony, A., Philosophy
Körösnyi, A., Political Science
Kukorelli, I., Constitutional Law
Lenkovits, B., Civil Law
Lévay, M., Criminology
Lőrincz, L., Public Administration Law
Mezei, B., Universal Legal and Political History
Pacsolay, P., Political Science
Pándi, G., Public Administration Law
Pokol, B., Political Science
Sájo, A., Civil Law
Sári, J., Constitutional Law
Schlett, I., Political Science
Stumpf, I., Political Science
Szabó, Márton, Political Science
Szabó, Máté, Political Science
Szilágyi, P., Theory of Law
Tamás, A., Theory of Law
Valki, L., International Law
Vékás, L., Civil Law

Faculty of Science (1088 Budapest, Rákoczi út 5):

Berczik, Á., Systematic Zoology and Ecology
Böddi, B., Biology
Bodzsár, É., Biology
Csányi, V., Behaviour Genetics
Csikor, F., Theoretical Physics
Demetrovics, J., Information Systems
Détári, L., Biology
Dózsa-Farkas, K., Biology
Erdei, A., Immunology
Farsang, Gy., Inorganic and Analytical Chemistry
Fodor, Z., Theoretical Physics
Frank, A., Operational Research
Galácz, A., Palaeontology

Gere, G., Biology
Geszti, T., Physics of Complex Systems
Gráf, L., Biochemistry
Gyenis, G., Biology
Gyurján, I., Plant Anatomy
Hegyi, G., Biology
Horváth, Z., Theoretical Physics
Kiss, A., Atomic Physics
Kiss, E., Mathematics
Komjáth, P., Computer Science
Kondor, I., Physics of Complex Systems
Kovács, J., Biology
Kürti, J., Physics
Laczkovich, M., Analysis
Láng, F., Biology
Lendvai, J., General Physics
Lovász, L., Computer Science
Nagy, D. L., Atomic Physics
Ormos, P., Physics
Orosz, L., Biology
Pálfy, P., Algebra and Number Theory
Palla, L., Theoretical Physics
Patkós, A., Atomic Physics
Podani, J., Biology
Polonyi, J., Atomic Physics
Sármay, G., Immunology
Sass, M., General Zoology
Szabó, K., Physical Chemistry
Szalay, S., Atomic Physics
Szathmári, E., Plant Taxonomy and Ecology
Szigeti, Z., Biology
Tél, T., Theoretical Physics
Tichy, G., Solid State Physics
Ungár, T., General Physics
Vesztergombi, G., Physics
Vicsek, T., Biological Physics
Vincze, I., Physics
Závodszky, P., Biological Physics

Institute and Postgraduate Centre for Sociology and Social Policy (1088 Budapest, Pollack Mihály tér 10):

Angelusz, R., Sociology
Csepeli, Gy., Social Psychology
Ferge, Zs., Social Policy
Huszár, T., Historical Sociology
Némedi, D., Social Theory
Pataki, F., Social Psychology
Somlai, P., Social Theory

Teacher-Training Faculty (1075 Budapest, Kazinczy u. 23–27):

Cs. Varga, I., Hungarian Language and Literature
Demeter, J., Hungarian Language and Literature
Druzsin, F., Hungarian Language and Literature
Dukkon, Á., Hungarian Language and Literature
Estók, J., History
Fried, I., Italian Language and Literature
Gaizer, F., Chemistry
Gödény, E., Hungarian Language and Literature
Grétsy, L., Hungarian Linguistics
Hajdu, P., Social Theory
Hegyvári, N., Mathematics
Heltai, P., English
Horváth, G., Geography
Jászó, A., Hungarian Linguistics
Madarász, I., Hungarian Linguistics
Milkovits, I., Biology
Németh, A., Educational Science
Salamon, K., History
Sapszon, F., Music
Siposné-Jáger, K., Biology
Uzonyi, P., German
Závodszky, G., History
Zirkuli, P., French Language and Literature

KAPOSVÁRI EGYETEM
(University of Kaposvár)

7401 Kaposvár, Guba Sándor u. 40
Telephone: (82) 505-910
Fax: (82) 505-896
E-mail: kszi@mail.atk.u-kaposvar.hu
Internet: www.u-kaposvar.hu
Founded 2000 from Faculty of Animal Husbandry of Pannon Agrártudományi Egyetem (Pannon Univ. of Agricultural Sciences) and Csokonai Vitéz Mihály Teacher-Training College
Incl. College Faculty of Art, not yet acccredited by the HAC (2009)
State control
Language of instruction: Hungarian
Academic year: September to June
Rector: Prof. Dr László Babinszky
Number of teachers: 250
Number of students: 4,800
Publication: *Acta Agraria Kaposváriensis* (4 a year)

DEANS

Faculty of Animal Science: Prof. István Holló
Faculty of Economic Science: Prof. Gyula Varga
Faculty of Pedagogy: Prof. István Rosta

PROFESSORS

Faculty of Animal Science (fax (82) 320-757; e-mail hollo@mail.atk.u-kaposvar.hu; internet www.atk.u-kaposvar.hu):

BABINSZKY, L., Animal Nutrition
BOGENFÜRST, F., Poultry Breeding
CSAPÓ, J., Biochemistry
DÉR, F., Plant Production
GYENIS, J., Process Engineering
HECKER, W., Academy of Equitation
HORN, P., Pig Production
HORVÁTH, GY., Social Sciences
KOVÁCS, M., Physiology and Animal Hygiene
PAÁL, J., Mathematics and Computer Science
REPA, I., Digital Imaging, Radiology
SARUDI, J., Chemistry and Biochemistry
STEFLER, J., Cattle Production
SZAKÁLY, S., Food Science
SZÉLES, GY., Farm Economics
SZENDRŐ, ZS., Animal Breeding
TAKÁTSY, T., Agricultural Engineering

ATTACHED INSTITUTE

Feed Crops Research Centre: 7095 Iregszemcse, Napraforgo u. 1; tel. (74) 481-127; fax (74) 481-253; e-mail tki.ireg@axelero.hu; Dir-Gen. Dr László Takács.

LISZT FERENC ZENEMŰVÉSZETI EGYETEM
(Ferenc Liszt Academy of Music)

1391 Budapest, POB 206, Liszt Ferenc tér 8
Telephone: (1) 462-4600
Fax: (1) 462-4648
Internet: www.liszt.hu
Founded 1875
State control
Academic year: September to June
Rector: Dr András Batta
Vice-Rector: Prof. László Tihanyi
Librarian: Dr. J. Kárpáti
Library of 187,000 vols
Number of teachers: 158
Number of students: 767.

ATTACHED INSTITUTES

Bartók Béla Zeneművészeti Szakközépiskola és Gimnázium (Béla Bartók Conservatory of Music and Secondary School): 1065 Budapest, Nagymező u.1; Dir T. Szabó.

Budapesti Tanárképző Intézet (Teacher Training Institute in Budapest): 1052 Budapest, Semmelweiss u. 12; Dir Prof. Lehel Both.

MAGYAR KÉPZŐMŰVÉSZETI EGYETEM
(University of Fine Arts)

1062 Budapest, Andrássy u. 69–71
Telephone: (1) 342-1738
Fax: (1) 342-1563
E-mail: rektor@mke.hu
Internet: www.mke.hu
Founded 1871
State control
Rector: Frigyes Kőnig
Vice-Rector: Károly Hantos
Int. Affairs: Zsófia Rudnay
Registrar: István Pongó
Librarian: Katalin Blaskó Majkó
Library of 60,000 vols, 90 periodicals
Number of teachers: 134
Number of students: 552

PROFESSORS

FARKAS, Á., Sculpture
KOCSIS, I., Graphic Art
MENRÁTH, P., Restoration
MOLNÁR, K., Applied Graphic Art
NAGY, G., Painting
PETERNÁK, M., Multimedia Studies
SZABADI, J., Art History
SZÉKELY, L., Stage and Costume Design
TÖLG-MOLNÁR, Z., Painting

MISKOLCI EGYETEM
(University of Miskolc)

3515 Miskolc-Egyetemváros
Telephone: (46) 565-111
Fax: (46) 565-014
E-mail: patko@uni-miskolc.hu
Internet: www.uni-miskolc.hu
Founded 1735, in Selmecbánya, Academy status 1770, moved 1919 to Sopron, reorganized 1949 in Miskolc
State control
Languages of instruction: Hungarian, English
Academic year: September to June
Rector: Prof. Dr Gyula Patkó
Vice-Rector for Educational Affairs: Prof. Judit Hell
Vice-Rector for Gen. Affairs: Prof. István Stipta
Vice-Rector for Int. Relations: Prof. Mihály Dobróka
Vice-Rector for Scientific Affairs and Int. Relations: Prof. Mihály Dobróka
Vice-Rector for Strategy and Devt: Dr Csaba Deák
Sec.-Gen.: Viktor Kovács
Librarian: Dr Erzsébet Burmeister
Library of 602,000 vols, 161,000 periodicals
Number of teachers: 750
Number of students: 12,828
Publications: *Miskolc Journal of International Law*, *Miskolci Egyetem Közleményei* (papers in Hungarian, irregular), *Publications of the University of Miskolc* (papers in German, English and Russian, irregular)

DEANS

College Faculty: Prof. László Hegedűs
Faculty of Arts: Dr Mária Kovács Illés
Faculty of Earth Science and Engineering: Prof. László Tihanyi
Faculty of Economics: Prof. György Kocziszky
Faculty of Health Care: Prof. László Barkai
Faculty of Law: Prof. Miklós Szabó

Faculty of Materials Science and Engineering: Prof. Zoltán Gácsi
Faculty of Mechanical Engineering and Informatics: Prof. Béla Illés

PROFESSORS

Faculty of Arts (tel. (46) 565-210; fax (46) 563-459; e-mail boldek@uni-miskolc.hu; internet www.bolcsesz.uni-miskolc.hu):

A. MOLNÁR, F., Hungarian Linguistics, History of Hungarian Linguistics
ANDRIK-HELL, J., Philosophy
BONA, G., Military History
CSEPELI, GY., Social Psychology
FERENCZI, L., Literature of the Enlightenment, Romanticism and Regional History
FORRAI, G., History of Philosophy
GYULAI, É., Cultural History and Museology
HELTAI, J., Old Hungarian Literature
ILLÉS-KOVÁCS, M., Hungarian Linguistics
KABDEBÓ, L., Contemporary Hungarian Literature
KECSKEMÉTI, G., Literary History, Old Hungarian Literature
KEMÉNY, G., Hungarian Linguistics, Stylistics
KNAUSZ, I., Science of Education
KOTICS, J., Cultural and Visual Anthropology
SCHWENDTNER, T., History of Philosophy, Science of Philosophy
SZABÓ, M., Political Science, Political Discourse
SZABÓ-TÓTH, K., Family Sociology
SZIGETI, J., Central European Literature and Culture
TÓTH, Z., Social History

Faculty of Earth Science and Engineering (tel. (46) 565-051; fax (46) 563-465; e-mail rekbdhiv@uni-miskolc.hu; internet www.mfk.uni-miskolc.hu):

BÓDI, T., Reservoir Engineering
BŐHM, J., Process Engineering
CSŐKE, B., Process Engineering
DOBOS, E., Geography and Environmental Science
DOBRÓKA, M., Geophysics
FÖLDESSY, J., Geology and Mineral Resources
GYULAI, Á., Geophysics
HAVASI, I., Geodesy and Mine Surveying
HEVESI, A., Geography and Environmental Sciences
KOCSIS, K., Human Geography
KOVÁCS, B., Hydrogeology and Engineering Geology
LADÁNYI, G., Equipment for Geotechnology
LAKATOS, I., Mining Chemistry
LESS, GY., Geology and Mineral Resources
MOLNÁR, J., Mining and Geotechnology
ORMOS, T., Geophysics
SOMOSVÁRI, ZS., Mining and Geotechnology
SZABÓ, I., Hydrogeology and Engineering Geology
SZAKÁLL, S., Mineralogy
SZŰCS, P., Hydrogeology and Engineering Geology
TAKÁCS, G., Petroleum Engineering
TIHANYI, L., Natural Gas Engineering

Faculty of Economics (tel. (46) 565-190; fax (46) 562-471; e-mail gazddek@uni-miskolc.hu; internet www.gtk.uni-miskolc.hu):

BENEDEK, J., Regional Policy
BESENYEI, L., Business Statistics and Forecasting
BOZSIK, S., Finance
CZABÁN, J., Business Economics
DANKÓ, L., International Marketing
ILLÉS, M., Business Economics
KOCZISZKY, GY., Regional Economics
KUNOS, I., Human Resources
NAGY, A., Economic Theory

NAGY, Z., World Economy and Comparative Economics
PÁL, T., Accounting
PELCZ-GÁLL, I., Entrepreneurship
PISKÓTI, I., Marketing Strategy and Communication
SZAKÁLY, D., Innovation and Technology Management
SZINTAY, I., Management
SZITA, K., Environment
VERES-SOMOSI, M., Organizational Behaviour

Faculty of Health Care:

BERKŐ, P., Gynaecology, Obstetrics
DÓZSA, C., Health Insurance, Health Management
FODOR, B., Nanobiotechnology, Nanomedicine
FORNET, B., Conventional Radiology, Ions Diagnostics
HARKÁNYI, Z., Radiology
KISS-TÓTH, E., Sociology, Socialpolicy
LOMBAY, B., Pediatrics, Radiology
MARTOS, J., Radiology, Neuroradiology
PAPP, M., Orthopedics
PEJA, M., Rehabilitation
RÁCZ, O., Physiology, Pathophysiology, Clinical Chemistry
SÁGODI, L., Pediatrics, Gynaecology, Pediatric Gynaecology
SZABÓ, L., Pediatrics, Nephrology
SZABÓ, Z., Surgery, Hand Surgery, Traumatology
SZÁNTÓ, A., Marketing, Business Studies
SZEBENI, J., Nanobiotechnology, Nanomedicine
ÚJSZÁSZY, L., Internal Medicine, Gastroenterology
VALIKOVICS, A., Neurology, Psychiatry
VELKEY, I., Pediatrics, Neurology, Pediatric Neurology
WINKLER, G., Internal Medicine, Endocrinology, Diabetology

Faculty of Law (tel. (46) 565-170; fax (46) 367-933; e-mail jogdekan@uni-miskolc.hu; internet www.jogikar.uni-miskolc.hu):

BARTA, J., Business Law
BIRÓ, GY., Civil Law
BRAGYOVA, A., Constitutional Law
CSÁK, CS., Labour Law and Agricultural Law
FARKAS, Á., Criminal Procedural Law and Law Enforcement
GÖRGÉNYI, I., Criminal Law and Criminology
JÁMBOR-RÓTH, E., Criminal Procedural Law and Law Enforcement
LÉVAY, M., Criminal Law and Criminology
LÉVAY-FAZEKAS, J., European and International Private Law
MAJTÉNYI, L., Information and Media Law
PÁSZTOR-ERDŐS, É., Financial Law
PÉTER, O., Roman Law
PETROVICH-WOPERA, ZS., Civil Procedural Law
PRUGBERGER, T., Labour Law and Agricultural Law
STIPTA, I., Legal History
SZABÓ, M., Legal Theory and Legal Sociology
TORMA, A., Administrative Law

Faculty of Materials Science and Engineering (tel. (46) 565-091; fax (46) 565-408; e-mail makdekani@uni-miskolc.hu; internet www .mak.uni-miskolc.hu):

BÁRÁNY, S., Chemistry
BÁRCZY, P., Polymer Engineering
DÚL, J., Foundry Engineering
GÁCSI, Z., Materials Science
GÖMZE, A. L., Ceramics and Silicate Engineering
KAPTAY, GY., Chemistry
KÁROLY, GY., Metallurgical and Foundry Engineering

KÉKESI, T., Metallurgy
MAROSSY, K., Polymer Technology
PALOTÁS, A. B., Combustion Technology and Thermal Energy
TÖRÖK, T., Metallurgy

Faculty of Mechanical Engineering and Informatics (tel. (46) 565-130; fax (46) 563-453; e-mail gkdh5@uni-miskolc.hu; internet www.gepesz.uni-miskolc.hu):

AJTONYI, I., Automation
BARANYI, L., Heat and Fluid Engineering
BERTÓTI, E., Mechanics
CZIBERE, T., Heat and Fluid Engineering
DÖBRÖCZÖNI, A., Machine Elements
DUDÁS, I., Production Engineering
ECSEDI, I., Mechanics
FARKAS, J., Materials Handling and Logistics
HORVÁTHNÉ VARGA, A., Mechanics
ILLÉS, B., Materials Handling and Logistics
JÁRMAI, K., Materials Handling and Logistics
JUHÁSZ, I., Descriptive Geometry
KACSUK, P., Automation
KOZÁK, I., Mechanics
KUNDRÁK, J., Production Engineering
LÉVAI, I., Materials Handling and Logistics
LUKÁCS, J., Mechanical Technology
MANG, B., Materials Handling and Logistics
NYÍRI, A., Heat and Fluid Engineering
PÁCZELT, I., Mechanics
PARIPÁS, B., Physics
PATKÓ, GY., Machine Tools
RONTÓ, M., Mathematical Analysis
SZABÓ, SZ., Heat and Fluid Engineering
SZALADNYA, S., Materials Handling and Logistics
SZARKA, T., Electrotechnology and Electronics
SZEIDL, GY., Mechanics
SZENTIRMAI, L., Electrotechnology and Electronics
SZIGETI, J., Mathematical Analysis
TAJNAFŐI, J., Machine Tools
TISZA, M., Mechanical Technology
TÓTH, L., Mechanical Technology
TÓTH, T., Information Engineering

ASSOCIATE INSTITUTES

Bela Bartók Music Institute: 3530 Miskolc, Bartók tér 1; tel. (46) 321-711; fax (46) 343-800; e-mail bolcsill@uni-miskolc.hu; internet www.uni-miskolc.hu/~bbziweb; Dir Dr ZOLTÁN SÁNDOR.

Comenius Teacher-Training College: 3950 Sárospatak, Eötvös u. 7; tel. (47) 513-000; fax (47) 312329; internet www.ctif.hu; Dir S. KOMÁROMY.

Institute of Health Care Studies: 3508 Miskolc, Mész u. 1; tel. (46) 366-560; fax (46) 366-961; e-mail rekefk@uni-miskolc.hu; internet www.uni-miskolc.hu/~wwweti; Dir Dr BARKAI LÁSZLÓ.

MOHOLY-NAGY MŰVÉSZETI EGYETEM
(Moholy-Nagy University of Arts)

1121 Budapest, Zugligeti ú. 9–25
Telephone: (1) 392-1193
Fax: (1) 392-1190
E-mail: international@mome.hu
Internet: w2.mome.hu

Founded 1880; fmrly Magyar Iparművészeti Egyetem; present name 2006
State control
Academic year: September to June

Rector: GÁBOR KOPEK
Vice-Rector: LÁSZLÓ ZSÓTÉR
Chancellor: Dr PÁL HATOS
Dir of Finance: BALÁZS KOHUT
Dir of Int. and Public Relations: ZSOLT PETRI
Librarian: KLÁRA LÉVAI

Library of 42,000 vols
Number of teachers: 98
Number of students: 570

Publications: *Diploma* (1 a year), *Kék Ég* (4 a year)

DIRECTORS OF INSTITUTES

Institute of Foundation Studies: Prof. JÓZSEF SCHERER
Institute of Humanities: Prof. GYULA ERNYEY
Institute for Manager Training: Prof. Dr ÁGNES KAPITÁNY

NYUGAT-MAGYARORSZÁGI EGYETEM
(University of West Hungary)

9400 Sopron, Bajcsy-Zs. u. 4
Telephone: (99) 518-100
Fax: (99) 311-103
E-mail: rectoro@nyme.hu
Internet: www.nyme.hu

Founded 2000 on merger of Soproni Egyetem (University of Sopron, f. 1762 as Academy of Mining and Forestry), Mosonmagyaróvár Faculty of Agriculture (f. 1818) of Pannon Agrártudományi Egyetem (Pannon University of Agricultural Sciences), Apáczai Csere János Teacher-Training College (f. 1778), and Benedek Elek College of Education (f. 1959)
State control
Language of instruction: Hungarian
Academic year: September to June

Rector: Prof. Dr SÁNDOR FARAGÓ
Pro-Rectors: Prof. Dr KÁROLY MÉSZÁROS, Prof. Dr RESZŐ SCHMIDT, Prof. Dr PÉTER TAKÁTS
Economic Dir: LÁSZLÓ HERCZEG
Admin. Officer: Dr MÁRIA MERÉNYI
Librarian: SÁNDOR SARKADY, Jr

Library of 380,000 vols
Number of teachers: 562
Number of students: 12,500

Publications: *Acta Agronomica Ovariensis* (2 a year, in Hungarian and English), *Acta Facultatis Forestalis* (in German and English), *Acta Facultatis Ligniensis* (in German and English), *Acta Silvatica & Lignaria Hungarica* (1 a year), *Apáczai Csere János Tanítóképző Főiskolai Kar Tanulmánykötet* (1 a year, in Hungarian), *Apáczai tanulmánykötetek* (1 a year, in Hungarian), *Benedek könyvek* (irregular, in Hungarian), *Bibliotheca Slavica Savariensis* (irregular, in Hungarian, English, Russian, Croatian and Slovenian), *Faipar* (Wood Science, 4 a year, in Hungarian with English summary), *Flora Pannonica* (Journal of Phytogeography and Taxonomy), *Folia Anthropologica* (1 a year, in Hungarian), *Gazdaság & Társadalom* (English abstracts, 4 a year, in Hungarian, German or English), *Kanitzia* (in Hungarian, 1 a year), *Karst Development* (1 a year, in English), *Karsztfejlődés* (1 a year, in Hungarian), *Magyar Apróvad Közlemények* (Hungarian Small Game Bulletin, 1 or 2 a year, in Hungarian and English), *Magyar Vízivad Közlemények* (Hungarian Waterfowl Publ., 1 or 2 a year, in Hungarian and English), *Tilia* (Journal of Botany, 1 or 2 a year, in Hungarian), *Studia Slavica Savariensia* (Journal of Linguistics and Literary Sciences, 1 a year, in Hungarian, English, German, Russian and Serbo-Croatian), *Tudomány Napja* (1 a year, in Hungarian)

DEANS AND DIRECTORS

Apáczai Csere János Teacher-Training College: Dr SÁNDOR CSEH
Benedek Elek College of Education: Dr ERZSÉBET ALPÁRNÉ SZÁLA
College of Geoinformatics: Dr BÉLA MÁRKUS

Faculty of Agricultural Sciences: Dr VINCE
ÖRDÖG
Faculty of Economic Sciences: Prof. Dr
ERZSÉBET GIDAI
Faculty of Forestry: Prof. Dr KÁROLY MÉS-
ZÁROS
Faculty of Wood Sciences: Prof. Dr SÁNDOR
MOLNÁR

PANNON EGYETEM
(University of Pannonia)

8200 Veszprém, Egyetem u. 10, POB 158

Telephone: (88) 422-022
Fax: (88) 423-866
E-mail: pr@uni-pannon.hu
Internet: www.uni-pannon.hu

Founded 1949; absorbed Georgikon Faculty
of Agriculture of the former Pannon
Agrártudományi Egyetem (Pannon Uni-
versity of Agricultural Sciences) 2000
State controlled
Languages of instruction: Hungarian, Eng-
lish
Academic year: September to June

Rector: Prof. Dr ÁKOS RÉDEY
Pro-Rector for Education and Accreditation:
Prof. Dr JÁNOS KRISTÓF
Pro-Rector for Int. Affairs: Prof. Dr ÁRPÁD
MIHALOVICS
Dir-Gen. of Economic Affairs: MÁRIA ZSIBOR-
ÁCS PETRÓ
Pro-Rector for Scientific Affairs: Prof. Dr
FERENC HUSVÉTH
Librarian: Dr M. EGYHÁZY

Library: see Libraries
Number of teachers: 435
Number of students: 6,794 (6,313 full-time,
481 part-time)

Publication: Hungarian Journal of Industrial Chemistry (4 a year)

DEANS

Faculty of Economics: Dr ANDRÁS JANCSIK
Faculty of Engineering: Dr OTTÓ HORVÁTH
Faculty of Humanities: Prof. Dr ISTVÁN
SZILÁGYI
Faculty of Information Technology: Prof. Dr
FERENC FRIEDLER
Faculty of Teacher Training: Prof. CSABA
FÖLDES
Georgikon Faculty of Agriculture: Prof.
KÁROLY DUBLECZ

PROFESSORS

ALMÁDI, L., Botany
ANDA, A., Water Management
BAKOS, J., Organic Chemistry
BÁRDOS, J., English Language
BENCZE, L., Organic Chemistry
BÉRES, I., Botany
BUDAI, L., English Language
BUZÁS, GY., Economics
FISCHL, G., Plant Pathology
FÖLDES, CS., German Language
FRIEDLER, F., Systems Engineering in Com-
puter Science
GAÁL, Z., Management and Economy
GÁBORJÁNYI, R., Plant Pathology
GYÖRI, I., Mathematics
HANGOS, K., Systems Engineering in Com-
puter Science
HLAVAY, J., Analytical Chemistry
HORVÁTH, A., Inorganic Chemistry
HORVÁTH, GY., Pedagogy and Psychology
HORVÁTH, J., Plant Pathology
HORVÁTH, O., Inorganic Chemistry
HUSVÉTH, F., Zoology
KANYÁR, B., Radiochemistry
KARDOS, Z., Economics
KARDOS, Z., Social Sciences
KISMÁNYOKI, T., Agronomy
KOCSONDI, J., Management and Economy
KOVÁCS, Z., Management and Economy

KOZMANN, GY., Informatics
KRISTÓF, J., Analytical Chemistry
LENGYEL, ZS., Applied Linguistics
LISZI, J., Physical Chemistry
LÖRINCZ, A., International Economics
MAJOR, I., Economics
MARTON, GY., Chemical Process Engineering
MÉSZÁROS, E., Environmental Sciences
MIHALOVICS, Á., French Language
MIHÁLYI, P., Economics
MINK, J., Analytical Chemistry
NAGY, I., Theatre Studies
PADISÁK, F., Limnology
PALKOVICS, M., Agricultural Economics
PAPP, S., Inorganic Chemistry
PUPOS, T,, Economics
RÉDEY, A., Chemical Technology, Environ-
mental Engineering
SOMOGYI, S., Management and Economics
SPEIER, G., Organic Chemistry
SUGÁR, L., Zoology
SZABÓ, F., Animal Husbandry
SZABÓ, F., Hungarian Linguistics
SZABÓ, I., Botany
SZABÓ T, A., Biology
SZILÁGYI, I., Social Sciences
SZIRDNYI, T., Image Processing and Neuro-
computing
SZOLGAY, P., Display Optics, Colour Image
Sensing
TÖRÖK, A., Economics
TUZA, ZS., Mathematics
UNGVÁRY, F., Organic Chemistry
VARGA, K., Radiochemistry
VÁRNAGY, L., Agricultural Hygiene
VERESS, G., Informatics and Control
VINCZE, L., Animal Nutrition
VINCZE, L., Inorganic Chemistry
ZSOLNAY, F., Pedagogy

PÉCSI TUDOMÁNYEGYETEM
(University of Pécs)

7622 Pécs, Vasvári Pál u. 4

Telephone: (72) 510-500
Fax: (72) 501-508
E-mail: rector@pte.hu
Internet: www.pte.hu

Founded 1367, re-f. 1923 as Janus Pannonius
Tudományegyetem (Janus Pannonius
Univ.); present name 2000 upon integra-
tion with Pécsi Orvostudományi Egyetem
(Pécs Univ. Medical School) and Illyés
Gyula Pedagógiai Főiskola (Gyula Illyés
College of Education)
State control
Academic year: September to May (two
terms)

Rector: Dr JÓZSEF BÓDIS
Sr Vice-Rector: Dr LÁSZLÓ I. KOMLÓSI
Vice Rector for Science and Innovation: Dr
GÁBOR KOVÁCS L.
Vice-Rector for Financial and Strategic
Affairs: Dr GYULA ZELLER
Chief Admin.Officer: Dr KATALIN URBÁN
Chief Librarian: Dr ÁGNES DÁRDAI

Number of teachers: 2,000
Number of students: 33,248

Publications: Pécsi Orvostudományi Egyetem
Évkönyve (1 a year), Specimina Fennica
(irregular), Specimina Geographica
(irregular), Specimina Nova Dissertatio-
num ex Institutio Historico (irregular),
Specimina Sibirica (irregular), Studia Iuridica Auctoritatae Universitatis Pécs Publicata (4 a year), Studia Oeconomica
Auctoritatae Universitatis Pécs Publicata
(4 a year), Studia Paedagogica Auctoritate
Universitatis Pécs Publicata (irregular),
Studia Philosophica et Sociologica Auctoritatae Universitatis Pécs Publicata (4 a
year), Szép Literatúrai Ajándék (4 a year),
Tudományos Dialóg (6 a year), Univ Pécs
(every 2 weeks)

DEANS

Faculty of Adult Education and Human
Resources Development: Dr DÉNES KOLTAI
Faculty of Business and Economics: Dr
GÁBOR RAPPAI
Faculty of Health Sciences: Prof. JÓZSEF
BETLEHEM
Faculty of Humanities: Dr FERENC FISCHER
Faculty of Law: Dr GYULA BERKE
Faculty of Music and Visual Arts: Prof. COLIN
FOSTER
Faculty of Sciences: Prof. ISTVÁN GERESDI
Illyés Gyula Faculty of Education: Dr BÉLA
HORVÁTH
Medical School: Prof. ATTILA MISETA
Mihály Pollack Faculty of Engineering: Dr
BÁLINT BACHMANN

PROFESSORS

Faculty of Business and Economics (7622
Pécs, Rákóczi u. 80; tel. (72) 501-599; fax (72)
501-553; e-mail rappai@ktk.pte.hu; internet
www.ktk.pte.hu):

BARAKONYI, K., Strategic Management
BÉLYÁCZ, I., Corporate Finance and
Accounting
BUDAY-SÁNTHA, A., Agricultural, Environ-
mental and Regional Economics
DOBAY, P., Business Informatics
FARKAS, F., Management
KOMLÓSI, S., Decision-making
LÁSZLÓ, GY., Corporate Finance and
Accounting
OROSZI, S., Economics
REKETTYE, G., Marketing
SIPOS, B., Strategic Management
TAKÁCS, B., Marketing
TÖRŐCSIK, M., Marketing
TÓTH, T., Economic History
VARGA, J., Decision-making
VÖRÖS, J., Decision-making

Faculty of Health Sciences (7621 Pécs,
Vörösmarty u. 4; tel. (72) 513-671; e-mail
dekan@etk.pte.hu):

BÓDIS, J., Obstetrics and Gynaecology
BUDA, J., Public Health
CHOLNOKY, P., Paediatrics
CSERE, T., Radiology
FARKAS, M., Nuclear Medicine
FIGLER, M., Gastroenterology
GYÓDI, GY., Paediatrics
HARTMANN, G., Physiology
HORVÁTH, B., Obstetrics and Gynaecology
ILLEI, GY., Obstetrics and Gynaecology
JEGES, S., Biostatistics
KELEMEN, J., Chemistry
KISS, T., Biology
KOMÁROMY, L., Biology
KOPA, J., Neurosurgery
KOVÁCS, L. G., Neuroendocrinology
KRÁNITZ, J., Orthopaedics
LAKY, R., Traumatology
ROZSOS, I., Surgery
SULYOK, E., Paediatrics
TAHIN, T., Medical Sociology
TÁRNOK, F., Gastroenterology

Faculty of Humanities (7624 Pécs, Ifjúság u.
6; tel. (72) 503-600; fax (72) 501-558; e-mail
dean@btk.pte.hu; internet www.btk.pte.hu):

ANDRÁSFALVY, B., Ethnography
BÓKAY, A., Literature and Culture of the
English-Speaking People
BOROS, J., History of Philosophy
ERÖS, F., Psychology
FISHER, F., Modern History
FONT, M., Medieval and Early Modern
History
FORRAY, R. K., Linguistics
HETESI, I., Classical Literary History and
Comparative Literature
KÁLMÁN, C. GY., Modern Literary History
and Theory of Literature
KARSAI, GY., Classical Philology
KASSAI, I., Linguistics

KÉZDI, B., Personality, Development and Clinical Psychology
KISBÁN, E., Ethnography
KOMLÓSI, L., English Linguistics
KUPA, L., Sociology and Social Policy
LÁSZLÓ, J., Psychology
NAGY, E., Sociology and Social Policy
NAGY, I., Classical Literary History and Comparative Literature
ORMOS, M., Modern History
PÓCS, É., Ethnography
ROHONYI, Z., Classical Literary History and Comparative Literature
SZÉPE, GY., Linguistics
TASSONI, L., Italian Studies
THOMKA, B., Modern Literary History and Theory of Literature
VARGYAS, P., Ancient History and Archaeology
VISY, ZS., Ancient History and Archaeology
WEISS, J., History of Philosophy
WILD, K., German Linguistics

Faculty of Law (7622 Pécs, 48-as tér 1; tel. (72) 501-563; fax (72) 215-148; e-mail berke@ajk.pte.hu; internet www.law.pte.hu):

ANDRÁSSY, GY., Political Science and Social Theory
BRUHÁCS, J., International and European Law
KAJTÁR, I., History of Law and Roman Law
KECSKÉS, L., Civil Law
KENGYEL, M., Civil Procedural Law and Sociology of Law
KISS, GY., Labour Law and Social Welfare Law
KISS, L., Administrative Law
KORINEK, L., Criminal Law
TÓTH, M., Criminal Law
TREMMEL, F., Criminal Procedural Law
VISEGRÁDY, A., Philosophy of Law and State

Faculty of Music and Visual Arts (7624 Pécs, Damjanich u. 30; tel. (72) 501-540; fax (72) 501-540; e-mail dekan@art.pte.hu; internet www.art.pte.hu):

BENCSIK, I., Sculpture
JOBBÁGY, V., Music
KESERÜ, I., Painting
KIRCS, L., Music
PINCZEHELYI, S., Painting
RÉTFALVI, S., Sculpture
TILLAI, A., Music
VIDOVSZKY, L., Theory of Art

Faculty of Sciences (7624 Pécs, Ifjúság u. 6; tel. (72) 501-512; fax (72) 501-527; e-mail szabgab@gamma.ttk.pte.hu; internet www.ttk.pte.hu):

AGÁRDI, P., Cultural Studies
BERGOU, J., Theoretical Physics
BORHIDI, A., Botany
CSOKNYA, M., Zoology and Neurobiology
ERDŐSI, F., Institute of Geography
FISCHER, E., Zoology and Neurobiology
HÁMORI, J., Zoology and Neurobiology
KLEIN, S., Human Resource Development
KOLLÁR, L., Inorganic Chemistry and Technology
KORPA, CS., Theoretical Physics
KŐSZEGFALVI, GY., Institute of Geography
KOZMA, L., Adult Education
LOVÁSZ, GY., Institute of Geography
MAJER, J., General and Applied Ecology
NAGY, G., General Physics and Chemistry
PESTI, M., General and Environmental Microbiology
SZABÓ, L., Botany
SZEIDL, L., Mathematics
TOMCSÁNYI, T., Genetics and Molecular Biology
TÓTH, J., Institute of Geography
UHRIN, B., Mathematics
VUICS, T., Institute of Geography

Illyés Gyula Faculty of Education (7100 Szekszárd, Rákóczi u. 1; tel. (74) 528-311; fax (74) 528-301; e-mail titkar@igyfk.pte.hu; internet www.igyfk.pte.hu):

ANDRÁSSY, GY., Philosophy
BAJNER, M., Foreign Languages
BORBÉLY, S., Hungarian Language and Literature
BÚS, I., Education
FUSZ, GY., Visual Education
HORVÁTH, B., Hungarian Language and Literature
KURUCZ, R., Education and Psychology
NAGY, J. T., Philosophy of Law
TOLNAI, GY., Social Policy
TOTHNÉ LITOVKINA, A., Foreign Languages
VÁRADY, Z., History of Science

Medical School (7624 Pécs, Szigeti u. 12; tel. (72) 536-200; fax (72) 536-104; e-mail dekani.hivatal@aok.pte.hu; internet www.aok.pte.hu):

ÁNGYÁN, L., Physiology
BAJNÓCZKY, I., Forensic Medicine
BARTHÓ, L., Pharmacology
BARTHÓNÉ SZEKERES, J., Medical Microbiology and Immunology
BELÁGYI, J., Central Research Laboratory
BELLYEI, A., Orthopaedics
BOGÁR, L., Anaesthesiology and Intensive Therapy
CZIRJÁK, L., Internal Medicine
CZOPF, J., Neurology
DÓCZI, T., Neurosurgery
EMBER, I., Public Health
EMŐDY, L., Microbiology
ERTL, T., Obstetrics and Gynaecology
FEKETE, M., Paediatrics
FISCHER, E., Pharmacology
GALLYAS, F., Neurosurgery
GÖTZ, F., Urology
GREGUS, Z., Pharmacology
HIDEG, K., Central Research Laboratory
HORVÁTH, L., Radiology
HORVÁTH ÖRS, P., Surgery
KAJTÁR, P., Paediatrics
KARÁTSON, A., Internal Medicine
KELÉNYI, G., Pathology
KELLERMAYER, M., Clinical Biochemistry
KETT, K., Surgery
KILÁR, F., Central Research Laboratory
KOLLÁR, L., Surgery
KOSZTOLÁNYI, GY., Paediatrics
KOVÁCS, B., Ophthalmology
KOVÁCS, S., Pathophysiology
KRÁNICZ, J., Orthopaedics
KROMMER, K., Obstetrics and Gynaecology
LÁZÁR, GY., Anatomy
LÉNÁRD, L., Physiology
LUDÁNY, A., Clinical Chemistry
MÉHES, K., Paediatrics
MEZŐNÉ FARKAS, B., Dermatology
MOLNÁR, D., Paediatrics
MÓZSIK, GY., Internal Medicine
NAGY, L., Family Medicine
NÉMETH, P., Immunology and Biotechnology
NYÁRÁDY, J., Traumatology
PAJOR, L., Pathology
PAPP, L., Cardiology
PÁR, L., Internal Medicine
PINTÉR, A., Paediatrics
PYTEL, J., Otorhinolaryngology
SÁNDOR, A., Biochemistry
SCHNEIDER, I., Dermatology
SÉTÁLÓ, GY., Anatomy
SOLTÉSZ, GY., Paediatrics
SOMOGYI, B., Biophysics
SÜMEGI, B., Biochemistry
SZABÓ, GY., Oral Medicine
SZABÓ, I., Behavioural Science
SZABÓ, I., Obstetrics and Gynaecology
SZEBERÉNYI, J., Biology
SZÉKELY, M., Pathophysiology
SZELÉNYI, Z., Pathophysiology
SZOLCSÁNYI, J., Pharmacology
TEKERES, M., Intensive Therapy and Anaesthesia

TÉNYI, J., Public Health
THAN, G., Obstetrics and Gynaecology
TÓTH, GY., Chemistry
TRIXLER, M., Psychiatry and Medical Psychology
VERECZKEI, L., Behavioural Science
VÉRTES, M., Physiology

Mihály Pollack Faculty of Engineering (7624 Pécs, Boszorkany u. 2; tel. (72) 211-968; fax (72) 214-682; e-mail mecsi@pmmk.pte.hu; internet pmmk.pte.hu):

ARADI, L., Public Utilities, Geodesy and Environmental Protection
ÁSVÁNYI, J., Automation
BACHMAN, Z., Design and Architecture
BÁRSONY, J., Statics and Supporting Structures
BUDAY, L., Education
CSÉBFALVI, GY., Statics and Supporting Structures
FÜLÖP, L., Building Structures
HÜBNER, M., Urban Development
JÓZSA, L., Electric Networks
KISS, E., Education
KISTELEGDI, I., Building Structures
KLINCSIK, M., Mathematics
LENKEI, P., Statics and Supporting Structures
ORBAN, F., Mechanical Engineering
ORBÁN, J., Materials, Geotechnics and Transport Engineering
TÓTH, Z., Urban Development
VAJDA, J., Building Construction
VARGA, L., Education
VÍG MIKLÓSNE, L. A., Mathematics

SEMMELWEIS EGYETEM
(Semmelweis University)

1085 Budapest VIII, Üllői u. 26

Telephone: (1) 459-1500
Fax: (1) 317-2220
E-mail: titkarsag.rektor@semmelweis-univ.hu
Internet: www.sote.hu

Founded 1769 as Medical Faculty of the Univ. of Nagyszombat, ind. 1951 as Semmelweis Orvostudományi Egyetem (Semmelweis Univ. of Medicine), present name 2000 upon integration with Haynal Imre Egészségtudományi (Imre Haynal Univ. of Health Sciences) and Magyar Testnevelési Egyetem (Hungarian Univ. of Physical Education)
State control
Languages of instruction: Hungarian, English, German
Academic year: September to June

Rector: Prof. Dr TIVADAR TULASSAY
Vice-Rector for Education and Int. Relations: Prof. Dr MIKLÓS KELLERMAYER
Vice-Rector for Gen. Affairs: Prof. Dr AGOSTON SLEL
Vice-Rector for Science and Innovation: Prof. Dr MIKLÓS TÓTH
Dir for Int. Relations: MARCEL POP
Librarian: Dr LIVIA VASAS

Library of 261,624 vols
Number of teachers: 1,171
Number of students: 11,143

Publication: Pathology Oncology Research (4 a year)

DEANS

Faculty of Dentistry: Prof. Dr PÁL FEJÉRDY
Faculty of Health and Public Sciences: Dr PÉTER GAÁL
Faculty of Health Sciences: Dr J. MÉSZÁROS (Dir-Gen.)
Faculty of Medicine: Prof. Dr ISTVÀN KARÁDI
Faculty of Pharmacy: Prof. Dr BÉLA NOSZAL
Faculty of Physical Education and Sport Sciences: Dr JÓZSEF TIHANYI

School of Doctoral Studies: Prof. Dr KÁROLY
RÀCZ (Pres.)

PROFESSORS

Faculty of Dentistry (tel. (1) 266-0453; fax (1)
266-1967; e-mail gera@szajseb.sote.hu):

BARABAS, J., Oral, Dental and Maxillofacial
Surgery
BOROS, I., Oral Biology
DIVINYI, T., Oral, Dental and Maxillofacial
Surgery
FÁBIÁN, T., Prosthodontics
FAZEKAS, Á., Preservation Dentistry
FEJÉRDY, P., Prosthetic Dentistry
GERA, I., Periodontics
NAGY, G., Oral Diagnostics
SIMON, GY., Oral Biology
SUBA, Z., Oral and Maxillofacial Surgery
SZABÓ, GY., Oral and Maxillofacial Surgery
VARGA, G., Oral Biology
ZELLES, T., Oral Biology

Faculty of Health Sciences (1088 Budapest,
Vas u. 17; tel. (1) 369-1241; fax (1) 369-1241;
e-mail meszarosj@seefk.hu):

CZINNER, A., Paediatrics
SZABOLCS, J., Dietetics

Faculty of Medicine (tel. (1) 317-9057; fax (1)
266-0441; e-mail vegan@rekhiv.sote.hu):

ÁCSÁDY, GY., Cardiovascular Surgery
ÁDÁM, É., Medical Microbiology
ÁDÁM, V., Medical Biochemistry
ALFÖLDY, F., Transplantation and Surgery
ARATO, A., Paediatrics
BANHEGY, G., Medical Chemistry
BIRKÁS, J., Military and Disaster Medicine
BITTER, J., Psychiatry and Psychotherapy
BODOR, E., Cardiovascular Surgery
BÖSZÖRMÉNYI NAGY, GY., Pulmonology
CSERMELY, P., Medical Chemistry, Molecu-
lar Biology and Pathobiochemistry
CSILLAG, A., Anatomy, Histology and
Embryology
DARVAS, K. I., Surgery
DE CHÂTEL, R., Internal Medicine
DEMETER, J., Internal Medicine
DZSINICH, CS., Cardiovascular Surgery
ENYEDI, P., Physiology
FALLER, J., Surgery
FALUDI, G., Psychiatry
FALUS, A., Biology
FARAGÓ, A., Medical Chemistry, Molecular
Biology and Pathobiochemistry
FARSANG, G., Internal Medicine
FEHÉR, E., Anatomy, Histology and Embry-
ology
FEKETE, B., Immunology
FEKETE, GY., Paediatrics
FIDY, J., Biophysics and Radiology
FLAUTNER, L., Surgery
FÜRST, ZS., Pharmacology
FÜST, GY., Internal Medicine
GÉHER, P., Pneumatology and Physiother-
apy
GERENDAI, I., Human Morphology and
Developmental Biology
GERGELY, P., Dermatology and Venereol-
ogy
GERŐ, L., Internal Medicine
GÖMÖR, B., Rheumatology and Physiother-
apy
GYIRES, K., Pharmacology and Pharma-
cotherapy
HORKAY, F., Cardiology
HORVÁTH, A., Dermatology and Venereol-
ogy
HUNYADY, L., Physiology
JÁRAY, J., Transplantation and Surgery
KÁDÁR, A., Pathology
KALABAY, L., Family Medicine
KÁLMÁNCHEY, R., Paediatrics
KARÁDI, I., Internal Medicine
KÁRPÁTH, S., Dermatology and Venereology
KELEMEN, Z., Urology
KELLER, E., Forensic Medecine

KELTAI, M., Cardiology
KEMPLER, P., Internal Medicine
KERPEL-FRONIUS, S., Pharmacology and
Pharmacotherapy
KOLLAI, M., Physiology and Experimental
Laboratory for Clinical Research
KOLLER, Á., Pathophysiology
KOPP, M., Behavioural Sciences
KOPPER, L., Pathology and Experimental
Cancer Research
KOVALSZKY, I., Pathology
KÖVES, K., Human Morphology and Devel-
opmental Biology
KUPCSULIK, P., Surgery
LAKATOS, P., Internal Medicine
LIGETI, E., Physiology
LIGETI, L., Physiology
LOSONCZY, GY., Pulmonology
MACHAY, T., Paediatrics
MAGYAR, P., Pulmonology
MANDL, J., Medical Chemistry, Molecular
Biology and Pathobiochemistry
MATOLCSY, A., Pathology and Experimental
Cancer Research
MORAVA, E., Public Health
MORVAI, V., Internal Medicine
MÓZES, T., Traumatology
NAGY, GY., Human Morphology and Devel-
opmental Biology
NAGY, P., Pathology
NAGY, Z., Cardiovascular Surgery
NEMES, A., Cardiovascular Surgery
NÉMETH, J., Ophthalmology
NYÁRY, I., Neurosurgery
OLÁH, I., Human Morphology and Devel-
opmental Biology
ONDREJKA, P., Surgery
PAJOR, A., Obstetrics and Gynaecology
PÁLÓCZI, K., Immunology
PAPP, J., Internal Medicine
PAPP, Z., Obstetrics and Gynaecology
PAULIN, F., Obstetrics and Gynaeology
PÉNZES, I., Anaesthesiology and Intensive
Therapy
PERNER, F., Transplantology and Surgery
POÓR, GY., Rheumatology and Physiology
PRÉDA, I., Cardiology
RÁCZ, K., Internal Medicine
RAJNA, P., Psychiatry and Psychotherapy
REGÖLY-MÉREI, J., Surgery
RÉPÁSSY, G., Otorhinolaryngology, Head
and Neck Surgery
RÉTHELYI, M., Anatomy, Histology and
Embryology
REUSZ, GY., Paediatrics
ROMICS, I., Urology
ROMICS, L., Internal Medicine
ROSIVALL, L., Pathophysiology
ROZGONYI, F., Microbiology
SALACZ, GY., Ophthalmology
SANDOR, J., Surgery
SÁNDOR, P., Human Physiology
SÁRVÁRY, A., Traumatology
SCHAFF, ZS., Pathology
SIKLÓSI, GY., Obstetrics and Gynaecology
SIMON, T., Public Health
SÓTONYI, P., Forensic Medicine
SPÄT, A., Physiology
SRÉTER, L., Internal Medicine
STAUB, M., Medical Chemistry, Molecular
Biology and Pathobiochemistry
SÜVEGES, I., Ophthalmology
SZAGO, A., Paediatrics
SZALAY, F., Internal Medicine
SZÁNTÓ, I., Surgery
SZÉKÁCS, B., Geriatrics
SZÉL, Á., Human Morphology and Devel-
opmental Biology
SZENDRŐI, M., Orthopaedics
SZIRMAI, I., Neurology
SZOLLÁR, L., Pathophysiology
TAMÁS, GY., Internal Medicine
TIHANYI, L., Paediatrics, Infectious Diseases
TOMPA, A., Public Health

TÓTH, M., Medical Chemistry, Molecular
Biology and Pathobiochemistry
TRINGER, L., Psychiatry and Psychotherapy
TULASSAY, T., Paediatrics
TULASSAY, ZS., Internal Medicine
UNGVÁRY, GY., Public Health
VEREBÉLY, T., Paediatrics
WENGER, T., Human Morphology and
Developmental Biology

Faculty of Pharmacy (tel. (1) 266-0449; fax
(1) 317-5340; e-mail nosbel@hogyes.sote.hu):

KLEBOVICH, J., Pharmaceutics
LEDNICZKY, L., Pharmacology
LIPTÁK, J., Medical Regulation
MARTON, S., Pharmaceutics
MÁTYUS, P., Organic Chemistry
NOSZÁL, B., Pharmaceutical Chemistry
PAÁL, T., Medical Regulation
SZŐKE, É., Pharmacognosy
TAKÁCSNÉ NOVÁK, K., Pharmaceutical
Chemistry
TEKES, K., Pharmacodynamics
TÖRÖK, T., Pharmacodynamics
VINCZE, Z., University Pharmacy, Phar-
macy Administration

Faculty of Physical Education and Sport
Sciences (1123 Budapest, Alkotás u. 44; tel.
(1) 487-9214; fax (1) 356-6337; e-mail
nyerges@mail.hupe.hu):

BERLLES, I., Sports Surgery
DOZSA, I., Rhythmic Dance and Aerobics
FÖLDESY, T., Social Sciences
GOMBOCZ, J., Theory and Teaching of
Physical Education
KERTÉSZ, I., Social Sciences
MÉSZAROS, J., Health Sciences and Sports
Medicine
NYAKAS, CS., Health Sciences and Sports
Medicine
PAVLIK, G., Health Sciences and Sports
Medicine
RADÁK, ZS., Sport Sciences Research
SIPOS, K., Psychology
TAKÁCS, F., Social Sciences
TIHANYI, J., Biomechanics

SZÉCHENYI ISTVÁN EGYETEM
(Széchenyi István University)

9026 Győr, Egyetem tér 1
Telephone: (96) 503-400
Fax: (96) 329-263
E-mail: sze@sze.hu
Internet: www.sze.hu

Founded 1968 as Széchenyi István Főiskola;
present name and status 2002
State control
Academic year: September to June

Rector: Dr TAMÁS SZEKERES
Vice-Rector: JÁNOS RECHNITZER
Vice-Rector for Institutional Devt: Prof. Dr
KÁROLY KARDOS
Dir of Int. Project Center: Prof. Dr CSABA
KOREN
Dir of Strategy and Devt: TAMÁS L. SZILASI
Sec.-Gen.: Prof. Dr BÉLA ÍRÓ
Library Dir: ANIKÓ FABULA
Library of 240,000 vols, 1,000 periodicals
Number of teachers: 360
Number of students: 10,600 (6,800 under-
graduate, 1,200 postgraduate, 2,600 dis-
tant learning)
Publications: *Acta Technica Jaurinensis*,
Hungarian Electronic Journal of Sciences
(online), *Law, State, Politics*, *Tudományos
Füzetek*

DEANS

Deák Ferenc Faculty of Law: Prof. Dr GYULA
SZALAY
Faculty of Technical Sciences: Prof. Dr
LÁSZLÓ KÓCZY T.

Kautz Gyula Faculty of Economics: Dr LÁSZLÓ JÓZSA

ATTACHED INSTITUTES

Petz Lajos Institute of Health and Social Studies: 9024 Győr, Szent Imre ut. 28; tel. (96) 507-940; fax (96) 507-940; e-mail nagysandor@petz.gyor.hu; Dir Prof. Dr SÁNDOR NAGY.

Varga Tibor Institute of Music: 9025 Győr, Kossuth ut. 5; tel. (96) 329-735; fax (96) 314-862; e-mail ruppert@sze.hu; Dir Prof. Dr ISTVÁN RUPPERT.

SZEGEDI TUDOMÁNYEGYETEM
(University of Szeged)

6720 Szeged, Dugonics tér 13
Telephone: (62) 544-001
Fax: (62) 546-371
E-mail: rekthiv@rekt.u-szeged.hu
Internet: www.u-szeged.hu

Founded 1872, refounded 1921; became József Attila Tudományegyetem (Attila József University) 1962; present name 2000 upon merger with Szent-Györgyi Albert Orvostudományi Egyetem (Albert Szent-Györgyi University of Medicine) and other instns
State control
Academic year: September to June

Rector: Prof. Dr GÁBOR SZABÓ
Vice-Rector for Education: Dr BÉLA PUKÁNSZKY
Vice-Rectors for Gen. Affairs: Prof. Dr IMRE MUCSI, Prof. Dr JÁNOS LONOVICS
Vice-Rector for Scientific Issues: Dr IMRE DÉKÁNY
Vice-Rector for Strategic Issues: Dr BÉLA RÁCZ
Vice-Rector for Student Issues: Dr ATTILA BADÓ
Librarian: PALOTÁSNÉ RÓZA PÁNTI
Library: see Libraries and Archives
Number of teachers: 2,279
Number of students: 31,478

Publications: *Acta Biologica Szegediensis, Acta Climatologica, Acta Cybernetica, Acta Scientarum Mathematicarum*

DEANS

Faculty of Agriculture: Prof. Dr IMRE MUCSI
Faculty of Arts: Prof. Dr ÁRPÁD BERTA
Faculty of Dentistry: Prof. Dr NAGY KATALIN
Faculty of Economics and Business Administrations: Dr BEÁTA FARKAS
Faculty of Engineering: Prof. Dr JÓZSEF FENYVESSY
Faculty of Health Sciences and Social Studies: Dr GYÖRGY BENEDEK
Faculty of Law: Prof. Dr IMRE SZABÓ
Faculty of Medicine: Prof. Dr MAGDOLNA POGÁNY
Faculty of Music: Prof. Dr FERENC KEREK
Faculty of Pharmacy: Prof. Dr GYÖRGY ISTVÁN FALKAY
Faculty of Science and Informatics: Prof. Dr GÁBOR MEZŐSI
Juhász Gyula Teacher Training Faculty: Prof. Dr GÁBOR GALAMBOS

PROFESSORS

Faculty of Agriculture (6800 Hódmezővásárhely, Andrássy u. 15; tel. (62) 246-466; e-mail bodnar@mgk.u-szeged.hu; internet www.mgk.u-szeged.hu):

PÉTER, J., Nutrition
SAS, B., Animal Husbandry
TANÁCS, L., Plant Protection

Faculty of Arts (6722 Szeged, Egyetem u. 2; tel. (62) 544-166; fax (62) 425-843; e-mail kelemen@arts.u-szeged.hu; internet www.arts.u-szeged.hu):

ANDERLE, Á., Hispanic Studies

BAKRÓ-NAGY, M., Finno-Ugrian Linguistics
BALÁZS, M., Early Hungarian Literature
BARNA, G., Ethnology
BASSOLA, P., German Linguistics
BERNÁTH, A., German Literature
CSAPÓ, B., Education
CSEJTEI, D., Philosophy
CSÚRI, K., Austrian Culture and Literature
FRIED, I., Comparative Literature
GYENGE, Z., Philosophy
IVANICS, M., Altaic Studies
J. NAGY, L., Modern World History and Mediterranean Studies
KARSAI, L., Modern World History
KENESEI, I., English and American Studies
KESERŰ, B., Early Hungarian Literature
KONTRA, M., Applied Linguistics
LEPAHIN, V., Russian Language and Literature
MAKK, F., Auxiliary Sciences of History
MARÓTI, E., Ancient History
MÁTÉ-TÓTH, A., Study of Religions
NAGY, J., Education
OLAJOS, T., Auxiliary Sciences of History
PÁL, J., Italian Language and Literature
PÁLFY, M., French Language and Literature
PENKE, O., French Language and Literature
RÓNA-TAS, A., Altaic Studies
SAJTI, E., Modern World History
SZAJBÉLY, M., Classic Hungarian Literature
SZŐNYI, G., English and American Studies
SZÖRÉNYI, L., Comparative Literature
TÓTH, I., Slavistics
VIDÁKOVICH, T., Education
VÍGH, É., Italian Language and Literature
WINKLER, I., Psychology
WOJTILLA, G., Ancient History

Faculty of Dentistry (6720 Szeged, Tisza L. krt. 64; tel. (62) 545-299; fax (62) 545-282; e-mail stoma@stoma.szote.u-szeged.hu; internet www.szote.u-szeged.hu/stoma):

FAZEKAS, A., Prosthodontics and Oral Biology
GORZÓ, I., Operative Dentistry and Endodontology
MARI, A., Operative Dentistry and Endodontology
NAGY, K., Dentistry, Oral Surgery
RAKONCZAY, Z., Prosthodontics and Oral Biology
SZENTPÉTERY, J., Prosthodontics and Oral Biology

Faculty of Economics and Business Administration (6722 Szeged, Honvéd tér 6; tel. (62) 544-485; fax (62) 544-499; e-mail bfarkas@eco.u-szeged.hu; internet www.eco.u-szeged.hu):

BENET, I., World Economics and European Economic Integration
BOTOS, K., Finance
DINYA, L., Marketing and Management
KOVÁCS, A., Finance
LENGYEL, I., Economics and Economic Development
REKETTYE, G., Marketing and Management

Faculty of Engineering:

BALOGH, S., Agricultural Economics and Rural Development
FENYVESSY, J., Food Technology
GÁBOR, M., Food Technology
HODÚR, C., Unit Operation and Environmental Techniques
KOVÁCS, E., Food Technology
MOLNÁR, P., Agricultural Economics and Rural Development
RAJKÓ, R., Unit Operation and Environmental Techniques
SZABÓ, G., Unit Operation and Environmental Techniques
VÉHA, A., Food Technology

Faculty of Health Sciences and Social Studies (6726 Szeged, Temesvári krt. 31; tel. (62) 545-024; fax (62) 545-515; e-mail poma@efk.u-szeged.hu; internet www.efk.u-szeged.hu):

BÁRÁNY, F., Social Work and Social Policy
BODA, M., Applied Medicine

Faculty of Law (6722 Szeged, Tisza L. krt. 54; tel. (62) 544-206; fax (62) 544-204; e-mail ajtk.dekani@juris.u-szeged.hu; internet www.juris.u-szeged.hu):

BADÓ, A., Philosophy and Sociology of Law
BALOGH, E., Legal History
BESENYEI, L., Civil Law and Civil Procedure
BLAZOVICH, L., Legal History
BLUTMAN, L., International Law
BODNÁR, L., International Law
CSÉKA, E., Criminal Law and Criminal Procedure
CZÚCZ, O., Social and Labour Law
HAJDÚ, J., Social and Labour Law
HERCZEG, J., Statistics and Demography
HOMOKI-NAGY, M., Legal History
JAKAB, É., Roman Law
KATONA, T., Statistics and Demography
MARTONYI, J., International Private Law
MOLNÁR, I., Roman Law
NAGY, F., Criminal Law and Criminal Procedure
NAGY, L., Economics
PACZOLAY, P., Political Sciences
POKOL, B., Philosophy and Sociology of Law
RUSZOLY, J., Legal History
STIPTA, I., Legal History
SZABÓ, I., Civil Law and Civil Procedure
TRÓCSÁNYI, L., Constitutional Law

Faculty of Medicine (6720 Szeged, Dóm tér 12; tel. (62) 545-015; fax (62) 426-529; e-mail aokdh@medea.szote.u-szeged.hu; internet www.szote.u-szeged.hu):

ÁBRAHÁM, G., Internal Medicine
BALOGH, Á., Clinical Surgery
BARI, F., Medical Physics and Informatics
BÁRTFAI, G., Tocology and Gynaecology
BARZÓ, P., Neurological Surgery
BÉLÁDI, I., Medical Microbiology and Immunology
BENDER, T., Orthopaedics
BENEDEK, G., Physiology
BODA, D., Neurological Surgery
BODOSI, M., Neurological Surgery
BOLDOGKŐI, Z., Medical Biology
BORBÉNYI, Z., Internal Medicine and Cardiology
BOROS, M., Experimental Surgery
CSANÁDY, M., Internal Medicine
CSERNAY, L., Nuclear Medicine
CSILLIK, B., Anatomy, Histology and Embryology
CSÖRGŐ BATA, Z., Dermatology and Allergology
CZIGNER, J., Otorhinolaryngology and Head and Neck Surgery
DÉSI, I., Public Health
DOBOZY, A., Dermatology and Allergology
DUDA, E., Medical Microbiology
DUX, L., Biochemistry
ENGELHARDT, J., Neurology
FARKAS, G., Surgery
FERDINANDY, P., Biochemistry
FORSTER, T., Internal Medicine and Cardiology
FRÁTER, L., Radiology
FÜZESI, K., Paediatrics
GAÁL MÉRAY, J., Anaesthesiology and Intensive Therapy
GELLÉN, J., Toxicology and Immunology
HAJNAL, F., Family Medicine
HAMMER, H., Ophthalmology
HANTOS, Z., Medical Physics and Informatics
HERCZEG VÁRKONYI, Á., Paediatrics
HORVÁTH, A., Laboratory Medicine

HUSZ, S., Dermatology and Allergology
IVÁNYI, B., Pathology
JANÁKY, M., Ophthalmology
JANCSÓ, G., Physiology
JANKA, Z., Neurology and Psychiatry
JÁRDÁNHÁZY, T., Neurology
JÓRI, J., Otorhinolaryngology and Head and Neck Surgery
JULESZ, J., Endocrinology
KAHÁN, Z., Oncotherapy
KÁLMÁN, J., Neurology and Psychiatry
KÁSA, P., Neurology and Psychiatry
KATONA, M., Paediatrics
KEMÉNY, L., Dermatology and Allergology
KÉRI, S., Physiology
KISS HŐGYE, M., Internal Medicine and Cardiology
KOLOZSVÁRI, L., Ophthalmology
KOVÁCS, G., Internal Medicine and Cardiology
KOVÁCS, L., Tocology and Gynaecology
LÁSZLÓ, A., Paediatrics
LÁZÁR, G., Pathophysiology
LÁZÁR, G., Surgery
LENCZ, L., Anaesthesiology and Intensive Therapy
LEPRÁN, I., Pharmacology and Pharmacotherapy
LONOVICS, J., Internal Medicine
MÁNDI, Y., Medical Microbiology and Immunology
MÉSZÁROS, T., Orthopaedics
MIHÁLY, A., Anatomy, Histology and Embryology
MIKÓ, T., Pathology
MOLNÁR, J., Anatomy, Histology and Embryology
MOLNÁR, J., Medical Microbiology and Immunology
MOLNÁR, Z., Anaesthesiology and Intensive Therapy
NAGY, E., Clinical Microbiology
NAGY, F., Internal Medicine
NAGY, S., Experimental Surgery
NAGYMAJTÉNYI, L., Public Health
OBÁL, F., Physiology
ORMOS, J., Pathology
PAJOR, L., Urology
PÁL, A., Tocology and Gynaecology
PALKÓ, A., Radiology
PAPP, G., Pharmacology and Pharmacotherapy
PÁVICS, L., Nuclear Medicine
PENKE, B., Medical Chemistry
PETRI, A., Surgery
PIFFKÓ, J., Oral And Maxillofacial Surgery
PINTÉR, S., Paediatrics
POKORNY, G., Rheumatology
PRÁGAI, B., Medical Microbiology and Immunology
PUSZTAI, R., Medical Microbiology and Immunology
RESCH, B., Tocology and Gynaecology
RUDAS, L., Anaesthesiology and Intensive Therapy
SCULTÉTY, S., Urology
SIMONKA, J., Traumatology
SOMFAY, A., Pulmonology
SZABAD, J., Medical Biology
SZABÓ, G., Pathophysiology
SZABÓ, J., Medical Genetics
SZARVAS, F., Internal Medicine
SZEKERES, L., Pharmacology and Pharmacotherapy
SZEMERE, G., Medical Genetics
SZILÁRD, J., Neurology and Psychiatry
SZTRIHA, L., Paediatrics
TAKÁCS, T., Internal Medicine
TELEGDY, G., Pathophysiology
TÉNYI, M., Internal Medicine and Cardiology
THURZÓ, L., Oncotherapy
TÓTH, G., Medical Chemistry
TÓTH, K., Orthopaedics
TUBOLY HORVÁTH, G., Physiology
TÚRI, S., Paediatrics

VARGA, E., Traumatology
VARGA, T., Forensic Medicine
VARRÓ, A., Pharmacology and Pharmacotherapy
VARRÓ, V., Internal Medicine
VAS, Á., Internal Medicine
VÉCSEI, L., Neurology
VÉGH, Á., Pharmacology and Pharmacotherapy
VIRÁG, I., Paediatrics
WITTMANN, T., Internal Medicine
ZARÁNDI, M., Medical Chemistry

Faculty of Music (6722 Szeged, Tisza L. krt. 79–81; tel. (62) 544-600; fax (62) 544-066; e-mail zfk@muzik.u-szeged.hu; internet www.muzik.u-szeged.hu):

KEREK, F., Piano
SZECSŐDI, F., Strings
TEMESI, M., Solo Singing

Faculty of Pharmacy (6720 Szeged, Zrinyi u. 9; tel. (62) 545-022; fax (62) 541-906; e-mail gytkdh@medea.szote.u-szeged.hu; internet www.szote.u-szeged.hu):

DOMBI, G., Pharmaceutical Analysis
ERŐS, I., Pharmaceutical Technology
FALKAY, G., Pharmacodynamics
FÜLÖP, F., Pharmaceutical Chemistry
GÁBOR, M., Pharmacodynamics
HÓDI, K., Pharmaceutical Technology
HOHMANN, J., Pharmacognosy
KATA, M., Pharmaceutical Technology
MÁTHÉ, I., Pharmacognosy
PAÁL, T., Drug Regulatory Affairs
RÉVÉSZ, P., Pharmaceutical Technology
SOÓS, G., Clinical Pharmacy
STÁJER, G., Pharmaceutical Chemistry
SZENDREI, K., Pharmacognosy

Faculty of Science and Informatics (6720 Szeged, Aradi vértanúk tere 1; tel. (62) 544-681; fax (62) 426-221; e-mail annuse@sci.u-szeged.hu; internet www.sci.u-szeged.hu):

BARTÓK, M., Chemistry
BECSEI, J., Geography
BENEDICT, M., Theoretical Physics
BOR, Z., Optics and Quantum Electronics
BOROS, I., Genetic and Molecular Biology
CZÉDLI, G., Algebra and Numeric Theory
CSÁKÁNY, B., Mathematics
CSÁNYI, L., Chemistry
CSENDES, T., Computational Optimization
CSIRIK, J., Computer Science
DÉKÁNY, I., Physical Chemistry and Material Science
DOMBI, A., Mechanic and Material Science
ERDEI, L., Plant Biology
ERDŐHELYI, A., Physical Chemistry and Material Science
ÉSIK, Z., Principles of Computer Science
FARKAS L, G., Biology
FEHÉR, L., Theoretical Physics
FEHÉR, O., Biology
FEJES, P., Chemistry
FEKETE, E., Comparative Physiology
FÜLÖP, Z., Principles of Computer Science
GAJDA, T., Inorganic and Analytical Chemistry
GALLÉ, L., Ecology
GÉCSEG, F., Computer Science
GULYA, K., Zoology and Cell Biology
GYIMÓTHY, T., Software Engineering
HANNUS, I., Applied and Environmental Chemistry
HATVANI, L., Analysis
HERNÁDI, K., Applied and Environmental Chemistry
HETÉNYI, M., Mineralogy, Geochemistry and Petrography
HEVESI, I., Physics
IGLÓI, F., Theoretical Physics
KÉRCHY, L., Analysis
KEVEI, I., Climatology and Landscape Ecology
KISS, T., Inorganic and Analytical Chemistry

KOVÁCS, K., Biotechnology
KOVÁCS, Z., Economic Geography
KRÁMLI, A., Applications of Analysis
KRISZTIN, T., Applied Numerical Mathematics
LEINDLER, L., Analysis
MAJOR, P., Applications of Analysis
MARÓTI, P., Medical Physics and Biophysics
MARÓY, P., Genetic and Molecular Biology
MÉSZÁROS, R., Economic Geography
MEZŐSI, G., Physical Geography and Geoinformatics
MÓCZÁR, L., Biology
MOLNÁR, B., Geography
MÓRICZ, F., Applications of Analysis
NEMCSÓK, J., Biochemistry
PAP, G., Applications of Analysis
PÉTER, A., Inorganic and Analytical Chemistry
RÁCZ, B., Optics and Quantum Electronics
SCHNEIDER, G., Chemistry
SOLYMOSI, F., Chemistry
SZABÓ, G., Optics and Quantum Electronics
SZATMÁRI, S., Experimental Physics
SZENDREI, Á., Algebra and Numeric Theory
SZENDREI, M., Algebra and Numeric Theory
SZENTE, M., Comparative Physiology
TAMÁS, G., Comparative Physiology
TOLDI, J., Comparative Physiology
TOMBÁCZ, E., Physical Chemistry and Material Science
TOTIK, V., Set Theory and Mathematical Logic
VÁGVÖLGYI, C., Microbiology
VINCZE, I., Chemistry
VISY, C., Physical Chemistry and Material Science
ZSOLDOS, F., Biology

Juhász Gyula Teacher Training Faculty (6722 Szeged, Boldogasszony sgt. 6; tel. (62) 546-050; fax (62) 420-953; e-mail galambos@jgytf.u-szeged.hu; internet www.jgytf.u-szeged.hu):

BÉKÉSI, I., Hungarian Language
GALAMBOS, G., Computer Science
LÁSZLÓ, F., Physical Education and Sports Science
NAGY, J., Hungarian Language
NÁNAI, L., Physics
PUKÁNSZKY, B., Education
RÁCZ, L., Applied Humanities
SERES, L., Chemistry
SZABÓ, T., Applied Humanities
VARGA, I., Education

SZENT ISTVÁN EGYETEM
(Szent István University)

2100 Gödöllő, Páter Károly u. 1

Telephone: (28) 522-000
Fax: (28) 410-804
E-mail: info@szie.hu
Internet: www.szie.hu

Founded 1945, as Gödöllői Agrártudományi Egyetem (Gödöllő University of Agricultural Sciences), merged with Allatorvostudomanyi Egyetem (University of Veterinary Science) (Budapest), Kertészeti és Élelmiszeripari Egyetem (University of Horticulture and Food Technology) (Budapest), Jászberényi Tanitóképző Főiskola (Jászberény Teacher-Training College) and Ybl Miklós Műszaki Főiskola (Miklós Ybl Polytechnic) in 2000, present status 2000
State control
Languages of instruction: Hungarian, English, German
Academic year: September to June
Rector: Dr SOLTI LÁSZLÓ

Vice-Rector for Education and Int. Relations:
Dr JÁNOS BEKE
Vice-Rector for Research: Dr LÁSZLÓ HORNOK
Library: attached libraries and archives in
Gödöllő, Budapest, Jászberény, Szarvas,
Gyula, Békéscsaba
Number of teachers: 663
Number of students: 16,978

DEANS

Faculty of Agricultural Engineering: Prof. Dr
CSÁNYI SÁNDOR
Faculty of Agricultural and Environmental
Sciences (Szarvas): Dr PUSKÁS JÁNOS
Faculty of Applied Arts (Jászberény): Dr
BARKÓ ENDRE
Faculty of Economics (Békéscsaba): Dr BOR-
ZÁN ANITA
Faculty of Economics and Social Sciences
(Gödöllő): Dr VILLÁNYI LÁSZLÓ
Faculty of the Food Industry: Prof. Dr
ANDRÁS FEKETE
Faculty of Horticulture: Dr JENŐ BERNÁTH
Faculty of Landscape Architecture: Dr ILONA
BALOGH ORMOS
Faculty of Mechanical Engineering (Gödöllő):
Dr SZABÓ ISTVÁN
Faculty of Pedagogy (Szarvas): Dr LIPCSEI
IMRE
Faculty of Veterinary Medicine: Prof. Dr
FODOR LÁSZLÓ
College Faculty of Jászberény: (vacant)
Ybl Miklós Faculty of Architecture and Civil
Engineering (Budapest): Dr MAKOVÉNYI
FERENC
Institute of Health Care and Environmental
Sanitation Studies (Gyula): Dr KÖTELES
LAJOS
Institute of Scientific Training: Dr PÉTER
SZENDRŐ

DIRECTORS

College Faculty of Agricultural Economics,
Gyöngygös: Dr SÁNDOR MAGDA

PROFESSORS

Faculty of Agricultural Engineering:
BARÓTFY, I., Environmental Engineering
BEER, GY., Agricultural Engineering
FARKAS, I., Physics
GYÜRK, I., Mechanics
JESZENSZKY, Z., Agricultural Engineering
KÓSA, A., Mathematics
SEMBERY, P., Food Engineering
SZENDRŐ, P., Agricultural Mechanization
SZÜLE, ZS., Agricultural Mechanization
VAS, A., Agricultural Engineering

Faculty of Agricultural and Environmental
Sciences:
ANDRÁS, D.
ERIKA, M.
ERZSÉBET, K.
FERENC, G.
FERENC, L.
FERENC, S.
FERENC, V.
GÁBOR, B.
GYÖRGY, F.
GYÖRGY, H.
GYÖRGY, V.
JÁNOS, K.
JÁNOS, T.
JÓZSEF, K.
JUDIT, D.
LAJOS, H.
LÁSZLÓ, B.
LÁSZLÓ, HESZKY
LÁSZLÓ, HORNOK
LÁSZLÓ, HORVÁTH
MÁRTA, B.
MÁRTON, J.
MIHÁLY, W.
MIKLÓS, M.
PÉTER GERGELY, P.
SÁNDOR, C.

ZOLTÁN, M.
ZOLTÁN, T.
Faculty of Agricultural, Water and Environ-
mental Management of Tessedik Samuel
College:
ISTVÁN, P.
ZOLTÁN, I.
Faculty of Economics and Social Sciences:
ANDRÁS, N.
BÁLINT CSABA, I.
CSABA, M.
CSABA, S.
GYÖRGY IVÁN, C.
IMRE, L.
ISTVÁN, F.
ISTVÁN, S.
JÓZSEF, L.
JÓZSEF, M.
JÓZSEF, V.
LAJOS, S.
LÁSZLÓ, H.
LÁSZLÓ, K.
LÁSZLÓ, V.
MAGDOLNA, C.
PÉTER, H.
TAMÁS, S.
TAMÁS, T.
TOMAY TAMÁS, S.
ZOLTÁN, S.

Faculty of Mechanical Engineering:
ATTILA, V.
CSIZMADIA BÉLA, M.
DEZSŐ, F.
GÁBOR, K.
ISTVÁN, B.
ISTVÁN, F.
ISTVÁN, H.
JÁNOS, B.
LAJOS, L.
LÁSZLÓ, F.
LÁSZLÓ, T.
PÉTER, S.
ZOLTÁN, V.
ZSOLT, S.

Faculty of Veterinary Medicine:
ENDRE, B.
GÁBOR, S.
JÁNOS, F.
JÁNOS, V.
JÁNOS LÁSZLÓ, V.
JÓZSEF ZSIGMOND, S.
LÁSZLÓ, F.
LÁSZLÓ, Z.
KÁROLY, V.
KATALIN, H.
MIKLÓS, R.
OTTÓ, S.
PÁL, R.
PÁL, S.
PÉTER, G.
PÉTER, L.
PÉTER, N.
PÉTER, S.
RÓBERT, F.
SÁNDOR, C.
SÁNDOR GYÖRGY, F.
TIBOR, G.
VILMOS LÁSZLÓ, F.

Ybl Miklós Faculty of Architecture and Civil
Engineering:
GÁBOR, T.
KÁROLY, Z.
RUDOLF, K.

PROFESSORS FROM THE FORMER UNIVERSITY OF
HORTICULTURE AND FOOD TECHNOLOGY

BALÁZS, S., Vegetable Production
BALOGH, S., Food Industry Economics
BÉKÁSSY-MOLNÁR, E., Food Technology
BERNÁTH, J., Medicinal Plants
BOROSS, L., Chemistry and Biochemistry
CSEMEZ, A., Landscape Architecture
CSEPREGI, P., Viticulture

DALÁNYI, L., Landscape Architecture
DEÁK, T., Microbiology
DIMÉNY, I., Agricultural Economics
DINYA, L., Economics and Marketing
EPERJESI, I., Oenology
ERDÉLYI, E., Food Technology
FARKAS, J., Food Preservation
FEKETE, A., Food Physics
FODOR, P., Chemistry and Biochemistry
GLITS, M., Plant Pathology
HARNOS, ZS., Mathematics
HORVÁTH, G., Plant Physiology
HOSCHKE, A., Brewing and Distillation
JÁMBOR, I., Landscape Architecture
KISS, I., Food Preservation
KÖRMENDY, I., Food Preservation
KOSÁRY, J., Chemistry and Biochemistry
LÁNG, Z., Technical Department
MÉSZÁROS, Z., Entomology
MŐCSÉNYI, M., Landscape Architecture
PAIS, I., Chemistry
PAPP, J., Fruit Growing
RIMÓCZI, I., Botany
SÁRAI, T., Food Technology
SÁRKÖZY, P., Agricultural Economics
SASS, P., Fruit Growing
SCHMIDT, G., Floriculture and Dendrology
SZABÓ, S. A., Food Chemistry
VARSÁNYI, I., Food Preservation
VELICH, I., Plant Genetics and Selection
VERMES, L., Agrometeorology and Water
Management

SZINHÁZ- ÉS FILMMŰVÉSZETI EGYETEM
(University of Drama and Film)

1088 Budapest, Vas u. 2c

Telephone: (1) 318-8111
Fax: (1) 338-4749
E-mail: xan6632@mail.iif.hu
Internet: www.filmacademy.hu
Founded 1865
State control

Rector: GÁBOR SZÉKELY
Vice-Rectors: LÁSZLÓ BABARCZY, ÁDÁM HOR-
VÁTH
Dir of Int. Relations: JÁNOS XANTUS
Sec.-Gen.: L. TISZEKER

Number of teachers: 97
Number of students: 269

ZRÍNYI MIKLÓS NEMZETVÉDELMI EGYETEM
(Zrínyi Miklós University of National Defence)

1101 Budapest, Hungária krt. 9-11

Telephone: (1) 432-9000
Fax: (1) 432-9012
E-mail: rektor@zmne.hu
Internet: portal.zmne.hu
State control

Rector: Dr JÁNOS SZABÓ.

Private Universities

ANDRÁSSY GYULA BUDAPESTI NÉMET NYELVŐ EGYETEM
(Andrássy Gyula University)

1464 Budapest, POB 1422
1088 Budapest, Pollack Mihály tér 3

Telephone: (1) 266-3101
Fax: (1) 266-3099
E-mail: uni@andrassyuni.hu
Internet: www.andrassyuni.hu
Private control
Language of instruction: German
Rector: Prof. Dr MASÁT ANDRÁS
Pro-Rector: Prof. Dr CHRISTIAN SCHUBEL
Library Dir: HEDVIG ZIMMERMANN

DEANS

Faculty of Comparative Law Studies: Prof. Dr ÓLIVER DIGGELMANN
Faculty of European Studies: Prof. Dr DIETER A. BINDER
Faculty of International Relations: Dr MARTINA ECKARDT

CENTRAL EUROPEAN UNIVERSITY

1051 Budapest, Nádor u. 9
Telephone: (1) 327-3000
Fax: (1) 327-3005
E-mail: public@ceu.hu
Internet: www.ceu.hu
Founded 1991
Private control
Language of instruction: English
Academic year: September to June

Pres. and Rector: Prof. JOHN SHATTUCK
Academic Pro-Rector: KATALIN FARKAS
Pro-Rector for Hungarian and EU Affairs: KAROLY BARD
Vice-Pres. for External Relations: ILDIKO MORAN
Vice-Pres. for Student Services: PETER JOHNSON

Library of 150,000 books, 1,500 periodicals
Number of teachers: 305
Number of students: 1,541

DEBRECENI REFORMÁTUS HITTUDOMÁNYI EGYETEM
(Debrecen University of Reformed Theology)

4044 Debrecen, Kálvin tér 16
Telephone: (52) 414-744
Fax: (52) 516-822
E-mail: info@drhe.drk.hu
Internet: www.drhe.drk.hu
Founded 1538
Private control

Rector: KÁROLY FEKETE

Library of 600,000 vols
Number of teachers: 36
Number of students: 306

EVANGÉLIKUS HITTUDOMÁNYI EGYETEM
(Evangelical-Lutheran Theological University)

1141 Budapest, Rózsavölgyi köz 3
Telephone: (1) 469-1050
Fax: (1) 363-7454
E-mail: teologia@lutheran.hu
Internet: teol.lutheran.hu
Founded 1557
Private control

Rector: Dr LAJOS SZABÓ

Library of 59,000 vols, 119 periodicals
Number of teachers: 15
Number of students: 160

KÁROLI GÁSPÁR REFORMÁTUS EGYETEM
(Gáspár Károli University of the Reformed Church in Hungary)

1092 Budapest, Ráday u. 28
Telephone: (1) 217-2403
Fax: (1) 217-2403
E-mail: dekani.hivvez.htk@kre.hu
Internet: www.kre.hu
Founded 1855
Private control

Rector: Prof. Dr. FERENC SZŰCS

Library of 2,000,000 vols
Number of teachers: 19
Number of students: 190

DEANS

Faculty of Humanities: (vacant): Dr SEPSI ENIKO
Faculty of Law: ANTALÓCZY PETER
Faculty of Teacher Training: Dr ISTVÁN NAGY
Faculty of Theology: Dr SÁNDOR BÉKÉSI

ATTACHED INSTITUTE

Institute of Kremlinology: tel. (1) 455-9060; e-mail kemoke@index.hu; Dir Prof. Dr MIKLÓS KUN.

ORSZÁGOS RABBIKÉPZŐ–ZSIDÓ EGYETEM
(Jewish Theological Seminary– University of Jewish Studies)

1084 Budapest, Bérkocsis u. 2
Telephone: (1) 317-2396
Fax: (1) 318-7049
E-mail: vzs@or-zse.hu
Internet: www.or-zse.hu
Founded 1877
Private control

Rector: Rabbi Dr Y. A. SCHÖNER

Library of 110,000 vols
Number of teachers: 87
Number of students: 264

Faculty of Rabbinical Studies; College Faculty/Paedagogium.

PÁZMÁNY PÉTER KATOLIKUS EGYETEM
(Péter Pázmány Catholic University)

1088 Budapest, Szentkirályi u. 28–30
Telephone: (1) 429-7211
Fax: (1) 318-0507
E-mail: rector@ppke.hu
Internet: www.ppke.hu
Founded 1635
Private control
Academic year: September to June

Rector: Rev. Dr GYÖRGY FODOR
Vice-Rector: Rev. Dr SZABOLCS ANZELM SZUROMI
Financial Dir: MIKLÓS RÓKA
Technical Dir: PÉTER BOROSS-TÓBY

Library of 400,000 vols
Number of teachers: 650
Number of students: 8,500

Publications: *Folia Canonica* (review of Eastern and Western Canon Law in five languages, 1 a year), *Folia Theologica* (in five languages, 1 a year), *Kánonjog* (Canon Law, in Hungarian, 2 a year), *Teológia* (in Hungarian, 4 a year), *VERBUM Analecta Neolatina* (in several European languages, 2 a year)

DEANS

Faculty of Humanities: Prof. IDA FRÖHLICH
Faculty of Information Technology: Prof. TAMÁS ROSKA
Faculty of Law and Political Science: Prof. GYULA BÁNDI
Faculty of Theology: Rev. Prof. ZOLTÁN ROKAY

Colleges

Apor Vilmos Katolikus Főiskola (Apor Vilmos Catholic College): 2600 Vác, Konstantin tér 1-5.; tel. (27) 511-140; fax (27) 511-141; e-mail avkf@avkf.hu; internet www.avkf.hu; Private control; Rector Dr PÁL BALÁZS.

Baptista Teológiai Akadémia (Baptist Theological Academy): 1068 Budapest, Benczúr u. 3; tel. (1) 342-0912; fax (1) 342-7534; internet www.bta.hu; Private control; Rector Dr TIBOR ALMÁSI.

Budapesti Gazdasági Főiskola (Budapest Business School): 1149 Budapest, Buzogány u. 11–13; tel. (1) 469-6600; fax (1) 469-6636; internet www.bgf.hu; f. 2000; State control; Rector Dr EVA SANDORNÉ-KRISZT; 17,796 students; Colleges of Commerce, Catering and Tourism; International Management and Business Studies; Finance and Accountancy.

Budapesti Kommunikációs és Üzleti Főiskola (Budapest School of Communication and Business): 1147 Budapest, Nagy Lajos kir.u. 1-9; tel. (1) 273-3090; fax (1) 273-3099; internet www.bkf.hu; Private control; Rector Dr LÁSZLÓ VASS; Librarian KORNÉLIA BÁNHEGYI KOLLÁR; Institutes of Economics and Business Sciences; European Studies; Journalism and Media Studies; Marketing and Business Communication; Social Sciences.

Budapesti Műszaki Főiskola (Budapest Tech (Polytechnical Institution)): 1034 Budapest, Doberdó u. 6; tel. (1) 250-0333; fax (1) 453-4149; e-mail rektor@bmf.hu; internet www.bmf.hu; f. 2000 as a result of the merger of Könnyüipari Műszaki Főiskola (College of Technology for Light Industry) (Budapest), Bánki Donát Gépipari Műszaki Főiskola (Donát Bánki Polytechnic) (Budapest), Kandó Kálmán Műszaki Főiskola (Kálmán Kandó College of Engineering) (Budapest) and other instns; State control; 417 teachers; 12,500 students; Rector Prof. Dr IMRE RUDAS; Librarian KRASZNAI MIHÁLYNÉ.

Dunaújvárosi Főiskola (Dunaújváros College): 2400 Dunaújváros Táncsics M. u. 1/A; tel. (25) 551-211; fax (25) 551-262; e-mail international@mail.duf.hu; internet www.duf.hu/english; f. 1969; State control; 111 teachers; 3,513 students; Dir-Gen. MÓNIKA RAJCSÁNYI-MOLNÁR.

International Business School, Budapest: 1021 Budapest, Tárogató u. 2–4; tel. (1) 391 2550; e-mail info@ibs-b.hu; internet www.ibs-b.hu; f. 1993; Private control; Chancellor Prof. ISTVÁN TAMÁS.

Károly Róbert Főiskola (Károly Róbert College): 320 Gyöngyös, 1 Mátrai u. 36; tel. (37) 518-305; fax (37) 313-170; internet www.karolyrobert.hu; Private control; Rector Dr SÁNDOR MAGDA; Colleges of Agriculture and Agricultural Management.

Kecskeméti Főiskola (Kecskemét College): 6000 Kecskemét, Izsáki u. 10B; tel. (76) 501-960; fax (76) 501-979; internet www.kefo.hu; State control; f. 2000 by merger of College of Mechanical Engineering and Automation, Teacher Training College and University of Horticulture and Food-Processing, Horticultural Faculty Kecskemét; 105 teachers; 6,000 students; Rector Dr JÓZSEF DANYI.

Magyar Táncművészeti Főiskola (Hungarian Dance Academy): 1145 Budapest, Columbus u. 87–89. POB 1372, Pf. 439; tel. (1) 273-3434; fax (1) 273-3444; e-mail info@mtf.hu; internet www.mtf.hu; f. 1950; State control; academic year September to June; library: 23,000 vols; 103 teachers; 600 students; Rector for Scientific and Admin. Issues Dr GÁBOR BOLVÁRI-TAKÁCS (acting); Rector for Artistic and Educational Issues GYÖRGY SZAKÁLY (acting); Dir Dr MÁRIA ZÓRÁNDI JAKAB; Finance Dir. GABRIELLA JAKUCS; Librarian IRÉN TÓTH BÍRÓ.

Nyíregyházi Főiskola (College of Nyíregyháza): 4401 Nyíregyháza, Sóstói u. 31b; tel. (42) 599-400; fax (42) 404-092; internet www.nyf.hu; State control; Rector Dr ZOLTÁN JÁNOSI.

Veszprémi Érseki Hittudományi Főiskola (Archiepiscopal Theological College of Veszprém): 8200 Veszprém, Jutasi u. 18/2; tel. (88) 426-116; fax (88) 426-865; internet www.vhf.hu; Private control; Rector Dr ISTVÁN VARGA.

ICELAND

The Higher Education System

The Icelandic higher education system dates back to the foundation of the University of Iceland in 1911. The University of Iceland remains the principal institution of higher learning in Iceland, but since the 1970s new institutions of higher education have emerged with a more specialized focus, providing greater diversity at that level. In 2007 there were nine higher education institutions in Iceland and some 17,728 students were enrolled in further and higher education.

Legislation on higher education institutions (the Universities Act, No. 136/1997) enacted in 1997 establishes the general framework for the activities of these institutions. In this Act, the term 'háskóli' is used to refer both to traditional universities and institutions that do not carry out research. Separate legislation for each public higher education institution, and the charters of privately run universities, define their engagement in research, internal organization, etc. Iceland is a signatory of the Bologna Declaration, and all legislative reforms and regulations are handled by a national Bologna follow-up group based in the Ministry of Education, Science and Culture. A two-cycle degree system that conforms to the Bologna regulations is well established for most courses' with the exception of medical-related subjects.

Public and private higher education institutions receive individual appropriations from the state budget. The administration of each public university is entrusted to the Senate, the rector, faculty meetings, faculty councils and deans, if the university is divided into faculties. The Senate issues final rulings in the affairs of the university and its institutions, formulates their overall policy and furthers their development. The Senate is the supreme decision-making body in each institution unless otherwise provided for explicitly in the relevant act. The state draws up performance-related contracts with all higher education institutions, defining how the institution intends to achieve its objectives and what the Government's financial contribution shall be.

Entry to undergraduate courses is based on the Stúdentspróf (matriculation examination). Many institutions have restricted admission based on the average mark obtained or marks in subjects that are deemed relevant. Mature students are not always required to hold the Stúdentspróf if they have specific work experience. Courses are assessed in terms of credits.

Short courses resulting in a certificate or diploma are available in a limited number of subjects. The Baccalaureatus (Bachelors degree), usually in arts, science or education, is three to four years in length (a minimum of 90 credits). The University of Iceland awards the Kandidatspróf (Candidatus degree), which is offered in professional subject areas (law, medicine, engineering, etc.) and is four to six years in length. A number of institutions provide one- to two-year programmes following the Baccalaureatus leading to postgraduate certificates in various subjects. The University of Iceland awards the Meistarapróf (Masters degree) after a two-year course for holders of the Baccalaureatus. In some cases, a first-class Baccalaureatus is required. The Magister Paedagogiae degree in education is only offered in Icelandic studies. All courses require completion of a major thesis or research project. The Iceland University of Education offers a two-year Master of Education course. There are two types of Doktorspróf (Doctorate degree) available either at the University of Iceland or the Iceland University of Education. The Doctor Philosophiae is three or four years in length and follows the Meistarapróf. The Doctor Scientiarum and the Doctor Medicinae degree courses are based on the Kandidatspróf or the Meistarapróf degrees. In exceptional circumstances, a holder of a good Baccalaureatus may be allowed to undertake a Doctorate degree; however, studies would have to last for four years. The course is completely research-based.

Specialized vocational schools, known as Sérskóli, offer courses for specialized employment. Since the 1990s many Sérskóli have been upgraded to the higher education level. Students are required to take 25 unit-credits in general academic subjects to complement their technical training. Apprentices completing their studies take the Sveinspróf (Journeyman's examination). Students may progress to become a Meistarabréf (Master Craftsman) after a period of work experience and advanced study. Alternatively, students may progress to university after a specified period of additional studies. The Meistarabréf gives the right to train apprentices, operate a business or manage an enterprise.

Icelandic students have a long tradition of studying abroad for their higher education. About 16% of Icelandic students in higher education study abroad, most of them in postgraduate studies.

Regulatory and Representative Bodies

GOVERNMENT

Ministry of Education, Science and Culture: Sölvhólsgötu 4, 150 Reykjavík; tel. 545-9500; fax 562-3068; e-mail postur@mrn.is; internet www.menntamalaraduneyti.is; Minister KATRÍN JAKOBSDÓTTIR.

ACCREDITATION

ENIC/NARIC Iceland: Office for Academic Affairs, Univ. of Iceland, Suðurgata, 101 Reykjavík; tel. 525-5452; fax 525-4317; e-mail ina@hi.is; internet www.naric-enic.hi.is; Dir of Academic Affairs ÞÓRÐUR KRISTINSSON.

NATIONAL BODIES

Samstarfsnefnd háskólastigsins (Standing Committee of the Rectors of Icelandic Higher Education Institutions): University of Iceland, Office of the Rector, Suðurgata, 101

Reykjavík; tel. 525-4302; fax 525-4038; e-mail thordrkri@hi.is; internet www.hi.is; f. 1987; 8 mems; Head KRISTÍN INGÓLFS-DÓTTIR; Dir of Academic Affairs ÞÓRÐUR KRISTINSSON.

Learned Societies

AGRICULTURE, FISHERIES AND VETERINARY SCIENCE

Bændasamtök Íslands (Farmers' Association of Iceland): Baendahöllinni við Hagatorg, 107 Reykjavík; tel. 563-0300; fax 562-3058; e-mail bondi@bondi.is; internet www.bondi.is; f. 1995; 3,500 farmer mems in 15 district asscns and 13 sector orgs; library of 10,000 vols; Chair. HARALDUR BENEDIKTSSON; Dir EIRÍKUR BLÖNDA; publs *Bændablaðið* (Farmers' News, 26 a year), *Freyr* (12 a year).

BIBLIOGRAPHY, LIBRARY SCIENCE AND MUSEOLOGY

Upplýsing—Félag bókasafns- og upplýsingafræða (Information—The Icelandic Library and Information Science Association): Lyngási 18, 210 Garðabæ; tel. 864-6220; e-mail upplysing@upplysing.is; internet upplysing.is; f. 2000; 600 mems; strengthens, encourages and works for the recognition of the importance of the services of libraries and information centres within Icelandic society; Pres. HRAFNHILDUR HREINS-DÓTTIR; Sec. INGIBJÖRG ÖSP ÓTTARSDÓTTIR; publs *Bókasafnið* (1 a year), *Fregnir* (3 a year).

FINE AND PERFORMING ARTS

Bandalag Íslenzkra Listamanna (Union of Icelandic Artists): POB 637, 121 Reykjavík; tel. 562-9700; e-mail bil@bil.is; internet www.bil.is; f. 1928; cooperative federation that aims to promote the role of artists and performers in the cultural and artistic development of society; 3,100 mems; Pres. KOL-BRÚN HALLDÓRSDÓTTIR.

Constituent Organizations:

Arkítektafélag Íslands (Icelandic Architects' Association): Engjateigi 9, 101 Reykjavík; tel. 551-1465; fax 562-0465; e-mail ai@ai.is; internet www.ai.is; 250 mems; Chair. SIGRÍÐUR MAGNÚSDÓTTIR.

Félag Íslenzkra Leikara (Icelandic Actors' Association): Lindargötu 6, 101 Reykjavík; tel. 552-6040; fax 562-7706; e-mail fil@fil.is; internet www.fil.is; Chair. RANDVER ÞORLÁKSSON; 400 mems.

Félag Íslenzkra Listdansara (Association of Icelandic Dance Artists): Lindargötu 6, 101 Reykjavík; e-mail dance@dance .is; internet www.dance.is; 111 mems; Chair. KAREN MARÍA JÓNSDÓTTIR.

Félag Íslenzkra Tónlistarmanna (Icelandic Musicians' Association): Lindargötu 46, 101 Reykjavík; fax 562-6455; e-mail fiston@fiston.is; internet www.fiston.is; 92 mems; Chair. MARGRÉT BÓASDÓTTIR.

Félag Kvikmyndagerðarmanna (Icelandic Film Makers' Association): POB 1652, 121 Reykjavík; e-mail formadur@ filmmakers.is; internet www.filmmakers .is; f. 1966; 150 mems; Chair. HRAFNHILDUR GUNNARSDÓTTIR.

Félag Leikstjóra á Íslandi (Icelandic Association of Stage Directors): Lindargötu 6, 101 Reykjavík; tel. 562-1025; e-mail leikstjorar@leikstjorar.is; internet www .leikstjorar.is; 87 mems; Chair. STEINUNN KNÚTSDÓTTIR.

Rithöfundasamband Íslands (Icelandic Writers' Association): Gunnarshúsi, Dyngjuvegi 8, 104 Reykjavík; tel. 568-3190; fax 568-3192; e-mail rsi@rsi.is; internet www .rsi.is; f. 1974; 380 mems; Chair. KRISTÍN STEINSDÓTTIR; Exec. Dir RAGNHEIÐUR TRYGGVADÓTTIR.

Samband Íslenzkra Myndlistarmanna (Icelandic Visual Artists' Association): Hafnarstræti 16, POB 1115, 121 Reykjavík; tel. 551-1346; fax 562-6656; e-mail sim@ simnet.is; internet www.sim.is; f. 2002; more than 350 mems; Chair. HRAFNHILDUR SIGURÐARDÓTTIR.

Samtök Kvikmundaleikstjóra (Guild of Icelandic Film Directors): Sudurgötu 14, 101 Reykjavík; e-mail skl-filmdirectors@ gmail.com; internet skl-filmdirectors.net; 53 mems; Chair. RAGNARI BRAGASYNI.

Tónskáldafélag Íslands (Society of Icelandic Composers): Laufásvegi 40, 101 Reykjavík; tel. 552-4972; internet www .listir.is; f. 1946; 130 mems; Chair. KJARTAN ÓLAFSSON.

Tónlistarfélagið (Music Society): Bjarmaland 19, 108 Reykjavík; f. 1930; operates a College of Music; affiliated societies in major towns; Chair. BALDVIN TRYGGVASON; Man. RUT MAGNÚSSON; Headmaster of College HALLDÓR HARALDSSON.

HISTORY, GEOGRAPHY AND ARCHAEOLOGY

Fornleifastofnun Íslands (Institute of Archaeology, Iceland): Bárugötu 3, 101 Reykjavík; tel. 551-1033; fax 551-1047; e-mail fsi@instarch.is; internet www.instarch.is; f. 1989; Pres. ADOLF FRIÐRIKSSON; publ. *Archaeologia Islandica.*

Sögufélag (Historical Society of Iceland): Fischersundi 3, 101 Reykjavík; tel. 551-4620; e-mail sogufelag@sogufelag.is; internet www .sogufelag.is; f. 1902; publ. of historical research and primary documents; 800 mems; Pres. Prof. ANNA AGNARSDÓTTIR; Sec. SÚSANNA MARGRÉT GESTSDÓTTIR; publ. *SAGA* (2 a year).

LANGUAGE AND LITERATURE

Hið Íslenzka bókmenntafélag (Icelandic Literary Society): Skeifan 3B, Reykjavík; tel. 588-9060; fax 581-4088; e-mail hib@islandia .is; internet www.hib.is; f. 1816; research work and publishing; 2,200 mems; Pres. SIGURÐUR LÍNDAL; Sec. REYNIR AXELSSON; publ. *Skírnir* (2 a year).

NATURAL SCIENCES

General

Vísindafélag Íslendinga (Icelandic Academy of Sciences and Letters): Bárugötu 3, 101 Reykjavík; f. 1918; 159 mems; Pres. SIGURÐUR STEINTHORSSON; publs *Ráðstefnurit* (irregular), *Rit.*

Biological Sciences

Íslenzka náttúrufrædifélag (Icelandic Natural History Society): POB 846, 121 Reykjavík; tel. 562-4757; fax 562-0815; f. 1889; publ. *Náttúrufrædingurinn* (Natural History, 4 a year).

Physical Sciences

Jöklarannsóknafélag Íslands (Iceland Glaciological Society): POB 5128, 125 Reykjavík; fax 552-1347; e-mail jorfi@jorfi.is; internet www.jorfi.is; f. 1950; 500 mems; Pres. MAGNÚS TUMI GUDMUNDSSON; Sec. ÞORSTEINN ÞORSTEINSSON; publ. *Jökull* (1 a year).

TECHNOLOGY

Verkfrædingafélag Íslands (Association of Chartered Engineers in Iceland): Engjateigi 9, 105 Reykjavík; tel. 535-9300; fax 535-9311; e-mail skrifstofa@verktaekni.is; internet www.vfi.is; f. 1912; 1,000 mems; Chair. JÓHANNA HARPA ARNADÓTTIR; Gen. Man. ÁRNI BJÖRN BJÖRNSSON; publ. *Arbók* (Yearbook).

Research Institutes

GENERAL

Rannsókna- og Þróunarmiðstöð (Research and Development Centre): Borgum v/Norðurslóð, 600 Akureyri; tel. 460-8900; fax 460-8919; e-mail rha@unak.is; internet www.rha.is; f. 1992; attached to Háskólinn á Akureyri (University of Akureyri); multi-disciplinary research into a wide array of fields, incl. aquaculture, economic devt, geography, management and sociology; Dir ÓLÍNA FREYSTEINSDÓTTIR.

ECONOMICS, LAW AND POLITICS

Alþjóðamálastofnun (Institute of International Affairs): Gimli við Sturlugötu, 101 Reykjavík; tel. 525-5262; fax 525-5841; e-mail ams@hi.is; internet stofnanir.hi.is/ ams/is; f. 1990; attached to Háskóli Íslands (University of Iceland); aims to strengthen the position of Iceland within the international community and to encourage cooperation and discussions between scholars and other parties interested in Icelandic foreign affairs and international politics; Dir PIA HANSSON.

Hagstofa Íslands (Statistics Iceland): Borgartúni 21A, 150 Reykjavík; tel. 528-1000; fax 528-1099; e-mail information@statice.is; internet www.statice.is; f. 1914; Dir-Gen. ÓLAFUR HJÁLMARSSON; Sec. ÞYRÍ MARTA BALDURSDÓTTIR; publs *Hagskýrslur Íslands* (Statistics of Iceland), *Hagtíðindi* (Statistics Monthly), *Landshagir* (Statistical Yearbook of Iceland).

Institute of Economic Studies: Oddi v/ Sturlugötu, 101 Reykjavík; tel. 525-4535; fax

525-4096; e-mail ioes@hi.is; internet www .ioes.hi.is; f. 1989; attached to Háskóli Íslands (University of Iceland); Chair. Prof. RAGNAR ÁRNASON.

Lagastofnun Háskóla Íslands (Institute of Law, University of Iceland): Lögbergi, 101 Reykjavík; tel. 525-5203; e-mail lagastofnun@hi.is; internet www .lagastofnun.hi.is; f. 2003; attached to Háskóli Íslands (University of Iceland); Chair. Prof. STEFÁN MÁR STEFÁNSSON; Dir MARÍA THEJLL.

HISTORY, GEOGRAPHY AND ARCHAEOLOGY

Stofnun Árna Magnússonar í Íslenskum Fræðum (Árni Magnússon Institute for Icelandic Studies): Árnagarði v/Suðurgötu, 101 Reykjavík; tel. 525-4010; fax 525-4035; e-mail arnastofnun@hi.is; internet www .arnastofnun.is; f. 1972 as Árni Magnússon Institute in Iceland; present name adopted 2006 following merger with Icelandic Language Institute, University of Iceland Institute of Lexicography, Sigurður Nordal Institute and Place-Name Institute of Iceland; attached to Háskóli Íslands (University of Iceland); practical and theoretical research pertaining to Icelandic culture, history, language and literature; library of 19,000 vols; Dir Prof. GUÐRÚN NORDA.

MEDICINE

Tilraunastöð Háskóla Íslands i meinafræði að Keldum (Institute for Experimental Pathology, University of Iceland): v/ Vesturlandsveg, 112 Reykjavík; tel. 585-5100; fax 567-3979; e-mail postur@keldur.is; internet www.keldur.is; f. 1948; attached to Háskóli Íslands (University of Iceland); library of 4,000 vols; Dir SIGURÐUR INGVARSSON; publ. *Icelandic Agricultural Sciences* (1–2 a year).

NATURAL SCIENCES

General

Rannsoknamidstod Íslands (The Icelandic Centre for Research): Laugavegur 13, 101 Reykjavík; tel. 515-5800; fax 552-9814; e-mail rannis@rannis.is; internet www .rannis.is; f. 1994; attached to Min. of Education, Science and Culture; advises the govt and Parliament on all aspects of science, technology and innovation, and promotes int. cooperation in science and technology; Dir-Gen. Dr HALLGRÍMUR JÓNASSON.

Attached Research Institutes:

Hafrannsóknastofnunin (Marine Research Institute): Skúlagötu 4, 121 Reykjavík; tel. 575-2000; fax 575-2001; e-mail hafro@hafro.is; internet www.hafro .is; attached to Min. of Fisheries; research into marine biological and oceanographic sciences; spec. divs for pelagic fish, demersal fish, flatfish, technology and fishing gear, hydrography, phytoplankton, zooplankton and benthos; Pres. FRIÐRIK MÁR BALDURSSON; Sec. JÓHANN GUÐMUNDSSON.

Idntæknistofnun Íslands (Technological Institute of Iceland): Keldnaholt, 112 Reykjavík; tel. 570-7100; fax 570-7111; internet www.randburg.com/is/iti/ attached to Min. of Industry; research and service institution for industry; research on raw materials, machinery and end products to improve quality and competitiveness of Icelandic industrial production; spec. divs for training and information, industrial devt, technical services and for research; Chair. MAGNÚS FRIÐGEIRSSON; Dir HALLGRÍMUR JÓNASSON.

Icelandic Building Research Institute (IBRI): Keldnaholt, 112 Reykjavík; tel.

570-7300; fax 570-7311; e-mail helpdesk@ rabygg.is; internet www.ibri.is; f. 1965; attached to Min. of Industry; scientific research and services for the construction and bldg industries; Dir HÁKON OLAFSSON; Gen. Man. OLAFUR H. WALLEVIK.

Rannsóknastofnun landbúnadarins (Agricultural Research Institute): Keldnaholt, 112 Reykjavík; tel. 577-1010; fax 577-1020; e-mail rala@rala.is; internet landbunadur.rala.is/landbunadur/wgrala .nsf/key2/english.html; f. 1965; attached to Min. of Agriculture; govt-financed research and experimental devt in agriculture; spec. divs for animal-breeding, ecology and cultivation and farming technology; Chair. SIGURÐUR ÞRÁINSSON; Dir ÞORSTEINN TÓMASSON.

Surtseyjarfélagið (Surtsey Research Society): POB 352, 121 Reykjavík; e-mail surtsey@ni.is; internet www.surtsey.is; f. 1965; promotes and coordinates scientific work in geo- and biological sciences on the island of Surtsey; Chair. HALLGRÍMUR JÓNASSON; Sec. KARL GUNNARSSON; publ. *Surtsey Research*.

Biological Sciences

Náttúrufrædistofnun Íslands (Icelandic Institute of Natural History): Urriðaholtsstræti 6–8, POB 125, 212 Garðabær Sími; tel. 590-0500; fax 590-0595; e-mail ni@ni.is; internet www.ni.is; f. 1889 by Íslenzka Náttúrufrædifélag (Icelandic Natural History Soc.) and maintained by this Soc. until 1946, taken over by the State 1947; library of 12,000 vols, 450 periodicals; Dir-Gen. JÓN G. OTTÓSSON; Sec. ELÍNBORG ÞORGRÍMSDÓTTIR; publs *Acta Botanica Islandica* (irregular), *Bliki* (irregular), *Fjölrit Náttúrufræðistofnunar* (irregular).

Physical Sciences

Vedurstofa Íslands (Icelandic Meteorological Office): Bústaðavegi 9, 150 Reykjavík; tel. 522-6000; fax 522-6001; e-mail office@ vedur.is; internet www.vedur.is; f. 1920; weather forecasts, climatology, aerology, sea ice, seismology, avalanches and landslides; library of 10,000 vols; Dir-Gen. ARNI SNORRASON; publs *Greinargerd* (Report, irregular), *Vedráttan* (12 a year).

PHILOSOPHY AND PSYCHOLOGY

Heimspekistofnun (Institute of Philosophy): Hugvísindastofnun, Sæmundargötu 2, 101 Reykjavík; tel. 525-4351; fax 552-1331; internet heimspekistofnun.hi.is; attached to Háskóli Íslands (University of Iceland); Dir SVAVAR HRAFN SVAVARSSON.

RELIGION, SOCIOLOGY AND ANTHROPOLOGY

ASÍS—The Icelandic Centre for Asian Studies: Aðalbygging v/Sæmundargötu, 101 Reykjavík; tel. 525-4400; fax 525-4410; e-mail geirs@hi.is; f. 2005; attached to Háskóli Íslands (University of Iceland); Dir GEIR SIGURÐSSON.

Mannfrædistofnun Háskóla Íslands (Institute of Anthropology, University of Iceland): Sæmundargötu 10, 101 Reykjavík; tel. 525-4165; fax 525-4179; e-mail krishar@hi.is; internet www.mannfraedistofnun.hi.is; f. 1974; attached to Háskóli Íslands (University of Iceland); Chair. Prof. UNNUR DÍS SKAPTADÓTTIR; Man. Dir KRISTÍN ERLA HARÐARDÓTTIR.

Libraries and Archives
Akureyri

Amtsbókasafnið á Akureyri (Akureyri Public Library): Brekkugötu 17, 602 Akureyri; tel. 460-1250; fax 460-1251; e-mail bokasafn@akureyri.is; internet www .akureyri.is/amtsbokasafn; f. 1827; 100,000 vols; Head Librarian GUÐRÚN KRISTÍN JÓNSDÓTTIR.

Hafnarfjörður

Bókasafn Hafnarfjarðar (Hafnarfjörður Public Library): Strandgötu 1, 220 Hafnarfjörður; tel. 585-5690; fax 585-5689; e-mail bokasafn@hafnarfjordur.is; internet www .hafnarfjordur.is/bokasafn; f. 1922; Head Librarian AÐALBJÖRG SIGÞÓRSDÓTTIR.

Ísafjörður

Bókasafn Ísafjarðar (Ísafjarðar Public Library): Gamlasjúkrahúsið, POB 138, 400 Ísafjörður; tel. 450-8220; fax 450-8229; e-mail bokasafn@isafjordur.is; internet www .isafjordur.is/bokasafn; f. 1889; 107,000 vols; Library Dir JÓNA SÍMONÍA BJARNADÓTTIR.

Reykjavík

Borgarbókasafn Reykjavíkur (City Library of Reykjavík): Tryggvagötu 15, 101 Reykjavík; tel. 411-6100; fax 411-6159; e-mail borgarbokasafn@borgarbokasafn.is; internet www.borgarbokasafn.is; f. 1923; 500,000 vols; Dir ANNA TORFADÓTTIR.

Landsbókasafn Íslands-Háskólabókasafn (National and University Library of Iceland): Arngrímsgötu 3, 107 Reykjavík; tel. 525-5600; fax 525-5615; e-mail upplys@landsbokasafn.is; internet www.landsbokasafn.is; f. 1994 by amalgamation of the Nat. Library of Iceland (f. 1818) and the Univ. Library (f. 1940); 900,000 books and journals, 16,000 MSS; Dir INGIBJÖRG STEINUNN SVERRISDÓTTIR.

Þjóðskjalasafn Íslands (National Archives of Iceland): Laugavegur 162–164, 105 Reykjavík; tel. 590-3300; fax 590-3301; e-mail upplysingar@skjalasafn.is; internet www .archives.is; f. 1882; colln of historical documents since 12th century; Nat. Archivist OLAFUR ÁSGEIRSSON.

Museums and Art Galleries
Húsavík

Hvalasafnið á Húsavík (Húsavík Whale Museum): Hafnarstétt 1, 640 Húsavík; tel. 414-2800; fax 464-2522; e-mail info@ whalemuseum.is; internet www .whalemuseum.is; f. 1997; provides information and education on the whale's biology, ecology and habitat, and the history of whaling in Iceland; Dir HERMANN BÁRÐARSON.

Reykjavík

Listasafn Einars Jónssonar (National Einar Jónsson Museum): Eiríksgötu, POB 1051, 121 Reykjavík; tel. 551-3797; fax 562-3909; e-mail skulptur@skulptur.is; internet www.skulptur.is; f. 1923; houses 300 sculptures and paintings by Einar Jónsson (1874–1954); Dir JÚLLIANA GOTTSKÁLKSDÓTTIR.

Þjóðminjasafn Íslands (National Museum of Iceland): Suðurgötu 41, 101 Reykjavík; tel. 530-2200; fax 530-2201; e-mail thjodminjasafn@thjodminjasafn.is; internet www.natmus.is; f. 1863; houses 2,000 objects, dating from the Settlement Age to the present; 1,000 photographs since beginning of 20th century; Dir MARGRÉT HALLGRÍMSDÓTTIR.

Vopnafjordur

Bustarfell Museum: Hofsárdalur, 690 Vopnafjordur; tel. 471-2211; e-mail bustarfell@ simnet.is; internet www.bustarfell.is; f. 1982; depicts the history of Icelandic farming and lifestyle changes from the start of the 18th century to the mid-20th century; Chair. BJÖRG EINARSDÓTTIR; Gen. Man. BERGHILDUR FANNEY HAUKSDÓTTIR.

Universities
HÁSKÓLI ÍSLANDS
(University of Iceland)

Sæmundargötu 2, 101 Reykjavík

Telephone: 525-4000
Fax: 552-1331
E-mail: hi@hi.is
Internet: www.hi.is

Founded 1911; merged with Kennarháskóli Íslands (Iceland Univ. of Education) 2008; attached to Min. of Education, Science and Culture
State control
Languages of instruction: English, Icelandic
Academic year: September to June

Rector: Prof. KRISTÍN INGÓLFSDÓTTIR
Pro-Rector for Academic Affairs: JÓN ATLI BENEDIKTSSON
Dir for Academic Affairs: ÞÓRÐUR KRISTINSSON
Dir for Finance: SIGURÐUR J. HAFSTEINSSON
Dir for Human Resources: GUÐRÚN JÓHANNA GUÐMUNDSDÓTTIR
Dir for Marketing and Public Relations: JÓN ÖRN GUÐBJARTSSON
Dir for Operations and Resources: GUÐMUNDUR R. JÓNSSON
Dir for Science and Research: HALLDÓR JÓNSSON
Library: see Libraries and Archives
Number of teachers: 2,840 (640 tenured, 2,200 non-tenured)
Number of students: 14,000
Publications: *Árbók Háskóla Íslands* (1 a year), *Ritaskrá Háskóla Íslands* (1 a year), *Tímarit Háskóla Íslands* (1 a year)

DEANS

Faculty of Education: Prof. JÓN TORFI JÓNASSON
School of Engineering and Natural Sciences: KRISTÍN VALA RAGNARSDÓTTIR
School of Health Sciences: Prof. SIGURÐUR GUÐMUNDSSON
School of Humanities: ÁSTRÁÐUR EYSTEINSSON
School of Social Sciences: OLAFUR Þ. HARÐARSON

HÁSKÓLINN Á AKUREYRI
(University of Akureyri)

Sólborg, Norðurslóð 2, 600 Akureyri

Telephone: 460-8000
Fax: 460-8999
E-mail: unak@unak.is
Internet: www.unak.is

Founded 1987
Languages of instruction: Icelandic, English
Academic year: August to June

Rector: Dr STEFÁNS B. SIGURÐSSONAR
Dir: OLAFUR HALLDÓRSSON

Number of teachers: 100
Number of students: 2,000

DEANS

School of Business and Science: Dr HANS KRISTJÁN GUÐMUNDSSON
School of Health Sciences: Dr ÁRÚN KRISTÍN SIGURÐARDÓTTIR

School of Humanities and Social Sciences: Dr SIGURDUR KRISTINSSON

HÁSKÓLINN Á BIFRÖST
(Bifröst University)

311 Borgarnes
Telephone: 433-3000
Fax: 433-3001
E-mail: bifrost@bifrost.is
Internet: www.bifrost.is
Founded 1918
Private, non-profit
Languages of instruction: Icelandic, English
Academic year: September to August
Rector: MAGNÚS ÁRNI MAGNÚSSON
Vice-Rector: BRYNDÍS HLÖÐVERSDÓTTIR
Librarian: ANDREA JÓHANNSDÓTTIR
Library of 10,000 vols
Number of teachers: 60
Number of students: 1,300

DEANS

Faculty of Business: STEFÁN KALMANSSON
Faculty of Law: BRYNDÍS HLÖÐVERSDÓTTIR
Faculty of Social Sciences: JÓN ÓLAFSSON

PROFESSORS

BJARNASON, A., Business
BLÖNDAL, E., Law
EINARSSON, A., Business
LINDAL, S., Law
ÓLAFSSON, J., Social Sciences
PAPANASTASSIOU, M., Business

HÁSKÓLINN Á HÓLUM
(Hólar University College)

Hólar i Hjaltadal, 551 Sauðárkrókur
Telephone: 455-6300
Fax: 455-6301
E-mail: holaskoli@holar.is
Internet: www.holar.is
Founded 1882 as Búnadarskólinn á Hólum i Hjaltadal (Hólar Agricultural School); univ. status acquired and present name adopted 2003
State control

Rector: Prof. SKÚLI SKÚLASON
Dir: HAUKUR JØRUNDARSON
Library of 6,000 vols
Number of teachers: 42
Number of students: 50

HEADS OF DEPARTMENT

Dept of Aquaculture and Fish Biology: Prof. BJARNI KRISTÓFER KRISTJÁNSSON
Dept of Equine Science: Prof. VÍKINGUR GUNNARSSON
Dept of Tourism: Prof. KRISTINA TRYSELIUS

HÁSKÓLINN Í REYKJAVÍK
(University of Reykjavík)

Menntavegi 1, 101 Reykjavík
Telephone: 599-6200
Fax: 599-6201
E-mail: ru@ru.is
Internet: www.ru.is
Founded 1998; absorbed Tækniskóli Íslands (Icelandic College of Engineering and Technology) 2005
Private control
Academic year: August to June
Rector: Dr ARI KRISTINN JÓNSSON
Provost: JOHN B. VANDER SANDE
Head Librarian: GUÐRÚN TRYGGVADÓTTIR
Number of teachers: 160
Number of students: 2,883

DEANS

School of Business: FRIÐRIK MÁR BALDURSSON
School of Computer Science: BJÖRN ÞÓR JÓNSSON
School of Health and Education: ÞORLÁKUR KARLSSON
School of Law: THÓRÐUR S. GUNNARSSON
School of Science and Engineering: GUNNAR GUÐNI TÓMASSON

LANDBUNAÐARHÁSKÓLI ÍSLANDS
(Agricultural University of Iceland)

Hvanneyri, 311 Borgarnes
Telephone: 433-5000
Fax: 433-5001

E-mail: lbhi@lbhi.is
Internet: www.lbhi.is
Founded 1889; univ. status acquired and present name adopted 2005
Rector: Dr ÁGÚST SIGURÐSSON,
Pro-rector for Education: BJÖRN ÞORSTEINSSON
Pro-rector for Research: ÁSLAUG HELGADÓTTIR
Library of 20,000 vols
Number of teachers: 30
Number of students: 250
Publication: *Fjölrit Bændaskólans* (1 a year)

DEANS

Faculty of Animal and Land Resources: ÁSLAUG HELGADÓTTIR
Faculty of Environmental Sciences: ÓLAFUR ARNALDS
Faculty of Vocational and Continuing Education: GUÐRÍÐUR HELGADÓTTIR

LISTAHÁSKÓLI ÍSLANDS
(Iceland Academy of Arts)

Skipholt 1, 105 Reykjavík
Telephone: 552-4000
Fax: 562-3629
E-mail: lhi@lhi.is
Internet: www.lhi.is
Founded 1998, following merger of Reykjavik College of Music, Icelandic College of Arts and Crafts, and Icelandic Drama School
Private control
Academic year: August to May
Depts of art, art education, design and architecture, music, and theatre and dance
Rector: HJÁLMAR H. RAGNARSSON
University Dir: BJÖRG JÓNA BIRGISDÓTTIR
Library Dir: LÍSA Z. VALDIMARSDÓTTIR
Library of 42,000 vols
Number of teachers: 40 full-time, 200 part-time
Number of students: 452

INDIA

The Higher Education System

The modern higher education system was established while India was under British rule. Among the oldest institutions are Presidency College (founded in 1817), Deccan College Post-graduate and Research Institute (founded in 1821) and Sanskrit College (founded in 1824). In 1857 major universities were founded at Mumbai (formerly Bombay), Madras and Kolkata (formerly Calcutta). The main representative body of Indian universities, the Association of Indian Universities, was founded in 1925 and re-established as a statutory body in 1947, when India gained its independence. In 1953 the University Grants Commission was created to act between the Government and States as the coordinating body on higher education. In the same year a National Council for Higher Education in Rural Areas was established. India had a total of 337 universities and institutions with university status in 2005/06, and some 13,413 university and affiliated colleges. University enrolment was about 14.5m.

Universities are autonomous institutions, mostly funded by the States' governments, except for the 'central' universities, which are funded by the central Government. Universities are classified as either 'unitary' or 'affiliating'. Unitary universities conduct all undergraduate and postgraduate teaching, while in affiliating universities the teaching of undergraduates is conducted by affiliated colleges. There are also two other types of universities, 'deemed' and 'institutions of national importance'. Deemed universities are single-discipline institutions that have been granted university status by the University Grants Commission, and the institutions of national importance are funded directly by the Government but are distinct from central universities. The States account for 90% of university funding, with the rest coming from central Government. Student fees account for a small percentage of universities' income. The National Assessment and Accreditation Council (founded 1994) is the national body responsible for accreditation and quality assurance.

Universities have broadly the same administrative structure. The Vice-Chancellor is both the administrative and the academic head of the university. The Senate or Court, Syndicate and Executive Council or Board of Management are the primary administrative bodies, responsible for institutional budgets and management. The Academic Council oversees all academic aspects of the institution, including teaching and research. Faculties are the most important academic divisions, and are headed by Deans. Boards of Study determine programmes of study.

Admission to higher education is on the basis of one of the different Higher Secondary School Certificates. Standard undergraduate Bachelors degrees last three years, although some programmes in professional fields of study last four years (engineering, dentistry and pharmacy) or five years (architecture). The Bachelors of Laws is either a five-year first degree or a two- to three-year second degree. The first postgraduate degree is the Masters. Admission to the Masters may vary depending on the institution; a Bachelors is the most common requirement, but institutions may also set an entrance examination, while applicants for Masters programmes in the fields of architecture, engineering, pharmacy and technology must sit the Graduate Aptitude Test in Engineering. Masters programmes are two to three years in length. Following the Masters, there is a pre-doctoral programme called the Master of Philosophy (MPhil), a one-and-a-half year course. Finally, the Doctorate (PhD) is awarded three years after the Masters and at least two years after the MPhil. The PhD consists of a thesis based on original research.

Technical and vocational education is overseen by several different bodies: the Central Apprenticeship Council, the National Council for Training in Vocational Trades, the National Council of Educational Research and Training, the Joint Council for Vocationalization of Education and the All India Council for Technical Education. The Joint Council for Vocationalization of Education was founded in 1990 and is the body tasked with implementing and maintaining the national standard of vocational education. Universities, polytechnics and colleges offer one- to four-year Diploma courses in most subjects.

In 2011 the Government was planning to establish new universities and colleges, but it was thought these would not be enough to meet demand. India's 11th five-year plan requires an additional 7m. new places in higher education by 2012 and a total of 16m. additional places in higher education by 2020.

Regulatory and Representative Bodies

GOVERNMENT

Bureau of University and Higher Education and Minority Education, Ministry of Human Resource Development: Shastri Bhavan, New Delhi 110 001; tel. (11) 23382298; fax (11) 23070036; e-mail skumar-mail@nic.in; internet education.nic.in; Min. of Human Resource Devt ARJUN SINGH; Jt Sec. (Additional charge) SUNIL KUMAR; Dirs R. D. SAHAY, ANUPAMA BHATNAGAR, UPAMANYU BASU, UMA SHANKAR.

Ministry of Culture: Room 334, 'C' Wing, Shastri Bhavan, Dr Rajendra Prasad Rd, New Delhi 110 001; tel. (11) fax (11) 23384867; e-mail js.culture@nic.in; internet indiaculture.nic.in; Min. AMBIKA SONI; Sec. JAWHAR SIRCAR; Jt Sec. N. C. GOYAL; publ. *Sanskriti.*

Ministry of Human Resource Development: Shastri Bhavan, New Delhi 110 001; tel. (11) 23782698; fax (11) 23382365; e-mail hrm@sb.nic.in; internet education.nic.in; Minister ARJUN SINGH.

ACCREDITATION

National Assessment and Accreditation Council: POB 1075, Nagarbhavi, Bangalore 560072, Karnataka; tel. (80) 23210261; fax (80) 23210270; e-mail naac@blr.vsnl.net.in; internet www.naacindia.org; Dir Prof. H. A. RANGANATH (acting).

FUNDING

University Grants Commission (UGC): Bahadur Shah Zafar Marg, New Delhi 110 002; tel. (11) 23232701; fax (11) 23231797; e-mail webmaster@ugc.ac.in; internet www.ugc.ac.in; f. 1953; attached to Dept of Higher Education, Min. of Human Resource Devt; library of 41,850 vols; Chair. Prof. S. K. THORAT; Sec. R. P. AGARWAL; publs *Bulletin of Higher Education, Journal of Higher Education, University Development in India* (annual statistical review).

NATIONAL BODIES

All India Council for Technical Education (AICTE): 7th Fl., Chanderlok Bldg, Janpath, New Delhi 110 001; tel. (11) 23724151; fax (11) 23724183; e-mail admin@aicte.ernet.in; internet www.aicte.ernet.in; f. 1945; Chair. of Ccl Prof. DAMODAR ACHARYA; Vice-Chair. of Ccl Dr R. A. YADAV; publ. *Technical Education in independent India 1999 (Compendium).*

Association of Indian Universities: AIU House, 16 Comrade Indrajit Gupta Marg (Kotla Marg), New Delhi 110 002; tel. (11) 23230059; fax (11) 23232131; e-mail info@aiuweb.org; internet www.aiuweb.org; f. 1925; library of 20,000 vols, 150 periodicals, annual reports, calendars, handbooks and Acts of the various univs and Supreme Court of India judgments in the field of education; Pres. Prof. A. M. PATHAN; Sec.-Gen. Prof. DAYANAND DONGAONKAR; publs *Equivalence of Foreign Degrees* (irregular), *Handbook of Computer Education* (1 a year), *Handbook of Distance Education* (1 a year), *Handbook of Engineering Education* (1 a year), *Handbook* *of Library and Information Science* (1 a year), *Handbook of Management Education* (1 a year), *Handbook of Medical Education* (1 a year), *Scholarships for Study Abroad and at Home* (1 a year), *Universities Handbook* (every 2 years).

Indian Adult Education Association: 17B Indraprastha Estate, New Delhi 110 002; tel. (11) 23379306; fax (11) 23378206; e-mail iaea_india@yahoo.com; internet www .iaea-india.org/; f. 1939 under the Indian Socs Registration Act 1860; 2,500 mems; library: Amarnath Jha Library (f. 1957) 23,500 books, 110 periodicals; Pres. Prof. K. C. CHOUDHARY; Gen.-Sec. Dr MADAN SINGH; publs *Indian Journal of Adult Education* (4 a year), *Indian Journal of Population Education* (4 a year), *Jago Aur Jagao* (in Hindi 12 a year), *Proudh Shiksha* (in Hindi, 12 a year).

National Council of Educational Research and Training: Sri Aurobindo Marg, New Delhi 110 016; tel. (11) 26560620; fax (11) 26868419; e-mail director .ncert@nic.in; internet www.ncert.nic.in; f. 1961 with the aim of improving school education; academic adviser to the Min. of Human Resource Devt; coordinates research and devt in all branches of education; organizes pre- and in-service training; publishes school textbooks, instructional material for teachers and educational surveys; 8 major constituent units: Nat. Institute of Education and Central Institute of Educational Technology in New Delhi, Central Institute of Vocational Education in Bhopal and 5 regional Institutes of Education at Ajmer, Bhopal, Bhubaneswar, Mysore and Shillong; Pres. The Union Min. of Human Resource Devt; Dir Prof. KRISHNA KUMAR; publs *Indian Educational Abstracts*, *Indian Educational Review* (2 a year), *Journal of Indian Education*, *Journal of Value Education*, *School Science* (4 a year), *The Primary Teacher*.

Learned Societies

GENERAL

India International Centre: 40 Lodi Estate, Max Mueller Marg, Lodhi Rd H.O., New Delhi 110003; tel. (11) 24619431; internet www.iicdelhi.nic.in; f. 1958; int. cultural organization for promotion of amity and understanding between the different communities in the world; programme of lectures, discussions, film evenings, etc.; mems: 3,746 individuals, 256 corporate (incl. 35 univs); library of 31,000 vols, also houses the India Collection of 3,500 rare documents on British India and the Himalayan Club Library of 900 vols; Pres. Dr KAPILA VATSYAYAN; Dir N. N. VOHRA; Sec. N. H. RAMACHANDRAN; publs *IIC Diary* (6 a year), *IIC Quarterly*.

Indian Council for Cultural Relations (ICCR): Azad Bhawan, Indraprastha Estate, New Delhi 110002; tel. (11) 23379309; fax (11) 23378639; e-mail president@iccrindia .org; internet www.iccrindia.org; f. 1950 to establish and strengthen cultural relations between India and other countries; branch offices in Mumbai, Kolkata, Madras, Bangalore, Chandigarh, Lucknow, Trivandrum and Hyderabad; cultural centres in Georgetown (Guyana), Paramaribo (Suriname), Moscow (Russia), Port Louis (Mauritius), Jakarta (Indonesia), Berlin (Germany), Cairo (Egypt), Tashkent (Uzbekistan), Almaty (Kazakhstan) and London (United Kingdom); activities incl. exchange visits between scholars, artists and people of eminence in the field of art and culture; exchange of exhibitions; int. confs and seminars, lectures

by renowned scholars incl. Azad Memorial Lectures; establishment of chairs and centres of Indian studies abroad and welfare of overseas students in India; admin. of Jawaharlal Nehru Award for Int. Understanding; presentation of books and Indian art objects to univs, libraries and museums in other countries; library: over 55,000 vols in India and other countries; Pres. Dr KARAN SINGH; Dir-Gen. PAVAN K. VARMA; publs interpretations of Indian art and culture and translations of Indian works into foreign languages, *African Quarterly* (in English, 4 a year), *Gagananchal* (Hindi, 4 a year), *Indian Horizons*, *Papeles de la India* (in Spanish, 4 a year), *Rencontre avec l'Inde* (in French, 4 a year), *Thaqafat-ul-Hind* (in Arabic, 4 a year).

Indian Institute of World Culture: No. 6 Shri B. P. Wadia Rd, Basavangudi, Bangalore 560004; tel. (80) 26678581; e-mail iiwc@ vsnl.net; internet www.ultindia.org/ indian_institute_of_world_c.html; f. 1945; a sister instn of ULT dedicated to further the first objective of the Theosophical Movement Universal Brotherhood of Humanity; Mumbai Office; provides opportunities for cultural and intellectual devt; promotes exchange of thought between India and other countries and raises the consideration of nat. and world problems to the plane of moral and spiritual values and to foster a sense of universal brotherhood; 3,100 mems; library of 40,000 vols, 400 periodicals; Pres. Justice M. N. VENKATACHALIAH; Vice-Pres. R. N. NAGARAJ; Hon. Sec. Y. M. BALAKRISHNA; publs *Bulletin* (12 a year), *Transactions*.

Jammu and Kashmir Academy of Art, Culture and Languages: Lal Mandi, Srinagar, Kashmir 190001; tel. (191) 2542640 (Jammu); tel. (8649) 232379 (Srinagar); fax (191) 2542640 (Jammu); fax (8649) 232379 (Srinagar); internet jkc.weebly.com/home .html; f. 1958; promotes arts, culture and languages of the State; library of 20,000 vols, 650 rare MSS, 250 laminated photographs, 90 opera and folk song recordings; collections of gramophone records, cassettes, paintings, jewellery, calligraphy, costumes, contemporary paintings and sculpture; Pres. Gen. K. V. KRISHNA RAO; Sec. ZAFFAR IQBAL KHAN MANHAS; publs *Encyclopaedia Kashmirana*, *Hamara Adab* (1 a year anthology in Urdu, Kashmiri, Gojri, Pahari, Dogri, Punjabi, Hindi, Ladakhi), *Sheeraza* (12 a year in Urdu, 6 a year in Kashmiri, Dogri, Punjabi and Hindi, 4 a year in Ladakhi, Pahari, Gojri and 1 a year in English and Balti).

AGRICULTURE, FISHERIES AND VETERINARY SCIENCE

Agri-Horticultural Society of India: 1 Alipore Rd, Kolkata 700027; tel. (33) 24791713; fax (33) 24793580; e-mail ahsi@ vsnl.net; internet www.agrihorticultureindia .com/; f. 1820; 1,300 mems; library of 400 vols; Pres. B. K. NAHATA; Sr Vice-Pres. GAURAV SWARUP; Vice-Pres. SHARAD KHAITAN; Sec. NIRUPOM SEN; publs *Encyclopedia of Himalayan Medicinal Flora*, *Horticultural Journal* (4 a year).

Agri-Horticultural Society of Madras: New-134 Cathedral Rd, Gopalapuram, Chennai 600086; tel. (44) 28116816; f. 1835; 3,410 mems; Patron HE The GOVERNOR OF TAMIL NADU; Chair. R. SADASIVAM; Hon. Sec. Prof. J. RAMCHANDRAN.

Crop Improvement Society of India: Dept of Plant Breeding and Genetics, Punjab Agricultural University, Ludhiana 141004, Punjab; tel. (161) 2401960; fax (161) 2400945; e-mail info@pau.edu; f. 1974; aims to disseminate knowledge on crop improvement through lectures, symposia, publications, to arrange excursions and

explorations, and to cooperate with national and international organizations; 200 mems; Pres. Dr G. S. SIDHU; Sec. Dr G. S. CHAHAL; publ. *Crop Improvement* (2 a year).

Indian Dairy Association: IDA House, Sector IV, R. K. Puram, New Delhi 110022; tel. (11) 26170781; fax (11) 26174719; e-mail ida@nde.vsnl.net.in; internet www .indairyasso.org; f. 1948; 3,000 mems; library: Mansingh Bhai Patel Library of 700 vols; 100 periodicals; Pres. Dr N. R BHASIN; Vice-Pres N. A. SHAIKH, ARUN NARKE; publs *Indian Dairyman* (12 a year), *Indian Journal of Dairy Science* (6 a year).

Indian Society of Agricultural Economics: Krishi Vikas Sadan, First Floor, (Near Dr Antonio Da Silva Technical High School) Veer Savarkar Marg, Dadar (W) Mumbai 400028; tel. (22) 24374789; fax (22) 24374790; e-mail isae@bom7.vsnl.net.in; internet www.isaeindia.org; f. 1939; promotes the study of social and economic problems of agriculture and rural areas, and technical competence for teaching and research in agricultural economics and allied subjects; 1,644 mems and subscribers; library of 22,349 vols; Pres. Dr C. RAMASAMY; Vice-Pres. Dr R. S. BAWA; Vice-Pres. Dr UTPAL GOSH; Vice-Pres. Prof. JASBIR SINGH; Vice-Pres. Dr R. P. SINGH; Vice-Pres. Dr KAMAL KUMAR DATTA; Hon. Sec. and Treas. Dr C. L. DADHICH; Hon. Jt Sec. VIJAYA VENKATESH; publs books, reports, papers, *Comparative Experience of Agricultural Development in Developing Countries of Asia and the South-East Since World War II (1972)*, *Evaluation of Land Reforms (with special reference to the Western Region of India)*, *The Indian Journal of Agricultural Economics* (4 a year).

Indian Society of Soil Science: First Fl, National Societies Block, National Agricultural Science Centre Complex, Dev Prakash Shastri Marg, Pusa, New Delhi 110012; tel. (11) 25841991; fax (11) 25841529; e-mail isss .secretary@gmail.com; internet www .isss-india.org/; f. 1934; cultivates and promotes soil science and its allied disciplines and disseminates knowledge of soil science and its applications; cooperation with Int. Soc. of Soil Science and similar orgs; organizes seminars symposia, confs, meetings, etc.; 2,350 mems; Pres. Dr A. K. SINGH; Vice-Pres Dr J. P. SHARMA, Dr B. P. SINGH; Sec. Dr R. K. RATTAN; publs *Bulletin* (irregular), *Journal* (4 a year).

ARCHITECTURE AND TOWN PLANNING

Indian Institute of Architects: Prospect Chambers Annexe, Dr D. N. Rd, Fort, Mumbai 400001; tel. (22) 22046972; fax (22) 22832516; e-mail iia@vsnl.com; internet www.iia-india.org; f. 1929; promotes aesthetic, scientific and practical efficiency of the architectural profession; sponsors architectural education; sets qualifying standards for the profession; provides a forum for discussing related subjects,; 10,233 mems, incl. 1,191 Fellows, 28 Hon. Fellows, 8,624 assocs, 95 Licentiates, 1,850 students, 65 retired; library of 3,000 vols; Pres. VINAY M. PARELKAR; Vice-Pres. PANDURANG POTNIS; Hon. Treas. DEBABRATA GHOSH; Jt Hon. Sec. VIJAY GARG; publ. *Journal* (12 a year).

BIBLIOGRAPHY, LIBRARY SCIENCE AND MUSEOLOGY

Indian Association of Special Libraries and Information Centres (IASLIC): P. 291, CIT Scheme No. 6M, Kankurgachi, Kolkata 700054, West Bengal; tel. (33) 23629651; e-mail iaslic@vsnl.net; internet www.iaslic.org.in; f. 1955; promotes study and research into special librarianship and information science; conducts short-term training courses on the subject, holds confs and coordinates activities among special libraries and spec. interest groups; publishes seminar and conf. papers and books on information and library science; translation and reprographic services; 2,500 mems; library of 3,600 vols, 50 current periodicals; Hon. Pres. Dr J. N. SATPATHI; Hon. Gen. Sec. Prof. PIJUSHKANTI PANIGRAHI; publs *Conference Proceedings, Journal of IASLIC (JIASLIC)* (4 a year), *Seminar Proceedings*.

Indian Library Association: A/40–41, Flat 201, Ansal Bldgs, Dr Mukherjee Nagar, Delhi 110009; tel. and fax (22) 27651743; internet www.ilaindia.org; f. 1933; 4,000 mems; library of 600 vols; Pres. Prof. C. R. KARISIDDAPPA; Sec. D. V. SINGH; publ. *ILA Bulletin* (4 a year).

Museums Association of India: c/o Dir, State Museum, Banarasi Bagh, Lucknow 226001; tel. (522) 2206157; fax (522) 2206158; f. 1865; professional discussions, seminars, conferences, exhibitions, courses in museology etc.; 700 individual and institutional mems; library of 25,000 books, 5,000 research journals; Dir Dr RAKESH TIWARI (acting); publ. *Bulletin of Museums and Archeology*.

National Book Trust, India: A-5, Green Park, New Delhi 110016; tel. (11) 26568052; fax (11) 26851795; e-mail nbtindia@ndb.vsnl .net.in; internet www.nbtindia.org.in; f. 1957; an autonomous body set up by the Govt; activities incl. publishing moderately priced books for general readers in 12 Indian languages and English, giving assistance to authors, illustrators and publishers for producing books for children, neo-literates and the higher education sector, organizing book fairs, exhibitions, seminars and workshops, and promoting Indian books abroad; Chair. Prof. BIPAN CHANDRA; Dir NUZHAT HASSAN.

ECONOMICS, LAW AND POLITICS

All India Bar Association: DS-423/424, New Rajinder Nagar, New Delhi 110060; tel. (11) 28743284; fax (11) 28743285; e-mail allindiabar@gmail.com; internet www .allindiabar.org; f. 1959; Chair. ADISH C. AGGARWALA.

Indian Council of World Affairs: Sapru House, Barakhamba Rd, New Delhi 110001; tel. (11) 23359159; fax (11) 23311208; internet www.icwa.in; f. 1943; non-governmental instn for the study of Indian and int. relations and world affairs; research library; 1,500 mems; library of 128,000 vols, 376 periodicals, UN and EU depository; Pres. HARCHARAN SINGH JOSH; Hon. Sec.-Gen. S. C. PARASHER; Chief Librarian CHHAYA SHARMA; publs *India Quarterly, Foreign Affairs* (12 a year).

Indian Economic Association: Delhi School of Economics, Delhi 110009; e-mail iejpanch@yahoo.co.in; f. 1918; Pres. Prof. G. K. CHADHA; Vice-Pres. Prof. L. K. MOHANA RAO; Hon. Sec. Dr ANIL KUMAR THAKUR; publ. *Indian Economic Journal*.

The Indian Law Institute: Opposite Supreme Court, Bhagwandas Rd, New Delhi 110001; tel. (11) 23386321; fax (11) 23782140; e-mail ili@ili.ac.in; internet www .ilidelhi.org; f. 1956; Deemed Univ.; promotes advanced studies and research in law and reform of admin. of law and justice; 3,500 mems; library of 75,000 vols; Pres. CHIEF JUSTICE OF INDIA; Dir Prof. D. S. SENGAR; Registrar DALIP KUMAR; publs *Annual Survey of Indian Law, Journal of Indian Law Institute* (4 a year).

Institute of Chartered Accountants of India: ICAI Bhawan, Indraprastha Marg, Post Box No. 7100, New Delhi 110002; tel. (11) 39893989; fax (11) 30110580; e-mail icaiho@icai.org; internet www.icai.org; f. 1949, a statutory body est. under an Act of Parliament; a statutory body for the regulation of the profession of chartered accountants in India; contributes in the fields of education, professional devt, maintenance of high accounting, auditing and ethical standards; 161,859 mems; library: Central Ccl Library 62,000 vols; Pres. AMARJIT CHOPRA; Vice-Pres. G. RAMASWAMY; publs *Gateway to International Trade-E Communiqué of the Committee on Trade Laws & WTO, ICAI Patrika, Management Accounting and Business Finance, The Chartered Accountant* (12 a year).

EDUCATION

All India Association for Educational Research: N1/55 IRC Village, Bhubaneswar 751015; tel. (674) 2550611; e-mail indianeducationalresearch@yahoo.co.in; internet www.aiaer.net; f. 1987; holds annual and periodical confs on various themes and publishes a journal, both print and online; 3,228 mems; Patron Prof. B. K. PASSI; Pres. Prof. SURAJ PRAKASH MALHOTRA; Gen. Sec. and Editor Prof. SUNIL BEHARI MOHANTY; Treas. DHRUBA CHARAN MISHRA; publ. *Journal of All India Association for Educational Research* (2 a year).

Hyderabad Educational Conference: 19 Bachelors' Quarters, Jawaharlal Nehru Rd, Hyderabad, Deccan; f. 1913; promotes academic research, assists needy students and furthers education in Andhra Pradesh; library: over 9,500 vols; Pres. SYED MASOOD ALI; Sec. GHOUSE MOHIUDDIN; publs *Educational Annual* (in Urdu), *Proceedings of Public Sessions* (in Urdu), *Ruh-e-tarraqui* (in Urdu).

J. N. Petit Institute: 312 Dr Dadabhoy Naoroji Rd, Fort, Mumbai 400001; tel. (22) 22048462; e-mail petitheritage_01@yahoo.co .in; f. 1856; organizes lectures and makes accessible literary, scientific and philosophic works; 4,210 mems; library: see Libraries and Archives; Pres. Sir DINSHAW M. PETIT; Hon. Secs RODA ANKALESARIA, N. M. PATEL.

National Bal Bhavan: Kotla Rd, New Delhi 110002; tel. (11) 23232672; e-mail nbb@bol .net.in; internet www.nationalbalbhavan.nic .in/; f. 1956; autonomous institution est. by Min. of Human Resource Devt; provides planned environment and creative activities based on Arts and Science to children between the ages of 5 and 16; provides leadership and guidance to teachers towards fostering a creative approach in teaching of art and science, organizes orientation courses for teachers and parents, runs a repertory theatre for children, the Nat. Children's Museum and a nat. training resource centre; library: children's library of 43,347 vols, reference library of 11,584 vols; Chair. Begum BILKES I. LATIF; Vice-Chair. ZENA BERNADETTE VIJAY KUMAR; Sec. AMITA SHAW; publ. *Akkar Bakkar and Akkar Bakkar Times* (booklet entirely produced by the children).

FINE AND PERFORMING ARTS

All-India Fine Arts and Crafts Society: 1 Rafi Marg, New Delhi 110001; tel. (11) 23711315; fax (11) 23715366; e-mail aifacsarts@yahoo.co.in; internet www.aifacs .org.in; f. 1928; holds art exhibitions incl. the All India Annual Art Exhibition of painting, photography, sculpture, graphics, traditional art and water colours and drawings, exhibitions of Indian art abroad and exhibitions of arts and crafts from foreign countries in India, talks and film shows on art; 550 mems; library of 5,300 vols; Pres. RAM V. SUTAR; Chair. Prof. PARAMJEET SINGH (acting); publs *Arts News* (12 a year), *Roopa Lekha* (1 a year).

Art Society of India: Sandhurst House, Shop 524 S.V.P. Rd, Bandra East, Mumbai 400051; tel. (22) 23888550; f. 1918; promotes art and artists all over India; colln of rare art books; 650 mems; library of 2,000 vols; Pres. P. DAHANUKAR; Hon. Sec. B. R. KULKARNI.

India International Photographic Council: 21 Bharti Artists Colony, Vikas Marg, New Delhi 110092; tel. (11) 65751099; e-mail iipc@mail.com; f. 1983; promotes art and science of photography; 4,000 mems; publ. *IIPC Photographic Journal* (12 a year).

Indian Society of Oriental Art (Calcutta): 15 Park St, Kolkata 700016; tel. (33) 22174805; f. 1907; 320 mems; promotes and researches all aspects of ancient and contemporary Indian and Oriental art; library of 3,500 vols; Sec. INDIRA NAG CHAUDHURI; publ. *Journal* (1 a year).

Lalit Kala Akademi/National Academy of Art: Rabindra Bhavan, Ferozshah Rd, New Delhi 110001; tel. (11) 23387241; e-mail lka@lalitkala.gov.in; internet lalitkala.gov .in; f. 1954; autonomous, govt-financed; sponsors nat. and int. exhibitions, such as the Nat. Exhibition of Art (annual) and Triennale-India; arranges seminars, lectures, films, etc.; Sec. Dr SUDHANAR SHARMA; publs *Lalit Kala Ancient* (2 a year), *Lalit Kala Contemporary* (4 a year), *Samkaleen Kala* (in Hindi, 4 a year).

National Academy of Music, Dance and Drama/Sangeet Natak Akademi: Rabindra Bhavan, Feroze Shah Rd, New Delhi 110001; tel. (11) 23381833; fax (11) 23385715; e-mail help@sangeetnatak.org; internet www.sangeetnatak.org; f. 1953; preserves and develops the performing arts of India; documents the performing arts through films, tapes and photographs; maintains a museum of musical instruments, costumes, masks and puppets; offers financial assistance to music, dance and theatre institutions; administers the Jawaharlal Nehru Manipur Dance Academy, Imphal, Kathak Kendra, Delhi, and Rabindra Rangashala, Delhi; conducts festivals, seminars; gives awards and fellowships for outstanding work; 66 mems; library of 22,000 vols and audio-visual library of tapes and discs; Chair. Dr RAM NIWAS MIRDHA; Sec. JAYANT KASTUAR; publ. *Sangeet Natak* (4 a year).

South India Society of Painters: No. 13, 111 Trust Cross, Chennai 600028.

The Bombay Art Society: Jehangir Art Gallery, Mahatma Gandhi Rd, Mumbai 400023; tel. (22) 22044058; e-mail contactus@bombayartsociety.org; internet www.bombayartsociety.org; f. 1888; 450 life mems; 150 ord. mems; 200 student mems; holds All India Annual Art Exhibition; Pres. VIJAY RAUT; Chair. VITTHAL LOKHANDKAR; Hon. Secs Prof. NARENDRA VICHARE, SURENDRA JAGTAP; Hon. Treas. CHANDRAJIT YADAV; publs *Art Journal*, illustrated catalogues of exhibitions.

HISTORY, GEOGRAPHY AND ARCHAEOLOGY

Bharata Itihasa Samshodhaka Mandala: 1321 Sadashiva Peth, Pune 411030; tel. (20) 24472581; f. 1910; collects, conserves and publishes historical materials; colln of 3,500 coins; 33,000 Persian, Sanskrit and Marathi MSS; 1,600,000 documents, about 1,200 old Indian paintings; 1,000 copperplates, sculptures and other antiquarian objects, museum of paintings; 675 mems; library of 40,000 vols; Pres. (vacant); Chair. Dr S. GOKHALE;

Sec. Dr S. M. BHAVE; publs *Journal* (4 a year), *Puraskrita Granthamala, Sviya Granthamala Series.*

Geographical Society of India: c/o Dept of Geography, Univ. of Calcutta, 35 Ballygunge Circular Rd, Kolkata 700019; tel. (33) 24753681; f. 1933; geographical lectures, seminars, excursions and exhibitions; encouragement of geographical research and training; 750 mems; library of 14,200 vols, 5,709 journals; Pres. S. P. DASGUPTA; Sec. DURGADAS SAHA; publ. *Geographical Review of India* (4 a year).

LANGUAGE AND LITERATURE

Academy of Sanskrit Research: Mandya Dist., Karnataka, Melkote, Karnataka 571431; tel. (8236) 48781; e-mail asrbng@vsnl.com; internet www.sanskritacademy.org; f. 1927; promotion and propagation of Sanskrit language, publication of studies and expositions of Sanskrit works, org. of oratorical and recitation competitions, regular lectures and seminars in Sanskrit and Tamil on well-known Sanskrit poets and philosophers by eminent scholars, occasional production of Sanskrit drama; library of 28,000 vols of philosophy, literature, culture, vedanta, aesthetics, agriculture, etc.; 200 mems; Dir and Jt Sec. Dr BHASHYAM SWAMY; publ. *Tattva Deepa* (1 a year).

Alliance Française: 2 Aurangzeb Rd, New Delhi 110001; tel. (11) 23014682; fax (11) 23014364; e-mail dgaf@afindia.org; internet www.afindia.org; offers courses and examinations in French language and culture and promotes cultural exchange with France; attached teaching centres in Ahmedabad, Bangalore, Bhopal, Chandigarh, Chennai, Coimbatore, Hyderabad, Indore, Jaipur, Karikal, Kochi, Kolkata, Madurai, Mahe, Mumbai, Panjim, Pondichery, Pune, Rajkot, Secunderabad and Trivandrum.

British Council: British High Commission, 17 Kasturba Gandhi Marg, New Delhi 110001; tel. (11) 23711401; fax (11) 23710717; e-mail delhi.enquiry@in.britishcouncil.org; internet www.britishcouncil.org/india; teaching centre; offers courses and exams in English language and British culture and promotes cultural exchange with the UK; attached offices in Hyderabad, Pune, Chandigarh, Bangalore, Chennai, Kolkata and Mumbai; library of 30,000 vols; Dir EDMUND MARSDEN.

Kendriya Hindi Nideshalaya (Central Hindi Directorate): Min. of Human Resource Devt, Dept of Education, West Block 7, R. K. Puram, New Delhi 110066; tel. (11) 26178454; fax (11) 26100758; e-mail pushplata_taneja@rediffmail.com; internet www.hindinidhalaya.nic.in; f. 1960; preparation and publ. of bilingual and trilingual dictionaries of Indian and foreign languages; teaching of Hindi by correspondence courses to Indians and foreigners; extension courses; c. 300 mems; library of 83,100 vols; Dir Dr K. VIJAY KUMAR; publs *Bhasha* (4 a year), *UNESCO DOOT* (12 a year), *Varshiki* (1 a year).

Linguistic Society of India: c/o Dept of Linguistics, Deccan College Postgraduate and Research Institute, Pune 411006; tel. (20) 26698744; e-mail secretaryil@gmail.com; internet www.lsi.org.in; f. 1928; 700 mems; library of 6,000 vols; Pres. K. RANGAN; Vice-Pres. ANVITA ABBI; publ. *Indian Linguistics* (1 a year).

Madras Literary Society: College Rd, Chennai 600006; tel. (44) 28279666; f. 1812, became Auxiliary of the Royal Asiatic Soc. of Great Britain and Ireland 1830; library of 150,000 vols, incl. 30,000 19th-century edns; Pres. M. GOPALAKRISHNAN; Hon. Sec. U.

RAMESH RAO; publs *Madras Journal of Literature and Science, Transactions of the Literary Society of Madras.*

Max Müller Bhavan (Goethe-Institut): 3 Kasturba Gandhi Marg, New Delhi 110001; tel. (11) 23329506; fax (11) 23325534; e-mail info@delhi.goethe.org; internet www.goethe.de/newdelhi; the 6 brs of the Goethe-Institut in India are named after the German Indologist Max Müller (1823–1900); offers courses and examinations in German language and culture and promotes cultural exchange with Germany; attached centres in Bangalore, Chennai, Mumbai, Kolkata and Pune; Dir for S Asia Region HEIKO SIEVERS.

Mythic Society: 2 Nrupathunga Rd, Bangalore 560002; tel. (80) 22215034; f. 1909; promotes the study of mythology, archaeology, indology and Karnataka history; 400 mems; library of 24,000 vols, incl. spec. collns of Mysore history; Pres. Dr SURYANATH U. KAMATH; Sec. Dr M. K. L. N. SASTRY; publ. *Journal* (4 a year).

PEN All-India Centre: Theosophy Hall, 40 New Marine Lines, Mumbai 400020; tel. (22) 22032175; e-mail india.pen@gmail.com; f. 1933; Founder SOPHIA WADIA; Pres. Dr DAUJI GUPTA; Sec.-Treas. RANJIT HOSKOTE (acting); publ. *The Indian PEN* (4 a year).

Sahitya Akademi/National Academy of Letters: Rabindra Bhavan, 35 Ferozeshah Rd, New Delhi 110001; tel. (11) 23387064; fax (11) 23382428; e-mail secy@ndb.vsnl.net.in; internet www.sahitya-akademi.org; f. 1954; devt of Indian literature, coordination of literary activities in the Indian languages and research in Indian languages and literature; publ. of literary works; promotion of cultural exchanges with other countries; awards annual prizes for original works and translations; organizes seminars, symposia and workshops on literary subjects; Gen. Ccl consists of 8 eminent persons in the field of letters elected in their personal capacity, nominees of the Central and State Govts, 20 reps of the univs and 1 rep. of each of the 22 languages of India recognized by the Akademi, and 1 rep. each of the Lalit Kala Akademi, the Sangeet Natak Akademi, the Indian Ccl for Cultural Relations, the Raja Rammohun Roy Library Foundation and the Indian Publishers' Asscns; library of 125,000 vols; Pres. Prof. SUNIL GANGOPADHYAY; Vice-Pres. SUTINDER SINGH NOOR; Sec. AGRAHARA KRISHNA MURTHY; publs *Indian Literature* (in English, 6 a year), *Samakaleena Bharatiya Sahitya* (in Hindi, 6 a year), *Sanskrita Pratibha* (in Sanskrit, 2 a year).

Tamil Nadu Tamil Development and Research Council: Fort St George, Chennai 600009; f. 1959; development of Tamil in all its aspects, especially as a modern language; library of 27,000 vols, 320 MSS, 85 periodicals; 16 teachers; 50 students; Chair. CHIEF MINISTER; Vice-Chair. MINISTER FOR EDUCATION; Sec. DIRECTOR OF TAMIL DEVELOPMENT; publ. *Tamil Nadu Tamil Bibliography.*

MEDICINE

All-India Ophthalmological Society: c/o Dr Lalit Verma, Dr R. P. Centre for Ophthalmic Sciences, All-India Institute of Medical Sciences, Ansari Nagar, New Delhi 110029; tel. (11) 26593187; fax (11) 26852919; e-mail lalitverma@yahoo.com; internet www.aios.org; f. 1930; cultivation and promotion of the study and practice of ophthalmic sciences with a view to render service to the community and to promote social contacts among ophthalmologists; 7,394 mems; Pres. Dr K. P. S. MALIK; Gen. Sec. Dr LALIT VERMA; publ. *Indian Journal of Ophthalmology* (4 a year).

Association of Medical Physicists of India: c/o Radiological Physics and Advisory Div., Bhabha Atomic Research Centre, CT & CRS Bldg, Anushaktinagar, Mumbai 400094; tel. (22) 24447077; e-mail office@ampi.org.in; internet www.ampi.org.in; f. 1976; organizes annual conf., workshops, lectures, awards, research grants, travel fellowships within India; 680 mems representing medical physicists, radiation oncologists and others interested in this field; Pres. Prof. S. K. KOUL; Vice-Pres. A. M. PENDSE; Sec. Dr R. M. NEHRU; publ. *Journal of Medical Physics* (4 a year).

Association of Surgeons of India: 21 Swamy Sivananda Salai, Chepauk, Chennai 600005; tel. (44) 25383459; fax (44) 25367095; e-mail asi@md5.vsnl.net.in; internet www.asiindia.org; f. 1938; 14,200 mems; library: approx. 12,000 vols; Pres. Dr B. K. SINHA; Pres.-Elect Dr RAMA KANT; Hon. Sec. Dr R. K. KARWASRA; publ. *Indian Journal of Surgery* (6 a year).

Bombay Medical Union: Blavatsky Lodge Bldg, Grant Rd, Mumbai 400007; tel. (22) 23612880; f. 1883; 250 mems; Pres. Dr U. N. BASTODKAR; Sec. Dr Smt. M. K. THACKER.

Federation of Obstetric & Gynaecological Societies of India: Model Residency CHS, Ground Fl., 605 Bapurao Jagtap Marg, Jacob Circle, Mahalaxmi East, Mumbai 400011; tel. (22) 23021648; fax (22) 23021383; e-mail fogsi2007@gmail.com; internet www.fogsi.org; f. 1950; organizes annual congress for the exchange of views in the various aspects of the subject; organizes workshops on family planning, etc.; medical education programme; holds periodic int. seminars; 25,000 mems; Pres. Dr P. C. MAHAPATRA; Sec.-Gen. Dr P. K. SHAH; publ. *Journal of Obstetrics & Gynaecology of India* (6 a year).

Helminthological Society of India: Dept of Parasitology, UP College of Veterinary Science and Animal Husbandry, Mathura; Pres. Prof. S. N. SINGH; Treas.-Sec. Prof. B. P. PANDE; publ. *Indian Journal of Helminthology* (2 a year).

Indian Association of Parasitologists: 110 Chittaranjan Ave, Kolkata 700012; Pres. Dr H. N. RAY; Sec. Dr A. B. CHAUDHURY.

Indian Cancer Society: Lady Ratan Tata Medical & Research Centre, M. Karve Rd, Cooperage, Mumbai 400021; tel. (22) 22029942; fax (22) 22872745; e-mail info@indiancancersociety.org; internet www.indiancancersociety.org; f. 1951; charitable trust subsisting on donations; supports cancer research; aids sufferers from cancer, improves facilities for diagnosis, treatment and rehabilitation; educates the public and the profession; and organizes nat. confs; diagnostic, treatment and research centre in South Mumbai (Lady Ratan Tata Medical and Research Centre); Chair. Dr S. H. ADVANI; Vice-Chair. NIHAL KAVIRATHE; Hon. Sec. and Man. Trustee Dr ARUN P. KURKURE; publ. *Indian Journal of Cancer* (4 a year).

Indian Medical Association: I.M.A. House, Indraprastha Marg, New Delhi 110002; tel. (11) 23370009; fax (11) 23379470; e-mail inmedici@vsnl.com; internet www.ima-india.org; f. 1928; 125,000 mems; Pres. Dr ASHOK ADHAO; Hon. Gen. Sec. Dr DHARAM PRAKASH; publs *Apka Swasthya* (12 a year), *Family Medicine India* (4 a year), *I.M.A. News* (12 a year), *Journal* (12 a year), *Your Health* (12 a year).

Indian Pharmaceutical Association: Kalina, Santacruz (East), Mumbai 400098; tel. (22) 26671072; fax (22) 26670744; e-mail ipacentre@ipapharma.org; internet www.ipapharma.org; f. 1939; 10,000 mems; Pres. Dr B. SURESH; Chair. for Industrial Pharmacy Div. and Vice-Pres. J. A. S. GIRI; Chair. for Community Pharmacy Div. and Vice-Pres. RAJ VAIDYA; Chair. for Regulatory Affairs Div. and Vice-Pres. A. KRISHNA DEV; Chair. for Education Div. and Vice-Pres. T. V. NARAYANA; Chair. for Hospital Pharmacy Div. and Vice-Pres. Dr R. N. GUPTA; Hon. Gen. Sec. S. D. JOAG; publs *Indian Journal of Pharmaceutical Sciences* (6 a year), *Pharma Times* (12 a year).

Indian Public Health Association: 110 Chittaranjan Ave, Kolkata 700073, West Bengal; tel. (33) 32913895; e-mail office@iphaonline.org; internet www.iphaonline.org; f. 1956; promotion of public health and allied sciences; 22 state and local brs; holds Annual Convention, meetings, confs, etc.; organizes training programme on various areas of interest of public health; 3,890 mems; Pres. Dr ASHOK KUMAR; Gen. Sec. Prof. Dr SANDIP K. RAY; publ. *Indian Journal of Public Health* (4 a year).

Indian Society for Medical Statistics: General Secretary, Tuberculosis Research Centre, Indian Council of Medical Research, Dept of Statistics, Chetpet, Chennai 600031; tel. (44) 28369638; e-mail secretaryisms@gmail.com; internet www.isms-india.com/; f. 1983; contributes to the devt of medical statistics and strengthens the application of statistics in medicine, health and related disciplines; organizes annual confs, refresher courses, symposia; 480 mems; Pres. Prof. AJIT SAHAI; Pres.-Elect Prof. ARVIND PANDEY; Gen. Sec. Dr P. VENKATESAN; publs *ISMS Bulletin*, proceedings of annual meetings.

Indian Society of Anaesthetists: c/o Dept of Anaesthesiology, K. E. M. Hospital, Parel, Mumbai 400012; e-mail isanational@gmail.com; internet www.isaweb.in; f. 1947; 4,000 mems; Pres. Dr MANJUSHREE RAY; Vice-Pres. Dr AJIT KUMAR; Hon. Sec. Dr S. S. C. CHAKRA RAO; publ. *Indian Journal of Anaesthesia* (6 a year).

Medical Council of India: Pocket 14, Sector 8, Dwarka Phase 1, New Delhi 110077; tel. (11) 25367033; fax (11) 25367024; e-mail mci@bol.net.in; internet www.mciindia.org; f. 1933; maintenance of uniform standards of medical education; reciprocity in mutual recognition of medical qualifications with other countries; maintenance of Indian Medical Register; Pres. Dr P. C. KESAVANKUTTY NAYAR (acting); Sec. Dr A. R. N. SETALVAD; publs *Indian Medical Register*, *MCI Bulletin of Information*, *Report of the Programme on Continuing Medical Education*.

National Academy of Medical Sciences: Ansari Nagar, Mahatma Gandhi Rd, New Delhi 110029; tel. (11) 26588718; fax (11) 26588992; e-mail nams_aca@yahoo.com; internet www.nams-india.org/; f. 1961; 2,039 mems (700 fellows, 1,339 ordinary mems); Pres. Dr PREMA RAMACHANDRAN; Vice-Pres. Dr R. MADAN; Sec. Prof. GITA SUBBA RAO; publs *Measurement of Insulin Resistance in Vivo, Metabolic Syndrome: From Inert Facts to Informed Action, Networking in Disaster Management, Oxidative Stress in the Development and Complications, The Emerging Epidemic of Obesity and Cardiometabolic Risk Factors*.

Pharmacy Council of India: 2nd Fl., Combined Councils' Bldg, Temple Lane, Kotla Rd, Aiwan-E-Ghalib Marg, New Delhi 110002; POB 7020, 110002 New Delhi; tel. (11) 23239184; fax (11) 23239184; e-mail pci@ndb.vsnl.net.in; internet pci.nic.in; f. 1949; attached to Min. of Health & Family Welfare, New Delhi; statutory body; sets and maintains educational standards for qualification and registration in pharmacy and coordinates the practice; Pres. Prof. B. SURESH; Vice-Pres. P. P. SHARMA; Sec. and

Registrar ARCHANA MUDGAL; Asst Sec. ANIL MITTAL.

NATURAL SCIENCES
General

Indian Academy of Sciences: CV Raman Ave, POB 8005, Sadashivanagar, Bangalore 560080, Karnataka; tel. (80) 23612546; fax (80) 23616094; e-mail office@ias.ernet.in; internet www.ias.ac.in; f. 1934; promotes the cause of science in its pure and applied forms; activities incl. publ. of scientific journals and special volumes, organizing meetings of the Fellowship and discussions on important topics, recognizing scientific talent, improvement of science education and supporting issues of concern to the scientific community; 1,073 full individual mems (970 fellows, 49 hon. fellows), 51 assoc. mems; library of 1,000 vols; Pres. Dr A. K. SOOD; Sec. Prof. DIPANKAR CHATTERJI; Sec. Prof. J. SRINIVASAN; Exec. Sec. G. CHANDRAMOHAN; publs *Bulletin of Materials Science* (6 a year), *Current Science* (24 a year), *Journal of Astrophysics and Astronomy* (4 a year), *Journal of Biosciences* (4 a year), *Journal of Chemical Sciences* (6 a year), *Journal of Earth System Science* (6 a year), *Journal of Genetics* (3 a year), *Pramana-journal of physics* (12 a year), *Proceedings Mathematical Sciences* (4 a year), *Resonance: Journal of Science Education* (12 a year), *Sadhana-engineering sciences* (6 a year), *Year Book*.

Indian National Science Academy (formerly National Institute of Sciences of India): Bahadur Shah Zafar Marg, New Delhi 110002; tel. (11) 23221931; fax (11) 23235648; e-mail esoffice@insa.nic.in; internet www.insa.ac.in; f. 1935; promotes scientific knowledge, coordination between scientific bodies, and safeguards the interests of scientists in India; adhering organization of ICSU; 676 Fellows, 104 Foreign Fellows; library of 21,000 vols; Pres. Dr S. VARADARAJAN; Secs Prof. N. APPAJI RAO, Prof. P. T. MANOHARAN; publs *Indian Journal of History of Science, Indian Journal of Pure and Applied Mathematics, Progress of Science in India*.

Indian Science Congress Association: 14 Dr Biresh Guha St, Kolkata 700017; tel. and fax (33) 22872551; e-mail iscacal@vsnl.net; internet sciencecongress.nic.in; f. 1914; advances and promotes science in India; holds annual congress; 12,001 mems; library of 8,000 vols, 60 periodicals; Pres. Dr T. RAMASAMI; Secs Prof. AVIJIT BANERJI, Dr ASHOK K. SAXENA; publs *Everyman's Science* (4 a year), *Proceedings* (1 a year, in 4 parts).

National Academy of Sciences, India: 5 Lajpatrai Rd, Allahabad 211002, Uttar Pradesh; tel. (532) 2640224; fax (532) 2641183; e-mail allahabad.nasi@gmail.com; internet www.nasi.nic.in; f. 1930; promotes research in all brs of science; 3,095 mems excluding 1,436 fellows, 29 honorary fellows and 84 foreign fellows; Pres. Prof. A. K. SHARMA; Gen. Sec Prof. KRISHNA MISRA; Gen. Sec Prof. JITENDRA PAUL KHURANA; Exec. Sec., CPIO and Vigilance Officer Dr NIRAJ KUMAR; publs *Annual Number* (1 a year), *National Academy of Sciences Letters* (6 a year), *Proceedings* in two sections— *Section A: Physical Sciences, Section B: Biological Sciences* (8 a year).

Biological Sciences

Academy of Zoology: Church Rd 2/95, Civil Lines, Agra 282002; f. 1954; 1,500 mems; library of 91,000 vols, exchange service with other zoological institutions; international organization and forum for the advancement

of zoology; Pres. and Sec. Dr D. P. S. BHATI; publ. *The Annals of Zoology*.

Association of Microbiologists of India: DDG Fisheries, ICAR, Krishi Bhavan, New Delhi 110001; tel. (11) 25846738; e-mail generalsecretaryami@yahoo.com; internet www.amiindia.info; f. 1938, registered under Socs Registration Act XXI of 1860; 1,500 mems; library of 3,000 vols; Pres. Dr S. AYYAPPAN; Gen. Sec. Prof. R. C. KUHAD; publ. *Indian Journal of Microbiology* (4 a year).

Bombay Natural History Society (BNHS): Hornbill House, Salim Ali Chowk, Shahid Bhagat Singh Rd, Mumbai 400001; tel. (22) 22821811; fax (22) 22837615; e-mail bnhs@bom4.vsnl.net.in; internet www.bnhs.org; f. 1883; studies natural history, ecology and conservation in Indian sub-continent; research programmes in field zoology; 5,000 mems; library of 20,000 vols; Pres. B. G. DESHMUKH; Hon. Sec. Dr ASHOK KOTHARI; Dir Dr ASAD R. RAHMANI; Librarian NIRMALA REDDY; publs *Hornbill, Journal*.

Indian Association of Biological Sciences: Life Science Centre, Calcutta University, Kolkata 700019; tel. (33) 224753681; f. 1968; 400 mems; Sec. and Editor Prof. T. M. DAS; publ. *Indian Biologist* (2 a year).

Indian Biophysical Society: c/o Sec., IBS Dept of Chemical Sciences, Tata Institute of Fundamental Research, Homi Bhabha Road, Colaba, Mumbai 400005; tel. (22) 22782278; fax (22) 22804610; internet www.tifr.res.in/~ibs; f. 1965; c. 200 mems; Pres. Prof. N. R. JAGANNATHAN; Sec. Prof. K. V. R CHARY; publ. *Proceedings* (1 a year).

Indian Botanical Society: Dept of Botany, University of Madras, Chepauk, Chennai 600005; f. 1920; Pres. K. S. THIND; Sec. Prof. K. S. BHARGAVA; publ. *Journal*.

Indian Phytopathological Society: Division of Plant Pathology, Indian Agricultural Research Institute, New Delhi 110012; tel. (11) 25848418; fax (11) 25843113; e-mail ipsdis@yahoo.com; internet www.ipsdis.org; f. 1947; 1,600 mems; virology, bacteriology, mycology, nematology and plant pathology; holds seminars, symposia, etc.; Pres. Dr C. MANOHARACHARY; Sec. Dr D. K. AGARWAL; publs *Indian Phytopathology* (4 a year), *IPS* (4 a year).

Indian Society of Genetics and Plant Breeding: F2, 1st Fl., NASC Comple, DPS Marg, New Delhi 110012; fax (11) 25843437; e-mail isgpb@rediffmail.com; f. 1942; plant breeding and genetic research; 1,600 mems; Pres. Dr M. C. KHARKWAL; Sec. S. M. S. TOMAR; publ. *Journal* (4 a year).

Marine Biological Association of India:; tel. (484) 2394420; fax (484) 2394909; e-mail mail@mbai.org.in; internet www.mbai.org.in/index.html; f. 1958; promotes research on marine sciences in the Asia-Pacific region; organizes lectures, symposia and seminars on specific subjects; offers requisite information to research workers and students undertaking research in marine biological sciences; Pres. Dr G. SYDA RAO; Vice-Pres. Prof. Dr N. R. MENON; Vice-Pres. Dr N. G. K. PILLAI; Sec. Dr K. SUNILKUMAR MOHAMED; publs *Journal of the Marine Biological Association of India* (2 a year), *Memoirs* (irregular), Proceedings of symposia (irregular).

Society of Biological Chemists, India: Indian Institute of Science, Bangalore 560012; tel. (80) 23601412; fax (80) 23601412; e-mail sbcihq@gmail.com; internet www.iisc.ernet.in/sbci/index.htm; f.

1930; symposia and annual meetings; sponsorships of symposia, seminar and workshops for nat. and int. scientists; 1,600 mems; Pres. Dr V. S. CHAUHAN; Vice-Pres. Dr D. N. RAO (local) Dr ALOK BHATTACHARYA (out station) Dr D. KARUNAGARAN (out station); publs *Biochemical Reviews* (1 a year), *Proceedings and Abstracts* (1 a year).

Mathematical Sciences

Allahabad Mathematical Society: 10 C. S. P. Singh Marg, Allahabad 211001; tel. (532) 2623553; fax (532) 2623221; e-mail ams10marg@gmail.com; internet www .amsallahabad.org; f. 1958, registered in 1962 under the Socs Registration Act XXI of 1860; furthers the cause of advanced study and research in various brs of mathematics, incl. theoretical physics and mathematical statistics; 270 mems; library of 5,000 vols; Pres. Dr MONA KHARE; publs *Bulletin* (1 a year), *Indian Journal of Mathematics* (3 a year).

Bharata Ganita Parisad: Dept of Mathematics and Astronomy, University, Lucknow 226007; tel. (522) 2740019; f. 1950; mathematics; 475 mems; library of 16,000 vols; Pres. Prof. J. B. SHUKLA; Gen. Sec. Prof. A. NIGAM; publ. *Ganita* (2 a year).

Calcutta Mathematical Society: Asutosh Bhavan, AE-374, Sector I, Saltlake City, Kolkata 700064; tel. (33) 23378882; fax (33) 23376290; e-mail cms@cal2.vsnl.net.in; f. 1908; lectures, seminars, symposia, workshops in mathematical sciences; research projects sponsored by various funding agencies; 1,120 mems; library of 23,002 vols; Pres. Prof. Dr B. K. DATTA; Sec. Prof. Dr U. C. DE; publs *Bulletin* (6 a year), *Journal* (2 a year), *News Bulletin* (12 a year), *Review Bulletin* (2 a year).

Indian Mathematical Society: Dept of Mathematics, Univ. of Pune, Pune, Maharashtra 411 007; e-mail sknimbhorkar@yahoo .com; internet www.indianmathsociety.org .in/; f. 1907; 1,400 mems; library of 4,000 vols; Pres. Prof. R. SREEDHARAN; Gen. Sec. Prof. V. M. SHAH; Treas. Prof. S. K. NIMBHORKAR; publs *Journal of the Indian Mathematical Society* (4 a year), *Mathematics Student* (4 a year).

Physical Sciences

Astronomical Society of India: ISRO Satellite Centre, Airport Road, Bangalore, Karnataka 560017; tel. (80) 25265628; fax (80) 25265407; e-mail pati@iiap.ernet.in; internet www.asindia.org/default.aspx; f. 1990; recognizes talented Indian individuals who have made significant contributions in fostering astronautics in India; 750 mems; Pres. G. MADHAVAN NAIR; Vice-Pres. K. V. S. S. PRASADA RAO; Exec. Sec. R. K. RANJANGAM; Treas. V. SUNDARARAMAIAH; publs *Bulletin* (4 a year), *Memoirs* (irregular).

Electrochemical Society of India: Indian Institute of Science Campus, Bangalore 560012; tel. (80) 23340977; fax (80) 23341683; e-mail mahesh@cedt.iisc.ernet.in; f. 1964; promotes the science and technology of electrochemistry, electro-deposition and plating, corrosion incl. high-temperature oxidation, electrometallurgy and metal finishing, semi-conductors and electronics, batteries, solid electrolytes, solid state electrochemistry, and protection of metals and materials against environmental attack; 670 mems; library of 4,000 vols; Pres. M. RAVINDRANATH; Sec. Dr G. ANANDA RAO; publ. *Journal* (4 a year).

Indian Association for the Cultivation of Science: 2A& 2B Raja S. C. Mallick Rd, Kolkata 700032; tel. (33) 24734971; fax (33) 24732805; e-mail helpdesk@iacs.res.in; internet www.iacs.res.in; f. 1876; promotes fundamental research in the developing areas of basic sciences; 703 mems (625 life, 50 ordinary, 10 assoc., 18 hon.); Pres. Dr T. RAMASAMI; publ. *Indian Journal of Physics* (12 a year).

Indian Chemical Society: University Science College Bldgs, 92 Acharya Prafulla Chandra Rd, Kolkata, West Bengal 700009; tel. (33) 23609497; fax (33) 23503478; e-mail indi3478@dataone.in; internet indianchemsoc.org/; f. 1924; 2,000 mems; library of 10,500 vols; Pres. Prof. RAMESH CHANDRA; Hon. Sec. Prof. P. L. MAJUMDER; publ. *Journal* (12 a year).

Optical Society of India: Dept of Applied Optics and Photonics, Applied Physics Bldg, Calcutta Univ., 92 Acharya Prafulla Chandra Rd, Kolkata 700009, West Bengal; tel. (33) 23522411; fax (33)25497701; e-mail info@osiindia.org; internet www.osiindia.org; f. 1965; promotes and diffuses the knowledge of optics in all its branches, pure and applied; organizes seminars, workshops and confs; 678 mems; library of 400 vols; Pres. T. K. ALEX; Gen. Sec. Dr KALLOL BHATTACHARYA; publ. *Journal of Optics* (4 a year).

RELIGION, SOCIOLOGY AND ANTHROPOLOGY

Anthropological Society of Mumbai: 209 Dr Dadabhai Naoroji Rd, Fort, Mumbai 400001; f. 1886; Pres. Dr J. F. BULSARA; Hon. Sec. SAPUR F. DESAI.

Asiatic Society: 1 Park St, Kolkata 700016; e-mail aslibcal@cal.vsnl.net.in; internet www .asiaticsocietycal.com; f. 1784; studies humanities and sciences in India; 1,292 mems, 64 research Fellows; library of 149,000 vols; 47,000 MSS in 26 languages, 80,000 journals, 24,000 old coins, 75 oil paintings; research on Indology and Oriental studies; Pres. Prof. BISWANATH BANERJI; Sec. Prof. RAMAKANTA CHAKRABARTY; publ. *Journal* (4 a year).

Asiatic Society of Mumbai: Town Hall, Shahid Bhagatsingh Marg, Fort Mumbai 400023, Maharashtra; tel. (22) 22660956; e-mail asml@mtnl.net.in; internet www .asiaticsociety.org; f. 1804 as Dr P. V. Kane Research Institute for Oriental Studies; investigates and encourages sciences, arts and literature in relation to Asia and India; 2,811 mems; library of 248,953 vols, 2,357 MSS, 10,443 old coins; Chief Patron HE THE GOVERNOR OF MAHARASHTRA; Pres. Dr AROON TIKEKAR; Hon. Sec. Dr VIDYA VENCATESAN; publs *Journal*, reports.

Indian Anthropological Association: Department of Anthropology, Univ. of Delhi, Delhi 110007; tel. (11) 27667329; e-mail iaadelhi@rediffmail.com; internet www .indiananthropology.org; f. 1964; 400 mems; Pres. Prof. Dr S. M. PATNAIK; Vice-Pres. S. N. RATHA; Gen. Sec. S. K. CHAUDHURY; publs *Directory of Anthropologists in India* (every 4–5 years), *Indian Anthropologist* (2 a year), *News Bulletin* (1 a year).

Indian Society for Afro-Asian Studies: 297 Sarswati Kunj, I.P. Ext., New Delhi 110092; tel. (11) 22722801; fax (11) 22725024; f. 1980; analyzes political, economic, social and cultural situation of Afro-Asian countries; 621 mems; Pres. LALIT BHASIN; Sec. Dr DHARAMPAL.

Theosophical Society: Int. HQs, Adyar, Chennai 600020; tel. (44) 24912474; e-mail intl.hq@ts-adyar.org; internet www.ts-adyar .org/; f. 1875 in New York, USA, Adyar Library & Research Centre 1886, present location 1986; forms a nucleus of the universal brotherhood of humanity without distinction of race, creed, sex, caste or colour; encourages the study of comparative religion, philosophy and science; investigates unexplained laws of nature and the powers latent in man; 32,000 mems throughout the world; library of 250,000 vols and 20,000 palm-leaf and paper MSS; Pres. RADHA BURNIER; Sec. MARY ANDERSON; publs *Adyar Library Bulletin* (1 a year), *The Theosophist* (12 a year).

TECHNOLOGY

Aeronautical Society of India: 13B, Indraprastha Estate, New Delhi 110002; tel. (11) 23370516; fax (11) 23370768; e-mail aerosoc@ bol.net.in; internet www.aerosocietyindia .com/; f. 1948; promotion and diffusion of knowledge of aeronautical sciences and aircraft engineering, and advancement of the aeronautical profession; 6,500 mems; library of 4,000 vols; Patron-in-Chief Hon'ble PRIME MINISTER OF INDIA; Pres. V. V. THULASIDAS; Pres.-Elect ASHOK K. BAWEJA; Vice-Pres RAVI MENON B. P. BALIGA, R. SAREEN, BABU PETER, V. P. AGRAWAL, ASHOK NAYAK; Hon. Sec.-Gen. ASHOK BHUSHAN; Officer on Special Duty for Admin. Gp Capt. (Retd) H. C. BHATIA; Sec. Gp Capt. (Retd) R. C. GOYAL; publs *Elastic Stability of Structural Elements*, *Journal* (4 a year).

Geological, Mining and Metallurgical Society of India: c/o Geology Dept, Univ. of Calcutta, 35 Ballygunge Circular Rd, Kolkata 700019; tel. (33) 24753681; e-mail boses_in@yahoo.com; f. 1924; 315 mems; Pres. Prof. A. K. GHOSH; Jt Sec. SANTANU BOSE; Jt Sec. P. SIKDAR; publs *Bulletin*, *Journal* (4 a year).

India Society of Engineers: 12B Netaji Subhas Rd, Kolkata 700001; f. 1934; library of 20,000 vols; 8,000 mems; Pres. A. C. SINHA; Gen. Sec. D. B. CHOWDHURY; publ. *Science and Engineering* (12 a year, in English).

Indian Association of Geohydrologists: c/o Geological Survey of India, 4 Chowringhee Lane, Kolkata 700016; f. 1964; 440 mems; Pres. V. SUBRAMANYAM; Hon. Sec. A. K. ROY; publ. *Indian Geohydrology*.

Indian Ceramic Society: c/o Central Glass and Ceramic Research Institute, Kolkata 700032; tel. (33) 24138878; fax (33) 24730957; e-mail info@incers.org; internet www.incers.org/home.html; f. 1928; 2,000 mems; Pres. Prof. F. D. GNANAM; Vice-Pres. SWAPAN KR. GUHA; Hon. Jt Secs S. CHAKRABARTI, Dr K. G. K. WARRIER; publ. *Transactions* (4 a year).

Indian Institute of Metals: Metal House, Plot 13/4, Block AQ, Sector V, Salt Lake, Kolkata 700091; tel. (33) 2367 9768; fax (33) 23675335; e-mail iiomcal@dataone.in; internet www.iim-india.net; f. 1947; chapters based in Katni, Delhi, Bhopal, Baroda, Burnpur, Coimbatore, Chittorgarh, Chennai, Bangalore, Hyderabad, Hisar, Jaipur, Kharagpur, Korba, Rourkela, Mysore, Roorkee, Raigarh, Varanasi, Trichy, Vijaynagar, Visakhapatnam, Udaipur, Trivandrum, Salem, Surathkal, Sunabeda, Paloncha, Poona, Nagpur, Mumbai, Kolkata, Kolar Fold Field, Keonjhar, Kalpakkam, Khetrinagar, Kanpur, Jamshedpur, Ichapur, Hazira, Ghatsila, Duburi, Durgapur, Chandigarh, Bhadravati, Bhilai, Bhubaneswar, Bokaro, Angul, Ambarnath; 9,000 mems; Pres. L. PUGAZHENTHY; Vice-Pres and Chair. Dr SANAK

MISHRA (Ferrous Division), Dr D. BANERJEE (Metal Sciences Division), M. NARAYANA RAO; Sec.-Gen. J. C. MARWAH; publs *IIM Metal News* (6 a year), *Transactions* (6 a year).

Indian National Academy of Engineering (INAE): 6th Fl., Vishwakarma Bhawan, Shaheed Jeet Singh Marg, New Delhi 110016; tel. (11) 2 6832635; fax (11) 26856635; e-mail inaehq@inae.org; internet www.inae.org/; f. 1987; promotes gen. advancement of engineering and technology and related sciences and disciplines; awards professorship, fellowship and scholarship; 299 Fellows; Pres. Dr P. S. GOEL; Vice-Pres. for Acad., Professional and Int. Affairs Dr BALDEV RAJ; Vice-Pres. for Fellowships, Awards and Corporate Communication Prof. PREM KRISHNA; Vice-Pres. for Finance and Establishment Dr M. J. ZARABI.

Indian Society of Mechanical Engineers (ISME): c/o Dept of Mechanical Engineering, Indian Institute of Technology, New Delhi 110016; tel. (11) 26311259; fax (11) 26311261; f. 1975; 480 mems; Pres. Prof. G. S. SEKHON; Sec. Dr S. G. DESHMUKH; publs *Journal of Engineering Design* (4 a year), *Journal of Engineering Production* (4 a year), *Journal of Thermal Engineering* (4 a year).

Institution of Electronics and Telecommunication Engineers (IETE): 2 Institutional Area, Lodi Rd, New Delhi 110003; tel. (11) 24631810; fax (11) 24649429; internet www.iete.org/; f. 1953; promotes the advancement of electronics and telecommunications engineering and related fields; 40,000 mems; Pres. Lt-Gen. ASHOK AGARWAL; Sec.-Gen. Brig. (Retd) V. K. PANDAY; publs *IETE Journal of Education* (4 a year), *IETE Journal of Research* (6 a year), *IETE Technical Review* (6 a year).

Institution of Engineers (India): 8 Gokhale Rd, Kolkata 700020; tel. (33) 22238230; fax (33) 22238345; e-mail sdg@ieindia.org; internet www.ieindia.org; f. 1920; engineering professional soc. in India imparting non-formal engineering education; inc. by Royal Charter 1935; 94 centres; 60 libraries; over 500,000 mems; Pres. Rear Admiral K. O. THAKARE; Sec. and Dir-Gen. Cmdr (retd) ARVIND K. POOTHIA; publs *Divisional Journals* (15 engineering journals) (12 a year), *Inter-Disciplinary* (2 a year), *Technorama* (2 a year).

Mineralogical Society of India: Manasa Gangotri, Mysore 6; f. 1959; advances knowledge of crystallography, mineralogy, petrology, etc., by means of research and the holding of confs, meetings and discussions; 400 mems; library of 1,500 vols; Pres. Dr VISWANATHIAH; Sec. Dr P. N. SATISH; publ. *The Indian Mineralogist.*

Systems Society of India: c/o The Deputy Director, Vikram Sarabhai Space Centre, Control Guidance and Simulation Entity, Thiruvananthapuram 695022; tel. (471) 2565516; fax (471) 2564080; e-mail ds_antuvan@vssc.gov.in; internet www.sysi .org; f. 1981; nat. professional org. for systems science and engineering; numerous chapters incl. Thiruvananthapuram Chapter, Kozhikkode Chapter, Kharagpur Chapter, Vellore Chapter, Manipal Chapter, Aligarh Chapter, Agra Chapter, Hyderabad Chapter; 1,800 mems; Pres. Dr BIJAN B. DAS; Vice-Pres Dr VISHAL SAHNI, Dr ZACHARIAH C. ALEX; Sec. Dr D. S. ANTUVAN; publ. *Journal of Systems Science and Engineering* (journal, 2 a year).

Research Institutes
GENERAL

Council of Scientific and Industrial Research: Anusandhan Bhawan, 2 Rafi Marg, New Delhi 110001; tel. (11) 23711251; fax (11) 23714788; internet www .csir.res.in; f. 1942; attached to Min. of Science and Technology; library of 20,000 vols; Pres. THE PRIME MIN.; Dir-Gen. Prof. SAMIR K. BRAHMACHARI; Jt Sec. for Admin. AJAY KUMAR; publ. *Technical Manpower Bulletin* (12 a year).

Attached Research Institutes:

Central Building Research Institute: Roorkee 247667, Uttar Pradesh; tel. (1332) 272243; fax (1332) 272272; e-mail general@ cscbri.ren.nic.in; f. 1947; research and devt in all aspects of building science and technology; work divided into 5 areas: shelter planning, new materials, structural and foundation engineering, disaster mitigation and process devt; library of 44,778 vols; Dir Dr R. NARAYANA IYENGAR; publ. *Bhavanika* (in Hindi, 4 a year).

Central Drug Research Institute: Chattar Manzil Palace, POB 173, Lucknow 226001; tel. (522) 2223286; fax (522) 2223405; e-mail director@cdri.res.in; internet www.cdriindia.org; f. 1951; biochemical, molecular biological, pharmacological, chemical, microbiological, endocrinological, biophysical, parasitological and medical research; library of 21,300 vols; Dir Dr TUSHAR KANTI CHAKRABORTY; publs *Industry Highlights* (4 a year), *Ocean Drugs Alert* (4 a year).

Central Electrochemical Research Institute: Karaikudi 630006, Tamil Nadu; tel. (4565) 222065; fax (4565) 222088; e-mail cecrik@cscecri.ren.nic.in; f. 1953; electrochemical and allied research; library of 31,755 vols; Dir Dr M. RAGHVAN; publ. *Bulletin of Electro-chemistry.*

Central Electronics Engineering Research Institute: Pilani, Rajasthan; tel. (1596) 242111; fax (1596) 242294; e-mail root@ceeri.ernet.in; f. 1953; design and construction of electronic equipment, components and test equipment; Dir Dr S. AHMAD; publ. *CEERI News* (4 a year).

Central Food Technological Research Institute: Cheluvamba Mansion, Food Technology PO, Mysore 570013; tel. (821) 2517760; fax (821) 2516308; e-mail director@nicfos.ernet.in; internet www .mylibnet.org.in/cftri/cftri.htm; f. 1950; library of 36,300 vols; Dir Dr V. PRAKASH; publs *Food Digest* (4 a year), *Food Patents* (4 a year), *Food Technology Abstracts* (12 a year), *Library Bulletin* (4 a year).

Central Glass and Ceramic Research Institute: 196 Raja S. C. Mullick Rd, Jadavpur, Kolkata 700032; tel. (33) 24735829; fax (33) 24730957; e-mail cscgcri@giascl.l.vsnl.net.in; f. 1950; fundamental and applied research on special kinds of glass, ceramics, sol-gel, refractories, ceramic coatings, composites and allied areas; library of 25,000 vols; Dir Dr H. S. MAITY.

Central Institute of Medicinal and Aromatic Plants: PO CIMAP, Lucknow 226015; tel. (522) 2359623; fax (522) 2342666; e-mail roor@cimap.sirnetd.ernet .in; f. 1959; co-ordination of activities in the devt of cultivation and use of medicinal and aromatic plants on organized basis; library of 2,688 vols; Dir Dr SUSHIL KUMAR; publs *Farm Bulletin* (irregular), *Journal of Medicinal and Aromatic Plant Sciences* (4 a year), *Yatharth* (4 a year).

Central Institute of Mining and Fuel Research: PO Fuel Research Institute, Digwadih, Dhanbad 828108, Jharkhand; tel. (326) 2296023; fax (326) 2296025; e-mail dcmrips@yahoo.co.in; f. 1945, fmrly known as Central Fuel Research Institute; research on coal, lignite, allied subjects and other sources of fuel; environmental management and waste utilization; library of 10,129 vols, 35,000 periodicals; Dir Dr AMALENDU SINHA; publ. *Fuel Science and Technology* (4 a year).

Central Leather Research Institute: Adyar, Chennai 600020; tel. (44) 24910846; fax (44) 24912150; e-mail clrim@giasmd01.vsnl.net.in; internet www .clri.org; f. 1948; library of 17,225 vols; Dir Dr T. RAMASAMI; publ. *Leather Science Abstract Services* (12 a year).

Central Mechanical Engineering Research Institute: Mahatma Gandhi Ave, Durgapur 713209, West Bengal; tel. (343) 2546749; fax (343) 2546745; e-mail root@cscmeri.ren.nic.in; internet www .cmeri.com; f. 1958; library of 60,000 vols; Dir Shri HARDYAL SINGH; publ. *Mechanical Engineering Bulletin* (4 a year).

Central Mining Research Institute: Barwa Rd, Dhanbad, 826001 Bihar; tel. (326) 2203043; fax (326) 2205028; e-mail director@csemri.ren.nic.in; f. 1956; research on safety, health and efficiency in mining; library of 26,382 vols; Dir Dr T. N. SINGH.

Central Road Research Institute: PO CRRI, Delhi-Mathura Rd, New Delhi 110020; tel. (11) 26848917; fax (11) 26845943; e-mail director@cscrri.ren.nic .in; f. 1952; research and devt in highway engineering, traffic and transportation, transport environment and safety, bridge engineering, pavement design; library of 90,000 vols; Dir Dr A. K. GUPTA; publs *CRRI Road Abstracts* (4 a year), *CRRI WIN Bulletin* (4 a year), *Highway Documentation* (12 a year), *Roadsearch Bulletin* (2 a year).

Central Salt and Marine Chemicals Research Institute: Waghawadi Rd, Bhavnagar 364002, Gujarat; tel. (278) 2569496; fax (278) 2566970; e-mail general@csmcri.ren.nic.in; f. 1954; preparation of salt, magnesium compounds, bromine and bromides, cultivation and use of marine algae, desalination of water by solar stills, electrodialysis and reverse osmosis, waste water treatment using membrane processes; library of 48,000 vols; Dir Dr P. K. GHOSH.

Central Scientific Instruments Organization: Sector 30-C, Chandigarh 160020; tel. (172) 2657190; fax (172) 2657267; e-mail root@cscsia.ren.nic.in; internet www.nio.org/csir/csio.htm; f. 1959; research, design, devt, repair and maintenance of scientific and industrial instruments; technical training and diploma courses in instrument technology; library of 38,700 vols, 180 periodicals; Dir Dr R. P. BAJPAI (acting); publ. *Communications in Instrumentation* (4 a year).

Centre for Biochemicals Technology: Mall Rd, Delhi Univ. Campus, Delhi 110007; tel. (11) 27257298; fax (11) 27257471; e-mail central@cbt.res.in; internet www.cbt.res.in; f. 1966; uses the results obtained in basic biological research to provide commercially viable technologies for health care; Dir SAMIR K. BRAHAMCHARI.

Centre for Cellular and Molecular Biology: Hyderabad; tel. (40) 27173487; fax (40) 27171195; e-mail lalji@ccmb.ap.nic .in; internet www.ccmbindia.org; f. 1977;

research in frontier areas and multi-disciplinary areas of modern biology with a view to aiding devt of biochemical and biotechnology in India by providing centralized facilities and training; Dir Dr LALJI SINGH; publ. *CCMB Highlights*.

Indian Institute of Chemical Biology: 4 Raja S. C. Mullick Rd, Jadavpur, Kolkata 700032; tel. (33) 24735197; fax (33) 24735197; e-mail iichbio@giascl01.vsnl.net .in; f. 1956; solution of medical problems through fundamental and applied research in the basic biological sciences, with emphasis on projects bearing directly on the country's current biological and medical needs; library of 30,000 vols; Dir Dr D. K. GANGULY (acting).

Indian Institute of Chemical Technology: Hyderabad 500007; tel. (40) 27173874; fax (40) 27173387; e-mail root@ csiict.ren.nic.in; f. 1944; agrochemicals, drugs and pharmaceuticals, inorganic chemicals and materials, organic coatings and polymers, design engineering of chemical plant, oils and fats, biotechnology; library of 40,000 vols, 500 periodicals; Dir Dr K. V. RAGHVAN; publ. *Bulletin* (4 a year).

Indian Institute of Petroleum: Dehradun 248005; tel. (135) 2624508; fax (135) 2671986; e-mail info1@iip.res.in; f. 1960; research and devt in the field of petroleum, natural gas, and petrochemicals and use of petroleum products; trains technical personnel; assists Bureau of Indian Standards in framing standards for petroleum products; library of 15,000 vols, 14,000 periodicals; the institute is a Patents Inspection Centre of the Indian Patents Office and is open to the public for studying patent specifications; Dir Dr M. O. GARG; publs *R & D Newsletter* (4 a year), *Vikalp* (4 a year).

Industrial Toxicology Research Centre: Mahatma Gandhi Marg, Lucknow 226001, Uttar Pradesh; tel. (522) 2221856; fax (522) 2228227; e-mail intox@itrc .sirnetd.ernet.in; f. 1965; studies the effects of industrial pollution; library of 25,200 vols; Dir Dr P. K. SETH.

Institute of Himalayan Bioresources Technology, Palampur: Dist. Kangra, 176061 Himachal Pradesh; tel. (1894) 230411; fax (1894) 230433; e-mail director@csihbt.ren.nic.in; f. 1983; biodiversity conservation, tea husbandry and manufacture, agro-technology, processing and post-harvest technologies for floriculture, aromatic and herbal plants; Dir Dr P. S. AHUJA.

Institute of Microbial Technology: Sector 39A, Chandigarh 160036; tel. (172) 2690785; fax (172) 2690585; e-mail root@ imtech.ernet.in; internet www.imtech .ernet.in; f. 1983; research and devt in genetic engineering and microbiology, protein engineering, immunology and fermentation technology; library of 15,809 vols; Dir Dr AMIT GHOSH.

Institute of Minerals and Materials Technology: Council of Scientific and Industrial Research, Bhubaneshwar, Orissa 751013; tel. (674) 2581636; fax (674) 5881637; e-mail bkm@immt.res.in; internet www.immt.res.in; f. 1964 fmrly Regional Research Laboratory; library of 35,000 vols; research in problems relating to minerals and materials resources and technology; Dir Prof. B. K. MISHRA; Librarian Dr D. B. RAMESH.

National Aerospace Laboratories: PB 1779, Kodihalli, Bangalore 560017; tel. (80) 25270584; fax (80) 25260862; e-mail viman@csnal.ren.in; internet www .cmmacs.ernet.in/nal; f. 1959; research and

devt in aircraft design, testing and operation, and support for nat. aerospace programmes; library of 110,000 vols; Dir Dr T. S. PRALAHAD.

National Botanical Research Institute: Rana Pratap Marg, Lucknow 226001; tel. and fax (522) 2282881; e-mail manager@nbri.sirnetd.ernet.in; f. 1953; research into economic botany and collection, introduction, propagation and improvement of ornamental and economic plants; 520 mems; library of 53,414 vols; Dir Dr P. PUSHPANGADAN; publ. *Applied Botany Abstracts* (4 a year).

National Chemical Laboratory: Dr Homi Bhabha Rd, Pune 411008; tel. (20) 25902600; fax (20) 25902601; e-mail director@ncl.res.in; internet www .ncl-india.org; f. 1950; advanced functional materials, biotechnology, catalysis, organic chemical technology, chemical engineering science and polymers; 770 mems; library of 138,452 vols; 700 students; Dir Dr SOURAV PAL; publ. *NCL Bulletin* (4 a year).

National Environmental Engineering Research Institute: Nehru Marg, Nagpur 440020, Maharashtra; tel. (712) 2249885; fax (712) 2249900; e-mail director@neeri.res.in; internet www.neeri .res.in; f. 1958; research and devt in environmental monitoring, environmental biotechnology, solid and hazardous waste management, environmental systems design, modelling and optimization, air and water pollution control, sewage and industrial wastewater treatment, instrumentation and environmental impact studies; library of 46,500 vols, journals, reports, conference proceedings, CDs and audiovisual films; 200 int. and nat. peer-reviewed current periodicals; online access to 3,000 scientific and technical journals; Dir Dr TAPAN CHAKRABARTI (acting); publs *Journal of Environmental Science and Engineering* (4 a year), *Paryavaran Patrika* (2 a year, in Hindi).

National Geophysical Research Institute: Uppal Rd, Hyderabad 500007; tel. (40) 27170141; fax (40) 27171564; e-mail postmast@csngri.ren.nic.in; internet www .ngri.com; f. 1961; basic and applied research into mineral exploration and investigation of the earth's interior through seismic, geomagnetic, electric, geochemical and paleogeophysical studies; library of 19,173 vols, 13,895 bound vols of journals, 120 subscribed journals; Dir Dr HARSH K. GUPTA.

National Institute of Oceanography: Miramar, Panaje, 403004 Goa; tel. (8251) 221322; fax (8251) 223340; e-mail ocean@ csnio.ren.nic.in; internet www.nio.org; f. 1966; investigates physical, chemical, geological and biological oceanography, also functions as the Nat. Oceanographic Data Centre; research on marine geophysics and instrumentation; maintenance of data pertaining to the Indian Ocean at Planning and Data Div.; library of 24,000 vols; Dir Dr E. DESA.

National Institute of Science, Technology and Development Studies: Hillside Rd, New Delhi 110012; tel. (11) 25743227; fax (11) 25754640; e-mail postmast@csnistad.ren.nic.in; f. 1981; research on technological and social change, and resource planning and use for regional devt; library of 15,000 vols, 250 periodicals; Dir Dr S. PRUTHI (acting); publs *CLOSS* (4 a year), *Report* (every 2 years).

National Metallurgical Laboratory: Jamshedpur 831007, Singhbhum District, Bihar; tel. (657) 2431131; fax (657)

2426527; e-mail nml@csnml.ren.nic.in; f. 1950; ore dressing, production, physical and chemical metallurgy; library of 43,875 vols; Dir Prof. P. R. RAO; publs *News Bulletin* (4 a year), *Technical Journal* (4 a year).

National Physical Laboratory: Hillside Rd, New Delhi 110012; tel. (11) 25741440; fax (11) 25752678; f. 1947; fundamental and applied research in physics; maintenance of standards; testing and calibration of equipment; library of 109,000 vols; Dir Prof. A. K. RAYCHAUDHARY; publs *Ionospheric Data* (4 a year), *Sameeksha* (4 a year).

North-East Institute of Science and Technology: Jorhat, 785006 Assam; tel. (376) 2370012; fax (376) 2370011; e-mail director@rrljorhat.res.in; f. 1961; research into coal, petroleum, pulp and paper, natural product chemistry, cement, drugs and pharmaceuticals, synthetic organic chemistry, essential oils and medicinal plants, general and earthquake engineering, biochemistry, biotechnology, material science, building materials, soil engineering, testing and analysis; library of 24,500 books, 22,000 back vols and standards, patents, reports and theses; Dir Dr P. G. RAO; Head B. C. SAIKIA; publs *Bioinformation up to date* (12 a year), *NEIST Highlights* (1 a year), *NEIST Jorhat Technologies* (irregular), *NEIST News* (6 a year).

Regional Research Laboratory: Canal Rd, Jammu-Tawi 180001, Jammu and Kashmir; tel. (191) 2546368; fax (191) 2548607; e-mail rrlj@nde.vsnl.net.in; f. 1957; drug and medicinal plants; introduction of exotic plants, particularly from temperate zones; plant chemistry, extraction and processing of drugs; library of 16,522 vols; Dir Prof. S. S. HANDA.

Regional Research Laboratory: Library Bldg, Hoshangabad Rd, Univ. of Bhopal, Habibganj Naka, Bhopal 462026; tel. (755) 2587105; fax (755) 2587042; e-mail root@rrlbpl.onp.nic.in; f. 1981; research and devt on minerals and materials with particular focus on aluminium; Dir Prof. T. C. RAO.

Regional Research Laboratory: Industrial Estate, Trivandrum; tel. (471) 2490324; fax (471) 2491712; e-mail root@ csrrltd.ren.nic.in; f. 1976 to develop technologies for the optimal use of regional resources, to help industry in the region through research, devt and technology transfer; Dir Dr G. V. NAIR.

Structural Engineering Research Centre: Chennai 600113; tel. (44) 22542139; fax (44) 22540508; e-mail director@sercm.org; internet www.sercm .org; f. 1965; wind engineering and experimentation and earthquake engineering; structural health monitoring and evaluation; forensic analysis; metal structure behaviour, transmission line towers and analysis design and testing; computational structural mechanics; sustainable materials and composites and structural engineering construction and technology; library of 13,500 vols, 146 periodicals; Dir Dr NAGESH R. IYER; publ. *Journal of Structural Engineering* (6 a year).

Structural Engineering Research Centre: Central Govt Enclave, Kamla Nehru Nagar, Ghaziabad 201002, Uttar Pradesh; tel. (575) 2721874; fax (575) 2721882; e-mail root@cssercg.ren.nic.in; f. 1965; research into various aspects of structural engineering, incl. problems connected with bridges and long-span structures and high-rise bldgs, natural disaster mitigations and materials science; library of 8,500 vols; Dir V. K. GHANEKAR; publ. *Journal* (4 a year).

AGRICULTURE, FISHERIES AND VETERINARY SCIENCE

Agro-Economic Research Centre: Visva-Bharati University, Santiniketan 731235, West Bengal; tel. (3463) 252751; fax (3463) 252672; e-mail aere@vbharat.ernet.in; f. 1954; conducts research in agricultural economics; library of 6,000 vols; Dir KAZI M. B. RAHIM.

Central Arid Zone Research Institute: Jodhpur 342003; tel. (291) 2786584; fax (291) 2788706; e-mail kprvittal@cazri.res.in; internet www.cazri.res.in; f. 1959; 7 divs: Resource Survey and Monitoring, Resource Management, Arable Cropping System, Perennial Cropping System, Animal Sciences and Rodent Control, Energy Management, Engineering and Product Processing; Outreach programme; Regional Research Stations in Pali, Bikaner, Jaisalmer, Bhuj; library of 19,000 books, 164 current journals, 1,990 reprints; Dir Dr K. P. R. VITTAL; publs *Annals of Arid Zone* (4 a year), *DEN News* (4 a year).

Central Inland Fisheries Research Institute: Barrackpore 700120, West Bengal; tel. (33) 25920177; fax (33) 25920388; e-mail cifri@vsnl.com; internet www.cifri.ernet.in; f. 1947; researches into ecology of rivers, production functions of inland water bodies in the country, reservoirs, flood plain wetlands, estuaries and lakes; appraisal of inland fisheries resources, fisheries management of selected rivers, reservoirs, ox-bow lakes and estuaries; pen culture of carp and prawns; biology of fish and prawns; water pollution studies, conservation and environmental modelling; fish diseases and their control; also conducts information and training programmes; library of 9,000 vols and 90 journals; Dir Prof. Dr ANIL PRAKASH SHARMA; publ. *Indian Fisheries Abstracts* (2 a year).

Central Rice Research Institute: Cuttack, 753006 Orissa; tel. (671) 2367757; fax (671) 2367663; e-mail crrictc@ori.nic.in; internet crri.nic.in; f. 1946; research on basic and applied aspects of all disciplines of rice culture; 530 mems; library of 12,000 vols, 200 periodicals; Dir Dr T. K. ADITYA; publs *Oryza* (4 a year), *Rice Research News* (4 a year).

Central Tobacco Research Institute: Rajahmundry 533105, Andhra Pradesh; tel. (883) 465995; fax (883) 64341; e-mail ctri@pol.net.in; internet www.indiantobacco.com/rd.php; f. 1947; library of 22,000 vols, 159 periodicals; under the Indian Council of Agric. Research (Ministry of Agriculture and Rural Reconstruction, Govt of India); applied and fundamental research on all types of tobacco grown in India; regional stations at Guntur, Vedasandur, Pusa, Hunsur, Dinhata, Jeelugumilli and Kandukur; 250 mems; Dir Dr KAPIL DEO SINGH.

Indian Agricultural Statistics Research Institute: Library Ave, Pusa Rd, New Delhi 110012; tel. (11) 25847121; fax (11) 25841564; e-mail director@iasri.res.in; internet www.iasri.res.in; f. 1959; part of ICAR; research in experimental designs, sample surveys, biometric techniques, forecasting techniques, econometrics and computer applications; conducts postgraduate courses and in-service training in agricultural statistics and computer application; provides advisory service to agricultural scientists; provides consultancy service in data processing; develops computer software and information systems; library of 26,240 vols, 8,561 journals, 40 online journals, 9,346 reports, 912 theses; Dir Dr V. K. BHATIA;

Nat. Prof. Dr V. K. GUPTA; publ. *Agricultural Research Data Book* (1 a year).

Indian Council of Agricultural Research (ICAR): Krishi Bhavan, Dr Rajendra Prasad Rd, New Delhi 110001; tel. (11) 23382629; e-mail mrai.icar@nic.in; internet www.icar.org.in; f. 1929; attached to Min. of Agriculture; promotes agricultural and animal husbandry research in conjunction with state govts, central and state research institutions; provides consultancy and information on agriculture, horticulture, resource management, animal sciences, agricultural engineering, fisheries, agricultural extension, agricultural education, home science and agricultural communication; coordinates agricultural research and devt programmes and develops links at nat. and int. level with related org. to enhance the quality of life of the farming community; research centres; human resource devt in the field of agricultural sciences; oversees numerous agricultural universities nationally; establishes Krishi Vigyan Kendras (farm training centres) responsible for training, research and demonstration of the latest agricultural technology; Pres. SHARAD PAWAR; Dir-Gen. Dr MANGALA RAI; Sec. A. K. UPADHYAY; publs *Indian Farming* (12 a year), *Indian Horticulture* (4 a year), *Indian Journal of Agricultural Sciences* (12 a year), *Indian Journal of Animal Sciences* (12 a year), *Kheti* (12 a year), *Krishi Chayanika* (4 a year), *Phal-Phool* (4 a year).

Indian Council of Forestry Research and Education: P.O. New Forest, Dehradun (Uttarakhand) 248006; tel. (135) 2759382; fax (135) 2755353; e-mail dg@icfre.org; internet www.icfre.org; f. 1906; library of 160,000 vols, 600 periodicals; Dir-Gen. JAGDISH KISHWAN; publs *ENVIS Forestry Bulletin*, *Indian Forest Records*.

Indian Plywood Industries Research and Training Institute: Post Bag 2273, Tumkur Rd, Yeshwanthpur, Bangalore 560022, Karnataka; tel. (80) 28394231; fax (80) 28396361; e-mail bdeviprasad@ipirti.gov.in; internet www.ipirti.gov.in; f. 1962; attached to Min. of Environment and Forests; researches on saw-milling, plywood-manufacturing techniques, preservative treatment of wood and wood-based panels, devt of synthetic and natural adhesives; testing of panel products; training in mechanical wood-processing technology; specialized short-term courses; library of 8,500 vols; Dir Dr C. N. PANDEY.

Indian Veterinary Research Institute: Izatnagar 243122, Uttar Pradesh; tel. (581) 2300096; fax (581) 2303284; e-mail dirivri@ivri.up.nic.in; internet www.ivri.nic.in; f. 1889, deemed univ. status 1983; campuses at Bangalore, Bhopal, Izatnagar, Kolkata, Mukteswar, Palampur and Srinagar; research divs of animal biochemistry, animal biotechnology, animal genetics and breeding, animal nutrition, animal physiology, avian diseases, biostatistics, livestock production and management, livestock products technology, poultry science, veterinary bacteriology, veterinary epidemiology, veterinary extension education, veterinary gynaecology and obstetrics, veterinary immunology, veterinary medicine, veterinary parasitology, veterinary pathology, veterinary pharmacology, veterinary public health, veterinary surgery, veterinary virology; library of 207,000 vols, 300 periodicals; Dir Dr R. S. CHAUHAN (acting); Dir for Academic and Dean Dr D. DAS; Registrar K. L. MEENA (acting).

National Dairy Research Institute: Karnal 132001, Haryana; tel. (184) 2252800; fax (184) 2250042; e-mail bnm@ndri.hry.nic.in;

internet www.ndri.res.in; f. 1923, deemed univ.; library of 75,000 vols and 22,000 periodicals; regional stations at Bangalore and Kalyani; research divs in animal biochemistry, animal biotechnology, dairy cattle breeding, dairy cattle nutrition, dairy cattle physiology, dairy chemistry, dairy econ., statistics and management, dairy engineering, dairy extension, dairy microbiology, dairy technology; Dir Dr A. K. SRIVASTAVA; Registrar RAMESHWAR SINGH; Dir of Library Services Dr B. R. YADAV; library of 92,555 vols, 350 periodicals; publ. *Dairy Samachar* (4 a year).

National Sugar Institute: PO NSI Kalyanpur, Kanpur 208017, Uttar Pradesh; tel. (512) 2570730; fax (512) 2570247; e-mail nsikanpur@nic.in; internet nsi.gov.in; f. 1936; attached to Min. of Consumer Affairs, Food and Public Distribution (Dept of Food and Public Distribution); undertakes research, teaching and consultancy activities in all aspects of sugar technology and allied industries; library of 7,836 vols; Dir Prof. SANDEEP KUMAR MITRA; publs *N.S.I. News*, *Sharkara*.

Rubber Research Institute of India: Kottayam 686009, Kerala; tel. (481) 2353311; fax (481) 2353324; e-mail rrii@rubberboard.org.in; internet www.rubberboard.org.in; f. 1955; promotes the devt of the industry; scientific, technological and economic research in improved methods of planting, cultivation, processing and consumption of natural rubber; library of 55,000 vols; Chair. SAJEN PETER; Dir of Research Dr JAMES JACOB; Documentation Officer MERCY JOSE; publs *Indian Rubber Statistics* (1 a year), *Natural Rubber Research* (2 a year), *Rubber* (in Malayalam, 12 a year), *Rubber Board Bulletin* (4 a year), *Rubber Growers' Companion* (4 a year), *Rubber Statistical News* (12 a year).

Vasantdada Sugar Institute: Manjari (Bk.), Tal. Haveli, Dist. Pune 412307, Maharashtra; tel. (20) 26902100; fax (20) 26902244; e-mail vsilib@vsnl.com; internet www.vsisugar.com; f. 1975; library of 18,000 vols; Dir-Gen. SHIVAJIRAO C. DESHMUKH; Librarian N. S. PATHAN; publ. *Bulletin* (4 a year).

BIBLIOGRAPHY, LIBRARY SCIENCE AND MUSEOLOGY

Documentation Research and Training Centre (Indian Statistical Institute): 8th Mile, Mysore Rd, R. V. College Post, Bangalore 560059; tel. (80) 28483002; fax (80) 28484265; e-mail drtc@isibang.ac.in; internet drtc.isibang.ac.in/drtc/dspace-india.html; f. 1962; conducts research in the fields of library science, documentation and information science; trains documentalists; provides an advisory service to industry, academic and research institutions; library of 20,000 vols; Head Prof. A. R. D. PRASAD; publ. *DRTC Annual Seminar*.

ECONOMICS, LAW AND POLITICS

Indian Institute of Public Administration: Indraprastha Estate, Ring Rd East, New Delhi 110002; tel. (11) 23702400; fax (11) 23702440; e-mail diriipa@bol.net.in; internet www.iipa.ernet.in; f. 1954; promotes the study of public admin.; research, training, consultancy; library of 192,000 vols, 400 periodicals; Dir Dr B. S. BASWAN; Registrar Dr NARESH KUMAR; publs *Documentation in Public Administration* (4 a year), *Nagarlok* (4 a year), *The Indian Journal of Public Administration* (4 a year).

Institute for Defence Studies and Analyses: 1 Development Enclave, Near USI, New Delhi 110010; tel. (11) 26717983; fax (11) 26154191; e-mail idsa@vsnl.com; internet

demic sessions every two years; Sec. Dr SAROJA BHATE; publ. *Proceedings of Sessions* (every 2 years).

Anjuman-i-Islam Urdu Research Institute: 92 Dr Dadabhoy Nowroji Rd, Mumbai 400001; tel. (22) 22620177; fax (22) 22621610; e-mail anjuman_uri@rediffmail .com; f. 1948; research in Urdu; PhD in Arabic, Persian, Urdu and Islamic Studies; library of 20,200 vols; Chair. SAMI KHATIB; Dir Dr ABDUS SATTAR DALVI; Librarian SAYED MOHAMMED TAHER; publ. *Nawa-e-Adab* (4 a year).

Bhandarkar Oriental Research Institute: 812, Shivajinagar, Law College Rd, Pune 411004; tel. (20) 25656932; fax (20) 25656932; e-mail bori1@vsnl.net; internet www.bori.ac.in; f. 1917; Sanskrit, Indological and Oriental studies; library of 110,000 vols books, 28,000 MSS; Hon. Sec. R. N. DANDEKAR; publ. *Annals of BORI* (1 a year).

Cama, K. R., Oriental Institute: 136 Mumbai Samachar Marg, Fort, Mumbai 400023; tel. (22) 22843893; fax (22) 22876593; e-mail krcamaoi@vsnl.com; f. 1916; library of 27,804 vols, 2,000 MSS, 199 journals; Pres. MUNCHERJI N. M. CAMA; Jt Hon. Sec. H. N. MODI; Jt Hon. Sec. Dr N. B. MODY; publ. *Journal* (1 a year).

Deccan College Postgraduate and Research Institute: Deccan College Rd, Yeravada, Pune 411006; tel. (20) 226683192; fax (20) 26692104; e-mail deccan.college@gems.vsnl.net.in; f. 1939; postgraduate research in linguistics, archaeology, history and Vedic Sanskrit; library of 150,000 books and periodicals, 12,000 rare MSS; Vice-Chancellor Prof. K. PADDAYYA; Registrar S. R. KASHIKAR.

Ganganatha Jha Kendriya Sanskrit Vidyapeetha (Central Sanskrit Research Institute): Azad Park, Allahabad 211002, Uttar Pradesh; f. 1943; research into Sanskrit and other Indological subjects; library of 60,000 vols, 50,000 MSS; Principal Dr G. C. TRIPATHI; publs *Quarterly Research Journal*, catalogues, bibliographies, Sanskrit texts and studies.

Gujarat Research Society: Dr Madhuri Shah Campus, Ramkrishna Mission Marg, Khar (W), Mumbai 400052; tel. (22) 26462691; fax (22) 26047398; f. 1936; organizes and coordinates research in social and cultural activities; teacher-training; library of 10,000 vols; Pres. K. P. HAZARAT; publ. *Journal* (4 a year).

International Academy of Indian Culture: J 22 Hauz Khas Enclave, New Delhi 110016; tel. (11) 22665495; f. 1935; studies India's artistic, literary and historic relations with other Asian countries; library of 200,000 vols, 40,000 MSS; Dir Dr LOKESH CHANDRA; publ. *Satapitaka Series*.

Kuppuswami Sastri Research Institute: 84 Thiru V. Kalayanasundaranar Rd, Mylapore, Chennai 600004; tel. (44) 24675281; fax (44) 24675282; e-mail info@ksrisanskrit.in; internet www.ksrisanskrit.in; f. 1944; govt-sponsored and affiliated to University of Madras; promotion of Oriental learning especially Indology; lectures, seminars and workshops; 400 mems; library of 30,000 vols (including palm-leaf manuscripts); Dir Dr S. S. JANAKI; publs *Journal of Oriental Research*, and numerous research publs.

Mumbai Marathi Granth Sangrahalaya: Dadar, Mumbai 400014; tel. (22) 24134211; f. 1898; research in Marathi language and literature; library of 185,020 vols; Pres. S. K. PATIL.

Oriental Institute of Indian Languages: Univ. of Mysore, Kautilya Circle, Mysore 570005, Karnataka; tel. (821) 2423136; pro-

motes inter-regional and inter-continental understanding through the study of languages; Dir Dr H. P. DEVAKI.

Oriental Research Institute: Univ. of Karnataka Mysore, 570005; tel. (81) 2420331; library of 28,300 vols and 50 periodicals; collection of 60,000 ancient MSS; Dir K. RAJAGOPALACHAR.

Sri Venkateswara University Oriental Research Institute: Tirupati 517502, Andhra Pradesh; tel. (877) 2289414; fax (877) 2289544; internet www.svuniversity .in; f. 1939, present bldg 1979, named the 'Tiruppan Alvar Bhavan' in memory of 9th-century Vaisnava St Tiruppan Alvar; given by T. T. DEVASTHANAMS to the Univ. in 1956; researches in language and literature, philosophy and religion, art and archaeology, ancient Indian history and culture; library of 42,000 vols, 16,948 palm-leaf and paper MSS; publs *Sri Venkateswara Oriental Series*, *SVU Oriental Journal*.

Vishveshvaranand Vedic Research Institute: Sadhu Ashram, Hoshiarpur 146021; tel. (1882) 223582; e-mail vvrinstitute@yahoo.co.in; f. 1903; academic and cultural studies on Indian literatures and religion; Pres. Prof. G. P. CHOPRA; Dir Prof. I. D. UNIYAL; publs *Research Bulletin* (1 a year, in English), *Vishva Jyoti* (cultural, Hindi 12 a year), *Vishva Samskritam* (cultural research, Sanskrit, 4 a year).

Attached Institute:

> **Vishveshvaranand Vishva Bandhu Institute of Sanskrit and Indological Studies:** Sadhu Ashram, Hoshiarpur 146021; tel. and fax (1882) 221002; e-mail vvbis@rediffmail.com; f. 1965; postgraduate teaching, research and study in Indology; Prak-Shastri and Shastri MA classes in Sanskrit; library of 80,000 vols, 3,000 ancient MSS; Chair. Prof. RAGHBIR SINGH; publs *Acharya Vishva Bandhu Memorial Lecture Series* (1 a year), *Panjab University Indological Series*, *Vishveshvaranand Indological Journal* (research, English and Sanskrit, 2 a year).

MEDICINE

Advanced Centre for Treatment, Research and Education in Cancer (ACTREC): Tata Memorial Centre, Kharghar, Navi Mumbai 410210; tel. (22) 27405000; fax (22) 27405085; e-mail mail@ actrec.gov.in; internet www.actrec.gov.in; f. 1952 as Cancer Research Centre; library: 5,481 books, 9,642 bound vols of journals, 51 current periodicals; Dir Dr R. SARIN; publ. *Scientific Report* (1 a year).

B. M. Institute of Mental Health: Ashram Rd, near Nehru Bridge, Maninagar, Ahmedabad 380009, Gujarat; tel. (79) 26578256; fax (79) 26578259; f. 1951; comprehensive mental health services, teaching, and research; psychiatric clinic for the emotionally disturbed; clinic for children with learning difficulties; occupational therapy and rehabilitation services; speech clinic; postgraduate training in psychodiagnostics and counselling; offers diploma in working with the developmentally handicapped; library of 6,484 vols; Dir Dr S. R. APTE; publ. *Mental Health Review* (1 a year).

Central Leprosy Teaching and Research Institute: Min. of Health & Family Welfare, Govt of India, Chengalpattu, Tamil Nadu 603001; tel. (44) 27426274; fax (44) 27429308; e-mail dircltri@dataone.in; f. 1955; a WHO regional training centre; library of 13,000 vols, 33 periodicals; Dir Dr P. K. OOMMEN; publ. *News Bulletin* (4 a year).

Central Research Institute: Kasauli, Himachal Pradesh; f. 1905; medical research,

graduate and postgraduate training, manufacture of biological products; Institute of the Govt of India; library of 30,000 vols; Dir Dr J. SOKHEY.

Haffkine Institute for Training, Research and Testing: Acharya Donde Marg, Parel, Mumbai 400012; tel. (22) 24160947; fax (22) 24161787; e-mail contact@haffkineinstitute.org; internet www .haffkineinstitute.org/; f. 1897; principal centre of research in communicable diseases, biomedical and allied sciences in India; library of 26,500 back vols of scientific journals, more than 10,500 books, 4,000 micro fiches and a CD-ROM colln; Dir Dr ABHAY CHOWDHARY; publs *Determination Of HIV Seroprevalence In Pulmonary Tuberculosis Patients And Study Of Their Cellular Responses To Recall Antigens*, *Evaluation of three 'ready to formulate' oil adjuvants for foot-and-mouth disease vaccine production*, *Synthesis and antimicrobial activity of 2,4-disubstituted thiazole derivatives containing 1,2,4-triazole ring systems*.

Indian Brain Research Association: Dept of Biochemistry, University of Calcutta, 35 Ballygunge Circular Rd, Kolkata 700019; f. 1964; 300 mems; library of 2,000 vols; Pres. and Ed. Sec. Prof. J. J. GHOSH; publ. *Brain News* (2 a year).

Indian Council of Medical Research: V. Ramalingaswami Bhawan, Ansari Nagar, New Delhi 110029; tel. (11) 26588895; fax (11) 26588662; e-mail icmrhqds@sansad.nic .in; internet www.icmr.nic.in; f. 1911; promotes, coordinates and funds medical research; maintains the National Institute of Nutrition (Hyderabad), National Institute of Virology (Pune), Tuberculosis Research Centre (Chennai), National Institute of Cholera and Enteric Diseases (Kolkata), Institute of Pathology (New Delhi), National Institute of Occupational Health (Ahmedabad), Institute of Immunohaematology (Mumbai), National Institute for Research in Reproductive Health (Mumbai), Entero Virus Research Centre (Mumbai), Vector Control Research Centre (Pondicherry), Central Jalma Institute for Leprosy (Agra), Malaria Research Centre (Delhi), Institute for Research in Medical Statistics (New Delhi), National Institute of Epidemiology (Chennai), Institute of Cytology and Preventive Oncology (New Delhi), Rajendra Memorial Research Institute of Medical Sciences (Patna), National AIDS Research Institute (Pune), National Centre for Laboratory Animal Sciences (Hyderabad), Food and Drug Toxicology Research Centre (both Hyderabad), Centre for Research in Medical Entomology (Madurai), ICMR Genetic Research Centre (Mumbai), and six Regional Medical Research Centres (Bhubaneswar, Dibrugarh, Jabalpur, Jodhpur, Port Blair, Belgaum); library of 20,000 vols; Dir-Gen. Dr VISHWA MOHAN KATOCH; publs *ICMR Bulletin* (12 a year), *ICMR Patrika* (in Hindi, 12 a year), *Indian Journal of Malariology* (4 a year), *Indian Journal of Medical Research* (12 a year, with supplements).

Institute of Child Health: 11 Dr Biresh Guha St, Kolkata 700017; internet www .ichcal.org/index.htm; f. 1956; affiliated to College for Child Health, Univ. of Calcutta; depts of biochemistry, clinical paediatrics, dermatology, ophthalmology and otorhinolaryngology, paediatric surgery, pathology, physiotherapy, preventive paediatrics, psychiatry, radiology; Dir Dr APURBA GHOSH.

King Institute of Preventive Medicine: Guindy, Chennai 600032; f. 1899; postgraduate training in microbiology; library of 20,137 vols; Dir Dr K. V. MURTHY.

National Institute of Communicable Diseases: Directorate Gen. of Health Services, Min. of Health and Family Welfare (GOI), 22 Sham Nath Marg, Delhi 110054; tel. (11) 23971272; fax (11) 23922677; e-mail dirnicd@bol.net.in; internet www.nicd.org; f. 1963, fmrly Malaria Institute of India (f. 1909); research and training centre in field of communicable and vector-borne diseases; brs at Alwar (Rajasthan), Coonoor (Tamil Nadu) and Jagdalpur (Madhya Pradesh) (all for research and training in epidemiology), Calicut (Kerala), Rajahmundry (Andhra Pradesh) and Varanasi (Uttar Pradesh) (all for research and training on helminthology), Patna (medical entomology and vector control), Bangalore (zoonosis); library of 32,000 vols of books and journals, 251 maps, 89 photocopies and 1,400 annual reports from various orgs; f. 1909; Dir Dr SHIV LAL; Jt Dir and HOD Dr S. VENKATESH (Epidemiology Division), Dr A. C. DHARIWAL (Helminthology Division), Dr V. K. SAXENA (Medical Entomology and Vector Division), S. M. KAUL (T & M Division), Dr VEENA MITTAL (Zoonosis Division), Dr S. T. PASHA (Biochemistry and Biotechnology Division); publs *CD Alert* (12 a year), *Health News Clipping* (12 a year).

Attached Institute:

National Anti-Malaria Eradication Programme: 22 Sham Nath Marg, Delhi 110054; tel. (11) 22918576; fax (11) 22518329; f. 1958; coordination, technical guidance, planning, monitoring and evaluation of a nationwide malaria control and eradication programme; library of 4,000 vols; Dir Dr SHIV LAL; publ. *Malaria Watch* (4 a year).

National Institute of Nutrition: Indian Council of Medical Research, Jamai-Osmania, Tarnaka, Hyderabad, 500007, Andhra Pradesh; tel. (40) 27197200; fax (40) 27019074; e-mail nin@ap.nic.in; internet www.ninindia.org; f. 1918 as Beri-Beri Enquiry Unit, Deficiency Disease Enquiry 1925, Nutrition Research Laboratories 1928; principal research and training centre for South and South-East Asia; incl. centres for Food and Drug Toxicology Research, Nat. Centre for Laboratory Animal Sciences and Nat. Nutrition Monitoring Bureau; library of 64,265 vols, 33,725 periodicals, 12,916 reports, 17,624 books; Dir Dr B. SESIKERAN; Sr Library and Information Officer DEVIDAS MAHINDRAKAR; publs *Nutrition* (4 a year), *Nutrition News* (6 a year).

National Jalma Institute for Leprosy and other Mycobacterial Diseases: POB 101, Dr M. Miyazaki Marg, Taj Ganj, Agra 282001, Uttar Pradesh; tel. (562) 2331756; fax (562) 2331755; e-mail jalma@sancharnet.in; internet www.jalma-icmr.org.in/; f. 1966 as India Centre of JALMA; centre officially handed over to the Govt of India and the Indian Ccl of Medical Research, named the Central JALMA Institute for Leprosy in 1976, present status and name in 2005; part of Indian Ccl of Medical Research; treatment, research and training on leprosy, tuberculosis and HIV/AIDS; library of 2,496 books, 40 journals; Dir Dr V. M. KATOCH; publ. *Quarterly Bulletin.*

National Tuberculosis Institute: Govt of India, 'Avalon', 8 Bellary Rd, Bangalore 560003; tel. (80) 23361192; fax (80) 23440952; e-mail ntiindia@blr.vsnl.net.in; internet ntiindia.kar.nic.in; f. 1959; research in epidemiology, applied tuberculosis bacteriology, sociological aspects and systems research with regard to tuberculosis control; training and control programme; information centre on tuberculosis; digital library of institute papers published in periodicals

and publs; 140 mems; Dir Dr PRAHLAD KUMAR; publ. *Bulletin* (2 a year).

Pasteur Institute and Medical Research Institute: Shillong, Meghalaya; f. 1915; library of 7,311 vols; Dir N. G. BANERJEE.

Pasteur Institute of India: Coonoor 643103 (Nilgiris), Tamil Nadu; tel. (423) 2231350; fax (423) 2231655; e-mail directorpiic@dataone.in; internet www .pasteurinstituteindia.com; f. 1907; production of DTP group of vaccines and tissue culture anti rabies vaccine; rabies diagnosis (RFFIT); library of 20,000 vols; Dir Dr B. SEKAR.

Vallabhbhai Patel Chest Institute: POB 2101, Univ. of Delhi, Delhi 110007; tel. and fax (11) 27667420; fax (11) 27666549; e-mail vpci@delnet.ren.nic.in; internet www.vpci .org.in; f. 1949; attached to Univ. of Delhi; postgraduate teaching and research in respiratory diseases and allied biomedical sciences; library of 30,000 vols; Dir Dr V. K. VIJAYAN; publ. *Indian Journal of Chest Diseases and Allied Sciences* (4 a year).

Vector Control Research Centre: Medical Complex, Indira Nagar, Pondicherry 605006; tel. (413) 2272396; fax (413) 2272041; e-mail vcrc@vsnl.com; internet vcrc.res.in/; f. 1975; attached to Indian Ccl of Medical Research; affiliated with Pondicherry Univ.; develops epidemiological surveillance tools and strategies for the prevention and control of vector-borne diseases, incl. malaria, filariasis and dengue fever; research and postgraduate training; library of 10,000 vols; Dir P. K. DAS.

NATURAL SCIENCES

General

Bose Institute: 93/1 Acharya Prafulla Chandra Rd, Kolkata 700009; tel. (33) 23502403; fax (33) 23506790; e-mail dbt@ boseinst.ernet.in; internet www.boseinst .ernet.in; f. 1917; advances the science and diffusion of knowledge; research undertaken by depts of biochemistry, biophysics, botany, chemistry, microbiology, physics; experimental stations at Falta, Shamnagar, Madhyamgram and Darjeeling; library of 24,883 vols; Dir Prof. SIBAJI RAHA; Registrar TUSHAR K. GHORUI; Information Officer KAJAL CHAUDHURI; publ. *Transactions.*

Indian Association for the Cultivation of Science (IACS): 2A& 2B Raja S C Mullick Rd, Kolkata 700032; tel. (33) 24734971; fax (33) 24732805; e-mail helpdesk@iacs.res.in; internet www.iacs.res.in; f. 1876; researches in theoretical physics, spectroscopy, material science, solid state physics, physical chemistry, biological chemistry, energy research unit, polymer science unit, organic and inorganic chemistry; library of 63,205 vols; Pres. Prof. S. K. JOSHI; Dir Prof. K. BHATTACHARYYA; publs *Bulletin of the IACS, Indian Journal of Physics.*

Raman Research Institute: C. V. Raman Ave, Sadashivanagar, Bangalore 560080, Karnataka; tel. (80) 23610122; fax (80) 23610492; e-mail root@rri.res.in; internet www.rri.res.in; f. 1948; astronomy and astrophysics, light and matter physics, soft condensed matter and theoretical physics; library of 26,035 books, 38,666 periodicals, 175 journals (incl. 100 online); Dir Prof. RAVI SUBRAHMANYAN; Librarian MANJUNATH M.

UNESCO Office New Delhi: B-5/29 Safdarjung Enclave, New Delhi 110029; tel. (11) 26713000; fax (11) 26713001; e-mail newdelhi@unesco.org; internet www.unesco .org/newdelhi; f. 1948; UNESCO's first decentralized office in Asia; acts as designated cluster office for four countries in South Asia (Bhutan, India, Maldives and Sri Lanka); science and technology pro-

grammes in 11 South and Central Asian countries and including communication, education and culture programmes; library: documentation and information centre, 30,000 UNESCO documents, reports, etc.; spec. collns: science and technology, education, social sciences, culture and communication; films library, posters, CD-ROMs, CDs; Dir ARMOOGUM PARSURAMEN.

Biological Sciences

Birbal Sahni Institute of Palaeobotany: 53 University Rd, Lucknow 226007; tel. (522) 2740008; fax (522) 2740485; e-mail director@ bsip.res.in; internet www.bsip.res.in/; f. 1946; scientific research on the fundamental and applied aspects of fossil plants and their bearing on the origins of life; evolutionary linkages; biostratigraphy; fossil fuel exploration; phytogeography and biodiagenesis; repository of fossil plants; library of 5,000 vols, 10,000 current periodicals, 35,000 reprints and 300 microfilms, etc.; Dir Prof. NARESH CHANDRA MEHROTRA; publ. *The Palaeobotanist* (3 a year).

Botanical Survey of India: CGO Complex, 3rd MSO Bldg, Block F (5th & 6th Floor), DF Block, Sector I, Salt Lake City, Kolkata 700064; tel. (33) 23344963; fax (33) 23346040; f. 1890; botanical surveys and research; Headquarters: Central Nat. Herbarium and Indian Botanic Garden at Howrah; Industrial Section, Indian Museum at Calcutta; regional circles at Allahabad, Pune, Coimbatore, Jodhpur, Port Blair, Shillong, Dehradun, Itanagar and Gangtok; library of more than 250,000 vols; 491 scientific staff; Dir Dr B. D. SHARMA; publ. *Indian Floras.*

Indian Association of Systematic Zoologists: c/o Zoological Survey of India, 34 Chittaranjan Ave, Kolkata 700012; f. 1947; Pres. Dr A. P. KAPUR.

Institute of Plant Industry: Indore, Madhya Pradesh; f. 1924; research in cotton genetics, and in crop improvement of cotton and rotation crops; Dir RAI BAHADUR R. L. SETHI.

Tropical Botanic Garden and Research Institute: Pacha-Palode, Thiruvananthapuram, 695562, Kerala; tel. (472) 2869246; fax (472) 2869646; e-mail tbgri@sancharnet .in; internet www.tbgri.in; f. 1979; botanical garden, an arboretum, a medicinal plant garden and laboratories for botanical, horticultural, plant biotechnical, ethnomedicinal, ethnopharmacological and phytochemical research; conservation of rare and endangered tropical plant species; promotion of research and devt studies of plants of medicinal and economic importance; herbarium of 17,800 mounted specimens and 30,000 duplicates of vascular plants; museum; library of 5,000 vols, 65 journals; Dir Prof. Dr A. SUBRAMONIAM; publs *Index Seminum, Information Brochures.*

Zoological Survey of India: Prani Vigyan Bhawan, M Block, New Alipore, Kolkata 700053; tel. (33) 24003925; fax (33) 24003238; internet zsi.gov.in/; f. 1916; activities incl. maintenance of Nat. Zoological Collns, conduct of faunistic surveys and research on systematic zoology, wildlife, environmental conservation, etc.; regional stations at Berhampur, Canning, Chennai, Dehradun, Digha, Hyderabad, Itanagar, Jabalpur, Jodhpur, Kozhikode, Patna, Port Blair, Pune, Shillong, Solan; library of 60,000 vols, 800 periodicals; Dir Dr RAMAKRISHNA; publs *Bibliography of Indian Zoology, Fauna of India, Handbooks, Memoirs, Occasional Papers, Records* (4 a year), *State Fauna Series.*

Mathematical Sciences

Institute of Mathematical Sciences: CIT Campus, Taramani, Chennai 600113; tel. (44) 22541856; fax (44) 22541586; internet www.imsc.res.in/; f. 1962; research in pure and applied mathematics, theoretical physics and theoretical computer science; library of 44,996 vols, 260 periodicals; Dir Prof. R. BALASUBRAMANIAN; Registrar SARASWATHI RAMARAJ; publ. *I.M.Sc. Reports*.

Physical Sciences

Alipore Observatory and Meteorological Office: Kolkata; f. 1877; publ. *The India Meteorological Department*.

Astronomical Observatory: Presidency College, Kolkata; f. 1898; Dir Dr P. CHOUDHURY.

Astronomical Observatory of St Xavier's College: 30 Mother Teresa Sarani, Kolkata 700016; tel. (33) 22551264; fax (33) 22879966; e-mail shiva@sxccal.edu; internet www.sxccal.edu/pg_physics; f. 1875; Dir Rev. Dr JOHN FELIX RAJ.

Bhabha Atomic Research Centre: Trombay, Mumbai 400085, Maharashtra; tel. (22) 25505050; fax (22) 25505151; e-mail director@barc.gov.in; internet www.barc.gov .in; f. 1944; nat. centre for research in and devt of atomic energy for non-military purposes; facilities incl. 3 research reactors; Van de Graaff accelerator; laboratories at Srinagar, Gulmarg, and Gauribidanur; isotope production unit; central workshops; pilot plants for production of heavy water, zirconium, titanium; uranium metal plant; food irradiation and processing laboratory; reactor engineering laboratory and test facilities; library of 200,000 vols, 1,200 technical journals, 450,000 technical reports; Dir Dr SRIKUMAR BANERJEE; publ. *Technical Reports*.

Central Seismological Observatory: Shillong; headquarters at New Delhi.

Geodetic and Research Branch, Survey of India: POB 77, Dehradun 248001; f. 1800; geodetic and allied geophysical activities, including development and research of instrumentation; library of 55,000 vols; Dir Dr M. G. ARUR; publs reports, and technical publications.

Geological Survey of India: 27 J. L. Nehru Rd, Kolkata 700016; tel. (33) 22861676; fax (33) 22496956; e-mail gsi_chq@vsnl.com; internet www.gsi.gov.in; f. 1851; devoted to surveying and mapping, mineral exploration, specialized investigations, other exploration, research and development, information dissemination, human resource development and project modernization and replacement; library of 5,003,500 vols; Dir-Gen. K. N. MATHUR; publs *Bulletin, Series A, B, C* (irregular), *Catalogue Series* (irregular), *Indian Minerals* (4 a year), *Manual Series* (irregular), *Memoirs of the Geological Survey of India* (irregular), *Miscellaneous Publications* (irregular), *Palaeontologica Indica* (irregular), *Records of the Geological Survey of India. Part I–VIII* (1 a year), *Special Publications* (irregular).

India Meteorological Department: Mausam Bhawan, Lodi Rd, New Delhi 110003; tel. (11) 24619415; fax (11) 24669216; internet www.imd.ernet.in/main_new.htm; f. 1875; 6 regional offices at New Delhi, Mumbai, Kolkata, Madras, Nagpur and Guwahati; 11 meteorological centres at Thiruvananthapuram, Bangalore, Hyderabad, Bhubaneshwar, Lucknow, Jaipur, Srinagar, Ahmedabad, Patna, Chandigarh and Bhopal; 10 cyclone detection radars; Positional Astronomy Centre at Kolkata; provides weather service; scientific activities cover research in all brs of meteorology, incl. agricultural and hydrometeorology, radio-meteorology, satellite and environmental meteorology, atmospheric electricity, seismology; New Delhi is Regional Telecommunication Hub and Regional Meteorological Centre under WMO World Weather Watch; Regional Specialised Meteorological Centre for Tropical Cyclones; also Regional Area Forecast Centre under ICAO; Dir-Gen. Dr AJIT TYAGI (acting); publs *Indian Astronomical Ephemeris* (1 a year), *Indian Weather Review*, *Mausam* (4 a year), occasional memoirs, *Regional/State Daily Weather Reports*, reviews.

Indian Bureau of Mines: 'Indira Bhavan', Civil Lines, Nagpur 440102; tel. (712) 2560041; fax (712) 2565073; e-mail cgibm@ ibm.mah.nic.in; internet ibm.nic.in; f. 1948; govt dept responsible for the conservation and devt of mineral resources and protection of mining environment; aid in mine and mineral devt; technical consultancy in mining and mineral-processing, colln and dissemination of mineral statistics and information, preparation of feasibility reports of mining projects, incl. benefication plants, and preparation of environmental management plans; conducts market surveys on minerals and mineral commodities; regional offices at Ajmer, Bangalore, Bhubaneswar, Chennai, Dehradun, Goa, Hyderabad, Jabalpur, Kolkata, Ranchi, Udaipur; mineral processing laboratory and pilot plant at Nagpur; library of 50,000 vols, 10,000 periodicals; Controller-Gen. A. N. BOSE; publs *Indian Minerals Yearbook, Monthly Statistics of Mineral Production, Mineral Industry at a Glance* (1 a year).

Indian Institute of Astrophysics: II Block, Koramangala, Bangalore 560034; tel. (80) 25530672; fax (80) 25534043; e-mail hasan@iiap.res.in; internet www.iiap.res.in; f. 1786 as private observatory in Madras; study of solar physics, stellar physics, solar system objects, theoretical astrophysics incl. ionosphere, cosmology, solar-terrestrial relationship and instrumentation; field stations at Gauribidanur, Hanle, Kavalur and Kodaikanal, and a research unit at Hosakote; library: more than 18,000 vols and access to 140 online journals; Dir Prof. S. S. HASAN; publ. *Reprints*.

Indian Institute of Geomagnetism: Kalamboli-Panvel Highway, New Panvel (W), New Mumbai 410218; tel. (22) 27484046; fax (22) 27480762; e-mail divyam@iigs.iigm.res.in; internet www.iigm .res.in; f. 1971; observatories in Alibag, Jaipur, Nagpur, Gulmarg, Shillong, Pondicherry, Rajkot, Silchar, Tirunelveli, Vishakapatnam; World Data Centre WDC-C2 for geomagnetism; operates geomagnetic observatory over Antarctica; basic research in upper atmospheric physics, solid earth geophysics and allied fields, environmental magnetism; research centres at Tirunelveli, Tamil Nadu (Equatorial Geophysical Research Laboratory) and at Allahabad, Uttar Pradesh (K. S. Krishnan Geomagnetic Research Laboratory); library: 20,000 vols (books, bound periodicals, reprints, reports, maps magnetic data and non-book material); Dir Prof. ARCHANA BHATTACHARYYA; publ. *Indian Magnetic Data* (1 a year).

Indian Space Research Organization (ISRO): Antariksh Bhavan, New BEL Rd, Bangalore 560094; tel. (80) 23415474; fax (80) 23412253; e-mail info@isro.gov.in; internet www.isro.gov.in; f. 1972; devt of satellites, launch vehicles and ground stations for satellite-based communications, resources survey and meteorological services; operates Vikram Sarabhai Space Centre, Space Applications Centre at Ahmedabad, ISRO Satellite Centre at Bangalore, SHAR Centre at Sriharikota Island, Liquid Propulsion System Unit at Trivandrum and Bangalore, Devt and Educational Communications Unit at Ahmedabad, ISRO Telemetry Tracking and Command Network at Bangalore, ISRO Inertial Systems Unit, Trivandrum, INSAT Master Control Facility, Hassan; Nat. Remote Sensing Agency at Hyderabad, Physical Research Laboratory at Ahmedabad and Nat. Mesosphere-Stratosphere-Troposphere Radar Facility at Gadanki; Chair. G. MADHAVAN NAIR; Man. Dir., Antrix Corp. Ltd (commercial arm of ISRO) K. R. SRIDHAR MURTHY; publs *Journal of Spacecraft Technology* (2 a year), *Space India* (4 a year).

Indira Gandhi Centre for Atomic Research: Dept of Atomic Energy, Kalpakkam 603102, Tamil Nadu; tel. (44) 27480267; fax (44) 27480060; e-mail dir@igcar.gov.in; internet www.igcar.gov.in; f. 1971; attached to Dept of Atomic Energy, Govt of India; researches in fast reactor technology and related disciplines; library of 65,000 vols, 820 journals, 200,000 research reports; Dir Dr BALDEV RAJ.

Institute for Plasma Research: Bhat, Gandhinagar, Gujarat 382428; tel. (79) 23962001; fax (79) 23962277; e-mail postmaster@ipr.res.in; internet www.ipr.res .in; f. 1986; research in plasma physics; library of 21,260 vols, 11,096 technical reports, 2,568 reprints, 105 periodicals; Dir P. K. KAW; publ. *Plasma Processing Update* (4 a year).

Inter-University Centre for Astronomy and Astrophysics: POB 4, Ganeshkhind, Pune Univ. Campus, Pune 411007; tel. (20) 25604100; fax (20) 25604699; e-mail root@ iucaa.ernet.in; internet www.iucaa.ernet.in; f. 1988; fundamental research and training in all aspects of astronomy and astrophysics; MSc and PhD, refresher courses, research workshops, etc.; Dir Prof. NARESH K. DADHICH; Dean Prof. T. PADMANABHAN (Core Academic Programmes), Prof. A. K. KEMBHAVI; publs *Khagol* (4 a year), *Lecture Notes*.

Mining, Geological and Metallurgical Institute of India: GN-38/4, Sector V, Salt Lake, Kolkata 700091; tel. (33) 23573987; fax (33) 23573482; e-mail mgmi@cal2.vsnl.net.in; internet www.mgmiindia.com; f. 1906; 3,000 mems from 16 brs; library of 3,500 vols; Pres. R. K. SAHA; Vice-Pres. T. K. LAHIRY; Hon. Sec. Dr D. SARKAR; Hon. Jt Sec. P. ROY; publ. *Transactions* (1 a year).

National Institute of Rock Mechanics: Champion Reefs P.O., Kolar Gold Fields 563117, Karnataka; tel. (8153) 275004; fax (8153) 275002; e-mail nirm@nirm.in; internet www.nirm.in/home.htm; f. 1989; library of 1,400 vols; Dir Dr P. C. NAWANI; publ. *Bulletin* (3 a year).

Nizamiah and Japal-Rangapur Observatories and Centre of Advanced Study in Astronomy: Dept of Astronomy, Osmania University, Hyderabad 500007; tel. (40) 27017306; e-mail pies@ouastr.ernet.in; f. 1908, transferred to control of Osmania Univ. 1919; library of 15,000 vols, 4,000 periodicals; Dir Prof. P. V. SUBRAHMANYAM; publ. *Astronomical*.

Physical Research Laboratory: Ahmedabad, Gujarat 380009; tel. (79) 26314000; fax (79) 26314900; e-mail info@prl.res.in; internet www.prl.res.in; f. 1947; atomic and molecular physics, nuclear and particle physics, laser physics and quantum optics, gravitational physics, non-linear dynamics and quantum chaos, optical and infrared astronomy, solar physics, astrophysics, atmospheric sciences and planetary aeronomy, oceanography and climate studies, solar system and geochronology, planetary science and exploration; library of 50,000 vols, 2,500 scientific reports and 1,200 maps; Dir

Prof. JITENDRA NATH GOSWAMI; Controller-cum-Registrar Y. M. TRIVEDI.

Saha Institute of Nuclear Physics: 1/AF, Bidhannagar, Kolkata 700064; tel. (33) 23375345; fax (33) 23374637; e-mail library@saha.ac.in; internet www.saha.ac.in/lib/www; f. 1950; 1,250 Institute mems; 500 external mems; conducts advanced research and teaching in nuclear science (radioactive ion beams, high-energy physics, quark gluon plasma); research in physics (atomic physics, condensed matter physics, high-energy physics, microelectronics, nuclear physics, plasmic physics, surface and general mathematical physics) and biophysical sciences (cell biology genetic toxicology, macromolecular crystallography, membrane biophysics, molecular genetics, nuclear and radiochemistry, photochemistry, radiation chemistry and biology, structural biology and biomolecular spectroscopy, ultrastructural research); library of 34,622 books, 49,753 journals, 25,000 reports, 901 CD-ROMs; Dir Prof. MILAN K. SANYAL; Registrar V. V. MALLIKARJUNA RAO.

PHILOSOPHY AND PSYCHOLOGY

Pratap Centre of Philosophy: Dept of Philosophy, Univ. of Pune, Amalner, District Jalgaon, Maharashtra 425401; tel. (2587) 222280; e-mail pratap.philosophy@gmail.com; f. 1916 as Indian Inst. of Philosophy, taken over by univ. and renamed 1972; comparative study of Indian and European philosophy; 3 fellowships awarded yearly for research; library of 6,000 vols; Dir Dr ARCHANA DEGAONKAR; publs *The Philosophical Quarterly* (4 a year), *Tatvadnyan Mandir* (in Marathi).

The Yoga Institute: Santa Cruz (East), Shri Yogendra Marg, Prabhat Colony, Mumbai 400055; tel. (22) 26122185; e-mail yogainstitute@gmail.com; internet www.theyogainstitute.org; f. 1918; promotes self-education, physical, mental, moral and psychic, aided by science of Yoga; conducts academic and scientific research in Yoga culture and technique; runs teacher training Inst. of Yoga and a Psychosomatic Clinic based on Yoga; library of 4,500 vols; Dir HANSA JAYADEVA YOGENDRA; publs *Cyclopaedia Yoga*, *Yoga and Total Health* (12 a year), *Yoga Studies*.

RELIGION, SOCIOLOGY AND ANTHROPOLOGY

Anjuman-i-Islam Urdu Research Association: 92 Dadabhoy Nowroji Rd, Mumbai 400001; library of 5,000 vols; Pres. Dr M. ISHAQUE JAMKHANAWALA; Dir Prof. N. S. GOREKAR; publ. 12 vols of research work on Islamic studies.

Anthropological Survey of India:; e-mail hohq@ansi.gov.in 27 Jawaharlal Nehru Rd, Kolkata 700016; tel. (33) 22861796; fax (33) 22861685; e-mail director@ansi.gov.in; internet www.ansi.gov.in; f. 1945; research in cultural and physical anthropology, human ecology, linguistics, psychology, folklore, biochemistry and radiology; library of 40,935 vols; Dir Dr V. R. RAO.

Applied Interdisciplinary Development Research Institute, Youth Entrepreneurship Development Organization (YEDO): 20 Thiruvenkadapuram Main Rd, Choolaimedu, Chennai 600094; tel. (44) 65317697; fax (44) 23741564; e-mail peteraidri@hotmail.com; f. 1985; 120 mems; library of 2,000 vols; interdisciplinary devt education, training, research, consultancy, information dissemination in fields of sustainable agricultural devt, youth empowerment, empowerment of street children, women's empowerment, indigenous know-ledge and local resources devt, environmental education, and entrepreneurship devt; Exec. Dir Dr A. PETER; publ. *Young Entrepreneurs Digest*.

Ethnographic and Folk Culture Society: C-24, K Rd, Mahanagar Extn, Lucknow 226006; tel. and fax (522) 2372362; e-mail efcs@sancharnet.in; internet www.efcsindia.com; f. 1945; research into anthropological sciences; museum of Folk Life and Culture; library; Pres. Prof. T. N. MADAN; Vice-Presidents Prof. R. K. KAR, Prof. P. VENKAT RAO, Prof. J. K. PUNDIR, Prof. R. B. S. VERMA, Prof. P. K. TEWARI; Hon. Gen. Sec. Dr SUKANT K. CHAUDHARY; publs *Indian Journal of Physical Anthropology and Human Genetics* (2 a year), *Manav* (in Hindi, 2 a year), *The Eastern Anthropologist* (4 a year).

Indian Council of Social Science Research (ICSSR): JNU Institutional Area, Aruna Asaf Ali Marg, New Delhi 110067; tel. (11) 26179849; fax (11) 26179836; e-mail info@icssr.org; internet www.icssr.org; f. 1969; sponsors and coordinates research in social science, provides financial assistance for research programmes, awards fellowships and grants; sponsors confs, seminars, training programmes and publs; provides partial support to 28 social science research institutes; collaborates with international bodies in research programmes; Nat. Social Science Documentation Centre (NASSDOC: see Libraries and Archives); Data Archives; regional centres in Mumbai, Kolkata, Chandigarh, Delhi, Hyderabad, and Shillong; library of 35,000 books, 150,000 periodicals; Chair. Prof JAVEED ALAM; Mem.-Sec. Dr RANJIT SINHA; Dir for Research Institute and Regional Centre Dr. S. N. M. KOPPARTY; Dir for Research Project and Research Fellowship Dr G. S. SAUN; Dir for Research Survey, Publications and Sales Dr RANJIT SINHA; Dir for NASSDOC Dr P. R. GOSWAMI; publs *ICSSR Journal of Abstracts and Reviews: Economics* (2 a year), *ICSSR Journal of Abstracts and Reviews: Geography* (2 a year), *ICSSR Journal of Abstracts and Reviews: Political Science* (2 a year), *ICSSR Journal of Abstracts and Reviews: Sociology and Social Anthropology* (2 a year), *Indian Psychological Abstracts and Reviews* (2 a year), *Indian Social Science Review*.

Institute of Applied Manpower Research: Sector A-7, Institutional Area, Narela, Delhi 110040; tel. (11) 27787214; fax (11) 27783467; e-mail iamrindia@nic.in; internet www.iamrindia.org; f. 1962; autonomous body under Planning Comm.; studies and disseminates information on the nature, characteristics and utilization of human resources in India; develops methodologies for forecasting demand and supply; compiles information on technical manpower; organizes seminars, confs, study courses and training programmes in techniques of manpower planning at nat. and int. levels and provides consultancy services; conducts degree and diploma courses in Human Resource Planning and Devt for int. participants in collaboration with Commonwealth Secretariat, London, United Kingdom; library of 26,250 vols, 150 journals; Pres. for Gen. Ccl MONTEK SINGH AHLUWALIA; Dir SANTOSH MEHROTRA; Librarian AJIT KUMAR; publs *Manpower Documentation* (12 a year), *Manpower Journal* (4 a year), *Manpower Profile India* (1 a year), *Technical Manpower Bulletin* (4 a year), *Technical Manpower Profile* (every 5 years).

Institute of Economic Growth: University of Delhi Enclave, North Campus, Delhi 110007; tel. (11) 27667288; fax (11) 27667410; e-mail system@iegindia.org; internet www.iegindia.org; f. 1958; an autonomous body recognized by the University of Delhi as a national-level multidisciplinary centre for advanced research and training, including PhD supervision in the fields of economic and social development; specialized library and documentation service; Dir Prof. KANCHAN CHOPRA; publs *Contributions to Indian Sociology: New Series* (2 a year), *Studies in Asian Social Development* (irregular), *Studies in Economic Development and Planning*.

Namgyal Institute of Tibetology/fmrly Sikkim Research Institute of Tibetology: Deorali, 737101 Gangtok, Sikkim; tel. and fax (3592) 281525; e-mail directornit@yahoo.com; internet www.tibetology.net; f. 1958; research centre for study of Mahayana (Northern Buddhism); museum of icons and art objects; library of 60,000 vols of Tibetan literature (canonical of all sects and secular) in MSS and xylographs; Pres. BALMIKI PRASAD SINGH; Dir TASHI DENSAPA; publ. *Bulletin of Tibetology* (2 a year).

National Institute of Rural Development: Rajendranagar, Hyderabad 500030; tel. (40) 24008526; fax (40) 24016500; e-mail dhiraj@nird.gov.in; internet www.nird.org.in; f. 1958; autonomous servicing and consultancy agency for central and state govts; training for govt and non-govt officials; a Centre on Rural Documentation (CORD) provides computerized library services; devt research into all facets of rural life; offers consultancy service to nat. and int. orgs; repackages govt and other literature on rural devt for wider dissemination; library of 95,000 vols; Dir-Gen. B. K. SINHA; Deputy Dir.-Gen. K. NARAYANA KUMAR; publs *CORD Abstracts* (6 a year), *CORD Alerts* (26 a year), *CORD Index* (12 a year), *Handbook of Rural Development Statistics* (1 a year), *Journal of Rural Development* (4 a year), *Recommendations of Seminars and Workshops* (1 a year), *Research Highlights* (1 a year).

Rural Development Organization: Lamsang Bazar, PO Lamsang, Manipur; tel. (85) 310961; f. 1975; research, socio-economic devt programme for the rural poor, skill training programme; Library and Documentation Centre, AIDS Prevention and Control Programme, Community Health Centre, Micro-credit scheme, rural bank, all set up with govt aid; library of 10,000 vols; Gen. Sec. W. BRAJABIDHU SINGH; publ. *Loyalam* (12 a year).

A. N. Sinha Institute of Social Studies: Patna 800001, Bihar; tel. (612) 2221395; fax (612) 2226226; e-mail root@ssaansi.ren.nic.in; internet www.ansiss.org; f. 1958 to undertake teaching and research in the social sciences, especially economics, sociology, social psychology and political science; library of 58,206 vols; Dir NAVIN VERMA; Sec. JITENDRA PANDEY; publ. *Journal of Social and Economic Studies* (4 a year).

Sri Aurobindo Centre: Adhchini, Junction of Sri Aurobindo Marg and Qutab Hotel Rd, New Mehrauli Rd, New Delhi 110017; e-mail mail@sabda.in; multi-disciplinary research and training in the integral study of Man; research in comparative religions, Indian cultural values; lectures, seminars, study groups, summer programmes; homeopathic dispensary; research facilities; library; Chair. DHARMA VIRA; Hon. Sec. K. M. AGARWALA.

V. V. Giri National Labour Institute: Sector 24, Gautam Budh Nagar, Noida 201301, Uttar Pradesh; tel. (120) 2411472; fax (120) 2411474; e-mail vvgnli@vsnl.com; internet www.vvgnli.org; f. 1964; research, training and consultancy; library of 50,000 vols; Dir S. K. DEV VERMAN; publs *Award Digest* (4 a year), *Labour and Development* (2 a year), *Shram Jagat* (6 a year), *Shram Vidhan* (6 a year).

TECHNOLOGY

Ahmedabad Textile Industries Research Association: PO Ambavadi Vistar, Ahmedabad 380015; tel. (79) 26307921; fax (79) 26304677; e-mail atiraad1@sancharnet.in; internet www.atira-rnd-tex.org; f. 1949; textile consultation, training and research, information and testing services; library of 41,000 vols; Dir Dr A. K. SHARMA; publs *ACT (ATIRA Communications on Textiles)* (4 a year), *TEXINCON* (4 a year).

The Automotive Research Association of India: POB 832 Pune 411004; Survey No. 102, Vetal Hill, Off Paud Rd, Kothrud, Pune 411038; tel. (20) 30231192; fax (20) 25434190; e-mail das.lib@araiindia.com; internet www.araiindia.com; f. 1966; research institution of the Automotive Industry with the Min. of Industry; provides facilities for research and development; product design; evaluation of equipment and standardization; certification for the Indian automotive and component industry; compilation and dissemination of technical information to the automotive and engineering industry; testing laboratories; library of 12,000 vols, 36 periodicals; Dir SHRIKANT R. MARATHE; publs *Automotive Abstracts* (12 a year), *ARAI Update* (4 a year).

Bengal Textile Institute: Serampore; f. 1904.

Berhampore Textile Institute: Berhampore; f. 1925.

Birla Research Institute for Applied Sciences: Birlagram 456331, Nagda, Madhya Pradesh; tel. (7366) 246760; fax (7366) 244114; e-mail bri@adityabirla.com; f. 1965; registered soc.; helps nat. industrial growth; research in pulp, cellulose fibre and pollution abatement; Pres. SHAILENDRA K. JAIN; Dir-Gen. A. N. SHRIVASTAVA; publ. *Bulletin* (4 a year).

The Bombay Textile Research Association: Lal Bahadur Shastri Marg, Ghatkopar (W), Mumbai 400086, Maharashtra; tel. (22) 25003651; fax (22) 25000459; e-mail btra@vsnl.com; internet www.btraindia.com; f. 1954; researches on process and product devts with emphasis on cleaner processing technologies; textile testing services; technical consultancy services in textile manufacturing; certification and training services; recognized for postgraduate studies by Univ. of Mumbai; library of 20,200 vols; Dir Dr ASHOK N. DESAI; publs *BTRA Bulletin* (12 a year), *BTRA Scan* (4 a year).

Bureau of Indian Standards (BIS): Manak Bhavan, 9 Bahadur Shah Zafar Marg, New Delhi 110002; tel. (11) 23230131; fax (11) 23234062; e-mail info@bis.org.in; internet www.bis.org.in/; f. 1947; library of 740,000 standards and technical publications and 416 periodicals; Dir-Gen. SHARAD GUPTA; Dir for Library Services ROMA ROY; publs *Current Published Information on Standardization, Standards India, Standards Worldover—Monthly Additions to Library*.

Central Institute for Research on Cotton Technology: Adenwala Rd, Matunga, Mumbai 400019; tel. (22) 24127273; fax (22) 24130835; e-mail circot@vsnl.com; internet www.circot.res.in; f. 1924; part of Indian Council of Agricultural Research; library of 11,800 vols; Dir Dr S. SREENIVASAN.

Central Water and Power Research Station: PO Khadakwasla Research Station, Pune 411024; tel. (20) 24103200; fax (20) 24381004; e-mail wapis@cwprs.gov.in; internet www.cwprs.gov.in; f. 1916; basic

and applied research in hydraulic engineering and allied subjects; activities in fields of hydrology and water resources analysis, river engineering, reservoir and appurtenant structures, coastal and offshore engineering, ship hydrodynamics, hydraulic machinery, foundations and structures, mathematical modelling, instrumentation and control, applied earth sciences; library of 70,779 vols, 200 periodicals; Dir Dr ISHWAR D. GUPTA; Jt Dirs A. C. GANGAL, A. R. CHAVAN, S. GOVINDAN, C. N. KANETKAR, F. T. MATHEW, S. G. PATNAIK, P. K. KHARE, B. S. KULKARNI, DHAYALAN S., R. K. KAMBLE, M. D. KUDALE, R. S. RAMTEKE, Dr C. B. SINGH, VIJAYAKUMAR B., R. S WADHWA.

Indian Institute of Natural Resins & Gums: Namkum, Ranchi 834010, Jharkhand; tel. (651) 2260117; fax (651) 2260202; e-mail iinrg@ilri.ernet.in; internet www.icar.org.in/; f. 1924, fmrly Indian Lac Research Institute; library of 40,128 vols; Dir Dr BANGALI BABOO.

Indian Rubber Manufacturers Research Association: Plot No. B–88, Rd No. 24/U–2, Wagle Industrial Estate, Thane 400604, Maharahstra; tel. (22) 25811348; fax (22) 25823910; e-mail rubberin@bom7.vsnl.net.in; internet www.irmra.org; f. 1959; research and devt relating to rubber and allied industries; 45 staff; Dir Dr S. K. CHAKRABORTY (acting); Deputy Dir P. R. CHOUDHURY; Sr Asst Dir P. K. DAS; Asst Dirs K. R. KRISHNAN, K. RAJKUMAR, Dr ARINDAM MUKHERJI.

Institute of Hydraulics and Hydrology: Poondi 602023, (Via) Trivellore, Chingleput District, Tamil Nadu; f. 1945; library of 8,000 vols and 5,870 journals; Dir K. SUBRAMANIAM.

Irrigation and Power Research Station: Amritsar; conducts research in fields of irrigation and hydraulic engineering; Dir J. NATH.

National Council for Cement and Building Materials: 34 Km-Stone, Delhi-Mathura Rd, Ballabgarh 121004, Haryana; tel. (129) 4192222; fax (129) 2242100; e-mail info@ncbindia.com; internet www.ncbindia.com; f. 1966; provides intensive and planned research and devt support to the cement, concrete and allied industries in the fields of new materials, technology devt and transfer, continuing education and industrial services; library of 46,220 vols, 100 periodicals; Dir-Gen. A. PAHUJA; publs *Cement Standards of the World, NCB Current Contents* (documentation list, 6 a year), *Research Reports*.

National Institute of Hydrology: Jalvigyan Bhawan, Roorkee, Uttarakhand 247667; tel. (1332) 272106; fax (1332) 272123; e-mail nihroal@nih.ernet.in; internet www.nih.ernet.in; f. 1978; under Min. of Water Resources; research in all aspects of water resources; library of 7,000 vols, 3,000 technical reports, 87 periodicals, etc.; Dir R. D SINGH; publs *Jal Vigyan Sameeksha, Research Reports*.

Pulp and Paper Research Institute: Jaykaypur 765017, Dist. Rayagada, Orissa; tel. (6856) 234077; fax (6856) 234078; e-mail contactpapri@gmail.com; f. 1971; researches in pulp and paper technology, forestry, environment and pigment; library of 6,340 vols, periodicals; Deputy Dir Dr J. C. PANIGRAHI; Librarian R. K. SAHOO; publ. *Abstract Index of Periodicals and Information Bulletin* (6 a year).

Research Designs and Standards Organization: Min.of Railways, Govt of India, Manak Nagar, Lucknow 226011; tel. (522) 2451221; fax (522) 2457125; e-mail dg@rdso.railnet.gov.in; internet www.rdso.gov.in; f. 1957; conducts studies on the design and standardization of all railway infrastructure

and equipment and tests and trials of new railway stock and other assets, and research into the economic and effective maintenance of operating practices; library of 154,000 vols, 130 periodicals; Dir-Gen. H. S. PANNU; Additional Dir-Gen. RAJEEV BHARGAV; publs *Indian Railway Technical Bulletin* (4 a year), *RDSO Highlights*, Research Reports, Technical Papers, etc.

Synthetic and Art Silk Mills Research Association: Sasmira, Sasmira Marg, Worli, Mumbai 400030; tel. (22) 24935351; fax (22) 24930225; e-mail sasmira@vsnl.com; internet www.sasmira.org; f. 1950; research and devt in man-made textiles; technical textiles; technical education (postgraduate and diploma courses) in the field of man-made fibres, textile technology, textile chemistry, knitting technology and retail, marketing and management; library of 26,000 vols; Pres. MAGANLAL H. DOSHI; Vice-Pres. MIHIR R. MEHTA; Dir U. K. GANGOPADHYAY; publ. *Man Made Textiles in India*.

Libraries and Archives

Ahmedabad

British Council Library: Bhakaka Bhavan, Law Garden Rd, Ellisbridge, Ahmedabad 380006; tel. (79) 26464693; fax (79) 26469493; e-mail bl.ahmedabad@in.britishcouncil.org; internet library.britishcouncil.org.in; f. 1979; 24,000 vols; adult lending, jr colln, English language devt colln, British home DVDs colln, select colln of magazines on contemporary Britain; Man. MOUMITA BHATTACHARYA.

Gujarat Vidyapeeth Granthalaya: Ahmedabad 380014; tel. (79) 40016260; fax (79) 27542547; e-mail libhod@gujaratvidyapith.org; internet www.gujaratvidyapith.org; f. 1920; Univ., State Central and Public Library combined; depository colln; 564,729 vols; Librarian BHARTI H. DESAI (acting).

Sheth Maheklal Jethabhai Pustakalaya (Free Public Library): Ellisbridge, Ahmedabad, Gujarat; tel. (79) 26578579; fax (79) 26586908; f. 1933; 25,012 mems; 178,317 vols; UNESCO programmes for children's libraries; Librarian SHANTIBHAI BHUDARDAS PATEL.

Allahabad

Allahabad Public Library: Rajkeeya Public Library, Chandra Shekher Azad Park (Alfred Park), Allahabad 211002; tel. (532) 2460197; f. 1864; 102,000 vols; old govt publs, parliamentary papers and blue books of the 19th century, old MSS and journals; reference and research service; Librarian Dr GOPAL MOHAN SHUKLA.

Bangalore

Bangalore State Central Library: Cubbon Park, Bangalore 560001, Karnataka; tel. (80) 22212128; f. 1914; 140,000 vols; State Librarian and Head of Public Libraries N. D. BAGERI.

British Council Library: Prestige Takt, 23 Kasturba Rd Cross, Opposite Visweswaraya Industrial and Technological Museum, Bangalore 560001; tel. (80) 22489220; fax (80) 22240767; e-mail bl.bangalore@in.britishcouncil.org; internet library.britishcouncil.org.in/profiles.asp?id=bl; f. 1960; 28,000 vols; Man. CHARU SAPRA.

Karnataka Government Secretariat Library: Room No. 11, Ground Floor, Vidhana Soudha, Bangalore 560001; tel. (80) 22033462; fax (80) 23425540; e-mail s_library@rediffmail.com; internet vslib.kar.nic.in; f. c. 1919; 126,400 vols, 20 newspapers, 74 periodicals; Chief Librarian ANANTH N. KASKAR.

Baroda

Central Library: Baroda 390006, Gujarat; f. 1910; 280,000 vols; State Librarian BAKU-LESH BHUTA; publ. *Granth Deep* (4 a year).

Chandigarh

British Library: SCO 183–187, Sector 9C, Madhya Marg, Chandigarh 160009; tel. (172) 2745195; fax (172) 2745199; e-mail bl .chandigarh@in.britishcouncil.org; f. 2000; 20,000 vols, 300 audio cassettes, 600 CD-ROMs, 2,500 children's books, 3,000 DVDs, 1,500 IT books; Man. BIPIN KUMAR.

Chennai

Adyar Library and Research Centre: International HQ, The Theosophical Soc., Adyar, Chennai 600020; tel. (44) 24913528; e-mail intl.hq@ts-adyar.org; internet www .ts-adyar.org/library.html; f. 1886; research in Indology; specializes in religion, philosophy, civilization; 200,000 vols, 18,000 MSS; Dir Dr S. SANKARANARAYANAN; Librarian Prof. C. A. SHINDE (acting); publ. *Brahmavidya* (1 a year).

Connemara (State Central) Public Library: Pantheon Rd, Egmore, Chennai 600008, Tamil Nadu; tel. (44) 28193751; internet www .connemarapubliclibrarychennai.com; f. 1896; deposit library from 1954 for all Indian publs; information centre for UN and allied agencies and for Asian Devt Bank; 556,003 vols; Librarian N. AVUDAIAPPAN; publ. *Tamil Nadu State Bibliography* (in Tamil, 12 a year and 1 a year).

Indian Institute of Technology Madras Central Library: Chennai 600036; tel. (44) 22574951; fax (44) 22570509; e-mail hchandra@iitm.ac.in; internet www.cenlib .iitm.ac.in; f. 1959; user education programmes; 242,720 vols, 1,384 current periodicals, 448 films, 1,600 microfilms and microfiches; colln of technical and scientific books (German and English); partial archive of scientific films; Chief Librarian Dr HARISH CHANDRA.

Madras Literary Society Library: Chennai 600006; f. 1812; 150,000 vols incl. 30,000 19th-century edns; Man. P. N. BALASUN-DARAM; Hon. Sec. S. V. B. ROW.

Tamil Nadu Government Oriental Manuscripts Library: University Bldg, Chepauk, Chennai 600005; tel. (44) 25365130; f. 1869; acquisition, preservation and publication of rare and important collection of MSS in Sanskrit, Islamic and South Indian languages; 25,373 vols, 72,314 MSS; Curator Dr S. SOUNDARAPANDIAN; publ. *Bulletin.*

Delhi

Central Archaeological Library: Second Floor, Annexe bldg of National Archives of India, Janpath, New Delhi 110001; tel. (11) 23387475; fax (11) 23385883; internet asi.nic .in/asi_ca_lib.asp; f. 1902; attached to Archaeological Survey of India; 102,180 vols, 5,776 maps, 85 current periodicals; Dir P. B. S. SENGAR.

Central Secretariat Library: Ministry of Culture, Govt of India, G Wing, Shastri Bhavan, New Delhi 110001; tel. (11) 23389684; fax (11) 23384846; e-mail csl@ delnet.ren.nic.in; f. 1890; lending, reference, reprographic divisions, background material on selected topics and biographies; 810,000 vols, 730 periodicals; spec. colln: area study, Indian official documents, foreign official documents, Hindi and Indian regional languages publs; Dir KALPANA DASGUPTA.

Delhi Public Library: H-Block, nr Main Market, Sarojini Nagar, Delhi 110023; tel. (11) 24101261; fax (11) 24673220; e-mail dpl@dpl.gov.in; internet www.dpl.gov.in; f. 1951 in association with UNESCO; est. as a model for public library devt in SE Asia; central library, 3 br. libraries, Braille section, 4 mobile libraries and 59 sub-br. and community libraries; 1,557,000 vols in English, Hindi, Urdu, Punjabi, Bengali, Sindhi and other Indian languages and in Braille; Dir Dr BANWARI LAL.

Indian Council of World Affairs Library: Sapru House, Barakhamba Rd, New Delhi 110001; tel. (11) 23317246; fax (11) 23310638; e-mail chhayasharma@icwa.in; internet www.icwa.in; f. 1943; research collns on social sciences with spec. reference to int. relations, int. law and int. economics; Press library; maps, microfilms and microfiches; UN and EU documents; 1,500 mems; 128,000 vols, 376 periodicals, 2,458,000 press clippings; Chief Librarian CHHAYA SHARMA; publ. *India Quarterly* (in-house journal).

Indira Gandhi National Centre for the Arts: 1 Central Vista Mess, Janpath, New Delhi 110001; tel. (11) 23384901; fax (11) 23381139; e-mail skojha@ignca.nic.in; internet ignca.nic.in; f. 1987; resource centre with reference material relating to Indian arts and culture; Academic Dir S. K. OJHA.

National Archives of India: Janpath, New Delhi 110001; tel. (11) 23383436; fax (11) 23384127; e-mail archives@nic.in; internet nationalarchives.nic.in; f. 1891 in Calcutta (Kolkata) as the Imperial Record Dept, transferred to New Delhi in 1911 and to present site in 1926; valuable collns of public records, maps, private papers and microfilm covering 35 km of shelf space; 200,000 vols 1,780,000 books and reports, 3,299 inscribed publications, 400 selections from vernacular native newspapers, 4,225 selections from Government of India and State Govt records, 4,590 vols of Indian parliamentary papers, 1,285 vols of Fort William College colln, 3,560 journals and periodicals, 1,778 gazettes, 2,960 publs in foreign languages; Dir-Gen. S. M. R. BAQAR; publs *Bulletin of Research Theses and Dissertations* (every 2 years), *Indian Archives* (2 a year).

National Institute of Science Communication and Information Resources: Dr K. S. Krishnan Marg, Pusa Campus, New Delhi 110012; tel. (11) 25841647; fax (11) 25847062; e-mail gp@niscair.res.in; internet www.niscair.res.in; f. 2002; attached to Ccl of Scientific and Industrial Research; nat. science library; disseminates scientific and technological information to the scientific community and the gen. public; provides networking services and network-based online services; bibliographical information retrieval from national and international online and CD-ROM databases; 178,000 vols; Dir Dr GANGAN PRATHAP; publs *Annals of Library and Information Studies* (4 a year), *Bharatiya Vaigyanic evam Audyogic Anusandhan Patrika* (2 a year, in Hindi), *Indian Journal of Biochemistry and Biophysics* (6 a year), *Indian Journal of Biotechnology* (4 a year), *Indian Journal of Chemical Technology* (6 a year), *Indian Journal of Chemistry, Sec A* (12 a year), *Indian Journal of Chemistry, Sec B* (12 a year), *Indian Journal of Engineering and Materials Sciences* (6 a year), *Indian Journal of Experimental Biology* (12 a year), *Indian Journal of Fibre and Textile Research* (4 a year), *Indian Journal of Marine Sciences* (4 a year), *Indian Journal of Pure and Applied Physics* (12 a year), *Indian Journal of Radio and Space Physics* (6 a year), *Indian Journal of Traditional Knowledge* (4 a year), *Indian Science*

Abstracts (26 a year), *Journal of Intellectual Property Rights* (6 a year), *Journal of Scientific and Industrial Research* (12 a year), *Medicinal and Aromatic Plants Abstracts* (6 a year), *Natural Product Radiance* (6 a year).

National Social Science Documentation Centre: 35 Ferozshah Rd, New Delhi 110001; tel. (11) 23385959; fax (11) 23383091; internet www.icssr.org; f. 1970; div. of Indian Ccl of Social Science Research (ICSSR); provides information and documentation service for social scientists, policymakers and others working in the academic and govt sectors, business and industry; provides library and reference services, document delivery and reprographic services, consultancy service, select bibliography service, training courses; 565 current periodicals, 150,000 serial vols, 5,000 PhD theses, 3,000 research projects and reports, 15,000 books, conf. papers, working papers; Dir Dr P. R. GOSWAMI; Deputy Dir SAVITRI DEVI; publs *Annotated Index of Indian Social Science Journals* (2 a year), *Bibliographic Reprints* (irregular), *Conference Alert* (4 a year).

Nehru Memorial Museum and Library: Teen Murti House, New Delhi 110011; tel. (11) 23015333; fax (11) 23793296; f. 1964; archival collections on modern Indian history with emphasis on Indian nationalism; research centre for interdisciplinary studies in modern Indian history and society; large collection of newspapers, microfilms, private papers, institutional records, photographs and oral history recordings; 226,603 vols; Dir K. JAYAKUMAR.

Dharamsala

Library of Tibetan Works and Archives: Gangchen Kyishong, Dharamsala 176215, Himachal Pradesh; tel. (1892) 222467; fax (1892) 223723; e-mail info@ltwa.net; internet www.ltwa.net; f. 1971; 80,000 vols 10,000 photographs, 25,000 hours of audio/video tape, 1,200 icons and artefacts; Dir Ven. Geshe LHAKDOR; publ. *The Tibet Journal* (4 a year).

Hyderabad

British Council Library: 5-9-22 Sarovar Centre, Secretariat Rd, Hyderabad 500063; tel. (40) 23483333; fax (40) 23483100; e-mail bl.hyderabad@in.britishcouncil.org; internet www.britishcouncilonline.org; f. 1979; library services; seminars; workshops; film screening on climate change and low carbon; 25,000 vols, 2,500 DVDs; information on higher education in the UK; Man. AJAY MERCHANT; Asst Man. EASWARAN NAMPOOTHIRI.

State Central Library: Afzalgunj, Hyderabad 500012, Andhra Pradesh; tel. (40) 24615621; fax (40) 24600107; f. 1891; 347,000 vols; Librarian T. V. VEDAMRUTHAM.

Kolkata

Centre for Asian Documentation: K-15, CIT Bldgs, Christopher Rd, POB 11215, Kolkata 700014; provides reference services; Dir S. CHAUDHURI; publs *Index Asia Series in Humanities* (irregular), *Index Indo-Asiasticus* (4 a year), *Index Internationalis Indicus* (every 3 years), *Indian Biography* (1 a year), *Indian Science index* (every 2 years).

National Library: Belvedere, Kolkata 700027, West Bengal; tel. (33) 24791381; fax (33) 24791462; e-mail nldirector@ rediffmail.com; internet www .nationallibrary.gov.in/index2.html; f. 1903 by the amalgamation of the Calcutta Public Library and the Imperial Library; depository and research library; 4,145 microfilms, 94,500 microfiches, 17,650 periodicals; incl. Central Reference Library, at the same address, compiles *Indian National Bibliography*, but does not hold a book colln; 2,186,500 vols, 84,952 maps, 3,127 MSS; Dir Dr R. RAMACHANDRAN; publs *Bibliographical Control in India, Bibliographies, Conservation of Library Materials, General Collection Author and Subject Catalogues, India's National Library—Systematization and Modernization, Indological Studies and South Asia Bibliography, Rabindra Grantha Suchi* (vol 1 part 1), *Reports, The National Library and Public Libraries in India.*

Lucknow

Acharya Narendra Dev Pustakalaya: 10 Ashoka Marg, Lucknow; f. 1959; public library, with special emphasis on social sciences; 79,636 vols; 150 periodicals; Librarian T. N. MISRA.

Ludhiana

Panjab University Extension Library: Civil Lines, Ludhiana, Punjab; tel. (161) 2449558; f. 1960; serves educational institutions within a radius of 60 km; 138,000 vols; Librarian PREM VERMA (acting).

Mumbai

Petit, J. N., Institute Library: 312 Dr Dadabhoy Naoroji Rd, Fort, Mumbai 400001; tel. (22) 22048463; e-mail petitheritage_01@ yahoo.co.in; f. 1856 as 'Fort Improvement Library'; 160,000 vols; Admin. J. R. MODY.

Patna

Bihar Secretariat Library: Patna 800015; f. 1885; 106,300 vols; Chief Librarian P. N. SINHA DOSHI.

Khuda Bakhsh Oriental Public Library: Ashok Rajpath, Patna 800004, Bihar; tel. (612) 2300209; fax (612) 2370315; e-mail pat_khopl@dataone.in; internet www .kblibrary.bih.nic.in; f. 1891; autonomous instn under Min. of Culture and declared as an instn of nat. importance; awards fellowships for PhD and D.Litt. students; designated as a MSS Resource Centre (MRC) and Manuscript Conservation Centre (MCC) by the Nat. Mission for MSS, Govt of India; contains more than 21,000 MSS in Arabic, Persian, Urdu, Pushto, Pali, Turkish, Hindi and Sanskrit, 278,187 vols, 39,395 bound periodicals, 1,980 audio and 1,030 video cassettes, 182 Slides, 2,195 microfilms of manuscripts; Mughal, Iranian, Central Asian and Rajput paintings; Dir Dr IMTIAZ AHMAD; Admin. Officer NAZIRUL HASNAIN; publ. *Khuda Bakhsh Quarterly Journals.*

Shrimati Radhika Sinha Institute and Sachchidananda Sinha Library (State Central Library, Bihar): G.P.O., Sinha Library Rd., Patna 800001; tel. (612) 2221674; f. 1924; admin. by State Govt; incl. a reading room, research room, and newspaper reading room; subscriptions to many foreign and Indian journals; books on literature, history, biography, philosophy, sociology; 175,000 vols, 600 periodicals; Librarian Dr R. S. P. SINGH.

Rajahmundry

Gowthami Regional Library: Rajahmundry 533104, Andhra Pradesh; tel. (883) 2476908; f. 1898, management transferred to Andhra Pradesh Govt in 1979; spec. colln of rare 19th-century periodicals in English and Telugu, rare colln of old Telugu books; research library of 58,643 vols, 428 palm-leaf MSS; Librarian VENNA POLI REDDY.

Trivandrum

Trivandrum Public Library (State Central Library): Palayam, Vikas Bhavan PO, Thiruvananthapuram, Kerala; tel. (471) 2322895; e-mail slscl@statelibrary.kerala .gov.in; internet www.statelibrary.kerala.gov .in/; f. 1829, declared the 'State Central Library' in 1958, given the status of a minor dept under admin. control of the Higher Education Dept with the State Librarian as HOD in 1988; 327,177 vols in English, Malayalam, Hindi, Tamil, Sanskrit in various disciplines; State Librarian P. SUPRABHA.

Museums and Art Galleries

Ahmedabad

Calico Museum of Textiles:; e-mail dsmehta@calicomuseum.com Sarabhai Foundation, Shahibag, Ahmedabad 380004; tel. (79) 22868172; fax (79) 22865759; e-mail info@calicomuseum.com; internet www .calicomuseum.com; f. 1948; colln of 17th- and 18th-century Indian textiles and costumes, shawls, large tents, carpets, religious textiles and artefacts, Indian miniature paintings, Indian bronzes, and reconstructed carved wooden façades from 17th to 19th centuries; Man. Trustee GIRA SARABHAI; Dir D. S. MEHTA; publ. *Historical Textiles of India at Calico Museum.*

Ajmer

Rajputana Museum: Ajmer 305001, Rajasthan; f. 1908; archaeology; rare sculptures, architectural carvings, old coins, epigraphs, Rajput paintings, arms and armour of Rajasthan; Curator R. D. SHARMA.

Banares

Bharat Kala Bhavan: Banaras Hindu University, Varanasi 221005; tel. (542) 316337; fax (542) 316337; e-mail bharatkalabhavan@ sify.com; internet www.bhu.ac.in/kala/ index_bkb.htm; f. 1920; attached to univ. since 1950; art objects, miniature paintings, sculpture, textiles, archaeology, seals; library: approx. 14,000 vols and periodicals, 26,511 MSS; Dir Prof. R. C. SHARMA; publs *Chhavi*, catalogues.

Bangalore

Government Museum: Kasturba Rd, Bangalore 560001, Karnataka; f. 1866; art, archaeology, industrial art and natural history; library of 2,000 vols; Curator (vacant).

Visvesvaraya Industrial and Technological Museum: Kasturba Rd, PMB 5216, Bangalore 560001, Karnataka; tel. (80) 22866200; fax (80) 22864009; e-mail vitm@ vsnl.com; internet www.vismuseum.org; f. 1962; aims to encourage interest in science and technology, and to explain the application of technology in industry and human welfare; library of 10,230 vols, also audio-visual materials; Dir K. V. BHATTA.

Baroda

Baroda Museum and Picture Gallery: Sayaji Bagh, Vadodra 390018, Gujarat; tel. (265) 2793801; fax (268) 2791959; e-mail barodamuseum@dataone.in; f. 1887, museum completed in 1894 and picture gallery in 1920; Indian archaeology; prehistoric and historic; Indian art: ancient, medieval and modern; numismatic collns; modern Indian paintings; industrial art; Asiatic and Egyptian collns; Greek, Roman, European civilizations and art; European paintings; ethnology, zoology, geology, economic botany; library of 19,000 vols; Dir R. D. PARMAR; Curator V. M. PATEL (Science); publ. *Museums in Gujarat.*

Bhubaneswar

Orissa State Museum: Bhubaneswar 751006, Orissa; f. 1932; archaeology, epigraphy, numismatics, armoury, arts and crafts, anthropology, palm-leaf MSS, natural history; library of 22,000 vols, 2,000 periodicals; Dir Dr H. C. DAS; publ. *Orissa Historical Research Journal.*

Bikaner

Government Museum: Bikaner 334001, Rajasthan; tel. (151) 2528894; f. 1937; collection of terracottas, sculptures, bronzes, coins, inscriptions, Rajasthani paintings, documents, arms and costumes, specimens of folk-culture; Superintendent P. C. BHARGAVA.

Bodh Gaya

Archaeological Museum: Archaeological Survey of India, Bodh Gaya, District Gaya, Bihar; tel. (631) 2200739; fax (631) 2200739; stone and bronze sculpture, etc.; Asst Superintending Archaeologist S. K. SINHA.

Chennai

Fort Museum: Archaeological Survey of India, Fort St George, Chennai 600009; tel. (44) 25671127; f. 1948; exhibits belong mainly to the days of the East India Co.; Asst Superintending Archaeologist P. S. SRIRAMAN.

Government Museum and National Art Gallery: Pantheon Rd, Egmore, Chennai 600008; tel. (44) 28193238; fax (44) 28193035; e-mail govtmuse@md4.vsnl.net .in; internet www.chennaimuseum.org; f. 1851; archaeology, ancient and modern Indian art, South Indian bronzes, Buddhist sculptures, numismatics, philately, anthropology, botany, zoology, geology, chemical conservation education, contemporary art, design and display; Dir THIRU M. A. SIDDIQUE; publ. *Madras Museum Bulletins.*

Delhi

Archaeological Museum Red Fort, Delhi: Mumtaz Mahal, Red Fort, 110006; tel. (11) 23267961; f. 1909; library of 420 vols; historical collns of the Mughal period; old arms, seals and signets, letters, MSS, coins, miniatures, Mughal dresses and relics of India's War of Independence; Asst Superintending Archaeologist V. D. JADHAV.

Crafts Museum: Pragati Maidan, Bhairon Rd, New Delhi 110001; tel. (11) 23371641; fax (11) 23371515; e-mail nhhm@vsnl.net; internet www.nationalcraftsmuseum.nic.in; f. 1952; attached to Ministry of Textiles; Indian traditional crafts and tribal arts; library of 11,000 vols; Dir Dr JYOTINDRA JAIN.

National Gallery of Modern Art: Jaipur House, India Gate, Sher Shah Rd, New Delhi 110003; tel. (11) 23386111; fax (11) 23384560; e-mail ngma@del3.vsnl.net.in; internet ngmaindia.gov.in/; f. 1954; contemporary art (paintings, sculpture, drawings, graphics, architecture, industrial design, photography, prints and minor arts); Dir Prof. RAJEEV LOCHAN.

National Gandhi Museum and Library: Rajghat, New Delhi 110002; tel. (11) 23310168; fax (11) 23311793; e-mail gandhimk@bol.net.in; internet www .gandhimuseum.org; f. 1953 by the Gandhi Memorial Museum Soc.; collects and displays Gandhi's records and mementos and promotes the study of his life and work; library of 45,000 vols, 25,000 documents, 80 periodicals, films and recordings, 9,000 photographs, large picture galleries; Chair. Prof. BIMAL PRASAD; Dir Dr SANGITA MALLIK; Head of Library S. K. BHATNAGAR.

National Museum of India: 1 Janpath, New Delhi 110011; tel. (11) 23018159; fax

(11) 23019821; internet www
.nationalmuseumindia.gov.in/; f. 1949; depts
of art, archaeology, anthropology, modelling,
presentation, preservation, publication,
library and photography; Indian prehistoric
tools, protohistoric remains from Harappa,
Mohenjodaro, etc., representative collns of
sculptures, terracottas, stuccos and bronzes
from 2nd century BC to 18th century AD;
illustrated MSS and miniatures; Stein Colln
of Central Asian murals and other antiquities; decorative arts; textiles, coins and illuminated epigraphical charts; armour; copperplate etchings; woodwork; library of 43,400
vols; Dir-Gen. R. C. MISHRA; Dirs U. DAS
(Colln and Admin.), Dr R. R. S. CHAUHAN
(Exhibition and Public Relation), S. P. SINGH;
publs Bulletin (1 a year), special publs on art
and archaeology.

National Museum of Natural History:
FICCI Museum Bldg, Barakhamba Rd, New
Delhi 110001; tel. (11) 23314849; e-mail
sksaraswat@yahoo.co.uk; internet nmnh.nic
.in; f. 1978; exhibits on natural history,
ecology, environment, conservation; educational programmes for children and other
groups, school loan service, mobile museum
for rural extension service; controls regional
museums of natural history in Mysore,
Bhopal and Bhubneshwar; library of 25,000
vols; Dir (vacant).

National Rail Museum: Chanakyapuri,
New Delhi 110021; tel. (11) 26881816; fax
(11) 26880804; e-mail smehranrm@yahoo.co
.in; internet www.nationalrailmuseum.org/
new_nrm; f. 1977; library of 5,000 vols; Dir
RAJESH AGRAWAL.

Rabindra Bhavan Art Gallery: 35 Feroze-
shah Rd, New Delhi; tel. (11) 23387241; fax
(11) 23782485; e-mail lka@bol.net.in; f. 1955;
permanent gallery of the Lalit Kala Akademi
(National Academy of Art), and venue of the
National Exhibition of Art and Triennale-
India (international art); Chair. Dr SARAYU
V. DOSHI; publs Lalit Kala Ancient (2 a year),
Lalit Kala Contemporary (4 a year), Samka-
leen Kala (in Hindi, 4 a year).

Shankar's International Dolls Museum:
Nehru House, 4 Bahadur Shah Zafar Marg,
New Delhi 110002; tel. (11) 23316970; fax
(11) 23721090; e-mail cbtnd@cbtnd.com;
internet www.childrensbooktrust.com; f.
1965; 6,000 exhibits from all over the world;
Advisor SHANTA SRINIVASAN.

Gauhati

Assam State Museum: Guwahati 781001,
Assam; f. 1940; indological and archaeo-
logical studies; library of 5,850 vols; Dir Dr
R. D. CHOUDHURY; publ. Bulletin (1 a year).

Guntur

Archaeological Museum: Nagarjunakonda
Zone, Vijayapuri South, District Guntur,
522439 Andhra Pradesh; tel. and fax (8642)
278107; e-mail asamnkonda@gmail.com; f.
1966; prehistoric and historical antiquities,
mainly sculptures belonging to Buddhism
(3rd–4th centuries AD) and Hinduism (15th–
16th centuries AD); Asst Superintending
Archaeologist CH. BABJI RAO.

Hyderabad

Andhra Pradesh State Museum: Hyderabad 500034; f. 1930; sculpture, epigraphy,
arms and weapons, bidriware, bronze objects,
miniatures and paintings, MSS, numismatics, European paintings (prints), decorative
and modern arts, textiles; excavations at
Yeleswaram Pochampal, Peddabankur; Dir
Dr V. V. KRISHNA SASTRY; publ. various on
numismatics.

Salar Jung Museum: Hyderabad 500002,
Andhra Pradesh; tel. (40) 24523211; fax (40)

24572558; e-mail salarjung@hotmail.com;
internet www.salarjungmuseum.in; f. 1951;
paintings, textiles, porcelain, jade, carpets,
MSS, antiques, ivory, glass, silver- and
bronze-ware; children's section; library of
60,000 vols incl. Persian, Arabic and Urdu
MSS; Dir Dr A. NAGENDER REDDY; publs
Research Journal (every 2 years), guidebook
and MSS catalogue.

Imphal

Manipur State Museum: Polo-ground,
Imphal, Manipur; general collection.

Jaipur

Maharaja Sawai Man Singh II Museum:
City Palace, Jaipur 302002, Rajasthan; tel.
(141) 2615681; fax (141) 2603880; f. 1959;
textiles and costumes, armoury, Mughal and
Rajasthani miniature paintings, Persian and
Mughal carpets, transport accessories,
regalia, historical documents, maps and
plans, MSS library of 10,000 Sanskrit, Persian, Hindi and Rajasthani MSS; Dir B. M. S.
PARMAR.

Kolkata

Asutosh Museum of Indian Art: Centenary Building, University of Calcutta, Kolkata
700073; f. 1937; library: over 2,000 vols and
periodicals; Curator NIRANJAN GOSWAMI;
publ. catalogues.

Birla Industrial and Technological
Museum: National Council of Science
Museums, Govt. of India, 19A Gurusaday
Rd, Kolkata 700019; tel. (33) 22877241; fax
(33) 22906102; e-mail bitm@cal2.vsnl.net.in;
internet www.bitmcal.org; f. 1959; administered by the Nat. Ccl of Science Museums;
portrays the history and development of
science and technology; 8 satellite centres
and 8 mobile science exhibition buses in rural
areas; educational programmes for students
and teachers and the gen. public; film and
CD library; archives; special collections on
history and development of science and
technology, arts, painting, museology, etc.;
library of 14,000 vols incl. periodicals; Dir Sk.
EMDADUL ISLAM; publ. Popscience (2 a year).

Indian Museum: 27 Jawaharlal Nehru Rd,
Kolkata 700016; tel. (33) 22861679; fax (33)
22495696; e-mail imbot@cal2.vsnl.net.in;
internet www.indianmuseumkolkata.org/; f.
1814; collns of archaeology, art, coins,
anthropology, geology, botany, zoology; herbarium; library of 45,000 vols; Dir Dr SAKTI
KALI BASU; Librarian Dr PATRA CHITTARAN-
JAN; publ. Bulletin (1 a year).

Victoria Memorial Hall: 1 Queens Way,
Kolkata 700071; tel. (33) 22231890; fax (33)
22235142; e-mail victomen@cal2.vsnl.net.in;
internet www.victoriamemorial-cal.org; f.
1906; museum of medieval Indian history
and culture, and British Indian history of the
late 18th and early 19th centuries; wide colln
of oil-paintings and watercolours by European artists of 18th and 19th centuries;
sketches, miniatures, engravings, photographs, sculptures, maps, MSS, furniture,
stamps, coins, medals, textiles, arms and
armour; library: almost 13,030 vols; Chair.
GOVERNOR OF WEST BENGAL; Sec. and Curator
Prof. CHITTARANJAN PANDA.

Lucknow

Uttar Pradesh State Museum: Banarasi-
bagh, Lucknow, Uttar Pradesh; tel. and fax
(522) 2206158; f. 1863; collns of sculptures,
terracottas, copper plates, numismatics,
paintings, MSS, textiles and natural history
specimens; anthropological colln; library of
15,000 vols; Dir R. C. TIWARI; publ. Bulletin
(2 a year).

Mathura

Government Museum: Dampier Nagar,
Mathura 281001, Uttar Pradesh; f. 1874;
40,000 items, dominated by sculptures, terracottas of Mathura School to Kushana and
Gupta period; coins, paintings, etc.; library:
reference library of 20,000 vols.

Mumbai

Chhatrapati Shivaji Maharaj Vastu San-
grahalay: 159–161 Mahatma Gandhi Rd,
Fort, Mumbai 400023; tel. (22) 22844484; fax
(22) 22045430; internet www
.bombaymuseum.org; f. 1905; fmrly Prince of
Wales Museum of Western India; sections:
Art, Painting, Archaeology, Natural History;
library of 25,000 vols; publs Bulletin, catalogues.

Dr Bhau Daji Lad Mumbai City
Museum: Rani Bagh, 19/A Dr B. Ambedkar
Rd, Byculla-East, Mumbai 400027; tel. (22)
23731234; fax (22) 23737942; e-mail
bdlmuseum@gmail.com; internet www
.bdlmuseum.org; f. 1855; reference library on
Indian and foreign art, archaeology, ethnology, geology, history, numismatics and
museology; exhibits of agriculture and village life, armoury, cottage industries, ethnology, fine arts, crafts, fossils, Indian coins,
minerals, misc. colln, Old Mumbai colln;
oldest museum in Mumbai; Man. Trustee
and Hon. Dir TASNEEM Z. MEHTA; Sr Asst
Curator PREEMA JOHN; publ. catalogues.

Nagpur

Central Museum: Civil Lines, Nagpur
440001 Maharashtra; tel. (712) 2546314; f.
1863; objects relating to archaeology, art,
tribal art and culture, natural history, sculpture, weapons and metal objects; Curator Y.
KATHANE.

Nalanda

Archaeological Museum: Archaeological
Survey of India, Nalanda, District Nalanda,
Bihar; tel. (6112) 281824; f. 1958; collns of
antiquities, specializing in Buddhist sculp-
tures; Asst Superintending Archaeologist K.
C. SRIVASTAVA.

Patna

Patna Museum: Patna-Gaya Rd, Buddha
Marg, Patna 800001, Bihar; tel. (612)
2235731; f. 1917; archaeology, bronzes, ethnology, geology, arms and armour, natural
history, art, coins, plaster casts, Tibetan
paintings; Dr Rajendra Prasad's colln (first
Pres. of India); Buddha Relic casket; publishes research on art, archaeology and
ethnology; seminars and lectures; Dir J. P.
AGRARWAL; Curator K. K. SHARMA.

Rajahmundry

Sri Rallabandi Subbarao Government
Museum (formerly the Andhra Historical
Research Society): Godavari Bund Rd, Rajah-
mundry, East Godavari District, Andhra
Pradesh 533101; f. 1967; art, archaeology,
epigraphy, history and numismatics; collec-
tion of coins, sculpture, pottery, terracotta,
palm-leaf MSS, inscriptions, etc.; Dir Dr V.
V. KRISHNA SASTRY; publ. Journal of the
AHRS.

Santiniketan

Rabindra-Bhavana (Tagore Museum and
Archives): Visva-Bharati, PO: Santiniketan,
Dist.: Birbhum, 731235, West Bengal; tel.
(3463) 262751; fax (3463) 262672; f. 1942;
colln of MSS, letters, books, newspaper clippings, gramophone records, photographs,
cine-film, paintings by Tagore and tape
recordings of his voice; inside the Uttarayan
Campus where the poet spent the last days of
his life; library of 40,000 books and over

12,000 bound journals; publ. *Rabindra-Viksa* (2 a year).

Sarnath

Sarnath Archaeological Museum: District Varanasi 221007, Uttar Pradesh; tel. (542) 2595095; archaeological site museum; f. 1904; Buddhist and Hindu collection from 3rd century BC to 12th century AD; Deputy Superintending Archaeologist A. JHA.

Srinagar

Sri Pratap Singh Museum: Lalmandi, Srinagar 190008-72078, Jammu and Kashmir; tel. (8649) 232374; f. 1898; general colln of Jammu and Kashmir; colln of excavated items incl. pottery, terracotta tiles, metal artifacts and stone objects dating back to different time periods, ranging from the 2nd to 12th centuries; also on display life-size statues of the Buddha, Lords Vishnu, Shiva and Brahma, in chronological order; other items incl. Sharda, Persian and Arabic stone inscriptions, 2nd-century terracotta tiles from Hoinar (Pahalgam) and 3rd-century Harwan tiles; library of 1,300 vols about cultural subjects; Curator M. S. ZAHID.

Trichur

Kerala State Museum:; f. 1885; incl. (1) State Museum and Zoo, Trichur, f. 1885; (2) Govt Museums and Zoological and Botanical Gardens, Trivandrum, f. 1857; natural history collns, Indian arts and crafts; (3) Art Gallery and Krishna-Menon Museum, Calicut, f. 1976; (4) Govt Botanical Garden, Olavanna, f. 1991; The Zoo has 315 animals in 46 species, Art Museum consists of antiques and other unique exhibits; Natural History Museum displays array of specimens of different kinds of animals.

Trivandrum

Sri Chitra Art Gallery, Gallery of Asian Paintings: Trivandrum 695001, Kerala; f. 1935; sections: Pure Indian Art, Rajput, Mughal and Persian, Tanjore, Tibetan, Chinese, Japanese, Balinese, Indo-European (watercolours and oils), etchings and woodcuts; Modern Indian Contemporary Art and Murals; library of 736 vols; Dir K. RAJENDRA BABU; publ. *Administration Report*.

Universities

There are three types of university in India: Affiliating and Teaching (most teaching done in colleges affiliated to the university, but some teaching, mostly postgraduate, undertaken by the university); Unitary (all teaching done on one campus); and Central (universities established by Acts of Parliament). It is not possible, for reasons of space, to give details of affiliated colleges.

ACHARYA N. G. RANGA AGRICULTURAL UNIVERSITY

Rajendranagr, Hyderabad 500030, Andhra Pradesh
Telephone: (40) 24015011
Fax: (40) 24015031
E-mail: angrau@ap.nic.in
Internet: www.angrau.net
Founded 1964 as Andhra Pradesh Agricultural Univ.; present name 1996
Languages of instruction: English, Telugu
Academic year: July to June
Composed of 9 Colleges, 58 Research Stations distributed in 9 Agro-climatic zones of the State, 8 Agricultural Polytechnics, 1 Horticultural Polytechnic, 1 Multipurpose Polytechnic, 22 District Agricultural Advisory

and Transfer of Technology Centres (DAATTCs), 12 Krishi Vigyan Kendras (Farmer Science Centres), 1 Agricultural Technology and Information Centre
Chancellor: HE THE GOVERNOR OF ANDHRA PRADESH
Vice-Chancellor: P. RAGHAVA REDDY
Dir of Extension: Dr L. G. GIRI RAO
Dir of Research: Dr G. LAKSHMI KANTHA REDDY
Dean of Student Affairs: Dr S. V. RAMAKRISHNA RAO
Comptroller: N. SRI KALA
Registrar: M. USHA RANI (acting)
Librarian: Dr K. VEERANJANEYULU
Library of 200,000 vols, 500 periodicals
Number of teachers: 1,035
Number of students: 3,853
Publication: *ANGRAU Journal of Research* (4 a year)

DEANS

Faculty of Agriculture: Dr M. SUDARSHAN REDDY
Faculty of Home Science: Dr P. RAJYA LAKSHMI
Postgraduate Studies: Dr SHAIK MOHAMMAD (acting)

ALAGAPPA UNIVERSITY

Alagappa Nagar, Karaikudi 630003, Tamil Nadu
Telephone: (4565) 228080
Fax: (4565) 225202
E-mail: registrar@alagappauniversity.ac.in
Internet: www.alagappauniversity.ac.in
Founded 1985
Academic year: July to April (2 terms)
Chancellor: HE THE GOV. OF TAMIL NADU
Pro-Chancellor: Dr K. PONMUDI
Vice-Chancellor: Dr P. RAMASAMY
Registrar: Dr A. SHENBAGAVALLI
Controller of Examinations: Dr V. MANICKAVASAGAM
Finance Officer: THIRU R. BOOMINATHAN
Dean of College Devt Ccl: Dr T. R. GURUMOORTHY
Dean of Student Welfare: Dr M. SELVAN
Librarian: Dr A. THIRUNAVUKKARASU
Library of 64,000 vols, 121 periodicals
Number of teachers: 150
Number of students: 1,545

DEANS

Faculty of Arts: Dr R. KRISHNARAJ
Faculty of Education: Dr P. PREMA
Faculty of Management: Dr R. M. CHIDAMBARAM
Faculty of Science: Dr P. NATARAJAN

ATTACHED CENTRES

Centre for Rural Development: tel. (4565) 225842; fax (4565) 225202; Dir Dr A. NARAYANAMOORTHY.
Centre for Gandhian Studies: Dir Dr V. S. S. KANNAN.
Centre for Nehru Studies: Dir Dr B. DHARMALINGAM.

ALIGARH MUSLIM UNIVERSITY

Aligarh 202002, Uttar Pradesh
Telephone: (571) 2700220
Fax: (571) 2700528
E-mail: vcamu@amu.ac.in
Internet: www.amu.ac.in
Founded 1875, as Anglo-Mohamedan Oriental College; univ. status 1920
Indian govt control
Language of instruction: English
Academic year: July to May
Chancellor: (vacant)

Pro-Chancellor: (vacant)
Vice-Chancellor: Prof. P. K. ABDUL AZIS
Registrar: Prof. Dr V. K. ABDUL JALEEL
Finance Officer: YASMIN JALAL BEG
Controller of Examinations: Prof. PERVEZ MUSTAJAB
Proctor: Prof. MUJAHID BAIG
Dean of Student's Welfare: Prof. AINUL HAQUE KHAN
Librarian: Prof. SHABAHAT HUSAIN
Library: 1.1m. vols; MSS in Arabic, Persian, Urdu and Hindi
Number of teachers: 1,101
Number of students: 17,954

DEANS

Faculty of Agriculture Sciences: Prof. FARZANA ALIM
Faculty of Arts: Prof. QAZI AFZAL HUSAIN
Faculty of Commerce: Prof. SIBGHATULLAH FAROOQUI
Faculty of Engineering and Technology: Prof. S. MAHDI ABBAS RIZVI
Faculty of Law: Prof. MOHAMMAD SHABBIR
Faculty of Life Sciences: Prof. MASOOD AHMAD
Faculty of Management Studies and Research: Prof. JAVAID AKHTAR
Faculty of Medicine: Prof. SYED ABRAR HASAN
Faculty of Science: Prof. ABHA LAKSHMI SINGH
Faculty of Social Sciences: Prof. C. P. S. CHAUHAN
Faculty of Theology: Prof. SYED ALI MOHAMMAD NAQVI
Faculty of Unani Medicine: Prof. SHAGUFTA ALEEM

ALLAHABAD UNIVERSITY

Allahabad 211002, Uttar Pradesh
Telephone: (532) 2461089
Fax: (532) 2545021
E-mail: mkc@allduniv.ac.in
Internet: www.allduniv.ac.in
Founded 1887
Unitary
Languages of instruction: English, Hindi
Academic year: July to April
Chief Rector: THE GOVERNOR OF UTTAR PRADESH
Chancellor: Dr VERGHESE KURIEN
Vice-Chancellor: Prof. RAJENDRA GOVIND HARSHE
Registrar: FIRDOUS A. WANI
Finance Officer: Prof. J. N. MISHRA
Controller of Examinations: Prof. H. S. UPADHYAYA
Librarian: Dr A. P. GAKHAR
Library of 710,000 vols
Number of students: 37,694

DEANS

Faculty of Arts: Prof. N. R. FAROOQI
Faculty of Commerce: Prof. RAMENDU ROY
Faculty of Law: Prof. L. R. SINGH
Faculty of Medicine: Prof. P. C. SAXENA
Faculty of Science: Prof. SATYA GURU PRAKASH

ATTACHED RESEARCH INSTITUTES

Centre for Behavioural and Cognitive Sciences: tel. (532) 2460738; e-mail office@cbcs.ac.in; internet www.cbcs.ac.in; f. 2002; Dir M. P. SHRIVASTAV.
Centre of Biomedical Magnetic Resonance: Sanjay Gandhi Postgraduate Institute of Medical Sciences Campus, Raebareli Road, Lucknow 226014, Uttar Pradesh; tel. (522) 2668700; fax (522) 2668215; e-mail cbmrlko@gmail.com; internet cbmr.res.in/; f. 2002; Dir Prof. C. L. KHETRAPAL.
Centre For Environmental Education and Research (CEEAR): Dir Dr D. R. MISHRA.

Centre of Mobile Communication for Developing Countries: tel. (532) 640012; Dir Prof. G. K. Mehta.

Motilal Nehru Institute of Research & Business Administration (MONIRBA): Chatham Lines Campus, Allahabad, Uttar Pradesh; tel. (532) 2250840; fax (532) 2644951; e-mail info@monirba.com; internet www.monirba.com; f. 1965.

National Centre of Experimental Mineralogy and Petrology (NCEMP): tel. (532) 2250840; fax (532) 2644951; e-mail ncempald@dataone.in; internet www.ncemp.org; f. 1996; Dir Prof. Alok Krishna Gupta.

ANDHRA UNIVERSITY

Visakhapatnam 530003, Andhra Pradesh
Telephone: (891) 2844444
Fax: (891) 2755324
E-mail: registrar@andhrauniversity.info
Internet: www.andhrauniversity.info
Founded 1926
Affiliating
Languages of instruction: English, Telugu
Academic year: July to March
Chancellor: HE The Governor of Andhra Pradesh
Vice-Chancellor: Dr Beela Satyanarayana
Rector: Dr B. Parvathiswara Rao
Registrar: Prof. Prasad Reddy
Dean of Academic Affairs: Prof. D. Harinarayana
Dean of College Devt Council: Prof. S. K. V. S. Raju
Dean of Postgraduate Examinations: Prof. E. Viswanatha Reddy
Dean of Student Affairs: Prof. O. S. R. U. Bhanu Kumar
Dean of Undergraduate Examinations: Prof. L. D. Sudhakara Babu
Dir of Press and Publs: Prof. U. Viplava Prasad
Librarian: Prof. C. Sasikala
Library of 431,800 vols
Number of teachers: 883
Number of students: 100,000.

CONSTITUENT COLLEGES

Autonomous College of Engineering: tel. (891) 2844999; fax (891) 2747969; e-mail principal@aucevizag.ac.in; 16 depts; centres of excellence incl. Int. Centre for Bioinformatics, Advanced Centre for Nano Technology, Centre for Biotechnology, Centre for Phase Equilibrium Thermodynamic, Centre for Energy Systems, Centre for Condition Monitoring and Vibration Diagnostics, Centre for Remote Sensing and Information System, Centre for Research on Off-Shore Structures; Principal Prof. P. S. N. Raju; Vice-Principal Prof. S. Rama Mohan Rao.

College of Arts and Commerce: tel. (891) 2844666; fax (891) 2550158; e-mail principal_arts@andhrauniversity.info; f. 1966; 237 teachers; 1,894 students; 28 depts; Principal Prof. L. K. Mohana Rao

DEAN/CHAIR.

Prof. M. Krishna Kumari, Faculty of Arts
Prof. B. Parvatheswara Rao, Faculty of Commerce
Prof. K. P. Subba Rao, Faculty of Education
Prof. V. Ramesh, Faculty of Fine Arts
Prof. Apada Rao, Faculty of Oriental Learning
N. Vijaya Mohan, Faculty of Physical Education
Prof. K. Madhu, Faculty of Yoga

College of Pharmaceutical Sciences: tel. (891) 2844922; f. 1975; Prin. Prof. K. P. R. Chowdary.

College of Science and Technology: tel. (891) 2844888; fax (891) 2550158; e-mail principal_science@andhrauniversity.info; f. 1931; 232 teachers; 2,000 students; Schools of Chemistry, Earth and Atmospheric Sciences, Life Sciences, Mathematical Sciences, Physics; 7 Research Centres; Prin. Prof. P. Rajendra Prasad; Asst Prins Prof. Y. V. Rao, Prof. K. Rajendra Prasad, Dr T. Siva Rao.

Dr B. R. Ambedkar College of Law: tel. (891) 2844502; f. 1945; Prin. Prof. A. Rajendra Prasad (acting).

The University also runs Bachelors of Education, undergraduate and postgraduate courses in East and West Godavari, Srikakulam, Visakhapatnam and Vizianagaram Districts

ANNA UNIVERSITY

Sardar Patel Rd, Guindy, Chennai 600025
Telephone: (44) 22351723
Fax: (44) 22350397
E-mail: vc@annauniv.edu
Internet: www.annauniv.edu
Founded 1978 as Perarignar Anna Univ. of Technology, name changed 1982
State control
Language of instruction: English
Academic year: July to May
Affiliating, with 225 self-financing engineering colleges, 6 govt colleges, 3 govt-aided engineering colleges located in various parts of Tamil Nadu
Vice-Chancellor: Prof. Dr P. Mannar Jawahar
Registrar: Dr S. Shanmugavel
Controller of Examinations: Dr V. Jayabalan
Dir of Admissions: Dr A. Ramalingam
Dir of Research: Dr V. Murugesan
Dir of Student Affairs: Dr S. Ganesan
Dir of Univ. Library: Dr K. Balu (acting)
Library of 202,503 vols, 615 periodicals
Number of teachers: 614
Number of students: 11,489

CHAIR.

Faculty of Architecture and Planning: Dr Ranee Maria Leonie Vedamuthu
Faculty of Civil Engineering: Dr K. Ilamparuthi
Faculty of Electrical Engineering: Dr M. R. Mohan
Faculty of Information and Communication Engineering: Dr T. V. Geetha
Faculty of Management Science: Dr L. Suganthi
Faculty of Mechanical Engineering: Dr S. Gowri
Faculty of Science and Humanities: Dr A. Vijayakumar
Faculty of Technology: Dr P. Gautam
Sports Board: Dr P. Ganesan

ANNAMALAI UNIVERSITY

Annamalai Nagar 608002, Tamil Nadu
Telephone: (4144) 238248
Fax: (4144) 238080
E-mail: info@annamalaiuniversity.ac.in
Internet: www.annamalaiuniversity.ac.in
Founded 1929 with a token deposit of 200 books along with Sri Meenakshi College, moved into its present location from the eastern wing of the admin. bldg in 1959
Unitary, residential
Languages of instruction: Tamil, English
Academic year: July to June
Chancellor: HE Governor of Tamil Nadu Thiru Surjit Singh Barnala
Pro-Chancellor: Dr M. A. M. Ramaswamy
Vice-Chancellor: Dr M. Ramanathan
Registrar: Dr M. Rathinasabapathi

Controller of Examinations: Dr R. Meenakshisundaram
Librarian: Dr M. Suriya
Library of 463,000 vols, palm-leaf MSS in Tamil and Sanskrit, gramophone records
Number of teachers: 2,000
Number of students: 18,567
Publications: *Annamalai University—A Short History*, *Annamalai University Research Journal*

DEANS

Faculty of Agriculture: Dr G. Kuppuswamy
Faculty of Arts: Dr S. Rajendran
Faculty of Dentistry: Dr C. R. Ramachandran
Faculty of Education: Dr K. Vaithianathan
Faculty of Engineering and Technology: Prof. B. Palaniappan
Faculty of Fine Arts: Prof. A. K. Palanivel
Faculty of Indian Languages: Dr P. L. Muthuveerappan
Faculty of Medicine: Dr N. Chidambaram
Faculty of Science: Dr Venugopal P. Menon

ASSAM AGRICULTURAL UNIVERSITY

Jorhat 785013, Assam
Telephone: (376) 3340008
Fax: (376) 3340001
E-mail: vc@aau.ren.nic.in
Internet: www.aau.ac.in
Founded 1969
Teaching, research and extension at undergraduate and postgraduate levels in Agriculture (Jorhat campus and Biswanath Chariali), Home Science (Jorhat campus), Veterinary Science (Khanapara campus and Azad, North Lakhimpur) and Fisheries Science (Raha); 6 regional research stations
Language of instruction: English
Autonomous control
Chancellor: HE The Governor of Assam
Vice-Chancellor: Dr B. C. Bhowmik (acting)
Registrar: Dr Krishna Gohain
Dir of Extension Education: Dr B. C. Bhowmick
Dir of Postgraduate Studies: Dr D. Das
Dir of Student Welfare: Dr D. Das (acting)
Dirs of Research: Dr N. N. Sarmah (Agriculture), Dr M. R. Borkakoty (Veterinary Sciences)
Chief Librarian: Dr T. C. Brahma
Library of 90,000 vols (main campus)
Number of teachers: 530
Number of students: 2,500
Publications: *Ghare-Pathare* (Assamese, 12 a year), *Journal of Research*, *Krishibikshan* (Assamese, 4 a year), *Package of Practices for Kharif Crops* (English, 2 a year), *Package of Practices for Rabi Crops* (English, 2 a year)

DEANS

Faculty of Agriculture: Dr L. K. Hazarika
Faculty of Home Science: Dr Minaxi Pathak
Faculty of Veterinary Science: Dr R. N. Goswami

ASSAM UNIVERSITY

Silchar 788011, Assam
Telephone: (3842) 270801
Fax: (3842) 270802
E-mail: auliba@sancharnet.in
Internet: www.assamuniversity.nic.in
Founded 1994
Central university
Academic year: July to June
Chief Rector: Governor of Assam, Lt-Gen. (Retd) A. Singh
Chancellor: Dr M. S. Swaminathan
Vice-Chancellor: Prof. Tapodhir Bhattacharjee

Pro Vice-Chancellor (Diphu Campus): Prof. B. MATE
Pro Vice-Chancellor (Silchar Campus): Prof. G. D. SHARMA
Finance Officer: Dr A. SEN (acting)
Controller of Examinations: Dr P. DEBNATH
Proctor: Dr M. DUTTA CHOUDHRY
Dir, CDC: Dr B. R. CHOUDHURY
Registrar: S. SENGUPTA
Librarian: V. D. SHRIVASTAVA
Library of 52,557 vols, 186 periodicals
Number of teachers: 140
Number of students: 1,446
Publications: *Journal of Assam University, Science in society: proceedings of regional symposium, Silchar: Problems of urban development of a growing city*

DEANS

School of Environmental Sciences: Prof. A. GUPTA
School of Humanities: Dr N. B. BISWAS
School of Information Sciences: Prof. G. P. PANDEY
School of Languages: Prof. S. DEVI
School of Life Sciences: Prof. G. D. SHARMA
School of Management Studies: Dr N. B. DEY
School of Physical Sciences: Prof. K. HEMA-CHANDRAN
School of Social Sciences: Prof. GOPALJI MISHRA
School of Technology: Prof. A. K. SEN

AWADHESH PRATAP SINGH UNIVERSITY

Rewa District Rewa 486003, Madhya Pradesh
Telephone: (7662) 230050
Fax: (7662) 242175
Internet: www.apsurewa.ernet.in
Founded 1968
Affiliating, Teaching and Research
Languages of instruction: Hindi, English
Academic year: July to June
Chancellor: HE THE GOVERNOR OF MADHYA PRADESH
Vice-Chancellor: Prof. A. D. N. BAJPAI
Registrar: Dr R. S. PANDEY
Librarian: G. K. SINGH
Library of 31,000 vols
Number of teachers: 841 (42 at univ., 799 at affiliated colleges)
Number of students: 47,254 (incl. affiliated colleges)
Publication: *Vindhya Bharati* (4 a year)

DEANS

Faculty of Arts: R. R. MATHUR
Faculty of Ayurveda: Dr R. V. SOHGUNRA
Faculty of Commerce: Prof. I. P. TRIPATHI
Faculty of Education: Dr RASHAMI SHUKLA
Faculty of Home Science: Dr A. K. SHRIVAS-TAVA
Faculty of Law: R. R. MATHUR
Faculty of Life Science: Dr R. N. SHUKLA
Faculty of Medicine: Dr M. K. RATHORE
Faculty of Prachya Sanskrit: Dr BHASHKAR-ACHARYA TRIPATHI
Faculty of Science: Dr S. K. NIGAM
Faculty of Social Science: Dr A. K. SHRIVAS-TAVA

There are 62 affiliated colleges

BABA FARID UNIVERSITY OF HEALTH SCIENCES

Sadiq Rd, Faridkot 151203, Punjab
Telephone: (1639) 256232
Fax: (1639) 256234
E-mail: generalinfo@bfuhs.ac.in
Internet: www.bfuhs.ac.in
Founded 1998

Affiliating
Faculties of Ayurveda, dental sciences, homeopathy, medical sciences, nursing sciences, physiotherapy; 133 affiliated and 4 constituent colleges
Chancellor: HE THE GOVERNOR OF PUNJAB
Vice-Chancellor: Dr SHIVINDER SINGH GILL
Registrar: Dr DARSHAN SINGH SIDHU
Librarian: Dr RAJEEV MANHAS
Library of 25,604 vols
Number of students: 21,332

DEANS

Faculty of Ayurveda: Dr RAVINDER KAUR SHUKLA
Faculty of Dental Sciences: Dr ANIL KOHLI
Faculty of Homeopathy: Dr TEJINDER PAL SINGH
Faculty of Medical Sciences: Dr J. L. GARGI
Faculty of Nursing Sciences: Dr KANWALJIT KAUR
Faculty of Physiotherapy: Dr SANJAY WADHWA

BABASAHEB BHIMRAO AMBEDKAR UNIVERSITY

Vidya Vihar, Rai Bareilly Rd, Lucknow 226025
Telephone: (522) 2440826
Fax: (522) 2440821
E-mail: info@bbauindia.org
Internet: www.bbauindia.org
Founded 1996
Central university
Academic year: July to June
Chancellor: Prof. U. R. RAO
Vice-Chancellor: Prof. B. HANUMAIAH
Finance Officer: D. K. JAIRAJ
Registrar: Prof. U. S. RAWAT
Librarian: K. L. MAHAWAR (acting)

DEANS

School of Ambedkar Studies: Prof. N. M. P. VERMA
School for Biosciences and Biotechnology: Prof. R. B. RAM
School for Environmental Sciences: Prof. D. P. SINGH
School for Home Sciences: Dr SUNITA MISHRA
School for Information Science and Technology: Prof. R. B. RAM
School for Legal Studies: Prof. S. K. BHATNA-GAR (acting)
Student Welfare: Dr K. L. MAHAWAR

BANARAS HINDU UNIVERSITY

Varanasi 221005, Uttar Pradesh
Telephone: (542) 2316558
Fax: (542) 2317074
E-mail: bhu@banaras.ernet.in
Internet: www.bhu.ac.in
Founded 1915
State control
Central univ. (residential and teaching)
Languages of instruction: Hindi, English
Academic year: July to April (three terms)
Visitor: PRES. OF THE REPUBLIC OF INDIA
Vice-Chancellor: Prof. D. P. SINGH
Rector: Prof. B. D. SINGH
Registrar: K. P. UPADHYAY
Finance Officer: PARAG PRAKASH
Controller of Examinations: K. P. UAPDHYAY
Dean of Students: S. K. SHARMA
Chief Proctor: Prof. H. C. S. RATHOR
Librarian: Prof. H. N. PRASAD
Library of 916,821 vols
Number of teachers: 1,085
Number of students: 16,105
Publications: *BHU Journal, Prajna*

DEANS

Faculty of Agriculture: Prof. R. P. SINGH
Faculty of Arts: Prof. S. N. PANDEY
Faculty of Ayurveda: Prof. M. DWIVEDI
Faculty of Commerce: Prof. S. CHANDRA
Faculty of Dental Science: Prof. N. MITTAL
Faculty of Education: Prof. B. D. SINGH
Faculty of Information Technology: Prof. J. N. SINHA
Faculty of Law: Dr M. N. P. SRIVASTAVA
Faculty of Management Studies: Prof. DEE-PAK BARMAN
Faculty of Medicine: Prof. P. SHARMA
Faculty of Performing Arts: Dr RITWIK SANYAL
Faculty of Sanskrit Vidya Dharma Vijnan Sankaya: Prof. K. K. SHARMA
Faculty of Science: Prof. S. C. LAKHOTIA
Faculty of Social Sciences: Prof. P. N. PANDEY
Faculty of Visual Arts: Dr MRIDULA SINHA

CONSTITUENT COLLEGE

Mahila Maha Vidyalaya: f. 1929; Principal Dr SUSHILA SINGH.

ATTACHED INSTITUTES

Institute of Agricultural Sciences: Dir Prof. S. R. SINGH.

Institute of Medical Sciences: Dir Prof. GAJENDRA SINGH

DEANS

Faculty of Ayurveda: Dr VINOD KUMAR JOSHI
Faculty of Dental Sciences: Prof. NEELAM MITTAL
Faculty of Modern Medicine: Prof. P. SHARMA
Institute of Technology: tel. (542) 2368106; fax (542) 2368428; e-mail director@itbhu.ac.in; internet www.itbhu.ac.in; Dir Prof. S. N. UPADHYAY.

4 affiliated colleges

BANGALORE UNIVERSITY

Jnana Bharathi Campus, Jnana Bharathi Post Bangalore 560056, Karnataka
Telephone: (80) 22961006
Fax: (80) 23219295
E-mail: registrar@bub.ernet.in
Internet: www.bub.ernet.in
Founded 1964
Affiliating
Languages of instruction: Kannada, English
Academic year: June to March
Chancellor: HE THE GOVERNOR OF KARNATAKA
Vice-Chancellor: Prof. A. N. PRABHUDEVA
Pro-Chancellor: ARAVIND LIMBAVALI
Finance Officer: SRI VENKATESHAPPA
Registrar: SANJAY VIR SINGH
Librarian: Dr P. V. KONNUR
Library of 315,000 vols
Number of teachers: 456
Number of students: 300,000
Publications: *Bash Bharathi* (2 a year), *Janapriya Vignana* (12 a year), *Sadhane* (Kannada, 4 a year), *Vidya Bharathi, Vignana Bharathi*

DEANS

Faculty of Arts: Dr G. S. SIVARAMAKRISHNAN
Faculty of Commerce: Dr PUSHPA D. BHATT
Faculty of Education: Dr M. NARAYANA SWAMY
Faculty of Engineering: Dr K. R. VENUGOPAL
Faculty of Law: Dr T. R. SUBRAMANYA
Faculty of Science: Dr H. T. RATHOD

UNIVERSITY COLLEGES

University College of Physical Education: Principal Dr M. S. TALWAR.

University Law College: Principal Dr K. M. HANUMANTHARAYAPPA.

University Visvesvaraya College of Engineering: f. 1917.

There are 400 affiliated colleges and 75 postgraduate depts

BARKATULLAH UNIVERSITY

Hoshangabad Rd, Bhopal 462026, Madhya Pradesh

Telephone: (755) 2491800

E-mail: buregistrar@yahoo.co.in

Internet: www.bubhopal.nic.in

Founded 1970 as Bhopal Univ., name changed 1989

Teaching and Affiliating; 170 affiliated colleges

Languages of instruction: English, Hindi

Chancellor: HE THE GOVERNOR OF MADHYA PRADESH

Vice-Chancellor: Prof. RAVINDRA JAIN

Proctor: Prof. P. K. MISHRA

Finance Officer: BUDHOLIYA

Dir for College Devt Council: H. S. YADAV

Dir for Public Relations: Dr V. S. BAIS

Dean for Student Welfare: Dr KALIKA YADAV

Registrar: Dr SANJAY P. TIWARI

Librarian: Dr ARVIND CHOUHAN

Library of 71,259 vols

Number of teachers: 1,100

Number of students: 40,000 (incl. affiliated colleges)

DEANS

Faculty of Arts: Prof. H. KHAN

Faculty of Commerce: Dr D. P. SHARMA

Faculty of Education: M. S. GUPTA

Faculty of Engineering: Dr A. S. MEHTA

Faculty of Law: H. L. JAIN

Faculty of Life Sciences: Dr S. D. BEBARE

Faculty of Management: Dr N. R. BHANDARI

Faculty of Science: Dr K. K. RAO

Faculty of Social Sciences: Dr H. S. YADAV

BENGAL ENGINEERING AND SCIENCE UNIVERSITY

PO Botanic Garden, Howrah 711103, West Bengal

Telephone: (33) 26684561

Fax: (33) 26682916

E-mail: vc@becs.ac.in

Internet: www.becs.ac.in

Founded 1856 as Civil Engineering College, Calcutta, 1992 deemed univ. status as Bengal Engineering College, 2004 univ. status and present name

Depts of applied mechanics, architecture, chemistry, civil, computer science and technology, electrical, electronics and telecommunications, geology, humanities, human resource management, information technology, mathematics, mechanical, metallurgy, mining, physics

Vice-Chancellor: Dr AJOY ROY

Dean of Research: Dr B. N. DATTA

Dean of Students: A. K. GHOSH

Registrar: Dr BIMAN BANDYOPADHYAY

Finance Officer: MANINDRA NATH SARKAR

Controller of Examinations: Dr BHASWATI MITRA

Librarian: Dr H. P. SHARMA

Library of 200,000 vols, 300 periodicals

Number of students: 2,500

DEANS

Faculty Councils for Postgraduate and Undergraduate Studies of Basic and Applied Sciences: Prof. BICHITRA KUMAR GUHA

Faculty Councils for Postgraduate and Undergraduate Studies of Engineering and Technology: Prof. AMIT KUMAR DAS

Faculty Councils for Postgraduate and Undergraduate Studies of Social and Management Sciences: Prof. MANAS KUMAR SANYAL

CONSTITUENT SCHOOLS

Purabi Das School of Information Technology: tel. (33) 26689312; fax (33) 26689313; internet pdsit.becdu.ac.in; Dir Prof. SURYA SARATHI BARAT.

School of Community Science and Technology (SOCSAT): Dir Dr BHASWATI MITRA.

School of Disaster Mitigation Engineering: Dir Prof. S. C. DUTTA.

School of Ecology Infrastructure and Human Settlement Management: Dir Prof. SOUVANIC ROY.

School of Management Science (SOMS): f. 2004; Dir Prof. S. C. SAHA.

School of Material Science and Engineering (SMSE): internet matsc.becs.ac.in; f. 2001; Dir Dr NIL RATAN BANDYOPADHYAY.

School of Mechatronics & Robotics: Dir Prof. S. R. BHADRA CHOUDHURI.

School of Safety & Occupational Health Engineering: Dir Prof. B. K. BHATTACHARYA.

School of VLSI Technology: Dir Prof. JAYA SIL.

BERHAMPUR UNIVERSITY

Berhampur 760007, Orissa

Telephone: (680) 2242172

Fax: (680) 2243322

Internet: bamu.nic.in

Founded 1967

Teaching and Affiliating

State control

Language of instruction: English

Academic year: June to May

Chancellor: HE THE GOVERNOR OF ORISSA

Vice-Chancellor: Prof. B. K. SAHU

Comptroller: P. K. RAUT

Controller of Examinations: Prof. A. K. MISHRA

Dir of College Devt Council: Prof. J. N. PANDA

Dir of Distance Education: Prof. B. B. KAR

Registrar: SURECH CH. PANDA

Librarian: J. PANIGRAHY (acting)

Library of 96,997 vols

Number of teachers: 168

Number of students: 31,550

Publication: *Research Journal* (1 a year)

PROFESSORS

ACHARYA, S., Oriya

BARAL, J. K., Political Science

DAS, D., Oriya

DAS, G. N., Linguistics

DAS, H. H., Political Science

DAS, N. C., Physics

KHAN, P. A., Botany

MAJHI, J., Electronics

MISHRA, S. K., English

MISRA, B. N., Botany

MISRA, D.

MISRA, P. M., Marine Science

MOHANTY, S. P., Physics

MOHAPATRA, N. C., Physics

PADHISHARMA, R., Economics

PANDA, C. S., Chemistry

PANDA, G. P., Law

PANDA, G. S., Business Administration

PANDA, J., Commerce

PANDA, P., Economics

PANIGRAHY, G. P., Chemistry

PARHI, N., Mathematics

PATI, S. C., Chemistry

PATNAIK, B. K., Zoology

PATRA, G. C., Industrial Relations and Labour Welfare

PRASAD, R., Zoology

RAO, E. R., English

RATH, D., Mathematics

SAHU, P. K., Commerce

SAMAL, J. K., History

VERMA, G. P., Zoology

There are 11 govt, 62 non-govt and 26 professional technical affiliated colleges

BHARATHIAR UNIVERSITY

Coimbatore 641046, Tamil Nadu

Telephone: (422) 2428100

Fax: (422) 2425706

E-mail: regr@b-u.ac.in

Internet: www.b-u.ac.in

Founded 1982

Teaching and Affiliating; incl. Bharathiar School of Management and Entrepreneur Devt and depts of applied mathematics, bio-informatics, bio-technology, botany, centre for life science, chemistry, commerce, communication and media studies, computer science, computer applications, economics, education, educational technology, electronics and instrumentation, English and foreign languages, environmental sciences, extension career guidance and student welfare, finance and accounting, information technology, library science, linguistics, mathematics, medical physics, microbial biotechnology, nanoscience and technology, physical education, physics, psychology, social work, sociology and population studies, statistics, Tamil, women's studies, zoology; 102 affiliated colleges and 19 affiliated research institutes

Academic year: July to April

Chancellor: HE THE GOVERNOR OF TAMIL NADU

Pro-Chancellor: HON'BLE MIN. FOR EDUCATION, GOVT OF TAMIL NADU

Vice-Chancellor: Dr C. SWAMINATHAN

Registrar: Dr P. THIRUMALVALAVAN

Controller of Examinations: Dr K. BALACHANDRAN

Dir (SDE): Dr N. BALASUBRAMANIAN

Finance Officer: K. RAMASUBRAMANIAN

Public Relations Officer: N. J. MURALI MOHAN

Dir of Research: Dr S. MANIAN

Dean of College Devt Ccl: Dr P. K. MANOHARAN

Librarian: Dr P. VINAYAKAMOORTHY

Library of 120,000 vols, 150 periodicals, 7,000 e-journals

Founded 1982

DEANS

Arts: Dr S. M. RAVICHANDRAN

Commerce: Dr G. GANESAN

Curriculum Development: Dr K. SWAMINATHAN

Education: Dr M. JAYAKUMAR

Research: Dr S. MANIAN

Science: Dr C. NAMASIVAYAM

Social Sciences: Dr R. VENKATAPATHY

BHARATHIDASAN UNIVERSITY

Palkalaiperur, Tiruchirappalli 620024, Tamil Nadu

Telephone: (431) 2407072

Fax: (431) 2407045

E-mail: office@bdu.ac.in

Internet: www.bdu.ac.in

Founded 1982

Affiliating; incl. 16 schools and 47 depts and centres; 106 affiliated colleges and 25 approved instns.

Languages of instruction: English, Tamil

State control

Academic year: June to April

Chancellor: HE THE GOVERNOR OF TAMIL NADU

Vice-Chancellor: Dr M. PONNAVAIKKO
Registrar: Dr T. RAMASWAMY (acting)
Finance Officer: THIRU S. SUBBURATHINAM
Controller of Examinations: Dr S. SRIDHARAN
Librarian: Dr S. SRINIVASA RAGAVAN (acting)
Library of 90,000 vols, 200 periodicals
Number of teachers: 2,779
Number of students: 99,802

DEANS

Arts: Dr K. PARTHASARATHY
Indian and Other Languages: Dr A. NOEL
 JOSEPH SEETHARAMAN
Science: Dr M. LAKSHMANAN

BHAVNAGAR UNIVERSITY

Gaurishanker Lake Rd, Bhavnagar 364002,
 Gujarat
Telephone: (278) 2430002
Fax: (278) 2426706
E-mail: drhc_trivedi@rediffmail.com
Internet: www.bhavuni.edu
Founded 1978
Teaching and Affiliating
State control
Language of instruction: Gujarati
Academic year: June to March (two terms)
Chancellor: HE THE GOVERNOR OF GUJARAT
Vice-Chancellor: Dr H. C. TRIVEDI
Registrar: RAMSINH H. RAJPUT
Controller of Examinations: K. L. BHATT
Dir of External Studies: B. N. DESAI
Librarian: Dr B. M. GOHEL
Library of 102,090 vols
Number of teachers: 400
Number of students: 20,959

DEANS

Faculty of Arts: Prof. VINOD H. JOSHI
Faculty of Commerce: Dr B. K. OZA
Faculty of Education: Dr J. P. MAIYANI
Faculty of Engineering: Prof. M. K. VORA
Faculty of Law: J. A. PANDYA
Faculty of Management: Dr A. KUMAR
Faculty of Medicine: Dr M. P. SINGH
Faculty of Rural Studies: SATISHBHAI PATEL
Faculty of Science: Dr MAYURIBEN PANDYA
There are 28 affiliated colleges

ATTACHED INSTITUTES

**B. V. Patel Pharmaceutical Education
and Research Institute:** Ahmedabad.
**Central Salt and Marine Chemicals
Research Institute:** see under Research
Institutes.
Dholakia School of Music: Sihor.
**K. K. Jani Institute of Medical Labora-
tory Technology:** Amargadh; Dir Dr R. M.
THAKKAR.
K. L. Institute for Deaf and Dumb:
Vidyanagar.
Perfect Foundation: Bhavnagar; Dir R. D.
MEHTA.

BHUPENDRA NARAYAN MANDAL
UNIVERSITY

Laloo Nagar, Madhepura 852113, Bihar
Telephone: (6476) 222059
Fax: (6476) 222068
Founded 1992
State control
Vice-Chancellor: Prof. QAMAR AHSAN
Registrar: B. P. YADAV
27 Constituent colleges, 24 affiliated colleges,
2 postgraduate centres.

BIDHAN CHANDRA KRISHI
VISWAVIDYALAYA

PO Krishi Viswavidyalaya, Mohanpur
 741252, Nadia, West Bengal
Telephone: (33) 25879772
Fax: (3473) 222275
E-mail: drbckv@vsnl.net
Internet: www.bckv.edu.in
Founded 1974
Residential
Academic year: July to June
Chancellor: HE THE GOVERNOR OF WEST
 BENGAL
Vice-Chancellor: Dr RANAJIT KUMAR SAMANTA
Registrar: ASOK BANERJEE
Dir of Extension Education: Dr P. BANDYO-
 PADHYAY
Dir of Farms: Dr T. K. KUMAR
Dir of Research: Prof. SAROJ SANYAL
Dean of Student Welfare: Prof. RANABIR
 CHATTERJEE
Asst Librarian: DIPIKA NEOGI
Library of 69,430 vols, 208 periodicals
Number of students: 466

DEANS

Faculty of Agriculture: Prof. A. K. DAS
Faculty of Horticulture: Prof. P. CHATTOPAD-
 HYAY
Postgraduate Studies: Prof. R. K. BISWAS

BIRSA AGRICULTURAL UNIVERSITY

Kanke, Ranchi 834006, Jharkhand
Telephone: (651) 2450500
Fax: (651) 2450850
E-mail: bau@bitsmart.com
Internet: www.baujharkhand.org
Founded 1981
Languages of instruction: English, Hindi
Academic year: July to June
Chancellor: HE THE GOVERNOR OF JHARKHAND
Vice-Chancellor: Dr N. N. SINGH
Dir of Research: Dr B. N. SINGH
Registrar: Dr S. M. PRASAD
Librarian: R. PRASAD
Library of 70,000 vols
Number of teachers: 200
Number of students: 700
Publication: *Journal of Research*

DEANS

Faculty of Agriculture: Dr A. K. SARKAR
Faculty of Forestry: Dr P. KAUSHAL
Faculty of Veterinary Science and Animal
 Husbandry: Dr A. K. SINHA

BUNDELKHAND UNIVERSITY

Jhansi 284003, Uttar Pradesh
Telephone: (510) 2320496; (510) 2320761
E-mail: admin@bujhansi.org
Internet: www.bujhansi.org
Founded 1975
Affiliating
Vice-Chancellor: Prof. V. K. MITTAL
Registrar: BHAGWAN SINGH
Finance Officer: K. C. VERMA
Dean of Student Welfare: Prof. V. P. KHARE
Proctor: Prof. V. K. SEHGAL
Librarian: Dr S. C. SROTIA
20 Affiliated colleges
Library of 10,000 vols
Number of teachers: 434
Number of students: 38,000

DEANS

Faculty of Agriculture: Dr B. D. PRAJAPATI
Faculty of Arts: Dr M. L. MAURYA
Faculty of Commerce: Prof. PANKAJ ATRI
Faculty of Education: Dr Y. KULSHRESTHA

Faculty of Engineering and Technology: Dr
 D. SINGH
Faculty of Law: Prof. D. P. GUPTA
Faculty of Medicine: Dr G. KUMAR
Faculty of Science: Prof. S. P. SINGH

UNIVERSITY CENTRE

**Veerangna Jhalkaribai Centre for
Women Studies and Development:** tel.
(510) 2321103; e-mail wsc_bu@rediffmail
.com; Dir Dr APARNA RAJ; publ. *International
Journal for Women and Gender Research* (2 a
year).

CENTRAL AGRICULTURAL
UNIVERSITY

Iroisemba, Imphal 795004, Manipur
Telephone: (385) 2415933
Fax: (385) 2415196
E-mail: snpuri04@yahoo.co.in
Internet: www.cic.nic.in/cicmanipur/html/
 cau.asp
Founded 1993
Central university
Academic year: August to July (two semes-
 ters)
Chancellor: V. L. CHOPRA
Vice-Chancellor: Dr S. N. PURI
Registrar: Dr M. PREMJIT SINGH
Library of 18,527 vols, 241 periodicals
Number of teachers: 103
Number of students: 437

DEANS

College of Agriculture: Prof. N. I. SINGH
College of Fisheries: Dr M. L. BHOWMIK
College of Home Science: Dr R. S. RAGHUVAN-
 SHI
College of Horticulture and Forestry: Prof. D.
 S. RATHORE
College of Veterinary Science and Animal
 Husbandry: Dr H. C. KALITA

PROFESSORS

BHATTACHARYA, D., Soil Science and Agricul-
 tural Chemistry
LAISHRAM, J. M., Plant Breeding and Genet-
 ics
MEITEI, W. I., Horticulture
NANDEESHA, M. C., Aquaculture
RAGHUVANSHI, R. S., Food and Nutrition
RATHORE, D. S., Pomology
SINGH, M. D., Animal Husbandry and Dairy-
 ing
SINGH, M. P., Agricultural Entomology
SINGH, M. R. K., Plant Breeding and Genetics
SINGH, N. I., Plant Pathology
SINGH, N. R., Agricultural Economics
SINGH, R. K. K., Soil Science and Agricultural
 Chemistry
SINGH, Y. J., Agricultural Engineering

CHANDRA SHEKHAR AZAD
UNIVERSITY OF AGRICULTURE AND
TECHNOLOGY

Nawabganj, Kanpur 208002, Uttar Pradesh
Telephone: (512) 2534156
Fax: (512) 2533808
E-mail: info@csauk.ac.in
Internet: www.csauk.ac.in
Founded 1975
State control
Languages of instruction: Hindi, English
Academic year: July to June
Chancellor: HE THE GOVERNOR OF UTTAR
 PRADESH
Vice-Chancellor: Prof. G. C. TEWARI
Comptroller: K. K. RAWAT
Dir of Agricultural Experiment Station: Dr L.
 P. TEWARI
Dir of Extension: Dr RAM CHARAN
Registrar: Dr V. P. KANAUJIA

Librarian: Dr C. L. MAURYA
Library of 64,300 vols, 4,481 periodicals
Number of teachers: 318
Number of students: 1,187

DEANS

Faculty of Agricultural Engineering and Technology: Dr M. P. YADAV
Faculty of Agriculture: Dr H. B. DWIVEDI
Faculty of Home Science: Dr POONAM SINGH

CHATRAPATI SHAHUJI MAHARAJ UNIVERSITY, KANPUR

Kalyanpur, Kanpur 208024, Uttar Pradesh
Telephone: (512) 2570450
Fax: (512) 2570006
Internet: www.kanpuruniversity.org
Founded 1966 as Kanpur University; present name 1997
Affiliating
State control
Languages of instruction: English, Hindi
Academic year: July to June
Chancellor: HE THE GOVERNOR OF UTTAR PRADESH
Vice-Chancellor: Dr H. K. SEHGAL
Registrar: MAHESH CHANDRA
Librarian: Dr S. P. SINGH
170 Affiliated colleges
Library of 47,000 vols
Number of students: 220,000

DEANS

Faculty of Agriculture: Dr A. K. SRIVASTAVA
Faculty of Arts: G. J. SRIVASTAVA
Faculty of Ayurvedic and Unani Medicine: Dr B. D. AGGARWAL
Faculty of Business Management: Prof. Y. C. MISHRA
Faculty of Commerce: Dr P. C. CHATURVEDI
Faculty of Education: Dr S. SHANTA
Faculty of Law: S. L. VIDYARTHI
Faculty of Life Sciences: Dr L. C. MISRA
Faculty of Medicine: Dr S. K. KATIYAR
Faculty of Science: Dr P. K. MATHUR
Faculty of Social Sciences: (vacant)
Univ. College of Dental Sciences: Prof. Y. C. MISHRA
Univ. Institute of Engineering and Technology: Prof. D. SARAN

CHAUDHARY CHARAN SINGH HARYANA AGRICULTURAL UNIVERSITY

Hissar 125004, Haryana
Telephone: (1662) 289326
Fax: (1662) 23495
E-mail: vc@hau.ernet.in
Internet: hau.ernet.in
Founded 1970
State control
Language of instruction: English
Academic year: July to June
Chancellor: HE THE GOVERNOR OF HARYANA
Vice-Chancellor: Dr DHARAM VIR (acting)
Registrar: Dr R. S. DALAL
Dir of Extension: Dr H. D. YADAV
Dir of Research: Dr S. S. PAHUJA
Controller of Examinations: Dr V. K. KALRA
Librarian: PREM SINGH
Library of 317,343 vols (218,000 books, 97,437 vols of periodicals)
Number of teachers: 730
Number of students: 650
Publications: Haryana Kheti (12 a year), HAU Journal of Research (2 a year)

DEANS

College of Agricultural Engineering and Technology: Dr M. K. GARG
College of Agriculture: Dr S. S. PAHUJA

College of Animal Sciences: Dr N. SINGH YADAV
College of Basic Sciences and Humanities: Dr V. K. CHOWDHURY
College of Home Science: Dr N. KHETARPAUL
College of Veterinary Science: Dr S. K. NAGPAL
Postgraduate Studies: Dr O. P. TOKY

CHAUDHARY CHARAN SINGH UNIVERSITY

Meerut 250005, Uttar Pradesh
Telephone: (121) 2760551
Fax: (121) 2760577
E-mail: vicechancellor@ccsuniversity.org
Internet: www.ccsum.com
Founded 1966 as Meerut University
Affiliating and Teaching
Languages of instruction: Hindi, English
Chancellor: HE THE GOVERNOR OF UTTAR PRADESH
Vice-Chancellor: Prof. S. P. OJHA
Registrar: Dr V. B. BANSAL
Library of 95,074 vols, 276 periodicals
Number of students: 125,365
Publications: Indian Journal of Political Science, Journal of Political and Public Administration

DEANS

Faculty of Agriculture: Prof. P. V. SINGH
Faculty of Arts: Prof. J. K. PUNDIR
Faculty of Commerce: Dr A. B. LAL
Faculty of Education: Prof. S. PAL
Faculty of Law: Dr C. SHEKAR
Faculty of Medicine: Dr U. SHARMA
Faculty of Science: Prof. D. PANDEY
Faculty of Technology: Prof. D. PANDEY

One constituent college and 63 affiliated colleges

CHAUDHARY DEVI LAL UNIVERSITY

Barnala Rd, Sirsa 125055, Haryana
Telephone: (1666) 247104
Internet: cdlu.edu.in
Founded 2003
Teaching and Affiliating
Language of instruction: English
Academic year: July to May (three terms)
Chancellor: HE THE GOVERNOR OF HARYANA
Vice-Chancellor: Dr K. C. BHARDWAJ
Registrar: Dr R. K SEHGAL
Dean of Academic Affairs: Dr R. K. SINGH
Finance Officer: Dr N. C. JAIN
Proctor: Dr R. CHANDER
Controller of Examinations: N. C. JAIN
Librarian: Dr D. P. WARNE

Faculties of Arts and Languages, Commerce and Management, Education, Engineering and Technology, Law, Physical Education, Social Sciences

DEANS

Faculty of Commerce and Management: Prof. SULTAN SINGH
Faculty of Education: Prof. SHAMSHER SINGH JANG BAHADUR
Faculty of Engineering and Technology: Prof. VIKRAM SINGH
Faculty of Humanities: Prof. ANU SHUKLA
Faculty of Law: Prof. HARBANSH
Faculty of Life Sciences: Prof. SURESH KUMAR GAHLAWAT
Faculty of Physical Sciences: Prof. PARVEEN AGHAMKAR
Faculty of Social Sciences: Dr RAJBIR SINGH DALAL

CHAUDHARY SARWAN KUMAR HIMACHAL PRADESH KRISHI VISHVAVIDYALAYA

Palampur 176062, Dist. Kangra, Himachal Pradesh
Telephone: (1894) 230521
Fax: (1894) 230465
E-mail: icuns@hillagric.ernet.in
Internet: www.hillagric.ernet.in
Founded 1978; fmrly Faculty of Agriculture of Himachal Pradesh University
State control
Language of instruction: English
Academic year: July to June
Chancellor: HE THE GOVERNOR OF HIMACHAL PRADESH
Vice-Chancellor: Dr TEJ PARTAP
Registar: NEERAJ KUMAR
Comptroller: B. R. DHIMAN (acting)
Dir of Education: Dr K. K. KATOCH
Dir of Research: Dr S. C. SHARMA
Registrar: RAJDEV SINGH JASROTIA
Librarian: Dr KAHAN BASSI (acting)
Library of 74,000 vols
Number of teachers: 367
Number of students: 792
Publication: Himachal Journal of Agricultural Research (2 a year)

DEANS

College of Agriculture (Palampur): Dr O. P. SHARMA (acting)
College of Basic Sciences: Dr R. G. SUD (acting)
College of Home Science: Dr P. K. SHARMA
College of Veterinary and Animal Sciences: Dr A. C. VARSHNEY (acting)
Postgraduate Studies: Dr P. K. SHARMA (acting)

ATTACHED REGIONAL RESEARCH STATIONS

Regional Research Centre, Bajaura: Bajaura, Dist. Kullu 175125, Himachal Pradesh; tel. (1905) 287235; Assoc. Dir H. L. THAKUR.

Regional Research Centre, Dhaulakuan: Dhaulakuan, Dist. Sirmour 173001, Himachal Pradesh; tel. (1704) 257421; Assoc. Dir V. KALIA.

Regional Research Centre, Kukumseri: Kukumseri, Dist. Lahoul and Spiti, Himachal Pradesh; tel. (1909) 222210; Assoc. Dir VIJAY SINGH THAKUR.

COCHIN UNIVERSITY OF SCIENCE AND TECHNOLOGY

Cochin 682022, Kerala
Telephone: (484) 2575396
Fax: (484) 2577595
E-mail: registrar@cusat.ac.in
Internet: www.cusat.ac.in
Founded 1971
State control
Language of instruction: English
Academic year: July to April
Chancellor: HE THE GOVERNOR OF KERALA
Pro-Chancellor: THE MINISTER FOR EDUCATION, KERALA
Vice-Chancellor: K. M. ABRAHAM
Registrar: Dr A. RAMACHANDRAN
Finance Officer: S. OUSEPH
Controller of Examinations: V. K. RAMACHANDRAN NAIR
Dir of Int. Relations and Academic Admissions: Dr K. SAJAN
Dir of Public Relations and Publs: S. ANILKUMAR
Librarian: Dr S. DEVI ANTHERJANAN
Library of 82,000 vols, 200 periodicals
Number of teachers: 197
Number of students: 2,100

Publications: *Indian Manager, Law Review, Statistical Methods*

DEANS

Faculty of Engineering: Prof. P. O. J. LEBBA
Faculty of Environmental Studies: Dr I. S. BRIGHT SINGH
Faculty of Humanities: Dr A. ARAVINDAKSHAN
Faculty of Law: Dr K. N. CHANDRASEKHARA PILLAI
Faculty of Marine Science: Dr K. MOHAN KUMAR
Faculty of Medical Science and Technology: Dr P. S. JOHN
Faculty of Science: Dr V. UNNIKRISHNAN NAIR
Faculty of Social Sciences: Dr D. RAJASENAN
Faculty of Technology: Dr V. P. NARAYANAN NAMPOORI

PROFESSORS

ALIYAR, S., Hindi
ARAVINDAKSHNAN, A., Hindi
BABU, T. J., Civil Engineering
BABU SUNDAR, S., Computer Application
BALACHAND, A. N., Physical Oceanography
BALAKRISHNAN, K. G., Electronics
CHACKO, J., Chemical Oceanography
CHANDRASEKHARAN, M., Biotechnology
CHANDRASEKHARAN, N. S., Legal Studies
CHANDRASEKHARAN PILLAI, K. N., Legal Studies
DAMODARAN, K. T., Marine Sciences
DAMODARAN, R., Marine Sciences
EASWARI, M., Hindi
FRANCIS, C. A., Management Studies
GEORGE, K. E., Polymer Science and Rubber Technology
GEORGE, K. K., Management Studies
GEORGE VARGHESE, K., Management Studies
GIRIJAVALLABHAN, C. P., Physics
GOPALAKRISHNA KURUP, P., Marine Sciences
HRIDAYANATHAN, C., Industrial Fisheries
JACOB, P. K., Computer Science
JATHAVEDAN, M., Mathematics
JOSEPH, R., Polymer Science and Rubber Technology
KORAKANDY, R., Industrial Fisheries
KRISHNAMURTHY, A., Mathematical Sciences
KRISHNANKUTTY, P., Ship Technology
KURIAKOSE, A. P., Polymer Science and Rubber Technology
KURIAKOSE, V. L., Physics
MADHUROADANA KENUP, B., Industrial Fisheries
MARY JOSEPH, T., Management Studies
MATHAI, E., Physics
MATHEW, K. T., Electronics
MATHEW, S., Industrial Fisheries
MATHEWS ABRAHAM, B., Civil Engineering
MOHAMMED YUSSUF, K., Applied Chemistry
MOHAN KUMAR, K., Atmospheric Science
MOHANAN, N., Hindi
MOHANAN, P., Electronics
MOHANDAS, A., Environmental Studies
MURALEEDHARAN NAIR, K. R., Statistics
MURUGESAN REDDIAR, K., German
NANDAKUMARAN, V. M., Photonics
NARAYANAN NAMPOOTHIRI, V. P., Photonics
PAVITHRAN, K. B., Management Studies
PHILIP, B., Marine Biology, Microbiology and Biochemistry
PHILIP, J., Instrumentation
PILLAI, P. R. S., Electronics
POULOSE JACOB, K., Computer Science
RADHAKRISHNAN, P., Photonics
RAJAN, C. K., Atmospheric Science
RAJAPPAN NAIR, K. P., Physics
RAJASENAN, D., Applied Economics
RAMACHANDRAN, A., Industrial Fisheries
RAMACHANDRAN NAIR, V. K., Statistics
RAM MOHAN, H. S., Marine Sciences
RAVINDRA-NATHA MENON, N. R., Marine Sciences
SABIR, M., Physics
SADASIVAN NAIR, G., Legal Studies
SAJAN, K., Marine Sciences

SALIH, M., Marine Biology, Microbiology and Biochemistry
SASIDHARAN, R., Hindi
SEBASTIAN, K. L., Applied Chemistry
SERALATHAN, P., Marine Geology and Geophysics
SHANMUGHAN, M., Hindi
SIVASANKARA PILLAI, V. N., Environmental Studies
SOMASEKHARAN NAIR, E. M., Ship Technology
SUDARSHANAN PILLAI, P., Management Studies
SUGUNAN, S., Applied Chemistry
SUKUMARAN NAIR, H. K., Applied Economics
SUKUMARAN NAIR, M. K., Applied Chemistry
SUNEETHA BAI, L., Hindi
THRIVIKRAMAN, T., Mathematical Sciences
UNNIKRISHNAN NAIR, N., Statistics
VALLABHAN, G., Photonics
VASUDEVAN, K., Electronics
VIJAYAKUMAR, K. P., Physics
WILSON, P. R., Management Studies
YUSUFF, M., Applied Chemistry

DEEN DAYAL UPADHYAY GORAKHPUR UNIVERSITY

Gorakhpur 273009, Uttar Pradesh
Telephone: (551) 2330767
Fax: (551) 2340459
E-mail: registrar@ddugu.edu.in
Internet: www.ddugu.edu.in

Founded 1958 as Gorakhpur Univ., present name 1997

Teaching and Affiliating; 4 professional and 82 affiliated colleges
Languages of instruction: Hindi, English
Academic year: July to April (two terms)
Chancellor: HE THE GOVERNOR OF UTTAR PRADESH
Vice-Chancellor: Prof. P. K. MAHANTY
Registrar: T. N. UPADHYAY
Librarian: J. L. UPADHYAY
Library of 387,100 vols, 800 periodicals
Number of teachers: 300
Number of students: 115,000 , incl. students of the colleges

DEANS

Baba Raghav Das Medical College: Dr R. B. VERMA
Faculty of Agriculture: Prof. A. B. MANI TRIPATHI
Faculty of Arts: Prof. A. K. SAXENA
Faculty of Commerce: Prof. T. P. N. SRIVASTAVA
Faculty of Education: Prof. S. N. TRIPATHI
Faculty of Law: Prof. A. KUMAR MISHRA
Faculty of Science: Prof. J. P. CHATRUWEDI

DEV SANSKRITI VISHWAVIDYALAYA

Gayatrikunj, Shantikunj, Hardwar 249411, Uttaranchal
Telephone: (1334) 261367
Fax: (1334) 260723
E-mail: administrator@dsvv.org
Internet: www.dsvv.org

Founded 2002
Academic year: July to May

Depts of computer science, English, holistic health management, human consciousness and yogic science, Indian culture and tourism studies, journalism and mass communication, psychology, rural management and entrepreneurship, theology

Chancellor: Dr PRANAV PANDYA
Vice-Chancellor: Dr S. P. MISHRA
Registrar: D. S. VISHWAVIDYALAY
Library of 25,000 vols
Number of teachers: 15
Number of students: 136

DEVI AHILYA VISHWAVIDYALAYA

Nalanda Parishar, Indore 452001, Madhya Pradesh
Telephone: (731) 2527532
Fax: (731) 2529540
E-mail: registrar.davv@dauniv.ac.in
Internet: www.dauniv.ac.in

Founded 1964 as University of Indore
Teaching and Affiliating
Languages of instruction: Hindi, English
State control
Academic year: July to May (three terms)
Chancellor: HE THE GOVERNOR OF MADHYA PRADESH
Vice-Chancellor: Dr BHAGIRATH PRASAD
Registrar: Dr R. D. MUSALGOANKAR
Librarian: Dr G. H. S. NAIDU
153 Affiliated colleges
Library of 117,210 vols
Number of teachers: 1,251
Number of students: 6,000 on campus; 120,000 in affiliated colleges

DEANS

Faculty of Arts: Dr C. DEOTALE
Faculty of Ayurved: Dr P. P. AGRAWAL
Faculty of Commerce: Dr D. D. MUNDRA
Faculty of Dentistry: Dr H. C. NEEMA
Faculty of Education: Dr S. VAIDYA
Faculty of Electronics: Dr RAJKAMAL
Faculty of Engineering: (vacant)
Faculty of Engineering Sciences: (vacant)
Faculty of Life and Home Sciences: Dr R. BHARADWAJ
Faculty of Management Studies: Dr R. D. PATHAK
Faculty of Medicine: Dr K. BHAGAWAT
Faculty of Pharmacy: Dr S. C. CHATURVEDI
Faculty of Physical Education: (vacant)
Faculty of Science: Dr K. K. PANDEY
Faculty of Social Sciences and Law: Dr B. Y. LALITHAMA

ATTACHED RESEARCH INSTITUTES

Institute of Engineering and Technology: tel. (731) 2462311; fax (731) 2764385; e-mail dir.iet@dauniv.ac.in; internet www.iet.dauniv.ac.in; Dir Dr M. CHANDWANI.

Institute of Management Studies: internet www.ims.dauniv.ac.in; f. 1969; Dir Dr P. N. MISHRA.

DHARMSINH DESAI UNIVERSITY

POB 35, College Rd, Nadiad 387001, Gujarat
Telephone: (268) 2520502
Fax: (268) 2520501
E-mail: vc@ddu.ac.in
Internet: www.ddu.ac.in

Founded 1968 as Dharmsinh Desai Institute of Technology; deemed univ. status 2000; state univ. status 2005

Pres.: Dr N. D. DESAI
Vice-Chancellor: Dr H. M. DESAI
Registrar: Dr T. R. SHAH
Library of 17,000 vols, 80 periodicals

DEANS

Faculty of Business Admin.: Prof. G. S. SHAH
Faculty of Commerce: Prof. M. K. TRIVEDI
Faculty of Dental Science: Dr B. S. JATHAL
Faculty of Pharmacy: Dr L. D. PATEL
Faculty of Technology: Dr P. A. JOSHI

DIBRUGARH UNIVERSITY

Dibrugarh 786004, Assam
Telephone: (373) 2370231
Fax: (373) 2370323
E-mail: info@dibru.ac.in
Internet: www.dibru.ac.in

Founded 1965

Affiliating and Teaching; depts of anthropology, applied geology, Assamese, chemistry, commerce, economics, education, English, history, life science, mathematics, petroleum technology, pharmaceutical sciences, physics, political science, sociology, statistics; 121 affiliated colleges
State control
Languages of instruction: Assamese, English
Academic year: January to December
Chancellor: HE THE GOVERNOR OF ASSAM
Vice-Chancellor: Dr K. K. DEKA
Registrar: Dr P. K. BHUYAN
Controller of Examinations: Dr S. GOGOI
Librarian: (vacant)
Library of 158,481 vols, 5,200 periodicals
Number of teachers: 181 (univ. depts)
Number of students: 58,850 (incl. affiliated colleges)
Publications: *Anthropology Bulletin, Assam Economic Journal, Assam Statistical Review, Dibrugarh University Journal of Education, Dibrugarh University Journal of English Studies, Journal of Historical Research, Life Sciences Bulletin, Mathematical Forum, Padartha Vigyan Patrika* (physics, in Assamese, 1 a year), *Pharmray, The North Eastern Research Bulletin.*

DR B. R. AMBEDKAR OPEN UNIVERSITY

Prof. G. Ram Reddy Marg, Rd 46, Jubilee Hills, Hyderabad 500033, Andhra Pradesh
Telephone: (40) 23544830
Fax: (40) 23544830
E-mail: info@braou.ac.in
Internet: www.braou.ac.in
Founded 1982
Academic year: July to June
Chancellor: HE THE GOVERNOR OF ANDHRA PRADESH
Vice-Chancellor: Prof. OBULREDDY RAMANJULA REDDY
Registrar: Dr B. SUNDER RAO
Controller of Examinations: Prof. V. C. RAO
Public Relations Officer: A. V. REDDY
Librarian: Dr G. SUJATHA
Library of 29,912 vols
Number of teachers: 63
Number of students: 63,575

DEANS

Faculty of Arts: Prof. K. S. RAMANA
Faculty of Commerce: Dr A. SUDHAKAR
Faculty of Science: Prof. S. V. RAJASEKHAR REDDY
Faculty of Social Sciences: A. VIDYAVATHI

PROFESSORS

CHANDRASEKHARA RAO, V., Library Science
DAMAYANTHI DEVI, I., Zoology
GNANAPRASUNA, K., Physics
HAYAT, S., Urdu
JADHAO, Y., Hindi
KIRANMAYI, Y. S., Business Management
KOTESWARA RAO, K., Commerce
KUPPUSWAMY RAO, K., Mathematics
NETHI, G., Zoology
PRASAD, V. S., Public Administration
PUSHPA RAMAKRISHNA, C., English
RAJASHEKAR REDDY, S. V., Geology
RAMACHANDRAIAH, G., Chemistry
RAMACHANDRAIAH, M., Botany
RAMAIAH, P., Economics
SRINIVASACHARYULU, G., Evaluation
SUNDARA RAO, B., Economics
UMAPATHI VARMA, Y. V., Educational Technology
VASUNADAN, R., Telugu
VENKAIAH, V., Business Management
VIDYAVATHI, A., Sociology
There are 140 Study Centres located in the state of Andhra Pradesh

DR BABASAHEB AMBEDKAR MARATHWADA UNIVERSITY

Aurangabad 431004, Maharashtra
Telephone: (240) 2400491
Fax: (240) 2403113
E-mail: registrar@bamu.net
Internet: www.bamu.net
Founded 1958
Teaching and Affiliating
Languages of instruction: English, Marathi
Academic year: June to April (two terms)
Chancellor: HE THE GOVERNOR OF MAHARASHTRA
Vice-Chancellor: Dr N. KOTTAPALLE
Registrar: Dr D. V. MULEY
Dir of Board of College and Univ.: Dr A. G. KHAN
Finance Officer: B. S. ANNASAHEB
Controller of Examinations: Dr M. G. GUMASTE
Librarian: Dr S. S. LOMATE
Library of 304,473 vols
Number of teachers: 3,275 (incl. affiliated colleges)
Number of students: 130,534

DEANS

Arts: N. A. LAVANDE
Ayurveda: D. V. KULKARNI
Commerce: S. R. MADAN
Education: G. V. SHETKAR
Engineering and Technology: P. A. DESHMUKH
Fine Art: D. D. BADE
Homeopathy: Dr S. M. DESARADA
Law: Dr S. P. PANDE
Management Science: Dr V. S. SAVANT
Physical Education: A. B. HUMBE
Science: Dr D. R. MANE
Social Science: P. N. PATIL
There are 146 affiliated colleges

DR BABASAHEB AMBEDKAR OPEN UNIVERSITY

Sarkhej-Gandhinagar Highway, Ahmedabad 380060, Gujarat
Telephone: (79) 27413747
Fax: (79) 27413751
E-mail: baouvc@yahoo.co.in
Internet: www.baou.org
Founded 1994
State control
Academic year: August to July
Schools of commerce and management, computer science, distance education and education technology, humanities and social sciences; 250 study centres
Chancellor: HE THE GOVERNOR OF GUJARAT
Vice-Chancellor: Prof. AVADHESH KUMAR SINGH
Registrar: S. H. BAROT.

DR BABASAHEB AMBEDKAR TECHNOLOGICAL UNIVERSITY

Vidyavihar, District Raigad, Lonere 402103, Maharashtra
Telephone: (2140) 275101
Fax: (2140) 275040
Internet: www.dbatechuni.org
Founded 1989
State control
Depts of chemical engineering, chemistry, computer engineering, electrical engineering, electronics and telecommunications engineering, information technology, mathematics, mechanical engineering. petrochemical engineering, physics
Chancellor: HE THE GOVERNOR OF MAHARASHTRA
Vice-Chancellor: Dr A. A. GHATOL

Registrar: Dr P. D. SATHE
Librarian: S. P. VAIDYA
Library of 51,000 vols, 114 periodicals.

DR BALASAHEB SAWANT KONKAN KRISHI VIDYAPEETH

Ratnagiri, Dapoli 415712, Maharashtra
Telephone: (2358) 282411
Fax: (2358) 282074
E-mail: root@kkv.ren.nic.in
Internet: www.dbskkv.org
Founded 1972
State control
Academic year: July to May
Language of instruction: English
Chancellor: HE THE GOVERNOR OF MAHARASHTRA
Vice-Chancellor: Dr V. MEHATA
Registrar: R. N. KULKARNI
Librarian: S. M. RODGE
Library of 32,384 vols, 128 periodicals
15 Research Stations

DEANS

Faculty of Agricultural Engineering: Dr A. G. PAWAR
Faculty of Agriculture: Dr V. B. MEHTA
Faculty of Fisheries: Dr P. C. RAJE

CONSTITUENT AND AFFILIATED COLLEGES

College of Agricultural Engineering and Technology: Manki-Palvan, Tal-Chiplun, Ratnagiri 415641; tel. (2355) 233181; fax (2352) 264830; e-mail caetmp@yahoo.co.in; f. 2003; Dir V. N. GAWANDE.

College of Agriculture: Saralgaon, Tal-Murbad, Thane 421401; tel. (2524) 240770; f. 2001.

College of Fisheries: Ratnagiri 415629, Maharashtra; tel. (2352) 232987; fax (2352) 232241; e-mail rtg_fishcoll@sancharnet.in; f. 1981.

College of Horticulture: Kharawate-Dahiwali, Ratnagiri 415606, Maharashtra; tel. (2355) 264017; fax (2355) 264830; f. 2001.

Govindraoji Nikam College of Agriculture: Mandki-Palvan. Tal-Chiplun, Ratnagiri 415629, Maharashtra; tel. (2355) 233181; fax (2355) 264830; e-mail gncamp@redifmail.com; f. 2001; Dir Dr T. L. CHORAGE.

DR BHIM RAO AMBEDKAR UNIVERSITY

Senate House, Paliwal Park, Agra 282004, Uttar Pradesh
Telephone: (562) 2820051
Fax: (562) 2520051
E-mail: info@dbrau.ac.in
Internet: www.dbrau.ac.in
Founded 1927 as Agra University; present name 1995
Affiliating and Teaching
Languages of instruction: English, Hindi
Academic year: July to May (one term)
Chancellor: HE THE GOVERNOR OF UTTAR PRADESH
Vice-Chancellor: Dr K. N. TRIPATHI
Registrar: Dr BALJI YADAV
Hon. Librarian: Dr SUNDER LAL
Library of 169,027 vols
Number of students: 123,000

DEANS

Faculty of Agriculture: Dr J. P. VERMA
Faculty of Commerce: Dr K. K. BANSAL
Faculty of Education: Dr CHANDER HANS PATHAK
Faculty of Fine Arts: Dr S. BHARGAVE
Faculty of Homeopathic Medicine: Dr MOTI LAL SHUKLA

Faculty of Home Science: Dr H. KUMAR
Faculty of Law: Dr V. K. KAUSHIK
Faculty of Medicine: Dr U. C. MISRA
Faculty of Science: Dr JAI SHANKER

CONSTITUENT INSTITUTES

Dau Dayal Institute of Vocational Education: Agra.

Deen Dayal Upadhyay Institute of Rural Development: Agra.

Institute of Basic Sciences: Agra.

Institute of Home Science: Agra; library of 10,218 vols; 10 teachers; Dir Dr H. KUMAR (acting).

Institute of Social Sciences: Agra; library of 18,000 vols; 14 teachers; Dir Dr S. V. PANDEY.

K. M. Institute of Hindi Studies and Linguistics: Agra; library of 39,000 vols; Dir Dr JAI SINGH NEERAD.

Lalit Kala Sansthan (Institute of Fine Arts): Agra.

School of Life Sciences: Agra.

Seth Padam Chandjain Institute of Commerce, Business Management and Economics: Agra; Dir Dr M. R. BANSAL (acting).

There are 144 affiliated colleges

DR HARI SINGH GOUR UNIVERSITY

Gour Nagar, University Campus, Sagar, Madhya Pradesh 470003
Telephone: (7582) 222574
Fax: (7582) 223236
E-mail: sagaruniversity@mp.nic.in
Internet: www.sagaruniversity.nic.in
Founded 1946
Teaching, Affiliating and Residential; 81 affiliated colleges
Languages of instruction: Hindi, English
Academic year: July to April (two terms)
Chancellor: HE THE GOVERNOR OF MADHYA PRADESH
Vice-Chancellor: Prof. D. P. SINGH
Rector: Prof. Dr K. S. PITRE
Registrar: Dr PARIKCHHIT SINGH
Dean of Student Welfare: Dr A. K. SHANDILYA
Finance Officer: P. N. SINGH
Librarian: MUKESH KUMAR SAHU (acting)
Library of 310,000 vols
Number of teachers: 300
Number of students: 80,000
Publication: *Madhya Bharti—Research Journal* (1 a year, Hindi and English)

DEANS

Faculty of Arts: Prof. A. K. AWASTHI
Faculty of Commerce: Prof. Y. S. THAKUR
Faculty of Education: Dr G. SHANKAR
Faculty of Engineering: Prof. R. K. TRIVEDI
Faculty of Law: Prof. P. K. RAI
Faculty of Life Sciences: Prof. D. C. ATRI
Faculty of Management: Prof. Y. S. THAKUR
Faculty of Science: Prof. D. C ATRI
Faculty of Social Sciences: Prof. P. K. RAI
Faculty of Technology: Prof. G. P. AGRAWAL

DR N. T. R. UNIVERSITY OF HEALTH SCIENCES, ANDHRA PRADESH

Vijayawada 520008, Andhra Pradesh
Telephone: (866) 2451206
Fax: (866) 2450463
E-mail: ntruhs@hotmail.com
Internet: 203.199.178.93
Founded 1986
Residential and teaching; faculties of dental sciences, indian systems of medicine, medical laboratory technology, modern medicine, nursing, nutrition and physiotherapy; 316 affiliated colleges
Language of instruction: English
State control
Academic year: July to June
Chancellor: HE THE GOVERNOR OF ANDHRA PRADESH
Vice-Chancellor: Prof. A. V. KRISHNAM RAJU
Registrar: Prof. T. VENUGOPAL RAO
Librarian: K. SRINIVASA RAO
Library: Library in process of formation
Number of teachers: 3,000
Number of students: 9,000 undergraduate, 3,000 postgraduate

DR PANJABRAO DESHMUKH AGRICULTURE UNIVERSITY

Krishi Nagar, Akola 444104, Maharashtra
Telephone: (724) 2258200
Fax: (724) 2258219
E-mail: vc@pdkv.mah.nic.in
Internet: pdkv.mah.nic.in
Founded 1969
State control
Languages of instruction: English, Marathi
Academic year: July to June
Chancellor: HE THE GOVERNOR OF MAHARASH-TRA
Pro-Chancellor: THE MIN. FOR AGRICULTURE, MAHARASHTRA
Vice-Chancellor: Dr V. M. MYANDE
Registrar: RAM CHIMURKAR
Library of 140,500 vols
Number of teachers: 650
Number of students: 3,650
Publications: *Krishi Patrika* (in Marathi, 12 a year), *PKV Research Journal* (2 a year), *Post Graduate Institute Research Journal* (1 a year)

DEANS

Faculty of Agricultural Engineering: Dr D. S. KHARCHE
Faculty of Agriculture: Dr V. D. PATIL

CONSTITUENT COLLEGES

College of Agricultural Engineering: Akola; f. 1970; Assoc. Dean Dr D. S. KHARCHE.

College of Agriculture: Akola; f. 1950; Assoc. Dean V. D. PATIL.

College of Agriculture: Nagpur; f. 1906; Assoc. Dean Dr C. S. CHOUDHARI.

College of Forestry: Akola; f. 2001; Assoc. Dean Dr J. S. ZOPE.

College of Horticulture: Akola; f. 2001; Assoc. Dean Dr V. K. MAHORKAR.

Postgraduate Institute: Akola; f. 1970; Assoc. Dean Dr R. B. SOMANI.

There are two affiliated colleges and 19 research stations

DR RAM MANOHAR LOHIA AVADH UNIVERSITY

PB 17, Faizabad 224001, Uttar Pradesh
Telephone: (5278) 246223
Fax: (5278) 246330
E-mail: edp@rmlau.ac.in
Internet: www.rmlau.ac.in
Founded 1975 as Avadh University
Teaching and Affiliating
Languages of instruction: English, Hindi
Academic year: July to June
Chancellor: HE THE GOVERNOR OF UTTAR PRADESH
Vice-Chancellor: Prof. ARUN KUMAR MITTAL (acting)
Registrar: K. N. PANDEY
Finance Officer: A. SRIVASTAVA
Librarian: S. K. SINGH
Number of teachers: 19 (univ.), 2,006 (affiliated colleges)
Number of students: 45,220 (univ. and affiliated colleges)

DEANS

Faculty of Agriculture: (vacant)
Faculty of Arts: Prof. S. P. TIWARI
Faculty of Commerce and Management: Dr H. P. PANDEY
Faculty of Dental Science: (vacant)
Faculty of Education: Dr RAKA SINHA
Faculty of Engineering and Technology: (vacant)
Faculty of Home Science: (vacant)
Faculty of Law: Dr U. SINGH
Faculty of Science: Prof. G. C. PANDEY
There are 33 affiliated colleges

DR YASHWANT SINGH PARMAR UNIVERSITY OF HORTICULTURE AND FORESTRY

Nauni (Solan) 173230, Himachal Pradesh
Telephone: (1792) 252219
Fax: (1792) 252009
E-mail: vc@yspuniversity.ac.in
Internet: www.yspuniversity.ac.in
Founded 1985
State control
Academic year: August to July
Chancellor: PRABHA RAO
Vice-Chancellor: Dr K. R. DHIMAN
Registrar: BALDEV RAM THAKUR
Librarian: Dr M. S. PATHANIA
Dir of Extension Education: Dr D. R. GAUTAM
Dir of Research: Dr S. K. SHARMA

Depts of basic sciences, biotechnology, entomology and apiculture, floriculture and landscaping, forest products, fruit breeding, mycology and plant pathology, pomology, post-harvest technology, silviculture and agroforestry, social sciences, soil science and water management, tree improvement and genetic resources, vegetable crops
Library of 57,206 vols
Number of teachers: 222
Number of students: 755

DEANS

College of Forestry: Dr S. D. SHARMA
College of Horticulture: Dr R. C. SHARMA

PROFESSORS

AGNIHOTRI, R. P., Regional Horticultural Research Station, Jachh
BARWAL, V. S., Post-harvest Technology
BAWA, R., Regional Centre, NAEB
BAWEJA, H. S., Directorate of Extension Education
BHALLA, R., Regional Horticultural Research Station, Mashobra
BHARDWAJ, M. L., Krishi Vigyan Kendra, Chamba
BHARDWAJ, S., Regional Horticultural Research Station, Mashobra
BHARDWAJ, S. S., Regional Horticultural Research Station, Bajarua
BHARDWAJ, S. V., Biotechnology
BHATIA, H. S., Regional Horticultural Research Station, Bajarua
BHATIA, R., Regional Horticultural Research Station, Jachh
CHAND, R., Forest Products
CHANDEL, J. S., Fruit Science
CHANDEL, R. P. S., Entomology and Apiculture
CHAUHAN, N. S., Forest Products
CHAUHAN, P. S., Regional Horticultural Research Station, Mashobra
CHAUHAN, U., Entomology and Apiculture
DORHOO, N. P., Directorate of Research
DUBEY, J. K., Directorate of Extension Education

GARG, R. C., Mycology and Plant Pathology
GUPTA, A. K., Mycology and Plant Pathology
GUPTA, B., Silviculture and Forestry
GUPTA, D., Entomology and Apiculture
GUPTA, J. K., Entomology and Apiculture
GUPTA, N. K., Silviculture and Forestry
GUPTA, P. R., Entomology and Apiculture
GUPTA, R., Directorate of Extension Education
GUPTA, S. K., Mycology and Plant Pathology
GUPTA, Y. C., Floriculture and Landscaping
JOSHI, A. K., Horticultural Research Station, Dhaulakuan
JOSHI, V. K., Post-harvest Technology
KANBID, B. R., Directorate of Extension Education
KANWAR, H. S., Seed technology and Production Centre
KANWAR, K., Biotechnology
KASHYAP, S. D., Silviculture and Forestry
KAUR, M., Basic Sciences
KAUR NATH, A., Biotechnology
KAUSHAL, P., Regional Centre (NAEB)
KHAJURIA, D. R., Regional Horticultural Research Station, Bajarua
KHAN, M. L., Entomology and Apiculture
KHANNA, A. S., Entomology and Apiculture
KHURANA, D. K., Tree Improvement and Genetic Resources
KORLA, B. N., Vegetable Science
KUMAR, J., Regional Horticultural Research Station, Bajarua
KUMAR, K., Fruit Breeding and Genetic Resources
KUMAR, P., Basic Sciences
KUMAR, R., Entomology and Apiculture
KUMARI, A., Directorate of Extension Education
MAHAJAN, S., Computer and Instrumentation Centre
MANKOTA, M. S., Regional Horticultural Research Station, Mashobra
MEHTA, K., Fruit Science
NARANG, M. L., Forest Protection Unit
NEGI, Y. S., Business Management
PRASHAR, R. S., Litchi and Mangro Research Station, Nagrota Bagwan
RAI, K., Forest Products
RAINA, J. N., Soil Science and Water Management
RAINA, R., Forest Products
RAM, V., Mycology and Plant Pathology
RANA, B. S., Entomology and Apiculture
RANA, S. S., Regional Horticultural Research Station, Jachh
RANDEV, A. K., Regional Horticultural Research Station, Mashobra
REHALIA, A. S., Pomology
SHAMET, G. S., Silviculture and Forestry
SHARMA, A. K., Regional Horticultural Research Station, Jachh
SHARMA, A. K., Basic Sciences
SHARMA, D. D., Fruit Science
SHARMA, D. D., Social Sciences
SHARMA, D. K., Regional Horticultural Research Station, Jachh
SHARMA, G. C., Horticultural Research Station, Kandaghat, Solan
SHARMA, G. K., Directorate of Extension Education
SHARMA, G. K., Fruit Breeding and Genetic Resources
SHARMA, H. R., Horticultural Research Station, Kandaghat, Solan
SHARMA, I. D., Entomology and Apiculture
SHARMA, I. M., Mycology and Plant Pathology
SHARMA, I. P., Soil Science and Water Management
SHARMA, J. N., Mycology and Plant Pathology
SHARMA, K. C., Temperate Horticultural Research Station, Kotkhai
SHARMA, K. D., Post-harvest Technology
SHARMA, L. R., Social Sciences
SHARMA, N., Fruit Science
SHARMA, O. P., Directorate of Extension Education

SHARMA, P. C., Post-harvest Technology
SHARMA, R., Social Sciences
SHARMA, R. C., Forest Protection Unit
SHARMA, R. L., Mycology and Plant Pathology
SHARMA, S. K., Biotechnology
SHARMA, S. K., Mycology and Plant Pathology
SHARMA, S. S., Basic Sciences
SHARMA, V., Basic Sciences
SHIRKOT, C. K., Basic Sciences
SHUKLA, Y. R., Vegetable Science
SINGH, N. B., Tree Improvement and Genetic Resources
SINGH THAKUR, A., Basic Sciences
SRIVASTAVA, D. K., Biotechnology
SUD, A., Regional Horticultural Research Station, Mashobra
SUMAN, B. C., Mycology and Plant Pathology
THAKUR, B. S., Krishi Vigyan Kendra, Kandaghat, Solan
THAKUR, K. S., Post-harvest Technology
THAKUR, M. C., Vegetable Science
THAKUR, P. D., Mycology and Plant Pathology
THAKUR, P. S., Silviculture and Forestry
THAKUR, S., Regional Horticultural Research Station, Jachh
THAKUR, V., Environmental Science
THAKUR, V. S., Regional Horticultural Research Station, Mashobra
THAPA, C. D., Mycology and Plant Pathology
TOMER, C. S., Fruit Science
TRIPATHI, D., Soil Science and Water Management
VERMA, K. S., Environmental Science

DRAVIDIAN UNIVERSITY

Chitoor District, Kuppam 517425, Andhra Pradesh
Telephone: (8570) 278220
Fax: (8570) 278230
Internet: www.dravidianuniversity.ac.in
Founded 1997

Teaching, Residential and Affiliating; depts of comparative Dravidian literature and philosophy, computers and allied sciences, Dravidian and computational linguistics, education and human resource devt, English and communication, folklore and tribal studies, history, archaeology and culture, Kannada language and translation studies, Tamil language and translation studies, Telugu language and translation studies

Academic year: July to June
Chancellor: HE THE GOVERNOR OF ANDHRA PRADESH
Vice-Chancellor: Prof. G. LAKSHMINARAYANA
Registrar: Prof. P. RAJASEKHARA REDDY
Dean of Academic Affairs: Prof. D. ANANDA NAIDU
Finance Officer: RAMA DAS
Library of 55,000 vols
Number of students: 165

EFL UNIVERSITY (ENGLISH AND FOREIGN LANGUAGES UNIVERSITY)

Hyderabad 500007, Andhra Pradesh
Telephone: (402) 7098131
Fax: (402) 7098402
E-mail: ciefors@ciefl.ac.in
Internet: www.efluniversity.ac.in
Founded 1958, deemed univ. status 1973; central univ. 2007
Academic year: June to May

Campuses at Lucknow, Shillong; schools of critical humanities, distance education, English language education, foreign languages, language sciences
Vice-Chancellor: Prof. ABHAI MAURYA
Registrar: Dr P. BAPAIAH

Library of 120,000 vols, 470 journals
Number of teachers: 98

Number of students: 2,276
Publications: *ESSAIS* (2 a year), *Journal of English and Foreign Languages* (2 a year), *Occasional Papers in Linguistics, Russian Philology* (1 a year)

DEANS

Academic: NIRUPAMA RASTOGI
Campus Development and Facilities: MEENAKSHI REDDY
Culture: K. G. VIJAYAKRISHNAN
English: T. SRIRAMAN
Examinations: P. MADHAVAN
Foreign Languages: MOHSIN USMANI
International Relations: ABHAI MAURYA
Non-Formal Courses and Resources: MALATHY KRISHNAN
Planning: LAKSHMI CHANDRA
Publications and Library: R. AMRITAVALLI
Research and Studies: M. MADHAVA PRASAD
Student Welfare: SATISH KUMAR PODUVAL
Technical Infrastructure: VINAY S. TOTAWAR

FAKIR MOHAN UNIVERSITY

Vyasa Vihar, Balasore 756019, Orissa
Telephone: (6782) 264244
Fax: (6782) 254881
Internet: www.fmuniversity.org
Founded 1999
Academic year: July to May

Depts of bioscience and biotechnology, business management, environment sciences, information and communication, population studies; 61 affiliated colleges

Chancellor: HE THE GOVERNOR OF ORISSA
Vice-Chancellor: Prof. SUKANTI PRIYA PATTNAIK
Registrar: Dr A. C. KAR
Controller of Finance: S. MARANDI

Library of 2,143 vols
Number of students: 23,542

GAUHATI UNIVERSITY

Main Campus, Gauhati 781014, Assam
Telephone: (3661) 2570415
Fax: (3661) 2570133

Kokrajhar Campus, PO Rangalikhata (Debargaon) Kokrajhar 783370, Assam
Telephone: (3661) 277183
E-mail: vc@gauhati.ac.in
Internet: www.gauhati.ac.in

Founded 1948

Teaching, Residential and Affiliating
Language of instruction: English
Academic year: July to May (three terms)
Chancellor: HE THE GOVERNOR OF ASSAM
Vice-Chancellor: Prof. O. K. MEDHI
Registrar: Dr UTTAM CHANDRA DAS
Controller of Examinations: Dr PRAFULLA K. DEKA
Treas.: HEM CHANDRA GAUTAM
Librarian: B. C. GOSWAMI

Library of 517,000 vols
Number of teachers: 281
Number of students: 118,213

DEANS

Faculty of Arts: Prof. UMESH DEKA
Faculty of Commerce: Prof. NAYAN BARUAH
Faculty of Engineering: Prof. D. BHATTACHARJEE
Faculty of Law: Prof. B. CHAKRAVERTY
Faculty of Medicine: Dr P. D. BORA
Faculty of Science: Prof. S. K. SARMA

CONSTITUENT COLLEGE

University Law College: Gauhati; Principal Dr B. K. CHAKRABORTY.

ATTACHED RESEARCH INSTITUTES
Population Research Centre: Hon. Dir Dr D. C. NATH.

Women's Studies Research Centre: Dir Dr ARCHANA SHARMA.

There are 194 affiliated colleges

GOA UNIVERSITY

Taleigao Plateau, 403203, Goa
Telephone: (832) 2451345
Fax: (832) 2451182
E-mail: registra@unigoa.ac.in
Internet: www.unigoa.ac.in
Founded 1985
Academic year: June to April
Vice-Chancellor: Prof. DILEEP DEOBAGKAR
Registrar: Dr DOHAN M. SANGODKAR
Finance Officer: DAMODAR J. NAIK
Controller of Examinations: G. J. S. TALAULIKAR
Librarian: P. V. KONNUR

46 Affiliated colleges
Library of 120,000 vols, 450 periodicals
Number of students: 7,080

DEANS
Faculty of Commerce: Dr B. RAMESH
Faculty of Design: (vacant)
Faculty of Education: Dr L. VERNAL
Faculty of Engineering: Prof. R. P. ADGAONKAR
Faculty of Languages and Literature: Dr K. S. BHAT
Faculty of Law: A. S. NADKARNI
Faculty of Life Science and Environment: Dr P. V. DESAI
Faculty of Management Studies: Dr P. R. SARODE
Faculty of Medicine: Prof. PRADEEP NAIK
Faculty of Natural Sciences: Dr J. B. FERNANDES
Faculty of Performing, Fine Art and Music: M. V. VENGURLEKAR
Faculty of Social Sciences: Prof. A. V. AFONSO

ATTACHED RESEARCH INSTITUTES
All India Institute of Local Self Government: tel. (832) 2226358; Principal A. G. KHANOLKAR.

Directorate of Archives and Archaelogy: tel. (832) 2226692; Principal M. L. DICHOLKAR.

Fisheries Survey of India: tel. (832) 2520957; Principal M. E. JOHN.

Malaria Research Centre: tel. (832) 2222444; Principal A. KUMAR.

National Centre for Antarctic and Ocean Research: tel. (832) 2520863; Principal RAVINDRA RASHIK.

National Institute of Oceanography: tel. (832) 2456700; Principal S. SHETYE.

Thomas Stephen's Konkani Kendra: tel. (832) 2415857; Principal P. NAIK.

Xavier Centre of Historical Research: tel. (832) 2414971; Principal D. MENDONCA.

GOVIND BALLABH PANT UNIVERSITY OF AGRICULTURE AND TECHNOLOGY

Udham Singh Nagar, Pantnagar 263145, Uttarakhand
Telephone: (5944) 233330
Fax: (5944) 233473
E-mail: vc@gbpuat.ernet.in
Internet: www.gbpuat.ac.in
Founded 1960
Languages of instruction: English, Hindi
State control
Academic year: July to June (two terms)

Accred. bodies: ICAR and AICTE; 10 constituent colleges and 72 teaching depts out of which 61 offer postgraduate degree programmes, univ. runs 13 on campus research centres/stations and 19 outstation research centres; farm service centres (Krishi Vigyan Kendra), 1 each in 11 dists of Uttarakhand, offer agriculture extension service
Chancellor: HE THE GOVERNOR OF UTTARAKHAND
Vice-Chancellor: Dr B. S. BISHT
Registrar: Dr T. C. THAKUR
Librarian: Dr S. P. JAIN
Library of 386,075 vols, 72,308 periodical titles
Number of teachers: 745
Number of students: 4,010 (2,400 males and 1,610 females)
Publications: *Indian Farmers Digest* (English, 12 a year), *Kisan BHARTI* (Hindi, 12 a year), *Pantnagar Journal of Research* (2 a year)

DEANS
College of Agribusiness Management: Dr V. B. K. SIKKA
College of Agriculture: Dr J. P. TIWARI
College of Basic Sciences and Humanities: Dr B. R. K. GUPTA
College of Fishery Sciences: Dr A. P. SHARMA
College of Home Science: Dr RITA SINGH RAGHUVANSHI
College of Technology: Dr M. P. SINGH
College of Veterinary and Animal Sciences: Dr G. K. SINGH
Hill Campus, Ranichauri: Dr M. C. NAUTIYAL
Postgraduate Studies: Dr J. K. SINGH
VCSG College of Horticulture, Bharsar: Dr P. S. BISHT

GUJARAT AYURVED UNIVERSITY

Chanakya Bhavan, Jamnagar 361008, Gujarat
Telephone: (288) 2556852
Fax: (288) 2555585
E-mail: info@ayurveduniversity.com
Internet: www.ayurveduniversity.edu.in
Founded 1967
Affiliating and Teaching
Languages of instruction: Gujarati, Hindi, English, Sanskrit
Academic year: June to April (two terms)
Chancellor: HE THE GOVERNOR OF GUJARAT
Vice-Chancellor: Dr M. L. SHARMA
Registrar: R. M. JHALA (acting)
Dir of Institute of Postgraduate Training and Research: Prof. M. S. BAGHEL
Dir of Pharmacy: (vacant): Dr P. K. PRAJAPATI
Librarian: S. M. JANI

12 Affiliated colleges
Library of 32,701 vols
Number of teachers: 369
Number of students: 2,456
Publications: *Ayu* (research at the University, 4 a year), *Traditional Medicine International* (4 a year).

CONSTITUENT COLLEGE
Shree Gulab Kunverba Ayurved Mahavidyalaya: Principal Dr M. N. GOHIL.

ATTACHED INSTITUTES
Institute of Ayurved Pharmaceutical Sciences: tel. (288) 2555746; fax (288) 2555966; e-mail iaps@ayurveduniversity.com; internet www.iaps.ac.in; f. 1999; Principal Dr SURESH CHANDRA DASH.

Maharishi Patanjali Institute for Yoga Naturopathy Education and Research: tel. (288) 2770103; e-mail info@ayuyoga.com; internet www.ayuyoga.com; f. 2000.

GUJARAT UNIVERSITY

Navrangpura, Ahmedabad 380009, Gujarat
Telephone: (79) 26301341
Fax: (79) 26302654
Internet: www.gujaratuniversity.org.in
Founded 1949
Teaching and Affiliating; 250 affiliated colleges, 15 recognized instns
Languages of instruction: Gujarati, Hindi, English
Academic year: June to April (two terms)
Chancellor: HE THE GOVERNOR OF GUJARAT
Vice-Chancellor: Dr P. H. TRIVEDI
Pro-Vice-Chancellor: Dr N. K. PATEL
Registrar: M. S. SHAH
Controller of Examinations: J. LILANI
Librarian: RAMANBHAI L. PATEL
Library of 334,110 vols
Number of teachers: 3,075
Number of students: 187,771 undergraduates; 36,505 postgraduates

DEANS
Faculty of Arts: Prof. K. B. DESAI
Faculty of Commerce: Principal: K. K. SHAH
Faculty of Engineering and Technology: Prof. H. V. TRIVEDI
Faculty of Law: Principal: R. S. DESAI
Faculty of Medicine: Dr H. P. BHALODIYA
Faculty of Science: Principal: R. G. BHATT

GULBARGA UNIVERSITY

Gulbarga 585106, Karnataka
Telephone: (8472) 263202
Fax: (8472) 263206
E-mail: reggug@rediffmail.com
Internet: www.gulbargauniversity.kar.nic.in
Founded 1980
State (Govt of Karnataka) control
Languages of instruction: English, Kannada
Academic year: June to March
Chancellor: H. R. BHARADWAJ
Pro-Chancellor: ARAVIND S. LIMBAVALI
Vice-Chancellor: Prof. B. G. MULIMANI
Registrar and Finance Officer: Prof. S. L. HIREMATH
Librarian: Dr R. B. GADDAGIMATH

305 Affiliated colleges, 43 univ. depts and postgraduate centres in Bellary, Bidar, Raichur, Sandur
Library of 320,000 vols, 410 journals, 9,500 e-journals
Number of students: 63,000

DEANS
Faculty of Arts: Prof. MOHD ABDUL HAMEED
Faculty of Commerce: Prof. B. M. KANAHALLI
Faculty of Education: Prof. SYEDA AKHTAR
Faculty of Law: Prof. S. S. PATIL
Faculty of Science and Technology: Prof. Y. M. JAYARAJ
Faculty of Social Science: Prof. B. S. MAHESHWARAPPA

GURU GHASIDAS UNIVERSITY

Bilaspur 495009, Chhattisgarh
Telephone: (7752) 260283
Fax: (7752) 260148
E-mail: csit@ggu.ac.in
Internet: www.ggu.ac.in
Founded 1983
Campus at Surguja (Ambikapur)
Vice-Chancellor: Prof. LAKSHMAN CHATURVEDI
Registrar: K. K. CHANDRAKAR
Finance Officer: UMESH AGRAWAL
Dir of College Devt Council: Dr M. S. K. KHOKAR
Dean of Student Welfare: Dr S. V. S. CHOUHAN
Librarian: Dr U. N. SINGH

139 Affiliated colleges
Library of 85,000 vols

DEANS

Faculty of Arts: Dr B. B. SHUKLA
Faculty of Education: A. KUJUR
Faculty of Engineering: Prof. S. M. SAHA
Faculty of Home Science: Dr J. SHARMA
Faculty of Law: Dr A. B. SONI
Faculty of Life Science: Prof. B. M. MUKHER-JEE
Faculty of Management and Commerce: Prof. L. M. MALVIYA
Faculty of Medical Science: Dr V. D. TIWARI
Faculty of Natural Resources: Prof. S. S. SINGH
Faculty of Physical Education: Prof. S. S. SINGH
Faculty of Science: Prof. A. K. SAXENA
Faculty of Social Science: Dr J. P. SHARMA

ATTACHED INSTITUTES

Chhattisgarh Institute of Medical Sciences: tel. (7752) 254300; fax (7752) 501684; f. 2001; Dean Prof. ANIL SARANGI

PROFESSORS

BADGAIYA, Y. D.
BEHARA, P. K., Biochemistry
CHHABRA, B., Anaesthesia
DHURIYA, A., Anatomy
HAJARI, S. K., Anatomy
JAINA, R. S., Orthopaedics
KAR, C. R., Surgery
MITRA, J. P., Microbiology
PANDA, B. K., Surgery
PATIL, S. K. B., Biochemistry
PATLE, D. R., Surgery
RATH, S. K., Obstetrics and Gynaecology
SARANGI, A., Dean
SHARMA, D. K., Physiology
SINGH, P. C., Venerology and Dermatology
SINGH, P. D., Pharmacology

Institute of Technology: Dir Prof. S. N. SAHA.

GURU GOBIND SINGH INDRAPRASTHA UNIVERSITY

Kashmere Gate, Delhi 110403
Telephone: (11) 23900166
Fax: (11) 23865941
E-mail: mail@ipu.edu
Internet: ipu.ac.in
Founded 1998
Teaching and Affiliating
Academic year: August to July
Chancellor: VIJAI KAPOOR
Vice-Chancellor: Prof. DILIP K. BANDYOPAD-HYAY
Registrar: VINOD K. JAIN
Controller of Examinations: Prof. YOGESH SINGH
Controller of Finance: VANDANA GUPTA
Dir of Corporate Affairs: Prof. O. P. GOYAL
Librarian: SUBHASH DESHMUKH
Library of 15,690 vols

DEANS

School of Basic and Applied Sciences: Prof. N. R. GARG
School of Biotechnology: Prof. P. C. SHARMA
School of Chemical Technology: Prof. S. S. SAMBI
School of Education: Prof. A. BENIWAL
School of Engineering and Technology: Prof. S. WADHWA
School of Environmental Management: Prof. J. K. GARG
School of Humanities and Social Sciences: Prof. A. BENIWAL
School of Information Technology: Prof. B. V. R. REDDY

School of Law and Legal Studies: Prof. S. GUPTA
School of Management Studies: Prof. A. S. LATHER
School of Planning and Architecture: Prof. B. V. R. REDDY

CHAIRMEN

University Centre for Disaster Management Studies: Dr A. KAUR
University Centre for IT Services and Infrastructure Management: Dr C. S. REDDY
University Centre for Media Studies: Prof. S. AGGARWAL

GURU JAMBESHWAR UNIVERSITY OF SCIENCE AND TECHNOLOGY

Delhi Rd, Hisar 125001, Haryana
Telephone: (1662) 263101
Fax: (1662) 276240
E-mail: gju_tech@yahoo.com
Internet: www.gju.ernet.in
Founded 1995
Chancellor: HE THE GOVERNOR OF HARYANA
Vice-Chancellor: Lt-Gen Dr D. D. S. SANDHU
Registrar: Prof. R. S. JAGLAN
Proctor: Prof. RAJESH MALHOTRA
Dean of Academic Affairs: Prof. H. L. VERMA
Dean of Student Welfare: Prof. NAWAL KISHORE
Controller of Examinations: Prof. R. S. JAGLAN
Librarian: Prof. J. K. SHARMA
Library of 73,732 vols, 184 periodicals

DEANS

Faculty of Engineering and Technology: Prof. D. KUMAR
Faculty of Management Studies: Prof. S. C. KUNDU
Faculty of Media Studies: Prof. S. GANDHI
Faculty of Medical Sciences: Prof. S. K. SHARMA
Faculty of Non-conventional Sources of Energy and Environmental Science: Prof. N. RAM
Faculty of Pharmaceutical Sciences: Prof. D. N. MISHRA
Faculty of Religious Studies: Prof. C. P. KAUSHIK
Faculty of Science and Technology Interface: Prof. K. BANSAL
Haryana School of Business: Prof. S. C. KUNDU

GURU NANAK DEV UNIVERSITY

Amritsar 143005, Punjab
Telephone: (183) 2258802
Fax: (183) 2258819
E-mail: reg_gndu@yahoo.com
Internet: www.gndu.ac.in
Founded 1969
Autonomous, partly funded by state government
Languages of instruction: English, Hindi, Punjabi
Academic year: July to June
Chancellor: HE THE GOVERNOR OF PUNJAB
Vice-Chancellor: Dr A. S. BRAR
Registrar: Dr INDERJIT SINGH
Library of 436,000 vols
Number of teachers: 311 (in univ. campus)
Number of students: 9,063
Publications: *Amritsar Law Journal* (1 a year), *Guru Nanak Journal of Sociology* (2 a year), *Indian Journal of Quantitative Economics* (2 a year), *Journal of Management Studies* (1 a year), *Journal of Regional History* (1 a year), *Journal of Sikh Studies* (English, 2 a year), *Journal of Sports Traumatology and Allied Sports Science* (1 a year), *Khoj Darpan* (Punjabi,

2 a year), *Personality Study and Group Behaviour* (1 a year), *Pradhikrit* (Hindi, 1 a year), *PSE Economic Analyst* (English, 2 a year), *Punjab Journal of English Studies* (1 a year), *Punjab Journal of Politics* (2 a year), *University Samachar* (4 a year)

DEANS

Faculty of Agriculture and Forestry: Dr J. S. BAL
Faculty of Applied Sciences: Dr NARPINDER SINGH
Faculty of Arts and Social Sciences: Dr RADHA SHARMA
Faculty of Economics and Business: Dr VIKRAM CHADHA
Faculty of Education: Dr SURINDERPAL KAUR DHILLON
Faculty of Engineering and Technology: Dr K. S. KAHLON
Faculty of Humanities and Religious Studies: Dr SHASHI BALA
Faculty of Languages: Dr BARKAT ALI
Faculty of Law: Dr RAJNIDERJIT KAUR PAWAR
Faculty of Life Sciences: Prof. Dr A. J. S. BHANWER
Faculty of Visual Arts and Performing Arts: Dr RAJINDERJIT KAUR PAWAR
Faculty of Physical Education: Dr SUKHDEV SINGH
Faculty of Physical Planning and Architecture: Eng. PARAMJIT SINGH MAHOORA
Faculty of Sciences: Dr RAKESH MAHAJAN
Faculty of Sport Medicine and Physiotherapy: Dr JASPAL SINGH SANDHU

HEMCHANDRACHARYA NORTH GUJARAT UNIVERSITY

University Rd, POB 21, Patan 384265, Gujarat
Telephone: (2766) 230427
Fax: (2766) 231917
E-mail: vc@ngu.ac.in
Internet: www.ngu.ac.in
Founded 1986
State control
Language of instruction: Gujarati
Academic year: June to April
Chancellor: HE THE GOV. OF GUJARAT
Vice-Chancellor: Dr KIRANKUMAR K. SHAH
Pro-Vice-Chancellor: Dr J. H. PANCHOLI
Registrar: B. J. RATHORE (acting)
Controller of Examinations: Dr B. J. RATHORE
Chief Accounts Officer: A. R. MAKWANA
Deputy Registrar for Academic Affairs: D. M. PATEL
Asst Registrar for Academic Affairs: K. N. PATEL
Asst Registrar for Examinations: DHRUV DAVE
Dir of Physical Eduction: Dr J. D. DAMOR (acting)
Nat. Social Scheme Coordinator: Dr J. D. DAMOR
Dean of Faculty: Prof. M. B. CHAUDHARY
Librarian: M. K. PRAJAPATI
Asst Librarian: Dr M. G. PATEL
248 Affiliated colleges
Library of 55,880 vols, 110 periodicals
Number of teachers: 1,829
Number of students: 43,080 (25,748 males and 17,332 females)
Publications: *Anart* (1 a year), *Udichya* (26 a year)

DEANS

Faculty of Arts: Dr J. N. BAROT
Faculty of Commerce: Prin.: S. H. PATEL
Faculty of Education: Dr B. D. DAVE
Faculty of Engineering: K .G. MARADIA
Faculty of Homeopathy: Prin.: Dr B. JAGN-NATHAN
Faculty of Law: Prin.: Dr J. U. NANAVATI

Faculty of Management Studies: N. H.
BHATT
Faculty of Pharmacy: Prin.: C. N. PATEL
Faculty of Rural Studies: A. B. PATEL
Faculty of Science: Dr B. L. PUNJANI

HEMWATI NANDAN BAHUGUNA GARHWAL UNIVERSITY

Srinagar (Garhwal) 246174, Uttaranchal

Telephone: (1370) 267795
Fax: (1346) 252174
E-mail: root@hnbgugrw.ren.nic.in
Internet: www.garhwaluniversity.org

Founded 1973, fmrly Garhwal University,
renamed 1989

Teaching and Affiliating
State control
Languages of instruction: Hindi, English
Academic year: July to May

Campuses at Chauras, Pauri, Tehri

Chancellor: HE THE GOVERNOR OF UTTAR
PRADESH
Vice-Chancellor: Dr N. NATARAJAN (acting)
Registrar: C. S. MEHTA
Hon. Librarian: Prof. B. S. SEMWAL

52 Affiliated govt colleges and 28 private
professional instns
Library of 280,000 vols
Number of teachers: 251
Number of students: 100,000 (incl. colleges)

DEANS

Faculty of Agriculture: Prof. N. D. TODARIYA
Faculty of Arts: Prof. B. M. KHANDURI
Faculty of Ayurveda: Dr PUJA BARDWAJ
Faculty of Commerce: Prof. ALOK SAKLANI
Faculty of Education: Prof. K. B. BUDHORI
Faculty of Engineering: Dr M. L. DEWAL
Faculty of Law: Dr S. K. MITTAL
Faculty of Medicine: Dr A. N. MEHROTRA
Faculty of Non-formal Education: Prof. A.
MISRA
Faculty of Science: Prof. R. D. GAUR

HIDAYATULLAH NATIONAL LAW UNIVERSITY

HNLU Bhawan, Civil Lines, Raipur 492001,
Chhattisgarh

Telephone: (771) 4080114
Fax: (771) 4080118
E-mail: registrar@hnlu.ac.in
Internet: www.hnlu.ac.in

Founded 2003

Residential; schools of Administration of
Justice, Continuing and Clinical Legal Edu-
cation (SAJCCLE), Business and Global
Trade Law Devt (SBGTLD), Constitutional
and Admin. Governance (SCAG), Int. Legal
Studies (SILS), Juridical and Social Sciences
(SJSS), Science, Technology and Sustainable
Devt (SSTSD); regional centre in Bilaspur

Vice-Chancellor: Prof. M. K. SRIVASTAVA
Dir for Bilaspur Centre: T. V. RAMAKRISHNAN.

HIMACHAL PRADESH UNIVERSITY

Summer Hill, Shimla 171005, Himachal
Pradesh

Telephone: (177) 2830890
Fax: (177) 2830775
E-mail: gad.hpu@gmail.com
Internet: hpuniv.nic.in

Founded 1970

Affiliating and Teaching
State control
Languages of instruction: English, Hindi
Academic year: July to May

Chancellor: HE THE GOVERNOR OF HIMACHAL
PRADESH
Vice-Chancellor: Prof. SUNIL KUMAR GUPTA

Registrar: Prof. SHASHI KANT SHARMA
Controller of Examinations: A. N. GUPTA
Dean of Students Welfare: Prof. Y. P. SHARMA
Dean of Studies: Prof. C. L. CHANDAN
Librarian: (vacant)

272 Affiliated colleges and instns
Library of 188,402 vols
Number of teachers: 260
Number of students: 6,461

DEANS

Faculty of Ayurveda: Dr Y. K. SHARMA
Faculty of Commerce and Management Stud-
ies: Dr SADHANA MAHAJAN
Faculty of Dental Sciences: Dr ASHU GUPTA
Faculty of Education: Prof. Y. K. SHARMA
Faculty of Engineering and Technology: Dr
NIRAJ SHARMA
Faculty of Languages: Prof. VIDYA SHARDA
Faculty of Law: Prof. SURESH KAPOOR
Faculty of Life Sciences: Prof. H. S. BANYAL
Faculty of Performing and Visual Arts: Dr
JEET RAM SHARMA
Faculty of Physical Science: Dr NIRAJ SHARMA
Faculty of Social Sciences: Dr B. S. MARH

ATTACHED RESEARCH INSTITUTE

Institute of Life Sciences: Gachibowli,
Hyderabad 500046; tel. (40) 66571500; fax
(40) 66571581; e-mail info@ilsresearch.org.

INDIRA GANDHI KRISHI VISHWAVIDYALAYA

Krishak Nagar, Raipur 492006, Madhya
Pradesh

Telephone: (771) 2443166
Fax: (771) 2442131
Internet: igau.edu.in

Faculties of agricultural eng., agriculture,
dairy technology, veterinary sciences and
animal husbandry

Chancellor: HE THE GOVERNOR OF CHHATTIS-
GARH
Vice-Chancellor: Dr C. R. HAZRA
Registrar: K. C. PAINKRA
Librarian: Dr R. K. MISHRA.

INDIRA GANDHI NATIONAL OPEN UNIVERSITY

Maidan Garhi, New Delhi 110068

Telephone: (11) 29532707
Fax: (11) 26862312
E-mail: vnr.pillai@ignou.ac.in
Internet: www.ignou.ac.in

Founded 1985

Central university
Autonomous control
Languages of instruction: English, Hindi
Academic year: January to December

Vice-Chancellor: Prof. V. N. RAJASEKHARAN
PILLAI
Pro-Vice-Chancellors: Prof. O. P. MISHRA,
Prof. P. SINCLAIR, Dr D. K. CHOUDHRY, Dr
L. PILLAI, Dr K. R. SRIVATHSAN
Registrar: K. LAXMAN
Librarian: S. K. ARORA

Library of 80,000 vols, 500 periodicals
Number of teachers: 255
Number of students: 594,227

Publication: *Indian Journal of Open Learning* (2 a year)

DIRECTORS

School of Agriculture: Prof. B. S. HANSRA
School of Communication: Prof. MADHULIKA
KAUSHIK
School of Computer and Information Science:
Prof. M. LAL
School of Continuing Education: Prof. A.
ANEJA
School of Education: Prof. M. L. KOUL

School of Engineering and Technology: Prof.
G. KANSAL
School of Health Sciences: Prof. S. B. ARORA
School of Humanities: Prof. J. M. PARAKH
School of Management Studies: Prof. N. V.
NARASIMHAM
School of Sciences: Prof. S. MALHOTRA
School of Social Sciences: Prof. U. KANJILAL

INDIRA KALA SANGIT VISHWAVIDYALAYA

Khairagarh 491881, Chhattisgarh

Telephone: (7820) 234232
Fax: (7820) 234108
E-mail: reg@iksvv.com
Internet: www.iksvv.com

Founded 1956

Teaching and affiliating; 6 affiliated centres
and 33 affiliated colleges
Languages of instruction: Hindi, English
Academic year: July to April (two terms)

Chancellor: HE THE GOVERNOR OF CHHATTIS-
GARH
Vice-Chancellor: Prof. GITA PAINTAL
Registrar: Prof. Dr T. UNNIKRISHNAN
Deputy Librarian: RAMESH PATEL

Library of 43,000 vols, 41 periodicals, 90 MSS
Number of teachers: 586
Number of students: 9,680

Publications: *Bharat Bhashyam, Bhatkhande Smriti Granth, Kala Saurabh, Ki
Sangit Yatra, Meri Dakshin Bharat, Sangit Suryodaya, Shiv Mangalam*

DEANS

Faculty of Arts: Prof. MRIDULA SHUKLA
Faculty of Dance: Prof. MANDAVI SINGH
Faculty of Folk Music and Arts: Prof. BHARAT
PATEL
Faculty of Music: Prof. PRAKASH MAHADIK
Faculty of Visual Arts: Prof. M. C. SHARMA

JADAVPUR UNIVERSITY

Main Campus, 188 Raja S. C. Mullick Rd,
Jadavpur, Kolkata 700032

Telephone: (33) 24146414
Fax: (33) 24137121

Salt Lake Campus, Plot 8, Blk LB, Sector 3,
Salt Lake City, Kolkata 700098

Telephone: (33) 23355215
E-mail: registrar@admin.jdvu.ac.in
Internet: www.jadavpur.edu

Founded 1955

Residential and Teaching; depts of architecture, bengali, chemical engineering, chemistry, civil engineering, comparative literature,
computer science and engineering, construction technology, economics, electrical engineering, electronics and telecommunication
engineering, English, film studies, food technology and biochemical engineering, geological science, history, information
technology, instrumentation and electronics
engineering, instrumentation science, international relations, library and information
science, life science and biotechnology, mathematics, mechanical engineering, metallurgical engineering, pharmaceutical
technology, philosophy, physical education,
physics, power engineering, printing engineering, production engineering, Sanskrit,
sociology; 20 interdisciplinary schools; 38
centres of research
Language of instruction: English
Academic year: July to June (two terms)

Chancellor: HE THE GOVERNOR OF WEST
BENGAL
Vice-Chancellor: Prof. P. N. GHOSH
Pro-Vice-Chancellor: Prof. S. DATTA
Dean of Students: Prof. R. RAY
Registrar: R. BANDYOPADHYAY

Controller of Examinations: Dr S. BHATTA-
CHARYYA
Finance Officer: G. K. PATTANAYAK
Chief Librarian: B. B. DAS
Library of 551,445 vols, 1,057 journals
Number of teachers: 662
Number of students: 9,441
Publications: *Essays and Studies* (2 a year),
Journal of Comparative Literature (1 a
year), *Journal of the Department of Ben-
gali* (1 a year), *Journal of History* (1 a
year), *Journal of International Relations* (1
a year), *Journal of Philosophy* (2 a year)

DEANS

Faculty of Arts: Prof. B. CHATTERJEE
Faculty of Engineering and Technology: Prof.
M. K. MITRA
Faculty of Science: Prof. Dr S. BHATTACHARYA

CENTRES FOR ADVANCED STUDIES

Centre for Ambedkar Studies: Prin. Prof.
A. K. BANERJI.
Centre for Cognitive Science: tel. (33)
24147620; e-mail cogsc@center.jdvu.ac.in;
internet www.ccsju.org; Prin. Prof. A. CHAT-
TERJEE.
Centre for European Studies: tel. (33)
24839962; e-mail europa_1997@rediffmail
.com; f. 1997; Prin. Prof. P. K. BHATTACHAR-
YYA.
Centre for Human Settlement Planning:
tel. (33) 4129520; fax (33) 4739852; e-mail
monideep@cal.vsnl.net.in; f. 1995; Prin. Prof.
M. CHATTERJEE.
Centre of Indology: tel. (33) 24146023;
Prin. Prof. M. BANERJEE.
Centre for Knowledge Based Systems:
tel. (33) 4736129; fax (33) 4727723; e-mail
ckbsjuin@vsnl.com; f. 1987; Prin. Prof. T. K.
GHOSHAL.
Centre for Marxian Studies: Prin. Prof. D.
CHAKRABORTY.
**Centre for Microprocessor Application
for Training, Education and Research:**
tel. (33) 24734866; f. 1983; Prin. Prof. D. K.
BASU.
**Centre for Mobile Computing and Com-
munication:** e-mail pkdas@ieee.org;
internet www.cmccju.org; f. 2003; Prin.
Prof. P. K. DAS.
Centre for Quality Management System:
tel. (33) 4832165; fax (33) 4831890; internet
www.cqmsju.org; f. 1994; Prin. Prof. S. K.
GHOSH.
Centre for Refugee Studies: tel. (33)
4835019; e-mail opmcrs@cal2.vsnl.net.in; f.
1997; Prin. Prof. O. MISHRA.
Centre for Surface Science: tel. (33)
4838411; e-mail cssju@yahoo.co.uk; f. 1992;
Prin. Prof. S. C. BHATTACHARYA.
Computer Aided Design Centre: tel. (33)
24146844; e-mail cadcentr@cadcentreju.org;
internet www.cadcentreju.org; Prin. Prof. R.
DUTTAGUPTA.
**Condensed Matter Physics Research
Centre:** tel. (33) 4138917; f. 1990; Prin.
Prof. D. ROY.
IC Design and Fabrication Centre: tel.
(33) 4721833; fax (33) 4732217; e-mail juicc@
vsnl.com; f. 1986; Prin. Prof. H. SAHA.
**Nuclear and Particle Physics Research
Centre:** tel. (33) 4138917; f. 2000; Prin. Prof.
D. GHOSH.
Plasma Studies Centre: tel. (33) 4731484;
fax (33) 4137902; e-mail mk@jufs.ernet.in; f.
1994; Prin. Prof. B. CHAKRABORTY.
**Relativity and Cosmology Research
Centre:** tel. (33) 24138917; e-mail asitb@
cal3.vsnl.net.in; f. 1994; Prin. Prof. Dr A.
BANERJEE.

**Sir C. V. Raman Centre for Physics and
Music:** Prin. Prof. Dr D. GHOSH.

JAGADGURU RAMANANDACHARYA
RAJASTHAN SANSKRIT UNIVERSITY

Rajasthan Textbook Board Bldg, 2–2A Jha-
lana, Dungri, Jaipur, Rajasthan
Telephone: (141) 2710047
Fax: (141) 2711050
E-mail: jrrsu@yahoo.com
Internet: www.jrrsanskrituniversity.ac.in
Founded 2001
Academic year: July to May
Chancellor: HE THE GOV. OF RAJASTHAN
Vice-Chancellor: Prof. YUGAL KISHORE MIS-
HRA
Registrar: MADAN MOHAN SHARMA
Publications: *Akshara*, *Wyakhyanmanimala*.

JAGADGURU RAMBHADRACHARYA
HANDICAPPED UNIVERSITY

Chitrakoot, Karwi, 210204 Uttar Pradesh
Telephone: (5198) 290454
Fax: (5198) 290111
E-mail: jrhuniversity@yahoo.com
Internet: www.jrhu.com
Founded 2001
Vice-Chancellor: Dr RAMDEO PRASAD SINGH
Registrar: Dr AVANISH C. MISHRA
Finance Officer: R. P. MISHRA

DEANS

Faculty of Humanities, Fine Art and Music:
Prof. YOGESH C. DUBEY
Faculty of Social Sciences, Computer Science, Information Technology and Education: Prof. KAPIL D. MISHRA

JAI NARAIN VYAS UNIVERSITY,
JODHPUR

Jodhpur 342001, Rajasthan
Telephone: (291) 2649733
Fax: (291) 2649733
E-mail: info@jnvu.edu.in
Internet: www.jnvu.edu.in
Founded 1962
Languages of instruction: English, Hindi
Academic year: July to April
Chancellor: HE THE GOVERNOR OF RAJASTHAN
Vice-Chancellor: Dr J. P. CHANDELIYA
Registrar: G. L. TIWARI
Finance Officer: NIRMLA MEENA
Librarian: Dr R. M. SHARMA
9 Affiliated colleges
Library of 277,229 vols
Number of teachers: 336
Number of students: 24,063
Publications: *The Beacons* (Engineering),
Annals of Economics, *International Jour-
nal of Finance and Economic Studies* (1 a
year), *Journal of Accounting and Control*
(1 a year)

DEANS

Faculty of Arts, Social Sciences and Educa-
tion: Dr A. MATHUR
Faculty of Commerce and Management Stud-
ies: Dr K. MATHUR
Faculty of Engineering and Architecture:
Prof. S. K. BHARGAVA
Faculty of Law: Dr M. K. BHANDARI
Faculty of Science: Dr A. BOHRA

DIRECTORS

Institute of Evening Studies: Dr P. S. BHATI
K. Nehru College for Women: Dr ANAND
MATHUR

PROFESSORS

BANERJI, K. K., Chemistry

BHANDARI, S., Mining Engineering
DHARIWAL, S. R., Physics
GUPTA, V. P., Civil Engineering
LALWANI, S. J., Commerce
MALI, S. L., Electrical Engineering
OHRI, M. L., Civil Engineering
SETRIA, M. R., Structural Engineering
SHARMA, D., Civil Engineering
SHARMA, U. S., Civil Engineering
SHEKHANAT, K. S., Rajasthani
SHRIVASTAVA, R. S., Sociology
SURANA, D. M., Mining Engineering
SURANA, P., Sociology
SURANA, S. L., Electrical Engineering
TIWARI, R. P., Mechanical Engineering

JAI PRAKASH VISHWAVIDYALAYA

Rahul Sankrityan Nagar, Chapra 841301,
Bihar
Telephone: (6152) 243898
Fax: (6152) 232607
Internet: jpv.bih.nic.in
Founded 1990
Languages of instruction: English, Hindi
Academic year: July to June
21 Constituent colleges and 10 affiliated
colleges
Vice-Chancellor: Dr DINESH PRASAD SINHA
Pro Vice-Chancellor: Dr DINESH PRASAD
SINHA
Dean of Student Welfare: Dr RAMANAND RAM
Proctor: Prof. BIJAY PRATAP KUMAR
Registrar: SONELAL SAHNI
Finance Officer: Dr GOPAL P. ARYA
Controller of Examinations: Dr GOPAL P.
ARYA

DEANS

Faculty of Commerce: (vacant)
Faculty of Humanities: Prof. Dr D. D.
SHARMA
Faculty of Science: Prof. Dr RAJESHWAR PD.
SINGH
Faculty of Social Sciences: Prof. Dr RAMA
SHANKAR SINGH

JAMIA MILLIA ISLAMIA

Maulana Mohammad Ali Johar Marg, Jamia
Nagar, New Delhi 110025
Telephone: (11) 26981717
Fax: (11) 26980229
E-mail: dir.cit@jmi.ac.in
Internet: jmi.nic.in
Founded 1920
Central university
Autonomous control (government financed)
Languages of instruction: Urdu, Hindi, Eng-
lish
Academic year: July to June
Chancellor: FAKHRUDDIN T. KHORAKIWALA
Vice-Chancellor: NAJEEB JUNG
Pro-Vice-Chancellor: Prof. S. M. RASHID
Registrar: Prof. S. M. SAJID
Finance Officer: Prof. SHAHID ASHRAF
Dean of Student Welfare: Prof. ZAHID HUSAIN
KHAN
Librarian: Dr GAYAS MAKHDUMI
Library of 324,870 vols, 3,000 periodicals,
448 MSS
Number of teachers: 933
Number of students: 14,264
Publications: *Islam and the Modern Age* (4 a
year, English), *Islam Aur Asr-e-Jadeed* (4 a
year, Urdu), *Jamia Risala* (4 a year,
Urdu), *Tadrees Nama* (4 a year, Urdu),
Third Frame (4 a year, English)

DEANS

Faculty of Architecture and Ekistics: Prof. S.
M. AKHTAR
Faculty of Dentistry: Prof. RAGINI

Faculty of Education: Prof. AEJAZ MASIH
Faculty of Engineering and Technology: Prof. KHALID MOIN
Faculty of Fine Arts: Prof. Z. A. ZARGAR
Faculty of Humanities and Languages: Prof. S. M. AZIZUDDIN HUSAIN
Faculty of Law: Prof. ROSE VARGHESE
Faculty of Natural Sciences: Prof. KHALIL AHMAD
Faculty of Social Sciences: Prof. KHAN MASOOD AHMAD

ATTACHED INSTITUTES

AJK Mass Communication Research Centre: tel. (11) 26987285; fax (11) 26986811; e-mail contact@ajkmcrc.org; internet ajkmcrc.org; f. 1982; Dir B. R. YADAV.

Centre for Culture Media and Governance: tel. (11) 6831717; Dir Prof. BISWAJIT DAS.

Centre for European and Latin American Studies: Dir Prof. SONYA SURABHI GUPTA.

Centre for Ghandian Studies: tel. (11) 26985473; e-mail gandhiancentre.jamia@gmail.com; Dir Dr A. P. SEN.

Centre for Interdisciplinary Research in Basic Sciences: tel. (11) 26981717; e-mail faizan_ahmad@yahoo.com; Dir Prof. FAIZAN AHMAD.

Centre for Jawaharlal Nehru Studies: e-mail dir.cjns@jmi.ac.in; Dir Prof. SHAKTI KAK.

Centre for Management Studies: e-mail furqanq@sify.com; Dir Prof. FURQAN QAMAR.

Centre for Physiotherapy and Rehabilitation Sciences: Dir Dr M. EJAZ HUSSAIN.

Centre for the Study of Comparative Religions and Civilizations: internet www.studyreligion.in; Dir Prof. I. H. AZAD FAROOQUI.

Centre for Theoretical Physics: e-mail ctp@jamia-physics.net; internet www.jmi.nic.in/ctp; Dir Prof. M. SAMI.

Centre for West Asian Studies: f. 2004; Dir Dr RAJENDRA M. ABHIYANKAR.

Dr K. R. Narayanan Centre for Dalit and Minorities Studies: Dir Prof. M. M. KHAN.

Dr Zakir Husain Institute of Islamic Studies: f. 1971; Dir Prof. AKHTARUL WASEY.

Maulana Mohamed Ali 'Jauhar' Academy of Third World Studies: f. 1988; Dir Prof. MUSHIRUL HASAN.

Nelson Mandela Centre for Peace and Conflict Resolution: tel. (11) 26985473; e-mail centreforpeace@rediffmail.com; internet www.jamia4peace.org; f. 2004; Dir Prof. RADHA KUMAR.

Sarojini Naidu Centre for Women Studies: tel. (11) 26981270; e-mail sncwsjmi@yahoo.co.in; f. 2000; Dir Prof. JANAKI RAJAN.

JAWAHARLAL NEHRU AGRICULTURAL UNIVERSITY

PB 80, Krishnagar, Jabalpur 482004, Madhya Pradesh
Telephone: (761) 2681778
Fax: (761) 2681389
E-mail: registrar_jnkvv@yahoo.co.in
Internet: www.jnkvv.nic.in

Founded 1964
Languages of instruction: Hindi, English
Academic year: July to June
Chancellor: HE THE GOVERNOR OF MADHYA PRADESH
Vice-Chancellor: Dr GAUTAM KALLOO
Registrar: Dr S. S. TOMAR
Comptroller: G. S. KURVETI
Dean of Student Welfare: Dr P. K. BISEN (acting)

Library of 202,000 vols, incl. periodicals
Number of students: 2,282
Publication: *JNKVV Research Journal* (4 a year)

DEANS

Faculty of Agricultural Engineering: Dr G. S. RAJPUT (acting)
Faculty of Agriculture: Dr V. S. TOMAR
Faculty of Veterinary Science and Animal Husbandry: Dr K. S. JOHAR

DIRECTORS

Extension and Instruction: Dr J. S. RAGHU
Farms: Dr S. K. RAO
Research: Dr V. S. TOMAR

CONSTITUENT COLLEGES

College of Agricultural Engineering, Jabalpur: Dean Dr S. S. TOMAR.

College of Agriculture, Ganj Basoda: Dean (vacant).

College of Agriculture, Gwalior: Dean Dr H. S. KUSHWAHA.

College of Agriculture, Indore: Dean Dr S. L. NAIK (acting).

College of Agriculture, Jabalpur: Dean Dr G. S. RAJPUT (acting).

College of Agriculture, Khandwa: Dean Dr R. A. SHARMA (acting).

College of Agriculture, Rewa: Dean Dr R. P. SINGH (acting).

College of Agriculture, Sehore: Dean Dr S. K. SHRIVASTAVA (acting).

College of Agriculture, Tikamgarh: Dean Dr R. K. PATHAK (acting).

College of Horticulture, Mandsaur: Dean Dr B. S. BAGHEL (acting).

College of Veterinary Science and Animal Husbandry, Jabalpur: Dean Dr R. P. S. BAGHEL (acting).

College of Veterinary Science and Animal Husbandry, Mhow: Dean Dr N. K. DIXIT (acting).

College of Veterinary Science and Animal Husbandry, Rewa: Dean (vacant).

JAWAHARLAL NEHRU TECHNOLOGICAL UNIVERSITY

Kukatpally, Hyderabad 500072, Andhra Pradesh
Telephone: (40) 23158661
Fax: (40) 23156184
E-mail: info@jntu.ac.in
Internet: www.jntu.ac.in

Founded 1972
State control
Academic year: July to April
Chancellor: HE THE GOVERNOR OF ANDHRA PRADESH
Vice-Chancellor: Dr D. NARASIMHA REDDY
Rector: Dr K. LAL KISHORE
Dir of Academics and Planning: Dr G. TULASIRAM DAS
Registrar: Dr E. SAIBABA REDDY
Librarian: Prof. B. SATYANARAYANA

192 Affiliated Engineering colleges, 12 Pharmacy Colleges, 3 Architectural Colleges
Library of 48,000 books, 128 periodicals
Number of teachers: 457
Number of students: 34,000 (incl. affiliated colleges).

CONSTITUENT COLLEGES

College of Engineering, Anantapur: f. 1946; Principal Dr K. RAJAGOPAL.

College of Engineering, Hyderabad: f. 1965; Principal Dr N. V. RAMANA RAO.

College of Engineering, Kakinada: f. 1946; Principal Dr N. S. V. GHANDI.

College of Fine Arts, Hyderabad: tel. (40) 3314282; f. 1940; Principal Prof. Y. RAO.

ATTACHED INSTITUTES

Bureau of Industrial Consultancy and Research and Development (BICARD), Hyderabad: tel. (40) 23321007; Dir Dr H. S. RAO.

Institute of Science and Technology: tel. (40) 23058729; f. 1989.

Oil Technological Research Institute, Anantapur: f. 1949.

School of Continuing and Distance Education: tel. (40) 3318055; fax (40) 23372662; e-mail scdejntu@hd2.dot.net.in; f. 1976; Principal Dr A. V. BABU.

School of Planning and Architecture, Hyderabad: tel. (40) 23317006; e-mail dir_spa_jntu@yahoo.com; f. 1940; Dir Dr PADMAVATHI.

JAWAHARLAL NEHRU UNIVERSITY

New Mehrauli Rd, New Delhi 110067
Telephone: (11) 26742676
Fax: (11) 26742580
E-mail: webmaster@mail.jnu.ac.in
Internet: www.jnu.ac.in

Founded 1969
Central university
Academic year: July to May
Chancellor: Prof. YASH PAL
Vice-Chancellor: Prof. B. B. BHATTACHARYA
Rectors: Prof. R. PRASAD, Prof. R. KUMAR
Registrar: AVAIS AHMAD (acting)
Dean of Student Welfare: Prof. R. K. KALE (acting)
Librarian: Dr K. GOPAL (acting)

Library of 484,702 vols, 700 periodicals
Number of teachers: 371
Number of students: 3,843
Publications: *Hispanic Horizon* (2 a year), *International Studies* (4 a year), *Journal of School of Languages* (2 a year), *Studies in History* (2 a year)

DEANS

School of Arts and Aesthetics: Prof. H. S. SHIVAPRAKASH
School of Biotechnology: Prof. A. DIXIT
School of Computer and Systems Sciences: Prof. N. PARIMALA
School of Environmental Sciences: Prof. V. K. JAIN
School of Information Technology: Prof. A. BHATTACHARYA
School of International Studies: Prof. P. PANT
School of Language, Literature and Culture Studies: Prof. V. SINGH
School of Life Sciences: Prof. P. K. YADAVA
School of Physical Sciences: Prof. R. GHOSH
School of Social Sciences: Prof. H. SINGH

ATTACHED CENTRES

Centre for the Study of Law and Governance: tel. (11) 26704021; fax (11) 26717506; e-mail dir_cslg@mail.jnu.ac.in; internet www.jnu.ac.in/cslg; Dir Prof. AMITA SINGH.

Special Centre for Molecular Medicine: Dir Dr RAKESH TYAGI.

Special Centre for Sanskrit Studies: tel. (11) 26714128; f. 2001; Dir Prof. VARYAM SINGH.

JAYPEE UNIVERSITY OF INFORMATION TECHNOLOGY

Waknaghat, PO Dumehar Bani, Via-Kandaghat, Dist. Solan, 173215, Himachal Pradesh
Telephone: (1792) 257999
Fax: (1792) 245362

Internet: www.juit.ac.in
Founded 2002
Private control
Language of instruction: English
Academic year: July to June
Chancellor: HE THE GOV. OF HIMACHAL PRADESH
Pro-Chancellor: Dr MANOJ GAUR
Vice-Chancellor: Prof. Y. MEDURY
Registrar: Brig. (Retd) BALBIR SINGH
Dean: Prof. T. S. LAMBA
Registrar: Brig. BALBIR SINGH
Librarian: SHRI RAM
Library of 26,000 vols
Number of teachers: 101
Number of students: 1,829

Depts of bioinformatics and biotechnology, civil engineering, computer science and engineering, electronics and communication engineering, information technology, management studies, mathematics, pharmacy, physics, professional devt and humanities

PROFESSORS

BHOOSAN, S. V., Electronics and Communication Engineering
CHAUDHURI, P., Computer Science and Information Technology
CHAUHAN, R. S., Biotechnology and Bioinformatics
GHRERA, S. P., Computer Science and Information Technology
GUPTA, A. K., Biotechnology and Bioinformatics
KATYAL, S. C., Physics
KULSHRESHTHA, D. C., Electronics and Communication Engineering
SINGH, H., Mathematics
SINGH, K., Mathematics

CONSTITUENT INSTITUTES

Jaypee Institute of Engineering and Technology: A-B Rd, Guna 473226, Madhya Pradesh; tel. (7544) 267051; fax (7544) 267011; e-mail contact@jiet.ac.in; internet www.jiet.ac.in; Dir Prof. N. J. RAO; Dean of Academic Affairs Prof. K. K. JAIN; Registrar Brig. S. K. S. NEGI.

Jaypee Institute of Information Technology: A-10, Sector 62, Noida 201307, Uttar Pradesh; tel. (120) 2400980; e-mail jp .gupta@jiit.ac.in; internet www.jiit.ac.in/jiit; Vice-Chancellor Prof. J. P. GUPTA; Registrar Col V. KUMAR.

JIWAJI UNIVERSITY

Vidya Vihar, Gwalior 474011, Madhya Pradesh
Telephone: (751) 2341896
Fax: (751) 2341450
E-mail: info@idejug.org
Internet: www.jiwaji.edu
Founded 1964
Teaching and Affiliating
Languages of instruction: Hindi, English
Academic year: July to June
Chancellor: HE THE GOVERNOR OF MADHYA PRADESH
Vice-Chancellor: Prof. A. K. KAPOOR
Registrar: Dr D. S. CHANDEL
Librarian: J. N. GAUTAM
Library of 140,000 vols
Number of students: 47,358
Publications: *Humanities* (2 a year), *Science* (2 a year)

DEANS

Faculty of Arts: Dr H. C. GUPTA
Faculty of Commerce and Management: Dr D. C. SHARMA
Faculty of Life Science: (vacant)
Faculty of Physical Education: (vacant)

Faculty of Science: (vacant)
Faculty of Social Sciences: Dr P. L. SABLOOK
There are over 100 affiliated colleges

KACHCHH UNIVERSITY

Mundra Rd, Kachchh 370001, Gujarat
Telephone: (2832) 290245
Fax: (2832) 235012
E-mail: info@kskvkachchhuniversity.org
Internet: kskvku.digitaluniversity.ac
Founded 2003
Faculties of arts, commerce, education, law, science, technology; 28 affiliated colleges
Number of teachers: 200
Number of students: 15,000
Vice-Chancellor: Dr K. V. GOR
Registrar: A. H. GOR
Controller of Examinations: A. P. MEJTA.

KAKATIYA UNIVERSITY

Vidyaranyapuri, Warangal 506009
Telephone: (8712) 277687
Fax: (8712) 278935
E-mail: registrar@kakatiya.ac.in
Internet: www.kakatiya.ac.in
Founded 1976
Teaching and Affiliating
Languages of instruction: English, Telugu, Urdu
Chancellor: HE THE GOVERNOR OF ANDHRA PRADESH
Vice-Chancellor: Prof. N. LINGAMURTHY
Registrar: Prof. SATYANARAIN NALLANI
Controller of Examinations: Prof. T. P. REDDY
Dean of College Devt Council: Prof. T. B. RAO
Deputy Librarian: K. RAMANAIAH
Library of 104,000 vols
Number of teachers: 248
Number of students: 90,000
Publication: *Kakatiya Journal of English Studies and Vimarshini*

DEANS

Faculty of Arts: Prof. K. KATYAYANI
Faculty of Commerce and Business Management: Prof. T. JOGA CHARY
Faculty of Education: Prof. G. RAMESH
Faculty of Engineering: Prof. R. V. CHALAM
Faculty of Law: Justice L. N. REDDY
Faculty of Pharmaceutical Sciences: Prof. A. V. N. APPA RAO
Faculty of Science: Prof. G. R. RAO
Faculty of Social Sciences: Prof. N. VIJAYA

CONSTITUENT COLLEGES

Institute of Advanced Studies in Education: Principal Prof. C. SAMMAIAH.

School of Distance Learning and Continuing Education: tel. (870) 2438S77; fax (870)2438000; e-mail info@sdlceku.ac.in; internet www.sdlceku.ac.in; Dir Prof. K. VENKATANARAYANA.

University Arts and Science College, Warangal: Principal Prof. G. S. REDDY.

University College of Engineering: Principal Prof. SHOWRY.

University College, Warangal: Principal Prof. C. SAMMAIH.

University College of Law, Warangal: Principal Dr K. SUDHAKAR.

University College of Pharmaceutical Sciences, Warangal: Principal Dr M. SARANGAPANI.

University Postgraduate College, Godavarikhani: Principal Dr VENKARAM REDDY.

University Postgraduate College, Karimnagar: Principal Dr BHARATH.

University Postgraduate College, Khammam: Principal Prof. M. RAO.

University Postgraduate College, Nirmal: Principal Prof. N. RAMULU.

University Postgraduate College, Warangal: Principal Prof. M. RAO.

KALYANI UNIVERSITY

Kalyani 741235, Nadia, West Bengal
Telephone: (33) 25828690
Fax: (33) 25828282
E-mail: registrar@klyuniv.ac.in
Internet: www.klyuniv.ac.in
Founded 1960
Teaching and Research
Language of instruction: English
Academic year: June to May
Chancellor: HE THE GOVERNOR OF WEST BENGAL
Vice-Chancellor: Prof. ARABINDA KUMAR DAS
Controller of Examinations: Dr PRADIP PRASAD KARURI
Dean of Student Welfare: Dr ASIT KUMAR DAS
Registrar: UTPAL BATTACHARYYA
Librarian: Dr ASITABHA DAS
36 Affiliated colleges
Library of 128,790 vols, 116 periodicals
Number of teachers: 217
Number of students: 4,000

DEANS

Faculty of Arts and Commerce: Dr SUBHAS CHANDRA SARKAR
Faculty of Education: Prof. SUDARSHAN BHOWMICK
Faculty of Engineering, Technology and Management: Dr JYOTSNA KUMAR MANDAL
Faculty of Science: Prof. D. K. BHATTACHARYYA

PROFESSORS

Bengali (tel. (33) 25828220 ext. 233):
  BANERJEE, R.
  CHOUDHURI, D.
  GHATAK, K.
  GHATAK, K. S.
  SHAW, R.
Biophysics and Biochemistry (tel. (33) 25828750):
  BHATTACHARYYA, D. K.
  ROY, P. K.
Botany (tel. (33) 25825750 ext. 317):
  BHATTACHARYYA, S.
  BISWAS, A. K.
  CHAUDHURI, S.
  GHOSH, P. D.
  SEN, T.
Chemistry (tel. (33) 25828220 ext. 305):
  DEY, K.
  GUHA, A.
  LAHIRI, S. C.
  MAJUMDER, K. C.
  MAJUMDER, M. N.
  MUKHERJEE, J.
  SARKAR, A. R.
Commerce (tel. (33) 25828750):
  BHATTACHARYYA, P. K.
  KONAR, D. N.
  MAJHI, M. M.
Ecology:
  SANTRA, S. C.
Economics (tel. (33) 25828750):
  BHATTACHARYYA, R. N.
  DUTTA, M.
  GHOSH, B.
  PAL, D. P.
Education (tel. (33) 25828750):
  BASU, M. K.
English (tel. (33) 25828750):
  BHATTACHARYYA, D. P.
  CHAKRABORTY, B.

WORLD OF LEARNING

DAS, N.
DEB, P. K.
Folklore and History:
CHAKRABORTY, B. K.
Mathematics (tel. (33) 25828750):
BASU, M.
CHAKRABORTY, H.
DAS, A. G.
DEY, U. C.
KONAR, A.
MUKHERJEE, S.
SANYAL, D. C.
SENGUPTA, P. R.
Physical Education (tel. (33) 25820184 ext. 232):
BANERJEE, A. K.
BHOWMICK, S.
GHOSH, S. R.
Physics (tel. (33) 25820184):
BHATTACHARYYA, A. B.
BISWAS, S.
CHAUDHURI, S.
DASGUPTA, P.
DEB, S. K.
ROY, A. C.
ROY, S.
RUDRA, P.
Political Science:
MUKHOPADHYAY, A.
Sociology:
DASGUPTA, H.
DASGUPTA, S. K.
MANNA, S.
Statistics:
DAS, P.
MITRA, T. K.
PANDA, R. N.
Zoology (tel. (33) 25828750):
BHATTACHARYYA, D. K.
CHAKRABORTY, S.
DEY, N. C.
HALDER, D. P.
JANA, B. B.
KHUDA BAX, A. R.
KONAR, S. K.
KUNDU, S.
MANNA, C. K.
MUKHERJEE, D. K.
SAHU, C. R.

KAMESHWAR SINGH DARBHANGA SANSKRIT UNIVERSITY

Darbhanga, Bihar 846004
Telephone: (6272) 222178; (6272) 222217
E-mail: info@ksdsu.edu.in
Internet: www.ksdsu.edu.in
Founded 1961
Teaching and Affiliating
Autonomous control
Languages of instruction: Sanskrit, Hindi
Academic year: July to June
Chancellor: HE THE GOVERNOR OF BIHAR
Vice-Chancellor: Dr KULAND JHA
Registrar: KANHALYA JEE CHOUBEY
Librarian: J. MAHTO
Library of 100,000 vols, 15,000 periodicals, 10,000 MSS
Number of students: 515,000
Publication: *Vishwa Maneesha* (4 a year)

DEANS

Faculty of Darshan: R. S. JHA
Faculty of Jyotish: R. C. JHA
Faculty of Puran: (vacant)
Faculty of Samaj Shstra: K. MISHRA
Faculty of Veda: S. MISHRA
Faculty of Vyakaran: V. MISHRA
There are 38 constituent colleges and 37 affiliated colleges

KANNADA UNIVERSITY HAMPI

Vidyaranya, Hospet (Taluk) 583276, Karnataka
Telephone: (8394) 241337
Fax: (8394) 241334
E-mail: mail@kannadauniversity.org
Internet: www.kannadauniversity.org
Founded 1991
Unitary and residential; faculties of fine arts, languages, sciences and social sciences
Vice-Chancellor: Dr A. MURIGEPPA
Registrar: Dr S. S. PUJAR
Publications: *Budakattu Karnataka* (Tribal Karnataka), *Janapada Karnataka* (Folklore of Karnataka), *Journal of Karnataka Studies* (in English), *Kannada Adhyayana*, (Kannada Studies), *Mahila Adhyayana* (Women Studies), *Namma Kannada* (Kannada Linguistics)

DEANS

Fine Arts: Prof. S. C. PATIL
Languages: Prof. RAHAMATH TARIKERE
Social Sciences: Dr T. R. CHANDRASHEKAR

KANNUR UNIVERSITY

Kannur 670567, Kerala
Telephone: (497) 2782351
Fax: (497) 2782190
E-mail: registrar@kannuruniversity.ac.in
Internet: www.kannuruniversity.ac.in
Founded 1996
105 Affiliated colleges; campuses at Kasaragod, Mananthavady, Mangattuparamba, Nileshwaram, Thalassery, Payyannur
Vice-Chancellor: Dr P. K. MICHAEL THARAKAN
Pro-Vice-Chancellor: Dr A. P. KUTTYKRISHNAN
Registrar: K. M. ABDUR RASHEED
Controller of Examinations: Dr S. PRADEEP KUMAR
Finance Officer: SHAJEE JOSE
Public Relations Officer: ACHUTHANANDAN KUNIYIL
Library of 26,980 vols, 151 periodicals

DEANS

Faculty of Ayurveda: Dr V. P. SADHANANDAN
Faculty of Commerce and Management: Dr M. BHASI
Faculty of Communication: Dr SUJETHA NAIR
Faculty of Education: Dr M. S. LALITHAMMA
Faculty of Engineering: Dr V. GOPAKUMAR
Faculty of Humanities: Dr K. V. KUNHIKRISHNAN
Faculty of Languages and Literature: Dr T. B. VENUGOPALA PANICKER
Faculty of Law: Dr D. RAJEEV
Faculty of Modern Medicine: Dr K. BHASKARAN
Faculty of Science: Dr P. K. VIJAYAN
Faculty of Social Science: Prof. DAMODARAN NAMBOOTHIRI

KARNATAK UNIVERSITY

Dharwad 580003, Karnataka
Telephone: (836) 2215252
Fax: (836) 2747884
E-mail: webmaster@kud.ernet.in
Internet: www.kud.ernet.in
Founded 1949
Teaching and affiliating; postgraduate centres in Belgaum, Bijapur, Haveri, Karwar; 246 affiliated colleges
Language of instruction: English
Academic year: June to April
Chancellor: HE THE GOVERNOR OF KARNATAKA
Vice-Chancellor: Prof. S. K. SAIDAPUR
Registrar: V. RANGASWAMY
Librarian: Dr S. B. PATIL

Library of 350,000 vols
Number of teachers: 310 postgraduate, 5,556 in colleges
Number of students: 3,779 (postgraduate)
Publications: *Bharati Vidyarthi* (4 a year), *Humanities, Journal of the Karnataka University—Science, Social Sciences; Karnataka Bharati* (4 a year)

DEANS

Faculty of Arts: Dr M. S. MULLA
Faculty of Commerce: Dr H. Y. KAMBLE
Faculty of Education: Dr N. N. GANIHAR
Faculty of Law: Dr K. R. AITHAL
Faculty of Management: Dr A. H. CHACHADI
Faculty of Science and Technology: Dr B. P. WAGHMARE
Faculty of Social Sciences: Dr A. S. BALASUBRAMANYA

CONSTITUENT COLLEGES

Karnatak Arts College: Dharwad; f. 1917; Prin. Dr VEENA SHANTESHWAR.
Karnatak Science College: Dharwad; f. 1919; Prin. Dr B. G. NADAKATTI.
University College of Education: f. 1962; Prin. Dr R. T. JANTALI.
University College of Law: f. 1962; Prin. C. S. PATIL.
University College of Music and Fine Arts: f. 1975; Prin. H. A. KHAN.

KARNATAKA STATE OPEN UNIVERSITY

Manasagangotri, Mysore 570006, Karnataka
Telephone: (821) 2512471
Fax: (821) 2500846
E-mail: registrarksou@gmail.com
Internet: www.ksoumysore.com
Founded 1969 as Institute of Correspondence Course and Continuing Education, present name and status 1996
Academic year: August to June
Vice-Chancellor: Dr B. A. VIVEKA RAI
Registrar: K. R. JAYAPRAKASH RAO
Dean of Academic Affairs: Dr JAGADEESH
Dean of Study Centres: Dr M. SUSHEELA URS
Regional Dirs: D. SHIVANNA (Davanagere): Dr K. G. SURESH (Bangalore): Dr KAMBLE ASHOK (Gulbarga): G. V. CHANDRA SHEKAR (Dharwad): Prof. HOOVAJAH GOWDA (Shimoga)
Library of 80,000 vols
Number of teachers: 60
Number of students: 30,000

CHAIRS OF DEPARTMENTS

Commerce and Management: Prof. JAGADEESHA
Economics: S. SHIVANNA
Education: Dr N. LAKSHMI
English: Y. ALIJAZ AHMED
Hindi: B. G. CHANDRALEKHA
History: Dr G. RAMANATHAN
Kannada: D. T. BASAVARAJ
Management: Dr JAGADEESH
Political Science and Public Administration: S. M. SEETHAMMA
Sanskrit: Dr N. RADHAKRISHNA BHAT
Sociology: N. DODDASIDIAH
Tamil: M. TAMILMARAN
Telugu: Dr A. RAMANATHAM NAIDU
Urdu: BALQUEES BANU

KARNATAKA STATE WOMEN'S UNIVERSITY

City Campus, Station Rd, Nr Dr B. R. Ambedkar Circle, Bijapur 586101, Karnataka
Toravi Campus, Toravi, Athani Rd, Bijapur 586109, Karnataka
Telephone: (8352) 240030

Fax: (8352) 242795
E-mail: wu_bij@kar.nic.in
Internet: www.kswubij.ac.in
Languages of instruction: Kannada, English
Academic year: July to June

Founded 2003

Vice-Chancellor: Prof. GEETHA BALI
Registrar: S. A. KAZI
Librarian: P. G. TADASAD

Library of 56,746 vols, 240 periodicals
Number of teachers: 46
Number of students: 16,027

66 Affiliated colleges

DEANS

Faculty of Arts: Dr VIJAYASHREE SABARAD
Faculty of Commerce: Dr S. B. KAMASHETTY
Faculty of Education: Dr T. M. GEETHA
Faculty of Science and Technology: Dr SHAR-ANAPPA HALASE
Faculty of Social Sciences: Dr S. A. KAZI

KARUNYA UNIVERSITY

Karunya Nagar, Coimbatore 641114, Tamil Nadu
Telephone: (42) 22614301
Fax: (42) 22615615
E-mail: ku@karunya.edu
Internet: www.karunya.edu

Founded 1986, deemed univ. status 2004, univ. status 2006

Language of instruction: English

Schools of biotechnology and health sciences, civil eng., computer science and technology, electrical sciences, food sciences and technology, management, mechanical sciences, science and humanities; depts of personality devt, value education

Library of 71,407 vols, 41,214 periodical titles, 254 journals
Number of teachers: 461
Number of students: 7,217

Publication: *Karunya Journal of Research*

Vice-Chancellor: Dr PAUL P. APPASAMY
Registrar: Dr ANNE MARY FERNANDEZ
Librarian: Dr J. DOMINIC
Dean for Academic Affairs: Dr S. DARIUS GNANARAJ
Dean for Devt and Collaborations: Dr ANNE MARY FERNANDEZ
Dean for Postgraduates: Dr T. MICHAEL N. KUMAR
Dir for Placement and Training: ANDRE AROUME
Dir for Projects and Training: Dr C. T. DEVADAS
Dir for Students: Dr NINAN P. JOHN.

KAVIKULGURU KALIDAS SANSKRIT VISHWAVIDYALAYA

Baghele Bhavan, Mouda Rd, District Nagpur, Ramtek 441106, Maharashtra
Telephone: (7114) 255549
Fax: (7114) 255549
E-mail: admin@sanskrituni.net
Internet: sanskrituni.net

Founded 1997
Academic year: July to May

Chancellor: HE THE GOVERNOR OF MAHARASHTRA
Vice-Chancellor: Dr PANKAJ CHANDE
Registrar: HARSHIDA DAVE (acting)
Dean of Faculty: Dr N. J. PURI
Librarian: Dr HARSHIDA DAVE

Undergraduate and postgraduate courses in Sanskrit

49 Affiliated colleges

Number of teachers: 22
Number of students: 1,148

KERALA AGRICULTURAL UNIVERSITY

Vellanikkara 680656, Thrissur, Kerala
Telephone: (487) 2371619
Fax: (487) 2370019
E-mail: registrar@kau.in
Internet: www.kau.edu

Founded 1972
Language of instruction: English
Academic year: June to March

Chancellor: HE THE GOVERNOR OF KERALA
Vice-Chancellor: K. R. VISWAMBHARAN
Registrar: JOBI V. PAUL
Comptroller: P. V. DEVDAS
Dir of Academic and Postgraduate Studies: Dr D. ALEXANDER
Dir of Extension: Dr M. K. SHEELA
Dir of Research: Dr P. K. ASHOKAN
Dir of Student Welfare: Dr JOSE J. CHUNGATH
Librarian: K. P. SATHIAN (acting)

10 Constituent colleges, 6 regional agricultural research stations, 26 research stations

Library of 115,000 vols
Number of teachers: 823
Number of students: 2,445

Publications: *Journal of Tropical Agriculture* (2 a year), *Journal of Veterinary and Animal Science* (2 a year)

DEANS

Faculty of Agricultural Engineering: Dr V. GANESAN
Faculty of Agriculture: Dr K. HARIKRISHNAN NAIR
Faculty of Fisheries: Dr MOHANA KUMARAN NAIR
Faculty of Veterinary and Animal Sciences: Dr E. NANU

CONSTITUENT COLLEGES

College of Agriculture, Padannakkad: Kasaragod 671328; tel. (467) 2280616; internet www.kau.edu/coapadnnakkad.htm.
College of Agriculture, Vellayani: Thiruvananthapuram 695522; tel. (471) 2381002; e-mail deanagri@kau.in; (formerly affiliated to University of Kerala).
College of Cooperation, Banking and Management: Thrissur 680656; tel. (487) 2370367; e-mail ccbm@kau.in; f. 1981.
College of Dairy Science and Technology, Idukki: Mannuthy, Thrissur 680651; tel. (487) 2372861; e-mail cdst@kau.in; f. 1994.
College of Fisheries: Panangad, Ernakulam 682651; tel. (484) 2700337; e-mail cofpanangad@kau.in; f. 1979.
College of Forestry: Thrissur 680656; tel. (487) 2370050; e-mail adforestry@kau.in.
College of Horticulture: Thrissur 680656; tel. (487) 2370790; e-mail adhort@kau.in; f. 1972.
College of Veterinary and Animal Science, Thrissur: Mannuthy, Thrissur 680651; tel. (487) 2370451; e-mail vetmannuthy@kau.in; (formerly affiliated to University of Calicut).
College of Veterinary and Animal Science, Wayanad: Pookot, Wayanad 673576; tel. (4936) 256340; e-mail vetpookot@kau.in; f. 1999.
Kelappaji College of Agricultural Engineering and Technology: Tavanur, Malappuram 679573; tel. (494) 2686009; e-mail kcaet@kau.in.

KUMAUN UNIVERSITY

Nainital 263001, Uttar Pradesh
Telephone: (5942) 235068; (5942) 235576
Internet: www.kumaununiversity.org

Founded 1973
Teaching and Affiliating; 3 campuses (Almora, Bhimtal, Nainital), 28 affiliated colleges
Languages of instruction: Hindi, English
Academic year: July to June (two terms)

Chancellor: HE THE GOVERNOR OF UTTARAKHAND
Vice-Chancellor: Prof. C. P. BARTHWAL
Registrar: B. C. JOSHI
Finance Officer: B. BANGYAL
Librarian: Prof. C. C. PANT

Library of 90,000 vols
Number of teachers: 573
Number of students: 75,000

DEANS

Faculty of Arts: Prof. N. K. SHAH
Faculty of Commerce and Management: Prof. B. D. AWASTHI
Faculty of Education: Prof. A. BHARTI
Faculty of Law: Prof. S. D. SHARMA
Faculty of Science: Prof. K. PANDEY

PROFESSORS

Faculty of Arts:
BISHT, H. S., Geography
BISHT, L. S., Economics
BISHT, L. S., Hindi
DUBE, M. P., Political Science
GUPTA, R. K., Hindi
PANDE, G. C., Economics
PANDEY, D. C., Economics
PATHAK, S., History
POKHARIA, D. S., Hindi
RAWAT, A. S., History
RUWALI, K. D., Hindi
SAH, N. K., Economics
SAHAI, V., History
SINGH, O. P., Geography
TRIPATHI, D. R., Sanskrit

Faculty of Commerce and Management:
BISHT, N. S., Business Administration
RANA, N. S., Commerce
TIWARI, J. C., Commerce

Faculty of Education:
DURGAPAL, S.
JOSHI, J. K.
JUYAL, P. D.
SHUKLA, S. C.

Faculty of Science:
BHATT, S. D., Zoology
BISHT, C. S., Mathematics
BISHT, G., Chemistry
BISHT, M., Zoology
CHANDRA, M., Chemistry
CHANDRA, S., Botany
DHAMI, H. S., Mathematics
JOSHI, G. C., Botany
JOSHI, L., Chemistry
KAUSHAL, B. R., Zoology
KHAMI, K. S., Chemistry
KHETWAL, K. S., Chemistry
KUMAR, S., Geology
KUMAR, S., Zoology
LOHANI, A. B., Mathematics
MATHELA, C. S., Chemistry
MATHPAL, K. N., Chemistry
MEHROTRA, R. M., Chemistry
MEHTA, S. P. S., Chemistry
MELKANI, K. B., Chemistry
MISHRA, V. N., Chemistry
PANDEY, K., Physics
PANDEY, K. N., Botany
PANDEY, S. B., Mathematics
PANGETI, Y. P. S., Botany
PANT, C. C., Geology
PANT, D. N., Mathematics
PANT, M. C., Physics
PANT, R. P., Mathematics
PANT, T. C., Physics
SHAH, L., Zoology
SINGH, R. P., Forestry

SINGH, S. P., Botany
VARMA, K. R., Botany

KURUKSHETRA UNIVERSITY

Kurukshetra 136119, Haryana
Telephone: (1744) 238039
Fax: (1744) 238277
E-mail: kulib@kuk.ernet.in
Internet: www.kuk.ac.in

Founded 1956

Teaching and affiliating; 3 constituent colleges, 213 affiliated colleges
State control
Languages of instruction: English, Hindi
Academic year: July to June

Chancellor: HE THE GOVERNOR OF HARYANA
Vice-Chancellor: Dr D. D. S. SANDHU
Registrar: Dr NAFA SINGH
Dean of Academic Affairs: Dr GIRISH CHOPRA
Dean of Colleges: Dr D. D. ARORA
Dean of Students: Dr R. TANWAR
Dir of Public Relations: Dr BRIJESH SAWHNEY
Librarian: Dr M. S. JAGLAN

Library of 354,549 vols, 350 periodicals and online journals
Number of teachers: 390
Number of students: 5,584

Publications: *Jeevanti* (in Hindi), *Journal of Haryana Studies* (in English), *Kalanidhi* (magazine, in Hindi), *Kuru Jyoti* (in English, Sanskrit and Hindi), *Kurukshetra Law Journal* (in English), *Praci Jyoti* (in English), *Research Journal for Arts and Humanities* (in English and Hindi), *Sambhawana* (in Hindi)

DEANS

Faculty of Arts and Languages: Dr MADHU BALA
Faculty of Commerce and Management: Dr D. D. ARORA
Faculty of Education: Dr O. P. GAHLAWAT
Faculty of Engineering and Technology: Dr P. K. SURI
Faculty of Indic Studies: Dr BHIM SINGH
Faculty of Law: Dr VARSHA RAZDAN
Faculty of Life Sciences: Dr SHARDA RANI
Faculty of Science: Dr P. K. SURI
Faculty of Social Sciences: Dr R. TANWAR

PROFESSORS

Faculty of Arts and Languages (tel. (1744) 234374):

GUPTA, L. C., Hindi
KAANG, A. S., Punjabi
SHARMA, S. D., English

Faculty of Commerce and Management:

BANSAL, M. L., Commerce
BHARDWAJ, D. S., Tourism
DWIVEDI, R. S., Management
GUPTA, S. L., Management
HOODA, R. P., Commerce
JAIN, M. K., Management
MITTAL, R. K., Commerce
SHARMA, V. D., Management

Faculty of Education:

MALHOTRA, S. P.
MAVI, N. S.
YADAV, D. S.

Faculty of Indic Studies (tel. (1744) 238347):

KUSHWAHA, S. K., Fine Arts
SAXENA, MADU BALA, Music
SHARMA, INDU BALA, ISIS
SINGH, A., Sanskrit

Faculty of Law:

AGGARWAL, V. K.
KUMARI, D.
VARANDANI, G.

Faculty of Science (tel. (1744) 239235):

ANEJA, K. R., Microbiology

ARYA, S. P., Chemistry
ASTHANA, V. K., Geography
CHATURVEDI, D. K., Physics
CHOPRA, G., Zoology
GEORGE, P. J., Electronics Science
GUPTA, S. C., Chemistry
KAKKAR, L. R., Chemistry
KUMARI, S., Statistics
LUNKAD, S. K., Geology
MATTA, N. K., Botany
MEHTA, J. R., Chemistry
MITTAL, I. C., Zoology
MUKHERJEE, D., Botany
NAND, LAL, Earth Sciences
RANI, S., Botany
ROHTASH, C., Zoology
SHARMA, N. D., Physics
SHARMA, V. K., Geography
SINGH, H., Biochemistry
SURI, P. K., Computer Science
TREHAN, K., Botany
VINOD KUMAR, Mathematics

Faculty of Social Sciences:

KUNDU, T. R., Economics
KHURANA, G., History
PATHANIA, S., History
SHARMA, P. D., Political Science
SHARMA, R. K., History
SINGH, H., Public Administration
TANWAR, R., History
TUTEJA, K. L., History
UPADHYAYA, R. K., Social Work
VASHIST, B. K., Economics

KUVEMPU UNIVERSITY

Jnana Sahyadri, Shankaraghatta 577451, Shimoga District, Karnataka
Telephone: (8282) 256221
Fax: (8282) 256262
E-mail: reg_admn@kuvempu.ac.in
Internet: www.kuvempu.ac.in

Founded 1987

Academic year: August to April

Affiliating; 57 postgraduate depts in arts, commerce, education and law, science; 4 constituent colleges (Sahyadri Arts And Commerce College; Sahyadri Science College, Shimoga; B. D. T. College Of Engineering, Davangere; Fine Arts College, Davangere); 3 BEd. colleges, 6 Law colleges and 30 BEd colleges in Shimoga, Chitradurga, Chikmagalur, Davangere; outlying regional postgraduate centres at Davangere and Kadur; 97 affiliated colleges

Chancellor: RAMESHWAR THAKUR
Vice-Chancellor: Prof. B. S. SHERIGARA
Registrar: R. UDAY KUMAR
Dir of College Devt Council: Prof. M. KRISH-NAPPA
Dir of Student Welfare: Dr BASAVARAJ NELLI-SARA
Librarian: Dr K. C. RAMAKRISHNEGOWDA

Library of 70,000 vols, 4,124 vols of periodicals
Number of teachers: 93
Number of students: 950 (postgraduate)

DEANS

Faculty of Arts: Prof. J. S. SADANANDA
Faculty of Commerce: Prof. V. MURUGAIAH
Faculty of Education: Prof. S. M. PRAKASH
Faculty of Engineering: Prof. K. REVANASID-DAPPA
Faculty of Law: Prof. B. S. REDDY
Faculty of Medicine: Dr C. M. RAMESH
Faculty of Science and Technology: Prof. M. KRISHNAPPA

LALIT NARAYAN MITHILA UNIVERSITY

Kameshwarnagar, POB 13, Darbhanga 846004, Bihar
Telephone: (6272) 222463; (6272) 222598
E-mail: vclnmu@indiatimes.com
Internet: lnmu.bih.nic.in

Founded 1972

Teaching and Affiliating; 43 constituent colleges, 24 affiliated colleges
Languages of instruction: Hindi, English
Academic year: June to May

Chancellor: HE THE GOVERNOR OF BIHAR
Vice-Chancellor: Dr SAMARENDRA PRATAP SINGH
Pro-Vice-Chancellor: (vacant)
Registrar: Dr BIMAL KUMAR
Librarian: (vacant)

Library of 186,859 vols, 54 journals
Number of teachers: 1,251
Number of students: 110,355

DEANS

Faculty of Humanities: Dr K. D. JHA
Faculty of Commerce: Dr N. C. PRASAD
Faculty of Education: Dr N. K. SINGH
Faculty of Law: (vacant)
Faculty of Medicine: Dr CHITTRANJAN ROY
Faculty of Science: Prof. JAIKER JHA
Faculty of Social Science: Dr N. K. SINGH

PROFESSORS

JHA, B. N., Mathematics
JHA, S. M., Maithili
LALL, G., Commerce
PANDEY, S., Zoology
PATHAK, R. K., Hindi
PRASAD, A. B., Botany
RAHMAN, M., Urdu
ROY, B. K., History
THAKUR, B., Economics
THAKUR, R. N., Political Science
THAKUR, Y., Chemistry

MADHYA PRADESH BHOJ (OPEN) UNIVERSITY

Kolar Rd, Raja Bhoj Marg, Damkheda, Chunabhatti Bhopal 462016, Madhya Pradesh
Telephone: (755) 2424670
Fax: (755) 2424670
Internet: www.bhojvirtualuniversity.com

Founded 1992

Academic year: July to June

Vice-Chancellor: Prof. K. SINGH
Registrar: Dr P. N. JOSHI
Librarian: J. P. SONI

Library of 7,000 vols

DIRECTORS OF REGIONAL CENTRES

Bhopal: Dr S. DWIVEDI
Bilaspur: Dr S. L. KOKA
Durg: Dr R. CHOUBEY
Gwalior: Dr A. P. S. CHOUHAN
Indore: Dr V. D. VARSHNEY
Jabalpur: Dr K. K. TIWARI
Jagdalpur: Dr A. ALI
Raipur: Dr S. K. SINGH
Rewa: Dr S. S. PARIHAR
Sagar: Dr R. S. KASANA
Satna: Dr R. TIWARI

PROFESSORS

DHAKAD, S. K.
DUBEY, S. K.
GARDE, V. D.
GOEL, R. M.
GREWAL, J. S.
MISRA, R. D.
SAXENA, M. C.
SESHADRI, C. S.
TOMAR, S. K.

MADURAI-KAMARAJ UNIVERSITY

Palkalai Nagar, Madurai 625021, Tamil Nadu

Telephone: (452) 2459455
Fax: (452) 2459181
E-mail: registrar@mkuniversity.org
Internet: www.mkuniversity.org

Founded 1966

Teaching and Affiliating
Languages of instruction: English, Tamil
Academic year: June to April

Chancellor: HE THE GOVERNOR OF TAMIL NADU
Vice-Chancellor: Dr R. KARPAGA KUMARAVEL
Registrar: Dr I. SINGARAM
Controller of Examinations: Dr S. SHANMU-GIAH
Dean of College Devt Council: Dr S. D. AMIRTHA RAJAN
Dean of Curriculum Devt: Dr G. SUBRAMA-NIAN
Dean of Endowment and Devt: Dr P. M. AJMALKHAN
Dean of Research and Devt: Dr K. VELUTHAMBI
Academic Dean: Dr K. IYAKUTTI
Librarian: A. SRIMURUGAN

18 Schools comprising 73 depts; 109 affiliated colleges (9 autonomous), 7 evening colleges
Library of 300,000 vols, 500 periodicals
Number of teachers: 377 (excluding affiliated colleges)
Number of students: 133,100 (including affiliated colleges)
Publication: *Journal of Biology Education* (4 a year)

PROFESSORS

School of Biological Sciences (tel. (452) 2458471 ext. 369):

GUNASEKARAN, P., Genetics
KANDULA, S., Immunology
MARIMUTHU, G., Animal Behaviour and Physiology
MUNAVAR, H., Molecular Biology
PALIWAL, K., Plant Morphology and Algology
SELVAM, G. S., Biochemistry
SHANMUGASUNDARAM, S., Microbial Technology
SUDHAKARSAMY, P., Plant Sciences

School of Biotechnology (tel. (452) 2458471 ext. 384):

DHARMALINGAM, K., Genetic Engineering
KRISHNASWAMY, S., Bioinformatics
PALANIVELU, P., Molecular Microbiology
VELUTHAMBI, K., Plant Biotechnology

School of Business Studies (tel. (452) 2458471 ext. 359):

ALAGAPPAN, V., Commerce
CHANDRAN, C., Management Studies
CHINNIAH, V., Management Studies
PANDIAN, P., Commerce
RAMAMOORTHY, K., Commerce
RAVICHANDRAN, K., Management Studies
SEKAR, P. C., Management Studies
SURYA RAO, U., Management Studies

School of Chemistry (tel. (452) 2458471 ext. 347):

ATHAPPAN, P. R., Inorganic Chemistry
GANDHIDASAN, R., Natural Products Chemistry
MURUGESAN, R., Physical Chemistry
MUTHUSUBRAMANIAN, S., Organic Chemistry
PERUMAL, S., Organic Chemistry
PITCHUMANI, K., Natural Products Chemistry
RAJAGOPAL., S., Physical Chemistry
RAMACHANDRAN, M. S., Physical Chemistry
RAMARAJ, R., Physical Chemistry
RAMESH, P., Natural Products Chemistry
RAMU, A., Inorganic Chemistry
SIVAKOLUNTHU, S., Inorganic Chemistry
VAIDYANATHAN, S., Physical Chemistry

School of Earth and Atmospheric Sciences (tel. (452) 2458471 ext. 245):

ILANGOVAN, P., Environmental Remote Sensing and Cartography
KRISHNAN, N., Environmental Remote Sensing and Cartography
LAKSHMI, K., Geography
PARTHASARATHY, G. R., Geography
SANTHAKUMARI, A., Geography
SHANMUGANANDAN, S., Geography

School of Economics (tel. (452) 2458471 ext. 353):

DEIVAMANI, K., Human Resources Devt Economics
DHULASI BIRUNDHA, V., Agricultural Economics
HARIDOSS, R., Mathematical Economics
HARIHARAN, S. V., Mathematical Economics
MANONMONEY, N., Industrial Economics
MUTHULAKSHMI, R., Rural Devt Economics
SARASWATHI, N., Rural Devt Economics
VIJAYALAKSHMI, S., Econometrics

School of Education (tel. (452) 2458471 ext. 356):

KRISHNAN, K., Education

School of Energy Environment and Natural Resources (tel. (452) 2458471 ext. 365):

KUMARAGURU, A. K., Environment Studies
MAHADEVAN, A., Futures Studies
PAULRAJ, S., Solar Energy
SUNDARAM, A., Futures Studies

School of English and Foreign Languages (tel. (452) 2458471 ext. 361):

CHELLIAH, S., English and Comparative Literature
PARAMESWARI, D., English and Comparative Literature
SANKARAKUMAR, A., English and Comparative Literature

School of Historical Studies (tel. (452) 2458471 ext. 354):

CHANDRA BABU, B. S., Medieval History
DANIEL, D., Modern History
GOPALKRISHNAN, P. B., Modern History
JAYARAJ, K. V., Modern History
RAMASWAMY, T., Ancient History

School of Indian Languages (tel. (452) 2458471 ext. 362):

GIRIPRAKASH, T. S., Telugu and Comparative Literature
HARIKRISHNA BHAT, B., Kannada

School of Information and Communication Sciences (tel. (452) 2458471 ext. 364):

MANONMANI, T., Communication
SANTHA, A., Journalism and Science Communication

School of Mathematics (tel. (452) 2458471 ext. 339):

ARIVARIGNAN, G., Applied Mathematics & Statistics
BASKARAN, R., Mathematics
KARUNAKARAN, V., Mathematics

School of Performing Arts (tel. (452) 2458471 ext. 248):

AYYANAR, V., Art History, Aesthetics and Fine Arts
MUTHIAH, I., Folklore
SETHURAMAN, G., Art History, Aesthetics and Fine Arts

School of Physics (tel. (452) 2458471 ext. 352):

ARUMUGAM, G, Computer Science
IYAKUTTI, K., Microprocessor and Computer
NATARAJAN, S., Computer Science
NAVANEETHAKRISHNAN, K., Theoretical Physics
RAMACHANDRAN, K., Theoretical Physics
RAMAKRISHNAN, V., Microprocessor and Computer
UMAPATHY, S., Theoretical Physics

School of Religions, Philosophy and Humanist Thought (tel. (452) 2458471 ext. 342):

AJMALKHAN, P. M., Islam and Islamic Tamil Studies
ANDIAPPAN, S., Gandhian Studies and Ramalinga Philosophy
JEYAPRAGASAM, S., Gandhian Studies and Ramalinga Philosophy
MUTHUMOHAN, N., Gurunanak Studies

School of Social Sciences (tel. (452) 2458471 ext. 360):

KANNAN, R., Sociology
MADHANAGOPAL, R., Political Science
NALINI, B., Sociology
PERIAKARUPPAN, P., Political Science
SINGARAM, I., Sociology
THARA BHAI, L., Sociology

School of Tamil Studies (tel. (452) 2458471 ext. 347):

ATHITHAN, A., Linguistics
MANIVEL, M., Manuscriptology, Tamilology
MOHAN, N. R., Comparative Literature
SARADHAMBAL, C., Comparative Literature
SASIREHA, S., Literary Criticism
THIRUMALAI, M., Literary Criticism
VENKATARAMAN, S., Modern Literature

MAGADH UNIVERSITY

Bodh-Gaya 824234, Bihar

Telephone: (631) 2200490
Fax: (631) 2222717
Internet: magadhuniversity.ac.in

Founded 1962

Teaching and Affiliating
Languages of instruction: English, Hindi
Academic year: June to May

Chancellor: HE THE GOVERNOR OF BIHAR
Vice-Chancellor: Prof. B. N. PANDEY
Pro-Vice-Chancellor: (vacant)
Registrar: Dr D. K. YADAV (acting)
Finance Officer: S. SRIVASTAVA
Controller of Examinations: Dr R. SINGH
Librarian: Prof. S. KUMAR

44 Constituent colleges, 60 affiliated colleges
Library of 162,161 vols, 10 journals, 1,381 MSS
Number of teachers: 5,000
Number of students: 170,500

DEANS

Faculty of Commerce: Dr V. K. SINGH
Faculty of Engineering: Dr K. P. SINGH
Faculty of Humanities: Dr I. K. MASIH
Faculty of Law: Dr D. N. MISHRA
Faculty of Management: Dr M. MURARI
Faculty of Medicine: Dr M. S. KUMAR
Faculty of Science: Dr R. L. PRASAD
Faculty of Social Science and Education: Dr B. SINGH

PROFESSORS

AGRAWAL, B. N., Political Science
AGRAWAL, N. C., Commerce
AMBASHTHA, A. V., Commerce
GUPTA, L. N., Commerce
JHA, B. K., Political Science
LAL, B. K., Philosophy
MISHRA, C. N., Sanskrit
NATH, B., Philosophy
PRASAD, B. K., Philosophy
PRASAD, B. N., Mathematics
PRASAD, N., English
ROY, L. M., Economics
ROY, P., Hindi
SAHAI, S., Ancient Indian and Asian Studies
SHRIVASTAVA, J. P., Chemistry
SINGH, A. N., Physics
SINGH, B. K., Psychology

SINGH, B. P., Political Science
SINGH, G. P., Physics
SINGH, H. G., Economics
SINGH, J. P., English
SINGH, R. C. P., Ancient Indian and Asian Studies
SINGH, S., Mathematics
SINGH, S. B., Zoology
SINHA, D. P., Zoology
SINHA, H. P., Philosophy
SINHA, N. C. P., Psychology
SINHA, S. P., Economics
SINHA, V. N., Philosophy
THAKUR, U., Ancient Indian and Asian Studies
TIWARY, P., Mathematics
VERMA, B. B., Commerce
VISHESHWARAM, S., Mathematics

ATTACHED INSTITUTES

Mishra, L. N., Institute of Economic Development and Social Change: Hon. Dir Dr CHAKERDHAR SINGH.

Nava Nalanda Mehavihar: Nalanda; postgraduate teaching in Pali and research in Pali literature with special reference to Buddhism; Dir Dr U. THAKUR.

Rajendra Memorial Research Institute of Medical Science: postgraduate research in conjunction with the Faculty of Medicine; Dir Dr LALA SURAYNANDAN PRASAD.

Sri D. K. Jain Orient Research Institute: Arrah; postgraduate research in Prakrit, Jain philosophy and religion; Hon. Dir Dr RAJA RAM JAIN.

MAHARAJA SAYAJIRAO UNIVERSITY OF BARODA

Vadodara 390002, Gujarat
Telephone: (265) 2795521
Fax: (265) 2792277
E-mail: registrar@msubaroda.ac.in
Internet: www.msubaroda.ac.in

Founded 1949

Residential and Teaching
Language of instruction: English
Academic year: June to April (two terms)

Vice-Chancellor: Dr RAMESH K. GOYAL
Pro-Vice-Chancellor: Prof. SHARADCHANDRA M. JOSHI
Registrar: A. V. GUPTA
Librarian: (vacant)

Library of 404,043 vols
Number of teachers: 1,230
Number of students: 35,000

Publications: *Journal of Animal Morphology and Physiology, Journal of Education and Psychology, Journal of Oriental Institute, Journal of Technology and Engineering* (1 a year), *Pavo, Swadhyaya*

DEANS

Faculty of Arts: Prof. NITIN J. VYAS
Faculty of Commerce: (vacant)
Faculty of Education and Psychology: Prof. S. KUMAR
Faculty of Family and Community Sciences: Prof. P. MOHITE
Faculty of Fine Arts: Prof. D. H. KANNAL
Faculty of Journalism and Communication: (vacant)
Faculty of Law: (vacant)
Faculty of Management Studies: Prof. G. C. MAHESHWARI
Faculty of Medicine: (vacant)
Faculty of Performing Arts: (vacant)
Faculty of Science: (vacant)
Faculty of Social Work: Prof. A. KHASGIWALA
Faculty of Technology and Engineering: Prof. B. S. PAREKH

PROFESSORS

Faculty of Arts:
CHOODAWAT, P. S., Sociology
JUNEJA, O. P., English
KAR, P., English
MEHTA, S. Y., Gujarati
MOHITE, D. H., Political Science
PANDYA, N. M., Economics
PANTHAM, T., Political Science
PAREKH, V. S., Archaeology
PATEL, K. H., Environmental Archaeology
PATEL, P. J., Sociology
REDE, L. A., Economics
SHAH, M. N., Economics
SIDDIQI, M. H., Persian
SONAWANE, V. H., Archaeology

Faculty of Commerce:
BHATT, A. S., Commerce and Business Administration
MOHITE, M. D., Cooperation
PANCHOLI, P. R., Business Economics
PATEL, B. S., Commerce and Business Administration
SANDHE, A. G., Commerce and Business Administration
SHAH, K. R., Economics
SINGH, S. K., Business Economics
SYAN, J. K., Banking and Business Finance
VYAS, I. P., Commerce and Business Administration

Faculty of Education and Psychology:
GOEL, D., Education
JOSHI, S. M., Educational Administration
YADAV, M. S., Education

Faculty of Fine Arts:
PANCHAL, R. R., Sculpture
PATEL, V. S., Graphic Arts

Faculty of Home Science:
BALKRISHNAIH, B., Clothing and Textiles
MANI, U. V., Foods and Nutrition
SARASWATI, T. S., Human Development and Family Studies
SHAH, A., Home Science Extension and Communication

Faculty of Law:
PARIKH, S. N., Law
RATHOD, J. C., Law

Faculty of Management Studies:
DADI, M. M., Management
DHOLAKIA, M. N., Management
JOSHI, K. M., Management
MAHESHWARI, G. C., Management

Faculty of Medicine:
BHOTI, S. J., Ophthalmology
BONDRE, K. V., Anatomy
BUCH, V. P., Radiology
CHANDWANI, S., Physiology
CHAUHAN, L. M., Obstetrics and Gynaecology
DESAI, M. R., Obstetrics and Gynaecology
GHOSH, S., Biochemistry
HATHI, G., Physiology
HEMAVATI, K. G., Pharmacology
JHALA, D. R., Paediatrics
JOSHI, G. D., Preventative and Social Medicine
KARELIA, L. S., Pathology
MAZUMDAR, U., Dentistry
MEHTA, J. P., Surgery
MEHTA, N. C., Medicine
PATHAK, K., Medicine
PATRA, B. S., Surgery
PATRA, S. B., Pathology
RAWAL, H. H., Anaesthesia
SAINATH, M., Ophthalmology
SANGHVI, N. G., Medicine
SAXENA, S. B., Microbiology
SHAH, A. U., Preventative and Social Medicine
SHAH, D. N., Preventative and Social Medicine
SHAK, K. D., Surgery

SHARMA, S. N., Plastic Surgery
SHETH, R. T., Ophthalmology
SHUKLA, G. N., Surgery
TIWARI, R. S., Ear, Nose and Throat
VAISHNAVI, A. J., Orthopaedics
VANKAR, G. K., Psychiatry
VOHRA, P. A., Radiology
VYAS, D. C., Anatomy

Faculty of Performing Arts:
BHONSLE, D. K., Vocal Music
SHAH, P., Dance

Faculty of Science:
AMBADKAR, P. M., Zoology
BHATTACHARYA, P. K., Chemistry
CHATTOO, B., Microbiology
CHHATPAR, H. S., Microbiology
DESAI, N. D., Geology
DESAI, S. J., Geology
DEVI, S. G., Chemistry
GOYAL, O. P., Mathematics
KATYARE, S. S., Biochemistry
MEHTA, T., Biochemistry
PADH, H., Biochemistry
PAREKH, L. J., Biochemistry
PATEL, H. C., Statistics
PATEL, M. P., Geology
PATEL, N. V., Mathematics
PILO, B., Zoology
RAKSHIT, A. K., Chemistry
RAMCHANDRAN, A. V., Zoology
RANGASWAMY, V. C., Geography
RAO, K. K., Microbiology
SHAH, A. C., Chemistry
SHREEHARI, M., Statistics
SOMAYAJULU, D. R. S., Physics
TELANG, S. D., Biochemistry

Faculty of Social Work:
ANJARIA, V. N., Social Work
NAVALE, A. S., Social Work
SAXENA, S. B., Social Work

Faculty of Technology and Engineering:
AGRAWAL, S. K., Metallurgical Engineering
AGRAWAL, S. R., Applied Mathematics
BALARAMAN, R., Pharmacy
BANGLORE, V. A., Textile Engineering
BASA, D. K., Metallurgical Engineering
BHAGIA, R. M., Applied Mechanics
BHATT, G. D., Mechanical Engineering
BHATT, R. D., Civil Engineering
BHAVNANI, H. V., Civil Engineering
BHAVSAR, N., Electrical Engineering
BIYANI, K. R., Applied Mechanics
CHUDASAMA, U. V., Applied Chemistry
DE, D. K., Textile Engineering
DESAI, P. B., Mechanical Engineering
DESHPANDE, S. V., Architecture
DIVEKAR, M. H., Chemical Engineering
ETHIRAJULU, K., Chemical Engineering
GADGEEL, V. I., Metallurgical Engineering
GOROOR, S. P., Water Management
GUHA, S., Textile Chemistry
GUPTE, S. G., Electrical Engineering
JOSHI, S. M., Electrical Engineering
JOSHI, T. R., Applied Physics
KANITKAR, S. A., Electrical Engineering
KAPADIA, V. H., Textile Engineering
LOIWAL, A. S., Mechanical Engineering
MISHRA, A. N. R., Pharmacy
MISHRA, S. H., Pharmacy
MODI, P. M., Water Management
MOINUDDIN, S., Chemical Engineering
MORTHY, R. S. R., Pharmacy
NANAVATI, J. I., Mechanical Engineering
PAI, K. B., Metallurgical Engineering
PAREKH, B. S., Computer Science
PARMAR, N. B., Civil Engineering
PATEL, A. A., Mechanical Engineering
PATEL, B. A., Electrical Engineering
PATEL, H. J., Computer Science
PATEL, N. M., Applied Mechanics
PATHAK, V. D., Applied Mathematics
PATODI, S. C., Applied Mechanics
POTBHARE, V. N., Applied Physics
PRAJAPATI, J. J., Civil Engineering

PURANIK, S. A., Chemical Engineering
PUTHANPURAYIL, P., Mechanical Engineering
RAJPUT, H. G., Training and Placement
SAVANI, A. K., Civil Engineering
SHAH, A. N., Civil Engineering
SHAH, D. L., Applied Mechanics
SHAH, S. G., Electrical Engineering
SHROFF, A. V., Applied Mechanics
SUBRAMANYAM, N., Chemical Engineering
SUKLA, H. J., Mechanical Engineering
SUNDAR MORTI, N. S., Metallurgical Engineering
SUTARIA, P. N., Civil Engineering
THAKUR, S. A., Electrical Engineering
TRIVEDI, A. I., Electrical Engineering
VASDEV, S., Chemical Engineering
VORA, R. A., Applied Chemistry
VYAS, J. K., Applied Mechanics
YADAV, R., Pharmacy

Centre for Continuing and Adult Education and Community Services:
PARALIKAR, K. R.

Oriental Institute:
NANAVATI, R. I.
WADEKAR, M. L.

CONSTITUENT COLLEGES

Baroda Sanskrit Mahavidyalaya: Vadodara; f. 1915; Prin. Y. B. OAZ.

Manibhai Kashibai Amin Arts and Science College and College of Commerce: Padra; f. 1965; Prin. G. S. PATEL.

Oriental Institute: tel. (265) 2425121; e-mail mlwadekar@hotmail.com; Dir Prof. M. L. WADEKAR.

Polytechnic: Vadodara; f. 1957; Prin. K. S. AGRAWAL.

ATTACHED CENTRE

Women's Studies Research Centre: tel. (265) 2792106; Dir Dr P. D. MUKHERJEE.

MAHARANA PRATAP UNIVERSITY OF AGRICULTURE AND TECHNOLOGY

Udaipur 313001, Rajasthan
Telephone: (294) 2471101
Fax: (294) 2470682
E-mail: vc@mpuat.ac.in
Internet: mpuat.digitaluniversity.ac.in
Founded 1999
Chancellor: HE THE GOVERNOR OF RAJASTHAN
Vice-Chancellor: Dr PRATAP NARAIN
Registrar: ASHOK YADAV
Dir of Extension Education: Dr P. M. JAIN
Dir of Research: Dr P. SINGH
Controller of Examinations: Dr S. C. BHANDARI
Librarian: Dr R. SWAMINATHAN
Library of 144,354 vols, 252 journals

DEANS

Rajasthan College of Agriculture: Dr V. N. JOSHI
College of Dairy and Food Science Technology: Dr N. S. RATHORE
College of Fisheries: Dr V. N. JOSHI
College of Home Science: Dr M. CHOUDHARY
College of Horticulture and Forestry (Jhalawar): Dr S. K. SHARMA
College of Technology and Engineering: Dr V. KUMAR

ATTACHED RESEARCH INSTITUTE

Land and Water Management Research Institute: Dir Dr RAJVEER SINGH.

MAHARASHTRA ANIMAL AND FISHERY SCIENCES UNIVERSITY

Seminary Hills, Nagpur 440006, Maharashtra
Telephone: (712) 2511784
Fax: (712) 2511282
E-mail: mafsudet@yahoo.co.in
Internet: www.mafsu.in
Founded 2000
Chancellor: HE THE GOV. OF MAHARASHTRA
Pro-Chancellor: MIN. FOR ANIMAL HUSBANDRY DAIRY DEVT AND FISHERY DEVT, MAHARASHTRA STATE
Vice-Chancellor: Dr A. S. NINAWE
Dir of Extension and Training: Dr S. Z. ALI
Dir of Instructions: Dr S. H. NARAYANKHEDKAR
Dir of Research and Registrar: Dr R. L. DHOBLE
Univ. Librarian: S. N. GAWANDE

DEANS

Faculty of Dairy Technology: Dr D. N. BAJAD
Faculty of Fishery Science: Dr D. R. KALORE
Faculty of Veterinary Science: Dr S. G. NARAYANKHEDKAR
Lower Education: Dr D. B. SARODE

CONSTITUENT COLLEGES

Bombay Veterinary College: Parel, Mumbai 400012; tel. (22) 24130162; fax (22) 24172301; e-mail vetsamad@yahoo.com; f. 1886; Dean Dr A. SAMAD.

College of Dairy Technology: Udgir, Dist. Latur 413517; tel. (2385) 257448; fax (2385) 2563506; e-mail cdkhedkar@gmail.com; f. 2008; Dean Dr C. D. KHEDKAR.

College of Dairy Technology: Warud (Pusat), Dist. Yavatmal 445204; tel. (7233) 247269; fax (7233) 247268; e-mail dtc@mafsu.in; f. 1992; Dean Dr D. N. BAJAD.

College of Fishery Science: Nagpur 440006; tel. and fax (712) 2567192; e-mail dewanandkalorey@rediffmail.com; f. 2007; Dean Dr D. R. KALORE.

College of Fishery Science: Udgir , Dist. Latur 413517; tel. (2385) 256672; fax (2385) 256690; e-mail adfish.udgir@gmail.com; f. 2006; Dean Dr B. R. KHARATMOL.

College of Veterinary and Animal Sciences, Parbhani: Parbhani 431402; tel. (2452) 220044; fax (2452) 226188; e-mail bhosle_ns@rediffmail.com; f. 1972; Dean Dr N. S. BHONSLE.

College of Veterinary and Animal Sciences, Udgir: Udgir, Dist. Latur 413517; tel. (2385) 257448; fax (2385) 2563506; e-mail udgirvet@yahoo.com; f. 1987; Dean Dr R. C. TAKARKHEDE.

Krantisinh Nana Patil College of Veterinary Science: Satara Dist., Shirval 412801; tel. (2169) 244227; fax (2169) 244243; e-mail deanknpvet@yahoo.co.in; f. 1988; Dean Dr A. G. KHARPE.

Nagpur Veterinary College: Seminary Hills, Nagpur 440006; tel. (712) 2511259; fax (712) 2510883; e-mail dean_nvc1@rediffmail.com; f. 1958; Dean Dr C. R. JANGDE.

Postgraduate Institute of Veterinary and Animal Sciences, Akola: Murtizapur Rd, Akola 444104; tel. (724) 2258643; fax (724) 2258644; e-mail drvhkalbande@rediffmail.com; f. 1970; Dean Dr V. H. KALBANDE.

MAHARASHTRA UNIVERSITY OF HEALTH SCIENCES

Vani-Dindori Rd, Mhasrul, Nashik 422004, Maharashtra
Telephone: (253) 2539292
Fax: (253) 2539295
E-mail: registrar@muhsnashik.com
Internet: www.muhsnashik.com
Founded 1998
Academic year: June to May
Faculties of allied health sciences, ayurveda, dentistry, homeopathy and medicine; 297 affiliated colleges
Chancellor: HE THE GOV. OF MAHARASHTRA
Vice-Chancellor: Dr NILIMA A. KSHIRSAGAR (acting)
Registrar: Dr SUNIL H. FUGARE

DEANS

Allied Health Sciences Faculty: Dr RESHMA DESAI
Ayurveda Faculty: Dr S. G. DESHMUKH
Dental Faculty: Dr M. G. PAWAR
Homeopathy Faculty: Dr A. N. BHASME
Medical Faculty: Dr S. D. DALVI

MAHARISHI MAHESH YOGI VEDIC VISHWAVIDYALAYA

Karaundi, Sihora, Paan Umariya, Katni 483332, Madhya Pradesh
Telephone: (7625) 280134
Fax: (761) 4007123
E-mail: mmyvv@mahaemail.com
Internet: www.mmyvv.com/mmyvv-e
Founded 1995
Academic year: July to June
Vice-Chancellor: Prof. BHUVNESH SHARMA
Registrar: ARVIND SINGH RAJPUT.

MAHARSHI DAYANAND SARASWATI UNIVERSITY

Ajmer 305001, Rajasthan
Telephone: (145) 2787055
Fax: (145) 2787049
Internet: www.mdsuajmer.com
Founded 1987 as Ajmer University; present name c. 1992
Vice-Chancellor: Prof. BHAGIRATH SINGH
Registrar: B. L. SUNARIA
There are 89 affiliated colleges

DEANS

Faculty of Commerce: Dr SHER SINGH DOCHANIYA
Faculty of Education: Dr V. G. JADHAV
Faculty of Fine Arts: Dr S. S. CHUG
Faculty of Law: MADAN LAL PEETLIYA
Faculty of Management Studies: Prof. MANOJ KUMAR
Faculty of Science: Dr SARVESH PALRIA
Faculty of Social Science: Dr R. P. JOSHI

PROFESSORS

BHARDWAJ, T. N., Botany
DUBE, S. N., Mathematics
JOSHI, R. P., Political Science
VASHISHTHA, V. K., History

MAHARSHI DAYANAND UNIVERSITY, ROHTAK

Rohtak 124001, Haryana
Telephone: (1262) 274327
Fax: (1262) 294133
E-mail: mduniversity@yahoomail.com
Internet: www.mdurohtak.com
Founded 1976
Languages of instruction: English, Hindi
Academic year: July to June
Chancellor: HE THE GOV. OF HARYANA
Vice-Chancellor: Prof. R. P. HOODA
Registrar: Dr S. P. VATS
Dean of College Devt Ccl: Prof. DALEEP SINGH
Dean of Student Welfare: Prof. RAJBIR SINGH
Dir of Distance Education: Prof. NARENDER KUMAR

Librarian: Dr PREM SINGH
Library of 325,292 vols, 400 periodicals
Number of teachers: 350
Number of students: 223,585
Publication: *Maharishi Dayanand University
Rohtak Research Journal (Arts)* (2 a year)

DEANS

Faculty of Commerce: Prof. Dr M. S. MALIK
Faculty of Education: Prof. Dr INDIRA DHULL
Faculty of Engineering and Technology: Prof.
S. P. KHATKAR
Faculty of Humanities: Prof. B. S. MEHRA
Faculty of Law: Prof. K. P. S. MAHALWAR
Faculty of Life Sciences: Prof. Dr S. N.
MISHRA
Faculty of Management Sciences: Prof. H. J.
GOSH ROY
Faculty of Performing and Visual Arts: Prof.
Dr BHARTI SHARMA
Faculty of Pharmaceutical Sciences: Prof.
ARUN NANDA
Faculty of Physical Sciences: Prof. ASHOK
KUMAR
Faculty of Social Sciences: Prof. Dr K. S.
SANGWAN

MAINTAINED INSTITUTE

Institute of Law and Management Studies, Gurgaon: tel. (124) 2580098; fax (124) 2383343; e-mail ilmsmdu@gmail.com; f. 2002; Dir Dr R. K. SABHARWAL, Law Programmes: Dr POONAM DATTA, Management Programmes.

MAHATAMA GANDHI ANTARRASHTRIYA HINDI VISHWAVIDYALAYA

Post Manas Mandir, Gandhi Hill, Wardha
442001, Maharashtra
Telephone: (7152) 230907
Fax: (7152) 230903
E-mail: info@hindivishwa.org
Internet: www.hindivishwa.org
Founded 1997
Academic year: July to May
Vice-Chancellor: Prof. VIBHUTI NARAIN RAI
Pro-Vice-Chancellor: Prof. NADEEM HASNAIN
Registrar: Dr K. G. KHAMARE
Finance Officer: M. S. KHAN

Publications: *Bahuvachan* (in Hindi, 4 a year), *Hindi: Language, Discourse, Writing* (in English, 4 a year), *Hindi Vishwa Samachar* (in Hindi, house journal), *Pustak Varta* (in Hindi, 24 a year)

DEANS

School of Culture: Prof. MANOJ KUMAR
School of Language: Prof. UMASHANKAR UPADHYAY
School of Literature: Prof. SURAJ PALIWAL
School of Translation and Interpretation:
Prof. A. P. SRIVASTAVA

CENTRES

Adult Continuing Education Extension and Field Outreach Centre: tel. (7151) 242812; e-mail klvp_k@yahoo.com; Dir Prof. K. VASWANI (acting).

Dr Babasaheb Ambedkar Dalit and Tribal Studies Centre: Dir Prof. L. KARUNYAKARA.

Distance Education Centre: Dir Prof. NADEEM HASNAIN.

Indian and Foreign Language Advanced Studies Centre.

Dr Bhadant Anand Kausalyayan, Buddhist Studies Centre: Dir M. L. KASARE.

Technology Studies Centre: e-mail mahendra@hindivishwa.org; Dean Prof. MAHENDRA KUMAR PANDEY.

Mahatma Gandhi Fuiji Guru Ji Peace Studies Centre: Dir Dr MANOJ KUMAR.

MAHATMA GANDHI CHITRAKOOT GRAMODAYA VISHWAVIDYALAYA

District Satna, Chitrakoot 485331, Madhya
Pradesh
Telephone: (7670) 265413
Fax: (7670) 265411
E-mail: mgcgv@rediffmail.com
Internet: www.ruraluniversity-chitrakoot
.org
Founded 1991
Academic year: July to June
Vice-Chancellor: Prof. G. SINGH
Registrar: Dr R. S. TRIPATHI
Librarian: Dr R. P. BAJPAL
Library of 32,644 vols, 54 journals

DEANS

Faculty of Agriculture and Animal Sciences:
Dr A. K. GUPTA
Faculty of Ayurveda: E. A. UPADHYAY
Faculty of Commerce: Dr Y. UPADHYAY
Faculty of Education: Dr S. R. S. SENGAR
Faculty of Fine Arts: Prof. K. D. MISHRA
Faculty of Humanities and Social Sciences:
Dr A. VERMA
Faculty of Rural Reconstruction: Dr R. C.
SINGH
Faculty of Science: Dr R. C. TRIPATHI

MAHATMA GANDHI KASHI VIDYAPEETH

Varanasi 221002, Uttar Pradesh
Telephone: (542) 2222689
Fax: (542) 2221268
E-mail: support@mgkvp.ac.in
Internet: www.mgkvp.ac.in
Chancellor: HE THE GOVERNOR OF UTTAR
PRADESH
Vice-Chancellor: NITIM RAMESH GOKARN
Registrar: BALJI YADAV
Finance Officer: Prof. NAND LAL
Controller of Examinations: PRABHAT RANJAN
Dean of Student Welfare: Dr K. PANDEY

DEANS

Faculty of Commerce and Management: Prof.
M. D. SHUKLA
Faculty of Education: Prof. M. K. DAS
Faculty of Humanities: Prof. R. K. RAI
Faculty of Law: Dr S. C. SINGH
Faculty of Medical Sciences: Dr P. N. DWIVEDI
Faculty of Science and Technology: Prof.
SATYA SINGH
Faculty of Social Sciences: Prof. O. P.
SRIVASTAVA
Faculty of Social Work: Prof. A. S. I. SHASTRI
Mahamana Madan Mohan Malviya Institute
of Hindi Journalism: Prof. O. P. SINGH

MAHATMA GANDHI UNIVERSITY

Priyadarshini Hills PO, Kottayam 686560,
Kerala
Telephone: (481) 2731050
Fax: (481) 2731009
E-mail: mgu@md2.vsnl.net.in
Internet: www.mguniversity.edu
Founded 1983 as Gandhiji Univ.
State control
Language of instruction: English
Academic year: June to March

21 Univ. depts, 27 engineering colleges, 1 law college, 4 medical colleges, 22 nursing colleges, 8 sme nursing insts, 3 centres of school of technology and applied sciences, 5 pharmacy colleges, 7 dental colleges, 3 ayurveda colleges, 2 homeopathic colleges, 3 allied medical education colleges, 1 music and fine

arts college; 127 affiliated arts and science colleges, 43 education training colleges and 12 univ. colleges of teacher education; 76 off-campus centres—62 centres within Kerala, 7 outside Kerala and 7 abroad; 10 interdisciplinary schools of teaching and research, 12 schools of higher learning in applied science and professional studies, with academic autonomy; 245 affiliating colleges of which 163 are in the unaided stream; central library and 21 deptl libraries
Chancellor: HE THE GOV. OF KERALA
Vice-Chancellor: Prof. Dr RAJAN GURUKKAL
Pro-Vice-Chancellor: Prof. Dr RAJAN VARUGHESE
Registrar: Prof. M. R. UNNI
Controller of Examinations: Dr THOMAS JOHN
MAMPRA
Finance Officer: ABRAHAM J. PUTHUMANA
Dir of College Devt Council: Dr B. THOMAS
Public Relations Officer: G. SREEKUMAR
Librarian: Dr R. R. NAIR

Library: 2,500 online nat. and int. journals
Number of teachers: 5,000
Number of students: 150,000

DEANS

Medical College: Dr J. JACOB K.
School of Behavioural Sciences: Dr R. PADMAM
School of Chemical Sciences: Dr M. PADMANABHAN,
School of Environmental Sciences: Dr A. P.
THOMAS
School of Gandhian Thought and Devt Studies: Dr M. MAHARAJAN
School of Indian Legal Thought: Prof. Dr K.
VIKRAMAN NAIR
School of Letters: Dr V. C. HARRIS
School of Management and Business Studies:
Dr K. SREERANGANATHAN
School of Medical Education: Prof. K. M.
MARIAM
School of Pedagogical Sciences: Prof. Dr P. J.
JACOB
School of Pure and Applied Physics: Dr C.
VENUGOPAL

MAHATMA JYOTIBA PHULE ROHILKHAND UNIVERSITY

Pilibhit by-pass Rd, Bareilly 243006, Uttar
Pradesh
Telephone: (581) 2527263
Fax: (581) 2523334
Internet: mjpru.ac.in
Founded 1975 as Rohilkhand Univ., present
name 1997
State control
Languages of instruction: Hindi, English
Academic year: July to June
130 Affiliated colleges
Chancellor: HE THE GOVERNOR OF UTTAR
PRADESH
Vice-Chancellor: Prof. SATYA P. GAUTAM
Registrar: B. K. PANDEY
Finance Officer: VIMAL PRAKASH SRIVASTAVA
Librarian: Prof. A. K. SINHA

Library of 27,000 vols, 140 periodicals
Number of teachers: 1,062
Number of students: 65,000

DEANS

Faculty of Advanced Social Sciences: Prof. R.
P. YADAV
Faculty of Agriculture: Dr P. VEER
Faculty of Applied Science: Prof. A. K. JAITLY
Faculty of Arts: Dr S. SHARMA
Faculty of Commerce: Dr B. N. CHAURASIA
Faculty of Dental Sciences: (vacant)
Faculty of Education: Dr B. R. GUPTA
Faculty of Engineering and Technology: Prof.
A. K. GUPTA
Faculty of Law: Dr S. K. SINGH

Faculty of Management: Prof. A. K. SARKAR
Faculty of Sciences: Prof. Y. K. GUPTA

MAHATMA PHULE KRISHI VIDYAPEETH

Rahuri, Ahmednagar Dist. 413722, Maharashtra
Internet: mpkv.mah.nic.in
Founded 1968
Academic year: July to May
Chancellor: HE THE GOVERNOR OF MAHARASHTRA
Pro-Chancellor: THE MINISTER FOR AGRICULTURE
Vice-Chancellor: Dr R. B. DESHMUKH
Registrar: BABASAHEB R. PARDHE
Librarian: A. G. KARANDE
Library of 62,864 vols
Number of students: 2,200
Publications: *Journal of Maharashtra Agricultural University* (in English, 3 a year), *Shi Suga* (in Marathi, 3 a year)

DEANS

Faculty of Agricultural Engineering: Prof. R. K. PARKALE
Faculty of Agriculture: Dr S. S. KADAM

CONSTITUENT COLLEGES

College of Agricultural Engineering, Rahuri: f. 1969; Assoc. Dean Prof. G. B. BANGAL.

College of Agriculture, Dhule: f. 1960; Assoc. Dean Dr Y. M. SHINDE.

College of Agriculture, Kolhapur: f. 1963; Assoc. Dean Prof. S. T. KANJALE.

College of Agriculture, Pune: f. 1906; library of 37,838 vols, 50 periodicals; Assoc. Dean Dr V. M. PAWAR.

Postgraduate Agricultural Institute, Rahuri: f. 1972; library of 80,000 vols; Assoc. Dean Dr S. S. KADAM.

MAKHANLAL CHATURVEDI RASHTRIYA PATRAKARITA VISHWAVIDYALAYA

POB RSN/560, Trilochan Singh Nagar, Shahpura, Bhopal 462016, Madhya Pradesh
Telephone: (755) 2725307
Fax: (755) 2561970
E-mail: query@mcu.ac.in
Internet: www.mcu.ac.in
Founded 1991
Academic year: August to July
Vice-Chancellor: ACHYUTANAND C. MISHRA
Dir: O. P. DUBEY
Registrar: ANIL CHOUBEY
Librarian: G. N. VYAS
Library of 15,000 vols
Publication: *Vidura* (in Hindi and English)
Depts of Broadcast Journalism, Communication and Public Relations, Computer Applications and Journalism, Library and Information Science.

MANGALORE UNIVERSITY

Mangalagangotri 574199, Karnataka
Telephone: (824) 2287276
Fax: (824) 2287367
E-mail: info@mangaloreuniversity.ac.in
Internet: www.mangaloreuniversity.ac.in
Founded 1980
Languages of instruction: English, Kannada
Academic year: June to April
25 Postgraduate depts; 2 constituent colleges; 4 law, 13 education, 5 autonomous and 119 affiliated colleges/instns

Chancellor: HE THE GOVERNOR OF KARNATAKA
Vice-Chancellor: Prof. K. M. KAVERIAPPA
Registrar: P. PREM KUMAR
Finance Officer: Prof. P. S. YADAPADITHAYA
Dir of College Devt Ccl: Dr W. LINDA CHRISTY
Dir of Student Welfare: Prof. K. CHINNAPPA GOWDA
Librarian: Dr M. K. BHANDI
Library of 150,428 vols
Number of teachers: 2,849
Number of students: 1,303 (university), 41,579 (affiliated colleges)

DEANS

Faculty of Arts: Prof. VISHWANATHA
Faculty of Commerce: Prof. P. S. YADAPADITHAYA
Faculty of Education: Dr H. NAGALINGAPPA
Faculty of Law: Dr K. VINODA RAI
Faculty of Science: K. KRISHNA BHAT

MANIPUR UNIVERSITY

Canchipur, Imphal 795003, Manipur
Telephone: (385) 2435143
Fax: (385) 2435145
E-mail: vcmu@sancharnet.in
Internet: manipuruniv.ac.in
Founded 1980
Central university 2005
Central control
Language of instruction: English
Academic year: July to June
Chief Rector: HE THE GOVERNOR OF MANIPUR
Chancellor: Prof. P. N. SRIVASTAVA
Vice-Chancellor: Prof. C. AMUBA SINGH
Registrar: Dr N. LOKENDRA SINGH
Finance Officer: M. BIREN SINGH
Controller of Examinatons: H. RAJAMANI SINGH
Dean of Student Welfare: Prof. TH. RATANKUMAR SINGH
Dir of College Devt Council: Prof. R. K. RANJAN SINGH
Librarian: Dr TH. KHOMDON SINGH
72 Affiliated colleges
Library of 156,811 vols, 205 nat. and 38 int. journals
Number of teachers: 163 (postgraduate depts only)
Number of students: 1,792 (postgraduate depts only)

DEANS

School of Humanities: Prof. S. SANATOMBI SINGHA
School of Human and Environmental Science: Prof. W. NABAKUMAR SINGH
School of Life Sciences: Prof. G. JITENDRA SHARMA
School of Mathematical and Physical Sciences: Prof. R. K. GARTIA
School of Medical Sciences: Prof. W. GYANESHWAR SINGH
School of Social Sciences: Prof. AMAR YUMNAM

CONSTITUENT COLLEGE

Manipur Institute of Technology (MIT): Principal Dr TH. KULACHANDRA SINGH.

ATTACHED CENTRES

Centre for Human Rights and Duties Education: Dir Prof. K. IBO SINGH.

Centre for Manipur Studies: f. 2005; Dir Prof. AMAR YUMNAM.

Centre for Myanmar Studies: f. 1989; Dir Prof. W. NABAKUMAR SINGH.

Centre for Social Exclusion & Inclusive Policy: Dir Prof. L. TOMBI SINGH.

Educational Multimedia Research Centre: f. 1989; Dir Dr N. PREMCHAND SINGH.

MANONMANIAM SUNDARANAR UNIVERSITY

Abishekapatti, Tirunelveli 627012, Tamil Nadu
Telephone: (462) 2333741
Fax: (462) 2334363
E-mail: tvl_regismsu@sancharnet.in
Internet: www.msuniversity.org.in
Founded 1990

Teaching and affiliating; depts of information technology and engineering, marine sciences and technology, chemistry, communication, computer science and engineering, criminology and criminal justice, English, environmental sciences, history, library and information science, management studies, mandatory disclosure of information, mathematics, physics, sociology, sports and physical education, statistics, Tamil; 70 affiliated colleges

Chancellor: HE THE GOVERNOR OF TAMIL NADU
Vice-Chancellor: Dr R. T. SABAPATHY MOHAN
Registrar: Dr S. GOPALAKRISHNAN
Finance Officer: S. RAMAKRISHNAN
Controller of Examinations: Dr N. ARUNACHALAM
Librarian: P. ALANGARABABU.

MARATHWADA AGRICULTURAL UNIVERSITY

Parbhani, 431402, Maharashtra
Telephone: (2452) 223801
Fax: (2452) 223582
E-mail: vcmau@rediffmail.com
Internet: mkv2.mah.nic.in
Founded 1972
State control
Language of instruction: English
16 Affiliated research stations
Academic year: June to May
Chancellor: HE THE GOVERNOR OF MAHARASHTRA
Vice-Chancellor: Dr S. S. KADAM
Registrar: Dr K. M. LAWANDE
Librarian: B. T. MUNDHE
Library of 62,405 vols, 229 periodicals
Number of teachers: 282
Number of students: 2,017
Publication: *Sheti Bhati* (Marathi, 12 a year)

PROFESSORS

Faculty of Agricultural Technology:
  KULKARNI, D. N., Food Science and Cereal Technology
  WANKHEDE, D. B., Biochemistry

Faculty of Agriculture:
  CHAVAN, B. N., Agronomy
  DHAVAN, A. S., Agricultural Chemistry and Soil Science
  GORE, K. P., Agricultural Engineering
  JANDHALE, S. G., Agricultural Extension
  KULKARNI, U. G., Plant Physiology
  NADRE, K. R., Agricultural Extension
  NARWADKAR, P. R., Horticulture
  PAWAR, N. D., Agricultural Economics and Statistics
  SHELKE, D. K., Agronomy
  SONTAKKE, M. B., Horticulture

Faculty of Home Science:
  MURALI, D., Home Management
  PATANAM, V., Child Development and Family Relations
  ROHINDEVI, P., Food and Nutrition

CONSTITUENT COLLEGES

College of Agricultural Engineering: Parbhani; Prin. Dr G. R. MORE.

College of Agricultural Technology: Parbhani; Prin. Dr D. B. WANKHEDE.

College of Agriculture, Ambajogai: Ambajogai; Prin. Dr B. K. DHANORKAR.

College of Agriculture: Badnapur; Prin. Dr H. N. PATIL.

College of Agriculture: Latur; Prin. Dr K. K. ZOTE.

College of Agriculture: Osmanabad; Prin. Dr V. G. REDDY.

College of Agriculture: Parbhani; Prin. Dr M. V. DHOBALE.

College of Home Science: Parbhani; Prin. Prof. D. MURALI.

College of Horticulture: Parbhani; Prin. Dr B. A. KADAM.

MAULANA AZAD NATIONAL URDU UNIVERSITY

Gochibowli, Hyderabad 500032, Andhra Pradesh

Telephone: (40) 23006612
Fax: (40) 23006603
E-mail: manuu@indiainfo.com
Internet: www.manuu.ac.in
Founded 1998
Central univ.
State control
Chancellor: Dr OBEID SIDDIQUI
Vice-Chancellor: Prof. A. M. PATHAN
Registrar: Prof. K. R. IQBAL AHMED
Finance Officer: Y. JAYANT RAO
Librarian: Dr ABBAS KHAN
Library of 14,500 vols, 54 periodicals
Number of students: 56,000
12 Depts, 104 study centres

DEANS

School of Education and Training: Prof. H. KHATIJA BEGUM
School of Languages, Linguistics and Indology: Prof. K. SAEED
School of Mass Communication and Journalism: Prof. A. NISAM
School of Political Science and Public Admin.: Prof. S. M. RAHMATULLAH

REGIONAL CENTRES

Bangalore Regional Centre—MANUU: Al-Ameen Commercial Complex, POB 27058, 2nd Fl., Hosur Rd, Bangalore 560027, Karnataka; tel. (80) 22228329; Dir KHAZI ZIAULLAH.

Bhopal Regional Centre—MANUU: 12 Ahmedabad Palace, Koh-e-Fiza, Bhopal, Madhya Pradesh; tel. (755) 2736930; Dir Dr MOHD AHSAN.

Darbhanga Regional Centre—MANUU: Super Market, Moula Ganj, Darbhanga 846 004, Bihar; tel. (6272) 258755; Dir Dr S. E. H. IMAM AZAM.

Delhi Regional Centre—MANUU: B-1/275, Ground Fl., Zaidi Apts, TIT Rd Okhla, Jamia Nagar, New Delhi, 110025; tel. (11) 26934762; fax (11) 26838260; Dir Dr SHAHID PERVEZ.

Kolkata Regional Centre—MANUU: Flat 5, 2nd Fl., 9A Lower Range, Kolkata 700017, West Bengal; tel. (33) 22894568; Dir SAHAB SINGH.

New Mumbai Regional Centre—MANUU: A-1, CHS Ltd, F-1/6, 2nd Fl., Dev Hotel, Sector 5, Vahsi, New Mumbai 400703, Maharashtra; tel. 22-27820515; Dir Dr M. ARSHAD EKBAL.

Patna Regional Centre—MANUU: 2nd Fl., Bihar State Co-operative Bank Bldg, Ashok Rajpath, Patna 800004, Bihar; tel. (612) 2300413; Dir Dr HASNUDDIN HAIDER.

Srinagar Regional Centre—MANUU: 18B Jawahar Nagar, Srinagar 190001, Jammu and Kashmir; tel. (914) 2310221; Dir Dr ABDUL GHANI.

MAULANA MAZHARUL HAQUE ARABIC AND PERSIAN UNIVERSITY

Sandal Nagar, Mahendru, Patna 800006
Vice Chancellor: AHMAD MUKHTARUDDIN.

MIZORAM UNIVERSITY

POB 190, Aizwal 796009, Mizoram
Telephone: (389) 2330654
Fax: (389) 2330642
E-mail: registrar@mzu.edu.in
Internet: www.mzu.edu.in
Founded 2000
Central univ.; depts of biotechnology, botany, chemistry, commerce, economics, education, electronic engineering, English, extension education and rural development, forest ecology and forestry, geography, geology, history and ethnography, horticulture, aromatic and medicinal plants, information technology, library and information science, management, mathematics and computer science, physics, political science, psychology, public administration, social work, zoology; 31 affiliated colleges
Academic year: August to July
Language of instruction: English
Vice-Chancellor: Prof. A. N. RAI
Registrar: I. D. A. S. BENJAMINA
Dir of College Devt Ccl: S. K. GHOSH
Librarian: A. S. CHANDEL
Library of 63,538 vols, 369 periodicals
Number of teachers: 129
Number of students: 1,237

DEANS

School of Earth Sciences and Natural Resource Management: Prof. H. LALRAMNGINGLOVA
School of Economics, Management and Information Sciences: Prof. LIANZELA
School of Education and Humanities: Prof. R. P. VADHERA
School of Engineering and Technology: Prof. R. P. TIWARI
School of Life Sciences: Prof. G. C. JAGETIA
School of Physical Sciences: Prof. R. P. TIWARI
School of Social Science: Prof. J. K. PATNAIK

CONSTITUENT SCHOOL

Pachhunga University College: College Veng, Aizawl; tel. (389) 2322257; fax (389) 2317524; f. 1958 as Aijal College; present name 1979; 2002 became constituent college; 84 teachers; 1,290 students; Prin. Dr TAWNENGA (acting).

MOHAN LAL SUKHADIA UNIVERSITY

Pratap Nagar, Udaipur 313001, Rajasthan
Telephone: (294) 2471035
Fax: (294) 2471150
E-mail: registrar@mlsu.org
Internet: www.mlsu.org
Founded 1962 as Rajasthan Agricultural University, present name 1982
Teaching and Affiliating
Autonomous control
Languages of instruction: English, Hindi
Academic year: July to June
Chancellor: HE THE GOVERNOR OF RAJASTHAN
Vice-Chancellor: ARPANA ARORA
Registrar: MOHAN LAL SHARMA
Dean of Postgraduate Studies: Prof. I. V. TRIVEDI
Dean of Student Welfare: Prof. S. R. VYAS
Librarian: Prof. M. S. SHARMA
110 Affiliated colleges

Library of 287,000 vols
Number of teachers: 264
Number of students: 47,209

DEANS

Faculty of Commerce: Prof. K. C. SODANI
Faculty of Humanities: Prof. S. R. VYAS
Faculty of Management: Dr P. K. JAIN
Faculty of Science: Prof. MADHU SUDAN SHARMA
Faculty of Social Sciences: Prof. R. N. VYAS

CONSTITUENT COLLEGES

College of Commerce and Management Studies: Udaipur; tel. (294) 2412009; Dean Prof. K. C. SODANI.

College of Law: Udaipur; tel. (294) 2470958; Dean Prof. VIJAY SHRIMALI.

College of Science: Udaipur; tel. (294) 2413955; Dean Prof. MADHU SUDAN SHARMA.

College of Social Sciences and Humanities: Udaipur; tel. (294) 2470143; Dean Prof. R. N. VYAS.

MOTHER TERESA WOMEN'S UNIVERSITY

Kodaikanal 624102, Tamil Nadu
Telephone: (4542) 241122
Fax: (4542) 241122
E-mail: registrar@motherteresawomenuniv.ac.in
Internet: www.motherteresawomenuniv.ac.in
Founded 1984
State control
Languages of instruction: English, Tamil
Academic year: June to May
Depts of biotechnology, computer science, economics, education, English, family life management, historical studies and tourism management, management, music, physics, sociology, Tamil, visual communication; 4 affiliated colleges
Chancellor: HE THE GOV. OF TAMIL NADU
Vice-Chancellor: Dr ARUNA SIVAKAMI ANANTHAKRISHNAN
Registrar: Dr S. MANI
Finance Officer: P. K. SUBRAMANYAN
Controller of Examinations: Dr S. SUNDARI
Asst Librarians: Dr K. P. PADMAVATHI, P. SEMBIANMADEVI
Library of 87,000 vols
Number of teachers: 34
Number of students: 1,000

PROFESSORS

ARAVANAN, T., Tamil
PHIL, M., Education

ATTACHED RESEARCH AND EXTENSION CENTRES

Chennai Centre: Teacher's Training College Campus, Saidapet, Chennai 600015; tel. (44) 24347222.

Madurai Centre: MMSSS Sancta Maria, Chokkalinga Nagar, Bye Pass Rd, Madurai 625010; tel. (452) 2387355.

CONSTITUENT COLLEGES

Government Arts College for Women: Nilakottai.

Mother Teresa Women's University College: Kodaikanal; f. 1985.

M. V. Muthiah Pillai Arts College for Women: Dindigul.

AFFILIATED COLLEGES

Arulmigu Palaniandavar Arts College for Women: Chinnakalayamputhur 624615 Palani Taluk, Dindigul Dist.; tel. and fax (4545) 255128; e-mail admin@apacwomen.ac.in; internet www.apacwomen.ac.in; f. 1970; library of 30,162 vols.; Prin. Dr G. THEMOZHI;

Librarian INDIRANI RAJAMANI; depts in commerce, economics, English, history, mathematics and sciences, Tamil.

Jeyaraj Annapakiyam College for Women: Periyakulam Theni 625601, Tamil Nadu; tel. and fax (4546) 231482; e-mail secretary@annejac.com; internet www.annejac.com; f. 1971; Pres. Mother Xavier MARIA THANGAM; Prin. Dr Sr Y. YESU THANGAM.

Nadar Saraswathi Arts and Science College for Women: POB 55, Vadapudupatty, Annanji Theni 625531; tel. (4546) 269297; fax (4546) 269000; e-mail nsc-principal@yahoo.com; internet www.nadarsaraswathicollege.com; f. 1996; library of 10,000 vols.; Pres. Dr A. S. R. JEYASEELAN; Prin. Dr K. GIRIJA.

St Antony's College of Arts and Science for Women: Dindigul.

Sri Adi Chunchanagiri Women's College: Cumbum.

NAGALAND UNIVERSITY

Lumami, Kohima 797001, Nagaland
Telephone: (370) 2290331
Fax: (370) 2290246
E-mail: nagalanduniversity@yahoo.co.in
Internet: www.nagauniv.org.in

Founded 1994
Central university
State control
Language of instruction: English
Academic year: September to August

Chief Rector: HE THE GOVERNOR OF NAGALAND
Chancellor: Prof. YOGINDER K. ALAGH
Vice-Chancellor: Prof. K. KANNAN
Registrar: T. VIHIENUO
Dean of Student Welfare: Dr B. V. RAO
Finance Officer: (vacant)
Librarian: LUCY BENDANG

Library of 32,916 vols, 75 periodicals
2 Further campuses at Kohima and Medziphema; 42 affiliated colleges
Number of teachers: 112
Number of students: 19,151 (18,349 undergraduate, 802 postgraduate)

DEANS

School of Agricultural Sciences and Rural Development: Prof. IMNAYONGDANG
School of Humanities and Education: Prof. IMTISUNGBA
School of Sciences: Prof. PARDESHI LAL
School of Social Sciences: Prof. A. K. MISHRA

NAGARJUNA UNIVERSITY

Nagarjuna Nagar 522510, Andhra Pradesh
Telephone: (863) 2293238
Internet: www.nagarjunauniversity.ac.in

Founded 1976
Language of instruction: English
Academic year: July to April
292 Affiliated colleges

Chancellor: HE THE GOV. OF ANDHRA PRADESH
Vice-Chancellor: Prof. Y. R. HARAGOPAL REDDY
Prin.: Prof. NIRMALA MARY TURAKA
Registrar: M. V. N. SARMA
Rector: Prof. K. VIYYANNA RAO
Librarian: J. RAMA RAO

Library of 100,000 vols, 331 periodicals
Number of teachers: 148
Number of students: 1,700

DEANS

Faculty of Commerce: Prof. G. N. BRAHMANANDAM
Faculty of Education: Dr G. BHUVANESWARA LAKSHMI

Faculty of Engineering: Prof. G. NAGESWARA RAO
Faculty of Humanities: Prof. G. KRUPACHARY,
Faculty of Law: Prof. A. SUBRAHMANYAM
Faculty of Natural Sciences: Prof. NIRMALA MARY TURAKA
Faculty of Pharmacy: Prof. N. RAMA RAO
Faculty of Physical Sciences: Prof. LAM PRAKASA RAO
Faculty of Social Sciences: C. S. N. RAJU

PROFESSORS

Faculty of Commerce:
  BRAHMANANDAM, G. N., Commerce
  DAKSHINA MURTHY, D., Commerce
  GANJU, M. K., Commerce
  HANUMANTHA RAO, K., Commerce
  NARASIMHAM, V. V. L., Commerce
  PRASAD, G., Commerce
  UMAMAHESWARA RAO, T., Commerce
  VIYYANNA RAO, K., Commerce
Faculty of Engineering:
  THRIMURTY, P., Computer Science and Engineering
Faculty of Humanities:
  BALAGANGADHARA RAO, Y., Telugu and Languages
  BHASKARA MURTHY, D., Ancient History and Archaeology
  KRUPACHARY, G., Telugu and Languages
  KUMARASWAMY, Y., Ancient History and Archaeology
  NIRMALA, T., Telugu and Oriental Languages
  PUNNA RAO, A., Telugu and Oriental Languages
  RAMA SASTRY, N. A., Telugu and Languages
  RAMALAKSHMI, P., Ancient History and Archaeology
  SARASWATHI, R., English
  SUBRAHMANYAM, B. R., Ancient History and Archaeology
Faculty of Law:
  HARAGOPAL REDDY, Y. R.
  RANGAIAH, N., Law
  VIJAYANARAYANA REDDY, D.
Faculty of Natural Sciences:
  BALAPARAMESWARA RAO, M., Aquaculture
  DURGA PRASAD, M. K., Zoology
  GOPALAKRISHNA REDDY, T., Zoology
  LAKSHMI, N., Botany
  MALLAIAH, K. V., Botany
  NARASIMHA RAO, P., Botany
  NIRMALA MARY, T., Botany
  RAMAMOHANA RAO, P., Botany
  RAMAMURTHY NAIDU, K., Botany
  RANGA RAO, V., Geology
  SANTHA KUMARI, D., Botany
  SHARMA, S. V., Zoology
Faculty of Physical Sciences:
  ANJANEYULU, Y., Chemistry
  GOPALA KRISHNA MURTHY, P. V., Physics
  HARANADH, C., Physics
  KOTESWARA RAO, G., Mathematics
  NARASIMHAM, V. L., Statistics
  NARAYANA MURTHY, P., Physics
  PRAKASA RAO, L., Mathematics
  PRAKASA RAO, N. S., Chemistry
  RAMA BADRA SARMA, I., Mathematics
  RAMAKOTAIAH, D., Mathematics
  RANGACHARYULU, H., Physics
  SATYANANDAM, G., Physics
  SATYANARAYANA, P. V. V., Chemistry
  SHYAM SUNDAR, B., Chemistry
  SIVA RAMA SARMA, B., Chemistry
  VENKATACHARYULU, P., Physics
  VENKATESWARA REDDY, Y., Mathematics
Faculty of Social Sciences:
  ASHEERVADH, N., Political Science
  BAPUJI, M., Political Science
  BHAVANI, V., Political Science
  NARAYANA RAO, C., Political Science

RAGHAVULU, C. V., Political Science and Public Administration
RAJA BABU, K., Economics
RAJU, C. S. N., Economics
SUDHAKARA RAO, N., Economics

NALANDA OPEN UNIVERSITY

Biscomaun Bhawan, Gandhi Maidan, Patna 800001, Bihar
Telephone: (612) 2201024
Fax: (612) 2201001
E-mail: nalopuni@sancharnet.in
Internet: www.nalandaopenuniversity.com

Founded 1987
Academic year: June to May

Chancellor: HE THE GOVERNOR OF BIHAR
Pro-Vice-Chancellor: Prof. K. K. SINGH
Vice-Chancellor: Prof. JITENDRA SINGH
Registrar: Dr S. P. SINHA

Library of 10,000 vols

HEADS OF SCHOOLS

School of Commerce and Social Sciences: Prof. R. P. SINGH RAHI
School of Computer and Information Sciences: A. N. PANDEY
School of Health and Environmental Sciences: Dr G. K. PRASAD
School of Management Studies and Physical Sciences: Prof. USHA SINGH
School of Indian Languages and Religions: Prof. P. C. PANDEY

NARENDRA DEVA UNIVERSITY OF AGRICULTURE & TECHNOLOGY

Narendranagar, Kumarganj, Faizabad 224229, Uttar Pradesh
Telephone: (5270) 262161
Fax: (5270) 262097
E-mail: nduat@up.nic.in
Internet: www.nduat.ernet.in

Founded 1974
State control
Languages of instruction: Hindi, English

Chancellor: HE THE GOVERNOR OF UTTAR PRADESH
Vice-Chancellor: Prof. BASANT RAM
Registrar: Prof. B. V. S. SISODIA

Library of 42,000 vols
Number of teachers: 67
Number of students: 432

Publication: *NDUAT News Bulletin*

DEANS

Faculty of Agricultural Engineering and Technology: Dr R. SINGH
Faculty of Agriculture: Dr M. R. VERMA
Faculty of Home Science: Dr SUMAN BHANOT
Faculty of Veterinary Science and Animal Husbandry: Dr R. SINGH

CONSTITUENT COLLEGE

Mahamaya College of Agricultural Engineering & Technology: Faizabad Ambedkar Nagar, Uttar Pradesh; f. 2003 as Engineering faculty of NDUAT.

NATIONAL ACADEMY OF LEGAL STUDIES AND RESEARCH UNIVERSITY (NALSAR)

3–4–761 Barkatpura, Hyderabad 500027, Andhra Pradesh
Telephone: (40) 27567955
Fax: (40) 27567310Justice City, Shameerpet, Rangareddy District, Hyderabad 500078, Andhra Pradesh
Telephone: (40) 23498107
Fax: (40) 245161
E-mail: admissions@nalsar.ac.in
Internet: www.nalsarlawuniv.ac.in

Founded 1998
Academic year: July to June
Vice-Chancellor: Prof. VEER SINGH
Registrar: Prof. K. V. S. SARMA
Library of 17,000 vols
Publication: *NALSAR Law Review* (2 a year).

NATIONAL LAW INSTITUTE UNIVERSITY

Bhopal Bhadbhada Rd, Barkheri Kalan, POB 369, Bhopal 462003, Madhya Pradesh
Telephone: (755) 2696965
Fax: (755) 2696965
E-mail: info@nliu.com
Internet: www.nliu.com
Founded 1998
Dir: Dr S. S. SINGH
Finance Officer: N. C. TEKAM
Registrar: C. M. GARG.

NATIONAL LAW UNIVERSITY

NH-65, Nagaur Rd, Mandor, Jodhpur 342304, Rajasthan
Telephone: (291) 2577530
Fax: (291) 2577540
E-mail: nlu-jod-rj@nic.in
Internet: www.nlujodhpur.ac.in
Founded 1999
State control
Language of instruction: English
Chancellor: Chief Justice of Rajasthan JAGDISH BHALLA
Vice-Chancellor: Justice N. N. MATHUR
Registrar: RATAN LAHOTI
Librarian: VINOD D.
Library of 10,500 books, 108 journals, 1,400 electronic journals
Number of teachers: 46
Number of students: 548
Publications: *Journal of Governance* (2 a year), *Scholasticus* (2 a year), *Trade Law and Development* (2 a year)

DEANS
Faculty of Law: Prof. Dr I. P. MASSEY
Faculty of Management: Prof. Dr U. R. DAGA
Faculty of Policy Science: Dr ALOK KUMAR GUPTA (acting)
Faculty of Science: Prof. Dr K. K. BANERJEE

NETAJI SUBHAS OPEN UNIVERSITY

1 Woodburn Park, Kolkata 700020, West Bengal
Telephone: (33) 22835157
Fax: (33) 22835082
E-mail: admin@wbnsou.com
Internet: www.wbnsou.com
Founded 1997
Language of instruction: Bengali
Undergraduate and postgraduate degree programmes in accountancy, Bengali, botany, chemistry, commerce, computer science, economics, education, English, environmental science, geography, history, management, mathematics, physics, political science, public administration, sociology, zoology; 6 campuses in Kolkata; 160 study centres
Chancellor: HE THE GOVERNOR OF WEST BENGAL
Vice-Chancellor: Prof. MANIMALA DAS
Registrar: TARUN KUMAR MANDAL
Dir of Humanities and Social Sciences: Dr UDAYBHANU BHATTACHARYA
Dir of Science: Prof. KAJAL DE
Dir of Study Centre: Prof. ASHIT BARAN AICH
Controller of Examinations: A. DAS
Number of students: 100,000

NIRMA UNIVERSITY OF SCIENCE AND TECHNOLOGY

Sarkhej Gandhinagar Highway, Village Chharodi, Ahmedabad 382481, Gujarat
Telephone: (2717) 241911
Fax: (2717) 241917
E-mail: asst_registrar@nirmauni.ac.in
Internet: www.nirmauni.ac.in
Founded 1994; present name and status 2003
Privately controlled by Nirma Education and Research Foundation
Vice-Chancellor: Dr N. V. VASANI
Exec. Registrar: D. P. CHHAYA

DEANS
Faculty of Law: Dr PURVI POKHARIYA (acting)
Faculty of Management: Prof. UPINDER DHAR
Faculty of Pharmacy: Dr AVANI AMIN (acting)
Faculty of Science: Dr SRIRAM SESHADRI (acting)
Faculty of Technology and Engineering: Prof. K. KOTECHA

CONSTITUENT INSTITUTES

Institute of Diploma Studies

Founded 1997
Prin.: Prof. H. N. PRAJAPATI
Registrar: D. P. CHHAYA
Depts of chemical engineering, computer engineering, electrical engineering, electronics and communication engineering, information technology, mechanical engineering, plastic engineering
Library of 60,000 vols, 400 print periodicals, 8,000 e-journals

Institute of Law

Founded 2007
Dir: Prof. V. S. MALLAR.

Institute of Management

E-mail: grnair@imnu.ac.in
Internet: www.imnu.ac.in
Founded 1996
Dir: Dr UPINDER DHAR
Librarian: Prof. H. ANIL KUMAR
Library of 23,000 vols, 185 periodicals

PROFESSORS
BAHL, S.
BHATTACHARYA, A.
CHUGAN, P. K.
DHANAK, D.
GUPTA, G. S.
GUPTA, P.
MAHAKUD, J.
MALLIKARJUN, M.
MUNCHERJI, N.
NATH, V. V.
PETHE, S.
SAHU, C.
SAHU, S.
SAXENA, S.
TRIVEDI, H.
YADAV, P. K.

Institute of Pharmacy

E-mail: rp.ip@nirmauni.ac.in
Founded 2004
Dir: Dr Y. K. AGRAWAL
Prin.: Dr AVANI F. AMIN
Library of 2,500 vols, 70 periodicals.

Institute of Science

E-mail: hs.is@nirmauni.ac.inn
Founded 2004
Dir: Dr Y. K. AGRAWAL
Postgraduate programmes in biochemistry and biotechnology
Library of 22,000 vols.

Institute of Technology

E-mail: director.it@nirmauni.ac.in
Founded 1995
Dir: Prof. A. B. PATEL
Depts of chemical engineering, civil engineering, electrical engineering, humanities, information technology and computer engineering, mathematics, mechanical engineering
Library of 22,000 vols.

NIZAM'S INSTITUTE OF MEDICAL SCIENCES

Punjagutta, Hyderabad 500082, Andhra Pradesh
Telephone: (40) 23489000
Fax: (40) 23310076
E-mail: nims@ap.nic.in
Internet: nims.ap.nic.in
Founded 1964 as Nizam's Orthopaedic Hospital; present name and status 1989
Residential; depts of anaesthesiology and intensive care, biochemisty, cardio-thoracic surgery, cardiology, chest clinic, clinical pharmacology and therapeutics, dental, dermatology, endocrinology and metabolism, gastroenterology, general medicine, gynaecology, medical oncology, microbiology, nephrology, neurology, neurosurgery, nuclear medicine, orthopaedics, paediatrics, pathology, physiotherapy, plastic surgery, radiation oncology, radiology and imageology, rheumatology, surgical gastroenterology, surgical oncology, transfusion medicine, urology, vascular surgery
Dir: Prof. D. PRASADA RAO
Dean: Prof. M. U. R. NAIDU
Medical Superintendent: Dr N. SATYANARAYANA
Exec. Registrar: Prof. M. SUDERSHANAM
Financial Controller: V. SRIDHAR
Number of teachers: 149

NORTH-EASTERN HILL UNIVERSITY

PO NEHU Campus, Shillong 793002
Telephone: (364) 2550101
Fax: (364) 2550076
Internet: www.nehu.ac.in
Founded 1973
Public control
Language of instruction: English
Academic year: July to June
Chancellor: Prof. M. G. K. MENON
Vice-Chancellor: Prof. A. N. RAI
Pro Vice-Chancellor: Prof. D. R. SYIEMLIEH
Registrar: LAMBHA ROY
Chief Finance Officer: TALIREMBA MAJHI
Controller of Examinations: Prof. K. ISMAIL
Dean of Student Welfare: Dr R. N. SHARAN
Dir of College Devt Council: Dr C. R. DIENGDOH
Librarian: Dr I. MAJAW
Library of 250,000 vols
Number of teachers: 342
Number of students: 32,000
Publication: *NEHU Journal of Social Sciences and Humanities* (4 a year)

DEANS

School of Education: Prof. P. K. GUPTA
School of Economics, Management and Information Science: Prof. P. NAYAK
School of Human and Environmental Sciences: Prof. B. S. MIPUN
School of Humanities: Prof. J. WAR
School of Life Sciences: Prof. B. K. SHARMA
School of Physical Sciences: Prof. H. K. MUKHERJEE
School of Social Sciences: Prof. L. S. GASSAH
School of Technology: Prof. S. CHOUDHURY

NORTH MAHARASHTRA UNIVERSITY

PB No. 80, Jalgaon 425002, Maharashtra
Telephone: (257) 2258405
Fax: (257) 2258406
E-mail: info@nmu.ac.in
Internet: www.nmu.ac.in
Founded 1990
State control
Academic year: July to April

Vice-Chancellor: Dr B. P. KHANDERAO
Registrar: Dr M. V. BARIDE
Dir of Public Relations: R. B. CHINCHOLAKAR
Librarian: Dr B. T. RAMCHANDRA

143 Affiliated colleges

Library of 28,728 vols, 85 periodicals
Number of teachers: 3,174
Number of students: 47,974

DIRS OF SCHOOLS

School of Chemical Sciences: Dr D. G. HUNDIWALE
School of Environmental and Earth Sciences: Dr S. T. INGLE
School of Life Sciences: Dr M. V. KULKARNI
School of Mathematical Sciences: Dr R. L. SHINDE
School of Physical Sciences: Dr P. P. PATIL

NORTH ORISSA UNIVERSITY

Sriram Chandra Vihar, Takatpur, Baripada, Mayurbhanj 757003, Orissa
Telephone: (6792) 255127
Fax: (6792) 255127
Internet: nou.nic.in
Founded 1998
State control
Academic year: June to May

Faculties of arts, commerce, computer applications, education, engineering, law, medicine, science, tribal studies; 81 affiliated colleges

Chancellor: HE THE GOV. OF ORISSA
Vice-Chancellor: Dr SHIBA PRASAD RATH
Registrar: Dr HARIPRASAD P. PANDA
Librarian: S. K. TANTI

Library of 2,647 vols
Number of students: 10,320

ORISSA UNIVERSITY OF AGRICULTURE AND TECHNOLOGY

District Khurda, Bhubaneswar 751003, Orissa
Telephone: (674) 2392677
Fax: (674) 2397780
E-mail: ouatmain@hotmail.com
Internet: ouat.ac.in
Founded 1962
Teaching and Research
State control
Language of instruction: English
Academic year: July to July

Chancellor: HE THE GOVERNOR OF ORISSA
Vice-Chancellor: Prof. D. P. RAY
Registrar: DUKHISHYAM SHATAPATHY
Dean of Extension Education: Dr S. S. NANDA
Dean of Research: Dr D. NAIK

Dean of Student Welfare: Dr D. K. DAS
Controller of Examinations: Dr BIRANCHI N. ROUTRAY
Librarian: Dr N. K. DHAL

7 Constituent colleges; Centre for Postgraduate Studies

Library of 900,000 vols, 133 periodicals
Number of teachers: 512
Number of students: 3,046

DEANS

College of Agricultural Engineering and Technology: Dr S. N. MOHANTY
College of Agriculture (Bhubaneswar): Dr P. K. MOHAPATRA
College of Agriculture (Chiplima): Dr S. K. MISHRA
College of Basic Science and Humanities: Dr M. CHAKRABORTY
College of Engineering and Technology: Dr B. S. PATRO
College of Fisheries: Dr S. K. MISHRA
College of Home Science: Prin.: Dr P. DAS
College of Veterinary Science and Animal Husbandry: Dr B. K. SAHOO

OSMANIA UNIVERSITY

Hyderabad 500007, Andhra Pradesh
Telephone: (40) 27098043
E-mail: registrar@osmania.ac.in
Internet: www.osmania.ac.in
Founded 1918
Teaching, Residential and Affiliating; 120 affiliated colleges and 16 Oriental colleges
Languages of instruction: English, Hindi, Telugu, Urdu, Marathi
Academic year: June to April (two terms)
Chancellor: HE THE GOV. OF ANDHRA PRADESH
Vice-Chancellor: Prof. T. TIRUPATI RAO
Registrar: Prof. Y. C. VENUDHAR
Dean of College Devt Ccl: Prof. P. JETTAIAH
Dean of Devt: Prof. M. NARSIMAHA CHARY
Dean of Student Affairs: Dr B. LAXMAIAH
Public Relations Officer: Prof. B. S. RAO
Librarian: V. REVATHI

Library of 422,000 vols
Number of students: 300,000
Publication: *Osmania Journal of English Studies*

DEANS

Faculty of Arts: Prof. M. MANVI
Faculty of Business Management: Prof. A. VIDYADHAR REDDY
Faculty of Commerce: Prof. K. V. ACHALAPATHI
Faculty of Education: Prof. B. VIJAYA LAKSHMI
Faculty of Engineering: Prof. R. RAMESH REDDY
Faculty of Informatics: Prof. A. VENUGOPAL REDDY
Faculty of Law: Justice L. NARSIMHA REDDY
Faculty of Oriental Languages: Dr M. A. JAMEEL KHAN
Faculty of Science: Prof. U. V. SUBHA RAO
Faculty of Social Sciences: Prof. P. V. LAKSHMI REDDY
Faculty of Technology: Prof. J. S. N. MURTHY

UNIVERSITY COLLEGES

Institute of Advanced Study in Education: f. 1918; Prin. Prof. K. SUBHASHCHANDRA REDDY.
University College of Arts and Social Sciences: tel. (40) 27098298; fax (40) 27091952; e-mail info@ouartscollege.com; internet ouartscollege.com; f. 1918; Prin. Prof. P. L. VISHWESHWER RAO.
University College of Commerce and Business Management: f. 1975; Prin. Prof. M. SHRI NIVAS.

University College of Engineering: tel. (40) 27098254; internet www.uceou.edu; f. 1929; Prin. Prof. D. N. REDDY.
University College of Law: tel. (40) 27098254; internet www.osmanialawcollege.org; f. 1960; Prin. Dr G. B. REDDY.
University College of Physical Education: tel. (40) 27090711; f. 1928; Prin. Prof. S. IBRAHIM.
University College of Science: f. 1918; Prin. Dr K. VEERA REDDY.
University College of Technology: tel. (40) 27682291; fax (40) 27098472; e-mail principal@ouct.org; f. 1969; Prin. Prof. S. VENKATESHWAR.

CONSTITUENT COLLEGES

Nizam College: Basheerbagh, Hyderabad; tel. (40) 23234231; fax (40) 23240806; e-mail principal@nizamcollege.ac.in; internet www.nizamcollege.ac.in; f. 1887; Prin. Prof. B. T. SEETHA.
Postgraduate College of Law, Hyderabad: f. 1954; Prin. G. MANCHAR RAO.
Postgraduate College of Science: Saifabad, Hyderabad; e-mail pgcss@rediffmail.com; internet oupgcollege.ac.in; f. 1951; Prin. Prof. K. SHANKARAIAH.
Postgraduate College, Secunderabad: Sadar Patel Rd, Secunderabad 500003; tel. (40) 27902169; fax (40) 27903688; e-mail principal@oupgcs.ac.in; internet www.oupgcs.ac.in; f. 1947; Prin. Prof. M. DEVA DASS.
University College for Women: Hyderabad; tel. (40) 24657813; fax (40) 24737692; e-mail oucwkoti@rediffmail.com; internet www.oucwkoti.ac.in; f. 1924; Prin. Prof. ZUBAIDA AZEEM.

District Postgraduate Colleges:

Postgraduate College, Biknoor: f. 1976; Prin. Dr U. UMESH KUMAR.
Postgraduate Centre, Mahaboobnagar: f. 1987; Head Dr N. ASHOK.
Postgraduate Centre, Mirzapur: f. 1980; Prin. Dr B. MANOHAR.
Postgraduate Centre, Nalgonda: f. 1987; Prin. Dr S. ANJAIAH.

PANDIT RAVISHANKAR SHUKLA UNIVERSITY, RAIPUR

Amanaka G. E. Rd, Raipur 492010, Chhattisgarh
Telephone: (771) 2262540
Fax: (771) 2262583
Internet: www.prsu.ac.in
Founded 1964
Teaching and Affiliating
Languages of instruction: Hindi, English
Private control
Academic year: July to June (two terms)
Chancellor: HE THE GOVERNOR OF CHHATTISGARH
Vice-Chancellor: Prof. SHIV KUMAR PANDEY
Registrar: INDU ANANT
Librarian: M. I. AHMED

180 Affiliated colleges

Library of 160,000 vols
Number of students: 125,000

DEANS

Faculty of Arts: Dr CHITTARANJAN KAR
Faculty of Ayurved: Dr D. K. KATARIA
Faculty of Commerce: AMIR CHAND JAIN
Faculty of Education: Dr B. K. MEHTA
Faculty of Engineering: Dr H. KUMAR
Faculty of Home Science: Dr V. RAJ
Faculty of Law: Dr A. A. KHAN
Faculty of Management: Dr R. P. DAS

Faculty of Science: Dr G. L. MUNDHRA
Faculty of Social Sciences: Dr M. A. KHAN
Faculty of Technology: Dr SHAILENDRA SARAF

CONSTITUENT SCHOOLS

Centre for Regional Studies and Research: f. 1993; Dir Prof. O. P. VERMA.

Centre for Woman Studies: f. 2001.

Institute of Management: f. 1993; Dir Dr R. P. DAS.

Institute of Pharmacy: tel. (771) 2262832; e-mail info@iopraipur.ac.in; internet www.iopraipur.ac.in; f. 2001; Dir Dr S. SARAF.

Institute of Teachers Education.

Institute of Tourism and Hotel Management: f. 2002; Dir Dr L. S. NIGAM.

School of Studies in Adult, Continuing Education and Extension: f. 1985; Dir Dr BINA PATHAK.

School of Studies in Ancient Indian History, Culture and Archaeology: f. 1971; Dir Prof. L. S. NIGAM.

School of Studies in Anthropology: f. 1965; Dir Dr MANJULA GUHA.

School of Studies in Biotechnology: f. 2003; Dir Dr K. L. TIWARI.

School of Studies in Chemistry: f. 1972; Dir Dr RAMA PANDE.

School of Studies in Comparative Religion and Philosophy: f. 1985; Dir Dr BHAGWANT SINGH.

School of Studies in Computer Science: e-mail dropvyas@gmail.com; internet www.prsu.ac.in/soscs.html; f. 1992; Dir Prof. O. P. VYAS.

School of Studies in Economics: f. 1971; Dir Dr USHA DUBEY.

School of Studies in Electronics: f. 1994; Dir Dr KAVITA THAKUR.

School of Studies in Geography: f. 1965; Dir Dr M. P. GUPTA.

School of Studies in Geology and Water Resource Management: f. 1984; Dir Dr M. W. Y. KHAN.

School of Studies in History: f. 1971; Dir Dr M. A. KHAN.

School of Studies in Law: f. 1982; Dir Dr A. ALIM KHAN.

School of Studies in Library and Information Science: f. 1971; Dir Dr A. K. VERMA.

School of Studies in Life Sciences: f. 1977; Dir Dr VIBHUTI RAI.

School of Studies in Literature and Languages: Dir Dr K. L. VERMA.

School of Studies in Mathematics: f. 1991; Dir Dr B. K. SHARMA.

School of Studies in Physical Education: f. 1972; Dir Dr RITA VENU GOPAL.

School of Studies in Physics: f. 1972; Dir Dr S. BHUSHAN.

School of Studies in Psychology: f. 1965; Dir Dr P. SINGH.

School of Studies in Sociology: f. 1965; Dir Dr P. K. SHARMA.

School of Studies in Statistics: f. 1977; Dir Dr GAURI SHANKAR.

PANJAB UNIVERSITY

Sector 14, Chandigarh 160014
Telephone: (172) 2541945
Fax: (172) 2541022
E-mail: regr@pu.ac.in
Internet: www.puchd.ac.in
Founded 1947
Teaching and affiliating; 115 affiliated colleges

Languages of instruction: English, Punjabi, Urdu, Hindi
Academic year: July to April
Chancellor: THE VICE-PRESIDENT OF INDIA
Vice-Chancellor: Dr R. C. SOBTI
Registrar: Prof. PARAMJIT SINGH
Librarian: A. R. SETHI

Library: Libraries of 590,000 vols
Number of teachers: 746
Number of students: 20,554

Publications: *Parakh, Parishodh, P. U. Research Journal* (science), *Social Sciences Research Journal*

DEANS

Faculty of Arts: Dr MADAN MOHAN PURI
Faculty of Business Management and Commerce: Prof. S. P. SINGH
Faculty of Design and Fine Arts: JOGINDER SINGH
Faculty of Education: NIRMAL KAUR
Faculty of Engineering and Technology: Prof. D. K. VOHRA
Faculty of Languages: Dr ANIRUDH JOSHI
Faculty of Law: GOPAL KRISHAN CHATRATH
Faculty of Medical Sciences: Dr K. S. CHUGH
Faculty of Pharmaceutical Sciences: Prof. V. K. KAPOOR
Faculty of Science: (vacant)

PATNA UNIVERSITY

Ashok Raj Path, Patna 800005, Bihar
Telephone: (612) 2670531; (612) 2670877
Internet: puonline.bih.nic.in

Founded 1917

Residential and teaching
Languages of instruction: Hindi, English
Academic year: June to May (three terms)
Chancellor: HE THE GOV. OF BIHAR
Vice-Chancellor: Prof. SHYAM LAL
Pro-Vice-Chancellor: Prof. SYED L. AHSON
Registrar: Dr VIBHASH KUMAR YADAV
Dean of Student Welfare: Dr EJAZ ALI ARSHAD
Controller of Examination: Dr SURENDRA PRASAD YADAV
Finance Office: Dr JATADHAR MISHRA
Librarian: Dr R. N. MISHRA

Library of 300,000 vols
Number of teachers: 895
Number of students: 11,000

Publication: *University of Patna Journal*

DEANS

Faculty of Commerce: Dr JYOTI SHEKHAR
Faculty of Education: G. K. PRAJAPATI
Faculty of Engineering: Dr P. K. SINHA
Faculty of Fine Arts: Dr N. K. P. SINGH
Faculty of Humanities: Dr R. R. SAHAY
Faculty of Law: Dr L. L. B. SHARAN
Faculty of Medicine: Dr B. K. SINGH
Faculty of Science: Dr S. N. GUHA
Faculty of Social Science: Dr SAVITRI SHARMA

PROFESSORS

ADHIKARI, S., Geography
AHMAD, S. U., Sociology
AKHTAR, M. M., Physics
ALAM, M. S., Persian
ALAM, P. A., Urdu
ARSHAD, E. A., Urdu
ARYA, R. S., Philosophy
ASHOK, S. M., English
AZAD, A., Urdu
AZAD, R., Chemistry
BANERJEE, N. N., Botany
BANERJEE, S., Political Science
BEGAM, S., Urdu
BHAKTA, C., Chemistry
BHATT, P., Zoology
BLAKTA, S., Mathematics
CHOUDHARY, A. K., Physics

CHOUDHARY, M. N., Hindi
CHOUDHARY, N. K., Economics
CHOUDHARY, R., Philosophy
CHOUDHARY, R. B., Sanskrit
CHOUDHARY, S., Political Science
DAS, R. N., Mathematics
DUBEY, G. R., Education
DUBEY, S., Psychology
DUBEY, V. S., Geology
DUTTA, P., History
DUTTA, S. A., English
GHOSH, A. K., Chemistry
GHOSH, P., History
GUHA, S. N., Physics
GUPTA, A. D., Sociology
GUPTA, A. K., Botany
GUPTA, F., Sanskrit
HASANARAN, S. J., Mechanical Engineering
JAISWAL, R., Mathematics
JHA, B., Maithili
JHA, H., Sociology
JHA, I., Education
JHA, K., Psychology
JHA, N. N., Physics
JHA, R., Ancient Indian History and Archaeology
JHA, R., English
JHA, S. M., Mathematics
JHA, U., Chemistry
KALIM, Z., English
KARAN, V., Maithili
KATHURIA, S., Botany
KHAN, S. A., Statistics
KUMAR, A., English
KUMAR, A., Sanskrit
KUMAR, B., Chemistry
KUMAR, B., Statistics
KUMAR, B. S., History
KUMAR, N., Mechanical Engineering
KUMAR, R. V., History
KUMAR, S., Civil Engineering
KUMAR, S., Sociology
KUMARI, A., Statistics
KUMARI, R., Sociology
KUMARI, S., Hindi
LAL, S., Chemistry
MAHTO, K., Geography
MAHTO, R. U., Commerce
MALTIYAR, K. K., Geography
MATHUR, K. N. L., Physics
MIRZA, K., Political Science
MISHRA, A., Statistics
MISHRA, B. K., Geology
MISHRA, H., English
MISHRA, J. S., History
MISHRA, N. M., Physics
MISHRA, R. G., Sanskrit
MISHRA, R. N., Statistics
MISHRA, R. S., Statistics
MISHRA, U., Commerce
MITRA, K. A., Physics
MOHAN, M., Zoology
MUKHERJEE, D., Physics
MUKHERJEE, I., Botany
MURARI, K., Economics
NATH, A., Zoology
NILIMA, N., Hindi
OJHA, G. P., Political Science
PADAMDEO, S. R., Botany
PANDEY, B. N., Commerce
PANDEY, M. K., Sanskrit
PANDEY, N. M., English
PANDEY, N. N., Physics
PASWAN, B., Hindi
PASWAN, K. N., Geography
PODAR, P. K., History
PRAJAPATI, G. K., Education
PRAKASH, D., Chemistry
PRASAD, A., Chemistry
PRASAD, A., Statistics
PRASAD, B., Mathematics
PRASAD, D., Mathematics
PRASAD, D., Sociology
PRASAD, K., Geology
PRASAD, K., History
PRASAD, R. D., Hindi

PRASAD, R. K., Chemistry
PRASAD, R. N., Philosophy
PRASAD, R. P., Chemistry
PRASAD, S. A. K., Mathematics
PRASAD, S. L., Geography
QUADRI, E. A., Civil Engineering
RAJGARHIA, C., Mathematics
RANI, P., Zoology
ROHATAGI, A. K., Geology
ROY, D. N., Bengali
ROY, R., English
ROY, R. B. R., Hindi
ROY, S., Chemistry
ROY, V. R., Psychology
RUDRA, S., Economics
SAHAY, R. R., Philosophy
SHARDENDU, Hindi
SHARMA, B., Mathematics
SHARMA, D. K., Mathematics
SHARMA, D. K., Physics
SHARMA, J. P., Education
SHARMA, M. D., Bengali
SHARMA, N. K., Hindi
SHARMA, P. L., History
SHARMA, R. N., Sociology
SHARMA, S., Psychology
SHARMA, S. N., Botany
SHARMA, S. N., Physics
SHARMA, S. N., Political Science
SHAW, G., Home Science
SHEKHAR, J., Commerce
SHREE, V., Philosophy
SHUKLA, H., Political Science
SHUKLA, K. N., Zoology
SHUKLA, P., Psychology
SHUKLA, R., Geology
SIDDIQUI, F. K., Arabic
SIDDIQUI, M. G., Persian
SIDDIQUI, M. O., Botany
SINGH, A., Economics
SINGH, A. K., Ancient Indian History and Archaeology
SINGH, A. K., History
SINGH, A. K., Psychology
SINGH, A. K. S., Hindi
SINGH, A. N., History
SINGH, B. P., Economics
SINGH, C., Commerce
SINGH, D. P., Hindi
SINGH, G., Hindi
SINGH, J., Physics
SINGH, J. M. P., Hindi
SINGH, J. P., Sociology
SINGH, K. N., Mechanical Engineering
SINGH, K. P., English
SINGH, K. S. P., Civil Engineering
SINGH, L. K. P., Geography
SINGH, N. K., Geology
SINGH, N. K., History
SINGH, N. N. P., History
SINGH, P., Philosophy
SINGH, P. D., Chemistry
SINGH, R. B. P., Geography
SINGH, R. P., Chemistry
SINGH, S., Botany
SINGH, S., Home Science
SINGH, S. C., History
SINGH, S. D. N., Sociology
SINGH, S. K., Mechanical Engineering
SINGH, S. K., Statistics
SINGH, S. K. P., Economics
SINGH, S. K. P., History
SINGH, S. N., Chemistry
SINGH, S. N., Economics
SINGH, S. P. Y., Hindi
SINGH, S. S., Ancient Indian History and Archaeology
SINHA, A. K., Civil Engineering
SINHA, A. K., Statistics
SINHA, A. P., Economics
SINHA, B. K., Mathematics
SINHA, G., Psychology
SINHA, H. B. P., Mathematics
SINHA, K., Economics
SINHA, K. S., Mathematics
SINHA, L., Political Science

SINHA, M., Psychology
SINHA, M., Sanskrit
SINHA, M. N., Geology
SINHA, M. P., Zoology
SINHA, M. R., English
SINHA, N., Geology
SINHA, P., Psychology
SINHA, P. K., Mathematics
SINHA, P. K., Mechanical Engineering
SINHA, R. C., Philosophy
SINHA, R. J., Chemistry
SINHA, R. K., Zoology
SINHA, R. M. P., Physics
SINHA, S., English
SINHA, S., Philosophy
SINHA, S. K., Civil Engineering
SINHA, S. S., Education
SINHA, U. K., Botany
SINHA, V., Psychology
SINHA, V. K., Zoology
SINHA, V. N. P., Geography
SIRKAR, J., Economics
SRINIVASAN, P., Physics
SRIVASTAVA, S. K., Zoology
SRIVASTAVA, U. K., Civil Engineering
SUKLA, B., Sociology
TAHAN, K., Persian
THAKUR, B. K., Geology
THAKUR, J., Physics
THAKUR, S. J., English
THAKUR, V. K., History
TIWARI, B., Hindi
TIWARY, N. P., Philosophy
TIWARY, P. N., History
TRIPATHY, A. N., Sanskrit
TULSIYAN, S. S., Economics
VARMA, M., Philosophy
VERMA, C., Zoology
VERMA, J., Psychology
VERMA, M., Economics
VERMA, P. C., Economics
VERMA, R. K., Mathematics
VERMA, S. P., Physics
VERMA, U., Geography
YADAV, A., Physics
YADAV, A. K. P., Physics
YASIN, S., Zoology

CONSTITUENT COLLEGES

Bihar College of Engineering: Mahendru, Patna; f. 1924; 4-year course; 46 teachers; 450 students; Prin. Dr A. K. SINHA.

Bihar National College: Bankipur, Patna 4; tel. (612) 2300619; f. 1917; 84 teachers; 1,263 students; Prin. Dr RAMESH PRASAD.

College of Arts and Crafts: Patna 800001; tel. (612) 2235348; f. 1938; 5 teachers; 150 students; Prin. Dr ANUNAY CHOUBEY.

Directorate of Distance Education: tel. (612) 2672941; e-mail contact@ddepu.org; internet www.ddepu.org; Dir Dr AMARENDRA MISHRA.

Institute of Library and Information Science: tel. (612) 2672941; Prin. Dr R. N. MISHRA.

Institute of Psychological Research and Service: tel. (612) 2690096; Prin. Dr PRABHA SHUKLA.

Institute of Public Administration: tel. (612) 2670284; Dir Dr KHALID MIRZA.

Magadh Mahila College: tel. (612) 2223454; fax (612) 2213738; e-mail info@magadhmahilacollege.org; internet www.magadhmahilacollege.org; f. 1946; 30 teachers; 918 students; Prin. Dr SUKHADA KUMARI.

National Institute of Technology: tel. (612) 2670631; Prin. Dr U. C. RAY.

Patna College: tel. (612) 2671589; f. 1863; the oldest college in the province, and the parent instn of 3 other colleges; 48 teachers; 2,363 students; Prin. Dr RANVIJAY KUMAR.

Patna Dental College: tel. (612) 2665130; Prin. Dr D. K. SINGH.

Patna Law College: tel. (612) 2670510; f. 1906; 20 teachers; 868 students; Prin. Dr RAKESH VERMA.

Patna Medical College: tel. (612) 2300343; f. 1925; under administrative control of the Govt of Bihar; 60 teachers; 900 students; Prin. Dr R. K. P. SINGH.

Patna Science College: tel. (612) 6453576; internet sciencecollege.bih.nic.in; f. 1927; 56 teachers; 1,002 students; Prin. Dr S. N. GUHA.

Patna Training College: tel. (612) 2302037; f. 1908; 10 teachers; 126 students; Prin. Dr JAGDISH PRASAD SHARMA.

Patna Women's College: tel. (612) 2531186; internet www.patnawomenscollege.in; f. 1940; 44 teachers; 2,309 students; Prin. Sister Dr DORIS D'SOUZA.

Vanijya Mahavidyalaya: tel. (612) 2670782; f. 1953; 12 teachers; 704 students; Prin. Dr SHAMBHU NATH SINGH.

Women's Training College: tel. (612) 2222809; f. 1951; 11 teachers; 244 students; Prin. Dr MONAWWAR JAHAN.

PERIYAR UNIVERSITY

Bangalore Main Rd Salem 636011, Tamil Nadu

Telephone: (427) 2345766
Fax: (427) 2345565
E-mail: info@periyaruniversity.ac.in
Internet: periyaruniversity.ac.in

Founded 1997
State control
Academic year: July to June
Languages of instruction: English, Tamil
Chancellor: HE THE GOVERNOR OF TAMIL NADU
Vice-Chancellor: Dr M. THANGARAJU
Registrar: Dr S. GUNASEKARAN
Controller of Examinations: Dr A. JAYAKUMAR
Univ. Librarian: Dr N. SUBRAMANIAN
Library of 48,000 vols, 168 periodicals
Number of teachers: 108
Number of students: 1,100

Faculties of Arts, Commerce, Education, Engineering, Languages and Science

There are 59 affiliated colleges.

PONDICHERRY UNIVERSITY

R. Venkataraman Nagar, Kalapet, Pondicherry 605014

Telephone: (413) 2655179
Fax: (413) 2655734
E-mail: registrar@pondiuni.edu.in
Internet: www.pondiuni.org

Founded 1985
Central university
State control
Languages of instruction: English, French, Tamil, Hindi, Malayalam, Telugu, Sanskrit
Academic year: July to June
Chancellor: HE THE VICE-PRESIDENT OF INDIA
Vice-Chancellor: Prof. J. A. K. TAREEN
Registrar: S. LOGANATHAN
Public Relations Officer: N. ARUNAGIRI
Controller of Examinations: Prof. T. J. SAHAYAM CHELLIAH
Librarian: R. SAMYUKTHA
Number of teachers: 140
Number of students: 1,217 (University), 15,909 (affiliated colleges and institutes)

Publication: *Journal of Social Sciences and Humanities*

DEANS
School of Humanities: Dr V. C. THOMAS

School of Life Sciences: Prof. PRIYA DAVIDAR
School of Management: Dr R. PANNEERSEL-VAM
School of Performing Arts: Prof. R. RAJU
School of Physical, Chemical and Applied Sciences: Dr S. BALAKRISHNAN
School of Social and Int. Studies: Prof. D. SAMBANDHAN
Ramanujam School of Mathematics and Computer Science: Dr H. P. PATIL
Subramania Bharathi School of Tamil Language and Literature: Dr A. ARIVUNAMBI

ATTACHED INSTITUTES

Bioinformatics Centre: tel. and fax (413) 2655211; e-mail bicpu2001@yahoo.co.in; internet www.bicpu.edu.in; Dir Dr P. P. MATHUR.

Centre for Human Rights: f. 1999; Dir Dr T. S. N. SASTRY.

Centre for Nehru Studies: Dir Dr B. KRISHNAMURTHY.

Centre for Pollution Control and Energy Technology: Dir Dr S. A. ABBASI.

Centre for Women's Studies: f. 1999; Dir Dr V. T. USHA.

Centre for Yoga Studies: f. 2000; Dir Dr D. SAKTHIGNANAVEL.

POTTI SREERAMULU TELUGU UNIVERSITY

Lalitha Kala Kshetram, Public Gardens, Nampally, Hyderabad 500004, Andhra Pradesh
Telephone: (40) 23230435
Fax: (40) 23236045
E-mail: info@teluguuniversity.ac.in
Internet: teluguuniversity.ac.in
Founded 1985
5 Campuses in Hyderabad, Kuchipudi, Rajahmundry, Sri Sailam, Warangal
Chancellor: HE The Gov. of Andhra Pradesh RAMESHWAR THAKUR
Vice-Chancellor: Prof. A. BHOOMAIAH
Registrar: Prof. T. GOWRISHANKER
Librarian: Dr C. M. KRISHANA
Library of 100,000 vols (55,000 Telugu, 43,000 English), 150 periodicals

DEANS

School of Comparative Studies: Prof. S. SUBRAHMANYAM
School of Fine Arts: Prof. BITTU VENKATESH-WARLU
School of Folk and Tribal Lore: Dr B. RAMESH
School of History, Culture and Archaeology: Prof. D. R. RAJU
School of Language Development: Prof. K. ASHIRVADAM
School of Social and Other Sciences: Prof. V.B. SUBRAHMANYAM
School of Telugu Literature: Prof. P. LEELA-VATHI

PUNJAB AGRICULTURAL UNIVERSITY

Ludhiana 141004, Punjab
Telephone: (161) 2401960
Fax: (161) 2400945
E-mail: info@pau.edu
Internet: www.pau.edu
Founded 1962
Teaching, Research and Extension
Autonomous control
Languages of instruction: English, Punjabi
Academic year: August to July (two terms)
Chancellor: HE THE GOVERNOR OF PUNJAB
Vice-Chancellor: Dr MANJIT SINGH KANG
Dir of Extension Education: Dr N. S. MALHI
Dir of Research: Dr PARAMJIT SINGH MINHAS

Dir of Student Welfare: Dr DULCHA SINGH BRAR
Dean of Postgraduate Studies: Dr SATWINDER K. MANN
Registrar: Dr V. K. SHARMA
Librarian: Dr J. K. SANGHA
Library of 257,724 vols, 6,849 journals, 36,043 theses, 101,311 periodicals, 22 e-books
Number of teachers: 1,182
Number of students: 2,067
Publications: *Changi Kheti* (in Punjabi, 12 a year), *Journal of Research* (in English, 4 a year), *Package of Practices for Crops of the Punjab* (2 a year), *Progressive Farming* (in English, 12 a year), *Punjab Agricultural Handbook* (1 a year)

DEANS

College of Agricultural Engineering: Dr P. K. GUPTA
College of Agriculture: Dr M. S. AULAKH
College of Basic Science and Humanities: Dr T. SINGH
College of Home Science: Dr N. GREWAL
College of Veterinary Science: Dr M. S. OBEROI

PUNJAB TECHNICAL UNIVERSITY

Ladowali Rd, Jalandhar 144001, Punjab
Telephone: (1822) 255506
Fax: (1822) 255507
E-mail: ptumail@ptu.ac.in
Internet: www.ptu.ac.in
Founded 1997
Courses in engineering, natural sciences and technology; affiliated colleges: 40 engineering, 56 management, 17 pharmacy, 6 architecture, 2 hotel management, 13 medical lab technology and IT
Chancellor: HE THE GOV. OF PUNJAB
Vice-Chancellor: Dr RAJNEESH ARORA
Registrar: SAROJINI GAUTAM SHARDA.

PUNJABI UNIVERSITY

Patiala 147002, Punjab
Telephone: (175) 3046030
Fax: (175) 2283073
E-mail: regpup@pbi.ac.in
Internet: www.punjabiuniversity.ac.in
Founded 1962
Languages of instruction: Punjabi, English
State control
166 Affiliated colleges
Academic year: July to May (three terms)
Chancellor: HE THE GOVERNOR OF PUNJAB
Vice-Chancellor: Dr JASPAL SINGH
Registrar: Dr S. S. KHEHRA
Dir of Public Relations: Dr GURMEET SINGH MAAN
Librarian: Dr SAROJ BALA
Library of 420,000 books, 50,000 journals
Number of students: 11,386
Publication: *Journal of Religious Studies* (4 a year)

DEANS

Faculty of Arts and Culture: Prof. GURNAM SINGH
Faculty of Business Studies: Dr A. S. CHAWLA
Faculty of Education and Information Science: Dr JAGTAR SINGH
Faculty of Engineering and Technology: Prof. M. S. SAINI
Faculty of Languages: Prof. B. S. KHEHRA
Faculty of Law: Dr C. SINGH
Faculty of Life Sciences: P. SINGHAL
Faculty of Medicine: Dr N. KAUR MULTANI
Faculty of Physical Sciences: Dr R. C. VERMA
Faculty of Social Sciences: Dr MANJU VERMA

ATTACHED RESEARCH INSTITUTE

Advanced Centre for Technical Development of Punjabi Language, Literature and Culture: ; tel. (175) 3046171; f. 2004; Dir Dr GURPREET SINGH LEHAL.

RABINDRA BHARATI UNIVERSITY

56A Barrackpore Trunk Rd, Kolkata 700050
Telephone: (33) 25568019
Fax: (33) 25568079
Internet: www.rabindrabharatiuniversity .net
Founded 1962
Languages of instruction: Bengali, English
State control
Academic year: June to May (three terms)
Chancellor: HE THE GOVERNOR OF WEST BENGAL
Vice-Chancellor: Prof. KARUNA SINDHU DAS
Registrar: Dr TAPATI MUKHERJEE
Finance Officer: AMIT MUKHERJEE
Public Relations Officer: SURANJANA BHATTA-CHARYA
Librarian: SATYABRATA GHOSAL
Library of 92,500 vols, 258 periodicals
Number of teachers: 165
Number of students: 6,759
Publications: departmental journals (1 a year: Bengali, Sanskrit, English, Education, Economics, Library and Information Science, Vedic Studies, Study and Research on Tagore, Rabindra Sangeet), *Rabindra Bharati Journal* (English, 1 a year), *Rabindra Bharati University Patrika* (Bengali, 1 a year)

DEANS

Faculty of Applied Arts: A. P. MITRA (acting)
Faculty of Arts: Prof. S. K. GHOSH
Faculty of Fine Arts: Prof. A. DUTT
Faculty of Visual Arts: Dr S. DHAR

RAJASTHAN AGRICULTURAL UNIVERSITY, BIKANER

Bikaner 334006, Rajasthan
Telephone: (151) 2250025
Fax: (151) 2250336
E-mail: reg@raubikaner.org
Internet: www.raubikaner.org
Founded 1988
Vice-Chancellor: Prof. PRATAP NARAIN
Registrar: RAM DEV GOYAL
Dean of Postgraduate Studies: Dr ANIL KUMAR
Controller of Examinations: Dr PRAN MEHRO-TRA
Dir of Distance Education: Dr A. K. PUROHIT
Dir of Extension Education: Dr R. N. GOS-WAMI
Dir of Student Welfare: Dr R. N. KACHHAWA
Dirs of Research: Dr S. B. S. YADAV, Dr M. P. SAHU
Librarian: CHETAN RAJPUROHIT
Library: Central Library of 10,000 vols
Number of teachers: 425
Number of students: 2,250

DEANS

College of Agriculture: Dr B. L. POONIA
College of Home Science: Dr M. GOYAL
College of Veterinary and Animal Science: A. K. GAHLOT
Institute of Agri-business Management: Prof. A. K. DAHAMA (Dir)

CONSTITUENT COLLEGES

College of Agriculture: tel. (151) 2250292; e-mail coa@agricolbikaner.org; internet www .agricolbikaner.org; f. 1988.

College of Home Science: tel. (151) 2250692; e-mail chsc_bkn@hotmail.com; internet www.hascraubikaner.org.

College of Veterinary and Animal Science: tel. (151) 2543419; fax (151) 2549348; internet www.bikanervetcol.org; publ. *Journal of Camel Practice and Research, Journal of Canine Development and Research, Veterinary Practitioner.*

Institute of Agribusiness Management (IABM): tel. (151) 2252981; e-mail director@ iabmbikaner.org; internet www.iabmbikaner .org; f. 2000.

S.K.N. College of Agriculture: Jobner; tel. (1425) 254022; Dir B. R. CHIPPA.

RAJASTHAN AYURVEDA UNIVERSITY

Jodhpur 342037, Rajasthan
Telephone: (291) 5153702
Fax: (291) 5153700
E-mail: rau_jodhpur@yahoo.co.in
Internet: www.raujodhpur.org
Founded 2003
Academic year: July to June
Languages of instruction: Sanskrit, Hindi, English
State Control

Vice-Chancellor: Prof. RAMESH KUMAR JAIN
Registrar: CHAIN SINGH PANWAR PANWAR
Librarian: Prof. RADHEYSHYAM SHARMA

44 Affiliated colleges
Library of 10,514 vols, 28 journals
Number of teachers: 33
Number of students: 6,948

DEANS

Faculty of Ayurved: Prof. RAJYAVARDHAN SINGH RAI
Faculty of Homeopathy: Dr H. P. TYAGI
Faculty of Unani: Prof. G. Q. CHISTI

RAJENDRA AGRICULTURAL UNIVERSITY

Pusa, Samastipur 848125, Bihar
Telephone: (6274) 240239
Fax: (6274) 240266
E-mail: info@pusavarsity.org.in
Internet: www.pusavarsity.org.in

Founded 1970
Languages of instruction: Hindi, English
Academic year: July to June (two terms)
Chancellor: HE THE GOV. OF BIHAR
Vice-Chancellor: Dr M. L. CHOUDHARY
Registrar: Dr A. K. P. SINGH
Librarian: Dr B. N. MISHRA

Library of 54,000 vols and 2,000 MSS
Number of teachers: 400
Number of students: 1,200

Publications: *Adhunik Kisan* (12 a year), *Research Journal* (4 a year)

DEANS

Faculty of Agricultural Engineering: Dr A. P. MISHRA
Faculty of Agriculture: Dr K. R. MAURYA
Faculty of Basic Science: Dr V. K. SHAHI
Faculty of Home Science: Dr M. SINGH
Faculty of Veterinary Science: Dr J. N. SINGH
Postgraduate Faculty: Dr V. S. VERMA

PROFESSORS

Faculty of Agricultural Engineering:
  KUMAR, A., Soil Conservation
  RAM, R. B., Farm Machinery
Faculty of Agriculture:
  CHOUDHARY, L. B., Plant Breeding
  MISHRA, S. S., Agronomy
  OJHA, K. L., Plant Pathology
  PRASAD, B., Soil Science
  SAKAL, R., Soil Science
  SHARMA, R. P. ROY, Agronomy
  SINGH, B. K., Agronomy
  SINGH, R. K., Seed Technology
  THAKUR, R., Plant Breeding
  YAZDANI, S. S., Entomology and Agricultural Zoology
Faculty of Veterinary Science:
  MOHAN, M., Animal Breeding and Genetics
  PRASAD, C. B., Veterinary Microbiology
  SINGH, M. K., Veterinary Pharmacology
  SINHA, R. R. P., Animal Nutrition
  SRIVASTAVA, P. S., Veterinary Parasitology

ATTACHED COLLEGES

Bihar Agriculture College: Sabour, Bhagalpur; f. 1908 as Bengal Provincial College; library of 24,835 vols, 70 periodicals; Prin. Dr S. K. CHANDRA.

Bihar Veterinary College: Patna; Prin. Dr S. R. SINGH.

College of Agricultural Engineering: f. 1983; depts of farm machinery, farm power and renewable energy, irrigation and drainage engineering, post-harvest technology and agricultural structures, soil and water conservation engineering; Dean Dr A. P. MISHRA.

College of Basic Sciences and Humanities: f. 1981; depts of biochemistry and chemistry, botany and plant physiology, genetics and molecular biology, language, mathematics and computer application, microbiology, physics, statistics; Dean Dr V. K. SHAHI.

College of Fisheries: Dholi; f. 1984; Prin. Dr S. C. RAI.

College of Home Science: Pusa; f. 1982; depts of child devt, clothing and textiles, family resource management, foods and nutrition; Dean Dr MEERA SINGH.

Sanjay Gandhi Institute of Dairy Technology: f. 1982; depts of dairy cattle breeding and production, dairy cattle nutrition and forage production, dairy chemistry, dairy economics, statistics and management, dairy eng., dairy microbiology, dairy technology, reproduction and physiology; Dir Dr C. PRASAD.

Tirhut College of Agriculture: Dholi, Muzaffarpur; f. 1960; Prin. Dr U. K. MISHRA.

RAJIV GANDHI PROUDYOGIKI VISHWAVIDYALAYA
(University of Technology of Madhya Pradesh)

Airport By-pass, Gandhi Nagar, Bhopal 462036, Madhya Pradesh
Telephone: (755) 2678890
Fax: (755) 2742002
E-mail: vc@rgtu.net
Internet: www.rgtu.net
Founded 1998
State Technological Univ.

156 Colleges of engineering, 44 colleges of MCA, 91 colleges of pharmacy, 3 colleges of architecture

Vice-Chancellor: Prof. PIYUSH TRIVEDI
Registrar: Dr A. K. S. BHADORIA
Controller of Examinations: Dr A. K. SINGH

Library of 24,720 vols
Number of students: 130,000

RAJIV GANDHI UNIVERSITY

Rono Hills, Doimukh 791112, Arunachal Pradesh
Telephone: (360) 2277253
Fax: (360) 2277889
E-mail: registrar@rgu.ac.in
Internet: www.rgu.ac.in

Founded 1984, as Arunachal Univ.; present name 2006
Public control
Language of instruction: English
Academic year: June to May

Chancellor: Prof. MRINAL MIRI
Vice-Chancellor: Prof. TAMO MIBANG
Registrar: A. MITRA
Asst Librarian: D. K. PANDEY

Library of 100,000 vols, 200 periodicals
Number of teachers: 100
Number of students: 500

DEANS

Faculty of Education: Prof. K. C. KAPOOR
Faculty of Environmental Sciences: Prof. R. S. YADAVA
Faculty of Languages: Prof. N. NAGARAJU
Faculty of Management: Prof. R. C. PARIDA
Faculty of Social Sciences: Prof. N. C. ROY

RAJIV GANDHI UNIVERSITY OF HEALTH SCIENCES, KARNATAKA

Bangalore 560041, Karnataka
Telephone: (80) 26961926
Fax: (80) 26961927
E-mail: drpsp@rguhs.ac.in
Internet: www.rguhs.ac.in
Founded 1996

Courses in anaesthesia, ayurveda, cardiology, dentistry, homeopathy, hospital management, medical laboratory technology, medicine, naturopathy and yogic sciences, nursing, perfusion technology, pharmacy, physiotherapy, psycho-social rehabilitation, radiography, renal dialysis technology, respiratory technology, surgery, unani medicine

Vice-Chancellor: Dr S. RAMANANDA SHETTY
Registrar: VASANTHA KUMAR S.
Librarian: Dr R. RAMA RAJ URS.

RANCHI UNIVERSITY

Shaheed Chowk Ranchi, 834001 Bihar
Telephone: (651) 2208553; (651) 2301077
E-mail: admin@ranchiuniversity.org.in
Internet: ranchiuniversity.org.in
Founded 1960

Teaching and affiliating; 23 postgraduate depts; 33 constituent colleges; 24 affiliated colleges

Chancellor: HE THE GOVERNOR OF BIHAR
Vice-Chancellor: Prof. A. A. KHAN
Registrar: Dr L. N. BHAGAT
Controller of Examinations: Dr A. K. MAHTO
Dean of Student Welfare: Dr C. S. P. LUGUN

Library of 100,000 vols
Number of teachers: c. 2,000
Number of students: 67,500

Publications: *Journal of Agricultural Science, Journal of Historical Research, Journal of Social Research, Political Scientist, Research Journal of Philosophy, The Geographical Outlook, The University Journal*

DEANS

Faculty of Commerce: Prof. S. N. L. DAS
Faculty of Education: Dr APARAJITA JHA
Faculty of Engineering: (vacant)
Faculty of Humanities: Prof. S. P. MISHRA
Faculty of Law: Dr B. N. JHA
Faculty of Medicine: Prof. Dr S. N. CHOUDHARY
Faculty of Science: Prof. G. P. SHARAN
Faculty of Social Sciences: Prof. S. P. MISHRA

RANI DURGAVATI VISHWAVIDYALAYA JABALPUR

Saraswati Vihar, Jabalpur 482001, Madhya Pradesh

Telephone: (761) 2600567
Fax: (761) 2603752
E-mail: cc@rdunijbpin.nic.in
Internet: www.rdunijbpin.org

Founded 1957 as Jabalpur University, name changed 1983

Teaching and Affiliating
Languages of instruction: Hindi, English
Academic year: July to April (four terms)
Chancellor: HE THE GOVERNOR OF MADHYA PRADESH
Vice-Chancellor: Dr S. M. P. KHURANA
Dir of College Devt Council: Dr KAMLESH MISHRA
Dean of Student Welfare: Dr R. D. BHARDWAJ
Registrar: M. K. RAI
Librarian: Y. L. CHOPRA
Library of 183,000 vols
Number of teachers: 1,053
Number of students: 95,000

DEANS

Faculty of Arts: (vacant)
Faculty of Ayurveda: Dr K. K. AGNIHOTRI
Faculty of Commerce: (vacant)
Faculty of Education: Dr B. K. SAHU
Faculty of Homeopathic Medicine and Surgery: (vacant)
Faculty of Home Science: (vacant)
Faculty of Law: Prof. A. SHRIVASTAVA
Faculty of Life Sciences: Prof. Y. K. BANSAL
Faculty of Management: (vacant)
Faculty of Mathematical Science: Prof. P. V. JAIN
Faculty of Medicine: Dr D. K. SAKALLE
Faculty of Science: Prof. A. SHRIVASTAVA
Faculty of Social Sciences: Dr C. S. S. THAKUR

There are 116 affiliated colleges

RASHTRASANT TUKADOJI MAHARAJ NAGPUR UNIVERSITY

Chhatrapati Shivaji Maharaj Admin. Premises, Rabindranath Tagore Marg, Nagpur 440001, Maharashtra

Telephone: (712) 2525417
Fax: (712) 2532841
E-mail: info@nagpuruniversity.org
Internet: www.nagpuruniversity.org

Founded 1923, fmrly Nagpur Univ.

Teaching and affiliating; 439 affiliated colleges
Languages of instruction: English, Hindi, Marathi
Academic year: June to March (two terms)
Chancellor: HE THE GOV. OF MAHARASHTRA
Vice-Chancellor: Dr S. N. PATHAN
Registrar: SUBHASH BELSARE
Librarian: Dr P. S. G. KUMAR
Library of 350,171 vols, including 14,313 MSS
Number of teachers: 4,074
Number of students: 95,664

DEANS

Faculty of Arts: A. K. DEY
Faculty of Ayurvedic Medicine: S. SHARMA
Faculty of Commerce: N. H. KHATRI
Faculty of Education: R. S. DAGAR
Faculty of Engineering and Technology: H. THAKARE
Faculty of Home Science: Dr A. G. MOHARIL
Faculty of Law: SUNDARAM
Faculty of Medicine: Dr W. B. TAYADE
Faculty of Science: Dr T. M. KARDE
Faculty of Social Sciences: V. H. GHORPADE

CONSTITUENT COLLEGES

B. R. Ambedkar College of Law: f. 1925; 10 teachers; 2,571 students; Prin. Dr J. L. APARAJIT.
Laxminarayan Institute of Technology: tel. (712) 2561107; fax (712) 2531659; e-mail rajumankar@rediffmail.com; internet www .litnagpur.info; f. 1942; 50 teachers; 510 students; Dir Dr R. B. MANKAR.
University College of Education: Nagpur; f. 1945; 16 teachers; 320 students; Prin. V. MANAPURE.

SAMBALPUR UNIVERSITY

PO Jyoti Vihar, Burla, Sambalpur 768019, Orissa

Telephone: (663) 2430157
Fax: (663) 2430158
E-mail: chairman@sambalpuruniversitypgc .in
Internet: www.sambalpuruniversitypgc.in

Founded 1967

Teaching and Affiliating
Language of instruction: English
Academic year: June to May
Chancellor: THE GOVERNOR OF ORISSA
Vice-Chancellor: Prof. ARUN K. PUJARI
Registrar: R. R. PADHEE
Dir of College Devt Council: Prof. S. MOHANTY
Librarian: Dr B. P. MOHAPATRA
179 Affiliated colleges
Library of 105,000 vols, 15,000 periodicals
Number of teachers: 1,653
Number of students: 36,225
Publications: *Journal* (Science, 1 a year), *Journal of Humanities* (1 a year), *Saptarshi* (12 a year)

DEANS

Faculty of Arts: Prof. S. NANDA
Faculty of Commerce: Prof. D. P. NAYAK
Faculty of Education: (vacant)
Faculty of Engineering: Dr R. K. MISHRA
Faculty of Law: Prof. G. K. RATH
Faculty of Medicine: Prof. A. K. SARANGI
Faculty of Science: Dr M. K. BEHERA

SAMPURNANAND SANSKRIT UNIVERSITY

Varanasi 221002, Uttar Pradesh

Telephone: (542) 2204089; (542) 2206617
Internet: ssvv.up.nic.in

Founded 1958

Teaching and affiliating; faculties of adhunika jnana vijnana, philsophy, sahitya Sanskrit, sramana vidya, veda-vedanga; 2 affiliated on-campus, and 1,998 off-campus colleges
Chancellor: THE GOV. OF UTTAR PRADESH
Vice-Chancellor: Prof. V. KUTUMB SHASTRI
Registrar: YOGANDRA NATH
Dir of Research: Dr RAJA RAM SHUKLA
Librarian: V. N. MISRA
Library of 262,000 vols
Number of students: 35,000

SARDAR PATEL UNIVERSITY

Vallabh Vidyanagar 388120, Gujarat

Telephone: (2692) 226812
Fax: (2692) 236475
Internet: www.spuvvn.edu

Founded 1955

Teaching and affiliating; 26 postgraduate depts, 1 constituent college, 71 affiliated colleges
Languages of instruction: Hindi, English, Gujarati

Academic year: June to April (two terms)
Chancellor: HE THE GOV. OF GUJARAT
Vice-Chancellor: Dr B. G. PATEL
Registrar: Dr B. NATRAJ
Librarian: Dr M. J. TRIVEDI
Library of 212,780 vols
Number of teachers: 172
Number of students: 43,912 , incl. 8,597 postgraduate
Publications: *Arth-Vikas* (Economics Journal), *Journal of Education and Psychology*, *Mimansa* (Journal of English Literature), *Prajna* (Journal of Basic Science), *Prajna* (Journal of Social Science and Business Studies), *Sheel Shrutam* (12 a year)

DEANS

Faculty of Arts: Dr R. P. PANDYA
Faculty of Business Studies: M. K. PATEL
Faculty of Education: Dr V. T. BHAMWARI
Faculty of Engineering and Technology: Prin.: F. S. UMRIGAR
Faculty of Home Science: Dr REMA SUBHASH
Faculty of Homoeopathy: Dr V. D. PATEL
Faculty of Law: APRURVA C. PATHAK
Faculty of Management: Dr NIKHIL M. ZAVERI
Faculty of Medicine: Dr S. H. SHRIVASTAV
Faculty of Pharmaceutical Science: Prof. A. K. SALUJA
Faculty of Science: Dr D. J. DESAI

SARDAR VALLABH BHAI PATEL UNIVERSITY OF AGRICULTURE AND TECHNOLOGY

Modipuram, Meerut 250110, Uttar Pradesh

Telephone: (121) 2411503
Fax: (121) 2411505
E-mail: university@svbpuniversitymerrut .org
Internet: www.svbpmeerut.ac.in

Founded 2000

Colleges of agriculture, agriculture business management, animal husbandry and veterinary science, basic sciences, biotechnology, engineering, home science, horticulture and agroforestry, information technology, postharvest technology and food processing, postgraduate studies
Chancellor: HE THE GOVERNOR OF UTTAR PRADESH
Vice-Chancellor: Dr M. P. YADAV
Registrar: Dr NARENDRA SHARMA
Dean of Student Welfare: Prof. P. L. SAROJ
Dir of Research: Prof. I. B. SINGH

DEANS

College of Agriculture: Prof. B. RAM (acting)
College of Biotechnology: Prof. D. SINGH (acting)
Postgraduate Studies: Prof. Y. P. SINGH

SARDARKRUSHINAGAR DANTIWADA AGRICULTURAL UNIVERSITY

District Banaskantha, Sardar Krushinagar 385506, Gujarat

Telephone: (2748) 278222
Fax: (2748) 278261
E-mail: vc@gauskn.guj.nic.in
Internet: www.sdau.edu.in

Founded 1972

Fmrly Gujarat Agricultural Univ.
Academic year: July to March
Chancellor: SUNDARSINGH BHANDARI
Vice-Chancellor: Dr RAVISH CHANDRA MAHESHWARI
Dir of Research and Dean of Postgraduate Studies: Dr S. B. S. TIKKA
Dir of Student Welfare: Dr VEER SINGH
Registrar: Dr H. N. KHER
Librarian: Dr L. D. PARMER
Library of 24,150 vols, 225 periodicals

Number of teachers: 1,336
Number of students: 2,181

DEANS

Faculty of Agricultural Engineering and Technology: Dr S. C. B. SIRIPURAPU
Faculty of Agriculture: Dr J. G. PATEL
Faculty of Dairy Science: Dr R. S. SHARMA
Faculty of Fisheries Science: Dr A. Y. DESAI (acting)
Faculty of Forestry and Horticulture: Dr B. M. PATEL (acting)
Faculty of Home Science: Dr K. SHREEDHARAN (acting)
Faculty of Veterinary Science and Animal Husbandry: Dr V. P. VADODARIA (acting)

CONSTITUENT COLLEGES

Aspee College of Home Science: Sardar Krushinagar; Prin. Dr M. M. PATEL (acting).

Aspee College of Horticulture and Forestry: Navsari; Prin. Dr B. M. PATEL (acting).

B. A. College of Agriculture: Anand; Prin. Dr D. J. PATEL.

College of Agricultural Engineering and Technology: Junagadh; Prin. Dr S. C. B. SIRIPURAPU.

College of Agriculture, Junagadh: Prin. Dr D. D. MALAVIA.

College of Agriculture, Sardar Krushinagar: Prin. Dr S. R. S. DANGE (acting).

College of Fisheries Science: Veraval; Prin. Dr A. Y. DESAI (acting).

College of Veterinary Science and Animal Husbandry, Anand: Prin. Dr M. B. PANDE (acting).

College of Veterinary Science and Animal Husbandry, Sardar Krushinagar: Prin. Dr M. C. DESAI.

Mansukhlal Chhaganlal College of Dairy Science: Anand; Prin. Dr R. S. SHARMA.

N. M. College of Agriculture: Navsari; Prin. Dr H. N. VYAS.

SAURASHTRA UNIVERSITY

University Campus, University Rd, Rajkot 360005, Gujarat
Telephone: (281) 2576347
Fax: (281) 2581385
E-mail: registrar@sauuni.ernet.in
Internet: www.saurashtrauniversity.edu
Founded 1967
Teaching and Affiliating
State control
Languages of instruction: Gujarati, Hindi, English
Academic year: June to March/April (two terms)
Chancellor: HE THE GOV. OF GUJARAT STATE
Vice-Chancellor: Dr KAMLESH P. JOSHIPURA
Pro-Vice-Chancellor: K. T. TRIVEDI
Registrar: G. M. JANI
Controller of Examinations: J. M. MAMTORA
Librarian: N. N. SONI
318 Affiliated colleges
Library of 171,577 vols, 230 periodicals
Number of teachers: 3,614 (incl. affiliated colleges)
Number of students: 140,234 (incl. affiliated colleges)

DEANS

Faculty of Architecture: (vacant)
Faculty of Arts: S. J. JHALA (acting)
Faculty of Business Management: Dr P. L. CHAUHAN
Faculty of Commerce: R. M. TALVANIA
Faculty of Education: B. R. RAMANUJ
Faculty of Engineering: S. PARIKH

Faculty of Home Science: V. CHHICHHIYA
Faculty of Homeopathy: Dr B. M. PANDA (acting)
Faculty of Law: N. C. SHUKLA (acting)
Faculty of Medicine: Dr D. K. SHAH
Faculty of Rural Studies: D. R. MARTHAK
Faculty of Science: Dr G. BHIMANI

SHER-E-KASHMIR UNIVERSITY OF AGRICULTURAL SCIENCES AND TECHNOLOGY JAMMU

Railway Rd, Jammu 180012, Jammu and Kashmir
Telephone: (191) 2263714
Fax: (191) 2262073
E-mail: vc@skuast.org
Internet: www.skuast.org
Founded 1999
State control
Language of instruction: English
Academic year: August to July
Chancellor: HE THE GOVERNOR OF JAMMU AND KASHMIR
Vice-Chancellor: Dr B. MISHRA
Registrar: B. B. GUPTA
Librarian: Dr V. SREENIVASULU
Library of 24,603 vols, 163 periodical titles
Number of teachers: 169
Number of students: 660

DEANS

Faculty of Agriculture: Dr AJAY KOUL
Faculty of Veterinary Sciences and Animal Husbandry: Dr A. R. NAZKI

SHER-E-KASHMIR UNIVERSITY OF AGRICULTURAL SCIENCES AND TECHNOLOGY OF KASHMIR

Shalimar Campus, Srinagar 191121, Jammu and Kashmir
Telephone: (194) 2462160
Fax: (194) 2462160
E-mail: vcskuastk@jk.nic.in
Internet: www.skuastkashmir.ac.in
Founded 1982
State control
Languages of instruction: English, Urdu
Academic year: August to July
Faculties of agriculture, fisheries, postgraduate studies, veterinary sciences and animal husbandry
Chancellor: HE THE GOVERNOR OF JAMMU AND KASHMIR
Vice-Chancellor: Dr TEJ PARTAP
Registrar: Dr F. A. ZAKI
Head of Library Services: BASHIR AHMAD
Library of 66,243 vols, 110 periodicals
Number of teachers: 420
Number of students: 928
Publication: *SKUAST-K Journal of Research*

DEANS

Faculty of Agriculture: Dr. M. YOUSF ZARGAR
Faculty of Fisheries: Dr. MASOOD-UL-HASAN BALKHI
Faculty of Veterinary Science and Animal Husbandry: Dr. ZAFFAR-ULLAH KHAN

SHIVAJI UNIVERSITY

Vidyanagar, Kolhapur 416004, Maharashtra
Telephone: (231) 2609000
Fax: (231) 2691533
E-mail: vcoffice@unishivaji.ac.in
Internet: www.unishivaji.ac.in
Founded 1962
Teaching and Affiliating
Languages of instruction: English, Marathi
Academic year: June to April (two terms)

Chancellor: HE THE GOVERNOR OF MAHARASH-TRA
Vice-Chancellor: Dr M. M. SALUNKHE
Registrar: Dr D. T. SHIRKE (acting)
Librarian: R. K. KAMAT (acting)
226 Affiliated colleges
Library of 244,729 vols, 6,923 MSS, 361 periodicals
Number of teachers: 3,483
Number of students: 194,314
Publication: *University Journal* (Humanities and Social Sciences sections)

DEANS

Faculty of Arts: Dr J. R. JADHAV
Faculty of Ayurvedic and Homeopathic Medicine: (vacant)
Faculty of Commerce: Dr B. S. SAWANT
Faculty of Education: K. N. SANGLE
Faculty of Engineering and Technology: A. N. JADHAV
Faculty of Law: Prin.: MANGLA S. PATIL
Faculty of Medicine: Dr RAMKRISHNA AYCHIT
Faculty of Science: Dr T. B. JAGTAP
Faculty of Social Sciences: Dr V. P. RASAM

CONSTITUENT CENTRES

Centre for Community Development: tel. (231) 2690571; Dir MANJUSHA DESHPANDE.

Centre of Gandhian Studies: f. 2000; Dir Dr R. B. PATIL.

Centre for Women's Studies: Dir Dr MEDHA NANIVADEKAR.

Shahu Research Centre: f. 1974; Dir Dr M. P. PATIL.

SHREEMATI NATHIBAI DAMODAR THACKERSEY WOMEN'S UNIVERSITY

1 Nathibai Thackersey Rd, Mumbai 400020, Maharashtra
Telephone: (22) 22031879
Fax: (22) 22018226
Internet: sndt.digitaluniversity.ac
Founded 1916
Teaching and affiliating; 210 affiliated colleges
State control
Languages of instruction: English, Gujarati, Marathi, Hindi
Academic year: June to March (two terms)
Chancellor: HE THE GOV. OF MAHARASHTRA
Vice-Chancellor: Dr CHANDRA KRISHNA-MURTHY
Pro-Vice-Chancellor: Prof. S. MANTHA
Registrar: Dr MADHU MADAN
Librarian: Dr SUSHAMA POWDWAL
Library of 335,000 vols
Number of teachers: 744 full-time, 238 part-time
Number of students: 50,000

DEANS

Faculty of Arts: Dr SHASHI KASHYAP
Faculty of Commerce: Dr KALYANI VENKA-TESHWARAN
Faculty of Education: Dr LEENA DESHPANDE
Faculty of Fine Arts: AVIRAJ TAYADE
Faculty of Home Sciences: Dr SHOBHA UDIPI
Faculty of Library Science: PARUL ZAVERI
Faculty of Nursing: NANCY FERNANDES
Faculty of Social Sciences: Dr MANGALA JUNGALE

CONSTITUENT COLLEGES

C. U. Shah College of Pharmacy: Sir Vithaldas Vidyavihar Juhu Rd, Mumbai 400049; tel. (22) 26608551; e-mail cuscp@yahoo.co.in; f. 1980; Prin. Dr S. Y. GABHE.

Janakidevi Bajaj Institute of Management Studies: Sir Vithaldas Vidyavihar Juhu Rd, Mumbai 400049; tel. (22) 26606626; e-mail jdbims@rediffmail.com;

internet www.jdbims.net; f. 1997; Dir GULNAR SHARMA.

Leelabai Thackersey College of Nursing: tel. (22) 22087422; e-mail ltcn@rediffmail.com; f. 1952; Prin. ALKA KALAMBI.

Premcoonverbai Vithaldas Damodar Thackersey College of Education for Women: tel. (22) 22063267; e-mail pvdtce@sndt.ac.in; f. 1959; Prin. Dr HARSHA MANCHANT.

Premlila Vithaldas Polytechnic: Sir Vithaldas Vidyavihar Juhu Rd, Mumbai 400049; tel. (22) 26608676; e-mail pvpelex@vsnl.com; internet www.pvpsndt.org; f. 1976; Prin. RAVINDRA KABNURKAR.

Shree Hansraj Pragji Thackersey School of Library Science: e-mail shptsndt@gmail.com; internet www.shpt-econtent.in; f. 1961; Prin. Prof. SUSHAMA POWDWAL.

Shreemati Nathibai Damodar Thackersey College of Arts, and Shreemati Champaben Bhogilal College of Commerce and Economics for Women: tel. (22) 22093789; internet drpradhansndtwcollege.com.in; f. 1931; Prin. Dr B. B. PRADHAN.

Shreemati Nathibai Damodar Thackersey College of Arts and Commerce for Women: Karve Rd, Maharshi Karve Vidyavihar, Pune 411038; f. 1916; Prin. (vacant).

Shreemati Nathibai Damodar Thackersey College of Education for Women: Karve Rd, Maharshi Karve Vidyarihar, Pune 411038; tel. (22) 25433416; e-mail sndt_education_pune@yahoo.co.in; f. 1964; Prin. Dr LEENA DESHPANDE.

Shreemati Nathibai Damodar Thackersey College of Home Science: Karve Rd, Maharshi Karve Vidyarihar, Pune 411038; tel. (22) 25432097; e-mail principal@sndthsc.com; internet www.sndthsc.com; f. 1968; Prin. (vacant).

Sir Vithaldas Thackersey College of Home Science: tel. (22) 26602504; e-mail computerlab@vsnl.net; internet www.svt.ac.in; f. 1959; Prin. Dr INDRAJIT MADAN (acting).

Usha Mittal Institute of Technology: Sir Vithaldas Vidyavihar Juhu Rd, Mumbai 400049; tel. (22) 26606040; e-mail umit@vsnl.net; internet www.umit.ac.in; Dir KUMUD VASNIK.

SHRI JAGANNATH SANSKRIT VISHWAVIDYALAYA

Srivihar, Puri 752003, Orissa
Telephone: (6752) 251663
Fax: (6752) 251073
E-mail: sjsv@ori.nic.in
Internet: sjsv.nic.in

Founded 1981

Depts of dharmashastra, nyaya, sahitya, sarvadarshan, veda, vedanta and vyakarana

Vice-Chancellor: Prof. ALEKHA CHANDRA SARANGI
Registrar: Dr BABAJI CHARAN PATTANAYAK
Librarian: MAHESHWAR MOHAPATRA
Library of 22,731 vols, 1,044 journals
Publication: *Jagannath Jyotih* (irregular).

SHRI MATA VAISHNO DEVI UNIVERSITY

SPO Kakryal, Katra 182320, Distrtict: REASI, Jammu and Kashmir
Telephone: (1991) 285535
Fax: (1991) 285694
E-mail: vc@smvdu.ac.in
Internet: www.smvdu.ac.in

Founded 1999

Residential and teaching
Chancellor: HE THE GOV. OF JAMMU AND KASHMIR
Vice-Chancellor: Prof. N. K. BANSAL
Registrar: Dr R. S. MISRA
Librarian: SUBRATA DEB
Library: approx. 20,000 vols, 1250 online periodicals and 94 print periodicals, e-resources: 500 CDs/DVDs, databases: ABI Inform Global, MathSciNet, EIS Statistical, Memberships: INDEST-AICTE CONSORTIUM, DELNET

DEANS

College of Engineering: Prof. M. L. GARG
College of Management: Prof. J. P. SINGH
College of Philosophy, Culture and Languages: Prof. R. S. MISRA
College of Sciences: Prof. V. VERMA

DIRECTORS

School of Applied Physics and Mathematics: Dr V. K. BHAT
School of Architecture and Landscape Design: Prof. C. L. RAZDAN
School of Business: Dr SUNIL GIRI (acting)
School of Economics: Dr SUPARN SHARMA (acting)
School of Electronics and Communication: Dr S. K. PURI
School of Infrastructure and Resource Management: RAKESH SHARMA (acting)
School of Languages: Dr VANDANA SHARMA (acting)
School of Mechanical Engineering: Dr SUDHIR KUMAR (acting)

SIDO KANHU MURMU UNIVERSITY

Santal Parganas, Dumka 814101, Jharkhand
Internet: skmu.edu.in

Founded 1992 as Siddhu Kanhu Univ., present name 2000

Academic year: June to May

13 Constituent colleges and 15 affiliated colleges

Vice-Chancellor: Dr VICTOR TIGGA
Pro-Vice-Chancellor: Dr ARVIND KUMAR
Dean of Student Welfare: Dr MANOJ KUMAR SINHA
Registrar: Dr A. N. PATHAK (acting)
Librarian: Dr AJIT KUMAR SINGH.

SIKKIM MANIPAL UNIVERSITY OF HEALTH, MEDICAL AND TECHNOLOGICAL SCIENCES

Fifth Mile, Tadong, Gangtok 737102, Sikkim
Telephone: (3592) 232041
Fax: (3592) 232041
E-mail: study@smu.edu.in
Internet: www.smu.edu.in

Founded 1995

Academic year: August to July

Chancellor: HE THE GOV. OF SIKKIM
Pro-Chancellor: Dr RAMDAS PAI
Vice-Chancellor: Dr K. JAYAKUMAR
Registrar: SHERAP SHENGA.

CONSTITUENT INSTITUTIONS

School of Basic and Applied Sciences: Majitar Rangpo 737132, East Sikkim; internet sbas.smu.edu.in.

Sikkim Manipal College of Nursing: Fifth Mile, Tadong, Gangtok 737102, Sikkim; internet cn.smu.edu.in; Principal MRIDULA DAS.

Sikkim Manipal College of Physiotherapy: Fifth Mile, Tadong, Gangtok 737102, Sikkim; internet cp.smu.edu.in; Principal Dr NIKITA JOSHI.

Sikkim Manipal Institute of Medical Science: Fifth Mile, Tadong, Gangtok 737102, Sikkim; Dean Dr P. G. SHIVANANDA.

Sikkim Manipal Institute of Technology: Majitar Rangpo 737132, East Sikkim; tel. (3592) 246353; fax (3592) 246112; internet smit.smu.edu.in; f. 1997; Dir Brig. Dr SOMNATH MISHRA; Dean Prof. Dr ACHINTYA CHOUDHURY.

SREE SANKARACHARYA UNIVERSITY OF SANSKRIT

Sree Sankarapuram, Ernakulam, Kalady 683574, Kerala
Telephone: (484) 2463380
Fax: (484) 2463480
E-mail: ssus@vsnl.com
Internet: www.ssus.ac.in

Founded 1994

Academic year: June to April

Faculties of arts, education, sanskrit studies and social sciences; regional Centres in Ettumanoor, Kalady, Koyilandy, Payyannur, Thrissur, Thuravoor and Tirur

Chancellor: HE THE GOV. OF KERALA
Vice-Chancellor: Dr J. PRASAD
Registrar: Dr S. PREMJITH
Prin. and Dean of Studies: Dr N. K. SANKARAN
Library of 53,000 vols, 125 periodicals, 200 MSS.

SRI KRISHNADEVARAYA UNIVERSITY

Sri Venkateswarapuram PO, Anantapur 515003, Andhra Pradesh
Telephone: (8554) 255700
Fax: (8554) 255804
E-mail: registrar@skuniversity.org
Internet: www.skuniversity.org

Founded 1967, univ. status 1981

Postgraduate teaching and research
Language of instruction: English
Academic year: December to October

Chancellor: HE THE GOVERNOR OF ANDHRA PRADESH
Vice-Chancellor: Prof. P. KUSUMA KUMARI
Prin.: Prof. T. PULLAIAH
Dean of College Devt Ccl: Prof. D. SARALA KUMARI
Controller of Examinations: T. K. SRINIVAS
Dir of Centre for Distance Education: Prof. V. REDDAPA REDDY
Registrar: Prof. Y. G. H. PHILIP
Librarian: Dr P. KAMAIAK

112 Affiliated colleges

Library of 114,000 vols, 190 periodicals
Number of teachers: 154
Number of students: 1,500

DEANS

Faculty of Engineering: (vacant)
Faculty of Languages and Literature: Prof. H. S. BRAHMANADA
Faculty of Law: Prof. S. SESHAIAH
Faculty of Life Sciences: Prof. K. RADHAKRISHNAIAH
Faculty of Management: Prof. C. R. REDDY RAO
Faculty of Physical Sciences: Prof. D. R. V. PRASAD RAO
Faculty of Social Sciences: Prof. C. U. MOHAN

PROFESSORS

ANKI REDDY, K. C., Mathematics
BASHA MOHIDEEN, M., Zoology
BRAHMAJI RAO, S., Chemistry
ENOCK, K., Telugu
GHOUSE, M., Law
GOPAL, B. R., History
KAMESWARA RAO, A.

KANTHA RAO, M. L., Economics
KOTESWARA RAO, T., Telugu
KRISHNA, D. V., Mathematics
MANOHARA MURTHY, N., Physics
NAIDU, V. T., Rural Development
NARAYANA, N., Economics
PRAKASHA RAO, C. G., Botany
RAGHUNATHA SARMA, S., Telugu
RAJGOPAL, E.
RAMA MURTHY, V., Physics
RAMAKRISHNA RAO, A., English
RAMAKRISHNA RAO, P., Biochemistry
RAMAKRISHNA RAO, T. V., Physics
RAMAVATHARAM, S. I., Law
SEETHARAMASWAMY, R., Mathematics
SHARMA, D. P., Commerce
SUBBA RAO, C., English
SUBBARAMAIAH, S., Economics
SUBBI REDDY, T., Commerce
SUBRAHMANYAM, S. V., Physics
SUDARSHAN RAO, T. P., Law
SWAMINATHAN, E., Geography
TIRUPATHI NAIDU, V., Rural Development
VENKATA REDDY, C., Economics
VENKATA REDDY, D., Chemistry
VENKATA REDDY, K., English
VENKATA REDDY, K., Rural Development
VENKATASIVA MURTHY, K. N., Mathematics

POSTGRADUATE CENTRE

SKU, Kurnool: f. 1977; library of 25,000 vols, 30 periodicals; courses in area planning and regional devt in economics, microprocessors in physics, MSc. computer science and management studies, natural products in chemistry, operations research and statistical quality control, telugu; Dir Prof. C. UMASANKAR.

SRI PADMAVATHI MAHILA VISVAVIDYALAYAM

Tirupati 517502, Andhra Pradesh
Telephone: (877) 2248417
Fax: (877) 2248417
E-mail: vcspmvv@yahoo.com
Internet: www.padmavatiwomen-univ.org
Founded 1983
Academic year: July to June

Schools of applied mathematics, business management, communication and information science, computer science, education, home science, legal studies and research, letters, life sciences, music and fine arts, pharmaceutical sciences, physical sciences, social sciences; Univ. College of Eng., Centre for Ambedkar Studies, Centre for Research Studies

Chancellor: HE THE GOV. OF ANDHRA PRADESH
Vice-Chancellor: Prof. G. SAROJAMMA
Rector: Prof. K. UMA DEVI
Registrar: Dr E. MANJUVANI
Deputy Librarian: Dr D. RAJESWARI

Library of 46,000 books, 8,000 vols of periodicals
Number of students: 1,032

SRI VENKATESWARA UNIVERSITY

Tirupati 517502, Andhra Pradesh
Telephone: (877) 2248374
Internet: www.svuniversity.in
Founded 1954 as Residential and Teaching; Affiliating since 1956
Languages of instruction: English, Telugu
Academic year: June to April (two terms)
Chancellor: HE THE GOVERNOR OF ANDHRA PRADESH
Vice-Chancellor: Prof. N. PRABHAKARA RAO
Registrar: Prof. K. RATHNAIAH
Dean of College Devt Council: Prof. M. A. K. SUKUMAR
Dir of Research: Prof. S. BUDDHUDU
Librarian: Dr M. R. CHANDRAN

Library: Libraries of 278,974 vols
Number of teachers: 400
Number of students: 5,000

DEANS

College of Arts: Prof. C. P. KASAIAH
College of Biological and Earth Sciences: Prof. P. SREENIVASULU
College of Commerce, Management and Information Sciences: Prof. S. BALARAMI REDDY
College of Education and Extension Studies: Prof. D. USHA RANI
College of Engineering: Prof. M. M. NAIDU
College of Humanities: Prof. S. G. D. CHANDRASEKHAR
College of Int. Studies: Prof. D. K. KRANTH CHOWDARY
College of Mathematical and Physical Sciences: Prof. C. SUBBARAMI REDDY

POSTGRADUATE CENTRES

Postgraduate Centre, Kadapa: f. 1977; library of 20,000 vols, 40 periodicals; Dir Prof. G. SIVA REDDY.

Postgraduate Centre, Kavali: f. 1929; library of 17,500 vols, 40 periodicals; Dir Prof. B. D. RAMI REDDY.

SWAMI RAMANAND TEERTH MARATHWADA UNIVERSITY

Vishnupuri, Nanded 431606, Maharashtra
Telephone: (2462) 229243
Fax: (2462) 229245
E-mail: nnd_vc@sancharnet.in
Internet: www.srtmun.ac.in
Founded 1994
Teaching and Affiliating
Academic year: June to April
Chancellor: HE THE GOV. OF MAHARASHTRA
Vice-Chancellor: Dr S. B. NIMSE
Registrar: Dr RAM B. WAGH
Dir of Student Welfare: D. D. PAWAR
Controller of Examinations: Maj. N. V. CHAVAN
Librarian: Dr S. P. SATARKAR
172 Affiliated colleges
Library of 40,000 vols, 123 nat. and 34 int. periodicals
Publication: *New Vision*

DEANS

Faculty of Arts: Dr B. S. JADHAV
Faculty of Commerce: Dr B. B. JADHAV
Faculty of Education: Dr B. M. GORE
Faculty of Physical Sciences: P. N. DESHMUKH
Faculty of Science: Dr G. D. BAGADE
Faculty of Social Sciences: Dr U. D. SAWANT

TAMIL NADU AGRICULTURAL UNIVERSITY

Coimbatore 641003, Tamil Nadu
Telephone: (422) 6611200
Fax: (422) 6611410
E-mail: registrar@tnau.ac.in
Internet: www.tnau.ac.in
Founded 1971
State control
Language of instruction: English
Academic year: July to June (two semesters)
10 Colleges; 34 research stations
Chancellor: HE THE GOV. OF TAMIL NADU
Pro-Chancellor: THE MIN. OF AGRICULTURE, GOVT OF TAMIL NADU
Vice-Chancellor: Dr C. RAMASAMY
Registrar: Dr S. D. SUNDAR SINGH
Controller of Admissions: Dr B. SANTHANAKRISHNAN
Deputy Librarian: K. PERUMALSAMY
Library of 161,146 vols, 380 periodicals

Number of teachers: 955
Number of students: 2,791

Publications: *Journal of Agriculture Resource Management* (in English, 2 a year), *Journal of External Education* (in English, 4 a year), *Madras Agricultural Journal* (in English, 12 a year), *South Indian Horticulture* (in English, 4 a year)

DEANS

Agricultural College and Research Institute, Coimbatore: Dr R. KRISHNASAMY
Agricultural College and Research Institute, Killikulam: Dr T. M. THIAGARAJAN
Agricultural College and Research Institute, Madurai: Dr N. KEMPUCHETTY
Agricultural Engineering College and Research Institute, Coimbatore: Dr R. MANIAN
Agricultural Engineering College and Research Institute, Kumulur: Dr C. T. DEVADAS
Anbil Dharmalingam Agricultural College and Research Institute, Tiruchirappalli: Dr S. ANTHONI RAJ
Forest College and Research Institute, Mettupalayam: Prof. K. S. NEELAKANDAN
Home Science College and Research Institute, Madurai: Dr K. SHEELA
Horticultural College and Research Institute, Coimbatore: Dr E. VADIVEL
Horticultural College and Research Institute, Periyakulam: Dr S. ANBU
School of Postgraduate Studies, Coimbatore: Dr S. KOMBAIRAJU

DIRECTORS

Centre for Agriculture and Rural Development Studies: Dr N. RAVEENDRAN
Centre for Plant Breeding and Genetics: Dr T. S. RAVEENDRAN
Centre for Plant Molecular Biology: Dr K. RAMASAMY
Centre for Plant Protection Studies: Dr T. MARIMUTHU
Extension Education: Dr G. DORAISWAMY
Open and Distance Learning: Dr V. ALAGESAN
Planning and Mentoring: Dr D. VEERARAGAVATHATHAM
Research: Dr S. RAMANATHAN
Soil and Crop Management Studies: Dr V. MURUGAPPAN
Student Welfare: Dr V. THANDAPANI
Tamil Nadu Rice Research Institute, Aduthurai: Dr B. CHANDRASEKARAN
Water Technology Centre: Dr K. PALANISAMI

CONSTITUENT COLLEGES

Agricultural College and Research Institute, Coimbatore: tel. (422) 6611210; fax (422) 6611410; e-mail deanagri@tnau.ac.in; internet www.tnau.ac.in/agcbe

Agricultural College and Research Institute, Killikulam: Killikulam, Vallanadu 628252, Tamil Nadu; tel. (4630) 2461226; fax (4630) 2461268; e-mail deankkm@tnau.ac.in; f. 1984; Dir Dr P. VIVEKANANDAN.

Agricultural College and Research Institute, Madurai: Madurai 625104; tel. (452) 2422956; e-mail deanagrimdu@tnau.ac.in; internet www.tnau.ac.in/agrimdu.html; ean Dr N. KEMBUCHETTY.

Agricultural Engineering College and Research Institute, Coimbatore: tel. (422) 5511255; fax (422) 2431672; e-mail deancaecbe@tnau.ac.in; internet www.tnau.ac.in/aecricbe; Dean Dr A. SAMPATHRAJAN.

Agricultural Engineering College and Research Institute, Kumulur: Tiruchirappalli 621712, Tamil Nadu; tel. and fax (431) 2541218; e-mail deancaekum@tnau.ac.in; f. 1972; Dean Dr C. T. DEVADAS.

Anbil Dharmalingam Agricultural College and Research Institute: Tiruchirappalli 620009, Tamil Nadu; f. 1992; Dean Dr A. ANTHONI RAJ.

Forest College and Research Institute: Mettupalayam 641301, Tamil Nadu.

Home Science College and Research Institute, Madurai: Madurai 625104; e-mail manimegalaigobalasamy@yahoo.co.in; f. 1980; Dean Dr G. MANIMEGALAI.

Horticultural College and Research Institute, Coimbatore: tel. (422) 5511371; fax (422) 2430781; e-mail deanhortcbe@tnau.ac.in; internet www.tnau.ac.in/horcbe; Dean Dr D. VEERARAGAVATHATHAM.

Horticultural College and Research Institute, Periyakulam: Periyakulam 625604, Tamil Nadu; tel. (4546) 231726; e-mail deanhcripkm@tnau.ac.in.

School of Postgraduate Studies, Coimbatore: e-mail deanspgs@tnau.ac.in; internet www.tnau.ac.in/pg; f. 1971.

TAMIL NADU DR AMBEDKAR LAW UNIVERSITY

5 Greenways Rd, Chennai 600028, Tamil Nadu

Telephone: (44) 24641212
Fax: (44) 24957414
E-mail: vc@tndalu.org
Internet: www.tndalu.org
Founded 1997
8 Affiliated law colleges
Chancellor: HE THE GOV. OF TAMIL NADU
Vice-Chancellor: Prof. S. SACHIDHANANDAM
Registrar: Dr D. GOPAL
Controller of Examinations: Prof. T. JOHNSON
Public Relations Officer: A. SHAJJATH HUSSAIN
Dean of Postgraduate Studies: Prof. A. RAGHUNATHA REDDY
Library of 13,960 vols
Number of students: 7,300
Publication: *Law Journal* (1 a year).

CONSTITUENT SCHOOLS

School of Excellence in Law: f. 2002; Dir Prof. Dr D. GOPAL.

Tamil Nadu Dr Ambedkar Law University Law College, Chengalpattu: f. 2003.

TAMIL NADU DR M. G. R. MEDICAL UNIVERSITY

69 Anna Salai, Guindy, Chennai 600032, Tamil Nadu

Telephone: (44) 22353574
Fax: (44) 22353698
E-mail: tnmmu@yahoo.com
Internet: www.tnmmu.ac.in
Founded 1987
Teaching and Affiliating
Chancellor: HE THE GOVERNOR OF TAMIL NADU
Vice-Chancellor: Dr K. M. M. HUSSAIN
Librarian: Dr N. C. JAYAMANI
226 Govt and private medical and paramedical instns affiliated

HEADS OF FACULTIES

Faculty of Ayurveda: Dr R. DEVADAS
Faculty of Basic Medical Sciences: Dr R. G. SUKUMAR
Faculty of Biomedical Sciences: Dr R. HARIHARAN
Faculty of Community Health, Social Sciences and History of Medicine: Dr RAJKUMAR
Faculty of Dentistry: Dr S. RAMACHANDRAN
Faculty of Homeopathy: Dr T. K. MOHANDAS

Faculty of Medicine and Medical Specialities: Dr M. THIRUNAVUKKARASU
Faculty of Naturopathy and Yogic Sciences: (vacant)
Faculty of Nursing: Dr M. GOWRI (acting)
Faculty of Obstetrics and Gynaecology and Related Specialities: Dr N. RAJAMAHESHWARI
Faculty of Paediatrics and Paediatric Specialities: Prof. K. M. M. HUSSEIN
Faculty of Pharmacy: Dr T. K. RAVI
Faculty of Siddha: Dr A. M. ABDUL KADHER
Faculty of Surgery and Surgical Specialities: Dr GOVHARDAN
Faculty of Unani: Dr K. R. AHMED

PROFESSORS

Faculty of Ayurveda:
  SESHADHRI, V.
Faculty of Basic Medical Sciences:
  BANUMATHY, S. P., Anatomy
  MANICKAVASAGAM, S.
  NALINI, A., Pharmacology
  RAJESWARI, C., Microbiology
  SHERIFF, Biochemistry
  VADIVELU, Forensic Medicine
Faculty of Biomedical Sciences:
  SAMUEL, N. M.
Faculty of Community Health, Social Sciences and History of Medicine:
  PRITHVI, A.
Faculty of Dentistry:
  JAGANNATHAN, J., Conservative Dentistry
  SWAMINATHAN, T. N., Prosthodontics
Faculty of Medicine and Medical Specialities:
  BHIRMANANDHAM, C. V., Cardiology
  JAGANNATHAN, K., Thoracic Medicine
  JAYANTHI, Gastroenterology
  PALANIAPPAN, V., Psychiatry
  PANCHAPAKESA RAJENDRAN, C., Rheumatology
  RAJAN, S. K., General Medicine
  RAVIKANNAN, Medical Oncology
  SENTHAMIL SELVI, G., Dermatology
  USMAN, N., Venerology
Faculty of Nursing:
  SAHU, G.
Faculty of Obstetrics and Gynaecology and Related Specialities:
  ANUSUYA, P., Obstetrics and Gynaecology
  MATHAI, M., Obstetrics and Gynaecology
  RAMACHANDRAN, M., Obstetrics and Gynaecology
  SAMBANDAN, S., Obstetrics and Gynaecology
  SOUNDARAM, K., Obstetrics and Gynaecology
  TAMILMANI, D., Obstetrics and Gynaecology
Faculty of Paediatrics and Paediatric Specialities:
  CHANDRASEKARAN, K., Paediatrics
  CHERIAN, T., Paediatrics
  SARKUNAM, C. S. R., Paediatrics
  TAMILARASU, P. T., Paediatrics
  TAMILVANAN, S., Paediatrics
Faculty of Pharmacy:
  PRAKASH, M. S.
  RAJENDRAN, A.
  RAO, G. S.
  SRIDHARAN, A.
Faculty of Siddha:
  GANAPATHY, G.
  IQBAL, P. I.
  PATRAYAN, A.
  RAJESWARI, A.
  SAKUNTHALA, P. R.
Faculty of Surgery and Surgical Specialities:
  CHANDRASEKARAN, M., Surgical Endocrinology
  DAMODARAN, S., Surgical Gastroenterology

JESUDASON, B., Surgery
PUSHPARAJ, K., Neurosurgery
RATHINAM, T., Ears, Nose and Throat

TAMIL NADU VETERINARY AND ANIMAL SCIENCES UNIVERSITY

Madhavaram Milk Colony, Chennai 600051, Tamil Nadu

Telephone: (44) 25551586
Fax: (44) 25551575
E-mail: tanuvas@vsnl.com
Internet: www.tanuvas.tn.nic.in
Founded 1989
State control
Academic year: July to June
Chancellor: HE THE GOV. OF TAMIL NADU
Vice-Chancellor: Dr P. THANGARAJU
Registrar: Dr N. D. JOY CHANDRAN
Number of teachers: 466
Number of students: 1,457
Publications: *Cheiron* (6 a year), *Tanuvas Newsletter* (12 a year), *Kalnadai Kathir* (6 a year), *Cheidhi Madal* (12 a year).

CONSTITUENT INSTITUTIONS

Centre for Animal Health Studies: Dir Dr B. MURALI MANOHAR.

Centre for Animal Production Studies: Dir Dr R. PRABHAKARAN.

Faculty of Basic Sciences: Dean Dr S. R. SRINIVASAN.

Fisheries College and Research Institute: Thoothukudi 628008, Tamil Nadu; Dean Dr V. K. VENKATARAMANI.

Institute of Animal Nutrition: LRS Campus, Kattankolathur PO, Kattupakkam 603203, Tamil Nadu; Dir Dr M. MURUGAN.

Institute of Food and Dairy Technology: Koduvalli, Chennai 600052, Tamil Nadu; Dir Dr ROBINSON J. J. ABRAHAM.

Madras Veterinary College: Depts of animal genetics and breeding, animal nutrition, animal reproduction, bioinformatics, dairy science, livestock production and management, meat science and technology, obstetrics and gynaecology, poultry science, veterinary anatomy and histology, veterinary and animal husbandry, extension and entrepreneurship, veterinary clinical medicine, ethics and jurisprudence, veterinary microbiology, veterinary parasitology, veterinary pathology, veterinary pharmacology and toxicology, veterinary physiology and biochemistry, veterinary preventive medicine and epidemiology and veterinary surgery, radiology; library of 60,363 vols, 162 periodicals; Dean Dr L. JOHN.

Veterinary College and Research Institute: Namakkal 637001, Tamil Nadu; library of 7,763 vols, 78 periodicals; Dean Dr C. CHANDRAHASAN.

TAMIL UNIVERSITY

Administrative Bldg, Trichy Rd, Thanjavur 613005, Tamil Nadu

Telephone: (4362) 227040
Fax: (4362) 227040
E-mail: contact@tamiluniversity.ac.in
Internet: www.tamiluniversity.ac.in
Founded 1981
Languages of instruction: Tamil, English
Academic year: July to April
Chancellor: HE THE GOV. OF TAMIL NADU
Vice-Chancellor: Dr M. RAJENDRAN
Registrar: Dr A. KARTHIKEYAN
Finance Officer: THIRU P. MOHAN
Public Relations Officer: Dr THIRU G. PANNEER SELVAM
Library Dir: Dr B. SUNDARESAN
Library of 136,324 vols, 393 periodicals

Number of teachers: 74
Number of students: 265

DEANS

Faculty of Arts: Dr M. RAMASAMY
Faculty of Developing Tamil: Dr H. CHITHIR-
APUTHIRAPILLAI
Faculty of Languages: Dr A. RAMANATHAN
Faculty of Manuscriptology: V. R. MADHAVAN
Faculty of Science: Dr G. DEIVANAYAGAM

ATTACHED INSTITUTES

Centre for Underwater Archaeology: Dir
(vacant).

School of Philosophy: research in philosophy; Dir Dr G. BASKARAN.

Tribal Research Institute: Dir Dr V.
CHIDAMBARANATHANPILLAI.

TEZPUR UNIVERSITY

Napaam, Tezpur 784028, Assam
Telephone: (3712) 267007
Fax: (3712) 267006
E-mail: administration@tezu.ernet.in
Internet: www.tezu.ernet.in
Founded 1994
Academic year: July to June
Central university
Vice-Chancellor: Prof. MIHIR K. CHAUDHURI
Registrar: Dr ALAK KUMAR BURAGOHAIN
Finance Officer: RABI RAM BORA
Controller of Examinations: Dr B. SAHARIA
Dean of Student Welfare: Prof. M. SARMA

Library of 25,000 vols
Number of teachers: 100
Number of students: 700

DEANS

School of Energy, Environment and Natural
Resources: Prof. K. K. BARUAH
School of Engineering: Prof. D. K. SAIKIA
School of Humanities and Social Sciences:
Prof. BIJAY KR. DANTA
School of Management Sciences: (vacant)
School of Science and Technology: Prof. B. K.
KONWAR

THIRUVALLUVAR UNIVERSITY

Fort Campus Vellore 632004, Tamil Nadu
Telephone: (416) 2217778
Fax: (416) 2221344
Internet: www.tvuni.in
Founded 2002

Depts of chemistry, economics, zoology; affiliated colleges in dists of Cuddalore, Thiru-
vannamalai, Vellore, Villupuram

Vice-Chancellor: Dr A. JOTHI MURUGAN
Registrar: Dr B. KRISHNAMURTHY
Controller of Examinations: Dr B. KRISHNA-
MURTHY.

TILKA MANJHI BHAGALPUR
UNIVERSITY

Bhagalpur 812007, Bihar
Telephone: (641) 2620100
Fax: (641) 2620353
E-mail: mustafams@yahoo.com
Internet: www.tmbu.org
Founded 1960 as Bhagalpur University; pre-
sent name 1991
Teaching and Affiliating
Academic year: June to May
Chancellor: HE THE GOVERNOR OF BIHAR
Vice-Chancellor: Dr PREMA JHA
Registrar: Dr V. K. DAS
Dean of Student Welfare: Dr B. N. SINGH

34 Univ. depts; 29 constituent colleges
Library of 140,000 vols, 125 periodicals
Number of teachers: 1,055

Number of students: 60,000

DEANS

Faculty of Commerce: Dr R. K. SINHA
Faculty of Education: HARENDRA P. SINGH
Faculty of Engineering: Dr C. R. PRATAP
Faculty of Humanities: Dr G. N. JHA
Faculty of Medicine: Dr ANIL KUMAR VERMA
Faculty of Science: Dr R. P. SAHAI
Faculty of Social Science: Dr R. D. SHARMA

TRIPURA UNIVERSITY

PO Suryamaninagar, Tripura West 799130,
Tripura
Telephone: (381) 2374801
Fax: (381) 2374802
E-mail: tripurauniversity@rediffmail.com
Internet: www.tripurauniversity.in
Founded 1987
State control
Teaching and Affiliating
Languages of instruction: English, Bengali
Academic year: June to May
Chancellor: HE THE GOVERNOR OF TRIPURA
Vice-Chancellor: Prof. ARUNODAY SAHA
Registrar: Dr K. B. JAMATIE
Controller of Examinations: B. C. SINHA
Librarian: D. K. RANA

21 Affiliated colleges
Library of 52,560 vols
Number of teachers: 63
Number of students: 19,000 (incl. affiliated
colleges)

DEANS

Arts and Commerce: Prof. M. CHOUDHURI
Science: Prof. BASANT KUMAR AGARWALA

PROFESSORS

AGGARWAL, B. K., Life Science
BHOWMIK, R. N., Mathematics
CHAUDHURIU, M., Bengali
CHAUDHURY, D. K., History
DEBNATH, P., Commerce
DEY, A., Mathematics
DEY, B. K., Physics
DEY, S. N., Sanskrit
DINDA, B., Chemistry
GHOSH, D., Life Science
HALDAR, P. K., Commerce
ROY, A. D., Life Science
SAHA, A., Economics
SRIVASTAVA, R. C., Life Science

UNIVERSITY OF AGRICULTURAL
SCIENCES, BANGALORE

Ghandi Krishni Vignan Kendra, Bellary Rd,
Bangalore 560065, Karnataka
Telephone: (80) 23330153
Fax: (80) 23330277
E-mail: registrar@uasbangalore.edu.in
Internet: www.uasbangalore.edu.in
Founded 1964
Residential
Languages of instruction: English, Kannada
State control
Academic year: September to August (two
terms)
Chancellor: HE THE GOVERNOR OF KARNATAKA
Pro-Chancellor: THE MINISTER OF AGRICUL-
TURE, KARNATAKA
Vice-Chancellor: Dr P. G. CHENGAPPA
Dir for Extension: Dr PRABHAKARA SETTY
Dir for Research: Dr H. SHIVANNA
Dir for Student Welfare: Dr K. P. RAMA
PRASANNA
Registrar: Dr B. RAJU
Librarian: Dr K. K. MANJUNATHA

Library of 169,835 vols
Number of teachers: 1,082

Number of students: 2,500 undergraduates
and 1,000 graduates
Publications: *Mysore Journal of Agricultural
Sciences* (4 a year), 10 series (UAS
Research, UAS Extension, UAS Education,
etc.)

PROFESSORS

ABDUL RAHMAN, S., Parasitology
ANANTHANARAYANA, R., Chemistry and Soils
ANILKUMAR, T. B., Plant Pathology
ASHOK, T. H., Horticulture
AVADHANI, K. K., Genetics and Plant Breed-
ing
BHAT, G. S., Dairy Chemistry
CHALLAIAH, Agricultural Extension
CHANDRAKANTH, M. G., Agricultural Econom-
ics
CHANDRAMOULI, K. N., Anatomy
CHANDRAPPA, H. M., Plant Breeding
CHANDRASHEKAR GUPTA, T. R., Fishery Ocean-
ography
CHANNAPPA, T. C., Agricultural Engineering
CHENGAPPA, P. G., Agricultural Marketing
CHIKKADEVAIAH, Seed Processing Engineer-
ing
CHOWDEGOWDA, M., Agricultural Engineering
DAS, T. K., Animal Nutrition
DEVEGOWDA, G., Poultry
ESHWARAPPA, G., Agricultural Extension
FAROOQ MOHAMMED, Veterinary Physiology
FAROOQI, A. A., Medicinal and Aromatic
Plants
GANGADHAR, K. S., Gynaecology and Obstet-
rics
GEETHA RAMACHANDRA, Biochemistry
GIRIJA, P. R., Psychology
GOPALA GOWDA, H. S., Agricultural Micro-
biology
GOPALAKRISHNA HEBBAR, Agricultural Eco-
nomics
GOPALAKRISHNA RAO, Agricultural Extension
GOVINDAIAH, M. G., Animal Genetics and
Breeding
GOVINDAN, R., Entomology
GOWDA, H., Pharmacology
GUNDURAO, D. S., Mathematics
GURUMURTHY, Statistics
GURURAJ HUNSIGI, Agronomy
HEGDE, S. V., Microbiology
HONNEGOWDA, Pharmacology
HUDDAR, A. G., Horticulture
JAGADISH, A., Entomology
JAGADISH KUMAR, Pharmacology
JAGANNATH, M. S., Parasitology
JANARDHANA, K. V., Crop Physiology
JAVAREGOWDA, S., Agricultural Engineering
JAYADEVAPPA, S. M., Surgery
JAYARAMAIAH, M., Sericulture
JOSEPH BHAGYARAJ, D., Agricultural Micro-
biology
JOSHI SHAMASUNDAR, Botany
KAILAS, M. M., Dairy Production
KARUNASAGAR, I., Fishery Microbiology
KATTEPPA, Y., Agricultural Extension
KESHAVAMURTHY, K. V., Plant Pathology
KESHAVANATH, P., Aquaculture
KHAN, M. M., Horticulture
KRISHNA, K. S., Agricultural Extension
KRISHNAPPA, A. M., Soil Science
KRISHNAPRASAD, Agricultural Entomology
KRISHNAPRASAD, P. R., Pathology
KRISHNEGOWDA, K. T., Agronomy
KULAKARNI, R. S., Agricultural Botany
KUMARASWAMY, A. S., Water Management
and Plant Breeding
LAKKUNDI, N. H., Agricultural Entomology
LOKANATH, G. R., Poultry for Meat
MALLIK, B., Acarology
MALLIKARJUNAIAH, R. R., Microbiology
MANJUNATH, A., Plant Breeding
MELANTA, R., Horticulture
MOHAN JOSEPH, Fishery Biology
MUNI LAL DUBEY, B., Gynaecology and
Obstetrics

MUNIYAPPA, T. V., Agricultural Extension
MUNIYAPPA, V., Plant Pathology
MUSHTARI BEGUM, J., Home Science
NAGARAJA SETTY, M. V., Plant Breeding
NAGARAJU, Animal Sciences
NANJEGOWDA, D., Nematology
NARASIMHAMURTHY, S., Mathematics
NARAYANA, K., Pharmacology
NARAYANA GOWDA, K., Agricultural Extension
NARAYANAGOWDA, J. V., Horticulture
NARENDRANATH, R., Physiology
PANCHAKSHARAIAH, S., Agronomy
PARAMASHIVAIAH, B. M., Animal Science
PARAMESWAR, N. S., Plant Breeding
PARASHIVAMURTHY, A. S., Soil Science
PARVATHAMMA, S., Mathematics
PARVATHAPPA, H. C., Soil Science and Agricultural Chemistry
PRABHAKAR HEGDE, B., Dairy Production
PRABHAKAR SETTY, T. K., Agronomy
PRABHUSWAMY, H. P., Agricultural Entomology
PRASAD, T. G., Crop Physiology
PRATAP KUMAR, K. S., Poultry Science
PUTTASWAMY, Entomology
RAGHAVAN, R., Veterinary Microbiology
RAJ, J., Microbiology
RAJAGOPAL, D., Apiculture
RAMACHANDRAPRASAD, T. V., Agronomy
RAMANJANEYULU, G., Dairy Technology
RAMAPRASANNA, K. P., Seed Technology
RANGANATHAIAH, K. G., Plant Pathology
RAVI, P. C., Agricultural Marketing
SAMIULLA, R., Horticulture
SATHYAN, B. A., Plant Breeding
SATHYANARAYANA RAO, G. P., Agricultural Extension
SESHADRI, V. S., Agricultural Extension
SHANBHOGUE, S. L., Fishery Biology
SHANKAR, P. A., Dairy Microbiology
SHANKAREGOWDA, B. T., Plant Sciences
SHANTHA JOSEPH, Fishery Economics
SHANTHA R. HIREMATH, Plant Breeding
SHANTHAMALLAIAH, N. R., Crop Production
SHARIEF, R. A., Plant Science
SHESHAPPA, D. S., Fishery Engineering
SHIVAPPA SHETTY, K., Microbiology
SHIVANNA, H., Plant Breeding and Genetics
SHIVARAJ, B., Agronomy
SHIVASHANKAR, K., Agronomy
SIDDARAMAIAH, A. L., Plant Pathology
SIDDARAMAIAH, B. S., Agricultural Extension
SIDDARAMAPPA, R., Soil Science
SIDDARAMEGOWDA, T. K., Biotechnology
SINGLACHAR, M. A., Agronomy
SOMASHEKARAPPA, G., Agricultural Extension
SRIDHARA, S., Zoology
SRIHARI, K., Zoology
SRIKAR, L. N., Biochemistry
SRINIVASA GOWDA, M. V., Economics
SRINIVASA GOWDA, R. N., Poultry Pathology
SURYA PRAKASH, S., Agricultural Economics
SUSHEELA DEVI, L., Soil Science and Agricultural Chemistry
THIMME GOWDA, S., Agronomy
UDAYAKUMAR, M., Crop Physiology
UPADHYA, A. S., Veterinary Microbiology
UTTAIAH, B. C., Horticulture
VAIDEHI, M. P., Home Science
VAJRANABAIAH, S. N., Crop Physiology
VASUDEVAPPA, Inland Fisheries
VEERABHADRAIAH, V., Agricultural Extension
VENKATASUBBAIAH, K., Botany
VENKATESH REDDY, T., Post-Harvest Technology
VENUGOPAL, Agricultural Extension
VENUGOPAL, N., Agricultural Meteorology
VIDYACHANDRA, B., Plant Breeding
VIJAYASARATHI, S. K., Veterinary Microbiology
VIRAKTHAMATH, C. A., Agricultural Entomology
VISHWANATH, D. P., Soil Science
VISWANATH, S., Virology
VISWANATHA, S. R., Plant Breeding

VISWANATHA REDDY, V. N., Gynaecology and Obstetrics
VISWANATHA SASTRY, K. M., Veterinary Medicine
YADAHALLI, Y. H., Agronomy

CONSTITUENT COLLEGES

College of Agriculture—Bangalore: e-mail diagri@bgl.vsnl.net.in; f. 1946; Dir Dr R. GOVINDAN.

College of Agriculture—Hassan: POB 39, Karekere 573201, Hassan; tel. (81) 72290517; e-mail diagri_hassan@rediffmail.co.in; f. 1996; Dir Dr A. S. KUMARA SWARMY.

College of Agriculture—Mandya: Mandya-Melkote Rd, Mandya, Kamataka; f. 1991; Dir Dr C. SHANKARAIAH.

College of Agriculture—Shimoga: f. 1990; Dir Dr K. KENCHAIAH.

College of Forestry: Kunda Rd, Ponnampet, Kodagu; tel. (82) 7449365; f. 1995; Dir Dr N. A. PRAKASH.

College of Horticulture: Mudigere 577132; tel. (82) 63228152; fax (82) 63228022; f. 1991; Dir Dr J. VENKATESHA.

College of Sericulture: Chinthamani; f. 1995; Dir Dr A. N. S. GOWDA.

UNIVERSITY OF BIKANER

Bikaner
Telephone: (151) 2200414
Fax: (151) 2522495
E-mail: info@bikaneruniversity.in
Internet: www.bikaneruniversity.in

Founded 2003

Affiliating; faculties of arts, commerce and management, education, law, science, social science; 69 affiliated colleges in Churu, Sriganganagar, Hanumangarh, Bikaner

Vice-Chancellor: Dr C. B. GENA
Registrar: S. S. RANKAWAT.

UNIVERSITY OF BURDWAN

Rajbati, Bardhaman 713104, West Bengal
Telephone: (342) 2533913
Fax: (342) 2530452
E-mail: pio@buruniv.ac.in
Internet: www.buruniv.ac.in

Founded 1960

Teaching and Affiliating
Languages of instruction: English, Bengali
Academic year: June to May
Chancellor: HE THE GOVERNOR OF WEST BENGAL
Vice-Chancellor: Prof. SUBRATA PAL
Registrar: Dr S. M. DAN
Finance Officer: P. N. GHOSH
Controller of Examinations: S. MUKHOPADHYAY
Librarian: A. M. MIDDA (acting)
Library of 210,481 vols
Number of teachers: 205
Number of students: 3,293

Publications: *Bengali Journal*, *English Journal*, *History Journal*, *Journal of Mass Communication*, *Law Review*, *Philosophy Journal*, *Political Science Journal*, *Sanskrit Journal*, *Science Journal*, *Socio-Political Journal*

PROFESSORS

BAGCHI, S., Chemistry
BAGCHI, S. B., Statistics
BANDOPADHYAY, D. N., English
BANDYOPADHYAY, M. K., Sanskrit
BANDYOPADHYAY, T. C., Zoology
BANERJEE, A. K., Economics
BANERJEE, C., Mathematics
BANERJEE, G., Mathematics
BANERJEE, K., Geography

BANERJEE, M., Chemistry
BASU, D. K., Philosophy
BASU, P. S., Botany
BASU, S., Bengali
BASU, S., Chemistry
BHATTACHARYYA, A., Philosophy
BHATTACHARYYA, A., Sanskrit
BHATTACHARYYA, A. K., Music
BHATTACHARYYA, A. K., Physics
BHATTACHARYYA, G. N., Sanskrit
BHATTACHARAYYA, K., Chemistry
BHATTACHARAYYA, K., Mathematics
BHATTACHARAYYA, P. K., Botany
BHATTACHARYYA, R. P., Sanskrit
BISWAS, S. C., Library and Information Science
BISWAS, S. K., Commerce
CHAKRABARTI, T., Sanskrit
CHAKRABORTY, B., Bengali
CHAKRABORTY, C. S., Zoology
CHAKRABORTY, K., Bengali
CHAKRABORTY, N. D., Mathematics
CHAKRABORTY, P., Economics
CHAKRABORTY, P., Zoology
CHAKRABORTY, P. C., English
CHAKRABORTY, P. K., Economics
CHAKRABORTY, S., Bengali
CHAKRABORTY, S., Zoology
CHAKRABORTY, S. K., Mathematics
CHATTERJEE, K. K., English
CHATTERJEE, S. K., Institute of Science Education
CHATTOPADHYAY, A., Statistics
CHATTOPADHYAY, K. C., Mathematics
CHATTOPADHYAY, N. C., Botany
CHATTOPADHYAY, R. R., Bengali
CHAUDHURY, M. K., Bengali
CHAUDHURY, P. K., Zoology
DAS, A. K., Chemistry
DAS, P., Commerce
DAS, T. K., Physics
DASGUPTA, S. S., Physics
DE, A. K., Bengali
DE, G. S., Chemistry
DE, N. K., Geography
DUTTA, D. M., Business Administration
GHOSH, B., Sociology
GUPTA, K., Botany
GUPTA, L. N., Bengali
HOQUE, A., Philosophy
HUI, A. K., English
KHAN, G. C., Philosophy
KUNDU, R. K., English
KUSHARI, D. P., Botany
MAHARATNA, A., Economics
MAJUMDAR, G., Zoology
MALLIK, A. K., Commerce
MALLIK, P., Physics
MALLIK, U. K., Commerce
MITRA, A., Sociology
MITRA, C., Geography
MONDAL, K. K., Mathematics
MONDAL, P. K., Philosophy
MUKHERJEE, A., Botany
MUKHERJEE, B., Sanskrit
MUKHERJEE, R. N., Mathematics
MUKHOPADHYAY, A. K., Botany
MUKHOPADHYAY, A. K., Chemistry
MUKHOPADHYAY, A. K., Political Science
MUKHOPADHYAY, R. N., Botany
MUKHOPADHYAY, S., Computer Science
NANDI, A. P., Zoology
NANDI, B., Botany
PRAMANIK, N. C., Political Science
PRASAD, N., Geography
RAY, A. B., Political Science
RAY, M. K., English
ROY, A., History
ROY, D., Business Administration
ROY, R. K., Physics
ROY, S., Zoology
ROY, S. K., Physics
ROY, S. K., Political Science
ROY CHOUDHURY, S. K., Mathematics
SAMAD, A., Mathematics
SAMANTA, B. C., Physics

SAMANTA, L. K., Physics
SARKAR, A. K., Zoology
SARKAR, B. C., Physics
SARKHEL, J., Commerce
SARMA, P., Botany
SENGUPTA, S. K., Business Administration
SIDDHANTA, U. K., Instrumentation Centre
SINGH, S. S., Law
SINHA, B. C., Hindi
THAKUR, S., Chemistry

There are 101 affiliated colleges

UNIVERSITY OF CALCUTTA

Senate House, 87/1, College St, Kolkata 700073, West Bengal
Telephone: (33) 22410071
Fax: (33) 22413222
E-mail: admin@caluniv.ac.in
Internet: www.caluniv.ac.in

Founded 1857

Teaching and Affiliating
Language of instruction: English
Academic year: July to June

Chancellor: GOVERNOR OF WEST BENGAL
Vice-Chancellor: Prof. ASIS KUMAR BANERJEE
Pro-Vice-Chancellor for Academic Affairs: Prof. SURANJAN DAS
Pro-Vice-Chancellor for Business and Finance: Prof. TAPAN KUMAR MUKHERJEE
Registrar: Dr BASAB CHAUDHURI
Librarian: Dr SOUMITRA SARKAR

Library of 795,000 vols
Number of teachers: 667
Number of students: 91,741

Publications: *Calcutta Review* (4 a year), *UNICAL* (4 a year)

DEANS

Faculty of Agriculture and Veterinary Science: Prof. R. K. SARKAR
Faculty of Arts: Prof. A. K. BANDYOPADHYAY
Faculty of Commerce, Social Welfare and Business Management: Prof. R. CHAKRABORTY
Faculty of Education, Journalism and Library Information Science: Prof. T. BASU
Faculty of Engineering and Technology: Prof. S. SEN
Faculty of Fine Arts, Music and Home Science: Prof. S. BANDYOPADHYAY
Faculty of Law: Prof. I. G. AHMED
Faculty of Science: Prof. D. CHATTOPADHYAY

PROFESSORS

University College of Agriculture (5 Ballygunge Circular Rd, Kolkata 700 019):
BASU, R. N.
BHATTACHARYYA, B.
GHOSH, K.
GUPTA, S. K.
MAJUMDAR, B. C.
MAJUMDAR, M. K.
SADHU, M. K.

University College of Arts (1 Reformatory St, Kolkata 700 027; tel. (33) 22410071; fax (33) 22413222):
ACHARYA, S. N., Sanskrit
ALQUADRI, S. M. S., Ancient Indian History and Culture
BANDYOPADHYAY, A., History
BANDYOPADHYAY, B. N., Sociology
BANDYOPADHYAY, S., Ancient Indian History and Culture
BANERJEE, A. K., Economics
BANERJEE, H., History
BANERJEE, H. K., Economics
BANERJEE, M., Philosophy
BANERJEE, S., Economics
BANERJEE, S., English
BASU, R., Sanskrit
BHATTACHARYA, A., Ancient Indian History and Culture

BHATTACHARYA, A., Philosophy
BHATTACHARYA, B., Pali
BHATTACHARYA, K., Linguistics
BHATTACHARYYA, S. K., Sociology
BHAUMIK, A. C., Museology
BURKE, I. K., Ancient Indian History and Culture
CHAKRABARTI, B., Library and Information Science
CHAKRABARTI, D., English
CHAKRABARTI, R., Ancient Indian History and Culture
CHAKRABARTI, R., Philosophy
CHAKRABARTI, S., English
CHATTERJEE, R., Islamic History and Culture
CHATTERJEE, R., Political Science
CHATTOPADHYAY, S.
CHATURVEDI, J., Hindi
CHAUDHURI, A., Economics
CHAUDHURI, B., South and South-East Asian Studies
CHOUDHURI, S., Islamic History and Culture
DAS, S., History
DASGUPTA, A., Economics
DASGUPTA, A., Library and Information Science
DE, B. B., Ancient
DUTTA, P. K., Political Science
DUTTA GUPTA, S., Political Science
GANGULY, M. K., Sanskrit
GANGULY, S. S., Bengali
GHOSH, D., Sanskrit
GHOSH, J., Bengali Language and Literature
GHOSH, P., South and South-East Asian Studies
GOSWAMI, K. R., Philosophy
GUPTA, C., Archaeology
GUPTA, D., Philosophy
KHAN, M., Bengali Language and Literature
MAHAPATRA, R., Tamil
MAITRA, J., Ancient Indian History and Culture
MAJUMDAR, M., Bengali Language and Literature
MALLIK, A., Economics
MUKHERJEE, B., Political Science
MUKHERJEE, B. K., Bengali Language and Literature
MUKHERJEE, S. K., Museology
MUKHOPADHYAY, B. K., Bengali Language and Literature
MUKHOPADHYAY, S. K., Political Science
NATH, M. K., Linguistics
PANDEY, C., Hindi
PARAMANIK, S. K., Sociology
RAY, A., Islamic History and Culture
RAY, J. K., History
ROY, A. K., South and South-East Asian Studies
ROY, D. K., Museology
ROY, S., English
SANYAL, J., English
SANYAL, K., Economics
SEN, K., Philosophy
SEN, P. K., Philosophy
SEN, R., Philosophy
SEN, S. K., Linguistics
SENGUPTA, S., Sanskrit
SHARMA, A., Hindi
SHAW, S., Hindi
SIKDAR, S. N., Economics
TAQI, Y. R., Urdi
VASUDEVAN, H. S., History

University College of Commerce, Social Welfare and Business Management (87/1 College St, Kolkata 700 073; tel. (33) 22410071; fax (33) 22413222):
BANERJEE, B.
BANERJEE, S.
SINHA, G. C.

University College of Law (51/1 Hazra Rd, Kolkata 700019; tel. (33) 24755801):
AHMED, I. G.

University College of Management (1 Reformatory St, Kolkata 700 027; tel. (33) 2479-1645):
CHAKRABARTI, R.
DHAR, S., Business Management
KHASNABIS, R., Business Management

University College of Science (35 Ballygunge Circular Rd, Kolkata 700 019
92 Acharya Prafulla Chandra Rd, Kolkata 700 009):
ACHARYA, S. K., Pure Mathematics
ADHIKARY, M. R., Pure Mathematics
BAGCHI, B., Applied Mathematics
BANDHYOPADHYAY, M. K., Geography
BANERJEE, A., Chemistry
BANERJEE, A. B., Biochemistry
BANERJEE, D., Physics
BANERJEE, J., Chemistry
BANERJEE, M., Botany
BANERJEE, S. B., Zoology
BASU, A., Statistics
BASU, S. R., Geography
BHATTACHARYYA, A., Zoology
BHATTACHARYYA, A., Marine Science
BHATTACHARYYA, A. K., Biochemistry
BHATTACHARYYA, C., Geology
BHATTACHARYYA, D. K., Pure Mathematics
BHATTACHARYYA, M., Anthropology
BHATTACHARYYA, P. K., Physics
CHAKRABARTI, B. C., Pure Mathematics
CHAKRABARTI, C. G., Applied Mathematics
CHATTERJEE, A., Botany
CHATTERJEE, N. B., Zoology
CHATTERJEE, P. K., Psychology
CHATTERJEE, S. P., Physiology
CHATTOPADHYAY, D., Biochemistry
CHOUDHURI, P. K., Applied Mathematics
CHOWDHURY, B., Anthropology
CHOWDHURY, U., Biophysics
DAS, J., Pure Mathematics
DAS, J. N., Applied Mathematics
DAS, K. C., Physics
DAS, K. P., Applied Mathematics
DAS, T. K., Physics
DASCHOWDHURY, A. B., Anthropology
DASGUPTA, C. K., Biophysics
DASGUPTA, U., Biophysics
DATTA GUPTA, A. K., Zoology
DE, S. S., Applied Mathematics
GANGULY, S., Pure Mathematics
GHATAK, K. P., Electronics Science
GHOSH, C. K., Biochemistry
GHOSH, P. N., Physics
GHOSH, S., Botany
LAHIRI, P., Zoology
MAITY, B. R., Zoology
MALLICK, R., Botany
MANNA, B., Zoology
MONDAL, A., Biochemistry
MUKHERJEE, D., Geology
MUKHERJEE, M., Biochemistry
MUKHERJEE, P., Botany
MUKHERJEE, S., Botany
MUKHERJEE, S., Geology
MUKHOPADHYAY, A. S., Zoology
MUKHOPADHYAY, S. C., Geography
NANDA, D. K., Zoology
PAL, S. G., Zoology
PAN, N. R., Physics
PRAMANIK, A. K., Applied Mathematics
PURAKAYASTHA, R., Botany
RAY, S., Botany
ROY, R., Anthropology
ROYCHAUDHURY, P., Applied Mathematics
ROYCHOUDHURY, D., Electronics Science
ROYCHOWDHURY, A., Physics
ROYCHOWDHURY, P., Physics
ROYCHOWDHURY, R., Botany
SAHA, G. B., Psychology
SAHA, P. K., Geography
SAMAJPATI, N., Botany

SAMANTA, B. K., Geology
SANYAL, A. B., Biophysics
SARKAR, S. K., Physics
SEN, R. N., Applied Mathematics
SEN, S., Botany
SENGUPTA, A., Geology
SENGUPTA, D., Biochemistry
SIRCAR, P. K., Botany
THAKUR, A. R., Biophysics

University College of Technology:

BANDHYOPADHYAY, S., Computer Science
BANIK, A. K., Chemical Engineering
BASU, A. K., Chemical Technology
BASU, D. K., Applied Physics
BASU, P. K., Radiophysics and Electronics
BHATTACHARJEE, A. K., Computer Science
BHATTACHARYYA, D. K., Chemical Technology
BHATTACHARYYA, S., Chemical Engineering
BHATTACHARYYA, T. K., Chemical Technology
CHAKRABORTY, A. K., Applied Physics
CHAKRABORTY, A. N., Radiophysics and Electronics
CHATTERJEE, N. K., Chemical Technology
CHATTOPADHYAY, D., Radiophysics and Electronics
DAS, V., Polymer Science and Technology
DASGUPTA, A. K., Radiophysics and Electronics
DAS PODDAR, P. K., Chemical Technology
DATTA, A. K., Applied Physics
DATTA, A. N., Radiophysics and Electronics
DATTA, B. K., Chemical Engineering
GHOSH, P., Polymer Science and Technology
GUPTA, S. N., Polymer Science and Technology
LAHIRI, C. R., Chemical Technology
MAJUMDER, R. N., Chemical Technology
MITRA, N. K., Chemical Technology
MITRA, T. K., Applied Physics
MUKHOPADHYAY, A. K., Applied Physics
NATH, N. G., Radiophysics and Electronics
PARIA, B. B., Chemical Engineering
PARIA, H., Radiophysics and Electronics
PURKAIT, N. N., Radiophysics and Electronics
RAKSHIT, P. C., Radiophysics and Electronics
ROY, P., Chemical Engineering
ROY, S. K., Radiophysics and Electronics
SAHA, P. K., Radiophysics and Electronics
SEN, A. K., Radiophysics and Electronics
SENGUPTA, P. K., Polymer Science and Technology

UNIVERSITY COLLEGES

University College of Agriculture: Kolkata; Sec. M. K. SENGUPTA.

University College of Arts: Kolkata; f. 1954; Sec. Dr D. P. DE.

University College of Commerce, Social Welfare and Business Management: Kolkata; f. 1954; Sec. Dr D. P. DE.

University College of Education, Journalism and Library Science: Sec. Dr A. K. CHAKRABORTI.

University College of Fine Arts, Music and Home Science: Sec. (vacant).

University College of Law: Kolkata; f. 1909; Sec. M. K. NAG.

University College of Medicine: Kolkata; f. 1957; Sec. Dr D. BAGCHI.

University College of Science: Kolkata; f. 1954; Sec. M. K. SENGUPTA.

University College of Technology: Kolkata; f. 1954; Sec. M. K. SENGUPTA.

CONSTITUENT COLLEGES

All India Institute of Hygiene and Public Health: Dir Dr B. N. GHOSH; see under Colleges.

Institute of Postgraduate Medical Education and Research: 244 Acharyya J. C. Bose Rd, Kolkata 700 020; Dir Prof. D. SEN.

Presidency College: 86/1 College St, Kolkata; f. 1817; Principal (vacant).

Sanskrit College: Bankim Chatterjee St, Kolkata; f. 1824; Principal B. P. BHATTACHARYYA.

School of Tropical Medicine: Kolkata; Dir Dr B. D. CHATTERJEE.

There are also 37 professional colleges and 207 affiliated colleges

UNIVERSITY OF CALICUT

PO Calicut University, Malappuram 673635, Kerala

Telephone: (494) 2401144
Fax: (494) 2400269
E-mail: reg@unical.ac.in
Internet: www.universityofcalicut.info

Founded 1968

Teaching and Affiliating
State control
Languages of instruction: English, Malayaam
Academic year: June to March
Chancellor: HE THE GOVERNOR OF KERALA
Vice-Chancellor: Prof. ANWAR JAHAN ZUBERI
Pro-Vice Chancellor: Dr C. GOBINATHAM PILLAI
Controller of Examinations: Dr T. K. NARAYANAN
Finance Officer: T. K. NARAYANAN (acting)
Dir of Public Relations: T. P. RAJEEVAN (acting)
Registrar: Dr T. K. NARAYANAN
Librarian: N. SUSHAMA

There are 285 affiliated colleges, incl. 115 Arts and Science Colleges, 53 Training Colleges, 23 Engineering/Technical Colleges, 5 Medical Colleges, 4 Ayurveda Colleges, 2 Law Colleges, 23 Oriental Title Colleges, 7 IHRD Centres, 1 Fine Arts College, 16 Nursing Colleges, 2 Dental Colleges, 8 Pharmacy Colleges, 1 Homeopathy College, 2 Hotel Management Colleges.
Library of 90,900 vols
Number of teachers: 166 (Univ. Depts), 5,920 (Affiliated Colleges)
Number of students: 305,000 (Univ. Depts and Affiliated Colleges)
Publications: *Calicut University Research Journal* (2 a year), *Interventions*, *Journal of South Indian History*, *Malabar*, *Malyala Vimarsam*

DEANS

Faculty of Ayurveda: Dr P. K. WARRIER
Faculty of Commerce and Management Studies: Dr E. P. SAINUL ABIDEEN
Faculty of Dentistry: Dr M. HARINDRANATH
Faculty of Education: Dr K. P. MANOJ
Faculty of Engineering: Dr M. P. CHANDRA SEKHARAN
Faculty of Fine Arts: Dr VAYALA VASUDEVAN PILLAI
Faculty of Health Science: T. SANKARAN NAIR
Faculty of Homeopathy: Dr M. P. PRAKASAN
Faculty of Humanities: Dr D. P. NAIR
Faculty of Journalism: Dr SYED AMJAD AMAMED
Faculty of Languages and Literature: Dr IQBAL AHAMMAD
Faculty of Law: Prof. K. V. NARAYANIKUTTY
Faculty of Medicine: Dr R. VELAYUDHAN NAIR
Faculty of Science: Dr P. RAMESAN

UNIVERSITY OF DELHI

Delhi 110007

Telephone: (11) 27667011
Fax: (11) 27667049

E-mail: vc@du.ac.in
Internet: www.du.ac.in

Founded 1922

Central univ.
Languages of instruction: English, Hindi
Academic year: July to April (three terms)
Chancellor: VICE-PRESIDENT OF INDIA
Pro-Chancellor: CHIEF JUSTICE OF INDIA
Vice-Chancellor: Prof. DEEPAK PENTAL
Pro-Vice-Chancellor: TANDON KUMAR
Registrar: Dr A. K. DUBEY
Dir of South Campus: Prof. DINESH SINGH
Dean of Colleges: Prof. NAYANJOT LAHIRI
Dean of Examinations: Prof. M. L. SINGHLA
Dean of Int. Relations: Prof. K. SREENIVAS
Dean of Research: Prof. K. N. TRIPATHI
Librarian: M. L. SAINI

Library of 1,450,000 vols, 1,290 journals
Number of teachers: 270
Number of students: 309,203

DEANS

Faculty of Applied Social Sciences and Humanities: Prof. S. K. VIJ
Faculty of Arts: Prof. S. PANJA
Faculty of Ayurvedic and Unani Medicine: K. K. SIJORIA
Faculty of Commerce and Business Studies: Prof. S. JAIN
Faculty of Education: Prof. B. BAJEVA
Faculty of Interdisciplinary and Applied Sciences: Prof. R. C. KUHAD
Faculty of Law: Prof. S. N. SINGH
Faculty of Management Studies: Prof. J. K. MITRA
Faculty of Mathematical Sciences: Prof. M. L. AGGARWAL
Faculty of Medical Sciences: Prof. U. RUSIA
Faculty of Music and Fine Arts: Prof. A. MITTAL
Faculty of Science: Prof. R. PAL
Faculty of Social Sciences: Prof. B. CHAKRABARTY
Faculty of Technology: Prof. P. KUMAR

CONSTITUENT COLLEGES

Atma Ram Sanatan Dharam College: New Delhi; f. 1959.

Bharati Mahila College: New Delhi; f. 1971.

Daulat Ram College: Delhi 7; f. 1960.

Gargi College: New Delhi; f. 1967.

Guru Gobind Singh College of Commerce: Delhi; f. 1984.

Gyan Devi Salwan College: New Delhi; f. 1970.

Hamdard College of Pharmacy: New Delhi; f. 1972.

Hamdard Tibbi College: Delhi; f. 1977.

Hans Raj College: Delhi; f. 1948.

Hindu College: Delhi; f. 1922.

Indraprastha College for Women: Delhi; f. 1925.

Institute of Home Economics: Delhi; f. 1969.

Janki Devi Mahavidyalaya: New Delhi; f. 1959.

Jesus and Mary College: New Delhi; f. 1968.

Kalindi College: New Delhi; f. 1967.

Kamla Nehru College: New Delhi; f. 1964.

Lady Irwin College: New Delhi; f. 1950.

Lady Shri Ram College for Women: New Delhi; f. 1956.

Lakshmibai College: Delhi; f. 1965.

Maitreyi College: New Delhi; f. 1967.

Mata Sundri College: New Delhi; f. 1967.

Moti Lal Nehru College: New Delhi; f. 1964.

P.G.D.A.V. College: New Delhi; f. 1957.

Rajdhani College: New Delhi; f. 1964.

St Stephen's College: Delhi; f. 1922.

Ramjas College: Delhi; f. 1917.

Satyawati Co-educational College: Delhi; f. 1972.

Shaheed Bhagat Singh College: New Delhi; f. 1967.

Shivaji College: New Delhi; f. 1961.

Shri Aurobindo College: New Delhi; f. 1972.

Shri Guru Teg Bahadur Khalsa College: Delhi; f. 1951.

Shri Ram College of Commerce: Delhi; f. 1926.

Shyam Lal College: Delhi; f. 1964.

Shyama Prasad Mukherjee College: New Delhi; f. 1969.

Sri Venkateswara College: New Delhi; f. 1961.

Swami Shardhanand College: Delhi; f. 1967.

Vivekanand Mahila College: Delhi; f. 1970.

Zakir Hussain College: Delhi; f. 1948.

UNIVERSITY MAINTAINED COLLEGES

College of Vocational Studies: New Delhi; f. 1972.

Deshbandhu College: Kalkaji, New Delhi; f. 1952.

Dyal Singh College: New Delhi; f. 1959.

Kirori Mal College: Delhi; f. 1954.

Miranda House for Women: Delhi; f. 1948.

School of Correspondence Courses and Continuing Education: Delhi; f. 1962.

University College of Medical Sciences: Delhi; f. 1971.

Vallabhbhai Patel Chest Institute: see under Research Institutes.

GOVERNMENT MAINTAINED COLLEGES

Ayurvedic and Unani Tabbia College: New Delhi; f. 1974.

College of Art: New Delhi; f. 1972.

College of Nursing: New Delhi; f. 1946.

College of Pharmacy: New Delhi; f. 1971.

Delhi College of Engineering: Kashmeri Gate, Delhi 6; f. 1959.

Delhi Institute of Technology: Delhi; f. 1983.

Lady Hardinge Medical College: New Delhi; f. 1949.

Maulana Azad Medical College: New Delhi; f. 1958.

ATTACHED RESEARCH CENTRES

Agricultural Economics Research Centre: tel. (11) 27667588; Dir P. S. VASHISHTHA.

Centre for Environmental Management of Degraded Ecosystem: tel. (11) 27662402; Dir Prof. INDERJIT.

Centre for Interdisciplinary Studies of Mountain and Hill Environment (CISMHE): f. 1990; Dir Dr V. KUMAR.

Developing Countries Research Centre (DCRC): tel. (11) 27666281; fax (11) 27667049; e-mail dcrc@dcrcdu.org; internet www.dcrcdu.org; f. 1993; Dir Prof. M. MOHANTY.

Dr B. R. Ambedkar Centre For Biomedical Research (ACBR): tel. (11) 27667151; Dir Prof. V. BRAHMACHARI.

Women Study Development Centre: tel. (11) 27667151; f. 1987; Dir Prof. V. CHATURVEDI.

UNIVERSITY OF HYDERABAD

Central University PO, Hyderabad 500046, Andhra Pradesh

Telephone: (40) 23132102
Fax: (40) 23010292
E-mail: yakkala@uohyd.ernet.in
Internet: www.uohyd.ernet.in

Founded 1974

Central university
State control
Language of instruction: English
Academic year: July to April
Chief Rector: HE THE GOVERNOR OF ANDHRA PRADESH
Chancellor: R. CHIDAMBARAM
Vice-Chancellor: Prof. S. E. HASNAIN
Pro-Vice-Chancellors: Prof. V. KANNAN, Prof. B. P. SANJAY
Registrar: Dr PRAKASH SARANGI
Public Relations Officer: A. J. THOMAS
Finance Officer: S. PARABRAHMAIAH
Controller of Examinations: Dr V. RAO
Librarian: Dr M. K. RAO
Library of 257,000 vols
Number of teachers: 200
Number of students: 2,000

DEANS

School of Chemistry: Prof. M. PERIASAMY
School of Engineering Sciences and Technology: Prof. A. T. BHATNAGAR
School of Humanities: M. G. RAMANAN
School of Life Sciences: Prof. A. S. RAGHAVENDRA
School of Management Studies: Prof. V. V. RAMANA
School of Mathematics and Computer and Information Sciences: Prof. T. AMARANATH
School of Medical Sciences: Prof. M. RAMANADHAM
School of Performing Arts, Fine Arts and Communication: Prof. V. PAVARALA
School of Physics: Prof. V. SRIVASTAVA
School of Social Sciences: Prof. E. HARIBABU

UNIVERSITY OF JAMMU

Baba Sahib Ambedkar Rd, Jammu (Tawi) 180006, Jammu and Kashmir

Telephone: (191) 2435248
Fax: (191) 2450014
E-mail: nodalpoint@jammuuniversity.in
Internet: www.jammuuniversity.in

Founded 1969

Affiliating and Teaching; 44 constituent colleges and 17 affiliated colleges
Languages of instruction: English, Hindi, Urdu, Sanskrit, Dogri, Punjabi
Academic year: July to March
Chancellor: HE THE GOVERNOR OF JAMMU AND KASHMIR
Vice-Chancellor: Prof. VARUN SAHNI
Registrar: Prof. O. S. SUDAN
Librarian: Prof. VERINDER GUPTA (acting)
Library of 340,810 vols, 250 periodicals
Number of teachers: 259
Number of students: 33,453
Publications: *Distance Education Journal, Social Sciences and Arts Journal*

DEANS

Faculty of Arts: Prof. N. SARAF
Faculty of Ayurveda: Dr C. R. GUPTA
Faculty of Behavioural Sciences: Prof. K. SUMBALI
Faculty of Commerce: Prof. S. P. GUPTA
Faculty of Engineering Technology: Dr R. N. SHARMA
Faculty of Law: Prof. S. K. SHARMA
Faculty of Life Sciences: Prof. V. K. ANAND
Faculty of Management Studies: Prof. J. R. DHOTRA
Faculty of Medicine: Dr ANIL GOSWAMY

Faculty of Music and Fine Arts: SAVITA BAKSHI
Faculty of Oriental Learning: Prof. K. H. SIDDIQUI
Faculty of Science: Prof. B. L. KALSOTRA
Faculty of Social Sciences: Prof. K. KOUR

PROFESSORS

AIMA, A., Management Studies
ANAND, V. K., Botany
BADYAL, S. K., Physics and Electronics
BANDHU, D., Distance Education
BHAT, B. L., Economics
CHARAK, P., English
CHOUDHARY, R., Political Science
DHAR, B. L., Geology
DHOTRA, J. R., Management Studies
DUTTA, S. P., Environmental Science
GANAI, N. A., Law
GOHIL, R. N., Botany
GUPTA, N., Hindi
GUPTA, R., Chemistry
GUPTA, R., Economics
GUPTA, S. C., Zoology
GUPTA, S. P., Commerce
GUPTA, V., Dogri
GUPTA, V. K., Physics and Electronics
HAMAL, I. A., Botany
JYOTI, M. K., Zoology
KAHN, S. R., Psychology
KALSOTRA, B. L., Chemistry
KAUR, K., Political Science
KESAR, A., Dogri Studies
KHOSA, S. K., Physics and Electronics
KOMAL, B. S., Mathematics
KOUL, G. L., Computer Science
KUMAR, R., Hindi
LANGER, A., Botany
MAGOTRA, L. K., Physics and Electronics
MAGOTRA, V. P., Law
MALHAN, I. V., Library Science
MANDOKA, R., English
MASOODI, G. S., Law
MOHD, J., History
OM, H., History
PANDA, J. R., Sociology
PARIHAR, L., Law
PRASAD, G. V. R., Geology
RANA, M. R., Management Studies
RAZDAN, K. B., English
SEHGAL, B. P. S., Law
SHARMA, I. B., Chemistry
SHARMA, K., Management Studies
SHARMA, N. R., Education
SHARMA, O. P., Economics
SHARMA, R. D., Commerce
SHARMA, R. L., Chemistry
SHARMA, S. K., Law
SIDDIQUI, K. H., Urdu
SINGH, A. P., Mathematics
SINGH, G., Computer Science
SINGH, G., Geography
SINGH, S., Law
SUDAN, C. S., Geology
SUMBLI, K., Education
SURI, S. P., Education
TIWARI, R. J., Statistics
VERMA, L., Education
WADAN, D. S., Punjabi
WAKHLU, A. K., Botany
WANGOO, C. L., Mathematics

ATTACHED CENTRES

Centre for History and Culture of Jammu and Ladakh Regions: f. 1994; Dir Dr ANITA BILLOWRIA.

Centre for New Literatures: Dir Prof. POSH CHARAK CHOUHAN.

Centre for Strategic and Regional Studies: e-mail csrs@jammuuniversity.in; f. 2002; Dir Dr SANGEETA THAPLIYAL.

Regional Centre for Field Operations and Research on Himalayan Glaciology: e-mail ganjoork@rediffmail.com; Dir Dr KESHAV SHARMA.

UNIVERSITY OF KASHMIR

Hazratbal, Srinagar 190006, Jammu and Kashmir

Telephone: (194) 2420078
Fax: (194) 2421357
E-mail: info@kashmiruniversity.net
Internet: www.kashmiruniversity.net

Founded 1948
Academic year: March to December

Teaching and Affiliating

Vice-Chancellor: Prof. RIYAZ PUNJABI
Registrar: Prof. S. FAYAZ AHMAD
Controller of Examinations: Prof. A. M. SHAH
Dean of Academics: Prof. ABDUL AZIZ UL AUZEEM
Dean of College Devt: Prof. NISAR AHMAD SHAH
Dean of Student Welfare: Prof. M. M. MASOODI
Public Relations Officer: SHOWKAT SHAFI
Librarian: REYAZ RUFAI

62 Affiliated colleges
Library of 375,000 vols
Number of teachers: 280
Number of students: 30,000 (incl. affiliated colleges)

Publication: *Journal of Himalayan Ecology and Sustainable Development*

DEANS

Faculty of Arts: Prof. A. H. TAK
Faculty of Commerce and Management Studies: Prof. G. M. DIN DAR
Faculty of Education: Prof. N. A. NADEEM
Faculty of Engineering: Prof. N. A. SHAH
Faculty of Law: Prof. M. A. MIR
Faculty of Medicine: Dr M. AHMAD
Faculty of Music and Fine Arts: Prof. A. AZIZ UL AUZEEM (acting)
Faculty of Oriental Learning: Prof. M. AHMAD KHAN
Faculty of Science: Prof. R. C. BHAGAT
Faculty of Social Science: Prof. N. BABA

PROFESSORS

ABDUL AZIZ, Mathematics
ALVI, W. A., Library and Information Science
AZURDAH, M. Z., Urdu
BABA, N. A., Political Science
BHAT, A. S., Law
BHAT, G. M., Economics
BHAT, M. I., Geology
BHAT, R. C., Zoology
CHANNA, A., Zoology
CHESTI, M. Z., Zoology
DABLA, B. A., Sociology
DHAR, R. L., Zoology
DHAR, T. N., English
DOST, M., Economics
FAROOQ, A., Physics
JAMWAL, K. S., Physics
JAVAID, A. Q., Urdu
KANT, T. A.
KAW, M. A., Central Asian Studies
KHAN, A. H., Distance Education
KHAN, A. M., Central Asian Studies
KHAN, A. R., Zoology
KHAN, B. A., Economics
KHAN, M. I., History
KURSHID, A., Management Studies
LONE, M. S., Kashmiri
MALIK, G. M., Education
MALIK, G. R., English
MALIK, N. A., Urdu
MASOODI, M. M., Persian
MATTOO, A. M., Central Asian Studies
MATTOO, A. R., Management Studies
MIR, A. A., Law
MIR, G. Q., Law
MIR, M., Law
MIR, M. A., Law
MUNSHI, A. H., Botany
MUZAMER, A. M., Urdu

NADEEM, N. A., Education
NIAZMAND, M. S., Persian
NISAR, A., Economics
PEER, M. A., Computer Science
PUNJABI, R., Distance Education
QUADRI, S. M. A., Law
QURESHI, A. W., Economics
QURESHI, M. A., Chemistry
RAFIQUI, A. Q., History
RAIS, A., Geography
RATHER, A. R., Education
SAPRU, B. L., Botany
SHAH, A. M., Environmental Services
SHAH, A. M., Management Studies
SHAH, G. M., Zoology
SHAH, N. A., Electronics
SIKANDAR, F., Botany
SOFI, M. A., Mathematics
SYED, F. A., Commerce
TAK, A. H., English
TANTRAY, G. N., Centre of Adult Continuing Education and Extension
WAFAI, B. A., Botany
WANI, M. A., History

RESEARCH CENTRES

Academic Staff Centre: tel. (194) 2420389; fax (194) 2421357; f. 1987; Dir Prof. MEHRAJ-UD-DIN.

Bioinformatics Centre: tel. (194) 2421353; fax (194) 2428723; e-mail andrabik@kashmiruniversity.net; internet www.bioinfoku.org; f. 2000; Dir Dr KHURSHID IQBAL ANDRABI.

Centre for Adult Continuing and Extension Education: f. 1978; Dir Prof. ALTAF AHMAD MIR.

Centre of Central Asian Studies: tel. (194) 2422553; fax (194) 2420923; e-mail mkaw@rediffmail.com; f. 1978; publ. *Journal of Central Asian Studies* (1 a year); Dir Prof. MUSHTAQ A. KHAN.

Centre of Distance Education: tel. (194) 2429810; e-mail disedu@kashmiruniversity.net; f. 1976; publ. *Communication* (1 a year), *Tarseel* (1 a year); Dir Dr SHAFIQA PRAVEEN.

Centre of Research for Development: f. 1979; Dir Prof. A. R. YOUSEF.

Educational Multimedia Research Centre: tel. (194) 2420610; e-mail emmrc@kashmiruniversity.net; f. 1992; Dir SHAHID RASOOL.

Iqbal Institute: tel. (194) 2410201; f. 1977; Dir Prof. B. A. NAHVI.

Population Research Centre: tel. (194) 2427541; fax (194) 2423091; e-mail prcsrinagar@rediffmail.com; f. 1985; Dir Prof. G. M. BHAT.

State Resource Centre: f. 1978; Dir Prof. B. A. WAFAI.

University Science Instrumentation Centre: tel. (194) 2410774; fax (194) 2420405; e-mail gmbhat_ku@yahoo.co.in; f. 1979; Dir Prof. G. M. BHAT.

UNIVERSITY OF KERALA

Thiruvananthapuram 695034, Kerala
Telephone: (471) 2306422
Fax: (471) 2307158
E-mail: kuinform@eth.net
Internet: www.keralauniversity.edu

Founded 1937

Teaching and Affiliating; 50 affiliated colleges, 25 professional colleges, 57 recognized research centres
Language of instruction: English
Academic year: June to May

Chancellor: HE THE GOVERNOR OF KERALA
Pro-Chancellor: THE MIN. FOR EDUCATION, GOVERNMENT OF KERALA

Vice-Chancellor: Dr A. JAYAKRISHNAN
Pro-Vice-Chancellor: Dr V. JAYAPRAKAS
Registrar: K. A. HASHIM
Controller of Examinations: Dr M. T. SULE-KHA
Dir of College Devt Ccl: Dr M. JAYAPRAKASH
Dir of Planning and Devt: Dr S. V. SUDHEER
Public Relations Officer: S. D. PRINS
Librarian: J. USHA

Library of 280,804 vols
Number of teachers: 5,799
Number of students: 123,310

DEANS

Faculty of Applied Sciences: Dr M. R. KAIMAL
Faculty of Arts: Dr J. BEEGUM
Faculty of Ayurveda: Dr M. R. VASUDEVAN NAMPOOTHIRI
Faculty of Commerce: Dr K. P. MURALEED-HARAN
Faculty of Dentistry: Dr K. J. KUMAR
Faculty of Education: Dr J. EXEMMAL
Faculty of Engineering and Technology: Dr R. IBRAHIMKUTTY
Faculty of Fine Arts: Dr V. V. PILLAI
Faculty of Homoeopathy: Dr T. M. SREEDEVI
Faculty of Law: Dr K. C. SUNNY
Faculty of Management Studies: Dr J. RAJAN
Faculty of Medicine: Dr D. DALUS
Faculty of Oriental Studies: Dr D. BENJAMIN
Faculty of Physical Education: Dr E. SUNIL
Faculty of Science: Dr P. INDRASENAN
Faculty of Social Sciences: Dr R. N. YESUDAS

UNIVERSITY CENTRES

Centre for Adult Continuing Education and Extension (CACEE): tel. (471) 2302523; e-mail cacee@keralauniversity.edu; Dir Prof. B. VIJAYAKUMAR.

Centre for Bioinformatics: tel. (471) 2412759; e-mail sankar.achuth@gmail.com; internet www.cbi.keralauniversity.edu; f. 2005; Dir Dr A. S. S. NAIR.

Centre for Canadian Studies: tel. (471) 306422; f. 1991; Dir Dr J. BEGUM.

Centre for Convergence Media Studies: tel. (471) 2301045; Dir M. VIJAYAKUMAR.

Centre for Gandhian Studies: f. 1970; Dir Dr J. M. RAHIM.

Centre for Marine Diversity: tel. (471) 2412434; e-mail k.padmakumar@vsnl.com; Dir Dr K. PADMAKUMAR.

Centre for Vedanta Studies: f. 1986; Dir Dr K. MAHESWARAN NAIR.

Centre for Women's Studies: tel. (471) 2441515; f. 1986; Dir Dr G. S. JAYASREE.

International Centre for Kerala Studies: tel. (471) 2412168; f. 1988; Dir Dr N. SAM.

Population Research Centre: tel. (471) 418796; f. 1983; Dir Dr K. KRISHNAKUMARI.

Sree Narayana Study Centre for Social Change: tel. (471) 2418421; f. 1996; Dir Dr K. VIJAYAN.

Survey Research Centre: f. 1979; Dir C. P. SURESH.

University Observatory: tel. (471) 2322732; f. 1837; Dir Dr V. K. VAIDYAN.

V. K. Krishna Menon Study Centre for International Relations: tel. (471) 2418307; Dir Dr G. GOPAKUMAR.

UNIVERSITY OF LUCKNOW

Badshah Bagh, Lucknow 226007, Uttar Pradesh
Fax: (522) 2740086
E-mail: info@lkouniv.ac.in
Internet: www.lkouniv.ac.in

Founded 1921

Residential and Teaching
Languages of instruction: English, Hindi
Academic year: July to April

Chancellor: HE The Governor of Uttar
  Pradesh
Vice-Chancellor: Prof. Ajaib Singh Brar
Pro-Vice-Chancellor: Prof. U. N. Dwivedi
Registrar: Dr G. P. Tripathi
Finance Officer: J. Prasad
Controller of Examinations: Prof. A. K. S.
  Chauhan
Dean of Student Welfare: Prof. N. Pandey
Library of 510,000 vols
Number of teachers: 661
Number of students: 48,625

DEANS

Faculty of Architecture: Nehru Lal
Faculty of Arts: Prof. V. D. Pandey
Faculty of Commerce: Prof. Vaishampayan
Faculty of Education: A. Choubey
Faculty of Fine Arts: Dr Rajiv Narain
Faculty of Law: A. K. Awasthi
Faculty of Science: Prof. V. K. Tandon

CONSTITUENT COLLEGES

College of Arts and Crafts: Lucknow; Prin.
J. K. Agarwal.

Government College of Architecture:
Lucknow; Prin. Prof. N. Lal.

**Institute of Engineering and Technol-
ogy:** Lucknow; Dir Prof. G. N. Pandey.

King George's Medical College: Lucknow;
f. 1911; 4-year postgraduate medical courses
have been established; Prin. Dr P. K. Mishra.

State College of Ayurveda: Lucknow; f.
1954; Prin. Prof. B. N. Singh.

ATTACHED INSTITUTES

Institute of Development Studies: Dir
Prof. A. K. Sengupta.

Institute of Management Sciences: tel.
(522) 2740032; Chair. Prof. A. S. Brar.

**Institute of Mass Communication in
Science and Technology:** f. 1995; Dir
Prof. D. Kumar.

Institute of Women's Studies: f. 1997; Dir
Prof. R. Chandra.

**Regional Centre for Urban and Envir-
onmental Studies:** tel. (522) 2740165;
e-mail directorrcueslko@gmail.com; internet
www.rcueslko.org; Dir Dr N. K. Rai.

UNIVERSITY OF MADRAS

Chepauk, Triplicane PO, Chennai 600005,
  Tamil Nadu
Telephone: (44) 25399778
Fax: (44) 25366693
E-mail: vcoffice@unom.ac.in
Internet: www.unom.ac.in
Founded 1857
Teaching and Affiliating
Languages of instruction: English, Tamil
Academic year: July to April
Chancellor: HE The Governor of Tamil
  Nadu
Vice-Chancellor: Prof. S. Ramachandran
Pro-Chancellor: Dr K. Ponmudi
Academic Dean: Dr P. Duraisamy
Dean of Research: Dr D. Velmurugan
Dir of Chepauk Campus: Dr P. T. Srinivasan
Dir of Guindy Campus: Dr H. Devaraj
Dir of Marina Campus: Dr Revathy
Dir of Taramani Campus: Dr N. Srinivasan
Registrar: Dr M. Ranganatham
Librarian: Dr R. Vengan (acting)
Library of 506,295 vols
Number of students: 107,518
Publication: *Annals of Oriental Research*

DEANS

Faculty of Arts: Dr R. Thandavan
Faculty of Fine Arts: Dr N. Ramanathan

Faculty of Indian and Other Languages: Dr
  V. Jayadevan
Faculty of Law: Dr N. Balu
Faculty of Science: Dr D. Lalitha Kumari
Faculty of Teaching: Dr D. Raja Ganesan
There are 276 affiliated colleges

UNIVERSITY OF MUMBAI

University Rd, Fort, Mumbai 400032,
  Maharashtra
Telephone: (22) 22704390
Fax: (22) 22652832
E-mail: vc@fort.mu.ac.in
Internet: www.mu.ac.in
Founded 1857 as Univ. of Bombay, present
  name 1996
Teaching and Affiliating
Language of instruction: English
Academic year: June to April (two terms)
Chancellor: HE The Gov. of Maharashtra
Vice-Chancellor: Dr Vijay Khole
Pro-Vice-Chancellor: Dr Arun D. Sawant
Registrar: K. Venkatramani
Controller of Examinations: V. B. Shinde
Librarian: Prof. Vijaya Rajhama

315 Constituent colleges and 79 recognized
postgraduate instns (mostly listed under
Research Institutes)
Library of 837,978 vols
Number of students: 262,350

Publications: *Journal of the University of
Bombay, Prakrit and Pali, Sanskrit, Uni-
versity of Bombay Studies, University Eco-
nomics Series, University Series in
Monetary and International Economics,
University Sociology Series*

DEANS

Faculty of Arts: Dr P. Venkatesh
Faculty of Commerce: Principal: M. G.
  Shirahatti
Faculty of Fine Arts: N. L. Keny
Faculty of Law: N. M. Rajadhyaksha
Faculty of Science: S. B. Patil
Faculty of Technology: Prof. S. Sahare

PROFESSORS

Faculty of Arts:

Abhedi, R. S. A., Urdu
Annakuty, V. K., German Literature and
  Russian
Bandivadekar, C. M., Comparative Litera-
  ture
Bharadwaj, M. A., Econometrics
Bharucha, N., Post-Colonial Literature
Bhat Nayak, V., Mathematics
Bhongle, N., 20th-Century Indian Litera-
  ture in English
Bokit, S. V., Industrial Policy and Devel-
  opment Banking
Bhowmik, S. K., Sociology
Chawathe, P. D., Graphs Theory
Correa, R., Economics
Dalvi, A. M. I., Urdu
Deshpande, J. V., Mathematics
Dossal, M., History
Giri, R. D., Mathematics
Guha, S. B., Geography
Gummadi, N., General Economics
Jadhav, A. S., Geography
Janwa, H. L., Algebra
Jogdand, P. G., Sociology
Joshi, S. A., Philosophy
Joshi, S. M., Statistical Inference
Kamath, P. M., American Studies
Khokle, V. S., Socio-linguistics
Kumaresan, S., Mathematics
Limaye, N. B., Mathematics
Lukmani, V. M., English
Mody, N. B., Civics and Politics
Mohanty, S. P., Social Demography
Momin, A. R., Cultural Anthropology

Mungekar, B. I., Economics
Nabar, S. P., Statistics
Nabar, V., Indo-English Literature
Nachane, D. N., Quantitative Economics
Nadkarni, M. G., Mathematics
Nemade, B. V., Comparative Literature
Pethe, A. M., Economics
Phadke, V. S., Geography
Rajhansa, V. P., Reference Service
Rao, M. J. M., General Economics
Sabnis, R. S., Monetary and Industrial
  Economics
Sandesara, J. C., Industrial Economics
Sane, S. S., Mathematics
Sawant, S. D., Agricultural Economics
Seeta Prabhu, K., Economics
Sen, M., Experimental Psychology
Sirdeshpande, M. R., French
Sriraman, S., Transport Economics
Tikekar, A. C., Library Science
Tiwari, R., Hindi
Vaidya, S. S., Marathi
Vanaja, N., Algebra
Vasant Karnik, A., Economics
Vasantkumar, T., Kannada Literature
Vyas, V. S., Music

Faculty of Commerce:

Anagol, M., Banking
Ghosh, P. K., Personnel Management
Iyer, V. R., Management
Manerikar, V. V., Research Methodology
Murthy, G. N., Finance and Accounts
Santanam, H., Operational Research

Faculty of Law:

Khodie, N., Mercantile Law
Rao, M., Law
Warke, P. C., Law

Faculty of Science:

Bagade, U. S., Life Sciences
Fulekar, M. H., Life Sciences
Gajbhiye, N. S., Physics
Gogavale, S. V., Experimental Electronic
  and Plasma Physics
Hosangadi, B. D., Organic Chemistry
Joshi, V. N., Computer Science
Kulkarni, A. R., Plant Sciences
Narayanan, P., Life Sciences
Narsale, A. M., Physics
Patel, S. B., Experimental Nuclear Phys-
  ics
Pratap, R., Electronics
Rangwala, A. A., Theoretical Physics
Shethna, Y. I., Life Sciences
Sivakami, S., Life Sciences
Vasanthakumar, T., Kannada

Faculty of Technology:

Akamanchi, K. G., Pharmaceutical Chem-
  istry
Athawale, V. D., Chemistry
Bhat, N. V., Physics
Chandalia, S. B., Chemical Engineering
Dixit, S. G., Physics
Joshi, J. B., Chemical Engineering
Kale, D. D., Polymer Technology
Kulkarni, P. R., Food Science and Tech-
  nology
Kulkarni, V. M., Medicinal Chemistry
Lokhande, H. T., Fibre Science
Malshe, V. C., Paint Technology
Mashraqui, S. H., Chemistry
Mhaskar, R. D., Chemical Engineering
Nyayadhish, V. B., Mathematics
Pai, J. S., Biochemical Engineering
Pangarkar, V. G., Chemical Engineering
Rajadyaksha, R. A., Physical Chemistry
Rao, H. M., Engineering
Seshadri, S., Dyestuffs Technology
Sharma, M. M., Chemical Engineering
Shenay, V. A., Textile Chemistry
Subramanian, V. V. R., Oil Technology
Teli, M. D., Fibre Science
Tiwari, K. K., Chemical Engineering
Tungare, S. A., Architecture
Varadarajan, T. S., Applied Physics

VENKATESEN, T. K., Oil Chemistry
YADAV, G. D., Chemical Engineering

UNIVERSITY OF MYSORE

POB 407, Mysore 570005, Karnataka
Telephone: (821) 2438666
Fax: (821) 2421263
E-mail: registrar@uni-mysore.ac.in
Internet: www.uni-mysore.ac.in

Founded 1916

Teaching and Affiliating
Languages of instruction: English, Kannada
Academic year: June to March (two terms)
Chancellor: HE THE GOV. OF KARNATAKA
Vice-Chancellor: Dr V. G. TALWAR (acting)
Registrar: B. J. HOSMATH
Registrar for Evaluation: B. RAMU
Finance Officer: M. K. SANNASWAMY
Dir of College Devt Ccl: Prof. K. SRIHARI
Librarian: Dr M. KRISHNAMURTHY

122 Affiliated colleges; 5 constituent colleges; 2 postgraduate centres at Hemagangotri and Mandya
Library of 800,000 vols, 2,400 journals
Number of students: 56,500

DEANS

Faculty of Arts: Prof. C. P. SIDDHASHRAMA
Faculty of Commerce: Prof. B. R. ANANTHAN
Faculty of Education: Prof. A. S. RAGHAVA KUMARI
Faculty of Engineering: Prof. CHENNA VENKATESH
Faculty of Law: Dr H. K. NAGARAJA
Faculty of Medicine: Dr KAMALA
Faculty of Science and Technology: Prof. Y. SRINIVASA REDDY

UNIVERSITY COLLEGES

College of Fine Arts for Women: Prin. Dr C. BHATT.

Maharaja's College: Prin. Dr C. SIDDARAJU.

University College of Physical Education: Prin. Dr M. CHANDRAKUMAR.

University Evening College: Prin. SARVAMANGALA BAI.

Yuvaraja's College: Prin. SUMINTHRA BAI.

ATTACHED INSTITUTES

Ambedkar Research Centre: Dir Dr A. SOMASHEKAR.

Centre for Information Science and Technology: Dir Prof. R. YUSADEV.

Educational Multimedia Research Centre: Dir Prof. A. BALASUBRAMANIAN.

Gandhi Bhavan: Dir Dr S. SHIVARAJAPPA.

Institute for Development Studies: f. 1971; Dir Dr K. S. ARUN KUMAR.

Oriental Research Institute: Dir Dr K. V. RAMESH.

Third Sector Research Resource Centre: e-mail info@tsr.uni-mysore.ac.in; internet tsr.uni-mysore.ac.in; Dir Dr Y. DONGRE.

University School of Design: Dir Prof. DAROGA.

UNIVERSITY OF NORTH BENGAL

PO North Bengal Univ., Raja Rammohunpur 734430, Darjeeling District, West Bengal
Telephone: (353) 2582099
Fax: (353) 2581212
E-mail: regnbu@sancharnet.in
Internet: www.nbu.ac.in

Founded 1962

Teaching and Affiliating; 23 postgraduate depts; 18 centres; 86 affilliated colleges
Academic year: July to June
Chancellor: HE THE GOV. OF WEST BENGAL

Vice-Chancellor: Prof. ARUNABHA BASUMAJUMDAR
Registrar: Dr DILIP K. SARKAR
Finance Officer: P. K. GHOSH
Librarian: M. MANDAL
Library of 180,000 vols, 700 periodicals
Number of teachers: 154
Number of students: 51,000

DEANS

Faculty of Arts, Commerce and Law: Prof. R. GHOSH
Faculty of Science: Prof. B. N. CHAKRABARTY

PROFESSORS

Arts, Commerce and Law:
  BHADRA, R. K., Sociology
  BHATTA, A., Bengali
  BHATTACHARJEE, C., Philosophy
  CHAKRABORTY, B. B., Philosophy
  CHAKRABORTY, U., English
  GHOSH, R., Philosophy
  MONDAL, SK. R., Centre for Himalayan Studies
  MUKHOPADHYAY, C., Economics
  MUKHOPADHYAY, R. S., Sociology
  ROY MOULIK, S. K., English
  SAHU, R., Centre for Himalayan Studies
  SENGUPTA, P. K., Political Science
  SENGUPTA, P. R., Commerce
  UPADHYAY, B. K., Nepali

Science:
  BOSE, M. K., Mathematics
  DAS, A. P., Botany
  DASGUPTA, D., Physics
  HAZRA, D. K., Chemistry
  KARANJAI, S. B., Mathematics
  MANNA, N. R., Computer Science and Applications
  MUKHOPADHYAY, A., Zoology
  NANDI, K. K., Mathematics
  ROY, A., Chemistry
  ROY, P. S., Chemistry
  SAHA, S. K., Chemistry
  SARKAR, P. K., Botany

UNIVERSITY OF PETROLEUM AND ENERGY STUDIES

PO Bidholi, Via-Prem Nagar, Dehradun 284006, Uttaranchal
Telephone: (135) 2102690
Fax: (135) 2694204
E-mail: info@upesindia.org
Internet: www.upesindia.org

Founded 2003

Private, Hydrocarbons Education and Research Soc.

Regional centre in Gurgaon; additional campus at Rajahmundry
Chancellor: Dr S. J. CHOPRA
Pro-Chancellor: Prof. G. C. TEWARI
Vice-Chancellor: Dr PARAG DIWAN
Registrar: SANDEEP MEHTA

Number of teachers: 20

DEANS

College of Engineering Studies: Dr B. P. PANDEY
College of Legal Studies: Dr R. H. GORANE
College of Management and Economic Studies: Prof. G. C. TEWARI

UNIVERSITY OF PUNE

Ganeshkhind Rd, Pune 411007, Maharashtra
Telephone: (20) 25696061
E-mail: regis@unipune.ernet.in
Internet: www.unipune.ernet.in

Founded 1949

Teaching and Affiliating

Languages of instruction: English (optional), Marathi
Academic year: June to March (two terms)
Chancellor: HE THE GOVERNOR OF MAHARASHTRA
Vice-Chancellor: Dr NARENDRA JADHAV
Registrar: Dr MANIK LAXMANRAO JADHAV
Librarian: Prof. S. K. PATIL

41 Postgraduate depts; 269 affiliated colleges; 129 research institutes
Library of 422,000 vols, 435 periodicals
Number of teachers: 288
Number of students: 96,000 (including affiliated colleges)

DEANS

Faculty of Arts: Prof. SUDHAKER PANDEY
Faculty of Ayurvedic Medicine: P. H. KULKARNI
Faculty of Commerce: Dr J. R. GODHA
Faculty of Education: Prof. S. V. KHER
Faculty of Engineering: Prof. H. M. GANESHRAO
Faculty of Law: VIJAYRAO MOHITE
Faculty of Medicine: Dr M. J. JOSHI
Faculty of Mental, Moral and Social Science: Dr D. B. KERUR
Faculty of Science: Dr S. C. GUPTE

ATTACHED INSTITUTES

Centre for Development of Advanced Computing: tel. (20) 25704100; fax (20) 25694004; internet www.cdac.in.

Inter-University Centre for Astronomy and Astrophysics: tel. (20) 25604100; fax (20) 25604699; e-mail nkd@iucaa.ernet.in; internet www.iucaa.ernet.in; Dir N. K. DADHICH.

National Centre for Cell Science: tel. (20) 25708000; fax (20) 25692259; Dir G. C. MISHRA.

National Centre for Radio Astrophysics: tel. (20) 25719000; fax (20) 25692149; e-mail www@ncra.tifr.res.in; Dir P. K. MANOHARAN.

UNIVERSITY OF RAJASTHAN

JLN Marg, Jaipur 302055, Rajasthan
Telephone: (141) 2711070
Fax: (141) 2709582
E-mail: info@uniraj.ernet.in
Internet: www.uniraj.ernet.in

Founded 1947

Teaching and Affiliating; 37 postgraduate depts; 206 affiliated colleges
Independent control
Languages of instruction: English, Hindi
Academic year: July to May (two terms)
Chancellor: HE THE GOV. OF RAJASTHAN
Vice-Chancellor: Dr NARENDRA KUMAR JAIN
Registrar: ALOK MATHUR
Controller of Examinations: N. N. GUPTA
Librarian: Prof. PRADEEP BHATNAGAR

Library of 371,500 vols, 65,000 bound periodicals
Number of teachers: 575
Number of students: 175,000

DEANS

Faculty of Arts: Prof. S. RAI
Faculty of Commerce: Dr J. K. TANDON
Faculty of Education: Dr R. ARORA
Faculty of Engineering and Technology: S. G. MODANI
Faculty of Fine Arts: Dr K. GARG
Faculty of Law: Prof. S. S. LAL
Faculty of Management Studies: Dr G. KAPOOR
Faculty of Science: Prof. S. L. KOTHARI
Faculty of Social Sciences: Prof. B. L. GUPTA

UNIVERSITY COLLEGES

Commerce College: f. 1956.

Evening Law College.
Law College.
Maharaja's College: f. 1944.
Maharani's College: f. 1944.
Rajasthan College: f. 1956.

RESEARCH CENTRES

Centre for Converging Technologies: Dir Prof. SARDAR SINGH.

Centre for Development of Physics Education: Dir Prof. SARDAR SINGH.

Centre for Gandhian Studies.

Centre for Jain Studies: Dir Dr P. C. JAIN.

Centre for Non-Conventional Energy Resources: e-mail jain-ip@uniraj.ernet.in; Dir Dr I. P. JAIN.

Indira Gandhi Centre for Human Ecology, Environmental and Population Studies: e-mail jamali-khan@uniraj.ernet.in; Dir Prof. T. I. K. JAMALI.

R. A. Podar Institute of Management: tel. (141) 2711349; Dir Dr RAJESH KOTHARI.

South Asia Studies Centre: e-mail sharma-ml@uniraj.ernet.in; Dir Dr M. L. SHARMA.

UTKAL UNIVERSITY

PO Vani Vihar, Bhubaneswar 751004, Orissa
Telephone: (674) 2581850
Fax: (674) 2581850
Internet: www.utkal-university.org

Founded 1943

Teaching and affiliating
State control
Languages of instruction: English, Oriya
Academic year: July to June
Chancellor: HE THE GOV. OF ORISSA
Vice-Chancellor: Prof. BINAYAK RATH
Registrar: Dr L. N. SAHOO
Dir of College Devt Ccl: Prof. H. K. PATRA
Dir of Student Welfare: Prof. BRAHMANANDA PADHI
Controller of Examinations: Dr BIMAL C. MISHRA
Comptroller of Finance: K. K. MOHANTY
Librarian: Dr P. K. MOHANTY (acting)
267 Affiliated colleges
Library of 237,695 vols, 236 periodicals
Number of teachers: 8,521
Number of students: 200,000

DEANS

Faculty of Arts: Prof. K. M. PATRA
Faculty of Commerce: Dr GUNANIDHI SAHOO
Faculty of Education: M. DAS
Faculty of Engineering: Dr NILAKANTHA PATTANAIK
Faculty of Law: INDRAJIT RAY
Faculty of Medicine: Dr R. N. DASH
Faculty of Science: Dr P. K. JESTHI

CONSTITUENT COLLEGES

Madhusudan Law College: Cuttack; f. 1949; Prin. Dr D. P. KAR.

University Law College: Vani Vihar, Bhubaneswar 751004; f. 1975; Prin. Dr P. K. PADHI.

UTKAL UNIVERSITY OF CULTURE

POB 4, Bhubaneswar 751001, Orissa
Telephone: (674) 2530213
Fax: (674) 2535486
E-mail: mail@utkaluniversityculture.org
Internet: www.utkaluniversityculture.org

Founded 1999

Teaching and affiliating; schools of architecture and archaeology, culture studies, language and literature, occupational studies, Orissan studies, performing arts, visual arts

Academic year: July to June
Chancellor: HE THE GOVERNOR OF ORISSA
Vice-Chancellor: Prof. Dr SADHU CHARAN PANDA
Registrar: Dr HARAPRASAD PARICHA PATNAIK
Finance Officer: R. K. PATRA
Library of 3,000 vols
27 Affiliated colleges (4 govt, 23 private).

UTTAR PRADESH RAJARSHI TANDON OPEN UNIVERSITY

17 Maharshi Dayanand Marg, Thornhill Rd, Allahabad 211001, Uttar Pradesh
Telephone: (532) 2621839
Fax: (532) 2624368
E-mail: contact@uprtou.org.in
Internet: www.uprtou.org.in

Founded 1998

Schools of computer and information technology, health sciences, humanities and languages, journalism and mass communication, management, social sciences, tourism and hotel management
Chancellor: HE THE GOV. OF UTTAR PRADESH
Vice-Chancellor: Prof. NAGESHWAR RAO
Registrar: M. L. KANAUJIA
Finance Officer: Dr S. K. GUPTA

DIRECTORS

School of Education: Prof. S. P. GUPTA
School of Humanities: Dr B. N. SINGH
School of Social Sciences: Dr M. N. SINGH

UTTAR PRADESH TECHNICAL UNIVERSITY

IET Campus, Sitapur Rd, Lucknow 226021, Uttar Pradesh
Telephone: (522) 2732194
Fax: (522) 2732189
Noida Office C-22, Sector 62, Noida 201301, Uttar Pradesh
Telephone: (120) 2400416
Fax: (120) 2400418
E-mail: registrar@uptu.ac.in
Internet: www.uptu.org

Founded 2000

Chancellor: HE THE GOVERNOR OF UTTAR PRADESH
Vice-Chancellor: Prof. PREM VRAT
Registrar: U. S. TOMER
Finance Officer: B. L. RATHORE
Controller of Examinations: Prof. V. K. SINGH
Number of students: 90,000
317 Affiliated colleges.

CONSTITUENT INSTITUTES

Institute of Engineering and Technology: Sitapur Rd, Lucknow; tel. (522) 2361692; e-mail director@ietlucknow.edu; internet ietlucknow.edu; Dir Prof. S. K. SRIVASTAVA.

Lucknow College of Architecture: Tagore Marg, Lucknow 226007; tel. (522) 2740236; e-mail principal@lcoarch.ac.in; internet www.foa.uptu.ac.in.

V. B. S. PURVANCHAL UNIVERSITY

Devkali Jasopur, Saraykhaja, Jaunpur 222001, Uttar Pradesh
Telephone: (5452) 252244
Fax: (5452) 252222
E-mail: registrar@vbspu.ac.in
Internet: vbspu.ac.in

Founded 1987

Residential and Affiliating; institutes of biological studies, business management, engineering and technology, pharmacy; depts of applied psychology, business economics,

financial studies, human resource devt, mass communication; 331 affiliated colleges
Vice-Chancellor: Prof. R. C. SARASWAT
Registrar: Dr B. L. ARYA
Finance Officer: RANJIT KUMAR SRIVASTAVA
Controller of Examinations: R. S. YADAV
Number of students: 380,000 (incl. affiliated colleges)

DEAN

Faculty of Science: Prof. D. D. DUBEY

VARDHAMAN MAHAVEER OPEN UNIVERSITY

Rawatbhata Rd, Akhelgarh, Kota 324010, Rajasthan
Telephone: (744) 2471254
Fax: (744) 2472525
E-mail: reg@vmoukota.in
Internet: vmou.ac.in

Founded 1987 as Kota Open Univ., present name 2002

Depts of commerce, computer science, economics, education, English, Hindi, history, Indian tradition and culture, journalism, law, library and information science, management and political science; regional centres in Ajmer, Bikaner, Jaipur, Jodhpur, Kota, Udaipur; 85 study centres
Chancellor: HE THE GOV. OF RAJASTHAN
Vice-Chancellor: Prof. NARESH DADHICH
Registrar: B. L. KOTHARI
Library: over 100,000 vols, 200 periodicals.

VEER KUNWAR SINGH UNIVERSITY

Arrah 802301, Bihar
Telephone: (6182) 223559
Fax: (6182) 223559
E-mail: registrar@vksu-ara.org
Internet: www.vksu-ara.org

Founded 1992

Academic year: June to May
20 Postgraduate depts, 17 constituent colleges, 3 Law colleges, 37 affiliated colleges
Chancellor: HE THE GOVERNOR OF BIHAR
Vice-Chancellor: Dr I. C. KUMAR
Registrar: Dr QAMAR AHSAN
Librarian: Dr J. P. SINGH

DEANS

Faculty of Commerce: Dr D. K. TIWARI
Faculty of Humanities: Dr R. P. RAI
Faculty of Science: Dr R. P. PANDEY
Faculty of Social Science: Dr GANDHIJEE RAI

VEER NARMAD SOUTH GUJARAT UNIVERSITY

Udhna-Magdalla Rd, Surat 395007, Gujarat
Telephone: (261) 2227141
Fax: (261) 2227312
E-mail: sgu@sgu.ernet.in
Internet: www.sgu.ernet.in

Founded 1967 as South Gujarat Univ., present name 2004

Teaching and Affiliating
State control
Language of instruction: Gujarati
Academic year: June to March (two terms); attached to Nat. Assessment and Accreditation Ccl, Bangalore
Chancellor: HE The Gov. of Gujarat PANDIT NAWAL KISHORE SHARMA
Vice-Chancellor: Prof. Dr B. A. PRAJAPATI
Registrar: J. R. MEHTA (acting)
Librarian: B. J. ANKUYA (acting)
140 Affiliated colleges
Library of 172,134 vols, 242 periodicals
Number of teachers: 105 (univ. postgraduate dept)

Number of students: 3,794 (univ. postgraduate dept)

DEANS

Faculty of Arts: G. P. SANADHYA
Faculty of Commerce: J. M. NAIK
Faculty of Education: Dr K. V. DESAI
Faculty of Law: Dr V. B. DESAI
Faculty of Management: Dr S. K. VAJPEYEE
Faculty of Medicine: Dr S. KUMAR
Faculty of Rural Studies: Dr V. J. SOMANI
Faculty of Science: N. B. MAHIDA

VIDYASAGAR UNIVERSITY

PO Vidyasagar Univ., West Midnapore 721102, West Bengal
Telephone: (32) 22275297
Fax: (32) 22275329
E-mail: registrar@vidyasagar.ac.in
Internet: www.vidyasagar.ac.in
Founded 1981
State control

Teaching and Affiliating; 53 affiliated colleges
Languages of instruction: English, Bengali
Academic year: July to June
Chancellor: HE THE GOV. OF WEST BENGAL
Vice-Chancellor: Prof. SWAPAN KUMAR PRA-MANICK
Registrar: Dr HIMANSU GHOSH
Librarian: AMIYA SARKAR (acting)
Library of 75,000 vols, 135 periodicals
Number of teachers: 105
Number of students: 36,500 (incl. affiliated colleges)

Publications: *Journal of Biological Sciences* (1 a year), *Journal of Commerce* (1 a year), *Journal of Library and Information Science* (1 a year), *Journal of Philosophy and the Life World* (1 a year), *Journal of Physical Sciences* (1 a year), *Politics and Society* (1 a year)

DEANS

Faculty of Arts and Commerce: Prof. SANKAR PRASAD SINGHA
Faculty of Science: Prof. SUSANTA KR. CHAK-RABORTY

PROFESSORS

BANERJEE, T. K., Political Science with Rural Administration
BATTACHARYA, T., Zoology
KHAN, L. A., Bengali
MAHAPATRA, P. K., Physics
MAITI, M., Applied Mathematics
MISRA, P. K., Philosophy and Life-World
MUKHOPADHAYA, S., Computer Science and Electronics
PATI, B. R., Microbiology
RANJAN DE, B., Chemistry and Chemical Technology
SAHA, S. C., Electronics

VIKRAM UNIVERSITY

University Rd, Ujjain 456010, Madhya Pradesh
Telephone: (734) 2514270
Fax: (734) 2514276
E-mail: info@vikramuniversity.ac.in
Internet: www.vikramuniversity.ac.in
Founded 1957
Teaching and Affiliating
Languages of instruction: Hindi, English
Academic year: July to June
Chancellor: HE THE GOVERNOR OF MADHYA PRADESH
Vice-Chancellor: Prof. RAM RAJESH MISHRA
Registrar: Dr M. K. RAI
Librarian: Prof. P. K. GOYAL

Two constituent colleges, 30 depts, 6 special centres
101 Affiliated colleges
Library of 191,793 vols, 48,000 vols of periodicals
Number of students: 31,472

DEANS

Faculty of Arts: Dr N. OBEROI
Faculty of Commerce: Dr R. SONI
Faculty of Education: Dr N. SHINDE
Faculty of Information Technology: Dr S. K. GHOSH
Faculty of Life Science: Dr S. K. BILLORE
Faculty of Management: Dr N. RAO
Faculty of Physical Science: Prof. V. W. BHAGWAT
Faculty of Social Science: Dr S. PANDE

VINOBA BHAVE UNIVERSITY

POB 31, Hazaribag 825301, Jharkhand
Telephone: (6546) 264279
Fax: (6546) 264279
E-mail: info@vbu.co.in
Internet: vbu.co.in
Founded 1992
State control
Academic year: July to May
17 Constituent colleges and 40 affiliated colleges
Chancellor: HE THE GOVERNOR OF JHARKHAND
Vice-Chancellor: Prof. Dr A. KUMAR
Pro-Vice-Chancellor: Dr J. L. ORAON
Registrar: Dr S. P. SINHA
Controller of Examinations: Dr M. K. SINGH
Librarian-in-charge: Dr PARMANAND MAHTO

DEANS

Faculty of Ayurveda: Dr H. P. PANDEY
Faculty of Education: Dr K. SINGH
Faculty of Engineering: Dr S. K. SINGH
Faculty of Homeopathy: Dr K. SINGH
Faculty of Humanities: Dr V. JHA
Faculty of Law: Dr D. K. SHARMA
Faculty of Medicine: Dr S. N. BAIROLIYA
Faculty of Science: Dr R. PRASAD
Faculty of Social Sciences: Dr S. N. SINGH

VISVA-BHARATI

PO Santiniketan, Birbhum 731235, West Bengal
Telephone: (3463) 261531
Fax: (3463) 261156
E-mail: registrar@visva-bharati.ac.in
Internet: www.visva-bharati.ac.in
Founded 1951
Central univ.; institutes of agricultural science, dance, drama and music, education, fine arts, humanities and social sciences, rural reconstruction, science, Tagore studies and research; 15 centres
Central Govt control
Languages of instruction: English, Bengali
Academic year: July to April (three terms)
Rector: HE THE GOV. OF WEST BENGAL
Chancellor: Dr MANMOHAN SINGH
Vice-Chancellor: Prof. RAJAT KANTA RAY
Registrar: Dr MANI MUKUT MITRA
Librarian: Prof. P. JASH (acting)
Library of 750,000 vols
Number of teachers: 516
Number of students: 6,357
Publications: *Visva-Bharati Patrika* (4 a year), *Journal of Philosophy*.

WEST BENGAL NATIONAL UNIVERSITY OF JURIDICAL SCIENCES

Dr Ambedkar Bhavan, 12 LB Block, Sector III, Salt Lake, Kolkata 700098, West Bengal
Telephone: (33) 23350534
Fax: (33) 23357422
E-mail: nujs@vsnl.com
Internet: www.nujs.edu
Founded 1999
State control
Schools of criminal justice and admin., economic and business laws, legal practice and devt, private laws and comparative jurisprudence, public law and governance, social sciences, technology, law and devt; centres for consumer protection and welfare, human rights and citizenship studies, studies in WTO laws, studies for women and law
Vice-Chancellor: Prof. MAHENDRA P. SINGH
Librarian: TUTU MUKHERJEE
Library of 100,000 vols, 124 journals.

VISVESWARAIAH TECHNOLOGICAL UNIVERSITY

Santhibastawad Rd, Machhe, Belgaum 590018, Karnataka
Telephone: (831) 2498100
Fax: (831) 2405467
E-mail: info@vtu.ac.in
Internet: www.vtu.ac.in
Founded 1994
Academic year: August to January, February to July (2 semesters)
Courses in chemical, civil, computer science, electrical, electronics, industrial production, mechanical, textile engineering; 175 affiliated colleges and regional centres in Bangalore, Belgaum, Gulbarga and Mysore; teaching and affiliating
Chancellor: HE THE GOV OF KARNATAKA
Pro-Chancellor: THE MIN. FOR HIGHER EDUCATION, KARNATAKA
Vice-Chancellor: Dr H. P. KINCHA
Registrar: Prof. K. V. A. BALAJI.

ATTACHED CENTRES

Bosch Rexroth Centre: GSSS Institute of Eng. and Tech., Metagalli Industrial Area, Kasaba Hobli, K. R. S. Rd, Mysore, Karnataka; fax (821) 2581977; e-mail vtubosch@vtu.ac.in.

E-Learning Centre: SJCE STEP SEED Bldg, SJCE Campus, Mysore, 570006; fax (8212) 413223; internet elearning.vtu.ac.in.

WEST BENGAL UNIVERSITY OF ANIMAL AND FISHERY SCIENCES

68 Kshudiram Bose Sarani, Kolkata 700037, West Bengal
Telephone: (33) 25563450
Fax: (33) 25571986
Internet: www.wbuafscl.ac.in
Founded 1995
State control
Academic year: July to June
Faculties of dairy technology, fishery sciences, and veterinary and animal sciences
Chancellor: HE THE GOV. OF WEST BENGAL
Vice-Chancellor: Prof. C. S. CHAKRABARTI
Registrar: Dr D. N. JANA
Librarian-in-charge: Dr RANAJIT KUMAR GHOSH

Library of 22,000 vols

DEANS

Faculty of Dairy Technology: Prof. AJIT K. MISRA

Faculty of Fishery Sciences: Prof. KUSHAN CH. DORA (acting)
Faculty of Veterinary and Animal Sciences: Prof. DIPAK DE

WEST BENGAL UNIVERSITY OF TECHNOLOGY

BF 142, Sector II, Salt Lake City, Kolkata, 700064, West Bengal
Telephone: (33) 2321-7578
Fax: (33) 2334-1030
E-mail: registrar@wbut.ac.in
Internet: www.wbut.net

Founded 2001
State control
Academic year: July to June
Language of instruction: English
Chancellor: HE THE GOVERNOR OF WEST BENGAL
Vice-Chancellor: Prof. SABYASACHI SENGUPTA
Pro Vice-Chancellor: P. K. MAHAPATRA
Registrar: Dr SYED RAFIKUL ISLAM
Finance Officer: ATRI BHOWMIK
Controller of Examinations: Prof. A. K. GUHA
Library of 30,000 vols, 60 periodicals, 8 e-journals
Number of teachers: 37
Number of students: 235

170 Affiliated colleges; offers 27 degrees in 79 courses.

YASHWANTRAO CHAVAN MAHARASHTRA OPEN UNIVERSITY

Nashik 422222, Maharashtra
Telephone: (253) 2231714
Fax: (253) 2231716
E-mail: registrar@ycmou.com
Internet: www.ycmou.com

Founded 1989
State control
Languages of instruction: English, Hindi, Marathi
Academic year: July to June
8 Regional centres and 2,500 recognized study centres
Chancellor: HE THE GOV. OF MAHARASHTRA
Vice-Chancellor: Dr RAJAN WELUKAR
Registrar: Dr NANASAHEB R. KAPADNIS
Library of 25,000 vols
Number of teachers: 4,300
Number of students: 400,000
Publications: *Dnyangangotri* (4 a year), *Mukta Vidya* (2 a year), *Wamvad* (12 a year)

DIRECTORS
School of Agricultural Science: Prof. SURYA GUNJAL
School of Commerce and Management: Prof. PANDIT PALANDE
School of Computer Science: Prof. RAMCHANDRA TIWARI
School of Continuing Education: Prof. RAJENDRA VADNERE
School of Education: Dr A. N. JOSHI
School of Health Sciences: Dr SHYAM ASHTEKAR
School of Humanities and Social Sciences: Dr RAMESH WARKHEDE
School of Science and Technology: MANOJ KILLEDAR

Institutes of National Importance

Institutes of National Importance are established, or so designated, through Acts of Parliament and are thereby granted degree-awarding powers.

ALL-INDIA INSTITUTE OF MEDICAL SCIENCES

Ansari Nagar, New Delhi 110029
Telephone: (11) 26588500
Fax: (11) 26588663
E-mail: director@aiims.ac.in
Internet: www.aiims.edu

Founded 1956
Depts of anaesthesiology, anatomy, biochemistry, biomedical engineering, biophysics, biostatistics, biotechnology, blood bank, cardiac anaesthesiology, cardiac biochemistry, cardiac pathology, cardiac radiology, cardiology, cardiothoracic and vascular surgery, dental surgery, dermatology and venereology, emergency medicine, endocrinology and metabolism, forensic medicine, gastroenterology and human nutrition, gastrointestinal surgery, haematology, histocompatibility and immunogenetics, hospital administration, laboratory medicine, microbiology, nephrology, neuro-anaesthesiology, neurology, neuropathology, neuro-radiology, neurosurgery, nuclear magnetic resonance, nuclear medicine, obstetrics and gynaecology, orthopaedics, otorhinolaryngology, paediatric surgery, paediatrics, pathology, pharmacology, physical medicine and rehabilitation, physiology, radio diagnosis, reproductive biology, surgical disciplines, urology

Dir: Dr T. D. DOGRA (acting)
Dean of Academics: Dr R. C. DEKA
Dean of Examinations: Dr T. D. DOGRA
Registrar: Dr SANDEEP AGARWALA
Librarian: Dr R. P. KUMAR
Library of 115,000 vols, 570 periodicals
Number of teachers: 475 .
Number of students: 1,000
Publication: *The National Medical Journal of India* (6 a year)

PROFESSORS
Anaesthesiology:
    ARORA, M. K.
    BATRA, R. K.
    CHANDERLEKHA
    DUREJA, G. P.
    JAYALAKSHMI, T. S.
    PAWAR, D. K.
    SAXENA, R.
Anatomy:
    AJMANI, M. L.
    KUCHERIA, K.
    KUMAR, R.
    MEHRA, R. D.
    SABHERWAL, U.
    WADHWA, S.
Biochemistry:
    RAO, D. N.
    SINGH, N.
    SINHA, S.
Biomedical Engineering:
    ANAND, S.
    RAY, A. R.
    SINGH, H.
    TANDON, S. N.
Biophysics:
    MISHRA, R. K.
    RAO, G. S.
    SINGH, T. P.
Biostatistics:
    SUNDARAM, K. R.
Biotechnology:
    PRASAD, H. K.
    SHARMA, Y. D.
    TYAGI, J. S.

Cardiology:
    BAHL, V. K.
    KOTHARI, S. S.
    REDDY, K. S.
    SAXENA, A.
Centre of Community Medicine:
    KAPOOR, S. K.
    PANDAV, C. S.
    REDDAIAH, V. P.
Dental Surgery:
    PARKASH, H.
    SHAH, N.
Dermatology and Venereology:
    KHANNA, N.
    SHARMA, V. K.
    VERMA, K. K.
Endocrinology and Metabolism:
    AMMINI, A. C.
Forensic Medicine:
    DOGRA, T. D.
Gastroenterology and Human Nutrition:
    ACHARYA, S. K.
    JOSHI, Y. K.
    KAPIL, U.
Gastrointestinal Surgery:
    CHATTOPADHYAY, T. K.
Haematology:
    CHOUDHRY, V. P.
    KUMAR, R.
    SAXENA, R.
Hospital Administration:
    CHAUBEY, P. C.
    SHARMA, R. K.
Laboratory Medicine:
    JAILKHANI, B. L.
    MUKHOPADHYAY, A. K.
Medicine:
    GULERIA, R.
    KUMAR, A.
    MISRA, A.
    SHARMA, S. K.
    SOOD, R.
Microbiology:
    BANERJEE, U.
    BROOR, S.
    SAMANTARAY, J. C.
    SETH, P.
Nephrology:
    DASH, S. C.
    TIWARI, S. C.
Nuclear Magnetic Resonance Imaging:
    JAGANNATHAN, N. R.
Nuclear Medicine:
    BANDOPADHYAYA, G. P.
    MALHOTRA, A.
    PANT, G. S.
Obstetrics and Gynaecology:
    KRIPLANI, A.
    KUMAR, S.
    MITTAL, S.
Orthopaedics:
    BHAN, S.
    JAYASWAL, A.
    KOTWAL, P. P.
    RASTOGI, S.
Otorhinolaryngology:
    BAHADUR, S.
    DEKA, R. C.
    SHARMA, S. C.
Paediatric Surgery:
    GUPTA, D. K.
    MITRA, D. K.
Paediatrics:
    ARORA, N. K.
    ARYA, L. S.

BHAN, M. K.
KALRA, V.
PAUL, V. K.
Pathology:
CHOPRA, P.
DAWAR, S.
KAPILA, K.
PANDA, S. K.
SARKAR, C.
SINGH, M. K.
VERMA, K.
VIJAYARAGHAVAN, M.
Pharmacology:
GROVER, J. K.
GUPTA, Y. K.
Physical Medicine and Rehabilitation:
SINGH, U.
Physiology:
BIJLANI, R. L.
KUMAR, V. M.
SENGUPTA, J.
Psychiatry and De-addiction Centre:
KHANDELWAL, S. K.
MEHTA, M.
RAY, R.
TRIPATHI, B. M.
Radio Diagnosis:
GUPTA, A. K.
MUKHOPADHYAY, S.
VASHIST, S.
Reproductive Biology:
KUMAR, A.
SARKAR, N. N.
Surgical Disciplines:
KUMAR, A.
MEHTA, S. N.
MISRA, M. C.
SRIVASTAVA, A.
Transplant Immunology and Immunogenetics:
MEHRA, N. K.
Urology:
GUPTA, N. P.
HERNAL, A. K.

ATTACHED CENTRES

Cardiothoracic Sciences Centre: f. 1982; Prin. Prof. A. SAMPATH.

Centre for Dental Education and Research: f. 2003; Prin. Dr NASEEM SHAH.

College of Nursing: e-mail mvatsa@aiims .ac.in; Prin. M. VATSA.

Dr R. P. Centre for Ophthalmic Sciences: tel. (11) 26589695; fax (11) 26593101; e-mail pschiefrpc@yahoo.com; f. 1967; Prin. Prof. S. GHOSE.

Jai Prakash Narayan Apex Trauma Centre.

National Drug Dependence Treatment Centre: Sector 19, Kamla Nehru Nagar, Ghaziabad, Uttar Pradesh; tel. (120) 2788974; fax (120) 2788979; e-mail nddtc .aiims@qmail.com; f. 1988; Prin. Dr RAJAT RAY.

Neurosciences Centre: f. 2003; Prin. Prof. H. H. DASH.

DAKSHINA BHARAT HINDI PRACHAR SABHA

Thanikachalam Rd, Chennai 600017, Tamil Nadu
Telephone: (44) 24341824
Fax: (44) 24388420
E-mail: info@dbhps-chennai.com
Internet: www.dbhps-chennai.com
Founded 1918, present name and status 1964
Academic year: July to June
Language of instruction: Hindi

20 Affiliated colleges
Chancellor: R. VENKATARAMAN
Vice-Chancellor: B. D. JATTI
Pro-Vice-Chancellor: V. A. SHARMA
Registrar: R. F. NEERLAKATTI
Registrar: Dr P. H. SETHUMADHAVA RAO
Library of 100,000 vols (within Nat. Hindi Research Library).

INDIAN INSTITUTE OF TECHNOLOGY, BOMBAY

Powai, Mumbai 400076, Maharashtra
Telephone: (22) 25722545
Fax: (22) 25723480
E-mail: director@iitb.ac.in
Internet: www.iitb.ac.in
Founded 1958
Language of instruction: English
Academic year: July to April

Residential; depts of aerospace engineering, bioscience and bioengineering, chemical engineering, chemistry, civil engineering, computer science and engineering, earth sciences, electrical engineering, energy science and engineering, humanities and social sciences, industrial design centre, mathematics, mechanical engineering, materials and metallurgical engineering, physics

Dir: Prof. DEVANG V. KHAKHAR
Registrar: B. S. PUNALKAR
Dean of Academic Programme: Prof. S. BISWAS
Dean of Alumni and Corporate Relations: Prof. A. Q. CONTRACTOR
Dean of Faculty: Prof. A. K. SURESH
Dean of Infrastructure Planning and Support: Prof. K. V. KRISHNA RAO
Dean of Int. Relations: Prof. SUBHASIS CHAUDHURI
Dean of Research and Devt: Prof. RANGAN BANERJEE
Dean of Student Affairs: Prof. PRAKASH GOPALAN
Librarian: Dr DAULAT JOTHWANI
Library of 414,475 vols, 1,442 periodicals
Number of teachers: 495
Number of students: 5,865.

ATTACHED RESEARCH CENTRES

Advanced Centre for Research in Electronics: tel. (22) 25767690; fax (22) 25723806; e-mail head.acre@iit.ac.in; Head Prof. RAMAN S. SRINIVASA.

Centre for Aerospace Systems Design and Engineering: tel. (22) 25767840; fax (22) 25729511; e-mail head.casde@iit.ac.in; Head Prof. P. M. MUJUMDAR.

Centre for Environmental Science and Engineering: tel. (22) 25767853; fax (22) 25764650; e-mail head.cese@iit.ac.in; Head Prof. S. R. ASOLEKAR.

Centre for Formal Design and Verification of Software: tel. (22) 25768700; fax (22) 25794290; e-mail head.cfdvs@iit.ac.in; Head Prof. G. SIVAKUMAR.

Centre for Studies in Resources Engineering: tel. (22) 25767263; fax (22) 25723190; e-mail head.csre@iit.ac.in; Head Prof. H. S. PANDALAI.

Centre for Technology Alternatives in Rural Areas: tel. (22) 25767500; fax (22) 25767874; e-mail head.ctara@iit.ac.in; Head Prof. A. W. DATE.

Computer Aided Design Centre: tel. (22) 25767796; fax (22) 25723480; e-mail head .cad@iit.ac.in; Head Prof. R. K. MALIK.

Industrial Design Centre: tel. (22) 25767819; fax (22) 25767803; e-mail head .idc@iit.ac.in; Head Prof. R. POOVAIAH.

Sophisticated Analytical Instrumentation Facility: tel. (22) 25767691; fax (22)

25723314; e-mail head.saif@iit.ac.in; Head Prof. A. R. KULKARNI.

ATTACHED SCHOOLS

Kanwal Rekhi School of Information Technology: tel. (22) 25767900; fax (22) 25720022; e-mail head.kresit@iit.ac.in; Head Prof. A. RANADE.

School of Biosciences and Bioengineering: tel. (22) 25767207; fax (22) 25726895; e-mail head.bio@iit.ac.in; Head Prof. K. K. RAO.

Shailesh J. Mehta School of Management: tel. (22) 25767781; fax (22) 25722872; e-mail head.som@iit.ac.in; Head Prof. K. JAIN.

INDIAN INSTITUTE OF TECHNOLOGY, DELHI

Hauz Khas, New Delhi 110016
Telephone: (11) 26582222
Fax: (11) 26582277
E-mail: webmaster@admin.iitd.ac.in
Internet: www.iitd.ac.in
Founded 1961, present status 1963
Academic year: July to May
Dir: Prof. SURENDRA PRASAD
Registrar: Dr A. L. VYAS (acting)
Dean of Alumni Affairs and Int. Programmes: Prof. ASHOK GUPTA
Dean of Industrial Research and Devt: Prof. S. N. SINGH
Dean of Postgraduate Studies and Research: Prof. K. GUPTA
Dean of Students: Prof. SHASHI MATHUR
Dean of Undergraduate Studies: Prof. SANTANU CHAUDHURY
Librarian: Dr JAGDISH ARORA
Library of 307,832 vols
Number of teachers: 421
Number of students: 4,931.

ATTACHED SCHOOLS

Amar Nath and Shashi Khosla School of Information Technology: tel. (11) 26591290; fax (11) 26868765; internet www .it.iitd.ac.in; Head Prof. H. SARAN.

Bharti School of Telecommunication Technology and Management: tel. (11) 6596200; internet www.iitd.ac.in/bsttm; f. 2000; Head Prof. S. PRASAD.

INDIAN INSTITUTE OF TECHNOLOGY, GUWAHATI

North Guwahati, Guwahati 781039, Assam
Telephone: (361) 2690401
Fax: (363) 2692321
E-mail: pro@iitg.ernet.in
Internet: www.iitg.ernet.in
Founded 1994

Depts of biotechnology, chemical engineering, chemistry, civil engineering, computer science and engineering, design, electronics and communication, humanities and social sciences, mathematics, mechanical engineering, physics

Dir: Prof. GAUTAM BARUA
Registrar: Dr BRAJENDRA NATH RAYCHOUDHURY
Dean of Academic Affairs: Prof. SUKUMAR NANDI
Dean of Admin.: (vacant)
Dean of Faculty Affairs: Prof. P. K. BORA
Dean of Research and Devt: Prof. P. S. ROBI
Dean of Student Affairs: Dr ARUP KUMAR SARMA

ATTACHED CENTRES

Centre for Educational Technology: tel. (361) 2582667; fax (363) 2690762; e-mail cet@ iitg.ernet.in; Dir Dr RAJIV TIWARI.

Centre for Energy: tel. (361) 2583150; fax (363) 2690762; e-mail dhirenh@iitg.ernet.in; f. 2004; Dir Dr PINAKESWAR MAHANTA.

Centre for the Environment: tel. (361) 2583050; fax (361) 2690762; e-mail evc_off@ iitg.ernet.in; Dir Dr CHANDAN MAHANTA.

Centre for Mass Media Communication: tel. (361) 2582456; Dir Prof. K. RAMACHAN-DRAN.

Centre for Nanotechnology: tel. (361) 2583075; fax (361) 2690762; e-mail nano_off@iitg.ernet.in; Dir Dr ARUN CHATTO-PADHYAY.

INDIAN INSTITUTE OF TECHNOLOGY, KANPUR

IIT PO, Kanpur 208016, Uttar Pradesh
Telephone: (512) 2597258
E-mail: doiitk@iitk.ac.in
Internet: www.iitk.ac.in
Founded 1960
State control
Language of instruction: English

Depts of engineering, humanities, science
Dir: Prof. S. G. DHANDE
Dean of Academic Affairs: Prof. R. K. THAR-EJA
Dean of Faculty Affairs: Prof. B. DEO
Dean of Research and Devt: Prof. K. MUR-ALIDHAR
Dean of Resource Planning and Generation: Prof. S. V. AGGARWAL
Dean of Student Affairs: Prof. P. SINHA
Registrar: S. S. KASHALKAR
Librarian: R. MISHRA

Library of 390,000 vols and 900 periodicals
Number of teachers: 319
Number of students: 2,061.

ATTACHED RESEARCH CENTRES

Advanced Centre for Materials Science: internet www.iitk.ac.in/acms; f. 1978; Head S. SANGAL.

Centre for Laser Technology: tel. (512) 3927766; e-mail utpal@iitk.ac.in; internet www.iitk.ac.in/celt; Head Prof. U. DAS.

Centre for Mechatronics: tel. (512) 2597995; internet www.iitk.ac.in/robotics; Head S. SEN.

Computer Aided Desgin: tel. (512) 597838; e-mail achat@iitk.ac.in; internet www.iitk.ac .in/cad; Head Prof. S. G. DHANDE.

National Information Centre of Earth-quake Engineering: tel. (512) 2597866; fax (512) 2597794; e-mail nicee@iitk.ac.in; internet www.nicee.org; Head Prof. S. K. JAIN.

National Wind Tunnel Facility: tel. (512) 2597843; e-mail kamal@iitk.ac.in; internet www.iitk.ac.in/nwtf; f. 1999; Head Dr K. PODDAR.

Samtel Centre for Display Technologies: tel. (512) 2597582; fax (512) 2597395; e-mail samtel_head@iitk.ac.in; internet www.iitk.ac .in/scdt; f. 2000; Head Prof. S. KUMAR.

SIDBI Innovation and Incubation Centre: tel. (512) 2596646; fax (512) 2597057; e-mail bvphani@iitk.ac.in; internet www.iitk.ac.in/siic; Head Dr B. V. PHANI.

INDIAN INSTITUTE OF TECHNOLOGY, KHARAGPUR

Kharagpur 721302, West Bengal
Telephone: (3222) 255221
Fax: (3222) 255303
E-mail: director@iitkgp.ernet.in
Internet: www.iitkgp.ac.in
Founded 1950
Academic year: July to April

Depts of aerospace engineering, agricultural and food engineering, architecture and regional planning, biotechnology, chemical engineering, chemistry, civil engineering, computer science and engineering, cryogenic engineering, electrical engineering, electronics and electrical communication engineering, geology and geophysics, humanities and social sciences, industrial engineering and management, information technology, materials science, mathematics, mechanical engineering, metallurgical and materials engineering, medical science and technology, mining engineering, ocean engineering and naval architecture, physics and meteorology
Dir: Prof. DAMODAR ACHARYA
Deputy Dir: M. CHAKRABORTY
Registrar: Dr D. GUNASEKARAN
Academic Dean: S. K. SOM
Dean of Continuing Education: A. CHAKRA-BORTY
Dean of Faculty and Planning: R. N. DATTA
Dean of Postgraduates and Research: P. K. J. MOHAPATRA
Dean of Student Affairs: D. K. TRIPATHY
Chair, Central Library: Prof. P. K. J. MAHA-PATRA

Library of 362,852 vols, 1,130 periodicals
Number of teachers: 431
Number of students: 3,604

INDIAN INSTITUTE OF TECHNOLOGY, MADRAS

IIT PO, Chennai 600036, Tamil Nadu
Telephone: (44) 22578100
Fax: (44) 22570509
E-mail: registrar@iitm.ac.in
Internet: www.iitm.ac.in
Founded 1959
State control

Residential; depts of aerospace engineering, applied mechanics, biotechnology, chemical engineering, chemistry, civil engineering, computer science and engineering, electrical engineering, engineering design, humanities and social sciences, management studies, mathematics, mechanical engineering, metallurgical and materials engineering, ocean engineering, physics
Language of instruction: English
Academic year: July to April
Dir: Prof. M. S. ANANTH
Dean for Academic Courses: Prof. K. RAMA-MURTHY
Dean for Academic Research: Prof. K. KRISH-NAIAH
Dean for Admin.: Prof. M. SINGAPERUMAL
Dean for Industrial Consultancy and Sponsored Research: Prof. JOB KURIEN
Dean for Planning: Prof. R. BHASKAR
Dean for Students: Prof. M. GOVARDHAN
Registrar: Dr M. THIRUMAVUKKARASU
Librarian: Dr H. CHANDRA

Library: see Libraries and Archives
Number of teachers: 477
Number of students: 5,232

Publications: *Journal of Mathematical and Physical Science* (6 a year), *Research Consultancy, Expertise and Facilities* (1 a year).

INDIAN INSTITUTE OF TECHNOLOGY, ROORKEE

Roorkee 247667, Uttaranchal
Telephone: (1332) 285311
Fax: (1332) 273560
E-mail: regis@iitr.ernet.in
Internet: www.iitr.ac.in
Founded 1847; fmrly Univ. of Roorkee

Depts of alternative hydro energy, architecture, biotechnology, chemical engineering, chemistry, civil engineering, earth sciences, earthquake engineering, electrical engineering, electronic and computer engineering, humanities, hydrology, management studies, mathematics, mechanical and industrial engineering, metallurgical engineering, paper technology engineering, physics, water resources
Dir: Prof. S. C. SAXENA
Dean of Admin.: Prof. S. C. JAIN
Dean of Alumni Affairs: Prof. H. SINVHAL
Dean of Faculty Affairs: Prof. D. K. PAUL
Dean of Finance and Planning: Prof. S. KUMAR
Dean of Postgraduate Studies and Research: Prof. H. O. GUPTA
Dean of Saharanpur Campus: Prof. R. P. AGARWAL
Dean of Sponsored Research and Industrial Consultancy: Prof. S. RAY
Dean of Student Welfare: Prof. V. K. GUPTA
Dean of Undergraduate Studies: Prof. G. S. SRIVASTAVA
Registrar: A. K. SRIVASTAVA
Librarian: Y. SINGH

Library of 320,000 vols.

INDIAN STATISTICAL INSTITUTE

203 Barrackpore Trunk Rd, Kolkata 700108, West Bengal
Telephone: (33) 25752001
Fax: (33) 25776680
E-mail: dean@isical.ac.in
Internet: www.isical.ac.in
Founded 1931
State control
Academic year: July to June

ISI regional centres located in Bangalore, Chennai, Coimbatore, Delhi, Giridih, Hyderabad, Mumbai, Pune, Vadodara
Dir: Prof. S. K. PAL
Dean of Studies: Prof. G. M. SAHA
Chief Librarian: Prof. D. DASGUPTA (acting)

Library of 215,000 vols

Publication: *Sankhya: The Indian Journal of Statistics*

HEADS OF DIVISIONS

Applied Statistics: Prof. A. N. BASU
Biological Sciences: Dr B. MUKHOPADHYAY
Computer Science and Communication Science: Prof. B. CHANDA
Physical and Earth Science: Prof. S. BHATTA-CHARYA
Social Sciences: Prof. T. KABIRAJ
Theoretical Statistics and Mathematics: Prof. G. MISRA

PROFESSORS

BAGCHI, B.
BAGCHI, D. K.
BAGCHI, S.
BAGCHI, S. C.
BANDYOPADHAY, S.
BHAT, B. V. R.
BHATIA, R.
BHATT, A. G.
BHATTACHARYA, B.
BHATTACHARYA, B. B.
BHATTACHARYA, S.
BHIMASANKARAM, P.
BOSE, A.
BOSE, M.
CHAKRAVARTY, S. R.
CHANDA, B.
CHANDA, S.
CHANDRA, T. K.
CHATTOPADHYAY, M.
CHAUDHURI, P.
CHOWDHURI, B. B.
COONDOO, D.
DANDAPAT, B. S.
DAS, A.

DAS, J.
DAS, N.
DAS, S.
DAS, S. P.
DASGUPTA, A. K.
DASGUPTA, D.
DASGUPTA, R.
DELAMPADY, M.
DEWANJI, A.
DEY, A.
DUTTA GUPTA, J.
GHOSE, M.
GOSWAMI, A.
GUPTA, M. R.
GUPTA, R.
JEGANATHAN, P.
KARANDIKAR, R. L.
KUNDU, M. K.
MAITI, P.
MAJUMDER, A.
MAJUMDER, H. P.
MAJUMDER, P. K.
MAJUMDER, P. P.
MAZUMDER, B. S.
MITRA, S.
MONDAL, B. N.
MUKHERJEA, K. K.
MURTHY, C. A.
MUTHURAMALINGAM, P. L.
NARAYANA, N. S. S.
PAL, N. R.
PARUI, S. K.
PAUL, M.
RAHA, A. B.
RAJEEV, B.
RAMACHANDRAN, V. K.
RAMAMURTHY, K.
RAMASUBRAMANIAM, S.
RAMASWAMY, B.
RAO, A. R.
RAO, I. K.
RAO, S. B.
RAO, T. J.
RAO, T. S. S. R. K.
RAY, K. S.
REDDY, B. M.
ROY, B. K.
ROY, P.
ROY, R.
ROY, S.
ROY CHOWDHURY, P.
SAHA, D.
SAHA, G. M.
SAMANTA, T.
SARBADHIKARI, H.
SARKAR, A.
SARKAR, N.
SASTRY, N. S. N.
SEN, A.
SENGUPTA, A.
SENGUPTA, D.
SIKDAR, K.
SINHA, B. P.
SINHA, K. B.
SITARAM, A.
SRIVASTAVA, S. M.
SWAMINATHAN, M.
THANGAVALU, S.
TRIPATHI, T. P.
VIJAYAN, K. S.

ATTACHED CENTRE

International Statistical Education Centre (ISEC): tel. (33) 25752521; fax (33) 25781834; e-mail isec@isical.ac.in; internet www.isical.ac.in/~isec; f. 1950; Principal Prof. M. PAL.

NATIONAL INSTITUTE OF PHARMACEUTICAL EDUCATION AND RESEARCH

Sector 67, SAS Nagar, Mohali 160062, Punjab

Telephone: (172) 2214682

Fax: (172) 2214692
E-mail: director@niper.nic.in
Internet: www.niper.nic.in

Founded 1991
Academic year: July to June

Depts of biotechnology, medicinal chemistry, natural products, pharmaceutical analysis, pharmaceutical management, pharmaceutical technology, pharmaceutics, pharmacology and toxicology, pharmacy practice

Dir: Prof. P. R. RAO
Dean: Prof. SARANJIT SINGH
Registrar: BHUPINDER SINGH (acting)
Library of 3,139 vols, 103 periodicals

Publication: *Current Research & Information on Pharmaceutical Sciences (CRIPS)* (4 a year)

PROFESSORS

BANERJEE, U. C., Pharmaceutical Technology
BANSAL, A. K., Pharmaceutics
BHUTANI, K. K., Natural Products
CHAKRABORTI, A. K., Medicinal Chemistry
DEY, C. S., Biotechnology
RAO, P. R., Pharmacology and Toxicology
SINGH, S., Pharmaceutical Analysis
TIWARI, P., Pharmacy Practice

POSTGRADUATE INSTITUTE OF MEDICAL EDUCATION AND RESEARCH

Sector 12, Chandigarh 160012

Telephone: (172) 2747585
Fax: (172) 2744401
E-mail: pgimer@chd.nic.in
Internet: www.pgimer.nic.in

Founded 1962
Academic year: January to December orJuly to June

Dir: Prof. K. K. TALWAR
Dean: Prof. VINAY SAKHUJA
Deputy Dir for Admin.: ANIL KUMAR GUPTA
Registrar: NARESH VIRDI
Library of 85,000 vols, 577 periodicals

PROFESSORS

BHANSALI, A., Endocrinology
CHAWLA, H. S., Oral Health Sciences
CHAWLA, Y. K., Hepatology
DHALIWAL, L. K., Obstetrics and Gynaecology
GILL, S. S., Orthopaedics
GUPTA, A., Ophthalmology
GUPTA, A. K., Hospital Administration
GUPTA, M., Anatomy
JINDAL, S. K., Pulmonary Medicine
JINDAL, S. K., Telemedicine
JOSHI, K., Histopathology
KANWAR, A. J., Dermatology, Venereology and Leprosy
KHANDELWAL, N., Radio Diagnosis and Imaging
KHANDUJA, K. L., Biophysics
KHOSLA, V. K., Neurosurgery
KOHLI, K. K., Biochemistry
KULHARA, P., Psychiatry
KUMAR, R., School of Public Health
MALLA, N., Parasitology
MANDAL, A. K., Urology
MARWAHA, N., Blood Transfusion
MINZ, M., Renal Transplant Surgery
NARANG, A., Paediatrics
PANDA, N. K., Otolaryngology
PANDHI, P., Pharmacology
PRABHAKAR, S., Experimental Medicine and Biotechnology
PRABHAKAR, S., Neurology
RAJWANSHI, A., Cytology and Gynaecological Pathology
RAO, K. L. N., Paediatric Surgery
RATHO, R. K., Virology
SAKHUJA, V., Nephrology
SHARMA, M., Medical Microbiology

SHARMA, R. K., Plastic Surgery
SHARMA, S. C., Radiotherapy
SINGH, D., Forensic Medicine
SINGH, K., Gastroenterology
TALWAR, K. K., Cardiology
VASISHTA, R. K., Immunopathology
VERMA, S., Internal Medicine
WADHWA, S., Physical and Rehabilitation Medicine
WIG, J., Anaesthesia
WIG, J. D., General Surgery

SANJAY GANDHI POSTGRADUATE INSTITUTE OF MEDICAL SCIENCES

Raebareli Rd, Lucknow 226014

Telephone: (33) 25752004
Fax: (522) 2668017
Internet: www.sgpgi.ac.in

Founded 1983
Autonomous, state funded

Depts of anaesthesiology, biostatistics, cardiology, cardiovascular and thoracic surgery, critical care medicine, endocrine surgery, endocrinology, gastroenterology, haematology, immunology, medical genetics, microbiology, nephrology, neurology, neurosurgery, nuclear medicine, pathology, radiodiagnosis, radiotherapy, surgical gastroenterology, transfusion medicine, urology

Dir: Prof. A. K. MAHAPATRA.

SREE CHITRA TIRUNAL INSTITUTE FOR MEDICAL SCIENCES AND TECHNOLOGY

Thiruvananthapuram 695011, Kerala

Telephone: (471) 2524400
Fax: (471) 2550728
E-mail: director@sctimst.ac.in
Internet: www.sctimst.ac.in

Founded 1973, present status 1980
Academic year: January to December

Depts and divs of anesthesiology, biochemistry, blood transfusion services, cardiology, cardiovascular and thoracic surgery, cellular and molecular cardiology, health science studies, microbiology, neurology, neurosurgery, pathology, radiology

Pres.: Dr R. CHIDAMBARAM
Dir: Dr K. RADHAKRISHNAN
Dean of Academic Affairs: Dr JAGAN MOHAN THARAKAN
Registrar: Dr A. V. GEORGE.

SRI VENKATESWARA INSTITUTE OF MEDICAL SCIENCES

Alipiri Rd, Tirupati 517507, Andhra Pradesh

Telephone: (877) 2287152
Fax: (877) 2286803
E-mail: svimshosp@yahoo.com
Internet: svimstpt.ap.nic.in

Founded 1993

Affiliating; depts of anaesthesiology, biochemistry, cardiology, cardiothoracic surgery, casuality, dietetics, endocrinolgy, gastroenterology, general medicine, genito urinary surgery, nephrology, nuclear medicine, neurology, neurosurgery, oncology, microbiology, pathology, physiotherapy radiology, transfusion medicine

Dir: G. SUBRAMANYAM.

Deemed Universities

Deemed Universities (also known as Deemed-to-be Universities) are institutions that have been conferred the status of a university by virtue of their long tradition of teaching, or specialization and excellence in a particular field of study.

Allahabad Agricultural Institute: Allahabad 211007, Uttar Pradesh; tel. (532) 2684281; fax (532) 2684394; e-mail registrar@aaidu.org; internet www.aaidu.org; f. 1910, deemed univ. status 2000; Faculties of agriculture, arts and culture, business studies, engineering and technology, health and medical sciences, humanities, science, social sciences, theology, veterinary science and animal husbandry; library: 40,000 vols; Chancellor Dr MANI JACOB; Pro-Chancellor Dr J. A. OLIVER; Vice-Chancellor Prof. RAJENDRA B. LAL; Pro-Vice-Chancellor Prof. HENRY SHEPHERD; Registrar Prof. A. K. A. LAWRENCE; Dir of Extension Prof. NAHAR SINGH; Dir of Finance STEPHEN DAS; Dir of Research Prof. S. B. LAL; Librarian S. P. MALLICK.

Amrita Vishwa Vidyapeetham: Ettimadai PO, Coimbatore 641105, Tamil Nadu; tel. (422) 2656422; fax (422) 2656274; e-mail univhq@amrita.edu; internet www.amrita.edu; f. deemed univ. status 2003; campuses at Amritapuri, Bangalore, Kochi, Mysore; schools of arts and sciences, ayurveda, biotechnology, business, dentistry, education, engineering, journalism, medicine, nursing, pharmacy; Centre for Nanosciences; Vice-Chancellor Dr P. VENKAT RANGAN; Dean of Admin. Dr S. KRISHNAMOORTHY; Dean of Corporate Relations Prof. C. PARAMESHWARAN.

Atal Bihari Vajpayee Indian Institute of Information Technology and Management: Morena Link Rd, Gwalior 474010, Madhya Pradesh; tel. (751) 2449702; fax (751) 2460313; e-mail director@iiitm.ac.in; internet www.iiitm.ac.in; f. 2001; Depts of computer science, electronics, finance, human resources, information technology, marketing and networking; Dir Prof. S. G. DESHMUKH.

Avinashilingam University for Women: Mettupalayam Rd, Coimbatore 641043, Tamil Nadu; tel. (422) 2440241; fax (422) 2438786; e-mail registrar@avinuty.ac.in; internet www.avinashilingam.edu; f. 1957, deemed univ. status 1988; Faculties of engineering, community education and entrepreneurship devt, home science, humanities, management studies, science; library: 130,000 vols; 4,436 students; Vice-Chancellor Dr SAROJA PRABHAKARAN; Registrar Dr GOWRI RAMAKRISHNAN

DEANS

Faculty of Business Administration: Dr SHANTHA B. KURUP
Faculty of Community College and Entrepreneurship Development: Dr VIJAYALAKSHMI PURUSHOTHAMAN
Faculty of Education: Dr R. CHANDRA
Faculty of Engineering: Dr S. MARAGATHAM NATRAJ
Faculty of Home Science: Dr SATHYAVATHIMUTHU
Faculty of Humanities: Dr D. LALITHA
Faculty of Science: Dr R. PARVATHAM.

Attached Centres:

Centre for Women's Studies: Avinashilingam University for Women, Coimbatore; tel. (422) 2435266; fax (422) 2433408; e-mail cws_auw@yahoo.com; internet www.cws-adu.org; f. 2000; Dir K. C. LEELAVATHY.

Gandhian Studies Centre: Avinashilingam University for Women, Coimbatore; f. 2005.

Banasthali Vidyapith (Banasthali University): *Banasthali Campus:* Banasthali

304022, Rajasthan; tel. (1438) 228348; fax (1438) 228365

Jaipur Campus: C-62, Sarojini Marg, C Scheme, Jaipur 302001, Rajasthan; tel. (141) 5118721; e-mail info@banasthali.ac.in; internet www.banasthali.ac.in; f. 1935, deemed univ. status 1983; Faculties of education, fine arts, home science, humanities, management, science, social sciences; library of 180,757 vols, 530 periodicals; 210 teachers; 4,182 students; Vice-Chancellor Prof. ADITYA SHASTRI; Pres. Prof. DIWAKAR SHASTRI; Sec. and Treas. Prof. CHITRA PUROHIT; Librarian Dr S. D. VYAS.

Bharath University: 173 Agharam Rd, Selaiyur, Chennai 600073, Tamil Nadu; tel. (44) 22290742; fax (44) 22293886; e-mail contact@bharathuniv.com; internet www.bharathuniv.com; f. 1984; deemed University status 2003; constituent instns: Bharath Institute of Science and Technology, Sree Balaji Dental College and Hospital, Sree Balaji Medical College and Hospital, Sree Lakshmi Narayana Institute of Medical Sciences; library of 75,000 vols, 80 periodicals; Chancellor Dr S. JAGATHRAKSHAKAN; Vice-Chancellor Dr K. P. THOOYAMANI; Registrar (vacant).

Bharati Vidyapeeth University: Lal Bahadur Shastri Marg, Pune 411030, Maharashtra; tel. (20) 24331317; fax (20) 24339121; e-mail bharati@vsnl.com; internet www.bharatividyapeeth.edu; f. 1964, deemed University status 1996; composed of 17 constituent instns: Medical College, Dental College and Hospital, College of Ayurved, Homoeopathic Medical College, College of Nursing, Yashwantrao Mohite College of Arts, Science and Commerce, New Law College, Yashwantrao Chavan Institute of Social Science Studies and Research, Social Science Centre, Research and Development Centre in Pharmaceutical Sciences and Applied Chemistry, Institute of Environment Education and Research, Pune College of Pharmacy, Institute of Management and Entrepreneurship Development, College of Engineering, College of Physical Education, Rajiv Gandhi Institute of Biotechnology and Information Technology, Interactive Research School for Health Affairs; library: total colln of 99,125 vols; 8,386 students; Vice-Chancellor Prof. SHIVAJIRAO KADAM; Registrar B. R. ARBAD.

Bhatkhande Music Institute University: 1 Kaiserbagh, Lucknow 226001, Uttar Pradesh; tel. (522) 2210318; fax (522) 2222926; e-mail info@bhatkhandemusic.edu.in; internet www.bhatkhandemusic.edu.in; f. deemed univ. status 2000; Faculties of dance, instrumental music, musicology, training and vocal music; Vice-Chancellor Prof. PURNIMA PANDE; Registrar Dr A. SRIVASTAVA.

Birla Institute of Technology, Ranchi:- Mesra 835215, Ranchi, Jharkhand; tel. (651) 2276249; fax (651) 2275401; e-mail birlatech@bitsmart.com; internet www.bitmesra.ac.in; f. 1955, deemed University status 1986; extension centres in Allahabad, Chennai, Jaipur, Kolkata, Lalpur, Noida and Patna; int. centres in Bahrain, Muscat and Ras Al Khaimah (UAE); depts of applied sciences, architecture, biotechnology, engineering and technology, hotel management and catering technology, management, pharmaceutical sciences; library of 112,470 vols, 100 periodicals; 149 teachers; 1,650 students; Vice-Chancellor Dr P. K. BARHAI; Registrar Dr R. K. VERMA (acting); Treas. S. S. JAJODIA (acting); Librarian Dr V. SREENIVASULU; publ. *Journal of Hospitality Application & Research* (1 a year), *Journal of Manufacturing Technology and Research* (4 a year), *PHARMBIT* (2 a year)

DEANS

Academic Coordination: Dr D. SASMAL
Academic Infrastructure: Dr USHA JHA
Admissions: Dr D. JAIRATH
Development Programme: Dr M. MUKHERJEE
Doctoral Research: Dr ASHOK MISRA
Examination: Prof. C. M. PRASAD
Extension Centres: Dr A. K. CHATTERJEE
Faculty Development: Dr GOPAL PATHAK
Finance: Dr P. C. JOSHI
Postgraduate Studies: Dr MOHAN VARMA
Research: Dr P. K. BARHAI
Undergraduate Studies: Prof. C. M. PRASAD

Birla Institute of Technology and Science: Vidhya Vihar Campus, Pilani 333031, Rajasthan; tel. (1596) 242192; fax (1596) 244183; e-mail mmsanand@bits-pilani.ac.in; internet discovery.bits-pilani.ac.in/index.html; f. 1964; Private; Accredited by Nat. Assessment and Accreditation Ccl; campuses in Goa, Hyderabad and Dubai (UAE); academic year July to May (2 terms); library of 223,810 vols, 535 periodicals; 535 teachers; 17,898 students; Chancellor Dr K. K. BIRLA; Vice-Chancellor Prof. L. K. MAHESHWARI; Deputy Dir of Academic Affairs Prof. G. RAGHURAMA; Deputy Dir of Admin. Prof. K. E. RAMAN; Dir of Dubai Campus Prof. M. RAMACHANDRAN; Dir of Goa Campus Prof. K. E. RAMAN; Dir of Hyderabad Campus Prof. V. S. RAO; Registrar Prof. M. M. S. ANAND; Librarian Dr M. I. BHAT; publ. *Journal of Cooperation among University, Research and Industrial Enterprises* (4 a year).

Central Institute of Fisheries Education: Seven Bungalows, University Rd, Anderi, Mumbai 400061, Maharashtra; tel. (22) 26361446; fax (22) 26361573; e-mail contact@cife.edu.in; internet www.cife.edu.in; f. 1961; deemed University status 1989; centres in Kolkata, Kakinada, Rohtak, Powerkheda; library of 27,326 vols; Dir Dr D. KUMAR; Registrar C. LAL.

Central Institute of Higher Tibetan Studies: Sarnath, Varanasi 221007, Uttar Pradesh; tel. (542) 2585148; fax (542) 2585150; e-mail ngawang_samten@yahoo.com; internet www.smith.edu/cihts; f. 1977, deemed univ. status 1988; faculties of Language and Literature, Philosophy, Social Science, Tibetan Fine Arts, Tibetan Medicine and Astrology; library of 56,000 vols on Buddhist, Tibetan, Indian and Himalayan Studies in Tibetan, Hindi, Sanskrit and other languages; publ. *Dhih – A Rare Buddhist Texts Research Journal*, 8 series of research vols; Dir NGAWANG SAMTEN; Registrar R. D. AGARWAL.

Datta Meghe Institute of Medical Sciences: Nyss Management Campus, Atrey Layaut, Pratap Nagar, Nagpur 440022; tel. (712) 3956552; fax (712) 2245318; e-mail info@dmims.org; internet www.dmims.org; Vice-Chancellor Dr VEDPRAKASH MISHRA; Dirs SAGAR MEGHE, SAMEER MEGHE; Registrar Dr VIDYA SAGAR

DEANS

Faculty of Ayurveda: (vacant)
Faculty of Dentistry: Dr A. J. PAKHAN
Faculty of Medicine: Dr S. S. PATEL

Dayalbagh Educational Institute: Dayalbagh, Agra 282005, Uttar Pradesh; tel. (562) 2801545; fax (562) 2801226; e-mail admin@dei.ac.in; internet www.dei.ac.in; f. 1981; faculties of arts, commerce, education, engineering, science and social sciences and technical college; library of 101,213 vols; 180 teachers; 2,493 students; Dir Prof. V. G. DAS; Registrar Prof. S. S. SRIVASTAVA; Treas. S. BIJLANI; publ. *Journal of Science and Engineering Research* (1 a year).

Deccan College Postgraduate and Research Institute: Yeravada, Pune 411006, Maharashtra; tel. (20) 26693794; fax (20) 26692104; e-mail deccan.college@gems.vsnl.net.in; internet www.deccancollegepune.org; f. 1821, deemed univ. status 1990; depts of archaeology, linguistics; library of 128,764 books, 31,647 vols of bound periodicals; 127 students; Dir Dr K. PADDAYYA; Librarian T. MORE.

Dr B. R. Ambedkar National Institute of Technology: Jalandhar 144004, Punjab; tel. (181) 2690301; fax (181) 2690320; e-mail admin@nitj.ac.in; internet www.nitj.ac.in; f. 1987, deemed univ. status 2002; depts of applied chemistry, applied mathematics, applied physics, chemical and biological engineering, civil engineering, computer science, electronics and communication engineering, humanities, industrial engineering, instrumentation and control engineering, leather technology engineering, management, mechanical engineering, textile technology eng.; Dir Prof. MOIN UDDIN; Registrar Dr A. L. SANGAL

DEANS

Academic Programmes: Prof. A AGNIHOTRI
Infrastructure Planning and Devt: Prof. S. P. SINGH
Research and Industrial Liaison: Prof. R. K. GARG
Students and Alumni: Prof. ARVINDER SINGH

Dr M. G. R. Educational and Research Institute:E. V. R. Periyar Salai (NH4 Highway), Maduravoyal, Chennai 600095, Tamil Nadu; tel. (44) 23782176; fax (44) 23783165; e-mail registrar@drmgrdu.ac.in; internet www.drmgrdu.ac.in; f. 1988, deemed univ. status 2003; faculties of engineering and technology, humanities and sciences, medicine and dental sciences; library of 50,000 vols, 302 periodicals; Vice-Chancellor Dr G. GOPALAKRISHNAN; Pro-Chancellor Prof. A .C. S. ARUN KUMAR; Dean of Admin. Prof. R. KALAVATHY; Exec. Dir Prof. G. C. KOTHANDAN; Managing Dir A. C. S. KUMAR; Registrar Prof. S. DINAKARAM.

Forest Research Institute University:-Kaulagarh Rd, Dehradun 248195, Uttaranchal; tel. (135) 2751826; fax (135) 2756865; e-mail dir_fri@icfre.org; internet friuniversity.icfre.gov.in; f. 1906, deemed univ. status 1991; MSc degree courses in environment management, forestry, wood science and technology; also offers postgraduate diploma courses and doctorate degree courses; library of 159,286 vols; 82 students; Dean Dr R. K. AIMA; Dir Dr S. S. NEGI; Registrar T. C. NAUTIYAL.

Gandhigram Rural Institute: Dindigul District, Gandhigram 624302, Tamil Nadu; tel. (451) 2452371; fax (451) 2453071; e-mail gricc@vsnl.com; internet www.ruraluniv.ac.in; f. 1956, deemed univ. status 1976; faculties of agriculture and animal husbandry, English and foreign languages, Indian languages, rural development, rural health and sanitation, rural oriented sciences, rural social sciences, Tamil and rural arts; library of 93,422 vols, 320 periodicals; 118 teachers; 2,024 students; Vice-Chancellor Dr M. R. KUBENDRAM; Registrar Dr M. S. VADIVELU; Librarian Dr J. ABRAHAM; library of 103,300 vols, 285 periodicals; publ. *Journal of Extension and Research* (2 a year)

DEANS

Faculty of Agriculture and Animal Husbandry: Dr R. UDHAYAKUMAR
Faculty of English and Foreign Languages: Dr M. R. KUBENDRAN

Faculty of Rural Development: Dr N. NARAYANASAMY
Faculty of Rural Health and Sanitation: Dr V. K. MUTHU
Faculty of Rural Oriented Sciences: Dr N. S. NAGARAJAN
Faculty of Rural Social Sciences: Dr M. WILLIAM BASKARAN
Faculty of Tamil, Indian Languages and Rural Arts: Dr A. PITCHAI

Gokhale Institute of Politics and Economics:BMCC Rd, Deccan Gymkhana, Pune 411004, Maharashtra; tel. (20) 25650287; fax (20) 25652579; e-mail gipelib@gipe.ernet.in; internet www.gipe.ernet.in; f. 1930, deemed univ. status 1993; postgraduate courses in politics and economics; library of 261,537 vols, 440 periodicals; Dir Dr A. SINHA; Registrar Dr N. BENJAMIN; publ. *Artha Vijanana* (in English, 4 a year).

Gujarat Vidyapith: Ashram Rd, Ahmedabad 380014, Gujarat; tel. (79) 40016200; fax (79) 27542547; e-mail registrar@gujaratvidyapith.org; internet www.gujaratvidyapith.org; f. 1920, deemed univ. status 1963; languages of instruction: Gujarati, Hindi; academic year June to April; campuses at Ahmedabad, Anand, Gandhinagar, Kheda, Valsad; Chancellor NARAYANBHAI DESAI; Vice-Chancellor SUDARSHAN AAYANGAR; Registrar Dr RAJENDRA KHIMANI (acting); Librarian BHARTIBEN DESAI (acting); library of 539,945 vols; 105 teachers; 1,774 students; publ. *Vidyapith* (4 a year)

DEANS

College of Education: Dr M. PATEL
College of Hindi Education: Dr K. C. PARMAR
M. D. College of Physical Education: Dr J. K. SAVALIA
M. D. College of Rural Service (Home Science), Randheja: Dr RAMILABEN PATEL
M. D. College of Rural Service, Sadra: KANUBHAI NAIK
M. D. College of Social Sciences: Dr MALTIBEN DUBEY

PROFESSORS

DUBEY, MALTIBEN, Hindi
JOSHI, BHARATBHAI H., Education
PANDYA, JAYAPRAKASH G., Education
PARMAR, KANTIBHAI C., Hindi Education
PATEL, ARTIBEN P., Education
PATEL, MOHANBHAI K., Education
SAVALIYA, JAMNADAS K., Physical Education
SHUKLA, NIMISHA, Rural Economics
UPADHYAY, USHA, Gujurati

Gurukul Kangri Vishwavidyalaya:PO Gurukul Kangri, Hardwar 249404, Uttar Pradesh; tel. (1334) 246811; fax (1334) 246366; e-mail queries@gkvharidwar.org; internet gkvharidwar.org; f. 1902, deemed univ. status 1962; library of 133,667 vols; 103 teachers; 1,558 students; Chancellor SUDERSHAN KUMAR SHARMA; Vice-Chancellor Prof. SWATANTRA KUMAR; Pro-Vice-Chancellor Prof. V. P. SHASTRI; Registrar Prof. A. K. CHOPRA; Librarian Dr J. P. VIDYALANKAR; library of 135,000 vols; publ. *Arya Bhatt* (4 a year), *Gurukula Patrika* (12 a year), *Prahlad* (4 a year), *Vedic Path* (4 a year).

Indian Agricultural Research Institute:-Pusa Campus, New Delhi 110012; tel. (11) 25847438; fax (11) 25846420; e-mail director@iari.res.in; internet www.iari.res.in; f. 1905, deemed univ. status 1958; postgraduate courses in all major branches of agriculture; schools of basic sciences, crop improvements, crop protection, resource management and social sciences; library of 600,000 vols; 360 teachers; 600 students; Dir Dr S. A. PATIL; Dir of Extension Dr B. SINGH; Dir of Research Dr K. R. KOUNDAL; Registrar

P. C. JACOB; Dean Dr H. S. GAUR; Librarian N. S. PAKHALE.

Indian Institute of Foreign Trade: Bhawan, B-21, Qutab Institutional Area, New Delhi 110016; tel. (11) 26965124; fax (11) 26853956; e-mail iift@iift.ac.in; internet www.iift.edu; f. 1963; attached research centres: Centre for International Trade in Technology, Centre for SME Studies, Centre for World Trade Organization Studies; library of 84,000 vols and 800 periodicals; Dir K. T. CHACKO; Registrar L. D. MAGO; Head (Kolkata Centre) Dr K. RANGARAJAN; publ. *Focus WTO, Foreign Trade Review*.

Indian Institute of Information Technology: Nehru Science Centre, Kamla Nehru Rd, Allahabad 211012, Uttar Pradesh; tel. (532) 2922000; fax (532) 2430006; e-mail contact@iiita.ac.in; internet www.iiita.ac.in; f. 1999; deemed University status 2000; undergraduate and postgraduate courses in information technology; Dean of Academic Affairs Dr M. D. TIWARI.

Indian Institute of Science: Bangalore 560012, Karnataka; tel. (80) 23600757; fax (80) 23600085; e-mail regr@admin.iisc.ernet.in; internet www.iisc.ernet.in; f. 1909; faculties of engineering and science; library of 411,676 vols; 434 teachers; 1,794 students; Dir Prof. P. BALARAM; Registrar J. LALITHA; Public Relations Officer V. THILAGAM; Librarian Dr S. VENKADESAN.

Indian Law Institute: Bhagwandas Rd, New Delhi 110001; tel. (11) 23387526; fax (11) 23782140; e-mail ili@ilidelhi.org; internet www.ilidelhi.org; f. 1956, deemed univ. status in 2004; courses in admin. law, alternative dispute resolution, corporate laws and management, cyber law, environmental law, human rights law, intellectual property rights law, int. trade law, labour law, securities and banking law, tax law; library of 75,000 vols, 270 periodicals; Dir Prof. S. SIVAKUMAR (acting); Registrar DALIP KUMAR; publ. *Journal of the Indian Law Institute*.

Indian School of Mines University: Dhanbad 826004, Jharkhand; tel. (326) 2296559; fax (326) 2296563; e-mail info@ismdhanbad.ac.in; internet www.ismdhanbad.ac.in; f. 1926; residential; depts of applied chemistry, applied geology, applied geophysics, applied mathematics, applied physics, computer science and engineering, electrical engineering, electronics engineering, fuel and mineral engineering, humanities and social science, management studies, mechanical engineering and mining machinery engineering, petroleum engineering; language of instruction: English; academic year July to June; library of 74,550 books, 550 journals, 3,000 online journals; 105 teachers; 1,035 students; Dir Prof. T. KUMAR; Dean of Academics and Research Prof. KAMPAN MUKHERJEE; Dean of Planning and Devt Prof. A. CHATTOPADHYAY; Dean of Student Welfare Prof. P. S. GUPTA; Registrar P. S. SANDHU; Librarian Dr PARTHA DE.

Indian Veterinary Research Institute: Izatnagar 243122, Uttar Pradesh; tel. (581) 2300096; fax (581) 2303284; e-mail dirivri@ivri.up.nic.in; internet www.ivri.nic.in; f. 1889, deemed univ. status 1983; campuses at Bangalore, Bhopal, Izatnagar, Kolkata, Mukteswar, Palampur and Srinagar; research divs of animal biochemistry, animal biotechnology, animal genetics and breeding, animal nutrition, animal physiology, avian diseases, biostatistics, livestock production and management, livestock products technology, poultry science, veterinary bacteriology, veterinary epidemiology, veterinary extension education, veterinary gynaecology and obstetrics, veterinary immunology, veterinary medicine, veterinary parasitology, veterinary pathology, veterinary pharmacology, veterinary public health, veterinary surgery, veterinary virology; library of 207,000 vols, 300 periodicals; Dir Dr R. S. CHAUHAN (acting); Dir for Academic and Dean Dr D. DAS; Registrar K. L. MEENA (acting).

Indira Gandhi Institute of Development Research: Gen. A. K.Vaidya Marg, Goregaon (E), Mumbai 400065, Maharashtra; tel. (22) 28400919; fax (22) 28402752; e-mail dean@igidr.ac.in; internet www.igidr.ac.in; f. 1987, deemed univ. status 1995; postgraduate courses in economics and devt studies; library of 40,000 vols, 460 periodicals; 30 teachers; Dir Dr D. M. NACHANE; Registrar T. V. SUBRAMANIAN; Librarian G. K. MANJU-NATH.

Institute of Advanced Studies in Education/IASE University: Gandhi Vidya Mandir, Sardarshahr 331401, Rajasthan; tel. (1564) 223054; fax (1564) 223682; e-mail info@iaseuniversity.org.in; internet www .iaseuniversity.org.in; f. 1950, deemed univ. status 2002; faculties of education, information technology, management, medicine; campuses at Bhunbeshwar and Bikaner; library of 95,000 vols; 10,000 students; Dir MILAP DUGAR; Registrar R. S. SUROLIA.

Institute of Armament Technology: Girinagar, Pune 411025, Maharashtra; tel. (20) 24389444; fax (20) 24389509; e-mail root@iat .ernet.in; f. 1952; deemed univ. status 1999; library of 42,000 vols, 250 periodicals; Dir Prof. G. S. MANI.

International Institute for Population Sciences: Govandi Station Rd, Deonar, Mumbai 400088, Maharashtra; tel. (22) 25563254; fax (22) 25563257; e-mail director@iips.net; internet www.iipsindia .org; f. 1956, deemed univ. status 1985; depts of devt studies, extramural studies and distance education, fertility studies, mathematical demography and statistics, migration and urban studies, population policies and programmes, public health and mortality studies; 30 teachers; 120 students; library of 76,962 books, 13,108 bound periodicals; Dir Dr FAUJDAR RAM; Registrar Dr M. K. KULKARNI; Librarian D. D. MESTRI.

International Institute of Information Technology: Gachibowli, Hyderabad 500032, Andhra Pradesh; tel. (40) 66531000; fax (40) 66531413; e-mail query@iiit.net; internet www.iiit.net; f. 1998; undergraduate and postgraduate courses in various disciplines of information technology; research centres in bioinformatics, building science, communications, earthquake engineering, education, data engineering, open software, technology consultancy, visual embedded systems technology, visual information technology; library of 6,000 vols; Dir Prof. RAJEEV SANGAL; Librarian V. PRABHAKAR SARMA.

Jain Vishva Bharati Institute: Dist. Nagaur, Ladnun 341306, Rajasthan; tel. (1581) 222110; fax (1581) 223472; e-mail registrar@jvbi.ac.in; internet jvbi.ac.in; f. 1970, deemed univ. status 1991; depts of Acharya Kalu Kanya Mahavidhyalaya, computer applications, education, jainology and comparative religion and philosophy, nonviolence and peace, prakrit and jain agama, science of living, preksha meditation and yoga, social work; library of 46,260 books, 116 periodicals, 6,000 MSS; Vice-Chancellor Dr SAMANI M. PRAJNA; Dir of Research Prof.

Dr BACHH R. DUGAR; Finance Officer RAKESH K. JAIN; Registrar Prof. Dr G. S. SHRIVASTAVA; Librarian H. C. R. SIDDAPPA.

Jamia Hamdard: Hamdard Nagar, New Delhi 110062; tel. (11) 26059688; fax (11) 26059663; e-mail inquiry@jamiahamdard .edu; internet www.jamiahamdard.edu; f. 1963, deemed univ. status 1989; faculties of allied health sciences, islamic studies and social science, management studies and information technology, medicine, nursing, pharmacy and science; library of 141,021 books, 124 periodicals, 5,000 MSS; 2,100 students; Vice-Chancellor Dr G. N. QAZI; Registrar Prof. NAUSHAD ALAM; Finance Officer C. L. GUPTA; Dean of Student Welfare Prof. R. K. KHAR; Provost Dr E. A. KHAN; Proctor Dr T. A. SIDDIQUI; Librarian K. K. FARUQI.

Janardan Rai Nagar Rajasthan Vidyapeeth: Pratap Nagar, Udaipur 313001, Rajasthan; tel. (294) 2490040; fax (294) 2492440; e-mail info@jrnrvpu.org; internet www.jrnrvu.org; f. 1937, deemed univ. status 1987; faculties of arts and commerce, computer science, management, medical science, science; 12 constituent institutions; library of 244,000 books, 140 periodicals; 5,300 students; Vice-Chancellor Prof. L. BHATT; Registrar Dr V. S. PANWAR; Dir of Distance Education Dr D. JOHAR; Librarian K. L. VAISHNAV.

CONSTITUENT COLLEGES:

Homeopathic Medical College and Hospital: Udaipur; e-mail homoeopathic@jrnrvpu.org.

Institute of Management Studies: Udaipur; tel. and fax (294) 2490632; e-mail imsjrnrvu_director@yahoo.co.in; internet www.fmsrvu.org; Dir Prof. RAJEEV JAIN.

Institute of Rajasthan Studies: Udaipur; e-mail rajasthanstudies@jrnrvpu.org.

Lokmanya Tilak College: Dabok, Udaipur; tel. (294) 2655327; fax (294) 2657753; e-mail info@lokmanyatilakcollege.org; internet www.lokmanyatilakcollege.org; faculty of education; Dean and Prin. Prof. DIVYA NAGAR.

M. V. Shramjeevi College: Town Hall Link Rd, Udaipur; e-mail shramjeevi@jrnrvpu.org; faculties of commerce, humanities and social sciences; Prin. Prof. N. K. PANDYA.

Udaipur School of Social Work: Dabok, Udaipur; e-mail social@jrnrvpu.org; Prin. (vacant).

Jawaharlal Nehru Centre for Advanced Scientific Research: Jakkur, Bangalore 560064, Karnataka; tel. (80) 22082900; fax (80) 22082766; e-mail admin@jncasr.ac.in; internet www.jncasr.ac.in; f. 1989; deemed univ. status 2002; library: 10,000 vols, 71 periodicals; 40 teachers; Pres. M. R. S. RAO; publs *Chemistry and Physics of Materials, Engineering Mechanics, Evolutionary and Organismal Biology, Geodynamics, Molecular Biology and Genetics, Theoretical Science.*

Kalinga Institute of Industrial Technology/KIIT University: Bhubaneshwar 751024, Orissa; tel. (674) 2725113; fax (674) 2725113; e-mail kiit@kiit.ac.in; internet www .kiit.ac.in; f. deemed univ. status 2004; schools of biotechnology, computer application, law, management, rural management, technology; constituent instns: Kalinga Institute of Medical Sciences, Kalinga Institute of Social Sciences, KIIT Int. School, KIIT Science College, Kalinga Polytechnic; Vice-Chancellor Prof. S. C. DE SARKAR; Pro-Vice-

Chancellor Prof. M. S. MISHRA; Registrar Dr A. K. JHA.

Lakshmibai National Institute of Physical Education: Mela Rd, Shakti Nagar, Gwalior 474002, Madhya Pradesh; tel. (751) 4000918; fax (751) 2340553; e-mail fo@lnipe .gov.in; internet www.lnipe.gov.in; f. 1957; Deemed University status 1995; library: 31,000 vols; depts of coaching, fitness and dance, computer science and applied statistics, health sciences and yoga therapy, research, devt and advanced studies, sports management and journalism, teacher education, youth affairs and sports; Vice-Chancellor Maj.-Gen. SHIBNATH MUKHERJEE; Registrar Dr L. N. SARKAR; Finance Officer VISHAL BANSAL; publs *Journal of Physical Education and Allied Sciences* (1 a year), *Journal of Physical Education and Sports Sciences* (1 a year)

PROFESSORS

DATTA, A. K.

DEBNATH, MONIKA

DEY, R. N., Research, Devt and Advance Studies

MAZUMDAR, INDU

MUKHERJEE, S., Teacher Education

PAL, RAMESH

PANDE, P. K., Health Sciences and Yoga Therapy

SINGH, JASRAJ

VERMA, J. P., Computer Science and Applied Statistics

Malaviya National Institute of Technology: Jaipur 302017, Rajasthan; tel. (141) 2529078; fax (141) 2529029; e-mail director@mnit.ac.in; internet www.mnit.ac.in; f. 1963, deemed univ. status 2002; depts of architecture, chemical engineering, chemistry, civil engineering, computer engineering, electrical engineering, electronics and communication engineering, humanities, mathematics, mechanical engineering, metallurgical engineering, physics, structural engineering; library: 133,600 vols; 150 teachers; 1,700 students; Dir Prof. R. P. DAHIYA; Dean of Academic Affairs Prof. P. R. SONI; Dean of Admin. Prof. G. AGARWAL; Dean of Faculty Affairs Prof. R. A. GUPTA; Dean of Research and Devt Prof. RAVINDRA NAGAR; Dean of Student Affairs Prof. SUDHIR KUMAR; Registrar P. S. DHAKHA; Librarian DEEP SINGH

PROFESSORS

BHARDWAJ, A. K., Management Studies

CHAURASIA, S. P., Chemical Engineering

GAUR, M. S., Computer Engineering

GUPTA, K. D., Chemistry

JAIN, R., Mathematics

JAIN, V. K., Electrical Engineering

MISRA, A., Structural Engineering

SHARMA, G., Civil Engineering

SHRINGI, R., Architecture

SONI, S. L., Mechanical Engineering

SWAMI, K. C., Physics

TANDON, N., Humanities

YADAV, R. K., Metallurgy and Materials

YADAV, R. P., Electronics and Communication

Manipal Academy of Higher Education: University Bldg, Madhav Nagar, Manipal 576104, Karnataka; tel. (820) 2571000; e-mail admissions@manipal.edu; internet www.manipal.edu; f. 1953, deemed univ. status 1993; privately controlled network of 50 instns run by the Manipal Group, incl. Kasturba Medical College, Manipal Centre for Information Sciences, Manipal College of Allied Health Sciences, Manipal College of Dental Sciences, Manipal College of Nursing, Manipal College of Pharmaceutical Sciences, Manipal Institute of Communication, Manipal Institute of Jewellery Management,

Manipal Institute of Management, Manipal Institute of Regenerative Medicine, Manipal Institute of Technology, Manipal Life Sciences Centre, Melaka Manipal Medical College, Welcomgroup Graduate School of Hotel Administration; depts of geopolitics, statistics; Manipal Advanced Research Group; off-campus BSc in animation; library: 50,000 vols, 600 periodicals; Chancellor Dr RAMDAS M. PAI; Pro-Chancellor Dr H. S. BALLAL; Vice-Chancellor Dr RAJ WARRIER; Registrar Dr H. VINOD BHAT.

Maulana Azad National Institute of Technology: Bhopal 462051, Madhya Pradesh; tel. (755) 5206006; fax (755) 2670562; e-mail info@manit.ac.in; internet www.manit.nic.in; f. 1960, deemed univ. status 2002; depts of architecture and planning, computer application, energy centre, eng., humanities, management, physical education, remote sensing and GIS, science; library: 107,923 vols, 100 journals; Dir Prof. K. S. PANDEY; Dean of Admin. Dr S. RANGNEKAR; Dean of Research and Devt Dr K. R. PARDASANI; Dean of Student Affairs Dr A. M. SHANDILYA; Registrar ARVIND MITTAL; Librarian AJAY PANDEY.

Meenakshi University: 12 Vembuli Amman Koil St, Chennai, 600078; tel. (44) 23643955; fax (44) 23643958; e-mail info@maher.ac.in; internet www.maher.ac.in; f. 2004; constituent colleges: Ammal Dental College and Hospital, College of Nursing, College of Physiotherapy, Dept of Eng. and Technology, Medical College and Research Institute; Vice-Chancellor Dr T. GUNASAGARAN; Dir Dr C. M. NANDAGOPAL; Registrar A. N. SANTHANAM.

CONSTITUENT COLLEGES:

Arulmigu Meenakshi Amman College of Nursing: Enathur, Kancheepuram.

Meenakshi Ammal Dental College and Hospital: Chennai 600095.

Meenakshi College of Nursing: Chennai 600095.

Meenakshi College of Occupational Therapy: Chennai 600095.

Meenakshi College of Physiotherapy: West K. K. Nagar, Chennai 600078.

Meenakshi Medical College and Research Institute: Enathur, Kancheepuram.

Mody Institute of Technology and Science: Dist. Sikar, Lakshmangarh 332311, Rajasthan; tel. (1573) 225001; fax (1573) 225042; e-mail contact@mitsuniversity.ac.in; internet www.mitsuniversity.ac.in; f. 1998, deemed univ. status 2004; faculties of arts, commerce and law, engineering and technology, management studies, science; library: 23,362 vols; 74 teachers; 1,250 students; Chancellor R. P. MODY; Vice-Chancellor Prof. SHAKTIDEV MUKHERJEE; Registrar Prof. AMAL KUMAR

DEANS

Faculty of Arts, Science and Commerce: Dr SHAKTI BAIJAL

Faculty of Engineering and Technology: Prof. P. K. DAS

Faculty of Juridical Sciences: Prof. SATISH C. SHASTRI

Faculty of Management Studies: Prof. K. V. S. M. KRISHNA

Motilal Nehru National Institute of Technology: Allahabad 211004; tel. (0532) 2445103; fax (0532) 2445101; internet www.mnnit.ac.in; f. 1961, deemed univ. status 2002; depts of applied mechanics, chemistry, civil engineering, computer science and engineering, electrical engineering, electronics and communications engineering, humanities and social science, management

studies, mathematics, mechanical engineering, physics; library: 95,409 vols, 268 journals; Dir Prof. A. B. SAMADDAR; Dean of Academic Affairs Dr N. ROY; Dean of Admin. Dr A. K. MISRA; Dean of Student Affairs Dr R. NARAIN; Librarian S. K. TIWARI.

Narsee Monjee Institute of Management Studies (NMIMS)/NMIMS University: V. L. Mehta Rd, Vile Parle (W), Mumbai 400056, Maharashtra; tel. (22) 26134577; fax (22) 26114512; e-mail enquiry@nmims.edu; internet www.nmims.edu; f. 1981, deemed univ. status 2003; schools of architecture, business management, commerce, distance learning, pharmacy, science, technology management and engineering; library: 42,000 books, 308 periodicals; Vice-Chancellor Dr RAJAN SAXENA (acting); Registrar V. K. SRIDHAR; Librarian VRUSHALI RANE; publ. *NMIMS Management Review* (2 a year)

DEANS

Balwant Sheth School of Architecture: TRILOCHAN M. CHHAYA

Mukesh Patel School of Technology Management and Engineering: Dr D. J. SHAH

School of Business Management: Dr RAMESH BHAT

School of Pharmacy and Technology Management: Dr R. S. GAUD

Technology Management: Dr PRADEEP KUMAR

National Brain Research Centre: NH 8, Manesar 122050, Haryana; tel. (124) 2338922; fax (124) 2338910; e-mail info@nbrc.ac.in; internet www.nbrc.ac.in; f. 2003, deemed univ.; main research areas: Molecular and Cellular Neuroscience, Systems Neuroscience, Computational Neuroscience; Dir Prof. VIJAYALAKSHMI RAVINDRANATH; Registrar K. V. S. KAMESWARA RAO; Chief Admin. Officer K. V. S. KAMESWARA RAO.

National Dairy Research Institute: Karnal 132001, Haryana; tel. (184) 2252800; fax (184) 2250042; e-mail bnm@ndri.hry.nic.in; internet www.ndri.res.in; f. 1923, deemed univ.; library: 75,000 vols and 22,000 periodicals; regional stations at Bangalore and Kalyani; research divs in animal biochemistry, animal biotechnology, dairy cattle breeding, dairy cattle nutrition, dairy cattle physiology, dairy chemistry, dairy econ., statistics and management, dairy engineering, dairy extension, dairy microbiology, dairy technology; Dir Dr A. K. SRIVASTAVA; Registrar RAMESHWAR SINGH; Dir of Library Services Dr B. R. YADAV; library: 92,555 vols, 350 periodicals; publ. *Dairy Samachar* (4 a year).

National Institute of Mental Health and Neurosciences: POB 2900, Hosur Rd, Bangalore 560029, Karnataka; tel. (80) 26995005; fax (80) 26564830; e-mail regt@nimhans.kar.nic.in; internet www.nimhans.kar.nic.in; f. 1974, deemed univ. status 1994; depts of biophysics, biostatistics, epidemiology, human genetics, mental health education, mental health and social psychology, neuroanaesthesia, neurochemistry, neuroimaging and interventional radiology, neurology, neuromicrobiology, neuropathology, neurophysiology, neurosurgery, neurovirology, nursing, psychiatric and neurological rehabilitation, psychiatric social work, psychiatry, psychopharmacology, speech pathology and audiology; library: 75,000 vols, 315 periodicals; Vice-Chancellor Prof. D. NAGARAJA; Dean Dr N. PRADHAN; Registrar M. V. SAVITHRI; Library and Information Officer Dr H. S. SIDDAMALLAIAH.

National Institute of Technology, Agartala: Barjala, Agartala 799055, Tripura (West); tel. (381) 2346630; fax (381) 2346360; e-mail nitagartala@yahoo.co.in;

internet www.tec.nic.in; f. 1965, fmrly Tripura Engineering College; depts of civil engineering, computer science and engineering, electrical engineering, electrical and electronics engineering, mechanical engineering, production engineering, transportation engineering; Prin. Dr S. C. SAHA; Vice-Prin. P. C. DAS; Academic Dean Dr SWAPAN BHAUMIK; Dean of Student Welfare Dr SAROJ K. DAS; Registrar Dr D. BHATTACHARJEE.

National Institute of Technology, Calicut: Calicut 673601, Kerala; tel. (495) 2286101; fax (495) 2287250; e-mail pvr@nitc.ac.in; internet www.nitc.ac.in; f. 1961, deemed univ. status 2002; library: 100,000 vols; depts of architecture and civil engineering, chemical engineering, computer science and engineering, electrical engineering, electronics engineering, humanities, mathematics, mechanical engineering, science; Dir Dr G. R. C. REDDY; Registrar P. ANANTHAKRISHNAN; Librarian Dr S. ASHOK.

National Institute of Technology, Durgapur: Mahatma Gandhi Ave, Durgapur 713209, West Bengal; tel. (343) 2546397; fax (343) 2547375; e-mail director@nitdgp.ac.in; internet www.nitdgp.ac.in; f. 1960, deemed univ. status 2002; depts of applied mechanics and drawing, biotechnology, chemical engineering, chemistry, civil engineering, computer science and engineering, electrical engineering, electronics and communication engineering, geology, humanities, information technology, management studies, mathematics, mechanical engineering, metallurgical and materials engineering, physics; library: 22,000 vols, 150 periodicals; 162 teachers; 1,800 students; Dir Prof. S. BHATTACHARYA; Admin. Dean Prof. A. K. MITRA; Registrar S. K. RAY; Librarian Dr M. MANDAL.

National Institute of Technology, Hamirpur: Hamirpur 177005, Himachal Pradesh; tel. (1972) 254001; fax (1972) 223834; e-mail director@nitham.ac.in; internet www.nitham.ac.in; f. 1986, deemed univ. status 2002; depts of applied science and humanities, architecture, computer science and engineering, civil engineering, electrical engineering, electronics and communications engineering, mechanical engineering; 68 teachers; 900 students; library: 55,870 vols; Dir Dr I. K. BHAT; Academic Dean Dr J. N. SHARMA; Registrar A. L. SHARMA; Librarian D. S. JASWAL.

National Institute of Technology, Jamshedpur: Jamshedpur 831014, Jharkhand; tel. (657) 2373392; fax (657) 2373246; e-mail director@nitjsr.ac.in; internet www.nitjsr.ac.in; f. 1960; depts of applied mechanics, chemistry, civil engineering, computer science and engineering, electrical engineering, electronics engineering, mathematics and humanities, mechanical engineering, metallurgical engineering and materials science, physics, production engineering and science; Dir Dr A. MISHRA; Dean of Academic Affairs Dr R. J. SINGH; Dean of Admin. Dr S. N. SINHA; Dean of Student Affairs N. K. NARAIN; Registrar Dr M. K. BANERJEE; Librarian Dr N. BHARTI.

National Institute of Technology, Karnataka: Surathkal, Dakshina Kannada, Srinivasnagar 575025, Karnataka; tel. (824) 2474000; fax (824) 2476033; e-mail registrar@nitk.ac.in; internet www.nitk.ac.in; f. 1960, deemed univ. status 2002; depts of applied mechanics, chemical engineering, chemistry, civil engineering, computer engineering, electronics and communication, humanities, social sciences and management, information technology, mathematical and computational sciences, metallurgical and materials engineering, mining engineering, physics; library: 100,000 vols; 195 teachers; Dir Dr S. SANCHETI; Dean of Academic Affairs Prof. K. HALEMANE; Dean of Admin. Affairs Prof. P. RAO; Dean of Planning and Devt Prof. S. G. MAYYA; Dean of Student Affairs Prof. V. R. SASTRY; Registrar Dr M. G. RAJ; Librarian M. K. MOHANDAS.

National Institute of Technology, Kurukshetra: Kurukshetra 136119, Haryana; tel. (1744) 238122; fax (1744) 238050; e-mail nit_kkr@rediffmail.com; internet www .nitkkr.ac.in; f. 1963, deemed univ. status 2002; depts of business administration, chemistry, civil engineering, computer engineering, electrical engineering, electronics and communication engineering, humanities and social sciences, mathematics, mechanical engineering, physics; library: 119,314 vols; Dir Dr M. N. BANDYOPADHYAY; Dean of Planning and Devt Dr S. P. JAIN; Academic Dean Dr R. K. BANSAL; Registrar R. P. S. LOHCHAB; Librarian KRISHAN GOPAL.

National Institute of Technology, Patna: Patna 799055, Bihar; tel. (381) 2346630; fax (381) 2346360; internet www.nitp.ac.in; f. 1886 as Pleaders Survey Training School, Bihar College of Engineering 1924, current status 2004; Autonomous; depts of civil engineering, computer science and engineering, electrical engineering, electronics and communications engineering, information technology, mechanical engineering; Dir Dr U. C. RAY; Registrar Dr VIDYA SAGAR.

National Institute of Technology, Raipur: Raipur 492010, Chhattisgarh; tel. (771) 2254200; fax (771) 2254600; internet www .nitrr.ac.in; f. 1963, fmrly Govt Engineering College, Raipur; depts of architecture, biomedical engineering, bio-technology, chemical engineering, civil engineering, computer science and engineering, electrical engineering, electronics and telecommunication engineering, information technology, mechanical engineering, mining engineering, metallurgical engineering; Dir Dr K. K. SUGHANDI

DEANS

Academic Affairs: Dr K. D. PERMAR
Administration: Dr K. K. SUGANDHI
Planing and Development: Prof. M. M. HAMBARDE
Research and Faculty Development: Dr A. M. RAWANI
Student's Welfare: Dr M. K. VERMA

National Institute of Technology, Rourkela: Rourkela 769008, Orissa; tel. (661) 2476773; fax (661) 2462999; e-mail info@ nitrkl.ac.in; internet www.nitrkl.ac.in; f. 1955, deemed univ. status 2002; depts of applied mathematics, biotechnolgy and medical engineering, ceramic engineering, chemical engineering, chemistry, civil engineering, computer science and engineering, electrical engineering, electronics and communication engineering, humanities and social sciences, mechanical engineering, metallurgical and materials engineering, mining engineering, physics; library: 150,000 vols; Dir Prof. SUNIL K. SARANGI; Dean of Academic Affairs Dr S. K. RATH; Dean of Admin. Dr J. K. SATAPATHY; Dean of Planning and Devt Dr U. K. MOHANTY; Dean of Research Dr R. K. SAHOO; Dean of Student Affairs Dr P. C. PANDA; Registrar S. K. UPADHYAY; Librarian Y. S. RAO.

National Institute of Technology, Silchar: Silchar 788010, Assam; tel. (3842) 233179; fax (3842) 233797; e-mail contactus@nits.ac.in; internet www.nits.ac .in; f. 1967; depts of chemistry, civil engineering, electrical engineering, electronics and telecommunication engineering, humanities and social sciences, mathematics, mechanical

engineering, physics; library: 45,000 vols, 150 periodicals; 880 students; Dir Prof. P. K. BANIK; Dean of Academic Affairs Prof. A. K. SIL; Dean of Planning and Devt Prof. A. K. ROY; Dean of Research Prof. R. GUPTA; Dean of Student Affairs Prof. A. K. SINHA; Registrar Dr FAZAL A. TALUKDAR.

National Institute of Technology, Srinagar: Hazratbal 190006, Jammu and Kashmir; tel. (194) 2422032; fax (194) 2420475; e-mail director@nitsri.net; internet www .nitsri.net; f. 1960, deemed univ. status 2003; depts of chemical engineering, chemistry, civil engineering, electrical engineering, electronics and communication engineering, humanities, mathematics, mechanical engineering, metallurgical engineering, physics; Dir Prof. R. K. WANCHOO; Registrar A. R. BHATT.

National Institute of Technology, Tiruchirapalli: Tanjore Main Rd, Nat. Highway 67, Tiruchirappalli 620015, Tamil Nadu; tel. (431) 2501801; fax (431) 2500133; e-mail deanac@nitt.edu; internet www.nitt.edu; f. 1964, deemed univ. status 2003; depts of architecture, chemical engineering, chemistry, civil engineering, computer applications, computer science and engineering, electrical and electronics engineering, electronics and communication engineering, english, humanities, instrumentation and control engineering, management studies, mathematics, mechanical engineering, metallurgical engineering, physics, production engineering; Centre for Energy and Environmental Science and Technology; library: 100,000 books, 15,943 bound periodicals, 200 current periodicals, 4,500 online journals; 2,190 undergraduates, 1,025 postgraduates; 192 teachers; Dir Prof. M. CHIDAMBARAM; Dean of Academic Programme Dr P. JAYABALAN; Dean of Admin. Dr M. UDAYAKUMAR; Dean of Industrial Consultancy and Sponsored Research Dr N. AMMASAI GOUNDEN; Dean of Students Dr S. KUMANAN.

National Institute of Technology, Warangal: Warangal 506004, Andhra Pradesh; tel. (870) 2459191; fax (870) 2459547; e-mail director@nitw.ernet.in; internet www.nitw .ac.in; f. 1959; depts of biotechnology, centre for management studies, chemical eng., chemistry, civil eng., computer science and eng., electrical eng., electronics and communication eng., mathematics and humanities, mechanical eng., metallurgical and materials eng., physical education, physics; library: 131,757 vols, 210 periodicals; 200 teachers; 3,000 students; Dir Prof. Y. V. RAO; Dean of Academic Affairs Prof. R. V. CHALAM; Dean of Admin. Prof. G. V. REDDY; Dean of Planning and Devt Prof. C. B. K. RAO; Dean of Student Affairs Prof. R. RAO; Registrar Prof. Y. N. REDDY; Public Relations Officers Dr D. S. K. RAO, Dr M. R. REDDY; Librarian R. S. REDDY.

National Law School of India University: Nagarbhavi, PB 7201, Bangalore 560242, Karnataka; tel. (80) 23213160; fax (80) 23160534; e-mail registrar@nls.ac.in; internet www.nls.ac.in; f. 1987; library: 18,000 books, 15,000 bound periodicals; 30 teachers; 400 students; Vice-Chancellor Prof. A. JAYAGOVIND; Registrar Prof. V. NAGARAJ; publs *Indian Journal of Law and Technology* (1 a year), *National Law School of India Review* (2 a year), *Socio-Legal Review* (1 a year).

Attached Research Institutes:

Centre for Child and the Law: NLSIU, PO 7201, Nagarbhavi, Bangalore 560072; tel. and fax (80) 23160528; e-mail ccl@nls .ac.in.

Centre for Environmental Education, Research and Advocacy: tel. (80) 23160527; e-mail ceera@nls.ac.in.

Centre for Intellectual Property Research and Advocacy: tel. (80) 23160535 ext. 235; e-mail cipra@nls.ac.in; internet www.iprlawindia.org.

Centre for Study of Casteism, Communalism and Law: tel. (80) 23160533.

Centre for Women and the Law: tel. (80) 23160532; e-mail cwl@nls.ac.in.

Institute of Law and Ethics in Medicine: e-mail tilem@nls.ac.in; tel. (80) 23160529.

National Institute for Alternate Disputes Resolution: tel. (80) 23160533.

National Institute of Human Rights: e-mail nihr@nls.ac.in; tel. (80) 23160533.

National Museum Institute of History of Art, Conservation and Museology: Janpath, New Delhi 110011; tel. (11) 23011901; fax (11) 23011899; e-mail dgnationalmuseum@gmail.com; internet nmi .gov.in; f. 1983, deemed univ. status 1989; postgraduate courses in conservation and restoration of works of arts, history of art, museology; library: 2,500 books, 60,000 slides; Vice-Chancellor R. C. MISHRA; Dean Prof. K. K. JAIN; Registrar K. K. KULSHRESHTHA; Librarian Dr B. N. SINGH.

National University of Educational Planning and Administration: 17-B Sri Aurobindo Marg, New Delhi 110016; tel. (11) 26863562; fax (11) 26853041; e-mail nuepa@ nuepa.org; internet www.nuepa.org; f. 1962, current status 2006; offers courses for education personnel of developing countries and district education officers; other in-service training courses; research in various aspects of educational planning and management; consultancy service for developing countries, State govts and other orgs; collaboration with UNESCO and other foreign agencies; Vice-Chancellor Prof. VED PRAKASH; Registrar Dr B. K. SINGH; Librarian DEEPAK MAKOL; library: 53,500 vols, 350 current journals; publs *Journal of Educational Planning and Administration* (4 a year), *Pariprakshya* (in Hindi).

Nava Nalanda Mahavihara (Nalanda University): PO Nalanda, Bihar 803111; tel. and fax (6112) 274820; internet navanalandamahavihara.org; f. 1951, deemed univ. status 2006; administered by Dept of Culture, Min. of Human Resources Devt; studies and research in Pali, Buddhism, philosophy, ancient Indian and Asian studies; diploma in languages: Chinese, Japanese, Tibetan, Hindi, Sanskrit and Pali; library: 36,000 vols; Dir Prof. Dr RAVINDRA PANTH; publs *Atthakatha, Pali Tipitaki*.

Padmashree Dr D. Y. Patil Vidyapeeth: Sector 15, CBD Belapur, Navi Mumbai 400614, Maharashtra; tel. (22) 39285999; fax (22) 39286197; e-mail info@dypatil.com; internet www.dypatil.in; f. 2002; Vice-Chancellor Prof. JAMES THOMAS; Registrar Dr F. A. FERNANDES; Controller of Examinations RADHA RAMAMURTHY; Finance Officer R. P. NALAWADE.

CONSTITUENT COLLEGES:

Dr D. Y. Patil Dental College and Hospital: Dental Hospital Bldg, Dr D. Y. Patil Vidyanagar, Sector 7, Nerul, Navi Mumbai 400706, Maharashtra; tel. (22) 27731599; fax (22) 27709591; e-mail dentistry@dypatil.edu.

Dr D. Y. Patil Medical College: New Medical College Bldg, Dr D. Y. Patil Vidyanagar, Sector 5 , Nerul, Navi Mumbai 400706, Maharashtra; tel. (22) 39215999; fax (22) 39215911; e-mail medicine@dypatil.edu.

Punjab Engineering College: Sector 12, Chandigarh 160012; tel. (172) 2753064; fax (172) 2745175; e-mail admissions@pec.ac.in; internet www.pec.ac.in; f. 1947; library: 106,000 vols; Dir Dr MANOJ DATTA; Dean of Academic Affairs Dr ASHWANI PRASHAR; Dean of Research and Planning Dr GURNAM SINGH; Dean of Student Welfare Prof. M. L. GUPTA; Head Librarian P. S. KANG.

Rashtriya Sanskrit Sansthan: 56-57 Institutional Area, Janakpuri, New Delhi 110058; tel. (11) 28524993; fax (11) 28521948; e-mail rsks@nda.vsnl.net.in; internet www.sanskrit .nic.in; f. 1970; campuses in Allahabad, Bhopal, Jaipur, Jammu, Lucknow, Mumbai, Puri, Sringeri and Trichur; library: total library colln of 213,581 vols, 51,133 MSS; Vice-Chancellor Prof. RADHAVALLABH TRI-PATHI; publ. *Sanskrit Vimarsh* (1 a year).

Rashtriya Sanskrit Vidyapeetha: Tirupati 517507, Andhra Pradesh; tel. (8574) 2286799; fax (8574) 2287809; e-mail registrar_rsvp@yahoo.com; internet rsvidyapeetha.ac.in; f. 1961; library: 60,000 vols and 5,000 MSS; Vice-Chancellor Prof. HAREKRISHNA SATAPATHY; Registrar A. GUR-UMURTHI; Dean of Academic Affairs Prof. K. E. GOVINDAN.

S. R. M. Institute of Science and Technology: *Head Office* 3 Veerasamy St, West Mambalam, Chennai 600033, Tamil Nadu; tel. (44) 24742836; fax (44) 24748925 *Kattankulathur Campus* SRM Nagar, Kattankulathur, Kancheepuram 603203, Tamil Nadu; tel. (44) 27452270; fax (44) 27452343 *Modi Nagar Campus* Delhi-Meerut Rd, Sikrikalan Modi Nagar, Gazhiabad 201204, Uttar Pradesh; tel. (1232) 248618; fax (1232) 245441 *Ramapuram Campus* Bharathi Salai, Ramapuram, Chennai 600089, Tamil Nadu; tel. (44) 43923042; fax (44) 22491777 *Trichy Campus* Irangalur Post, Mannachanallur Taluk, Tiruchirapalli Dist 621105; tel. (431) 2910599; e-mail registrar@srmuniv.ac.in; internet www.srmuniv.ac.in; f. 1985 as S. R. M. Engineering College, deemed univ. status 2002; faculties of engineering, management, medicine, science and humanities; campuses at Kattankulathur, Modi Nagar, Ramapuram; Chancellor T. R. PACHAMUTHU; Vice-Chancellor P. SATHYANARAYANAN.

Sardar Vallabhbhai National Institute of Technology: Ichhchha Nath, Surat 395007, Gujarat; tel. (261) 2223606; fax (261) 2228394; e-mail director@svnit.ac.in; internet www.svnit.ac.in; f. 1961; library: 100,000 vols; depts of applied mechanics, applied science and humanities, chemical engineering, computer engineering, electrical engineering, electronics engineering, mechanical engineering, production engineering; Dir Dr P. D. POREY; Dean of Admin. Dr H. S. PATIL; Registrar H. A. PARMAR; Librarian T. B. GHOSH.

Sathyabama University: Jeppiaar Nagar, Old Mamallapuram Rd, Chennai 600119, Tamil Nadu; tel. (44) 24503150; fax (44) 24502344; e-mail admissions@ sathyabamauniv.ac.in; internet www .sathyabamauniv.ac.in; f. 1987, deemed univ. status 2001; depts of architecture, bioinformatics, biomedical engineering, biotechnology, chemical engineering, civil engineering, computer application, computer science and engineering, electrical and electronics engineering, electronics and communication engineering, electronics and control engineering, electronics and instrumentation engineering, electronics and telecommunication engineering, information technology, management sciences, mechanical engineering, production engineering, science and visual communication; library: 50,000 vols, 290 periodicals; Vice-Chancellor Prof. V. S. R. K. MOULY;

Registrar Dr S. S. RAU; Controller of Examinations Prof. K. V. NARAYANAN; Dean of Academic Research Dr P. E. SANKARANARAYA-NAN; Dean of Postgraduate Studies Dr N. MANOHARAN.

School of Planning and Architecture: 4 Block B, Indraprastha Estate, New Delhi 110002; tel. (11) 23702382; fax (11) 23702383; e-mail regspa@indiatimes.com; internet www.spa.ac.in; f. 1955; depts of architectural conservation, architecture, building engineering and management, environmental planning, housing, industrial design, landscape architecture, physical planning, regional planning, transport planning, urban design, urban planning; library: 74,759 vols; 62 teachers; 694 students; Dir Prof. RANJIT MITRA KUMAR; Dean of Studies Prof. A. K. SHARMA; Registrar D. R. BAINS; Librarian NAJMA RIZVI; publ. *SPACE* (4 a year).

Shanmugha Arts, Science, Technology and Research Academy: Shanmugha Campus, Tirumalaisamaduram, Thanjavur 613402, Tamil Nadu; tel. (4362) 264101; fax (4362) 264120; e-mail admissions@sastra .edu; internet www.sastra.edu; f. 1984, deemed univ. status 2001; schools of chemical engineering and biotechnology, civil engineering, computing, electrical and electronics engineering, humanities and sciences, management, mechanical engineering; 600 teachers; 8,000 students; Vice-Chancellor Prof. R. SETHURAMAN; Registrar N. ANANTHARAMAN; Dean of Student Affairs Prof. M. NARAYANAN; Dean of Research Dr T. R. SIVARAMAKRISHNAN.

ATTACHED CENTRES:

Centre for Advanced Research in Indian System of Medicine: internet www.sastra.edu/carism; Dean Dr G. VIC-TOR RAJAMANICKAM.

Centre for Nanotechnology and Advanced Biomaterials: tel. (4362) 304000; fax (4362) 264120; internet www .sastra.edu/centab; Dir Dr S. SWAMI-NATHAN.

Shri Lal Bahadur Shastri Rashtriya Sanskrit Vidyapeetha: Qutub Institional Area, New Delhi 110016; tel. (11) 46060606; fax (11) 26533512; e-mail info@slbsrsv.ac.in; internet www.slbsrsv.ac.in; f. 1962; deemed univ. status 1987; library: 65,000 vols, 17 periodicals; Vice-Chancellor Prof. VACHASPATI UPADHYAYA; Registrar B. K. MOHAPATRA.

Sri Chandrasekharenda Saraswathi Viswa Mahavidyalaya: Sri Jayendra Saraswathi St, Enathur 631561, Tamil Nadu; tel. (44) 27264301; fax (44) 27264285; e-mail registrar@kanchiuniv.ac.in; internet www .kanchiuniv.ac.in; f. 1993; library: 200,000 vols; depts of ayurvedic medicine, Sanskrit and Indian culture, science and humanities, electrical engineering, mechanical engineering, computer science and engineering, electronics and communications, management studies; Vice-Chancellor Prof. B. VISWA-NATHAN; Registrar Prof. Dr V. S. VISHNU-POTTY; Dean for Academics G. SUBBA RAO; Dean for Research K. P. V. RAMANA KUMAR.

Sri Ramachandra University: No.1, Ramchandra Nagar, Porur, Chennai 600116, Tamil Nadu; tel. (44) 24768403; fax (44) 24767008; e-mail registrar@srmc.edu; internet www.srmc.edu; f. 1985, deemed univ. status 1994; depts of anaesthesiology, cardiac care, chest and tuberculosis, dermatology, emergency, trauma and critical care, endocrinology, ears, nose and throat, general medicine, general surgery, medical gastroenterology, nephrology, neurology, neurosurgery, obstetrics and gynaecology, ophthalmology, orthopaedics, paediatric

medicine, paediatric surgery, paediatric urology, plastic and reconstructive surgery, psychiatry, radiology and imaging sciences, surgical gastroenterology and urology; library: 23,000 vols, 350 periodicals; 3,500 students; Chancellor V. R. VENKATAACHALAM; Vice-Chancellor Dr S. RANGASWAMI; Chief Executive Director RADHA VENKATACHALAM; Dean of Faculties Dr K. V. SOMASUNDARAM.

Sri Sathya Sai University: Prasanthi Nilayam Campus, Anantapur District, Andhra 515134, Andhra Pradesh; tel. (8555) 287239; fax (8555) 287390; e-mail registrar@ sssu.edu.in; internet sssu.edu.in; depts of accounting and finance, biosciences, chemistry, commerce, economics, education, English language and literature, history and Indian culture, home sciences, management, mathematics and computer science, philosophy, physics, political science, Telugu language and literature; campuses at Anantapur, Bangalore; f. 1981; library: 150,000 vols; 115 teachers; 1,100 students; Vice-Chancellor Prof. VISWANATH PANDIT; Registrar Prof. A. V. LAKSHMINARASIMHAM; Controller of Examinations Prof. M. NANJUNDAIAH; Prin. (Prasanthi Nilayam Campus) Prof. U. S. RAO; Prin. (Anantapur Campus) SANJAY SAHNI; Prin. (Brindavan Campus) Dr DWARAKA RANI RAO; publs *Bulletin of Pure and Applied Sciences* (4 a year), *International Journal of Modern Physics* (4 a year), *Journal of Applied Mathematics and Stochastic Analysis* (4 a year), *Third Concept: An International Journal of Ideas* (6 a year).

Swami Vivekananda Yog Anusandhana Samsthana: Bangalore 560019, Karnataka; e-mail info@svyasa.org; internet www.svyasa .org; divs of yoga and humanities, yoga and life sciences, yoga and management studies, yoga and physical sciences, yoga and spirituality; Vice-Chancellor Prof. H. R. NAGENDRA.

Symbiosis International Education Centre: Senapati Bapat Rd, Pune 411004, Maharashtra; tel. (20) 25652444; fax (20) 25659209; e-mail siec@vsnl.net; internet www.symbiosis.ac.in; f. 1979; deemed univ. status 2002; constituent institutes: Centre for Information Technology, Centre for Management and Human Resource Development, Centre for Management Studies, College of Nursing, English Language Teaching Institute, Institute of Business Management, Institute of Computer Studies and Research, Institute of Design, Institute of Foreign and Indian Languages, Institute of Geo-informatics, Institute of Health Sciences, Institute of International Business, Institute of Management Studies, Institute of Mass Communication, Institute of Operations Management, Institute of Telecom Management, Law College; 217 teachers (43 full-time, 7 part-time, 167 visiting); 45,000 students; Vice-Chancellor Dr M. S. RASTE; Dir Dr VIDYA YERAVDEKAR; Registrar V. S. POL.

Tata Institute of Fundamental Research: Homi Bhabha Rd, Mumbai 400005, Maharashtra; tel. (22) 22782000; fax (22) 22804610; e-mail webmaster@tifr .res.in; internet www.tifr.res.in; f. 1945, deemed univ. status 2003; attached research centres: National Centre for Biological Sciences (Bangalore), National Centre for Radio Astrophysics (Pune), Homi Bhabha Centre for Science Education (Mumbai); attached field stations: Balloon Facility (Hyderabad), High Energy Gamma Ray Observatory (Panchmarhi), Radio Astronomy Centre (Ooty), TIFR Centre Maths (Bangalore), TIFR Gravitation Laboratory (Gauribidanur); schools of mathematics, natural sciences, technology and computer science; Dir Prof. MUSTANSIR BARMA.

Tata Institute of Social Sciences: POB 8313, Deonar, Mumbai 400088, Maharashtra; tel. (22) 25563289; fax (22) 25562912; e-mail sparasuraman@tiss.edu; internet www.tiss.edu; f. 1936, deemed univ. status 1964; schools of health systems studies, management and labour studies, rural devt, social sciences, social work; independent centres for lifelong learning, media and cultural studies, research methodology, Jamsetji Tata Centre for Disaster Management; library: 105,000 vols; 106 students; Dir Prof. S. PARASURAMAN; Registrar Dr SANDEEP CHATTERJEE; Librarian Dr M. KOGANURAMATH; publ. *The Indian Journal of Social Work*.

TERI University: India Habitat Centre, Lodi Rd, New Delhi 110003; Plot No 10, Institutional Area, Vasant Kunj, New Delhi; tel. (11) 26122222; fax (11) 26122874; e-mail registrar@teri.res.in; internet www .teriuniversity.ac.in; f. 1998, deemed univ. status 1999; faculties of applied sciences, policy and planning; Chancellor Dr R. K. PACHAURI; Vice-Chancellor Dr P. P. BHOJVAID (acting); Registrar RAJIV SETH.

Thapar University: POB 32 Patiala 147004, Punjab; tel. (175) 2393021; fax (175) 2364498; e-mail registrar@tiet.ac.in; internet www.tiet.ac.in; f. 1956, deemed univ. status 1985; schools of chemistry and biotechnology, management and social sciences, mathematics and computer applications, physics and material science; library: 55,000 vols; 102 teachers; 1,340 students; Dir Dr ABHIJIT MUKHERJEE; Registrar Brig. PARAMJIT SINGH; Registrar B. P. CHAUHAN; Dean of Academic Affairs Dr R. K. SHARMA; Dean of Research and Sponsored Projects Dr SUSHEEL MITTAL; Dean of Student Affairs Dr N. K. VERMA.

Tilak Maharashtra Vidyapeeth: Vidyapeeth Bhavan, Gultekdi, Pune 411037; tel. (20) 24261856; fax (20) 24266068; e-mail timavee@pn2.vsnl.net.in; internet www.tmv .edu.in; f. 1921; faculties of arts and fine arts, ayurveda, education, modern sciences and professional skills, moral and social sciences; campuses at Aurangabad, Delhi, Mumbai; library: 77,674 vols; 35 teachers; 5,508 students; Vice-Chancellor Dr DEEPAK TILAK; Registrar Dr UMESH KESKAR; Finance Officer PRADIP A. KHATAVKAR; Controller of Examinations JAGDISH SALVE; Librarian REVATI DESHMUKH.

Vinayaka Missions Research Foundation: NH-47 Sankari Main Rd, Ariyanoor, Salem 636308, Tamil Nadu; tel. (427) 3987000; fax (427) 2477903; e-mail vmtrust@vinayakamission.com; internet www.vinayakamission.com; f. 2001; faculties of allied health sciences, arts and sciences, dentistry, education, engineering technology and management sciences, homeopathy, int. dentistry, int. medicine, medicine, nursing, pharmacy, physical education, physiotherapy; 13 constituent colleges in Chennai, Karaikal, Pondicherry, Salem; Chancellor Dr A. SHANMUGASUNDARAM; Vice-Chancellor Prof. Dr V. R. RAJENDRAN; Controller of Examinations Dr A. BALASUNDARAM.

Visvesvaraya National Institute of Technology: South Ambazari Rd, Nagpur 440011, Maharashtra; tel. (712) 2226240; fax (712) 2223230; e-mail registrar@vnit.ac .in; internet www.vnitnagpur.ac.in; f. 1960, deemed univ. status 2002; depts of applied chemistry, applied mechanics, applied physics, architecture, civil engineering, electrical engineering, electronics and computer science, humanities, mathematics, mechanical engineering, metallurgical engineering, mining engineering; library: 90,838 vols, 166 periodicals; 1,500 undergraduates, 200 post-

graduates; Dir Dr S. S. GOKHALE; Registrar B. M. GANVEER; Librarian Dr H. T. THORAT.

Colleges
BUSINESS

Administrative Staff College of India: Bella Vista, Raj Bhavan Rd, Khairabad, Hyderabad 500082; tel. (40) 66533000; fax (40) 23312954; internet www.asci.org.in; f. 1956; conducts post-experience management devt programmes for officials in govt, execs and mans in industry and non-govt orgs; undertakes research and consultancy assignments for nat. and int. orgs; library: 74,000 vols, 500 periodicals, online databases; Dir-Gen. Dr S. K. RAO; Dean of Research and Consultancy Prof. M. CHANDRASEKHAR; Dean of Training and Confs Dr PARAMITA DAGUPTA; Registrar and Sec. Col (Retd) TEJINDER SINGH; Librarian Dr N. G. SATISH; publ. *ASCI Journal of Management* (2 a year).

Indian Institute of Management, Ahmedabad: Vastrapur, Ahmedabad 380015; tel. (79) 66324599; fax (79) 26306896; e-mail director@iimahd.ernet.in; internet www .iimahd.ernet.in; f. 1962; 2-year postgraduate, 4-year doctoral programme in management; gen. and functional management programmes for practising managers, and special programmes for govt officials, univ. teachers and sectors such as agriculture, public systems; undertakes project research and consulting in the field of management; 80 teachers; 400 postgraduate programme students; 50 PhD-level students; library: 148,600 vols; Chair. Dr VIJAYPAT SINGHANIA; Dir Prof. SAMIR K. BARUA; publ. *Vikalpa* (4 a year).

Indian Institute of Management, Bangalore: Bannerghatta Rd, Bangalore 560076; tel. (80) 26582450; fax (80) 26584050; e-mail info@iimb.ernet.in; internet www.iimb.ernet .in/iimb; f. 1973; postgraduate programmes; library: 209,000 vols, 34 online databases, 695 print journals, 850 electronic journals; 80 teachers; 425 students; Dir Prof. PANKAJ CHANDRA; publ. *IIMB Management Review* (2 a year).

Indian Institute of Management, Calcutta: Diamond Harbour Rd, Joka, Kolkata 700104, West Bengal; tel. (33) 24678310; fax (33) 24678307; e-mail director@iimcal.ac.in; internet www.iimcal.ac.in; f. 1961 to promote improvement in management through education, research and consultancy; 2-year MBA course in Computer-Aided Management, 3-year part-time MBA in business management; doctoral and extension courses; centres for studies in human values, devt and environment policy, rural devt and environment management; executive devt; faculty devt through research and consulting services; library: Dr B. C. Roy Memorial library of 125,000 vols; 77 teachers; 669 students; Dir Dr SHEKHAR CHAUDHURI; publs *Decision, Journal on Human Values* (2 a year).

Indian Institute of Management, Indore: Prabandh Shikhar, Pithampur Rd, Rau, Indore 453331, Madhya Pradesh; tel. (731) 4228400; fax (731) 4228800; e-mail webman@ iimidr.ac.in; internet www.iimidr.ac.in; f. 1997; library: 15,000 vols and 425 periodicals; 27 teachers; Dir Prof. N. RAVICHANDRAN; Chief Admin. Officer K. R. NARENDRA BABU; Librarian KISHOR SATPATHY; publ. *International Journal of Management Practices and Contemporary Thought (IMPACT)*.

Indian Institute of Management, Kozhikode: IIMK Campus P.O., Kozhikode 673570, Kerala; tel. (495) 2803001; fax (495)

2803010; e-mail director@iimk.ac.in; internet www.iimk.ac.in; f. 1996; library: 7,000 books, 1,120 periodicals; Dir Dr KRISHNA KUMAR; Librarian Dr M. G. SREEKUMAR.

Indian Institute of Management, Lucknow: Prabandh Nagar, Off Sitapur Rd, Lucknow 226013, Uttar Pradesh; tel. (522) 2734101; fax (522) 2734025; e-mail admission@iiml.ac.in; internet www.iiml.ac .in; f. 1984; 2-year postgraduate programme in agri-business management, exec. devt programmes; undertakes research and consulting projects in the field of management; main areas: agriculture, health, education, rural development, state public enterprises, corporate management, information technology and systems, entrepreneurship, corporate communication and media relations, leadership and human values; centre for entrepreneur devt and new venture management, agricultural management centre; library: Gyanodaya Library of 60,000 documents; 66 teachers; 480 postgraduate students; Dir Prof. PREM C. PURWAR; Dean of Academic Affairs Prof. YOGESH AGARWAL; Dean of Planning and Development Prof. SUKUMAR NANDI; publ. *Metamorphosis* (2 a year).

EDUCATION

National Institute of Educational Planning and Administration: 17-B Sri Aurobindo Marg, New Delhi 110016; tel. (11) 26863562; fax (11) 26853041; f. 1962; diploma courses for education personnel of developing countries and district education officers; other in-service training courses; research in various aspects of educational planning and management; consultancy service for developing countries, State govts and other orgs; collaboration with UNESCO and other foreign agencies; library: 45,963 vols, 350 current journals; Dir Prof. KULDEEP MATHUR; publs *Journal of Educational Planning and Administration* (4 a year), *Pariprakshya* (in Hindi).

GENERAL

Christ College Bangalore: Hosur Rd, Bangalore; tel. (80) 40129100; fax (80) 40129000; e-mail principal@christcollege .edu; internet www.christcollege.edu; depts of commerce/management, humanities, sciences, social sciences; College of Education, College of Law; library: 77,500 vols, 173 journals; Prin. Dr THOMAS C. MATHEW; Vice-Prin. Fr ABRAHAM.

Fergusson College: Pune 411004; tel. (20) 25654212; e-mail principal@fergusson.edu; internet www.fergusson.edu; f. 1885; affiliated to Univ. of Pune; library: 300,000 vols; Prin. Dr R. G. PARDESHI; Vice-Prin. Prof. D. V. KULKAMI.

Hans Raj College: Mahatma Hans Raj Marg, Malka Ganj, Delhi 110007; tel. (11) 27667747; fax (11) 27666338; e-mail principal@hrc.du.ac.in; internet www .hansrajcollege.com; f. 1948; Autonomous; BA in economics, English, Hindi, history, mathematics, Sanskrit; BSc in botany, chemistry, computer science, physics, zoology; constituent college of Univ. of Delhi; Prin. Dr S. R. ARORA; Librarian G. R. SHARMA.

Lady Shri Ram College for Women: Lajpat Nagar-IV, New Delhi 110024; tel. (11) 26434459; fax (11) 26216951; e-mail lsrc@vsnl.com; internet www.lsrcollege.org; f. 1956; depts of commerce, economics, education, English, Hindi, history, journalism, mathematics, philosophy, physical education, political science, psychology, Sanskrit, sociology, statistics; constituent college of

Delhi Univ.; 2,000 students; Prin. Dr MEENAKSHI GOPINATH; Librarian A. P. YADAV.

Loyola College: Chennai 600034, Tamil Nadu; tel. (44) 28178200; fax (44) 28175566; e-mail helpdesk@loyolacollege.edu; internet www.loyolacollege.edu; Autonomous; f. 1925; depts of advanced zoology and biotechnology, chemistry, commerce, computer science, economics, English, foreign languages, history and applied history, mathematics, oriental languages, philosophy, physical education, physics, plant biology and biotechnology, social work, sociology, statistics, Tamil, visual communication; Institutes of Dialogue with Cultures and Religions, Entomology Research, Frontier Energy, Industrial and Social Science Research, People Studies, Vocational Education; 116 teachers; 7,021 students; Prin. Fr A. ALBERT MUTHUMALAI; Dean of Students Prof. K. S. ANTONYSAMY; Controller of Examinations Prof. D. P. VENUGOPALAN; Librarian Prof. K. T. DILLI.

Madras Christian College: Tambaram, Chennai 600059, Tamil Nadu; tel. (44) 22397731; internet www.mcc.edu.in; f. 1837; Autonomous; depts of chemistry, commerce, economics, English, history, languages, mathematics, philosophy, physics, public admin., social work, statistics, Tamil; Prin. Dr V. J. PHILIP.

Presidency College, Chennai: Chennai; tel. (44) 28544894; fax (44) 28510732; e-mail info@presidencychennai.com; internet www.presidencychennai.com; f. 1840; Autonomous; faculties of arts and commerce, languages, science; library: 150,000 vols, 95 journals; Prin. Prof. M. DHANUSHKODI; Librarian K. V. RAMALINGAM.

Presidency College, Kolkata: 86/1 College St, Kolkata 700073, West Bengal; tel. (33) 22412738; e-mail contact@presidencycollegekolkata.ac.in; internet www.presidencycollegekolkata.ac.in; f. 1817 as Hindoo College, present name 1885; depts of Bengali, botany, chemistry, economics, English, geography, geology, Hindi, history, mathematics, philosophy, physics, physiology, political science, sociology, statistics, zoology; Prin. MAMATA RAY; Librarian DEBNARAYAN CHAKRABARTI.

St Joseph's College: PB 27094, 36 Lalbagh Rd, Bangalore 560027; tel. (80) 22211429; fax (80) 22272299; e-mail principal@sjc.ac.in; internet www.sjc.ac.in; Autonomous; f. 1882; Principal Dr. Fr AMBROSE PINTO; Vice-Principal Fr CLARENCE D'SOUZA.

St Stephen's College: University Enclave, Delhi 110007; tel. (11) 27667271; fax (11) 27667965; e-mail info@ststephens.edu; internet www.ststephens.edu; f. 1881; depts of chemistry, computer science, economics, English, history and political science, mathematics, philosophy, physics, Sanskrit and Hindi, Urdu, Persian; constituent college of Delhi Univ.; library: 12,000 vols; Prin. Rev. VALSON THAMPU; Vice-Prin. Dr M. S. FRANK; Dean NANDITA NARAIN; Dean of Academic Affairs Dr VIJAY TANKHA.

St Xavier's College, Ahmedabad: Navaranpura, Ahmedabad, Gujarat; internet www.stxavierscollege.net; depts of biochemistry, biology, chemistry, computer science, economics, electronics, English, Gujarati and Hindi, mathematics, physics, psychology, Sanskrit, statistics; Pres. Fr WILLIAM K. ABRANCHES; Vice-Pres. Fr AMALRAJ SEBASTIAN; Librarian HARBHAM JADEJA.

INSTITUTIONS:

Katha Xavier's Centre for Translation: f. 2003; conducts seminars on autobiographies of Gujarati mainstream writers; socially and politically marginalized figures in Gujarat's history; storytelling trad-

itions, myths, fables, fantasy tales, partition literature; Muslim narratives in Gujarati; research on literature of marginal communities of Dalits, Tribals, documentation of narratives by Parsis and Kutchis; Dir Dr RITA KOTHARI.

Xavier Research Foundation: f. 1995.

St Xavier's College, Kolkata: 30 Park St, Kolkata 700016; tel. (33) 22875995; fax (33) 22879966; e-mail principal@sxccal.edu; internet www.sxccal.edu; Autonomous; language of instruction: English; f. 1860; faculties of arts, business administration, commerce, education, science; library: 18,800 vols; Rector Rev. Fr GEORGE PONODATH; Prin. Rev. Fr Dr FELIX RAJ; Librarian Fr FELIX RAJ.

St Xavier's College, Mumbai: 5 Mahapalika Marg, Mumbai 400001; tel. (22) 22620661; fax (22) 22620665; e-mail admin@xaviers.edu; internet www.xaviers.edu; f. 1860; affiliated to Univ. of Mumbai; faculties of arts, business management, commerce, mass media, science; Institutes of Communication, Counselling, Management and Research, Social Research and Action; library: 12,000 vols; Prin. Fr FRAZER MASCARENHAS; Librarian MEDHA TASKAR.

Symbiosis College of Arts and Commerce: Senapati Bapat Marg, Pune 411004; tel. (20) 25653903; fax (20) 25651850; e-mail info@symbiosiscollege.org; internet www.symbiosiscollege.org; f. 1983; affiliated to Symbiosis Int. Univ.; Liberal Arts college; Dir Dr S. B. MUJUMDAR.

LANGUAGES

Central Institute of Indian Languages: Department of Higher Education, Language Bureau, Ministry of Human Resource Development, Government of India, Manasagangothri, Hunsur Rd, Mysore 570006; tel. (821) 2345031; fax (821) 2515032; e-mail udaya@ciil.stpmy.soft.net; internet www.ciil.org; f. 1969; assisting and coordinating the devt of Indian languages; preparation of grammars and dictionaries of tribal and border languages; inter-disciplinary research; preparation of materials for teaching and learning; 290 academic and technical staff; 7 Regional Language Centres in Mysore (languages: Kannada, Telugu, Malayalam, Tamil), Bhubaneswar (languages: Assamese, Bengali, Oriya), Pune (languages: Marathi, Gujarati, Sindhi), Patiala (languages: Urdu, Punjabi, Kashmiri), Solan (Urdu), Lucknow (Urdu) and Guwahati (north-eastern languages); centres for creative writing and lexicography, educational technology and media studies, excellence in classical languages, human resource development, information on language sciences, language planning, language technology, linguistic and cultural documentation, materials production, speech sciences, testing and evaluation, tribal and endangered languages; library: 63,000 vols and 250 periodicals; Dir Prof. UDAYA NARAYANA SINGH; Head, Centre for Applied Language Sciences Dr J. C. SHARMA; Head, Centre for Language Planning and Development Dr K. P. ACHARYA; Head, Centre for Language Technology Dr A. K. BASU; Head, Centre for Material Production, Testing and Evaluation B SYAMALA KUMARI; Head, Centre for Translation, Lexicography and Extension Dr P. N. DATTA BARUAH; publ. *New Language Planning Newsletter* (4 a year).

LAW

Amity Law School: *Delhi Campus* Yasho Bhawan (Adj. Escorts Heart Institute), Okhla Marg, New Delhi 110025; *Noida Campus* Sector 44 Noida (NCR), Uttar

Pradesh; tel. (11) 26325901; fax (11) 26325903; internet www.amity.edu/als; affiliated to Guru Gobind Singh Indraprastha Univ.; f. 2000; library: 150,000 vols, 80 periodicals; Dir (Delhi) Prof. M. K. BALACHANDRAN; Dir (Noida) Prof. S. P. SINGH.

Government Law College: A Rd, Churchgate, Mumbai 400020, Maharastra; tel. (22) 22041707; fax (22) 22851315; e-mail principal@glc.edu; internet www.glc.edu; f. 1855; library: 36,000 vols, 38 journals; publs *Journal of Law and Society*, *Law Review*; Prin. P. R. RAO.

ILS Law College: Law College Rd, Pune 411004, Maharashtra; tel. (20) 25678678; fax (20) 25658665; e-mail ilslaw@vsnl.com; internet www.ilslaw.edu; f. 1923; 3-year and 5-year LLB degree; Masters in Labour Laws, Labour Welfare; diploma in Taxation Laws; 1,600 students; library: 45,000 vols, 100 periodicals; Pres. Y. V. CHANDRACHUD; Vice-Pres. R. SHINDE; Prin. VAIJAYANTI JOSHI.

Indian Academy of International Law and Diplomacy: 9 Bhagwan Dass Rd, New Delhi 110001; tel. (11) 23384458; fax (11) 23383783; e-mail isil@giasdl01.vsnl.net.in; internet www.isil-aca.org/indian-academy-intl-law.htm; f. 1964; part of the Indian Society of International Law; includes a research institute and library; offers courses in int. law and diplomacy, human rights, int. humanitarian and refugee laws, int. trade and business law, law of air transport and aviation liability, int. law and law of int. instns; library: 25,000 vols; Pres. RAM NIWAS MIRDHA; publ. *Indian Journal of International Law* (4 a year).

Symbiosis Law School: Senapati Bapat Rd, Pune 411004; tel. (20) 25655114; fax (20) 25671711; e-mail info@symlaw.ac.in; internet www.symlaw.ac.in; f. 1977; constituent of Symbiosis Int. Univ.; Chancellor Dr S. B. MUJUMDAR; Vice-Chancellor Dr M. S. RASTE; Prin. Dr SHASHIKALA GURPUR; Librarian KALPANA JADHAV.

MEDICINE

All India Institute of Hygiene and Public Health: 110 Chittaranjan Ave, Kolkata 700073; tel. (33) 315286; f. 1932; constituent college of University of Calcutta; administered by Directorate-General of Health Services and Ministry of Health and Family Welfare; facilities for postgraduate work and medical research; depts of behavioural sciences, biochemistry and nutrition, epidemiology and health education, maternal and child health, microbiology, occupational health, public health administration, public health nursing, sanitary engineering, social and preventive medicine, statistics and demography, veterinary public health; Rural Health and Training Centre, Urban Health and Training Centre; offers diploma, certificate, and orientation courses; academic year July to June; 112 teachers (incl. 14 professors); 300 students; library: 85,000 vols, 250 current periodicals; Dir Prof. K. J. NATH.

Armed Forces Medical College: Wanowrie, Pune 411040; internet afmc.nic.in; f. 1948; library: 20,000 bound journals; Dir and Commandant Lt-Gen. S. K. SHARMA; Dean Maj.-Gen. G. RAVINDRANATH; publ. *Medical Journal Armed Forces of India (MJAFI)*.

Christian Medical College: Vellore 632004, Tamil Nadu; tel. (416) 2222102; fax (416) 2232035; e-mail directorate@cmcvellore.ac.in; internet www.cmch-vellore.edu; f. 1948; graduate courses in laboratory technology, medical records science, medicine, occupational therapy, physiotherapy; 11 postgraduate medical diploma courses; 23

postgraduate degree courses; 11 higher specialty courses; variety of allied health sciences diploma programmes; Dir Dr SURANJAN BHATTACHARJI; Dean, College of Nursing BHARATHI JACOB.

Jawaharlal Institute of Postgraduate Medical Education: Dhanvantri Nagar, Pondicherry 605006; tel. (413) 2272380; fax (413) 2272067; e-mail director@jipmer.edu .in; internet www.jipmer.edu; f. 1823 as Ecole de Medicine de Pondicherry, present name 1964; Govt control; affiliated to Pondicherry Univ.; depts of anaesthesiology, anatomy, biochemistry, cardiology, cardiothoracic and vascular surgery, dermatology, dentistry, ear, nose and throat, emergency medical services, forensic medicine and toxicology, medicine, medical education, microbiology, neurology, obstetrics and gynaecology, ophthalmology, orthopaedics, paediatrics, pathology, plastic surgery, pharmacology, physiology, preventive and social medicine, psychiatry, radiodiagnosis, radiotherapy, sexually transmitted diseases, surgery, tb and chest diseases, urology; Dir Dr SUBBA RAO; Dean Dr K. S. REDDY.

Kasturba Medical College, Manipal: Manipal Univ., Manipal 576104, Karnataka; tel. (820) 2922367; fax (820) 2571927; e-mail office.kmc@manipal.edu; internet www .manipal.edu; f. 1953; part of Manipal Univ.; depts of anatomy, ayurvedic medicine, biochemistry, biotechnology, community medicine, dermatology, ear, nose and throat, forensic medicine, hospital admin., laser spectroscopy, medical education, nephrology, obstetrics and gynaecology, ophthalmology, orthopaedics, paediatric surgery, pathology, plastic surgery, psychiatry, radiodiagnosis and imaging, surgery, tb and respiratory diseases, urology, yoga; Dean Dr P. SRIPATHI RAO; Librarian Dr SHIVANANDA BHAT.

Lady Hardinge Medical College: New Delhi 110001; e-mail lhmc@vsnl.com; f. 1914; library: 25,000 vols, 18,000 bound and 148 current periodicals; affiliated to Univ. of Delhi; depts of anaesthesiology, anatomy, biochemistry, ear, nose and throat, forensic medicine, microbiology, obstetrics and gynaecology, ophthalmology, orthosurgery, paediatrics, pathology, pharmacology, physiology, psychiatry, radiology, radiotherapy, skin, surgery, venereal diseases; Prin. Dr G. K. SHARMA.

Maulana Azad Medical College: Bahadur Shah Zafar Marg, New Delhi 110002; tel. (11) 23239271; e-mail info@mamc.ac.in; internet www.mamc.ac.in; f. 1959; depts of anaesthesia, anatomy, biochemistry, community medicine, dentistry, dermatology and sexually transmitted diseases, ear, nose and throat, forensic medicine, microbiology, obstetrics and gynaecology, orthopaedics, paediatrics, pathology, pharmacology, physiology, radiodiagnosis, radiotherapy, surgery; Dean Dr A. K. AGARWAL; Registrar S. M. HAIDER.

National Institute of Health and Family Welfare (NIHFW): Baba Gang Nath Marg, Munirka, New Delhi 110067; tel. (11) 26165959; fax (11) 26101623; e-mail director@nihfw.org; internet www.nihfw.org; f. 1977; in-service training, MD course in community health administration, biomedical research, research and consultancy; regional centre for health management; documentation and reprographic services; library: specialized library of 41,000 vols and 308 periodicals; Dir Prof. DEOKI NANDI;

publs *NIHFW Journal* (4 a year), Technical Report series.

TECHNOLOGY

See Institutes of National Importance for details of Indian Institutes of Technology.

Government College of Engineering and Ceramic Technology: 73, Abinash Chandra Banerjee Lane, Kolkata 700010, West Bengal; tel. (33) 23701264; fax (33) 23701264; e-mail gcect@rediffmail.com; internet www .gcect.ac.in; f. 1941 as Bengal Ceramic Institute, Calcutta; renamed the College of Ceramic Technology in 1962; present status in 2001; Prin. Dr ASIS KUMAR BANDYOPADHYAY.

Institute of Radiophysics and Electronics, University of Calcutta: 92 Acharya Prafulla Chandra Rd, Kolkata 700009, West Bengal; tel. (33) 23509115; fax (33) 23515828; e-mail bbandy@vsnl.com; internet www.irpel .org; f. 1949; houses postgraduate teaching and research dept of Univ. of Calcutta, Faculty of Technology; 3-year post-BSc integrated course leading to BTech. degree, and two-year post-BTech./BE course leading to MTech. degrees in radiophysics and electronics and in information technology; conducts training programmes; research facilities in ionosphere, radio wave propagation, radio astronomy, solid state and microwave electronics, millimetre wave technology, solid state devices, plasma and quantum electronics, optoelectronics, control systems and micro-computers, communication theory and systems, microelectronics and VLSI technology; maintains ionosphere field station at Haringhata and radio astronomy field station at Kalyani; recognized as a Centre of Advanced Study by the University Grants Commission; 36 teachers; 240 students; library: 18,000 vols, 5,000 journal issues; Head Dr BIJOY BANDYOPADHYAY.

National Institute of Fashion Technology: Hauz Khas, Near Gulmohar Park, New Delhi 110016; tel. (11) 26965080; fax (11) 26851198; e-mail admission@nift.ac.in; internet www.nift.ac.in; f. 1986; undergraduate and postgraduate diploma courses relevant to the textiles and clothing industries; library of 17,000 books and docs; campuses in New Delhi, Bangalore, Mumbai, Kolkata, Gandhinagar, Hyderabad, Chennai, Rae Bareli; Dir KALPANA SWAMY; Dean of Academics Prof. ASHA BAXI; Registrar MUNISH GIRIDHAR; publ. *Fashion and Beyond* (4 a year).

Schools of Art and Music

Academy of Architecture: 278 Shankar Ghanekar Marg, Prabhadevi, Mumbai 400025, Maharashtra; f. 1955; 5-year Govt Diploma courses in architecture; library: 5,600 vols and 2,000 slides; Prin. P. P. AMBERKAR.

Bharatiya Vidya Bhavan: Munshi Sadan, Bhartiya Vidya Bhavan Chowk, Kulapati Munshi Rd, Mumbai 400007, Maharashtra; tel. (22) 23631261; fax (22) 23630058; e-mail bhavan@bhavans.info; internet www .bhavans.info; f. 1938; revitalizes ancient Indian values to suit modern needs; postgraduate courses in Indology; colleges of arts, science, commerce and engineering; runs schools, Academy of Foreign Languages, College of Sanskrit; dept of Ancient Insights and Modern Discoveries; Ayurveda Research

Centre; Institute of Communication and Management; Institute of Management and Research; schools of music, dancing, dramatic art; library: 76,688 vols and 1,404 MSS; 31,450 mems; Pres. SURENDRALAL G. MEHTA; Vice-Pres MURLI S. DEORA B. N. SRIKRISHNA; Dir-Gen. and Exec. Sec. H. N. DASTUR; publs *Astrological Journal* (English and Gujarati, 1 a year), *Bharatiya Vidya* (Sanskrit, 4 a year), *Bhavan's Dimdima* (English, 12 a year children's magazine), *Bhavan's Journal* (26 a year), *Navneet* (Hindi, 12 a year), *Navneet-Samarpan* (Gujarati, 12 a year), *Samvid* (Sanskrit, quarterly), 11 vols of the *History and Culture of the Indian People*, and various series.

ATTACHED COLLEGE:

Bhavan's Sardar Patel College of Engineering: Munshi Nagar, Andheri (West), Mumbai 400058, Maharashtra; tel. (22) 26289777; fax (22) 26237819; e-mail spce01@bom2.vsnl.net.in; internet www.spce.ac.in; f. 1962; depts of civil, electrical, mechanical and structural engineering; Exec. Chair and Dean Dr M. L. SHRIKANT; Principal Dr S. Y. MHAISKAR; Librarian SANJAY JAYARAM SAWANT; library of 44,000 vols.

There are 12 affiliated colleges and 33 other institutions.

Kalakshetra Foundation: Tiruvanmiyur, Chennai 600041, Tamil Nadu; tel. (44) 24524057; fax (44) 24524359; e-mail director@kalakshetra.in; internet www .kalakshetra.in; f. 1936; centre for education in classical music, dancing, theatrical art, painting and handicrafts; maintains a weaving centre for the production of silk and cotton costumes in traditional design and a Kalamkari Unit for dyeing and hand-block printing with vegetable dyes; Dr U. V. Swaminatha Aiyar library noted for classical MSS and literature in Tamil; library: 10,000 books on dance, music, painting, literature and religion; Dir LEELA SAMSON; Sec R. V. RAMANI.

Music Academy: 168 T. T. K. Rd, Royapettah, Chennai 600014, Tamil Nadu; tel. (44) 28112231; fax (44) 42359362; e-mail music@ musicacademymadras.com; internet www .musicacademymadras.in; f. 1927; research and study of Indian music; directs the Teachers' College of Music; library: 5,300 vols; Pres. N. MURALI; Vice-Pres HABIBULLAH BADSHA, C. V. KARTHIK NARAYANAN, L. VISWANATHAN, P. OBUL REDDY, R. SESHSAYEE, R. SRINIVASAN; publ. *Journal*.

National School of Drama: Bahawalpur House, 1 Bhagwandas Rd, New Delhi 110001; tel. (11) 23382821; fax (11) 23384288; e-mail info@nsd.gov.in; internet nsd.gov.in; f. 1959; 3-year diploma course for a maximum of 20 students in each class, short-term theatre training workshops; Theatre-in-Education Company working with and performing for children; library: 28,000 vols, 2,500 slides, records, etc.; 16 teachers; 60 students; Dir Dr ANURADHA KAPUR; Registrar D. R. SARIN; publs *Rang Prasang* (in Hindi, 2 a year), *Theatre India* (in English, 2 a year).

Sri Varalakshmi Academies of Fine Arts: Ramavilas, Kashipathy Agarahar, Chamaraja Double Rd, Mysore 4; f. 1945; educational and cultural research instn; gives advanced courses of study in Karnataka music; library: 5,000 vols; Prin. Vidwan C. V. SRIVATSA; Head Research Dept Prof. R. SATHYANARAYANA.

INDONESIA

The Higher Education System

The oldest institution of higher education is the Institut Teknologi Bandung (Bandung Institute of Technology), which was founded in 1920 when Indonesia was part of the Dutch East Indies. In 1949 Indonesia gained independence from the Netherlands. The Portuguese colony of Timor-Leste (formerly East Timor) was annexed in 1975 and administered as a province of Indonesia until 1999, when it was transferred to a UN transitional administration before achieving sovereign independence in 2002. Higher education facilities consist of different types of institutions, which include public and private universities (universitas), higher colleges (sekolah tinggi), teacher training institutes (institut keguruan dan ilmu pendidikan), Islamic universities (universitas Islam), Christian universities (universitas Kristen), academies (akademi) and polytechnics (politeknik). Universities (including the three technical institutes) offer a full range of undergraduate and postgraduate degrees; teacher training institutes and Islamic universities have degree-awarding powers; academies are specialized institutions of higher education related to a particular profession; and polytechnics are technical and vocational institutions offering diploma-level education. In 2007/08 there were 2,680 tertiary institutions with a total enrolment of 3,805,287 students. The Directorate-General of Higher Education is the government body responsible for overall control of higher education, but the Directorate of Islamic Higher Education is responsible for the Islamic universities.

Admission to public universities is on the basis of the Entrance Examination to State Universities (Ujian Masuk Perguruan Tinggi Negeri), while admission to polytechnics requires the applicant to complete secondary education and sit an entrance examination (Ujian Masuk Politeknik). The Entrance Examination to State Universities is divided into two streams, social sciences and natural sciences. Institutions may also make an offer of admission based on Interest and Ability Tracing (Penelusuran Minat dan Kemampuan), a system for monitoring secondary school students.

Indonesia operates a US-style 'credit semester' system for awarding undergraduate and postgraduate degrees, divided into three stages (sarjana). The first stage is the undergraduate degree (Sarjana Satu), the course for which lasts a minimum of eight semesters (four years) and requires 144–160 credits. Degrees in professional fields, such as medicine, dentistry, veterinary science and engineering, may last for an additional one to three years. The second stage (and first postgraduate degree) is the Magister, a course of study requiring 36–50 credits and lasting at least four semesters (two years). The third and last stage is the Doktor, also lasting at least four semesters (two years) and requiring a further 40–60 credits.

Post-secondary technical and vocational education is offered by polytechnics and academies. Students are awarded one of four diplomas (D1–D4) depending on length of course (one to four years) or area of specialization. The diploma D4 is regarded as equivalent to the Sarjana Satu. There are also two 'specialist' vocational qualifications, Ijazah Spesialis (SP1), awarded after two years and requiring 26–50 credits, and Ijazah Spesialis (SP2), awarded after 40–50 credits have been accrued following SP1.

The National Accreditation Board for Higher Education (Badan Akreditasi Nasional Perguruan Tinggi) was founded in 1994 as part of the Directorate-General of Higher Education and is the body responsible for accrediting both public and private institutions of higher education. Courses are ranked on a scale A–D, with A being 'very good' and D 'unsatisfactory'. C is the minimum requirement for accreditation. The board started piloting institutional accreditation by early 2008.

Regulatory and Representative Bodies

GOVERNMENT

Direktorat Jenderal Pendidikan Tinggi (Directorate-General of Higher Education): Ditjen DIKTI, Jl. Pintu Timur Senayan, Jakarta; e-mail dikti@dikti.go.id; internet www.dikti.go.id; Dir-Gen. Prof. Dr BAMBANG SUDIBYO.

Ministry of Culture and Tourism: Sapta Pesona Bldg, Jl. Medan Merdeka Barat 17, Jakarta 10110; tel. (21) 3838167; fax (21) 3849715; e-mail pusdatin@budpar.go.id; internet www.budpar.go.id; Min. JERO WATJIK.

Ministry of National Education: Jl. Jenderal Sudirman, Senayan, Jakarta 12070; tel. (21) 57950226; fax (21) 5701088; e-mail pengaduan@kemdiknas.go.id; internet www.kemdiknas.go.id; Min. MOHAMMAD NUH.

ACCREDITATION

Badan Akreditasi Nasional Perguruan Tinggi (National Accreditation Board for Higher Education): Komplek Ditjen Jend. Mandikdasmen, Depdiknas RI, Gd D, Lantai 1, Jl. RS. Fatmawati Cipete, Jakarta 12410; tel. and fax (21) 7668690; e-mail sekretariat.banpt@gmail.com; internet ban-pt.depdiknas.go.id; f. 1994; Chair. Prof. KAMANTO SUNARTO.

Learned Societies

GENERAL

Jajasan Kerja-Sama Kebudajaan (Foundation for Cultural Cooperation): Jl. Gajah Mada 13, Bandung 40115; promotes cooperation and mutual understanding between the countries of Western Europe and Indonesia; Rep. for Indonesia A. KOOLHAAS.

BIBLIOGRAPHY, LIBRARY SCIENCE AND MUSEOLOGY

Asosiasi Museum Indonesia (Indonesian Museum Association): c/o Museum Nasional, Jl. Merdeka Barat 12, Jakarta 10110; tel. (21) 3868172; fax (21) 3811076; e-mail asosiasi_museum_indonesia@yahoo.com; internet www.asosiasimuseumindonesia.or.id; f. 2004; Chair. Drs SOETRISNO.

Ikatan Pustakawan Indonesia (Indonesian Library Association): Jl. Salemba Raya 28A, Jakarta 10430; tel. and fax (21) 7872353; f. 1954; Pres. DADY P. RACHIMANANTA; Sec.-Gen. H. ZULFIKAR ZEN.

EDUCATION

UNESCO Office Jakarta and Regional Science Bureau for Asia and the Pacific: Jl. Galuh (II) No. 5, Kebayoran Baru, POB 1273/JKT, Jakarta 12110; tel. (21) 7399818; fax (21) 72796489; e-mail jakarta@unesco.org; internet www.unesco.or.id; represents Brunei, Indonesia, Malaysia, Philippines and Timor-Leste; Dir Dr HUBERT GIJZEN.

LANGUAGE AND LITERATURE

Alliance Française: Jl. Raya Puputan I, 13A, Denpasar 80235; tel. and fax (361) 234143; e-mail info@afdenpasar.org; internet www.afdenpasar.org; offers courses and examinations in French language and culture and promotes cultural exchange with France; centres in Balikpapan, Bandung, Denpasar, Lampung, Manado, Medan, Padang and Semarang; Dir AUDREY LAMOU; Librarian FEYBE I. MOKOGINTA.

British Council: S. Widjojo Centre, Jl. Jenderal Sudirman Kav 71, Jakarta 12190; tel. (21) 2524115; fax (21) 2524129; e-mail information@britishcouncil.or.id; internet www.britishcouncil.org/indonesia; teaching centre; offers courses and examinations in English language and British culture and promotes cultural exchange with the UK; attached office in Surabaya; library of 18,000 vols; Dir Dr PATRICK BRAZIER; Man., English Language Services SIMON COLLEDGE.

Goethe-Institut: Jl. Sam Ratulangi 9–15, POB 3640, Jakarta 10350; tel. (21) 23550208; fax (21) 23550021; e-mail info@jakarta.goethe.org; internet www.goethe.de/jakarta; f. 1961; offers courses and examinations in German language and culture and promotes cultural exchange with Germany; attached centre in Bandung; library of 8,500 vols,

1,600 audiovisual items, 40 periodicals; Dir FRANZ XAVER AUGUSTIN.

MEDICINE

Ikatan Dokter Indonesia (Indonesian Medical Association): Jl. Dr Sam Ratulangi 29, Menteng, Jakarta 10350; tel. (21) 3150679; fax (21) 3900473; e-mail pbidi@ idola.net.id; internet www.idionline.org; f. 1950; 45,131 mems; Chair. Prof. Dr FACHMI IDRIS; Sec.-Gen. Dr SLAMET BUDIARTO; publs BIDI (26 a year), Majalah Kedokteran Indonesia (12 a year).

NATURAL SCIENCES

Physical Sciences

Astronomical Association of Indonesia: Jakarta Planetarium, Cikini Raya 73, Jakarta 10330; tel. (21) 2305146; fax (21) 2305147; f. 1920; promotes advancement of astronomical science; Chair. Prof. Dr BAMBANG HIDAYAT; Sec. Drs S. DARSA; Treas. Dr WINARDI SUTANTYO.

TECHNOLOGY

Persatuan Insinyur Indonesia (Indonesian Institute of Engineers): 39 Jl. Halimun, Jakarta 12980; tel. (21) 8352180; fax (21) 83700663; e-mail info@pii.or.id; internet www.pii.or.id; 27,000 mems; Pres. ABURIZAL BAKRIE; Sec.-Gen. I. SUCIPTO UMAR.

Research Institutes

GENERAL

Lembaga Ilmu Pengetahuan Indonesia (Indonesian Institute of Sciences): Jl. Jendral Gatot Subroto 10, Jakarta 12710; tel. (21) 5251542; fax (21) 5207226; e-mail kepala@ lipi.go.id; internet www.lipi.go.id; f. 1967; govt agency; promotes the devt of science and technology; serves as the nat. centre for regional and int. scientific cooperation; organizes nat. research centres; library of 150,000 titles; Head Prof. Dr UMAR ANGGARA JENIE; publs Annales Bogorienses (2 a year), Berita Biologi (4 a year), Berita Iptek (4 a year), IPT Technical Journal (4 a year), Jurnal Kimia Terapan Indonesia (3 a year), Journal of Tropical Ethnobiology (2 a year), Jurnal Ekonomi dan Pembangunan (2 a year), Jurnal Elektronika dan Pembangunan (6 a year), Jurnal Masyarakat dan Budaya (2 a year), Jurnal Penduduk dan Pembangunan (2 a year), Jurnal Teknologi Informasi (3 a year), Korosi: Majalah Ilmu dan Teknologi (2 a year), Limnotek (2 a year), Majalah Perencanaan LIPI (2 a year), Majalah Widyariset (12 a year), Masyarakat Indonesia: Majalah Ilmu-ilmu Sosial Indonesia (2 a year), Oseanologi dan Limnologi di Indonesia (6 a year), Prosea Newsletter (4 a year), Reinwardtia: A Journal on Taxonomic Botany, Plant Sociology and Ecology (irregular), Riset Geologi dan Pertambangan, Telaah: Berkala Ilmu Pengetahuan dan Teknologi (2 a year), Treubia: Journal on Zoology of the Indo-Australian Archipelago (irregular), Warta Biotek (4 a year), Warta KIM (12 a year), Warta Kimia Analitik (2 a year), Warta Oseanografi (4 a year).

AGRICULTURE, FISHERIES AND VETERINARY SCIENCE

Badan Penelitian dan Pengembangan Kehutanan (Forestry Research and Development Agency): Manggala Wanabakti Bldg, Blk 1, 11 Fl., Jl. Jend. Gatot Subroto, Jakarta 10270; tel. (21) 5730392; fax (21) 5720189; e-mail datinfo@forda-mof.org; internet www .forda-mof.org; f. 1983; attached to Kementerian Kehutanan (Min. of Forestry); 390

research scientists; library of 34,005 vols, 2,848 vols in reference colln, 6,321 textbooks; Dir-Gen. TACHRIR FATHONI; Sec. PUTERA PARTHAMA; Sec.-Gen. BOEN M. PURNAMA; publs Journal of Forestry Research (2 a year), Journal of Forestry Policy Analysis (series, 3 a year), Journal of Forest and Nature Conservation Research (5 or 6 a year), Journal of Forest Products Research (4 a year), Forest Product Bulletin (2 a year), Forestry Socio Economic Journal (4 a year), Info Hutan (4 or 6 a year), Info Sosial Ekonomi Kehutanan (magazine, 4 a year), Mitra Hutan Tanaman (3 a year), Plantation Forest Research Journal (3 a year), Tekno Hutan Tanaman (3 a year).

Balai Besar Industri Agro (Centre for Agro-Based Industry): Jl. Ir H. Juanda 11, Bogor 16122; tel. (251) 8324068; fax (251) 8323339; e-mail cabi@bbia.go.id; internet www.bbia.go.id; f. 1909; attached to Min. of Industry; provides services for agriculture-based industry through training, consultancy, chemical and microbiological testing, research and devt, certification, environmental management, technical inspection, design engineering on food processing and calibration; Dir YANG YANG SETIAWAN; publ. Warta IHP (Journal of Agro-Based Industry, 2 a year).

Balai Besar Penelitian Veteriner Bogor (Indonesian Research Centre for Veterinary Science (IRCVS), Indonesian Agency for Agricultural Research and Development (IAARD), Ministry of Agriculture): Jl. R. E. Martadinata 30, POB 151, Bogor 16164; tel. (251) 8331048; fax (251) 8336425; e-mail balivet@indo.net.id; internet bbalitvet .litbang.deptan.go.id; f. 1908; depts of bacteriology, toxicology and mycology, parasitology, pathology, virology, balitvet culture colln (BCC), BSL-3 Modular Laboratory; library of 12,627 vols, 92 e-books and 1,119 journals; Head Dr HARDIMAN.

Balai Penelitian Bioteknologi Perkebunan Indonesia (Indonesian Biotechnology Research Institute for Estate Crops): Jl. Salak 1A, Bogor 16151; tel. (251) 8333382; fax (251) 8315985; e-mail ipardboo@indo.net .id; internet www.ipard.com; f. 1933; supportive research in plant molecular biology and immunology, microbes and bioprocessing; library of 13,493 vols, 1,597 periodicals, 3,109 reprints, 70 theses; Head of Unit Dr Ir DARMONO TANIWIRYONO; publ. Menara Perkebunan (in English and Indonesian, 2 a year).

Pusat Penelitian dan Pengembangan Hortikultura (Indonesian Centre for Horticulture Research and Development (ICHORD)): Jl. Raya Ragunan 29A, Pasarminggu, Jakarta 12520; tel. (21) 7805768; fax (21) 7805135; e-mail puslitbanghorti@litbang .deptan.go.id; internet hortikultura.litbang .deptan.go.id; research and devt of horticultural crops; Dir Dr YUSDAR HILMAN; publs IPTEK (1 a year), Jurnal Hortikultura (4 a year), Katalog (1 a year).

Attached Institutes:

Balai Penelitian Tanaman Buah Tropika (Indonesian Tropical Fruit Research Institute): Jl. Raya Solok-Aripan Km 8.

Pusat Penelitian dan Pengembangan Peternakan (Central Research Institute for Animal Sciences Research and Development): Jl. Raya Pajajaran, Kav E-59, Bogor, West Java 16151; tel. (251) 322185; fax (251) 328283; e-mail criansci@indo.net.id; internet peternakan.litbang.deptan.go.id; f. 1950; researches into farm animals and animal parasites and diseases; library of 14,000 vols, 1,199 periodicals; Dir Dr BESS TIASNAMURTI; publs Ilmu Peternakan dan Veteriner (4 a year), Indonesian Journal of Animal and Veterinary Sciences, Proceedings of the

National Seminar (1 a year), Wartazoa (4 a year).

Pusat Penelitian dan Pengembangan Tanaman Pangan (Centre for Food Crops Research and Development): Jl. Merdeka 147, Bogor 16111; tel. (251) 334089; fax (251) 312755; internet www.puslittan.bogor .net; f. 1961; food crops research and devt; library of 3,000 vols; Dir Dr ACHMAD M. FAGI; publ. Contributions of CRIFC (4–6 a year).

Attached Institutes:

Balai Penelitian Bioteknologi Tanaman Pangan (Research Institute for Biotechnology of Food Crops): Jl. Tentara Pelajar 3A, Bogor 16111; tel. (251) 337975; fax (251) 338820; Dir Dr DJOKO S. DAMARDJATI; publs Buletin Penelitian (Research Bulletin, 2–4 a year), Penelitian Pertanian (Agricultural Research, 3–4 a year, in Indonesian and English).

Balai Penelitian Tanaman Jagung dan Serealia Lain (Research Institute for Maize and Other Cereals): Jl. Ratulangi, Kotak Pos 173, Maros 90511, Ujung Pandang, Sulawesi Selatan Telp; tel. (411) 371016; fax (411) 318148; Dir Dr MARSUM DAHLAN; publ. Agrikam: Buletin Penelitian Pertanian (Agricultural Research Bulletin, 2–4 a year, with English summary).

Balai Penelitian Tanaman Kacang-kacangan dan Umbi-umbian Malang (Research Institute for Legumes and Root Crops): Jl. Raya Kendal Payak, Kotak Pos 66, Malang, Jawa Timur 65101; tel. (341) 81468; fax (341) 318148; Dir Dr SUYAMTO; publ. Penelitian Palawija (Palawija Research, 2 a year, in Indonesian, and abstract in English).

Balai Penelitian Tanaman Padi (Research Institute for Rice): Jl. Raya 9, Sukamandi—Tromol Pos 11, Cikampek Subang, Jawa Barat 41255; tel. (264) 520157; fax (264) 520158; Dir Dr ANDI HASANUDDIN; publ. Media Sukamandi (Research at Sukamandi, 2–4 a year, with English summary).

Balai Penelitian Tanaman Pangan Lahan Rawa (Research Institute for Food Crops on Swampy Areas): Jl. Kebun Karet, Lok Tabat, Kotak Pos 31, Kalimantan, Selatan Banjarbaru 70712; tel. (511) 4772534; fax (511) 4773034; Dir ACHMADI; publ. Pemberitaan Penelitian (2–4 a year, in Indonesian and English).

Pusat Penelitian Kelapa Sawit (Indonesian Oil Palm Research Institute): Jl. Brigjen Katamso 51, Medan 20158; tel. (61) 7862477; fax (61) 7862488; e-mail admin@iopri.org; internet www.iopri.org; f. 1916; promotes agricultural improvement on the member estates; library of 11,000 vols, 20,000 periodicals; Dir Dr Ir WITJKSANA; publs Berita (in Indonesian), Bulletin (4 a year, in Indonesian with English summaries), Oil Palm Statistics (in Indonesian), Rainfall Records (in Indonesian).

Pusat Penelitian Perkebunan Gula Indonesia (Indonesian Sugar Research Institute): Jl. Pahlawan 25, Pasuruan 67126; tel. (343) 421086; fax (343) 421178; e-mail puslitgula@ipard.com; f. 1887; 150 staff; library of 15,000 vols; Dir Dr MIRZAWAN PDN; publs Berita (Communications), Bulletin (2 a year, in Indonesian), Majalah Penelitian Gula (Sugar Journal, 4 a year).

Pusat Penelitian Tanah dan Agroklimat (Soil and Agricultural Climate Research Centre): Jl. Ir H. Juanda 98, Bogor 16123; f. 1905; library of 4,000 vols; Dir Dr SYARIFUDDIN KARAMA.

ARCHITECTURE AND TOWN PLANNING

Research Institute for Human Settlements and United Nations Regional Centre for Research on Human Settlements: Jl. Panyawungan, Cileunyi, Wetan, Kab. Bandung 40393; tel. (22) 798393; fax (22) 798392; e-mail inge@bdg.centrin.net.id; f. 1953; researches on housing, bldgs, etc.; library of 29,000 vols; Dir SUTIKUI UTORO; publs *Buku Petunjuk Pedesaan* (in Bahasa Indonesian), *Jurnal Penelitian Pemutiman* (4 a year, in Bahasa Indonesian), *Masalah Bangunan* (4 a year, in English).

ECONOMICS, LAW AND POLITICS

Badan Pusat Statistik (BPS Statistics Indonesia): Jl. Dr Sutomo 6–8, Jakarta 10710; tel. (21) 3841195; fax (21) 3857046; e-mail bpshq@bps.go.id; internet www.bps.go.id; f. 1960; library of 60,000 vols, 1,100 periodicals; Dir Dr SOEDARTI SURBAKTI.

Centre for Strategic and International Studies: Jakarta Post Bldg, Third Fl., Jl. Palmerah Barat 142–243, Jakarta 10270; tel. (21) 53654601; fax (21) 53654607; e-mail csis@csis.or.id; f. 1971; policy-oriented studies in int. and nat. affairs in collaboration with industry, commerce, and the political, legal and journalistic communities; library of 50,000 vols, 377 journals and 20 newspapers; Exec. Dir Dr HADI SOESASTRO; publs *Analisis CSIS* (4 a year), *The Indonesian Quarterly* (in English).

Indonesian Institute of World Affairs: c/o University of Indonesia, Jakarta; Chair. Prof. SUPOMO; Sec. SUDJATMOKO.

Lembaga Administrasi Negara (National Institute of Public Administration): Jl. Veteran 10, Jakarta 10110; tel. (21) 3868201; fax (21) 3848792; e-mail humas@lan.go.id; internet www.lan.go.id; f. 1957; library of 16,712 vols; Chair. Dr ASMAWI REWANSYAH; publs *Jurnal Administrasi Negara*, *Jurnal Administrasi Publik*, *Jurnal Administrator Borneo*, *Jurnal Diklat Aparatur*, *Jurnal Ilmu Administrasi*, *Manajemen Pembangunan*.

Lembaga Pers dan Pendapat Umum (Press and Public Opinion Institute, Ministry of Information): Pegangsaan Timur 19B, Jakarta; f. 1953; audience research of press, film and radio; library of 4,500 vols; Dir Dr MARBANGUN.

HISTORY, GEOGRAPHY AND ARCHAEOLOGY

Dinas Intelijen Medan & Geografi Jawatan Topografi TNI-AD (Geographical Institute): Jl. Dr Wahidin 1/11, Jakarta; Dir Capt. AMARUL AMRI.

Direktorat Perlindungan dan Pembinaan Peninggalan Sejarah dan Purbakala (Directorate for the Protection and Development of the Historical and Archaeological Heritage): Jl. Cilacap 4, POB 2533, Jakarta; Dir UKA TJANDRASASMITA.

Pusat Penelitian Arkeologi (Research Centre of Archaeology): Jl. Raya Condet Pejaten 4, Pasar Minggu, Jakarta 12510; tel. (21) 7988131; fax (21) 7988187; e-mail arkenas@bit.net.id; brs in Yogyakarta, Denpasar, Palembang, Bandung, Banjarmasin, Makassar, Manado, Ambon and Jayapura; library of 15,000 vols; Dir Dr HARIS SUKENDAR; publs *Aspects*, *Amerta*, *Bulletin*, *Kalpataru*.

LANGUAGE AND LITERATURE

Pusat Bahasa. Departemen Pendidikan Nasional (Language Centre of the Ministry of National Education): POB 6259, Jl. Daksinapati Barat IV, Rawamangun, Jakarta 13220; tel. (21) 4706678; fax (21) 4750407; e-mail masterfbs@bahasa-sastra.web.id; f. 1975; language-planning policies, research in linguistics and vernaculars, compiling of dictionaries, coordinating and supervising language devt and cultivation, applied research in language education; library of 20,000 vols; Dir DENDY SUGONO; publs *Bahasa dan Sastra* (6 a year), *Informasi Pustaka Kebahasaan* (4 a year), *Lembar Komunikasi* (6 a year).

MEDICINE

Badan Pengawas Obat dan Makanan (National Agency of Drug and Food Control): Jl. Percetakan Negara 23, Jakarta 10560; tel. (21) 42883309; fax (21) 42889117; e-mail informasi@pom.go.id; internet www.pom.go.id; f. 2000; legislation, regulation and standardization of drug and food industries; licensing and certification of pharmaceutical industry; evaluation of products; sampling and laboratory testing of products; inspection of production and distribution facilities; investigation and law enforcement; auditing of product advertising and promotion; research on drug and food policy implementation; public communication, information and education; Head Dra KUSTANTINAH; Sec. Dr M. HAYATIE AMAL.

Central Institute for Leprosy Research: Jl. Kimia 17, Jakarta; f. 1935; incl. clinic and laboratory; Dir MOH. ARIF.

Laboratorium Kesehatan Daerah (Pathological Laboratory, Ministry of Health): Jl. Rawasari Slt 2, Jakarta 10510; tel. (21) 4247408; f. 1906; investigation and control of contagious and endemic diseases in Sumatra; library of 3,000 vols; Dir Dr ISKAK KOIMAN.

Laboratorium Kesehatan Pusat Lembaga Eijkman (Eijkman Institute): Library, Clinical Pathology Dept, Medical Faculty of the University of Indonesia, Ciptomangunkusumo Hospital, Jl. Diponegoro 69–71, Jakarta 10010; tel. (21) 332265; fax (21) 3147713; f. 1888; bacteriological-serological dept, chemical dept and virus division; publs reports, papers; Head Dr HENDRO JOEWONO.

Lembaga Malaria (Malaria Institute, Ministry of Health): Jl. Percetakan Negara 29, Jakarta; tel. (21) 417608; fax (21) 4207807; f. 1920; Dir Dr P. R. ARBANI.

Perusahaan Negara Bio-Farma (Pasteur Institute): Jl. Pasteur 9, POB 47, Bandung 40161; Dir M. S. NASUTION.

Pusat Penelitian dan Pengembangan Pelayanan dan Technologi Kesehatan (Health Services and Technology Research and Development Centre): Jl. Indrapura 17, Surabaya 60176; tel. (31) 3528748; fax (31) 3528749; internet www.litbang.depkes.go.id/p4tk Jl. Percetakan Negara 23A, Jakarta 10560; tel. (21) 4243314; fax (21) 4211013; f. 1975; library of 14,500 books, 750 magazine titles; Dir Dr H. SUWANDI MAKMUR; publs *Bulletin of Health System Research* (2 a year), *Warta JIP* (4 a year).

Unit Diponegoro (Nutrition Institute): c/o Nutrition Centre, Seameo Tropmed–U.I., Campus University of Indonesia, Salemba 4, Jakarta; f. 1937; Dir Dradjat D. PRAWIRANEGARA.

NATURAL SCIENCES

General

Institut de Recherche pour le Développement (IRD): Wisma Anugraha, Jl. Taman Kemang 32B, Jakarta 12730; tel. (21) 71792114; fax (21) 71792179; e-mail ird-indo@rad.net.id; internet www.id.ird.fr; f. 1944; (see main entry under France); agroforestry, agronomy, anthropology, aquaculture, archaeology, ethno-ecology, fisheries, geography; Dir Dr PATRICE LEVANG.

Biological Sciences

Pusat Penelitian Biologi (Research Centre for Biology): Jl. Raya Jakarta, Bogor Km 46, Cibinong, Bogor 16911; tel. and fax (21) 8797612; e-mail biologi@mail.lipi.go.id; internet biologi.lipi.go.id; f. 1817; 424 mems; library of 49,180 vols, 4,393 bound periodicals, c. 600 current periodicals, 24,587 reprints, 4,377 unpublished reports, 7,155 newspaper clippings, 2,463 maps; Dir Dr SITI NURAMALIATI PRIJONO; publs *Berita Biologi*, *Reinwardtia*, *Treubia*, *Laporan Tahunan*, *Laporan Teknik* (1 a year), *Laporan Kemajuan* (4 a year), *Warta Kita* (6 a year), *pamphlets*.

Attached Institutes:

Balai Penelitian dan Pengembangan Botani (Research and Development Institute for Botany): Jl. Raya Juanda 22, Bogor; f. 1884; Head Dr JOHANIS PALAR MOGEA.

Balai Penelitian dan Pengembangan Mikrobiologi (Research and Development Institute for Microbiology): c/o Kebun Raya Indonesia; f. 1884; Head Dr SUBADRI ABDULKADIR.

Balai Penelitian dan Pengembangan Zoologi (Research and Development Institute for Zoology): Jl. Raya Juanda 3, Bogor; Head Drs MOHAMAD AMIR.

UPT Balai Pengembangan Kebun Raya (Bogor Botanical Gardens):; f. 1817; Head Dr SUHIRMAN; publs *Alphabetical List of Plant Species*, *Buletin Kebun Raya* (4 a year), *Index Seminum* (1 a year), *Warta Kebun Raya* (irregular).

Physical Sciences

Badan Meteorologi Klimatologi dan Geofisika (Meteorology, Climatology and Geophysics Agency): Jl. Angkasa 1, No. 2, Kemayoran, POB 3540, Jakarta 10720; tel. (21) 4246321; fax (21) 4246314; internet www.bmkg.go.id; drafting nat. policies relating to meteorology, climatology and geophysics; data and information services; research and devt; Dir-Gen. Dr WORO B. HARIJONO.

Dinas Geodesi, Jawatan Topografi TNI-AD (Geodetic Section, Army Topographic Service): Jl. Bangka 1, Bandung; f. 1855; library of 2,000 vols, 2,500 periodicals; Dir MOH TAWIL.

Badan Tenaga Nuklir Nasional (National Atomic Energy Agency): Jl. Kuningan Barat, Mampang Prapatan, POB 4390, Jakarta 12710; tel. (21) 5251109; fax (21) 5251110; e-mail humas@batan.go.id; internet www.batan.go.id; Dir-Gen. DJALI AHIMSA.

Observatorium Bosscha (Bosscha Observatory): Jl. Peneropongan Bintang, Lembang, Java; tel. and fax (22) 2786001; e-mail kunjungan@as.itb.ac.id; internet bosscha.itb.ac.id; f. 1925; since 1951 the observatory has been part of the Dept of Astronomy, Bandung Institute of Technology, Bandung; Dir Dr BAMBANG HIDAYAT; publs *Annals* (irregular), *Contributions* (irregular).

Pusat Penelitian Oseanografi (Research Centre for Oceanography): Jl. Pasir Putih 1, Ancol Timur, POB 4801/JKTF, Jakarta 14430; tel. (21) 64713850; fax (21) 64711948; e-mail p30.lipi@jakarta.wasantara.net.id; internet www.oseanologi.lipi.go.id; f. 1905; library of 2,000 vols, 250 periodical titles; Dir Dr Ir KURNAN SUMADHIHARYA; publs *Marine Research in Indonesia* (irregular), *Oseana* (4 a year), *Oseanologi di Indonesia* (irregular).

Pusat Survei Geologi (Centre for Geological Survey): Jl. Diponegoro 57, Bandung 40122; tel. and fax (22) 7218482; e-mail contact@grdc.esdm.go.id; internet www.grdc.esdm.go.id; f. 1979; geological and geophysical research and systematic mapping; library: see Libraries; Dir Dr A. DJUMARMA WIRAKUSUMAH; publs *Buletin*, *Geofisika dan Tematik*, *Geosurvey Newsletter*, *Journal of Geology and Mineral Resources*, *Peta Geologi*, *Publikasi Khusus* (spec. publs), *Publikasi Teknik* (Technical Papers: Geophysics, Palaeontology Series).

TECHNOLOGY

Akademi Teknologi Kulit (Academy of Leather Technology): Jl. Ateka Bangunharjo, Sewon, Bantul, POB 1186, Yogyakarta 55187; tel. and fax (274) 383727; e-mail info@atk.ac.id; internet www.atk.ac.id; Dir Ir JULI ASTUTI.

Balai Besar Kerajinan dan Batik (Batik and Handicraft Research Institute): Jl. Kusumanegara 7, Yogyakarta; tel. (274) 546111; fax (274) 543582; internet www.batik.go.id; f. 1951; research, testing, and training courses; 108 mems; library of 1,792 vols; Dir SOEPARMAN S. TEKS.

Balai Besar Kulit, Karet dan Plastik (BBKKP) (Centre for Leather, Rubber and Plastic (CLRP)): Jl. Sokonandi 9, Yogyakarta 55166; tel. (274) 563939; fax (274) 563655; e-mail bbkkp@bbkkp.go.id; internet www.bbkkp.go.id; f. 1927; library of 4,000 vols; Dir RAMELAN SUBAGYO.

Balai Fotogrametri (Institute of Photogrammetry): Jl. Gunung Sahar 90, Jakarta; f. 1937; attached to Min. of Defence; researches on problems relating to photogrammetry, aerotriangulization, topographical maps, etc.; library of 1,500 books and periodicals; Head Maj. R. E. BEAUPAIN.

Dinas Hidro-Oseanografi (Naval Hydro-Oceanographic Office): Jl. Pantai Kuta V1, Jakarta 14430; f. 1947; hydrographical survey of Indonesia; staff of 700; publishes Tide Tables, etc.; Dir Col P. L. KATOPPO.

Direktorat Metrologi (Directorate of Metrology): Jl. Pasteur 27, Bandung 40171; tel. (22) 4203597; fax (22) 4207035; e-mail ditmet@bdg.centrin.net.id; f. 1923; Dir of Metrology AMIR SAHARUDDIN SJABRIAL.

Institut Teknologi Tekstil (Institute of Textile Technology): Jl. Jond. A. Yani 318, Bandung; f. 1922; Dir Maj. JON SEORJOSEO-JARSO.

Jajasan Dana Normalisasi Indonesia (Indonesian Standards Institution): Jl. Braga 38, (Atas) Bandung; f. 1920; Chair. Prof. R. SOEMONO; Sec. GANDI.

Lembaga Research dan Pengujian Materiil Angkatan Darat (Military Laboratory for Research and Testing Material, Ministry of Defence): Jl. Ternate 6–8, Bandung; f. 1865; library of 1,500 vols; Dir Brig.-Gen. N. A. KUSOMO.

Pusat Penelitian dan Pengembangan Sumber Daga Air (Research Institute for Water Resources): Jl. Ir. H. Juanda 193, POB 841, Bandung 40135; tel. (22) 2504053; fax (22) 2500163; e-mail pusair@bdg.centrin.net.id; internet www.pusair.domainvalet.com; f. 1966; attached to Agency for Research and Devt, Min. of Settlement and Regional Infrastructure; surveys, investigates and researches in the field of water resources devt; comprises experimental stations for hydrology, water resources, the environment, hydraulic structures and geotechnics, irrigation, swamps and coastal regions, rivers and sabo; library of 6,000 vols, 3,000 reports, 9,000 periodicals; Dir DYAH RAHAYU PANGESTI; publs *Bulletin Pusair* (2 a year),

Jurnal Penelitian dan Pengembangan Pengairan (2 a year), *Technical and Research Report* (1 a year).

Libraries and Archives

Jakarta

Arsip Nasional Republik Indonesia (National Archives): Jl. Ampera Raya 7, Jakarta 12560; tel. (21) 7805851; fax (21) 7805812; e-mail info@anri.go.id; internet www.anri.go.id; f. 1892; preserves documents as a nat. heritage and nat. account of the planning, execution and performance of the nat. life; provides records for govt and public activities; supervises the management of current operational records and the colln, storage, preservation, safe-keeping and use of historical archives; c. 25 km archives; 8,437 vols of books and other publs, 48,000 films, 10,000 video recordings, 4,000 oral history recordings, 1.6m. photographs; Dir Dr DJOKO UTOMO; publs *Berita Arsip Nasional RI* (2 a year), *Lembaran Berita Sejarah Lisan Arsip Nasional RI* (irregular), *Penerbitan Sumber Sejarah* (irregular), *Penerbitan Sumber Sejarah Lisan* (irregular).

Central Documentation and Library of the Ministry of Information: Medan Merdeka Barat 9, Jakarta; f. 1945; specializes in mass communication, social and political subjects, and supplies regional br. offices; press-cutting service from Indonesian newspapers since 1950; temporarily acting as Exchange Centre for govt publs and official documents; 10,000 vols; Head Drs P. DALI-MUNTHE; Librarian SAMPOERNO.

Perpustakaan Bagian Pathologi Klinik R. S. 'Dr Tjipto Mangunkusumo' (Dr Tjipto Mangunkusumo Hospital Library): Jl. Diponegoro 69, Jakarta; 3,000 vols; medicine, public health; Dir Prof. Dr JEANNE LATU.

Perpustakaan Dewan Perwakilan Rakyat Republik Indonesia (Library of Indonesian Parliament): Jl. Jenderal Gatot Subroto, Jakarta 10270; tel. (21) 5715220; fax (21) 584804; f. 1946; 200,000 vols; Librarian ROEMNINGSIH.

Perpustakaan Nasional (National Library of Indonesia): Jl. Salemba Raya 28A, POB 3624, Jakarta 10002; Jl. Merdeka Selatan 11, Pusat, Jakarta 10002; tel. (21) 3922669; fax (21) 3103554; internet www.pnri.go.id; f. 1980, by a merger of four libraries; depository library of Indonesia; 750,000 vols; spec. collns: Indonesian newspapers since 1810, Indonesian periodicals since 1779, Indonesian maps since 17th century, Indonesian dissertations, Indonesian monographs since 17th century; Dir MASTINI HARDJO PRAKOSO; publs *Bibliografi Nasional Indonesia* (4 a year), *Indeks artikel suratkabar* (Press Index, 4 a year), *subject bibliographies*, *catalogues*.

Perpustakaan Sejarah Politik dan Sosial (Library of Political and Social History): Medan Merdeka Seletan 11, Jakarta; f. 1952; 65,000 vols; incl. the Nat. Bibliographic Centre (Kantor Bibliografi Nasional) deposit library; Librarian Drs SOEKARMAN; publs *Berita Bulanan* (Bulletin, 12 a year), *Checklist of Serials in the Libraries of Indonesia*, *Publications—Indonesia*, *Regional Bibliography of Social Sciences*.

Pusat Dokumentasi dan Informasi Ilmiah—Lembaga Ilmu Pengetahuan Indonesia (PDII-LIPI) (Indonesian Scientific Knowledge Centre): Jl. Jendral Gatot Subroto 10, POB 4298, Jakarta 12042; tel. (21) 5733465; fax (21) 5733467; e-mail admin@pdii.lipi.go.id; internet www.pdii.lipi.go.id; f. 1965; 58,552 books, 4,783 periodicals, 14,022 theses and dissertations, 75,000 microforms, 40,000 research reports, 11,679 patents; Head Dra JUSNI DJATIN; publs *Abstract of Research and Survey Reports* (irregular), *Baca* (Read, 3 a year), *Daftar Terbitan Berkala Indonesia yang Telah Mempunyai ISSN* (Indonesian Serials with ISSN, irregular), *Directory of Special Libraries and Information Sources in Indonesia* (irregular), *FOKUS* (issues covering 17 subjects, 6 a year), *Index of Indonesian Learned Periodicals*, *Index to Papers Submitted to Seminars* (irregular), *Union Catalog of Serials* (irregular).

UPT Perpustakaan dan Dokumentasi, Biro Pusat Statistik (Library and Statistical Documentation, Central Bureau of Statistics): POB 1003, Jl. Dr Sutomo 8, Jakarta; tel. (21) 3810291; fax (21) 3857046; 60,000 vols; Librarian DAME MUNTHE.

South Sulawesi

Perpustakaan Umum Makassar (Makassar Public Library): Jl. Madukelleng 3, POB 16, Ujung Pandang 90112; f. 1969; organizes lending library services in brs throughout South Sulawesi Province; film and music programmes; foreign-language courses; children's library services; exhibitions and talks; 42,000 vols; Dir (vacant).

UPT Perpustakaan Universitas Hasanuddin (Hasanuddin University Library): Kampus UNHAS Tamalanrea, Jl. Perintis Kemerdekaan km 10, Ujung Pandang 90245; tel. (411) 587027; fax (411) 510088; e-mail library@unhas.ac.id; internet www.unhas.ac.id/perpustakaan; f. 1956; open to public; 122,000 vols, 3,821 periodicals, 23,421 dissertations and theses; Head Dra NOER JIHAD SALEH; publs *Iaporan Tahunan*, *Info Pustaka*, *Warta Perpustakan*.

West Java

Perpustakaan Pusat Institut Teknologi Bandung (Central Library, Bandung Institute of Technology): Jl. Ganesha 10, Bandung 40132; tel. (22) 2500089; fax (22) 2500089; e-mail info@lib.itb.ac.id; internet www.lib.itb.ac.id; f. 1920; colln of rare books, pamphlets and reports on Indonesia; colln on science, technology, fine arts and business; 227,000 vols, 791 current periodicals, 40,000 bound vols; Dir Dr YANNES MARTINUS PASARIBU; publ. *ITB Proceedings*.

Perpustakaan Pusat Penelitian dan Pengembangan Geologi (Library of Geological Research and Development Centre): Jl. Diponegoro 57, Bandung 40122; tel. (22) 772601; fax (22) 702669; e-mail grdc@melsa.net.id; 11,000 vols, 904 periodicals, 4,609 maps, 11,021 reports, 9,034 reprints, 400 microfiches; Chief Librarian RINI H. MARINO.

Perpustakaan (Pusat) Universitas Indonesia: Kampus UI, Depok 16424; tel. (21) 7864134; fax (21) 7863469; e-mail libserv@ui.edu; internet www.lib.ui.ac.id; Head of Library Dra LUKI WIJAYANTI.

Pusat Perpustakaan Angkatan Darat (Central Military Library): Jl. Kalimantan 6, Bandung; 36,000 vols in Central Library, and about 20,000 vols in departmental, territorial and college and office libraries; Dir Brig.-Gen. SOESATYO.

Pusat Perpustakaan Pertanian dan Komunikasi Penelitian (Indonesian Centre for Agricultural Library and Technology Dissemination): Jl. Ir Haji Juanda 20, Bogor 16122; tel. (251) 8321746; fax (251) 8326561; e-mail pustaka@pustaka-deptan.go.id; internet www.pustaka-deptan.go.id; f. 1842; 400,000 vols; Dir Ir FARID HASAN BAKTIR; publs *Abstrak Hasil Penelitian Per-*

tanian Indonesia (Indonesian Agricultural Research Abstract, 2 a year), *Indek Biologi dan Pertanian Indonesia* (Indonesian Biology and Agricultural Index, 3 a year), *Indonesian Journal of Agriculture* (2 a year), *Indonesian Journal of Agricultural Science* (2 a year), *Jurnal Bioteknologi Pertanian* (Indonesian Journal of Agricultural Biotechnology, 2 a year), *Jurnal Penelitian dan Pengembangan Pertanian* (Indonesian Journal of Agricultural Research and Development, 2 a year).

UPT Perpustakaan Institut Pertanian Bogor (Bogor Agricultural University Library): Kampus Darmaga, POB 199, Bogor 16680; tel. (251) 8621073; fax (251) 8623166; e-mail perpustakaan@bima.ipb.ac.id; internet perpustakaan.ipb.ac.id; f. 1963; 159,000 vols, 3,500 periodicals; Head Librarian TOHA NURSALAM; publs *Forum Pasca Sarjana*, *Indonesian Journal of Tropical Agriculture*.

Yogyakarta

Perpustakaan Islam (Islamic Library): c/o Min. of Religious Affairs, Jl. Lapangan Banteng Barat 3–4, Jakarta 10710; Jl. P. Mangkubumi 38, Yogyakarta; internet www.perpustakaan-islam.com; f. 1942; attached to Min. of Religious Affairs; 70,000 vols; MSS and periodicals; Dir Drs H. ASYHURI DAHLAN; Librarian MOH. AMIEN MANSOER.

Perpustakaan Jajasan Hatta (Hatta Foundation Library): Malioboro 85, Yogyakarta; 43,000 vols; Librarian R. SOEDJAT-MIKO.

Perpustakaan Wilayah (Regional Library): Malioboro 175, Yogyakarta; f. 1949; 120,000 vols; Librarian ST. KOSTKA SOEGENG.

Museums and Art Galleries

Aceh

Museum Nanggroe Aceh Darussalam: Jl. Sultan Alaidin Mahmudsyah 12, Baiturrahman, Banda Aceh 23241; tel. (651) 23144; fax (651) 21033; f. 1915, as the House of Aceh, present name and status 2002; weaponry, household furnishings, ceremonial costumes, gold jewellery and calligraphy.

Museum Nangguor Pidie: Jl. Teuku Cik Ditiro, Sigli, Pidie Regency.

Museum Perjuangan Iskandar Muda: Jl. Kelurahan Penniti, kecamatan Baiturrahman, Banda Aceh.

Bali

Blanco Renaissance Museum: POB 80571, Ubud, Bali; tel. (361) 975502; fax (361) 975551; e-mail a-blanco@indo.net.id; internet www.blancomuseum.com; f. 1998, fmr studio of artist Antonio Blanco; collns of paintings.

Museum Bali: Jl. Letnan Kolonel Wisnu 1, Denpasar, Bali; f. 1932; exhibits of Bali culture; library of 1,970 vols, 1,605 magazines, 1,023 transcriptions of lontars (palm leaves); Dir Drs PUTU BUDIASTRA; publs *Karya Widia tak berkala*, *Majalah Saraswati*.

Museum Gedong Kirtya: Jl. Veteran 20, Singaraja; tel. (362) 22645; f. 1928; collns incl. ancient Balinese letters, chronicles and *kakawin* (Balinese poetry) written on palm leaves.

Museum Puri Lukisan: Jl. Raya Ubud, Ubud, Bali; tel. (361) 971-159; fax (361) 975-136; e-mail info@museumpurilukisan.com; internet www.mpl-ubud.com; f. 1956, admin. by Yayasan Ratna Wartha foundation (f.

1953); colln incl. Balinese paintings and woodcarvings.

Museum Seni Agung Rai (Agung Rai Museum of Art): Jl. Pengosekan, Ubud, Gianyar 80571; tel. (361) 975742; fax (361) 975332; e-mail info@armamuseum.com; internet www.armamuseum.com; f. 1996; colln of paintings; special temporary exhibitions; theatre performances; dance, music, and painting classes; bookshop, library and reading room; cultural workshops; seminars and training programmes; centre for visual and performing arts; Chair. AGUNG RAI.

Neka Art Museum: Jl. Raya Campuhan, Kedewatan Village, Ubud, Gianyar 80571; tel. (361) 975074; fax (361) 97563; e-mail info@museumneka.com; internet www.museumneka.com; f. 1982; Dir SUTEJA NEKA.

Rudana Museum: Jl. Cok Rai Pudak 44 Peliatan, Ubud, Bali 80571; tel. (361) 975779; fax (361) 975091; e-mail info@museumrudana.com; internet www.museumrudana.com; f. 1995; Man. Dir PUTU SUPADMA RUDANA.

Central Java

Museum Jawa Tengah Ronggowarsito: Jl. Abdulrahman Saleh 1, Semarang; tel. and fax (6224) 760238; e-mail cs@museumronggowarsito.org; internet www.museumronggowarsito.org; f. 1989; collns in art, archaeology, biology, geology, ceramics and technology; Head Drs PUJI JOHARNOTO.

Museum Masjid Agung Demak: Jl. Sultan Fatah 57, Demak; tel. and fax (291) 685532; f. 1975.

Museum Soesilo Soedarman: Gentasari-Kroya, Cilacap; tel. and fax (282) 494400; f. 2000; collns of rifles, pistols and machine-guns.

Museum Tosan Aji Purworejo: Jl. Mayjend Sutoyo 10, Purworejo; collns of prehistoric artefacts in stone mortar, Hindu religious statues, yonis, statues of Shiva-Parvati.

Jakarta

Fine Art and Ceramic Museum: Jl. Pos Kota 2, West Jakarta; tel. (21) 6907062; f. built 1870, f. as Fine Arts Gallery 1976; colln of 400 items: sculpture, graphics, wood totems and batik paintings; spec. collns incl. masterpieces of Indonesian artists Hendra Gunawan, Raden Saleh; collns of ceramics from various regions.

Jakarta History Museum: Jl. Taman Fatahillah 1, West Jakarta 11110; tel. (21) 6929101; fax (21) 6902387; exhibits from prehistoric Jakarta; est. of Jayakarta in 1527; 16th-century Dutch colonization to independence of Indonesia.

Museum Listrik dan Energi Baru (Electricity and Renewable Energy Museum): Jl. Raya Taman Mini, Jakarta 13560; tel. and fax (21) 8413451; e-mail museumlistrik@yahoo.com; internet www.museumlistrik.com; history, outdoor exhibits of electric technology; Dir Drs SOETRISNO.

Museum Nasional (National Museum): Jl. Merdeka Barat 12, Pusat Jakarta; tel. 360796; e-mail museumnasional@indo.com; internet www.museumnasional.org; f. 1778, fmrly Museum Pusat; library of 360,000 vols (now part of Nat. Library); depts of ceramics, ethnography, prehistory, classical archaeology, anthropology, MSS and education; publs subject catalogues; Dir Dr ENDANG SRI HARDIATI.

Museum Wayang (Puppet Museum): Jl. Pintu Besar Utara 27, Tamansari, West Jakarta 11110; tel. (21) 6929560; e-mail info@museumwayang.com; displays leather and wood puppets; colln of 4,000 puppets.

Textile Museum: Jl. Aipda K. S. Tubun 4, Central Jakarta; tel. (21) 5606613; f. 1975; displays traditional *kain* (skirt worn by Indonesian men and women).

North Sumatra

Museum Deli Serdang: Lubuk Pakam Kompleks Perkantoran Pemda Deli Serdang, Kelurahan Desa Jati Sari, Kecamatan, Lubuk Pakam, Deli Serdang; f. 2003; attached to Min. of Culture and Tourism.

Museum Karo Lingga: Desa Lingga Kabupaten Karo, Kelurahan Desa Lingga, Kecamatan Simpang Empat, Karo; f. 1977.

Museum Negeri Propinsi Sumatra Utara (State Museum of North Sumatra): Jl. H. M. Joni No. 51, Medan 20217; tel. (61) 7366792; fax (61) 7322220; e-mail info@museum-sumut.org; f. 1982; Museum Head Drs HARTINI.

Museum Simalungun: Jl. Sudirman 20 Pematang Siantar, Kelurahan Proklamasi, Kecamatan Siantar Barat, Siantar; tel. (622) 21954; f. 1940.

Papua

Museum Loka Budaya: Jl. Raya Abeoura-Setani, Kelurahan Hedam, Kecamatan Abepura, Kabupaten Jayapura; f. 1970; colln of 2,000 ethnographic objects of tribes in Papua.

Museum Negeri Provinsi Papua (Papua State Museum): Jl. Raya Sentani Km 17, 8 Waena-Jayapura Kelurahan Waena, Kecamatan Abepura, Kabupaten Jayapura; f. 1981; colln of 3,447 items: geology, biology, ethnography, archaeology, history, numismatics, physiology, ceramics, fine arts, human profiles, maps and dioramas.

Riau

Museum Daerah Riau Sang Nila Utama (Riau Regional Museum of Nila Utama): Jl. Jend. Sudirman 194; tel. (761) 33466; fax (761) 40195; historical relics of the Riau Province.

Museum Sultan Syarif Kasim: Jl. Jend. Sudirman, Bengkalis; collns incl. royal jewellery, hand-woven embroidery, batik fabrics.

South Sumatra

Monumen Perjuangan Rakyat (MONPERA) Sumatera Bagian Selatan (People's Struggle Monument of South Sumatera): Jl. Merdeka, Palembang 30132; tel. (711) 358450; f. 1988; library of 356 titles; Guide and Admin. Staff LIDYA ELIZA.

Museum Negeri Propinsi Sumatra Selatan (State Museum of South Sumatra): Jl. Srijaya 288, Km 5.5, Kecamatan Sukaramai, Palembang 30139; tel. (711) 411382; fax (711) 412636.

Museum Pahlawan Nasional Dr A. K. Gani (Museum of National Hero Dr A. K. Gani): Jl. MP Mangkunegara 1/RT01, Sukamaju Sako, Palembang 30168; tel. and fax (711) 824046; e-mail museum_akgani@yahoo.com; f. 2006, govt undertaking 2008; exhibits related to life of Adenan Kapau Gani, leader of nat. freedom movement; Sec. SURAWIJAYA GANI.

Museum Sultan Mahmud Badaruddin II: Jl. Sultan Mahmud Badaruddin II 2; tel. (711) 358450; fax (711) 352573; f. 1823, present status 2004, fmrly official home of the Dutch resident in Palembang; collns incl. numismatics, ceramics and fine arts.

West Sumatra

Museum Kereta Api Sawahlunto: Jl. Kampung Teleng, Kelurahan Pasar, Kecamatan Lembah Segar, Sawahlunto; tel. and fax (754) 61023; collns of cars, steam locomotives, communication devices; photo documentation.

Museum Mande Rubiah: Kampung Lubuk Sitepung, Nagari Lunang, Kecamatan Lunang Silaut, Kabupaten Pesisir Selatan; collns of MSS, coins, weapons, kitchen utensils, ceremonial tools, traditional wear, porcelain dishes, lamps and canes.

Museum Perjuangan Tridaya Eka Dharma: Jl. Panorama 24 Kelurahan Kayu Kubu, Kecamatan Guguk Panjang, Kecamatan Bukittinggi; collns incl. traditional tools and weapons.

Museum Rumah Kelahiran Bung Hatta: Jl. Soekarno, Hatta 37, Bukit Tinggi; tel. (752) 23503; birth home of Mohammad Hatta.

Yogyakarta

Museum Dewantara Kirti Griya: Jl. Tamansiswa 31, Yogyakarta; tel. (274) 389208; fax (274) 377120; f. 1970.

Museum Geoteknologi Mineral UPN 'Veteran' Yogyakarta: Jl. Babarsari 2, Tambakbayan, Yogyakarta; tel. (274) 486991; fax (274) 487147; e-mail museummgmt@upnyk.ac.id; internet museum.upnyk.ac.id; f. 1988.

Museum Monumen Pergerakan Wanita Indonesia (Museum of the Women's Movement): Jl. Laksda Adisucipto 88, Yogyakarta; tel. (274) 587818; fax (274) 520360; displays household appliances and kitchen equipment.

Museum Pusat AD 'Dharma Wiratama' (Central Army Museum): Jl. Jend. Sudirman 47, Yogyakarta; tel. and fax (274) 561417; f. 1956, present location 1982; collns of weapons, inventory, optical and communications equipment; spec. travelling exhibitions; lectures and workshops.

Museum Rumah Jawa Tembi Bantul: Jl. Parang Tritis, Km 8.4 Tembi, Timbulharjo, Sewon, Bantul, Yogyakarta; tel. (274) 368004; fax (274) 368001; f. 1999.

Museum Wayang Kekayon Yogyakarta (Kekayon Puppet Museum Yogyakarta): Jl. Yogya Wonosari, Km 7 no. 277, Yogyakarta; tel. (274) 513218; puppet masks and clothing.

Ullèn Sentalu (Javanese Culture and Art Museum): Jl. Boyong Kaliurang, Sleman, Yogyakarta; tel. (274) 880158; fax (274) 881743; internet www.ullensentalu.com; f. 1994; art heritage wealth, culture and history from the Javanese civilization.

State Universities

INSTITUT PERTANIAN BOGOR
(Bogor Agricultural University)

Jl. Lingkar Akademik, Kampus IPB Darmaga, Bogor 16680

Telephone: (251) 622642
Fax: (251) 622708
Internet: www.ipb.ac.id

Founded 1963
State control
Languages of instruction: Indonesian, English(for foreign visiting professors)
Academic year: September to June (two semesters)

Rector: Dr Ir HENRY SUHARDIYANTO
Vice-Rector for Academic Affairs and Student Affairs: Prof. Dr Ir H. YONNY KUSMARYONO
Vice-Rector for Business and Communication: Dr Ir H. ARIF IMAN SUROSO
Vice-Rector for Resources and Devt: Prof. Dr Ir HERMANTO SIREGAR
Vice-Rector for Research and Collaboration: Dr Ir H. MIFTAH ANAS FAUZI
Registrar: Dr SETYO PERTIWI
Administrator: Ir UDIN M. WAHJUDIN

Librarian: Ir TOHA NURSALAM
Number of teachers: 1,327
Number of students: 19,440

Publications: *Buletin Hama dan Penyakit Tumbuhan, Buletin Ilmu Tanah, Communication Agriculture, Feed and Nutrition Journal, Forum Pasca Sarjana, Gema Penelitian, Indonesian Journal of Tropical Agriculture, Jurnal Ilmu Pertanian Indonesian, Jurnal Primatologi, Media Konservasi, Media Peternakan, Media Veteriner, Teknologi*

DEANS

Faculty of Agriculture: Prof. Dr M. CHOSIN
Faculty of Agricultural Technology: Prof. Dr M. BAMBANG PRAMUDYA NOORACHMAT
Faculty of Animal Science: Prof. Dr H. SOEDARMADI
Faculty of Economics and Management: Prof. Dr BUNASOR SANIM
Faculty of Fisheries and Marine Science: Dr E. HARIS
Faculty of Forestry: Prof. Dr YUSUF SUDOHADI
Faculty of Mathematics and Natural Sciences: Dr SISWADI
Faculty of Veterinary Medicine: Dr F. H. PASARIBU

INSTITUT SENI INDONESIA SURAKARTA
(Indonesia Institute of the Arts Surakarta)

Jl. ki Hajar Dewantara 19, Kentingan, Jebres, Surakarta 57126

Telephone: (271) 647658
Fax: (271) 646175
E-mail: direct@isi-ska.ac.id
Internet: www.isi-ska.ac.id

Founded 1965 as Akademi Seni Karawitan Indonesia (ASKI), merged with Akademi Seni Tari Indonesia (ASTI) to form Sekolah Tinggi Seni Indonesia Surakarta 1983, present status 2006
Public control

Rector: Prof. Dr T. SLAMET SUPARNO

Library of 36,588 vols
Number of teachers: 203
Number of students: 852

INSTITUT SENI INDONESIA YOGYAKARTA
(Indonesia Institute of the Arts Yogyakarta)

Jl. Parangtritis Km 6.5, POB 1210, Yogyakarta 55188

Telephone: (274) 373659
Fax: (274) 371233
E-mail: arts@isi.ac.id
Internet: www.isi.ac.id

Founded 1984, univ. status, fmrly known as Institut Seni Indonesia Yogyakarta
Language of instruction: Indonesian
Academic year: September to June

Rector: Drs SOEPRAPTO SOEDJONO
Vice-Rector for Academic Affairs: Prof. Dr A. M. HERMIN KUSMAYATI
Vice-Rector for Admin. and Financial Affairs: Drs SISWADI
Vice-Rector for Students Affairs: Drs SYAFRUDDIN
Registrar: G. BUDI PRIYATMO
Librarian: Dra HERLIN NOVIAR SUBARYANTI

Library of 44,368 vols
Number of teachers: 329
Number of students: 1,922

Publications: *ARS, Visual Arts Journal, EKSPRESI, Research Journal, FENOMEN, Research Journal, RESITAL, Performing Arts Journal, REKAM, Recorded Media Arts Journal, SENI, Journal for the Arts* (4 a year), *SURYA SENI, Postgraduate Journal*

DEANS

Faculty of Performing Arts: Drs TRIYONO BRAMANTYO PAMUDJO SANTOSO
Faculty of Recorded Media Arts: Drs ALEX ANDRI LUTHFI R.
Faculty of Visual Arts: Dr M. AGUS BURHAN

INSTITUT TEKNOLOGI BANDUNG
(Bandung Institute of Technology)

Jl. Tamansari 64, Bandung 40116
Jl. Ganesha 10, Bandung 40132

Telephone: (22) 2500935
E-mail: webmaster@itb.ac.id
Internet: www.itb.ac.id

Founded 1920, present form 1959 as a merger of the faculties of mathematics, natural sciences and engineering of the Univ. of Indonesia
State control
Language of instruction: Indonesian
Academic year: August to July

Rector: Prof. Dr Ir DJOKO SANTOSO
Vice-Rector for Academic Affairs: Dr Ir ADANG SURAHMAN
Vice-Rector for Gen. Admin.: Prof. Dr Ir DJOKO SANTOSO
Vice-Rector for Devt, Planning, Admin. and Information Systems: Dr Ir RIZAL ZAINUDDIN TAMIN
Librarian: Dr Ir ROBERT MANURUNG
Number of teachers: 1,263
Number of students: 15,031

Publications: *Akta Farmasetika Indonesia* (12 a year), *Buletin Geologi* (3 a year), *Geodesi dan Surveying* (2 a year), *Journal of Mathematics and Science* (2 a year), *Journal Pusat Pengembangan Perencanaan Wilayah Kota* (1 a year), *Jurnal Atap* (1 a year), *Jurnal Teknik dan Manajemen Industri* (3 a year), *Jurnal Teknik Lingkungan* (2 a year), *Jurnal Teknik Sipil* (4 a year), *Jurnal Teknologi Mineral* (3 a year), *Kontribusi Fisika* (4 a year), *Maalah Ilmiah Himpunan Matematika Indonesia* (2 a year), *Majalah Ilmiah Teknik Electro* (3 a year), *Majalah Mesin* (3 a year)

DEANS

Faculty of Civil Engineering and Planning: Prof. Dr Ir TOMMY FIRMAN
Faculty of Fine Arts and Design: Drs SETIAWAN SABANA
Faculty of Industrial Technology: Prof. Dr Ir DJOKO SUJARTO
Faculty of Mathematics and Natural Sciences: Dr Ing. CYNTHIA LINAYA RADIMAN
Faculty of Mineral Technology: Prof. Dr Ir MADE EMMY RELAWAT
Graduate Programme: Prof. Dr Ir SOELARSO (Dir)
School of Business and Management: Prof. Dr SURNA TJAHJA DJAJADININGRAT

PROFESSORS

ACHMAD, S. A., Chemistry
AGOES, G., Pharmacy
ALGAMAR, K., Environmental Engineering
ANSJAR, M., Mathematics
ARIFIN, A., Mathematics
ARISMUNANDAR, W., Mechanical Engineering
ASIKIN, S., Geology
BAGIASNA, K., Mechanical Engineering
BARMAWI, M., Physics
BINTORO, S. B., City Planning
BRODJONEGRO, S. S., Mechanical Engineering
BROTOSISWOJO, B. S., Physics
CHATIB, B., Environmental Engineering
DHANUTIRTO, H., Pharmacy
DIRAN, O., Mechanical Engineering

DJAJADININGRAT, A. H., Environmental Engineering
DJAJADININGRAT, S. T., Industrial Engineering
DJAJAPUTRA, A. A., Civil Engineering
DJAJASUGITA, F. A., Electrical Engineering
DJALARI, Y. A., Design
DJAUHARI, M. A., Mathematics
DJOJODIHARDJO, H., Mechanical Engineering
FIRMAN, K., Pharmacy
FIRMAN, T., City Planning
GANI, A. Z., Industrial Engineering
GDE RAKA, I. D., Industrial Engineering
HANDOJO, A., Engineering Physics
HARAHAP, F., Mechanical Engineering
HARJOSUPARTO, S., Chemical Engineering
HARLANDJA, B., Civil Engineering
HAROEN, Y., Electrical Engineering
HARSOKOESOEMO, D., Mechanical Engineering
HENDRADJAYA, L., Physics
HIDAYAT, B., Astronomy
JENJIE, S. D., Mechanical Engineering
KAHAR, J., Geodesy
KAMIL, S., Mechanical Engineering
KANA, J. C., Petroleum Engineering
KARSA, K., Electrical Engineering
KOESOEMADINATA, R. P., Geology
KUSBIANTORO, City Planning
LIANG, O. B., Chemistry
LIONG, T. H., Physics
MANGUNWIJAYA, A., Mining Engineering
MARDIHARTANTO, F. X., Industrial Engineering
MARDISEWOJO, P., Petroleum Engineering
MARTODJOJO, S., Geology
MARTOJO, W., Mining Engineering
MERATI, I. G. W., Civil Engineering
MIRA, S., Geodesy
NABANAN, S. M., Mathematics
ON, T. M., Physics
PADMAWINATA, K., Pharmacy
PIROUS, A. D., Design
PRINGGOPRAWIRO, H., Geology
PRINGGOPRAWIRO, M., Physics
PRODJOSOEMARTO, P., Mining Engineering
PULUNGGONO, A., Geology
RAHAYU, S. I., Chemistry
RAIS, J., Geodesy
RELAWATYI, S. E., Geology
RIDWAN, A. S., Civil Engineering
SAMADIKUN, S., Electrical Engineering
SAMPURNO, Geology
SANTOSO, D., Geophysics
SAPIIE, S., Electrical Engineering
SASMOJO, S., Chemical Engineering
SASTRAMIHARDJA, I., Chemical Engineering
SASTRODIHARDJO, S., Biology
SATIADARMA, K., Pharmacy
SEMBIRING, R. K., Mathematics
SILABAN, P., Physics
SIRAIT, K. T., Electrical Engineering
SIREGAR, C., Pharmacy
SIREGAR, H. P. S., Petroleum Engineering
SISWOSUWARNO, M., Mechanical Engineering
SJAFRUDDIN, A., Civil Engineering
SJUIB, F., Pharmacy
SLAMET, J. S., Environmental Engineering
SOEDIRO, I., Pharmacy
SOEDJITO, B. B., City Planning
SOEGIJANTO, R. M., Engineering Physics
SOEGIJOKO, S., Electrical Engineering
SOELARSO, Mechanical Engineering
SOEMARTO, S., Environmental Engineering
SOEMINTAPOERA, K., Electrical Engineering
SOEMODINOTO, W., Mining Engineering
SOENARKO, B., Engineering Physics
SOEPANGKAT, H. P., Physics
SOERIA-ATMADJA, R., Geology
SOERIAATMADJA, R. E., Biology
SUDARWATI, S., Biology
SUDIRMAN, I., Industrial Engineering
SUDRADJAT, I., Architecture
SUHARTO, D., Mechanical Engineering
SUHUD, R., Civil Engineering
SUJARTO, D., City Planning

SUKARMADIJAYA, H., Environmental Engineering
SULE, D., Mining Engineering
SUMAWIGANDA, S., Civil Engineering
SURAATMADJA, D., Civil Engineering
SURDIA, N. M., Chemistry
SURDIA, T., Metallurgical Engineering
SUTJIATMO, B., Mechanical Engineering
SUWONO, A., Mechanical Engineering
TABRANI, P., Design
TAROEPRATJEKA, H., Industrial Engineering
TJAHJATI, S. B., City Planning
TOHA, I. S., Industrial Engineering
TUAH, H., Civil Engineering
UMAR, F., Mining Engineering
WANGSADINATA, W., Civil Engineering
WARDIMAN, A., Engineering Physics
WAWOROENTOE, W. J., City Planning
WIDAGDO, Design
WIDODO, R. J., Electrical Engineering
WIRASONJAYA, S., Architecture
WIRJOMARTONO, S. H., Mechanical Engineering
WIRJOSUMARTO, H., Mechanical Engineering
WISJNUPRAPTO, Environmental Engineering
ZAINUDDIN, I. M., Design
ZEN, M. T., Geology

INSTITUT TEKNOLOGI SEPULUH NOPEMBER
(Technology Institute of Sepuluh Nopember)

POB 900/SB, Surabaya 60008, East Java
Located at: Kampus ITS, Sukolilo, Surabaya 60111, East Java

Telephone and fax (31) 5923411
E-mail: int_off@its.ac.id
Internet: www.its.ac.id

Founded 1960
State control
Language of instruction: Indonesian
Academic year: September to June

Rector: Dr Ir PRIYO SUPROBO
Vice-Rector for Academic Affairs: Prof. Ir NOOR ENDAH B. MOCTAR
Vice-Rector for Admin.: Ir R. SYARIF WIDJAYA
Vice-Rector for Student Affairs: Dr Ir ACHMAD JAZIDIE
Head of the Academic Admin. and Student Affairs Bureau: Drs HARRY SANTOSO
Head of the Admin. Planning and Information System Bureau: Ir ARIE KISMANTO
Head of the Gen. Admin. and Finance Bureau: NURIJATI HAMID
Librarian: Drs ACHMAD

Library of 45,994 vols
Number of teachers: 1,043
Number of students: 17,384

Publications: Berita ITS, Iptek, various faculty bulletins

DEANS

Faculty of Civil Engineering and Planning: Prof. Dr Ir PRIYO SUPROBO
Faculty of Industrial Technology: Dr Ir TRIYOGI YUWONO
Faculty of Information Technology: Prof. Ir ARIEF DJUNAIDI
Faculty of Mathematics and Sciences: Prof. Dr SUASMORO
Faculty of Ocean Engineering: Ir ASJHAR IMRON

DIRECTORS

Polytechnic of Electronics: Dr Ir TITON DUTONO
Polytechnic of Ship Building: Ir SUWARNO TAHID
Research and Public Service Institute: Prof. Ir I. NYOMAN SUTANTRA

PROFESSORS

ALTWAY, A., Chemical Engineering

ANWAR, N., Civil Engineering
BAKTIR, A., Chemical Engineering
DJANALI, S., Informatics Engineering
DJUNAIDY, A., Information System Engineering
ERSAM, T., Chemical Engineering
HADI, W., Environmental Engineering
KOESTALAM, P., Civil Engineering
LINUWIH, S., Statistics
MOCHTAR, I. B., Civil Engineering
MOCHTAR, N. E., Civil Engineering
NUH, M., Electrical Engineering
NURSUHUD, D., Mechanical Engineering
PENANGSANG, H. O., Electrical Engineering
PRATIKTO, W. A., Ocean Engineering
PURNOMO, M. H., Electrical Engineering
PURWONO, R., Structural Engineering
PUTU RAKA, I. G., Civil Engineering
RACHIMOELLAH, M., Chemistry
RAMELAN, R., Mechanical Engineering
RENANTO, Chemical Engineering
SANTOSA, M., Architecture
SANTOSO, H. R., Architecture
SARNO, R., Informatics Engineering
SILAS, J., Architecture
SOEBAGIO, Electrical Engineering
SOEGIONO, Ocean Engineering
SUASMORO, H., Physics
SUKARDJONO, S., Electrical Engineering
SUPROBO, P., Civil Engineering
SUTANTRA, N., Mechanical Engineering
SUTRISNO, H., Electrical Engineering
SUWARNO, J., Chemical Engineering
SUWARNO, N., Chemical Engineering
TJANDRASA, H., Informatics Engineering
WAHYUDI, H., Civil Engineering

UNIVERSITAS AIRLANGGA
(Airlangga University)

Jl. Mulorejo, Kampus C, Surabaya 60115

Telephone: (31) 5914042
Fax: (31) 5981841
E-mail: sekretaris_ua@unair.ac.id
Internet: www.unair.ac.id

Founded 1954
Language of instruction: Indonesian
Academic year: September to August

Rector: Prof. Dr Dr D. H. FASICH
Vice-Rector for Academic and Learning, Research and Public Service: Prof. Dr MUHAMAD ZAINUDDIN
Vice-Rector for General Admin.: Dr MUSLICH ANSHORI
Vice-Rector for Information and Student Affairs: Dr SUNARKO SETYAWAN
Chief, Bureau for General Academic Admin. and Student Affairs: Dr ZAINAL ARIFIN
Chief, Bureau for General Admin.: Dra Hj. SUNARTI
Chief, Bureau for Planning Admin. and Information Systems: ROSMELYANI
Librarian: RR. RATNANINGSIH

Number of teachers: 1,434
Number of students: 20,719

Publications: Buletin Toraks Kardiovaskular Indonesia (4 a year), Folia Medika Indonesiana (4 a year), Majalah Kedokteran Gigi (4 a year), Majalah Kedokteran Surabaya (4 a year), Majalah Kedokteran Tropis Indonesia (4 a year), Majalah Kesehatan Masyarakat (4 a year), Majalah Masyarakat Kebudayaan Politik (4 a year), Surabaya Journal of Surgery (4 a year), Yuridika (4 a year)

DEANS

Faculty of Dentistry: Prof. Dr Drg. MOHAMAD RUBIANTO
Faculty of Economics: Drs KARJADI MINTAROEM
Faculty of Law: H. MACHSOEN ALI
Faculty of Letters: Prof. HERU SUPRIYADI

Faculty of Mathematics and Natural Sciences: Drs H. ABDUL LATIEF BURHAN
Faculty of Medicine: Prof. Dr Dr H. M. S. WIYADI
Faculty of Pharmacy: Prof. Dr NOOR CHOLIES ZAINI
Faculty of Psychology: Prof. Dr H. M. ZAINUDIN
Faculty of Public Health: Dr Dr TJIPTO SUWANDI
Faculty of Social and Political Sciences: Dr Drs HOTMAN SIAHAAN
Faculty of Veterinary Medicine: Dr Drh. ISMUDIONO
Postgraduate Programmes: Prof. Dr Dr H. MUHAMMAD AMIN

UNIVERSITAS ANDALAS

Kampus Limau Manis, Padang 25163
Telephone: (751) 71181
Fax: (751) 71508
Internet: www.unand.ac.id

Founded 1956
Language of instruction: Indonesian
Academic year: September to June

Rector: MARLIS RAHMAN
Vice-Rector for Academic Affairs: AMIRMUSLIM MALIK
Vice-Rector for Admin. and Finance: DJASWIR ZEIN
Vice-Rector for Student Affairs: FIRMAN HASAN
Head Librarian: MARAMIS

Number of teachers: 1,396
Number of students: 13,009

Publications: *Andalas Medical Journal, Jurnal Antropologi, Jurnal Ekonomi Manajemen, Jurnal Matematika dan Ilmu Pengetahuan Alam, Jurnal Pembangunan dan Perubahan Sosial Budaya, Jurnal Penelitian Andalas, Jurnal Peternakan dan Lingkungan, Jurnal Teknologi Pertanian* (Journal of Agricultural Technology), *Justisia, Lingua: Jurnal Bahasa dan Sastra, Potetika, Teknika, Warta Pengabdian Andalas*

DEANS

Faculty of Agriculture: BUJANG RUSMAN
Faculty of Animal Husbandry: AZINAR KAMARUDDIN
Faculty of Arts: SYAFRUDDIN SULAIMAN
Faculty of Economics: SJAFRIZAL
Faculty of Engineering: DAHNIL ZAINUDDIN
Faculty of Law and Social Science: AZHAR RAUF
Faculty of Mathematics and Natural Sciences: HAZLI NURDIN
Faculty of Medicine: RUSDAN DJAMIL
Faculty of Political and Social Sciences: DAHRUL DAHLAN
Polytechnic of Agriculture: MASRUL JALAL
Polytechnic of Engineering: ALIZAR HASAN

UNIVERSITAS BENGKULU
(University of Bengkulu)

Jl. Raya Kandang Limun, Bengkulu 38371
Telephone: (736) 21170
Fax: (736) 22105
E-mail: rektorat@unib.ac.id
Internet: www.unib.ac.id

Founded 1982

Rector: Prof. Dr Ir ZAINAL MUKTAMAR
Chief Admin. Officer: Drs BOKO SUSILO
Librarian: Ir BAMBANG GONGGO M.

Library of 20,600 vols
Number of teachers: 726
Number of students: 10,477

DEANS

Faculty of Agriculture: TOEKIDJO MARTOREJO
Faculty of Economics: Dr RIDWAN NURAZI

Faculty of Education: Prof. Drs SAFNIL
Faculty of Law: HERLAMBANG
Faculty of Social Sciences: Drs PANJI SUMINAR
Faculty of Technology: Prof. Dr Ir M. SYAIFUL

UNIVERSITAS BRAWIJAYA

Jl. Veteran, Malang, Jawa Timur 65145
Telephone: (341) 575777
Fax: (341) 565420
E-mail: rektorat@brawijaya.ac.id
Internet: www.brawijaya.ac.id

Founded 1963
State control
Language of instruction: Indonesian
Academic year: September to August

Rector: Prof. Dr Ir YOGI SUGITO
Vice-Rector: Prof. Dr BAMBANG SUHARTO
Vice-Rector: Drs WARKUM SUMITRO
Vice-Rector: Prof. Dr H. R. B. AINURRASYID
Head of Gen. Admin. Bureau: GOERID HARDJITO
Head of Planning and Information Systems Bureau: Dra Hj. SITI ROMLAH
Head of Student and Academic Admin. Bureau: Dra Haja SITI ROMLAH
Librarian: Dra WELMIN SUNYI ARININGSIH

Number of teachers: 1,271
Number of students: 28,105

Publications: *Administrator* (12 a year), *Agrivita* (12 a year), *Agrotek* (4 a year), *Aqua* (4 a year), *Arena Hukum* (12 a year), *Buletin* (12 a year), *Canopy* (12 a year), *Dian* (12 a year), *Diagnostika* (1 a year), *Febra* (12 a year), *Habitat* (3 a year), *Indicus* (12 a year), *Indikator* (12 a year), *Jurnal* (2 a year), *Jurnal Administrasi Bisnis* (2 a year), *Jurnal Administrasi Negara* (2 a year), *Jurnal Ilmu Peternakan* (2 a year), *Jurnal Penelitian Ilmu—Ilmu Hayati* (2 a year), *Jurnal Penelitian Ilmu—Ilmu Sosial* (2 a year), *Jurnal Penelitian Ilmu—Ilmu Teknik* (2 a year), *Jurnal Teknik* (3 a year), *Jurnal Teknologi Pertanian* (2 a year), *Lintasan Ekonomi* (2 a year), *Mafaterna* (2 a year), *Majalah Kedokteran Universitas Brawijaya* (3 a year), *Manifest* (2 a year), *Media Karya Ilmiah* (2 a year), *Mimbar Universitas Brawijaya* (6 a year), *Mitra Akademika* (2 a year), *Natural Jurnal* (2 a year), *Prasetya* (48 a year), *Solid* (2 a year), *Techno* (2 a year), *Wartamina* (6 a year)

DEANS

Faculty of Administrative Sciences: Dr SUHADAK
Faculty of Agriculture: Prof. Dr Ir SYEKHFANI
Faculty of Agricultural Technology: Prof. Dr Ir SIMON BAMBANG WIDJANARKO
Faculty of Animal Husbandry: Prof. Dr Ir IFAR SUBAGIYO
Faculty of Economics: Prof. Dr BAMBANG SUBROTO
Faculty of Engineering: Ir IMAM ZAKY
Faculty of Fisheries: Ir SUKOSO
Faculty of Law: WARKUM SUMITRO
Faculty of Medicine: Dr HARIJANTO
Faculty of Natural Science and Mathematics: Ir ADAM WIRYAWAN
Faculty of Polytechnic: Ir BUDI TJAHJONO
Postgraduate Studies Programme: Prof. Dr Dr DJANGGAN SARGOWO

PROFESSORS

ACHMAD, H., Medicine
ACHMADY, Z. A., Administration
ACHMANU, Animal Husbandry
ALHABSJI, T., Administration
ALI, M. M., Medicine
ARIFFIN, Aeroclimatology
ASHARI, M. S., Agriculture
ASTUTI, M. S., Law

BAISOENI, H., Mathematics
CHUZAEMI, S., Animal Husbandry
FADJAR, A. M., Law
FANANI, Z., Animal Husbandry
FAUZI, A., Administration
GINTING, E., Animal Husbandry
GURITNO, B., Agriculture
HADIASTONO, T., Agriculture
HAIRIAH, K., Agriculture
HAKIM, L., Animal Husbandry
HANDAYANTO, E., Agriculture
HARIJONO, Agricultural Technology
HARSONO, O. S. H., Economics
HIDAYAT, A., Medicine
HIDAYAT, M., Medicine
ICHSAN, M., Administration
IDRUS, M. S., Economics
ISLAMY, M. I., Administration
ISMANI, Administration
KALIM, H., Medicine
KIPTIYAH, S. M., Economics
KOENTJOKO, Animal Husbandry
KUMALANINGSIH, S., Agricultural Technology
LOEKITO, R. M., Medicine
LUTH, T., Law
MARTAWIJAYA, S., Economic Development
MIMBAR, S. M., Agriculture
MISMAIL, B., Electrical Engineering
MOELJADI, H., Economics
MOENANDIR, J., Agriculture
MUNIR, M., Agriculture
MUNIR, M., Law
MUSTADJAB, M. M., Agriculture
NIMRAN, U., Administration
NUGROHO, W. H., Mathematics
PURNOMO, H., Animal Husbandry
RASYID, Y., Agriculture
RUBAI, M., Law
SALEH, M., Economics
SARGOWO, D., Medicine
SASTRAHIDAYAT, I. R., Agriculture
SEMAOEN, M. I., Agriculture
SITOMPUL, S. M., Agriculture
SJAMSUDDIN, S., Administration
SODIKI, A., Law
SOEBAKTININGSIH, Medicine
SOEBARINOTO, Animal Husbandry
SOEHONO, L. A., Mathematics
SOEKARTAWI, Agriculture
SOEMARNO, Agriculture
SOEPARMAN, S., Engineering
SOEPRAPTO, R., Administration
SOETANTO, H., Animal Husbandry
SOEWARTO, S., Medicine
SUBROTO, B., Accounting
SUDARMA, M. S., Accounting
SUGIJANTO, Agriculture
SUGITO, Y., Agriculture
SUHARDJONO, Research Methodology
SUHARTO, B., Agricultural Technology
SUKESI, K., Agriculture
SULISTYOWATI, L., Agriculture
SUMITRO, S. B., Agricultural Technology
SUNUHARYO, B. S., Administration
SUPRIYANTO, E., Fisheries
SUSANTO, M. H., Economics
SUSANTO, T., Agricultural Technology
SYAFRADJI, M. S., Economics
SYAMSIDI, S. R. C., Agriculture
SYAMSULBAHRI, Agriculture
SYEKHFANI, Agriculture
THANTAWI, Economics
TRIADJI, B., Economics
TRISUNUWATI, P., Epidemiology
TROENA, E. A., Economics
UTOMO, W. H., Agriculture
WAHAB, S. A., Administration
WARDANA, N. G., Engineering
WARDIYATI, T., Agriculture
WIDJANARKO, S. B., Agricultural Technology
WIDODO, M. A., Medicine
ZAIN, D., Economics

UNIVERSITAS CENDERAWASIH

Jl. Kamp Wolker, Kampus UNCEN Waena, Jayapura, Papua 99358

Telephone: (967) 572108
Fax: (967) 572102
E-mail: uncen@uncen.ac.id
Internet: www.uncen.ac.id

Founded 1962
Language of instruction: Indonesian
Academic year: September to July

Rector: Ir FRANS A. WOSPAKRIK
Vice-Rector: Drs ISAAK AJOMI
Vice-Rector: Drs DAAN DIMARA
Vice-Rector: Ir ROBERT LALENOH
Gen. Admin. Officer: Ir H. SUMANTO
Academic and Student Admin. Officer: Drs M. HATTU
Librarian: Drs A. C. SUNGKANA HADI

Library of 56,000 vols
Number of teachers: 519
Number of students: 6,789

Publications: *Bulletin of Irian Jaya Development*, *Tifa Agro*

Faculties of agriculture, civil engineering, economics, education and teacher training, law, mathematics, natural sciences, social and political sciences.

UNIVERSITAS DIPONEGORO
(Diponegoro University)

Jl. Prof. Sudarto, Tembalang, Semarang 50275

Telephone: (24) 7460014
Fax: (24) 7460013
Internet: www.undip.ac.id

Founded 1956
Academic year: September to August

Rector: Prof. Ir EKO BUDIHARDJ
Vice-Rector for Academic Affairs: Prof. Dr S. P. HADI
Vice-Rector for Admin. and Finance: Prof. Dr Ir Y. S. DARMANTO
Vice-Rector for Devt and Collaboration: Dr Dr SUSILO WIBOWO
Vice-Rector for Student Affairs: Dr Ir BAMBANG TRIONO BASUKI
Head of Admin. and Academic Bureau: Drs PRIYO SANTOSO
Head of Gen. Admin. Bureau: Dra KUSRINI
Head of Planning Admin. and Information Systems Bureau: Dra ISMARTINI
Head of Student Admin. Bureau: Dra PRANTIKASIH
University Librarian: Dra ARI WIDJAYANTI

Library of 191,224 vols
Number of teachers: 1,618
Number of students: 38,522

Publications: *Berita Penelitian, Berita UNDIP, Bhakti, Buletin Fekom, Bulletin Dharma Wanita, Bulletin Fakultas Peternakan & Perikanan, Cakranaka, Edent, Forum, Gallery, Gema, Gema Keadilan, Gema Teknologi, Hayam Wuruk, Ilmiah Politeknik, Info, Kinetika, Konsolidasi, Lembaran Imu Sastra, Mahaprika, Majalah, Majalah Kedokteran, Manunggal, Masalah-Masalah Hukum, Masalah Teknik, Media, Media Ekonomi & Bisnis, Nuansa, Opini, Prasasti, Publica, Pulsa, Respect, Teknis, Transient, Warta Perpustakaan, Zigma*

DEANS

Faculty of Animal Husbandry: Dr Ir BAMBANG SRIGANDONO
Faculty of Economics: Dr H. M. CHABACHIB
Faculty of Engineering: Prof. Ir EKO WAHYUNI
Faculty of Fisheries and Marine Science: Prof. Dr Ir YOHANES HUTALIRAT
Faculty of Law: ACHMAD BUSRO
Faculty of Letters: Prof. Dr RAHAYU PRIHATMI

Faculty of Mathematics and Natural Sciences: Dr Drs WALIYU SETIA RUDI
Faculty of Medicine: Prof. Dr KABULRACHMAN
Faculty of Public Health: Dr LUDFI SANTOSO
Faculty of Social and Political Sciences: Drs WARSITO

DIRECTORS

Community Service Institute: Drs SUWARSO
Education Development Institute: Drs YUSMILARSO
Research Institute: Prof. Dr Dr I. RIWANTO

PROFESSORS

ANGGORO, S., Aquatic Biology
ATMOMARSONO, U., Animal Science
BUDIHARDJO, E., Architecture
BUDI PRAYITNO, S., Aquaculture
DARMANTO, Y. S., Fisheries Resources
DARMONO, S., Nutrition
DJOKO MOELJANTO, S., Internal Medicine
DJULIATI SUROYO, A. M., Social and Economic History
FAIK HEYDER, A., Surgery
FATIMA MUIS, S., Nutrition
GHOZALI, I., Methodology
HADIHARDAJA, J., Steel Construction
HADISAPUTRO, S., Public Health
HARRY KISTANO, N., Letters
HARTONO, B., Neurology
HARTONO, S. R., Commercial Law
HUTABARAT, S., Oceanography
HUTABARAT, Y., Aquatic Culture
KABULRACHMAN, Dermatovenerology
KARYANA, S., Traditional Javanese Culture
KELIB, A., Islamic Law
KRISTIANTI, L., Paediatrics
MANGUNWIHARDJO, S., Financial Management
MIYASTO, Economics
MULADI, H., Criminal Law
MUSTAFID, Mathematics
NASUTION, I., Pharmacology and Theraputics
NAWAWI ARIEF, B., Criminal Law
NOTOATMOJO, H., Paediatrics
PARSUDI ABDULROCHIM, I., Internal Medicine
P. HADI, S., Environmental Studies
PRAMONO, N., Obstetrics and Gynaecology
PRAPTOHARDJO, U., Gynaecology and Obstetrics
PRIHATMI, M. S. R., Literature
RACHMATULLAH, P., Physiology
RAHAYU PRIHATMI, S., Literature
REDJEKI, H. S., Law
RIWANTO, Surgery
SARJADI, H., Anatomy, Pathology
SATOTO, Nutrition
SERIKAT PUTRAJAYA, N., Criminal Law
SOEBOWO, Anatomy, Pathology
SOEDARSONO, Animal Production
SOEDJARWO, Indonesian Literature
SOEDJATI, Linguistics
SOEJOENOES, A., Obstetrics and Gynaecology
SOEMANTRI, A., Paediatrics, Haematology
SOENARTO, S., Internal Medicine
SOETOMO, I., Linguistics
SOETOMO, S., Planology
S. TRASTOTENOJO, M., Paediatrics
SUDARYONO, Linguistics
SUDIGBIA, Paediatrics
SUGANGGA, Proscriptive Law
SULTANA, A., Histology
SUNARJO, S., Anaesthiology
SUNARTI, D., Animal Production
SUPRIHARYONO, A., Fisheries
SURYANTO, B., Agribusiness Management
SUSANTO, I. S., Criminal Law
SUTRISNO, I., Animal Husbandry
SYA'RANI, L., Fisheries
WARASIH, E., Law and Society
WARELLA, Y., Sociology and Politics
WIBOWO, S., Andrology
WILARDJO, S., Ophthalmology

UNIVERSITAS GADJAH MADA

Bulaksumur, Yogyakarta 55281

Telephone: (274) 588688
Fax: (274) 565223
E-mail: rektor@ugm.ac.id
Internet: www.ugm.ac.id

Founded 1949
Language of instruction: Indonesian
Academic year: September to June

Rector: Prof. Ir SUDJARWADI
Sr Vice-Rector for Academic, Research, and Community Service: Prof. Dr Ir SUDJARWADI
Sr Vice-Rector for Admin., Finance and Human Resources Devt: Ir AINUN NA'IM
Vice-Rector for Students, Alumni and Business Devt: Prof. Dr Ir ZAENAL BACHARUDDIN
Exec. Sec.: Drs DJOKO MOERDIYANTO

Number of teachers: 2,273
Number of students: 55,000

Publications: *Agritech* (agricultural technology, 4 a year), *Berita Kedokteran Masyarakat* (medicine, 4 a year), *Berkala Ilmiah MIPA* (mathematics and natural sciences, 2 a year), *Berkala Ilmu Kedokteran* (medicine, 4 a year), *Biologi* (biology, 2 a year), *Buletin Kehutanan* (forestry, 4 a year), *Buletin Peternakan* (animal husbandry, 4 a year), *Forum Teknik* (engineering, 3 a year), *Humaniora* (humanities, 4 a year), *Indonesian Food and Nutrition Progress* (2 a year), *Indonesian Journal of Geography* (2 a year), *Jurnal Fisika Indonesia* (mathematics and natural sciences, 4 a year), *Majalah Farmasi Indonesia* (pharmacy, 4 a year), *Majalah Geografi Indonesia* (geography, 2 a year), *Manusia dan Lingkungan* (environmental studies, 3 a year), *Media Teknik* (engineering, 4 a year), *Perlindungan Tanaman Indonesia* (agricultural technology, 2 a year), *Warta Pengabdian* (community service, 3 a year)

DEANS

Faculty of Agricultural Technology: Dr Ir DJAGAL WISESO MARSENO
Faculty of Agriculture: Prof. Ir TRIWIBOWO YUWONO
Faculty of Animal Science: Prof. Dr Ir TRI YUWANTA
Faculty of Biology: Dr RETNO PENI SANCAYANINGSIH
Faculty of Cultural Sciences: Dr IDA ROCHANI ADI
Faculty of Dentistry: Drg. SOEHARDONO
Faculty of Economics: Prof. MARWAN ASRI
Faculty of Engineering: Ir TUMIRAN
Faculty of Forestry: Prof. Dr Ir MOCHAMMAD NA'IEM
Faculty of Geography: Prof. Dr SURATMAN
Faculty of Law: Prof. Dr MARSUDI TRIATMODJO
Faculty of Mathematics and Natural Sciences: Dr CHAIRIL ANWAR
Faculty of Medicine: Prof. Dr ALI GHUFRON MUKTI
Faculty of Pharmacy: Prof. Dr MARCHABAN
Faculty of Philosophy: Dr M. MUKHTASAR SYAMSUDDIN
Faculty of Psychology: Prof. Dr FATUROCHMAN
Faculty of Social and Political Sciences: Prof. Dr PRATIKNO
Faculty of Veterinary Medicine: Prof. Dr Drh. BAMBANG SUMIARTO MOECHAROM
Graduate Programmes: Prof. Dr HARTONO

UNIVERSITAS HALUOLEO

Kampus Bumi Tridharma Anduonohu, Kendari, Sulawesi Tenggara 93232

Telephone: (401) 25104
Fax: (401) 22006

Founded 1981

Academic year: September to June

Rector: Prof. Dr Ir H. SOLEH SOLAHUDDIN
Vice-Rector: Drs SULEMAN
Vice-Rector: Drs H. AHMAD BAKKARENG
Vice-Rector: Drs LA ODE MUH. ARSYAD TENO
Vice-Rector: Drs H. ALIBAS YUSUF
Librarian: Drs L. HAISU

Library of 43,342 vols
Number of teachers: 452
Number of students: 9,029

Publications: *Agri Plus* (6 a year), *Gema Pendidikan* (6 a year), *Journal Haluoleo* (4 a year), *Majalah Ekonomi* (6 a year), *Sosial Politik* (6 a year)

DEANS

Faculty of Agriculture: Ir H. MAHMUD HAMUNDU
Faculty of Economics: HASAN AEDY
Faculty of Education: Drs H. MUHAMMAD GAZALI
Faculty of Social and Political Sciences: Drs H. M. NUR RAKHMAN

UNIVERSITAS HASANUDDIN

Jl. Perintis Kemerdekaan, Kampus Unhas Tamalanrea, Makassar 90245

Telephone: (411) 584002
Fax: (411) 585188
E-mail: cio@unhas.ac.id
Internet: www.unhas.ac.id

Founded 1959
Academic year: September to February

Rector: Prof. Dr Dr IDRUS A. PATURUSI
Deputy Rector for Academic Affairs: Prof. Dr DJABIR HAMZAH
Deputy Rector for Admin. and Financial Affairs: Prof. Dr Ir H. A. SYAMSUL ARIFIN P.
Deputy Rector for Student and Alumni Affairs: Prof. Dr Ir AMBO ALA
Deputy Rector for Cooperative and Devt Affairs: Prof. Dr Ir A. MAPPADJANTJI AMIEN
Registrar: Dra RATNA ARDJO
Librarian: Dr SYARIFUDDIN ATTJE (acting)

Number of teachers: 1,684
Number of students: 20,816

Publications: *Identitas UNHAS* (12 a year), *Interaski/LPPM* (3 a year), *Jupiter/Perpustakaan* (2 a year)

DEANS

Faculty of Agriculture and Forestry: Prof. Dr Ir SYAWAL
Faculty of Animal Husbandry: Prof. Dr Ir H. BASIT WELLO
Faculty of Dentistry: Dr M. AMIN KANSI
Faculty of Economics: Dr H. FATTAH KADIR
Faculty of Engineering: Dr Ir SALEH PALLU
Faculty of Law: ABDUL RAZAK
Faculty of Letters: Dr H. M. DARWIS
Faculty of Marine Sciences and Fisheries: Ir HAMZAH SUNUSI
Faculty of Mathematics and Natural Sciences: Prof. Dr ALFIAN NOOR
Faculty of Medicine: Prof. Dr Dr IDRUS A. PATURUSI
Faculty of Public Health: Prof. Dr Dr RAZAK THAHA
Faculty of Social and Political Sciences: Prof. Dr HAFIED CANGARA

DIRECTORS

Central Workshop: Dr Ir DUMA HASAN
Language Centre: Dr ETTY BAZERGAN
Postgraduate Studies Programme: Prof. Dr Ir H. M. NATSIR NESSA
UNHAS Information Centre: Dr Ir MUH. IVAN AZIS

UNIVERSITAS INDONESIA

Main Campus Kampus UI Depok Jakarta 16424
Jl. Salemba Raya no. 4, Jakarta 10430
Telephone: (21) 7867222
Fax: (21) 78849060
E-mail: io-ui@ui.ac.id
Internet: www.ui.ac.id

Founded 1849 as School for Javanese Doctor
Public control
Languages of instruction: Indonesian, English
Academic year: August to June (2 semesters)

Pres.: Prof. Dr GUMILAR RUSLIWA SOMANTRI
Vice-Pres. for Academic Affairs and Student Affairs: Prof. Dr Ir MUHAMMAD ANIS
Vice-Pres. for Human Resources, Finance, and Gen. Admin. Affairs: TAFSIR NURCHAMID
Vice-Pres. for Research, Devt and Industrial Cooperation: SUNARDJI
Univ. Sec.: Prof. Dr I. KETUT SURAJAYA
Head of Academic Quality Assurance Body: Prof. Dr HANNA BACHTIAR ISKANDAR
Librarian: Prof. Dr Ir RIRI FITRI SARI

Library: 5m. vols
Number of teachers: 6,694
Number of students: 49,183

Publication: *Antropologi Indonesia*
Publication: *Asean Marketing Journal*
Publication: *CIVIC, Journal for Civil Society Empowerment*
Publication: *EBAR (Economic Business Accounting Review)*
Publication: *Ekonomi dan Keuangan Indonesia (Economics and Finance in Indonesia)*
Publication: *EKSIS: Jurnal Ekonomi Keuangan dan Bisnis Islami*
Publication: *Gifted Review, Jurnal Keberbakatan dan Kreativitas*
Publication: *Glasnost, Jurnal Kajian Slavia - Rusia*
Publication: *GLOBAL, Jurnal Politik Internasional*
Publication: *Indonesian Capital Market Review*
Publication: *Indonesian Journal of Dentistry*
Publication: *JAKASTRA: Jurnal Aplikasi Kajian Stratejik*
Publication: *Jurnal Akutansi dan Keuangan Indonesia*
Publication: *Jurnal Bisnis & Birokrasi*
Publication: *Jurnal Ekonomi dan Pembangunan Indonesia*
Publication: *Jurnal Hukum Internasional (Indonesian Journal of International Law)*
Publication: *Jurnal Ilmu Komputer dan Teknologi Informasi (ICIS)*
Publication: *Jurnal Kajian Timur Tengah dan Islam*
Publication: *Jurnal Kajian Wilayah Eropa*
Publication: *Jurnal Kajian Pengembangan Perkotaan*
Publication: *Jurnal Keperawatan Indonesia*
Publication: *Jurnal Kriminologi Indonesia*
Publication: *Jurnal Lingkungan dan Pembangunan (Environment & Development)*
Publication: *Jurnal MTI (Magister Teknologi Informasi)*
Publication: *Jurnal Polisi Indonesia*
Publication: *Journal of Population* (2 a year)
Publication: *Jurnal Psikologi Sosial*
Publication: *Jurnal Sains Indonesia*
Publication: *Jurnal Studi Amerika*
Publication: *Jurnal TEKNOLOGI: Journal of Technology*

Publication: *KESMAS, Jurnal Kesehatan Masyarakat Nasional*
Publication: *KILAS*
Publication: *Majalah Ilmu Kefarmasian*
Publications: *Makara* (Health Sciences edn) (2 a year), *Makara* (Science edn) (2 a year), *Makara* (Social Sciences and Humanities edn) (2 a year), *Makara* (Technology edn) (2 a year), and various faculty bulletins
Publication: *MASYARAKAT: Jurnal Sosiologi*
Publication: *Medical Journal of Indonesia*
Publication: *The South East Asian Journal of Management*
Publication: *Thesis, Jurnal Penelitian Ilmu Komunikasi*
Publication: *Wacana, Jurnal Ilmu Pengetahuan Budaya*

DEANS

Faculty of Computer Sciences: Dr Prof. T. BASARUDIN
Faculty of Dentistry: Prof. BAMBANG IRAWAN
Faculty of Economics: Prof. FIRMANZAH
Faculty of Engineering: Dr Ir BAMBANG SUGIARTO
Faculty of Humanities: Dr BAMBANG WIBAWARTA
Faculty of Law: Prof. SAFRI NUGRAHA
Faculty of Mathematics and Sciences: Dr Prof. ADI BASUKRIADI
Faculty of Medicine: Dr RATNA SITOMPUL
Faculty of Nursing: Prof. Dra DEWI IRAWATI
Faculty of Psychology: Dr WILMAN DAHLAN MANSOER
Faculty of Public Health: Prof. Dr BAMBANG WISPRIYONO
Faculty of Social and Political Sciences: Dr BAMBANG SHERGI LAKSMONO
Graduate Studies: Prof. CHANDRA WIJAYA (Dir)

UNIVERSITAS ISLAM NEGERI SYARIF HIDAYATULLAH JAKARTA (Syarif Hidayatullah State Islamic University (UIN) Jakarta)

Jl. Ir H. Juanda, 95 Ciputat, Banten 15412
Telephone: (21) 7401925
Fax: (21) 7402982
E-mail: info@uinjkt.ac.id
Internet: www.uinjkt.ac.id

Founded 1960, as the State Academy of Islamic Studies, renamed the Syarif Hidayatullah State Institute of Islamic Studies 1998, univ. status 2002
State control

Rector: Prof. Dr KOMARUDDIN HIDAYAT
Vice-Rector for Academic Affairs: Dr JAMHARI
Vice-Rector for Gen. Admin.: Prof. Dr AMSAL BACHTIAR
Vice-Rector for Institutional Development: Dr SUDARNOTO ABDUL HAKIM
Vice-Rector for Students Affairs: Prof. Dr THIB RATA

DEANS

Faculty of Adab and Humanities: Dr H. ABDUL CHOIR
Faculty of Da'wa and Communication: Dr ARIEF SUBHAN
Faculty of Dirasat Islamiya: Prof. Dr ABUDDIN NATA
Faculty of Economics and Social Science: ABDUL HAMID
Faculty of Medicine and Health Sciences: Prof. Dr Dr M. K. TAJUDIN
Faculty of Psychology: Dr YAHYA UMAR
Faculty of Shari'a and Law: Prof. Dr M. AMIN SUMA
Faculty of Science and Technology: Dr Ir SYOPIANSYAH JAYA PUTRA

Faculty of Tarbiya and Teaching Sciences:
Prof. Dr DEDE ROSYADA
Faculty of Usul-al Din and Philosophy: Dr
AMIN NURDIN

UNIVERSITAS JAMBI

Kampus Universita Jambi, Jl. Raya Jambi,
Muara Bulian, Km 15 Mendalo, Jambi
36361
Telephone: (741) 583377
Fax: (741) 583111
E-mail: unja@unja.ac.id
Internet: www.unja.ac.id
Founded 1963
Language of instruction: Indonesian
Academic year: September to August
Rector: H. KEMAS ARSYAD SOMAD
Vice-Rector for Academic Affairs: Drs H.
ARDINAL
Vice-Rector for Admin.: Dr Ir. A. RAHMAN
Vice-Rector for External and Internal
Affairs: Dr AULIA TASMAN
Vice-Rector for Student Affairs: Dr Drs
MAIZAR KARIM
Head of Bureau of Academic Admin., Student
Affairs, Planning and Information Sys-
tems: Drs IBRAHIM
Head of Bureau of Gen. Admin. and Finance:
Drs H. A. GANI
Librarian: SYAFRI SYAM
Library of 140,000 vols
Number of teachers: 696
Number of students: 13,563
Publication: Berita UNJA (12 a year)

DEANS

Faculty of Agriculture: Dr Ir ZILKIFLI
Faculty of Animal Husbandry: Ir AFZALANI
Faculty of Economics: Dr AFRIZAL
Faculty of Education: Drs AFFAN MALIK
Faculty of Law: TAUFIK YAHYA
Postgraduate Programmes: Dr SURATNO

UNIVERSITAS JEMBER

Jl. Kalimantan 37, Jember 68121
Telephone and fax (331) 331042
Internet: www.unej.ac.id
Founded 1964
State control
Languages of instruction: Indonesian, Eng-
lish, French
Academic year: July to June
Rector: Prof. Dr H. KABUL SANTOSO
Vice-Rector for Academic Affairs: Dr Ir IDHA
HARIYANTO
Vice-Rector for Admin. and Finance: Prof.
Drs KADIMAN
Vice-Rector for Student Affairs: PURNOMO
Registrar: Drs MADE PEDUNGAN SARDHA
Dir of Agricultural Polytechnic: Ir H.
SUHARJO WIDODO
Dir of Univ. Research Institute: Drs LIAKIP
Librarian: Drs MAHFUD A.
Library of 117,441 vols
Number of teachers: 783
Number of students: 12,933
Publications: Argopuro, Dian Wanita, Gema
Universitas

DEANS

Faculty of Agricultural Technology: Ir
WAGITO
Faculty of Agriculture: Ir Hj. SITI HARTANTI
Faculty of Dentistry: Drg. BOB SOEBIJANTORO
Faculty of Economics: Drs H. SUKUSNI
Faculty of Law: SAMSI KUSAIRI
Faculty of Letters: Drs SUDJADI
Faculty of Social and Political Sciences: Prof.
Drs H. BARIMAN
Faculty of Teacher Training & Educational
Sciences: Drs SUKARDJO

UNIVERSITAS JENDERAL SOEDIRMAN

Jl. H. R. Boenyamin 708, Purwokerto, Cen-
tral Java
Telephone: (281) 635292
Fax: (281) 631802
E-mail: info@unsoed.ac.id
Internet: www.unsoed.ac.id
Founded 1963
Language of instruction: Indonesian
Academic year: September to August (two
semesters)
Rector: Prof. RUBIJANTO MISMAN
Vice-Rector for Academic Affairs: Dr SUD-
JARWO
Vice-Rector for Admin. Affairs: Prof. Dr H.
KAMIO
Vice-Rector for Student Affairs: KOMARI
Chief Registrar: Ir BAMBANG PURNOMO
Librarian: Drs CHAMDI
Number of teachers: 750
Number of students: 13,000
Publications: Journal of Rural Development
(4 a year), Majalah Ilmiah Unsoed (bio-
logical scientific journal, 4 a year)

DEANS

Faculty of Agriculture: Ir SUMIRAT BRONTO
WALUYO
Faculty of Animal Husbandry: Prof. Dr Ir
SWANDIARINI
Faculty of Biology: Prof. Dr Haji TRIANI
HARDIYATI
Faculty of Economics: Drs GATOT SUPRIHANTO
Faculty of Law: ABDUL AZIS NASIHUDIN
Faculty of Social Sciences and Politics: Drs
SUHARI

UNIVERSITAS LAMBUNG MANGKURAT

Kampus UNLAM, Jl. Brigjen H. Hasan
Basry, POB 279, South Kalimantan, Ban-
jarmasin 70123
Telephone and fax (511) 54177
E-mail: pr4@unlam.ac.id
Internet: www.unlam.ac.id
Founded 1958 as private univ., state control
1960
Public control
Language of instruction: Indonesian
Academic year: September to August
Rector: Prof. Dr I H. MUHAMMAD RUSLAN
Vice-Rector for Academic Affairs: Prof. Dr H.
MUHAMMAD HADIN MUHJAD
Vice-Rector for Admin. Affairs: Prof. Dr H.
AKHMAD GAZALI
Vice-Rector for Student Affairs: Prof. Dr Ir H.
IDIANNOR MAHYUDDIN
Vice-Rector for Planning and Cooperation
Affairs: Prof. Dr H. SUTARTO HADI
Head of Planning Administration and Infor-
mation Systems: Drs H. ARY ACHDYANI
Head of General Admin., Financial and
Employee Affairs: HERRY SUPRIYANTO
Head of Admin., Academic and Students
Affairs: Dra H. FITRIYANI A. KUSASI
Number of teachers: 1,042
Number of students: 17,144
Publications: Kalimantan Agriculture (4 a
year), Kalimantan Scientiae (2 a year),
Orientasi (4 a year), Vidya Karya (2 a year)

DEANS

Faculty of Agriculture: Ir H. RODINAH
Faculty of Economics: Drs H. FAHMI RIZANI,
MM, AK.
Faculty of Engineering: Ir H. NORMAN RUS-
LAN
Faculty of Fisheries: Ir RISWANDI BANDUNG
Faculty of Forestry: Ir SUNARDI, MS
Faculty of Law: HELMI, SH, MH
Faculty of Medicine: Dr H. HASYIM FACHIR

Faculty of Social and Political Sciences: Drs
SALADDIN GHALIB
Faculty of Teacher-Training and Education:
Drs H. AHMAD SOFYAN

UNIVERSITAS LAMPUNG
(University of Lampung)

Jl Prof. Dr Soemantri Brojonegoro No. 1,
Bandar Lampung 35145
Telephone: (721) 709611
Fax: (721) 702767
E-mail: info@unila.ac.id
Internet: www.unila.ac.id
Founded 1965
State control
Languages of instruction: Indonesian, Eng-
lish
Academic year: August to June (2 terms)
Rector: Prof. Dr Ir SUGENG P. HARIANTO
Vice-Rector I for Academic Affairs: Prof. Dr
Ir HASRIADI MAT AKIN
Vice-Rector II for Admin. and Finance
Affairs: Ir SULASTRI RAMLI
Vice-Rector III for Student Affairs: Dr D. M.
SUNARTO
Vice-Rector IV for Cooperation, Planning and
Information Affairs: Dr SATRIA BANGSAWAN
Admin. Gen. and Finance Bureau Leader:
HARSONO SUCIPTO
Admin. Planning, Management Information
System and Cooperation Bureau Leader:
Drs MARDI SYAHPERI
Research Centre Leader: Prof. JOHN HENDRI
Public Service Leader: Dr BUDI KOESTORO
Man. Dir: Prof. Dr Ir ABDUL KADIR SALAM
Library Dir: Drs SUGIANTA
Number of teachers: 1,173
Number of students: 25,944
Publications: Buletin Penelitian, Warta Pen-
gabdian pada Masyarakat

DEANS

Faculty of Agriculture: Prof. WAN ABBAS
ZAKARIA
Faculty of Economics: TOTO GUNARTO
Faculty of Education and Teacher Training:
Prof. Dr SUDJARWO
Faculty of Engineering: Dr LUSMELIA
Faculty of Law: ADIUS SEMENGUK
Faculty of Mathematics and Natural Science:
Dr SUTYARSO
Faculty of Social and Political Sciences: Drs
AGUS HADIAWAN

DIRECTORS

Bureau of Legal Consultation and Aid: M.
PULUNG
Centre of Languages: Drs DEDI SUPRIYADI
Centre of Public Services: Drs KANTAN
ABDULLAH
Institute of Demography: MUCHSIN BADAR
Institute of Environmental Studies: Prof. Dr
K. E. S. MANIK
Institute of Management: SUDANAR
Lampungnese Culture Studies: Dr VIVIT
BARTOVEN
Research Centre: Dr FADDEL DJAUHAR

UNIVERSITAS MALIKUSSALEH

Jl. Tgk Chik Ditiro, 26 Lancang Garam
Lhokseumawe, Aceh
Telephone: (645) 41373
Fax: (645) 44450
E-mail: info@unimal.ac.id
Internet: www.unimal.ac.id
Founded 1969
State control
Faculties of agriculture, economics, engin-
eering and law
Rector: Prof. A. HADI ARIFIN
Vice-Rector I: RASYIDIN
Vice-Rector II: AIYUB

Vice-Rector III: BAKHTIAR
Vice-Rector IV: M. AKMAL.

UNIVERSITAS MATARAM

Jl. Majapahit 62, Nusa Tenggara Barat,
Mataram 83125
Telephone: (370) 633007
Fax: (370) 636041
E-mail: rektorat@unram.org
Internet: www.unram.ac.id
Founded 1962
Public control
Language of instruction: Bahasa
Academic year: September to August
Rector: Dr SUNARPI
Vice-Rector for Academic Affairs: Dr L. SAPTA
  KARYADI
Vice-Rector for Admin. Affairs: Dr HAILUDIN
Vice-Rector for External Cooperation:
  SUWARDJI
Vice-Rector for Student Affairs: Dr NASRUDIN
Registrar: MUHIBAH NASRUDIN
Admin. Officer: SYAMSUDIN
Librarian: LALU BUDIMAN
Library of 87,557 vols
Number of teachers: 1,018
Number of students: 17,457
Publications: *Agroteksos* (4 a year), *Komuni-
  tas* (2 a year), *Research Institution Journal*
  (3 a year)

DEANS

Faculty of Agriculture: Prof. Dr M. SARJAN
Faculty of Animal Science: Prof. Dr YUSUF A.
  SUTARYONO
Faculty of Economics: Prof. Dr THATOK
  ASMUNY
Faculty of Education and Teaching: Prof. Dr
  MAHSUN
Faculty of Engineering: FATURACHMAN
Faculty of Law: Prof. Dr GALANG ASMARA
Faculty of Medicine: Prof. Dr MULYANTO

UNIVERSITAS MULAWARMAN

Kampus Gunung. Kelua, East Kalimantan,
  Samarinda 75119
Telephone: (541) 741118
Fax: (541) 732870
E-mail: rektorat@unmul.ac.id
Internet: www.unmul.ac.id
Founded 1962 as Mulawarman School of
  Higher Learning, present status 1963
Academic year: September to August
Rector: Prof. Dr ARIFFIEN BRATAWINATA
Vice-Rector for Academic Affairs: Prof. Dr
  MAMAN SUTISNA
Vice-Rector for Admin. and Finance:
  SUYATNO WIJOYO
Vice-Rector for Devt and Cooperation: Prof.
  Dra Hj. RUSMILAWATI
Vice-Rector for Student Affairs: Prof. Drs
  EDDY SUBANDRIJO
Head of Gen. Admin. and Finance Bureau:
  MASRIANI
Library Dir: SUBIANTORO
Number of teachers: 856
Number of students: 26,746
Publication: *Frontir* (2 a year)

DEANS

Faculty of Agriculture: GUSTI HAFIZIANSYAH
Faculty of Economics: Prof. ZAMRUDDIN HASID
Faculty of Education and Teacher Training:
  Drs ICHRAR ASBAR
Faculty of Engineering: Ir H. DHARMA
  WIDADA
Faculty of Fisheries and Marine Science: Dr
  H. HELMINUDDIN
Faculty of Forestry: Prof. Dr AFIF RUCHAEMI
Faculty of Law: LA SINA

Faculty of Mathematics and Natural Sci-
  ences: Drs SUDRAJAT
Faculty of Medicine: Dr EMIL BACHTIAR
  MOERAD
Faculty of Pharmacy: LAODE RIJAI
Faculty of Public Health: Dra SITI BADRAH
Faculty of Social and Political Sciences: D. B.
  PARANOAN

UNIVERSITAS NEGERI GORONTALO

Jl. Jend. Sudirman, 6 Kota, Gorontalo
Telephone: (435) 821125
Fax: (435) 821752
Internet: www.ung.ac.id
Founded 1963
State control
Rector: Prof. Dr Ir H. NELSON POMALINGO
Vice-Rector I: Dr SYAMSU QAMAR BADU
Vice-Rector II: Drs NAWIR SUNE
Vice-Rector III: Drs HAMZAH UNO
Vice-Rector IV: Dr MAHLUDIN BARUADI

DEANS

Faculty of Agriculture: Ir ZULZAIN ILAHUDE
Faculty of Education: Drs SAMATOWA USMAN
Faculty of Engineering: Drs NAWIR SUNE
Faculty of Health Sciences and Sports: Dra
  RAMA P. HIOLA
Faculty of Literature and Culture: Dra HJ.
  MALABAR SAYAMA
Faculty of Mathematics and Natural Sci-
  ences: Dr RAMLI UTINA
Faculty of Social Sciences: Drs MOONTI
  USMAN

UNIVERSITAS NEGERI JAKARTA
(State University of Jakarta)

Jl. Rawamangun Muka, Jakarta 13220
Telephone: (21) 4890046
Fax: (21) 4893726
E-mail: administrator@unj.ac.id
Internet: www.unj.ac.id
Founded 1957
State control
Faculties of economy, engineering, languages
and arts, mathematics and natural sciences,
science and education, social sciences, sports
Rector: Dr BEDJO SUJANTO
Vice-Rector I: Dr ZAINAL RAFLI
Vice-Rector II: Dr SYARIFUDIN
Vice-Rector III: Drs FACHRUDDIN ARBAH
Vice-Rector IV: Dr SOEPRIJANTO.

UNIVERSITAS NEGERI MAKASSAR
(State University of Makassar)

Jl. A. P. Pettarani, Makassar 90222
Telephone: (411) 869854
E-mail: admin@unm.ac.id
Internet: www.unm.ac.id
Founded 1961
State control
Faculties of arts and design, economics,
education, engineering, languages and lit-
erature, mathematics and natural sciences,
psychology, sports science
Rector: Prof. Dr H. ARISMUNANDAR
Vice-Rector I: Prof. Dr SOFYAN SALAM
Vice-Rector II: Prof. Dr ANDI ICHSAN
Vice-Rector III: Prof. Dr HAMSU ABDUL GANI
Vice-Rector IV: Dr NURDIN NONI.

UNIVERSITAS NEGERI MALANG
(State University of Malang)

Jl. Semarang 5, Malang 65145
Telephone: (341) 551312
Fax: (341) 551921
E-mail: info@um.ac.id
Internet: um.ac.id
Founded 1954

State control
Languages of instruction: English, Indone-
  sian
Academic year: July to June
Rector: Prof. Dr H. SUPARNO (acting)
Vice-Rector I: Dr H. KUSMINTARDJO
Vice-Rector II: Prof. Dr H. AH. ROFI'UDDIN
Vice-Rector III: Drs H. KADIM MASJKUR
Vice-Rector IV: Drs H. ISNANDAR
Library of 56,251 vols
Number of teachers: 929
Number of students: 25,100
Publications: *Jurnal Bahasa dan Seni, Jur-
  nal Ilmu Pendidikan, Jurnal Pendidikan
  dan Pembelajaran, Jurnal Sekolah Dasar,
  TEFLIN*

DEANS

Faculty of Economy: Dr. ERY TRI DJATMIKA
  RUDIANTO WAHJU WARDHANA
Faculty of Education: Prof. Dr. M.Pd H.
  HENDYAT SUTOPO
Faculty of Engineering: Prof Dr Ir H.DJOKO
  KUSTONO
Faculty of Letters: Prof. Dr. H. DAWUD
Faculty of Science and Mathematics: Dr. H.
  ISTAMAR SYAMSURI
Faculty of Social Sciences: Prof. Dr. HAR-
  IYONO
Faculty of Sports Science: Dr. ROESDIYANTO
Programme of Postdoctoral Studies: Prof. Dr
  MARTHEN PALI

UNIVERSITAS NEGERI MANADO
(State University of Manado)

Tondano, Manado
Internet: www.unima.ac.id
Founded 1955
State control
Rector: Prof. Dr PHILOTEUS E. A. TUERAH.

UNIVERSITAS NEGERI MEDAN
(State University of Medan)

Jl. Willem Iskandar Pasar V, Medan 20221
Telephone: (61) 6613365
Fax: (61) 6613319
E-mail: sekretariat@unimed.ac.id
Internet: www.unimed.ac.id
Founded 1956
State control
Rector: SYAWAL GULTOM.

UNIVERSITAS NEGERI PAPUA
(Papua State University)

Manokwari
Internet: www.unipa.ac.id
Founded 2000
State control
Faculties of agriculture and agricultural
technology, animal husbandry, economics,
fisheries and marine science, forestry, math-
ematics and natural sciences
Rector: Prof. Dr Ir FRANS WANGGAI.

UNIVERSITAS NEGERI SEMARANG
(State University of Semarang)

Semarang
Internet: www.unnes.ac.id
Founded 1961
State control
Faculty of economics and law, education,
engineering, languages and arts, mathemat-
ics and natural sciences, social sciences,
sports
Rector: Prof. Dr H. SUDIJONNO SASTROAT-
  MODJO
Vice-Rector for Academic Affairs: Prof. Dr
  SUPRIADI RUSTAD
Vice-Rector for Gen. Admin.: Drs WAHYONO

Vice-Rector for Devt and Cooperation: Prof. Dr FATHUR ROKHMAN

Vice-Rector for Student Affairs: Dr MASRU-KHI.

UNIVERSITAS NEGERI SURABAYA
(State University of Surabaya)

Jl. Ketintang, Surabaya

Telephone: (31) 828009

Fax: (31) 828080

E-mail: rektor@um.ac.id

Internet: www.unesa.ac.id

Founded 1960

State control

Rector: Prof. Dr H. SUPARNO.

UNIVERSITAS NEGERI YOGYAKARTA

Karangmalang, Yogyakarta 55281

Telephone: (274) 586168

Fax: (274) 542185

E-mail: humas@uny.ac.id

Internet: www.uny.ac.id

Founded 1964

State control

Rector: Prof. SUGENG MARDIYONO.

UNIVERSITAS NUSA CENDANA
(Nusa Cendana University)

Jl. Adisucipto, Penfui, Nusa Tenggara Timur, Kupang 85001

Telephone: (380) 881580

Fax: (380) 881586

E-mail: puskomundana@undana.ac.id

Internet: www.undana.ac.id

Founded 1962

State control

Languages of instruction: Indonesian, English

Academic year: July to June

Rector: Prof. Ir FRANS UMBU DATTA

Vice-Rector for Academic Affairs: Drs DAVID PANDIE

Vice-Rector for Admin. Affairs: Drs DOPPY ROY NENDISSA

Vice-Rector for Cooperation Affairs: Ir FABIAN HARRY LAWALU

Vice-Rector for Student Affairs: Ir MAXIMI-LIAN KAPA

Chief Admin. Officer for Academic, Students and Information Systems: Drs DAUD U. Z. KAMURI

Chief Admin. Officer for Finance and Facilities: Drs JOSEPH WULAGENING

Librarian: Drs GORIS SABON

Number of teachers: 900

Number of students: 15,000

Publications: *Liguminesa Journal* (4 a year), *Media Eksakta Journal* (4 a year), *Nusa Cendana Journal* (4 a year), *Sinergia* (12 a year), *Warta Undana* (12 a year)

DEANS

Faculty of Agriculture: Dr MARTHEN PELO-KILLA

Faculty of Animal Husbandry: Ir AGUS KONDA MALIK

Faculty of Law: Dr SUKARDAN ALOVSIUS

Faculty of Medicine: Dr HERU TJAHYONO

Faculty of Public Health: Ir GUSTAF OEMATAN

Faculty of Science and Engineering: Dr MANGGADAS LUMBAN GAOL

Faculty of Social and Political Sciences: Prof. Dr ALOYSIUS LILIWERI

Faculty of Teacher Training and Education: Drs LUKAS BILI BORA

UNIVERSITAS PADJADJARAN

Jl. Dipati Ukur 35, Bandung 40132

Telephone: (22) 2503271

Fax: (22) 2534498

E-mail: info@unpad.ac.id

Internet: www.unpad.ac.id

Founded 1957

State control

Languages of instruction: Indonesian, English

Academic year: August to July (two semesters)

Rector: Prof. Dr H. A. HIMENDRA WARGAHADI-BRATA

Vice-Rector for Academic Affairs: Prof. Dr H. PONPON S. IDJRADINATA

Vice-Rector for Admin.: M. WAHYUDIN ZARKA-SYI

Vice-Rector for Cooperation: Prof. Dr H. USMAN HARDI

Vice-Rector for Planning, Information Systems and Supervision: Prof. T. SUGANDA

Vice-Rector for Student Affairs: SYARIF A. BARMAWI

Librarian: Prof. Dr I. NURPILIHAN

Library of 178,441 vols

Number of teachers: 1,868

Number of students: 40,482

Publications: *Agrikulture* (Agriculture, 3 a year), *Bionatura* (Sciences, 3 a year), *Jurnal Ekonomi* (Economics, 2 a year), *Jurnal Kedokteran Bandung* (Medicine, 3 a year), *Jurnal Keperawatan* (Nursing, 2 a year), *Puslitbangkum* (Law, 2 a year), *Sosiohumaniora* (Social Sciences, 3 a year)

DEANS

Faculty of Agriculture: Prof. Dr SADELI NATASASMITA

Faculty of Animal Husbandry: Prof. Dr NASIPAN USRI

Faculty of Communication Science: Drs SOLEH SOEMIRAT

Faculty of Dentistry: Dr SETIAWAN NATASA-MITA

Faculty of Economics: Prof. Dr H. SURIPTO SAMID

Faculty of Law: Prof. Dr MAN SUPARMAN SASTRAWIDJAJA

Faculty of Letters: Prof. Dr H. EDI SUHARDI EKADJATI

Faculty of Mathematics and Natural Sciences: Prof. Dr SUPRIATNA

Faculty of Medicine: Dr FIRMAN FUAD WIR-AKUSUMAH

Faculty of Psychology: Dr H. SURYANA SUMANTRI

Faculty of Social and Political Science: Drs TACHJAN

UNIVERSITAS PALANGKARAYA

Jl. Yos Sudarso, Kotak Pos 2, Palangka Raya, Kalimantan Tengah 73112

Telephone: (536) 26878

Fax: (536) 21722

E-mail: info@universitaspalangkaraya.ac.id

Internet: www.upr.ac.id

Founded 1963

Language of instruction: Indonesian

Academic year: July to June

Rector: Drs NAPA J. AWAT

Vice-Rector I: Drs HERIYANTO M. GARANG

Vice-Rector II: Drs DADANG LORIDA

Vice-Rector III: H. M. DAMIRI

Vice-Rector IV: Prof. Dr H. AHMADI ISA

Academic and Students' Admin. Officer: Drs LEUNHARD BAN YEN

Librarian: Dra ISTIRAHAYU

Number of teachers: 501

Number of students: 5,265

Publications: *Garantung* (12 a year), *Optimal* (12 a year), *Suara Tunjung Nyaho* (12 a year), *Wahana* (12 a year)

DEANS

Faculty of Agriculture: Ir SINTO R. NOEHAN

Faculty of Economics: Drs EFENDY D. TIM-BANG

Faculty of Education and Teacher Training: Drs HENRY SINGARASA

UNIVERSITAS PATTIMURA AMBON

POB 95, Jl. Ir M. Putuhena Poka, Ambon 97233

Telephone: (911) 322626

Fax: (911) 322691

E-mail: sisdiksat@unpatti.ac.id

Internet: www.unpatti.ac.id

Founded 1956, present status 1962

Language of instruction: Indonesian

Academic year: August to July

Rector: Dr Ir J. L. NANERE

Vice-Rector for Academic Affairs: Prof. P. J. SIWABESSY

Vice-Rector for Admin. and Finance: J. LEIWAKABESSY

Vice-Rector for Student Affairs: Ir J. J. TUHUMURY

Registrar: Drs E. LEUWOL

Librarian: ALI ZAWAWI

Number of teachers: 636

Number of students: 7,516

Publication: *Media Unpatti* (12 a year)

DEANS

Faculty of Agriculture: Ir J. PUTINELLA

Faculty of Economics: Drs L. A. RASJID

Faculty of Fisheries: Ir J. M. NANLOHY

Faculty of Law: C. M. PATTIRUHU

Faculty of Social and Political Sciences: Drs M. RENUR

Faculty of Teacher Training and Education: Drs T. J. A. UNEPUTTY

Faculty of Technology: Ir J. ASTHENU

DIRECTORS

Institute of Community Service: Dr MUS. HULISELAN

Institute of Research: Dr Ir P. SITIAPESSY

UNIVERSITAS PENDIDIKAN GANESHA SINGARAJA

Bali

Telephone: (362) 22570

Fax: (362) 25735

E-mail: humas@undiksha.ac.id

Internet: www.undiksha.ac.id

State control

Faculties of education, languages and arts, mathematics and natural sciences, social education, sports and health, technical and vocational education

Rector: Dr I NYOMAN SUDIANA

Vice-Rector I: Dr I GUSTI PUTU SUHARTA

Vice-Rector II: Dr I NYOMAN JAMPEL

Vice-Rector III: Drs I PUTU SUHARTA

Vice-Rector IV: Dr I KETUT SEKEN

Library of 37,818 vols, 4275 titles.

UNIVERSITAS PENDIDIKAN INDONESIA

Jl. Dr Setiabudhi 229, Bandung 40154

Telephone: (22) 2013161

Fax: (22) 2013651

Internet: www.upi.edu

Founded 1954 as Perguruan Tinggi Pendidikan Guru (Teacher's Education College), reformed as Bandung Institute of Teaching and Educational Sciences 1964, present status 1999

State control

Faculties of educational sciences, language and art, science, social studies, sports and health, technology

Rector: Prof. SUNARYO KARTADINATA
Number of teachers: 1,302
Number of students: 22,700

UNIVERSITAS RIAU

Kampus Bina Widya Km 12.5, Simpang
Baru, Pekanbaru, Sumatra 28293

Telephone: (761) 63266
Fax: (761) 63279
E-mail: rektor@unri.ac.id
Internet: www.unri.ac.id

Founded 1962
Public control
Language of instruction: Indonesian
Academic year: September to July

Rector: Prof. Dr MUCHTAR AHMAD
Vice-Rector for Academic Affairs: Prof. Dr
DADANG ISKANDAR
Vice-Rector for Admin.: Drs AMIR HASAN
Vice-Rector for Planning and Cooperation: Ir
SUWARDI LOCKMAN
Vice-Rector for Student Affairs: Ir ARIFIEN
MANSYOER
Librarian: Dr NURHAYATI

Number of teachers: 919
Number of students: 24,643

Publications: *Dawat* (journal of Malay language and culture, 4 a year), *Jurnal
Agritek* (agricultural technology, 2 a
year), *Jurnal Ekonomi* (economics, 4 a
year), *Jurnal Ilmu Sosial dan Politik*
(social and political sciences, 4 a year),
Jurnal Natur Indonesia (2 a year), *Jurnal
Penelitian* (general scientific research, 4 a
year), *Jurnal Perikanan dan Ilmu Kelau-
tan* (fisheries and marine science, 2 a year),
Terubuk (fisheries bulletin, 4 a year)

DEANS

Faculty of Agriculture: Prof. Dr USAMAN PATO
Faculty of Economics: Drs KENNEDY
Faculty of Engineering: Dr BAHRI
Faculty of Fisheries: Prof. Dr BUSTARI
Faculty of Law: H. B. GUSLIANA
Faculty of Medicine: Dr TASWIN YACOB
Faculty of Natural Sciences and Mathemat-
ics: Prof. Dr ADEL ZAMRI
Faculty of Politics and Social Science: Drs
ALI YUSRI
Faculty of Teacher Training and Education:
Prof. Dr ISJONI

PROFESSORS

ADAM, D., Government and Law
AHMAD, M., Marine Sciences and Fisheries
DAHRIL, T., Planktonology and Water Quality
DIAH, M., Education
HASAN, K., Education
IMRAN, A., Islamology
ISKANDAR, D., Physics
KASMY, M. F., Physics
KASRY, A., Aquatic Resources Management
MAHMUD, S., Education
MARZUKI, S., History Education
RAB, T., Enzymology
RAHMAN, M., Mathematics
RASYAD, A., Agriculture
SAAD, M., Rural Sociology
SAMAD, R., Education
SUWARDI, History
UMAR, S. M., Education
USMAN, F., Agriculture

UNIVERSITAS SAM RATULANGI

Kampus UNSRAT Bahu, North Sulawesi,
Manado 95115

Telephone: (431) 863886
Fax: (431) 822568
E-mail: rektorat@unsrat.ac.id
Internet: www.unsrat.ac.id

Founded 1961
State control

Language of instruction: Indonesian
Academic year: starts September

Rector: Prof. Dr DONALD A. RUMOKOY
Vice-Rector: Prof. Dr J. SH POLIL MANDANG
Vice-Rector: Prof. Dr PAULUS KINDANGEN
Vice-Rector: Prof. Dr B. H. R. KALRUPAN
Vice-Rector: Prof. Dr DAVID A. KALIGIS
Vice-Rector: Prof. Dr Ir JEFREY I KINDANGEN
Vice-Rector: Prof. Drs MAJID ABDULLAH
Head of Bureau for Academic and Student
Admin.: H. J. MEWENGKANG
Head of Central Library: D. SILANGEN

Number of teachers: 1,496
Number of students: 12,526

Publication: *Palakat-Inovasi*

DEANS

Faculty of Agriculture: Dr Ir D. T. SEMBEL
Faculty of Animal Husbandry: Prof. Dr D. A.
KALIGIS
Faculty of Economics: Prof. NY. I. NAJOEN
Faculty of Engineering: R. J. M. MANDAGI
Faculty of Fisheries and Maritime Sciences:
Prof. Dr S. BERHIMPON
Faculty of Law: Prof. ADOLF DAPU
Faculty of Letters: Drs ROBERT TANDI
Faculty of Mathematics and Natural Science:
Dr S. RONDONUWU
Faculty of Medicine: Dr J. W. SIAGIAN
Faculty of Public Health: Prof. Dr JOOTJE
M.L. UMBOH
Faculty of Social Sciences and Politics: Drs J.
J. LONTAAN

PROFESSORS

ALAMSJAH, Soil Physics
BUDIARSO, Technology
DUNDU, B., Microbiology
JAN, H., Statistics
KAKAUHE, R. P. L., Management Accounting
KAPOJOS-MONGULA, I. C. R., Civil Law
KARINDA, D. S., English and Dutch
KASINEM-S., Commercial Law
KORAH, M. W., Marketing Management Sci-
ence
MANDANG, J. H. A., Ahli Mata
MUNIR, M., Paediatrics
MUSA, A., Modern Indonesian History
MUSA KARIM, Indonesian Literature
PALAR, W. T., Agrarian Studies
PALENEWEN, J. L., Ecology
PANDA, H. O., Surgery
PUNUH-GO, S., Civil Law
ROGI, M., Economic Development
SALEH, M., Indonesian Government System
SINOLUNGAN, J. M., Medical Psychology
SOEPENO, Customary Law
SUPIT, J. T., Sociology
TANGKUDUNG, R. S., Civil Administration
TIMBOELENG, K. W., Physics and Research
Methodology
TUSACH, N. A., Civil Law
WANTASEN, D., Soil Physics
WAWOROENTOE, S. A., Physics
WAWOROENTOE, W. J., Urban and Regional
Planning
WILAR, A. F., Veterinary Science
WOKAS, F. H. M., Plant Protection
WOWOR, G. E., Gynaecology
WUMU, J., History of Economics

UNIVERSITAS SEBELAS MARET
SURAKARTA
(Sebelas Maret University Surakarta)

Jl. Ir Sutami 36A, Surakarta 57126

Telephone and fax (271) 646994
E-mail: io@uns.ac.id
Internet: www.uns.ac.id

Founded 1976
State control
Language of instruction: Indonesian
Academic year: August to July

Rector: Prof. Dr H. MOHAMMED SYAMSULHADI

Vice-Rector for Academic Affairs: Prof. Dr
RAVIK KARSIDI
Vice-Rector for Admin. Affairs: Prof. Dr Ir
SHOLAHUDDIN
Vice-Rector for Cooperation Affairs: Prof. Dr
ADI SULISTYONO
Vice-Rector for Student Affairs: Drs DWI
TIYANTO
Librarian: Drs HARMAWAN

Library of 288,024 vols
Number of teachers: 1,571
Number of students: 30,020

Publications: *Issues In Social and Environmental Accounting* (journal), *Mediator*
(student magazine, 12 a year)

DEANS

Faculty of Agriculture: Prof. Dr Ir H. SUN-
TORO
Faculty of Economics: Prof. Dr BAMBANG
SUTOPO
Faculty of Engineering: Ir MUKAHAR
Faculty of Law: MOCH. YAMIN
Faculty of Letters and Arts: Drs SUDARNO
Faculty of Mathematics and Natural Sci-
ences: Prof. Dr SUTARNO
Faculty of Medicine: Prof. Dr A. A. SUBIYANTO
Faculty of Social and Political Science: Drs
SUPRIYADI
Faculty of Teacher Training and Education:
Prof. Dr M. FURQON HIDAYATULLAH
Postgraduate Programme: Prof. Drs SURANTO

UNIVERSITAS SRIWIJAYA

Jl. Jaksa Agung R. Suprapto, Palembang,
South Sumatra

Telephone: (711) 26004
E-mail: yadiutama@ilkom.unsri.ac.id
Internet: www.unsri.ac.id

Founded 1960
State control
Language of instruction: Indonesian
Academic year: July to June

Rector: Prof. Dr BADIA PERIZADE
Vice-Rector I: Dr ZULFIKARI DAHLAN
Vice-Rector II: KENCANA DEWI
Vice-Rector III: H. ANIS SAGAF
Vice-Rector IV: Dr ABDUL HAMID RASYID
Admin. Bureau: Drs HERMAN MURSAL
Librarian: Dra CHUZAIMAH DIEM

Number of teachers: 540 full-time, 617 part-
time
Number of students: 8,427

Publications: *Majalah Universitas Sriwijaya*
(3 a year), and faculty bulletins

DEANS

Faculty of Agriculture: ZULJATI SYAHRUL
Faculty of Dentistry: Prof. Dr ARSUAD
Faculty of Economics: BADIA PERIZADE
Faculty of Education: Dr ZULKIFLI DAHLAN
(acting)
Faculty of Engineering: Dr HASAN BASRI
Faculty of Law: SOFYAN HASAN
Faculty of Teacher Training: Prof. Dr DJAHIR
BASIR

PROFESSORS

HALIM, A., Linguistics
HARDJOWIJONO, G., Paediatrics
MUKTI, H. D., Advanced Management
MUSLIMIN, A., Administrative Law
SOELAIMAN, M., Adat Law

UNIVERSITAS SUMATERA UTARA
(University of Sumatera Utara)

Jl. Dr. T. Mansur No. 9, Kampus USU, North
Sumatera Medan 20155

Telephone: (61) 8216575
Fax: (61) 8219411
E-mail: usu@karet.usu.ac.id
Internet: www.usu.ac.id

Founded 1952
State control
Languages of instruction: Indonesian, English
Academic year: August to July
Rector: Prof. CHAIRUDDIN P. LUBIS
Vice-Rector for Academic Affairs: Prof. Dr SUMONO
Vice-Rector for Administrative Affairs: Dr SUBHILHAR
Vice-Rector for Asset Management: Ir ISMAN NURIADI
Vice-Rector for Planning, Cooperation and Foreign Affairs: Prof. Dr SUKARIA SINU-LINGGA
Vice-Rector for Student Affairs: Dr LINDA MAAS
Head of Library and Information System: Drs A. RIDWAN SIREGAR
Library of 500,000 vols
Number of teachers: 1,750
Number of students: 28,000

DEANS

Faculty of Agriculture: Dr ZULKIFLI NASUTION
Faculty of Dentistry: Prof. ISMET D. NASUTION
Faculty of Economics: Drs JHON T. RITONGA
Faculty of Engineering: Dr NAWAWY LOEBIS
Faculty of Law: Prof. Dr RUNTUNG
Faculty of Letters: Prof. BAHREN UMAR SIREGAR
Faculty of Mathematics and Sciences: Prof. EDDY MARLIANTO
Faculty of Medicine: Dr T. BAHRI ANWAR
Faculty of Political and Social Science: Drs M. ARIF NASUTION
Faculty of Public Health: (vacant)
School of Postgraduate Studies: Dr T. CHAIRUN NISA

UNIVERSITAS SYIAH KUALA

Jl. Darussalam, Kopelma Darussalam Banda Aceh 23111
Telephone: (651) 7410250
E-mail: rektor@unsyiah.ac.id
Internet: www.unsyiah.ac.id
Founded 1961
State control
Language of instruction: Indonesian
Academic year: August to June
Rector: DARNI
Vice-Rector I: Dr SAMSUL RIZAL
Vice-Rector II: Dr EDDY NUR ILYAS
Vice-Rector III: Drs RUSLI YUSUF
Vice-Rector IV: DARUSMAN
Chief Academic Admin. Officer: Drs BACH-TIAR EFENDI
Chief Admin. Officer: Drs MUSTAFA USMAN
Librarian: Drs SANUSI
Number of teachers: 1,278
Number of students: 16,715

Publications: Agripet (2 a year), Agrista, Ekobis, Jurnal Kedokteran Syiah Kuala, Jurnal Teknik Sipil (3 a year), Kanun Fakultas Hukum, Managemen dan Bisnis, Medica Veterinaria, Mekanikal Komputasi & Numerical, Mon Mata (4 a year), Nat-ural, Rekayasa Elektrika, Rekayasa Kimia & Lingkungan, Teknorama, Telaah dan Riset, Wacana Pendidikan (4 a year), Warta Unsyiah

DEANS

Faculty of Agriculture: Ir ISMAYANI
Faculty of Economics: Prof. Dr SAID MUHAM-MAD
Faculty of Engineering: Prof. Dr Ir HUSAINI
Faculty of Law: MAWARDI ISMAIL
Faculty of Mathematical and Natural Sci-ences: Dr MUSTANIR
Faculty of Medicine: Dr SYAHRUL
Faculty of Teacher Training and Education: Dr M. YUSUF AZIZ

Faculty of Veterinary Science: Dr MAHDI ABRAR

UNIVERSITAS TADULAKO

Kampus Bumi, Tadulako Tondo, Sulawesi, Palu 94118
Telephone: (451) 422611
Fax: (451) 422844
E-mail: lemlit@untad.ac.id
Internet: www.untad.ac.id
Founded 1981
Rector: Drs MOHAMMAD RASYID
Vice-Rector: T. A. M. TILAAR
Vice-Rector: ARIFUDDIN BIDIN
Vice-Rector: SAHABUDDIN MUSTAPA
Vice-Rector: Dr MAIN LABASO
Head of General Admin. Bureau: RAFIGA PONULELE
Librarian: Drs MUH. ASRI HENTE
Library of 30,042 vols
Number of teachers: 660
Number of students: 6,500

DEANS

Faculty of Agricultural Sciences: Ir MASRIL BUSTAMI
Faculty of Economics: ARSYAD MAARDANIN
Faculty of Law: ISMAIL KASIM
Faculty of Social and Political Sciences: Drs ZAINUDDIN BOLONG
Faculty of Teacher Training: Drs H. TJATJO THAHA
Diploma Programme for Technical Sciences: Ir GALIB ISHAK

UNIVERSITAS TANJUNGPURA

Jl. Ahmad Yani Pontianak, Kalbar, Pontia-nak 78124
Telephone and fax (561) 739636
E-mail: untan@untan.ac.id
Internet: www.untan.ac.id
Founded 1959
Language of instruction: Indonesian
Academic year: begins September
Rector: Prof. Hj. ASNIAR ISMAIL
First Vice-Chancellor: Prof. Dr HENDRO S. SUDAGUNG
Registrar: RADJALI HADIMASPUTRA
Head of Gen. Admin. Bureau: MAYARANA RANITA
Librarian: SUTARMIN
Number of teachers: 734
Number of students: 9,305

DEANS

Faculty of Agriculture: Prof. Ir ALAMSYAH
Faculty of Economics: ASNIAR SUBAGYO
Faculty of Engineering: Ir Haji PONY SEDYA-NINGSIH
Faculty of Law: Prof. ANWAR SALEH
Faculty of Social and Political Sciences: Prof. Dr Sy. IBRAHIM ALKADRIE
Faculty of Teaching and Education: Prof. Drs JAWADI HASID

UNIVERSITAS TERBUKA
(Indonesian Open Learning University)

Jl. Cabe Raya, Pondok Cabe, Pamulang Tangerang Selatan-Banten 15418
Telephone: (21) 7490941
Fax: (21) 7490147
E-mail: humas@ut.ac.id
Internet: www.ut.ac.id
Founded 1984
State control
Language of instruction: Indonesian
Rector: Prof. Dr Ir TIAN BELAWAT
Vice-Rector: Dr YUNI TRI HEWINDATI
Vice-Rector: Ir NADIA SRI DAMAJANTI
Vice-Rector: HASMONEL

Vice-Rector: Drs MAXIMUS GORKY SEMBIRING
Registrar: Drs ACHMAD RAZAD
Librarian: Dr EFFENDI WAHYONO
Library of 42,311 vols
Number of teachers: 791
Number of students: 639,049

Publications: Journal of Open and Distance Learning (5 a year), Journal of Education (5 a year), Journal of Indonesian Studies (2 a year), Journal of Mathematics, Science and Technology (5 a year), Journal of Management Organization (5 a year), Komunika (4 a year), Suara Terbuka (4 a year)

DEANS

Faculty of Economics: Dr YUN ISWANTO
Faculty of Education and Teacher Training: Dr RUSTAM
Faculty of Mathematics and Natural Science: Dr NURAINI SOLEIMAN
Faculty of Social and Political Science: Dr DARYONO

UNIVERSITAS TRUNOJOYO MADURA

Bangkalan, East Java
Telephone: (31) 3014091
Fax: (31) 3014463
E-mail: humas@trunojoyo.ac.id
Internet: www.trunojoyo.ac.id
Founded 2001
State control
Rector: Prof. Dr Ir H. ARIFFIN
Vice-Rector I: Drs BAMBANG SABARIMAN
Vice-Rector II: Dr Ir SLAMET SUBARI
Vice-Rector III: H. BOED MUSTIKO

DEANS

Faculty of Agriculture: Ir MOH. FAKHRY
Faculty of Economics: Prof. IWAN TRIYUN-WONO
Faculty of Engineering: Ir SOEPRAPTO
Faculty of Law: H. MOH. AMIR HAMZAH

UNIVERSITAS UDAYANA
(Udayana University)

Bukit Jimbaran Campus, Badung 80361
Telephone: (361) 701954
Fax: (361) 701907
E-mail: info@unud.ac.id
Internet: www.unud.ac.id
Founded 1962
State control
Academic year: August to December
Language of instruction: Indonesian
Pres.: Prof. Dr I. MADE BAKTA
Deputy Pres. for Academic Affairs: Prof. Dr I. KOMANG GDE BENDESA
Deputy Pres. for Admin. Affairs: Prof. Dr DEWA PUTU SUTJANA
Deputy Pres. for Cooperation and Informa-tion Affairs: Prof. Dr Ir I. G. P. WIRAWAN
Deputy Pres. for Student Affairs: Prof. Dr Ir I. NYOMAN SUTJIPTA
Librarian: Drs I. GUSTI NYOMAN TIRTAYASA
Library of 21,390 vols
Number of teachers: 1,702
Number of students: 16,304

Publications: Berita Udayana (12 a year), Majalah Ilmiah Universitas Udayana (4 a year), Majalah Kedokteran Unud (4 a year)

DEANS

Faculty of Agricultural Technology: I GUSTI NGURAH AGUNG
Faculty of Agriculture: NENGAH ARTHA
Faculty of Animal Husbandry: TJOKORDA GDE OKA SUSULA
Faculty of Economics: Dr MADE KEMBAR SRI BUDHI
Faculty of Engineering: Dr I WAYAN REDANA

Faculty of Law: I. KETUT RAI SETIA BUDHI
Faculty of Letters (Arts): Prof. Dr I. WAYAN ARDIKA
Faculty of Medicine: Prof. Dr D. P. WIDJANA
Faculty of Sciences: Prof. Dr I. WAYAN KASA
Faculty of Veterinary Science: Dr Drh. I MADE DAMRI YASA

PROFESSORS

ADIPUTRA, N., Occupational Health
ARDANA, G. G., History
ARDIKA, W., Archaeology
ARGA, Agricultural Economics
ARHYA, N., Biochemistry
ARKA, B., Veterinary Science
ARYANTA, W. R., Food Microbiology
ASTININGSIH, K., Poultry Production
ASTITI, T. I. P., Custom Law
ATMAJA, D. G., Law
BAGUS, G. N., Indonesian Language
BAGUS, G. N., Social Anthropology
BAKTA, M., Internal Medicine
BAWA, W., Indonesian Language
BHINAWA, N., Animal Production
BUDHA, K., Surgery
BUNGAYA, G., Management
DJAGRA, I. B., Animal Production
KALAM, A. A. R., Arts and Design
LANA, K., Animal Nutrition
LANANG, O., Genetics
MANIK, G., Animal Husbandry
MANUABA, I. B. A., Human Physiology
MARDANI, N. K., Biology (Environmental Studies)
MASTIKA, M., Animal Nutrition
MATRAM, R. B., Veterinary Physiology
NALA, G. N., Human Physiology
NEHEN, K., Economic Devt
NETRA SUBADIYASA, N., Soil Science
NITIS, M., Animal Nutrition
OKA, I. B., Pharmacology
PANGKAHILA, J. A., Sexology
PUTHERA, G. A. G., Human Histology
PUTRA, D. K. H., Animal Physiology
RATA, I. B., Archaeology
RIKA, K., Forage Science
SAIDI, H. S., Islamology
SIRTA, N., Custom Law
SOEWIGIONO, S., Gastroenterology
SUARNA, I. M., Forage Science
SUATA, I. K., Microbiology
SUDHARTA, T. R., Sanskrit Language
SUDJATHA, W., Food and Technology
SUKARDI, E., Human Anatomy
SUKARDIKA, K., Microbiology
SURAATMAJA, S., Paediatrics
SURYADHI, N. T., Public Health
SUTAWAN, N., Social and Agricultural Economics
SUTER, K., Food Technology
SUTHA, G. K., Law
SUTJIPTA, N., Social and Agricultural Economics
SUWETA, G. P., Veterinary Science
SUYATNA, G., Social Economics
TJITARSA, I. B., Public Health
WIDNYANA, M., Law
WINAYA, P. D., Soil Fertility
WIRAWAN, D. N., Public Health
WITA, W., Cardiology

Private Universities

MAHASARASWATI DENPASAR UNIVERSITY

Jl. Kamboja 11A, Denpasar, Bali
Telephone and fax (361) 227019
E-mail: info@unmas.ac.id
Internet: www.unmas.ac.id
Founded 1962
Private control
Languages of instruction: English, Indonesian

Academic year: September to June
Vice-Rector: Dr Ir N UTARI VIPRIYANTI
Number of teachers: 165
Number of students: 5,760
Publications: *Ekonomi Pembangunan, Santiaji Pendidikan*

DEANS

Agriculture: PUTU SUJANA
Dentistry: MAHENDRI KUSUMAWATI
Technology: NGURAH SUNATHA

PETRA CHRISTIAN UNIVERSITY

Jl. Siwalankerto 121–131, Surabaya 60236
Telephone: (31) 8439040
Fax: (31) 8436418
E-mail: info@peter.petra.ac.id
Internet: www.petra.ac.id
Founded 1961
Private control
Languages of instruction: Indonesian, English
Academic year: August to July (2 semesters)
Rector: Prof. Ir Dr ROLLY INTAN
Vice-Rector for Academic Affairs: Dr Ir HANNY HOSIANA TUMBELAKA
Vice-Rector for Finance and Admin.: Dra JUALIANA ANGGONO
Vice-Rector for Student Affairs: Drs FREDERICK JONES SYARANAMUAL
Registrar: Dra WIDIARTI SUPRAPTO
Librarian: LIAUW TOONG TJIEK
Library: 141,806 books, 11,866 audiovisual items
Number of teachers: 642
Number of students: 6,960
Publications: *Accounting and Finance Journal* (2 a year), *Architecture Dimension* (2 a year), *Civil Engineering Dimension* (2 a year), *Electrical Journal* (2 a year), *Industrial Engineering Journal* (industrial engineering dept, 2 a year), *Informatic Journal* (2 a year), *K@TA* (language and literature, 2 a year), *Management and Entrepreneur Journal* (2 a year), *Mechanical Engineering Journal* (2 a year), *Nirmana* (visual communication design dept, 2 a year), (published by The Institute of Research and Community Outreach in collaboration with Communication Science Dept)

DEANS

Faculty of Art and Design: Ir ANDRIAN DEKTISA HAGIJANTO (acting)
Faculty of Civil Engineering and Planning: Ir HANDOKO SUGIHARTO
Faculty of Communication Studies: Drs FELICIA GOENAWAN (acting)
Faculty of Economics: Drs DIAH DHARMAYANTI
Faculty of Industrial Technology: Prof. Ir DJONI HARYADI SETIABUDI
Faculty of Letters: Drs RIBUT BASUKI

UNDIKNAS UNIVERSITY

Jl. Bedugul 39 Sidakarya, Denpasar 80225
Telephone: (361) 723868
Fax: (361) 723077
E-mail: info@undiknas.ac.id
Internet: www.undiknas.ac.id
Founded 1969
Private control
Rector: Prof. Dr GEDE SRI DAMA

DEANS

Faculty of Administrative Science and Communication: Dr I NYOMAN SUBANDA
Faculty of Economics and Business: Prof. Dr IDA BAGUS RAKA SUARDANA

Faculty of Information and Engineering: I WAYAN SUTAMA
Faculty of Law: Prof. Dr I NYOMAN BUDIANA
Faculty of Social Science and Political Science: Dr I NYOMAN SUBANDA

UNIVERSITAS 17 AGUSTUS 1945, JAKARTA
(17 August 1945 University, Jakarta)

Jl. Sunter Permai Raya Sunter Agung, Podomoro, Jakarta Utara 14350
Telephone and fax (21) 6410287
E-mail: untag@untag-jkt.org
Internet: www.untag-jkt.org
Founded 1945
Private control
Faculties of administration, economics, engineering, law, pharmacy, social and political science
Rector: Dr THOMAS NOACH PEEA.

UNIVERSITAS 17 AGUSTUS 1945, SURABAYA
(17 August 1945 University, Surabaya)

Telephone: (31) 5931800
Fax: (31) 5927817
E-mail: info@untag.ac.id
Internet: www.untag-sby.ac.id
Founded 1958
Language of instruction: Indonesian
Academic year: September to August
Faculties of agricultural science, economics, law, letters, psychology, social and political sciences.

UNIVERSITAS AL-AZHAR

Complex of Al-Azhar Mosque, Jakarta 12110
Telephone: (211) 7279275
Fax: (211) 7244767
Internet: www.uai.ac.id
Founded 2000
Private control
Rector: Prof. Dr Ir ZUHAL
Vice-Rector for Corporate Devt: DJOKOSANTOSO MOELJONO
Vice-Rector for Public Admin. and Human Resources: Drs MUHSIN LUBIS
Vice-Rector for Student Affairs and Academic Div.: Dr Ir AHMAD H. LUBIS

DEANS

Faculty of Economics: Prof. Dr SAYUTI HASIBUAN
Faculty of Engineering: Prof. Dr Ir SARDY
Faculty of Islamic Religion: Dr NURHAYATI DJAMAS
Faculty of Law: Prof. Dr ERMAN RAJAGUKGUK
Faculty of Mathematics and Science: Dr Ir WITONO BASUKI
Faculty of Psychology: Prof. HARSONO WIRYOSUMARTO
Faculty of Social and Political Sciences: Prof. Dr YAHYA A. MUHAIMIN

UNIVERSITAS ATMA JAYA YOGYAKARTA

Campus Bldg II, Thomas Aquinas Rd, Babarsari 44, Yogyakarta 55281
Telephone: (274) 487711
Fax: (274) 487748
E-mail: admisi@mail.uajy.ac.id
Internet: www.uajy.ac.id
Founded 1965
Private control
Rector: Ir A. KOESMARGONO
Vice-Rector for Admin., Finance and Human Resources: LUDDY INDRA PURNAMA.

UNIVERSITAS BAITURRAHMAH

Jl. Raya by-pass Km 15, Aie Pacah, Padang
Telephone: (751) 463069
Fax: (751) 463068
Internet: www.unbrah.ac.id
Founded 1979
Private control

DEANS

Faculty of Dentistry: R. RAMA PUTRANTO
Faculty of Economics: Dr H. YANDI SUKRI
Faculty of Medicine: Prof. H. AMIRMUSLIM
  MALIK
Faculty of Public Health: Dr WINARDI

UNIVERSITAS BALIKPAPAN

Jl. Pupuk Raya, Gn. Bahagia, Balikpapan
Telephone: (542) 765442
Fax: (542) 764205
E-mail: info@uniba-bpn.ac.id
Internet: www.uniba-bpn.ac.id
Private control
Rector: Prof. Dr ELLYANO S. LASAM

DEANS

Faculty of Economics: Drs HAIRUL ANAM
Faculty of Law: Drs MUHAMAD MUHDAR
Faculty of Sastras: Dra SITI HAFSAH
Faculty of Technology: Ir POEGOEH

UNIVERSITAS BATANGHARI JAMBI

Jl. Slamet Riyadi Broni, Jambi
Telephone: (741) 60673
Fax: (741) 64930
E-mail: rektorat@unbari.ac.id
Internet: www.unbari.ac.id
Private control
Rector: H. FACHRUDDIN RAZI

DEANS

Faculty of Agriculture: Ir M. SUGIHARTONO
Faculty of Economics: OSRITA HAPSARA
Faculty of Law: M. ZEN ABDULLAH
Faculty of Technology: Ir AZWARMAN

UNIVERSITAS BINA DARMA

Jl. Jend. Ahmad Yani, Palembang
Internet: www.binadarma.ac.id
Founded 1993
Private control
Faculties of communication, computer science, economy, engineering, language and literature, psychology
Pres.: Prof. Ir BUCHORI RACHMAN.

UNIVERSITAS BINA NUSANTARA
(Bina Nusantara University)

Kampus Anggrek, Jl. Kebon Jeruk Raya No.
  27, Kebon Jeruk, Jakarta Barat 11530
Telephone: (21) 53696969
Fax: (21) 5300244
E-mail: publicrelations@binus.edu
Internet: www.binus.ac.id
Founded 1974
Private control
Rector: Prof. Dr Ir HARJANTO PRABOWO
Vice-Rector for Academic Devt: IMAN HER-
  WIDIANA KARTOWISASTRO
Vice-Rector for Collaboration and Institu-
  tional Devt: WAYAH S. WIROTO
Vice-Rector for Operation and Resources: S.
  KOM. NELLY
Vice-Rector for Student Affairs and Commu-
  nity: Drs ANDREAS CHANG.

UNIVERSITAS BORNEO TARAKAN
(Borneo University)

Jl. Amal Lama 1, POB 170, Tarakan 77123
Telephone: (551) 5507023
E-mail: ubt@borneo.ac.id
Internet: www.borneo.ac.id
Founded 1999
Private control
Rector: ABDUL JABARSYAH
Faculties of agriculture, economics, fisheries, law, technology.

UNIVERSITAS BUNG HATTA

Jl. Sumatra Ulak Karang, Padang, Sumatra
  Barat 25133
Telephone: (751) 7051678
Fax: (751) 55475
E-mail: rektorat@bung-hatta.ac.id
Founded 1981
Private control
Rector: Prof. Dr HAFRIZAL SJANDRI

DEANS

Faculty of Civil Engineering and Planning: Ir
  HENRI WARMAN
Faculty of Fisheries and Marine Science: Ir
  H. YEMPITA EFENDI
Faculty of Industrial Technology: Dr Ir
  SAIFUL JAMAAN
Faculty of Law: BOY YENDRA TAMIN

UNIVERSITAS DWIJENDRA

Jl. Kamboja 17, Denpasar, Bali
Telephone: (361) 224383
Fax: (361) 233974
E-mail: info@undwi.ac.id
Internet: www.undwi.ac.id
Founded 1982
Private control
Rector: I KETUT WIRAWAN
Vice-Rector I: Ir PUTU GDE ERY SUARDANA
Vice-Rector II: Dra NI MADE SUARNINGSIH
Vice-Rector III: Drs IDA BAGUS RAI

DEANS

Faculty of Agriculture: Ir GEDE SEDANA
Faculty of Engineering: Ir IDA BAGUS GDE
  MANUABA
Faculty of Law: PUTU DYATMIKAWATI
Faculty of Science Communication: Dra IDA
  AYU RATNA WESNAWATI
Faculty of Teaching and Science Education:
  Drs I MADE SILA

UNIVERSITAS EKASAKTI

Jl. Veteran Dalam, 26B, Padang, Sumatera
  Barat 25131
Telephone and fax (2751) 28859
E-mail: agussikki@yahoo.com
Internet: www.univ-ekasakti-pdg.ac.id
Founded 1973
Private control
Rector: Prof. Dr ANDI MUSTARI
Vice-Rector I: Dr AGUSSALIM MANGULUANG
Vice-Rector II: Prof. Dr NASRUN
Vice-Rector III: NURFAN AGUS
Librarian: Dra SAUFNI CHALID
Library of 8,648 titles

DEANS

Faculty of Agriculture: I KETUT BUDARAGA
Faculty of Computer Management Informa-
  tion: JUSMITA WERIZA
Faculty of Economics: TETI CHANDRAYANTI
Faculty of Engineering: Ir ABU RIZAL
Faculty of Law: Dr OTONG ROSADI
Faculty of Sastras: RAFLIS
Faculty of Social Science and Political Sci-
  ence: SUMARTONO

Faculty of Teacher Training: FEBY MEUTHIA
YUSUF

UNIVERSITAS HKBP NOMMENSEN
(Huria Kristen Batak Protestan Nommensen University)

Jl. Sutomo 4A, POB 1133, Medan
Telephone: (61) 4522922
Fax: (61) 4571426
E-mail: uhn@nommensen.org
Internet: www.nommensen.org
Founded 1954
Private control: Batak Christian Protestant
  Church
Language of instruction: Indonesian
Academic year: September to July
Rector: Ir B. RICSON SIMARMATA
Vice-Rector for Academic Affairs: Drs RAFLES
  D. TAMPUBOLON
Vice-Rector for Financial Affairs: Drs PANTAS
  SILABAN
Vice-Rector for Student Affairs: Ir HOTMAN
  MANURUNG
Dir of Community Service: Ir B. T. SIMANJOR-
  ANG
Dir of Research: Dr Ir JONGKER TAMPUBOLON
Number of teachers: 310
Number of students: 7,549
Publication: *VISI* (scientific magazine)

DEANS

Faculty of Agriculture: Ir P. PARLIN LUMBAN-
  RAJA
Faculty of Animal Husbandry: Ir HERLINA
  SARAGI
Faculty of Arts: Drs BEN M. PASARIBU
Faculty of Economics: Drs ADANAN SILABAN
Faculty of Education: Dr TAGOR PANGARIBUAN
Faculty of Engineering: Ir SINDAK HUTAURUK
Faculty of Law: TULUS SIAMBATON
Faculty of Public and Business Admin.: Drs
  MONANG SITORUS

UNIVERSITAS IBN CHALDUN JAKARTA

Jl. Pemuda, Kav. 97, POB 1224, Rawaman-
  gun, Jakarta 13220
Telephone: (21) 4722059
Fax: (21) 4702563
E-mail: humas@ibnuchaldun.com
Internet: www.ibnuchaldun.com
Founded 1956
Languages of instruction: Indonesian, Eng-
  lish, Arabic
Academic year: September to June
Rector: Prof. Drs QOMARI ANWAR
Vice-Rector: Dr HARTINI SALAMAH
Vice-Rector: ANAS YANUN
Vice-Rector: ANTHONY HILMAN
Registrar: ERWINA
Librarian: Ir M. FERYZAL
Number of teachers: 115
Number of students: 10,000
Publications: *Muqaddimah* (Learning about
  Islam), *Editorial Campus*

DEANS

Faculty of Agriculture: Ir SAPRI
Faculty of Communication: Drs NARSO
Faculty of Economics: Drs URHEN LUKMAN
Faculty of Islamic Religion: SUHARDIN
Faculty of Law: NURLELY DARWIS
Faculty of Social and Political Science: Drs
  AIDIL FITRI
Institute of Social Research: Dr ASDIH CHA-
  NIAGO

UNIVERSITAS IBN KHALDUN BOGOR

Jl. K. H. Sholeh Iskandar Km 2, POB 172, Bogor 16162

Telephone and fax (251) 356884
E-mail: rector@mail.uika-bogor.ac.id
Internet: www.uika-bogor.ac.id

Founded 1961
Private control
Language of instruction: Indonesian

Chancellor: Prof. Dr Ir H. AFFENDI ANWAR
Rector: Dr Ir SUNSUN SAEFULHAKIM
Head of Academic Admin.: Dra HERAWATI
Head of Gen. Admin.: Hj. TITING SUHARTI
Librarian: Dra TATI TARSITI

Number of teachers: 300
Number of students: 4,293

Publication: *Islamic Journal of Technology, Institutional and Humanity Development* (2 a year)

DEANS

Faculty of Economics: H. AHMAD MUBAROK
Faculty of Education: Drs YUSUF SHOBIRI
Faculty of Engineering: Dr Ir PRAWOTO
Faculty of Islamic Studies: Drs H. E. BAHRUDDIN
Faculty of Law: BARLY
Graduate School of Islamic Studies: Dr K. H. DIDIN HAFIDHUDDIN

UNIVERSITAS ISLAM INDONESIA
(Islamic University of Indonesia)

Gedung Rektorat, Jl. Kaliurang Km 14.5, Yogyakarta 55584

Telephone: (274) 898444
Fax: (274) 898459
E-mail: rektorat@uii.ac.id
Internet: www.uii.ac.id

Founded 1945
Private control
Language of instruction: Indonesian
Academic year: July to June

Rector: Dr LUTHFI HASAN
Vice-Rector for Academic Affairs: Dr S. F. MARBUN
Vice-Rector for Admin. and Financial Affairs: Dr H. MUQODIM
Vice-Rector for Collaborative Affairs: Dr A. AKHYAR ADNAN
Vice-Rector for Student Affairs: Ir H. BACHNAS
Chief Admin. Officer: Drs H. SYAFARUDDIN ALWI
Librarian: Dra MURYANTI

Library of 73,000 vols
Number of teachers: 365
Number of students: 18,375

Publication: *UII News* (12 a year)

DEANS

Faculty of Civil Engineering and Planning: Prof. Dr Ir. WIDODO
Faculty of Economics: Drs SUWARSONO
Faculty of Industrial Technology: Ir H. BACHRUN SUTRISNO
Faculty of Islamic Science: Drs H. MUDHOFAR AKHWAN
Faculty of Law: Dr JAWAHIR THONTOWI
Faculty of Mathematics and Science: JAKA NUGRAHA
Faculty of Medical Science: Prof. Dr Dr RUSDI LAMSUDDIN
Faculty of Psychology: Dr SUKARTI

PROFESSORS

AHMAD ANTONO, Concrete Structures
ASYMUNI, H., Islamic Court
ATMADJA, M. K., International Law
BAHARUDDIN LOPA, Criminal Law
BERNADIB, S. I., Methods of Educational Evaluation, Educational Philosophy
CHOTIB, H. A., Ushl al-Fiqh

DAHLAN, H. Z., Principles of Islamic Law
FATKHURRAHMAN, History of Islam and Islamic Law
HADITONO, S. R., Individual Psychology
HARDJOSO, R., Irrigation
HASAN POERBOHADIWIDJAJA, Environmental Planning
KOESNOE, H. M., Private Procedural Law
KUSNADI HARDJOSUMANTRI, Environment Law
MOCHTAR YAHYA, H., General Philosophy
MUH ZEIN, Method and Evaluation of Islamic Education
MULADI, Politics of Law
PARLINDUNGAN, A. P., Agrarian Law
PARTADIREDJA, H. A., Indonesian Economy
PRAGNYONO, R., Fluid Mechanics
PURNOMO, B., Criminal Law
RIYANTO, B., Development Economy
SATJIPTO RAHARDJO, Sociology of Law
SITI RAHAYU, Psychology
SOEDIKNO MERTOKOESOEMO, Civil Law, Jurisprudence
SOEDIRDJO, Educational Counselling, Curriculum Advancement
SOEKANTO, Business Policy
SOELISTYO, International Economy
SOEPARNO, Analytical Geometry
SRI SUMANTRI, Constitutional Law
SUNARDJO, R., Irrigation Technology
SUYUTI, H. Z., Statistics
SYACHRAN BASAH, Administrative Law
SYAFI'I MA'ARIF, A., Islamic Cultural History
TUGIMAN, N., Indonesian Language
UMAR, H. M., Modern Islamic Ideology
UMAR ASSASUDDIN, English
WARSITO, Polymer Chemistry
YUSUF, H. H., Hadiths I, II, III

UNIVERSITAS ISLAM INDONESIA CIREBON
(Islamic University of Indonesia in Cirebon)

Jl. Kapten Samadikun 31, Cirebon
Pres.: SA'DILLAH FATHONI
Sec.: M. Z. ABIDIEN

DEANS

Faculty of Economics: Drs ROSYADI
Faculty of Law: S. PRAWIRO
Faculty of Theology: H. MAS'OED

UNIVERSITAS ISLAM JAKARTA

Jl. Balai Takyat, Utan Kayu, Jakarta 13120
Telephone: (21) 8566451
Fax: (21) 8504818
E-mail: informasi@uid.ac.id
Internet: www.uid.ac.id

Founded 1951

Pres.: Prof. Dr SOEMEDI
Rector: SOEDJONO HARDJOSOEDIRO
Registrar: RASJIDI OESMAN
Librarian: ZAINAL ABIDIN

Number of teachers: 34
Number of students: 309

DEANS

Faculty of Economics: TAHER IBRAHIM
Faculty of Education: H. M. NUR ASJIK
Faculty of Law and Social Sciences: Drs H. NAZARUDIN

UNIVERSITAS ISLAM NUSANTARA

Jl. Soekarno-Hatta 530, POB 1579, Bandung 40286
Telephone: (22) 7509655
E-mail: humus@uninus.ac.id
Internet: www.uninus.ac.id

Founded 1959 as Universitas Nahdlatul Ulama, present name 1976
Academic year: September to August

Chancellor: Mayjen H. ACHMAD RUSTANDI

Rector: Dr H. DEDI MULYASANA
Deputy Rector: Drs SUHENDRA YUSUF
Deputy Rector: WAHDI SUARDI
Deputy Rector: H. RUBI ROBANA
Registrar: Drs RUSLI
Librarian: Drs UNDANG SUDAR SANA

Number of teachers: 402
Number of students: 6,574

Publications: *Literat* (4 a year), *Suara UNINUS* (4 a year)

DEANS

Faculty of Agriculture: Ir RUBI ROBANA
Faculty of Communication Sciences: Drs H. S. INSAR MARTADIKUSUMAH
Faculty of Economics: Drs KUSMANA
Faculty of Education and Literature: Dr DIDIN WAHIDIN
Faculty of Engineering: Ir AGUS EDY PRANOTO
Faculty of Islamology: Drs HANAFI
Faculty of Law: Drs ENJANG SURACHMAN

PROFESSORS

Faculty of Agriculture:
  AISYAH, H., Pedology
  SADELI, H.
Faculty of Communication Sciences:
  HUSEIN, S. I., Communications Sciences
Faculty of Economics:
  SURACHMAN, H., Management Economics
Faculty of Education and Literature:
  EFFENDY, E. R., Mathematics
  EMUH, Arabic
  FAISAL, Y. A., Indonesian Literature
  RUSYANA, Y., Indonesian Literature
  SLAMET, H. A., Indonesian Language
  SOEHARTO, B., Non-Formal Education
  SYAMSUDDIN, Curriculum Development and Methodology
Faculty of Engineering:
  HANDALI, D., Mathematics
  SUMARNO, Mathematics
Faculty of Islamology:
  DJATNIKA, H. R., Islamology
  HELMY, H., Islamology
  SALIMUDDIN, Islamology
Faculty of Law:
  BASYAH, S., Public Administration Law
  RASYIDI, L., Family Law
  SANUSI, H. A., Law, Public Administration and Education

UNIVERSITAS ISLAM RIAU
(Islamic University of Riau)

Jl. Kaharuddin Nasution 113, Perhentian, Marpoyan, Pekanbaru, Riau 28284

Telephone and fax (761) 674834
Internet: www.unri.ac.id

Founded 1962
Academic year: July to June

Rector: Prof. Dr MUCHTAR AHMAD
Vice-Rector I: Prof. Dr DADANG ISKANDAR
Vice-Rector II: AMIR HASAN
Vice-Rector III: ARIFFIEN MANSYOER
Vice-Rector IV: Drs SUARDI LOEKMAN
Librarian: FIRDAUS

Library of 5,150 vols
Number of teachers: 660 (160 full-time, 500 part-time)
Number of students: 7,391

Publications: *Alam* (4 a year), *Dinamika Pertanian* (4 a year), *Presfektif* (2 a year), *Saintis* (2 a year), *Siasat* (2 a year)

DEANS

Faculty of Agriculture: Ir T. ISKANDAR JOHAN
Faculty of Economics: Drs SHAHDANUR
Faculty of Education: Drs NAZIRUN
Faculty of Engineering: ALI MUSNAL

Faculty of Islamic Theology: ALI NUR
Faculty of Law: ARIFIN BOER
Faculty of Political and Sociological Sciences: ZAINI ALI

UNIVERSITAS ISLAM SUMATERA UTARA
(Islamic University of North Sumatra)

Campus Munawarah, Teladan, Medan 20217
Telephone and fax (61) 716790
Internet: www.uisu.ac.id
Founded 1952
Private control
Language of instruction: Indonesian
Academic year: July to June
Chancellor: Brig.-Gen. (retd) H. A. MANAF LUBIS
Rector: Drs H. M. YAMIN LUBIS
Registrar: Drs ABDUL HAKIM SIREGAR
Librarian: Drs SUDIAR SUDARGO
Number of teachers: 808
Number of students: 10,000
Publications: *Al Jamiah-UISU* (3 a year), *Buletin Fakultas Hukum* (6 a year), *Buletin Fakultas Pertanian* (4 a year)

DEANS

Faculty of Agriculture: Ir MEIZAL
Faculty of Economics: Drs AHMAD GHAZALI
Faculty of Education and Teaching: Drs H. ADLIN AHMAD
Faculty of Engineering: Ir H. M. ICHWAN NASUTION
Faculty of English: Drs MISRAN SUDIONO
Faculty of Islamic Communication: Drs MUS-TAFA KAMIL
Faculty of Islamic Education: H. MAHMUD AZIZ SIREGAR
Faculty of Islamic Law: Drs SAID ALHINDUAN
Faculty of Law: AMRIZAL PULUNGAN
Faculty of Medicine: Prof. Dr H. HABIBAH HANUM NASUTION
Faculty of Political Science: Drs DANAN JAYA

UNIVERSITAS JAYABAYA

Campus A Jl. Pulomas Selatan kav 23, Jakarta Timur 13210
Telephone: (21) 4700877
Fax: (21) 4700893
Campus C Jl. Raya Bogor km 28, Cimanggis, Jakarta Timur 13210
Telephone: (21) 8719958
E-mail: info@jayabaya.ac.id
Internet: www.jayabaya.ac.id
Founded 1958
Chancellor: Dr H. MOESLIM TAHER
Rector: Prof. H. AMIR SANTOSO
Vice-Rector I: Hj. POPON SJARIF ARIFIN
Vice-Rector II: Drs H. SYAHID SUHANDI AZIS
Vice-Rector III: MANSYUR KARDI
Number of teachers: 782
Number of students: 15,000

DEANS

Faculty of Communication Science: DARMA SETIAWAN
Faculty of Economics: Prof. Dr Hj. MIRRIAM
Faculty of Law: Prof. Dr H. YUDHA BHAKTI
Faculty of Law and Management: H. INDAR-TONO RIVAI
Faculty of Political and Social Sciences: H. AMIR SANTOSO
Faculty of Technology: DARMA SETIAWAN

UNIVERSITAS KADER BANGSA PALEMBANG

Kampus A Jl. Mayjend. H. M. Ryacudu 88, Palembang
Telephone: (711) 510173*Kampus B* Jl. Jend.

Sudirman 1077–1088, Palembang
Telephone: (711) 318311
Internet: www.ukb.ac.id
Founded 2000
Private control
Programmes in engineering, health studies, legal studies, midwifery, pharmacy
Rector: H. T. WATHAN
Vice-Rector I: FERRY PRESCA
Vice-Rector II: Dr Hj. IRZANITA
Vice-Rector III: AHMAD DINAR.

UNIVERSITAS KATOLIK INDONESIA ATMA JAYA

Semanggi Campus Jl. Jend. Sudirman 51, Jakarta 12930
Telephone: (21) 5703306
Fax: (21) 5708811
Pluit Campus Jl. Pluit Raya 2, Jakarta 14440
Telephone: (21) 6691944
Fax: (21) 6606122
E-mail: rek@atmajaya.ac.id
Internet: www.atmajaya.ac.id
Founded 1960
Languages of instruction: Indonesian, English
Academic year: July to June
Chair. of Board: Drs R. DJOKOPRANOTO
Rector: Prof. Dr BERNADETTE N. SETIADI
Vice-Rector: Ir ST. NUGROHO KRISTONO
Vice-Rector: Dr MARCELLINUS MARCELLINO
Vice-Rector: Drs PETRUS PIUS SALAMIN
Vice-Rector: Dr LILIANA SUGIHARTO
Librarian: Dr DIAO AI LIEN
Library of 70,260 vols
Number of teachers: 1,071
Number of students: 13,452
Publications: *Atma nan Jaya* (science, 3 a year), *Gloria Juris* (law and human rights, 2 a year), *Jurnal Administrasi dan Bisnis* (administration and business, 4 a year), *Jurnal Ekonomi dan Bisnis* (economics and business, 2 a year), *Majalah Kedokteran* (medical science, 3 a year), *Metris* (science and technology, 4 a year), *Respons* (social ethics, 2 a year)

DEANS

Faculty of Business Administration: Dr POL A. Y. AGUNG NUGROHO
Faculty of Economics: Drs SOFIAN SUGIOKO
Faculty of Engineering: Dr M. M. LANNY W. PANDJAITAN
Faculty of Law: ANTONIUS P. S. WIBOWO
Faculty of Medicine: Dr SATYA JOEWANA
Faculty of Psychology: Dr ENGELINA TANZIL BONANG
Faculty of Teacher Training and Education: Dr LAURA F. N. SUDARNOTO
Faculty of Technobiology: Prof. Dr ANTONIUS SUWANTO
Graduate School: Dr ALOISIUS AGUS NUGROHO

UNIVERSITAS KATOLIK PARAHYANGAN
(Parahyangan Catholic University)

Ciumbuleit 94, Bandung 40141
Telephone: (22) 2032655
Fax: (22) 2031110
E-mail: humas@home.unpar.ac.id
Internet: www.unpar.ac.id
Founded 1955
Private control
Languages of instruction: Indonesian, English
Academic year: August to June
Chair. for Board of Trustees: Prof. Dr Ir B. S. KUSBIANTORO
Rector: Dr CECILIA LAUW JADE SWAN

Vice-Rector for Academic and Student Affairs: Prof. Dr Ir PAULUS P. RAHARDJO
Vice-Rector for Financial Affairs: Dra CATHARINA TAN
Vice-Rector for Organization and Personnel: Dr R. ISMADI BEKTI SANTOSO
Librarian: Dra SISKA TOBING
Number of teachers: 1,321 (334 full-time, 687 part-time)
Number of students: 9,781
Publications: *Bina Ekonomi* (4 a year), *Integral* (4 a year), *Jurnal Administrasi Publik* (2 a year), *Jurnal PACIS* (2 a year), *Melintas* (4 a year), *Profil* (4 a year), *Pro Justitia* (4 a year), *Potensia* (4 a year), *Rekasaya* (4 a year), *Research Journal* (2 a year)

DEANS

Faculty of Economics: Dra ELIZABETH MANURUNG
Faculty of Engineering: Dr Ir CAROLINE SUTANDI
Faculty of Industrial Technology: Dr Ir PAULUS SUKAPTO
Faculty of Law: BAYU SETO
Faculty of Information Technology and Sciences: Dr J. DHARMA LESMONO
Faculty of Philosophy: Dr FABIANUS HEATUBUN
Faculty of Social and Political Sciences: Dr ULBER SILALAHI
Graduate School: Prof. Dr Ir BAMBANG SURYOATMONO

PROFESSORS

BROTOSISWOJO, B. S., Computer Physics
DIRJOSISWORO, S., Law
DJAJAPUTERA, A., Civil Engineering
NIMPOENO, J. S., Psychology
RAHARDJO, P. P., Geotechnology
SIDHARTA, B. A., Law
SIREGAR, S., Architecture
SJAFRUDDIN, A., Law
SOELARNOSIDJI, D., Geotechnology in Civil Engineering
SUHARTO, IGN., Chemical Engineering
SUNDJAJA, R. S., Management
SURJOATMONO, B., Civil Engineering
WINARDI, Economics

UNIVERSITAS KLABAT

Airmadidi, Manado 95371
Telephone: (431) 891035
Fax: (431) 891036
E-mail: email@unklab.ac.id
Internet: www.unklab.ac.id
Founded 1965
Private control
Rector: A. B. SEPANG.

UNIVERSITAS KRISNADWIPAJANA

Jl. Raya Jati Waringin, Pondok Gede, Jakarta 13077
Telephone: (21) 8462229
Fax: (21) 8462461
E-mail: humas@unkris.ac.id
Founded 1952
Language of instruction: Indonesian
Academic year: February to December
Rector: Dr LODEWIJK GULTOM
Vice-Rector I: PUGUH SANTOSO
Vice-Rector II: Hj. LINDA ISMAIL
Vice-Rector III: Drs EDWARD DOLOKSARIBU
Dir of Postgraduate Programmes: Prof. Dr RUSLI RAMLI
Sec.: WAYAN SUGIYANA
Librarian: Dr DASPAN
Number of teachers: 128
Number of students: 2,000

DEANS

Faculty of Economics: Drs MUHADI RIYANTO
Faculty of Law: Dr LODEWIJK GULTOM
Faculty of Science Administration: Drs JACK R. SIDABUTAR
Faculty of Technology: RUSJDI HADJERAT

UNIVERSITAS KRISTEN INDONESIA
(Christian University of Indonesia)

Jl. Mayjen Sutoyo 2, Cawang, Jakarta 13630
Telephone: (21) 8092425
Fax: (21) 80886882
E-mail: humas-uki@uki.ac.id
Internet: www.uki.ac.id
Founded 1953
Rector: Prof. Dr K. TUNGGUL SIRAIT
Vice-Rector for Academic Affairs: Dr A. S. L. RAMPEN
Vice-Rector for Admin. Planning and Devt: E. GUNAWAN
Vice-Rector for Student Affairs: A. SIREGAR
Number of teachers: 739
Number of students: 8,000
Publications: *Dialektika, Dinamika Pendidikan, Emas, Honeste Vivere, Jurnal Ekonomi, Logos, UKI Bulletin*

DEANS

Faculty of Economics: Drs A. ZABUA
Faculty of Education: TOGAP LINANJUNTAK
Faculty of English Language and Literature: Dr L. S. BANGUN
Faculty of Law: Dr BERNARD HUTABARAK
Faculty of Medicine: Dr S. M. L. TORUAN
Faculty of Social and Political Science: Prof. Dr PAYUNG BANGUN
Faculty of Technology: Dr A. SOEBAGIO

UNIVERSITAS KRISTEN MARANATHA
(Maranatha Christian University)

Jl. Prof. Suria Sumantri 65, Bandung 40164
Telephone: (22) 2012186
Fax: (22) 2015154
E-mail: humas@maranatha.edu
Internet: www.maranatha.edu
Founded 1965
Language of instruction: Indonesian
Academic year: September to August
Rector: Prof. Dr Ir H. P. SEPTORATNO SIREGAR
Vice-Rector I: Ir RUDY WAWOLUMAJA
Vice-Rector II: Ir NOEK SULANDARI
Vice-Rector III: Pdt. FERLY DAVID
Vice-Rector IV: Dr FELIX KASIM
Number of teachers: 500
Number of students: 12,000
Publications: *Journal Kedoktoran* (Medicine Journal, 1 a year), *Majalah Ilmiah Maranatha* (Maranatha Scientific Magazine, 4 a year), *Media Komunikasi Maranatha* (Maranatha Communication Media, 3 a year)

DEANS

Faculty of Art and Design, Undergraduate Programme: Dr GAI SUHARJA
Faculty of Economics, Undergraduate Programme: TEDY WAHYUSAPUTRA
Faculty of Engineering, Undergraduate Programme: Prof. Dr Ir BENJAMIN SOENARKO
Faculty of Information Technology, Undergraduate Programme: RADIANT VICTOR IMBAR
Faculty of Letters, Undergraduate Programme: Drs EDWARD ALDRICH LUKMAN
Faculty of Medicine, Undergraduate Programme: Dr SURJA TANURAHARDJA
Faculty of Psychology, Undergraduate Programme: Drs R. SANOESI SUSANTO
Master of Accounting, Postgraduate Programme: RIKI MARTUSA

Master of Management, Postgraduate Programme: Dra IKA GUNAWAN
Master of Psychology, Postgraduate Programme: Dr PARWATI SUPANGAT

UNIVERSITAS KRISTEN SATYA WACANA
(Satya Wacana Christian University)

Jl. Diponegoro 52–60, Salatiga 50711
Telephone: (298) 321212
Fax: (298) 321433
Internet: www.uksw.edu
Founded 1956
Languages of instruction: Indonesian, English(for special programmes only)
Academic year: August to July
Rector: Prof. Dr KRIS HERAWAN TIMOTIUS
Asst Rector I: Dr Ir DANIEL DAUD KAMEO
Asst Rector II: HARIJONO
Asst Rector III: UMBU RAUTA
Asst Rector IV: AGNA SULIS KRAVE
Registrar: SUDI WINARNO
Librarian: Drs DJASMANI
Number of teachers: 306 (full-time)
Number of students: 9,325
Publications: *Citra Wacana* (4 a year), *Dian Ekonomi* (2 a year), *Kritis* (3 a year)

DEANS

Faculty of Agriculture: Ir SUPRIHATI
Faculty of Biology: Drs AGNA SULIS KRAVE
Faculty of Economics: Prof. HENDRAWAN SUPRATIKNO
Faculty of Education and Teacher Training: Drs AUGUS HERMAN NAIOLA
Faculty of Languages and Letters: Drs URIP SUTIYONO
Faculty of Law: J. DANNY ZACHARIAS
Faculty of Pedagogy: Dr LOBBY LUKMONO
Faculty of Performing Arts: Drs AGASTYA RAMA LISTYA
Faculty of Psychology: Dra HARI SUTJININGSIH
Faculty of Science and Mathematics: Dr AGUS KRISTIJANTO
Faculty of Social and Political Sciences: Dr KUTUT SUWONDO
Faculty of Technology: Ir BUDIHARDJA MURTIANTA
Faculty of Theology: Drs DANIEL NUHAMARA
Professional Programmes: LINA SINATRA
Postgraduate Programmes: Prof. DANIEL DAUD KAMEO

UNIVERSITAS MAHAPUTRA MUHAMMAD YAMIN SOLOK

Jl. Raya Koto Baru 7, Solok 27361
Telephone: (755) 20128
Fax: (755) 20127
Private control
Programmes in accounting, agribusiness, agrotechnology, biology, economic development, legal studies, livestock, management and mathematics.

UNIVERSITAS MEDAN AREA

Campus 1 Jl. Kolam 1, Medan 20223
Telephone: (61) 7366878
Fax: (61) 736068
Campus 2 Jl. Jend Gatot Subroto 395, Medan 20118
Telephone: (61) 4567330*Campus 3* Jl. Sei Serayu 70A, Medan 20118
Telephone: (61) 8214875
E-mail: uma001@indosat.net.id
Internet: www.universitasmedanarea.com
Founded 1983
Private control
Faculties of agriculture, engineering, law, social and political sciences and psychology.

UNIVERSITAS METHODIST INDONESIA

Campus 1 Jl. Hang Tuah 8, Medan 20152
Telephone: (61) 4536735
Fax: (61) 4567533
Campus 2 Jl. Setia Budi Pasar II, Tg. Sari
Internet: umi-medan.info
Founded 1969
Private control
Rector: Dr THOMSON P. NADAPDAP
Vice-Rector I: Prof. Dr J. NAIBAHO
Vice-Rector II: Dr P. SIMANJUNTAK
Vice-Rector III: Drs OCTAVIAN RAGNAR SITORUS

DEANS

Faculty of Agriculture: Ir BERTON E. LUMBANTOBING
Faculty of Computer Science: Drs LISTON SIHITE
Faculty of Economics: Drs RAFIDIN HUTAPEA
Faculty of Literature: Drs P. SIMANJUNTAK
Faculty of Medicine: Dr HOPHOPTUA SIAHAAN

UNIVERSITAS MUHAMMADIYAH ACEH

Jl. Muhammadiyah 91, Desa Bathoh Lueng Bata, Banda Aceh 23245
Telephone: (651) 31583
Fax: (651) 34092
Founded 1969
Private control
Library of 1,300 titles.

UNIVERSITAS MUHAMMADIYAH JAKARTA

Campus A Jl. K. H. Ahmad Dahlan, Cirendeu Ciputat, Jakarta Selatan
Telephone: (21) 7401894
Fax: (21) 7430756
Campus B Jl. Cempaka Putih Tengah 27, Jakarta Pusat
Telephone: (21) 4256024
E-mail: info@umj.ac.id
Internet: www.umj.ac.id
Rector: AGUS SUNARTO
Faculties of agriculture, economics, law, medicine, religion, social and political sciences, technology.

UNIVERSITAS MUHAMMADIYAH KUPANG

Jl. K. H. Ahmad Dahlan 17, Kupang, Nusa Tengarra Timur
Telephone: (380) 833693
Fax: (380) 25333
Founded 1987
Private control
Rector: Drs DARSYAD ANTJO
Library of 5,282 vols, 15,882 periodicals.

UNIVERSITAS MUHAMMADIYAH MALANG
(Muhammadiyah University of Malang)

Jl. Raya Tlogomas 246, Malang 65144
Telephone: (341) 464318
Fax: (341) 460782
E-mail: webmaster@unix.umm.ac.id
Internet: www.umm.ac.id
Founded 1966
Languages of instruction: Indonesian, English
Academic year: September to June
Rector: Drs H. MUHADJIR EFFENDY
Vice-Rector for Academic Affairs: Ir H. MUH. HAMZAH

Vice-Rector for Financial Affairs: Drs H. WAKIDI

Vice-Rector for Student Affairs: Ir H. ALI SAIFULLAH

Chief of Academic Admin.: Ir DAMAT

Chief of Public Admin.: Drs H. FAUZAN

Librarian: WAHJOE DWI PRIJONO

Number of teachers: 816

Number of students: 20,274

Publications: *Bestari Journal* (4 a year), *Bestari Tabloid* (12 a year)

DEANS

Faculty of Agriculture: Ir MISBAH RUHIYAT

Faculty of Animal Husbandry: Ir ABDUL MALIK

Faculty of Economics: Drs WAHYU HIDAYAT RIYANTO

Faculty of Engineering: Ir SUNARTO

Faculty of Islamic Education: Drs MOH. NURHAKIM

Faculty of Law: MOKH. HAJIH

Faculty of Medicine: Ir H. MUH. HAMZAH (acting)

Faculty of Psychology: Drs LATIPUN

Faculty of Social and Political Science: Dra VINA SALVIANA

Faculty for Teacher Training and Education: Drs AHSANUL IN'AM

UNIVERSITAS MUHAMMADIYAH MATARAM

Jl. K. H. A. Dahlan 1, Pegesangan, Mataram

Telephone: (370) 633723

Founded 1980

Private control

Rector: Ir H. SUHARTO TJITROHADJONO

Library of 8,500 titles

Number of teachers: 80

Number of students: 1,930

UNIVERSITAS MUHAMMADIYAH SUMATERA UTARA

Jl. Kapt. Mukhtar Basri 3, Medan 20238

Telephone: (61) 6619056

Fax: (61) 6625474

Internet: www.umsu.ac.id

Founded 1957

Private control

Rector: H. BAHDIN NUR TANJUNG

Vice-Rector I: Drs H. ARMANSYAH

Vice-Rector II: H. SUHARWADI K. LUBIS

Vice-Rector III: Drs AGUSSANI

DEANS

Faculty of Agriculture: Ir ALRIDIWIRSAH

Faculty of Economics: PASARIBU ZULASPAN TUPTI

Faculty of Engineering: RAHMATULLAH

Faculty of Islamic Religion: AKRIM

Faculty of Law: FARID WAJDI

Faculty of Medicine: TAUFIQ

Faculty of Social and Political Sciences: R. KUSNADI

Faculty of Teacher Training and Education: Hj. NUR'AIN LUBIS

UNIVERSITAS MUHAMMADIYAH TAPANULI SELATAN DI PADANG SIDEMPUAN

Jl. Sutan Moch. Arief 32, Padang Sidempuan, Tapanuli Selatan 22716

Telephone: (634) 21696

Founded 1983

Private control

Rector: H. MARAGINDA HARAHAP.

UNIVERSITAS MUSLIM NUSANTARA AL-WASHLIYAH

Medan

E-mail: admin@umnaw.com

Internet: www.umnaw.com

Private control

Rector: Prof. Hj. Sri SULISTYAWATI

DEANS

Faculty of Agriculture: Ir ERNITA

Faculty of Economics: ARBY BACHTIAR

Faculty of Law: PURBA NELVITIA

Faculty of Mathematics and Natural Sciences: PANDAPOTAN NASUTION

Faculty of Sastras: S. S. SUFATMI

Faculty of Teacher Training and Education: Drs ULIAN BARUS

UNIVERSITAS NAHDLATUL WATHAN MATARAM

Jl. Kaktus 1–3, Mataram 82137

Telephone: (370) 641275

Fax: (370) 641275

Private control.

UNIVERSITAS NASIONAL

Jl. Sawo Manila, Pasar Minggu, Jakarta 12520

Telephone: (21) 7806700

Fax: (21) 7802718

E-mail: info@unas.ac.id

Internet: www.unas.ac.id

Founded 1949

Private control

Language of instruction: Indonesian

Academic year: October to August

Rector: Drs EL AMRY BERMAWI PUTERA

Vice-Rector for Academic Affairs: Dr MOCH. RUM ALIM

Vice-Rector for Research and Devt Community Services: Drs ERNAWATI SINAGA

Vice-Rector for Financial and Gen. Admin. Affairs: Drs EKO SUGIYANTO

Vice-Rector for Int. Cooperation and Students Affairs: Drs FALDY RASYIDIE

Univ. Librarian: Drs FATHUDDIN

Library of 32,181 vols, 20,206 books, 205 magazines and journals, 12 bulletins, 11,695 theses

Number of teachers: 683

Number of students: 7,000

Publications: *Ilmu Dan Budaya* (social science, 12 a year), *Jurnal Poelitik* (political science), *Jurrnal Sawo Manila* (literature)

DEANS

Faculty of Agriculture: Ir TRI WALUYO

Faculty of Biology: Drs IMRAN S. L. TOBING

Faculty of Economics: SURYONO EFENDI

Faculty of Engineering and Science: Ir AJAT SUDRAJAT

Faculty of Health Science: Dr ROSMAWATY LUBIS

Faculty of Informatics, Communications and Technology: Dr ISKANDAR FITRI

Faculty of Law: SURAJIMAN

Faculty of Literature and Languages: Drs WAHYU WIBOWO

Faculty of Social and Political Science: Prof. Drs H. B. TAMAM ACHDA

UNIVERSITAS NGURAH RAI DENPASAR

Jl. Padma Penatih, Denpasar, Timur

Telephone and fax (361) 468349

E-mail: fisip@unr.ac.id

Internet: www.unr.ac.id

Founded 1981

Private control.

UNIVERSITAS PAKUAN

Jl. Pakuan, POB 452, Bogor 16143

Telephone: (251) 8312206

Fax: (251) 356927

Internet: www.unpak.ac.id

Founded 1961

Chancellor: Dr H. MASHUDI

Rector: ACHMAD SUBROTO

Sec.: R. H. NATANEGARA

Number of teachers: 60

Number of students: 350

DEANS

Faculty of Economics: Drs USMAN ZAKARIA

Faculty of Law: BINTATAR SINAGA

Faculty of Mathematics and Natural Science: Ir SOEDARSONO

Faculty of Technology: DJAUHARI NOOR

UNIVERSITAS PANCASILA

Srengseng Sawah, Jagakarsa, Pasar Minggu, Jakarta Selatan 12640

Telephone: (21) 7270086

Fax: (21) 7271868

E-mail: info@univpancasila.ac.id

Internet: www.univpancasila.ac.id

Founded 1966

Language of instruction: Indonesian

Academic year: September to August

Chair.: Dr Ir SISWONO YUDOHUSODO

Rector: Dr EDIE TOET HENDRATNO

Vice-Rector for Academic Affairs: Ir SUHARSO

Vice-Rector for Finance and Admin.: Dra DEWI TRIRAHAYU

Vice-Rector for Student Affairs: Dr MUHAMMAD IBRAHIM

Vice-Rector for Cooperation and Venture: Drs SUROTO

Library of 30,906 vols

Number of teachers: 472

Number of students: 8,000

Publications: *Jurnal Farmasi, Jurnal Teknik, Media Humas, Retorika, Suara Ekonomi*

DEANS

Faculty of Communication: Prof. Dr ANDI MUHAMMAD

Faculty of Economy: Dr TRI WIDYASTUTI

Faculty of Engineering: Ir FAUZRI FAHIMUDDIN

Faculty of Law: Dr INDAH HARLINA

Faculty of Pharmacy: Drs I. WAYAN REDJA

Faculty of Tourism: Dr RIADIKE MASTRA

UNIVERSITAS PEMBANGUNAN PANCABUDI

Jl. Jend. Gatot Subroto, Km 4, 5 Simpang Sei Sikambing, Medan, Sumatera Utara 20122

Telephone: (61) 8455571

Fax: (61) 4514808

E-mail: unpab@pancabudi.ac.id

Internet: www.pancabudi.ac.id

Founded 1961

Private control

Academic year: July to June

Rector: Mag. H. MUHAMMAD ISA INDRAWAN

Vice-Rector for Academic Affairs: Mag. SAMRIN

Vice-Rector for Admin. and Finance: Mag. SAIMARA SEBAYANG

Vice-Rector for Student Affairs: Mag. RIADIONO

Vice-Rector for Cooperation and Business: Mag. INDRAJAYA LUBIS

Number of teachers: 191

Number of students: 6,000

DEANS

Faculty of Agriculture: Mag. MARAHADI SIR-
EGAR
Faculty of Economic: Mag. MUHAMAD TOYIB
DAULAY
Faculty of Islamic: Mag. MUHAMMAD JAMIL
Faculty of Law: Mag. RIADIONO
Faculty of Metaphysics: Mag. M. JAMIL
Faculty of Technology: Mag. LENI MARLINA

UNIVERSITAS PGRI KUPANG

Jl. Anggur 10 Naikoten I, Kupang 85118
Telephone and fax (380) 821824
E-mail: pgrintt@yahoo.com.

UNIVERSITAS SAMAWA

Jl. Raya Sering, Sumbawa, Besar
Telephone: (371) 625848
E-mail: unsasumbawa@yahoomail.com
Private control.

UNIVERSITAS SERAMBI MEKKAH

Jl. Tengku Imum Lueng Bata Desa Bathoh,
Banda Aceh 23249
Telephone: (651) 26160
Founded 1985
Private control
Rector: Prof. Dr M. ISA SULAIMAN.

UNIVERSITAS SISINGAMANGARAJA XII TAPANULI UTARA DI SIBORONG-BORONG

North Tapanuli, Siborongborong
Telephone and fax (633) 41017
Founded 1987
Private control
Rector: Ir ADRIANI SIAHAAN
Vice-Rector: Ir ARVITA SIHALOHO
Vice-Rector: Ir T. B. PAKPAHAN
Vice-Rector: Drs MAULIATE SIMORANGKIR

DEANS

Faculty of Agriculture: ELSERIA SIBURIAN
Faculty of Economics: Dr AGUSNI PASARIBU
Faculty of Engineering: Ir M. SIAHAAN
Faculty of Law: TUNGGUL SIMORANGKIR
Faculty of Teacher Training and Education:
Drs DONVER PANGGABEAN

UNIVERSITAS SULTAN AGENG TIRTAYASA

Jl Raya Jakarta KM 4, Pakupatan, Serang,
Banten
Telephone: (254) 280330
Fax: (254) 281254
E-mail: info@untirta.ac.id
Internet: www.untirta.ac.id
Founded 2001
Private control
Rector: Ir RAHMAN ABDULLAH
Faculties of economics, engineering.

UNIVERSITAS TABANAN

Jl. Wagimin 8, Kediri, Tabanan, Bali
Telephone: (361) 811605
Founded 1981
Private control
Rector: Ir IDA BAGUS GDE WIRAKUSUMA
Library of 1,901 vols, 2,356 periodicals.

UNIVERSITAS TRIKARYA

Jl. Gaperta Ujung 58, Perladangan Helvetia,
Medan Helvetia, Medan 20124
Telephone: (61) 8450419
E-mail: univ_trikarya@plasa.com

Founded 2002
Private control.

UNIVERSITAS TRISAKTI

Jl. Kyai Tapa 1, Grogol, Jakarta 11440
Telephone: (21) 5663232
Fax: (21) 5644270
E-mail: sekun@trisakti.ac.id
Internet: www.trisakti.ac.id
Founded 1965
Language of instruction: Indonesian
Academic year: September to August
Rector: Prof. Dr THOBY MUTIS
Vice-Rector for Academic Affairs: Prof. Dr
H.YUSWAR Z BASRI,
Vice-Rector for Cooperation and Human
Resources: Ir ASRI NUGRAHANTI
Vice-Rector for Personnel, Admin. and
Finance: Prof. Dr ITJANG D. GUNAWAN
Vice-Rector for Student Affairs: H. I. KOMANG
SUKA'ARSANA
Secretariat: H. SOFAN
Head of Library: Dra FARIDA SALIM
Number of teachers: 2,681 (1,691 full-time,
701 part-time)
Number of students: 30,754
Publication: *Masyarakat Kampus* (24 a year)

DEANS

Faculty of Art and Design: Prof. Drs YUSUF
AFFENDI DJALARI
Faculty of Civil Engineering and Planning:
Dr Ir EKA SEDIADI RASYAD
Faculty of Dentistry: Dr BAMBANG S. TREN-
GGONO
Faculty of Earth and Energy Technology: Ir
H. MOH THAMRIN
Faculty of Economics: Prof. Dr FARIDA JASFAR
Faculty of Industrial Technology: Ir DOCKY
SARASWATI
Faculty of Landscape Architecture and
Environmental Technology: Ir IDA BAGUS
RABINDRA
Faculty of Law: ENDAR PULUNGAN
Faculty of Medicine: Prof. JULIUS E. SURYA-
WIDJAJA

UNIVERSITAS VETERAN REPUBLIK INDONESIA

Jl. Baruga Raya Kampus II, Ujung Pandang
Telephone: (411) 491203
Faculties of education, history, law.

UNIVERSITAS WARMADEWA

Denpasar, Bali
Internet: www.warmadewa.ac.id
Founded 1983
Private control
Rector: Prof. Dr I. MADE SUKARSA
Vice-Rector I: Drs I. MADE YUDHIANTARA
Vice-Rector II: IDA BAGUS UDAYANA PUTRA
Vice-Rector III: Ir A. A. NGURAH MAYUN
WIRAJAYA

DEANS

Faculty of Economics: Drs I. WAYAN ARJANA
Faculty of Engineering: I. GUSTI MADE S.
DIASA
Faculty of Law: NI LUH MADE MAHENDRAWATI
Faculty of Literature: Drs NYOMAN SUJAYA

Institutes

ABFI Institute Perbanas: Jl. Perbanas,
Karet Kuningan, Setiabudi, Jakarta 12940;
tel. (21) 5252533; fax (21) 5228460; e-mail
info@perbanasinstitute.ac.id; internet www
.perbanasinstitute.ac.id; f. 2007, by merger of
Sekolah Tinggi Ilmu Ekonomi (College of
Economics, f. 1969) and Sekolah Tinggi
Manajemen Informatika dan Komputer (College of Information Management and Computers, f. 1993); offers programmes in
banking, general management and risk management; Rector Dr Ir FATCHUDIN; Vice-Rector for Academic Affairs Dr STEPH SUBANIDJA;
Vice-Rector for Graduate Programmes Prof.
Dr ADLER HAYMANS MANURUNG; Vice-Rector
for Human Resource Devt Dr WILSON R.
LUMBANTOBING; Vice-Rector for Student and
Alumni Affairs Dr DAVID SITUMORANG.

**Balai Pengkajian Teknologi Pertanian
Jawa Barat** (West Java Research Institute
for Agricultural Technology): Jl. Kayuambon
80, Lembang, Bandung 40391; tel. (22)
2786238; fax (22) 2789846; e-mail
bptp-jabar@litbang.deptan.go.id; internet
jabar.litbang.deptan.go.id; f. 1994.

**Institut Filsafat Theologi dan Kepemim-
pinan Jaffray (IFTK Jaffray Jakarta)**
(Institute for Theological and Leadership
Philosophy Jaffray): Jl. Jatinegara Timur II
35, Jakarta 13350; tel. (21) 8570986; fax (21)
8570988; e-mail iftkj@centrin.net.id; internet
www.iftk-jaffray.com; f. 1932, present name
and status 1991; Rector Dr Drs JERRY
RUMAHLATU; Vice-Rector for Academic Affairs
NASOKHILI GIAWA; Vice-Rector for Admin. and
Finance Dr MAGDALENA TOMATALA; Vice-Rector for Student Affairs PHILEMON INDAKRAY.

**Institut Ilmu Sosial dan Ilmu Politik
Jakarta** (Institute of Social and Political
Sciences): Jl. Raya Lenteng Agung 32,
Jakarta Selatan 12610; tel. (21) 7806223;
fax (21) 7817630; e-mail admin@iisip.ac.id;
internet www.iisip.ac.id; f. 1953; faculties of
administration, communication, social and
political sciences; Rector MASLINA W. HUTA-
SUHUT.

**Institut Keguruan dan Ilmu Pendidikan
Budi Utomo:** Jl. Simpang Arjuno 14B,
Malang; tel. (341) 326019; fax (341) 335070;
e-mail info@budiutomo.ac.id; f. 1984; offers
programmes in economics, English, history
and sociology, mathematics, sports and
health.

**Institut Keguruan dan Ilmu Pendidikan
Mataram** (Institute of Teacher Training and
Education): Gedung Dwitya Jl. Pemuda 59,
Mataram; tel. (370) 632082; internet
ikipmataram.ac.id; f. 1967; Rector H. LALU
SAID RUHPINA; Head Librarian A. SUNANDAR.

**Institut Keguruan dan Ilmu Pendidikan
PGRI Bali:** Jl. Seroja, Tonya, East Denpasar, Denpasar; tel. (361) 431434; fax (361)
701128; f. 1983; library: 3,100 titles; Rector
REDHA GUNAWAN.

**Institut Keguruan dan Ilmu Pendidikan
PGRI Jember:** Jl. Jawa 10, Jember; tel.
(331) 335823; fax (331) 335977; internet www
.ikip-jember.org; f. 1979; Rector Drs H. M.
ARIFIN.

**Institut Keguruan dan Ilmu Pendidikan
PGRI Madiun:** Jl. Setiabudi 85, Madiun;
tel. (351) 462986; fax (351) 459400; e-mail
rektorat@ikippgri-madiun.ac.id; internet
ikippgri-madiun.ac.id; Rector Drs PARJI.

**Institut Keguruan dan Ilmu Pendidikan
PGRI Semarang:** Jl. Cipto Lontar 1, Semarang; tel. (24) 8316377; fax (24) 8448217;
internet ikip-pgrismg.net; faculties of language and literature, mathematics and science education; library: 10,771 titles, 35,244
theses; Rector MUHDI.

**Institut Keguruan dan Ilmu Pendidikan
Saraswati Tabanan:** Jl. Pahlawan 2, Delod
Peken, Tabanan 82113; tel. (362) 811267.

Institut Pertanian STIPER Yogyakarta:
Jl. Nangka II, Maguwoharjo, Depok, Sleman,
Yogyakarta 55282; tel. and fax (247) 885479;
e-mail info@instiper.ac.id; internet www
.instiper.ac.id; f. 1958; faculties of agricul-

tural technology, agriculture, forestry; library: 789 reference titles, 327 journals; Rector Dr Ir PURWADI; Vice-Rector Dr Ir HARSAWARDANA; Vice-Rector I Dr Ir A. SIH AYIEK SAYEKTI.

Institut Sains dan Teknologi AKPRIND Yogyakarta: Jl. Kalisahak 28, Komplek, Balapan 55222; tel. (274) 563029; fax (274) 563847; e-mail ista@indo.net.id; internet www.akprind.ac.id; faculties of applied science, industrial technology and mineral technology.

Institut Sains dan Teknologi TD Pardede: Jl. Dr. TD Pardede 8, Kecamatan, Medan 20153; tel. and fax (61) 4569877; e-mail mail@istp.ac.id; internet www.istp.ac.id; f. 1987; faculties of civil engineering and planning, mineral technology and industrial technology; Rector Ir RUDOLF SITORUS; Vice-Rector I Drs L. SIHOMBING; Vice-Rector II Ir OMNY PARNGARIBUAN; Vice-Rector III Ir SIBARANI.

Institut Teknologi Adhi Tama Surabaya: Jl. Arief Rachman Hakim 100, Surabaya; tel. (31) 5945043; fax (31) 5994620; internet www .itats.ac.id; library: 19,165 book titles; Rector HADI SETIYAWAN; Vice-Rector I ARIEF RACHMAN; Vice-Rector II KUNTO EKO SUSILO; Vice-Rector III BAMBANG SETYONO.

Institut Teknologi Indonesia: Jl. Raya Puspiptek Serpong, Tangerang, Banten 15320; tel. and fax (21) 7561102; internet www.iti.ac.id.

Institut Teknologi Medan: Jl. Gedung Arca 52, Medan 20217; tel. and fax (61) 7363771; e-mail itm@itm.ac.id; internet www .itm.ac.id; f. as Akademi Teknik Dwiwarna, name changed to Institut Teknologi Sumatera 1963, Sekolah Tinggi Teknik Medan 1976, present name and status 1984; Rector Ir MAHRIZAL MASRI; Vice-Rector I Ir ILMI ABDULLAH; Vice-Rector II MUNAJAT; Vice-Rector III MAHYUZAR MASRI.

Institut Teknologi Nasional (National Institute of Technology): Mustafa 23, Bandung 40124; tel. (22) 7272215; internet www .itenas.ac.id; f. 1972 as Akademi Teknologi Nasional, present name and status 1984; Rector Prof. Dr Ir HARSONO TAROEPRATJEKA; Vice-Rector for Academic and Student Affairs

Ir SYAHRIL SAYUTI; Vice-Rector for Finance and Gen. Admin. Ir YANTI HELIANTY; Vice-Rector for Planning and Cooperation Dr IMAM ASCHURI.

Higher Colleges

Sekolah Tinggi Bahasa Asing (STBA) Yapari-ABA Bandung: Jl. Cihampelas 194, Bandung 40131; tel. (22) 2035426; fax (22) 2036765; e-mail info@stbayapariaba.ac .id; internet stbayapariaba.ac.id; Private control.

Sekolah Tinggi Filsafat Driyarkara (School of Philosophy Driyarkara): Jl. Cempaka Putih Indah 100A, Jembatan Serong Rawasari, Jakarta 10520; tel. (21) 4247129; fax (21) 4224866; e-mail stfd@dnet.net.id; internet www.driyarkara.ac.id; f. 1969; offers programmes in philosophy and science theology; 316 students; Chair. Prof. Dr A. EDDY KRISTIYANTO; publ. *Driyarkara* (4 a year).

Sekolah Tinggi Ilmu Ekonomi Malangkuçeçwara (Malangkuçeçwara School of Economics): Jl. Terusan Candi Kalasan, Blimbing, Malang 65142; tel. (341) 491813; e-mail info@stie-mce.ac.id; internet www .stie-mce.ac.id; f. 1971; depts of accounting and finance; Pres. NEVI DANILA; Vice-Pres. Drs BUNYAMIN; Vice-Pres. Drs TACHJUDDIN; Vice-Pres. Drs KADARUSMAN.

Sekolah Tinggi Ilmu Ekonomi Pasundan (Higher College for Economics Pasundan): Jl. Usman Ambon 4, Kacang Pedang, Pangkalpinang 33125; tel. (717) 438735; fax (717) 438736; e-mail info@stie-ibek.ac.id; internet stiepas.ac.id; f. 2000; offers programmes in accounting and management; Chair. YOLANDA PUSPASARI.

Sekolah Tinggi Ilmu Ekonomi Solusi Bisnis Indonesia (Higher College for Economics and Business Solutions Indonesia): Jl. Ring Rd Utara 17, Condong Catur, Yogyakarta 55283; tel. and fax (274) 887984; internet stie-sbi.ac.id; programmes in accounting and management; Chair. LUCIA IKA FITRIASTUTI.

Sekolah Tinggi Ilmu Sosial dan Ilmu Politik Kebangsaan–Masohi (College of Social and Political Science): Jl. Christina Martha Tiahahu 15, Masohi; tel. (914) 22057; internet www.stisipkebangsaanmasohi.com; f. 1999; administered by Yayasan Perguruan Tinggi Kebangsaan (Nat. Higher Education Foundation) Masohi; Chair. Drs J. KAPRESSY.

Sekolah Tinggi Manajemen Informatika dan Teknik Komputer (STIKOM) Surabaya (Higher College of Information Management and Computer Engineering Surabaya): Jl. Kedung Baruk 98, Surabaya; tel. (31) 8721731; e-mail info@stikom.edu; internet www.stikom.edu; f. 1983.

Sekolah Tinggi Teknik Poliprofesi Medan: Jl. Sei Batanghari 3–4, Medan; tel. (61) 8446729; e-mail layanan@ sttp-poliprofesi.ac.id; internet sttp-poliprofesi.ac.id; f. 2002; Dir AKMAN DAULAY.

Sekolah Tinggi Teknologi Jakarta: Jl. Jatiwaringin Raya 278, Pondok Gede, Jakarta; tel. (21) 8462316; fax (21) 8463692; e-mail stj@cbn.net.id; internet www.sttj.ac .id; f. 1972; Chair. ROSSI SETIADJI.

Sekolah Tinggi Teknologi Nuklir– BATAN (Higher College for Nuclear Technology): Jl. Babarsari POB 6101 YKBB, Yogyakarta 55281; tel. (247) 484085; fax (247) 489715; internet www.sttn-batan.ac .id; f. 1982; research and devt of nuclear technology.

Schools of Art and Music

Akademi Seni Karawitan Indonesia Padang Panjang (Academy for Traditional Music and Dance): Jl. Puti Bungsu 35, Padang Panjang, Sumatra Barat; tel. (752) 82077; fax (752) 82803; f. 1966; offers diploma courses in ballet, dance, music and music performance; library: 6,196 vols; 62 teachers; 428 students; Dir Prof. MARDJANI MARTAMIN; Registrar BAHRUL PADEK; Librarian Drs ANNAS HAMIR.

IRAN

The Higher Education System

The first modern institution of higher education was the Dar al-Fanun, a technical institute founded in 1851. In 1928 two more technical institutes were founded, now known as Iran University of Science and Technology and K. N. Toosi University of Technology. In 1934 Dar al-Fanun was incorporated into the newly established University of Tehran, the first multi-disciplinary institution of higher education. Universities were closed following the Islamic revolution in 1979 but gradually reopened from 1983. Public universities and colleges are administered by the Ministry of Science, Research and Technology, and medical universities (which are classified separately) are controlled by the Ministry of Health and Medical Education. In 1982 an 'open' university, Islamic Azad University, was founded, which now has 80 centres in cities and towns. It is not funded by central government, it administers its own entrance examination and charges tuition fees. Payame Noor University was founded in 1987 and offers correspondence courses and continuing adult education. There are 54 state-operated universities, and by 2008 there were over 3.5m. students enrolled, with 8,50,000 of these at the Islamic Azad University. Other higher education institutions include general and professional colleges, technological institutes and vocational establishments.

To enter higher education, students must gain the Pre-University Certificate and sit the National Entrance Examin-ation. (Islamic Azad University administers its own entrance examination—Kunkur.) Iranian higher education is based on a 'credit semester' system; one credit is gained following 17 hours of taught classes, 34 hours of laboratory work or 51 hours of practical ('workshop') experience. The first undergraduate qualification is the Associate degree, awarded after four semesters (two years) and requiring 67–72 credits. Colleges of Further Education offer an equivalent degree known as Kardani. The Bachelors is the second (and main) undergraduate degree, lasting eight semesters (four years) and requiring 130–35 credits. First degrees offering professional titles are available in pharmacy, medicine, dentistry and veterinary science; these last for 11 semesters (six years). A student with the Bachelors may progress to postgraduate education, which consists of the Masters (Karshenasi-Arshad or Fogh-Licence) and Doctorate. The Masters is a course lasting four semesters (two years) and requiring 28–32 credits (of which the thesis accounts for four to 10 units). The final university degree is the Doctorate, which consists of two stages: first, the student must complete 12–30 credits of classroom-based learning; second, a period of original research leading to submission of a thesis is required. The course lasts a total of four to five years.

University courses must be accredited by either the Ministry of Science, Research and Technology Directorate of Development or the Ministry of Health and Medical Education.

Regulatory Bodies

GOVERNMENT

Ministry of Culture and Islamic Guidance: Baharestan Sq., Tehran; tel. (21) 32411; fax (21) 33117535; e-mail info@ershad.gov.ir; internet www.ershad.gov.ir; Minister MUHAMMAD HOSSEIN SAFFAR-HAR-ANDI.

Ministry of Education: Si-e-Tir St, Emam Khomeini Sq., Tehran; tel. (21) 32421; fax (21) 675503; e-mail info@medu.ir; internet www.medu.ir; Minister AI REZA ALI AHMADI.

Learned Societies

GENERAL

UNESCO Office Tehran: Bahman Bldg, Sa'ad Abad Palace Complex, Tehran 19894; tel. (21) 22751315; fax (21) 22751318; e-mail tehran@unesco.org; internet www.unesco.org/tehran; designated Cluster Office for Afghanistan, Iran, Pakistan and Turkmenistan; Dir QUNLI HAN.

ECONOMICS, LAW AND POLITICS

Iran Management Association: POB 15855-359, Tehran; Karimkhan Blvd 1 corner of Asjodi St, Tehran; tel. (21) 8827878; fax (21) 8835278; e-mail info@iranmanagement.org; internet www.iranmanagement.org; f. 1960; promotes sound management principles and techniques for the improvement of management in Iran, and to create understanding and cooperation among managers in Iran and other countries; 200 individual and 300 institutional mems; library of 8,000 vols; Sec.-Gen. PARVIZ BAYAT; publs *Management Magazine* (in Persian, with summary in English, 12 a year), *Modiriat* (Management, 6 a year).

HISTORY, GEOGRAPHY AND ARCHAEOLOGY

Ancient Iran Cultural Society: Jomhorie Eslamie Ave, Shahrokh St, Tehran; f. 1961; Man. Dir A. QUORESHI.

British Institute of Persian Studies: c/o The British Acad., 10 Carlton House Terrace, London, SW1Y 5AH, United Kingdom; tel. (20) 7969-5203; fax (20) 7969-5401; e-mail bips@britac.ac.uk *Tehran:* 1553, Khiaban-e Dr Ali Shariati, Qolhak, Tehran 19396–13661; tel. (21) 22601937; fax (21) 22604901; e-mail bips@parsonline.net; internet www.bips.ac.uk; f. 1961; cultural institute, with special emphasis on history, archaeology and all aspects of Iranian studies; 400 mems; library of 10,000 books and MSS; Hon. Sec. (London Office) PETER DAVIES; Librarian (Tehran Office) FARIBA RAYHANPOUR; publ. *Iran* (1 a year).

LANGUAGE AND LITERATURE

British Council: North Entrance British Embassy Compound, Shariati St, Qholhak, Tehran 19396-13661; tel. (21) 2001222; fax (21) 2007604; e-mail info@ir.britishcouncil.org; internet www.britishcouncil.org/iran; offers courses and exams in English language and British culture and promotes cultural exchange with the UK; Dir ANDREW MURRAY.

MEDICINE

Iranian Society of Microbiology: Department of Microbiology and Immunology, Faculty of Medicine, University of Tehran; tel. (21) 88955810; e-mail ijmicrobiology@gmail.com; internet www.ism.ir; f. 1940; 185 mems; Gen. Sec. G. H. NAZARI; publ. *Iranian Journal Microbiology*.

NATURAL SCIENCES

Mathematical Sciences

Iranian Mathematical Society: POB 13145-418, Tehran; tel. (21) 8808855; fax (21) 8807775; e-mail iranmath@ims.ir; internet www.ims.ir; f. 1971; 2,750 mems; Pres. E. S. MAHMOODIAN; publs *Bulletin* (2 a year), *Farhang va Andishaye Riyazi* (2 a year).

Research Institutes

GENERAL

Institute for Humanities and Cultural Studies (IHCS): 64 St, Seyyed Jamal-eddin Ave, Tehran 14374; tel. (21) 88048037; fax (21) 88036317; e-mail info@ihcs.ac.ir; internet www.ihcs.ac.ir; f. 1981; research faculties: cultural studies, literature, history, history and philosophy of science, religious studies, linguistics, social sciences; languages of instruction: Arabic, English, Persian; library of 120,000 vols; Dir Dr HAMID AYATOLLAHI; publs *Afaq al-Hizarah al-Islamiyyah* (2 a year), *Journal of Humanities* (4 a year), *Science and Religion Bulletin* (2 a year), *The Farhang* (4 a year).

AGRICULTURE, FISHERIES AND VETERINARY SCIENCE

Agricultural Biotechnology Research Institute of Iran (ABRII): POB 4119, Mardabad Ave, Karaj 31585; tel. (261) 2708282; fax (261) 2704539; e-mail khayam@abrii.ac.ir; internet www.abrii.ac.ir; f. 1983 as the Plant Biotechnology Department of Seed and Plant Improvement

Institute; depts of cellular and molecular biology, genetics, genomics, microorganisms and biosafety, physiology and proteomics, technical services and research support and tissue culture and gene transformation; Dir-Gen. Dr MOJTABA KHAYYAM NEKOUEI.

Animal Science Research Institute: POB 31585-1483, Karaj, Tehran; tel. (261) 4430010; fax (261) 4413258; e-mail info@asri.ir; internet www.asri.ir; f. 1933; research on cattle, water buffalo, sheep, goats, poultry and honeybees; library of 6,425 books, 176 periodicals; Gen. Dir Dr MOHAMMAD ALI KAMALI; publ. *Animal Husbandry Research Institute*.

Plant Pests and Diseases Research Institute: POB 19395-1454, Evin/Tabnak St, Tehran; tel. (21) 2403012; fax (21) 2403691; e-mail info@ppdri.ac.ir; internet www.ppdri.ac.ir; f. 1943; research on pests and diseases of agricultural crops, botany, entomology, biological control, pesticides and agricultural zoology; library of 55,000 vols (English and Farsi), 480 periodicals (English and Farsi); Dir Dr G. A. ABDOLLAHI; publs *Applied Entomology and Phytopathology* (1 a year, in Farsi and English), *Iranian Journal of Plant Pathology* (1 a year, in Farsi and English), *Journal of the Entomological Society of Iran* (1 a year, in Farsi and English), *Rostaniha—Botanical Journal of Iran* (1 a year, in Farsi and English).

Razi Vaccine and Serum Research Institute: POB 31975–148, Karaj 31976-19751; tel. (261) 4570038; fax (261) 4552194; e-mail admin@rvsri.com; internet www.rvsri.com; f. 1930; epizootological and ecological studies of animal diseases and human and animal biology; research and preparation of all veterinary vaccines, some human vaccines and therapeutic sera; postgraduate courses in virology and microbiology; languages of instruction: Persian, English; library of 13,000 books, 800 periodicals; Gen. Dir Prof. ABDOLHOSSEIN DALIMI; publ. *Archives of the Razi Institute* (in English, 1 a year).

ECONOMICS, LAW AND POLITICS

Institute for Political and International Studies (IPIS): Shahid Bahonar Ave, Shahid Aghaee St, POB 19395-1793, Tehran; tel. (21) 22802671; fax (21) 22802649; e-mail cominfo@ipis.ir; internet www.ipis.ir; f. 1983; acts as a research and information centre on int. relations, law, economics and Islamic studies, with emphasis on the Middle East, the Persian Gulf and Central Asia; holds conferences and seminars on contemporary int. issues; library of 200,000 vols; Pres. ALI AHANI; Dir-Gen. Dr SEYED R. MOSAVI; publs *Amyu Darya* (in English and Russian), *Central Asia and Caucasus Review Quarterly* (in Farsi), *Foreign Policy Quarterly* (in Farsi), *Iranian Journal of International Affairs Quarterly* (in English), *Islam and International Relations* (in Farsi), *Journal of Alalaghat Aliranieh* (in Arabic).

Institute for Trade Studies and Research: 240 North Kargar St, POB 14185-671, Tehran 14187; tel. (21) 6622378; fax (21) 66938374; e-mail info@itsr.ir; internet www.itsr.ir; f. 1980; library of 70,000 vols; Pres. MAHMOOD DODANGEH; publs *Commercial Surveys* (6 a year), *Iranian Journal of Trade Studies (IJTC)* (4 a year).

HISTORY, GEOGRAPHY AND ARCHAEOLOGY

Institut Français de Recherche en Iran: Ave Shahid Nazari, 52 rue Adib, POB 15815-3495, Tehran 94371; tel. (21) 66401192; fax (21) 6405501; e-mail ifri@ifriran.org; internet www.ifriran.org; f. 1897, present name 1983; research into Iranian civilization, contact between French and Iranian scholars; library of 42,000 vols; Dir CHRISTOPHE BALAIJ; publs *Abstracta Iranica* (1 a year), *Cahiers de la DAFI, Bibliothéque Iranienne*.

National Cartographic Centre: POB 13185-1684, Azadi Sq., Meraj Ave, Tehran; tel. (21) 6000031; fax (21) 6001971; internet www.ncc.org.ir; f. 1953; library of 4,000 vols, 2,500 reports; Dir Dr M. MADAD; publ. *Naghshebardari* (Journal of Surveying, 4 a year).

MEDICINE

Institut Pasteur: 69 Pasteur Ave, Tehran; tel. (21) 66953311; fax (21) 66465132; e-mail office@pasteur.ac.ir; internet www.pasteur.ac.ir; f. 1921; vaccines, research in microbiology, biochemistry, biopharmaceuticals, biotechnology and human genetics, molecular biology, parasitology and mycology, physiology and pharmacology; teaching and postgraduate training; Dir-Gen. Dr ABDOLHOSSEIN ROUHOL AMINI NAJAFABADI; publ. *Iranian Biomedical Journal*.

NATURAL SCIENCES

Institute for Research in Fundamental Sciences: POB 19395-5746, Niavaran Bldg, Niavaran Sq., Tehran; tel. (21) 22287013; fax (21) 22290151; e-mail ipminfo@ipm.ir; internet www.ipm.ir; f. 1989; schools of astronomy, cognitive sciences, computer science, mathematics, nanoscience, particles and accelerators, philosophy, physics; Dir M. J. A. LARIJANI; publ. *Akhbar* (4 a year).

RELIGION, SOCIOLOGY AND ANTHROPOLOGY

Anthropological Research Institute: Azadi Ave, Zanjan Int., POB 13445-719, Tehran; tel. (21) 6016367; fax (21) 6018628; f. 1937; attached to Iranian Cultural Heritage Organization; Dir MOHAMMAD MIRSHOKRAEE.

Islamic Research Foundation, Astan Quds Razavi: POB 91735-366, Mashhad; tel. (511) 2232501; fax (511) 2230005; e-mail intrelation@islamic-rf.ir; internet www.islamic-rf.ir; f. 1984; research into Islamic subjects: the Qu'ran, the Hadith, jurisprudence, scholastic theology, Islamic text editing, translating Islamic books, study of Islamic arts, production of Islamic CDs; nat. and int. seminars; library of 78,000 vols; Man. Dir Prof. ALI AKBAR ELAHI KHORASANI; publ. *Meshkat* (4 a year).

TECHNOLOGY

Electric Power Research Centre: POB 15745-448, Shahrak Ghods, Pounak Bakhtari Blvd, Tehran; tel. (21) 8079401; fax (21) 8094774; f. 1983; attached to Min. of Energy; library of 12,000 vols, 151 periodicals; Pres. S. M. TABATABAEE; publ. *Journal of Electrical Science and Technology* (4 a year).

Libraries and Archives

Isfahan

Municipal Library: Shahied Nikbakht St, POB 81638, Isfahan; tel. (31) 621200; fax (31) 621100; f. 1991; 60,000 vols.

University of Isfahan Library: Isfahan; internet book.ui.ac.ir/cgi-bin/lib; 112,150 vols, half in Persian and Arabic, the remainder in European languages; Persian MSS and incunabula; Dir Dr HOSSEIN HARSIJ.

Mashhad

Ferdowsi University of Mashhad Information Centre and Central Library: POB 331-91735, Mashhad; tel. (511) 8789263; fax (511) 8796822; e-mail cent-lib@um.ac.ir; internet c-library.um.ac.ir; f. 1971; 539,609 vols; Dir of Information Centre and Central Library Prof. Dr MEHRDAD MOHRI.

Organizations of Libraries, Museums and Documents Center of Astan-e Quds-e Razavi: POB 91735-177, Mashhad; tel. (511) 2216555; fax (511) 2220845; e-mail info@aqlibrary.org; internet www.aqlibrary.org; f. 15th century; general library and assistance for researchers, 33 br. libraries, document centre, museums; 2m. vols, 65,000 MSS and 6m. other documents; 78,200 vols of foreign books (in 64 languages); Gen. Dir Dr ALI MUHAMMAD BARADRAN RAFIEI.

Tabriz

Tabriz Public Library (Ketabkhaneh Melli Tabriz): Tabriz; 12,816 vols; Dir SEYYED MASOUD NAQIB.

Tarbiat Library: Daneshsara Sq., Tabriz; tel. (41) 5222190; f. 1921; 29,750 vols; Dir HOSSEIN ASADI.

University of Tabriz Central Library and Documentation Centre: Tabriz; tel. (411) 3344705; fax (411) 3355993; e-mail a-assadzadeh@tabrizu.ac.ir; internet www.2tabrizu.ac.ir; f. 1967; 95,871 vols, 6,231 microfiches, 4,300 maps, 6,231 microfilms, 1,643 periodicals, 647 tapes; Librarian A. ASSADZADEH.

Tehran

Central Library and Documentation Centre of Shahid Beheshti University: Evin, Tehran 19834; tel. (21) 293155; f. 1960; 315,529 vols, 3,190 periodicals; Librarian Dr ZAHRA GOOYA; publs *Sourat Ketabhaye Fehrest Shodeh, Tazebaye Ketabkhaneh*.

Central Library and Documentation Centre of University of Tehran: Enghelab Ave, Tehran; tel. (21) 61112362; fax (21) 66495388; e-mail libpublic@ut.ac.ir; internet library.ut.ac.ir; f. 1949, re-housed 1970; Central Library of 850,000 vols, faculty libraries of 950,000 vols; Librarian Dr A. A. ENAYATI.

Centre for Socio-Economic Documentation and Publications: Baharestan Sq., Tehran 11365; tel. 3271; fax 301135; f. 1962, reorganized 1982; attached to Planning and Budget Org.; brs in 6 divs: technical services, information services and network affairs, libraries (Central Library, Archive for Devt Maps and Projects and 25 regional libraries), editing, graphics and production, distribution; libraries: 49,000 vols, 576 periodicals, 1,627 titles microforms, 16,000 titles devt projects, 18,000 maps and plans, databases of selected articles; Dir GHAFOUR BABAEI; publ. *Periodical Index to Socio-Economic Articles* (4 a year).

Institute for Political and International Studies Library and Documentation Centre: POB 19395-1793, Tajrish, Tehran; tel. (21) 2571010; fax (21) 2802643; internet www.ipis.ir; f. 1983; attached to the Foreign Ministry; spec. library and assistance for researchers; 20,000 vols on Islamic science, history, politics, economics, law, geography, diplomacy, military studies; 400 periodicals; Dir-Gen. Dr S. M. K. SAJJADPOUR; publs *African Studies Journal* (2 a year), *Al-Alaaghaat* (4 a year), *Amu Darya* (4 a year), *Asiyaje Miyaneh va Ghofghaaz* (4 a year), *Iranian Journal of International Affairs* (4 a year), *Siyasat-e-Khare* (Journal of Foreign Policy, 4 a year).

Iran Bastan Museum Library: Khiaban-e Imam Khomeini, Khiaban-e Sium-e Tir, Tehran 11365; f. 1964; 17,000 vols; Dir M. R. RIYAZI KESHE.

Iran University of Medical Sciences and Health Services Central Library and

Documentation Centre: POB 14155-6439, Tehran; tel. (21) 8058644; fax (21) 8054360; e-mail centrlib@iums.ac.ir; internet www .iums.ac.ir; f. 1975; 35,000 books, 1,323 current periodicals, 9,355 theses, 3,000 audiovisual titles; Dir SUSSAN ERTEJAEI.

Iranian Cultural Heritage Organization Documentation Centre: POB 13445-1594, Tehran; tel. (21) 6003126; fax (21) 6003126; e-mail info@ichodoc.ir; internet www.ichodoc .ir; f. 1994; 36,000 vols, 237 periodicals, 15,667 research reports, 2,030 films, 22,180 maps, 70,000 photographs, 155,560 slides, 125,000 negatives, 122 video cassettes, 204 audio cassettes, 771 CDs, 923 posters, 4,000 microfiches; Dir FARIBA FARZAM.

Iranian Information and Documentation Centre (IRANDOC): 1090 Englab St, POB 13185-1371, Tehran; tel. (21) 66494980; fax (21) 66462254; e-mail info@irandoc.ac.ir; internet www.irandoc.ac.ir; f. 1968; attached to Min. of Higher Education; research; training; information and knowledge management services; work in the fields of basic sciences, agriculture, medical sciences, humanities and technology; advises and assists in the establishment of specialized information centres and acts as the nat. reference centre; organizes, processes and disseminates scientific and technologic documents; key role in nat. and ministerial orgs; 24,000 vols, 210 current periodicals, 70,000 student dissertations; Dir SEYYED OMID FATEMI; publs *Abstracts of Scientific/Technical Papers* (4 a year), *Current Research in Iranian Universities and Research Centres* (4 a year), *Directory of Scientific Meetings held in Iran* (4 a year), *Dissertation Abstracts of Iranian Graduates Abroad* (4 a year), *Ettela s Resani* (Technical Bulletin, 4 a year), *Information Science & Technology Journal*, *Iranian Dissertation Abstracts* (4 a year), *Iranian Government Reports* (4 a year), *Iranian Scholars and Experts* (1 a year), *Science Thesauri*.

Library of the Bank Markazi Jomhouri Islami Iran (Central Bank of the Islamic Republic of Iran): Pegah St, Mirdamad Blvd, POB 11365-8531, Tehran; tel. (21) 29953263; fax (21) 29953290; e-mail libinfoservices@cbi .ir; internet lib.cbi.ir/libcbi; f. 1960; 110,000 books and reports; Dir MAHROKH LOTFI.

Malek Library: Melale Mottahed Ave, Janb e Vezarat Omour Kharege, Tehran; tel. (21) 66743744; fax (21) 66705974; e-mail khoddari@yahoo.com; f. 1937; 70,000 vols covering the sciences, 19,000 titles, 6,400 MSS; attached to the Malek Museum; Museum Dir and Head of Research Dept SAEID KHODDARI NAEINI.

National Library and Archives of Iran: National Library Blvd, Haqani Expressway (West–East), POB 15875-3693, Tehran 1537614111; tel. (21) 88644080; fax (21) 88644082; e-mail pria@nlai.ir; internet www .nlai.ir; f. 1937; 684,465 books (510,479 in Farsi and Arabic, 173,986 in other languages), 1m. periodicals, 172,000 MSS documents and patchworks, 14,729 Arabic and Farsi MSS, 67,280 pamphlets and sheets, 9,848 lithographic prints, 320,093 non-book items; maintains library higher education centre for library science; Dir KAZEM MOOSAVI BOJNOURDI; publ. *Iranian National Bibliography* (online and CD-ROM, 1 a year).

Parliament Library (1): Ketabkhane-ye Majles-e Shora-ye Eslami 1, Baharestan Sq., POB 11365-866, Tehran; tel. (21) 33126092; fax (21) 33130919; internet www .majlislib.com; f. 1912; 272,000 books, 28,000 bound vols of 5,000 Persian, Arabic and Latin periodicals, 24,000 manuscripts vols, 12m. national and historical documents, 10,000 photographs, 460 magnetic tapes, 90 old

maps, 17,500 manuscripts on microfilm, 3,000 CDs of manuscripts, 27 vols of theses and dissertations, 12,000 government reports, 300 microfilms and 250 CDs of old Iranian periodicals; UN depository; museum (see Museums and Art Galleries); Dir SEYYED MOHAMMAD ALI AHMADI ABHARI; publs *Name-ye Baharestan* (2 a year), *Payam-e Baharestan* (12 a year).

Attached Library:

Parliament Library (2): Ketabkhaneh Majles-e Shora-ye Eslami 2, Emam Khomeini Ave, Tehran 13174; tel. (21) 6135335; fax (21) 3130919; f. 1959; spec. colln on Iranian, Islamic and Oriental studies: 49,554 printed books, 5,166 bound vols of 395 Persian, Arabic and Latin periodicals; Dir SEYYED MOHAMMAD ALI AHMADI ABHARI.

Museums and Art Galleries

Isfahan

Armenian Museum of All Saviour's Cathedral: POB 81735-115, Julfa, Isfahan; tel. (311) 6243471; fax (311) 6270999; e-mail sourbv@yahoo.com; internet www.newjulfa .org; f. 1930, rehoused 1971 with additions; under the supervision of the Diocesan Council of the Armenians in Julfa; 750 ancient MSS, 570 paintings, miniatures and antique church vestments, tomb portraits; library of 25,000 vols.

Chehel Sotun Museum: Isfahan; Dir KARIM NIKZAD.

Mashhad

Astan-e Qudse Razavi Museums: Sahn-e Kausar, Mashhad 91348-43388; tel. (511) 2241105; fax (511) 2224570; e-mail info@ aqlibrary.org; internet www.aqm.ir; f. 1937, inaugurated 1945; Anthropology Museum, Central Museum, Weapons Museum, Koran Museum, Stamp Museum, Astronomical Instruments and Clocks Museum, Natural Objects and Shells Museum, Crystal and Porcelain Museum, Coins and Medals Museum, Carpet Museum, Museum of Holy Qur'an and Precious Objects presented by His Eminence Ayatollah Khamenei, History of Mashhad Museum and Paintings Museum; Dir MOHSEN AMIRY NIA.

Qom

Qom Museum: Eram St, Qom; tel. 7741491; f. 1936; under the supervision of the Archaeological Service; Dir B. YOSEFZADEH.

Shiraz

Pars Museum: Shiraz; tel. (11) 24151; f. 1938; exhibits incl. manuscripts, earthenware, ancient coins; Dir MOHAMMAD HOSSEIN ESTAKHR; Curator HASRAT ZADEH SORUDE.

Tehran

Golestan Palace Museum: Maidan Panzdah Khordad, POB 11365-4595, Tehran 11149; tel. (21) 3113335; fax (21) 3111811; e-mail info@golestanpalace.org; internet www.golestanpalace.ir; f. 1894; Dir PARVIN SADR SEGHT-OL-ESLAMI.

Iran Bastan Museum: Khiaban-e Imam Khomeini, Khiaban-e Sium-e Tir, Tehran 11364; tel. (21) 6672061; f. 1946; archaeological and cultural research; conservation, repair and exhibition of cultural material; 4 depts; library of 15,924 vols; Dir J. GOLSHAN.

Malek Museum: Melale Mottahed Ave, Tehran; tel. (21) 66726613; fax (21) 66717364; e-mail khoddari@yahoo.com;

internet www.aqmlm.ir; f. 1937, opened new bldg in 1997; various objects of historical interest: coins, paintings, metalwork and woodwork, royal decrees, carpets, philatelic colln; library: see Libraries and Archives; Museum Dir and Head of Research Dept Dr SAID KHODDARI NAINI.

Mardom Shenassi Museum (Ethnological Museum): Maidan Panzdah Khordad, POB 11365-9595, Tehran 11149; tel. (21) 3110653; fax (21) 3111811; f. 1888; Dir ALIREZA ANISI.

Parliament Museum: Muze-ye Majles-e Shora-ye Eslami, POB 11365-866, Baharestan Sq., Tehran; tel. and fax (21) 3130919; internet www.majlislib.com; f. 1999; 294 old Iranian paintings, 714 artistic and traditional handicrafts and gifts presented to the speakers of the Islamic Consultative Assembly by foreign dignitaries, 150 rolls of old carpets, 70 chairs and tables, small colln of antiques; Dir SEYYED MOHAMMAD ALI AHMADI ABHARI.

Tehran Museum of Contemporary Art: N Karegar Ave, Laleh Park, Tehran; tel. (21) 98951324; fax (21) 88965664; e-mail info@ tmoca.com; internet www.tmoca.com; f. 1977; library of 24,000 vols in formation; Dir MAHMOOD SHALOOEI.

Universities

AHWAZ JONDISHAPOUR UNIVERSITY OF MEDICAL SCIENCES

Golestan-bol, University City Central Bldg, Ahwaz 61357-15794

Telephone: (611) 3339092
Fax: (611) 3335200
E-mail: info@ajums.ac.ir
Internet: www.ajums.ac.ir

Founded 1988, fmrly part of Shahid Chamran Univ.
Academic year: September to June
Pres.: Dr HAYAT MOMBEINI
Registrar: Dr M. E. MOTLAQ
Librarian: B. DASHTBOZORGI
Number of teachers: 408
Number of students: 5,276

Publications: *Jondishapour Journal of Pharmaceutical Sciences* (2 a year), *Scientific Medical Journal* (4 a year)

DEANS

College of Dentistry: Dr M. SHOKRI
College of Health: M. LATIFI
College of Nursing: Z. ABBASPOUR
College of Pharmacology: Dr A. HEMATI
College of Physiotherapy: Dr M. J. SHATERZADEH
Medical College: Dr M. FEGHHI
Paramedicine College: Dr M. KARANDISH

PROFESSORS

ASHNAGHAR, A.
BEHROOZ, M.
KALANTARI, H.
MAKVANDI, M.
MARAGHI, S.
MOGHADAM, A. Z.
PEDRAM, M.
ZANDIAN, K.

AL-ZAHRA UNIVERSITY

Vanak, Tehran 19938-91176
Telephone: (21) 88035187
Fax: (21) 88044040
E-mail: office@alzahra.ac.ir
Internet: www.alzahra.ac.ir

Founded 1965, name changed 1981
State control
Language of instruction: Persian

Academic year: September to June
Chancellor: Dr MAHBOUBEH MIBASHERI
Vice-Chancellor for Academic Affairs: Dr YADOLLAH ORDUKHANI
Vice-Chancellor for Admin. and Finance: Dr MAHNAZ MOLLANAZARI
Vice-Chancellor for Research: Dr SIMIN HOS-SEINIAN
Vice-Chancellor for Student Affairs: SHAHIN GHAHREMAN IZADI
Dir of Int. Relations: Dr AZAM SAZVAR
Librarian: Dr QODSI ZIARANI MOHAMMADI
Library of 121,569 vols
Number of teachers: 600
Number of students: 7,932
Publications: *Journal of Art 'Jelveye Honar'*, *Journal of Hadith and Qu'ran Studies*, *Journal of Humanities*, *Journal of Science*, *Journal of Women Studies*

DEANS

Faculty of Engineering: Dr JAFAR BAGHERI NEJAD
Faculty of Fine and Applied Arts: Dr ABUL-QASEM DADVAR
Faculty of Literature, Foreign Languages and History: Dr ENSIEH KHAZALI
Faculty of Physical Education and Sports Science: Dr PARVANEH NAZAR ALI
Faculty of Psychology and Education: Dr MOJDEH VAZIRI
Faculty of Sciences: Dr REZA SABET DARIYANI
Faculty of Social Sciences and Economics: Dr SUSAN BASTANI
Faculty of Theology: Dr ZAHRA RABBANI

ATTACHED RESEARCH CENTRE

Women's Research Centre: tel. (21) 8049809; fax (21) 8049809; e-mail golkhoo@ alzahra.ac.ir; Dir Dr SHEKOOFEH GOLKHOO.

ALLAMEH TABATABA'I UNIVERSITY

POB 15815-3487, Tehran
Telephone: (21) 8901521
Fax: (21) 8902536
Internet: web.atu.ac.ir
Founded 1984, following merger of Univ. Complex for Literature and Humanities and Univ. Centre for Public and Business Administration
State control
Languages of instruction: English, Persian
Academic year: September to June
Pres.: Dr SEYED SADRODDIN SHARIATI
Vice-Chancellor for Academic Affairs: Prof. Dr AHMAD TAMIMDARI
Vice-Chancellor for Admin. and Finance: Prof. Dr JAFAR BABAJANI
Vice-Chancellor for Research and Int. Relations: Prof. Dr HOSSEIN RAHMANSERESHT
Vice-Chancellor for Student Affairs: Prof. Dr HOSSEIN SALIMI
Registrar: Ms SEPEHRI
Chief Librarian: Dr ZAHRA SEIFKASHANI
Number of teachers: 361 (full-time)
Number of students: 12,177
Publication: Each faculty publishes its own journal

DEANS

Faculty of Economics: Prof. Dr HAMID SHOR-AKA
Faculty of Law and Politics: Asst Prof. Dr GHOLAM-ALI CHEGENIZADE
Faculty of Management and Accounting: Asst Prof. Dr ABULFAZL KAZZAI
Faculty of Persian Literature and Foreign Languages: Prof. Dr SAEED VAEZ
Faculty of Psychology and Education: MORTEZA AMINFAR
Faculty of Social Sciences: Asst Prof. Dr MAHAMMAD ZAHEDIASL

ATTACHED RESEARCH INSTITUTES

Center for Studies on Iranian Economy (CSIE): Dean Asst Prof. Dr SAEED MOSHIRI.
International Centre for Insurance Education and Research (ICIER): Dean Asst Prof. Dr MOHAMMAD-GHOLI YOSEFI.

AMIRKABIR UNIVERSITY OF TECHNOLOGY

424 Hafez Ave, Tehran 15875-4413
Telephone: (21) 64540-1
Fax: (21) 66413969
E-mail: intoff1@aut.ac.ir
Internet: www.aut.ac.ir
Founded 1958 as Tehran Polytechnic
State control
Academic year: September to June
Pres.: Dr ALIREZA REHAI
Vice-Pres. for Academic Affairs: Dr MOHAM-MAD HASAN SEBT
Vice-Pres. for Admin. and Finance Affairs: Dr ALI MOHAMMAD KIMIAGARI
Vice-Pres. for Research and Technology: Dr REZA SAFABAKHSH
Vice-Pres. for Student Affairs: Dr BEHROOZ AREZOO
Dir of Int. Affairs: Dr F. SHARIF
Librarian: Dr OROUJALIAN
Number of teachers: 450
Number of students: 9,100
Depts of aerospace engineering, chemical engineering, civil engineering, computer and information technology, electrical engineering, industrial engineering, marine engineering, mathematics, medical engineering, mining and metallurgical engineering, physics, polymer engineering, textile engineering
Publication: *Amirkabir Journal of Science and Technology* (4 a year).

ATTACHED RESEARCH INSTITUTES

Advanced Textiles Materials and Technology Research Institute: internet atmt .aut.ac.ir.
Concrete Technology and Durability Research Centre: tel. (21) 64543074; fax (21) 64543074; e-mail concrete@aut.ac.ir; internet www.aut.ac.ir/ctdr; Dir Prof. ALI AKBAR RAMEZANIANPOUR.
Energy Research Centre: tel. (21) 64542611; fax (21) 64542611; e-mail erc@ aut.ac.ir; internet www.aut.ac.ir/research/ erc/home.htm; Dir Prof. BAHRAM DABIR.
Synthetic Fibres and Textile Research Centre: Dir Dr MOHAMMAD REZA BABAEI.

UNIVERSITY OF ART

POB 11155-655, Tehran
58 Sarhang Sakhai St, Hafez Ave., Tehran 11368-13518
Telephone: (21) 66734001
Fax: (21) 66734002
E-mail: art-university@art.ac.ir
Internet: www.art.ac.ir
Founded 1980, by merger with Conservatory of Music, College of Decorative Arts, College of Dramatic Arts, College of Nat. Music and Farabi Univ., present name 1991; attached to Min. of Science, Research & Technology
State control
Language of instruction: Farsi
Academic year: October to September
Pres.: Dr SAEED KASAN FALLAH
Vice-Pres. for Admin. and Finance: AHMAD RAHBARI
Vice-Pres. for Instruction: Dr MAJID SALEHI
Vice-Pres. for Research: Dr MOHAMMADREZA HOSNAI

Vice-Pres. for Student Affairs: Dr SAEED MAJIDI
Library of 50,000 vols
Number of teachers: 405 (105 full-time, 300 part-time)
Number of students: 3,500
Publications: *Dastavard* (4 a year), *Honarna-meh* (4 a year)

DEANS

Architecture and Urban Planning: Dr MOS-TAFA KIANI
Cinema and Theatre: Dr SHAHAB ADEL
Faculty of Applied Arts: Dr AHMAD TONDI
Music: Dr MOHAMMADREZA AZADEHFAR
Visual and Applied Arts: Dr JAVAD SALIMI

BU-ALI SINA UNIVERSITY

Shariati Ave, University Sq., Hamadan 65174
Telephone: (811) 8273952
Fax: (811) 8272046
Internet: www.basu.ac.ir
Founded 1973
State control
Academic year: September to June
Pres.: Dr M. GHOLAMI
Vice-Pres. for Admin. and Finance: Dr A. KAREGAR BIDEH
Vice-Pres. for Devt: M. R. TAHMASEBI
Vice-Pres. for Education: Dr G. R. KHANLARI
Vice-Pres. for Research: Dr S. J. SABOUNCHI
Vice-Pres. for Student Affairs: Dr M. SHAR-IFIAN
Librarian: Dr M. S. GHAEMIZADEH
Number of teachers: 272
Number of students: 7,450
Publication: *Agricultural Research* (2 a year)

DEANS

Faculty of Agriculture: Dr M. J. SOLEIMANI
Faculty of Engineering: Dr M. NILI
Faculty of Letters and Humanities: Dr F. MIRZAII
Faculty of Science: Prof. H. ILUKHANI
Faculty of Teacher Training (Malayer): Dr M. JALALI
Faculty of the Veterinary College: Dr H. SHOKRIAN

FERDOWSI UNIVERSITY OF MASHHAD

Azadi Sq., Ferdowsi Univ. Campus, Mashhad 91779-48974
Telephone: (511) 8836037
Fax: (511) 8836056
E-mail: intr@um.ac.ir
Internet: www.um.ac.ir
Founded 1949
State control
Language of instruction: Persian
Academic year: September to June (two semesters)
Chancellor: Prof. ALI REZA ASHOURI
Vice-Chancellor for Academic Affairs: Dr MAHDI KHAJAVI
Registrar: Dr MAHMOOD REZAI ROKN ABAD
Dir of the Int. Relations Office: Dr ABEDIN VAHEDIAN
Librarian: Dr BEHROOZ MAHRAM
Library of 536,312 vols
Number of teachers: 661
Number of students: 19,600
Publications: *Ferdowsi Review: An Iranian Journal of English Language* (in English), *Iranian Journal of Animal Biosystematics* (in English), *Iranian Journal of Animal Science Studies*, *Iranian Journal of Health and Physical Activity* (in English), *Iranian Journal of Veterinary Science and Technology* (4 a year), *Journal of Agricultural*

Machinery Engineering (JAME), Journal of Agroecology, Journal of Applied Sciences in Mechanics, Journal of Arabic Language and Literature (in Arabic), *Journal of Cell and Molecular Research, Journal of Civil Engineering* (in Persian), *Journal of Economics and Agricultural Development* (in Persian), *Journal of Educational and Psychological Studies* (in Persian), *Journal of Evolution Management, Journal of Historical Research and Studies, Journal of History and Culture, Journal of Horticulture Science, Journal of Iranian Field Crop Research, Journal of Iranian Grain Research, Journal of Islamic Philosophy and Thoughts, Journal of Jurisprudence (Fiqh) and Islamic Foundations, Journal of Knowledge and Development, Journal of Knowledge and Technology, Journal of Language and Translation, Journal of Linguistics and Khorasani Dialects, Journal of Metallurgical and Material Engineering, Journal of Plant Protection, Journal of Qur'anic Sciences and Hadith, Journal of Separation and Transport Phenomena, Journal of Social Sciences, Journal of the School of Economics and Business Administration* (4 a year), *Journal of Water and Soil, Mashhad Research Journal of Mathematical Sciences* (in English)

DEANS

Faculty of Administration and Economics: Dr M. SALIMI FAR
Faculty of Agriculture: Dr REZA VALIZADEH
Faculty of Architecture and Urban Engineering: Dr. A. SHOOSHTARI
Faculty of Education and Psychology: Dr M. SAEEDI REZVANI
Faculty of Engineering: Dr HOSSAIN NOEEI BAGHBAN
Faculty of Letters and Humanities: Dr A. TALEBZADEH SHOOSHTARI
Faculty of Mathematical Sciences: Dr A. ERFANIAN MOSHIRI NEZHAD
Faculty of Natural Resources and Environment: Dr. SH. DANESH
Faculty of Physical Education: A. HASHEMI JAVAHERI
Faculty of Sciences: Dr M. RAHIMI ZADEH
Faculty of Theology: Dr H. NAGHI ZADEH
Faculty of Veterinary Science: Dr M. MALEKI
Nishabour School of Fine Arts: Dr G. HASANI DARAMIAN
Shirvan School of Agriculture: Dr A. KHOSHNOUD YAZDI

UNIVERSITY OF GILAN

POB 1841, Mellat Street, Rasht
Telephone: (131) 3221999
Fax: (131) 3227022
E-mail: khazar@cd.gu.ac.ir
Internet: www.gu.ac.ir
Founded 1977
State control
Language of instruction: Farsi
Academic year: September to June (two semesters)

Chancellor: Dr DAWOUD AHMADI DASTJERDI
Vice-Chancellor for Academic Affairs: Dr REZA FOTOUHI GHAZVINI
Vice-Chancellor for Finance and Admin.: ESMAEIL MAGHSODI
Vice-Chancellor for Research Affairs: Dr ABOLFAZL DARVIZEH
Vice-Chancellor for Student Affairs: Dr MALEK-MOHAMMAD RANJBAR
Office of Int. and Scientific Relations: Dr MASOUD VAHABI MOGHADDAM
Office of Public Relations: Dr HASSAN TAJIK
Librarian: Dr REYHANEH SARIRI

Number of teachers: 308
Number of students: 6,705

Publication: *Mahnameh* (12 a year, in Farsi)

DEANS

Faculty of Agriculture: Dr AHAD SAHRAGARD
Faculty of Engineering: Dr HOSSEIN HAFTH-CHENARI
Faculty of Fine Arts and Architecture: HAMZEH GHOLAM-ALI-ZADEH
Faculty of Fishery and Aquatic Animals: Dr MSOUD SATTARI
Faculty of Humanities: Dr MOHAMMAD KAZEM YOUSEFPOUR
Faculty of Natural Resources: Dr ZYAEDDIN MIRHOSSEINI
Faculty of Physical Education: Dr ARSALAN DAMIRCHI
Faculty of Sciences: Dr ESMAEIL ANSARI

IRAN UNIVERSITY OF MEDICAL SCIENCES AND HEALTH SERVICES

Crossroads of Shahid Hemmat and Shahid Chamran Expressways, POB 15875-6171, Tehran 144961-4535
Telephone: (21) 98052193
Fax: (21) 88054393
E-mail: ofintrel@iums.ac.ir
Internet: www.iums.ac.ir
Founded 1974 as Iran Medical Centre
State control
Language of instruction: Persian
Academic year: September to June

Chancellor: Dr S. A. HASSANI
Vice-Chancellor for Education: Dr A. PAZOUKI
Vice-Chancellor for Food and Pharmaceutical Affairs: Dr M. BEYGLAR
Vice-Chancellor for Health Affairs: Dr F. EMAMI
Vice-Chancellor for Management Devt and Resources: Dr S. A. RAZAVI
Vice-Chancellor for Research: Dr S. A. MOTEVALIAN
Vice-Chancellor for Student and Cultural Affairs: Dr A. AMIRFARHANGI
Registrar: Dr M. AFKARI
Head of Central Library: B. JAMEI
Library of 45,244 vols, 3,681 journals, 14,623 theses, 202 research projects
Number of teachers: 684
Number of students: 6,572

Publications: *Annals of Iranian Medicine* (4 a year), *Five Star Doctor* (4 a year), *Iran Journal of Nursing* (4 a year), *Iranian Journal of Pharmacology and Therapeutics* (4 a year, online), *Iranian Journal of Psychiatry and Clinical Psychology* (4 a year), *Journal of Health Management* (4 a year), *Journal of Iran University of Medical Sciences* (4 a year), *Journal of Medical Laboratory Sciences* (4 a year), *Journal of Medical Management* (4 a year), *Journal of Students* (12 a year), *Journal of Thought and Behavior* (4 a year), *Medical Education* (4 a year), *Rehabilitation Message* (4 a year)

DEANS

School of Allied Medical Sciences: Dr A. KAZEMI
School of Management and Medical Information: Dr SH. TOFIGHI
School of Medicine: Dr R. FARASATKISH
School of Nursing and Midwifery: Dr F. HAGHDOOST OSKOUEI
School of Public Health: Dr M. H. TAGHDISI
School of Rehabilitation Sciences: Dr M. S. GHASEMI

PROFESSORS

AGHAKHANI, K., Forensic Medicine
AKBARIAN-NIA, M., Neurology
ARAB MOHAMMAD HOSSEONI, A., Paediatrics
AZAR, M., Neurosurgery
BIDARI, A., Emergency Medicine

BOLOURI, B., Biophysics
DANESHI, A., Otorhinolaryngology
FIROUZRAY, M., Biochemistry
GHAFFARPOUR, G., Dermatology
GHALEHBANDI, M., Psychiatry
HADIZADEH, H., Radiology
HASHEMI, F., Pathology
HASHEMI, M., Ophthalmology
HEYDARI, M., Surgery
HOMAYOUNFAR, H., Physiology
IMANI, F., Anaesthesiology
JAFARI, D., Orthopaedics
JAVAD MOUSSAVI, S. A., Internal Medicine
JOGHATAEI, M. T., Anatomy
KASHANIAN, M., Obstetrics and Gynaecology
KAZAMI, A., Reconstructive Surgery
MAHMOUDIAN, M., Pharmacology
MAJIDPOUR, A., Infectious Diseases
MOLAVI NOJOUMI, M., Social Medicine
MOVAHHED, M., Nuclear Medicine
OURMAZDI, H., Parasitology
RASTEGAR LARI, A., Microbiology
SALEKMOGHADDAM, A., Immunology
SHAHROKH, H., Urology
YEKKEH YAZDANDOUST, R., Clinical Psychology

IRAN UNIVERSITY OF SCIENCE AND TECHNOLOGY

Narmak, Tehran 16846-13114
Telephone: (21) 77240303
Fax: (21) 77491031
E-mail: interiust@iust.ac.ir
Internet: www.iust.ac.ir
Founded 1928
State control
Language of instruction: Farsi
Academic year: September to June

Chancellor: Dr MOHAMMAD SAEED JABALAMELI
Vice-Chancellor for Admin. and Finance: Dr BIJAN GHAFFARI
Vice-Chancellor for Education: Dr MOHAMMAD FATHIAN
Vice-Chancellor for Research and Technology: Dr MOHAMMAD HASSAN BAZIAR
Vice-Chancellor for Student and Cultural Affairs: Dr ROUHOLLAH TALEBI
Dir of the Office of Int. and Scientific Cooperation: Dr SAEED MIRZAMOHAMMADI
Head of Graduate Studies: Dr MOHAMMAD REZA MOGHBELI
Registrar: Dr SEYED HOSSEIN RAZAVI
Librarian: Dr SEYED MAHDI ALAVI AMLASHI
Library of 120,000 vols, 1,054 journals, more than 1,400 subscriptions to academic magazines, more than 23,000 titles of thesis
Number of teachers: 369
Number of students: 12,909

Publications: *International Journal of Architecture and Urban Planning* (4 a year, in English), *International Journal of Civil Engineering* (4 a year, in English), *International Journal of Industrial Engineering and Production Management* (4 a year, in Persian), *International Journal of Industrial Engineering and Production Research* (4 a year, in English), *Iranian Journal of Electrical and Electronic Engineering* (4 a year, in English), *Iranian Journal of Materials Science and Engineering* (4 a year, in English)

DEANS

Arak Branch-Iran University of Science and Technology: Dr ABOLFAZL AHMADI
Behshahr Branch-Iran University of Science and Technology: Dr MOHAMMAD MOHAMMADPOUR OMRAN
Dept of Chemistry: Dr RAHMATOLLAH RAHIMI
Dept of Foreign Languages: Dr SEYED MAHMOOD MIR TABATABAEI

School of Architecture and Urban Design: Eng. ABDOLHAMID NOGHREH KAR

School of Automotive Engineering: Dr MOHAMMAD HASSAN SHOJAEE FARD

School of Chemical Engineering: Dr MOHAMMAD TAGHI SADEGHI

School of Civil Engineering: Dr GHOLAMREZA GHODRATI AMIRI

School of Computer Engineering: Dr NASER MOZAYANI

School of Electrical Engineering: Dr AHMAD CHELDAVI

School of Industrial Engineering: Dr ALIREZA MOINI

School of Mathematics: Dr GHOLAMHOSSEIN YARI

School of Mechanical Engineering: Dr MORTEZA MONTAZERI

School of Metallurgy and Materials Engineering: Dr SEYED MOHAMMAD-ALI BOUTORABI

School of Physics: Dr SEYED ROUHOLLAH AGHDAEE

School of Railway Engineering: Dr PARISA HOSSEINI TEHRANI

PROFESSORS

ABOUTALEBI, M.-R., School of Metallurgy and Materials Engineering

AFSHAR, A., School of Civil Engineering

AHMADIAN, H., School of Mechanical Engineering

AMINI, F., School of Civil Engineering

ARABI, H., School of Metallurgy and Materials Engineering

ARYANEZHAD, M.-B.-Q., School of Industrial Engineering

AYATOLLAHI, M. R., School of Mechanical Engineering

BAZIAR, M. H., School of Civil Engineering

BEHBAHANI, H., School of Civil Engineering

BEITOLLAHI, A., School of Metallurgy and Materials Engineering

BOUTORABI, S. M.-A., School of Metallurgy and Materials Engineering

CHELDAVI, AHMAD, School of Electrical Engineering

DANESHJOU, K., School of Mechanical Engineering

ESRAFILIAN, E., School of Mathematics

FALLAHI, M., Department of Foreign Languages

FARMAN, H., School of Physics

GHASEMZADEH, R., School of Metallurgy and Materials Engineering

GHODRATI AMIRI, G., School of Civil Engineering

GOLESTANI-FARD, F., School of Metallurgy and Materials Engineering

HABIBNEJAD KORAYEM, M., School of Mechanical Engineering

HASHEMINEJAD, S. M., School of Mechanical Engineering

HEDJAZI, J., School of Metallurgy and Materials Engineering

HODJAT KASHANI, F., School of Electrical Engineering

JASBI, A., School of Industrial Engineering

JAVADPOUR, J., School of Metallurgy and Materials Engineering

KAVEH, A., School of Civil Engineering

KHARRAZI, Y., School of Metallurgy and Materials Engineering

MAJIDI, H., School of Physics

MALEK NEJAD, K., School of Mathematics

MARGHUSSAIN, V., School of Metallurgy and Materials Engineering

MIRDAMADI, S., School of Metallurgy and Materials Engineering

MOHAMMAD MORADI, A., School of Architecture & Environmental Design

MOHAMMAD NEJAD, S., School of Electrical Engineering

MOHAMMADI, K., School of Electrical Engineering

MOHAMMADI, T., School of Chemical Engineering

NOOROSSANA, R., School of Industrial Engineering

ORAIZI, H., School of Electrical Engineering

RAZAVIZADEH, H., School of Metallurgy and Materials Engineering

REZAIE, H., School of Metallurgy and Materials Engineering

ROEENTAN, G., School of Electrical Engineering

SADJADI, S. J., School of Industrial Engineering

SAIDI MEHRABAD, M., School of Industrial Engineering

SANAEI, E., School of Civil Engineering

SEYED SADJADI, S., Dept of Chemistry

SEYED-HOSSEINI, S. M., School of Industrial Engineering

SHABESTARI, S. G., School of Metallurgy and Materials Engineering

SHAYANFAR, H., School of Electrical Engineering

SHAYGANMANESH, A., School of Mathematics

SHIDFAR, A., School of Mathematics

SHOJAEEFARD, M. H., School of Automotive Engineering

SHOKRIEH, M. M., School of Mechanical Engineering

SHOULAIE, A., School of Electrical Engineering

SOLEIMANI, M., School of Electrical Engineering

TAEB, A., School of Chemical Engineering

ATTACHED RESEARCH INSTITUTES

Asphalt Concrete Mixture and Bitumen Research Centre: tel. (21) 77240281; fax (21) 77240089; Dir Dr HASSAN ZIARI.

Automotive Engineering Research Center: tel. and fax (21) 77491224; Dir Dr MOHAMMAD HASSAN SHOJAEEFARD.

Cement Research Centre: tel. (21) 77240475; fax (21) 77240397; Dir Dr ALI ALLAHVERDI.

Center of Excellence for Advanced Materials and Processing: tel. (21) 77240291; fax (21) 77240480; Dir Dr FARHAD GOLESTANI FARD.

Center of Excellence for Fundamental Studies in Structural Engineering: tel. (21) 77240399; fax (21) 77240398; Dir Dr ALI KAYEH.

Center of Excellence for Power Systems Automation and Operation: tel. and fax (21) 77240585; Dir Dr SHAHRAM JADID.

Electronic Research Centre: tel. (21) 77240487; fax (21) 77240486; Dir Dr SATTAR MIRZAKUCHAKI.

Green Research Centre: tel. (21) 77491223; fax (21) 77491242; e-mail jadid@iust.ac.ir; Dir Dr SHAHRAM JADID.

Information Technology Research Centre: tel. (21) 77491192; fax (21) 77491193; e-mail akbari@iust.ac.ir; Dir Dr AHMAD AKBARI.

Iran Aluminium Research Centre: tel. (21) 77240599; fax (21) 77240500; Dir Dr MOHAMMAD-TAGHI SALEHI.

Iran Composites Institute: tel. and fax (21) 77491206; e-mail shokrieh@iust.ac.ir; internet www.irancomposits.org; Dir Dr MAHMOOD MEHRDAD SHOKRIEH.

Technology Incubator of IUST: tel. (21) 77497788; fax (21) 77899955; Dir Dr MOHAMMAD REZA JAHED MOTLAGH.

Transportation Research Centre: tel. (21) 77240399; fax (21) 77240398; Dir Dr AFSHIN SHARIAT.

UNIVERSITY OF ISFAHAN

Isfahan, Darvazeh Shiraz 81746-73441

Telephone: (311) 7932001
Fax: (311) 6687396
E-mail: int-office@ui.ac.ir
Internet: www.ui.ac.ir

Founded 1946, present status 1958
State control
Language of instruction: Persian
Academic year: September to July

Chancellor: Dr MOHAMMAD HOSSEIN RAMESHT
Vice-Chancellor for Academic Affairs and Graduate Studies: Dr MOHAMMAD HOSSIN ESTEKI
Vice-Chancellor for Finance and Admin.: Dr ALI REZA ABDELAHI
Vice-Chancellor for Research and Technology: Dr MOHAMMAD RABANI
Vice-Chancellor for Student and Cultural Affairs: Dr ALI AKBAR KAJBAF
Dir for Int. Relations: Dr ARASH SHAHIN
Librarian: Dr MOZAFAR CHESHMEHSOHRABI

Library of 484,863 vols
Number of teachers: 509
Number of students: 15,000

Publications: *Comparative Theology* (2 a year), *Geography and Environmental Planning* (4 a year), *Geography Researches* (4 a year), *Historical Researches* (4 a year), *International Economics* (2 a year), *Iranian Journal of Petrology* (4 a year), *Iranian Journal of Plant Biology* (2 a year), *Journal of Financial Accounting Research* (2 a year), *Journal of Persian Language and Literature (GOHARE GOYA)* (4 a year), *Journal of Regional and Urban Planning* (4 a year), *Journal of Researches in Linguistics* (4 a year), *Literature Arts* (4 a year), *Metaphysic* (4 a year), *Practical Sociology* (4 a year), *Researches in Sedimentary and Cryptology* (4 a year), *Researches on Persian Language Literature* (4 a year), *Taxonomy and Biosystematics* (2 a year)

DEANS

Faculty of Administrative Sciences and Economics: Dr SEYYED JAVAD EMAM JOMEH ZADEH

Faculty of Educational Sciences and Psychology: Dr HOSSEIN SAMAVATIAN

Faculty of Engineering and Technology: Dr MOHAMMAD SADEGH HATAMIPOOR

Faculty of Foreign Languages: Dr MAHMOUD REZA GASHMARDI

Faculty of Literature and Humanities: Dr ASGHAR MONTAZEROLGHAEM

Faculty of Mathematics and Computer Studies, Khansar: Dr HESHMATOLLAH YAVARI

Faculty of Physical Education and Sports Sciences: Dr SEYYED MOHAMMAD MARANDI

Faculty of Pure Sciences: SHAHRAM TANGESTANI NEJAD

Faculty of Sciences and New Technology: Dr MOJITABA MOSTAJABODDAVATI

ISFAHAN UNIVERSITY OF MEDICAL SCIENCES

Hezar-Jerib Ave, Isfahan

Telephone: (311) 7923077
Fax: (311) 6687898
E-mail: international@mui.ac.ir
Internet: www.mui.ac.ir

Founded 1950
State control
Language of instruction: Persian
Academic year: September to June

Chancellor: Dr SHAHIN SHIRANI
Vice-Chancellor for Academic Affairs: Dr SEYED ALI MOUSAVI
Vice-Chancellor for Finance and Admin.: Dr BAHRAM GOODARZI

Vice-Chancellor for Research and Technology Affairs: Dr PEYMAN ADIBI
Vice-Chancellor for Student Affairs: MOJTABA KARBASI
Registrar: MOHAMMAD JAVAD ALE-MOKHTAR
Head of Libraries: H. RASTEGARI
Number of teachers: 659
Number of students: 6,205
Publications: *ARYA Atherosclerosis* (4 a year), *Dental Research Journal*, *Iranian Journal of Nursing and Midwifery Research* (4 a year), *Iranian Journal of Pediatrics*, *Iranian Red Crescent Medical Journal*, *Journal of Medical School* (4 a year), *Journal of Preventive Medicine*, *Journal of Research in Medical Sciences* (6 a year), *Journal of Research in Pharmaceutical Sciences* (4 a year), *Journal of Skin and Leishmaniasis*

DEANS

Faculty of Dentistry: Dr A. KHADEMI
Faculty of Health: Dr MOHAMMAD ENTEZARI
Faculty of Management and Information Services: Dr SAEED KARIMI
Faculty of Medicine: Dr HASSAN RAZMJOO
Faculty of Nursing and Midwifery: Dr FARIBA TALEGHANI
Faculty of Pharmacy: Dr SEYED ABOLFAZL MOSTAFAVI
Faculty of Rehabilitation Sciences: Dr JAVID MOSTMAND

ISFAHAN UNIVERSITY OF TECHNOLOGY

Isfahan 84156-83111
Telephone: (311) 3912505
Fax: (311) 3912511
E-mail: isco@cc.iut.ac.ir
Internet: www.iut.ac.ir
Founded 1977
State control
Language of instruction: Persian
Academic year: September to July
Pres.: Dr G. R. GHORBANI
Vice-Pres. for Academic Affairs: Dr MOJTABA AZHARI
Vice-Pres. for Finance and Admin.: Dr MOHAMMAD HASSAN ABBASI
Vice-Pres. for Research: Dr SEYED HASAN GHAZIASKAR
Vice-Pres. for Student Affairs: Dr ALI AKBAR ALEM RAJABI
Registrar: Dr SOROUSH ALIMORADI
Library Dir: Dr MOSTAFA KARIMAIAN EGHBAL
Library of 88,000 vols, 2,500 periodicals
Number of teachers: 440
Number of students: 9,000
Publications: *Esteghlal* (Journal of Engineering, 2 a year), *Iranian Journal of Physics Research*, *Journal of Sciences and Technology of Agriculture and Natural Resources*

DEANS

College of Agriculture: Dr MORTEZA ZAHEDI
Faculty of Chemical Engineering: Dr GH. ETEMAD
Faculty of Chemistry: Dr S. H. GHAZIASKAR
Faculty of Civil Engineering: Dr M. M. SAADATPOUR
Faculty of Electrical and Computer Engineering: Dr M. A. MONTAZERI
Faculty of Industrial Engineering: Dr GH. A. RAISSI ARDALI
Faculty of Materials Engineering: Dr M. A. GOLOZAR
Faculty of Mathematics: Dr H. R. ZOHOURI-ZANGENAH
Faculty of Mechanical Engineering: Dr A. SABONCHI
Faculty of Mining Engineering: Dr J. TAJA-DOD

Faculty of Natural Resources: Dr A. JALALIAN
Faculty of Physics: Dr H. AKBARZADEH
Faculty of Textile Technology: Dr S. H. AMIRSHAHI

PROFESSORS

AKBARZADEH, H., Physics
AMINI, S. M., Computational Physics
AMINZADEH, A., Chemistry
BASSIR, H., Mining Engineering
HAGHANY, A., Pure Mathematics
HAJRASOOLIHA, SH., Soil Science
KALBASI, M., Soil Science
MALLAKPOUR, S. E., Chemistry
MOLKI, M., Mechanical Engineering
MOUSAVI, S. F., Agriculture
PARSAFAR, GH., Chemistry
PARSIAN, A., Statistics
REZAEI, A., Plant Breeding, Cytogenetics
ROSTAMI, A. A., Mechanical Engineering
SAADATPOUR, M. M., Civil Engineering
TAHANI, V., Electronic Engineering

ISLAMIC AZAD UNIVERSITY

4th Golestan St, Pasdaran Ave, Tehran 16669-76113
Telephone: (21) 22565149
Fax: (21) 22547787
E-mail: info@intl.iau.ir
Internet: www.azad.ac.ir
Founded 1982
Academic year: September to September
Colleges of agricultural engineering, arts, civil engineering, humanities, medicine and basic sciences; each of the University's 350 brs, which are located throughout Iran, offers a selection of the courses run by the univ.
Pres.: Dr A. JASSBI
Vice-Pres. for Academic Affairs: Dr H. SADE-GHISHOJA
Vice-Pres. for Construction and Devt: A. SHAHRAKI
Vice-Pres. for Coordination Affairs: M. S. KALHOR
Vice-Pres. for Cultural Affairs: M. PIRAYAN-DEH
Vice-Pres. for Financial and Admin. Affairs: M. ZAHABION
Vice-Pres. for Int. Affairs: Dr PAYMAN MAHASTI
Vice-Pres. for Medical Affairs: Dr H. YAHYAVI
Vice-Pres. for Non-profit Schools: M. MIR-SHAMSI
Vice-Pres. for Parliamentary Affairs: Dr F. FARMAND
Vice-Pres. for Research: Dr F. LARIJANI
Vice-Pres. for Student Affairs: Dr J. AZIZIAN
Librarian: P. MAHASTI SHOTORBANI
Library: 4.9m. vols
Number of teachers: 25,310
Number of students: 850,000
Publications: *Armane-e-Pazhouhesh*, *Bassirat* (Vision, 4 a year), *Daneshnameh* (4 a year), *Danesh va Pezhouhesh* (4 a year), *Economics and Management* (4 a year), *Ensan Va Andishe* (Man and Thought, 4 a year), *Geographic Space* (4 a year), *Jelve-gahe-do-payam* (4 a year), *Journal of Agricultural Sciences* (4 a year), *Journal of Medical Sciences* (4 a year), *Journal of Sciences* (4 a year), *Koushk* (4 a year), *Mobin* (4 a year), *Namaye Pazhoohosh* (4 a year), *Nedaye-Daneshgah* (4 a year), *Nedaye Golestan* (4 a year), *Nourolelm* (4 a year), *Omran* (4 a year), *Pazhoheshna-meh I* (4 a year), *Pazhuhesh–DINI* (4 a year), *Peyke Dime* (4 a year), *Pooyesh* (4 a year), *Pouya* (4 a year), *Rah-avar, Rahavard* (4 a year), *Rouyesh* (4 a year), *Scientific-Cultural Letter of Research* (4 a year), *Scientific Research Journal* (4 a year), *Scientific Research Periodical* (4 a year), *Scientific Research Quarterly*, *Sedaye*

Didar (4 a year), *Selselat-Al-Zahab* (4 a year), *Sokhane Ashna* (4 a year), *Tazeha* (4 a year), *Tolu-e-Andishe* (4 a year), *Yeganeh* (4 a year), *Zakaria Razi* (4 a year).

K. N. TOOSI UNIVERSITY OF TECHNOLOGY

POB 15875-4416, 470 Mirdamad Ave W, 19697-64499 Tehran
Telephone: (21) 88881003
Fax: (21) 88882997
E-mail: oisc@kntu.ac.ir
Internet: www.kntu.ac.ir
Founded 1928, present name 1987
State control
Languages of instruction: Farsi, English
Academic year: September to June
Pres.: Dr SEYED MOHAMMAD TAGHI BATHAEE
Vice-Pres. for Admin. and Finance: Dr FARID NAJAFEE
Vice-Pres. for Education: Dr A. SHAHANI
Vice-Pres. for Research: Dr HAMID ABRISHAMI MOGHADAM
Vice-Pres. for Student Affairs: Dr HASSAM KARIMI MAZRAE
Librarian: Dr M. VARSHOSAZ
Library of 44,506 vols
Number of teachers: 233
Number of students: 5,587
Publications: *Abangan Magazine* (4 a year), *Journal of Robotics*, *Olum-o-Mohandesi'ye Nasir* (2 a year)

DEANS

Faculty of Aerospace Engineering: Dr M. MOSAVI NAIENIAN
Faculty of Civil Engineering: Dr MOGHADAS TAFRESHI
Faculty of Electrical and Computer Engineering: Dr AHMADIAN
Faculty of Geodesy and Geomatics Engineering: Dr VOSOOGHI
Faculty of Industrial Engineering: Dr KHOSHALHAN
Faculty of Mechanical Engineering: Dr Z. BASHAR HAGH
Faculty of Science: Dr SALEH KOOTAHI

KERMANSHAH UNIVERSITY OF MEDICAL SCIENCES

Shahid Beheshti Blvd, Kermanshah
Telephone: (831) 8354434
Fax: (831) 8356433
E-mail: info@kums.ac.ir
Internet: www.kums.ac.ir
Founded 1986, fmrly part of Razi Univ.
State control
Academic year: September to July
Chancellor: Dr SAMAD NORIZAD
Vice-Chancellor for Admin. and Financial Affairs: Dr EBRAHIM SHAKIBA
Vice-Chancellor for Education and Research: Dr HAMIDREZA OMRANI
Vice-Chancellor for Food and Drugs: Dr REZA TAHVILIAN
Vice-Chancellor for Health: Dr HAHAB MOINI MOSTOFI
Vice-Chancellor for Research: Dr FARID NAJAFI
Vice-Chancellor for Treatment: Dr TUORAJ AHMADI JUOYBARI
Librarian: SAYED JALAL KAZEMI OSKUEE
Library of 96,000 vols
Number of teachers: 228
Number of students: 3,072
Publications: *Behbood* (scientific quarterly, 4 a year), *Journal of Injury and Violence Research*

DEANS

Faculty Of Dentistry: Dr HAMID REZA MOZA-
FARI
Faculty of Health: Dr YAHYA SAFARI
Faculty of Medicine: Dr SAYED HAMID MADANI
Faculty of Nursing: Dr ALIREZA KHATONI,
Faculty of Pharmacy: Dr BABAK GHOLAMIN
Faculty of Pormedical: FATEME DARABI

MASHHAD UNIVERSITY OF MEDICAL SCIENCES

Daneshghah Ave, POB 91375-345, Mashhad
Telephone: (511) 8433528
Fax: (511) 8430249
E-mail: info.en@mums.ac.ir
Internet: www.mums.ac.ir
Founded 1945
Academic year: October to July
Pres.: Dr MASOUD MALEKI
Vice-Pres. for Admin. and Financial Affairs:
Dr AMANOLLAH KARIMI
Vice-Pres. for Education: Dr AKBAR DARAKH-
SHAN
Vice-Pres. for Food and Drug Affairs: Dr
NASER VAHDATI
Vice-Pres. for Health: Dr MOHAMMADREZA
MAJDI
Vice-Pres. for Research: Dr JALIL TAVAKKOL
AFSHARI
Vice-Pres. for Student Affairs: Dr NASER
SARGOLZAIE
Vice-Pres. for Treatment Affairs: Dr GHOLA-
MALI MAEMOORI
Librarians: P. MODIRAMANI, Z. JANGI
Library of 100,000 vols
Number of teachers: 554
Number of students: 5,688
Publications: *Iranian Journal of Basic Med-
ical Sciences* (4 a year), *Iranian Journal of
Otorhinolaryngology* (4 a year), *Journal* (4
a year)

DEANS

Faculty of Dentistry: Dr MOHAMMAD HASSAN
ZARABI
Faculty of Health and Paramedical Sciences:
Dr J. MOVAFFAGH
Faculty of Medicine: Dr MOHAMMAD TAGHI
RAJABI MASHHADI
Faculty of Nursing and Midwifery: Dr
ABBASS HEIDAN
Faculty of Pharmacy: Dr H. HOSSEINZADEH

MAZANDARAN UNIVERSITY

POB 416, Pasdaran St, Babolsar 47415
Telephone: (11252) 32095
Fax: (11252) 33702
E-mail: um@umz.ac.ir
Internet: www.umz.ac.ir
Founded 1975 as Reza Shah Kabir Univer-
sity, name changed 1980
State control
Language of instruction: Farsi
Academic year: September to June
Pres.: Dr GHASEM ALIZADEH AFROUZI
Vice-Pres. for Academic Affairs: Dr SAEED
MIRZANEJAD
Vice-Pres. for Admin. and Finance: Dr BAH-
RAM SADEGHPOUR
Vice-Pres. for Research: Dr AHMAS JAFARI
SAMIMI
Vice-Pres. for Student Affairs: Dr MORTEZA
ALAVIAN
Registrar: Dr ALI BAGHERI KHALILI
Librarian: Dr REZA NOORZAD
Number of teachers: 320
Number of students: 11,280

DEANS

Faculty of Art and Architecture: Dr GHOLAM-
REZA MALEKSHAHI

Faculty of Basic Sciences: Dr YAHYA TALEBI
Faculty of Economics and Admin. Sciences:
Dr ALIREZA POURFARAJ
Faculty of Humanities and Social Sciences:
Dr GHOLAMREZA PIROUZ
Faculty of Law and Political Science: Dr
KIOMARS KALANTARI
Faculty of Physical Sciences: Dr SHADMEHR
MIRDAR

PAYAME NOOR UNIVERSITY

POB 19395-4697, Lashkarak Rd, Tehran
19569
Telephone: (21) 22442042
Fax: (21) 22441511
E-mail: int@pnu.ac.ir
Internet: www.pnu.ac.ir
Founded 1987
State control
Languages of instruction: Persian, English
Academic year: September to July (two
terms)
Pres.: Prof. HASSAN ZIARI
Vice-Pres. for Admin. and Finance: Dr MAH-
MOUD REZA KAYMANESH
Vice-Pres. for Education and Assessment: Dr
ABDOLLAH MOTAMEDI
Vice-Pres. for Information Technology: Dr
REZA HAJI HOSSEINI (acting)
Vice-Pres. for Planning and Devt: MAHMOUD
REZA KAYMANESH
Vice-Pres. for Research: Dr SEYED AHMAD
MIRSHOKRAIE
Vice-Pres. for Student Affairs and Culture:
Dr ALIREZA AZHDAR
Dir of the Int. Office: Dr HOSSEIN SALEHZADEH
Librarian: Dr SEYED ALI ALAMOLHODA
Library: 1.4m. vols (total for all centres)
Number of teachers: 3,500 1.1m.
Publications: *Journal of Basic Sciences* (4 a
year), *Journal of Humanities* (4 a year),
Peyke Noor Journal (6 a year)

DEANS

Faculty of Agricultural Sciences: Dr MOHSEN
SHOOKAT FADAEE
Faculty of Art and Media: Dr HOOSHANG
KHOSROBEIGI
Faculty of Basic Sciences: Prof. SEYED AHMAD
MIRSHOKRAIE
Faculty of Economics and Social Sciences: Dr
MOHAMMAD TAGHI AMINI
Faculty of Engineering: Dr HASSAN FALLAH
Faculty of Humanities: Dr FATEMEH KOUPA
Faculty of Theology: Dr ABEDIN MO'MENI

PETROLEUM UNIVERSITY OF TECHNOLOGY

569 Hafez Ave, Tehran 15996-45313
Telephone: (21) 8804272
Fax: (21) 8807687
E-mail: info@put.ac.ir
Internet: www.put.ac.ir
Founded 1939 as Abadan Institute of Tech-
nology
State control, under Ministry of Petroleum
Languages of instruction: English, Farsi
Academic year: September to June
Chancellor: Dr D. H. PANJESHAHI
Vice-Chancellor for Academic Affairs: Dr M.
R. SHISHESAZ
Vice-Chancellor for Finance and Admin.: A.
ALIMORADY
Vice-Chancellor for Research Affairs: Dr B.
ROUZBEHANI
Vice-Chancellor for Research and Postgradu-
ate Studies: Dr A. EMAMZADEH
Vice-Chancellor for Student Affairs: Dr N.
NABHANI
Registrar: Dr M. FARZAM
Number of teachers: 100
Number of students: 1,500

DEANS

Faculty of Accounting and Finance (Tehran):
Dr A. EMAMZADEH
Faculty of Chemical and Petrochemical
Engineering (Abadan): Dr T. JADIDI
Faculty of Petroleum Engineering (Ahwaz):
Dr K. SALAHSHOOR

ATTACHED INSTITUTE

**Mahmood-Abad Institute for Marine
Sciences:** POB 161, Mahmood-Abad; Dir H.
RAZAEE.

RAZI UNIVERSITY

Kermanshah Azadi Sq., Kermanshah
Telephone: (831) 4277603
E-mail: info@razi.ac.ir
Internet: www.razi.ac.ir
Founded 1974
State control
Languages of instruction: English, Persian
Academic year: January to September
Chancellor: Prof. MOHAMMAD MEHDI KHODAEI
Vice-Chancellor for Academic Affairs: Dr ALI
BIDMESHKIPOUR
Vice-Chancellor for Research Affairs: Dr
SAEED JALALI HONARMAND
Vice-Chancellor for Student Affairs: Dr
ABDOLALI CHALE-CHALE
Number of teachers: 350
Number of students: 13,000

DEANS

School of Agriculture: Dr SAEED JALALI
HONARMAND
School of Engineering: Dr NAJAF BIGLARI
School of Literature and Humanities: Dr
VAHID SABZIANPOUR
School of Physical Education: Dr VAHID
TADIBI
School of Science: Dr REZA HASHEMI
School of Social Science: Dr MASOUD AKHA-
VANKAZEMI
School of Veterinary Medicine: Dr ABDOL ALI
CHALECHALE

SEMNAN UNIVERSITY OF MEDICAL SCIENCES

POB 35195-163, Molavi Blvd, Semnan
Telephone: (231) 3320112
Fax: (231) 3321622
E-mail: info@sem-ums.ac.ir
Internet: www.sem-ums.ac.ir
Founded 1988 as Semnan College of Medical
Sciences; present name and status 1990
Academic year: September to June (two
semesters)
Works in collaboration with seven hospitals
in the Semnan province
Chancellor: Dr ALI RASHIDI-POUR
Vice-Chancellor for Academic and Research
Affairs: Dr VAHID SEMNANI
Vice-Chancellor for Drugs and Food: Dr
SIAMAK YAGHMAIAN
Vice-Chancellor for Financial and Admin.
Affairs: Dr BEHPOUR YOUSEFI
Vice-Chancellor for Health Affairs: Dr JAFAR
JANDAGHI
Vice-Chancellor for Student Affairs: Dr
MOHAMMAD AMOUZADEH KHALILI
Vice-Chancellor for Treatment: Dr MOHAM-
MAD BAGHER SABERI ZAFARGHANDI
Head Librarian: Dr GHOLAMREZA IRAJIAN
Library of 41,863 vols, 125 current period-
icals, 417 theses
Number of teachers: 119
Number of students: 1,420
Publications: *Avay-e-Elm* (medical research,
in Persian, 2 or 3 a year), *Health commu-
nicators, focus on Health* (in Persian, 2 a
year), *Health magazine* (in Persian, 2 a

year), *Koomesh Medical Journal* (in Persian, 4 a year)

DEANS

Faculty of Health: MOHAMMAD BAGHER DEL-KHOSH
Faculty of Medicine: Dr MOHAMMAD E. AMIN-BEIDOKHTI
Faculty of Nursing and Paramedical Sciences: SAEED HAJIAGHAJANI
Faculty of Rehabilitation: Dr AMIR H. BAKH-TIARI

SHAHED UNIVERSITY

POB 15875-5794, 115 North Kargar Ave, Tehran
Telephone: (21) 6413734
Fax: (21) 6419568
Internet: www.shahed.ac.ir
Founded 1989
State control
Academic year: September to June

Chancellor: Dr MAHMOOD NOORISAFA
Vice-Chancellor for Academic Affairs: Dr SEIYED KAZEM FOROOTAN
Vice-Chancellor for Admin. and Financial Affairs, and Devt: Dr MOSTAFA KIAIE
Vice-Chancellor for Cultural Affairs: Dr ALI AZAM KHOSRARI
Vice-Chancellor for Research: Dr SOGHRAT FAGHIHZADEH
Vice-Chancellor for Student Affairs: Dr KAM-RAR SAGHAFI
Librarian: ABFOLREZA NOROOZI CHACOLI
Library of 215,000 vols, 240 periodicals
Number of teachers: 215
Number of students: 3,000
Publication: *Daneshvar* (4 a year)

DEANS

Faculty of Agriculture: Dr MASOOD ISFAHANI
Faculty of Art: ALI ASGAR SHIRAZI
Faculty of Basic Sciences: Dr IRAJ RASOOLI
Faculty of Dentistry: Dr SEIYED SHOJAEDDIN SHAYEGH
Faculty of Engineering: Dr JALAL NAZARZA-DEH
Faculty of Humanities and Literature: Dr MOHAMMAD REZA IMAM
Faculty of Medical Sciences: Dr SEIYED SAEID SEIYED MORTAZ

SHAHID BAHONAR UNIVERSITY OF KERMAN

POB 76169-133, Kerman
Telephone: (341) 3220041
Fax: (341) 3220065
E-mail: sbuk@mail.uk.ac.ir
Internet: www.uk.ac.ir
Founded 1974, teaching commenced 1975
State control
Languages of instruction: Farsi, English
Academic year: September to June

Colleges of agriculture, art, basic sciences, engineering, literature and human sciences, management and economics, mathematics and computer science, physical education and sport science, veterinary sciences; faculties of agriculture (Jiroft), higher education (Bam), mining (Zarand), technology (Sirjan)

Pres.: AHMAD AMIRI KHORASANI
Vice-Pres. for Admin. and Finance: AKBAR HOSSEINI POUR
Vice-Pres. for Education: HOSSEIN MOHEBI
Vice-Pres. for Research: MOHAMMAD RANJBAR HAMGHAVANDI
Vice-Pres. for Student Affairs: MANSOUR SAHEBZAMANI
Registrar: Dr M. A. VALI
Librarian: M. SHAFIIE
Library of 150,000 vols

Number of teachers: 400
Number of students: 12,500

SHAHID BEHESHTI UNIVERSITY

Evin, 19834 Tehran 19839-63113
Telephone: (21) 29901
Fax: (21) 22431919
E-mail: info@sbu.ac.ir
Internet: www.sbu.ac.ir
Founded 1960 as Nat. Univ. of Iran; present name 1983
State control
Language of instruction: Farsi
Academic year: September to June

Pres.: Prof. AHMAD SHAABANI
Vice-Pres. for Admin. and Finance: Dr BEH-ROOZ DORI
Vice-Pres. for Education and Graduate Studies: Dr BAHMAN HONARI
Vice-Pres. for Information and Communication Technology: Dr FEREIDOON SHAMS
Vice-Pres. for Research and Technology: Dr PEYMAN SALEHI
Vice-Pres. for Student and Cultural Affairs: Dr MORTEZA SAMNOON MAHDAVI
Dir of Collegiate Relations and Int. Scientific Cooperations: Dr HOSSEIN POUR AHMADI
Dir of Public Relations: HADI SALEHI ZADEH
Registrar: Dr MASOOD SHARIFI
Library: see Libraries and Archives
Number of teachers: 500
Number of students: 13,576
Publications: *Ayeneh Isar*, *Ayeneh Ma'refat* (Research Journal of Philosophy and Discourse), *Daneshnameh*, *Journal of Earth Sciences*, *Journal of Family Research*, *Journal of Human Sciences*, *Management Excellence*, *Management Perspective*, *Rahyaft* (Political and International Approaches, 4 a year), *Quarterly Applied Psychology*, *Revue de Recherche Juridique*, *Soffeh* (architecture)

DEANS

Faculty of Architecture and Urban Planning: Dr AKBAR HAJ EBRAHIM ZARGAR
Faculty of Biological Sciences: Dr MASSOD SHEIDAI
Faculty of Earth Sciences: Dr HASSAN LASH-KARI
Faculty of Economics and Political Sciences: Dr MOHAMMAD NASER SHERAFAT JAHROMI
Faculty of Education and Psychology: HAMID REZA POURETAMAD
Faculty of Electrical and Computer Engineering: Dr SEYED EBRAHIM AFJEII
Faculty of Law: Dr GOODARZ EFTEKHAR JAHROMI
Faculty of Letters and Human Sciences: Dr AKBAR MAJDODINE
Faculty of Management and Accounting: Dr MOHAMMAD ESMAEIL FADAEI
Faculty of Mathematical Sciences: Dr MOHAMMAD ZOKAEI
Faculty of New Technologies and Energy Engineering: Dr ABAS SAIDI
Faculty of Physical Education and Sports Sciences: Dr KHOSRO EBRAHIM
Faculty of Sciences: Dr MEHRDAD FARHOUDI
Faculty of Theology and Religions: Dr HAS-SAN SAEEDI

PROFESSORS

ABASSI, A., Literature and Human Sciences
ABBAS ZADEGAN, S. M., Education and Psychology
ABBASPOUR, M., Electrical and Computer Engineering
ABDI DANESHPOUR, Z., Architecture and Urban Planning
ABDOLAHI, M., Environmental Sciences Research Institute

ABDOLI, A., Environmental Sciences Research Institute
ABDOLI, B., Physical Education and Sport Sciences
ABEDIN, A., Education and Psychology
ABEDIN, A., Family Research Institute
ABOLGHASEMI, M., Education and Psychology
ABOLGHASEMI, S. M., Literature and Human Sciences
ADABI, M. H., Earth Sciences
ADIB RAD, N., Education and Psychology
ADIBZADEH, B., Architecture and Urban Planning
AFJEI, S. E., Electrical and Computer Engineering
AGHDAEE, M., Physical Education and Sport Sciences
AHARI, Z., Architecture and Urban Planning
AHMAD ZADEH, F., Environmental Sciences Research Institute
AHMADI, F., Architecture and Urban Planning
AHMADI, S. H., Literature and Human Sciences
AHMADZADEH, S., Literature and Human Sciences
AKBARI, M. A., Literature and Human Sciences
AKBARI GHAMSARI, A., Literature and Human Sciences
AKBARIAN, M., Management and Accounting
ALAEI, A., Architecture and Urban Planning
ALAMOL HODA, J., Education and Psychology
ALASKARI, Z., Literature and Human Sciences
ALAVI, S. A., Earth Sciences
ALAVINIA, S., Literature and Human Sciences
ALBORZ, M., Mathematical Sciences
ALEM TABRIZ, A., Management and Accounting
ALIREZAEI, S., Earth Sciences
ALSHAHIR BIFARHANG MAJDODDIN, A., Literature and Human Sciences
AMINI, M., Law
AMINI HOURA, M., Architecture and Urban Planning
AMIR ARJOMAND, A., Law
ANSARINIA, S., Architecture and Urban Planning
ARAB MAZAR, A., Economic and Political Sciences
ARABMAZAR YAZDI, M., Management and Accounting
ARBABI, M., Law
ARBABIAN, A., Management and Accounting
ARDEBILI, M. A., Law
ARDEBILI, M. H., Management and Accounting
AREFI, M., Education and Psychology
ASADI, G., Management and Accounting
ASGHARI, A. H., Mathematical Sciences
ASGHARIAN JEDDI, A., Architecture and Urban Planning
ASHTIANI, M., Education and Psychology
ASLANKHANI, M., Physical Education and Sport Sciences
ASSADI, B., Economic and Political Sciences
AVANI, G., Literature and Human Sciences
AYATOLLAHZADEH SHIRAZI, M. M., Mathematical Sciences
AZADEH, A. A., Mathematical Sciences
AZARI, H., Mathematical Sciences
AZGHANDI, A., Economic and Political Sciences
BA EZAT, F., Education and Psychology
BABAPOOR, M. M., Department of Islamic Teachings
BADIEI, M., Architecture and Urban Planning
BAGHERIAN, F., Education and Psychology
BAHADORI BARCHELOEI, M., Electrical and Computer Engineering
BAHADORIFAR, M., Earth Sciences
BAHAR NEJAD, Z., Department of Islamic Teachings
BAHARI ARDESHIRI, A. A., Literature and Human Sciences
BAHER, G., Management and Accounting

BANA RAZAVI, M., Economic and Political Sciences
BARGH JELVE, S., Environmental Sciences Research Institute
BEHESHTI AVAL, S. B., Architecture and Urban Planning
BEHZAD, M., Mathematical Sciences
BEHZADI SHIRKALA, M., Earth Sciences
BEIGZADEH, E., Law
BERANJEH TORABI, D. M., Literature and Human Sciences
BLACK, J. E., Environmental Sciences Research Institute
BOZORGAN NIA, M. A., Literature and Human Sciences
CHALABI, M., Literature and Human Sciences
CHENARI, A. A., Literature and Human Sciences
CHIME, N., Family Research Institute
DADASHI, M. S., Physical Education and Sport Sciences
DADGAR, U., Law
DADKAN, M. H., Physical Education and Sport Sciences
DANESH, E., Education and Psychology
DANESHPOUR PARVAR, F., Literature and Human Sciences
DARABKOLAIE, E., Department of Islamic Teachings
DARABPOUR, M., Law
DARGAHI, A., Electrical and Computer Engineering
DARGAHI, H., Economic and Political Sciences
DARIUSH HAMEDANI, H., Mathematical Sciences
DARKOOSH, S. A., Economic and Political Sciences
DAVOODI, P., Economic and Political Sciences
DEHGAN, A., Department of Islamic Teachings
DEHGHAN, M., Family Research Institute
DEHZAD, B., Earth Sciences
DELSHAD, S., Literature and Human Sciences
DEYHIMFARD, R., Environmental Sciences Research Institute
DEZFOULIAN, K., Literature and Human Sciences
DIDARI, R., Literature and Human Sciences
DORRI, B., Management and Accounting
EBRAHIM, K., Physical Education and Sport Sciences
EBRAHIMI, M. M., Mathematical Sciences
EBRAHIMI VARKIANI, M., Department of Islamic Teachings
EFTEKHAR JAHROMI, G., Law
EJTEHADI, M., Literature and Human Sciences
EMADZADEH, G., Literature and Human Sciences
ESHGHI, M., Electrical and Computer Engineering
ESLAHCHI, C., Mathematical Sciences
ESLAMI, R., Law
ESMAEILI, J., Electrical and Computer Engineering
ESMAILPOUR MOTLAGH, A., Literature and Human Sciences
ESPANDAR, R., Earth Sciences
ESTARAMI, E., Literature and Human Sciences
ETEZADI, L., Architecture and Urban Planning
FADAEI NEJAD, M. E., Management and Accounting
FAGHIHI, M. R., Mathematical Sciences
FAKHARI, A. H., Law
FAKHARI TEHRANI, F., Architecture and Urban Planning
FALLAHI, A., Architecture and Urban Planning
FALSAFI, H., Law
FANNI, Z., Earth Sciences
FARDANESH, M. A., Economic and Political Sciences
FARSIJANI, H., Management and Accounting
FARZAD, F., Management and Accounting

FATEMI JAHROMI, S. A., Literature and Human Sciences
FATHI VAJAR GAH, K., Education and Psychology
FATTAH, A., Electrical and Computer Engineering
FERDOSI, S., Education and Psychology
FEYZOLLAHZADEH, A., Literature and Human Sciences
FOROOZESH, N., Mathematical Sciences
FOYOZAT, E., Literature and Human Sciences
GADAK, A., Law
GANJALI, M., Mathematical Sciences
GHADIMI, H., Architecture and Urban Planning
GHADIRI, F., Family Research Institute
GHAEM, G., Architecture and Urban Planning
GHAFFARI, A., Architecture and Urban Planning
GHAFOORI, M., Economic and Political Sciences
GHAHREMANI, M., Education and Psychology
GHANAATSHOAR, M., Laser and Plasma Research Institute
GHANBARI, M. J., Law
GHANBARI MAMAN, H., Economic and Political Sciences
GHAREHCHEH, M., Management and Accounting
GHARI SEYED FATEMI, M., Law
GHASEMI HAMED, A., Law
GHASEMPOUR, A., Environmental Sciences Research Institute
GHASEMZADEH, A., Management and Accounting
GHAVAM, A., Economic and Political Sciences
GHAVAMI ZADEH, R., Electrical and Computer Engineering
GHAVIMI, M., Literature and Human Sciences
GHOAMREZAEI, M., Literature and Human Sciences
GHORBANI, M., Earth Sciences
GHOUCHANI, F., Management and Accounting
GOLDOOST JOUYBARI, R., Law
GOLKAR, K., Architecture and Urban Planning
GOOYA, Z., Mathematical Sciences
HADDADI, S. M., Literature and Human Sciences
HADIZADEH, A., Management and Accounting
HAGHIGHAT, R., Earth Sciences
HAGHIGHI, M., Management and Accounting
HAJ EBRAHIM ZARGAR, A., Architecture and Urban Planning
HAJ JABBARI, S., Mathematical Sciences
HAJI GHASEMI, K., Architecture and Urban Planning
HAJI KARIMI, A., Management and Accounting
HAJI MIR ARAB, M., Economic and Political Sciences
HAJIABOLHASAN, H., Mathematical Sciences
HAJI-YOUSEFI, A. M., Economic and Political Sciences
HAMIDIZADEH, M. R., Management and Accounting
HAMIDREZA, G., Laser and Plasma Research Institute
HANAEI KASHANI, M. S., Literature and Human Sciences
HANJANI, S. A., Law
HASAN ZADE KIABI, B., Environmental Sciences Research Institute
HASHEMI, S. A., Economic and Political Sciences
HASHEMI, S. H., Environmental Sciences Research Institute
HASHEMI, S. M., Law
HASHEMIPOUR, O., Electrical and Computer Engineering
HASSANI, A., Literature and Human Sciences
HASSANI, M., Earth Sciences
HEKMAT, N., Literature and Human Sciences
HERAVI, I., Management and Accounting
HERAVI, M., Architecture and Urban Planning

HESHMATZADEH, M. B., Economic and Political Sciences
HEYDARI, M., Education and Psychology
HEYDARI, M., Family Research Institute
HEYDARIAN., M. T., Literature and Human Sciences
HOJJAT, M., Department of Islamic Teachings
HONARI, B., Mathematical Sciences
HOSHI, A., Management and Accounting
HOSSEINABADI, A., Law
HOSSEINALIPOUR, S., Architecture and Urban Planning
HOSSEINI, S. M., Management and Accounting
HOSSEINI BARMAEI, S. F., Law
HOSSEINI BARZI, M., Earth Sciences
HOSSEINPOUR KAZEMI, M., Economic and Political Sciences
HOSSEINZADEH, M., Management and Accounting
HOVANLO, F., Physical Education and Sport Sciences
HOZHABR KIANI, K., Economic and Political Sciences
ILKHANI, M., Literature and Human Sciences
ILKHANI, S. C., Literature and Human Sciences
JABERIPOUR, G., Electrical and Computer Engineering
JAFARI ROHANI, B., Mathematical Sciences
JAHANKHANI, A., Management and Accounting
JALALI, A., Electrical and Computer Engineering
JALALI, M., Architecture and Urban Planning
JAVIDRUZI, M., Architecture and Urban Planning
JOUDAT, M. R., Architecture and Urban Planning
KAFAIE, S. M. A., Economic and Political Sciences
KANANI, M. R., Environmental Sciences Research Institute
KARIMIAN, F., Literature and Human Sciences
KASSAEE, M., Management and Accounting
KHAKZAD, A., Earth Sciences
KHALATBARI, A., Literature and Human Sciences
KHALEDI, S., Earth Sciences
KHALFEH SHOUSHTARI, M. E., Literature and Human Sciences
KHALIGHI, A., Literature and Human Sciences
KHANSARI MOUSAVI, S., Literature and Human Sciences
KHATAMI, A., Literature and Human Sciences
KHATAMI, M. J., Architecture and Urban Planning
KHATTAT, N. K., Literature and Human Sciences
KHEYRANDISH, A., Environmental Sciences Research Institute
KHLLAT, F., Mathematical Sciences
KHODA PANAHI, M. K., Education and Psychology
KHODADADI, A., Mathematical Sciences
KHODAI KALATEBAI, N., Literature and Human Sciences
KHODAIAN, S., Earth Sciences
KHOMAMIZADEH, F., Law
KHORASANI ZADEH, M., Architecture and Urban Planning
KHORSAND, H., Electrical and Computer Engineering
KHORSHIDI, G., Management and Accounting
KHOSH KONESH, A., Education and Psychology
KHOSHBAKHT, K., Environmental Sciences Research Institute
KOOSHA, J., Law
KOUCHAKZADE, M., Environmental Sciences Research Institute
LAJEVARDI, M., Earth Sciences
LAJEVARDI, S. J., Management and Accounting

LARI, A., Physical Education and Sport Sciences
LASHKARI, H., Earth Sciences
LATIFI, H., Laser and Plasma Research Institute
LESSAN PEZESHKI, H., Literature and Human Sciences
LIAGHATI, H., Environmental Sciences Research Institute
LOTF ABADI, H., Education and Psychology
LOTFALIKANI, A., Earth Sciences
MAHDAVI, M. S., Literature and Human Sciences
MAHDAVI DAMGHANI, A. M., Environmental Sciences Research Institute
MAHDAVI HERSINI, S. E., Education and Psychology
MAHMOUDI, H., Environmental Sciences Research Institute
MAHMOUDI, M., Mathematical Sciences
MAJIDI KHAMENEH, B., Earth Sciences
MAKHZAN MOUSAVI, S. A., Literature and Human Sciences
MANAVI TEHRAN, A., Economic and Political Sciences
MANI, M. A., Economic and Political Sciences
MANSOORBAKHT, G., Literature and Human Sciences
MANSOUR, L., Education and Psychology
MARANDI, M. R., Department of Islamic Teachings
MASHAYEKH FARIDANI, S., Architecture and Urban Planning
MASOUDI, R., Laser and Plasma Research Institute
MASOUMZADEH KIAEI, M. A., Economic and Political Sciences
MAZAHERI TEHRANI, M. A., Education and Psychology
MAZAHERI TEHRANI, M. A., Family Research Institute
MAZLOOMNEZHAD, B., Electrical and Computer Engineering
MEHRA, N., Law
MEHRDAD, S. M., Environmental Sciences Research Institute
MEHRPOUR MOHAMMADABADI, H., Law
MEHRSHAHI, E., Electrical and Computer Engineering
MEMARIAN, A., Architecture and Urban Planning
MESGARI, A. A., Literature and Human Sciences
MESHKANI, M. R., Mathematical Sciences
MILANI, V., Mathematical Sciences
MINA KARI, M., Education and Psychology
MINOUEI, S., Environmental Sciences Research Institute
MIR JALILI, M. H., Environmental Sciences Research Institute
MIR RIAHI, S., Architecture and Urban Planning
MIR SHAMS SHAHSHAHANI, S., Literature and Human Sciences
MIRI, S., Architecture and Urban Planning
MIRMOHAMMAD SADEGHI, H., Law
MOEINI, M., Physical Education and Sport Sciences
MOGHIM ESLAM, G., Laser and Plasma Research Institute
MOGHISEH, H., Department of Islamic Teachings
MOHAGHEGH AHMADABADI (DAMAD), S. M., Law
MOHAJERANI, A., Laser and Plasma Research Institute
MOHAMMADI, H. R., Earth Sciences
MOHAMMADZADEH, H., Earth Sciences
MOHSENI ARMAKI, S. M., Laser and Plasma Research Institute
MOMAYEZ, A., Architecture and Urban Planning
MOMENI, I., Earth Sciences
MOMENI, M., Earth Sciences
MOMTAZ, F., Literature and Human Sciences
MONIRI, M., Mathematical Sciences
MONSHIZADEH, R., Earth Sciences

MORTAZAVI, S., Education and Psychology
MOSADEGH RASHTI, A. A., Literature and Human Sciences
MOSHARAFOLMOLK, M., Literature and Human Sciences
MOSHIRI, F., Architecture and Urban Planning
MOSTAFAVI, H., Environmental Sciences Research Institute
MOSTAFAVI KASHANI, S. M., Law
MOSTAFAVI NIA, S. M. K., Department of Islamic Teachings
MOTTAGHI, H., Management and Accounting
MOUSA POUR, N., Education and Psychology
MOUSAVI, M. R., Earth Sciences
MOUTABI, F., Family Research Institute
NADIMI, H., Architecture and Urban Planning
NADIMI, H., Literature and Human Sciences
NAHREYNI, F., Law
NAJAFI ABRANDABADI, H., Law
NAJAFIAN, B., Earth Sciences
NAMAZI, H., Economic and Political Sciences
NAMAZIAN, A., Architecture and Urban Planning
NAMAZIZADEH, M., Physical Education and Sport Sciences
NAMVAR GHAREH SHIRAN, E., Electrical and Computer Engineering
NASSERY, H. R., Earth Sciences
NAVAEI, K., Architecture and Urban Planning
NAVI, K., Electrical and Computer Engineering
NAZARI, A., Architecture and Urban Planning
NAZEMI, E., Electrical and Computer Engineering
NEJAD EBRAHIMI, S., Environmental Sciences Research Institute
NEMATOLLAHI, V., Literature and Human Sciences
NIKBAKHT, H. R., Law
NIKNAM, A., Laser and Plasma Research Institute
NIKPEY, A., Law
NILI, M. Y., Architecture and Urban Planning
NOBAHAR, R., Law
NOFARASTI, M., Economic and Political Sciences
NOJOUMIAN, A. A., Literature and Human Sciences
NOOR BALOOCHI, S., Mathematical Sciences
NOORI NAEINI, S., Economic and Political Sciences
NOURANI POUR, R., Education and Psychology
NOURBAHA, R., Law
NOURI ROUDSARI, O., Environmental Sciences Research Institute
NOURSHAHI, M., Physical Education and Sport Sciences
ORKAMANI AZAR, F., Electrical and Computer Engineering
OSSEINION, S. A., Mathematical Sciences
PADIDAR, M., Architecture and Urban Planning
PAKDAMAN, S., Education and Psychology
PAKZAD, J., Architecture and Urban Planning
PALIZBAN, F., Literature and Human Sciences
PANAGHI, L., Family Research Institute
PARCHAMI, D., Literature and Human Sciences
PARDAKHTCHI, M., Education and Psychology
PARSA, M. A., Architecture and Urban Planning
PARVIN JAHROMI, K., Mathematical Sciences
PAZUKI, A., Architecture and Urban Planning
POOR KAZEMI, M. H., Economic and Political Sciences
POORBARAT, M., Mathematical Sciences
POORSINA, M., Department of Islamic Teachings
POUR AHMADI MIEBODI, H., Economic and Political Sciences
POUR ETEMAD, H. R., Education and Psychology

POUR KERAMATI, V., Architecture and Urban Planning
POUR KERMANI, M., Earth Sciences
POUR MOAFI, S. M., Earth Sciences
POURETEMAD, H., Family Research Institute
POURKIANI, M., Physical Education and Sport Sciences
RAFATI, H., Environmental Sciences Research Institute
RAFIPOOR, F., Literature and Human Sciences
RAHGOSHAI, M., Earth Sciences
RAHMANI, B., Earth Sciences
RAHMANI FAZLI, A., Earth Sciences
RASA, I., Earth Sciences
RASEKH, M., Law
RASHIDIAN, A., Literature and Human Sciences
RASI, M., Literature and Human Sciences
RASOULI NARAGHI, G., Architecture and Urban Planning
RASTKAR, A. R., Laser and Plasma Research Institute
RAZAVI ZADEH, G., Electrical and Computer Engineering
RAZAVIAN, M. T., Earth Sciences
RAZJOUYAN, M., Architecture and Urban Planning
RAZMGAH, F., Architecture and Urban Planning
REZA, M. T., Environmental Sciences Research Institute
REZAEIAN, A., Management and Accounting
REZAZADE VALUJERDI, A., Electrical and Computer Engineering
ROHANI RANKOUHI, M. T., Electrical and Computer Engineering
ROOZBEHAN, M., Economic and Political Sciences
ROSHAN, M., Family Research Institute
ROSOULI, H., Literature and Human Sciences
ROUSTA, A., Management and Accounting
SABAHI, H., Environmental Sciences Research Institute
SABBAGHIAN, Z., Education and Psychology
SADAT KYAIE, M., Department of Islamic Teachings
SADEGHI, A., Earth Sciences
SADEGHI, A., Law
SADEGHI PEY, N., Architecture and Urban Planning
SADJADI, S. A. M., Literature and Human Sciences
SADOOGH VANINI, H., Earth Sciences
SADR, S. K., Economic and Political Sciences
SADRIA, A., Architecture and Urban Planning
SAEIDI, A., Earth Sciences
SAFFAR, M. J., Law
SAFFARI, A., Law
SAHBA YAGHMAEI, M., Laser and Plasma Research Institute
SAIDI, H., Department of Islamic Teachings
SAJADI, J., Earth Sciences
SALAHI MALEK, Y., Economic and Political Sciences
SALEHI, P., Environmental Sciences Research Institute
SALEHI ZADEH, H., Department of Islamic Teachings
SALEHPOUR, Y., Family Research Institute
SALEMI, A., Environmental Sciences Research Institute
SAMNON, M., Department of Islamic Teachings
SAMSAMI, H., Economic and Political Sciences
SANEI DAREHBIDI, M., Literature and Human Sciences
SANIEI, N., Electrical and Computer Engineering
SARAFI, M., Earth Sciences
SARIOLGHALAM, M., Economic and Political Sciences
SARTIPI POUR, M., Architecture and Urban Planning
SAVARAEI, P., Law

SAVOJI, M. H., Electrical and Computer Engineering
SEIFI, S. J., Law
SEIFI, Z., Law
SERVAT, M. M., Literature and Human Sciences
SERVATI, M. R., Earth Sciences
SEYED HASHEMI, S. E., Department of Islamic Teachings
SEYED MIRZAEI, S. M., Literature and Human Sciences
SHABANI, N., Environmental Sciences Research Institute
SHABANI, R., Literature and Human Sciences
SHAEGHI, A. A., Environmental Sciences Research Institute
SHAFIE HOLIHI, K., Mathematical Sciences
SHAH HOSSEINI, H., Electrical and Computer Engineering
SHAHBAZI, E., Environmental Sciences Research Institute
SHAHIDA, M. R., Earth Sciences
SHAHIDI, S., Education and Psychology
SHAHLAEE, A., Mathematical Sciences
SHAHNI KARAMAZADEH, N., Mathematical Sciences
SHAHRIARI, S., Earth Sciences
SHAHSHAHANI, S., Literature and Human Sciences
SHAHVARANI, A., Mathematical Sciences
SHAMLOO, B., Law
SHAMS, A., Law
SHAMSFARD, M., Electrical and Computer Engineering
SHARIF TEHRANI, S. R., Architecture and Urban Planning
SHARIFI, M., Education and Psychology
SHARIFI, M., Family Research Institute
SHARIFI, M. J., Electrical and Computer Engineering
SHEIKH, M. A., Literature and Human Sciences
SHEIKHHASSANI, G. H., Earth Sciences
SHEMIRANI, A., Earth Sciences
SHERAFAT, M. N., Economic and Political Sciences
SHOEIBI, A., Architecture and Urban Planning
SHOKRI, B., Laser and Plasma Research Institute
SIMBAR, F., Economic and Political Sciences
SOHEIL, K., Literature and Human Sciences
SOKHANVAR, J., Literature and Human Sciences
SOLEIMANI, D., Literature and Human Sciences
SONBOLI, A., Environmental Sciences Research Institute
TABARSA, G., Management and Accounting
TABATABEI, S., Electrical and Computer Engineering
TAFAZOLI, F., Economic and Political Sciences
TAGHI, Z., Architecture and Urban Planning
TAHBAZ, M., Architecture and Urban Planning
TAHMASBIAN, K., Family Research Institute
TAJIK, M. R., Economic and Political Sciences
TALEB ZADEH, M., Education and Psychology
TALEBI, D., Management and Accounting
TAVAKKOLI, M., Department of Islamic Teachings
TAVAKOLI, A., Economic and Political Sciences
TAVAKOLINIA, J., Earth Sciences
TAVASOLI, S. H., Laser and Plasma Research Institute
TAVASSOLIZADEH, N., Law
TEHRANCHI, M. M., Laser and Plasma Research Institute
THOMAS ZADEH, R., Literature and Human Sciences
TOUSI ARDEKANI, M., Mathematical Sciences
VAEZ IRAVANI, F., Electrical and Computer Engineering
VAEZI, A., Literature and Human Sciences

VAHDANI MOGHADAM, M., Laser and Plasma Research Institute
VAHID DOSTJERDI, F., Literature and Human Sciences
VAHIDI, T., Architecture and Urban Planning
VAHIDI ASL, M. Q., Mathematical Sciences
VATANKHAH, M., Economic and Political Sciences
VAZIRI FARAHANI, B., Architecture and Urban Planning
VAZIRI FARAHANI, P., Architecture and Urban Planning
VIZEH FAYAZ, O., Literature and Human Sciences
VOSOOGHI ABEDINI, M., Earth Sciences
YAMANI DOUZI SORKHABI, M., Education and Psychology
YAVARI, M. E., Economic and Political Sciences
YAZDI, M., Earth Sciences
YOSOFI, S. A., Mathematical Sciences
ZADE MOHAMMADI, A., Family Research Institute
ZAKER ALHOSSEINI, A., Electrical and Computer Engineering
ZAKERZADEH, A., Literature and Human Sciences
ZAND, E., Environmental Sciences Research Institute
ZAREI, M. H., Law
ZEKAVAT, K., Architecture and Urban Planning
ZIATAVANA, M. H., Earth Sciences
ZOKAEI, M., Mathematical Sciences

SHAHID BEHESHTI UNIVERSITY OF MEDICAL SCIENCES AND HEALTH SERVICES

POB 4139-19395, Shahid Chamran Highway, Evin, Tehran
Telephone: (21) 2401022
Fax: (21) 2400052
E-mail: icrd@sbmu.ac.ir
Internet: www.sbmu.ac.ir
Founded 1961 as Melli University; present name 1986
State control
Language of instruction: Farsi
Academic year: September to June

Chancellor: Dr HABIBOLLA PEYRAVI
Vice-Chancellor for Academic Affairs: Dr D. YADEGARI
Vice-Chancellor for Admin. and Finance: Dr R. ABOUFAZELI
Vice-Chancellor for Curative and Pharmaceutical Affairs: Dr S. S. RAZAVI
Vice-Chancellor for Health: Dr A. RAMEZAN-KHANI
Vice-Chancellor for Research: Dr M. JORJANI
Vice-Chancellor for Student and Cultural Affairs: Dr M. HOSSEINI KHAMENE
Dir of Int. Relations and Congress Management: Dr F. OKHOVATIAN
Librarian: A. MOHADES RAAD

Library of 5,458 vols, 3,000 current journals, 60 e-books
Number of teachers: 1,039
Number of students: 5,961

Publications: *Bina* (Journal of Ophthalmology, 4 a year), *Digestive Disease Digest* (12 a year), *International Journal of Endocrinology and Metabolism* (4 a year), *Iranian Journal of Infectious Disease and Tropical Medicine* (4 a year), *Iranian Journal of Plastic and Reconstructive Surgery* (4 a year), *Iranian Journal of Urology* (4 a year), *Journal of Dentistry* (4 a year), *Journal of Medical Education* (4 a year), *Journal of the Pharmaceutical Research Centre* (4 a year), *Pejouhandeh*, *Research in Medical Subjects* (in Farsi, 4 a year), *Tanaffos* (Respiration, 4 a year)

DEANS

Faculty of Allied Medicine: Dr S. H. MOGHA-DAM-NIA
Faculty of Dentistry
Faculty of Medicine: Dr M. MARDANI
Faculty of Nutrition and Food Industrial Sciences: Dr N. KALANTARI
School of Nursing and Midwifery: Dr M. YAZDJERDI
Faculty of Pharmacy: Dr M. MOSADEGH
School of Public Health: Dr H. KHATAMI
Faculty of Rehabilitation: Dr M. GHASSEMY BOROMAND

SHAHID CHAMRAN UNIVERSITY

Ahvaz, Khouzestan
Telephone: (611) 3330022
Fax: (611) 3332040
E-mail: webmaster@cua.ac.ir
Internet: www.scu.ac.ir
Founded 1955 as Jundi Shapur University, present name 1983
State control
Language of instruction: Farsi
Academic year: September to June

Chancellor: Dr MORTEZA ZARGAR SHOOSHTARI NOURI
Vice-Chancellor for Academic Affairs: Dr M. A. FIROOZI
Vice-Chancellor for Admin. and Finance: Dr GHOMESHI
Vice-Chancellor for Research and Technology: Dr H. R. GHAFOURI
Vice-Chancellor for Student Affairs: M. MOGHBELAL-HOSSEIN
Dir of Int. Affairs: Mr SADROS-SADAT
Registrar: M. JANNEJAD
Librarian: Dr A. FARAJPAHLOU

Number of teachers: 518
Number of students: 13,308

Publications: *Journal of Education and Psychology* (in Farsi, 4 a year), *Journal of Engineering* (in Farsi, 1 a year), *Journal of Literature and Islamic Studies* (in Farsi, 1 a year), *Journal of Veterinary Medicine* (in Farsi, 1 a year), *Scientific Journal of Agriculture* (in Farsi, 4 a year), *University Journal of Science* (in Farsi, 1 a year)

DEANS

Faculty of Agriculture: Dr NABIPOUR
Faculty of Arts: M. KOLLAHKAJ
Faculty of Economic and Social Science: Dr NABAVI
Faculty of Education and Psychology: Dr M. KOUKABI
Faculty of Engineering: Dr M. JOORABIAN
Faculty of Geology and GIS: G. RANGZAN
Faculty of Literature and Humanities: Dr MOVAHED
Faculty of Mathematics and Computer Science: H. HARIZAVI
Faculty of Physical Education: Dr A. H. HABIBI
Faculty of Science: Dr M. CHITSAZAN
Faculty of Theology and Islamic Studies: Dr A. MATOORI
Faculty of Veterinary Science: Dr M. GHOR-BANPOUR
Faculty of Water Science Engineering: Dr S. M. KASHEFIPOUR

SHAHID SADOUGHI UNIVERSITY OF MEDICAL SCIENCES

POB 89195-734, 2 Bouali Ave, Yazd
Telephone: (351) 82470171
Fax: (351) 8245446
E-mail: info@ssu.ac.ir
Internet: www.ssu.ac.ir
Founded 1983
State control
Language of instruction: Farsi

Academic year: September to June
Chancellor: Dr AHMAD HAERIAN
Vice-Chancellor for Academic Affairs: Dr MR. MANSORIAN
Vice-Chancellor for Admin. and Financial Affairs: Dr MH. EHRAMPOUSH
Vice-Chancellor for Health: Dr M. KARIMI
Vice-Chancellor for Research Affairs: Dr S. M. YASSINI
Vice-Chancellor for Student Services: Dr HOSSEINI
Dir of Int. Affairs: Dr SM. KALANTAR
Registrar: A. M. ALI HEIDARI
Library of 40,000 vols, 278 journals
Number of teachers: 236
Number of students: 1,800

DEANS

Faculty of Dentistry: Dr TALEBI
Faculty of Medicine: Dr RAFIEAN
Faculty of Nursing and Midwifery: Dr SEYED HASSANI
Faculty of Paramedicine: Dr KHALILI
Faculty of Public Health: Dr EHRAMPOUSH

SHAHREKORD UNIVERSITY OF MEDICAL SCIENCES

POB 88184, Kashany Ave, Shahrekord
Telephone: (381) 34590
Fax: (381) 34588
Internet: www.skums.ac.ir

Founded in 1986
State control
Language of instruction: Persian

Pres.: Dr M. HASHEMZADEH
Vice-Chancellor for Admin. and Financial Affairs: F. SHARAFATI
Vice-Chancellor for Curative, Drug and Food Affairs: Dr E. NOORIAN
Vice-Chancellor for Education and Research: Dr M. R. SAMIEY NASAB
Vice-Chancellor for Student and Cultural Affairs: Dr H. DAVOODPOUR
Librarian: Dr A. AMINI

Library of 33,000 vols
Number of teachers: 130
Number of students: 1,357

DEANS

Faculty of Medicine: Dr M. ROGHANY
Faculty of Nursing and Midwifery: M. RAHIMY
Broujen Faculty of Nursing: S. BANAEYAN

SHARIF UNIVERSITY OF TECHNOLOGY

POB 11365-8639, Tehran
Telephone: (21) 66005419
Fax: (21) 66012983
E-mail: scientia@sharif.edu
Internet: www.sharif.edu

Founded 1965 as Aryamehr University, present name 1979
State control
Languages of instruction: Farsi, English
Academic year: September to May

Depts of aerospace engineering, chemical engineering and petroleum, chemistry, civil engineering, computer engineering, electrical engineering, industrial engineering, management and economics, materials science and engineering, mathematical sciences, mechanical engineering, philosophy of science, physics

Pres.: Prof. SAEED SOHRABPOUR
Vice-Pres. for Admin. and Finance: Prof. SEYED ALI AKBAR EKRAMI
Vice-Pres. for Education and Graduate Studies: Prof. ALI MEGHDARI
Vice-Pres. for Planning and Budget: ALI ASGHAR ESKANDAR BAYATI

Vice-Pres. for Research: Dr REZA ROOSTA AZAD
Vice-Pres. for Student Affairs: Dr BIJAN VOSOOGHI VAHDAT
Chair. of Office of Int. and Scientific Cooperation (OISC): Prof. ABOLHASSAN VAFAI
Dean of Assessment: ALI KARIMI TAHERI
Dean of Education: ABOL GHASEM DOLATI
Dean of Extra Curriculum: MOHAMMAD MIRZAI
Dean of Financial Affairs: MOHAMMAD FOROOTAN
Dean of Graduate Studies: AMIR DANESHGAR
Dean of Human Resources: HAMID REZA MADAAH HOSSEINI
Dean of Industrial Cooperation: SEYYED JAMALEDIN HASHEMIAN
Dean of Research Affairs: MASOUD TAJRISHI
Dean of Student Affairs: SEYED REZA NAGHINASAB
Librarian: Prof. HAMID MEHDIGHOLI

Library of 242,000 vols (130,000 in English, 12,000 in Farsi), 100,000 periodicals
Number of teachers: 300
Number of students: 8,000 , incl. 2,000 Masters and 400 PhD students

Publications: *Scientia Iranica* (6 a year, in English), *Sharif* (scientific and research, 4 a year, in Farsi).

ATTACHED RESEARCH CENTRES

Advanced Communications Research Institute: tel. (21) 6165910; fax (21) 6036002; e-mail acri@sharif.edu; internet acri.sharif.ir.

Advanced Information and Communication Technology Centre: internet www.aictc.com; Dir Dr HAMID REZA RABIEE.

Advanced Manufacturing Research Centre (AMRC): Dir MOJTABA TAHMOURES.

Centre of Excellence in Earthquake Engineering: Dir Prof. M. T. KAZEMI.

Centre of Excellence in Energy Conversion: Azadi St, Tehran; tel. (21) 66165549; fax (21) 66000021; internet sina.sharif.edu; languages of instruction: Farsi, English; Dir Dr S. K. HANNANI.

Electronics Research Centre: tel. (21) 66005517; fax (21) 66030318; e-mail erc@sina.sharif.edu; internet www.sharif-erc.com; Dir Prof. MAHMOUD TABIANI.

Institute for Nanoscience and Nanotechnology: tel. (21) 66164123; fax (21) 66164119; e-mail inst@sharif.edu; internet nano.sharif.ir; Dir Prof. AZAM IRAJI ZAD.

Institute for Transportation Studies and Research: Dir Dr HOSSEIN POURZAHEDI.

Sharif Applied Physics Research Centre: tel. (21) 616-4542; fax (21) 6602-2711; e-mail appliedphysics@mehr.sharif.edu; internet physics.sharif.edu/~appliedphysics; Dir Dr AHMAD AMJADI.

Sharif Energy Research Institute: Dir Dr YADDOLLAH SABOUHI.

Water Energy Research Centre: tel. (21) 66005118; fax (21) 66164651; e-mail torkian@sina.sharif.ac.ir; internet sharif.ir/~werc; Dir Dr AYOOB TORKIAN.

SHIRAZ UNIVERSITY

Jam-e-Jam Ave, Shiraz 71946-84636
Telephone: (71) 6286416
Fax: (71) 6286419
E-mail: sadeghi@shirazu.ac.ir
Internet: www.shirazu.ac.ir

Founded 1946 as Pahlavi University, present name 1979
State control
Languages of instruction: Farsi, English

Academic year: October to July (two semesters)

Chancellor: Dr MOHAMMAD HADI SADEGHI
Vice-Chancellor for Academic Affairs: Dr ABDOLHOSAIN JAHANMIRI
Vice-Chancellor for Admin. and Financial Affairs: Dr EBRAHIM HADIAN
Vice-Chancellor for Research Affairs: Dr GHOLAMHOSEIN ZAMANI
Vice-Chancellor for Student and Cultural Affairs: Dr MOHAMMAD MOAZZENI
Dir of Public Relations: MOJTABA TOOBAEI
Librarian: Dr ZAHIR HAYATI

Number of teachers: 573
Number of students: 12,446

Publications: *Iran Agricultural Research Journal of Social Sciences and Humanities*, *Iranian Journal of Science and Technology*

DEANS

School of Agriculture: Dr YAHYA EMAM
School of Arts and Architecture: Dr MAHYAR ARDSHIRI
School of Education and Psychology: Dr MOHSEN KHADEMI
School of Engineering: Dr SEYYED SHAHABEDIN AYATOLAHI
School of Law: Dr PARVIZ AMERI
School of Literature and Human Sciences: Dr ABDULMAHDI RIAZI
School of Science: Dr NOZAR SAMANI
School of Veterinary Medicine: Dr SEYYED SHAHRAM SHEKARFOROUSH
Junior Agricultural College, Darab: SAMAD ERFANIFAR
Teacher Training College, Kazeroon: SEYYED MOHTASHAM MOHAMMADI

UNIVERSITY OF SISTAN AND BALUCHISTAN

POB 98135-987, Zahedan
Telephone: (541) 2445981
Fax: (541) 2446771
Internet: www.usb.ac.ir

Founded 1974
State control
Language of instruction: Farsi
Academic year: September to July (two semesters)

Chancellor: Dr A. AKBARI
Vice-Chancellor for Academic Affairs: M. H. SANGTARASH
Vice-Chancellor for Admin. and Finance: Dr AMIN REZA KAMALYAN
Vice-Chancellor for Research: Dr RAHBAR RAHIMI
Vice-Chancellor for Student Affairs: Dr A. A. MORYDI FARIMANI
Registrar: Dr ABDOLLAH WASIGH ABBASI
Dir of Central Library: Dr RAHMATOLLAH LASHKARIPOUR

Number of teachers: 300
Number of students: 12,000

Publications: *Applied Engineering* (in Farsi, 2 a year), *Divine and Law* (in Farsi, 2 a year), *Geography & Development* (in Farsi, 2 a year), *History and Archaeology* (in Farsi, 2 a year), *Iranian Journal of Fuzzy System* (2 a year), *Journal of Engineering and Science* (in Farsi, 2 a year), *Journal of Humanities* (in Farsi, 4 a year), *Persian Language and Literature* (in Farsi, 2 a year), *Train Science and Psychology* (in Farsi, 2 a year)

DEANS

College of Humanities (Iranshar): Eng. AZARAG
College of Humanities (Zahedan): Dr A. A. AHANGAR
Engineering College: Dr S. FARAHAT
Fine Arts College: Dr M. MEHRAN

Science College: Dr A. A. MIRZAIE

PROFESSORS

AKBARI, A., Agricultural Economics
ATASHI, H., Chemical Engineering
AZIMI, P., Mathematics
ESHGI, H., Chemistry
KHOSHNOODI, M., Chemical Engineering
LASHKARIPOUR, G. R., Geology
MANSORI-TORSHIZI, H. M., Chemistry
NOORA, A. A., Mathematics
RAHIMI, R., Chemical Engineering
REZVANI, A. R., Chemistry
SARDASHTI, A. R., Chemistry
SHARIATI, H., Mathematics
TORMANZAHI, A., Agriculture
VALIZADEH, J., Agriculture
YAZDANI, B.-O., Humanities

TABRIZ UNIVERSITY OF MEDICAL SCIENCES

Golgasht Ave, Tabriz
Telephone: (411) 3347345
Fax: (411) 3347345
E-mail: iro@tbzmed.ac.ir
Internet: www.tbzmed.ac.ir
Founded 1985, fmrly part of University of Tabriz
State control
Languages of instruction: Farsi, English
Academic year: October to July
Chancellor: Dr A. R. JODATI
Vice-Chancellor for Admin. and Finance: Dr A. JAVAD ZADEH
Vice-Chancellor for Education: Dr J. HANAEE
Vice-Chancellor for Food and Medicines: Dr A. GARJANI
Vice-Chancellor for Health Services: Dr A. R. NIKNIAZ
Vice-Chancellor for Research: Dr RASHIDI
Vice-Chancellor for Student Affairs: Dr A. A. TAHER AGDAM
Vice-Chancellor for Treatment: Dr M. KHOSH-BATEN
Registrar: Dr M. VARSCHOCHI
Librarian: Mrs MASOOMI
Number of teachers: 500
Number of students: 4,664
Publications: *Journal of Basic Science in Medicine, Journal of Nursing and Obstetrics, Medical Journal, Pharmaceutical Science, Research Journal*

DEANS

Faculty of Dentistry: Dr J. YAZDANI
Faculty of Medical Rehabilitation Science: Dr R. KHANDAGI
Faculty of Medicine: Dr M. BARZEGAR
Faculty of Nursing and Obstetrics: Dr Z. MAYABI
Faculty of Paramedical Sciences: Dr A. RAFI
Faculty of Pharmacy: Dr M. H. ZARRINTAN
Faculty of Public Health and Nutrition: Dr M. R. SIYAHI

ATTACHED RESEARCH CENTRES

Biotechnology Research Center: tel. (411) 3364038; fax (411) 3379420; e-mail brc .info@tbzmed.ac.ir; internet www.tbzmed.ac .ir/biotechnology; Dir Prof. SIAVOUSH DAST-MALCHI.

Haematology Oncology Research Center: tel. (411) 3343811; fax (411) 3343844; e-mail irajkermani@hotmail.com; internet horc.tbzmed.ac.ir; Dir Dr IRAJ ASVADI KER-MANI.

Research Centre for Pharmaceutical Nanotechnology: tel. (411) 3367914; fax (411) 3367929; e-mail yomidi@tbzmed.ac.ir; internet nano.tbzmed.ac.ir; Dir Dr YADOLLAH OMIDI.

Tuberculosis and Lung Disease Center: tel. (411) 3364901; fax (411) 3364901; e-mail

ansarink@tbzmed.ac.ir; internet www .tbzmed.ac.ir/tlrc; Dir Dr KHALIL ANSARIN.

UNIVERSITY OF TABRIZ

29th Bahman Blvd, Tabriz 51666-14766
Telephone: (411) 3355994
Fax: (411) 3344272
E-mail: international@tabrizu.ac.ir
Internet: www.tabrizu.ac.ir
Founded 1946, fmrly Univ. of Azarabadegan
State control
Language of instruction: Farsi
Academic year: September to June (two semesters)
Chancellor: Prof. S. M. T. ALAVI
Vice-Chancellor for Academic and Post-Graduate Studies: Dr H. R. GHASSEMZADEH
Vice-Chancellor for Finance and Admin. Affairs: Dr M. T. ALAMI
Vice-Chancellor for Cultural Affairs: Dr R. IZADI
Vice-Chancellor for Research Affairs: Prof. A. ROSTAMI
Vice-Chancellor for Student Affairs: Dr H. NAVID
Registrar: Dr A. HOSSEINZADEH DALIR
Dir of Int. Academic Collaboration: Dr A. MOHAMMAD KHORSHIDDOUST
Librarian: Dr M. MAHDIPOUR
Library of 85,751 vols
Number of teachers: 528
Number of students: 14,482
Publications: *Journal of Agricultural Sciences* (4 a year), *Journal of English Language Teaching and Learning* (2 a year), *Journal of the Faculty of Engineering* (4 a year), *Journal of the Faculty of Humanities and Social Sciences* (4 a year), *Pazhoohesh* (Record of University Research Activities, 2 a year)

DEANS

Ahar College of Agriculture: Prof. A. BABAI-AHARI
Faculty of Agriculture: Dr A. BABAEI-AHARI
Faculty of Chemistry: Dr M. GH. HOSSEINI
Faculty of Civil Engineering: Prof A. HADIDI
Faculty of Education and Psychology: Dr M BEIRAMI
Faculty of Electrical and Computer Engineering: Dr Z. DAEI KOOZEHKONANI
Faculty of Humanities and Social Sciences: Dr M. R. NIKJOU
Faculty of Mathematical Sciences: Dr H. EMAMALIPOUR
Faculty of Mechanical Engineering: Dr M. T. SHERVANI-TABAR
Faculty of Natural Sciences: Dr M. MOAYYED
Faculty of Persian Literature and Foreign Languages: Dr F. FARROKHI
Faculty of Physics: Dr S. ASHRAFI
Faculty of Theology and Islamic Sciences: Dr N. FOROUHI
Marand Faculty of Engineering: Dr R. JOMEIRI
Research Institute for Applied Physics and Astronomy: Dr M. SAHRAI BARENJI
School of Engineering Emerging Technologies: Prof. A. ROSTAMI

PROFESSORS

Faculty of Agriculture (tel. (411) 3341316; fax (411) 3345332; e-mail agri-dean@tabrizu .ac.ir):

MASSIHA, S., Horticulture
MOGHADDAM-VAHED, M., Plant Breeding
PEYGHAMIE, E., Plant Pathology
RAHIMZADEH KHOEI, F., Agronomy
VALIZADEH, M., Genetics and Breeding

Faculty of Chemistry (tel. (411) 3355998; fax (411) 3340191; e-mail chemfac@tabrizu.ac .ir):

BLOURCHIAN, S. M., Organosilicon Chemistry
DJOZAN, DJ., Analytical Chemistry
ENTEZAMI, A. A., Polymer Chemistry
GOLABI, S. M., Electroanalytical Chemistry
MANZOORI, J., Analytical Chemistry, Spectroscopy
POURNAGHI AZAR, M. H., Electroanalytical Chemistry
SOROURADDIN ABADI, M. H., Analytical Chemistry
ZAFARANI-MOATTAR, M. T., Physical Chemistry

Faculty of Education and Psychology (tel. (411) 3341133; fax (411) 3356009):

HOSSEINI-NASAB, D., Training Psychology

Faculty of Engineering (tel. (411) 3356022; fax (411) 3346287; e-mail joeng@tabrizu.ac .ir):

BEHRAVESH, A., Structural Engineering
DILMAGHANI, S., Civil Engineering
HASANZADEH, Y., Heat and Fluid Transfer Engineering
HOSSEINI, S. H., Power Electronics
KEYANVASH, A., Metallurgy
KHANMOHAMMADI, S., Automatic Engineering
KHOSHRAVAN-AZAR, M. E., Heat Transfer Engineering
PIROUZ-PANAH, V., Internal Combustion Engines

Faculty of Humanities and Social Sciences (tel. (411) 3344286; fax (411) 3356013):

BANIFATEMEH, H., Social Sciences
ESFAHANIYAN, D., History
HARIRI-AKBARI, M., Political Sociology
RAJAEI ASL, A. H., Physical Geography

Faculty of Mathematics (tel. (411) 3356032; fax (411) 3344015):

MEHRVARZ, A. A., Algebra
N-DEHGAN, Y., Mathematical Analysis
SHAHABI, M. A., Mathematics
TOOMANIAN, A., Differential Geometry

Faculty of Natural Sciences (tel. (411) 3356027; fax (411) 3341244):

HOSSEINPOUR FEIZI, M. A., Radiobiology

Faculty of Persian Literature and Foreign Languages (tel. (411) 3341150; fax (411) 3356017):

BAGHERI, M., Culture and Ancient Languages
EJLALI, A. P., Persian Language and Literature
IRANDOOST, R., French Language and Literature
LOTFIPOUR SAEDI, K., Applied Linguistics
NAVALI, M., Philosophy
SARKARATI, B., Ancient Iranian Languages

Faculty of Physics (tel. (411) 3356030; fax (411) 3341244):

BIDADI, H., Solid-state Physics
JAFARIZADEH, M., Physics of Elementary Particles
KALAFI, M., Solid-state Physics
MOHAMMAD-ZADEH JASSUR, D., Atomic Physics
SOBHANIAN, S., Atomic Physics, Plasma
TAJALLI SAIFI, H., Atomic Physics, Lasers

ATTACHED COLLEGES

College of Engineering (Bonab Campus): Dir M. R. A. PARSA.

College of Engineering (Marand Campus): Dir S. HOSSEINI.

College of Veterinary Medicine: Dir Dr H. KARIMIE.

TARBIAT MODARRES UNIVERSITY

POB 14155-4838, Intersection of Chamran and Ale-Ahmad Highways, Tehran
Telephone: (21) 8011001
Fax: (21) 8006544
E-mail: intl@modares.ac.ir
Internet: www.modares.ac.ir
Founded 1982
Academic year: September to June
Pres.: Dr FARHAD DANESHJOO
Vice-Pres. for Academic Affairs: Dr M. T. AHMADY
Vice-Pres. for Admin. and Financial Affairs: Dr H. BAHRAMI
Vice-Pres. for Research: Dr M. F. MOUSAVI
Vice-Pres. for Student Affairs: Dr A. MALEKI MOGHADDAM
Librarian: Dr AHMAD ZAVARAN HOSEINI
Library of 80,000 vols, 2,552 periodicals
Number of teachers: 433
Number of students: 3,595

DEANS

Faculty of Agriculture: Dr T. TAVAKOLI
Faculty of Arts: Dr M. R. POORJAAFAR
Faculty of Basic Medical Sciences: Dr M. RASAEE
Faculty of Basic Sciences: Dr H. NADERIMA-NESH
Faculty of Engineering: Dr SHOJAOSSADATI
Faculty of Humanities: Dr S. AYEENEVAND
Faculty of Natural Resources and Marine Sciences: Dr SAHARI

TEHRAN UNIVERSITY OF MEDICAL SCIENCES AND HEALTH SERVICES

23 Dameshgh Ave, Vali-e-Asr St, Tehran 14155-14167
Telephone: (21) 8896692
Fax: (21) 8898532
E-mail: iro@sina.tums.ac.ir
Internet: www.tums.ac.ir
Founded 1935 following devolution of medical schools from the University of Tehran and merger with other Tehran-based medical institutions
Chancellor: Dr BAGHER LARIJANI
Vice-Chancellor for Research: Dr AKBAR FOTOUHI
Number of teachers: 1,300
Number of students: 13,000
Publications: *Acta Medica* (4 a year), *Daru* (4 a year), *Journal of Dentistry* (4 a year)
Schools of Advanced Medical Technologies, Allied Medical Services, Dentistry, Medicine, Nursing and Midwifery, Pharmacy, Public Health, Rehabilitation
Research centres: science and technology in medicine, rheumatology, auditory, digestive diseases, skin diseases and leprosy, trauma, haematology and oncology, cardiovascular diseases, endocrinology and metabolism, reproductive health, urology, immunology, asthma and allergies, ethics and medical history, cancer, addiction, bank of transplantation products of Iran; 11 Educational and Health Research Centres in 10 provinces, 15 teaching hospitals; 40 br. libraries and one digital library with access to more than 5,000 full-text medical journals.

UNIVERSITY OF TEHRAN

Enghelab Ave, Tehran 14174
Telephone: (21) 61113358
Fax: (21) 6409348
E-mail: international@ut.ac.ir
Internet: www.ut.ac.ir
Founded 1934

Language of instruction: Farsi
Academic year: September to July (2 semesters)
Pres.: Dr FARHAD RAHBAR
Vice-Pres. for Academic Affairs: Dr S. M. GHAMSARI
Vice-Pres. for Admin.: Dr S. M. MOGHIMI
Vice-Pres. for Int. Affairs: Dr S. MOHAMMAD ALI MOUSAVI
Vice-Pres. for Planning: Dr S. R. AMELI
Vice-Pres. for Research and Technology: Dr M. JAFARI
Vice-Pres. for Student and Cultural Affairs: Dr M. GHAMSARI
Univ. Librarian: Dr F. FAHIMNIA
Library: see Libraries and Archives
Number of teachers: 2,359
Number of students: 38,445

DEANS

College of Agriculture and Natural Resource: Dr M. HOSSEIN OMID
College of Engineering: Dr MAHMOOD KAMAR-EIEE
College of Fine Arts: Dr M. AZIZI
Faculty of Economics: Dr MANSOOR KHALILI ARAGHI
Faculty of Geography: Dr POOR AHMAD
Faculty of Law and Political Science: Dr S. FAZELLOLLAH MOOSAVI
Faculty of Literature and Foreign Languages: Dr S. FARIDE ALAVI
Faculty of Literature and Humanities: Dr KARIMI DOOSTAN
Faculty of Management and Business Administration: Dr S. REZA S. JAVADIN
Faculty of Physical Education: Dr GOODARZI
Faculty of Psychology and Educational Science: Dr G. ALI AFROOZ
Faculty of Science: Dr ALI MAGHARI
Faculty of Social Science: Dr G. REZA GAMSHIDIHA
Faculty of Theology and Islamic Studies: Dr S. M. REZA EMAM
Faculty of Veterinary Medicine: Dr PARVIZ TAJIK
Graduate Faculty of Environmental: Dr G. REZA NABI BIDHENDI

URMIA UNIVERSITY

POB 165, Urmia 57153
Telephone: (441) 3448131
Fax: (441) 3443443
E-mail: chancellor@urmia.ac.ir
Internet: www.urmia.ac.ir
Founded 1965
Academic year: September to July
Chancellor: Dr GOUDARZ SADEGHI-HASHJIN
Vice-Chancellor for Devt: Dr ESFANDYAR MARDANI
Vice-Chancellor for Education: Dr ESMAIL AYAN
Vice-Chancellor for Personnel and Finance: GHOLAMREZA MANSOORFAR
Vice-Chancellor for Research: Dr MOHAMMAD MEHDI BARADARANI
Vice-Chancellor for Student Affairs: Dr MAHMOOD RAZAZADEH
Registrar: Dr ALIREZA MOZAFFARI
Librarians: Dr FARHAD FARROKHI ARDEBILI, MOHAMMADREZA FARHADPOOR
Library of 58,000 vols
Number of teachers: 284
Number of students: 8,431
Publications: *Neda* (12 a year), *Pajoohesh-garan* (4 a year)

DEANS

Faculty of Agriculture: Dr ASGHAR KHOSROW-SHAHI

Faculty of Engineering: Dr IRAJ MIRZAEE
Faculty of Literature and Humanities: Dr ABDOLLAH TOLOEE-AZAR
Faculty of Science: Prof. M. NOJAVAN ASHGARI
Faculty of Veterinary Medicine: Dr B. DALIR NAGHADEH

YAZD UNIVERSITY

POB 89195-741, Yazd
Telephone: (351) 8211827
Fax: (351) 8211829
E-mail: president-office@yazduni.ac.ir
Internet: www.yazduni.ac.ir
Founded 1988
State control
Languages of instruction: Farsi, English
Academic year: September to June
Pres.: Dr SEYYED ALI MOHAMMAD MIRMOHAM-MADI MEYBODI
Vice-Pres. for Education: Dr AHMAD SOHAN-KAR ESFAHANI
Vice-Pres. for Finance and Admin.: Dr FAZLOLLAH ADIBNIYA
Vice-Pres. for Research: Dr MOHAMMAD HAS-SAN KHADEMI
Vice-Pres. for Student Affairs: Dr MOHAMMAD ALI AMROLLAHI
Registrar: Dr ALI AKBAR DEHGHAN
Librarian: TAHMASEBI MOHAMMAD
Library of 201,470 vols (incl. Farsi and Latin vols)
Number of teachers: 330
Number of students: 10,100
Publications: *Bulletin*, *Kavoshnameh* (humanities research, 2 a year)

DEANS

Faculty of Art and Architecture: Dr K. MANDEGARI
Faculty of Engineering: Dr K. BARKHORDARI
Faculty of Humanities: Dr M. MALEKSABET
Faculty of Natural Resources and Desert Studies: Dr M. TAGHI DASTOORANI
Faculty of Science: Dr M. REZA NOORBALA

RESEARCH CENTRES

Desert and Dryland Research Institute: tel. (351) 8211670; fax (351) 82110317; e-mail ddri@yazduni.ac.ir; f. 1998.

Engineering and Applied Science Research Center: tel. (351) 8211670; fax (351) 8210699; e-mail easr@yazduni.ac.ir.

Colleges

There are c. 50 colleges of higher education in Iran, and c. 40 technological institutes, of which the following are a selection only.

College of Surveying: POB 1844, Azadi Sq., Tehran; f. 1965; national training centre for surveyors; 80 students; affiliated to National Cartographic Centre; Dir Dr H. NAHAVANDCHI.

Iran Banking Institute: POB 19395-4814, 207 Pasdaran Ave, Tehran; tel. (21) 2848000; fax (21) 2842618; internet www.ibi.ac.ir; f. 1963; 4-year BA degree courses in Banking, Accounting and Computer Science, and MA degree courses in Banking, Accounting and Law; library: 24,000 vols; 2,450 students; Chancellor Dr MEHDI EMRANI.

Military Academy: Sepah Ave, Tehran; depts of general engineering science, international relations and treaties, military armaments, military history, military science and tactics, nuclear warfare, physics and electronics.

IRAQ

The Higher Education System

The University of Baghdad (founded 1957) is the oldest university in Iraq. As a result of increasing petroleum revenues in the 1970s, the higher education sector expanded significantly, and in addition to the universities a large number of technical institutes were established. However, during the 1980s and 1990s higher education was affected by economic privations caused by war with Iran (1980–88) and sanctions imposed by the international community following Iraq's invasion of Kuwait in 1990 and defeat by a US-led coalition in 1991. In March–April 2003 another US-led coalition invaded Iraq, captured Baghdad and toppled the Baathist regime of Saddam Hussein. Since 2003 higher education has been subject to reform, including the establishment of new universities; however, many academics have been killed, moved abroad or taken permanent leave of absence, student numbers have fallen, and in some areas Islamist groups have imposed segregated classes or forced female students to adopt Islamic forms of dress. The Ministry of Higher Education and Scientific Research oversees the administration of the 20 public universities and other colleges and technical institutes. In 2002/03 there were approximately 240,000 undergraduates attending 65 institutions of higher education; however, it was reported in 2006 that a growing number of students were failing to attend school or university as a result of the worsening security situation in many parts of the country.

Students must complete secondary education to be admitted to public universities. Each year the Ministry of Higher Education and Scientific Research determines entry requirements, which vary from programme to programme. The main undergraduate degree is the Bachelors, which lasts four years, although longer periods of study are required for pharmacy, architecture, dentistry, veterinary medicine (all five years) and medicine (six years). The first postgraduate degree is the Masters, lasting two to three years and incorporating both taught and research elements. The final university degree is the Doctor of Philosophy, which also includes both taught and research elements, with students required to pass examinations based on classroom-based work before proceeding to the research element.

Technical and vocational education is dominated by technical colleges and institutes, most of which were founded during the 1970s. The Commission for Technical Education is the government body responsible for administering these institutions and technical degrees and diplomas. The Technician Diploma is a two-year course offered by technical institutes, of which there were 37 in 2004. (Some technical institutes are directly affiliated to government ministries, depending on the area of specialization.) Holders of the Technician Diploma can gain direct entry to the second year of the four-year Bachelor of Technology programme, offered by technical colleges. The majority of these courses are in the fields of engineering and medicine. Following the Bachelor of Technology, technical colleges offer a two-year Higher Diploma of Technology, mainly in engineering disciplines. The Master of Technology is similar to the Higher Diploma of Technology, but contains a greater element of research.

During the US-led military campaign to oust the regime of Saddam Hussein in early 2003, and in the subsequent period of social unrest, damage and looting were reported at a number of Iraq's public institutions.

Regulatory Bodies

GOVERNMENT

Ministry of Culture: POB 624, Qaba bin Nafi Sq., Sadoun St, Baghdad; tel. (1) 5383171; Minister SAADOUN AL-DULAIMI.

Ministry of Education: Saad State Enterprises Bldg, nr the Convention Centre, Baghdad; tel. (1) 8832571; Min. MUHAMMAD TAMIM.

Ministry of Higher Education and Scientific Research: Baghdad; tel. (1) 2806315; e-mail ministry@moheiraq.org; internet www.moheiraq.org; Minister ALI AL-ADIB.

Learned Societies

EDUCATION

Arab Literacy and Adult Education Organization (ARLO): POB 3217, 113 Abu Nawas St, Baghdad; tel. 7186246; f. 1966 by ALECSO to promote co-operation in all aspects of literacy and adult education between the Arab states; all Arab states are mems; library of 14,700 vols; Dir HASHIM ABU ZEID EL-SAFI (acting); publ. *The Education of the Masses* (2 a year).

FINE AND PERFORMING ARTS

Iraqi Artists' Society: Damascus St, Baghdad; f. 1956; exhibitions and occasional publs; Pres. NOORI AL-RAWI; Sec. AMER ALU-BIDI.

LANGUAGE AND LITERATURE

British Council: 10 Spring Gardens, London, SW1A 2BN, United Kingdom; tel. (161) 957-7755; fax (161) 957-7762; e-mail iraq@britishcouncil.org; internet www.britishcouncil.org/iraq; f. 1940; offers courses and exams in English language and promotes cultural exchange with the UK; based in London until further notice; Chief Exec. MARTIN DAVIDSON.

Iraqi Academy: Waziriya, Baghdad; tel. (1) 4224202; fax (1) 4222066; e-mail iraqacademy@yahoo.com; internet www.iraqacademy.org; f. 1947 with the aims of maintaining the Arabic language and heritage, supporting research in Arabic and Muslim history, the history of Iraq and Arabic language and heritage, maintaining Kurdish and Assyrian languages; 37 mems; Pres. Prof. Dr AHMED MATLOUB; publ. *Majallat al-Mejmah al-Ilmi* (literary, 4 a year).

MEDICINE

International Iraqi Medical Association: e-mail adilmahd@emirates.net.ae; internet www.iimaonline.net; NGO supporting Iraqi physicians at home and abroad; annual conf.; Pres. Dr ALI HARJAN; Dir of Public Relations Dr ADIL AL-MANSOURI; publ. *Journal.*

Iraqi Medical Association: Maari St, al-Mansoor, Baghdad; tel. (1) 5374209; fax (1) 5372193; e-mail nfo@ima-iq.org; internet www.ima-iq.org; f. 1920; Pres. Prof. Dr NADHIM A. KASIM; publ. *Iraqi Medical Journal* (2 a year, in Arabic and English).

NATURAL SCIENCES

General

Federation of Arab Scientific Research Councils: POB 13027, Baghdad; tel. (1) 8881709; fax (1) 8867511; f. 1976; strengthens collaboration among scientific research ccls, instns, centres and univs in all Arab states; plans jt research projects among Arab states, especially those related to Arab devt plans; 15 mem. states; library of 800 vols, 600 periodicals, 1,100,000 patent documents from USA, EPO, WIPO; Sec.-Gen. Prof. Dr TAHA T. AL-NAIMI; publs *Federation News, Journal of Computer Research.*

Research Institutes

GENERAL

Scientific Research Council: POB 2441, Jadiriya, Baghdad; f. 1963; Pres. Dr NAJIH M. KHALIL.

Attached Research Centres:

Agriculture and Water Resources Research Centre: Fudhailiyah; Dir Dr SAMIR A. AL-SHAKER.

Biological Research Centre: Jadiriya; Dir Dr AZWAR N. KHALAF.

Building Research Centre: Jadiriya; Dir Dr M. AL-IZZI.

Educational Studies and Psychological Research Center: Jadiriya; tel. 7785162; e-mail psychocenter@hotmail.com; internet www.psychocenteriraq.com;

f. 1986; library of 3,358 vols; Dir Dr GHASSAN H. SALIM; publ. *Psychological Sciences*.

Electronics and Computer Research Centre: Jadiriya; Dir Dr M. N. BEKIR.

Genetic Engineering and Biotechnology Research Centre: Jadiriya; Dir Dr FARUQ YASS AL-ANI.

Petroleum Research Centre: Jadiriya; Dir Dr A. H. A. K. MOHAMMED.

Scientific Affairs Office: Jadiriya; Dir Dr RADHWAM K. A. HALIM.

Scientific Documentation Centre: Jadiriya; library: see under Libraries.

Solar Energy Research Centre: Jadiriya; Dir N. I. AL-HAMDANY.

Space Research Centre: Jadiriya; Dir Dr ALI AL-MASHAT.

AGRICULTURE, FISHERIES AND VETERINARY SCIENCE

Agriculture and Water Resources Research Centre: POB 2416, Karada al-Sharkiya, Baghdad; tel. (1) 7512080; f. 1980 to carry out research to improve and develop water and agricultural resources; 75 researchers; library of 6,000 vols, 450 periodicals; Dir-Gen. Dr SAMIR A. H. AL-SHAKIR; publ. *Journal of Agriculture and Water Resources Research*.

EDUCATION

Centre for Educational and Psychological Research: Univ. of Baghdad, 9 Waziriya, Baghdad; e-mail edu-psychological@uob.edu.iq; f. 1966; educational and psychological research studies to make education an effective power for the acceleration of economic and social devt; library of 6,000 vols; Dir Dr MOHAMMED ALI KHALAF; publ. *Journal of Educational Psychological Research* (2 a year).

HISTORY, GEOGRAPHY AND ARCHAEOLOGY

British Institute for the Study of Iraq: 10 Carlton House Terrace, London, SW1Y 5AH, United Kingdom; tel. (20) 7969-5274; fax (20) 7969-5401; e-mail bisi@britac.ac.uk; internet www.bisi.ac.uk; f. 1932 as the British School of Archaeology; present name 2007; promotes, supports and undertakes research in Iraq and neighbouring countries; covers the subjects of archaeology, history, anthropology, geography, language and other related domains from earliest times to the present; grants are available for research; 800 mems; library: the library is currently housed by the British embassy in Baghdad, the number of vols is unknown; Chair. Prof. ROGER MATTHEWS; Vice-Chair. Dr HARRIET CRAWFORD; publs *Iraq* (1 a year), *The International Journal of Contemporary Iraqi Studies* (3 a year).

PHILOSOPHY AND PSYCHOLOGY

Psychological Research Center: Univ. of Baghdad Complex, Jaderiyah, Baghdad; tel. (1) 7786678; fax (1) 7785162; e-mail psychocenter@hotmail.com; internet www.psychocenteriraq.com; psychological and parapsychological research and training; library of 3,070 vols (1,992 Arabic, 1,078 English); publs *Journal of Psyche and Life* (6 a year, incl. section in English), *Journal of Psychological Sciences* (4 a year, in Arabic and English), *Psychological Health* (4 a year, in Arabic).

TECHNOLOGY

Department of Scientific and Industrial Research: Directorate-General of Industry, Baghdad; f. 1935; staff 42; Dir-Gen. of Industry SHEETH NA'AMANN; publ. *Technical Bulletin*.

Nuclear Research Centre: Tuwaitha, Baghdad; f. 1967; fmr main establishment of Iraq Atomic Energy Commission, now under control of International Atomic Energy Agency; administrative responsibility assumed by the Iraqi Ministry of Science and Technology.

Libraries and Archives

Arbil

University of Salahaddin Central Library: Kirkuk St, Arbil; tel. (66) 2260089; e-mail library@usalah.org; f. 1968; 263,705 vols, 530 current periodicals; Dir Dr MOHAMMAD MUSTAFA.

Baghdad

Al-Awqaf Central Library (Ministry of Endowments and Religious Affairs Central Library): POB 14146, Baghdad; f. 1928; library building looted and burnt down April 2003; library staff were able to preserve approx. 5,250 of the total collection of 7,000 MSS; Contact HASAN FREIH; publ. *Al-Rissala-al-Islamiya*.

Al-Mustansiriya University Library: POB 14022, Waziriya, Baghdad; e-mail library@uomustansiriyah.edu.iq; f. 1963; 311,800 vols, 30,000 vols of periodicals, 330 rolls of film, 280 current periodicals; also 11 college libraries with 33,000 vols, 850 periodicals; part of the colln was looted 2003; Dir FAISAL ANWAN AL-TAEE.

Arab Gulf States Information and Documentation Center: POB 5063, Baghdad; tel. (1) 5433914; f. 1981; affiliated to the Board of Ministers of Information of the Arab Gulf States; aims to gather information from many sources, and to systematize, analyse and exchange it; supports the basic structure of existing information services; seven mem. states; provides a consultancy service; databases, microfilms; specialized library of 8,000 vols; Dir-Gen. HAYFA A. JAJAWI.

Educational Documentation Library: Ministry of Education, Educational Campus, Baghdad; tel. (1) 8860000-2178; f. 1921; 37,000 vols, 73 periodicals; Librarian Dr KADHIM G. AL-KHAZRAJI.

Ibn Hayyan Information House: Iraqi Atomic Energy Commission, POB 765, Tuwaitha, Baghdad; up-to-date references, reports, pamphlets, microcards, magazines and film reels; Dir ISAM ATTA AJAJ.

Iraqi Academy Library: Waziriya, Baghdad; f. 1947; 60,000 vols, 32 original MSS, 1,600 copied MSS, 1,500 microfilms; Librarian SABAH NOAH.

Iraqi Museum Library: Salhiya Quarter, Baghdad West; tel. (1) 8840876; f. 1934; archaeology, history of civilization, art, architecture, cultural heritage; evacuation of colln undertaken before the US-led military intervention of 2003, currently in storage; 229,000 vols, 34,000 MSS; Dir ZAINAT AL-SAMAKRI; publ. *Al-Maskukat*.

National Archives of Iraq: POB 594, Baghdad; f. 1964; attached to the Min. of Culture; bldg looted and burnt down April 2003; colln subsequently subject to flooding and is currently frozen to prevent deterioration.

National Library: POB 594, Baghdad; tel. (1) 4164190; f. 1961; building looted and burnt down April 2003; 500,000 vols destroyed in fire; some holdings were subsequently subject to flooding and are currently frozen to prevent deterioration; legal deposit centre and national bibliographic centre; Dir-Gen. SAAD ESKANDER.

Scientific Documentation Centre: Abu Nuas Rd, POB 2441, Baghdad; tel. (1) 7760023; f. 1972; scientific information services to researchers at the institutes/centres of the Scientific Research Council (q.v.), and to others working in Iraqi laboratories, incl. UNDP experts; seven libraries are being developed, each attached to a research centre of the Council, incl. the Central Science Library; in-service training for students of Library Science and Documentation and librarians; 20 staff mems; Dir Dr FAIK ABDUL S. RAZZAQ.

University of Baghdad Central Library: POB 47303, Jadiriya, Baghdad; e-mail maktaba.unive@yahoo.com; f. 1959; section in Al-Waziriya looted and some stock stolen April 2003; major reconstruction under way; govt and UN depository library; acts as Exchange and governmental Bibliographical Centre; publ. *Current Contents of Iraqi Universities' Journals* (temporarily ceased publication).

Basrah

University of Basrah Central Library: Basrah; f. 1964; 200,000 vols, 700 MSS, 1,400 current periodicals; Librarian Dr TARIK AL-MANASSIR; publ. catalogue (irregular).

Mosul

University of Mosul Central Library: Mosul; tel. 810162; fax 814765; f. 1967; looted April 2003, although its collns were left intact; 24 br. libraries; 140,000 vols, 3,500 periodicals, depository of UN and Iraqi govt publs; Dir MAHMUD JIRJIS; publs *Adab Al-Rafidarn* (irregular), *Al-Rafidain Engineering* (irregular), *Annals of the College of Medicine-Mosul* (irregular), *Catalogue* (1 a year), *Iraqi Journal of Veterinary Sciences* (irregular), *Journal of Education and Science* (irregular), *Journal of Rafidain Development* (irregular), *Mesopotamia Journal of Agriculture* (irregular), *Research Work of University Faculty Members* (1 a year).

Museums and Art Galleries

Arbil

Arbil Museum: Arbil; tel. (66) 522273; objects from Iraqi history up to Arabic-Islamic period.

Babylon

Babylon Museum: Babylon; f. 1949; contains models, pictures and paintings of the remains at Babylon; the museum is situated among the ruins.

Baghdad

Abbasid Palace Museum: Baghdad; tel. (1) 4164950; a restored palace dating back to the late Caliphs of the Abbasid dynasty (13th century AD); an exhibition of Arab antiquities and scale models of important Islamic monumental buildings in Iraq. Opened as a Museum in 1935.

Baghdad Museum: Sahat al Risafi, Baghdad; tel. (1) 4165317; f. 1970; museum of folklore and costumes, natural history; photographic exhibition on history of Baghdad; Memorial Exhibition, containing the royal relics of King Faisal I; picture gallery; Dir ALAE AL-SHIBLI.

Iraq Military Museum: A'dhamiya, Baghdad; f. 1974 by merger of Arms Museum (f. 1940) and Museum of War (f. 1966); contains old Arabian weapons, Othmanic fire-arms and contemporary Iraqi weapons.

Iraq National Museum: Salhiya quarter, Baghdad West; internet www .theiraqmuseum.org; f. 1923; looted April 2003, resulting in theft or destruction of approx. 15,000 items; closed until Feb. 2009 when it was re opened to select groups; colln incl. antiquities dating from the early Stone Age to the beginning of the 18th century AD, incl. large colln of Islamic objects; Al-Sarraf gallery contains Islamic coins; library: see Libraries; Dir AMIRA EIDAN; publs *Al-Maskukat* (2 a year), *Sumer* (1 a year).

Iraq Natural History Research Centre and Museum: Bab al Muadham, Baghdad; tel. (1) 4165790; f. 1946; attached to the University of Baghdad; incl. sections on zoology, botany and geology; research work in natural history; exhibitions of animals, plants, rocks and minerals pertaining to Iraq; organizes cultural, educational and scientific training programmes; library of 31,000 vols, 850 periodicals; Dir H.-A. ALI; publs *Bulletin of the Iraq Natural History Research Centre, Iraq Natural History Research Centre Publications* (series of scientific papers, in English (with Arabic summaries), dealing with the natural history of Iraq and neighbouring countries).

National Museum of Modern Art: Al-Nafoura Square, Bal Al-Sharqi, Baghdad; f. 1962; Supervisor AMER AL UBAIDI.

Basrah

Natural History Museum of the University of Basrah: Corniche St, POB 432, Basrah; tel. (40) 213494; f. 1971; study of flora and fauna of the marshes of South Iraq and the Arabian Gulf; sections on mammals, birds, reptiles and amphibia, and fishes; scientific collns in all sections accessible to specialists and exhibits open to public; Dir Dr KHALAF AL ROBAAE.

Mosul

Mosul Museum: Dawassa, Mosul; tel. (60) 2430; f. 1951; collns of Assyrian antiquities of the 9th and 8th centuries BC found at Nimrud, objects uncovered in the ruins of Hatra dating from the 2nd century BC to the 2nd century AD, agricultural tools and pottery vessels from 5000–4000 BC, photographs of excavated buildings at Tepe Gawra, maps of the Assyrian Empire, Nimrud and Hatra; Prehistoric and Islamic exhibits; assists in discovery and maintenance of several archaeological sites; library: c. 2,000 vols; Dir HAZIM A. AL HAMEED.

Nasiriya

Nasiriya Museum: Nasiriya; tel. (42) 233851; Sumerian and other archaeological objects found in Ur, Al-Abeed and Aridu; Dir ABDUL AMIR HAMDANI.

Samarra

Samarra Museum: Samarra; tel. (21) 722114; f. 1936; it is housed in one of the old city gates, and contains objects excavated in the ruins of ancient Samarra; also historic maps, writings, pictures.

Universities

UNIVERSITY OF AL ANBAR

Ramadi, al Anbar governorate
Telephone: (1) 8864814
Fax: (1) 8178849
E-mail: anb.unv@uruklink.net
Founded 1987
State control

Pres.: ABDUL HADI RAJEB HABEEB (acting)
Vice-Pres. for Admin. and Scientific Affairs: ABDUL MAJEED ABOUL HAMEED ALI AL ANNI (acting)
Number of teachers: 464

AL MUSTANSIRIYA UNIVERSITY

POB 14022, Waziriya, Baghdad
Telephone: (1) 4168501
Fax: (1) 4165521
E-mail: mustuni@uruklink.net
Founded 1963
State control
Languages of instruction: Arabic, English
Academic year: September to June
Pres.: Dr IHSAN K. AL KURSHY (acting)
Vice-Pres. for Admin.: ADEL H. AL BAGHDADI (acting)
Vice-Pres. for Scientific Affairs: Dr KANAN A. ABDUL RAZAK (acting)
Librarian: MAISOON A. AL OBIADY
Library: see Libraries
Number of teachers: 1,555
Number of students: 23,748

Publications: *Al Mustansiriya Journal of Science, Al Mustansiriya Literary Review, Journal of Administration and Economics, Journal of the College of Education, Journal of the College of Teachers, Journal of Dialah Education, Journal of Engineering and Pollution, Journal of the Founding Leader for National and Socialist Studies, Journal of Medical Research, Journal of Middle Eastern Studies*

DEANS

College of Administration and Economics: Dr ALI J. AL OBIADY
College of Arts: Dr MUHAMED O. AL SHEMARY
College of Dental Studies: Dr RAAD M. JADOA
College of Education: Dr SABAH A. ATTY
College of Engineering: Dr ALI M. AL ATHARY
College of Medicine: Dr MUHAMED H. AL WAN
College of Science: Asst Prof. KADUM H. AL MOSSAWI
College of Sports: Asst Prof. Dr SAMEER M. ALAWE

AL NAHRAIN UNIVERSITY

POB 64074, Jadiriyah, Baghdad
Telephone: (1) 7767810
Fax: (1) 7763592
E-mail: saduni@uruklink.net
Internet: www.alnahrain-university.org
Founded 1993 as Saddam Univ.; present name 2003
Pres.: MAHMOOD H. HAMMASH (acting)
Vice-Pres. for Admin.: FAYEK J. AL AZZAWI
Librarian: ZAINAB H. RASHID
Library of 65,963 vols
Number of teachers: 285
Number of students: 1,180

DEANS

College of Engineering: Dr MAZIN A. KADHIM
College of Law: Dr BASIM M. SALEH
College of Medicine: Dr MAHMOOD H. HAMASH
College of Political Sciences: Dr MAZIN I. AL RAMADANI
College of Science: Dr FALAH A. ATTAWI

UNIVERSITY OF AL QADISIYA

POB 88, Diwaniya, al Qadisiya governorate
Telephone: (36) 628066
Fax: (1) 8164160
E-mail: unv.qadisia@uruklink.net
Founded 1988
State control
Pres.: Dr MOHAMMAD H. AL JABIRI (acting)
Vice-Pres. for Admin.: D. HIKMAT (acting)

Library of 2,000 vols
Number of teachers: 407

UNIVERSITY OF AL TA'AMEEM

Baghdad Rd, Kirkuk, al Ta'ameem governorate
Telephone: 418531
E-mail: fqislam@uruklink.net
Founded 2003
State control
Pres.: KAMAK OTHMAN OMEAR (acting)
Vice-Pres. for Admin.: ABRAHIM ATEA SALIH (acting)
Vice-Pres. for Scientific Affairs: NAJAT QADIR OMEAR (acting)
Number of teachers: 60

UNIVERSITY OF BABYLON

POB 4, Hilla, Babylon
Telephone: (30) 246562
Fax: (30) 8851398
E-mail: unihead@babylon-uni.com
Internet: www.babylon-uni.com
Founded 1991
State control
Colleges of agriculture, art, basic education, dentistry, economics and administration, education, engineering, fine arts, law, materials engineering, medicine, nursing, physical education, science, veterinary science; Science College for Girls
Pres.: Prof. Dr NABEEL H. AL A'ARAGI (acting)
Vice-Pres. for Admin.: HAMDIA ABBAS (acting)
Vice-Pres. for Scientific Affairs: ABD-AMEER AL GANEMI (acting)
Number of teachers: 450

UNIVERSITY OF BAGHDAD

POB 17635, Jadiriya, Baghdad
Telephone: (1) 7787819
Fax: (1) 7763592
E-mail: info@univofbaghdad.com
Internet: www.univofbaghdad.org
Founded 1957
State control
Languages of instruction: Arabic, English
Academic year: September to June
Pres.: MOSA JAWAD AZIZ AL MOSAWE
Vice-Pres. for Admin.: Dr NIHAD M. ABDUL RAHMAN
Vice-Pres. for Scientific Affairs: Dr RIYADH AZIZ HADI
Registrar: Dr HUSEIN KUDHAIR ABDUL-HUSEIN
Librarian: Dr MAJID ABDUL-KAREEM
Library: see Libraries and Archives
Number of teachers: 3,517
Number of students: 85,000

Publications: *Ibn al Haitham Journal for Pure and Applied Sciences* (2 a year), *Iraqi Journal of Pharmaceutical Sciences* (4 a year), *Iraqi Journal of Science* (4 a yeary), *Iraqi Journal of Veterinary Medicine* (2 a year), *Iraqi Natural History Museum Bulletin* (4 a year), *Journal of Agricultural Sciences* (2 a year), *Journal of Legal Sciences* (4 a year), *Journal of Political Science* (4 a year), *Journal of Sports Education* (irregular), *Journal of the College of Administration and Economics* (4 a year), *Journal of the College of Dentistry* (irregular), *Journal of the College of Education for Women* (2 a year), *Journal of the College of Languages* (1 a year), *Journal of the College of Shari'a* (2 a year), *Journal of Engineering* (irregular), *Journal of the Faculty of Medicine* (4 a year), *Statistical Bulletin* (1 a year), *The Academic* (4 a year), *The Professor* (4 a year)

DEANS

College of Administration and Economics: Dr
   MUHAMMAD AL-MA'AMOORI
College of Agriculture: Dr HAMZA AL-ZUBAIDI
College of Arts: Dr FLAIH AL-RIKABI
College of Dentistry: Dr ALI AL-KAFAJI
College of Education (Ibn al Haitham): Dr
   ABDUL-JABBAR ABDUL-QADIR MUKHLIS
College of Education (Ibn Rushd): Dr OHOOD
   ABDUL-WAHID ABDUL-SAMAD
College of Education for Women: Dr AMIR
   MUHAMMAD ALI
College of Engineering: Dr QASSIM MUHAM-
   MAD DOS
College of Fine Arts: Dr AQEEL MAHDI
College of Islamic Sciences: Dr MUHAMMAD
   SALIH
College of Languages: Dr TALIB AL-QURAISHI
College of Law: Dr ALI AL-RUFAE
College of Medicine: Dr FADHIL AL-JANABI
College of Nursing: MOHAMMAD FADHIL KHA-
   LIFA
College of Pharmacy: Dr ALAA ABDUL-HUS-
   SEIN
College of Political Science: Dr AMIR JABBAR
   FAYADH
College of Science: Dr SALIH MOHAMMAD ALI
College of Sports Education: Dr RIYADH
   KHALIL KHAMAS
College of Veterinary Medicine: Dr FAREED
   AL-TAHAN

AFFILIATED CENTRES

**Astronomical Research Unit (attached
to the College of Science):** Dir Dr HAMEED
MIJWIL AL NIAIMI.

**Centre for International Studies
(attached to the College of Political
Science):** Dir Dr ABDUL GHAFOUR KARIM ALI.

**Centre for Palestinian Studies
(attached to the College of Political
Science):** Dir Dr KHLDOUN NAJI MAROUF.

**Centre for the Revival of Arab Scientific
Heritage:** Dir NABILA ABDUL MUNIM.

**Centre for Urban and Regional Plan-
ning (Postgraduate studies):** Dir Dr WAD-
HAH SAID YAHYA.

**Educational and Psychological
Research Centre (attached to the Col-
lege of Education, Ibn Rushd):** Dir MAHDI
AL SAMARRAE.

UNIVERSITY OF BASRAH

POB 49, Basrah
Telephone: (1) 8868520
Fax: (1) 8862998
E-mail: basrauniversity@satline.net
Founded 1964
State control
Languages of instruction: Arabic, English
Academic year: September to June
Pres.: DAWOOD SULEIMAN
Vice-Pres.: (vacant)
Librarian: Dr AMER ABID MUHSIN AL SAAD
Library of 169,586 vols, 59,000 periodicals
Number of teachers: 1,033
Number of students: 19,781

Publications: *Arab Gulf Journal, Basrah
Journal of Agricultural Sciences, Basrah
Journal of Sciences, Basrah Journal of
Surgery, Economic Studies, Gulf Econom-
ics Journal, Iraqi Journal of Polymers,
Journal of Arts, Journal of Basrah
Research, Journal of Physical Education,
Marina Mesopotamica, Medical Journal of
Basrah University*

DEANS

Faculty of Administration and Economics: Dr
   JALIL S. THAMAD
Faculty of Agriculture: Dr NAZAR A. SHUKRI
Faculty of Arts: Dr RAAD ZAHRAW AL MUSAWI

Faculty of Education: Dr GALIB BAKIR M.
   GALIB
Faculty of Education (at Theequar): Dr
   MAHDI ORYBY HUSSAIN AL DAKHIL
Faculty of Engineering: Dr ABDULAMIR S.
   RESAN
Faculty of Fine Arts: MUAYAD ABDULSAMAD
Faculty of Law: Prof. Dr ABDULMAHDI SALEEM
   AL MUDHAFFAR
Faculty of Medicine: Prof. Dr ALIM ABDULHA-
   MID YACOUB
Faculty of Physical Education: Dr SALAH
   ATTYA KADHUM
Faculty of Science: Prof. Dr GOURGIS ABIDAL
   ADAM
Faculty of Teacher-Training: Dr HAMEED
   HASSAN TAHIR
Faculty of Veterinary Science: Dr ABDULMUT-
   TALIB Y. YOUSIF

DIRECTORS

Centre for Arab Gulf Studies: Dr OWDA
   SULTAN
Centre for Marine Sciences: Dr ABDULRAZAK
   MAHMOOD
Computer Centre: Dr WALEED A. J. MOHAM-
   MAD ALI
Medical Centre: Dr ABDULKHALIQ Z. BNAYAN

UNIVERSITY OF DIYALA

POB 2, Baquba Post Office, Baqubah, Diyala
   governorate, Al-Muradia, Old Baquba-
   Baghdad Way
Telephone: (790) 1978420
Fax: (5) 8853610
E-mail: diyala_university@yahoo.com
Internet: www.uodiyala.edu.iq
Languages of instruction: Arabic, English
Founded 1999
State control
Pres.: Prof. Dr MAHMOUD SHAKER RASHEED
   (acting)
Vice-Pres. for Admin. Affairs: Dr AYAD AL
   AJEELY
Vice-Pres. for Scientific Affairs: Dr AMER M.
   IBRAHIM (acting)
Number of teachers: 867
Number of students: 14,782

Publication: *Al Afaak Al Jadida* (in Arabic)

DEANS

College of Administration and Economics: Dr
   MUHSIN HASSAN ALWAN
College of Agriculture: Dr ADEL NORI GOMA'A
College of Basic Education: Dr ABBAS FADIL
   GAWAD
College of Education (Al-Razi): Dr ABBAS
   ABOOD FARHAN
College of Education (Al-Asmaee): Dr MAH-
   MOUD FAIAD HUMMADI
College of Engineering: Dr ADEL KHALEEL
   MAHMOUD
College of Islamic Sciences: AHMED ABID AL
   SATTAR GASIM
College of Law: Dr ABID AL-AZIZ SHAABAN
   KHALID
College of Medicine: Dr KHUDHAIR KH. IBRA-
   HIM
College of Science: Dr DHAHIR ABID AL-HADI
College of Sport Education: Dr MAHIR ABID
   AL-LATEEF
College of Veterinary Medicine: Dr ABID AL
   RAZZAQ SHAFEEQ

UNIVERSITY OF DUHOK

Zakho rd 38, Kurdistan Region, Dohuk
   governorate
Telephone: (62) 7227060
E-mail: relations@uod.ac
Internet: www.uod.ac
Founded 1992; attached to Min. of Higher
   Education

State control
Languages of instruction: Arabic, English,
   Kurdish
Academic year: September to August
Pres.: Dr ASMAT MOHAMMED KHALID (acting)
Vice-Pres. for Admin. Affairs: Dr SALEEM H.
   HAJI (acting)
Vice-Pres. for Scientific Affairs: Dr HASAN
   AMEEN MOHAMMED (acting)
Vice-Pres. for Int. Relations: Dr DAWOOD S.
   ATRUSHI
Library of 11,770 vols
Number of teachers: 791
Number of students: 9,100

Publication: *Govara Zankoya*

DEANS

College of Law and Politics: Dr NADHIM
   YOUNS OTHMAN
College of Medicine: Dr FARHAD KHURSHEED
   MOHAMMED
College of Nursing: Dr AHMED MOHAMMED
   SALIH
College of Physical Education: Dr ODEAT
   ODISHO
College of Science: Dr AHMED MOHAMMED
   SALIH
College of Veterinary Medicine: Dr NADHIM
   SULAIMAN A. AZIZ
Faculty of Agriculture: Dr MOAFAQ SULAIMAN
Faculty of Education: Prof. AUDIATE ODISHO
Faculty of Engineering and Applied Science:
   Prof. NAZAR M. S. NUMAN
Faculty of Evening Studies: Prof. ELIAS
   KHALAF
Faculty of Humanities: Dr MOSA
Facutly of Medicine: Dr ARIF YOUNIS BALATI
Higher Institute of Learning: Dr ASMAT
   MOHAMMED KHALID (Head)
Scientific Research Centre: JALADET JUBREAL
   (Head)

ISLAMIC UNIVERSITY

Adhmai, Habiet Khatoun, Baghdad
Telephone: (1) 4254257
E-mail: islamicuniversitybag@yahoo.com
Internet: www.iubaghdad.com
Founded 1989
State control
Language of instruction: Arabic
Academic year: September to August
Pres.: Prof. Dr ZIYAD M. RASHEED AL ANI
   (acting)
Vice-Pres. for Admin. Affairs: Dr ANMMAR
   AHMED MOHAMED
Vice-Pres. for Scientific Affairs: Prof. Dr
   IBRAHEEM ABID SAIL
Librarian: Dr KAIS ABDULLATIF AHMED
Library of 24,715 vols, 2,467 periodical titles
Number of teachers: 573
Number of students: 10,299

Publication: *Al-khaber*

DEANS

College of Art: Dr ABDULLAH HASAN AL-
   HADITHI
College of Economics and Administration: Dr
   HIKMET FARIS TA'AAN
College of Education: Dr ADNAN ADNAN ALI
   AL-FARAJI
College of Education for Girls: Dr OMER
   MAJEED AID SALEH
College of Law: Dr ZIYAD HAMED ABAAS AL-
   SUMAYDAAI
College of Mass Media: Dr HASHIM AHMED
   NGHEEMISH
College of Religions' Fundamentals: Prof. Dr
   SUBHI FANDI AL-KUBEISI
College of Shari'a: Dr ABDULMUNAEM KHALIL
   AL-HITI

UNIVERSITY OF KARBALA

Al Dhbbat district, Karbala, Karbala governorate

Telephone: (32) 321364
E-mail: info@uokerbala.edu.iq
Internet: www.uokerbala.edu.iq

Founded 2002
State control
Academic year: September to July

Colleges of administration and economics,
agriculture, education, engineering, law,
medicine, pharmacy, science

Pres.: A. H. ALWAN (acting)

Library of 25,000 vols
Number of teachers: 222
Number of students: 5,000

UNIVERSITY OF KUFA

Kufa, POB 21, Najaf, al Najaf governorate

Telephone: (33) 346094
E-mail: info@kuiraq.com
Internet: www.kuiraq.com

Founded 1987; attached to Min. of Higher
Education and Scientific Research
Public control
Languages of instruction: Arabic, English
Academic year: September to June

Pres.: Prof. RAZAK AL-ESSA (acting)
Vice-Pres. for Admin.: Asst Prof. ABDUL-
SAHIB AL-BAGHDADY
Vice-Pres. for Scientific Affairs: Prof. MUHSIN
AL-DHALEMI

Library of 23,500 vols
Number of teachers: 1,425
Number of students: 18,519

Publications: *Al-Ghary Journal for Econom-
ical and Administrative Researches, Al-
Kufa Journal for Agricultural Sciences, Al-
Kufa Journal for Legal and Political Sci-
ences, Al-Kufa Journal for Medical and
Veterinary Sciences, Al-Kufa Journal for
Nursing Science, Arabic Language and Its
Arts, Biology Journal, Chemical Sciences
Journal, College of Education Journal for
Human Sciences, College of Jurisprudence
Journal, Geographic Researches Journal,
Kufa Engineering Journal, Kufa Journal
of Arts, Kufa Medical Journal, Kufa Stud-
ies Center Journal, Mathematics and Com-
puters Journal, Physics Journal*

DEANS

College of Agriculture: Prof. SADOON SADOON
College of Athletic Education: Asst Prof.
QASEM HASSAN
College of Basic Education: Asst Prof. IBTI-
SAM AL-MADANY
College of Dentistry: Asst Prof. ABBAS AL-
HWEIZY
College of Economy and Administration:
Prof. MAZIN ESSA
College of Education: Asst Prof. BASEM BAQER
College of Education for Girls: Asst Prof.
SAAD AZIZ
College of Engineering: Asst Prof. ALAA
MAHDI
College of Jurisprudence: Prof. SABAH UNOUZ
College of Law and Political Sciences: Asst
Prof. ALI AL-SHUKRI
College of Mathematics and Computer Sci-
ences: Asst Prof. YAHYA AL-MAYALI
College of Medicine: Prof. MUHAMMED SAEED
College of Nursing: Asst Prof. ABDUL-KAREEM
ABDULLAH
College of Pharmacy: Asst Prof. RAHEEM AL-
SAEDI
College of Sciences: Prof. ABDUL-MAJEED AL-
SAADI
College of Veterinary Medicine: Prof. AHMED
AL-AZZAM

PROFESSORS

ABAS ALSAED SALMAN, J., Agriculture Sci-
ences
ABDUL-AMEER AL-DALEMY, M., Abdominal
Medicine
ABDUL-HAMSA AL-SHAMARY, P., Micro Alive
ABDUL-RASSWL AL-GHAKANEI, N., Economy
ABOUD AL-KAFAF, A., Geography
ABU HAMD AL-ALI, R., Economy
ABU RAHEAL AL-FATLAWEI, A., Geography
ADEA EASSA AL-MHANA, J., Medicine and
Surgery
AKAB AL-WAIALY, T., Modern History
ALEASA, A., Biochemistry
ALI ALHAKEMI, H., History
ALI SAMEA AL-ALI, M., Geography
ALI AL-FEDAWEE, A., Paediatrics
ALI AL-SAKEAR, M., Arabic Language
ALMOUSA AL-ASADI, K., Geography Natural
AL-HASSENI, H., Mathematics
AL-HASSNWEI, S., Pharmacy
AL-JUMAILI, S., Biology
AL-KHALIDI, A., Turkish
AL-KUTUBI, S., Mathematics
AL-SAEEDI, A., Biology
AL-SHARMANY, M., Agriculture Sciences
ALWAN AL-FATLAWI, A., Arabic Language
ASER MOSSA AL-GORATEI, H., Arabic Litera-
ture
HAFAD AL-KAFAGEI, A., Arabic Literature
HAMOD AL-SHAMA, Y., Physiology
HUSSEIN AL-KUFEE, A., Diseases Medicine
HUSSEIN AL-ZAMALY, N., Medicines
HASSAN AL-SNEAD, A., Physics
HASSAN AL-ENASSI, T., History
JALEEL ABDUL-HASSAN AL-GHALEBEI, A.,
Economy
KADEM THEDAN AL-FATLAWEI, K., Economy
MERZA AL-HUMAIRI, T., Biology
MHASSEN ALBU-AREBI, N., Philosophy
MOHAMED AL-ATHAREI, A., Economy
MOHAMED AL-JANABI, H., Abdominal Medi-
cine
MUHSIN AL-YASIRI, A., Arabic Language
RADEE ABUOD NASAR, M., Islamic Sciences
RAKBAN AL-KAFAGEI, A., Law
RESHED JABBER AL-ABEADI, H., Nutriments
Sciences
RWAH ALI AL-MUOSWEAI, S., Administrations
SADAK ALSHIKE RADEA, M., Economy
SADDON AJEAL AL-AJEALI, S., Agriculture
Sciences
TALAB AL-MUOSWEA, A., Geography
TARASH ZAOARI AL-JANABI, H., Micro Alive

UNIVERSITY OF MOSUL

Al Majmoa Al Thaqafia, Mosul

Telephone: (60) 810733
Fax: (60) 815066
E-mail: president@uomosul.edu.iq
Internet: www.uomosul.edu.iq

Founded 1967 as a separate univ., fmrly part
of the Univ. of Baghdad
State control
Languages of instruction: Arabic, English
Academic year: September to June (2 terms)

Pres.: OBAY S. AL DEWACHI (acting)
Vice-Pres. for Admin.: Dr ADNAN ALSAFAWI
(acting)
Vice-Pres. for Scientific Affairs: Dr NAZAR
MAJEED QIBI (acting)
Librarian: Dr NASSER ABDUL RAAZAQ MULLA
JASSIM

Library of 335,816 vols, 2,540 periodicals
Number of teachers: 4,343
Number of students: 35,766

Publications: *Adab al Rafidian* (4 a year), *Al
Rafidian Engineering Sciences* (4 a year),
Al Rafidain Dental Journal (4 a year), *Al
Rafidain Journal of Computer Science* (4 a
year), *Al Rafidain Journal of Earth Science* (4 a year), *Al Rafidain Journal of Law*
(4 a year), *Al Rafidain Journal of Science*
(4 a year), *Al Rafidain Journal of Statistical Science* (4 a year), *Al Rafidain Sports
Science Journal* (4 a year), *Annals of The
Medical College* (4 a year), *College of Basic
Education Research Journal* (4 a year),
Iraq Journal of Agricultural Science (4 a
year), *Iraqi Journal of Pharmacy* (4 a
year), *Iraqi Journal of Veterinary Medicine*
(4 a year), *Journal of Education and
Science* (4 a year), *Regional Studies* (4 a
year), *Studies Mosulia* (4 a year), *Tanmiat
al Rafidain* (4 a year)

DEANS

College of Administration: Dr FAWAZ GAR-
ALLA AL DOLUMY
College of Agriculture: Prof. Dr NAHIL
MOHAMMED ALI
College of Archeology: Prof. Dr ALI YASIN
ALJUBURI
College of Arts: MUHAMMAD BASIL AL AZZAWI
College of Basic Education: Dr FADHIL KHALIL
IBRAHIM
College of Dentistry: Dr TAHANI A. A. AL
SANDOOK
College of Education: Dr ABDL WAHID DH.
TAHA
College of Education for Girls: Prof. Dr
KHAWLA AHMED AL-FLAEH
College of Electronic Engineering: Dr BASIL
SH. MAHMOOD
College of Engineering: Dr FAROOQ KHALIL
AMOORI
College of Environmental Science and Tech-
nology: Prof. Dr MOAATH HAMID MUSTAFA
College of Fine Arts: Dr ADEL SAEED al SAFAR
College of Islamic Sciences: Prof. Dr ABDULLA
FATHI AL DHAHIR
College of Law: Prof. Dr AKRAM MAHMOOD
HUSSEIN
College of Mathematics and Computer Sci-
ence: Dr THAFER RAMATHAN MUTTAR
College of Medicine: Dr MUZAHIM FATAH AL
CHETACHI
College of Medicine (Nineveh): Prof. Dr FARIS
BAKIR AL SAWAF
College of Nursing: Dr SUBHE HUSEIN al
GUBORE
College of Pharmacy: Prof. Dr BASIL MOHAM-
MED AL KHAYAT
College of Physical Education: Dr YASSIN
TAHA MOHAMMAD ALI
College of Political Science: Dr MUFEED TH.
YOUNIS
College of Science: Dr IHSAN A. MUSTAFA AL
ABDULLAH
College of Veterinary Medicine: Dr FOUAD
KASIM MOHAMMAD

UNIVERSITY OF SALAHADDIN

Karkuk St, Runaki 235–323, Erbil, Kurdistan region

Telephone: (66) 2230409
E-mail: presedent-office@salahaddin-ac.com
Internet: www.salahaddin-ac.com

Founded 1968 in Sulaimaniya as University
of Sulaimaniya; present name and location
1981
State control
Languages of instruction: Arabic, English,
Kurdish
Academic year: September to June (two
terms)

Pres.: Dr MOHAMMAD S. MOHAMMAD
Vice-Pres. for Scientific Affairs: Dr AHMAD
ANWAR AMIN DEZAYE
Librarian: Dr MOHAMMAD MUSTAFA

Library: see Libraries
Number of teachers: 800
Number of students: 10,965 (10,597 under-
graduate, 368 postgraduate)

Publications: *Statistical Abstract* (1 a year),
University News (12 a year, in Arabic),

Zanco (scientific journal, in Arabic and English)

DEANS

College of Administration and Economics: Asst Prof. Dr DLER ISMAIL HAQI
College of Agriculture: Asst Prof. Dr FARHAD HASSAN AZEEZ
College of Arts: Prof. Dr AZAD MUHAMMAD AMEEN NAQISHBANDI
College of Dentistry: Dr DASHTI BAIZ DZAYI
College of Education: Prof. Dr KAREEM SALIH ABDUL
College of Engineering: Dr FARAYDOON HADI MAROUF
College of Law: NAJDAT SABRI AQRAWI
College of Medicine: Asst Prof. Dr HAMA NAJIM JAFF
College of Nursing: Dr FARHAD JALEEL KHAYAT
College of Pharmacy: Dr TAFUR JALAL KHLEL
College of Physical Education: IIDREES MUHAMMAD TAHIR
College of Political Science: Dr AHMED MUS-TAFA SULAIMAN
College of Science: Asst Prof. ROSTEM KAREEM SAED
College of Teacher Training: Asst Prof. Dr AZAD JALAL SHAREEF

UNIVERSITY OF SULAIMANIYA

2/3/205 Kani-Askan, Sulaimaniya
Telephone: (53) 2127453
E-mail: info@univsul.com
Internet: www.univsul.org
Founded 1968
State control
Languages of instruction: Arabic, English, Kurdish
Colleges of administration and economics, agriculture, dentistry and commerce, education, engineering, fine arts, humanities, languages, nursing, physical education, law, medicine, science, veterinary medicine
Pres.: KAMAL KHOSHNAW (acting)
Vice-Pres. for Admin.: SHAWNM ABDUL QADIR (acting)
Vice-Pres. for Scientific Affairs and Post-graduate Research: NAZAR M. MUHAMMAD AMIN (acting)
Library of 24,689 vols
Number of teachers: 489
Number of students: 8,000

UNIVERSITY OF TECHNOLOGY

al Sinah St, Baghdad
Telephone: (1) 7746532
Fax: (1) 7199446
E-mail: shekhly@uruklink.net
Internet: www.uotiq.org
Founded 1975; fmrly the College of Engineering Technology of the University of Baghdad
State control
Languages of instruction: Arabic, English
Academic year: October to July
Pres.: Dr WAIL NOORALDEN AL RIFAIE (acting)
Vice-Pres. for Admin. and Scientific Affairs: KRIKOR SIROB (acting)
Registrar: Dr ABDU AL HUSAIN SAKHI
Librarian: AYAD J. SHAMIS ELDEN
Library of 25,000 vols
Number of teachers: 961 (668 full-time, 293 part-time)
Number of students: 7,752

PROFESSORS

AL HADEETHI, A., Structural Engineering
AL HAIDARY, J. T., Production Engineering and Metallurgy
AL MUTALIB IBRAHIM, A., Applied Sciences
AL SAMAUI, A., Structural Engineering
AL SAMRAAI, J. M. A., Electrical Engineering
AL TOORNAJI, M., Production Engineering and Metallurgy
HAMMUDI, W. KH., Applied Sciences
KHAIRI, W., Computer and Control Engineering
KHORSEED, N., Structural Engineering
MAJEED, J., Mechanical Engineering
TAWFICK, H., Mechanical Engineering

UNIVERSITY OF THI-QAR

Nasiriya, Thi-Qar governorate
Internet: www.unidhiqar.com
Founded 2002
State control
Pres.: ISMAIL OBEID ALSNAVI (acting)
Vice-Pres. for Admin.: QASIM MOHAMMAD (acting)
Vice-Pres. for Scientific Affairs: ABBAS HUS-SEIN (acting)
Number of teachers: 155
Number of students: 5,639

DEANS

College of Arts: FADEL KAZEM SADIK
College of Education: MOHAMED JASSIM MOHAMMED
College of Engineering: HAIDAR SAAD REFINERY
College of Medicine: NAJI MAJID
College of Sciences: NAJAH RASSOL AL JABBRAI

UNIVERSITY OF TIKRIT

POB 42, Salah al Din, Tikrit
Telephone: (21) 825743
Fax: (21) 825384
E-mail: tikrituniversity@hotmail.com
Founded 1987
State control
Languages of instruction: Arabic, English
Academic year: September to June
Pres.: Prof. Dr MAHER S. AL JUBORI (acting)
Librarian: SABAH S. KHALEFE
Number of teachers: 701
Number of students: 6,824
Publications: *Iraqi Journal of Educational and Psychological Sciences and Sociology* (4 a year), *Surra Min Raa Journal* (4 a year), *Tikrit Journal of Agricultural Sciences* (4 a year), *Tikrit Journal of Economic Sciences* (4 a year), *Tikrit Journal of Engineering Sciences* (4 a year), *Tikrit Journal of Humanities* (4 a year), *Tikrit Journal of Pharmaceutical Sciences* (4 a year), *Tikrit Journal of Pure Sciences* (4 a year), *Tikrit Medical Journal* (4 a year)

DEANS

College of Administration and Economics: Asst Prof. Dr SABAH F. MAHMOOD
College of Agriculture: Prof. Dr ABDULLAH AHMED AL SAMARRAIE
College of Dentistry: Prof. Dr ADNAN H. MOHAMMED
College of Education: Asst Prof. Dr ALI SALIH HUSSEIN
College of Education (Samarra): Asst Prof. Dr MUHAMMAD IBRAHIM HUSSEIN
College of Education for Women: Asst Prof. Dr JAID Z. MUKHLIF
College of Engineering: Asst Prof. Dr HAYDAR SAAD YASEEN AL JUBAIR
College of Law: Asst Prof. Dr DHAMIN HUSSEIN
College of Medicine: Asst Prof. Dr ABID AHMAD SALMAN
College of Pharmacy: Prof. Dr ALI ISMAIL UBEID
College of Science: Asst Prof. Dr SUBHI ATIA MAHMOOD

PROFESSORS

ABDOON, H. F., Islamic Jurisprudence
ABDULLAH, A. A.-M., Veterinary Science
ALAAH, M. M., Microbiology
AL AZIZ, M. A., Veterinary Science
AL BAYDHANI, I. S., Modern History
AL HUSSEIN, S. A., Biology
AL JUBURI, A. H. M., Arabic Language
AL NAJAFEE, H. M., Civil Engineering
AL OMER, A. K., Arabic Language
ALI, A. A.-G. M., Medicine
ALI, K. I., Politics
ALI, N. H., Physical Education
AL-JUBURI, M. S. A., Arabic Language
AL JUMAILI, S. H. A., Arabic Language
AL-KUTUBI, S. H., Mathematics
ALRAHMAN, Y. A. A., Medicine
AL SAMARRAIE, A. A.-K. M., Physical Education
AL SAMARRAIE, A. A.-M. H., Chemistry
AL SHIQARCHI, S. T., Chemistry
AL TAAI, A. A. H., Arabic Language
AUBED, A. I., Pharmacology and Toxicology
AZIZ, A. A., Chemistry
DAWOOD, A. S., Plant Protection
DAWOOD, I. S., Biology
DEKRAAN, S. B., Chemistry
GHANIM, Y. M.-A., Medicine
HAMAD, G. Q., Arabic Language
HANTOSH, F. G., Chemistry
HUSEIN, M. H., Civil Engineering
KAMEL, A. A.-M., Modern History
KAMEL, F. M., Food Technologies
LATEEF, R. A., Crops
MAHMOUD, S. A., Chemistry
MOHAMMED, A. H., Dentistry
MOHAMMED, A. H., Economics
MOHAMMED, M. M., Medicine
MUKHIF, J. Z., Arabic Language
MUSA, M. M., Veterinary Science
RASEED, A. A-M., Economics
SAIED, J. M., Animal Production
SHIHAB, A. F., Biology
WADY, A. A.-R. A., History

UNIVERSITY OF WASSIT

Kut, Wassit governorate
Telephone: (23) 313861
Internet: www.uowasit.edu.iq
Founded 2003
State control
Pres.: Dr JABBAR YASSER AL MAYAH
Number of teachers: 109

Colleges

Al Imam al A'dham College: Karkh, Baghdad; f. 1967, affiliated to Baghdad Univ. 1978; degree course in Islamic studies; 34 teachers; 516 students; Dean Dr SUBHI MOHAMMAD JAMIL AL KHAYYAT; publ. *Journal* (1 a year).

Foundation for Technical Institutes: Baghdad; f. 1972; attached to the Min. of Higher Education and Scientific Research; groups all the institutes of technology; Pres. H. M. S. ABDUL WAHAB.

Incorporated Institutes:

Institute of Administration: Rissafa, Baghdad; f. 1964; Dean A. S. AL MASHAT.
Institute of Administration, Karkh (Baghdad): f. 1976; Dean T. SHAKER.
Institute of Applied Arts: Baghdad; f. 1969; Dean A. NOOR-EDDIN.
Institute of Technology: Baghdad; f. 1969; Dean N. S. MUSTAFA.
Technical Institute, Basrah: f. 1973; UNDP/UNESCO project; technology and

admin.; 1,660 students; Dean H. I. MOHAM-MED.

Technical Institute, Hilla: f. 1976; technology and admin.; Dean S. B. DERWISH.

Technical Institute, Kirkuk: f. 1976; technology and admin.; Dean M. ABDUL RAHMAN.

Technical Institute, Mosul: f. 1976; technology and admin.; Dean M. S. SAFFO.

Technical Institute, Missan: f. 1979; technology and admin.

Technical Institute, Najaf: f. 1978; technology and admin.; Dean M. A. JASSIM.

Technical Institute, Ramadi: f. 1977; technology and admin.; Dean J. M. AMIN.

Technical Institute, Sulaimaniya: f. 1973; medical technology and admin.; Dean R. M. ABDULLAH.

Technical Institute of Agriculture: Abu-Ghraib, Baghdad; f. 1964; Dean S. A. HASSAN.

Technical Institute of Agriculture, Arbil: Aski-Kalak, Arbil; f. 1976; Dean M. S. ABBASS.

Technical Institute of Agriculture, Kumait: Kumait, Missan; f. 1976; Dean H. L. SADIK.

Technical Institute of Agriculture, Mussaib-Babylon: Mussaib-Babylon; f. 1979.

Technical Institute of Agriculture, Shatra-Thi Qar: Shatra-Thi Qar; f. 1979.

Technical Institute of Medicine: Baghdad; f. 1964; Dean A. S. AL MASHAT.

IRELAND

The Higher Education System

Higher education in Ireland dates from the foundation of the University of Dublin Trinity College in 1592; the next oldest institutions are the Royal College of Physicians of Ireland (founded 1654) and the National University of Ireland, Maynooth (formerly St Patrick's College, founded 1795). Until 1920 the 32 counties of Ireland were part of the United Kingdom; however, in that year Ireland was partitioned: the six north-eastern counties remained part of the United Kingdom, and the 26 southern counties sought independence. In 1922 the southern counties achieved dominion status, under the British Crown, as the Irish Free State. Ireland achieved full sovereignty within the Commonwealth in 1937, and the Republic of Ireland was declared in 1949. There are seven universities, as well as other institutions of higher education including colleges, institutes of technology, schools of art and music, and professional establishments. Under the Universities Act (1997) and the Qualifications Act (1999), Ireland participates in the Bologna Process. In 2006/07 82,488 full-time students were enrolled at universities and Higher Education Authority Institutions, and 53,358 students were enrolled at technology colleges.

Admission to higher education is administered by the Central Applications Office. In accordance with the Bologna Process, the university awards system consists of Bachelors, Masters and Doctorate degrees. The Bachelors is the main undergraduate degree and lasts for three to four years. However, degrees in some disciplines, such as dentistry, veterinary medicine, architecture (all five years) and medicine (six years), may last longer. Following the Bachelors, a student may take the Masters, the first postgraduate degree. The Masters is a one-to two-year programme of study, and may be either a taught or a research degree. The second postgraduate degree (and final university-level award) is the Doctor of Philosophy, which is a research-based course lasting two to five years. In addition to the universities, higher education is offered by other types of institution, including Institutes of Technology and so-called 'Designated' Institutions. Awards from these establishments are assured by the Higher Education and Training Awards Council (founded 2001). Quality assurance of universities is organized through the independent Irish Universities Quality Board, which was established in 2002, however the devolved statutory responsibility is with the universities. The Higher Education Authority also has a statutory right to review the quality assurance procedures in the universities, having consulted with the universities and the National Qualifications Authority of Ireland.

Technical and vocational education is offered by colleges, the Dublin Institute of Technology and Industrial Training Authority centres. The Higher Education and Training Awards Council oversees all continuing and adult education and administers a wide range of certificated courses. The most prominent vocational award is the National Vocational Certificate (Levels 1–3).

Regulatory and Representative Bodies

GOVERNMENT

Department of Education and Skills: Marlborough St, Dublin 1; tel. (1) 8892162; fax (1) 8786712; e-mail info@education.gov.ie; internet www.education.ie; Minister MARY COUGHLAN.

Department of Tourism, Culture and Sport: 23 Kildare St, Dublin 2; tel. (1) 6313800; fax (1) 6611201; e-mail maryhanafin@tcs.gov.ie; internet www.tcs.gov.ie; Minister MARY HANAFIN.

ACCREDITATION

Accreditation Commission on Colleges of Medicine (ACCM): tel. (87) 2388502; fax (1) 2868660; e-mail office@accredmed.org; internet www.accredmed.org; f. 1995; accreditation of medical colleges; brs in Sint Maarten, Island Territory of Saba, Cayman Islands and Nevis Island; Chair. Prof. RAYMOND FITZGERALD; Hon. Sec. and Treas. JOYCE TIMMS.

ENIC/NARIC Ireland: Nat. Qualifications Authority of Ireland, 5th Floor, Jervis House, Jervis St, Dublin 1; tel. (1) 8871500; fax (1) 8871595; e-mail info@qualificationsrecognition.ie; internet www.qualrec.ie; Co-Mans of Operations, Qualifications Recognition LAURA CARRIGAN, NIAMH LENEHAN.

Higher Education and Training Awards Council: 26–27 Denzille Lane, Dublin 2; tel. (1) 6441500; fax (1) 6441577; e-mail info@hetac.ie; internet www.hetac.ie; f. 2001 under the Qualifications (Education and Training) Act 1999; develops higher education outside the univ. system in the Republic of Ireland; approves and recognizes courses; grants and confers nat. awards (degrees, diplomas, certificates); coordinates courses within and between institutions; successor to the Nat. Council for Educational Awards (NCEA—f. 1972); may delegate authority to make awards to recognized institutions under the Qualifications (Education and Training) Act 1999; Chair. Prof. W. J. SMYTH; Chief Exec. GEARÓID Ó CONLUAIN; Sec. TADHG Ó HÉALAITHE.

National Qualifications Authority of Ireland: Jervis House, 5th Fl., Jervis St, Dublin 1; tel. (1) 8871500; fax (1) 8871595; e-mail info@nqai.ie; internet www.nqai.ie; f. 2001; objects: the establishment and maintenance of a framework of qualifications for the devt, recognition and award of qualifications based on standards of knowledge, skill or competence to be acquired by learners; the establishment and promotion of the maintenance and improvement of the standards of awards of the further and higher education and training sector, other than in the existing univs; the promotion and facilitation of access, transfer and progression throughout the span of education and training provision; the Authority is not an awarding body; Chair. PAUL HARAN; Chief Exec. Dr PADRAIG WALSH.

State Examinations Commission: Cornamaddy, Athlone, Co Westmeath; tel. (90) 6442700; fax (90) 6442744; e-mail sec.pressoffice@examinations.ie; internet www.examinations.ie; f. 2003; responsible for the provision and quality of the Irish State Examinations; aims to deliver an efficient, fair and accessible examination and assessment system in conjunction with school authorities and education providers; Chair. RICHARD LANGFORD; CEO PÁDRAIC MCNAMARA.

FUNDING

Higher Education Authority: Brooklawn House, Crampton Ave, Shelbourne Rd, Dublin 4; tel. (1) 2317100; fax (1) 2317172; e-mail info@hea.ie; internet www.hea.ie; statutory planning and devt body for higher education and research in Ireland; has wide advisory powers throughout the whole of the tertiary education sector; funding authority for univs and a number of designated higher education instns; Chair. JOHN HENNESSY; Chief Exec. TOM BOLAND.

Science Foundation Ireland: Wilton Park House, Wilton Pl., Dublin 2; tel. (1) 6073200; fax (1) 6073201; e-mail info@sfi.ie; internet www.sfi.ie; f. 2000; national funding body for research in the fields of science and engineering; three key areas of interest: biotechnology, information and communications technology, and sustainable energy and energy-efficient technologies; Dir-Gen. Prof. FRANK GANNON; Sec. and COO DONAL KEANE.

NATIONAL BODIES

Central Applications Office: Tower House, Eglinton St, Galway; tel. (91) 509800; fax (91) 562344; internet www.cao.ie; f. 1976; processes applications for first-year undergraduate courses offered by the higher-education instns in the Republic of Ireland; CEO IVOR GLEESON.

Further Education and Training Awards Council: East Point Plaza, East Point Business Park, Dublin 3; tel. (1) 8659500; fax (1) 8650067; e-mail information@fetac.ie; internet www.fetac.ie; f. 2001; makes quality-assured awards in accordance with nat. standards within the nat. framework, creating opportunities for all learners in further education and training to have their achievements recognized and providing access to systematic progression pathways; Chief Exec. STAN MCHUGH.

Irish Universities Association: 48 Merrion Sq., Dublin 2; tel. (1) 6764948; fax (1) 6622815; e-mail info@iua.ie; internet www .iua.ie; the rep. body of the heads of the 7 Irish univs; seeks to advance univ. education and research through the formulation and pursuit of collective policies and actions on behalf of the Irish univs thereby contributing to Ireland's social, cultural and economic wellbeing; Pres. Prof. JOHN HUGHES; Chief Exec. NED COSTELLO; publ. *IUA Review* (irregular).

Irish Universities Quality Board: 10 Lower Mount St, Dublin 2; tel. (1) 6449774; fax (1) 6612449; internet www.iuqb.ie; f. 2002; supports and promotes a culture of quality in Irish universities; independently evaluates the effectiveness of quality processes; mem. of the European Quality Assurance Register and the European Asscn for Quality Assurance in Higher Education; Chair. Justice CATHERINE MCGUINNESS; CEO and Sec. Dr PADRAIG WALSH.

National Centre for Technology in Education: Dublin City University, Dublin 9; tel. (1) 7008200; fax (1) 7008210; e-mail info@ ncte.ie; internet www.ncte.ie; f. 1998 under Dept of Education and Science (renamed the Dept of Education and Skills in 2010); oversees, and gives advice and support with regard to, the use of information and communications technology (ICT) within education, with the aim of achieving a high-quality ICT infrastructure to support learning and teaching; Dir JEROME MORRISSEY.

National Council for Special Education: 1–2 Mill St, Trim, Co Meath; tel. (46) 9486400; fax (46) 9486404; e-mail ops@ncse .ie; internet www.ncse.ie; f. 2003; restructured 2005; plans and coordinates provision of education and support services to persons (particularly children) with special educational needs arising from disabilities; Chair. SYDNEY BLAIN.

Learned Societies

GENERAL

Royal Dublin Society: Anglesea Rd, Ballsbridge, Dublin 4; tel. (1) 6680866; fax (1) 6604014; e-mail info@rds.ie; internet www .rds.ie; f. 1731; advancement of agriculture, industry, science and the arts; 6,000 mems; library: see Libraries and Archives; Pres. Dr TONY SCOTT; Chief Exec. MICHAEL DUFFY; Registrar EILEEN BYRNE; publ. *Minerva* (3 a year).

Royal Irish Academy: Academy House, 19 Dawson St, Dublin 2; tel. (1) 6762570; fax (1) 6762346; e-mail info@ria.ie; internet www .ria.ie; f. 1785; acad. for the sciences and humanities in the Republic of Ireland; promotes excellence in scholarship, recognizes achievements in learning and undertakes research projects; advises on and contributes to public debate and public policy formation in science, technology and culture; maintains a library; the largest Irish publisher of scholarly and scientific journals, books and monographs; 489 mems (424 ordinary, 65 hon.); library of 35,000 vols, 31,000 pamphlets, 1,800 sets of current periodicals, 2,500 MSS; Pres. Prof. NICHOLAS P. CANNY; Sec. Prof. THOMAS BRAZIL; Exec. Sec. PATRICK BUCKLEY; publs *Biology and Environment Proceedings* (3 a year), *Eriu* (1 a year), *Irish Journal of Earth Sciences* (1 a year), *Irish*

Studies in International Affairs (1 a year), *Mathematical Proceedings* (2 a year), *Proceedings Section C* (Archaeology, Celtic Studies, History, Linguistics, Literature, 1 a year).

AGRICULTURE, FISHERIES AND VETERINARY SCIENCE

Royal Horticultural Society of Ireland: Cabinteely House, The Park, Cabinteely, Dublin 18; tel. and fax (1) 2353912; e-mail info@rhsi.ie; internet www.rhsi.ie; f. 1816; 1,000 mems; Pres. MAEVE KEARNS; Sec. CORA KENNEDY.

Society of Irish Foresters: Glenealy, Co Wicklow; tel. (404) 44204; e-mail info@ societyofirishforesters.ie; internet www .societyofirishforesters.ie; f. 1942; advances and spreads the knowledge of forestry in all its aspects; promotes professional standards in forestry and the regulation of the forestry profession in Ireland; annual study tour, field days, annual symposium, lectures; continuous professional development programme; 700 mems; Pres. PAT FARRINGTON; Sec. CLODAGH DUFFY; publ. *Irish Forestry* (2 a year).

Veterinary Council: 53 Lansdowne Rd, Ballsbridge, Dublin 4; tel. (1) 6684402; fax (1) 6604373; e-mail info@vci.ie; internet www .vci.ie; f. 1931; 2,370 registered mems; Registrar VALERIE BEATTY.

ARCHITECTURE AND TOWN PLANNING

Architectural Association of Ireland: Office 1, 43–44 Temple Bar, Dublin 2; tel. (1) 6761703; e-mail contact@ architecturalassociation.ie; internet www .architecturalassociation.ie; f. 1896 to promote the practice and study of architecture, and to foster cooperation among architects; 450 mems; Pres. HUGO LAMONT; Hon. Sec. DOUGLAS CARSON; publ. *Building Material* (6 a year).

Royal Institute of the Architects of Ireland: 8 Merrion Sq., Dublin 2; tel. (1) 6761703; fax (1) 6610948; e-mail info@riai .ie; internet www.riai.ie; f. 1839; 3,300 mems; Pres. PAUL KEOGH; Dir JOHN GRABY; publs *Architecture Ireland* (6 a year), *House* (2 a year).

Society of Chartered Surveyors: 5 Wilton Pl., Dublin 2; tel. (1) 6765500; fax (1) 6761412; e-mail info@scs.ie; internet www .scs.ie; constituent body of the Royal Instn of Chartered Surveyors; Dir-Gen. CIARA MURPHY.

BIBLIOGRAPHY, LIBRARY SCIENCE AND MUSEOLOGY

Library Association of Ireland (Cumann Leabharlann na hEireann): 53 Upper Mount St, Dublin 2; tel. (53) 9124922; fax (1) 6762346; e-mail president@ libraryassociation.ie; internet www .libraryassociation.ie; f. 1928, incorporated 1952; courses: continuing professional devt, Assoc. of the Library Asscn of Ireland (ALAI), Fellow of the Library Asscn of Ireland (FLAI); holds conferences; lobbies govt; 560 mems; Pres. FIONNUALA HANRAHAN; Hon. Sec. KIERAN SWORDS; publ. *An Leabharlann: The Irish Library* (2 a year).

ECONOMICS, LAW AND POLITICS

Institute of Chartered Accountants in Ireland: Chartered Accountants House, 47–49 Pearse St, Dublin 2; Belfast Office: 32–38 Linenhall St, Belfast, BT2 8BG, UK; tel. (1) 6377200; fax (1) 6680842; e-mail ca@icai.ie; internet www.charteredaccountants.ie; inc. by Royal Charter 1888; 18,000 mems; library of 20,000 vols; Pres. PAUL O'CONNOR; Chief

Exec. PAT COSTELLO; publ. *Accountancy Ireland* (6 a year).

King's Inns, Honorable Society of: Henrietta St, Dublin 1; tel. (1) 8744840; fax (1) 8726048; e-mail info@kingsinns.ie; internet www.kingsinns.ie; f. 1542; provides training course to enable students to be admitted to the degree of barrister-at-law; 4,000 mems; library of 100,000 vols; Dean of School of Law MARY FAULKNER; Registrar MARCELLA HIGGINS; publ. *Irish Student Law Review* (1 a year).

Law Society of Ireland: Blackhall Pl., Dublin 7; tel. (1) 6724800; fax (1) 6724801; e-mail general@lawsociety.ie; internet www .lawsociety.ie; f. 1852; 12,000 mems; library of 14,000 vols; Pres. GERARD DOHERTY; Dir-Gen. KEN MURPHY; publs *Gazette* (12 a year), *Law Directory* (1 a year).

Statistical and Social Inquiry Society of Ireland: c/o Seán Lyons, Economic & Social Research Institute, Whitaker Sq., Sir John Rogerson's Quay, Dublin 2; tel. (1) 8632019; e-mail info@ssisi.ie; internet www.ssisi.ie; f. 1847; promotes the study of social and economic developments; c. 500 mems; Pres. Prof. P. SWEENEY; Hon. Secs T. N. CAVEN, P. WALSH, S. LYONS; publ. *Journal* (1 a year).

EDUCATION

Church Education Society: c/o Church of Ireland House, Church Ave, Rathmines, Dublin 6; tel. (1) 4978422; fax (1) 4978821; e-mail ces@ireland.anglican.org; f. 1839; Asst Sec. and Treas. JENNIFER BYRNE.

FINE AND PERFORMING ARTS

Aosdána: 70 Merrion Sq., Dublin 2; tel. (1) 6180200; fax (1) 6761302; e-mail aosdana@ artscouncil.ie; internet www.aosdana .artscouncil.ie; f. 1981; attached to the Arts Council; an affiliation of artists engaged in literature, music and visual arts; membership limited to 250 mems; Registrar TOBY DENNETT.

Arts Council: 70 Merrion Sq., Dublin 2; tel. (1) 6180200; fax (1) 6761302; e-mail info@ artscouncil.ie; internet www.artscouncil.ie; f. 1951; Irish Govt agency for devt of the arts; promotes and assists the artists; in addition to organizing and promoting exhibitions and other activities itself, the Council gives grant-aid to many organizations including the theatre, opera, arts centres, arts festivals, exhibitions and publishers; also awards bursaries and scholarships to individual artists; offers advice and information on arts to Govt, individuals and orgs; Chair. PAT MOYLAN.

Irish Recorded Music Association: IRMA House, 1 Corrig Ave, Dun Laoghaire, Co Dublin; tel. (1) 2806571; fax (1) 2806579; e-mail irma_info@irma.ie; internet www .irma.ie; f. 1948; trade asscn for record companies, works to promote and protect the welfare and interests of the Irish record industry; 55 mems; Chair. WILLIE KAVANAGH; Dir-Gen. DICK DOYLE; publs *Music Events Diary*, *Policy Statement of Music Education*.

Royal Hibernian Academy: 15 Ely Pl., Dublin 2; tel. (1) 6612558; fax (1) 6610762; e-mail info@rhagallery.ie; internet www .royalhibernianacademy.ie; f. 1823; painting, sculpture, installation and mixed media; 5 galleries; 66 mems (13 hon., 44 acads, 9 assoc.); Pres. DES MCMAHON; Sec. DAVID CRONE.

HISTORY, GEOGRAPHY AND ARCHAEOLOGY

Cork Historical and Archaeological Society: c/o Hon. Treasurer, 13 Lislee Rd, Maryborough, Douglas, Cork; tel. (21)

541076; internet www.ucc.ie/chas; f. 1891; 400 mems; Pres. Dr KEVIN O'SULLIVAN; Hon. Sec. ANN EGAN; publ. *Journal* (1 a year).

Folklore of Ireland Society: c/o UCD Delargy Centre for Irish Folklore and the Nat. Folklore Colln, School of Irish, Celtic Studies, Irish Folklore and Linguistics, Newman Bldg, Belfield, Dublin 4; tel. (1) 7168216; fax (1) 7161144; e-mail eolas@bealoideas.ie; internet www.bealoideas.ie; f. 1927; 650 mems; Pres. ANRAÍ Ó BRAONÁIN; Sec. RÓNÁN Ó GEALBHÁIN; publ. *Béaloideas* (1 a year).

Geographical Society of Ireland: c/o GSI Secretary, School of Geography, Planning and Environmental Policy, E001 Newman Bldg, University College Dublin, Belfield, Dublin 4; tel. (1) 7168179; internet www .geographical-society-ireland.org; f. 1934; seeks to provide information and promote discussion about a wide range of topics of geographical interest, within Ireland and abroad; organizes lectures and seminars, field trips; 200 mems; Pres. Prof. MARK BOYLE; Sec. DAVID MEREDITH; publ. *Irish Geography* (3 a year).

Military History Society of Ireland: University College Dublin, Newman House, 86 St Stephen's Green, Dublin 2; tel. (1) 2985617; fax (1) 7067211; e-mail alanoif@ indigo.ie; internet www.mhsi.ie; f. 1949; 1,000 mems; Pres. HARMAN MURTAGH; Hon. Sec. for Correspondence Dr PATRICK MCCARTHY; Hon. Sec. for Records Capt. PADRAIC KEANE; publ. *The Irish Sword* (2 a year).

Old Dublin Society: 44 Warrenhouse Rd, Baldoyle, Dublin 13; e-mail olddublinsociety@dublin.ie; internet www .olddublinsociety.ie; f. 1934; promotes study of history and antiquities of Dublin; 325 mems; library of 1,300 vols (reference only; access by appointment); Pres. Rev. DUDLEY A. LEVISTONE COONEY; Hon. Secs BARRY FARRELL, BRIAN DYSON, NOEL HEALY; publ. *Dublin Historical Record* (2 a year).

Royal Society of Antiquaries of Ireland: 63 Merrion Sq., Dublin 2; tel. (1) 6761749; e-mail rsai@rsai.ie; internet www.rsai.ie; f. 1849; 1,100 mems; library of 13,000 vols (reference only); Pres. CHARLES DOHERTY; Hon. Gen. Secs Dr NIALL BRADY, Dr KELLY FITZGERALD; publ. *Journal* (1 a year).

LANGUAGE AND LITERATURE

Alliance Française: 1 Kildare St, Dublin 2; tel. (1) 6761732; fax (1) 6764077; e-mail info@ alliance-francaise.ie; internet www .alliance-francaise.ie; offers courses in general French, French conversation, specialized French, French for primary schools; also offers diploma courses and corporate courses; promotes French culture; attached offices in Cork, Galway, Kilkenny, Limerick, Waterford and Wexford; Dir CLAIRE BOURGEOIS.

British Council: Newmount House, 22–24 Lower Mount St, Dublin 2; tel. (1) 6764088; fax (1) 6766945; e-mail info@ie.britishcouncil .org; internet www.britishcouncil.org/ ireland; offers courses and examinations in English language and British culture and promotes cultural exchange with the UK; promotes creative and knowledge economy of the UK; Dir MATT BURNEY.

Conradh na Gaeilge (Gaelic League): 6 Harcourt St, Dublin 2; tel. (1) 4757401; fax (1) 4757844; e-mail eolas@cnag.ie; internet www.cnag.ie; f. 1893; 200 brs; Sec.-Gen. JULIAN DE SPÁINN; publs *An tUltach* (12 a year), *Feasta* (12 a year).

Goethe-Institut: 37 Merrion Sq., Dublin 2; tel. (1) 6611155; fax (1) 6611358; e-mail info@ dublin.goethe.org; internet www.goethe.de/ dublin; offers courses and examinations in German language and culture and promotes cultural exchange with Germany; library of 12,000 vols; Dir ROLF STEHLE.

Instituto Cervantes: Lincoln House, Lincoln Pl., Dublin 4; tel. (1) 6311500; fax (1) 6311599; e-mail cendub@cervantes.es; internet dublin.cervantes.es; f. 1991; offers courses and examinations in Spanish language and culture and promotes cultural exchange with Spain and Spanish-speaking Latin and Central America; library of 11,000 vols; Dir ROSA LEÓN CONDE.

Irish PEN: c/o United Arts Club, 3 Upper Fitzwilliam St, Dublin 12; e-mail info@ irishpen.com; internet www.irishpen.com; f. 1921; 62 mems; Pres. BRIAN FRIEL; Chair. JOE ARMSTRONG.

Irish Texts Society: c/o Hon. Secretary, 69A Balfour St, London, SE17 1PL, UK; e-mail hon.secretary@irishtextssociety.org; internet www.irishtextssociety.org; f. 1898 to advance public education by promoting the study of Irish literature, and to publish texts in the Irish language, with translations, notes, etc.; 640 mems; library: archives of the Society have been placed in the Univ. College Cork Library; Pres. Prof. PÁDRAIG Ó RIAIN; Hon. Sec. SEÁN HUTTON; publs *Main Series: 63 vols of Irish-language texts with English translation*, *Subsidiary Series: 20 vols.*

MEDICINE

Dental Council: 57 Merrion Sq., Dublin 2; tel. (1) 6762069; fax (1) 6762076; e-mail info@ dentalcouncil.ie; internet www.dentalcouncil .ie; f. 1928 as the Dental Board, superseded by the Dental Council in 1985; registers dentists and controls standards of education and conduct among dentists in Ireland; Pres. Dr MARTIN HOLOHAN; Chief Officer and Registrar DAVID O'FLYNN.

Irish Medical Organisation: IMO House, 10 Fitzwilliam Pl., Dublin 2; tel. (1) 6767273; fax (1) 6612758; e-mail imo@imo.ie; internet www.imo.ie; f. 1936; 6,000 mems; Pres. Prof. SEÁN TIERNEY; CEO GEORGE MCNEICE; publ. *Irish Medical Journal* (10 a year).

Medical Council: Kingram House, Kingram Pl., Dublin 2; tel. (1) 4983100; fax (1) 4983102; e-mail nfo@mcirl.ie; internet www .medicalcouncil.ie; f. 1978; 17,000 mems; Pres. Prof. KIERAN MURPHY; CEO CAROLINE SPILLANE.

Pharmaceutical Society of Ireland: 18 Shrewsbury Rd, Ballsbridge, Dublin 4; tel. (1) 2184000; fax (1) 2837678; e-mail info@ pharmaceuticalsociety.ie; internet www .pharmaceuticalsociety.ie; f. 1875; reorganized 2007; Pres. NOELEEN HARVEY; Registrar and CEO Dr AMBROSE MCLOUGHLIN; publ. *The Irish Pharmacy Journal* (irregular).

Royal Academy of Medicine in Ireland: Frederick House, 4th Floor, 19 S Frederick St, Dublin 2; tel. (1) 6334820; fax (1) 6334918; e-mail secretary@rcpi.ie; internet www.rami.ie; f. 1882; 1,200 fellows/mems; Pres. Dr FENTON HOWELL; Gen. Sec. and Treas. Dr JOHN O'CONNOR; publ. *Irish Journal of Medical Science* (4 a year).

NATURAL SCIENCES

Biological Sciences

Dublin University Biological Association: POB 14, Regent House, Trinity College, Dublin; e-mail biosoc@csc.tcd.ie; internet www.tcdbiosoc.com; f. 1874; hosts lectures and discussion groups on medical topics and arranges booksales and social events; 550 mems; library of 200 vols, access by request; Pres. Prof. JOHN O'LEARY; Chair. ANNA FEENEY; Treas. GABRIEL BEECHAM; Sec. DANIELLE COURTNEY; publ. *Trinity Student Medical Journal* (online, www.tcd.ie/tsmj).

Dublin Zoo: Phoenix Park, Dublin 8; tel. (1) 4748900; fax (1) 6771660; e-mail info@ dublinzoo.ie; internet www.dublinzoo.ie; f. 1830; 9,000 mems; Dir LEO OOSTERWEGHEL.

Physical Sciences

Institute of Chemistry of Ireland: POB 9322, Cardiff Lane, Dublin 2; e-mail info@ instituteofchemistry.org; internet www .chemistryireland.org; f. 1950; organizes meetings and confs; promotes chemistry at all levels, from school competitions and local events to EC meetings; 800 mems; Pres. Dr B. A. MURRAY; Hon. Sec. J. P. RYAN; publ. *Irish Chemical News* (2 a year).

Institute of Physics in Ireland: c/o Department of Experimental Physics, University College Dublin, Belfield, Dublin 4; tel. (1) 7162216; fax (1) 2837275; e-mail alison .hackett@iop.org; internet www.iopireland .org; f. 1964 as the Irish Branch of the Institute of Physics; learned society and professional body for the advancement of physics and physics education on the island of Ireland; 1,700 mems; Co-Chair. Prof. ROBERT BOWMAN, Dr KEVIN MCGUIGAN; Sec. Dr CRÉIDHE O'SULLIVAN; publ. *Physics World* (12 a year).

Irish Astronomical Society: POB 2547, Dublin 14; tel. (1) 2981268; e-mail ias1937@ hotmail.com; internet www.irishastrosoc.org; f. 1937; 150 mems; library: video cassette and book libraries; Pres. MICHAEL MURPHY; Treas. DAVID BRANIGAN; Sec. (vacant); publs *Orbit* (6 a year), *Sky High* (1 a year).

PHILOSOPHY AND PSYCHOLOGY

Psychological Society of Ireland: CX House, 2A Corn Exchange Pl., Poolbeg St, Dublin 2; tel. (1) 4749160; fax (1) 4749161; e-mail info@psihq.ie; internet www.psihq.ie; f. 1970 to advance psychological knowledge and research in Ireland, to ensure maintenance of high standards of professional training and practice, to seek the devt of psychological services; 2,000 mems; Pres. NIALL PENDER; Hon. Sec. MARK LATIMER; publs *The Irish Journal of Psychology*, *The Irish Psychologist*.

Theosophical Society in Ireland: 31 Pembroke Rd, Dublin 4; tel. (1) 6602517; e-mail duffer@dublin.ie; internet www .theosophyireland.com; f. 1919; encourages the study of comparative religion, philosophy and science; Pres. JOHN DOHERTY; Sec. MARIE HARKNESS; publ. *Bulletin* (12 a year).

University Philosophical Society: Graduate Memorial Bldg, Trinity College, Dublin 2; tel. (87) 2108423; fax (1) 6778996; e-mail president@tcdphil.com; internet www.tcdphil .com; f. 1684, re-founded 1854; 'Major Society' for composition, reading and discussion of papers on literary, political, philosophical and scientific subjects; regular guest speakers; 7,500 mems; Pres. EOIN O'LIATHAIN; Sec. LORCAN CLARKE; publs *Laws*, *Philander* (1 a year).

TECHNOLOGY

Biomedical/Clinical Engineering Association of Ireland: c/o Dept of Biomedical Engineering, Cork University Hospital, Bishopstown Rd, Wilton, Cork; tel. (21) 4922849; e-mail noel.murphy@hse.ie; internet www.beai.ie; f. 1992; Chair. BERNARD MURPHY; Sec. NOEL MURPHY; publ. *BEAI Spectrum* (4 a year).

Engineers Ireland: 22 Clyde Rd, Ballsbridge, Dublin 4; tel. (1) 6651300; fax (1) 6685508; e-mail info@engineersireland.ie; internet www.engineersireland.ie; f. 1835; fmrly the Institution of Engineers of Ireland; promotes knowledge and advancement of the engineering profession, conducts examinations and confers the designations 'Chartered Engineer', 'Associate Engineer' and 'Engineering Technician'; 18,000 mems; Pres. MARTIN LOWERY; Dir-Gen. JOHN POWER; publ. *Engineers Journal* (10 a year).

Institution of Civil Engineers (Republic of Ireland Division): 8 Ardglas, Dundrum, Dublin 16; tel. (1) 2224260; internet www.ice .org.uk/nearyou/europe/rep-of-ireland; f. 1818; 881 mems; library of 130,000 vols; Chair. DON N. MCENTEE; publs *Municipal Engineer* (4 a year), *New Civil Engineer* (52 a year).

Institution of Engineering and Technology (Republic of Ireland Division): ESB National Grid, Lower Fitzwilliam St, Dublin 2; e-mail erc@ucd.ie; internet www.theiet .org/local/emea/europe/ireland; f. 2006 following merger of the Institution of Electrical Engineers and the Institution of Incorporated Engineers; Chair. PAT KIDNEY; Hon. Sec. MARK NEEDHAM.

Research Institutes
GENERAL

National Centre for Sensor Research: Research and Engineering Bldg, Dublin City University, Glasnevin, Dublin 9; tel. (1) 7008821; fax (1) 7008021; e-mail ncsr@dcu .ie; internet www.dcu.ie/~ncsr; f. 1999; attached to Dublin City University; multidisciplinary facility that aims to develop future sensory technologies for economic and societal benefit for application in, *inter alia*, health monitoring and diagnostics, environmental monitoring and nanomedicine; Dir Prof. DERMOT DIAMOND.

Science Policy Research Centre: Faculty of Commerce, Univ. College Dublin, Belfield, Dublin 4; tel. (1) 7068263; fax (1) 7061132; e-mail joe.cogan@ucd.ie; f. 1969 to carry out research and to undertake commissioned studies in areas related to technology and innovation policy; small private library; Dir Prof. D. J. COGAN.

AGRICULTURE, FISHERIES AND VETERINARY SCIENCE

Teagasc (Agriculture and Food Development Authority): Oak Park, Carlow; tel. (59) 9170200; fax (59) 9182097; e-mail info@ teagasc.ie; internet www.teagasc.ie; f. 1988; nat. body providing advisory, research, education and training services to the agriculture and food industry; activities are integrated and managed through 6 divs; Chair. Dr NOEL CAWLEY; Dir Prof. GERRY BOYLE; publs *Irish Journal of Agricultural and Food Research* (2 a year), *Today's Farm* (6 a year), *TResearch* (4 a year).

Divisions:

Ashtown Food Research Centre: Ashtown, Dublin 15; tel. (1) 8059500; fax (1) 8059550; e-mail declan.troy@teagasc.ie; internet www.teagasc.ie/ashtown; centre providing research, devt and consultancy services for all aspects of food production (except dairy products), food safety and nutrition, and market studies; Head Dr DECLAN TROY.

Kildalton College of Agriculture: Piltown, Co Kilkenny; tel. (51) 643105; fax (51) 643797; e-mail mgalvin@kildalton .teagasc.ie; nat. crops div. and headquarters for advisory and training services in Teagasc South; Dir MICHAEL GALVIN.

Kinsealy Research Centre: Malahide Rd, Dublin, 17; tel. (1) 8460644; fax (1) 8460524; e-mail bfarrell@grange.teagasc .ie; nat. beef div.; headquarters for advis-

ory and training services in Teagasc North; Dir DONAL CAREY.

Moorepark Research and Development Division (Teagasc): Fermoy, Co Cork; tel. (25) 42222; fax (25) 42340; nat. centre for research in dairying and pig production; Head of Dairy Husbandry Dr PATRICK DILLON; Head of Pig Husbandry BRENDAN LYNCH.

National Dairy Products Research Centre: Moorepark, Fermoy, Co Cork; tel. (25) 42222; fax (25) 42340; e-mail ldonnelly@moorepark.teagasc.ie; nat. centre providing research, devt and consultancy services; Dir Dr PATRICK DILLON.

Rural Development Division (Teagasc): Athenry, Co Galway; tel. (91) 845845; fax (91) 845847; e-mail pseery@ athenry.teagasc.ie; nat. centre for rural devt; Dir PETER SEERY.

BIBLIOGRAPHY, LIBRARY SCIENCE AND MUSEOLOGY

Irish Manuscripts Commission: 45 Merrion Sq., Dublin 2; tel. (1) 6761610; fax (1) 6623832; e-mail support@irishmanuscripts .ie; internet www.irishmanuscripts.ie; f. 1928; publishes primary manuscript sources for Irish history located in public and private archives in Ireland and abroad; 21 mems; Chair. Prof. JAMES MCGUIRE; publ. *Analecta Hibernica* (irregular).

ECONOMICS, LAW AND POLITICS

Economic and Social Research Institute: Whitaker Sq., Sir John Rogerson's Quay, Dublin 2; tel. (1) 8632000; fax (1) 8632100; e-mail admin@esri.ie; internet www.esri.ie; f. 1960; library of 40,000 vols; Dir Prof. FRANCES RUANE; publs *Medium Term Review* (every 2 years), *Quarterly Economic Commentary*, *The Economic and Social Review* (4 a year).

Geary Institute: Geary Bldg, Belfield, Dublin 4; tel. (1) 7164615; fax (1) 7161108; e-mail geary@ucd.ie; internet www.ucd.ie/ geary; f. 1999; attached to University College Dublin; supports frontier methods of investigation and provides objective analysis and solutions that address the economic and social challenges facing policy makers; Dir Prof. COLM HARMON.

HISTORY, GEOGRAPHY AND ARCHAEOLOGY

Office of the Chief Herald of Ireland: 2 Kildare St, Dublin 2; tel. (1) 6030311; fax (1) 6621062; e-mail herald@nli.ie; internet www .nli.ie; f. 1552; granting, confirming and registering of armorial bearings; 1,000 MSS since the 16th century, 100,000 archive items since 1800; Chief Herald and Keeper COLETTE O'FLAHERTY.

LANGUAGE AND LITERATURE

Instiúid Teangeolaíochta Éireann/Linguistics Institute of Ireland: 31 Fitzwilliam Pl., Dublin 2; tel. (1) 6765489; fax (1) 6610004; f. 1972; research in applied linguistics with special reference to the Irish language and teaching and learning of languages generally; 30 mems; library of 10,000 books, 151 periodicals; Chair. CLÍONA DE BHALDRAITHE MARSH; Dir EOGHAN MAC AOGÁIN; publs *Language, Culture and Curriculum* (3 a year), *Teangeolas* (2 a year).

MEDICINE

Health Research Board: 73 Lower Baggot St, Dublin 2; tel. (1) 2345000; fax (1) 6612335; e-mail hrb@hrb.ie; internet www .hrb.ie; f. 1986 by merger of the Medico-Social Research Board and the Medical

Research Council of Ireland; Chair. REG SHAW.

Molecular Medicine Ireland: Newman House, 85A St Stephen's Green, Dublin 2; tel. and fax (1) 4779823; e-mail info@ molecularmedicineireland.ie; internet www .molecularmedicineireland.ie; f. 2002 as the Dublin Molecular Medicine Centre; present name adopted 2008; collaboration between National University of Ireland Galway, Royal College of Surgeons in Ireland, Trinity College Dublin, University College Cork and University College Dublin; aims to accelerate the translation of biomedical research into improved health care diagnostics and therapies; Chair. Dr DAMIAN O'CONNELL; Chief Exec. Dr RUTH BARRINGTON.

NATURAL SCIENCES
Physical Sciences

Dunsink Observatory: School of Cosmic Physics, Castleknock, Dublin 15; tel. (1) 8387911; fax (1) 8387090; e-mail astro@ dunsink.dias.ie; internet www.dunsink.dias .ie; f. 1785; part of Dublin Institute for Advanced Studies; library of 5,000 vols, 75 periodicals; Dir Prof. EVERT MEURS; Sec. CAROL WOODS.

Marine Institute: Rinville, Oranmore, Co Galway; tel. (91) 387200; fax (91) 387201; e-mail institute.mail@marine.ie; internet www.marine.ie; f. 1991; assesses and realizes the economic potential of Ireland's marine resources, promotes the sustainable development of marine industry through strategic funding programmes and essential scientific services, and safeguards the marine environment through research and environmental monitoring; Chair. JIM FENNELL; publ. *Irish Fisheries Bulletin* (irregular).

National Institute for Bioprocessing Research and Training: Engineering Bldg, Belfield, Dublin 4; tel. (1) 7161946; fax (1) 7161873; e-mail info@nibrt.ie; internet www.nibrt.ie; f. 2006; collaborative project between Dublin City University, Institute of Technology Sligo, Trinity College Dublin and University College Dublin; Chair. JOE HARFORD; CEO Dr MAURICE TREACY.

National Institute for Cellular Biotechnology: Dublin City University, Ballymun Rd & Collins Ave, Dublin 9; tel. (1) 7005700; fax (1) 7005484; e-mail nicb@dcu.ie; internet www.nicb.dcu.ie; f. 2001; attached to Dublin City University; collaboration between Dublin City University, Institute of Technology Tallaght and National University of Ireland, Maynooth; Dir Prof. MARTIN CLYNES.

Libraries and Archives
Cork

Cork City Libraries: 57–61 Grand Parade, Cork; tel. (21) 4924900; fax (21) 4275684; e-mail libraries@corkcity.ie; internet www .corkcitylibraries.ie; f. 1892; 420,017 vols, incl. extensive local studies and reference collns in books, newspapers and journals; large music colln in Rory Gallagher Music Library; City Librarian LIAM RONAYNE.

Cork County Library: Cork County Library and Arts Service, County Library Bldg, Carrigrohane Rd, Cork; tel. (21) 4546499; e-mail corkcountylibrary@corkcoco .ie; internet www.corkcoco.ie/library; 1,080,000 vols, 90 periodicals; 28 brs, 6 mobile libraries; Librarian (vacant).

Cork Institute of Technology Bishopstown Library: Rossa Ave, Bishopstown, Cork; tel. (21) 4326501; fax (21) 4326714; e-mail library.info@cit.ie; internet library.cit .ie; brs at Cork School of Music and Crawford

College of Art and Design; 60,000 vols; Librarian DERRY DELANEY.

University College Cork Library: Boole Library, University College Cork, College Rd, Cork; tel. (21) 4902794; fax (21) 4273428; e-mail library@ucc.ie; internet booleweb.ucc .ie; f. 1849; 700,000 vols, incl. Irish MSS colln (microfilm), Senft (philosophy), Torna (Irish), Cooke (travel), John E. Cummings Memorial Colln (humour), Langlands Colln (Africa); Postgraduate Research Library currently under construction; EU documentation centre; Irish copyright privilege; Librarian JOHN FITZGERALD.

Dublin

Central Catholic Library: 74 Merrion Sq., Dublin 2; tel. (1) 6761264; e-mail catholiclibrary@imagine.ie; internet www .catholiclibrary.ie; f. 1922; controlled by the Central Catholic Library Asscn; open to the public; lending and reference depts containing material on every aspect of Catholicism, on other Christian denominations and other religions, Irish history and culture, philosophy; 100,000 vols, incl. large journal colln, spec. colln of 2,000 vols on Christian art, Ireland Colln; Librarian Dr TERESA WHITINGTON; Hon. Librarian PETER COSTELLO.

Chester Beatty Library: Dublin Castle, Dublin 2; tel. (1) 4070750; fax (1) 4070760; e-mail info@cbl.ie; internet www.cbl.ie; f. 1953; donated to the Irish nation by Sir Alfred Chester Beatty in 1968; contains one of the world's leading collns of Islamic and East Asian art, important Western and Biblical MSS and miniatures; incunabula and other printed books; Dir Dr MICHAEL RYAN.

Dublin City Public Libraries: 138–144 Pearse St, Dublin 2; tel. (1) 6744800; fax (1) 6744879; e-mail dublinpubliclibraries@ dublincity.ie; internet www .dublincitypubliclibraries.ie; f. 1884; 2,400,000 vols; spec. collns incl. early Dublin printing and fine binding, incunabula, political pamphlets and cartoons, Dublin periodicals and 18th-century plays, Abbey Theatre material, Swift and Yeats material; extensive local history colln in books, newspapers and pictures; representative holdings of modern Dublin presses; spec. music library; language learning centre; City Librarian MARGARET HAYES.

Irish Theatre Archive: c/o Dublin City Library and Archive, 138–144 Pearse St, Dublin 2; tel. (1) 6744800; fax (1) 6744881; e-mail cityarchives@dublincity.ie; internet www.dublincity.ie; f. 1981; collects and preserves Ireland's theatre heritage; colln incl. programmes, posters, play-scripts, promptbooks, etc.; organizes lecture series, exhibitions; Archivist Dr MARY CLARK.

Law Library of Ireland: Four Courts, Dublin 7; tel. (1) 8175000; fax (1) 8175150; e-mail barcouncil@lawlibrary.ie; internet www.lawlibrary.ie; controlled by The Bar Council of Ireland; open to mems of the Irish Bar only; 100,000 vols; Chair., Professional Services Cttee RODERICK MAGUIRE; publ. *The Bar Review* (irregular).

Library Council: 53–54 Upper Mount St, Dublin 2; tel. (1) 6761167; fax (1) 6766721; e-mail info@librarycouncil.ie; internet www .librarycouncil.ie; f. 1947 by Public Libraries Act; advises local authorities and the Min. for the Environment, Heritage and Local Govt on the devt of public library services; provides an information service on libraries and librarianship; operates the inter-library lending system for Ireland, and provides the Secretariat for the Cttee on Library Cooperation in Ireland; operates Public Lending Remuneration Office est. by the Copyright and Related Rights (Amendment) Act 2007; Dir NORMA MCDERMOTT; publ. *Irish Library News* (11 a year).

Marsh's Library: St Patrick's Close, Dublin 8; tel. and fax (1) 4543511; e-mail keeper@ marshlibrary.ie; internet www.marshlibrary .ie; f. 1701; 25,000 vols and 300 MSS; Keeper Dr MURIEL MCCARTHY.

National Archives of Ireland: Bishop St, Dublin 8; tel. (1) 4072300; fax (1) 4072333; e-mail mail@nationalarchives.ie; internet www.nationalarchives.ie; f. 1988 (merger of Public Record Office, f. 1867, and State Paper Office, f. 1702), under the Nat. Archives Act; preserves and makes accessible the records of Depts of State, courts, other public service orgs and private donors; 50,000 linear m of archives; Dir Dr DAVID CRAIG.

National Library of Ireland: Kildare St, Dublin 2; tel. (1) 6030200; fax (1) 6612523; e-mail info@nli.ie; internet www.nli.ie; f. 1877; 8,000,000 vols incl. Irish printing colln, pamphlets, periodicals, newspapers, 70,000 MSS, incl. 1,200 Gaelic MSS, 630,000 photographic negatives, 90,000 prints and drawings, ephemera and music; Dir FIONA ROSS; Keeper of Manuscripts and Chief Herald COLETTE O'FLAHERTY; publ. *National Library of Ireland News* (3 a year).

Oireachtas Library and Research Service: Leinster House, Dublin 2; tel. (1) 6184701; fax (1) 6184109; e-mail library.and .research@oireachtas.ie; internet www .oireachtas.ie; f. 1922; information and research services to support the work of both Houses of the Oireachtas (Parliament), cttees and individual mems of Parliament; Head of Library and Research Service MADELAINE DENNISON; publ. *Spotlight* (12 a year).

Representative Church Body Library: Braemor Park, Churchtown, Dublin 14; tel. (1) 4923979; fax (1) 4924770; e-mail library@ ireland.anglican.org; internet www.library .ireland.anglican.org; f. 1932; theological library controlled by the Representative Body of the Church of Ireland; 40,000 vols, mainly theology, history, ethics and education; Church of Ireland archives; MSS colln, mainly ecclesiastical; Librarian and Archivist Dr RAYMOND REFAUSSÉ.

Royal College of Surgeons in Ireland Library (The Mercer Library): Mercer St Lower, Dublin 2; tel. (1) 4022407; fax (1) 4022457; e-mail library@rcsi.ie; internet www.rcsi.ie/library; f. 1784; 75,000 vols; spec. collns: archives of RCSI and Dublin hospitals, 10,000 rare books, medical pamphlets from 17th century; Chief Librarian KATE KELLY.

Royal Dublin Society Library (RDS Library): Merrion Rd, Ballsbridge, Dublin 4; tel. (1) 2407254; fax (1) 6604014; e-mail librarydesk@rds.ie; internet www.rds.ie/ library; f. 1731; 100,000 vols, incl. more than 4,000 relating to Ireland, many of them old and rare; 6,000 works and pamphlets on all branches of agricultural science up to 1920, incl. 1,500 works of equestrian interest; reference collection of more than 2,000 vols, incl. the 'Thoms Street' directory on Dublin, since the 1840s; the scientific and private correspondence of Professor George Francis Fitzgerald (1851–1901), physicist at Trinity College, Dublin, who first suggested a method of producing radio waves) of which there are more than 1,000 letters; Irish local history colln and genealogical information; Dublin horse show archives, incl. the Maymes Ansell archive of equestrian photographs, archival colln incl. the written and visual heritage of the Society manuscript material from 1731, rare first edns of science publs, the papers of Dr Horace H. Poole, Richard M. Barrington and John Edmund Carew; the records of the Radium Institute and the Maymes Ansell Archive of Equestrian Photographs; Dir of Library JOANNA QUINN; Librarian GERARD WHELAN.

Trinity College Library: College St, Dublin 2; tel. (1) 8961127; fax (1) 6719003; e-mail dutylibrarian@tcd.ie; internet www .tcd.ie/library; f. 1592; Univ. and British/ Irish legal deposit library; 5,000,000 printed vols, 6,000 MSS, incl. the Book of Kells and other medieval MSS; collns of 17th- and 18th-century French printed materials and caricatures; extensive colln of music scores and maps; visitor centre; Librarian and College Archivist ROBIN ADAMS; publ. *Long Room* (1 a year).

University College Dublin Library: Belfield, Dublin 4; tel. (1) 7167583; fax (1) 2837667; e-mail library@ucd.ie; internet www.ucd.ie/library; f. 1908; 5 brs; 1,200,000 vols, 8,000 periodicals; spec. collns incl. pre-1850 imprints, Baron Palles (Law) Library of 2,500 vols, Zimmer (Celtic) Library of 2,000 vols, C. P. Curran (Irish literature), John McCormack (music), Colm Ó Lochlainn (Irish printing), F. J. O'Kelley (Irish printing) and John L. Sweeney (Literature) collns; MSS colln; literary archives and papers incl. those of Sean O'Riordain, Patrick Kavanagh, Mary Lavin, Maeve Binchy and Frank McGuinness; Univ. Librarian Dr JOHN BROOKS HOWARD.

Galway

Galway City Library: St Augustine St, Galway; tel. (91) 561666; fax (91) 566852; e-mail info@galwaylibrary.ie; internet www .galwaylibrary.ie; f. 1927; 3 brs; Librarian PATRICK MCMAHON.

Galway County Libraries: Island House, Cathedral Sq., Galway; tel. (91) 562471; fax (91) 565039; e-mail info@galwaylibrary.ie; internet www.galwaylibrary.ie; f. 1927; 7 full-time and 20 part-time brs; 350,000 vols; County Librarian PATRICK MCMAHON.

James Hardiman Library, National University of Ireland, Galway: National University of Ireland, University Rd, Galway; tel. (91) 493399; fax (91) 522394; e-mail library@nuigalway.ie; internet www.library .nuigalway.ie; f. 1849; 463,000 vols; 350 archival collns in areas of theatre, literature, politics and history; Librarian MARIE REDDAN.

Limerick

Limerick City Library: The Granary, Michael St, Limerick; tel. (61) 407510; fax (61) 411506; e-mail citylib@limerickcity.ie; internet www.limerickcorp.ie/library; 3 br. libraries; Librarian DOLORES DOYLE.

Limerick County Library: Lissanalta House, Dooradoyle Rd, Co Limerick; tel. (61) 496526; fax (61) 583135; e-mail libinfo@ limerickcoco.ie; internet www.lcc.ie/library; 21 brs; Librarian DAMIEN BRADY.

Maynooth

John Paul II Library, National University of Ireland, Maynooth: Maynooth, Co Kildare; tel. (1) 7083884; fax (1) 6286008; e-mail library.information@nuim.ie; internet library.nuim.ie; f. 1795; 643,437 vols (incl. 337,795 electronic books and 43,089 electronic journals); Librarian CATHAL MCCAULEY.

Waterford

Waterford City Council Central Library: Lady Lane, Waterford; tel. (51) 849975; fax (51) 850031; e-mail library@waterfordcity.ie; internet www.waterfordcity.ie/library; 3 brs; audio-listening and language-learning facilities, e-books, e-audio books; Librarian JANE CANTWELL.

Waterford County Library Headquarters: Ballyanchor Rd, Lismore, Co Waterford; tel. (58) 21370; e-mail libraryhq@waterfordcoco.ie; internet www.waterfordcountylibrary.ie; 8 brs; County Librarian JEAN WEBSTER (acting); Exec. Sec. ANNE WALSH.

Museums and Art Galleries

Cork

Cork Public Museum: Fitzgerald Park, The Mardyke, Cork; tel. (21) 4270679; fax (21) 4270931; e-mail museum@corkcity.ie; internet www.corkcity.ie/services/recreationamenityculture/museum; f. 1910; sections devoted to Irish history and archaeology, also municipal, social and economic history, Cork glass, silver and lace; items of special interest include the Cork helmet horns, the Garryduff gold bird, the Roche silver collar, civic maces, municipal oar, freedom boxes and Grace Cup of Cork Corporation; Curator STELLA CHERRY.

Dublin

Civic Museum: 58 South William St, Dublin 2; tel. (1) 6794260; f. 1953; attached to Dublin Public Libraries; original exhibits of antiquarian and historical interest pertaining to Dublin; subjects in the permanent colln incl. streets and buildings of Dublin, traders, industry, transport, political history, maps; Curator THOMAS P. O'CONNOR.

Dublin City Gallery, The Hugh Lane: Charlemont House, Parnell Sq. North, Dublin 1; tel. (1) 2225550; fax (1) 8722182; e-mail info.hughlane@dublincity.ie; internet www.hughlane.ie; f. 1908; works of Irish, English and European schools of painting, and pictures from the Sir Hugh Lane colln; sculptures; Dir BARBARA DAWSON.

Dublin Writers Museum: 18 Parnell Sq., Dublin 1; tel. (1) 8722077; fax (1) 8722231; e-mail writers@dublintourism.ie; internet www.writersmuseum.com; f. 1991; history of Irish literature; library; Operations Man. NYRÉE LANDRY; Curator ROBERT NICHOLSON.

Irish Museum of Modern Art: Royal Hospital, Military Rd, Kilmainham, Dublin 8; tel. (1) 6129900; fax (1) 6129999; e-mail info@imma.ie; internet www.imma.ie; f. 1991; works by Irish and non-Irish artists since the beginning of the 20th century; Chair. EOIN MCGONIGAL; Dir ENRIQUE JUNCOSA (acting).

James Joyce Museum: Joyce Tower, Sandycove, Co Dublin; tel. and fax (1) 2809265; e-mail joycetower@dublintourism.ie; f. 1962; papers and personal effects of the writer (1882–1941) and critical works about him; library of 550 vols; Curator ROBERT NICHOLSON.

National Botanic Gardens Glasnevin: Glasnevin, Dublin 9; tel. (1) 8040300; fax (1) 8360080; e-mail botanicgardens@opw.ie; internet www.botanicgardens.ie; f. 1795; incl. Irish National Herbarium; visitor centre combines a lecture hall, restaurant and display area with exhibits relating to the history and purpose of the gardens; library of 40,000 vols, incl. collns of illustrated botanical works, periodicals and rare books; Dir Dr MATTHEW JEBB; publ. *Glasra–Contributions from the National Botanic Gardens, Glasnevin* (1 a year).

National Gallery of Ireland: Merrion Sq. W and Clare St, Dublin 2; tel. (1) 6615133; fax (1) 6615372; e-mail info@ngi.ie; internet www.nationalgallery.ie; f. 1854; nat., historical and portrait galleries; continental European, British and Irish masters since the 14th century; 2,500 oil paintings, 300 sculptures, 5,200 drawings and watercolours, 3,000 prints; library of 70,000 vols; research services comprise the Fine Art Library (50,000 vols), NGI Archive, Diageo Print Room, ESB Centre for the Study of Irish Art and the Yeats Archive; Dir RAYMOND KEAVENEY.

National Museum of Ireland: Kildare St, Dublin 2; tel. (1) 6777444; fax (1) 6777450; e-mail marketing@museum.ie; internet www.museum.ie; f. 1877 by the Science and Arts Museums Act; incl. (1) Irish Antiquities Div. (Keeper EAMONN P. KELLY); (2) Art and Industrial Div. (Keeper MICHAEL KENNY); (3) Irish Folklife Div. (Keeper TONY CANDON); (4) Natural History Div., which incl. zoological and geological sections (Keeper NIGEL MONAGHAN); Dir Dr PATRICK F. WALLACE.

Royal College of Surgeons in Ireland Museum: St Stephen's Green, Dublin 2; f. 1820; Asst Curator Prof. DOROTHY BENSON.

Galway

Galway Arts Centre: 47 Dominick St, Galway; tel. (91) 565886; fax (91) 568642; e-mail info@galwayartscentre.ie; internet www.galwayartscentre.ie; f. 1982; houses national and international contemporary art works; also provides classes in art, writing and photography; Man. Dir PARAIC BREATHNACH.

Galway City Museum: Spanish Parade, Galway; tel. (91) 532460; fax (91) 532467; e-mail museum@galwaycity.ie; internet www.galwaycitymuseum.ie; f. 1976; 1,000 objects of cultural heritage related to the city of Galway and its people, past and present; also carries a varied selection of artwork; Dir SARAH GILLESPIE.

Limerick

Limerick City Gallery of Art: c/o Istabraq Hall, Limerick City Council, Merchants Quay, Limerick; tel. (61) 310633; fax (61) 310228; e-mail artgallery@limerickcity.ie; internet gallery.limerick.ie; f. 1948 as the Limerick Free Art Gallery; contemporary art works, incl. prominent colln (numbering 831 works) of Irish art from 18th–20th centuries; also holds the Nat. Colln of Contemporary Drawing and the Michael O'Connor Int. Poster Colln comprising more than 2,800 works of international design; Curator MARIAN LOVETT (acting).

Maynooth

National Science Museum: Maynooth Campus, Maynooth, Co Kildare; e-mail niall.mckeith@may.ie; internet www.nuim.ie/museum; f. 1934; attached to St Patrick's College Maynooth; houses ecclesiastical and scientific artefacts; Curator Dr NIALL MCKEITH.

Strokestown

Strokestown Park House Garden and Famine Museum: Strokestown Park, Strokestown, Co Roscommon; tel. (78) 9633013; fax (78) 9633712; e-mail info@strokestownpark.ie; internet www.strokestownpark.ie/museum.html; f. 1994; collns related to the history of the Great Irish Famine of the 1840s; Man. JOHN O'DRISCOLL.

Waterford

Waterford County Museum: St Augustine St, Dungarvan, Co Waterford; tel. (58) 45960; e-mail website@dungarvanmuseum.org; artefacts pertaining to the history of Dungarvan and the western Waterford area from medieval times through to the 20th century; collections incl. militaria, coins, photographs and video footage; Curator WILLIE FRAHER.

Universities

DUBLIN CITY UNIVERSITY

Ballymun Rd & Collins Ave, Dublin 9

Telephone: (1) 7005000

Fax: (1) 8360830

E-mail: public.affairs@dcu.ie

Internet: www.dcu.ie

Founded 1980 as National Institute for Higher Education, Dublin; university status 1989

State control

Academic year: September to May

Pres.: Prof. BRIAN MACCRAITH

Vice-Pres. for Learning Innovation: Prof. RICHARD O'KENNEDY

Vice-Pres. for Research: Prof. EUGENE KENNEDY

Deputy-Pres. and Registrar: Prof. ANNE SCOTT

Sec.: MARTIN CONRY

Dir of Library Services: PAUL SHEEHAN

Library of 250,000 vols

Number of teachers: 1,762

Number of students: 11,442 (8,909 full-time, 1,579 part-time, 954 distance learning)

DEANS

Dublin City University Business School: Prof. BERNARD PIERCE

Faculty of Engineering and Computing: JIM DOWLING

Faculty of Humanities and Social Sciences: Prof. EITHNE GUILFOYLE

Faculty of Science and Health: Prof. MALCOLM SMYTH

Oscail–National Distance Education Centre: Dr RONNIE SAUNDERS

ATTACHED INSTITUTE

National Distance Education Centre: Beo Orpen Bldg, Glasnevin, Dublin 9; tel. (1) 7005924; fax (1) 7005494; e-mail oscail.student@dcu.ie; internet www.oscail.ie; f. 1982; Faculty of the university; exec. arm of the Nat. Distance Education Ccl; Academic Dir SEAMUS FOX.

ATTACHED COLLEGES

Mater Dei Institute of Education: Clonliffe Rd, Dublin 3; tel. (1) 8086500; fax (1) 8370776; e-mail info@materdei.dcu.ie; internet www.materdei.ie; f. 1966; College of the University since 1999; courses in Irish Studies and Theology; 50 teachers; 545 students; library of 160,000 vols; Pres. DERMOT A. LANE; Dir ANDREW G. MCGRADY; Registrar ANNABELLA STOVER; publ. *Religion, Education and the Arts* (1 a year).

St Patrick's College: Drumcondra, Dublin 9; tel. (1) 8842000; fax (1) 8376197; e-mail presidents.office@spd.dcu.ie; internet www.spd.dcu.ie; f. 1875; College of the University since 1993; 58 teachers; 2,000 students; library of 100,000 vols; Pres. Dr PÁURIC TRAVERS; Registrar OLIVIA BREE; publ. *Studia Hibernica* (1 a year), *The Irish Journal of Education* (irregular).

NATIONAL UNIVERSITY OF IRELAND (NUI)

49 Merrion Sq., Dublin 2

Telephone: (1) 4392424

Fax: (1) 4392466

E-mail: registrar@nui.ie

Internet: www.nui.ie

Founded 1908

Abolition of the univ. announced by Minister for Education and Science in Jan. 2010;

however, no date for such action specified, and situation remained unclear at mid-2011

Chancellor: Dr MAURICE MANNING
Vice-Chancellor: Prof. HUGH BRADY
Registrar: Dr ATTRACTA HALPIN

Publication: *Éigse: A Journal of Irish Studies* (irregular).

CONSTITUENT COLLEGES

National University of Ireland, Galway

Galway
Telephone: (91) 524411
Fax: (91) 525700
E-mail: info@nuigalway.ie
Internet: www.nuigalway.ie

Founded 1845 as Queen's College, Galway; became Univ. College, Galway in 1908; present name 1997
Languages of instruction: English, Irish
Academic year: September to June

Pres.: Dr JAMES BROWNE
Deputy Pres. and Registrar: Prof. AN TOLLAMH NOLLAIG MACCONGÁIL (acting)
Vice-Pres. for Capital Projects: KEITH WARNOCK
Vice-Pres. for Innovation and Performance: Prof. CHRIS CURTIN
Vice-Pres. for Research: Prof. TERRY SMITH
Vice-Pres. for the Student Experience: MARY O'RIORDAN
Sec. for Academic Affairs: Dr AN TUASAL GEARÓID Ó CONLUAIN
Bursar: Dr MARY DOOLEY

Library: see Libraries and Archives
Number of teachers: 550
Number of students: 16,000

DEANS

College of Arts, Social Sciences and Celtic Studies: Dr EDWARD HERRINGL
College of Business, Public Policy and Law: Prof. WILLIAM GOLDEN
College of Engineering and Informatics: Prof. GERRY LYONS
College of Medicine, Nursing and Health Sciences: B. G. LOFTUS
College of Science: Prof. TOM SHERRY
School of Medicine: Prof. GERARD LOFTUS

PROFESSORS

Faculties of Arts and Celtic Studies:

BARRY, K., English
BRADLEY, D., Spanish
CANNY, N. P., History
CURTIN, C. A., Political Science and Sociology
ERSKINE, A. W., Classics
JAMES, J., Psychology
MAC CRAITH, M., Modern Irish
NÍ DHONNCHADHA, M., Old and Middle Irish and Celtic Philology
O'BRIEN, C., Italian
Ó GORMAILE, P., French
RICHARDSON, W., German
SCHMIDT-HANISSA, H., German
STROHMAYER, U., Geography
WADDELL, J., Archaeology
WORNER, M. H., Philosophy

Faculty of Commerce:

COLLINS, J. F., Accountancy and Finance
CUDDY, M. P., Economics
GREEN, R. H., Management
WARD, J. J., Marketing

Faculty of Engineering:

CUNNANE, C., Hydrology
LYONS, G. J., Information Technology
MCNAMARA, J. F., Mechanical Engineering
O'DONOGHUE, P. E., Civil Engineering
WILCOX, D., Electronic Engineering

Faculty of Law:

O'MALLEY, W. A., Business Law

QUINN, G., Law
SCHABAS, W., Human Rights Law

Faculty of Science:

BUTLER, R., Chemistry
COLLERAN, E., Microbiology
GUIRY, M. D. R., Botany
HINDE, J. P., Statistics
HURLEY, T. C., Mathematics
KANE, M. T., Physiology
LOWNES, N., Biochemistry
RICHARDSON, W., Spanish
RYAN, P. A., Geology
SMITH, T. J., Biomedical Engineering and Science
WALTON, P. W., Applied Physics

School of Medicine:

CALLAGY, G., Pathology
CANTILLON, P., General Practice
CORMICAN, M., Bacteriology
DOCKERY, P., Anatomy
EGAN, L., Pharmacology and Therapeutics
KERIN, M., Surgery
LAFFEY, J., Anaesthesia
LOFTUS, B. G., Paediatrics
MCCARTHY, P. A., Radiology
MCDONALD, C., Psychiatry
MORRISON, J., Obstetrics and Gynaecology
O'BRIEN, T., Medicine
WHEATLEY, A., Physiology

National University of Ireland, Maynooth

Maynooth, Co Kildare
Telephone: (1) 7086000
E-mail: admissions@nuim.ie
Internet: www.nuim.ie

Founded 1795 as St Patrick's College, Maynooth, which divided in 1997 into Nat. Univ. of Ireland, Maynooth, and a continuing St Patrick's College, Maynooth
State control
Languages of instruction: Irish, English
Academic year: September to June

Pres.: Prof. JOHN G. HUGHES
Vice-Pres. for Innovation: Dr JAMES A. WALSH
Registrar: DAVID REDMOND
Librarian: CATHAL MCCAULEY

Library: see Libraries and Archives
Number of teachers: 256
Number of students: 7,300

Publications: *ReSearch Magazine*, *The Bridge Alumni Magazine*

DEANS

Faculty of Arts, Celtic Studies and Philosophy: Dr THOMAS O'CONNOR
Faculty of Science and Engineering: Prof. BERNARD P. MAHON
Faculty of Social Sciences: Dr ROWENA PECCHENINO

University College Cork

Western Rd, Cork
Telephone: (21) 4903000
Fax: (21) 4273428
E-mail: registrar@ucc.ie
Internet: www.ucc.ie

Founded 1845 as Queen's College, Cork; changed to above in 1908
Academic year: October to September

Pres.: Dr MICHAEL MURPHY
Vice-Pres. for Academic Affairs and Registrar: Prof. PAUL GILLER
Vice-Pres. for External Relations: ÉAMONN P. SWEENEY
Vice-Pres. for Research Policy and Support: Prof. MICHAEL PETER
Vice-Pres. for the Student Experience: CON O'BRIEN
Vice-Pres. for Teaching and Learning: Prof. GRACE NEVILLE

Sec.: MICHAEL FARRELL
Chief Financial Officer and Bursar: DIARMUID COLLINS
Librarian: JOHN A. FITZGERALD
Number of teachers: 2,280 (539 full-time, 1,741 part-time)
Number of students: 17,000 full-time

Publication: *Chimera* (1 a year)

DEANS

College of Arts, Celtic Studies and Social Sciences: Prof. CAROLINE FENNELL
College of Business and Law: Prof. IRENE LYNCH-FANNON
College of Medicine and Health: Prof. GERALDINE MCCARTHY (acting)
College of Science, Engineering and Food Science: Prof. PATRICK FITZPATRICK

University College Dublin

Belfield, Dublin 4
Telephone: (1) 7167777
Fax: (1) 7161160
E-mail: communications@ucd.ie
Internet: www.ucd.ie
Languages of instruction: English, Irish
Founded 1854
Academic year: September to May

Pres.: Dr HUGH BRADY
Registrar, Deputy Pres. and Vice-Pres. for Academic Affairs: Dr PHILIP NOLAN
Vice-Pres. for Devt: AÍNE GIBBONS
Vice-Pres. for Research: Prof. DESMOND FITZGERALD
Vice-Pres. for Staff: EAMON DREA
Vice-Pres. for Students: Dr MARTIN BUTLER
Vice-Pres. for Univ. Relations: Dr PÁDRAIC CONWAY
Librarian: Dr JOHN B. HOWARD

Library: see Libraries and Archives
Number of teachers: 1,047 FTE
Number of students: 24,000

Publication: *Irish University Review* (2 a year)

DEANS

Arts and Celtic Studies, Prin. of College: Prof. MARY E. DALY
Business and Law, Prin. of College: TOM BEGLEY
Engineering, Mathematical and Physical Sciences, Prin. of College: Prof. NICK QUIRKE
Human Sciences, Prin. of College: Prof. BRIGID LAFFAN
Life Sciences, Prin. of College: Prof. MAURICE BOLAND

PROFESSORS

(Many professors are members of more than one faculty; entry here is shown under one faculty only)

College of Arts and Celtic Studies (Newman Bldg, Belfield, Dublin 4; tel. (1) 7168101; e-mail artsceltic@ucd.ie):

BARNES, J. C., Italian
BARTLETT, T., Modern Irish History
BREATNACH, P. A., Classical Irish
CALDICOTT, C. E. J., French
CLAYTON, M., Old and Middle English
CRUICKSHANK, D. W., Spanish
FANNING, J. R., Modern History
KIBERD, D., Anglo-Irish Literature and Drama
MCCARTHY, M. J., History of Art
MAYS, J. C. C., Modern English and American Literature
MEIKLE, J. L., American Studies
NÍ CATHÁIN, M. P., Early (incl. Medieval) Irish Language and Literature
Ó CATHÁIN, S., Irish Folklore
RAFTERY, B., Celtic Archaeology
RIDLEY, H. M., German

SMITH, A., Classics
WATSON, S., Modern Irish Language and Literature
WHITE, H., Music

College of Business and Law (Carysfort Ave, Blackrock, Dublin 4; tel. (1) 7168852; fax (1) 7168954):

BOURKE, P., Banking and Finance
BRADLEY, M. F., International Marketing
BRENNAN, N., Management
CASEY, J. P., Law
DEEGAN, A., Management Information Systems
HOURIHAN, A. P., Management of Financial Institutions
KELLY, W. A., Business Administration
LAMBKIN, M. V., Marketing
O'BRIEN, F. J., Accountancy
OSBOROUGH, W. N., Jurisprudence and Legal History
ROCHE, W. K., Industrial Relations and Human Resources
WALSH, E., Accounting

College of Engineering, Mathematical and Physical Sciences (UCD Engineering and Materials Science Centre, Belfield, Dublin 4; tel. (1) 7161864; fax (1) 7161155; e-mail engscience@ucd.ie):

BOLAND, P.
BRAZIL, T.
BYRNE, G., Mechanical Engineering
DINEEN, S.
GARDINER, S. J.
GRUNEWALD, M.
IVANKOVIC, A.
KEALY, L., Architecture
LYNCH, P.
MACELROY, J. M. D.
O'BRIEN, E. J., Civil Engineering
OTTEWILL, A.
SHANNON, P. M.
SMYTH, B.

College of Human Sciences (Newman Bldg (Room G210), Belfield, Dublin 4; tel. (1) 7168619; fax (1) 7168355; e-mail mary.buckley@ucd.ie):

BENSON, C., Psychology
BOLAND, P. J., Statistics
BURKE, M., Library and Information Studies
BUTTIMER, A., Geography
DINEEN, S., Mathematics
DRUDY, S., Education
GARVIN, T. C., Politics
LAFFAN, B., European Politics
LAFFEY, T. J., Mathematics
MENNELL, S., Sociology
MORAN, D., Philosophy
NEARY, J. P., Political Economy
OUHALLA, J., Linguistics
WALSH, B. M., National Economics of Ireland and Applied Economics

College of Life Sciences (Belfield, Dublin 4; tel. (1) 7162684; fax (1) 7162685; e-mail life-sciences@ucd.ie):

BAIRD, A., Veterinary Physiology and Biochemistry
BANNIGAN, J. G., Anatomy
BELLENGER, C. R., Veterinary Surgery
BOLAND, M. P., Animal Husbandry
BRADY, H. R., Medicine and Therapeutics
BRESNIHAN, B., Rheumatology
BURY, G., General Practice
CARRINGTON, S., Veterinary Anatomy
CASEY, P. R., Clinical Psychiatry
COLLINS, J. D., Farm Animal Clinical Studies
CURRY, J., Agricultural Zoology
CUSACK, D. A., Legal Medicine
DAWSON, K. A., Physical Chemistry
DERVAN, P. A., Pathology
DRUMM, B., Paediatrics
DUKE, E., Zoology
ENGEL, P. C., Biochemistry

ENNIS, J. T., Radiology
FITZGERALD, M. X., Medicine
FITZPATRICK, C., Child and Adolescent Psychiatry
FITZPATRICK, J. M., Surgery
GARDINER, J. J., Forestry
GREEN, A., Medical Genetics
HALL, W. W., Medical Microbiology
HEGARTY, A. F., Organic Chemistry
HENNERTY, M. J., Horticulture
JONES, B. R., Small Animal Clinical Studies
KEANE, M., Computer Science
KENNEDY, M. J., Geology
MACERLEAN, D. P., Radiology
MCKENNA, B., Food Science
MCKENNA, T. J., Investigative Endocrinology
MCNICHOLAS, F., Child and Adolescent Psychiatry
MORIARTY, D. C., Anaesthesiology
O'BRIEN, C., Ophthalmology
O'CALLAGHAN, E., Mental Health Research
O'HERLIHY, C., Obstetrics and Gynaecology
O'HIGGINS, N. J., Surgery
POWELL, D., Investigative Endocrinology
QUINN, P. J., Veterinary Microbiology and Parasitology
ROCHE, J. F., Animal Husbandry and Production
RYAN, M. P., Pharmacology
SHEAHAN, B., Veterinary Pathology
STEER, M., Botany
TREACY, M. M., Nursing
WALSH, E., Crop Science

ATTACHED SCHOOL

Michael Smurfit Graduate School of Business: tel. (1) 7168934; e-mail smurfitschool@ucd.ie; internet www.smurfitschool.ie; Dean Prof. TOM BEGLEY.

RECOGNIZED COLLEGES OF THE UNIVERSITY

Institute of Public Administration: 57–61 Lansdowne Rd, Ballsbridge, Dublin 4; tel. (1) 2403600; fax (1) 6689135; e-mail information@ipa.ie; internet www.ipa.ie; Dir-Gen. BRIAN CAWLEY; 1,500 individual mems; library of 40,000 vols, 300 periodicals; 1,400 students; publ. *Administration* (4 a year), *Personnel & Industrial Relations Directory* (every 2 years).

Milltown Institute of Theology and Philosophy: Milltown Park, Ranelagh, Dublin 6; tel. (1) 2776300; fax (1) 2692528; e-mail info@milltown-institute.ie; internet www.milltown-institute.ie; Pres. Dr CON CASEY (acting); Registrar Dr ANTHONY WHITE (acting)

DEANS

Philosophy: Prof. SANTIAGO SIA
Theology and Spirituality: Dr THOMAS WHELAN

National College of Art and Design: 100 Thomas St, Dublin 8; tel. (1) 6364200; fax (1) 6364207; e-mail fios@ncad.ie; internet www.ncad.ie; f. 1746; faculties of design, education, fine art, and history of art and design and complementary studies; Dir DECLAN MCGONAGLE; 75 teachers; 1,500 students (incl. part-time)

HEADS OF FACULTIES

Design: Prof. ANGELA WOODS
Education: Prof. GARY GRANVILLE
Fine Art: PHILIP NAPIER
Visual Culture: Prof. NIAMH O'SULLIVAN

Royal College of Surgeons in Ireland: 123 St Stephens Green, Dublin 2; tel. (1) 4022100; fax (1) 4022464; e-mail info@rcsi.ie; internet www.rcsi.ie; f. 1784; faculties of dentistry, nursing, radiologists, sports science and exercise medicine; college of anaesthetists; Pres. Prof. ELLIS MCGOVERN; Vice-

Pres. PATRICK J. BROE; CEO and Registrar Prof. CATHAL KELLY; 125 teachers; 900 students; publ. *Journal* (4 a year)

DEANS

School of Medical and Health Services: HANNAH MCGEE
School of Postgraduate Studies: Prof. KEVIN NOLAN

PROFESSORS

BRADFORD, A., Physiology
CLARKE, T., Paediatrics
COLLINS, P. B., Biochemistry
COLLUM, L. M., Ophthalmology
COWMAN, S., Nursing
CROKE, D., Biochemistry
CUNNINGHAM, A., Anaesthesia and Critical Care
FARRELL, M., Clinical Neurological Sciences
GRAHAM, I., Epidemiology and Preventive Medicine
HARBISON, J., Forensic Medicine and Toxicology
HILL, C., Clinical Surgery
HUMPHREYS, H., Clinical Microbiology
KELLY, J., Pharmacy
KENNY, D., Cardiovascular Biology
LEADER, M., Pathology
LEE, M., Radiology
LEE, T., Anatomy
MCCONKEY, S., International Health and Tropical Medicine
MCGEE, H., Psychology
MCMENAMIN, J., Paediatrics
MALONE, F., Obstetrics and Gynaecology
MURPHY, K., Psychiatry
NICHOLSON, A., Paediatrics
NOLAN, K., Pharmaceutical and Medicinal Chemistry
PREHN, J., Physiology
WADDINGTON, J., Clinical Neuroscience
WALSH, M. A., Otolaryngology

St Angela's College of Education: Lough Gill, Sligo; tel. (71) 9143580; fax (71) 9144585; e-mail mcapilitan@stacs.edu.ie; internet college.stangelas.ie; Bachelors degree courses in education, home economics and nursing; Pres. Dr ANNE TAHENY.

Shannon College of Hotel Management: Shannon International Airport, Shannon, Co Clare; tel. (61) 712210; fax (61) 475160; e-mail info@shannoncollege.com; internet www.shannoncollege.com; Dir PHILLIP J. SMYTH.

TRINITY COLLEGE DUBLIN, THE UNIVERSITY OF DUBLIN

College Green, Dublin 2
Telephone: (1) 8961000
Internet: www.tcd.ie

Founded 1592
Academic year: July to August
Chancellor: MARY TERESE WINIFRED ROBINSON,
Pro-Chancellor: Sir ANTHONY O'REILLY
Pro-Chancellor: T. D. SPEARMAN
Pro-Chancellor: VINCENT JOHN SCATTERGOOD
Provost: Dr JOHN HEGARTY
Vice-Provost: PATRICK JOHN PRENDERGAST
Registrar: JÜRGEN BARKHOFF
Sec.: (vacant): A. FITZGERALD
Librarian: ROBIN ADAMS

Library: see Libraries and Archives
Number of teachers: 1,843 (incl. academic research staff)
Number of students: 16,215 (13,594 full-time, 2,621 part-time incl. postgraduate)
Publication: *Hermathena* (2 a year)

DEANS

Faculty of Arts, Humanities and Social Sciences: Prof. MICHAEL ANTHONY MARSH

Faculty of Engineering, Mathematics and Science: Prof. DAVID CLIVE WILLIAMS
Faculty of Health Sciences: Prof. COLM ANTOINE O'MORÁIN
Graduate Studies: Prof. CAROL ANN O'SULLIVAN
Research: Dr DAVID GEORGE LLOYD
Students: Prof. GERARD FRANCIS WHYTE

PROFESSORS

AHMAD, K., Computer Science
ANWYL, R., Neurophysiology
BACIK, I., Criminal Law, Criminology and Penology
BARNES, L., Dermatology
BARRY, F., International Business and Development
BARRY, J., Population Health Medicine
BEGLEY, C., Nursing and MidwiferyBENOIT, K., Quantitative Social Sciences
BERGIN, C., Infectious Diseases
BINCHY, W., Law
BLAU, W., Physics of Advanced Materials
BOLAND, J., Chemistry Research
BRADLEY, D., Population Genetics
BYRNE, M., Cognitive Science
CAFFREY, M., Membrane Structural and Functional Biology
CAHILL, V., Computer Science
CAMPBELL, N., Speech and Communication Technology
CASSIDY, L., Ophthalmology
CHAHOUD, A., Latin
CLAFFEY, N., Periodontology
COAKLEY, D., Medical Gerontology
COEY, J., Natural and Experimental Philosophy
COFFEY, U. C., Electrical Engineering
COLEMAN, D., Oral and Applied Microbiology
CONLON, K., Surgery
CUNNINGHAM, E., Animal Genetics
DASILVA, L, Telecommunications
DORMAN, C., Microbiology
DRURY, L., Astronomy
DYER, M., Construction Innovation
FALLON, P., Translational Immunology
FEARSON, P., Psychiatry
FITZGERALD, M., Child and Adolescent Psychiatry
FITZPATRICK, D., Modern History
FITZPATRICK, J., Mechanical Engineering
FLINT, S., Oral Medicine
FOSTER, T., Molecular Microbiology
FRODL, T., Integrated Neuroimaging
GALLAGHER, M., Comparative Politics
GILL, M., Psychiatry
GILLIGAN, R., Social Work and Social Policy
GRAHAM, I., Cardiovascular Medicine
GRATTON, J., French
GREENE, S., Childhood Research
GRENE, N., English Literature
GRIMSON, J., Health Informatics
GUNNLAUGSSON, T., Chemistry
HARDIMAN, O., Neurology
HASLETT, J., Statistics
HEGNER, M., Physics
HINTON, J., Microbial Pathogenesis
HOGAN, L., Ecumenics
HOLLYWOOD, D., Clinical Oncology
HORNE, J., Modern European History
HUMPHRIES, P., Medical Molecular Genetics
JONES, M., Botany
KEARNEY, C., International Business
KELLEHER, D., Medicine
KELLY, J., Chemistry
KENNEDY, H., Forensic Psychiatry
KENNY, R., Geriatric Medicine
KRAMER, A., European History
LANE, S., Physiology
LANE, S., Respiratory Medicine
LAWLOR, B., Old Age Psychiatry
LUCEY, J., Psychiatry
LYNCH, M., Cellular Neuroscience
MARSH, M., Comparative Political Behaviour
MARTIN, S., Medical Genetics
MCCANN, S., Haematology

McCONNELL, D., Genetics
McGILP, J., Surface and Interface Optics
McGING, B., Greek
McGOWAN, M., Germanic Studies
McLOUGHAN, D., Psychiatry
McMANUS, P., Early Irish
MEAMY, J., Radiology
MILLS, K., Experimental Immunology
MURPHY, D., Obstetrics
MURRAY, J., Business Studies
NORMAND, C., Health Policy and Management
NUNN, J., Special Care Dentistry
O'BYRNE, K., Oncology
O'CONNELL, B., Restorative Dentistry
O'CONNOR, H., Gastroenterology
O'DOWD, T., General Practice
O'FARRELLY, C., Comparative Immunology
O'HAGAN, J., Economic Policy Studies
O'HALPIN, E., Contemporary Irish History
O'KEANNE, V., Psychiatry
O'KELLY, F., General Practice
O'LEARY, J., Pathology
O'MAHONY, M., Civil Engineering
O'MARA, S., Psychology
O'MORÁIN, C., Medicine
O'NEILL, L., Biochemistry
O'ROURKE, K., Economics
PETHICA, J., Physics
PRENDERGAST, P., Bio-Engineering
RAMASWAMI, M., Neurogenetics
REILLY, R., Neural Engineering
REYNOLDS, J., Surgery
ROBERTSON, I., Psychology
ROBINSON, I., History
ROGERS, T., Clinical Microbiology
ROSS, I., Eighteenth-Century Studies
ROWAN, M., Neuropharmacology
SCOTT, D., Textual and Visual Studies
SENGE, M., Organic Chemistry
SHATASHVILI, S., Natural Philosophy
SHVETS, I., Applied Physics
SIMONS, P., Moral Philosophy
SMITH, O., Haematology
STALLEY, R., History of Art
STASSEN, L., Oral and Maxillofacial Surgery
SWANWICK, G., Psychiatry
TAYLOR, D., Geography
TAYLOR, D., Materials Engineering
TIMON, C., Otolaryngology
VIJ, J., Electronic Materials
WALSH, J., Clinical Medicine
WOLFE, K., Genome Evolution

RECOGNIZED COLLEGES

Church of Ireland College of Education: 96 Upper Rathmines Rd, Dublin 6; tel. (1) 4970033; fax (1) 4971932; e-mail info@cice.ie; internet www.cice.ie; 3-year course leading to Bachelor of Education pass degree; Principal Dr ANNE LODGE.

Coláiste Mhuire, Marino: Griffith Ave, Dublin 9; tel. (1) 8057700; fax (1) 8335290; e-mail info@mie.ie; internet www.mie.ie; 3-year course leading to Bachelor of Education pass degree; Principal Dr ANNE O'GARA.

Froebel College of Education: Sion Hill, Blackrock, Co Dublin; tel. (1) 2888520; fax (1) 2880618; e-mail marie.mcloughlin@froebel.ie; internet www.froebel.ie; 3-year course leading to Bachelor of Education pass degree; Principal MARIE MCLOUGHLIN.

Irish School of Ecumenics (Trinity College Dublin): Bea House, Milltown Park, Dublin 6; tel. (1) 2601144; fax (1) 2601158; e-mail isedir@tcd.ie; internet www.tcd.ie/ise; Dir J. D. A. MAY.

St Catherine's College of Education for Home Economics: Sion Hill, Blackrock, Co Dublin; tel. (1) 2884989; f. 1929; 4-year course leading to Bachelor of Education (home economics) honours degree; Pres. MADELEINE MULRENNAN.

UNIVERSITY OF LIMERICK

Limerick
Telephone: (61) 202700
Fax: (61) 330316
Internet: www.ul.ie
Founded 1972 as Nat. Institute for Higher Education, Limerick, univ. status 1989
State control
Language of instruction: English
Academic year: September to May
Pres. and Vice-Chancellor: Prof. DON BARRY
Vice-Pres. for Academics and Registrar: Prof. PAUL MCCUTCHEON
Vice-Pres. for Admin. and Sec.: (vacant)
Vice-Pres. for Research: Prof. BRIAN FITZGERALD
Dir for Finance: JOHN FIELD
Library of 300,000 vols
Number of teachers: 514
Number of students: 11,300
Publications: *Research Works*, *UL Links*

DEANS

Faculty of Arts, Humanities and Social Sciences: Prof. PAT O'CONNOR

Faculty of Education and Health Sciences: Prof. MARY O'SULLIVAN

Faculty of Science and Engineering: Prof. KIERAN HODNETT

Graduate School: Dr HUW LEWIS

Kemmy Business School: Prof. DONAL A. DINEEN

University-Level Institutions

DUBLIN INSTITUTE FOR ADVANCED STUDIES

10 Burlington Rd, Dublin 4
Telephone: (1) 6140100
Fax: (1) 6680561
E-mail: registrar@admin.dias.ie
Internet: www.dias.ie
Founded 1940
Chair. of Council: V. CUNNANE
Registrar: CECIL KEAVENEY.

CONSTITUENT SCHOOLS

School of Celtic Studies: Dir Prof. FERGUS KELLY

SENIOR PROFESSORS

BREATNACH, L.
BREATNACH, P.

School of Cosmic Physics: Dir Prof. L. DRURY

SENIOR PROFESSORS

JONES, A. G.
MEURS, E. J. A.

School of Theoretical Physics: Dir Prof. W. NAHM

SENIOR PROFESSORS

DORLAS, T. C.
O'CONNOR, D.

ROYAL COLLEGE OF PHYSICIANS OF IRELAND

Frederick House, 19 S Frederick St, Dublin 2
Telephone: (1) 8639700
Fax: (1) 6724707
E-mail: college@rcpi.ie
Internet: www.rcpi.ie
Founded 1654
President: JOHN DONOHOE
Registrar: Prof. FRANK MURRAY

CEO: LEO KARNS

Faculties of obstetrics and gynaecology, occupational medicine, paediatrics, pathology, public health medicine; Postgraduate Diploma courses; also awards Fellowships and Memberships

DEANS

Dr STEPHEN PATCHETT
Dr BERNARD SILKE, Higher Medical Training

Institutes of Technology

Athlone Institute of Technology: Dublin Rd, Athlone, Co Westmeath; tel. (90) 6468000; fax (90) 6468148; e-mail info@ait .ie; internet www.ait.ie; f. 1970; two-year Higher Certificate courses, three- and one-year Higher Diploma courses, four-year degree/professional courses, one-year post-Higher Diploma degree courses, Postgraduate Diploma courses, Masters degree courses, postgraduate research; library: 50,000 vols; 300 teachers; 4,000 students; Pres. Prof. CIARÁN Ó CATHÁIN; Registrar Dr JOSEPH RYAN; Sec. JOHN MCKENNA.

Cork Institute of Technology: Rossa Ave, Bishopstown, Cork; tel. (21) 4326100; internet www.cit.ie; f. 1912; library: 65,000 vols, 550 periodicals; 1,237 teachers (471 full-time, 766 part-time); 12,000 students (6,000 full-time, 6,000 part-time); Pres. Dr BRENDAN J. MURPHY; Vice-Pres. for Academic Affairs and Registrar Dr BARRY O'CONNOR; Vice-Pres. for Development MICHAEL DELANEY; Vice-Pres. for Finance and Admin. PAUL GALLAGHER.

Attached Centres:

Centre for Advanced Manufacturing and Management Systems: Dir M. COTTERELL.

Centre for Clean Technology: Dir D. CUNNINGHAM.

Centre for Educational Opportunities: Dir M. BERMINGHAM.

Centre for Innovation in Education: Dir R. P. COUGHLAN.

Centre for Nautical Enterprise: Dir G. TRANT.

Centre for Surface and Interface Analysis: Dirs E. M. CASHELL, L. MCDONNELL.

Constituent Schools:

Cork School of Music: Union Quay, Cork; tel. (21) 4807310; internet www.cit .ie/citcorkschoolofmusic; f. 1878; Dir Dr GEOFFREY SPRATT.

Crawford College of Art and Design: Sharman Crawford St, Cork; tel. (21) 4335200; internet www.cit.ie/ citcrawfordcollegeofartanddesi1; f. 1884; Principal ORLA FLYNN (acting).

National Maritime College: Ringaskiddy, Co Cork; tel. (21) 4970600; fax (21) 4970601; e-mail reception@nmci.ie; internet www.nmci.ie; Head Capt. JOHN CLARENCE.

Dublin Institute of Technology: 143–149 Rathmines Rd, Dublin 6; tel. (1) 4023000; fax (1) 4023399; internet www.dit.ie; f. 1978 by bringing together 6 established colleges; formally established 1993; academic year September to June; 1,500 teachers, (incl. part-time); 25,000 students, (incl. part-time); Pres. Prof. B. NORTON; Dir of Academic Affairs Dr F. MCMAHON; Dir of Finance and Physical Resources P. FLYNN; Dir of Human Resources D. CAGNEY; Dir of Research and Enterprise Dr E. HAZELKORN; Registrar Dr T. DUFF.

Dun Laoghaire Institute of Art, Design and Technology: Carraiglea Park, Kill Ave, Dun Laoghaire, Co Dublin; tel. 2394000; fax 2394700; e-mail info@iadt.ie; internet www .iadt.ie; f. 1997; Higher Certificate, Postgraduate Diploma and Bachelor and Masters degree programmes; Chair. DAVID HARVEY; Dir JIM DEVINE; Registrar Dr ANNIE DOONA; Sec. BERNARD MULLARKEY.

Dundalk Institute of Technology: Dublin Rd, Dundalk, Co Louth; tel. (42) 9370200; fax (42) 9333505; e-mail info@dkit.ie; internet www.dkit.ie; f. 1970; Higher Certificate, Higher Diploma and Bachelor, Masters and Doctoral degree courses; library: 30,000 vols; Pres. DENIS CUMMINS; Dir SEAN MCDONAGH; Registrar S. MCMANUS.

Galway-Mayo Institute of Technology: Dublin Rd, Galway; tel. (91) 753161; fax (91) 751107; internet www.gmit.ie; f. 1972; Bachelor and Masters degree, Higher and Postgraduate Diploma, and Higher Certificate courses; Pres. MARION COY; Registrar BERNARD O'HARA; Librarian MARGARET WALDRON; library: 100,000 vols; 375 teachers; 9,000 students (5,000 full-time, 4,000 part-time incl. postgraduate).

Institute of Technology Blanchardstown: Blanchardstown Rd North, Dublin 15; tel. (1) 8851000; fax (1) 8851001; e-mail info@itb.ie; internet www.itb.ie; f. 1999; Bachelor and Masters degree, Higher Certificate, and Higher and Postgraduate Diploma courses; 67 teachers; 1,060 students (626 full-time, 356 part-time, 78 apprentices); Pres. Dr MARY MEANEY; Librarian AIDIN O'SULLIVAN; publ. *Journal* (2 a year).

Institute of Technology Carlow: Kilkenny Rd, Carlow; tel. (59) 9175000; fax (59) 9175005; e-mail info@itcarlow.ie; internet www.itcarlow.ie; f. 1970; Higher Certificate and Bachelor degree courses; library: 25,000 vols; 200 teachers; 4,000 students; Dir Dr RUAIDHRÍ NEAVYN; Registrar BRIAN L. BENNETT.

Institute of Technology Sligo: Ash Lane, Ballinode, Sligo; tel. (71) 9155222; fax (71) 9160475; e-mail info@itsligo.ie; internet www .itsligo.ie; f. 1970; Higher Certificate, Postgraduate Diploma, and Bachelor and Masters degree courses; also offers professional courses; library: 23,000 vols; 495 full-time teachers; 4,300 full-time students; 250 apprentices; Pres. Prof. TERRI SCOTT; Registrar BRENDAN MCCORMACK; Sec. and Financial Controller JOHN COSGROVE.

Institute of Technology Tallaght: Tallaght, Dublin 24; tel. (1) 4042000; fax (1) 4042700; e-mail info@ittdublin.ie; internet www.it-tallaght.ie; f. 1992; Higher Certificate, and ordinary and honours Bachelor degree courses; Pres. PAT MACLAUGHLIN (acting); Registrar JOHN VICKERY; Sec. THOMAS STONE; Librarian GILLIAN KERINS.

Institute of Technology Tralee: Clash, Tralee, Co Kerry; tel. (66) 7145600; fax (66) 7125711; e-mail info@ittralee.ie; internet www.ittralee.ie; f. 1977; full-time Higher Certificate, Higher Diploma, and Bachelor, Masters and Doctoral degree courses, and part-time degree courses; library: 30,000 vols; 250 teachers; 3,500 students (incl. part-time); Pres. MICHAEL CARMODY.

Letterkenny Institute of Technology: Port Rd, Letterkenny, Co Donegal; tel. (74) 9186000; fax (74) 9186005; e-mail reception@ lyit.ie; internet www.lyit.ie; Higher Certificate, Higher and Postgraduate Diploma, and Bachelor and Masters degree courses in engineering, science, design and business studies; library: 30,000 vols; 200 teachers; 2,500 students; Pres. PAUL HANNIGAN; Registrar DANIEL BRENNAN; Sec. COLIN MORROW; Librarian JOHN DEVLIN.

Limerick Institute of Technology: Moylish Park, Limerick; tel. (61) 208208; fax (61) 208209; e-mail information@lit.ie; internet www.lit.ie; f. 1852; 500 teachers; 6,000 students; Pres. Dr MARIA HINEFELAAR; Registrar TERRY TWOMEY (acting); Sec. JIMMY BROWNE.

Waterford Institute of Technology: Cork Rd, Waterford; tel. (51) 302000; fax (51) 378292; e-mail info@wit.ie; internet www .wit.ie; f. 1969; Higher Certificate, Higher and Postgraduate Diploma, and Bachelor, Masters and Doctoral degree courses; library: 90,000 vols, 400 periodicals; 200 full-time teachers; 9,000 students (6,000 full-time, 3,000 part-time); Dir Prof. KIERAN R. BYRNE; Registrar P. DOWNEY; Sec. TONY MCFEELY.

Other Higher Education Providers

National College of Ireland: Mayor St Dublin 1; tel. (1) 4498500; fax (1) 44972200; e-mail info@ncirl.ie; internet www.ncirl.ie; f. 1951; Doctoral and Masters degrees, Postgraduate and Higher Diplomas, and Higher Certificate courses, full-time and part-time; also short courses; specialist areas: human resource management, personnel management, industrial relations, trade union studies, accountancy, business management, languages and European studies, computing, information technology law, management of change, leadership, community-based learning; 350 teachers (130 full-time, 220 part-time); 5,000 students; Pres. Dr PHILLIP MATTHEWS.

St Patrick's College, Maynooth: Maynooth, Co Kildare; tel. (1) 7084700; fax (1) 7083959; e-mail president@spcm.ie; internet www.maynoothcollege.ie; f. 1795; comprises National Seminary and Pontifical University; Bachelors, Masters and Doctoral degrees, Higher and Postgraduate Diplomas, and Licentiates; library: 65,000 vols; 8,000 students (incl. part-time); Pres. Right Rev. Mgr HUGH G. CONNOLLY; Vice-Pres. and Registrar Rev. MICHAEL MULLANEY; Sec. Rev. DONAL O'NEILL; Librarian CATHAL MCCAULEY.

Tipperary Institute: Nenagh Rd, Thurles, Co Tipperary; tel. (504) 28000; fax (504) 28001; e-mail info@tippinst.ie; internet www.tippinst.ie; f. 1998; Bachelors degrees and Higher Certificates; library: 17,479 vols, 330 periodicals; 600 students; Chief Exec. MICHAEL O'CONNELL (acting); Dir for Corporate Affairs SHEILA MCCARTHY; Dir for Development and Academic Affairs GARY PROSSER.

Schools of Art and Music

Burren College of Art: Newton Castle, Ballyvaughan, Co Clare; tel. (65) 7077200; fax (65) 7077201; e-mail anna@burrencollege .ie; internet www.burrencollege.ie; f. 1993; Masters degree, Postgraduate Diploma and post-baccalaureate courses; Pres. MARY HAWKES-GREEN; Dir for Graduate Studies Prof. TIMOTHY EMLYN JONES.

National College of Art and Design: see under National University of Ireland–Recognized Colleges of the University.

Royal Irish Academy of Music: 36–38 Westland Row, Dublin 2; tel. (1) 6764412; fax (1) 6622798; e-mail info@riam.ie; internet www.riam.ie; f. 1848, incorporated 1889; 75 teachers; 1,000 students; Dir JOHN O'CONOR; Sec. DOROTHY SHIEL.

ISRAEL

The Higher Education System

The earliest institutions of higher education were founded when Palestine was a province of the Ottoman Turkish Empire, and tended to be religious, technical or arts schools. The oldest specialist institution is the Etz Hayim, General Talmud, Torah and Grand Teshivah (founded 1847), and the oldest university-level institution is Technion—Israel Institute of Technology (founded 1912; inaugurated 1924). Following the First World War (1914–18), Palestine became a League of Nations mandate under British administration and increased Jewish immigration led to the expansion of the higher education sector: the Hebrew University of Jerusalem was founded in 1918 and inaugurated in 1925. The Arab and Jewish communities began to develop parallel forms of communal government, including separate education systems. In May 1948 the United Kingdom terminated its Palestinian mandate, and an independent Jewish State of Israel was declared. Several university-level institutions were established shortly after, including the Weizmann Institute of Science (founded 1949), Bar-Ilan University (founded 1953; inaugurated 1955) and Tel-Aviv University (founded 1953; inaugurated 1956). In addition to the eight universities, other institutions of higher education include colleges and higher institutes. The Council for Higher Education Law (1958) established the Council for Higher Education to oversee Israeli higher education, including accreditation of institutions and quality assurance. There is a three-stage process of accreditation. First, the institution is allowed to advertise programmes of study, invite applications from students and start teaching courses; however, the institution is not allowed to award degrees or other qualifications. Secondly, an institution is permitted to be opened and maintained as a provisional institution of higher education but without accreditation and without awarding the relevant qualifications. Thirdly, and finally, the institution is accredited as an institution of higher education and authorized to award degrees.

In 2005/06 there were 209,500 students in institutions of higher education compared with 76,000 in 1990. In addition, there were 41,150 students in the Open University compared with 13,000 in 1990. In 2006 there were 41,800 studying for a Masters degree. Studies for the Doctoral degree are offered only in the research universities. The number of doctoral students increased steadily from 3,910 in 1990 to 9,835 in 2006.

The school leavers' certificate or bagrut (matriculation) is the main criterion for admission to higher education. Applicants may also be required to undergo psychometric testing and attend a personal interview, depending on the institution. The Bachelors degree is the standard university-level undergraduate qualification, and the course usually lasts three years. However, some disciplines require longer periods of study, such as nursing (four years) and medicine (six years). Bachelors degrees from non-university institutions, usually Colleges and Higher Institutes, tend to be awarded in conjunction with a professional title or indicate the area of specialization. The first postgraduate-level degree is the Masters, a one- to two-year programme of study that may or may not include a thesis component. A Masters with a thesis component (Type A) allows admission to doctoral studies; a Masters without a thesis (Type B) does not. The second (and highest) postgraduate qualification is the Doctorate (most commonly a PhD) and lasts two years.

Technical and vocational education at the post-secondary level is offered by technical colleges and non-university institutions of higher education. The first qualification at this level is the Technai (Qualified Technician), which lasts one year. The other main qualification is the Handassai (Practical Engineer), which is divided into two tracks, Type A and Type B. Handassai (Type A) is a one-year programme of study, and Handassai (Type B) lasts two years. Admission to Technai and Handassai courses requires a bagrut or completion of 12 years of education.

The proportion of ultra-Orthodox adults outside the labour force increased steadily over much of the late 20th and early 21st centuries. In 2010 the Council for Higher Education formulated a plan to encourage these ultra-Orthodox adults into higher education in order to improve their employability. This formed part of a five-year plan for the whole higher education system.

Regulatory and Representative Bodies

GOVERNMENT

Ministry of Education: POB 292, 34 Shivtei Israel St, 91911 Jerusalem; tel. (2) 5602222; fax (2) 5602223; e-mail info@education.gov.il; internet www.education.gov.il; Minister GIDEON SA'AR.

Ministry of Science and Technology: POB 49100, Kiryat Hamemshala, Hamizrachit, Bldg 3, 91490 Jerusalem; tel. (2) 5411171; fax (2) 5811613; e-mail minister@most.gov.il; internet www.most.gov.il; f. 1982; Min. Prof. DANIEL HERSHKOWITZ.

ACCREDITATION

Council for Higher Education: POB 4037, 91040 Jerusalem; tel. (2) 5679911; fax (2) 5679955; internet www.che.org.il; f. 1958; recommends to the Govt the granting of licences to higher education institutes, and accreditation, and authorizes awarding of degrees; 24 mems; Chair. THE MINISTER OF EDUCATION; Dir-Gen. STEVEN G. STAV.

ENIC/NARIC Israel: Dept for Evaluation of Foreign Academic Degrees, Ministry of Education, 2 Devora Haneviah St, 91911 Jerusalem; tel. (2) 5603702; fax (2) 5603876; e-mail diplomot@education.gov.il; Dir TZIPY WEINBERG.

Quality Assessment Unit: 38 Keren Hayesod St, cnr of 2 Jabotinsky St, David Brothers Bldg, 4th Fl., Jerusalem; tel. (2) 5669938; fax (2) 5611914; e-mail michal@che.org.il; internet www.che.org.il; f. 2004 to improve the quality of higher education, increase awareness of the quality assessment process, and develop systems in higher education instns for the continual evaluation of academic quality; periodical assessment of study programmes; Head MICHAL NEUMAN.

Learned Societies

GENERAL

Israel Academy of Sciences and Humanities: POB 4040, 91040 Jerusalem; tel. (2) 5676222; fax (2) 5666059; e-mail academy@academy.ac.il; internet www.academy.ac.il; f. 1959; sections of Humanities and Natural Sciences; academic centre in Cairo, Egypt; 87 mems; Pres. Prof. MENAHEM YAARI; Vice-Pres. Prof. RUTH ARNON; Exec. Dir Dr MEIR ZADOK; Chair. of Humanities Prof. YOHANAN FRIEDMANN; Chair. of Natural Sciences Prof. RAPHAEL MECHOULAM.

BIBLIOGRAPHY, LIBRARY SCIENCE AND MUSEOLOGY

Israel Librarians' Association: POB 303, 61002 Tel-Aviv; f. 1952; gen. organization of librarians, archivists and information specialists; promotes the interests and advances the professional standards of librarians; professional and examining body; 850 mems; Chair. BENJAMIN SCHACHTER; Sec. NAAMA RAVID; publs *Meida La Sefran*, *Yad-La-Kore* (Libraries and Archives Magazine).

Israel Society of Libraries and Information Professionals (ASMI): 8 Blum St, 44253 Kefar Saba; tel. (77) 2151800; fax (77) 2151800; e-mail asmi@asmi.org.il; internet www.asmi.org.il; f. 1966; promotes the utilization of recorded knowledge by disseminating information in the fields of science, technology and the humanities, and facilitates written and oral communication; 400 mems; Chair. Dr SHAHAF HAGAFNI; publs

Igeret (irregular), *Information and Librarianship* (1 a year).

Israeli Center for Libraries: POB 3251, 51103 Benei Berak; tel. (3) 6180151; fax (3) 5798048; e-mail icl@icl.org.il; internet www .icl.org.il; f. 1965; provides centralized processing and other services for libraries; organizes non-academic librarianship courses; Chair. JACOB AGMON; Dir ORLY ONN; publs *Basifriyot* (12 a year), *Yad Lakore* (1 a year).

Museums Association of Israel: POB 7, 75100 Rishon Le-Zion; tel. (3) 9565977; fax (3) 9565788; e-mail secretariat@icom.org.il; internet www.icom.org.il; f. 1964 to foster public interest in museums and cooperation among asscn members; affiliated to International Council of Museums (ICOM); 55 mems; Chair. ITZHAK BRENNER.

ECONOMICS, LAW AND POLITICS

International Association of Jewish Lawyers and Jurists: 10 Daniel Frish St, 64731 Tel-Aviv; tel. (3) 6910673; fax (3) 6953855; e-mail iajj@goldmail.net.il; internet www.intjewishlawyers.org; f. 1969 to contribute towards establishing int. order based on law and the promotion of human rights; examines legal problems related to Jewish communities; holds int. congresses and seminars; 10 centres (in Israel and abroad); affiliated with the World Jewish Congress (WJC); Pres. ALEX HERTMAN; Exec. Dir RONIT GIDRON-ZEMACH; publ. *Justice* (4 a year).

Israel Bar: 10 Daniel Frish St, 64731 Tel-Aviv; tel. (3) 6362200; fax (3) 6918696; e-mail vaadmerkazi@israelbar.org.il; internet www .israelbar.org.il; f. 1961; autonomous statutory body to incorporate and represent lawyers in Israel; 16,000 mems; Pres. YORI GEIRON; Gen. Dir LINDA SHAFIR; Chair., Nat. Council AMOS VAN EMDEN; publs *Hapraklit* (12 a year), *Orech Hadin* (2 a year).

Attached Organizations:

David Rotlevi National Mediation Institute of the Israel Bar:tel. (3) 6362221; fax (3) 6091641; Jt Chairs SHAY SEGAL, MOSHE TCHETCHIK.

Institute for Continuing Legal Studies: 82 Menachem Begin Rd, 67138 Tel Aviv; tel. (3) 5616550; fax (3) 5616551; e-mail machon@israelbar.org.il; Jt Chairs Dr YORAM DANZIGER, Prof. AHARON NAMDAR.

International Association of Jewish Lawyers and Jurists Secretariat:tel. (3) 6910673; fax (3) 6953855; e-mail iajlj@ goldmail.net.il; internet www .intjewishlawyers.org; Man. ARIEL AINBINDER.

Israel Political Science Association: c/o Dept of Political Studies, Bar-Ilan University, 52900 Ramat Gan; tel. (3) 5318578; fax (3) 9234511; e-mail ispsa.mail@gmail.com; internet www.ispsa.org; 100 mems; Chair. Prof. SAM LEHMAN WILZIG.

FINE AND PERFORMING ARTS

ACUM (Society of Authors, Composers and Music Publishers in Israel): ACUM House, 9 Tuval St, POB 1704, 52117 Ramat Gan; tel. (3) 6113400; fax (3) 6122629; e-mail acum@acum.org.il; internet www.acum.org .il; f. 1936; copyright; promotion of music and literature; 4,000 mems; Chief Exec. Officer YORIK BEN-DAVID.

Israel Music Institute: 55 Menachem Begin Rd, POB 51197, 67138 Tel-Aviv; tel. (3) 6247095; fax (3) 5612826; e-mail musicinst@bezeqint.net; internet www.imi .org.il; f. 1961; publishes and promotes Israeli music and musicological works throughout the world; produces CDs on Israeli music celebration festival; Israel Music Information Centre; Central Library of Israeli Music; mem. of the Int. Asscn of Music Information Centres and Int. Fed. of Serious Music Publishers; library: 2,500 scores, 2,000 audio recordings; Chair. DANIELA RABINOWITZ; Dir PAUL LANDAU; publ. *IMI News* (3 a year).

Israel Painters and Sculptors Association: 9 Alharizi St, 64244 Tel-Aviv; tel. (3) 5246685; fax (3) 5226433; e-mail artassoc@ netvision.net.il; f. 1934 to advance plastic arts in Israel and protect artists' interests; affiliated to the International Association of Art; organizes group exhibitions and symposia; provides assistance to immigrant artists; maintains a gallery for members' exhibitions; graphic arts workshop and materials supply store; 3 brs; 2,000 mems; Chair. RACHEL SHAVIT.

HISTORY, GEOGRAPHY AND ARCHAEOLOGY

Historical Society of Israel: 2 Betar St, POB 4179, 91041 Jerusalem; tel. (2) 5650444; fax (2) 6712388; e-mail info@shazar.org.il; internet www.shazar.org.il; f. 1926; promotes the study of general and Jewish history; 1,000 mems; library: Library of Jewish History, Judaica, 25,000 vols; Chair. Prof. MICHAEL HEYD; Sec.-Gen. ZVI YEKUTIEL; publs *Historia* (general history, 2 a year, in Hebrew, with summary in English), *Zion* (Jewish history, 4 a year, in Hebrew with summary in English).

Israel Antiquities Authority: POB 586, 91004 Jerusalem; tel. (2) 6204622; fax (2) 6289066; internet www.antiquities.org.il; f. 1948; govt authority; engages in archaeological excavations and surveys, inspection and preservation of antiquities and ancient sites, scientific publs; custodianship of all antiquities; Dir of Antiquities SHUKA DORFMAN; Sec. H. MENAHEM; publs *Archaeological Survey of Israel* (irregular), *Atiqot* (irregular), *Excavations and Surveys in Israel* (2 a year).

Israel Geographical Association: c/o Dept of Geography, Bar-Ilan University, 52900 Ramat-Gan; internet www.geography.org.il; f. 1961; 650 mems; Pres. YEHUDA CRADUS; Sec. Dr GABI LIPSHITZ; publ. *Ofakim*.

Israel Prehistoric Society: POB 1502, Jerusalem; tel. (2) 5666611; f. 1958; 100 mems; incl. the 'M. Stekelis' Museum of Prehistory; Chair A. GOPHER; Sec. N. GOREN; publ. *Mitekufat Haeven* (1 a year).

Jerusalemer Institut der Görres-Gesellschaft (Jerusalem Institute of the Görres Society): Notre Dame of Jerusalem Center, POB 4595, 91044 Jerusalem; tel. (2) 6271170; f. 1908; fmrly Orientalisches Institut der Görres-Gesellschaft; art, history, archaeology, biblical studies, Christian iconography; library, photo archive, computerized index of Christian monuments in the Holy Land; Pres. Prof. WOLFGANG BERGSDORF.

LANGUAGE AND LITERATURE

Academy of the Hebrew Language: Givat Ram Campus, 91904 Jerusalem; tel. (2) 6493555; fax (2) 5617065; e-mail acad2u@ huji.ac.il; internet hebrew-academy.huji.ac .il; f. 1953; studies the vocabulary, structure and history of the Hebrew language and is the official authority for its devt; is compiling a historical dictionary of the Hebrew language; library: library specializing in Hebrew and Semitic languages; 38 mems (23 full, 15 advisory); Pres. Prof. M. BAR-ASHER; Chief Scientific Sec. R. GADISH; publs *Leshonenu* (4 a year), *Leshonenu La'am* (4 a year), *Zikhronot*.

Association of Religious Writers: POB 7440, Jerusalem; tel. (2) 5660478; fax (2) 5660478; f. 1963; Chair. Dr ZAHAVA BEN-DOV; publ. *Mabua*.

British Council: Crystal House, 12 Hahilazon St, Ramat Gan, 52136 Tel-Aviv; tel. (3) 6113600; fax (3) 6113640; e-mail info@ britishcouncil.org.il; internet www .britishcouncil.org/israel; promotes cultural relations between the UK and other countries by offering opportunities for inter-cultural dialogue and knowledge sharing in science, education, English language, sports and arts; offers preparation and testing for International English Language Testing System (IELTS) and administers various British professional and academic exams; attached offices in Nazareth and W Jerusalem; Dir JIM BUTTERY; Head of English Language Testing HELEN SYKES.

Goethe-Institut: 15 Sokolov St, 92144 Jerusalem; tel. (2) 5610627; fax (2) 5618431; e-mail info@jerusalem.goethe.org; internet www.goethe.de/jerusalem; offers courses and exams in German language and culture and promotes cultural exchange with Germany; attached centre in Tel-Aviv; Dir Dr FRIEDRICH DAHLHAUS.

Hebrew Writers Association in Israel: POB 7111, Tel-Aviv; tel. (3) 6953256; fax (3) 6919681; f. 1921; 400 mems; publ. *Moznayim* (12 a year).

Instituto Cervantes: Shulamit 7, 64371 Tel Aviv; tel. (3) 5279992; fax (3) 5299558; e-mail centel@cervantes.es; internet telaviv .cervantes.es; offers courses and exams in Spanish language and culture and promotes cultural exchange with Spain and Spanish-speaking Latin and Central America; library of 14,000 vols; Dir ROSA MARÍA MORO DE ANDRÉS.

Palestinian PEN Centre: Wadi al-Juz, Al-Khaldi St 4, Jerusalem; tel. (2) 6262970; fax (2) 6280103; f. 1992; 50 mems; Pres. HANAN AWWAD.

MEDICINE

Israel Gerontological Society: POB 2371, 55000 Kiryat Ono; tel. (3) 5357161; fax (3) 6359399; e-mail igs@netvision.net.il; internet www.gerontology.org.il; f. 1956; 600 mems; Chair. Prof. JACOB LOMRANZ; Vice-Chair. Dr YITSHAL BERNER; publ. *Gerontology* (4 a year).

Israel Medical Association: POB 3604, 52136 Ramat Gan; 35 Jabotinsky St, 2 Twin Towers, Level 11, 52136 Ramat Gan; tel. (3) 6100444; fax (3) 5753303; e-mail tguvot@ima .org.il; internet www.ima.org.il; f. 1912; Pres. Dr YORAM BLACHAR; publs *Harefuah* (26 a year, in Hebrew, abstracts in English), *Israel Medical Association Journal* (12 a year).

Israel Society for Neuroscience: POB 666, 75106 Rishon Le Zion; tel. (3) 9694126; fax (3) 9660841; e-mail michal.gilady@isfn .org.il; internet www.isfn.org.il; Pres. ILIANA GOZES.

Israel Society of Internal Medicine: Dept of Internal Medicine, Meir Medical Centre, 44281 Kfar Sava; tel. (9) 7472534; fax (9) 7460781; e-mail rozado@clalit.org.il; internet www.isim.org.il; f. 1958; 4 regional centres; a division of the Israel Medical Association (IMA), and affiliated to the International Society of Internal Medicine (ISIM); organizes scientific meetings and congresses; participates in the planning of postgraduate education in internal medicine and improving conditions of internal medicine practitioners; 750 mems; Chair. Prof. MORDECHAI RAVID; Sec. Dr MEIR LAHAV.

Society for Medicine and Law in Israel: 30 Arlozerov St, Petach-Tikva; tel. (3) 9231047; e-mail acarmi@research.haifa.ac.il; f. 1972; 3 brs; affiliated to the World Association for Medical Law (WAML); examines and recommends amendments to medical laws; organizes int. conferences; 1,600 mems; Pres. A. CARMI; publ. *Refuah U Mishpat* (Medicine & Law, 4 a year, in Hebrew).

NATURAL SCIENCES
General

Association for the Advancement of Science in Israel: c/o Prof. M. Jammer, Dept of Physics, Bar-Ilan University, 52100 Ramat-Gan; tel. (3) 5318433; fax (3) 5353298; f. 1953; 5,200 mems; Pres. Prof. M. JAMMER; publ. *Proceedings of Congress of Scientific Societies*.

Biological Sciences

Entomological Society of Israel: POB 6, 50250 Bet-Dagan; tel. (3) 9683729; fax (3) 9604428; e-mail vtada@volcani.agri.gov.il; internet entomology.org.il; f. 1962; promotes, improves and disseminates the science of entomology (incl. acarology) in Israel; holds 1 full-day meeting per year; 224 mems; Pres. Prof. ADA RAFAELI; Sec. Dr VICTORIA SOROKER; publ. *Israel Journal of Entomology*.

Israel Society of Plant Sciences: c/o Hebrew University of Jerusalem, 76100 Rehovot; tel. (4) 9489443; fax (4) 9489899; e-mail ispb@post.tau.ac.il; internet www.tau.ac.il/lifesci/ispb; f. 1936; aims to promote the advancement of the fundamental and applied branches of botanical science; conducts research, organizes lectures and field work; over 300 mems; Pres. Dr SHAHAL ABBP; publ. *Israel Journal of Plant Sciences*.

Israel Society of Biochemistry and Molecular Biology: POB 9095, 52 190 Ramat Efal; tel. (3) 6355038; fax (3) 5351103; e-mail isbmb1@gmail.com; internet www.tau.ac.il/lifesci/isbmb; 350 mems; Pres. Prof. MICHAEL EISENBACH; Sec. Prof. ORNA ELROY-STEIN.

Society for the Protection of Nature in Israel: 4 Hashfela St, 66183 Tel-Aviv; tel. (3) 5375063; fax (3) 5377695; internet www.teva .org.il; f. 1953; promotes nature conservation and quality of the environment; operates 24 local brs, 26 field-study centres, 7 biological information centres; research centres on birds, mammals, reptiles, insects, plants and caves; maintains close cooperation with the Nature Reserves Authority, the Environmental Protection Service and the Council for Beautiful Israel; organizes int. seminars on nature conservation education; 100,000 mems; Chair. YOAV SAGI; Exec. Dir EITAN GEDALIZON; publs *Eretz Magazine* (6 a year, in English), *Pashosh* (children's, 12 a year, in Hebrew), *Teva Va'aretz* (Nature & Land, 6 a year, in Hebrew).

Zoological Society of Israel: c/o Dept of Zoology, Tel-Aviv University Ramat Aviv; internet telem.openu.ac.il/zoosoc; f. 1940; 300 mems; Chair. B. S. GALIL.

Mathematical Sciences

Israel Mathematical Union: c/o Israel Mathematical Union, Faculty of Mathematics and Computer Sciences, Weizmann Institute, 76100 Rehovot; fax (8) 9344278; e-mail imu@imu.org.il; internet imu.org.il; f. 1953; 210 mems; Pres. HARRY DYM; Sec. UZI VISHNE.

Physical Sciences

Israel Chemical Society: POB 26, 76100 Rehovot; tel. (8) 9343829; fax (8) 9344142; e-mail ics.sec@gmail.com; internet www

.weizmann.ac.il/ics; a scientific and professional asscn; holds two conventions each year and organizes lectures and symposia in various parts of Israel; the society represents Israel in the International Union of Pure and Applied Chemistry; Pres. Prof. HERBERT BERNSTEIN; Sec. Prof. MOSHE KOL.

Israel Geological Society: POB 1239, 91000 Jerusalem; e-mail gsi@igs.org.il; internet www.igs.org.il; f. 1951; 400 mems; Pres. ARIEL HEIMANN; Vice-Pres. DOV AVIGAD; publ. *Israeli Journal of Earth Sciences*.

Israel Physical Society: c/o Dept of Physics, Technion, 32000 Haifa; tel. (3) 5318431; fax (3) 5353298; e-mail dekel@phys.huji.ac; internet physics.technion.ac.il/~ips; f. 1954; 250 mems; Pres. Prof. AVISHAI DEKEL; Sec. Prof. AVRAHAM SCHILLER; publ. *Annals of the IPS*.

PHILOSOPHY AND PSYCHOLOGY

Israel Psychological Association: 74 Frishman St, POB 11497, 61114 Tel-Aviv; tel. (3) 5239393; fax (3) 5230763; e-mail psycho@zahav.net.il; internet www .psychology.org.il; f. 1958; 2,623 mems; Chair. DAN ZAKAY.

RELIGION, SOCIOLOGY AND ANTHROPOLOGY

Israel Oriental Society: The Hebrew University, Jerusalem; tel. (2) 5883633; f. 1949; aims to promote interest in and knowledge of history, politics, economics, culture and life in the Middle East; arranges lectures and symposia to study all aspects of contemporary Middle Eastern, Asian and African affairs; Chair. NEHEMIA LEVTZION; Sec. NIMROD GOREN; publ. *Hamizrah Hehadash* (The New East, 1 a year).

TECHNOLOGY

Association of Engineers and Architects in Israel: 200 Dizengoff Rd, POB 6429, 61063 Tel-Aviv; tel. (3) 5240274; fax (3) 5235993; e-mail eng-1@aeai.org.il; internet www.engineers.org.il; f. 1922; brs in Tel-Aviv, Jerusalem, Haifa, Beersheba; 20,000 mems; Pres. Prof. Y. NEEMAN; Chair. Eng. E. COHEN-KAGAN; publs *Chemical Engineering* (6 a year), *Electrical Engineers* (6 a year), *Journal of Engineering and Archaeology* (12 a year, in Hebrew with English summaries).

Israel Society of Aeronautics and Astronautics: POB 2956, 61028 Tel-Aviv; e-mail biaf@aerospace.org.il; internet www .aerospace.org.il; f. 1951 as Israel Soc. of Aeronautical Sciences, merged 1968 with Israel Astronautical Soc.; lectures and confs to foster the growth of aerospace science; 300 mems; Chair. Prof. OVADIA HARARI; Sec. Gen. YEHUDA BOROVIK; publ. *BIAF-Israel Aerospace e-Magazine* (4 a year).

Society of Electrical and Electronics Engineers of Israel: 200 Dizengoff St, Tel-Aviv; e-mail seeei@bezeqint.com; internet www.seeei.org.il; f. 1937; 120 mems; Pres. Ing. J. KOEN; Sec. Ing. J. KORNBLUM; publ. *Electricity and People* (6 a year, in Hebrew).

Research Institutes
GENERAL

Samuel Neaman Institute for Advanced Studies in Science and Technology: Technion City, 32000 Haifa; tel. (4) 8292329; fax (4) 8231889; e-mail info@neaman.org.il; internet www.neaman.org.il; f. 1978; independent public policy institute researching nat. problems in science and

technology, education, and economic, health and social devt; Dir Prof. MOSHE MOSHE.

Technion Research and Development Foundation Ltd: Senate House, Technion City, 32000 Haifa; tel. (4) 8292497; fax (4) 8320186; e-mail oshmu@cs.technion.ac.il; internet www.trdf.co.il; f. 1952; operates Industrial Testing Laboratories (building materials, geodetic research, soils and roads, hydraulics, chemistry, metals, electro-optics, vehicles); administers sponsored research at Technion—Israel Institute of Technology (see under Universities) in aeronautical, agricultural, biomedical, chemical, civil, computer, electrical, food and biotechnology, industrial, management and mechanical engineering; biology, chemistry, mathematics and physics (sciences); and architecture and town planning, education in technology and science, general studies, medicine; 22 subsidiaries in fields of electronics, energy, agriculture, food and medicine; Man. Dir Prof. ODED SHMUELI.

AGRICULTURE, FISHERIES AND VETERINARY SCIENCE

Agricultural Research Organization: Volcani Center, POB 6, 50250 Bet-Dagan; tel. (3) 9683226; fax (3) 9665327; e-mail research@volcani.agri.gov.il; internet www .agri.gov.il; f. 1921; fundamental and applied research in agriculture; numerous scientific projects at 7 institutes and 3 experiment stations; part of the Min. of Agriculture and Rural Devt; library of 30,000 vols and periodicals; Dir Prof. YITZHAK SPIEGEL; publ. *Israel Agresearch* (Hebrew with English summaries and captions).

Attached Institutes:

Institute of Agricultural Engineering: tel. (3) 9683303; fax (3) 9604704; Dir Dr ZE'EV SCHMILOVITCH.

Institute of Animal Science: Volcani Center, POB 6, 50250 Bet-Dagan; tel. (8) 9484400; fax (8) 9475075; e-mail harpaz@volcani.agri.gov.il; internet www.agri.gov.il/en/units/institutes/3.aspx; basic and practical research to support Israeli animal breeders and farmers; depts (i) Poultry and Aquaculture, (ii) Ruminant Science and Genetics; Head of Institute Prof. SHEENAN HARPAZ.

Institute of Plant Protection: tel. (3) 9683437; fax (3) 9604180; e-mail frtir@volcani.agri.gov.il; Dir Prof. ABED GERA.

Institute of Plant Sciences: tel. (3) 9683482; fax (3) 9669583; e-mail vcfield@volcani.agri.gov.il; Dir Prof. ITAMAR GLAZER.

Institute of Soils, Water and Environmental Sciences: tel. (3) 9683640; fax (3) 9604017; e-mail etty@volcani.agri.gov.il; Dir Dr MENACHEM BEN-HUR.

Institute for Technology and the Storage of Agricultural Products: tel. (3) 9683588; fax (3) 9604428; e-mail gadit@volcani.agri.gov.il; Dir Prof. ELAZAR FALLIK.

Beth Gordon, A. D. Gordon Agriculture, Nature and Kinnereth Valley Study Institute: Deganya A, 15120 Emeq Ha-Yarden; tel. (6) 750040; f. 1935; inaugurated 1941; regional and research centre and museum of natural history and agriculture and history of the Kinneret (Lake of Galilee) Region; library of 60,000 vols; Dir S. BEN NOAM; Curator of Archaeology Z. VINOGRADOV; Curator of Natural History S. LULAV.

ECONOMICS, LAW AND POLITICS

International Institute for Counter-Terrorism (ICT): Interdisciplinary Center Herzliya, POB 167, 46150 Herzliya; tel. (9)

9527277; fax (9) 9513073; e-mail webmaster@
ict.org.il; internet www.ict.org.il; f. 1996;
global research on terrorism and counter-
terrorism; Chair. SHABTAI SHAVIT; Exec. Dir
Dr BOAZ GANOR; Deputy Dir Dr EITAN AZANI.

Jerusalem Institute for Israel Studies:
20 Radak St, 92186 Jerusalem; tel. (2)
5630175; fax (2) 5639814; internet www.jiis
.org.il; f. 1981; independent non-profit organization to study policy issues and social,
economic and political processes in Jerusalem in order to facilitate and improve public
policy-making; and to study and disseminate
research and environmental policy issues in
Israel; Dir ORA AHIMEIR; Exec. Dir Prof.
JAACOV BAR SIMON TOV.

**Research Institute of the Yitzhak Rabin
Centre for Israel Studies:** 77 Rokach Blvd,
POB 17538, 61175 Tel-Aviv; tel. (3) 7453333;
fax (3) 7453355; e-mail info@rabincenter.org
.il; internet www.rabincenter.org.il; f. 1997;
history, society and culture of the State of
Israel; associated Rabin archive, library and
museum; Chair. Prof. YAAKOV NEEMAN; Exec.
Dir of Research Institute YOSSI LAHMANY.

Weitz Center for Development Studies:
POB 12, 76100 Rehovot; tel. (8) 9474111; fax
(8) 9475884; e-mail training@netvision.net.il;
internet www.weitz-center.org; f. 1963;
research, training and planning activities
related to the promotion of rural regional
devt, tourism and entrepreneurship in Israel
and the developing world; library of 50,000
vols, World Bank depository library; Gen. Dir
JULIA MARGULIES.

EDUCATION

**Henrietta Szold Institute—National
Institute for Research in the Behavioural Sciences:** 9 Columbia St, Kiryat
Menachem, Jerusalem; tel. (2) 6494444; fax
(2) 6437698; e-mail szold@szold.org.il;
internet www.szold.org.il; f. 1941; non-profit
organization undertaking research on psychology, psychometry, sociology and education;
information retrieval centre for the social
sciences in Israel; database of 40,000 records;
Dir Prof. ISAAC FRIEDMAN; publ. *Megamot—
Behavioral Sciences Quarterly*.

HISTORY, GEOGRAPHY AND ARCHAEOLOGY

**Albright, William Foxwell, Institute of
Archaeological Research in Jerusalem:**
26 Salah ed-Din St, POB 19096, Jerusalem;
tel. (2) 6288956; fax (2) 6264424; e-mail
director@albright.org.il; internet www.aiar
.org; f. 1900 as the American School of
Oriental Research; research projects in Semitic languages, literatures, and history; archaeological surveys and excavations; library of
30,000 vols; Pres. J. EDWARD WRIGHT; Dir S.
GITIN.

Israel Exploration Society: Avida St 5,
POB 7041, 91070 Jerusalem; tel. (2) 6257991;
fax (2) 6247772; e-mail ies@vms.huji.ac.il;
internet israelexplorationsociety.huji.ac.il; f.
1913 as the Soc. for the Reclamation of
Antiquities; excavations and allied research
into the history, archaeology and geography
of Israel; publishes excavation reports, books,
research results; educates the public in these
matters by means of congresses, general
meetings, etc.; Pres. JOSEPH AVIRAM; Chair.
of Exec. Cttee Prof. E. STERN; Dir HILLEL
GEVA; Deputy Dir ALAN PARIS; publs *Eretz-
Israel* (every 3 years, in Hebrew and English), *Israel Exploration Journal* (2 a year, in
English), *Qadmoniot* (2 a year, in Hebrew).

**Joe Alon Centre for Regional and Folk-
lore Studies:** Kibbutz Lahav, 85335 Negev;
tel. (8) 9913322; fax (8) 9919889; e-mail
joealon@lhv.org.il; internet www.joealon.org
.il; f. 1972; centre for research, study and

survey of the Southern Shefelah (the hilly
region between Jerusalem and Beersheba);
incl. an Archaeological Museum, a Museum
of Bedouin Culture, a Museum for the New
Jewish Settlement in the Negev, the Fehalin
Exhibit, housed in a restored dwelling cave
complex, at the foot of a major site; awards
grants for research in the region; library of
900 vols, 3,500 slides; Exec. Dir UZZI HALAM-
ISH.

Kenyon Institute: POB 19283, 91192 Jerusalem; tel. (2) 5828101; fax (2) 5323844;
e-mail kenyon@cbrl.org.uk; internet www
.britac.ac.uk/institutes/cbrl/; f. 1920 as British School of Archaeology in Jerusalem; part
of the Council for British Research in the
Levant (see parent institution in Research
Institutes in Jordan); undertakes and promotes study of all aspects of the archaeology,
history and culture of the Levant from
prehistoric times to the present; library and
hostel; library of 10,000 vols, 100 periodicals;
Dir Dr JAIMIE LOVELL; Research Scholar
CHLOE MASSEY.

Leo Baeck Institute Jerusalem: 33 Bus-
tenai St, Jerusalem; tel. (2) 5633790; fax (2)
5669505; e-mail leobaeck@leobaeck.org;
internet www.leobaeck.org; f. 1955; research
and publs on history and culture of Central
European Jewry; academic and cultural
events, maintenance of library and archives;
library: library and archive of items in German, English and Hebrew; special colln:
microfilm archive of Jewish newspapers;
publs *Bridges*, *Innovations in the Study of
German Jewry*, *Juedischer Almanach*, *Studies in the History of German and Central
European Jewry*.

MEDICINE

Sheba Medical Center: 52621 Tel Hasho-
mer; tel. (3) 5302473; fax (3) 5356851;
internet eng.sheba.co.il; f. 1948; Dir Prof.
ZEEV ROTSTEIN; research centres in regenera-
tive medicine, neuroscience, cancer, heart
disease and genetics; incl. Israel National
Center for Health Policy and Epidemiology
Research, Israel National Center for Medical
Simulation, Middle East Pediatric Congeni-
tal Heart Center, Israel Center for Newborn
Screening, Israel National Center for
Rehabilitation.

NATURAL SCIENCES

General

Israel Science Foundation: Albert Einstein Sq., 43 Jabotinsky St, 91040 Jerusalem;
tel. (2) 5885412; fax (2) 5635782; e-mail
tamar@isf.org.il; internet www.isf.org.il; f.
1995; Dir Dr TAMAR JAFFE-MITTWOCH.

Biological Sciences

Israel Institute for Biological Research:
POB 19, 74100 Ness-Ziona; tel. (8) 9381656;
fax (8) 9401404; internet www.iibr.gov.il; f.
1952; conducts biomedical research in drug
design, synthesis of fine chemicals and devt
of newly advanced products and processes in
biotechnology; three research divs: Chemistry, Biology and Environmental Sciences;
370 scientists and supporting staff; library
of 50,000 vols and 800 periodicals; Head of
Biological Sciences Dr ARIE ORDENTLICH;
Head of Medicinal Chemistry Dr SHAI KEND-
LER; Head of Environmental Sciences Dr GAD
FRISHMAN; publ. *OHOLO Annual International Scientific Conference*.

**National Institute for Psychobiology in
Israel:** Hebrew University, Givat Ram Campus, 91904 Jerusalem; tel. (2) 6584086; fax
(2) 5635267; e-mail psychobi@cc.huji.ac.il;
internet www.psychobiology.org.il; f. 1971
with funds from the Charles E. Smith Family
Foundation, to create a network of scientists

engaged in research in psychobiology, to
further co-operative programmes between
existing institutions, and to train personnel
in the field of psychobiology; administers
Charles E. Smith Family Laboratory for
Collaborative Research in Psychobiology;
operates through the Research and Development Authority of the Hebrew University;
Pres. DAVID BRUCE SMITH; Dir Prof. SHAUL
HOCHSTEIN; Chair. Prof. ELLIOT GERSHON.

Physical Sciences

**Earth Sciences Research Administra-
tion:** 30 Malkhei Israel, 95501 Jerusalem;
tel. (2) 5314246; fax (2) 5380688; e-mail
mbeyth@gsi.gov.il; f. 1949; attached to Min.
of National Infrastructure; defines scientific
issues involved in energy, environment and
infrastructure; Dir-Gen. HEZI KUGLER.

Subordinate Institutions:

Geological Survey of Israel: 30 Malkhei
Israel St, 95501 Jerusalem; tel. (2)
5314211; fax (2) 5380688; e-mail ask_gsi@
gsi.gov.il; internet www.gsi.gov.il; f. 1949;
geological mapping, research and exploration of mineral, water and energy
resources; environmental geology; mitigation of earthquake hazards; Dir Dr ORA
SHAPIRA.

Geophysical Institute of Israel: POB
182, 71100 Lod; tel. (8) 9785888; fax (8)
9208811; internet www.gii.co.il; f. 1957;
activities devoted chiefly to the exploration
of petroleum, water and mineral resources
and to engineering studies in Israel and
abroad, using geophysical methods; documentation unit; data-processing centre;
monitoring and mitigation of earthquake
hazards; Dir Dr Y. ROTSTEIN.

**Israel Oceanographic and Limnologi-
cal Research:** POB 1793, 31000 Haifa; tel.
(4) 8526639; fax (4) 8511911; e-mail
barak@ocean.org.il; internet www.ocean
.org.il; f. 1967; physical, chemical and
biological oceanography and limnology;
aquaculture; Dir Prof. BARAK HERUT.

Israel Meteorological Service: POB 25,
50250 Bet Dagan; tel. (3) 9682121; fax (3)
9604065; e-mail ims@ims.gov.il; internet
www.ims.gov.il; f. 1936; provides general
service to public and detailed service to
various orgs; library; various publs; Dir Z.
ALPERSON.

RELIGION, SOCIOLOGY AND ANTHROPOLOGY

**Harry Fischel Institute for Research in
Talmud and Jewish Law:** Bucharim Quarter, 14 David St (Corner Fischel St), POB
5289, 91052 Jerusalem; tel. (2) 5322517; fax
(2) 5326448; e-mail harry_@netvision.net.il;
f. 1932; seminary for Rabbis and Rabbinical
Judges; legislation and research publs; codification of Jewish law; Jewish adult education
centre; 80 mems; Chancellor Chief Rabbi
SHEAR-YASHUV COHEN.

World Jewish Bible Center: POB 7024,
Jerusalem; tel. (2) 6255965; f. 1957; aims to
disseminate a knowledge of the Bible and of
Bible research by publications, lectures and
exhibitions; Chair. S. J. KREUTNER; publ. *Beit
Mikra* (4 a year, in Hebrew).

Yad Izhak Ben-Zvi: POB 7660, 91076
Jerusalem; tel. (2) 5398888; fax (2) 5638310;
e-mail ybz@ybz.org.il; internet www.ybz.org
.il; f. 1964; encourages research into the
history of Israel and Jerusalem; promotes
the study of Jewish communities in the
Middle East, Izhak Ben-Zvi and the Zionist
and labour movements of Israel; library;
library of 65,000 vols; Dir Dr ZVI ZAMERET;
publs *Cathedra* (4 a year), *Et-mol* (6 a year),

Pe'amim (4 a year), *Sefunot* (irregular), *Shalem* (irregular).
Subordinate Institutions:

Ben-Zvi Institute for the Study of Jewish Communities in the East: POB 7660, 91076 Jerusalem; tel. (2) 5398844; fax (2) 5612329; e-mail mbz@ybz.org.il; internet www.ybz.org.il; f. 1947; operated jtly with the Hebrew Univ. of Jerusalem; sponsors research into the history and culture of Jewish communities in Muslim countries since the 7th century; maintains a large colln of MSS, and other historical documents; library; Chair. Prof. YOM TOV ASSIS; publs *Ginzei Qedem—Genizah Research Annual* (1 a year, in Hebrew and English), *Jewish Communities in the East in the 19th and 20th centuries*, *Pe'amim* (4 a year, in Hebrew), *Sefunot* (irregular, in Hebrew).

Institute for Research of Eretz Israel: POB 7660, 91076 Jerusalem; tel. (2) 5398888; fax (2) 5638310; e-mail ybz@ybz.org.il; internet www.ybz.org.il; promotes research on the history of Eretz Israel from Biblical times to the mid-20th century, and publishes studies on the history and culture of the Jewish people in Israel from the destruction of the Second Temple to the first years of the State of Israel's existence; research and studies based on the work of scientists at the main univs; Dir Prof. URI BIALER.

TECHNOLOGY

Israel Atomic Energy Commission: POB 7061, 61070 Tel-Aviv; 26 Rehov Chaim Levanon, Ramat Aviv, Tel-Aviv; tel. (3) 6462922; fax (3) 6462570; internet www.iaec.gov.il; f. 1952; advises the Government on long-term policies and priorities in the advancement of nuclear research and devt; supervises the implementation of policies approved by the Govt, incl. the licensing of nuclear power plants; promotion of technological industrial applications; represents Israel in relations with scientific instns and organizations abroad (Israel is a mem. of IAEA); Chair. The PRIME MINISTER; Dir-Gen. G. FRANK.

Attached Research Centres:

Negev Nuclear Research Centre: Dimona; natural uranium-fuelled and heavy water-moderated reactor IRR-2 of 26 MW thermal; Dir MICHA DAPHT.

Soreq Nuclear Research Centre: 81800 Yavne; tel. (8) 9434290; internet www.soreq.gov.il; f. 1958; swimming-pool research reactor IRR-1 of 5 MW thermal; Dir URI HALAVEE.

Office of the Chief Scientist—Industrial Research Administration, Ministry of Industry and Trade: 5 Bank Israel St, POB 3166, 91036 Jerusalem; tel. (2) 6662486; fax (2) 6662928; f. 1970; promotes industrial research and devt in industry, research institutes and higher education institutes by financing projects; encourages establishment of science-based industrial parks near universities and research institutes; proposes policies to promote innovative industry through legislation, developing physical and technical infrastructure and intergovernmental industrial research and development (R&D) agreements; Chief Scientist ELI OPER.

Associated Institutions:

Institutes for Applied Research, Ben-Gurion University of the Negev: POB 1025, 84110 Be'ersheva; tel. (8) 5778382; f. 1956; engages in applied research in water desalination, membrane and ion-exchange technologies, chemical technologies, irrigation with brackish and seawater, develop-

ment of salt- and drought-resistant crops and ornamentals, natural products from higher plants and algae, devt of mechanical and electromechanical products, utilization of non-conventional energy sources; 120 staff; library of 13,200 vols; Dir Prof. A. SHANI; publ. *Scientific Activities* (2 a year).

Israel Ceramic and Silicate Institute: Technion City, 32000 Haifa; tel. (4) 8222107; fax (4) 8325339; e-mail isracer@actcom.co.il; internet www.isracer.org; f. 1962; provides the local ceramic industry with technical assistance and with research and devt into advanced and new fields in ceramics technology; 12 staff; Dir Dr ADRIAN GOLDSTEIN.

Israel Fiber Institute: POB 8001, 91080 Jerusalem; tel. (2) 5707377; fax (2) 5245110; attached to Technion—Israel Institute of Technology; f. 1953; advances textile, polymer, paper, leather and related industries; applied research and development (R&D), testing services, quality control, training courses for engineers and technicians, MSc and PhD courses in conjunction with the Hebrew Univ.; 45 staff; library of 4,000 vols and 30 periodicals; Dir Dr HILDA GUTTMAN.

Israel Institute of Metals: Technion City, 32000 Haifa; tel. (4) 8294473; f. 1962; serves industry in metallurgy and powder technology, foundry, corrosion and coating technology, vehicle and mechanical engineering; Dir Prof. A. ROSEN.

Israel Institute of Plastics: POB 7293, 31072 Haifa; tel. (4) 8225174; fax (4) 8225173; f. 1981; research and development (R&D) and information centre for promoting the plastic industry; Dir Dr S. ABRAHAMI.

Israel Wine Institute: POB 2329, 4 Ha-Raz St, 76310 Rehovot; tel. (8) 9475693; f. 1957; improves the country's wines by means of quality control and applied research and promotes their export; Dir SHLOMO COHEN.

National Physical Laboratory: Hebrew Univ., Danziger A Bldg, Givat Ram Campus, 91904 Jerusalem; tel. (2) 6303501; fax (2) 6303516; attached to Min. of Industry, Trade and Labour; f. 1950; applied research with industrial orientation, basic physical and chemical standards, energy saving, ecology, solar energy; Dir Dr ILYA KUSELMAN.

Rubber Research Association Ltd: Technion City, 32000 Haifa; tel. (4) 8222147; fax (4) 8227582; f. 1951; the advancement of the rubber industry in Israel; Dir D. CZIMERMAN.

Standards Institution of Israel: POB 39020, 61390 Tel-Aviv; tel. (3) 5454154; fax (3) 5419683; internet www.iso.co.il; f. 1923; tests the compliance of commodities with the requirements of standards and specifications; grants standards mark; conducts technological research; publishes the Nat. Standards Specifications and Codes; 550 staff; library of 300,000 standards; Dir-Gen. ELI HADAR; publ. *Mati* (4 a year).

Libraries and Archives
Be'ersheva

Ben Gurion University of the Negev Aranne Library: POB 653, 84105 Be'er Sheva; tel. (8) 6461413; fax (8) 6472940; e-mail yaatz@bgu.ac.il; internet www.bgu.ac.il/aranne; f. 1966; 1,000,000 vols, 25,000 current periodicals incl. e-journals, 3,200 microfilms, 300 audiovisual cassettes, 76 DVDs, 1,200 CD-ROMs and books, 1,500

online theses; spec. collns; David Tuviyahu Archives of the Negev; Isaiah Berlin Room; Dir HAYA ASNER.

Haifa

Borochov Library: c/o Haifa Labour Council, POB 5226, Haifa; f. 1921; 40,000 vols, in central library, 60,000 vols in 24 brs; Chief Librarian EZECHIEL OREN.

Haifa AMLI Library of Music: 23 Arlosoroff St, POB 4811/25, Haifa; tel. (4) 8644485; fax (4) 8644485; f. 1958; lending library incl. books, scores, records and cassettes; Librarian LEAH MARCUS.

Pevsner Public Library: 54 Pevsner St, POB 5345, Haifa; tel. (4) 8667766; f. 1934; 200,000 vols covering all fields of literature and science, in Hebrew, English and German; 15 brs; Chief Librarian Dr S. BACK.

Technion—Israel Institute of Technology, Library System: Technion City, 32000 Haifa; tel. (4) 8292507; fax (4) 8295662; e-mail ddalia@tx.technion.ac.il; internet library.technion.ac.il; f. 1925; science, technology, architecture and medicine; Elyachar (Central) Library, 17 departmental libraries; 1,000,000 vols, 12,700 current periodicals, 281 databases, 695 electronic books; Dir DALIA DOLEV.

University of Haifa Library: Mount Carmel, 31905 Haifa; tel. (4) 8240289; fax (4) 8257753; e-mail libmaster@univ.haifa.ac.il; internet lib.haifa.ac.il; f. 1963; 1,050,000 vols, 17,000 periodical titles; 8,000 current periodicals; 480,000 micro-fiches and -films; 27,000 maps; 168,000 slides; 5,600 films (incl. video cassettes); special collns incl. integrated law colln, rare books, media centre, laboratory for children's librarianship; Dir OREN WEINBERG; Admin. Dir. HUMI REKEM.

Jerusalem

Archive and Library of Ashkenaz House Synagogue Memorial: 58 King George St, POB 7440, 91073 Jerusalem; tel. (2) 6233225; fax (2) 6233226; e-mail synagog@netvision.net.il; internet www.ashkenazhouse.org; f. 1988; research into German communities and synagogues destroyed during 'Kristallnacht' in Germany, November 1938; collects material about Ashkenaz Jewry and docs relating to 'Kristallnacht'; ongoing compilation of a series of memorial books in German (of which 5 have already appeared in print), documenting the synagogues and Jewish communities destroyed in the early 20th century in greater Germany; preparation of English-language memorial books on the above subjects, for the American public; research into history of the ship *Exodus* and the subsequent deportation of holocaust survivors back to Europe; Founder and Dir-Gen. Prof. em. Dr MEIER SCHWARZ.

Awkaf Supreme Council Library: c/o Supreme Muslim Council, POB 19859, Jerusalem; Haram al-Sharif, Jerusalem; f. 1931; contains Arabic and Islamic MSS.

Bibliothèque de l'Ecole Biblique et Archéologique Française de Jérusalem: POB 19053, 6 Nablus Rd, 91190 Jerusalem; tel. (2) 6264468; fax (2) 6282567; e-mail biblio@ebaf.edu; internet www.ebaf.edu; f. 1890; 145,000 vols; archaeology and epigraphy of the ancient Near East, biblical studies; Dir Dr HERVÉ PONSOT; Librarian Rev. PAWEL TRZOPEK; publs *Cahiers de la Revue Biblique*, *Etudes Bibliques*, *Revue Biblique* (4 a year).

Central Archives for the History of the Jewish People (formerly Jewish Historical General Archives): POB 39077, 91390 Jerusalem; tel. (2) 6586249; fax (2) 6535426; e-mail archives@vms.huji.ac.il; internet sites .huji.ac.il/archives; f. 1969; Dir HADASSAH ASSOULINE; 13,000 vols on Jewish history,

1,600 community archives, 12,000 photographs, 8,000 statutes; intended to serve as the central archives of Jewish history.

Central Zionist Archives: POB 92, Jerusalem; tel. (2) 6204800; fax (2) 6204837; e-mail cza@wzo.org.il; internet www .zionistarchives.org.il; f. 1919; official repository of the World Zionist Org., the Jewish Agency, the Jewish Nat. Fund Keren Hayesod and the World Jewish Congress; 70,000 books, 10,000m. original documents, 900,000 photographs and negatives, 70,000 maps, 26,000 posters and announcements, 6,000 newspaper titles; 500 audio recordings, 2m. genealogical records; Admin. Dir GILI SIMHA; Deputy Dir for Archival Matters ROCHELLE RUBINSTEIN.

Gulbenkian Library: Armenian Patriarchate, POB 14106, 91140 Jerusalem; tel. (2) 6282331 ext. 222; e-mail ibrary@ armenian-patriarchate.org; f. 1929; donated by the late Calouste Gulbenkian; one of the three great Armenian libraries in the diaspora, the others being the Mekhitarist Fathers' Library in Venice, Italy and another in Vienna, Austria; public library of 100,000 vols, of which one-third are in Armenian and the rest in foreign languages, primarily English and French; receives more than 360 newspapers, magazines, periodicals (of which more than one-half are Armenian) from foreign countries; collns of newspapers and magazines since the 1850s; a copy of the first printed Armenian Bible (1666); 3,890 Armenian MSS; Dir Rev. Fr NORAYR KAZAZIAN; Sec. RINA DJERNAZIAN; Librarian MALINA ZAKIAN LA-PORTA; publ. *Sion* (official organ of the Armenian Patriarchate, 12 a year).

Israel Antiquities Authority Archives Branch: POB 586, 91004 Jerusalem; tel. (2) 6204680; fax (2) 6271173; e-mail arieh@ israntique.org.il; internet www.antiquities .org.il; f. 1920; written, computerized, photographic and digitized records, maps and plans; Head of Archives Branch BARUCH BRANDL; Asst to Head of Archives Branch ARIEH ROCHMAN-HALPERIN.

Israel State Archives: Prime Minister's Office, Kiryat Ben-Gurion, 91950 Jerusalem; tel. (2) 5680680; fax (2) 6793375; e-mail research@archives.gov.il; internet www .archives.gov.il; f. 1949; comprises 7 sections: Department of Files and Manuscripts, Library Department, Records Management, Supervision Department of Public and Private Archives, Services to the Public, Technical Services Department and Publication of State Papers; holdings incl. files occupying 30 kilometres of shelving, 150,000 printed items and 25,000 books; administrative records, incl. foreign relations, are available after 30 years and records on defence after 50 years; State Archivist E. FRIESEL; Dir M. MOSSEK; publs *Documents on the Foreign Policy of Israel, Israel Government Publications* (bibliography, 1 a year).

Jerusalem City (Public) Library: POB 1409, Jerusalem; tel. (2) 6256785; fax (2) 6255785; f. 1961; 750,000 vols; 20 brs and 2 Bookmobiles; Dir ABRAHAM VILNER.

Library of the Central Bureau of Statistics: 66 Kanfei Nesharm St, POB 34525, 95464 Jerusalem; tel. (2) 6592666; fax (2) 6521340; internet www.cbs.gov.il; f. 1948; 40,000 vols; spec. collns: all publs of (British) Palestine Dept of Statistics (due to be transferred to the Israel State Archives); most publs available for exchange; Librarian MARIAN ROMAN.

Library of the Knesset: Knesset, 91950 Jerusalem; tel. (2) 6753333; fax (2) 6662733; internet www.knesset.gov.il; f. 1949; principally for members' use; 150,000 vols, incl. books, bound periodicals and colln of all

Israeli Govt publs, UN publs and foreign parliamentary papers; Librarian NAOMI KIMHI.

Library of the Studium Biblicum Franciscanum: POB 19424, Monastery of the Flagellation, Via Dolorosa, 91193 Jerusalem; tel. (2) 6270485; fax (2) 6264519; e-mail secretary@studiumbiblicum.org; f. 1924; 50,000 vols chiefly on archaeology, judaeo-christianism, biblical and patristic studies, 420 periodicals; 20 mems; Librarian LOCHE GIOVANNI.

Muriel and Philip Berman Medical Library, Hebrew University of Jerusalem: POB 12272, 91120 Jerusalem; tel. (2) 6758795; fax (2) 6410974; e-mail mdlibinfo@ savion.huji.ac.il; internet library.md.huji.ac .il; f. 1919; serves faculty and students of the Hebrew Univ. of Jerusalem Faculty of Medicine, Faculty of Dental Medicine, School of Pharmacy, Nursing School and School of Public Health and the Hadassah-Hebrew Univ. Hospital; 400,000 vols, 45,000 print and electronic book titles, 8,000 electronic journals in health sciences; history of medicine colln and museum; Dir SHARON LENGA.

Schocken Library: 6 Balfour St, 92102 Jerusalem; tel. (2) 5631288; fax (2) 5636857; e-mail jtspress@schocken-jts.org.il; internet www.schocken-jts.org.il; f. 1900; 55,000 vols, 200 MSS, 20,000 photostats (Hebrew Liturgy and Poetry); Dir Dr SHMUEL GLICK; Bibliographer and Research Librarian DAVID KERSCHEN.

Supreme Court Library: Supreme Court of Israel, Rehov Sha'arei Mishpat, Kiryat Ben Gurion, 91 950 Jerusalem; tel. (2) 6759665; e-mail liba@supreme.court.gov.il; internet www.court.gov.il; f. 1949; 85,000 vols; Dir LIBA BORCK.

The National Library of Israel: POB 39105, 91390 Jerusalem; tel. (2) 6584651; fax (2) 6511771; e-mail orenw@savion.huji.ac .il; internet www.jnul.huji.ac.il; f. 1892; 10,000 MSS; 49,000 microfilmed Hebrew MSS; microfilms of Jewish and Israeli newspapers; 200 incunabula (120 Hebrew and 80 in other languages); 15,000 current periodicals; special collns incl. the Abraham Schwadron Colln of Jewish Autographs and Portraits, the Harry Friedenwald Colln on the History of Medicine, the National Sound Archives and the Jacob Michael Colln of Jewish Music, the Sidney M. Edelstein Colln on the History of Chemistry, the Eran Laor Cartographic Colln, the Archives of Albert Einstein; 5,000,000 vols, incl. those in departmental libraries; Dir OREN WEINBERG; Chief Librarian RIVKA SHVEIKY; publs *Index of Articles on Jewish Studies* (1 a year), *Kiryat Sefer* (bibliography, 4 a year).

Kfar Giladi

Kfar Giladi Library: 12210 Kfar Giladi, Upper Galilee; f. 1934; 35,000 vols, 110 periodicals; Librarian SHULAMIT ROSENTHAL.

Kiryat Shmona

Library of Tel-Hai Academic College: Upper Galilee, 12210, nr Kiryat Shmona; tel. (4) 8181785; fax (4) 8181787; e-mail sagim@telhai.ac.il; internet www.telhai.ac.il; incl. the Calvary Colln, the Ofer Colln, the Kapeliuk Middle East colln, Dvir Colln in Environmental Studies, the Lubin art colln and the Gail Chasin art colln, Littauer Judaic Colln, Silvia Sheim Colln; 80,000 vols, 600 periodicals, 1,200 videotapes, 4,200 e-Journals; Library Dir IRIS CHAI.

Nahariya

Municipal Library in Memory of William and Chia Boorstein: 61 Herzl St, Nahariya; tel. (4) 9879870; f. 1946; under the

supervision of the Min. of Education, Jerusalem; 70,000 vols; Chief Librarian SHOSHANA GIBLEY.

Ramat-Gan

Bar-Ilan University Library System: Central Library, 52900 Ramat-Gan; tel. (3) 5318165; fax (3) 5353116; e-mail tchiya .dagan@mail.biu.ac.il; internet www.biu.ac .il/lib; f. 1955; serves faculties of humanities, Judaica, law, social sciences, exact sciences, and life sciences; 1,000,000 vols, 4,500 current journals, spec. collns incl. the Mordecai Margulies colln of rare 16th and 17th century Hebrew books and 800 Hebrew Oriental MSS, Berman colln of early E European Hebrew imprints, rare Latin and German books on Jewish studies, Old Testament criticism, material on the Dead Sea Scrolls and the Samaritans; a colln of material on the devt of Religious Zionism; colln of Responsa and Jewish studies; Moussaieff colln of 220 Kabbalistic MSS; Head Periodicals Dept T. DAGAN; publs *Hebrew Subject Headings* (online), *Index to Literary Supplements of the Daily Hebrew Press* (online).

'Dvir Bialik' Municipal Central Public Library: Hibat-Zion St 14, Ramat-Gan; f. 1945; 400,000 vols, incl. special Rabbinic literature and Social Sciences colln; maintains 11 brs; Chief Librarian HADASSAH PELACH.

Rehovot

Hebrew University of Jerusalem, The Library of Agricultural, Food and Environmental Quality Sciences: POB 12, 76100 Rehovot; tel. (8) 9489906; fax (8) 9361348; e-mail suzanag@savion.huji.ac.il; internet www.agri.huji.ac.il/library/menu .html; f. 1960; br. in Koret School of Veterinary Medicine: The Lubetzky-Americus Library of Veterinary Medicine; Nat. Agricultural Library, operated jtly by the Volcani Centre of the Min. of Agriculture's Agricultural Research Org. and the Hebrew Univ. Faculty of Agriculture; maintains exchange relations all over the world; regional libraries at Gilath, Dor and N've Ya'ar; 300,000 vols, 3,200 current periodicals and serials, 180,000 docs; Dir SUSANA GURMAN.

Weizmann Archives: POB 26, 76100 Rehovot; tel. (8) 9343390; fax (8) 9344176; internet www.weizmann.ac.il/wis-library/archive .htm; f. 1973; contains assembled letters, papers, photographs, and other docs relating to political and scientific activities of Dr Chaim Weizmann, first President of Israel; approx. 180,000 items; Archivist ORNA ZELTZER.

Weizmann Institute of Science Libraries: POB 26, 76100 Rehovot; tel. (8) 9343873; fax (8) 9344176; e-mail hedva.milo@ weizmann.ac.il; internet www.weizmann.ac .il/library; f. 1934, as Ziff Institute Libraries; renamed 1949; central library, 3 faculty libraries, 1 deptl library and approx. 50 deptl collns; 260,000 vols, incl. bound periodicals and 1,032 current print periodicals in science and technology, and access to several databases and several thousand electronic journals; Chief Librarian HEDVA MILO.

Tel-Aviv

Felicja Blumental Music Center and Library: 26 Bialik St, 61048 Tel-Aviv; tel. (3) 6201185; fax (3) 6201323; e-mail info@ fbmc.co.il; internet www.fbmc.co.il; f. 1950; 75,920 vols, 64 periodicals, 18,000 records, 3,446 compact discs, 170 video cassettes; Bronislav Huberman archive, Joachim Stutschewsky archive, Shulamith Conservatory (1910), Beit Levi'im (1919), etc.; Dir IRIT SCHÖNHORN.

General Archives of the City of Tel-Aviv-Yafo: City Hall, Kikar Malkhei Israel, 64162 Tel-Aviv; tel. (3) 6438554; f. 1967; Archivist JUDITH Z. FASTOVSKY.

Library of the Kibbutzim College of Education: 149 Namir Rd, 62507 Tel-Aviv; tel. (3) 6902323; fax (3) 6992791; internet www.smkb.ac.il; f. 1940; 75,000 vols; Librarian EDNA NAAMAN.

Sourasky Central Library, Tel-Aviv University: POB 39038, Ramat-Aviv, 61930 Tel-Aviv; tel. (3) 6408745; fax (3) 6407833; e-mail miril@tauex.tau.ac.il; internet www.cenlib .tau.ac.il; f. 1954; 880,000 vols, 4,800 current periodicals and 96,000 microforms; 7 specialized br. libraries; 788,000 vols; incl. the Pevsner Colln of Hebrew Press, the Faitlovitch colln, the Colln of Yiddish Literature and Culture in memory of Benzion and Pearl Margulies, the Wiener Library colln, which concerns the Second World War, spec. the Holocaust, and the history of anti-Semitism, the Herbert Cohen colln of rare books, the Dr Horodisch colln on the history of books and the Jaffe colln of Hebrew poetry; Dir MIRA LIPSTEIN.

Tel-Aviv Central Public Library 'Shaar Zion': 25 King Saul Blvd, POB 33235, Tel-Aviv; tel. (3) 6910141; fax (3) 6919024; internet www.tel-aviv.gov.il/english/culture/ariela.htm; f. 1922; 900,000 vols (in 25 brs); General Library in 8 languages; spec. collns: Rambam Library, Ahad ha-Am Library (history and geography of Eretz Israel), Dance Library, Graphoteque (lending library of artist prints), Legal Library; Dir ORA NEBENZAHL.

Museums and Art Galleries

Acre

Okashi Art Museum, Acre: Old City of Akko, El-Jazz'ar St, Acre; permanent exhibition of works by Avsalom Okashi (1916–1980); temporary exhibitions by Israeli artists.

Be'ersheva

Negev Museum: 60 Ha'atsmaut Rd, POB 5188, 84100 Be'ersheva; tel. (7) 6206570; fax (7) 6206536; e-mail br7museum@br7.org.il; f. 1954; exhibits from regional excavations, mainly from the Chalcolithic, Israelite, Roman and Byzantine periods; exhibitions of Israeli contemporary art; Dir GALIA GAVISH.

Haifa

Haifa Museum of Art: 26 Shabbetai Levy St, 33043 Haifa; tel. (4) 8523255; fax (4) 8552714; e-mail curator@hma.org.il; internet www.hma.org.il; f. 1951; collns of Israeli and world contemporary art, prints, art posters, paintings and sculptures; library of 10,000 vols; Curator Dir TAMI KATZ-FREIMAN.

National Maritime Museum: 198 Allenby Rd, POB 44855, 31447 Haifa; tel. (4) 8536622; fax (4) 8539286; e-mail curator@nmm.org.il; internet www.nmm.org.il; f. 1954; large colln of artefacts and ship models illustrating 5,000 years of navigation and shipbuilding, old maps and engravings, undersea archaeology, a Hellenistic bronze ram, and stamps and ancient coins connected with seafaring and maritime symbols; archaeology and civilizations of ancient peoples; scientific instruments; library: research history of 6,000 vols; Dir-Gen. NISSIM TAL; publ. *Sefunim.*

Tikotin Museum of Japanese Art: 89 Hanassi Ave, 34642 Haifa; tel. (4) 8383554;

fax (4) 8379824; e-mail curator@tmja.org.il; internet www.tmja.org.il; f. 1960; paintings, prints, drawings, textiles, netsuke, lacquer work, ceramics, metalwork, colln of Mingei (folk art); courses for children and adults; library of 3,000 vols; Chief Curator Dr ILANA SINGER.

Jerusalem

Archaeological (Rockefeller) Museum: POB 71117, 91710 Jerusalem; tel. (2) 6282251; fax (2) 6708906; e-mail fawziib@imj.org.il; internet www.imj.org.il; f. 1938; fmrly Palestine Archaeological Museum; archaeology of Israel from earliest times up until end of Islamic period; largely material found in excavations before 1948; Dir JAMES S. SNYDER.

Beit Ha'Omanim (Jerusalem Artists' House): 12 Shmuel Hanagid St, Jerusalem; tel. (2) 6253653; fax (2) 6258594; e-mail artists@zahav.net.il; f. 1965; Israeli and foreign contemporary art exhibitions and permanent gallery of works by Israeli artists; Dir RUTH ZADKA.

Bible Lands Museum Jerusalem: POB 4670, 91046 Jerusalem; 25 Granot St, 93706 Jerusalem; tel. (2) 5611066; fax (2) 5638228; e-mail contact@blmj.org; internet www.blmj .org; f. 1992; ancient Near Eastern history and Biblical archaeology; Chair. BATYA BOROWSKI; Dir AMANDA WEISS; Deputy Dir ORIT LEV-SEGEV.

Israel Museum: POB 71117, 91710 Jerusalem; tel. (2) 6708811; fax (2) 5631833; e-mail info@imj.org.il; internet www.imj.org.il; f. 1965; fine art, Judaica and archaeology from Biblical times to the present; Shrine of the Book housing Dead Sea Scrolls; Billy Rose Sculpture Garden; a renovation project to extend the museum bldgs is to be completed by the end of 2009; library of 65,000 vols; Dir JAMES S. SNYDER; publ. *Journal* (1 a year).

Mayer, L. A., Museum for Islamic Art: POB 4088, 2 Hapalmach St, 91040 Jerusalem; tel. (2) 5661291; fax (2) 5619802; e-mail islamart@netvision.net.il; internet www .islamicart.co.il; f. 1974; colln of Islamic art: metalwork, glass, miniatures, ceramics, ivories, jewellery; Sir David Salomons colln of antique clocks and watches; educational activities in Jewish and Arab sectors; photographs and slides; library of 14,000 vols, 50 periodicals; Dir RACHEL HASSON.

Museum of Prehistory, Institute of Archaeology, Hebrew University: Mt Scopus Campus, Jerusalem; tel. (2) 5882099; fax (2) 5825548; internet archaeology.huji.ac.il; f. 1955; large colln of objects from prehistoric sites in Israel; library.

Museum of Taxes: 42 Agripas St, POB 3100, 91036 Jerusalem; tel. (2) 6257597; fax (2) 6252381; e-mail misim@mof.gov.il; internet ozar.mof.gov.il/museum; f. 1964; 5 sections: artefacts from the Land of Canaan and environs, taxes levied specifically on Jews in the Diaspora, gen. section for tax-related items from all over the world, taxation in Israel, prevention of smuggling and importation of illegal goods and other customs-related issues; Dir MIRA DROR; publ. *Israeli Tax Review* (4 a year).

Museum of the Studium Biblicum Franciscanum: POB 19424, Monastery of the Flagellation, Via Dolorosa, Jerusalem; tel. (2) 6270456; fax (2) 6270498; e-mail secretary@studiumbiblicum.org; internet 198.62.75.1/www1/ofm/sbf/sbfmuse.html; f. 1902; Palestinian archaeology: city coins of Palestine, Roman-Byzantine-Crusader pottery and objects; ancient model of Holy Sepulchre, Bethlehem treasure, bronze objects, seals,

Egyptian findings, Mesopotamian colln, glassware, weights, amulets, antiphonaries, picture-gallery, Pharmacy of St. Saviour's, Numismatic colln and inscriptions; Curator Prof. EUGENIO ALLIATA; Sec. ROSARIO PIERRI; publ. *SBF Museum.*

Yad Vashem, Holocaust Martyrs' and Heroes' Remembrance Authority: POB 3477, Mount of Remembrance, 90435 Jerusalem; tel. (2) 6443400; fax (2) 6443409; e-mail general.information@yadvashem.org .il; internet www.yadvashem.org; f. 1953; the Jewish people's nat. memorial to the Holocaust; Holocaust History museum: permanent exhibition of photographs, documents, artefacts and testimonies; Hall of Names; Hall of Remembrance; Children's Memorial; Valley of the Communities; Memorial to the Deportees; Ave and Garden of the Righteous Among the Nations; Holocaust art museum; Int. Institute for Holocaust Research is responsible for expanding academic and research activities; Int. School for Holocaust Studies organizes seminars and develops teaching materials; library of 123,000 vols; world's largest repository of archival and documentary information on the Holocaust: approx. 68m. pages of documents, microfilms, testimonies, diaries, artefacts; Chair. AVNER SHALEV; publ. *Yad Vashem Studies.*

Kibbutz Hazorea

Wilfrid Israel Museum of Oriental Art and Studies: Kibbutz Hazorea, 30060 Post Hazorea; f. 1947; opened 1951 in memory of the late Wilfrid Israel; a cultural centre for study and art exhibitions incl. modern art and all areas of the plastic arts; houses the Wilfrid Israel colln of Near and Far Eastern art and cultural materials; local archaeological exhibits from neolithic to Byzantine times; art library; Dir EHUD DOR.

Kibbutz Lahav

Museum of Bedouin Culture: Joe Alon Centre, Kibbutz Lahav, 85335 Negev D. N.; tel. (8) 9913322; fax (8) 9919889; e-mail joealon@lhv.org.il; internet www.joealon.org .il; f. 1985; part of the Colonel Joe Alon Centre for Regional and Folklore Studies; exhibition of contemporary arts and crafts, educational lectures and guided tours, photographs, demonstrations of Bedouin life (weaving, cooking, etc.); museum of Jewish settlement in the Negev; art gallery; museum of the Bar-Kokba Rebellion; awards grants for research in Bedouin and regional studies; library of 150 vols, 3,000 slides; Gen. Dir RACHEL ALON-MARGALIT.

Kiryat Shmona

Tel Hai Museum: 12210 Tel Hai, Upper Galilee; tel. (4) 6951333; reconstruction of a Jewish settlement from the beginning of the 20th century; documents of Joseph Trumpeldor and his defence of the region in 1920.

Ma'ayan Baruch

Ma'ayan Baruch Prehistory Museum of the Huleh Valley: 12220 Ma'ayan Baruch, Upper Galilee; tel. (4) 523791649; fax (4) 6950724; f. 1952; prehistory of the Huleh Valley from the Palaeolithic (incl. large colln of Ashulian handaxes) to the Chalcolithic period; locally excavated Bronze Age and Roman-Byzantine objects; colln of stone grain mills and oil presses; the Earliest Dog in the World, buried with a woman from the Natufian period (10,000 BC); plaster skull from Neolithic era (7000 BC); world ethnographic exhibition of tools fashioned by people who still live as in prehistoric times; Dir A. ASSAF.

Nazareth

Terra Sancta Museum: Terra Sancta Monastery, POB 23, 96100 Nazareth; tel. (4) 6572501; fax (4) 6460203; f. 1920; Byzantine (and later) remains, coins, Roman and Byzantine glass; colln of antiquities from excavations made in the monastery compound; Vicar of Monastery Rev. P. José Montalverne de Lancastre.

Safad

Israel Bible Museum: c/o POB 1396, Safed; tel. (4) 6999972; internet www .israelbiblemuseum.com; f. 1984; exhibition of the biblical art of Phillip Ratner; permanent and changing exhibitions incl. Kabbalah and art for children; Dir Ami Shoshan.

Sha'ar Ha-Golan

Museum of Prehistory: Sha'ar Ha-Golan, Jordan Valley; f. 1950; large number of exhibits from the neolithic Yarmukian culture excavated in the region; Dir Y. Roth.

Tel-Aviv

Ben-Gurion House: 17 Ben-Gurion Blvds, 63454 Tel-Aviv; tel. (3) 5221010; fax (3) 5247293; f. 1974; residence of David Ben-Gurion, first Prime Minister of the State of Israel; museum and research and study centre; library of 20,000 vols and periodicals on history of Zionist movement, land and state of Israel, ancient peoples, cultures, religions and philosophies, gen. and military history; Dir Hanni Hermolin.

Beth Hatefutsoth (The Nahum Goldmann Museum of the Jewish Diaspora): POB 39359, 61392 Tel-Aviv; tel. (3) 7457890; fax (3) 7457831; e-mail armoni@bh.org.il; internet www.bh.org.il; f. 1978; permanent exhibition tells the story of Jewish survival and life in the Diaspora; temporary exhibitions portray Jewish communities all over the world; seminars and youth educational activities; photographic and film archives; Jewish Genealogy and music centre; CEO Avinoam Armoni.

Eretz-Israel Museum: 2 Chaim Levanon St, POB 17068, Ramat Aviv, 61170 Tel-Aviv; tel. (3) 6415244; fax (3) 6412408; internet www.eretzmuseum.org.il; Tel-Aviv region archaeology and history, Jewish ethnography and folklore, ceramics, ancient glass, numismatics, history of Jewish theatre, tools and technology, planetarium; library of 40,000 vols.

Tel-Aviv Museum of Art: POB 33288, 27 Shaul Hamelech Blvd, 64329 Tel-Aviv; tel. (3) 6077000; fax (3) 6958099; e-mail cliffs@tamuseum.com; internet www.tamuseum.com; f. 1932; art colln consisting of works since 16th century; Israeli art; library: art library of 60,000 vols, periodicals, microfiches, databases; Dir and Chief Curator Prof. Mordechai Omer.

Tiberias

Municipal Museum of Antiquities: Lake Front, Tiberias; f. 1953; colln of antiquities from Tiberias and region, mainly of the Roman, Byzantine and Arab periods; Dir Elisheva Ballhorn.

Universities

BAR-ILAN UNIVERSITY

52900 Ramat-Gan
Telephone: (3) 5318111
Fax: (3) 5344622
E-mail: director-general.office@mail.biu.ac.il
Internet: www.biu.ac.il

Founded 1953; inaugurated 1955

State control
Language of instruction: Hebrew
Academic year: October to June
Pres.: Prof. Moshe Kaveh
Vice-Pres. for Research: Prof. Harold Basch
Assoc. Vice-Pres.: Judith Haimoff
Rector: Prof. Joseph Menis
Dir-General: Haim Glick
Academic Registrar: M. Mishan
Librarian: (vacant)
Library: see Libraries and Archives
Number of teachers: 1,350
Number of students: 31,678

Four regional colleges; Ashkelon College, Jordan Valley College, Safed College, Western Galilee College; 76 research centres

Publication: *Philosophia* (4 a year)

DEANS

Faculty of Exact Sciences: Prof. A. Amir
Faculty of Humanities: Prof. B. Abrahamov
Faculty of Jewish Studies: Prof. M. Orfali
Faculty of Law: Prof. A. Reich
Faculty of Life Sciences: Prof. H. Breitbart
Faculty of Social Sciences: Prof. S. Sandler

PROFESSORS

Faculty of Exact Sciences (tel. (3) 5318585; fax (3) 5344766; e-mail exacts@mail.biu.ac.il; internet www.esc.biu.ac.il):

Agronovsky, M., Mathematics
Amir, A., Computer Science
Basch, H., Chemistry
Berkowitz, R., Physics
Deutsch, M., Physics
Ehrenberg, B., Physics
Eisenberg, L., Mathematics
Freulikher, V., Physics
Freund, Y., Physics
Friedman, L., Mathematics
Frimer, A., Chemistry
Gedanken, A., Chemistry
Goldschmidt, Z., Chemistry
Gordon, A., Chemistry
Halpern, H., Physics
Havlin, S., Physics
Hochberg, K., Mathematics
Hoz, S., Chemistry
Kantor, I., Physics
Kaveh, M., Physics
Kay, K., Chemistry
Kessler, D., Physics
Krauss, S., Computer Science
Krushkal, S., Mathematics
Margel, S., Chemistry
Margolis, S., Mathematics
Marzbach, E., Mathematics
Nudelman, A., Chemistry
Orbach, D., Chemistry
Persky, A., Chemistry
Rabin, I., Physics
Rappaport, D., Physics
Rosenbluh, M., Physics
Rowen, L., Mathematics
Shapira, B., Physics
Shlimak, I., Physics
Shnider, S., Mathematics
Sukenik, H., Chemistry
Teicher, M., Mathematics
Ulman, A., Chemistry
Yeshurun, Y., Physics
Zalcman, L., Mathematics

Faculty of Humanities (tel. (3) 5318370; fax (3) 5347601; e-mail segalil@mail.biu.ac.il; internet www.biu.ac.il/hu):

Abrahamov, B., Arabic
Fine, J., English
Halamish, M., Philosophy
Handelman, S., English
Harvey, S., Philosophy
Hassine, J., Comparative Literature
Katzoff, R., Classical Studies
Koren, R., French Culture
Langerman, Z., Arabic

Perl, J., English
Reichelberg, R., Comparative Literature
Rothstein, S., English
Saguy, A., Philosophy
Schwartz, D., Philosophy
Spolsky, E., English
Widoker, D., Philosophy

Faculty of Jewish Studies (tel. (3) 5318233; fax (3) 5351233; e-mail jsfcty@mail.biu.ac.il; internet www.biu.ac.il/js):

Bar Tikvah, B., Literature of the Jewish People
Baumgarten, A., Jewish History
Cohen, M., General History
Cohen, T., Literature of the Jewish People
Dishon, Y., Literature of the Jewish People
Feiner, S., Jewish History
Genizi, H., General History
Havlin, S. Z., Talmud and Information Sciences
Hazan, E., Literature of the Jewish People
Kasher, R., Bible
Kloner, A., Land of Israel Studies
Kogel, J., Bible
Lipsker, A., Literature of the Jewish People
Michman, D., Jewish History
Milikowski, H., Talmud
Orfali, M., Jewish History
Rosman, M., Jewish History
Safrai, Z., Land of Israel Studies
Schwartz, J., Land of Israel Studies
Schwartzwald, O., Hebrew Language
Sharvit, S., Hebrew Language
Sokoloff, M., Hebrew and Semitic Languages
Sperber, D., Talmud
Spiegel, Y., Talmud
Tabori, Y., Talmud
Tauber, E., History of the Middle East
Toaff, A., Jewish History
Vargon, S., Bible
Weiss, H., Literature of the Jewish People

Faculty of Law (tel. (3) 5318417; fax (3) 5351856; e-mail olmertr@mail.biu.ac.il; internet www.law.biu.ac.il):

Cohen, Z.
Lerner, S.

Faculty of Life Sciences (tel. (3) 5318721; fax (3) 7369928; e-mail landmar@mail.biu.ac.il; internet life-sciences.biu.ac.il):

Achituv, Y.
Breitbart, H.
Brodie, C.
Cohen, Y.
Haas, E.
Kislev, M.
Malik, Z.
Mayevsky, A.
Sampson, S.
Shainberg, A.
Shoham, Y.
Sredni, B.
Steinberger, J.
Susswein, A.

Faculty of Social Sciences (tel. (3) 5318452; fax (3) 5351825; e-mail socials@mail.biu.ac.il; internet www.biu.ac.il/soc):

Adad, M., Criminology
Alperovitch, G., Economics
Babkoff, H., Psychology
Cohen, S., Political Science
Don-Yehieh, E., Political Science
Friedman, M., Sociology
Gaziel, H., School of Education
Goldreich, Y., Geography
Greilsammer, I., Political Studies
Halevy-Spiro, M., Social Work
Hillmann, A., Economics
Inbar, E., Political Science
Iram, Y., Education
Jaffe, E., Business Administration
Katz, J., Geography

KLEIN, P., Education
KOSLOWSKY, M., Psychology
KRAWITZ, S., Psychology
LAUTERBACH, B., School of Business Administration
LAVEE, H., Geography
LEVI-SHIFF, R., Psychology
MENIS, J., Education
MEVARECH, Z., Education
MIKULINCER, M., Psychology
NACHSHON, I., Criminology
NITZAN, S., Economics
ORBACH, I., Psychology
RABINOWITZ, J., Social Work
SANDLER, S., Political Science
SCHWARZWALD, J., Psychology
SHULMAN, S., Psychology
SILBER, J., Economics
TAPIERO, C., Economics
TZURIEL, D., School of Education
VAKIL, E., Psychology
WELLER, A., Psychology
WOLF, Y., Criminology
YEHUDA, S., Psychology
YITZCHAKI, H., Social Work
ZIDERMAN, A., Economics
ZISSER, B., Political Science

BEN GURION UNIVERSITY OF THE NEGEV

POB 653, 84105 Be'ersheva
Telephone: (8) 6461223
Fax: (8) 6479434
E-mail: rector@bgu.ac.il
Internet: www.bgu.ac.il

Founded 1965
Languages of instruction: English, Hebrew
Academic year: October to June

Pres.: Prof. RIVKA CARMI
Rector: Prof. JIMMY WEINBLATT
Vice-Pres. and Dir-Gen.: DAVID BAREKET
Vice-Pres. and Dean for Research and Devt: Prof. MORDECHAY HERSKOWITZ
Vice-Pres. for External Affairs: Prof. AMOS DRORY
Dir of Public Affairs: NINA PERLIS
Librarian: AVNER SCHMUELEVITZ

Library: see Libraries and Archives
Number of teachers: 1,000
Number of students: 17,000

Publications: *Geography Research Forum*, *HAGAR—International Social Science Review*, *Israel Social Science Research Journal*, *Israel Studies*, *JAMA'A—Interdisciplinary Journal for the Study of the Middle East*, *MIKAN—Research Journal of Hebrew Literature*, *Shvut—Studies in Russian and East European Jewish History and Culture*

DEANS

Faculty of Engineering Sciences: Prof. GABI BEN-DOR
Faculty of Health Sciences: Prof. SHAUL SOFER
Faculty of Humanities and Social Sciences: Prof. MOSHE JUSTMAN
Faculty of Natural Sciences: Prof. AMIR SAGI
Guilford Glazer School of Business and Management: Prof. ARIE REICHEL
Kreitman School of Advanced Graduate Studies: Prof. RAMY BRUSTEIN

PROFESSORS

Faculty of Engineering Sciences (tel. (8) 6479270; fax (8) 6479401; e-mail offcdean@bgumail.bgu.ac.il; internet cmsprod.bgu.ac.il/eng/engn):

AHARONI, H., Electrical and Computer Engineering
ALFASSI, Z., Nuclear Engineering
APELBLAT, A., Chemical Engineering
ARAZI, B., Electrical and Computer Engineering

BEN-DOR, G., Mechanical Engineering
BEN-YAAKOV, S., Electrical and Computer Engineering
CENSOR, D., Electrical and Computer Engineering
DARIEL, M., Materials Engineering
DINSTEIN, I., Electrical and Computer Engineering
DUBI, A., Nuclear Engineering
EILON, A., Electrical and Computer Engineering
ELIEZER, D., Materials Engineering
ELPERIN, T., Mechanical Engineering
FINGER, N., Industrial Engineering and Management
FUKS, D., Materials Engineering
GALPERIN, A., Nuclear Engineering
GOTTLIEB, M., Chemical Engineering
HAVA, S., Electrical and Computer Engineering
HERSKOWITZ, M., Chemical Engineering
IGRA, O., Mechanical Engineering
JACOB, I., Nuclear Engineering
KAPLAN, B., Electrical and Computer Engineering
KOPEIKA, N., Electrical and Computer Engineering
KOST, J., Chemical Engineering
LADANY, S., Industrial Engineering and Management
LETAN, R., Mechanical Engineering
MENIPAZ, E., Industrial Engineering and Management
MERCHUK, J., Chemical Engineering
MOND, M., Mechanical Engineering
PERL, M., Mechanical Engineering
PLISKIN, J., Industrial Engineering and Management
PLISKIN, N., Industrial Engineering and Management
PORTMAN, V., Mechanical Engineering
RONEN, Y., Nuclear Engineering
ROTMAN, S., Electrical and Computer Engineering
SCHULGASSER, K., Mechanical Engineering
SEGEV, R., Mechanical Engineering
SHACHAM, M., Chemical Engineering
SHANI, G., Nuclear Engineering
SHER, E., Mechanical Engineering
SHINAR, D., Industrial Engineering and Management
SHUVAL, P., Information Systems Engineering
SINUANI-STERN, Z., Industrial Engineering and Management
SLONIM, M., Electrical and Computer Engineering
TALYANKER, M., Materials Engineering
TAMIR, A., Chemical Engineering
VILNAY, O., Construction Engineering
VOLLICH, D., Electrical and Computer Engineering
WISNIAK, J., Chemical Engineering
ZARETSKY, E., Mechanical Engineering

Faculty of Health Sciences (tel. (8) 6477409; fax (8) 6477632; e-mail rtemes@bgumail.bgu.ac.il; internet www.fohs.bgu.ac.il):

ABOUD, M., Microbiology and Immunology
ALKAN, M., Internal Medicine
APPELBAUM, A., Cardiology
APTE, R., Microbiology and Immunology
BASHAN, N., Clinical Biochemistry
BENJAMIN, J., Psychiatry
BUSKILA, D., Internal Medicine
CARMEL, S., Health Sociology
CARMI, R., Clinical Genetics
CLARFIELD, M., Geriatrics
FRASER, D., Epidemiology
GROSSMAN, Y., Physiology
GURMAN, G., Anaesthesiology
HALEVI, S., Dermatology
HALLAK, M., Gynaecology
HELDMAN, E., Physiology
HERZANO, Y., Radiology
ILIA, R., Cardiology

ISAKOV, N., Microbiology and Immunology
KATZ, M., Gynaecology
LEVY, R., Biochemistry
LEVY, Y., Biochemistry
LUNENFELD, E., Gynaecology
MARGULIS, C., Medical Education
MAZOR, M., Gynaecology
MEYERSTEIN, N., Physiology
MORAN, A., Physiology
NAGGAN, L., Epidemiology
NEUMANN, L., Epidemiology
PIURA, B., Gynaecology
PORATH, A., Internal Medicine
POTASHNIK, G., Gynaecology
RAGER, B., Microbiology and Immunology
SCHLESINGER, M., Paediatrics
SCHVARTZMAN, P., Family Medicine
SEGAL, S., Microbiology and Immunology
SHARONI, Y., Clinical Biochemistry
SCHLAEFFER, F., Internal Medicine
SHANY, SH., Clinical Biochemistry
SIKULER, E., Internal Medicine
SOFER, S., Paediatrics
SUKENIK, S., Internal Medicine
TAL, A., Paediatrics
WEINSTEIN, J., Microbiology
WHITE, E., Morphology

Faculty of Humanities and Social Sciences (tel. (8) 6461105; fax (8) 6472945; e-mail henik@bgumail.bgu.ac.il; internet www.bgu.ac.il/html/academics.html):

ALEXANDER, T., Hebrew Literature
BAR-ON, D., Behavioural Sciences
BENZION, U., Economics
BLIDSTEIN, G., Jewish Thought
BORG, A., Hebrew Language
BOWMAN, D., Geography and Environmental Development
BRAVERMAN, A., Economics
BREGMAN, D., Hebrew Literature
CASPI, D., Communication Studies
DANZINGER, L., Economics
DREMAN, S., Behavioural Sciences
EINY, E., Economics
GELMAN, Y., Philosophy
GILAD, I., Bible and Ancient Near-Eastern Studies
GORDON, D., Education
GORDON, H., Education
GORODETSKY, M., Education
GRADUS, Y., Geography and Environmental Development
GRIES, Z., Jewish Thought
GRUBER, I., Bible and Ancient Near-East Studies
HENIK, A., Behavioural Sciences
HOCHMAN, O., Economics
HUROWITZ, V., Bible and Ancient Near-Eastern Studies
ISRALOWITZ, R., Social Work
JUSTMAN, M., Economics
KRAKOVER, S., Geography and Environmental Development
KREISEL, H., Jewish Thought
LARONNE, J., Geography and Environmental Development
LASKER, D., Jewish Thought
LAZIN, F., Behavioural Sciences
LIBERLES, R., History
LURIE, Y., Philosophy
MEIR, A., Geography and Environmental Development
MORRIS, B., Middle East Studies
OREN, E., Bible and Ancient Near-Eastern Studies
PARUSH, A., Philosophy
POZNANSKI, R., Politics and Government
PRIEL, B., Behavioural Sciences
QIMRON, E., Hebrew Language
REGEV, U., Economics
ROSEN, S., Bible and Ancient Near-Eastern Studies
SALMON, Y., History
SHAROT, S., Behavioural Sciences
SHINAR, D., General Studies

SIVAN, D., Hebrew Language
STERN, E., Geography and Environmental Development
TALSHIR, Z., Bible and Ancient Near-East Studies
TOBIN, I., Foreign Languages and Literature
TROEN, I., History
TSAHOR, Z., History
TSOAR, H., Geography and Environmental Development
TZELGOV, Y., Behavioural Sciences
VINNER, S., Science and Technology Education
WEINBLATT, J., Economics

Faculty of Natural Sciences (tel. (8) 6461633; fax (8) 6472954; e-mail mia@math.bgu.ac.il; internet www.bgu.ac.il/html/academics .html):

ABRAHAM, U., Mathematics
ABRAMSKY, Z., Life Sciences
ALPAI, D., Mathematics
ALTSHULER, A., Mathematics
AVISHAI, Y., Physics
BAHAT, D., Geological and Environmental Sciences
BAND, Y., Chemistry
BARAK, Z., Life Sciences
BECKER, J., Chemistry
BELITSKI, H., Mathematics
BEREND, D., Mathematics
BERNSTEIN, J., Chemistry
BITTNER, S., Chemistry
BRUSTEIN, R., Physics
CHIPMAN, D., Life Sciences
COHEN, M., Mathematics
DAVIDSON, A., Physics
EFRIMA, S., Chemistry
EICHLER, D., Physics
EISENBERG, T., Mathematics
FEINTUCH, A., Mathematics
FONF, V., Mathematics
FUHRMANN, P. A., Mathematics
GEDALIN, M., Physics
GERSTEN, A., Physics
GLASER, R., Chemistry
GOLDSHTEIN, V., Mathematics
GOREN, S., Physics
GORODETSKY, G., Physics
GRANOT, Y., Life Sciences
HODORKOVSKY, V., Chemistry
HOROVITZ, B., Physics
HOROWITZ, Y., Physics
KISCH, H., Geological and Environmental Sciences
KOJMAN, M., Mathematics
KOST, D., Chemistry
LIN, M., Mathematics
MEIR, Y., Physics
MIZRAHI, Y., Life Sciences
MOALEM, A., Physics
MORDECHAI, S., Physics
MOREH, R., Physics
OWEN, D., Physics
PAROLA, A., Chemistry
POLAK, M., Chemistry
PRIEL, Z., Chemistry
PROSS, A., Chemistry
RABINOVITSCH, A., Physics
ROSENWAKS, S., Physics
RUBIN, M., Mathematics
SCHARF, B., Chemistry
SEGEV, Y., Mathematics
SHOSHAN-BARMATZ, V., Life Sciences
SHUKER, R., Physics
TKACHENKO, V., Mathematics
ZARITSKY, A., Life Sciences

Guilford Glazer School of Business and Management (tel. (8) 6472190; fax (8) 6472868; e-mail sompr@nihul.bgu.ac.il; internet www.bgu.ac.il/som):

BAR-ELI, M., Business Administration
DRORY, A., Business Administration
GIDRON, B., Business Administration
MALACH-PINES, A., Business Administration
PREISS, K., Business Administration
REICHEL, A., Hotel and Tourism Management

ATTACHED RESEARCH INSTITUTES

Ben-Gurion Research Institute for the Study of Israel: tel. (8) 6596936; fax (8) 6596939; e-mail moreshet@bgu.ac.il; internet cmsprod.bgu.ac.il/eng/centers/bgi; f. 1976; publ. *Israel Studies* (3 a year), *Iyunim Bitkumat Israel* (1 a year); Dir MICHAL MOUYAL.

Homeland Security Research Institute: tel. (8) 6596936; fax (8) 6596939; e-mail doronhav@bgu.ac.il; internet cmsprod.bgu.ac .il/eng/centers/hsri; Dir Prof. DORON HAVAZALET.

Jacob Blaustein Institute for Desert Research: Sde Boker Campus, 84990 Be'ersheva; tel. (8) 6596777; fax (8) 6596703; e-mail bidr@bgu.ac.il; internet www.bgu.ac .il/bidr; f. 1974; Dir Prof. AVIGAD VONSHAK.

National Institute for Biotechnology in the Negev: tel. (8) 6461963; fax (8) 6472983; e-mail vardasb@bgu.ac.il; internet cmsprod .bgu.ac.il/eng/centers/nibn; Dir Prof. VARDA SHOSHAN BARMATZ.

Research Institute for Jewish and Israeli Literature and Culture: tel. (8) 6596936; e-mail heksher@bgu.ac.il; internet cmsprod.bgu.ac.il/eng/centers/heksherim; f. 2001; Dir Prof. YIGAL SCHWARTZ.

UNIVERSITY OF HAIFA

Mount Carmel, 31905 Haifa
Telephone: (4) 8240111
Fax: (4) 8342104
E-mail: rector@univ.haifa.ac.il
Internet: www.haifa.ac.il

Founded 1963
Independent
Language of instruction: Hebrew
Academic year: October to June

Pres.: Prof. AARON BEN-ZE'EV
Rector: Prof. DAVID FARAGGI
Vice Rector: Prof. BATIA LAUFER
Vice-Pres. for Admin.: Prof. BARUCH MARZAN
Vice-Pres. for External Relations and Resource Devt: AMOS GAVER
Vice-Pres. and Dean of Research: Prof. MAJID AL-HAJ
Registrar: RUTH RABINOWITZ
Academic Sec.: SHOSHANA LANDMAN
Dean of Graduate Studies: Prof. YITZHAK HARPAZ

Number of teachers: 1,125
Number of students: 16,000

Publications: *Dappim—Research in Literature* (1 a year, Hebrew, with English abstracts), *Jewish History* (every 2 years), *JTD Haifa University Studies in Theatre and Drama* (1 a year), *Mishpat Umimshal Law and Government in Israel* (every 2 years, Hebrew), *Studies in Children's Literature* (1 a year, Hebrew), *Studies in Education* (every 2 years, Hebrew)

DEANS AND HEADS OF SCHOOLS

Faculty of Education: Prof. OFRA MAYSELLES
Faculty of Humanities: Prof. REUVEN SNIR
Faculty of Law: Prof. NIVA ELKIN-KOREN
Faculty of Natural Sciences: Prof. GAL RICHTER-LEVIN
Faculty of Social Sciences: Prof. AVI SAGI-SCHWARTZ
Faculty of Social Welfare and Health Sciences: Prof. SHAI LINN
School of Political Sciences: Prof. ERAN VIGODA GADOT
School of Social Work: Prof. FAISAL AZAIZA

Graduate School of Management: Prof. SHEIZAF RAFAELI

PROFESSORS

Faculty of Education (tel. (4) 8240726; fax (4) 8240911; internet www.edu.haifa.ac.il):

ALEXANDER, H., Education
BARAK, A., Education
BEN-PERETZ, M., Education
BREZNITZ, Z., Education
COHEN, A., Education
EIZIKOVITS, R., Education
HERTZ-LAZAROWITZ, R., Education
KATRIEL, T., Education
KLINGMAN, A., Education
LINN, R., Education
NESHER, P., Education
REITER, S., Education
SALOMON, G., Education
SCHECHTMAN, Z., Education
SEGINER, R., Education
SFARD, A., Education
SHARE, D., Education
SHIMRON, J., Education
YERUSHALMY, M., Education
ZEIDNER, M., Education

Faculty of Humanities (tel. (4) 8240125; fax (4) 8240128; e-mail pfientu1@univ.haifa.ac.il; internet hcc.haifa.ac.il):

ARTZY, M., Maritime Civilizations
AVISHUR, Y., Hebrew Language
AZAR, M., Hebrew Language
BARAM, A., Middle Eastern History
BARNAI, J., Land of Israel Studies
BAR-YITZHAK, H., Hebrew and Comparative Literature
BEN-ARTZI, Y., Land of Israel Studies
BEN-DOV, N., Hebrew and Comparative Literature
CHETRIT, J., French
CHISICK, H., History
DAVID, E., General History
DIMANT, D., Jewish History
DOLGOPOLSKY, A., Hebrew Language
DORCHIN, Y., Art
ERDINAST-VULCAN, D., English
ELBAZ, R., French
ELDAR, I., Hebrew Language
EVRON, M., Archaeology
FREEDMAN, W., English
FIRRO, K., Middle-East History
GELBER, Y., Land of Israel Studies
GILBAR, G., Middle-East History
GILEAD, A., Philosophy
GINAT, J., Land of Israel Studies
GOLDSTEIN, Y., Land of Israel Studies
GOODITCH, M., General History
GRABOIS, A., History
HAHLILI, R., Archaeology
HELTZER, M., Bible
HOFFMAN, J., Hebrew Language
HON, G., Philosophy
KAGAN, Z., Hebrew and Comparative Literature
KANAZI, G., Arabic Language and Literature
KATZ, A., Art
KELLNER, M., Jewish History
KOCHAVI, A., History
KURZON, D., English
KUSHNIR, D., Middle East History
LAUFER, M., English
LUZ, E., Jewish Thought
MALUL, M., Biblical Studies
MANSOUR, J., Hebrew Language
MART, Y., Maritime Civilizations
MELAMED, A., Jewish History
MENACHE, S., General History
MICHEL, J., French
MYHILL, J., English
NEVO, J., Middle-East History
ODED, B., Jewish History
ORKIN, M., Theatre, English Literature
PECHTER, M., Jewish History
RAPPAPORT, U., Jewish History

REICH, R., Archaeology
ROBIN, R., General History
RONEN, A., Archaeology
ROZEN, M., Jewish History
SANDLER, W., English
SCHATZKER, C., Jewish History
SEGAL, A., Archaeology
SHENHAR, A., Hebrew and Comparative Literature
SHICHOR, Y., Multidisciplinary Studies
SHOHAM, R., Hebrew and Comparative Literature
SMILANSKY, S., Philosophy
SNIR, R., Arabic
SOBEL, M., History
SPANIER, E., Maritime Civilizations
STATMAN, D., Philosophy
STOW, K., Jewish History
TOBI, J., Hebrew and Comparative Literature
WARBURG, G., Middle Eastern History
YARDENI, M., History
YEHOSHUA, A. B., Hebrew and Comparative Literature
ZINGUER, I., French

Faculty of Law (tel. (4) 8240633; fax (4) 8249247; internet law.haifa.ac.il):

BEN-OLIEL, R., Law
EDREY, Y., Law
GROSS, E., Law

Faculty of Natural Sciences (tel. (4) 8288076; fax (4) 8288108; e-mail mgoldbe1@univ.haifa.ac.il; internet science.haifa.ac.il):

BUTNARIO, D., Mathematics
CARO, Y., Mathematics
CENSOR, Y., Mathematics
DAFNI, A., Biology
FAHIMA, T., Evolution
GOLAN, J., Mathematics
GORDON, A., Physics
HAIM, A., Biology
KOZENIKOV, A., Mathematics
LEV, S., Science Education—Biology
LEV-YADUN, S., Science Education—Biology
MORAN, G., Mathematics
NEVO, E., Biology
REISNER, S., Mathematics
RUBINSTEIN, Z., Mathematics
SKOLNICK, A., Biology
SOKER, N., Physics
TEMPLETON, A., Evolution
VAISMAN, I., Mathematics
WASSER, S., Biology
WEIT, I., Mathematics
YITZHAKI, I., Biology
YUSTER, R., Mathematics
ZACKS, J., Mathematics
ZOLLER, U., Chemistry

Faculty of Social Sciences (tel. (4) 8240331; fax (4) 8246814; e-mail ssmooha@univ.haifa.ac.il; internet hevra.haifa.ac.il):

AL-HAJ, M., Sociology
ARAZY, J., Mathematics and Computer Science
ARIAN, A., Political Science
BARAK, A., Psychology
BAR-GAL, Y., Geography
BAR-LEV, S., Statistics
BEIT-HALLAHMI, B., Psychology
BEN-DOR, G., Political Science
BERG, M., Statistics and Business Administration
BERMAN, E., Psychology
BIGER, N., Business Administration
BRAUN, A., Mathematics and Computer Science
BREZNITZ, S., Psychology
CENSOR, Y., Mathematics and Computer Science
DAFNI, A., Biology
EDEN, B., Economics
FARAGGI, D., Statistics
FELZENTAL, D., Political Science

FISHMAN, G., Sociology
FROSTIG, E., Statistics
GOLAN, J., Mathematics and Computer Science
GOLOMBIC, M., Computer Science
GROSS, M., Political Science
GUIORA, A. Z., Psychology
HARPAZ, Y., Sociology and Business Administration
HAYUTH, Y., Geography
INBAR, M., Geography
ISHAI, Y., Political Science
KATRIEL, T., Communication
KELLERMAN, A., Geography
KEREN, G., Psychology
KIMCHI, R., Psychology
KIPNIS, B., Geography
KLIOT, N., Geography
KORIAT, A., Psychology
KRAUS, V., Sociology
KUTIEL, H., Geography
LANDAU, G., Computer Science
LANDSBERGER, M., Economics
LANDSMAN, Y., Statistics
LANGBERG, N., Statistics
LIEBERMAN, O., Economics
MAKOV, E., Land of Israel Studies
MATTRAS, Y., Sociology
MELNIK, A., Economics
MESHIULAM, I., Business Admin.
MILLER, B., Political Science
MINTZ, A., Political Science
MORAN, G., Mathematics and Computer Science
NAVON, D., Psychology
NEVO, B., Psychology
NEWMAN, I., Computer Science
PERRY, D., Statistics
RAFAELI, S., Business Admin.
RAKOVER, S., Psychology
RATNER, A., Sociology and Anthropology
REISER, B., Statistics
RICHTER-LEVIN, G., Psychology
ROITMAN, M., Mathematics
ROSENFELD, H., Sociology
ROSNER, M., Sociology
ROZENBLATT, M., Business Admin.
RUBIN, S., Psychology
RUBINSTEIN, Z., Mathematics and Computer Science
SAFIR, M., Psychology
SAGI-SCHWARTZ, A., Psychology
SAMUEL, Y., Sociology
SHECHTER, M., Economics
SHITOVITZ, B., Economics
SHLIFER, E., Business Admin.
SMOOHA, S., Sociology
SOBEL, Z., Sociology
SOFFER, A., Geography
VAINSHTEIN, A., Mathematics and Computer Science
VAISMAN, I., Mathematics and Computer Science
WATERMAN, S., Geography
WEIMAN, G., Sociology and Communication
WEISS, G., Statistics
WEIT, I., Mathematics and Computer Science
ZAKS, J., Mathematics and Computer Science

Faculty of Social Welfare and Health Sciences (tel. (4) 8249950; fax (4) 8249946; e-mail werner@research.haifa.ac.il; internet hw.haifa.ac.il):

ATTIAS, J., Speech Therapy
DICKSTEIN, R., Physiotherapy
EISIKOVITS, Z., Social Work
GILBAR, O., Social Work
GUTTMAN, D., Social Work
LEV-WIESEL, R., Social Work
LINN, S., Public Health
LOEWENSTEIN, A., Gerontology
RIMMERMAN, A., Social Work
SHARLIN, S., Social Work
WEISS, T., Occupational Therapy

WERNER, P., Gerontology

HEBREW UNIVERSITY OF JERUSALEM

Mt Scopus, 91905 Jerusalem
Telephone: (2) 6585111
Fax: (2) 5322545
E-mail: admission@savion.huji.ac.il
Internet: www.huji.ac.il

Founded 1918, inaugurated 1925
Private control, partially supported by the Govt
Academic year: October to June
Language of instruction: Hebrew

Chair., Bd of Govs: MICHAEL FEDERMANN
Pres.: Prof. MENACHEM BEN-SASSON
Vice-Pres. and Dir-Gen.: BILLY SHAPIRA
Vice-Pres. for External Relations: CARMI GILLON
Vice-Pres. and Chair. of the Authority for Research and Devt: Prof. ISAIAH ARKIN
Rector: Prof. SARA STROUMSA
Vice-Rectors: Prof. YAACOV SCHUL, Prof. ODED NAVON
Dean of Students: Prof. ESTHER SHOHAMI

Number of teachers: 1,200
Number of students: 23,250

Publications: *ACTA-Analysis of Current Trends in Antisemitism* (research papers, 2–3 a year, in English), *Aleph: Historical Studies in Science and Judaism* (1 a year, in English), *Antisemitism International* (1 a year, in English), *Edah Velashon* (Publn of the Hebrew Univ. Jewish Oral Traditions Research Centre, 1 a year, Hebrew), *Hispania Judaica Bulletin* (History, Culture, Thought, Literature, Art and Language of Jews in the Iberian Peninsula, in English), *Hukim-journal on Legislation*, *Israel Journal of Mathematics* (6 a year, in English), *Israel Law Review* (3 a year, in English), *Italia* (History, Culture and Literature of the Jews of Italy, 1 a year, multilingual), *Iyyun* (Journal of Philosophy, 4 a year, 2 a year in Hebrew and 2 in English), *Jerusalem Review of Legal Studies*, *Jerusalem Studies in Arabic and Islam (JSAI)* (1 a year, mostly with English contributions but also French, German and Arabic), *Jerusalem Studies in Hebrew Language* (1 a year, in Hebrew), *Jerusalem Studies in Hebrew Literature* (1 a year, in Hebrew), *Jerusalem Studies in Jewish Folklore* (1 a year, in Hebrew), *Jerusalem Studies in Jewish Thought* (1 a year, in Hebrew), *Jewish Law Annual*, *Jews in Russia Eastern Europe* (in English, published in co-operation with the Leonid Nevzlin Research Centre), *Journal d'Analyse Mathématique* (3 a year, in English), *Journal of Experimental Criminology* (4 a year, in English), *Massorot* (Studies in Language Traditions of Hebrew and Aramaic, 1 a year, in Hebrew), *Mishpatim* (Law, 3 a year, in English and Hebrew), *Partial Answers* (Journal of Literature and the History of Ideas, in English), *Perspectives* (Humanistic Studies, in particular Literature, History and Arts, 1 a year, in French), *Politika* (Journal of Israeli political science and int. relations, in Hebrew), *QAEDEM: Monographs of the Institute of Archaeology* (1–2 a year, in English), *QEDEM Reports* (Archaeology, 1–2 a year, in English), *Shnaton Hamishpat Haivri* (Jewish Law, in Hebrew), *Shnaton: Annual for Biblical and Ancient Near Eastern Studies* (1 a year, Hebrew), *Studies in Contemporary Jewry* (Studies in Contemporary Jewry, 1 a year, in English published in conjunction with Oxford Univ. Press), *Studies in Jewish Education* (Multi-disciplinary, 1 a year, bi-lingual

(English, Hebrew)), *Tarbiz* (Jewish studies, 4 a year, in Hebrew), *Yearbook of Jewish Law*

DEANS AND DIRECTORS

Faculty of Dental Medicine: Prof. ADAM STABHOLZ
Faculty of Humanities: Prof. REUVEN AMITAI
Faculty of Law: Prof. BARAK MEDINA
Faculty of Mathematics and Natural Science: Prof. GAD MAROM
Faculty of Medicine: Prof. ERAN LEITERSDORF
Faculty of Social Sciences: Prof. AVNER DE-SHALIT
Jerusalem School of Business Admin.: Prof. DAN GALAI
Paul Baerwald School of Social Work and Social Welfare: Prof. JOHN GAL
Robert H. Smith Faculty of Agriculture, Food and Environment: Prof. RONNIE FRIEDMAN

PROFESSORS

Faculty of Agricultural, Food and Environmental Science
(incl. the School of Nutritional Sciences and the Koret School of Veterinary Medicine)

ADAM, Z., Plant Sciences and Genetics in Agriculture
ADIN, A., Soil and Water Sciences
CAHANER, A., Plant Sciences and Genetics in Agriculture
CHEN, Y., Soil and Water Sciences
CZOSNEK, H., Sciences and Genetics in Agriculture
FEINERMAN, E., Agricultural Economics
FRIEDMAN, A., Animal Sciences
GUTNICK, J. M., School of Veterinary Medicine
HADAR, Y., Plant Pathology and Microbiology
KIGEL, J., Plant Sciences and Genetics in Agriculture
LERMAN, Z., Agricultural Economics
MADAR, Z., Biochemistry, Food Science and Nutrition
MAHRER, Y., Soil and Water Sciences
MEIDAN, R., Animal Sciences
MUALEM, Y., Soil and Water Sciences
NAIM, H., Food Science and Nutrition
NUSSINOVITCH, A., Biochemistry, Food Science and Nutrition
OKON, Y., Plant Pathology and Microbiology
RUBIN, B., Plant Sciences and Genetics in Agriculture
SAGUY, I., Biochemistry, Food Science and Nutrition
TEL-OR, E., Plant Sciences and Genetics in Agriculture
TSUR, Y., Agricultural Economics
VAINSTEIN, A., Plant Sciences and Genetics in Agriculture
WALLACH, R., Soil and Water Sciences
WEISS, D., Plant Sciences and Genetics in Agriculture
WOLF, S., Plant Sciences and Genetics in Agriculture
WOLFENSON, D., Animal Sciences
YARDEN, O., Plant Pathology and Microbiology
YUVAL, B., Entomology
ZAMIR, D., Plant Sciences and Genetics in Agriculture

Faculty of Dental Medicine (En Karem Campus, POB 12272, 91120 Jerusalem; tel. (2) 6158595; fax (2) 6439219; e-mail dentistry_sa@savion.huji.ac.il; internet dental.huji.ac.il):
(Hebrew Univ.—Hadassah School of Dental Medicine)

BAB, I., Oral Pathology
CHEVION, M., Biochemistry

DEUTSCH, D., Oral Biology
GAZIT, D., Oral Pathology
HOROWITZ, M., Physiology
MANN, J., Community Dentistry
NITZAN, D., Oral and Maxillofacial Surgery
SCHWARTZ, Z., Periodontics
SELA, J., Oral Pathology
SELA, M., Maxillofacial Rehabilitation
SELA, M., Oral Biology
SHAPIRA, L., Periodontics
SOSKOLNE, A., Periodontics
STABHOLZ, A., Endodontics
TAL, M., Anatomy and Cell Biology

Faculty of Humanities
(the Joseph and Ceil Mazer Centre for the Humanities, incl. the Asian and African Studies; Archaeology; Contemporary Jewry; Languages, Literatures and Art; Philosophy and History; Institutes of: Jewish Studies)

AMITAI, R., Islamic and Middle Eastern Studies
ASCHHEIM, S., History
ASSIS, Y.-T., Jewish History
BAR-ELLI, G., Philosophy
BARTAL, I., Jewish History
BAR YAFFE, Y., Spanish and Latin American Studies
BELFER-COHEN, A., Archaeology
BEN-MENAHEM, Y., Philosophy, History and Philosophy of Science
BEN-SASSON, M., Jewish History
BESSERMAN, L., English Literature
BRODY, R., Talmudic Studies
BUDICK, E., American Studies
BUDICK, S., English Literature
BUNIS, D., Hebrew Language
COHEN, E., History
COHEN, R., Jewish History
COTTON, H., History and Classics
DELLA PERGOLA, S., Contemporary Jewry
DINER, D., History
ELIOR, R., Jewish Thought
ELIZUR, S., Hebrew Literature
GAFNI, I., Jewish History
GOLOMB, J., Philosophy
GOREN-INBAR, N., Archaeology
HALBERTAL, M., Jewish Thought and Philosophy
HARVEY, Z., Jewish Thought
HASAN-ROKEM, G., Hebrew Literature and Folklore
HEVER, H., Hebrew Literature
HEYD, D., Philosophy
HEYD, M., History
HOPKINS, S. A., Arabic Language and Literature
IDEL, M., Jewish Thought
KADISH, A., History
KAHANA, M., Talmudic Studies
KAPLAN, S., Comparative Religion and African Studies
KAPLAN, Y., Jewish History
KISTER, M., Jewish Studies
KÜHNEL, B., Art History
LECKER, M., Arabic Language and Literature
MAMAN, A., Hebrew Language
MAZAR, A., Archaeology
MENDELS, D., History
PATRICK, J., Archaeology
PITOWSKY, I., History and Philosophy of Science
POZY, C., Philosophy
RAPPAPORT-HOVAV, M., English Literature
RAVITZKY, A., Jewish Thought
RICCI, D., American Studies and Political Science
ROJTMAN, B., French Language and Literature, General and Comparative Literature
ROSENTHAL, D., Talmudic Studies
SCHULMAN, D., Indian Studies and Comparative Religion

SCHWARTZ, D., Jewish History
SCOLNICOV, S., Education, Philosophy
SEROUSSI, E., Musicology
SHESHA-HALEVY, A., General and Egyptian Philology
SHINAN, A., Hebrew Literature
STEINER, M., Philosophy
STEWART, F., Islamic Studies
STROUMSA, G., Comparative Religion
STROUMSA, S., Jewish Thought, Arabic Language and Literature
SZEINTUCH, Y., Yiddish
TAUBE, M., Linguistics and Slavic Studies
TIMENCHIK, R., Russian and Slavic Studies
TOCH, M., History
TOKER, L., English Literature
TOV, E., Bible
WISTRICH, R., History, Jewish History
WOLOSKY, S., English Literature
YAHALOM, Y., Hebrew Literature
YUVAL, I., History of Jewish Studies
ZAKOVITCH, Y., Bible
ZIMMERMANN, M., History

School of Education:

BABAD, E., Education
GATI, I., Education, Psychology
KAREEV, Y., Education
NURIT, Y., Education, Psychology
RAPOPORT, T., Education, Social Work
RITOV, I., Education
SCOLNICOV, S., Education, Philosophy
ULLMAN-MARGALIT, E., Education
WEXLER, P., Education

Faculty of Law (tel. (2) 5882528; fax (2) 5823042; e-mail law_sa@savion.huji.ac.il; internet law.mscc.huji.ac.il):
(incl. the Harry Sacher Institute for Legislative Research and Comparative Law, the Israel Matz Institute for Research in Jewish Law)

BEN-MENAHEN, H., Jewish Law, Philosophy of Law
DOTAN, Y., Public Law
FASSBERG, C., Private International Law, Comparative Law, Legal History
GAVISON, R., Philosophy of Law and Public Law
GILEAD, I., Tort Law
GUR-ARYE, M., Criminal Law
HAREL, A., Jurisprudence, Theory of Rights, Economic Analysis of Law
KREMITZER, M., Criminal and Constitutional Law
LIBSON, G., Islamic Law
LIFSCHITZ, B., Jewish Law
SHETREET, S., Public Law and the Judiciary
WEISBURD, D., White Collar Crime, Policing
ZAMIR, E., Contract Law

Faculty of Medicine
(the Hebrew Univ.—Hadassah Medical School, incl. the Hadassah-Henrietta Szold School of Nursing, the School of Occupational Therapy, the School of Pharmacy, School of Social Medicine and Public Health)

ABRAMSKY, O., Neurology
ARGOV, A., Neurology
ARIEL, I., Pathology
BACH, G., Genetics
BARENHOLZ, Y., Biochemistry
BEERI, E., Public Health, Nutrition
BELLER, U., Obstetrics
BEN-CHETRIT, E., Medicine
BEN-EZRA, D., Ophthalmology
BEN-NERIAH, Y., Immunology
BEN-SASSON, Z., Immunology
BEN-YEHUDA, D., Haematology
BENITA, S., Pharmacy
BERCOVIER, H., Clinical Microbiology
BERGMAN, H., Physiology
BERGMAN, Y., Experimental Medicine, Cancer Research

BIALER, M., Pharmacology
BRANSKY, D., Paediatrics
BRENNER, T., Neurology
BREUER, R., Medical Imaging
BREZIS, M., Medicine
CEDAR, H., Cellular Biochemistry, Human Genetics
CHAJEK-SHAUL, T., Internal Medicine
DOMB, A., Medicinal Chemistry
EILAT, D., Immunology, Internal Medicine
ELIDAN, J., Laryngology
ELPELEG, O., Paediatrics
FAINSOD, A., Cellular Biochemistry and Human Genetics
FIBACH, E., Experimental Haematology
FREUND, H., Surgery
FRIEDLANDER, Y., Epidemiology, Public Health
FRIEDMAN, G., Medicine, Geriatrics
FRIEDMAN, M., Pharmacy
GABIZON BARCHILOM, A., Oncology
GALUN, E., Gene Therapy
GLASER, B., Endocrinology
GOLDBERG, I., Microbiology, Molecular Genetics
GOLOMB, G., Pharmaceutics
GOMORI, M. (acting), Radiology
GRANOT, E., Paediatrics
GRETZ, D., Anatomy
HANANI, M., Surgery
HANSKY, E., Microbiology
HEMERMAN, C., Paediatrics
HEYMAN, S., Internal Medicine
HONIGMAN, A., Virology
ILAN, Y., Medicine
JAFFE, C., Parasitology
KAEMPFER, R., Molecular Virology
KAISER, N., Endocrinology
KALCHEIM, C., Anatomy
KANNER, B. I., Biochemistry
KAPLAN, M., Paediatrics
KARK, J., Social Medicine
KEDAR, E., Immunology
KEREM, E., Paediatrics
KEREN, A., Cardiology
KESHET, E., Molecular Biology
KOHEN, R., Pharmacy
LAUFER, N., Obstetrics and Gynaecology
LEWIN, A., Obstetrics and Gynaecology
LIBSON, Y., Medical Imaging
LEITERSDORF, E., Internal Medicine
LERER, B., Psychiatry
LEV-TOV, A., Anatomy and Cell Biology
LEVY-SHAFFER, F., Pharmacology
LICHTENSTEIN, D., Physiology
LIEBERGALL, M., Orthopaedic Surgery
MANNY, J., Surgery
MARGALIT, H., Genetics
MAYER, M., Clinical Biochemistry
MEYUCHAS, O., Biochemistry
MILGROM, CH., Orthopaedics
MINKE, B., Physiology
MITRANI-ROSENBAUM, S., Molecular Biology, Gene Therapy
NAPARSTEK, J., Internal Medicine
ORNOY, A., Anatomy
PANET, A., Virology
PEER, J., Ophthalmology
PERETZ, T., Oncology
RAZ, I., Internal Medicine
RAZIN, E., Biochemistry
RECHES, A., Neurology
ROTSHENKER, S., Anatomy
RUBINSTEIN, A., Psychiatry
SAMUELOFF, A., Obstetrics
SHALEV, A., Psychiatry
SHOUVAL, D., Internal Medicine
SHPIRA, S., Medical Management
SHLOMAI, J., Molecular Biology
SHOHAMI, E., Pharmacology
SIEGAL, T., Neurology and Neuro-Oncology
SILVER, J., Nephrology
SPRUNG, CH. L., Medicine
STEINER, I., Neurology
TOVITO, E., Pharmacology
TZIVONI, D., Medicine, Cardiology

UMANSKY, F., Neurosurgery
VAADIA, E., Physiology
VARON, D., Haematology
VLODAVSKY, I., Oncology
WEINSTEIN, D., Obstetrics and Gynaecology
WEISSMAN, CH., Anaesthesiology
YAARI, E., Physiology
YAGEL, S., Obstetrics and Gynaecology
YANAI, J., Anatomy and Embryology
YEDGAR, S., Biochemistry
YEFENOF, E., Immunology

Faculty of Science
(incl. the Amos de Shalit Science Teaching Centre; Alexander Silberman Institute of Life Sciences; Heinz Schteinitz Interuniversity; Institute of Computer Science; Institute of Earth Sciences; Institute for Marine Biological Research; Institute of Mathematics Institute of Chemistry; Racah Institute of Physics)

AGMON, N., Chemistry
AGRANAT, A., Applied Physics
AIZENSHTAT, Z., Applied Chemistry
ARKIN, I., Biological Chemistry
ASSCHER, M., Physical Chemistry
ATLAS, D., Biological Chemistry
AVNIR, D., Organic Chemistry
BAER, R., Physical Chemistry
BALBERG, Y., Experimental Physics
BANIN, U., Physical Chemistry
BARAK, A., Computer Science
BECKENSTEIN, Y., Theoretical Physics
BEERI, C., Computer Science
BELKIN, S., Life Sciences
BEN-ARTZI, M., Mathematics
BEN-OR, M., Computer Science
BEN-SHAUL, A., Theoretical Chemistry
BENVENISTY, N., Life Sciences
BIALI, S., Organic Chemistry
BINO, A., Theoretical and Analytical Chemistry
BUCH, V., Chemistry
CABANTCHIK, Y., Biophysics
CAMHI, J. M., Cell and Animal Biology
COHEN, A., Atmospheric Sciences
COHN, D., Applied Chemistry
DAVIDOV, D., Experimental Physics
DEKEL, A., Theoretical Physics
DE-SHALIT, E., Mathematics
DEVOR, M., Zoology
DOLEV, D., Computer Science
DROR-FARJOUN, E., Mathematics
ELITZUR, S., Theoretical Physics
ENZEL, Y., Earth Sciences
EREL, Y., Geology
EREZ, J., Oceanography
FARKAS, H., Mathematics
FEINBERG, J., Physics
FELDMAN, Y., Applied Physics
FELNER, I., Experimental Physics
FRIEDLAND, L., Theoretical Physics
FRIEDMAN, N., Computer Science
GAL, A., Theoretical Physics
GARTI, N., Applied Chemistry
GENIN, A., Ecology and Oceanography
GERBER, R. B., Theoretical Chemistry
GIVEON, A., Physics
GLABERSON, W., Experimental Physics
GRUENBAUM, Y., Genetics
HART, S., Mathematics
HIRSCHBERG, J., Genetics
HOCHSTEIN, S., Neurobiology
HRUSHOVSKI, E., Mathematics
JOSKOWICZ, L., Computer Science
KALAI, G., Mathematics
KAPLAN, A., Plant Sciences
KEREM, B., Life Sciences
KHAIN, A., Atmospheric Sciences
KHAZDAN, D., Mathematics
KIFER, Y., Mathematics
KOSLOFF, R., Physical Chemistry
KUPFERMAN, O., Computer Science
LEV, O., Ecology
LEVIN, G., Mathematics

LEVITAN, A., Physics
LEVITSKI, A., Biological Chemistry
LEWIS, A., Applied Physics
LINIAL, M., Biological Chemistry
LINIAL, N., Computer Science
LIVNE, R., Mathematics
LUBOTZKY, A., Mathematics
LURIA, M., Applied and Environmental Science
LUZ, B., Plant Sciences
MAGDASSI, S., Applied Chemistry
MAGIDOR, M., Mathematics
MANDELZWEIG, V., Theoretical Physics
MANDLER, D., Chemistry
MAROM, G., Applied Chemistry
MATTHEWS, A., Geology
MEERSON, B., Experimental Physics
MILO, O., Physics
MOSHEIOV, G., Statistics
MOZES, S., Mathematics
NAVON, O., Geology
NECHUSHTAI, R., Plant Sciences
NELKEN, I., Neurobiology
NEYMAN, A., Mathematics and Economics
NISAN, N., Computer Science
OREN, A., Ecology
ORLY, J., Biological Chemistry
OVADYAHU, Z., Experimental Physics
PALDOR, N., Plant Sciences
PAUL, M., Experimental Physics
PELEG, S., Computer Science
PIRAN, Z., Theoretical Physics
POST, A., Molecular Ecology
RABINOVICI, E., Theoretical Physics
RIPS, E., Mathematics
ROSENFELD, D., Plant Sciences
ROSENSCEIN, J., Computer Science
RUBINSKY, B., Bioengineering
RUHMAN, S., Chemistry
SAGIV, Y., Computer Science
SARI, R., Physics
SASSON, Y., Applied Chemistry
SCHULDINER, S., Microbial Ecology
SEGEV, I., Neurobiology
SELA, Z., Mathematics
SHAIK, S. S., Organic Chemistry
SHALEV, A., Mathematics
SHASHUA, A., Computer Science
SHELAH, S., Mathematics
SHMIDA, A., Botany
SOLOMON, S., Theoretical Physics
SOMPOLINSKY, H., Physics
SOREQ, H., Biological Chemistry
SPIRA, M., Neurobiology
TIKOCHINSKY, Y., Physics
TISHBY, N., Computer Science
WEINSHALL, D., Computer Science
WEISS, B., Mathematics
WERMAN, M., Computer Science
WILLNER, I., Organic Chemistry
YAROM, Y., Neurobiology
ZIGLER, A., Physics

Faculty of Social Sciences:
BAR-SIMAN-TOV, Y., Int. Relations
BEN-ARI, E., Sociology, Anthropology
BEN-SHAKHAR, G., Psychology
BEN-YEHUDA, N., Sociology
BENTIN, S., Psychology and Education
BIALER, U., Int. Relations
BIENSTOCK, M., Economics
BILO, Y., Psychology and Sociology
BORNSTEIN, G., Psychology
COHEN, A., Psychology
COHEN, R., Int. Relations
DAYAN, U., Geography
DE-SHALIT, A., Political Sciences
EBSTEIN, R., Psychology
EZRAHI, Y., Political Science
FROST, R., Psychology
GALNOOR, I., Political Science
GATI, I., Psychology and Education
GILULA, Z., Statistics and Social Work
HART, S., Economics
HASSON, S., Geography and Urban Studies
HAVIV, M., Statistics

ILOUZ, E., Sociology
KARK, R., Geography
KELLA, O., Statistics
LAVIH, V., Economics
LIEBES, T., Communication
LIEBLICH, A., Psychology
METZER, J., Economics
MOSHEIOV, G., Statistics
NINIO, A., Psychology
OMAN, S., Statistics
PERRY, M., Economics, Rationality Centre
PFEFFERMAN, D., Statistics
POLLAK, M., Statistics
RICCI, D., Political Science
RINOTT, Y., Statistics
RITOV, Y., Statistics
RUBIN, R., Geography
SALOMON, I., Geography and Urban Studies
SCHUL, Y., Psychology
SHAMIR, B., Sociology, Anthropology
SHANON, B., Psychology
SHAVIT, Y., Psychology
SHEFFER, G., Political Science
TEUBAL, M., Economics
VERTZBERGER, Y., Int. Relations
WINTER, E., Economics
WOLFSFELD, G., Political Science
YERMIYA, R., Psychology
YIRMIYA, N., Psychology
YITZHAKI, S., Economics
ZUCKER, D., Statistics

Jerusalem School of Business Administration (tel. (2) 5883235; fax (2) 5881576; internet bschool.huji.ac.il):

BAR-YOSEF, S., Accounting
GALAI, D., Banking
KORNBLUTH, J., Business Admin.
LANDSKRONER, Y., Business Admin.
MAZURZKY, O., Marketing
MOSHEIOV, G., Business Admin., Statistics
VENEZIA, I., Business Admin.

Paul Baerwald School of Social Work and Social Welfare (tel. (2) 5881477; fax (2) 5823587; e-mail social-work@savion.huji.ac.il; internet www.sw.huji.ac.il):

AUSLANDER, G.
BENBEMISHTY, R.
LITWIN, H.
RAPOPORT, T.
SCHMID, H.

RESEARCH CENTRES AND INSTITUTES

Alexander Silberman Institute of Life Sciences: Givat Ram, 91904 Jerusalem; tel. (2) 65854314; fax (2) 6586103; e-mail rnathan@cc.huji.ac.il; internet www.bio.huji.ac.il; Chair. Prof. RAN NATHAN.

Alex Grass Center for Drug Design and Synthesis of Novel Therapeutics: The School of Pharmacy, Hebrew Univ. of Jerusalem, POB 12065 Jerusalem; tel. (2) 6758683; fax (2) 6757076; e-mail malkan@savion.huji.ac.il; Dir Prof. GIL LEIBOWITZ.

Asper Centre for Entrepreneurship: Jerusalem School of Business Admin., Jerusalem; tel. (2) 5882994; fax (2) 5883685; e-mail shellyk@savion.huji.ac.il; internet bschool.huji.ac.il; Dir Prof. DAVID MAZUKSKY.

Benjamin Triwaks Bee Research Centre: Hebrew Univ. of Jerusalem, POB 12, 76100 Rehovot; tel. (8) 9489401; fax (8) 9489842; e-mail shafir@agri.huji.ac.il; internet departments.agri.huji.ac.il/entomology/staff_pages/shafir.html; Dir Dr SHARONI SHAFIR.

Ben-Zvi Institute for the Study of Jewish Communities in the East: POB 7660, Jerusalem; tel. (2) 5398844; fax (2) 5612329; e-mail bzi@ybz.org.il; internet www.ybz.org.il; Chair. Prof. YOM TOV ASSIS.

Brettler Center for Research in Molecular Pharmacology and Therapeutics: The Institute for Drug Research, Hebrew

Univ. of Jerusalem, POB 12065 Jerusalem; tel. (2) 6758743; fax (2) 6758741; e-mail ruths@savion.huji.ac.il; internet pharmacy.huji.ac.il; Dir Prof. FRANCESCA LEVI-SHAFFER.

Centre for Agricultural Economic Research: Hebrew Univ. of Jerusalem, POB 12, 76100 Rehovot; tel. (8) 9489230; fax (8) 9466267; e-mail kimhi@agri.huji.ac.il; Dir Prof. AYAL KIMHI.

Centre for Diabetes Research: Hebrew Univ., Hdassah Medical Centre, 2nd Fl., Main Bldg; tel. (2) 6776788; fax (2) 6437940; e-mail gleib@hadassah.org.il; Chair. Prof. GIL LEIBOWITZ.

Centre for Integrated Pest Management: Hebrew Univ. of Jerusalem, POB 12, 76100 Rehovot; tel. (8) 9489223; fax (8) 9466768; e-mail coll@agri.huji.ac.il; Dir Dr MOSHE COLL.

Centre for Jewish Art: Faculty of Humanities, Mt Scopus, Jerusalem; tel. (2) 5882281; fax (2) 5400105; e-mail cja@vms.huji.ac.il; internet cja.huji.ac.il; Dir Dr RINA TALGAM.

Centre for Literary Studies: Faculty of Humanities, Mt Scopus, Jerusalem; tel. (2) 5883925; fax (2) 5880203; e-mail cis@savion.huji.ac.il; Dir Dr JON DAVID WHITMAN.

Centre for Nanoscience and Nanotechnology: Givat Ram, Jerusalem; tel. (2) 6586948; fax (2) 6584340; e-mail porath@chem.huji.ac.il; internet www.nanoscience.huji.ac.il; Dir Prof. DANNY PORATH.

Centre for Rationality and Interactive Decision Theory: Givat Ram, Jerusalem; tel. (2) 6584514; fax (2) 6513681; e-mail mseyal@mscc.huji.ac.il; internet www.ratio.huji.ac.il; Dir Prof. EYAL WINTER.

Centre for Research in Plant Sciences in Agriculture: HU POB 12, 76100 Rehovot; tel. (8) 9489812; fax (8) 3489899; e-mail samach@agri.huji.ac.il; Dir Dr ALON SAMACH.

Centre for Research on Dutch Jewry: Rabin Bldg, Mt Scopus, Jerusalem; tel. (2) 5880242; fax (2) 5880241; e-mail dutchjew@cc.huji.ac.il; internet dutchjewry.huji.ac.il; Dir Prof. YOSEF KAPLAN.

Centre for Research on Romanian Jewry: Rabin Bldg, Mt Scopus, Jerusalem; tel. (2) 5881672; fax (2) 5881673; e-mail rumjewry@vms.huji.ac.il; Dir Dr ODED IR-SHAI.

Centre for the Study of Christianity: Faculty of Humanities, Mt Scopus, Jerusalem; tel. (2) 5883827; fax (2) 5883819; e-mail centerc@savion.cc.huji.ac.il; Dir Dr BROURIA BITTON-ASHKELONY.

Centre for the Study of Jewish Languages and Literature: Rabin Bldg, Mt Scopus, Jerusalem; tel. (2) 5880244; fax (2) 5881206; e-mail otirosh@mscc.huji.ac.il; Dir Dr OFRA TIROSH-BECKER.

Centre for the Study of Pain: tel. (2) 6758456; fax (2) 6757451; e-mail talm@ekmd.huji.ac.il; internet paincenter.huji.ac.il/tal.htm; Dir Prof. MICHAEL TAL.

Chais Centre for Jewish Studies in Russian: Rabin Bldg, Mt Scopus, Jerusalem; tel. (2) 5881770; fax (2) 5881795; e-mail chais_center@savion.huji.ac.il; Dir Dr SEMION GOLDIN.

Cherrick Centre for the Study of Zionism, the Yishuv and the State of Israel: Cherrick Centre, Mt Scopus, Jerusalem; tel. (2) 5882867; fax (2) 5882986; e-mail cherrick@mscc.huji.ac.il; internet cherrick.huji.ac.il; Dir Dr UZI REBHUN.

D. Walter Cohen DDS Middle East Centre for Dental Education: tel. (2) 6758596; fax (2) 6439219; e-mail hujident@cc.huji.ac.il; Dir Dr DORON ARFAMIAN.

David R. Bloom Centre for Pharmacy: The Institute for Drug Research, POB 12065 Jerusalem; tel. (2) 6758743; fax (2) 6758741; e-mail ruths@savion.huji.ac.il; internet pharmacy.huji.ac.il; Dir Prof. ISRAEL RINGEL.

Dinur Centre for Research in Jewish History: Rabin Bldg, Mt Scopus, Jerusalem; tel. (2) 5884894; fax (2) 5883894; e-mail dinurcenter@mscc.huji.ac.il; internet www.dinur.org; Dir Dr ODED IR-SHAI.

Edmund Landau Minerva Centre for Research in Mathematical Analysis and Related Areas: Institute of Mathematics, Givat Ram, Jerusalem; tel. (2) 6586868; fax (2) 5630702; e-mail ylast@math.huji.ac.il; internet www.ma.huji.ac.il; Dir Prof. YORAM LAST.

Eliezer Ben-Yehudah Research Centre for History of Hebrew, The: Faculty of Humanities, Mt Scopus, Jerusalem; tel. (2) 5883550; fax (2) 5881206; e-mail yreshef@mscc.huji.ac.il; internet www.hum.huji.ac.il/benyehuda; Dir Dr YAEL RESHEF.

European Forum at the Hebrew University: tel. (2) 5883286; fax (2) 5881535; e-mail mseuro@mscc.huji.ac.il; internet www.ef.huji.ac.il; Dir Prof. BIANCA KUHNEL.

Fishman-JEC Center for Finance, Entrepreneurship and Real Estate: Jerusalem School of Business Admn, 76100 Jerusalem; tel. (2) 5883224; fax (2) 5883685; e-mail shellyk@savion.huji.ac.il; internet bschool.huji.ac.il; Dir Prof. ZVI WIENER.

Folklore Research Centre: Rabin Bldg, Mt Scopus, Jerusalem; tel. (2) 5881797; e-mail hasan@mscc.huji.ac.uk; Dir Prof. GALIT HASAN-ROKEM.

Franz Rosenzweig Centre for the Study of German Culture and Literature: Rabin Bldg, Mt Scopus, Jerusalem; tel. (2) 5881909; fax (2) 5811369; e-mail yfaatw@pluto.mscc.huji.ac.il; Dir Prof. YFAAT WEISS.

Fritz Haber Research Centre for Molecular Dynamics: Institute of Chemistry, Givat Ram, Jerusalem; tel. (2) 6586114; fax (2) 6513742; e-mail roi.baer@huji.ac.il; internet www.chemistry.huji.ac.il; Dir Prof. ROIE BAER.

G. W. Leibnitz Minerva Centre for Research in Computer Sciences: School of Computer Science and Engineering, Jerusalem; tel. (2) 6585730; fax (2) 6585261; e-mail noam.nisan@gmail.com; internet www.cs.huji.ac.il; Dir Prof. NOAM NISSAN.

Gal-Edd Centre for Industrial Development: Jerusalem School of Business Admin., Jerusalem; tel. (2) 5883224; fax (2) 5883685; e-mail shellyk@savion.huji.ac.il; internet bschool.huji.ac.il; Dir Dr NIRON HASHAI.

Gilo Citizenship, Democracy and Civil Education Centre: tel. (2) 5882267; fax (2) 5881532; e-mail gilocenter@mscc.huji.ac.il; internet www.gilocenter.huji.ac.il; Dir Dr JEFF MACY.

Goldie Rotman Centre for Cognitive Science in Education: School of Education, Mt Scopus, Jerusalem; tel. (2) 5882102; fax (2) 5881311; e-mail kareev@vms.huji.ac.il; Dir Prof. YAAKOV KAREEV.

Halbert Centre for Canadian Studies: tel. (2) 5881344; fax (2) 5826267; e-mail mscanada@mscc.huji.ac.il; Dir Prof. NACHMAN BEN-YEHUDA.

Harry and Michael Sacher Institute for Legislative Research and Comparative Law: tel. (2) 5882535; fax (2) 5882565; e-mail sacher.institute@gmail.com; internet law.mscc.huji.ac.il/law1/sache; Dir Prof. MICHAEL KARAYANNI.

Harry S. Truman Research Institute for the Advancement of Peace: tel. (2) 5882300; fax (2) 5828076; e-mail truman@

savion.huji.ac.il; internet truman.huji.ac.il; Dir Prof. STEVEN KAPLAN.

Hebrew University Bible Project: Rabin Bldg, Mt Scopus, Jerusalem; tel. (2) 5880246; fax (2) 5880248; e-mail rzer@mscc.huji.ac.il; Dir Dr MICHAEL SEGAL.

Herb and Frances Brody Centre for Food Sciences: Hebrew Univ. of Jerusalem, POB 12, 76100 Rehovot; tel. (8) 9489292; fax (8) 9462384; e-mail fridman@agri.huji.ac.il; Dir Prof. RONNIE FRIEDMAN.

Hubert H. Humphrey Centre for Experimental Medicine and Cancer Research: tel. (2) 6758350; fax (2) 6414583; e-mail ruthyn@savion.huji.ac.il; Dir Prof. ODED BEHAR.

Institute for Advanced Studies: Givat Ram, 91904 Jerusalem; tel. (2) 6584735; fax (2) 6523429; e-mail advance@vms.huji.ac.il; internet www.as.huji.ac.il; Dir Prof. ELIEZER RABINOVICI.

Institute for Dental Sciences: tel. (2) 6757595; fax (2) 6439219; e-mail apalmon@cc.huji.ac.il; Dir Prof. AARON PALMON.

Institute for Medical Research: POB 12272, 91120 Jerusalem; tel. (2) 6757527; fax (2) 6757529; e-mail davidli@ekmd.huji.ac.il; internet medicine.huji.ac.il; Dir Prof. DAVID LICHTSTEIN.

International Centre for University Teaching of Jewish Civilization: Faculty of Humanities, Mt Scopus, Jerusalem; tel. (2) 5881773; fax (2) 5819096; e-mail msjewciv@mscc.huji.ac.il; internet jewishcivilization.huji.ac.il; Dir Prof. CYRIL ASLANOV.

Israel Matz Institute for Research in Jewish Law: tel. (2) 5882501; fax (2) 5882567; e-mail jewishlaw@savion.cc.huji.ac.il; internet law.mscc.huji.ac.il/law1/newsite/hebrew.html; Dir Prof. BERACHYAHU LIFSHITZ.

Jewish Music Research Centre: POB 39105, 91390 Jerusalem; tel. (2) 6585059; fax (2) 5611156; e-mail jmrc_inf@savion.huji.ac.il; internet www.jewish-music.huji.ac.il; Dir Prof. EDWIN SEROUSSI.

Jewish Oral Traditions Research Centre: Rabin Bldg, Mt Scopus, Jerusalem; tel. (2) 5881828; e-mail dornirit@zahav.net.il; Dir Prof. AHARON MAMAM.

K Mart International Retail and Marketing Centre: Jerusalem School of Business Admin., Jerusalem; tel. (2) 5883224; fax (2) 5883685; e-mail shellyk@savion.huji.ac.il; internet bschool.huji.ac.il; Dir Prof. JACOB GOLDENBERG.

Kennedy Leigh Centre for Horticultural Research: Hebrew Univ. of Jerusalem, POB 12, 76100 Rehovot; tel. (8) 9489251; fax (8) 9489899; e-mail shimony@agri.huji.ac.il; internet departments.agri.huji.ac.il/horticulture/kennedy.html; Dir Prof. ADAM ZACH.

Knune Minerva Farkas Centre for the Study of Light Induced Processes: Institute of Chemistry, Givat Ram, Jerusalem; tel. (2) 6585326; fax (2) 5618033; e-mail sandy@fh.huji.ac.il; internet www.chemistry.huji.ac.il; Dir Prof. SANFORD RUCHMAN.

Krueger Centre for Finance: Jerusalem School of Business Admin., Jerusalem; tel. (2) 5883224; fax (2) 5883685; e-mail shellyk@savion.huji.ac.il; internet bschool.huji.ac.il; Dir Prof. YISHAY YAFFE.

Kubin Centre for Study of Infectious and Tropical Diseases: Faculty of Medicine, Hebrew Univ., POB 12272, 91120 Jerusalem; tel. (2) 6758089; fax (2) 6727425; e-mail josephs@ekmd.huji.ac.il; internet kuvin.huji.ac.il; Dir Prof. JOSEPH SHLOMAI.

Lafer Centre for Women and Gender Studies: tel. (2) 5883455; fax (2) 5883364;

e-mail mslaferc@mscc.huji.ac.il; internet www.lafer.huji.ac.il; Dir Prof. NURIT YERMIA.

Lautenberg Centre for General and Tumour Immunology: Faculty of Medicine, POB 12272, 91120 Jerusalem; tel. (2) 6758726; fax (2) 6430834; e-mail daniellak@savion.huji.ac.il; internet immunology.huji.ac.il; Dir Prof. EITAN YEFE-NOF.

Leo Picard Groundwater Research Centre: tel. (8) 9489174; fax (8) 9475181; e-mail chefetz@agri.huji.ac.il; Dir Prof. BENNY CHEFETZ.

Leonard Davis Institute for International Relations: tel. (2) 5882312; fax (2) 5825534; e-mail msdavis@mscc.huji.ac.il; internet davis.huji.ac.il; Dir Prof. AVRAHAM SELA.

Leonid Nevzlin Research Centre for Russian and East European Jewry: Rabin Bldg, Mt Scopus, Jerusalem; tel. (2) 5881959; fax (2) 5881950; e-mail merkaznev@savion.huji.ac.il; internet www.nevzlin.huji.ac.il; Dir Dr JONATHAN DEKEL-CHEN.

Levi Eshkol Institute for Economic, Social and Political Research: tel. (2) 5883032; fax (2) 5324339; e-mail eshkol@mscc.huji.ac.il; internet eshkol.huji.ac.il; Dir Prof. MICHAEL SHALEV.

Levin Centre for the Study of Normal Child and Adolescent Development: tel. (2) 5883370; fax (2) 5881159; e-mail levinc@mscc.huji.ac.il; internet psychology.mscc.huji.ac.il; Dir Prof. NURIT YIRMIA.

Lisa Meitner-Minerva Centre for Computational Quantum Chemistry: Institute of Chemistry, Givat Ram, Jerusalem; tel. (2) 6585909; fax (2) 6585345; e-mail sason@yfaat.ch.huji.ac.il; internet www.chemistry.huji.ac.il; Dir Prof. SASSON SHAIK.

Liverant Centre for the study of Latin America, Spain, Portugal and their Jewish Communities: Rabin Bldg, Mt Scopus, Jerusalem; tel. (2) 5881633; fax (2) 5881633; e-mail literantc@mscc.huji.ac.il; internet www.hum.huji.ac.il/site/liwerant; Dir Prof. ISRAEL YUVAL.

Louis Frieberg Centre for East Asian Studies, The: Faculty of Humanities, Mt Scopus, Jerusalem; tel. (2) 5881371; fax (2) 5881371; e-mail eacenter@mscc.huji.ac.il; internet www.eacenter.huji.ac.il; Dir Dr GIDEON SHELACH.

Minerva Centre for Human Rights: tel. (2) 5881156; fax (2) 5819371; e-mail mchr@savion.huji.ac.il; internet law.mscc.huji.ac.il/law1/minerva/english; Dir Dr TOMER BROUDE.

Misgav Yerushalaim Centre for the Study of Sephardi and Oriental Jewry: Rabin Bldg, Mt Scopus, Jerusalem; tel. (2) 5883962; fax (2) 5815460; e-mail yaronbn@mscc.huji.ac.il; internet www.hum.huji.ac.il/misgav/index2.htm; Dir Dr YARON BEN-NAEH.

Mordechai Zagagi Centre for Finance and Accounting: Jerusalem School of Business Admin., Jerusalem; tel. (2) 5883224; fax (2) 5883685; e-mail shellyk@savion.huji.ac.il; internet bschool.huji.ac.il; Dir Prof. MOSHE LEVY.

Moshe Shilo Centre for Marine Biogeochemistry: Institute of Life Sciences, Givat Ram, Jerusalem; tel. (8) 6585561; fax (8) 6585318; e-mail zeev@vms.huji.ac.il; internet www.ivi-eilat.ac.il; Dir Prof. ZEEV AIZENSH-TAT.

Multi-Disciplinary Centre for Environmental Research: tel. (8) 9489916; fax (8) 9467763; e-mail kigel@agri.huji.ac.il; internet www.sites.huji.ac.il/cfer; Dir Prof. JAIME KIGEL.

National Council of Jewish Women Research Institute for Innovation in Education: tel. (2) 5882015; fax (2) 5882174; e-mail ayalab@savion.huji.ac.il; internet ncjw.res.mscc.huji.ac.il; Dir Dr MEIR BUZAGLO.

National Institute for Psychobiology in Israel: Life Sciences Bldg, Givat Ram, 91904 Jerusalem; tel. (2) 6584086; fax (2) 5635267; e-mail psychobi@cc.huji.ac.il; internet psychobiology.org.il; Dir Prof. SHAUL HOCHSTEIN.

Nehemia Levzion Centre for Islamic Studies: Faculty of Humanities, Mt Scopus, Jerusalem; tel. (2) 5881541; fax (2) 5880258; e-mail islamic@mscc.huji.ac.il; internet islam-center.huji.ac.il; Dir Dr MEIR HATINA.

Niznick Dental Implant and Research Centre: tel. (2) 6776193; fax (2) 6776175; e-mail ervinw@cc.huji.ac.il; internet www.hadassah.org.il; Dir Prof. E. WEISS.

Nutrigenomics & Functional Food Research Centre: HU POB 12, 76100 Rehovot; tel. (8) 9489746; fax (8) 9363208; internet froy@agri.huji.ac.il; Dir Prof. OREN FROY.

Orion Centre for the Study of the Dead Sea Scrolls and Associated Literature, The: Rabin Bldg, Mt Scopus, Jerusalem; tel. (2) 5881966; fax (2) 5883584; e-mail msdss@mscc.huji.ac.il; internet orion.mscc.huji.ac.il; Dir Prof. MENAHEM KISTER.

Otto Warburg Minerva Centre for Agricultural Biotechnology: Hebrew Univ. of Jerusalem, POB 12, 76100 Rehovot; tel. (8) 9489973; fax (8) 9363882; e-mail ingel@agri.huji.ac.il; internet departments.agri.huji.ac.il/biotech; Dir Prof. EDOUARD JURKEVITCH.

Philip and Muriel Berman Centre for Biblical Archaeology: Institute of Archaeology, Hebrew Univ., 91905 Jerusalem; tel. (2) 5882403; fax (2) 5825548; Dir Prof. YOSEF GARFINKEL.

Recanati Centre for Research in Business Administration: Jerusalem School of Business Admin., Jerusalem; tel. (2) 5883224; fax (2) 5883685; e-mail shellyk@savion.huji.ac.il; internet bschool.huji.ac.il; Dir Prof. ZVI WIENER.

Research Centre for Agriculture, Environment and Natural Resources (RCAENR): HU POB 12, 76100 Rehovot; tel. (8) 9489384; fax (8) 9475181; e-mail chefetz@agri.huji.ac.il; Dir Prof. BENNY CHEFETZ.

Research Centre for Sustainable Animal Health and Husbandry: HU POB 12, 76100 Rehovot; tel. (8) 9489988; fax (2) 9465763; e-mail sivan@agri.huji.ac.il; Dir Prof. BERTA LEVAVI-SIVAN.

Richard Koebner Centre for German History: Faculty of Humanities, Mt Scopus, Jerusalem; tel. (2) 5883766; fax (2) 5816501; e-mail mskoeb@pluto.mscc.huji.ac.il; Dir Prof. MOSCHE ZIMMERMAN.

Robert H. and Clarice Smith Centre for Art History: Hebrew Univ., Faculty of Humanities, Mt Scopus, 91905 Jerusalem; tel. (2) 5883872; fax (2) 5883944; e-mail milstein@huji.ac.il; internet www.smithcenter.huji.ac.il; Dir Prof. RACHEL MILSTEIN.

Ronald E. Goldstein DDS Research Centre for Dental Materials and Aesthetics in Dentistry: Faculty of Dental Medicine, Hebrew Univ., POB 12272, 91120 Jerusalem; tel. (2) 6776193; fax (2) 6429683; e-mail nitzan@bichacho.net; Dir Prof. NITZAN BICHACHO.

Sanford F. Kuvin Centre for the Study of Infectious and Tropical Diseases: Institute for Medical Research, POB 12272, 91120

Jerusalem; tel. (2) 6758089; fax (2) 6727425; e-mail josephs@ekmd.huji.ac.il; internet kuvin.huji.ac.il; Dir Prof. JOSEPH SHLOMAI.

Scheinfeld Centre for Human Genetics in the Social Sciences: tel. (2) 536855; fax (2) 536853; e-mail ebstein@mscc.huji.ac.il; Dir Prof. RICHARD EBSTEIN.

Scholion Interdisciplinary Research Centre in Jewish Studies: Rabin Bldg, Mt Scopus, Jerusalem; tel. (2) 5882430; fax (2) 5881196; e-mail scholion@savion.huji.ac.il; internet scholion.huji.ac.il; Dir Prof. ISRAEL J. YUVAL.

Seagram Centre for Soil and Water Sciences: Hebrew Univ. of Jerusalem, POB 12, 76100 Rehovot; tel. (8) 9489340; fax (8) 9475181; e-mail soil@agri.huji.ac.il; internet departments.agri.huji.ac.il/soils; Dir Prof. BENNY CHEFETZ.

S. H. Bergman Centre for Philosophical Studies: Faculty of Humanities, Mt Scopus, Jerusalem; tel. (2) 5883762; fax (2) 5880148; Dir Prof. DAVID HEYD.

Shasha Centre for Strategic Studies: tel. (2) 5881988; fax (2) 5881200; e-mail saritf@savion.huji.ac.il; Dir EFRAIM HALEVY.

Shaine Centre for Research in the Social Sciences: tel. (2) 5883032; fax (2) 5324339; e-mail msschein@mscc.huji.ac.il; Dir Prof. GAD YAIR.

Sidney M. Edelstein Centre for the History and Philosophy of Science, Technology and Medicine: Safra Campus, 91905 Jerusalem; tel. (2) 6585652; fax (2) 6586709; e-mail travis@cc.huji.ac.il; Dir Prof. YEMIMA BEN-MENAHEM.

Sigmund Freud Centre for Study and Research in Psychoanalysis: tel. (2) 5883380; fax (2) 5322132; e-mail msfreud@pluto.mscc.huji.ac.il; internet atar.mscc.huji.ac.il/%7efreud; Dir Prof. GABY SHEFLER.

Smart Family Foundation Communication Institute: tel. (2) 5883210; fax (2) 5817008; e-mail msmartc@mscc.huji.ac.il; internet smart.huji.ac.il; Dir Prof. MENACHEM BLONDHEIM.

Sturman Centre for Human Development: tel. (2) 5883409; fax (2) 5881159; e-mail msmerava@mscc.huji.ac.il; Dir Prof. RAM FROST.

Sudarsky Centre for Computational Biology: Givat Ram, Jerusalem; tel. (2) 6585425; fax (2) 6586103; e-mail michall@cc.huji.ac.il; internet www.cbc.huji.ac.il; Dir Prof. MICHAL LINEAL.

Vidal Sassoon International Centre for the Study of Antisemitism: Faculty of Humanities, Mt Scopus, Jerusalem; tel. (2) 5882494; fax (2) 5881002; e-mail sicsa@mscc.huji.ac.il; internet sicsa.huji.ac.il; Dir Prof. ROBERT WISTRICH.

Zigi and Lisa Daniel Swiss Centre: tel. (2) 5883056; fax (2) 5880004; e-mail crmr@savion.huji.ac.il; internet www.crmr.huji.ac.il; Dir Prof. ILANA RITOV.

OPEN UNIVERSITY OF ISRAEL

108 Ravutski St, POB 808, 43107 Raanana

Telephone: (9) 7780778

Fax: (9) 7780642

E-mail: president@openu.ac.il

Internet: www.openu.ac.il

Founded 1974, fmrly Everyman's Univ., present name 1989

Language of instruction: Hebrew

Academic year: September to June (two semesters) and summer semester

A distance-learning institution serving students on a nationwide basis; academic and general adult education using written material and integrating technology (incl. online and satellite transmission) in a self-study system supplemented by tutorial instruction; offers 700 courses in the arts, culture, cognition, computer science and natural sciences, communication, democracy, education, economics, management, history, Judaic studies, life sciences, literature, language, mathematics, philosophy, philosophy of science, political science, psychology, sociology, culture, technology; undergraduate and graduate degrees

Chancellor: Lord WOOLF

Deputy Chancellor: Lord ROTHSCHILD

Vice-Chancellor: Prof. ABRAHAM GINZBURG

Pres.: Prof. HAGIT MESSER-YARON

Vice-Pres. for Academic Affairs: Prof. JUDITH GAL-EZER

Dir-Gen.: AMIT SHTREIT

Dean of Academic Studies: Prof. SONIA ROCAS

Dean of Devt and Technology: Prof. YOAV YAIR

Dean of Research: Prof. ANAT BARNEA

Dean of Students: Dr HAIM SAADOUN

Dir of the Library: HAVA MUSTIGMAN

Library of 75,000 vols, 500 e-books, 92 databases, 20,000 electronic periodicals

Number of teachers: 1,693 (80 senior faculty members, 428 junior faculty mems and 1,210 tutors throughout Israel teaching in 50 study centres)

Number of students: 42,295 , 3,276 graduate students, 4,000 students in countries of the fmr USSR

TEL-AVIV UNIVERSITY

POB 39040, 69978 Tel-Aviv

Telephone: (3) 6408111

Fax: (3) 6408601

E-mail: tauinfo@post.tau.ac.il

Internet: www.tau.ac.il

Founded 1953; inaugurated 1956

Private control, partially supported by the Govt

Language of instruction: Hebrew

Academic year: October to June (2 terms)

Pres.: Prof. JOSEPH KLAFTER

Vice-Pres. for Public Affairs: Dr GARY SUSSMAN

Vice-Pres. for Research and Devt: Prof. EHUD GAZIT

Vice-Pres.: Col (Res.) YEHIEL BEN-ZVI

Rector: Prof. DANY LEVIATAN

Vice-Rector: Prof. ARON SHAI

Dir-Gen.: MORDEHAI KOHN

Academic Sec.: SARA KINEL

Dean of Students: Prof. YOAV ARIEL

Library: see Libraries and Archives

Number of teachers: 2,200

Number of students: 29,000

Publications: *Hasifrut* (4 a year), *Iunei Mishpat* (4 a year), *Poetics Today* (4 a year), *Zemanim* (4 a year), *Mideast File* (4 a year), *Middle East Contemporary Survey* (1 a year), *Jahrbuch des Instituts für Deutsche Geschichte* (1 a year), *Dinei Israel* (1 a year), *Israel Yearbook in Human Rights* (1 a year), *Studies in Zionism* (2 a year), *Mediterranean Historical Review* (2 a year), *Michael* (8 every 18 months), *Shvut* (9 a year), *Studies in Educational Evaluation* (4 a year), *International Perspective on Education and Society* (1 a year), *Theoretical Inquiries in Law* (2 a year), *Israeli Society* (in Hebrew), *Kesher*

DEANS

Yolanda and David Katz Faculty of Arts: Prof. HANNAH NAVEH

Iby and Aladar Fleischman Faculty of Engineering: Prof. EHUD HEYMAN

Raymond and Beverly Sackler Faculty of Exact Sciences: Prof. HAIM WOLFSON

Lester and Sally Entin Faculty of Humanities: Prof. EYAL ZISSER

Buchmann Faculty of Law: Prof. HANOCH DAGAN

George S. Wise Faculty of Life Sciences: Prof. YOEL KLOOG

Faculty of Management (Leon Recanati Graduate School of Business Administration): Prof. ASHER TISHLER

Sackler Faculty of Medicine: Prof. YOSEPH MEKORI

Gershon H. Gordon Faculty of Social Sciences: Prof. NOAH LEWIN-EPSTEIN

PROFESSORS

AARONSON, J., Mathematics

ABBOUD, S., Biomedical Engineering

ABRAMOWICZ, H., Physics

AHARONOWITZ, Y., Microbiology

AHARONY, A., Physics

AHITUV, N., Management

AKSELROD, S., Physics

ALGOM, D., Psychology

ALON, N., Mathematics

ALONI, R., Botany

ALPERT, P., Geophysics and Planetary Sciences

AMIRAV, A., Chemistry

AMIT, Y., Bible

AMOSSY, R., French Literature

ANDELMAN, D., Physics

ANILY, S., Management

APTER, A., Psychiatry

ARBEL, A., Industrial Engineering

ARBEL, B., History

ARBER, N., Medicine

ARON, S., History

ASHKENAZI, S., Paediatrics

AVERBUCH, A., Computer Sciences

AVRON, A., Computer Sciences

AYALON, A., History of the Middle East and Africa

AZAR, Y., Computer Sciences

AZRIEL, P., Anaesthiology and Intensive Care

BANKS-SILLS, L., Mechanical Engineering

BAR-KOCHVA, B., History of the Jewish People

BAR-MEIR, S., Medicine

BAR-NAVI, E., History

BAR-NUN, A., Planetary Sciences

BAR-TAL, D., Education

BARBASH, G., Preventive Medicine, Social Medicine

BARKAI, R., History

BARNEA, D., Mechanical Engineering

BARZILAY, Z., Paediatrics

BATTLER, A., Cardiology

BE'ERY, Y., Electrical Engineering

BEER, S., Plant Sciences

BELHASSEN, B., Cardiology

BELKIN, A., Theatre Arts

BELKIN, M., Ophthalmology

BEN, E. S., Psychology

BEN-AVRAHAM, Z., Geophysics

BEN-BASSAT, I., Haematology

BEN-DAVID, Y., Anatomy and Anthropology

BEN-JACOB, E., Physics

BEN-RAFAEL, E., Sociology and Anthropology

BEN-RAFAEL, Z., Gynaecology and Obstetrics

BEN-ZVI, A., Political Science

BEN-ZVI, L., Theatre Arts

BENAYAHU, Y., Zoology

BENJAMINI, Y., Statistics

BENNINGA, S., Management

BENVENISTE, Y., Mechanical Engineering

BENVENISTI, E., Law

BERECHMAN, J., Urban Planning

BERGMAN, D., Physics

BERNHEIM, J., Medicine

BERNSTEIN, J., Mathematics

BIDERMAN, S., Philosophy

BIXON, M., Chemistry

BOXMAN, R., Electrical and Electronic Engineering

BRACHA, B., Law

BRAUNER, N., Mechanical Engineering

BREIMAN, A., Plant Sciences

BUCHNER, A., Oral Pathology
CARMELI, S., Physics
CASHER, A., Physics
CHEN, R., Physics
CHESHNOVSKY, O., Chemistry
CHESKIS, S., Chemistry
CHOR, B., Computer Sciences
COHEN, A., Communication
COHEN, G., Molecular Microbiology and Biotechnology
COHEN, J., History of the Jewish People
COHEN, N., Law
CUKIERMAN, A., Economics
DAGAN, H., Law
DASCAL, M., Philosophy
DASCAL, N., Physiology
DAVIDSON, M., Psychiatry
DAYAN, D., Oral Pathology
DAYAN, T., Zoology
DEKEL, E., Economics
DERSHOWITZ, N., Computer Sciences
DEUTCH, M., Law
DINARI, G., Paediatrics
DOR, J., Obstetrics and Gynaecology
DRAZEN, A., Economics
DREYFUS, T., Teaching of Science
DYN, N., Applied Mathematics
ECKSTEIN, Z., Economics
EDEN, D., Management
EINAV, S., Biomedical Engineering
ELAD, D., Biomedical Engineering
ELDAR, M., Cardiology
ENTIN, O., Physics
EPEL, B. L., Botany
ESHEL, I., Statistics
EVEN, U., Chemistry
EVEN-ZOHAR, I., Theory of Literature
FABIAN, I., Cell Biology and Histology
FAINARU, M., Medicine
FARBER, M., Mathematics
FARFEL, Z., Medicine
FEDER, M., Electrical Engineering
FERSHTMAN, CH., Economics
FIAT, A., Computer Sciences
FINKELBERG, M., Classics
FINKELSTEIN, I., Archaeology
FISHELSON, Z., Cell and Development Biology
FISHER, M., Classical Archaeology
FLEUROV, V., Physics
FRANKFURT, L. L., Physics
FREEMAN, A., Biotechnology
FRENK, H., Psychology
FRENKEL, J., Economics
FRENKEL, N., Cell Research and Immunology
FRIEDLAND, N., Psychology
FRIEDMAN, M. A., Talmud
FUCHS, C., Statistics
FUCHS, M., Mechanical Engineering
GADOTH, N., Neurology
GAFTER, U., Medicine
GANS, CH., Law
GANZACH, Y., Management
GAT, A., Political Sciences
GAZIT, A., Human Microbiology
GERCHAK, Y., Industrial Engineering
GERSHONI, I., History of the Middle East
GERSHONI, Y., Cell Research and Immunology
GILBOA, I., Management, Economics
GINSBURG, D., Mathematics
GITIK, M., Mathematics
GLASNER, S., Mathematics
GLAZER, J., Management
GLEZERMAN, M., Obstetrics and Gynaecology
GLUSKIN, E., Mathematics
GOFER, A., Archaeology
GOLANI, I., Zoology
GOLDBERG, I., Chemistry
GOLDBOURT, U., Preventive Medicine, Social Medicine
GOLDHIRSCH, I., Mechanical Engineering
GOLDMAN, B., Genetics
GORODETSKY, G., History
GOVER, A., Electrical and Electronic Engineering
GOZES, I., Clinical Biochemistry
GRAUR, D., Zoology

GREEN, M., Preventive Medicine, Social Medicine
GREENSTEIN, E., Bible
GRODEZINSKY, Y., Psychology
GROSSMAN, E., Medicine
GUREVITZ, M., Plant Sciences
GUTNIK, D., Microbiology
HALKIN, H., Medicine
HALPERN, Z., Medicine
HAMMEL, I., Pathology
HARAN, D., Mathematics
HARATS, D., Medicine
HARDY, A., Electrical and Electronic Engineering
HASSIN, R., Statistics
HATIVA, N., Education
HAZAN, H., Sociology and Anthropology
HEFETZ, A., Zoology
HENIG, M., Management
HENIS, Y., Biochemistry
HERSHKOVITZ, I., Anatomy and Anthropology
HEYMAN, E., Electrical Engineering
HILDESHEIMER, M., Communication Disorders
HIZI, A., Cell Biology
HOCHBERG, Y., Statistics
HOFFMAN, Y., Bible
HOLZMAN, A., Hebrew Literature
HOMBURG, R., Obstetrics and Gynaecology
HORNIK, J., Management
HOROWITZ, A., Geology
HOROWITZ, M., Cell Research and Immunology
HUPPERT, D., Chemistry
ICHILOV, O., Education
ISAAC, B., Classics
ITZCHAK, Y., Diagnostic Radiology
IZRE'EL, S., Semitic Linguistics
JARDEN, M., Mathematics
KAFFE, I., Oral Radiology
KAHANE, Y., Management
KALAY, A., Management
KALDOR, U., Chemistry
KANDEL, SH., Management
KANTOR, Y., Physics
KARLINER, M., Physics
KARNIOL, R., Psychology
KASHMAN, Y., Chemistry
KATZ, D., History
KATZIR, A., Physics
KAUFMAN, G., Biochemistry
KEISARI, Y., Human Microbiology
KENAAN-KEDAR, N., History of Arts
KEREN, G., Cardiology
KIT, E., Mechanical Engineering
KLAFTER, J., Chemistry
KLEIN, A., Mathematics
KLEIN, S., Jewish Philosophy
KLIEMAN, A., Political Science
KLOOG, Y., Biochemistry
KORCZYN, A., Neurology
KORENSTEIN, R., Physiology
KOSLOFF, D., Geophysics
KREITLER, S., Psychology
KRONFELD, I., Geophysics and Planetary Sciences
KUPIEC, M., Microbiology
LAMED, R., Biotechnology
LANDMAN, F., Linguistics
LANGHOLZ, G., Electrical Engineering
LAOR, D., Hebrew Literature
LAOR, N., Psychiatry
LASS, Y., Physiology
LAVI, S., Cell Biology
LEDERMAN, E., Law
LEHRER, E., Statistics
LEIBOWITZ, E., Physics and Astronomy
LEIDERMAN, L., Economics
LESSING, J., Gynaecology and Obstetrics
LEVANON, N., Electrical and Electronic Engineering
LEVIATAN, D., Mathematics
LEVIN, D., Applied Mechanics
LEVIN, E., Physics
LEVIN, Z., Atmospheric Sciences
LEVO, Y., Medicine
LEVY, A., Physics

LEVY, S., Theatre Arts
LEWIN, N., Sociology and Anthropology
LIBERMAN, U. A., Statistics
LICHTENBERG, D., Pharmacology
LICHTENSTADT, J., Physics
LITSYN, S., Electrical Engineering
LIVSHITS, Z., Anatomy and Anthropology
LOBEL, T., Psychology
LOTAN, I., Physiology
LOYA, Y., Zoology
MAIMON, O., Industrial Engineering
MALKIN, I., Ancient History
MANSOUR, Y., Computer Sciences
MAOZ, D., Physics and Astronomy
MAOZ, Z., Political Science
MARGALIT, M., Education
MARGALIT, R., Biochemistry
MATZKIN, H., Surgery
MAUTNER, M., Law
MAZEH, T., Physics
MEDIN, Z., History
MEILIJSON, I., Statistics
MEKORI, Y., Medicine
MELAMED, E., Neurology
MENASHIRI, D., History of the Middle East
MESSER, H., Electrical Engineering
MEVARECH, M., Microbiology
MICHAELSON, D., Biochemistry
MILMAN, V., Mathematics
MILOH, T., Engineering
MIMOUNI, F., Paediatrics
MINTS, R., Physics
MOHR, R., Surgery
MOTRO, M., Cardiology
MULLER, E., Management
NAAMAN, N., History of the Jewish People
NADLER, A., Psychology
NAOR, Z., Biochemistry
NAVON, R., Human Genetics
NELSON, N., Biochemistry
NETZER, H., Physics
NEVO, D., Education
NITZAN, A., Chemistry
NUSSINOV, R., Biochemistry
NUSSINOV, S., Physics
OFEK, I., Human Microbiology
OFER, A., Management
OLEVSKII, A., Mathematics
OPPENHEIMER, A., History of the Jewish People
OR, U. G., Surgery
ORON, U., Zoology
ORON, Y., Pharmacology
OVADIA, M., Zoology
PASSWELL, J., Paediatrics
PAZ, G., Physiology
PELED, E., Chemistry
PHILLIP, M., Paediatrics
PIASETZKY, E., Physics
PICK, E., Immunology
PITARU, S., Oral Biology
PODOLACK, M., Planetary Science
POLAK, F., Bible
POLTEROVICH, L., Mathematics
PORAT, A., Law
PORTUGALI, J., Geography
RABEY, M., Neurology
RABINOVICH, I., History of the Middle East
RABINOWITZ, B., Cardiology
RAK, Y., Anatomy and Anthropology
RAVID, M., Medicine
RAVIV, A., Psychology
RAZ, A., Biochemistry
RAZ, J., East Asian Studies
RAZ, T., Management
RAZI, Z., History
RAZIN, A., Economics
RECHAVI, G., Haematology
REHAVI, M., Pharmacology
REIN, R., History
REPHAELI, Y., Physics
RISHPON, J., Biotechnology
ROKEM, F., Theatre Arts
ROLL, I., Classical Archaeology
RON, E., Microbiology
RON-EL, R., Gynaecology and Obstetrics

RONEN, B., Management
ROSENAU, P., Applied Mathematics
ROSENBAUM, M., Psychology
ROSENBERG, M., Human Microbiology
ROSENMAN, G., Electrical Engineering
ROSSET, SH., Mathematics
ROZEN, S., Chemistry
RUBIN, U., Arabic Language and Literature
RUBIN, Z., History
RUBINSTEIN, A., Economics
RUBINSTEIN, E., Medicine
RUDNICK, Z., Mathematics
RUPIN, E., Computer Science
RUPIN, E., Physiology
RUSCHIN, SH., Electrical Engineering
SABAR, B., Education
SADAN, J., Islamic Culture, Arabic Literature
SADKA, E., Economics
SAFRA, Z., Management
SAMET, D., Management
SAND, SH., History
SARNE, Y., Physiology
SAVION, N., Clinical Biochemistry
SCHMEIDLER, D., Statistics and Economics
SCHWARTZ, M., Physics
SEMYONOV, M., Sociology
SHACHAM-DIAM, Y., Electrical Engineering
SHAI, A., History
SHAKED, U., Electrical and Electronic Engin-
eering
SHALGI, R., Embryology
SHAMIR, M., Political Science
SHAMIR, R., Computer Sciences
SHAMIR, Z., Hebrew Literature
SHANI, M., Health Systems Management
SHAPIRA, A., History of the Jewish People
SHAPIRA, Y., Electrical and Electronic Engin-
eering
SHAPIRO, Y., Physiology
SHARIR, M., Computer Sciences
SHAVIT, Y., History of the Jewish People
SHAVIT, Y., Sociology and Anthropology
SHAVIT, Z., Semiotics and Cultural Research
SHEMER, J., Medicine
SHEMER, L., Mechanical Engineering
SHENKMAN, L., Medicine
SHILOH, Y., Human Genetics
SHOENFELD, Y., Medicine
SHOHAMY, E., Education
SHOHAT, M., Paediatrics
SHUSTIN, E., Mathematics
SIDI, Y., Medicine
SINGER, I., Cultures of the Ancient East
SINGER, S., Electrical Engineering
SIVASHINSKY, G., Applied Mathematics
SKORNICK, Y., Surgery
SKUTELSKY, E., Pathology
SNEH, B., Botany
SNYDERS, I., Electrical Engineering
SODIN, M., Mathematics
SOLOMON, B., Biotechnology
SOLOMON, Z., Social Work
SOUDRY, D., Mathematics
SPIEGLER, I., Management
STAVY, R., Teaching of Science
STEINBERG, B., Electrical Engineering
STERN, N., Medicine
STERNBERG, A., Physics
STERNBERG, M., Theory of Literature
STONE, L., Zoology
STRAUSS, S., Educational Psychology
TAL, H., Periodontology
TAMARKIN, M., History of Africa
TAMIR, A., Statistics
TAMSE, A., Endodontology
TARSI, M., Computer Sciences
TAUMAN, Y., Management
TEBOULLE, M., Operation Research and Stat-
istics
TE'ENI, D., Management
TEICHMAN, M., Psychology
TEICHMAN, Y., Psychology
TERKEL, J., Zoology
TIROSH, D., Teaching of Science
TISHLER, A., Management
TODER, V., Embryology

TOLEDANO, E., History of the Middle East
TOURY, G., Theory of Literature, Compara-
tive Literature
TSAL, Y., Psychology
TSIRELSON, B., Statistics
TUR, M., Electrical and Electronic Engineer-
ing
TUR-KASPA, R., Medicine
TURKEL, E., Mathematics
TYANO, S., Psychiatry
URBAKH, M., Chemistry
VERED, T., Cardiology
VIDNE, B., Surgery
VOLKOV, S., History
WEINER, I., Psychology
WEINSTEIN, E., Electrical and Electronic
Engineering
WEISMAN, Y., Paediatrics
WEISS, A., Electrical Engineering
WEISS, Y., Economics
WEIZMAN, A., Psychiatry
WEIZMAN, R., Psychiatry
WIENTROUB, S. H., Orthopaedic Surgery
WOLFSON, H., Computer Sciences
YAKAR, J., Archaeology
YANKIELOWICZ, S., Physics
YAROSLAVSKY, L., Electrical Engineering
YASSIF, E., Hebrew Literature
YEHUDAI, A., Computer Sciences
YINON, U., Physiology
YOGEV, A., Sociology of Education
YOM-TOV, Y., Zoology
ZADOK, R., History of the Jewish People and
Cultures of the Ancient East
ZAGAGI, N., Classical Studies
ZAHAVI, J., Management
ZAKAY, D., Psychology
ZALTZMAN, N., Law
ZANG, I., Management
ZILCHA, I., Economics
ZISAPEL, N., Biochemistry
ZONNENSCHEIN, J., Physics
ZWICK, U., Computer Sciences

TECHNION—ISRAEL INSTITUTE OF TECHNOLOGY

32000 Haifa
Telephone: (4) 8292111
Fax: (4) 8292000
E-mail: pard@tx.technion.ac.il
Internet: www.technion.ac.il
Founded 1912; inaugurated 1924
State control
Language of instruction: Hebrew
Academic year: October to July
Pres.: Prof. PERETZ LAVIE
Sr Exec. Vice-Pres.: Prof. PAUL D. FEIGIN
Exec. Vice-Pres. and Dir-Gen.: Dr AVITAL
STEIN
Exec. Vice-Pres. for Academic Affairs: Prof.
MOSHE SIDI
Exec. Vice-Pres. for Research: Prof. ODED
SHMUELI
Vice-Pres. for Resource Devt and External
Relations: Prof. RAPHAEL ROM
Dean of Undergraduate Studies: Prof. YAA-
COV MAMANE
Dean of Graduate School: Prof. MOSHE
SHPITALNI
Dean of Students: Prof. MICHAL GREEN
Library: see Libraries and Archives
Number of teachers: 993
Number of students: 12,665 (9,401 under-
graduate, 3,264 postgraduate)
Publications: *HaTechnion* (3 a year), *Shlomo
Kaplansky Memorial Series* (inc. in *Israel
Journal of Technology*), *The Joseph
Wunsch Lectures* (1 a year)

DEANS

Faculty of Aerospace Engineering: Prof.
YORAM TAMBOUR
Faculty of Architecture and Town Planning:
Prof. YERACH DOYTSHER

Faculty of Biology: Prof. GADI SCHUSTER
Faculty of Biotechnology and Food Engineer-
ing: Prof. BEN ZION LEVI
Faculty of Chemical Engineering: Prof.
YACHIN COHEN (Chair.)
Schulich Faculty of Chemistry: Prof. MORIS
EISEN
Faculty of Civil and Environmental Engin-
eering: Prof. ARNON BENTUR
Faculty of Computer Science: Prof. ELI BIHAM
Faculty of Electrical Engineering: Prof. ADAM
SHWARTZ
Faculty of Industrial Engineering and Man-
agement: Prof. BOAZ GOLANY
Faculty of Materials Engineering: Prof.
WAYNE D. KAPLAN
Faculty of Mathematics: Prof. JACOB RUBIN-
STEIN
Faculty of Mechanical Engineering: Prof.
PINHAS BAR-YOSEPH
Ruth and Bruce Rappaport Faculty of Medi-
cine: Prof. IDO PERLMAN
Faculty of Physics: Prof. NOAM SOKER
Dept of Biomedical Engineering: Dr DAN
ADAM (Head)
Dept of Education in Technology and Sci-
ence: Assoc. Prof. M. MOORE (Head)
Dept of Humanities and Arts: Prof. CHAR-
LOTTE SCHAPIRA (Head)

PROFESSORS

Faculty of Aerospace Engineering (tel. (4)
8292308; fax (4) 8292030; e-mail aerdean@
aerodyne.technion.ac.il; internet ae-www
.technion.ac.il):

  BAR-ITZHACK, I., Navigation, Guidance and
    Control
  DURBAN, D., Aerospace Structure
  GANY, A., Rocket Propulsion
  GIVOLI, D., Aerospace Structures, Compu-
    tational Mechanics
  GREENBERG, B., Combustion Theory
  GUELMAN, M., Space Engineering
  KARPEL, M., Aeroelasticity, Optimization
  RAND, O., Rotary Wings, Aerospace Struc-
    tures
  ROSEN, A., Rotary Wings, Aerospace Struc-
    ture
  TAMBOUR, Y., Combustion of Fuel Sprays
  WEIHS, D., Fluid Mechanics, Bio-Mechan-
    ics and Stability Theory
  WELLER, T., Aerospace Structures, Smart
    Structures Technology

Faculty of Architecture and Town Planning
(tel. (4) 8294001; fax (4) 8294617; e-mail
deanarc@tx.technion.ac.il; internet
architecture.technion.ac.il):

  ALTERMAN, R., Land Development
  AMIR, S., Regional Planning
  BURT, M., Ocean Architecture
  CARMON, N., Social Policy
  CHURCHMAN, A., Environmental Psych-
    ology
  SHAVIV, E., Energy and Architecture
  SHEFER, D., Urban and Regional Econom-
    ics

Faculty of Biology (tel. (4) 8294211; fax (4)
8225153; e-mail ddafna@tx.technion.ac.il;
internet biology.technion.ac.il):

  CASSEL, D., G-Proteins and Membrane
    Traffic
  SCHUSTER, G., Molecular Biology

Department of Biomedical Engineering (tel.
(4) 8294129; fax (4) 8294599; e-mail office@
bm.technion.ac.il; internet www.bm.technion
.ac.il):

  DINNAR, U., Cardiovascular Fluid Dynam-
    ics, Minimal Invasive Diagnosis
  LANIR, Y., Tissues Mechanics and Struc-
    ture, Cardiac Mechanics, Coronary Cir-
    culation
  MIZRAHI, J., Orthopaedic and Rehabilita-
    tion Biomechanics

Faculty of Biotechnology and Food Engineering (tel. (4) 8293068; fax (4) 8293399; e-mail biotech@tx.technion.ac.il; internet biotech .technion.ac.il):

COGAN, U., Food Chemistry
LEVI, B. Z., Mammalian Cell Biotechnology, Transcriptional Regulation, Innate Immunity
MILTZ, J., Packaging Engineering
SHOHAM, Y., Biochemical Engineering, Industrial Microbiology, Applied Enzymology

Faculty of Chemical Engineering (tel. (4) 8292820; fax (4) 8295672; e-mail chemeng@ technion.ac.il; internet chemeng.technion.ac .il):

COHEN, Y., Polymer Science and Engineering
GRADER, G., Ceramic Materials, Sol-Gel Systems
LEWIN, D. R., Process Design and Control
MARMUR, A., Interfaces and Colloids
NIR, A., Fluid Mechanics, Transport Phenomena
SEMIAT, R., Process Development, Separation Processes, Desalination, Electro-Optical Techniques for Fluid-Flow
SHEINTUCH, M., Chemical Reaction Engineering, Catalysis, Non-linear Dynamics
TALMON, Y., Complex Liquids, Electron Microscopy

Faculty of Chemistry (tel. (4) 8293727; fax (4) 8295860; e-mail chsabine@tx.technion.ac.il; internet schulich.technion.ac.il):

APELOIG, Y., Organosilicon and Computational Chemistry
BAASOV, T., Bio-organic Chemistry, Enzymology
EISEN, M., Polymer Chemistry, Organometallic Chemistry
GROSS, Z., Catalysis, Inorganic Chemistry, Bioinorganic Chemistry
KAFTORY, M., Chemical Crystallography
KEINAN, E., Biocatalysis, Organic Synthesis, Molecular Computing
KOLODNEY, E., Molecular Beams, Surface Chemistry
MAREK, I., Organic Synthesis
MOISEYEV, N., Quantum Chemistry
SCHLECTER, I., Analytical Chemistry
SPEISER, S., Laser Photophysics

Faculty of Civil and Environmental Engineering (tel. (4) 8293066; fax (4) 8220133; e-mail deansecr@technion.ac.il; internet cee .technion.ac.il):

BENTUR, A., Cementitious and Composite Building Materials
CEDER, A., Transportation Planning and Operation
DOYTSHER, Y., Mapping and Geo-Information Engineering
EISENBERGER, M., Computational Mechanics-Static, Dynamics, Stability Analysis
FROSTIG, Y., Sandwich Structures, Prestressed Concrete, Retrofitting of Concrete Structures, Tile-Wall Systems
FRYDMAN, S., Geotechnical Engineering
KIRSCH, U., Structural Engineering
LAUFER, A., Project Management
MAMANE, Y., Air Pollution Meteorology, Atmospheric Aerosols
MURAVSKI, G., Soil Structure Interaction
NEUMANN, P. M., Plant Physiology
POLUS, A., Traffic Flow and Congestion Modelling, Safety of Transportation Systems
RUBIN, H., Contaminant Hydrology
SHEINMAN, I., Post-Buckling, Dynamics, Static, Damage, Vibration Induced by People
STIASSNIE, M., Water Waves
UZAN, J., Pavement Engineering

YANKELEVSKY, D., Impact Engineering, Mechanics of Reinforced Concrete, Earthquake Engineering
ZIMMELS, Y., Environmental and Process Engineering

Faculty of Computer Science (tel. (4) 8294313; fax (4) 8294353; e-mail itai@cs .technion.ac.il; internet www.cs.technion.ac .il):

BARAM, Y., Pattern Recognition, Artificial Neural Network
BIHAM, E., Cryptology
BRUCKSTEIN, A., Image Processing
BSHOUTY, N., Computational Learning Theory
FRANCEZ, N., Semantics and Verification, Computational Linguistics
GRUMBERG, O., Formal Verification
ISRAELI, M., Scientific Computing, Numerical Methods, Computational Linguistics
ITAI, A., Analysis of Algorithms and Data Structures, Computational Linguistics
KUSHILEVITZ, E., Complexity and Cryptography
MAKOWSKY, J., Mathematical Logic Computability and Complexity, Combinatorial Algorithms, Database Theory
MORAN, S., Search Methods on the Web
ROTH, R., Coding Theory
SIDI, A., Theoretical Numerical Analysis and Scientific Computing
SHMUELI, O., Databases: Systems and Theory
UNGARISH, M., Modelling and Numerical Simulation of Fluid Flows
ZAKS, S., Distributed Computing and Communication Networks

Faculty of Electrical Engineering (tel. (4) 8294680; fax (4) 8295757; e-mail eedean@ee .technion.ac.il; internet www.ee.technion.ac .il):

CIDON, I., Communication Networks
EISENSTEIN, G., Optoelectronics
FEUER, A., Automatic Control
FINKMAN, E., Quantum Hetrostructure
FISCHER, B., Optoelectronics
LEVIATAN, Y., Electromagnetic Waves
MALAH, D., Digital Signal Processing of Speech and Images
MERHAV, N., Information Theory
ROM, R., Communication Networks
SALZMAN, J., Optoelectronics
SCHIEBER, D., Energy Conversion
SEGALL, A., Computer Networks
SHAMAI, S., Information Theory
SHWARTZ, A., Large Deviations Theory
SIDI, M., Computer Networks
TANNENBAUM, A., Robust Control Theory
ZEEVI, Y., Vision and Image Sciences
ZEITOUNI, Z., Large Deviations Theory
ZIV, J., Statistical Communication, Information Theory

Faculty of Industrial Engineering and Management (tel. (4) 8294444; fax (4) 8295676; e-mail iedean@ie.technion.ac.il; internet iew3.technion.ac.il):

ADLER, R., Stochastic Processes
BEN-TAL, A., Non-linear Optimization
EREV, I., Behavioural Sciences and Experimental Economics
EREZ, M., Organizational Psychology
DE-HAAN, U., Entrepreneurship
FEIGIN, P., Applied Statistics
GOLANY, B., Industrial Engineering
GOPHER, D., Human Factors
KASPI, H., Probability and Stochastic Processes
MANDELBAUM, A., Operations Research, Stochastic Processes and their Applications
MONDERER, D., Game Theory
NEMIROVSKY, A., Optimization Complexity Theory
NOTEA, A., Non-Destructive Testing

ROTHBLUM, U. G., Operations Research
RUBINSTEIN, R., Stochastic Systems
SHTUB, A., Project Management
TENNENHOLTZ, M., Artificial Intelligence
WEISSMAN, I., Probability and Statistics

Faculty of Materials Engineering (tel. (4) 8294591; fax (4) 8295677; e-mail oilana@tx .technion.ac.il; internet materials.technion .ac.il):

EIZENBERG, M., Electronic Materials
GUTMANAS, E., Processing of High-Performance Material
KOMEM, Y., Electronic Materials
LIFSHITZ, Y., Nanostructured Inorganic Materials
SHECHTMAN, D., Properties and Microstructure of Intermetallic Compounds
SIEGMANN, A., Polymers and Plastic Structuring
ZOLOTOYABKO, E., X-Ray Diffraction

Faculty of Mathematics (tel. (4) 8223071; fax (4) 8324654; e-mail mathsee@tx.technion.ac .il; internet www.math.technion.ac.il):

AHARONI, R., Combinatorics
AHARONOV, D., Complex Analysis
BENYAMINI, Y., Banach Spaces
BERMAN, A., Matrix Theory
BSHOUTY, D., Complex Analysis, Probability Theory, Mathematical Statistics
CHILLAG, D., Algebra Group Theory
CWIKEL, M., Functional Analysis and Interpolation Space
GOLDBERG, M., Numerical Analysis
GORDON, Y., Functional Analysis
HERSHKOWITZ, D., Matrix Theory
IOFFE, A., General Theory of Sub-differentials
KATCHALSKI, M., Combinatorial Geometry
LERER, L., Linear Algebra, Operator Theory
LIRON, N., Applied Mathematics
LOEWY, R., Linear Algebra
MARCUS, M., Partial Differential Equations, Non-linear Analysis
NEPOMNYASHCHY, A., Fluid Mechanics
PINKUS, A., Approximation Theory
PINSKY, R., Probability and Stochastic Processes, Partial Differential Equations
REICH, S., Non-linear Analysis
RUBINSTEIN, J., Applied Mathematics
SOLEL, B., Operator Theory, Functional Analysis
SONN, J., Algebraic Number Theory
WAJNRYB, B., Algebraic Geometry
ZEITOUNI, O., Probability and Stochastic Processes
ZIEGLER, Z., Theory of Approximation

Faculty of Mechanical Engineering (tel. (4) 8292079; fax (4) 8295710; e-mail iritg@ technion.ac.il; internet meeng.technion.ac.il):

ALTUS, E., Micro-Mechanics of Solids
BAR-YOSEPH, P., Finite Element Analysis
BEN-HAIM, Y., Decisions under Uncertainty, Reliability
DEGANI, D., Computational Fluid Dynamics
ELIAS, E., Thermohydraulics, Nuclear Engineering
ETSION, I., Tribology, Lubrication
GROSSMAN, G., Thermodynamics, Heat Pumps, Cooling and Air-Conditioning
GUTMAN, S., Relative Stability of Linear Dynamic Systems
HABER, S., Particulate Systems
PALMOR, Z., Digital Control of Industrial and Mechanical Systems
RUBIN, M., Continuum Mechanics
SHAPIRO, M., Porous Media, Aerosols
SHITZER, A., Bio-Heat Transfer
SHOHAM, M., Robotics and Medical Robotics
SHPITALNI, M., CAD/CAM, Manufacturing
TIROSH, J., Fracture Mechanics
YARIN, A., Rheology, Fluid Mechanics
YARIN, L. P., Two-Phase Flow, Combustion

ZVIRIN, Y., Solar Energy, Internal Combustion Engines

Faculty of Medicine (POB 9649, Bat Galim, 31096 Haifa; tel. (4) 8292111; fax (4) 8517008; e-mail md@tx.technion.ac.il; internet md.technion.ac.il):

AVIRAM, M., Lipid Research Laboratory
BENJAMIN, B., Haematology
BEYAR, R., Invasive Cardiology
CIECHANOVER, A., Intercellular Breakdown of Proteins
ETZIONI, A., Paediatrics and Immunology
FINBERG, J., Neuropharmacology
FINSOD, M., Neurosurgery
FRY, M., Enzymology of DNA Replication
GAVISH, M., Molecular Pharmacology
HASIN, Y., Cardiology
HERSHKO, A., Intracellular Protein Degradation
ITSKOVITZ, J., Human Embryonic Stem Cells
KRAUSZ, M., General Surgery
LAVIE, P., Psychobiology, Sleep Research
LEWIS, B., Cardiology
NEUFELD, G., Angiogenesis
PALTI, Y., Physiology and Biophysics
PERLMAN, I., Vision Neurophysiology
PRATT, H., Behavioural Sciences
ROWE, Y., Haematology
SHALEV, E., Obstetrics and Gynaecology
SKORECKI, K., Nephrology, Molecular Medicine
VOLDAVSKY, I., Vascular and Tumour Biology, Biochemistry
YOUDIM, M., Neuropharmacology

Faculty of Physics (tel. (4) 8293909; fax (4) 8295755; e-mail office@physics.technion.ac.il; internet physics.technion.ac.il):

AKKERMANS, E., Theory of Condensed Matter Physics, Mesoscopic Quantum
AUERBACH, A., Condensed Matter Theory
AVRON, J., Mathematical Physics
BRAUN, E., Biophysics, Non-linear Dynamics of Systems out of Equilibrium
COHEN, E., Spectroscopic Properties of Laser Materials
DADO, S., High-Energy Physics Experimentation
DAR, A., Astroparticle Physics
EHRENFREUND, E., Semiconducting Quantum Structures and Polymers
EILAM, G., Elementary Particle Physics
FELSTEINER, J., Condensed Matter Physics, Plasma Physics
FISHMAN, S., Quantum Chaos
GERSHONI, D., Semiconducting Quantum Heterostructures
GRONAU, M., Theoretical High Energy Physics
KALISH, R., Ion-Implantation—Hyperfine Interactions
KOREN, G., Superconductivity and Lasers
LIPSON, S., Low Temperature Physics
MANN, A., Theoretical Physics
MOSHE, M., Theoretical High Energy Physics
ORI, A., General Relativity, Black Holes, Gravitational Radiation
POLTURAK, E., High Temperature Superconductors
REGEV, O., Astrophysics
RIESS, I., Solid State Electrochemistry
SEGEV, M., Nonlinear Optics
SHAPIRO, B., Theory of Condensed Matter
SHAVIV, G., Astrophysics
SIVAN, U., Mesoscopic Physics, Bio-Electronics
SOKER, N., Astrophysics Theory

WEIZMANN INSTITUTE OF SCIENCE

POB 26, 76100 Rehovot
Telephone: (8) 9342111
Fax: (8) 9344107
E-mail: news@weizmann.ac.il
Internet: www.weizmann.ac.il

Founded 1949, incl. the Daniel Sieff Research Institute (f. 1934).

Private non-profit corporation for fundamental and applied research in the natural and exact sciences; the Feinberg Graduate School offers MSc and PhD courses

Pres.: Prof. DANIEL ZAJFMAN
Vice-Pres.: Prof. HAIM GARTY
Vice-Pres. for Admin. and Finance: Dr ISAAC SHARIV
Vice-Pres. for Resource Devt and Public Affairs: Prof. ISRAEL BAR-JOSEPH
Vice-Pres. for Technology Transfer: Prof. MORDECHAI SHEVES
Chief Librarian: Mrs I. POLLACK
Library: see Libraries and Archives
Number of teachers: 300
Number of students: 785 postgraduates

DEANS

Faculty of Biochemistry: Prof. ZVI LIVNEH
Faculty of Biology: Prof. MICHAL NEEMAN
Faculty of Chemistry: Prof. YEHIAM PRIOR
Faculty of Mathematics and Computer Science: Prof. DAVID PELEG
Faculty of Physics: Prof. YOSEF NIR
Feinberg Graduate School: Prof. LIA ADDADI

DIRECTORS OF CENTRES

Faculty of Biochemistry:

Avron-Wilstätter Minerva Center for Research in Photosynthesis: Prof. A. SCHERZ
Charles W. and Tillie K. Lubin Center for Plant Biotechnology: Prof. AVRAHAM LEVY
Crown Human Genome Center: Prof. DORON LANCET
David and Fela Shapell Family Center for Genetic Disorders Research: Prof. YORAM GRONER
Dr Joseph Cohn Minerva Center for Biomembrane Research: Prof. EITAN BIBI
Harry and Jeanette Weinberg Center for Plant Molecular Genetics Research: Prof. AVRAHAM LEVY
Kekst Family Center for Medical Genetics: Prof. YORAM GRONER
Leo and Julia Forchheimer Center for Molecular Genetics: Prof. YOSEF SHAUL
M. D. Moross Institute for Cancer Research: Prof. YORAM GRONER
Mel Dobrin Center for Nutrition: Prof. AVRAHAM LEVY
Y. Leon Benoziyo Institute for Molecular Medicine: Prof. ZVI LIVNEH

Faculty of Biology:

Belle S. and Irving E. Meller Center for Biology of Ageing: Prof. YAIR REISNER
Carl and Micaela Einhorn-Dominic Institute for Brain Research: Prof. YADIN DUDAI
Gabrielle Rich Center for Transplantation Biology Research: Prof. YAIR REISNER
Helen and Martin Kimmel Institute for Stem Cell Research: Prof. DOV ZIPORI
Kirk Center for Childhood Cancer and Immunological Disorders: Prof. BENJAMIN GEIGER
Murray H. and Meyer Grodetsky Center for Research of Higher Brain Functions: Prof. AMIRAM GRINVALD
Nella and Leon Benoziyo Center for Neurological Diseases: Prof. ANTHONY H. FUTERMAN
Nella and Leon Benoziyo Center for Neurosciences: Prof. YADIN DUDAI
Norman and Helen Asher Center for for Brain Imaging: Prof. YADIN DUDAI
Wilner Family Center for Vascular Biology: Prof. NAVA DEKEL
Women's Health Research Center: Prof. VARDA ROTTER

Yad Abraham Research Center for Cancer Diagnostics and Therapy: Prof. VARDA ROTTER

Faculty of Chemistry:

Center for Energy Research: Prof. JACOB KARNI
Fritz Haber Center for Physical Chemistry: Prof. LUCIO FRYDMAN
Gerhardt M. J. Schmidt Minerva Center for Supermolecular Architecture: Prof. DAVID CAHEN
Helen and Martin Kimmel Center for Archaeological Science: Prof. STEPHEN WEINER
Helen and Martin Kimmel Center for Molecular Design: Prof. DAVID MILSTEIN
Helen and Martin Kimmel Center for Nanoscale Science: Prof. RESHEF TENNE
Helen and Milton A. Kimmelman Center for Biomolecular Structure and Assembly: Prof. ADA E. YONATH
Ilse Katz Institute for Material Sciences and Magnetic Resonance Research: Prof. YEHIAM PRIOR
Joseph and Ceil Mazer Center for Structural Biology: Prof. ZIPPORA SHAKKED
Moskowitz Center for Nano and Bio-nano Imaging: Prof. ABRAHAM MINSKY
Sussman Family Center for the Study of Environmental Sciences: Prof. BRIAN BERKOWITZ

Faculty of Mathematics and Computer Science:

Arthur and Rochelle Belfer Institute of Mathematics and Computer Science: Prof. DAVID PELEG
Ida Kohen Centre for Mathematics: Prof. DAVID PELEG
John von Neumann Minerva Center for the Development of Reactive Systems: Prof. DAVID HAREL

Faculty of Physics:

Albert Einstein Minerva Center for Theoretical Physics: Prof. MORDEHAI MILGROM
Benoziyo Center for Astrophysics: Prof. ELI WAXMAN
Center for Experimental Physics: Prof. YOSEF NIR
Crown Photonics Center: Prof. YARON SILBERBERG
Joseph H. and Belle R. Braun Center for Submicron Research: Prof. MOTY HEIBLUM
Maurice and Gabriela Goldschleger Center for Nanophysics: Prof. MOTY HEIBLUM
Minerva Center for Non-linear Physics of Complex Systems: Prof. ITAMAR PROCACCIA
Nella and Leo Benoziyo Center for High Energy Physics: Prof. GIORA MIKENBERG

Feinberg Graduate School:

Aharon Katzir-Katchalsky Center: Prof. LIA ADDADI
Dwek Family Research School of Chemical Science: Prof. GILAD HARAN
Ekard Research School of Biological Science: Prof. ARI ELSON
Lorry I. Lokey Research School of Biochemical Science: Prof. ARI ELSON
Moross Research School of Mathematics and Computer Science: Prof. RAN RAZ
Research School of Physical Science: Prof. SHIMON LEVIT

Colleges and Higher Institutes

Academic Centre Ruppin: PO Academic Center Ruppin, 40250 Emek Hefer; tel. (9) 8983005; fax (9) 8983021; e-mail rani@ruppin .ac.il; internet www.ruppin.ac.il; f. 1949;

three-year degree courses in accounting, business admin. and behavioural sciences, economics; two-year courses in architecture, basic trades, computers, electrical engineering, industrial management, landscape architecture, megatronics, soil and water engineering; short courses in accounting and mechanics, basic economics; school of engineering: electrical, industrial and computer science; library: 30,000 vols; 350 teachers; 5,000 students; Pres. Prof. SHOSH ARAD; Dir ZVIKA LEVIN.

Academic Centre of Law and Business: 26 Ben Gurion St, 52275 Ramat-Gan; tel. (3) 6000800; fax (3) 6000801; e-mail info@rg-law .ac.il; internet www.clb.ac.il; depts of communication and technology, criminal law and criminology and law, human rights; 1,000 students; Dean Prof. PINHAS SHIFMAN.

Academic College of Tel-Aviv-Yaffo: 4 Antokolsky St, POB 16131, 61161 Tel-Aviv; tel. (3) 5211840; fax (3) 5211870; e-mail mirsham@mta.ac.il; internet www.mta.ac.il; Bachelors of Arts degrees in computer science, behavioural science, management, society and politics.

Bezalel Academy of Arts and Design: Mount Scopus, POB 24046, 91240 Jerusalem; tel. (2) 5893333; fax (2) 5823094; e-mail mail@bezalel.ac.il; internet www.bezalel.ac .il; f. 1906; degree courses in architecture, design, animation, ceramics and glass design, fine arts, Gold- and Silver-smithin-gindustrial design, jewellery and fashion accessories design,photography, visual communication, video and computer imaging; library: 35,000 vols; 300 teachers; 1,600 students; Pres. Prof. ARNON ZUCKERMAN.

Ecole Biblique et Ecole Archéologique Française: 6 Nablus Rd, POB 19053, 91190 Jerusalem; tel. (2) 6264468; fax (2) 6282567; e-mail directeur@ebaf.edu; internet ebaf.op .org; f. 1890; research, Biblical and Oriental studies, exploration and excavation in Palestine; 14 professors; library, see Libraries; Dir PAULINE BOILARD; publs Cahiers de la Revue Biblique, Etudes Annexes, Etudes Bibliques, Littératures anciennes du Proche Orient, Revue Biblique (4 a year).

Hadassah College: 37 Hanevi'im St, POB 1114, 91010 Jerusalem; tel. (2) 6291911; fax (2) 6250619; e-mail info@hadassah.ac.il; internet www.hadassah.ac.il; f. 1970; comprises Hadassah Academic College (depts of communication disorders, computer sciences, medical laboratory sciences, optometry, , Hadassah College of Technology (depts of dental technology, cinema and television production, hotel management, photography and digital media, industrial design, printing and computer graphics, technical software engineering), Tachlit Centre for Lifelong Learning; Pres. Prof. NAVA BEN ZVI.

Hebrew Union College—Jewish Institute of Religion: 13 King David St, 94101 Jerusalem; tel. (2) 6203333; fax (2) 6251478; e-mail mzakai@huc.edu; internet www.huc .edu; f. 1963; br. of the same instn in the United States of America; the first year of graduate rabbinic studies, Jewish education, cantorial training and programme in biblical archaeology, incl. summer excavations; Rabbinic programme for Israel Reform (Progressive); English 'Lehrhaus' study programmes in classical Jewish Literature for gen. public (Bet Midrash); Skirball Museum of Biblical Archaeology; library: Abramov library of 40,000 vols; microfilm colln from American Jewish Archives; 35 teachers; 150 students; Pres. Dr DAVID ELLENSON; Dean Rabbi MICHAEL MARMUR.

International Institute of Histadrut: Beit Berl, 44905 Kfar Saba; tel. (9) 7612303; fax (9) 7456962; e-mail info@peoples.org.il; internet www.peoples.org.il; f. 1958 to train labour and cooperative movements, professional assocs and women's and youth orgs; candidates nominated by trade unions, cooperatives, univs, int. labour orgs, etc.; courses and seminars in fields of labour, social and economic devt and cooperative studies in Arabic, English, French, Russian and Spanish; 41,400 graduates from 140 countries; library: 15,000 vols, and monographs and periodicals; 8 teachers; 1,400 students; Dir-Gen. MICHAEL FROHLICH; Academic Dir SERDIO GRYN.

Jerusalem Academy of Music and Dance: Givat Ram Campus, 91904 Jerusalem; tel. (2) 6759911; fax (2) 6512824; e-mail schul@jamd.ac.il; internet www.jamd.ac.il; f. 1947; performing arts, composition, conducting and theory, music education, dance; awards BMus., BEdMus., Dance and Artists' Diplomas; courses leading to BAMus., MAMus. and MMus. in cooperation with the Hebrew University; Conservatory and High School (Music and Dance); 190 teachers; 550 students; library: 60,000 vols; colln of musical instruments; electroacoustic laboratory; Pres. Prof. ILAN SCHUL; Dir-Gen MICHA TAL.

Jerusalem College of Technology: 21 Havaad Haleumi St, POB 16031, 91160 Jerusalem; tel. (2) 6751111; fax (2) 6751068; e-mail pr@jct.ac.il; internet www.jct.ac.il; f. 1969; 4-year first degree courses; library: 20,000 vols; 106 teachers (66 full-time, 40 part-time); 2,660 students; Pres. Prof. JOSEPH S. BODENHEIMER; Rector Prof. MENACHEM STEINER; Librarian ZVI SOBEL.

Jerusalem University College: POB 1276, Mount Zion, 91012 Jerusalem; tel. (2) 6718628; fax (2) 6732717; e-mail paulwright@juc.edu; internet www.juc.edu; f. 1957; also known as American Institute of Holy Land Studies; Christian study centre at univ. level; graduate and undergraduate courses in the geography, history, languages, religions and cultures of Israel in the Middle East context; field trips and archaeological excavation programme; 20 teachers; 200 students; Pres. Dr PAUL WRIGHT.

Mosad Harav Kook: POB 642, Jerusalem; tel. (2) 6526231; fax (2) 6526968; internet www.mosadharavkook.com; f. 1937 to educate and train young men for research in the field of Torah Literature and to infuse the original Hebrew culture in all classes of the people; library: Rav Maimon Library of Judaica; religious Zionist Archives; publs Torah-Science books, incl. the printing of MSS of previously unpublished Rishonim works that are still retained in Genizah form, popular commentary to the entire Bible; incorporates Institute for Chasiduth; Dir Rabbi JOSEPH MOVSHOVITZ.

ORT Braude College: POB 78, 21982 Karmiel; tel. (4) 9901911; fax (4) 9901715; e-mail rishum@braude.ac.il; internet www .braude.ac.il; f. 1988; B.Tech degree programmes in Biotechnology Engineering, Electrical and Electronics Engineering, Mechanical Engineering, Industrial and Management Engineering, and Software Engineering; also Practical Engineering 2-year degree programmes; library: 50,000 vols; 320 teachers; 1,200 undergraduate students; Pres. Prof. YOHANAN ARZI.

Pontifical Biblical Institute: POB 497, 3 Paul-Emile Botta St, 91004 Jerusalem; tel. (2) 6252843; fax (2) 6241203; e-mail admipib@gmail.com; internet www.biblico.it/ jerusalem.html; f. 1913 as a br. of the Pontifical Biblical Institute of Rome, Italy; fosters the study of Biblical geography and archaeology; provides courses for students and graduates of Roman Institute; Prehisto-rical Museum containing discoveries of Tele-ilat Ghassul, a chalcolithic site in the Jordan valley, excavated by the Institute; library: 26,000 vols for biblical studies; Dir Rev. JOSEPH DOAN CÔNG NGUYÊN.

Shenkar College of Engineering and Design: 12 Anne Frank St, 52526 Ramat-Gan; tel. (3) 6110045; fax (3) 7521141; e-mail info@shenkar.ac.il; internet www.shenkar.ac .il; f. 1970; Bachelors degrees and research in industrial management and marketing, computer science, plastics engineering, industrial chemistry, industrial engineering, fashion design, textile and interior design, jewellery design, industrial design; library: 20,000 vols, 250 periodicals; 50 teachers; 2,180 students (680 full-time, 1,500 part-time); Pres. Prof. AMOTZ WEINBERG; Man. Dir GUY PERETZ.

Studium Biblicum Franciscanum: POB 19424, Monastery of the Flagellation, 91193 Jerusalem; tel. (2) 6270485; fax (2) 6264519; e-mail secretary@studiumbiblicum.org; internet www.custodia.org/sbf; f. 1927; centre of archaeological research sponsored by the Franciscan Custody of the Holy Land, biblical and archaeological faculty of the Pontificium Athenaeum Antonianum, Rome, for degrees of Bachelors in theology, Licentiate and Doctorate in biblical sciences and archaeology, and diploma in oriental biblical studies and archaeology and in biblical formation; 15 teachers; 80 students; Dean G. C. BOTTINI; publs Analecta, Collectio Maior, Collectio Minor, Liber Annuus, Museum.

Tel Hai Academic College: 12210 Upper Galilee; tel. (4) 8181785; fax (4) 6900919; e-mail telhai@telhai.ac.il; internet www .telhai.ac.il; f. 1957; Bachelors degree courses in biotechnology and environmental sciences, nutrition sciences, education, economics and management, social work, computer science, multidisciplinary studies; Diploma courses in architecture, construction, electronics and electricity, computers, mechanics and machinery, industrial management, telemedia and communication, drama therapy; art institute courses in sculpture, drawing, ceramics, photography and ethnic crafts; 500 teachers; 4,000 students; Pres. Prof. ZEKI BERK; Vice-Pres. for Academic Affairs Prof. SHMUEL SHAMAI.

Ulpan Akiva Netanya, International Hebrew Study Centre: POB 6086, 42160 Netanya; tel. (9) 8352312; fax (9) 8652919; e-mail ulpanakv@netvision.net.il; internet www.ulpan-akiva.org; f. 1951; basic and supplementary courses in Arabic and Hebrew; cultural studies; 45 teachers; Dir ESTHER PERRON.

Yeshivat Dvar Yerushalayim (Jerusalem Academy of Jewish Studies): 53 Katzenellenbogen, Har Nof, POB 34580, 344 Jerusalem; tel. (2) 6522817; fax (2) 6522827; e-mail dvar@dvar.org.il; internet www.dvar.org.il; f. 1970; runs courses in English, French, Spanish, Russian and Hebrew on the Bible, Hebrew, Talmud, philosophy, ethics and Halacha; 500 mems; library: 5,000 vols; 7 teachers; 70 students; Dean Rabbi B. HOROVITZ; Exec. Dir Rabbi E. ALTHEIM; publ. Jewish Studies Magazine (1 a year).

Zinman College of Physical Education and Sport Sciences at the Wingate Institute: 42902 Netanya; tel. (9) 8639222; fax (9) 8650960; e-mail zinman@wincol.macam.ac.il; internet www.wincol.ac.il; f. 1944; four-year BEd programme, M.P.E. programme at the college, MA programme in conjunction with Haifa Univ.; in-service training; library: 52,000 vols, 180 periodicals; 450 teachers; 950 regular students, 3,000 students on other courses; Rector Prof. Dr MICHAEL SAGIV.

ITALY

The Higher Education System

Italy's first universities were established during the 10th to the 13th century and are among the oldest in Europe; in fact, Università degli Studi di Parma (AD 962) is Europe's oldest university, and other long-established universities include Università di Bologna (founded 1088), Università degli Studi di Modena e Reggio Emilia (founded 1175) and Università degli Studi di Perugia (founded 1200). Several universities date from the 14th to the 16th century. In 2006/07 there were 1.8m. undergraduate students in higher education in Italy; the largest universities were La Sapienza in Rome, with around 170,000 students, and Bologna, with more than 100,000 students. In 2005/06 there were 74 institutes of higher education. Italian universities operate on the European Credit Transfer System (ECTS), and Italy also participates in the Bologna Process to establish a European Higher Education Area. The Ministry of Universities and Research is the government agency responsible for higher education. In addition to universities, there are four other types of State-recognized institutions of higher education: academies of arts education, higher institutes of applied arts, the national school for cinema studies and national institutes or schools for cultural restoration and preservation.

Admission to higher education is primarily based on the higher secondary school certificate (Diploma di Esame di Stato), though institutions may also administer entrance examinations. Since the implementation of the Bologna Process in 1999 the universities have adopted a two-tier Bachelors and Masters degree system. The Bachelors degree (Laurea) is a three-year programme that requires 180 credits. Undergraduates in specialized or professional fields that require longer periods of study, such as medicine (six years), pharmacy, architecture and law (all five years), may carry credits over into the Laurea Specialistica. Alternatively, the Laurea Specialistica may be awarded as a conventional Masters-type degree after one to three years study following the Laurea. Dottorato di Ricerca is the standard doctoral degree programme, and admission is on the basis of the Laurea Specialistica and institutional requirements.

A decree was made in 2008 allowing universities to become private sector foundations, though by 2010 none had yet taken up the option.

Regulatory and Representative Bodies

GOVERNMENT

Ministry of Cultural Heritage and Activities: Via del Collegio Romano 27, 00186 Rome; tel. 06-67231; fax 06-6798441; e-mail urp@beniculturali.it; internet www.beniculturali.it; Minister SANDRO BONDI.

Ministry of Education, Universities and Research: *Education Section:* Viale Trastevere, 76A, 00153 Rome; *Universities and Research Section:* Piazza Kennedy 20, 00144 Rome; tel. *Education Section:* 06-58491; tel. *Universities and Research Section:* 06-97721; e-mail urp@istruzione.it; internet www.istruzione.it; Minister MARIASTELLA GELMINI.

ACCREDITATION

Comitato Nazionale per la Valutazione del Sistema Universitario (National Committee for the Evaluation of the University System): Piazzale Kennedy 20, 00144 Rome; tel. 06-97726401; fax 06-97726480; e-mail valuniv@miur.it; internet www.cnvsu.it; Pres. Prof. LUIGI BIGGERI.

ENIC/NARIC Italy/Centro di Informazione sulla Mobilità e le Equivalenze Accademiche (Information Centre on Academic Mobility and Equivalence): Viale Ventuno Aprile 36, 00162 Rome; tel. 06-86321281; fax 06-86322845; e-mail cimea@fondazionerui.it; internet www.cimea.it; f. 1984; Dir Dott. CARLO FINOCCHIETTI.

Istituto Nazionale per la Valutazione del Sistema Educativo di Istruzione e di Formazione (National Institute for the Assessment of the Educational System): Villa Falconieri, Via Borromini 5, 00044 Frascati; tel. 06-941851; fax 06-94185215; e-mail biblioteca@invalsi.it; internet www.invalsi.it; f. 1974; library of 9,500 vols, 235 current periodicals; Dir ANTONIO PILEGGI; Head Librarian RITA MARZOLI.

NATIONAL BODIES

Conferenza dei Rettori delle Università Italiane (Italian University Rectors' Conference): Palazzo Rondanini, Piazza Rondanini 48, 00186 Rome; tel. 06-684411; fax 06-68441399; e-mail segreteriacrui@crui.it; internet www.crui.it; f. 1963; Pres. Prof. ENRICO DECLEVA; Exec. Dir Dott. EMANUELA STEFANI.

Consiglio Universitario Nazionale (National University Council): Piazzale Kennedy 20, 00144 Rome; tel. 06-97727502; fax 06-97726031; e-mail cun@miur.it; internet www.cun.it; f. 1997; 57 mem. univs; Pres. Prof. ANDREA LENZI; Sec. Dott. ANTONIO VALEO.

Istituto per la Cooperazione Universitaria Onlus (Institute for University Co-operation): Viale G. Rossini 26, 00198 Rome; tel. 06-93938367; fax 06-1786034698; e-mail info@icu.it; internet www.icu.it; f. 1967 to promote cultural relations between different countries, chiefly through univ. cooperation, int. meetings and study groups; int. technical cooperation by sending volunteers and experts to developing countries; Pres. GIOVANNI DIANA; Gen. Sec. ANDREA VIGEVANI; publs *Educazione e Sviluppo* (irregular), *SIPE—Servizio Stampa Educazione e Sviluppo* (6 a year).

Fondazione Rui: Viale XXI Aprile 36, 00162 Rome; tel. 06-86321281; fax 06-86322845; e-mail info@fondazionerui.it; internet www.fondazionerui.it; f. 1959; library of 3,000 vols; Pres. Prof. CRISTIANO CIAPPEI; Dir Dr FABIO MONTI; publs *Fondazione Rui* (4 a year), *Universitas*.

Learned Societies

GENERAL

Accademia delle Scienze dell'Istituto di Bologna (Academy of Sciences of the Bologna Institute): Via Zamboni 31, 40126 Bologna; tel. 051-222596; fax 051-265249; e-mail accademiascienze@libero.it; internet www.unibo.it/portale/ateneo/divulgazione+scientifica/accademia/default.htm; f. 1711; organizes national and international conventions and conferences; promotes studies of art restoration and art history; 60 mems; 200 corresp. mems; Pres. Prof. ILLIO GALLIGANI; Sec. Prof. RUGGERO BORTOLAMI.

Accademia delle Scienze di Ferrara (Academy of Sciences of Ferrara): Via de Romei 3, 44100 Ferrara; tel. 0532-205209; fax 0532-205209; e-mail info@accademiascienze.ferrara.it; internet www.accademiascienze.ferrara.it; f. 1823; sections of Medical Sciences, Mathematics, Physics, Chemistry and Natural Sciences, Law, Economics, History and Moral Sciences; 270 mems; library of 12,500 vols; Pres. Prof. ROBERTO TOMATIS; Sec. Avv. VINCENZO CAPUTO; publ. *Atti*.

Accademia delle Scienze di Torino (Academy of Sciences of Turin): Via Maria Vittoria 3, 10123 Turin; tel. 011-5620047; fax 011-532619; e-mail presidenza@accademia.csi.it; internet www.accademiadellescienze.it; f. 1783; sections of Physics, Mathematics and Natural Sciences, Moral Sciences, History and Philology; 310 mems; library: see Libraries and Archives; Pres. Prof. PIETRO ROSSI; publs *Atti* (edns for physical, mathematical and natural sciences, and for moral sciences, history and philology, 1 a year each), *Memorie* (edns for physical, mathematical and natural sciences, and for moral sciences, history and philology, 1 a year each), *Quaderni* (irregular).

Accademia Etrusca (Etruscan Academy): Palazzo Casali, Piazza Signorelli 9, 52044 Cortona; tel. 0575-637248; fax 0575-637248; e-mail accademia_etrusca@libero.it; internet www.accademia-etrusca.org; f. 1727; promotes knowledge of the culture and history of the Cortona area and of Etruscan archaeological discoveries; 80 mems; 50 hon. mems; 80 corresp. mems; Pres. Dott. GIOVANNANGELO CAMPOREALE; Vice-Pres. and Sec. Prof. EDOARDO MIRRI; publs *Annuario* (every

2 years), *Cortona Francescana*, *Fonti e Testi*, *Note e Documenti*.

Accademia Gioenia di Catania: Via Fragalà 10, 95100 Catania; e-mail malber@unict.it; internet www.unict.it/gioenia; f. 1824; sections of Natural Sciences, Physics, Chemistry and Mathematics, and Applied Sciences; 56 mems, 57 corresp. mems; library of 20,000 vols, 400 periodicals; Pres. Prof. SALVATORE FOTI; Gen. Sec. Prof. GIORGIO MONTAUDO; publs *Atti della Accademia Gioenia di Scienze Naturali in Catania*, *Bollettino delle Sedute della Accademia Gioenia di Scienze Naturali in Catania*.

Accademia Ligure di Scienze e Lettere (Ligurian Academy of Sciences and Letters): Piazza G. Matteotti 5, 16123 Genoa; tel. 010-565570; fax 010-566080; e-mail accademialigure@fastwebnet.it; f. 1798; 180 mems (30 ordinary and 50 corresp. in each class; 20 hon.); library of 60,000 vols; Pres. Profa PAOLA MASSA PERGIOVANNI; Sec.-Gen. Dott. G. P. PELOSO; publs *Atti* (1 a year), *Studi e Ricerche*.

Accademia Nazionale dei Lincei: Palazzo Corsini, Via della Lungara 10, 00165 Rome; tel. 06-680271; fax 06-6893616; e-mail segreteria@lincei.it; internet www.lincei.it; f. 1603; sections of Physical, Mathematical and Natural Sciences (Academic Secs Prof. GIANCARLO SETTI, Prof. ANNIBALE MOTTANA), Moral, Historical and Philological Sciences (Academic Secs Prof. ANTONIO GIULIANO, Prof. FULVIO TESSITORE); 540 mems (180 nat., 180 corresp., 180 foreign); library: see Libraries and Archives; Pres. Prof. LAMBERTO MAFFEI; Vice-Pres. Prof. ALBERTO QUADRIO CURZIO; Academic Administrator Prof. LUCIANO MARTINI; Academic Administrator Prof. PIETRO RESCIGNO; publs *Memorie: Classe di Scienze Morali, Storiche e Filologiche* (irregular), *Memorie Lincee, Classe di Scienze Morali, Storiche e Filologiche* (4 a year), *Memorie Lincee, Matematica e Applicazioni* (irregular), *Memorie Lincee, Scienze Fisiche e Naturali* (irregular), *Notizie degli Scavi di Antichità*, *Rendiconti: Classe di Scienze Morali, Storiche e Filologiche* (4 a year), *Rendiconti Lincei: Matematica e Applicazioni* (4 a year), *Rendiconti Lincei: Scienze Fisiche e Naturali* (4 a year).

Accademia Nazionale di San Luca (National Academy of San Luca): Piazza dell'Accademia di San Luca 77, 00187 Rome; tel. 06-6798850; fax 06-6789243; e-mail segreteria@accademiasanluca.it; internet www.accademiasanluca.it; f. 14th century; sections of Painting, of Sculpture, of Architecture; 54 mems; 90 corresp. mems; 30 foreign mems; 47 cultural and hon. mems; library: see Libraries and Archives; Pres. NICOLA CARRINO; Sec.-Gen. GIORGIO CIUCCI.

Accademia Nazionale di Santa Cecilia (National Academy of Santa Cecilia): Auditorium Parco della Musica, Largo Luciano Berio 3, 00196 Rome; tel. 06-80242501; fax 06-80242301; e-mail info@santacecilia.it; internet www.santacecilia.it; f. 1566; promotes symphonic concert music, has own symphony orchestra and chorus, carries out professional music training; 100 mems (70 nat., 30 foreign); Pres. Prof. BRUNO CAGLI; publs *E. M. Rivista degli Archivi di Etnomusicologia* (1 a year), *Studi Musicali* (2 a year).

Accademia Nazionale Virgiliana di Scienze, Lettere e Arti (Virgilian National Academy of Sciences, Literature and Arts): Via dell'Accademia 47, 46100 Mantua; tel. 0376-320314; fax 0376-222774; e-mail mantua@accademiavirgiliana.191.it; internet www.accademiavirgiliana.it; f. early 17th century, present name 1981; 170 mems (90 full, 20 hon., 60 corresp.); library: see Libraries and Archives; Pres. GIORGIO

ZAMBONI; Sec. EUGENIO CAMERLENGHI; publ. *Atti e Memorie N. S.* (1 a year).

Accademia Petrarca di Lettere, Arti e Scienze di Arezzo (Petrarch Academy of Literature, Arts and Science): Via dell'Orto 28, 52100 Arezzo; tel. 0575-24700; fax 0575-298846; e-mail info@accademiapetrarca.it; internet www.accademiapetrarca.it; f. 1810; 413 mems; library of 15,000 vols; Pres. Prof. GIULIO FIRPO; Sec. Prof. ANTONIO BATINTI; publs *Atti e Memorie* (1 a year), *Studi Petrarcheschi* (1 a year).

Accademia Pugliese delle Scienze (Puglia Academy of Sciences): Palazzo dell'Ateneo, Piazza Umberto I, 70121 Bari; tel. and fax 080-5714578; e-mail accademia.pugliese@ateneo.uniba.it; internet www.ateneo.uniba.it/accademiapugliese; f. 1925; divided into two classes: physical, medical and natural sciences, and moral sciences; library of 6,600 vols, 270 periodical titles; 120 ordinary mems, 200 corresp. mems and 20 hon. mems; Pres. Prof. VITTORIO MARZI; Sec. GIOVANNA PANEBIANCO; publ. *Atti e Relazioni* (1 a year).

Accademia Roveretana degli Agiati di Scienze, Lettere ed Arti: Piazza Rosmini 5, 38068 Rovereto; tel. 0464-436663; fax 0464-487672; e-mail segreteria@agiati.org; internet www.agiati.org; f. 1750; fosters the development of sciences, literature and art; 330 mems; library of 50,000 vols; Pres. Prof. FABRIZIO RASERA; Sec. Dott. CARLO ANDREA POSTINGER; publs *Atti* (Series A (human sciences, literature, art), online), *Atti* (Series B (mathematics, physics, natural science), online).

Accademia Tiberina: Via del Vantaggio 22, 00186 Rome; tel. 06-3610212; e-mail info@accademiatiberina.it; internet www.accademiatiberina.it; f. 1813; 200 mems and 2,000 assoc., corresp., resident and hon. mems; applied sciences, psychology, arts, hygiene and health, anthropology, Yoga-Vedanta centre; library of 10,000 vols; Pres. Mgr Prof. FERNANDO MARIOTTI; Sec. FRANCO ANTONIO PINARDI.

Accademia Toscana di Scienze e Lettere 'La Colombaria' (La Colombaria Tuscan Academy of Science and Literature): Via S. Egidio 23, 50122 Florence; tel. 055-2396628; fax 055-2396628; e-mail segreteria@colombaria.it; internet www.colombaria.it; f. 1735; library of 30,000 vols; Pres. Prof. FRANCESCO ADORNO; Administrator Prof. PIERO TANI; publs *Atti e Memorie* (1 a year), *Corpus dei papiri filosofici greci e latini* (irregular), *Studi* (4 or 5 a year).

Fondazione Internazionale Premio E. Balzan—'Premio': Piazzetta U. Giordano 4, 20122 Milan; tel. (2) 76002212; fax (2) 76009457; e-mail balzan@balzan.it; internet www.balzan.org; f. 1957; awards Balzan Prizes for worldwide promotion of arts and sciences; library of 4,500 vols; Pres. Amb. B. BOTTAI; Sec.-Gen. Dr S. WERDER; publs *Balzan Prizes* (1 a year), *Annual Balzan Lecture* (1 a year).

Istituto Lombardo Accademia di Scienze e Lettere: Via Borgonuovo 25, 20121 Milan; tel. 02-864087; fax 02-86461388; e-mail istituto.lombardo@unimi.it; internet www.istitutolombardo.it; f. 1802; divided into 2 classes: Mathematics and Natural Sciences (Sec. Prof. FIORENZA DE BERNARDI); Moral Sciences (Sec. Profa ISABELLA GUALANDRI);; 120 mems; 193 corresp. assocs; 80 foreign mems; library of 495,000 vols, 330 Italian periodicals, 600 foreign periodicals; Pres. Prof. GIANNANTONIO SACCHI LANDRIANI; publs *Cicli di Lezioni* (1 a year), *Memorie della Classe di Scienze Matematiche e Naturali*, *Memorie della Classe di Lettere e Scienze Morali*, *Rendiconti–Classe di Lettere*

e Scienze Morali e Storiche, *Rendiconti–Classe di Scienze Matematiche e Naturali*, *Rendiconti–Parte Generale e Atti Ufficiali*.

Istituto Veneto di Scienze, Lettere ed Arti (Venetian Institute of Sciences, Literature and Arts): Campo S. Stefano 2945, 30124 Venice; tel. 041-2407711; fax 041-5210598; e-mail ivsla@istitutoveneto.it; internet www.istitutoveneto.it; f. 1838; functions as academy; also organizes postdoctoral courses; sections of Physical, Mathematical and Natural Sciences (Academic Sec. Prof. ANDREA RINALDO), Moral Sciences, Literature and Arts (Academic Sec. Prof. GHERARDO ORTALLI); 69 mems; 119 corresp. mems; 33 foreign mems; library of 200,600 vols; Pres. Prof. GIAN ANTONIO DANIELI; Administrator Prof. LORENZO FELLIN; publs *Atti* (Proceedings (moral sciences series), 4 a year), *Atti* (Proceedings (physical sciences series), 4 a year), *Memorie*.

Società di Letture e Conversazioni Scientifiche (Scientific Society): Palazzo Ducale ammezzato ala est, Piazza Matteotti 5, Genoa; tel. 010-565141; fax 010-565141; e-mail info@letturescientifiche.it; internet www.letturescientifiche.it; f. 1866; holds conferences and debates on scientific, historical, literary and political topics; library of 11,000 vols; Pres. UMBERTO COSTA.

Società Nazionale di Scienze, Lettere ed Arti in Napoli (National Society for Sciences, Literature and Art): Via Mezzocannone 8, 80134 Naples; tel. 081-5527549; fax 081-5527549; e-mail socnazsla@virgilio.it; internet www.socnazsla.unina.it; f. 1808; sections of Physical and Mathematical Sciences (Academic Sec. ANTONIO GIUDITTA), Moral and Political Sciences (Academic Sec. FRANCA ASSANTE), Archaeology, Literature and Fine Arts (Academic Sec. MARCELLO ROTILI), ,Medical Sciences and Surgery (Academic Sec. ERNESTO CATENA); library of 35,000 vols; Pres. Prof. FULVIO TESSITORE; Sec.-Gen. Prof. CARLO SBORDONE.

UNESCO Office in Venice–UNESCO Regional Bureau for Science and Culture in Europe (BRESCE): 4930 Castello–Palazzo Zorzi, 30122 Venice; tel. 041-2601511; fax 041-5289995; e-mail veniceoffice@unesco.org; internet www.unesco.org/venice; f. 1988; science policy, education and research throughout SE Europe; environmental policy in local govt (incl. management of water resources and prevention of natural disasters); devt of cultural activities and identifying priorities in SE Europe, such as protection and promotion of cultural heritage; training programmes for cultural conservation; promotes cultural dialogue and artistic creation, and handicraft as a symbol of cultural diversity; library of 2,000 UNESCO publs; Dir Dr ENGELBERT RUOSS.

AGRICULTURE, FISHERIES AND VETERINARY SCIENCE

Accademia di Agricoltura di Torino (Academy of Agriculture of Turin): Via Andrea Doria 10, 10123 Turin; tel. 011-8127470; fax 011-8127470; e-mail to0323@biblioteche.reteunitaria.piemonte.it; internet web.tiscali.it/accagri; f. 1785; 155 mems; library of 26,000 vols, 50 current periodicals; Pres. ORAZIO SAPPA; publs *Annali Dell'Accademia di Agricoltura di Torino* (1 a year), *Nuovo Calendario Georgico* (1 a year).

Accademia dei Georgofili (Academy of Georgofili): Logge Uffizi Corti, 50122 Florence; tel. 055-212114; fax 055-2302754; e-mail accademia@georgofili.it; internet www.georgofili.it; f. 1753; promotes the application of sciences to agriculture and environmental protection, and the development of rural areas; 522 mems; library of

70,000 vols; Pres. Prof. FRANCO SCARAMUZZI; publs *Atti* (1 a year), *Quaderni*, *Rivista di Storia della Agricoltura*.

Accademia Italiana di Scienze Forestali (Italian Academy of Forest Sciences): Piazza Edison 11, 50133 Florence; tel. 055-570348; fax 055-575724; e-mail info@aisf.it; internet www.aisf.it; f. 1951; 327 mems; library of 6,000 vols; Pres. Prof. O. CIANCIO; publs *Annali* (1 a year), *L'Italia Forestale e montana* (6 a year).

Accademia Nazionale di Agricoltura (National Academy of Agriculture): Via Castiglione 11, 40124 Bologna; tel. 051-268809; fax 051-263736; e-mail segreteria@accademia-agricoltura.it; internet www.accademia-agricoltura.unibo.it; f. 1807; 80 mems and 140 corresponding mems; library of 20,000 vols; Pres. Prof. GIORGIO AMADEI; Sec. GUALTIERO BARALDI; publ. *Annali* (4 a year).

Istituto Agronomico per l'Oltremare (Agronomic Institute for Overseas): Via Antonio Cocchi 4, 50131 Florence; tel. 055-50611; fax 055-5061333; e-mail iao@iao.florence.it; internet www.iao.florence.it; f. 1904; 50 mems; library of 133,000 vols, 800 current periodicals; Dir-Gen. GIOVANNI TOTINO; publ. *Journal of Agriculture and Environment for International Development* (4 a year).

Società Italiana delle Scienze Veterinarie (Italian Society of Veterinary Sciences): Via Istria 3B, 25125 Brescia; tel. 030-223244; fax 030-2420569; e-mail sisvet@fondiz.it; internet www.sisvet.it; f. 1947; 1,700 mems; Pres. Prof. ANTONIO PUGLIESE; Gen. Sec. Prof. MASSIMO DE MAJO; publ. *Atti*.

Società Italiana di Economia Agraria (Italian Agrarian Economics Society): c/o Dott. Annalisa Zezza – INEA, Via Barberini 36, 00187 Rome; e-mail zezza@inea.it; internet ilo.unimol.it/sidea; f. 1962; 300 mems; Pres. Prof. GIOVANNI CANNATA; Sec. Dott. ANNALISA ZEZZA; publ. *Atti* (1 a year).

ARCHITECTURE AND TOWN PLANNING

Centro Internazionale di Studi di Architettura 'Andrea Palladio' (Andrea Palladio International Centre for the Study of Architecture): Palazzo Barbaran da Porto, contra' Porti 11, CP 835, 36100 Vicenza; tel. 0444-323014; fax 0444-322869; e-mail segreteria@cisapalladio.org; internet www.cisapalladio.org; f. 1958 to make known the work of Andrea Palladio, born Padua 1508, and to encourage the study of Palladianism and of Venetian architecture of all ages; library of 30,000 vols; Pres. AMALIA SARTORI; publ. *Annali* (online, 1 a year).

Istituto Nazionale di Architettura (IN-ARCH) (National Architectural Institute): Via Crescenzio 16, 00193 Rome; tel. 06-68802254; fax 06-6868530; e-mail inarch@inarch.it; internet www.inarch.it; f. 1959; organizes meetings, debates and exhibitions; 2,000 mems; Pres. Ing. ADOLFO GUZZINI.

Istituto Nazionale di Urbanistica (INU) (National Institute of Town Planning): Piazza Farnese 44, 00186 Rome; tel. 06-68801190; fax 06-68214773; e-mail segreteria@inu.it; internet www.inu.it; f. 1930; 2,654 mems (960 ordinary, 1,694 assoc.); Pres. FEDERICO OLIVA; Sec. SIMONE OMBUEN; publs *Urbanistica* (3 a year), *Urbanistica Dossier* (12 a year), *Urbanistica Informazioni* (6 a year).

Italia Nostra—Associazione Nazionale per la Tutela del Patrimonio Storico, Artistico e Naturale della Nazione (Italia Nostra—National Association for the Preservation of the Historical, Artistic and Natural Heritage of the Nation): Viale Liegi, 33, 00198 Rome; tel. 06-8537271; fax 06-85350596; e-mail italianostra@italianostra.org; internet www.italianostra.org; f. 1955; 20,000 mems, subscribers, delegates; library of 4,500 vols; brs in 206 towns; Pres. ALESSANDRA MOTTOLA MOLFINO; Sec.-Gen. ANTONELLO ALICI; publ. *Italia Nostra* (9 a year).

BIBLIOGRAPHY, LIBRARY SCIENCE AND MUSEOLOGY

Associazione Italiana Biblioteche (Italian Library Association): CP 2461, Ufficio Roma 158, Via Marsala 39, 00185 Rome; c/o Biblioteca nazionale centrale, Viale Castro Pretorio 105, 00185 Rome; tel. 06-4463532; fax 06-4441139; e-mail aib@aib.it; internet www.aib.it; f. 1930 to support the org. and devt of libraries and a library service in Italy, and to act as a professional representative in all cultural, scientific, technical, legal and legislative spheres; 4,500 mems; library of 8,000 vols, 500 journals; Pres. Prof. MAURO GUERRINI; Sec. GIOVANNA FRIGIMELICA; publs *AIB Notizie* (6 a year), *Bollettino AIB* (4 a year).

Associazione Nazionale dei Musei Italiani (National Association of Italian Museums): Piazza San Marco 49, 00186 Rome; tel. 06-6791343; fax 06-6791343; Pres. Prof. D. BERNINI; Sec. Dott. L. BARBACINI; publ. *Musei e Gallerie d'Italia*.

Istituto Centrale per il Restauro e la Conservazione del Patrimonio Archivistico e Librario (Central Institute for the Restoration and Conservation of Archives and Libraries): Via Milano 76, 00184 Rome; tel. 06-482911; fax 06-4814968; e-mail icapl@beniculturali.it; internet www.icpal.beniculturali.it; f. 2007 by merger of Istituto Centrale per la Patologia del Libro (ICPL) with Centro di Fotoriproduzione Legatoria e Restauro Degli Archivi di Stato (CFLR); attached to Italian Min. of Cultural Heritage and Activities; book and document restoration and preservation; research on the safeguarding and conservation of library and archival heritage; 77 mems; library of 15,000 vols, 170 current periodicals; Dir CRISTINA MISITI.

ECONOMICS, LAW AND POLITICS

Accademia Italiana di Economia Aziendale (Academy of Business Economics): Via Farini 14, 40124 Bologna; tel. 051-558798; fax 051-6492446; e-mail redazione@accademiaaidea.it; internet www.accademiaaidea.it; f. 1813; divided into 3 classes; 375 national mems; 50 foreign mems; 10 hon. mems; reps from all Italian universities; Pres. Prof. ROBERTO CAFFERATA; Vice-Pres. Prof. GIORGIO INVERNIZZI; Vice-Pres. Prof. LUCIANO MARCHI.

CIRGIS (International Centre for Juridical Research and Scientific Initiatives): Via Manzoni 45, 20121 Milan; tel. 02-6552167; fax 02-6570144; e-mail segreteria@cirgis.it; internet www.cirgis.it; f. 1979 to promote cultural relations between scholars of Italian and foreign law; aims for the realization of exchanges of thought and experience between Italian and foreign jurists, the knowledge of laws and institutions of different countries through meetings, publs, etc.; c. 400 mems; Pres. Avv. Prof. FRANCESCO OGLIARI; International Sec. Avv. GIUSEPPE AGLIALORO.

Istituto di Diritto Romano e dei Diritti dell'Oriente Mediterraneo (Institute of Roman Law and Laws of the Near East): Facoltà di Giurisprudenza, Piazzale Aldo Moro 5, 00185 Rome; tel. 06-49910232; fax 06-49910241; e-mail marilena.zanatatritto@uniroma1.it; f. 1937; library of 70,000 vols, 80 current periodicals; Dir Prof. ANDREA DI PORTO; Academic Sec. Dott. MARILENA ZANATA TRITTO.

Società Italiana degli Economisti (Italian Economists' Society): Piazzale Martelli, 8, 60121 Ancona; tel. 071-2207111; fax 071-200494; e-mail sie@univpm.it; internet www.sie.univpm.it; f. 1950; 594 mems; Pres. Prof. ALESSANDRO RONCAGLIA; Gen. Sec. Prof. ALBERTO ZAZZARO; publs *Bollettino dei Soci*, *Lettera* (1 a year), *Rivista Italiana degli Economisti*.

Società Italiana di Economia, Demografia e Statistica: Piazza Tommaso de Cristoforis 6, 00159 Rome; tel. 06-43589008; fax 06-43589008; e-mail sieds@tin.it; internet www.sieds.it; f. 1938; c. 600 mems; Pres. GIOVANNI MARIA GIORGI; Sec.-Gen. GIOVANNI CARIANI; publ. *Rivista Italiana di Economia, Demografia e Statistica* (4 a year).

Società Italiana di Filosofia del Diritto: c/o Ist. di Filosofia del Diritto, Facoltà di Giurisprudenza, Università La Sapienza, 00185 Rome; tel. 06-490489; fax 06-49910951; internet www.sifd.it; f. 1936; 200 mems; Pres. Prof. FRANCESCO VIOLA; publ. *Rivista internazionale di filosofia del diritto* (4 a year).

Società Italiana di Statistica (Italian Statistics Society): Salita de' Crescenzi 26, 00186 Rome; tel. 06-6869845; fax 06-6540742; e-mail sis@caspur.it; internet www.sis-statistica.it; f. 1939; 1,000 mems; 300 associates; statistics and demography; Pres. Prof. MAURIZIO VICHI; Sec. Profa CECILIA TOMASSINI; publs *Statistical Methods and Applications* (4 a year; in English), *Statistica e Società* (online), *SISmagazine* (online), *SIS-Informazioni* (12 a year).

Società Italiana per l'Organizzazione Internazionale (SIOI) (UN Association for Italy): Piazza di S. Marco 51, 00186 Rome; tel. 06-6920781; fax 06-6789102; e-mail sioi@sioi.org; internet www.sioi.org; f. 1944; sections in Milan, Naples, Turin; library: see Libraries; Pres. UMBERTO LA ROCCA; Sec.-Gen. FABIO MIGLIORINI; publ. *La Comunità Internazionale* (4 a year).

EDUCATION

Associazione Pedagogica Italiana (Italian Educational Association): Via Zamboni 34, 40126 Bologna; tel. 051-2098442; fax 051-228847; e-mail info@aspei.it; internet www.aspei.it; f. 1950; aims to promote the development of schools in general and all other institutions of education, also studies and research in education; 50 brs; 5,000 mems; Pres. SIRA SERENELLA MACCHIETTI; Sec.-Gen. ALDO D'ALFONSO; publ. *Bollettino* (4 a year).

FINE AND PERFORMING ARTS

Accademia di Francia (French Academy in Rome): Villa Medici, Viale Trinità dei Monti 1, 00187 Rome; tel. 06-67611; e-mail standard@villamedici.it; internet www.villamedici.it; f. 1666; organizes exhibitions, concerts, symposia and seminars on artistic and literary topics, and on their history; library of 32,000 vols; Dir ERIC DE CHASSEY; Gen. Sec. SIDNEY PEYROLES.

Accademia Raffaello: Via Cesare Battisti 54, 61029 Urbino; tel. 0722-329695; fax 0722-378466; e-mail segreteria@accademiaraffaello.it; internet www.accademiaraffaello.it; f. 1869; promotes fine art; 260 mems; library of 16,000 vols; Pres. Prof. GIORGIO CERBONI BAIARDI; publs *Accademia Raffaello. Atti e studi*, *Rivista Accademia Raffaello* (2 a year).

Fondazione Istituto Italiano per la Storia della Musica (Italian Institute for the History of Music): c/o Accademia Nazio-

LEARNED SOCIETIES

nale di Santa Cecilia, Via Vittoria 6, 00187
Rome; tel. 06-36000146; fax 06-36000146;
e-mail info@iism.it; internet www.iism.it; f.
1938; Pres. Prof. AGOSTINO ZIINO.

Istituto Nazionale di Studi Verdiani
(National Institute of Verdi Studies): Via
Melloni 1B, 43100 Parma; tel. 0521-285273;
e-mail direzione@studiverdiani.it; internet
www.studiverdiani.it; f. 1960 under the patronage of the International Music Council
and the Italian Ministry of Culture to study
the life and works of Giuseppe Verdi; library
of 15,000 vols, archives of 16,000 documents;
Pres. MARIA MERCEDES CARRARA VERDI; Dir
PIERLUIGI PETROBELLI; publs *Carteggi Verdiani*, *Premio Internazionale Rotary Club di
Parma 'Giuseppe Verdi'*, *Proceedings of Congresses*, *Quaderni*, *Studi Verdiani* (1 a year).

**Istituto Universitario Olandese di
Storia dell'Arte** (Dutch University Institute
for the History of Art): Viale Torricelli 5,
50125 Florence; tel. 055-221612; fax 055-
221106; e-mail iuo@iuo.iris.firenze.it;
internet niki.meyson.net; f. 1958; library of
50,000 vols; Dir Dr MICHAEL W. KWAKKEL-
STEIN.

**Kunsthistorisches Institut in Florenz–
Max-Planck-Institut/Istituto di Storia
dell'Arte di Firenze** (Institute for the History of Art in Florence): Via Giuseppe Giusti
44, 50121 Florence; tel. 055-249111; fax 055-
2491155; internet www.khi.fi.it; f. 1897,
became Max-Planck Institute 2002; 60
mems; library of 270,000 vols, 2,600 periodicals and 600,000 reproductions; spec. collns
incl. art in Italy; Dir Prof. Dr GERHARD WOLF;
Dir Prof. Dr ALESSANDRO NOVA; publs *Kleine
Schriftenreihe des KHI* (1 a year), *Mitteilungen* (1 a year), *Studi e ricerche* (conference
proceedings).

Real Academia de España en Roma
(Royal Spanish Academy in Rome): Piazza
San Pietro in Montorio 3, 00153 Rome; tel.
06-5812806; fax 06-5818049; e-mail info@
raer.it; internet raer.it; f. 1873; Dir ENRIQUE
PANÉS; Gen. Sec. FERNANDO VALERO.

**Società d'Incoraggiamento d'Arti e Mes-
tieri** (Society for the Encouragement of Arts
and Crafts): Via Santa Marta 18, 20123
Milan; tel. 02-86450125; fax 02-86452542;
e-mail segreteria@siam1838.it; internet www
.siam1838.it; f. 1838; education in mechanics,
electronics, electrotechnics, chemistry, information technology; library of 6,000 vols;
Pres. BRUNO SORESINA; Gen. Sec. ALBERTO
PIANTA.

Società Italiana di Musicologia (Italian
Musicological Society): CP 7256, Ag. Roma
Nomentano, 00162 Rome; Via dei Greci 18,
00187 Rome; tel. 338-1957796; e-mail
segreteria@sidm.it; internet www.sidm.it; f.
1964; 800 mems; Pres. GUIDO SALVETTI; Sec.
SARA CICCARELLI; publs *Bollettino* (2 a year),
Fonti Musicali Italiane (1 a year), *Rivista
Italiana di Musicologia* (2 a year).

**Società Italiana Musica Contempora-
nea:** Via Domenichino 12, 20149 Milan; tel.
02-468157; fax 02-468157; e-mail simc@
fastwebnet.it; internet www.simc-italia.it;
Pres. DAVIDE ANZAGHI; Sec. GABRIELE ROTA;
publ. *Newsletter* (online).

HISTORY, GEOGRAPHY AND ARCHAEOLOGY

Associazione Archeologica Romana
(Roman Archaeological Society): Piazza Benedetto Cairoli 117, 00186 Rome; tel. 06-
6865647; fax 06-6865647; e-mail
assoarcheologicaromana@tin.it; internet
www.associazionearcheologicaromana.it; f.
1902; 400 mems; library of 3,000 vols; Pres.
Prof. CLAUDIO STRINATI; Sec. Dott. PAOLA
MANETTO; publ. *Romana Gens* (4 a year).

Istituto Geografico Militare (Military
Geographical Institute): Via Cesare Battisti
10, 50122 Florence; tel. 055-27321; fax 055-
282172; e-mail info@geomil.esercito.difesa.it;
internet www.igmi.org; f. 1872; geodetic and
topographical surveying; official cartography; library of 120,000 vols, 700 atlases,
22,000 cartographic items; Dir-Gen. Gen.
ANTONIO DE VITA; publs *Bollettino di Geode-
sia e Scienze Affini* (3 a year), *L'Universo* (6 a
year).

Istituto Italiano di Numismatica (Italian
Numismatics Institute): Palazzo Barberini,
Via Quattro Fontane 13, 00184 Rome; tel. 06-
4743603; fax 06-4743603; e-mail istituto@
istitutoitalianonumismatica.it; internet www
.istitutoitalianonumismatica.it; f. 1936;
library of 22,000 vols; Dir Prof. SARA SORDA;
publ. *Annali* (1 a year).

**Istituto Italiano di Paleontologia
Umana** (Italian Institute of Human Palaeontology): Piazza Mincio 2, 00198 Rome; tel.
06-8557598; e-mail info@isipu.org; internet
www.isipu.org; f. 1913; quaternary environment, geology, palaeontology, palaeoanthropology, archaeology; 250 mems; library of
5,800 vols, 31 periodicals; extensive offprints
series; Pres. RAFFAELE SARDELLA; publs *Memorie* (irregular), *Quaternaria* (1 a year).

Istituto Italiano per la Storia Antica
(Italian Institute for Ancient History): Via
Milano 76, 00184 Rome; tel. 06-4880597; fax
06-4880597; e-mail storia.antica@virgilio.it;
internet www.storiaantica.eu; f. 1935; library
of 18,000 vols, 82 current periodicals; Pres.
Prof. ANDREA GIARDINA; publs *Miscellanea
Greca e Romana*, *Studi pubblicati dall'Istituto Italiano per la Storica Antica*.

**Istituto Nazionale di Archeologia e
Storia dell'Arte** (National Institute of
Archaeology and History of Art): Piazza San
Marco 49, 00186 Rome; tel. 06-6780817; fax
06-6798804; e-mail inasa@inasa-roma.it;
internet www.inasa-roma.it; f. 1918; library
of 500,000 vols; Pres. Prof. ADRIANO LA
REGINA; publ. *RIASA - Rivista dell'Istituto
Nazionale di Archeologia e Storia dell'Arte* (1
a year).

**Istituto Nazionale di Studi Etruschi ed
Italici** (National Institute for Etruscan and
Italic Studies): Via Romana 37A, 50125
Florence; tel. 055-2207175; fax 055-2207175;
e-mail studietruschi@interfree.it; internet
studietruschi.org; f. 1932; 233 mems; library
of 16,000 vols; Pres. Prof. GIOVANNANGELO
CAMPOREALE; Gen. Sec. Prof. LUIGI DONATI;
publ. *Studi Etruschi* (1 a year).

**Istituto per la Storia del Risorgimento
Italiano** (Institute for the History of the
Italian Revival): Museo Centrale del Risorgimento, Complesso del Vittoriano, Piazza
Venezia, 00186 Rome; tel. 06-6793598; fax
06-6782572; e-mail ist.risorgimento@
tiscalinet.it; internet www.risorgimento.it; f.
1936; 3,400 mems; Pres. Prof. ROMANO
UGOLLINI; Gen. Sec. Prof. SERGIO LA SALVIA;
publs *Atti* (irregular), *Edizione scritti Garibaldi* (irregular), *Fonti* (irregular), *Memorie*
(irregular), *Rassegna Storica del Risorgimento dal 1914* (online).

**Istituto Storico Italiano per il Medio
Evo** (Italian Institute of Medieval History):
Piazza dell'Orologio 4, 00186 Rome; tel. 06-
68802075; fax 06-68195963; e-mail
amministrazione@isime.it; internet www
.isime.it; f. 1883; library of 100,000 vols; Pres.
Prof. MASSIMO MIGLIO; publs *Bullettino*, *Fonti
per la storia dell'Italia medievale*, *Nuovi
Studi Storici*, *Repertorium Fontium Historiae Medii Aevi*.

**Istituto Storico Italiano per l'Età Mod-
erna e Contemporanea** (Italian Historical
Institute for the Contemporary and Modern
Era): Via Michelangelo Caetani 32, 00186

Rome; tel. 06-68806922; fax 06-6875127;
e-mail iststor@libero.it; internet www.icbsa
.it; f. 1934; historical research and publications; library of 35,000 vols; Pres. Prof. LUIGI
LOTTI; publ. *Annuario*.

Società di Minerva: Piazza Hortis 4, 34123
Trieste; tel. 040-660245; fax 040-661030;
e-mail societadiminerva@gmail.com;
internet www.societadiminerva.it; f. 1810;
studies history, art and culture of Trieste,
Istria and Gorizia; 150 mems; Pres. Prof.
arch. GINO PAVAN; Sec. Dott. GIULIANA MAR-
INI; publs *Archeografo Triestino* (1 a year),
Extra serie dell'Archeografo Triestino
(irregular), *Quaderni di Minerva* (irregular).

Società di Studi Geografici (Society for
Geographical Studies): Via San Gallo 10,
50129 Florence; tel. 055-2757956; fax 055-
2757956; e-mail info@societastudigeografici
.it; internet www.societastudigeografici.it; f.
1895; Devt of geographic, territorial and
regional geography through seminars, workshops, int. confs, journal publs; 500 mems;
library of 25,000 vols; Pres. Prof. LIDIA
SCARPELLI; Vice-Pres. Prof. LEONARDO ROM-
BAI; Sec. Prof. CAPINERI CRISTINA; publs
Memorie geografiche Nuova Serie (1 a year),
Rivista Geografica Italiana (4 a year).

Società Geografica Italiana: Palazzetto
Mattei in Villa Celimontana, Via della Navicella 12, 00184 Rome; tel. 06-7008279; fax 06-
77079518; e-mail segreteria@
societageografica.it; internet www
.societageografica.it; f. 1867; library: see
Libraries and Archives; Pres. Prof. FRANCO
SALVATORI; publs *Bollettino* (4 a year),
Ricerche e Studi.

Società Napoletana di Storia Patria
(Neapolitan Society of Italian History):
Maschio Angioino, Piazza Municipio, 80133
Naples; tel. 081-5510353; fax 081-5510353;
e-mail snsp@unina.it; internet www
.storiapatrianapoli.it; f. 1875; library of
350,000 vols, 900 current periodicals; 650
mems; Pres. Prof. RENATA DE LORENZO; Vice-
Pres. Prof. AURELIO MUSI; Librarian FRAN-
CESCA RUSSO; publ. *Archivo Storico per le
Province Napoletane*.

Società Romana di Storia Patria (Roman
Society of Italian History): Piazza della
Chiesa Nuova 18, 00186 Rome; tel. 06-
68307513; fax 06-68307513; e-mail
segreteria@srsp.it; internet www.srsp.it; f.
1876; c. 100 mems; Pres. LETIZIA ERMINI
PANI; Sec. ALBERTO BARTOLA; publs *Archivio
della Società* (1 a year), *Codice diplomatico
di Roma e della Regione Romana* (irregular),
Miscellanea della Società (irregular).

Società Storica Lombarda (Lombardy
Historical Society): Via Morone 1, 20121
Milan; tel. and fax 02-860118; e-mail
storica@tiscalinet.it; internet www
.societastoricalombarda.it; f. 1873; 450
mems; library of 27,000 vols; Pres. GIAN
BATTISTA ORIGONI DELLA CROCE; Sec. Dott.
LUIGI OROMBELLI; publ. *Archivio Storico
Lombardo* (1 a year).

LANGUAGE AND LITERATURE

Accademia della Crusca: Villa Medicea di
Castello, Via di Castello 46, 50141 Florence;
tel. (55) 454277; fax (55) 454279; e-mail
edizioni@crusca.fi.it; internet www
.accademiadellacrusca.it; f. 1583; library of
122,000 vols; Pres. Prof. NICOLETTA MAR-
ASCHIO; Dir of Philological Studies ROSANNA
BETTARINI; Dir of Lexicographical Studies
Prof. LUCA SERIANNI; Dir of Grammatical
Studies Prof. TERESA POGGI SALANI; Sec.
PIERO FIORELLI; publs *La Crusca Per Voi* (2
a year), *Studi di Filologia Italiana* (1 a year),
Studi di Grammatica Italiana (1 a year),
Studi di Lessicografia Italiana (1 a year).

Alliance Française: Via Giulia 250, 00186 Rome; tel. 06-6892461; fax 06-4456370; e-mail assistant-dgaf@alliancefr.it; internet www.alliancefr.it; offers courses and exams in French language and culture and promotes cultural exchange with France; attached teaching centres in 30 locations incl. Aosta, Bari, Bologna, Catania, Catanzaro, Genoa, La Spezia, Lecce, Messina, Padua, Potenza, San Marino, Sassari, Trieste, Turin, Venice and Verona; Dir CHARLES DE TINGUY DE LA GIROULIÈRE.

British Council: Via di San Sebastianello, 16, 00187 Rome; tel. 06-478141; fax 06-4814296; e-mail corsi.roma@britishcouncil .it; internet www.britishcouncil.org/italy; teaching centre; offers courses and exams in English language and British culture and promotes cultural exchange with the UK; attached teaching centres in Milan and Naples; Dir, Italy PAUL DOCHERTY.

Goethe-Institut: Via Savoia 15, 00198 Rome; tel. 06-8440051; fax 06-8411628; e-mail info@rom.goethe.org; internet www .goethe.de/it/rom/deindex.htm; offers courses and exams in German language and culture and promotes cultural exchange with Germany; attached centres in Genoa, Milan, Naples, Palermo, Rome, Trieste and Turin; library of 29,000 vols; Dir SUSANNE HÖHN.

Instituto Cervantes: Via di Villa Albani 14–16, 00198 Rome; tel. 06-8537361; fax 06-8546232; e-mail cenrom@cervantes.es; internet roma.cervantes.es; f. 1992; offers courses and exams in Spanish language and culture and promotes cultural exchange with Spain and Spanish-speaking Latin and Central America; attached centres in Milan, Naples and Palermo; library of 32,000 vols; Dir MARIO GARCÍA DEL CASTRO.

PEN Club Italiano: Via Daverio 7, 20122 Milan; tel. 0335-7350966; fax 0363-350654; e-mail segreteria@penclub.it; internet www .penclub.it; promotes freedom of expression; 250 mems; Pres. SEBASTIANO GRASSO; Sec.-Gen. GIORGIO MANNACIO; publ. *Rivista* (4 a year).

Società Dante Alighieri: Palazzo di Firenze, Piazza Firenze 27, 00186 Rome; tel. 06-6873694; fax 06-6873685; e-mail segreteria@ ladante.it; internet www.ladante.it; f. 1889; promotes Italian language and culture throughout the world; Sec.-Gen. Comm. Dott. ALESSANDRO MASI; publ. *Pagine della Dante* (3 a year).

Società Dantesca Italiana (Italian Dante Society): Palagio dell'Arte della Lana, Via Arte della Lana 1, 50123 Florence; tel. 055-287134; fax 055-211316; e-mail sdi@dantesca .it; internet www.dantesca.it; f. 1888; library of 25,000 vols, 1,500 microfilms; Pres. Prof. ENRICO GHIDETTI; publs *Collana, Dantesca, Edizione Nazionale delle Opere di Dante Alighieri, Manoscritti Danteschi e d'Interesse Dantesco, Quaderni degli Studi Danteschi, Quaderni del Centro di Studi e Documentazione Dantesca e Medievale, Rivista Annuale, Studi Danteschi.*

Società Filologica Romana: Dipartimento di Studi Europei e Interculturali, Sapienza Università di Roma, Facoltà di Scienze Umanistiche, Piazzale Aldo Moro 5, 00185 Rome; tel. 06-49913071; fax 06-490450; e-mail roberto.antonelli@uniroma1.it; internet w3.uniroma1.it/studieuropei/sfr; f. 1901; library of 8,000 vols; Pres. Prof. ROBERTO ANTONELLI; Sec. GIOVANNELLA DESIDERI; publ. *Studj Romanzi.*

Società Italiana degli Autori ed Editori (SIAE) (Italian Authors' and Publishers' Society): Viale della Letteratura 30, 00144 Rome; tel. 06-59901; fax 06-59647050; e-mail sam.urp@siae.it; internet www.siae.it; f. 1882; protects authors' and publishers'

rights; 90,000 mems; administers the Biblioteca e Museo Teatrale del Burcardo (35,000 vols); Pres. LORENZO FERRERO (acting); Gen. Dir Dr GAETANO BLANDINI; publs *Annuario dello Spettacolo, SiaeNews.*

Società Letteraria di Verona (Verona Literary Society): Piazzetta Scalette Rubiani 1, 37121 Verona; tel. 045-595949; fax 045-595949; e-mail societaletteraria@ societaletteraria.it; internet www .societaletteraria.it; f. 1808; promotes appreciation of sciences, literature and art; 540 mems; library of 100,000 vols; Pres. DANIELA BRUNELLI; publ. *Bollettino* (1 a year).

MEDICINE

Accademia delle Scienze Mediche di Palermo: c/o Policlinico universitario Paolo Giaccone, Dip. di Biopatologia e Metodologia Biomediche, corso Tukory 211, 90134 Palermo; tel. 091-6552456; fax 091-6555901; e-mail accademiascienze@unipa.it; internet www.unipa.it/accademiascienze; f. 1621; library; Pres. Prof. A. SALERNO; Sec. Prof. ALFREDO DI JESÙ; publ. *Atti* (1 a year).

Accademia di Medicina di Torino (Turin Academy of Medicine): Via Po 18, 10123 Turin; tel. and fax 011-8179298; e-mail accademia.medicina@unito.it; internet www .accademiadimedicina.unito.it; f. 1846; 120 ordinary mems, 30 hon. mems, 29 corresp. mems; library of 11,761 vols; Pres. Prof. NICOLA RICCARDINO; Sec.-Gen. Prof. GIOVANNI CARLO ISAIA; publ. *Giornale* (2 a year).

Accademia Medica di Roma: Policlinico Umberto I, Viale del Policlinico, 00161 Rome; tel. 06-4957818; f. 1875; 400 mems; Pres. Prof. ANDREA SCIACCA; Sec. Prof. LUIGI TRAVIA; publ. *Bolletino ed Atti* (1 a year).

Associazione Italiana di Dietetica e Nutrizione Clinica (Italian Association for Dietetics and Clinical Nutrition): Via dei Sassoni 16, 01030 Monterosi (VT); tel. 0761-699511; e-mail adicentral@libero.it; internet www.adiitalia.com; f. 1950; education and training; application of research in nutrition; 200 mems; Pres. Prof. MARIA ANTONIA FUSCO; Gen. Sec. Dr GIUSEPPE FATATI; publs *ADI Magazine* (4 a year), *Attualità in Dietetica e Nutrizione Clinica* (2 a year), *Mediterranean Journal of Nutrition and Metabolism.*

Associazione Italiana di Medicina Aeronautica e Spaziale (Italian Association for Aeronautical and Space Medicine): Università degli Studi di Roma 'La Sapienza', Istituto di Medicina Legale, Viale Regina Elena 336, 00161 Rome; tel. 0347-9401715; fax 06-99331577; e-mail segreteria@aimas.it; internet www.aimas.it; f. 1963; Pres. MANLIO CARBONI; Gen. Sec. PAOLA VERDE; publ. *Bollettino* (irregular).

Fondazione Luigi Villa: Via Pace 9, 20122 Milan; tel. 02-5510709; fax 02-54100125; e-mail info@fondazioneluigivilla.org; internet www.fondazioneluigivilla.org; f. 1969; prevention and treatment of the haemorrhagic and thrombotic diseases; library of 9,500 vols; Pres. Prof. PIERMANNUCCIO MANNUCCI; Sec. Prof. FLORA PEYVANDI.

Società Italiana di Anestesia, Analgesia, Rianimazione e Terapia Intensiva (Italian Society for Anaesthesia, Analgesia, Resuscitation and Intensive Therapy): Corso Bramante 83, 10126 Turin; tel. 011-678282; fax 011-674502; e-mail siaarti@unipg.it; internet www.siaarti.it; f. 1934; 2,000 mems; Pres. VITO ALDO PEDUTO; Sec./Treas. FABIO GORI; publ. *Minerva Anestesiologica* (12 a year).

Società Italiana di Cancerologia (Italian Society of Cancerology): Via G. Venezian, 1, 20133 Milan; tel. 02-23902675; fax 02-2664342; e-mail sic@istitutotumori.mi.it;

internet www.cancerologia.it; f. 1952; Pres. ALFREDO FUSCO; publ. *Tumori* (6 a year, online).

Società Italiana di Chirurgia (Italian Society for Surgery): Viale Tiziano, 19, 00196 Rome; tel. 06-3221867; fax 06-3220676; e-mail sic@sichirurgia.org; internet www.sichirurgia.org; f. 1882; Pres. Prof. GIANLUIGI MELOTTI; Gen. Sec. Prof. ROCCO BELLANTONE; publ. *Chirurgia Italiana* (6 a year).

Società Italiana di Farmacologia (Italian Pharmacological Society): Viale Abruzzi 32, 20131 Milan; tel. 02-29520311; fax 02-29520179; e-mail sifcese@comm2000.it; internet www.sifweb.org; f. 1939 to develop pharmacological studies and their applications; 1,152 mems (1,115 ordinary, 13 hon., 24 assoc.); Pres. Prof. CARLO RICCARDI; Sec. Prof. LIBERATO BERRINO; publs *Pharmacological Research* (12 a year), *Quaderni della SIF* (4 a year, online).

Società Italiana di Ginecologia ed Ostetricia (Italian Society for Gynaecology and Obstetrics): Via dei Soldati 25, 00186 Rome; tel. 06-6875119; fax 06-6868142; e-mail federazione@sigo.it; internet www.sigo.it; f. 1892; 5,300 mems; Pres. GIORGIO VITTORI; Sec. FABIO SIRIMARCO; publs *Atti* (4 a year), *Italian Journal of Gynaecology and Obstetrics* (4 a year), *SIGO Notizie* (3 a year).

Società Italiana di Medicina Interna (Italian Society for Internal Medicine): Viale dell'Università 25, 00185 Rome; tel. 06-44340373; fax 06-44340474; e-mail info@ simi.it; internet www.simi.it; f. 1887; annual nat. congress; 2,710 mems; Pres. Prof. FRANCESCO VIOLI; Sec. Prof. NICOLA MONTANO; publ. *Internal and Emergency Medicine* (official journal, in English).

Società Italiana di Medicina Legale e delle Assicurazioni (Italian Society for Legal Medicine and Assurance): Dipartimento di Scienze Anatomiche, Istologiche, Medico Legali e dell'Apparato Locomotore, Università degli Studi di Roma 'La Sapienza', Piazzale Aldo Moro 5, 00185 Rome; e-mail paola.frati@fastwebnet.it; internet www .simlaweb.com; f. 1897; Pres. Prof. PAOLO ARBARELLO; Sec. Prof. PAOLA FRATI; publ. *Rivista Italiana di Medicina Legale.*

Società Italiana di Odontostomatologia e Chirurgia Maxillo-Facciale (Italian Society for Odontostomatology and Maxillofacial Surgery): Via Eugubina 42A, 06122 Perugia; tel. 075-5729867; fax 075-5737378; e-mail siocmf@tin.it; internet main .netemedia.net/siocmf; f. 1957; 2,000 mems; Pres. Prof. PIERLUIGI SAPELLI; Sec.-Gen. and Treas. Prof. MAURIZIO PROCACCINI; publ. *Minerva Stomatologica* (12 a year).

Società Italiana di Ortopedia e Traumatologia (Italian Society for Orthopaedics and Traumatology): Via Nicola Martelli 3, 00197 Rome; tel. 06-80691593; fax 06-80687266; e-mail segreteria@siot.it; internet www.siot .it; f. 1906; 3,100 mems; Pres. Prof. PIETRO BARTOLOZZI; Sec. Dott. ANDREA PICCIOLI.

Società Italiana di Radiologia Medica: Via della Signora 2, 20122 Milan; tel. 02-76006094; fax 02-76006108; e-mail segreteria@sirm.org; internet www.sirm.org; f. 1913; Pres. ANTONIO ROTONDO; Sec. LUCA BRUNESE; publ. *La Radiologia Medica* (in Italian and English).

Società Italiana di Reumatologia (Italian Society for Rheumatology): Via Turati 40, 20121 Milan; tel. 02-7382330; fax 02-7385763; e-mail segreteria@reumatologia.it; internet www.reumatologia.it; f. 1950; 915 mems; Pres. CARLOMAURIZIO MONTECUCCO; Gen. Sec. SILVANA ZENI; publ. *Reumatismo* (4 a year, in Italian and English).

Società Italiana di Traumatologia della Strada (Italian Society for Road Accident Traumatology): Via Monte delle Gioie 1/D, 00199 Rome; tel. 06-49982399; fax 06-49982553; e-mail socitras@socitras.org; internet www.socitras.org; f. 1984; studies on road trauma, safety campaigns, dissemination of knowledge, training courses; 200 mems; Pres. Prof. ANDREA COSTANZO; Sec.-Gen. Dr ROBERTO SAPIA.

Società Medica Chirurgica di Bologna (Society of Medicine and Surgery): Palazzo dell'Archiginnasio, Piazza Galvani 1, 40124 Bologna; tel. 051-231488; fax 051-231488; e-mail info@medchir.bo.it; internet www.medchir.bo.it; f. 1802; holds scientific meetings; 250 mems; library of 15,000 vols; Pres. Prof. LUIGI BOLONDI; Sec. RITA GOLFIERI; Dir of Library Prof. STEFANO ARIETI; publ. *Bullettino delle Scienze Mediche*.

NATURAL SCIENCES
General

Accademia Nazionale delle Scienze, detta dei XL (National Academy of Sciences, known as the Forty): Via L. Spallanzani 7, 00161 Rome; tel. 06-44250054; fax 06-44250871; e-mail segreteria@accademiaxl.it; internet www.accademiaxl.it; f. 1782 as the Italian Society; 65 mems (40 Italian, 25 foreign); Pres. Prof. G. T. SCARASCIA MUGNOZZA; Sec. Profa EMILIA CHIANCONE; publs *Annuario* (every 2 years), *Memorie di Matematica* (1 a year), *Rendiconti: Memorie Scienze Fisiche e Naturali* (1 a year), *Scritti e Documenti* (irregular).

Federazione delle Associazioni Scientifiche e Tecniche (Federation of Scientific and Technological Associations): Piazzale R. Morandi 2, 20121 Milan; tel. 02-77790304; fax 02-782485; e-mail fast@fast.mi.it; internet www.fast.mi.it; f. 1897; aims at fostering cultural debate and promotion of the fields of science policy, technological and industrial research and development, with particular reference to: energy and resources, chemistry and materials, electronics and information, biotechnology, technological research and innovation, ecology and environment, training, professionalism and job organization; mems: 40 scientific orgs, 55,000 individuals; Pres. Prof. ADOLFO COLOMBO; Gen. Sec. Dr ALBERTO PIERI; publ. *Scienza e Tecnica* (4 a year, online).

Società Adriatica di Scienze (Adriatic Society of Sciences): CP 1029, 34100 Trieste; e-mail adriscie@univ.trieste.it; internet www.units.it/~adriscie; f. 1874; 200 mems; library of 27,000 vols; Pres. Prof. FRANCO CUCCHI; Sec. BERNARDINO CRESSERI; publ. *Bollettino* (1 a year).

Società Italiana di Scienze Naturali (Italian Society of Natural Sciences): Museo Civico di Storia Naturale, Corso Venezia 55, 20121 Milan; tel. 02-795965; fax 02-795965; e-mail info@scienzenaturali.org; internet www.scienzenaturali.org; f. 1857; promotes and carries out scientific research; organizes meetings to present and discuss members' research results; study groups on vertebrates in the wild, exobiology and biological optimization; 1,000 mems; library: library of 1,600 periodicals; Pres. CARLO VIOLANI; Sec. CLAUDIO BELLANTE; publs *Atti* (2 a year), *Memorie*, *Natura* (2 a year), *Paleontologia Lombarda*, *Rivista Italiana di Ornitologia* (2 a year).

Società Italiana per il Progresso delle Scienze (Italian Society for Scientific Progress): Viale dell'Università 11, 00185 Rome; tel. 06-4451628; fax 06-4451628; e-mail sips@sipsinfo.it; internet www.sipsinfo.it; f. 1839; library of 30,000 vols; Pres. Prof. MAURIZIO CUMO; Sec. ENZO CASOLINO; publs *Atti Riunioni SIPS* (1 a year), *Scienza e Tecnica* (12 a year).

Società Toscana di Scienze Naturali (Tuscan Society of Natural Sciences): Via S. Maria 53, 56126 Pisa; e-mail info@stsn.it; internet www.stsn.it; f. 1847; 412 mems; library of 75,000 vols, 300 current periodicals; Pres. Prof. STEFANO MERLINO; Gen. Sec. Prof. FRANCO RAPETTI; Librarian CHIARA SORBINI; publs *Atti—Memorie serie A (abiologica)* (online, 1 a year), *Atti—Memorie serie B (biologica)* (online, 1 a year), *Palaeontographia Italica* (1 a year).

Biological Sciences

Società Botanica Italiana Onlus (Italian Botanical Society Onlus): Via Giorgio La Pira 4, 50121 Florence; tel. 055-2757379; fax 055-2757467; e-mail sbi@unifi.it; internet www.societabotanicaitaliana.it; f. 1888; 1,300 mems; library of 9,000 vols; Pres. Prof. FRANCESCO MARIA RAIMONDO; Sec. Prof. CONSOLATA SINISCALCO; publs *Informatore Botanico Italiano* (2 a year with supplements), *Plant Biosystems* (4 a year).

Società Entomologica Italiana (Italian Entomological Society): Via Brigata Liguria 9, 16121 Genoa; tel. (10) 586009; e-mail socentomit.info@alice.it; internet www.socentomit.it; f. 1869; pure and applied entomology; library (Corso Torino 19/4 sc. A. Genoa); 700 mems; library of 1,100 vols; Pres. Prof. A. VIGNA TAGLIANTI; Sec. ROBERTO POGGI; publs *Bollettino* (3 a year), *Memorie* (1 a year).

Società Italiana di Biochimica Clinica e Biologia Molecolare Clinica (Italian Society of Clinical Biochemistry and Clinical Molecular Biology): Via Libero Temolo 4, 20126 Milan; tel. 02-87390041; fax 02-87390077; e-mail segreteria@sibioc.it; internet www.sibioc.it; f. 1968; 2,500 mems; mem. of Int. Federation of Clinical Chemistry; Pres. Dott. COSIMO OTTOMANO; Sec. GIUSEPPE AGOSTA; publ. *Biochimica Clinica* (6 a year).

Società Italiana di Biochimica e Biologia Molecolare (Italian Society for Biochemistry and Molecular Biology): Centro di Cultura Scientifica 'Alessandro Volta', Villa Olmo, Via Cantoni 1, 22100 Como; tel. 031-579815; fax 031-573395; e-mail segreteriasib@centrovolta.it; internet www.biochimica.it; f. 1951; has 16 scientific interest groups; 1,100 mems; Pres. Prof. ANTONIO DE FLORA; Sec. Prof. LUCIANA AVIGLIANO.

Società Italiana di Ecologia (SItE) (Italian Ecological Society): c/o Dipartimento di Scienze Ambientali 'G. Sarfatti', Via Mattioli 4, 53100 Siena; tel. 0577-232887; fax 0577-232930; e-mail info@ecologia.it; internet www.ecologia.it; f. 1976; aims to promote theoretical and applied ecological research, to disseminate knowledge of ecology, encourage the devt of cultural exchange among researchers, and to facilitate nat. and int. cooperation; operates working groups, congresses, etc.; 705 mems; Pres. Prof. PIERLUIGI VIAROLI; Sec. ANTONIO MAZZOLA; publ. *SITE Atti* (proceedings of congresses and symposia, 1 a year).

Società Italiana di Microbiologia (Italian Microbiological Society): Via Sannio 4, 20137 Milan; tel. 02-59902320; fax 02-59900758; e-mail sim@societasim.org; internet www.societasim.org; f. 1962; promotes the study of microbiology, holds congresses and conventions; Pres. GIUSEPPE NICOLETTI; Sec. and Treas. S. RIPA.

Physical Sciences

Associazione Geofisica Italiana (Italian Geophysical Association): c/o CNR, V.le dell'Università 11, 00185 Rome; tel. 06-44702989; fax 06-44702989; e-mail info@associazionegeofisica.it; internet www.associazionegeofisica.it; f. 1951; promotes, coordinates and disseminates knowledge, studies and research on pure and applied geophysics; 200 mems; library of 1,500 vols; Pres. Prof. Dr M. COLACINO; Sec. Dr M. AVERSA; publ. *Bollettino Geofisico* (4 a year).

Associazione Geotecnica Italiana (Italian Geotechnical Association): Viale dell'Università 11, 00185 Rome; tel. 06-44704349; fax 06-44361035; e-mail agiroma@iol.it; internet www.associazionegeotecnica.it; f. 1947; independent; aims to encourage, carry out and support geotechnical studies and research in Italy through publications, conferences, scholarships, etc.; 1,100 mems; Pres. Prof. Ing. STEFANO AVERSA; Sec. Dott. Ing. CLAUDIO SOCCODATO; publ. *Rivista Italiana di Geotecnica* (4 a year).

Associazione Italiana Nucleare: Corso Vittorio Emanuele II 244, 00186 Rome; tel. 06-94005401; fax 06-94005314; e-mail info@assonucleare.it; internet www.assonucleare.it; f. 1998 by merger of ANDIN (Associazione Italiana di Ingegneria Nucleare e Sicurezza Impiantistica), FIEN (Forum Italiano dell'Energia Nucleare) and SNI (Società Nucleare Italiana); promotes debate and research into the role of nuclear power, in order to promote the peaceful and safe use of nuclear technology, in the national interest; Pres. Ing. ENZO GATTA; Sec. Ing. UGO SPEZIA.

Società Astronomica Italiana (Italian Astronomical Society): Largo E. Fermi 5, 50125 Florence; tel. and fax 055-2752270; e-mail sait@arcetri.astro.it; internet www.sait.it; f. 1920; 700 mems; Pres. Prof. ROBERTO BUONANNO; Sec. Dr FABRIZIO MAZZUCCONI; publs *Giornale di Astronomia* (print and electronic versions, 4 a year), *Memorie* (4 a year).

Società Chimica Italiana (Italian Chemical Society): Viale Liegi 48/C, 00198 Rome; tel. 06-8549691; fax 06-8548734; e-mail soc.chim.it@agora.it; internet www.soc.chim.it; f. 1909; organizes confs and publs; promotes chemical culture by any event able to put in contact chemists with civil society; 5,000 mems; library of 2,300 vols; Pres. Prof. VINCENZO BARONE; publs *La Chimica e l'Industria* (12 a year), *La Chimica nella Scuola* (6 a year).

Società Geologica Italiana (Italian Geological Society): c/o Dipartimento di Scienze della Terra, Università degli Studi di Roma 'La Sapienza', Piazzale Aldo Moro 5, 00185 Rome; tel. (6) 4959390; fax (6) 49914154; e-mail info@socgeol.it; internet www.socgeol.it; f. 1881; 1,700 mems; Pres. Prof. CARLO DOGLIONI; Sec. Dott. ACHILLE ZUCCARI; publs *Italian Journal of Geosciences* (3 a year), *Memorie* (irregular), *Rendiconti* (irregular).

Società Italiana di Fisica (Italian Physics Society): Via Saragozza 12, 40123 Bologna; tel. 051-331554; fax 051-581340; e-mail sif@sif.it; internet www.sif.it; f. 1897; 1,500 mems; library of 6,500 vols; Pres. LUISA CIFARELLI; publs *EPJ Plus* (online), *European Physical Journal A—Hadrons and Nuclei* (12 a year, also online), *European Physical Journal B—Condensed Matter and Complex Systems* (24 a year, also online), *European Physical Journal C—Particles and Fields* (12 a year, also online), *European Physical Journal D—Atomic, Molecular, Optical and Plasma Physics* (12 a year, also online), *European Physical Journal E—Soft Matter and Biological Physics* (12 a year, also online), *Europhysics Letters* (24 a year, also online), *Giornale di Fisica* (4 a year, also online), *Il Nuovo Cimento C—Colloquia on Physics* (6 a year, also online), *Il Nuovo Saggiatore* (4 a year, also online), *Quaderni* di Storia della Fisica (irregular, also online), Rivista del Nuovo Cimento (12 a year, also online).

PHILOSOPHY AND PSYCHOLOGY

Società Filosofica Italiana (Italian Philosophical Society): c/o Dip. di Studi Filosofici ed Epistemologici, Università di Roma 'La Sapienza', Villa Mirafiori, Via Nomentana 118, 00161 Rome; tel. and fax 06-8604360; e-mail sfi@sfi.it; internet www.sfi.it; f. 1902; ind. org.; promotes philosophical research on a scientific level; safeguards the professional status of philosophy lecturers; encourages contact and collaboration in Italy and internationally between philosophic disciplines; helps set up local centres of study; 1,350 mems; Pres. STEFANO POGGI; Sec. and Treas. Prof. CARLA GUETTI; publ. Bollettino (3 a year).

Società Italiana di Psicologia: Via Tagliamento 76, 00198 Rome; tel. 06-8845136; fax 06-8845136; e-mail e@sips.it; internet www.sips.it; f. 1910; carries out activities in conjunction with university institutions for study and research; organizes national congresses every 3 years; Pres. ANTONIO LO IACONO; publ. Psicologia Italiana (3 a year).

RELIGION, SOCIOLOGY AND ANTHROPOLOGY

Fondazione Marco Besso (Marco Besso Foundation): Largo di Torre Argentina 11, 00186 Rome; tel. 06-6865611; fax 06-68216313; e-mail segreteriadue@fondazionemarcobesso.it; internet www.fondazionemarcobesso.it; f. 1918; promotes development of Roman cultural world; library: see Libraries and Archives; Pres. GLORIA SONAGLIA LUMBROSO; Dir ANTONIO MARTINI.

Gruppo Interdisciplinare per la Ricerca Sociale (Interdisciplinary Group for Social Research): Facoltà di Scienze Statistiche, Demografiche e Attuariale, Piazzale Aldo Moro 5, 00185 Rome; tel. 06-4453828; f. 1937; Italian section of Int. Institute of Sociology; library of 8,000 vols, 100 current periodicals; Pres. Prof. AMMASSARI.

Società Italiana di Antropologia e Etnologia: Via del Proconsolo 12, 50121 Florence; tel. 055-2396449; fax 055-219438; e-mail info@antropologiaetnologia.it; internet www.antropologiaetnologia.it; f. 1871; 200 mems; library of 5,760 vols, 70 periodicals; Pres. Prof. PIERO MANNUCCI; Librarian MARIA EMANUELA FRATI; publ. Archivio per l'Antropologia e la Etnologia (1 a year).

TECHNOLOGY

Associazione Idrotecnica Italiana (Italian Water Resources Association): Via di Santa Costanza 7, 00198 Rome; tel. 06-8845064; fax 06-8852974; e-mail info@idrotecnicaitaliana.it; internet www.idrotecnicaitaliana.it; f. 1923; study of problems concerning the utilization and management of water resources, and the safeguarding of the environment; 1,500 mems; library of 200 vols; Pres. MASSIMO VELTRI; Gen. Sec. FRANCESCO BOSCO; publ. L'Acqua (6 a year).

Associazione Italiana di Aeronautica e Astronautica (Italian Association of Aeronautical and Space Sciences): Casella Postale 227, 00187 Rome; tel. and fax (6) 88346460; e-mail info@aidaa.it; internet www.aidaa.it; f. 1920; promotes and coordinates research in aeronautical and space sciences; cooperates with nat. and int. bodies in this field; 400 mems in 8 sections; Pres. Prof. FRANCO PERSIANI; Gen. Sec. Prof. ANTONIO CASTEL-

LANI; Treas. Prof. LUIGI BALIS CREMA; publ. Aerotecnica Missili e Spazio (4 a year).

Associazione Italiana di Metallurgia (Italian Metallurgical Association): Piazza R. Morandi 2, 20121 Milan; tel. 02-76021132; fax 02-76020551; e-mail aim@aimnet.it; internet www.metallurgia-italiana.net; f. 1946; promotes and develops all aspects of science, technology and use of metals and materials closely related to metals; 2,000 mems; Pres. VINCENZO CRAPANZANO; Gen. Sec. Dott. FEDERICA BASSANI; publ. La Metallurgia Italiana (12 a year).

Associazione Italiana Nucleare (Italian Nuclear Association): Corso Vittorio Emanuele II 244, 00186 Rome; tel. 06-94005401; fax 06-94005314; e-mail info@assonucleare.it; internet www.assonucleare.it; f. 2005; Pres. Ing. ENZO GATTA; Gen. Sec. Ing. UGO SPEZIA.

Comitato Elettrotecnico Italiano (CEI) (Italian Electrotechnical Committee): Via Saccardo 9, 20134 Milan; tel. 02-210061; fax 02-21006210; e-mail cei@ceiweb.it; internet www.ceiweb.it; f. 1909; Pres. Dr Ing. UGO NICOLA TRAMUTOLI; Gen. Dir. Dr Ing. ROBERTO BACCI.

Comitato Termotecnico Italiano (CTI) (Italian Thermotechnical Committee): Via Scarlatti 29, 20124 Milan; tel. 02-2662651; fax 02-26626550; e-mail cti@cti2000.it; internet www.cti2000.it; f. 1933; Pres. Prof. Ing. CESARE BOFFA; Gen. Sec. Prof. Ing. GIOVANNI RIVA; publ. La Termotecnica (10 a year).

Ente Nazionale Italiano di Unificazione (UNI) (Italian National Standards Association): Via Sannio 2, 20137 Milan; tel. 02-700241; fax 02-70024375; e-mail uni@uni.com; internet www.uni.com; f. 1921; Pres. PAOLO SCOLARI; Exec. Vice-Pres. Dr Ing. ENRICO MARTINOTTI; publ. Unificazione (4 a year).

Federazione Italiana di Elettrotecnica, Elettronica, Automazione, Informatica e Telecomunicazioni (AEIT) (Italian Federation for Electrotechnology, Electronics, Automation, Information Technology and Telecommunications): Central Office, Via Mauro Macchi 32, 20124 Milan; tel. 02-87389960; fax 02-66989023; e-mail aeit@federaeit.it; internet www.aei.it; f. 1896; Pres. Ing. GIANFRANCO VEGLIO; Sec. IVANA SARTORI; publs AEIT—Federazione di Elettrotecnica, Elettronica, Automazione, Informatica e Telecomunicazioni (12 a year), L'Energia Elettrica (6 a year), Mondo Digitale (12 a year).

Istituto di Studi Nucleari per l'Agricoltura (ISNA) (Institute of Nuclear Studies applied to Agriculture): Via IV Novembre 152, 00187 Rome; tel. 06-6784991; fax 06-6782994; f. 1959; Pres. Avv. Prof. GIUSEPPE GESUALDI; Sec.-Gen. Prof. M. L. SCARSELLI; publs Agricoltura d'Italia (12 a year), Il Corriere di Roma, Quaderni ISNA.

Istituto Italiano del Marchio di Qualità (IMQ) (Italian Institute of the Quality Mark): Via Quintiliano 43, 20138 Milan; tel. 02-50731; fax 02-5073271; e-mail luigi.paleari@imq.it; internet www.imq.it; f. 1951; tests electrical and gas products to grant the IMQ safety mark; undertakes EU Directives conformity assessment and certifies company quality and management systems as part of the CSQ scheme; Pres. Ing. GIORGIO SCANAVACCA; Man. Dir Ing. GIANCARLO ZAPPA; publs Gruppo IMQ Informa (1 a year, online), IMQ Notizie (News, 2 a year, online).

Istituto Italiano della Saldatura (Italian Welding Institute): Lungobisagno Istria 15, 16141 Genoa; tel. 010-83411; fax 010-8367780; e-mail iis@iis.it; internet www.iis

.it; f. 1948; consultancy training, research, standardization, certification, laboratory tests and diploma courses in welding; 800 mems; library of 15,000 vols; Sec.-Gen. Dott.-Ing. MAURO SCASSO.

Research Institutes
GENERAL

Consiglio Nazionale delle Ricerche (CNR) (National Research Council of Italy): Piazzale Aldo Moro 7, 00185 Rome; tel. 06-49931; fax 06-4461954; e-mail urp@urp.cnr.it; internet www.cnr.it; f. 1923; research is carried out by 110 institutes in 11 depts: Agri-Food (Dir Dott. A LCIDE B ERTANI); Cultural Heritage (Dir vacant); Cultural Identity (Dir vacant); Earth and Environmental Sciences (Dir G IUSEPPE C AVARRETTA); Energy and Transport (Dir C LAUDIO B ERTOLI); Information and Communications Technology (Dir Prof. F RANCESCO B ELTRAME); Life Sciences (Dir G IUSEPPE M ARTINI); Materials and Devices (Dir Prof. M ASSIMO I NGUSCIO); Medicine (Dir Prof. G IANLUIGI C ONDORELLI); Molecular Design (Dir S ESTO V ITICOLI); and Production Systems (Dir C LAUDIO B ERTOLI); Pres. Prof. LUCIANO MAIANI; Gen. Man. Dott. FABRIZIO TUZI; publs Almanacco della Scienza (26 a year, online), Ricerca e Futuro (print and online versions, 4 a year), Notiziario Neutroni e Luce di Sincrotrone (print and online versions, in English, 2 a year).

Agri-Food:

Istituto di Biologia e Biotecnologia Agraria (Institute of Agricultural Biology and Biotechnology): Via Edoardo Bassini 15, 20133 Milan; tel. 02-23699403; fax 02-23699411; e-mail direttore@ibba.cnr.it; internet www.ibba.cnr.it; f. 2001; Dir Dott. ROBERTO BOLLINI.

Istituto di Biometeorologia (Institute for Biometeorology): Via Giovanni Caproni 8, 50145 Florence; tel. 055-3033711; fax 055-308910; e-mail a.raschi@ibimet.cnr.it; internet www.ibimet.cnr.it; f. 2000; Dir Dott. ANTONIO RASCHI.

Istituto di Diritto Agrario Internazionale e Comparato/Centro di Responsabilità Scientifica IDAIC (Institute of International and Comparative Agricultural Law): Via La Marmora 29, 50121 Florence; tel. 055-579558; fax 055-5047100; e-mail idaic@fi.191.it; internet www.idaic.it; f. 1957; Man. Dir Prof. ALBERTO GERMANO; publ. Rivista di Diritto Agrario.

Istituto di Genetica Vegetale (Institute of Plant Genetics): Via Giovanni Amendola 165/A, 70126 Bari; tel. 080-5583400; fax 080-5587566; e-mail domenico.pignone@igv.cnr.it; internet www.igv.cnr.it; f. 2001; Dir Dott. DOMENICO PIGNONE.

Istituto di Scienza dell'Alimentazione (Institute of Food Science): Via Roma 52 a/c, 83100 Avellino; tel. 0825-299111; fax 0825-781585; e-mail direttore@isa.cnr.it; internet www.isa.cnr.it; f. 2001; Dir Prof. RAFFAELE COPPOLA.

Istituto di Scienze delle Produzioni Alimentari (Institute of Food Production Sciences): Via Amendola 122/O, 70126 Bari; tel. 080-5929333; fax 080-5929373; e-mail angelo.visconti@ispa.cnr.it; internet www.ispa.cnr.it; f. 2001; Dir Dott. ANGELO VISCONTI.

Istituto di Virologia Vegetale (Institute of Plant Virology): Strada delle Cacce 73, 10135 Turin; tel. 011-3977911; fax 011-343809; e-mail direttore@ivv.cnr.it;

internet www.ivv.cnr.it; f. 2001; Dir Dott. JOZSEF BURGYAN.

Istituto per i Sistemi Agricoli e Forestali del Mediterraneo (Institute for Mediterranean Agriculture and Forest Systems): CP 101, 80040 S. Sebastiano al Vesuvio; Via Patacca 85, 80056 Ercolano; tel. 081-7717325; fax 081-7718045; e-mail segreteria@isafom.cnr.it; internet www .isafom.cnr.it; f. 2001; Dir Dr RICCARDO D'ANDRIA.

Istituto per il Sistema Produzione Animale in Ambiente Mediterraneo (Institute for Animal Production in the Mediterranean Environment): Via Argine 1085, 80147 Naples; tel. 081-5966006; fax 081-5965291; e-mail leopoldo.iannuzzi@ ispaam.cnr.it; internet www.ispaam.cnr.it; f. 2001; Dir Prof. LEOPOLDO IANNUZZI.

Istituto per la Protezione delle Piante (Plant Protection Institute): Via Madonna del Piano 10, 50019 Sesto Fiorentino; tel. 055-5225589; fax 055-5225666; e-mail f .loreto@ipp.cnr.it; internet www.ipp.cnr.it; f. 2001; Dir Dott. FRANCESCO LORETO.

Cultural Heritage:

Istituto di Studi sulle Civiltà dell'Egeo e del Vicino Oriente (Institute for Aegean and Near Eastern Studies): Via Giano della Bella 18, 00162 Rome; tel. 06-4416131; fax 06-44237724; e-mail direzione@icevo.cnr.it; internet www.icevo .cnr.it; f. 1968, present status in 2001; library of 15,000 vols; Aegean and Early Greek Civilization; Aegean Archaeology; Mycenaean Philology; Cretan Archaeology; Cypriot Archaeology; Mediterranean Protohistory; Anatolian and Near Eastern Civilization; Near Eastern Archaeology; Anatolian Archaeology; Iranian Archaeology; Hittitology; Hurritology; Urartian Civilization; Assyriology; 13 mems; Dir Dr MARIE-CLAUDE TRÉMOUILLE (acting); publ. *Studi Micenei ed Egeo Anatolici*.

Istituto di Studi sulle Civiltà Italiche e del Mediterraneo Antico (Institute for the Study of the Italic and Ancient Mediterranean Civilizations): Via Salaria Km 29.3, CP10, 00016 Monterotondo; tel. 06-90672284; fax 06-90672818; e-mail direttore@iscima.cnr.it; internet soi.cnr.it/ iscima; f. 2001; Dir Dott. PAOLA SANTORO.

Istituto per i Beni Archeologici e Monumentali (Institute of Archaeological Heritage—Monuments and Sites): Prov.le Lecce-Monteroni, 73100 Lecce; tel. 0832-422200; fax 0832-422225; e-mail segreteria@ibam.cnr.it; internet www .ibam.cnr.it; f. 2001; Dir Dott. ANTONELLA PELLETTIERI.

Istituto per la Conservazione e Valorizzazione dei Beni Culturali (Institute for the Conservation and Promotion of Cultural Heritage): Via Madonna del Piano 10, Edificio C, 50019 Sesto Fiorentino; tel. 055-5225484; fax 055-5225403; e-mail direttore@icvbc.cnr.it; internet www.icvbc .cnr.it; f. 2001; Dir Prof. PIERO FREDIANI.

Istituto per le Tecnologie Applicate ai Beni Culturali (Institute for Technologies Applied to Cultural Heritage): Via Salaria Km. 29.3, CP 10, 00016 Monterotondo Stazione; tel. 06-90625274; fax 06-90672684; e-mail itabc@itabc.cnr.it; internet www.itabc.cnr.it; f. 2001; Dir Dott. SALVATORE GARRAFFO.

Cultural Identity:

Istituto di Linguistica Computazionale 'Antonio Zampolli' (Institute of Computational Linguistics): Via Giuseppe Moruzzi 1, 56124 Pisa; tel. 050-3152872; fax 050-3152839; e-mail direttore@ilc.cnr

.it; internet www.ilc.cnr.it; f. 2001; Dir Dott. ANDREA BOZZI.

Istituto di Ricerca sui Sistemi Giudiziari (Institute for Research on Judicial Systems): Via Zamboni 26, 40126 Bologna; tel. 051-2756211; fax 051-260250; e-mail direttore@irsig.cnr.it; internet www.irsig .cnr.it; f. 2002; Dir Dott. MARCO FABRI.

Istituto di Ricerca sull'Impresa e lo Sviluppo (Institute of Research on Business Firms and Development): Via Real Collegio 30, 10024 Moncalieri; tel. 011-6824911; fax 011-6824966; e-mail segreteria@ceris.cnr.it; internet www.ceris .cnr.it; f. 1956; Dir Dott. SECONDO ROLFO.

Istituto di Ricerche sulla Popolazione e le Politiche Sociali (Institute for Research on Population and Social Policies): Via Palestro 328, 00185 Rome; tel. 06-492724200; fax 06-49383724; e-mail info@irpps.cnr.it; internet www.irpps.cnr .it; f. 2001; Dir Dott. SVEVA AVVEDUTO.

Istituto di Ricerche sulle Attività Terziarie (Institute for Service Industry Research): Via Michelangelo Schipa 91, 80122 Naples; tel. 081-2470953; fax 081-7618265; e-mail a.morvillo@irat.cnr.it; internet www.irat.cnr.it; f. 2001; Dir Dott. ALFONSO MORVILLO.

Istituto di Scienze e Tecnologie della Cognizione (Institute of Cognitive Sciences and Technologies): Via S. Martino della Battaglia 44, 00185 Rome; tel. 06-44595246; fax 06-44595243; e-mail direzione.istc@istc.cnr.it; internet www .istc.cnr.it; f. 2001; Dir Prof. CRISTIANO CASTELFRANCHI.

Istituto di Storia dell'Europa Mediterranea (Institute of Mediterranean European History): Via G. B. Tuveri 128, 09129 Cagliari; tel. 070-403635; fax 070-498118; e-mail codignola@isem.cnr.it; internet www.isem.cnr.it; f. 2001; Dir Prof. LUCA CODIGNOLA BO.

Istituto di Studi Giuridici Internazionali (Institute for International Legal Studies): Via dei Taurini 19, 00185 Rome; tel. 06-49937660; fax 06-44340025; e-mail segreteria@isgi.cnr.it; internet www.isgi .cnr.it; f. 1986, present name 2001; research in international law; the international protection of human rights; international environmental law; library of 2,000 vols; Dir Prof. SERGIO MARCHISIO.

Istituto di Studi sui Sistemi Regionali Federali e sulle Autonomie 'Massimo Severo Giannini' (Institute for the Study of Regionalism, Federalism and Self-Government): Via dei Taurini 19, 00185 Rome; tel. 06-49937740; fax 06-490704; e-mail segreteria@issirfa.cnr.it; internet www .issirfa.cnr.it; f. 2001; Dir Prof. STELIO MANGIAMELI.

Istituto di Studi sulle Società del Mediterraneo (Institute of Studies on Mediterranean Societies): Via Pietro Castellino 111, 80131 Naples; tel. 081-6134086; fax 081-5799467; e-mail istituto@issm.cnr.it; internet www.issm .cnr.it; f. 2001; growth, convergence and divergence in Mediterranean economies in the past and present; 30 mems; library of 15,000 vols; Dir Prof. PAOLO MALANIMA; publ. *Global environment*.

Istituto di Teoria e Tecniche dell'Informazione Giuridica (Institute of Legal Information Theory and Techniques): Via dei Barucci 20, 50127 Florence; tel. 055-43995; fax 055-4399605; e-mail ittig@ittig .cnr.it; internet www.ittig.cnr.it; f. 2001; Dir Dott. COSTANTINO CIAMPI.

Istituto Opera del Vocabolario Italiano (The Italian Dictionary): Via di

Castello 46, 50141 Florence; tel. 055-452841; fax 055-452843; e-mail beltrami@ ovi.cnr.it; internet www.ovi.cnr.it; f. 2001; Dir Prof. PIETRO BELTRAMI.

Istituto per il Lessico Intellettuale Europeo e la Storia delle Idee (Institute for the European Intellectual Lexicon and the History of Ideas): Villa Mirafiori, Via Nomentana, 118, 00161 Rome; tel. 06-86320527; fax 06-49917215; e-mail iliesi@ iliesi.cnr.it; internet www.iliesi.cnr.it; f. 1964; 25 mems; library of 4,600 microfilms; Dir Prof. RICCARDO POZZO; publs *Bruniana and Campanelliana*, *Elenchos*.

Istituto per la Storia del Pensiero Filosofico e Scientifico Moderno (Institute for the History of Philosophical and Scientific Thought in the Modern Age): Via Porta di Massa 1, 80133 Naples; tel. 081-2535580; fax 081-2535515; e-mail sanna@ unina.it; internet www.ispf.cnr.it; f. 2001; Dir Dott. MANUELA SANNA.

Istituto per le Tecnologie Didattiche (Institute for Educational Technology): Via de Marini 6, Torre di Francia, 16149 Genoa; tel. 010-6475303; fax 010-6475300; e-mail itd@itd.cnr.it; internet www.itd.cnr .it; f. 2001 by merging of Istituto per le Tecnologie Didattiche, based in Genoa and founded in 1970, and the Istituto Tecnologie Didattiche e Formative, established in 1993 in Palermo; research in educational technology; computer science, engineering, mathematics, physics, pedagogy, psychology, languages; library of 5,000 vols; Dir Dr ROSA BOTTINO; publ. *TD-Tecnologie Didattiche* (Italian, abstract in English, 3 a year).

Earth and Environment:

Istituto di Biologia Agro-ambientale e Forestale (Institute of Agro-environmental and Forest Biology): Viale Guglielmo Marconi 2, 05010 Porano; tel. 0763-374911; fax 0763-374980; e-mail ibaf@pec.cnr.it; internet www.ibaf.cnr.it; f. 2001; Dir Dott. ENRICO BRUGNOLI.

Istituto di Geologia Ambientale e Geoingegneria (Institute of Environmental Geology and Geoengineering): Via Salaria Km 29.3, CP 10, 00016 Monterotondo Stazione; tel. 06-90672600-595; fax 06-90672733; e-mail giovannimaria .zuppi@igag.cnr.it; internet www.igag.cnr .it; f. 2001; Dir Prof. GIOVANNI MARIA ZUPPI.

Istituto di Geoscienze e Georisorse (Institute of Geosciences and Earth Resources): Via Giuseppe Moruzzi 1, 56124 Pisa; tel. 050-3152372; fax 050-3152323; e-mail igg@igg.cnr.it; internet www.igg.cnr.it; f. 2001; Dir Dott. GIOVANNI GIANELLI.

Istituto di Metodologie per l'Analisi Ambientale (Institute of Methodologies for Environmental Analysis): Contrada S. Loja, CP 27, 85050 Tito Scalo (PZ) Basilicata; tel. 0971-427111; fax 0971-427264; e-mail maa@pec.cnr.it; internet www.imaa .cnr.it; f. 2001; Dir Dott. VINCENZO LAPENNA.

Istituto di Ricerca per la Protezione Idrogeologica (Research Institute for Geo-hydrological Protection): Via Madonna Alta 126, 06128 Perugia; tel. 075-5014411; fax 075-5014420; e-mail segreteria@irpi .cnr.it; internet www.irpi.cnr.it; f. 2001; Dir Dott. FAUSTO GUZZETTI.

Istituto di Ricerca sulle Acque (Water Research Institute): Via Salaria Km 29.3, CP 10, 00015 Monteredondo Stazione; tel. 06-90672850; fax 06-90672787; e-mail direzione@irsa.cnr.it; internet www.irsa .cnr.it; f. 2001; Dir Dott. MAURIZIO PETTINE.

Istituto di Scienze dell'Atmosfera e del Clima (Institute of Atmospheric Sciences and Climate): Via Piero Gobetti 101, 40129 Bologna; tel. 051-6399619; fax 051-6399658; e-mail direttore@isac.cnr.it; internet www.isac.cnr.it; f. 2000; Dir Dott. CRISTINA SABBIONI.

Istituto di Scienze Marine (Institute of Marine Sciences): Arsenale Tesa 104, Castello 2737/F, 30122 Venice; tel. 041-2407927; fax 041-2407940; e-mail direttore@ismar.cnr.it; internet www .ismar.cnr.it; f. 2001; Dir Dott. FABIO TRINCARDI.

Istituto per la Dinamica dei Processi Ambientali (Institute for the Dynamics of Environmental Processes): Calle Larga Santa Marta 2, 30123 Venice; tel. 041-2348547; fax 041-2578549; e-mail pietro .mario.rossi@idpa.cnr.it; internet www .idpa.cnr.it; f. 2001; Dir Dott. PIETRO MARIO ROSSI.

Istituto per l'Ambiente Marino Costiero (Institute for the Coastal Marine Environment): Calata Porta di Massa, 80133 Naples; tel. 081-5423804; fax 081-5423887; e-mail direttore@iamc.cnr.it; internet www.iamc.cnr.it; f. 2001; Dir Dott. SALVATORE MAZZOLA.

Istituto per la Valorizzazione del Legno e delle Specie Arboree (Tree and Timber Institute): Via Madonna del Piano 10, 50019 Sesto Fiorentino; tel. 055-52251; fax 055-5225507; e-mail direttore@ ivalsa.cnr.it; internet www.ivalsa.cnr.it; f. 2002; Dir Prof. ARIO CECCOTTI.

Istituto per lo Studio degli Ecosistemi (Institute of Ecosystem Study): Largo Vittorio Tonolli 50, 28922 Pallanza Verbania; tel. 0323-518300; fax 0323-556513; e-mail direzione@ise.cnr.it; internet www .ise.cnr.it; f. 2001; Dir Dott. ROSARIO MOSELLO.

Istituto sull'Inquinamento Atmosferico (Institute for Atmospheric Pollution Research): Via Salaria Km 29.3, CP 10, 00016 Monterotondo; tel. 06-90625349; fax 06-90672660; e-mail pirrone@iia.cnr.it; internet www.iia.cnr.it; f. 2001; Dir Dott. NICOLA PIRRONE.

Energy and Transport:

Istituto di Fisica del Plasma 'Piero Caldirola' (Institute for Plasma Physics): Via Roberto Cozzi 53, 20125 Milan; tel. 02-66173238; fax 02-66173239; e-mail direttore@ifp.cnr.it; internet www.ifp.cnr .it; f. 1974; library of 3,000 vols, 100 periodical titles; Dir Dott. MAURIZIO LONTANO.

Istituto di Ricerche sulla Combustione (Institute for Research on Combustion): Piazzale Vincenzo Tecchio 80, 80125 Naples; tel. 081-7682245; fax 081-5936936; e-mail ciajolo@irc.cnr.it; internet www.irc .cnr.it; f. 2001; Dir Dott. ANNA CIAJOLO.

Istituto di Tecnologie Avanzate per l'Energia 'Nicola Giordano' (Institute for Advanced Energy Technologies): Via Salita S. Lucia sopra Contesse 5, 98126 Messina; tel. 090-624246; fax 090-624247; e-mail gaetano.cacciola@itae.cnr.it; internet www.itae.cnr.it; f. 2000; Dir Dott. Ing. GAETANO CACCIOLA.

Istituto Gas Ionizzati/Consorzio RFX (Institute of Ionized Gas): Corso Stati Uniti 4, 35127 Padua; tel. 049-8295000; fax 049-8700718; e-mail segrgen@igi.cnr.it; internet www.igi.cnr.it; f. 2001; Dir Prof. FRANCESCO GNESOTTO.

Istituto Motori (Motors Institute): Via Marconi 8, 80125 Naples; tel. 081-7177131; fax 081-2396097; e-mail direttore@im.cnr

.it; internet www.im.cnr.it; f. 2001; Dir Ing. PAOLA BELARDINI.

Istituto per l'Energetica e le Interfasi (Institute for Energetics and Interphases): Corso Stati Uniti 4, 35127 Padua; tel. 049-8295850; fax 049-8295853; e-mail s.daolio@ ieni.cnr.it; internet www.ieni.cnr.it; f. 2000; Dir Dott. SERGIO DAOLIO.

Information and Communications Technology:

Istituto di Analisi dei Sistemi ed Informatica 'Antonio Ruberti' (Institute for Systems Analysis and Computer Science): Viale Manzoni 30, 00185 Rome; tel. 06-77161; fax 06-7716461; e-mail bertolai@iasi.cnr.it; internet www.iasi.cnr .it; f. 2001; Dir Dott. PAOLA BERTOLAZZI.

Istituto di Calcolo e Reti ad Alte Prestazioni (Institute for High-performance Computing and Networking): Via Pietro Bucci, Cubo 41C, 87036 Rende (CS); tel. 0984-831720; fax 0984-839054; e-mail cosenza@icar.cnr.it; internet www .icar.cnr.it; f. 2001; Dir Prof. DOMENICO TALIA.

Istituto di Elettronica e di Ingegneria dell'Informazione e delle Telecomunicazioni (Institute of Electronics, Computer and Telecommunications Engineering): Corso Duca degli Abruzzi 24, 10129 Turin; tel. 011-5645400; fax 011-5645429; e-mail direttore@ieiit.cnr.it; internet www.ieiit.cnr.it; f. 2001; Dir Dott. RICCARDO TASCONE.

Istituto di Informatica e Telematica (Institute for Informatics and Telematics): Via Giuseppe Moruzzi 1, 56124 Pisa; tel. 050-3152112; fax 050-3152113; e-mail domenico.laforenza@iit.cnr.it; internet www.iit.cnr.it; f. 2001; Dir Dott. DOMENICO LAFORENZA.

Istituto di Matematica Applicata e Tecnologie Informatiche (Institute of Applied Mathematics and Information Technology): Via Ferrata 1, 27100 Pavia; tel. 0382-548211; fax 0382-548300; e-mail direttore@imati.cnr.it; internet www.imati .cnr.it; f. 2000; Dir Prof. FRANCO BREZZI; Librarian M. GRAZIA FUSARI.

Istituto di Scienza e Tecnologie dell'Informazione 'Alessandro Faedo' (Institute of Information Science and Technology 'Alessandro Faedo'): Via Giuseppe Moruzzi 1, 56124 Pisa; tel. 050-3152878; fax 050-3152811; e-mail direttore@isti.cnr .it; internet www.isti.cnr.it; f. 2000; Dir Dr CLAUDIO MONTANI.

Istituto per il Rilevamento Elettromagnetico dell'Ambiente (Institute for Electromagnetic Sensing of the Environment): Via Diocleziano 328, 80124 Naples; tel. 081-5707999; fax 081-5705734; e-mail bucci.om@irea.cnr.it; internet www.irea .cnr.it; f. 2001; active microwave remote sensing; passive remote sensing in optics; modelling of electromagnetic interaction processes; multi source data fusion and integration for environmental monitoring; sensors and techniques for electromagnetic diagnostics; biological effects and clinical diagnostic and therapy applications related to electromagnetic fields; 36 mems; Dir Prof. OVIDIO MARIO BUCCI.

Life Sciences:

Istituto di Biochimica delle Proteine (Institute of Protein Biochemistry): Via Pietro Castellino 111, 80131 Naples; tel. 081-6132273; fax 081-6132277; e-mail d .corda@ibp.cnr.it; internet www.ibp.cnr.it; f. 2001; Dir Dott. DANIELA CORDA.

Istituto di Biologia e Patologia Molecolari (Institute of Molecular Biology and Pathology): Piazzale Aldo Moro 5, 00185

Rome; tel. (6) 4940543; fax (6) 4440062; e-mail info@ibpm.cnr.it; internet www .ibpm.cnr.it; f. 2001; Dir Prof. EMILIA CHIANCONE.

Istituto di Biomembrane e Bioenergetica (Institute of Biomembrane and Bioenergetics): Via Giovanni Amendola 165/A, 70126 Bari; tel. 080-5443389; fax 080-5443317; e-mail g.pesole@ibbe.cnr.it; internet www.ibbe.cnr.it; f. 2001; Dir Dott. GRAZIANO PESOLE.

Istituto di Genetica delle Popolazioni (Institute of Population Genetics): Traversa La Crucca 3, Reg. Baldinca, 07100 Sassari; tel. 079-2841301; fax 079-2841399; e-mail c.lamon@igp.cnr.it; f. 2001; Dir Dott. MARIO PIRASTU.

Istituto di Genetica e Biofisica 'Adriano Buzzati Traverso' (Institute of Genetics and Biophysics): Via Pietro Castellino 111, 80131 Naples; tel. 081-6132698; fax 081-6132706; e-mail baldini@igb.cnr.it; internet www.igb.cnr.it; f. 2000; Dir Prof. ANTONIO BALDINI.

Istituto per l'Endocrinologia e l'Oncologia 'Gaetano Salvatore' (Institute for Experimental Endocrinology and Oncology): Via Sergio Pansini 5, 80131 Naples; tel. 081-7463602; fax 081-2296674; e-mail a .fusco@ieos.cnr.it; internet www.ieos.cnr .it; f. 2001; Dir Prof. ALFREDO FUSCO.

Materials and Devices:

Istituto dei Sistemi Complessi (Institute for Complex Systems): Via dei Taurini 19, 00185 Rome; tel. 06-49937495; fax 06-49937442; e-mail segreteria@isc.cnr.it; internet www.isc.cnr.it; f. 2004; Dir Prof. LUCIANO PIETRONERO.

Istituto di Biofisica (Institute of Biophysics): Via De Marini 6, Torre di Francia, 16149 Genoa; tel. 010-6475577; fax 010-6475500; e-mail direttore@ge.ibf.cnr.it; internet www.ibf.cnr.it; f. 2001; Dir Dott. FRANCO GAMBALE.

Istituto di Cibernetica 'Edoardo Caianiello' (Cybernetics Institute): Via Campi Flegrei 34, 80078 Pozzuoli; tel. 081-8675111; fax 081-8675128; e-mail m .russo@cib.na.cnr.it; internet www.cib.na .cnr.it; f. 2001; Dir MAURIZIO RUSSO.

Istituto di Fisica Applicata 'Nello Carrara' (Institute of Applied Physics): Via Madonna del Piano, 10 50019 Sesto Fiorentino (FI); tel. 055-5226436; fax 055-5226477; e-mail r.salimbeni@ifac.cnr.it; internet www.ifac.cnr.it; f. 2001; Dir Dott. RENZO SALIMBENI.

Istituto di Fotonica e Nanotecnologie (Institute for Photonics and Nanotechnologies): Via Cineto Romano 42, 00156 Rome; tel. 06-4152221; fax 06-41522220; e-mail evangelisti@ifn.cnr.it; internet www.ifn .cnr.it; f. 2000; study and development of photonics from points of view of radiation-matter interaction and of developing materials, devices and systems; study and development of nanotechnologies for the fabrication of nanoscale-size devices; development of microelectronic and micromechanical devices; Dir Prof. FLORESTANO EVANGELISTI.

Istituto di Metodologie Inorganiche e dei Plasmi (Institute of Inorganic Methodologies and Plasmas): Via Salaria Km 29.3, CP 10, 00016 Monterotondo Scalo; tel. 06-906721; fax 06-90672238; e-mail direttore@imip.cnr.it; internet www.imip .cnr.it; f. 2000; Dir Dott. MARIO CACCIATORE.

Istituto di Struttura della Materia (Institute for the Structure of Matter): Via del Fosso del Cavaliere 100, 00133 Rome; tel. 06-49934476; fax 06-49934153;

e-mail direttore@ism.cnr.it; internet www .ism.cnr.it; f. 2000; Dir Dott. DINO FIORANI.

Istituto Nanoscienze (Nanoscience Institute): Piazza San Silvestro 12, 56127 Pisa; tel. 050-509418; fax 050-509417; e-mail segreteria@nano.cnr.it; internet www .nano.cnr.it; f. 2010; Dir Dott. LUCIA SORBA.

Istituto Nazionale di Ottica (INO) (National Institute of Applied Optics): Largo Enrico Fermi 6, 50125 Florence; tel. 055-23081; fax 055-2337755; e-mail direttore@ino.it; internet www.ino.it; f. 1927; quantum, instrumental and physiological optics; library of 7,000 vols; Pres. Dott. PAOLO DE NATALE; Gen. Dir Dr CARLO CASTELLINI.

Istituto Nazionale per la Fisica della Materia/Centro di Responsabilità Scientifica INFM (National Institute for the Physical Sciences of Matter): Corso Perrone 24 , 16152 Genoa; tel. 010-6598750; fax 010-6506302; e-mail sede@ infm.it; internet www.infm.it; f. 2005; Dir Prof. ELISA MOLINARI.

Istituto Officina dei Materiali (Institute of Materials Workshop): S.S. 14, Km. 163.5, 34149 Trieste; tel. 040-3756411; fax 040-226767; e-mail iom@pec.cnr.it; internet www.iom.cnr.it; f. 2010; conducts interdisciplinary research based on knowledge of the physical properties of materials and complex systems at the atomic scale and their functionality; Dir Prof. ALBERTO MORGANTE.

Istituto per i Processi Chimico-Fisici (Institute for Chemical and Physical Processes): Via Giuseppe Moruzzi 1, 56124 Pisa; tel. 050-3152233; fax 050-3152230; e-mail direttore@ipcf.cnr.it; internet www .ipcf.cnr.it; f. 2000; Dir Dott. CIRINO SALVATORE VASI.

Istituto per la Microelettronica e Microsistemi (Institute for Microelectronics and Microsystems): Ottava strada, 5 (Zona Industriale), 95121 Catania; tel. 095-5968211; fax 095-5968312; e-mail corrado.spinella@imm.cnr.it; internet www.imm.cnr.it; f. 2000; Dir Dott. CORRADO SPINELLA.

Istituto per le Applicazioni del Calcolo 'Mauro Picone' (Institute for Applied Mathematics): Viale dei Taurini 19, 00185 Rome; tel. 06-49270921; fax 06-4404306; e-mail bertsch@iac.rm.cnr.it; internet www.iac.cnr.it; f. 2000; Dir Prof. MICHIEL BERTSCH.

Istituto Superconduttori, Materiali Innovativi e Dispositivi (Institute for Superconductors, Innovative Materials and Devices): Corso F. Perrone, 16152 Genoa; tel. 010-6598750; fax 010-6598750; e-mail segreteria@spin.cnr.it; internet www.spin.cnr.it; f. 2010; Dir Prof. RUGGERO VAGLIO.

Medicine:

Istituto di Bioimmagini e Fisiologia Molecolare (Institute of Molecular Bioimaging and Physiology): Via Fratelli Cervi 93, 20090 Segrate; tel. 02-21717514; fax 02-21717558; e-mail direzione@ibfm.cnr.it; internet www.ibfm.cnr.it; f. 2001; Dir Prof. MARIA CARLA GILARDI.

Istituto di Biologia Cellulare (Institute of Cell Biology): Via E. Ramarini 32, 00015 Monterotondo Scalo; tel. 06-90091207; fax 06-90091261; e-mail emma@emmanet.org; internet www.emma.cnr.it; f. 1969; research areas in functional genomics, systems of signal transduction, molecular aspects of the construction logic and the functioning of complex organisms, RNA, molecular aspects of the relationship between parasite and host in tropical dis-

eases, construction of mutant strains and phenocopies of mice, cryo-conservation, rederivation, distribution of mutant strains, production and telematic distribution of databases of mutant strains; Dir Prof. GLAUCO TOCCHINI-VALENTINI.

Istituto di Biomedicina e di Immunologia Molecolare 'Alberto Monroy' (Institute of Biomedicine and Molecular Immunology): Via Ugo La Malfa 153, 90146 Palermo; tel. 091-6809194; fax 091-6809122; e-mail segreteria@ibim.cnr.it; internet www.ibim.cnr.it; f. 2001; Dir Dott. GIOVANNI VIEGI.

Istituto di Fisiologia Clinica (Institute of Clinical Physiology): Via Giuseppe Moruzzi 1, 56124 Pisa; tel. 050-3152216; fax 050-3152166; e-mail picano@ifc.cnr.it; internet www.ifc.cnr.it; f. 2001; Dir Dott. EUGENIO PICATO.

Istituto di Genetica Molecolare (Institute of Molecular Genetics): Via Abbiategrasso 207, 27100 Pavia; tel. 0382-5461; fax 0382-422286; e-mail biamonti@igm.cnr .it; internet www.igm.cnr.it; f. 2000; Dir Dott. GIUSEPPE BIAMONTI.

Istituto di Ingegneria Biomedica (Institute of Biomedical Engineering): Corso Stati Uniti 4, 35127 Padua; tel. 049-8295702; fax 049-8295763; e-mail mbox@isib.cnr.it; internet www.isib.cnr.it; f. 2001; Dir Dott. FERDINANDO GRANDORI.

Istituto di Neurobiologia e Medicina Molecolare (Institute of Neurobiology and Molecular Medicine): Via del Fosso di Fiorano 64, Località Prato Smeraldo, 00143 Rome; tel. 06-501703025; fax 06-501703311; e-mail segreteria@inmm.cnr.it; f. 2000; Dir Dott. DELIO MERCANTI.

Istituto di Neurogenetica e Neurofarmacologia (Institute of Neurogenetics and Neuropharmacology): Cittadella Universitaria di Cagliari, 09042 Monserrato CA Sardinia; tel. 070-6754543; fax 070-6754652; e-mail c.flore@inn.cnr.it; f. 2001; Dir Prof. FRANCESCO CUCCA (acting).

Istituto di Neuroscienze (Neuroscience Institute): Via Giuseppe Moruzzi 1, 56124 Pisa; tel. 050-3152207; fax 050-3153210; e-mail segreteria@in.cnr.it; internet www .in.cnr.it; f. 2001; Dir Prof. TULLIO POZZAN.

Istituto di Scienze Neurologiche (Institute of Neurological Sciences): Contrada Burga 44, 87050 Mangone; tel. 0984-98011; fax 0984-969306; e-mail a.quattrone@isn .cnr.it; internet www.isn.cnr.it; f. 2001; Dir Prof. ALDO QUATTRONE.

Istituto di Tecnologie Biomediche (Institute of Biomedical Technologies): Via Fratelli Cervi 93, 20090 Segrate; tel. 02-26422702; fax 02-26422770; e-mail luigi .zecca@itb.cnr.it; internet www.itb.cnr.it; f. 2001; Dir Dott. LUIGI ZECCA.

Istituto per i Trapianti d'Organo e Immunocitologia (Organ Tranplantation and Immunology Institute): Piazzale Collemaggio, 67100 L'Aquila; tel. 0862-27129; fax 0862-410758; e-mail d.adorno@itoi.cnr .it; f. 2001; Dir Prof. DOMENICO ADORNO.

Molecular Design:

Istituto di Biostrutture e Bioimmagini (Institute of Biostructure and Bioimaging): Via Pansini 5, 80131 Naples; tel. 081-2203187; fax 081-2296117; e-mail direttore@ibb.cnr.it; internet www.ibb.cnr .it; f. 2001; Dir Dott. BRUNO ALFANO.

Istituto di Chimica Biomolecolare (Institute of Biomolecular Chemistry): Via Campi Flegrei 34, 80078 Pozzuoli; tel. 081-8675018; fax 081-8041770; e-mail direzione@icb.cnr.it; internet www.icb.cnr .it; f. 2001; Dir Dott. AGATA GAMBACORTA.

Istituto di Chimica dei Composti Organo Metallici (Institute of Organometallic Compounds Chemistry): Via Madonna del Piano 10, 50019 Sesto Fiorentino (Firenze); tel. 055-5225280; fax 055-5225203; e-mail claudio.bianchini@iccom .cnr.it; internet www.iccom.cnr.it; f. 2001; Dir Dott. CLAUDIO BIANCHINI.

Istituto di Chimica del Riconoscimento Molecolare (Institute of Chemistry of Molecular Recognition): Via Mario Bianco 9, 20131 Milan; tel. 02-28500024; fax 02-28901239; e-mail segreteria@icrm .cnr.it; internet www.icrm.cnr.it; f. 2001; Dir Dott. SERGIO RIVA.

Istituto di Chimica e Tecnologia dei Polimeri (Institute of Polymer Chemistry and Technology): Via Campi Flegrei 34, 80078 Pozzuoli; tel. 081-8675111; fax 081-8675230; e-mail secr@ictp.cnr.it; internet www.ictp.cnr.it; f. 2001; Dir Prof. COSIMO CARFAGNA.

Istituto di Chimica Inorganica e delle Superfici (Institute of Inorganic and Surface Chemistry): Corso Stati Uniti 4, 35127 Padua; tel. 049-8295611; fax 049-8295951; e-mail info@icis.cnr.it; internet www.icis .cnr.it; f. 2000; Dir Dott. GILBERTO ROSSETTO.

Istituto di Cristallografia (Institute of Crystallography): Via Giovanni Amendola 122/O, 70126 Bari; tel. 080-5929148; fax 080-5929170; e-mail segreteria@ic.cnr.it; internet www.ic.cnr.it; f. 2001; Dir Dott. MICHELE SAVIANO.

Istituto di Metodologie Chimiche (Institute of Chemical Methodologies): Via Salaria Km 29.3, CP 10, 00016 Montelibretti; tel. 06-90625111; fax 06-90672519; e-mail direttore@imc.cnr.it; internet www .imc.cnr.it; f. 2001; Dir Dott. GIANCARLO ANGELINI.

Istituto di Scienze e Tecnologie Molecolari (Institute of Molecular Science and Technologies): Via Camillo Golgi 19, 20133 Milan; tel. 02-50314276; fax 02-50313927; e-mail s.alocci@istm.cnr.it; internet www .istm.cnr.it; f. 2000; Chair. Dott. RINALDO PSARO.

Istituto per i Materiali Compositi e Biomedici (Institute for Composite and Biomedical Materials): Piazzale Vincenzo Tecchio 80, 80125 Naples; tel. 081-7682508; fax 081-2425932; e-mail segreteria@imcb.cnr.it; internet www.imcb .cnr.it; f. 2001; Dir Ing. LUIGI AMBROSIO.

Istituto per la Sintesi Organica e la Fotoreattività (Institute for Organic Syntheses and Photoreactivity): Via Piero Gobetti 101, 40129 Bologna; tel. 051-6399770; fax 051-6399844; e-mail direzione@isof.cnr.it; internet www.isof .cnr.it; f. 2000; Dir Dott. ROBERTO ZAMBONI.

Istituto per la Tecnologia delle Membrane (Institute for Membrane Technology): Via P. Bucci, Cubo 17C, 87036 Rende (CS); tel. 0984-492050; fax 0984-402103; e-mail l.giorno@itm.cnr.it; internet www .itm.cnr.it; f. 2001; devt of membrane science and technology at nat. and int. level; Dir Dott. LIDIETTA GIORNO.

Istituto per lo Studio dei Materiali Nanostrutturati (Institute of Nanostructured Materials): Via dei Taurini 19, 00185 Rome; tel. 06-90672484; fax 06-90672372; e-mail mariaester.moresi@ismn.cnr.it; internet www.ismn.cnr.it; f. 2000; Dir Dr. GIUSEPPINA PADELETTI.

Istituto per lo Studio delle Macromolecole (Institute for Macromolecular Studies): Via Edoardo Bassini 15, 20133 Milan; tel. 02-23699373; fax 02-70636400; e-mail bolognesi@ismac.cnr.it; internet www

.ismac.cnr.it; f. 2000; Dir Dott. ALBERTO BOLOGNESI.

Production Systems:

Istituto dei Materiali per l'Elettronica ed il Magnetismo (Institute of Materials for Electronics and Magnetism): Parco Area delle Scienze 37A, 43100 Parma; tel. 0521-26911; fax 0521-269206; e-mail direttore-imem@imem.cnr.it; internet www.imem.cnr.it; f. 2001; library of 1,300 vols; Dir Dott. SALVATORE IANNOTTA.

Istituto di Acustica e Sensoristica'Orso Mario Corbino' (Institute of Acoustics and Sensors): Via del Fosso del Cavaliere 100, 00133 Rome; tel. 06-45488482; fax 06-45488061; e-mail segreteria@idasc.cnr.it; internet www.idasc.cnr.it; f. 2001; Dir CLAUDIO RAFANELLI.

Istituto di Scienza e Tecnologia dei Materiali Ceramici (Institute of Ceramics Science and Technology): Via Granarolo 64, 48018 Faenza; tel. 0546-699711; fax 0546-699719; e-mail istec@istec.cnr.it; internet www.istec.cnr.it; f. 2001; Dir Dott. ALIDA BELLOSI.

Istituto di Studi sui Sistemi Intelligenti per l'Automazione (Institute of Intelligent Systems for Automation): Via Giovanni Amendola 122/D-O, 70126 Bari; tel. 080-5929429; fax 080-5929460; e-mail distante@ba.issia.cnr.it; internet www.issia.cnr.it; f. 2001; Dir Dott. ARCANGELO DISTANTE.

Istituto di Tecnologie Industriali e Automazione (Institute of Industrial Technologies and Automation): Via Bassini 15, 20133 Milan; tel. 02-23699995; fax 02-23699941; e-mail itia.milano@itia.cnr.it; internet www.itia.cnr.it; f. 2000; Dir Prof. TULLIO TOLIO.

Istituto per le Macchine Agricole e Movimento Terra (Institute for Agricultural and Earth-moving Machines): Via Canal Bianco 28, 44124 Ferrara; tel. 0532-735611; fax 0532-735666; e-mail info@imamoter.cnr.it; internet www.imamoter.cnr.it; f. 2001; Dir Ing. ROBERTO PAOLUZZI.

Istituto per le Tecnologie della Costruzione (Construction Technologies Institute): Viale Lombardia 49, 20098 San Giuliano Milanese; tel. 02-9806301; fax 02-98280088; e-mail roberto.vinci@itc.cnr.it; internet www.itc.cnr.it; f. 2001; Dir Ing. ROBERTO VINCI.

AGRICULTURE, FISHERIES AND VETERINARY SCIENCE

Consiglio per la Ricerca e la Sperimentazione in Agricoltura (CRA) (Agricultural Research Council): Via Nazionale 82, 00184 Rome; tel. 06-478361; fax 06-47836320; e-mail cra@entecra.it; internet sito.entecra.it; f. 1999; supervised by the Ministry of Agriculture, Food and Forests; gathers findings of 28 agricultural research institutes and 54 related operational units; depts of Vegetal Biology and Production, Animal Biology and Production, Transformation and Valorization of Agro-Industrial Products, Agronomy, Forestry and Land Use, Quality, Certification and Referenzation; Pres. Prof. ROMUALDO COVIELLO; Gen. Dir Dott. GIOVANNI LO PIPARO.

Istituto Sperimentale per la Zoologia Agraria (Experimental Institute of Agricultural Zoology): Via Lanciola 12A, Cascine del Riccio, 50125 Florence; tel. 055-24921; fax 055-209177; e-mail isza@isza.it; internet www.isza.it; f. 1875; library of 55,000 vols; Dir Dott. MARCO VITTORIO COVASSI; publ. *Redia* (1 a year).

Ufficio Centrale di Ecologia Agraria (Meteorological and Ecological Centre): Via del Caravita 7A, 00186 Rome; tel. 06-695311; fax 06-69531215; e-mail ucea@ucea.it; internet www.ucea.it; f. 1876; controls 100 observatories; 18 mems; Dir Dott. DOMENICO VENTO; publs *Bollettino Agrometeorologico Nazionale* (12 a year), *Bollettino Avversità Meteo*, *Osservazioni Meteo Collegio Romano* (electronic, 1 a year), *Indici Agroclimatici: Velocità e direzione del vento*.

ECONOMICS, LAW AND POLITICS

Centre for Studies on Technologies in Distributed Intelligence Systems (TeDIS): Isola di San Servola, 30100 Venice; tel. 041-2719511; fax 041-2719510; e-mail stefano.micelli@univiu.org; internet www.univiu.org/research-training/research-tedis; f. 1999; attached to Venice Int. Univ.; conducts research on industrial districts, technologies and networks, SMEs, local clusters and internationalization, creativity, design and innovation, innovation in public administration, e-government and e-democracy, transport logistics and supply chain management; Pres. ENZO RULLANI; Dir STEFANO MICELLI.

Centre for Thematic Environmental Networks (TEN): Isola de San Servolo, 30100 Venice; tel. 041-2719511; fax 041-2719510; e-mail ten@univiu.org; internet www.univiu.org/research-training/research-ten; f. 2003; attached to Venice Int. Univ.; promotes the exchange of knowledge and information in the field of the environment and offers tools and supplementary approaches in order to solve environmental issues with specific reference to sustainable devt; Pres. Prof. IGNAZIO MUSU; Dir Dott. ALESSANDRA FORNETTI.

Centro di Ricerche Economiche e Sociali (CERES) (Centre for Economic and Social Research): Via Po 102, 00198 Rome; tel. 06-8541016; fax 06-85355360; internet www.ce-res.org; f. 1970 as an autonomous body promoted by a trade union (CISL); improves economic and social conditions of workers; fosters contact and collaboration between nat. and int. centres and institutes interested in problems of economic and social devt; Pres. Prof. RENATA LIURAGHI; Sec.-Gen. Prof. GABRIELLA PAPPADA; publs *Benessere degli Anziani* (12 a year), *Quaderni di Economia del Lavoro* (3 a year).

Centro Speciale sulla Sicurezza Internazionale (Insubria Centre on International Security (ICIS)): Palazzo Natta, Via Natta 14, 22100 Como; tel. 031-579825; fax 031-570174; e-mail icis@uninsubria.it; attached to Università degli Studi dell'Insubria; Dir Prof. MAURIZIO MARTELLINI.

Fondazione Giangiacomo Feltrinelli: Via Romagnosi 3, 20121 Milan; tel. 02-874175; fax 02-86461855; e-mail segretaria@fondazionefeltrinelli.it; internet www.fondazionefeltrinelli.it/feltrinelli-cms; f. 1949; history of int. socialism, communism and the labour movement; economic and social history; library of 200,000 vols, 317 current periodicals, 2,500 microforms; Pres. CARLO FELTRINELLI.

Istituto Affari Internazionali (Institute of International Affairs): Via Angelo Brunetti 9, 00186 Rome; tel. (6) 3224360; fax (6) 3224363; e-mail iai@iai.it; internet www.iai.it; f. 1965; promotes understanding of the problems of int. politics through studies, research, meetings and publs; library of 25,000 vols; Pres. STEFANO SILVESTRI; Exec. Vice-Pres. GIANNI BONVICINI; Dir and Legal Rep. ETTORE GRECO; Librarian ALESSANDRA BERTINO; publs *Affari Internazionali* (online, in Italian), *IAI Quaderni* (4 a year, in English

and Italian), *La politica estera dell'Italia* (yearbook, in Italian), *The International Spectator* (4 a year, in English).

Istituto di Studi Europei 'Alcide De Gasperi': Via Poli 29, 00187 Rome; tel. 06-6784262; fax 06-6794101; e-mail kipsc@tin.it; internet www.ise-ies.org; f. 1953; promotes research and organizes meetings on legal, economic, political and social issues in the field of European co-operation and integration, and within a broader pan-European context; the Postgraduate School of European Studies organizes courses of varying duration and specialized seminars; courses are also held on the specialized English and French terminology of European int. orgs; library of 5,000 vols; Pres. Prof. GIUSEPPE SCHIAVONE; Admin. Officer CLAUDIA BATTISTI.

Istituto Italiano di Studi Legislativi (Italian Institute for Legislative Studies): Via del Corso 267, 00186 Rome; tel. 06-69941306; fax 06-69941306; e-mail gianpierorsello@inwind.it; f. 1925 to promote the scientific and technical studies of legislation; Pres. Prof. GIAN PIERO ORSELLO; Gen. Sec. Dott. FRANCA CIPRIGNO; publs *L'Italia e l'Europa*, *Yearbook of Comparative Law and Legislative Studies*.

Istituto Nazionale di Statistica (National Institute of Statistics): Via Cesare Balbo 16, 00184 Rome; tel. 06-46731; fax 06-46733107; e-mail dgen_s@istat.it; internet www.istat.it; f. 1926; library of 500,000 vols, 2,700 current periodicals; Pres. ENRICO GIOVANNINI; Gen. Dir GIOVANNI FONTANAROSA; publ. *Rivista di statistica ufficiale* (4 a year, print and online versions).

Istituto per gli Studi di Politica Internazionale (Institute for the Study of International Politics): Palazzo Clerici, Via Clerici 5, 20121 Milan; tel. 02-8633131; fax 02-8692055; e-mail ispi.segreteria@ispionline.it; internet www.ispionline.it; f. 1934; public and private funding; aims to provide information and analysis of the great global issues of today, to identify opportunities for more effective Italian participation in int. affairs, to identify the domestic factors that constrain or enhance Italy's int. role; research in int. politics and economics, strategic problems and the history of foreign relations, European integration, int. economic cooperation, consolidation of peace and security among nations, strengthening of political freedoms and democratic instns; library of 80,000 vols, historical archive, press archive; postgraduate training courses; organizes conferences, lectures, etc.; Pres. BORIS BIANCHERI; Dir Dott. PAOLO MAGRI; publs *ISPI Relazioni Internazionali* (3 a year, online), *Quaderni di Relazioni Internazionali* (3 a year, online), *Annuario sulla Politica Estera Italiana* (1 a year).

Istituto per le Relazioni tra l'Italia e i Paesi dell'Africa, America Latina, Medio ed Estremo Oriente (IPALMO) (Institute for Relations between Italy and the Countries of Africa, Latin America and the Middle and Far East): Via Ennio Quirino Visconti 8, 00193 Rome; tel. 06-32699701; fax 06-32699730; e-mail ipalmo@ipalmo.com; internet www.ipalmo.com; f. 1971; promotes and develops political, economic and cultural relations between countries in these regions; research and promotion of information at all levels of Italian society; to organize confs, seminars, etc.; library of 20,000 vols, 500 periodicals; Pres. GIANNI DE MICHELIS; Gen. Sec. CRISTINA GAGGIO; publ. *Politica Internazionale* (6 a year).

UNICEF Innocenti Research Centre: Piazza SS. Annunziata 12, 50122 Florence; tel. 055-20330; fax 055-2033220; e-mail florence@unicef.org; internet www.unicef-irc .org; f. 1988; conducts research vital to the work of the United Nations Children's Fund (UNICEF), especially in the field of children's rights; addresses emerging issues in areas of social and economic policies and implementation of int. standards for children in all countries; Dir GORDON ALEXANDER.

EDUCATION

Istituto per Ricerche ed Attività Educative (Institute for Educational Research and Activity): Riviera di Chiaia 264, 80121 Naples; tel. 081-2457074; e-mail ipe@ ipeistituto.it; internet www.ipeistituto.it; f. 1979; aims to give young people access to education, culture and jobs; offers grants, promotes study and research in education; 32 mems; library of 6,500 vols; Pres. Prof. RAFFAELE CALABRÒ; Gen. Sec. Dott. LORENZO BURDO; publ. *IPEnews* (2 a year).

FINE AND PERFORMING ARTS

Istituto Internazionale per la Ricerca Teatrale (International Institute for Theatre Research): Casa di Goldoni, S. Tomà 2794, 30124 Venice; tel. 041-714883; f. 1953 by the Int. Fed. for Theatre Research; library of 30,000 vols; spec. collns: critical works, Italian and foreign dramatic works, Venetian musical theatre scores, periodicals, edns of the playwright Carlo Goldoni, Maddelena (miscellany), Ortolani miscellany, Vendramin Archive; Chair. Prof. CARMELO ALBERTI; Gen. Sec. Doc. MARIA IDA BIGGI.

Istituto Superiore per la Conservazione ed il Restauro (Institute for Conservation and Restoration): Via di San Michele 23, 00153 Rome; tel. 06-67236300; e-mail is-cr@ beniculturali.it; internet iscr.beniculturali.it; f. 1939; research on the influence of environment on cultural property and on prevention of deterioration; studies formulation of rules on theory of conservation and restoration and on techniques to be used; advises institutes of the Min. of Cultural Assets and Activities, and regional organizations; in-service teaching and refresher courses; carries out restoration of complex works or those of interest in research and teaching; library of 35,000 vols, 650 periodicals; Dir GISELLA CAPPONI; publ. *Bollettino ICR* (2 a year).

Villa I Tatti/Harvard University Center for Italian Renaissance Studies: Via di Vincigliata 26, 50135 Florence; tel. 055-603251; fax 055-603383; e-mail info@itatti .it; internet www.itatti.it; f. 1961; fmr residence of Bernard Berenson, who left his library and art colln to Harvard; offers postdoctoral study of the Italian Renaissance: history of art, political, economic and social history, history of philosophy and religion, history of literature, music and science; library of 150,000 vols, 500 current periodicals, 300,000 photographs; Dir JOSEPH CONNORS; publ. *I Tatti Studies* (every 2 years).

HISTORY, GEOGRAPHY AND ARCHAEOLOGY

Academia Belgica (Belgian Academy in Rome): Via Omero 8, 00197 Rome; tel. 06-203986303; fax 06-3208361; e-mail walter .geerts@academiabelgica.it; internet www .academiabelgica.it; f. 1939; research centre and residence; congress centre; promotion of science and culture from Belgium and its regions; library of 80,000 vols; Dir Prof. WALTER GEERTS; publs *Belgian Historical Institute in Rome* (series and annual bulletin since 1919), *Bibliotheca Cumontiana, Etudes de Philologie, d'Archéologie et d'Histoire Ancienne* (irregular).

Accademia di Danimarca (Danish Institute of Science and Art in Rome): Via Omero 18, 00197 Rome; tel. 6-3265931; fax 6-3222717; e-mail accademia@acdan.it; internet www.acdan.it; f. 1956; archaeology, philology, art and architecture, history of art, history of music, literature; library of 24,000 vols; Dir Prof MARIANNE PADE (acting); Sec. BENTE RASMUSSEN; publ. *Analecta Romana Instituti Danici.*

Accademia Tedesca (German Academy in Rome): Villa Massimo, Largo di Villa Massimo 1–2, 00161 Rome; tel. 06-44259311; fax 06-44259355; e-mail info@villamassimo.de; internet www.villamassimo.de/it/ demnaechst/index.html; Dir Dr JOACHIM BLÜHER.

American Academy in Rome: Via Angelo Masina 5, 00153 Rome; tel. 06-58461; fax 06-5810788; e-mail info@aarome.org; internet www.aarome.org; f. 1894; fellowships for independent study and advanced research in fine arts, classical studies, art history, Italian studies and archaeology; library of 135,000 vols; Pres. and CEO ADELE CHATFIELD-TAYLOR; Dir CHRISTOPHER CELENZA.

British Institute of Florence: Piazza Strozzi 2, 50123 Florence; tel. 055-26778200; fax 055-26778222; e-mail info@ britishinstitute.it; internet www .britishinstitute.it; f. 1917; develops cultural understanding between the UK and Italy through the teaching of their respective languages and cultures; offers a range of Italian language and history of art courses, and an extensive programme of English language courses for the host population; a number of special programmes are run in conjunction with British and American univs; archive containing material relating to the British community in Tuscany in 19th and early 20th centuries incl. the Waterfield family, Susan Horner, Maquay family, Edward Gordon Craig and Edward Hutton; Vernon Lee colln contains a number of books from her library with her annotations; library of 50,000 vols; 1,700 students; Dir VANESSA HALL-SMITH.

British School at Rome: Via Gramsci 61, 00197 Rome; tel. 06-3264939; fax 06-3221201; e-mail info@bsrome.it; internet www.bsr.ac.uk; f. 1901, inc. by Royal Charter 1912; postgraduate residential centre for higher research in the humanities and for the practice of the fine arts and architecture; 40 residents; library of 60,000 vols, 600 current periodicals; Dir Prof. CHRISTOPHER SMITH.

Canadian Academic Centre in Italy: Via Zara 30, 00198 Rome; tel. 06-4404329; fax 06-4404331; e-mail caci@caspur.it; internet www.acadita.it/caci.html; f. 1978; assists Canadian researchers and scholars in Italy and promotes their work through lectures, conferences and publications; fosters academic exchanges between Italy and Canada; library of 3,000 vols; Dir EGMONT LEE.

Centro Camuno di Studi Preistorici (Centre for Prehistoric Studies): Via Marconi 7, 25044 Capo di Ponte (Brescia); tel. 0364-42091; fax 0364-42572; e-mail ccspreist@tin .it; internet www.ccsp.it; f. 1964; research centre specializing in prehistoric rock art; archaeological research, early religions, anthropology and ethnology; seminars, int. symposia, individual tutoring in prehistoric and tribal art; coordinator of World Archives of Rock Art; provides advisers and consultants on conservation, exhibition and evaluation of prehistoric and tribal art; park and museum planning; field research in Europe, Asia and Australia; Valcamonica summer school; library of 40,000 vols, 300,000 photographs; Dir Prof. EMMANUEL ANATI; publs

Archivi, BCSP: The World Journal of Prehistoric and Tribal Art.

Centro Italiano di Studi sul Basso Medioevo – Accademia Tudertina: Via Ciuffelli 31, 06059 Todi (Perugia); tel. 075-8942521; f. 1986; all aspects of late medieval civilization; Pres. Prof. TULLIO GREGORY; Dir Prof. ENRICO MENESTÒ.

Deutsches Archäologisches Institut Rom (German Archaeological Institute Rome): Via Curtatone, 00185 Rome; tel. 06-4888141; fax 06-4884973; e-mail sekretariat@rom.dainst.org; internet www .dainst.org; f. 1829; library of 220,000 vols, 1,200 current periodicals; Dirs Prof. Dr HENNER VON HESBERG, Prof. Dr KLAUS S. FREYBERGER; Sec. ALESSANDRA RIDOLFI; publs *Römische Mitteilungen* (1 a year), *Sonderschriften des Deutschen Archäologischen Instituts Rom.*

Fondazione Centro Italiano di Studi sull'Alto Medioevo (Central Italian Foundation for Studies on Early Medieval Civilization): Palazzo Ancaiani, Piazza della Libertà 12, 06049 Spoleto; tel. 0743-225630; fax 0743-49902; e-mail cisam@cisam.org; internet www.cisam.org; f. 1952; promotes research, conferences and scientific publications on all aspects of early medieval civilization; library of 3,000 vols; Pres. Prof. ENRICO MENESTÒ; publs *Bizantinistica* (1 a year), *Franciscana* (1 a year), *Medioevo e Rinascimento* (1 a year).

Ecole Française de Rome/Scuola Francese di Roma (French School in Rome): Piazza Farnese 67, 00186 Rome; tel. 06-68601333; fax 06-6874834; e-mail dirsecr@ efrome.it; internet www.efrome.it; f. 1875; French school of archaeology and history, specializing in Rome and medieval and modern Italy; library of 205,000 vols, 2,000 periodicals and 32,000 offprints; Dir MICHEL GRAS; Dirs of Studies JEAN-FRANÇOIS CHAUVARD, STÉPHANE GIOANNI, YANN RIVIÈRE; publ. *Mélanges de l'Ecole Française de Rome* (series *Antiquité, Moyen Age, Italie et Méditerranée*).

Escuela Española de Historia y Arqueología, CSIC Roma (Spanish School of History and Archaeology in Rome): Via di Torre Argentina 18-3°, 00186 Rome; tel. 06-68100021; fax 06-68309047; e-mail escuela@ csic.it; internet www.eehar.csic.es; f. 1910; history of Italian-Spanish interaction; organizes confs, seminars; research programmes and support for Spanish historians and archaeologists in Italy; 15 mems; library of 20,000 vols; special collns: Monumenta Albornotiana, documents on Spanish music in Italy; Dir Prof. RICARDO OLMOS ROMERA; publ. *Noticias EEHAR* (1 a year, online).

Institutum Romanum Finlandiae: Passeggiata del Gianicolo 10, 00156 Rome; tel. 06-68801674; fax 06-68802349; e-mail info@ irfrome.org; internet www.irfrome.org; f. 1954; Classical and Italian studies; library of 17,000 vols; Dir KATARIINA MUSTAKALLIO; publ. *Acta Instituti Romani Finlandiae.*

Istituto di Norvegia in Roma (Norwegian Institute in Rome): Viale Trenta Aprile 33, 00153 Rome; tel. 06-58391007; fax 06-5880604; e-mail mejohansen@roma.uio.no; internet www.hf.uio.no/dnir/; f. 1959; library of 25,000 vols; Head of Dept TURID KARLSEN SEIM; publ. *Acta ad Archaeologiam et Artium Historiam Pertinentia* (1 a year).

Istituto Ellenico di Studi Bizantini e Postbizantini di Venezia (Hellenic Institute of Byzantine and Post-Byzantine Studies of Venice): Castello 3412, 30122 Venice; tel. 041-5226581; fax 041-5238248; e-mail info@istitutoellenico.org; internet www .istitutoellenico.org; f. 1951; library of 30,000 vols, and archives containing 200,000 documents from 16th–19th centuries relating to the Greek Orthodox community of Venice; Dir CHRYSSA MALTEZOU; Sec. FILIPPOS TRIK-KAS; Librarian Dr DESPINA VLASSI; publ. *Thesaurismata* (1 a year).

Istituto Italiano di Studi Germanici (Italian Institute for Germanic Studies): Via Calandrelli 25, 00153 Rome; tel. 06-588811; fax 06-5888139; e-mail chiarini@studigermanici.it; internet www.studigermanici.it; f. 1932; library of 80,000 vols, 200 periodicals; Dir Prof. PAOLO CHIAR-INI; publs *Atti, Poeti e prosatori tedeschi, Strumenti, Studi e ricerche, Studi Germanici* (3 a year), *Wissenschaftliche Reihen: Testi e Materiali*.

Istituto Italiano per gli Studi Storici (Italian Institute for Historical Studies): Via Benedetto Croce 12, 80134 Naples; tel. 081-5512390; fax 081-5514813; e-mail istituto@iiss.it; internet www.iiss.it; f. 1947; studies and teaching in history, philosophy and the humanities; awards 20 student grants annually and offers scholarships to Italian and non-Italian postgraduates; library of 135,000 vols, 1,500 periodicals, 400 current periodicals; Pres. Prof. NATALINO IRTI; Dir Prof. GENNARO SASSO; Gen. Sec. Dott.ssa MARTA HERLING; Librarian Dott.ssa ELLI CATELLO; publs *Annali* (1 a year), *Carteggi di Benedetto Croce* (2 a year), *Collana delle monografie* (2 a year), *Inventari* (1 a year), *Ristampe Anastatiche* (4 a year), *Saggi e Studi, Testi storici filosofici e letterari* (1 a year).

Istituto Nazionale di Studi Romani (National Institute of Roman Studies): Piazza dei Cavalieri di Malta 2, 00153 Rome; tel. 06-5743442; fax 06-5743447; e-mail segreteria@studiromani.it; internet www.studiromani.it; f. 1925; promotes the study of Rome from ancient to modern times in all aspects; 120 mems; library of 26,000 vols, 1,500 periodicals; Pres. Prof. PAOLO SOMMELLA; Dir LETIZIA LANZETTA; publs *Rassegna d'Informazioni* (12 a year), *Studi Romani* (4 a year).

Istituto Nazionale di Studi sul Rinascimento (National Institute of Renaissance Studies): Palazzo Strozzi, 50123 Florence; tel. 055-287728; fax 055-280563; e-mail insr@iris.firenze.it; internet www.insr.it; f. 1938; publishes critical texts and results of research; 10-mem. ccl; library of 45,000 vols, 500 periodicals, special colln 'Machiavelli-Serristori', art photo library of 78,000 items, 700 microfilms; Pres. Prof. MICHELE CILIBERTO; publ. *Rinascimento* (1 a year).

Istituto Papirologico 'Girolamo Vitelli' (Papyrological Institute): Borgo degli Albizi 12–14, 50122 Florence; tel. 055-2478969; fax 055-2480722; e-mail guido.bastianini@unifi.it; internet vitelli.ifnet.it; f. 1908; study of Greek and Latin papyri; library of 25,000 vols; colln of papyri; Scientific Dir Prof. GUIDO BASTIANINI; publs *Comunicazioni* (every 2 years), *Notiziario di Studi e Ricerche in Corso, Papiri Greci e Latini*.

Istituto Siciliano di Studi Bizantini e Neoellenici 'B. Lavagnini' (Sicilian Institute for Byzantine and Neo-hellenic Studies): Via Noto 34, 90141 Palermo; tel. 091-6259541; fax 091-308996; e-mail segreteria@issbi.org; internet www.issbi.org; f. 1952; 120 mems (60 ordinary, 60 corresp.); library of 10,000 vols; Pres. Prof. VINCENZO ROTOLO; Sec.-Gen. Prof. RENATA LAVAGNINI.

Istituto Storico Austriaco Roma (Austrian Historical Institute in Rome): Viale Bruno Buozzi 111–113, 00197 Rome; tel. 06-36082601; fax 06-3224296; e-mail info@oehirom.it; internet www.oehirom.it; f. 1881; library of 87,000 items; Dir Prof. RICHARD

BÖSEL; publ. *Römische Historische Mitteilungen* (1 a year).

Istituto Storico Germanico di Roma/Deutsches Historisches Institut in Rom (German Historical Institute in Rome): Via Aurelia Antica 391, 00165 Rome; tel. 06-6604921; fax 06-6623838; e-mail verwaltung@dhi-roma.it; internet www.dhi-roma.it; f. 1888; medieval, modern and contemporary history; history of music; library of 222,300 vols, 861 current periodicals; Dir Prof. Dr MICHAEL MATHEUS; Head Librarian Dr THOMAS HOFMANN; publs *Analecta musicologica, Bibliographische Informationen zur neuesten Geschichte Italiens, Bibliothek des Deutschen Historischen Instituts, Quellen und Forschungen aus italienischen Archiven und Bibliotheken, Ricerche dell'Istituto Storico Germanico di Roma*.

Svenska Institutet i Rom (Swedish Institute of Classical Studies in Rome): Via Omero 14, 00197 Rome; tel. 06-3201596; fax 06-3230265; e-mail info@isvroma.org; internet www.isvroma.it; f. 1926; library of 65,000 vols, 300 current periodicals; Swedish courses for students of classical archaeology and history of art; fellowships in classical philology, archaeology, architecture, history of art and conservation; excavations at various sites in Italy; Dir Prof. BARBRO SANTILLO FRIZELL; Librarian ASTRID CAPOFERRO; publs *Acta Instituti Romani Regni Sueciae* (irregular), *Opuscula* (1 a year), *Suecoromana*.

Real Colegio Mayor de San Clemente de los Españoles (Royal College of Spain): Via Collegio di Spagna 4, 40123 Bologna; tel. 051-330408; fax 051-3370004; e-mail segreteria@bolonios.it; internet www.bolonios.it; f. 1364 under Will of Cardinal Don Gil de Albornoz; study centre for 20 Spanish postgraduates; library of 25,000 vols; Rector JOSÉ GUILLERMO GARCÍA VALDECASAS; publ. *Studia Albornotiana* (irregular).

Reale Istituto Neerlandese a Roma (Royal Netherlands Institute): Via Omero 10–12, 00197 Rome; tel. 06-3269621; fax 06-3204971; e-mail info@knir.it; internet www.knir.it; f. 1904; classical archaeology, history of art, history of Rome and Italy; residence for scholars from Dutch univs; library of 50,000 vols; Dir Prof. Dr BERNARD STOLTE; publ. *Fragmenta* (1 a year).

MEDICINE

Istituto di Ricerche Farmacologiche 'Mario Negri' (Institute of Pharmacological Research): Via La Masa 19, 20156 Milan; tel. 02-390141; fax 02-3546277; e-mail mnegri@marionegri.it; internet www.marionegri.it; f. 1961; non-profit org. for research and education in pharmacology and biomedicine; library of 5,000 vols, 250 periodicals; Chair. Dott. PAOLO MARTELLI; publs *Negri News* (12 a year), *Research and Practice* (6 a year).

Istituto Nazionale di Ricerca per gli Alimenti e la Nutrizione (National Institute for Research on Food and Nutrition): Via Ardeatina 546, 00178 Rome; tel. 06-514941; fax 06-51494550; e-mail segreteriadg@inran.it; internet www.inran.it; f. 1936 as part of CNR, independent 1958 on budget of Min. of Agricultural Resources, supported by contracts and grants from Min. of Health, CNR and int. bodies; biological research in human nutrition, analyses and surveys on composition and nutritive value of foods; Gen. Dir Dott. SALVATORE PETROLI.

Istituto Nazionale per la Ricerca sul Cancro (National Institute for Cancer Research): Largo Rosanna Benzi 10, 16132 Genoa; tel. 010-56001; fax 010-358032; e-mail direzione.generale@istge.it; internet www.istge.it; f. 1978; research in all fields of cancer prevention, diagnosis, cure and

rehabilitation; holds conferences, seminars, training courses; library of 1,808 books, 148 periodicals; Gen. Dir Dott. GIAN FRANCO CIAPPINA; Scientific Dir Prof. RICCARDO ROSSO.

Istituto Superiore di Sanità (Higher Institute of Health): Viale Regina Elena 299, 00161 Rome; tel. 06-49901; fax 06-49387118; e-mail web@iss.it; internet www.iss.it; f. 1934; aims to promote public health through scientific research, surveys, controls and analytical tests in the various fields of health sciences; library of 200,000 vols, 3,500 current periodicals; Pres. Prof. ENRICO GARACI; Dir-Gen. MONICA BETTONI; publs *Annali* (4 a year, online), *Istisan Congressi* (5 a year, online), *Notiziario* (12 a year, online), *Rapporti ISTISAN* (40 a year, online), *Strumenti di Riferimento* (irregular, online).

NATURAL SCIENCES

General

Istituto per l'Interscambio Scientifico/Fondazione ISI (Institute for Scientific Interchange): Viale S. Severo 65, 10133 Turin; tel. 011-6603090; fax 011-6600049; e-mail isi@isi.it; internet www.isi.it; f. 1982; promotes basic research in molecular biology, chemistry, computer sciences, economics, mathematics, theoretical physics; Pres. MARIO RASETTI.

Biological Sciences

Herbarium Universitatis Florentinae—Sezione Botanica, Museo di Storia Naturale dell'Università di Firenze: Via La Pira 4, 50121 Florence; tel. 055-2757462; fax 055-289006; e-mail musbot@unifi.it; f. 1842; systematic botany, plant geography, history of botanical collns; Dir Dr CHIARA NEPI; publ. *Pubblicazioni del Museo Botanico*.

Stazione Zoologica 'Anton Dohrn' (Zoological Station 'Anton Dohrn'): Villa Comunale, 80121 Naples; tel. (81) 5833111; fax (81) 7641355; e-mail stazione.zoologica@szn.it; internet www.szn.it; f. 1872; conducts biological research on marine organisms and marine ecosystems; library of 90,000 vols, 159 periodicals, 1,000 electronic resources; Pres. Prof. ROBERTO DI LAURO; Gen. Dir Ing. MARCO CINQUEGRANI; publs *History and Philosophy of Life Sciences* (3 a year), *Marine Ecology*.

Mathematical Sciences

Istituto Nazionale di Alta Matematica Francesco Severi (National Institute of Higher Mathematics): Piazzale Aldo Moro 5, 00185 Rome; tel. 06-490320; fax 06-4462293; e-mail indam@altamatematica.it; internet www.altamatematica.it; f. 1939; promotes training of researchers in mathematics, conducts research in pure and applied mathematics; Pres. Prof. VINCENZO ANCONA.

Physical Sciences

Comitato Glaciologico Italiano (Italian Glaciological Committee): Corso Massimo D'Azeglio 42, 10125 Turin; tel. 011-3977251; fax 011-6707155; e-mail comitato@glaciologia.it; internet www.glaciologia.it; f. 1895; glaciology and alpine climatology; library of 700 books, 15,000 photographs; Pres. Prof. CARLO BARONI; Gen. Sec. Dr GIOVANNI MORTARA; publ. *Geografia Fisica e Dinamica quaternaria* (2 a year).

Dipartimento di Ingegneria Nucleare, Centro Studi Nucleari Enrico Fermi (CESNEF) (E. Fermi Centre for Nuclear Studies): Politecnico di Milano, Via Ponzio 34/3, 20133 Milan; tel. 02-23996300; fax 02-23996309; e-mail dipnuc@polimi.it; internet www.cesnef.polimi.it; f. 1957; a division of the Department of Energy of the Politecnico di Milano; trains technical personnel in the fields of nuclear energy, physics of materials, and electronics; library of 7,000 vols, 31 current periodicals; Head of Dept Prof. CARLO BOTTANI.

Istituto Gemmologico Italiano (Italian Gemmological Institute): Piazza San Sepolcro, 1, 20123 Milan; tel. 02-80504992; fax 02-80505765; e-mail info@igi.it; internet www.igi.it; f. 1973; courses in gemmology, laboratory analysis, research; 1,500 mems; Pres. PAOLO VALENTINI.

Istituto Idrografico della Marina (Naval Institute of Hydrography): Passo dell'Osservatorio 4, 16100 Genoa; tel. 010-24431; fax 010-261400; e-mail iim.sre@marina.difesa.it; internet www.marina.difesa.it; f. 1872; library of 35,000 vols; Dir Contrammiraglio FRANCO FAVRE.

Istituto Italiano di Speleologia: Dip. Scienze della Terra e Geologico-Ambientali, Via Zamboni 67, 40126 Bologna; tel. 051-2094543; fax 051-2094522; e-mail dewaele@geomin.unibo.it; f. 1929; exploration and scientific research in natural caves; 5 mems; library of 65,000 vols; Dir Prof. PAOLO FORTI; publ. *Memorie* (irregular).

Istituto Nazionale di Astrofisica: Viale del Parco Mellini 84, 00136 Rome; tel. 06-355331; fax 06-35533219; e-mail inaf@inaf.it; internet www.inaf.it; promotes, carries out and co-ordinates research in the fields of astronomy, radioastronomy, spatial astrophysics and cosmic physics; has observatories in: Bologna, Cagliari, Catania, Florence, Milan, Naples, Padua, Palermo, Rome, Teramo, Trieste and Turin; finances the Telescopio Nazionale Galileo (*q.v.*) located on La Palma, Canary Islands; has a part ownership in the Large Binocular Telescope at the Mount Graham Int. Observatory (*q.v.*), AZ, USA; Chair. Prof. TOMMASO MACCACARO; Dir of Research Prof. ANTONIO NAVARRO.

Istituto Nazionale di Fisica Nucleare (INFN) (National Institute of Nuclear Physics): Via Enrico Fermi 40, 00044 Frascati (Rome); tel. 06-94031; fax 06-68307924; e-mail prot_ac@inf.infn.it; internet www.infn.it; f. 1951; promotes and undertakes research in fundamental nuclear physics; consists of: Central Administration (Frascati), 19 divisions, 4 National Laboratories (Frascati, Legnaro, Gran Sasso (L'Aquila), Catania, the National Centre for Informatics and Networking (CNAF Bologna) and 11 groups; the divisions are at the Institutes of Physics at the Universities of Turin, Milan, Padua, Genoa, Trieste, Bologna, Pisa, Pavia, Florence, Rome, Rome II, Rome III, Naples, Bari, Catania, Cagliari, Ferrara, Perugia, Lecce; the groups are at the Institutes of Physics at the Universities of Alessandria, Trento, Udine, Brescia, Parma, Siena, Salerno, Messina, L'Aquila, Cosenza, Sanità; Pres. Prof. ROBERTO PETRONZIO.

Istituto Nazionale di Geofisica e Vulcanologia (National Institute of Geophysics and Volcanology): Via di Vigna Murata 605, 00143 Rome; tel. 06-518601; fax 06-5041181; e-mail info@ingv.it; internet www.ingv.it; f. 1936; seismology, tectonophysics, geomagnetism, aeronomy, environmental geophysics; has important additional facilities in Bologna, Catania, Milan, Naples, Palermo and Pisa; library of 8,000 vols, 150 current periodicals; Pres. Prof. ENZO BOSCHI; Gen. Dir Dott. TULLIO PEPE; publs *Annali di Geofisica* (6 a year), *Annuario geomagnetico*, *Bollettino dei valori istantanei alle ore 0*, *Bollettino indici K* (12 a year), *Bollettino ionosferico* (12 a year), *Bollettino macrosismico* (1 a year), *Bollettino sismico* (4 a year), *Tavole di previsione ionosferica* (26 a year), *2* (3 a year).

Istituto Nazionale di Oceanografia e di Geofisico Sperimentale (National Institute for Oceanography and Experimental Geophysics): Borgo Grotta Gigante 42/C, 34010 Sgonico (TS); tel. 040-21401; fax 040-327307; e-mail mailbox@ogs.trieste.it; internet www.ogs.trieste.it; f. 1958; library of 3,000 vols; Chair. Prof. IGINIO MARSON; Gen. Dir Dott. TIZIANA MAIER; publ. *Bollettino di Geofisica Teorica e Applicata* (4 a year).

PHILOSOPHY AND PSYCHOLOGY

Centro Superiore di Logica e Scienze Comparate (Centre for Logic and Comparative Science): Via Belmeloro 3, 40126 Bologna; f. 1969; promotes the study of logic and contributes to research in this field; 1,250 mems; library and archives; Pres. Prof. FRANCO SPISANI.

Istituto di Studi Filosofici 'Enrico Castelli' (Institute of Philosophy): Via Carlo Fea 2T, 00161 Rome; tel. 06-44238062; internet www.filosofia.uniroma1.it; f. 1939; Pres. JEAN-LUC MARION; Dir Prof. PIERLUIGI VALENZA; publs *Archivio di Filosofia* (4 a year), *Bibliografia filosofica Italiana*, *Edizione Naz. A. Rosmini*, *Edizione Naz. dei Classici del pensiero italiano*, *Edizione Naz. V. Gioberti*, *Settimana di studi filosofici internazionali* (1 a year).

RELIGION, SOCIOLOGY AND ANTHROPOLOGY

Centro Internazionale di Ricerca per le Storie Locali e le Diversità Culturali (International Research Centre for Local History and Cultural Diversities): Via Ravasi 2, 21100 Varese; tel. 0332-219800; fax 0332-219809; e-mail info@cslinsubria.it; internet www.cslinsubria.it; attached to Università degli Studi dell'Insubria; Pres. Prof. RENZO DIONIGI; Dir Dott. FILADELFO FERRI.

Fondazione di Ricerca 'Istituto Carlo Cattaneo' ('Istituto Carlo Cattaneo' Research Foundation): Via Santo Stefano 11, 40125 Bologna; tel. 051-239766; fax 051-262959; e-mail istitutocattaneo@cattaneo.org; internet www.cattaneo.org; f. 1965; studies and researches in the field of social science with particular regard to education, electoral behaviour, politics, crime, terrorism, family, immigration and public policy; Pres. Prof. RAIMONDO CATANZARO; Dir Prof. GIANCARLO GASPERONI; Deputy Dir Prof. GIANFRANCO BALDINI; publs *Cattaneo* (irregular), *Cultura in Italia* (1 a year), *Elezioni, Governi, Democrazia* (irregular), *Italian Politics—A Review* (1 a year), *Misure / Materiali di ricerca dell'Istituto Carlo Cattaneo* (irregular), *Polis-Ricerche e studi su società e politica in Italia* (3 a year), *Stranieri in Italia* (irregular).

Istituto Italiano di Antropologia (Italian Institute of Anthropology): Università di Roma 'La Sapienza', Dipart. di Biologia Animale e dell'Uomo, P.le Aldo Moro 5, 00185 Rome; tel. 06-49912273; fax 06-49912771; e-mail isita@isita-org.com; internet www.isita-org.com; f. 1893 as Società Romana di Antropologia; adopted current name in 1937; promotes interdisciplinary approach to anthropology, which encompasses a synthesis of the biological, social and cultural aspects of human evolution; organizes scientific meetings; runs courses and seminars; 120 mems; library of 6,500 vols; Pres. BERNARDINO FANTINI; Sec. Assoc. Prof. GIOVANNI DESTRO-BISOL; publ. *Journal of Anthropological Sciences* (1 a year, in print and online).

Istituto Italiano per l'Africa e l'Oriente (IsIAO) (Italian Institute for Africa and the East): Via Ulisse Aldrovandi 16, 00197 Rome;

tel. 06-328551; fax 06-3225348; e-mail info@isiao.it; internet www.isiao.it; f. 1995; library of 140,000 vols, 500 current periodicals; Pres. Prof. GHERARDO GNOLI; Gen. Dir Dr UMBERTO SINATTI; a museum of oriental art is attached to the Institute; publs *Africa* (4 a year), *Cina* (1 a year), *East and West* (in English, 4 a year), *Il Giappone* (1 a year), *Reports and Memoirs*, *Rome Oriental Series*.

Istituto Luigi Sturzo: Via delle Coppelle 35, 00186 Rome; tel. 06-6840421; fax 06-68404244; e-mail segretaria@sturzo.it; internet www.sturzo.it; f. 1951; sociological and historical research; library of 120,000 vols; Pres. Dott. ROBERTO MAZZOTTA; Sec.-Gen. Dott. FLAVIA NARDELLI; publs *Civitas* (3 a year), *Sociologia* (3 a year).

Istituto per l'Oriente C. A. Nallino: Via Alberto Caroncini 19, 00197 Rome; tel. (6) 8084106; fax (6) 8079395; e-mail ipocan@ipocan.it; internet www.ipocan.it; f. 1921; researches on modern and ancient Near East; library of 35,000 vols, 300 periodicals; Pres. Prof. CLAUDIO LO JACONO; publs *Eurasian Studies* (2 a year), *Oriente Moderno* (2 a year), *Quaderni di Studi Arabi* (1 a year), *Rassegna di Studi Etiopici* (1 a year).

TECHNOLOGY

Agenzia Nazionale per le Nuove Tecnologie, l'Energia e lo Sviluppo Economico Sostenible (ENEA) (National Agency for New Technology, Energy and Sustainable Economic Development): Lungotevere Thaon di Revel 76, 00196 Rome; tel. 06-36271; fax 06-36272591; internet www.enea.it; f. 1960; scientific research and technological devt, implementing advanced research programmes and conducting complex projects for Italy's social and economic devt; library of 250,000 vols; Commissioner Dott. GIOVANNI LELLI; publs *Energia, Ambiente e Innovazione* (6 a year), *Rapporto Energia e Ambiente* (1 a year, online).

Centro Radioelettrico Sperimentale 'Guglielmo Marconi' (Marconi Experimental Radio-electric Centre): Dipartimento di Ingegneria Elettronica, Università di Tor Vergata, Via del Politecnico 1, 00133 Rome; e-mail luglio@uniroma2.it; internet www.centromarconi.it; f. 1933; research on radio waves; Pres. GIOVANNI CANCELLIERI.

Centro Sviluppo Materiali SpA: Via di Castel Romano 100, 00128 Rome; tel. 06-50551; fax 06-5050250; e-mail info@c-s-m.it; internet www.c-s-m.it; f. 1963; reference centre for innovation in materials and in related production, design and application technologies; library of 40,000 vols; Chair. Dott. ROBERTO BRUNO; CEO MAURO PONTREMOLI.

Fondazione Guglielmo Marconi (Guglielmo Marconi Foundation): Via Celestini 1, 40037 Pontecchio Marconi (BO); tel. 051-846121; fax 051-846951; e-mail fgm@fgm.it; internet www.fgm.it; f. 1938; research in telecommunications; library of 3,500 vols; Chair. Prof. GABRIELE FALCIASECCA.

Istituto Nazionale per Studi ed Esperienze di Architettura Navale (National Institute of Naval Architecture Studies and Experiments): Via di Vallerano 139, 00128 Rome; tel. 06-502991; fax 06-5070619; e-mail secretary@insean.it; internet www.insean.it; f. 1927; library of 3,500 vols; Pres. GIANO PISI; Gen. Dir Dott. EMILIO F. CAMPANA; publ. *Quaderni* (1 a year).

SORIN Biomedica SpA: Via Benigno Crespi 17, 20159 Milan; tel. (02) 69969711-509; internet www.sorin.com; f. 1956; applied research in biomedicine; production and development of radiopharmaceuticals and immunodiagnostic kits (using radioactive and enzymatic tracers), pacemakers, artificial cardiac valves (mechanical and biological), oxygenators, dialysers, haemodialysis and haemoperfusion accessories; 3,600 staff; Chair. ROSARIO BIFULCO; CEO ANDRÉ-MICHEL BALLESTER.

Libraries and Archives

Alessandria

Biblioteca Civica: Piazza Vittorio Veneto 1, (ang. Via Machiavelli), 15100 Alessandria; tel. 0131-515911; e-mail biblioteca.civica@ comune.alessandria.it; internet www .comune.alessandria.it; f. 1806; 180,000 vols, 217 current periodicals; Dir (vacant).

Ancona

Archivio di Stato di Ancona: Via Maggini 80, 60127 Ancona; tel. 071-2800356; fax 071-2818785; e-mail as-an@archivi.beniculturali .it; internet archivi.beniculturali.it/asan; f. 1941; provincial archives dating from before Italian unification; 8,000 vols, 280 periodicals; Dir Dott. GIOVANNA GIUBBINI; publ. *Archivio di Stato-Ancona* (series, irregular).

Biblioteca Comunale Luciano Benincasa: Via Bernabei 32, 60121 Ancona; tel. 71-2225020; fax 71-2225027; e-mail aiaale@ comune.ancona.it; f. 1669; 145,000 vols, 62 incunabula, 124 periodicals, 241 MSS, 3,000 *cinquecentine*; Dir EMANUELA IMPICCINI.

Arezzo

Biblioteca della Città di Arezzo: Palazzo Pretorio, Via dei Pileati 8, 52100 Arezzo; tel. 0575-22849; fax 0575-370419; e-mail direzione@bibliotecaarezzo.it; internet www .bibliotecarezzo.it; f. 1603; 265,000 vols, pamphlets and miscellanea, 548 MSS and 197 incunabula; Dir Dott. MANUELA FABBRINI.

Ascoli Piceno

Biblioteca Comunale 'Giulio Gabrielli': Polo Culturale S. Agostino, Corso Mazzini, 90, 63100 Ascoli Piceno; tel. 0736-248650; fax 0736-248657; e-mail protocollo@comune .ascolipiceno.it; internet /www.comune .ascolipiceno.it; f. 1849; 200,000 vols, 300 incunabula, 900 MSS, 3,000 *cinquecentine*, 340 periodicals; Dir Dott. FABIO EMIDIO ZEPPILLI.

Avellino

Biblioteca Provinciale Scipione e Giulio Capone: Corso Europa 41, 83100 Avellino; tel. 0825-790513; fax 0825-790529; e-mail info@mediateca.avellino.it; internet www .culturacampania.rai.it; f. 1913; 200,000 vols; Dir Dott. PASQUALE DI SALVIO.

Bari

Archivio di Stato di Bari: Via Pietro Oreste 45, 70125 Bari; tel. 080-099311; fax 080-099322; e-mail as-ba@beniculturali.it; internet www.archiviodistatodibari .beniculturali.it; f. 1835; 6,192 vols, 224 periodicals, 139 MSS; Dir Dott. EUGENIA VANTAGGIATO.

Biblioteca Nazionale 'Sagarriga-Visconti-Volpi': Via Pietro Oreste 45, 70121 Bari; tel. 080-2173111; fax 080-2173444; e-mail bn-ba@beniculturali.it; internet www .bibliotechepubbliche.it; f. 1865; 300,000 vols, 55 incunabula, 460 MSS, 2,196 *cinquecentini*, 450 current periodicals; Dir Dott. MARINA PANETTA.

Bergamo

Civica Biblioteca 'Angelo Mai': Piazza Vecchia 15, 24129 Bergamo; tel. 035-399430; fax 035-240655; e-mail info@ bibliotecamai.org; internet www

.bibliotecamai.org; f. 1760; 650,000 vols, 9,380 MSS, 22,000 parchments, 2,140 incunabula, 12,000 *cinquecentine*; Dir Dott. GIULIO ORAZIO BRAVI.

Bologna

Archivio di Stato di Bologna: Piazza dei Celestini 4, 40123 Bologna; tel. 051-223891; fax 051-220474; e-mail as-bo@beniculturali .it; internet www.archiviodistatobologna.it; f. 1874; 245,592 items; 23,000 vols, 331 periodicals; Dir ELISABETTA ARIOTI.

Biblioteca Carducci: Piazza Carducci 5, 40125 Bologna; tel. 051-347592; fax 051-4292820; e-mail casacarducci@comune .bologna.it; internet www.casacarducci.it/ htm/home.htm; given to the commune of Bologna in 1907 by Marguerite of Savoy, inaugurated in 1921; the library preserves the surroundings of the poet Giosuè Carducci and contains his collected works, as well as many rare editions of other works; 35,000 items; Dir PIERANGELO BELLETTINI.

Biblioteca Comunale dell'Archiginnasio: Piazza Galvani 1, 40124 Bologna; tel. 051-276811; fax 051-261160; e-mail archiginnasio@comune.bologna.it; internet www.archiginnasio.it; f. 1801; 951,535 vols (incl. 2,500 incunabula, 20,000 16th-century edns), 12,000 MSS, 500,000 letters and documents; Dir Dott. PIERANGELO BELLETTINI; publ. *L'Archiginnasio—Bollettino della Biblioteca Comunale di Bologna* (1 a year).

Biblioteca del Dipartimento di Scienze Giuridiche 'A. Cicu': Via Zamboni 27–29, 40126 Bologna; tel. 051-2099626; fax 051-2099624; e-mail dipscgiur.biblioteca@unibo .it; internet www.giuridico.unibo.it; f. 1926; 215,000 vols, 1,042 current periodicals; Chief Librarian Dott. ANNA PRAMSTRAHLER.

Biblioteca San Domenico: Piazza San Domenico 13, 40124 Bologna; tel. 051-6400493; fax 051-6400492; e-mail biblsand@ iperbole.bologna.it; internet www.comune .bologna.it/iperbole/biblsand; f. 1218; more than 75,000 vols, incunabula and MSS; spec. collns incl. philosophy and theology; Dir ANGELO PIAGNO.

Biblioteca Universitaria di Bologna: Via Zamboni 33–35, 40126 Bologna; tel. 051-2088300; fax 051-2088385; e-mail direzione@bub.unibo.it; internet www.bub .unibo.it; f. 1712; 1,371,366 vols, 15,238 *cinquecentini*, 311,875 pamphlets, 12,875 MSS, 1,021 incunabula, 77,481 microforms, 867 current periodicals; Dir Dott. BIANCASTELLA ANTONINO; publs *BUBLife* (3 a year), *In Bub : ricerche e cataloghi sui fondi della biblioteca Universitaria di Bologna* (1 a year).

Brescia

Biblioteca Queriniana: Via Mazzini 1, 25121 Brescia; tel. 030-2978200; fax 030-2400359; e-mail queriniana@comune.brescia .it; internet queriniana.comune.brescia.it; f. 1747; 526,000 vols; Dir Dott. ENNIO FERRAGLIO.

Cagliari

Archivio di Stato di Cagliari: Via Gallura 2, 09125 Cagliari; tel. 070-669450; fax 070-653401; e-mail as-ca@beniculturali.it; internet www.archiviostatocagliari.it; f. 19th century; 29,525 vols, 2,690 periodicals, 21 MSS, 407,000 microfiches; Dir Dott.ssa ANNA PIA BIDOLLI.

Biblioteca Universitaria: Via Università 32A, 09123 Cagliari; tel. 070-661021; fax 070-652672; e-mail bu-ca@beniculturali.it; internet www.sardegna.beniculturali.it/ index.php?it/267/biblioteche/22/biblioteca-universitaria-di-cagliari; f. 1792; 460,470 vols; 6,000 MSS, 236 incunabula, 5,000 *cinquecen-*

tini, Gabinetto delle Stampe 'Anna Marongiu Pernis' contains 4,541 etchings; Dir ESTER GESSA.

Campobasso

Archivio di Stato di Campobasso: Via Orefici 43, 86100 Campobasso; tel. 0874-411488; fax 0874-411525; e-mail as-cb@ beniculturali.it; internet www.archivi .beniculturali.it/ascb; f. 1818; 19,000 vols, 802 periodicals, 29 MSS; Dir Dott. DANIELA DI TOMMASO.

Catania

Archivio di Stato di Catania: Via Vittorio Emanuele 156, 95131 Catania; tel. 095-7159860; fax 095-7150465; e-mail as-ct@ beniculturali.it; internet archivi .beniculturali.it/asct; f. 1854; 161,790 items; 11,700 vols; Dir Dott. ALDO SPARTI.

Biblioteca Regionale Universitaria: Piazza Università 2, 95124 Catania; tel. 095-7366111; fax 095-326862; f. 1755; 350,000 vols, 116 incunabula, 522 MSS, 2,710 *cinquecentini*; Dir MARIA GRAZIA PATANÈ.

Biblioteche Riunite Civica e A. Ursino Recupero: Via Biblioteca 13, 95124 Catania; tel. 095-316883; fax 095-497599; internet www.comune.catania.it; f. 1931 as municipal library, fmrly a Benedictine monastery library, nationalized in 1867; 210,000 vols, specializing in Sicily and Catania, 1,696 parchments, 2,000 MSS, 132 incunabula and 4,000 *cinquecentine*; Dir Dott. RITA ANGELA CARBONARO.

Cesena

Istituzione Biblioteca Malatestiana: Piazza Bufalini 1, 47521 Cesena; tel. 0547-610892; fax 0547-21237; e-mail malatestiana@sbn.provincia.ra.it; internet www.malatestiana.it; f. 1452; 300,000 vols, 287 incunabula, 4,000 *cinquecentine* 1,753 MSS; Dir Dott. DANIELA SAVOIA.

Como

Biblioteca Comunale: Piazzetta Venosto Lucati 1, 22100 Como; tel. 031-270187; fax 031-240183; e-mail biblioteca@comune.como .it; internet bibliotecacomunale.comune.como .it; f. 17th century; 380,000 vols; Dir RICCARDO TERZOLI.

Cremona

Biblioteca del Seminario Vescovile: Via Milano 5, 26100 Cremona; tel. 03-72458289; fax 03-7229135; e-mail biblio.seminario@ gmail.com; internet biblioseminariocremona .wordpress.com; f. 1592; 100,000 vols, 400 MSS, 20 incunabula, 1,300 *cinquecentine*; Dir ANDREA FOGLIA.

Biblioteca Statale: Via Ugolani Dati 4, 26100 Cremona; tel. 0372-495611; fax 0372-495615; e-mail bs-cr@beniculturali.it; f. c. 1600; 700,000 vols, 2,380 MSS, 18,600 letters and documents, 374 incunabula, 6,000 16th-century editions; Dir Dr STEFANO CAMPAGNOLO; publs *Annali*, *Fonti e Sussidi*, *Mostre*.

Fermo

Biblioteca Civica 'Romolo Spezioli': Piazza del Popolo 63, 63023 Fermo; tel. 0734-284310; fax 0734-284482; e-mail biblioteca.orientamento@comune.fermo.net; internet cultura.fermo.net; f. 1688; 350,000 vols and pamphlets, incl. 681 incunabula, 15,000 *cinquecentine*; 110 current periodicals, 3,000 MSS; Dir Dott. MARIA CHIARA LEONORI.

Ferrara

Biblioteca Comunale Ariostea: Via Scienze 17, 44121 Ferrara; tel. 0532-418200; fax 0532-204296; e-mail info.ariostea@

comune.fe.it; internet www.artecultura.fe.it; f. 1753; 430,257 vols; Dir Dott. ENRICO SPINELLI.

Florence

Archivio di Stato di Firenze: Viale Giovine Italia 6, 50122 Florence; tel. 055-263201; fax 055-2341159; e-mail as-fi@beniculturali.it; internet www.archiviodistato.firenze.it; f. 1852; 790,000 items; 51,000 vols, 350 periodicals; Dir CARLA ZARRILLI.

Biblioteca degli Uffizi: Loggiato degli Uffizi, 50122 Florence; tel. 055-2388647; fax 055-2388648; e-mail biblioteca@polomuseale.firenze.it; internet www.polomuseale.firenze.it/biblioteche/bib_uffizi.asp; f. 1770; 78,600 titles, incl. 470 MSS, 192 *cinquecentine*, 140 current periodicals; Dir Dott. CLAUDIO DI BENEDETTO.

Biblioteca del Gabinetto Scientifico Letterario G. P. Vieusseux: Palazzo Strozzi, Piazza Strozzi, 50123 Florence; tel. 055-288342; fax 055-2396743; e-mail biblioteca@vieusseux.it; internet www.vieusseux.fi.it; f. 1819; 450,000 vols; Dir LAURA DESIDERE; publs *Antologia Vieusseux* (New Series, 4 a year), *Il Vieusseux* (4 a year).

Attached Archive:

Archivio Contemporaneo 'Alessandro Bonsanti': Palazzo Corsini-Suarez, Via Maggio 42, 50125 Florence; tel. 055-290131; fax 055-213188; e-mail archivio@vieusseux.it; internet www.vieusseux.fi.it/archivio_contemporaneo.html; f. 1975; 500,000 documents, 50,000 vols; Man. GLORIA MANGHETTI.

Biblioteca Marucelliana: Via Cavour 43–47, 50129 Florence; tel. 055-2722200; fax 055-294393; e-mail b-maru@beniculturali.it; internet www.maru.firenze.sbn.it; f. 1752; 630,000 vols and pamphlets, incl. 490 incunabula and 7,995 *cinquecentine*; 2,927 MSS, 3,200 drawings, 53,000 prints, 10,065 periodicals; Dir Dott. MONICA MARIA ANGELI.

Biblioteca Medicea-Laurenziana: Piazza S. Lorenzo 9, 50123 Florence; tel. 55-210760; fax 55-2302992; e-mail b-mela@beniculturali.it; internet www.bmlonline.it; f. 1571; contains the private Medici Library, collns of MSS from the Medici family, the Grand Dukes of Lorena, S. Croce, S. Marco, Badia Fiesolana, cathedral of Florence, and private family collns; 15th- and 16th-centuries first edns; 14,000 MSS of the 5th–19th century; 2,500 papyri, 80 ostraca, 150,000 vols; Dir Dr MARIA PRUNAI FALCIANI.

Biblioteca Moreniana: Via dei Ginori 10, 50123 Florence; tel. 055-2760331; fax 055-2761249; e-mail moreniana@provincia.fi.it; internet www.provincia.fi.it/palazzo-medici-ricciardi/biblioteca-moreniana; f. 1869; 34,000 vols, c. 2,000 MSS, specializing in ancient Tuscan history; Dir MASSIMO TARASSI.

Biblioteca Nazionale Centrale: Piazza Cavalleggeri 1, 50122 Florence; tel. 055-249191; fax 055-2342482; e-mail info@bncf.firenze.sbn.it; internet www.bncf.firenze.sbn.it; f. 1747; 6,000,000 vols, pamphlets, 120,000 periodicals (15,000 current), 25,000 MSS, 4,000 incunabula, 29,000 *cinquecentine*; Dir MARIA LETIZIA SEBASTIANI; publ. *Bibliografia nazionale italiana* (12 a year, 1 a year accumulations, 4 a year CD-ROM).

Biblioteca Pedagogica Nazionale: c/o Biblioteca di Documentazione Pedagogica, Palazzo Gerini, Via M. Buonarroti 10, 50122 Florence; tel. 055-2380364; fax 055-2380330; e-mail biblioteca@indire.it; internet www.indire.it/chisiamo/biblio_patrimonio.html; f. 1941; 85,000 vols, 1,600 periodicals,

rare books, drawings; data banks on education; Dir Dott. PAMELA GIORGI; publs *Schedario* (review of children's literature, 3 a year), *Segnalibro* (review of literature for young people, 1 a year).

Biblioteca Riccardiana: Via dei Ginori 10, 50123 Florence; tel. 055-212586; fax 055-211379; e-mail b-ricc@beniculturali.it; internet www.riccardiana.firenze.sbn.it; f. 1815; 63,833 vols, 4,450 MSS, 725 incunabula, 3,865 *cinquecentine*, 258 periodicals; Dir Dott. GIOVANNA LAZZI.

Biblioteca Umanistica dell' Università: Piazza Brunelleschi 4, 50121 Florence; tel. 055-2757811; fax 055-243471; e-mail floriana.tagliabue@unifi.it; internet www.sba.unifi.it/biblio/umanistica; f. 1959; 1,600,000 vols; sections on philosophy, geography, literature, psychology, education, art history, and North American history and literature; Dir Dott. FLORIANA TAGLIABUE.

Forlì

Biblioteca Comunale 'Aurelio Saffi': Corso della Repubblica 72, 47100 Forlì; tel. 0543-712600; fax 0543-712616; e-mail biblioteca-saffi@comune.forli.fc.it; internet www.cultura.comune.forli.fc.it; 490,000 vols, 250 incunabula, 8,000 16th-century editions, 2,000 MSS, 2,200 periodicals; Dir Dr FRANCO FABBRI.

Genoa

Archivio di Stato di Genova: Piazza S. Maria in Via Lata, 7, 16128 Genoa; tel. 010-537561; fax 010-5375636; e-mail as-ge@beniculturali.it; internet archivi.beniculturali.it/asge/asge.htm; f. 1817; 13,000 vols, 145 periodicals; Dir PAOLA CAROLI.

Biblioteca Durazzo Giustiniani: Via XXV Aprile 12, 16123 Genoa; tel. 010-2476232; fax 010-2474122; f. 1760–1804; 20,000 17th- and 18th-century vols, 1,000 *cinquecentine*, 448 incunabula, 300 MSS; Curator Dott.ssa SANDRA MACCHIAVELLO.

Biblioteca di Storia dell'Arte: Via ai Quattro Canti di San Francesco 49/51, 16121 Genoa; tel. 010-5574957; fax 010-5574970; e-mail biblarte@comune.genova.it; internet www.museidigenova.it/spip.php?article313; f. 1908; attached to Centro di Documentazione per la Storia, l'Arte, l'Immagine di Genova; 51,000 vols, 207 current periodicals; specialized library relating to Italian and Genoese fine arts (since 11th century); Dir Dr ELISABETTA PAPONE; publ. *Bollettino dei Musei Civici Genovesi*.

Biblioteca Universitaria: Via Balbi 3 e 38B, 16126 Genoa; tel. 010-254641; fax 010-2546420; e-mail bu-ge@beniculturali.it; internet www.bibliotecauniversitaria.ge.it; f. 18th century; 617,109 vols, 1,039 incunabula, 1,949 MSS, 19,287 letters and documents; Dir Reg. SIMONETTA BUTTÒ.

Gorizia

Biblioteca Statale Isontina di Gorizia: Via Mameli 12, 34170 Gorizia; tel. 0481-580211; fax 0481-580260; e-mail bs-ison@beniculturali.it; internet www.isontina.librari.beniculturali.it; f. 1629; lending and reference library; bibliographical information service; 371,000 vols, 41 incunabula, 934 *cinquecentine*, 1,074 current periodicals, 862 MSS, 1,181 microfiches; Dir Prof. MARCO MENATO; publ. *Studi Goriziani* (2 a year).

Imola

Biblioteca Comunale: Via Emilia 80, 40026 Imola; tel. 0542-602636; fax 0542-602602; e-mail bim@comune.imola.bo.it; internet bim.comune.imola.bo.it; f. 1761;

470,000 vols, 1,692 MSS, 140 incunabula; Dir Dott. MARINA BARUZZI.

L'Aquila

Biblioteca Provinciale 'Salvatore Tommasi': Via Niccolò Copernico, Bazzano, 67100 L'Aquila; tel. 0862-61964; fax 0862-61964; e-mail biblioteca.reference@provincia.laquila.it; internet www.provincia.laquila.it/biblioteca; f. 1848; 260,000 vols, 230 current periodicals, 131 incunabula, 911 MSS, 3,500 *cinquecentine* (rare 16th-century editions); Dir Dott. PAOLO COLLACCIANI.

Livorno

Biblioteca Labronica - Villa Fabbricotti: Viale della Libertà 30, 57123 Livorno; tel. 0586-264511; e-mail labronica@comune.livorno.it; f. 1816; 120,000 vols incl. 2,000 *cinquecentine*, 1,500 MSS, 117 incunabula and 60,000 letters and documents; Dir Dott. DUCCIO FILIPPI; publ. *Quaderni della Labronica* (4 a year).

Attached Libraries:

Biblioteca Labronica – Bottini dell'Olio: Via del Forte di San Pietro 15, 57123 Livorno; tel. 0586-219265; fax 0586-219151; e-mail bottinidellolio@comune.livorno.it; internet www.comune.livorno.it/_livo/pages.php?id=127; 61,000 vols; Dir Dott. DUCCIO FILIPPI.

Biblioteca Labronica - Sezione Emeroteca: Via del Toro 8, 57123 Livorno; tel. 0586-892059; fax 0586-894147; e-mail emeroteca@comune.livorno.it; 3,950 periodicals, 750 current periodicals; Dir Dott. DUCCIO FILIPPI.

Lucca

Biblioteca Statale di Lucca: Via S. Maria Corteorlandini 12, 55100 Lucca; tel. 0583-491271; fax 0583-496770; e-mail bs-lu@beniculturali.it; internet www.bslu.librari.beniculturali.it; f. 1794; 449,200 vols, 594 current periodicals, 10,000 *cinquecentine*, 835 incunabula, 4,321 MSS, 19,462 letters and documents; Dir Dott. MARCO PAOLI.

Macerata

Biblioteca Comunale Mozzi-Borgetti: Piazza Vittorio Veneto 2, 62100 Macerata; tel. 0733-256360; fax 0733-256338; e-mail biblioteca@comune.macerata.it; internet www.comune.macerata.it/entra/engine/raservepg.php3/p/2508110417; f. 1773; 350,000 vols, 10,000 MSS, 300 incunabula, 20,000 photographs; Dir Dott.ssa ALESSANDRA SFRAPPINI.

Mantua

Biblioteca Comunale Teresiana: Via Roberto Ardigò 13, 46100 Mantua; tel. 0376-321515; fax 0376-17084080; e-mail biblioteca.comunale@domino.comune.mantova.it; internet www.bibliotecateresiana.it; f. 1780; 330,000 vols, 1,375 MSS, 1,425 incunabula, 8,500 *cinquecentine*; Dir Dr CESARE GUERRA.

Biblioteca dell' Accademia Nazionale Virgiliana: Via dell'Accademia 47, 46100 Mantua; tel. 0376-320314; fax 0376-222774; e-mail mantua@accademiavirgiliana.191.it; internet ww.accademiavirgiliana.it/menubiblioteca.html; f. early 17th century; 30,000 vols; Librarian Prof. MARIO VAINI; publs *Atti e Memorie* (1 a year), *Nuova Serie* (1 a year).

Messina

Biblioteca Regionale Universitaria di Messina: Via I Settembre 117, 98122 Messina; tel. 090-771908; fax 090-771909; e-mail brs.me@regione.sicilia.it; internet www.regione.sicilia.it/beniculturali/brum/index.htm; f. 1731; 449,926 vols, 461 current periodicals, 1,307 MSS, 423 incunabula, 3,637 *cinquecentine*; Dir Arch. ROCCO GIOVANNI SCIMONE.

Milan

Archivio di Stato di Milano: Via Senato 10, 20121 Milan; tel. 02-7742161; fax 02-774216230; e-mail as-mi@beniculturali.it; internet www.archiviodistatomilano.it; f. 1886; 27,096 vols and pamphlets, 18,814 periodicals; Dir Dott. MARIA BARBARA BERTINI.

Archivio Storico Civico e Biblioteca Trivulziana: Castello Sforzesco, 20121 Milan; tel. 02-88463690; fax 02-88463698; e-mail c.ascbibliotrivulziana@comune.milano.it; internet www.comune.milano.it; f. 1872 as Archivio Storico Civico, renamed Biblioteca Trivulziana 1935; 170,000 vols, 1,500 MSS dating from the 8th century, 2,000 incunabula, and rare edns of works on history and literature, local historical artefacts; Dir Dott.ssa ISABELLA FIORENTINI; publ. *Libri E Documenti* (1 a year).

Biblioteca Archeologica e Numismatica: Castello Sforzesco, 20121 Milan; tel. 02-88463772; fax 02-88463800; e-mail c.bibliocasva@comune.milano.it; internet www.comune.milano.it/casva; f. 1808; prehistoric, Roman, Etruscan, Greek and Egyptian archaeology; coins and medals; library and historical archives; 26,930 vols, 17,650 periodicals, 240 current periodicals; Dir Dr RINA LA GUARDIA.

Biblioteca Centrale di Ingegneria–Leonardo: Piazza Leonardo da Vinci 32, 20133 Milan; tel. 02-23992550; fax 02-23992560; internet www.biblio.polimi.it/biblioteche; f. 1863; 192,100 vols, 350 MSS, 3,780 periodicals, 173 current periodicals; Head of Library MARINELLA TRENTA.

Biblioteca Comunale 'Sormani': Palazzo Sormani, Corso di Porta Vittoria 6, 20122 Milan; tel. 02-88463397; fax 02-88463353; e-mail c.bibliocentrale@comune.milano.it; internet www.comune.milano.it/biblioteche; f. 1886; 640,000 vols, 20,000 periodicals, 2,300 current periodicals, 32,500 audio and video items, 500 electronic resources; Dir Dott. ANNA MARIA ROSSATO.

Biblioteca d'Arte: Castello Sforzesco, 20121 Milan; tel. 02-88463737; fax 02-88463819; e-mail c.biblioarte@comune.milano.it; internet www.comune.milano.it/casva; f. 1930; art history, applied arts, museology, graphics, design, visual arts; art library; 118,525 vols, 1661 periodicals, 256 current periodicals; Dir RINA LA GUARDIA.

Biblioteca d'Ateneo dell'Università Cattolica del Sacro Cuore: Largo Gemelli 1, 20123 Milan; tel. 02-72342230; fax 02-72342701; e-mail biblioteca.direzione-mi@unicatt.it; internet www.unicatt.it/library; f. 1921; linked to libraries in three other locations: Brescia, Piacenza and Cremona, and Rome and Campobasso; 1,373,000 vols and pamphlets, 32,520 periodicals, 12,800 electronic journals, 270 online and CD-ROM-based databases; Head of Library Dott. ELLIS SADA.

Biblioteca del Centro Nazionale di Studi Manzoniani: Via Morone 1, 20121 Milan; tel. 02-86460403; fax 02-875618; e-mail cnsm@tiroli.it; f. 1937; 25,000 vols; Dir Prof. GIANMARCO GASPARI; Vice-Pres. Prof. ANGELO STELLA; publs *Annali*, *Bollettino Bibliografico*, *Edizione Nazionale ed Europea delle Opere di Alessandro Manzoni*.

Biblioteca del Conservatorio 'Giuseppe Verdi': Via Conservatorio 12, 20122 Milan; tel. 02-762110219; fax 02-76003097; e-mail biblioteca@consmilano.it; internet www.consmilano.it; f. 1808; 500,000 items; 50,000 MSS, 30,000 books on music, 400 periodicals; Librarian LICIA SIRCH.

Biblioteca dell' Istituto Lombardo Accademia di Scienze e Lettere: Via Borgonuovo 25, 20121 Milan; tel. 02-864087; fax 02-86461388; e-mail istituto.lombardo@unimi.it; internet www.istitutolombardo.it/biblioteca.html; f. 1802; 495,000 vols, 2,600 periodicals; Dir Dott. ADELE BIANCHI ROBBIATI.

Biblioteca dell' Università Commerciale Luigi Bocconi: Via Gobbi 5, 20136 Milan; tel. 02-58365027; fax 02-58365100; e-mail library.staff@unibocconi.it; internet lib.unibocconi.it; f. 1903; borrowing and reference services, user instruction services; European Documentation Centre; Asian Devt Bank Repository; 500,000 vols, 6,000 paper periodicals, 13,324 e-journals, 48,763 theses, 52 databases, 1,662 ancient books (from 16th to 18th centuries); Head Librarian Dott. MARISA SANTARSIERO.

Biblioteca della Facoltà di Agraria: Università degli Studi di Milano, Via G. Celoria 2, 20133 Milan; tel. 02-50316428; fax 02-50316427; e-mail bib.agraria@unimi.it; internet users.unimi.it/biblioteche/agraria; f. 1871; 35,000 vols and periodicals; Scientific Dir Profa VINCENTINA ANDREONI; Librarian Dott. ANGELO BOZZOLA.

Biblioteca delle Facoltà di Giurisprudenza e di Lettere e Filosofia dell' Università: Via Festa del Perdono 7, 20122 Milan; tel. 02-50312468; fax 02-50312598; e-mail info.bglf@unimi.it; internet www.sba.unimi.it/biblioteche/bglf/1864.html; f. 1925; 360,000 vols, 1,379 current periodicals, 1,034 online periodicals; Dir LIDIA CATERINA DIELLA.

Biblioteca Nazionale Braidense: Via Brera 28, 20121 Milan; tel. 02-86460907; fax 02-72023910; e-mail b-brai@beniculturali.it; internet www.braidense.it; f. 1770; 1,500,000 vols, 17,149 periodicals, 26,455 autographs, 2,107 MSS; Dir Dott. AURELIO AGHEMO.

Civiche Raccolte Storiche di Milano, Biblioteca e Archivio: Palazzo De Marchi, Via Borgonuovo 23, 20121 Milan; tel. 02-88464180; fax 02-88464181; e-mail francesco.basile@comune.milano.it; internet www.civicheraccoltestoriche.mi.it/biblioteca.php; f. 1884; 130,000 vols, periodicals and pamphlets, 3,825 files of documents since 1750; Dir CLAUDIO SALSI.

Veneranda Biblioteca Ambrosiana: Piazza Pio XI 2, 20123 Milan; tel. 02-806921; fax 02-80692212; e-mail info@ambrosiana.it; internet www.ambrosiana.eu; f. 1607, opened to the public in 1609; 900,000 vols and rare prints, 36,000 MSS mostly Latin, Greek, and Oriental, 3,0000 incunabula, 12,000 parchments, 22,500 prints, 20,000 letters, 22,000 engravings; Dir Dott. GIANANTONIO BORGONOVO; publ. *Accademia Ambrosiana. Studia Borromaica* (1 a year).

Modena

Biblioteca Estense Universitaria: Palazzo dei Musei, Largo Porta S. Agostino 337, 41121 Modena; tel. 059-222248; fax 059-230195; e-mail b-este@beniculturali.it; internet www.cedoc.mo.it/estense; 556,889 vols, 11,025 MS vols, 158,464 loose MSS, 1,662 incunabula, 15,966 *cinquecentine*, 128,610 pamphlets, 8,582 periodicals; Dir Dott. LUCA BELLINGERI; Librarian ANNALISA BATTINI.

Naples

Archivio di Stato di Napoli: Piazzetta del Grande Archivio, 80138 Naples; tel. 081-5638111; fax 081-5638300; e-mail as-na@beniculturali.it; internet www .archiviodistatonapoli.it; f. 1808; 544,000 items; 25,000 vols; Dir Dott. IMMA ASCIONE.

Biblioteca del Conservatorio S. Pietro a Majella: Via S. Pietro a Majella 35, 80138 Naples; tel. (81) 5644427; fax (81) 5644415; e-mail biblioteca@sanpietroamajella.it; internet www.sanpietroamajella.it/it/bl_introduzione_w.html; f. 1791; 300,000 vols, 18,000 MSS, 10,000 costume designs, 8,000 opera libretti, 10,000 letters, 200 *cinquecentine*; Dir Dr FRANCESCO MELISI.

Biblioteca della Facoltà di Agraria dell' Università degli Studi di Napoli Federico II: Via Università 100, 80055 Portici; tel. 081-2539321; fax 081-7760229; e-mail giovanna.ameno@unina.it; internet biblioteca.agraria.unina.it; f. 1872; 65,000 vols, 3,511 periodicals, 363 current periodicals; Dir Dott. GIOVANNA AMENO.

Biblioteca della Pontificia Facoltà Teologica dell' Italia Meridionale, sezione 'San Tommaso d'Aquino': Viale Colli Aminei 2, 80131 Naples; tel. 081-7410000; fax 081-7437580; e-mail presidenzapftim@libero.it; internet www.teologia.it/pftim; f. 1687; 120,000 vols; 11 incunabula, 600 MSS, 1,000 periodicals, 450 current periodicals; Dir Prof. ANTONIO PORPORA.

Biblioteca della Società Napoletana di Storia Patria: Piazza Municipio, Maschio Angioino, 80133 Naples; tel. 081-5510353; fax 081-5510353; e-mail bibl.snsp@libero.it; internet www.storia.unina.it/snsp; f. 1875; 350,000 vols, 2,400 MSS, 2,955 periodicals, 900 current periodicals, 1,300 *cinquecentine*, 59 incunabula; Librarian MARIA CONCETTA VILLANI; publ. *Archivio Storico per le Province Napoletane*.

Biblioteca di Castelcapuano: Piazza Tribunali 1, 80138 Naples; tel. 081-269416; fax 081-282367; e-mail info@bibliotecademarsico.it; f. 1848; 80,000 vols and pamphlets, 1,100 documents; Dir Dott. RAFFAELLO ROSSI BUSSOLA.

Biblioteca Nazionale 'Vittorio Emanuele III': Piazza del Plebiscito 1, 80132 Naples; tel. 081-7819111; fax 081-403820; e-mail bn-na@beniculturali.it; internet www .bnnonline.it; f. 1804; 1,800,000 vols, 19,000 MSS, 8,300 periodicals, 4,563 incunabula, 1,792 papyri from Herculaneum; Dir Dott. MAURO GIANCASPRO.

Biblioteca Statale Oratoriana del Monumento Nazionale dei Girolamini: Via Duomo 114, 80138 Naples; tel. 081-294444; fax 081-294444; e-mail bmn-gir@beniculturali.it; internet www.girolamini.it; f. 1586; 169,000 vols, 120 incunabula, 5,000 *cinquecentine*, 485 periodicals, 57 current periodicals; Dir GIOVANNI FERRARA.

Biblioteca Universitaria di Napoli: Via G. Paladino 39, 80138 Naples; tel. 081-5517025; fax 081-5528275; e-mail bu-na@beniculturali.it; internet www.bun.unina.it; f. 1816; 776,211 vols, 5,820 periodicals, 3,654 *cinquecentine*, 462 incunabula, 144 MSS; open to the public; Dir Dott. ORNELLA FALANGOLA.

Novara

Biblioteca Civica 'Carlo Negroni': Corso Felice Cavallotti 4, 28100 Novara; tel. 0321-3702800; fax 0321-3702851; e-mail biblioteca.negroni@comune.novara.it; internet www.comune.novara.it/citta/biblioteca/biblioteca.php; f. 1848; 300,000 vols, 3,052 periodicals, 2,000 *cinquecentine*, 130 incunabula, 771 microfilms, 420 MSS, maps, 6,500 discs, tapes and cassettes; Dir Dott. M. CARLA UGLIETTI.

Padua

Biblioteca Antoniana: Via Orto Botanico 11, 35123 Padua; tel. 049-8751492; fax 069-

1275425; e-mail info@bibliotecaantoniana
.191.it; internet biblioteca.antoniana.net; f.
13th century; 85,000 vols, 800 MSS; Dir
ALBERTO FANTON.

Biblioteca Civica: Via Altinate 71, 35121
Padua; tel. 049-8204811; fax 049-8204804;
e-mail biblioteca.civica@comune.padova.it;
internet www.padovanet.it/biblioteche; f.
1858; art, Italian literature, history, local
history (Padua and Veneto); 500,000 vols,
5,500 MSS, 385 incunabula, 2,000 periodicals, 1300 DVDs; Head Librarian Dr GILDA
P. MANTOVANI; publ. *Bollettino del Museo
Civico di Padova*.

**Biblioteca del Seminario Vescovile di
Padova-della Facoltà Teologica del Tri-
veneto-dell'Istituto Filosofico Aloisia-
num:** Via Seminario 29, 35122 Padua; tel.
049-8230013; fax 049-8761934; e-mail biblio
.seminariopda@unipd.it; internet www
.seminariopadova.it; f. 1671; 300,000 vols,
1,135 MSS, 417 incunabula, 800 periodicals;
Dir Prof. RICCARDO BATTOCCHIO; Librarian Dr
ACHILLE CANTAMESSA; Librarian Dr MARIA
CRISTINA FAZZINI.

Biblioteca Universitaria: Via S. Biagio 7,
35121 Padua; tel. 049-8240211; fax 049-
8762711; e-mail info.bupd@unipd.it;
internet www.bibliotecauniversitariapadova
.it; f. 1629; 676,982 vols; 2,798 MSS, 1,283
incunabula, 1,530 music scores, 1,055 maps,
6,681 periodicals, 592 current periodicals,
9,622 *cinquecentine*, 3,000 prints and engravings; Dir Dott. FRANCESCO ALIANO.

Palermo

Archivio di Stato di Palermo: Corso
Vittorio Emanuele 31, 90133 Palermo; tel.
091-2510634; fax 091-5080681; e-mail as-pa@
beniculturali.it; internet www
.archiviodistatodipalermo.it; f. 1814; 386,918
items; 22,000 vols; Dir CLAUDIO TORRISI.

**Biblioteca Centrale della Regione Sicili-
ana:** Corso Vittorio Emanuele 429–431,
90134 Palermo; tel. 091-7077642; fax 091-
7077644; e-mail bcrs@regione.sicilia.it;
internet www.regione.sicilia.it/beniculturali/
bibliotecacentrale; f. 1782; 682,000 vols;
1,930 MSS, 1,044 incunabula, 5,907 periodicals, 15,000 letters and documents, 5,066
rare books, 4,125 maps, prints and engravings, 47,664 microforms, 3,541 photographs
and slides; Dir FRANCESCO VERGARA.

Biblioteca Comunale: Piazza Casa Pro-
fessa 1, 90134 Palermo; tel. 091-7407940;
fax 091-7407948; e-mail
sistemabibliotecario@comune.palermo.it;
internet librarsi.comune.palermo.it; f. 1760;
330,000 vols, 5,000 MSS, 1,038 incunabula,
6,000 *cinquecentine*; Dir Dott. FILIPPO GUT-
TUSO.

Parma

Biblioteca Palatina: Strada alla Pilotta 3,
43121 Parma; tel. 0521-220411; fax 0521-
235662; e-mail b-pala@beniculturali.it;
internet www.bibliotecapalatina
.beniculturali.it; f. 1761; 715,000 vols, 6,671
MSS, 556 periodicals, 3,044 incunabula,
52,601 engravings and drawings; Dir ANDREA
DE PASQUALE.

**Biblioteca Palatina–Sezione Musicale
presso il Conservatorio di Musica 'A.
Boito':** Via del Conservatorio 27, 43121
Parma; tel. 0521-289429; fax 0521-235662;
internet www.bibpal.unipr.it; f. 1889;
167,000 items; 167,000 vols, 16,288 MSS, 40
periodicals; Dir Dr ANDREA DE PASQUALE.

Pavia

Biblioteca Civica 'Carlo Bonetta': Piazza
Petrarca 2, 27100 Pavia; tel. 0382-21635; fax
0382-307386; e-mail fbonetta@comune.pv.it;
internet www.comune.pv.it/on/home/

canalitematici/arteecultura/bibliotecacivica-
bonetta.html; f. 1887; Dir Dott. FELICE
MILANI.

Biblioteca Universitaria: Corso Strada
Nuova 65, 27100 Pavia; tel. 0382-24764; fax
0382-25007; e-mail bu-pv@beniculturali.it;
internet siba.unipv.it/buniversitaria; f.
1763; 497,077 vols, 2,556 MSS, 691 incunabula, 6,102 periodicals, 718 current periodicals, 7,000 *cinquecentine*, 11,021 microfilms,
4,000 engravings; Dir Dott. ALESSANDRA
BRACCI.

Perugia

**Biblioteca Augusta del Comune di Per-
ugia:** Palazzo Conestabile della Staffa, Via
delle Prome 15, 06122 Perugia; tel. 075-
5772500; fax 075-5722231; e-mail augusta@
comune.perugia.it; internet www.comune
.perugia.it/canale.asp?id=2822; f. 1615;
380,000 vols, 3,380 MSS, 1,330 incunabula,
3,800 periodicals, 16,500 *cinquecentine*; Dir
Dott. MAURIZIO TARANTINO.

Pesaro

Biblioteca e Musei Oliveriani: Via Mazza
Domenico 97, 61121 Pesaro; tel. 0721-33344;
fax 0721-370365; e-mail biblio.oliveriana@
provincia.ps.it; internet www.oliveriana.pu
.it/index.php?id=14525; f. 1793; 354,000 vols
on general culture and local history; Dir
MARCELLO DI BELLA; publ. *Studia Oliveriana*
(1 a year).

Piacenza

Biblioteca Comunale Passerini Landi:
Via Carducci 14, 29121 Piacenza; tel. 0532-
492410; fax 0532-492400; e-mail biblio
.reference@comune.piacenza.it; internet /
passerinilandi.biblioteche.piacenza.it; f.
1774; 50,000 vols, 1,000 incunabula, 5,000
cinquecentine; Dir Dott. ANTONELLA GIGLI.

Pisa

Biblioteca Universitaria: Via Curtatone e
Montanara 15, 56100 Pisa; tel. 050-913411;
fax 050-42064; e-mail bu-pi@beniculturali.it;
internet www.pisa.sbn.it; f. 1742; 600,000
vols, 1,389 MSS, 24,087 documents, 161
incunabula, 4,357, periodicals, 1,030 current
periodicals, 7,022 *cinquecentine*; Dir Dott.
ALESSANDRA PESANTE.

Pistoia

Biblioteca Comunale Forteguerriana:
Piazza della Sapienza 5, 51100 Pistoia; tel.
0573-24348; fax 0573-371466; e-mail
forteguerriana@comune.pistoia.it; internet
www.comune.pistoia.it/forteguerriana/index
.html; f. 1696; 220,000 vols, 1,290 periodicals,
1,000 MSS, 126 incunabula, 3,000 *cinquecentine*; Dir MARIA STELLA RASETTI.

Portici

**Biblioteca del Dipartimento di Entomo-
logia e Zoologia Agraria, Università
degli Studi di Napoli Federico II:** Via
Università 100, 80055 Portici; tel. 081-
2539188; fax 081-7755145; e-mail
bibliodeza@unina.it; f. 1872; applied entomology and biological control; 100,000 vols;
Dir CINZIA STELLATO; publ. *Bollettino del
Laboratorio di Entomologia Agraria 'Filippo
Silvestri'*.

Potenza

Archivio di Stato di Potenza: Via Nazario
Sauro 1, 85100 Potenza; tel. 0971-56144; fax
0971-56223; e-mail aspz@aspz.it; internet
aspz.it; f. 1818; 10,000 linear miles of records
(since the 11th century); administrative and
judicial archives since 1687; notarial archives since 1524; archives of religious houses
dissolved in the 19th century; private and
feudal archives since 1500; collns of parch-

ments (since the 10th century) and municipal
statutes; also archives of ecclesiastical bodies
incl. those of the Venosa cathedral chapter
(since the 11th century); 17,000 vols, 2,500
periodicals; Dir Dott.ssa VALERIA VERRASTRO.

Biblioteca Nazionale: Via del Gallitello
103, 85100 Potenza; tel. 0971-54829; fax
0971-55071; e-mail bn-pz@beniculturali.it;
internet www.bibliotecanazionale.potenza.it;
f. 1985; functions as univ. library (Univ. della
Basilicata) and regional library; 300,000 vols,
1,681 periodicals; Dir FRANCESCO SABIA.

Ravenna

Istituzione Biblioteca Classense: Via
Baccarini 3, 48121 Ravenna; tel. 0544-
482112; fax 0544-482104; e-mail
informazioni@classense.ra.it; internet www
.classense.ra.it; f. 1707–1711; 800,000 items,
incl. 800 incunabula, 8,000 *cinquecentine*,
750 MSS, 10,000 prints; Dir Dott. DONATINO
DOMINI; publ. *Letture Classensi*.

Reggio Emilia

Biblioteca Panizzi: Via Farini 3, 42121
Reggio Emilia; tel. 0522-456084; fax 0522-
456081; e-mail panizzi@municipio.re.it;
internet panizzi.comune.re.it; f. 1796;
500,000 vols, 10,000 MSS; Dir GIORDANO
GASPARINI.

Rimini

Biblioteca Civica Gambalunga: Via Gambalunga 27, 47921 Rimini; tel. 0541-704486;
fax 0541-704480; e-mail gambalunghiana@
comune.rimini.it; internet www
.bibliotecagambalunga.it; f. 1619; 220,000
vols (incl. 7,000 *cinquecentine*), 382 incunabula, 1,350 MSS, 2,545, periodicals, 400 current periodicals, 1,960 bound periodicals,
8,000 drawings and engravings, 80,000
photographs; Dir ORIETTA BAIOCCHI.

Rome

Archivio Centrale dello Stato: Piazzale
degli Archivi 27, 00144 Rome; tel. 06-545481;
fax 06-5413620; e-mail acs@beniculturali.it;
internet www.archiviocentraledellostato
.beniculturali.it; f. 1875; 110 shelf-km of
documents; political, administrative, cultural
and judicial archives of the Kingdom of Italy
and Italian Republic; Dir AGOSTINO ATTANA-
SIO.

Archivio di Stato di Roma: Corso del
Rinascimento 40, 00186 Rome; tel. 06-
6819081; fax 06-68190871; e-mail as-rm@
beniculturali.it; internet www
.archiviodistatoroma.beniculturali.it; f. 1871;
conservation of archives produced by the
central offices of the Papal State from the
Middle Ages to 1870, together with documents produced by other agencies in the
Rome area; papal provincial treasuries (incl.
Avignon and Benevento); archives of religious orders since the 14th century and of
brotherhoods, academies, corporate bodies,
the University of Rome and notary registers
since the 13th century; conservation of govt
office records of the Italian State with seat in
Rome; School of Archival Science, Latin
Palaeography and Diplomatics; 52,000 vols,
with 3 important collns: Statutes, MSS,
Decrees; Dir Prof. EUGENIO LO SARDO.

Biblioteca Angelica: Piazza Sant'Agostino
8, 00186 Rome; tel. 06-6840801; fax 06-
68408053; e-mail b-ange@beniculturali.it;
internet www.biblioangelica.it; f. 1605;
15th–18th-century literature; Augustinian,
Jansenist, Reformation and counter-Refor-
mation collns; 220,000 vols, 2,704 MSS, 1,156
incunabula; Dir Dott.ssa FIAMMETTA TERLIZZI.

Biblioteca Casanatense: Via S. Ignazio 52,
00186 Rome; tel. (6) 6976031; fax (6)
69920254; e-mail casanatense@biblioroma
.sbn.it; internet www.casanatense.it; f. 1701;

preserves and enhances the collns of Cardinal Girolamo Casanate; 400,000 vols; spec. collns: MSS colln, 6,000 vols of great value incl. exultet, liturgical codes, medical-scientific texts, Oriental and Hebraic codes, famous autographs incl. that of Niccolò Paganini; Incunabula colln, 2,200 vols incl. unique first edns and plaques; Engravings colln, 30,000 engravings incl. Abbot Antonio Ricci's donation and endowment of the Chamber of Calligraphy; Musical works colln, 1,700 MSS and 2,000 published works; Theatre colln, 7,000 copies of dramatic works and musical librettos, Edicts and Bans colln, 70,000 from 1550 to 1870, esp. from the Pontiff State; Periodicals: colln, 2,000 titles (220 current subscriptions) incl. Roman and Pontifical State journals; Heraldry colln, 1,200 works; Sanctification actions colln, Decisions of the Sacred Rota and other ecclesiastical tribunals; the library's holdings are currently being increased by the acquisition of antiquarian materials and new publs; Dir IOLANDA OLIVIERI.

Biblioteca Centrale del Consiglio Nazionale delle Ricerche (Central Library of National Research Council): Piazzale Aldo Moro 7, 00185 Rome; tel. 06-49933221; fax 06-49933858; e-mail biblioce@bice.rm.cnr.it; internet www.bice.rm.cnr.it; f. 1927; 1,000,000 vols, 10,000 periodicals (6,000 online), EU depository library; scientific and technical subjects; Dir Prof. BRUNELLA SEBAS-TIANI.

Biblioteca Centrale del Ministero dell'Interno: Palazzo del Viminale, Via Agostino Depretis, 00184 Rome; tel. 06-46525703; fax 06-46536689; internet www.interno.it/mininterno/export/sites/default/it/sezioni/ministero/biblioteche/la_biblioteca_centrale; f. 1872; 110,000 vols; Dir ARTURO LETIZIA.

Biblioteca Centrale Giuridica del Ministero della Giustizia: Palazzo di Giustizia, Piazza Cavour, 00193 Rome; tel. 06-68834900; e-mail bcg@giustizia.it; internet www.giustizia.it/giustizia/it/mg_7.wp; f. 1866; 200,000 vols, 2,300 periodicals, 1,000 current periodicals; Dir Dr ORAZIO FRAZZINI.

Biblioteca del Ministero degli Affari Esteri: Piazzale della Farnesina 1, 00194 Rome; tel. 06-36913279; fax 06-36912701; e-mail giorgetta.troiano@esteri.it; internet www.esteri.it/mae/it/ministero/servizi/italiani/archivi_biblioteca/biblioteca.htm; f. 1850; 200,000 vols, 1,500 periodicals, 168 current periodicals; international relations, contemporary history; Dir Dott. MARIA ADE-LAIDE FRABOTTA.

Biblioteca del Senato 'Giovanni Spadolini': Piazza della Minerva, 38, 00186 Rome; tel. 06-67063717; fax 06-67064338; e-mail bibliotecaminerva@senato.it; internet www.senato.it/biblioteca; f. 1848; 600,000 vols, 3,200 periodicals, 200 current periodicals, 850 MSS, 80 incunabula, 2,000 *cinquecentine*; chiefly works on law, history and politics; medieval statutes; Head of Library Dott. SANDRO BULGARELLI.

Biblioteca dell'Accademia Nazionale dei Lincei e Corsiniana: Via della Lungara 10, 00165 Rome; tel. 06-6861983; fax 06-68027343; e-mail biblioteca@lincei.it; internet www.lincei.it; f. 1883; 552,000 vols on history of arts, sciences and culture, 7,000 periodicals, 4,600 MSS, 2,307 incunabula; oriental section on Arabic and Islamic civilization, with 35,000 books, 350 periodicals, 500 MSS; online catalogue for modern collection; Dir Dott. MARCO GUARDO; Librarian (Ancient Printed Books) Dott. EBE ANTETO-MASO; Librarian (Modern Printed Books) Dott. ALESSANDRO ROMANELLO; Librarian (Oriental Section) Dott. VALENTINA SAGARIA ROSSI; Librarian (Oriental Section and Inter-

library Loans) Dott. ANDREA TRENTINI; Librarian (Reading Room and Loan Service) ANDREA DIBITONTO.

Biblioteca della Camera dei Deputati: Via del Seminario 76, 00186 Rome; tel. 06-67603476; fax 06-6786886; e-mail bib_segretaria@camera.it; f. 1848 in Turin; 1,000,000 vols, 10,000 bound periodicals, 2,500 current periodicals; Dir Dr ANTONIO CASU; publ. *Bollettino Nuove Accessioni* (12 a year).

Biblioteca della Fondazione Marco Besso: Largo di Torre Argentina 11, 00186 Rome; tel. 06-68192984; fax 06-68216313; e-mail biblioteca@fondazionemarcobesso.it; internet www.fondazionemarcobesso.it/nuovobesso; f. 1918; 60,000 vols and 5,000 pamphlets; special collections: Rome, Dante, Proverbs, Tuscia; Curator ANTONIO MARTINI.

Biblioteca della Società Geografica Italiana: Villa Celimontana, Via della Navicella 12, 00184 Rome; tel. 06-7008279; fax 06-77079518; e-mail biblioteca@societageografica.it; internet www.societageografica.it/archivio/biblioteca/index.htm; f. 1867; 400,000 vols; Library Counsellor LINA MARIA VITALE; publs *Bollettino della Società geografica italiana*, *Memorie della Società geografica italiana*, *Ricerche e studi*.

Biblioteca della Società Italiana per l'Organizzazione Internazionale (SIOI): Piazza di S. Marco 51, Palazzetto di Venezia, 00186 Rome; tel. 06-6920781; fax 06-6789102; e-mail sioi@sioi.org; internet www.sioi.org/la_biblioteca.htm; f. 1944; 70,000 vols, 800 periodicals, 500,000 UN documents; Dir Dott. SARA CAVELLI.

Biblioteca della Soprintendenza alla Galleria Nazionale d'Arte Moderna e Contemporanea: Viale delle Belle Arti 131, 00196 Rome; tel. 06-32298246; fax 06-3221579; e-mail biblio.gnam@arti.beniculturali.it; internet www.ufficignam.beniculturali.it/index.php?it/107/biblioteca; f. 1945; 70,000 vols, 1,500 periodicals, 40,000 miscellaneous items on art since the 19th century; Dir Prof. LEANDRO VENTURA; Librarian Dott. DINA MACERA; publ. *Bollettino mensile delle nuove accessioni* (12 a year, online).

Biblioteca di Archeologia e Storia dell'Arte: Piazza Venezia 3, 00187 Rome; tel. 06-6977001; fax 06-6781167; e-mail b-asar@beniculturali.it; internet www.archeologica.librari.beniculturali.it; f. 1922; 370,000 vols, 3,900 periodicals, 1,600 MSS, 16 incunabula, 66,000 microfiches, 740 *cinquecentine*, and 20,700 engravings, drawings and photographs; Dir MARIA CONCETTA PETROLLO.

Biblioteca di Storia Moderna e Contemporanea: Via M. Caetani 32, 00186 Rome; tel. 06-6828171; fax 06-68807662; e-mail b-stmo@beniculturali.it; internet www.bsmc.it; f. 1917; 450,000 vols, 11,000 MSS, 7,200 bound periodicals, 600 current periodicals, 3,000 microfilms and microfiches; Dir STEFA-NIA MURIANNI.

Biblioteca Istituto Italo-Latino Americano: Piazza Benedetto Cairoli 3, 00186 Rome; tel. 06-68492241; fax 06-6872834; e-mail biblioteca@iila.org; internet www.iila.org; f. 1966; specializes in contemporary Latin-American life; services offered: offsets of any item in library, in-service library loans, information service; 80,000 vols, 1,000 periodicals, 100 CD-ROMs; Librarian Prof. RICCARDO CAMPA.

Biblioteca Lancisiana: Borgo Santo Spirito 3, 00193 Rome; tel. 06-68352449; fax 06-68352470; e-mail segreteria.biblioteca@lancisiana.it; internet www.lancisiana.it; f. 1711; history of medicine, history of science; 18,013 vols, 374 MSS, 60 incunabula, 2,000

cinquecentine; Dir Dott. SAVERIO MARCO FIORILLA; Currently closed for repairs and renovation work.

Biblioteca Medica Statale: Viale del Policlinico 155, 00161 Rome; tel. 06-490778; fax 06-4457265; e-mail bs-medi@beniculturali.it; internet bms.beniculturali.it; f. 1925; 145,000 vols, 1,193 periodicals; Dir Dr GIO-VANNI ARGANESE; publ. *Bollettino bimestrale nuove accessioni*.

Biblioteca Musicale del Conservatorio 'Santa Cecilia': Via dei Greci 18, 00187 Rome; tel. 06-36096736; fax 06-36001800; internet www.conservatoriosantacecilia.it; f. 1875; 300,000 vols, 10,000 MSS, 100 current periodicals; Dir Prof. DOMENICO CARBONI.

Biblioteca Nazionale Centrale di Roma: Viale Castro Pretorio 105, 00185 Rome; tel. 06-4989318; fax 06-4457635; e-mail bnc-rm@beniculturali.it; internet www.bncrm.librari.beniculturali.it; f. 1876; 6,000,000 vols, 8,000 MSS, 2,000 incunabula, 25,000 *cinquecentine*, 20,000 maps, 50,000 periodicals, 10,000 prints and drawings; Dir Dott. OSVALDO AVALLONE.

Biblioteca Storica e Centro Multimediale del Ministero dell'Economia e delle Finanze: Via XX Settembre 97, 00187 Rome; tel. 06-47613120; fax 06-47614779; e-mail biblioteca.storica@tesoro.it; internet www.dag.mef.gov.it/le_persone/cittadini/biblioteca_storica_presentazione; f. 1857; 100,000 vols; Head Dott. PATRIZIA FEMORE.

Biblioteca Storica Nazionale dell'Agricoltura: Via XX Settembre 20, 00187 Rome; tel. 06-46652519; fax 06-46652519; e-mail bibliotecastorica@politicheagricole.gov.it; internet www.politicheagricole.it/biblioteca; f. 1860; 1,000,000 vols, 300 current periodicals; Dir Dott. GIOVANNI PIERO SANNA.

Biblioteca Universitaria Alessandrina: Piazzale Aldo Moro 5, 00185 Rome; tel. 06-44740220; fax 06-44740222; e-mail alessandrina@librari.beniculturali.it; internet www.alessandrina.librari.beniculturali.it; f. 1667; 1,000,000 vols, 452 MSS, 674 incunabula, 15,000 *cinquecentine*; Dir MARIA CRISTINA DI MARTINO.

Biblioteca Vallicelliana: Piazza della Chiesa Nuova 18, 00186 Rome; tel. 06-68802671; fax 06-6893868; e-mail b-vall@beniculturali.it; internet www.vallicelliana.it; f. 1581; 150,000 vols, 2,659 MSS, 404 incunabula; also contains library of 'Società Romana di Storia Patria' (50,000 vols); Dir Dr MARIA CONCETTA PETROLLO PAGLIARANI.

Bibliotheca Hertziana—Max-Planck-Institut für Kunstgeschichte: Via Gregoriana 28, 00187 Rome; tel. 06-69993227; fax 06-69993333; e-mail institut@biblhertz.it; internet www.biblhertz.it; f. 1913; 289,000 vols on history of Italian art, 1,139 periodicals, 2,559 bound periodicals, 809,000 photographs of Italian art; Librarian Dr ANDREAS THIELEMANN; publs *Römisches Jahrbuch der Bibliotheca Hertziana*, *Römische Forschungen der Bibliotheca Hertziana*, *Römische Studien der Bibliotheca Hertziana*, *Studi della Bibliotheca Hertziana*.

Cineteca Nazionale: Via Tuscolana 1524, 00173 Rome; tel. 06-72294278; fax 06-7211619; e-mail biblioteca@fondazionecsc.it; internet www.snc.it/ct_home.jsp?id_link=129&area=29; f. 1935; includes the National Film Archive and the Luigi Chiarini Library; 92,000 vols and documents, 10,976 scenarios, 871 bound periodicals, 170 current periodicals; Gen. Dir MARCELLO FOTI; Library Dir Dott.ssa FIAMMETTA LIONTI; publ. *Bianco e Nero* (3 a year).

David Lubin Memorial Library, Food and Agriculture Organization (FAO) of

the United Nations: Viale delle Terme di Caracalla, 00153 Rome; tel. 06-57053784; fax 06-57052002; e-mail fao-library-reference@fao.org; internet www.fao.org/library; f. 1946; reference and information services, briefings and seminars, and electronic reproduction of FAO documents; technical services for institutional repository; 1,000,000 vols and more than 8,000 current journals, of which 2,500 electronic; Head Librarian PATRICIA MERRIKIN.

Istituto Centrale per i Beni Sonori ed Audiovisivi (Central Institute for Sound and Audiovisual Heritage): Via M. Caetani 32, 00186 Rome; tel. 06-68406901; fax 06-6865837; e-mail ic-bsa@beniculturali.it; internet www.icbsa.it; f. 1928; collection of recordings of eminent Italians; 220,000 records of classical and light music, jazz; 25,000 records and tapes on anthropology and folklore; collection of sound reproduction equipment; 13,000 vols, 150 current periodicals, 2,000 opera librettos; Dir Dott. MASSIMO PISTACCHI; Librarian MARIA CARLA ZOU.

Istituto Centrale per il Catalogo Unico delle Biblioteche Italiane e per le Informazioni Bibliografiche (Central Institute of the Union Catalogue of Italian Libraries and Bibliographical Information): Viale Castro Pretorio 105, 00185 Rome; tel. 06-4989425; fax 06-4959302; e-mail ic-cu@beniculturali.it; internet www.iccu.sbn.it; f. 1951; Dir ROSA CAFFO.

Rovigo

Pinacoteca dell'Accademia dei Concordi: Piazza V. Emanuele II 14, 45100 Rovigo; tel. 0425-27991; fax 0425-27993; e-mail concordi@concordi.it; internet www.concordi.it; f. 1580; Egyptian and Roman colln; numismatic colln of 2,000 items; colln of paintings from 15th–19th centuries; 250,000 vols.

Sassari

Biblioteca Universitaria: Piazza Università 21, 07100 Sassari; tel. 079-235179; fax 079-235787; e-mail bu-ss@beniculturali.it; internet sba.uniss.it; f. between 1558 and 1562; 200,000 vols, 1,200 bound periodicals, 1,000 current periodicals, 1,500 MSS, 1,431 microfilms, 71 incunabula, 3,500 *cinquecentine*; Dir ELISABETTA PILIA.

Siena

Biblioteca Comunale degli Intronati: Via della Sapienza 3, 53100 Siena; tel. 0577-280704; fax 0577-44293; e-mail biblioteca@biblioteca.comune.siena.it; internet www.bibliotecasiena.it; f. 1758; 386,419 vols, 3,679 bound periodicals, 1,091 current periodicals, 5,699 MSS, 1,038 incunabula, 20,000 prints, 5,810 microfiches, 32,500 slides; Dir Dott. DANIELE DANESI.

Teramo

Biblioteca Provinciale 'Melchiorre Dèlfico': Via Dèlfico 16, 64100 Teramo; tel. 0861-252744; fax 0861-254197; e-mail biblioteca@provincia.teramo.it; internet www.provincia.teramo.it/biblioteca; f. 1816; 260,000 vols, 5,000 bound periodicals, 600 current periodicals, 1,200 *cinquecentine*, 55 incunabula, 15,000 MSS, 100,000 photographs; Dir LUIGI PONZIANI.

Trento

Biblioteca dell' Archivio di Stato di Trento: Via Maestri del Lavoro 4, 38100 Trento; tel. 0461-829008; fax 0461-828981; e-mail as-tn@beniculturali.it; internet www.icar.beniculturali.it/biblio; f. 1919; administered by the Ministero per i Beni Culturali e Ambientali; cultural function and to promote historical research; 7,141 vols, 100 period-

icals, holds archives of state offices from pre-unification Italy and single documents and archives belonging to or deposited with the State; Dir GIOVANNI MARCADELLA.

Biblioteca Comunale: Via Roma 55, 38100 Trento; tel. 0461-275521; fax 0461-275552; e-mail tn.viaroma@biblio.infotn.it; internet www.bibcom.trento.it; f. 1856; 751,609 vols, 536 incunabula and 4,244 16th-century edns, music section of 20,000 vols; 25,250 MSS, 8,450 periodicals, 10,341 maps; colln of 171,132 vols on history and culture of Trentino-Alto Adige; Austrian Library (8,128 vols); Dir Dr FABRIZIO LEONARDELLI; publs *A TUTTO BIB—Novita per Ragazzi* (4 a year), *BIB—Notiziario della Biblioteca Comunale di Trento* (4 a year), *Pubblicazioni Trentine* (1 a year), *Studi Trentini* (4 a year), *Trentine* (1 a year).

Treviso

Biblioteca Borgo Cavour: Borgo Cavour 20, 31100 Treviso; tel. 0422-545342; fax 0422-583066; e-mail info@bibliotecatreviso.it; internet www.bibliotecatreviso.it; f. 1770; 450,000 vols, 5,000 MSS, 800 incunabula, 13,000 prints; Dir Dott. EMILIO LIPPI; publ. *Studi Trevisani*.

Trieste

Archivio di Stato di Trieste: Via A. La Marmora 17, 34139 Trieste; tel. 040-390020; fax 040-9380033; e-mail as-ts@beniculturali.it; internet www.archivi.beniculturali.it/asts; f. 1926; 45,250 vols, 1,116 periodicals; Dir Dott. GRAZIA TATÒ; Librarian CARMELO BIANCO.

Biblioteca Civica 'A. Hortis': Via Madonna del Mare 13, 34124 Trieste; tel. 040-6758200; fax 040-6758199; e-mail bibcivica@comune.trieste.it; internet www.retecivica.trieste.it/triestecultura/new/bibliotecacivica/default.asp; f. 1793; 400,000 vols, 401 MSS, drawings and maps; Petrarch, Piccolomini, Svevo and Joyce sections and historical archives; Dir Dott. ADRIANO DUGULIN.

Biblioteca Statale di Trieste: Largo Papa Giovanni XXIII 6, 34123 Trieste; tel. 040-300725; fax 040-301053; e-mail bs-ts@beniculturali.it; internet www.bsts.librari.beniculturali.it; f. 1956; 200,000 vols; Dir Dott. SABINA MAGRINI.

Narodna in študijska knjižnica v Trstu (Slovene National Study Library): Via S. Francesco 20, 34133 Trieste; tel. 040-635629; fax 040-3484684; e-mail bibslo@spin.it; internet www.nsk-trst.sik.si; f. 1947; 100,000 vols, 500 periodicals.

Turin

Archivio di Stato di Torino: Piazza Castello 209, 10124 Turin; tel. (11) 540382; fax (11) 546176; e-mail as-to@beniculturali.it; internet www.archiviodistatotorino.it; f. 12th century, bldg 1731; houses documents of House of Savoy (county, duchy, kingdom) up to 1861, and those of provincial state admins of 19th century; archives: 81 shelf-km; 50,000 vols, MSS collns; Dir Dr MARCO CARASSI.

Biblioteca dell' Accademia delle Scienze di Torino: Via Maria Vittoria 3, 10123 Turin; tel. 011-5620047; fax 011-532619; e-mail biblioteca@accademia.csi.it; internet www.accademiadellescienze.it; f. 1783; a conservation library covering most fields of the sciences and humanities; rare books dating from the 15th–19th centuries; colln of books, letters and MSS from the late 18th–19th centuries; 200,000 vols, 418 current periodicals and 4,780 others, 35,000 letters, MSS; online catalogue; Head Librarian Dott. ELENA BORGI; publs *Atti della Accademia* (1

a year), *Memorie della Accademia* (1 a year), *Quaderni della Accademia* (1 a year).

Biblioteche Civica Centrale: Via Cittadella 5, 10122 Turin; tel. 011-4429812; fax 011-4429830; e-mail biblioteche.civiche@comune.torino.it; internet www.comune.torino.it/cultura/biblioteche; f. 1869; 524,553 vols, 67 incunabula, 2,000 MSS, 1,600 *cinquecentine*, 18,762 rare vols, 7,721 microfilms, 1,247 current periodicals; 14 br. libraries; Dir Dott. PAOLO MESSINA.

Sistema Bibliotecario del Politecnico di Torino: Corso Duca degli Abruzzi 24, 10129 Turin; tel. 011-0906709; fax 011-0906799; e-mail direttore.bibli@polito.it; internet www.biblio.polito.it; 15,000 vols; Dir Dott. MARIA VITTORIA SAVIO.

Biblioteca Reale: Piazza Castello 191, 10122 Turin; tel. 011-543855; fax 011-5178259; e-mail b-real@beniculturali.it; internet www.bibliotecareale.beniculturali.it; f. 1831; 200,000 vols, 4,500 MSS, 1,500 parchments, 3,055 drawings, 1,112 periodicals, 187 incunabula, 5,019 *cinquecentine*; library of the Savoy family; historical documents on heraldry, military matters, the Sardinian States, the *Risorgimento* and the Piedmont; Dir CLARA VITULO.

Biblioteca Speciale di Matematica 'Giuseppe Peano': Dipartimento di Matematica, Università degli Studi di Torino, Via Carlo Alberto 10, 10123 Turin; fax 011-6702824; f. 1883; 70,000 vols; Dir Prof. FERDINANDO ARZARELLO.

Udine

Biblioteca Civica 'Vincenzo Joppi': Piazza Marconi 8, 33100 Udine; tel. 0432-271583; fax 0432-271580; e-mail bcu@comune.udine.it; internet www.udinecultura.it; f. 1864; 526,000 vols, 10,000 MSS, 124 incunabula, 3,000 *cinquecentine*; Dir Dott. ROMANO VECCHIET.

Urbino

Biblioteca Universitaria: Via Aurelio Saffi 2, 61029 Urbino; tel. 0722-305212; fax 0722-305286; e-mail fabio@uniurb.it; internet www.uniurb.it/bib/home.htm; f. 1720; 550,000 vols, 5,300 periodicals, 3,950 *cinquecentine*; Dir Dott. GOFFREDO MARANGONI.

Venice

Biblioteca dell' Accademia Armena di S. Lazzaro dei Padri Mechitaristi: Isola S. Lazzaro, 30126 Venice; tel. 041-5260104; fax 041-5268690; f. 1701; 170,000 vols, 4,500 MSS; Dir Dr SAHAK DJEMDJEMIAN.

Biblioteca del Civico Museo Correr: Piazza S. Marco 52, Procuratie Nuove, 30124 Venice; tel. 041-2405211; fax 041-5200935; e-mail biblioteca.correr@fmcvenezia.it; internet www.museiciviciveneziani.it; f. 1830; specializes in history of art and Venetian history; 116,933 vols, 1,022 periodicals, 13,018 MSS, 700 MSS on microfiche; Dir GIANDOMENICO ROMANELLI.

Biblioteca Nazionale Marciana: Piazzetta San Marco 7, 30124 Venice; tel. 041-2407211; fax 041-5238803; e-mail biblioteca@marciana.venezia.sb.it; internet marciana.venezia.sbn.it; f. 1468; 1,000,000 vols, 3,731 periodicals, 2,883 incunabula, 24,055 *cinquecentine*, 13,000 MSS; Dir Dott. MARIA LETIZIA SEBASTIANI.

Fondazione Scientifica Querini-Stampalia: Castello 5252, 30122 Venice; tel. (41) 2711411; fax (41) 2711445; e-mail biblioteca@querinistampalia.org; internet www.querinistampalia.it/biblioteca; f. 1869; 300,000 vols, 400 current periodicals; Dir ENRICO ZOLA.

Verona

Biblioteca Civica: Via Cappello 43, 37121 Verona; tel. 045-8079700; fax 045-8079727; e-mail bibliotecacivica@comune.verona.it; internet biblioteche.comune.verona.it; f. 1792; 700,000 vols; 1,188 incunabula; 3,477 MSS; Dir Dott. REN GABRIELE.

Vicenza

Biblioteca Civica Bertoliana: Contrà Riale 5, 36100 Vicenza; tel. 0444-578211; fax 0444-578234; e-mail consulenza@ bibliotecabertoliana.it; internet www .bibliotecabertoliana.it; f. 1696; 800,000 vols, 852 incunabula, 3,565 MSS, 750 periodicals, 8,000 *cinquecentine*; Librarian Dott. GIORGIO LOTTO.

Museums and Art Galleries

Ancona

Museo Archeologico Nazionale delle Marche: Palazzo Ferretti, Via Ferretti 6, 60121 Ancona; tel. 071-202602; e-mail mara .silvestrini@beniculturali.it; fax 071-2083233; internet www.archeomarche.it/ musarch.htm; f. 1906; prehistoric and Roman archaeology; large colln from Iron Age Picene and Celtic cultures; Dir Dott. MARA SILVES-TRINI.

Aquileia

Museo Archeologico Nazionale: Via Roma 1, 33051 Aquileia; tel. 0431-91016; fax 0431-919537; e-mail archeologico@ museoarcheo-aquileia.it; internet www .museoarcheo-aquileia.it; f. 1882; collection of Roman architecture, sculpture, inscriptions, mosaics, etc. from excavations in the town; library of 10,000 vols; Dir Dott. FRANCA MASELLI SCOTTI; publ. *Aquileia Nostra* (1 a year).

Attached Museum:

Museo Paleocristiano: Via Monastero, 33051 Aquileia; tel. 0431-91035; fax 0431-919537; e-mail paleocristiano@ museoarcheo-aquileia.it; internet www .museoarcheo-aquileia.it; f. 1961; mosaics and inscriptions from the palaeo-Christian era; Dir Dott. FRANCA MASELLI SCOTTI.

Ardea

Raccolta Manzù: Via Laurentina Km 32.8, 00040 Ardea; tel. 06-9135022; e-mail mcossu@arti.beniculturali.it; internet www .museomanzu.beniculturali.it; f. 1969; paintings and sculptures by Giacomo Manzù (b. 1908 in Bergamo); part of Nat. Gallery of Modern Art in Rome; Chief Dir MARCELLA COSSU; Technical Dir ALESSANDRO MARIA LIGUORI.

Arezzo

Museo Archeologico Nazionale 'Gaio Cilnio Mecenate': Via Margaritone 10, 52100 Arezzo; tel. 0575-20882; fax 0575-20882; internet www.mega.it/archeo .toscana/samuar.htm; f. 1832; Etruscan, Greek and Roman antiquities, coralline vases of Augustan period, sarcophagi, mosaics, coins and bronzes; Dir Dott. P. ZAMARCHI.

Museo Statale d'Arte Medievale e Moderna: Via San Lorentino 8, 52100 Arezzo; tel. 0575-409050; fax 0575-299850; internet www .sbappsae-ar.beniculturali.it/index.php?it/ 179/museo-statale-darte-medievale-e-moderna; f. 1957; Italian paintings from 13th–19th centuries, Majolica ware, glass, ivories, seals and coins; Curator Dott. STEFANO CASCIU.

Assisi

Museo del Tesoro della Basilica di S. Francesco in Assisi: Piazza S. Francesco, 2, 06081 Assisi; tel. 075-819001; fax 075-8190035; e-mail museosc@gmail.com; internet www.sanfrancescoassisi.org; f. 1927; historical and artistic collns relating to the Basilica church of St Francis, F. M. Perkins colln of 13th–15th-century European art; Dir Fr LUIGI MARIOLI.

Bari

Museo Archeologico: Palazzo dell'Ateneo, Piazza Umberto I, 70121 Bari; tel. 080-5211559; internet www.archeologia .beniculturali.it/pages/atlante/s89.html; f. 1882; library of 2,500 vols; Dir Dott. GIUSEPPE ANDREASSI.

Pinacoteca Provinciale: Via Spalato 19, 70121 Bari; tel. 080-5412421; fax 080-5583401; e-mail pinacotecaprov.bari@tin.it; f. 1928; Apulian, Venetian and Neapolitan paintings and sculpture from 11th to 19th centuries; paintings from the 'Macchiaioli'; library of 3,000 vols; Dir Dott.ssa CLARA GELAO.

Bergamo

Accademia Carrara di Belle Arti–Museo: Accademia Carrara di Belle Arti, Piazza Giacomo Carrara 82/A, 24121 Bergamo; tel. 035-399640; fax 035-224510; e-mail accademiacarrara@comune.bg.it; internet www.accademiacarrara.bergamo.it; f. 1796; colln incl. paintings by Bellini, Raffaello, Pisanello, Mantegna, Botticelli, Beato Angelico, Previtali, Tiepolo, Lotto, Moroni, Baschenis, Galgario; drawings, prints and sculptures since 15th century; Dir FRANCESCO ROSSI.

Bologna

Museo Civico Archeologico: Via dell'Archiginnasio 2, 40124 Bologna; tel. 051-2757211; fax 051-266516; e-mail cristiana.morigigovi@ comune.bologna.it; internet www.comune .bologna.it/bologna/museoarcheologico; f. 1881; prehistoric, Egyptian, Greek, Roman, Villanovan, Etruscan and Celtic antiquities; numismatic colln; library of 15,000 vols, 631 periodicals, 128 current periodicals; Dir Dott. PAOLA GIOVETTI; Curator MARINELLA MARCHESI.

Pinacoteca Nazionale: Via Belle Arti 56, 40126 Bologna; tel. 051-4209411; fax 051-251368; e-mail sbsae-bo@beniculturali.it; internet www.pinacotecabologna.it; f. 1808; Bolognese paintings and other Italian schools from 14th–18th centuries; German and Italian engravings; Dir Dott. GIANPIERO CAMAROTA.

Bolzano

Museo Archeologico dell'Alto Adige/ Südtiroler Archäologiemuseum (South Tyrol Museum of Archaeology): Via Museo 43, 39100 Bolzano; tel. 0471-320100; fax 0471-320122; e-mail museo@iceman.it; internet www.iceman.it; history and archaeology of the South Tyrol region from the Palaeolithic to the Carolingian period (AD 800); also 'Ötzi', 5,000-year old mummified man discovered in the Schnalstal Glacier in 1991; Dir Dr ANGELIKA FLECKINGER.

Museo Civico di Bolzano: Via Cassa di Risparmio 14, 39100 Bolzano; tel. 0471-997967; fax 0471-997964; e-mail museo .civico@comune.bolzano.it; internet www .comune.bolzano.it/cultura_context.jsp?i-d_link=750&area=48; f. 1902; history of art since medieval period; archaeology, numismatics, furniture, liturgical items; library of 30,000 vols, 428 periodicals; Dir Dott. STEFAN DEMETZ.

Brescia

Fondazione Brescia Musei: Via Musei 55, 25121 Brescia; tel. 030-2400640; fax 030-2990267; internet www.bresciamusei.com; Dir Dott. RENATA STRADIOTTI.

Constituent Museums and Galleries:

Museo delle Armi 'Luigi Marzoli': Via Castello 9, 25121, Brescia; tel. 030-293292; f. 1988; 14th- to 18th-century arms.

Museo del Risorgimento: Via Castello 9, 25121 Brescia; tel. 030-293292; f. 1959; 19th-century historical exhibits.

Pinacoteca Tosio Martinengo: Piazza Moretto 4, 25121 Brescia; tel. 030-3774999; f. 1906; art from the 13th to 18th centuries.

Santa Giulia–Museo della Città: Via dei Musei 81/bis, 25121 Brescia; tel. 030-2977834; f. 1882; art and archaeology and 3 churches; incl. colln of the former Museo Romano (prehistoric, pre-Roman and Roman artefacts).

Museo Civico di Scienze Naturali: Via Ozanam 4, 25128 Brescia; tel. 030-2978672; fax 030-3701048; e-mail museo.scienze@ comune.brescia.it; internet www.comune .brescia.it/museoscienzenaturali; f. 1949; botanical, geological, zoological and palaeoethnographical collns; library of 60,000 vols, 150 current periodicals; Dir MARCO TONON; publs *Annuario Civica Specola Cidnea*, *Natura Bresciana*.

Museo Diocesano: Via Gasparo da Salò 13, 25122 Brescia; tel. 030-40233; fax 030-3751064; e-mail seo@diocesi.brescia.it; internet www.diocesi.brescia.it/ museodiocesano; f. 1978; Dir GIUSEPPE FUSARI.

Cagliari

Museo Archeologico Nazionale: Cittadella dei Musei, Piazza Arsenale 1, 09124 Cagliari; tel. 070-655911; fax 070-658871; e-mail sba-ca@beniculturali.it; f. 1806; Sardinian antiquities (prehistorical, Punic, Roman periods); library of 8,000 vols; Dir Dr VINCENZO SANTONI.

Capua

Museo Provinciale Campano: Via Roma, 81043 Capua; tel. 0823-620076; fax 0823-620035; e-mail museocampano@provincia .caserta.it; internet www.provincia.caserta .it/museocampano; f. 1870; library of 70,000 vols, 2,956 MSS; Pres. ON. DOMENICO ZINZI; Dir (vacant).

Chieti

Museo Archeologico Nazionale d'Abruzzo: Via Villa Comunale 2, 66100 Chieti; tel. 0871-331668; fax 0871-330955; e-mail maria.ruggeri-01@beniculturali.org; internet www.archeoabruzzo.beniculturali .it/manda1.html; f. 1959; pottery, weapons and ornaments from 9th to 4th century BC, burial sites, sculpture from 6th and 5th centuries BC; Dir Dott. MARIA RUGGERI.

Cividale

Museo Archeologico Nazionale: Piazza del Duomo 13, 33043 Cividale del Friuli; tel. 0432-700700; fax 0432-700751; e-mail museoarcheocividale@beniculturali.it; f. 1817; prehistoric, Roman and medieval archaeology, jewellery and miniatures, MSS; library of 15,000 vols and archives; Dir Dott.ssa SERENA VITRI; publ. *Forum Iulii* (1 a year).

Faenza

Museo Internazionale delle Ceramiche: Viale Baccarini 19, 48018 Faenza; tel. 0546-697311; fax 0546-27141; e-mail info@ micfaenza.org; internet www.micfaenza.org; f. 1908; history, art and techniques of ceramics; library of 53,000 vols; Pres. Dr PIER ANTONIO RIVOLA; publ. *Faenza* (6 a year).

Ferrara

Gallerie d'Arte Moderna e Contemporanea: Corso Porta Mare 9, 44100 Ferrara; tel. 0532-243415; fax 0532-205035; e-mail artemoderna@comune.fe.it; internet www.artecultura.fe.it; Dir Dott. ANDREA BUZZONI.

Constituent Galleries:

Palazzo dei Diamanti: Corso Ercole I d'Este 21, 44121 Ferrara; tel. 0532-244949; fax 0532-203064; e-mail diamanti@comune.fe.it; internet www.palazzodiamanti.it; incl. Gallerie d'Arte Moderna e Contemporanea; opens in occasion of temporary exhibitions.

Palazzo Massari: Corso Porta Mare 9, 44100 Ferrara; tel. 0532-244949; fax 0532-203064; e-mail artemoderna@comune.fe.it; incorporates Museo d'Arte Moderna e Contemporanea 'Filippo de Pisis', Museo dell'Ottocento, Museo G. Boldini, Padiglione d'Arte Contemporanea.

Museo Archeologico Nazionale di Ferrara: Via XX Settembre 122 (Palazzo di Ludovico il Moro), 44100 Ferrara; tel. 0532-66299; fax 0532-741270; e-mail sba-ero.museoarchferrara@beniculturali.it; internet www.archeobo.arti.beniculturali.it/ferrara; f. 1935; Greco-Etruscan vases, statuettes, bronzes and gold ornaments from the graves of Spina; Dir Dott. CATERINA CORNELIO.

Florence

Comune di Firenze–Direzione Cultura–Servizio Musei: Via delle Conce 28, 50122 Florence; tel. 055-2625961; fax 055-2625943; e-mail gestione.musei@comune.fi.it; internet www.museicivicifiorentini.it; Dir ELENA PIANEA.

Attached Museums and Galleries:

Cappella Brancacci: Piazza del Carmine 14, 50124 Florence; tel. 055-2382195; frescoes in the Church of Santa Maria del Carmine painted by Masolino (1383–1447) and Masaccio (1401–28), and completed by Filippino Lippi (1457–1504).

Collezioni del Novecento: Forte di Belvedere, Via San Leonardo 1, Florence; tel. 055-2340849; fax 055-2001486; c. 250 works donated by Alberto della Ragione in 1970; Italian art 1914–60.

Fondazione Salvatore Romano: Piazza Santo Spirito 29, 50125 Florence; tel. 055-287043; colln of sculptures given by Salvatore Romano; incl. 2 pieces by Tino di Camaino, and 2 fragments attributed to Donatello.

Galleria Rinaldo Carniel: Piazza Savonarola 3, 50132 Florence; works by the sculptor Rinaldo Carniel (1853–1910).

Museo Firenze com'era: Via dell'Oriuolo 24, 50122 Florence; tel. 055-2616545; depicts the history of the city.

Museo di Palazzo Vecchio: Quartieri Monumentali, Piazza della Signoria, 50122 Florence; tel. 055-2768325; paintings, furnishings; frescoes by Ghirlandaio, Salviati, Bronzino, Vasari; Michelangelo's 'Victory' statue.

Museo di Santa Maria Novella: Piazza S. Maria Novella, 50123 Florence; tel. 055-282187; museum built in part of a Dominican church; 15th-century frescoes of the Genesis story by Paolo Uccello, Dello Delli; 14th-century frescoes by Andrea di Bonaiuto depicting the Dominican order and the Church Triumphant.

Museo Stefano Bardini: Via dei Renai 37, 50125 Florence; tel. 055-2342427; f. 1925; paintings by Pollaiuolo, Beccafumi, Lucas Cranach, Mirabello Cavalori, Giovanni da S. Giovanni, Cecco Bravo, Guercino, Carlo Dolci, Luca Giordano, Il Volterano; sculptures by Nicola and Giovanni Pisano, Tino di Camaino, Andrea della Robbia, Donatello, Michelozzo; oriental rugs, bronzes, arms, furniture, medals, etc.

Gabinetto Disegni e Stampe degli Uffizi: Via della Ninna 5, 50122 Florence; tel. 055-2388671; fax 055-2388624; e-mail ua@polomuseale.firenze.it; internet www.polomuseale.firenze.it/musei/disegni; Dir MARZIA FAIETTI.

Galleria d'Arte Moderna: Piazza Pitti 1, 50125 Florence; tel. 055-2388601; fax 055-2654520; e-mail gam@polomuseale.firenze.it; internet www.polomuseale.firenze.it/musei/artemoderna; f. 1914; paintings and sculptures since the 19th century; library of 2,000 vols on the history of art; Dir ANNAMARIA GIUSTI.

Galleria degli Uffizi: Piazzale degli Uffizi, 50122 Florence; tel. 055-2388651; fax 055-2388694; e-mail direzione.uffizi@polomuseale.firenze.it; internet www.polomuseale.firenze.it/uffizi; f. 16th century; Florentine Primitive and Renaissance paintings and sculpture, and paintings by German, Dutch and Flemish masters; library of 64,000 vols, 470 MSS relating to the Florentine collections, 5 incunabula, 996 bound periodicals, 140 current periodicals; Dir ANTONIO NATALI.

Galleria dell' Accademia: Via Ricasoli 58–60, 50122 Florence; tel. 055-2388609; fax 055-2388764; e-mail galleriaaccademia@polomuseale.firenze.it; internet www.polomuseale.firenze.it; f. 1784; contains the most complete colln of Michelangelo's statues in Florence and works of art of 13th–19th-century masters, mostly Tuscan; colln of musical instruments from the Medici and Lorena families; Dir Dott.ssa FRANCA FALLETTI.

Galleria Palatina e Appartamenti Reali: Piazza Pitti 1, 50125 Florence; tel. 055-2388614; fax 055-2388613; e-mail galleriapalatina@polomuseale.firenze.it; internet www.polomuseale.firenze.it/musei/palatina; f. 18th and 19th centuries; Italian and European masterpieces from the 16th and 17th centuries, incl. works by Raphael, A. del Sarto, Carvaggio, Titian, Rubens, Correggio and Van Dyck; Dir ALESSANDRO CECCHI.

Museo Archeologico Nazionale: Via della Colonna 36, 50121 Florence; tel. 055-23575; fax 055-242213; internet www.firenzemusei.it/archeologico; f. 1870; Egyptian, Etruscan and Greco-Roman archaeology; Dir Dott. ANGELO BOTTINI.

Museo degli Argenti: Piazza Pitti 1, 50125 Florence; tel. 055-2388709; fax 055-2388710; e-mail argenti@polomuseale.firenze.it; internet www.polomuseale.firenze.it/musei/argenti; summer state apartments of the Medici Grand Dukes; collns of gold, silver, enamel, *objets d'art*, hardstones, ivory, amber, cameos and jewels, principally from the 15th–18th centuries; Dir MARIA SFRAMELI.

Attached Gallery:

Galleria del Costume: Piazza Pitti 1, 50125 Florence; tel. 055-2388763; fax 055-2388763; e-mail costume.pitti@polomuseale.firenze.it; internet www.polomuseale.firenze.it/musei/costume; period costumes, principally since the 18th century, shown in the neo-classical Meridiana wing of the Pitti Palace; Dir CATERINA CHIARELLI.

Museo dell' Opera di Santa Maria del Fiore: Via della Canonica 1, 50122 Florence; tel. 055-2302885; fax 055-2302898; e-mail opera@operaduomo.firenze.it; internet www.operaduomo.firenze.it; f. 1891; Administrator PATRIZIO OSTICRESI.

Museo della Casa Buonarroti: Via Ghibellina 70, 50122 Florence; tel. 055-241752; fax 055-241698; e-mail fond@casabuonarroti.it; internet www.casabuonarroti.it; f. 1858; works by Michelangelo and others; large collection of drawings by Michelangelo, sculptures, majolica and archaeological items from the Buonarroti family collections; library of 10,000 vols, 41 periodicals, 44 *cinquecentine*, Buonarotti Archive of 169 vols; Dir PINA RAGIONIERI.

Museo delle Porcellane: Piazza Pitti 1, 50125 Florence; tel. 055-2388709; fax 055-2388710; e-mail argenti@polomuseale.firenze.it; internet www.polomuseale.firenze.it/musei/porcellane; collection of European porcelain from c. 1720–1850; Dir ORNELLA CASAZZA.

Museo di Palazzo Davanzati (Antica Casa Fiorentina): Via di Porta Rossa 13, 50122 Florence; tel. 055-2388610; fax 055-289805; e-mail museo.davanzati@polomuseale.firenze.it; internet www.polomuseale.firenze.it/davanzati; f. 1956; applied arts, specializing in lace and ceramics; Dir MARIA GRAZIA VACCARI.

Museo di S. Marco: Piazza San Marco 3, 50121 Florence; tel. 055-2388608; fax 055-2388704; e-mail museosanmarco@polomuseale.firenze.it; internet www.polomuseale.firenze.it/musei/sanmarco; f. 1869; contains the largest existing colln of paintings by Fra Angelico; Dir Dott.ssa MAGNOLIA SCUDIERI.

Museo Galileo—Istituto e Museo di Storia della Scienza: Piazza dei Giudici 1, 50122 Florence; tel. 055-265311; fax 055-2653130; e-mail info@museogalileo.it; internet www.museogalileo.it; f. 1927; museum of scientific instruments and institute dedicated to the research, documentation and dissemination of the history of science; library of 110,000 vols; Dir Prof. PAOLO GALLUZZI; publs *Galilaeana* (1 a year), *Nuncius Annali di Storia della Scienza* (2 a year).

Museo Horne: Via dei Benci 6, 50122 Florence; tel. 055-244661; fax 055-2009252; e-mail info@museohorne.it; internet www.museohorne.it; furniture and works of art from the 14th–16th centuries; library of 5,000 vols; Dir Dott. ELISABETTA NARDINOCCHI.

Museo Marino Marini: Piazza San Pancrazio, 50123 Florence; tel. 055-219432; fax 055-289510; e-mail info@museomarinomarini.it; internet www.museomarinomarini.it; f. 1988; 183 sculptures, paintings, drawings by the sculptor Marino Marini (1901–80) in a permanent exhibition; Pres. CARLO SISI.

Museo Nazionale del Bargello: Via del Proconsolo 4, 50122 Florence; tel. 055-2388606; fax 055-2388756; e-mail museobargello@polomuseale.firenze.it; internet www.polomuseale.firenze.it/musei/bargello; f. 1859; medieval and modern sculpture and *objets d'art*; organizes exhibitions, research and concerts; Dir BEATRICE PAOLOZZI STROZZI.

Museo Stibbert: Via F. Stibbert 26, 50134 Florence; tel. 055-486049; fax 055-475721; e-mail info@museostibbert.it; internet www.museostibbert.it/web.it; f. 1908; Etruscan, Roman and medieval arms and armour; European and Oriental arms from 15th to 19th centuries; holy objects and vestments; European and Oriental costumes, etc., from

18th to 19th centuries; Flemish tapestries from 15th to 17th centuries, Italian and foreign paintings and furniture from 14th to 19th centuries; library of 3,500 vols; Dir KIRSTEN ASCHENGREEN PIACENTI.

Forlì

Forlì Cultura—Musei e Gallerie: Comune di Forlì, Piazza Saffi 8, 47100 Forlì; tel. 0543-712111; internet www.cultura.comune.forli.fc.it.

Attached Museums and Galleries:

Armeria Albicini: Corso della Repubblica 72, 47121 Forlì; tel. 0543-712606; fax 0543-712618; e-mail servizio.pinacoteca.musei@comune.forli.fc.it; 500 arms and pieces of armour from the 15th century to the 19th century; colln of arms from Congo.

Museo Archeologico: Palazzo del Merenda, Corso della Repubblica 72, 47121 Forlì; tel. 0543-712606; fax 0543-712618; e-mail servizio.pinacoteca.musei@comune.forli.fc.it; f. late 19th century; exhibits from the Lower Palaeolithic to the seventh century AD.

Museo Etnografico Romagnolo 'B. Pergoli': Palazzo del Merenda, Corso della Repubblica 72, 47121 Forlì; tel. 0543-712609; fax 0543-712618; e-mail servizio.pinacoteca.musei@comune.forli.fc.it; exhibits depicting rural work and crafts, home environments, workshops relating to various trades.

Museo del Risorgimento 'A. Saffi': Corso G. Garibaldi 96, 47121 Forlì; tel. 0543-21109; fax 0543-712618; e-mail servizio.pinacoteca.musei@comune.forli.fc.it; artefacts from the Napoleonic era to World War II.

Museo Romagnolo del Teatro: Corso Garibaldi, 96, 47121 Forlì; tel. 0543-21109; fax 0543-712618; e-mail servizio.pinacoteca.musei@comune.forli.fc.it; theatrical memorabilia, musical instruments.

Museo Storico 'Dante Foschi': Via Piero Maroncelli 4, 47121 Forlì; tel. 0543-32328; e-mail servizio.pinacoteca.musei@comune.forli.fc.it; 20th-century uniforms, arms, medals, awards, coins, military decorations and badges, postcards, books, furniture.

Pinacoteca Civica 'Melozzo degli Ambrogi': Piazza Guido da Montefeltro 12, 47100 Forlì; tel. 0543-712659; fax 0543-712658; e-mail museisandomenico@comune.forli.fc.it; f. 1838; paintings on wood and canvas, frescoes, sculptures and tapestries.

Istituti Culturali ed Artistici: Corso della Repubblica 72, 47100 Forlì; tel. 0543-712600; fax 0543-712616; comprises a picture gallery, collection of prints and engravings, archaeological and ethnographical museums, ceramics, sculpture and local history; Piancastelli collection of paintings, medals and coins; Dir Dr FRANCO FABBRI.

Pinacoteca e Musei del Comune: Corso della Repubblica 72, 47100 Forlì; tel. 0543-712606; fax 0543-712618; e-mail servizio.pinacoteca.musei@comune.forli.fc.it; internet www.cultura.comune.forli.fc.it; f. 1838; Dir LUCIANA PRATI.

Genoa

Comune di Genova Direzione Cultura, Sport e Turismo—Settore Musei: Largo Pertini 4, 16121 Genoa; tel. 010-5574700; fax 010-5574701; e-mail museicivici@comune.genova.it; internet www.comune.genova.it/turismo/musei/welcome.htm; f. 1908; library of 40,000 vols; Dir GUIDO GANDINO; publ. *Bollettino dei Musei Civici Genovesi* (4 a year).

Attached Museums and Galleries:

Archivio Storico del Comune di Genova: Palazzo Ducale, Piazza Matteotti 10, 16123 Genoa; tel. 010-5574808; fax 010-5574823; e-mail archiviostorico@comune.genova.it; internet www.archiviostoricogenova.it; f. 1906; documents since 15th century; coins, weights and measures; Curator RAFFAELLA PONTE.

Castello D'Albertis Museo delle Culture del Mondo: Corso Dogali 18, 16136 Genoa; tel. 010-2723820; fax 010-2721456; e-mail castellodalbertis@comune.genova.it; internet www.castellodalbertis.museidigenova.it; f. 2004; housed in a Neo-Gothic castle with archaeological and ethnological collns from pre-Columbian civilizations of Central and South America, Indians of North American plains, Hopi of Arizona, cultures of Oceania and Africa; also houses Museo delle Musiche dei Popoli (Folk Music Museum) that preserves musical instruments from all over the world; Curator MARIA CAMILLA DE PALMA.

Centro di Documentazione per la Storia, l'Arte, l'Immagine di Genova: Via ai 4 Canti di San Francesco 59–61 r, 16124 Genoa; tel. 010-5574956; fax 010-5574970; e-mail archiviofotografico@comune.genova.it; internet www.museidigenova.it; f. 2005; art library; topographic colln; 200,000 photographs (1860–1946) on Genoese customs and history, 19th-century landscapes, war damage, Italian and Genoese art and architecture 11th–19th centuries; photographs of museum collns; topographical and cartographical documents on Genoa and Liguria; library of 50,000 vols, 200,000 photos, 7,000 documents; Dir ELISABETTA PAPONE.

Civico Museo di Storia e Cultura Contadina Genovese e Ligure: Salita al Garbo 47, 16159 Genoa Rivarolo; tel. 010-7401243; fax 010-5574701; f. 1983; colln of tools and utensils relating to local rural life since 19th century; Curator PATRIZIA GARIBALDI.

Galata Museo del Mare: Calata de Mari 1, Darsena, Porto Antico, 16128 Genoa; fax 010-2345655; e-mail info@galatamuseodelmare.it; internet www.galatamuseodelmare.it; maritime history of the city; exhibits incl. 17th-century galleon, arsenal, docks, ancient atlases and naval instruments.

Galleria di Palazzo Bianco: Via Garibaldi 11, 16124 Genoa; tel. 010-5572193; fax 010-5572269; e-mail museidistradanuova@comune.genova.it; internet www.museidigenova.it; f. 1889; paintings by Genoese and Flemish masters and other schools (16th–18th centuries); Dir PIERO BOCCARDO; Curator RAFFAELLA BESTA.

Galleria di Palazzo Rosso: Via Garibaldi 18, 16124 Genoa; tel. 010-2476351; fax 010-2475357; e-mail museopalazzorosso@comune.genova.it; internet www.museopalazzorosso.it; f. 1874; the fine art colln of a noble Genoese family: paintings and sculpture, frescoes and stuccos, nativity models, ceramics; also a colln of textiles; Curator PIERO BOCCARDO.

Museo di Archeologia Ligure: Villa Durazzo-Pallavicini, Via Pallavicini 11, 16155 Genoa–Pegli; tel. 010-6981048; fax 010-6974040; e-mail archligure@mail.it; f. 1892; Ligurian archaeology of the periods up to the Roman era; colln of Greek and Roman antiquities; Curators PATRIZIA GARIBALDI, GUIDO ROSSI.

Museo d'Arte Contemporanea Villa Croce: Via Jacopo Ruffini 3, 16128 Genoa; tel. 010-585772; fax 010-532482; e-mail museocroce@comune.genova.it; internet www.museovillacroce.it; f. 1985; works by key Italian artists; documentation on artistic research in Genoa and Liguria from the Second World War onwards; sculpture by Genoese and Ligurian artists; specialized library and archive open to the public; library of 20,000 books and exposition catalogues; Curator SANDRA SOLIMANO.

Museo d'Arte Orientale 'Edoardo Chiossone': Villetta di Negro, Piazzale Mazzini 4N, 16122 Genoa; tel. 010-542285; fax 010-580526; e-mail museochiossone@comune.genova.it; internet www.chiossone.museidigenova.it; f. 1905; Japanese works of art from 11th–19th centuries (about 20,000 pieces), collected in Japan during the Meiji period by Edoardo Chiossone; Dir DONATELLA FAILLA.

Museo Civico di Storia Naturale 'Giacomo Doria': Via Brigata Liguria 9, 16121 Genoa; tel. 010-564567; fax 010-566319; e-mail museodoria@comune.genova.it; internet www.museodoria.it; f. 1867; zoology, botany and geology; library of 89,000 vols; Dir Dr ROBERTO POGGI; publs *Annali* (every 2 years), *Doriana* (irregular).

Museo 'Giannettino Luxoro': Via Mafalda di Savoia 3, 16167 Genoa–Nervi; tel. 010-322673; fax 010-322396; f. 1945; Flemish and Genoese paintings of the 17th and 18th centuries, furniture, ceramics and pottery in the rooms of an early 20th-century villa; Curator LOREDANA PESSA.

Museo Navale: Villa Doria, Piazza Bonavino 7, 16156 Genoa–Pegli; tel. 010-6969885; fax 010-5574701; f. 1930; models of ships, nautical instruments, navigation maps, prints; Curator PIERANGELO CAMPODONICO.

Museo del Risorgimento e Istituto Mazziniano: Casa di Mazzini, Via Lomellini 11, 16124 Genoa; tel. 010-2465843; fax 010-2541545; e-mail museorisorgimento@comune.genova.it; internet www.istitutomazziniano.it; f. 1934; exhibits illustrating life and work of Mazzini, 19th-century documents and arms, specialized library containing works since 18th century; Curator LEO MORABITO.

Museo di Sant'Agostino: Piazza Sarzano 35r., 16128 Genoa; tel. 010-2511263; fax 010-2464516; e-mail museosagostino@comune.genova.it; internet www.museosantagostino.it; f. 1939, closed due to damage sustained during the Second World War, reopened 1984; sculpture from 10th–18th centuries, architecture and paintings; Curator ADELMO TADDEI.

Museo del Tesoro della Cattedrale di San Lorenzo: Piazza San Lorenzo, 16123 Genoa; tel. 010-2471831; fax 010-5574701; e-mail info@arti-e-mestieri.it; internet www.museosanlorenzo.it; f. 1892; gold and silver objects; Curator CLARIO DI FABIO.

Padiglione del Mare e della Navigazione: Porto Antico—Magazzini del Cotone, 16126 Genoa; tel. 010-2463678; fax 010-2467746; f. 1996; maritime colln; works of art, models and reproductions; Curator PIERANGELO CAMPODONICO.

Raccolte Frugone in Villa Grimaldi: Villa Grimaldi Fassio, Via Capolungo 9, Nervi, 16167 Genoa; tel. 010-322396; fax 010-3724405; e-mail raccoltefrugone@comune.genova.it; internet www.raccoltefrugone.it; f. 1993; colln of sculpture and paintings by Italian and int.

artists since 19th century; Curator MARIA FLORA GIUBILEI.

Galleria Nazionale di Palazzo Spinola: Piazza Pellicceria 1, 16123 Genoa; tel. 010-2705300; fax 010-2705322; e-mail palazzospinola@beniculturali.it; internet www.palazzospinola.it; f. 1958; Dir Dott.ssa FARIDA SIMONETTI; publ. *Quaderni* (1 a year).

Soprintendenza per i Beni Archeologici della Liguria: Palazzo Reale, Via Balbi 10, 16126 Genoa; tel. 010-27181; fax 010-2465925; e-mail sba-lig@beniculturali.it; internet www.archeoge.arti.beniculturali.it; f. 1939; preservation of monuments and excavations of Liguria (prehistoric, Roman and medieval); conservation of the ancient city of Luni, prehistoric caves of Balzi Rossi and archeological area of Varignano Vecchio; library of 15,000 vols; Superintendent Dott. FILIPPO MARIA GAMBARI; Librarian MARTA PUPPO.

Grosseto

Museo Archeologico e d'Arte della Maremma: Piazza Baccarini 3, 58100 Grosseto; tel. 0564-488750; fax 0564-488753; e-mail maam@gol.grosseto.it; internet www.gol .grosseto.it/puam/comgr/museo/museo.php; f. 1865; archaeological and medieval findings from the Maremma; library of 3,000 vols; Dir Dott. VALERIO FUSI.

L'Aquila

Museo Nazionale d'Abruzzo: Castello Cinquecentesco, Via Colecchi 1, 67100 L'Aquila; tel. 0862-633303; fax 0862-413096; e-mail calcedonio.tropea@beniculturali.it; internet www.museonazionaleabruzzo.beniculturali .it; f. 1949; art from the early Middle Ages to contemporary times; Dir Dott. CALCEDONIO TROPEA.

Lecce

Museo Provinciale 'Sigismondo Castromediano': Viale Gallipoli 28, 73100 Lecce; tel. 0832-683503; fax 0832-304435; e-mail acassiano@provincia.le.it; internet eneaportal.unile.it/sul_cammino_di_enea_it/ lecce/cultura/musei; f. 1868; archaeology and art gallery; library of 5,500 vols, 2,500 pamphlets and offprints; Dir ANTONIO CASSIANO.

Lucca

Museo e Pinacoteca Nazionale di Palazzo Mansi: Via Galli Tassi 43, 55100 Lucca; tel. 0583-55570; fax 0583-312221; internet www.tuscanypass.com/ tuscany_attractions/9281_museo-nazionale--di-palazzo-mansi-e-pinacoteca-nazionale .html; f. 1868; paintings by Titian, Tintoretto, etc., and Tuscan, Venetian, French and Flemish Schools; Dir Dott. MARIA TERESA FILIERI.

Museo Nazionale di Villa Guinigi: Villa Guinigi, Via della Quarquonia, 55100 Lucca; tel. 0583-496033; fax 0583-496033; e-mail luccamuseinazionali@libero.it; internet www .luccamuseinazionali.it/content.php?p=vg_e-dificio; colln of Roman and late Roman sculptures and mosaics; Romanesque, Gothic, Renaissance and Neoclassical sculpture; paintings from the 12th–18th centuries incl. Fra Bartolomeo and Vasari; wood inlays, textiles, medieval goldsmiths' art; Dir Dott. MARIA TERESA FILIERI.

Mantua

Palazzo Ducale e Castello di San Giorgio: Piazza Sordello 40, 46100 Mantua; tel. 0376-352100; fax 0376-366274; e-mail sbsae-mn@beniculturali.it; internet www .mantovaducale.it; incorporates Museo e Galleria di Pittura (13th–18th-century paint-

ings) and Museo Statuario d'Arte Greca e Romana; Dir Dott. FABRIZIO MAGANI.

Matera

Museo Nazionale D. Ridola: Via D. Ridola 24, 75100 Matera; tel. 0835-310058; internet www.archeologia.beniculturali.it/pages/ atlante/s201.html; f. 1910; local prehistory; funerary items from 6th–4th centuries BC, bronzes; Dir Dott. MARIA LUISA NAVA.

Messina

Museo Regionale: Viale della Libertà 465, 98121 Messina; tel. 090-361292; fax 090-361294; internet www.regione.sicilia.it/ beniculturali/dirbenicult/database/page_mu-sei/pagina_musei.asp?id=5&idsito=43; f. 1922; local art and culture from 12th–18th centuries; Dir Dott. CARMELA ANGELA DI STEFANO.

Milan

Circuito dei Musei del Centro di Milano: Palazzo De Marchi, Via Borgonuovo 23, 20121 Milan; tel. 02-88464180; fax 02-88464181; internet www.museidelcentro.mi .it; f. 1884; library of 130,000 vols; Dir CLAUDIO SALSI.

Attached Museums and Galleries:

Casa del Manzoni: Via Moroni 1, 20121 Milan; tel. 02-86460403; internet www .casadelmanzoni.mi.it; fmr home of the writer Manzoni.

Museo Bagatti Valsecchi: Via Gesù 5, 20121 Milan; tel. 02-76006132; fax 02-76014859; e-mail segreteria@ museobagattivalsecchi.org; internet www .museobagattivalsecchi.org; f. 1994; fmr 19th-century residence containing paintings, wood carvings, weapons and armour, ceramics, glassware, gold and ivory artifacts, decorative metal objects, tapestries.

Museo di Milano: Via Moroni 1, 20121 Milan; tel. 02-86460403; fax 02-88465736; internet www.museodimilano.mi.it; colln of prints, paintings, sculpture; 18th-century home decoration, furniture and objects.

Museo del Risorgimento: Via Borgonuovo 23, 20121 Milan; tel. 02-88464180; fax 02-88464181; internet www .museodelrisorgimento.mi.it; f. 1885; collns of prints, paintings, sculpture, drawings, arms and memorabilia illustrate the period 1796–1870 in Italian history.

Museo Teatrale alla Scala: Largo Ghiringhelli 1, Piazza Scala, 20121 Milan; tel. 02-88792473; internet www .museidelcentro.mi.it/frameset_scala.htm; f. 1913; library of 140,000 vols; instruments from the 17th century, paintings, ceramics, memorabilia, costumes, posters.

Galleria d'Arte Moderna: Via Palestro 16, 20121 Milan; tel. 02-88445947; fax 02-88445951; internet www.gam-milano.com; f. 1861; painting and sculpture from Neo-Classical period until late 19th century; incl. the Grassi and Vismara collns and Museo Marino Marini; Dir CLAUDIO SALSI.

Museo Civico di Storia Naturale di Milano: Corso Venezia 55, 20121 Milan; tel. 02-88463280; fax 02-88463281; internet www.comune.milano.it/museostorianaturale; f. 1838; all brs of natural history; depts of vertebrate palaeontology, invertebrate palaeontology, mineralogy, vertebrate zoology, invertebrate zoology, entomology, botany; library of 140,000 vols; Dir Dr ENRICO BANFI; publs *Atti della Società Italiana di Scienze Naturali e del Museo Civico di Storia Naturale di Milano* (2 a year), *Memorie della Società Italiana di Scienze Naturali e del Museo Civico di Storia Naturale di Milano* (irregular), *Natura* (2 a year).

Raccolte Artistiche, Raccolte Grafiche e Fotografiche: Castello Sforzesco, 20121 Milan; tel. 02-88463700; fax 02-88463650; f. 1878; sculpture from the middle ages to the 16th century, incl. the *Pietà* of Michelangelo; paintings, incl. works by Mantegna, Foppa, Lippi, Bellini, Lotto, Tintoretto, Tiepolo, Guardi; furniture, silver, bronzes, ivories, ceramics, musical instruments, tapestries by Bramantino, Bertarelli stamp colln; library of 41,000 vols; Dir Dr CLAUDIO SALSI (engravings, drawings); Dir Dr FRANCESCA TASSO (art collns).

Museo Nazionale della Scienza e della Tecnologia 'Leonardo da Vinci': Via San Vittore 21, 20123 Milan; tel. 02-48555558; fax 02-48010055; e-mail museo@ museoscienza.org; internet www .museoscienza.org; f. 1953; scientific and technical activities, displaying relics, models and designs, with particular emphasis on Leonardo's work; library of 32,000 vols, mostly history of science and technology, 150 *cinquecentine*, large section on Leonardo, including facsimile of every MS; Dir FIORENZO GALLI; publ. *Museoscienza* (2 a year).

Museo Poldi Pezzoli: Via A. Manzoni 12, 20121 Milan; tel. 02-796334; fax 02-45473811; e-mail info@museopoldipezzoli.it; internet www.museopoldipezzoli.it; f. 1881; paintings from 14th–19th centuries; armour, tapestries, rugs, jewellery, porcelain, glass, textiles, furniture, clocks and watches, etc.; library of 5,500 vols; Dir Dott. ANNALISA ZANNI.

Pinacoteca Ambrosiana: Piazza Pio XI 2, 20123 Milan; tel. 02-806921; fax 02-80692210; e-mail info@ambrosiana.it; internet www.ambrosiana.eu; f. 1618; paintings by Raphael, Botticelli, Titian, Luini, Jan Brueghel, Leonardo da Vinci, Jacobo Bassano, Bramantino, etc.; miniatures, enamels, ceramics and medallions; Dir Dott. FRANCO BUZZI.

Pinacoteca di Brera: Via Brera 28, 20121 Milan; tel. 02-722631; fax 02-72001140; e-mail sbsae-mi.brera@beniculturali.it; internet www.brera.beniculturali.it; f. 1809; pictures of all schools, especially Lombard and Venetian; paintings by Mantegna, Bellini, Crivelli, Lotto, Titian, Veronese, Tintoretto, Tiepolo, Foppa, Bergognone, Luini, Piero della Francesca, Bramante, Raphael, Caravaggio, Rembrandt, Van Dyck, Rubens; also 20th-century works, mostly Italian; Dir SANDRINA BANDERA.

Modena

Galleria, Museo e Medagliere Estense: Palazzo dei Musei, Piazza Sant' Agostino 337, 41121 Modena; tel. 059-4395711; fax 059-230196; e-mail sbsae-mo@beniculturali .it; internet www.spsae-mo.beniculturali.it; f. 15th century in Ferrara, transferred to Palazzo Ducale, Modena, 1598, to Palazzo dei Musei 1894; collns incl. about 2,000 paintings and drawings from 14th to 18th centuries, sculpture, engravings, medals; library of 15,000 vols; Superintendent Dott. STEFANO CASCIU.

Museo Civico Archeologico Etnologico: Palazzo dei Musei, Viale Vittorio Veneto 5, 41100 Modena; tel. 059-2033100; e-mail museo.archeologico@comune .modena.it; internet www.comune.modena.it/ museoarcheologico; f. 1871; prehistory and ethnology; library of 5,000 vols, 2,700 pamphlets; Curator Dott. ILARIA PULINI; publ. *Quaderni.*

Museo Civico d'Arte: Viale Vittorio Veneto 5, 41124 Modena; tel. 059-2033100; fax 059-2033110; e-mail museo.arte@comune .modena.it; internet www.comune.modena.it/ museoarte; f. 1871; paintings, sculpture, decorative arts; history and culture of Modena from 12th–20th centuries; library of 7,500 vols, 3,500 pamphlets; Dir Dott. FRANCESCA PICCININI.

Museo Lapidario Estense: Palazzo dei Musei, Piazza Sant' Agostino 337, 41121 Modena; tel. 059-4395711; fax 059-230196; e-mail sbsae-mo@beniculturali.it; internet www.spsae-mo.beniculturali.it; f. 1828; Roman and medieval archaeological collns; Superintendent Dott. STEFANO CASCIU.

Naples

Museo Archeologico Nazionale: Piazza Museo Nazionale 19, 80135 Naples; tel. 081-292823; fax 081-440013; e-mail ssba-na@beniculturali.it; internet museoarcheologiconazionale.campaniabeniculturali.it; f. 18th century; Greek, Roman, Italian and Egyptian antiquities; Superintendent Prof. Dr PIETRO GIOVANNI GUZZO; publ. *Rivista di studi pompeiani* (1 a year).

Museo Civico 'Gaetano Filangieri': Via Duomo 288, 80138 Naples; tel. 081-203211; fax 081-203175; internet filangieri.sbpsaena.campaniabeniculturali.it; f. 1888; paintings, furniture, archives, photographs, majolica, arms and armour; library of 30,000 vols, and coin collection of Neapolitan history; Dir ANTONIO BUCCINO GRIMALDI.

Museo 'Duca di Martina' alla Floridiana: Via Cimarosa 77, 80127 Naples; tel. 081-5788418; e-mail martina.artina@beniculturali.it; f. 1931; decorative art; exhibits donated by the Duke; spec. colln of oriental art; Dir Dr LUISA AMBROSIO.

Museo e Gallerie Nazionali di Capodimonte: Via Miano 2, 80131 Naples; tel. 081-7499111; fax 081-7445032; e-mail capodimonte.artina@arti.beniculturali.it; internet museodicapodimonte .campaniabeniculturali.it; f. 1738; paintings from 13th–19th centuries; sculpture from 19th century; contemporary art; colln of arms and armour; medals and bronzes of the Renaissance; porcelain; library of 2,000 vols; Dir Prof. MARIELLA UTILI.

Museo Nazionale di S. Martino: Largo San Martino 5, 80129 Naples; tel. and fax 081-5781769; e-mail sanmartino.artina@artibeniculturali.it; internet museosanmartino .campaniabeniculturali.it; f. 1872; ancient church of S. Martino with 16th–18th century pictures, 13th–19th century sculpture, majolica and porcelain, Neapolitan historical records and topographical colln, naval colln, arms and military costumes, opaline glass, section of modern painting, prints and engravings; Dir Dott. ROSSANA MUZII.

Soprintendenza Archeologica di Pompei: Via Villa dei Misteri 2, 80100 Pompei; tel. 081-8575111; fax 081-8613183; e-mail sba-pomp@beniculturali.it; internet www .pompeiisites.org; f. 1982; Superintendent Prof. JEANNETTE PAPADOPOULOS.

Supervised Sites:

Antiquarium Nazionale di Boscoreale: Via Settetermini 15, Loc. Villa Regina, 80041 Boscoreale; tel. 081-5368796; fax 081-8613183; e-mail sba-pomp@beniculturali.it; internet www .pompeiisites.org; Dir Dott. GRETE STEFANI.

Scavi di Ercolano: Corso Resina, 80056 Ercolano; tel. 081-7324311; fax 081-8613183; e-mail sba-pomp@beniculturali.it; internet www.pompeiisites.org; Dir Dott. MARIA PAOLA GUIDOBALDI.

Scavi di Oplontis: Via Sepolcri, 80058 Torre Annunziata; tel. 081-8621755; fax 081-8613183; e-mail sba-pomp@beniculturali.it; internet www .pompeiisites.org; Dir Dott. LORENZO FERGOLA.

Scavi di Pompei: Via Villa dei Misteri 2, 80045 Pompei; tel. 081-8575111; fax 081-8613183; e-mail sba-pomp@beniculturali.it; internet www.pompeiisites.org; f. 2008; Dir Prof. TERESA ELENA.

Scavi di Stabia: Via Passeggiata Archeologica, 80053 Castellammare di Stabia; tel. 081-8714541; fax 081-8613183; e-mail sba-pomp@beniculturali.it; internet www .pompeiisites.org; Dir Dott. GIOVANNA BONIFACIO.

Padua

Musei Civici di Padova: Piazza Eremitani 8, 35121 Padua; tel. 049-8204551; fax 049-8204585; e-mail musei@comune.padova.it; internet padovacultura.padovanet.it/homepage-6.0/2010/09/complesso_eremitani_1.html; f. 1825; Dir DAVIDE BANZATO; publ. *Bollettino del Museo Civico di Padova*.

Constituent Institutions:

Cappella degli Scrovegni: Piazza Eremitani 8, 35121 Padua; tel. 49-8204551; fax 49-8204585; e-mail musei@comune.padova .it; internet padovacultura.padovanet.it/homepage-6.0/2010/12/cappella_degli_scrovegni.html; f. 1300; hall with presbytery, on altar Madonna and child with 2 angels, by 14th-century sculptor Giovanni Pisano; Giotto frescoes; Dir DAVIDE BANZATO.

Museo Archeologico: c/o Musei Civici, Piazza Eremitani 8, 35121 Padua; tel. 049-8204551; fax 049-8204585; e-mail zampierig@comune.padova.it; internet padovacultura.padovanet.it/homepage-6.0/2004/02/museo_archeologico_2.html; f. 1825; pre- and early historic and Roman finds; Dir DAVIDE BANZATO.

Museo d'Arte Medioevale e Moderna: c/o Musei Civici, Piazza Eremitani 8, 35121 Padua; tel. 049-8204551; fax 049-8204585; e-mail musei@comune.padova.it; internet padovacultura.padovanet.it/homepage-6.0/2004/02/museo_darte_medioevale_e_moder.html; f. 1825; works from 14th and 15th centuries; Venetian paintings from 14th to the 16th centuries; sculptures from 14th to the 18th centuries; decorative and architectural fragments of inscribed stone tablets; Dir DAVIDE BANZATO.

Museo di Arte Applicate: Corso Garibaldi 33, 35122 Padua; tel. 049-665567; fax 049-8774671; e-mail musei@comune .padova.it; internet padovacultura .padovanet.it/musei/archivio/000147.html; glass, carvings, ceramics, silver, ivory, jewellery, textiles and furniture; paintings, architectural fragments from 9th to 10th centuries, coats of arms of Venetian families; Dir DAVIDE BANZATO.

Museo Bottacin: Palazzo Zuckermann, Corso Garibaldi 33, 35122 Padua; tel. 049-8766959; fax 049-8774671; internet padovacultura.padovanet.it/musei/archivio/000148.html; f. 1865; Graeco-Roman, Paduan, Venetian, Italian, Napoleonic coins, seals and medals, 19th-century sculptures and paintings; Curator Dott. ROBERTA PARISE.

Palazzo della Ragione 'Il Salone': Piazza delle Erbe, 35122 Padua; tel. 049-8205006; fax 049-8204566; e-mail musei@comune.padova.it; internet padovacultura .padovanet.it/homepage-6.0/2010/12/palazzo_della_ragione.html; f. 1218; works by Fra Giovanni degli Eremitani, frescoes by Nicolò Miretto and Stefano Da Ferrara; Dir DAVIDE BANZATO.

Palermo

Museo Archeologico Regionale 'A. Salinas': Piazza Olivella 24, 90100 Palermo; tel. 091-6116805; fax 091-6110740; e-mail urpmuseopa@regione.sicilia.it; internet www .regione.sicilia.it/beniculturali/salinas; f. 1866; prehistoric, Egyptian, Greek, Punic, Roman and Etruscan antiquities; library of 25,000 vols and pamphlets; Dir AGATA VILLA.

Parma

Galleria Nazionale: Piazzale della Pilotta 15, 43100 Parma; tel. 0521-233309; fax 0521-206336; e-mail sbaspr@libero.it; internet www.artipr.arti.beniculturali.it/htm/galleria .htm; f. 1752, later reconstructed and added to; paintings from 13th–19th centuries, incl. works by Correggio, Parmigianino, Cima, El Greco, Piazzetta, Tiepolo, Holbein, Van Dyck, Mor, Nattier, and several painters of the school of Parma; 19th-century paintings by Parmesan painters; library of 15,000 vols; Superintendent LUCIA FORNARI SCHIANCHI.

Museo Archeologico Nazionale: Piazza della Pilotta 5, 43100 Parma; tel. 0521-233718; fax 0521-386112; e-mail sba-ero .museoarchparma@beniculturali.it; internet www.archeobologna.beniculturali.it/parma; f. 1760; archaeological collection of sculptures and other monuments from Veleia; Prehistoric and Bronze Age collections; Roman monuments from province of Parma; Egyptian, Greek, Etruscan and Roman art documents; Dir Dott. MARIA BERNABÒ BREA.

Museo Bodoniano: c/o Biblioteca Palatina, Palazzo della Pilotta 3A, 43121 Parma; tel. 0521-220411; fax 0521-235662; e-mail museobodoni@beniculturali.it; internet www .museobodoni.beniculturali.it; f. 1963; dedicated to art of printing: punches, original matrices and moulds (approx. 80,000) from Bodoni's printing works; rare edns, technical manuals, press and tools of 'the prince of printers'; Dir ANDREA DE PASQUALE; Curator CATERINA SILVA; publ. *Crisopoli. Bollettino del museo Bodoniano di Parma* (1 a year).

Pavia

Civici Musei—Castello Visconteo: Viale XI Febbraio 35, 27100 Pavia; tel. 0382-33853; fax 0382-303028; e-mail museicivici@comune .pv.it; internet www.museicivici.pavia.it; f. 1838; library of 24,500 vols; Dir Dott. SUSANNA ZATTI; Librarian ANGELA MACELLI.

Perugia

Galleria Nazionale dell'Umbria: Palazzo dei Priori, Corso Vannucci 19, 06123 Perugia; tel. 075-586681415; fax 075-58668400; e-mail gallerianazionaleumbria@beniculturali.it; internet www.gallerianazionaleumbria.it; f. 1918; paintings of Umbrian school, 13th–19th centuries; also sculptures and jewellery; library of 5,300 vols; Dir Dott.ssa VITTORIA GARIBALDI.

Museo Archeologico Nazionale dell'Umbria: Piazza Giordano Bruno 10, 06121 Perugia; tel. 075-5727141; fax 075-5728651; e-mail sba-umb@beniculturali.it; internet www.archeopg.arti.beniculturali.it; f. 1948; prehistoric, Roman, Hellenistic and Etruscan remains; primitive pottery, bone tools, funerary urns, amulets, archaic bronzes, coins; Dir MARISA SCARPIGNATO.

Pesaro

Musei Civici di Pesaro (Pinacoteca e Museo delle Ceramiche): Piazza Toschi Mosca 29, 61121 Pesaro; tel. (721) 387541; fax (721) 387524; e-mail musei@comune .pesaro.ps.it; internet www .museicivicipesaro.it; f. 1936; art gallery and ceramics and decorative arts museum; Coordinator ERIKA TERENZI.

Pisa

Museo Nazionale di San Matteo: Piazza San Matteo in Soarta 1, 56126 Pisa; tel. 050-541865; fax 050-542640; e-mail dario .matteoni@beniculturali.it; internet www

.sbappsae-pi.beniculturali.it/index.php?it/ 146/pisa-museo-nazionale-di-san-matteo; f. 1949; sculptures by the Pisanos and their school; colln of the Pisan school from the 12th–14th centuries, and paintings and sculpture from the 15th to 17th centuries (works by Simone Martini, Masaccio, Beato Angelico, Benozzo Gozzoli, Ghirlandaio, Donatello, Della Robbia), 10th–17th-century ceramics, colln of coins and medals; Dir DARIO MATTEONI.

Portoferraio

Museo Napoleonico di Villa S. Martino: San Martino, 57037 Portoferraio; tel. 0565-914688.

Ravenna

Museo Nazionale di Ravenna: Via Benedetto Fiandrini, 48121 Ravenna; tel. 0544-543711; fax 0544-543732; e-mail sbap-ra .museonazionale@beniculturali.it; internet soprintendenzaravenna.beniculturali.it; f. 1885; State property since 1885; art, numismatics and archaeology; Dir Dott. CETTY MUSCOLINO.

Reggio Calabria

Museo Nazionale: Piazza De Nava 26, 89122 Reggio Calabria; tel. 0965-812255; fax 0965-25164; e-mail sba-cal@ beniculturali.it; internet www .museonazionalerc.it; f. 1958; archaeological objects from Calabria from prehistoric era to Roman times; also Antiquarium di Locri (Locri), Museo Archaeologico (Vibo Valentia), Museo Archaeologico (Crotone), Museo della Sibaritide (Sibari); art gallery; library of 10,000 vols; Dir Dott. ELENA LATTANZI; publ. *Klearchos* (1 a year).

Rome

Galleria Borghese: Piazzale del Museo Borghese, 5, 00197 Rome; tel. 06-8413979; e-mail info.servizimusei@libero.it; internet www.galleriaborghese.it; f. c. 1616; picture gallery, collections of classical and Baroque sculpture; Dir Dott. ALBA COSTAMAGNA.

Galleria Nazionale d'Arte Antica di Palazzo Barberini: Via delle Quattro Fontane 13, 00184 Rome; tel. 06-4824184; fax 06-4880560; internet www.galleriaborghese.it; Italian and European paintings from 12th–18th centuries, Baroque architecture; Corsini colln at Galleria Corsini, Via della Lungara 10; Dir Dott. SIVIGLIANO ALLOISI.

Istituto Nazionale per la Grafica: Calcografia, Via della Stamperia 6, 00187 Rome; tel. 06-69980242; fax 06-69921454; e-mail s .papaldo@inggrafica.it; internet www.grafica .arti.beniculturali.it; f. 1895; Italian and foreign prints and drawings from 14th century onwards; collection of matrices since 16th century; Dir Dott. SERENITA PAPALDO.

Keats-Shelley House: Piazza di Spagna 26, 00187 Rome; tel. (6) 6784235; fax (6) 6784167; e-mail info@keats-shelley-house .org; internet www.keats-shelley-house.org; f. 1903; access by appointment and dependent upon a letter of recommendation from an academic instn or publisher; Dir's permission required prior to consulting books published before 1900; library: reference library of 9,000 vols; Dir CATHERINE PAYLING; publ. *The Keats-Shelley Review*.

Mausoleo di Cecilia Metella: Viale Appia Antica 161, 00179 Rome; tel. 06-39967700; internet www.medioevo.roma.it/html/ architettura/torri-ext/tex-castello_caetani .htm#01; f. AD 20–30; funeral monument.

Musei Capitolini: Piazza del Campidoglio 1, 00186 Rome; tel. 06-67102475; fax 06-6785488; e-mail info.museicapitolini@ comune.roma.it; internet www

.museicapitolini.org; f. 1471; archaeology, art history; Dir CLAUDIO PARISI PRESICCE.

Museo Barracco: Corso Vittorio Emanuele 168, 00186 Rome; tel. and fax 06-68806848; e-mail info.museobarracco@comune.roma.it; internet en.museobarracco.it; f. 1905; evolution of sculpture from Egyptian to Roman styles; Dir Dott.ssa MADDALENA CIMA.

Museo della Civiltà Romana: Piazza G. Agnelli 10, 00144 Rome; tel. 06-5926041; fax 06-5926135; e-mail info .museociviltaromana@comune.roma.it; internet www.museocivilaromana.it; f. 1952; history of Rome from its origins; Curator CLAUDIO PARISI PRESICCE.

Museo di Palazzo Venezia: Via del Plebiscito 118, 00186 Rome; tel. 06-69994284; fax 06-69994394; internet museopalazzovenezia .beniculturali.it; f. 1921; 13th–16th century paintings; bronze, marble and terracotta sculptures; medieval and Renaissance decorative art; 16th–17th century ceramics; furniture, prints, textiles; Dir ROSSELLA VODRET.

Museo di Roma: Piazza San Pantaleo 10 (Piazza Navona), 00186 Rome; tel. 06-67108346; fax 06-67108303; e-mail museodiroma@comune.roma.it; internet www.museodiroma.it; f. 1930; topographic, cultural, social, historical and artistic development of Rome since medieval times; Dir CLAUDIO PARISI PRESICCE.

Museo Nazionale d'Arte Orientale: Palazzo Brancaccio, Via Merulana 248, 00185 Rome; tel. 06-46974815; fax 06-46974837; e-mail mn-ao.direzione@ beniculturali.it; internet www.museorientale .beniculturali.it; f. 1957; library of 10,000 vols; Dir MARIAROSARIA BARBERA.

Istituto Centrale per la Demoetnoantropologia Museo Nazionale delle Arti e Tradizioni Popolari: Piazza Marconi 8/10, 00144 Rome; tel. 06-5926148; fax 06-5911848; internet ic-d@beniculturali.it; f. 1923; library of 30,000 vols; archives of musical, spoken and photo-cinematographic material; Dir Dott.ssa DANIELA PORRO.

Museo Nazionale di Castel Sant'Angelo: Lungotevere Castello 50, 00193 Rome; tel. 06-6819111; fax 06-68191196; e-mail sspsae-rm.santangelo@beniculturali.it; internet castelsantangelo.beniculturali.it; f. 1925; ancient armoury; architectural and monumental remains, frescoes, sculptures, pictures and period furniture; library of 13,000 vols, 60 periodicals; Dir MARIA GRAZIA BERNARDINI.

Museo Nazionale di Villa Giulia: Piazzale di Villa Giulia 9, 00196 Rome; tel. 06-3226571; fax 06-3202010; e-mail sba-em@ beniculturali.it; internet villagiulia .beniculturali.it; f. 1889; Etruscan and Italian antiquities; Dir Dott. FRANCESCA BOITANI.

Museo Nazionale Preistorico Etnografico 'Luigi Pigorini': Piazzale G. Marconi 14, 00144 Rome; tel. 06-549521; fax 06-54952310; e-mail pigorini@arti.beniculturali .it; internet www.pigorini.arti.beniculturali .it; f. 1875; prehistory and ethnology; library of 70,000 vols, 500 bound periodicals, 500 current periodicals; Superintendent LUIGI LA ROCCA; publ. *Bullettino di Paletnologia Italiana* (1 a year).

Ostia Antica: Viale dei Romagnoli 717, 00119 Ostia Antica, Rome; tel. 06-56358099; fax 06-5651500; internet archeoroma .beniculturali.it/siti%20archeologici/ostia/ ostia%20antica; Roman antiquities, monuments, paintings, sculptures, mosaics; Dir ANGELO PELLEGRINO.

Soprintendenza alla Galleria Nazionale d'Arte Moderna e Contemporanea: Viale

delle Belle Arti 131, 00196 Rome; tel. 06-322981; fax 06-3221579; e-mail ss-gnam@ beniculturali.it; internet /www.ufficignam .beniculturali.it; Superintendent MARIA VITTORIA MARINI CLARELLI.

Attached Sites:

Galleria Nazionale d'Arte Moderna e Contemporanea: Viale delle Belle Arti 131, 00197 Rome; tel. 06-322981; fax 06-3221579; e-mail s-gnam@beniculturali.it; internet www.gnam.arti.beniculturali.it; f. 1883; art since 19th century; library of 70,000 vols, 1,500 periodicals; Dir MARIA VITTORIA MARINI CLARELLI.

Museo Boncompagni Ludovisi: Via Boncompagni 18, 00187 Rome; tel. and fax (6)-42824074; e-mail museoboncompagni.info@beniculturali.it; internet www.museoboncompagni .beniculturali.it; f. 1995; modern decorative arts and fashion; Dir MARIASTELLA MARGOZZI.

Museo Hendrik Christian Andersen: Via Pasquale Stanislao Mancini, 20 (Piazzale Flaminio), 00196 Rome; tel. 06-3219089; e-mail s-gnam.museoandersen@ beniculturali.it; internet www .museoandersen.beniculturali.it; f. 1998; paintings and sculpture by Hendrik Christian Andersen (1872–1940); Dir ELENA DI MAJO.

Museo Mario Praz: Palazzo Primoli, Via Zanardelli 1, 00186 Rome; tel. 06-6861089; fax 06-6861089; e-mail museopraz@ museopraz.191.it; internet www .museopraz.beniculturali.it; f. 1995; furniture, paintings, sculpture, carpets, miniatures and objects made of bronze, crystal, porcelain, silver and marble collected by Mario Praz (1896–1982); Dirs PATRIZIA ROSAZZA.

Raccolta Manzù: Via Laurentina Km 32, 00040 Ardea; tel. 06-9135022; e-mail mcossu@arti.beniculturali.it; internet www.museomanzu.beniculturali.it; f. 1981; work by the sculptor Manzù; Chief Dir MARCELLA COSSU.

Soprintendenza Speciale per i Beni Archeologici di Roma: Piazza dei Cinquecento 67, 00185 Rome; tel. 06-48020205; fax 06-4880445; e-mail ssba-rm@beniculturali.it; internet archeoroma.beniculturali.it; Superintendent Dott. ANNA MARIA MORETTI.

Attached Sites:

Il Colosseo (The Colosseum): Piazza del Colosseo 1, 00184 Rome; tel. 06-39967700; internet archeoroma.beniculturali.it/ siti-archeologici/colosseo; f. AD 80; Dir ROSSELLA REA.

Domus Aurea (Golden House): Via della Domus Aurea 1, 00184 Rome; tel. 06-39967700; internet archeoroma .beniculturali.it/siti%20archeologici/centro/domus%20aurea; remains of Nero's villa built after the great fire of AD 64; Dir FEDORA FILIPPI.

Foro Romano e Palatino (Roman Forum and Palatine Hill): Piazza Santa Maria Nova 53, 00186 Rome; tel. 06-39967700; internet archeoroma.beniculturali.it/ siti%20archeologici/centro/foro%20romano; history of Rome from 8th century BC; Dir MARIA ANTONIETTA TOMEI.

Museo Nazionale dell'Alto Medioevo (National Museum of the Early Middle Ages): Viale Lincoln 3, Esposizione Universale, 00144 Rome; tel. 06-54228124; internet archeoroma.beniculturali.it/ musei/museo-nazionale-dell-alto-medioevo; f. 1967; exhibits dateable between the 4th and 14th centuries, coming mainly from Rome and central Italy; weapons, jewels, ivories, glassware and vessels in bronze and ceramic, marble reliefs, furnishings, Coptic colln of reliefs and textiles, marble inlay; Dir MARGHERITA TATA BEDELLO.

Museo della Via Ostiense (Via Ostiense Museum): Via Raffaele Persichetti, 00153 Rome; tel. 06-5743193; internet archeoroma.beniculturali.it/museo_della_-via_ostiense; f. 1967; plastic reconstructions of the ancient city of Ostia, and of nearby ports in the 1st and 2nd centuries AD, paintings; Man. ANGELO PELLEGRINO.

Terme di Caracalla: Viale delle Terme di Caracalla, 00153 Rome; tel. 06-39967700; internet archeoroma.beniculturali.it/siti-archeologici/terme-caracalla; f. AD 216; remains of large complex of Roman baths; Dir MARINA PIRANOMONTE.

Villa dei Quintili: Via Appia Nuova 1092, 00178 Rome; tel. 06-39967700; internet archeoroma.beniculturali.it/siti%20archeo-logici/suburbio/villa%20dei%20quintili; f. 2nd century AD; extensive villa with rooms for masters and servants, bath quarters; Dir RITA PARIS.

Museo Nazionale Romano: Piazza dei Cinquecento 79, 00185 Rome; tel. 06-483617; fax 06-4814125; internet archeoroma.beniculturali.it/museo-nazio-nale-romano; f. 1889; Greek, Hellenistic and Roman sculpture and bronzes, paintings and mosaics, numismatics; archaeological colln; Dir Prof. ADRIANO LA REGINA.

Constituent Centres:

Crypta Balbi: Via delle Botteghe Oscure 31, 00186 Rome; tel. 06-39967700; internet archeoroma.beniculturali.it/musei/museo--nazionale-romano-crypta-balbi; f. 13BC; remains of an arcaded courtyard and theatre; material and tools from a 7th-century workshop; Man. LAURA VENDITTELLI.

Palazzo Altemps: Piazza di Sant'Apollinare 46, 00186 Rome; tel. 06-39967700; internet archeoroma.beniculturali.it/musei/museo-nazionale-romano-palaz-zo-altemps; f. 1997; Greek and Roman sculpture; Mans ALESSANDRA CAPODIFERRO, MATILDE DE ANGELIS.

Terme di Diocleziano (Baths of Diocletian): Via Enrico de Nicola 79, 00185 Rome; tel. 06-39967700; internet archeoroma.beniculturali.it/musei/museo-nazionale-r-omano-terme-diocleziano; f. 3rd century AD; museum f. 1889; sculpture, sarcophagi, inscriptions, mosaics and frescoes; Man. ROSANNA FRIGGERI.

Palazzo Massimo: Largo di Villa Peretti, 00185 Rome; tel. 06-39967700; internet archeoroma.beniculturali.it/musei/museo--nazionale-romano-palazzo-massimo; f. 1998; statues, mosaic pavement, numismatics, frescoes, bronzes and jewellery from 1st century BC to 4th century AD; Man. RITA PARIS.

Villa Farnesina: Via della Lungara 230, 00165 Rome; tel. 06-68027267; fax 06-68027513; e-mail farnesina@lincei.it; internet www.lincei.it/modules .php?name=content&pa=showpage&pid=8; now the property of the Accademia Nazionale dei Lincei; built 1509 by Peruzzi; decorated by Raphael, Peruzzi and others; Curator Geom. RODOLFO DONZELLI.

Rovereto

Museo Civico di Rovereto: Borgo Santa Caterina 41, 38068 Rovereto; tel. 0464-452800; fax 0464-439487; e-mail museo@museocivico.rovereto.tn.it; internet www.museocivico.rovereto.tn.it; f. 1851; sections on archaeology, art history, astronomy, bot-

any, earth sciences, numismatics and zoology; Dir FRANCO FINOTTI.

Rovigo

Pinacoteca dell'Accademia dei Concordi e del Seminario Vescovile: Palazzo Roverella, Via Laurenti 8/10, 45100 Rovigo; tel. 0425-460093; fax 0425-27993; e-mail info@palazzoroverella.com; internet www .palazzoroverella.com/pinacoteca.php; contains 650 Venetian paintings from the 15th–18th centuries; colln of Flemish paintings.

Sarsina

Museo Archeologico Nazionale: Via Cesio Sabino 39, 47027 Sarsina; tel. 0547-94641; internet www.comune.sarsina.fo.it/museoarch/museo.htm; f. 1890; exhibition of archaeological remains from the Roman age; Dir Dott. CHIARA GUARNIERI.

Sassari

Museo Nazionale Archeologico Etnografico 'G. A. Sanna': Via Roma, 64 07100 Sassari; tel. 079-272203; fax 079-271524; e-mail museosanna@beniculturali.it; internet www.archeossnu.beniculturali.it; f. 1931; archaeology, medieval and modern art, ethnography; Dir Dott.ssa GABRIELLA GASPERETTI.

Siena

Museo Archeologico: Piazza Duomo 1, 53100 Siena; tel. 0577-534511; fax 0577-534543; e-mail infoscala@sms.comune.siena .it; internet www.santamariadellascala.com; antiquities from the local area; Etruscan section; numismatic collection; Dir TATIANA CAMPIONI.

Museo Aurelio Castelli: Strada dell'Osservanza 7, 53100 Siena; tel. 0577-332444; fax 0577-335705; internet www.sienaonline.it/aurelio_castelli.html; 14th–15th-century sculpture; paintings and drawings from the 15th–18th centuries; library of 25,000 vols.

Pinacoteca Nazionale: Palazzo Buonsignori, Via San Pietro 29, 53100 Siena; tel. 0577-286143; fax 0577-286143; e-mail pinacoteca.siena@libero.it; internet www .spsae-si.beniculturali.it/index.php?it/77/musei; f. 1930; 650 Sienese paintings of the 13th–16th centuries; Dir Dott. ANNA MARIA GUIDUCCI.

Syracuse

Museo Archeologico Regionale 'Paolo Orsi': Viale Teocrito 66, 96100 Syracuse; tel. 0931-464022; fax 0931-462347; e-mail museo.orsi@tin.it; internet www.siracusaweb .com/main/siracusa/cultura/museo-archeolo-gico-regionale-paolo-orsi.html; f. 1886; prehistory, statuary and antiques from the excavations of the Greco-Roman city and from prehistoric and classical sites of Eastern Sicily; Dir CONCETTA CIURCINA.

Taranto

Museo Archeologico Nazionale: Corso Umberto 141, 74100 Taranto; tel. 099-4532112; fax 099-4594946; e-mail info@museotaranto.it; internet www .museotaranto.it; f. 1887; local prehistory and Greco-Roman remains; Dir ANTONIETTA DELL'AGLIO.

Tarquinia

Museo Archeologico Nazionale Tarquiniense: Palazzo Vitelleschi, Piazza Cavour, 01016 Tarquinia; tel. 0766-856036; e-mail info@tarquiniaturismo.it; internet www .tarquiniaturismo.it/?p=170&lang=en; f. 1924; Etruscan sarcophagi from the 4th and 3rd centuries BC, Etruscan and Greek vases,

bronzes, ornaments; Etruscan paintings; Dir Dott. MARIA CATALDI.

Trento

Castello del Buonconsiglio–Monumenti e Collezioni Provinciali: Via Bernardo Clesio 5, 38122 Trento; tel. 0461-233770; fax 0461-239497; e-mail info@buonconsiglio .it; internet www.buonconsiglio.it; f. 1924; ancient, medieval and modern art; Dir Dott. FRANCO MARZATICO.

Trieste

Civici Musei di Storia ed Arte: Via Rossini 4, IV Piano, 34121 Trieste; tel. 040-6754035; e-mail dugulin@comune.trieste.it; internet www.retecivica.trieste.it/triestecultura; Dir Dott. ADRIANO DUGULIN.

Constituent Museums and Galleries:

Castello di San Giusto e Civico Museo del Castello, Lapidario Tergestino: Piazza della Cattedrale 3, 34121 Trieste; tel. 040-309362; fax 040-6754065; e-mail cmsa@comune.trieste.it; internet www .retecivica.trieste.it/triestecultura/new/musei/sangiusto; f. 1936, Lapidario 2001; Dir Dott. ADRIANO DUGULIN.

Civico Aquario Marino: Molo Pescheria 2, 34139 Trieste; tel. 040-306201; fax 040-302563; e-mail museisci@comune.trieste.it; internet www.retecivica.trieste.it/triestecultura/new/musei_scientifici/aqua-rio; f. 1933; Dir Dott. ADRIANO DUGULIN.

Civico Museo d'Arte Orientale: Via San Sebastiano 1, 34121 Trieste; tel. 040-6754068; e-mail museoarteorientale@comune.trieste.it; internet www.retecivica .trieste.it/triestecultura/new/musei/museo_orientale; f. 2001; Dir Dott. ADRIANO DUGULIN.

Civico Museo di Guerra per la Pace 'Diego de Henriquez': Via delle Milizie 16, 34139 Trieste; tel. 040-948430; fax 040-944390; e-mail museodehenriquez@comune.trieste.it; internet www.retecivica .trieste.it/triestecultura/new/musei/museo_henriquez; f. 1998; Dir Dott. ADRIANO DUGULIN.

Civico Museo del Mare: Via Campo Marzio 5, 34139 Trieste; tel. 040-304885; e-mail museomare@comune.trieste.it; internet www.retecivica.trieste.it/triestecultura/new/musei_scientifici/mare; f. 1968; Dir Dott. ADRIANO DUGULIN.

Civico Museo Sartorio: Largo Papa Giovanni XXIII 1, 34123 Trieste; tel. 040-301479; e-mail cmsa@comune.trieste.it; internet www.retecivica.trieste.it/triestecultura/new/musei/museo_sartorio; f. 1947; Dir Dott. ADRIANO DUGULIN.

Civico Museo di Storia ed Arte e Orto Lapidario: Piazza della Cattedrale 1, 34121 Trieste; tel. 040-308686; fax 040-300687; e-mail cmsa@comune.trieste.it; internet www.retecivica.trieste.it/triestecultura/new/musei/museo_storiae-darte; f. Orto Lapidario 1843, Civico Museo di Storia 1873; Dir Dott. ADRIANO DUGULIN.

Civico Museo di Storia Naturale: Via dei Tominz 4, 34139 Trieste; tel. 040-6758658; fax 040-6758230; e-mail sportellonatura@comune.trieste.it; internet www.retecivica.trieste.it/triestecultura/new/musei_scientifici/stor-ia_naturale; f. 2010; Dir Dott. ADRIANO DUGULIN.

Civico Museo di Storia Patria—Civico Museo Morpurgo de Nilma: Via Imbriani 5, 34122 Trieste; tel. 040-636969; fax 040-636969; e-mail cmsa@comune.trieste.it; internet www.retecivica .trieste.it/triestecultura/new/musei/museo_storiapatria; f. Museo Morpurgo

1947, Civico Museo di Storia Patria 1950; Dir Dott. ADRIANO DUGULIN.

Civico Museo Teatrale 'Carlo Schmidl': Via Rossini, 4, 34122 Trieste; tel. 040-6754072; fax 040-6754030; e-mail museoschmidl@comune.trieste.it; internet www.retecivica.trieste.it/triestecultura/new/musei/museo_schmidl; f. 1950; Conservator STEFANO BIANCHI.

Civico Orto Botanico: Via Marchesetti 2, 34139 Trieste; tel. 040-360068; fax 040-360068; e-mail ortobotanico@comune.trieste.it; internet www.retecivica.trieste.it/triestecultura/new/musei_scientifici/orto_botanico; f. 1842; Curator MASSIMO PALMA.

Museo Ferroviario di Trieste Campo Marzio: Via Giulio Cesare 1, 34123 Trieste; tel. 040-3794185; fax 040-312756; e-mail info@museoferroviariotrieste.it; internet www.museoferroviariotrieste.it; Dir Dott. ADRIANO DUGULIN.

Museo Joyce: Via Madonna del Mare 13, 34121 Trieste; tel. 040-3593606; fax 040-3593625; e-mail museojoyce@comune.trieste.it; internet www.museojoycetrieste.it; f. 2004; Dir Dott. ADRIANO DUGULIN.

Museo Petrarchesco Piccolomineo: Via Madonna del Mare 13, 34123 Trieste; tel. 040-6758184; fax 040-6758199; e-mail museopetrarchesco@comune.trieste.it; internet www.retecivica.trieste.it/triestecultura/new/musei/museo_petrarchesco; f. 2003; Dir ALESSANDRA SIRUGO.

Museo Postale e Telegrafico della Mitteleuropa: Piazza Vittorio Veneto 1, 34132 Trieste; tel. 040-6764264; fax 040-6764570; e-mail simonchi@posteitaliane.it; internet www.retecivica.trieste.it/triestecultura/new/musei/museo_postale; f. 1997, in association with Poste Italiane S.p.A.; Dir Dott. ADRIANO DUGULIN.

Museo Revoltella – Galleria d'Arte Moderna: Via Diaz 27, 34123 Trieste; tel. 040-6754350; fax 040-6754137; e-mail revoltella@comune.trieste.it; internet www.museorevoltella.it; f. 1872; library of 17,000 vols, 426 periodicals, 34 current periodicals; Dir Dott. MARIA MASAU DAN.

Museo della Risiera di San Sabba—Monumento Nazionale: Via Giovanni Palatucci 5, 34148 Trieste; tel. 040-826202; fax 040-8330974; e-mail risierasansabba@comune.trieste.it; internet www.retecivica.trieste.it/triestecultura/new/musei/risiera_san_-sabba; f. 1975; Dir Dott. ADRIANO DUGULIN.

Museo del Risorgimento e Sacrario Oberdan: Via XXIV Maggio 4, 34133 Trieste; tel. 040-361675; fax 040-300687; e-mail cmsa@comune.trieste.it; internet www.retecivica.trieste.it/triestecultura/new/musei/museo_risorgimento; f. 1934; Dir Dott. ADRIANO DUGULIN.

Museo Sveviano: Via Madonna del Mare 13, 34123 Trieste; tel. 040-3593606; fax 040-6758199; e-mail museosveviano@comune.trieste.it; internet www.retecivica.trieste.it/svevo; f. 1997; Dir Dott. ADRIANO DUGULIN.

Turin

Armeria Reale: Piazza Castello 191, 10123 Turin; tel. 011-543889; fax 011-5087799; e-mail armeriareale@artito.arti.beniculturali.it; internet www.artito.arti.beniculturali.it; f. 1837; colln of arms; includes the equestrian armour of Otto Heinrich and works by Pompeo della Chiesa, Etienne Delaune and the engravers of the Munich school, Emanuel Sadeler, Daniel Sadeler and Caspar Spät; Dir ALESSANDRA GUERRINI.

Fondazione Torino Musei: Corso Vittorio Emanuele II 78, 10121 Turin; tel. 011-4436901; fax 011-4436917; e-mail info@fondazionetorinomusei.it; internet www.comune.torino.it/musei; Sec.-Gen. and Administrative Dir ADRIANO DA RE.

Attached Museums:

Borgo e Rocca Medioevale: Parco del Valentino, Viale Virgilio 107, 10126 Turin; tel. 011-4431701; fax 011-4431719; e-mail borgomedievale@fondazione torinomusei.it; internet www.borgomedievaletorino.it; Dir ENRICA PAGELLA.

Galleria Civica d'Arte Moderna e Contemporanea: Via Magenta 31, 10128 Turin; tel. 011-5629911; fax 011-4429550; e-mail gam@fondazionetorinomusei.it; internet www.gamtorino.it; f. 1953; Dir DANILO ECCHER.

Museo d'Arte Orientale (Museum of Oriental Art): Via San Domenico 11, 10122 Turin; tel. 011-4436927; fax 011-4436918; e-mail mao@fondazionetorinomusei.it; internet www.maotorino.it; f. 2008; Dir FRANCO RICCA.

Palazzo Madama—Museo Civico d'Arte Antica: Piazza Castello, 10122 Turin; tel. 011-4433501; fax 011-4429929; e-mail palazzomadama@fondazionetorinomusei.it; internet www.palazzomadamatorino.it; f. 1863; Dir ENRICA PAGELLA.

Museo Civico Pietro Micca e dell'assedio di Torino del 1706 (Pietro Micca and 1706 Siege of Turin Civic Museum): Via Guicciardini 7A, 10121 Turin; tel. 011-546317; fax 011-533772; internet www.museopietromicca.it; f. 1961; Hon. Curator and Dir-Gen. SEBASTIANO PONSO.

Galleria Sabauda: Via Accademia delle Scienze 6, 10123 Turin; tel. (11) 5617776; fax (11) 5069814; e-mail galleriasabauda@museitorino.it; internet www.museitorino.it/galleriasabauda; f. 1832; one of principal Flemish and Dutch collns, and early Italian, also Bronzino, Veronese, Tiepolo and Lombard and Piedmontese schools, furniture, sculpture and jewellery; Dir Dott. PAOLA ASTRUA.

Museo di Antichità: Via XX Settembre 88C, 10122 Turin; tel. 011-5211106; fax 011-5213145; e-mail info@museoarcheologico.it; internet www.museoantichita.it; f. 1940; Piedmontese prehistory; Etruscan, Sardinian and Gallo-Roman remains; Greek and Cypriot ceramics; Roman statues; silverware; Dir Dott. LILIANA MERCANDO.

Museo Egizio: Via Accademia delle Scienze 6, 10123 Turin; tel. 011-5617776; fax 011-5623157; e-mail info@museoegizio.org; internet www.museoegizio.org; f. 1824; Pharonic, Ptolemaic and Coptic antiquities; entire furnishings of the tomb of architect Kha and his wife from Deir el-Medina, Temple of Ellesija (reconstructed Nubian temple of 18th dynasty) presented by the Egyptian Govt; objects from Droveth colln and Schiaparelli excavations in Egypt; Dir ELENI VASSILIKA.

Udine

Civici Musei e Gallerie di Storia ed Arte: Colle del Castello, Piazza Libertà, 33100 Udine; tel. 0432-271591; fax 0432-271982; e-mail vania.gransinigh@comune.udine.it; internet www.comune.udine.it/opencms/opencms/release/comuneudine/cittavicina/cultura/info/musei/civici_musei_e_gallerie_-di_storia_ed_arte; f. 1866; history, art; Dir Dott. VANIA GRANSINIGH.

Urbino

Galleria Nazionale delle Marche—Palazzo Ducale: Piazza Duca Federico 107, 61029 Urbino; tel. 0722-2760; fax 0722-4427; e-mail info.servizimusei@libero.it; internet www.galleriaborghese.it/nuove/einfourbino.html; f. 1912; medieval and Renaissance works of art originating in the town of Urbino and the provinces of Marche; Dir Dott. LORENZA MOCHI ONORI.

Venice

Biennale di Venezia: Ca' Giustinian, San Marco 1364/A, 30124 Venice; tel. 041-5218711; fax 041-2728329; e-mail info@labiennale.org; internet www.labiennale.org; f. 1895; an autonomous body; organizes artistic and cultural events throughout the year: visual arts, architecture, cinema, theatre, music, dance; the Biennale owns historical archives of contemporary art; library of 130,000 vols and catalogues, photographs, etc.; Pres. PAOLO BARATTA; Gen. Dir ANDREA DEL MERCATO.

Gallerie dell'Accademia: Campo della Carità, Dorsoduro 1050, 30100 Venice; tel. 041-5222247; fax 041-5212709; e-mail sspsae-ve.accademia@beniculturali.it; internet www.polomuseale.venezia.beniculturali.it/index.php?it/3/gallerie-dellaccademia; f. 1807; Venetian painting 1310–1700; Dir MATTEO CERIANA.

Galleria Giorgio Franchetti alla Ca' d'Oro: Cannaregio 3932, 30126 Venice; tel. (41) 5222349; fax (41) 5238790; e-mail sspsae-ve.franchetti@beniculturali.it; internet www.polomuseale.venezia.beniculturali.it/index.php?it/4/galleria-giorgio-franchetti-alla-ca-doro; f. 1928; sculpture, bronzes, medals, coins, tapestries, ceramics, and Venetian, central Italian and Flemish art; Deputy Dir Dott. CLAUDIA CREMONINI; Curator Dott. CLAUDIA CREMONINI; Ceramics Curator Dott. FRANCESCA SACCARDO; Paintings Restorer Dott. GLORIA TRANQUILLI.

Musei Civici Veneziani: Piazza San Marco 52, 30124 Venice; tel. 041-5225625; fax 041-5200935; e-mail info@fmcvenezia.it; internet www.museicivicivenezaini.it; Dir Prof. GIANDOMENICO ROMANELLI.

Constituent Institutions:

Ca' Rezzonico: Dorsoduro 3136, 30123 Venice; tel. 041-2410100; e-mail info@fmcvenezia.it; internet www.museicivicivenezaini.it; f. 1935; 18th-century Venetian art, sculpture, etc.

Casa di Carlo Goldoni: San Polo 2794, 30125 Venice; tel. 041-2759325; fax 041-2440081; e-mail mkt.musei@comune.venezia.it; internet www.museicivicivenezaini.it; house of the comic playwright (1707–93).

Galleria Internazionale d'Arte Moderna di Ca' Pesaro: Santa Croce 2076, 30135 Venice; tel. 041-5240695; fax 041-5241075; e-mail mkt.musei@comune.venezia.it; internet www.museicivicivenezaini.it; f. 1897; works of art since the 19th century.

Museo Correr: Piazza San Marco 52, 30124 Venice; tel. 041-2405211; fax 041-5200935; e-mail info@fmcvenezia.it; internet www.museicivicivenezaini.it; f. 1830 by Teodoro Correr who bequeathed his collns to the City; Venetian art (13th–16th centuries) and history of the Serenissima, Renaissance coins, ceramics; publ. *Bollettino* (4 a year).

Museo Fortuny: San Marco 3780, 30124 Venice; tel. 041-5200995; fax 041-5223088; e-mail mkt.musei@comune.venezia.it; internet www.museicivicivenezaini.it; closed for restoration.

Museo del Merletto: Piazza Galuppi 187, 30012 Burano; tel. 041-730034; fax 041-735471; e-mail mkt.musei@comune .venezia.it; internet www .museiciviciveneziani.it; f. 1981; examples of lace since 19th century in the former Lace School.

Museo di Storia Naturale: Santa Croce 1730, 30125 Venice; tel. 041-2750206; fax 041-7210000; e-mail mkt.musei@comune .venezia.it; internet www .museiciviciveneziani.it; f. 1923; natural history; entomology, malacology, ornithology, icthyology, African ethnology; library of 10,000 vols.

Museo del Vetro: Fondamenta Giustinian 8, 30121 Murano; tel. 041-739586; e-mail mkt.musei@museiciviciveneziani.it; internet www.museiciviciveneziani.it; f. 1861; Venetian glass from middle ages to the present; also collns of Roman glass from 1st century AD, Spanish, Bohemian and English collns; archives and photographic colln; spec. exhibitions and educational projects.

Palazzo Ducale (Doge's Palace): Piazza San Marco 1, 30124 Venice; tel. 041-2715911; fax 041-5285028; e-mail mkt .musei@comune.venezia.it; internet www .museiciviciveneziani.it; f. 1340; doge's apartments, institutional chambers, armoury and prisons.

Palazzo Mocenigo: Santa Croce 1992, 30126 Venice; tel. 041-721798; fax 041-5241614; e-mail mkt.musei@comune .venezia.it; internet www .museiciviciveneziani.it; palace of the noble Venetian family that provided several of the doges; colln of fabrics and costumes; library on history of fashion.

Planetario di Venezia: Ass.Astrofili Veneziani, Casella Postale 36, Venice Lido; tel. 041-731518; e-mail planetario@ astrovenezia.net; internet www .astrovenezia.net.

Torre Civica di Mestre: Piazza Erminio Ferretto, 30174 Mestre; tel. 041-2749062; fax 041-2749049; internet www .museiciviciveneziani.it/frame .asp?pid=996; f. 13th century.

Torre dell'Orologio (Clock Tower): Piazza San Marco, 30124 Venice; tel. 041-2715911; fax 041-5285028; e-mail mkt .musei@comune.venezia.it; internet www .museiciviciveneziani.it; f. 15th century; closed for restoration.

Museo Archeologico Nazionale: Piazza S. Marco 52, 30124 Venice; tel. 041-5225978; fax 041-5225978; e-mail sspsae-ve .archeologico@beniculturali.it; internet www .polomuseale.venezia.beniculturali.it/index .php?it/6/museo-archeologico-nazionale; f. 1523, reorganized 1923–26 and again after 1945; Greek and Roman sculpture, gems and coins, mosaics and sculptures from the 5th century BC–11th century AD; library of 3,000 vols; Curator MARIA CRISTINA DOSSI.

Museo d'Arte Orientale: Sestiere di Santa Croce 2076, 30100 Venice; tel. 041-5241173; fax 041-5241173; e-mail sspsae-ve.orientale@ beniculturali.it; internet www.polomuseale .venezia.beniculturali.it/index.php?it/5/ museo-darte-orientale; 17th–19th-century decorative arts from the Far East; Dir Dott. FIORELLA SPADAVECCHIA.

Museo della Fondazione Querini Stampalia: Santa Maria Formosa, Castello 5252, 30122 Venice; tel. 041-2711411; fax 041-2711445; e-mail museo@querinistampalia .org; internet www.querinistampalia.it; f. 1869; 14th- to 19th-century Italian paintings, 18th- and 19th-century furniture, china;

library of 330,000 vols, 400 periodicals; Dir Dott. ENRICO ZOLA.

Museo Storico Navale: Riva S. Biasio Castello 2148, 30122 Venice; tel. 041-5200276; fax 041-5200276; f. 1919; library of 3,000 vols; Dir Amm. Div. LORENZO SFERRA.

Peggy Guggenheim Collection (Solomon R. Guggenheim Foundation, New York): Palazzo Venier dei Leoni, 701 Dorsoduro, 30123 Venice; tel. 041-2405411; fax 041-5206885; e-mail info@guggenheim-venice.it; internet www.guggenheim-venice.it; f. 1980; permanent colln includes masterpieces of cubism, futurism, metaphysical painting, European abstraction, surrealism, and American abstract expressionism; Italian futurist works on loan from the Gianni Mattioli collection; sculpture garden; Dir PHILIP RYLANDS.

Pinacoteca Manfrediniana: Dorsoduro 1, 30123 Venice; tel. 041-2411018; fax 041-2743998; e-mail seminario@patriarcato .venezia.it; internet www.marcianum.it; f. 1827; paintings and sculpture of the Roman, Gothic, Renaissance, Baroque, Neo-classical periods; library of 80,000 vols; Dir Prof. Mgr LUCIO CILIA.

Verona

Galleria d'Arte Moderna Palazzo Forti: Via A. Forti 1, 37121 Verona; tel. 045-8001903; fax 045-8003524; e-mail palazzoforti@comune.verona.it; internet www.palazzoforti.it; f. 1982; Dir Prof. G. ROSSI CORTENOVA.

Musei Civici d'Arte di Verona: Corso Castelvecchio 2, 37121 Verona; tel. 045-8062611; fax 045-8010729; e-mail castelvecchio@comune.verona.it; internet portale.comune.verona.it/nqcontent .cfm?a_id=582; f. 1857; Dir Dott. PAOLA MARINI.

Constituent Museums and Galleries:

Museo degli Affreschi 'Giovanni Battista Cavalcaselle' alla Tomba di Giulietta: Via del Pontiere 35, 37122 Verona; tel. 045-8000361; e-mail castelvecchio@ comune.verona.it; f. 1973; Dir Dott. PAOLA MARINI.

Museo Archeologico al Teatro Romano: Regaste Redentore 2, 37129 Verona; tel. 045-8000360; fax 045-8010587; e-mail castelvecchio@comune .verona.it; f. 1924; Dir Dott. PAOLA MARINI.

Museo di Castelvecchio: Corso Castelvecchio 2, 37121 Verona; tel. 045-8062611; fax 045-8010729; e-mail castelvecchio@ comune.verona.it; library of 42,000 vols, 500 periodicals; Dir Dott. PAOLA MARINI.

Museo Lapidario Maffeiano: Piazza Brà 28, 37121 Verona; tel. 045-590087; fax 045-8010729; f. 1745; Curator Dott. MARGHERITA BOLLA.

Vicenza

Musei Civici Vicenza: Palazzo Chiericati, Piazza Matteotti 37–39, 36100 Vicenza; tel. 0444-222811; fax 0444-546619; internet www .museicivicivicenza.it; Dir Dott. MARIA ELISA AVAGNINA.

Attached Museums:

Museo Naturalistico Archeologico: Chiostri di Santa Corona, contrà Santa Corona 4, 36100 Vicenza; tel. 0444-320440; e-mail museonatarcheo@comune.vicenza .it; internet www.museicivicivicenza.it/it/ mna/index.php; f. 1991; fossils, flora and fauna; Palaeolithic and local Roman remains; Dir Dott. ANTONIO DAL LAGO; publ. *Natura Vicentina* (1 a year).

Museo del Risorgimento e della Resistenza: Villa Guiccioli, Viale X Giugno 115,

36100 Vicenza; tel. 0444-222820; e-mail museorisorgimento@comune.vicenza.it; internet www.museicivicivicenza.it/it/mrr/ index.php; Dir Dott. MAURO PASSARIN.

Museo Civico Pinacoteca: Palazzo Chiericati, Piazza Matteotti 37–39, 36100 Vicenza; tel. 0444-321348; e-mail museocivico@comune.vicenza.it; internet www.museicivicivicenza.it/it/mcp/index .php; f. 1855; 13th–19th century paintings and sculpture by artists incl. Montagna, Veronese, Tintoretto and Tiepolo; MSS, drawings, prints and coins; Dir Dott. MARIA ELISA AVAGNINA.

Viterbo

Museo Civico: Piazza Francesco Crispi 2, 01100 Viterbo; tel. 0761-348275; fax 0761-340810; e-mail museocivico@comune.viterbo .it; internet www.comune.viterbo.it/ museocivico; f. 1912; archaeology, art history; Dir ORSOLA GRASSI.

Volterra

Museo Diocesano d'Arte Sacra: Palazzo Vescovile, Via Roma 13, 56048 Volterra; tel. 0588-86290; fax 0588-86290; e-mail museoartesacravolterra@nemail.it; internet www.comune.volterra.pi.it/museiit/musart .html; f. 1932; sculpture, paintings, costumes, ornaments; Dir Dott. UMBERTO BAVONI.

Museo Etrusco Guarnacci: Via Don Minzoni 15, 56048 Volterra; tel. 0588-86347; fax 0588-90987; e-mail a.furiesi@comune .volterra.pi.it; internet www.comune.volterra .pi.it/english/museiit/metru.html; f. 1761; Roman and Etruscan coins, urns, bronzes, etc.; Dir Dr ALESSANDRO FURIESI.

State Universities

POLITECNICO DI BARI

Via E. Orabona 4, 70125 Bari
Telephone: 080-5962111
Fax: 080-5962510
E-mail: rettore@poliba.it
Internet: www.poliba.it
Founded 1990
State control

Rector: Prof. NICOLA COSTANTINO
Deputy Rector: Prof. CLAUDIO CHERUBINI
Admin. Dir: Dott. MARCO RUCCI

Library of 200,000 and journals

DEANS

Faculty of Architecture: Prof. Arch. CLAUDIO D'AMATO GUERRIERI
I Faculty of Engineering (in Bari and Foggia): Prof. Ing. ANTONIO DELL'AQUILA
II Faculty of Engineering (in Taranto): Prof. Ing GREGORIO ANDRIA

POLITECNICO DI MILANO

Piazza Leonardo da Vinci 32, 20133 Milan
Telephone: 02-23991
Fax: 02-23992106
Internet: www.polimi.it
Founded 1863
Academic year: November to October

Rector: Prof. GIOVANNI AZZONE
Vice-Rector: Prof. ALESSANDRO BALDUCCI
Gen. Dir: GRAZIANO DRAGONI
Librarian: SONIA PASQUALIN

Number of teachers: 1,355
Number of students: 25,952

Publication: *Politecnico* (4 a year)

DEANS

First School of Architecture (Architecture and Society): Prof. PIERCARLO PALERMO
Second School of Architecture (Civil Architecture): Prof. ANGELO TORRICELLI
School of Design: Prof. ARTURO DELL'ACQUA BELLAVITIS
First School of Engineering (Civil, Environmental and Territorial Engineering): Prof. FEDERICO PEROTTI
Second School of Engineering (Systems Engineering): Prof. ALESSANDRO POZZETTI
Third School of Engineering (Industrial Process Engineering): Prof. MAURIZIO MASI
Fourth School of Engineering (Industrial Engineering): Prof. GIOVANNI LOZZA
Fifth School of Engineering (Information Engineering): Prof. ROBERTO NEGRINI
Sixth School of Engineering (Construction Engineering/Architecture): Prof. EMILIO PIZZI

POLITECNICO DI TORINO

Corso Duca degli Abruzzi 24, 10129 Turin
Telephone: 011-5646100
Fax: 011-5646329
E-mail: rettore@polito.it
Internet: www.polito.it
Founded 1859
Public control
Languages of instruction: English, Italian
Higher Institute of Engineering and Architecture
Academic year: November to October
Rector: Prof. FRANCESCO PROFUMO
Vice-Rector: Prof. MARCO GILLI
Admin. Dir: ENRICO PERITI
Library Dir: Dott. MARIA VITTORIA SAVIO
Library of 382,898 vols
Number of teachers: 814
Number of students: 29,000

DEANS

First School of Architecture: Prof. FERRUCCIO ZORZI
Second School of Architecture – Architecture and Environment: Prof. ROCCO CURTO
First School of Engineering: Prof. DONATO FIRRAO
Third School of Engineering – Information Technologies: Prof. PAOLO ENRICO CAMURATI
Fourth School of Engineering – Economics and Management: Prof. SERGIO ROSSETTO
Graduate School: Prof. MARIO RASETTI (Dir)

SAPIENZA UNIVERSITÀ DI ROMA

Piazzale Aldo Moro 5, 00185 Rome
Telephone: 06-49911
Fax: 06-49910348
E-mail: rettore@uniroma1.it
Internet: www.uniroma1.it
Founded 1303 by Pope Boniface VIII, with the Papal Bull 'In Supremae praeminentia dignitatis'
Rector: Prof. LUIGI FRATI
Vice-Rector: Prof. FRANCESCO AVALLONE
Deputy Rector for Accomplishment and Implementation of the Rector's Programme and for Relations with the Admin.: Prof. ADRIANO REDLER
Deputy Rector for Applied Research, Technology Transfer and Relations with the Business World: Prof. LUCIANO CAGLIOTI
Deputy Rector for Cooperation and Int. Relations: Prof. ANTONELLO BIAGINI
Deputy Rector for Devt of Research and Educational Activities: Prof. BARTOLOMEO AZZARO
Deputy Rector for Relations with Confederate Univs: Prof. FULCO LANCHESTER

Deputy Rector for Strategic Planning: Prof. GIUSEPPINA CAPALDO
Head of Admin.: CARLO MUSTO D'AMORE
Librarian: Prof. GIOVANNI CICLOTTI
Number of teachers: 4,500
Number of students: 140,000

DEANS

Faculty of Architecture: Prof. RENATO MASIANI
Faculty of Civil and Industrial Engineering: Prof. FABRIZIO VESTRONI
Faculty of Economics: Prof. ATTILIO CELANT
Faculty of Engineering, Information Technology and Statistics: Prof. LUIGIA CARLUCCI AIELLO
Faculty of Jurisprudence: Prof. MARIO CARAVALE
Faculty of Mathematics, Physics and Natural Science: Prof. PIERO NEGRINI
Faculty of Medicine and Dentistry: Prof. ADRIANO REDLER
Faculty of Medicine and Psychology: Prof. VINCENZO ZIPARO
Faculty of Pharmacy and Medicine: Prof. EUGENIO GAUDIO
Faculty of Philosophy, Arts, Humanities and Oriental Studies: Prof. MARTA FATTORI
Faculty of Political Science, Sociology and Communication: Prof. GIANLUIGI ROSSI

ATTACHED CENTRES

Interdepartmental Research Centre of European and International Studies: internet www.eco.uniroma1.it/europe; Dir Prof. GIUSEPPE BURGIO.

Interuniversity Research Centre on Developing Countries (CIRPS): internet www.cirps.it; Dir Prof. VINCENZO NASO.

SECONDA UNIVERSITÀ DEGLI STUDI DI NAPOLI

Viale Beneduce 10, 81100 Caserta
Telephone: 0823-274901
Fax: 0823-327589
E-mail: rettoratoce@unina2.it
Internet: www.unina2.it
Founded 1991
State control
Rector: Prof. FRANCESCO ROSSI
Vice-Rector: Prof. MARIO DE ROSA
Admin. Dir: Dott. VINCENZO LANZA
Number of students: 30,000

DEANS

Faculty of Architecture: Prof. CARMINE GAMBARDELLA
Faculty of Economics: Prof. CLELIA MAZZONI
Faculty of Engineering: Prof. MICHELE DI NATALE
Faculty of Environmental Sciences: Prof. PAOLO VINCENZO PEDONE
Faculty of Law: Prof. LORENZO CHIEFFI
Faculty of Letters and Philosophy: Prof. ROSANNA CIOFFI
Faculty of Mathematical, Physical and Natural Sciences: Prof. AUGUSTO PARENTE
Faculty of Medicine and Surgery: Prof. GIUSEPPE PAOLISSO
Faculty of Political Studies: Prof. GIAN MARIA PICCINELLI
Faculty of Psychology: Prof. ALIDA LABELLA

UNIVERSITÀ CA' FOSCARI VENEZIA

Dorsoduro 3246, 30123 Venice
Telephone: 041-2348111
Fax: 041-2348321
E-mail: help@unive.it
Internet: www.unive.it
Founded 1868, formerly Istituto Universitario di Economia e Commercio e di Lingue e Letterature Straniere

Academic year: November to October
Rector: Prof. CARLO CARRARO
Pro-Rector: Prof. ERASMO SANTESSO
Admin. Dir: Dott. STEFANIA TORRE
Librarian: EUGENIO BURGIO
Number of teachers: 494
Number of students: 17,427
Publications: *Annuario*, *Cafoscariappuntamenti* (6 a year), *Cafoscarinotizie* (4 a year)

DEANS

Faculty of Economics: Prof. ANTONELLA BASSO
Faculty of Foreign Languages and Literature: Prof. ALIDE CAGIDEMETRIO
Faculty of Letters and Philosophy: Prof. FILIPPO MARIA CARINCI
Faculty of Mathematical, Physical and Natural Sciences: Prof. ALVISE BENEDETTI

UNIVERSITY CENTRES AND SCHOOLS

Administrative Computer Centre: Dorsoduro 2169, Santa Marta, 30123 Venice; Pres. Dott. G. BUSETTO.

Computer Centre: Dorsoduro 3861, 30123 Venice; tel. 5229823; Pres. Prof. G. PACINI.

Interdepartmental Experimental Centre: Dorsoduro 2137, 30123 Venice; tel. 5298111; Pres. Prof. G. A. MAZZOCCHIN.

Interfaculty Linguistics Centre: Santa Croce 2161, 30125 Venice; tel. 5241642; Dir Prof. G. CINQUE.

Interuniversity Centre for Venetian Studies: San Marco 2945, Ca' Loredan, 30124 Venice; tel. 5200996; Dir Prof. G. PADOAN.

Statistical Documentation Centre: Dorsoduro 3246, 30123 Venice; tel. 5298111; Dir Prof. R. VEDALDI.

UNIVERSITÀ DEGLI STUDI 'GABRIELE D'ANNUNZIO' CHIETI PESCARA

Via dei Vestini 31, 66013 Chieti Scalo
Telephone: 0871-3551
Fax: 0871-3556007
E-mail: segreteriarettore@unich.it
Internet: www.unich.it
Founded 1965 as a private univ.; became a state univ. 1982
State control
Rector: Prof. FRANCO CUCCURULLO
Gen. Dir: Dr MARCO NAPOLEONE
Number of students: 19,000

DEANS

Faculty of Architecture: Prof. ALBERTO CLEMENTI
Faculty of Arts: Prof. STEFANO TRINCHESE
Faculty of Economics: Prof. ANNA MORGANTE
Faculty of Education: Prof. GAETANO BONETTA
Faculty of Foreign Languages and Literature: Prof. CARLO CONSANI
Faculty of Management: Prof. GIUSEPPE PAOLONE
Faculty of Mathematical, Physical and Natural Sciences: Prof. LEANDRO D'ALESSANDRO
Faculty of Medicine and Surgery: Prof. CARMINE DI ILIO
Faculty of Pharmacy: Prof. MICHELE VACCA
Faculty of Psychology: Prof. RAFFAELE CIAFARDONE
Faculty of Social Sciences: Prof. MICHELE CASCAVILLA
Faculty of Sports Science: Prof. MARIO FELACO

UNIVERSITÀ DEGLI STUDI 'MAGNA GRÆCIA' DI CATANZARO

Viale Europa, Località Germaneto, 88100 Catanzaro
Telephone: 0961-3694001
E-mail: rettore@unicz.it
Internet: www.unicz.it

Founded 1998
State control

Rector: Prof. FRANCESCO SAVERIO COSTANZO
Vice-Rector: Prof. LUIGI VENTURA
Admin. Dir: Dott. LUIGI GRANDINETTI
Number of students: 11,000

DEANS

Faculty of Law: Prof. LUIGI GRANDINETTI
Faculty of Medicine and Surgery: Prof. GIOVAMBATTISTA DE SARRO
Faculty of Pharmacy: Prof. DOMENICANTONIO ROTIROTI

UNIVERSITÀ DEGLI STUDI DEL MOLISE

Via de Sanctis, 86100 Campobasso
Telephone: 0874-4041
Fax: 0874-317259
Internet: www.unimol.it

Founded 1982
Academic year: October to September

Rector: Prof. GIOVANNI CANNATA
Vice-Rector: Prof. SALVATORE PASSARELLA
Admin. Dir: Dott. VINCENZO LUCCHESE
Library Dir: Dott. VINCENZO LUCCHESE
Number of students: 10,331

DEANS

Faculty of Agriculture: Prof. EMANUELE MARCONI
Faculty of Economics: Prof. PAOLO DE VITA
Faculty of Engineering: Prof. DONATELLA CIALDEA
Faculty of Health Sciences: Prof. MAURIZIO TAGLIALATELA
Faculty of Human and Social Sciences: Prof. PAOLO MAURIELLO
Faculty of Law: Prof. GIANMARIA PALMIERI
Faculty of Mathematical, Physical and Natural Sciences: Prof. VINCENZO DE FELICE
Faculty of Medicine: Prof. GIOVANNANGELO ORIANI

UNIVERSITÀ DEGLI STUDI DEL SANNIO

Piazza Guerrazzi 1, 82100 Benevento
Telephone: 0824-305001
Fax: 0824-23648
E-mail: rettore@unisannio.it
Internet: www.unisannio.it

Founded 1998
State control

Rector: Prof. FILIPPO BENCARDINO
Admin. Dir: Dott. GAETANO TELESIO
Library of 28,000 , 350 journals

DEANS

Faculty of Economics and Business: Prof. MASSIMO SQUILLANTE
Faculty of Engineering: Prof. FILIPPO DE ROSSI
Faculty of Law: Prof. ANNA CLARA MONTI
Faculty of Mathematical, Physical and Natural Sciences: Prof. FRANCESCO MARIA GUADAGNO

UNIVERSITÀ DEGLI STUDI DELL'AQUILA

Via Giovanni Falcone 25, 67100 Coppito (AQ)
Telephone: 0862-432030
Fax: 0862-432033
E-mail: webmaster@cc.univaq.it

Internet: www.univaq.it

Founded 1952

Rector: Prof. FERDINANDO DI ORIO
Admin. Dir: Dott. FILIPPO DEL VECCHIO

Library of 171,356 vols
Number of teachers: 600
Number of students: 20,000

DEANS

Faculty of Arts: Prof. GIANNINO DI TOMMASO
Faculty of Biotechnologies: Prof. SILVIA BISTI
Faculty of Economics: Prof. FABRIZIO POLITI
Faculty of Education: Prof. ANTONELLA GASBARRI
Faculty of Engineering: Prof. PIER UGO FOSCOLO
Faculty of Mathematical, Physical and Natural Sciences: Prof. PAOLA INVERARDI
Faculty of Medicine and Surgery: Prof. MARIA GRAZIA CIFONE
Faculty of Psychology: Prof. FERNANDA AMICARELLI
Faculty of Sports Science: Prof. LEILA FABIANI

UNIVERSITÀ DEGLI STUDI DELL'INSUBRIA

Via Ravasi 2, 21100 Varese
Telephone: 0332-219001
Fax: 0332-219009
E-mail: rettore@uninsubria.it
Internet: www.uninsubria.eu

Founded 1998

Rector: Prof. RENZO DIONIGI
Vice-Rector in Como: Prof. GIORGIO CONETTI
Administrative Director: Dr MARINO BALZANI
Library Dir: ALESSANDRA BEZZI

Library of 81,570 vols, 648 journals, 13,000 electronic journals
Number of teachers: 393
Number of students: 9,546

DEANS

Faculty of Economics: Prof. MATTEO ROCCA
Faculty of Law: Prof. MARIA PAOLA VIVIANI SCHLEIN
Faculty of Medicine in Varese: Prof. FRANCESCO PASQUALI
Faculty of Sciences in Como: Prof. STEFANO SERRA CAPIZZANO
Faculty of Sciences in Varese: Prof. ALBERTO COEN PORISINI

UNIVERSITÀ DEGLI STUDI DELLA BASILICATA

Via Nazario Sauro 85, 85100 Potenza
Telephone: 0971-201111
Fax: 0971-202102
E-mail: segreteriarettore@unibas.it
Internet: www.unibas.it

Founded 1982

Rector: Prof. MAURO FIORENTINO
Vice-Rector: Prof. GIOVANNI CARLO DI RENZO
Admin. Dir: Dott. MARIO GIANNONE CODIGLIONE
Librarians: Prof. CARLO MARIA SIMONETTI, Prof. GABOR KORCHMAROS

Library of 85,000 vols
Number of teachers: 307
Number of students: 4,845

Publications: *Basilicata Università*, *Collana 'Atti e Memorie'*, *Collana 'Strutture e Materiali'*, *Quaderni*

DEANS

Faculty of Agriculture: Prof. MICHELE PERNIOLA
Faculty of Engineering: Prof. IGNAZIO MARCELLO MANCINI
Faculty of Humanities and Philosophy: Prof. PASQUALE FRASCOLLA

Faculty of Mathematical, Physical and Natural Sciences: Prof. ONOFRIO MARIO DI VINCENZO
Faculty of Pharmacy: Prof. FAUSTINO BISACCIA

UNIVERSITÀ DEGLI STUDI DELLA TUSCIA

Via. S. Maria in Gradi 4, 01100 Viterbo
Telephone: 0761-3571
Fax: 0761-321771
E-mail: infoperme@unitus.it
Internet: www3.unitus.it

Founded 1979
State control
Academic year: November to October

Rector: Prof. MARCO MANCINI
Vice-Rector: Prof. STEFANO GREGO
Admin. Dir: Dr GIOVANNI CUCULLO

Number of teachers: 320
Number of students: 10,000

DEANS

Faculty of Agriculture: Prof. BRUNO RONCHI
Faculty of Conservation of Cultural Heritage: Prof. ALFIO. CORTONESI
Faculty of Economics: Prof. ALESSANDRO RUGGIERI
Faculty of Mathematics, Physics and Natural Sciences: Prof. LUIGI BOSCO
Faculty of Modern Languages and Literature: Prof. GAETAO PLATANIA
Faculty of Political Sciences: Prof. MAURIZIO RIDOLFI

UNIVERSITÀ DEGLI STUDI DI BARI 'ALDO MORO'

Piazza Umberto I 1, 70121 Bari
Telephone: 080-311111
Internet: www.uniba.it

Founded 1924

Rector: Prof. CORRADO PETROCELLI
Vice-Rector: Prof. AUGUSTO GARUCCIO
Admin. Dir: Dott. GIORGIO DE SANTIS

Number of teachers: 700
Number of students: 42,439

DEANS

Faculty of Agriculture: Prof. VITO NICOLA SAVINO
Faculty of Arts: Prof. GRAZIA DISTASO
Faculty of Biotechnology: Prof. LUIGI PALMIERI
Faculty of Economics: Prof. VITTORIO DELL'ATTI
Faculty of Economics (Taranto): Prof. BRUNO NOTARNICOLA
Faculty of Education: Prof. GIUSEPPE ELIA
Faculty of Foreign Languages and Literature: Prof. PASQUALE GUARAGNELLA
Faculty of Law: Prof. MARIO GIOVANNI GAROFALO
Faculty of Law (Taranto): Prof. ANTONIO FELICE URICCHIO
Faculty of Mathematical, Physical and Natural Sciences: Prof. PAOLO SPINELLI
Faculty of Mathematical, Physical and Natural Sciences (Taranto): Prof. SILVIA ROMANELLI
Faculty of Medicine and Surgery: Prof. ANTONIO QUARANTA
Faculty of Pharmacy: Prof. ROBERTO PERRONE
Faculty of Politics: Prof. ENNIO TRIGGIANI
Faculty of Veterinary Medicine: Prof. BUONAVOGLIA CANIO

UNIVERSITÀ DEGLI STUDI DI BERGAMO

Via Salvecchio 19, 24129 Bergamo
Telephone: 035-2052111
Fax: 035-243054

E-mail: postmaster@unibg.it
Internet: www.unibg.it

Founded 1968

Rector: Prof. STEFANO PALEARI
Vice-Rector: Prof. VALERIA UGAZIO
Admin. Dir: Dott. GIUSEPPE GIOVANELLI
Librarian: Dott. ENNIO FERRANTE

Library of 200,000 vols, 1,200 journals
Number of teachers: 211
Number of students: 6,317

DEANS

Faculty of Economics: Prof. LAURA VIGNANÒ
Faculty of Education: Prof. IVO LIZZOLA
Faculty of Engineering: Prof. PAOLO RIVA
Faculty of Foreign Languages and Literature: Prof. BRUNO CARTOSIO
Faculty of Humanities: Prof. CLAUDIO VILLA
Faculty of Law: Prof. BARBARA PEZZINI

PROFESSORS

Faculty of Economics:

AMADUZZI, A., Business Administration
ARCUCCI, F., International Trade and Finance
BERTOCCHI, M. I., Financial Mathematics
BIFFIGNANDI, S., Statistics Applied to Economics
FENGHI, F., Commercial Law
FERRI, P. E., Economic Analysis
GAMBARELLI, G., General Mathematics
GRAZIOLA, G., Economics of Enterprise
LEONI, R., Labour Economics
MASINI, M., Banking
RENOLDI, A., Value Management
SACCHETTO, C., Tax Law
SPEDICATO, E., Operations Research
TAGI, G., Industrial Operations Management
TAGLIARINI, F., Commercial Penal Law

Faculty of Engineering:

BUGINI, A., Industrial Management of Quality
COLOMBI, R., Statistics and Probability
PERDICHIZZI, A., Energetic Powerplants
RIVA, R., Theoretical and Applied Mechanics
SALANTI, A., Economics

Faculty of Foreign Languages and Literature:

BELLER, M., German Language and Literature
CASTOLDI, A., French Language and Literature II
CERUTI, M., Epistemology
CORONA, M., Anglo-American Languages and Literature
GOTTI, M., History of the English Language
LOCATELLI, A., English Language and Literature
MARZOLA, A., English Language and Literature
MIRANDOLA, G., French Language and Literature I
MOLINARI, M. V., Germanic Philology
MORELLI, G., Spanish Language and Literature
PAPA, E., Modern and Contemporary History
VILLA, C., Medieval and Humanist Philology

UNIVERSITÀ DEGLI STUDI DI BRESCIA

Piazza del Mercato 15, 25121 Brescia

Telephone: 030-29881
Fax: 030-2988329
Internet: www.unibs.it

Founded 1982

Rector: Prof. SERGIO PECORELLI
Vice-Rector: Prof. DANIELE MARIOLI

Admin. Dir: Dott. ENRICO PERITI
Librarians: EUGENIO PELIZZARI (Economics and Law), Dott. MARCO BAZZOLI (Engineering), ENRICA VERONESI (Medicine and Surgery)

Number of teachers: 573
Number of students: 14,132

DEANS

Faculty of Economics: Prof. CLAUDIO TEODORI
Faculty of Engineering: Prof. ALDO ZENONI
Faculty of Law: Prof. ANTONELLO CALORE
Faculty of Medicine and Surgery: Prof. STEFANO MARIA GIULINI

UNIVERSITÀ DEGLI STUDI DI CAMERINO

Piazza Cavour 19/f, 62032 Camerino

Telephone: 0737-4011
Fax: 0737-402007
E-mail: segreteria.rettore@unicam.it
Internet: www.unicam.it

Founded 1336; University status 1727
Academic year: November to October

Rector: Prof. FULVIO ESPOSITO
Vice-Rector: Prof. IPPOLITO ANTONINI
Deputy Rector for Int. Research: Prof. FLAVIO CORRADINI
Deputy Rector for Teaching: Prof. LUCIANO MISICI
Deputy Rector for Student Affairs: Prof. DANIELA ACCILI
Admin. Dir: Dott. LUIGI TAPANELLI
Librarian: SONIA CAVIRANI

Number of teachers: 301
Number of students: 10,055

DIRECTORS

School of Advanced Studies: Prof. CRISTINA MICELI
School of Architecture and Design: Prof. UMBERTO CAO
School of Bioscience and Biotechnology: Prof. CLAUDIO GUALERZI
School of Environmental Science: Prof. CARLO RENIERI
School of Law: Prof. IGNAZIO BUTI
School of Pharmaceutical Sciences and Health Products: Prof. SAURO VITTORI
School of Science and Technology: Prof. ROBERTO BALLINI
School of Veterinary Medicine: Prof. GIACOMO RENZONI

ATTACHED INSTITUTES

School of Specialization in Animal Health, Livestock and Animal Production: Dir Prof. ANDREA SPATERNA.

School of Specialization in Civil Law: Dir Prof. LUCIA RUGGERI.

School of Specialization in Clinical Biochemistry: Dir Prof. ROSALIA TACCONI.

School of Specialization in Hospital Pharmacy: Dir Prof. CARLO POLIDORI.

School of Specialization for the Legal Professions: Dir Prof. Avv. MAURIZIO CINELLI.

UNIVERSITÀ DEGLI STUDI DI CASSINO

Via G. Marconi 10, 03043 Cassino (Frosinone)

Telephone: 0776-2991
Fax: 0776-310562
E-mail: info@unicas.it
Internet: www.unicas.it

Founded 1979
State control

Rector: CIRO ATTAIANESE
Vice-Rector: FRANCO DE VIVO
Admin. Dir: ASCENZO FARENTI

Number of teachers: 334
Number of students: 11,415

DEANS

Faculty of Arts and Philosophy: SEBASTIANO GENTILE
Faculty of Economics: Prof. ENRICA IANNUCCI
Faculty of Engineering: Prof. GIOVANNI BETTA
Faculty of Law: Prof. EDOARDO ALES
Faculty of Sports Sciences: Prof. GIOVANNI CAPELLI

UNIVERSITÀ DEGLI STUDI DI CATANIA

Piazza dell' Università 2, 95124 Catania

Telephone: 095-321112
Fax: 095-325194
E-mail: rettore@unict.it
Internet: www.unict.it

Founded 1434

Rector: Prof. ANTONINO RECCA
Vice-Rector: Prof. MARIA LUISA CARNAZZA
Admin. Dir: Dott. LUCIO MAGGIO

Number of teachers: 1,517
Number of students: 53,674

DEANS

Faculty of Agriculture: Prof. AGATINO RUSSO
Faculty of Architecture: Prof. CARLO TRUPPI
Faculty of Arts: Prof. ENRICO IACHELLO
Faculty of Economics: Prof. CARMELO BUTTÀ
Faculty of Education: Prof. FEBRONIA ELIA
Faculty of Engineering: Prof. LUIGI FORTUNA
Faculty of Foreign Languages and Literature: Prof. NUNZIO FAMOSO
Faculty of Law: Prof. VINCENZO DI CATALDO
Faculty of Mathematical, Physical and Natural Sciences: Prof. GUIDO LI VOLSI
Faculty of Medicine and Surgery: Prof. FRANCESCO BASILE
Faculty of Pharmacy: Prof. GIUSEPPE RONSISVALLE
Faculty of Political Science: Prof. GIUSEPPE BARONE

UNIVERSITÀ DEGLI STUDI DI FIRENZE

Piazza San Marco 4, 50121 Florence

Telephone: 055-27571
Fax: 055-264194
E-mail: urp@unifi.it
Internet: www.unifi.it

Founded 1321
Academic year: September to August

Rector: Prof. ALBERTO TESI
Vice-Rector for Finance: Prof. GIACOMO POGGI
Vice-Rector for Scientific Research: Prof. ELISABETTA CERBAI
Vice-Rector for Teaching and Student Affairs: Prof. ANNA NOZZOLI
Vice-Rector for Technological Transfer: Prof. MARCO BELLANDI
Admin. Dir: Dott. MICHELE OREFICE
Dir of Library System: Dott. GIULIA MARAVIGLIA

Number of teachers: 2,236
Number of students: 59,847

DEANS

Faculty of Agriculture: Prof. GIUSEPPE SURICO
Faculty of Architecture: Prof. SAVERIO MECCA
Faculty of Arts: Prof. RICCARDO BRUSCAGLI
Faculty of Economics: Prof. FRANCESCO GIUNTA
Faculty of Education: Prof. SIMONETTA ULIVIERI
Faculty of Engineering: Prof. STEFANO MANETTI
Faculty of Law: Prof. PAOLO CAPPELLINI
Faculty of Mathematical, Physical and Natural Sciences: Prof. EMILIO MARIO CASTELLUCCI

Faculty of Medicine and Surgery: Prof. GIAN FRANCO GENSINI
Faculty of Pharmacy: Prof. SERGIO PINZAUTI
Faculty of Political Sciences: Prof. FRANCA MARIA ALACEVICH
Faculty of Psychology: Prof. ANDREA SMORTI

UNIVERSITÀ DEGLI STUDI DI FOGGIA

Via A. Gramsci 89/91, 71122 Foggia
Telephone: 08831-338446
E-mail: urp@unifg.it
Internet: www.unifg.it
Founded 1999
State control
Rector: Prof. GIULIANO VOLPE
Deputy Rector: Prof. ANDREA DI LIDDO
Admin. Dir: Dott. COSTANTINO QUARTUCCI
Library of 80,000 , 780 journals, 4,300 online journals
Number of teachers: 198
Number of students: 11,000

DEANS

Faculty of Agriculture: Prof. AGOSTINO SEVI
Faculty of Arts and Philosophy: Prof. GIOVANNI CIPRIANI
Faculty of Economics: Prof. ISABELLA VARRASO
Faculty of Education: Prof. FRANCA PINTO MINERVA
Faculty of Law: Prof. MAURIZIO RICCI
Faculty of Medicine and Surgery: Prof. MATTEO DI BIASE

UNIVERSITÀ DEGLI STUDI DI GENOVA

Via Balbi 5, 16126 Genoa
Telephone: 010-20991
Fax: 010-2099227
E-mail: orientamento@unige.it
Internet: www.unige.it
Founded 1670
Academic year: November to October
Rector: Prof. GIACOMO DEFERRARI
Vice-Rector: Prof. MAURIZIO MARTELLI
Admin. Dir: ROSA GATTI
Number of teachers: 1,719
Number of students: 40,125
Publications: *Annuario dell'Università di Genova* (sections on research and teaching units, each annual), *Genuense Atenaeum* (6 a year)

DEANS

Faculty of Architecture: STEFANO FRANCESCO MUSSO
Faculty of Arts: FRANCESCO SURDICH
Faculty of Economics: PIER MARIA FERRANDO
Faculty of Education: GUIDO FRANCO AMORETTI
Faculty of Engineering: PAOLA GIRDINIO
Faculty of Foreign Languages and Literature: SERGIO POLI
Faculty of Law: PAOLO COMANDUCCI
Faculty of Mathematical, Physical and Natural Sciences: GIANCARLO ALBERTELLI
Faculty of Medicine and Surgery: GIANCARLO TORRE
Faculty of Pharmacy: ALESSANDRO BALBI
Faculty of Political Sciences: GIOVANNI BATTISTA VARNIER

UNIVERSITÀ DEGLI STUDI DI MACERATA

Piaggia della Torre 8, 62100 Macerata
Telephone: 0733-2581
Fax: 0733-2582689
E-mail: rettorato@unimc.it
Internet: www.unimc.it

Founded 1290
Rector: Prof. LUIGI LACCHÈ
Vice-Rector: Prof. ROSA MARISA BORRACCINI
Admin. Dir: Dott. MAURO GIUSTOZZI
Number of teachers: 300
Number of students: 15,000

DEANS

Faculty of Communication Sciences: Prof. BARBARA POJAGHI
Faculty of Cultural Heritage: Prof. ENZO CATANI
Faculty of Economics: Prof. ANTONELLA PAOLINI
Faculty of Education: Prof. GIUSEPPE ROSSI
Faculty of Humanities and Philosophy: Prof. GIANFRANCO PACI
Faculty of Law: Prof. ALBERTO FEBBRAJO
Faculty of Political Science: Prof. FRANCESCO ADORNATO

UNIVERSITÀ DEGLI STUDI DI MESSINA

Piazza Salvatore Pugliatti 1, 98122 Messina
Telephone: 090-6761
Fax: 090-6764274
E-mail: rettorato@unime.it
Internet: www.unime.it
Founded 1548
Academic year: November to June
Rector: Prof. FRANCESCO TOMASELLO
Deputy Vice-Rector: Prof. RITA DE PASQUALE
Admin. Dir: GIUSEPPE CARDILE
Number of teachers: 1,300
Number of students: 40,000

DEANS

Faculty of Arts and Humanities: Prof. VINCENZO FERA
Faculty of Economics: Prof. LUIGI FERLAZZO NATOLI
Faculty of Education: Prof. ANTONINO PENNISI
Faculty of Engineering: Prof. SIGNORINO GALVAGNO
Faculty of Law: Prof. SALVATORE BERLINGÒ
Faculty of Mathematics, Physics and Natural Sciences: Prof. MARIO GATTUSO
Faculty of Medicine: Prof. EMANUELE SCRIBANO
Faculty of Pharmacy: Prof. GIUSEPPE BISIGNANO
Faculty of Politics: Prof. ANDREA ROMANO
Faculty of Veterinary Medicine: Prof. VINCENZO CHIOFALO

UNIVERSITÀ DEGLI STUDI DI MILANO

Via Festa del Perdono 7, 20122 Milan
Telephone: 02-503111
Fax: 02-50312508
E-mail: webmaster@unimi.it
Internet: www.unimi.it
Founded 1923
Public control
Academic year: October to September
Rector: Prof. ENRICO DECLEVA
Vice-Rector: Prof. DARIO CASATI
Vice-Rector for Research: Prof. ALBERTO MANTOVANI
Pro-Rector for Postgraduate Education and Int. Affairs: Prof. MARINO REGINI
Pro-Rector for Research: Prof. ALBERTO MANTOVANI
Admin. Dir: ALBERTO SILVANI
Library Dir: Dott. MAURIZIO DI GIROLAMO
Number of teachers: 716
Number of students: 63,000
Publication: *Sistema Università* (4 a year; online at www.unimi.it/news/38106.htm)

DEANS

Faculty of Agriculture: Prof. MARISA PORRINI
Faculty of Arts: Prof. GIULIANA ALBINI
Faculty of Law: Prof. ALESSANDRO ALBISETTI
Faculty of Mathematical, Physical and Natural Sciences: Prof. PAOLA CAMPADELLI
Faculty of Medicine and Surgery: Prof. VIRGILIO FERRUCCIO FERRARIO
Faculty of Motor Sciences: Prof. ARSENIO VEICSTEINAS
Faculty of Pharmacy: Prof. CESARE SIRTORI
Faculty of Political Sciences: Prof. DANIELE CHECCHI
Faculty of Veterinary Medicine: Prof. GIORGIO POLI

PROFESSORS

Faculty of Agriculture (Via Celoria 2, 20133 Milan; tel. 02-50316500; fax 02-50316508; e-mail preside.agraria@unimi.it; internet www.unimi.it/ateneo/facol/agraria.htm):
ANDREONI, V., Agricultural Microbiology
BASSI, D., Fruit Farming
BELLI, G., Plant Pathology
BIANCO, P. A., Plant Pathology
BODRIA, L., Agricultural Mechanics
BONOMI, F., Biochemistry
CASATI, D., Agrofood Economy
CASTELLI, G., Agricultural Mechanics
CASTROVILLI, C. M., Zooculture
COCUCCI, M., Physiology of Farmed Plants
CORTESI, P., Plant Pathology
CROVETTO, G. M., Animal Nutrition and Foodstuffs
DE WRACHIEN, D., Irrigation and Drainage
DESIMONI, E., Analytical Chemistry
DURANTI, M. M., Biochemistry
ECCHER, T., General Arboriculture
ELIAS, G., Environmental Technical Physics
FRISIO, D. G., Rural Economics and Surveying
GALLI, A., Foods Microbiology
GANDOLFI, C., Agricultural and Forest Hydraulics
GARLASCHI, F. M., Vegetable Physiology
GASPARETTO, E., Agricultural Mechanization
GAVAZZI, G., Plant Genetic Improvement
GENEVINI, P., Soil Chemistry
GIURA, R., Agricultural Hydraulics
GREPPI, M., Hydraulic Systems, Forestry
LOCATELLI, D. P., General and Applied Entomology
LOZZIA, G. C., General and Applied Entomology
LUCISANO, M., Food Science and Technology
MAGGIORE, T., Herbaceous Farming
MANACHINI, P., General Microbiology
MANNINO, S., Chemico-Physical and Sensory Analysis of Food
MERLINI, L., Organic Chemistry
MONDELLI, R., Organic Chemistry
PAGANI, S., Enzymology
PELLEGRINO, L. M., Food Science and Technology
PIERGIOVANNI, L., Food Science and Technology
POLELLI, M., Rural Evaluation
POMPEI, C., Food Technology Processes
PORRINI, M., Physiology
PRETOLANI, R., Rural Economics and Surveying
QUARONI, S., Vegetable Pathology
RAGG, E. M., Organic Chemistry
RESMINI, P., Agricultural Industry
ROSSI, M., Food Science and Technology
SACCHI, G. A., Organic Chemistry
SALAMINI, F., Genetics and Biotechnology
SANGIORGI, F., Rural and Forest Construction
SCHIRALDI, A., Physical Chemistry
SCIENZA, A., General Arboriculture and Tree Cultivation

SORLINI, C., Agricultural and Forest Microbiology
SUCCI, G., Special Animal Husbandry
SÜSS, L., Agricultural Entomology
TANO, F., Herbaceous Farming
TATEO, F., Food Science and Technology
TESTOLIN, G., Human Food and Nutrition
TOCCOLINI, A., Rural and Forest Construction
VOLONTERIO, G., Agricultural Industry
ZOCCHI, G., Food Science and Technology

Faculty of Law (Via Festa del Perdono 7, 20122 Milan; tel. 02-50312400; fax 02-50312653; e-mail presidenza .giurisprudenza@unimi.it; internet www .unimi.it/ateneo/facol/giurisp.htm):

ALBISETTI, A., Ecclesiastical Law
AMODIO, E., Procedural Penal Law
ANGIOLINI, V., Constitutional Law
BARIATTI, S., International Law
BENATTI, F., Institutions of Private Law
BOSCHIERO, N., International Law
CANDIAN, A., Comparative Private Law
CANTARELLA, E., Institutions of Roman Law
CARINCI, M. T., Labour Law
CARNEVALI, U., Institutions of Private Law
CASTAGNOLA, A., Civil Procedural Law
CASUSCELLI, G., Ecclesiastical Law
CAVALLONE, B., Civil Procedural Law
CONDINANZI, M., International Law
D'AMICO, M. E., Constitutional Law
DE NOVA, G., Civil Law
DENOZZA, F., Commercial Law
DI RENZO, M. G., History of Italian Law
DOLCINI, E., Penal Law
DOMINIONI, O., Procedural Penal Comparative Law
FERRARI, E., Administrative Law
FERRARI, S., Canon Law
FERRARI, V., Sociology of Law
FLORIDA, G., Comparative Public Law
FRASSI, P. A., Commercial Law
GAFFURI, G., Tributary Law
GALANTINI, M. N., Procedural Penal Law
GAMBARO, A., Comparative Private Law
GITTI, G., Institutions of Private Law
GNOLI, F., Roman Law
GOISIS, G., Political Economy
GRECO, G., Administrative Law
GREZZI, M. L., Philosophy of Law
GUERCI, C. M., Political Economy
JAEGER, P., Commercial Law
JORI, M., Philosophy of Law
LANCELLOTTI, E., Financial Science
LUZZATI, C. R., Philosophy of Law
LUZZATTO, R., International Law
MARINUCCI, G., Penal Law
MASSETTO, G., History of Italian Law
MERLIN, E., Civil Procedural Law
MORELLO, U. M., Private Law
NASCIMBENE, B., European Community Law
PADOA SCHIOPPA, A., History of Italian Law
PALIERO, C., Penal Law
PARISI, F., Institutions of Private Law
PELOSI, A. C., Institutions of Private Law
PERICU, G., Administrative Law
PISANI, M., Procedural Penal Law
POCAR, F., International Law
POLARA, G., Institutions of Roman Law
RICCI, E., Bankruptcy Law
RIMINI, E., Commercial Law
ROSSIGNOLI, B., Economics of Credit Institutions
SACCHI, R., Commercial Law
SALETTI, A., Civil Procedural Law
SANTA MARIA, A., International Law
SPAGNUOLO VIGORITA, L., Labour Law
TENELLA SILLANI, C., Institutions of Private Law
TREVES, T., International Private and Procedural Law
TRIMARCHI, F., Administrative Law
TRIMARCHI, P., Civil Law
VIGANÒ, F., Penal Law

VILLA, G., Institutions of Private Law
VILLATA, R., Administrative Law
VIOLINI, L., Constitutional Law
VITALI, E. G., Ecclesiastical Law
ZANON, N., Constitutional Law

Faculty of Letters and Philosophy (Via Festa del Perdono 7, 20122 Milan; tel. 02-50312701; fax 02-50312543; e-mail elio .franzini@unimi.it; internet www.unimi.it/ ateneo/facol/letfil.htm):

ALBINI, G., Medieval History
ANTONIELLI, L., History of Political Institutions
ANZI, A., History of the English Theatre
BARONI, M. F., Palaeography
BEJOR, G., Classical Archaeology
BERRA, C., Italian Literature
BIANCHI, E., Geography
BIGALLI, D., History of Philosophy
BIGNAMI, M., English Language and Literature
BOCCALI, G., Sanskrit Language and Literature
BOELLA, L., Moral Philosophy
BOLOGNA, M., Archives, Bibliography and Library Science
BOLOGNA, M. P., Glottology and Linguistics
BONOMI, A., Philosophy of Language
BONOMI, I., Italian Linguistics
BOSISIO, P., Dramatic Arts
BRAMBILLA, E., Modern History
BRIOSCHI, F., History of Literary Criticism
BROGI, G., History of the Russian Language
BRUTI LIBERATI, L., Modern History
CADIOLI, A. V., Contemporary Italian Literature
CAIZZI, F., History of Ancient Philosophy
CANAVERO, A., Modern History
CANZIANI, G., History of Philosophy
CAPRA, C., Modern History
CASALEGNO, P., Philosophy and Theory of Languages
CATTANEO, M. T., Spanish Language and Literature
CAVAJONI, G., Latin Language and Literature
CERCIGNANI, F., German Language and Literature
CHIAPPA, M. L., Medieval History
CHITTOLINI, G., Medieval History
CIANCI, G., English Language and Literature
CICALESE, M. L., Theory and History of Historiography
COLOMBO, M., French
COMBA, R., Medieval History
COMETTA, M., German Philology
CONCA, F., History of the Greek Language
CORDANO, F., Greek History
D'AGOSTINO, A., Romance Philology
DAVERIO, G., Greek History
DE ANGELIS, V., Humanistic Philology
DECLEVA, E., Contemporary History
DE FRANCESCO, A., Modern History
DEGRADA, F., History of Modern and Contemporary Music
DE MARINIS, R. C., Early and Recorded History
DEVECCHI, P., History of Modern Art
DI SALVO, M. G., Slavonic Philology
DOGLIO, M., French Literature
DONATI, C., History of the Ancient Italian States
DONINI, P., History of Ancient Philosophy
FIACCADORI, G., Christian and Medieval Archaeology
FORABOSCHI, D., Roman History
FRANZINI, E., Aesthetics
FUMAGALLI, M. J., History of Medieval Philosophy
GALLAZZI, C., Papyrology
GIACOMELLI, R., Glottology and Linguistics
GIORELLO, G., Philosophy of Science
GORI, G., History of Modern Philosophy

GUALANDRI, I., Latin Literature
IAMARTINO, G., English
LANARO, G. V., History of Philosophy
LEHNUS, L. A., Classical Philology
MARI, M., Italian Literature
MASINI, A., Italian Linguistics
MAZZOCCA, F., Museology, Art Criticism and Restoration Criticism
MENEGHETTI, M. L., Romance Philology
MERLO, G., History of the Medieval Church and Heresy
MERZARIO, R., Economic History
MICHELI, G., History of Science and Technology
MILANINI, C., Italian Literature
MODENESI, M., French Literature
MONTALEONE, C., Moral Philosophy
MONTECCHI, G., Bibliography and Archive and Library Science
MORGANA, S., Italian Language History
NEGRI, A., History of Modern Art
NISSIM, L., French Language and Literature
ORLANDI, G., Medieval Latin Literature
PAGETTI, C., English Language and Literature
PERASSI, E., Hispano-American Languages and Literatures
PETTOELLO, R., History of Philosophy
PEYRONEL, S., Medieval and Early Modern History
PIACENTINI, P., Egyptology and Coptic Civilization
PIRETTO, G. P., Slavic Studies
PIVA, P., History of Medieval Art
PUNZO, M., Modern History
RAMBALDI, E., Moral Philosophy
ROSA, G., Contemporary Italian Literature
RUMI, G., Contemporary History
SAMPIETRO, L., Anglo-American Languages and Literatures
SAPELLI, G., Economic History
SCARAMELLINI, G., Geography
SCARAMUZZA, G., Aesthetics
SCARAMUZZA, M. E., Spanish Literature
SINI, C., Theoretical Philosophy
SPAGGIARI, W., Italian Literature
SPERA, F., Italian Literature
TREVES, A. L., Geography
VALOTA, B., History of Eastern Europe
VISMARA, P., History of Christianity and the Churches
ZANETTO, G., Greek Language and Literature
ZECCHI, S., Aesthetics
ZERBI, M. C., Geography

Faculty of Medicine (Via Festa del Perdono 7, 20122 Milan; tel. 02-50312360; fax 02-50312365; e-mail preside.medicina@unimi .it; internet www.unimi.it/ateneo/facol/ medchir.htm):

AGUS, G. B., Vascular Surgery
ALESSI, E., Dermatology
ALLEGRA, L., Diseases of the Respiratory System
ALLEVI, P., Biochemistry
ALTAMURA, A. C., Psychiatry
ALTOMARE, G., Dermatology
ANASTASIA, M., Chemistry and Biochemical Propaedeutics
AUSTONI, E., Urology
AUXILIA, F., Hygiene
BA, G., Psychiatry
BALDISSERA, F. G., Human Physiology
BALSARI, A., General Pathology
BEK PECCOZ, P., Endocrinology
BELLINI, T., Applied Physics (Arts, Environment, Biology and Medicine)
BERTAZZI, P. A., Industrial Medicine
BIANCHI PORRO, G., Gastroenterology
BIGLIOLI, P., Cardiac Surgery
BLASI, F. B., Diseases of the Respiratory System
BOCK, G., History of Medicine
BOLIS, G., Obstetrics and Gynaecology

BORTOLANI, E., General Surgery
BRAGA, P., Pharmacology
BRESOLIN, N., Neurology
BRESSANI DOLDI, S., General Surgery
BRUSATI, R., Maxillofacial Surgery
BUSACCA, M., Obstetrics and Gynaecology
CABITZA, P., Orthopaedics and Traumatology
CAIRO, G., General Pathology
CAJONE, F., General Pathology
CANTALAMESSA, L., Internal Medicine
CAPETTA, P., Obstetrics and Gynaecology
CAPPELLINI, M. D., Internal Medicine
CAPUTO, R., Dermatology
CARACCIOLO, E., Clinical Psychology
CARRASSI, A., Special Odontostomatological Pathology
CARRUBA, M., Pharmacology
CATTANEO, M. N., Internal Medicine
CAVAGNA, G., Human Physiology
CAVAGNINI, F., Endocrinology
CAVALLARI, P., Physiology
CESARANI, A., Audiology
CESTARO, B. A., Biological Chemistry
CHIESARA, E., Toxicology
CHIGORNO, V. L., Clinical Biochemistry and Molecular Biology
CIANCAGLINI, R., Clinical Gnathology
CICARDI, M., Internal Medicine
CLEMENTI, F., Cellular and Molecular Pharmacology
CLERICI, M. S., General Pathology
COGGI, G., Pathological Anatomy and Histology
COLOMBI, A., Industrial Medicine
COLOMBO, M., Internal Medicine
COMI, P., General Pathology
CONTE, D., Gastroenterology
CORNALBA, G., Imaging and Radiotherapy Diagnostics
CORTELLARO, M., Internal Medicine
CORTI, M., Medical Physics
CROSIGNANI, P., Obstetrics and Gynaecology
CROSTI, C., Dermatology
CUSI, D. M., Nephrology
D'ANGELO, E., Human Physiology
DE FRANCHIS, R., Gastroenterology
DECARLI, A., Medical Statistics
DELLE FAVE, A., General Psychology
DESIDERIO, M. A., General Pathology
DI FIORE, P. P., General Pathology
DI GIULIO, A. M., Pharmacology
DONATELLI, F., Cardiac Surgery
DUBINI, F., Microbiology
FANTINI, F., Rheumatology
FARGION, S. R., Internal Medicine
FARNETI, A., Forensic Medicine
FARRONATO, G., Odontostomatological Diseases
FASSATI, L. R., General Surgery
FEDELE, L., Obstetrics and Gynaecology
FERRARIO, V. F., Human Anatomy
FERRERO, M. E., General Pathology
FIORENTINI, C., Cardiology
FOÀ, V., Industrial Hygiene
FOSCHI, D., General Surgery
GABRIELLI, L., Vascular Surgery
GAINI, S. M., Neurosurgery
GALLI, M., Infectious Diseases
GALLI, M. G., Hygiene
GALLUS, G. V., Medical Statistics and Biometrics
GATTINONI, L., Anaesthesiology and Resuscitation
GELMETTI, C., Dermatology
GHIDONI, R., Biological Chemistry
GIANNI, A., Medical Oncology
GINELLI, E., General Biology
GIOIA, M. A., Human Anatomy
GIOVANNINI, M., Paediatrics
GRANDI, M. A., Forensic Medicine
GROPPETTI, A., Pharmacology
GUAZZI, M., Cardiology
GUIDOBONO CAVALCHIN, F., Pharmacology
IAPICHINO, G., Anaesthesiology

INVERNIZZI, G., Psychiatry
LAMBERTENGHI DELILIERS, G., Internal Medicine
LARIZZA, L., Medical Genetics
LEDDA, M., Histology
LENTI, C., Child Neuropsychiatry
LEONETTI, G., Medical Semiology and Methodology
LODI, F., Forensic Toxicology
LUCIGNANI, G., Imaging and Radiotherapy Diagnostics
MAGRINI, F., Internal Medicine
MALCOVATI, M., Molecular Biology
MALLIANI, A., Internal Medicine
MANNUCCI, P. M., Internal Medicine
MANTOVANI, A., General Pathology
MARIANI, C., Neurology
MARIOTTI, M., Physiology
MARONI, M., Industrial Medicine
MASSIMINI, F., General Psychology
MATTINA, R., Microbiology
MATTURRI, L., Pathological Anatomy and Histology
MELZI D'ERIL, G., Clinical Biochemistry and Molecular Biology
MEOLA, G., Neurology
MERONI, P., Internal Medicine
MEZZETTI, M., Thoracic Surgery
MILANESI, G., Cellular Biology
MILANI, F., Radiotherapy
MOJA, G., General Psychology
MONTORSI, M., General Surgery
MORABITO, A., Medical Statistics
MORACE, G., Microbiology and Clinical Microbiology
MORGANTI, A., Internal Medicine
MORONI, M. E., Infectious Diseases
MÜLLER, E., Pharmacology
NICOLIN, A. N., Pharmacology
ORECCHIA, R., Radiotherapy
ORZALESI, N., Ophthalmology
OTTAVIANI, F., Otorhinolaryngology
PAGANI, M., Internal Medicine
PAGANO, A., Hygiene
PARDI, G., Obstetrics and Gynaecology
PELICCI, P. G., General Pathology
PERETTI, G., Orthopaedics and Traumatology
PERRELLA, M., Physical Biochemistry
PODDA, M., Internal Medicine
POLI, M., General Psychology
PONTIROLI, A., Internal Medicine
PRINCIPI, N., Paediatrics
RATIGLIA, R., Ophthalmology
RIVA, E., General and Specialist Paediatrics
ROCCO, F., Urology
RONCALLI, M., Pathological Anatomy
RONCHETTI, F., Chemistry and Biochemical Propaedeutics
RONCHI, E., Forensic Medicine
ROVIARO, G. C., General Surgery
SALVATO, A., Orthognathodontics
SAMBATARO, G., Otorhinolaryngology
SANTAMBROGIO, L., Thoracic Surgery
SANTANIELLO, E., Chemistry and Biochemical Propaedeutics
SANTORO, F., Odontostomatology
SCALABRINO, G., General Pathology
SCARONE, S., Psychiatry
SCORZA, R., Clinical Immunology and Allergology
SCORZA, R., General Surgery
SETTEMBRINI, P., Vascular Surgery
SICCARDI, A., General Biology
SMIRNE, S., Neurology
SONNINO, S., Biological Chemistry
SPINNLER, H., Neurology
STEFANI, M., Anatomy and Pathological Histology
STROHMENGER, L., Pedodontics
SURACE, A., Orthopaedics and Traumatology
TAROLO, G. L., Nuclear Medicine
TASCHIERI, A., General Surgery
TEALDI, D. G., Vascular Surgery

TENCHINI, M. L. G., General Biology
TETTAMANTI, G., Human Systematic Biochemistry
TRABUCCHI, E., General Surgery
VAGO, G., Pathological Anatomy
VERGANI, C., Gerontology and Geriatrics
VIALE, G., Pathological Anatomy and Histology
VICENTINI, L., Pharmacology
VILLA, M. L., Immunology
WEINSTEIN, R., Parodontology
ZANETTI, A., Hygiene
ZOCCHI, L., Physiology

Faculty of Motor Sciences (Via Kramer 4A, 20129 Milan; tel. 02-50315151; fax 02-50315152; e-mail scienze.motorie@unimi.it; internet www.unimi.it/ateneo/facol/scmot .htm):

CARANDENTE, F., Internal Medicine
FIORILLI, A., Applied Dietetics
LUZI, L., Physiology
PETRUCCIOLI, M. G., Human Anatomy
PIZZINI, G., Human Anatomy
SFORZA, C., Human Anatomy
VEICSTEINAS, A., Physiology
VENERANDO, B., Biochemistry

Faculty of Pharmacy (Viale Balzaretti 9, 20133 Milan; tel. 02-50318402; fax 02-50318266; e-mail presidenza.farmacia@ unimi.it; internet www.unimi.it/ateneo/facol/ farmacia.htm):

ABBRACHIO, M. P., Pharmacology
ALBINATI, A., General and Inorganic Chemistry
BARLOCCO, D., Pharmaceutical Chemistry
BECCALLI, E., Organic Chemistry
BERINGHELLI, T., General and Inorganic Chemistry
BERRA, B., Biological Chemistry
BOMBIERI, G., Drug Analysis
CARINI, M., Pharmaceutical Chemistry
CASTANO, P., Human Anatomy
CATAPANO, A. L., Pharmacology
CATTABENI, F., Applied Pharmacology
CATTANEO, E., Pharmacology
CELOTTI, F., General Pathology
CESAROTTI, E., General and Inorganic Chemistry
COLONNA, S., Organic Chemistry
CORSINI, A., Pharmacology
D'ALFONSO, G., General and Inorganic Chemistry
DALLA CROCE, P., Heterocyclic Chemistry
DE AMICI, M., Pharmaceutical Chemistry
DE GIULI MORGHEN, C., General Microbiology
DE MICHELI, C., Pharmaceutical and Toxicological Chemistry
DEL PRA, A., General and Inorganic Chemistry
FERRI, V., Pharmaceutical and Toxicological Chemistry
FOLCO, G., Pharmacology and Pharmacognosy
FRANCESCHINI, G., Pharmacology
GALLI, C., Pharmacological Tests and Measuring
GALLI, C. L., Pharmacology
GAVEZZOTTI, A., Physical Chemistry
GAZZANIGA, A., Applied Pharmaceutical Technology
GELMI, M. L., Organic Chemistry
MAFFEI FACINO, R., Drug Analysis
MAGGI, A. C., Pharmacology
MONTANARI, L., Pharmaceutical Technology, Socioeconomy and Legislation
MOTTA, M., General Physiology
PALLAVICINI, M., Pharmaceutical Chemistry
PIVA, F., Physiology
POCAR, D., Organic Chemistry
RACAGNI, G., Pharmacology and Pharmacognosy
SIRTORI, C., Clinical Pharmacology
SPARATORE, A., Pharmacological Chemistry

STRADI, R., Physical Methods in Organic Chemistry
TARAMELLI, D., General Pathology
TOMÈ, F., Pharmaceutical Biology
TREMOLI, E., Pharmacology
VALOTI, E., Pharmaceutical Chemistry

Faculty of Political Sciences (Via Conservatorio 7, 20122 Milan; tel. 02-50321000; fax 02-50321005; e-mail presidenza.scienze .politiche@unimi.it; internet www.unimi.it/ ateneo/facol/scpol.htm):

ALBERICI, A., Economics of Credit Institutions
ANTONIOLI, M., Contemporary History
BARBA NAVARETTI, G., Political Economy
BECCALLI, B. Z., Sociology of Economic and Labour Processes
BERNAREGGI, G. M., Public Economy
BESUSSI, A., Political Philosophy
BILANCIA, P., Institutions of Public Law
BOGNETTI, G., Financial Sciences
BORDOGNA, L., Sociology of Economic and Labour Processes
CAFARI PANICO, R., European Community Law
CALVI, M. V., Spanish Language and Translation
CELLA, G. P., Economic Sociology
CHECCHI, D., Political Economy
CHIARINI, R., History of Political Parties and Political Movements
CHIESI, A. M., General Sociology
CLERICI, R., International Private Law
DE CARLI, P. G., Economics and Law
DE MARCO, E., Institutions of Public Law
DONZELLI, F., Political Economy
ESCOBAR, R., Political Philosophy
FACCHI, A., Philosophy of Law
FERRARA, M., Political Science
FERRARI, A., Contemporary History
FERRARI, P. A., Statistics
FLORIO, M., Financial Science
FRIGO, M., International Law
GALEOTTI, M. D., Political Economy
GANINO, M., Comparative Public Law
GARAVELLO, O., Economic Politics
GARZONE, G. E., English
ICHINO, P., Labour Law
ISENBURG, T., Political and Economic Geography
ITALIA, V., Institutions of Public Law
JULLION, M. C., French Language and Translation
LACAITA, G. C., Contemporary History
LAMBERTI ZANARDI, P., International Law
LAVAGNINO, A., Chinese and South East Asian Languages and Literatures
LEONINI, L., Sociology of Cultural and Communicative Processes
LIVORSI, F., History of Political Doctrine
LUPONE, A. M. G., International Law
MARAFFI, M., General Sociology
MARTELLI, P., Political Science
MARTINELLI, A., Political Science
MAURI, A., Economics of Credit Institutions
MAZZOLENI, F., Sociology of Cultural and Communicative Processes
MISSALE, A., Political Economy
MOIOLI, A., Economic History
MOLTENI, C., Japanese and Korean Languages and Literatures
MOSS, D. M., Demo-etno-anthropology
NICOLINI, G., Statistics
OLLA, M. P., History of International Relations
PEDRAZZI, M., International Law
PILOTTI, L., Economics and Management Studies
REGALIA, I., Sociology of Economic and Labour Processes
REGINI, M., Industrial Relations
REGONINI, G., Political Science
RIMINI, C. P., Institutions of Private Law
RIOSA, A., Contemporary History
RIVOLTA, G. C., Commercial Law

RONFANI, P., Juridical Sociology of Deviance and Social Change
RUFFINI, M. L., Comparative Private Law
SALVATI, M. A., Political Economy
SANTONI, M., Public Economy
SEGATTI, P., Political Phenomena and Sociology
TURSI, A., Labour Law
VENTURINI, G., International Law
VIARENGO, I., International Law
VIVAN, I., English Literature
ZICCARDI, F. E., Comparative Private Law

Faculty of Sciences (Via Saldini 50, 20133 Milan; tel. 02-50316001; fax 02-50316004; e-mail presidenza.scienze@unimi.it; internet www.unimi.it/ateneo/facol/smfn.htm):

ACERBI, E., Physics Experiments
ANNUNZIATA, R., Organic Chemistry
APOLLONI, B., Informatics
ARDIZZONE, S., Physical Chemistry
ARTIOLI, G., Mineralogy
BAMBUSI, D. P., Mathematical Physics
BELLINI, B., Physics Experiments
BELLOBONO, I. R., General and Inorganic Chemistry
BELLONE, E., History of Science and Technology
BERETTA, G. P., Applied Geology
BERTIN, G., Astronomy and Astrophysics
BERTINO, E., Database and Information Systems
BERTOLINI, M., Geometry
BERTONI, A., Theoretical Computer Science
BIRATTARI, C., Physics
BLASI, A., Mineralogy
BOLOGNESI, M., Biochemistry
BONETTI, R., Nuclear and Sub-Nuclear Physics
BONIFACIO, R., Institutions of Theoretical Physics
BORIANI, A., Petrography
BORTIGNON, P. F., Nuclear and Sub-Nuclear Physics
BOTTAZZINI, U., Complementary Mathematics
BRACCO, A., Physics Experiments
BROGLIA, R. A., Theory of Nuclear Structures
BRUSCHI, D., Informatics
CAMPADELLI, P., Informatics
CANDIA, M. D., Zoology
CANUTO, G., Geometry
CAPASSO, V., Mathematical Statistics
CARACCIOLO, S., Theoretical Physics and Mathematical Models and Methods
CASTANO, S., Computer Science
CAVALLINI, G., General Pedagogy
CENINI, S., General and Inorganic Chemistry
CESA BIANCHI, N. A., Informatics
CIANI, G. F., Inorganic Chemistry
CINQUINI, M., Organic Chemistry
COLOMBO, R., Cytology and Histology
COTTA RAMUSINO, P., Theoretical Physics and Mathematical Models and Methods
COZZI, F., Organic Chemistry
DAMIANI, E., Informatics
DANIELI, B., Physical Methods in Organic Chemistry
D'ANTONA, O., Informatics
DE BERNARDI, F., Zoology
DEDÒ, M., Geometry
DE FALCO, D., Calculus of Probability and Mathematical Statistics
DEGLI ANTONI, G., Applied Computer Science (Programming)
DEHÒ, G., Genetics
DEJANA, E., General Pathology
DE MICHELIS, M., Plant Physiology
D'ESTE, G., Algebra
DESTRO, R., Physical and Chemical Laboratory
DI FRANCESCO, D., General Physiology
ERBA, E., Palaeontology and Palaeoecology
FAELLI, A., General Physiology

FERRAGUTI, M., Zoology
FERRARI, R., Statistical Mechanics
FERRARIO, A., Mineral Deposits
FERRUTI, P., Macromolecular Chemistry
FOIANI, M., Molecular Biology
FORNI, L., Physical Chemistry
FORNILI, S. L., Physics
FORTE, S., Theoretical Physics and Mathematical Models and Methods
GADIOLI, E., Nuclear Physics
GAETANI, M., Geology
GALASSI, S., Ecology
GALGANI, L., Pure Mechanics
GALLI, E. A., General Microbiology
GARLASCHELLI, L., General and Inorganic Chemistry
GENNARI, C., Organic Chemical Laboratory
GHILARDI, S., Logic and Philosophy of Science
GIANINETTI, E., Theoretical Chemistry
GIAVINI, E., Comparative Anatomy
GIGLIO, M., Physics Experiments
GORLA, M., Genetics
GOSSO, G., Structural Geology
GRAMACCIOLI, C., Physical Chemistry
GREGNANIN, A., Petrography
HAUS, G., Computer Science
JADOUL, F., Regional Geology
JENNINGS, R., Photobiology
LANDINI, D., Industrial Chemistry
LANTERI, A., Geometry
LANZ, L., Institutions of Theoretical Physics
LICANDRO, E., Physical Chemistry
LONGHI, P., Electrochemistry
LONGO, C., Botany
LORENZI, A., Mathematical Analysis
MAIORANA, S., Organic Chemistry
MANDELLI, L., General Physics
MANITTO, P. M., Chemistry of Natural Organic Substances
MANTOVANI, R., Genetics
MARANESI, P., Electronics
MARTELLA, G., Information Systems
MERONI, E., Experimental Physics
MILANI, P., Material Structure
MILAZZO, M., Physical Methodology in the Arts
MOSCA, A., Clinical Biochemistry and Molecular Biology
MUSSINI, T., Electrochemistry
MUSSIO, P., Informatics
NALDI, G., Numerical Analysis
NICOLA, P. C., Mathematical Economics
NICORA, A., Palaeontology and Palaeoecology
ORSINI, F., Organic Chemistry
PAGANONI, L., Mathematical Analysis
PALLESCHI, M., Institutions of Advanced Geometry
PANERAI, A., Pharmacology
PAULMICHL, M., Physiology
PAVARINO, L. F., Numerical Analysis
PAVERI, F. S., Institutions of Mathematics
PEROTTI, M. E., Cytology and Histology
PESOLE, G., Molecular Biology
PIGHIZZINI, G., Computer Science
PIGNANELLI, M., Institutions of Nuclear and Subnuclear Physics
PIURI, V., Information Processing Systems
PIZZOTTI, M., General and Inorganic Chemistry
PLEVANI, P., Molecular Biology
POLI, S., Petrology and Petrography
POZZOLI, R., Material Structure
PREMOLI SILVA, I., Micropalaeontology
PROVINI, A., Ecology
RAGAINI, V., Chemical Industrial Processes and Systems
RAGUSA, A., Experimental Physics
RAIMONDI, M., Physical Chemistry
REATTO, L., Material Structure
RIGOLI, M., Geometry
ROSSI, G. P., Informatics
ROSSI, M., General and Inorganic Chemistry

RUF, B., Mathematical Analysis
RUSSO, G., Organic Chemistry
SABADINI, R., Terrestrial Physics
SAINO, N., Ecology
SALA, F., Botany
SAMARATI, P., Computer Science
SANNICOLÒ, F., Organic Chemistry
SCARABOTTOLO, N., Computer Science
SCOLASTICO, C., Organic Chemistry
SEGALE, A., Rural Economics and Surveying
SERRA, E., Mathematical Analysis
SIRONI, A., General and Inorganic Chemistry
SIRONI, G., Genetics
SMIRAGLIA, C., Physical Geography and Geomorphology
SOAVE, C., Plant Physiology
SPERANZA, G., Organic Chemistry
STURANI, E. P., Cellular Biochemistry
TANTARDINI, G. F., Physical Chemistry
TINTORI, A., Palaeontology and Palaeoecology
TONELLI, C., Genetics
TRASATTI, S., Electrochemistry
TUCCI, P., History of Physics
UGO, R., General Inorganic Chemistry
VALLE, G., Computer Science
VAN GEEMAN, L., Geometry
VANONI, M. A., Biochemistry
VERDI, C., Institutions of Mathematics
VITELLARO, L., Comparative Anatomy and Cytology
ZAMBELLI, V., Algebra
ZANETTI, G., Biological Chemistry
ZANON, D., Theory of Physics, Mathematical Models and Methods

Faculty of Veterinary Medicine (Via Celoria 10, 20133 Milan; tel. 02-50318002; fax 02-50318004; e-mail presveter@unimi.it; internet www.unimi.it/ateneo/facol/medvet.htm):

ADDIS, F., Clinical Veterinary Surgery
BALDI, A., Animal Nutrition and Foodstuffs
BELLOLI, A. G., Medical Veterinary Semiology
BERETTA, C., Pharmacology, Pharmacodynamics and Veterinary Pharmacy
BONIZZI, L., Veterinary Microbiology and Immunology
BONTEMPO, V., Animal Nutrition and Diet
CAIROLI, F., Clinical Obstetrics and Veterinary Gynaecology
CANTONI, C. A., Animal Food Products Inspection and Control
CARENZI, C., Morpho-Functional Evaluation of Animal Production
CARLI, S., Veterinary Pharmacology and Toxicology
CATTANEO, P., Animal Food Products Inspection and Control
CLEMENT, M. G., Veterinary Physiology
CODAZZA, D. M., Infectious Diseases of Domestic Animals
CORINO, C., Animal Foodstuffs and Nutrition
CREMONESI, F., Veterinary Obstetrics and Gynaecology
CRIMELLA, C., Special Zootechnics
DE GRESTI DI SANLEONARDO, A., Surgical Veterinary Semiology
DELL' ORTO, V., Animal Foodstuffs and Nutrition
DOMENEGHINI, C., Systematic and Comparative Veterinary Anatomy
FERRANDI, B., Systematic and Comparative Veterinary Anatomy
FERRO, E., Clinical Veterinary Medicine
FINAZZI, M., Veterinary Pathological Anatomy
FONDA, D., Surgical Veterinary Semiology
GALLAZI, D., Infectious Diseases of Domestic Animals
GANDOLFI, F., Anatomy of Domestic Animals

GENCHI, C., Parasitic Diseases
GUIDOBONO CAVALCHINI, A., Mechanization of Farming Processes.
GUIDOBONO CAVALCHINI, L., Aviculture
LANFRANCHI, P., Veterinary Parasitology
LAURIA, A., Veterinary, Systematic and Comparative Anatomy
MORTELLARO, C., Veterinary Surgical Pathology
NAVAROTTO, P., Rural and Forest Construction
PAGNACCO, G., Animal Genetic Improvement and General Husbandry
PEZZA, F., Clinical Veterinary Medicine
PIRANI, A., Rural Economics and Surveying
POLI, G., Veterinary Microbiology and Immunology
POMPA, G., Veterinary Toxicology
PONTI, W., Infectious Diseases of Domestic Animals
PORCELLI, F., General and Special Histology and Embryology
POZZA, O., Pathology of Domestic Animals
RONCHI, S., Biochemistry
RUFFO, G., Infectious Diseases, Prophylaxis and Veterinary Inspection
SALA, V., Infectious Diseases of Domestic Animals
SARTORELLI, P., Veterinary General Pathology and Pathological Anatomy
SAVOINI, G., Foodstuffs Technology
SCANZIANI, E., General and Veterinary Anatomical Pathology
SECCHI, C. L., Biochemistry
VALFRÈ, F., Supply, Markets and Rural Industries
VERGA, M., Specialized Zootechnics
ZECCONI, A., Infectious Diseases of Domestic Animals

UNIVERSITÀ DEGLI STUDI DI MILANO-BICOCCA

Piazza dell'Ateneo Nuovo 1, 20126 Milan
Telephone: 02-64481
E-mail: international.office@unimib.it
Internet: www.unimib.it
Founded 1998
Academic year: October to September
Rector: Prof. MARCELLO FONTANESI
Vice-Rector: Prof. SUSANNA MANTOVANI
Admin. Dir: CANDELORO BELLANTONI
Number of teachers: 910
Number of students: 35,689

DEANS

Faculty of Economics: Prof. MASSIMO SAITA
Faculty of Education: Prof. SILVIA KANIZSA
Faculty of Law: Prof. BRUNO BOSCO
Faculty of Mathematical, Physical and Natural Sciences: Prof. FRANCESCO NICOTRA
Faculty of Medicine and Surgery: Prof. ANDREA STELLA
Faculty of Psychology: Prof. LAURA D'ODORICO
Faculty of Sociology: Prof. ANTONIO DE LILLO
Faculty of Statistics: Prof. GIOVANNI CORRAO

UNIVERSITÀ DEGLI STUDI DI MODENA E REGGIO EMILIA

Via Università 4, 41121 Modena
Telephone: 059-2056511
Fax: 059-245156
E-mail: rettore@unimore.it
Internet: www.unimore.it
Founded 1175
Academic year: November to October
Rector: Prof. ALDO TOMASI
Vice-Rector (Modena Campus): Prof. SERGIO PABA
Vice-Rector (Reggio Emilia Campus): Prof. LUIGI GRASSELLI
Admin. Dir: Dott. STEFANO RONCHETTI

Library Dir: Dott. MARIA RAFFAELLA INGROSSO
Library of 294,000 vols
Number of teachers: 700
Number of students: 14,564

DEANS

Faculty of Agriculture: Prof. DOMENICO PIETRO LO FIEGO
Faculty of Arts: Prof. MARINA BONDI
Faculty of Biosciences and Biotechnology: Prof. SERGIO FERRARI
Faculty of Communications and Economics: Prof. GIOVANNA GALLI
'Marco Biagi' Faculty of Economics: Prof. EUGENIO CAPERCHIONE
Faculty of Education: Prof. GIORGIO ZANETTI
'Enzo Ferrari' Faculty of Engineering: Prof. GIUSEPPE CANTORE
Faculty of Engineering (Reggio Emilia): Prof. EUGENIO DRAGONI
Faculty of Law: Prof. RENZO LAMBERTINI
Faculty of Mathematical, Physical and Natural Sciences: Prof. CARLO MARIA BERTONI
Faculty of Medicine and Surgery: Prof. GABRIELLA AGGAZZOTTI
Faculty of Pharmacy: Prof. ALBERTINO BIGIANI

PROFESSORS

Faculty of Agricultural Science and Technology (Via Kennedy 17, 42100 Reggio Emilia; tel. 0522-383232; fax 0522-304217; internet www.rcs.re.it/corsi/agraria.htm):

BIANCHI, U., Genetics
GIUDICI, P., Agroalimentary and Environmental Microbiology
PELLEGRINI, M., Applied Geology
TONGIORGI, P., Zoology

Faculty of Arts and Philosophy (Via Berengario 51, 41100 Modena; tel. 059-2056911; fax 059-2056917):

BONDI, M., English Linguistics
DRUMBL, J., German Linguistics
TOCCI, G., Modern History

Faculty of Economics (Via Berengario 51, 41100 Modena; tel. 059-2056911; fax 059-2056917; e-mail preside.economia@unimo.it; internet www.economia.unimo.it):

BISONI, C., Professional and Banking Procedures
BOSI, P., Finance and Financial Law
BRUSCO, S., Economics and Industrial Policy
BURSI, T., Industrial and Commercial Techniques
FERRARI, A., Stock Exchange Techniques
GINZBURG, A., Economic and Financial Policy
GOLZIO, L. E., Work Study
GRANDORI, A., Personnel Management
LANE, D. A., Statistics
RICCI, G., Financial Mathematics

Faculty of Engineering (Via Campi 213/A, 41100 Modena; tel. 059-2055107; fax 059-366293; e-mail preside.ingegneria@unimo.it; internet www.ing.unimo.itViale Allegri 15, 42100 Reggio Emilia; tel. 0522-406356; fax 0522-496466; e-mail preside.ingre@unimo.it; internet www.ingre.unimo.it):

ALBERIGI, A., Electronics
ANDRISANO, A. O., Industrial Design
BAROZZI, G. S., Technical Physics
BERGAMASCHI, S., Information Elaboration Systems
BISI, O., General Physics
CAMPI, S., Mathematical Analysis
CANALI, C., Applied Electronics
CANNAROZZI, M., Construction Theory
CANTORE, G.
CECCHI, R., Environmental Sanitary Engineering
FANTINI, F., Industrial Electronics
FRANCESCHINI, V., Rational Mechanics

GRASSELLI, L., Geometry
IMMOVILLI, G., Electronic Communications
NANNARONE, S., Physics
PELLACANI, G. C., General and Inorganic Chemistry
PILATI, F., Macromolecular Chemistry
RIMINI, B., Industrial Plant Mechanics
SANDROLINI, S., Hydraulic Machinery
STROZZI, A.
TIBERIO, P., Information Elaboration Systems
ZOBOLI, M.

Faculty of Jurisprudence (tel. 059-2056589; fax 059-417522; e-mail preside .giurisprudenza@unimo.it; internet www .giurisprudenza.unimo.it):

ALESSANDRINI, S., Economic Policy
ANTONINI, A., Navigation Law
BIONE, M., Commercial Law
BONFATTI, S., Banking Law
BORGHESI, D., Law of Civil Procedure
CALANDRA BUONAURA, V., Commercial Law
DONINI, M., Penal Law
GALANTINO, L., Labour Law
GASPARINI CASARI, V., Administrative Law
GIANOLIO, R. C., Administrative Law
GUERZONI, L., Ecclesiastical Law
LAMBERTINI, R., Institutions of Roman Law
LUBERTO, S., Anthropology and Criminology
MARANI, F., General Private Law
PANFORTI, M. D., Comparative Private Law
SILINGARDI, G., Transport Law
VIGNUDELLI, A., Constitutional Law

Faculty of Mathematics, Physics and Natural Sciences (Via Campi 213/A, 41100 Modena; tel. 059-371834; fax 059-270809; e-mail preside.scienze@unimo.it; internet www .scienze.unimo.it):

ACCORSI, C. A., Phytogeography
BERTOLANI, R., Zoology
BERTONI, C. M., Theoretical Physics
BONI, M., Mathematical Analysis
BORTOLANI, V., Solid State Physics
CALANDRA BUONAURA, C., Structure of Materials
CAPEDRI, S., Petrography
CAVICCHIOLI, A., Institutes of Advanced Geometry
CHITI, G., Mathematical Analysis
CREMA, R., Ecology
DEL PRETE, C., Botany
DIECI, G., Micropalaeontology
FANTIN, A. M., Histology and Embryology
FAZZINI, P., Geology
FUNARO, D., Numerical Analysis
GAGLIARDI, C., Geometry II
JACOBONI, C., Atomic Physics
LARATTA, A., Numerical Analysis and Programming
LAZZERETTI, P., Physical Chemistry
LEVONI, S., Foundations of Mathematical Physics
MAGHERINI, P. C., General Physiology
MARINI, M., Comparative Anatomy
MENABUE, L., General and Inorganic Chemistry
MESCHIARI, M., Geometry
MIRONE, P., Physical Chemistry
MOMICCHIOLI, F., Physical Chemistry
OTTAVIANI, E., Comparative Anatomy and Cytology
OTTAVIANI, G., Physics (Preparation of Experiments)
PAGLIAI, A. M., Zoology
PAGNONI, U. M., Organic Chemistry
PALYI, G., Chemical Composition
PANIZZA, M., Physical Geography
PASSAGLIA, E., Mineralogy
PRUDENZIATI, M., Applied Electronics
QUATTROCCHI, P., Advanced Elementary Mathematics
RIVALENTI, G., Metamorphic Petrography
RUSSO, A., Palaeoecology
SANTANGELO, R., Terrestrial Physics

SEGRE, U., Electrochemistry
SERPAGLI, E., Palaeontology
SIGHINOLFI, G., Geochemistry
TADDEI, F., Advanced Organic Chemistry
TORRE, G., Organic Chemistry

Faculty of Medicine and Surgery (Via del Pozzo 71, 41100 Modena; tel. 059-422398; fax 059-374037; e-mail preside.medicina@unimo .it; internet wwww.medicina.unimo.it):

AGGAZZOTTI, G., Hygiene and Dentistry
AGNATI, L. F., Human Physiology
ALBERTAZZI, A., Nephrology
ARTIBANI, W., Urology
BAGGIO, G. G., Pharmacology
BALLI, R., Otorhinolaryngology
BARBOLINI, G., Anatomy, Histology and Pathology
BEDUSCHI, G., Forensic Medicine
BERGOMI, M., Hygiene and Odontology
BERNASCONI, S., Paediatrics
BERTOLINI, A., Pharmacology
BLASI, E., Microbiology
BOBYLEVA, V., General Pathology
BON, L., Human Physiology
BORELLA, P., General and Applied Hygiene
CALANDRA BUONAURA, S., General Pathology
CANÉ, V.
CARULLI, N., Medical Pathology and Clinical Methodology
CAVAZZUTI, G. B., Clinical Paediatrics
CELLI, L., Orthopaedics and Traumatology
CONSOLO, U., Odontostomatological Special Surgery
CORAZZA, R., Human Physiology
CORTESI, N., General Clinical Surgery and Surgical Therapy
CORTI, A., Biological Chemistry
CURCI, P., Psychiatry
DE BERNARDINIS, G., General Surgery
DE FAZIO, F. A., Forensic and Insurance Medicine
DE GAETANI, C., Foundations of Medicine and Histological Pathology
DELLA CASA, L., Infectious Diseases
ESPOSITO, R., Infectious Diseases
FABBRI, L., Respiratory Diseases
FABIO, U., Microbiology
FAGLIONI, P., Clinical Neurology
FERRARI, F., Pharmacology
FERRARI, S., Applied Biology
FERRARI, S., Biological Chemistry
FORABOSCO, A., Histology and Embryology
GALETTI, G., Clinical Otorhinolaryngology
GIANNETTI, A., Clinical Dermatology
GUARALDI, G. P., Clinical Psychiatry
GUERRA, R., Clinical Ophthalmology
JASONNI, V. M., Obstetrics and Gynaecology
LODI, R. G., Thoracic Surgery
MANENTI, F., Gastroenterology
MAROTTI, G., Human Anatomy
MATTIOLI, G., Cardiology
MODENA, M. G., Cardiology
MONTI, M. G., Biological Chemistry
MORUZZI, M. S., Chemical Biology
MUSCATELLO, U., General Pathology
PASETTO, A., Anaesthesiology
PONZ DE LEON, M., Internal Medicine
PORTOLANI, M., Virology
ROMAGNOLI, R., Radiology
SALVIOLI, G., Surgical Pathology
SAVIANO, M., Surgical Pathology
SEIDENARI, S., Allergological Dermatology
SILINGARDI, V., Special Medical Pathology and Clinical Methodology
STELLA, A., Vascular Surgery
STERNIERI, E., Clinical Pharmacology
TOMASI, A., General Physiopathology
TORELLI, G., Haematology
TORELLI, U., General Clinical Medicine and Therapy
TRENTINI, G. P., Anatomy and Pathological History

VENTURA, E., General Clinical Medicine and Therapy
VIVOLI, G., Hygiene
VOLPE, A., Physiopathology of Human Reproduction
ZENEROLI, M. L., Semiotics
ZINI, I., Human Physiology

Faculty of Pharmacy (Via Campi 183, 41100 Modena; tel. 059-2055169; fax 059-373602; e-mail preside.farmacia@unimo.it; internet www.farmacia.unimo.it):

ALBASINI, A., Applied Pharmaceutical Chemistry and Toxicology
BARALDI, M., Pharmacology
BERNABEI, M. T., Pharmaceutical Procedures and Legislation
BRASILI, L., Pharmaceutical and Toxicological Chemistry
CAMERONI, R., Applied Pharmaceutical Chemistry
FORNI, F., Pharmaceutical Procedures and Legislation
GALLI, E., Mineralogy
GAMBERINI, G., Pharmaceutical Chemical Analysis
MELEGARI, M., Pharmaceutical Chemical Analysis II
MONZANI, V. A., Pharmaceutical Chemical Analysis
PECORARI, P., Pharmaceutical Chemical Analysis
PIETRA, P., General Physiology
QUAGLIO, G., Hygiene

UNIVERSITÀ DEGLI STUDI DI NAPOLI 'FEDERICO II'

Corso Umberto I, 80138 Naples
Telephone: 081-2531111
Fax: 081-2537330
E-mail: webint@unina.it
Internet: www.unina.it
Founded 1224

Rector: Prof. MASSIMO MARRELLI
Pro-Rector: Prof. GAETANO MANFREDI
Admin. Dir: Dott. MARIA LUIGIA LIGUORI
Library of 1,200,000 vols, 18,000 journals
Number of teachers: 1,483
Number of students: 94,510

DEANS

Faculty of Agriculture: Prof. PAOLO MASSI
Faculty of Architecture: Prof. CLAUDIO CLAUDI DE SAINT MIHIEL
Faculty of Arts: Prof. ARTURO DE VIVO
Faculty of Biotechnology: Prof. GENNARO PICCIALLI
Faculty of Economics: Prof. ACHILLE BASILE
Faculty of Engineering: Prof. PIERO SALATINO
Faculty of Law: Prof. LUCIO DE GIOVANNI
Faculty of Mathematical, Physical and Natural Sciences: Prof. ROBERTO PETTORINO
Faculty of Medicine and Surgery: Prof. GIOVANNI PERSICO
Faculty of Pharmacy: Prof. GIUSEPPE CIRINO
Faculty of Political Science: Prof. MARCO MUSELLA
Faculty of Sociology: Prof. GIANFRANCO PECCHINENDA
Faculty of Veterinary Medicine: Prof. LUIGI ZICARELLI

UNIVERSITÀ DEGLI STUDI DI NAPOLI – L'ORIENTALE

Via Partenope 10/A, 80121 Naples
Telephone: 081-7643230
Fax: 081-6909112
Internet: www.iuo.it
Founded 1732

Chancellor: Prof. LIDA VIGANONI
Vice-Chancellor: Prof. GIUSEPPE CATALDI
Pro-Rector for Teaching: Prof. ELDA MORTICCHIO

Admin. Dir: Dott. CLAUDIO BORRELLI
Library of 673,000 vols

DEANS

Faculty of Arabian-Islamic and Mediterranean Studies: Prof. AGOSTINO CILARDO
Faculty of Arts: Prof. AMNERIS ROSELLI
Faculty of Foreign Languages and Literature: Prof. AUGUSTO GUARINO
Faculty of Political Science: Prof. GIORGIO AMITRANO

UNIVERSITÀ DEGLI STUDI DI PADOVA

Via 8 Febbraio 2, 35122 Padua
Telephone: 049-8275111
Fax: 049-8273009
E-mail: rettore@unipd.it
Internet: www.unipd.it
Founded 1222
Rector: Prof. GIUSEPPE ZACCARIA
Vice-Rector: Prof. FRANCESCO GNESOTTO
Admin. Dir: Arch. GIUSEPPE BARBIERI
Librarian: Dott. MAURIZIO VEDALDI
Number of teachers: 1,382
Number of students: 60,000

DEANS

Faculty of Arts: Prof. MICHELE CORTELAZZO
Faculty of Agriculture: Prof. GIANCARLO DALLA FONTANA
Faculty of Economics: Prof. ENRICO RETTORE
Faculty of Education: Prof. GIUSEPPE MICHELI
Faculty of Engineering: Prof. PIERFRANCESCO BRUNELLO
Faculty of Law: Prof. GHERARDO BERGONZINI
Faculty of Mathematical, Physical, and Natural Sciences: Prof. RENATO BOZIO
Faculty of Medicine and Surgery: Prof. GIORGIO PALÙ
Faculty of Pharmacy: Prof. GIULIANO BANDOLI
Faculty of Political Science: Prof. GIANNI RICCAMBONI
Faculty of Psychology: Prof. PIETRO BOSCOLO
Faculty of Statistical Sciences: Prof. GIANPIERO DALLA ZUANNA
Faculty of Veterinary Medicine: Prof. MASSIMO CASTAGNARO

UNIVERSITÀ DEGLI STUDI DI PALERMO

Piazza Marina 61, 90133 Palermo
Telephone: 091-270111
E-mail: info@unipa.it
Internet: www.unipa.it
Founded 1777
Rector: Prof. ROBERTO LAGALLA
Vice-Rector: Prof. ENNIO CARDONA
Admin. Dir: Dott. ANTONIO VALENTI
Number of teachers: 1,300
Number of students: 70,000
Publications: Annali del Seminario Giuridico, Circolo Giuridico 'L. Sampolo'

DEANS

Faculty of Agriculture: Prof. GIUSEPPE GIORDANO
Faculty of Arts: Prof. MARIO GANDOLFO GIACOMARRA
Faculty of Architecture: Prof. ANGELO MILONE
Faculty of Economics: Prof. FABIO MAZZOLA
Faculty of Education: Prof. MICHELE COMETA
Faculty of Engineering: Prof. Ing. FABRIZIO MICARI
Faculty of Law: Prof. ANTONIO SCAGLIONE
Faculty of Arts: Prof. MARIO GANDOLFO GIACOMARRA
Faculty of Mathematical, Physical and Natural Sciences: Prof. ROBERTO BOSCAINO

Faculty of Medicine and Surgery: Prof. GIACOMO DE LEO
Faculty of Pharmacy: Prof. GIROLAMO CIRRINCIONE
Faculty of Politics: Prof. ANTONELLO MIRANDA
Faculty of Sports Science: Prof. GIUSEPPE LIOTTA

UNIVERSITÀ DEGLI STUDI DI PARMA

Via Università 12, 43121 Parma
Telephone: 0521-032111
Fax: 0521-034357
E-mail: protocollo@pec.unipr.it
Internet: www.unipr.it
Founded 962
Academic year: October to September
Rector: Prof. GINO FERRETTI
Deputy Rector: Prof. CARLO CHEZZI
Admin. Dir: Dott. RODOLFO POLDI
Number of teachers: 1,100
Number of students: 30,000

DEANS

Faculty of Agriculture: Prof. ERASMO NEVIANI
Faculty of Architecture: Prof. IVO IORI
Faculty of Economics: Prof. GIAN PIERO LUGLI
Faculty of Engineering: Prof. ANTONIO MONTEPARA
Faculty of Humanities: Prof. ROBERTO GRECI
Faculty of Law: Prof. LAURA PINESCHI
Faculty of Mathematical, Physical and Natural Sciences: Prof. GIAN LUIGI ROSSI
Faculty of Medicine and Surgery: Prof. LORIS BORGHI
Faculty of Pharmacy: Prof. PAOLO COLOMBO
Faculty of Politics: Prof. ALESSANDRO DUCE
Faculty of Psychology: Prof. SILVIA PERINI
Faculty of Veterinary Medicine: Prof. ATTILIO CORRADI

UNIVERSITÀ DEGLI STUDI DI PAVIA

Corso Strada Nuova 65, 27100 Pavia
Telephone: 0382-9811
Fax: 0382-504529
E-mail: rettore@unipv.it
Internet: www.unipv.eu
Founded 1361 by Emperor Charles IV
Academic year: November to October
Rector: Prof. ANGIOLINO STELLA
Admin. Dir: Dr GIOVANNI COLUCCI
Number of teachers: 1,120
Number of students: 23,000
Publication: Annuario (online)

DEANS

Faculty of Arts and Philosophy: Prof. ELISA ROMANO
Faculty of Economics: Prof. CARLUCCIO BIANCHI
Faculty of Engineering: Prof. Ing. CARLO CIAPONI
Faculty of Law: Prof. ETTORE DEZZA
Faculty of Mathematical, Physical and Natural Science: Prof. LUCIO TOMA
Faculty of Medicine and Surgery: Prof. ANTONIO DAL CANTON
Faculty of Musicology: Prof. GIANCARLO PRATO
Faculty of Pharmacy: Prof. AMEDEO MARINI
Faculty of Political Sciences: Prof. FABIO RUGGE

UNIVERSITÀ DEGLI STUDI DI PERUGIA

Piazza dell' Università 1, 06100 Perugia
Telephone: 075-5851
Fax: 075-5852067
E-mail: gestione@unipg.it
Internet: www.unipg.it

Founded 1276
State control
Academic year: November to October
Rector: Prof. FRANCESCO BISTONI
Admin. Dir: Dott.ssa ANGELA MARIA LACAITA
Pro-Rector: Prof. ANTONIO PIERETTI
Librarian: PAOLO BELLINI
Number of teachers: 312
Number of students: 31,746
Publications: La Salute Umana, L'Università, Rivista di Biologia, Rivista di Dermatologia, Rivista di Idrobiologia

DEANS

Faculty of Agriculture: Prof. FRANCESCO PENNACCHI
Faculty of Economics: Prof. PIERLUIGI DADDI
Faculty of Education: Prof. ROMANO UGOLINI
Faculty of Engineering: Prof. GIANNI BIDINI
Faculty of Law: Prof. MAURO BOVE
Faculty of Humanities: Prof. GIORGIO BONAMENTE
Faculty of Mathematical, Physical and Natural Sciences: Prof. FAUSTO ELISEI
Faculty of Medicine and Surgery: Prof. LUCIANO BINAGLIA
Faculty of Pharmacy: Prof. CARLO ROSSI
Faculty of Political Science: Prof. GIORGIO EDUARDO MONTANARI
Faculty of Veterinary Medicine: Prof. FRANCO MORICONI

PROFESSORS

Faculty of Agrarian Science:
ABBOZZO, P., Farm Evaluation
BENCIVENGA, M., Systematic Agricultural Botany
BERNARDINI BATTAGLINI, M., Animal Husbandry
BIANCHI, A. A., Herbaceous Cultivation
BIN, F., Biological Techniques
BONCIARELLI, F., Cultivation of Special Herbaceous Plants
BUSINELLI, M., Soil Chemistry
CIRICIOFOLO, E., Biology, Production and Technology of Seeds
COSTANTINI, F., Animal Nutrition and Feeding
COVARELLI, G., Weed Control
DURANTI, E., Physiology of Animals in Stockbreeding
FALCINELLI, M., Genetic Improvement in Cultivated Plants
FANTOZZI, P., Alimentation
FATICHENTI, F., Agrarian and Arboreal Microbiology
GIOVAGNOTTI, C.
LORENZETTI, F., Agrarian Genetics
MANNOCCHI, F., Agrarian Hydraulics
MARTE, M., Plant Pathology
MARTINI, A., Agrarian Microbiology
MARUCCHINI, C., Introductory Agrarian Chemistry
MENNELLA, V. G., Agricultural and Forestry Planning
MONOTTI, M., General Agriculture
MONTEDORO, G., Agricultural Industries
PENNACCHI, F., Agrarian Economics
RAGGI, V., Plant Pathology
ROMANO, B., Morphology and Plant Physiology
ROSSI, A. C., Economics and Agrarian Policy
ROSSI, J., Dairy Food Microbiology
SARTI, D. M., Stockbreeding
SCARPONI, L., Agrarian Biochemistry
SOLINAS, M., Agricultural Entomology
STANDARDI, A., Specialist Fruit Growing
TOMBESI, A., General Fruit Growing
VERONESI, F., Genetic Biotechnology
ZAZZERINI, A., Phytotherapy

Faculty of Economics:
BORGIA, R., Institutions of Private Law
BRACALENTE, B., Economics Statistics

CALZONI, G., Political Economy
CAVAZZONI, G., Accountancy
CHIARELLE, R., Institutions of Public Law
CICCHITELLI, G., Statistics
CORALLINI, S., Banking
FORCINA, A., Statistics
GRASSELLI, P. M., Political Economy
MEZZACAPO, V., Banking Legislation
MORICONI, F., Mathematics
PAGLIACCI, G., General Mathematics
PERONI, G., Marketing
RIDOLFI, M., Political Economy
SEDIARI, T., Agrarian Economics and Politics
SEVERINO, P., Commercial Penal Law

Faculty of Education:

BALDINI, M., History of Philosophy
BUCCI, S., General Education
DOTTI, U., Italian Language and Literature
FINZI, C., History of Political Doctrine
FISSI MIGLIORINI, R., Dantesque Philology
FURIOZZI, G. B., History of Umbria
MANCINI, F. F., History of Umbrian Art
MIRRI, E., Philosophy
PERUGI, M., Romance Philology
PETRONI, F., History of Modern and Contemporary Italian Literature
RICCIOLI, G., French Language and Literature
ROSATI, L., Teaching
SANTINI, C., Latin Language and Literature
SETAIOLI, A., Latin Grammar
UGOLINI, R., Contemporary History
ZURLI, L., Latin Philology

Faculty of Engineering:

BALLI, R., Applied Mechanics
BASILI, P., Electromagnetic Fields
BATTISTON, R., Physics
BERNA, L., Urban Technology
BIDINI, G., Machines
BORRI, A., Construction Theory
BRANDI, P., Mathematical Analysis
BURRASCANO, P., Electrotechnology
CANDELORO, D., Mathematical Analysis I
CONTI, P., Industrial Technical Drawing
CORRADINI, C., Technical Hydrology
FELLI, M., Technical Physics
LA CAVA, M., Automatic Controls
LIUTI, G., Chemistry
MAZZOLAI, F. M., Physics
PALMIERI, L., Physics
PARDUCCI, A., Construction Technology
PUCCI, E., Advanced Mechanical Engineering
SOCINO, G., Physics
SOLETTI, A. C., Design
SORRENTINI, R., Electromagnetic Fields
TACCONI, P., Applied Geology
VECCHIOCATTIVI, F., Chemistry

Faculty of Jurisprudence:

AZZARITI, G., Constitutional Law
BADIALI, G., International Law
BARBERINI, G., Ecclesiastical Law
CAPRIOLI, S., History of Modern Italian Law
CARDI, E., Procedural Law
CAVALAGLIO, A., Bankruptcy Law
CAVALLO, B., Administrative Law
CINELLI, M., Labour Law
DALLERA, G. F., Finance and Financial Law
GAITO, A., Penal Law
MIGLIORINI, L., Administrative Law
MORSELLI, E., Penal Law
PALAZZO, A., Institutions of Private Law
PALAZZOLO, N., History of Roman Law
PEPPE, L., Roman Law
SALVI, C., Civil Law
SASSANI, M., Civil Procedural Law
TALAMANCA, A., Canon Law
TINELLI, G., Tax Law
VOLPI, M., Constitutional Comparative Law

Faculty of Letters and Philosophy:

AGOSTINIANI, L., Linguistics
BONAMENTE, G., Roman History
CARANCINI, G. L., European Protohistory
COARELLI, F., Greek and Roman Antiquity
DI PILLA, F., French Language and Literature
FALASCHI, G., Italian Literature
FROVA, C., Medieval History
GIORDANI, R., Christian Archaeology
ISOLA, A., Ancient Christian Literature
MADDOLI, G., Greek History
MELELLI, A., Geography
MENESTÒ, E., Medieval Latin Literature
MORETTI, G., Italian Dialectology
PICCINATO, S., Anglo-American Literature
PIERETTI, A., Theoretical Philosophy
PIZZANI, U., Latin Literature
PRIVITERA, G. A., Greek Literature
RONCALLI DI MONTORIO, F., Etruscan Studies and Italic Antiquity
RUFINI, S., English Language and Literature
SANTACHIARA, U., Church History
SCARPELLINI PANCRAZI, P., History of Medieval Art
SEPPILLI, T., Cultural Anthropology
SPAGGIARI PERUGI, B., Romance Philology
TORELLI, M., Archaeology and History of Greek and Roman Art
TORTI, A., English Language and Literature

Faculty of Mathematical, Physical and Natural Sciences:

ALBERTI, G., Inorganic Chemistry
AMBROSETTI, P. L., Palaeontology
ANTONIELLI, M., Plant Physiology
AQUILANTI, V., General and Inorganic Chemistry
AVERNA, A.
BARSI, F., Theory and Application of Mechanical Calculation
BARTOCCI, U., Geometry
CATALIOTTI, R. S., Physical Chemistry
CIOFI DEGLI ATTI, C., Institutions of Nuclear Physics
CIONINI, P. G., Botany
CIROTTO, C., Cytology and Histology
CLEMENTI, S., Organic Chemistry
COLETTI, G., Institutions of Mathematics
DE TOLLIS, B. A., Institutions of Theoretical Physics
DI GIOVANNI, M. V., Zoology
FAINA, G., Geometry
FAVARO MAZZUCATO, G., Physical Chemistry
FRINGUELLI, F., Organic Chemistry
GAINO, E., Zoology
GIANFRANCHESCHI, G. L., General Physiology
GRANETTI, B., Botany
GUAZZONE, S., Algebra
IORIO, A. M., Virology
LAGANÀ, A., General and Inorganic Chemistry
LARICCIA, P., Physics Laboratory
MAFFEI, P., Astrophysics
MANTOVANI, G., General Physics
MARINO, G., Organic Chemistry
MAZZUCATO, U., Physical Chemistry
MONTANINI MEZZASOMA, I., Biochemistry
MOROZZI, G., Hygiene
MORPURGO, G. P., Genetics
NAPPI, A., General Physics
ONORI, G., Physics
ORLACCHIO, A., Biochemistry
PASCOLINI, R., Comparative Anatomy
PASSERI, L., Sedimentology
PECCERILLO, A., Petrography
PERUZZI, M. I., General Physics
PIALLI, G., Geology
PIOVESANA, O., General and Inorganic Chemistry
PUCCI, P., Mathematical Analysis
RINALDI, R., Mineralogy

SACCHETTI, F., Solid State Physics
SANTUCCI, S., Physics Laboratory
SAVELLI, G., Organic Chemistry
SGAMELLOTTI, A., Inorganic Chemistry
SRIVASTAVA YOGENDRA, N., Quantum Theory
TATICCHI, A., Organic Chemistry
TATICCHI, M. I., Ecology
TULIPANI, S., Computer Science
VERDINI, L., Structure of Matter
VOLPI, G., General and Inorganic Chemistry
ZANAZZI, P. F., Crystallography

Faculty of Medicine and Surgery:

ABBRITTI, G., Industrial Medicine
AMBROSIO, G., Cardiology
ARIENTI, G., Biological Chemistry
BARTOLI, A., General Surgery
BECCHETTI, E., Histology
BINAGLIA, L., Chemistry and Biomedicine
BISTONI, F., Microbiology
BOLIS, G. B., Anatomy and Pathological Histology
BOLLI, G., Metabolic Diseases
BORRI, P. F., Psychiatry
BRUNETTI, P., Internal Medicine
BUCCIARELLI, E., Anatomy and Pathological Histology
CALANDRA, P., Dermatology
CAPRINO, G., Radiology
CASALI, L., Diseases of the Respiratory System
DADDI, G., Surgical Pathology and Clinical Propaedeutics
DELOGU, A., Ophthalmology
D'ERRICO, P., Dental Prosthesis
DONATO, R. F., Neuroanatomy
FABRONI, F., Forensic Medicine
FALORNI, A., Paediatrics
FIORE, C., Physiopathological Optics
FRONGILLO, R. F., Infectious Diseases
FURBETTA, M., Preventive and Social Paediatrics
GALLAI, V., Neurology
GIOVANNINI, E., General Biology
GORACCI, G. F., Biological Chemistry
GRIGNANI, F., Internal Medicine
LATINI, P., Radiotherapy
LAURO, V., Gynaecology and Obstetrics
LIOTTI, F. S., General Biology
LISI, P., Dermatology
MAGNI, F., Human Physiology
MAIRA, G., Neurosurgery
MANNARINO, E., Internal Medicine
MARCONI, P., Immunology
MARTELLI, M. F., Haematology
MASTRANDREA, V., Hygiene
MODOLO, M. A., Hygiene
MOGGI, L., General Surgery
MORELLI, A., Gastroenterology
NEGRI, P. L., Paradontology
NENCI, G. G., Internal Medicine
NORELLI, G. A., Forensic Medicine
PALUMBO, R., Nuclear Medicine
PAULUZZI, S., Infectious Diseases
PECORELLI, F., Orthopaedics and Traumatology
PEDUTO, V. A., Anaesthesia and Resuscitation
PETTOROSSI, V. E., Human Physiology
PORENA, M., Urology
PUXEDDU, A., Internal Medicine
RIBACCHI, R., Anatomy and Pathological Histology
RICCARDI, C., Pharmacology
RINONAPOLI, E., Orthopaedics and Traumatology
ROSI BARBERINI, G., Cellular Biology
ROSSI, R., General Pathology
SALVADORI, P., Physics
SANTEUSANIO, F., Endocrinology
SENIN, U., Geriatrics and Gerontology
STAFFOLANI, N., Oral Surgery
STAGNI, G., Infectious Diseases
TRISTAINO, B., General Surgery

VACCARO, R., Paediatrics
VALORI, C., Internal Medicine
VILLANI, C., Oncological Gynaecology
VIOLA MAGNI, M. P., General Pathology

Faculty of Pharmacy:

CORSANO LEOPIZZI, S., Pharmaceutical and Toxicological Chemistry
COSTANTINO, U., General and Inorganic Chemistry
DAMIANI, P., Food Science Chemistry
FIORETTI CECCHERELLI, M. C., Pharmacology and Pharmacognosy
FLORIDI, A., Biochemistry
FRAVOLINI, A., Pharmaceutical and Toxicological Chemistry
GRANDOLINI, G., Socioeconomic Technology and Pharmaceutical Legislation
MENGHINI, A., Pharmaceutical Botany
PELLICCIARI, R., Pharmaceutical and Toxicological Chemistry
PUCCETTI, P., Pharmacology
ROSSI, C., Applied Pharmaceutical Chemistry
SCASSELLATI, S. G., Hygiene
TESTAFERRI, L., Organic Chemistry
TIECCO, M., Organic Chemistry
VECCHIARELLI, A., Microbiology

Faculty of Political Science:

BONO, S., History and Institutions of Afro-Asian Countries
CARINI, C., History of Political Doctrine
COMPARATO, V. I., Modern History
CRESPI, F., Sociology
D'AMOJA, F., History of International Relations
DI GASPARE, G., Economic Law
GALLI DELLA LOGGIA, E., History of Political Parties and Movements
GROHMANN, A., Economic History
MARCHISIO, S., International Law
MELOGRANI, P., Contemporary History
MERLONI, F., Administrative Justice
RAVERAIRA, M., Institutions of Public Law
TEODORI, M., American History
TOSI, L., History of Treaties and International Politics
TRAMONTANA, A., Finance

Faculty of Veterinary Medicine:

ASDRUBALI, G., Pathology of Birds
AVELLINI, G., Clinical Veterinary Medicine
BATTISTACCI, M., Clinical Veterinary Surgery
BEGHELLI, V., Veterinary Physiology and Ethology
BELLUCCI, M., Veterinary Radiology and Nuclear Medicine
BOITI, C., Veterinary Physiology and Ethology
CASTRUCCI, G., Infectious Diseases and Prophylaxis
CECCARELLI, P., Topographical Veterinary Anatomy
CHIACCHIARINI, P., Obstetrics and Gynaecology
DEBENEDETTI, A., Endocrinology of Domestic Animals
DI ANTONIO, E., Inspection and Control of Foodstuffs of Animal Origin
FRUGANTI, G., Veterinary Medical Pathology
GAITI, A., Biochemistry
GARGIULO BERSIANI, A. M., Histology and General Embryology
LORVIK, S., Anatomy of Domestic Animals
MALVISI, J., Pharmacology and Pharmacodynamics
MANGILI PECCI, V., Laboratory Diagnosis
MANOCCHIO, I., Pathological Anatomy
MORICONI, F., Veterinary Surgical Pathology
OLIVIERI, O., Animal Nutrition
POLIDORI GIROLAMO, A. B., Veterinary Parasitology

RANUCCI, S., Veterinary Medical Semiology and Clinical Methodology
SILVESTRELLI, M., Special Stockbreeding
VALENTE, C., Infectious Diseases
VITELLOZZI, G., Veterinary Pathological Anatomy

UNIVERSITÀ DEGLI STUDI DI PISA

Lungarno Pacinotti 43, 56126 Pisa
Telephone: 050-2212111
Fax: 050-40834
E-mail: rettore@unipi.it
Internet: www.unipi.it
Founded 1343
State control
Academic year: November to October

Rector: Prof. MASSIMO MARIO AUGELLO
Deputy Rector: Prof. NICOLETTA DE FRANCESCO
Vice-Rector for Applied Research and Innovation: Prof. PAOLO FERRAGINA
Vice-Rector for Budgetary Policy: Prof. ADA CARLESI
Vice-Rector for Infrastructure: Assoc. Prof. SANDRO PACI
Vice-Rector for Internationalization: Assoc. Prof. ALESSANDRO GUIDI
Vice-Rector for Legal Matters: Prof. FRANCESCO DEL CANTO
Vice-Rector for Research: Prof. PAOLO BARALE
Vice-Rector for Student Affairs: Dott. ROSALBA TOGNETTI
Vice-Rector for Teaching: Prof. PAOLO MANCARELLA
Vice-Rector for University Relations: Assoc. Prof. MARIA ANTONELLA GALANTI
Chief Admin. Officer: Dott. RICCARDO GRASSO
Librarian: Dott. RENATO TAMBURRINI

Number of teachers: 1,767
Number of students: 52,648

DEANS

Faculty of Agriculture: Dott. STEFANO FANTI
Faculty of Economics: Prof. DIANORA POLETTI
Faculty of Engineering: Prof. Ing. PIERANGELO TERRENI
Faculty of Foreign Languages and Literature: Prof. BRUNO MAZZONI
Faculty of Law: Prof. EUGENIO RIPEPE
Faculty of Letters and Philosophy: Prof. ALFONSO MAURIZIO IACONO
Faculty of Mathematical, Physical and Natural Sciences: Prof. PAOLO ROSSI
Faculty of Medicine and Surgery: Prof. MARIO PETRINI
Faculty of Pharmacy: Prof. CLAUDIA MARTINI
Faculty of Political Science: Prof. CLAUDIO PALAZZOLO
Faculty of Veterinary Medicine: ALESSANDRO POLI

UNIVERSITÀ DEGLI STUDI DI ROMA 'FORO ITALICO'
(Italian University of Sport and Movement)

Piazza Lauro de Bosis 15, 00194 Rome
Telephone: 06-36733599
Fax: 06-3613065
E-mail: rettorato@iusm.it
Internet: www.uniroma4.it
Founded 1998
State control

Rector: Prof. PAOLO PARISI
Vice-Rector: Prof. FABIO PIGOZZI
Admin. Dir: Dott. GIULIO GORIA

Number of teachers: 60
Number of students: 2,000

Depts of human movement and sport sciences, training for physical activities and sports, health sciences.

UNIVERSITÀ DEGLI STUDI DI ROMA 'TOR VERGATA'

Via Orazio Raimondo 18, 00173 Rome
Telephone: 06-72591
Fax: 06-7234368
Internet: web.uniroma2.it
Founded 1985

Rector: Prof. RENATO LAURO
Deputy Rector: Prof. GIUSEPPE SANTONI
Admin. Dir: Dr ERNESTO NICOLAI

Number of teachers: 1,538
Number of students: 43,000

Publications: I Quaderni di Tor Vergata, L'Osservatorio

DEANS

Faculty of Economics: Prof. MICHELE BAGELLA
Faculty of Engineering: Prof. VITTORIO ROCCO
Faculty of Law: Prof. GIAN PIERO G. MILANO
Faculty of Literature and Philosophy: Prof. LAZZARO CAPUTO
Faculty of Mathematical, Physical and Natural Sciences: Prof. MAURIZIO PACI
Faculty of Medicine and Surgery: Prof. GIUSEPPE NOVELLI

UNIVERSITÀ DEGLI STUDI DI SALERNO

Via Ponte don Melillo, 84084 Fisciano (Salerno)
Telephone: 089-961111
E-mail: urp@unisa.it
Internet: www.unisa.it
Founded 1970

Rector: Prof. RAIMONDO PASQUINO
Vice-Rector: Prof. MARIA GALANTE
Admin. Dir: Dott. GIUSEPPE PADUANO

DEANS

Faculty of Economics: Prof. DANIELA VALENTINO
Faculty of Education: Prof. LUIGI REINA
Faculty of Engineering: Prof. VITALE CARDONE
Faculty of Foreign Languages and Literature: Prof. ILEANA PAGANI
Faculty of Law: Prof. ENZO MARIA MARENGHI
Faculty of Letters and Philosophy: Prof. LUCA CERCHIAI
Faculty of Mathematical, Physical and Natural Sciences: Prof. MARIA TRANSIRICO
Faculty of Pharmacy: Prof. RAFFAELE RICCIO
Faculty of Political Science: Prof. LUIGINO ROSSI

UNIVERSITÀ DEGLI STUDI DI SASSARI

Piazza Università 21, 07100 Sassari, Sardinia
Telephone: 079-228211
Fax: 079-228211
E-mail: direzione@uniss.it
Internet: www.uniss.it
Founded 1562
State control
Academic year: November to October

Rector: Prof. ATTILIO MATINO
Vice-Rector: Prof. LAURA MANCA
Admin. Di: Dott. GUIDO CROCI
Librarian: Dott. ELISABETTA PILIA

Number of teachers: 604
Number of students: 16,319

DEANS

Faculty of Agriculture: Prof. PIETRO LUCIANO
Faculty of Architecture: Prof. GIOVANNI MACIOCCO
Faculty of Economics: Prof. ENRICO GROSSO

Faculty of Foreign Languages and Literature: Prof. GIULIA PISSARELLO
Faculty of Law: Prof. FRANCESCO SINI
Faculty of Letters and Philosophy: Prof. ALDO MARIA MORACE
Faculty of Mathematical, Physical and Natural Sciences: Prof. MASSIMO CARPINELLI
Faculty of Medicine and Surgery: Prof. GIUSEPPE MAEDDU
Faculty of Pharmacy: Prof. MARIA ANTONIETTA ZORODDU
Faculty of Political Science: Prof. VIRGILIO MURA
Faculty of Veterinary Medicine: Prof. SALVATORE NAITANA

UNIVERSITÀ DEGLI STUDI DI SIENA

Via Banchi di Sotto 55, 53100 Siena
Telephone: 0577-232111
Fax: 0577-298202
E-mail: info@unisi.it
Internet: www.unisi.it
Founded 1240
Rector: Prof. ANGLEO RICCABONI
Registrar: Dott. INES FABBRO
Library Dir: Dott. GUIDO BADALAMENTE
Number of teachers: 514
Number of students: 19,093

Publication: *Annuario Accademico*

DEANS

Faculty of Arts and Humanities: Prof. ROBERTO VENUTI
Faculty of Arts and Humanities (Arezzo): Prof. WALTER BERNARDI
Faculty of Economics: Prof. GUIDO GHELLINI
Faculty of Engineering: Prof. ENRICO MARTINELLI
Faculty of Law: Prof. ROBERTO GUERRINI
Faculty of Mathematical, Physical and Natural Sciences: Prof. DONATO DONATI
Faculty of Medicine and Surgery: Prof. GIAN MARIA ROSSOLINI
Faculty of Pharmacy: Prof. MAURIZIO BOTTA
Faculty of Political Science: Prof. LUCA VERZICHELLI

UNIVERSITÀ DEGLI STUDI DI TERAMO

Viale Crucioli 122, 64100 Teramo
Telephone: 0861-2661
Fax: 0861-245350
E-mail: protocollo@pec.unite.it
Internet: www.unite.it
Founded 1993, upon independence of Teramo campus of Università degli Studi 'Gabriele D'Annunzio'
Rector: Prof. RITA TRANQUILLI LEALI
Pro-Rector: Prof. FULVIO MARSILIO
Admin. Dir: Dott. LUIGI RENZULLO
Librarian: Dott. VALERIA DE BARTOLOMEIS
Library of 119,760 vols
Number of teachers: 251
Number of students: 8,747

Publication: *Trimestre* (2 a year)

DEANS

Faculty of Agriculture: Prof. DINO MASTROCOLA
Faculty of Communication Studies: Prof. LUCIANO D'AMICO
Faculty of Law: Prof. FLORIANA CURSI
Faculty of Political Science: Prof. ENRICO DEL COLLE
Faculty of Veterinary Medicine: Prof. FULVIO MARSILIO

UNIVERSITÀ DEGLI STUDI DI TORINO

Via Verdi 8, 10124 Turin
Telephone: 011-6706111
Fax: 011-6702218
E-mail: rettore@unito.it
Internet: www.unito.it
Founded 1404
Academic year: October to September
Rector: Prof. EZIO PELIZZETTI
Pro-Rector: Prof. SERGIO RODA
Admin. Dir: LOREDANA SEGRETO
Number of teachers: 4,000
Number of students: 70,000

DEANS

Faculty of Agriculture: Prof. ELISABETTA BARBERIS
Faculty of Arts and Humanities: Prof. LORENZO MASSOBRIO
Faculty of Economics: Prof. SERGIO BORTOLANI
Faculty of Education: Profa RENATO GRIMALDI
Faculty of Law: Prof. GIANMARIA AJANI
Faculty of Mathematical, Physical and Natural Sciences: Prof. ALBERTO CONTE
Faculty of Medicine and Surgery 'San Luigi Gonzaga': Prof. PIER MARIA FURLAN
Faculty of Modern Languages and Literature: Prof. LIBORIO TERMINE
Faculty of Pharmacy: Prof. MICHELE TROTTA
Faculty of Political Sciences: Prof. FABIO ARMAO
Faculty of Psychology: Prof. FERDINANDO ROSSI
Faculty of Veterinary Medicine: Prof. BARTOLOMEO BIOLATTI

UNIVERSITÀ DEGLI STUDI DI TRENTO

Via Belenzani 12, 38122 Trento
Telephone: 461-881111
Fax: 461-881258
E-mail: direzione.generale@unitn.it
Internet: www.unitn.it
Founded 1962
State control (since 1982)
Academic year: October to September
Pres.: Dott. INNOCENZO CIPOLLETTA
Rector: Prof. DAVIDE BASSI
Vice-Rector: Prof. GIOVANNI PASCUZZI
Deputy Rector for Admin. Staff Affairs, Collective Bargaining and Business Relationships: Prof. ALBERTO MOLINARI
Deputy Rector for Int. Relations: Prof. CARLA LOCATELLI
Deputy Rector for Scientific Research: Prof. ANTONIO SCHIZZEROTTO
Gen. Dir: Dott. GIANCARLA MASÈ
Librarian: Dott. PAOLO BELLINI
Library of 416,655 vols and 13,035 periodicals
Number of teachers: 577
Number of students: 15,226

DEANS

Faculty of Arts and Philosophy: Prof. MAURIZIO GIANGIULIO
Faculty of Cognitive Science: Prof. FRANCO FRACCAROLI
Faculty of Economics: Prof. PAOLO COLLINI
Faculty of Engineering: Prof. MARCO TUBINO
Faculty of Law: Prof. LUCA NOGLER
Faculty of Mathematical, Physical and Natural Sciences: Prof. ANDREA CARANTI
Faculty of Sociology: Prof. BRUNO DALLAGO
School of International Studies: Prof. PAOLO COLLINI (Dir)
School on Local Development: Prof. BRUNO DALLAGO (Dir)

UNIVERSITÀ DEGLI STUDI DI TRIESTE

Piazzale Europa 1, 34127 Trieste
Telephone: 040-5587111
Fax: 040-5583000
E-mail: rettore@units.it
Internet: www.units.it
Founded 1924
Rector: Prof. FRANCESCO PERONI
Vice-Rector: Prof. SERGIO PAOLETTI
Admin. Dir: Dott. ANTONINO DI GUARDO
Librarian: M. LUISA NESBEDA
Number of teachers: 1,200
Number of students: 24,500

Publication: *Piazzale Europa News* (3 a year, online)

DEANS

Advanced School of Modern Languages for Interpreters and Translators: Prof. NADINE CELOTTI
Faculty of Architecture: Prof. GIOVANNI FRAZIANO
Faculty of Economics: Prof. GIANLUIGI GALLENTI
Faculty of Education: Prof. GIUSEPPE BATTELLI
Faculty of Engineering: Prof. ROBERTO CAMUS
Faculty of Humanities: Prof. MARIA CRISTINA BENUSSI
Faculty of Law: Prof. PAOLO GIANGASPERO
Faculty of Mathematics, Physics and Natural Sciences: Prof. RINALDO RUI
Faculty of Medicine and Surgery: Prof. NICOLÒ DE MANZINI
Faculty of Pharmacy: Prof. ROBERTO DELLA LOGGIA
Faculty of Political Science: Prof. ROBERTO SCARCIGLIA
Faculty of Psychology: Prof. WALTER GERBINO

UNIVERSITÀ DEGLI STUDI DI UDINE

Palazzo Florio, Via Palladio 8, 33100 Udine
Telephone: 0432-556111
Fax: 0432-507715
E-mail: urp@uniud.it
Internet: www.uniud.it
Founded 1978
State control
Rector: Prof. CRISTIANA COMPAGNO
Pro-Rector: Prof. LEONARDO ALBERTO SECHI
Admin. Dir: Dott. DANIELE LIVON
Librarian: Prof. FRANCO FABBRO
Library of 810,400 vols, 3,850 journals
Number of teachers: 735
Number of students: 16,336

DEANS

Faculty of Agriculture: Prof. ROBERTO PINTON
Faculty of Economics: Prof. MARINA BROLLO
Faculty of Education: Prof. GIAN LUCA FORESTI
Faculty of Engineering: Prof. ALBERTO FELICE DE TONI
Faculty of Humanities: Prof. ANDREA TABARRONI
Faculty of Law: Prof. DANILO CASTELLANO
Faculty of Mathematical, Physical and Natural Sciences: Prof. FRANCO PARLAMENTO
Faculty of Medicine and Surgery: Prof. MASSIMO BAZZOCCHI
Faculty of Foreign Languages and Literature: Prof. ANTONELLA RIEM NATALE
Faculty of Veterinary Medicine: Prof. BRUNO STEFANON

UNIVERSITÀ DEGLI STUDI DI URBINO 'CARLO BO'

Via Aurelio Saffi 2, 61029 Urbino
Telephone: 0722-3051
Fax: 0722-374242

E-mail: rettore@uniurb.it
Internet: www.uniurb.it

Founded 1506
State control
Academic year: November to October

Rector: Prof. STEFANO PIVATO
Vice-Rector: Prof. GIANCARLO FERRERO
Admin. Dir: Dott. LUIGI BOTTEGHI

Library: see Libraries
Number of teachers: 483
Number of students: 17,000

Publications: *Documents de Travail* (semiotics, in 6 series), *Fonti e Documenti* (history), *Hermeneutica* (philosophy), *Le Carte* (history), *Notizie da Palazzo Albani* (art review), *Quaderni dell'Istituto di Filosofia* (philosophy), *Quaderni di Hermeneutica* (philosophy), *Quaderni Urbinati di Cultura Classica* (philology), *Storie Locali* (history), *Studi Urbinati—A* (law and economics), *Studi Urbinati—B* (history, philosophy and literature)

DEANS

Faculty of Economics: Prof. MASSIMO CIAMBOTTI
Faculty of Education: Prof. DOMENICO LOSURDO
Faculty of Foreign Languages and Literature: Prof. ANNA TERESA OSSANI
Faculty of Law: Prof. EDUARDO ROZO ACUNA
Faculty of Letters and Philosophy: Prof. SETTIMIO LANCIOTTI
Faculty of Pharmacy: Prof. ORAZIO CANTONI
Faculty of Political Sciences: Prof. MARCO CANGIOTTI
Faculty of Science and Technology: Prof. STEFANO PAPA
Faculty of Sociology: Prof. BERNARDO VALLI
Faculty of Sports Science: Prof. VILBERTO STOCCHI

PROFESSORS

(Some staff serve in more than one faculty)

Faculty of Economics (Via Saffi 42, 61029 Urbino; tel. 0722-305500; fax 0722-305566; e-mail presecon@uniurb.it; internet www.econ.uniurb.it):

ANTONELLI, G., Marketing of Agroindustrial Products
CIAMBOTTI, M., Economic Planning and Auditing
FERRERO, G., Marketing
GARDINI, L., Mathematics for Economic Applications
GIAMPAOLI, A., Banking
MARCHINI, I., Business Economics
PAOLONI, M., General and Applied Accountancy
PENCARELLI, T., Economics and Management
POLIDORI, G., Transport Economics
RINALDI, R., Financial Law
STEFANINI, L., General Mathematics

Faculty of Education (Via Bramante 17, 61029 Urbino; tel. 0722-327628; fax 0722-327628; e-mail lisa@uniurb.it; internet www.uniurb.it/sciform/home.htm):

BALDACCI, M., General Pedagogy
CUBELLI, R., General Psychology
FILOGRASSO, N., General Pedagogy
LOSURDO, D., History of Philosophy
PERSI, P., Geography
PIRANI, P., Educational Psychology
RIPANTI, G., Theoretical Philosophy
ROSSI, S., Theory and Techniques of Psychological Discourse
SALA, G., Dynamic Psychology

Faculty of Environmental Sciences (Località Crocicchia, 61029 Urbino; tel. 0722-304271; fax 0722-305265; e-mail sc.ambientali@uniurb.it; internet www.uniurb.it/sa/index.html):

CECCHETTI, G., Principles of Environmental Protection
CONFORTO, G., Laboratory of General Physics
MAGNANI, F., Environmental Chemistry
WEZEL FORESE, C., Stratigraphy
ZUMINO, M. E., Biogeography

Faculty of Foreign Languages (Piazza Rinascimento 7, 61029 Urbino; tel. 0722-328506; fax 0722-328506; e-mail pres.facolta.lingue@uniurb.it):

BOGLIOLO, G., French Literature
MORISCO, G., Anglo-American Languages and Literatures
MULLINI, R., English Literature
OSSANI, A. T., Italian Literature
PIVATO, S., Contemporary History
SAURIN DE LA IGLESIA, M. R., Spanish Literature
VENTURELLI, A., History of German Culture
ZAGANELLI, G., Romance Philology

Faculty of Law (Via Matteotti 1, 61029 Urbino; tel. 0722-3031; fax 0722-2955; e-mail presidigiur@giur.uniurb.it; internet www.uniurb.it):

DONDI, A., Civil Procedural Law
FANTAPPIÈ, C., History of Canon Law
FERRONI, L., Institutes of Private Law
GILIBERTI, G., Roman Law
MARI, L., International Law
MOROZZO DELLA ROCCA, P., Civil Law
ROZO ACUNA, E., Comparative Public Law

Faculty of Letters and Philosophy (Piano S. Lucia 6, 61029 Urbino; tel. 0722-320125; fax 0722-320125; e-mail preslet@lettere.uniurb.it):

ARBIZZONI ARTUSI, G., Philosophy of Italian Literature
BERNARDINI, P., Greek Language and Literature
BOLDRINI, S., Latin Language and Literature
CECCHINI, E., Humanist Medieval Latin Literature
CECCHINI, F. M., Contemporary History, History of the Risorgimento
CERBONI BAIARDI, G., Italian Literature
CUBEDDU, I., Theoretical Philosophy
FRANCHI, A., Glottology and Linguistics
GORI, F., History of Christianity and the Church
GUERCIO, M., Archives, Bibliography and Librarianship
ILLUMINATI, A., History of Philosophy
LANCIOTTI, S., Latin Language and Literature
PERINI, G., Museum Organization and Art and Restoration Criticism
PERUSINO, F., Greek Language and Literature
QUESTA, C., Classical Philology
RAFFAELLI, R., Latin Language and Literature
RINALDI TUFI, S., Classical Archaeology
SCODITTI, G., Anthropological Demoethnic Studies
TAROZZI, G., Logic and Philosophy of Science

Faculty of Mathematics, Physics and Natural Sciences (Località Crocicchia, 61029 Urbino; tel. 0722-304283; fax 0722-304240; e-mail scienze.mmffnn@uniurb.it):

ATTANASI, O. A., Organic Chemistry
BALSAMO, M., Zoology
BERETTA, E., Mathematical Analysis
COCCIONI, R., Micropalaeontology
COLANTONI, P., Sedimentology
DEL GRANDE, P., Comparative Anatomy
GAZZANELLI, G., Cytochemistry and Histochemistry
GORI, U., Applied Geology
MAGNANI, M., Biological Chemistry
MICHELONI, M., General and Inorganic Chemistry

NINFALI, P., Comparative Biochemistry
PAPA, S., Human Anatomy
PERRONE, V., Stratigraphic Geology

Faculty of Pharmacy (Via Saffi 2, 61029 Urbino; tel. 0722-329881; fax 0722-2737; e-mail farmacia@uniurb.it):

ACCORSI, A., Biological Chemistry
CANTONI, O., Pharmacotherapy
DACHÀ, M., Applied Biochemistry
PIATTI, E., Food Science
TARZIA, G., Pharmaceutical Chemistry and Toxicology
VETRANO, F., Physics

Faculty of Physical Education and Health (Via Oddi 14, 61029 Urbino; tel. 0722-3517278; fax 0722-328829; e-mail presid.smotorie@uniurb.it):

FALCIERI, E., Human Anatomy
STOCCHI, V., Applied Biochemistry

Faculty of Political Sciences (Via Bramante 17, 61029 Urbino; tel. 0722-328557; fax 0722-328656; e-mail sc.politiche@uniurb.it):

DELLA CANANEA, G., Administrative Law
GREGOIRE, R., History of Christianity
GUDERZO, M., History of International Relations
MAZZONI, R., Political Economy
PARLATO, V., Canon Law
TENELLA-SILLANI, C., Institutes of Private Law

Faculty of Sociology (Via Saffi 15, 61029 Urbino; tel. 0722-327343; fax 0722-322343; e-mail presidenza@soc.uniurb.it; internet www.soc.uniurb.it):

ALFIERI, L., Political Philosophy
DEI, M., Sociology of Education
DEL TUTTO, L., General Linguistics
DIAMANTI, I., Political Science
FRANCI, A., Social Statistics
GRASSI, P., Philosophy of Religions
MAGGIONI, G., Sociology of Law
MAZZOLI, G., Communication Sociology
NEGROTTI, M., Methodology in Human Sciences
PIAZZI, G., Sociological Theory
VALLI, B., Mass-Media Sociology

UNIVERSITÀ DEGLI STUDI DI VERONA

Via dell'Artigliere 8, 37129 Verona
Telephone: 045-8028111
Fax: 045-8098255
Internet: www.univr.it

Founded 1982

Rector: Prof. ALESSANDRO MAZZUCCO
Pro-Rector: Prof. BETTINA CAMPEDELLI
Admin. Dir: Dott. ANTONIO SALVINI
Library Dir: Dott. FABRIZIO BERTOLI

Number of teachers: 258
Number of students: 13,087

DEANS

Faculty of Economics: Prof. FRANCESCO ROSSI
Faculty of Education: Prof. MARIO LONGO
Faculty of Foreign Languages and Literature: Prof. ALESSANDRA TOMASELLI
Faculty of Humanities and Philosophy: Prof. GUIDO AVEZZÙ
Faculty of Law: Prof. STEFANO TROIANO
Faculty of Mathematical, Physical and Natural Sciences: Prof. ROBERTO GIACOBAZZI
Faculty of Medicine and Surgery: Prof. MICHELE TANSELLA
Faculty of Motor and Sports Science: Prof. CARLO MORANDI

UNIVERSITÀ DEGLI STUDI ROMA TRE

Via Ostiense 159, 00154 Rome
Telephone: 06-57332403
Fax: 06-57332300

E-mail: segr_ret@uniroma3.it
Internet: www.uniroma3.it

Founded 1992
State control

Rector: Prof. GUIDO FABIANI
Deputy Rector: Prof. MARIO MORGANTI
Admin. Dir: Dott. PASQUALE BASILICATA

Library of 500,000 , 2,500 journals, 6,500
online journals
Number of teachers: 870
Number of students: 40,000

DEANS

Faculty of Architecture: Prof. FRANCESCO
CELLINI
Faculty of Economics: Prof. CARLO MARIA
TRAVAGLINI
Faculty of Education: Prof. GAETANO DOME-
NICI
Faculty of Engineering: Prof. PAOLO MELE
Faculty of Humanities: Prof. FRANCESCA
CANTÙ
Faculty of Law: Prof. PAOLO BENVENUTI
Faculty of Mathematical, Physical and Nat-
ural Sciences: Prof. SETTIMIO MOBILIO
Faculty of Political Sciences: Prof. FRANCESCO
GUIDA

UNIVERSITÀ DEL SALENTO

Piazza Tancredi N7, 73100 Lecce
Telephone: 0832-291111
Fax: 0832-292204
E-mail: rettore@unisalento.it
Internet: www.unisalento.it

Founded 1956; current name 2006
Academic year: November to October

Rector: Prof. DOMENICO LAFORGIA
Admin. Dir: Dott. INNOCENZO SANTORO
Librarian: Dott. MARIA GRAZIA D'ALOISIO

Library of 1,000,000 vols, 600 journals
Number of teachers: 750
Number of students: 28,000

DEANS

Faculty of Cultural Heritage: Prof. REGINA
POSO
Faculty of Economics: Prof. STEFANO ADAMO
Faculty of Education: Prof. GIOVANNI INVITTO
Faculty of Engineering: Prof. Ing. VITO
DATTOMA
Faculty of Foreign Languages and Litera-
ture: Prof. ALIZIA ROMANOVIC
Faculty of Humanities: Prof. ROSARIO COLUC-
CIA
Faculty of Industrial Engineering: Prof. Ing.
ANTONIO FICARELLA
Faculty of Law: Prof. RAFFAELE DE GIORGI
Faculty of Science: Prof. CARLO SEMPI
Faculty of Social and Political Science: Prof.
MARCELLO STRAZZERI

UNIVERSITÀ DELLA CALABRIA

Via P. Bucci, 87036 Arcavacata di Rende
Telephone: 0984-4911
Fax: 0984-493616
E-mail: diramm@unical.it
Internet: www.unical.it

Founded 1972
Academic year: November to October

Rector: Prof. GIOVANNI LaTorre
Admin. Officer: Dott. BRUNA ADAMO

Library of 400,000 vols
Number of teachers: 865 (incl. professors
and researchers)
Number of students: 34,266

DEANS

Faculty of Economics: Prof. FRANCO RUBINO
Faculty of Engineering: Prof. PAOLO VELTRI
Faculty of Letters and Philosophy: Prof.
RAFFAELE PERRELLI

Faculty of Mathematical, Physical and Nat-
ural Sciences: Prof. GINO MIROCLE CRISCI
Faculty of Pharmacy, Nutrition and Health:
Prof. SEBASTIANO ANDÒ
Faculty of Political Sciences: Prof. GUERINO
D'IGNAZIO

UNIVERSITÀ DI BOLOGNA

Via Zamboni 33, 40126 Bologna
Telephone: 051-2099111
Fax: 051-2099372
Internet: www.unibo.it

Founded 1088
Languages of instruction: English, Italian,
Spanish
Academic year: October to July

Rector: Prof. IVANO DIONIGI
Deputy Rector: Prof. EMILIO FERRARI
Vice-Rector for Int. Relations: Dr CARLA
SALVATERRA
Vice-Rector for Research: Prof. DARIO BRAGA
Vice-Rector for the Romagna campuses: Prof.
GUIDO SARCHIELLI
Vice-Rector for Students: Prof. ROBERTO
NICOLETTI
Vice-Rector for Teaching and Education:
Prof. GIANLUCA FIORENTINI
Admin. Dir: Dott. GIUSEPPE COLPANI

Library of 1,250,000 vols and 400 video
cassettes, 65 libraries
Number of teachers: 3,001
Number of students: 83,000

DEANS

Advanced School of Modern Languages for
Interpreters and Translators: Prof. RAFAEL
LOZANO MIRALLES
Faculty of Agriculture: Prof. ANDREA SEGRÈ
Faculty of Architecture 'Aldo Rossi': Prof.
GINO MALACARNE
Faculty of Arts and Humanities: Prof. CARLA
GIOVANNINI
Faculty of Economics: Prof. GIANLUCA FIOR-
ENTINI
Faculty of Economics, Forlì: Prof. GIULIO
ECCHIA
Faculty of Economics, Rimini: Prof. CORRADO
BENASSI
Faculty of Education: Prof. LUIGI GUERRA
Faculty of Engineering: Prof. PIER PAOLO
DIOTALLEVI
Faculty of Engineering II: Prof. Ing. ENRICO
SANGIORGI
Faculty of Exercise and Sport Sciences: Prof.
CARLO BOTTARI
Faculty of Foreign Languages and Litera-
ture: Prof. DANIELA GALLINGANI
Faculty of Industrial Chemistry: Prof.
FRANCO MAGELLI
Faculty of Law: Prof. GIOVANNI LUCHETTI
Faculty of Mathematical, Physical and Nat-
ural Sciences: Prof. BRUNO MARANO
Faculty of Medicine and Surgery: Prof.
SERGIO STEFONI
Faculty of Pharmacy: Prof. CLAUDIO GALLETTI
Faculty of Political Science: Prof. FABIO
GIUSBERTI
Faculty of Political Science 'Roberto Ruffilli':
Prof. MARIA SERENA PIRETTI
Faculty of Preservation of the Cultural Heri-
tage: Prof. PIERFRANCESCO CALLIERI
Faculty of Psychology: Prof. FIORELLA GIUS-
BERTI
Faculty of Statistical Sciences: Prof. ANGELA
MONTANARI
Faculty of Veterinary Medicine: Prof. SAN-
TINO PROSPERI

UNIVERSITÀ DI CAGLIARI

Via Università 40, 09124 Cagliari, Sardinia
Telephone: 070-6751
Fax: 070-669425
E-mail: rettore@unica.it

Internet: www.unica.it

Founded 1606 by Pope Paul V

Rector: Prof. GIOVANNI MELIS
Vice-Rector: Prof. GIOVANNA MARIA LEDDA
Admin. Dir: Dott. FABRIZIO CHERCHI
Librarian: Dott. DONATELLA TORE

Number of teachers: 1,000
Number of students: 18,000

Publication: Studi economico-giuridici and
publs from each faculty

DEANS

Faculty of Architecture: Prof. ANTONELLO
SANNA
Faculty of Economics: Prof. ERNESTINA GIU-
DICI
Faculty of Education: Prof. ANTONIO
CADEDDU
Faculty of Engineering: Prof. GIORGIO MAS-
SACCI
Faculty of Foreign Languages and Litera-
ture: Prof. GIUSEPPE MARCI
Faculty of Law: Prof. MASSIMO DEIANA
Faculty of Letters and Philosophy: ROBERTO
CORONEO
Faculty of Mathematical, Physical and Nat-
ural Sciences: Prof. LUCA FANFANI
Faculty of Medicine and Surgery: Prof.
MARIO PIGA
Faculty of Pharmacy: Prof. FILIPPO PIRISI
Faculty of Political Science: Prof. PAOLA
PIRAS

UNIVERSITÀ DI FERRARA

Via Savonarola 9, 44121 Ferrara
Telephone: 0532-293111
Fax: 0532-293031
E-mail: urp@unife.it
Internet: www.unife.it

Founded 1391
Academic year: November to October

Rector: Prof. PASQUALE NAPPI
Admin. Dir: Dott. CLARA COVIELLO

Number of teachers: 714
Number of students: 16,752

Publications: Annali dell' Università, Ateneo
(6 a year)

DEANS

Faculty of Architecture: Prof. GRAZIANO
TRIPPA
Faculty of Arts: Prof. MATTEO GALLI
Faculty of Economics: Prof. CATERINA
COLOMBO
Faculty of Engineering: Prof. PIERO OLIVO
Faculty of Law: Prof. GIANGUIDO BALANDI
Faculty of Mathematical, Physical and Nat-
ural Sciences: Prof. ROBERTO CALABRESE
Faculty of Medicine and Surgery: Prof.
ALBERTO LIBONI
Faculty of Pharmacy: Prof. SEVERO SALVA-
DORI

PROFESSORS

Faculty of Architecture (Via Quartieri 8,
44100 Ferrara; tel. 0532-293613; fax 0532-
293611; e-mail faf@unife.it; internet
architettura.fe.infn.it):

ACOCELLA, A., Architectural Technology
ALESSANDRI, C., Construction Theory
CECCARELLI, P., Urban Planning
DI FEDERICO, I., Industrial Technical Phys-
ics
LAUDIERO, F., Construction Methods
MINARDI, B., Urban and Architectonic
Composition
TRIPPA, G., Architectural Technology

Faculty of Economics (Vicolo del Gregorio
13–15, 44100 Ferrara; tel. 0532-293000; fax
0532-293012; internet www.economia.unife
.it):

BIANCHI, P., Applied Economics

CALAMANTI, A., Economics of Financial Mediators
COCOZZA, F., Economic Law
PINI, P., Political Economy
POLA, G., Finance
SEGALA, F., Mathematical Analysis

Faculty of Engineering (Via Saragat 1, 44100 Ferrara; tel. 0532-974871; fax 0532-760162; internet www.unife.it/facolta/facolta-300076 .htm):

BEGHELLI, S., Automatic Controls
BETTOCCHI, R., Energy and Environmental Systems
DAL CIN, R., Stratigraphic and Sedimentological Geology
DALPIAZ, G., Applied Machine Mechanics
DEL PIERO, G., Construction Theory
FERRETTI, P., Experimental Physics
FRANCHINI, M., Hydraulic and Marine Hydraulic Engineering
FRONTERA, F., Experimental Physics
LAMMA, E., Information Processing Systems
OLIVO, P., Electronics
PADULA, M., Mathematical Physics
PIVA, S., Industrial Technical Physics
POMPOLI, R., Environmental Technical Physics
RUSSO, P., Topography and Cartography
TRALLI, A., Construction Theory
ZUCCHI, F., Chemical Foundations of Technology

Faculty of Law (Corso Ercole I d'Este 37, 44100 Ferrara; tel. 0532-205521; fax 0532-200188; e-mail infogiur@unife.it; internet www.giuri.unife.it):

ADAMI, F. E., Canon and Ecclesiastical Law
BALANDI, G. G., Labour Law
BERNARDI, A., Penal Law
BIN, R., Constitutional Law
BORGHI, P., Agrarian Law
BRUNELLI, G., Institutions of Public Law
BRUZZO, A., Political Economy
CARIELLO, V., Commercial Law
CASAROTTO, G., Agrarian Law
CAZZETTA, G., History of Medieval and Modern Law
CIACCIA, B., Civil Procedure Law
COSTATO, L., Agrarian Law
DE GIORGI, M. V., Private Law
GRIPPO, G., Commercial Law
MANFREDINI, A., Roman Law and Laws of Antiquity
NAPPI, P., Agrarian Law
PASTORE, B., Philosophy of Law
PELLIZZER, F., Administrative Law
PUGIOTTO, A., Constitutional Law
SALERNO, F., International Law
SCARANO USSANI, V., Roman Law and Laws of Antiquity
SOMMA, A., Comparative Private Law
ZAMORANI, P., Roman Law and Laws of Antiquity

Faculty of Letters and Philosophy (Via Savonarola 38, 44100 Ferrara; tel. 0532-293416; fax 0532-202689; internet www .unife.it/facolta/facolta-300035.htm):

BELLATALLA, L., History of School and Educational Institutions
BOLLINI, M., Roman History
CAMPI, C. A., Geography
CHERCHI, P., Italian Literature
FABBRI, P., Musicology and Musical History
FAVA, E., Glottology and Linguistics
FOLLI, A., Contemporary Italian Literature
GALLI, M., German Literature
GENOVESI, G., General and Social Pedagogy
MATARRESE, S., Italian Language
MAZZI, M. S., Medieval History
MAZZOCCHI, G., Spanish Literature
MERCI, P., Romance Philology and Linguistics
NESPOR, M. A., Glottology and Linguistics

PANCERA, C., History of Schools and Educational Institutions
RICCI, G., Modern History
SECHI, S., Contemporary History
TEMPERA, M., English Literature
TROVATO, P., Italian Language
VARESE, R., History of Modern Art
ZANOTTI, A., General Sociology

Faculty of Mathematical, Physical and Natural Sciences (Via Luigi Borsari 46, 44100 Ferrara; tel. 0532-291347; fax 0532-291348; internet www.unife.it/facolta/facolta-275017 .htm):

ABELLI, L., Comparative Anatomy and Cytology
ALBERTI, A., Mineralogy
BARBUJANI, G., Genetics
BECCALUVA, L., Petrology and Petrography
BERNARDI, F., Biochemistry
BIASINI, L., Numerical Analysis
BIGNOZZI, C. A., General and Inorganic Chemistry
BOSELLINI, A., Stratigraphic and Sedimentological Geology
BROGLIO, A., Anthropologyy
CANESCHI, L., Theoretical Physics and Mathematical Models and Methods
CIMIRAGLIA, R., Physical Chemistry
COLTORTI, M., Petrology and Petrography
CORALLINI, A., General Microbiology
DALPIAZ, P., General Physics
DEL CENTINA, A., Geometry
DI CAPUA, E., Experimental Physics
DONDI, F., Analytical Chemistry
DONDONI, A., Organic Chemistry
ELLIA, P., Geometry
FAGIOLI, F., Environmental and Conservation Chemistry
FASULO, M. P., General Botany
FIORENTINI, G., Nuclear and Subnuclear Physics
FOA', A. G., Zoology
GERDOL, R., Environmental and Applied Botany
GILLI, G., Physical Chemistry
LASCU, A., Geometry
MARTINELLI, G., Experimental Physics
MASSARI, U., Mathematical Analysis
MENINI, C., Algebra
NANNI, T., Applied Geology
NIZZOLI, F., Solid-State Physics
PEPE, L., Complementary Mathematics
PERETTO, C., Anthropology
PICCOLINO, M., Physiology
PRODI, F., Earth Physics
ROSSI, R., Ecology
RUGGIERO, V., Numerical Analysis
SACCHI, O., Physiology
SACERDOTI, M., Mineralogy
SALVATORELLI, G., Comparative Anatomy and Cytology
SCANDOLA, F., General and Inorganic Chemistry
SCHIFFRER, G., Theoretical Physics and Mathematical Models and Methods
SIENA, F., Petrology and Petrography
SOLONNIKOV, V., Mathematical Physics
TRAVERSO, O., General and Inorganic Chemistry
TRIPICCIONE, R., Theoretical Physics and Mathematical Models and Methods
ZANGHIRATI, L., Mathematical Analysis

Faculty of Medicine and Surgery (Via Fossato di Mortara 64/b, 44100 Ferrara; tel. 0532-291545; fax 0532-291546; e-mail preside.medicina@unife.it; internet unife.it/ facolta/medicina):

AVATO, F. M., Forensic Medicine
AZZENA, G. F., General Surgery
BERGAMINI, C., Clinical Biochemistry and Clinical Molecular Biology
BERTI, G., General Pathology
BOREA, P. A., Pharmacology
BORGNA, C., General and Specialized Paediatrics

CALURA, G., Odontostomatological Diseases
CALZOLARI, E., Medical Genetics
CAPITANI, S., Human Anatomy
CARUSO, A., Histology
CASSAI, E., Microbiology and Clinical Microbiology
CASTOLDI, G. L., Haematology
CAVAZZINI, L., Anatomical Pathology
CIACCIA, A., Diseases of the Respiratory Tract
CONCONI, F., Biochemistry
CROCE, C. M., Medical Oncology
DALLOCCHIO, F. P. F., Biochemistry
DE ROSA, E., Industrial Medicine
DEGLI UBERTI, E., Endocrinology
DEL SENNO, L., Molecular Biology
DI VIRGILIO, F., General Pathology
DONINI, I. G., General Surgery
DURANTE, E., General Surgery
FAVILLA, M., Physiology
FELLIN, R., Internal Medicine
FERRARI, R., Cardiovascular Diseases
GRANIERI, E., Neurology
GRAZI, E., Biochemistry
GREGORIO, P., General and Applied Hygiene
GUALDI, E., Anthropology
LIBONI, A., General Surgery
LONGHINI, C., Internal Medicine
MANNELLA, P., Imaging and Radiotherapy Diagnostics
MARTINI, A., Audiology
MOLINARI, S., Clinical Psychology
MOLLICA, G., Obstetrics and Gynaecology
NENCI, I., Anatomy and Pathological Histology
PASTORE, A., Otolaryngology
PINAMONTI, S., Applied Biology
RAMELLI, E., Psychiatry
REGOLI, D., Pharmacology
SEBASTIANI, A., Eyesight Diseases
SICILIANI, G., Odontostomatological Diseases
SPIDALIERI, G., Physiology
TOGNON, M., Applied Biology
TRAINA, G. C., Ambulatory Diseases
TROTTA, F., Rheumatology
TURINI, D., Urology
VIGI, V., General and Specialized Paediatrics
VIRGILI, A., Skin and Venereal Diseases

Faculty of Pharmacy (Via Fossato di Mortara 17/19, 44100 Ferrara; tel. 0532-291265; fax 0532-291296; e-mail farmline@unife.it; internet web.unife.it/facolta/farmacia):

BARALDI, P. G., Pharmaceutical Chemistry
BIANCHI, C., Pharmacology
BIONDI, C., Physiology
BRANDOLINI, V., Food Chemistry
BRUNI, A., Pharmocological Biology
GAMBACCINI, M., Applied Physics (Conservation, Environmental, Biological and Medical)
GAMBARI, R., Biochemistry
MANFREDINI, S., Pharmaceutical Chemistry
MANSERVIGI, R., Microbiology and Clinical Microbiology
MENEGATTI, E., Applied Pharmaceutical Technology
POLLINI, G. P., Organic Chemistry
RIZZUTO, R., General Pathology
SALVADORI, S., Pharmaceutical Chemistry
SCATTURIN, A., Applied Pharmaceutical Chemistry
SIMONI, D., Pharmaceutical Chemistry
TANGANELLI, S., Pharmacology
TOMATIS, R., Pharmaceutical Chemistry
TRANIELLO, M. S., Biochemistry

UNIVERSITÀ IUAV DI VENEZIA

Santa Croce 191, Tolentini, 30135 Venice
Telephone: 041-2571720
Fax: 041-2571760
E-mail: rettorato@iuav.it

Internet: www.iuav.it
Founded 1926
Public control
Language of instruction: Italian
Academic year: November to October

Rector: Prof. AMERIGO RESTUCCI
Vice-Rector: Prof. DONATELLA CALABI
Admin. Dir: ALDO TOMMASIN
Librarian: Dott. LAURA CASAGRANDE

Library of 123,000 vols, 2,500 periodicals
Number of teachers: 517
Number of students: 12,000

DEANS

Faculty of Architecture: Prof. GIANCARLO
 CARNEVALE
Faculty of Arts and Design: Prof. MEDARDO
 CHIAPPONI
Faculty of Regional Planning: Prof. MATELDA
 REHO

UNIVERSITÀ MEDITERRANEA DI REGGIO CALABRIA

Via Diana 3, 89125 Reggio Calabria
Telephone: 0965-872912
Fax: 0965-332201
E-mail: amministrazione@pec.unirc.it
Internet: www.unirc.it
Founded 1982

Rector: Prof. MASSIMO GIOVANNINI
Pro-Rector: Prof. FRANCESCO RUSSO
Admin. Dir: ANTONIO ROMEO
Number of students: 9,697

DEANS

Faculty of Agriculture: Prof. SANTO MAR-
 CELLO ZIMBONE
Faculty of Architecture: Prof. FRANCESCA
 FATTA
Faculty of Engineering: Prof. ADOLFO SANTINI
Faculty of Law: Prof. ATTILIO GORASSINI

UNIVERSITÀ POLITECNICA DELLE MARCHE

Piazza Roma 22, 60121 Ancona
Telephone: 071-2201
Fax: 071-2202324
E-mail: info@univpm.it
Internet: www.univpm.it
Founded 1969
Academic year: November to October

Rector: Prof. MARCO PACETTI
Vice-Rector: Prof. LEANDRO PROVINCIALI
Admin. Dir: Dott. LUISIANA SEBASTIANELLI
Librarian: Dott. SILVIA SOTTILI

Library of 26,000 vols
Number of teachers: 430
Number of students: 13,000

DEANS

Faculty of Agriculture: Prof. RODOLFO SANTI-
 LOCCHI
Faculty of Economics: Prof. GIANLUCA GRE-
 GORI
Faculty of Engineering: Prof. GIOVANNI
 LATINI
Faculty of Medicine and Surgery: Prof.
 ANTONIO BENEDETTI
Faculty of Sciences: Prof. ETTORE OLMO

Other Universities, Colleges and Institutes

AMERICAN UNIVERSITY OF ROME

Via Pietro Roselli 4, 00153 Rome
Telephone: 06-58330919
Fax: 06-58330992
E-mail: admissions@aur.edu

Internet: www.aur.edu
Founded 1969
Language of instruction: English
Academic year: August to July

Pres.: Dr ANDREW THOMPSON
Provost: Dr MAURIZIO MAMORSTEIN
Dir of First Year Program and Coordinator of
 Special Projects: DIANE FRANCES HYETT
Assoc. Dean of Enrolment Services and
 Registrar: STEFANIA IORIO
Dir of Library and Information Services:
 JAMES L. WEINHEIMER

Library of 15,000 vols
Number of teachers: 69
Number of students: 500

BOLOGNA CENTER OF THE JOHNS HOPKINS UNIVERSITY PAUL H. NITZE SCHOOL OF ADVANCED INTERNATIONAL STUDIES (SAIS)

Via Belmeloro 11, 40126 Bologna
Telephone: 051-2917811
Fax: 051-228505
E-mail: admission@jhubc.it
Internet: www.jhubc.it
Founded 1955
Language of instruction: English
Academic year: September to May

Dir: Prof. KENNETH KELLER
Dir of Finance and Admin.: BART DRAKULICH
Registrar: BERNADETTE O'TOOLE
Librarian: GAIL MARTIN

Library of 85,000 vols
Number of teachers: 50
Number of students: 185

Publication: Bologna Center Journal of International Affairs (1 a year).

ENI CORPORATE UNIVERSITY— SCUOLA ENRICO MATTEI

Via S. Salvo 1, 20097 San Donato Milanese
Telephone: 02-52057907
Fax: 02-59822141
E-mail: info.scuolamattei@eni.it
Internet: www.enicorporateuniversity.it/
 scuolamattei/
Founded 1957
Academic year: September to June

Dean: Prof. PIERANGELO CIGNOLI

Library of 15,000 vols
Number of teachers: 50
Number of students: 55 new students per
 year

Publication: Quaderni (3 a year)

Economic and management studies; higher
degrees in energy and environmental economics, and petroleum engineering.

EUROPEAN UNIVERSITY INSTITUTE

Via dei Roccettini 9, 50014 San Domenico di
 Fiesole, (FI)
Telephone: 055-46851
Fax: 055-4685298
Internet: www.eui.eu
Founded 1972 by the member states of the
 European Communities (present-day EU)
Academic year: September to June
Language of instruction: EU languages

Pres.: JOSEP BORRELL FONTELLES
Sec.-Gen.: Dott. MARCO DEL PANTA RIDOLFI
Librarian: VEERLE DECKMYN

Library of 500,000 vols, 3,000 journals
Number of teachers: 50 (full-time)
Number of students: 600 (postgraduate)

Publications: EUI Review, EUI Working
 Papers, European Foreign Policy Bulletin,
 European Journal of International Law,
 European Law Journal, President's

Annual Report, Robert Schuman Centre
Newsletter

Depts of economics, history and civilization,
law, and political and social sciences.

ATTACHED INSTITUTIONS

Academy of European Law: Advanced-
level summer courses in human rights law
and EU law; Dirs Prof. LOÏC AZOULAI, Prof.
MARISE CREMONA, Prof. FRANCESCO FRAN-
CIONI.

**Robert Schuman Centre for Advanced
Studies:** Research on Europe and the processes of European integration. Core themes
are: European instns, governance and democracy; migration; economic and monetary
policy; competition policy and market regulation; energy policy; int. and transnational
relations of the EU; Dir Prof. STEFANO
BARTOLINI.

FREIE UNIVERSITÄT BOZEN/LIBERA UNIVERSITÀ DI BOLZANO (Free University of Bozen/Bolzano)

Piazza Università 1, 39100 Bolzano
Telephone: 0471-011000
Fax: 0471-011009
E-mail: info@unibz.it
Internet: www.unibz.it
Founded 1997
Provincial state control
Languages of instruction: German, Italian,
 English

President: Dr KONRAD BERGMEISTER
Rector: Prof. WALTER A. LORENZ
Vice-Rector for Intercultural Communica-
 tion: Prof. JOHANN DRUMBL
Vice-Rector for Research: Prof. YURIY
 KANIOVSKYI
Head of Library: ELISABETH FRASNELLI

Library of 77,300 books, 1,036 periodicals,
 4,250 online journals, 68 databases
Number of teachers: 25
Number of students: 1,965

DEANS

Faculty of Computer Science: Prof. GIAN-
 CARLO SUCCI
School of Economics and Management: Prof.
 MAURIZIO MURGIA
Faculty of Education: Prof. Dr FRANZ COM-
 PLOI
Faculty of Design and Art: Prof. Dr phil.
 habil. GERHARD GLÜHER
Faculty of Science and Technology: Prof.
 MASSIMO TAGLIAVINI

IMT INSTITUTE FOR ADVANCED STUDIES

Piazza San Ponziano 6, 55100 Lucca
Telephone: 0583-4326561
Fax: 0583-4326565
E-mail: info@imtlucca.it
Internet: www.imtlucca.it

Dir: FABIO PAMMOLLI
Deputy Dir: UGO MONTANARI

Four doctoral programs are available: computer science and engineering, management
and devt of cultural heritage, political systems and institutional change, and economics, markets, institutions.

ISTITUTO ITALIANO DI SCIENZE UMANE (SUM)

Palazzo Strozzi, Piazza degli Strozzi, 50123
 Florence
Telephone: 055-2673300
Fax: 055-2673350
Internet: www.sumitalia.it
State control

Dir: Prof. MARIO CITRONI
Admin. Dir: Dott. ANTONIO CUNZIO

Master's course in local govt; doctoral courses in political science, European private law; scholarships for post-doctoral research in humanities.

ISTITUTO REGIONALE DI STUDI E RICERCA SOCIALE

Piazza S. Maria Maggiore 7, 38100 Trento
Telephone: 0461-273611
Fax: 0461-233821
E-mail: emma.stefano@irsrs.tn.it
Internet: irsrs.isite.it
Founded 1947; until c. 1993, Scuola Superiore Regionale di Servizio Sociale
Pres.: Dott. ITALO MONFREDINI
Dir: Dott. LAURA RAVANELLI
Library of 15,000 vols, 825 journals, 300 current journals
Number of teachers: 350
Number of students: 6,000
Publication: *Annali* (1 a year)

Two-year course for health workers.

CONSTITUENT INSTITUTE

Università della Terza Età e del Tempo Disponibile (Open University): training for social workers, and adult education.

ISTITUTO UNIVERSITARIO DI STUDI EUROPEI
(University Institute of European Studies)

Via Maria Vittoria 26, 10123 Turin
Telephone: 011-8394660
Fax: 011-8394664
E-mail: info@iuse.it
Internet: www.iuse.it
Founded 1952

Offers postgraduate courses and researches in law and int. econ.

Pres.: Prof. RAFFAELE CATERINA
Library of 50,000 vols, incl. books, periodicals, official pubs from EU and other int. orgs.

ISTITUTO UNIVERSITARIO DI STUDI SUPERIORI (IUSS)

Viale Lungo Ticino Sforza 56, 27100 Pavia
Telephone: 0382-375811
Fax: 0382-375899
E-mail: external.relations@iusspavia.it
Internet: www.iusspavia.it
Founded 1997
Languages of instruction: Italian, English
Dir: Prof. ROBERTO SCHMID

Ordinary courses in humanities, social sciences, science and technology, biomedical sciences; master's and higher education courses in management of complex systems, media science and technology, materials science, seismic engineering, nuclear technology, developmental cooperation, exec. program in int. economic integration, int. design seminar; doctoral courses offered in asscn with the Università degli Studi di Pavia.

ITALIAN UNIVERSITY LINE (IUL)

Via M. Buonarroti 10, 50122 Florence
E-mail: segreteria@iuline.it
Internet: www.iuline.it
Founded 2005
Private control
Rector: Prof. STEFANIA FUSCAGNI
Offers distance learning.

JOHN CABOT UNIVERSITY

Via della Lungara 233, 00165 Rome
Telephone: 06-6819121
Fax: 06-6832088
E-mail: info@johncabot.edu
Internet: www.johncabot.edu
Office in USA: 14100 Walsingham Rd, Suite 36, #10, Largo, FL 33774, USA
E-mail: usoffice@johncabot.edu
Founded 1972
Independent, four-year institution of liberal arts
President: FRANCO PAVONCELLO
Vice-President and Dean of Academic Affairs: MARY MERVA
Vice-President for Operations and Finance: ANDREA GIUMMARRA
Registrar: CARMEN SCARPATI
Head Librarian: ELISABETTA MORANI
Library: Frohring Library: reference material, curriculum-related items, newspapers, 1,000 online journals
Number of teachers: 100
Number of students: 850

PROFESSORS

CREAGAN, J. F., International Relations
GRAY, L. E., Political Science

LIBERA UNIVERSITÀ DEGLI STUDI DI ENNA 'KORE' (UKE)

Cittadella Universitaria, 94100 Enna (SI)
Telephone: 0935-536342
Fax: 0935-536907
E-mail: rettore@unikore.it
Internet: www.unikore.it
Founded 2004
Private control with public participation
Pres.: Prof. CATALDO SALERNO
Rector: Prof. SALVO ANDÒ
Admin. Dir: Dott. SALVATORE BERRITTELLA

DEANS

Faculty of Arts and Communication: Prof. LIBORIO TERMINE
Faculty of Economic and Social Sciences: Prof. GIACOMO MULÉ
Faculty of Engineering and Architecture: Prof. GIOVANNI TESORIERE
Faculty of Law: Prof. GIUSEPPE DI CHIARA
Faculty of Psychology and Educational Sciences: Prof. VALERIA SCHIMMENTI
Faculty of Sports Science and Wellbeing: Prof. MARIO LIPOMA

LIBERA UNIVERSITÀ DEGLI STUDI PER L'INNOVAZIONE E LE ORGANIZZAZIONI (LUSPIO)

Via delle Sette Chiese 139. 00145 Rome
Telephone: 06-5107771
Fax: 06-5122416
E-mail: info@luspio.it
Internet: www.luspio.it
Founded 1996
Private control
Rector: Prof. GIUSEPPE ACOCELLA
Deputy Rector: Prof. GIANDOMENICO BOFFI
Admin. Dir: Dott. CRISTIANO NICOLETTI

DEANS

Faculty of Economics: Prof. GUIDO PAGGI
Faculty of Interpretation and Translation: Prof. NOVELLA NOVELLI
Faculty of Political Sciences: Prof. OLGA MARZOVILLA
Higher School of Advanced Studies: Prof. ROBERTO GUIDA (Dir)

LIBERA UNIVERSITÀ DI LINGUE E COMUNICAZIONE IULM

Via Carlo Bo 1, 20143 Milan
Telephone: 02-891411
Fax: 02-891414000
E-mail: iulm.orienta@iulm.it
Internet: www.iulm.it
Founded 1968
Academic year: October to May
Rector: Prof. GIOVANNI A. PUGLISI
Vice-Rector: Prof. MARIO NEGRI
Library Dir: Dott. GIOVANNI MOSCATI
Library of 190,000 vols, 1,350 journals
Number of teachers: 350
Number of students: 8,500

DEANS

Faculty of Arts, Markets and Cultural Heritage: Profa MARIO NEGRI
Faculty of Communications, Public Relations and Advertising: Prof. GIAN BATTISTA CANOVA
Faculty of Interpreting, Translation, and Language and Cultural Studies: Profa PAOLO PROIETTI
Faculty of Tourism: Prof. ALBERTO ABRUZZESE

LIBERA UNIVERSITÀ INTERNAZIONALE DEGLI STUDI SOCIALI 'GUIDO CARLI'
(Independent International University of Social Studies)

Viale Pola 12, 00198 Rome
Telephone: 06-852251
Fax: 06-85225300
E-mail: direzionegenerale@luiss.it
Internet: www.luiss.it
Founded 1945, recognized by the Government 1966
Pres.: Dott. EMMA MARCEGAGLIA
Exec. Vice-Pres.: ALESSANDRO LATERZA
Rector: Prof. MASSIMO EGIDI
Gen. Dir: PIER LUIGI CELLI
Librarian: Dr BEATRIZ VILLAGRASA HERNANDEZ
Library of 118,000 vols and 2,133 periodicals
Number of teachers: 1,070
Number of students: 7,494

DEANS

Faculty of Economics: Prof. GIORGIO DI GIORGIO
Faculty of Law: Prof. ROBERTO PESSI
Faculty of Political Science: Prof. SEBASTIANO MAFFETONE

LIBERA UNIVERSITÀ MARIA SS. ASSUNTA

Via della Traspontina 21, 00193 Rome
Telephone: 06-684221
Fax: 06-6878357
E-mail: lumsa@lumsa.it
Internet: www.lumsa.it
Founded 1939
Academic year: October to July
Rector: Prof. GIUSEPPE DALLA TORRE DEL TEMPIO DI SANGUINETTO
Vice-Rector: Prof. GIUSEPPE IGNESTI
Admin. Dir: Dott. GIANNINA DI MARCO
Librarian: Dott. GIUSEPPINA D'ALESSANDRO
Library of 100,000 vols
Number of teachers: 350
Number of students: 5,200
Publications: *I Quaderni della Lumsa* (1 a year), *Nuovi Studi Politici* (4 a year)

DEANS

Faculty of Eduction: Prof. CONSUELO CORRADI
Faculty of Law: Prof. ANGELO RINELLA

Faculty of Letters and Philosophy: Prof. LOREDANA LAZZARI

LIBERA UNIVERSITÀ MEDITERRANEA 'JEAN MONNET'

S.S. 100 Km 18, Casamassima (BA)
Telephone: 080-6978111
Fax: 080-6977122
E-mail: info@lum.it
Internet: www.lum.it
Founded 1995
Private control
Rector: EMANUELE DEGENNARO
Admin. Dir: FELICE GNAGNARELLA
Library of 11,000 , 160 journals, 30 online journals

DEANS
Faculty of Economics: Prof. ANTONELLO GARZONI
Faculty of Law: Prof. ROBERTO MARTINO

SCUOLA INTERNAZIONALE SUPERIORE DI STUDI AVANZATI

Via Bonomea 265, 34136 Trieste
Telephone: 040-3787111
Fax: 040-3787249
Internet: www.sissa.it
Founded 1978; sponsored by the Italian Government
Languages of instruction: English, Italian
Academic year: November to October
Director: GUIDO MARTINELLI
Admin. Dir: LUCA BARDI
Library of 20,000 vols, 120 journals, 7,000 online journals
Number of teachers: 62
Number of students: 220
Higher degrees in physics, mathematics and neuroscience; research; fellowships for students from developing countries.

SCUOLA NORMALE SUPERIORE DI PISA

Piazza dei Cavalieri 7, 56126 Pisa
Telephone: 050-509111
Fax: 050-563513
E-mail: info@pec.sns.it
Internet: www.sns.it
Founded 1810
State control
Dir: Prof. FABIO BELTRAM
Admin. Dir: Dott. ANNA MARIA GAIBISSO
Library Dir: Dott. ENRICO MARTELLINI
Library of 100,000,000 vols
Number of teachers: 40
Number of students: 280
Publications: Annali (Arts series, Science series), Appunti, Bibliotheca, Colloquia, CRM Series (mathematical research), Seminari e convegni, Strumenti, Studi, Tesi, Testi e commenti

DEANS
Faculty of Arts: Prof. DANIELE MENOZZI
Faculty of Sciences: Prof. RICCARDO BARBIERI

SCUOLA SUPERIORE DI STUDI UNIVERSITARI E DI PERFEZIONAMENTO 'SANT'ANNA'

Piazza Martiri della Libertà 33, 56127 Pisa
Telephone: 050-883111
Fax: 050-883225
E-mail: urp@sssup.it
Internet: www.sssup.it
Founded 1987
Private control
Pres.: Prof. RICCARDO VARALDO

Dir: Prof. MARIA CHIARA CARROZZA
Admin. Dir: MARIO GARZELLA
Library of 70,000 , 200 current journals, 30,000 online journals
Number of teachers: 103
Number of students: 1,810
Admission to the courses is by public competitive examination. Programmes in economics, law, political sciences, agriculture, medicine, industrial and information engineering. Standard courses, university and int. Masters degree courses, PhD programmes and doctorates, and advanced education are offered

DEANS
Academic Class of Experimental Sciences: Prof. ENRICO BONARI
Academic Class of Social Sciences: Prof. EMANUELE ROSSI

UNIVERSITÀ CAMPUS BIO-MEDICO DI ROMA

Via Álvaro del Portillo, 21, 00128 Rome
Telephone: 06-225411
Fax: 06-22541456
E-mail: info@unicampus.it
Internet: www.unicampus.it
Founded 1991
Private control
Pres.: Prof. PAOLO ARULLANI
Rector: Prof. VINCENZO LORENZELLI
Admin. Dir: Ing. PAOLO SORMANI

DEANS
Faculty of Engineering: Prof. LUIGI MARRELLI
Faculty of Medicine and Surgery: Prof. VINCENZO DENARO

UNIVERSITÀ CARLO CATTANEO— LIUC

Corso Matteotti 22, 21053 Castellanza (VA)
Telephone: 0331-5721
Fax: 0331-572511
E-mail: info@liuc.it
Internet: www.liuc.it
Founded 1991
Private control
Rector: ANDREA TARONI
Gen. Dir: PIERLUIGI RIVA

DEANS
Faculty of Economics: Prof. VALTER LAZZARI
Faculty of Engineering: Prof. GIACOMO BUONANNO
Faculty of Law: Prof. MARIO ZANCHETTI

UNIVERSITÀ CATTOLICA DEL SACRO CUORE
(Catholic University of the Sacred Heart)

Largo A. Gemelli 1, 20123 Milan
Telephone: 02-72341
Fax: 02-72343796
E-mail: seg.prorettori@unicatt.it
Internet: www.unicattolica.it
Founded 1920; recognized by the Government 1924
Rector: Prof. LORENZO ORNAGHI
Admin. Dir: Prof. MARCO ELEFANTI
Librarian: Dott. ELLIS SADA
Library of 2,000,000 vols, 32,000 journals, 12,000 online journals
Number of teachers: 1,400
Number of students: 42,000
Publication: various, published by individual faculties

DEANS
Faculty of Agriculture: Prof. LORENZO MORELLI
Faculty of Banking, Finance and Insurance Sciences: Prof. MARIO ANOLLI
Faculty of Economics (Milan and Rome): Prof. DOMENICO BODEGA
Faculty of Economics (Piacenza): Prof. MAURIZIO LUIGI BAUSSOLA
Faculty of Education: Prof. MICHELE LENOCI
Faculty of Law (Milan): Prof. GABRIO FORTI
Faculty of Law (Piacenza): Prof. ROMEO ASTORRI
Faculty of Letters and Philosophy: Prof. ANGLEO BIANCHI
Faculty of Linguistic Sciences and Foreign Literatures: Prof. LUISA CAMAIORA
Faculty of Mathematical, Physical and Natural Sciences: Prof. ALFREDO MARZOCCHI
Faculty of Medicine and Surgery: Prof. ROCCO BELLANTONE
Faculty of Political Sciences: Prof. CARLO BERETTA
Faculty of Psychology: Prof. EUGENIA SCABINI
Faculty of Sociology: Prof. MAURO MAGATTI

UNIVERSITÀ COMMERCIALE LUIGI BOCCONI

Via Sarfatti 25, 20136 Milan
Telephone: 02-58361
Fax: 02-58362000
Internet: www.unibocconi.eu
Founded 1902; private control
Academic year: November to October
Pres.: Prof. MARIO MONTI
Rector: Prof. GUIDO TABELLINI
Vice-Pres.: Prof. LUIGI GUATRI
Man. Dir: Dott. BRUNO PAVESI
Number of teachers: 971
Number of students: 12,600
Publications: Azienda Pubblica, Commercio, Economia delle Fonti di Energia, Economia e Management, Economia e Politica Industriale, Finanza Marketing e Produzione, Giornale degli Economisti e Annali di Economia, Sviluppo e Organizzazione

DEANS
SDA Bocconi School of Management: Prof. ALBERTO GRANDO
Graduate School: Prof. FRANCESCO SAITA
School of Law: Prof. GIOVANNI IUDUCA
PhD School: Prof. ALFONSO GAMBARDELLA
Undergraduate School: Prof. GIOVANNI VALOTTI

PROFESSORS
AIROLDI, G., Business Administration
ALESSANDRI, A., Commercial Law
AMATORI, F., Economic History
AMIGONI, F., Business Administration
ARTONI, R., Public Finance
BATTIGALLI, P., Economics
BELTRATTI, A., Economics
BERTONI, A., Corporate Finance
BIANCHI, L. A., Company and Business Law
BINI, M., Corporate Finance
BORGONOVI, E., Public Administration
BRUGGER, G., Corporate Finance
BRUNETTI, G., Business Administration
BRUNI, F., International Monetary Theory and Policy
BUSACCA, B., Business Administration and Management
CASTAGNOLA, A., Civil Law
CASTAGNOLI, E., Mathematics
CATTINI, M., Economic History
CIFARELLI, D. M., Statistics
CODA, V., Business Administration
DE PAOLI, L., Business Administration and Management
DEMATTÈ, C., Financial Intermediaries
FABRIZI, P. L., Securities Market

FAVERO, C. A., Monetary Economics
FERRARI, G., Monetary Economics
FILIPPINI, C., Economic Development
FORESTIERI, G., Financial Intermediaries
FRACCHIA, F., Administrative Law
FROVA, A., Corporate Finance
GIAVAZZI, F., Economics
GOLFETTO, F., Business Administration and Management
GRANDORI, A., Corporate Organization
GUARNERI, A., Comparative Civil Law
INVERNIZZI, G., Business Administration
IUDICA, G., Civil Law
LIEBMAN, S., Labour Law
MALERBA, F., Business Administration
MARCHETTI, P., Industrial Law
MASSARI, M., Capital Budgeting
MONTESANO, A., Economics
MONTI, M., Economics
MOTTURA, P., Financial Intermediaries
MULIERE, P., Statistics
ONIDA, F., International Economics
PACI, S., Management of Insurance Companies and Savings Institutions
PECCATI, L., Mathematics for Economics and Finance
PERRONE, V., Organization Theory
PEZZANI, F., Business Administration
PIVATO, S., Industrial Management
PODESTÀ, S., Commercial Management
PORTA, A., Monetary Theory and Policy
PROVASOLI, A., Cost Accounting and Management Control Systems
ROMANI, A., Economic History
RUOZI, R., Banking
SACERDOTI, G., International Law
SALVEMINI, S., Human Resources Management
SECCHI, C., Economics of the European Communities
SENN, L., Regional Economics
SITZIA, B., Econometrics
TABELLINI, G., Economics
URBANI, G., Political Science
VALDANI, E., Marketing
VALOTTI, G., Business Administration
VERONESE, P., Statistics
VICARI, S., Management of Industrial Companies
VIGANO, A., Cost Accounting and Management Control Systems

UNIVERSITÀ DEGLI STUDI DI SCIENZE GASTRONOMICHE
(University of Gastronomic Sciences)

Piazza Vittorio Emanuele 9, fraz. Pollenzo, 12042 Bra (CN)
Telephone: 0172-458511
Fax: 0172-458500
E-mail: info@unisg.it
Internet: www.unisg.it
Founded 2004
Private control

Rector: Prof. VALTER CANTINO
Vice-Rector: Prof. ALBERTO CAPATTI
Admin. Dir: CARLO CATANI
Number of teachers: 15

Undergraduate course in gastronomic sciences; graduate course in gastronomy and food communications; masters courses in Italian gastronomy and tourism, and food culture and communications; Advanced School in Sustainability and Food Policies.

UNIVERSITÀ DEGLI STUDI E-CAMPUS

Via Isimbardi 10, 22060 Novedrate (CO)
Telephone: 031-7942500
Fax: 031-792631
E-mail: info@uniecampus.it
Internet: www.uniecampus.it
Founded 2006

Private control
Pres.: Prof. LANFRANCO ROSATI
Offers distance learning

COORDINATORS
Faculty of Arts: Prof. PAOLO TROVATO
Faculty of Economics: Prof. ELISABETTA BERTACCHINI
Faculty of Engineering: Prof. CARLO MARIA BARTOLINI

UNIVERSITÀ DEGLI STUDI SUOR ORSOLA BENINCASA

Corso Vittorio Emanuele 292, 80135 Naples
Telephone: 081-2522111
E-mail: f.desanctis@unisob.na.it
Internet: www.unisob.na.it
Founded 1864
Private control

Rector: Prof. FRANCESCO DE SANCTIS
Deputy Rector: Prof. LUCIO D'ALESSANDRO
Admin. Dir: Dott. ANTONIO CUNZIO

DEANS
Faculty of Arts: Prof. EMMA GIAMMATTEI
Faculty of Education: Prof. LUCIO D'ALESSANDRO
Faculty of Law: Prof. FRANCO FICHERA

UNIVERSITÀ DELLA VALLE D'AOSTA/ UNIVERSITÉ DE LA VALLÉE D'AOSTE

Strada Cappuccini 2A, 11100 Aosta
Telephone: 0165-306711
Fax: 0165-32835
E-mail: info@univda.it
Internet: www.univda.it
Founded 2000
Private control
Languages of instruction: Italian, English, French, Spanish, German
Rector: Prof. PIETRO PASSERIN D'ENTRÈVES
Admin. Dir: Dott. FRANCO VIETTI

DEANS
Faculty of Economics and Management: Prof. CHIARA MAURI
Faculty of Education: Prof. TERESA GRANGE
Faculty of Languages and Communication: Prof. CARLO MARIA BAJETTA
Faculty of Political Sciences: Prof. MICHELE VELLANO
Faculty of Psychology: Prof. MARIA GRAZIA MONACI

UNIVERSITÀ EUROPEA DI ROMA

Via degli Aldobrandeschi 190, 00163 Rome
Telephone: 06-665431
Fax: 06-66543840
E-mail: rettorato@unier.it
Internet: www.universitaeuropeadiroma.it
Founded 2004
Private control
Rector: Prof. Padre PAOLO SCARAFONI
Gen. Sec.: Padre JESÚS PARREÑO

Undergraduate courses in economics, history, law, psychology.

UNIVERSITÀ PER STRANIERI 'DANTE ALIGHIERI'

Via del Torrione 95, 89125 Reggio di Calabria
Telephone: 0965-312593
Fax: 0965-323640
E-mail: rettore@unistrada.it
Internet: www.unistrada.it
Founded 1984
Private control
Rector: Prof. SALVATORE BERLINGÒ
Pro-Rector: Prof. ANTONINO ZUMBO

Admin. Dir: ALESSANDRO ZOCCALI

Undergraduate courses in social sciences, literature, foreign languages and literature; graduate courses in planning and management of policies and social sciences, int. marketing; European master's degree course.

UNIVERSITÀ PER STRANIERI DI PERUGIA

Piazza Fortebraccio 4, 06123 Perugia
Telephone: 075-57461
Fax: 075-5732014
E-mail: diramm@unistrapg.it
Internet: www.unistrapg.it
Founded 1921
Academic year: January to December
Rector: Prof. STEFANIA GIANNINI
Vice-Rector: Prof. MARCO IMPAGLIAZZO
Admin. Dir: Dott. ANTONELLA BIANCONI
Library of 70,000 vols
Number of teachers: 100
Number of students: 7,000
Publication: Annali dell'Università

DEANS
Faculty of Italian Language and Culture: Prof. PAOLA BIANCHI DE VECCHI
Dept of Comparative Cultures: Prof. NORBERTO CACCIAGLIA (Dir)
Dept of Languages: Prof. DANIELLA GAMBINI (Dir)

ATTACHED CENTRES
Centre for Language Evaluation and Certification: Dir Prof. GIULIANA GREGO BOLLI.
WARREDOC: internet warredoc.unistrapg.it; Carries out teaching, research, organizational and documentation activities in the sphere of water resources, environment, natural disasters management and sustainable devt; Dir Prof. ROBERTO CHIONNE.

UNIVERSITÀ PER STRANIERI DI SIENA

Piazza Carlo Rosselli 27–28, 53100 Siena
Telephone: 0577-240100
Fax: 0577-281030
E-mail: info@unistrasi.it
Internet: www.unistrasi.it
Founded 1917
State control
Rector: Prof. MASSIMO VEDOVELLI
Pro-Rector: Prof. MARINA BENEDETTI
Admin. Dir: Dott. ALESSANDRO BALDUCCI
Number of students: 4,599

DEANS
Faculty of Italian Language and Culture: Prof. MASSIMO PALERMO
Dept of Humanities: Prof. PIETRO CATALDI (Dir)
Dept of Languages and Cultures: Prof. MARIA LUCIA STRAPPINI (Dir)

UNIVERSITÀ TELEMATICA 'GIUSTINO FORTUNATO'

Viale Raffaele Delcogliano 12, 82100 Benevento
Telephone: 0824-316057
Fax: 0824-351887
E-mail: info@unifortunato.eu
Internet: www.unifortunato.eu
Founded 2006
Private control
Rector: Prof. AUGUSTO FANTOZZI
Admin. Dir: Dott. MARIA VINCENZA RIVELLINI

Offers distance learning. Masters degrees in law, business law, Roman law, tax law.

UNIVERSITÀ TELEMATICA 'LEONARDO DA VINCI'

Piazza San Rocco, 66010 Torrevecchia Teatina (CH)
Telephone: 0871-361658
Fax: 0871-361658
E-mail: info@unidav.it
Internet: www.unidav.it

Founded 2004 jointly by the Università degli Studi 'Gabriele D'Annunzio' and the Fondazione Università 'Gabriele d'Annunzio'
Private control

Rector: Prof. FABIO CAPANI

Offers distance learning. Faculties of cultural heritage, education, law, management, medicine and surgery, psychology.

UNIVERSITÀ TELEMATICA 'UNIVERSITAS MERCATORUM'

Via Appia Pignatelli 62, 00178 Rome
Telephone: 06-78052327
Fax: 06-7842136
E-mail: segreteria@unimercatorum.it
Internet: www.unimercatorum.it

Founded 2006
Private control

Rector: Prof. GIORGIO MARBACH

Offers distance learning; undergraduate courses in company management, human resources management.

UNIVERSITÀ TELEMATICA DELLE SCIENZE UMANE UNISU

Via Casalmonferrato 2B, 00182 Rome
Telephone: 06-70304302
E-mail: info@unisu.it
Internet: www.unisu.it

Founded 2006
Private control

Rector: Prof. Avv. GIOVANNI PUOTI
Gen. Dir: DANIELA SASANELLI
Admin. Dir: LUIGI PELUSO CASSESE

Offers distance learning. Faculties of economics, education, law, politics.

UNIVERSITÀ TELEMATICA INTERNAZIONALE UNINETTUNO

Corso V. Emanuele II 39, 00186 Rome
Telephone: 06-69207670
E-mail: info@uninettunouniversity.net
Internet: www.uninettunouniversity.net

Founded 2005
Private control

Rector: Prof. MARIA AMATA GARITO
Admin. Dir: STEFANO FRIGERI

Offers distance learning

DEANS

Faculty of Arts: Prof. TATIANA KIROVA
Faculty of Communication Sciences: Prof. ALBERTO ABRUZZESE
Faculty of Economics: Prof. GENNARO OLIVIERI
Faculty of Engineering: Prof. BERNARDINO CHIAIA
Faculty of Law: Prof. GIOVANNI CABRAS
Faculty of Psychology: Prof. JOOST LOWYCK

UNIVERSITÀ TELEMATICA PEGASO

Via Vittoria Colonna 14, Angolo Piazza Amedeo, 80121 Naples
Telephone: 081-19567975
Fax: 081-1954330
Internet: www.unipegaso.it

Founded 2006
Private control

Rector: Prof. RICCARDO FRAGNITO

Gen. Dir: Dott. ELIO PARIOTA

Offers distance learning. Faculties of humanities, law.

UNIVERSITÀ TELEMATICA SAN RAFFAELE ROMA

Via di Val Cannuta 247, 00166 Rome
Telephone: 02-36696110
Fax: 02-36696112
Internet: www.uni-tel.it

Founded 2006
Private control

Rector: Prof. GIUSEPPE ROTILIO

Offers distance learning. Faculties of architecture and industrial design, sport sciences, agriculture.

UNIVERSITÀ TELEMATICA UNITELMA

Viale Regina Elena 295, 00161 Rome
Telephone: 06-69190797
E-mail: segreteria@unitelma.it
Internet: www.unitelma.it

Founded 2004
Private control

Rector: Prof. ANIELLO CIMITILE
Admin. Dir: Dott. MICHELE OREFICE

Offers distance learning

DEANS

Faculty of Economics: Prof. SERGIO SCIARELLI
Faculty of Law: Prof. ANIELLO CIMITILE

UNIVERSITÀ VITA-SALUTE 'SAN RAFFAELE'

Via Olgettina, 58, 20132 Milan
Telephone: 02-26433802
Fax: 02-26433803
E-mail: segreteria.studenti@unisr.it
Internet: www.unisr.it

Founded 1996
Private control

Rector: Sac. Prof. LUIGI M. VERZÉ
Gen. Dir: Dott. RAFFAELLA VOLTOLINI

DEANS

Faculty of Philosophy: Prof. MICHELE DI FRANCESCO
Faculty of Medicine and Surgery: Prof. MASSIMO CLEMENTI
Faculty of Psychology: Prof. LUCIO SARNO

VENICE INTERNATIONAL UNIVERSITY

Isola di San Servolo, 30100 Venice
Telephone: 041-2719511
Fax: 041-2719510
E-mail: viu@univiu.it
Internet: www.univiu.org

Founded 1997
Academic year: September to May

Pres.: UMBERTO VATTANI
Dean: STEFANO MICELLI
Admin. Dir: ALESSANDRO SPEZZAMONTE
Dir of School of Humanities and Social Sciences: LUCA PES

Staff and students provided by the constituent univs.

Schools of Music and Art
MUSIC

Accademia Filarmonica Romana (Rome Philharmonic Academy): Via Flaminia 118, 00196 Rome; tel. 06-3201752; fax 06-3210410; e-mail info@filarmonicaromana .org; internet www.filarmonicaromana.org; f. 1821; library: 1,500 vols; Pres. PAOLO BARATTA; Artistic Dir SANDRO CAPPELLETTO.

Accademia Musicale Chigiana: Via di Città 89, 53100 Siena; tel. 0577-22091; fax 0577-288124; e-mail accademia.chigiana@ chigiana.it; internet www.chigiana.it; f. 1932; master classes, seminars, lectures, concerts, operas, international research conventions; 26 teachers; 351 students; Artistic Director Maestro ALDO BENNICI.

Conservatorio 'Claudio Monteverdi' di Bolzano: Piazza Domenicani 19, 39100 Bolzano; tel. 0471-978764; e-mail info@ conservatoriobolzano.it; internet www .conservatoriobolzano.it; f. 1940; library: 10,000 vols; international Busoni Piano Competition held annually; Dir Prof. FELIX RESCH; Admin. Dir Dott. MARIO BELLI.

Conservatorio di Musica 'Arrigo Boito' di Parma: Via del Conservatorio 27A, 43121 Parma; tel. 0521-381911; fax 0521-200398; e-mail direttore@conservatorio.pr.it; internet www.conservatorio.pr.it; f. 1825; library: 70,000 vols; 140 teachers; 800 students; Dir ROBERTO CAPPELLO.

Conservatorio di Musica 'Benedetto Marcello': Palazzo Pisani, San Marco 2810, 30124 Venice; tel. 041-5225604; fax 041-5239268; e-mail direttoreamministrativo@ conseve.it; internet www.conseve.it; f. 1877; 90 teachers; 480 students; library: 50,000 vols, 70 periodicals; Dir Prof. MASSIMO CONTIERO.

Conservatorio di Musica di Napoli 'San Pietro a Majella': Via San Pietro a Majella 35, 80138 Naples; tel. 081-5644411; fax 081-5644415; e-mail direzioneamministrativa@ sanpietroamajella.it; internet www .sanpietroamajella.it; Dir PATRIZIO MARRONE; Admin. Dir CLOTILDE PUNZO.

Conservatorio di Musica 'Giovan Battista Martini': Piazza Rossini 2, 40126 Bologna; tel. 051-221483; fax 051-223168; e-mail segreteria@conservatorio-bologna .com; internet www.conservatorio-bologna .com; f. 1804; Dir DONATELLA PIERI.

Conservatorio di Musica 'Giuseppe Tartini': Via Ghega 12, 34132 Trieste; tel. 040-6724911; fax 040-370265; e-mail rosanna .corsi@conts.it; internet www.conservatorio .trieste.it; f. 1903; 93 teachers; 630 students; Dir MASSIMO PAROVEL; Admin. Dir ROSANNA CORSI.

Conservatorio di Musica 'Giuseppe Verdi': Via Conservatorio 12, 20122 Milan; tel. 02-762110216; fax 02-76020259; e-mail segreteriadirezione@consmilano.it; internet www.consmilano.it; f. 1808; library: see Libraries; Dir SONIA BO.

Conservatorio di Musica 'Niccolò Piccinni': Via Cifarelli 26, 70124 Bari; tel. 080-5740022; fax 080-5794461; e-mail diramm@ conservatoriopiccinni.it; internet www .conservatoriopiccinni.it; f. 1959; library: 11,000 vols; Dir Maestro FRANCESCO MONOPOLI; Admin. Dir Dott. ANNAMARIA SFORZA.

Conservatorio di Musica 'Vincenzo Bellini' di Palermo: Via Squarcialupo 45, 90133 Palermo; tel. 091-580921; fax 091-586742; e-mail paconsediwin@hotmail.com; internet www.conservatoriobellini.it; f. 1721; library: 40,000 vols, collection of 18th- and 19th-century MSS; Dir Maestro CARMELO CARUSO; Admin. Dir Dott. RAIMUNDO CIPOLLA; publ. Quaderni del Conservatorio (irregular).

Conservatorio 'Santa Cecilia': Via dei Greci 18, 00187 Rome; tel. 06-36096720; internet www.conservatoriosantacecilia.it; Dir Maestro EDDA SILVESTRI.

Conservatorio Statale di Musica 'G. Rossini': Piazza Olivieri 5, 61100 Pesaro; tel. 0721-33671; fax 0721-35295; e-mail segreteria@conservatoriorossini.it; internet www.conservatoriorossini.it; f. 1882; library: 25,000 vols; Dir MAURIZIO TARSETTI.

Conservatorio Statale di Musica 'Giovanni Pierluigi da Palestrina': Piazza E. Porrino 1, 09128 Cagliari; tel. 070-493118; fax 070-487388; e-mail dir.amministrativo@conservatoriocagliari.it; internet www.conservatoriocagliari.it; f. 1939; Dir Prof. M. GABRIELLA ARTIZZU; Admin. Dir Dott. FRANCESCA BASILONE.

Conservatorio Statale di Musica 'Giuseppe Verdi': Via Mazzini 11, 10123 Turin; tel. 011-8178458; fax 011-885165; internet www.conservatoriotorino.eu; f. 1867; Dir MARIA LUISA PACCIANI.

Conservatorio Statale di Musica 'Luigi Cherubini': Piazzetta delle Belle Arti 2, 50121 Florence; tel. 055-2989311; fax 055-2396785; e-mail info@conservatorio.firenze.it; internet www.conservatorio.firenze.it; f. 1861; 107 teachers; 702 students; Dir Prof. PAOLO BIORDI; Chief Admin. Officer Dott. ROBERTO VOLPI.

ART

Accademia Albertina delle Belle Arti di Torino: Via Accademia Albertina 6, 10123 Turin; tel. 011-889020; fax 011-8125688; e-mail info@accademialbertina.torino.it; internet www.accademialbertina.torino.it; f. 1652; 70 teachers; 550 students; Pres. Dott. MARCO ALBERA; Dir Prof. GUIDO CURTO.

Accademia di Belle Arti di Bologna (Academy of Fine Arts of Bologna): Via Belle Arti 54, 40126 Bologna; tel. 051-4226411; fax 051-253032; e-mail info@accademiabelleartibologna.it; internet www.accademiabelleartibologna.it; f. 1710; library: 15,000 vols; Dir Prof. ADRIANO BACCILIERI; Librarian CRISTINA PRATI; publ. *Prontuario* (1 a year).

Accademia di Belle Arti di Brera (Academy of Fine Arts of Brera): Palazzo di Brera, Via Brera 28, 20121 Milan; tel. 02-869551; fax 02-86403643; e-mail accademia@accademiadibrera.milano.it; internet www.accademiadibrera.milano.it; f. 1776; library: 25,000 vols; 400 teachers; 3,500 students; Pres. Dott. SALVATORE CARRUBBA; Dir Prof. GASTONE MARIANI.

Accademia di Belle Arti di Carrara (Academy of Fine Arts): Via Roma 1, 54033 Carrara; tel. 0585-71658; e-mail info@accademiacarrara.it; internet www.accademiacarrara.it; courses in painting, sculpture and scene-painting; Dir Prof. MARCO BAUDINELLI; Admin. Dir Dr GUIDO RAFFAELE.

Accademia di Belle Arti di Firenze (Academy of Fine Arts of Florence): Via Ricasoli 66, 50122 Florence; tel. 055-215449; fax 055-2396921; e-mail segreteria@accademia.firenze.it; internet www.accademia.firenze.it; f. 1801; library: 22,000 vols; Pres. Avv. GAETANO VICICONTE; Dir Prof. GIULIANA VIDETTA.

Accademia di Belle Arti di Lecce (Academy of Fine Arts of Lecce): Via Libertini 3, 73100 Lecce; tel. 0832-258611; fax 0832-301490; e-mail accademialecce@libero.it; internet www.accademiabelleartilecce.com; Dir Prof. Arch. GIACINTO LEONE.

Accademia di Belle Arti di Napoli (Academy of Fine Arts of Naples): Via Costantinopoli 107, 80138 Naples; tel. 081-444245; fax 081-444245; e-mail napoli_accademia@libero.it; internet www.accademianapoli.it; f. 1838; library: 7,000 vols; Dir Prof. ALFREDO SCOTTI.

Accademia di Belle Arti di Palermo (Academy of Fine Arts of Palermo): Via Papireto 1, 90134 Palermo; tel. 091-580876; fax 091-583746; e-mail amministrazione@accademiadipalermo.it; internet www.accademiadipalermo.it; f. 1780; Dir Prof. UMBERTO DE PAOLA.

Accademia di Belle Arti di Ravenna (Academy of Fine Arts of Ravenna): Via delle Industrie 76, 48122 Ravenna; tel. 0544-453125; fax 0544-451104; e-mail accademia@comune.ra.it; internet www.accademiabellearti.ra.it; f. 1827; library: 10,000 vols; Dir Prof. MAURO MAZZALI; Admin. Dir Dott.ssa ORIELLA GARAVINI.

Accademia di Belle Arti di Roma (Academy of Fine Arts of Rome): Via Ripetta 222, 00186 Rome; tel. 06-3227025; fax 06-3218007; e-mail direzione@accademiabelleartiroma.it; internet www.accademiabelleartiroma.it; f. 1873; 2,000 students; Pres. Dr CESARE ROMITI; Dir Prof. GERARDO LO RUSSO.

Accademia di Belle Arti di Venezia (Academy of Fine Arts of Venice): Dorsoduro 423, 30123 Venice; tel. 041-2413752; fax 041-5230129; e-mail info@accademiavenezia.it; internet www.accademiavenezia.it; f. 1750; 96 teachers; 870 students; Dir CARLO DI RACO.

Accademia di Belle Arti 'Pietro Vannucci' di Perugia (Academy of Fine Arts of Perugia): Piazza San Francesco al Prato 5, 06123 Perugia; tel. 075-5730631; fax 075-5730632; e-mail direzione@abaperugia.org; internet www.abaperugia.org; f. 1573; 96 Academicians, 143 Hon. Academicians; collections of paintings, engravings, drawings, etc.; library: 13,330 vols; Pres. Avv. MARIO RAMPINI; Dir Prof. GIULIANO GIUMAN.

Istituto Statale d'Arte: Via Bramante 20, 61029 Urbino; tel. 0722-329892; fax 0722-4830; e-mail ia.scuolalibro@provincia.ps.it; internet www.isaurbino.it; f. 1865; engraving techniques, cartoon drawing, ceramics, photography, editorial graphics, publicity art; library: 20,000 vols; 110 teachers; 714 students; Pres. Prof. MAURIZIA RAGONESI.

Istituto Statale d'Arte 'Enrico e Umberto Nordio': Via di Calvola 2, 34143 Trieste; tel. 040-300660; fax 040-311646; e-mail info@isanordio.it; internet www.isanordio.it; f. 1955; courses in architecture, design and printing of textiles, interior decorating; library: 5,450 vols; Dir Prof. TEODORO GIUDICE.

Istituto Statale d'Arte 'Filippo Figari': Piazza d'Armi 16, CP 105, 07100 Sassari; tel. 079-234466; fax 079-2012665; e-mail sssd020006@istruzione.it; f. 1935; woodwork, metalwork, weaving, painting, ceramics, graphic art and architecture; Pres. Prof. NICOLÒ MASIA.

Istituto Statale d'Arte 'G. Ballardini': Corso Baccarini 17, 48018 Faenza; tel. 0546-21091; fax 0546-680093; e-mail iaballardini@provincia.ra.it; internet www.ceramicschool.it; f. 1916; basic courses in ceramic art and technology; higher courses in stoneware, ceramic building coatings, porcelain, restoration, technology of special ceramics, traditional ceramics.

DANCE AND DRAMA

Accademia Nazionale d'Arte Drammatica 'Silvio d'Amico': Via Vincenzo Bellini 16, 00198 Rome; tel. 06-8543680; fax 06-8542505; e-mail segreteria.direttore@silviodamico.it; internet www.silviodamico.it; f. 1935; 45 teachers; 100 students; Dir Prof. LUIGI MARIA MUSATI.

Accademia Nazionale di Danza: Largo Arrigo VII 5, 00153 Rome; tel. 06-5717621; fax 06-5780994; e-mail sd@accademianazionaledanza.it; internet www.accademianazionaledanza.com; f. 1948; Pres. BRUNO BORGHI; Dir MARGHERITA PARRILLA.

JAMAICA

The Higher Education System

The University of Technology, Jamaica (formerly Jamaica Institute of Technology) was founded in 1958, while Jamaica was under British colonial administration. In 1962 Jamaica achieved full independence within the Commonwealth, and in the same year the University of the West Indies (founded 1948), which has a campus on the island at Mona, was elevated to university status. In 2003/04 there were 15 institutions providing tertiary education with 11,600 students enrolled. By 2005 the University of the West Indies alone had over 13,000 students. The Tertiary Unit of the Ministry of Education is the Government agency responsible for higher education.

Admission to higher education is on the basis of two or more GCE A-Levels. The Bachelors is the standard undergraduate degree and lasts three years, followed by the Masters, the first postgraduate degree. The University of the West Indies offers either a two-year, coursework-based Masters programme or a research-based Master of Philology (MPhil). The highest university degree is the Doctorate, which lasts for two years after award of the Masters.

Technical and vocational education at the post-secondary level is supervised by the Human Employment and Resource Training Agency and National Council on Technical and Vocational Education and Training. The Human Employment and Resource Training Agency runs several academies and vocational training centres and the National Council on Technical and Vocational Education and Training is the official body responsible for awarding the National Vocational Qualification of Jamaica (Levels 1–4). A three-year Associate of Science degree is offered by the College of Agriculture, Science and Education.

The University Council of Jamaica is responsible for quality assurance and accreditation of higher education institutions.

Regulatory and Representative Bodies

GOVERNMENT

Ministry of Education: 2 National Heroes Circle, Kingston 4; tel. 922-1400; fax 948-7755; e-mail maria.jones@moey.gov.jm; internet www.moey.gov.jm; Minister ANDREW HOLNESS.

Ministry of Information, Culture, Youth and Sports: Jamaica House, Kingston 6; tel. 927-9941; e-mail maria.jones@moey.gov.jm; Minister OLIVIA GRANGE.

ACCREDITATION

University Council of Jamaica: 6B Oxford Rd, Kingston 5; tel. 929-7299; fax 929-7312; e-mail ucj@cwjamaica.com; internet www.universitycouncilja.com; f. 1987 to increase the availability of univ.-level training in Jamaica, through accreditation of instns, courses and programmes for recognition and acceptability; has the power to confer degrees, diplomas, certificates and other academic awards and distinctions on those who have pursued courses approved by the Council at associated tertiary instns; Chair. Dr LLOYD BARNETT; Exec. Dir Dr ETHLEY D. LONDON.

Learned Societies

GENERAL

Institute of Jamaica: 12–16 East St, Kingston; tel. 922-0620; fax 922-1147; internet www.instituteofjamaica.org.jm; f. 1879; comprises the National Library of Jamaica (see Libraries); two Junior Cultural Centres; Natural History Division; Arawak (Indian) Museum; Jamaica Folk Museum; Military Museum; Maritime Museum; the National Gallery of Jamaica; the African-Caribbean Institute/Jamaica Memory Bank; Institute of Jamaica Publications; Exec. Dir. VIVIAN CRAWFORD (acting); publ. *Jamaica Journal*.

UNESCO Office Kingston: 3rd Fl., The Towers, 25 Dominica Drive, Kingston 5; tel. 929-7087; fax 929-8468; e-mail kingston@unesco.org; internet www.unescocaribbean .org; designated Cluster Office for Antigua and Barbuda, Bahamas, Barbados, Belize, Dominica, Grenada, Guyana, Jamaica, St Christopher and Nevis, St Lucia, St Vincent and the Grenadines, Suriname, Trinidad and Tobago; Dir HELENE-MARIE GOSSELIN.

AGRICULTURE, FISHERIES AND VETERINARY SCIENCE

Jamaican Association of Sugar Technologists: c/o Sugar Industry Research Institute, Kendal Rd, Mandeville; tel. 962-2241; fax 962-1288; f. 1937 by the local sugar industry to conduct research and investigate technical problems of the Jamaican sugar industry; 266 mems; uses library of Sugar Industry Research Institute; Pres. MICHAEL G. HYLTON; Sec. H. M. THOMPSON; publ. *JAST Journal* (1 a year).

ARCHITECTURE AND TOWN PLANNING

Jamaican Institute of Architects: POB 251, Kingston 10; 2A Oxford Park Ave, Kingston 5; tel. 926-8060; fax 920-3589; e-mail jia@cwjamaica.com; internet www.jia .org.jm; f. 1957; 71 mems (56 full, 15 assoc.); Pres. CHRISTOPHER WHYMS-STONE; Vice-Pres. LAURIE FERRON; Hon. Sec. VIDAL DOWDING; publ. *Jamaica Architect* (1 a year).

BIBLIOGRAPHY, LIBRARY SCIENCE AND MUSEOLOGY

Library and Information Association of Jamaica: POB 125, Kingston 5; tel. and fax 970-6578; e-mail liajapresident@yahoo.com; internet www.liaja.org.jm; f. 1949, as Jamaica Library Asscn; 227 mems; Pres. PAULINE NICHOLAS; Sec. ANDREA ROBINS; publs *LIAJA Bulletin* (1 a year), *LIAJA News* (2 a year).

HISTORY, GEOGRAPHY AND ARCHAEOLOGY

Jamaica National Heritage Trust: POB 8934, 79 Duke St, Kingston CSO; tel. 922-1287; fax 967-1703; e-mail jnht@cwjamaica .com; internet www.jnht.com; f. 1958; protection, preservation, restoration and promotion of Jamaica's material and cultural heritage, particularly through declaration of national monuments and designation of protected national heritage; Chair. Rev. DEVON DICK; Exec. Dir SUSANNE LYON.

LANGUAGE AND LITERATURE

Alliance Française: 12B, Lilford Ave (off Lady Musgrave Rd), Kingston 10; tel. 978-4622; fax 978-1836; e-mail alliance .francaisekingston@laposte.net; offers courses and examinations in French language and culture and promotes cultural exchange with France.

British Council: The British High Commission, 28 Trafalgar Rd, Kingston 10; tel. 929-7090; fax 960-3030; e-mail bcjamaica@ britishcouncil.org.jm; internet www .britishcouncil.org/caribbean; offers courses and examinations in English language and British culture and promotes cultural exchange with the UK; Man. NICOLA JOHNSON.

MEDICINE

Medical Association of Jamaica: 19A Windsor Ave, Kingston 5; tel. 946-1105; fax 946-1102; internet www.medicalassnjamaica .com; f. 1877 as br of British Medical Asscn; ind. body 1966; for the promotion of medical and allied sciences and of the medical profession; 707 mems; Pres. Dr ALVERSTON BAILEY; Hon. Sec. Dr ANN JACKSON-GIBSON; publ. *Journal* (1 a year).

TECHNOLOGY

Jamaica Institution of Engineers: 2 Winchester Rd, Kingston 10; tel. 929-6741; fax 929-4655; e-mail jie@anngel.com.jm; internet www.jieng.org; f. 1960, present name 1977; to promote the advancement of the engineering profession and the practice and science of engineering, and to facilitate the exchange of information and ideas on those subjects among the mems and others; Pres. HOWARD CHIN; Hon. Sec. HERMON EDMONSON; publ. *JIE Advisor* (12 a year).

Research Institutes

AGRICULTURE, FISHERIES AND VETERINARY SCIENCE

Sugar Industry Research Institute: Kendal Rd, Mandeville; tel. 962-2241; fax 962-1288; e-mail sirijam@jamaicasugar.org; internet www.jamaicasugar.org; f. 1973; research into sugar cane cultivation and environmental management; library of 660 vols, 2,500 bound vols of periodicals; Dir of Research EARLE ROBERTS.

ECONOMICS, LAW AND POLITICS

Planning Institute of Jamaica: 16 Oxford Rd, POB 634, Kingston 5; tel. 960-9339; fax 906-5011; e-mail info@pioj.gov.jm; internet www.pioj.gov.jm; f. 1955, fmrly the Central Planning Unit, present name in 1984; policy advice on economic, social and sustainable devt issues to the govt; Dir-Gen. Dr PAULINE KNIGHT; publs *Economic and Social Survey,- Jamaica* (1 a year), *Economic Update and Outlook* (4 a year), *JA People Magazine* (1 a year), *Jamaica Survey of Living Conditions* (1 a year), *The Labour Market Information Newsletter* (2 a year).

MEDICINE

Caribbean Food and Nutrition Institute (CFNI): Jamaica Centre, POB 140, Mona, Kingston 7; tel. 927-1540; fax 927-2657; e-mail e-mail@cfni.paho.org; internet www.cfni.paho.org; f. 1967; conducts research and training courses and provides technical advisory services to 18 govts of the English-speaking Caribbean on matters relating to food and nutrition; library of 5,700 vols; there is a centre in Trinidad; Dir Dr FITZROY HENRY; publs *Cajanus* (4 a year), *Nyam News* (24 a year).

Medical Research Council Laboratories: University of the West Indies, Mona, Kingston 7; tel. 927-2471; fax 927-2984; e-mail grserjnt@uwimona.edu.jm; f. 1974; attached to Medical Research Council, London; research into sickle-cell disease; 20 staff; Dir G. R. SERJEANT.

NATURAL SCIENCES

General

Scientific Research Council: POB 350, Kingston 6; tel. 927-1771; fax 927-1990; e-mail adminsrc@toj.com; internet www.src-jamaica.org; f. 1960; undertakes, fosters and coordinates scientific research in the island; library of 10,000 vols; Exec. Dir Dr AUDIA BARNETT; publs *Conference Proceedings* (1 a year), *Jamaican Journal of Science and Technology* (1 a year).

Libraries and Archives

Kingston

Jamaica Library Service: POB 58, 2 Tom Redcam Dr., Kingston 5; tel. 926-3310; fax 926-2188; internet www.jamlib.org.jm; f. 1948; provides an island-wide network of 656 service points, including 13 parish libraries, and 121 branch libraries; oversees 925 school and higher education libraries; total bookstock 2,711,000 vols, 70 periodicals; 1,121,000 vols in primary schools and 428,000 vols in secondary schools; Dir PATRICIA ROBERTS; publ. *Statistical Report of the Jamaica Library Service* (1 a year).

National Library of Jamaica: 12 East St, POB 823, Kingston; tel. 967-2494; fax 922-5567; e-mail nljresearch@cwjamaica.com; internet www.nlj.gov.jm; f. 1979; 47,000 printed items, 29,600 maps and plans, 4,400 serials, 27,100 photographs, 3,150 MSS, 2,550 items of audiovisual material on Jamaica and the West Indies; Exec. Dir WINSOME HUDSON; publs *Jamaica National Bibliography* (1 a year), *National Library News* (2 a year).

University of the West Indies Library: Mona, Kingston 7; tel. 512-3569; fax 927-1926; e-mail main.library@uwimona.edu.jm; internet www.mona.uwi.edu/library; f. 1948; 518,981 vols incl. 6,349 current and 6,495 non-current periodicals in the Main Library and 2 br. libraries for the Medical (32,896 vols) and Scientific (97,634 vols) Collns; Campus Librarian NORMA Y. AMENU-KPODO.

Spanish Town

Jamaica Archives and Records Department: cnr King and Manchester Sts, Spanish Town, St Catherine; tel. 984-2581; fax 984-8254; e-mail jarchives@jard.gov.jm; internet www.jard.gov.jm; f. 1659, present status 1955; nat. archives of Jamaica; spec. colln of ecclesiastical and private records of historical value; Govt Archivist CLAUDETTE THOMAS.

Museum

Kingston

Institute of Jamaica Museum: see Institute of Jamaica.

Universities

UNIVERSITY OF TECHNOLOGY, JAMAICA

237 Old Hope Rd, Kingston 6
Telephone: 927-1680
Fax: 927-4388
E-mail: regist@utech.edu.jm
Internet: www.utechjamaica.edu.jm
Public control

Accredited by University Council of Jamaica

Founded 1958 as Jamaica Institute of Technology; became College of Arts, Science and Technology 1959; present name and status 1995

Academic year: August to May

Chancellor: Sir WILLIAM MORRIS
Pro-Chancellor: EDWARD SEAGA
Pres.: Prof. ERROL MORRISON
Vice-Pres. for Academic Affairs and Quality Assurance: GEORGE ROPER
Vice-Pres. for Admin. and Univ. Registrar: DIANNE MITCHELL
Vice-Pres. for Devt: Dr NEVILLE SADDLER
Vice-Pres. for Finance, IT and Business Services: KOFI NKRUMAH-YOUNG
Vice-Pres. for Graduate Studies, Research and Entrepreneurship: Prof. GOSSETT OLIVER
Hon. Treasurer: VIVIAN CRAWFORD
Univ. Librarian: HERMINE SALMON
Univ. Orator: PAMELA KELLY

Number of teachers: 600
Number of students: 10,000

Serves Antigua and Barbuda, Anguilla, Barbados, Bahamas, Belize, British Virgin Islands, Dominica, Grenada, Guyana, Jamaica, St Lucia, St Vincent, Trinidad and Tobago, and Turks and Caicos Islands

Publication: *Journal*

DEANS

Faculty of the Built Environment: Dr CAROL ARCHER (acting)
Faculty of Business and Management: GARTH KIDDOE

Faculty of Education and Liberal Studies: Dr HALDANE JOHNSON
Faculty of Engineering and Computing: CHARMAINE DELISSER
Faculty of Health and Applied Science: Dr EUGENIE BROWN-MYRIE

UNIVERSITY OF THE WEST INDIES, MONA CAMPUS

Mona, Kingston 7
Telephone: 927-1661
Fax: 927-2765
E-mail: oadmin@uwimona.edu.jm
Internet: www.mona.uwi.edu

Founded 1948, University 1962

Serves 16 territories: Jamaica, Anguilla, Bahamas, Belize, British Virgin Islands, Cayman Islands, Barbados, Antigua and Barbuda, Dominica, Grenada, Montserrat, St Christopher and Nevis, St Lucia, Turks and Caicos, St Vincent and the Grenadines, Trinidad and Tobago. The faculties of humanities and education, medical sciences and social sciences are located on all three campuses. The faculty of law is in Barbados, agriculture and engineering in Trinidad, and the faculties of pure and applied sciences are in Barbados and Jamaica

Academic year: August to July

Chancellor: Sir GEORGE ALLEYNE
Vice-Chancellor: Prof. NIGEL HARRIS
Prin.: Prof. KENNETH HALL
University Registrar: GLORIA BARRETT-SOBERS
Librarian: STEPHNEY FERGUSON

Number of teachers: 400
Number of students: 11,000

Publications: *Arts Review* (2 a year), *Caribbean Journal of Criminology and Social Psychology* (2 a year), *Caribbean Journal of Education*, *Caribbean Law Bulletin* (2 a year), *Caribbean Law Review* (2 a year), *Caribbean Quarterly*, *Journal of Tropical Agriculture* (4 a year), *Social Economics Studies* (4 a year), *West Indian Journal of Engineering* (2 a year), *West Indian Law Journal* (1 a year), *West Indian Medical Journal* (4 a year)

DEANS AT MONA

Faculty of Humanities and Education: Prof. AGGREY BROWN
Faculty of Medical Sciences: Prof. ARCHIBALD McDONALD
Faculty of Pure and Applied Sciences: Prof. RONALD YOUNG
Faculty of Social Sciences: MARK FIGUEROA

PROFESSORS

AHMAD, M., Biotechnology
BAILEY, W., Geography and Geology
BAIN, B., Community Health and Psychiatry
BENNETT, F., Pathology
BORNHOP, D., Applied Chemistry
BRANDAY, J., Surgery, Radiology, Anaesthesia and Intensive Care
BROWN, A., Mass Communication
BURTON, E., Medicine
CAMPBELL, C., History
CHEN, A., Physics
CHEVANNES, B., Social Anthropology
CHRISTIE, C., Obstetrics, Gynaecology and Child Health
DASGUPTA, T., Inorganic Chemistry
DENBOW, C., Medicine
DEVONISH, H., Language, Linguistics and Philosophy
DONOVAN, S., Palaeozoology
DURRANT, F., Library and Information Studies
FLETCHER, P., Clinical Surgery
FORRESTER, T., Tropical Medicine
FREEMAN, B., Ecology

HANCHARD, B., Anatomical Pathology
HICKLING, F., Psychiatry
JACKSON, T., Igneous Petrology
JACOBS, H., Chemistry
JONES, E., Public Administration
LENNARD, J., English and American Literature
LEO-RHYNIE, E., Women and Development Studies
LEWIS, R., Political Thought
MILLER, E., Teacher Education
MORGAN, O., Medicine
MOORE, B., History
MORRIS, M., Creative Writing and West Indian Literature
MORRISON, E., Biochemistry
MUNROE, T., Government and Politics
NETTLEFORD, R. N., Continuing Studies
REICHGELT, J., Computer Science
REID, H., Clinical Haemorheology
ROBINSON, E., Geology
SHIRLEY, G., Management Studies
SPENCER, H., Cardiothoracic Surgery
THOMAS-HOPE, E., Environmental Development
UCHE, C., Sociology and Social Work
WALKER, S., Epidemiology
WARNER-LEWIS, M., African Caribbean Language and Orature
WILKS, R., Epidemiology
WINT, A., International Business
YOUNG, R., Physiology

ATTACHED INSTITUTES

Biotechnology Centre: Dir Prof. M. AHMAD.

Caribbean Institute of Media and Communication: Dir Drs M. DE BRUIN.

Centre for Environment and Development: Dir Prof. A. BINGER.

Centre for Gender and Development Studies: Dir Dr B. BAILEY.

Centre for Management Development: Dir Dr J. COMMA.

Centre for Marine Sciences: Dir Dr G. WARNER.

Chronic Disease Research Centre: Dir Prof. H. FRASER.

Institute of Caribbean Studies: Dir J. PEREIRA.

Institute of Education: Dir J. TUCKER.

International Centre for Environment and Nuclear Sciences: Dir Prof. G. C. LALOR.

Philip Sherlock Centre for Creative Arts: Mona, Kingston 7; f. 1967; term-to-term activity in painting, sculpture, dance, theatre, writing, exhibitions, readings, etc.; acting as the home for ICC Week activities; the mounting of a small Caribbean Arts Festival; Sec. CAROLYN ALLEN.

School of Business: Dir Prof. G. SHIRLEY.

School of Continuing Studies: Mona, Kingston 7; Dir Prof. L. CARRINGTON.

Sir Arthur Lewis Institute for Social and Economic Studies: Mona, Kingston 7; tel. 927-2409; applied research relating to the Caribbean; Dir Prof. N. DUNCAN (Mona; Dir Prof. A. DOWNES (Cave Hill; Dir Prof. S. RYAN (St. Augustine.

Trade Union Education Institute: Mona, Kingston 7; Dir of Studies Prof. L. CARRINGTON.

Tropical Medicine Research Institute: Mona, Kingston 7; Dir Prof. TERRENCE FORRESTER.

AFFILIATED INSTITUTIONS

Caribbean Institute for Meteorology and Hydrology: Dir Dr COLIN DEPRADINE.

Mico Teachers' College: Dir Dr CLAUDE PACKER.

St John Vianney and the Uganda Martyrs: Dir Rev. MICHAEL DE VERTEUIL.

St Michael's Seminary: Mona, Kingston 7; awards degrees of the Univ. of the West Indies; Director Sr THERESA LOWE CHING.

United Theological College of the West Indies: Mona, Kingston 7; awards degrees and licentiates of the Univ. of the West Indies; Pres. Dr LEWIN WILLIAMS (acting).

College

College of Agriculture, Science and Education: POB 170, Passley Gardens, Port Antonio, Portland; tel. 993-3246; fax 993-2208; internet www.case.edu.jm; f. 1995 by merger of College of Agriculture and Passley Gardens Teachers' College; two-year degree course in all aspects of agriculture; 47 faculty mems; 533 full-time students; 86 part-time; 24 evening; faculties of agriculture, education and science; community college and continuing education programmes; library: 35,000 vols, spec. colln: UN publs, West Indian works, Jamaica Govt publs; Pres. Dr PAUL IVEY (acting); Registrar PATRICIA WRIGHT-CLARKE.

JAPAN

The Higher Education System

Higher education in Japan consists of four categories of institution: universities (daigaku), junior colleges (tanki-dai-gaku), vocational colleges and technology colleges (koto-sen-mongakko) and professional graduate schools (the latter since 2003). Institutions are either publicly or privately adminis-tered. In 2005 there were 726 universities and graduate schools, with 2.9m. students, and 551 junior and technical colleges, with 278,515 students. Universities offer the full range of undergraduate and postgraduate degrees, and since incorporation in 2004 have become autonomous from the Ministry of Education, Culture, Sports, Science and Technology with regard to decisions about finance, staffing and self-assessment. Junior colleges specialize in two- or three-year Associate Degrees (Jun-Gakushi), credits from which may be accepted towards completion of the university Bachelors degrees. Technology colleges offer five-year training pro-grammes in specialist fields of engineering and technology, and professional graduate schools, first established in 2003, offer two-year programmes of study aimed at bridging the gap between formal education and professional experience. The Ministry of Education, Culture, Sports, Science and Technology is responsible for education at all levels, sets the centrally compiled curriculum guidelines and authorizes textbooks. The Japan University Accreditation Association (JUAA) carries out the Certified Evaluation System, whereby all universities are evaluated periodically by a Ministry-approved third party. (The JUAA was originally established in 1947 and had voluntary membership.)

Admission to university is a three-stage process, based on completion of secondary education, results in the Unified First Stage Examination, administered by the National Centre for University Entrance, and each institution's entrance examin-ation. Applicants can only take an institution's entrance examination depending upon their results in the Unified First Stage Examination. The Bachelors (Gakushi) is the under-graduate degree, and is awarded on a 'credit' system following four (or up to six, for some subjects) years of study. Students must accrue at least 124 credits in 'major' and 'minor' subjects. The two-year Associate Degree offered by junior colleges requires a minimum of 62 credits and the three-year Associate Degree 93 credits. The first postgraduate degree is the Masters (Shushui), and is only available at university postgraduate schools (daigaku-in). The Masters is mainly a research-based degree, lasting two years and requiring 30 credits. The Doctorate (Hakushi) is the second postgraduate degree and highest university-level qualification. It is an entirely research-based programme of study, culminating in the submission of a thesis.

Technical and vocational education qualifications include the Special Training School Advanced Course Certificate (Senshu gakko Senmon-ka shuryo shosho), Special Training School Upper Secondary Certificate (Senshu gakko koto-ka sotsugyuo menjo), Technical Associate Degree or Diploma from a Special Training College (Senmonshi) and Vocational Training Certifi-cate or Diploma (awarded by Vocational Training College of the Ministry of Labour).

In 2005 a report entitled The Future of Higher Education in Japan was published. The report identified that as from 2007 university capacity would be at saturation point. It specified a number of goals including increased funding and quality assurance, a review of undergraduate liberal arts education and the introduction of a system for approving new institutions and departments.

The economic downturn since 2009, and Japan's long-term economic problems, may accelerate higher education reforms but are unlikely to reshape them in any significant way. Reforms include a plan to reduce government funding for national and city-controlled universities, subsidization of pri-vate institutions, and a series of targeted programmes—including a university excellence initiative, an evolving quality assurance programme, and an effort to recruit foreign students.

Regulatory and Representative Bodies

GOVERNMENT

Ministry of Education, Culture, Sports, Science and Technology: 3-2-2, Kasumi-gaseki, Chiyoda-ku, Tokyo 100-8959; tel. (3) 5253-4111; fax (3) 3595-2017; internet www.mext.go.jp; Minister KISABURO TOKAI.

ACCREDITATION

Daigaku Kijun Kyokai (Japan University Accreditation Association): 2-7-13, Ichigaya Sadohara-cho, Sinjuku-ku, Tokyo 162-0842; tel. (3) 5228-2020; fax (3) 5228-2323; internet www.juaa.or.jp; f. 1947; promotes the quali-tative improvement of univs in Japan through the voluntary efforts and mutual assistance of mem. univs; Pres. HIROMI NAYA.

Daigaku-hyoka Gakui-juyo Kiko (National Institution for Academic Degrees and University Evaluation (NIAD-UE)): 1-29-1 Gakuen-nishimachi, Kodaira-shi, Tokyo 187-8587; tel. (42) 307-1500; fax (42) 307-1552; e-mail dir-intl@niad.ac.jp; internet www.niad.ac.jp; f. 1991; ind. agency conduct-ing evaluations of teaching and research activities at univs, junior colleges, colleges of technology and inter-univ. research insti-tutes to raise the quality of education and research; awards academic degrees to learn-ers recognized as having fulfilled required academic standards; Pres. SHIN-ICHI HIRANO.

NATIONAL BODIES

Chuo Kyoiku Shingikai (Central Council for Education): Min. of Education, Culture, Sports, Science and Technology, 3-2-2, Kasu-migaseki, Chiyoda-ku, Tokyo 100-8959; tel. (3) 5253-4111; internet www.mext.go.jp; f. 1952; advises the Minister; carries out research and considers issues relating to the promotion of education, lifelong learning and sports; has 5 working groups concerned with: education systems, lifelong learning, elementary and lower secondary education, univs, and sports and youth; Chair. MASA-KAZU YAMAZAKI.

Kokuritsu Daigaku Kyokai (Japan Asso-ciation of National Universities): 4F, Nat. Center of Sciences Bldg, 1-2, Hitotsubashi 2-chome, Chiyoda-ku, Tokyo 101-0003; tel. (3) 4212-3506; fax (3) 4212-3509; e-mail info@janu.jp; internet www.janu.jp; Pres. HIROSHI KOMIYAMA.

Kokuritu Kyoiku Seisaku kenkyu Sho (National Institute for Educational Policy Research): 3-2-2 Kasumigaseki, Chiyoda-ku, Tokyo 100-8951; tel. (3) 6733-6833; e-mail info@nier.go.jp; internet www.nier.go.jp; f. 1949; conducts research on specific issues for use in the planning and formulation of educational policy; carries out research into social education; conducts jt int. initiatives (incl. research studies) in the education field; Dir-Gen. SHIGENORI YANO.

Koritsu Daigaku Kyokai (Japan Associ-ation of Municipal and Prefectural Colleges and Universities): Toranomon-Yoshiara Bldg, 9th Floor, 1-6-13 Nishi-Shimbashi, Minato-ku, Tokyo 105-0003; tel. (3) 3501-3336; fax (3) 3501-3337; e-mail jimu@kodaikyo.jp; internet www.kodaikyo.jp; f. 1949; 74 mems; Pres. TAKAO KODAMA.

Nihon Shiritsu Daigaku Kyokai (Associ-ation of Private Universities of Japan): Shigakukaikan Bekkan 9F, 4-2-25 Kudan-kita, Chiyoda-ku, Tokyo 102-0073; tel. (3) 3261-7048; fax (3) 3261-0769; e-mail koei@shidaikyo.or.jp; internet www.shidaikyo.or.jp; f. 1946; 384 private univs and colleges; Chair. Dr SUNAO ONUMA; Sec.-Gen. HIDEBUMI KOIDE; publ. Kyoikugakujutsu.

Learned Societies

GENERAL

Nihon Gakujutsu Kaigi (Science Council of Japan): 22–34 Roppongi 7-chome, Minato-ku, Tokyo 106; tel. (3) 3403-6291; fax (3) 3403-

6224; internet www.scj.go.jp; f. 1949; governmental org. coordinating Japan's scientific research; divisions of Agriculture, Commerce and Business Administration, Dentistry and Pharmacology, Economics, Engineering, Law and Political Science, Literature, Medicine, Pedagogy, Philosophy, Psychology, Pure Science, Sociology and History; 210 mems; library: see Libraries and Archives; Pres. Dr ICHIRO KANAZAWA; Sec.-Gen. YASUHIKO NAGASHIMA.

Nihon Gakujutsu Shinko-kai (Japan Society for the Promotion of Science): 6 Ichibadncho, Chiyoda-ku, Tokyo 102-8471; tel. (3) 3263-1722; fax (3) 3221-2470; internet www.jsps.go.jp; f. 1932; independent admin. institution and funding agency; administers grants-in-aid for scientific research, research fellowships for young scientists, univ./industry cooperation, scientific outreach, etc.; has cooperative agreements with 82 overseas orgs; operates JSPS overseas offices in 10 cities; 99 mems; Pres. MOTOYUKI ONO; publs *Japanese Scientific Monthly, JSPS Quarterly*.

Nippon Gakushiin (Japan Academy): 7–32 Ueno Park, Taito-ku, Tokyo 110-0007; tel. (3) 3822-2101; fax (3) 3822-2105; e-mail international@japan-acad.go.jp; internet www.japan-acad.go.jp; f. 1879; 150 mems; Pres. Prof. MASAAKI KUBO; Vice-Pres. Prof. TAKASHI SUGIMURA; Section Chair. (Humanities and Social Sciences) Prof. EIICHI HOSHINO; Section Chair. (Pure and Applied Sciences) Prof. YOSHIHIDE KOZAI; publs *Proceedings* (2 series, 10 a year), *Nippon Gakushiin Kiyo* (3 a year).

AGRICULTURE, FISHERIES AND VETERINARY SCIENCE

Engei Gakkai (Japanese Society for Horticultural Science): Business Center for Academic Societies Japan, 16–9 Honkomagome 5-chome, Bunkyo-ku, Tokyo 113; tel. (3) 5814-5801; fax (3) 5814-5820; f. 1923; 2,795 mems; Pres. ICHIRO KAJIURA; Sec. TADASHI BABA; publ. *Journal* (6 a year).

Nihon Ikushu Gakkai (Japanese Society of Breeding): c/o Faculty of Agriculture, University of Tokyo, Bunkyo-ku, Tokyo 113-8657; tel. (3) 5841-5065; fax (3) 5841-5063; e-mail kishima@abs.agr.hokudai.ac.jp; internet www.nacos.com/jsb/e; f. 1951; 2,300 mems; Pres. ATSUCHI HIRAI; publs *Breeding Science* (4 a year), *Ikushugaku Kenkyu* (4 a year).

Nihon Ju-í Gakkai (Japanese Society of Veterinary Science): Tokyo RS Bldg, 8th Fl., 6-26-12 Hongo, Bunkyo-ku, Tokyo 113-0033; tel. (3) 5803-7761; fax (3) 5803-7762; e-mail office@jsvs.or.jp; internet www.soc.nii.ac.jp/jsvs; f. 1885; 4,100 mems; Pres. KUNIO DOI; publ. *The Journal of Veterinary Medical Science* (12 a year).

Nihon Oyo Toshitsu Kagaku Kai (Japanese Society of Applied Glycoscience): c/o National Food Research Institute, 2-1-2 Kannondai, Tsukuba, Ibaraki 305; tel. (298) 38-7991; fax (298) 38-8005; internet www.soc .nii.ac.jp/jsag; f. 1952; 1,147 mems; Pres. YASUHITO TAKEDA; Vice-Pres. HIROKAZU MATSUI, KENJI YAMAMOTO, TAKASHI KURIKI; publ. *Journal of Applied Glycoscience* (4 a year).

Nihon Sanshi Gakkai (Japanese Society of Sericultural Science): c/o Nat. Institute of Agrobiological Sciences, 1-2 Ohwashi, Tsukuba, Ibaraki 305-8634; tel. and fax (29) 838-6056; e-mail jsss@silk.or.jp; internet www .soc.nii.ac.jp/jsss2; f. 1930; 557 mems; Pres. Prof. MICHIHIRO KOBAYASHI; Man. HIDETOSHI TERAMOTO; publs *Journal of Insect Biotechnology and Sericology* (3 a year), *Journal of Sericultural Science of Japan* (Sanshi Konchu Biotec, 3 a year).

Nippon Seibutsu-Kogaku Kai (Society for Biotechnology, Japan): c/o Faculty of Engineering, Osaka Univ., 2–1 Yamadaoka, Suita, Osaka 565-0871; tel. (6) 6876-2731; fax (6) 6879-2034; e-mail sbbj@bio.eng.osaka-u.ac .jp; internet www.sbj.or.jp; f. 1923; provides training and development opportunities for students and young researchers; 3,500 mems; Pres. Prof. SHINJI IIJIMA; publs *Journal of Bioscience and Bioengineering* (in English, 12 a year), *Seibutsu-kogaku Kaishi* (in Japanese, 12 a year).

Nihon Shinringakkai (Japanese Forestry Society): c/o Japan Forest Technical Association, Rokubancho 7, Chiyoda-ku, Tokyo; tel. and fax (3) 3261-2766; f. 1914; forestry research; 2,900 mems; Pres. KAZUMI KOBAYASHI; publs *Journal* (6 a year), *Shinrin Kagaku* (bulletin, 3 a year).

Nippon Chikusan Gakkai (Japanese Society of Animal Science): 201 Nagatani Corporas, Ikenohata 2-9-4, Taito-ku, Tokyo 110-0008; tel. (3) 3828-8409; fax (3) 3828-7649; e-mail tikusan@blue.ocn.ne.jp; internet www .soc.nii.ac.jp/jszs; f. 1924; animal science; 2,706 mems; Pres. HIDEO YANO; publs *Animal Science Journal* (6 a year), *Nihon Chikusan Gakkaihou* (4 a year).

Nippon Dojo-Hiryo Gakkai (Japanese Society of Soil Science and Plant Nutrition): 26-10-202 Hongo, 6 chome, Bunkyo-ku, Tokyo; tel. (3) 3815-2085; fax (3) 3815-6018; e-mail jsspm@wwwsoc.nii.ac.jp; f. 1914; 2,300 mems; Pres. TADAKATU YONEYAMA; publs *Journal* (6 a year), *Soil Science and Plant Nutrition* (6 a year).

Nippon Nougei Kagaku Kai (Japan Society for Bioscience, Biotechnology and Agrochemistry): 4–16 Yayoi 2-chome, Bunkyo-ku, Tokyo 113-0032; fax (3) 3815-1920; e-mail shomu-b@jsbba.or.jp; internet www.jsbba.or .jp; f. 1924; 12,546 mems; library of 742,010 vols; Pres. Prof. SAKAYU SHIMIZU; publs *Bioscience, Biotechnology and Biochemistry* (in English, 12 a year), *Nippon Nōgeikagaku Kaishi* (in Japanese, 12 a year), *Kagaku To Seibutsu* (in Japanese, 12 a year).

Nippon Sakumotsu Gakkai (Crop Science Society of Japan): 2F Shin-Kyoritsu Bldg, Shinkawa 2-22-4, Chuo-ku, Tokyo 104-0033; fax (3) 3553-2047; e-mail cssj-jim@bridge.ocn .ne.jp; internet www.soc.nii.ac.jp/cssj; f. 1927; 1,500 mems; Pres. Dr SHIGEMI AKITA; Sec. YUSEKE GOTO; publs *Japanese Journal of Crop Science* (4 a year), *Plant Production Science* (4 a year).

Nippon Shokubutsu-Byori Gakkai (Phytopathological Society of Japan): Shokubo Bldg, Komagome 1-43-11, Toshima-ku, Tokyo 170; tel. (3) 3943-6021; fax (3) 3943-6021; internet www.ppsj.org; f. 1916 to promote research on plant diseases; 1,880 regular mems; Pres. SHINJI TSUYUMU; Vice-Pres. TOMONORI SHIRAISHI; publ. *Journal* (4 a year).

Nippon Suisan Gakkai (Japanese Society of Fisheries Science): c/o Tokyo University of Fisheries, 4-5-7 Konan, Minato-ku, Tokyo 108-8477; tel. (3) 3471-2165; fax (3) 3471-2054; f. 1932; research in fishing science and technology, mariculture, aquaculture, marine environmental science and related fields; 4,879 mems; library of 69 vols; Pres. Prof. T. WATANABE; publs *Fisheries Science* (in English, 6 a year), *Nippon Suisan Gakkaishi* (6 a year).

Nogyokikai Gakkai (Japanese Society of Agricultural Machinery): c/o BRAIN, 1-40-2 Nisshin-cho, Saitama 331-8537; tel. (48) 652-4119; fax (48) 652-4119; e-mail jsam@iam .brain.go.jp; internet www.soc.nii.ac.jp/jsam; f. 1937; 1,500 mems; Pres. TOMOHIKO ICHIKAWA; publ. *Journal of the Japanese Society of Agricultural Machinery* (6 a year).

ARCHITECTURE AND TOWN PLANNING

Nihon Zoen Gakkai (Japanese Institute of Landscape Architecture): Zoen Kaikan, 6th Fl., 1-20-11 Jinnan, Shibuya-ku, Tokyo 150-0041; tel. (3) 5459-0515; fax (3) 5459-0516; e-mail info@landscapearchitecture.or.jp; internet www.landscapearchitecture.or.jp; f. 1924; 1,800 mems; Pres. AKIRA HOMMA; publ. *Journal*.

Nihon Zosen Gakkai (Japanese Society of Naval Architects and Ocean Engineers):internet www.jasnoe.or.jp; f. 2005 by merger of Society of Naval Architects of Japan, Kansai Society of Naval Architects, Japan, and the West-Japan Society of Naval Architects; publ. *Kanrin*.

Nippon Toshi Keikaku Gakkai (City Planning Institute of Japan): Ichibancho-West Building 6F, Ichibancho 10, Chiyoda-ku, Tokyo 102-0082; tel. (3) 3261-5407; fax (3) 3261-1874; internet wwwsoc.nii.ac.jp/cpij; f. 1951; 5,349 mems; Pres. TAKASHI ONISHI; publ. *City Planning Review* (6 a year).

BIBLIOGRAPHY, LIBRARY SCIENCE AND MUSEOLOGY

Gakujutsu Bunken Fukyu-Kai (Association for Science Documents Information): c/o Tokyo Institute of Technology, 2-12-1 Ookayama, Meguro-ku, Tokyo 152-8550; fax (3) 3726-3118; e-mail gakujyutubunken@ mvd.biglobe.ne.jp; f. 1933; Pres. SHU KANBARA; publ. *Reports on Progress in Polymer Physics in Japan* (English, 1 a year).

Information Processing Society of Japan: Kagaku-kaikan (Chemistry Hall) 4F, 1–5 Kanda-Surugadai, Chiyoda-ku, Tokyo 101-0062; tel. (3) 3518-8374; fax (3) 3518-8375; e-mail somu@ipsj.or.jp; internet www.ipsj.or.jp; f. 1960; 30,000 mems; Pres. Dr HAJIME SASAKI; publ. *Journal of Information Processing*.

Joho-Jigyo, Kagaku-Gijutsu Shinko Kiko (S&T Information Services, Japan Science and Technology Agency (JST)): 5-3 Yonban-cho, Chiyoda-ku, Tokyo 102-0081; tel. (3) 5214-8402; fax (3) 5214-8400; e-mail sti@jst.go.jp; internet sti.jst.go.jp; f. 1957; an integrated org. of S&T; prepares abstracts, online and manual search services, translation and photo-duplication service, library service, computer processing; 470 mems; Pres. K. KITAZAWA; publs *Current Bibliography on Science and Technology* (Abstracts from about 16,200 journals, 12 series), *Journal of Information Processing and Management* (12 a year), *Current Science and Technology Research in Japan* (in English and Japanese), *JST Thesaurus, JST Holding List of Serials and Proceedings* (online).

Joho Kagaku Gijutsu Kyokai (Information Science and Technology Association): Sasaki Bldg, 5–7 Koisikawa 2, Bunkyo-ku, Tokyo 112; tel. (3) 3813-3791; fax (3) 3813-3793; e-mail infosta@infosta.or.jp; internet www.infosta.or.jp; f. 1950; 2,020 mems; Pres. T. GONDOH; publ. *Journal* (1 a year).

Nihon Hakubutsukan Kyokai (Japanese Association of Museums): Shoyu-Kaikan 3-3-1, Kasumigaseki, Chiyoda-ku, Tokyo 100-8925; tel. (3) 3591-7190; fax (3) 3591-7170; e-mail webmaster@j-muse.or.jp; internet www.j-muse.or.jp; f. 1928; Gen. Man. YOKO NIIZUMA; 1,280 mems; publ. *Museum Studies* (12 a year).

Nihon Toshokan Kyokai (Japan Library Association): 1-11-14, Shinkawa, Chuo-ku, Tokyo 104-0033; tel. (3) 3523-0811; fax (3) 3523-0841; e-mail info@jla.or.jp; internet www.jla.or.jp; f. 1892; all aspects of library development; 8,900 mems; library of 10,000 vols; Sec.-Gen. KATSURA YOKOYAMA; publs *Gendai no Toshokan* (4 a year), *Nihon no*

Sankotosho Shikiban (4 a year), *Nihon no Toshokan* (1 a year), *Toshokan Nenkan* (1 a year), *Toshokan Zasshi* (12 a year).

Nippon Toshokan Joho Gakkai (Japan Society of Library and Information Science): c/o Graduate School of Library and Information Science, Univ. of Tsukuba, 1–2 Kasuga, Tsukuba-shi, Ibaraki-ken 305-8550; fax (29) 859-1380; e-mail jslis-info@slis.tsukuba.ac .jp; internet www.soc.nii.ac.jp/jslis; f. 1953; 750 mems; Pres. SHUICHI UEDA; Sec. YUKO YOSHIDA; publ. *Journal* (4 a year).

ECONOMICS, LAW AND POLITICS

Aziya Seikei Gakkai (Japan Association for Asian Studies): c/o Ochanomizu University, 2-1-1 Otsuka, Bunkyo-ku, 112-8610; tel. 5976-1478; e-mail jaas-info@ npo-ochanomizu.org; internet www.jaas.or .jp; f. 1953; 900 mems; Pres. SATOSHI AMAKO; publ. *Aziya Kenkyu* (Asian Studies, 4 a year).

Hikaku-ho Gakkai (Japan Society of Comparative Law): c/o Faculty of Law, Tokyo University, Hongo, Bunkyo-ku, Tokyo 113; internet www.soc.nii.ac.jp/jscl; f. 1950; studies in comparative law; holds conferences; issues publications; 780 mems; Pres. H. TANAKA; publ. *Hikakuhô Kenkyû* (Comparative Law Journal, 1 a year).

Hogaku Kyokai (Jurisprudence Association): Faculty of Law, University of Tokyo, Hongo, Bunkyo-ku, Tokyo; tel. (3) 3812-2111; f. 1884; 600 mems; Pres. TAKESHI SASAKI; publs *Hogaku Kyokai Zasshi*, *Journal*.

Hosei-shi Gakkai (Japan Legal History Association): Kyoto University, Yoshida-hommachi, Sakyo-ku, Kyoto 606-8501; tel. (75) 753-3235; fax (75) 753-3290; e-mail jalha@wwwsoc.nii.ac.jp; internet wwwsoc.nii .ac.jp/jalha; f. 1949; 495 mems; Pres. H. TERADA; publ. *Legal History Review* (1 a year).

Hosokai (Lawyers' Association): 1, 1-chome, Kasumigaseki, Chiyoda-ku, Tokyo; tel. (3) 3581-2146; internet www.hosokai.or.jp; f. 1891; 20,000 mems; library of 30,000 vols; Pres. RYOHACHI KUSABA; Dir ISAO IMAI; publ. *Hoso Jiho*.

Japan Institute of International Affairs: Toranomon Mitsui Bldg, 3rd Fl., 3-8-1 Kasumigaseki, Chiyodaku, Tokyo 100-0013; tel. (3) 3503-7261; fax (3) 3503-7292; e-mail jiiajoho@jiia.or.jp; internet www.jiia.or.jp; f. 1956; 512 mems; Pres. YOSHIJI NOGAMI; Deputy Dir-Gen. NAOKO SAIKI; publ. *Kokusai Mondai* (International Relations, in Japanese, 4 a year).

Japan Institute of Public Finance: c/o Institute of Statistical Research, Japan Life Insurance Bldg, 7th Fl., 1-18-16 Shinbashi Minatoku, Tokyo 105-0004; tel. (3) 3591-8496; fax (3) 3595-2220; e-mail zaisei@isr.or .jp; internet wwwsoc.nii.ac.jp/jipf; f. 1940 as Japanese Association of Fiscal Science; 1,000 mems; publ. *Zaisei Kenkyu* (1 a year).

Keizai Riron Gakkai (Japan Society of Political Economy): Faculty of Economics, Rikkyo University, 3 Ikebukuro, Toshima-ku, Tokyo; internet www.jspe.gr.jp; f. 1959; 865 mems; Pres. H. OOUCHI; publ. *Political Economy Quarterly*.

Keizaigaku-shi Gakkai (Japan Society for the History of Economic Thought): Dept of Economics, Tohoku University, Kawauchi, Sendai; tel. (22) 217-6275; fax (22) 217-6231; e-mail mawatari@econ.tohoku.ac.jp; internet society.cpm.ehime-u.ac.jp/shet/shet .html; f. 1949; 810 mems; Pres. SHOHKEN MAWATARI; publ. *History of Economic Thought*, *Society Newsletter*.

Kokusaiho Gakkai (Association of International Law): Faculty of Law, Univ. of Tokyo, Hongo, Bunkyo-ku, Tokyo; tel. (3)

3812-2111; f. 1897; 804 mems; Pres. M. OTSUKA; publs *Kokusaiho Gaiko Zasshi*, *Journal of International Law and Diplomacy*.

Labour Lawyers Association of Japan: 4F Sohyo-Kaikan, 3-2-11 Kanda-Surugadai Chiyoda-ku, Tokyo; tel. (3) 3251-5363; fax (3) 3258-6790; f. 1957; 1,400 mems; publ. *Rodosha no Kenri* (Workers' Rights, 4 a year).

Nichibei Hougakukai (Japanese American Society for Legal Studies): c/o Faculty of Law, Univ. of Tokyo, Hongo, Bunkyo-ku, Tokyo 113-0033; f. 1964; seeks and develops mutual understanding of Japanese and American law and legal scholarship, especially through cooperation of members of the legal profession; 800 mems; Dir M. OTSUKA; publ. *Amerika Hō* (Law in the USA, 2 a year).

Nihon Keizai Gakkai (Japanese Economics Association): c/o The Institute of Statistical Research, 1-18-16 Shimbashi, Minato-ku, Tokyo 102-0072; tel. (3) 5211-5707; fax (3) 5211-5065; e-mail office@jeaweb.org; internet www.jeaweb.org; f. 1934; 3,398 mems; Pres. TOSHIHIRO IHORI; publ. *Japanese Economic Review* (4 a year).

Nihon Kinyu Gakkai (Japan Society of Monetary Economics): 1-2-1 Nihonbashi Hongokucho, Chuo-ku, Tokyo 103-0021; tel. (3) 3231-1372; fax (3) 3241-3649; e-mail jsme@d8.dion.ne.jp; internet www.soc.nii.ac .jp/jsme; f. 1943; 1,365 mems; Pres. Prof. HIDEO FUJIWARA; publ. *Review of Monetary and Financial Studies* (2 a year).

Nihon Koho Gakkai (Japan Public Law Association): Univ. of Tokyo, 7-3-1 Hongo, Bunkyo-ku, Tokyo; f. 1948; 1,200 mems; Pres. K. TAKAHASHI; publ. *Koho-Kenkyu* (Public Law Review, 1 a year).

Nihon Minji Soshoho Gakkai (Japan Association of Civil Procedure Law): c/o Faculty of Law, Osaka City University, 3-3-138 Sugimoto, Sumiyoshi-ku, Osaka; tel. (6) 6605-2327; fax (6) 6605-2920; f. 1949; 815 mems; Pres. H. MATSUMOTO; publ. *Journal of Civil Procedure* (1 a year).

Nihon Tokei Gakkai (Japan Statistical Society): c/o SINFONICA, Nohgakushorin Bldg 5F, 3-6 Kanda Jimboucho Chiyoda-ku, Tokyo 101-0051; tel. (3) 3234-7738; fax (3) 3234-7738; internet www.jss.gr.jp; f. 1931; 1,312 mems; Pres. Prof. YASUTO YOSHIZOE; Pres. Prof. MANABU IWASAKI; publ. *Journal* (2 a year).

Nippon Hoshakai Gakkai (Japan Association of Sociology of Law): University of Tokyo, Hongo, Bunkyo-ku, Tokyo; internet wwwsoc.nii.ac.jp/hosha; f. 1947; 805 mems; Pres. N. TOSHITANI; publ. *Sociology of Law* (1 a year).

Nippon Hotetsu-Gakkai (Japan Association of Legal Philosophy): Chiba University, Faculty of Law and Economics, 1-33, Yayoicho, Inage-ku, Chiba-shi, Chiba 263-8522; tel. (43) 290-2362; fax (43) 290-2362; e-mail jalp@wwwsoc.nii.ac.jp; internet wwwsoc.nii .ac.jp/jalp; f. 1948; 486 mems; Pres. Prof. ITARU SHIMAZU; publ. *The Annals of Legal Philosophy*.

Nippon Keiei Gakkai (Japan Society of Business Administration): Hitotsubashi Univ., 2-1 Naka, Kunitachi, Tokyo 186-8601; tel. (42) 580-8571; internet www.soc .nii.ac.jp/jsba; f. 1926; 2,160 mems; Pres. T. TAKAHASHI; publs *Annual Review of Business Administration*, *Journal of Business Management*.

Nippon Keiho Gakkai (Criminal Law Society of Japan): University of Tokyo, Hongo, Bunkyo-ku, Tokyo; f. 1949; 1,000 mems; Pres. K. SHIBAHARA; publ. *Journal* (4 a year).

Nippon Keizai Seisaku Gakkai (Japan Economic Policy Association): School of Political Science and Economics, Waseda University, 1-6-1 Nishiwaseda, Shinjuku-ku, Tokyo 169-8050; tel. (3) 5286-2193; fax (3) 5286-2193; e-mail jepa-mail@list.waseda.jp; internet wwwsoc.nii.ac.jp/jepa; f. 1940; 1,150 mems; Pres. Prof. YASUMI MATSUMOTO; publ. *International Economic Policy Studies*.

Nippon Seizi Gakkai (Japanese Political Science Association): Faculty of Law, Rikkyo University, 3-34-1, Nishi-Ikebukuro, Toshima-ku, Tokyo 171; fax (3) 3705-4530; e-mail ykobayas@hs.catv.ne.jp; internet www.soc.nii.ac.jp/jpsa2; 820 mems; Sec.-Gen. Dr YOSHIAKI KOBAYASHI; publ. *Annals* (1 a year).

Nippon Shogyo Gakkai (Japan Society of Commercial Sciences): Meiji University, Surugadai Kanda, Chiyoda-ku, Tokyo; f. 1951; 980 mems; Pres. K. FUKUDA.

Private International Law Association: Chuo University Faculty of Law, 742-1 Higashinakano Hachioji-shi, Tokyo 192-0393; tel. (42) 674-3154; fax (42) 674-3133; f. 1949; 244 mems; Pres. KORESUKE YAMAUCHI.

Tokyo Daigaku Keizai Gakkai (Society of Economics): Faculty of Economics, Univ. of Tokyo, 7-3-1 Hongo, Bunkyo-ku, Tokyo 113-0033; f. 1922; 200 mems; Pres. HIROSHI YOSHIKAWA; publ. *Journal of Economics* (4 a year).

EDUCATION

Asia–Pacific Cultural Centre for UNESCO (ACCU): 6 Fukuromachi, Shinjuku-ku, Tokyo 162-8484; tel. (3) 3269-4435; fax (3) 3269-4510; e-mail general@accu.or.jp; internet www.accu.or.jp; f. 1971; adult learning materials, children's books, literacy materials development, music, personnel exchange programmes, photo contest, protection of cultural heritage, training programmes and other regional cultural activities; library of 29,000 vols; Pres. KAZUO SUZUKI; Dir-Gen. KOJI NAKANISHI; publs *Activity Report* (1 a year), *ACCU News* (Japanese, 6 a year), *Asian/Pacific Book Development* (English, 4 a year).

Nihon Gakko-hoken Gakkai (Japanese Association of School Health): Dept of Health Education, Faculty of Education, University of Tokyo, Hongo 7-3-1, Bunkyo-ku, Tokyo 113; tel. (3) 3812-2111; fax (3) 5991-3741; e-mail jash@shobix.co.jp; internet www.soc .nii.ac.jp/jash; f. 1954; 1,500 mems; Pres. ATSUHISA EGUCHI; publ. *Gakko-hoken Kenkyu* (Japanese Journal of School Health, 12 a year).

Nihon Hikaku Kyoiku Gakkai (Japan Comparative Education Society): c/o Dept of Education, Graduate School of Human Environment Studies, Kyushu University, 6-19-1, Hakozaki, Higashi-ku, Fukuoka City, Fukuoka Prefecture 812-8581; tel. and fax (92) 632-8426; f. 1965; 905 mems; Pres. K. MOCHIDA; Sec.-Gen. H. TAKEKUMA; publs *Comparative Education* (2 a year), *Newsletter* (2 a year).

Nihon Kyoiku Gakkai (Japanese Educational Research Association): 2-29-3-3F Hongo, Bunkyo-ku, Tokyo 113-0033; tel. (3) 3818-2505; fax (3) 3816-6898; e-mail jsse@ oak.ocn.ne.jp; f. 1941; 3,300 mems; Pres. HIDENORI FUJITA; publs *Educational Studies in Japan: International Yearbook*, *The Japanese Journal of Educational Research* (4 a year).

Nihon Kyoiku-shakai Gakkai (Japan Society of Educational Sociology): Faculty of Education, University of Tokyo, Hongo 7-3-1, Bunkyo-ku, Tokyo 113; tel. (3) 3907-3750; fax

(3) 5907-6364; e-mail jses2@wwwsoc.nii.ac
.jp; internet www.soc.nii.ac.jp/jses2; f. 1949;
1,200 mems; Pres. HIDENORI FUJITA; publ.
Journal of Educational Sociology (2 a year).

Nihon Kyoiku-shinri Gakkai (Japanese
Association of Educational Psychology):
Hongo Ohara Bldg, 7th Fl., Hongo 5-24-6,
Bunkyo-ku, Tokyo 113-0033; tel. (3) 3818-
1534; fax (3) 3818-1575; internet www.soc.nii
.ac.jp/jaep; f. 1952; 7,100 mems; Pres. YUJI
MORO; publ. *Japanese Journal of Educa-
tional Psychology* (4 a year).

Nippon Kagaku Kyoiku Gakkai (Japan
Society for Science Education): c/o Nakanishi
Printing Co. Ltd., Shimotachiuri Ogawa-
Higashi, Kamikyo-ku, Kyoto 602 8048; tel.
(75) 41-53-661; fax (75) 41-53-662; e-mail
jsse@nacos.com; internet www.jsse.jp; f.
1977; science and mathematics education
and educational technology; 1,200 mems;
Pres. J. YOSHIDA; publs *Journal* (4 a year),
Letter (6 a year), *Proceedings of Annual
Meeting*.

Nippon Sugaku Kyoiku Gakkai (Japan
Society of Mathematical Education): POB 18,
Koishikawa, Tokyo 112-8691; tel. (3) 3946-
2267; fax (3) 3946-3736; internet www.sme.or
.jp; f. 1919; 3,334 mems; Pres. Prof. T.
SAWADA; publs *Journal* (12 a year), *Supplementary issue* (report on mathematical education, 2 a year), *Yearbook* (1 a year).

Nippon Taiiku Gakkai (Japanese Society
of Physical Education, Health and Sport
Sciences): Kishi Memorial Hall (Rm 508),
Jinnan 1-1-1, Shibuya-ku, Tokyo 150; tel. (3)
3481-2427; fax (3) 3481-2428; internet www
.soc.nii.ac.jp/jspe3; f. 1950; 6,752 mems; Pres.
Dr JUJIRO NARITA; publ. *International Journal of Sport and Health Science* (4 a year).

FINE AND PERFORMING ARTS

Bijutsu-shi Gakkai (Japanese Art History
Society): c/o Tokyo National Research Insti-
tute of Cultural Properties, 13–27 Ueno
Park, Taito-ku, Tokyo 110; internet www
.soc.nii.ac.jp/jahs2; f. 1949; 2,300 mems; publ.
Journal (4 a year).

Nihon Engeki Gakkai (Japanese Society
for Theatre Research): Waseda University, 1-
6-1 Nishi-Waseda, Shinjuku-ku, Tokyo 169-
8050; tel. (3) 3203-4141; f. 1949; Pres. T.
MORI.

Nippon Ongaku Gakkai (Musicological
Society of Japan): 3-3-3-201 Iidabashi,
Chiyoda-ku, 102-0072 Tokyo; tel. (3) 3288-
5616; f. 1952; 1,350 mems; Pres. T. ISOYAMA;
publ. *Ongaku Gaku* (Journal, 3 a year).

HISTORY, GEOGRAPHY AND ARCHAEOLOGY

Keizai Chiri Gakkai (Japan Association of
Economic Geographers): Institute of Economic Geography, Faculty of Economics,
East Bldg, Hitotsubashi University, Naka 2-
1, Kunitachi-shi, Tokyo 186; tel. (425) 72-
1101, ext 5374; fax (425) 71-1893; internet
wwwsoc.nii.ac.jp/jaeg; f. 1954; 700 mems;
Pres. K. TAKEUCHI; publ. *Annals* (4 a year).

Nihon Kokogakkai (Archaeological Society
of Japan): c/o Tokyo National Museum, Ueno
Park, Taito-ku, Tokyo; f. 1895; 2,200 mems;
Pres. Dr FUJITA KUNIO; publ. *Kokogaku
Zasshi* (4 a year).

Nippon Kokogaku Kyokai (Japanese
Archaeological Association): 5-15-5, Hirai,
Edogawa-ku, Tokyo 132-0035; tel. (3) 3618-
6608; fax (3) 3618-6625; internet www.soc.nii
.ac.jp/jaa2; f. 1948; 4,072 mems; library of
37,790 vols; Pres. TADASHI NISHTANI; publ.
Nihon Kōkogaku (journal).

Nippon Oriento Gakkai (Society for Near
Eastern Studies in Japan): Tokyo-Tenrikyo-
kan 9, 1-chome 9, Kanda Nishiki-cho,

Chiyoda-ku, Tokyo 101-0054; tel. (3) 3291-
7519; fax (3) 3291-7519; f. 1954; 800 mems;
Pres. KOJI KAMIOKA; publs *Oriento* (in Japanese, 2 a year), *Orient* (in European languages, 1 a year).

Nippon Seibutsuchiri Gakkai (Biogeographical Society of Japan): c/o Prof. Dr S. Sakai,
2-26-12 Sendagi, Bunkyo-ku, Tokyo 113; tel.
(3) 3828-0445; fax (3) 3828-0445; e-mail
qyv04336@nifty.ne.jp; internet wwwsoc.nii
.ac.jp/tbsj; f. 1928; 300 mems; Pres. Prof. Dr
SEIROKU SAKAI; publs *Bulletin*, *Biogeographica*, *Fauna Japonica*.

Nippon Seiyoshigakukai (Japanese Society of Western History): Dept of Western
History, Graduate School of Letters, Osaka
Univ., 1–5 Machikaneyama-cho, Toyonaka,
Osaka 560-8532; tel. (6) 6850-5105; fax (6)
6850-5105; e-mail seiyousihgaku@mti
.biglobe.ne.jp; f. 1948; 880 mems; Pres. Prof.
A. EGAWA; publ. *Studies in Western History* (4
a year).

Shigaku-kai (Historical Society of Japan):
University of Tokyo, Hongo, Bunkyo-ku,
Tokyo 113; f. 1889; c. 2,470 mems; Pres.
OSAMU NARUSE; publ. *Shigaku-Zasshi* (His-
torical Journal of Japan).

Tokyo Chigaku Kyokai (Tokyo Geographical Society): 12–2 Nibancho, Chiyoda-ku,
Tokyo 102-0084; tel. (3) 3261-0809; fax (3)
3263-0257; e-mail chigaku@abox9.so-net.ne
.jp; internet www.soc.nii.ac.jp/tokyogeo; f.
1879; 810 mems; Pres. ISAMU KOBAYASHI;
publ. *Journal of Geography* (6 a year, and 1
special issue a year).

Toyoshi-Kenkyu-Kai (Society of Oriental
Researches): Kyoto University, Sakyo-ku,
Kyoto City; tel. (75) 753-2790; internet
wwwsoc.nii.ac.jp/toyoshi/index.html; f. 1935;
1,400 mems; Pres. I. MIYAZAKI; publ. *Toyoshi-
Kenkyu* (Journal of Oriental Researches, 4 a
year).

LANGUAGE AND LITERATURE

Alliance Française: Imamura Bldg, 9th Fl.,
2-2-11 Tenjinbashi, Kita-Ku, Osaka 530-
0041; tel. (6) 358-7391; fax (6) 358-7393;
e-mail info@calosa.com; internet www
.calosa.com; offers courses and examinations
in French language and culture and promotes cultural exchange with France;
attached teaching centres in Nagoya, Sapporo, Sendai and Tokushima; Dir ERIC
GALMARD.

British Council: 1–2 Kagurazaka, Shinjuku-ku, Tokyo 162-0825; tel. (3) 3235-8031;
fax (3) 3235-8040; e-mail enquiries@
britishcouncil.or.jp; internet www
.britishcouncil.org/japan; teaching centre;
offers courses and examinations in English
language and British culture and promotes
cultural exchange with the UK; attached
teaching centres in Kyoto, Nagoya and
Osaka; Dir, Japan JOANNA BURKE.

Goethe-Institut: Doitsu Bunka Kaikan, 7-
56 Akasaka, Minato-ku, Tokyo 107-0052;
tel. (3) 3584-3201; fax (3) 3586-3069; e-mail
info@tokyo.goethe.org; internet www.goethe
.de/os/tok/deindex.htm; offers courses and
examinations in German language and culture and promotes cultural exchange with
Germany; attached centres in Kyoto and
Osaka; library of 10,000 vols, 40 periodicals;
Dir RAIMUND WOERDEMANN.

**Japan Comparative Literature Associ-
ation:** Aoyamagakuin University, Shibuya-
ku, Tokyo; tel. (3) 5421-3238; fax (3) 5421-
3238; internet wwwsoc.nii.ac.jp/jcla; f. 1948;
400 mems; Pres. KEN INOUE; Sec.-Gen. Prof.
TAKASHI ARIMITSU; publ. *Journal* (1 a year).

Japanese Centre of International PEN:
20-3 Kabuto-cho, Nihonbashi, Chuo-ku,
Tokyo 103-0026; e-mail secretariat01@

japanpen.or.jp; internet www.japanpen.or.jp;
f. 1935; Pres. KAZUNARI YOSHIZAWA.

Kokugogakkai (Society for the Study of
Japanese Language): Faculty of Letters,
University of Tokyo, Hongo, Bunkyo-ku,
Tokyo 113; fax 5802-0615; e-mail office@
jpling.gr.jp; internet wwwsoc.nii.ac.jp/jpling;
f. 1944; 1,500 mems; Pres. ETSUTARO IWABU-
CHI; publ. *Studies in the Japanese Language*
(4 a year).

Manyo Gakkai (Society for Manyo Studies):
3-3-138 Sugimotocho Sumiyoshiku, Osaka
558-0022; tel. (6) 6605-2414; f. 1951; 810
mems; publ. *The Manyo* (4 a year).

Nihon Dokubungakkai (Japanese Society
of German Literature): c/o Ikubundo, Hongo
5-30-21, Bunkyo-ku, Tokyo 113-0033; tel. (3)
3813-5861; fax (3) 3813-5861; e-mail jgg@
tokyo.email.ne.jp; internet wwwsoc.nii.ac.jp/
jgg; f. 1947; 2,600 mems; Pres. Prof. TERUAKI
TAKAHASHI; publs *Doitsu Bungaku / German
Literature* (2 a year), *Doitsugo Kyoiku /
Deutschunterricht in Japan* (1 a year).

Nihon Eibungakkai (English Literary
Society of Japan): 501 Kenkyusha Bldg, 9
Surugadai 2-chome, Kanda, Chiyoda-ku,
Tokyo 101-0062; tel. (3) 3293-7528; fax (3)
3293-7539; e-mail ejimu@elsj.org; internet
www.elsj.org; f. 1928; 4,000 mems; Pres.
YOSHIYUKI FUJIKAWA; publ. *Studies in Eng-
lish Literature* (3 a year).

Nihon Esperanto Gakkai (Japan Esperanto Institute): Waseda-mati 12-3, Sinzyuku-
ku, Tokyo 162-0042; tel. (3) 3203-4581; fax (3)
3203-4582; e-mail chb71944@biglobe.ne.jp; f.
1919; 1,435 mems; linguistics; Pres. YAMA-
SAKI SEIKÔ; Sec. ISINO YOSIO; publ. *La Revuo
Orienta* (12 a year).

Nihon Gengogakkai (Linguistic Society of
Japan): Shimotachiuri Ogawa Higashi, Kami
Kyoku, Kyoto 602-8048; tel. (75) 415-3661;
fax (75) 415-3662; e-mail lsj@nacos.com;
internet www.tooyoo.l.u-tokyo.ac.jp/~lsj/jap;
f. 1938; 2,050 mems; publ. *Gengo Kenkyu*
(Journal, 2 a year).

Nippon Onsei Gakkai (Phonetic Society of
Japan): National Institute for Japanese Language, 10–2 Midori-cho, Tachikawa, Tokyo
190-8561; tel. (42) 540-4515; fax (42) 540-
4524; e-mail psj@nacos.com; internet www
.psj.gr.jp; f. 1926; study of sound phenomena
of human speech; 780 mems; library of
30,000 vols; Pres. SHOSUKE HARAGUCHI;
publ. *Journal* (3 a year).

Nippon Seiyo Koten Gakkai (Classical
Society of Japan): Dept of Classics, Faculty
of Letters, Kyoto Univ., Kyoto 606-8501; tel.
(75) 753-2767; e-mail hiroyuki.takahashi@
bun.kyoto-u.ac.jp; internet www.bun.kyoto-u
.ac.jp/classics/csj/csj.html; f. 1950; 500 mems;
Pres. Dr TETSUO NAKATSUKASA; Sec. HIROYUKI
TAKAHASHI; publ. *Journal of Classical Studies* (1 a year).

MEDICINE

Japanese Society for the Study of Pain:
Department of Anaesthesiology, Nihon University School of Medicine, 30-1, Oyaguchi-
kamicho, Itabashi-ku, Tokyo 173-8610; tel.
(3) 3972-8111; fax (3) 5917-4766; e-mail
s-ogawa@med.nihon-u.ac.jp; f. 1973; research
into pain mechanism and pain management;
698 mems; Pres. Prof. K. IWATA; publ. *Pain
Research* (4 a year).

Nihon Eisei Gakkai (Japanese Society for
Hygiene): Osaka University, Graduate
School of Medicine, Dept of Social and
Environmental Medicine, 2-2 Yamada-oka,
Suita, Osaka 565-0871; tel. (6) 6879-3922; fax
(6) 6879-3928; internet www.nacos.com/jsh; f.
1929; 2,750 mems; Pres. Prof. KANEHISA
MORIMOTO; publs *Environmental Health and
Preventive Medicine* (in English, 4 a year),

Japanese Journal of Hygiene (in Japanese, 4 a year).

Nihon Hinyokika Gakki: (Japanese Urological Association); Saito Bldg, 5F, 2-17-15 Yushima, Bunkyo-ku, Tokyo 113-0034; f. 1912; 7,200 mems; Pres. Prof. SEIJI NAITO; publs *International Journal of Urology* (12 a year), *Japanese Journal of Urology* (6 a year).

Nihon Hotetsu Shika Gakkai (Japan Prosthodontic Society): 1-43-9 Komagome, Toshima-ku, Tokyo; tel. (3) 5940-5451; fax (3) 5940-5630; e-mail hotetsu-gakkai01@max .odn.ne.jp; internet www.hotetsu.com; f. 1931; meetings, confs, seminars; researches on new prosthodontics; liaisons with other prosthodontic societies worldwide; 6,611 mems; Pres. Prof. KEIICHI SASAKI; Vice-Pres. and Pres. Elect KIYOSHI KOYANO; Vice-Pres. YOSHINOBU TANAKA; Gen. Affairs HIDEO MATSUMURA; publs *Journal of Prosthodontic Research* (4 a year), *Nihon Hotetsu Shika Gakkai zasshi* (Journal of Japan Prosthodontic Society, 4 a year).

Nihon Ishi-Kai (Japan Medical Association): Bunkyo-ku, Tokyo 113; f. 1916; 121,514 mems; Pres. Y. KARASAWA; publs *Japan Medical Association Journal* (in English, 6 a year), *Journal* (in Japanese, 12 a year).

Nihon Junkanki Gakkai (Japanese Circulation Society): 8th Fl., CUBE OIKE Bldg, 599 Bano-cho Karasuma Aneyakoji, Nakagyo-ku, Kyoto 604-8172; tel. (75) 257-5830; fax (75) 213-1675; e-mail admin@j-circ.or.jp; internet www.j-circ.or.jp; f. 1935; cardiology; 21,096 mems; Chief Dir AKIRA TAKESHITA; publs *Circulation Journal* (in English, 12 a year; supplement in Japanese, 3 a year), *Journal of Board of Certified Members of the Japanese Circulation Society* (in Japanese, 2 a year).

Nihon Kakuigakukai (Japanese Society of Nuclear Medicine): c/o Japan Radioisotope Association, 2-28-45 Honkomagome, Bunkyo-ku, Tokyo 113-0021; tel. (3) 3947-0976; fax (3) 3947-2535; e-mail anm@xvg.biglobe.ne.jp; internet www.jsnm.org; f. 1963; 3,500 mems; Pres. Dr NAGARA TAMAKI; publs *Annals of Nuclear Medicine* (10 a year), *Japanese Journal of Nuclear Medicine* (4 a year).

Nihon Koku Eisei Gakkai (Japanese Society for Dental Health): c/o Koku Hoken Kyokai 43-9, Komagome 1-chome Toshima-ku, Tokyo 170-0003; tel. (3) 3947-8891; fax (3) 3947-8341; internet www.kokuhoken.or.jp/ jsdh; f. 1952; 2,500 mems; Pres. M. YONEMITSU; publ. *Journal* (4 a year).

Nihon Koku Geka Gakkai (Japanese Society of Oral and Maxillofacial Surgeons): Seven-Ster Mansion Takanawa (2nd floor), 20-26-202 Takanawa 2-chome, Minato-Ku, Tokyo; tel. (3) 5791-1791; fax (3) 5791-1792; internet www.jsoms.org; f. 1952; 8,500 mems; Gen. Sec. Dr KAN-ICHI SETO; publ. *Japanese Journal of Oral and Maxillofacial Surgery* (12 a year).

Nihon Kokuka Gakkai (Japanese Stomatological Society): Department of Oral Surgery, School of Medicine, University of Tokyo, 7-3-1 Hongo, Bunkyo-ku, Tokyo 113-8549; tel. (3) 5803-5400; fax (3) 5803-0101; f. 1947; 3,600 mems; Dir ICHIRO YAMASHITA; publ. *Journal* (4 a year).

Nihon Kyosei Shikagakkai (Japan Orthodontic Society): c/o Koku Hoken Kyokai, 1-44-2 Komagome, Toshima-ku, Tokyo 170-0003; tel. (3) 3947-8891; fax (3) 3947-8341; e-mail info@jos.gr.jp; internet www.jos.gr.jp; f. 1932; 4,200 mems; Pres. Dr KUNIMICHI SOMA; publ. *Orthodontic Waves* (in English and Japanese, 6 a year).

Nihon Masuika Gakkai (Japan Society of Anaesthesiologists): TY Bldg 6F, 18-11 Hongo 3-chome, Bunkyo-ku, Tokyo 113-0033; tel. (3) 3815-0590; fax (3) 3814-0464; internet www.anesth.or.jp; f. 1954; 8,677 mems; Pres. K. HANAOKA; Sec. Y. SHIMIDA; publs *Masui* (12 a year), *Journal of Anaesthesia* (4 a year).

Nihon Naika Gakkai (Japanese Society of Internal Medicine): 28–8, 3-chome, Bunkyo-ku, Tokyo 113-8433; fax (3) 3818-1556; e-mail iminfo@naika.or.jp; internet www.naika.or .jp; f. 1903; 73,000 mems; Chief Dir ICHIRO KANAZAWA; publs *Internal Medicine* (in Japanese, 12 a year), *Internal Medicine* (in English, 12 a year).

Nihon No-Shinkei Geka Gakkai (Japan Neurosurgical Society): Ishikawa Bldg 4F, 5-25-16 Hongo, Bunkyo-ku, Tokyo; tel. (3) 3812-6226; fax (3) 3812-2090; e-mail jns@ss .iij4u.or.jp; internet jns.umin.ac.jp; f. 1948; 8,088 mems; Chair. TAKASHI YOSHIMOTO; publ. *Neurologia Medico-Chirurgica* (in English, 12 a year).

Nihon Ronen Igakukai (Japan Geriatrics Society): Kyorin Bldg No 702, 4-2-1 Yushima, Bunkyo-ku, Tokyo 113; internet www .jpn-geriat-soc.or.jp; f. 1959; 4,500 mems; Chair. Prof. H. ORIMO; publ. *Japan Journal of Geriatrics* (6 a year).

Nihon Seishin Shinkei Gakkai (Japanese Society of Psychiatry and Neurology): Wing Bldg 52, 5-25-18 Hongo, Bunkyo-ku, Tokyo 113-0033; tel. (3) 3814-2991; fax (3) 3814-2992; e-mail info@jspn.or.jp; internet www .jspn.or.jp; 8,200 mems; Pres. Dr TAKUYA KOJIMA; publ. *Seishin Shinkeigaku Zasshi* (in Japanese, 12 a year).

Nihon Shika Hoshasen Gakkai (Japanese Society for Oral and Maxillofacial Radiology): c/o Hitotsubashi Printing Co. Ltd, Gakkai Business Center, 2-4-11 Fukagawa, Koutouku, Tokyo 135-0033; tel. (3) 5620-1953; fax (3) 5620-1960; e-mail tsuchimochi@ngt.ndu.ac .jp; f. 1951; 1,200 mems; Sec.-Gen. S. KANDA; publs *Dental Radiology* (in Japanese, 4 a year), *Oral Radiology* (in English, 2 a year).

Nihon Shika Igakkai (Japanese Association for Dental Science): 4-1-20 Kudankita, Chiyoda-ku, Tokyo; tel. (3) 3262-9214; fax (3) 3262-9885; internet www.jads.jp; f. 1949; 94,000 mems; 39 mem. socs; Pres. Prof. K. ETO; publs *Journal of Japanese Association for Dental Science* (1 a year), *Japanese Dental Science Review* (2 a year).

Nihon Shokaki-byo Gakkai (Japanese Society of Gastroenterology): Ginza Orient Bldg, 8F, Ginza 8-9-13, Chuo-ku, Tokyo; tel. (3) 3573-4297; fax (3) 3289-2359; e-mail info@ jsge.or.jp; internet www.jsge.or.jp; f. 1898; 25,000 mems; Pres. KENJI FUJIWARA; publs *Journal of Gastroenterology* (in English, 12 a year), *Nihon Shokaki-byo Gakkai Zasshi* (in Japanese, 12 a year).

Nihon Shonika Gakkai (Japan Paediatric Society): 4F Daiichi Magami Bldg, 1-1-5 Koraku, Bunkyo-ku, Tokyo 112-0004; tel. (3) 3818-0091; fax (3) 3816-6036; internet www.jpeds.or.jp; f. 1896; 16,311 mems; Pres. Dr SHUMPEI YOKOTA; Sec. Gen. Dr MAKIKO OKUYAMA; publs *Paediatrics International* (in English, 6 a year), *Journal of the Japan Paediatric Society* (in Japanese, 12 a year).

Nihon Syoyakugakkai (Japanese Society of Pharmacognosy): Business Centre for Academic Societies, 4–16, Yayoi 2-chome, Bunkyo-ku, Tokyo 113; tel. (3) 5206-6007; fax (3) 5206-6008; e-mail shoyaku@asas.or.jp; internet www.jsphcg.gr.jp; f. 1946; 1,027 mems; Pres. M. KONOSHIMA; publ. *Japanese Journal of Pharmacognosy* (4 a year).

Nihon Teii Kinou Shinkei Geka Gakkai (Japan Society for Stereotactic and Functional Neurosurgery): c/o Dept of Neurological Surgery, School of Medicine, Nihon University, 30-1 Ohyaguchi Kamimachi, Itabashi-ku, Tokyo 173-8610; tel. (3) 3972-8111, ext. 2481; fax (3) 3554-0425; e-mail teii@med .nihon-u.ac.jp; internet jssfn.umin.ac.jp; f. 1963; 518 mems; Sec.-Gen. Dr C. FUKAYA; publ. *Functional Neurosurgery* (2 a year).

Nihon Yakuri Gakkai (Japanese Pharmacological Society): Yayoi 2-4-16, Bunkyo-ku, Tokyo 113-0032; tel. (3) 3814-4828; fax (3) 3814-4809; e-mail society@pharmacol.or.jp; internet www.pharmacol.or.jp; f. 1927; 6,100 mems; Chair. NOROI MATUKI; publs *Folia Pharmacologica Japonica* (in Japanese, 12 a year), *Journal of Pharmacological Sciences* (in English, 13 a year).

Nippon Bitamin Gakkai (Vitamin Society of Japan): NIhon Italia kyoto Kaikan, Yoshida Ushinomiya, Sakyo-ku, Kyoto 606-8302; tel. (75) 751-0314; fax (75) 751-2870; e-mail vsojkn@mbox.kyoto-inet.or.jp; internet web.kyoto-inet.or.jp/people/vsojkn; f. 1947; 2,000 mems; Pres. KENJI FUKUZAWA; Chief Sec. TAKESHI MATUMOTO; publs *Journal of Nutritional Science and Vitaminology* (in English, 6 a year), *Vitamins* (in Japanese, 12 a year).

Nippon Byorigakkai (Japanese Society of Pathology): New Akamon Bldg 4F, 2-40-9 Hongo, Bunkyo-ku, Tokyo 113-0033; tel. (3) 5684-6886; fax (3) 5684-6936; internet jsp .umin.ac.jp; f. 1911; 4,200 mems; Chair. SHIGEO MORI; publs *Annual of Pathological Autopsy Cases in Japan* (in Japanese), *Pathology International* (in English, 12 a year), *Proceedings* (in Japanese).

Nippon Gan Gakkai (Japanese Cancer Association): c/o Cancer Institute, Kami-Ikebukuro 1-37-1, Toshima-ku, Tokyo 170-0012; tel. (3) 3918-0111, ext. 4231; fax (3) 3918-5776; f. 1907; 16,976 mems; Pres. Dr TOMOYUKI KITAGAWA; publs *Japanese Journal of Cancer Research* (12 a year), *Gann Monograph on Cancer Research* (irregular).

Nippon Ganka Gakkai (Japanese Ophthalmological Society): 2-4-11-402, Sarugaku-cho, Chiyoda-ku, Tokyo 101-8346; fax (3) 3293-9384; internet www.nichigan.or.jp; f. 1897; 13,690 mems; Pres. MAKOTO ARAIE; publs *Japanese Journal of Ophthalmology* (6 a year), *Journal of Japanese Ophthalmological Society* (12 a year).

Nippon Geka Gakkai (Japan Surgical Society): World Trade Center Bldg, 2-4-1 Hamamatsu-cho, Minato-ku, Tokyo 105-6108; tel. (3) 5733-4094; fax (3) 5473-8864; e-mail info@jssoc.or.jp; internet www.jssoc.or .jp; f. 1899; 37,405 mems; Pres. TAKASHI KANEMATSU; publ. *Surgery Today* (12 a year).

Nippon Hifu-ka Gakkai (Japanese Dermatological Association): CosmosHongo Bldg 6F, 1-4, Hongo 4-chome, Bunkyo-ku, Tokyo 113-0033; tel. (3) 3811-5099; fax (3) 3812-6790; e-mail gakkai@dermatol.or.jp; internet www.dermatol.or.jp; f. 1901; 8,567 mems; Pres. S. HARADA; publs *Japanese Journal of Dermatology* (in Japanese, 14 a year), *Journal of Dermatology* (in English, 12 a year).

Nippon Hoi Gakkai (Medico-Legal Society of Japan): Dept of Forensic Medicine, Faculty of Medicine, Univ. of Tokyo, 7-3-1 Hongo, Bunkyo-ku, Tokyo 113; tel. (3) 5800-5416; fax (3) 5800-5416; e-mail legalmed@m.u-tokyo.ac .jp; internet web.sapmed.ac.jp/jslm; f. 1914; 1,400 mems; Pres. Dr KENJI KAMIYA; publs *Japanese Journal of Legal Medicine* (2 a year), *Legal Medicine* (4 a year).

Nippon Hoshasen Eikyo Gakkai (Japan Radiation Research Society): National Institute of Radiological Sciences, 9-1 Anagawa-4, Inage-ku, Chiba 263-8555; tel. (43) 251-2111; fax (43) 251-4531; f. 1959; 1,052 mems; Pres.

KENJI KAMIYA; publ. *Journal of Radiation Research* (4 a year).

Nippon Igaku Hōshasen Gakkai (Japan Radiological Society): NP-II Bldg, 5-1-16 Hongo, Bunkyo-ku, Tokyo 113-0033; tel. (3) 3814-3077; fax (3) 5684-4075; e-mail qa@radiology.or.jp; internet www.radiology.jp; f. 1950; 7,500 mems; Pres. Dr OSAMU MATSUI; publ. *Radiation Medicine*.

Nippon Jibi-Inkoka Gakkai (Otorhinolaryngological Society of Japan, Inc.): 3-25-22 Takanawa, Minato-ku, Tokyo 108-0074; tel. (3) 3443-3085; fax (3) 3443-3037; e-mail office@jibika.or.jp; internet www.jibika.or.jp; f. 1893; 10,500 mems; Pres. TAKUYA UEMURA; publ. *Nippon Jibi-Inkoka Gakkai Kaiho (Tokyo)* (12 a year).

Nippon Kaibo Gakkai (Japanese Association of Anatomists): c/o Oral Health Institute, 1-43-9 Komagome, Toshima-ku, Tokyo; tel. (3) 3947-8891; e-mail gakkai24@kokuhoken.or.jp; internet www.anatomy.or.jp; f. 1893; 2,450 mems; Pres. Dr KUNIAKI TAKATA; publ. *Anatomical Science International* (4 a year).

Nippon Kansenshoh Gakkai (Japanese Association for Infectious Diseases): Nichinai Bldg, 2F, 3-28-8, Hongo, Bunkyo-ku, Tokyo 113-0033; tel. (3) 5842-5845; fax (3) 5842-5846; e-mail info@kansensho.or.jp; internet www.kansensho.or.jp; f. 1926; 10,500 mems; Pres. AIKICHI IWAMOTO; publs *Journal of the Japanese Association for Infectious Diseases* (online, 6 a year), *Journal of Infection and Chemotherapy* (online).

Nippon Kekkaku-byo Gakkai (Japanese Society for Tuberculosis): 1-24, Matsuyama 3-chome, Kiyose-shi, Tokyo 204-8533; tel. 0424-92-2091; fax 0424-91-8315; f. 1923; 3,000 mems; Chair. Dr K. AOKI; publ. *Kekkaku* (12 a year).

Nippon Ketsueki Gakkai (Japanese Society of Haematology): c/o Kinki Chiho Invention Center, 14 Kawahara-cho, Yoshida, Sakyo-ku, Kyoto 606-8305; tel. (75) 752-2844; fax (75) 752-2842; e-mail info@jshem.or.jp; internet www.jshem.or.jp; f. 1937; academic year September to August; organizes research, symposia, seminars; 7,500 mems; Pres. Prof. YUZURU KANAKURA; publs *International Journal of Hematology* (12 a year), *The Japanese Journal of Clinical Hematology* (12 a year).

Nippon Kisei-chu Gakkai (Japanese Society of Parasitology): Dept of Tropical Medicine and Parasitology, Keio University School of Medicine, 35 Shinanomachi Shinjuku-ku, Tokyo 160-8582; tel. (3) 3353-1211; fax (3) 3353-5958; internet jsp.tm.nagasaki-u.ac.jp; f. 1929; 998 mems; Pres. Prof. T. HORII; Chair Prof. T. TAKEUCHI; publ. *Parasitology International* (4 a year).

Nippon Koshu-Eisei Kyokai (Japan Public Health Association): Koei Bldg, 1-29-8, Shinjuku, Shinjuku-ku, Tokyo 160-0022; tel. (3) 3352-4281; fax (3) 3352-4605; e-mail info@jpha.or.jp; internet www.jpha.or.jp; f. 1883; 5,000 mems; Pres. MINORU SEIJO; publs *Japanese Journal of Public Health*, *Public Health Information* (12 a year).

Nippon Rai Gakkai (Japanese Leprosy Association): 4-2-1, Aoba-cho, Higashimurayama-shi, Tokyo 189-0002; tel. (42) 391-8085; fax (42) 394-9092; e-mail jla-hp-admin@hansen-gakkai.jp; internet www.hansen-gakkai.jp; f. 1927; 355 mems; Pres. NORIHASA ISHII; publ. *Japanese Journal of Leprosy* (3 a year).

Nippon Saikingakkai (Japanese Society for Bacteriology): c/o Oral Health Association of Japan, 1-44-2 Komagome, Toshima-ku, Tokyo 170; tel. (3) 3947-8891; fax (3) 3947-8341; e-mail gakkai@kokuhiken.or.jp;

internet wwwsoc.nii.ac.jp/jsb; f. 1927; 3,400 mems; Pres. Dr HIDEO HAYASHI; publs *Japanese Journal of Bacteriology* (4 a year), *Microbiology and Immunology* (12 a year).

Nippon Sanka-Fujinka Gakkai (Japan Society of Obstetrics and Gynaecology): Twin View Ochanomizu Bldg, 2-3-9 Hongo, Bunkyo-ku, Tokyo 113-0033; tel. (3) 5842-5452; fax (3) 5842-5470; e-mail nissanfu@jsog.or.jp; internet www.jsog.or.jp; f. 1949; 15,434 mems; Chair. Prof. YASUNORI YOSHIMURA; publ. *Acta Obstetrica et Gynaecologica Japonica* (12 a year).

Nippon Seikei Geka Gakkai (Japanese Orthopaedic Association): 2-40-18, Hongo, Bunkyo-ku, Tokyo 113-8418; tel. (3) 3816-3671; fax (3) 3818-2337; internet www.joa.or.jp; f. 1926; 20,742 mems; Pres. Prof. HIROSHI YAMAMOTO; publs *Journal* (in Japanese, 12 a year), *Journal of Orthopaedic Science* (in English, 6 a year).

Nippon Seiri Gakkai (Physiological Society of Japan): 3-30-10 Hongo, Bunkyo-ku, Tokyo 113-0033; tel. (3) 3815-1624; fax (3) 3815-1603; e-mail psj@qa2.so-net.ne.jp; internet int.physiology.jp; f. 1922; 3,700 mems; Pres. YASUNOBU OKADA; publs *Journal of the Physiological Society of Japan* (in Japanese, 12 a year), *Journal of the Physiological Society of Japan* (in English, 6 a year).

Nippon Shika Hozon Gakkai (Japanese Society of Conservative Dentistry): c/o Oral Health Association of Japan (Koku Hoken Kyokai), Komagome TS Bldg, 1-43-9 Komagome, Toshima-ku, Tokyo 170-0003; tel. (3) 3947-8891; fax (3) 3947-8341; e-mail gakkai8@kokuhoken.or.jp; internet wwwsoc.nii.ac.jp/jscd; f. 1955; 4,540 mems; Pres. HIDEAKI SUDA; publ. *Journal of Conservative Dentistry* (6 a year).

Nippon Shinkei Gakkai (Japanese Society of Neurology): Ichimaru Bldg 31-21, Yushima 2-chome, Bunkyo-ku, Tokyo 113-0034; tel. (3) 3815-1080; fax (3) 3815-1931; internet www.neurology-jp.org; f. 1960; 6,895 mems; Chair. ICHIRO KANAZAWA; publ. *Clinical Neurology* (12 a year).

Nippon Shinkeikagaku Gakkai (Japan Neuroscience Society): Hongo Bldg 9F 2-2, Hongo 7-chome, Bunkyo-ku, Tokyo 113-0033; tel. (3) 3813-0272; fax (3) 3813-0296; e-mail office@jnss.org; internet www.jnss.org; f. 1974; 4,000 mems; Pres. Dr YASUSHI MIYASHITA; publs *Neuroscience Research* (12 a year), *News*.

Nippon Tonyo-byo Gakkai (Japan Diabetes Society): 5-25-18, Hongo, Bunkyo-ku, Tokyo 113-0033; tel. (3) 3815-4364; fax (3) 3815-7985; f. 1958; 15,533 mems; Pres. KOICHI YOKONO; publ. *Journal* (12 a year).

Nippon Uirusu Gakkai (Society of Japanese Virologists): Business Centre for Academic Societies, 5-16-9 Honkomagome, Bunkyo-ku, Tokyo 113; f. 1953; 3,000 mems; Pres. Dr HIROSHI YOSHIKURA; publs *Microbiology and Immunology* (12 a year), *Virus* (Japanese text with English summary, 2 a year).

Nippon Yakugaku-Kai (Pharmaceutical Society of Japan): 12-15, Shibuya 2-chome, Shibuya-ku, Tokyo 150-0002; tel. (3) 3406-3321; fax (3) 3498-1835; e-mail doi@pharm.or.jp; internet www.pharm.or.jp; f. 1880; 21,541 mems; Pres. O. YONEMITSU; Exec. Dir M. OHZEKI; publs *Biological and Pharmaceutical Bulletin* (12 a year), *Chemical and Pharmaceutical Bulletin* (12 a year), *Farumashia* (12 a year), *Japanese Journal of Toxicology and Environmental Health* (6 a year).

Nippon Yuketsu Gakkai (Japan Society of Blood Transfusion): Metropolitan Tokyo Red Cross Blood Centre, 1-31-4 Hiroo, Shibuya-

ku, Tokyo; tel. (3) 5485-6020; fax (3) 5466-3111; internet www.yuketsu.gr.jp; f. 1954; 3,000 mems; Pres. TAKEO JUJI; publ. *Japanese Journal of Transfusion Medicine* (6 a year).

Oto-Rhino-Laryngological Society of Japan: 3-25-22 Takanawa, Minato-Ku, Tokyo 108-0074; tel. (3) 3443-3085; fax (3) 3443-3037; f. 1893 as the Tokyo Oto-Rhino-Laryngological Society; 1947 present name; 10,604 mems; Chair GINICHIRO ICHIKAWA; publs *Auris Nasus Larynx*, *Nippon Jibiinkoka Gakkai Kaiho* (12 a year).

NATURAL SCIENCES
General

Nihon Kagakushi Gakkai (History of Science Society of Japan): Shimazu Bldg 202, 2-13-1 Hirakawa-cho, Chiyoda-ku, Tokyo 102-0093; tel. and fax (3) 3239-0545; internet www.soc.nii.ac.jp/jshs; f. 1941; 1,000 mems; Pres. TATSUMASA DOUKE; publs *Kagakushi Kenkyu* (4 a year), *Historia Scientiarum* (3 a year).

Biological Sciences

Nihon Hassei Seibutsu Gakkai (Japanese Society of Developmental Biologists): Center for Developmental Biology, RIKEN Kobe, 2-2-3 Minatojima-minami Chuo-ku, Kobe, Hyogo 650-0047; tel. and fax (78) 306-3072; e-mail jsdbadmin@jsdb.jp; internet www.jsdb.jp; f. 1968; 1,400 mems; Pres. KIYOKAZU AGATA; publ. *Development, Growth and Differentiation* (in English, 9 a year).

Nihon Jinrui Iden Gakkai (Japan Society of Human Genetics): Dept of Medical Genomics, Tokyo Medical and Dental University, 1-5-45 Yushima, Bunkyo-ku, Tokyo 113-8510; tel. (3) 5803-5820; fax (3) 5803-0244; internet jshg.jp; f. 1956; 1,046 mems; Pres. YU-SUKE NAKAMURA; publ. *Journal* (4 a year).

Nihon Kairui Gakkai (Malacological Society of Japan): National Science Museum, 3-23-1, Hyakunin-cho, Shinjuku-ku, Tokyo 169-0073; tel. (3) 3364-7124; e-mail msj_manager@hotmail.com; f. 1928; scientific research on molluscs; 900 mems; Pres. T. OKUTANI; publs *Chiribotan* (in Japanese with English abstract, 4 a year), *Venus* (4 a year).

Nihon Kontyû Gakkai (Entomological Society of Japan): c/o Dept of Zoology, National Science Museum (Natural History), 3-23-1 Hyakunin-cho, Shinjuku, Tokyo 169; e-mail ueno@kintaro.grt.kyushu-u.ac.jp; f. 1917; 1,300 mems; Pres. HIROSHI SHIMA; publs *Entomological Science*, *Insects of Japan* (irregular).

Nihon Mendel Kyokai (Japan Mendel Society): Editorial and Business Office, Cytologia, c/o Toshin Bldg, Hongo 2-27-2, Bunkyo-ku, Tokyo 113-0033; fax (3) 3814-5352; f. 1929; 1,100 mems; Pres. HIDEO HIROKAWA; publ. *Cytologia* (4 a year).

Nihon Seitai Gakkai (Ecological Society of Japan): 1–8 Nishihanaikecho, Koyama, Kitaku Kyoto 603-8148; tel. and fax (75) 384-0250; e-mail office@mail.esj.ne.jp; internet www.esj.ne.jp/esj; f. 1953; research in all aspects of ecology; 4,000 mems; Pres. T. NAKASHIZUKA; Sec.-Gen. T. TAKADA; publs *Japanese Journal of Ecology* (in Japanese, 3 a year), *Ecological Research* (in English, 6 a year), *Japanese Journal of Conservation Ecology* (in Japanese, 2 a year).

Nihon Shokubutsu Bunrui Gakkai (Japanese Society for Plant Systematics): Faculty of Symbiotic Systems Science, Fukushima University, Fukushima 960-1296; internet wwwsoc.nii.ac.jp/jsps; f. 2001; 900 mems; plant taxonomy and phytogeography; Pres. JIN MURATA; Sec. TAKAHIDAE

KUROSAWA; publ. *Acta Phytotaxonomica et Geobotanica* (3 a year).

Nippon Chô Gakkai (Ornithological Society of Japan): c/o National Museum of Nature and Science, 3-23-1 Hyakunin-cho, Shinjuku-ku, Tokyo 169-0073; tel. (3) 3364-7131; fax (3) 3364-7104; e-mail nihon-chogakkai@lagopus .com; internet www.soc.nii.ac.jp/osj; f. 1912; 1,300 mems; library of 600 vols; Pres. HIROSHI NAKAMURA; Vice-Pres. ISAO NISHIUMI; publs *Japanese Journal of Ornithology* (in Japanese, 2 a year), *Ornithological Science* (in English, 2 a year).

Nihon Dobutsu Gakkai (Zoological Society of Japan): Toshin Bldg, Hongo 2-27-2, Bunkyo-ku, Tokyo 113-0033; tel. (3) 3814-5461; fax (3) 3814-6216; e-mail zsj-society@zoology .or.jp; internet www.zoology.or.jp; f. 1878; 2,500 mems; Pres. YOSHITAKA NAGAHAMA; Sec.-Gen. YUKO NAGAI; publ. *Zoological Science* (12 a year).

Nippon Eisei-Dobutu Gakkai (Japanese Society of Medical Entomology and Zoology): c/o Dept of Parasitology, School of Medicine, Aichi Medical University, Nagakute, Aichi 480-1195; tel. (561) 62-3311; fax (561) 63-3645; internet www.jsmez.gr.jp; f. 1943; 750 mems; Pres. Prof. YASUO CHINZEI; publ. *Medical Entomology and Zoology* (4 a year).

Nippon Iden Gakkai (Genetics Society of Japan): National Institute of Genetics, 1, 111 Yata, Mishima, Shizuoka 411-8540; tel. 55-981-6736; fax 55-981-6736; e-mail japgenet@ lab.nig.ac.jp; internet wwwsoc.nii.ac.jp/gsj3; f. 1920; 1,500 mems; Pres. SADAO ISHIWA; publ. *Genes and Genetic Systems* (6 a year).

Nippon Kin Gakkai (Mycological Society of Japan): c/o Forest Health Group, Kansai Research Center, Forestry and Forest Products Research Institute, Nagai-Kyutaro 68, Momoyama-cho, Fushimi-ku, Kyoto 612-0855; tel. (75) 366-9912; fax (75) 611-1207; e-mail msj_office@remach.kais.kyoto-u.ac.jp; internet wwwsoc.nii.ac.jp/msj7; f. 1956; 1,600 mems; Pres. MAKOTO KAKISHIMA; publ. *Mycoscience* (4 a year).

Nippon Kumo Gakkai (Arachnological Society of Japan): c/o Faculty of Education, Kumamoto Univ., Kurokami 2-chome 40-1, Kumamoto 860-8555; tel. (96) 342-2532; e-mail tanabe@gpo.kumamoto-u.ac.jp; f. 1936; 300 mems; Pres. Dr NOBUO TSURUSAKI; Sec. TSUTOMU TANABE; publ. *Acta Arachnologica* (2 a year).

Nippon Oyo-Dobutsu-Konchu Gakkai (Japanese Society of Applied Entomology and Zoology): c/o Japan Plant Protection Association, 43-11, 1-chome, Komagome, Toshima-ku, Tokyo 170; internet odokon .org; f. 1957; 2,000 mems; Pres. Prof. KENJI FUJISAKI; Exec. Dir HIROSHI HONDA; publs *Applied Entomology and Zoology* (in English, 4 a year), *Japanese Journal of Applied Entomology and Zoology* (in Japanese with English synopsis, 4 a year).

Nippon Rikusui Gakkai (Japanese Society of Limnology): c/o School of Environmental Science, University of Shiga Prefecture, 2500 Hassaka-cho, Hikone, Shiga 522-8533; tel. (749) 28-8307; fax (749) 28-8463; e-mail ban@ ses.usp.ac.jp; internet wwwsoc.nii.ac.jp/jslim; f. 1931; 1,288 mems; Pres. Dr NORIO OGURA; Gen. Sec. Dr OSAMU MITAMURA; publs *Japanese Journal of Limnology* (3 a year), *Limnology* (3 a year).

Nippon Shokubutsu Gakkai (Botanical Society of Japan): c/o Toshin Bldg, 2-chome 27-2 Hongo, Bunkyo-ku, Tokyo; tel. (3) 3814-5675; fax (3) 3814-5352; e-mail bsj@bsj.or.jp; internet bsj.or.jp; f. 1882; 2,100 mems; Pres. H. FUKUDA; publ. *Journal of Plant Research* (6 a year).

Nippon Shokubutsu Seiri Gakkai (Japanese Society of Plant Physiologists): Shimotachiuri Ogawa Higashi, Kamikyoku, Kyoto 602-8048; tel. (75) 415-3661; fax (75) 415-3662; e-mail jspp@nacos.com; internet www .nacos.com/jspp; f. 1959; 3,201 mems; Pres. KIYOTAKA OKADA; Sec.-Gen. AKIRA NAGATANI; publ. *Plant and Cell Physiology* (12 a year).

Mathematical Sciences

Nihon Sugaku Kai (Mathematical Society of Japan): 34–8, Taito 1-chome, Taito-ku, Tokyo 110-0016; tel. (3) 3835-3483; fax (3) 3835-3485; f. 1877; 5,000 mems; Pres. SADAYOSHI KOJIMA; publs *Journal* (4 a year), *Sugaku* (4 a year), *Sugaku-Tsushin* (bulletin, 4 a year), *Japanese Journal of Mathematics* (2 a year), *MSJ Memoirs* (irregular), *Advanced Studies in Pure Mathematics* (irregular).

Physical Sciences

Butsuri Tansa Gakkai (Society of Exploration Geophysicists of Japan): 2F MK5 Bldg, 1-5-6 Higashikanda, Chiyoda-ku, Tokyo 101-0031; tel. (3) 6804-7500; fax (3) 6804-7500; e-mail office@segj.org; internet www.segj .org; f. 1948; 1,420 mems; Pres. S. ROKUGAWA; publ. *Butsuri Tansa* (Geophysical Exploration, 6 a year).

Chigaku Dantai Kenkyu-kai (Association for Geological Collaboration in Japan): Kawai Bldg, 2-24-1, Minami-Ikebukuro, Toshima-ku, Tokyo 171-0022; tel. (3) 3983-3378; fax (3) 3983-7525; e-mail chidanken@ tokyo.email.ne.jp; internet wwwsoc.nii.ac.jp/ agcj/index.html; f. 1947; study of geology, mineralogy, palaeontology and related earth sciences; 1,500 mems; Pres. TSUTOMU OHTSUKA; Sec. YOSHIAKI KANAI; publs *Sokuhō* (News, 12 a year), *Chikyu-Kagaku* (Earth Science, 6 a year), *Senpō* (Monograph, irregular), *Chigaku Kyoiku To Kagaku-undo* (Education of Earth Science, 2 a year).

Chikyu-Denjiki Chikyu-Wakuseiken Gakkai (Society of Geomagnetism and Earth, Planetary and Space Science): Edocho 85-1, Kobe, Chuo-ku, Tokyo 650-0033; tel. (78) 332-3703; fax (78) 332-2506; e-mail sgepss@pac.ne.jp; internet www.kurasc .kyoto-u.ac.jp/sgepss; f. 1947; frmly Nippon Chikyu Denki Ziki Gakkai; 695 mems; Pres. Prof. RYOICHI FUJII; publ. *Earth, Planets and Space* (12 a year).

Japan Weather Association: Sunshine 60 Bldg 3-1-1, Higashi-Ikebukuro, Toshima-ku, Tokyo 170-6055; tel. (3) 5958-8161; fax (3) 5958-8162; e-mail webmaster@jwa.go.jp; internet www.jwa.or.jp; f. 1950; Pres. MICHIHIKO MATSUO; publs *Geophysical Magazine*, *Journal of Meteorological Research* (12 a year), *Kisho*, *Oceanographical Magazine* (4 a year).

Japanese Society of Microscopy: Akihabara Konoike Bldg 3F, 1-25 Kanda-sakuma Cho, Chiyoda-ku, Tokyo 101-0025; fax (3) 702-8816; e-mail kenbikyo@realize-se.co.jp; internet wwwsoc.nii.ac.jp/jsm/; f. 1949; 2,690 mems; Pres. KAZUO OGAWA; publ. *Journal of Electron Microscopy* (4 a year).

Kobunshi Gakkai (Society of Polymer Science, Japan): Shintomicho Tokyu Bldg, 3-10-9 Irifune, Chuo-ku, Tokyo 104-0042; tel. (3) 5540-3771; fax (3) 5540-3737; e-mail intnl@ spsj.or.jp; internet www.spsj.or.jp; f. 1951; 12,598 mems; Pres. MITSUO SAWAMOTO; publs *Kobunshi* (High Polymers, 12 a year), *Kobunshi Ronbunshu* (Journal of Polymer Science and Technology, abstracts in English, 12 a year), *Polymer Journal* (in English, 12 a year), *Polymer Preprints* (CD-ROM, in English, 2 a year).

Nihon Bunseki Kagaku-Kai (Japan Society for Analytical Chemistry): Gotanda San-

haitsu, 26-2, Nishigotanda 1-chome, Shinagawa-ku, Tokyo 141-0031; tel. (3) 3490-3351; fax (3) 3490-3572; e-mail analytsci@jsac.or.jp; internet www.soc.nii.ac .jp/jsac; f. 1952; 9,108 mems; Pres. M. TANAKA; Sec.-Gen. Dr TADASHI FUJINUKI; publs *Bunseki Kagaku* (12 a year), *Analytical Sciences* (6 a year).

Nihon Kobutsu Kagaku Kai (Japan Association of Mineralogical Sciences): c/o Graduate School of Science, Tohoku Univ., Sendai 980-8578; tel. (22) 224-3852; fax (22) 224-3852; e-mail kyl04223@nifty.ne.jp; internet wwwsoc.nii.ac.jp/jams3/jmps.htm; f. 2007, by merger of Japanese Association of Mineralogists, Petrologists and Economic Geologists (f. 1929) and The Mineralogical Society of Japan; 1,000 mems; library of 16,000 vols; Pres. Dr EIJI OHTANI; Sec. MASUMI MIYACHI; publs *Japanese Magazine of Mineralogical and Petrological Sciences* (6 a year), *Journal of Mineralogical and Petrological Sciences* (6 a year).

Nihon Nensho Gakkai (Combustion Society of Japan): c/o Department of Mechanical Engineering, Osaka Prefecture University, 1-1 Gakuen-cho, Sakai, Osaka 599-8531; tel. (72) 255-7037; fax (72) 255-7037; e-mail office@combustionsociety.jp; internet combustionsociety.jp; f. 1953; 700 mems; Pres. TOSHIKAZU KADOTA; publ. *Journal* (4 a year).

Nihon Nogyo-Kisho Gakkai (Society of Agricultural Meteorology of Japan): c/o Yokendo Co. Ltd., 5-30-15 Hongo, Bunkyo-ku, Tokyo 113-0033; tel. (3) 3814-0915; fax (3) 3814-2615; e-mail nogyo-kisho@yokendo.co .jp; internet www.soc.nii.ac.jp/agrmet; f. 1942; studies protected cultivation, agricultural meteorology and resources of food production; 787 mems; Pres. Prof. MASUMI OKADA; publs *Journal of Agricultural Meteorology* (4 a year), *Seibutsu to Kisho* (e-journal).

Nihon Seppyo Gakkai (Japanese Society of Snow and Ice): 3rd Fl., Kagaku-Kaikan, Kanda Surugadai 1-5, Chiyoda-ku, Tokyo 101-0062; tel. (3) 5259-5245; fax (3) 5259-5246; e-mail jimu@seppyo.org; internet www .seppyo.org; f. 1939; 950 mems; Pres. Dr YOSHIYUKI FUJII; publs *Seppyo* (Journal of the Japanese Society of Snow and Ice, in Japanese and English, 6 a year), *Bulletin of Glaciological Research* (in English, 1 a year), occasional papers and bibliography.

Nippon Bunko Gakkai (Spectroscopical Society of Japan): c/o Industrial Hall, 1-13, Kanda-Awaji-cho, Chiyoda-ku, Tokyo 101; tel. (3) 3253-2747; fax (3) 3253-2740; f. 1951; 1,300 mems; Pres. M. TASUMI; Sec. Y. F. MIZUGAI; publ. *Bunko Kenkyu* (6 a year).

Nippon Butsuri Gakkai (Physical Society of Japan): 5th Fl., Eishin-kaihatsu Bldg, 5-34-3 Shimbashi, Minato-ku, Tokyo 105-0004; tel. (3) 3434-2671; fax (3) 3432-0997; e-mail jps-office@jps.or.jp; internet wwwsoc.nii.ac .jp/jps; f. 1946; 18,223 mems; Pres. SUKEKATSU USHIODA; publs *Butsuri* (in Japanese, 12 a year), *Journal of the Physical Society of Japan* (12 a year), *Physics Education in Universities* (in Japanese, 3 a year), *Progress of Theoretical Physics* (12 a year).

Nippon Chishitsu Gakkai (Geological Society of Japan): Igeta Bldg, 8-15 Iwamoto-cho 2-chome, Chiyoda-ku, Tokyo 101-0032; tel. (3) 5823-1150; fax (3) 5823-1156; e-mail main@geosociety.jp; internet www.geosociety .jp; f. 1893; stratigraphy, petrology, tectonics, volcanology, etc; 5,000 mems; library of 10,000 vols; Pres. ASAHIKO TAIRA; publ. *Journal* (12 a year).

Nippon Dai-Yonki Gakkai (Japan Association for Quaternary Research): 3rd Fl., Rakuyo Bldg, Waseda-Tsurumaki-cho 519, Shinjuku, Tokyo 162-0041; tel. (3) 5291-6231;

fax (3) 5291-2176; e-mail daiyonki@
shunkosha.com; internet wwwsoc.nii.ac.jp/
qr/index.html; f. 1956; 1,800 mems; Sec. of
Exec. Cttee SUMIKO KUBO; publ. *Quaternary
Research* (5 a year).

Nippon Kagakukai (Chemical Society of
Japan): 1-5 Kanda-Surugadai, Chiyoda-ku,
Tokyo 101-8307; tel. (3) 3292-6161; fax (3)
3292-6318; e-mail info@chemistry.or.jp;
internet www.csj.jp; f. 1878; 31,000 mems;
Pres. Prof. YASUHIRO IWASAWA; Man. HIROKO
IHIDA; publs *Bulletin of the Chemical Society
of Japan* (12 a year), *Chemistry: An Asian
Journal* (12 a year), *Chemistry Letters* (12 a
year), *Chemical Record* (6 a year).

Nippon Kaisui Gakkai (Society of Sea
Water Science, Japan): c/o Sea Water Science
Research Laboratory, Salt Industry Centre of
Japan, 4-13-20, Sakawa, Odawara-shi, Kana-
gawa; f. 1950; 414 mems; Pres. SHINICHI
NAKAO; publ. *Journal*.

Nippon Kaiyo Gakkai (Oceanographic
Society of Japan): MACAS, 9th Fl., Palace-
side Bldg, 1-1-1 Hitotsubashi, Chiyoda-ku,
Tokyo 100-0003; tel. (3) 3211-1412; fax (3)
3211-1413; e-mail jos@mycom.co.jp; internet
wwwsoc.nii.ac.jp/kaiyo; f. 1941; 2,379 mems;
Pres. ISAO KOIKE; publs *Journal of Oceanography* (6 a year), *Umi no Kenkyu* (Oceanography in Japan, 6 a year).

Nippon Kazan Gakkai (Volcanological
Society of Japan): c/o Earthquake Research
Institute, University of Tokyo, 1-1-1 Yayoi,
Bunkyo-ku, Tokyo 113-0032; tel. (3) 3813-
7421; fax (3) 5684-7421; e-mail kazan@khaki
.plala.or.jp; internet wwwsoc.nii.ac.jp/kazan;
f. 1932; 1,200 mems; Pres. TADAHIDE UI; publ.
Bulletin (6 a year).

Nippon Kessho Gakkai (Crystallographic
Society of Japan): Nissei Bldg, 3-11-6 Otuka,
Bunkyo-ku, Tokyo 112-0012; tel. (3) 5940-
7640; fax (3) 5940-7980; internet wwwsoc.nii
.ac.jp/crsj/index.html; f. 1950; 1,000 mems;
Pres. KAZUMAZA OHSUMI; Sec-Gen. MASAKI
TAKATA; publ. *Journal* (6 a year).

Nippon Kisho Gakkai (Meteorological
Society of Japan): c/o Japan Meteorological
Agency, 1-3-4 Ote-machi, Chiyoda-ku, Tokyo
100-0004; tel. (3) 3212-8341; fax (3) 3216-
4401; e-mail metsoc-j@aurora.ocn.ne.jp;
internet wwwsoc.nii.ac.jp/msj; f. 1882; 4,300
mems; Pres. T. ASAI; publs *Journal* (6 a year),
Tenki (in Japanese, 12 a year).

Nippon Kokai Gakkai (Japan Institute of
Navigation): c/o Tokyo University of Mercantile Marine, 2-1-6 Etchujima, Koto-ku,
Tokyo; tel. (3) 3630-3093; fax (3) 3630-3093;
internet homepage2.nifty.com/navigation; f.
1948; 1,011 mems; Pres. Prof. S. KUWASIMA;
publs *Journal* (2 a year), *Navigation* (4 a
year).

Nippon Koseibutsu Gakkai (Palaeontological Society of Japan): 4th Fl., Hongo MT
Bldg, 7-2-2 Hongo, Bunkyo-ku, Tokyo 113-
0033; tel. (3) 3814 5490; fax (3) 3814 6216;
e-mail psj-office@world.ocn.ne.jp; internet
www.soc.nii.ac.jp/psj5; f. 1935; 1,050 mems;
Pres. TOMOKI KASE; publs *Paleontological
Research* (4 a year), *Fossils* (2 a year).

Nippon Onkyo Gakkai (Acoustical Society
of Japan): Nakaura 5th Bldg, 2-18-20 Soto-
kanda, Chiyoda-ku, Tokyo 101-0021; fax (3)
5256-1022; e-mail asj-www@asj.gr.jp;
internet www.asj.gr.jp; f. 1936; 4,530 mems;
Pres. T. SONE; publs *Acoustical Science and
Technology* (12 a year, online), *Reports of
Spring and Autumn Meetings* (2 a year).

Nippon Sokuchi Gakkai (Geodetic Society
of Japan): c/o Japanese Association of Surveyors, 1-3-4 Koishikawa, Bunkyo-ku, Tokyo,
112-0002; tel. (3) 5684-3358; fax (3) 5684-
3366; e-mail nihonsokuchi@jsurvey.jp;
internet wwwsoc.nii.ac.jp/geod-soc; f. 1954;

studies astronomy, crustal activity, earth
tide, geodesy, geomagnetism, gravity, etc;
600 mems; library of 5,000 vols; Pres. Dr
SHUHEI OKUBO; publ. *Journal* (4 a year).

Nippon Temmon Gakkai (Astronomical
Society of Japan): National Astronomical
Observatory, 2-21-1 Osawa, Mitaka-shi,
Tokyo 181-8588; tel. (422) 31-1359; fax (422)
31-5487; e-mail jimu@asj.or.jp; internet www
.asj.or.jp; f. 1908; 2,640 mems; Pres. Y.
UCHIDA; publs *Publications* (6 a year), *The
Astronomical Herald* (in Japanese, 12 a
year).

Nippon Yukagaku Kai (Japan Oil Chemists' Society): 7th Floor, Yushi Kogyo Kaikan,
13-11, Nihonbashi 3-chome, Chuo-ku, Tokyo
103-0027; tel. (3) 3271-7463; fax (3) 3271-
7464; e-mail yukagaku@jocs-office.or.jp;
internet www.soc.nii.ac.jp/jocs; f. 1951;
2,426 mems; Pres. ISAO IKEDA; publ. *Journal
of Oleo Science* (12 a year).

Sen-i Gakkai (Society of Fibre Science and
Technology, Japan): 3-3-9-208 Kamiosaki,
Shinagawa-ku, Tokyo 141; tel. (3) 3441-
5627; fax (3) 3441-3260; e-mail office@fiber
.or.jp; internet www.fiber.or.jp; f. 1943; c.
3,000 mems; Pres. HIROSHI INAGAKI; publ.
Journal (12 a year).

Shokubai Gakkai (Catalysis Society of
Japan): 1-5 Kanda Surugadai, Chiyoda-ku,
Tokyo 101-0062; tel. (3) 3291-8224; fax (3)
3291-8225; e-mail catsj@pb3.so-net.ne.jp;
internet www.shokubai.org; f. 1958; 2,370
mems; Pres. Y. MOROOKA; publ. *Shokubai*
(Catalyst, 8 a year).

Zisin Gakkai (Seismological Society of
Japan): 6-26-12 Tokyo RS Building, Hongo,
Bunkyo-ku, Tokyo 113-0033; tel. (3) 5803-
9570; fax (3) 5803-9577; e-mail zisin@tokyo
.email.ne.jp; internet wwwsoc.nii.ac.jp/ssj; f.
1929; 2,400 mems; Chair. MASAKAZU OHTAKE;
publs *Zisin* (Journal, 4 a year), *Earth Planets
and Space* (12 a year), *Newsletter* (6 a year).

PHILOSOPHY AND PSYCHOLOGY

Bigaku-Kai (Japanese Society for Aesthetics): Kyoto Univ., Graduate School of Human
and Environmental Studies, Prof. Shinohara's Room, Yoshida-Nihonmatsu-Cho,
Sakyo-ku, Kyoto 606-8501; e-mail
bigakukai@nifty.ne.jp; internet wwwsoc.nii
.ac.jp/bigaku; f. 1950; 1,500 mems; Pres.
MOTOAKI SHINOHARA; publs *Aesthetics* (every
2 years), *Bigaku* (in Japanese, 2 a year).

Moralogy Kenkyusho (Institute of Moralogy): 2-1-1, Hikarigaoka, Kashiwa-shi,
Chiba-ken 277-8654; tel. (4) 7173-3252; fax
(4) 7173-3263; e-mail rc@moralogy.jp;
internet rc.moralogy.jp; f. 1926; 236 mems;
library of 70,753 vols; Gen. Sec. T. NAGAI;
publ. *Studies in Moralogy* (2 a year).

Nihon Rinrigakukai (Japanese Society for
Ethics): Dept of Ethics, Faculty of Letters,
University of Tokyo, Bunkyo-ku, Tokyo 113;
tel. (3) 727-147; e-mail jse@logos.tsukuba.ac
.jp; internet jse.trustyweb.jp; f. 1950; 800
mems; Pres. YÔKICHI YAZIMA; Man. MASAHIRO
NAKAGAWA; publ. *Rinrigakunenpo* (1 a year).

Nippon Dobutsu Shinri Gakkai (Japanese Society for Animal Psychology): c/o K. &
U. Co. Ltd, MSK Bldg 3F, 3-32-7 Hongo,
Bunkyo-ku, Tokyo 113-0033; tel. (3) 3815-
4800; fax (3) 3815-4807; e-mail
dousin-gakkai@umin.ac.jp; internet www.soc
.nii.ac.jp/jsap2; f. 1933; 400 mems; Pres.
MASATAKA WATANABE; publ. *The Japanese
Journal of Animal Psychology* (2 a year).

Nippon Shakai Shinri Gakkai (Japanese
Society of Social Psychology): c/o International Academic Printing Co. Ltd, 4-4-19
Takadanobaba, Shinjuku-ku, Tokyo 169-
0075; tel. (3) 5389-6217; fax (3) 3368-2822;
e-mail jssp-post@bunken.co.jp; internet

wwwsoc.nii.ac.jp/jssp; f. 1950; 1,896 mems;
Pres. IKUO DAIBO; publs *Japanese Journal of
Social Psychology*, *Bulletin* (3 a year).

Nippon Shinri Gakkai (Japanese Psychological Association): 5-23-13-7F, Hongo, Bunkyo-ku, Tokyo 113; tel. (3) 3814-3953; fax (3)
3814-3954; internet www.psych.or.jp; f. 1927;
7,000 mems; Pres. KEIICHIRO TSUJI; publs
Japanese Journal of Psychology (6 a year),
Japanese Psychological Research (4 a year).

RELIGION, SOCIOLOGY AND
ANTHROPOLOGY

**Japanese Society of Cultural Anthropol-
ogy:** 2-1-1-813 Mita, Minato-ku, Tokyo 108-
0073; tel. (3) 5232-0920; fax (3) 5232-0922;
e-mail hoya@jasca.org; internet wwwsoc.nii
.ac.jp/jasca; f. 1934; 2,000 mems; publ. *Bun-
kajinruigaku* (Japanese Journal of Cultural
Anthropology, 4 a year).

Nihon Indogaku Bukkyôgakukai (Japanese Association of Indian and Buddhist
Studies): Hongo Bldg 2F, 3-33-5 Hongo,
Bunkyo-ku, Tokyo 113-0033; e-mail jaibs@l
.u~tokyo.ac.jp; f. 1951; 2,350 mems; Pres.
KIYOTAKA KIMURA; publ. *Indogaku Bukkyô-
gaku Kenkyû* (Journal of Indian and Buddhist Studies).

Nihon Shūkyō Gakkai (Japanese Association for Religious Studies): 1-29-7-205
Hongo, Bunkyo-ku, Tokyo 113-0033; tel. (3)
5684-5473; fax (3) 5684-5474; internet
wwwsoc.nii.ac.jp/jars; f. 1930; 2,100 mems;
Pres. FUJIO IKADO; publ. *Journal of Religious
Studies* (4 a year).

Nippon Dokyo Gakkai (Japan Society of
Taoistic Research): Tokyo University, Faculty of Letters, 5-28-20 Hakusan, Bunkyo-
ku, Tokyo 112-8606; tel. (3) 3945-7557; f.
1950; 650 mems; Pres. TOSHIAKI YAMADA;
publ. *Journal of Eastern Religions* (2 a year).

Nippon Jinruigaku Kai (Anthropological
Society of Nippon): 3-21-10 3F Urbano,
Ootsuka Kita Otsuka, Tokyo 170-0004; tel.
(3) 5814-5801; fax (3) 5814-5820; e-mail
g002jinrui-mng@ml.galileo.co.jp; internet
www.soc.nii.ac.jp/jinrui; f. 1884; 700 mems;
Pres. TASUKU KIMURA; publs *Anthropological
Science* (4 a year), *Anthropological Science
(Japanese Series)* (2 a year).

Nippon Shakai Gakkai (Japanese Sociological Society): Dept of Sociology, Faculty of
Letters, Univ. of Tokyo, 7-3-1 Hongo, Bunkyo-ku, Tokyo 113-0033; tel. (3) 5841-8933;
fax (3) 5841-8932; e-mail jss@wwwsoc.nii.ac
.jp; internet www.gakkai.ne.jp/jss; f. 1923;
3,600 mems; Pres. SHUJIRO YAZAWA; publs
International Journal of Japanese Sociology
(in English, 1 a year), *Shakaigaku Hyóron* (4
a year).

Tōhō Gakkai (Institute of Eastern Culture):
4-1, Nishi Kanda 2-chome, Chiyoda-ku,
Tokyo 101-0065; tel. (3) 3262-7221; fax (3)
3262-7227; e-mail iec@tohogakkai.com;
internet www.tohogakkai.com; f. 1947; Asian
studies; 1,600 mems; Chair. YOSHIO TOGAWA;
Sec.-Gen. HIDEO KAWAGUCHI; publs *Acta
Asiatica* (bulletin, 2 a year), *Tōhōgaku* (Eastern Studies, 2 a year), *Transactions of the
International Conference of Eastern Studies*
(1 a year).

TECHNOLOGY

Denki Gakkai (Institute of Electrical
Engineers of Japan (IEEJ)): Homat Horizon
Bldg, 6-2 Goban-cho, Chiyoda-ku, Tokyo 102-
0076; tel. (3) 3221-7256; fax (3) 3221-3704;
e-mail jimkyoku@iee.or.jp; internet www.iee
.or.jp; f. 1888; 26,000 mems; Pres. HISAO OKA;
publs *IEEJ Transactions on Electronics,
Information and Systems* (in Japanese and
English, 12 a year), *IEEJ Transactions on
Fundamentals and Materials* (in Japanese

and English, 12 a year), *IEEJ Transactions on Industry Applications* (in Japanese and English, 12 a year), *IEEJ Transactions on Power and Energy* (in Japanese and English, 12 a year), *IEEJ Transactions on Sensors and Micromachines* (in Japanese and English, 12 a year), *Journal of the IEEJ* (in Japanese, 12 a year).

Denshi Joho Tsushin Gakkai (Institute of Electronics, Information and Communication Engineers): Kikai-Shinko-Kaikan Bldg, 5-8, Shibakoen 3-chome, Minato-ku, Tokyo 105-0011; tel. (3) 3433-6691; fax (3) 3433-6659; f. 1917; 40,000 mems; Pres. HISASHI KANEKO; publs *Journal*, *Transactions* (9 series, incl. *Original Contributions in English and Abstracts in English from the Transactions*, 12 a year).

Doboku-Gakkai (Japan Society of Civil Engineers): Yotsuya 1-chome, Shinjuku-ku, Tokyo; tel. (3) 3355-3452; fax (3) 5379-2769; e-mail iad@jsce.or.jp; internet www.jsce-int.org; f. 1914; 40,742 mems; library of 45,000 vols; Pres. Dr TORU KONDO; Exec. Dir. MORIYASU FURUKI; publ. *Journal* (12 a year), *Coastal Engineering in Japan* (in English, 2 a year), *Transactions* (12 a year), *Civil Engineering, JSCE* (1 a year).

Keikinzoku Gakkai (Japan Institute of Light Metals): Tukamoto-Sazan Bldg, 2–15, Ginza 4-chome, Chuo-ku, Tokyo 104-0061; tel. (3) 3538-0232; fax (3) 3538-0226; e-mail jilm1951@jilm.or.jp; internet www.jilm.or.jp; f. 1951; 2,222 mems; Pres. AKIHIKO KAMIO; publ. *Journal* (in Japanese and synopsis in English, 12 a year).

Keisoku Jidouseigyo Gakkai SICE (Society of Instrument and Control Engineers): 1-35-28-303, Hongo, Bunkyo-ku, Tokyo 113-0033; tel. (3) 3814-4121; fax (3) 3814-4699; internet www.sice.or.jp; f. 1962; 9,183 mems; Pres. SUSUMU TACHI; Vice-Pres RYOICHI TAKAHASHI, KAZUO KYUMA; publ. *Journal* (12 a year).

Kuki-Chowa Eisei Kogakkai (Society of Heating, Air-conditioning and Sanitary Engineers of Japan): 8-1, 1-chome, Kitashinjuku, Shinjuku-ku, Tokyo; f. 1917; 17,000 mems; Pres. M. KAMATA; publs *Journal* (12 a year), *Transactions* (12 a year).

Nihon Genshiryoku Gakkai (Atomic Energy Society of Japan): Shimbashi 2-3-7, Minato-ku, Tokyo 105-0004; tel. (3) 3508-1261; fax (3) 3581-6128; e-mail atom@aesj.or.jp; internet wwwsoc.nii.ac.jp/aesj; f. 1959; peaceful uses of atomic energy; 7,700 mems; Pres. Dr M. TAKUMA; Sec.-Gen. Y. TARUISHI; publs *Journal of Nuclear Science and Technology* (12 a year), *Nihon-Genshiryoku-Gakkai Shi* (12 a year), *Transactions of the Atomic Energy Society of Japan* (4 a year).

Nihon Kasai Gakkai (Japanese Association for Fire Science and Engineering): 3F Gakkai Center Bldg, 2-4-16 Yayoi, Bunkyo-ku, Tokyo 113-0032; tel. (3) 3813-8308; fax (3) 5689-3577; e-mail kasai50@sepia.ocn.ne.jp; f. 1951; 2,000 mems; Pres. TAKAO WAKAMATU; publ. *Kasai* (Fire, 6 a year).

Nihon Kikai Gakkai (Japan Society of Mechanical Engineers): Shinanomachi-Rengakan 5F, 35 Shinanomachi, Shinjuku-ku, Tokyo 160-0016; tel. (3) 5360-3500; fax (3) 5360-3508; e-mail wwwadmin@jsme.or.jp; internet www.jsme.or.jp; f. 1897; 40,000 mems; Pres. MASAKI SHIRATORI; publs *Journal* (12 a year), *JSME International Journal* (in English, 12 a year, online), *Transactions* (12 a year).

Nippon Kinzoku Gakkai (Japan Institute of Metals): 1-14-32 Ichibancho, Aoba-ku, Sendai 980-8544; tel. (22) 223-3685; fax (22) 223-6312; e-mail secgnl@jim.or.jp; f. 1937; 10,000 mems; Pres. KIYOHITO ISHIDA; publs

Bulletin (12 a year), *Journal* (12 a year), *Materials Transactions* (in English, 12 a year).

Nippon Kogakukai (Japan Federation of Engineering Societies): Kaikan Bldg 6th Fl., 5-26-20 Shiba, Minato-ku, Tokyo 108-0014; tel. (3) 5765-8002; fax (3) 5765-3219; internet www.jfes.or.jp; f. 1879.

Nippon Koku Ūchu Gakkai (Japan Society for Aeronautical and Space Sciences): c/o Meiko Bldg, Bekkan, 1-18-2 Shinbash, Minato-ku, Tokyo 105-0004; tel. (3) 3501-0463; fax (3) 3501-0464; e-mail office@jsass.or.jp; internet www.jsass.or.jp; f. 1934; 4,400 mems; Pres. Prof. KANICHIROU KATO; publs *Journal* (12 a year), *Transactions* (4 a year).

Nippon Seramikusu Kyoukai (Ceramic Society of Japan): 22-17, 2-chome, Hyakunin-cho, Shinjuku-ku, Tokyo 169-0073; fax (3) 3362-5714; e-mail information@cersj.org; internet www.ceramic.or.jp; f. 1891; 5,546 mems; Pres. YOSHINORI KOKUBU; publs *Journal*, *Ceramics Japan* (Bulletin).

Nippon Shashin Gakkai (Society of Photographic Science and Technology of Japan): Tokyo Polytechnic Institute, 2-9-5 Hon-cho, Nakano-ku, Tokyo 164-8678; tel. (3) 3373-0724; fax (3) 3299-5887; internet www.spstj.org; f. 1925; 1,550 mems; Pres. T. WAKABAYASHI; publ. *Journal* (6 a year).

Nippon Tekko Kyoukai (Iron and Steel Institute of Japan): Niikura Building, 2-Kanda-Tsukasacho 2-chome, Chiyoda-ku, Tokyo 101-0048; tel. (3) 5209-7011; fax (3) 3257-1110; internet www.isij.or.jp; f. 1915; 9,274 mems; Exec. Dir Dr AKIRA KOJIMA; publs *Ferrum* (bulletin, in Japanese, 12 a year), *ISIJ International* (in English, 12 a year), *Tetsu-to-Hagané* (Iron and Steel, in Japanese, 12 a year).

Nippon Toribologi Gakkai (Japanese Society of Tribologists): c/o Kikai Shinko Kaikan No. 407-2, 3-5-8, Shibakoen, Minato-ku, Tokyo 105-0001; tel. (3) 3434-1926; fax (3) 3434-3556; e-mail jast@tribology.jp; internet www.tribology.jp; f. 1956; 3,044 mems; Pres. TAKASHI YAMAMOTO; publs *Journal of Japanese Society of Tribologists* (12 a year), *Tribology* (online).

Nogyo-Doboku Gakkai (Japanese Society of Irrigation, Drainage and Reclamation Engineering): Nogyo Doboku-Kaikan, 34-4 Shinbashi 5-chome, Tokyo 105-0004; tel. (3) 3436-3418; fax (3) 3435-8494; e-mail suido@jsidre.or.jp; internet www.jsidre.or.jp; f. 1929; 13,000 mems; Pres. Prof. TSUYOSHI MIYAZAKI; publs *Journal* (12 a year), *Journal of Rural and Environmental Engineering* (in English, 2 a year), *Transactions* (6 a year).

Seisan Gijutsu Kenkyusho (Institute of Industrial Science): c/o University of Tokyo, 4-6-1 Komaba, Meguro-ku, Tokyo 153-8505; tel. (3) 5454-6024; fax (3) 5452-6094; e-mail kokusai@iis.u-tokyo.ac.jp; internet www.iis.u-tokyo.ac.jp; f. 1949; Dir-Gen. Prof. S. NISHIO; publ. *Seisan-Kenkyu* (12 a year).

Shigen Sozai Gakkai (Mining and Materials Processing Institute of Japan): Nogizaka Bldg, 9-6-41 Akasaka, Minato-ku, Tokyo 107-0052; tel. (3) 3402-0541; fax (3) 3403-1776; e-mail info@mmij.or.jp; internet www.mmij.or.jp; f. 1885; 2,030 mems; Sec.-Gen. SUSUMU OKABE; publs *Journal of MMIJ* (9 a year), *MMIJ Proceedings* (2 a year).

Sisutemu Seigyo Jyouhou Gakkai (Institute of Systems, Control and Information Engineers): 14 Yoshidakawaharacho, Sakyo-ku, Kyoto City, Kyoto 606-8305; tel. (75) 751-6413; fax (75) 751-6037; e-mail shomu@iscie.or.jp; internet www.iscie.or.jp; f. 1957; 2,744 mems; Pres. MINORU ABE; publ. *Systems, Control and Information* (12 a year).

Yosetsu Gakkai (Japan Welding Society): 1-11 Sakuma-cho, Kanda, Chiyoda-ku, Tokyo; tel. (3) 3253-0488; fax (3) 3253-3059; internet wwwsoc.nii.ac.jp/jws; f. 1925; 5,000 mems; Pres. Dr SHUZO SUSEI; publ. *Journal* (12 a year).

Research Institutes

GENERAL

Kokusai Nihon Bunka Kenkyu Center (International Research Center for Japanese Studies): 3–2 Oeyama-cho, Goryo, Nishikyo-ku, Kyoto 610-1192; tel. (75) 335-2222; fax (75) 335-2091; e-mail www-admin@nichibun.ac.jp; internet www.nichibun.ac.jp; f. 1987; attached to Nat. Institutes for the Humanities (an Inter-Univ. Research Institute Corporation); interdisciplinary and comprehensive research on Japanese studies, and research cooperation; library of 420,000 vols, 6,700 periodicals; Dir-Gen. Dr TAKENORI INOKI; publs *Japan Review* (in English), *Nihon Kenkyu* (in Japanese).

Sogo Kenkyu Kaihatsu Kiko (National Institute for Research Advancement): POB 5004, 34F Yebisu Garden Place Tower, 4-20-3 Ebisu, Shibuya-ku, Tokyo 150-6034; tel. (3) 5448-1700; fax (3) 5448-1743; e-mail info@nira.or.jp; internet www.nira.or.jp; f. 1974 under parliamentary legislation to promote and conduct interdisciplinary research that focuses on the problems facing modern society and their alleviation; conducts its own research, also commissions and subsidizes research by other bodies; promotes international exchange of research affecting policy-making around the world; research results are made public through lectures, symposia or publication of reports; Chair. YOTARO KOBAYASHI; Pres. MOTOSHIGE ITO; Executive Vice-Presidents YOSHIO EZAKI YASUO SAWAI; publs *Almanac of Think Tanks in Japan*, *NIRA Kenkyu Hokokusho*, *NIRA News*, *NIRA Research Output* (in English), *NIRA Review* (in English), *NIRA Seisaku Kenkyu*, *NIRA's World Directory of Think Tanks* (in English).

AGRICULTURE, FISHERIES AND VETERINARY SCIENCE

Forest and Forest Products Research Institute: 1 Matsunosato, Tsukuba Ibaraki 305-8687; tel. (29) 873-3211; fax (29) 874-3720; internet www.ffpri.affrc.go.jp; f. 1878; library of 386,000 vols (incl. br. stations); Pres. KAZUO SUZUKI; publ. *Bulletin* (4 a year).

National Agriculture Research Centre: 3-1-1 Kannondai, Tsukuba, Ibaraki 305-8666; tel. (29) 838-8481; fax (29) 838-8484; e-mail www@narc.affrc.go.jp; internet narc.naro.affrc.go.jp; f. 1981; library of 62,000 vols, 5,800 periodicals; Dir AKIHIRO SASAKI.

National Food Research Institute: 2-1-12 Kannondai, Tsukuba, Ibaraki 305-8642; tel. (29) 838-7971; fax (29) 838-7996; internet www.nfri.affrc.go.jp; f. 1934; food processing, chemistry, technology, storage, engineering, distribution, nutrition; applied microbiology, analysis, radiation, etc.; 121 mems; library of 40,000 vols; Dir Dr S. TANIGUCHI; publs *Report of the National Food Research Institute*, *Food Science and Technology*.

National Institute for Rural Engineering: 2-1-6 Kannondai, Tsukuba-shi, Ibaraki-ken 305-8609; tel. (298) 38-7513; fax (298) 38-7609; internet www.nkk.affrc.go.jp; f. 1988; research on engineering technologies for agriculture and rural community areas; 115 mems; library of 38,000 vols; Dir-Gen. HIROSHI SATO; publs *Bulletin* (12 a year), *Technical Report* (irregular).

National Institute of Agrobiological Sciences (NIAS): 2-1-2 Kannondai, Tsukuba, Ibaraki 305-8602; tel. (298) 38-7406; fax (298) 38-7408; e-mail niasl@nias.affrc.go.jp; internet www.nias.affrc.go.jp; f. 2001 by merger of National Institute of Agrobiological Resources (NIAR) and National Institute of Sericultural and Entomological Sciences (NISES); life science research on plants, animals and insects to facilitate the devt of Japan's domestic agricultural industry; 400 mems; library of 75,000 vols; Pres. TERUO ISHIGE; publ. *Gamma Field Symposia* (1 a year).

National Institute of Animal Health: 3-1-5, Kannondai, Tsukaba-shi, Ibaraki 305-0856; tel. (29) 838-7708; fax (29) 838-7907; e-mail ref-niah@ml.affrc.go.jp; internet niah.naro.affrc.go.jp; f. 1921; animal husbandry, biology, veterinary medicine; 3 br. laboratories; library of 21,422 vols, 2,465 serial titles; Dir-Gen. Dr TAKAFUMI HAMAOKA; publs *Animal Health* (research report, 1 a year), *Bulletin* (1 a year).

National Institute of Crop Science: 2-1-18 Kannondai, Tsukuba, Ibaraki 305-8518; tel. (298) 38-8260; fax (298) 38-7488; e-mail www-nics@naro.affrc.go.jp; internet nics.naro.affrc.go.jp; f. 1893; library of 130,000 vols; publ. *Bulletin* (irregular).

National Institute of Fruit Tree Science: 2-1 Fujimoto, Tsukuba, Ibaraki 305-8605; tel. (29) 838-6451; fax (29) 838-6437; e-mail www-fruit@naro.affrc.go.jp; internet fruit.naro.affrc.go.jp; f. 1902; library of 60,000 vols; Dir Dr YOSHINORI HASEGAWA.

National Institute of Livestock and Grassland Science: 2 Ikenodai, Kukizaki, Ibaraki 305-0901; tel. (298) 38-8612; fax (298) 38-8628; e-mail nilgs-libchief@ml.affrc.go.jp; internet www.nilgs.naro.affrc.go.jp; f. 1916; library of 51,000 vols; Librarian KIRIKO HASHIMOTO; publ. *Bulletin* (irregular).

National Institute of Vegetable and Tea Science: 360 Kusawa, Ano, Age Mie 514-2392; tel. (59) 268-4621; fax (59) 268-1339; internet vegetea.naro.affrc.go.jp; f. 1902; publ. *Bulletin* (1 a year).

Policy Research Institute, Ministry of Agriculture, Forestry and Fisheries: 2-2-1 Nishigahara, Kita-ku, Tokyo; tel. (3) 3910-3946; fax (3) 3940-0232; e-mail www@primaff.affrc.go.jp; internet www.primaff.affrc.go.jp; f. 1946; library of 331,495 vols; Dir T. SHINOHARA; publ. *Journal of Agricultural Policy Research* (in Japanese).

ECONOMICS, LAW AND POLITICS

Chuto Chosakai (Middle East Institute of Japan): Sanko Park Bldg, 5th Fl., 7-3-1 Nishi-Shinjuku-ku, Tokyo 160-0023; tel. (3) 3371-5798; fax (3) 3371-5799; internet www.meij.or.jp; f. 1960; government-aided; exchanges information with other countries; research activities in 4 areas: political and diplomatic affairs, industry, economy, natural resources; library in process of formation; Chair. KOSAKU INABA; publs *Chuto Kenkyu* (Journal of Middle East Studies, 12 a year), *Chuto Kitaafurika Nenkan* (Yearbook of the Middle East and North Africa).

Japan Center for International Exchange: 4-9-17 Minami-Azabu, Minato-ku, Tokyo 106-0047; tel. (3) 3446-7781; fax (3) 3443-7580; e-mail admin@jcie.or.jp; internet www.jcie.or.jp; f. 1971 to promote dialogue between Japan and the rest of the world; int. conferences and seminars, overseas programme planning, promotion of policy studies and exchange programmes among philanthropic organizations; Japanese Secretariat of the Trilateral Commission; Pres. TADASHI YAMAMOTO.

Japan Economic Research Institute: 6th Floor, Kowa 32 Bldg, 2-32, Minami-Azabu 5-chome, Minato-ku, Tokyo 106-0047; tel. (3) 3442-9400; fax (3) 3442-9403; e-mail web@nikkeicho.or.jp; internet www.nikkeicho.or.jp; f. 1962; research and study of domestic and foreign economic and business management; library of 8,000 vols; Exec. Dir KATSUZO YAMADA; Chair. KENJIRO NAGASAKA; publ. research reports.

Japan Maritime Development Association: Kaiun Bldg, 6-4, 2-chome, Hirakawacho, Chiyoda-ku, Tokyo; tel. (3) 3265-5231; fax (3) 3265-5035.

Kabushikikaisha Mitsubishi Sogo Kenkyusho (Mitsubishi Research Institute, Inc.): 3-6, Otemachi 2-chome, Chiyoda-ku, Tokyo 100-8141; tel. (3) 3270-9211; fax (3) 3279-1308; internet www.mri.co.jp; f. 1970; aims to meet new social, economic and industrial requirements in an age of advanced information systems and internationalization; research on nat. and int. scale to serve the needs of government agencies and industry in the fields of economic, political, industrial and management affairs, techno-economics, social engineering, technology and data processing; 900 mems; library of 63,000 vols, 1,000 periodicals; Chair. TAKESHI YANO; Pres. MASAYUKI TANAKA; publs *Outlook for the Japanese Economy* (2 a year), *Journal* (2 a year), *MRI Analysis of Japanese Corporations* (2 a year).

National Institute of Population and Social Security Research: 6th Fl., Hibiya Kokusai Bldg, 2-2-3 Uchisaiwaicyo, Chiyoda-ku, Tokyo 100-0011; tel. (3) 3595-2984; fax (3) 3591-4816; e-mail soumuka@ipss.go.jp; internet www.ipss.go.jp; f. 1939; part of Ministry of Health and Welfare; library of 16,000 vols; Dir TAKANOBU KYOGOKU; publ. *Journal of Population Problems* (4 a year).

Nihon Boeki Shinkokiko Ajia Keizai Kenkyusho (Institute of Developing Economies, Japan External Trade Organization): 3-2-2 Wkaba, Mihama-ku, Chiba-shi, Chiba 261-8454; tel. (43) 299-9500; fax (43) 299-9724; e-mail info@ide.go.jp; internet www.ide.go.jp; f. 1960; library of 600,000 vols; 400 mems; researches on economic, political and social issues in developing economies to support Japan's expansion of harmonious trade and investment; provision of int. economic cooperation focused on developing economies; Chair. and CEO YASUO HAYASHI; Pres. TAKASHI SHIRAISHI; publs *Ajia Keizai* (in Japanese, 12 a year), *The Developing Economies* (in English, 4 a year), *Ajiken World Trend* (in Japanese, 12 a year).

Nihon Keizai Kenkyu Center (Japan Center for Economic Research): Nikkei Kayabacho Bldg, 2-6-1 Nihombashi-kayabacho, Chuo-ku, Tokyo 103; tel. (3) 3639-2801; fax (3) 3639-2839; e-mail jcernet@jcer.or.jp; internet www.jcer.or.jp; f. 1963; 372 institutional, 280 individual mems; library of 45,813 vols, 920 periodicals; Pres. S. TOSHIDA; publ. *Asian Economic Policy Review.*

Nippon Keidanren (Japan Business Federation): 1-9-4, Otemachi, Chiyoda-ku, Tokyo 100-8188; tel. (3) 5204-1500; fax (3) 5255-6255; internet www.keidanren.or.jp; f. 2002 by merger of Keidanren (Japan Federation of Economic Organizations) and Nikkeiren (Japan Federation of Employers' Associations); 1,662 mems; library of 100,000 vols; Chair. FUJIO MITARAI.

Nippon Research Center Ltd: 2-7-1 Nihonbashi-honchou, Chuo-ku, Tokyo 103-0023; tel. (3) 6667-3400; fax (3) 6667-3470; internet www.nrc.co.jp; f. 1960 by interdisciplinary researchers and businessmen to meet the needs of industrial and economic circles; marketing and public opinion research, marketing consultancy, public relations, economic forecasting and urban and regional development; 96 staff; library of 3,000 vols; Pres. INAHIRO SUZUKI; publ. *Bulletin of Marketing Research* (in Japanese, 1 a year).

Rôdô Kagaku Kenkyusho (Institute for Science of Labour): 2-8-14, Sugao, Miyamae-ku, Kawasaki-shi, Kanagawa-ken 216-8501; tel. (44) 977-2121; fax (44) 977-7504; internet www.isl.or.jp; f. 1921; systems safety, chemical health risk management, employment and working life conditions, human–technology interaction, human work environment management, local industries, occupational epidemiology, systems safety, welfare support, work stress, participatory training for occupational safety and health; Pres. TAKAFUSA SHIOYA; Dir Dr KAZUHIRO SAKAI; publs *Rôdô Kagaku* (Journal of Science of Labour, 6 a year), *Rôdô no Kagaku* (Digest of Science of Labour, 12 a year).

EDUCATION

Kokuritsu Kyoiku Seisaku Kenkyujo (National Institute for Educational Policy Research): 6-5-22 Shimomeguro, Meguro-ku, Tokyo 153-8681; tel. (3) 5721-5150; fax (3) 3714-7073; e-mail info@nier.go.jp; internet www.nier.go.jp; f. 1949; conducts basic research on specific issues for use in the planning and formulation of education policy and also pursues a wide range of activities such as providing academic sectors with information about educational studies, conducting research studies in conjunction with schools, pursuing practical research into social education, and conducting joint int. initiatives (incl. research studies) in the education field; library: see Libraries; Dir-Gen. SHIGERU YOSHIDA; publs *Bulletin* (in Japanese, annual; in English, irregular), *Kenkyushuroku* (in Japanese, 2 a year), *Koho* (in Japanese, 6 a year), *Unesco-NIER Newsletter* (in English, 3 a year).

FINE AND PERFORMING ARTS

Tokyo Bunkazai Kenkyu-jo (Tokyo National Research Institute of Cultural Properties): 13–43 Ueno Park, Taito-ku, Tokyo 110-8713; tel. (3) 3823-2241; fax (3) 3828-2434; internet www.tobunken.go.jp; f. 1930; depts incl. Intangible Cultural Heritage, Research Programming; also Center for Conservation Science and Restoration Techniques, Japan Center for Int. Co-operation in Conservation and Div. of General Affairs; library of 110,000 vols; Dir-Gen. SUZUKI NORIO; publs *Bijutsu Kenkyu* (Journal of Art Studies, 4 a year), *Hozon Kagaku* (Science for Conservation, 1 a year), *Nihon Bijutsu Nenkan* (Year Book of Japanese Art), *Proceedings of the International Symposium on the Conservation and Restoration of Cultural Property* (1 a year).

Tôyô Ongaku Gakkai (Society for Research in Asiatic Music): No. 307 Miharu Building 3-6-3 Ueno, Taitô-ku, Tokyo 110-0005; tel. (3) 3823-5173; fax (3) 3823-5174; e-mail len03210@nifty.com; internet wwwsoc.nii.ac.jp/tog; f. 1936; aims to promote research in Japanese and other Asian music and ethnomusicology; 750 mems; Pres. KAZUYUKI TANIMOTO; publ. *Tôyô Ongaku Kenkyū* (1 a year).

HISTORY, GEOGRAPHY AND ARCHAEOLOGY

Geospatial Information Authority of Japan: Kitasato-1, Tsukuba, Ibaraki 305-0811; tel. (29) 864-1111; fax (29) 864-8087; internet www.gsi.go.jp; f. 1869; National Survey and Mapping Org.; library of 32,000 vols; Dir YOSHIHISA HOSHINO; publ. *Bulletin* (1 a year).

LANGUAGE AND LITERATURE

Kokubungaku Kenkyu Siryokan (National Institute of Japanese Literature): Midorityou 10-3 Tachikawa, Tokyo 190-0014; tel. (50) 5533-2900; fax (42) 526-8604; e-mail so-mu@nijl.ac.jp; internet www.nijl.ac.jp; f. 1972 by the Min. of Education, Science and Culture at the recommendation of the Japan Science Council and in response to requests for a centre for the preservation of Japanese classical literature; surveys, collects (largely in microfilm), studies, processes, preserves and provides access to MSS and old printed books relating to Japanese literature before 1868; also undertakes research in this field; provides scholarly community with facilities for consultation and reproduction of materials; historical documents division collects and preserves documents of *kinsei* (1600–1867); library: see Libraries; Dir-Gen. Dr YUICHIRO IMANISHI; publs *Bulletin* (1 a year), *Bibliographic Reports* (1 a year), *Bibliography of Research in Japanese Literature* (1 a year), *Proceedings of the International Conference on Japanese Literature in Japan* (1 a year).

Kokuritu Kokugo Kenkyuzyo (National Institute for Japanese Language): 10-2 Midorimachi, Tachikawa, Tokyo; tel. (42) 540-4300; fax (42) 540-4333; internet www.kokken.go.jp; f. 1948; library of 105,000 vols; Pres. SEIJU SUGITO; Dir MICHITERU TOKUSHIGE; publs *Kokugo Nenkan* (Japanese Language Studies, 1 a year), *Nihongo Kagaku* (Japanese Linguistics), *Nihongo Kyouiku Ronshu* (Japanese Language Education, 1 a year).

MEDICINE

Cancer Institute, Japanese Foundation for Cancer Research: 3-10-6 Ariake, Kotoku, Tokyo, 135-8550; tel. (3) 3520-0111; fax (3) 3520-0141; internet www.jfcr.or.jp; f. 1908; departments of biochemistry, cancer chemotherapy, cell biology, experimental pathology, gene research, human genome analysis, pathology, physics, molecular biotherapy and viral oncology; library of 5,000 vols, 10,000 periodicals; Cancer Chemotherapy Center, Cancer Institute Hospital and Genome Center attached; Dir Dr TETSUO NODA; publ. *Japan Journal for Cancer Research* (12 a year).

Institute of Brain and Blood Vessels: 6-23 Ootemachi, Isezaki-city, Gumma; tel. (270) 24-3355; fax (270) 24-3359; f. 1963; clinical and basic research on cerebrovascular disease; 356 mems; Dir Dr TATSURU MIHARA; publ. *Nosotchu No Kenkyu* (Studies on Apoplexy).

Institute of Chemotherapy: 6-1-14 Kohnodai, Ichikawa-city, Chiba; tel. (473) 75-1111; fax (473) 73-4921; f. 1939; Dir Prof. TSUGUO HASEGAWA; publ. *Bulletin of the Institute of Chemotherapy.*

Kekkaku Yobo Kai Kekkaku Kenkyujo (Research Institute of Tuberculosis, Japan Anti-Tuberculosis Association): 3-1-24 Matsuyama Kiyose-shi, Tokyo 204-8533; tel. (424) 93-5711; fax (424) 92-4600; internet www.jata.or.jp; f. 1939; research on health education campaign against tuberculosis: information, surveillance and training center: tuberculosis and respiratory diseases; 56 mems; library of 15,000 vols; Dir Dr NOBUKATSU ISHIKAWA; publs *Information and Review of Tuberculosis and Respiratory Disease Research* (in Japanese, 4 a year), *Red Double-Barred Cross* (in Japanese, 6 a year), *Review of Tuberculosis for Public Health Nurses* (in Japanese, 2 a year).

Kitasato Institute Research Center for Biologicals: 6-111 Arai, Kitamoto-shi, Saitama 108; tel. (3) 3444-6161; internet www.kitasato.ac.jp; f. 1914; research on the cause, prevention and therapy of various diseases; 1,100 mems; library of 86,000 vols; Dir S. OMURA.

Kohno Clinical Medicine Research Institute: 1-28-15 Kita-Shinagawa, Shinagawa-ku, Tokyo; tel. (3) 472-4630; fax (3) 474-1355; internet kcmi.or.jp; f. 1951; 62 staff; library of 3,000 vols; Dir M. KOHNO; publs *Archives, Bulletin.*

Miyake Medical Institute: 1-3 Tenjin-mae, Takamatsu-city, Kagawa; internet www.miyake.or.jp; f. 1949; Dir T. MIYAKE.

National Cancer Center: 5-1-1 Tsukiji, Chuo-ku, Tokyo 104-0045; tel. (3) 3542-2511; fax (3) 3542-3567; e-mail www-admin@ncc.go.jp; internet www.ncc.go.jp; f. 1962; diagnosis, treatment and research of cancer and allied diseases; Dept of Ministry of Health, Labour and Welfare; 800 staff; library of 56,000 vols, 17,000 monographs, 500 periodicals; Pres. SETSUO HIROHASHI; Dirs RYOSUKE TSUCHIYA (Hospital), KEIJI WAKABAYASHI (Research Institute); publs *Collected Papers of Hospital* (in Japanese and English, 1 a year, distributed free to libraries), *Collected Papers of Research Inst.* (in English, 1 a year, distributed free to libraries), *Tumour Registration of Bone, Lung, Stomach, Blood, Brain, etc.* (in Japanese, distributed free to libraries).

National Institute of Genetics: 1111, Yata, Mishima-city, Shizuoka 411-8540; tel. (55) 981-6707; fax (55) 981-6715; e-mail shomuka@lab.nig.ac.jp; internet www.nig.ac.jp/home.html; f. 1949; part of Ministry of Education, Culture, Sports, Science and Technology; library of 20,000 vols; Dir Dr YOSHIKI HOTTA.

National Institute of Health and Nutrition: 1-23-1 Toyama, Shinjuku-ku, Tokyo 162-8636; tel. (3) 3203-5721; fax (3) 3202-3278; e-mail eiken-office@nih.go.jp; internet www.nih.go.jp; f. 1920; part of Ministry of Health, Labour and Welfare; library of 30,000 vols; Dir NOBUAKI SHIBAIKE; publ. *Japanese Journal of Nutrition* (in Japanese, every 2 months).

National Institute of Health Sciences: 1-18-1 Kamiyoga, Setagaya, Tokyo 15-8501; tel. (3) 3700-1141; fax (3) 3707-6950; internet www.nihs.go.jp; f. 1874; research in connection with the cosmetics, drugs, environmental chemicals, medical devices and regulation of foods; Dir MASAHIRO NISHIJIMA; publ. *Bulletin* (1 a year).

National Institute of Occupational Safety and Health: 6-21-1, Nagao Tamaku, Kawasaki-city, Kanagawa 214-8585; tel. (44) 865-6111; fax (44) 865-6124; e-mail info@niih.go.jp; internet www.jniosh.go.jp/en/; f. 1956; part of Ministry of Health, Labour and Welfare; library of 26,000 vols; Dir YUTAKA MAEDA; publ. *Industrial Health* (6 a year).

National Institute of Public Health: 2-3-6 Minami, Wako-shi, Saitama 351-0197; internet www.niph.go.jp; f. 2002; by merger of Institute of Public Health, National Institute of Health Services Management and part of the Dept of Oral Science in National Institute of Infectious Disease; depts of education and training technology, environmental health, epidemiology, facility sciences, health promotion, healthy building and housing, human resources development, management sciences, oral health, policy sciences, public health nursing, social services, technology assessment and biostatistics, water supply engineering; library of 80,000 books, 4,000 journals; publ. *Hoken Iryo Kagaku*.

National Institute of Infectious Diseases: Toyama 1-23-1, Shinjuku-ku, Tokyo 162-8640; tel. (3) 5285-1111; fax (3) 5285-1150; e-mail info@nih.go.jp; internet www.nih.go.jp/niid; f. 1947; part of Ministry of Health, Labour and Welfare; research on communicable diseases, including an AIDS Research Centre; assay of biological products and antibiotics; library of 30,000 vols; Dir TATSUO MIYAMURA; publ. *The Japanese Journal of Infectious Diseases* (6 a year).

National Institute of Mental Health, National Center of Neurology and Psychiatry: 4-1-1 Higashimaci, Kodairashi, Tokyo 187-8553; tel. (42) 341-2711; fax (42) 346-1944; internet www.ncnp.go.jp/nimh; f. 1952; part of Ministry of Health, Labour and Welfare; Dir A. FUJINAWA; publ. *Journal of Mental Health* (1 a year).

Neuropsychiatric Research Institute: 91 Benten-cho, Shinjuku-ku, Tokyo; tel. (3) 3260-9171; fax (3) 3260-9191; internet www.seiwa-hp.com; f. 1951; research on sleep disorders, mood disorders; art therapy; Chief Dir T. HIROSE.

Nukada Institute for Medical and Biological Research: 5-18 Inage-cho, Chiba-city, Chiba; f. 1939; Dir Dr H. NUKADA; publ. *Report* (irregular).

Ogata Institute for Medical and Chemical Research: 2-10-14 Higashi-Kanda, Chiyoda-ku, Tokyo 101-0031; tel. (3) 3865-7500; fax (3) 3865-7510; f. 1962; library of 12,000 vols; Pres. MASAHIDE ABE; publ. *Igaku to Seibutsugaku* (Medicine and Biology, 12 a year).

Tokyo Metropolitan Institute of Medical Science: Honkomagome 3-18-22, Bunkyoku, Tokyo 113-8613; tel. (3) 3823-2105; fax (3) 3823-2965; e-mail ui@rinshoken.or.jp; internet www.rinshoken.or.jp; f. 1975; research in aetiology and pathogenesis of intractable diseases and application of molecular and cellular biology to the aetiology of these diseases; library of 30,000 vols; Dir KEIJI TANAKA; publ. *Rinshoken News* (in Japanese, 12 a year).

NATURAL SCIENCES

General

Kokuritsu Kyokuchi Kenkyujyo (National Institute of Polar Research): Midoricho 10-3, Tokyo 190-8518; tel. (42) 512-0648; fax (42) 528-3146; e-mail shomu@nipr.ac.jp; internet www.nipr.ac.jp; f. 1973; attached to Joho Shisutemu Kenkyu Kiko (Research Organization of Information Systems); replaces the former Polar Research Centre of the National Science Museum; government-sponsored; implements programmes of the Japanese Antarctic Research Expeditions (JARE), organizes postgraduate courses in polar subjects, offers research facilities to national and foreign universities and individual researchers; library of 51,000 vols and bound periodicals51 full-time staff; Dir-Gen. Prof. YOSHIYUKI FUJII; Librarian YORIKO HAYAKAWA; publs *Antarctic Geological Map Series, Antarctic Record, Arctic Data Reports, JARE Data Reports* (8 a year), *Journal* (irregular), *Memoirs of the National Institute of Polar Research* (Special Issue), *Polar Science.*

Biological Sciences

Kihara Institute for Biological Research: Yokohama City University, Maioka-cho 641, Totsuka-ku, Yokohama 244; tel. (45) 820-1900; fax (45) 820-1901; f. 1942; library of 20,000 vols; Dir KAORU MIYAZAKI; publs *Seiken Ziho* (1 a year), *Wheat Information Service* (2 a year).

Osaka Bioscience Institute: 6-2-4 Furuedai, Suita-shi, Osaka 565-0874; tel. (6) 6872-4812; fax (6) 6872-4818; e-mail office@obi.or .jp; internet www.obi.or.jp; f. 1987; library of 15,000 vols; Dir Dr SHIGETADA NAKANISHI; Librarian ATSUKO TAKIKAWA.

Tokyo Biochemical Research Institute: Kyobashi NS Bldg, 2-5-21 Kyobashi, Chuo-ku, Tokyo 104-0031; tel. (3) 3562-5705; fax (3) 3562-5730; e-mail asia@tokyobrf.or.jp; internet www.tokyobrf.or.jp; f. 1950; Dir M. OKADA.

Mathematical Sciences

Institute of Statistical Mathematics: 4-6-7 Minami Azabu, Minato-ku, Tokyo 106-8569; tel. (3) 5421-8719; fax (3) 5421-8719; internet www.ism.ac.jp; f. 1944; Nat. Inter-Univ. Research Institute; research in statistics; library of 52,000 vols, 2,250 periodicals; Dir Prof. GENSHIRO KITAGAWA; publs *Annals* (4 a year), *Proceedings* (2 a year).

Physical Sciences

Fukada Geological Institute: 2-13-12 Hon-Komagome, Bunkyo-ku, Tokyo 113-0021; tel. (3) 3944-8010; fax (3) 3944-5404; e-mail fgi@fgi.or.jp; internet www.fgi.or.jp; f. 1954; Chair TADASHI SATO; publs *Fukadaken Library* (10 a year), *Nenpo* (in Japanese or English, both with English abstract, 1 a year).

Institute of Physical and Chemical Research (RIKEN): 2–1 Hirosawa, Wakoshi, Saitama 351-0198; tel. (48) 462-1111; fax (48) 462-1554; e-mail koho@riken.jp; internet www.riken.go.jp; f. 1917; studies related to science and technology; 621 mems; library of 100,000 vols; Pres. RYOJI NOYORI; publs *RIKEN Accelerated Progress Report* (1 a year), *RIKEN Review* (6 a year).

Japan Atomic Energy Agency (JAEA): 4–49 Muramatsu, Tokai-mura, Naka-gun, Ibaraki 319-1184; tel. (29) 282-1122; internet www.jaea.go.jp; f. 2005 by merger of Japan Atomic Energy Research Institute (JAERI) and Japan Nuclear Cycle Development Institute (JNC); library of 36,000 vols; Pres. TOSHIO OKAZAKI; Exec. Dir ICHIRO NAKAJIMA.

Kobayasi Institute of Physical Research: 3-20-41 Higashi-Motomachi, Kokubunji, Tokyo 185-0022; tel. (42) 321-2841; fax (42) 322-4698; e-mail info@ kobayasi-riken.or.jp; internet www .kobayasi-riken.or.jp; f. 1940; acoustics (noise and vibration, acoustic material, piezoelectric material); Pres. M. YAMASHITA; Dir K. YAMAMOTO.

Meteorological Research Institute: 1–1 Nagamine, Tsukuba, Ibaraki 3050052; tel. (29) 853-8546; fax (29) 853-8545; www.mri-jma.go.jp; f. 1942; 174 mems; meteorology, geophysics, seismology, oceanography, geochemistry; Dir-Gen. H. ITOH; publ. *Papers in Meteorology and Geophysics* (4 a year).

National Astronomical Observatory, Mizusawa VERA Observatory: 2-12 Hoshigaoka-cho, Oshu-shi Mizusawa, Iwate-ken 023-0861; tel. (197) 22-7111; fax (197) 22-7120; internet www.miz.nao.ac.jp; f. 1899; astronomy, geophysics, geodesy; part of Institute of Natural Sciences; library of 68,400 vols; Prof. H. KOBAYASHI; publ. *National Astronomical Observatory Technical Reports of the Mizusawa Kansoku Centre.*

National Institute for Materials Science: 1-2-1 Sengen, Tsukuba, Ibaraki 305-0047; tel. (29) 859-2000; e-mail info@nims.go.jp; internet www.nims.go.jp; f. 2001; management of basic research and devt of materials science and advancement of expertise in field; 1,450 mems; Pres. Prof. SUKEKATSU USHIODA.

Space Activities Commission: 2-2-1 Kasumigaseki, Chiyoda-ku, Tokyo 100-8966; tel. (3) 3581-5271; fax (3) 3503-2570; f. 1968; contributes to a comprehensive and streamlined execution of government programmes on space development, incl. organization of administrative agencies, planning of general policies and outlining training programmes for researchers and technicians; Chair. SADAKAZU TANIGAKI.

RELIGION, SOCIOLOGY AND ANTHROPOLOGY

Okura Institute for the Study of Spiritual Culture: 706 Futoo-cho, Kohoku-ku, Yokohama; tel. (45) 542-0050; fax (45) 542-0051; f. 1929; Dir N. SASAI; publ. *Okuravama Ronshu.*

TECHNOLOGY

Building Research Institute: 1 Tachihara, Tsukuba-shi, Ibaraki Pref.; tel. (29) 864-2151; fax (29) 864-2989; e-mail bri@kenken .go.jp; internet www.kenken.go.jp; f. 1946; 101 mems; building design and use, building economics, building materials, construction techniques, earthquake engineering, environmental engineering, fire safety, structural engineering, town planning; library of 50,000 vols; Dir-Gen. H. YAMANOUCHI; publ. *BRI Research Papers.*

Civil Engineering Research Institute of Hokkaido/Hokkaido Development Agency: Hiragishi 1-3, Toyohira-ku, Sapporo 062-8602; internet www.ceri.go.jp; f. 1937; library of 36,000 vols; Pres. TOMONORI SAITO; publ. *Report* (4 a year).

Communications Research Laboratory: 4-2-1 Nukui-Kitamachi, Koganei, Tokyo 184-8795; tel. (42) 327-5392; fax (42) 327-7587; e-mail publicity@crl.go.jp; internet www.crl .go.jp; f. 1952; next-generation information-communication networks, radio, space and optical communication, space weather forecasting, and related fields; library of 160,000 vols; Dir T. IIDA; publs *CRL Annual Bulletin* (in Japanese), *CRL News* (in Japanese, 12 a year), *Ionospheric Data in Japan* (12 a year), *Journal* (4 a year), *Review* (in Japanese, 4 a year).

Engineering Research Institute: Faculty of Engineering, University of Tokyo, 11-16, Yayoi 2-chome, Bunkyo-ku, Tokyo; f. 1939; 67 staff; library of 6,747 vols; Dir YOICHI GOSHI.

Institute for Fermentation, Osaka: 17-85, Juso-honmachi 2-chome, Yodogawaku, Osaka 532; tel. (6) 6300-6555; fax (6) 6300-6814; e-mail desk@ifo.or.jp; internet www.ifo .or.jp; f. 1944; preservation and distribution of micro-organisms and animal cells; 23 staff; library of 800 vols; Dir Dr TORU HASEGAWA; publs *List of Cultures*, *IFO Research Communications* (every 2 years).

Institute for Future Technology: Tomiokabashi Bldg, 2-6-11 Fukagawa, Koto-ku, Tokyo; tel. (3) 5245-1011; fax (3) 5245-1061; internet www.iftech.or.jp; f. 1971; research in the fields of technology forecasting, technology assessment and other socio-economic research in future technologies (electronics, telecommunications, space and energy); library of 15,000 vols; Pres. HIROEI FUJIOKA; Chief Sec. TAKAMITSU KOSHIKAWA; publ. *Kenkyu Seika Gaiyo* (research results, in Japanese, 1 a year).

Institute of Energy Economics, Japan: Inui Bldg, 13–1 Kachidoki 1-chome, Chuo-ku, Tokyo 104-0054; tel. (3) 5547-0211; fax (3) 5547-0223; e-mail otoiawase@tky.ieej.or.jp; internet eneken.ieej.or.jp; f. 1966; coordinates information related to energy, its use, supply, conservation and economic aspects; provides material as basis for planning and policy formation by govt and private business; int. cooperation on energy projects; 200 mems incl. energy-related industries and research instns; library of 56,450 vols; Chair. and CEO MASAKAZU TOYODA; Man. Dirs MASAKI CHIBA, KOKICHI ITO, KENSUKE KANEKIYO KENJI KOBAYASHI HIDEKI OKAMOTO, TSUTOMU TOICHI, Dr KEN KOYAMA, Dr KOICHIRO TANAKA AKIHIRO KUROKI; publs *IEEJ Energy Journal* (in English, 4 a year), *EDMC Handbook of Energy & Economic Statistics in Japan* (in English, 1 a year), *EDMC Energy Trend* (in Japanese, 12 a year).

Institute of Research and Innovation, Japan: 1-6-8 Yushima, Bunkyo-ku, Tokyo 113; tel. (3) 5689-6356; fax (3) 5689-6350; f. 1959; fmrly Industrial Research Institute, Japan; independent; research and development in technology and socio-technology, including alternative energy sources, nuclear technologies and related innovative problems; 70 research staff; library of 2,000 vols; Pres. SHO NASU; Dir JIRO MIYAMOTO; publ. *Bulletin* (in Japanese, 4 a year).

International Association of Traffic and Safety Sciences: 6-20, 2-chome, Yaesu, Chuo-ku, Tokyo 104-0028; f. 1974; aims to contribute to the realization of a better traffic soc. through the practical application of research conducted in a variety of fields; research surveys on traffic and its safety; colln and retrieval of information on traffic-related sciences; sponsorship of domestic and int. symposia and study meetings; provision of awards; IATSS Forum, human resource devt programme for south-east Asian countries; Exec. Dir HIROSHI ISHIZUKI; publs *IATSS Research* (in English, 2 a year), *IATSS Review* (in Japanese with English abstracts, 4 a year), *Statistics: Road Accidents in Japan* (in English, 1 a year), *White Paper on Traffic Safety* (in English, 1 a year).

Japan Aerospace Exploration Agency (JAXA): 1-6-4 Marunouchi, Chiyoda-ku, Tokyo 100-0005; tel. (3) 6266-6400; fax (3) 6266-6910; internet www.jaxa.jp; f. 2003 by merger of Institute of Space and Astronautical Science (ISAS), National Aerospace Laboratory of Japan (NAL) and National Space Development Agency of Japan (NASDA); Pres. KEIJI TACHIKAWA.

Japan Construction Method and Machinery Research Institute: 3154 Obuchi, Fuji-shi, Shizuoka-ken; tel. (545) 35-0212; fax (545) 35-3719; e-mail nakashima@ cmi.or.jp; f. 1964; construction machine testing and associated research; Dir HIDESUKE NAKASHIMA.

Kokudo Gijyutsu Seisaku Sougou Kenkyujo (National Institute for Land and Infrastructure Management, Ministry of Land, Infrastructure and Transport): 1 Asahi, Tsukuba-shi, Ibaraki-ken 305-0804; tel. (29) 864-4593; fax (29) 864-4322; e-mail kokusai@nilim.go.jp; internet www.nilim.go .jp; f. 2001; 43 research divisions; 386 staff; research on advanced information technology, airports, building, coastal and marine environments, disaster risk management, environment, harbours, housing, land and construction management, ports, rivers, roads, water quality control, and urban planning; library of 193,000 vols; Dir TSUNEYOSHI MOCHIZUKI; publ. *NILIM News Letter* (in English).

National Institute of Advanced Industrial Science and Technology: Tokyo Headquarters, 1-3-1, Kasumigaseki Chiyoda-ku, Tokyo 100-8921; tel. (3) 5501-0900; e-mail presec@m.aist.go.jp; internet www.aist.go.jp; f. 2001; government-sponsored research institute; Dir Dr HIROYUKI YOSHIKAWA.

National Marine Research Institute: 6-38-1, Shinkawa, Mitaka, Tokyo 181-0004; tel. (422) 41-3015; fax (422) 41-3247; e-mail info2@nmri.go.jp; internet www.nmri.go.jp; f. 1916; 2001 present name; attached to Ministry of Transport; shipbuilding and marine engineering; library of 68,000 vols; Pres. SHIRO INOUE; publ. *Papers* (6 a year).

National Research Institute for Earth Science and Disaster Prevention (NIED): 3-1 Tennodai, Tsukuba-shi, Ibaraki-ken 305-0006; tel. (29) 851-1611; fax (29) 851-1622; e-mail toiawase@bosai.go.jp; internet www.bosai.go.jp; f. 1963; library of 71,232 vols; Dir YOSHIMITSU OKADA; publs *Report of the NIED* (2 a year), *Technical Note of the NIED, Disaster Research Report of the NIED, Strong-motion Earthquake Records in Japan* (1 a year), *Prompt Report of Strong-motion Earthquake Records* (irregular).

Branches:

Nagaoka Institute of Snow and Ice Studies: 187-16, Maeyama, Suyoshi Omachi, Nagaoka-shi, Niigata-ken 940; study of techniques for the prevention of snow damage.

Shinjyo NIED Branch of Snow and Ice Studies: 1400, Takadan, Toka-machi, Shinjo-shi, Yamagata-ken 996; study of the prevention of disasters caused by snow and ice.

National Research Institute of Brewing: 2-6-30 Takinogawa, Kita-ku, Tokyo 114-0023; tel. (3) 3910-6237; fax (3) 3910-6236; e-mail info@nrib.go.jp; internet www.nrib.go.jp; f. 1904; Pres. JYUNICHI HIRAMATSU; Exec. Dir YASUZOU KIZAKI.

Noguchi Institute: 1-8-1 Kaga, Itabashi-ku, Tokyo 173-0003; tel. (3) 3961-3255; fax (3) 3964-4071; internet www.noguchi.or.jp; f. 1941; research into carbohydrate chemistry, solid-state catalysts for ecoprocess; Pres. KAGEYASU AKASHI.

Port and Airport Research Institute: 3-1-1 Nagase, Yokosuka, Kanagawa 239-0826; fax (468) 44-5010; fax (468) 44-1274; internet www.pari.go.jp; f. 1962 as Port and Harbour Research Institute; later reorganized into 2 institutes: National Institute for Land and Infrastructure Management and Port and Airport Research Institute; attached to Ministry of Transport; research on all aspects of port, harbour and airport construction technology; library of 20,000 vols; Exec. Researcher Dr SHIGEO TAKAHASHI; publs *Report* (4 a year), *Technical Notes* (4 a year).

Railway Technical Research Institute: 2-8-38 Hikari-cho, Kokubunji-shi, Tokyo 185-8540; tel. (425) 73-7258; fax (425) 73-7356; internet www.rtri.or.jp; f. 1907; research in railway engineering and magnetic levitated vehicles; 530 mems; library of 350,000 vols; Chair. YOSHIJI MATSUMOTO; Pres. HIROUMI SOEJIMA; publs *Quarterly Report of RTRI, Railway Research Review* (in Japanese, 12 a year), *Souken Hokoku* (RTRI Report, in Japanese, 12 a year).

Research Institute for Production Development: 15 Shimo Kamomori Honmachi, Sakyo-ku, Kyoto 606-0805; tel. (75) 781-1107; fax (75) 791-7659; f. 1947; Pres. TAKAO YAMAMURO.

Research Institute of Printing Bureau: 6-4-20 Sakawa, Odawara, Kanagawa; tel. (465) 49-4246; f. 1891; Dir H. NONAKA; publ. *Research Bulletin* (2 a year).

Shobo-kenkyujo (National Research Institute of Fire and Disaster): 35-3, Jindaiji-Higashicho 4-chome, Chofu, Tokyo 182-8508; tel. (422) 44-8331; fax (422) 42-7719; e-mail toiawase2008@fri.go.jp; internet www.fri.go.jp; f. 1948; library of 17,500 vols; Dir AKIRA TERAMURA; publs *Shobo-kenkyujo Hokoku, Shoken Syuho* (1 a year).

Tensor Society: c/o Kawaguchi Institute of Mathematical Sciences, Matsu-ga-oka 2-7-15, Chigasaki 253; fax (467) 86-4713; e-mail tensorsociety@ybb.ne.jp; f. 1937; undertakes original research in the field of tensor analysis and its applications; library of 23,000 vols; Pres. Prof. Dr T. KAWAGUCHI; Sec. Prof. Dr H. KAWAGUCHI; publ. *Tensor* (3 a year).

Libraries and Archives

Akita

Akita Prefectural Library: 14-31 Sannou-sinmati, Akita-shi, Akita 010-0952; tel. (18) 866-8400; fax (18) 866-6200; e-mail apl@apl.pref.akita.jp; internet www.apl.pref.akita.jp; f. 1899; 403,162 vols; Librarian N. FUJITA.

Chiba

Chiba Prefectural Central Library: 11-1 Ichibacho Chuo-ku, Chiba City 260-8660; tel. (43) 222-0116; internet www.library.pref.chiba.lg.jp; 268,488 vols; Librarian S. TATEISHI.

Hakodate

Hakodate City Library: 17-2 Aoyagi-cho, Hakodate City; tel. (138) 22-7447; fax (138) 22-0837; 122,500 vols (including branch library); Librarian I. FUKUDA.

Hiroshima

Hiroshima Prefectural Library: 3-7-47 Senda-machi, Naka-ku, Hiroshima City; tel. (82) 241-4995; fax (82) 241-9799; f. 1951; public library; 399,957 vols; Librarian K. HATAKEYAMA.

Ise

Jingu Bunko: 1711 Kodakushimoto-cho, Ise, Mie Prefecture 516-0016; tel. (596) 222737; fax (596) 225066; internet www.isejingu.or.jp/bunka/bunbody4.htm; 260,000 vols on Shinto; Librarian KUNIO KOBORI.

Kagoshima

Kagoshima Prefectural Library: 1-1 Shiroyama-machi, Kagoshima City; 222,357 vols; Librarian H. KUBOTA.

Kanazawa

Kanazawa City Libraries: 2-20 Tamagawa-cho, Kanazawa City 920; internet www.lib.kanazawa.ishikawa.jp; 510,000 vols; Librarian N. YOSHIMOTO.

Kanazawa Municipal Izumino Library: 22-22, 4-chome Izumino-machi, Kanazawa City 921-8034; tel. (76) 280-2345; fax (76) 280-2342; e-mail m-m@lib.kanazawa.ishikawa.jp; internet www.lib.kanazawa.ishikawa.jp; f. 1995; 360,000 vols; Dir S. KIDO.

Kobe

Kobe City Library: 7-2 Kununoki-cho, Ikuta, Kobe; f. 1911; 240,000 vols; Librarian S. AKAI.

Kobe University Library: Rokkodai-cho, Nada-ku, Kobe; tel. (78) 803-7315; fax (78) 803-7320; e-mail kikaku@lib.kobe-u.ac.jp; internet www.lib.kobe-u.ac.jp; f. 1908; 2,958,000 vols; Dir TAKESHI SASAKI.

Kochi

Kochi Prefectural Library: 3 Marunouchi, Kochi City; 141,927 vols; Librarian N. SHIMESHINO.

Kyoto

Institute for Research in Humanities Library: Yoshida-Honmachi, Sakyo-ku, Kyoto 606-8501; attached to Kyoto University; 564,000 vols; institute divided into 2 sections: humanities and oriental studies; Dir Prof. NAOKI MIZUNO.

Kyoto Prefectural Library and Archives: 1-4 Hangi-cho, Shimogamo, Sakyo-ku, Kyoto-shi, Kyoto 606-0823; tel. (75) 723-4831; fax (75) 791-9466; internet www.pref.kyoto.jp/shiryokan; f. 1898; 350,000 vols; Dir MINORU SHIBATA.

Kyoto University Library: Yoshida Honmachi, Sakyo-ku, Kyoto 606-8501; tel. (75) 753-2613; fax (75) 753-2629; e-mail kikaku@kulib.kyoto-u.ac.jp; internet www.kulib.kyoto-u.ac.jp; f. 1899; 6,358,815 vols; central library and 54 libraries of 15 graduate schools and 13 research institutes; Dir Dr JOJI FUJII; publ. *Seishu* (Library Bulletin, 4 a year).

Ryukoku University Library: 67 Tsukamoto-cho, Fukakusa, Fushimi-ku, Kyoto 612; tel. (75) 645-7885; fax (75) 641-7955; e-mail f-lib@ad.ryukoku.ac.jp; internet opac.lib.ryukoku.ac.jp; f. 1639; 1,800,000 vols; 3 brs: Fukakusa, Omiya and Seta libraries; Librarian JITSUZO SHIGETA.

Matsuyama

Matsuyama University Library: 4-2 Bunkyo-cho, Matsuyama 790; tel. (89) 925-7111; fax (86) 926-9116; e-mail mu-libs@matsuyama-u.jp; internet www.matsuyama.ac.jp; f. 1923; 540,000 vols; collection of rare books, including first editions of 18th- and 19th-century works on political economy; Librarian Prof. K. SHISHIDO.

Nagoya

Nagoya City Tsuruma Central Library: 43 Tsurumai-cho, Tsurumai 1-1-155, Showa-ku, Nagoya City; tel. (52) 741-3131; fax (52) 732-9872; internet www.tsuruma-lib.showa.nagoya.jp; f. 1923; 1,040,400 vols; Librarian Y. WADA.

Nagoya University Library: Furo-cho, Chikusa-ku, Nagoya 464-8601; tel. (52) 789-3678; fax (52) 789-3694; e-mail wwwadmin@nul.nagoya-u.ac.jp; internet www.nul.nagoya-u.ac.jp; f. 1939; central library and 23 libraries of 13 graduate schools and 3 institutes; 3,112,036 vols; Dir Prof. Y. MATSUURA; Exec. Dir SHINYA KATO; publ. *Kanto* (4 a year).

Naha

Ryukyu Islands Central Library: Central Library Building, Naha, Okinawa; f. 1950; 45,926 vols; central deposit library.

Nara

Nara Prefectural Library: 48 Nobori Oojicho, Nara City 630-8135; tel. (742) 34-2111; fax (742) 34-5514; e-mail info@library.pref.nara.jp; internet www.library.pref.nara.jp; f. 1909; 296,000 vols; Librarian KATSUKO TOYODA; publ. *Untei.*

Niigata

Niigata Prefectural Library: 3-1-2 Meike Minami, Niigata City; tel. (25) 284-6001; fax (25) 284-6832; f. 1915; 610,000 vols; Librarian K. SHIBUYA.

Niigata University Library: 8050 Ikarashi 2-nocho, Nishi-ku, Niigata City 950-2181; f. 1949; 1,672,410 vols; Dir T. YATA.

Nishinomiya

Kwansei Gakuin University Library: 1-1-155 Uegahara, Nishinomiya, Hyogo 662-8501; tel. (798) 54-6121; fax (798) 54-6448; internet library.kwansei.ac.jp; f. 1889; 1,200,000 vols, nearly 40% in foreign languages; br. libraries for 8 schools, 11 graduate schools, 2 satellite campuses; Dean of

University Library Services TAKUTOSHI INOUE; publ. *Tokeidai* (Bulletin).

Okayama

Okayama University Library: 1-1 Naka 3-chome, Tsushima, Okayama City 700-8530; tel. (86) 252-1111; fax (86) 251-7314; internet www.lib.okayama-u.ac.jp; f. 1949; 2 br. libraries; 1,870,000 vols; Dir H. INOUE; publ. *Kai* (Library News, 2 a year).

Osaka

Kansai University Library: 3-3-35 Yamate-cho, Suita-shi, Osaka; tel. (6) 368-1121; fax (6) 330-1464; internet www .kansai-u.ac.jp/english/library; f. 1914; 2,028,000 vols; Librarian K. URANISHI.

Osaka Prefectural Nakanoshima Library: 1-2-10 Nakanoshima, Kita-ku, Osaka 530-0005; tel. (6) 6203-0474; fax (6) 6203-4914; internet www.library.pref.osaka .jp; f. 1903; 545,000 vols; Head Librarian HIROKAZU OMOKI; publ. *Osaka Furitsu Tosyokan Kiyou* (1 a year).

Sapporo

Hokkaido University Library: Kita 8 Nishi 5, Kita-ku, Sapporo 060-0808; tel. (11) 716-2111; fax (11) 747-2855; internet www .lib.hokudai.ac.jp/index_e.html; f. 1876; 20 br. libraries; 3,688,129 vols (incl. 1,798,649 foreign language texts); spec. collns on Slavic studies and N Eurasian culture studies; Librarian Dr MASAAKI HEMMI; publ. *Yuin* (4 a year).

Sendai

Tohoku University Library: Kawauchi, Aoba-ku, Sendai 980-77; internet www .library.tohoku.ac.jp; f. 1911; 2,247,000 vols, incl. Kano Colln (108,000 vols) in Japanese and Chinese, the Tibetan Buddhist Canons (6,652 vols), Wundt Colln (15,800 vols) and several other special collns; Dir Prof. KEICHI NOE.

Shizuoka

Shizuoka Prefectural Central Library: 53–1 Yada, Shizuoka City; tel. (54) 262-1242; fax (54) 264-4268; e-mail mailmaster@ tosyokan.pref.shizuoka.jp; internet www .tosyokan.pref.shizuoka.jp; f. 1925; 430,000 vols, 7,500 periodicals, 4,000 films and videotapes; Librarian YOSHIHIKO SUZUKI; publs *Aoi* (1 a year), *Toshokan-Dayori* (6 a year).

Tenri

Tenri Central Library: 1050 Somanouchi, Tenri, Nara 632-8577; tel. (743) 63-9200; fax (743) 63-7728; e-mail info@tcl.gr.jp; internet www.tcl.gr.jp; f. 1930; 2m. vols (incl. 480,000 in foreign languages); spec. libraries: Yorozuyo Library on Christian Missions (incl. Jesuit mission printings in Japan), Kogido Library of Africana Colln (6,000 items), Ito Jinsai on Confucian Studies, Wataya Library on Renga and Haikai Collns (20,000 items); Dir Prof. KEIICHIRO MOROI; publ. *Biblia* (in Japanese, 2 a year).

Tokyo

Chuo University Library: 742-1 Higashi-nakano, Hachioji-shi, Tokyo 192-0393; tel. (4) 2674-2511; fax (4) 2674-2514; f. 1885; 2m. vols (577,826 in foreign languages), 14,561 periodicals; Librarian Prof. NOBUO YASUI.

Hitotsubashi University Library: Naka 2-1, Kunitachi-city, Tokyo 186-8601; tel. (42) 580-8237; fax (42) 580-8251; internet www .lib.hit-u.ac.jp; f. 1887; 1,815,793 vols, 16,225 periodicals; Librarian MASAO WATANABE; houses br. library for Institute of Economic Research; f. 1940; 242,500 vols; Dir Y. KIKOKAWA.

Imperial Household Agency Library: 1–1 Chiyoda, Chiyoda-ku, Tokyo; tel. (3) 3213-1111; fax (3) 3214-2792; e-mail information@ kunaicho.go.jp; f. 1948; 87,946 vols; Librarian Mr MOMOTA.

International Christian University Library: 10-2 Osawa 3-chome, Mitaka-shi, Tokyo 181-8585; tel. (422) 33-3301; fax (422) 33-3305; e-mail library@icu.ac.jp; internet www-lib.icu.ac.jp; f. 1953; 685,655 vols (incl. 326,327 foreign), 2,105 periodicals; Dir TAMAMI HATAKEYAMA (acting); Man. FUJIKI YUKO.

Japan Meteorological Agency Library: 1-3-4 Ote-machi, Chiyoda-ku, Tokyo 100-8122; e-mail jma-library@met.kishou.go.jp; f. 1875; 110,000 vols; Chief Librarian EIJU TAKAHASI.

Keio University Media Center: 2-15-45 Mita, Minato-ku, Tokyo 108; Chair. S. SUGIYAMA.

Kokugakuin University Library: 4-10-28 Higashi, Shibuya-ku, Tokyo; f. 1882; 1,087,663 vols; Librarian Prof. TOSHIO SAWA-NOBORI; publ. *Kokugakuin Daigaku Toshokan Kiyo* (Library Journal).

Kokuritsu Kobunshokan (National Archives): 3-2 Kitanomaru Park, Chiyoda-ku, Tokyo 102-0091; tel. (3) 3214-0621; fax (3) 3212-8806; internet www.archives.go.jp; f. 1971; attached to Cabinet office; archives, Cabinet Library of 480,000 vols, and government records of 725,000 vols; Pres. MASAYA TAKAYAMA; publs *Kitanomaru* (1 a year), *Archives* (3 a year).

Kokuritsu Kyoiku Seisaku Kenkyujo, Kyoiku Kenkyu Joho Senta, Kyoiku Toshokan (Library of Education, Educational Resources Research Centre, National Institute for Educational Research of Japan): 3-2-2 Kasumigaseki, Chiyoda-ku, Tokyo 100-8951; tel. (3) 6733-6536; fax (3) 6733-6957; e-mail library@nier.go.jp; internet www.nier .go.jp/library; f. 1949; 500,000 vols; Chief librarian HISAO SUNAOSHI; publ. *Kyoiku Kenkyu Ronbun Sakuin* (Education Index, online, 4 a year).

Ministry of Foreign Affairs Library: 2-2 Kasumigaseki, Chiyoda-ku, Tokyo 100; 90,638 vols and 175 periodicals; Librarian YOSHIMASA KIMURA.

Ministry of Justice Library: 1-1, 1-chome, Kasumigaseki, Chiyoda-ku, Tokyo 100-8977; f. 1928; 300,000 vols; Chief Librarian T. OYAMA.

National Diet Library: 1-10-1 Nagatacho, Chiyoda-ku, Tokyo 100-8924; tel. (3) 3506-5147; fax (3) 3508-2934; e-mail kokusai@ndl .go.jp; internet www.ndl.go.jp; f. 1948; deposit library for Japanese publs and publs of the UN, UNESCO, ILO, WHO, ICAO, WTO, etc.; IFLA PAC centre for Asia, ISSN centre for Japan; is divided into 1 bureau and 6 depts: Acquisitions, Admin., Books, Research and Legislative Reference, Serials, Special Materials and Library Co-operation; consists of the Main Library, Detached Library in the Diet, Int. Library of Children's Literature, Toyo Bunko (Oriental) Library and 27 br. libraries in the Exec. and Judicial agencies of the Govt; 33,639,985 items, 8,833,407 books; 502,838 maps; 598,900 audio materials and CDs; 12,957,816 items of microform materials; 63,921 optical discs; 472,447 Japanese doctoral dissertations; 276,509 manuscripts; other catalogued items; subscriptions: 11,848,762 serials (periodicals and newspapers); Librarian MAKOTO NAGAO; publs *National Diet Library Newsletter* (online, in English, 6 a year), *CDNLAO Newsletter* (online, in English, 3 a year), *Books on Japan* (online, in English, 4 a year), *National Bibliography Weekly List* (online, in Japanese), *Current Awareness* (online and print, most issues Japanese, a few English), *Japanese National Library monthly bulletin* (online, in Japanese).

National Institute of Japanese Literature Library: Midorityou 10-3, Tachikawa Tokyo 190-0014; tel. (50) 553-32926; fax (42) 526-8607; e-mail service@nijl.ac.jp; internet www.nijl.ac.jp; f. 1972; 188,397 vols; microforms of woodcuts, old printed books and MSS; 46,434 reels of microfilm, 57,358 sheets of microfiche, 74,362 vols of paper copy, 6,773 titles of serials; archives for Japanese historical documents: 500,000 items; Dir N. YAMA-SHITA.

Norin Suisansho Toshokan: (Ministry of Agriculture, Forestry and Fisheries Library): 1-2-1, Kasumigaseki, Chiyoda-ku, Tokyo 100-8950; tel. (3) 3910-3978; fax (3) 3940-0232; e-mail ref-primaff@ml.affrc.go.jp; f. 1948; 275,000 vols; Librarian TATEKI ARAI; publs *Norin Suisan Tosho Shiryo Geppo* (12 a year, review of publs on agriculture, forestry and fisheries), *Norin Suisan Bunken Kaidai* (1 a year, annotated bibliography).

Ochanomizu University Library: 1-1 Otsuka 2-chome, Bunkyo-ku, Tokyo 112-8610; tel. (3) 5978-5839; fax (3) 5978-5933; e-mail lib-ref@cc.ocha.ac.jp; internet www.lib .ocha.ac.jp; f. 1874, reorganized 1949; 563,000 (including 179,000 foreign) vols; Dir YUJIRO OGUCHI.

Science Council of Japan Library: 22-34, Roppongi 7-chome, Minato-ku, Tokyo 106; tel. (3) 3403-6291; internet www.scj.go.jp; f. 1949; 54,000 vols; Librarian MASATO OKA-MOTO.

Seikado Bunko Library and Art Museum: 2-23-1 Okamoto, Setagaya-ku, Tokyo; tel. (3) 3700-0007; internet www .seikado.or.jp; 200,000 vols of Chinese and Japanese classics; Librarian MAKO NARI-SAWA.

Sophia (Jôchi) University Library: 7-1 Kioi-cho, Chiyoda-ku, Tokyo 102-8554; tel. (3) 3238-3511; fax (3) 3238-3268; f. 1913; 920,000 vols, 10,500 periodicals; Librarian MIKITO HAYASHI.

Statistical Library, Statistics Bureau, Management and Coordination Agency: 19-1, Wakamatsu-cho, Shimjuku-ku, Tokyo 162; tel. (3) 3202-1111; internet www.stat.go .jp; f. 1946; 400,000 vols; Librarian KENJI OKADA; publs numerous reports, statistical handbooks.

Supreme Court Library: 4-2 Hayabusa-cho, Chiyoda-ku, Tokyo 102-8651; f. 1949; 260,000 vols; Librarian M. UEMURA.

Tokyo Geijutsu Daigaku Toshokan (Tokyo University of the Arts Library): Ueno Park 12–8, Taito-ku, Tokyo 110-8714; tel. (50) 5525-2420; fax (50) 5525-2531; internet www.lib.geidai.ac.jp; f. 1887; over 365,377 vols, 2,212 microfilms, 4,359 microfiches; also music and audiovisual collns (97,722 scores, 19,831 records, 6,290 CDs, 3,396 video recordings); Dir E. TAGUCHI.

Tokyo Metropolitan Central Library: 5-7-13 Minami-Azabu, Minato-ku, Tokyo 106-8575; tel. (3) 3442-8451; fax (3) 3447-8924; internet www.library.metro.tokyo.jp; f. 1972; research and reference centre, centre of library co-operation in Tokyo; 1,471,000 vols and 10,000 periodicals; Morohashi Colln (Chinese classics), Sanetoh Colln (Chinese literature), Yedo Colln, Kaga Colln (rare books of the Yedo Era) and others; Dir TETSUYA SAITO; publs *Hibiya*, *Library Science Bulletin* (1 a year).

Tokyo University of Foreign Studies Library: 3-11-1 Asahicho, Fuchu-shi, Tokyo 183-8534; tel. (42) 330-5193; fax (42) 330-5199; e-mail www-lib@tufs.ac.jp; internet

www.tufs.ac.jp/common/library/index-e
.html; f. 1899; 785,006 vols (incl. 420,413
foreign); Dir H. KURITA; publ. *Castalia: Tokyo
University of Foreign Studies Library Bulletin*.

**Tokyo University of Marine Science and
Technology Library:** Konan 4-5-7, Minato-
ku, Tokyo 108-8477; tel. (3) 5463-0444; fax (3)
5463-0445; e-mail to-joho@s.kaiyodai.ac.jp;
internet lib.s.kaiyodai.ac.jp; f. 1888; 296,000
vols (including 74,000 foreign); Chief Librarian HIROSHI OKADA; publ. *Journal* (1 a year).

Toyo Bunko (Oriental Library): Honkomagome 2-28-21, Bunkyo-ku, Tokyo 113-0021;
tel. (3) 3942-0121; fax (3) 3942-0258; e-mail
webmaster@toyo-bunko.or.jp; internet www
.toyo-bunko.or.jp; f. 1924; 898,542 vols;
research library specializing in Asian studies; special collections: Iwasaki collection of
old and rare Japanese and Chinese books
and manuscripts, Kawaguchi collection of
Tibetan and Buddhist classics, Morrison collection of Western books on Asia; Dir YOSHI-
NOBU SHIBA; publs *Toyo Gakuho* (4 a year),
*Memoirs of the Research Department of the
Toyo Bunko* (1 a year, jt publ. with National
Diet Library).

University of Tokyo Library System:
Hongo 7-3-1, Bunkyo-ku, Tokyo 113-0033;
tel. (3) 5841-2612; fax (3) 5841-2636; e-mail
kikaku@lib.u-tokyo.ac.jp; internet www.lib
.u-tokyo.ac.jp; f. 1877; 8,120,000 vols, incl.
Nanki colln (96,000 vols) and several other
spec. collns; general library, Komaba library,
Kashiwa library and 52 faculty and institute
libraries; Dir K. SAIGO; publ. *Bulletin*.

Waseda University Library: 1-6-1 Nishi-
waseda, Shinjuku-ku, Tokyo 169-8050; fax
(3) 5272-2061; e-mail info@wul.waseda.ac.jp;
internet www.wul.waseda.ac.jp; f. 1882;
5,404,970 vols; Dir SHOZO IIJIMA; publ. *Bulletin* (1 a year).

Toyonaka

Osaka University Library: 1–4, Machikaneyama-cho, Toyonaka, Osaka 560-0043; tel.
(6) 6850-5045; fax (6) 6850-5052; internet
www.library.osaka-u.ac.jp; f. 1931; 3,050,000
vols; main library and 2 branch libraries; Dir
MINORU KAWAKITA.

Utsunomiya

Tochigi Prefectural Library: 1-2-23
Hanawada, Utsunomiya, Tochigi 320-0027;
tel. (28) 622-5111; fax (28) 624-7855; e-mail
tochilib@lib.pref.tochigi.jp; internet www.lib
.pref.tochigi.jp; 196,579 vols; Librarian T.
IZUMI.

Yamaguchi

Yamaguchi Prefectural Library: 150–1
Matsue, Ushirogawa, Yamaguchi City 753-
0083; tel. (3) 924-2111; fax (3) 932-2817;
internet library.pref.yamaguchi.lg.jp; f.
1903; 389,104 vols; Librarian TANAKA HIR-
OSHI; publ. *Toshokan Yamaguchi*.

Yamaguchi University Library: 1667-1
Yoshida, Yamaguchi-shi, Yamaguchi 753-
8511; tel. (3) 933-5182; e-mail toshokan@
yamaguchi-u.ac.jp; f. 1949; 2 br. libraries;
1,552,323 vols, 29,501 periodicals.

Yokohama

Kanagawa Prefectural Library: 9-2
Momijigaoka, Nishi-ku, Yokohama City; f.
1954; 76 mems; 540,875 vols; Librarian M.
ANDO; publ. *Kanagawa Bunka* (6 a year).

Yokohama National University Library:
79-6 Tokiwadai, Hodogayaku, Yokohama
240-8501; tel. (45) 339-3217; fax (45) 339-
3229; e-mail libref@ynu.ac.jp; internet www
.lib.ynu.ac.jp; f. 1949; 1,401,234 vols; Dir
Prof. H. FUKUTOMI.

Museums and Art
Galleries

Abashiri

Abashiri Kyodo Hakubutsukan (Abashiri
Municipal Museum): Katsuramachi 1-1-3,
Abashiri-shi, Hokkaido 093-0041; tel. (152)
43-3090; fax (152) 61-3020; f. 1936; 600 local
products, 25,000 articles of historical, geographical and archaeological interest, and
1,800 ethnological objects; Dir HIDEAKI
WADA.

Atami

MOA Museum of Art: 26-2, Momoyama,
Atami 413-8511; tel. (557) 84-2511; fax (557)
84-2570; internet www.moaart.or.jp; f. 1957,
reorganized 1982 by Mokichi Okada Asscn;
Japanese and Oriental fine arts: paintings,
ceramics, lacquers, calligraphy and sculp-
tures; library of 25,000 vols; Dir YOJI
YOSHIOKA; publs *Digest Catalogue*, *MOA
Museum Members Club* (4 a year), *Selected
Catalogue* (5 vols).

Gora

Hakone Museum of Art: 1300 Gora, Kanagawa Pref.; tel. (460) 2-2623; fax (460) 2-
0124; internet www.moaart.or.jp/english/
hakone; f. 1952; private collection of Japanese ceramic works of art belonging to Okada
Mokichi; Dir YOJI YOSHIOKA (Director of MOA
Foundation).

Hakodate

Hakodate City Museum: 21-7 Suehiro-cho,
Hakodate City; tel. (138) 22-4128; f. 1879;
oldest local museum in Japan; Dir M.
ISHIKAWA.

Hiraizumi

Chuson-ji Sanko-zo (Chuson-ji Temple
Sanko Repository): Hiraizumi-machi, Nishi-
Iwai-gun; internet www.chusonji.or.jp; f.
1955 to preserve treasures and possessions
of the Fujiwara family who were important
in the late Heian period (801–1185).

Hiroshima

Hiroshima Children's Museum: 5-83,
Moto-machi, Naka-ku, Hiroshima City 730;
tel. (82) 222-5346; fax (82) 502-2118; e-mail
riyou-annai@pyonta.city.hiroshima.jp; internet www.pyonta.city.hiroshima.jp; f. 1980;
scientific and cultural programmes; planetarium; exhibits on science, transport, astronomy; Dir HIROSHI OKIMOTO; publs *Kagakukan
Dayori* (12 a year), *Planetarium* (4 a year).

Ikaruga

Hōryūji (Hōryūji Temple): Aza Hōryūji,
Ikaruga-cho, Ikoma-gun, Nara Prefecture; a
large number of Buddhist images and paint-
ings; the buildings date from the Asuka,
Nara, Heian, Kamakura, Ashikaga and
Tokugawa periods.

Ise

Jingu Chokokan (Jingu Historical
Museum): 1754-1 Koda-kushimoto, Ise-city,
Mie 516-0016; tel. (596) 22-1700; fax (596) 22-
5515; internet www.isejingu.or.jp/museum;
1,734 exhibits, incl. treasures of the Grand
Shrine of Ise (Naiku Shrine and Geku
Shrine) and many objects of historical inter-
est; library of 1,082 vols, MSS and pictures;
Dir and Chief of Cultural Section of the
Grand Shrine of Ise YASUJI AKIOKA.

Jingu Nogyokan (Agricultural Museum):
1754-1 Koda-kushimoto-cho, Ise, Mie 516-
0016; tel. (596) 22-1700; fax (596) 22-5515;
internet www.isejingu.or.jp/museum; f. 1905;
9,583 exhibits connected with agriculture,

forestry, and fishing (incl. colln of over 40
species of shark); Dir YASUJI AKIOKA.

Itsukushima

Itsukushima Jinja Homotsukan (Treasure Hall of the Itsukushima Shinto Shrine):
Miyajima-cho, Saeki-gun; f. 1934; 4,000
exhibits of paintings, calligraphy, sutras,
swords, and other ancient weapons; Curator
and Chief Priest MOTOYOSHI NOZAKA.

Kamakura

Kamakura Kokuhokan (Kamakura
Museum): 2-1-1 Yukinoshita, Kamakura
City, Kanawaga; tel. (467) 22-0753; fax
(467) 23-5953; internet www.city.kamakura
.kanagawa.jp/kokuhoukan/index.htm; f.
1928; Japanese art and history in the Middle
Ages; 3,521 valuable specimens of Japanese
fine arts; 12 mems; library of 6,587 vols; Dir
TATSUTO NUKI; publ. *Kokuhokan-zuroku*.

Museum of Modern Art, Kamakura: 2-1-
53 Yukinoshita, Kamakura, Kanagawa 248-
0005; tel. (467) 22-5000; fax (467) 23-2464;
e-mail kinbi.4313@pref.kanagawa.jp;
internet www.planet.pref.kanagawa.jp/city/
kinbi.htm; f. 1951; modern and contemporary
art in Japan and Europe; Dir TADAYASU
SAKAI.

Kobe

Hakutsuru Bijitsukan (Hakutsuru Fine
Art Museum): 6-1-1 Sumiyoshiyamate, Higashinada-ku, Kobe 658-0063; tel. (78) 851-
6001; fax (78) 851-6001; f. 1934; 1,300 specimens of fine art, incl. noted Chinese ceramics, old bronze vases and silverware, and
oriental carpets; library of 10,000 vols; Dir
HIDEO KANO.

Kobe City Museum: 24 Kyo-machi, Chuo-
ku, Kobe 650-0034; tel. (78) 391-0035; fax
(78) 392-7054; internet www.city.kobe.jp/
cityoffice/57/museum; f. 1982; theme of
museum is the historical view of international cultural intercourse, especially contact between Eastern and Western cultures;
38,000 items including 21 national treasure
items, important collections of Namban and
Kohmoh arts, 17th–19th-century maps, also
historical and archaeological items; library of
55,000 vols; Sec.-Gen. KAZUO KOBAYASHI;
publs *Yearbook*, *Museum Tayori* (newsletter,
3 a year), *Bulletin* (1 a year).

Kochi

Kochi Kaitokukan (Kochi Castle): 1-2-1
Marunouchi, 780-0850 Kochi City, Kochi
Prefecture; tel. (888) 24-5701; fax (888) 24-
9931; internet www.pref.kochi.jp/~kochijo; f.
1913; 800 exhibits, including autographs and
material of interest in Japanese historical
research; Dir YUTAKA KONDO.

Kotohira

Kotohira-gü Hakubutsukan (Museum in
the Kotohira Shrine): Kotohira-gü Shrine,
Kotohira-machi, Nakatado-gun; 3,011
exhibits; Chair. MITSUSHIGE KOTOOKA; Sec.
HAZIME HIRAO KOTOHIRA.

Kumamoto

Kumamoto Arts and Crafts Museum: 3–
35 Chibajo-machi, Kumamoto City 860-0001;
tel. (96) 324-4930; f. 1982; traditional arts
and crafts; 3,000 ancient and contemporary
items.

Kurashiki

Ohara Bijutsukan (Ohara Museum of Art):
1-1-15 Chuo, Kurashiki City; tel. (86) 422-
0005; fax (86) 427-3677; e-mail info@ohara.or
.jp; internet www.ohara.or.jp; f. 1930; Western paintings since the 19th century and
contemporary arts; modern Japanese ceramics and fabrics; modern Japanese oil paint-

ings; Asiatic art; artwork from Ancient Egypt and Medieval Islam; Dir SHUJI TAKASHINA.

Kushiro

Kushiro-shiritsu Hakubutsukan (Kushiro City Museum): Harutori Park 1-7, Shunkodai, Kushiro; tel. (154) 41-5809; fax (154) 42-6000; e-mail ku7011@city.kushiro .hokkaido.jp; internet www.city.kushiro .hokkaido.jp; f. 1936; 12,130 earthenware articles, natural history museum; Dir FUMIO NISHIYAMA; publs *Memoirs of the Kushiro City Museum* (1 a year), *Science Report of the Kushiro City Museum* (4 a year).

Kyoto

Chishakuin (Treasure Hall of the Chishakuin Temple): 964 Higashi-Kawaramachi, Higashiyama-ku, Kyoto; tel. (75) 541-5361; fax (75) 541-5364; Buddhist equipment and utensils, old documents, paintings, calligraphy, sutras, and books in Japanese and in Chinese.

Daigoji Reihokan (Treasure Hall of the Daigoji Temple): Daigo, Fushimi-ku, Kyoto; tel. (75) 571-0002; fax (75) 571-0101; f. 1936; contains 1,500 old art objects and 120,000 historical documents relating chiefly to Buddhism.

Jishoji (Ginkakuji) (Silver Temple): Ginkakuji-cho, Sakyo-ku, Kyoto; f. 1482 by Yoshimasa, eighth Shogun of Ashikaga, as 12 separate bldgs in the grounds of his villa; only the Ginkaku or Silver Hall, and the Togudo are now left; Curator R. ARIMA.

Kitano Temmangu Homotsuden (Treasure Hall of Kitano-Temmangu shrine): Kitano Bakuro-cho, Kamigyo-ku, Kyoto; tel. (75) 461-0005; fax (75) 461-6556; internet www.kitanotenmangu.or.jp; shrine dedicated to Michizane Sugawara, statesman and great scholar of Heian period; exhibits of treasure hall include the 'Kitano-Tenjin' history picture scrolls and an ancient copy of the 'Nihon Shoki'.

Korūji Reihōden (Treasure Museum of the Koryuji Temple): Koryuji Temple, Uzumasa, Ukyo-ku, Kyoto; f. 1922; many Buddhist images and pictures, including the two images of 'Miroku Bosatsu'; Curator EIKO KIYOTAKI.

Kyoto Kokuritsu Hakubutsukan (Kyoto National Museum): 527 Chaya-machi, Higashiyama-ku, Kyoto; tel. (75) 541-1151; fax (75) 531-0263; e-mail welcome@kyohaku.go .jp; internet www.kyohaku.go.jp; f. 1897 as Imperial Kyoto Museum; 52,692 books and 188,528 research photographs; 11,513 exhibits, incl. fine art and applied art exhibits and historical materials of Asia, chiefly of Japan; Dir Dr JOHEI SASAKI; Chief Curator MINORU NISHIGAMI; publs *Bulletin* (Research journal in Japanese, 1 a year), *Ueno Memorial Foundation for the Study of Buddhist Art* (in Japanese, 1 a year).

Kyoto-shi Bijutsukan (Kyoto Municipal Museum of Art): Okazaki Park, Sakyo-ku, Kyoto 606-8344; tel. (75) 771-4107; fax (75) 761-0444; internet www.city.kyoto.jp/bunshi/ kmma; f. 1933; contemporary fine art objects (mostly Japanese); Dir MITSUGI UEHIRA.

Myōhōin (Treasure House of the Myōhōin Temple): Myohoin-maegawa-cho, Higashiyama-ku, Kyoto; possessions of Toyotomi-Hideyoshi and many other national treasures.

National Museum of Modern Art, Kyoto: Enshoji-cho, Okazaki, Sakyo-ku, Kyoto; tel. (75) 761-4111; fax (75) 752-0509; e-mail info@ momak.go.jp; internet www.momak.go.jp; f. 1963; Nihonga (Japanese-style painting), Yōga (Western-style painting), prints, sculpture, crafts (ceramics, textiles, metalworks, wood and bamboo works, lacquers and jew-

ellery), photography and modern art; Dir MASAAKI OZAKI; Chief Curator HIDETSUGU YAMANO; publs *Museum News* (6 a year), *Membership* (4 a year).

Ninnaji Reihóden (Treasure Hall of the Ninnaji Temple): Ninnaji Temple, Omuro Daimon-cho, Ukyo-ku, Kyoto.

Rengeoin (Sanjusangendo) (Treasure House of the Rengeoin Temple): Mawaricho, Higashiyama-ku, Kyoto; 'One Thousand Images' and many other Buddhist images.

Rokuonji (Treasures of the Rokuonji Temple): Kinkakuji-cho, Kita-ku, Kyoto; famed for its garden and gold pavilion.

Shoren-in (Treasure House of the Shōren-in Temple): Sanjōbō-machi, Awadaguchi, Higashiyama-ku, Kyoto; internet www.shorenin .com; f. 1153; Dir JIKO HIGASHIFUSHIMI; library of 5,000 vols; rare books, writings, paintings, etc.

Taiten Kinen Kyoto Shokubutsuen (Kyoto Prefectural Museum Botanical Garden): Hangi-cho, Shimogamo, Sakyô-ku, Kyoto 606-0823; tel. (75) 701-0141; fax (75) 701-0142; 120,000 plants and 5,500 botanical specimens.

Toyokuni Jinja Hómotsuden (Treasure Hall of the Toyokuni Shrine): Shomen Chaya-machi Yamato-Ooji, Higashiyama-ku, Kyoto; treasures and possessions of Toyotomi-Hideyoshi, incl. paintings, painted screens, swords, etc.

Yogen-In (Treasure Hall of the Yōgen-In Temple): Sanju-sangendō-mae, Yamato-ōji Shichijō Higashi Iru, Higashiyama-ku, Kyoto.

Yūrinkan (Yurinkan Collection): 44 Okazaki-Enshōjichyô, Sakyō-ku, Kyoto 606-8344; tel. (75) 761-0638; f. 1926; privately owned by the Fujii Foundation; rare antique Chinese fine arts and curios, incl. bronze and jade ware, porcelain, seals, Buddhist images, pictures, and calligraphy; Dir Z. FUJII.

Matsue

Koizumi-Yakumo Kinenkan (Lafcadio Hearn Memorial Museum): 322 Okudanimachi, Matsue City 690-0872; tel. (852) 21-2147; fax (852) 21-2156; f. 1933; collection of items belonging to Lafcadio Hearn; library of 492 vols (works by and on Hearn); Dir TOSHIO UCHIDA.

Shimane Prefectural Museum: 1 Tonomachi, Matsue City; tel. (852) 22-6727; fax (852) 22-6728; e-mail kodai@izm.ed.jp; internet www2.pref.shimane.jp/kodai; f. 1959; bronze bells, bronze swords and other ancient heritage; Dir SYO KATSUBE; publs *Ancient Culture in Shimane* (1 a year), *News of the Institution for Ancient Study* (4 a year), *Studies of Ancient Culture* (1 a year).

Matsumoto

Matsumoto City Museum: 4-1 Marunouchi, Matsumoto City, Nagano 390-0873; tel. (263) 32-0133; fax (263) 32-8974; e-mail mcmuse@city.matsumoto.nagano.jp; internet www.city.matsumoto.nagano.jp; f. 1906; folklore, history, archaeology, star festival dolls, popular belief tools, fine art, agricultural tools; Dir KENICHI KUMAGAI.

Minobu

Minobusan Homotsukan (Treasury of the Kuonji Temple): Kuonji Temple, Minobumachi, Minami-Koma-gun; 300 articles, examples of the fine arts, and materials connected with the history of the Nichiren Sect of Buddhism, the biography of Saint Nichiren.

Mount Koya

Kōyasan Reihōkan (Museum of Buddhist Art on Mount Kōya): Kōyasan, Kōya-cho, Ito-gun; f. 1921; 50,000 exhibits, incl. Buddhist paintings and images, sutras and old documents, some of them registered National Treasures and Important Cultural Properties; a centre of Buddhism in Japan; Dir CHIKYŌ YAMAMOTO.

Nagoya

Nagoya Castle Donjon: 1-1 Hon-maru, Naka-ku, Nagoya; tel. (52) 231-1700; built in 1612 by Ieyasu Tokugawa; destroyed by fire 1945; restored to its original form 1959; exhibition rooms, galleries and observatory; 1,049 paintings of the Kano school on sliding doors and ceilings; armoury and swords.

Nara

Kasugataisha Homotsuden (Treasure Hall of the Kasugataisha Shrine): Kasugataisha Shrine, 160 Kasugano-cho, Nara City; f. 1934; the ancient, curvilinear style of architecture is called 'Kasuga Zukuri' after this shrine; Shrine Master CHIKATADA KASANNOIN.

Museum Yamato Bunkakan: 1-11-6 Gakuen-minami, Nara; tel. (742) 45-0544; fax (742) 49-2929; internet www.kintetsu.jp/ kouhou/yamato; f. 1960; art objects of East Asia, chiefly Japan, China and Korea; library of 20,000 vols; Dir Prof. SHUGO ASANO; publs *Yamato Bunka* (2 a year), *Catalogues of the Museum Collection* (in English), *Bi-no-Tayori* (4 a year).

Nara National Museum: 50 Nobori-oji-cho, Nara-shi 630-8213; tel. (742) 22-7771; fax (742) 26-7218; internet www.narahaku.go.jp; f. 1895; Buddhist sculptures, paintings, applied arts, calligraphy, archaeological objects, etc.; also special exhibitions; library of 59,750 vols; Dir KENICHI YUYAMA.

Neiraku Museum: Isuien Park, 74 Suimoncho, Nara City; tel. (742) 22-2173; fax (742) 25-0781; f. 1939; ancient Chinese bronze mirrors, seals, etc., and Korean potteries; Dir JUNSUKE NAKAMURA.

Todaiji: 406-1 Zōshi-cho, Nara; tel. (742) 22-5511; fax (742) 22-0808; f. 752; HQ of Kegonshū Buddhist sect; Daibutsuden: Main Hall of the Todaiji Temple, the largest wooden edifice in the world, the world-famous Great Image of Buddha and 2 Bodhisattvas; attached bldgs are the Hokkedō, Kaidanin, Nigatsudō, which contain many famous images of Buddha and Bodhisattva; library of 70,000 vols, 10,000 manuscripts; Dir D. UENO; publ. *Nanto Bukkyō: Journal of the Nanto Society for Buddhist Studies* (1 a year).

Yakushiji (Yakushiji Temple): 457 Nishi-no-Kyō-machi, Nara City 630-8563; tel. (742) 33-6001; fax (742) 33-6004; e-mail yksj8@ mahoroba.or.jp; internet www .nara-yakushiji.com; f. 697; famous bronze images of the Yakushi Trinity; a pagoda 1,300 years old; Dir Lord Abbot S. MATSUKUBO.

Narita

Naritasan Reikokan Museum (Treasure Hall of the Naritasan-Shinshoji Temple): Narita Park, Narita-City, Chiba Pref. 286-0023; tel. (476) 22-2111; fax (476) 24-2210; internet www.naritasan.or.jp; f. 1947; contains treasures dedicated to the shrine and archaeological pieces from the region, 12,113 MSS and books, sculptures, botanical specimens; Curator SHOSEKI TSURUMI.

Omishima

Oyamazumi Jinja Kokuhokan (Treasure Hall of the Oyamazumi Shrine): Oyamazumi

Shrine, Omishima Town, Ochigun; f. AD 1; 2,000 exhibits, incl. a large colln of ancient armour, swords, and the oldest mirrors in Japan; library of 20,000 vols; Curator YASU-HISA MISHIMA.

Osaka

National Museum of Ethnology: 10-1 Senri Expo Park, Suita, Osaka 565-8511; tel. (6) 6876-2151; fax (6) 6875-0401; internet www.minpaku.ac.jp; f. 1974; 256,436 artefacts from Japan and abroad; conducts anthropological research and promotes general understanding and awareness of peoples, societies and cultures around the world; established as Inter-Univ. Research Institute; library of 587,115 vols, 15,586 journals, 69,325 audiovisual items; Dir-Gen. KEN'ICHI SUDO; publs *Bulletin* (in Japanese, English, French, Spanish, Russian, Chinese and German, 4 a year), *Minpaku Anthropology Newsletter* (2 a year, in English), *Minpaku Tsushin* (newsletter, in Japanese), *Senri Ethnological Reports* (irregular), *Senri Ethnological Studies* (in English and selected other European languages, irregular).

Osaka Municipal Museum of Art: 1–82 Chausuyama-cho, Tennoji-ku, Osaka 543-0063; tel. (6) 6771-4874; fax (6) 6771-4856; internet www.city.osaka.jp/museum-art; f. 1936; Chinese, Korean and Japanese fine art; library of 11,000 vols; Dir YUTAKA MINO; publ. *Miotsukushi* (Bulletin, 2 a year).

Osaka Museum of Natural History: Nagai Park, Higashisumiyoshi-ku, Osaka 546-0034; tel. (6) 6697-6221; fax (6) 6697-6225; internet www.mus-nh.city.osaka.jp; f. 1952; botany, entomology, geology, palaeontology and zoology; Dir TAKAYOSHI NASU; Head Curator MOTOHARU OKAMOTO; publs *Bulletin*, *Nature Study*, *Occasional Paper* (1 a year), *Special Publications* (1 a year).

Tenri

Tenri University Sankokan Museum: 250 Morimedo-cho, Tenri City, Nara Prefecture 632-8540; tel. (743) 63-8414; fax (743) 63-7721; internet www.sankokan.jp; f. 1930; attached to Tenri University; ethnographic and archaeological items from all parts of the world.

Tokyo

Ancient Orient Museum: 1–4 Higashi Ikebukuro 3-chome, Toshima-ku, Tokyo 170-8630; tel. (3) 3989-3491; fax (3) 3590-3266; e-mail museum@orientmuseum.com; internet www.sa.il24.net; f. 1978; archaeology and art history of Middle and Near East, Egypt, India and Central Asia; library of 17,000 vols; Dir Dr ICHIRO NAKATA; Curator K. ISHIDA; publ. *Bulletin of the Ancient Orient Museum* (1 a year).

Bridgestone Museum of Art, Ishibashi Foundation: 10-1, Kyobashi 1-chome, Chuo-ku, Tokyo 104-0031; tel. (3) 3563-0241; fax (3) 3561-2130; f. 1952 by Shojiro Ishibashi; private museum of 19th- and 20th-century European paintings and modern Japanese Western-style paintings; Dir NORIO SHIMADA.

Gotoh Museum: 9–25 3-chome Kaminoge, Setagaya-ku, Tokyo; tel. (3) 3703-0662; fax (3) 3703-0440; internet www.gotoh-museum.or.jp; f. 1960; Japanese, Chinese and Korean art; c. 4,000 exhibits, incl. the 'Tales of Genji' scroll and the 'Diary of Lady Murasaki' scroll; Curator FUKUSHIMA OSAMU.

Inokashira Onshi Koen Shizen Bunkaen (Natural Science Park in Inokashira Park): 1-17-6 Gotenyama, Musashinoshi, Tokyo; zoo, botanical garden, research room, marine biology room.

Kokuritsu Kagaku Hakubutsukan (National Museum of Nature and Science):

Ueno Park 7–20, Taito-ku, Tokyo 110-8718; tel. (3) 3822-0111; fax (3) 5814-9898; e-mail webmaster@kahaku.go.jp; internet www.kahaku.go.jp; f. 1877, merged with Research Institute for Natural Resources in 1971; exhibits of natural history, physical science and engineering; colln of over 3.6m. specimens; library of 105,234 vols; Dir SHINJI KONDO; publs *Bulletin* (in 5 series), *Memoirs* (irregular), *Monographs* (irregular).

Kotsu Hakubutsukan (Transportation Museum): 25 1-chome, Kanda-Sudacho, Chiyoda-ku, Tokyo; tel. (3) 3251-8481; fax (3) 3251-8489; e-mail gakugei@kouhaku.or.jp; internet www.kouhaku.or.jp; f. 1921; aircraft, electric equipment, locomotives, motor-cars, ships, etc.; Dir TATSUHIKO SUGA.

Meguro Parasitological Museum: 4–1-1 Shimomeguro, Meguro-ku, Tokyo 153-0064; tel. (3) 3716-1264; fax (3) 3716-2322; internet kiseichu.org; f. 1953; science of parasites; Dir MASAAKI MACHIDA.

Meiji Jingu Homotsuden (Meiji Shrine Treasure Museum): Yoyogi, Shibuya-ku, Tokyo; f. 1921; 102 treasures and possessions of Emperor Meiji and 74 objects belonging to Empress Shoken; there is also a Memorial Picture Gallery.

Mori Art Museum: 53rd Fl., Roppongi Hills, Mori Tower, 6-10-1 Roppongi, Minato-ku, Tokyo; tel. (3) 5777-8600; fax (3) 6406-9351; internet www.mori.art.museum; f. 2003; Dir FUMIO NANJO.

Museum of Contemporary Art, Tokyo: Metropolitan Kiba Park, 4-1-1 Miyoshi Koto-ku, Tokyo 135-0022; tel. (3) 5245-4111; fax (3) 5777-8600; internet www.mot-art-museum.jp; Japanese and foreign art since 1945.

National Museum of Modern Art, Tokyo: 3–1 Kitanomaru Koen, Chiyoda-ku, Tokyo 102-8322; tel. (3) 5777-8600; internet www.momat.go.jp; f. 1952; art museum and crafts gallery; colln of modern artworks, and related references dating from the beginning of the 20th century to present; art museum incls paintings, sculptures, prints, watercolours, drawings, photographs and other works; crafts gallery incls textiles, glass, lacquer, wood, bamboo and metalwork, dolls, industrial and graphic design; also nat. film centre holding films and non-film materials; Dir KAMOGAWA SACHIO; publs *Gendai no Me* (in Japanese, 6 a year), *National Film Center Newsletter* (in Japanese, 6 a year).

National Museum of Western Art: 7-7 Ueno-koen, Taito-ku, Tokyo 110-0007; tel. (3) 5777-8600; fax (3) 3828-5135; e-mail wwwadmin@nmwa.go.jp; internet www.nmwa.go.jp; f. 1959 (building designed by Le Corbusier); 19th-century European paintings and sculptures collected by the late Kojiro Matsukata and new acquisitions of old masters; Dir Dr MASANORI AOYAGI.

Nezu Institute: 6-5-1 Minami-Aoyama Minato-ku, Tokyo 107-0062; tel. (3) 3400-2536; fax (3) 3400-2436; e-mail nezu@nezu-muse.or.jp; internet www.nezu-muse.or.jp; f. 1940; private colln by Nezu Kaichiro Sr. and donations of approx. 7,000 paintings, calligraphy, sculpture, swords, ceramics, lacquer-ware, archaeological exhibits; 7 items of nat. treasures, 87 items of cultural properties; Dir NEZU KOICHI; Chief Curator SHIRAHARA YUKIKO.

Nippon Mingeikan (Japan Folk Crafts Museum): 4-3-33 Komaba, Meguro-ku, Tokyo 153-0041; tel. (3) 3467-4527; fax (3) 3467-4537; internet www.mingeikan.or.jp; f. 1936; Japanese traditional folk craft and craft from around the world; spec. collns from founding mems of Mingei Movement: Soetsu Yanagi, Kanjiro Kawai, Shoji Hamada, Keisuke Serizawa, Bernard Leach, Shiko Munakata,

Kenkichi Tomimoto and others; Dir YOTARO KOBAYASHI; publ. *Mingei* (12 a year).

Okura Cultural Foundation Okura Shukokan Museum: 2-10-3, Toranomon, Minato-ku, Tokyo; f. 1917; 1,700 articles of fine arts; library of 36,000 vols of Chinese classics; Pres. NOBORU NISHITANI.

Shitamachi Museum: 2–1 Ueno-koen, Taito-ku, Tokyo; tel. (3) 3823-7451; internet www.taitocity.net/taito/shitamachi; f. 1980; re-creation of the old commercial district of Tokyo; incl. typical street, wooden houses, life-size figures, furniture, pictures, books and letters, religious material, domestic utensils, Second World War items, games and musical instruments, cosmetics and accessories, etc.; Dir HIDENOBU HIROSE.

Shodo Hakubutsukan (Calligraphy Museum): 2-10-4 Negishi, Taito-ku, Tokyo 110-0003; tel. (3) 3872-2645; f. 1936; colln of the calligrapher, the late F. Nakamura; 1,000 rubbed copies of the stone tablets and 'hōjō', ancient texts of calligraphy (10,000 articles).

Tokyo Daigaku Rigaku Kenkyu-ka Fuzoku Shokubutsuen (Botanical Gardens, Graduate School of Science, University of Tokyo): 7-1, Hakusan 3, Bunkyo-ku, Tokyo 112; tel. (3) 3814-2625; fax (3) 3814-0139; f. 1684, transferred to Univ. 1877; Nikko br.; research in systematic botany and conservation of plants; 6,000 kinds of plants; 2,500 in Nikko; associated with the herbarium TI with approx. 700,000 specimens; library of 20,000 vols; Dir Prof. Dr JIN MURATA.

Tokyo Kokuritsu Hakubutsukan (Tokyo National Museum): 13-9 Ueno Park, Taito-ku, Tokyo 110-8712; tel. (3) 5405-8686; fax (3) 3822-2081; internet www.tnm.jp; f. 1872; largest museum in Japan; Japanese and E fine arts, incl. paintings, calligraphy, sculpture, metalwork, ceramic art, textiles, lacquer-ware, archaeological exhibits; Dir-Gen. MASAMI ZENIYA; publs *Museum* (12 a year), *Tokyo National Museum News* (12 a year).

Tokyo-to Bijutsukan (Tokyo Metropolitan Art Museum): Ueno Park 8–36, Taito-ku, Tokyo; tel. (3) 3823-6921; fax (3) 3823-6920; e-mail tobi@tobikan.jp; internet www.tobikan.jp; f. 1926; ancient and modern art exhibition, educational service, art library and gallery for group exhibitions; closed from April 2010 to March 2012 for renovation; Dir YOSHITAKE MAMURO; Curator ATSUKO TAKEUCHI; publ. *Bulletin* (1 a year).

University Art Museum, Tokyo University of the Arts: Ueno Park, Taito-ku, Tokyo 110-8714; tel. (3) 5525-2200; fax (3) 5525-2532; internet www.geidai.ac.jp/museum; paintings, sculptures and applied art of Japan, China and Korea.

Waseda Daigaku Tsubouchi Hakase Kinen Engeki Hakubutsukan (Tsubouchi Memorial Theatre Museum, Waseda University): 1-6-1 Nishi-Waseda, Shinjuku-ku, Tokyo 169-8050; tel. (3) 5286-1829; fax (3) 5276-4398; e-mail enpaku@list.waseda.jp; internet www.waseda.jp/enpaku; f. 1928; library of 200,000 vols, 46,700 woodblock colour prints and 343,000 pictures; Dir MIKIO TAKEMOTO; publs *Studies in Dramatic Art*, *Theatre Museum*.

Yasukuni Jinja: Kudan Kita, 3-1-1, Chiyoda-ku, Tokyo 102-8246; tel. (3) 3261-8326; fax (3) 3261-0081; internet www.yasukuni.or.jp; f. 1869; nat. shrine dedicated to the war dead; museum displays items from wars fought by Japan since the establishment of the shrine.

Ueno

Iga-ryu Ninja Museum: 117-13-1 Ueno-marunouchi, Iga City, Mie Prefecture; tel. (595) 23-0311; fax (595) 23-0314; e-mail ninpaku@ict.ne.jp; internet www.iganinja.jp; history and exhibits on Ninjas, spies who played an important role during periods of civil war in medieval Japan.

Yokohama

Kanagawa Prefectural Kanazawa Bunko Museum: 142 Kanazawa-cho, Kanazawa-ku, Yokohama; tel. (45) 701-9069; fax (45) 788-1060; internet www.planet.pref .kanagawa.jp/city/kanazawa.htm; f. 1972; nat. treasures (figure of Hojo-Sanetoki, etc.); library: f. 1275; 20,000 old books and 4,149 documents; Curator MAKOTO NAGAMURA.

National Universities

AICHI PREFECTURAL UNIVERSITY

1522-3 Ibaragabasama, Kumabari, Nagakute-cho, Aichi-gun, Aichi 480-1198

Telephone: (561) 64-1111
E-mail: jim@bur.aichi-pu.ac.jp
Internet: www.aichi-pu.ac.jp

Founded 1947

Pres.: MASAO MORI

Library of 450,000 vols

PROFESSORS

Faculty of Foreign Studies:

HAYAMIZU, Y., Department of French Studies
HIOKI, M., Department of German Studies
KICHISE, S., Department of British and American Studies
KURAHASHI, M., Department of Chinese Studies
SHIGA, I., Department of Spanish and Latin American Studies

Faculty of Information Science and Technology:

HANDA, N., Department of Applied Information Science and Technology
SAKURAI, K., Department of Information Systems

Faculty of Letters:

KAWAGUCHI, A., Department of Childhood Education
KOTANI, S., Department of Japanese Language and Letters
SHIMIZU, K., Department of Social Welfare
TOUYAMA, I., Department of English
YAMADA, M., Department of Japanese History and Culture

ASAHIKAWA MEDICAL COLLEGE

2-1-1-1 Midorigaoka, Asahikawa 078-8510

Telephone: (166) 65-2111
Fax: (166) 66-0025
E-mail: ipc@asahikawa-med.ac.jp
Internet: www.asahikawa-med.ac.jp

Founded 1973

Independent (National University Corporation)

Academic year: April to March

Pres.: SUNAO YACHIKU
Exec. Dirs: HIYOSHI SHIONO, MUTSUO ISHIKAWA
Exec. Sec.-Gen.: SUSUMU OHTA
Library Dir: KATSUHIRO OGAWA

Library of 139,000 vols
Number of teachers: 263
Number of students: 953 (845 undergraduate, 108 postgraduate)

Publication: *Asahikawa Medical College* (1 a year).

BUNKYO UNIVERSITY

3-2-17 Hatanodai, Shinagawa-ku, Tokyo 142-0064

Telephone: (3) 3783-5511
Fax: (3) 3783-8300
E-mail: iec@stf.bunkyo.ac.jp
Internet: www.bunkyo.ac.jp

Founded 1927

Pres.: TSUNEYOSHI ISHIDA

Number of teachers: 226
Number of students: 8,649
Library of 546,000 vols

Faculties of Culture, Education, Human Science, Information and Communications, International Studies, Language and Literature.

CHIBA UNIVERSITY

1-33 Yayoi-cho, Inage-ku, Chiba-shi, Chiba 263-8522

Telephone: (43) 251-1111
Fax: (43) 290-2041
E-mail: kokusai@office.chiba-u.jp
Internet: www.chiba-u.jp

Founded 1949

Public control

Languages of instruction: English, Japanese
Academic year: April to March

Pres.: Prof. YASUSHI SAITO
Vice-Pres. for Planning Affairs: Prof. KEIJI YAMAMOTO
Vice-Pres. for Education and Student Affairs: Prof. SEIJI NAGASAWA
Vice-Pres. for Research and International Affairs: Prof. TAKESHI TOKUHISA
Vice-Pres. for Planning and Human Resources: Prof. ITARU SHIMAZU
Vice-Pres. for General Affairs: TERUSHI IKEDA
Dir-Gen.: TETSUO YAMANE
Library Dir: SYUN TUTIYA

Library of 1,401,043 vols
Number of teachers: 1,223
Number of students: 15,178

Publications: *Bulletin of the Faculty of Education* (1 a year), *Chemical Analysis Centre Research Achievements*, *Chiba University Social Sciences and Humanities* (1 a year), *Economics Journal* (4 a year), *HortResearch* (1 a year), *International Research and Education* (in Japanese, 1 a year), *Journal of Humanities* (1 a year), *Journal of Law and Politics* (4 a year), *Journal of the School of Nursing* (1 a year), *Journal on Public Affairs* (1 a year), *Laboratory Waste Treatment Plant Bulletin* (1 a year), *Marine Biosystems Research* (1 a year), *Outline of the Research Centre for Pathogenic Fungi and Microbial Toxicoses* (every 2 years), *Record of Research Activities of the Faculty of Pharmaceutical Science*, *Research Activities and Interests of the Faculty of Engineering* (2 a year), *Research Report of the Centre for Co-operative Research*, *Studies on Humanities and Social Sciences of Chiba University* (in Japanese, 2 a year), *Technical Bulletin of the Faculty of Horticulture* (1 a year), *Technical Reports of Mathematical Sciences* (1 a year)

DEANS

Faculty of Education: Prof. FUMIO TAKIZAWA
Faculty of Engineering: Prof. AKIHIDE KITAMURA
Faculty of Horticulture: Prof. TAKATO KOBA
Faculty of Law and Economics: Prof. SHOICHI OGANO
Faculty of Letters: Prof. MASARU YAMADA
Faculty of Pharmaceutical Sciences: Prof. ATSUSHI NISHIDA
Faculty of Science: Prof. KAZUYO OHASHI

Graduate School of Advanced Integration Science: Prof. SHOJI TOMINAGA
Graduate School of Humanities and Social Sciences: Prof. HIROSHI NAKAGAWA
Graduate School of Medical and Pharmaceutical Sciences: Prof. TOMOKO YAMAMOTO
Law School: Prof. TSUTOMU YASUMURA
School of Medicine: Prof. HARUAKI NAKAYA
School of Nursing: Prof. HARUE MASAKI

PROFESSORS

Centre for Environment, Health and Field Sciences (6-2-1 Kashiwanoha, Kawashi-shi, Chiba 277-0882; tel. (4) 7134-8401; fax (4) 7134-8437):

ANDO, T., Ornamental Plant Science
KOZAI, T., Environmental Control Engineering
KURIYAMA, T., Respirology
NOMA, Y., Experimental Farms
OHGAMA, T., Wood Science and Technology
TOKUYAMA, I., Sports Pedagogy

Centre for Environmental Remote Sensing (tel. (43) 290-3832; fax (43) 290-3857; internet www.cr.chiba-u.jp):

MIWA, T., Dept of Geoinformation Analysis
NISHIO, H., Dept of Database Research
SUGIMORI, Y., Dept of Geoinformation Analysis
TAKAMURA, T., Dept of Sensor and Atmospheric Radiation
TAKEUCHI, N., Dept of Sensor and Atmospheric Radiation

Centre for Foreign Languages:

BOSWELL, P. D., Psychology of Teaching
KUBOTA, M., Linguistics
MIKOSHIBA, M., Russian Intellectual History
SHIINA, K., Methodology for English Teaching
TABATA, T., Linguistics, Phonology
YAMAOKA, K., French Literature

Centre for Frontier Science (1–33 Yayoi-cho, Inage-ku, Chiba-shi, Chiba 263-8522; tel. (43) 290-3522; fax (43) 290-3523; e-mail info@cfs.chiba-u.jp; internet www.cfs.chiba-u .ac.jp):

HANAWA, T., Astrophysics
OHTAKA, K., Applied Physics

Graduate School of Science and Technology:

ANDO, A., Proteins Engineering
ASANO, Y., Environmental Plant Science
FUJIKAWA, T., XAFS Theory
FURUYA, T., Applied Geomorphology
HATTORI, M., Architectural Design Study
HIRATA, H., Systems Engineering
ICHIKAWA, A., Knowledge Engineering
INABA, T., Differential Topology
IWADATE, Y., Physics and Chemistry of Liquids and Amorphous Materials
KOHMOTO, S., Organic Photochemistry
MAJIMA, T., Mechanics and Strength of Materials
MATSUDA, T., Electronic Commerce and Agribusiness
NATSUME, Y., Condensed Matter Theory
NISHIKAWA, K., Physical Chemistry
OHNO, T., Imaging Materials
SATO, T., Plant Molecular Biology
SHIGA, H., Complex Manifolds
SHIMAKURA, S., Fundamentals of Electrical and Electronic Engineering
SUGIYAMA, K., Design Systems Planning
TAGAWA, A., Agricultural Process Engineering
TAMURA, T., Molecular Biology
UESUGI, H., Fireproofing of Buildings
YAHAGI, T., Digital Signal Processing
YOSHIDA, H., Complex Analysis

Faculty of Education (fax (43) 290-2519; e-mail hd2504@office.chiba-u.jp; internet www.e.chiba-u.jp):

ABE, A., Physical Education and School Health Education
AKASHI, Y., Sociology of Education
AMAGAI, Y., Developmental Clinical Psychology
AMAGASA, S., School Management
FUJII, T., Constitutional Law
FUJIKAWA, D., Development of Teaching
FUJISAWA, H., Art Education
FUSHIMA, Y., Psychology of School Learning
HIRAIDE, S., English and American Literature
HOSAKA, T., Clinical Studies in School Education
INABA, H., Physical Chemistry
INAGAKI, K., Early Childhood Education
INOUE, T., Sociology
ISAKA, J., Japanese Linguistics
ISHII, K., Food and Cookery Science
ISOBE, K., Orthopaedics
ISOZAKI, I., Political Science
IWAGAKI, O., Teaching Methods
IWATA, M., Developmental Psychology
IWATSUKI, K., Educational Psychology
KAMIYA, N., Musical Expression in Early Childhood Education
KAMO, H., Philosophy
KANAMORI, R., Painting
KATAOKA, Y., Sports Physiology
KATAYAMA, T., Sports Management
KATO, S., Chinese Literature
KENMOCHI, N., Analysis and Applied Mathematics
KIKUCHI, T., Teaching Methods of Physical Education and Sports
KOBAYASHI, K., Theory of School Nursing and School Health
KOMIYAMA, T., Motor Control
KOSHIKAWA, H., Differential Topology
KUMABE, T., Mechanics
KURANO, M., Analysis and Applied Mathematics
KUSAKARI, H., Nuclear Physics
MISAWA, M., Climatology
MIWA, S., School Management
MIYAMOTO, M., Sociology of the Family
MIYANO, M., Teaching of Music
MIYASHITA, K., Adolescent Psychology
MIZUUCHI, H., Curriculum Development
MOROTOMI, Y., Educational Counselling
MURAMATSU, S., Sports and Nutrition
NAGANE, M., School Psychology
NAGASAWA, S., Social Education
NAGATA, K., Comparative Theory of Art
NAKAZAWA, J., Developmental Psychology
NUKUI, M., Teaching of Science
OASHI, O., Psychology of Learning
OHGAMA, T., Wood Science and Technology
OHKOCHI, N., Agriculture Education
OHTA, T., Special Education
OI, K., English Pedagogy
OKAMOTO, K., Solid State Physics
OKI, T., Industrial Design
OTSUKA, T., English Linguistics
SADAHIRO, S., Educational Administration
SATO, F., Home Economics Education
SATO, K., Ethics
SATO, M., Children's Literature
SATO, M., Movement Theory of Sport
SHIBATA, M., Aesthetics of Costume
SHIMADA, K., Teaching of Mathematics
SHIMIZU, T., English and American Literature in School Education
SHUTO, H., Japanese Language Education
SUGITA, K., Paediatric Neurology
SUZUKI, A., Physiology and Ecology of Fungi
TAKEUCHI, H., Teaching of Social Studies
TAKIZAWA, F., Philosophy of Physical Education and Sport
TAMURA, T., Greek History

TANAKA, T., Teaching of Social Studies
TERAI, M., Japanese Language Education
TERAKADO, Y., Housing and the Living Environment
TOKUYAMA, I., Sports Pedagogy
TOZAKI, K., Physics
TSURUOKA, Y., Science Education
UENO, H., Sculpture
UESUGI, K., Moral Education
UKAWA, M., Music Education (Piano)
UMETANI, T., Psychology of Handicapped Children
URANO, T., Teaching of Calligraphy
WATANABE, S., Vocal Music
YAMAMURA, J., Human Geography
YAMANO, Y., Electrical Engineering
YAMAUCHI, K., Group Representation Theory
YAMAZAKI, Y., Geology
YODA, A., Technology Education

Faculty of Engineering:

AKUTSU, F., Synthetic Polymer Chemistry
ANDO, M., Construction and Production of Buildings
AOKI, H., Materials Planning for Design
AOYAGI, S., Bio-organic Chemistry
FUJITA, T., Synthetic Organic Chemistry
FUKASAWA, A., Communication and Information Networks
FUKUKAWA, Y., Urban Planning and Design, Historic Conservation
HASEGAWA, A., Photophysics
HATTORI, T., Ceramic Sciences
HIBINO, H., Design Psychology and Colour Science
HIROHASHI, M., Materials Science
HISIDA, M., Heat Engine Engineering
HONDA, T., Optical Engineering, Image Processing
HOTTA, A., Industrial Design
IKEDA, H., Computer Science
ITO, K., Antenna Engineering
KAGEGAWA, K., Inorganic Material
KAMAIKE, M., Product Design
KATO, H., Optimization of Manufacturing
KATSUURA, T., Ergonomics
KITAHARA, T., City Planning
KITAMURA, A., Fundamentals of Materials Science
KITAMURA, T., Electronic Image Processing
KOBAYASHI, H., Organic Memory and Display Materials
KOTERA, H., Printing Image Processing
KUDO, K., Physical Electronics
KURYU, A., Architectural Design
LIU, H., Biomechanical Engineering
MAENO, K., Thermofluid Dynamics
MATSUBA, I., Engineering of Information Processing
MIYAKE, Y., Measurement and Analysis of Image Information
MIYATA, T., Interior Design
MIYAZAKI, K., Philosophy and History of Design
MIYAZAKI, M., Visual Communication Design
MORITA, H., Laser Chemistry on Nanomaterials
MORITA, K., Structural Planning
NAKAHARA, T., Polymer Chemistry
NAKAI, S., Disaster Prevention
NAKAMOTO, T., Micro Machining
NAKAMURA, M., Plastic Working
NISHIKAWA, N., Fluids Engineering
NOGUCHI, K., Visual Perception
NONAMI, K., Control and Robotics
OCHIAI, Y., Advanced Device Materials
OGUMA, K., Analytical Chemistry
OGURA, K., Synthetic Organic Chemistry
OKAMOTO, H., Optical Properties of Semiconductors
OTANI, S., Earthquake Engineering
OTSUBO, Y., Rheology
SAITO, O., Semiconductor Rhotonics
SHIMIZU, T., Environmental Design

SUGITA, K., Information Recording Materials
TAMAI, T., History of Architecture
TANAKA, K., Physical Electronics
TATEDA, M., Opto-electronics
TATSUMOTO, H., Systems Design in Water and Wastewater Treatment
UEMATSU, T., Industrial Physical Chemistry
UENO, N., Molecular Quantum Assemblies
UNO, M., Architecture and Urban Design
WATANABE, T., Micro-machine Elements
YAGUCHI, H., Visual Science
YAMAGUCHI, M., Electrical Circuits
YAMAMOTO, M., Synthetic Organic Chemistry
YAMAOKA, T., Imaging Materials
YASHIRO, K., Microwave Theory and Technology
YOSHIKAWA, A., Quantum Electronics

Faculty of Horticulture (648 Matsudo, Matsudo-shi, Chiba 271-8510; tel. (47) 308-8706; fax (47) 308-8720; e-mail n8703@office .chiba-u.jp; internet www.h.chiba-u.ac.jp):

AMANO, H., Applied Entomology and Zoology
AMEMIYA, Y., Green Space Environmental Technology
AMEMIYA, Y., Plant Pathology
ANDO, T., Ornamental Plant Science
FUJII, T., Microbial Engineering
HARADA, K., Genetics and Plant Breeding
HONJO, T., Planting Design
IIMOTO, M., Plant Production Engineering
INUBUSHI, K., Soil Science
KEINO, S., Agricultural Marketing
KIKUCHI, M., Agricultural Economics
KON, H., Green Space Meteorology
KOZAI, T., Environmental Control Engineering
MASADA, M., Biochemistry
MATSUI, H., Fruit Science
MII, M., Plant Cell Technology
MINAMIDA, S., Horticultural Management and Information
MOTOYAMA, N., Pesticide Toxicology
NAGATA, Y., Molecular Biology
NAKAGAWA, H., Biotechnology of Agroresources
NAKAMURA, O., Town and Country Planning
OHE, Y., Horticultural Information Science
OKITSU, S., Forest Ecology
ONO, S., Garden Design
SAITO, O., Farm Business Management
SANADA, H., Food and Nutrition
SHINOHARA, Y., Vegetable Science
TASHIRO, Y., Urban Landscape Design
WATANABE, Y., Plant Nutrition
YAMAUCHI, S., Humanistic Study on Environment

Faculty of Law and Economics:

ABE, K., International Economics
ABIKO, S., Contemporary Economic Theory
AKIMOTO, E., American Economic History
AMANO, M., Monetary Economics, Business Cycles
AMEMIYA, A., German Socio-economic History
AOTAKE, S., Corporate Law
ENDOH, Y., Commercial Law, Anti-monopoly Law
FURUUCHI, H., Modern European Economic History
HANDA, Y., Civil Law
HAYASHI, W., International Cooperation Law, Anglo-Japanese Alliance Relations
HAYASHI, Y., Criminal Law
HIROI, Y., Social and Health Policy
INABA, H., Econometrics
IWAMA, A., Constitutional Law, Parliamentary System
IWATA, M., Comparative Economic Systems, Yugoslav Politics and Political Economy

KAKIHARA, K., Macroeconomics
KAMANO, K., Civil Law, Environmental Law
KINPARA, K., Religion and Law, Civil Procedure
KUDO, H., History of Social Thought
KURITA, M., Economic Law, Competition Law
MARUYAMA, E., Condominium Law, Housing Law, Urban Law, Property Law, Civil Law
MATSUDA, C., Public Finance
MIYAZAKI, R., Japanese Government and Politics
MURAYAMA, M., Sociology of Law
MUSASHI, T., Industrial Organization
NAKAHARA, H., International Research and Development, Company Management
NAKAKUBO, H., Labour and Employment Law
NOMURA, Y., Mathematical Economics
NOZAWA, T., History of Political Economy
OGANO, S., Civil Law, Environmental Law, Property Law
OKUMOTO, Y., Economic Statistics, Seasonal Adjustment
OMORI, W., Public Administration, Local Government
SAKAKIBARA, K., Macroeconomics, Money, Constitutional Economics
SAKAMOTO, T., Japanese Legal History
SHIMAZU, I., Philosophy of Law
SHINDO, M., Public Administration
SUZUKI, T., Administrative Law, Local Government Law
TAGAYA, K., Information Law, Administrative Law
TEZUKA, K., Foreigners and Law, Employment Security in Japan, Germany and USA
UEKI, S., Comparative Studies of Civil Law, Contracts and Torts
WATANABE, Y., Constitutional Law
YUMOTO, K., Political Consciousness in the Chinese Republican Era
YOSHIZUMI, Y., Financial Accounting

Faculty of Letters:

AKIYAMA, K., Comparative Literature, French Modern Literature, Japanese Modern Literature
CHOI, K., History of Korea
GORYO, K., Psychology
IIDA, N., Ethics, Bioethics
INUZUKA, S., Industrial Sociology, Theory of Organization
JITSUMORI, M., Comparative Cognition, Animal Learning
KUROSAWA, K., Social Psychology, Law and Psychology, Personality Psychology
MAEDA, S., German and Austrian Literature, Narratology
MARUYAWA, T., German Studies
MATSUMOTO, H., Japanese Linguistics (Grammar, Dialectology)
MINAMIZUKA, S., History of Europe, History of Hungary, Rural Society
MITSUI, Y., 18th-century French Literature, Philosophy of the Enlightenment
MIURA, S., Japanese Ancient Literature, Japanese Oral Literature
MIYAKE, A., Modern Japanese History, Labour History
MIYANO, H., Psychology
MIZUKAMI, T., German Literature
NAGAI, H., Contemporary Western Philosophy
NAKAGAWA, H., Linguistics, Oral Literature, Ainu Language and Literature
NISHIMURA, Y., Comparative Studies of Modern Art and Literature
OGATA, T., Labour Sociology, Foreign Worker Problems, Sociology of Traffic Problems
OGIHARA, S., Cultural Anthropology of Northern Asia, Ethnology of the Ainu, Oral Traditions of the Ainu and the Northern Peoples
OGURA, M., Medieval English Philology
OKAMOTO, T., Japanese Archaeology
ONO, K., American Literature
OZAWA, H., Modern and Contemporary History of Europe
SAKURAI, A., Life—History Approach, Sociology of Social Problems, Research of Japanese Minorities (Buraku People, etc.)
SATO, H., History
SUGAHARA, K., History of Tokugawa Shogunate
TAKAGI, G., Japanese Early Modern Literature
TAKAHASHI, K., Ancient Philosophy
TAKEI, H., Medical Anthropology, Cultural Anthropology, Amazonian Aboriginal Culture
TAKITO, M., Modern Japanese Literature
TOKIZANE, S., American Literature, Novel, Theory of Literature
TUTIYA, S., Philosophy, Ethics, Cognitive Science, Spoken Dialogue Studies, Document Processing
YAMASHINA, T., Middle High German
YANAGISAWA, S., Prehistory of Japan
YASUDA, H., Modern Japanese Literature

Faculty of Science:

FUNABASHI, M., Carbohydrate Chemistry
HINO, Y., Mathematical Analysis
HIROI, Y., Metamorphic Petrology
IMAMOTO, T., Organic Chemistry
INOUE, A., Clay Mineralogy
ISEZAKI, N., Geophysics
ISIMURA, R.
ITO, M., Sedimentology
ITO, T., Structural Geology
KANEKO, K., Surface Solid State Chemistry, Molecular Science, Adsorption Science
KIMURA, T., High Energy Physics
KITAZUME, M., Finite Group Theory, Algebraic Combinatorics
KOBAYASHI, K., Cell Biology
KOHORI, Y., Low-temperature Physics
KOSHITANI, S., Algebra
KOYAMA, N., Biochemistry
KURASAWA, H., Nuclear Physics
MATSUMOTO, R., Astrophysics
NAGISA, M., Operator Algebra
NAKAGAMI, J., Statistics, Mathematical Programming
NAKAMURA, K., Coding Theory, Cryptography and Information Security
NAKANO, M., Biochemistry
NAKAYAMA, T., Nanoscience
NISHIDA, T., Mineralogy
NOZAWA, S., Algebra
OBINATA, T., Developmental Biology
OGAWA, K., Nuclear Physics
OHARA, S., Environmental Geology
OHASHI, K., Cell Physiology
SAKURA, Y., Hydrogeology
TAGURI, M., Statistics
TAKAGI, R., Geometry
TAKEDA, Y., Coordination Chemistry, Solution Chemistry
TSUJI, T., Computer Software, Theory of Programmes
TUTIYA, T., Echophysiology
YAMADA, I., Solid State Physics
YAMAMOTO, K., Molecular Physiology
YANAGISAWA, A., Organic Chemistry
YASUDA, M., Statistics
WATANO, Y., Plant Biosystems, Molecular Ecology

Graduate School of Medical and Pharmaceutical Sciences:

CHIBA, T., Neurobiology

Graduate School of Medicine (1-8-1 Inohana, Chuo-Ku, Chiba-shi, Chiba 260-8670; tel. (43) 222-7171; fax (43) 226-2005; e-mail g5004@office.chiba-u.jp; internet www.m.chiba-u.ac.jp):

BUJO, H., Genome Research and Clinical Application
FUJISAWA, T., Thoracic Surgery
FUKUDA, Y., Autonomic Physiology
HARIGAYA, K., Molecular and Tumour Pathology
HATA, A., Public Health
HATTORI, T., Neurology
HIRASAWA, H., Emergency and Critical Care Medicine
ICHINOSE, M., Plastic Surgery
ISHIKURA, H., Molecular Pathology
ITO, H., Radiology
ITO, H., Urology
IWASE, H., Legal Medicine
IYO, M., Psychiatry
KIMURA, S., Biochemistry and Molecular Pharmacology
KOHNO, Y., Paediatrics
KOMURO, I., Cardiovascular Science and Medicine
KOSEKI, H., Molecular Embryology
KURIYAMA, T., Respirology
KUWAKI, T., Molecular and Integrative Physiology
MIYAZAKI, M., General Surgery
MORI, C., Bioenvironmental Medicine
MORIYA, H., Orthopaedic Surgery
NAKAYA, H., Pharmacology
NAKAYAMA, T., Medical Immunology
NISHINO, T., Anaesthesiology
NODA, M., Molecular Infectology
NOGAWA, K., Occupational and Environmental Medicine
NOMURA, F., Molecular Diagnosis
OCHIAI, T., Academic Surgery
OHNUMA, N., Paediatric Surgery
OKAMOTO, Y., Otorhinolaryngology
SAISHO, H., Medicine and Clinical Oncology
SAITO, T., Molecular Genetics
SAITO, Y., Clinical Cell Biology
SEKIYA, S., Reproductive Medicine
SHINKAI, H., Clinical Biology of Extracellular Matrix
SHIRASAWA, H., Molecular Virology
SUZUKI, N., Environmental Biochemistry
TAKIGUCHI, M., Biochemistry and Genetics
TANIGUCHI, M., Molecular Immunology
TANZAWA, H., Clinical Molecular Biology
TOKUHISA, T., Developmental Genetics
TOSHIMORI, K., Anatomy and Developmental Biology
YAMAMOTO, S., Ophthalmology and Visual Science
YAMAURA, A., Neurological Surgery
YANO, A., Infection and Host Disease

Graduate School of Pharmaceutical Sciences (1-33 Yayoi-cho, Inage-ku, Chiba-shi, Chiba 263-8522; tel. (43) 251-1111; fax (43) 290-2974):

AIMI, N., Molecular Structure and Biological Function
ARANO, Y., Radiopharmaceutical Chemistry
CHIBA, K., Pharmacology and Toxicology
HAMADA, Y., Pharmaceutical Chemistry
HORIE, T., Biopharmaceutics
IGARASHI, K., Clinical Biochemistry
ISHIBASHI, M., Natural Products Chemistry
ISHIKAWA, T., Medicinal Organic Chemistry
KOBAYASHI, H., Biochemistry
MURAYAMA, T., Chemical Pharmacology
NEYA, S., Physical Chemistry
NISHIDA, A., Synthetic Organic Chemistry
SAITOH, K., Molecular Biology and Biotechnology
SUZUKI, K. T., Toxicology and Environmental Health
TOIDA, T., Bio-analytical Chemistry
UEDA, S., Drug Information and Communication
UENO, K., Geriatric Pharmacology and Therapeutics

YAMAGUCHI, N., Molecular Cell Biology
YAMAMOTO, K., Pharmaceutical Technology
YAMAMOTO, T., Microbiology and Molecular
　Genetics
YANO, S., Molecular Pharmacology and
　Pharmacotherapeutics
Health Sciences Centre (1-33 Yayoi-cho,
Inage-ku, Chiba-shi, Chiba 263-8522; tel.
(47) 290-2210; fax (47) 290-2220; e-mail
inf@hsc.chiba-u.ac.jp; internet hschome-gw
.hsc.chiba-u.ac.jp):

NAGAO, K., Internal Medicine
Institute of Media and Information Technology (1–33 Yayoi-cho, Inage-ku, Chiba-shi,
Chiba 263-8522; tel. (43) 290-3535; fax (43)
290-3581; internet www.imit.chiba-u.jp):

KOMORI, Y., Mathematical Logic
SOHMIYA, Y., German Linguistics, Seman-
　tics, Corpus Linguistics
ZEN, H., Intelligent Information Media
International Student Centre (tel. (43) 290-
2197; fax (43) 290-2198; e-mail bm2198@
office.chiba-u.jp):

HATA, H., Teaching Japanese as a Second
　Language
NIIKURA, R., Cross-cultural Psychology
Marine Biosystems Research Centre (1
Uchiura, Amatsu-kominato-cho, Awagun,
Chiba 299-5502; tel. (47) 095-2201; fax (47)
095-2271; internet www-es.s.chiba-u.ac.jp/
kominato/index_eng.html):

MIYAZAKI, T., Aquatic Ecology
YAMAGUCHI, T., Palaeobiology
School of Nursing (1-8-1 Inohana, Chuo-Ku,
Chiba-shi, Chiba 260-8672; tel. (43) 222-
7171):

FUNASHIMA, N., Nursing Education
HONDA, A., Continuing Nursing
ISHIGAKI, K., Home Care Nursing
IWASAKI, Y., Psychiatric Nursing
KITAIKE, T., Health Science
MASAKI, H., Gerontological Nursing
MIYAZAKI, M., Community Health Nursing
MORI, M., Maternity Nursing
NAKAMURA, N., Child Nursing
OHTA, S., Gerontological Nursing
OMURO, R., Nursing Administration
SATO, R., Adult Nursing
TESHIMA, M., Hospital Nursing Care
YAMADA, S., Physiology and Biochemistry
YOSHIMOTO, T., Geriatric Community
　Nursing, Care Systems Management
Research Centre for Frontier Medical Engin-
eering:

HACHIYA, H., Medical Image Processing
IGARASHI, T., Surgical Device Design
ITO, K., Antenna Engineering
SHIMOYAMA, I., Human Neurophysiology
TATKSUOKA, H., Neuroscience
Research Centre for Pathogenic Fungi and
Microbial Toxicology (1-8-1 Inohana, Chuo-
ku, Chiba 260-8670; tel. (43) 222-7171; fax
(43) 226-2486; internet www.pf.chibau.ac.jp;
f. 1946; Dir: YUZURU MIKAMI):

FUKUSHIMA, K., Division of Fungal
　Resources and Development
KAMEI, K., Division of Fungal Infection
MIKAMI, Y., Division of Molecular Biology
　and Therapeutics
NISHIMURA, K., Division of Phylogenetics
TAKEO, K., Division of Ultrastructure and
　Function
University Hospital (1-8-1 Inohana, Chuo-
ku, Chiba-shi, Chiba 260-8670; tel. (43) 222-
7171; fax (43) 224-3830; e-mail wad6005@
office.chiba-u.jp; internet www.ho.chiba-u
.jp):

IKUSAKA, M., Dept of General Medicine
KITADA, M., Pharmacy
KOUZU, T., Dept of Endoscopic Diagnostics
　and Therapeutics
SATOMURA, Y., Medical Informatics

TONABE, M., Postgraduate Education
Centre

CHUKYO UNIVERSITY
101-2 Yagoto Honmachi, Showa-ku, Nagoya-
shi, Aichi-ken 466-8666
Telephone: (52) 835-7111
E-mail: ic@mng.chukyo-u.ac.jp
Internet: www.chukyo-u.ac.jp
Founded 1954
Pres.: KAORU KITAGAWA
Chancellor and Chair. of the Board of Dirs:
　KIYOHIRO UMEMURA
Dir of the Library: HITOSHI YASUMURA
Dir, Admin. Bureau: KAZUHIRO HANAMURA

DEANS

Faculty of English: HIROSHI YOSHIKAWA
Faculty of Economics: KIYOHIDE UMEMURA
Faculty of Law: YUKIO HIYAMA
Faculty of Letters: SUMIAKI MORISHITA
Faculty of Psychology: MAREHIRO MUKAI
Faculty of Sociology: NOBORU MATSUDA
School of Health and Sport Sciences: KAGE-
　MOTO YUASA
School of Information Science and Technol-
　ogy: HIROYASU KOSHIMIZU
School of International Liberal Studies: SUS-
　UMU ITO
School of Management: MASAAKI NAKAMURA
School of Policy Design: NOBUHIRO OKUNO

CHUO GAKUIN UNIVERSITY
451 Kujike, Abiko, Chiba 270-1196
Telephone: (4) 7183-6501
Fax: (4) 7183-6502
Internet: www.cgu.ac.jp
Founded 1900
President: TERUO OKUBO
Faculties of Commerce and Law.

EHIME UNIVERSITY
10-13 Dogo-Himata, Matsuyama City 790-
8577
Telephone: (89) 927-9000
Fax: (89) 927-9025
Internet: www.ehime-u.ac.jp
Founded 1949
Independent
Academic year: April to March (2 terms)
Pres.: MASAYUKI KOMATSU
Admin. Officer: I. KUBONIWA
Dean of Students' Affairs Office: T. SAITO
Library Dir: KOJI SANUKI
Library of 1,144,000 vols
Number of teachers: 976 full-time
Number of students: 9,858

DEANS

Faculty of Agriculture: MASAYA. SHIRAISHI
Faculty of Education: YASUNOBU KINTO
Faculty of Engineering: KOICHI SUZUKI
Faculty of Law and Arts: MOTOJI IMAIZUMI
Faculty of Medicine: KOJI HASHIMOTO
Faculty of Science: YASUNOBU YANAGISAWA
United Graduate School of Agricultural Sci-
　ences: TADAAKI WAKIMOTO

FUKUI UNIVERSITY
9-1 Bunkyo 3-chome, Fukui City 910-8507
Telephone: (776) 23-0500
Fax: (776) 27-8030
E-mail: kaiho@sec.icpc.fukui-u.ac.jp
Internet: www.fukui-u.ac.jp
Founded 1949
Independent
Academic year: April to March
Pres.: SHINPEI KOJIMA
Dir of Admin.: YUZO SATO

Librarian: TOSHIYUKI KODAIRA
Library of 453,403 vols
Number of teachers: 367
Number of students: 4,159

DEANS

Faculty of Education and Regional Studies:
　YOSHIHIKO HAYATA
Faculty of Engineering: SHINGO TAMAKI

FUKUSHIMA UNIVERSITY
1 Kanayagawa, Fukushima 960-1296
Telephone: (24) 548-8084
Fax: (24) 548-3180
E-mail: hpc@fukushima-u.ac.jp
Internet: www.fukushima-u.ac.jp
Pres.: TOSHIO KONNO
Number of students: 4,309
Faculties and Graduate Schools of Adminis-
tration and Social Sciences, Economics and
Business Administration, Human Develop-
ment and Culture, Symbiotic Systems Sci-
ence.

FUKUYAMA UNIVERSITY
985-1 Aza-Sanzou, Higashimuracho,
　Fukuyama-shi, Hiroshima 729-0292
Telephone: (84) 936-2111
Fax: (84) 936-2213
E-mail: soumu@fucc.fukuyama-u.ac.jp
Internet: www.fukuyama-u.ac.jp
Founded 1975
Chancellor: TAKASHI MIYACHI
Pres.: TAIZO MUTA
Vice-Pres: HIRAKU SHIMADA, RYUUSUKE YOSHI-
　HARA
Librarian: TOSHIRO KATAOKA
Library of 222,700 vols
Number of teachers: 240
Number of students: 5,500

DEANS

Faculty of Economics: ISAO OOKUBO
Faculty of Engineering: KAZUO KOBAYASHI
Faculty of Human Cultures: FUMIKO MAT-
　SUDA
Faculty of Life Science and Biotechnology:
　KIYOSHI SATOUCHI
Faculty of Pharmacy: SATOSHI HIBINO

GIFU UNIVERSITY
1-1 Yanagido, Gifu-shi, Gifu-ken 501-1193
Telephone: (58) 230-1111
Fax: (58) 230-2021
E-mail: gjea04007@jim.gifu-u.ac.jp
Internet: www.gifu-u.ac.jp
Founded 1949
Independent
Pres.: T. KINJOH
Sec.-Gen.: Y. KIJIMA
Librarian: T. UNO
Library of 822,409 vols, 13,000 periodicals
Number of teachers: 738 full-time
Number of students: 5,995

DEANS

Faculty of Agriculture: T. NAKAMURA
Faculty of Education: YOSHIMI SASAKI
Faculty of Engineering: H. SHIMIZU
Faculty of Regional Studies: Y. MATSUDA
School of Medicine: Y. NOZAWA

GUNMA UNIVERSITY
4–2 Aramaki-machi, Maebashi City, Gunma
371-8510
Telephone: (27) 220-7111
E-mail: s-research@jimu.gunma-u.ac.jp
Internet: www.gunma-u.ac.jp
Founded 1949

Academic year: April to March
President: MAMORU SUZUKI
Vice-Pres. for General, Financial Affairs and Facilities: HIROYUKI SHIRAI
Vice-Pres. for Research: SEIJI OZAWA
Vice-Pres. for Student Affairs: KIMIO NAKAMURA
Dir of University Hospital: YASUO MORISHITA
Dir of Management: MOTOHARU IUE
Admin.: TADEDNORI IKENOUE
Librarian: YOUICHI NAKAZATO

Library of 651,576 vols
Number of teachers: 849 full-time
Number of students: 7,021

Publication: *Journal of Social and Information Studies* (1 a year)

DEANS

Faculty of Education: TADASHI MATSUDA
Faculty of Engineering: TAKAYUKI TAKARADA
Faculty of Medicine: FUMIO GOTO
Faculty of Social and Information Studies: NOBUTAKA OCHIAI
Institute of Molecular and Cellular Regulation: ITARU KOJIMA

HIROSAKI UNIVERSITY

1 Bunkyo-cho, Hirosaki 036-8560

Telephone: (172) 36-2111
Fax: (172) 37-6594
E-mail: webmaster@cc.hirosaki-u.ac.jp
Internet: www.hirosaki-u.ac.jp

Founded 1949
Independent
Academic year: April to March

Pres.: MASAHIKO ENDO
Vice-Pres.: Y. MIZUNE
Registrar: R. SHIBATA
Librarian: E. OKAZAKI
Dir of the Hospital: S. HARATA

Number of teachers: 692
Number of students: 5,512

Publication: *School Outline* (1 a year)

DEANS

Faculty of Agriculture and Life Science: K. TOYOKAWA
Faculty of Education: H. OZAWA
Faculty of Humanities: T. TANNO
Faculty of Science and Technology: H. OHNUKI
School of Medicine: M. ENDO

PROFESSORS

Faculty of Agriculture and Life Science (3 Bunkyo-cho, Hirosaki 036-8561; internet nature.cc.hirosaki-u.ac.jp):

ANDO, Y., Entomology
AOYAMA, M., Soil Science
ARAKAWA, O., Pomology
ASADA, Y., Applied Microbiology, Microbial Technology
BOKURA, T., Agricultural Meteorology
FUKUDA, H., Horticulture
HARADA, Y., Plant Pathology
ISHIGURO, S., Biochemistry of the Eye, Developmental Biology
KANDA, K., Cooperative Study
KUDO, A., Irrigation, Drainage and Hydraulic Engineering
MAKITA, H., Vegetation Geography, Environmental Science
MIYAIRI, K., Biochemistry
MOTOMURA, Y., Science of Horticultural Bioproducts
MUTO, A., Molecular Engineering
NAKAMURA, S., Biochemical Engineering
NIIZEKI, M., Plant Breeding and Genetics
OBARA, Y., Cytogenetics
OHMACHI, T., Molecular Biology, Applied Microbiology

OKUNO, T., Organic Chemistry and Biochemistry
SASAKI, C., Agricultural Land Engineering
SAWADA, S., Plant Ecophysiology
SAWARA, Y., Animal Behaviour
SHIOZAKI, Y., Pomology
SUGIYAMA, K., Virology, Molecular Biology
SUGIYAMA, S., Crop Science, Plant Evolutionary Biology
TAKAHASHI, H., Regional Economy
TAKAMURA, K., Morphogenesis
TAKEDA, K., Microbial Ecology
TANIGUCHI, K., Rural Planning
TOYOKAWA, K., Feeds and Feeding
UNO, T., Agricultural Economics
YURUGI, M., Structural Mechanics, Construction Materials, Concrete

Faculty of Education (internet siva.cc .hirosaki-u.ac.jp):

ANDO, F., Education for Children with Disabilities
ANNO, M., Japanese History
ASANO, K., Piano
FUMOTO, N., Psychology of Sport and Physical Activity
GION, Z., Social Studies Education
HAGA, T., Clothing Science
HANDA, S., Mathematics Education
HAYAKAWA, M., Health Education
HIKAGE, Y., Home Economics Education, Laundering and Finishing
HIRAKI, K.
HIRAOKA, K., Adolescent Development, Learning Theory
HONMA, M., Movement Theory
HORIUCHI, H., Earth Materials Science
HOSHI, K., Art Education
HOSHINO, H., Condensed Matter Physics
IMAI, T., Musicology
ITOH, S., Analysis
IWAI, Y., Oil Painting, Tempera and Etching
KAMADA, K., Sedimentology
KAMIYA, K., Rural Sociology
KATO, Y., Food Chemistry
KITADA, T., Harmonic Analysis
KON, M., Differential Geometry
MARUYAMA, M., Japanese Literature
MENZAWA, K., School Health Education and Safety Education, School Health Promotion
MORI, A., School Health Education
MORI, R., Home Economics Education
MURAKAMI, O., Animal Physiology
MURAYAMA, M., Educational Methodology
NANBA, K., Algebra, Foundations of Mathematics, Discrete Mathematics
OHSHIMA, Y., Biomechanics
OHTAKA, A., Animal Taxonomy
OKADA, K., Sculpture, Clay Working (Pottery)
OKUNO, T., English Linguistics
OTA, S., Mathematics Education
OTSUBO, S., Sociology of Education
OYAMA, S., Health and Physical Education
OZAWA, H., Educational System and Administration
SAITO, S., Science Education, Phycology, Limnology
SAITO, T., History of Medieval Japan
SATO, K., Exercise Physiology
SATO, S., Adult Education
SATO, Y., Paediatrics
SATOH, Y., Magnetics
SEKI, H., Photochemistry
TAKANASHI, T., English Teaching Methodology
TANDOH, S., Educational Psychology
TOYOSHIMA, A., Social Clinical Psychology
UEDA, K., Timber Engineering
WATANABE, K., Voice
YAJIMA, T., Philosophy
YAMAGUCHI, S., Sinology
YOSHINO, H., Developmental Psychology, Psychology of Personality

Faculty of Humanities (internet human.cc .hirosaki-u.ac.jp):

AKAGI, K., Public Economics, Law and Economics
ARAI, K., Behavioural Accounting
CARPENTER, V., International Politics
FUJINUMA, K., Japanese Archaeology
FUJITA, M., Business Behaviour, Public Utilities
FUNAKI, Y., Statistics and Operations Research
HASEGAWA, S., Early Modern Japanese History
HORIUCHI, T., Constitutional Law
HOSHINO, Y., Accounting and Control
IGARASHI, Y., Ethics
ISHIDOU, T., English, American Literature, American Studies, Robert Frost, Mark Twain, McCarthyism
KATORI, K., Science of Information and Systems
KITAJIMA, S., Regional Economy and Regional Policy
MOROOKA, M., Science of Religion
MURAMATSU, K., Political Theory
MURATA, S., English Literature
NAKAZAWA, K., Western Economic History
NITTA, S., Modern German Literature
OKAZAKI, E., Philosophy
OKUNO, K., Linguistics
PHILIPS, J. E., History of Africa, America and Islam
SAKUMICHI, S., Social Psychology, Anthropology
SATO, N., English Literature
SATOH, K., Japanese Linguistics
SHIMUZU, A., Philosophy of Information
SHINOMIYA, T., Business History
SUDO, H., History of Art
SUGIYAMA, Y., Cultural Anthropology
SUZUKI, K., Economic Theory
TANAKA, I., German Literary Arts
TERADA, M., French Literature
UEKI, H., Chinese Classical Literature
USUDA, S., Japanese Literature
WARASHINA, K., Japanese Language
YASUDA, M., Marketing

Faculty of Science and Technology (3 Bunkyo-cho, Hirosaki 036-8561; internet www.st .hirosaki-u.ac.jp):

AMENOMORI, M., Cognitive Science, Superhigh Energy Physics
ARAKI, T., Applied Electronics
FUKASE, M., VLSI Computer
FURUYA, Y., Intelligent Materials Design and Systems, Materials Processing, Solid State Sensors and Actuators, Non-destructive Evaluation
GOTO, T., Applied Chemistry
IIKURA, Y., Instrumentation Physics, Remote Sensing
INAMURA, T., Spray Engineering and Combustion, Propulsion Engineering
ITO, A., Combustion, Fire Science, Multiple Phase Flow
ITO, S., Organic Syntheses
KATO, H., Solid State Physics, Synchrotron-Radiation Science
KAWAGUCHI, S., Cosmic-ray Physics
KURAMATA, A., Space Physics
KURATSUBO, S., Harmonic Analysis
MAKINO, E., Micro Electromechanical Systems
MASHITA, M., Thin Film and Surface Physics
MIYATA, H., Solid Mechanics, Fracture Mechanics, Strength Evaluation Systems
MORI, T.
MOTOSE, K., Algebra
NAKAZATO, H., Functional Analysis
NANJO, H., High Energy Astrophysics
NENCHEV, D. N., Robotics
OHZEKI, K., Analytical Chemistry

RIKIISHI, K., Physical Oceanography, Meteorology, Glaciology
SAITO, M., Computational Science Approach to Biomolecular Recognition
SAKISAKA, Y., Solid State Physics, Synchrotron-radiation Science
SASAKI, K., Surface Physics
SATO, H., Phase Transformation, Plastic Deformation
SATO, T., Raman Spectra
SATO, T., Seismology
SHIBA, M., Disaster Prevention Geology
SHIMIZU, T., Bioinformatics, Biophysics
SUDO, S., Physical Chemistry
SUTO, S., Physical Chemistry of Polymers
TAJIRI, A., Organic Physical Chemistry
TAKAGUCHI, M., Matrix Analysis
TAKEGAHARA, K., Theoretical Solid State Physics
TANAKA, K., Physical Vulcanology, Seismology
TSURUMI, M., Environmental Chemistry, Geochemistry
UJIIE, Y., Petroleum Geology, Organic Geology
YOSHIOKA, Y., Computer Networks, Computer Architecture
YOSHIZAWA, A., Organic Materials Science

School of Medicine (53 Hon-cho, Hirosaki 036-8563; internet hippo.med.hirosaki-u.ac.jp):

ABE, Y., Radiation Oncology
ENDO, M., Glycobiology of Glycoconjugates
HADA, R., Medical Informatics
HANADA, K., Sun Protection, Laser Therapy, Atopic Dermatitis, Photodynamic Therapy
ICHIMARU, T., Medical Apparatus and Engineering
ICHINOHE, T., Paediatric Nursing, Guidance in Nursing Practice
ITO, E., Paediatric Haematology and Oncology
IWASAKI, A., Medical (Radiation) Physics
KACHI, T., Anatomy
KAGIAYA, A., Obstetrics and Gynaecology
KAMIYA, H., Immunopathology of Parasitic Infection
KANEKO, S., Epiteptology, Clinical and Basic Neuropsychopharmacology
KAWAHARA, R., Gerontological Nursing
KIKUCHI, H., Endocrinology
KIMURA, H., Oral and Maxillo-facial Surgery
KIMURA, K., Nursing of Adults
KUDO, H., Tumour Pathology
KURATA, K., Neurophysiology
KURODA, N., Forensic Pathology
MATSUKI, A., Anaesthesiology, Intensive Care, Pain Clinic
MATSUMOTO, M., Neurophysiology
MATSUNAGA, M., Clinical Neurology, Neuroepidemiology
MINAGAWA, T., Cancer Nursing
MITA, R., Public Health
MIURA, H., Existence Philosophy, Medical Philosophy and Ethics
MIURA, T., Orthopaedic Surgery, Rehabilitation Medicine
MIZUSHIMA, Y., Respirology, Gerontology
MOTOMURA, S., Cardiovascular Pharmacology
MUNAKATA, A., Gastroenterology
MUNAKATA, H., Paediatric Surgery
NAKAMURA, T., Chronic Pancreatitis, Pancreatic Steatorrhoea, Pancreatic Diabetes, Gastric Emptying, Clinical Laboratory Medicine
NAKANE, A., Bacteriology, Immunology
NAKAZAWA, M., Basic and Clinical Research for Retinal Diseases
NIKARA, T., Physiology
OHGUSHI, Y., Nursing Science
OKUMURA, K., Internal Medicine, Cardiology

SASAKI, J., Tumour Immunology, Pathogenic Bacteriology, Food Science
SASAKI, M., Surgery for Digestive Diseases, Hepato-pancreaticobiliary Surgery, Liver Transplantation
SATO, T., Pathology
SATO, Y., Neuroscience
SATOH, K., Basic Studies on the Pathogenesis of Cerebrovascular Diseases
SATOH, K., Biochemistry, Enzymology, Chemical Larcinogenesis
SAWADA, Y., Study of Wound Healing, Burns, Hypertrophic Scan and Keloids, Microcirculation of the Flap
SEIMIYA, Y., Analysis of Daily Activity
SHINKAWA, H., Inner and Middle Ear Morphology, Middle Ear Surgery
SHOMURA, K., Neural Anatomy
SUDA, T., Endocrinology and Metabolism
SUGAMARA, K., Pharmacological and Pharmaceutical Drugs Interaction
SUGAWARA, K., Physical Fitness, Nutrition, Immunology
SUZUKI, S., Neurosurgery, Cerebrovascular Diseases
SUZUKI, T., Oncology of the Urogenital Region
TAKAHASHI, G., Microscopic Anatomy, Cell Biology
TATEISHI, T., Clinical Pharmacology, Pharmacokinetics and Pharmacodynamics
TSUCHIDA, S., Cancer Biochemistry, Biochemical Pharmacology
TSUSHIMA, H., Physical Therapy
WADA, K., Clinical Research in Adult Epilepsy
WAKABAYASHI, K., Neuropathology
WAKUI, M., Cellular Physiology
WAKUI, M., Physiology I
YAGIHASHI, S., Pathology
YAMABE, H., Nephrology
YAMADA, C., Community Health, Public Health, International Health, International Cooperation
YASUJIMA, M., Laboratory Medicine, Hypertension
YODONO, H., Research of Interventional Radiology
YONESAKA, S., Paediatric Cardiology

ATTACHED RESEARCH INSTITUTES

Center for Computing and Communications: 3 Bunkyo-Cho, Hirosaki 036-8561; Dir Y. YOSHIOKA.

Center for Education and Research of Lifelong Learning: 1 Bunkyo-cho, Hirosaki 036-8560; Dir S. SATO.

Center for Educational Research and Practice: 1 Bunkyo-cho, Hirosaki 036-8560; Dir K. FUKIGAI.

Center for Joint Research: 3 Bunkyo-cho, Hirosaki 036-8561; Dir A. TAJIRI.

Earthquake and Volcano Observatory: 3 Bunkyo-cho, Hirosaki 036-8561; Dir K. TANAKA.

Gene Research Center: 3 Bunkyo-cho, Hirosaki 036-8561; Dir M. NIIZEKI.

Institute of Brain Science: 5 Zaifu-cho, Hirosaki 036-8562; Dir M. MATSUNAGA.

Institute for Experimental Animals: 5 Zaifu-cho, Hirosaki 036-8562; Dir H. KAMIYA.

University Farms: 7-1 Shitafukuro, Fujisaki-machi, Aomori-ken 038-3802; Dir T. NOMURA.

HIROSHIMA UNIVERSITY

3-2 Kagamiyama 1-chome, Higashi-Hiroshima 739-8511

Telephone: (82) 422-7111
Fax: (82) 424-6179
E-mail: inquiry@office.hiroshima-u.ac.jp

Internet: www.hiroshima-u.ac.jp/index-j.html

Founded 1949
Independent
Academic year: April to March (2 semesters)

Pres.: TOSHIMASA ASAHARA
Exec. Vice-Pres. for Education: M. SAKAKOSHI
Exec. Vice-Pres. for Research: E. TSUCHIYA
Exec. Vice-Pres. for Public Relations and Academic Information: T. OKAMOTO
Exec. Vice-Pres. for International Affairs: Y. YAMANE
Exec. Vice-Pres. for Medical Affairs: M. OCHI
Exec. Vice-Pres. for Finance and General Affairs: T. KAWAMOTO
Vice-Pres. for Student Support: N. KAWASAKI
Vice-Pres. for Library: K. TOMINAGA

Library of 3,367,718 vols, incl. 1,305,786 in foreign languages
Number of teachers: 1,766
Number of students: 15,463

Publications: *Agricultural and Fisheries Economics of Hiroshima University, Bulletin of Setouchi Field Science Centre Graduate School of Biosphere Science Hiroshima University, Bulletin of the Department of Teaching Japanese as a Second Language, Bulletin of the Faculty of Education, Bulletin of the Faculty of School Education, Bulletin of the Graduate School of Education, Bulletin of the Graduate School of Engineering, Bulletin of the Graduate School of Integrated Arts and Sciences, Bulletin of the Institute for the Cultural Studies of the Seto Inland Sea, Bulletin of Training and Research Centre for Clinical Psychology, Bulletin of Research Centre for Educational Study and Practice, Bulletin of the Research Centre for the Technique of Representation, Daigaku ronshu: Research in Higher Education, Essay on Modern Literature, Etudes de Langue et Littérature françaises de l'Université de Hiroshima, Hiroshima Forum for Psychology, Hiroshima Interdisciplinary Studies in the Humanities, Hiroshima Journal of Ethnological Studies, Hiroshima Journal of Mathematics Education, Hiroshima Journal of Medical Sciences, Hiroshima Law Review, Hiroshima Papers on Society and Culture, Hiroshima Peace Science, Hiroshima Psychological Research, Hiroshima Studies in English Language and Literature, Hiroshima Studies in Language and Language Education, Hiroshima University Management Review, IPSHU Research Report Series, Journal of Health Sciences, Journal of Hiroshima University Archives, Journal of International Cooperation in Education, Journal of International Development and Cooperation, Journal of Japan Academy of Neonatal Nursing, Journal of Learning and Curriculum Development, Journal of Learning Science, Journal of the Faculty of Applied Biological Science, Hiroshima University, Journal of the Graduate School of Biosphere Science, Journal of the Hiroshima University Curriculum Research and Development Association, The Annals of Educational Research, The Annals of the Research Project Centre for the Comparative Study of Logic, The Annual of research on Early Childhood, The Bulletin of the Centre for Research on Regional Economic Systems, The Bulletin of the Centre for Special Needs Education Research and Practice, The Economic Studies, The Hiroshima Economic Review, The Hiroshima Economic Studies, The Hiroshima Law Journal, The Hiroshima University studies, Faculty of Letters, The Hiroshima University studies, Graduate School of Letters, The Journal of Ethical Studies, The Journal of Hiroshima University Dental Soci-*

ety, *The Journal of Social and Cultural Studies on Asia, The Review of the Study of History, Medical journal of Hiroshima Universtiy, Memoirs of the Faculty of Integrated Arts and Sciences, Reviews in Higher Education, Review of Japanese Studies, Scientific report of the Laboratory for Amphibian Biology, Seikei Ronso: The Journal of Politics and Economics of Hiroshima University, Studies in European and American Culture*

DEANS

Faculty of Dentistry: Prof. T. TAKATA
Faculty of Medicine: Prof. M. YOSHIZUMI
Faculty of Pharmaceutical Sciences: Prof. H. OTSUKA
Graduate School of Advanced Sciences of Matter: Prof. T. TAKABATAKE
Graduate School of Biomedical Sciences: Prof. M. KOBAYASHI
Graduate School of Biosphere Sciences: Prof. M. ESAKA
Graduate School of Education: Prof. K. TANAHASHI
Graduate School of Engineering: Prof. F. YOSHIDA
Graduate School of Health Sciences: Prof. S. KAWAMATA
Graduate School of of Integrated Arts and Sciences: Prof. O. KASHIHARA
Graduate School for International Development and Cooperation: Prof. H. IKEDA
Graduate School of Letters: Prof. H. YAMAUCHI
Graduate School of Science: Prof. H. DEGUCHI
Graduate School of Social Sciences: Prof. S. TOMIOKA
Hiroshima University Hospital: Prof. K. CHAYAMA (Dir)
Hiroshima University Law School: Prof. M. KINOSHITA

PROFESSORS

Faculty of Integrated Arts and Sciences (7-1 Kagamiyama 1-chome, Higashi-Hiroshima 739-8521; tel. (82) 422-7111; fax (82) 424-0751; e-mail souka-bucho-sien@office .hiroshima-u.ac.jp; internet home .hiroshima-u.ac.jp/souka/e/ias.html):

Division of Area Studies:

FUJITA-SANO, M., Cultural Anthropology, American Studies
IIDA, M., English Literature and Culture
ITOH, S., American Literature and Culture
KASHIHARA, O., Modern Japanese Literature
KOHATA, F., Biblical Studies
KUSUNOSE, M., Modern Chinese History
MIKI, N., Contemporary Chinese Culture
OKAMOTO, M., American Social History
SATAKE, A., Japanese History and Culture
SATO, M., History of German Literature, Everyday Life and Customs in the Early Modern Age
TAKATANI, M., Cultural Anthropology, Southeast Asian Studies

Division of Behavioural and Biological Sciences:

ANDO, M., Integrative Physiology
FURUKAWA, Y., Neurobiology
HORI, T., Psychophysiology
IWATA, K., Comparative Politics and Diplomacy
KAWAHARA, A., Developmental Biology
KUSUDO, K., History of Sport
SEIWA, H., Psychology of Personality
TSUTSUI, K., Brain Science
URA, M., Social Psychology
WADA, M., Biochemistry of Exercise
YAMASAKI, M., Exercise Physiology

Division of Creative Arts and Sciences:

GOLDSBURY, P. A., Philosophy of Language, Comparative Culture

HARA, M., Comparative Philosophy and Music Aesthetics
KOTOH, T., Comparative Philosophy
MURASE, N., French Theatre, French Studies
NAKAMURA, H., Shakespeare, Cinema Studies, Cultural Semiotics
SAITO, T., Modern Science and Mysticism
TAKAHASHI, N., Ancient Greek Philosophy

Division of Language and Culture:

ANIYA, S., Linguistics
HIGUCHI, M., English Philology
IMAZATO, C., History of the English Language, Lexicography
INOUE, K., Linguistics
KOBAYASHI, H., Applied Linguistics, TESOL
NISHIDA, T., Applied Linguistics
OGAWA, Y., Comparative Study of Japanese and Chinese
SKAER, P. M., Linguistics
TANAKA, S., German Literature
YAMADA, J., Psycholinguistics
YOON, K. B., Korean Literature
YOSHIDA, M., Linguistics

Division of Materials Science:

FUKAMIYA, N., Bioactive Natural Products Chemistry
HATAKENAKA, N., Theoretical Condensed Matter Physics
HIKOSAKA, M., Soft Materials Physics
HOSHINO, K., Condensed Matter Physics
ITOH, T., Molecular Spectroscopy and Quantum Chemistry
KOJIMA, K., Condensed Matter Physics
KOMINAMI, S., Biophysical Chemistry
NAGAI, K., Theoretical Solid State Physics
TAKEDA, T., Condensed Matter Physics
UDAGAWA, M., Condensed Matter Physics

Division of Mathematical and Information Sciences:

AGAOKA, Y., Differential Geometry
HARADA, K., Geometry Graphics
KUWADA, M., Experimental Design
MIZUTA, Y., Function Theory
YOSHIDA, K., Applied Analysis

Division of Natural Environmental Sciences:

FUKUOKA, M., Research of Earth Resources
HAYASE, K., Environmental Sciences
HONDA, K., Chemical Ecology
HORIKOSHI, T., Microbiology
KAIHOTSU, I., Hydrology
NAKAGOSHI, N., Landscape Ecology
NARISADA, K., Science Studies
OHO, Y., Environmental Geology
SAKURAI, N., Environmental Plant Physiology
TOGASHI, K., Applied Ecology

Division of Socio-Environmental Studies:

AKIBA, S., Rural Sociology
FUKIHARA, S., Regions and Economy
ICHIKAWA, H., History of Technology
YASUNO, M., Contemporary History

Graduate School of Biosphere Sciences:

NAKANE, K., Environmental Ecosystem Ecology
SAKUGAWA, H., Environmental Chemistry

Graduate School of Education (1-1 Kagamiyama 1-chome, Higashi-Hiroshima 739-8524; tel. (82) 422-7111; fax (82) 422-7171; e-mail kyoiku-kyo-sien@office.hiroshima-u .ac.jp; internet www.ed.hiroshima-u.ac.jp/ index.html):

Doctoral Programme in Learning and Curriculum Development; and Master's Programme in Learning Science—Learning Development Major:

DOBASHI, T., Lifespan Developmental Education
HIGUCHI, S., Philosophy and Aesthetics of Learning
ISHII, S., Environmental Psychology

MORI, T., Psychology of Learning
NISHINE, K., Sociology of Education
TAKAHASHI, S., Social Psychology

Doctoral Programme in Learning and Curriculum Development; and Master's Programme in Learning Science—Curriculum and Instruction Development Major:

KIHARA, S., Physical Education
KIMURA, H., Social Studies Education
KUROSE, M., Keyboard Music
MAEDA, S., Human Geography
MATSUDA, Y., Psychology of Physical Education
MOCHIZUKI, T., Food Science
MORITA, N., Japanese Language Education
SHIBA, K., Science Education
TAINOSHO, J., Home Economics Education
WAKAMOTO, S., Art Education

Doctoral Programme in Learning and Curriculum Development; and Master's Programme in Special Education:

FUNATSU, M., Psychology of Children with Disabilities
HAYASAKA, K., Speech and Language Pathology
OCHIAI, T., Special Educational Systems, Inclusive Education
SHIMIZU, Y., Audiology and Education of Children with Hearing Impairment
YAMANASHI, M., Methods of Teaching Children with Visual Impairment

Doctoral Programme in Arts and Science Education; and Master's Programme in Science, Technology and Science Education—Science Education Major:

FURUKAWA, Y., Solid State Chemistry, Magnetic Resonance
HAYASHI, T., Regional Geology, Geoinformatics, Earth Science Education
KADOYA, S., Science Education
MAEHARA, T., Particles and Fields, Physics Education
SUZUKI, M., Petrology
TANAKA, H., Inorganic Chemistry
TOKUNAGA, T., Solid State Physics
TORIGOE, K., Zoology, Biology Education
TSUTAOKA, T., Solid State Physics
YAMASHITA, Y., Nuclear Physics, Physics Education

Doctoral Programme in Arts and Science Education; and Master's Programme in Science, Technology and Science Education—Mathematics Education Major:

IMAOKA, M., Geometry
IWASAKI, H., Mathematics Education
KAGEYAMA, S., Statistics and Combinatorics
MARUO, O., Algebra
NAKAHARA, T., Mathematics Education

Doctoral Programme in Arts and Science Education; and Master's Programme in Science, Technology and Science Education—Technology and Information Education Major:

BANSHOYA, K., Woodworking
MONDEN, Y., Computer Science
TASHIMA, S., Mechanical Processing
UEDA, K., Technology Educations
YAMAMOTO, T., Computer Control Technology

Doctoral Programme in Arts and Science Education; and Master's Programme in Science, Technology and Science Education—Social Studies Education Major:

IKENO, N., Social Studies Education
KATAKAMI, S., Social Studies Education
KOBARA, T., Social Studies Education
MIYAKE, T., Modern Japanese History
NAKAYAMA, T., Medieval Japanese History
OBI, T., Eastern History
SATO, S., Western History

SHIMOMUKAI, T., Ancient and Medieval Japanese History
TANAHASHI, K., Social Studies Education

Doctoral Programme in Arts and Science Education; and Master's Programme in Language and Culture Education—Japanese Language and Culture Education Major:

EBATA, Y., Japanese Language
IWASAKI, F., Japanese Literature
TAKAHASHI, K., Linguistic Geography
TAKEMURA, S., Japanese Literature
YOSHIDA, H., Japanese Language Education

Doctoral Programme in Arts and Science Education; and Master's Programme in Language and Culture Education—English Language and Culture Education Major:

FUKAKAWA, S., Pragmatics, Classroom Research
HAMAGUCHI, O., American Literature
MIURA, S., English Language Education
NAKAO, Y., English Philology and Linguistics
TANAKA, M., Language Testing in English Language Teaching

Doctoral Programme in Arts and Science Education; and Master's Programme in Language and Culture Education—Japanese Pedagogy, Linguistics and Culture Studies Major:

KURACHI, A., Intercultural Education
MACHI, H., Study of Japanese Composition and Style
MIZUMACHI, I., Educational Language Technology
MIZUSHIMA, H., Comparative Cultures and Comparative Literature
NAKAMURA, S., Japanese Intellectual History
NUIBE, Y., Japanese Language Pedagogics
NUMOTO, K., Historical Study of Japanese Language
SAKODA, K., Second Language Acquisition
TAWATA, S., Japanese Linguistics and Japanese Language Education

Doctoral Programme in Arts and Science Education; and Master's Programme in Lifelong Activities Education—Health and Sports Sciences Education Major:

ESASHI, Y., Physical Education
KUROKAWA, T., Sports Training
KUSUDO, K., History of Sport
MATSUOKA, S., Physical Education
WATANABE, K., Physiology, Sports Biomechanics
YANAGIHARA, E., Kinematical Analysis in Sport (Ball Games)

Doctoral Programme in Arts and Science Education; and Master's Programme in Lifelong Activities Education—Human Life Sciences Education Major:

HIRATA, M., Management of Life
IKAWA, Y., Science of Food Preparation
IWASHIGE, H., House Environment Science
MIYAMOTO, S., Clothing Science
SHIBA, S., Home Economics Education

Doctoral Programme in Arts and Science Education; and Master's Programme in Lifelong Activities Education—Music Culture Education Major:

CHIBA, J., Musicology
KUROSE, M., Keyboard Music
OKANO, S., Piano
OKUDA, M., Vocal Music
YOSHITOMI, K., Music Education

Doctoral Programme in Arts and Science Education; and Master's Programme in Lifelong Activities Education—Art Education Major:

ESAKI, A., Product Design
SUGAMURA, T., Science of Arts (History of Japanese Arts)

UCHIDA, M., Drawing and Painting

Doctoral Programme in Education and Human Science; and Master's Programme in Educational Studies:

KOGA, K., Educational Administration and Policy
KOHNO, K., Studies of Educational Leadership
KOIKE, G., Adult and Continuing Education
NAKANO, K., Curriculum Research
NINOMIYA, A., Comparative Education
OKATO, T., Educational Management
OTSUKA, Y., Comparative Education
SAKAKOSHI, M., Educational Thought and Philosophy in Germany
SATOH, H., History of Japanese and Eastern Education
TORIMITSU, M., Early Childhood Education
YAMASAKI, H., Sociology of Higher Education
YASUHARA, Y., History of Western Education

Doctoral Programme in Education and Human Science; and Master's Programme in Psychology:

FUKADA, H., Social Psychology
KODAMA, K., Clinical Psychology
MAEDA, K., Developmental Psychology
MIYATANI, M., Cognitive Psychology
OKAMOTO, Y., Developmental Clinical Psychology
TOSHIMA, T., Neuropsychology
YAMAZAKI, A., Child Psychology

Doctoral Programme in Education and Human Science; and Master's Programme in Higher Education Research and Development:

ARIMOTO, A., Sociology of Higher Education
DAIZEN, T., Sociology of Higher Education
HATA, T., History of Higher Education in Japan
KITAGAKI, I., Education Technology, Fuzzy Science
YAMAMOI, A., Sociology of Higher Education

Graduate School of Advanced Sciences of Matter (3-1 Kagamiyama 1-chome, Higashi-Hiroshima 739-8530; tel. (82) 422-7111; fax (82) 424-7000; internet www.hiroshima-u.ac.jp/en/adsm/):

Department of Molecular Biotechnology:

HIRATA, D., Molecular Biology
KATO, J., Molecular Environmental Biotechnology
KINASHI, H., Microbiology and Natural Product Chemistry
KURODA, A., Biochemistry
MIYAKAWA, T., Molecular Biotechnology in Yeast
NISHIO, N., Environmental Bioengineering
ONO, K., Molecular Biochemistry
TSUCHIYA, E., Molecular Cell Biology
YAMADA, T., Plant/Microbe Interactions

Department of Quantum Matter:

ENDO, I., Photon Physics
JO, T., Theory of Condensed Matters
KADOYA, Y., Solid State Quantum Optics
OGUCHI, T., Computational Physics
OKAMOTO, H., Beam Physics
SERA, M., Experimental Researches of Strongly Correlated Electron Systems
SUZUKI, T., Low Temperature Physics
TAKABATAKE, T., Magnetism and Magnetic Materials
TAKAHAGI, T., Nanotechnology

Department of Semiconductor Electronics and Integration Science:

IWATA, A., Integrated Circuits
MIURA-MATTAUSCH, M., Semiconductor Device Technology
MIYAZAKI, S., Semiconductor Electronics

Graduate School of Biomedical Sciences (2-3 Kasumi 1-chome, Minami-ku, Hiroshima 734-8513; tel. (82) 257-5555; fax (82) 257-5278; e-mail bimes-kyou@office.hiroshima-u.ac.jp; internet www.hiroshima-u.ac.jp/bimes/):

Programmes for Applied Biomedicine:

AKAGAWA, Y., Advanced Prosthodontics, Implantology
EBOSHIDA, A., Public Health and Health Policy, Health Science, Epidemiology, Environmental Health
HAMADA, T., Geriatric Dentistry, Prosthodontics, Stomatognathic Dysfunction
HIRAKAWA, K., Otorhinolaryngology, Head and Neck Surgery and Oncology, Rhinology
INAI, K., Pathology, Tumour Pathology
ITO, K., Radiology, Diagnostic Imaging, Interventional Radiology
KAMATA, N., Oral and Maxillofacial Surgery
KANBE, M., Clinical Laboratory Medicine, Clinical Physiology, ME, Medical Informatics, Gene Engineering
KAWAHARA, M., Dental Anaesthesiology, Pain Clinic
KIMURA, K.
KOBAYASHI, M., Paediatrics, Child Health
KOHNO, N., Molecular and Internal Medicine, Respiratory Diseases, Cancer Therapeutics
KOZAI, K., Paediatric Dentistry
KUDO, Y., Obstetrics and Gynaecology
MAEDA, N., Oral Growth and Developmental Biology, Development of Masticatory System
MORIKAWA, N., Clinical Pharmacotherapy, Pharmacokinetics, Therapeutic Drug Monitoring
OCHI, M., Orthopaedic Surgery, Sports Medicine, Knee Surgery
OZAWA, K., Pharmacotherapy, Clinical Pharmacology
SUEDA, T., Surgery, Thoracic and Cardiovascular Surgery, Bioengineering
TAKAHASHI, I., Preventive Dentistry, Mucosal Immunology
TANIGAWA, K., Emergency and Critical Care Medicine, Cardiopulmonary Resuscitation, Airway Management, Free Radicals and Reperfusion Injury
TANIMOTO, K., Oral and Maxillofacial Radiology, Dysphagia
TANNE, K., Orthodontics and Craniofacial Developmental Biology, Biomechanics
YAJIN, K., Otorhinolaryngology, Head and Neck Surgery, Head and Neck Oncology, Rhinology
YOSHIZAWA, K., Infectious Disease Control and Prevention, Seroepidemiology of Viral Hepatitis
YUGE, O., Anaesthiology and Critical Care

Programmes for Biomedical Research:

AOYAMA, H., Anatomy and Developmental Biology
ASAHARA, T., Surgery, Gastroenterological Surgery, Organ Transplantation
CHAYAMA, K., Medicine and Molecular Science, Gastroenterology, Hepatology
DOHI, T., Dental Pharmacology
HAZEKI, O., Physiological Chemistry, Cellular Signal Transduction
HIDE, M., Dermatology, Allergology and Immunopharmacology in Skin
IDE, T., Cellular and Molecular Biology
KANNO, M., Immunology, Parasitology, Molecular Immunology
KATAOKA, K., Histology and Cell Biology, Histochemistry and Cell Biology of the Digestive Organs
KATO, Y., Dental and Medical Biochemistry, Biochemistry and Oral Biology
KIKUCHI, A., Biochemistry, Intracellular Signal Transduction

KURIHARA, H., Periodontal Medicine, Periodontal Tissue Regeneration, Endodontology

KURISU, K., Neurosurgery, Neuro-oncology, Neuroradiology, Surgery of Brain Tumours and Cerebro-vascular Disease, Skull Base Surgery

MASUJIMA, T., Analytical Molecular Medicine and Devices, Videonanoscopes, Cell Dynamics, Pharmaco-dynamics, Bioanalysis

MATSUMOTO, M., Clinical Neuroscience and Therapeutics, Neurology, Strokology, Gerontology

MISHIMA, H., Ophthalmology and Visual Science, Glaucoma, Ocular Cell Biology, Ocular Pharmacology, Retinal Disease

OGATA, N., Neurophysiology

OHTA, S., Xenobiotic Metabolism and Molecular Toxicology, Neurochemistry, Drug Metabolism

OKAMOTO, T., Molecular Oral Medicine and Maxillofacial Surgery

OKAZAKI, M., Biomaterials Science, Dental Materials

SAKAI, N., Molecular and Pharmacological Neuroscience, Molecular Neurobiology, Neuropharmacology

SHIBA, Y., Oral Physiology

SUGAI, M., Bacteriology, Oral Microbiology

SUGIYAMA, M., Molecular Microbiology and Biotechnology, Antibiotics, Enzymology, Molecular Genetics, Applied Microbiology

TAKATA, T., Oral Maxillofacial Pathobiology, Oral Oncology, Periodontal Tissue Engineering, Diagnostic Pathology

UCHIDA, T., Oral Biology, Oral Anatomy

USUI, T., Urology, Andrology, Oncology, Endo-urology

YAMAWAKI, S., Psychiatry and Neurosciences, Biological Psychiatry, Psychopharmacology, Affective Disorders, Neuroleptic Malignant Syndrome, Psychosomatic Medicine, Liaison Psychiatry, Psycho-oncology

YASUI, W., Molecular Pathology, Molecular Pathology of Gastrointestinal Cancer

YOSHIDA, T., Virology, Paramyxovirus, Bacteriology

YOSHIZUMI, M., Cardiovascular Physiology and Medicine, Cardiology and Vascular Biology

Programmes for Pharmaceutical Sciences:

KOIKE, T., Functional Molecular Sciences, Medicinal Chemistry, Bioinorganic Chemistry

NAKATA, Y., Pharmacology, Neuropharmacology, Molecular Pharmacology

OOTSUKA, H., Pharmacognosy and Natural Product Chemistry, Molecular Pharmaceutics

TAKANO, M., Pharmaceutics and Therapeutics, Drug Transporters and Metabolizing Enzymes, Drug Delivery Systems

TAKEDA, K., Synthetic Organic Chemistry, Mechanistic Organic Chemistry, Synthetic Methodology

Graduate School of Biosphere Sciences (4-4 Kagamiyama 1-chome, Higashi-Hiroshima 739-8528; tel. (82) 424-7905; fax (82) 424-2459; e-mail sei-bucho-sien@office .hiroshima-u.ac.jp; internet home .hiroshima-u.ac.jp/gsbstop/english/top/ index-e.html):

Department of Bioresource Science and Technology:

ESAKA, M., Function and Biosynthesis of Ascorbic Acid in Plants

FUJITA, M., Environmental Physiology of Farm Animals

FURASAWA, S., Basic and Applied Immunobiology

GOTO, N., Enology and Viticulture

GUSHIMA, K., Foraging Ecology of Coral Reef Fishes

HORI, K., Structures, Functions and Applications of Lectins from Marine Organisms

IEFUJI, H., Environmental and Food Biotechnology

IMABAYASHI, H., Larval Settlement of Benthic Organisms

KATO, N., Nutrition and Cancer

KONO, K., Cellular Immunology

MATSUDA, H., Chicken Monoclonal Antibodies

MITANI, K., Holistic Management of Farm Animals

MIZUTA, K., Molecular and Cellular Biology of Yeast

NAGAMATSU, Y., Applied Biochemistry of Microbial Proteins

NAKANO, H., Behaviour and Control of Foodborne Bacterial Pathogens

NISHIMURA, T., Structure and Function of Proteases in Muscle Foods

OHTA, T., Physiological Phenomena and Molecules, Identification and Mechanism Analysis

SATO, K., Physical Chemistry of Lipids

SUZUKI, K., Emulsifying Characteristics and Properties of Food Emulsions

SUZUKI, N., Bio-organic Chemistry, Active Oxygen, Antioxidative Activity, Bio- and Chemiluminescence

TANIGUCHI, K., Ruminant Nutrition and Feeding

TERADA, T., Nuclear Transfer in the Bovine and Porcine Embryo

TSUDUKI, M., Animal Breeding and Genetics

YOSHIMURA, Y., Endocrine Control of Avian Reproductive Functions

Department of Environmental Dynamics and Management:

FUJITA, K., Source–Sink Relationship

HOSHIKA, Y., Mechanism of Material Circulation and its Control in Coastal Seas

ISEKI, K., Marine Ecology and Biogeochemical Cycle

KONO, K., Biology and Fertility of Soils

MARAYAMA, T., Biology of Symbiotic Relationships between Marine Invertebrates and Micro-organisms, Biology of Hyperthermophiles

MASAOKA, Y., Enhancement of Metal Stress Tolerance in Plants

NAKANE, K., Environmental Chemistry

SAKUGAWA, H., Environmental Ecosystem Ecology

TAKASUGI, Y., Monitoring and Diagnosis of the Physical Environment in Semi-enclosed Sea

UYE, S., Production Ecology of Marine Zooplankton

YAMAMOTO, K., Microbial Ecology and Marine Ecology

YAMAMOTO, T., Aquatic Environmental Management

YAMAUCHI, M., Development of Ecophysiological Soil and Water Management Technology for Environmental Protection

Department of Sciences for Biospheric Co-existence:

NAKAI, T., Fish-pathogenic Bacteria and Viruses

TANAKA, H., Consumer Food Cooperatives

UEMATSU, K., Neural Basis for Fish Swimming

YAMAO, M., Locally Based Coastal Resource Management in Asia, Sustainable Coastal Fisheries Management and 'Code of Conduct for Responsible Production', People's Participation in Community Development and their Responsibility, Development and

Export-oriented Food Production and its Impact on the Resource Environment

Graduate School of Engineering (4-1 Kagamiyama 1-chome, Higashi-Hiroshima 739-8527; tel. (82) 422-7111; fax (82) 422-7039; internet www.eden.hiroshima-u.ac.jp):

Mechanical Systems Engineering:

ISHIZUKA, S., Combustion Science and Technology

KIKUCHI, Y., Heat Transfer, Biomass Energy, Carbon Nanotube

KUROKI, H., Powder Metallurgy and Ceramics

MAEKAWA, H., Fluid Engineering

NAGAMURA, K., Machine Elements, Gear Design and Vibration, Tribology

NAKAGAWA, N., Dynamics of Machines

NAKASA, K., Strength and Fracture of Materials, Vibration and Sound, Acoustic Energy

OBA, F., Manufacturing Systems

SAEKI, M., Automatic Control

SAWA, T., Strength of Material, Elasticity, Solid Mechanics

SHINOZAKI, K., Welding and Joining

SHIZUMA, K., Quantum Energy Applications

TAKI, S., Reactive Gas Dynamics

TAKIYAMA, K., Plasma Spectroscopy

YAMANE, Y., Machining, Machine Tools and Mechatronics

YANAGISAWA, O., Control of Material Properties

YOSHIDA, F., Engineering Elasto-Plasticity

Artificial Complex Systems Engineering:

HINAMOTO, T., Electronic Control, Digital Signal Processing

IWASE, K., Mathematical Statistics and Data Analysis

KADO, T., Nano-electronics

KANEKO, M., Robotics, Active Sensing

NAKANO, K., Computer Engineering

NISHIZAKI, I., Decision Analysis and Game Theory

SAKAWA, M., Systems Optimization

SHIBATA, T., Differential Equations and their Application

TAKAHASHI, K., Production Systems Engineering

TSUJI, T., Biological Systems Engineering

YOKOGAWA, K., Computational Materials Science

YORINO, N., Electric Power System Engineering

Information Engineering:

DOHI, T., Systems Reliability Engineering

HARADA, K., Graphics Geometry

HIRASHIMA, T., Computer-based Learning Environment

KUBO, F., Algebraic Deformation Theory

KUWADA, M., Experimental Designs

MORITA, K., Theoretical Computer Science

SHIBA, M., Complex Analysis and its Applications

WATANABE, T., Computer Science and Information Technology

Chemistry and Chemical Engineering:

ASAEDA, M., Separation and Purification Technology

HARIMA, Y., Materials Physical Chemistry

HIROKAWA, T., Applied Instrumental Analysis

KUNAI, A., Organic Materials Chemistry

OKADA, M., Environmental Chemical Engineering

OKUYAMA, K., Thermal Fluids Engineering

OTSUBO, T., Applied Organic Chemistry

SAKOHARA, S., Polymer Technology

SHIONO, T., Advanced Polymer Chemistry

TAKISHIMA, S., Chemical Engineering Thermodynamics

YAMANAKA, S., Applied Inorganic Materials Chemistry

YOSHIDA, H., Fine Particle Technology

Social and Environmental Engineering:

DOI, Y., Marine Hydrodynamics
FUJIKUBO, M., Strength of Structures
FUJIMOTO, Y., Reliability of Structures and Systems
KANEKO, A., Ocean–Atmosphere Environment
KAWAHARA, Y., Hydraulic Engineering
KITAMURA, M., Computational Mechanics for Structural Design
KOSE, K., Management of Human-Technology–Environment Systems
MATSUO, A., Building Structures
MIURA, K., Building Disasters Prevention
MURAKAWA, S., Community Environmental Science
NAKAMURA, H., Structural Engineering
OHKUBO, T., Building Materials and Components
SASAKI, Y., Soil Mechanics and Earthquake Geotechnical Engineering
SATO, R., Concrete and Concrete Structural Engineering
SUGANO, S., Earthquake Engineering
SUGIE, Y., Transportation Planning
SUGIMOTO, T., Architectural History and Design Theory
TAKAKI, M., Ocean Space Engineering
TSUCHIDA, T., Geotechnical and Geo-environmental Engineering
YASUKAWA, H., Naval Architecture
YOKOBORI, H., Architecture, Urban Planning and International Cooperation

Graduate School for International Development and Co-operation (5-1 Kagamiyama 1-chome, Higashi-Hiroshima 739-8529; tel. (82) 424-6905; fax (82) 424-6904; e-mail idec@hiroshima-u.ac.jp; internet home.hiroshima-u.ac.jp/idec):

Division of Development Science:

FUJIWARA, A., Transportation Planning, Environmental Engineering
HIGO, Y., Ocean Engineering
KINBARA, T., Management and Organization
KOMATSU, M., Development Economics
MATSUOKA, S., Environmental Economics
NAKAZONO, K., International Relations
NOHARA, H., Comparative Study of Industrial Organizations
SAITO, K., Marine Development Technology
TOMINAGA, K., Disaster Prevention on Geotechnical Engineering

Division of Educational Development and Cultural and Regional Studies:

IKEDA, H., Content-based Science Education (Biology Education), International Cooperation in Science Education
KASAI, T., Motor Neurophysiology and Motor Rehabilitation Medicine
TABATA, Y., Educational Administration (Educational System, Teacher Education)
UEHARA, A., Intercultural Communication

Graduate School of Letters (2-3 Kagamiyama 1-chome, Higashi-Hiroshima 739-8522; tel. (82) 422-7111; fax (82) 424-0315; e-mail bun-kyo-sien@office.hiroshima-u.ac.jp; internet home.hiroshima-u.ac.jp/bungaku/index.html):

ARIMOTO, N., Modern and Contemporary Japanese Literature
FURUSE, K., Archaeology
HARANO, N., French Language and Literature
ICHIKI, T., Chinese Philosophy
IMADA, Y., Linguistics
ITOH, K., Medieval Japanese Literature
ITOH, S., American Literature and Culture
IWAI, T., Ancient History of Europe
JIMURA, A., English Language Studies

KANO, M., Chinese Linguistics
KATSUBE, M., Japanese Modern History
KAWAHARA, T., German Plays and Opera
KISHIDA, H., Ancient and Medieval Japanese History
KONDO, Y., History of Ethical Thought
KUBOTA, K., Modern and Contemporary Japanese Literature
MATSUI, F., History of Ethical Thought, Bioethics
MATSUMOTO, M., Japanese Language Studies
MATSUMOTO, Y., French Language and Literature
MIURA, M., History of Japanese Architecture
MIZUTA, H., History of Western Philosophy
NAKAMURA, H., Shakespeare, Cinema Studies, Cultural Semiotics
NISHIBEPPU, M., Ancient History of Japan
NOMA, F., History of Ancient and Medieval Chinese Thought
OCHI, M., Ethics
OKAHASHI, H., Human Geography, Regional Geography
OKAMOTO, A., Modern and Contemporary Western History
OKUMURA, K., Physical Geography, Quaternary Geology
SATO, T., Chinese Literature
SODA, S., Modern Chinese History
TANAKA, H., Modern Contemporary American Literature
TOMINAGA, K., Chinese Literature
UEDA, Y., Linguistics
UEKI, K., English Literature
UEMURA, Y., Asian History
YAMASHIRO, H., Medieval Western History
YAMAUCHI, H., Western Philosophy
YOSHINAKA, T., English Literature

Graduate School of Medicine (2-3 Kasumi 1-chome, Minami-ku, Hiroshima 734-8553; tel. (82) 257-5555; fax (82) 257-5278; e-mail bimes-kyou@office.hiroshima-u.ac.jp; internet www.hiroshima-u.ac.jp/hsc/):

Health Sciences:

INAMIZU, T., Sports Medicine and Sciences
INOUE, M., Gastroenterology, Gastrointestinal Physiology and Treatment of Acid-related Diseases
KAKEHASHI, M., Health Science, Health Statistics, Mathematical Modelling, Public Health
KATAOKA, T., Health Care for Adults
KAWAMATA, S., Anatomy of Musculoskeletal System, Anatomy of Calcified Tissue
KINJYO, T., Geriatric Nursing
KOBAYASHI, T., Health Development
MATSUKAWA, K., Physiology, Neural Control of the Cardiovascular System, Motor Control
MIYAGUCHI, H., Occupational Behavioural Science Laboratory
MIYAKOSHI, Y., Fundamentals of Nursing Theory and Practice, Nursing Management and Education
MORIYAMA, M., Medical–Surgical Nursing, Adult Health Nursing
MURAKAMI, T., Rheumatoid Surgery, Elbow Surgery, Sports Medicine
OKAMURA, H., Psycho-oncology, Psychosocial Rehabilitation
ONO, M., Community Health and Home Care Nursing
SHIMIZU, H., Science of Occupational Therapy
SHINKODA, K., Physical Therapy, Kinesiology
TANAKA, Y., Paediatrics, Health Science, Nursing Education
TOBIMATSU, Y., Rehabilitation Medicine and Science for the Elderly and People with Disabilities
TSUSHIMA, H., Community and School Health Nursing

URABE, Y., Athletic Rehabilitation
YAMAKATSU, H., Occupational Therapy for Physical Dysfunction and ADL Disorder
YOKOO, N., Neonatal Nursing, Maternal and Child Health Nursing, Midwifery
YUGE, R., Nerve and Muscle Regeneration

Graduate School of Science (3-1 Kagamiyama 1-chome, Higashi-Hiroshima 739-8526; tel. (82) 422-7111; fax (82) 424-0709; e-mail ri-bucho-sien@office.hiroshima-u.ac.jp; internet www.sci.hiroshima-u.ac.jp/english):

Mathematics:

ENOMOTO, H., Graph Theory, Discrete Mathematics
KAMADA, S., Knots, Topology
MATSUMOTO, M., Galois Group, Arithmetic Fundamental Group, Random Number Generation
MATUMOTO, T., Topology
MIZUTA, Y., Potential Theory
MORITA, T., Dynamic Systems, Ergodic Theory
NAGAI, T., Differential Equations
TSUZUKI, N., Arithmetic Geometry, Number Theory
YOSHINO, M., Differential Equations

Physical Science:

HASHIMOTO, E., Physics of Perfect Crystals, Synchrotron Radiation Physics
HIRAYA, A., Molecular Photophysics and Photochemistry
HORI, T., Particle Accelerator Physics, Synchrotron Radiation Physics
KOJIMA, Y., Theory of Relativity and Astrophysics
MARUYAMA, H., Solid State Physics, X-Ray Spectroscopy
NAMATAME, H., Solid State Physics, Synchrotron Radiation Physics
OHSUGI, T., High Energy Particle Physics, Gamma-ray Astrophysics
OKAWA, M., Elementary Particle Theory, Lattice QCD
SUGITATE, T., High Energy Nuclear Physics
TANAKA, K., Photochemistry and Photophysics
TANIGUCHI, M., Solid State Physics, Synchrotron Radiation Science

Chemistry:

AIDA, M., Quantum Chemisty
EBATA, T., Laser Chemistry and Molecular Spectroscopy
FUJIWARA, T., Analytical Chemistry
FUKAZAWA, Y., Organic Stereochemistry
INOUE, K., Molecular Magnetism
MIYOSHI, K., Coordination and Organometallic Chemistry
OHKATA, K., Synthesis and Isolation of Natural Products
OHNO, K., Physical Chemistry and Vibrational Spectroscopy
YAMAMOTO, Y., Organic Main Group Element Chemistry
YAMASAKI, K., Chemical Kinetics and Dynamics

Biological Science:

DEGUCHI, H., Plant Taxonomy and Ecology, Bryology
HOSOYA, H., Cell Biology, Signal Transduction
MICHIBATA, H., Molecular Physiology
SUZUKI, K., Molecular Genetics, Yeast and Agrobacterial Genetics
TAKAHASHI, Y., Plant Molecular Biology
YOSHIZATO, K., Developmental Biology, Regeneration Biology

Earth and Planetary Systems Science:

HIDAKA, H., Isotope Geochemistry
SHIMIZU, H., Trace Element Geochemistry
TAJIMA, F., Solid Earth Geophysics
WATANABE, M., Ore Petrology and Ore Genesis

Mathematical and Life Sciences:

GEKKO, K., Physical Chemistry of Biopolymers

HIRATA, T., Biological Chemistry and Biotechnology

IDE, H., DNA Damage and Repair

KOBAYASHI, R., Self-organization in Material and Life Science

MORIKAWA, H., Molecular Plant Biology

NISHIMORI, H., Complex Systems and Nonlinear Dynamics

SAKAMOTO, K., Dynamical Systems

TANIMOTO, Y., Magneto-science

YAMAMOTO, T., Molecular Developmental Biology

YOSHIDA, K., Partial Differential Equations

Marine Biological Laboratory:

YASUI, K., Development and Bio-history of Marine Deuterostomes

Miyajima Natural Botanical Garden:

DEGUCHI, H., Plant Taxonomy and Ecology, Bryology

Institute for Amphibian Biology:

KASHIWAGI, A., Endocrine Disruptors, Space Biology, Apoptosis, Transgenesis

SUMIDA, M., Evolutionary Genetics, Molecular Phylogeny

YAOITA, Y., Developmental Biology, Metamorphosis, Programmed Cell Death

Laboratory of Plant Chromosome and Gene Stock:

KONDO, K., Plant Demography, Chromosome Science and Gene Resources

Graduate School of Social Sciences (Higashi-Hiroshima Campus: 2-1 Kagamiyama 1-chome, Higashi-Hiroshima 739-8525 Higashi-Senda Campus: 1-89 Higashisenda-machi 1-chome, Hiroshima 730-0053; tel. (82) 422-7111 (Higashi-Hiroshima), (82) 542-7014 (Higashi-Senda); fax (82) 424-7212 (Higashi-Hiroshima), (82) 542-6964 (Higashi-Senda); e-mail syakai-bucho-sien@office.hiroshima-u.ac.jp):

AGAOKA, Y., Medieval Western History
AIZAWA, Y., Private International Law
EGASHIRA, D., Sociology
FUKIHARU, T., Microeconomics
FUTAMURA, H., Public Finance
GINAMA, I., Macroeconometrics
HINO, S., Product Development Theory
HOSHINO, I., Financial Accounting
INOUE, Z., Management (Strategy Theory)
ISHIDA, M., International Finance
ITOH, T., Economic Policy
KAN, T., Fiscal Policy
KANNO, R., Finance
KATOH, F., Occidental Economic History
KAWASAKI, N., Public Administration
MAEKAWA, K., Financial Econometrics
MAKINO, M., Political History
MATSUDA, M., Political Economy
MATSUMIZU, Y., World Economic Conditions
MATSUIKE, H., Criminal Law
MATSUURA, K., Finance and Econometrics
MORIBE, S., Japanese Politics
MORIOKA, T., Labour Economics
MORITA, K., Comparative Economic Systems
MURAMATSU, J., Marketing Theory
NISHIMURA, H., Constitutional Law
NISHITANI, H., International Law
NOMOTO, R., Industrial Organization
ODAKI, M., Statistics
OKAMURA, M., International Economics, Applied Microeconomics
OTANI, T., Sociology of Law
SAKAGUCHI, K., Management Accounting
SAKANE, Y., Economic History of Japan
TAKAHASHI, H., Civil Law
TAKI, A., Industrial Relations
TERAMOTO, Y., Diplomacy and Diplomatic History

TODA, T., Regional Development Policy
TOMIOKA, S., Economic History
TSUBAKI, Y., Information Resource Management
TSUJI, H., Labour Law
UEDA, Y., Public Choice and Institutional Economics
WAKIMOTO, S., Economic Policy
WATANABE, M., Social Policy
YAMADA, S., History of Political Thought
YANO, J., Macroeconomics
YOSHIDA, O., Asian Politics
YOSHIHARA, T., Legal History

Law School (1-89 Higashisenda 1-chome, Hiroshima 730-0053; tel. (82) 542-7014; fax (82) 542-6964; e-mail senda-bk-sien@office.hiroshima-u.ac.jp; internet www.law.hiroshima-u.ac.jp/lawschool/ls-top.htm):

GOTOH, K., Commercial Law
HIRANO, T., Legal Philosophy
KAMITANI, Y., Civil Law
KATAGI, H., Commercial Law
KINOSHITA, M., Commercial Law
KOHAMA, S., Civil Law
KOHARI, Y., International Law
MITSUI, M., Labour Law
MONDEN, T., Constitutional Law
NAKA, T., Administrative Law
ODA, N., Criminal Law
OHKUBO, T., Criminal Procedure
OKAMOTO, T., Civil Law
SAEKI, Y., Administrative Law
TANABE, M., Civil Procedure
TORIYABE, S., Civil Law

Research Institute for Radiation Biology and Medicine (2-3 Kasumi 1-chome, Minami-ku, Hiroshima 734-8553; tel. (82) 257-5555; fax (82) 255-8339; e-mail bimes-gen@office.hiroshima-u.ac.jp; internet www.rbm.hiroshima-u.ac.jp/index.html):

HONDA, H., Developmental Biology
HOSHI, M., Radiation Biophysics
INABA, T., Molecular Oncology, Haematology
KAMIYA, K., Radiation Biology, Oncology
KIMURA, A., Haematology and Oncology
MATSUURA, S., Human Genetics
MIYAGAWA, K., Molecular Oncology
NISHIYAMA, M., Molecular Oncology, Preclinical Development
OHTAKI, M., Biometrics, Environmetrics
SUZUKI, F., Radiation Biology
TAKIHARA, Y., Stem Cell Biology, Haematology, Regenerative Medicine
TASHIRO, S., Molecular Cell Biology

ATTACHED INSTITUTES

Beijing Research Centre: College of International Education, Capital Nomal University, 105 Xisanhuan Beilu, Beijing 00037, China; Dir T. SATO.

Centre for the Study of International Co-operation in Education: 5-1 Kagamiyama 1-chome, Higashi-Hiroshima 739-8529; Dir A. NINOMIYA.

Collaborative Research Centre: 10-31 Kagamiyama 3-chome, Higashi-Hiroshima 739-0046; Dir Y. YAMANE.

Community Co-operation Centre: 3-2 Kagamiyama 1-chome, Higashi-Hiroshima 739-8511; Dir T. ANDO.

Environmental Research and Management Centre: 5-3 Kagamiyama 1-chome, Higashi-Hiroshima 739-8513; Dir S. OTA.

Health Service Centre: 7-1 Kagamiyama 1-chome, Higashi-Hiroshima 739-8511; Dir M. YOSHIHARA.

Hiroshima Synchrotron Radiation Centre: 313 Kagamiyama 2-chome, Higashi-Hiroshima 739-8526; Dir M. TANIGUCHI.

Information Media Centre: 4-2 Kagamiyama 1-chome, Higashi-Hiroshima 739-8526; Dir T. WATANABE.

Institute for Peace Science: 1-89, Higashisenda-machi 1-chome, Naka-ku, Hiroshima 730-0053; Dir M. MATSUO.

International Student Centre: 1-2 Kagamiyama 1-chome, Higashi-Hiroshima 739-8523; Dir S. TAWADA.

Natural Science Centre for Basic Research and Development: 3-1 Kagamiyama 1-chome, Higashi-Hiroshima 739-8526; Dir I. YAMASHITA.

Research Centre for Nanodevices and Systems: 4-2 Kagamiyama 1-chome, Higashi-Hiroshima 739-8527; Dir A. IWATA.

Research Centre for Regional Geography: 2-3 Kagamiyama 1-chome, Higashi-Hiroshima 739-8522; Dir H. OKAHASHI.

Research Institute for Higher Education: 2-2 Kagamiyama 1-chome, Higashi-Hiroshima 739-8521; Dir A. ARIMOTO.

Saijo Seminar House: Misonou, Saijo-cho, Higashi-Hiroshima 739-0024; Dir S. TAKAHASHI.

HITOTSUBASHI UNIVERSITY

2-1 Naka, Kunitachi-city, Tokyo 186-8601
Telephone: (42) 580-8000
Fax: (42) 580-8006
Internet: www.hit-u.ac.jp
Independent
Founded 1875
Academic year: April to March
Pres.: HIROMITSU ISHI
Vice-Pres.: JYURO TERANISHI
Dir-Gen.: SAKASHI KAMATA
Dean of Students: TAKEHIKO SUGIYAMA
Librarian: MAKOTO IKEMA
Library of 1,739,884 vols
Number of teachers: 465 full-time
Number of students: 6,429

Publications: *The Hitotsubashi Review* (12 a year), *Hitotsubashi Journal of Commerce and Management* (1 a year), *Hitotsubashi Journal of Economics* (2 a year), *Hitotsubashi Journal of Law and Politics* (1 a year), *Hitotsubashi Journal of Social Studies* (2 a year), *Hitotsubashi Arts and Sciences* (1 a year), *Gengo Bunka—Cultura Philologica* (1 a year)

DEANS

Graduate School and Faculty of Commerce and Management: K. ITO
Graduate School and Faculty of Economics: E. TAJIKA
Graduate School and Faculty of Law: T. YAMAUCHI
Graduate School and Faculty of Social Sciences: N. TASAKI
Graduate School of International Corporate Strategy: H. TAKEUCHI
Graduate School of Language and Society: Y. SANO

ATTACHED INSTITUTES

Institute of Economic Research: Tokyo; f. 1940; 41 teachers; Dir M. KUBONIWA; publ. *Economic Review* (4 a year).

Institute of Innovation Research: Tokyo; f. 1997; 11 teachers; Dir S. NAGAOKA; publ. *Hitotsubashi Business Review* (4 a year).

HOKKAIDO UNIVERSITY

Kita 8 Nishi 5, Kita-ku, Sapporo 060-0808
Telephone: (11) 706-8027
Fax: (11) 706-8036
E-mail: info@oia.hokudai.ac.jp
Internet: www.hokudai.ac.jp
Founded 1876
Independent
Academic year: April to March

Pres.: Prof. HIROSHI SAEKI
Vice-Pres.: Prof. MASAAKI HEMMI
Vice-Pres.: Prof. TADAYUKI HAYASHI
Vice-Pres.: Prof. HISATAKE OKADA
Vice-Pres.: Prof. MINORU WAKITA
Vice-Pres.: Prof. TAKEO HONDOH
Dir-Gen.: KAZUO SHIMANUKI
Dir of Univ. Library: Prof. TAKAHIKO NITTA
Dir of Univ. Hospital: Prof. SATOSHI FUKUDA
Library of 3,795,300 vols
Number of teachers: 2,093
Number of students: 18,226
Publication: *Hokudai Jiho* (12 a year)

DEANS

Faculty of Advanced Life Science: ISAO
TANAKA
Faculty of Fishery and Fisheries Sciences:
NAOTSUNE SAGA
Faculty of Pharmaceutical Sciences: AKIRA
MATSUDA
Graduate School and Faculty of Education:
SHINICHI TOKORO
Graduate School and Faculty of Science:
KEIZO YAMAGUCHI
Graduate School and Research Faculty of
Agriculture: AKIHITO HATTORI
Graduate School of Chemical Sciences and
Engineering: NOBORU KITAMURA
Graduate School of Dental Medicine: YASU-
NORI TOTSUKA
Graduate School of Economics and Business
Administration: KAZUO MACHINO
Graduate School of Engineering: TAKASHI
MIKAMI
Graduate School of Environmental Science
and Faculty of Environmental Earth Sci-
ence: TOSHIO IWAKUMA
Graduate School of Health Sciences and
Faculty of Health Sciences: SEIICHI
KOBAYASHI
Graduate School of Information Science and
Technology: MASAHITO KURIHARA
Graduate School of International Media,
Communication and Tourism Studies and
Research Faculty of Media and Communi-
cation: SHYUUICHI SUGIURA
Graduate School of Law: NOBUHISA SEGAWA
Graduate School of Letters: KAZUYORI
YUHAZU
Graduate School of Life Science: AKIRA
MATSUDA
Graduate School of Medicine: KAZUNORI
YASUDA
Graduate School of Veterinary Medicine:
SHIGEO ITO
Public Policy School: KENICHI NAKAMURA

PROFESSORS

Faculty and School of Fisheries Science (3-1-
1 Minato-cho, Hakodate; tel. (13) 840-5505;
fax (13) 843-5015; e-mail shomu@fish
.hokudai.ac.jp; internet www.fish.hokudai.ac
.jp):

ABE, S., Aquagenomics and Resources
Management
ADACHI, S., Molecular Cell Biology and
Histology
ARAI, K., Genetics, Genomics and Develop-
mental Biology
GOSHIMA, S., Marine Ecology; Behaviour;
Benthos
GOTO, A., Evolutionary Biology of Fishes
HARA, A., Comparative Biochemistry of
Fish Serum Protein
HIROYOSHI, K., Fisheries Business Econom-
ics
IIDA, K., Underwater Acoustics; Fisheries
and Plankton Acoustics; Bio-Acoustics
IKEDA, T., Zooplankton Ecology
ISSHIKI, K., Food Safety; Food Protection
ITABASHI, Y., Lipid Chemistry and Chro-
matography
KAERIYAMA, M., Conservation Ecology; Sal-
monology; Fish Ecology

KAWAI, Y., Food Preservation; Food Chem-
istry; Food Hygiene
KIMURA, N., Fishing Informatics; Seakeep-
ing Qualities of Fishing Vessels
KISHI, J., Numerical Modelling of Marine
Ecosystems
KONNO, K., Marine Food Science
KUMA, K., Chemical Oceanography and
Marine Biogeochemistry
MEGURO, T., Marine Biology
MIURA, T., Scientific Gears for Fish Sam-
pling
MIYASHITA, K., Liquid Oxidation and Anti-
oxidant
MONTANI, S., Biogeochemical Oceanog-
raphy
NAKAYA, K., Phylogeny; Taxonomy; Sharks
OJIMA, T., Molecular Biology and Biotech-
nology of Marine Organisms
OKAMOTO, J., Fisheries Policy
SAEKI, H., Health Benefit of Marine Food
Proteins and Marine Food Allergy
SAGA, N., Marine Biology; Developmental
Biology
SAITOH, S., Satellite Oceanography
SAKURAI, Y., Marine Ecology; Reproductive
Ecology of Marine Fish and Cephalopods
SIGA, N., Zooplankton Taxonomy and Ecol-
ogy
TAKAGI, Y., Mechanism of Biomineraliza-
tion
TAKAHASHI, K., Conversion of Fisheries By-
products into Value Added Products
TAKAHASHI, T., Life History of Righteye
Flounders
YABE, M., Systematic Ichthyology
YANADA, M., Marine Organic Chemistry
YOSHIMIZU, M., Viral and Bacterial Fish
Diseases
YOSHIMURA, Y., Control and Design of
Fishing Boats and Fisheries Machinery

Faculty of Advanced Life Science (Kita 10,
Nishi 8, Kita-ku, Sapporo; tel. (11) 716-3026;
fax (11) 756-1244; e-mail shomu@sci.hokudai
.ac.jp; internet www.lfsci.hokudai.ac.jp):

AYABE, T., Innate Intestinal Immunity
DEMURA, M., Membrane Protein NMR and
Bioinformatics
IGARASHI, Y., Sphingolipid Biology and
Biochemistry
KAMO, N., Biophysical Chemistry
KODA, T., Molecular Biology
KOIKE, T., Molecular and Cellular Neuro-
biology
NAITO, S., Molecular Genetics
NISHIMURA, S., Advanced Chemical Biology
OBUSE, C., Molecular and Cellular Biology
SEYA, T., Microbiology and Immunology
SUGAHARA, K., Glycoscience and Glycobiol-
ogy
TAKAHASHI, T., Reproductive Biology
TANAKA, I., Protein Crystallography
YAMASHITA, M., Reproductive Biology
YAMAGUCHI, J., Plant Biology and Biochem-
istry
YAZAWA, M., Biochemistry

Faculty of Education (Kita 11, Nishi 7, Kita-
ku, Sapporo; tel. (11) 707-6586; fax (11) 706-
4951; e-mail shomu@edu.hokudai.ac.jp;
internet www.hokudai.ac.jp/educat):

ANEZAKI, Y., Higher and Continuing Edu-
cation
AOKI, O., Education and Poverty
CHEN, S., Developmental Psychology of
Infancy
KAWAGUCHI, A., Prevention and Health
MIYAZAKI, T., Adult Education
MIZUNO, M., Muscle Physiology
MUROHASHI, H., Clinical Cognitive Neu-
roscience
NISHIO, T., History of Physical Education
and Sport
OHTSUKA, Y., Health Resort Medicine
ONAI, T., Sociology of Education
SATO, K., Psychology of Learning

SHINDO, S., Teaching Methods for Physical
Education
SUDA, K., Teaching Methods for Math-
ematics
SUZUKI, T., Community Adult Education
TANAKA, Y., Developmental Psychopathol-
ogy
TOKORO, S., Comparative History of Edu-
cation
TSUBOI, Y., Educational Administration
YANO, T., Physiology of Exercise

Faculty of Environmental Earth Science
(Kita 10, Nishi 5, Kita-ku, Sapporo; tel. (11)
728-4715; fax (13) 706-4867; e-mail somu@
ees.hokudai.ac.jp; internet www.ees.hokudai
.ac.jp):

FUGETSU, B., Ion/Membrane Interactions
HASEBE, F., Weather/Oceanic Physics/
Hydrology; Environmental Dynamic
Analysis
HIGASHI, S., Animal Ecology
HIRAKAWA, K., Landform Development
under Periglacial and Glacial Environ-
ment; Active Tectonics and Paleo-mega-
tsunamis
IKEDA, M., Effects of Ocean and Sea Ice on
Climate Variability
IWAKUMA, T., Ecology/Environment; Envir-
onmental Dynamic Analysis; Resource
Maintenance Studies
KIMURA, M., Ecology/Environment; Animal
Physiology/Behaviour Heredity/Genome
Dynamics
KOHYAMA, T., Maintenance Mechanisms of
Species Diversity; Scale Issue of Forest
Ecosystem Response to Global Change
KUBOKAWA, A., Weather/Oceanic Physics/
Hydrology
MATSUDA, F., Synthetic Organic Chemistry
and Natural Product Chemistry
MINAGAWA, M., Isotope Biogeochemistry
MORIKAWA, M., Applied Microbiology; Liv-
ing Organism Molecular Science
NAKAMURA, H., Organic Chemistry/Phys-
ical Chemistry/Analytical Chemistry
NORIKI, S., Analytical Chemistry; Earth
Astrochemistry; Environmental
Dynamic Analysis
OHARA, M., Evolution of Life History of
Plants and Conservation
OKUHARA, T., Environmental Catalyst
ONO, Y., Environmental Geography
SAKAIRI, N., Synthetic Carbohydrate
Chemistry
SHIMAZU, K., Environmental Chemistry;
Functional Material Chemistry
SUGIMOTO, A., Environmental Dynamic
Analysis; Earth Astrochemistry; Wea-
ther/Oceanic Physics/Hydrology
TANAKA, S., Analytical Chemistry; Envir-
onmental Technology/Environmental
Material
TAKADA, T., Ecology/Environment
YAMAZAKI, K., Weather/Oceanic Physics/
Hydrology
YOSHIKAWA, H., Environmental Dynamic
Analysis; Weather/Oceanic Physics/
Hydrology

Faculty of Pharmaceutical Sciences (Kita 12,
Nishi 6, Kita-ku, Sapporo; tel. (11) 706-3486;
fax (11) 706-4989; e-mail shomu@pharm
.hokudai.ac.jp; internet www.pharm.hokudai
.ac.jp):

ARIGA, H., Molecular Biology
HARASHIMA, H., Molecular Design of Phar-
maceutics
HASHIMOTO, S., Synthetic and Industrial
Chemistry
INAGAKI, F., Structural Biology
ISEKI, K., Clinical Pharmaceutics and
Therapeutics
KOBAYASHI, J., Natural Products Chemis-
try
MATSUDA, A., Medicinal Chemistry
MATSUDA, T., Hygienic Chemistry

MINAMI, M., Pharmacology
MIURA, T., Analytical Chemistry
SATO, Y., Fine Synthetic Chemistry
SHUTO, S., Organic Chemistry for Drug Development
SUZUKI, T., Neuroscience
YOKOSAWA, H., Biochemistry

Faculty of Public Policy (Kita 9, Nishi 7, Kita-ku, Sapporo; tel. (11) 706-3074; fax (11) 706-4948; e-mail shomu@juris.hokudai.ac.jp; internet www.hops.hokudai.ac.jp):

ISHII, Y., Regional Policy
KEN ENDO, I., International Politics
KURATA, K., Technology Policy
MATSUURA, M., Japanese Political History
MIYAWAKI, A., Public Administration
NAKAMURA, K., International Politics
NAKATSUJI, T., Transportation and Traffic Engineering
SASAKI, T., International Political Economy
SHIBATA, F., Social Security Administration
SHUNJI KANIE, S., Structural Mechanics
WATARI, T., Administrative Law
YAMADA, H., Macroeconomic Policy
YAMAGUCHI, J., Public Administration
YAMAZAKI, M., Local Government and Politics
YOSHIDA, F., Environmental Economics

Faculty of Science (Kita 10, Nishi 8, Kita-ku, Sapporo; tel. (11) 716-3026; fax (11) 756-1244; e-mail shomu@sci.hokudai.ac.jp; internet www.sci.hokudai.ac.jp):

AIKAWA, H., Potential Theory
AMITSUKA, H., Condensed Matter Physics
ARAI, A., Mathematical Physics
FUJIMOTO, M., Theoretical Physics
FUJINO, K., Mineralogy
GONG, J., Polymer Science
HAYASHI, M., Function Theory
HEKI, K., Space Geodesy
HINATSU, Y., Solid State Chemistry
HORIGUCHI, T., Phycology and Protistology
IDO, M., Solid State Physics
IKEDA, R., Geophysical Hydrology
INABE, T., Solid State Chemistry
ISHIKAWA, G., Geometry
ISHIKAWA, K., Theoretical Physics
ISHIMORI, K., Structural Chemistry
IZUMIYA, S., Geometry
JIMBO, S., Applied Analysis, Partial Differential Equations
KASAHARA, M., Seismology and Geodesy
KATAKURA, H., Speciation of Terrestrial Invertebrates
KATO, A., Plant Molecular Genetics
KATO, K., Nuclear Physics
KATO, M., Coordination Chemistry
KAWABATA, K., Biophysics
KAWAMOTO, N., Theoretical Physics
KAWANO, K., Structural Biology
KISHIMOTO, A., Operator Algebra
KITAMURA, N., Analytical Chemistry
KOIKE, K., Solid State Physics
KOYAMA, J., Solid Earth Science
KOZASA, T., Astrophysics and Planetary Science
KUMAGAI, K., Solid State Physics
KURAMOTO, K., Planetary Science
MATSUOU, M., Philosophy of Science
MAWATARI, S., Taxonomy of Invertebrates
MINOBE, S., Physical Oceanography, Climate and Meteorology
MOGI, T., Subsurface Geophysics
MURAKOSHI, K., Material Chemistry
NAGASAKA, Y., Theory of Function
NAKAGAWA, M., Volcanology and Petrology
NAKAMURA, G., Inverse Problems, Partial Differential Equations
NAKAMURA, I., Algebraic Geometry
NAKAZI, T., Functional Analysis
NOMURA, K., Solid State Physics
OHKAWA, F., Theoretical Physics
OIKAWA, H., Bio-organic Chemistry
ONO, K., Differential Geometry and Topology

ONODERA, A., Solid State Physics
OZAWA, T., Partial Differential Equations
SAKAGUCHI, K., Biological Chemistry
SASAKI, N., Tissue Science and Mechanobiology
SAWAMURA, M., Organometallic Chemistry
SUGIYAMA, S., History of Science
SUZUKI, N., Molecular Cell Biology
SUZUKI, N., Organic Geochemistry
SUZUKI, T., Physical Organic Chemistry
TAKAHATA, M., Behavioural Physiology
TAKEDA, S., Physical Chemistry
TAKESHITA, T., Structural Geology and Tectonics
TAKETSUGU, T., Quantum Chemistry
TANINO, K., Synthetic Organic Chemistry
TERAO, H., Combinatorics, Singularities
UOSAKI, K., Physical Chemistry
URANO, A., Neuroendocrinology
WATANABE, S., Planetary Atmosphere
YAMAGUCHI, K., Differential Geometry
YAMAMOTO, K., Plant Physiology
YAMAMOTO, S., Condensed-Matter Theory
YAMASHITA, H., Representation Theory
YOMOGIDA, K., Seismology
YOSHIDA, T., Group Theory and Combinatorics
YURI, M., Complex Systems and Ergodic Theory
YURIMOTO, H., Geochemistry

Graduate School of Dental Medicine (Nishi 7, Kita 13, Kita-ku, Sapporo 060-8586; tel. (11) 706-4313; fax (11) 706-4919; e-mail d-syomu@jimu.hokudai.ac.jp; internet www.den.hokudai.ac.jp):

FUKUSHIMA, K., Oral Pathobiological Science
IIDA, J., Oral Functional Science
INOUE, N., Oral Health Science
KAWANAMI, M., Oral Health Science
KITAGAWA, K., Oral Pathobiological Science
MORITA, M., Oral Health Science
NAKAMURA, M., Oral Pathobiological Science
OHATA, N., Oral Functional Science
SANO, H., Oral Health Science
SHIBATA, K., Oral Pathobiological Science
SHINDOH, M., Oral Pathobiological Science
SUZUKI, K., Oral Pathobiological Science
TAMURA, M., Oral Health Science
TOTSUKA, Y., Oral Pathobiological Science
WATARI, F., Oral Health Science
YAWAKA, Y., Oral Functional Science
YOKOYAMA, A., Oral Functional Science

Graduate School of Economics and Business Administration (Kita 9, Nishi 7, Kita-ku, Sapporo; tel. (11) 706-4058; fax (11) 706-4947; e-mail keizai@pop.econ.hokudai.ac.jp; internet www.econ.hokudai.ac.jp/en05):

HAMADA, Y., Money and Banking
HASEGAWA, H., Econometrics
INOUE, H., International Investment and Finance
ITAYA, J., Public Economics
IWATA, S., Corporate Behaviour
KANDA, K., Disclosure System and Financial Accounting
KANIE, A., Auditing
KIMURA, T., Operations Research
KOJIMA, H., Management of Non-Profit Organizations
KOYAMA, K., Public Finance
MACHINO, K., Applied Game Theory
MIYAMOTO, K., Economic History of Asia
MOHRI, S., Management by Networking
NISHIBE, M., Evolutionary Economics
OKABE, H., Social Economy
SASAKI, K., History of Economics
SEKIGUCHI, Y., Managerial Informatics
SONO, S., Foundations of Statistics
TANAKA, S., Socioeconomic History
UCHIDA, S., Macroeconomics
YONEYAMA, Y., Financial Accounting
YOSHIMI, H., Auditing and Public Sector Accounting

YOSHINO, E., Comparative Socioeconomic Systems

Graduate School of Engineering (Kita 13, Nishi 8, Kita-ku, Sapporo; tel. (11) 716-8832; fax (11) 706-7895; e-mail shomu@eng.hokudai.ac.jp; internet www.eng.hokudai.ac.jp):

AKERA, H., Quantum Matter Physics
ARAI, M., Chemical Engineering
ASAKURA, K., Atmospheric and Terrestrial Engineering
BABA, N., Optical Science and Technology
CHIKAHISA, T., Applied Energy Systems
ENAI, M., Planning and Performances for Built Environment
FUJII, Y., Geoenvironmental Engineering
FUJIKAWA, S., Materials and Fluid Mechanics
FUJITA, O., Space Systems Engineering
FUNAMIZU, N., Water Metabolic System
FURUICHI, T., Policy for Engineering and Environment
FURUSAKA, M., Applied Quantum Beam Engineering
GOHARA, K., Complex Material Physics
GOTO, Y., Building Science and Space Planning
HABAZAKI, H., Functional Materials Chemistry
HARA, S., Industrial Organic Chemistry
HAYASHIKAWA, T., Sustainable Infrastructure System
HINO, T., Plasma Science and Engineering
ICHIKAWA, T., Functional Materials Chemistry
IGUCHI, M., Ecological Materials
IKEGAWA, M., Micromechanical Systems
ISHIMASA, T., Complex Material Physics
ITAGAKI, M., Plasma Science and Engineering
IZUMI, N., Hydraulic and Aquatic Environment Engineering
KADO, Y., Human Settlement Design
KAGAYA, S., Construction Engineering for Cold Regional Environment
KAGIWADA, T., Biomechanics and Robotics
KAKUCHI, T., Chemistry of Functional Molecules
KAMIDATE, T., Chemistry of Functional Molecules
KANEKO, K., Atmospheric and terrestrial Engineering
KIKKAWA, S., Inorganic Materials Chemistry
KIYANAGI, Y., Applied Quantum Beam Engineering
KOBAYASHI, H., Human Settlement Design
KOBAYASHI, Y., Biomechanics and Robotics
KONNO, H., Functional Materials Chemistry
KOSHIZAWA, A., Planning and Performances for Built Environment
KUDO, K., Micromechanical Systems
MASUDA, T., Chemical Engineering
MATSUI, Y., Water Metabolic System
MATSUTO, T., Solid Waste Resources Engineering
MATSUURA, K., Materials Design
MIDORIKAWA, M., Structural and Urban Safety Design
MIKAMI, T., Construction Engineering for Cold Regional Environment
MITACHI, T., Geoenvironmental Engineering
MIURA, S., Geoenvironmental Engineering
MIYAURA, N., Industrial Organic Chemistry
MOHRI, T., Materials Design
MORITA, R., Optical Science and Technology
MUKAI, S., Chemical Engineering
MUNEKATA, M., Biotechnology
MUTO, S., Solid State Physics and Engineering

NAGANO, K., Planning and Performances for Built Environment

NAGATA, H., Space Systems Engineering

NAKAMURA, T., Materials and Fluid Mechanics

NAKANO, T., Chemistry of Functional Molecules

NAKAYAMA, T., Quantum Matter Physics

NARABAYASHI, T., Nuclear and Environmental Systems

NARITA, Y., Micromechanical Systems

NAWA, T., Solid Waste Resources Engineering

OGAWA, H., Applied Energy Systems

OHKUMA, T., Industrial Organic Chemistry

OHNUKI, S., Energy Materials

OHNUMA, H., Construction Engineering for Cold Regional Environment

OHTA, S., Atmospheric and Terrestrial Engineering

OHTSUKA, T., Ecological Materials

ORIHARA, H., Complex Material Physics

OSHIMA, N., Space Systems Engineering

SASAKI, K., Materials and Fluid Mechanics

SASATANI, T., Structural and Urban Safety Design

SATO, S., Nuclear and Environmental Systems

SATOH, K., Policy for Engineering and Environment

SENBU, O., Building Science and Space Planning

SHIMADA, S., Inorganic Materials Chemistry

SHIMAZU, Y., Nuclear and Environmental Systems

SHIMIZU, Y., Policy for Engineering and Environment

SUGIYAMA, K., Nuclear and Environmental Systems

SUGIYAMA, T., Sustainable Infrastructure System

SUMIYOSHI, T., Applied Quantum Beam Engineering

SUZUKI, R., Ecological Materials

TADANO, S., Biomechanics and Robotics

TAGUCHI, S., Biotechnology

TAKAGI, M., Biotechnology

TAKAHASHI, H., Materials Design

TAKAHASHI, J., Inorganic Materials Chemistry

TAKAHASHI, M., Hydraulic and Aquatic Environment Engineering

TAKEDA, Y., Applied Energy Systems

TAMURA, S., Solid State Physics and Engineering

TANAKA, K., Solid State Physics and Engineering

TANDA, S., Quantum Matter Physics

TSUNEKAWA, M., Solid Waste Resources Engineering

UEDA, M., Structural and Urban Safety Design

UEDA, T., Sustainable Infrastructure System

UKAI, S., Energy Materials

WATANABE, Y., Water Metabolic System

WRIGHT, O., Quantum Matter Physics

YAMASHITA, M., Optical Science and Technology

YAMASHITA, T., Hydraulic and Aquatic Environment Engineering

YOKOYAMA, S., Planning and Performances for Built Environment

YONEDA, T., Geoenvironmental Engineering

Graduate School of Information Science and Technology (Kita 14, Nishi 9, Kita-ku, Sapporo; tel. (11) 706-6514; fax (11) 706-7890; e-mail jimusitu@ist.hokudai.ac.jp; internet www.ist.hokudai.ac.jp):

AMEMIYA, Y., Integrated Systems Engineering

ARAKI, K., Information Media Science and Technology

ARIMURA, H., Knowledge Software Science

ENDO, T., Bioinformatics

FUKUI, T., Integrated Systems Engineering

FURUKAWA, M., Complex Systems Engineering

HARAGUCHI, M., Knowledge Software Science

HASEYAMA, M., Information Media Science and Technology

HOMMA, T., Informatics for System Synthesis

IGARASHI, H., Informatics for System Synthesis

KANAI, S., Informatics for System Creation

KANEKO, S., Informatics for System Creation

KAWAHARA, K., Biomedical Systems Engineering

KITA, H., Informatics for System Synthesis

KOSHIBA, M., Information Communication Systems

KUDO, M., Mathematical Information Science

KURIHARA, M., Complex Systems Engineering

MISHIMA, T., Advanced Electronics

MIYAKOSHI, M., Mathematical Information Science

MIYANAGA, Y., Information Communication Systems

MOTOHISA, J., Integrated Systems Engineering

NOJIMA, T., Information Communication Systems

OGASAWARA, S., Informatics for System Synthesis

OGAWA, Y., Information Communication Systems

OHUCHI, A., Complex Systems Engineering

ONOSATO, M., Informatics for System Creation

SAKAI, Y., Integrated Systems Engineering

SATO, Y., Mathematical Information Science

SHIMIZU, K., Biomedical Systems Engineering

SUEOKA, K., Advanced Electronics

TAKAHASHI, Y., Advanced Electronics

TANAKA, Y., Knowledge Software Science

WADA, M., Complex Systems Engineering

WATANABE, H., Bioinformatics

YAMAMOTO, K., Biomedical Systems Engineering

YAMAMOTO, M., Advanced Electronics

YAMAMOTO, T., Information Media Science and Technology

YAMASHITA, Y., Informatics for System Creation

ZEUGMANN, T., Knowledge Software Science

Graduate School of Law (Kita 9, Nishi 7, Kita-ku, Sapporo; tel. (11) 706-3074; fax (11) 706-4948; e-mail shomu@juris.hokudai.ac.jp; internet www.juris.hokudai.ac.jp):

DOKO, T., Labour Law

FUJIWARA, M., Civil Law

GONZA, T., History of Political Theory

HASEGAWA, K., Philosophy of Law

HAYASHI, T., Commercial Law

HAYASHIDA, S., Economic Analysis of Law

HIENUKI, T., Economic Law

HITOMI, T., Administrative Law

ICHIRO Ozaki, S.

IKEDA, S., Civil Law

IMAI, H., Philosophy of Law

KOMORI, T., International Law

MACHIMURA, Y., Law of Civil Procedure

MATSUHISA, M., Civil Law

MIYAMOTO, T., Comparative Political Economy

MURAKAMI, H., Administrative Law

NAGAI, C., Criminal Law

NAKAYAMA, H., Law of Criminal Procedure

OHTSUKA, R., Commercial Law

OKADA, N., Constitutional Law

ONAGI, A., Criminal Law

SASADA, E., Constitutional Law

SEGAWA, N., Civil Law

SHIRATORI, Y., Law of Criminal Procedure

SORAI, M., Modern Political Analysis

SUZUKI, K., Asian Law

TAGUCHI, M., Western Legal History

TAKAMI, S., Law of Civil Procedure

TAMURA, Y., Intellectual Property Law

TANAKA, H., Legal Ethics

TSUJI, Y., Political Theory

TSUNEMOTO, T., Constitutional Law

YAMAMOTO, T., Commercial Law

YAMASHITA, R., Administrative Law

YOSHIDA, K., Civil Law

Graduate School of Letters (Kita 10, Nishi 7, Kita-ku, Sapporo; tel. (11) 726-7728; fax (11) 706-4803; e-mail wwwadmin@let.hokudai.ac.jp; internet www.hokudai.ac.jp/letters):

ABE, J., Psychology

AKASHI, M., Occidental History

ANDO, A., Western Literature

ANZAI, M., Western Literature

CHIBA, K., Philosophy

FUJII, K., Religious Studies and Indian Philosophy

GOTO, Y., Japanology

HANAI, K., Philosophy

HISHITANI, S., Psychology

HOSODA, N., Religious Studies and Indian Philosophy

IKEDA, S., Linguistics Sciences

IKEDA, T., Regional Sciences

INOUE, K., Japanese History

IRIMOTO, T., Northern Culture Studies

KADOWAKI, S., Linguistic Sciences

KAMEDA, T., Behavioural Sciences

KANEKO, I., Sociology

KITAMURA, K., Theory and History of Art

KURYUZAWA, T., Occidental History

KUWAYAMA, T., History and Anthropology

MATSUOKA, M., Sociology

MIKI, S., Asian History

MISAKI, H., Japanology

MIYATAKE, K., History and Anthropology

MOCHIZUKI, T., Linguistics and Western Languages

NAKA, M., Psychology

NAKATOGAWA, K., Philosophy

NAMBU, N., Japanese History

NITTA, T., Ethics and Applied Philosophy

ONO, Y., Linguistics Sciences

OTA, K., History and Anthropology

SAKURAI, Y., Sociology

SATO, R., Sinology

SOTO, J., Filmology and Cultural Studies of Representation

SEKI, T., Regional Sciences

SHIMIZU, M., Linguistics and Western Languages

SHIRAKIZAWA, A., Japanese History

SUTO, Y., Sinology

TAKAHASHI, H., Linguistics and Western Languages

TAKAHEI, H., Philosophy

TAKEDA, M., Sinology

TAKIGAWA, T., Psychology

TAYAMA, T., Psychology

TOMITA, Y., Japanology

TSUMAGARI, T., Northern Culture Studies

TUDA, Y., Asian History

URAI, Y., Linguistics and Western Languages

UTSUNOMIYA, T., Religious Studies and Indian Philosophy

WADA, H., Psychology

YAMADA, T., Philosophy

YAMADA, T., Western Literature

YAMAGISHI, T., Behavioural Sciences

YUHAZU, K., Sinology

Graduate School of Medicine (Kita 15, Nishi 7, Kita-ku, Sapporo; tel. (11) 716-5003; fax (11) 717-5286; e-mail shomu@med.hokudai.ac.jp; internet www.med.hokudai.ac.jp):

AKITA, H., Medical Oncology

ARIGA, T., Paediatrics
ARIKAWA, J., Infectious Disease
CHIBA, H., Biomedical Informatics
DAIGUJI, M., Clinical Occupational Therapy
DATE, H., Medical Engineering and Science
FUJITA, H., Environmental Biology
FUKUDA, S., Otolaryngology, Head and Neck Surgery
FUKUSHIMA, J., Basic Physical Therapy
FUKUSHIMA, K., Sensorimotor and Cognitive Research
GANDO, S., Acute and Critical Care Medicine
HATAKEYAMA, S., Medical Chemistry
HATTA, T., Clinical Occupational Therapy
HONMA, K., Chronobiology
IMAMURA, M., Haematology and Oncology
INOUE, K., Basic Occupational Therapy
ISHIZU, A., Clinical Pathophysiology
IWANAGA, T., Histology and Cytology
IWASAKI, Y., Neurosurgery
IWATA, G., Maternal Nursing and Child Nursing
KAMIYA, H., Neurobiology
KASAHARA, M., Pathology
KAWAGUCHI, H., Laboratory Medicine
KISHI, R., Public Health
KOBAYASHI, S., Biomedical Informatics
KOIKE, T., Clinical Immunology
KONDO, S., Surgical Oncology
KOYAMA, T., Psychiatry
MAEZAWA, M., Healthcare Research and Quality
MATSUNO, K., Clinical Pathophysiology
MATSUSHITA, M., Adult and Gerontological Nursing
MIKAMI, T., Clinical Pathophysiology
MINAKAMI, H., Obstetrics
MINAMI, A., Orthopaedic Surgery
MIWA, S., Cellular and Molecular Pharmacology
MIYAMOTO, K., Clinical Physical Therapy
MORIMOTO, Y., Anaesthesia and Perioperative Medicine
MORISHITA, S., Fundamental Nursing
MORIYAMA, T., Biomedical Informatics
MURATA, W., Basic Occupational Therapy
NISHIMURA, M., Respiratory Medicine
NISHIOKA, T., Radiological Technology
NONOMURA, K., Renal and Genito-urinary Surgery
OGASAWARA, K., Medical Engineering and Science
OHMIYA, Y., Photobiology
OHNO, S., Ophthalmology
SAEKI, K., Community Health Nursing
SAGAWA, T., Maternal Nursing and Child Nursing
SAITO, T., Community Health Nursing
SAKAI, M., Radiological Technology
SAKURAGI, N., Reproductive Endocrinology and Oncology
SAKURAI, T., Medical Informatics
SASAKI, F., Paediatric Surgery
SASAKI, H., Neurology
SATO, Y., Maternal Nursing and Child Nursing
SHIMIZU, H., Dermatology
SHIMIZU, T., Radiological Technology
SHIRATO, H., Radiology
TAKANAMI, S., Community Health Nursing
TAKEDA, N., Basic Physical Therapy
TAMAKI, N., Nuclear Medicine
TAMASHIRO, H., Global Health and Epidemiology
TERAZAWA, K., Forensic Medicine
TODO, S., General Surgery
TSUTSUI, H., Cardiovascular Medicine
WATANABE, M., Anatomy and Embryology
YAMAGUCHI, H., Biomedical Informatics
YAMAMOTO, T., Medical Engineering and Science
YAMAMOTO, Y., Plastic Surgery
YAMANAKA, M., Clinical Physical Therapy

YASUDA, K., Sports Medicine and Joint Reconstruction Surgery
YOKOSAWA, K., Medical Engineering and Science
YOSHIMURA, S., Fundamental Nursing
YOSHIOKA, M., Neuropharmacology

Graduate School of Veterinary Medicine (Kita 18, Nishi 9, Kita-ku, Sapporo; tel. (11) 706-5173; fax (11) 706-5190; e-mail syomu@ vetmed.hokudai.ac.jp; internet www.vetmed .hokudai.ac.jp):

AGUI, T., Disease Control
FUJINAGA, T., Veterinary Clinical Sciences
FUJITA, S., Environmental Veterinary Sciences
HABARA, Y., Biomedical Sciences
HORIUCHI, M., Prion Diseases
INABA, M., Veterinary Clinical Sciences
INANAMI, O., Environmental Veterinary Sciences
ITO, S., Biomedical Sciences
KATAKURA, K., Disease Control
KIDA, H., Disease Control
KIMURA, K., Biomedical Sciences
KON, Y., Biomedical Sciences
TAKAHASHI, Y., Veterinary Clinical Sciences
TAKASHIMA, I., Environmental Veterinary Sciences
TSUBOTA, T., Environmental Veterinary Sciences
UMEMURA, T., Veterinary Clinical Sciences

Research Faculty of Agriculture (Kita 9, Nishi 9, Kita-ku, Sapporo; tel. (11) 706-4123; fax (11) 706-4893; e-mail shomu@agr .hokudai.ac.jp):

ARIGA, S., Environmental Molecular Bioscience
ASANO, K., Applied Microbiology
BANDO, H., Applied Molecular Entomology
DEMURA, K., Agricultural and Environmental Policy
FUJIKAWA, S., Woody Plant Biology
HARA, H., Nutritional Biochemistry
HASEGAWA, S., Soil Conservation
HASHIDOKO, Y., Ecological Chemistry
HATANO, R., Soil Science
HATTORI, A., Meat Science
HIRAI, T., Timber Engineering
HIRANO, T., Environmental Informatics
IIZAWA, R., Agricultural Marketing
IWAMA, K., Crop Science
KAKIZAWA, H., Forest Policy
KAWABATA, J., Food Biochemistry
KIMURA, A., Molecular Enzymology
KIMURA, T., Agricultural and Food Process Engineering
KITAMURA, K., Plant Genetics and Evolution
KOBAYASHI, Y., Animal Nutrition
KODA, Y., Crop Physiology
KOIKE, T., Silviculture and Forest Ecology
KONDO, S., Animal Production System
KONDO, T., Environmental Horticulture and Landscape Architecture
KUROKAWA, I., Farm Management
MARUTANI, T., Earth Surface Processes and Land Management
MASUDA, K., Plant Functional Biology
MASUTA, C., Cell Biology and Manipulation
MATSUDA, J., Agricultural Circulative Engineering
MATSUI, H., Biochemistry
MIKAMI, T., Genetic Engineering
NABETA, K., Natural Product Chemistry
NAGASAWA, T., Land Improvement and Management
NAITO, S., Molecular Biology
NAKAMURA, F., Animal By-product Science
NAKAMURA, F., Forest Ecosystem Management
NOGUCHI, N., Vehicle Robotics
OSAKI, M., Plant Nutrition
OSANAMI, F., Agricultural Development
SAITO, Y., Animal Ecology

SAKASHITA, A., Agricultural Cooperative
SANO, Y., Plant Breeding
SHIMAZAKI, K., Dairy Food Science
SUZUKI, M., Horticultural Science
UBUKATA, M., Wood Chemistry
URANO, S., Agricultural and Environmental Physics
UYEDA, I., Pathogen–Plant Interactions
WATANABE, T., Animal Breeding and Reproduction
YAJIMA, T., Forest Resource Biology
YOKOTA, A., Microbial Physiology

Research Faculty of Media and Communication (Kita 17, Nishi 8, Kita-ku, Sapporo; tel. (11) 716-2111; fax (11) 706-7801; e-mail soumu@ilcs.hokudai.ac.jp; internet www .hokudai.ac.jp/imcts/rfmc.html):

Most of the Professors in this Faculty also belong to the Foreign Language Education Center.

EGUCHI, Y., German
HASHIMOTO, H., English
ISHIBASHI, M., German
ISHIKAWA, K., German
KOBAYAKAWA, M., International Public Relations
KOGA, H., Italian
MIYASHITA, M., English
NAGAI, Y., Chinese
NISHI, M., French
NOZAWA, Y., Chinese
OGAWA, Y., English
OHIRA, T., French
OHNO, K., English
SATOH, S., German
SONODA, K., English
STAPLETON, P., English
SUGIURA, S., Russian
TAKAHASHI, Y., German
TAKAI, K., Chinese
TAKEMOTO, K., English
TAKENAKA, M., French
TERADA, T., German
TSUKUWA, M., German
UEDA, M., English
USAMI, S., Russian
YAMADA, K., Russian
YAMADA, Y., English
YOSHIDA, T., German

ATTACHED RESEARCH INSTITUTES

Admission Center: f. 2005; Dir MINORU WAKITA.

Catalysis Research Center: f. 1989; Dir WATARU UEDA.

Center for Advanced Research of Energy Conversion Materials: f. 2004; Dir KAZUYA KUROKAWA.

Center for Advanced Tourism Studies: f. 2006; Dir SHUZO ISHIMORI.

Center for Ainu and Indigenous Studies: f. 2007; Dir TERUKI TSUNEMOTO.

Center for Experimental Research in Social Sciences: f. 2007; Dir TOSHIO YAMAGISHI.

Center for Instrumental Analysis: f. 1979; Dir TOSHIAKI MIURA.

Center for Research and Development in Higher Education: f. 1995; Dir MINORU WAKITA.

Central Institute of Radioisotope Science: f. 1978; Dir NAGARA TAMAKI.

Creative Research Initiative 'Sousei': f. 2005; Dir HISATAKE OKADA.

Environmental Preservation Center: f. 1995; Dir MASAYA SAWAMURA.

Field Science Center for the Northern Biosphere: f. 2001; Dir KAICHIRO SASA.

Foreign Language Education Center: f. 2007; Dir YUTAKA EGUCHI.

Health Administration Center: f. 1972; Dir MANABU MUSASHI.

Hokkaido University Archives: f. 2005; Dir MASAAKI HEMMI.

Hokkaido University Museum: f. 1999; Dir SHUNSUKE MAWATARI.

Information Initiative Center: f. 2003; Dir TSUYOSHI YAMAMOTO.

Institute for Genetic Medicine: f. 2000; Dir TOSHIMITSU UEDE; publ. *Collected Papers* (1 a year).

Institute of Low Temperature Science: f. 1941; Dir AKIRA KOUCHI.

International Student Center: f. 1991; Dir TAKEO HONDOH.

Meme Media Laboratory: f. 1996; Dir YUZURU TANAKA.

Research and Education Center for Brain Science: f. 2003; Dir SHINYA KURIKI.

Research Center for Integrated Quantum Electronics: f. 2001; Dir TAKASHI FUKUI.

Research Center for Zoonosis Control: f. 2005; Dir HIROSHI KIDA.

Research Institute for Electronic Science: f. 1943; Dir KEIJI SASAKI.

Slavic Research Center: f. 1990; Dir KIMITAKA MATSUZATO; publ. *Acta Slavica Iaponica* (1 a year).

IBARAKI UNIVERSITY

1-1, Bunkyo 2-chome, Mito-Shi, Ibaraki-ken 310-8512

Telephone: (29) 228-8007
Fax: (29) 228-8019
Internet: www.ibaraki.ac.jp
Founded 1949
Independent
Academic year: April to March

Pres.: TAKEO MIYATA
Admin.: T. MIYATA
Dean of Student Affairs: F. IKEYA
Librarian: Y. ASANO

Library of 939,000 vols
Number of teachers: 584 full-time
Number of students: 8,864

Publications: Bulletins (in Japanese), Journals of the faculties (in Japanese)

DEANS

Faculty of Education: R. KIKUCHI
Faculty of Engineering: K. YAMAGATA
Faculty of Humanities: T. MURANAKA
Faculty of Science: T. WATANABE
School of Agriculture: T. MATUDA

PROFESSORS

Faculty of Education:

ADACHI, K., School Education
AKISAKA, M., Clinical Medicine
AKUTA, N., Clinical Psychology
ARAKAWA, C., Housing and Domestic Science
EBATA, H., School Education
FUJIHIRA, S., German Literature
HASEGAWA, S., Vocal Music
HASHIURA, H., Japanese Literature
HATTORI, K., Physical Activity Science
HAYAKAWA, K., Composition
HAYAKAWA, T., Geomorphology
HONNDA, T., Information Education
IKEYA, F., European History
INABA, K.
INAMI, Y., Computer Science
KAIZU, S., Applied Mathematics
KAJIWARA, S., Instrumental Music
KANEKO, K., Art Education
KIKUCHI, R., Adult Education
KIMURA, K., Philosophy
KOIZUMI, S., Art History

KOJIMA, H., Information Education
KOMURO, K., Technical Education
KUSAKA, Y., Physical Education
MAEKAWA, Y., Sinology
MAKINO, Y., Geology
MATSUDA, M., Art Education
MATSUI, M., Information Sciences
MATSUMURA, T., Education for Handicapped Children
MATSUZAKA, A., Health and Physical Education
MIURA, T., Health and Physical Education
NAGASAWA, K., English Language Teaching
NAKAMURA, T., Health Education
NAMIKI, T., English Morphology
OGATA, T., Health and Physical Education
OKAMOTO, K., Physical Education
ONO, Y., Mycology
ONODERA, A., Historical Geography
OSHIMA, K., Earth Science
OTA, S., Physical Education
OTAKE, H., Women's Studies
OTANI, A., School Nursing
OTSUKI, I., Economic History of Modern Japan
OUCHI, Z., Language Ethics Education
OZAKI, H., Physiology for Handicapped Children
SASAKI, Y., Japanese Language Teaching
SATO, A., Musicology
SATO, E., Mathematical Education
SATO, H., Technical Education
SOGA, H., Mathematical Science
SOGO, M., Painting
SUGANUMA, K., Clinical Psychology
SUZUKI, E., Social Studies Teaching
TAKIZAWA, T., Hygienics
TANAKA, K., Music Education
TANIGUCHI, T., School Education
TASHIRO, T., School Education
TATSUMI, N., Physical Education
TERAMOTO, T., Industrial Arts
TOGASHI, T., Physical Education
TOSHIYASU, Y., Science Education
YAMAMOTO, H., Organic Chemistry
YAMAMOTO, K., Household Management Education
YAMANE, S., Insect Ecology
YAMASHITA, T., School Education
YANAGIDA, N., Mathematics
YASUDA, K., Home Economics Education
YOSHIDA, H., Home Economics Education

Faculty of Engineering:

ABE, O., Ceramics Engineering
ARAKI, T., Computer Science
EDA, H., Production Engineering and Machine Tools
ENOMOTO, M., Materials Physics
FUJII, K., Laser and Plasma
FUKUZAWA, K., Concrete Engineering
HAMAMATSU, Y., Modelling and Simulation
HARIU, T., Electronic Material Systems
HOSHI, T., Systems Information and Remote Sensing
ICHIMURA, M., Materials Physics
IGARASHI, S., Analytical Chemistry
IKEHATA, T., Plasma Science
IMAI, Y., Communication Engineering
INUI, M., Systems Engineering
ISHIGURO, M., Computer Applications
ITO, G., Plastic Working Science
KAGOSHIMA, K., Antennas
KAMINAGA, H., Energy Conversion
KANO, M., Discrete Mathematics and its Application
KAZITANI, S., Energy Conservation
KIKUMA, I., Electronic Materials
KISHI, Y., Intelligent Systems
KOBAYASHI, M., Systems Information
KOBIYAMA, M., Electromagnetic Systems
KOUNOSU, S., Design Engineering
KOYAMADA, Y., Photonic Systems
KOYANAGI, T., Landscape Planning and Design
KUROSAWA, K., Plasma Science

MAEKAWA, K., Materials Science and Engineering
MASUI, M., Electronic Materials
MASUZAWA, T., Dynamics of Machines
MIMURA, N., Global Environment Engineering
MOMOSE, Y., Surface Chemistry
MOTOHASHI, Y., Materials Science and Engineering
MURANOI, T., Electronic Materials for Functionality
NAITO, K., Analytical Chemistry
NAKAMOTO, R., Functional Analysis
NARA, K., Electrical Power Systems
NIIMURA, N., Physics
NIREI, H., Environmental Asset Science
NUMAO, T., Architecture
OGUCHI, K., Dynamics of Machines
OKADA, Y., Dynamics of Machines
ONO, K., Polymer Science
ONUKI, J., Materials Technology
OZAWA, S., Computational Physics
SASAKI, Y., Foundation and Design of Precision Engineering
SENBA, I., Computer Science
SHIRAISHI, M., Systems and Controls
SIOHATA, K., Design Engineering
SUGITA, R., Electrical and Electronics Engineering
SUZUKI, H., Mechanical Design
SUZUKI, T., Energy Conversion
TAKAHASHI, M., Organic Chemistry
TAKEUCHI, M., Electrical Materials
TAZUKE, Y., Applied Physics
TOMODA, Y., Mechanical Metallurgy
TOZUNE, A., Electric Machines
TURUTA, K., High Voltage and Plasma Science
WU, Z., Structural Engineering
YAMANAKA, K., Systems and Controls
YASUHARA, K., Geotechnical Engineering
YOKOYAMA, K., Structural Engineering
ZYOU, M., CAD/CAM/CAE

Faculty of Humanities:

AIZAWA, Y., English and American Culture
AMEMIYA, S., Politics
AOKI, K., French
ARIIZUMI, S., Economic Structure
ARITOMI, M., Psychology
ASANO, Y., Human Geography
CHEANG, K., Linguistics
FUJII, F., Linguistics
FUKAYA, N., Law
FUKAZAWA, Y., European History
FUSHIMI, K., German
IIZUKA, K., Law
IIJIMA, H., Management Science
KAMATA, A., Social Structure
KAMIYA, T., Social Structure
KANAMOTO, S., Japanese Education
KANOU, Y., Asian Culture
KATAYAMA, Y., Philosophy
KIMURA, M., Southeast Asia Area Study
KISHIMOTO, N., Linguistics
KOIDO, M., French and European Culture
KOIZUMI, Y., English and American Culture
KOMIYAJI, M., Business Administration
LIENG, J., Sinology
MATUMURA, N., Social Structure
MAYANAGI, M., Oriental History
MOGI, M., Comparative Culture
MORIYA, S., Logic
MORIYA, T., Sociology
MURANAKA, M., Sociology
NAKURA, B., Economic Structure
NOSAKA, M., Law
OHATA, K., English and American Culture
OKUBO, N., French Culture
SAITO, M., Regional Societies
SAITO, Y., Local Administration
SANO, H., Media Studies
SASAKI, H., History
SASAKURA, S., English
SATO, K., Economic Structure

SATO, K., German Culture
SIBUYA, A., Sociology
SIMAOKA, S., English
SUGII, K., Oriental History
SUGISHITA, T., International Cooperation Theory
SUMIKAWA, H., European and American Economy Theory
SUZUKI, T., Communication
SUZUKI, Y., Psychology
SUZUKI, Y., German
TAKAHASHI, T., English
TAMURA, T., Law
TANAKA, S., Regional Societies
TATEWAKI, I., Regional Societies
TATEYAMA, Y., International Economics
TOKUE, K., Economic Policy
UENO, H., Social Anthropology
UMEDA, T., Law
WATANABE, K., European Culture
YAMAMOTO, H., Asian Economics

Faculty of Science:
AMANO, T., Science of Cosmic Matter
FUJII, Y., Coordination Chemistry
FUJIWARA, T., Physics
HORI, Y., Botany
HORIUCHI, T., Analysis
ICHIMASA, M., Cell Biology
ICHIMASA, Y., Physiology
IKEDA, Y., Geochemistry
IMURA, H., Analytical Chemistry
ISIZUKA, T., Astrophysics
IZUOKA, A., Physical Chemistry
KANEKO, M., Chemistry
KANNO, S., Atomic Physics
KAWADA, Y., Chemistry
KIMURA, M., Geochemistry
KOJIMA, J., Entomology
MATSUDA, R., Algebra
MISHIMA, S., Biology
MIWA, I., Biology
MORINO, H., Systematics
NAKANO, Y., Structural Chemistry
NISHIHARA, Y., Magnetism and Superconductivity
NODA, F., Theoretical High Energy
OHASHI, K., Analytical Chemistry
ONISHI, K., Applied Mathematics
ONOSE, H., Statistics
ORIYAMA, T., Organic Chemistry
OSHIMA, H., Topology
SAKATA, F., Mathematical Science
SAKUMA, T., Solid-State Physics
TAGIRI, M., Earth and Planetary Physics
TAKANO, K., Mathematics
URABE, T., Geometry
WATANABE, T., Earth Science
YAMADA, M., Physics
YAMAGAMI, S., Quantum Physics
YANAGIDA, R., Cosmic Ray Physics
YOKOSAWA, M., Astrophysics

School of Agriculture:
AKUTSU, K., Plant Pathology
GOTO, T., Applied Physics
KARUBE, J., Farmland Engineering
KASHIWAGI, M., Regional Planning Science
KINOSE, K., Hydraulic Engineering
KODAMA, O., Bio-regulation Chemistry
KOSUGIYAMA, M., Animal Breeding
KOUNO, Y., Chemical Ecology
KUBOTA, M., Soil Science and Plant Nutrition
KURUSU, Y., Industrial Microbiology
MACHIDA, T., Agricultural Systems
MARUBASHI, W., Plant Breeding
MASAKI, T., Enzymatic Chemistry
MATSUDA, T., Horticulture
MATSUZAWA, Y., Animal Husbandry and Behaviour
MORIIZUMI, S., Agricultural Machinery
NAKAGAWA, M., Agricultural Economics
NAKAJIMA, M., Farm Science
NAKAMURA, Y., Feed Science
NAKANE, K., Algebra

NAKASONE, H., Agricultural and Environmental Engineering
OTA, H., Microbial Ecology
SAGO, R., Cultivation Science
SHIO, K., Information Science
SHIRAI, M., Molecular Microbiology
TAKAHARA, H., Bioresource Engineering
TSUKIHASHI, T., Horticulture
YONEKURA, M., Crop Production

IWATE UNIVERSITY

3-18-8 Ueda, Morioka, Iwate 020-8550
Telephone: (19) 621-6006
Fax: (19) 621-6014
E-mail: ssomu@iwate-u.ac.jp
Internet: www.iwate-u.ac.jp
Founded 1949
Independent
Academic year: April to March
Pres.: KENICHI HIRAYAMA
Chief Admin. Officer: TOSHIAKI KIKUCHI
Librarian: YOSHIYA NAKASHIMA
Library of 760,434 vols
Number of teachers: 835
Number of students: 6,218
Publications: *Journal of the Faculty of Agriculture, Report on Technology of Iwate University, Artes Liberales*

DEANS
Faculty of Agriculture: YOSHINOBU OTA
Faculty of Education: TAKAO FUJIWARA
Faculty of Technology: KUNIO MORI
College of Humanities and Social Sciences: TATSUYUKI TAKATSUKA

JAPAN ADVANCED INSTITUTE OF SCIENCE AND TECHNOLOGY

1-1 Asahidai, Nomi, Ishikawa 923-1292
Telephone: (761) 51-1111
Fax: (761) 51-1088
E-mail: kouhou@jaist.ac.jp
Internet: www.jaist.ac.jp
Founded 1990
State control
Languages of instruction: English, Japanese
Academic year: April to March
Pres.: TAKUYA KATAYAMA
Vice-Pres.: YASUSHI HIBINO
Vice-Pres.: YUSUKE KAWAKAMI
Vice-Pres.: KOZO SUGIYAMA
Dir of the Library: ATSUKO MIYAJI
Library of 134,735 vols
Number of teachers: 167
Number of students: 970
Publication: *JAIST NOW* (2 a year)

DEANS
School of Information Science: MASATO AKAGI
School of Knowledge Science: SUSUMU KUNIFUJI
School of Materials Science: HIDEKI MATSUMURA

KAGAWA UNIVERSITY

1-1 Saiwai-cho, Takamatsu-shi 760-8521
Telephone: (87) 832-1025
Fax: (87) 832-1053
E-mail: kokusait@jimu.ao.kagawa-u.ac.jp
Internet: www.kagawa-u.ac.jp
Founded 1949
Independent
Academic year: April to March
Pres.: Dr YOSHITSUGU KIMURA
Vice-Pres: Dr HIROAKI TAKEUCHI, Dr TAKUMI YOSHIZAWA
Sec.-Gen.: KUNIO SEKI
Librarian: MASAYUKI SATO
Library of 650,000 vols

Number of teachers: 473 (incl. teachers at attached schools)
Number of students: 5,261

DEANS
Faculty of Agriculture: MASAHIKO ICHII
Faculty of Economics: MICHIYO IHARA
Faculty of Education: YOSHIMASA KANO
Faculty of Engineering: HIROSHI ISHIKAWA
Faculty of Law: SADAMI UEMURA
Faculty of Medicine: AKINOBU OKABE

KAGOSHIMA UNIVERSITY

1-21-24, Korimoto, Kagoshima 890-8580
Telephone: (992) 85-7111
Internet: www.kagoshima-u.ac.jp
Founded 1949
State control
Pres.: HIROKI YOSHIDA
Dir.-Gen.: CHIKARA MORIMOTO
Library of 1,338,169 vols
Number of teachers: 1,200 full-time
Number of students: 11,000

DEANS
Faculty of Agriculture: I. IWAMOTO
Faculty of Dentistry: K. SUGIHARA
Faculty of Education: A. TAKEKUMA
Faculty of Fisheries: T. NORO
Faculty of Law, Economics and the Humanities: H. ISHIKAWA
Faculty of Medicine: Y. EIZURU
Faculty of Science: S. KIYOHARA
Graduate School of Health Science: A. YOSHIDA
Graduate School of Medical and Dental Sciences: T. MATSUYAMA
Graduate School of Science and Engineering: Y. FUKUI
Law School: H. UNIEME
Professional Graduate School of Clinical Psychology: T. ABE
United Graduate School of Agricultural Sciences: T. SUGANUMA

KANAGAWA UNIVERSITY

3-27-1 Rokkakubashi, Kanagawaku, Yokohama 221-8686
Telephone: (45) 491-1701
Fax: (45) 481-6011
E-mail: kohou-info@kanagawa-u.ac.jp
Internet: www.kanagawa-u.ac.jp
Founded 1949
Library of 1,110,000 vols
Number of students: 19,129
Faculties of Business Administration, Economics, Engineering, Foreign Languages, Law, Science.

KANAZAWA UNIVERSITY

Kakuma-machi, Kanazawa-shi 920-1192
Telephone: (76) 264-5111
Fax: (76) 234-4010
E-mail: now@kanazawa-u.ac.jp
Internet: www.kanazawa-u.ac.jp
Founded 1949
Independent
Academic year: April to March
Pres.: SHIN-ISHI NAKAMURA
Vice-Pres. for Finance and Hospital: M. FURUKAWA
Vice-Pres. for General Affairs and Human Resources: N. WAKISAKA
Vice-Pres. for Education and Student Affairs: Y. KASHIMI
Vice-Pres. for Information: S. SAKURAI
Vice-Pres. for Research and Int. Affairs: I. NAGANO
Library of 1,786,038 vols
Number of teachers: 1,082

Number of students: 10,443

DEANS

College of Human and Social Sciences: S. IKUTA

College of Medical, Pharmaceutical and Health Sciences: H. YAMAMOTO

College of Science and Engineering: K. YAMAZAKI

Graduate School of Education: H. OKUBO

Graduate School of Human and Socio-environmental Studies: H. INOUE

Graduate School of Medical Science: O. MATSUI

Graduate School of Natural Science and Technology: Y. FUKUMORI

Law School: S. OJIMA

DIRECTORS

Advanced Science Research Centre: M. ASANO

Cancer Research Institute: N. MUKAIDA

Centre for Innovation: N. YOSHIKUNI

Centre for Regional Collaboration: H. KAMIYA

Environment Preservation Centre: H. NAKAMURA

Foreign Language Institute: S. SAWADA

Information Media Centre: K. AOKI

Institute of Nature and Environmental Technology: K. NAKAMURA

International Student Centre: M. SHIMURA

Research Centre for Child Mental Devt: H. HIGASHIDA

Research Centre for Higher Education: N. NISHIYAMA

University Hospital: K. TOMITA

University Library: M. SHIBATA

PROFESSORS

Advanced Science Research Centre (13-1 Takara-machi, Kanazawa, Ishikawa; tel. (76) 265-2771; fax (76) 234-4537; e-mail yamaguti@kenroku.kanazawa-u.ac.jp; internet web.kanazawa-u.ac.jp/~asrc):

ASANO, M., Experimental Animal Science

MORI, H., Nuclear Medicine

YAMAGUCHI, K., Molecular Genetics

Cancer Research Institute (13-1 Takara-machi, Kanazawa, Ishikawa; tel. (76) 265-2799; fax (76) 234-4527):

HARADA, F., Molecular and Cellular Biology

HIRAO, A., Molecular and Cellular Biology

MINAMOTO, T., Basic and Clinical Oncology

MUKAIDA, N., Molecular Oncology

MURAKAMI, S., Molecular Genetics

SATO, H., Molecular Oncology

SAWABU, N., Basic and Clinical Oncology

SUDA, T., Molecular and Cellular Immunology

TAKAKURA, N., Molecular and Cellular Biology

YAMAMOTO, K., Molecular and Cellular Biology

YOSHIOKA, K., Molecular and Cellular Biology

Centre for Co-operative Research (tel. (76) 264-6111; fax (76) 234-4019):

SERYO, K., Mechanical Engineering

YOSHIKUNI, N., Intellectual Property Management

Faculty of Economics (tel. (76) 264-5440; fax (76) 264-5444):

BENNOU, S., Economic History of Modern China

GOKA, K., Labour Economics

HORIBAYASHI, T., Theory of Economic Planning

IKARIYAMA, H., Public Finance

KAMIJO, I., History of Economic Thought

MAEDA, T., Modern Economics

MARUYAMA, K., Comparative Social Philosophy

MIYATA, M., Banking and Financial Systems

MURAKAMI, K., Principles of Economics

NAKASHIMA, K., World-System Theory and the Financial History of Medieval and Modern Europe

NAMU, S., Education

NISHIDA, Y., Japanese Contemporary Agricultural History

NISHIJIMA, Y., Contrastive Sociolinguistics

NOMURA, M., History of Social Thought

SAWADA, M., Industrial Relations and Human Resource Management in Japan and the USA, General Theory of Business Management

SHIRAISHI, H., Business Administration

TSURUZONO, Y., Korean History

UNNO, Y., Economic Policy

YOKOYAMA, T., Social Security

YOSHINO, Y., Sports Science

Faculty of Education (tel. (76) 264-5555; fax (76) 234-4100):

DEMURA, S., Lifelong Sports

EMORI, I., Pedagogy

GOMI, T., Historical Geography

HATANAKA, H., Magnetic Resonance

IHARA, Y., Inorganic Chemistry

IKEGAMI, K., Developmental Psychology

ISHIMURA, U., Physical Education

ITOH, S., Geography and Planning

IZUMI, N., Dielectrics

KATAGIRI, K., Developmental Neuropsychology of Mental Retardation

KATOH, K., Japanese Linguistics

KAWABATA, K., Freshwater Biology

KAYAHARA, M., Clinical Psychology

KIMURA, M., Education for the Handicapped

KONDOH, A., Japanese Linguistics

KUJIRA, Y., Crop Science

KUROBORI, T., Applied Optics

MAEDA, H., Modern Japanese Literature

MATSUBARA, M., Teaching of Science

MATSUDAIRA, M., Textile Science

MATSUNAKA, H., Instrumental Music

MATSUSHITA, R., Philosophy of Education

MATSUURA, N., Graphic Design

MIYASHITA, T., History of European Art

MIYOSHI, Y., Information Science

MORI, E., Japanese Literature

MOROOKA, K., Teaching Methods

MURAI, A., Research on Methods of Teaching Social Studies

OHTSUKA, I., English Linguistics

OI, M., Communication Disorders

OKAZAKI, F., Philosophy

OKUBO, H., History of Physical Education and Sports

OKUDA, H., Japanese History

SAKAYORI, A., Igneous Petrology

SASAK, T., Materials Science and Engineering

SHINOHARA, H., Music Education

SUGIMOTO, M., Geology

SUNADA, R., Practice and Research for Clinical Psychology and Education

TANABE, S., Educational Administration and Management

UEDA, J., Chemistry

YAKURA, K., Plant Molecular Biology

YAMAGISHI, M., Housing Science

YAMAMOTO, H., Biomechanics in Sports

YAMAMOTO, H., Classic Japanese Literature

YAMAMOTO, T., Teaching Methods

YASUKAWA, T., History of Foreign Education

Faculty of Law (tel. (76) 264-5403; fax (76) 264-5405):

CHEN, I., Conflict of Laws

INOUE, H., Social Security Law

KASHIMA, M., International Relations

KUSUNE, S., International Communication

MAEDA, T., Labour Law

NAKAMASA, M., Social Philosophy

NAKAMURA, M., Chinese Legal History

NAKAYAMA, H., Criminal Procedure

NISHIMURA, S., Political Sociology

SAKURAI, T., European Legal History

TAKAHASHI, R., Sociology

TOKUMOTO, S., Civil Law

UMEDA, Y., Japanese Legal History

YAMAGATA, K., Developmental Psychology

Faculty of Letters (tel. (76) 264-5360; fax (76) 264-5362):

FUJII, S., Prehistory of the Near East

FURUHATA, T., Oriental History

HASHIMOTO, K., Sociology

HONMA, T., American Literature

IKUTA, S., English Literature

IWATA, R., Chinese Linguistics

KAGAMI, H., Cultural Anthropology

KAJIKAWA, S., Russian History

KAJIKAWA, Y., Geography

KAMIYA, H., Geography

KASAI, J., Japanese History

KASUYA, Y., French Literature

KIGOSHI, O., Japanese Literature

KUBOTA, I., German Literature

KUBUKI, S., Comparative Culture

MATSUKAWA, J., Cognitive Psychology

MIZOBE, A., Sociology

MOCHII, Y., Oriental History

MURAKAMI, K., American Literature

NAKABAYASHI, N., Cultural Anthropology

NAKAMURA, Y., English Language

NISHIMURA, S., Japanese Literature

NITTA, T., Linguistics

OHTAKI, S., Chinese Language

SASAKI, T., Archaeology

SHIBATA, M., Philosophy

SHIMA, I., Comparative Culture

SUNAHARA, Y., Philosophy

TAKADA, S., English Literature

TAKAHAMA, S., Archaeology

TAKEUCHI, Y., German Linguistics

TOHDA, M., British History

TSUGE, Y., Linguistics

UCHIDA, H., French Literature

UEDA, M., Japanese Literature

YASUMURA, N., Classical Greek and Latin Literature

Faculty of Medicine (5-11-80 Kodatsuno, Kanazawa, Ishikawa; tel. (76) 265-2500; fax (76) 234-4351):

AMANO, R., Radiochemistry and Radiobiology

ASAI, H., Physical Therapy

HASEGAWA, M., Mental Health and Psychiatric Nursing

HOSO, M., Pathology and Anatomy

HOSOMI, H., Ethics and Bioethics

HOSONO, R., Neurobiology

IKUTA, M., Human Activity Analysis

INAGAKI, M., Fundamental Nursing and Division of Health Science

IZUMI, K., Gerontological and Rehabilitation Nursing

KARASAWA, T., Bacterial Pathogenesis

KAWAHARA, E., Pathology

KAWAI, K., Radiopharmaceutical Chemistry

KIDO, T., Occupational and Environmental Health

KIKUCHI, Y., Radiation Oncology

KIMURA, R., Child Development and Paediatric Nursing

KOJIMA, K., Medical Electronics and Information Sciences

KOSHIDA, K., Medical Radiation Protection

KOYAMA, Y., Psychiatry and Neuropsychology

MIZUKAMI, Y., Radiation Pathology

NAKASHIMA, H., Bioinformatics

NAKATANI, T., Anatomy and Biology of Cutaneous Wounds

NEMOTO, T., Medical Engineering, Bioengineering, Biomedical Measurement

NOTOYA, M., Neuropsychology and Speech Pathology

OGIWARA, S., Physical Therapy
OHTAKE, S., Haematology and Oncology
SAEKI, K., Community Health Nursing
SAKAI, A., Maternal and Child Nursing and Midwifery
SANADA, S., Radiological Technology and Medical Physics
SEKI, H., Child and Adolescent Health
SHIMADA, K., Women's Health and Midwifery
SHOSAKU, T., Neurophysiology
SOMEYA, F., Rehabilitation Medicine
SUZUKI, M., Neuroradiology
TACHINO, K., Rehabilitation Medicine
TAKATA, S., Clinical Physiology
TAKAYAMA, T., Nuclear Medicine Technology
TANAKA, J., Virology
YACHIE, A., Immunology and Host Defence

Graduate School of Medical Science (13-1 Takara-machi, Kanazawa, Ishikawa; tel. (76) 265-2100; fax (76) 234-4202):

FUJIWARA, K., Human Movement and Health
FUKUDA, R., Molecular Genetics (Dept. of Biochemistry)
FURUKAWA, M., Otorhinolaryngology, Head and Neck Surgery
HASHIMOTO, T., Laboratory Medicine
HIGASHIDA, H., Biophysical Genetics
ICHIMURA, H., Viral Infection and International Health
INABA, H., Emergency Medical Science (Department of Emergency and Critical Care Medicine)
INOUE, A., Molecular Reproductive Biology
ISEKI, S., Histology and Embryology
KANEKO, S., Cancer Gene Regulation, Gastroenterology and Nephrology
KANO, M., Cellular Neurophysiology
KATO, S., Molecular Neurobiology
KOIZUMI, S., Angiogenesis and Vascular Development (Department of Paediatrics)
KOSHINO, Y., Psychiatry and Neurobiology
MATSUI, O., Radiology
NAKANISHI, Y., Molecular and Cellular Biochemistry
NAKANUMA, Y., Morpho-Functional Pathology (Department of Human Pathology)
NAKAO, S., Cellular Transplantation Biology (Haemato-oncology and Respiratory Medicine)
NAMIKI, M., Integrative Cancer Therapy and Urology
OGAWA, S., Biotargeting
OGINO, K., Environmental and Preventive Medicine
OHSHIMA, T., Forensic and Social Environmental Medicine
OOI, A., Molecular and Cellular Pathology
SAIJOH, K., Environmental and Molecular Bio-informatics
SHIMIZU, T., Bacteriology
SUGIYAMA, K., Ophthalmology
TAKEHARA, K., Angiogenesis and Connective Tissue Metabolism (Department of Dermatology)
TAKUWA, Y., Molecular Vascular Physiology
TANAKA, S., Anatomy and Neuroembryology
TOMITA, K., Restorative Medicine of Neuromusculoskeletal System (Department of Orthopaedic Surgery)
TONAMI, N., Biotracer Medicine (Department of Nuclear Medicine)
WATANABE, G., Thoracic, Cardiovascular and General Surgery (Department of Surgery I)
YAMADA, M., Neurology and Neurobiology of Ageing
YAMAMOTO, E., Oral and Maxillofacial Surgery

YAMAMOTO, H., Biochemistry and Molecular Vascular Biology
YAMAMOTO, K., Organ Function Restoratology (Department of Anaesthesiology and Intensive Care Medicine)
YOKOI, T., Drug Metabolism and Molecular Toxicology
YOKOTA, T., Stem Cell Biology
YOSHIMOTO, T., Molecular and Medical Pharmacology

Graduate School of Natural Science and Technology (tel. (76) 264-6821; fax (76) 234-6844):

ADACHI, M., Optical Metrology
ANDO, T., Biophysics
AOKI, K., Theoretical Physics
ARAI, S., Petrology
CHIKATA, Y., Bridge Maintenance Management
ENDO, K., Theoretical Chemistry
FUJIMAGARI, T., Mathematical Analysis
FUJISHITA, H., Quantum Physics of Condensed Matter
FUJIWARA, N., Systems and Control
FUKUMORI, Y., Physiological Chemistry
FUNADA, T., Vehicle Automation
FURUMOTO, M., Geophysics
HASHIMOTO, H., Visual Communication, Video Coding, Multimedia Processing
HATANE, I., Numerical Analysis, Computational Physics and Mathematics
HAYAKAWA, K., Hygienic Chemistry
HAYASHI, Y., Separation Engineering
HIRAO, M., Production Engineering
HIROSE, Y., Computational Mechanics
HIWATARI, Y., Theory of Material Physics
HOJO, A., Strength of Materials
HONJO, T., Analytical Chemistry
ICHINOSE, T., Functional Analysis
IKEDA, O., Electrochemistry
INOMATA, K., Organic Chemistry
ISHIBASHI, H., Synthetic Organic Chemistry
ISHIDA, H., Coastal Engineering
ISHIWATARI, A., Geology and Petrology
ISOBE, K., Inorganic Chemistry
ITO, H., Differential Equations
ITO, S., Discrete Dynamical System and its Application
ITO, T., Algebraic Combinatorics
IWAHARA, M., Power Electronics, Applied Magnetics
IWATA, Y., Dynamics of Machinery
KAJIKAWA, Y., Structural Engineering
KAMIYA, Y., Robotics
KANJIN, Y., Harmonic Analysis
KANOH, S., Synthetic Polymer Chemistry
KASUE, A., Geometry
KATO, M., Stratigraphy and Palaeontology
KAWAKAMI, M., Urban and Regional Planning
KIHARA, K., Mineralogy and Crystallography
KIMATA, N., Infrastructure Planning, System Simulation
KIMURA, H., Artificial Intelligence
KIMURA, K., Drug Management and Policies
KIMURA, S., Fluid Mechanics and Thermal Sciences
KINOSHITA, H., Organic Chemistry
KITAGAWA, K., Mechanical Properties of Engineering Materials
KITAGAWA, M., Deformation and Strength of Man-made and Naturally Produced Materials
KITAURA, M., Earthquake Engineering
KODAMA, A., Geometry
KOMURA, A., Electrochemistry
KUBO, J., Theoretical Physics
KUMEDA, M., Electronic Materials
KUNIMOTO, K., Bio-organic Chemistry, Environmental Technology
MAEGAWA, K., Structural Engineering
MAGAI, T., Defects in Solids

MASUYA, H., Structural Engineering
MATSUDA, Y., Integrated Circuits
MATSUMOTO, T., Pile Foundations, Pile Dynamics, Numerical Analysis
MATSUNAGA, T., Molecular Human Genetics
MATSUURA, K., Instrumentation by Image Processing
MIKAGE, M., Herbal Medicine and Natural Resources
MIYAGISHI, S., Applied Physical Chemistry
MIYAJIMA, M., Earthquake Engineering
MIYAKAWA, T., Partial Differential Equations
MONZEN, R., Metallic Materials
MORI, S., Heat and Mass Transfer
MORIMOTO, A., Electronic Materials
MOTOI, M., Organic Chemistry of Polymers
MUKAI, C., Pharmaceutical and Organic Chemistry
MURAKAMI, T., Astrophysics
MURAMOTO, K., Image Information Systems
NAGANO, I., Radio Wave Engineering
NAKAGAKI, R., Physical Chemistry
NAKAMOTO, Y., Polymer Chemistry
NAKANISHI, T., Radiochemistry
NAKAO, S., Applied Mathematics
NAKAYAMA, K., Adaptive Systems
NAOE, S., Optical Properties of Materials
NISHIKAWA, K., Digital Signal Processing
NISHIKAWA, K., Theoretical Chemistry
NITTA, K., Polymer Physics
ODA, J., Bionic Design
OHASHI, N., Molecular Physics
OHGISHI, M., Cognitive Engineering
OHKUMA, S., Biochemistry and Molecular Cell Biology
OHTA, T., Pharmacognosy and Chemistry of Natural Products
OKUNO, M., Mineralogy and Non-crystalline Material Science
OMATA, S., Partial Differential Equations and Numerical Analysis
OTANI, Y., Aerosol Technology
SAITOU, M., Computational Materials Science
SAKURAI, S., Developmental Biology
SAKURAI, T., Biochemistry
SATO, H., Non-linear Vibration
SATO, Y., Organic Physical Chemistry
SEKI, H., Environmental Engineering
SEKIZAKI, M., Physical Chemistry of Crystals
SENDA, H., Coordination Chemistry
SHIMADA, K., Clinical Analytical Sciences
SHINTAKU, S., Textile Machinery
SOMEI, M., Chemistry
SUGANO, T., Algebra
SUZUKI, H., Solid State Physics
SUZUKI, M., Coordination Chemistry
SUZUKI, N., Holistic Pharmacotherapy
TAGO, Y., Computational Science
TAKAHASHI, K., Photo-function Material Chemistry
TAKAMIYA, S., Microwave/Optoelectronic Semiconductor Devices
TAKANOBU, S., Stochastic Analysis
TAKAYAMA, J., Traffic Engineering and Transport Planning
TAKIMOTO, A., Heat and Mass Transfer, Energy Conversion and Environmental Conservation
TAMAI, N., River Engineering, River Planning
TAMURA, K., Chemical Engineering Fundamentals and Thermodynamics
TANAKA, I., History of Science and Technology
TAZAKI, K., Environmental Earth Science
TORII, K., Civil Engineering Materials
TSUCHIYA, M., Mathematics (Theory of Stochastic Processes)
TSUJI, A., Innovative Pharmaceutics

UCHIYAMA, Y., Tribology (Friction and Wear Mechanisms of Rubbers and Plastics)
UEDA, K., Phylogenetics
UEDA, K., Separation and Analytical Chemistry
UEDA, T., Precision Machining, Laser Processing
UENO, H., Fluid Machinery, Fluid Power
UESUGI, Y., Plasma Science, Fusion Plasma Engineering
USUDA, M., Materials Working
YAJIMA, T., Ecology
YAMADA, K., Neuropsychopharmacology
YAMADA, M., Combinatorics
YAMADA, M., Opto-electronics
YAMADA, T., Polymer Processing, Reaction Engineering and Phase Equilibria
YAMADA, Y., Mechanical Properties of Materials
YAMAKOSHI, K., Biomedical Engineering
YAMANE, S., Computer Science
YAMAZAKI, K., Structural Optimization
YATOMI, C., Non-linear Continuum Mechanics
YOKOI, T., Drug Metabolism and Molecular Toxicology
YONEDA, Y., Molecular Pharmacology
YONEYAMA, T., Metal Forming, Machine Design

Law School (tel. (76) 264-5968; fax (76) 234-4167):

ATARASHI, M., Constitutional Law
FURITSU, T., Criminal Law
HASEGAWA, T., Civil Law
HATA, Y., Comparative Constitutional Law
HIGASHI, I., Criminal Procedure
HOSOKAWA, T., Administrative Law
KASHIMI, Y., Civil Law
NAKAJIMA, F., Commercial Law
NAKO, M., Labour Law
NISHIMURA, S., Criminal Law
NOSAKA, Y., Civil Law
OJIMA, S., Family Law
SATO, M., Criminal Procedure
TAJIMA, J., Civil Law

Environmental Preservation Centre (tel. (76) 234-6893; fax (76) 234-6895):

OHTA, T., Chemical Engineering Thermodynamics

Extension Institute (tel. (76) 264-5271; fax (76) 234-4045):

HATTORI, E., Adult Education (Life-long Education), Extramural Education

Foreign Language Institute (tel. (76) 264-5760; fax (76) 264-5993):

AISAWA, K., German
KANEKO, Y., German
KIKUCHI, E., German
KUWANO, H., English
MIKAMI (KIMURA), J., French
OYABU, K., English
SANBAI, R., English
SAWADA, S., English
WATANABE, A., English
YABUCHI, T., Chinese

Health Service Centre (tel. (76) 264-5251; fax (76) 234-4044; e-mail nakabaya@kenroku.kanazawa-u.ac.jp):

NAKABAYASHI, H., Endocrinology and Metabolism

Information Media Centre (tel. (76) 264-6911; fax (76) 234-6918):

SHAKO, M., Network Security
SUZUKI, T., Computational Physics, Particle Physics

Institute for Nature and Environmental Technology (tel. (76) 264-6141; fax (76) 234-4016):

IWASAKA, Y.
KASHIWAYA, K., Hydro-geomorphology

KIMURA, S., Heat Transfer and Fluid Mechanics
KOMURA, K., Environmental Radioactivity
NAKAMURA, K., Ecology
SASAYAMA, Y., Biodiversity
SHIMIZU, N., Bioengineering
YAMADA, S., Magnetic Technology
YAMAMOTO, M., Nuclear Geochemistry

International Student Centre (tel. (76) 264-5188; fax (76) 234-4043):

MATSUSHITA, M., Psychology
MIURA, K., Japanese Language Education
OKAZAWA, T., Insect Ecology

Research Centre for Higher Education (tel. (76) 264-5837; fax (76) 234-4172):

AONO, T., Medical Law
HAYATA, Y., Evaluation

University Hospital (13-1 Takara-machi, Kanazawa, Ishikawa; tel. (76) 265-2000; fax (76) 234-4320):

KOIZUMI, J., Department of General Medicine
MIYAMOTO, K., Department of Hospital Pharmacy

KITAMI INSTITUTE OF TECHNOLOGY

165 Koen-cho, Kitami, Hokkaido 090-8507
Telephone: (157) 26-9106
Fax: (157) 26-9117
Internet: www.kitami-it.ac.jp

Founded 1960
Independent
Academic year: April to March (2 semesters)
Pres.: HIDEYUKI TSUNEMOTO
Vice-Pres: KOICHI AYUTA, NOBUO TAKAHASHI
Dir of Admin.: AKIHIRO SHIBAZAKI
Library Dir: TOSHIYUKI OSHIMA

Number of teachers: 150 full-time
Number of students: 2,103

Publication: *Memoirs of Kitami Institute of Technology*.

KOBE UNIVERSITY

1-1 Rokkodai-cho, Nada-ku, Kobe 657-8501, Hyogo
Telephone: (78) 881-1212
E-mail: www-admin@kobe-u.ac.jp
Internet: www.kobe-u.ac.jp

Founded 1902
Independent
Academic year: April to March
Pres.: TOMOYUKI NOGAMI
Dirs: KUNIO SAKAMOTO, MASAHIRO TAKASAKI, MASAYUKI SUZUKI, OSAMI NISHIDA, SADAO KAMIDONO, SHIGEYUKI MAYAMA, SHINZO KITAMURA, SHOJI NISHIJIMA
Dir of Admin.: KUNIO SAKAMOTO
Library Dir: KENICHI SUDO

Library of 3,365,000 vols
Number of teachers: 1,674 full-time
Number of students: 17,598

Publications: *Law Review* (1 a year), *Economic Review* (1 a year), *Business Research* (irregular), *Journal of Mathematics* (2 a year), *Kobe Journal of Medical Sciences* (6 a year), *Bulletin of Allied Medical Sciences* (1 a year), *Memoirs of the Graduate School of Science and Technology* (1 a year), *Journal of International Cooperation Studies* (3 a year), *Economic and Business Review* (1 a year), *Journal of Economics and Business Administration* (12 a year), *Kobe Economic and Business Review* (1 a year)

DEANS

Faculty of Agriculture: CHIHARU NAKAMURA
Faculty and Graduate School of Letters: TAKAJI MATSUSHIMA

Faculty of Cross-cultural Studies: SATOSHI MUNAKATA
Faculty of Human Development: SUSUMU WADA
Faculty and Graduate School of Law: EIJI TAKIZAWA
Faculty and Graduate School of Economics: TAKASHI NAKATANI
Faculty and Graduate School of Business Administration: HISAKATSU SAKURAI
School and Graduate School of Medicine: SAKAN MAEDA
Faculty of Engineering: HIROMOTO USUI
Faculty of Maritime Sciences: KINZO INOUE
Faculty of Science: HIROSHI TAKEDA
Graduate School of Cultural Studies and Human Science: SUSUMU WADA
Graduate School of Humanities and Social Sciences: TAKAJI MATSUSHIMA
Graduate School of International Cooperation Studies: YUTAKA KATAYAMA
Graduate School of Science and Technology: HIDEKI FUKUDA
Research Institute for Economics and Business Administration: HIDETOSHI YAMAJI

PROFESSORS

Biosignal Research Center (tel. (78) 803-5332; fax (78) 803-5972; e-mail drkikaku@ofc.kobe-u.ac.jp; internet inherit:biosig.kobe-u.ac.jp/biosignal/english/index.html):

KIKKAWA, U., Biochemistry
ONO, Y., Biology of Living Functions
SAITO, N., Pharmacology
YONEZAWA, K., Biochemistry

Faculty of Agriculture (1-1 Rokkodai-cho, Nada-ku, Kobe 657-8501; tel. (78) 803-5921; fax (78) 803-5931; e-mail ashomu@ofc.kobe-u.ac.jp; internet www.ans.kobe-u.ac.jp/indexe.html):

AE, N., Soil Science and Plant Nutrition
AOKI, K., Applied Biofunctional Chemistry
ASHIDA, H., Applied Biofunctional Chemistry
HASEGAWA, S., Animal Nutrition, Morphology and Microbiology
HATA, T., Regional and Environmental Engineering
HORIO, H., Biosystems Engineering
HOSAKA, K., Food Resources Education and Research Centre
HOSHI, N., Animal Nutrition, Morphology and Microbiology
INAGAKI, N., Horticultural Science
KAKO, T., Food and Environmental Economics
KAMIJIMA, O., Plant Breeding and Production Science
KANAZAWA, K., Biofunctional Molecules
KAWAMURA, T., Biosystems Engineering
MAYAMA, S., Plant Protection
MIYAKE, H., Biofunctional Chemistry
MIYANO, T., Animal Breeding and Reproduction
MIZUNO, M., Plant Resource Science
MUKAI, F., Animal Breeding and Reproduction
NAITO, T., Plant Protection
NAKAMURA, C., Plant Genetics and Physiology
NAKANISHI, T., Horticultural Science
OHNO, T., Biofunctional Molecules
OHSAWA, R., Animal Science
OKAYAMA, T., Applied Biofunctional Chemistry
SHIMIZU, A., Animal Nutrition, Morphology and Microbiology
SUGITOMO, T., Genetics and Physiology
SUGIMOTO, Y., Applied Biofunctional Chemistry
TAKADA, O., Food and Environmental Economics
TANAKA, T., Regional and Environmental Science
TERAI, H., Horticultural Science

TOYODA, K., Biosystems Engineering
UCHIDA, K., Regional and Environmental Science
UCHIDA, N., Plant Breeding and Production Science
YAMAGATA, H., Biofunctional Molecules
YASUDA, T., Plant Genetics and Physiology

Faculty of Cross-cultural Studies (1-2-1 Tsurukabuto, Nada-ku, Kobe 657-8501; tel. (78) 803-7515; fax (78) 803-7509; e-mail shomudai@ofc.kobe-u.ac.jp; internet ccs.cla.kobe-u.ac.jp/kohou/eigo):

AMANO, K., Comtemporary Culture and Society Division
CHO, S., Comtemporary Culture and Society Division
FUJINO, K., Contemporary Culture and Society Division
GODA, T., Intercultural Communication Division
HAYASHI, H., Human Communication and Information Science Division
ICHIDA, Y., Comtemporary Culture and Society Division
ISHIHARA, K., Area Studies Division
ISHIKAWA, T., Area Studies Division
ISHIZUKA, H., Area Studies Division
KABURAGI, M., Human Communication and Information Science Division
KAGEYAMA, S., Area Studies Division
KIBA, H., Intercultural Communication Division
KINOSHITA, M., Area Studies Division
KOMURASAKI, S., Intercultural Communication Division
LU, X., Area Studies Division
MIKAMI, T., Contemporary Culture and Society Division
MIKIHARA, H., Comtemporary Culture and Society Division
MIURA, N., Intercultural Communication Division
MIZUGUCHI, S., Human Communication and Information Science Division
MIZUTA, K., Comtemporary Culture and Society Division
MORIMOTO, M., Intercultural Communication Division
MORISHITA, J., Human Communication and Information Science Division
MUNAKATA, S., Comtemporary Culture and Society Division
NOTANI, K., Intercultural Communication Division
OHTSUKI, K., Human Communication and Information Science Division
SADANOBU, T., Human Communication and Information Science Division
SAKAMOTO, C., Area Studies Division
SAKANO, T., Intercultural Communication Division
SASAE, O., Area Studies Division
SHIBATA, Y., Intercultural Communication Division
SONE, H., Area Studies Division
SUDO, K., Area Studies Division
SUZAKI, S., Area Studies Division
TANIMOTO, S., Area Studies Division
TERAUCHI, N., Area Studies Division
TODA, M., Intercultural Communication Division
UCHIDA, M., Intercultural Communication Division
UOZUMI, K., Contemporary Culture and Society Division
UTSUKI, N., Human Communication and Information Science Division
WANG, K., Area Studies Division
YAMAZAKI, Y., Contemporary Culture and Society Division
YOKOYAMA, R., Area Studies Divison
YOSHIDA, N., Contemporary Culture and Society Division
YOSHIOKA, M., Intercultural Communication Division

Faculty of Engineering (tel. (78) 803-6333; fax (78) 803-6396; e-mail kousyomu@ofc.kobe-u.ac.jp; internet www.eng.kobe-u.ac.jp/index.html):

ADACHI, H., Theory and History of Architecture
DEKI, S., Applied Inorganic Chemistry
FUJII, S., Energy Conversion Engineering
FUJITA, I., Hydraulic Engineering
HAYASHI, S., Mathematical Theory of Programming
HIRASAWA, S., Heat Transfer and Thermal Engineering
KAKUDA, Y., Mathematical Logic and Mathematical Design Theory
KANKI, H., Machine Dynamics and Control
KAWATANI, M., Structural Dynamics
KAYA, N., Space Solar Power Systems
KIKYO, H., Mathematical Logic and Computer Science
KONDO, A., Biochemical Engineering
KURODA, K., Transportation Engineering and Infrastructure Planning
MASUDA, S., Algorithms and Data Structures
MATSUYAMA, H., Membrane Technology
MICHIOKU, K., River Hydraulics
MITANI, I., Ultimate Design of Steel and Composite Structures
MIYOSHI, T., Quantum Electronics
MORII, M., Information Theory, Computer Networks, Internet Security and Cryptography
MORIMOTO, M., Environmental Acoustics
MORIWAKI, T., Intelligent Manufacturing Systems and Ultraprecision Machining
MORIYAMA, M., Architectural and Urban Environmental Engineering
NAGAO, T., Design and Performance of Building Structures
NAKAGIRI, S., Control and Identification of Distributed Systems
NAKAI, Y., Fatigue and Fracture of Engineering Materials
NAMBU, T., Control of PDE
NISHINO, T., Polymer Chemistry
NUMA, M., VLSI Design and CAD
OGAWA, M., Semiconductor Electronics
OHI, K., Quake-proof Structural Engineering
OHMAE, N., Micro- and Nano-Tribology and Surface Engineering
OHMURA, N., Transport Science
OHTA, Y., Control Engineering
OKUBO, M., Polymer Colloid Chemistry
OSUKA, K., Advanced Control Engineering
SHIBUYA, S., Geotechnical Engineering
SHIGEMURA, T., Urban and Architectural Design
SHIOZAKI, Y., Urban and Housing Study
SHIRASE, K., Autonomous Machine Tools and Intelligent Manufacturing Systems
TADA, Y., Optimum Design of Systems
TAKADA, S., Earthquake Engineering
TAKENAKA, N., Multiphase Flow Engineering
TAKI, K., Computer Science and Engineering
TOMITA, Y., Solid Mechanics
TOMIYAMA, A., Energy and Environmental Engineering
TSUKAMOTO, M., Computer Systems and Networking
TSURUYA, S., Catalytic Chemistry
UEDA, Y., Applied Physical Chemistry
USUI, H., Non-Newtonian Fluid Mechanics
WADA, O., Optoelectronic Materials and Devices
YASAKA, Y., Plasma Science and Power Engineering
YASUDA, C., Architectural Planning and Urban Design
YASUDA, H., Nanomaterials Science
YOSHIMOTO, M., VLSI System Engineering

YOSHIMURA, T., Applied Optics and Image Processing

Faculty of Letters (tel. (78) 803-5591; fax (78) 803-5589; e-mail lsoumu@lit.kobe-u.ac.jp; internet www.lit.kobe-u.ac.jp):

DONOHASHI, A., Art History
EDAGAWA, M., French Literature
FUJI, M., Sociology
FUJITA, H., Geography
FUKUNAGA, S., Japanese Literature and Language
HASEGAWA, K., Geography
HISHIKAWA, E., British and American Literature
IWASAKI, N., Sociology
KAMATANI, T., Chinese Language and Literature
KAZASHI, N., Philosophy
KUBOZONO, H., Linguistics
MATSUDA, H., French Literature
MATSUDA, T., Philosophy
MATSUMOTO, Y., Linguistics
MATSUSHIMA, T., Psychology
MOHRI, A., European and American History
MORI, N., Asian History
NAGANO, J., Art Theory
NISHIMITSU, Y., Linguistics
OGURA, T., Psychology
OHTSURU, A., European and American History
RINBARA, S., Japanese Literature and Language
SAITO, S., British and American Literature
SASAKI, M., Sociology
SUZUKI, Y., Japanese Literature and Language
TAKAHASHI, M., Japanese History
YAMAGUCHI, K., German Literature
YAMAMOTO, M., Philosophy
YUI, K., Sociology

Faculty of Human Development (3-11 Tsurukabuto, Nada-ku, Kobe 657-8501; tel. (78) 803-7905; fax (78) 803-7939; e-mail info@h.kobe-u.ac.jp; internet www.h.kobe-u.ac.jp):

AMAKAWA, T., Sciences for the Natural Environment
AOKI, T., Human Life Environment
ASANO, S., Studies of Social Environment
EBINA, K., Sciences for the Natural Environment
ENOMOTO, T., Sciences for the Natural Environment
FUNAKI, T., Educational Science
FUNAKOSHI, S., Childhood Development and Education
GOMI, K., Childhood Development and Education
HAMAGUCHI, H., Human Life Environment
HIRAKAWA, K., Sports Science
HIRAYAMA, Y., Human Life Environment
HIROKI, K., Childhood Development and Education
HOUNOKI, K., Adult Learning
ICHIHASHI, H., Human Life Environment
IMATANI, N., Studies of Social Environment
INAGAKI, N., Educational Science
ISHIKAWA, T., Health Education
ITO, K., Development Psychology
IWAI, M., Music
JOH, H., Human Life Environment
KAWABATA, T., Health Education
KAWABE, S., Sports Science
KISHIMOTO, H., Childhood Development and Education
MARUYA, N., Human Life Environment
MIKAMI, K., Educational Science
NAKABAYASHI, T., Developmental Psychology
NAKAGAWA, K., Sciences for the Natural Environment
NAKAMURA, K., Developmental Psychology
NAKAYAMA, S., Art and Design
NINOMIYA, A., Studies of Social Environment

ODA, T., Behavioural Development Studies
ODAKA, N., Art and Design
OGAWA, M., Educational Science
OKADA, S., Behavioural Development Studies
SAIDA, Y., Music
SAITO, K., Sciences for the Natural Environment
SATO, M., Developmental Psychology
SHIBA, M., Sports Performance
SHIRAKURA, T., Mathematics and Computer Studies
SUEMOTO, M., Adult Learning
SUGINO, K., Developmental Psychology
TAINOSHO, Y., Sciences for the Natural Environment
TAKAHASHI, J., Mathematics and Computer Studies
TAKAHASHI, M., Mathematics and Computer Studies
TAKAHASHI, T., Mathematics and Computer Studies
TANAKA, Y., Health Education
TERAKADO, Y., Sciences for the Natural Environment
TSUCHIYA, M., Educational Science
TSUKAWAKI, J., Art and Design
UEZI, S., Sciences for the Natural Environment
WADA, S., Studies of Social Environment
WAKAO, Y., Music
YAMAGUCHI, Y., Sport Sciences
YAMASAKI, T., Studies of Social Environment
YANAGIDA, Y., Sport Sciences
YANO, S., Human Life Environment

Faculty of Maritime Sciences (5-1-1 Fukae-minamimachi, Higashinada-ku, Kobe 658-0022; tel. (78) 431-6206; fax (78) 431-6355; e-mail mssoumu@ofc.kobe-u.ac.jp; internet www.maritime.kobe-u.ac.jp):

AZUKIZAWA, T., Marine Mechatronics
FUKUDA, K., Maritime Energy Engineering
FUKUOKA, T., Machine Design Engineering
FUKUSHI, K., Analytical Chemistry
FURUSHO, M., Seamanship and Traffic Psychology at Sea
HASHIMOTO, M., Internal Combustion Engines
HAYASHI, Y., Ship Navigation
IMAI, A., Logistics Planning
INOUE, K., Marine Traffic Engineering and Maritime Safety Management
INOUE, T., Network and Communication Systems Engineering
ISHIDA, H., Marine Meteorology
ISHIDA, K., Disaster Science
ISHIDA, T., Marine Power and System Engineering
ISOGAI, T., Statistical Science and Quality Management
KATO, E., Functional Polymer Materials Science
KIMURA, R., Acoustical Engineering and Maintenance Engineering
KITAMURA, A., Particle Beam Engineering
KOBAYASHI, E., Maritime Science and Naval Architecture
KOGUCHI, N., Navigation
KOZAI, K., Satellite Oceanography
MARUO, K., Partial Differential Equations
NISHIDA, O., Energy and Environmental Engineering
NISHIO, S., Naval Architecture
NISHIOKA, T., Fracture Mechanics, Computational Mechanics, Experimental Mechanics
ODA, K., Radiation Dosimetry and Applications
OTSUJI, T.
SADAKANE, H., Naval Architecture
SAKAMOTO, K., Power Electronics
SATO, M., Material Chemistry for Transportation

SHIOTANI, S., Numerical Ship Hydrodynamics
SIMADA, H., Cognitive Science
SUGITA, H., Management for Marine Power Plants
SUZUKI, S., Marine Traffic Laws
TAKAHASHI, R., Statistics
TANAKA, S., Fluid Mechanics of Engineering
YAMAMURA, S., Information Engineering
YOSHIDA, S., Shipping Economics

Faculty of Science (tel. (78) 803-5761; fax (78) 803-5770; e-mail rishomu@ofc.kobe-u.ac.jp; internet www.sci.kobe-u.ac.jp):

FUKE, K., Physical Chemistry
FUKUDA, Y., Optical Physics
FUKUYAMA, K., Analysis
GUNJI, Y., Planetary Science
HARIMA, H., Condensed Matter Theory
HAYASHI, F., Biology of Living Functions
HAYASHI, M., Organic Chemistry
HIGUCHI, Y., Applied Mathematics
HIMENO, S., Inorganic Chemistry
IKEDA, H., Applied Mathematics
KADONO, Y., Biology of Living Structures
LIM, C. S., High Energy Theory
MATSUDA, T., Planetary Science
MIMURA, T., Biology of Living Structures
MIYATA, T., Earth Science
NAKAGAWA, Y., Planetary Science
NAKAMURA, N., Planetary Science
NAKANISHI, Y., Algebra and Geometry
NORO, M., Applied Mathematics
ONISHI, H., Physical Chemistry
OTOFUJI, Y., Earth Science
SAITO, M., Algebra and Geometry
SAKAMOTO, H., Biology of Living Functions
SASAKI, T., Algebra and Geometry
SATO, H., Earth Science
SETSUNE, J., Inorganic Chemistry
TAKANO, K., Analysis
TAKAYAMA, N., Analysis
TAKEDA, H., Particle Physics
TOMEOKA, K., Planetary Science
TSUCHIYA, T., Biology of Living Functions
WADA, S., Condensed Matter Physics
WATANABE, K., Biology of Living Structures
YAMADA, Y., Analysis
YAMAMURA, K., Organic Chemistry
YAMAZAKI, T., Algebra and Geometry

Graduate School of Business Administration (2-1 Rokkodai-cho, Nada-ku, Kobe, 657-8501; tel. (78) 803-7256; fax (78) 803-6969; e-mail bwebmstr@kobe-u.ac.jp; internet www.b.kobe-u.ac.jp):

DEI, F., International Economics, International Investments
FUJIWARA, K., Money and Financial Systems
GOTOH, M., Financial Reporting and Accounting Systems
HARADA, T., Industrial Organization
ISHII, J., Marketing Management and Business Strategy
KAGONO, T., Business Strategy and Corporate Behaviour
KANAI, T., Organizational Behaviour
KATO, H., Finance
KATO, Y., Management Accounting
KOGA, T., International Accounting
KOKUBU, K., Social and Environmental Accounting
KOMBAYASHI, N., Human Resource Management
KOU, L., Marketing
KUTSUNA, K., Entrepreneurial Finance
KUWAHARA, T., Business History
MARUYAMA, M., Applied Microeconomics, Distribution Systems
MATSUO, H., Supply Chain Management, Production Planning and Scheduling
MIZUTANI, F., Public Utility Economics and Regulatory Economics
NAITO, F., Financial Accounting and Auditing

NAKANO, T., Accounting Systems and History
OGAWA, S., Marketing
SAKAKIBARA, S., Corporate Finance and Portfolio Management
SAKASHITA, A., Organizational Behaviour and Corporate Culture
SAKURAI, H., Financial Accounting, Financial Statement Analysis
SHOJI, K., Transport Economics and Policy
TAKAO, A., Insurance Industry Analysis
TAKASHIMA, K., Marketing and Distribution Systems
TANI, T., Management Accounting and Control

Graduate School of Economics (2-1 Rokkodai-cho, Nada-ku, Kobe 657-8501; tel. (78) 803-7246; fax (78) 803-7293; e-mail esoumu@ofc.kobe-u.ac.jp; internet www.econ.kobe-u.ac.jp):

ADACHI, M., Social Policy
AMANO, M., Modern Japanese Economic History
FUJITA, S., International Monetary System
FUKUDA, W., Economic System Theory
HAGIWARA, T., Contemporary Technology Theory
HAMORI, S., Statistical Analysis of Economic Time Series Data
HARA, M., International Investment Theory
HARUYAMA, T., Economic Growth Theory
IRITANI, J., Public Finance Policy
ISHIGURO, K., International Politics and Economics
ISHIKAWA, M., Environmental Economics
JINUSHI, T., American Economy
KATO, H., Chinese Economy
KUBO, H., European Economy
MARUYA, R., Theory of Economic Policy
MATSUBAYASHI, Y., Empirical Analysis of International Macroeconomy
MITANI, N., Labour Economics
NAKAMURA, T., Macroeconomics, Investment Theory
NAKANISHI, N., International Economics
NAKATANI, T., Macrodynamic Theory
OHKUBO, H., Monetary Policy
OHTANI, K., Theory of Statistical Inference
OKUNISHI, T., European Economic History
OSHIO, T., Social Security
SHIGETOMI, K., Economic History of Modern Britain
TAKAHASHI, S., World Economic Geography
TAKIGAWA, Y., Monetary Economics
TANAKA, Y., Theory of Economic Structure
TANIZAKI, H., Estimation and Test in Simulation-base Econometrics
UEMIYA, S., History of Economic Theory
URANAGASE, T., Japanese Economic History
YAMAGUCHI, M., Agricultural Policy
YANAGAWA, T., Industrial Organization
YOSHII, M., Comparative Economics

Graduate School of Cultural Studies and Human Science (3-1-1 Tsurukabuto, Nada-ku, Kobe 657-8501; tel. (78) 803-7905; fax (78) 803-7939; e-mail inkouhou@ccs.cla.kobe-u.ac.jp; internet www.cla.kobe-u.ac.jp/sojinka):

HARIMA, T., Clinical Psychology
HOUNOKI, K., Human and Community Empowerment
KAWABATA, T., Human and Community Empowerment
SUEMOTO, M., Human and Community Empowerment

Graduate School of Humanities and Social Sciences (1-1 Rokkodai-cho, Nada-ku, Kobe 657-8501; tel. (78) 803-5591; fax (78) 803-5589; e-mail lsoumo@lit.kobe-u.ac.jp; internet www.lit.kobe-u.ac.jp/index_bunka.html):

IWASAKI, N., Theory of Social Risks

Graduate School of International Cooperation Studies (2-1 Rokkodai-cho, Nada-ku, Kobe 657-8501; tel. (78) 803-7265; fax (78) 803-7295; e-mail kokusomu@ofc .kobe-u.ac.jp; internet www.kobe-u.ac.jp/ ~gsics/indexj.html):

ALEXANDER, R. B., Endogenous Security
CHEN, K., Economic Development and Regional Inequality
FUKUI, S., Development Microeconomics
IGARASHI, M., International Law
KATAYAMA, Y., Political Development in Southeast Asia
KIMURA, K., Nation-building and State Formation in Korea
MATSUNAGA, N., International Trade and Economic Growth
MATSUNAMI, J., Comparative Study on Deregulation, Privatization and Local Government
MIZUNO, T., Review and Future Assessment on International Issues
NISHINA, K., Development Finance
OHTA, H., Applied Microeconomics
SHIBATA, A., International Law
SURUGA, T., Economic Development and Employment
TAKADA, H., Local Public Administration and Finance
TAKAHASHI, M., African Economics
TATEBAYASHI, M., Policy Activities of Political Elites in Japan
TOSA, H., Critical Theory and its Application in International Relations
UCHIDA, Y., Social Sector Management in Developing Countries
UENO, H., Transition Economy Policies

Graduate School of Law (2-1 Rokkodai-cho, Nada-ku, Kobe 657-850; tel. (78) 803-7232; fax (78) 803-7292; e-mail j1shomu@ofc .kobe-u.ac.jp; internet www.law.kobe-u.ac .jp):

AKASAKA, M., Constitutional Law
AMIYA, R., Western Political History
BABA, K., Sociology of Law
FUJIWARA, A., Japanese Legal History
HAMADA, F., Labour Law
HASUNUMA, K., Philosophy of Law
HATA, M., Civil Procedure
IIDA, F., Political Theory
INOUE, N., Constitutional Law
INOUE, Y., Intellectual Property Law
IOKIBE, M., Japanese Political History, Comparative Politics
ISHIKAWA, T., Professional Legal Education
ISOMURA, T., Civil Law
ITO, M., Comparative Politics
JI, W. D., Chinese Law, Comparative Studies in Legal Culture
KASHIMURA, S., Sociology of Law
KIKKAWA, G., International Relations
KOMURO, N., International Economic Law
KONDO, M., Commercial Law, Securities Regulation
KUBOTA, A., Civil Law
MARUYAMA, E., Anglo-American Law, Medical Law
MASUJIMA, K., International Relations
MORISHITA, T., Russian Law, Principles of Social Sciences
NAKAGAWA, T., Administrative Law
NAKANISHI, M., Civil Procedure
NAKANO, S., Private International Law, International Civil Procedure
NEGISHI, A., Economic Law
OSHIMA, S., Professional Legal Education
OTSUKA, H., Criminal Law
OUCHI, S., Labour Law
SAITO, A., International Trade Law, Private International Law
SAKAMOTO, S., International Law
SATO, H., Tax Law
SENSUI, F., Economic Law
SHINADA, Y., Political Data Analysis, Election System

SHITANI, M., Commercial Law
SUDO, M., Professional Legal Education
TAKIZAWA, E., Western Legal History, Roman Law
TEJIMA, Y., Civil and Medical Law
TSUKIMURA, T., International Relations
USHIMA, K., Criminal Law
YAMADA, S., Civil Law
YAMADA, T., Professional Legal Education
YAMAMOTO, H., Civil Procedure
YAMAMOTO, K., Civil Law
YASUNAGA, M., Civil Law
YONEMARU, T., Administrative Law
YUKIZAWA, K., Commercial Law, Commercial Transactions

Graduate School of Science and Technology (tel. (78) 803-5332; fax (78) 803-5349; e-mail drkikaku@ofc.kobe-u.ac.jp; internet www .scitec.kobe-u.ac.jp/english/index.html):

ABE, S., Function Control
ARAI, T., Information Mathematics
ASAKURA, Y., Space Formation Engineering
BOKU, S., Environmental Science of Bio-resource Production
FUKUDA, H., Applied Molecular Assembly
KANAZAWA, Y., Bioresource and Energy Creation
KATO, S., Material Production Process Engineering
KITAGAWA, H., Relational Biosystems
KOJIMA, F., Structural Design
MAEKAWA, S., Bioinformation
MATSUSHITA, T., Fire Safety Engineering, Thermal Environmental Engineering in Building
MIYAKE, M., Biosystem Applications
MUKAI, T., Space and Planetary Materials
NAKAYAMA, A., Regional Environment
NANBA, T., Material Functions
NOUMI, M., Mathematical Structures
NOZAKI, M., Material Structures
ODANI, M., Urban Transportation Planning, Urban and Regional Planning
OHKAWA, T., Intelligent Bioinformatics
ONO, M., Food Marketing
SASAKI, M., Organic Chemistry
TABUCHI, M., Creation of Spatial Systems
TAKEDA, M., Molecular Cellular Science
TAKEUCHI, T., Molecular Structure and Function
TANAKA, S., Theoretical Life Science and Computational Molecular Biology
TAURA, T., Intelligent Artificial Systems
TSUBAKI, M., Functional Molecular Assembly
TSUTAHARA, M., Biological Resource Utilization
UEHARA, K., Media Technology and its Production
YAMANAKA, M., Earth Sciences

International Student Center (tel. (78) 803-5265; fax (78) 803-5289; e-mail ryugaku@ofc .kobe-u.ac.jp; internet www.kobe-u.ac.jp/ ~kisc):

NAKANISHI, Y., Education in Japanese Language
SEGUCHI, I., Intercultural and Transcultural Education

Medical Center for Student Health (tel. (78) 803-5245; fax (78) 803-5254; e-mail healthy@ kobe-u.ac.jp; internet www.kobe-u.ac.jp/ medicalc):

BABA, H., Internal Medicine, Biosignal Pathophysiology

Molecular Photoscience Research Center (tel. (78) 803-5761; fax (78) 803-5770; e-mail rishomu@ofc.kobe-u.ac.jp; internet www .kobe-u.ac.jp/mprc):

OHTA, H., Condensed Matter Physics
TOMINAGA, K., Condensed Phase Dynamics

Research Center for Environmental Genomics (tel. (78) 803-5332; fax (78) 803-5349; e-mail drkikaku@ofc.kobe-u.ac.jp; internet www.rceg.biosig.kobe-u.ac.jp/hpj.html):

FUKAMI, Y., Biology of Living Structures
NANMORI, T., Plant Molecular Biology
OONO, K., Plant Cell Biology

Research Center for Inland Seas (tel. (78) 803-5761; fax (78) 803-5770; e-mail rishomu@ ofc.kobe-u.ac.jp; internet www.kobe-u.ac.jp/ kurcis):

HYODO, M., Earth Science
KAWAI, H., Marine Biology
NAGATA, S., Environmental Biochemistry

Research Center for Urban Safety and Security (tel. (78) 803-6437; fax (78) 803-6394; e-mail rcuss@kobe-u.ac.jp; internet www .kobe-u.ac.jp/~tosi):

ARIKI, Y., Media Engineering
IIZUKA, A., Geo-environmental Engineering and Geoinformatics
ISHIBASHI, K., Seismotectonics
KAMAE, I., Health Informatics and Decision Sciences
OKIMURA, T., Slope Stability and Geotechnical Engineering
TANAKA, Y., Soft Ground Engineering and Earthquake Geotechnical Engineering

Research Institute for Economics and Business Administration (2-1 Rokkodai-cho, Nada-ku, Kobe 657-8501; tel. (78) 803-7270; fax (78) 803-7059; e-mail office@rieb.kobe-u .ac.jp; internet www.rieb.kobe-u.ac.jp):

GOTO, J., International Economy and Business
IGAWA, K., International Economy and Business
ISOBE, T., International Economy and Business
IZAWA, H., International Economy and Business
KAMIHIGASHI, T., Information Economy and Business
KATAYAMA, S., International Economy and Business
KOJIMA, K., Information Economy and Business
KONISHI, Y., Information Economy and Business
LEE, H., Information Economy and Business
MIYAO, R., RIEB Liaison Centre
NISHIJIMA, S., International Economy and Business
NOBEOKA, K., RIEB Liaison Centre
SHIMOMURA, K., Information Economy and Business
TOMITA, M., International Economy and Business
YAMAJI, H., Information Economy and Business

Research Institute for Higher Education (1-2-1 Tsurukabuto, Nada-ku, Kobe 657-8501; tel. (78) 803-7522; fax (78) 803-7539; e-mail dakaikei@ofc.kobe-u.ac.jp; internet www .kurihe.kobe-u.ac.jp):

KAWASHIMA, T., Sociology of Education
MAIYA, K., Experimental Psychology
YAMANOUCHI, K., Sociology of Education

School and Graduate School of Medicine (7-5-1 Kusunoki-cho, Chuo-ku, Kobe 650-0017; tel. (78) 382-5111; fax (78) 382-5050; e-mail webmst@med.kobe-u.ac.jp; internet www .med.kobe-u.ac.jp/welcomej.html):

AIBA, A., Cell Biology
AKITA, H., General Medical Science
ANDO, H., Basic Allied Medicine
AZUMA, T., Polygenic Disease Research
CHIHARA, K., Endocrinology; Metabolism, Neurology and Haematology; Oncology
FUJIMARA, M., Urology
FURUKAWA, H., Applied Occupational Therapy

GU, E., Advanced Medical Research and Treatment
HASHIMOTO, T., Basic Occupational Therapy
HAYASHI, Y., Molecular Medicine and Medical Genetics
HOTTA, H., Microbiology and Genomics
ISHII, N., Disaster and Emergency Medicine
ISHIKAWA, Y., Health Sciences and Basic Nursing
KASUGA, M., Diabetes, Digestive and Kidney Diseases
KATAOKA, T., Molecular Biology
KAWABATA, M., International Health
KAWAGUCHI, Y., Psychiatric Nursing and Mental Health
KAWAMATA, T., Applied Occupational Therapy
KITA, A., Maternal Nursing and Midwifery
KOHMURA, E., Neurosurgery
KOMORI, T., Oral and Maxillofacial Functional Science
KUMAGAI, S., Clinical Pathology and Immunology
KUNO, T., Molecular Pharmacology and Pharmacogenomics
KURODA, Y., Gastroenterological Surgery
KUROSAKA, M., Orthopaedic Surgery
MAEDA, K., Psychiatry and Neurology
MAEDA, S., Molecular Pathology
MARUO, T., Women's Medicine
MATSUDA, N., Community Health Nursing
MATSUMURA, S., Biochemistry
MATSUO, H., Maternity Nursing
MATSUO, M., Paediatrics
MIKI, A., Basic Physical Therapy
MINAMI, Y., Biomedical Regulation and Parasitology
MURATA, K., Clinical Nursing
NAKAMURA, S., Biochemistry
NAKAZONO, N., Applied Medical Technology
NEGI, A., Ophthalmology
NIBU, K., Otorhinolaryngology—Head and Neck Surgery
NISHIGORI, C., Dermatology
NISHIO, H., Public Health
NISHIYAMA, K., Basic Medical Technology
OBARA, H., Perioperative Medicine and Pain Management
OKAMURA, H., Molecular Brain Science
OKITA, Y., Cardiovascular, Thoracic and Paediatric Surgery
OKUMURA, K., Clinical Pharmacokinetics
RYO, R., Applied Medical Technology, Haematology and Blood Transfusion Medicine
SAKAMOTO, N., Medical Informatics
SEINO, S., Cell Biology and Neurophysiology
SEKI, K., Applied Occupational Therapy
SHIMADA, T., Applied Physical Therapy
SHIOZAWA, S., Rheumatology
SUGIMURA, K., Radiology
TABUCHI, Y., Clinical Oncology and Surgical Nursing
TAHARA, S., Plastic Surgery
TAKADA, S., Maternal and Child Health Science
TAMURA, Y., Basic Nursing
TERASHIMA, T., Developmental Neurobiology
TSUTOU, A., Basic Allied Medicine
UENO, Y., Legal Medicine
UGA, S., Parasitology
USAMI, M., Basic Medical Technology, Surgical Metabolism and Nutrition
WATANABE, M., Applied Medical Technology
YADA, M., Clinical Nursing
YAMAGUCHI, M., Applied Occupational Therapy
YAMAMURA, H., Proteomics
YAMAZAKI, I., Applied Occupational Therapy

YOKONO, K., Internal and Geriatric Medicine
YOKOYAMA, M., Cardiovascular and Respiratory Internal Medicine
YOKOZAKI, H., Surgical Pathology

School of Languages and Communication (1-2-1 Tsurukabuto, Nada-ku, Kobe 657-8501; tel. (78) 803-7522; fax (78) 803-7539; e-mail dakaikei@ofc.kobe-u.ac.jp; internet solac.cla.kobe-u.ac.jp):

GREER, T., Conversation Analysis, Applied Linguistics, Bilingualism
IGUCHI, J., Applied Linguistics
ISHIKAWA, S., Applied Linguistics
KASHIWAGI, H., English Language Education
KATO, M., English Education
MASUDA, Y., German Linguistics
MIKI, Y., European Maritime Culture
MURATA, R., The Later Enlightenment in Germany
NAKAGAWA, M., Contrastive Linguistics
OKIHARA, K., Applied Linguistics and English Language Education
SHIMAZU, A., American Literature
TSUJIMOTO, Y., British Journalism of the 18th and 19th centuries
URITA, S., English Literature
YOKOKAWA, H., Psycholinguistics
ZHU, C., Phonetics and Foreign Language Education

KUMAMOTO UNIVERSITY

39-1 Kurokami 2-chome, Kumamoto-shi 860-8555
Telephone: (96) 344-2111
Fax: (96) 342-3110
E-mail: message@svml.jimu.kumamoto-u.ac.jp
Internet: www.kumamoto-u.ac.jp
Founded 1949
Independent
Academic year: April to March (2 terms)
Pres.: Dr TATSURO SAKIMOTO
Dir of Admin. Bureau: MASAHARU CHOKI
Vice-Pres: Prof. CHIUCHI HIRAYAMA, Prof. TOMOMICHI ONO
Librarian: Prof. NAKAMASA IWAOKA
Number of teachers: 1,022
Number of students: 9,836
Publications: *Kumamoto Journal of Culture and Humanities* (1 a year), *Kumamoto Law Review* (4 a year), *Kumamoto Journal of Mathematics* (1 a year), *Kumamoto Journal of Science (Earth Sciences)* (1 a year), *Memoirs of the Faculty of Engineering* (2 a year), *Physics Report of Kumamoto University* (every 2 years), *Cryogenics Report of the Shockwave and Condensed Matter Research Center* (1 a year), *Kumamoto University Studies in Social and Cultural Sciences* (1 a year)

DEANS

Faculty of Education: Prof. SHOICHI ISHIHARA
Faculty of Engineering: Prof. ISAO TANIGUCHI
Faculty of Law: Prof. YATARO YOSHINAGA
Faculty of Letters: Prof. MASATO MORI
Faculty of Medical and Pharmaceutical Sciences: Prof. NOBUO SAKAGUCHI
Faculty of Science: Prof. MITSUHIKO KOHNO
Graduate School of Science and Technology: Prof. KATSUHIKO SUGAWARA
Graduate School of Social and Cultural Sciences: Prof. YASUTOSHI YUKAWA
School of Law: Prof. ITARU YAMANAKA

PROFESSORS

Faculty of Education (40-1 Kurokami 2-chome, Kumamoto 860-8555; tel. (96) 342-2514; fax (96) 342-2510; e-mail kyo-somu@jimu.kumamoto-u.ac.jp; internet www.educ.kumamoto-u.ac.jp):

ASAKAWA, M., Food
BABA, K., Biology
CHIKUMA, Y., Educational Philosophy
FUKUSHIMA, K., Physics
HARADA, I., Electricity
HIGASHI, T., Electricity
HIRAMINE, Y., Algebra
HIRAWA, T., Vocal Music
HORIHATA, M., Japanese Linguistics
ICHIMURA, K., School Health
ISHIHARA, S., Sculpture
ITOH, J., Algebra
KAWAMINAMI, H., Teaching of Social Studies
KIMURA, M., School Health
KIYOZUMI, M., School Health
KOGA, N., Sociology
KUWAHATA, M., Teaching of Domestic Sciences
MAEDA, K., Teaching of Science
MASAMOTO, K., Biology
MIYAMOTO, M., Teaching of Social Studies
NAGATA, N., Teaching of School Health
NAKATA, Y., Educational Administration
NAKAYAMA, T., Theory and History of Music
NISHIKAWA, M., English Linguistics
OGATA, A., Psychology of Handicapped Children
OGAWA, K., Japanese Literature
OGO, K., Exercise and Hygiene
SHIBAYAMA, K., Clinical Psychology
SHIN, K., Education of Handicapped Children
SHINOHARA, H., Educational Psychology
SUGI, S., Teaching of Japanese
SUGOU, H., History of Handicraft Education
SUZUKI, R., English and American Literature
SUZURIKAWA, S., Social Welfare
TAKAGI, N., Teaching of English
TAKAMORI, H., Clothing
TANIGUCHI, K., Physiology of Exercise
TODA, T., English Linguistics
TORIKAI, K., Home Management
TSURUSHIMA, H., History
TSUZINO, T., Mechanics
UMEDA, M., Design and Crafts
WATANABE, K., Earth Science
YAMAMOTO, S., Teaching of Mathematics
YAMANAKA, M., Economics
YANAGI, H., Educational Sociology
YOKOYAMA, S., Geography
YONEMURA, K., Clinical Medicine and Nursing
YOSHIDA, M., Group Dynamics
YOSHIKAWA, N., Theory and History of Art
YOSHINAGA, S., Teaching of Music

Faculty of Engineering (39-1 Kurokami 2-chome, Kumamoto 860-8555; tel. (96) 342-3513; fax (96) 342-3510; internet www.eng.kumamoto-u.ac.jp/english/index.htm):

AKIYAMA, H., Electrical Energy Systems
EBIHARA, K., Electrical Energy Systems
FURUKAWA, K., Water Environmental Engineering
GOTO, M., Bio-related Molecular Science
HARADA, H., Intelligent Systems Engineering
HIROE, T., High Pressure Science and Materials Processing
HIROSE, T., Biochemical Engineering
IHARA, H., Bio-related Molecular Science
IKEGAMI, T., Advanced Technology of Electrical and Computer Systems
IKUNO, H., Electronic and Communication Systems
IMURA, H., Thermal and Fluid Energy Systems
INOUE, T., Electronic and Communication Systems
ISHIHARA, O., Regional Planning and Management
IWAI, Z., Intelligent Systems for Measurement and Control

JYO, A., Chemistry of Molecular Engineering
KASHIWAGI, H., Intelligent Systems for Measurement and Control
KAWAJI, S., Computer Science and Engineering
KAWAMURA, Y., Advanced Materials Technology
KITANO, T., Regional Planning and Management
KITAZANO, Y., Water Environmental Engineering
KOBAYASHI, I., Water Environmental Engineering
KURODA, N., Advanced Materials Technology
MACHIDA, M., Chemistry for Molecular Engineering
MAKINO, Y., Architectural Planning and Design
MAZDA, T., Structural Engineering
MITA, N., Advanced Technology of Electrical and Computer Systems
MITSUI, Y., Architectural Planning and Design
MIYAHARA, K., Electronic and Communication Systems
MIZOKAMI, S., Disaster Prevention Engineering
MOROZUMI, M., Regional Planning and Management
MURAYAMA, N., Advanced Technology of Electrical and Computer Systems
NAITOU, K., Mathematical Science
NAKAMURA, R., Intelligent Systems Engineering
NAKAMURA, Y., Advanced Technology of Electrical and Computer Systems
NISHIDA, M., Advanced Materials Technology
NONAKA, T., Chemistry for Material Science
OBARA, Y., Geotechnical Engineering
ODA, I., Intelligent Machine Design and Manufacturing
OGAWA, K., Architectural Planning and Design
OHMOTO, T., Water Environmental Engineering
OHNO, Y., Materials Development Systems
OHTANI, J., Water Environmental Engineering
OSHIMA, Y., Mathematical Science
SADATOMI, M., Thermal and Fluid Energy Systems
SAISHO, M., Disaster Prevention Engineering
SAKURADA, K., Disaster Prevention Engineering
SATONAKA, S., Intelligent Machine Design and Manufacturing
SHOSENJI, H., Chemistry for Molecular Engineering
SUEYOSHI, T., Computer Science and Engineering
SUZUKI, A., Geotechnical Engineering
TAKADA, Y., Mathematical Science
TANIGUCHI, I., Bio-related Molecular Science
TONDA, H., Materials Development Systems
TORII, S., Intelligent Machine Design and Manufacturing
UCHIYAMA, O., Architectural Planning and Design
UMENO, H., Computer Science and Engineering
USAGAWA, T., Intelligent Systems Engineering
WATANABE, J., Thermal and Fluid Energy Systems
YAMAO, T., Structural Engineering
YANO, T., Structural Engineering
YASUI, H., Intelligent Machine Design and Manufacturing
YOKOI, Y., Mathematical Science

Faculty of Law (40-1 Kurokami 2-chome, Kumamoto 860-8555; tel. (96) 342-2315; fax (96) 342-2310; e-mail jsj-somu@jimu .kumamoto-u.ac.jp; internet www.law .kumamoto-u.ac.jp):

FUKAMATI, K., International Law
HAYASHI, I., International Law
INADA, T., Criminal Procedure
ITO, H., Politics
IWAOKA, N., Politics
KAWAMOTO, T., English Literature
KITAGAWA, K., Philosophy
KIZAKI, Y., Civil Law
MORI, M., German Literature
NAKAMURA, N., Philosophy of Law
OHSAWA, H., Politics
SATO, M., Economic Policy
SUZUKI, K., Politics
WAKASONE, K., European Legal History
YAMASHITA, T., Economics
YAMAZAKI, K., Tax Law
YOSHIDA, I., Sociology of Law
YOSHINAGA, Y., Social Law

Faculty of Letters (40-1 Kurokami 2-chome, Kumamoto 860-8555; tel. (96) 342-2313; fax (96) 342-2310; e-mail bun-somu@jimu .kumamoto-u.ac.jp; internet www.let .kumamoto-u.ac.jp/let/index.html):

FUKAHORI, K., German Literature
FUKUZAWA, K., Linguistics
HOHGETSU, T., Geography
IHARA, S., Japanese Language
IKEDA, M., Cultural Anthropology and Medical Humanities
KAMIMURA, N., German Language
KINOSHITA, N., Archaeology
KOMATSU, H., Cultural History
KOMOTO, M., Archaeology
KUMAMOTO, S., English Language
MARUYAMA, S., Regional Sociology
MORI, M., Japanese Literature
OGINO, K., German Language
OKABE, T., Aesthetics
OOKUMA, K., French Literature
SAKATA, M., German Literature
SHINOZAKI, S., Ethics
SUGITANI, K., German Literature
TAGUCHI, H., Sociology
TAKAHASHI, T., Ethics
TANAKA, Y., German Literature
TANIKAWA, N., English Literature
TERADA, M., French Literature
TOKUNO, S., Regional Sociology
TONE, T., Psychology
WATANABE, I., Psychology
YASUDA, M., Folklore
YOSHIKAWA, E., Chinese Language
YOSIMURA, T., Japanese History

Faculty of Medical and Pharmaceutical Sciences (1-1 Honjo 1-chome, Kumamoto 860-8556; tel. (96) 373-5904; fax (96) 373-5906; e-mail iys-somu@jimu.kumamoto-u.ac.jp; internet www.medphas.kumamoto-u.ac.jp):

ARAKI, E., Metabolic Medicine
EKINO, S., Histology
ENDO, F., Paediatrics
FUTATUKA, M., Public Health
GOTO, M., Structure-Function Physical Chemistry
HARADA, S., Medical Virology
HARANO, K., Computational Molecular Design
HORIUCHI, S., Medical Biochemistry
IMAI, T., Drug Metabolism and Disposition
INOMATA, Y., Paediatric Surgery
IRIE, T., Clinical Chemistry and Informatics
ITO, T., Pathology and Experimental Medicine
KAI, H., Molecular Medicine
KAMASUJI, M., Cardiovascular Surgery
KIKAWA, K., General Medicine
KINOSHITA, Y., Aggressology and Critical Care Medicine

KITAMURA, T., Clinical Behavioural Sciences
KODAMA, K., Anatomy
KURATSU, J., Neurosurgery
MIIKE, T., Child Development
MITSUYA, H., Haematology
MITSUYAMA, S., Pharmacology and Molecular Therapeutics
MIURA, R., Molecular Enzymology
MIYATA, T., Chemico-Pharmacological Sciences
MIZUSHIMA, T., Pharmaceutical Microbiology
MORI, M., Molecular Genetics
NAKAGAWA, K., Pharmacology and Therapeutics
NAKAJIMA, M., Organic Chemistry
NAKANISHI, H., Molecular Pharmacology
NAKAYAMA, H., Molecular Cell Function
NISHIMURA, Y., Immunogenetics
NOHARA, T., Natural Medicines
OGAWA, H., Cardiovascular Medicine
OGAWA, H., Sensory and Cognitive Physiology
OHTSUKA, M., Bio-organic Medicinal Chemistry
OKABE, H., Diagnostic Medicine
OKAMURA, H., Reproductive Medicine and Surgery
OTAGIRI, M., Biopharmaceutics
SAITO, H., Pharmacy
SAKAGUCHI, N., Immunology
SASAKI, Y., Gastroenterology and Hepatology
SAYA, H., Tumour Genetics and Biology
SHIGA, K., Molecular Physiology
SHINOHARA, M., Oral and Maxillofacial Surgery
SHOJI, S., Pharmaceutical Biochemistry
TAKAHAMA, K., Environmental and Molecular Health Sciences
TAKEYA, M., Cell Pathology
TANAKA, H., Developmental Neurobiology
TANIHARA, H., Ophthalmology and Visual Science
TERASAKI, H., Anaesthesiology
TOMITA, K., Nephrology
TSUNENARI, S., Forensic Medicine
UCHINO, M., Neurology
UEDA, M., Pharmaceutical Microbiology
UEDA, S., Urology
UEKAWA, K., Physical Pharmaceutics
UNO, T., Analytical and Biophysical Chemistry
YAMAGATA, Y., Structural Biology
YAMAMOTO, T., Molecular Pathology
YAMASHITA, Y., Diagnostic Imaging
YOSHIHARA, H., Medical Informatics
YUMOTO, E., Otolaryngology—Head and Neck Surgery

Faculty of Science (39-1 Kurokami 2-chome, Kumamoto 860-8555; tel. (96) 342-3314; fax (96) 342-3320; e-mail rig-some@jimu .kumamoto-u.ac.jp; internet www.sci .kumamoto-u.ac.jp/index.html):

ABE, S. I., Developmental Biology
ANIYA, M., Fundamental Physics
ARAI, K., Fundamental Physics
FUJII, A., Solid State Spectroscopy
FURUSHIMA, M., Algebra and Geometry
HAMANA, Y., Probability Theory
HARAOKA, Y., Analysis and Applied Analysis
HASE, Y., Palaeobotany and Environmental Science
HASEGAWA, S., Palaeontology and Environmental Science
HASENAKA, T., Volcanology and Igneous Petrology
ICHIKAWA, F., Superconductivity
ICHIMURA, K., Physical Chemistry
IMAFUKU, K., Organic Chemistry
ISHIDA, A., Dynamics of Environments
ITOH, K., Magnetic Thin Films
KIMURA, H., Analysis and Applied Analysis

KOBAYASHI, O., Algebra and Geometry
KOHNO, M., Analysis and Applied Analysis
MATSUMOTO, N., Inorganic Chemistry
MATSUSAKA, T., Dynamics of Environments
MATSUZAKI, S., Physical Chemistry
MITSUNAGA, M., Quantum Optics
MOMOSHIMA, N., Environmental Analysis
MOTOYOSHI, A., Fundamental Physics
NISHINO, H., Organic Chemistry
NISHIYAMA, T., Petrology, Mineralogy and
  Geodynamics
NOHDA, S., Environmental Analysis
OHWAKI, S., Integrated Mathematics
SAKAMOTO, N., Polymer Chemistry
SANEMASA, I., Environmental Analysis
SHIBUYA, H., Palaeomagnetism and Geody-
  namics
SHIMADA, J., Groundwater Circulation
SHIODA, M., Molecular Cell Biology
TANI, T., Molecular Biology
UCHINO, A., Dynamics of Environments
WATANABE, A., Algebra and Geometry
YAMAKI, H., Algebra and Geometry
YOSHIASA, A., Geodynamics and Condensed
  Matter Physics

**Graduate School of Social and Cultural Sci-
ences** (40-1 Kurokami 2-chome, Kumamoto
860-8555; tel. (96) 342-2313; fax (96) 342-
2130; e-mail bun-somu@jimu.kumamoto-u.ac
.jp; internet www.let.kumamoto-u.ac.jp/
gsscs/index_e.html):

YAMANAKA, S., Geography
YUKAWA, Y., Linguistics

Graduate School of Science and Technology
(39-1 Kurokami 2-chome, Kumamoto 860-
8555; tel. (96) 342-3013; fax (96) 342-3010;
e-mail dcjimu@gpo.kumamoto-u.ac.jp;
internet 133.95.161.1/index-en.html):

HASEGAWA, S., Natural Environmental Sci-
  ences
HIYAMA, T., Energy Systems
ICHIMURA, K., Basic Chemistry and Physics
  for Materials Sciences
IKI, K., Human-Environmental Engineer-
  ing
ISHITOBI, M., Intelligent Manufacturing
  Systems
KAWAHARA, M., Materials Science and
  Technology
KIDA, K., Applied Chemistry for Materials
  and Life Sciences
MATSUMOTO, Y., Applied Chemistry of
  Materials
OHBA, H., Mechanical Systems Design
OHTSU, M., Disaster-preventive Structural
  Engineering
OKUNO, Y., Electrical and Computer
  Engineering
SUGAWARA, K., Environmental Conserva-
  tion Engineering
UCHIMURA, K., Intelligent Systems and
  Computer Science
YAMAKI, H., Mathematics
YOSHITAMA, K., Bioinformational Science

School of Law (40-1 Kurokami 2-chome,
Kumamoto 860-8555; tel. (96) 342-2315; fax
(96) 342-2310; e-mail jsj-somu@jimu
.kumamoto-u.ac.jp; internet www
.kumamoto-ua.ac.jp/lawschool):

FUKUYAMA, M., Law
HARADA, T., Law
HASHIMOTO, M., Civil Law
HAYASHI, M., Local Government Law
HIRATA, H., Criminal Procedure
ISHIBASHI, H., Social Law
KUBOTA, M., Commercial Law
MATSUBARA, H., Civil Procedure Law
NAKAGAWA, Y., Administrative Law
NAKAMURA, S., Criminal Law
ONO, Y., Civil Law
ONODERA, M., Prosecutor
SAWATARI, K., Law
TADA, N., International Private Law
YAMAMOTO, E., Constitutional Law

YAMANAKA, I., Legal Theory and History

Center for AIDS Research (2-1 Honjo 2-
chome, Kumamoto 860-0811; tel. (96) 373-
6531; fax (96) 373-6532; internet www.caids
.kumamoto-u.ac.jp):

MATSUSHITA, S., Clinical Retrovirology and
  Infectious Diseases
OKADA, S., Haematopoiesis
TAKIGUCHI, M., Viral Immunology

Center for Marine Environment Studies (39-
1 Kurokami, 2-chome, Kumamoto 860-8555;
tel. (96) 342-3448; fax (96) 342-3448; internet
www.engan.dc.kumamoto-u.ac.jp/index
.html):

HENMI, Y., Analysis of Cyclization Systems
  for Natural Resources
TAKIKAWA, K., Hydro- and Geosphere
  Environments
TAKIO, S., Conservation and Development
  of Natural Resources

**Center for Multimedia and Information
Technologies** (39-1 Kurokami 2-chome,
Kumamoto 860-8555; tel. (96) 342-3824; fax
(96) 342-3829; internet www.cc.kumamoto-u
.ac.jp):

IRIGUCHI, N.
NAKANO, Y.
SUGITANI, K.

Co-operative Research Center (2081-7
Tabaru, Mashiki-machi, Kumamoto 861-
2202; tel. (96) 286-1212; fax (96) 286-1067;
internet www.kcr.kumamoto-u.ac.jp/index-j
.html):

HIROSUE, H., Liaison between University
  and Industry
MATSUSHITA, H., Technology Transfer
  between University and Industry

**Institute of Molecular Embryology and Gen-
etics** (24-1 Kuhonji 4-chome, Kumamoto 862-
0976; tel. (96) 344-2111; fax (96) 373-6638;
e-mail imeg@kaiju.medic.kumamoto-u.ac.jp;
internet www.imeg.kumamoto-u.ac.jp):

KUME, S., Stem Cell Biology
NAGAFUCHI, A., Cellular Interactions
NAKAO, M., Organ Development
NISHINAKAMURA, R., Integrative Cell Biol-
  ogy
OGAWA, M., Cell Differentiation
OGURA, T., Molecular Cell Biology
OKUBO, H., Molecular Neurobiology
SHIMAMURA, K., Morphogenesis
TAGA, T., Cell Fate Modulation
YAMAIZUMI, M., Cell Genetics
YAMAMURA, K., Developmental Genetics
YOKOUCHI, Y., Pattern Formation

**Institute of Resource Development and
Analysis** (2-2-1 Honjo, Kumamoto 860-0811;
tel. (96) 373-6637; fax (96) 373-6638; e-mail
iys-senter@jimu.kumamoto-u.ac.jp):

NAKAGATA, N., Reproductive Engineering
URANO, T., Microbiology and Genetics
YAMADA, G., Transgenic Technology

International Student Center (40-1 Kurokami 2-chome, Kumamoto 860-8555; tel.
(96) 342-2133; fax (96) 342-2130; e-mail
gji-ryugaku@jimu.kumamoto-u.ac.jp; internet center.ryu.kumamoto-u.ac.jp/index_e
.html):

KOWAKI, M., Linguistics (Semitic Languages)

Research Center for Higher Education (40-1
Kurokami 2-chome, Kumamoto 860-8555; tel.
(96) 342-2716; fax (96) 342-2710; e-mail
gak-kyomu@jimu.kumamoto-u.ac.jp; internet www.ge.kumamoto-u.ac.jp):

OHMORI, F., Education Policy
SUGAWARA, T., Educational Evaluation
YAMADA, M., Advanced and Applied Edu-
  cation of European History

Research Center for Lifelong Learning (40-1
Kurokami 2-chome, Kumamoto 860-8555; tel.

(96) 342-3281; fax (96) 342-3281; e-mail
sos-tiiki@kumamoto-u.ac.jp; internet www
.lifelong.kumamoto-u.ac.jp):

SAGA, T., Philosophy, Bio-ethics
UENO, S., Political Science
YANAGI, H., Educational Sociology

**Shock Wave and Condensed Matter Research
Center** (39-1 Kurokami 2-chome, Kumamoto
860-8555; tel. (96) 342-3299; fax (96) 342-
3293; internet www.shocomarec
.kumamoto-u.ac.jp):

FUJII, A., Low Temperature Science
ITO, S., Shock Processing and its Applica-
  tions
KUBOTA, H., Solid State Physics under
  Multi-Extreme Conditions

KYOTO INSTITUTE OF TECHNOLOGY

Hashigami-cho, Matsugasaki, Sakyo-ku,
Kyoto 606-8585

Telephone: (75) 724-7111
Fax: (75) 724-7010
E-mail: webmaster@adm.kit.ac.jp
Internet: www.kit.ac.jp

Founded 1949
Public control
Academic year: April to March

Pres.: YOSHIMICHI EJIMA
Vice-Pres.: MASAO FURUYAMA
Vice-Pres.: MUTSUO TAKENAGA
Dir-Gen.: KIMIO MURAMATSU
Librarian: SHIGEYUKI YAMAGUCHI

Library of 378,000 vols
Number of teachers: 301
Number of students: 4,068

Publications: *Memoirs of the Faculty of
  Engineering and Design—JINBUN* (Series
  of Science and Technology, 1 a year),
  Bulletin of the Faculty of Textile Science
  (1 a year)

DEANS

Faculty of Engineering and Design: RIKUO
  OTA
Faculty of Textile Science: SHIGERU KUNUGI

KYOTO UNIVERSITY

Yoshida-Honmachi, Sakyo-ku, Kyoto 606-
8501

Telephone: (75) 753-7531
E-mail: koryu52@mail.adm.kyoto-u.ac.jp
Internet: www.kyoto-u.ac.jp

Founded 1897
Independent
Academic year: April to March

Pres.: HIROSHI MATSUMOTO
Exec. Vice-Pres. for Student Affairs: AKIHIKO
  AKAMATSU
Exec. Vice-Pres. for Education: TOSHIYUKI
  AWAJI
Exec. Vice-Pres. for Finance and Facilities:
  NOBORU NISHISAKA
Exec. Vice-Pres. for Gen. Affairs and Person-
  nel: KOHEI SHIOTA
Exec. Vice-Pres. for Planning and Evalu-
  ation: NOBUYOSHI ESAKI
Exec. Vice-Pres. for Research: KIYOSHI YOSHI-
  KAWA
Exec. Vice-Pres. for External Affairs and
  Alumni Relations: YUZO OHNISHI

Library: see Libraries and Archives
Number of teachers: 3,296
Number of students: 22,559

DEANS

College of Medical Technology: (vacant)
Graduate School of Agriculture and Faculty
  of Agriculture: TAKASHI ENDO
Graduate School of Asian and African Area
  Studies: TAKASHI SUGISHIMA

Graduate School of Biostudies: SHIN YONE-HARA

Graduate School of Economics and Faculty of Economics: HIDEO TANAKA

Graduate School of Education and Faculty of Education: MASASHI TSUJIMOTO

Graduate School of Energy Science: HIRO-HIKO TAKUDA

Graduate School of Engineering and Faculty of Engineering: SATORU KOMORI

Graduate School of Global Environmental Studies: SHINTARO KOBAYASHI

Graduate School of Human and Environmental Studies and Faculty of Integrated Human Studies: YASUHIKO TOMIDA

Graduate School of Informatics: YOSHIMASA NAKAMURA

Graduate School of Law and Faculty of Law: TAKASHI MURANAKA

Graduate School of Letters and Faculty of Letters: AKIHIRO SATO

Graduate School of Management: KIYOSHI KOBAYASHI

Graduate School of Medicine and Faculty of Medicine: NAGAHIRO MINATO

Graduate School of Pharmaceutical Sciences and Faculty of Pharmaceutical Sciences: HIDEO SAJI

Graduate School of Science and Faculty of Science: JUICHI YAMAGIWA

Law School: YOSHIO SHIOMI

School of Government: MASARU MABUCHI

School of Public Health: (vacant)

PROFESSORS

Graduate School of Agriculture and Faculty of Agriculture (Kitashirakawa, Oiwake-cho, Sakyo, Kyoto, 606-8502; tel. (75) 753-6490; fax (75) 753-6020; internet www.kais.kyoto-u.ac.jp):

ADACHI, S., Bioengineering
AOYAMA, S., Agricultural Facility Engineering
AZUMA, J., Forest Biochemistry
ENDO, T., Plant Genetics
FUJISAKI, K., Insect Ecology
FUJITA, M., Structure of Plant Cells
FUJIWARA, T., Fisheries, Oceanography
FUSHIKI, T., Nutrition Chemistry
FUTAI, K., Environmental Mycoscience
HIRATA, T., Marine Bioproducts Technology
HIROOKA, H., Animal Science
HORIE, T., Crop Science
IMAI, H., Animal Reproduction
INOUYE, K., Enzyme Chemistry
IWAI, Y., Forest Resources and Society
KAGATSUME, M., Regional Environmental Economics
KANO, K., Bioelectroanalytical Chemistry
KAWACHI, T., Water Resources Engineering
KAWADA, T., Food Biochemistry
KITA, K., Bioenergy Conversion
KITABATAKE, N., Food and Environmental Science
KOSAKI, T., Soil Science
KUME, S., Environmental Physiology
MATSUMOTO, T., Fibrous Biomaterials
MATSUMURA, Y., Quality Analysis and Assessment
MITSUNO, T., Irrigation, Drainage and Hydrological Environment Engineering
MIYAGAWA, H., Bioregulation Chemistry
MIZUYAMA, T., Erosion Control
MORIMOTO, Y., Landscape Architecture
MURATA, K., Molecular Biotechnology
NAKAHARA, H., Marine Microbial Ecology
NAKATSUBO, F., Chemistry of Biomaterials
NIIYAMA, Y., Farm Management
NISHIDA, R., Chemical Ecology
NISHIO, Y., Chemistry of Composite Materials
NISHIOKA, T., Biofunction Chemistry
NOBUCHI, T., Forest Utilization

NODA, K., Comparative Agricultural History
ODA, S., Farm Management Information and Accounting
OHIGASHI, H., Organic Chemistry in Life Science
OHNISHI, O., Crop Evolution
OHTA, S., Tropical Forest Resources and Environments
OIDA, A., Agricultural Systems Engineering
OKUMURA, S., Wood Processing
OKUNO, T., Plant Pathology
SAKO, Y., Marine Microbiology
SAKUMA, M., Behavioural Physiology and Chemical Ecology of Insects
SAKURATANI, T., Tropical Agriculture
SASAKI, Y., Animal Breeding and Genetics
SEKIYA, J., Plant Nutrition
SHIMIZU, S., Fermentation Physiology and Applied Microbiology
SUEHARA, T., Principles of Agricultural Science
TAKAFUJI, A., Ecological Information
TAKEBE, T., Agricultural and Environmental Policy
TAKEDA, H., Forest Ecology
TANAKA, M., Fish Biology
TANI, M., Forest Hydrology
TANISAKA, T., Plant Breeding
TOMINAGA, T., Weed Ecology
UEDA, K., Cellular Biochemistry
UEDA, M., Biomacromolecular Chemistry
UMEDA, M., Field Robotics
UTSUMI, S., Food Quality Design and Development
YAMADA, T., Plant Production Management
YAMASUE, Y., Physiological Aspects of Agricultural Systems
YANO, H., Animal Nutrition
YAZAWA, S., Vegetable and Ornamental Horticulture
YONEMORI, K., Pomology
YOSHIDA, M., Forest Policy and Economics
YOSHIKAWA, M., Physiological Function of Food

Graduate School of Asian and African Area Studies (46 Shimoadachi-cho, Yoshida, Sakyo-ku, Kyoto 606-8501; tel. (75) 753-7302; fax (75) 753-7350; e-mail soumu@cseas.kyoto-u.ac.jp; internet www.asafas.kyoto-u.ac.jp):

ADACHI, A., The Hindu World
ARAKI, S., Agricultural Ecology
HIRAMATSU, K., Natural Hisory
ICHIKAWA, M., Socio-ecological History
KAJI, S., Culture and Ethnicity
KAKEYA, M., Livelihood and Economy
KOBAYASHI, S., Environmental Ecology
KOSUGI, Y., The Islamic World
OHTA, I., Nature–Human Interaction
SHIMADA, S., Socio-cultural Integration
SUGISHIMA, T., Comparative Social Transformation

Graduate School of Biostudies:

INABA, K., Laboratory of Science Communication and Bioethics
INOUE, T., Laboratory of Gene Biodynamics
ISHIKAWA, F., Laboratory of Cell Cycle Regulation
KAKIZUKA, A., Laboratory of Functional Biology
KOCHI, T., Laboratory of Plant Molecular Biology
KOZUTUMI, Y., Laboratory of Membrane Biochemistry and Biophysics
MINATO, N., Laboratory of Immunology and Cell Biology
NAGAO, M., Laboratory of Biosignals and Response
NEGISHI, M., Laboratory of Molecular Neurobiology
NISHIDA, E., Laboratory of Signal Transduction

SATO, F., Laboratory of Molecular and Cellular Biology of Totipotency
TAKEYASU, K., Laboratory of Plasma Membrane and Nuclear Signalling
UEMURA, T., Laboratory of Cell Recognition and Pattern Formation
YAMAMOTO, K., Laboratory of Molecular Biology of Bioresponse
YONEHARA, S., Laboratory of Molecular and Cellular Biology

Graduate School of Economics and Faculty of Economics (tel. (75) 753-3400; fax (75) 753-3492; e-mail kyoumu@econ.kyoto-u.ac.jp; internet www.econ.kyoto-u.ac.jp):

FUJII, H., International Accounting
FURUKAWA, A., Money and Finance
HIOKI, K., Organization Theory
HISAMOTO, N., Labour Economics
HORI, K., Economic History
IMAKUBO, S., Economic Policy
IWAMOTO, T., International Economics
KAZUSA, Y., Managerial Accounting
KIJIMA, M., Financial Engineering
KOJIMA, H., Principles of Economics
MORIMUNE, K., Econometrics
MOTOYAMA, Y., World Economy
NARIU, T., Applied Economics
NEI, M., Modern Economics
NISHIMURA, S., Applied Economics
NISHIMUTA, Y., Business History
OHNISHI, H., Economic Statistics
OKADA, T., Regional Economy
SHIMOTANI, M., Japanese Economy
SHIOJI, H., Japanese Economy
TACHIBANAKI, T., Economic Policy
TANAKA, H., History of Social Thought
TAO, M., Business Policy
TOKUGA, Y., Accounting for Venture Business
UETA, K., Public Finance
UNI, H., Economic Theory
WAKABAYASHI, Y., Marketing
YAGI, K., Economic Theory
YAMAMOTO, H., Chinese Economy
YOSHIDA, K., Contemporary Economics

Graduate School of Education and Faculty of Education (tel. (75) 753-3010; fax (75) 753-3025; e-mail kyoumu@kyoumu.educ.kyoto-u.ac.jp; internet www.educ.kyoto-u.ac.jp):

FUJIWARA, K., Clinical Psychology
INAGAKI, K., Sociology of Education
ITOH, Y., Clinical Psychology
IWAI, H., Sociology of the Course of Life
KAWAI, T., Clinical Psychology
KAWASAKI, Y., Library and Information Science
KOYASU, M., Cognitive Psychology in Education
MAEHIRA, Y., Lifelong Education
OKADA, Y., Clinical Personality Psychology
SUGIMOTO, H., Comparative Education
SUZUKI, S., Pedagogy
TAKAMI, S., Educational Finance
TANAKA, K., Curriculum Development and Assessment
TSUJIMOTO, M., Japanese History of Education
YAMADA, Y., Developmental Psychology
YANO, S., Clinical Pedagogy
YOSHIKAWA, S., Cognitive Psychology in Education

Graduate School of Energy Science (tel. (75) 753-4871; fax (75) 753-4745; internet www.energy.kyoto-u.ac.jp/index-eng.html):

HOSHIDE, T., Fracture Mechanics for System Integrity
ISHIHARA, K., Social Engineering of Energy
ISHII, R., Space Energy and Resources
ISHIYAMA, T., Combustion Engine Technology
IWASE, M., Physical Chemistry of Iron- and Steelmaking and Related High-Temperature Processes

KASAHARA, M., Atmospheric Environmental Engineering
KONDO, K., Plasma Diagnostics
MABUCHI, M., Materials Science and Engineering
MAEKAWA, T., Plasma Physics
MATSUMOTO, E., Non-linear Continuum Mechanics
NOZAWA, H., Physics and Technology of VLSI
SAKA, S., Ecosystems of Biomass for Energy Use
SHIOJI, M., Combustion Science and Engineering
SHIOTSU, M., Thermal Hydraulics in Energy Systems
TAKUDA, H., Advanced Processing of Resources and Energy
TEZUKA, T., Energy Economics
YAO, T., Solid-state Energy Chemistry
YOSHIKAWA, H., Man–Machine Systems

Graduate School of Engineering and Faculty of Engineering:

AOKI, K., Rarefied Gas Dynamics
AOKI, K., Resources Development Engineering
AOYAMA, Y., Biorecognition
AOYAMA, Y., Urban and Regional Planning
ARAKI, M., Control Engineering
ASAKURA, T., Tunnel Engineering
ASHIDA, Y., Exploration Geophysics
AWAKURA, Y., Materials Electrochemistry
CHUJO, Y., Polymerization Chemistry
EGUCHI, K., Catalyst Science and Catalyst Design Engineering
FUJII, S., Division of Environmental Quality Control
FUKUYAMA, A., Basic Quantum Engineering
HAGIWARA, T., Automatic Control Engineering
HAMACHI, I., Bio-organic Chemistry
HASEBE, S., Process Systems Engineering
HAYASHI, Y., Disaster Risk Management of Built Environment
HIGASHITANI, K., Surface Control Engineering
HIGUCHI, T., Landscape and Environmental Planning
HIKIHARA, T., Power Conversion and Control Laboratory
HIRAO, K., Inorganic Structural Chemistry
HIYAMA, T., Organic Chemistry of Natural Products
HOJO, M., Continuum Mechanics
HOKOI, S., Thermal Analysis and Design
HOSODA, T., River Engineering
ICHIKAWA, A., Systems and Control
IEMURA, H., Earthquake Engineering
IMAHORI, H., Applied Molecular Science
IMANAKA, T., Biotechnology
INAMURO, T., Fluid Dynamics
INOUE, K., Space Development and Structural Systems
INOUE, K., Energy Conversion Chemistry
INUI, H., Intermetallic Alloys for Structural and Functional Uses
ISHIKAWA, J., Charged Particle Devices
ITO, S., Polymer Structure and Function
ITOH, A., Applied Beam Materials Engineering
ITOH, S., Urban Sanitary Engineering
KAKIUCHI, T., Functional Solution Chemistry
KATO, N., Architectural Information Systems
KAWAI, J., Process Chemical Physics
KIDA, S., Fluid Dynamics
KIMURA, K., Mesoscopic Materials Engineering
KIMURA, S., Design of Functional Materials
KITAGAWA, S., Functional Chemistry
KITAMURA, R., Transport Planning and Engineering

KITAMURA, T., Mechanical Behaviour of Materials
KITANO, M., Quantum Optical Engineering
KOBAYASHI, K., Civil Engineering Systems Analysis
KOBAYASHI, T., Biomedical Engineering
KOMORI, S., Fluids Engineering
KOTERA, H., Mechanical Systems
KUBO, A., Machine Design
MAE, K., Environmental Process Engineering
MAEDA, T., Theory of Architecture and Environmental Design
MAKI, T., Mechanical Properties of Steel
MAKINO, T., Thermophysical Properties of Materials
MASUDA, H., Powder Technology
MASUDA, T., Polymer Physics and Rheology
MATSUBARA, A., Precision Measurement and Machining
MATSUBARA, E., Structural Characterization by X-ray Diffraction
MATSUHISA, H., Vibration Engineering
MATSUMOTO, M., Wind Engineering
MATSUOKA, T., Engineering Geology
MATSUSHIGE, K., Molecular Nano-electronics
MITSUDO, T., Catalysis
MIURA, K., Environmental Process Engineering
MIYAGAWA, T., Durability of Reinforced Concrete
MIYAHARA, M., Fluids Confined in Nanospace Order Formation by Nano-colloids
MIYAZAKI, N., Computational Solid Mechanics
MONNAI, T., Architecture and Human Environmental Planning
MORI, Y., Molecular Biology
MORISAWA, S., Environmental Risk Analysis
MORISHIMA, N., Neutron Science
MORIYAMA, H., Nuclear Materials
MUNEMOTO, J., Architectural Planning
MURAKAMI, M., Organometallic Chemistry
MURAKAMI, M., Thin Film Metallurgy
NAGATA, M., Gas Dynamics
NAKATSUJI, H., Quantum Chemistry
NEZU, I., Fluid Mechanics and Hydraulics
NISHIMOTO, S., Excited-state Hydrocarbon Chemistry
NODA, S., Quantum Optoelectronics Engineering
OGUMI, Z., Electrochemistry
OHE, K., Organometallic Chemistry
OHNISHI, Y., Rock Mechanics
OHSAWA, Y., Electric Power System Engineering
OHSHIMA, M., Materials Process Engineering
OKA, F., Soil Mechanics
ONO, K., Propulsion Engineering
OSAMURA, K., Science of Materials
OSHIMA, K., Organic Reaction Chemistry
OTSUKA, K., Analytical Chemistry of Materials
SAITO, T., Mining and Rock Mechanics
SAKAI, T., Coastal Engineering
SAKAKI, S., Quantum Molecular Science and Technology
SAWAMOTO, M., Living Cationic Polymerization
SAWARAGI, T., Design Systems Engineering
SCAWTHORN, C., Natural Hazard Risk Management
SERIZAWA, A., Nuclear Reactor Engineering
SHIMA, S., Engineering Plasticity
SHIMASAKI, M., Computational Electromagnetic Field Analysis
SHIRAKAWA, M., Biophysical Chemistry
SUGIMURA, H., Nanoscopic Surface Architecture
SUGINOME, M., Organic Synthesis and System Design
SUZUKI, M., Integrated Function Engineering

TABATA, O., Micro Electro-Mechanical Systems
TACHIBANA, A., Quantum Theory of Condensed Matter
TACHIBANA, K., Plasma Physics and Technology
TAKADA, M., Housing and Environmental Design
TAKAHASHI, H., Architectural Design and Theory
TAKAHASHI, Y., History of Architecture
TAKAMATSU, S., Architectural Design
TAKAOKA, G., Ion Engineering, Cluster Science
TAKEDA, N., Solid Waste Management
TAKEWAKI, I., Earthquake Resistant Engineering
TAKIGAWA, T., Physics of Polymer Materials
TAMON, H., Separation Engineering
TAMURA, K., Structural Properties of Materials
TAMURA, M., Environmental Remote Sensing
TAMURA, T., Applied Mechanics
TANAKA, F., Polymer Core Physical Chemistry
TANAKA, H., Environmental Evaluation
TANAKA, I., Ceramic Materials Science
TANAKA, K., Inorganic Solid-State Chemistry
TANAKA, K., Molecular Energy Conservation
TANAKA, T., Molecular Science and Technology of Catalysis
TANIGUCHI, E., Urban Infrastructure Systems
TSUCHIYA, K., Dynamics and Control of Space Vehicles
TSUNO, H., Water Quality Conservation
UCHIYAMA, I., Environmental Health
UETANI, K., Mechanics of Building Structures
WADA, O., Circuit Theory and Applications
WATANABE, F., Reinforced and Pressed Concrete Structures
YAMAMOTO, K., Quantum Physics
YAMASHINA, H., Computer-integrated Manufacturing
YOSHIDA, H., Urban Environment and Safety Engineering
YOSHIDA, J., Organic Chemistry
YOSHIKAWA, T., Robotics
YOSHIMURA, M., Knowledge and Information Systems
YOSHIZAKI, T., Polymer Statistical Mechanics
YOSIDA, H., Thermal Systems Engineering

Graduate School of Global Environmental Studies (tel. (75) 753-9167; fax (75) 753-9187; internet www.adm.kyoto-u.ac.jp/ges):

KAMON, M., Environmental Infrastructure Engineering
KAWASAKI, M., Environmental Atmospheric Chemistry
KOBAYASHI, M., Global Environment Architecture
KOBAYASHI, S., Regional Planning
KOSAKI, T., Terrestrial Ecosystems Management
MATSUI, S., Environmentally Friendly Industries for Sustainable Development
MATSUOKA, Y., Global Integrated Assessment Modelling
MATSUSHITA, K., Global Environmental Policy
MIMURO, M., Environmental Biotechnology
MORIMOTO, Y., Landscape Ecology and Planning
NAKAHARA, H., Conservation of Coastal Ecosystems
OGAWA, T., Philosophical Theory of Human and Environmental Symbiosis
SHIIBA, M., Circulation of Environmental Resources

TAKEBE, T., Global Resource Economics
TAMURA, R., Environmental Materials Science
UETA, K., Global Ecological Economics
YOKOYAMA, T., Towards a Theory of Global Civilization

Graduate School of Human and Environmental Studies and Faculty of Integrated Human Studies (Yoshida Nihonmatsu-cho, Sakyo, Kyoto; tel. (75) 753-2950; fax (75) 753-2957; internet www.adm.kyoto-u.ac.jp/jinkan):

ADACHI, Y., Socio-cultural Environments
ATSUJI, T., Chinese Linguistics
BECKER, C., Comparative Religion, Ethics, Death and Dying
EDA, K., History of Modern China
FUKUI, K., Cultural Anthropology of Ethiopia
FUKUOKA, K., American Literature
FUNAHASHI, S., Neurophysiology
HATTORI, F., Linguistics and Slavonic Languages
HORI, T., Natural Environments
INAGAKI, N., Modern French Literature
ISHIDA, A., Modern German Philology and Literature
ISHIHARA, A., Neurochemistry and Physiology
IYORI, T., Common Environmental System
KAMATA, H., Volcanology
KANASAKA, K., Human Societies
KATO, M., Coexisting Systems of Nature and Human Beings
KAWASHIMA, A., Modern British History
KIMURA, T., Russian Literature
KIWAMOTO, Y., Plasma Physics
KOYAMA, S., History of Japanese Education
KUJIRAOKA, T., Human Development
MAEGAWA, S., Low Temperature Magnetism
MAMIYA, Y., Common Environmental System
MARUHASHI, Y., English Drama
MATSUDA, K., History of Western Learning in Japan
MATSUI, M., Systematic Zoology
MATSUMARU, M., Neurophysiology
MATSUURA, S., History of North-Eastern Asia
MICHIHATA, T., German Literature
MIHARA, O., German Literature
MITANI, K., Slavic Linguistics
MIYAMOTO, Y., Polymer Physics
MORIMOTO, Y., Theory of Partial Differential Equations
MORITANI, T., Environmental Conservation and Development
MOTOKI, Y., Medieval History of Japan
MURANAKA, S., Solid State Chemistry
NAGAYA, M., History and Theory of Social Statistics
NAKANISHI, T., International Relations
NISHII, M., Environmental Conservation and Development
NISHIMURA, M., History of Western Law
NISHIWAKI, T., History of Chinese Philosophy
NISHIYAMA, R., Ancient History of Japan
NIWA, T., American Literature
OKADA, A., Art History and Criticism
OKADA, K., Pedagogy
OKI, M., Linguistics and French Language
ONO, S., Middle High German Literature
OTAGI, H., History of Medieval China
SAEKI, K., Social-environmental System
SAITO, H., Comparative Linguistics and German Language
SAKAGAMI, M., Gravity and Relativity
SHIKAYA, T., Philosophy of Aesthetics
SHIMADA, M., Contemporary History of the United States
SHINGU, K., Fundamental Human Ontology
SHINOHARA, M., Aesthetics and Philosophy

SUGAWARA, K., Social Anthropology and Communication
SUGIMAN, T., Group Dynamics
SUZUKI, M., 18th-century English Culture and Literature
TAKAHASHI, Y., Environmental Conservation and Development
TAKASAKI, K., Algebraic Analysis and Mathematical Physics
TAMADA, O., Environmental Conservation and Development
TANABE, R., German Literature
TOGO, Y., French Linguistics
TOMIDA, Y., Philosophy and History of Philosophy
TOMITA, H., Statistical Physics
TORISSEN, E., Comparative Culture
TSUDA, K., Internal Medicine
UCHIDA, M., Grammar of the Japanese Language
USHIKI, S., Coexisting Systems of Nature and Human Beings
YAMADA, M., Urban Geography
YAMADA, T., Anthropology and Cognition, Shamanism and Ethnicity
YAMAGUCHI, R., Coexisting Systems of Nature and Human Beings
YAMAMOTO, Y., Organic Chemistry
YAMANASHI, M., Cognitive Linguistics
YASUI, K., Human Development
YODA, Y., Shakespeare

Graduate School of Informatics (tel. (75) 753-3599; fax (75) 753-5379; e-mail jimu-soumu@i.kyoto-u.ac.jp; internet www.i.kyoto-u.ac.jp):

EIHO, S., Image Processing Systems
FUJISAKA, H., Non-equilibrium Dynamics
FUKUSHIMA, M., Systems Optimization
FUNAKOSHI, M., Nonlinear Dynamics
GOTOH, O., Bioinformatics
INUI, T., Cognitive Science
ISHIDA, T., Global Information Network
ISO, Y., Analysis of Inverse Problems
IWAI, T., Dynamical Systems Theory
IWAMA, K., Logic Circuits, Algorithms and Complexity Theory
KATAI, O., Symbiotic Systems
KATAYAMA, T., Control Systems Theory
KIGAMI, J., Nonlinear Analysis
KOBAYASHI, S., Biological Information
KUMAMOTO, H., Human Systems
MATSUDA, T., Biomedical Engineering
MATSUYAMA, T., Visual Information Processing
MORIHIRO, Y., Integrated-media Communications
MORIYA, K., Bioresource Informatics
MUNAKATA, T., Physical Statistics
NAKAMURA, Y., Applied Mathematical Analysis
NAKAMURA, Y., Processor Architecture and Systems Synthesis
NISHIDA, T., Artificial Intelligence
NOGI, T., Fundamentals of Complex Systems
OKUNO, H. G., Speech Media Processing
ONODERA, H., Integrated Circuits Design Engineering
SAKAI, H., Mathematical Systems Theory
SAKAI, T., Environmental Informatics
SATO, M., Foundations of Software Science
SATO, T., Advanced Signal Processing
SUGIE, T., Mechanical Systems Control
TAKAHASHI, T., Intelligent Communication Networks
TAKAHASHI, Y., Information Systems
TANAKA, K., Digital Library
TOMITA, S., Computer Architecture
YAMAMOTO, A., Foundations of Artificial Intelligence
YAMAMOTO, Y., Intelligent and Control Systems
YOSHIDA, S., Digital Communications
YUASA, T., Computer Software

Graduate School of Law and Faculty of Law (fax (75) 753-3290; internet www.kyodai.jp/i-english.htm):

AKIZUKI, K., Public Administration
ASADA, M., International Law
DOI, M., Constitutional Law
HATTORI, T., German Law
HAYASHI, N., Roman Law
IDA, R., Law of International Organizations
ITO, T., Japanese Legal History
ITO, Y., Political and Diplomatic History of Japan
KAMEMOTO, H., Legal Philosophy
KARATO, T., Political and Diplomatic History
KASAI, M., Law of Civil Procedure
KAWAHAMA, N., Economic Law
KAWAKAMI, R., European Legal History
KIMURA, M., Comparative Politics
KINAMI, A., Anglo-American Law
KITAMURA, M., Commercial Law
MABUCHI, M., Public Policy
MAEDA, M., Commercial Law
MATOBA, T., Political Science
MATSUOKA, H., Civil Law
MORI, T., Constitutional Law
MORIMOTO, S., Commercial Law
MURANAKA, T., Labour Law
NAKAMORI, Y., Criminal Law
NAKANISHI, H., International Politics
NISHIGORI, S., Civil Law
NISHIMURA, K., Social Security Law
OISHI, M., Constitutional Law
OKAMURA, S., Administrative Law
OKAMURA, T., Tax Law
ONO, N., History of Political Thought
OTAKE, H., Political Process
SAKAI, H., International Law
SAKAMAKI, T., Criminal Law
SAKUMA, T., Civil Law
SAKURADA, Y., Private International Law
SHIBAIKE, Y., Administrative Law
SHINKAWA, T., Political Process
SHIOMI, J., Criminal Law
SHIOMI, Y., Civil Law
SHIYAKE, M., Constitutional Law
SUZUKI, H., Commercial Law
SUZUKI, M., International Politics and Economy
TAKAYAMA, K., Criminal Law
TANAKA, S., Legal Philosophy
TANASE, T., Sociology of Law
TERADA, H., Oriental Legal History
TOKUDA, K., Law of Civil Procedure
YAMAMOTO, K., Civil Law
YAMAMOTO, K., Law of Civil Procedure
YAMAMOTO, Y., Civil Law
YOKOYAMA, M., Civil Law
YOSHIOKA, K., Criminology

Graduate School of Letters and Faculty of Letters:

AKAMATSU, A., History of Indian Philosophy
FUJII, J., Japanese History
FUJITA, K., Psychology
FUJITA, M., Japanese Philosophy
FUMA, S., Oriental History
HAMADA, M., Asian History
HATTORI, Y., European History
HAYASHI, S., Humanistic Informatics
HIRATA, S., Chinese Language and Literature
IKEDA, S., History of Chinese Philosophy
ISHIKAWA, Y., Geography
ITO, K., Philosophy
ITO, K., Sociology
IWAKI, K., Aesthetics and Art History
IZUMI, T., Archaeology
KAMADA, M., Japanese History
KATAYANAGI, E., Christian Studies
KATSUYAMA, S., Japanese History
KAWAI, K., Chinese Language and Literature

KAWAZOE, S., History of Western Medieval Philosophy
KETA, M., Philosophy of Religion
KIDA, A., Japanese Language and Literature
KIHIRA, E., Contemporary History
KINDA, A., Geography
KOBAYASHI, M., History of Western Philosophy
MATSUDA, M., Sociology
MIMAKI, K., Buddhist Studies
MINAMIKAWA, T., European History
MIYAUCHI, H., English Language and Literature
NAGAI, K., Contemporary History
NAKAMURA, K., American Literature
NAKAMURA, T., Art History
NAKATSUKASA, T., Greek and Latin Classics
NEDACHI, K., Aesthetics and Art History
NISHIMURA, M., German Language and Literature
OCHIAI, E., Sociology
OSAKA, N., Psychology
OTANI, M., Japanese Language and Literature
SAITO, Y., Italian Language and Literature
SAKURAI, Y., Psychology
SATO, A., Slavic Languages and Literature
SHOGAITO, M., Linguistics
SUGIMOTO, Y., 20th Century Studies
SUGIURA, K., Geography
SUGIYAMA, M., Oriental History
TAGUCHI, N., French Language and Literature
TAKAHASHI, H., Greek and Latin Classics
TAKUBO, Y., Linguistics
TOKUNAGA, M., Sanskrit Language and Literature
UCHII, S., Philosophy and History of Science
UEHARA, M., Archaeology
WAKASHIMA, T., English Language and Literature
YOSHIDA, J., French Language and Literature
YOSHIDA, K., Linguistics
YOSHIMOTO, M., Oriental History

Graduate School of Medicine and Faculty of Medicine (Yoshida konoe-cho, Sakyo-ku, Kyoto 606-8501; tel. (75) 753-4300; fax (75) 753-4348; e-mail shomu06@mail.adm .kyoto-u.ac.jp; internet www.med.kyoto-u.ac .jp):

CHIBA, T., Gastroenterology and Hepatology
FUJII, S., Gynaecology and Obstetrics
FUJITA, J., Clinical Molecular Biology
FUKUDA, K., Anaesthesia
FUKUHARA, S., Epidemiology and Health Care Research
FUKUI, T., Clinical Epidemiology
FUKUSHIMA, M., Pharmacoepidemiology
FUKUYAMA, H., Functional Brain Imaging
HASHIMOTO, N., Neurosurgery
HAYASHI, T., Psychiatry
HIRAIDE, A., Center for Medical Education
HIRAOKA, M., Radiation Oncology and Image-applied Therapy
HONJO, T., Immunology and Genomic Medicine
ICHIYAMA, S., Clinical Laboratory Medicine
IDE, C., Anatomy and Neurobiology
IMANAKA, Y., Healthcare Economics and Quality Management
INAGAKI, M., Metabolism and Clinical Nutrition
INUI, K., Pharmacy
ITO, J., Otolaryngology, Head and Neck Surgery
KANEKO, T., Morphological Brain Science
KAWANO, K., Integrative Brain Science
KIHARA, M., Global Health and Socio-Epidemiology
KITA, T., Cardiovascular Medicine

KOIZUMI, A., Health and Environmental Sciences
KOMEDA, M., Cardiovascular Surgery
KOSUGI, S., Biomedical Ethics
MAEKAWA, T., Transfusion Medicine and Cell Therapy
MANABE, T., Diagnostic Pathology
MATSUDA, F., Genome Epidemiology
MIMORI, T., Rheumatology and Clinical Immunology
MINATO, N., Immunology and Cell Biology
MISHIMA, M., Respiratory Medicine
MITSUYAMA, M., Microbiology
MIYACHI, Y., Dermatology
NABESHIMA, Y., Pathology and Tumour Biology
NAKAHARA, T., Public Health and International Health
NAKAHATA, T., Paediatrics
NAKAMURA, T., Orthopaedic and Musculo-skeletal Surgery
NAKANISHI, S., Biological Sciences
NAKAO, K., Medicine and Clinical Science
NARUMIYA, S., Cell Pharmacology
NODA, M., Molecular Oncology
NOMA, A., Physiology and Biophysics
OGAWA, O., Urology
OHMORI, H., Physiology and Neurobiology
SAKAMOTO, J., Epidemiological and Clinical Research Information Management
SATO, T., Biostatistics
SERIKAWA, T., Laboratory Animals
SHIMIZU, A., Human Genome Analysis
SHINOHARA, T., Molecular Genetics
SHIOTA, K., Anatomy and Developmental Biology
SHIRAKAWA, T., Health Promotion and Human Behaviour
SUZUKI, S., Plastic and Reconstructive Surgery
TAKAHASHI, R., Neurology
TAKEDA, S., Radiation Genetics
TAKETO, M., Pharmacology
TAMAKI, K., Legal Medicine
TANAKA, K., Transplantation and Immunology
TOGASHI, L., Diagnostic Imaging and Nuclear Medicine
TSUKITA, S., Cell Biology
UCHIYAMA, T., Haematology and Oncology
WADA, H., Thoracic Surgery
YOKODE, M., Clinical Innovative Medicine
YOSHIHARA, H., Medical Informatics
YOSHIMURA, N., Ophthalmology and Visual Sciences

Graduate School of Pharmaceutical Sciences and Faculty of Pharmaceutical Sciences (46-29 Yoshida Shimoadachi-cho, Sakyo-ku, Kyoto 606-8501; tel. (75) 753-4510; fax (75) 753-4502; internet www.pharm.kyoto-u.ac .jp):

AKAIKE, A., Pharmacology
FUJII, N., Bio-organic Medicinal Chemistry
HANDA, T., Biosurface Chemistry
HASHIDA, M., Drug Delivery Research
HONDA, G., Pharmacognosy
ITOH, N., Genetic Biochemistry
KANEKO, S., Molecular Pharmacology
KATO, H., Structural Biology
KAWAI, A., Molecular Microbiology
SAJI, H., Patho-Functional Bioanalysis
TAKAKURA, Y., Biopharmaceutics and Drug Metabolism
TAKEMOTO, Y., Organic Chemistry
TOMIOKA, K., Synthetic Medicinal Chemistry
TSUJIMOTO, G., Genomic Drugs Discovery

Graduate School of Science and Faculty of Science:

AGATA, K., Developmental Biology
AOYAMA, H., Theory of Elementary Particles
ARUGA, T., Surface Chemistry
AWAJI, T., Physical Oceanography
FUJIYOSHI, Y., Molecular Biophysics

FUKAYA, K., Geometry
HANADA, T., Inorganic Materials Chemistry
HARA-NISHIMURA, I., Plant Cell Biology
HATA, H., Theoretical Particle Physics
HAYASHI, T., Organic Chemistry
HIRAJIMA, T., Petrology
HIRANO, T., Neurobiology
HORI, M., Animal Ecology
HORIUCHI, H., Theoretical Nuclear Physics
IKAWA, M., Partial Differential Equations
IMAFUKU, M., Ethology
IMAI, K., Experimental Nuclear Physics
IMANISHI, H., Foliation and Symplectic Geometry
INAGAKI, S., Astrophysics
IYEMORI, T., Solar Terrestrial Physics
KAJIMOTO, O., Physical Chemistry
KATAYAMA, K., Biological Anthropology
KATO, K., Number Theory
KATO, S., Representation Theory
KATO, S., Theoretical Chemistry
KAWAI, H., Theoretical Particle Physics
KIDA, H., Climate Physics
KITAMURA, M., Mineralogy
KONO, A., Topology
KOYAMA, K., Cosmic Ray Physics
KUROKAWA, H., Solar Physics
MACHIDA, S., Geomagnetism and Space Physics
MAIHARA, T., Astrophysics
MARUOKA, K., Synthetic Organic Chemistry
MARUYAMA, M., Algebraic Geometry
MASUDA, F., Stratigraphy and Sedimentology
MATSUDA, Y., Solid State Physics
MATSUKI, T., Lie Groups
MIKI, K., Structural Biochemistry and Protein Crystallography
MIWA, T., Algebraic Analysis
MIZUSAKI, T., Low-Temperature Physics
MORI, K., Molecular Biology
MORIWAKI, A., Algebraic Geometry
NAGATA, T., Astrophysics
NAGATANI, A., Plant Physiology
NAKAJIMA, H., Representation Theory and Geometry
NAKAMURA, T., Nuclear Astrophysics
NISHIDA, G., Algebraic Topology
NISHIKAWA, K., Experimental High Energy Physics
NISHIWADA, K., Differential Equations, Financial Mathematics
OBATA, M., Petrology
OIKE, K., Seismology and Physics of the Earth's Interior
OKADA, A., Active Tectonics and Geomorphology
OKADA, K., Plant Molecular Genetics
ONUKI, A., Statistical Physics
OSUKA, A., Organic Chemistry
SAITO, G., Organic Solid State Chemistry
SAITO, H., Number Theory
SASAO, N., Experimental High Energy Physics
SATOH, N., Developmental Genomics
SETOGUCHI, T., Vertebrate Palaeontology
SHIBATA, K., Solar and Cosmic Plasma Physics
SHICHIDA, Y., Molecular Physiology
SHIGEKAWA, I., Probability Theory
SHIMAMOTO, T., Structural Geology and Rock Rheology
SHIRAYAMA, Y., Marine Biology
SHISHIKURA, M., Dynamical System
SUGIYAMA, H., Chemical Biology, Bio-organic Chemistry
TAKEMOTO, S., Geodesy
TAKEMURA, K., Quaternary Geology and Geothermal Sciences
TAKADA, S., Developmental Biology
TANAKA, K., Solid State Spectroscopy, Laser Spectroscopy
TANAKA, Y., Volcano Magnetism
TANIMORI, T., Cosmic Ray Physics

TANIMURA, Y., Theoretical Chemical Physics

TERAO, T., Chemical Physics

TERAZIMA, M., Physical Chemistry, Biophysical Chemistry

TOBE, H., Plant Systematics and Evolution

TSUTSUMI, Y., Nonlinear Partial Differential Equations

UE, M., Low-dimensional Topology

UEDA, T., Complex Analysis in Several Variables

UEMATSU, T., Theory of Elementary Particles

UENO, K., Theory of Complex Manifolds

YAMADA, K., Theory of Condensed Matter

YAMAGIWA, J., Primatology and Anthropology

YAMAUCHI, J., Physical Chemistry and Electron Spin Resonance

YAMAUCHI, M., Number Theory

YAO, M., Physics of Disordered Systems

YODEN, S., Meteorology

YONEI, S., Radiation Biology

YOSHIDA, H., Number Theory

YOSHIKAWA, K., Chemical Physics, Biological Physics

YOSHIMURA, K., Inorganic Chemistry, Solid State Chemistry and Physics, Nuclear Magnetic Resonance

YUSA, Y., Hydrology and Geothermal Sciences

School of Health Sciences, Faculty of Medicine (53 Syogoin Kawahara-cho, Sakyo-ku, Kyoto 606-8507):

AMANO, S., Experimental Epileptology and Neuropathology

EGAWA, T., Diabetes, Teaching Renal Failure, Foot Care

FUJITA, M., Cardiology

FUKUDA, K., Nuclear Magnetic Resonance

FUKUDA, Y., Hepatology, Clinical Immunology

FUNATO, T., Laboratory Medicine and Molecular Diagnostics

HAYASHI, Y., Adult Health Nursing

HINOKUMA, F., Maternal Nursing, Midwifery

INAMOTO, T., Surgery and Clinical Oncology

KABEYAMA, K., Midwifery, Mother and Child Nursing, Women's Health

KATSURA, T., Preventive Nursing, Community Health Nursing

KAWASAKI, N., Biochemistry and Glycobiology

KONISHI, N., Occupational Therapy, Developmental Delay

MITANI, A., Rehabilitation and Brain Science

MIYAJIMA, A., Environmental Health Nursing

NARUKI, H., Community Health Nursing

NOMURA, S., Neuroanatomy and Functional Human Anatomy

SAITO, Y., Basic Nursing, Hospital Infection Control

SAKURABA, S., Psychiatric and Mental Health Nursing

SASADA, M., Haematology and Infectious Diseases

SUGA, S., Clinical Psychology

TOICHI, M., Psychiatry, Cognitive Neuroscience

TSUBOYAMA, T., Orthopaedics, Musculoskeletal Oncology, Bone Metabolism

TSUKITA, S., Cell Biology

UMEMURA, S., Biomedical Ultrasonics

YAMANE, H., Occupational Therapy for Mental Disorders

Law School (fax (75) 753-3290; internet www.kyodai.jp/i-ls.htm):

ASADA, M., International Law

DOI, M., Constitutional Law

ENDO, K., Law Practice Unit

HAMAMOTO, S., Law Practice Unit

HATTORI, T., German Law

HAYASHI, N., Roman Law

HONDA, M., Law Practice Unit

IDA, R., International Law

IIMURA, Y., Law Practice Unit

ITO, T., Japanese Legal History

ITO, Y., Political and Diplomatic History of Japan

KAMEMOTO, H., Legal Philosophy

KAMIKO, A., Law Practice Unit

KASAI, M., Law of Civil Procedure

KAWAHAMA, N., Economic Law

KAWAKAMI, R., European Legal History

KINAMI, A., Anglo-American Law

KITAGAWA, K., Law Practice Unit

KITAMURA, M., Commercial Law

MAEDA, M., Commercial Law

MATSUDA, K., Law Practice Unit

MATSUOKA, H., Civil Law

MORI, T., Constitutional Law

MORIKAWA, S., Law Practice Unit

MORIMOTO, S., Commercial Law

MURAKAMI, K., Law Practice Unit

MURANAKA, T., Labour Law

NAKAGAWA, H., Law Practice Unit

NAKAMORI, J., Criminal Law

NISHIGORI, S., Civil Law

NISHIMURA, K., Social Security Law

OISHI, M., Constitutional Law

OKAMURA, S., Administrative Law

OKAMURA, T., Tax Law

SAKAI, H., International Law

SAKAMAKI, T., Criminal Law

SAKUMA, T., Civil Law

SAKURADA, Y., Private International Law

SHIBAIKE, Y., Administrative Law

SHIMIZU, M., Law Practice Unit

SHIOMI, J., Criminal Law

SHIOMI, Y., Civil Law

SHIYAKE, M., Constitutional Law

SUZAKI, H., Commercial Law

TAKAYAMA, K., Criminal Law

TANASE, T., Sociology of Law

TERADA, H., Oriental Legal History

TOKUDA, K., Law of Civil Procedure

YAMAGAMI, K., Law Practice Unit

YAMAMOTO, K., Law of Civil Procedure

YAMAMOTO, K., Civil Law

YAMAMOTO, Y., Civil Law

YASUKI, K., Law Practice Unit

YOKOYAMA, M., Civil Law

YOSHIOKA, K., Criminology

ATTACHED RESEARCH INSTITUTES

Academic Center for Computing and Media Studies: Yoshida-Honmachi, Sakyo-ku, Kyoto; f. 2002; Dir Prof. T. MATSUYAMA.

Center for African Area Studies: Shimoadachi-cho 46, Yoshida, Sakyo-ku, Kyoto; f. 1986; Dir Prof. Dr S. ARAKI.

Center for Archaeological Operations: Yoshida Honmachi, Sakyo-ku, Kyoto; f. 1977; Dir Prof. Dr M. UEHARA.

Center for Ecological Research: 509-3 2-chome, Hirano, Otsu, Shiga 520-2113; f. 1991; Dir Prof. Y. TSUBAKI.

Center for Southeast Asian Studies: Shimoadachi-cho 46, Yoshida, Sakyo-ku, Kyoto; f. 1965; Dir Prof. Dr K. TANAKA; publ. *Southeast Asian Studies* (4 a year), *Kyoto Review of Southeast Asia* (in English).

Center for the Promotion of Excellence in Higher Education: Yoshida-nihonmatsu-cho, Sakyo-ku, Kyoto; f. 2003; Dir Prof. Dr T. TANAKA.

Disaster Prevention Research Institute: Gokasho, Uji City, Kyoto; f. 1951; Dir Prof. K. ISHIHARA.

Environment Preservation Center: Yoshida Honmachi, Sakyo-ku, Kyoto; f. 1977; Dir Prof. K. OSHIMA.

Field Science Education and Research Center: Oiwake-cho, Kitashirakawa, Sakyo-ku, Kyoto; f. 2003; Dir Prof. M. TANAKA.

Fukui Institute for Fundamental Chemistry: Takanonishihiraki-cho, Sakyo-ku, Kyoto; f. 2002; Dir Prof. H. NAKATSUJI.

Institute of Advanced Energy: Gokasho, Uji City, Kyoto; f. 1941; Dir Prof. A. KOHYAMA.

Institute for Chemical Research: Gokasho, Uji City, Kyoto; f. 1926; Dir Prof. N. ESAKI.

Institute of Economic Research: Yoshida Honmachi, Sakyo-ku, Kyoto; f. 1962; library of 75,722 vols; Dir Prof. Dr T. SAWA.

Institute for Frontier Medical Sciences: 53 Kawahara-cho, Shogoin, Sakyo-ku, Kyoto 606-8507; f. 1998; Dir Prof. N. NAKATSUJI.

Institute for Research in Humanities: Ushinomiya-cho, Yoshida, Sakyo-ku, Kyoto; f. 1939; Dir Prof. B. KIN; publ. *Journal of Oriental Studies* (1 a year), *Journal of Humanities Studies* (in Japanese, annual), *Annual Bibliography of Oriental Studies*, *Annals ZINBUN* (in European languages, irreg.).

Institute for Virus Research: Kawara-cho, Shogoin, Sakyo-ku, Kyoto; f. 1956; Dir Prof. R. KAGEYAMA.

Kyoto University Archives: Yoshida Honmachi, Sakyo-ku, Kyoto; f. 2000; Dir Prof. Dr J. SASAKI.

Kyoto University International Innovation Center: Kyoto-Daigaku-katsura, Nishikyo-ku, Kyoto; f. 2001; Dir Prof. K. MAKINO.

Kyoto University Museum: Yoshida Honmachi, Sakyo-ku, Kyoto; f. 1997; Dir Prof. Dr I. YAMANAKA.

Primate Research Institute: Kanrin 41-2, Inuyama City, Aichi Prefecture; f. 1967; Dir Prof. N. SHIGEHARA.

Radiation Biology Center: Yoshida Konoecho, Sakyo-ku, Kyoto; f. 1976; research and postgraduate training in radiation biology; Dir Prof. T. MATSUMOTO.

Radioisotope Research Center: Yoshida Konoecho, Sakyo-ku, Kyoto; f. 1971; Dir Prof. Dr Y. ISOZUMI.

Research Center for Low Temperature and Materials Science: Oiwake-cho, Kitashirakawa, Sakyo-ku, Kyoto; f. 2002; Dir Prof. T. MIZUSAKI.

Research Institute for Mathematical Sciences: Kitashirakawa, Sakyo-ku, Kyoto; f. 1963; research and postgraduate training in mathematical sciences; library of 78,931 vols; Dir Prof. Y. TAKAHASHI.

Research Institute for Sustainable Humanosphere: Gokasho, Uji City, Kyoto; f. 2004; Dir Prof. S. KAWAI.

Research Reactor Institute: Kumatori-cho, Sennan-gun, Osaka; f. 1963; library of 45,300 vols; Dir Prof. S. SHIROYA.

Yukawa Institute for Theoretical Physics: Kitashirakawa, Sakyo-ku, Kyoto; f. 1953; Dir Prof. T. KUGO; publ. *Progress of Theoretical Physics* (12 a year).

KYUSHU INSTITUTE OF DESIGN

Shiobaru 4-9-1, Minami-ku, Fukuoka-shi 815-8540

Telephone: (92) 553-4407

Fax: (92) 553-4593

E-mail: syomuka@kyushu-id.ac.jp

Internet: www.kyushu-id.ac.jp

Founded 1968

Independent

Academic year: April to March (2 semesters)

Pres.: SHO YOSHIDA

Dir-Gen.: MAKOTO OHYA

Dean of Students: MASAMICHI OHKUBO

Library Dir: RYUZO TAKIYAMA

Number of teachers: 96
Number of students: 1,208 (929 undergraduate, 279 postgraduate)

PROFESSORS

Department of Environmental Design:

DOI, Y., History of Architecture and Industrial Design
HIROKAWA, S., Theory of Environmental Design
ISHII, A., Environmental Systems, Building and Environment Engineering
KATANO, H., Environmental Systems and Building Construction
KATO, H. M., Environmental Planning and Design
MIYAMOTO, M., Environmental Planning and Design
OHKUBO, M., Environmental Systems and Structural Engineering
SHIGEMATSU, T., Theory of Environmental Design

Department of Industrial Design:

FUKATA, S., Intelligent Mechanics and Control
ISHIMURA, S., Industrial History
ITOI, H., Industrial Design
MORITA, Y., Public Space and Element Design
SAKATA, T., Mathematical Statistics
SAKI, K., Tribology
SATO, H., Ergonomics
TOCHIHARA, Y., Environmental Ergonomics
YASUKOUCHI, A., Physiological Anthropology

Department of Visual Communication Design:

FUKUSHIMA, S., Artificial Intelligence
GENDA, E., Image Design
NAGASHIMA, K., Image Engineering
SATO, M., Research and Design on Sign Communication
URAHAMA, K., Image Information Processing
WAKIYAMA, S., Visual Image Design
YAMASHITA, S., Vision Science and Neurobiology
YAMASHITA, Y., Vision Science and Psychophysics

Department of Acoustic Design:

FUJIEDA, M., Science of Sound Culture
FUJIWARA, K., Science of Acoustical Environment
IWAMIYA, S., Science of Acoustical Environment
KAWABE, T., Science of Acoustical Environment
NAKAJIMA, Y., Science of Acoustic Information
NAKAMURA, S., Science of Sound Culture
YOSHIKAWA, S., Science of Acoustic Information

Department of Art and Information Design:

FUJIMURA, N., Media Design
KUROSAWA, S., Media Art and Culture
OHNISHI, S., Media Art and Culture
OTA, S., Information Environment Sciences
SASABUCHI, S., Information Environment Sciences

KYUSHU INSTITUTE OF TECHNOLOGY

1-1 Sensui-sho, Tobata-ku, Kitakyushu-shi, Fukuoka 804-8550

Telephone: (93) 884-3008
Fax: (93) 884-3015
E-mail: sou-kikaku@jimu.kyutech.ac.jp
Internet: www.kyutech.ac.jp

Founded 1909
Independent
Language of instruction: Japanese

Academic year: April to March
Pres.: TERUO SHIMOMURA
Registrar: MAKOTO YOSHIDA
Librarian: MORIO MATSUNAGA
Library of 489,867 vols
Number of teachers: 636 full-time
Number of students: 6,307
Publications: Bulletin, Memoirs

DEANS

Faculty of Computer Science and Systems Engineering: T KODAMA
Faculty of Engineering: T. KOBAYASHI
Graduate School of Computer Science and Systems Engineering: H. TSUKAMOTO

KYUSHU UNIVERSITY

6-10-1 Hakozaki, Higashi-ku, Fukuoka 812-8581

Telephone: (92) 642-2111
Fax: (92) 642-2113
Internet: www.kyushu-u.ac.jp

Founded 1911
Independent
Languages of instruction: English, Japanese
Academic year: April to March
Pres.: Dr SETSUO ARIKAWA
Exec. Vice-Pres.: Dr KATSUMI IMAIZUMI
Exec. Vice-Pres.: Dr HIDETOSHI OCHIAI
Exec. Vice-Pres.: Dr KOTOKU KURACHI
Exec. Vice-Pres.: Dr RYOICHI TAKAYANAGI
Exec. Vice-Pres.: Dr YUKIO FUJIKI
Exec. Vice-Pres.: Dr SHUNICHI MARUNO
Exec. Vice-Pres.: Dr HIROTO YASUURA
Exec. Vice-Pres. and Dir-Gen.: AKIYOSHI MOTOKI
Librarian: YOSHIAKI KAWAMOTO
Library of 4,016,028 vols, 92,741 serials
Number of teachers: 2,186
Number of students: 18,765

DEANS

Faculty of Agriculture: A. YOSHIMURA
Faculty of Dental Science: H. NAKANISHI
Faculty of Design: S. ISHIMURA
Faculty of Economics: Y. KAWANAMI
Faculty of Engineering: S. HINO
Faculty of Engineering Sciences: H. HONJO
Faculty of Human–Environment Studies: A. KAWANO
Faculty of Humanities: A. TAKAGI
Faculty of Information Science and Electrical Engineering: K. TOKO
Faculty of Languages and Cultures: K. YAMASHITA
Faculty of Law: M. DOI
Faculty of Mathematics: M. KANEKO
Faculty of Medical Sciences: M. KATANO
Faculty of Pharmaceutical Sciences: K. INOUE
Faculty of Sciences: M. ARATONO
Faculty of Social and Cultural Studies: Y. TANAKA
Graduate School of Integrated Frontier Sciences: K. SHIOTSUGU
Graduate School of Systems Life Sciences: Y. FUKUMAKI
Law School (Professional Graduate School): M. MATSUO
School of Education: H. MINAMI

MIE UNIVERSITY

1515 Kamihama-cho, Tsu-shi, Mie 514
Telephone: (592) 32-1211
Fax: (592) 31-9000
Internet: www.mie-u.ac.jp
Founded 1949
Independent
Academic year: April to March
Pres.: RYUICHI YATANI
Chief Admin. Officer: KATSUYUKI KUROSAKI

Librarian: HIROYUKI NODA
Library of 783,000 vols
Number of teachers: 1,740
Number of students: 7,505
Publications: Outline of Mie University (every 2 years), The Journal of Law and Economics (Hōkei Ronsō), various faculty bulletins

DEANS

Faculty of Bioresources: HITOSHI OBATA
Faculty of Education: TAKESHI KINOSHITA
Faculty of Engineering: GORO SAWA
Faculty of Humanities and Social Sciences: HIDEKAZU HIROSE
School of Medicine: RYUICHI YATANI
College of Medical Sciences: KATSUMI DEGUCHI

UNIVERSITY OF MIYAZAKI

1-1 Gakuen Kibanadai Nishi, Miyazaki-shi, Miyazaki 889-2192

Telephone: (985) 58-7104
Fax: (985) 58-2896
E-mail: kokusai@miyazaki-u.ac.jp
Internet: www.miyazaki-u.ac.jp

Founded 1949; present name and status 2003 following integration of Miyazaki Medical College
Independent
Academic year: April to March (2 semesters)
Pres.: A. SUMIYOSHI
Registrar: K. OHTANI
Librarian: C. TAMURA

Number of teachers: 624
Number of students: 5,450

Publications: Bulletins and memoirs of the faculties

DEANS

Faculty of Agriculture: S. KOBAYE
Faculty of Education and Culture: T. IWAMOTO
Faculty of Engineering: K. HIRANO
Miyazaki Medical College: H. KANNAN

MURORAN INSTITUTE OF TECHNOLOGY

Mizumoto-cho 27-1, Muroran 050-8585, Hokkaido

Telephone: (143) 46-5022
Fax: (143) 46-5033
Internet: www.muroran-it.ac.jp

Founded 1949
Independent
Academic year: April to March

Pres.: HIROAKI TAGASHIRA
Admin. Officer: YASHUTO UEMARA
Chief Librarian: KEN-ICHI MATSUOKA

Library of 284,300 vols
Number of teachers: 360
Number of students: 3,500

Publication: Memoirs (1 a year).

NAGAOKA UNIVERSITY OF TECHNOLOGY

1603-1 Kamitomioka, Nagaoka, Niigata 940-2188

Telephone: (258) 46-6000
Fax: (258) 47-9000
E-mail: syomugroup@jcom.nagaokaut.ac.jp
Internet: www.nagaokaut.ac.jp

Founded 1976
State control
Languages of instruction: English, Japanese
Academic year: April to March
President: Prof. YO KOJIMA
Vice-Pres. for Academic Affairs: Prof. YASUNORI MIYATA

Vice-Pres. for Evaluation: Prof. IKUZO NISHI-GUCHI

Vice-Pres. for Graduate School: Prof. YASU-NOBU INOUE

Vice-Pres. for Industry–Academia Cooperation and Information: ATSUSHI KAWASAKI

Vice-Pres. for International Affairs: Prof. KOZO ISHIZAKI

Vice-Pres. for Research, Admission and Student Affairs: Prof. KYUICHI MARUYAMA

Dir of Admin.: SATO MASARU

Library of 140,000 vols
Number of teachers: 212
Number of students: 2,469

Departments of Bioengineering, Civil and Environmental Engineering, Electrical Engineering, Management and Information System Science, Materials Science and Technology, Mechanical Engineering, System Safety

DEANS

Graduate School of Engineering: Prof. YASU-NOBU INOUE

Graduate School of Management of Technology: Prof. YASUNORI MIYATA

School of Engineering: Prof. YASUNOBU INOUE

NAGASAKI UNIVERSITY

1-14 Bunkyo-machi, Nagasaki 852-8521
Telephone: (95) 819-2042
Fax: (95) 819-2044
E-mail: www_admin@ml.nagasaki-u.ac.jp
Internet: www.nagasaki-u.ac.jp
Founded 1949
Academic year: April to March
Independent

Pres.: HIROSHI SAITO
Vice-Pres: TSUYOSHI SAKIYAMA, HARUHIKO MASAKI, SHIGERU KATAMINE
Dir-Gen.: SYUSUKE MORITA
Library Dir: TAKATOSHI OKABAYASHI

Library of 1,078,347 vols
Number of teachers: 1,067 full-time
Number of students: 8,935

Publications: *Bulletin of the Faculty of Education*, *Journal of Business and Economics* (4 a year), *Annual Review of South East Asian Studies*, *Annual Review of Economics*, *Nagasaki Medical Journal* (4 a year), *Acta Medica Nagasakiensia* (2 a year), *Report of the Faculty of Engineering* (2 a year), *Journal of Environmental Studies* (2 a year), *Bulletin of the Faculty of Fisheries*, *Bulletin of the School of Allied Medical Sciences*, *Seasonal Report of the Education and Research Centre for Life-long Learning*

DEANS

Faculty of Economics: Prof. TOSHIO SUGIHARA
Faculty of Education: Prof. TATEO HASHIMOTO
Faculty of Engineering: Prof. JUN OYAMA
Faculty of Environmental Studies: Prof. YOSHIHIKO INOUE
Faculty of Fisheries: Prof. MUTSUYOSHI TSU-CHIMOTO
Graduate School of Biomedical Sciences: Prof. KOHTARO TANIYAMA
Graduate School of Science and Technology: Prof. TADASHI ISHIHARA
Institute of Tropical Medicine: Prof. YOSHIKI AOKI
School of Allied Medical Sciences: Prof. AKEMI TERASAKI
School of Dentistry: Prof. MITSURU ATSUTA
School of Medicine: Prof. TAKASHI KANEMATSU
School of Pharmaceutical Sciences: Prof. KENICHIRO NAKASHIMA

DIRECTORS

Animal Research Center: Prof. MICHIO NAKA-MURA

Atomic Bomb Disease Institute: Prof. MASAO TOMONAGA
Center for Educational Research and Training: Prof. AKIFUMI FUKUI
Center for Frontier Life Sciences: Prof. HIROSHI SATO
Center for Instrumental Analysis: Prof. SUSUMI HATAKEYAMA
Division of Comparative Medicine: HIROSHI SATO
Division of Functional Genomics: NORIO NIIKAWA
Division of Radiation Biology and Protection: Prof. YUTAKA OKUMURA
Education and Research Center for Life-long Learning: Prof. KAGEHIRO ITOYAMA
Environmental Protection Center: Prof. TAKEHIRO TAKEMASA
Garden for Medicinal Plants: Prof. ISAO KONO
Health Center: Prof. NOBUKO ISHII
International Student Center: Prof. YOSHIHIRO MATSUMURA
Joint Research Center: Prof. MAKOTO EGA-SHIRA
Marine Research Institute: Prof. HIDEAKI NAKATA
Research and Development Center for Higher Education: Prof. SHIGERU KATAMINE
Research Center for Tropical Infectious Diseases: Prof. MASAAKI SHIMADA
Science Information Center: Prof. HIDEO KURODA
University Hospital attached to School of Dentistry: Prof. HIROYUKI FUJII
University Hospital attached to School of Medicine: Prof. KOJI SUMIKAWA

PROFESSORS

Faculty of Economics (4-2-1 Katafuchi, Nagasaki 850-8506; tel. (95) 820-6300; fax (95) 820-6370; internet www.econ.nagasaki-u.ac.jp):

AOYAMA, S., Development Economics
BASU, D., International Economics
FUJINO, T., Japanese Corporations and Management
FUJITA, W., Economics of Natural Resources and Energy
FUKAURA, A., Monetary Economics
FUKUZAWA, K., Labour Economics
FURUYAMA, M., Law and Finance
GUNN, G., International Relations
IDE, K., Modern Asian Economies
IMADA, T., Accounting
KANKE, M., Business Management
KASAHARA, T., Business Enterprise and Human Evolution
KAWAMURA, Y., Corporate Planning of Financial Institutions, Investment Banking
KIHARA, T., Cooperation among Nations and International Economics
KOREEDA, M., Microeconomics
MARUYAMA, Y., Decision Making
MATSUMOTO, M., Economic History of the British Empire
MATSUNAGA, A., Small Business Administration
MIHARA, Y., Human Resource Management
MURATA, S., Microeconomics
MURATA, Y., Mathematics
OKADA, H., Financial Accounting
SHIBATA, K., Japanese Economic History
SUGIHARA, T., Management Engineering
SUSAI, M., International Finance
TAGUCHI, N., International Investment
TAKAHASHI, Y., Intellectual Property and Licensing
TAKAKURA, Y., Political Economy
TATEYAMA, S., Business Enterprises and Asian Economics
UCHIDA, S., Monetary Economics
UENO, K., Financial Accounting
UNOTORO, Y., Japanese Economy
YAJIMA, K., Derivative Securities

Faculty of Education (fax (95) 819-2265; internet www.edu.nagasaki-u.ac.jp):

ADACHI, K., Analysis and Applied Mathematics
AIKAWA, K., School for Intellectually Impaired Children
AKASAKI, M., Teaching of Home Economics
ARITA, Y., Teaching of Social Studies
AZUMA, M., Biology
FUKUI, A., Music Education
FUKUYAMA, Y., Physics
FUNAKOE, K., Law
FURUYA, Y., Materials Science and Engineering
GOTO, Y., Early Childhood Education and Care
HAMASAKI, K., German Literature
HARADA, J., Educational Psychology
HASHIMOTO, T., Science Education
HIGUCHI, S., Analytical Chemistry
HORIUCHI, I., Pianoforte Playing
IIZUKA, T., Philosophy
IKAWA, S., Painting
INOUE, I., American Literature
ITOYAMA, K., Teaching of Technology
IYAMA, K., Social Education
JINNO, N., Biology
KABASHIMA, S., Physics
KAMIZONO, K., Moral and Philosophy Education
KATSUMATA, T., Japanese Literature
KITAMURA, Y., Analysis
KOGA, M., Solid State Physics
MATUNAGA, J., Teaching of Health and Physical Education
MIYAZAKI, M., Developmental Psychology
MURATA, Y., Developmental Psychology
NAKAMURA, M., American Literature
NAKAMURA, Y., English and American Literature
NAKANISHI, H., Biology
NISHIZAWA, S., Physical Fitness
OBARA, T., Exercise Physiology
ODA, M., Design
OSAKI, Y., Astronomy
OTSUBO, Y., Teaching of English
SATO, K., Sculpture
SINNO, T., Psychological Study of Preschool Children's Play
SINOHARA, S., Philosophy
SUGAWARA, M., Exercise Physiology
SUGAWARA, T., Geometry
SUGIYAMA, S., Woodworking
TAHARA, Y., School Health and Sports Physiology
TAKAHASHI, S., International Law, Constitutional Law
TAKAHASHI, S., Sociology
TAMARI, M., Food and Nutritional Chemistry
TANIGAWA, M., Politics
TOMONAGA, S., Psychology
WASHIO, T., Algebra
YAMAGUCHI, T., History
YAMAMOTO, T., Teaching of Japanese
YAMANO, S., Theory of Music
YAMAUCHI, M., Physical Education
YANAGIDA, Y., Educational Sociology
YASUKOUCHI, Y., Teaching of Japanese
YOKOYAMA, M., Politics
YOSHIOKA, H., Educational Psychology

Faculty of Engineering (fax (95) 849-4999; internet www.eng.nagasaki-u.ac.jp):

AOYAGI, H., Biochemistry
EGASHIRA, M., Materials Chemistry
FUJIYAMA, H., Plasma Science
FUKUNAGA, H., Magnetics
FURUMOTO, K., Hydraulics
HARADA, T., Reinforced and Prestressed Concrete Structures
HASAKA, M., Materials Physics and Engineering
IMAI, Y., Fracture Mechanics
ISHIMATSU, T., Measurement and Control Engineering

IWANAGA, H., Analysis of Crystal Structure
IWAO, M., Synthetic Organic Chemistry
KAGAWA, A., Metal Science
KANEMARU, K., Heat Transfer
KAWAZOE, T., Tribology
KISU, H., Computational Mechanics
KOBAYASHI, K., Network Systems
KODAMA, Y., Fluid Dynamics
KUDO, A., Algebra
KUDO, T., Solid State Electrochemistry
MATSUDA, H., Structural and Engineering Mechanics
MATSUO, H., High-voltage Engineering
MIYAHARA, S., Pattern Recognition and Information Retrieval Systems
NOGUCHI, M., Hydraulics
OGURI, K., Computer and Information Science
OKABAYASHI, T., Dynamics and Control of Structures
ONISHI, M., Coordination Chemistry
OYAMA, J., Electrical Machinery
SAKIYAMA, T., Structural Analysis
SETOGUCHI, K., Fatigue
SHIGECHI, T., Thermal Engineering
SHUGYO, M., Inelastic Behaviour of Steel Structures
TAKAHASHI, K., Structural Vibration
TAKENAKA, T., Electromagnetic Wave Theory
TAMARU, Y., Organic Chemistry
TANABASHI, Y., Soil Mechanics
TANAKA, K., Engineering Optics
TSUJI, M., Electrical Control Systems
UCHIYAMA, Y., Ceramics Science and Technology

Faculty of Environmental Studies (fax (95) 819-2716; internet www.env.nagasaki-u.ac.jp/mainj.shtml):

ARAO, K., Meteorology and Climatology
FUKUSHIMA, K., Anthropology of Religion
GOTO, N., Solid State Physics
HAMA, T., Labour Environment
HAYASE, T., Environmental Politics
HIMENO, J., History of Economics
IDE, Y., Environmental Business Management
IKENAGA, T., Plant Functional Science
IKUNO, M., Civil Law
INOUE, Y., Philosophy
ISHIZAKI, K., Environmental Engineering
KOHRA, S., Environmental Chemistry
MASAKI, H., Oriental Philosophy and Bioethics
MIYA, Y., Crustacean Taxonomy
NAKAMURA, T., Biostatistics and Risk Analysis
NAKAMURA, T., Coastal Oceanography
ONO, T., Environment Economics
SAKUMA, T., Japanese Intellectual History
SONODA, N., German Literature
TAIMURA, A., Exercise Physiology
TAKAZANE, Y., French Culture and Culture Exchange
TAKEMASA, T., Soil Physics
TANIMURA, K., Living Environment
TSUCHIYA, K., Environmental Physiology
UEDA, K., Peptide Chemistry
WAKAKI, Y., Japanese Literature
YAMAZAKI, S., Environmental Biochemistry
YOSHIDA, M., Greek Philosophy
YOSHIKAWA, I., Radiation Genetics

Faculty of Fisheries (fax (95) 819-2799; internet www.fish.nagasaki-u.ac.jp/index .htm):

ARAKAWA, O., Marine Food Hygiene
GODA, M., Navigation, Nautical Instruments
HARA, K., Biochemistry
HASHIMOTO, J., Deep-sea Biology
ISHIHARA, T., Aquatic Biochemistry
ISHIMATSU, A., Fish Physiology
ISHIZAKA, J., Biological Oceanography, Ocean Colour Remote Sensing
KATAOKA, C., Marine Social Science

KITAMURA, H., Marine Chemical Ecology, Effects of Pollution on Marine Life
MATSUBAYASHI, N., Colloid and Interface Science
MATSUOKA, K., Micropalaeontology and Coastal Environment Science
MATSUYAMA, M., Limnology and Oceanography
MORII, H., Ecology and Physiology of Marine and Food Bacteria
NAKATA, H., Fisheries Oceanography and Coastal Oceanography
NATSUKARI, Y., Fisheries Biology, Invertebrates, Cephalopoda
NISHINOKUBI, H., Fishing Boat Seamanship, Fishing Gear Engineering
NOZAKI, Y., Chemistry and Technology of Marine Food Materials
ODA, T., Marine Biochemistry
TACHIBANA, K., Nutritional Chemistry of Marine Food
TAKEMURA, A., Acoustical Behaviour of Marine Animals, Life History of Marine Mammals and Sharks
TAMAKI, A., Ecology of Marine Benthos
TSUCHIMOTO, M., Nutritional Physiology of Marine Food
YAMAGUCHI, Y., Fishing Technology Science, Fishing Ground Ecology
YOSHIKOSHI, K., Fish Pathology

Graduate School of Science and Technology (fax (95) 819-2491; internet www.seisan .nagasaki-u.ac.jp):

FUJITA, Y., Marine Phycology
FURUKAWA, M., Polymer Science
GOTOH, K., Remote Sensing
HAGIWARA, A., Marine Invertebrate Zoology, Live Food Science, Applied Planktology
ISHIDA, M., Diesel Combustion Engineering
KURODA, H., Computer and Information Science
MATSUO, H., Electronic and Digital Control
NAKASHIMA, N., Chemistry and Materials Science of Nanocarbons
YOSHITAKE, Y., Vibration of Structures

Institute of Tropical Medicine (1-12-4 Sakamoto, Nagasaki 852-8523; tel. (95) 849-7800; fax (95) 849-7805; internet www.tm .nagasaki-u.ac.jp):

AOKI, Y., Parasitology
HIRAYAMA, K., Molecular Immunogenetics
HIRAYAMA, T., Bacteriology
IWASAKI, T., Pathology
KANBARA, H., Protozoology
MIZOTA, T., Social Environment
MOJI, K., Human Ecology
MORITA, K., Virology
NAGATAKE, T., Internal Medicine
NAKAMURA, M., Biochemistry
SHIMADA, M., Eco-epidemiology
TAKAGI, M., Medical Entomology
YAMAMOTO, N., Preventive Medicine and AIDS Research

School of Dentistry (1-7-1 Sakamoto, Nagasaki 852-8588; tel. (95) 849-7600; fax (95) 849-7608; internet www.de.nagasaki-u.ac .jp):

ATSUTA, M., Fixed Prosthodontics
FUJII, H., Removable Prosthodontics
FUJIWARA, T., Paediatric Dentistry
HARA, Y., Periodontology
HAYASHI, Y., Endodontics and Operative Dentistry
HISATSUNE, K., Dental Materials Science
INOKUCHI, T., Oral and Maxillofacial Surgery II
KATO, Y., Dental Pharmacology
MIZUNO, A., Oral and Maxillofacial Surgery I
NAKAMURA, T., Radiology and Cancer Biology
NAKAYAMA, K., Oral Bacteriology
NEMOTO, T., Oral Biochemistry

OI, K., Dental Anaesthesiology
ROKUTANDA, A., Oral Anatomy
SHINSHO, F., Preventive Dentistry
TAKANO, K., Oral Histology
TODA, K., Oral Physiology
YAMAGUCHI, A., Oral Pathology
YOSHIDA, N., Orthodontics

School of Medicine (1-12-4 Sakamoto, Nagasaki 852-8523; tel. (95) 849-7000; fax (95) 849-7166; internet www.med.nagasaki-u.ac .jp):

AIKAWA, T., Physiology of Visceral Function and Body Fluid
AOYAGI, K., Preventive Health Sciences and Community Health
EGUCHI, K., Immunology, Endocrinology and Metabolism
EISHI, K., Cardiovascular Surgery
FUNASE, K., Human Motor Control, Exercise Physiology
HAMANO, K., Foundations of Nursing
HAYASHI, K., Radiological Science
ISHIHARA, K., Adult Nursing, Cancer Nursing
ISHIMARU, T., Obstetrics and Gynaecology
ITO, T., Biochemistry
KAMIHIRA, S., Laboratory Medicine
KANEMATSU, T., Surgery
KANETAKE, H., Nephro-urology
KATAMINE, S., Cellular and Molecular Biology
KATAYAMA, I., Dermatology
KATO, K., Anatomy of Locomotor Systems, Physical Anthropology
KOHNO, S., Molecular and Clinical Microbiology
KOJI, T., Histology and Cell Biology
KONDO, T., Clinical Biochemistry and Molecular Biology in Ageing-related Vascular Diseases and Cancer
MATSUMOTO, T., Paediatrics
MATSUSAKA, N., Rehabilitation Medicine, Orthopaedic Surgery
MATSUYAMA, T., Cytokine Signalling
MIYASHITA, H., Child Nursing, Rehabilitation
MORISHITA, M., Community Health Nursing
MORIUCHI, H., Medical Virology
NAGAO, T., Occupational Therapy, Assistive Technology
NAGASHIMA, S., Macroscopic Morphology
NAGATA, I., Clinical Neuroscience, Neurology and Neurosurgery
NAKAGOMI, O., Molecular Epidemiology
NAKAJIMA, H., Gynaecological Oncology, Obstetrics
NAKAZONO, I., Forensic Pathology and Science
NIIKAWA, N., Human Genetics
NIWA, M., Neurosensory Pharmacology
OHISHI, K., Midwifery
OHTA, Y., Psychiatry, Mental and Physical Health
OKUMURA, Y., Radiation Biophysics
SATO, H., Comparative Medicine
SEKINE, I., Molecular Pathology
SENJYU, H., Physical Therapy, Pulmonary Rehabilitation
SHIBATA, Y., Radiation Epidemiology
SHIMOKAWA, I., Pathology and Gerontology
SHINDO, H., Orthopaedic Pathomechanism
SHINOHARA, K., Physiology
SUMIKAWA, K., Anaesthesiology
TAGAWA, Y., Thoracic Surgery and Cytometry
TAGUCHI, T., Pathology
TAHARA, H., Physical Therapy, Quality of Life
TAKAHASHI, H., Otorhinolaryngology
TANIYAMA, K., Pharmacology and Therapeutics
TASHIRO, T., Respirology, Infectious Diseases
TERASAKI, A., Adult Health Nursing

TOKUNAGA, M., Public Health Nursing
TOMONAGA, M., Molecular Medicine and Haematology
URATA, H., Adult Nursing, Surgical Nursing
YAMASHITA, S., Molecular Medicine
YANO, K., Cardiovascular Medicine
YOSHIMURA, T., Neurology (Morphology in Neuromuscular Diseases)
YUI, K., Immunology

School of Pharmaceutical Sciences (fax (95) 819-2412; internet www.ph.nagasaki-u.ac.jp/indexj.html):

FUJITA, K., Pharmaceutical Chemistry
HATAKEYAMA, S., Pharmaceutical Organic Chemistry
KAI, M., Chemistry of Biofunctional Molecules
KOBAYASHI, N., Molecular Biology of Diseases
KOHNO, M., Cell Regulation
KOUNO, I., Pharmacognosy
KURODA, N., Analytical Chemistry for Pharmaceutics
MURATA, I., Pharmacotherapeutics
NAKAMURA, J., Pharmaceutics
NAKASHIMA, K., Analytical Research for Pharmacoinformatics
NAKAYAMA, M., Hygienic Chemistry
NATSUMARA, Y., Synthetic Chemistry for Pharmaceutics
UEDA, H., Molecular Pharmacology and Neuroscience
WATANABE, M., Radiation and Life Science
YOSHIMOTO, T., Biotechnology

NAGOYA INSTITUTE OF TECHNOLOGY

Gokiso-cho, Showa-ku, Nagoya 466-855
Telephone: (52) 735-5000
Fax: (52) 735-5009
Internet: www.nitech.ac.jp
Founded 1949
Independent
Language of instruction: Japanese
Academic year: April to March
Pres.: HIROAKI YANAGIDA
Vice-Pres: IWATA AKIRA, NOBUYUKI MATSUI, TETSUMI HORIKOSHI
Dir-Gen.: HIDESHI SUDA
Dir for Univ. Library: KOICHIRO KAWASHIMA
Library of 463,169 vols
Number of teachers: 372
Number of students: 6,516
Publication: *Bulletin* (1 a year).

ATTACHED INSTITUTES

Center for Information and Media Studies: Gokiso-cho, Showa-ku, Nagoya 466-8555; e-mail staff@center.nitech.ac.jp; Dir YUKIE KOYAMA.

Ceramics Research Laboratory: 6–29 Asahigaoka 10-chome, Tajimi, Gifu; Dir SUGURU SUZUKI.

Co-operative Research Center: Gokiso-cho, Showa-ku, Nagoya; Dir KOICHI NAKAMURA.

Instrument and Analysis Center: Gokiso-cho, Showa-ku, Nagoya 466-8555; Dir YOSHI-HARU TSUJITA.

Research Center for Micro-structure Devices: Gokiso-cho, Showa-ku, Nagoya; Dir MASAYOSHI UMENO.

NAGOYA UNIVERSITY

Furo-cho, Chikusa-ku, Nagoya 464-8601
Telephone: (52) 789-2044
Fax: (52) 789-2045
E-mail: ised@post.jimu.nagoya-u.ac.jp
Internet: www.nagoya-u.ac.jp
Founded 1939

Independent
Language of instruction: Japanese
Academic year: April to March (two semesters)
Pres.: MICHINARI HAMAGUCHI
Vice-Pres and Trustees: TAKASHI MIYATA, HARUO SABURI, HIROYUKI SUGIYAMA, ICHIRO YAMAMOTO, RYOICHI FUJII
Vice-Pres. for Hospital Management: SEIICHI MATSUO
Vice-Pres. for Research and Int. Planning: YOSHIHITO WATANABE
Vice-Pres. for Evaluation and Gen. Planning: YUSHU MATSUSHITA
Dir-Gen. for Admin.: MAKOTO TAKAHASHI
Dir of the Library: YOSHITO ITOH
Library: see Libraries and Archives
Number of teachers: 1,716 full-time
Number of students: 14,977 full-time
Publication: *Nagoya University Bulletin*

DEANS

Graduate School of Bioagricultural Sciences: T. MATSUDA
Graduate School of Economics: MAKOTO TAWADA
Graduate School of Education and Human Development: MISAO HAYAKAWA
Graduate School of Engineering: N. SAWAKI
Graduate School of Environmental Studies: YASUSHI YAMAGUCHI
Graduate School of Information Science: NOBUAKI KOGA
Graduate School of International Development: KATSUFUMI NARITA
Graduate School of Languages and Culture: K. KONDO
Graduate School of Law: H. SABURI
Graduate School of Letters: TOSHIHIRO WADA
Graduate School of Mathematics: Y. NAMI-KAWA
Graduate School of Medicine: M. HAMAGUCHI
Graduate School of Science: I. OHMINE
School of Agricultural Sciences: T. MATSUDA
School of Economics: MAKOTO TAWADA
School of Education: MISAO HAYAKAWA
School of Engineering: N. SAWAKI
School of Informatics and Sciences: M. SANO
School of Law: H. SABURI
School of Letters: TOSHIHIRO WADA
School of Medicine: M. HAMAGUCHI
School of Science: I. OHMINE

DIRECTORS

Bioscience and Biotechnology Center: TSU-KASA MATSUDA
Center for Asian Legal Exchange: MASANORI AIKYO
Center for Chronological Research: TOSHIO NAKAMURA
Center for Cooperative Research in Advanced Science and Technology: G. OBINATA
Center for Developmental Clinical Psychology and Psychiatry: S. HONJO
Center for Gene Research: M. ISHIURA
Center for Information Media Studies: I. YAMAMOTO
Center for Studies of Higher Education: MOTOKAZU KIMATA
EcoTopia Science Institute: TSUNEO MATSUI
Education Center for International Students: YUKIO ISHIDA
Hydrospheric Atmospheric Research Center: HIROSHI UYEDA
Information Technology Center: T. WATA-NABE
Institute for Advanced Research: KONDO TAKAO
International Cooperation Center for Agricultural Education: AKIRA YAMAUCHI
Kobayashi–Maskawa Institute for the Origin of Particles and the Universe: TOSHIHIDE MASKAWA (Dir-Gen.)
Nagoya University Museum: M. ADACHI

Radioisotope Research Center: K. NISHIZAWA
Research Center for Materials Science: RYOJI NOYORI (Supervisor)
Research Center of Health, Physical Fitness and Sports: K. SHIMAOKA
Research Institute of Environmental Medicine: I. KODAMA
Solar–Terrestrial Environment Laboratory: YUTAKA MATSUMI
University Hospital: A. IGUCHI

PROFESSORS

Center for Gene Research (Furo-cho, Chikusa-ku, Nagoya 464-8602; tel. (52) 789-3080; fax (52) 789-3081; internet www.gene.nagoya-u.ac.jp/index-e.html):

ISHIURA, M., Genome Biology, Molecular Biology
SUGITA, M., Plant Molecular Biology

Center for Studies of Higher Education (tel. (52) 789-5696; fax (52) 789-5695; e-mail webmaster@cshe.nagoya-u.ac.jp; internet www.cshe.nagoya-u.ac.jp):

NATSUME, T., Comparative Study on Higher Education

Radioisotope Research Center (Furo-cho, Chikusa-ku, Nagoya 464-8602; tel. (52) 789-2563; fax (52) 789-2567; internet www.ric.nagoya-u.ac.jp):

NISHIZAWA, K., Radiation Protection

Nagoya University Museum (Furo-cho, Chikusa-ku, Nagoya 464-8601; tel. (52) 789-5767; fax (52) 789-5896; internet www.num.nagoya-u.ac.jp):

ADACHI, M., Sedimentation and Tectonics
NISHIKAWA, T., Taxonomy and Phylogeny of Marine Invertebrates

Center for Co-operative Research in Advanced Science and Technology (tel. (52) 789-3921; fax (52) 789-3922; internet www.ccrast.nagoya-u.ac.jp):

IWATA, S., Magnetic Materials and Magnetic Devices
KASAHARA, K., Quantum Electronics, Optical Communication
MORI, S., Environment Process Technology
OBINATA, G., Modelling and Control in Robotics, Human–Robot Interfaces, Biocybernetics
OGAWA, M., Semiconductor Devices
TAKAHASHI, H., Copyright

Center for Information Media Studies (tel. (52) 789-3903; fax (52) 789-3900; internet www.media.nagoya-u.ac.jp):

NAGAO, K., Digital Content Technology, Media Informatics, Image and Language Processing, Agent Technology, Artificial Intelligence

Center for Chronological Research (Furo-cho, Chikusa-ku, Nagoya 464-8602; tel. (52) 789-2579; fax (52) 789-3092; internet www.nendai.nagoya-u.ac.jp/en/index.html):

NAKAMURA, T., Geochemistry and Radio-chronometry
SUZUKI, K., Petrology and Geochronology

Bioscience and Biotechnology Center (tel. (52) 789-5194; fax (52) 789-5195; internet www.agr.nagoya-u.ac.jp/~nubs/index.html):

HATTORI, T., Plant Cell Function
KITAJIMA, K., Animal Cell Function
KITANO, H., Plant Bioresources
MATSUOKA, M., Plant Molecular Breeding
UOZUMI, T., Molecular Biosystems
WAKAMATSU, Y., Freshwater Fish Stocks

Hydrospheric–Atmospheric Research Center (tel. (52) 789-3466; fax (52) 789-3436; e-mail koho@hyarc.nagoya-u.ac.jp; internet www.hyarc.nagoya-u.ac.jp/hyarc):

NAKAMURA, K., Satellite Meteorology
SAINO, T., Ocean Climate Biology
UYEDA, H., Meteorology

YASUNARI, T., Meteorology, Climate System Study

Center for Asian Legal Exchange (tel. (52) 789-2325; fax (52) 789-4902; e-mail cale@nomolog.nagoya-u.ac.jp; internet www.nomolog.nagoya-u.ac.jp):

AIKYO, M., Asian Law

Information Technology Center (tel. (52) 789-4352; fax (52) 789-4385; internet www.itc.nagoya-u.ac.jp):

ISHII, K., Computational Fluid Dynamics
MASE, K., Computer Mediated Communication
MIYAO, M., Ergonomics
YOSHIKAWA, M., Database Systems

Center for Developmental Clinical Psychology and Psychiatry (tel. (52) 789-2656; fax (52) 789-5059):

HONJO, S., Child Psychiatry
TSURUTA, K., School Counselling
UJIIE, T., Clinical Support of the Mother–Child Relationship

Education Center for International Students (tel. (52) 789-2198; fax (52) 789-5100; internet www.ecis.nagoya-u.ac.jp):

KASHIMA, T., Phonetics, Teaching Pronunciation of Japanese as a Foreign Language
MATSUURA, M., International Student Advisory and Resource Services
MURAKAMI, K., Teaching Japanese as a Foreign Language
NOMIYA, T., Instrumental Analytical Chemistry, Student Exchange Programme Education
OZAKI, A., Teaching Japanese as a Foreign Language

EcoTopia Science Institute (tel. (52) 789-5262; fax (52) 789-5265; e-mail jimu@esi.nagoya-u.ac.jp; internet www.esi.nagoya-u.ac.jp):

ENOKIDA, Y., Nuclear Fuel Engineering
FUJISAWA, T., High Temperature Physical Chemistry
HASEGAWA, T., Environmental Thermo-Fluid Technologies
HASEGAWA, Y., Energy Science
ICHIHASHI, M., Electron Optics
ITHO, H., Solid Waste Treatment
KATAYAMA, A., Bioremediation and Bioreclamation
KATAYAMA, M., Communication and Information Systems
KITAGAWA, K., Advanced Energy Conversion Systems and Technologies
NAGASAKI, T., Materials Science
OKUBO, H., Electric Power Engineering
SUZUKI, K., Environmental Research
TAKAI, O., Materials Science and Engineering
TANAKA, N., High Resolution Electron Microscopy and Electron Diffraction of Clusters, Wires and Think-Film Related to Nanotechnology
TATEISHI, K., Structural Engineering
TONOIKE, T., Linguistics, Lexicology and Optimality Theory
WATANABE, T., Fluid Informatics and Computational Fluid Dynamics
YOGO, T., Materials Chemistry

Graduate School of Environmental Studies (tel. (52) 789-3454; fax (52) 789-3452; internet www.env.nagoya-u.ac.jp):

AGETA, Y., Glaciology
ANDO, M., Seismology and Geodesy
ENAMI, M., Metamorphic Petrology and Rock-forming Mineralogy
FUJII, N., Volcanology and Planetary Physics
FUKUWA, N., Earthquake Engineering
HATTA, T., Neuropsychology
HAYASHI, N., Economic and Urban Geography

HAYASHI, Y., Sustainable Transport and Spatial Development
HIBINO, T., Electrochemistry
HIRAHARA, K., Seismology
HIROSE, Y., Environmental Social Psychology
HOSHINO, M., Surface Material Systems
IKADATSU, Y., Jurisprudence
IMURA, H., Environmental Systems Analysis and Planning
ISHII, K., Associative Learning
ITAKURA, T., Sociology
ITO, Y., Counselling and Clinical Psychology (Person-centered Approach and Focusing-oriented Psychotherapy)
KAI, M., Meteorology, Climatology and Remote Sensing
KAINUMA, J., Sociology
KANZAWA, H., Meteorology
KATAGI, A., Architectural Design and Theory
KAWABE, I., REE Geochemistry, Geochemical Earthquake Prediction
KAWADA, M., History of Political Thought in Japan
KAWAGUCHI, J., Cognitive Psychology, Human Memory
KAWAI, T., Environmental Science
KAWASAKI, S., Economics
KUNO, S., Environmental Engineering, Environmental Psychology
KURODA, T., Urban Economics, Regional Science, Economic Theory
MASUZAWA, T., Inorganic Biogeochemistry
MATSUBARA, T., Environmental Science, Microbiology, Biochemistry
MATSUMOTO, E., Geochemistry
MIZOGUCHI, T., Historical Geography, Regional Study of South Asia
MORIKAWA, T., Transport Planning
MORIMOTO, H., Mathematical Biology
MURATA, S., Organic Chemistry, Physical Organic Chemistry, Environmental Materials Science
NISHIHARA, K., Sociology, Phenomenological Sociology, Social Theory
OHKAWA, M., Constitutional Law, Environmental Law
OHMORI, H., Structural Mechanics and Computational Analysis
OKAMOTO, K., Geography, Behavioural Geography, Urban Geography
OKUMIYA, M., Optimization of Energy Supplies in Building and Urban Scale
OZAWA, T., Geobiology, Evolutionary Biology
SANO, M., Fuel Cell, Secondary Battery, Energy Systems
SHIMIZU, H., Architectural Planning and Design, Theatre Planning and Administration
SUGIMOTO, T., Heterocyclic Chemistry
SUZUKI, Y., Active Tectonics
TANAKA, S., Urban Sociology
TANAKA, T., Isotope Geochemistry
TANOUE, E., Marine Biogeochemistry
TESHIGAWARA, M., Reinforced Concrete Structures
UMITSU, M., Geomorphology, Quaternary Geology, Geo-environmental Studies
YAMADA, I., Seismology and Planetary Physics
YAMADA, K., Structural Engineering, Bridge Engineering
YAMAGUCHI, Y., Remote Sensing for Environmental Monitoring

Graduate School of International Development (tel. (52) 789-4952; fax (52) 789-4951; e-mail webmaster@gsid.nagoya-u.ac.jp; internet www.gsid.nagoya-u.ac.jp):

EZAKI, M., Development Information Systems
FUTAMURA, H., Drug Trafficking in Latin America
HIROSATO, Y., Educational Development

KIMURA, H., Dynamics of Regional Politics, International Cooperation Policy I, II, Dynamics of Regional Politics
KINOSHITA, T., Second Language Acquisition, Learning, Language Assessment, TESOL and Applied Linguistics
NAKANISHI, H., International and Regional Politics, Organization for International Cooperation
NISHIMURA, Y., Development Management
OHASHI, A., South-east Asian Studies
OMURO, T., Dynamic Theory of Language
OSADA, H., Integrated Development Planning
OTSUBO, S., International Development Economics
SAKURAI, T., Theory of Intercultural Communication
SUGIURA, M., Second Language Acquisition
TAKAHASHI, K., Multiculturalism I, Social Change during Modernization
YASUDA, N., Comparative Asian Legal Systems, Introduction to Law and Development Studies

Graduate School of Languages and Cultures (tel. (52) 789-4881; fax (52) 789-4873; e-mail lcoffice@lang.nagoya-u.ac.jp; internet www.lang.nagoya-u.ac.jp):

ANDO, S., 16th- and 17th-century English Poetry
ARIKAWA, K., German Literature in the Age of the Enlightenment
FUKUDA, M., Comparative Literature and Culture, Medical History
HIGH, P., Intellectual History of Japanese Film
IIDA, H., Contrastive Study of Japanese, Korean and English
INOUE, I., English Linguistics
KAMIYA, O., Modern Chinese Language
KATO, S., American Literature, Japanese and American Environmental Literature
KONDO, K., Language Typology
KOSAKA, K., Contrastive Linguistics
MAENO, M., Cultural History of Early Modern Europe
MATSUMOTO, I., Women's Studies
MATSUOKA, M., Victorian Literature
MURANUSHI, K., William Shakespeare
NAGAHATA, A., American Literature
NAKAI, M., Trend of Thought in Modern Chinese Literature
NAKAJIMA, T., German Lyric Poems of the 19th Century
OCHI, K., Obliteration of Feminine in the Western Culture
SHIBATA, S., Modern Literature in Japan and Germany
SUZUKI, S., Emblems and Religious Poetry in the 16th and 17th Centuries
TADOKORO, M., Comparative Literature and Culture
TANO, I., Modern American Literature and Culture
YANAGISAWA, T., Language Typology, North-western Caucasian Languages
YOSHIMURA, M., English Romanticism

Graduate School of Mathematics (Furo-cho, Chikusa-ku, Nagoya 464-8602; tel. (52) 789-2429; fax (52) 789-2829; internet www.math.nagoya-u.ac.jp/en):

FUJIWARA, K., Algebraic Geometry
GYOJA, A., Representation Theory
KANAI, M., Geometry and Dynamic Systems
KANNO, H., Mathematical Physics
KIMURA, Y., Fluid Dynamics
KOBAYASHI, R., Differential Geometry
KONDO, S., Algebraic Geometry
MATSUMOTO, K., Number Theory
MIYAKE, M., Partial Differential Equations
NAMIKAWA, Y., Algebraic Geometry
NAYATANI, S., Conformal Geometry
OHSAWA, T., Complex Analysis
SATO, H., Geometry

SHIOTA, M., Real Algebraic Geometry
SHOJI, T., Representational Theory
TSUCHIYA, A., Geometry and Mathematical Physics
UMEMURA, H., Algebraic Geometry
UZAWA, T., Representational Theory

International Cooperation Center for Agricultural Education (tel. (52) 789-4225; fax (52) 789-4222; e-mail iccae@agr.nagoya-u.ac.jp; internet www.agr.nagoya-u.ac.jp/~iccae/index-j.html):

ASANUMA, S., Network Development
MATSUMOTO, T., Project Development

Research Center for Materials Science (Furo-cho, Chikusa-ku, Nagoya 464-8602; tel. (52) 789-5902; fax (52) 789-5902; internet www.rcms.nagoya-u.ac.jp/intro/):

IMAE, T., Physical Chemistry
KITAMURA, M., Synthetic Organic Chemistry
SEKI, K., Physical Chemistry
TATSUMI, K., Inorganic Chemistry

Research Center of Health, Physical Fitness and Sports (tel. (52) 789-3946; fax (52) 789-3957; internet www.htc.nagoya-u.ac.jp):

HIRUTA, S., Workload in Care Services
IKEGAMI, Y., Biomechanical Analysis of Human Movement
ISHIDA, K., Cardio-respiratory Responses during Exercise
IZUHARA, Y., Class Work Study of Physical Education
KONDO, T., Exercise and Gastrointestinal Function, Pancreatic Diseases, Breath and Skin Gas in Health and Diseases
NISHIDA, T., Achievement Motivation in Physical Education and Sports
OGAWA, T., Phenomenological Psychopathology, Psychoanalytic Psychotherapy of Adolescents
OSHIDA, Y., Exercise for Insulin Resistance
SHIMAOKA, K., Teaching of Exercise in Health Promotion Programmes
SHIMAOKA, M., Health and Physical Fitness in Workers
YAMAMOTO, Y., Motor Control and Learning from a Dynamical System Approach

Research Institute of Environmental Medicine (tel. (52) 789-3886; fax (52) 789-3887; internet www.riem.nagoya-u.ac.jp/e/index.html):

KAMIYA, K., Molecular and Genomic Regulation of the Heart
KODAMA, I., Molecular and Cellular Cardiology
KOMATSU, Y., Synaptic Plasticity in the Visual Cortex
MIZUMURA, K., Neurophysiology of Pain
MURATA, Y., Molecular Genetics
SAWADA, M., Molecular and Cellular Neuroscience
SEO, H., Molecular Mechanism of Hormone Action
SUZUMURA, A., Neuroimmunology
YASUI, K., Bioinformation Analysis

School of Agricultural Sciences and Graduate School of Bioagricultural Sciences (tel. (52) 789-5266; fax (52) 789-4005; e-mail info@agr.nagoya-u.ac.jp; internet www.agr.nagoya-u.ac.jp):

AOI, K., Polymer Chemistry
DOKE, N., Plant Pathology
EBIHARA, S., Animal Behavioural Physiology
FUKUSHIMA, K., Forest Chemistry
FUKUTA, K., Animal Morphology and Function
HATTORI, K., Plant Genetics and Breeding
HATTORI, S., Forest Resources Utilization
HIRASHIMA, Y., Biomaterials Engineering
ISOBE, M., Organic Chemistry
KIMURA, M., Soil Biology and Chemistry
KITAGAWA, Y., Stem Cell Engineering

KOBAYASHI, M., Biodynamics of Insect–Virus Interactions
KOBAYASHI, T., Gene Regulation
MAEDA, K., Reproductive Science
MAESHIMA, M., Cell Dynamics
MAKI, M., Molecular and Cellular Regulation
MATSUDA, T., Molecular Bioregulation
MIYAKE, H., Plant Resources and Environment
MIZUNO, T., Molecular Biology and Molecular Genetics
MORI, H., Developmental Signalling Biology
NAKAMURA, K., Biological Chemistry
NAKANO, H., Molecular Biotechnology
NAMIKAWA, T., Animal Genetics
NOGUCHI, T., Molecular Physiological Chemistry
OHTA, T., Forest Meteorology and Hydrology
OJIKA, M., Molecular Function Modelling
OMATA, T., Molecular Plant Physiology
OSAWA, T., Food and Biodynamics
SAKAGAMI, Y., Bioactive Natural Products Chemistry
SHIBATA, E., Forest Protection
SHIMADA, K., Animal Physiology
SOMIYA, H., Animal Information Biology
TAKABE, T., Biosphere Symbiosis
TAKENAKA, C., Forest Environment and Resources
TAKEYA, H., Socioeconomic Science of Food Production
TANAKA, T., Applied Entomology
TOMARU, N., Forest Ecology and Physiology
TSUCHIKAWA, S., Mechanical Engineering for Biological Materials
TSUGE, T., Microbes and Plant Production
YAGINUMA, T., Sericulture Entomological resources
YAMAUCHI, A., Biosphere Resources Cycling
YAMAKI, S., Horticultural Science
YOKOTA, H., Animal Feeds and Production
YOSHIMURA, T., Biomacromolecules

School and Graduate School of Economics (tel. (52) 789-4920; fax (52) 789-4921; internet www.soec.nagoya-u.ac.jp):

ANDO, T., History of European Economic Thought
ARAYAMA, Y., Agricultural Policy and Economic Growth
HIRAKAWA, H., Asian Economics
KANAI, Y., British Monetary History during the Inter-war Period
KIMURA, S., Management Accounting
KISIDA, T., Organization
MINAGAWA, T., Microeconomic Foundations of Macroeconomics
NABESHIMA, N., History of Economic Thought, Political Economy
NAGAO, S., History of Economic and Social Thought, Political Economy
NAKANISHI, S., Japanese Economic History
NEMOTO, J., Applied Econometrics and Productivity Analysis
NOGUCHI, A., Financial Accounting
OHTA, S., Labour Economics
OKUMURA, R., Intertemporal Open-economy Macroeconomics
SATO, M., Conceptual Framework of Business Accounting
TAKAKUWA, S., Business Administration
TAKEUCHI, J., Comparative Study on Economic Development
TAKEUCHI, N., Stabilization Policy
TAMARU, M., Globalization and Japanese Economy
TAWADA, M., International Trade Theory
TOMOSUGI, Y., Management Audit
TSUKADA, H., Mathematical Finance
WAGO, H., Econometrics Analysis
YAMAMOTO, T., Financial Statement Analysis

YAMORI, N., Monetary Economics and Banking Theory

School and Graduate School of Education and Human Development (tel. (52) 789-2602; fax (52) 789-2666; internet www.educa.nagoya-u.ac.jp):

HAYAKAWA, M., Philosophy of Human Becoming
HAYAMIZU, T., Psychology of Personality
IMAZU, K., Sociology of Education
KAGEYAMA, H., School Psychology
KANAI, A., Clinical Psychology
KATOH, S., History of Education
MATOBA, M., Methods of Education
MATUSHITA, H., Philosophy of Human Becoming
MORITA, M., Family Psychology
MURAKAMI, T., Psychometrics
NAKAJIMA, T., Educational Administration
NISHINO, S., Comparative Education
NOGUCHI, H., Psychometrics
OKADA, T., Cognitive Psychology
OTANI, T., Technologies in Education
TAKAGI, Y., School Environment
TERADA, M., Vocational and Technical Education
UEDA, T., Educational Management
YOSHIDA, T., Social Psychology

School and Graduate School of Engineering (Furo-cho, Chikusa-ku, Nagoya 464-8603; tel. (52) 789-3405; fax (52) 789-3100; internet www.engg.nagoya-u.ac.jp):

ANDO, H., Mathematical Information Systems
ASAI, S., Electromagnetic Processing of Materials
ASAOKA, A., Soil Mechanics
BABA, Y., Applied Analytical Chemistry
FUJIMAKI, A., Integrated Quantum Devices Engineering
FUKUDA, T., Micro-nano System Control Engineering
FURUHASHI, T., Complex Systems
HAYAKAWA, Y., Intelligent Mechatronics
HIRASAWA, M., Nano-integration Engineering
HONDA, H., Bio-process Engineering
HOSOE, S., Mechatronics Control
ICHIMIYA, A., Fundamental Quantum Engineering
IGUCHI, T., Quantum Beam Measurement and Instrumentation
IIDA, T., Energy Environmental Safety Engineering
IIJIMA, S., Molecular Biology and Genetic Engineering
IKUTA, K., Biomedical Micro- and Nano-mechatronics
INOUE, J., Solid State Engineering
IRITANI, E., Mechanical Separation Process Engineering
ISHIDA, Y., Intelligent Manufacturing Machinery
ISHIHARA, K., Chemistry of Biologically Active Materials
ISHIKAWA, T., Deformation Processing of Materials
ITOH, Y., Infrastructure System Design
KAMIGAITO, M., Organic Chemistry of Macromolecules
KANEDA, Y., Computational Fluid Mechanics
KANETAKE, N., Structure and Morphology Control Engineering
KAWAIZUMI, F., Diffusional Process Engineering
KITANO, T., Radiation Chemistry
KODA, S., Chemical Physics of Condensed Matters
KONO, A., Optical Electronics
KOUMOTO, K., Solid State Materials
KUKITA, Y., Energy Transport Engineering
KURODA, K., Nano-material Characterization

KURODA, S., Quantum Material Physics and Engineering
KUWABARA, M., Materials Reaction Process Engineering
MATSUDA, H., Thermal Energy Engineering
MATSUDA, I., Design of Catalytic Reactions
MATSUI, M., Magnetism of Materials and Magnetics
MATSUI, T., Energy Functional Materials Engineering
MATSUMOTO, T., Knowledge-based Design
MATSUMURA, T., High Current and Power Engineering
MATSUSHITA, Y., Physical Chemistry of Materials
MITAKU, S., Biophysical Engineering
MITSUYA, Y., Micro- and Nano-instrumentation Engineering
MIYATA, T., Fatigue and Fracture of Materials
MIZUTANI, N., Coastal and Maritime Engineering
MIZUTANI, T., Quantum Nano-devices Engineering
MORINAGA, M., Materials Design
MURAMATSU, N., Human System Engineering
MUTO, S., Energy Materials Science under Extreme Conditions
NAKAMURA, A., Optical Physics
NAKAMURA, H., Concrete Materials and Structures
NAKAMURA, M., Resources and Environment
NAKAMURA, Y., Fluid Dynamics
NAKAZATO, K., Intelligent Devices
NIIMI, T., Micro Thermofluid Engineering
NISHIYAMA, H., Selective Organic Synthesis
NOMURA, H., Casting and Solidification Process Engineering
OHNO, N., Computational Solid Mechanics
OKIDO, M., Surface-interface Engineering
OKUMA, S., Information and Control Systems
ONOGI, K., Process Systems Engineering
SAITO, Y., Nano-structure Analysis
SAKAI, Y., Statistical Fluid Engineering
SAKATA, M., Structural Physics Engineering
SATO, K., Micro- and Nano-process Engineering
SATO, K., Communication Networks
SATSUMA, A., Catalyst Design
SAWADA, Y., Disaster Prevention, Geotechnical Engineering
SAWAKI, N., Semiconductor Electronics
SEKI, T., Molecular Assembly, Systems Engineering
SHAMOTO, E., Ultra-precision Engineering
SHIMADA, T., Super-microcomputing
SHINODA, T., Fabrication of Materials Engineering
SODA, K., Quantum Beam Materials Engineering
SOGA, T., Physical Gas Dynamics
SUGAI, H., Plasma Electronics
SUZUOKI, Y., Energy System and Engineering
TAGAWA, T., Chemical Reaction Engineering
TAKAGI, K., Functional Crystalline Chemistry
TAKAI, Y., Energy Device Engineering
TAKAMURA, S., Plasma Science and Technology
TAKEDA, K., Physical Chemistry of Materials
TAKEDA, Y., Nano-materials and Devices
TANAKA, E., Biomechanics
TANAKA, K., Materials and Mechanics
TANIGUCHI, G., Architectural Planning
TANIMOTO, M., Visual Information
TORIMOTO, T., Material Design Chemistry
TSUBAKI, J., Processes for the Functional Development of Materials

TSUJIMOTO, T., River, Coastal and Estuarine Hydro-morphodynamics
TSUNASHIMA, S., Spin Electronics
UEDA, T., Structural Mechanics
UMEHARA, N., Manufacturing Process Technology
UMEMURA, A., Propulsion Energy Systems Engineering
URITANI, A., Applied Nuclear Physics
USAMI, T., Structural Analysis
YAMADA, K., Control Systems Engineering
YAMAMOTO, I., Energy Materials Recycling Engineering
YAMANE, T., Protein Crystallography and Structural Biology
YAMANE, Y., Reactor Physics and Engineering
YAMASHITA, H., Heat Transfer and Combustion
YAMAZAKI, K., Energy Materials Science Engineering
YASHIMA, E., Polymer Materials Design
YOSHIKAWA, N., Aerospace Microsystems
ZAIMA, S., Nano-structured Electronic Device Engineering

School and Graduate School of Law (tel. (52) 789-4910; fax (52) 789-4900; e-mail info@nomolog.nagoya-u.ac.jp; internet www.nomolog.nagoya-u.ac.jp):

AIKYO, K., Constitutional Law
AKANE, T., Criminal Procedure
CHIBA, E., Civil Law
FUJITA, S., Role of the Attorney in Legal Practice
FUKE, T., Public Finance Law and Tax Law
HACHISUKA, T., Role of the Attorney in Legal Practice
HAMADA, M., Corporate Law
HASEGAWA, Y., Civil Procedure
HASHIDA, H., Criminal Law
HONMA, Y., Civil Procedure
ICHIHASHI, K., Administrative Law
ISHII, M., Western Legal History
ISOBE, T., History of Western Political Thought
JIMBO, F., Japanese Legal History
KAGAYAMA, S., Civil Law
KAMINO, K., Administrative Law
KATO, H., Environmental Law
KATO, M., Civil Law
KAWANO, M., Civil Procedure
KITAZUMI, K., Western Political History
KOBAYASHI, R., Commercial Law
MAKINO, J., Business Law Practice
MASUDA, T., Japanese Political History
MATSUURA, Y., Legal Informatics, History of Legal Thought
MORI, H., Constitutional Law
MORIGIWA, Y., Jurisprudence
MOTO, H., Constitutional Law
NAKAHIGASHI, M., Corporate Law
NAKAYA, H., Civil Law
OBATA, K., International Law
OHSAWA, Y., Criminal Procedure
ONO, K., Political Science
SABURI, H., International Law
SADAKATA, M., International Politics
SINDO, H., Urban Politics
SUGAWARA, I., Sociology of Law
SUGIURA, K., Russian Law
SUZUKI, M., Intellectual Property Law
URABE, N., Constitutional Law
USHIRO, F., Public Administration
WADA, H., Labour Law
YAMAMOTO, T., Criminal Law

School and Graduate School of Letters (tel. (52) 789-2202; fax (52) 789-2272; internet www.lit.nagoya-u.ac.jp):

ABE, Y., Anthropology, Study of Religions and the History of Japanese Thought
AMANO, M., English Linguistics
EMURA, M., Asian History
HAGA, S., Japanese History
IKEUCHI, S., Japanese History
INABA, N., Japanese History

INOUE, S., Asian History
KAMIO, M., English and American Literature
KAMITSUKA, Y., Chinese Philosophy
KANAYAMA, Y., Philosophy
KASUGA, Y., Japanese Culture
KIMATA, M., Aesthetics and Art History
KUGINUKI, T., Japanese Linguistics
MACHIDA, K., Linguistics
MATSUZAWA, K., French Literature
MIYAJI, A., Aesthetics and Art History
ODA, Y., Japanese Culture
OGAWA, M., Classics
SATO, S., Western History
SHIMADA, Y., Anthropology, Study of Religions and the History of Japanese Thought
SHIMIZU, S., German Literature
SHIOMURA, K., Japanese Literature
SUGIYAMA, H., Chinese Literature
SUTO, Y., Western History
TAKAHASHI, T., Japanese Literature
TAKEUCHI, H., Chinese Philosophy
TAKIKAWA, M., English and American Literature
TAMURA, H., Philosophy
TSUBOI, H., Japanese Culture
WADA, T., Indian Studies
WAZAKI, H., Anthropology, Study of Religions and the History of Japanese Thought
YAMADA, H., Philosophy
YAMAMOTO, N., Archaeology
YOSHIDA, J., Chinese Philosophy

School and Graduate School of Medicine (65 Tsurumai-cho, Showa-ku, Nagoya 466-8550; tel. (52) 744-2500; fax (52) 744-2428; internet www.med.nagoya-u.ac.jp):

ANDO, H., Paediatric Surgery
ANDO, S., Clinical Nursing
AOYAMA, A., International Health
AOYAMA, T., Basic Radiological Technology
ASANO, M., Human Development Nursing and Midwifery
BAN, N., Family and Community Medicine
FUJIMOTO, T., Molecular Cell Biology
FURUKAWA, K., Molecular and Cellular Biology
GOTO, H., Therapeutic Medicine
GOTO, S., Fundamentals of Nursing
HAMAGUCHI, M., Molecular Pathogenesis
HAMAJIMA, N., Preventive Medicine
HIRAI, M., Public Health and Home Care Nursing
HIROSE, K., Cell Physiology
HOSHIYAMA, M., Basic Occupational Therapy
IDA, K., Basic Physical Therapy
IGUCHI, A., Geriatrics
IKEMATSU, Y., Clinical Nursing
ISHIGAKI, T., Radiology
ISHIGURE, N., Medical Radiological Technology
ISHIGURO, N., Orthopaedics
ISOBE, K., Immunology
ITO, H., Basic Medical Technology
ITO, K., Medical Administration and Politics
ITO, S., Basic Radiological Technology
KAIBUCHI, K., Cell Pharmacology
KAJITA, E., Public Health and Home Care Nursing
KATSUMATA, Y., Legal Medicine and Bioethics
KAWAMURA, M., Basic Physical Therapy
KAWATSU, Y., Fundamentals of Nursing
KIKKAWA, F., Obstetrics and Gynaecology
KIKUCHI, A., Molecular Mycology and Medicine
KIUCHI, T., Transplant Surgery
KOBAYASHI, K., Basic Physical Therapy
KODERA, Y., Medical Radiological Technology
KOIKE, Y., Medical Laboratory Technology
KOJIMA, S., Paediatrics

KOJIMA, T., Medical Laboratory Technology
KOMORI, K., Vascular Surgery
MAEDA, H., Medical Radiological Technology
MAEKAWA, A., Public Health and Homecare Nursing
MATSUMURA, Y., Clinical Nursing
MATSUO, S., Clinical Immunology
MIYATA, T., Cell Biology
MIZUTANI, M., Clinical Nursing
MORI, N., Biological Response
MORITA, S., Human Development Nursing and Midwifery
MURATE, T., Medical Laboratory Technology
MUROHARA, T., Cardiology
NABESHIMA, T., Clinical Pharmacy
NAGASE, F., Medical Laboratory Technology
NAKAMURA, S., Clinical Pathophysiology
NAKAO, A., Gastroenterological Surgery
NAKASHIMA, T., Otorhinolaryngology
NAOE, T., Haematology
NARAMA, M., Human Development Nursing and Midwifery
NASU, T., Occupational and Environmental Health
NIMURA, Y., Surgical Oncology
NISHIYAMA, Y., Molecular Virology
OBATA, Y., Medical Radiological Technology
OHNO, K., Neurogenetics and Bioinformatics
OHTA, M., Molecular Bacteriology
OISO, Y., Diabetology and Endocrinology
OTA, K., Fundamentals of Nursing
OZAKI, N., Psychiatry
SAKAKIBARA, H., Public Health and Home Care Nursing
SHIMADA, Y., Anaesthesiology
SHIMAMOTO, K., Medical Radiological Technology
SHIMOKATA, K., Clinical Preventive Medicine
SOBUE, G., Neurology
SOKABE, M., Cell Biophysics
SUGIMURA, K., Basic Occupational Therapy
SUZUKI, K., Basic Occupational Therapy
SUZUKI, K., Human Development Nursing and Midwifery
SUZUKI, S., Applied Physical Therapy
TABUSHI, K., Basic Radiological Technology
TACHIKAWA, K., Hospital and Healthcare Business Management
TAGAWA, Y., Applied Occupational Therapy
TAKAGI, K., Basic Medical Technology
TAKAHASHI, M., Tumour Pathology
TAKAHASHI, T., Molecular Carcinogenesis
TAKAMATSU, J., Transfusion Medicine
TAKEZAWA, J., Emergency and Critical Care Medicine
TERASAKI, H., Protective Care for Sensory Disorders
TOMITA, Y., Dermatology
TORII, S., Plastic and Reconstructive Surgery
TOYOSHIMA, H., Public Health
UEDA, M., Maxillofacial Surgery
UEDA, Y., Cardio-thoracic Surgery
WAKUSAWA, S., Basic Medical Technology
WATANABE, N., Clinical Nursing
YAMADA, S., Applied Physical Therapy
YAMAUCHI, K., Medical Information and Management Science
YAMAUCHI, T., Fundamentals of Nursing
YOKOI, T., Medical Laboratory Technology
YOSHIDA, J., Neurosurgery

School and Graduate School of Science (Furocho, Chikusa-ku, Nagoya 464-8602; tel. (52) 789-2394; fax (52) 789-2800; internet www.sci.nagoya-u.ac.jp/index.html):

AIBA, H., Molecular Biology
AWAGA, K., Materials Chemistry
ENDO, T., Biochemistry
FUKUI, Y., Astrophysics

HIRASHIMA, D., Condensed Matter Physics
HOMMA, M., Bioenergetics
HORI, H., Evolutionary Genetics
IIO, T., Biophysics
ISHII, K., Theoretical Biology
ITOH, M., Solid State Physics
ITOH, S., Biophysics, Bioenergetics
KATOU, K., Physiology of Plant Growth
KONDO, S., Pattern Formation
KONDO, T., Plant Physiology
KOUYAMA, T., Biophysics
KUNIEDA, H., Astrophysics
KUROIWA, A., Developmental Biology
MACHIDA, Y., Molecular Biology
MATSUMOTO, K., Molecular Biology
MORI, I., Molecular Neurobiology
NAKANISHI, T., Nuclear and Particle Physics
NISHIDA, Y., Animal Development
NIWA, K., Nuclear and Particle Physics
NOZAKI, K., Nonlinear Physics
ODA, Y., Developmental Biology
OHMINE, I., Physical Chemistry
OHSAWA, Y., Plasma Physics
OHSHIMA, T., Nuclear and Particle Physics
OKAMOTO, Y., Theoretical Biophysics
OWARIBE, K., Cell Adhesion and Cytoskeleton
SANDA, I., Particle Physics and Fields
SATO, M., Solid State Physics
SATO, S., Astrophysics
SAWADA, H., Marine Biochemistry
SHIBAI, H., Astrophysics
SHINOHARA, H., Physical Chemistry
SUGAI, S., Solid State Physics
SUZUMURA, Y., Solid State Physics
TOMIMATSU, A., Theory of Gravitation
UEMURA, D., Organic Chemistry
WADA, N., Low Temperature Physics
WATANABE, Y., Bioinorganic Chemistry
YAMAGUCHI, S., Organic Chemistry
YAMAWAKI, K., Elementary Particle Physics and Fields

School of Informatics and Sciences and Graduate School of Information Science (tel. (52) 789-4716; fax (52) 789-4800; e-mail syomuk@info.human.nagoya-u.ac.jp; internet www.is.nagoya-u.ac.jp):

AGUSA, K., Information Engineering
ARITA, T., Complex Systems Science
AZEGAMI, H., Complex Systems Science
HAYAKAWA, Y., Complex Systems Science
HIRATA, T., Computer Science and Mathematical Informatics
HIROKI, S., Complex Systems Science
ISHII, K., Systems and Social Informatics
JINBO, S., Computer Science and Mathematical Informatics
KOGA, N., Complex Systems Science
MATSUBARA, Y., Computer Science and Mathematical Informatics
MATSUMOTO, H., Computer Science and Mathematical Informatics
MATSUO, S., Complex Systems Science
MITSUI, T., Computer Science and Mathematical Informatics
MIWA, K., Media Science
MORI, M., Complex Systems Science
MORI, T., Complex Systems Science
MURASE, H., Media Science
NAGAOKA, M., Complex Systems Science
OHNISHI, N., Media Science
SAITO, H., Media Science
SAKABE, T., Information Engineering
SAKAI, M., Computer Science and Mathematical Informatics
SASAI, M., Complex Systems Science
SUENAGA, Y., Media Science
SUGIYAMA, Y., Complex Systems Science
TAKADA, H., Information Engineering
TAKAGI, N., Information Engineering
TAKAHAMA, M., Information Engineering
TAKEDA, K., Media Science
TODAYAMA, K., Systems and Social Informatics

WATANABE, T., Systems and Social Informatics
YASUDA, T., Systems and Social Informatics
YASUMOTO, M., Computer Science and Mathematical Informatics
YOKOI, S., Systems and Social Informatics
YOKOSAWA, H., Complex Systems Science
YONEYAMA, M., Systems and Social Informatics

Solar–Terrestrial Environment Laboratory (Honohara 3-13, Toyokawa, Aichi Pref., 442-8507; tel. (533) 86-3154; fax (533) 86-0811; internet www.stelab.nagoya-u.ac.jp):

FUJII, R., Space Science (Magnetosphere and Ionosphere Physics
ITOW, Y., Cosmic Ray, Dark Matter and Neutrino Physics
KAMIDE, Y., Solar–Terrestrial Physics
KIKUCHI, T., Solar–Terrestrial Physics
KOJIMA, M., Interplanetary Space Physics
MATSUMI, Y., Atmospheric Photochemistry and Chemical Kinetics
MIZUNO, A., Atmospheric Chemistry and Radio Astronomy
MURAKI, Y., Solar Cosmic Ray Physics
OGAWA, T., Upper Atmosphere Physics
OGINO, T., Space Plasma Physics

NARA WOMEN'S UNIVERSITY

Kita-Uoya-Higashi-Machi, Nara City 630-8506

Telephone: (742) 20-3204
Fax: (742) 20-3205
E-mail: admin@jimu.nara-wu.ac.jp
Internet: www.nara-wu.ac.jp

Founded 1908
Independent
Academic year: April to March

Pres.: MASAKO NIWA
Sec-Gen.: MASAMI KOTANI
Librarian: NANAKO SHIGESADA

Library of 514,000 vols
Number of teachers: 222
Number of students: 2,746

Publications: *Studies in Home Economics*, *Graduate School of Human Culture*

DEANS

Faculty of Human Life and Environment: Prof. M. MIYOSHI
Faculty of Letters: Prof. T. HIRAI
Faculty of Science: Prof. Y. TAKAGI
Graduate School of Human Culture (Doctorate Course): Prof. N. FUJIWARA

NIIGATA UNIVERSITY

8050 Ikarashi Ni-no-cho, Nishi-ku, Niigata 950-2181

Telephone: (25) 262-6246
Fax: (25) 262-7519
E-mail: kokusai@adm.niigata-u.ac.jp
Internet: www.niigata-u.ac.jp

Founded 1949
Independent
Academic year: April to March

Pres.: AKIRA HASEGAWA
Vice-Pres: MASAHIRO SHIMADA, SHOJI KOHNO, SUKEO FUKASAWA, TADAO ITO, TAKEHIKO BANDO
Dir of Univ. Library: TAKASHI OOKUMA

Library: see Libraries and Archives
Number of teachers: 1,226
Number of students: 12,901

DEANS

Faculty of Agriculture: T. OHYAMA
Faculty of Dentistry: T. MAEDA
Faculty of Economics: Y. SUGAHARA
Faculty of Education and Human Sciences: T. MORITA

Faculty of Engineering: H. OHKAWA
Faculty of Humanities: H. HONDA
Faculty of Law: T. KATO
Faculty of Medicine: M. UCHIYAMA
Faculty of Science: K. SHUTO
Graduate School of Education: T. MORITA
Graduate School of Health Sciences: M. TAKAHASHI
Graduate School of Management of Technology: M. MASUDA
Graduate School of Medical and Dental Sciences: M. UCHIYAMA
Graduate School of Science and Technology: T. HASEGAWA
Graduate School of the Study of Modern Society and Culture: Y. SUZUKI
School of Law: K. HONMA

OBIHIRO UNIVERSITY OF AGRICULTURE AND VETERINARY MEDICINE

Inada-cho, Obihiro, Hokkaido 080-8555
Telephone: (155) 49-5111
Fax: (155) 49-5229
E-mail: soumu@obihiro.ac.jp
Internet: www.obihiro.ac.jp
Founded 1941
Independent
Academic year: April to March
Pres.: NAOYOSHI SUZUKI
Dir of Admin. Bureau: M. KIKUCHI
Dir of Univ. Library: T. KAWABATA
Library of 190,426 vols
Number of teachers: 149
Number of students: 1,431

Department of Agro-Environmental Science: JUNKO MARUYAMA
Department of Applied Veterinary Science: TOSHIKAZU SHIRAHATA
Department of Basic Veterinary Science: JUNZO YAMADA
Department of Clinical Veterinary Science: TAKAO SARASHINA
Department of Pathobiological Science: MASAKAZU NISHIMURA
Research Unit of Animal Physiology and Function: IKICHI ARAI
Research Unit of Animal Production Science: MIKAMI MASAYUKI
Research Unit of Engineering in Agricultural and Biological Systems: KENICHI ISHIBASHI
Research Unit of Environmental and Rural Engineering: FUJIO TSUCHIYA
Research Unit of Farm Management: ICHIO SASAKI
Research Unit of Food and Resource Economics: SHIGERU ITO
Research Unit of Molecular Cell-Regulation Science: HIROSHI MASUDA
Research Unit of Plant Bioscience: SOUHEI SAWADA
Research Unit of Socio-Environmental Science: MASARU UMETSU

Publication: *Research Bulletin* (on Natural Sciences and on Humanities and Social Sciences, each 2 a year).

OCHANOMIZU UNIVERSITY

2-1-1, Otsuka, Bunkyo-ku, Tokyo 112-8610
Telephone: (3) 5978-5106
Fax: (3) 5978-5890
E-mail: soumu2@cc.ocha.ac.jp
Internet: www.ocha.ac.jp
Founded 1874; reorganized 1949 as Nat. Univ.
Independent
Language of instruction: Japanese
Academic year: April to March
Pres.: Dr SAWAKO HANYU
Admin.: KAZUFUMI YOSHIDA
Librarian: SARUMARU MAKIKO

Library of 633,703 vols
Number of teachers: 362
Number of students: 3,271

Publications: *Natural Science Report of the Ochanomizu University* (2 a year), *Ochanomizu University Studies in Art and Culture* (1 a year)

DEANS

Faculty of Human Life and Environmental Science: SUGITA TAKAO
Faculty of Letters and Education: Dr MIURA TORU
Faculty of Science: Dr MOGAMI YOSHIHIRO
Graduate School of Humanities and Sciences: ISHIGUCHI AKIRA

OITA UNIVERSITY

700 Dannoharu, Oita City
Telephone: (97) 569-3311
Fax: (97) 554-7413
E-mail: webmaster@ad.oita-u.ac.jp
Internet: www.oita-u.ac.jp
Founded 1949
Independent
Language of instruction: Japanese
Academic year: April to March (2 semesters)
Pres.: IWAO NAKAYAMA
Dir-Gen. of Admin. Bureau: TAKANOBU IRIE
Dir of Univ. Library: KOICHI OBA
Library of 541,000 vols
Number of teachers: 569
Number of students: 5,802

DEANS

Faculty of Economics: MINORU UNO
Faculty of Education and Welfare Science: MAKOTO OSHIMA
Faculty of Engineering: TADAO EZAKI
Graduate School of Social Service Administration: TAKATOMI NINOMIYA

ATTACHED INSTITUTE

Tsurumi Seaside Research Institute: Aza-Hirama, Oaza-Ariakeura, Tsurumi-machi, Minamiamabe-gun, Oita 876-1204; tel. (972) 33-1133.

OKAYAMA UNIVERSITY

1-1-1, Tsushima-Naka, Okayama 700-8530
Telephone: (86) 252-1111
Fax: (86) 254-6104
E-mail: ace7038@adm.okayama-u.ac.jp
Internet: www.okayama-u.ac.jp
Founded 1949
Independent
Academic year: April to March (2 semesters)
Pres.: IICHIRO KONO
Vice-Pres: KYOZO CHIBA, KIICHI MATSUHATA, HIROKAZU OSAKI, HAJIME INOUE
Dir-Gen.: T. ABE
Library: see Libraries and Archives
Number of teachers: 1,341 full-time
Number of students: 14,091

Publication: *Okayama University Bulletin*

DEANS

Dental School: T. WATANABE
Faculty of Agriculture: T. SHIRAISHI
Faculty of Economics: T. MATSUMOTO
Faculty of Education: N. MORIKAWA
Faculty of Engineering: H. TOTSUJI
Faculty of Environmental Science and Technology: T. ADACHI
Faculty of Law: S. TANI
Faculty of Letters: F. TAKAHASHI
Faculty of Pharmaceutical Sciences: T. KIMURA
Faculty of Science: K. KASE
Graduate School of Environmental Science (Doctorate Course): F. NAKASUJI

Graduate School of Humanities and Social Sciences (Doctorate Course): T. TAKAHASHI
Graduate School of Medicine, Dentistry and Pharmaceutical Science (Doctorate Course): H. KUMON
Medical School: K. OGUMA
School of Law: M. OKADA, Graduate School of Natural Science and Technology (Doctorate Course): J. TAKADA

PROFESSORS

Faculty of Agriculture (tel. (86) 251-8273; fax (86) 251-8388):

BABA, N., Chemistry of Biological Functions
ICHINOSE, Y., Genetic Engineering
INABA, A., Postharvest Agriculture
INAGAKI, K., Applied Biochemistry and Biotechnology
IZUMIMOTO, M., Animal Food Technology
KAMIMURA, K., Microbial Function
KANZAKI, H., Chemistry and Biochemistry of Bioactive Compounds
KIMURA, Y., Bioapplied Enzymology
KOMATSU, Y., Farm Management and Data Processing Methods
KONDO, Y., Animal Physiology and Pharmacology
KUBOTA, N., Horticultural Crop Production
KUNIEDA, T., Animal Genetics
KURODA, T., Crop Production Science
MASUDA, M., Olericulture
MIYAMOTO, T., Animal Food Function
NAKAJIMA, S., Chemistry and Biochemistry of Bioactive Compounds
NAKASUJI, F., Integrated Pest Management
NIWA, K., Animal Reproduction
OIKAWA, T., Animal Genetics and Breeding
OKAMOTO, G., Pomology
OKUDA, K., Animal Reproduction
SAKAGUCHI, E., Animal Nutrition
SAKAMOTO, K., Applied Plant Ecology
SASAKAWA, H., Rhizosphere Biological Chemistry
SATO, K., Animal Genetics and Breeding
SATOH, T., Resources Management
SHIMOISHI, Y., Biological Information of Chemistry
SHIRAISHI, T., Plant Pathology
SUGIO, T., Microbial Function
TADA, M., Biological Chemistry of Foods
TAHARA, M., Cell Engineering
TSUDA, M., Crop Whole-plant Physiology
YOKOMIZO, I., Farm Management and Date Processing Methods
YOSHIKAWA, K., Physiological Plant Ecology

Faculty of Economics (tel. (86) 251-7345; fax (86) 251-7350):

CHINO, T., Health Economics
ENOMOTO, S., Strategic Management
GENKA, T., Comparative Economic Systems
HARUNA, S., Industrial Organization
HIRANO, M., Local Public Finance
KONISHI, N., Accounting
KOYAMA, Y., Financial Management
KUROKAWA, K., Economic History of the United States
MATSUDA, Y., Organizational Behaviour and Organizational Change
MATSUMOTO, T., Economic History of Modern Asia
NAGAHATA, H., Statistics, Information Science
NAKAMURA, R., Urban and Regional Economics
NIIMURA, S., History of Economic Thought
OTA, Y., History of Economic Thought
SHIMONO, K., Economic History of Modern Japan
TAKEMURA, S., Theory of the Firm, Industrial Organisation
WADA, Y., Social Economics
YOSHIDA, T., Social Statistics, Econometrics
ZHANG, X., Economic Statistics

Faculty of Education (tel. (86) 251-7584; fax (86) 251-7755):

ARIYOSHI, H., Teacher Training
DOI, Y., Algebra
FUCHIGAMI, K., School Organizational Psychology
FUJITA, R., Housing and Living Design
FUKUNAGA, S., British Literature
FURUICHI, Y., Educational Psychology
IDO, K., Music Education
IKEDA, A., Geometry
INADA, T., Japanese Literature
INOUE, S., Educational Psychology
KAGA, M., Biomechanics
KANETA, Y., Composition
KANI, K., Material Engineering
KASAI, Y., Science of Food Preparation
KAWATA, T., Food Science
KISHIMOTO, H., Political Science
KITA, H., Chemistry
KITAGAMI, M., School Management
KONDO, I., Information Technology
KOSAKO, M., English Philology
KUSACHI, I., Mineralogy
MATSUOKA, Y., Clinical Psychology
MIZUNO, M., Developmental Psychology
MONDEN, S., Education for School Health Care
MORI, K., Chinese Philosophy
MORIKAWA, N., Pedagogy
MUSHIAKI, M., Vocal Music
NAKAO, Y., Chemistry
NII, I., Arts and Crafts Education
NISHIYAMA, M., Paintings
NOBE, M., Sociology
OGAWA, T., Paintings
OGURA, H., Biology
OHASHI, K., Manufacturing Education
OHASHI, Y., Physical Education
OKU, S., Music Education
ONO, H., Curriculum Development
ONOYAMA, K., Ceramics
SAKATA, N., Physical Education
SANADA, S., Education for Handicapped Children
SANEKATA, N., Mathematical Analysis
SUGAHARA, M., Japanese Education
SUGIHARA, R., Clothing Science
TAKAHASHI, K., Medicine for School Health Care
TAKAHASHI, T., Mathematics Education
TAKATSUKA, S., English Language Teaching
TAKAYAMA, Y., Social Studies Education
TANAKA, K., Science Education
TANAKA, K., Social Psychology
TANAKA, M., European History
TOKUNAGA, T., Sport Education
UEHARA, K., History
YAMAGUCHI, H., Computer Education
YAMAGUCHI, S., Psychology of Pre-school Children
YAMAMOTO, H., Musicology
YAMAMOTO, H., Systems Engineering
YAMAMOTO, T., Clinical Psychology
YAMANAKA, Y., History of Japanese Education
YAMASHITA, N., Solid State Spectroscopy
YANAGIHARA, M., Psychology of Handicapped Children
YOSHIDA, N., Japanese Language

Faculty of Engineering (tel. (86) 251-8004; fax (86) 251-8021):

FUNABIKI, N., Distributed Systems
GOFUKU, A., Systems Applications
GOTO, K., Functional Materials Chemistry
HASHIGUCHI, K., Foundations of Information Science
HATA, M., Distributed Systems
INABA, H., Energy Engineering
INOUE, A., Systems Theory
KAMIURA, Y., Electronics
KANATANI, K., Foundations of Information Science

KISHIMOTO, A., Functional Materials Chemistry
KOGA, R., Network Architecture
KONISHI, M., Electrical Engineering
MASAKI, A., Information-based Engineering Systems
MIYAZAKI, S., Systems Intelligence
MORIKAWA, Y., Foundations of Information and Communication
NAKANISHI, K., Biotechnology
NARA, S., Electronics
NOGI, S., Electronics
NORITSUGU, T., Systems Control
OHMORI, H., Applied Bioscience
OSAKA, A., Bioactive Materials
SAITO, S., Bioactive Materials
SAKAI, H., Biotechnology
SAKAI, T., Molecular Transformation Chemistry
SAKATA, Y., Functional Materials Chemistry
SENUMA, T., Control of Material Properties
SHAKUNAGA, T., Artificial Intelligence
SHIMAMURA, K., Functional Materials Chemistry
SISHIDO, M., Biomolecular Engineering
SUGIYAMA, Y., Foundations of Information and Communication
SUZUKI, K., Systems Theory
SUZUMORI, K., Systems Control
TADA, N., Material Engineering
TAKADA, J., Functional Materials Chemistry
TAKAHASHI, N., Electrical Engineering
TAKAI, K., Molecular Transformation Chemistry
TANAKA, H., Molecular Transformation Chemistry
TANAKA, Y., Systems Applications
TANIGUCHI, H., Information Based Engineering Systems
TOMITA, E., Energy Engineering
TORAYA, T., Applied Bioscience
TORII, T., Materials Engineering
TOTSUJI, H., Electronics
TUKADA, K., Electronics
TUKAMOTO, S., Manufacturing Engineering
UNEYAMA, K., Molecular Transformation Chemistry
UNO, Y., Design and Manufacturing Technology
WASHIO, S., Engineering Measurement
YAMADA, H., Biomolecular Engineering
YAMASAKI, S., Artificial Intelligence
YANASE, S., Engineering Measurement
YOKOHIRA, T., Network Architecture
YOSHIDA, A., Design and Manufacturing Technology

Faculty of Law (tel. (86) 251-7345; fax (86) 251-7350):

ARAKI, M., Western Political History
ATAKA, K., Local Tax and Finance Law
HARANO, A., Administrative Law
HATANO, S., European Legal History
KAWAHARA, Y., International Politics
KOYAMA, H., Administrative Law
KUROKAMI, N., Law of International Organizations
NAKAMURA, M., Information Law and Policy
NAKATOMI, K., Constitutional Law
NISHIHARA, J., Civil Law
OBATA, T., Japanese Political History
SANO, M., Private International Law
TANI, S., Political Process
TONAI, K., Labour Law
YAMAGUCHI, K., Constitutional Law
YONEYAMA, K., Commercial Law
ZHANG, H., Chinese Law

Faculty of Letters (tel. (86) 251-7345; fax (86) 251-7350):

EGUCHI, Y., Japanese Linguistics
HASEGAWA, Y., Psychology
HISANO, N., History of Japanese Culture
INADA, T., Archaeology

INAMURA, S., Ethics
JIANG, K., Modern History of Japanese Culture
KANASEKI, T., Comparative Study of Cultures
KITAMURA, K., Cultural Anthropology
KITAOKA, T., Religious Philosophy
KOBAYASHI, T., Sociology
KURACHI, K., History of Japanese Culture
MATSUMOTO, M., English Historical Linguistics
MIYAKE, S., Operatic Studies
NAGASE, H., French Literature
NAGATA, R., European History
NIIMURA, Y., History of Chinese Culture
NIIRO, I., Archaeology
NISHIMAE, T., American Literature
SHIMOSADA, M., Chinese Literature
TAKAHASHI, F., Ethics
TAKAHASHI, T., Old German Language and Literature
TAKUMA, F., Modern German History
TANAKA, T., Psychology
TAYA, R., Psychology
TERAOKA, T., History of German Literature
TSUJI, S., Linguistics
UCHIDA, K., Geography
WADA, M., Linguistics
WATANABE, M., Japanese Literature
YAMAGUCHI, K., Aesthetics
YAMAGUCHI, N., History of French Thought
YOSHIOKA, F., English Literature

Faculty of Pharmaceutical Sciences (tel. (86) 251-7913; fax (86) 251-7926):

HARAYAMA, T., Synthetic and Medicinal Chemistry
HIROTA, T., Pharmaceutical Chemistry
KAMEI, C., Pharmacology
KAWASAKI, H., Clinical Pharmaceutical Science
KIMURA, T., Pharmaceutics
KUROSAKI, Y., Pharmaceutics
MORIYAMA, Y., Neurochemistry
NARIMATSU, S., Health Chemistry
OKAMOTO, K., Bio-organic Chemistry
SAITO, Y., Pharmaceutical Analytical Chemistry
SASAKI, K., Pharmaceutical Fundamental Science
SHINODA, S., Environmental Hygiene
TAMAGAKE, K., Pharmaceutical Physical Chemistry
TSUCHIYA, T., Microbiology
WATAYA, Y., Medicinal Information
YAMAMOTO, I., Immunochemistry
YAMAMOTO, S., Molecular Microbiology
YOSHIDA, T., Pharmacognosy

Faculty of Science (tel. (86) 251-7764; fax (86) 251-7777):

ASAMI, M., Petrology
CHIBA, H., Isotope Geochemistry
HARADA, I., Theoretical Physics
HIROKAWA, M., Mathematical Physics
ISHIDA, H., Structural Chemistry
IWAMI, M., Thin Films and Surface Physics
KAGAWA, H., Molecular Biology
KAMADA, T., Molecular Cell Biology
KASE, K., Resources Geology
KAWAGUCHI, K., Molecular Spectroscopy
KIMURA, M., Organic Function Chemistry
KIYOHARA, K., Differential Geometry
KOBAYASHI, T., Physics of Strongly Correlated Systems
KOJIMA, M., Coordination Chemistry
KURODA, Y., Inorganic Chemistry
KUTSUKAKE, K., Molecular Genetics
MACHIDA, K., Mathematical Physics
MOTOMIZU, S., Analytical Chemistry
NAGAO, M., Surface Chemistry
NAKAMURA, H., Number Theory
NAKANO, I., High Energy Physics
NARAOKA, H., Organic Cosmogeochemistry
NOGAMI, Y., Low Dimensional Material Physics
ODA, H., Seismology

OSHIMA, K., Physics of Quantum Materials
ONO, F., Physics of Materials under Extreme Conditions
SAKAI, T., Differential Geometry
SAKAMOTO, T., Marine Biology
SAKUDA, M., Neutrino Physics
SATAKE, K., Organic Chemistry
SATO, R., Analysis
SAWADA, A., Quantum Electromagnetic Physics
SHEN, J.-R., Plant Physiology and Structural Biology
SHIBATA, T., Geology
SHIMAKAWA, K., Petrology and Marine Geology
SUZUKI, I., Geophysics
TAKAGI, K., Synthetic Organic Chemistry
TAKAHASHI, S., Endocrinology
TAKAHASHI, T., Plant Molecular Genetics
TAKAHASHI, Y., Plant Physiology and Plant Molecular Biology
TAMURA, H., Analysis
TANAKA, H., Theoretical Chemistry
TOMIOKA, K., Chronobiology
TSUKAMOTO, O., Atmospheric Science
UEDA, H., Molecular and Developmental Biology
YAMADA, H., Representation Theory
YAMAMOTO, H., Organic Chemistry
YAMAMOTO, S., Physical Chemistry
YAMAMOTO, Y., Plant Physiology and Biochemistry
YOKOYA, T., Photo-emission Condensed Matter Physics
YOSHIKAWA, Y., Inorganic Chemistry
YOSHIMURA, H., Particle Physics-based Cosmology
YOSHINO, Y., Algebra
ZHENG, G.-Q., Low Temperature Condensed Matter Physics

Graduate School of Medicine, Dentistry and Pharmaceutical Sciences:
ABE, K., Neuroscience
AWAYA, T., Legal Medicine and Bioethics
DATE, I., Neuroscience
FUKUI, K., Oral Pathobiology
GOHDA, E., Immunochemistry
HARAYAMA, T., Synthetic and Medicinal Chemistry
HATANO, T., Natural Product Chemistry
HIRAMATSU, Y., Obstetrics and Gynaecology
HIROTA, T., Pharmaceutical Chemistry
HUH, N., Basic Oncology
ISHIZU, H., Legal Medicine and Bioethics
IWATSUKI, K., Sensory and Locomotory Function Medicine
KAMEI, C., Pharmacology
KANAZAWA, S., Radiology and Laboratory Medicine
KATO, N., Basic Oncology
KATSU, T., Pharmaceutical Physical Chemistry
KAWAKAMI, N., Social Medicine and Environmental Health Sciences
KAWASAKI, H., Clinical Pharmaceutical Science
KIMATA, Y., Sensory and Locomotory Function Medicine
KIMURA, I., Pharmaceutics
KISHI, K., Oral and Maxillofacial Surgery and Diagnostic Medicine
KITAYAMA, S., Oral Pathobiology
KOIDE, N., Radiology and Laboratory Medicine
KUBOKI, T., Oral Functional Reconstruction
KUMON, H., Basic and Clinical Pathophysiology
KURODA, S., Basic and Clinical Neuroscience
KUROSAKI, Y., Pharmaceutics
MAKINO, H., Basic and Clinical Pathophysiology

MATSUI, H., Basic and Clinical Neuroscience
MATSUO, R., Oral Biology
MINAGI, S., Oral Functional Reconstruction
MIYOSHI, S., Environmental Hygiene
MORISHIMA, T., Obstetrics and Gynaecology
MORITA, K., Anaesthesiology and Emergency Medicine
MORIYAMA, Y., Neurochemistry
NAGAI, N., Oral Pathobiology
NAKAYAMA, E., Infection and Immunology
NARIMATSU, S., Health Chemistry
NINOMIYA, Y., Human Biology
NISHIZAKI, K., Sensory and Locomotory Function Medicine
OGAWA, N., Basic and Clinical Neuroscience
OGUMA, K., Infection and Immunology
OHE, T., Cardiovascular Medicine
OHTSUKA, A., Human Biology
OHTSUKA, Y., Basic and Clinical Neuroscience
OKAMOTO, K., Bio-organic Chemistry
SAITO, Y., Pharmaceutical Analytical Chemistry
SANO, S., Cardiovascular Pathophysiology
SASAKI, A., Oral and Maxillofacial Surgery and Diagnostic Medicine
SASAKI, J., Anatomy
SASAKI, K., Pharmaceutical Fundamental Science
SHIMADA, M., Oral and Maxillofacial Surgery and Diagnostic Medicine
SHIMIZU, K., Basic Oncology
SHIMIZU, N., Basic and Clinical Pathophysiology
SHIMONO, T., Oral Health, Growth and Development
SHIRATORI, Y., Basic and Clinical Pathophysiology
SUGAHARA, T., Oral and Maxillofacial and Diagnostic Medicine
SUGIMOTO, T., Oral Biology
SUZUKI, K., Oral Functional Reconstruction
TAKASHIBA, S., Oral Health, Growth and Development
TAKEI, K., Human Biology
TAKIGAWA, M., Oral Biology
TANAKA, N., Basic and Clinical Pathophysiology
TANIMOTO, M., Basic and Clinical Pathophysiology
TSUCHIYA, T., Microbiology
TSUTSUI, K., Human Biology
WATANABE, T., Oral Health, Growth and Development
WATAYA, Y., Medicinal Information
YAMADA, M., Infection and Immunology
YAMAMOTO, S., Molecular Microbiology
YAMAMOTO, T., Oral Biology
YAMAMOTO, T., Oral Health, Growth and Development
YASUDA, T., Basic and Clinical Pathophysiology
YOSHINO, T., Basic and Clinical Pathophysiology
YOSHIYAMA, M., Oral Functional Reconstruction

Medical School:
AKIMOTO, N., Adult Nursing
ARAO, Y., Clinical Biology
ASARI, S., Adult Nursing
FUJINO, F., Adult Nursing
FUKAI, K., Human Nursing
IKEDA, S., Clinical Pathology
JOJA, I., Medical Radiotechnology
KAGEYAMA, J., Adult Nursing
KANDA, A., Community Health Nursing
KATAOKA, M., Clinical Biology
KATO, H., Medicinal Radioscience
KATO, K., Human Nursing
KAWASAKI, S., Medical Radioscience
KURAZONO, H., Clinical Biology
KUSACHI, S., Clinical Pathology

NAKAGIRI, Y., Medical Radiotechnology
NAKATA, Y., Clinical Pathology
NISHIDA, M., Adult Nursing
ODA, M., Maternal and Child Health Nursing
OHTA, N., Maternal and Child Health Nursing
OKA, H., Clinical Biology
OKAMOTO, M., Clinical Biology
OKANO, H., Community Health Nursing
OKUDA, H., Maternal and Child Health Nursing
ONO, K., Maternal and Child Health Nursing
SENDA, Y., Adult Nursing
SUMIMOTO, T., Medical Radioscience
TAKAHASHI, K., Clinical Pathology
TAGUCHI, T., Medical Radiotechnology
TAKEDA, Y., Medical Radiotechnology
YAMAMOTO, Y., Medical Radioscience
YAMAOKA, K., Medical Radioscience
YOKOYAMA, Y., Community Health Nursing

School of Law (tel. (86) 251-7345; fax (86) 251-7350):
AKAMATSU, H., Civil Law
FUJITA, H., Civil Law
FUJIWARA, K., Criminal Procedure
HAGA, R., Commercial Law
HAGIWARA, S., Criminal Law
IGUCHI, F., Constitutional Law
KITAGAWA, K., Criminal Law
MATSUMURA, K., Civil Procedure
MIURA, O., Commercial Law
OKADA, M., Administrative Law
SATO, S., Investigative Law
UEDA, S., Criminal Procedure

ATTACHED INSTITUTES

Institute for Study of the Earth's Interior: 827, Yamada, Misasa-cho, Tohaku-gun, Tottori 682-0193; tel. (858) 43-1215; fax (858) 43-2184; f. 1985; Dir Prof. E. NAKAMURA.

Research Institute for Bioresources: 2-20-1, Chuo, Kurashiki, Okayama 710-0046; tel. (86) 424-1661; fax (86) 434-1249; f. 1914; affiliated 1951; Dir Prof. K. TAKEDA.

OPEN UNIVERSITY OF JAPAN

2-11 Wakaba, Mihama-ku, Chiba City 261-8586

Telephone: (43) 276-5111
Fax: (43) 298-4378
Internet: www.u-air.ac.jp
Founded 1983

Chair.: YASUSHI MITARAI
Pres.: HIROMITSU ISHI
Vice-Pres: YOICHI OKABE, HIROSHI OGINO, HIROFUMI HONMA
Dir-Gen.: MITSUHIRO IKEHARA
Librarian: HITOSHI ABE
Library of 630,643 vols
Number of teachers: 94
Number of students: 87,169

OSAKA UNIVERSITY

1-1 Yamadaoka, Suita, Osaka 565-0871
Telephone: (6) 6877-5111
Fax: (6) 6879-7106
E-mail: kokusai-ina@ml.office.osaka-u.ac.jp
Internet: www.osaka-u.ac.jp
Founded 1931, merged with Osaka University of Foreign Studies 2007
Public control
Academic year: April to March
Pres.: KIYOKAZU WASHIDA
Vice-Pres (Trustees): TAKEFUMI DOI, JUNJI KOIZUMI, MORITO MONDEN, SHOGO NISHIDA, SHOJIRO NISHIO, SHINNOSUKE OYAMA, EIICHI TAKASUGI, KIICHIRO TSUJI
Chief Dir-Gen. of Admin. Bureau: KOICHI KITAMI

Dir of Univ. Library: HIRONOBU NAKAMURA
Library: see Libraries and Archives
Number of teachers: 3,864
Number of students: 23,702
Publications: *Bulletin of Graduate School of Human Sciences* (1 a year), *Engekigaku Ronso* (1 a year), *GALLIA* (french language and literature community magazine, 1 a year), *Handai Comparative Literature* (1 a year), *Handai Law Review* (6 a year), *Handai Nihongo Kenkyu* (1 a year), *Handai Ongakugakuho* (1 a year), *International Economic Review* (4 a year), *International Public Policy Studies* (2 a year), *Machikaneyama Ronso* (1 a year), *Memoir of Kaitokudo Center* (1 a year), *Memoirs of the Graduate School of Letters* (1 a year), *Memoirs of the Institute of Scientific and Industrial Research* (1 a year), *Nihon Gakuho* (1 a year), *Osaka Economic Papers* (4 a year), *Osaka Journal of Mathematics* (4 a year), *Osaka University Law Review* (1 a year), *Osaka University Papers in English Linguistics* (1 a year), *Philokalia* (1 a year), *Public History* (1 a year), *Studies in Aesthetics & Art Criticism* (1 a year), *Studies in Language and Culture* (1 a year), *Transactions of JWRI* (2 a year)

DEANS

Graduate School and Faculty of Medicine: YOSHIHIRO YONEDA
Graduate School and School of Dentistry: SATOSHI WAKISAKA
Graduate School and School of Economics: KENZO ABE
Graduate School and School of Engineering: AKIO BABA
Graduate School and School of Engineering Science: YOSHITO TOBE
Graduate School and School of Human Sciences: TOSHIO TOMOEDA
Graduate School and School of Letters: TSUYOSHI KATAYAMA
Graduate School and School of Pharmaceutical Sciences: MOTOMASA KOBAYASHI
Graduate School and School of Science: KIYOSHI HIGASHIJIMA
Graduate School of Frontier Biosciences: KEIICHI NAMBA
Graduate School of Information Science and Technology: MAKOTO IMASE
Graduate School of Language and Culture: SHIGEO KIMURA
Graduate School of Law: SETSUO TANIGUCHI
Graduate School of Law and Politics and School of Law: TOSHIMITSU NAKAO
Osaka School of International Public Policy: TOSHIYA HOSHINO
United Graduate School of Child Development: MASAYA TOHYAMA

PROFESSORS

Graduate School and Faculty of Medicine (2-2 Yamadaoka, Suita, Osaka 565-0871; fax (6) 6879-3070; internet www.med.osaka-u.ac.jp):

AOZASA, K., Molecular Pathology
ARAKIDA, M., Health Promotion Science
ASO, Y., Health Promotion Science
BEPPU, S., Functional Diagnostic Physics
FUJIKADO, T., Applied Visual Science
FUJIWARA, C., Child and Reproductive Health
FUJIWARA, H., Medical Physics and Engineering
FUKUZAWA, M., Paediatric Surgery
HARUNA, M., Medical Physics and Engineering
HATAZAWA, J., Nuclear Medicine
HAYAKAWA, K., Health Promotion Science
HAYASHI, N., Molecular Therapeutics
HIRANO, T., Immunology and Molecular Biology
HORI, M., Cardiovascular Medicine

HOSOKAWA, K., Plastic Surgery
INAGAKI, S., Bioinformatics
INOUE, O., Medical Physics and Engineering
INOUE, T., Radiation Oncology
IWATANI, Y., Bioinformatics
JOHKOH, T., Functional Diagnostic Science
KANAKURA, Y., Haematology and Oncology
KANEDA, Y., Gene Therapy Science
KANOH, M., Cellular Neuroscience
KATAYAMA, I., Dermatology
KAWANO, S., Functional Diagnostic Science
KAWASE, I., Respirology
KIDO, Y., Evidence-based Clinical Nursing
KINOSHITA, H., Biomechanic and Motor Control
KUBO, T., Otorhinolaryngology
KURACHI, Y., Pharmacology
KUROKAWA, N., Pharmacy
MAKIMOTO, K., Evidence-based Clinical Nursing
MASHIMO, T., Anaesthesiology and Critical Care Medicine
MATOBA, R., Legal Medicine
MATSUURA, N., Functional Diagnostic Science
MIKAMI, H., Health Promotion Science
MIYASAKA, M., Immunodynamics
MIYAZAKI, J., Stem Cell Regulation Research
MONDEN, M., Surgery
MORIMOTO, K., Hygiene and Preventive Medicine
MURASE, K., Medical Physics and Engineering
MURATA, Y., Obstetrics and Gynaecology
NAGAI, T., Child and Reproductive Health
NAGATA, S., Genetics
NAKAMURA, H., Radiology
NAKAMURA, T., Molecular Regenerative Medicine
NAKANO, T., Stem-cell Biology
NOGUCHI, S., Surgical Oncology
OGASAWARA, C., Health Promotion Science
OGIHARA, T., Geriatric Medicine
OGINO, S., Evidence-based Clinical Nursing
OHASHI, K., Child and Reproductive Health
OHIRA, Y., Applied Psychology
OHNO, Y., Health Promotion Science
OKAMOTO, M., Molecular Physiological Chemistry
OKUMIYA, A., Evidence-based Clinical Nursing
OKUYAMA, A., Urology
OZONO, K., Paediatrics
SAKODA, S., Neurology
SATO, H., Cognitive Neuroscience
SHIMADA, M., Child and Reproductive Health
SHIMOMURA, I., Internal Medicine
SHIRAKURA, R., Organ Transplantation
SOBUE, K., Neuroscience
SUGIMOTO, H., Traumatology and Acute Critical Medicine
SUGIMOTO, N., Applied Bacteriology
SUGIYAMA, H., Functional Diagnostic Science
SUZUKI, S., Evidence-based Clinical Nursing
TODA, T., Clinical Genetics
TAKAI, Y., Molecular Biology and Biochemistry
TAKEDA, H., Medical Information Science
TAKEDA, J., Environmental Genetics
TAKEDA, M., Psychiatry
TAMURA, S., Interdisciplinary Image Analysis
TANIGUCHI, N., Biochemistry
TANO, Y., Ophthalmology
TESHIMA, T., Medical Physics and Engineering
TOHYAMA, M., Anatomy and Neuroscience
TSUJIMOTO, Y., Molecular Genetics
UCHIYAMA, Y., Cell Biology and Neuroscience

YAMAMOTO, Y., Bioinformatics
YAMAMURA, T., Bioinformatics
YAMATODANI, A., Medical Physics and Engineering
YANAGIDA, T., Physiology and Biosignalling
YONEDA, Y., Anatomy and Cell Biology
YORIFUJI, S., Functional Diagnostic Science
YOSHIDA, T., Applied Psychology
YOSHIKAWA, H., Orthopaedic Surgery
YOSHIMINE, T., Neurosurgery

Graduate School and School of Dentistry (1-8 Yamadaoka, Suita, Osaka 565-0871; fax (6) 6879-2832; internet www.dent.osaka-u.ac.jp/index-e.html):

AMANO, A., Oral Science Methodology
EBISU, S., Endodontology
FURUKAWA, S., Oral and Maxillofacial Radiology
KAMISAKI, Y., Pharmacology
KAN, Y., Oral Physiology
KOGO, M., Management of Oral and Maxillofacial Diseases
MAEDA, Y., Interdisciplinary Dentistry
MORISAKI, I., Nursing Dentistry
MURAKAMI, S., Periodontology
NIWA, H., Dental Anaesthesiology
NOKUBI, T., Oromaxillofacial Prosthodontics
OHSHIMA, T., Paediatric Dentistry
SHIZUKUISHI, S., Preventive Dentistry
TAKADA, K., Orthodontics and Dentofacial Orthopaedics
TOYOSAWA, S., Oral Pathology
WAKISAKA, S., Oral Anatomy and Developmental Biology
YATANI, H., Occlusion, TMD and Advanced Prosthodontics
YONEDA, T., Molecular and Cellular Craniofacial Biology
YOSHIDA, A., Oral Anatomy and Neurobiology
YURA, Y., Oral and Maxillofacial Oncology

Graduate School and School of Economics (1-7 Machikaneyama-cho, Toyonaka, Osaka 560-0043; tel. (6) 6850-6111; fax (6) 6850-5205):

ABE, K., Economics
ABE, T., Historical Analysis
ASADA, T., Business Information
BAN, K., Economics
DOME, T., Political Analysis
FUKUSHIGE, M., Management of Technology
FUTAGAMI, K., Economics
HONDA, Y., Policy Analysis
HONMA, M., Economics
IMAI, Y., Theoretical Analysis
KANAI, K., Business Information
KOBAYASHI, T., Business Information
MINO, K., Theoretical Analysis
MIYAMOTO, M., Historical Analysis
NAGATANI, H., Theoretical Analysis
NAKAJIMA, N., Business
OHNISHI, M., Business
OHYA, K., Business Analysis
SAITO, S., Policy Analysis
SAMURA, T., Historical Analysis
SAWAI, M., Historical Analysis
SUGIHARA, K., Economics
TABATA, Y., Business Analysis
TAKAO, N., Business
TAKEDA, E., Business Analysis
YAMADA, M., Theoretical Analysis

Graduate School and School of Engineering (2-1 Yamadaoka, Suita, Osaka 565-0871; fax (6) 6879-7210; internet www.eng.osaka-u.ac.jp):

Department of Advanced Science and Biotechnology:

AONO, M., Applied Surface Science
FUKUI, K., Dynamic Cell Biology
FUKUZUMI, S., Physical Chemistry for Life Science
HARASHIMA, S., Molecular Genetics

ITO, K., Applied Optics and Optical Information Processing
KANAYA, S., Biological Extremity Engineering
KOBAYASHI, A., Cell Technology
MIYATA, M., Molecular Recognition Chemistry
OHTAKE, H., Biochemical Engineering
SHIOYA, S., Bioprocess Systems Engineering
TAKAI, Y., Theoretical Computation Physics
URABE, I., Enzyme Engineering
YOKOYAMA, M., Molecular System Engineering

Department of Applied Chemistry:

AKASHI, M., Industrial Organic Chemistry
BABA, A., Resources Chemistry
CHATANI, N., Molecular Interaction Chemistry
HIRAO, T., Material Synthetic Chemistry
IMANAKA, N., Material Synthetic Chemistry
INOUE, Y., Molecular Interaction Chemistry
KAI, Y., Structural Physical Chemistry
KAMBE, N., Synthesis and Catalysis
KOMATSU, M., Synthetic Organic Chemistry
KUROSAWA, H., Organometallic Chemistry
KUWABATA, S., Applied Chemistry
OHSHIMA, T., Theoretical Organic Chemistry
UYAMA, H., Theoretical Organic Chemistry

Department of Materials Chemistry:

HIRAO, T., Materials Synthetic Chemistry
IMANAKA, N., Materials Synthetic Chemistry
KAI, Y., Structural Physical Chemistry
KOMATSU, M., Synthetic Organic Chemistry
KUWABATA, S., Applied Electrochemistry
OSHIMA, T., Theoretical Organic Chemistry
UYAMA, H., Structural Organic Chemistry

Department of Biotechnology:

FUKUI, K., Dynamic Cell Biology
HARASHIMA, S., Molecular Genetics
KOBAYASHI, A., Cell Technology
OTAKE, H., Biochemical Engineering
SHIOYA, S., Bioprocess Systems Engineering
URABE, I., Enzyme Engineering

Department of Precision Science, Technology and Applied Physics:

HIROSE, K., Computational Physics
KASAI, H., Materials Physics Theory
KATAOKA, T., Quantum Measurement and Instrumentation
KAWAKAMI, N., Condensed Matter Physics and Statistical Physics
MASUHARA, H., Laser Photochemistry and Microspectroscopy
MORITA, M., Scientific Hardware Systems
SUGAWARA, Y., Engineering Physics
YAGI, A., Non-linear Analysis and its Applications
YAMAUCHI, K., Ultra-precision Machining
YASUTAKE, K., Atomically-controlled Processes
YOSHII, K., Functional Materials

Department of Applied Physics:

KASAI, H., Materials Physics Theory
KAWAKAMI, N., Condensed Matter Physics and Statistical Physics
MASUHARA, H., Laser Photochemistry and Microspectroscopy
SUGAWARA, Y., Engineering Physics
YAGI, A., Nonlinear Analysis and its Applications

Department of Adaptive Machine Systems:

ASADA, M., Emergent Robotics
ISHIGURRO, H., Evolution Dynamics
MINAMINO, Y., Intelligent Materials

NAKATANI, A., Microdynamics
OHJI, T., Advanced Materials Processing
YASUDA, H., Materials Processing and Devices

Department of Mechanophysics Engineering:

FUJITA, K., Design and Manufacturing Engineering
HURUSHO, J., Real-world Active Intelligence
IKEDA, M., Control Engineering
INABA, T., Morphology in Machine Phenomena
KAJISHIMA, T., Fluid Engineering and Thermohydrodynamics
KATAOKA, I., Quantum Measurement
KUBO, S., Materials and Structures Evaluation
MINOSHIMA, K., Intelligent Materials
MIYOSHI, T., Production and Measurement Systems Engineering
MORI, N., Complex Fluid Mechanics
OTA, Y., Control Engineering
SHIBUTANI, Y., Solid Mechanics
TAKEISHI, K., Thermal Science and Engineering
TAKEUCHI, Y., Design and Manufacturing Engineering
TANAK, T., Mechanical Systems Analysis and Solid Mechanics
TSUJI, Y., Complex Fluid Mechanics
UMEDA, Y., Design and Manufacturing Engineering

Department of Mechanical Engineering and Systems:

KUBO, S., Materials and Structures Evaluation
MINOSHIMA, K., Materials and Structures Evaluation
MIYOSHI, T., Production and Measurement Systems Engineering
SHIBUTANI, Y., Solid Mechanics
TANAKA, T., Mechanical Systems Analysis and Solid Mechanics

Department of Computer-controlled Mechanical Systems:

FUJITA, K., Design and Manufacturing Engineering
FURUSHO, J., Real-world Active Intelligence
IKEDA, M., Control Engineering
OTA, Y., Control Engineering
SHIRAI, Y., Real-world Active Intelligence
TAKEUCHI, Y., Design and Manufacturing Engineering

Department of Materials Science and Processing:

ARAI, E., Advanced Manufacturing Systems
FUJIMOTO, K., Micro-nano Systems
FUJIMOTO, S., Environmental Materials and Surface Processing
FUJIWARA, Y., Crystal Growth
HIRATA, Y., Intelligent Materials Processing Systems
HIROSE, K., Computational Physics
HUJIMOTO, S., Environmental Materials and Surface Processing
KAKESHITA, T., Quantum Physics of Solids
KOBAYASHI, K., Smart Materials Processing
MATSUO, S., Intelligent Materials Processing
MINAMI, F., Materials Evaluation for Structuring
NISHIMOTO, K., Materials Joining
TANAKA, T., Interface Science and Technology
TOYODA, M., Strength/Fracture Evaluation for Manufacturing
USUI, T., Materials Processing and Metallurgy
YAMAMOTO, M., Physics of Surface and Interface
YAMASHITA, H., Thermophysics of Materials

Department of Materials Science and Engineering:

FUJIWARA, Y., Crystal Growth
KAKESHITA, T., Quantum Physics of Solids
YAMAMOTO, M., Physics of Surface and Interface

Department of Manufacturing Science:

ARAI, E., Advanced Manufacturing Systems
FUJIMOTO, K., Micro-nano Systems
HIRATA, Y., Intelligent Materials Processing Systems
KOBAYASHI, K., Smart Materials Processing
MINAMI, F., Materials Evaluation for Structuring
MIYAMOTO, I., Intelligent Materials Processing Systems
NISHIMOTO, K., Materials Joining
TOYODA, M., Strength/Fracture Evaluation for Manufacturing

Department of Communications Engineering:

BABAGUCHI, N., Telecommunications and Systems Engineering
IIDA, T., Fusion Engineering
ISE, T., Systems and Electric Power Engineering
ITO, T., Electro-materials Engineering
KAWASAKI, Z., Fundamentals for Communications Engineering
KODAMA, R., Laser Engineering
KOMAKI, S., Microwave and Optical Communication Systems
KUMAGAI, S., Control Engineering
MORITA, S., Microscopic Quantum Engineering
NISHIKAWA, M., Supra-high-temperature Engineering
SANPEI, S., Telecommunication and Systems Engineering
SASAKI, T., Applied Electrophysics
SUGINO, T., Science and Technology of Electrical Materials
SUHARA, T., Integrated Electronic Engineering
TAKINE, T., Advanced Communications and Photonic Networks
TANAKA, K., Laser Engineering
TANIGUCHI, K., Quantum Devices
TANINO, T., Systems Analysis and Optimization
TSUJI, K., Systems Engineering
YAGI, T., Control System Engineering

Department of Sustainable Energy and Environmental Engineering:

HORIIKE, H., Neutronics and Nuclear Instrumentation
KAGA, A., Engineering for the Atmospheric Environment
MIZUNO, M., Environment and Energy Systems
MORIOKA, T., Environmental Management
NISHIJIMA, S., Nuclear Chemical Engineering
SAWAKI, M., Environmental Management
TAKEDA, T., Nuclear Reactor Physics
YAMANAKA, S., Nuclear Fuels

Department of Global Architecture:

DEGUCHI, I., Social Systems Engineering
HASEGAWA, K., Naval Architecture
IMAI, K., Regional Environment and Global Transport
KATO, N., Naval Architecture
KOHZU, I., Structural Engineering
MATSUI, S., Structural and Geotechnical Engineering
NAITO, S., Marine Systems Engineering
NAKATSUJI, K., Social Systems Engineering
NITTA, Y., Social Systems Engineering
OHNO, Y., Structural Engineering
SAGARA, K., Architectural Design
TACHIBANA, E., Structural Engineering

TANIMOTO, C., Sustainable Development and Strategy
TOKIDA, K., Structural and Geotechnical Engineering
YAMAGUCHI, K., Sustainable Development and Strategy
YAO, T., Naval Architecture

Department of Environmental Engineering:

FUJITA, M., Water Science and Environmental Biotechnology
KAGA, A., Engineering for the Atmospheric Environment
MIZUNO, M., Environment and Energy Systems
MORIOKA, T., Environmental Management

Department of Management for Industry and Technology:

NARUMI, S., Management of Technology Knowledge
SATO, T., Technology Design
YAMAMOTO, T., Management of Technology Knowledge
ZAKO, M., Technology Design

Science Center for Atoms, Molecules and Ions Control:

FUKUDA, T., Plasma Particle Control Division
HAMAGUCHI, S., Plasma Particle Control Division
NAKATANI, R., Micro-composite Research Division
OKADA, S., Plasma Particle Control Division
SHIRAI, Y., Micro-structures Division

Research Center for Ultra-Precision Science and Technology:

ENDO, K., Precision Science and Technology

Graduate School and School of Engineering Science (1-3 Machikaneyama-cho, Toyonaka, Osaka 560-8531; tel. (6) 6850-6111; fax (6) 6850-6151; internet www.es.osaka-u.ac.jp/index-e.html):

Department of Materials Engineering Science:

HIRAI, T., Solar Energy Chemistry
HIRATA, Y., Environment and Energy System
HIYAMIZU, S., Quantum Physics of Nanoscale Materials
IMOTO, N., Quantum Physics of Nanoscale Materials
INOUE, Y., Environment and Energy System
ITOH, T., Dynamics of Nanoscale Materials
IWAI, S., Molecular Organization Chemistry
KANEDA, K., Chemical Reaction Engineering
KITAOKA, Y., Frontier Materials
KITAYAMA, T., Synthetic Chemistry
KUBOI, R., Bioprocess Engineering
MASHIMA, K., Synthetic Chemistry
MATSUMURA, M., Solar Energy Chemistry
MIYAKE, O., Electron Correlation Physics
MIYASAKA, H., Dynamics of Nanoscale Materials
NAKANO, M., Chemical Reaction Engineering
NAKATO, Y., Molecular Organization Chemistry
NAOTA, T., Synthetic Chemistry
OHGAKI, K., Environment and Energy System
SHIMIZU, K., Quantum Science in Extreme Conditions
SUGA, S., Electron Correlation Physics
SUZUKI, N., Frontier Materials
SUZUKI, Y., Electron Correlation Physics
TADA, H., Quantum Physics of Nanoscale Materials
TAYA, M., Bioprocess Engineering
TOBE, Y., Frontier Materials

UEYAMA, K., Chemical Reaction Engineering
YOSHIDA, H., Quantum Science in Extreme Conditions

Department of Mechanical Science and Bioengineering:

ARAKI, T., Biomedical and Biophysical Measurements
HIRAO, M., Mechanics of Solid Materials
KOBAYASHI, H., Mechanics of Solid Materials
MIYAZAKI, F., Mechano-informatics
NOMURA, T., Biophysical Engineering
OHSHIRO, O., Biomedical and Biophysical Measurements
OSAKADA, K., Mechano-informatics
SUGIMOTO, N., Mechanics of Fluids and Thermo-fluids
TANAKA, M., Biomedical Engineering
TSUJIMOTO, Y., Propulsion Engineering
WAKABAYASHI, K., Biophysical Engineering

Department of Systems Innovation:

AIDA, S., Mathematical and Statistical Finance
AKASAKA, Y., Solid-State Electronics
ARAI, T., Intelligent Systems
FUJII, T., System Theory
IIGUNI, Y., System Theory
INAGAKI, N., Mathematical and Statistical Finance
INUIGUCHI, M., Theoretical Systems Science
ITOSAKI, H., Advanced Quantum Devices and Electronics
KANO, Y., Statistical Science
KITAGAWA, M., Advanced Quantum Devices and Electronics
KOBAYASHI, T., Optical Electronics
NAGAI, H., Mathematical and Statistical Finance
NAWA, H., Mathematical Modelling
NISHIDA, S., Intelligent Systems
OKAMOTO, H., Solid-State Electronics
OKAMURA, Y., Optical Electronics
OKUYAMA, M., Solid-State Electronics
SATO, K., Intelligent Systems
SHIRAHATA, S., Statistical Science
SUZUKI, T., Mathematical Modelling
URABE, S., Optical Electronics
USHIO, T., Theoretical Systems Science
YACHIDA, M., Intelligent Systems

Graduate School and School of Human Sciences (1-2 Yamadaoka, Suita, Osaka 565-0871; tel. (6) 6877-5111; fax (6) 6879-8010; internet www.hus.osaka-u.ac.jp/english):

ABE, A., Educational Policy and Administration
ADACHI, K., Behavioural Data Science
DAIBO, I., Social Psychology
FUJIOKA, J., Educational Psychology
FUJITA, A., Clinical Thanatology and Geriatric Behavioural Science
HINOBAYASHI, T., Comparative and Developmental Psychology
HIRASAWA, Y., Lifelong Education
IMURA, O., Clinical Psychology
KASUGA, N., People and Culture
KAWABATA, A., Advanced Empirical Sociology
KIMAE, T., Sociology of Modern Society
KOIZUMI, J., Cultural and Social Anthropology
KONDO, H., Sociology of Education
KOTO, Y., Sociological Theory
KUGIHARA, N., Social Psychology
KUMAKURA, H., Biological Anthropology
KURIMOTO, E., Cultural and Social Anthropology
KUWANO, S., Environmental Psychology
MAESAKO, T., Communication and Media
MINAMI, T., Comparative and Developmental Psychology
MIURA, T., Applied Cognitive Psychology
MIYATA, K., Clinical Psychology

MORIKAWA, K., Fundamental Psychology
MUTA, K., Sociology of Communication
NAKAGAWA, S., Cultural and Social Anthropology
NAKAMURA, T., Quantitative Psychology of Expression and Cognition
NAKAMURA, Y., International Collaboration
NAKAYAMA, Y., Logical Studies, Foundation of Science
NAOI, A., Information Technology and Human Sciences
OIMATSU, K., Clinical Psychology
ONODA, M., Educational Policy and Administration
SHIMIZU, K., Cultural Studies of Education
SUGAI, K., Educational Technology
SUGENO, T., Philosophical Anthropology
TSUTSUMI, S., Social Policy and Community Empowerment Studies
USUI, S., Human Risk Studies
UTSUMI, S., International Collaboration
YAMAMOTO, T., Behavioural Physiology

Graduate School and School of Letters (1-5 Machikaneyama-cho, Toyonaka, Osaka 560-8532; tel. (6) 6850-6111; fax (6) 6850-5091; e-mail web-admin@www.let.osaka-u.ac.jp; internet www.let.osaka-u.ac.jp):

AKITA, S., Western History
AMANO, F., Theatre Studies
AOKI, N., Japanese Linguistics
ARAKAWA, M., Central Asian History
EGAWA, A., Western History
ENOMOTO, F., Indian Philosophy and Buddhist Studies
FUJIKAWA, T., Western History
FUJITA, H., Environmental Aesthetics
FUKUNAGA, S., Archaeology
GOTO, A., Japanese Language and Literature
HACHIYA, M., Japanese Language and Literature
HAYASHI, M., German Literature
IIKURA, Y., Japanese Language and Literature
IKAI, T., Japanese History
IRIE, Y., Philosophy and History of Philosophy
IZUHARA, T., Japanese Language and Literature
KAMIKURA, T., Aesthetics
KASHIWAGI, T., French Literature
KATAYAMA, T., Asian History
KAWAMURA, K., Historical Studies of Cultural Exchanges
KINSUI, S., Japanese Language and Literature
KOBAYASHI, S., Human Geography
KODERA, T., Art History
KUDO, M., Japanese Linguistics
MOMOKI, S., Asian History
MORIOKA, Y., American Literature
MORIYASU, T., Central Asian History
MURATA, M., Japanese History
NAGATA, Y., Theatre Studies
NAITO, T., Comparative Literature
NAKAOKA, N., Clinical Philosophy and Ethics
NEGISHI, K., Musicology
OBA, Y., English Linguistics
OHASHI, R., Philosophy and Aesthetics
OKUDAIRA, S., Art History
SANADA, S., Japanese Linguistics
SUGIHARA, T., Historical Studies of Cultural Exchanges
SURO, N., Philosophy, Modern Thought and Cultural Studies
TAIRA, M., Japanese History
TAKAHASHI, B., Chinese Literature
TAKENAKA, T., Western History
TAMAI, A., English Literature
TOKI, S., Japanese Linguistics
UENO, O., Philosophy and History of Philosophy
UMEMURA, T., Japanese History
WADA, A., French Literature

WAKAYAMA, E., Art History
WASHIDA, K., Clinical Philosophy and Ethics
YUASA, K., Chinese Philosophy

Graduate School and School of Pharmaceutical Sciences (1-6 Yamadaoka, Suita, Osaka 565-0871; fax (6) 6879-8154; internet www.phs.osaka-u.ac.jp):

AZUMA, J., Clinical Evaluation of Medicines and Therapeutics
BABA, A., Molecular Neuropharmacology
DOI, T., Protein Molecular Engineering
HIRATA, K., Environmental Bioengineering
IMANISHI, T., Bioorganic Chemistry
KITA, Y., Synthetic Organic Chemistry
KOBAYASHI, M., Natural Product Chemistry
MAEDA, M., Biochemistry and Molecular Biology
MATSUDA, T., Medicinal Pharmacology
MURAKAMI, N., Medicinal Plant Resource Exploration
NAKAGAWA, S., Biopharmaceutics
NASU, M., Environmental Science and Microbiology
NISHIKAWA, J., Environmental Biochemistry
OHKUBO, T., Biophysical Chemistry
TAKAGI, T., Pharmaceutical Information Science
TANAKA, K., Toxicology
TANAKA, T., Medicinal and Organic Chemistry
UNO, T., Analytical Chemistry
YAGI, K., Bio-functional Molecular Chemistry
YAMAMOTO, H., Immunology

Graduate School and School of Science (1-1 Machikaneyama-cho, Toyonaka, Osaka 560-0043; tel. (6) 6850-6111; fax (6) 6850-5288; internet www.sci.osaka-u.ac.jp):

AKAI, H., Quantum Physics
AKUTSU, Y., Quantum Physics
AOSHIMA, S., Polymer Synthesis
ASAKAWA, M., Hadronic Physics
DOI, S., Analysis
FUJIKI, A., Global Geometry and Analysis
FUKASE, K., Natural Product Chemistry
FUKUYAMA, K., Structural Biology
HARADA, A., Supermolecular Science
HASE, S., Organic Biochemistry
HAYASHI, N., Applied Mathematics
HIGASHIJIMA, K., Particle Physics
HOSOTANI, Y., Fundamental Physics
IBUKIYAMA, T., Algebra
INABA, A., Structural Thermodynamics
KAIZAKI, S., Inorganic Chemistry
KANAZAWA, H., Molecular Biology
KASAI, T., Reaction Dynamics, Molecular Thermodynamics
KATAKUSE, I., Interdisciplinary Physics
KAWAMURA, H., Solid-State and Statistical Physics
KAWARAZAKI, S., Solid-State Physics
KISHIMOTO, T., Particle and Nuclear Physics
KOISO, N., Geometry
KONNO, K., Algebra
KONNO, T., Coordination Chemistry
KOTANI, S., Analysis
KUNO, Y., Elementary Particle Physics
KURAMITSU, S., Biophysical Chemistry
MABUCHI, T., Global Mathematics
MASUKATA, H., Molecular Genetics
MATSUDA, J., Planetary Science
MUNAKATA, T., Chemistry
MURATA, M., Biomolecular Chemistry
NAKASHIMA, S., Physical Geochemistry
NAKAZAWA, Y., Condensed Matter Physical Chemistry
NAMIKAWA, Y., Algebra
NISHIDA, H., Development Biology
NISHITANI, T., Analysis
NOMACHI, M., Quark Nuclear Physics
NORISUYE, T., Polymer Solutions
NOZUE, Y., Condensed Matter Physics

OGAWA, T., Quantum Physics
OGIHARA, S., Cell Biology
OHSHIKA, K., Geometry
ONUKI, Y., Condensed Matter Physics
SATO, T., Polymer Chemical Physics
SHIMODA, T., Nuclear Physics
SHINOHARA, A., Nuclear Chemistry
SUGITA, H., Analysis
SUZUKI, S., Bioinorganic Chemistry
TAJIMA, S., Condensed Matter Physics
TAKAHARA, F., Theoretical Astrophysics
TAKEDA, S., Condensed Matter Physics
TAKISAWA, H., Molecular Cell Biology
TERASHIMA, I., Plant Ecophysiology
TOKUNAGA, F., Extreme-environment Biology
TSUCHIYAMA, A., Experimental Planetology
TSUNEKI, K., Comparative Zoology
TSUNEMI, H., Astrophysics
UMEHARA, M., Global Mathematics
USUI, S., Algebra
WATANABE, T., Algebra
WATARAI, H., Analytical Chemistry
YAMAGUCHI, K., Quantum Chemistry, Physical Chemistry of Condensed Matter
YAMANAKA, T., High Energy Physics
YAMANAKA, T., Physics of Matter
YONESAKI, T., Microbial Genetics

Graduate School of Information Science and Technology (1-5 Yamadaoka, Suita, Osaka 565-0871; tel. (6) 6877-5111; fax (6) 6879-4570; internet www.ist.osaka-u.ac.jp):

Department of Pure and Applied Mathematics:

DATE, E., Mathematical Science
HIBI, T., Combinatorics
KAWANAKA, N., Discrete Structures
MATSUMURA, A., Applied Analysis
ODANAKA, S., Computer-assisted Mathematics
SAKANE, Y., Applied Geometry

Department of Information and Physical Sciences:

ISHII, H., Operations Research
MORITA, H., Computing with Complexity and Nonlinearity
NUMAO, M., Architecture for Intelligence
TANIDA, J., Physical Sciences
UOSAKI, K., Nonlinear Systems, Modelling and Optimization

Department of Computer Science:

HAGIHARA, K., Supercomputing Engineering
INOUE, K., Software Engineering
KUSOMOTO, S., Software Science
MASUZAWA, T., Algorithm Engineering
YAGI, Y., Intelligent Media Systems

Department of Information Systems Engineering:

CHIBA, T., Advanced System Architecture
IMAI, M., Integrated System Design
KAWATA, T., Advanced Systems Architecture
KIKUNO, T., Dependability Engineering
ONOYE, T., Information Systems Synthesis
TAKEMURA, H., Integrated Media Environment

Department of Information Networking:

HIGASHINO, T., Mobile Computing
IMASE, M., Information Sharing Platform
MURAKAMI, K., Intelligent Networking Systems
NAKANO, H., Advanced Network Architecture
OBASHI, Y., Cyber Communication
SATO, T., Cyber Communication

Department of Multimedia Engineering:

FUJIWARA, T., Information Security Engineering
KATAGIRI, Y., Multimedia Agent Systems
KISHINO, F., Human Interface Engineering

KOGURE, K., Multimedia Agent Systems
KOMODA, N., Business Information Systems
NISHIO, S., Multimedia Data Engineering
SHIMOJO, S., Applied Media Engineering

Department of Bioinformatic Engineering:

AKAZAWA, K., Human Information Engineering
KASHIWABARA, T., Bio-network Engineering
MATSUDA, H., Genome Information Engineering
SHIMIZU, H., Metabolic Engineering

Graduate School of Language and Culture (1-8 Machikaneyama-cho, Toyonaka, Osaka 560-0043; tel. (6) 6850-6111; fax (6) 6850-5865):

DYUBOVSKI, A., Language and Technology
HARUKI, Y., Language and Communication
HAYASHI, Y., Language and Information Science
HUKAZAWA, Y., Language and Communication
IWANE, H., Language and Technology
KANASAKI, H., Area Studies in Language and Culture
KANEKO, M., Area Studies in Language and Culture
KIMURA, K., Area Studies in Language and Culture
KIMURA, S., Interdisciplinary Cultural Studies
KITAMURA, T., Interdisciplinary Cultural Studies
NAKA, N., Language and Culture in International Relations
NAKANO, Y., Language and Culture in International Relations
NARITA, H., Education in Language and Culture
OKADA, N., Education in Language and Culture
OKITA, T., Education in Language and Culture
SENBA, Y., Language and Technology
TAKAOKA, K., Language and Culture in International Relations
TSUDA, A., Language and Communication
TSUKUI, S., Area Studies in Language and Culture
WATANABE, S., Language and Information Science
YOKOTA, G., Interdisciplinary Cultural Studies

Graduate School of Law (1-6 Machikaneyama-cho, Toyonaka, Osaka 560-0043; tel. (6) 6850-6111; fax (6) 6850-5091):

AOE, H., Legal Practice
AOTAKA, S., Legal Practice
CHAEN, S., Legal Practice
HIRATA, K., Legal Practice
IKEDA, T., Legal Practice
KOJIMA, N., Legal Practice
KOSUGI, S., Legal Practice
MATSUI, S., Legal Practice
MATSUKAWA, T., Legal Practice
MATSUMOTO, K., Legal Practice
MISAKA, Y., Legal Practice
MIZUTANI, N., Legal Practice
MURAKAMI, T., Legal Practice
SAKUMA, O., Legal Practice
SHIMOMURA, M., Legal Practice
SUENAGA, T., Legal Practice
SUZUKI, H., Legal Practice
TANIGUTCHI, S., Legal Practice
YOSHIDA, M., Legal Practice
YOSHIMOTO, K., Legal Practice

Graduate School of Frontier Biosciences (1-3 Yamadaoka, Suita, Osaka 565-0871; fax (6) 6879-4420; internet www.fbs.osaka-u.ac.jp):

FUJITA, I., Neuroscience
HAMADA, H., Organismal Biosystems
HANAOKA, F., Integrated Biology
HIRANO, T., Organismal Biosystems
KAWAMURA, S., Nanobiology

KINOSHITA, S., Biophysical Dynamics
KONDOH, H., Biomolecular Networks
KURAHASHI, T., Biophysical Dynamics
MURAKAMI, F., Neuroscience
NAGATA, S., Integrated Biology
NAKANO, T., Integrated Biology
NAMBA, K., Nanobiology
NORIOKA, S., Biophysical Dynamics
OGURA, A., Neuroscience
OHZAWA, I., Neuroscience
OKAMOTO, M., Biomolecular Networks
SHIMOMURA, I., Organismal Biosystems
SUGINO, A., Biomolecular Networks
TANAKA, K., Organismal Biosystems
YAGI, T., Integrated Biology
YAMAMOTO, N., Neuroscience
YANAGIDA, T., Nanobiology
YONEDA, Y., Biomolecular Networks

Graduate School of Law and Politics and School of Law (1-6 Machikaneyama-cho, Toyonaka, Osaka 560-0043; tel. (6) 6850-6111; fax (6) 6850-5091):

HAYASHI, T., Comparative Law and Politics
KAWATA, J., Center for Legal and Political Practice
KUNII, K., Comparative Law and Politics
MITSUNARI, K., Independent Study Center
NAKAO, T., Comparative Law and Politics
NAKAYAMA, R., Governance and Law
OKUBO, N., Governance and Law
SAKAMOTO, K., Governance and Law
TAGO, K., Governance and Law
TAKADA, A., Governance and Law
TAKAHASHI, A., Independent Study Course
TAKENAKA, Y., Independent Study Course
TAKIGUCHI, T., Comparative Law and Politics
YAMASHITA, M., Comparative Law and Politics
YOON, K. C., International and Comparative Law Course

Osaka School of International Public Policy (1-31 Machikaneyama-cho, Toyonaka, Osaka 560-0043; tel. (6) 6850-6111; fax (6) 6850-5208):

HASHIMOTO, Y., Comparative Public Policy
HOSHINO, T., Systems Integration
KOHSAKA, A., Systems Integration
KOJIMA, N., Comparative Corporate Behaviour
KUROSAWA, M., International Public System
MATSUSHIGE, H., Systems Integration
MURAKAMI, M., International Public System
NAKANO, T., Comparative Corporate Behaviour
NOMURA, Y., Systems Integration
SAITO, S., Comparative Economic Development
SAWAI, M., Comparative Economic Development
SUGIHARA, S., Contemporary Japanese Law and Economy
TAKENAKA, H., International Trade Relations
TANIGUCHI, S., International Trade Relations
TOKOTANI, F., Comparative Public Policy
YAMAUCHI, N., Contemporary Japanese Law and Economy
YONEHARA, K., Contemporary Japanese Law and Economy

ATTACHED INSTITUTES

Institute for Protein Research: Suita Campus, Yamadaoka, Suita, Osaka; Dir HIDEO AKUTSU.

Institute of Scientific and Industrial Research: Suita Campus, Mihogaoka, Ibaraki, Osaka; Dir TOMOJI KAWAI.

Institute of Social and Economic Research: Suita Campus, Mihogaoka, Ibaraki, Osaka; Dir SHINSUKE IKEDA.

Joining and Welding Research Institute: Suita Campus, Mihogaoka, Ibaraki, Osaka; Dir KIYOSHI NOGI.

Research Institute for Microbial Diseases: Suita Campus, Yamadaoka, Suita, Osaka; Dir TAROH KINOSHITA.

OTARU UNIVERSITY OF COMMERCE

3-5-21, Midori, Otaru, 047-0851, Hokkaido
Telephone: (134) 27-5200
Fax: (134) 27-5213
E-mail: inl@office.otaru.ac.jp
Internet: www.otaru-uc.ac.jp
Founded 1949
Independent
Pres.: IEMASA YAMADA
Chief Admin. Officer: HIROSHI AIBA
Librarian: YOICHIRO YUKI
Library of 420,000 vols
Number of teachers: 134
Number of students: 2,260

Depts of economics, commerce, law, information and management sciences, teacher-training programme in commerce and graduate school

PROFESSORS

Department of Commerce: HAJIME ITOH
Department of Economics: HAJIME IMANISHI
Department of Information Technology: HARUHIKO OGASAWARA
Department of Law: MASAHIRO MICHINO

UNIVERSITY OF THE RYUKYUS

1 Senbaru, Nishihara-cho, Okinawa 903-0213
Telephone: (98) 895-2221
Fax: (98) 895-8037
E-mail: webmaster@www.u-ryukyu.ac.jp
Internet: www.u-ryukyu.ac.jp
Founded 1950
Academic year: April to March
Independent
Language of instruction: Japanese
Pres.: TERUO IWAMASA
Vice-Pres. for Financial, Facilities and Hospital Management: HAYAO MIYAGI
Vice-Pres. for Gen. Affairs: TAKASHI MARUYAMA
Vice-Pres. for Planning and Management Strategy: HAJIME OSHIRO
Vice-Pres. for Research Education and Student Affairs: RISHUN SHINZATO
Vice-Pres. for Research Outreach and Int. Affairs: KEISUKE TAIRA
Dean of Students: KATSUMA YAGASAKI
Library Dir: K. OYAKAWA
Library of 930,000 vols
Number of teachers: 879
Number of students: 8,195

DEANS

Faculty of Agriculture: S. GIBO
Faculty of Education: T. NAKAMURA
Faculty of Engineering: T. YAMAKAWA
Faculty of Law: K. UEZATO
Faculty of Medicine: Y. SATO
Faculty of Science: M. TSUCHIYA
Faculty of Tourism Sciences and Industrial Management: T. HESHIKI
Graduate School of Health Sciences: T. HOKAMA
Graduate School of Law: T. TAKARA

PROFESSORS

Faculty of Agriculture:

AKINAGA, T., Postharvest Handling
CHINEN, I., Applied Biochemistry
GIBO, S., Land Conservation
HAYASHI, H., Woody Materials and Processing

HIGA, T., Tropical Horticulture
HIGOSHI, H., Animal Hygiene
HIRATA, E., Forestry Measurement
HONGO, F., Chemistry of Animal Products and Applied Bioresource Utilization
ISHIMINE, Y., Economic Plants
IWAHASHI, O., Insect Ecology
KAWASHIMA, Y., Comparative Anatomy
KOBAMOTO, N., Applied Biophysics
KOKI, Z., Preventive Forestry Engineering
KURODA, T., Environmental Information Sciences
MIYAGI, N., Soil Engineering
MURAYAMA, S., Crop Science
NAKADA, T., Animal Reproduction
NAKASONE, Y., Food Chemistry
OSHIRO, S., Animal Science, Environmental Physiology
SATO, S., Genetics and Breeding of Rice Plants
SHINJO, A., Animal Breeding
SHINJO, T., Geomechanics
SHINOHARA, T., Forest Policy and Economics
TAWATA, S., Pesticide Chemistry
TOKASHIKI, Y., Soil Science
UENO, M., Agricultural Engineering
UESATO, K., Floricultural Plant Science
YAGA, S., Wood Chemistry and Wood Preservation
YAMASHIRO, S., Agricultural Engineering
YASUDA, M., Food Microbiology
YONAHA, T., Plant Pathology
YOSHIDA, S., Agricultural Marketing Theory

Faculty of Education:

AIZAWA, T., Chinese Literature
ARATA, Y., Biophysics Engineering
FUJIE, T., Homemaking Education, Aesthetics in Costume
FUJIWARA, Y., Didactics
HAMAMOTO, M., Sports Methodology
HANASHIRO, R., Consumer Education
HIGA, Z., Technical Education
HIGASIMORI, K., Food Science
HIRATA, E., Education for the Handicapped
IKEDA, K., Judo
INOUE, K., Lifelong Education
ISHIGURO, E., Optics
ISHIKAWA, K., Social Development in Children
ITOKAZU, T., Educational Music of Wind Instruments
IZUMI, K., Vocal Music
KAKAZU, T., Psychology
KAMIYAMA, T., Woodcut
KAMIZONO, S., Developmental Psychology of Mentally Retarded and Handicapped Children
KATO, M., Complex Analysis
KAWANA, T., Physical Geography
KINJO, M., Mathematics Education
KINJO, S., Culinary Science
KINJO, Y., Inorganic Chemistry
KOBASHIGAWA, H., Sports Psychology
KOBAYASHI, M., Theory and History of Art
KOJIMA, Y., Japanese Literature
KOYANAGI, M., Physical Chemistry
MAEHARA, H., Discrete Geometry
MAEHARA, T., Psychology
MAESHIRO, R., Regional Economics
MATSUMOTO, S., Mathematical Physics
MIZUNO, M., Criminal Law
NAGAYAMA, T., Piano Playing
NAKAMURA, I., Meteorology
NAKAMURA, T., Education for the Handicapped
NAKAMURA, T., Theory of Music
NAKASONE, Y., Ecology
NAKAZATO, H., Algebra
NISHIMURA, S., Sculpture
NISHIZATO, K., History of East Asia
NOHARA, T., Palaeontology
OKUDA, M., Ceramic Art
OZAWA, Y., Japanese Literature

SEKINE, H., Electricity and Electrical Engineering
SHIMABUKURO, Z., English Linguistics
SHIMOJANA, M., Animal Ecology and Taxonomy (especially spiders)
SHINZATO, R., Clinical Psychology
SHINZATO, S., Kinematics and Dynamics of Mechanisms
SIMABUKURO, T., Psychology of Personality
TAIRA, K., Health Promotion
TAIRA, T., Physical Education
TAKASHIMA, N., Social Studies
TAKEDA, H., International Peace Studies
TAMAKI, A., Physical Education
TOMINAGA, D., Psychophysiology
UEZU, E., Nutrition and Physiology
YAMAUTI, S., TESL/TEFL
YONEMORI, T., Educational Information Technology

Faculty of Engineering:
AMANO, T., Wind Engineering for Building Structures
ASHARIF, M. R., Adaptive Digital Signal Processing, Speech in Images
FUKUSHIMA, S., Architectural Planning
IKEDA, T., Urban and Regional Planning
KANESHIRO, H., Fatigue Fracture
KINA, S., Sanitary Engineering
KODAMA, M., Microwave
MEKARU, S., Plastic Working
MIYAGI, H., Intelligent Systems
MIYAGI, K., High Velocity Impact
MORITA, D., Conservation Science and Environmental Planning for Architecture
NAGAI, M., Mechanics and Fluid Engineering
NAGATA, T., Thermal Engineering
NAKAMURA, I., Electronic Circuits
NAKAO, Z., Mathematical Informatics
OSHIRO, T., Structural Analysis and Materials
OYAKAWA, K., Heat Transfer Augmentation
SHINZATO, T., Thermal Engineering
TAKAHASHI, H., Power Systems Engineering and Surge Analysis
TAKARA, T., Spoken Language Processing
TAMAKI, S., Digital Control
TOGUCHI, M., Electronic Materials
TSUKAYAMA, S., Coastal Engineering
TSUTSUI, S., Coastal Engineering
UEZATO, K., Electric Machinery
YABUKI, T., Bridge and Structural Engineering
YAFUSO, T., Strength of Materials
YAMAKAWA, T., Reinforced Concrete Structures
YAMAMOTO, T., Neuro-control
YAMASHIRO, Y., Electrical Materials
YARA, H., Welding Engineering
YOSHIYA, K., Intelligent Information Processing
ZUKERAN, C., Multiple-valued Logic Circuit

Faculty of Law and Letters:
AKAMINE, K., American Literature
AKAMINE, M., Japanese Folklore
AKAMINE, M., Modern Chinese History, Modern Okinawa History
ANDO, Y., Sociology
ARAKAKI, S., Civil Law
ASHITOMI, T., Civil Law
CHINEN, S., Monetary Economics
CHINEN, Y., Public Finance
EGAMI, T., Science of Public Administration, Comparative Politics
ENDO, M., Cognitive Psychology
GABE, M., International Relations
HAMASAKI, M., Greek Philosophy
HESHIKI, T., International Marketing
HIYANE, T., History of Political Thought, Political Science
HOSAKA, H., Journalism
IHA, M., Marketing
IKEDA, Y., Japanese Archaeology, Museography

IKEMIYA, M., Ryukyuan Literature
IMURA, O., Clinical Psychology
INABA, Y., Criminal Procedure
IREI, T., Human Resources Management, Business Administration
ISHIKAWA, T., Regional Geography, Human Geography
ISHIMINE, K., Constitutional Law
KABIRA, N., Economic History
KARIMATA, S., Japanese Linguistics, Study of Ryukyuan Dialects
KAWASOE, M., Social Services for the Aged
KOMATSU, M., Economic History
KUDEKEN, K., Community Development in Social Welfare
MACHIDA, M., Settlement Geography, Geographical Information Systems
MAEKADO, A., Geomorphology
MIYARA, S., Linguistics
NAKACHI, H., Administrative Law
NAKACHI, K., American Literature
NAKAHARA, T., Business and Corporation Laws
NAKAHODO, M., Modern Japanese Literature
NAKAMURA, T., Social Psychology
NAMIHIRA, T., Political Philosophy and Theory, Political Science
NISHIKAWA, H., Contemporary Philosophy
OSABE, Y., Asian History
OSHIRO, H., International Economics
OSHIRO, I., Theoretical Economics
OSHIRO, M., Managerial Finance
OSHIRO, T., Regional Development Policy
OYAKAWA, T., Linguistics
SAKIMA, N., European History
SHIMABUKURO, S., Human Geography
SHIMABUKURO, T., Commercial Law, Law of Securities Regulation
SHIMIZU, K., Criminal Law
SHIMOJI, Y., English Linguistics
SHIMURA, K., Quality Management
SUZUKI, N., International Sociology
TAIRA, M., American Literature
TAIRA, T., Applied Linguistics
TAKARA, K., Ryukyuan History
TAKARA, K., Constitutional Law, Administrative Law
TAMAKI, I., Civil Procedure Law
TAMAKI, M., Ryukyuan Literature
TANAKA, H., Economic Statistics
TOMA, S., Theoretical Economics
TOMINAGA, H., Econometrics
TOYOOKA, T., Accounting Information Theory, Accounting Systems
TSUHA, T., Social Anthropology
TSUNODA, M., Civil Law, European Private Law
UEZATO, K., Chinese Literature
UEZU, Y., Accounting
YAMAZATO, J., Japanese History
YAMAZATO, K., American Literature
YOGI, K., Linguistics
YONAHARA, T., Strategic Management
YOSHII, K., German
YOSHIMURA, K., English Literature
YOSHIZAWA, T., Sociology of Education

Faculty of Medicine:
ANIYA, Y., Biochemical Pharmacology
ARAKI, K., Haematology
ARIIZUMI, M., Preventive Medicine
FUKUNAGA, T., Virology
HOKAMA, T., Health Care
IMAMURA, T., Bacteriology
ISHIZU, H., Mental Health Science
ISIDA, H., Anatomy
ITO, E., Pathology
IWAMASA, T., Pathology
IWANAGA, M., Bacteriology
KANAYA, F., Hand Surgery, Microsurgery
KANAZAWA, K., Gynaecological Oncology, Reproductive Immunology
KARIYA, K., Biochemistry
KOJA, K., Surgery

KONO, S., Obstetrics and Gynaecology, Endocrinology
KOSUGI, T., Physiology, Haematology
MAEHIRA, F., Clinical Biochemistry, Biochemistry
MIYAGI, I., Medical Entomology
MIYAZAKI, T., Forensic Medicine
MURAYAMA, S.
MUTO, Y., Digestive Surgery
NAKA, K., Health Administration
NODA, Y., Otorhinolaryngology, Head and Neck Surgery
NONAKA, S., Dermatology, Photobiology
OGAWA, Y., Urology
OGURA, C., Neuropsychiatry
OHTA, T., Paediatrics
SAITO, A., Internal Medicine
SAKANASHI, M., Pharmacology
SAKIHARA, S., Health Sociology, Community Health
SATO, Y., Parasitology
SAWAGUCHI, S., Ophthalmology
SHIMADA, K., Human Pathology
SHIMAJIRI, S., Maternal Nursing
SUGAHARA, K., Anaesthesiology
SUNAGAWA, Y., Adult Nursing, Geriatric Nursing
SUNAKAWA, H., Oral and Maxillofacial Surgery
TAKASU, N., Internal Medicine
TANAKA, T., Biochemistry
TERASHIMA, S., Physiology
UZA, M., Health Care
YAMANE, N., Laboratory Medicine
YASUZUMI, F., Anatomy
YOSHII, Y., Neurosurgery

Faculty of Science:
FUKUHARA, C., Inorganic Chemistry
GINOZA, M., Condensed Matter Physics
GOYA, E., Functional Analysis
HAGIHARA, A., Forest Ecophysiology
HAYASHI, D., Structural Geology
HENNA, J., Mathematical Statistics
HIDAKA, M., Coral Biology
HIGA, M., Organic Chemistry
HIGA, T., Marine Natural Products Chemistry
HOSOYA, M., Computer Physics
IKEHARA, N., Physiology and Biochemistry
ISA, E., Calcification
ISHIJIMA, S., Atmospheric Science
KAKAZU, K., Mathematical Physics
KATO, Y., Petrology
KIMURA, M., Marine Geology
KODAKA, K., Functional Analysis
KUNIYOSHI, M., Marine Natural Products Chemistry
MAEDA, T., Algebraic Geometry
MAEHARA, R., Topology
MATAYOSHI, S., Quantum Physics
MIYAGI, Y., Molecular Spectroscopy
NAKAMURA, S., Cytology
NIKI, H., Solid State Physics
NISHISHIRAHO, T., Approximation Theory
OHMURA, Y., Condensed Matter Physics
OOMORI, T., Marine Geochemistry
SHIGA, H., Topology
SHOKITA, S., Fisheries Biology
SUZUKI, T., Number Theory
TAIRA, H., Analytical Chemistry
TAKUSHI, E., Solid State Optics
TEZUKA, M., Topology
TOKUYAMA, A., Environmental Chemistry
TOMOYOSE, T., Solid State Physics
TSUCHIYA, M., Ecology
UEHARA, T., Embryology
UEHARA, Y., Physical Chemistry
YAGASAKI, K., Solid State Physics
YAMAGUCHI, M., Coral-reef Biology
YAMAMOTO, S., Sedimentology
YAMAZATO, M., Probability Theory
YOGI, S., Organic Chemistry
YONASHIRO, K., Condensed Matter Physics

Education and Research Center for Lifelong Learning (Senbaru, Nishihara-cho, Okinawa):

DAIZEN, T., Sociology of Schooling, Sociology of Higher Education

Okinawa–Asia Research Center of Medical Science (Uehara, Nishihara-cho, Okinawa):

JINNO, Y., Molecular Genetics
TANAKU, Y.

Tropical Biosphere Research Center:

ARAMOTO, M., Terrestrial Resources
FUJIMORI, K., Cell Biology
KUMAZAWA, N., Environmental Microbiology Epidemiology
MURAI, M., Animal Ecology
NAKAMURA, M., Reproductive Biology
TAKASO, T., Plant Morphology

University Hospital (Uehara, Nishihara-cho, Okinawa):

HIROSE, Y., Hospital Information System, Knowledge-base System
HOBARA, N., Pharmacokinetic Drug Interaction, Quality Control of Medicine

ATTACHED INSTITUTES

Academic Museum (Fujukan): Senbaru, Nishihara-cho, Okinawa; Dir Y. KAWASHIMA.

Center for Cooperative Research: Senbaru, Nishihara-cho, Okinawa; Dir H. YARA.

Center for Educational Research and Practice: Senbaru, Nishihara-cho, Okinawa; Dir T. YONEMORI.

Center for Educational Research and Training of Handicapped Children: Senbaru, Nishihara-cho, Okinawa; Dir S. KAMIZONO.

Computing and Networking Center: Senbaru, Nishihara-cho, Okinawa; Dir H. MIYAGI.

Education and Research Center for Lifelong Learning: Senbaru, Nishihara-cho, Okinawa; Dir T. YOSHIZAWA.

Environmental Science Center: Senbaru, Nishihara-cho, Okinawa; Dir Y. MIYAGI.

Gene Research Center: Senbaru, Nishihara-cho, Okinawa; Dir N. KOBAMOTO.

Health Administration Center: Senbaru, Nishihara-cho, Okinawa; Dir H. TAKARA.

Institute for Animal Experiments: Uehara, Nishihara-cho, Okinawa; Dir E. ITO.

Instrumental Research Center: Senbaru, Nishihara-cho, Okinawa; Dir Y. UEHARA.

Language Center: Senbaru, Nishihara-cho, Okinawa; Dir Y. SHIMOJI.

Low Temperature Center: Senbaru, Nishihara-cho, Okinawa; Dir H. NIKI.

Okinawa–Asia Research Center of Medical Science: Uehara, Nishihara-cho, Okinawa; Dir K. NARITOMI.

Radioisotope Laboratory: Senbaru, Nishihara-cho, Okinawa; Dir E. ISA.

Research Laboratory Center: Uehara, Nishihara-cho, Okinawa; Dir M. SAKANASHI.

Tropical Biosphere Research Center: Senbaru, Nishihara-cho, Okinawa; Dir K. FUJIMORI.

Attached Stations:

Iriomote Station: Uehara Taketomi-cho, Yaeyama Okinawa; Chief T. TAKASO.

Sesoko Station: Sesoko Motobu-cho, Okinawa; Chief M. MURAI.

University Education Center: Senbaru, Nishihara-cho, Okinawa; Dir H. NAKACHI.

University Experimental Farm: Senbaru, Nishihara-cho, Okinawa; Dir Y. ISHIMINE.

University Experimental Forest: Yona, Kunigami-son, Okinawa; Dir E. HIRATA.

University Hospital: Uehara, Nishihara-cho, Okinawa; Dir K. KANAZAWA.

SAGA UNIVERSITY

Honjo-cho 1, Saga City 840
Telephone: (952) 28-8168
Fax: (952) 28-8819
Internet: www.saga-u.ac.jp
Founded 1949
Academic year: April to March
Pres.: HARUO UEHARA
Vice-Pres: GUNJI ARAMAKI, YASUHISA SHINTOMI
Dir of Gen. Admin. Bureau: TOSHIJI UEDA
Dir of Univ. Library: KEIICHI MIYAJIMA
Library of 600,341 vols
Number of teachers: 471
Number of students: 595 graduate, 5,808 undergraduate
Publication: various faculty reports and bulletins

DEANS

Faculty of Agriculture: TAKAYUKI KOJIMA
Faculty of Culture and Education: KENJI TSUJI
Faculty of Economics: KAZAFUMI KOGA
Faculty of Science and Engineering: AKIRA HASEGAWA

DIRECTORS

Analytical Research and Development Center: KEIICHI WATANABE
Coastal Bioenvironment Center: OSAMU KATO
Computer and Network Center: YOSHIAKI WATANABE
Institute of Lowland Technology: SHIGENORI HAYASHI
Institute of Ocean Energy: MASANORI MONDE
International Student Center: TATSUYA KOMOTO
Joint Research and Development Center: KOHEI ARAI
Synchrotron Light Application Center: HIROSHI OGAWA
Venture Business Laboratory: MASAYOSHI AIKAWA

SAITAMA UNIVERSITY

255 Shimo-Okubo, Sakura-ku, Saitama City, Saitama 338-8570
Telephone: (48) 858-9624
Fax: (48) 858-9675
E-mail: kokusai@gr.saitama-u.ac.jp
Internet: www.saitama-u.ac.jp
Founded 1949
Independent
Academic year: April to March
Pres.: YOSHIHIKO KAMII
Exec. Dirs: TAKASHI MARUYAMA
Exec. Dir: YASUTAKE KATO
Exec. Dir: MASAAKI KAWAHASHI
Exec. Dir: MAKOTO HORI
Library of 841,134 vols, 20,732 periodicals
Number of teachers: 557
Number of students: 9,001
Publications: *Asian Economy and Social Environment* (1 a year), *Research Report of Department of Civil and Environmental Engineering* (1 a year), *Saitama Mathematical Journal* (1 a year)

DEANS

Faculty of Economics: OSAMU ITO
Faculty of Education: KAZUTAKA YAMAGUCHI
Faculty of Liberal Arts: EIJI TAKAGI
Graduate School of Cultural Science: EIJI TAKAGI
Graduate School of Economic Science: OSAMU ITO

Graduate School of Education: KAZUTAKA YAMAGUCHI
Graduate School of Science and Engineering: HIROKI YAMAGUCHI
School of Engineering: YUICHI SATO
School of Science: SEIICHIRO NAKABAYASHI

SHIGA UNIVERSITY

1-1-1 Banba, Hikone, Shiga 522-8522
Telephone: (749) 27-1172
Fax: (749) 27-1174
E-mail: koho@biwako.shiga-u.ac.jp
Internet: www.shiga-u.ac.jp
Founded 1949
Independent
Academic year: April to March
Pres.: KENICHI MIYAMOTO
Vice-Pres: SEIJI OGURI, HIDEKI SUMIOKA
Admin. Dir: OSAHIRO TODOROKI
Librarian: TAKEO TERAYOKO
Library of 550,208 vols
Number of teachers: 315
Number of students: 3,981
Publications: *Fuzoku-shiryo-kan Kenkyu-Kiyo* (Bulletin of the Archival Museum, 1 a year), *Kenkyu-Nenpo* (Annals of Human and Social Sciences, 1 a year), *The Hikone Ronso* (economics, irregular), *Kyoiku-Gakubu Kiyo* (Memoirs of the Faculty of Education, 1 a year), *Shiga-Eibun-Gakkai-Ronbunshu* (English Studies Review, every 2 years)

DEANS

Faculty of Economics: HIROAKI KITAMURA
Faculty of Education: SHOBU SATO
Graduate School of Economics: HIROAKI KITAMURA
Graduate School of Education: SHOBU SATO

ATTACHED RESEARCH INSTITUTES

Archives Museum: Dir HIDEKI USAMI.

Center for Educational Research and Practice: 2-5-1 Hiratsu, Otsu, Shiga 520-0862; Dir TSUTOMU KUBOSHIMA.

Center for Environmental Education and Lake Science: 2-5-1 Hiratsu, Otsu, Shiga 520-0862; Dir SHUICHI ENDO.

Institute for Economic and Business Research: Dir NAOKI UMEZAWA.

Information Processing Center: Dir SABURO HORIMOTO.

Joint Research Center: Dir ISAO OGAWA.

Research Center for Lifelong Learning: 2-5-1 Hiratsu, Otsu, Shiga 520-0862; Dir OSAMU UMEDA.

SHIMANE UNIVERSITY

1060 Nishikawatsu-cho, Matsue-shi, Shimane-ken 690-8504
Telephone: (852) 32-6100
Fax: (852) 32-6019
E-mail: webinfo@jn.shimane-u.ac.jp
Internet: www.shimane-u.ac.jp
Founded 1949
Independent
Academic year: April to March
Pres.: YUICHI HONDA
Registrar: T. KAMADA
Librarian: S. WATANABE
Library of 692,000 vols
Number of teachers: 500
Number of students: 5,550

DEANS

Faculty of Education: M. YAMASHITA
Faculty of Law and Literature: Y. MATSUI
Faculty of Life and Environmental Sciences: H. YAMAMOTO

Faculty of Science and Engineering: A. TAKUNA

SHINSHU UNIVERSITY

Asahi 3-1-1, Matsumoto, 390-8621 Nagano-ken

Telephone: (263) 35-4600
Fax: (263) 36-6769
E-mail: shinhp@shinshu-u.ac.jp
Internet: www.shinshu-u.ac.jp

Founded 1949
Independent

Pres.: KIYOHITO YAMASAWA
Number of teachers: 1,150 full-time
Number of students: 11,446 (9,364 undergraduates, 2,082 in Graduate School)

DEANS

Faculty of Agriculture: SOICHIRO NAKAMURA
Faculty of Arts: HIDEO WATANABE
Faculty of Economics: JOJI TOKUI
Faculty of Education: YOSHINAO HIRANO
Faculty of Engineering: MASAYUKI OKAMOTO
Faculty of Science: MITSUO TAKEDA
Faculty of Textile Science and Technology: KUNIHIRO HAMADA
School of Medicine: KEISHI KUBO

SHIZUOKA UNIVERSITY

Ohya 836, Shizuoka-shi 422-8529

Telephone: (54) 238-4407
Fax: (54) 237-0089
E-mail: koho@gene1.adb.shizuoka.ac.jp
Internet: www.shizuoka.ac.jp

Founded 1949
Independent

Pres.: YOSHIMITSU AMAGISHI
Vice-Pres: NOBUYUKI ARAKI, HIROKAZU NAKAI
Dir-Gen.: SHIGENOBU MORI
Dir of Univ. Library: KIMIO BAMBA

Number of teachers: 744 full-time
Number of students: 11,112

DEANS

Faculty of Agriculture: KIYOSHI OKAWA
Faculty of Education: SHOJI KANAI
Faculty of Engineering: HITOSHI ISHII
Faculty of Humanities and Social Sciences: YOSHIHIKO YAMAMOTO
Faculty of Information Sciences: HIROYUKI TOKUYAMA
Faculty of Science: KATSUTOSHI ISHIKAWA

DIRECTORS

Center for Education and Research Lifelong Learning: KINJI TAKI
Center for Joint Research: NAOMICHI OKA-MOTO
Information Processing Center: NAOKAZU YAMAKI
Institute for Genetic Research and Biotechnology: KOICHI YOSHINAGA
International Student Center: TAKASHIGE HONDA
Research Institute of Electronics: KENZO WATANABE
Satellite Venture Business Laboratory: NOR-IHIRO INAGAKI

TOHOKU UNIVERSITY

1-1 Katahira, 2-chome, Aoba-ku, Sendai 980-8577

Telephone: (22) 217-4844
Fax: (22) 217-4846
E-mail: kokusai@bureau.tohoku.ac.jp
Internet: www.tohoku.ac.jp/english

Founded 1907
Public control
Languages of instruction: English, Japanese
Academic year: April to March

Pres.: AKIHISA INOUE
Vice-Pres. for Management of Univ. Hospital: SUSUMU SATOMI
Exec. Vice-Pres. for General Affairs and Dir, Office of the Pres.: YUKIHISA KITAMURA
Exec. Vice-Pres. for Education and Information System: YOSHIAKI NEMOTO
Exec. Vice-Pres. for Financial Affairs: TOSHIYA UEKI
Exec. Vice-Pres. for Human Resources and Personnel Admin., Campus Environment and Gender Equality: MASAMICHI KONO
Exec. Vice Pres. for Public Relations, Alumni Assoc., and Academic Information: KEIICHI NOE
Exec. Vice-Pres. for Research and Environmental Security: TOSHIO IJIMA
Dir of Main Library: KEIICHI NOE
Vice Pres. for Legal Affairs: EIJI HYODO
Exec. Vice-Pres.: MASAHARU HINO
Exec. Vice-Pres. for Industry–Univ. Cooperation: HIROSHI KAZUI

Library: see Libraries and Archives
Number of teachers: 2,892
Number of students: 18,167

Publications: *Annals of nanoBME* (1 a year), *Annual Research Bulletin of the Graduate School of Pharmaceutical Sciences* (1 a year), *Bulletin of the Tohoku University Museum* (1 a year), *CYRIC annual report / Cyclotron and Radioisotope Center, Tohoku University* (1 a year), *Discussion paper / Tohoku Management & Accounting Research Group. Department of Economics. Tohoku University* (irregular), *Explorations in English linguistics: EEL/Tohoku University. Department of English Linguistics* (1 a year), *Graduate School of Engineering and Faculty of Engineering* (1 a year), *Interdisciplinary Information Science* (2 a year), *Journal of Integrated Field Science* (1 a year), *Northeast Asian Study* (1 a year), *Reports of the Institute of Fluid Science* (1 a year), *Research Report of the Laboratory of Nuclear Science* (1 a year), *The science reports of the Tohoku University* (2 a year), *Tohoku Journal of Agricultural Research* (2 a year), *Tohoku Journal of Experimental Medicine* (12 a year), *Tohoku Mathematical Journal. Second Series* (4 a year), *Tohoku Mathematical Publications* (irregular), *Tohoku Psychologica Folia* (1 a year)

DEANS

Graduate School of Biomedical Engineering: HIDETOSHI MATSUKI
Graduate School of Educational Informatics, Educational Division: SHINICHI WATABE
Graduate School of Educational Informatics, Research Division: SHINICHI WATABE
Graduate School of Environmental Studies: KAZUYUKI TOHJI
Graduate School of Information Sciences: MICHITAKA KAMEYAMA
Graduate School of International Cultural Studies: FUMIO KOBAYASHI
Graduate School of Life Sciences: HIDEYUKI TAKAHASHI
Graduate School of Agricultural Science and Faculty of Agriculture: TOMOYUKI YAMAYA
Graduate School and Faculty of Arts and Letters: KEN-ICHI OHBUCHI
Graduate School and School of Dentistry: KEIICHI SASAKI
Graduate School of Economics and Management and Faculty of Economics: SEIICHI OHTAKI
Graduate School and Faculty of Education: EIICHI MIYAKOSHI
Graduate School and School of Engineering: MASARU UCHIYAMA
Graduate School and School of Law: NORIKO MIZUNO

Graduate School and School of Medicine: MASAYUKI YAMAMOTO
Graduate School of Pharmaceutical Sciences and Faculty of Pharmacy and Pharmaceutical Sciences: YOSHITERU OSHIMA
Graduate School and Faculty of Science: HIROSHI FUKUMURA

PROFESSORS

Botanical Gardens (12-2 Kawauchi, Aoba-ku, Sendai 980-0862; tel. (22) 795-6760; fax (22) 795-6766; e-mail garden-tu@biology.tohoku.ac.jp; internet www.biology.tohoku.ac.jp/garden):

SUZUKI, M., Plant Anatomy

Center for Interdisciplinary Research (Aoba, Aramaki, Aoba-ku, Sendai 980-8578; tel. (22) 795-5757; fax (22) 795-5756; e-mail office@cir.tohoku.ac.jp; internet www.cir.tohoku.ac.jp):

KASUYA, A., Materials Science
SUEMITSU, M., Materials Science
YAMANE, H., Solid-state Chemistry
YAO, T., Department of Applied Physics

Center for Low-temperature Science (2-1-1 Katahira, Aoba-ku, Sendai 980-8577; tel. (22) 215-2181; fax (22) 215-2184; e-mail ltcenter@imr.tohoku.ac.jp; internet www.clts.tohoku.ac.jp):

AOKI, H., Low-temperature Physics

Center for North-east Asian Studies (41 Kawauchi, Aoba-ku, Sendai 980-8576; tel. (22) 795-6009; fax (22) 795-6010; e-mail asiajimu@cneas.tohoku.ac.jp; internet www.cneas.tohoku.ac.jp/index-j.html):

HIRAKAWA, A., Political Economy
ISOBE, A., Cultural Studies
KIKUCHI, E., Regional Ecosystem Studies
KUDOH, J., North Asian Societies
KURIBAYASHI, H., Linguistic Studies
MIYAMOTO, K., Socio-economic Studies on the Environment
SATO, M., Environmental and Resources Survey
SEGAWA, M., Social Ecology
TANIGUCHI, H., Geochemistry
YAMADA, K., Social Structure

Center for the Advancement of Higher Education (41 Kawauchi, Aoba-ku, Sendai 980-8576; tel. (22) 795-7551; fax (22) 795-7647; e-mail center@high-edu.tohoku.ac.jp; internet www.he.tohoku.ac.jp/index.html):

HIDA, W., Respiratory Medicine
HORIE, K., Linguistic Typology and Japanese–Korean Contrastive Linguistics
NAWATA, T., Applied Research Section
SAITOH, K., Applied Research Section
SEKIUCHI, T., Basic Research Section
SHIZUYA, H., Theoretical Computer Science
SUZUKI, T., Applied Clinical Psychology
YOSHIMOTO, K., Formal Linguistics, Cognitive Science

Cyclotron Radioisotope Center (6-3 Aoba, Aramaki, Aoba-ku, Sendai 980-8578; tel. (22) 795-7800; fax (22) 795-7997; e-mail admin@cyric.tohoku.ac.jp; internet www.cyric.tohoku.ac.jp):

BABA, M., Radiation Physics
ITOH, M., Nuclear Medicine
IWATA, R., Radioisotope Production and Radiopharmaceutical Chemistry
OKAMURA, H., Nuclear Physics

Graduate School of Educational Informatics, Research Division (Kawauchi, Aoba-ku, Sendai 980-8576; tel. (22) 795-6103; fax (22) 795-6110; internet www.ei.tohoku.ac.jp):

HAGIHARA, T., Theory of an Open University
IWASAKI, S., Information Technology Educational Architecture
MURAKI, E., Information Technology Education System Theory

WATABE, S., Information Technology Cognitive Science

Graduate School of Environmental Studies (Aobayama, Sendai 980-8579; tel. (22) 795-4504; fax (22) 795-4309; e-mail s-ara@bureau.tohoku.ac.jp; internet www.kankyo.tohoku.ac.jp):

ARAI, K., Environmental Chemical Engineering
ASANO, Y., East Asian Philosophy
CHIDA, T., Geoenvironmental Remediation
ENOMOTO, H., Environmental Processing for Energy Resources
HATTORI, T., Environmentally Benign Sythesis
HOSHINO, H., Analytical Environmental Chemistry
ISHIDA, H., Environmentally Harmonized Materials
KAYA, K., Environmental Ecology Design
KIMUTA, Y., Middle Eastern and Central Asian Studies
MARUYAMA, K., Structural Materials for Eco-friendly Systems
MATSUE, T., Environmental Bioengineering
MATSUKI, K., Environmental Geomechanics
NAGASAKA, T., Environmental Impact Assessment
NARISAWA, M., Korean Ethnoculture
NIITSUMA, H., Earth System Monitoring and Instrumentation
SAITO, T., Urban Environment
SAKAIDA, K., Physical Environmental Geography
SATAKE, M., International Economic and Environmental Studies
TAKAHASHI, H., Earth Exploitation Environmental Studies
TANIGUCHI, S., Materials Process for Circulatory Society
TOHJI, K., Design of Eco-nanomaterials
TSUCHIYA, N., Environmental Geochemistry
YAMASAKI, N., Environmental Hydrothermal Processes
YOSHIOKA, T., Recycling Chemistry

Graduate School of Information Sciences (Aoba, Aramaki, Aobu-ku, Sendai 980-8579; tel. (22) 795-5813; fax (22) 795-5815; e-mail is-syom@bureau.tohoku.ac.jp; internet www.is.tohoku.ac.jp):

ADACHI, Y., Media and Semiotics
AKAMATSU, T., Road Transportation and Traffic
ANDO, A., Econometric System Analysis
AOKI, T., Computer Structures
DEGUCHI, K., Image Analysis
EBISAWA, H., Physical Fluctuomatics
FUKUCHI, H., Verbal Text Analysis
HASHIMOTO, K., Intelligent Control Systems
HIAI, F., Mathematical Systems Analysis III
HIDA, W., Health Informatics
HORIGUCHI, S., Firmware Science
INAMURA, H., International and Intermodal Transportation
ITOI, K., Information Biology
IWASAKI, S., Cognitive Psychology
KAMEYAMA, M., Intelligent Integrated Systems
KANEKO, M., Mathematical Structures II
KATO, N., Information Technology
KINOSHITA, T., Communication Software Science
KOBAYASHI, H., Ultra-high-speed Information Processing Algorithm
KOBAYASHI, K., Theory of Social Structure and Change
KOBAYASHI, N., Foundations of Software Science
KUDOH, J., Environmental Informatics
MARUOKA, A., Computation Theory

MORISUGI, H., Regional and Urban Planning
MUNEMASA, A., Mathematical Structures I
NAKAJIMA, K., Brain Function Integration
NAKAMURA, T., Computer Architecture
NAKAO, M., Biomodelling
NEMOTO, Y., Communication Science
NISHIZEKI, T., Algorithm Theory
NUMASAWA, J., Information Storage Systems
OBATA, N., Mathematical Systems Analysis II
OBAYASHI, S., Fusion Flow Informatics
OHORI, A., Logic for Information Science
OZAWA, M., Mathematical Structures III
SASAKI, K., Socio-economic Analysis of Urban Systems
SASOH, S., Flow System Informatics
SEKIMOTO, E., Media and Culture
SHINOHARA, A., System Information Sciences
SHIOIRI, S., Visual Recognition and Systems
SHIRATORI, N., Communication Theory
SHIZUYA, H., Information Security
SONE, H., Information Network Systems
SUNOUCHI, C., Mathematical Structures IV
SUZUKI, Y., Acoustic Information
TADOKORO, S., Human–Robot Informatics
TAKEUCHI, O., Philosophy of Human Information
TOKUYAMA, T., Design and Analysis of Information Systems
TOYAMA, Y., Logic for Information Science
TSUBOKAWA, H., Life Fluctuomatics
URAKAWA, H., Mathematical Systems Analysis I
YAMAMOTO, H., Political Analysis of the Information Society
YAMAMOTO, S., Mathematical Modelling

Graduate School of International Cultural Studies (Kawauchi, Aoba-ku, Sendai 980-8576; tel. (22) 795-7541; fax (22) 795-7583; internet www.intcul.tohoku.ac.jp):

ASAKAWA, T., Language System
ASANO, Y., Asian Cultural Studies
FUJITA, M., Comparative Cultural Studies
FUJIWARA, I., Comparative Cultural Studies
HOLDEN, T., Multicultural Societies
ICHIKAWA, M., Cultural Uses of Language
IGAWA, M., American Studies
ISHIHATA, N., Cultural Uses of Language
ISHIKAWA, H., Asian Cultural Studies
KAWAHIRA, Y., Language Generation
KITAGAWA, S., Islamic Areas and Cultural Studies
KOBAYASHI, F., European Cultural Studies
KUSUDA, I., Language Systems
NUNOTA, T., European Cultural Studies
SASAKI, K., Linguistic Communication
SATO, K., Language Systems
SATO, S., Language Generation
SHIGAKI, M., Language Education
SUZUKI, M., Cultural Uses of Language
TAKAHASHI, R., Science, Technology and Environment
TAKENAKA, K., American Studies
TANAKA, T., Multicultural Societies
TATSUYOSHI, T., Monetary Economics
YAMAGUCHI, N., Linguistic Function
YAMASHITA, H., Multicultural Societies
YOKOKAWA, K., International Economic Relations
YONEYAMA, C., Linguistic Function

Graduate School of Life Sciences (tel. (22) 795-5702; fax (22) 795-5704; internet www.lifesci.tohoku.ac.jp/index.html):

ARIMOTO, H., Biostructrual Chemistry
HIGASHITANI, A., Genomic Reproductive Biology
IDE, H., Organogenesis
IIJIMA, T., Systems Neuroscience
KATOW, H., Developmental Biology
KAWATA, M., Evolutionary Biology

KUMAGAI, T., Genetic Ecology in Critical Environments
KUSANO, T., Plant Molecular and Cellular Biology
MAEDA, Y., Control of Growth and Differentiation
MINAMISAWA, K., Environmental Microbiology
MIZUNO, K., Molecular Cell Biology
MURAMOTO, K., Functional Biomolecules
NAKAMURA, H., Molecular Neurobiology
NISHITANI, K., Plant Physiology
OHSHIMA, Y., Bio-organic Chemistry
SASAKI, M., Biostructural Chemistry
SOGAWA, K., Gene Regulation
TAKAGI, T., Molecular Diversity
TAKAHASHI, H., Space and Adaptation Biology
TSUDA, M., Microbial Genetics
URABE, J., Community and Ecosystem Ecology
WATANABE, M., Plant Reproductive Biology
WATANABE, T., Organella Research
YAMAMOTO, D., Neurogenetics
YAMAMOTO, K., Molecular Genetics
YAWO, H., Molecular and Cellular Neurosciences

Information Synergy Center (6-3 Aoba, Aramaki, Aoba-ku, Sendai 980-8578; tel. (22) 795-3407; fax (22) 795-6098; internet www.isc.tohoku.ac.jp):

KINOSHITA, T., Knowledge Engineering
KOBAYASHI, H., High-performance Computer Systems
SONE, H., Communication Networks
YOSHIZAWA, M., Communication Networks

Institute for Materials Research (2-1-1 Katahira, Aoba-ku, Sendai 980-8577; tel. (22) 215-2181; fax (22) 215-2184; e-mail imr-som@imr.tohoku.ac.jp; internet www.imr.tohoku.ac.jp):

CHEN, M., International Frontier Center for Advanced Materials
FUKUYAMA, H., International Frontier Center for Advanced Materials
GOTO, T., Multifunctional Materials Science
HASEGAWA, M., Irradiation Effects in Nuclear and Related Materials
INOUE, A., Non-equilibrium Materials
IWASA, Y., Low-temperature Condensed State Physics
KAWASAKI, M., Superstructured Thin Film Chemistry
KAWAZOE, Y., Materials Design by Computer Simulation
KOBAYASHI, N., Low-temperature Physics
MAEKAWA, S., Theory of Solid State Physics
MATSUI, H., Nuclear Materials Engineering
MATSUOKA, T., Advanced Electronic Materials
NAKAJIMA, K., Crystal Physics
NOJIRI, H., Magnetism
SAKURAI, T., Surface and Interface Research
SATO, Y., Non-equilibrium Materials
SHIKAMA, T., Nuclear Materials Science
SHIOKAWA, Y., Radiochemistry of Metals
TAKANASHI, K., Magnetic Materials
UDA, S., Crystal Chemistry
WAGATSUMA, K., Analytical Science
WATANABE, K., High Field Laboratory for Superconducting Materials
YAMADA, K., Neuron and Gamma-ray Spectroscopy on Condensed Matters

Institute of Development, Ageing and Cancer (4-1 Seiryo-machi, Aoba-ku, Sendai 980-8575; tel. (22) 717-8443; fax (22) 717-8452):

FUKUDA, H., Radiation Medicine
FUKUMOTO, M., Pathology
ISHIOKA, C., General Internal Medicine, Gastroentorology, Molecular Biology

KONDO, T., Thoracic Surgery, Lung Cancer, Lung Transplantation
MATSUI, Y., Developmental Biology
NUKIWA, T., Chest Physician, Molecular Biology
OBINATA, M., Cell Biology
OGURA, T., Developmental Neurobiology, Developmental Biology, Molecular Biology
SATAKE, M., Molecular Biology
SATO, Y., Vascular Biology
TAKAI, T., Experimental Immunology
TAMURA, S., Biochemistry and Molecular Biology
TSUCHIYA, S., Paediatrics
YAMAMOTO, T., Molceular Biology, General Medical Chemistry, Pathological Medical Chemistry
YAMBE, T., Artificial Organs, Cardiovascular Medicine
YASUI, A., DNA Repair and Ageing

Institute of Fluid Science (2-1-1 Katahira, Aoba-ku, Sendai 980-8577; tel. (22) 795-5302; fax (22) 795-5311; e-mail shomu@ifs.tohoku .ac.jp; internet www.ifs.tohoku.ac.jp):

FUJISHIRO, I., Complex Dynamics
HAYASE, T., Super-real-time Medical Engineering
HAYASHI, K., Molten Geomaterials
IKOHAGI, T., Complex Flow Systems
INOUE, O., Advanced Computational Fluid Dynamics
ISHIMOTO, J., Reality-coupled Computation
KOBAYASHI, H., Complex Dynamics
KOHAMA, Y., Ultimate Flow Environment
MARUYAMA, S., Heat Transfer Control
NANBU, K., Gaseous Electronics
NISHIYAMA, H., Electromagnetic Intelligent Fluids
OBAYASHI, S., Integrated Fluid Informatics
OHARA, T., Molecular Heat Transfer
OHIRA, K., Cryogenic Flow
OTA, M., Biofluids Control
QIU, J., Intelligent Systems
SAMUKAWA, S., Intelligent Nano-process
SASOH, A., Ultra-high Enthalpy Flow
SUN, M., Interdisciplinary Shockwave Research
TAKAGI, T., Advanced Systems and Materials Evaluation
TAKEUCHI, S., Advanced Systems
TOKUYAMA, M., Theoretical Fluid Dynamics
TSUCHIYAMA, T., Advanced Technology for Environment and Energy

Institute of Multidisciplinary Research for Advanced Materials (2-1-1 Katahira, Aoba-ku, Sendai 980-8577; tel. (22) 795-5202; fax (22) 795-5211; internet www.tagen.tohoku.ac .jp):

AJIRI, T., Organic Resources Chemistry
ARIMA, T., Strongly Correlated Electron Systems
HARADA, N., Chemistry of Molecular Chirality
ISSHIKI, M., High Purity Materials
ITAGAKI, K., Nonferrous Chemical Metallurgy
ITO, O., Photochemistry
KAINO, T., Materials Chemistry
KAKIHANA, M., Chemical Engineering
KASAI, E., Iron and Steel Engineering
KAWAMURA, J., Solid State Ion Physics
KITAKAMI, O., Magnetic Materials and Devices
KITAMURA, S., Ferrous Process Metallurgy
KOMEDA, T., Molecular Chemistry
KONO, S., Surface Physics
KOYAMA, T., Biochemistry
KURIHARA, K., Surface Forces
KYOTANI, T., Applied Chemistry
MIYASHITA, T., Materials Chemistry
MIZUSAKI, J., Solid State Ion Devices
MURAMATSU, A., Solid State Chemistry
NAKAMURA, T., Physical Process Engineering

NAKANISHI, H., Materials Chemistry
NODA, Y., Electronic Properties of Solids
OKA, Y., Solid State Spectroscopy
OTSUKA, Y., Catalytic and Chemical Processes
SAITO, F., Chemical Engineering, Powder Technology
SAITO, M., Chemistry
SATO, S., Metal Industrial Engineering
SATO, T., Inorganic Materials Chemistry
SHIMIZU, T., Bio-inorganic Chemistry
SINDO, D., Atomic Scale Morphology Analysis
SODEOKA, M., Chemistry
SUITO, H., Physico-chemical Metallurgy
SUZUKI, S., Physical Metallurgy
TERAUCHI, M., Electronic Diffraction and Spectrology
TERO, S., Physical Chemistry
TOCHIYAMA, O., Atomic Energy Engineering
TSAI, A., Materials Control
UDAGAWA, Y., X-ray Physics
UEDA, K., Molecular Physics
UMETSU, Y., Aqueous Processing, Physical Chemistry of Metals
YAMAMOTO, M., Soft X-ray Microscopy
YAMAUCHI, S., Physical Chemistry
YANAGIHARA, M., Soft X-ray Microscopy
YOKOYAMA, T., Chemical Engineering

International Exchange Center (Kawauchi, Aoba-ku, Sendai 980-8576; tel. (22) 795-7776; fax (22) 795-7826; e-mail ryugaku@bureau .tohoku.ac.jp; internet www.insc.tohoku.ac .jp):

HORIE, K., Linguistic Typology and Japanese–Korean Comparative Linguistics
KASUKABE, Y., Development of the Short-term Student Exchange Programme
SATO, S., Japanese Language Teaching
SHIGENO, Y., Technologies of Resource and Material Processing
UEHARA, S., Linguistics and Phonetics
YOSHIMOTO, K., Formal Syntax and Japanese Intonation

New Industry Creation Hatchery Center (Aoba 6-6-10, Aramaki, Aoba-ku, Sendai 980-8579; tel. (22) 795-7105; fax (22) 795-7985; e-mail liaison-office@niche.tohoku.ac .jp; internet www.niche.tohoku.ac.jp):

ICHIE, M., Music and Acoustical Medicine
ISHIDA, K., Advanced Materials based on Computer-aided Design and Microstructural Control
KAWASHIMA, R., Functional Brain Imaging
KOHNO, M., Research and Development on Genomics-protemics Technology and Free Radical Control
MIYAMOTO, A., Quantum Design of Nanofunctional Materials
OHMI, T., DIIN (New Intelligence for IC Differentiation) Project
TAKAHASHI, M., Development of Self-assembled Monodisperse Nano-particles, Thin-film Media for Terabit Recording
TERASAKI, T., Drug Discovery and Development
UEMATSU, Y., Development of Technology for Preserving the Environment and Reducing Wind-induced Disaster
YAMANAKA, K., Advanced Ultrasonic Non-destructive Evaluation and Sensing
YOKOYAMA, H., Ultrabroadband Coherent Light Sources

Research Institute of Electrical Communication (2-1-1 Katahira, Aobaku, Sendai 980-8577; tel. (22) 795-5420; fax (22) 795-5426; e-mail shomu@jm.riec.tohoku.ac.jp; internet www.riec.tohoku.ac.jp/index-j.html):

AOI, H., Information Storage Systems
CHO, Y., Dialectic Nano-devices
EDAMATSU, K., Quantum Optics and Optical Spectroscopy

HANYU, T., Next-generation VLSI Computing
ITO, H., Quantum and Optoelectronics
MASUOKA, F., Electron Devices
MATSUOKA, H., Advanced Practical Information Technology Development
MIZUNO, K., Electron Devices
MURAOKA, H., Information Recording Devices
MUROTA, J., Atomically Controlled Processing
NAKAJIMA, K., Intelligent Integrated Systems
NAKAMURA, Y., Information Storage Engineering
NAKAZAWA, M., Ultra High Speed Optical Communication
NIWANO, M., Molecular Electronics, Silico-bioelectronics
NUMAZAWA, J., Video Storage Systems
OHNO, H., Compound Semiconductors, Quantum Structures and Spintronics
OHORI, A., Computer Science
OTSUJI, H., Ultrafast and Ultrabroadband Electronics
SHIRAI, M., Advanced Functional Materials
SHIRATORI, N., Information Communication Systems
SIOIRI, S., Visual Cognition and Systems
SUGIURA, A., Electromagnetic Compatibility
SUZUKI, Y., Acoustic Signal Processing
TAKAGI, T., Wireless Mobile Systems
TANEICHI, M., Advanced Practical Information Technology Development
TOYAMA, Y., Computer Science
TSUBOUCHI, K., Wireless Internet System, Circuits and Devices
YANO, M., Informatics in Biological Systems

School and Graduate School of Arts and Letters (Kawanchi, Aoba-ku, Sendai 980-8576; tel. (22) 795-6003; fax (22) 795-6086; e-mail art-syom@bureau.tohoku.ac.jp; internet www.sal.tohoku.ac.jp/index-j.html):

ABE, H., Western Literature and Languages
AKOSHIMA, K., Japanese History and Archaeology
CHIGUSA, S., Linguistics
GOTO, H., Linguistics
GOTO, T., Indology and History of Indian Buddhism
GYOBA, J., Psychology
HANATO, M., Sinology
HARA, E., Western Literature and Languages
HARA, J., Behavioural Science
HARA, K., Western Literature and Languages
HASEGAWA, K., Sociology
IMAIZUMI, T., Japanese History and Archaeology
KANEKO, Y., Western Literature and Languages
KAWAI, Y., Oriental History
KOBAYASHI, T., Japanese Linguistics
KUMAMOTO, T., Oriental History
MASAMURA, T., Sociology
MATSUMOTO, N., European History
MIURA, S., Sinology
MORIMOTO, K., Western Literature and Languages
NAKAOKA, R., History of Fine Arts
NAKAJIMA, R., Sinology
NAKAMURA, M., Western Literature and Languages
NIHEI, M., Japanese Literature and History of Japanese Philosophy
NIHEI, Y., Psychology
NOE, K., Philosophy and Ethics
NUMAZAKI, I., Cultural Anthropology and Science of Religions
OHBUCHI, K., Psychology

OHTO, O., Japanese History and Archaeology
ONO, Y., European History
OZAKI, A., History of Fine Arts
SAITA, I., Applied Japanese Linguistics
SAITO, M., Japanese Linguistics
SAITO, Y., Western Literature and Languages
SAKURAI, M., Indology and History of Indian Buddhism
SATO, H., Japanese Literature and History of Japanese Philosophy
SATO, M., European History
SATO, N., Japanese Literature and History of Japanese Philosophy
SATO, Y., Behavioural Science
SHIMA, M., Cultural Anthropology and Science of Religions
SHIMIZU, T., Philosophy and Ethics
SHINO, K., Philosophy and Ethics
SUTO, T., Japanese History and Archaeology
SUZUKI, A., Applied Japanese Linguistics
SUZUKI, I., Cultural Anthropology and Science of Religions
TAKAGI, K., Sociology
UMINO, M., Behavioural Science
YOSHIHARA, N., Sociology
ZAKOTA, Y., Philosophy and Ethics

School and Graduate School of Dentistry (4-1 Seiryo-machi, Aoba-ku, Sendai 980-8575; tel. (22) 717-8244; fax (22) 717-8279; e-mail den-syom@bureau.tohoku.ac.jp; internet www.ddh.tohoku.ac.jp/index.html):

ECHIGO, S., Oral Surgery
HAYASHI, H., Oral Physiology
IGARASHI, K., Oral Dysfunction Science
KAWAMURA, H., Maxillofacial Surgery
KIKUCHI, M., Oral and Craniofacial Anatomy
KIMURA, K., Fixed Prosthodontics
KOMATSU, M., Operative Dentistry
KOSEKI, T., Preventive Dentistry
MAYANAGI, H., Paediatric Dentistry
OKUNO, O., Dental Biomaterials
ŌOYA, K., Oral Pathology
OSAKA, K., International Oral Health
SASAKI, K., Advanced Prosthetic Dentistry
SASANO, T., Oral Diagnosis and Radiology
SASANO, Y., Craniofacial Development and Regeneration
SHIMAUCHI, H., Periodontology and Endodontology
SHINODA, H., Dental Pharmacology
SUGAWARA, S., Oral Molecular Bioregulation
SUZUKI, O., Craniofacial Function Engineering
TAKADA, H., Oral Microbiology
TAKAHASHI, M., Dento-oral Anaesthesiology
TAKAHASHI, N., Oral Ecology and Biochemistry
WATANABE, M., Ageing and Geriatric Dentistry

School and Graduate School of Economics and Management (27-1 Kawauchi, Aoba-ku, Sendai 980-8576; tel. (22) 795-6263; fax (22) 795-6270; e-mail webmaster@econ.tohoku.ac.jp; internet www.econ.tohoku.ac.jp/indexj.html):

AKITA, J., International Finance
AOKI, K., Comparative Economic Systems
AOKI, M., Cost Accounting
DOLAN, D., Business Communication
FUJII, T., International Accounting
FUKAI, T., Auditing
HASEBE, H., History of Japanese Economy
HAYASHIYAMA, Y., Environmental Economics
HINO, S., Modern Political Economy
HIRAMOTO, A., Japanese Economy
HOSOYA, Y., Econometrics
IPPOSHI, N., Accounting
ITO, T., Information Systems Management

KAMOIKE, O., Money and Banking
KANAZAKI, Y., Financial Management
KOHNO, D., Business Administration
KOHNO, S., Personnel Administration
KWEON, K. C., Research and Development Management
MASUDA, S., Regional Planning
MIYAKE, M., Macroeconomics
MORI, K., Political Economy
NAKAGAWA, T., International Management
NISHIZAWA, A., Policies for New Venture Creation
NOMURA, M., Social Policy
ODONAKA, N., Socio-intellectual History
OMURA, I., Political Economy
OTAKI, S., Business Policy
OTOMASA, S., Corporate Governance
SARUWATARI, K., Comparative Business Studies
SATO, H., International Economics
SEKITA, Y., Welfare Information System
SHIMOMURA, H., Tax Law
SUZUKI, T., Business History
TANIGUCHI, A., Types of Business Enterprise
TERUI, N., Marketing
TSUGE, N., Agricultural Economics
TSUKUDA, Y., Business Statistics
YASUDA, K., Management Information System

School and Graduate School of Education (Kawauchi, Aoba-ku, Sendai 980-8576; tel. (22) 795-6103; fax (22) 795-6110; internet www.sed.tohoku.ac.jp/index-j.html):

AKINAGA, Y., Sociology of Education
ARAI, K., Educational Policy and Planning
HASEGAWA, K., Clinical Psychology
HONGO, K., Psychology and Disability
HOSOKAWA, T., Developmental Disorders
IKUTA, K., Philosophy of Education
KAJIYAMA, M., History of Japanese Education
KATO, M., History of Foreign Education
KAWASUMI, R., Compensation and Welfare of Disabilities
KIKUCHI, T., Developmental Psychology
KOIZUMI, S., Educational Process Studies
MIYAKOSHI, E., Comparative Educational Systems
MIZUHARA, K., Curriculum Studies
NAKAZIMA, N., Socio-cultural Study of Sport
OMOMO, T., Educational Administration
ONODERA, T., Educational Psychology
TAKAHASHI, M., Adult Education
UENO, T., Clinical Community Psychology
UNO, S., Educational Psychology

School and Graduate School of Engineering (6-6-04, Aramaki Aza Aoba, Aoba-ku, Sendai 980-8579; tel. (22) 795-5817; fax (22) 795-5824; e-mail dean@eng.tohoku.ac.jp; internet www.eng.tohoku.ac.jp):

ABE, H., Urban Design
ABE, K., Fusion Reactor Engineering
ADACHI, F., Communication Systems
ANZAI, K., Casting and Advanced Solidification Processing
ASAI, H., Experimental Aerodynamics
ASAI, K., Solid State Physical Chemistry
ASO, H., Network Theory
CHONAN, S., Biomechatronics
EMURA, T., Intelligent Mechatronics
ESASHI, M., Micromachines
FUKINISHI, Y., Fluid Mechanics
FUKUNAGA, H., Space Structures
GALSTER, W., Energy Physics Engineering
HAMAJIMA, T., Applied Power Systems Engineering
HANE, K., Mechanoptics Design
HARA, N., Materials Electrochemistry
HARAYAMA, Y., Technology Policy
HASHIDA, T., Complex Fracture Systems Design
HASHIZUME, H., Fusion and Electromagnetic Engineering

HATAKEYAMA, R., Basic Plasma Engineering
HINO, M., Ferrous Process Metallurgy
HOKKIRIGAWA, K., Intelligent Systems Engineering
HOSHIMIYA, N., Biomedical Electronics
ICHINOKURA, O., Power Electronics
IGUCHI, Y., Socio-engineering
IIBUCHI, K., History of Architecture
IKEDA, K., Mathematical Systems Design
IMAMURA, F., Tsunami Engineering
INOMATA, H., Supercritical Fluid Technology
INOMATA, K., Spin-electronics Materials
INOUE, K., Machine Design
INOUE, N., Structural Engineering
INOUE, Y., Applied Organic Synthesis
INUTAKE, M., Magneto-Plasma-Dynamics Engineering
ISHIDA, K., Computational Microstructure Design
ISHII, K., Radiation Science and Engineering
ITAYA, K., Electrochemical Science and Technology
ITO, T., Solid State Electronics
IWAKUMA, T., Structural Mechanics
IWASAKI, S., Engineers Education and Educational Informatics
KAJITANI, T., Applied X-ray and Neutron Spectroscopy
KANAI, H., Electronic Control Engineering
KANNO, M., Architectural Planning
KATO, K., Tribology
KAWAMATA, M., Intelligent Electronic Circuits
KAWASAKI, A., Micro-power Processing and Systems
KAZAMA, M., Geotechnical Engineering
KISHINO, Y., Mechanics of Materials
KIYONO, S., Nanosystem Engineering
KOIKE, J., Device Reliability Science and Engineering
KOIKE, Y., Low Temperature Physics and Superconductivity Physics
KOKAWA, H., Interface Science and Engineering of Joining
KONNO, M., Material Processing
KOSUGE, K., System Robotics
KOYANAGI, M., Advanced Bio-nano Devices
KUMAGAI, I., Protein Technology
KURIYAGAWA, T., Nanoprecision Mechanical Fabrication
KUSHIBIKI, J., Instrumentation and Ultrasonic Micro-spectroscopy Network
KUWANO, H., Informative Nanotechnology
MAKINO, S., Intelligent Communication Engineering
MANO, A., Disaster Potential Research
MASUYA, G., Aerospace Systems
MATSUBARA, F., Applied Mathematical Physics
MATSUKI, H., Bio-electromagnetics
MATSUMOTO, S., Process Control
MIHASHI, H., Building and Materials Science
MIMURA, H., Nuclear Energy Flow, Environmental Engineering
MIURA, H., Fracture Control of Microstructures
MIURA, T., Energy Process Engineering
MIYAZAKI, T., Magnetism and Magnetic Materials
MIZOGUCHI, T., Environmental Chemistry
MOTOSAKA, M., Earthquake Engineering
NAGAHIRA, A., Management of Technology
NAKAHASHI, K., Aerodynamic Design
NAKAMURA, K., Acoustic Physics Engineering
NISHIMURA, O., Ecological Engineering
NISHIZAWA, M., Biomicromachine Engineering
NISINO, T., Applied Life Chemistry
NOIKE, T., Environmental Protection Engineering
NITTA, J., Materials Quantum Science

OHMI, T., Urban Planning and Analysis
OHTSU, H., Applied Nuclear Medical Engineering
OKADA, M., Energy Materials
OMURA, T., Water Quality Engineering
OOJI, A., Energy Conversion Technology
OTA, T., Control of Heat Transfer
OUCHI, C., Biomedical Materials
OYAMA, Y., Opto-electronic Materials
SAHASHI, M., Magnetic Microelectronics
SAITOH, H., Engineering for Information Society
SAKA, M., Mechanics of Materials Systems
SAKUMA, A., Solid-state Physics
SASAO, M., Fusion Plasma Diagnostics
SATO, M., Cell Biomechanics
SAWADA, K., Computational Aerodynamics
SAWAMOTO, M., Hydro-environment Systems
SAWAYA, K., Electromagnetic Wave Engineering
SEKINE, H., Smart System for Materials and Structures
SHINDO, Y., Mechanics and Design of Material Systems
SHODA, S., Functional Macromolecular Chemistry
SHOJI, K., Precision Machining
SMITH, R. L., Supercritical Fluid Technology
SOYAMA, H., Intelligent Sensing of Materials
SUGAWA, S., Advanced Functional Systems Engineering
SUGIMURA, Y., Structural Mechanics
SUZUKI, M., Structural Design Engineering
SUZUKI, M., Physicochemistry of Biomolecular Systems
TAKIZAWA, H., Synthetic Chemistry of Advanced Materials
TANAKA, H., Environmental Hydrodynamics
TOCHIYAMA, O., Nuclear Fuel Engineering
UCHIDA, S., Science and Engineering of Particle Beams
UCHIDA, T., Image Electronics
UCHIYAMA, M., Science and Engineering of Particle Beams
UEMATSU, Y., Wind Engineering
WADA, H., Biomechanical Engineering
WAKABAYASHI, T., Foundation of Risk Assessment and Management
WAKABAYASHI, T., Nuclear Energy Systems Safety Engineering
WATANABE, T., Material Design and Interface Engineering
YAMADA, M., Hydrocarbon Chemistry
YAMADA, M., Architectural Disaster Prevention Engineering
YAMADA, Y., Particle-beam Substance Reaction Engineering
YAMAGUCHI, M., Electromagnetic Theory
YAMAGUCHI, T., Computational Biomechanics
YAMAMURA, T., Physics and Chemistry of Fluids
YAMANAKA, K., Materials Evaluation and Sensing
YOKOBORI, T., Materials Design and Interface Engineering
YONEMOTO, T., Reaction Process Engineering
YOSHIDA, K., Space Exploration
YOSHINO, H., Building Environmental Engineering
YOSHINOBU, T., Biomedical Electronics
YUGAMI, H., New Energy Engineering

School and Graduate School of Law (27-1 Kawauchi, Aoba-ku, Sendai 980-8576; tel. (22) 795-6173; fax (22) 795-6249; e-mail law-jm@bureau.tohoku.ac.jp; internet www .law.tohoku.ac.jp):

AOI, H., Jurisprudence
ARIKAWA, T., Constitutional Law
HIRATA, T., European Political History

IKUTA, O., Land Law
INABA, K., Administrative Law
KAISE, Y., International Civil Procedure
KAWAKAMI, S., Civil Law
KAWATO, S., Political Science, Modern Political Analysis
KOGAYU, T., Civil Law
MIZUNO, N., Civil Law, Family Law
MORITA, K., Administrative Law
OHNISHI, H., International Politics
OKAMOTO, M., Criminal Law
OUCHI, T., Western Legal History
OZAKI, K., International Law
SAITO, T., Criminology
SAKATA, H., Civil Procedure
SERIZAWA, H., Anglo-American Law, Transnational Law of Information
SHIBUYA, M., Tax Law
TSUJIMURA, M., Constitutional Law, Comparative Constitutional Law
UEKI, T., International Law
UEMURA, T., Current Japanese Administration
YAGYU, K., History of Political Theory
YAMAMOTO, H., Constitutional Law, Comparative Constitutional Law
YOSHIDA, M., Japanese Legal History
YOSHIHARA, K., Commercial Law, Commercial Law

School and Graduate School of Medicine (2-1 Seiryo-machi, Aoba-ku, Sendai 980-8575; tel. (22) 717-8005; fax (22) 717-8021; e-mail med-som@bureau.tohoku.ac.jp; internet www.med.tohoku.ac.jp/index-j.html):

ABE, T., Clinical Cell Biology
AIBA, S., Dermatology
ARAI, Y., Urology
DODO, Y., Anatomy and Anthropology
DOHURA, K., Prion Biology
FUKUDO, S., Behavioural Medicine
FUNAYAMA, M., Forensic Medicine
HANDA, Y., Restorative Neuromuscular Rehabilitation
HATTORI, T., Allergy and Infectious Diseases
HAYASHI, Y., Paediatric Surgery
HONGO, M., Comprehensive Medicine (University Hospital)
HORII, A., Molecular Pathology
IGARASHI, K., Biochemistry
ITOH, S., Nephrology, Endocrinology and Vascular Medicine
ITOH, T., Immunology and Embryology
ITOYAMA, Y., Neurology
IZUMI, S., Physical Medicine and Rehabilitation
KAKU, M., Molecular Diagnostics
KASAI, N., Institute for Animal Experimentation
KATAGIRI, H., Advanced Therapeutics for Metabolic Diseases
KATOH, M., Anaesthesiology
KITAMOTO, T., Creutzfeldt–Jakob Disease Science and Technology
KOBAYASHI, T., Otolaryngology, Head and Neck Surgery
KOHZUKI, M., Internal Medicine and Rehabilitation Science
KOINUMA, N., Health Administration and Policy
KOKUBUN, S., Orthopaedic Surgery
KONDO, H., Histology
KONDO, Y., Medical Informatics
MARUYAMA, Y., Physiology I
MATSUBARA, Y., Medical Genetics
MATSUOKA, H., Psychiatry
MORI, E., Behavioural Neurology and Cognitive Neuroscience
NAGATOMI, R., Medicine and Science in Sport and Exercise
NAKAYAMA, K., Developmental Genetics
NODA, T., Molecular Genetics
OHUCHI, N., Surgical Oncology
OKA, Y., Molecular Metabolism and Diabetes

OKAMURA, K., Obstetrics
ONO, T., Genome and Radiation Biology
OSUMI, N., Developmental Neuroscience
SAIJO, Y., Molecular Medicine
SASAKI, I., General Surgery, Biological Regulation and Oncology
SASAKI, T., Rheumatology and Haematology
SASANO, H., Anatomical Pathology
SATOH, H., Environmental Health Sciences
SATOMI, S., Advanced Surgical Science and Technology
SHIBAHARA, S., Molecular Biology and Applied Physiology
SHIMOSEGAWA, T., Gastroenterology
SHINOZAWA, Y., Emergency and Critical Care Medicine
SHIRATO, K., Cardiovascular Medicine
SORA, I., Psychobiology
SUGAMURA, K., Immunology
TABAYASHI, K., Cardiovascular Surgery
TAKAHASHI, A., Neuroendovascular Therapy
TAKAHASHI, S., Diagnostic Radiology
TAKESHIMA, H., Biochemistry and Molecular Biology
TOMINAGA, T., Neurosurgery
TSUJI, I., Epidemiology
UEHARA, N., International Health
YAEGASHI, N., Gynaecological Oncology
YAMADA, A., Plastic and Reconstructive Surgery
YAMADA, S., Therapeutic Radiology
YAMAMURO, M., Pain Control
YANAGISAWA, T., Molecular Pharmacology
YANAI, K., Pharmacology
YOSHIMOTO, T., Neurosurgery

School and Graduate School of Pharmaceutical Sciences (Aoba, Aramaki, Aoba-ku, Sendai 980-8578; tel. (22) 795-6801; fax (22) 795-6805; e-mail ph-som@bureau.tohoku.ac.jp; internet www.pharm.tohoku.ac.jp):

ANZAI, J., Pharmaceutical Physicochemistry
ENOMOTO, T., Molecular Cell Biology
FUKUNAGA, K., Pharmacology
IHARA, M., Medicinal Chemistry
IMAI, Y., Clinical Pharmacology and Therapeutics
IWABACHI, Y., Synthetic Chemistry
KONDO, Y., Molecular Transformation
KOSUGI, H., Organoreaction Chemistry
NAGANUMA, A., Molecular and Biochemical Toxicology
NAKAHATA, N., Cellular Signaling
OHIZUMI, Y., Pharmaceutical Molecular Biology
OHUCHI, K., Pathophysiological Biochemistry
OSHIMA, Y., Natural Products Chemistry
SAKAMOTO, T., Heterocyclic Chemistry
TAKEUCHI, H., Bio-structural Chemistry
TERASAKI, T., Membrane Transport and Drug Targeting
YAMAGUCHI, M., Organometallic Chemistry
YAMOZOE, Y., Drug Metabolism and Molecular Toxicology

School and Graduate School of Science (6-3 Aoba, Aramaki, Aoba-ku, Sendai 980-8578; tel. (22) 795-6346; fax (22) 795-6363; e-mail sci-syom@bureau.tohoku.ac.jp; internet www .sci.tohoku.ac.jp):

AOKI, S., Atmospheric Physics
ASANO, S., Atmospheric Radiation, Physical Climatology
BANDO, S., Differential Geometry
CHIBA, M., Astrophysics
EZAWA, Z. F., Theoretical High Energy Physics, Condensed Matter Physics
FUJIMAKI, H., Geochemistry and Petrology
FUJIMOTO, H., Geodynamics of Subduction Zones
FUJIMURA, Y., Theoretical Chemistry
FUKUMURA, H., Physical Chemistry
FUKUNISHI, H., Upper Atmosphere Physics

FUTAMASE, T., Cosmology, General Relativity
HAMA, H., Beam Physics
HANAMURA, M., Algebraic Geometry
HANAWA, K., Physical Oceanography
HASEGAWA, A., Seismology
HASHIMOTO, O., Experimental Nuclear Physics
HATTORI, T., Mathematical Physics
HIKASA, K., Theoretical High Energy Physics
HINO, M., Human Geography
HIRAMA, M., Organic Chemistry
IGARASHI, G., Volcanology and Planetary Science
IMAIZUMI, T., Active Tectonics
INOUE, K., Experimental Particle Physics
ISHIDA, M., Algebraic Geometry
ISHIHARA, T., Solid State Photophysics
IWASAKI, T., Atmospheric Science
KABUTO, K., Organic Chemistry
KAIHO, K., Palaeontology
KASAGI, J., Nuclear Physics
KAWAKATSU, T., Physics of Soft Materials
KAWAMURA, H., Satellite Oceanography
KENMOTSU, K., Differential Geometry
KIRA, M., Organometallic Chemistry
KOBAYASHI, N., Functional Molecular Chemistry
KOBAYASHI, T., Experimental Nuclear Physics
KOZONO, H., Functional Analysis
KUDOH, Y., Mineralogy and Crystallography
KURAMOTO, Y., Theoretical Condensed Matter Physics
MIKAMI, N., Physical Chemistry
MINOURA, K., Palaeontology
MIYASE, H., Experimental Nuclear Physics
MORIOKA, A., Planetary Space Science
MORITA, N., Organic Chemistry
MORITA, Y., Number Theory
MURAKAMI, Y., Solid State Physics
NAKAMURA, T., Number Theory
NAKAZAWA, T., Atmospheric Physics
NIIZEKI, K., Theoretical Condensed Matter Physics
NISHIKAWA, S., Differential Geometry
ODA, M., Micropalaeontology
OGAWA, T., Partial Differential Equations and Applied Analysis
OHKI, K., Biophysics
OHNO, K., Physical Chemistry
OHTANI, E., Geochemistry and Planetology
OKAMOTO, H., Atmospheric Radiation
OKANO, S., Planetary Spectroscopy
ONO, T., Planetary Plasma Physics
ONODERA, H., Microscopic Research on Magnetism
OTSUKI, K., Tectonics and Structural Geology
SAIKAN, S., Non-linear Laser Spectroscopy
SAIO, H., Astrophysics
SAITO, R., Solid State Theory Nanotube
SATO, H., Seismology
SATOH, T., Experimental Ultra Low Temperature Physics
SEKI, M., Astrophysics
SHIMIZU, H., Nuclear Physics
SUTO, S., Surface Physics
SUZUKI, A., Experimental Particle Physics
SUZUKI, M., Plant Anatomy
TAKAGI, I., Partial Differential Equations
TAKAHASHI, T., Photoemission Solid State Physics
TAKAHASHI, T., Number Theory
TAKEDA, M., Probability Theory
TAKIGAWA, N., Theoretical Nuclear Physics
TAMURA, S., Astronomy
TANAKA, K., Mathematical Logic and Foundations of Mathematics
TANIGAKI, K., Solid State Physics
TERAMAE, N., Analytical Chemistry
TOBITA, H., Inorganic Chemistry
TOSA, M., Astronomy
TOYOTA, N., Molecular Metals

TSUBOTA, H., Experimental Nuclear Physics
UEDA, M., Natural Product Chemistry
UMINO, N., Seismotectonics
YAMAGUCHI, A., Experimental High Energy Physics
YAMAMOTO, H., Experimental High Energy Physics
YAMAMOTO, Y., Organic Chemistry
YAMASHITA, M., Coordination Chemistry
YANAGIDA, E., Partial Differential Equations
YASUDA, N., Meteorology
YOSHIDA, T., Volcanology and Petrology
YOSHIFUJI, M., Organic Chemistry
YUKIE, A., Number Theory

School of Agriculture and Graduate School of Agricultural Science (1-1 Tsutsumidori-Amamiyamachi, Aoba-ku, Sendai 981-8555; tel. (22) 717-8603; fax (22) 717-8607; e-mail agr-syom@bureau.tohoku.ac.jp; internet www.agri.tohoku.ac.jp):

AKIBA, Y., Animal Nutrition
GOMI, K., Microbial Biotechnology
HASEBE, T., Environmental Economics
IKEDA, I., Food and Biomolecular Science
IKEGAMI, M., Plant Pathology
KAMIO, Y., Applied Microbiology
KANAHAMA, K., Horticultural Science
KATSUMATA, R., Animal Microbiology
KIJIMA, A., Ecological Genetics (Field Science Center)
KOKUBUN, M., Crop Science
KOMAI, M., Nutrition
KUDO, A., Farm Business Management
KUWAHARA, S., Applied Bio-organic Chemistry
MAE, T., Plant Nutrition and Function
MATSUDA, K., Insect Science and Bioregulation
MINAMI, T., Fisheries Biology and Ecology
MIYAZAWA, T., Biodynamic Chemistry
MOROZUMI, K., Regional Planning
MUROGA, K., Aquacultural Biology
NAKAI, Y., Animal Health and Management
NANZYO, M., Soil Science
NISHIDA, A., Animal Breeding and Genetics
NISHIMORI, K., Molecular Biology
NISHIO, T., Plant Breeding and Genetics
OBARA, Y., Animal Physiology
OHKAMA, K., Agricultural and Resource Economics
OMORI, M., Fisheries Biology and Ecology
SAIGUSA, M., Environmental Crop Science (Field Science Center)
SAITO, G., Remote Sensing (Field Science Center)
SAITO, T., Animal Products Chemistry
SATO, E., Animal Reproduction
SATO, M., Marine Biochemistry
SATO, S., Land Ecology
SEIWA, K., Forest Ecology
SUZUKI, T., Marine Biotechnology
TANIGUCHI, A., Biological Oceanography
TANIGUCHI, K., Applied Aquatic Botany
TANIGUCHI, N., Applied Population Genetics
TORIYAMA, K., Environmental Biotechnology
YAMAGUCHI, T., Functional Morphology
YAMASHITA, M., Biophysical Chemistry
YAMAYA, T., Plant Cell Biochemistry
YONEKURA, H., Resource Management and Development Policy

School of Health Science, Faculty of Medicine (2-1 Seiryo-machi, Aoba-ku, Sendai 980-8575; tel. (22) 717-7903; fax (22) 717-7910; e-mail cms-syom@bureau.tohoku.ac.jp; internet www.cms.tohoku.ac.jp):

HAYASHI, S., Molecular Oncology
ISHIDA, M., Management of Nursing
ITAGAKI, K., Fundamental Nursing
KOBAYASHI, K., Clinical Investigation
KUROKAWA, T., Microbiology

MARUOKA, S., Nuclear Medicine
MASUDA, T., Pathology
MORI, I., Medical Imaging
NEMOTO, R., Adult Nursing
OISHI, M., Image Engineering
OOTAKA, T., Haematology
SAITO, H., Community Health Nursing
SAITO, H., Psychiatry
SAITO, K., Midwifery
SHINDOH, C., Respiratory Physiology
SHIWAKU, H., Child Health Nursing
TAKABAYASHI, T., Maternity Investigation
TAMURA, H., Neuroradiology
ZUGUCHI, M., Diagnostic Radiology

Tohoku University Museum (Aoba 6-3, Aramaki, Aoba-ku, Sendai 980-8578; tel. (22) 795-6767; fax (22) 795-6767; e-mail staff@museum.tohoku.ac.jp; internet www.museum.tohoku.ac.jp):

EHIRO, M., Geology and Palaeontology
YANAGIDA, T., Archaeology

UNIVERSITY OF TOKUSHIMA

2-24 Shinkura-cho, Tokushima 770-8501
Telephone: (88) 656-7000
Fax: (88) 656-7012
E-mail: hibunsyok@jim.tokushima-u.ac.jp
Internet: www.tokushima-u.ac.jp
Founded 1949
National University Corporation
Academic year: April to March
Pres.: TOSHIHIRO AONO
Vice-Pres: HIROSHI NAKAMURA, HIROSHI KAWAKAMI, HISASHI KITAJIMA, MASAYUKI SHIBUYA, YASUHIRO KURODA
Sec.-Gen.: HIROSHI NAKAMURA
Dir of Univ. Library: KAZUO HOSOI

Number of teachers: 895 full-time
Number of students: 7,744

Publications: *Bulletin of the Faculty of Engineering* (1 a year), *Journal of Human Sciences* (1 a year), *Journal of Human Sciences and Arts* (1 a year), *Journal of Language and Literature* (1 a year), *Journal of Mathematics* (1 a year), *Journal of Medical Investigation* (2 a year), *Natural Science Research* (1 a year), *Social Sciences Research* (1 a year)

DEANS

Faculty of Dentistry: EIICHI BANDO
Faculty of Engineering: YONEO YANO
Faculty of Integrated Arts and Sciences: MAKOTO WADA
Faculty of Medicine: SABURO SONE
Faculty of Pharmaceutical Sciences: TAKSAHI YAMAUCHI
Institute of Health Biosciences, Graduate School: SABURO SONE

PROFESSORS

Faculty of Dentistry, Graduate School of Oral Sciences and Institute of Health Biosciences (3-18-15 Kuramoto-cho, Tokushima 770-8504; tel. (88) 633-9100; fax (88) 631-4215; e-mail isysoumu2k@jim.tokushima-u.ac.jp):

ASAOKA, K., Biomaterials and Bio-engineering
BANDO, E., Fixed Prosthodontics
HANEJI, T., Anatomy and Histology
HAYASHI, Y., Oral Molecular Pathology
HONDA, E., Oral and Maxillofacial Radiology
HOSOI, K., Molecular Oral Physiology
ICHIKAWA, T., Removable Prosthodontics and Oral Implantology
KAWANO, F., Oral Care and Clinical Education
KITAMURA, S., Anatomy
MATSUO, T., Conservative Dentistry
MIYAKE, Y., Microbiology
MORIYAMA, K., Orthodontics and Dentofacial Orthopaedics

NAGATA, T., Periodontology and Endodontology

NAGAYAMA, M., Oral and Maxillofacial Surgery

NAKAJO, N., Dental Anaesthesiology

NISHINO, M., Paediatric Dentistry

NOMA, T., Molecular Biology

SATO, M., Oral and Maxillofacial Surgery and Oncology

YOSHIMOTO, K., Molecular Pharmacology

Faculty of Engineering (2-1 Minamijosanjima-cho, Tokushima 770-8506; tel. (88) 656-7304; fax (88) 656-7328; e-mail kgsoumuk@jim.tokushima-u.ac.jp; internet www.e .tokushima-u.ac.jp/english/main.html):

AKAMATSU, N., Neural Networks and Speech Recognition

AOE, J., Intelligent Systems Engineering

FUKUI, M., Optoelectronics

FUKUTOMI, J., Fluid Engineering and Turbomachinery

HANABUSA, T., Production Systems Engineering

HASHIMOTO, C., Construction Materials

HASHINO, M., Stochastic Hydrology, Water Resources Engineering

HIRAO, K., Structural Engineering and Seismic Design

HORI, H., Biological Science

IMAEDA, M., Process Dynamics and Control

IMAI, H., Mathematics and Applied Mathematics

INOUE, K., Applied Superconductivity and High-Field Generation

INOUE, T., Crystal Growth and Crystal Engineering

IRITANI, T., Spread Spectrum Communications

ISAKA, K., Electric Energy Engineering

IWATA, T., Applied Spectroscopy and Optical Measurement

KAIEDA, Y., Plastic Forming and Powder Metallurgy

KANESHINA, S., Biological Science

KAWAMURA, Y., Organic Chemistry

KAWASHIRO, K., Enzyme Engineering

KINOUCHI, Y., Biomedical Electronics

KITAYAMA, S., Digital Signal Processing

KONAKA, S., Integrated Circuits

KONDO, A., Geotechnical Engineering

KONISHI, K., Robot and Computer Vision

KORAI, H., Microbiology and Microbiological Control

MASUDA, S., Synthetic and Polymer Chemistry

MIWA, K., Combustion Engineering and Energy Conversion

MIZUGUCHI, H., Urban Planning and Landscape Design

MOCHIZUKI, A., Foundations Engineering and Soil Mechanics

MORIOKA, I., Heat Transfer

MOTONAKA, J., Analytical Chemistry

MURAKAMI, H., Risk and Environmental Assessment

MURAKAMI, R., Metal Fatigue, Surface Modification

NAGAMACHI, S., Mathematics and Applied Mathematics

NIKI, N., Medial Imaging, Pattern Recognition

NISHIDA, N., Optical Information Science

NOJI, S., Molecular Biology and Devlopmental Biology

OHNO, T., Nuclear Magnetic Resonance

OHNO, Y., Electron Devices

OKABE, T., River Engineering, Environmental Hydraulics

ONISHI, T., Power Engineering

ONO, N., Multi-agent Systems and Reinforcement Learning

OOSHIMA, T., Enzymology and Genome Engineering

OUSAKA, A., Thermal Engineering, Multiphase Flow

OYA, K., Particle-surface Collisions and Nuclear Fusion

REN, F., Computer Science Technology, Natural Language Processing

SAKAI, S., Semiconductor Photonic Devices

SAWADA, T., Structural Engineering, Earthquake Engineering

SHIMOMURA, T., Soft Engineering, Algorithnic Debugging

SUEDA, O., Well-being Engineering and Assistive Engineering

TAJIMA, K., All-optical Devices

TAKEUCHI, T., Numerical Analysis

TAMESADA, T., Design and Test of Electronic Circuits

TAMURA, K., Biophysical Chemistry

TANAKA, H., Polymer Synthesis and Functional Organic Materials

TOMIDA, T., Chemical Processes Engineering

TSUJI, A., Biochemistry and Protein Engineering

TSUKAYAMA, M., Synthetic and Polymer Chemistry

YAMADA, K., Elasticity and Micromechanics

YAMAGAMI, T., Geotechnical and Landslide Engineering

YAMANAKA, H., Urban Transport Planning and Design

YANO, Y., Intelligent Systems Engineering

YOSHIDA, K., Material Evaluation and Acoustic Emission

YOSHIMURA, T., Vehicle Suspensions and Fuzzy Control

Faculty of Integrated Arts and Sciences (1-1 Minamijosanjima-cho, Tokushima 770-8502; tel. (88) 656-7103; fax (88) 656-7298; e-mail sksoumks@jim.tokushima-u.ac.jp; internet www.ias.tokushima-u.ac.jp):

ABE, E., Kimono Cloth Shrinkage and Repair

ANDO, M., Chinese Literature

ARAKI, H., Motor and Behavioural Physiology

ARIMA, T., Philosophy of the Qin and Han Dynasties

AZUMA, K., Calligraphy

AZUMA, U., Asian Archaeology

BABA, T., German Language and Literature

GOTO, T., Comparative Biochemistry and Physiology

HAMADA, J., Visual Perception

HARAMIZU, T., Japanese Literature

HAYASHI, H., Environmental Biology

HAYASHI, K., Constitutional Law

HIOKI, Z., Theoretical High Energy Physics

HIRAI, S., Historical Geography

HIRAKI, M., Study of Painting Expression

IMAI, S., Applied Spectrocopy, Atomic Spectrometry and Trace Analysis

INOUE, N., English Corpus Linguistics, English Lexicography

ISHIDA, K., Microfossil Geology

ISHIDA, M., Philosophy of the Mind–Body Problem

ISHIHARA, T., Differential Geometry

ISHII, K., Image Conservation Techniques

ISHIKAWA, E., German Language and Literature

ITO, M., Partial Differential Equations

ITO, T., Computational Mathematics and Sciences

ITO, Y., Functional Analysis

KATAOKA, K., Musicology

KATAYAMA, S., Algebraic Number Theory

KATSURA, S., German Language and Literature

KAWAKAMI, S., German Language and Literature

KISHIE, S., Japanese Dialects

KOORI, N., Nuclear Physics

KOYAMA, K., Solid-State Physics

KUWABARA, M., Japanese History

KUWABARA, R., Global Analysis

MAEDA, S., Applied Mathematics

MASUDA, T., Bio-organic Chemistry

MATOBA, H., Exercise Physiology

MATSUMOTO, M., Physical Chemistry

MATSUO, Y., Genetics

MATSUSHITA, M., English Literature

MAYUMI, K., Environmental Economics

MIKI, M., Financial Accounting

MITSUI, A., Industrial Technology

MIURA, T., Physical Education

MIYAZAKI, T., English Literature

MIYAZAWA, K., Composition, Music using Computers

MIZUSHIMA, T., Middle Eastern Economics

MORI, Y., Psychotherapy

MORIOKA, Y., English Linguistics

MOTOKI, Y., English Linguistics

MURATA, A., Geology

NAKAGAWA, H., Marine Physiology and Biochemistry

NAKAJIMA, M., Economic History

NAKAMURA, H., Physical Education

NAKAYAMA, S., Nuclear Physics

NISHIDE, K., American History

OBARA, S., Exercise Physiology

OHASHI, M., Mathematical Programming

OHASHI, M., Immunobiology

OHBUCHI, A., Algebraic Geometry

OYAMA, Y., Analytical Cytology

SAKUMA, R., Social and Imperial History of Modern Britain

SANO, K., Physiological Psychology

SEKIZAWA, J., Risk Assessment for Environmental Protection and Safety

SENBA, M., Japanese Linguistics

SEO, I., English Literature

SHIOTA, Y., Geology

TACHIBANA, Y., Economic Theory

TAJIMA, T., French Literature

TAKEDA, Y., Natural Products Chemistry

TERAO, H., Inorganic Chemistry

UENO, K., Sociology of Social Problems

WADA, M., Organic Chemistry

YAMADA, K., Labour Law

YAMAMOTO, M., Developmental Disorders

YOKOIGAWA, K., Applied Microbiology

YOSHIDA, H., Theoretical Sociology

YOSHIDA, S., Ancient Greek Philosophy

YOSHIMORI, K., Chinese Medieval History

Faculty of Medicine, Graduate School of Medical Sciences and Institute of Health Biosciences (3-18-15 Kuramoto-cho, Tokushima 770-8503; tel. (88) 633-9116; fax (88) 633-9028; e-mail isysoumu1k@jim.tokushima-u .ac.jp; internet www.hosp.med.tokushima-u .ac.jp/university/servlet/index):

ADACHI, A., Virology

ARASE, S., Dermatological Science

DOI, T., Clinical Biology and Medicine

FUKUI, Y., Anatomy and Developmental Neurobiology

IRAHARA, M., Gynaecology and Obstetrics

ISHIMURA, K., Anatomy and Cell Biology

ITO, S., Digestive and Cardiovascular Medicine

IZUMI, K., Molecular and Environmental Pathology

KAJI, R., Clinical Neuroscience

KITAGAWA, T., Cardiovascular Surgery

KISHI, K., Nutritional Physiology

KUBO, S., Legal Medicine

MATSUMOTO, T., Medicine and Bioregulatory Sciences

MIYAMOTO, K., Nutritional Biochemistry

MORITA, Y., Integrative Physiology

NAGAHIRO, S., Neurosurgery

NAKAHORI, Y., Human Genetics and Public Health

NAKANISHI, H., Plastic and Reconstructive Surgery

NAKAYA, Y., Nutrition and Metabolism

NISHITANI, H., Radiology

OHMORI, T., Psychiatry

OSHITA, S., Anaesthesiology

OTA, F., Food Microbiology
SANO, T., Human Pathology
SASAKI, T., Biochemistry
SHIOTA, H., Ophthalmology and Visual Science
SONE, S., Internal Medicine and Molecular Therapeutics
TAKEDA, E., Clinical Nutrition
TAKEDA, N., Otorhinolaryngology and Communicative Neuroscience
TAMAKI, T., Pharmacology
TASHIRO, S., Digestive and Paediatric Surgery
TERAO, J., Food Science
YAMAMOTO, S., Applied Nutrition
YASUI, N., Orthopaedic Surgery
YASUMOTO, K., Immunology and Parasitology
YOSHIZAKI, K., Physiology

Faculty of Pharmaceutical Sciences and Graduate School of Pharmaceutical Sciences (1-78-1 Shomachi, Tokushima 770-8505; tel. (88) 633-7245; fax (88) 633-9517; e-mail isysoumu3k@jim.tokushima-u.ac.jp; internet www.ph.tokushima-u.ac.jp):

ARAKI, T., Drug Metabolism and Therapeutics
BABA, Y., Molecular and Pharmaceutical Biotechnology
CHUMAN, H., Molecular and Analytical Chemistry
FUKUI, H., Molecular Pharmacology
FUKUZAWA, K., Health Chemistry
HIGUCHI, T., Molecular Cell Biology and Medicine
ITO, K., Medicinal Biotechnology
KIHARA, M., Pharmaceutical Information Science
KIWADA, H., Pharmacokinetics and Biopharmaceutics
KUSUMI, T., Marine Medicinal Resources
NAGAO, Y., Molecular Medicinal Chemistry
OCHIAI, M., Pharmaceutical Organic Chemistry
SHIMABAYASHI, S., Physical Pharmacy
SHISHIDO, K., Organic Synthesis
TAKAISHI, Y., Pharmacognosy
TAKIGUCHI, Y., Clinical Pharmacology
YAMAUCHI, T., Biochemistry

School of Health Sciences (3-18-15 Kuramoto-cho, Tokushima 770-8503; tel. (88) 633-9003; fax (88) 633-9015; e-mail isysoumu4k@jim.tokushima-u.ac.jp; internet www2.medsci.tokushima-u.ac.jp):

FUJII, M., Neuroradiology
HARADA, M., Neuroradiology
KAGAWA, N., Human Pathology
KAWANISHI, C., Fundamental Nursing
KONDO, H., Fundamental Nursing
KONDO, T., Nutritional Biochemistry
MAEZAWA, H., Radiation Medicine
MORIMOTO, T., Breast Surgery
NAGAMINE, I., Clinical Neurpsychiatry
NAGASHINO, H., Biomedical Engineering
NINOMIYA, T., Psychosomatic Medicine
ONISHI, C., Adult and Gerontological Nursing
ONO, T., Bacterial Genetics
SAITOH, K., Cardiology
SEKIDO, K., Dermatological Science
TADA, T., Gerontological Nursing
TAKEGAWA, Y., Radiotherapy
TAMURA, A., Adult Nursing
TERAO, T., Maternal Health
UENO, J., Diagnostic Radiology
YAMANO, S., Artificial Reproductive Technology
YOSHINAGA, T., Medical Image Reconstruction

Center for Advanced Information Technology (2-1 Minamijosanjima-cho, Tokushima 770-8506; tel. (88) 656-7555; fax (88) 656-9122; e-mail kokusai1@jim.tokushima-u.ac.jp; internet www.ait.tokushima-u.ac.jp):

KITA, K., Computer Science, Information Retrieval, Natural Language Processing
OE, S., Image Processing and Visual Pattern Processing

Center for University Extension (1-1 Minamijosanjima-cho, Tokushima 770-8502; tel. (88) 656-7276; fax (88) 656-7277; e-mail kygakusk@jim.tokushima-u.ac.jp; internet www.cue.tokushima-u.ac.jp):

HIROWATARI, S., Adult and Continuing Education
MORITA, H., Analytical Chemistry
SODA, K., Function of Narrative
WAKAIZUMI, S., High Energy Physics
YOSHIDA, A., Educational Technology

Institute for Animal Experimentation, Institute of Health Biosciences (3-18-15 Kuramoto-cho, Tokushima 770-8503; tel. (88) 633-9116; fax (88) 633-9028; e-mail isysoum1k@jim.tokushima-u.ac.jp; internet www.anex.med.tokushima-u.ac.jp):

SASAKI, T., Biochemistry

Institute for Enzyme Research (3-18-15 Kuramoto-cho, Tokushima 770-8503; tel. (88) 633-9420; fax (88) 633-9422; e-mail kenkyu@jim.tokushima-u.ac.jp; internet mms1.ier.tokushima-u.ac.jp/index2.html):

EBINA, Y., Molecular Genetics
FUKUI, K., Gene Regulatorics
KIDO, H., Molecular Enzyme Chemistry
MATSUMOTO, M., Informative Cytology
SUGINO, H., Molecular Cytology
TANIGUCHI, H., Molecular Enzyme Physiology

Institute for Genome Research (3-18-15 Kuramoto-cho, Tokushima 770-8503; tel. (88) 633-9420; fax (88) 633-9422; e-mail kenkyu@jim.tokushima-u.ac.jp; internet www.genome.tokushima-u.ac.jp):

HARA, E., Division of Protein Information
ITAKURA, M., Division of Genetic Information
SHINOHARA, Y., Division of Gene Expression
SIOMI, H., Division of Gene Function Analysis
TAKAHAMA, Y., Division of Experimental Immunology

Institute for Medicinal Resources, Institute of Health Biosciences (1-78-1 Shomachi, Tokushima 770-8505; tel. (88) 633-7245; fax (88) 633-9517; e-mail isysoum3k@jim.tokushima-u.ac.jp; internet www.ph.tokushima-u.ac.jp):

ITO, K., Medicinal Biotechnology

International Student Center (1-1 Minamijosanjima-cho, Tokushima 770-8502; tel. (88) 656-7082; fax (88) 656-9873; e-mail ryugakuk@jim.tokushima-u.ac.jp; internet www.isc.tokushima-u.ac.jp):

JIN, C. H., Computing Science
MISUMI, T., Teaching Japanese as a Foreign Language
OISHI, Y., Teaching Japanese as a Foreign Language

Radioisotope Center (3-18-15 Kuramoto-cho, Tokushima 770-8503; tel. (88) 633-9416; fax (88) 633-9417; e-mail kenkyu@jim.tokushima-u.ac.jp; internet ricb.ri.tokushima-u.ac.jp/rirc.html):

ADACHI, A., HIV/AIDS treatment

TOKYO INSTITUTE OF TECHNOLOGY

2-12-1, Ookayama, Meguro-ku, Tokyo 152-8550

Telephone: (3) 5734-3827
Fax: (3) 5734-3685
E-mail: kenkyusha@jim.titech.ac.jp
Internet: www.titech.ac.jp

Founded 1881
Independent

Academic year: April to March
Pres.: KENICHI IGA
Exec.Vice-Pres. for Education: AKIO SAITO
Exec.Vice-Pres. for Finance: HIROMITSU MUTA
Exec.Vice-Pres. for Planning: ICHIRO OKURA
Exec.Vice-Pres. for Research: TATSUO IZAWA
Dir-Gen. of Admin. Bureau: DAISUKE IKEDA
Dir of Institute Library: EIJI FUJIWARA

Library of 886,484 vols
Number of teachers: 1,149
Number of students: 6,477

DEANS

School of Bioscience and Biotechnology: TOMOYA KITAZUME
School of Engineering: KEN OKAZAKI
School of Science: MAKOTO OKA
Graduate School of Bioscience and Biotechnology: TOMOYA KITAZUME
Graduate School of Decision Science and Technology: HIROMITSU MUTA
Graduate School of Engineering: KEN OKAZAKI
Graduate School of Information Science and Engineering: YUKIO TAKAHASHI
Graduate School of Innovation Management: TAKAO ENKAWA
Graduate School of Science and Engineering: MAKOTO OKA
Interdisciplinary Graduate School of Science and Engineering: SACHIHIKO HARASHINA

DIRECTORS

Chemical Resources Laboratory: MASASUKE YOSHIDA
Materials and Structures Laboratory: KENICHI KONDOU
Precision and Intelligence Laboratory: SHINICHI YOKOTA
Research Laboratory for Nuclear Reactors: MASAO OGAWA

PROFESSORS

Graduate School of Bioscience and Biotechnology:

AKAIKE, T., Biomaterial Design
AONO, R., Microbial Physiology, Genetic Engineering
FUJIHIRA, M., Biomolecular Processes
HAMAGUCHI, Y., Cell Biology
HANDA, H., Biotechnology
HASHIMOTO, H., Bio-organic Chemistry
HIROSE, S., Biochemistry
ICHINOSE, H., Neurochemistry and Neuropharmacology
IKAI, A., Biodynamics
INOUE, Y., Enzyme Functions
ISHIKAWA, T., Biofunctional Engineering
KISHIMOTO, T., Cell and Developmental Biology
KITAMURA, N., Molecular Biology
KITAZUME, T., Bio-organic Chemistry
KUDO, A., Molecular Immunology
MOTOKAWA, T., Animal Physiology
NAKAMURA, S., Genetic Engineering
OKADA, N., Molecular Evolution
OKAHATA, Y., Fundamentals of Biomolecules
OKURA, I., Biophysical Chemistry, Enzyme Chemistry
SATO, F., Molecular Design of Biological Importance
SEKINE, M., Bio-organic Chemistry
SHISHIDO, K., Molecular Biology
TAKAMIYA, K., Plant Physiology
TANAKA, N., Protein Crystallography
UENO, A., Bio-organic Chemistry, Molecular Recognition
UNNO, H., Biochemistry

Graduate School of Decision Science and Technology:

ENKAWA, T., Production Management
HASHIZUME, D., Sociology

HAYASAKA, M., History of Politics (Slavic Studies)
HIDANO, N., Regional Planning and Infrastructure Project Appraisal
HIGUCHI, Y., Socioeconomic Networks
IGUCHI, T., Japanese Literature
IIJIMA, J., Systems Theory
IMADA, T., International Relations
ISHII, M., Sports Psychology
ITO, K., Ergonomics, Production Control
KIJIMA, K., Management Systems
KIMOTO, T., History of Technology
KUWAKO, T., Philosophy
KYOMOTO, N., Intellectual Property Strategy, Licensing, Software Protection
MAYEKAWA, S., Psychometrics, Educational Statistics, Multivariate Data Analysis
MIYAJIMA, M., Industrial Management
MIYAKAWA, M., Applied Statistics, Quality Control
MIZUNO, S., Operations Research
MURAKI, M., Process Management
MUTA, H., Educational Planning, Economics of Education
MUTO, S., Game Theory
NAKAGAWA, M., Educational Psychology
NAKAHARA, Y., Exercise Physiology
NAKAI, N., Urban Planning
SAIKI, T., Patenting of Pharmaceutical Inventions
SAITO, T., Sociometrics
SAITO, U., Regional Landscape Planning and Design
TANAKA, Z., Political Science
WARAGAI, T., Philosophy, Logic
WATANABE, C., Technology Policy, Technology Management
YAMAMURO, K., Document Analysis
YAMATO, T., Economic Theory
YAMAZAKI, M., History of Science
YANO, M., Social Planning

Graduate School of Information Science and Engineering:
FUJII, S., Environmental Engineering
FUJIWARA, E., Coding Theory, Computer Systems
FURUI, S., Speech Recognition, Human Interfaces
HIGUCHI, Y., Socioeconomic Networks
HIROSE, S., Applied Solid Mechanics, Ultrasonic Nondestructive Evaluation, Numerical Analysis using Boundary Element Method
KIMEI, H., Geophysical Prospecting
KIMURA, K., Vibration, Stochastic Dynamics, Nonlinear Dynamics
KOJIMA, M., Mathematical Programming
KOJIMA, S., Geometry and Topology
MASE, S., Spatial Statistics
MORI, K., Computer Systems, Distributed Computing
NADAOKA, K., Environmental Systems Analysis, Coastal and Ocean Engineering, Mesoscale Meteorology, Applied Remote Sensing, Coastal-space Design, Applied Fluid Dynamics
NAKAJIMA, M., Computer Graphics, Image Processing
NAKAMURA, H., Strength of Materials
OGAWA, H., Pattern Recognition, Image Processing
SAEKI, M., Software Engineering
SASAJIMA, K., Precision Engineering, Measuring Systems
SASSA, M., Computer Software, Programming Environments
SATO, T., Artificial Intelligence and Logic Programming
SHIBAYAMA, E., Software Science, Parallel and Distributed Computing
SHIMIZU, M., Biomechanics, Fluid Dynamics
TAKAHASHI, W., Functional Analysis and its Applications

TAKAHASHI, Y., Applied Probability, Operations Research
TAKIGUCHI, K., Mechanics of Building Structures, Disaster Prevention Systems, Concrete Engineering
TANAKA, H., Natural Language Processing
TOKUDA, T., Software Engineering
UJIHASHI, S., Biomechanics, Sports Engineering, Safety Engineering
WATANABE, O., Theory of Computation
YONEZAKI, N., Applied Logic, Software Science

Graduate School of Science and Engineering:
ABE, M., Electronic Properties of Matter
AKAGI, H., Power Engineering, Power Electronics, Electrical Machines
ANDO, I., Polymer Structure, NMR Spectroscopy, Electronic Structure of Polymers
ANDO, M., Antennas, Electromagnetic Wave Theory
ANDO, T., Physics, Condensed Matter Theory, Quantum Hall Effect, Semiconductor Quantum Structures
AOKI, Y., Urban Planning
ARAKI, K., Coding Theory, Digital Communication Systems
ASAHI, K., Experimental Nuclear Physics
DAIMON, M., Cement Chemistry, Porous Materials, Hydrochemical Synthesis
ENDO, M., Solid Vibrations
ENOKI, T., Physical Chemistry
FUJII, N., Electronic Circuits and Networks
FUJIMOTO, Y., Bio-organic Chemistry
FUJIOKA, H., History of Architecture, Architectural Design
FUJITA, T., Algebraic Geometry
FURUYA, K., Optical and Quantum Electronics
FUTAKI, A., Differential Geometry
HAGIWARA, I., Collaboration Engineering
HANNA, J., Imaging Materials
HASHIMOTO, T., Polymer Processing, Thermal Properties of Polymers
HIGUCHI, Y., Exercise Physiology
HINODE, H., Inorganic Synthesis of Solids, Inorganic Industrial Chemistry
HIRAO, A., Polymer Syntheses
HIROSE, S., Robotics, Biomechanics
HONKURA, Y., Geophysics
HOSOYA, A., Theoretical Cosmology
ICHIMURA, T., Molecular Spectroscopy
IGUCHI, I., Condensed Matter Physics and Superconducting Electronics
IIO, K., Experimental Condensed Matter Physics
IKARIYA, T., Homogeneous Catalysis, Synthetic Organic Chemistry
IKEDA, K., Hydraulics and Environmental Fluid Mechanics
INOU, N., Biomechanics, Autonomous Decentralized Systems, Robotics
INOUE, A., Singularity, Algebraic Geometry
INOUE, T., Physical Chemistry of Polymer Materials
ISHII, S., Singularity and Bifurcation
ISHII, S., Electric Power Engineering, Plasma
ISHIZU, K., Polymer Syntheses, Polymer Reactions
IWAMOTO, M., Electronic Materials
IWASAWA, N., Synthetic Organic Chemistry
IWATSUKI, N., Robotics
KAIZU, Y., Coordination Chemistry
KAJIUCHI, T., Biochemical Engineering, Environmental Chemical Engineering
KAKIMOTO, F., Experimental Cosmic Ray Physics
KAKIMOTO, M., Polymer Syntheses, Thin Polymer Films
KAKINUMA, K., Bio-organic Chemistry
KAWAI, N., Astrophysics
KAWAMURA, K., Physics, Inorganic Chemistry, Mineral Physics
KAWASAKI, J., Mass Transfer Operations

KAWASHIMA, K., Earthquake Engineering
KIKUTANI, T., Fibre and Polymer Processing, Physical Properties of Polymers
KISHIMOTO, K., Strength of Materials, Computational Mechanics
KITAGAWA, A., Fluid Power Control
KOBAYASHI, A., Industrial Measurement
KOBAYASHI, H., Fracture Mechanics and Fatigue
KONAGAI, M., Semiconductors
KOSHIHARA, S., Materials Science
KOUCHI, N., Physical Chemistry of Atomic and Molecular Processes
KUMAZAWA, I., Human Interface
KUNIEDA, H., Integrated Circuits, Signal Processing
KURODA, C., Process Information Systems
KUROKAWA, N., Number Theory
KUSAKABE, O., Geotechnical Engineering
KYOGOKU, K., Tribology, Machine Elements
MARUYAMA, S., Geology, Tectonics
MARUYAMA, T., Physical Chemistry in Advanced Materials
MATSUI, Y., Advanced Thermo-fluid Dynamics
MASUKO, M., Tribology, Applied Surface Chemistry
MATSUO, T., Physical Metallurgy of Iron and Steels, High Temperature Deformation in Alloys
MATSUO, Y., Mechanical Properties of Ceramics
MATSUZAWA, A.
MIKI, C., Structural Mechanics and Engineering
MIMACHI, K., Special Functions, Material Physics, Representation Theory, Holonomic Systems
MINAMI, F., Solid State Physics and Laser Spectroscopy
MITA, T., Control Theory, Applications of Control Theory, Robotics
MIYAUCHI, T., Fluid Dynamics, Reactive Gas Dynamics
MIYAZAKI, K., Technology Strategy and Diffusion
MIZUTANI, N., Advanced Ceramics, Ceramic Processing, Electro-ceramics, Thin Films
MOCHIMARU, Y., Computational Fluid Dynamics
MORIIZUMI, T., Bioelectronics
MUNEKATA, H., Applied Physics of Property and Crystallography
MURAI, T., Wanderology
MURAKAMI, H., Workshop Processes and Production Engineering
MURATA, M., Differential Equations
NAGAHASHI, H., Image Processing
NAGAI, T., Solar–Terrestrial Physics
NAGATA, K., High Temperature Physical Chemistry and Electronic Materials
NAKAHARA, T., Lubrication Technology, Two-Phase Flow, Oil Hydraulics
NAKAJIMA, K., Chemical Engineering
NAKAMURA, Y., Diffraction Crystallography, Magnetic Thin Film
NAKASHIMA, S., Experimental Physical Geochemistry, Geochemical Spectroscopy and Kinetics, Physicochemical Properties of Water in the Earth, Organic–Inorganic Interactions and the Origin of Life, Geochemistry of Resources and the Environment
NAKAZAWA, K., Planetary Physics
NISHI, T., Polymer Alloys, Soft Materials, Polymer Nanotechnology
NISHIDA, N., Experimental Condensed Matter Physics, Low Temperature Physics
NISHIMORI, H., Statistical Physics
NIWA, J., Structural Concrete
OBIKAWA, T., Machining, Materials Science, Mechanical Processing Systems
OGAWA, K., Mechanical Operations

OGAWA, T., Steel and Shell Structures
OGUNI, M., Physical Inorganic Chemistry
OHASHI, H., Power Semiconductor Devices
OHASHI, Y., Crystal Chemistry
OHTA, H., Geotechnical Engineering
OHTAGUCHI, K., Biochemical Reaction Engineering
OKA, M., Theoretical Nuclear Physics
OKADA, K., Ceramic Raw Materials, Mineralogical Science
OKADA, T., Analytical Chemistry
OKAZAKI, K., Thermal and Environmental Engineering
OKUDA, Y., Low Temperature Physics
OKUI, N., Organic Thin Films, Physical Properties of Polymers
OKUMA, M., Dynamics, Optimum Design
OKUTOMI, M., Computer Vision
ONO, K., Dynamics of Machinery
ONZAWA, T., Welding and Materials Science
OTSUKA, K., Heterogeneous Catalysis, Electrocatalysis
OTSUKI, N., Construction Materials, Environmental Materials Design
SAITO, A., Thermal Engineering
SAITO, S., Theoretical Condensed Matter Physics
SAITO, Y., Manufacturing Engineering, CAD, CAM, Computer Intelligent Manufacturing
SAJI, T., Electrochemistry, Surface Chemistry
SAKAI, N., Theoretical Elementary Particle Physics
SAKAI, Y., Communication Systems
SAKAMOTO, K., Architectural Design
SAKANIWA, K., Communication Theory
SAMPEI, M., Control Theory (Linear and Non-linear) and its Application, Nonholonomic Systems
SATO, T., Materials Development, Magnetic Materials, Amorphous Metals
SATOH, I., Thermal Engineering, Heat Transfer Measurement
SENDA, M., Environmental Design
SHIBATA, S., Inorganic Materials Engineering
SHIBATA, T., Experimental Nuclear Physics
SHIBUYA, K., Physical Chemistry
SHIGA, H., Complex Analysis
SHIGA, T., Stochastic Processes
SUMITA, M., Solid Structure and Physical Properties of Organic Materials, Polymer Composites
SUSA, M., Physical Chemistry of Materials
SUZUKI, H., Organometallic Chemistry
SUZUKI, H., Radio Communications Engineering
SUZUKI, K., Organic Chemistry
SUZUKI, M., Plasma Engineering, Nuclear Chemical Engineering
SUZUMURA, A., Joining, High Temperature Materials
TAKAGI, S., Analogue Integrated Circuits, Analogue Signal Processing
TAKAHASHI, E., Petrology, Geochemistry, Solid Geophysics
TAKAHASHI, T., Synthetic Organic Chemistry, Synthetic Processes for Natural Products
TAKATA, T., Supramolecular and Polymer Chemistry
TAKAYANAGI, K., Diffraction, Crystal Physics, Surface Physics
TAKEZOE, H., Optical and Electrical Properties of Organic Materials
TANIOKA, A., Physical Chemistry of Organic Materials, Membrane Science
TOKIMATSU, K., Geotechnical Engineering
TOKURA, H., Processing Technologies
TSUDA, K., Chemical Plant Materials
TSUNAKAWA, H., Geophysics
TSURU, T., Chemistry of Metal Surfaces, Electrochemistry, Corrosion and Passivity of Metals

TSURUMI, T., Electrical Properties and Structure of Inorganic Materials
UCHIYAMA, K., Stochastic Processes and Applied Probability
UEDA, M., Condensed Matter Theory, Quantum Optics
UEDA, M., Polymer Syntheses
UEDA, M., Wave Information Processing
UENO, S., Theory of Parallel and VLSI Computation
UYEMATSU, T., Information Theory, Data Compression
WAKIHARA, M., Inorganic Solid-State Chemistry
WATANABE, J., Structure and Properties of Polymer Liquid Crystals
WATANABE, Y., Experimental Particle Physics
YABE, T., Laser Nuclear Fusion, Computational Fluid Dynamics
YAGI, K., Experimental Condensed Matter Physics, Crystal and Surface Physics
YAI, T., Transport Planning and Engineering
YAMAJI, A., Materials Science
YOSHIDA, T., Topology
YOSHINO, J., Experimental Condensed Matter Physics

Interdisciplinary Graduate School of Science and Engineering (4259 Nagatsuta-cho, Midori-ku, Yokohama 226-8502; tel. (45) 922-1111):

AOYAGI, Y., Information Devices
ASADA, M., Quantum Electronics
DEGUCHI, H., Polymer Synthesis
DOI, Y., Polymer Synthesis
FUCHIGAMI, T., Catalytic Chemistry
HARA, M., Nanotechnology
HARASHINA, S., Environmental Planning, Conflict Resolution
HATORI, Y., Visual Communication System, Network Interface
HIROTA, K., Information Systems
HORIOKA, K., High Power Beam Technology, Laser Engineering
HOTTA, E., Plasma Engineering, Pulsed Power Technology
HOYANO, A., Urban and Building Environment
ISHIKAWA, T., Hydraulics and Hydrology
ISHIWARA, M., Nanomaterials
ITO, K., Computational Brain Science, Design and Control of Robotics and Prostheses
KABASHIMA, Y., Information and Communication Engineering
KANNO, R., Lithium Battery, Solid-State Ionics, Inorganic Materials Chemistry, Solid State Electrochemistry, High Pressure and Thin-film Synthesis
KATO, M., Fracture and Deformation
KINUGASA, Y., Earthquake Geology, Environmental Geology
KOBAYASHI, S., Knowledge Information Processing
KOBAYASHI, T., Digital Signal Processing
KOHNO, T., Nuclear Physics, Heavy Ion-Beam Science
KOSUGI, Y., Neural Networks
KUMAI, S., Nano-electronics
MAEJIMA, H., Microprocessors, Special Purpose Processors, On-chip Systems
MIDORIKAWA, S., Earthquake Engineering
MISHIMA, Y., Physical Metallurgy and Alloy Design
NAKAMURA, K., Computational Neuroscience
NAKANO, Y., Environmental Engineering, Separation Process Engineering
NITTA, K., Artificial Intelligence, Regal Reasoning
ODAWARA, O., Electrochemistry of Metals
OHMACHI, T., Earthquake Engineering
OHNO, R., Architectural Design and Planning, Environmental Psychology

OHSAKA, T., Molten Salt Chemistry, Electrochemistry, Electroanalytical Chemistry, Bioelectrochemistry
OHTSU, M., Opto-quantum Electronics
OKAMURA, T., Cryogenic and Energy Conversion Engineering
ONAKA, S., Mechanical Properties of Materials
SAKAI, T., Semiconductor Devices
SASANO, S., History of Urban and Architectural Design
SATO, A., Strengthening Mechanism and Lattice Imperfections
SEO, K., Engineering Seismology
TAMURA, T., Environmental Atmospheric Turbulence, Urban Wind Climate, Aerodynamic Control
TEHRANO, T., Intelligent Informatics
UCHIKAWA, K., Visual Information Processing
WATANABE, M., Physical Geography
YAI, T., Transport Planning and Engineering
YAMAMURA, M., DNA Computing
YAMASAKI, H., Energy Conversion Engineering
YAMAZAKI, Y., Solid-State Physics and Chemistry
YOKOYAMA, M., Automated Machine Design
YOSHIKAWA, K., High Temperature Energy Conversion, Environmental Fluid Dynamics

Chemical Resources Laboratory:

AKITA, M., Organometallic Chemistry
DOMEN, K., Surface Chemical Reaction
FUJII, M.
IKEDA, T., Polymer Chemistry and Photochemistry
ISHIDA, M., Chemical Engineering and Chemical Environmental Process Design
IWAMOTO, M., Heterogeneous Catalysis
IYODA, T., Functional Molecular Materials, Nano-structured Materials, Materials Electrochemistry
NAKA, Y., Process Systems Engineering
OSAKADA, K., Coordination and Organometallic Chemistry
SHODA, M., Biochemical Engineering, Applied Microbiology
TANAKA, M., Industrial Organic Chemistry
YAMAMOTO, T., Inorganic and Organometallic Chemistry
YAMASE, T., Photochemistry and Photoelectrochemistry
YOSHIDA, M., Biochemistry

Materials and Structures Laboratory:

ATAKE, T., Materials Science, Physical Chemistry
HAYASHI, S., Structural Engineering
ITOH, M., Physical Properties of Inorganic Materials
KASAI, K., Structural Engineering, Earthquake Engineering
KONDO, K., Inorganic Materials and Properties, Applied Physics of Property and Crystallography
SASAKI, S., Synchrotron Radiation Science, X-Ray Crystallography, Solid-State Physics
TANAKA, K., Inorganic Materials and Properties, Building Materials
WAKAI, F., Inorganic Materials and Properties
YAMAUCHI, H., Materials Science, Applied Physics of Property and Crystallography, Strongly Correlated Electron Materials, Superconducting Oxides
YASUDA, E., Ceramic Base Composites, Carbon Alloys and Materials
YOSHIMURA, M., Inorganic Materials and Properties, Soft Processing, Advanced Ceramics

Precision and Intelligence Laboratory:

HATSUZAWA, T., Precise Measurement
HIGO, Y., Physical Metallurgy, Nondestructive Evaluation
HORIE, M., Kinematics of Machinery
HOUJOH, H., Acoustic Measurement, Machine Dynamics
KAGAWA, T., Process Control
KOBAYASHI, K., Opto-electronics, Optical Communications, Photonic Integrated Semiconductor Devices
KOYAMA, F., Optical Semiconductor Devices
MASU, K., Advanced Microdevices
OHTSUKI, S., Bio-medical Ultrasonics, Acoustic Engineering
SATO, M., Pattern Recognition Image Processing
SHINNO, H., Ultraprecision Machining, Machine Tool Engineering
SIMOKOBE, A., Dynamics and Control of Precision Mechanisms
UEHA, S., Ultrasonic Engineering, Applied Optics
WAKASHIMA, K., Materials Science, Micromechanics of Composites
WATANABE, S., Mathematics and Information Science
YOKOTA, S., Fluid Power Control

Research Laboratory for Nuclear Reactors:

ARITOMI, M., Nuclear Thermal Engineering
FUJII, Y., Fusion Fuel Chemistry, Tritium Chemistry
HATTORI, T., Accelerator Physics, Heavy Ion Inertial Fusion
KATO, Y., Advanced Nuclear Reactor Systems Design, Complex Flow Computer Simulation
NINOKATA, H., Reactor Safety, Reactor Physics
OGAWA, M., Beam Plasma Sciences, Nuclear Fusion, Nuclear Physics
SEKIMOTO, H., Neutronics, Nuclear Reactor Design
SHIMADA, R., Fusion Reactor Control, Plasma Engineering
TORII, H., Energy Policy
YANO, T., Composite Materials and their Properties
YOSHIZAWA, Y., Thermal Engineering, Energy System, Combustion

TOKYO MEDICAL AND DENTAL UNIVERSITY

5-45, Yushima 1-chome, Bunkyo-ku, Tokyo 113

Telephone: (3) 3813-6111
E-mail: webmaster.isc@tmd.ac.jp
Internet: www.tmd.ac.jp
Founded 1946
Independent
Academic year: April to March (2 semesters)
Pres.: AKIO SUZUKI
Dir-Gen.: O. KIKUKAWA
Dir for Univ. Library: KEIICHI OHYA
Library of 334,132 vols
Number of teachers: 696
Number of students: 2,921
Publications: *Bulletin, Bulletin of the Department of General Education, Reports of the Medical Research Institute, Reports of the Institute for Medical and Dental Engineering*

DEANS

College of Liberal Arts and Sciences: SAKUMI ITABASHI
Faculty of Dentistry: KAZUHIRO ETO
Faculty of Medicine: KATSUIKU HIROKAWA
Graduate School of Allied Health Sciences: RYUICHI KAMIYAMA

ATTACHED INSTITUTES

Institute for Medical and Dental Engineering: 3-10, Kandasurugadai 2-chome, Chiyoda-ku, Tokyo 101; Dir T. TOGAWA.
Medical Research Institute: 3-10, Kandasurugadai 2-chome, Chiyoda-ku, Tokyo 101; Dir A. SAKUMA.

TOKYO NATIONAL UNIVERSITY OF FINE ARTS AND MUSIC

12-8 Ueno Park, Taito-ku, Tokyo 110-8714

Telephone: (3) 5685-7500
Fax: (3) 5685-7760
Internet: www.geidai.ac.jp
Founded 1949
Pres.: IKUO HIRAYAMA
Dir of Univ. Library: HIROMICHI UENO
Sec.-Gen.: YOSHIYUKI OTAWA
Library: see Libraries and Archives
Number of teachers: 218 full-time
Number of students: 2,785

DEANS

Faculty of Fine Arts: KIJO ROKKAKU
Faculty of Music: AKIO SONODA

DIRECTORS

Media Art Center: TAKAMICHI ITO
Performing Arts Center: TERUO SANBAYASHI
Training centre for Foreign Languages and Declamation: SHUN'ICHIRO HATA
University Art Museum: JUNICHI TAKEUCHI

UNIVERSITY OF TOKYO

7-3-1 Hongo, Bunkyo-ku, Tokyo 113-8654

Telephone: (3) 3812-2111
Fax: (3) 5689-7344
E-mail: kokusai@ml.adm.u-tokyo.ac.jp
Internet: www.u-tokyo.ac.jp
Founded 1877
Independent
Academic year: April to March
Pres.: Dr JUNICHI HAMADA
Univ. Librarian: KAZUHIKO SAIGO
Library: see Libraries and Archives
Number of teachers: 4,165
Number of students: 29,000

DEANS

Graduate School of Agricultural and Life Sciences and Faculty of Agriculture: SHIN-ICHI SHOGENJI
Graduate School of Arts and Sciences and College of Arts and Sciences: SUSUMU YAMAKAGE
Graduate School of Economics and Faculty of Economics: HIROSHI YOSHIKAWA
Graduate School of Education and Faculty of Education: M. SATOH
Graduate School of Engineering and Faculty of Engineering: TAKEHIKO KITAMORI
Graduate School of Frontier Sciences: HIROYUKI YAMATO
Graduate School of Humanities and Sociology and Faculty of Letters: KAZUHISA TAKAHASHI
Graduate School of Information Science and Technology: M. TAKEICHI
Graduate School for Law and Politics: MASAHITO INOUYE
Graduate School of Mathematical Sciences: TOSHIO OSHIMA
Graduate School of Medicine and Faculty of Medicine: TAKAO SHIMIZU
Graduate School of Pharmaceutical Sciences and Faculty of Pharmaceutical Sciences: TETSUO NAGANO
Graduate School of Public Policy: KUNIAKI TANABE
Graduate School of Science and Faculty of Science: TOSHIO YAMAGATA

Interfaculty Initiative in Information Studies and Graduate School of Interdisciplinary Information Studies: T. HANADA

PROFESSORS

Graduate School of Agricultural and Life Sciences and Faculty of Agriculture (1-1-1 Yayoi, Bunkyo-ku, Tokyo 113-8657; tel. (3) 5841-5486; fax (3) 5841-8122; e-mail oice@ofc.a.u-tokyo.ac.jp; internet www.a.u-tokyo.ac.jp/english/index.html):

ABE, H., Biochemistry of Aquatic Animals
ABE, K., Biological Function Development
AIDA, K., Fish Physiology
AKASHI, H., Veterinary Microbiology
ANDO, N., Wood-based Materials and Timber Engineering
AOKI, I., Fisheries Biology
CHIDA, K., Cell Regulation
DOI, K., Veterinary Pathology
FUKUDA, K., Biological Function Development
FUKUI, Y., Biological Chemistry
FUKUYO, Y., Aquatic Biology
FURUYA, K., Fisheries Oceanography
HAYASHI, Y., Veterinary Anatomy
HIGUCHI, H., Wildlife Biology
HINO, A., Aquaculture Biology
HOGETSU, T., Plant Physiology and Plant Ecology, Silviculture
HONMA, M., Economics
HORI, S., Landscape and Sustainable Tourism
HORINOUCHI, S., Microbiology and Fermentation
IDE, Y., Forestry Gene Science
IGARASHI, Y., Applied Microbiology
INOUE, M., Forest Policy
ISOGAI, A., Pulp and Paper Sciences
ITOH, K., Veterinary Public Health
IWAMOTO, N., Agricultural History and History of Agricultural Sciences
IZUMIDA, Y., International Food System
KISHINO, H., Biometrics and Statistical Genetics
KITAHARA, T., Organic Chemistry
KOBAYASHI, H., Forest Utilization
KOBAYASHI, K., Agricultural Ecosystems
KUGA, S., Structural Biopolymers
KUMAGAI, S., Veterinary Public Health
KUMAGAI, Y., Evaluation of the Natural Environment
KURATA, K., Bio-environmental Engineering
KUROHMARU, M., Veterinary Anatomy
KUROKURA, H., Aquatic Biology
MASAKI, H., Molecular and Cellular Breeding
MATSUNAGA, S., Aquatic Natural Products Chemistry
MESHITSUKA, G., Wood Chemistry and Pulping Chemistry
MIYAZAKI, T., Soil Physics and Soil Hydrology
MORI, Y., Veterinary Ethology
NAGASAWA, H., Bio-organic Chemistry
NAGATA, S., Forest Ecology and Society
NAGATO, Y., Plant Breeding and Genetics
NAKANISHI, T. M., Radio–Plant Psychology
NANBA, S., Bioresource Technology
NISHIHATA, M., Veterinary Physiology
NISHIYAMA, M., Cell Biotechnology
NISHIZAWA, N. K., Plant Nutrition and Biotechnology
OGAWA, H., Veterinary Emergency Medicine
OGAWA, K., Fish Pathology
OHSHITA, S., Bioprocess Engineering
OHSUGI, R., Crop Physiology
OHTA, A., Cellular Genetics
OHTA, M., Wood-based Materials and Timber Engineering, Wood Physics
OMASA, K., Biological and Environmental Information Engineering
ONO, H., Polymeric Materials

ONO, K., Veterinary Clinical Pathobiology
ONODERA, T., Molecular Immunology
OYAIZU, H., Soil Science
OZAKI, H., Veterinary Pharmacology
SAGARA, Y., Food Informatics and Engineering
SAKAI, H., Forest Utilization
SAKAI, S., Animal Breeding
SAMEJIMA, M., Forest Chemistry
SASAKI, N., Veterinary Surgery
SATO, R., Food Chemistry
SENOO, K., Soil Microbiology
SHIMADA, T., Insect Genetics and Bioscience
SHIMIZU, K., Bioinformation Engineering
SHIMIZU, M., Food Chemistry
SHIMOMURA, A., Forest Landscape Planning and Design
SHIOTA, K., Cellular Biochemistry
SHIOZAWA, S., Physical Planning and Environmental Engineering
SHIRAISHI, N., Forest Management
SHIRAKO, Y., RNA Virology
SHOGENJI, S., Food and Resource Economics
SHOUN, H., Enzymology and Applied Microbiology
SUGIYAMA, N., Horticultural Science
SUZUKI, M., Forest Hydrology and Erosion Control
TAKAHASHI, N., Nutritional Biochemistry
TAKEUCHI, K., Landscape Ecology and Planning
TANAKA, T., Water Environmental Engineering
TANGE, T., Forest Ecophysiology
TANIGUCHI, N., Agricultural Structure and Policy
TANOKURA, M., Food Engineering
TATSUKI, S., Applied Entomology
TOJO, H., Applied Genetics
TSUBONE, H., Comparative Pathophysiology
TSUJIMOTO, H., Veterinary Internal Medicine
TSUTSUMI, N., Plant Molecular Genetics
WASHITANI, I., Conservation Ecology
WATABE, S., Aquatic Molecular Biology and Technology
WATANABE, H., Organic Chemistry
YAGI, H., Farm Business Management
YAMAGUCHI, I., Pesticide and Natural Products Chemistry
YAMAGUCHI-SHINOZAKI, L., Plant Molecular Biology
YAMAMOTO, H., Forest Planning
YAMANE, H., Environmental Biochemistry
YATAGAI, M., Plant Material Sciences
YODA, K., Microbiology Biotechnology
YOKOYAMA, S., Biomass Energy Conversion Technology
YONEYAMA, T., Plant Nutrition and Fertilizers
YOSHIKAWA, Y., Laboratory Animal Science
YOSHIMURA, E., Plant Molecular Physiology

Graduate School of Arts and Sciences and College of Arts and Sciences (3-8-1 Komaba, Meguro-ku, Tokyo 153-8902; tel. (3) 5454-6827; fax (3) 5454-4319; e-mail info-komaba@adm.c.u-tokyo.ac.jp; internet www.c.u-tokyo.ac.jp):

ADACHI, H., History of Japanese Technology
ADACHI, N., Area Studies
AIZAWA, T., German, German History
AOKI, M., German
ARAI, Y., Human Geography
ARAMAKI, K., International Finance
ASASHIMA, M., Developmental Biology
ATOMI, Y., Sports Sciences
BOCCELLARI, J., English, Comparative Literature
ELLIS, T., Japanese as a Foreign Language
ENDO, Y., American Studies
ENDO, Y., Physical Chemistry

ERIGUCHI, Y., Astrophysics
FUKAGAWA, Y., Development Studies, Korean Studies
FUNABIKI, T., Cultural Anthropology
GOTO, N., Environmental Economics
HASEGAWA, T., Behavioural Ecology
HAYAKAMA, S., Law
HAYASHI, F., American Literature
HIKAMI, S., Statistical Physics
HIROMATSU, T., Statistics
HYODO, T., Physics
IKEDA, N., German
IKEGAMI, S., European Medieval History
IKEUCHI, M., Biology
IMAI, T., Philosophy
ISHIDA, A., International Relations
ISHIDA, Y., German History, Comparative Genocide Studies
ISHII, A., International Relations
ISHII, N., Sports Sciences
ISHII, Y., French
ISHIMITSU, Y., German Literature
ISHIURA, S., Neuroscience
ISOZAKI, Y., Earth Science
ITO, A., Cultural Anthropology
ITOH, T., English
IWASA, T., French, Contemporary Art
IWASAWA, Y., International Law
KADOWAKI, S., Philosophy
KAGOSHIMA, S., Solid-State Physics
KAJI, T., German
KANEKO, K., Nonlinear Physics, Statistical Physics
KARIMA, F., Chinese
KATO, M., Architectural Composition Theory
KAWAI, S., Graphics
KAWANAGO, Y., German, History of Christian Thought
KAWATO, S., Biophysics
KAZAMA, Y., Theory of Elementary Particles
KIBATA, Y., English, British History
KIMURA, H., Anthropology
KITAGAWA, S., Philosophy
KOBAYASHI, K., Sports Sciences
KOBAYASHI, Y., French, Modern Thought
KODA, K., German
KOJIMA, N., Chemistry
KOJO, Y., Political Science
KOMAKI, K., Radiation Physics
KOMIYAMA, S., Theory of Solid-State Physics
KOMORI, Y., Japanese Literature
KONDOH, A., Japanese
KONOSHI, T., Japanese Literature
KOTERA, A., International Law
KUBOTA, S., Sports Science
KUGA, T., Quantum Electronics, Quantum Optics
KURODA, R., Biochemistry of DNA
KUROZUMI, M., Ethics, Japanese Intellectual History
LAMARRE, C., Linguistic Analysis
MABUCHI, I., Biochemistry and Biophysics
MARUYAMA, M., Economics
MASUDA, K., French, French Philosophy
MASUDA, S., Chemistry
MATSUBARA, R., Economic Thought, Social Economics
MATSUI, T., Theoretical Nuclear Physics
MATSUO, N., Environmental and Analytical Chemistry
MATSUOKA, S., Japanese Literature
MATSUURA, H., Multimedia Analysis
MISUMI, Y., Japanese Literature
MITANI, H., Japanese History
MIYAMOTO, H., Philosophy
MIYASHITA, S., French
MORI, M., Political and Social Philosophy
MOTOMURA, R., European History
MURATA, J., Philosophy
MURATA, M., Cell Biology and Biophysics
MURATA, Y., China Studies
NAGATA, T., Physical Chemistry
NAKAI, K., International Relations

NAKANISHI, T., Economics
NAKAZAWA, H., Crosscultural Communication
NAMIKI, Y., Chinese History
NISHINAKAMURA, H., Russian
NIWA, K., Research Management
NOMURA, T., Japanese
NOTOJI, M., American Literature
OE, H., International Relations, Human Security
OGOSHI, N., Korean
OHTA, K., Theoretical Nuclear Physics
OKA, H., English
OKABE, Y., German, Comparative Literature
OKOSHI, Y., Criminal Law
ONAKA, M., Catalysis Chemistry
ONUKI, T., Hellenistic and Early Christian Literature
OTSUKI, T., Sports Sciences
ROSSITTER, P., English
SAKAHARA, S., French
SAKAI, T., Political Science
SASAKI, C., History and Philosophy of Science
SATO, N., Plant Biology
SATO, Y., English, American Literature
SATO, Y., Law, Dispute Processing, Peace Building
SATOMI, D., Biology
SHIBA, N., Serbo-Croat, History
SHIBATA, T., History of Political Thought
SHIGEMASU, K., Bayesian Statistics
SHIMADA, M., Population and Evolutionary Ecology
SHIMOI, M., Inorganic Chemistry, Coordination Chemistry
SHIROTA, T., Chinese Literature
SUGAWARA, K., English
SUGAWARA, T., Physical Organic Chemistry
SUGIHASHI, Y., German, Literature and Aesthetics
SUGITA, H., Arabic
SUTOH, K., Molecular Cell Biology
SUYAMA, A., Biophysics
SUZUKI, H., English and Music
SUZUKI, K., French
SUZUKI, K., Graphics
TAJIRI, M., German
TAKADA, Y., English Literature
TAKAHASHI, H., History
TAKAHASHI, N., Political Science
TAKAHASHI, S., German Literature
TAKAHASHI, T., Philosophy
TAKATSUKA, K., Theoretical Molecular Science
TAKEUCHI, N., French, Comparative Literature
TAKITA, Y., English
TAMAI, T., Software Engineering
TANIUCHI, T., Human Geography
TANJI, A., English Literature
TOMODA, S., Organic Chemistry
TSUNEKAWA, K., Political Science
UCHIDA, R., Contemporary Society
UEDA, H., Spanish
URA, M., Russian Literature
USUI, R., German
WAKABAYASHI, M., Chinese, Modern History of East Asia
WILSON, B., English
YAMADA, H., French Literature, Psychoanalytic Criticism
YAMAKAGE, S., International Relations
YAMAMOTO, S., English
YAMAMOTO, T., Philosophy
YAMAMOTO, Y., Culture and Social Change
YAMASHITA, S., Cultural Anthropology
YAMAUCHI, M., Asian History
YAMAWAKI, N., History of Social Thought
YAMAZAKI, Y., Atomic Physics
YONEYA, T., Theoretical Physics
YOSHIE, A., Japanese History
YOSHIOKA, D., Theory of Solid-State Physics
YUASA, H., French

YUI, D., American and International History

Graduate School of Economics and Faculty of Economics (7-3-1 Hongo, Bunkyo-ku, Tokyo 113-0033; tel. (3) 5841-5543; fax (3) 5841-5521; e-mail advisefs@e.u-tokyo.ac.jp; internet www.e.u-tokyo.ac.jp):

ABE, M., Marketing

ARAI, T., Corporate Finance, Securities Investment

BABA, S., Economic History of the Western World, History of Industrialization and Urbanization in Germany

DAIGO, S., Financial Accounting

FUJIMOTO, T., Technology and Operations Management

FUJIWARA, M., Applied Microeconomics

FUKUDA, S., Money and Banking, Macroeconomics

HANNAH, L., Comparative Business History

HAYASHI, F., Applied Econometrics, Macroeconomics

HIROTA, I., Economic History of Modern France

ICHIMURA, H.

IHORI, T., Public Finance and Economics

ITO, T., International Finance, Finance and Macroeconomics

ITOH, MASANAO, Japanese Economy, Financial History in Japan

ITOH, MOTOSHIGE, International Economics

IWAI, K., Economic Theory

IWAMI, T., International Economics

IWAMOTO, Y., Public Economics, Macroeconomics

JINNO, N., Public Finance

KAMIYA, K., Microeconomics, Mathematical Programming

KANDORI, M., Microeconomic Theory, Game Theory

KANEMOTO, Y., Urban Economics

KOBAYASHI, T., Theory of Investments and Capital Markets

KUBOKAWA, T., Mathematical Statistics

KUNITOMO, N., Statistics, Econometrics and Financial Econometrics

MATSUI, A., Game Theory, Information Economics, Monetary Theory

MATSUSHIMA, H., Microeconomics, Game Theory, Theory of Finance, Informational Economics

MIWA, Y., Economics of Regulations, Corporate Governance, Law and Economics

MOCHIDA, N., Public Finance, Intergovernmental Fiscal Relations

MORI, T., Industrial Relations

OBATA, M., Economic Theory

OKAZAKI, T., Japanese Economic History

OKUDA, H., Russian Economic History

ONOZUKA, T., Economic History of the Western World

SAGUCHI, K., Industrial Relations

SHIBATA, T., Modern Capitalism, Institutional Economics

TABUCHI, T., Urban Economics

TAKAHASHI, N., Organization Theory

TAKEDA, H., Japanese Economic History

TAKENOUCHI, M., International Economics

UEDA, K., Macroeconomics, Financial Theory, Theory of International Finance

WADA, K., Comparative Business History

YAJIMA, Y., Statistics and Econometrics

YOSHIKAWA, H., Macroeconomics

Graduate School of Humanities and Sociology and Faculty of Letters (7-3-1 Hongo, Bunkyo-ku, Tokyo 113-0033; tel. (3) 5841-3705; fax (3) 5841-3817; e-mail shomu@l.u-tokyo.ac.jp; internet www.l.u-tokyo.ac.jp):

AKIYAMA, H., Social Psychology of Ageing

AMANO, M., Philosophy

FUJII, S., Modern Chinese Literature

FUJITA, K., Aesthetics

FUJITA, S., Early Modern Japanese History

FUJIWARA, K., Japanese Literature of Heian Era

FUKASAWA, K., History of Early Modern Europe

GOMI, F., Medieval Japanese History

GOTO, T., Japanese Archaeology

HASEMI, K., Russian and Polish Literature

HATTORI, T., Korean Studies (Sociology)

HAYASI, T., Turkic Languages

HIRAISHI, T., American Literature

HIRANO, Y., German Language and Literature

ICHIKAWA, H., History of Religion, the Bible and Judaism

IKEDA, K., Political Behaviour and Communication, Social Reality and Mediated Communication

IMAMURA, K., Japanese and Asian Archaeology

IMANISHI, N., English Linguistics and Syntax Theory

ISHII, N., History of Modern Europe

ITUMI, K., Classical Languages and Literature

KANAZAWA, M., Russian Literature

KANNO, K., Japanese Ethical Thoughts

KATAYAMA, H., Classical Languages and Literature

KAWAHARA, H., History of the Science of Chance

KIMURA, H., Chinese Language

KINOSHITA, N., Cultural Resource Studies

KISHIMOTO, M., Chinese History

KOJIMA, T., Medieval Japanese Literature

KOMATSU, H., Central Asian History

KONDO, K., History of Modern Europe

KONO, M., History of Japanese Art

KUMAMOTO, H., Indo-European Linguistics

MARUI, H., Indian Philosophy

MATSUMOTO, M., Sociology of Science and Technology, Environmental Sociology

MATSUMURA, K., Uralic Linguistics

MATSUNAGA, S., Philosophy

MATSUURA, J., German Language

MIZUSHIMA, T., South Asian History

MURAI, S., Medieval Japanese History

NAGAMI, S., Italian Language and Literature

NAGASHIMA, H., Early Modern Japanese Literature

NAKAJI, Y., French Language and Literature

NISHIMURA, K., Aesthetics

NITAGAI, K., Urban Sociology

NUMANO, M., Russian and Polish Literature

OHASI, Y., English Literature

ONUKI, S., East Asian Archaeology

OSANO, S., History of Western Art

SAITO, A., Indian Philosophy

SAKURAI, M., Ancient Greek History

SAKURAI, Y., Southeast Asian History

SATO, M., Ancient Japanese History

SATO, S., Intellectual History of Modern China

SATO, T., Visual Perception

SATO, Y., Ethics and Social Thought

SATO, Y., History of Japanese Art

SEIYAMA, K., Mathematical Sociology

SEKINE, S., Occidental Ethical Thought

SHIBATA, M., American Literature

SHIGETO, M., German Linguistics

SHIMAZONO, S., Japanese Religious Thought

SHIOKAWA, T., French Language and Literature

SHITOMI, Y., West Asian History

SUEKI, F., Japanese Buddhism

SUZUKI, T., Japanese Language

TACHIBANA, M., Visual Neuroscience

TADA, K., Ancient Japanese Literature

TAKAHASHI, K., English Literature

TAKAHASHI, T., Dravidian Language and Literature

TAKANO, Y., Cognitive Psychology

TAKAYAMA, H., Medieval European History

TAKAYAMA, M., Philosophy

TAKEGAWA, S., Sociology of Social Policy

TAKESHITA, M., Islamic Studies

TAKEUCHI, S., Japanese Ethical Thought

TAMURA, T., French Language and Literature

TOKURA, H., Chinese Literature

TSUCHIDA, R., Sanskrit Language and Literature

TSUKIMURA, T., French Language and Literature

TSUNODA, T., Australian Aboriginal Linguistics

TSURUOKA, Y., Christian Mysticism

UENO, C., Family and Gender Studies

UTAGAWA, H., East Asian Archaeology

UWANO, Z., Accentology and Dialectology

WATANABE, H., Aesthetics

YAMAGUCHI, S., Experimental Social Psychology

YOSHIDA, M., Korean History

YOSHIDA, N., Early Modern Japanese History

Graduate School of Education and Faculty of Education (7-3-1 Hongo, Bunkyo-ku, Tokyo 113-0033; tel. (3) 5841-3904; fax (3) 5841-3914; e-mail edushomu@p.u-tokyo.ac.jp; internet www.p.u-tokyo.ac.jp/index-j.html):

AKITA, K., Action Research on Training

ETO, T., Health Education

HAEBARA, T., Educational Measurement

HIJIKATA, S., History of Japanese Education

HIROTA, T., Sociology of Education

ICHIKAWA, S., Cognitive Psychology

KAMEGUCHI, K., Clinical Psychology

KANAMORI, O., Methods of Education

KANEKO, M., Higher Education

KARIYA, T., Sociology of Education

KAWAMOTO, T., History of Western Education

MUTOH, Y., Physical Education

NAKADA, M., Methods of Education

NEMOTO, A., Library and Information Science

OGAWA, M., Educational Administration

SASAKI, M., Methods of Education

SATOH, K., Lifelong Learning

SATOH, M., Action Research on Teaching

SHIMOYAMA, H., Clinical Psychology

SHIOMI, T., Science of Education

SHIRAISHI, S., Anthropology of Education

TANAKA, C., Clinical Psychology

WATANABE, H., Educational Measurement

YAMAMOTO, Y., Physiology of Education

YANO, M., Higher Education

Graduate School of Engineering and Faculty of Engineering (7-3-1 Hongo, Bunkyo-ku, Tokyo 113-8656; tel. (3) 5841-7662; fax (3) 5841-7446; e-mail octo@t-adm.t.u-tokyo.ac.jp; internet www.t.u-tokyo.ac.jp):

AIDA, T., Macromolecular Chemistry, Supramolecular Chemistry, Bioinorganic Chemistry

AOKI, T., Aerospace Structures, Mechanics of Composite Materials, Smart Structures

ARAI, T., Automatic Assembly, Robotics, Artificial Intelligence and Service Engineering

ARAKAWA, Y., Electric Propulsion

DOI, M., Soft Matter Physics, Polymer Physics, Rheology

DOMEN, K., Heterogeneous Catalysis

FUJIMOTO, K., Deformation and Fracture of Solids, Tribology

FUJINO, Y., Structural Engineering, Dynamics, Control and Monitoring of Structures and Bridges, Wind and Earthquake

FUJITA, M., Organic Coordination Chemistry

FUJITA, T., Mineral and Material Processing, Recycling Technology, Intelligent Fluid

FUJIWARA, T., Solid-State Physics, Electronic Structure in Condensed Matter

FURUMAI, H., Urban Drainage and Water Quality Management

FURUTA, K., Cognitive Systems Engineering, Technology for Safe and Secure Society

GONOKAMI, M., Non-linear Optics, Quantum Optics, Quantum Electronics, Optical Processes in Solids

HANAKI, K., Urban and Global Environmental Management, Urban Environment Systems

HARATA, N., Urban Transport Planning

HASHIMOTO, K., Intelligent Materials

HASHIMOTO, T., Science and Technology Studies

HIDAKA, K., High Voltage Engineering, Electrical Insulation, Electrical Discharge and Plasma Physics

HIGUCHI, T., Mechatronics, Micro Electromechanical Systems

HIRAO, K., Theoretical Chemistry and Electronic Structure Theory

HORI, K., Artificial Intelligence

HORII, H., Sociotechnology, Rock Mechanics, Applied Mechanics

HOTATE, K., Photonic Sensing, Photonic Signal Processing, Optical Devices

ICHIKAWA, M., Semiconductor Nano-science and Technology

IEDA, H., Transport and City Planning

IIZUKA, Y., Systems Analysis and Design, Structured Knowledge Engineering, Health Care Social System Engineering

IKUHARA, Y., Interface and Grain Boundary Engineering

ISHIHARA, K., Biomaterials

ISHIHARA, S., Nanomechanics, Nanofabrication

ITO, T., Urban and Architectural History

KAGEYAMA, K., Composite Materials Engineering, Smart Material and Structure Systems

KAMATA, M., Equipment and Environmental Engineering

KAMATA, M., Noise and Vibration Control, Vehicle Engineering, Assistive Technology

KANEKO, S., Flow-induced Vibration, Vibration Control, Micro Gas Turbine Engineering

KANNO, M., Metallic Materials

KANODA, K., Experimental Physics of Low-dimensional Correlated Electronic Systems

KASAGI, N., Thermal and Fluids Engineering, Energy Systems Engineering, Turbulence Engineering

KATAOKA, K., Biomaterials and Drug Delivery Systems

KATO, T., Materials Chemistry, Polymer Chemistry, Supramolecular Chemistry

KATO, T., Surface Engineering, Tribology, Nanotribology

KATSUMURA, Y., Radiation Chemistry, Applied Radiation Chemistry

KAWACHI, K., Flight Dynamics, Biokinetics, Helicopter Engineering

KIMURA, F., Design Engineering, CAD/CAM, Manufacturing Systems, Computer-aided Technology in Manufacturing Engineering

KISHIO, K., Solid-State Chemistry, Ionic and Electronic Transport in Solids, Superconductivity

KITAMORI, T., Integration of Micro Chemical Systems, Micro Space Chemistry

KOBAYASHI, I., Environmental Information Network, Light Communications

KOIDE, O., Evaluation of Regional Risks and Multimedia Database System for Historical Disasters

KOIKE, T., Hydrology and Water Resources, Remote Sensing

KOMIYAMA, H., Global Environmental Engineering, Materials Science and Engineering

KOSAKO, T., Radiation Safety, Radiation Shielding, Radiation Dosimetry

KOSEKI, T., Metals and Alloys

KOSHI, M., Chemical Reaction Kinetics, Laser-induced Chemistry

KOSHIZUKA, S., Computational Fluid Dynamics

KUBO, T., Structural and Earthquake Engineering, Reinforced Concrete Structures

KUWAMURA, H., Structural Engineering, Steel Structures, Welding Mechanics, Reliability Analysis and New Materials

MABUCHI, K., Advanced Biomedical Engineering and Life Sciences

MADARAME, H., Nuclear Safety

MAEDA, K., Defects in Solids, Nanoscopic Analysis

MAEKAWA, K., Concrete Engineering, Modelling of Concrete Performance

MARUYAMA, S., Science and Technology of Carbon Nanotubes, Nanoscale Thermal Engineering

MATSUMOTO, Y., Fluid Engineering, Molecular Dynamics

MATSUSHIMA, K., Business and Innovation Modelling

MITSUISHI, M., Intelligent Manufacturing Systems, Network-based Manufacturing Systems, Active Thermal Compensation for High-speed Machine Tools

MIYATA, H., Computational Fluid Dynamics, Systems Design, Technology Management

MIZUNO, N., Catalytic Chemistry, Inorganic Chemistry

MOHRI, N., Manufacturing Systems Control, Precision Machining

MORISHITA, E., High-speed Gas Dynamics

NAGAMUNE, T., Biotechnology, Biochemical Engineering, Protein Engineering

NAGAOSA, N., Condensed Matter Theory, Superconductivity

NAGASAKI, S., Safety Research on the Nuclear Fuel Cycle

NAGASAWA, Y., Architectural Planning and Design

NAGASHIMA, T., Aerospace Propulsion

NAGASUKA, S., Space Engineering

NAITO, H., Architectural Design, Landscape Design

NAKAO, M., Nano-micro Manufacturing, Information Instrument Design, Mechanical Engineering for Science

NAKAO, S., Membrane Science and Technology

NAKAZAWA, M., Radiation Measurement, Quantum Beam Engineering

NAMBA, K., Sustainable Design in Architecture and Urban Space

NAWATA, K., Econometrics, Statistics

NISHIMURA, Y., Urban Conservation Planning, Urban Design

NITTA, T., Applied Superconductivity, Electrical Machinery, Power Systems

NOZAKI, K., Organometallic Chemistry, Homogeneous Catalysis

ODA, T., Electrostatics, Plasma Application for Environmental Protection and Magnetic Separation

OHASHI, H., Thermal Hydrodynamics, Advanced Models for Complex Phenomena

OHBA, Z., Education Systems Project

OHGAKI, S., Environmental Engineering

OHTSU, M., Nanophotonics

OKA, Y., Nuclear Reactor Design and Analysis

OKABE, A., Urban and Regional Analysis, Geographical Information Science

OKABE, Y., Information Devices, Superconductive Electronics, Brain Computer

OKAMOTO, K., Visualization, Micro- ,Nano- and Biofluids

OKATA, J., Urban Planning

OKUBO, S., Mining Machinery, Rock Mechanics

OKUDA, H., Computational Mechanics, Digital Value Engineering

OSHIMA, M., Semiconductor Surface Chemistry, Synchrotron Radiation Science

OZAWA, K., Construction, Project and Infrastructure Management

RINOIE, K., Aircraft Design, Separated Flow Aerodynamics

ROKUGAWA, S., Exploration Geophysics, Earth Observing Systems

SAKAI, S., Strength of Materials, Life Cycle Assessment, Fracture Mechanics

SAKAMOTO, I., Building Construction, Timber Structures

SAKAMOTO, Y., Environmental Control Engineering, Air Conditioning

SATO, K., Petroleum Engineering

SATO, S., Coastal and Environmental Engineering

SEKIMURA, N., Maintenance Engineering, Nuclear Materials, Effects of Radiation on Materials

SHIBATA, T., Semiconductor Devices and Integrated Circuits, Integrated Human Intelligence Systems

SHIMIZU, E., Geoinformatics, Regional Planning

SHINOHARA, O., Landscape Planning and Civic Design

SHIOYA, T., Aerospace Materials, Mechanical Behaviour of Materials

SUGA, T., Microsystem Integration and Packaging, Eco-design

SUZUKI, H., Computer-aided Design and Manufacture, Geometric Modelling

SUZUKI, H., History of Architecture, History of Modern Architecture

SUZUKI, H., Structural Engineering, Ocean Engineering

SUZUKI, S., Flight Mechanics, Control Engineering

SUZUKI, T., Systems Engineering in Materials Science

TAIRA, K., RNA as Origin of Life and RNA Technology

TAKADA, T., Structural Reliability, Earthquake Engineering, Computational Mechanics, Risk Analysis, Decision Theory

TAKAHASHI, H., Digital Signal Processing

TAKAMASU, K., Precision Metrology, Nanometer Measurement, Coordinate Metrology

TAMAKI, K., Marine Geology

TANAKA, M., Materials and Device Physics, Spintronics

TANAKA, S., Fusion Engineering, Nuclear Waste Management

TARUCHA, S., Electronic Properties of Semiconductor Nanostructures

TERAI, T., Materials Science for Nuclear Systems, Fusion Reactor Engineering, Synthesis and Property Control of Advanced Materials by High-energy Particle Processing

TOKURA, Y., Materials Physics

TORIUMI, A., Advanced Devices Engineering

TOWHATA, I., Geotechnical Engineering

UEDA, T., Cost-Benefit Analysis, Infrastructure Economics

UESAKA, M., Quantum Beam Engineering and Applied Electro-Magnetics

WADA, K., Microphotonics

WASHIZU, M., Bio-nanotechnology

WATANABE, S., Computational Engineering of Nanomaterials

YAGI, O., Applied Microbiology

YAMADA, I., Lifestyle and Environmental Information Technology, Network Sensing, Telecommunication Energy Systems

YAMAGUCHI, H., Polar Environment Engineering, Cavitation

YAMAGUCHI, S., Solid-State Ionics

YAMAGUCHI, Y., Nanomaterials Technology, Chemical System Engineering

YAMAJI, K., Energy Systems Engineering

YAMASHITA, K., Theoretical Chemistry and Chemical Reaction Dynamics, Computational Molecular Engineering

YAMATOMI, J., Rock Engineering and Mining Engineering

YOKOYAMA, A., Power Systems Engineering, Control Engineering

YOSHIDA, M., Education Systems Project

YOSHIDA, T., Plasma Materials Engineering

YUHARA, T., Energy Engineering and Policy, Engineering for Naval Architecture and Ocean Engineering, Management of Engineering Projects

Graduate School of Frontier Sciences (5-1-5 Kashiwanoha, Kashiwa-shi, Chiba 277-8562; tel. (4) 7136-5506; fax (4) 7136-4021; e-mail souiki@k.u-tokyo.ac.jp; internet www.k.u-tokyo.ac.jp):

AIDA, H., High-quality Networking, Parallel and Distributed Processing

AIZAWA, K., Image Processing, Multimedia Technologies

AMEMIYA, Y., X-ray Physics and Instrumentation

ASAI, K., Stochastic Models in Bioinformatics

CHIKAYAMA, T., Information Engineering

FUJIMORI, A., Condensed Matter Physics

FUJIWARA, H., Insect Molecular Biology

HAMANO, Y., Content Production

HARATA, N., Urban Transport Planning, Environmental Information Systems in Spatial Planning and Policy

HASEZAWA, S., Plant Cell Biology

HIHARA, E., Refrigeration Engineering, Heat Transfer, Multi-phase Flows

HIROSE, K., Speech Information Processing

HISADA, T., Finite Element Method, Biomechanics

HOSAKA, H., Information Mechatronics and Microdynamics

IBA, H., Evolutionary Computation, Evolutionary Robotics, Genome Informatics

ISOBE, M., Coastal Environment

ITO, K., Polymer Physics

ITO, T., Functional Genomics

IWATA, S., Design Science, Environmental Studies

KAGEMOTO, H., Environmental Hydrodynamics

KAJI, M., Forest Ecology

KANDA, J., Structural Engineering

KATAOKA, H., Biochemistry

KAWAI, M., Surface Science, Nano-Science

KAWANO, S., Molecular Cell Biology

KIMURA, K., Nano-space Function Design, Applied Solid-State Physics

KITOH, S., Environmental Ethics

KOBAYASHI, I., Laboratory of Social Genome Sciences

KOJI, O., Environmental Visualization

KONO, M., Energy Conversion, Aerospace Propulsion

KUMAGAI, Y., Landscape Architecture, Forest Landscape Planning and Design

KUNISHIMA, M., International Infrastructure Development and Management

MATSUHASHI, R., Environment Systems and Economics

MATSUI, T., Comparative Planetology

MINO, T., Water Environment Control, Environmental Biotechnology

MITANI, H., Molecular Genetics, Radiation Biology

MIYAMOTO, Y., Molecular Physiology

MORISHITA, S., Computational Biology, Bioinformatics, Data Mining, Database Systems, Computational Logic

NAGATA, M., Insect Pathology

NAKAYAMA, M., Weather Resources Management and Regional Planning

NAMBA, S., Molecular Plant-Microbe Interactions

NISHITA, T., Computer Graphics

OHMORI, H., Natural Environmental Structures

OHNO, H., Living Environmental Design

OHSAWA, M., Plant Ecology

OHYA, Y., Signal Transduction

OKADA, M., Brain Science Information Theory and Physics

ONABE, K., Semiconductor Materials Engineering

SAIGO, K., Synthetic Organic Chemistry, Synthetic Macromolecular Chemistry

SAIKI, K., Surface Science

SAKUMA, I., Biomedical Engineering, Computer-aided Surgery, Precision Engineering

SASAKI, K., Mechatronics, Signal Processing

SHIBATA, T., Semiconductor Electronics

SUGANO, S., Functional Genomics

SUGIURA, S., Cardiology, Physiology of Cardiac Muscle

TAKAGI, H., Solid-State Physics and Chemistry

TAKAGI, S., Semiconductor Device Engineering

TAKAGI, T., Computational Biology

TAKAGI, Y., Development Economics

TAKASE, Y., Plasma Physics

TAKEDA, N., Smart Structures and Composite Materials

TAKEDA, T., Brain Science

TORIUMI, M., Petrology, Structural Geology

TORO, S., Ocean Environmental Engineering

TSUJI, S., Environmental Archaeology and Ethnology

TSUJI, T., Biomedical Engineering, Cardiovascular Surgery, Biomaterials

TSUKIHASHI, F., Physical Chemistry of Materials

UEDA, T., Molecular Biology

WADA, H., Magneto-Science and Technology

WATANABE, S., Natural Environment Formation

WATANABE, T., Molecular Oncology, Human Retrovirology

YAMAJI, E., Agro-environmental Engineering

YAMAJI, K., Energy Systems Analysis

YAMAMOTO, H., Information Theory and Cryptology

YAMAMOTO, K., Glycobiology

YAMATO, H., Industrial Information Systems and Environment

YANAGISAWA, Y., Chemical Analysis of Air and Indoor Air Pollution, Systems Analysis of Global Environment

YANAGITA, T., International Monetary Economics

YOSHIDA, T., Transnational Infrastructure Management

YOSHIDA, Z., Plasma Physics and Nonlinear Sciences

YOSHIMURA, S., Simulation and Virtual Environment

Graduate School of Information Science and Technology (7-3-1 Hongo, Bunkyo-ku, Tokyo 113-8656; tel. (3) 5841-7662; fax (3) 5841-7446; e-mail octo@t-adm.t.u-tokyo.ac.jp; internet www.i.u-tokyo.ac.jp):

ANDO, S., Sensors, Measurement, Image Processing

AOYAMA, T., Communication Networks and Systems

DOHI, T., Computer-aided Surgery

ESAKI, H., Computer Networks, Internet Architecture

FUJII, M., Economics and Finance

HAGIYA, M., Formal Verification, Programming Languages, Biocomputing

HARA, S., Control Theory, Learning and Optimization

HARASHIMA, H., Human Communications Engineering

HIRAKI, K., Parallel Processing, Computer Architecture, High Speed Networks

HIROSE, K., Speech Information Processing

HIROSE, M., Virtual Reality, Human Interface

IMAI, H., Alogorithms, Optimization, Complexity, Quantum Computing

ISHIKAWA, M., Robotics, Vision, VLSI, Optics in Computing

ISHIZUKA, M., Artificial Intelligence, Multimodal Lifelike Agents, WWW Intelligence

KANZAKI, R., Neural Mechanisms of Behaviour

MABUCHI, K., Advanced Biomedical Engineering and Life Science

MUROTA, K., Discrete Mathematics

NAKAMURA, Y., Robotics, Mechatronics, Automatic Control

NANYA, T., Dependable Computing and VLSI Design

OKABE, Y., Time Series Analysis and Financial Technology

OTSU, N., Real-world Intelligence, Pattern Recognition

OYANAGI, Y., Numerical Analysis, Parallel Processing

SAGAYAMA, S., Speech Recognition, Signal Processing, Spoken Dialogue System, Music Information Processing

SAKAI, S., Computer Systems and Applications

SATO, T., Intelligent Mechanics Human Machine Systems, Human Cooperative Robotics

SHIMOYAMA, I., Micro Electromechanical Systems, Robotics

SUGIHARA, K., Computational Geometry, Robust Scientific Computation

SUGIHARA, M., Numerical Analysis

TACHI, S., Advanced Robotics, Virtual Reality, Telexistence and Retro-reflective Projection Technology

TAKEICHI, M., Programming Language Theory and its Implementation

TAKEUCHI, I., Real-time Distributed Cooperative Systems

TAKEMURA, A., Statistical Science

YONEZAWA, A., Foundation for Computer Software, Programming Language, Software Security

Graduate School for Law and Politics (7-3-1 Hongo, Bunkyo-ku, Tokyo 113-0033; tel. (3) 5841-3104; fax (3) 5841-3291; e-mail jshomu@j.u-tokyo.ac.jp; internet www.j.u-tokyo.ac.jp):

AIHARA, R., Litigation, Finance and Corporate Law

ARAKI, T., Labour and Employment Law

ASAKA, K., Anglo-American Law

BABA, Y., European Political History

CH'EN, P. H.-C., Principles of Comparative Law, Chinese Legal System

DOGAUCHI, H., Civil Law, Trust Law

EBIHARA, A., German Law

EGASHIRA, K., Commercial Law

FOOTE, D. H., Sociology of Law

FUJITA, T., Commercial Law

FUJIWARA, K., International Politics, Southeast Asian Studies

FURUE, Y., Criminal Procedure

HASEBE, Y., Constitutional Law

HIBINO, T., Constitutional Theory

HIGUCHI, N., Anglo-American Law

HIROSE, H., Consumer Law

IGARASHI, T., Comparative Politics

INOUE, T., Philosophy of Law

INOUYE, M., Criminal Procedure

ISHIGURO, K., Private International Law, Conflict of Laws

ISHIKAWA, K., Constitutional Law

ITO, M., Civil Procedure
ITO, Y., European Law
IWAHARA, S., Corporation Law, Regulation of Financial Institutions
IWAMURA, M., Social Security Law
KABASHIMA, I., Japanese Politics
KANDA, H., Commercial Law
KANSAKU, H., Commercial Law
KATO, J., Comparative Politics
KAWAIDE, Y., History of Western Political Thought
KITAMURA, I., French Law
KOBA, A., Roman Law
KOBAYAKAWA, M., Administrative Law
KOKETSU, H., Administrative Law
KUBO, F., American Government and History
MASUI, Y., Tax Law
MATSUSHITA, J., Insolvency Law
MIYASAKO, Y., International Business Law
MORITA, A., Public Administration
MORITA, H., Civil Law
MORITA, O., Civil Law
NAKATANI, K., International Law
NAKAYAMA, N., Intellectual Property Law
NAKAZATO, M., Tax Law
NISHIDA, N., Criminal Law
NISHIKAWA, Y., Occidental Legal History
NITTA, I., Japanese Legal History
NOMI, Y., Civil Law, Trust Law
NOZAKI, K., General Legal Practice
OBUCHI, T., Intellectual Property Law
OCHIAI, S., Commercial Law
OHGUSHI, K., Latin American Politics
OKUWAKI, N., International Law
OMURA, A., Civil Law
ONUMA, Y., International Law
OTA, S., Law and Social Science, Law and Economics, Civil Dispute Resolution, Legal Negotiation
SAEKI, H., Criminal Law
SAITO, M., Administrative Law, Law of Local Government
SHIOKAWA, N., Russian and Post-Soviet Politics
SHIRAISHI, T., Competition Law
TAKAHARA, A., Politics of East Asia
TAKAHASHI, H., Civil Procedure
TAKAHASHI, K., Constitutional Law
TAKAHASHI, S., History of International Politics
TAKATA, H., Civil Procedure
TANABE, K., Policy Studies
TERAO, Y., Anglo-American Law
UCHIDA, T., Civil Law
UGA, K., Administrative Law
USUI, M., Public Finance Law
WATANABE, H., History of Japanese Political Thought
YAMAGUCHI, A., Criminal Law
YAMAMOTO, R., Administrative Law
YAMAMURO, M., Criminal Procedure
YAMASHITA, T., Commercial Law

Graduate School of Science and Faculty of Science (7-3-1 Hongo, Bunkyo-ku, Tokyo 113-0033; tel. (3) 5841-4570; fax (3) 5841-8776; e-mail shomu@adm.s.u-tokyo.ac.jp; internet www.s.u-tokyo.ac.jp):

AIHARA, H., High Energy Physics
AKASAKA, K., Evolutional and Developmental Biology
AOKI, H., Theoretical Condensed-matter Physics
AOKI, K., Population Biology
EGUCHI, T., Theoretical Particle Physics
FUKADA, Y., Biochemistry and Molecular Biology
FUKUDA, H., Plant Cell Biology
GELLER, R., Seismology
HAMAGUCHI, H., Physical Chemistry
HAMANO, Y., Earth Dynamics
HASEGAWA, T., Solid-State Chemistry
HATSUDA, T., Theoretical Hadron Physics
HAYANO, R., High Energy Nuclear Physics Experiment

HIBIYA, T., Ocean Dynamics
HIRANO, H., Evolutionary Genetics
HOSHINO, M., Space Physics
IWASAWA, Y., Surface Chemistry and Catalysis
KAMIYA, R., Cell Biology
KAWASHIMA, T., Organic Chemistry
KIMURA, G., Tectonics, Structural Geology
KOBAYASHI, A., Materials Chemistry, Structural Chemistry
KOBAYASHI, T., Quantum Electronics
KOMAMIYA, S., Experimental Elementary Particle Physics
KOMEDA, Y., Plant Molecular Genetics
KUBO, T., Physiological Chemistry, Molecular Biology
KUBONO, S., Nuclear Physics, Nuclear Astrophysics
KUWAJIMA, K., Biophysics
MAKISHIMA, K., Experimental High Energy Astrophysics
MATSUMOTO, R., Sedimentology and Geochemistry
MATSU'URA, M., Earthquake Physics, Tectonics
MINOWA, M., Experimental Particle Physics without Accelerators
MIYAMOTO, M., Evolution of Planetary Material
MIYASHITA, S., Statistical Mechanics, Magnetism, Condensed Matter
MURAKAMI, T., Environmental Mineralogy
MURATA, J., Plant Systematics
NAGAHARA, H., Petrology, Planetary Science
NAGAO, K., Geochemistry
NAGATA, T., Plant Physiology and Plant Molecular Biology
NAKADA, Y., Stellar Astrophysics
NAKAMURA, E., Organic Chemistry
NAKANO, A., Developmental Cell Biology
NARASAKA, K., Synthetic Organic Chemistry
NISHIHARA, H., Inorganic Chemistry
NOMOTO, K., Theoretical Astrophysics
NONAKA, M., Molecular Immunology
NOTSU, K., Geochemistry
OHTA, T., Solid-State Physical Chemistry
OKA, Y., Neurobiology
OKAMURA, S., Extragalactic Astronomy
ONAKA, T., Astrophysics
OTSUKA, T., Nuclear Theory
OZAWA, K., Petrology
SAIGO, K., Molecular Biology
SAKAI, H., Nuclear Physics
SAKANO, H., Molecular Biology
SANO, M., Nonlinear Dynamics, Fluid Dynamics
SATO, K., Astrophysics and Cosmology
SHIBAHASHI, H., Theoretical Astrophysics
SHIMOURA, S., Nuclear Physics
SHIONOYA, M., Bioinorganic Chemistry
SOFUE, Y., Radio Astronomy
SUGIURA, N., Planetary Science
TACHIBANA, K., Chemistry of Natural Products
TADA, R., Sedimentology and Palaeoceanography
TAJIMA, F., Molecular Population Genetics
TAKEDA, H., Developmental Genetics
TANABE, K., Palaeontology
TERASAWA, T., Space and Magnetospheric Physics
TOHE, A., Yeast Genetics
TSUBONO, K., Experimental Relativity
UCHIDA, S., Solid-State Physics, High-Temperature Superconductivity
UEDA, S., Human Molecular Evolution
UMEZAWA, Y., Analytical Chemistry
URABE, T., Chemical Geology, Economic Geology
WADATI, M., Statistical Physics and Condensed-matter Physics
YAMAGATA, T., Ocean–Atmosphere Dynamics
YAMAGISHI, A., Clay Mineralogy

YAMAMOTO, M., Molecular Genetics
YAMAMOTO, S., Astrophysics, Astrochemistry, Molecular Spectroscopy
YAMANOUCHI, K., Physical Chemistry
YANAGIDA, T., Elementary Particle Physics
YOKOYAMA, J., Cosmology and Astrophysics
YOKOYAMA, S., Biophysics, Biochemistry and Molecular Biology
YOSHII, Y., Galactic Astronomy

Graduate School of Mathematical Sciences (3-8-1 Komaba, Meguro-ku, Tokyo 153-8914; tel. (3) 5465-7014; fax (3) 5465-7012; e-mail suriso@ms.u-tokyo.ac.jp; internet www.ms.u-tokyo.ac.jp):

ARAI, H., Real Analysis, Harmonic Analysis, Theory of Function Spaces
FUNAKI, T., Probability Theory
FURUTA, M., Global Analysis, Low-dimensional Topology
GIGA, Y., Nonlinear Analysis
HORIKAWA, E., Algebraic Geometry
JIMBO, M., Integrable Systems, Representation Theory
KATAOKA, K., Partial Differential Equations
KATSURA, T., Algebraic Geometry
KAWAHIGASHI, Y., Operator Algebras
KAWAMATA, Y., Algebraic Geometry and Complex Manifolds
KIKUCHI, F., Numerical Analysis
KOHNO, T., Three-manifolds, Quantum Groups
KUSUOKA, S., Probability Theory and its Application
MATANO, H., Nonlinear Partial Equations, Dynamical Systems
MATSUMOTO, Y., Topology
MIYAOKA, Y., Algebraic Geometry
MORITA, S., Topology of Manifolds
NAKAMURA, S., Differential Equations and Mathematical Physics
NOGUCHI, J., Complex Analysis in Several Variables, Complex Geometry
ODA, T., Number Theory
OKAMOTO, K., Differential Equations Complex Analysis
OSHIMA, T., Algebraic Analysis, Theory of Unitary Representations
SAITO, S., Arithmetic Geometry, Algebraic Geometry
SAITO, T., Arithmetic Geometry
TOKIHIRO, T., Mathematical Physics, Solid-State Physics
TSUBOI, T., Foliations, Diffeomorphism Groups
YOSHIDA, N., Mathematical Statistics, Stochastic Analysis

Graduate School of Medicine and Faculty of Medicine (7-3-1 Hongo, Bunkyo-ku, Tokyo 113-0033; tel. (3) 5841-3303; fax (3) 5841-3670; e-mail liaison@m.u-tokyo.ac.jp; internet www.m.u-tokyo.ac.jp):

AKABAYASHI, A., Biomedical Ethics
ANDO, J., Systems Physiology
ARAIE, M., Ophthalmology
ETO, F., Rehabilitation Medicine
FUJITA, T., Nephrology and Endocrinology
FUKAYAMA, M., Human Pathology and Diagnostic Pathology
HANAOKA, K., Anaesthesiology and Pain Medicine
HASHIZUME, K., Paediatric Surgery
HIROKAWA, N., Cell Biology and Anatomy
IGARASHI, T., Paediatrics
IHARA, Y., Neuropathology
IINO, M., Cellular and Molecular Pharmacology
KADOWAKI, T., Nutrition and Metabolism
KAGA, K., Otorhinolaryngology, Head and Neck Surgery
KAI, I., Social Gerontology
KAMINISHI, M., Gastrointestinal Surgery, Surgical Sensory Motor Neuroscience, Metabolic Care and Endocrine Surgery
KANDA, K., Nursing Administration

KATO, N., Neuropsychiatry

KAZUMA, K., Adult Nursing; Terminal and Long-term Care Nursing

KIRINO, T., Neurosurgery

KITA, K., Biomedical Chemistry

KITAMURA, T., Urology

KIUCHI, T., Medical Information Network Research

KOBAYASHI, Y., Public Health

KOIKE, K., Infection Control and Prevention

KOSHIMA, I., Plastic and Reconstructive Surgery

KURIHARA, H., Physiological Chemistry and Metabolism

MAKUUCHI, M., Hepatobiliary Pancreatic Surgery, Artificial Organ and Transplantation

MATSUSHIMA, K., Molecular Preventive Medicine

MISHINA, M., Molecular Neurobiology

MIYASHITA, Y., Physiology

MIYAZONO, K., Molecular Pathology

MORI, K., Cellular and Molecular Physiology

MURASHIMA, S., Community Health Nursing

NAGAI, R., Cardiology

NAGASE, T., Respiratory Medicine

NAGAWA, H., Surgical Oncology

NAKAMURA, K., Orthopaedic Surgery

NOMOTO, A., Microbiology

OHASHI, Y., Biostatistics; Epidemiology and Preventive Health Sciences

OHE, K., Medical Informatics and Economics

OHTOMO, K., Diagnostic Radiology

OKAYAMA, H., Molecular Biology

OMATA, M., Gastroenterology

OUCHI, Y., Ageing Science, Geriatric Medicine

OYAMA, H., Clinical Bioinformatics

SANADA, H., Gerontological Nursing

SHIMIZU, T., Cellular Signalling

SUZUKI, H., Pharmaceutical Services

TAKAHASHI, K., Transfusion Medicine

TAKAHASHI, T., Neurophysiology

TAKAMOTO, S., Cardiothoracic Surgery

TAKATO, T., Oral and Maxillofacial Surgery

TAKETANI, Y., Obstetrics and Gynaecology

TAMAKI, K., Dermatology

TANIGUCHI, T., Immunology

TOHYAMA, C., Disease Biology and Interpretative Medicine

TOKUNAGA, K., Human Genetics

TSUJI, S., Neurology

TSUTSUMI, O., Obstetrics and Gynaecology

UENO, S., Bioimaging and Biomagnetics

USHIDA, T., Biomedical Materials and Systems

USHIJIMA, H., Developmental Medical Sciences

WAKAI, S., International Community Health

WATANABE, C., Human Ecology

YAHAGI, N., Emergency and Critical Care Medicine

YAMAMOTO, K., Allergology and Rheumatology

YAMAZAKI, T., Clinical Bioinformatics

YATOMI, Y., Clinical Laboratory Medicine

YOSHIDA, K., Forensic Medicine

Graduate School of Pharmaceutical Sciences and Faculty of Pharmaceutical Sciences (7-3-1 Hongo, Bunkyo-ku, Tokyo 113-0033; tel. (3) 5841-4878; fax (3) 5841-4711; e-mail adviser@mol.f.u-tokyo.ac.jp; internet www.f .u-tokyo.ac.jp/index-e.html):

ARAI, H., Health Chemistry

EBIZUKA, Y., Natural Products Chemistry

FUKUYAMA, T., Synthetic Natural Products Chemistry

FUNATSU, T., Biophysics

ICHIJO, H., Cell Signalling

IRIMURA, T., Cancer Biology and Molecular Immunology

IWATSUBO, T., Neuropathology and Neuroscience

KATADA, T., Physiological Chemistry

KIRINO, Y., Neurobiophysics

KOBAYASHI, S., Organic and Organometallic Chemistry

MATSUKI, N., Neuropharmacology and Neuroscience

MIURA, M., Molecular Neurobiology

NAGANO, T., Chemical Biology and Medicinal Chemistry

OHWADA, T., Organic and Medicinal Chemistry

SATOW, Y., Protein Structural Biology

SEKIMIZU, K., Biochemistry, Molecular Biology

SHIBASAKI, M., Synthetic Organic Chemistry

SHIMADA, I., Structural Biology, NMR Spectroscopy, Physical Chemistry

SUGIYAMA, Y., Molecular Pharmacokinetics

Graduate School of Public Policy (7-3-1 Hongo, Bunkyo-ku, Tokyo 113-0033; tel. (3) 5841-3104; fax (3) 5841-3291; e-mail ppin@j .u-tokyo.ac.jp; internet www.pp.u-tokyo.ac .jp):

HAYASHI, R., Economic Policy

ICHIMURA, H., Econometrics

IHORI, T., Public Finance, Public Economics

ITO, T., International Finance, Macroeconomics

KANEMOTO, Y., Urban Economics

KAWAI, M., Basic Macroeconomics

MORITA, A., Public Management

OKUWAKI, N., International Law and Organization, Law of the Sea, Air and Outer Space

TANABE, K., Politics, Policy Analysis, Policy Process

Interfaculty Initiative in Information Studies and Graduate School of Interdisciplinary Information Studies (7-3-1 Hongo, Bunkyo-ku, Tokyo 113-0033; tel. (3) 5841-5900; fax (3) 3811-5970; e-mail info@iii.u-tokyo.ac.jp; internet www.iii.u-tokyo.ac.jp):

ARAKAWA, C., Computational Fluid Dynamics, Simulation

BABA, A., Historical Informatics, Japanese Early Modern Economic History, Digital Archive Science

EINCO, S., Indian Philology, Ritual and Religion in India

HAMADA, J., Information Law and Policy

HANADA, T., Media Studies

HARA, Y., Economic Development Theory, Southeast Asian Economics

HARASHIMA, H., Communication Engineering and Face Studies

HASHIMOTO, Y., Social Psychology

HIROI, O., Social Psychology, Sociology of Disasters

IKEUCHI, K., Computer Vision

ISHIDA, H., Information Semiotics

KAN, S., Investigation of Possibilities for Regional Union in North-east Asia

KAWAGUCHI, Y., Computer Art

KUNIYOSHI, Y., Intelligent Systems and Informatics

NISHIGAKI, T., Information and Media Studies

SAKAMURA, K., Computer Architecture

SASAKI, M., Ecological Psychology

SUDOH, O., Economics of the Knowledge-based Society

TSUJII, J., Computational Linguistics, Natural Language Processing

YAMAGUCHI, Y., Graphics

YOSHIMI, S., Popular Culture and Media Events

ATTACHED RESEARCH INSTITUTES

Asian Natural Environmental Science Center: 1-1-1 Yayoi, Bunkyo-ku, Tokyo 113-8657; f. 1995; Dir K. TAKEUCHI.

Biotechnology Research Center: 1-1-1 Yayoi, Bunkyo-ku, Tokyo 113-8657; f. 1993; Dir S. HORINOUCHI.

Center for Climate System Research: 5-1-5 Kashiwanoha, Kashiwa-shi, Chiba 277-8568; f. 1991; Dir T. NAKAJIMA.

Center for Collaborative Research: 4-6-1 Komaba, Meguro-ku, Tokyo 153-8505; f. 1996; Dir H. YOKOI.

Center for Research and Development of Higher Education: 7-3-1 Hongo, Bunkyo-ku, Tokyo 113-0033; f. 1996; Dir K. OKAMOTO.

Center for Spatial Information Science: 5-1-5 Kashiwanoha, Kashiwa-shi, Chiba 277-8568; f. 1998; Dir R. SHIBASAKI.

Cryogenic Center: 2-11-16 Yayoi, Bunkyo-ku, Tokyo 113-0032; f. 1967; Dir M. MINOWA.

Earthquake Research Institute: 1-1-1 Yayoi, Bunkyo-ku, Tokyo 113-0032; f. 1925; Dir S. OKOBU; publ. *Bulletin of the Earthquake Research Institute* (4 a year).

Environmental Science Center: 7-3-1 Hongo, Bunkyo-ku, Tokyo 113-0033; f. 1975; Dir K. YAMAMOTO.

Health Service Center: 7-3-1 Hongo, Bunkyo-ku, Tokyo 113-0033; f. 1967; Dir (vacant); publ. *Kenko Kanri Gaiyo* (1 a year).

High Temperature Plasma Center: 5-1-5 Kashiwanoha, Kashiwa-shi, Chiba 277-8568; f. 1999; Dir Y. OGAWA.

Historiographical Institute: 7-3-1 Hongo, Bunkyo-ku, Tokyo 113-0033; f. 1869; Dir M. HOTATE; publ. *Shiryo Hensan—Sho Ho* (1 a year), *Shiryo Hensan—Jo Kenkyu Kiyo* (1 a year).

Information Technology Center: 2-11-16 Yayoi, Bunkyo-ku, Tokyo 113-8658; f. 1999; Dir Y. OKABE.

Institute for Cosmic Ray Research: 5-1-5 Kashiwanoha, Kashiwa-shi, Chiba 277-8582; f. 1953; Dir Y. SUZUKI; publ. *ICRR Report* (irregular), *ICRR News* (4 a year), *ICRR Hokoku.*

Institute of Industrial Science: 4-6-1 Komaba, Meguro-ku, Tokyo 153-8505; f. 1949; Dir M. MAEDA; publ. *Seisan-Kenkyu* (12 a year).

Institute of Medical Science: 4-6-1 Shirokanedai, Minato-ku, Tokyo 108-8639; f. 1892; Dir T. YAMAMOTO.

Institute of Molecular and Cellular Biosciences: 1-1-1 Yayoi, Bunkyo-ku, Tokyo 113-0032; f. 1953; Dir A. MIYAJIMA.

Institute of Oriental Culture: 7-3-1 Hongo, Bunkyo-ku, Tokyo 113-0033; f. 1941; Dir A. TANAKA; publ. *Memoirs* (2 a year), *Oriental Culture* (1 a year).

Institute of Social Science: 7-3-1 Hongo, Bunkyo-ku, Tokyo 113-0033; f. 1946; Dir A. KOMORIDA; publ. *Shakai Kagaku Kenkyu* (Journal of Social Science, 6 a year), *Social Science Japan Journal* (2 a year), *Social Science Japan* (newsletter, 3 a year).

Institute for Solid-State Physics: 5-1-5 Kashiwanoha, Kashiwa-shi, Chiba 277-8581; f. 1957; Dir K. UEDA; publ. *Technical Report* (irregular).

Intelligent Modelling Laboratory: 2-11-16 Yayoi, Bunkyo-ku, Tokyo 113-8656; f. 1996; Dir K. HIRAO.

International Center: 7-3-1 Hongo, Bunkyo-ku, Tokyo 113-8654; f. 1990; Dir G. MESHITSUKA; publ. *Bulletin* (1 a year), *News* (4 a year).

International Center for Elementary Particle Physics: 7-3-1 Hongo, Bunkyo-ku, Tokyo 113-0033; f. 2004; Dir S. KOMAMIYA.

International Research Center for Medical Education: 7-3-1 Hongo, Bunkyo-ku, Tokyo 113-0033; f. 2000; Dir K. KAGA; publ. *Newsletter* (2 a year).

Komaba Open Laboratory: 4-6-1 Komaba, Meguro-ku, Tokyo 153-8904; f. 1998; Dir T. NANYA.

Molecular Genetics Research Laboratory: 7-3-1 Hongo, Bunkyo-ku, Tokyo 113-0033; f. 1983; Dir M. YAMAMOTO.

Ocean Research Institute: 1-15-1 Minamidai, Nakano-ku, Tokyo 164-8639; f. 1962; Dir M. TERAZAKI; publ. *Bulletin*, *Preliminary Cruise Report* (irregular).

Radioisotope Center: 2-11-16 Yayoi, Bunkyo-ku, Tokyo 113-0032; f. 1970; Dir Y. MAKIDE.

Research Center for Advanced Science and Technology: 4-6-1 Komaba, Meguro-ku, Tokyo 153-8904; f. 1987; Dir K. HASHIMOTO.

Research into Artifacts Center for Engineering: 5-1-5 Kashiwanoha, Kashiwa-shi, Chiba 277-8568; f. 1992; Dir K. UEDA.

VLSI Design and Education Center: 2-11-16 Yayoi, Bunkyo-ku, Tokyo 113-8656; f. 1996; Dir K. ASADA.

University Museum: 7-3-1 Hongo, Bunkyo-ku, Tokyo 113-0033; f. 1965; Dir S. TAKAHASHI; publ. *Ouroboros* (newsletter, 3 a year), *Bulletin* (irregular), *Material Reports* (irregular), *UMUT Monograph* (irregular).

TOKYO UNIVERSITY OF AGRICULTURE AND TECHNOLOGY

2-8-1 Harumi-cho, Fuchu-shi, Tokyo 183

Telephone: (423) 64-3311
Fax: (423) 60-7376
Internet: www.tuat.ac.jp

Founded 1949
Independent
Language of instruction: Japanese
Academic year: April to March

Pres.: HIDEFUMI KOBATAKE
Vice-Pres: TADASHI MATSUNAGA, TAKAHIKO ONO, AKIRA SASAO, HIROFUMI TAKEMOTO
Library Dir: HIROYUKI OHNO

Library of 524,018 vols
Number of teachers: 442
Number of students: 5,966 (4,032 undergraduate, 1,934 graduate)

Publication: faculty bulletins (1 a year)

DEANS

Faculty of Agriculture: YASUHISA KUNIMI
Faculty of Technology: AKINORI KOKITSU
Graduate School of Bio-applications and Systems Engineering: MASANORI OKAZAKI
Graduate School of Technology Management: HIDEO KAMEYAMA
United Graduate School of Agricultural Science: YUTARO SENGA

TOKYO UNIVERSITY OF FISHERIES

5-7 Konan 4, Minato-ku, Tokyo 108-8477

Telephone: (3) 5463-0400
Fax: (3) 5463-0359
E-mail: www-master@tokyo-u-fish.ac.jp
Internet: www.tokyo-u-fish.ac.jp

Founded 1888
Academic year: April to March

Pres.: Dr FUMIO TAKASHIMA
Vice-Pres: Dr K. SATO, Dr R. TAKAI
Admin. Dir: M. SATO
Librarian: Dr E. WATANABE

Library of 268,000 vols
Number of teachers: 171
Number of students: 1,745

Publication: *Journal of the TUF* (2 a year)

HEADS OF LABORATORIES

Aquatic Biosciences:

Aquatic Biology: Dr K. FUJITA, Prof. M. OMORI, Dr S. SEGAWA, Prof. J. TANAKA, Dr S. WATANABE
Aquaculture: Dr T. TAKEUCHI, Dr M. NOTOYA, Dr N. OKAMOTO, Dr T. WATANABE, Dr H. FUKUDA
Genetics and Biochemistry: Dr T. AOKI

Fisheries Resource Management:

Fisheries Resource Management System: Dr T. KITAHARA, Dr S. YAMADA, Dr K. TAYA, Y. SATO, Dr K. UENO, Prof. Y. SATO
Ecology and Economics of Fisheries Resources: Dr Y. NAKAI, Dr A. OHNO, Dr R. ISEDA, Dr N. KOIWA, Prof. Y. NAKAI
International Economics of Fisheries and Food Industries: Dr K. SAKURAI

Food Science and Technology:

Food Chemistry: Dr T. SUZUKI, Dr T. FUJII, Dr S. WADA, Dr M. TANAKA
Food Engineering: Dr H. WATANABE, Prof. T. MIHORI, Dr R. TAKAI
Marine Biochemistry: Dr S. KIMURA, Dr K. SHIOMI, Dr H. YAMANAKA, Dr T. HAYASHI, Dr T. WATANABE
Applied Microbiology: Dr E. WATANABE

International and Interdisciplinary Studies:

English: Dr S. MIURA
Ethics: T. AMEMIYA
French: T. SHIMANO
History: O. KANAMORI
Psychology: Dr K. NAKAMURA

Marine Science and Technology:

Fishing Science and Technology: Dr T. ARIMOTO, Dr C. ITOSU, Dr H. KANEHIRO, Dr T. TOKAI
Ocean Systems Engineering: Dr T. AKITA, Prof. Y. NAKAMURA, Dr K. SATOHH, Dr M. FURUSAWA, Dr S. YADA, Dr S. MURAMATSU

Ocean Sciences:

Marine Ecosystem Studies: Dr T. ISHIMARU, Dr M. MAEDA, Dr M. NAMIKOSHI, Dr Y. YAMAGUCHI
Physics and Environmental Modelling: Prof. Y. ANDO, Dr K. KIHARA, Dr M. MATSUYAMA, Dr T. MORINAGA, Dr H. NAGASHIMA, Dr H. OHASHI, Dr N. SHIOTANI

TOKYO UNIVERSITY OF FOREIGN STUDIES

3-11-1 Asahicho, Fuchu-shi, Tokyo 183-8534

Telephone: (42) 330-5126
Fax: (42) 330-5140
E-mail: ml-zhenhp@tufs.ac.jp
Internet: www.tufs.ac.jp/index-j.html

Founded 1899; reorganized 1949
Semi-private institution

Pres.: SETSUHO IKEHATA
Dir-Gen.: M. KOTANI
Library Dir: N. TOMIMORI

Library: see Libraries and Archives
Number of teachers: 241 full-time
Number of students: 4,282

Publication: *Area and Culture Studies* (2 a year)

DEANS

Faculty of Foreign Studies: AKIRA BABA

ATTACHED INSTITUTE

Research Institute for Languages and Cultures of Asia and Africa: 3-11-1 Asahicho, Fuchu-shi, Tokyo 183-8534; tel. (42) 330-5600; fax (42) 330-5610; f. 1964; Dir Dr K. MIYAZAKI; publ. *Journal of Asian and African Studies* (2 a year), *Newsletter* (3 a year).

TOKYO UNIVERSITY OF MERCANTILE MARINE

2-1-6 Etchujima, Koto-ku, Tokyo 135-8533

Telephone: (3) 5245-7312
Internet: www.tosho-u.ac.jp

Founded 1875
Independent

Pres.: AKIO M. SUGISAKI
Dir of Admin. Bureau: TAKAO OKA
Library Dir: SUUSHIN SATO

Number of teachers: 110 full-time
Number of students: 1,093

Publication: *Journals* (natural sciences, humanities and social sciences)

PROFESSORS

Electric Power: YOSHIHIRO HATANAKA
Floating Facilities: KUNIAKI SHOJI
Information Systems Engineering and Navigation Systems: HAYAMA IMAZU
Internal Combustion Engines: HIROSHI OKADA
International Cultural Studies: TAKAKO NIWA
Logistics Engineering: IWAO TAMINAGA
Machinery and Equipment: TOSHIHIKO FUJITA
Marine Engineering and Guidance Control: KOHEI OHTSU
Marine Science and Technology: HIROSHI YAMAGISHI
Mathematical Science: OSAMU MATSUSHITA
Navigational Electronics: SHOGO HAYASHI
Nuclear Power: TOMOJI KAWAMASA
Power Systems Engineering and Steam Power: MASAHIRO OSAKABE

UNIVERSITY OF ELECTRO-COMMUNICATIONS

1-5-1 Chofugaoka, Chōfu City, Tokyo 182-8585

Telephone: (424) 43-5014
Fax: (424) 43-5108
E-mail: kenkyo-k@office.uec.ac.jp
Internet: www.uec.ac.jp

Founded 1949
Independent
Academic year: April to March

Pres.: M. KAJITANI
Dir of Secretariat: I. ISHIOKA
Library Dir: T. MIKI

Number of teachers: 360 full-time
Number of students: 5,452 (4,347 undergraduate, 1,105 postgraduate)

Publication: *Bulletin* (2 a year)

DEANS

Computer and Media Science: KAZUHIKO OZEKI
Department of Applied Physics and Chemistry: K. HAKUTA
Department of Computer Science: RIKIO ONAI
Department of Electronic Engineering: KIMURA TADAMASA
Department of Human Communications: HARUYUKI INOUE
Department of Mechanical Engineering and Intelligent Systems: S. KURODA
Department of Systems Engineering: MASAYUKI MATSUI
Information and Communications Systems: TAKASHI S. FUKUDA
Information Photonics and Wave Signal Processing: YOSHIO KAMI
Information Transfer: Theory and Practice: KIYOSHI ANDO

TOTTORI UNIVERSITY

4-101 Minami, Koyama-cho, Tottori City 680-0945

Telephone: (857) 31-5010
Fax: (857) 31-5018
E-mail: net_adm@jim.tottori-u.ac.jp
Internet: www.tottori-u.ac.jp
Founded 1949
Academic year: April to March
Pres.: MASANORI MICHIUE
Dir-Gen. of Admin.: Y. SUZUKI
Librarian: K. KOSAKA
Number of teachers: 762 full-time
Number of students: 6,090

DEANS

Faculty of Agriculture: M. IWASAKI
Faculty of Education and Regional Sciences: M. NAGAYAMA
Faculty of Engineering: H. KIYAMA
Faculty of Medicine: T. NOSE

TOYAMA UNIVERSITY

3190 Gofuku, Toyama City 930-8555
Telephone: (764) 45-6011
E-mail: info@toyama-u.ac.jp
Internet: www.toyama-u.ac.jp
Founded 1949; Toyama Medical and Pharmaceutical University, Takaoka National College and Toyama University merged May 2003
Academic year: April to March (2 terms)
Pres.: HIROSHI TAKIZAWA
Chief Admin. Officer: O. IMADA
Librarian: H. FUJITA
Library of 965,300 vols
Number of teachers: 445 full-time
Number of students: 7,400

DEANS

Faculty of Economics: S. YOSHIHARA
Faculty of Education: M. KASE
Faculty of Engineering: M. TOKIZAWA
Faculty of Humanities: N. KOTANI
Faculty of Science: K. MATSUMOTO

TOYOHASHI UNIVERSITY OF TECHNOLOGY

Tempaku, Toyohashi, Aichi 441-8580
Telephone: (532) 47-0111
Fax: (532) 44-6509
Internet: www.tut.ac.jp
Founded 1976
Independent
Academic year: April to March
Pres.: Dr TATAU NISHINAGA
Vice-Pres: TOSHIRO KOBAYASHI, HIROYUKI MATSUI
Dir-Gen. of Admin. Bureau: TAKASHI NORIZUKI
Librarian: HIROO YONEZU
Library of 170,000 vols
Number of teachers: 213
Number of students: 2,144

DEANS

Department of Architecture and Civil Engineering: AKIRA OHGAI
Department of Ecological Engineering: TOSHIHIRO KITADA
Department of Electrical and Electronic Engineering: AKIO OOTA
Department of Humanities, Management, Science and Engineering: JUN YAMAMOTO
Department of Information and Computer Sciences: SEIICHI NAKAGAWA
Department of Knowledge-based Information Engineering: YOSHIMASA TAKAHASHI
Department of Materials Science: KATSUYUKI AOKI

Department of Mechanical Engineering: MASAO UEMURA
Department of Production Systems Engineering: MASAHIRO KAWAKAMI

UNIVERSITY OF TSUKUBA

1-1-1 Tennodai, Tsukuba, Ibaraki-ken 305-8577

Telephone: (29) 853-2056
Fax: (29) 853-2059
E-mail: koryuka@sakura.cc.tsukuba.ac.jp
Internet: www.tsukuba.ac.jp
Founded 1973
Independent
Language of instruction: Japanese
Academic year: April to March
Pres.: NOBUHIRO YAMADA
Vice-Pres.: KAZUHIKO SHIMIZU
Vice-Pres.: MASAFUMI AKAHIRA
Vice-Pres.: KIYOSHI NISHIKAWA
Vice-Pres.: YUTAKA TSUJINAKA
Vice-Pres.: KOUICHI MORIMOTO
Vice-Pres.: HISATOSHI SUZUKI
Vice-Pres.: AKIRA UKAWA
Vice-Pres.: TETSUYA IGARASHI
Vice-Pres.: TERUO HIGASHI
Dir of Univ. Hospital: TETSUYA IGARASHI
Dir of Education Bureau of the Laboratory Schools: TERUO HIGASHI
Dir of Univ. Library: SUMIO HATANO
Library of 2,548,405 vols, 29,213 periodicals
Number of teachers: 1,788
Number of students: 16,797

PROVOSTS AND DEANS

Undergraduate Programmes
    School of Art and Design:
SHINICHI TAMAGAWA (Provost)
    College of Humanities: MAKOTO ITOH (Dean)
    College of Comparative Culture: HIROSHI YAMANAKA (Dean)
    College of Japanese Language and Culture: YURIKO SUNAKAWA (Dean)
School of Health and Physical Education:
TAIJI AZEGAMI (Provost)
    School of Humanities and Culture:
MICHIYOSHI AE (Provost)
    College of Social Sciences: SOON-HEE WHANG (Dean)
    College of International Studies: TATSUO AKANEYA (Dean)
    School of Human Sciences:
TOSHIKI OGAWA (Provost)
    School of Informatics:
SHIN-ICHI NAKAYAMA (Provost)
    College of Education: SHINJI KUBOTA (Dean)
    College of Media Arts, Science and Technology: MIKIO YAMAMOTO (Dean)
    College of Psychology: TAMAKI HATTORI (Dean)
    College of Disability Sciences: KAZUNORI TAKEDA (Dean)
School of Life and Environmental Sciences:
AKIRA TABAYASHI (Provost)
    College of Biological Sciences: TAKEO HAMA (Dean)
    College of Agro-Biological Resource Sciences: SUMINORI TOKUNAGA (Dean)
    College of Geoscience: KEN-ICHIRO HAYASHI (Dean)
School of Medicine and Medical Sciences:
FUJIO OTSUKA (Provost)
    School of Medicine: AKIRA HARA (Dean)
    School of Nursing: YUKA SAEKI (Dean)
    School of Medical Sciences: TADAO ARINAMI (Dean)

School of Science and Engineering:
EIJI KITA (Provost)
    College of Mathematics: HIROSHI ISOZAKI (Dean)
    College of Physics: YASUHIRO HATSUGAI (Dean)
    College of Chemistry: KAZUYA SAITO (Dean)
    College of Engineering Sciences: KEN-ICHI HINO (Dean)
    College of Engineering Systems: NORIYUKI HORI (Dean)
    College of Policy and Planning Sciences: YUICHIRO KANAZAWA (Dean)
School of Social and International Studies:
MIYOKO MOTOZAWA (Provost)
    College of Information Science: YOSHINORI YAMAGUCHI (Dean)
    College of Media Arts, Science and Technology: CHIEKO MIZOUE (Dean)
    College of Knowledge and Library Sciences: MAKOTO MATSUMOTO (Dean)
Masters Degree Programmes:
KAZUHIKO SHIMIZU (Provost)
Doctoral Degree Programmes
    Graduate School of Business Sciences:
YASUAKI KAWANABE (Provost)
Graduate School of Comprehensive Human Sciences:
SADAO UEMATSU (Provost)
Graduate School of Humanities and Social Sciences:
TOSHIHARU OMUKA (Provost)
Graduate School of Library, Information and Media Studies:
YOSHIHIRO SHIRAIWA (Provost)
Graduate School of Life and Environmental Sciences:
YASUO MIAKE (Provost)
    Graduate School of Pure and Applied Sciences:
YUICHI OHTA (Provost)
Graduate School of Systems and Information Engineering:
JIRO TANAKA (Provost)

UTSUNOMIYA UNIVERSITY

350 Mine-machi, Utsunomiya-shi, Tochigi 321-8505

Telephone: (286) (36) 1515
Internet: www.utsunomiya-u.ac.jp
Founded 1949
Independent
Language of instruction: Japanese
Academic year: April to March
Pres.: HIROTO TABARA
Vice-Pres: HIDEKI KASUYA, SHIGERU KITAJIMA
Dir of Univ. Library: HIROTAKA KOIKE
Library of 551,376 vols
Number of teachers: 476
Number of students: 5,411

DEANS

Faculty of Agriculture: TADATAKE MIZUMOTO
Faculty of Education: KIYOSHI NAKAMURA
Faculty of Engineering: YASUSHI NISHIDA
Faculty of International Studies: KAZUKO FUJITA

WAKAYAMA UNIVERSITY

Sakaedani 930, Wakayama-shi 640-8510
Telephone: (73) 454-0361
Fax: (73) 457-7000
Internet: www.wakayama-u.ac.jp
Founded 1949
Academic year: April to March
Pres.: S. MORIYA
Chief Admin. Officer: M. TANIGUCHI

Librarian: H. Tachibana
Library of 741,765 vols
Number of teachers: 371
Number of students: 4,460
Publications: *Bulletin of the Faculty of Education, The Wakayama Economic Review*

DEANS

Faculty of Economics: T. Kinouchi
Faculty of Education: K. Morisugi
Faculty of Systems Engineering: O. Otsuki

YAMAGATA UNIVERSITY

1-4-12, Koshirakawa-machi, Yamagata 990-8560
Telephone: (23) 628-4006
Fax: (23) 628-4013
Internet: www.yamagata-u.ac.jp
Founded 1949
Independent
Academic year: April to March (2 semesters)
Pres.: Fujiro Sendo
Sec.-Gen.: Daisuke Ikeda
Librarian: Masanobu Hayakawa
Library of 991,330 vols
Number of teachers: 1,800
Number of students: 9,436
Publications: *Bulletin of Humanities* (1 a year), *Bulletin of Social Sciences* (2 a year), *Bulletin of Educational Science* (1 a year), *Bulletin of Natural Sciences* (1 a year), *Medical Journal* (2 a year), *Bulletin of Engineering* (1 a year), *Bulletin of Agricultural Science* (1 a year)

DEANS

Faculty of Agriculture: Takeshi Sassa
Faculty of Education: Tsuneo Ishijima
Faculty of Engineering: Takeshi Endo
Faculty of Literature and Social Sciences: Koichi Takagi
Faculty of Science: Seigo Kato
School of Medicine: Masao Endoh

YAMAGUCHI UNIVERSITY

1677-1 Yoshida, Yamaguchi 753-8511
Telephone: (83) 933-5026
Fax: (83) 933-5029
E-mail: sh033@office.cc.yamaguchi-u.ac.jp
Internet: www.yamaguchi-u.ac.jp
Founded 1949
National University Corporation
Academic year: April to March
Pres.: Hiroshi Kato
Vice-Pres: Kyosuke Sakate, Osamu Fukumasa, Shinya Kawai Takuya Marumoto Yoshikazu Sugihara
Sec.-Gen.: Yutaka Matsuyama
Dir of Univ. Library: Osamu Fukumasa
Library: see Libraries and Archives
Number of teachers: 889
Number of students: 10,785 (9,099 undergraduates, 1,686 postgraduates)

DEANS

Faculty of Agriculture: Daizo Koga
Faculty of Economics: Osamu Takiguchi
Faculty of Education: Issei Yoshida
Faculty of Engineering: Toshikatsu Miki
Faculty of Humanities: Susumu Tanaka
School of Medicine: Tokuhiro Hiroshi Ishihara
Faculty of Science: Hiroyuki Mashiyama
Graduate School of East Asian Studies: Noriko Otani
Graduate School of Innovation and Technology Management: Ken Kaminishi
United Graduate School of Veterinary Science: Toshiharu Hayashi

UNIVERSITY OF YAMANASHI, NATIONAL UNIVERSITY CORPORATION

4-4-37 Takeda Kofu, Yamanashi 400-8510
Telephone: (55) 220-8004
Fax: (55) 220-8024
Internet: www.yamanashi.ac.jp
Founded 1949
Independent
Academic year: April to March
Pres.: Yoji Yoshida
Registrar: Kenji Tamaru
Dean of Students: Kunio Oohara
Librarian: Toshiaki Otomo
Library of 556,439 vols
Number of teachers: 600
Number of students: 5,150
Publications: *Bulletin of the Faculty of Education and Human Sciences* (2 a year), *Report of the Faculty of Engineering* (1 a year), *Journal of Applied Educational Research* (1 a year), *Report of the Faculty of Medicine*

DEANS

Faculty of Education: Tetsuo Hori
Faculty of Engineering: Koki Yokotsuka
Faculty of Medicine: Hideaki Nukui

ATTACHED INSTITUTES

Center for Crystal Science and Technology: attached to the Faculty of Engineering.
Center for Instrumental Analysis: 4-3-11 Takeda, Kofu 400-8511.
Center for Life Science Research: 1110 Shimokato, Tamaho-cho, Nakakoma-gun 409-3898.
Clean Energy Research Center: 7 Miyamae-cho, Kofu 400-0021.
Cooperative Research and Development Center: 4-3-11 Takeda, Kofu 400-8511.
Institute of Enology and Viticulture: attached to the Faculty of Engineering.
Integrated Information Processing Center: 4-3-11 Takeda, Kofu 400-8511; Dir Koji Iwanuma.
International Student Center: 4-4-37 Takeda, Kofu 400-8510.

YOKOHAMA NATIONAL UNIVERSITY

79-1 Tokiwadai, Hodogayaku, Yokohama 240-8501
Telephone: (45) 339-3036
Fax: (45) 339-3039
E-mail: international@nuc.ynu.ac.jp
Internet: www.ynu.ac.jp
Founded 1949
National University Corporation
Language of instruction: Japanese
Academic year: April to March (2 semesters)
Pres.: Kunio Suzuki
Exec. Dir and Exec. Vice-Pres.: Y. Kokubun
Exec. Dir and Exec. Vice-Pres.: S. Mizoguchi
Exec. Dir and Exec. Vice-Pres.: K. Matsuoka
Exec. Dir and Exec. Vice-Pres.: N. Takeshita
Exec.Vice-Pres.: H. Yamada
Library: see Libraries and Archives
Number of teachers: 608 full-time
Number of students: 10,134

DEANS

Faculty of Business Administration: H. Izumi
Faculty of Economics: T. Kamikawa
Faculty of Education and Human Sciences: Y. Ono
Faculty of Engineering: O. Ishihara
Graduate School of Education and Human Sciences: Y. Ono
International Graduate School of Social Sciences: Y. Fukuda

Graduate School of Engineering Science: O. Ishihara
Graduate School of Environment and Information Sciences: S. Morishita
Graduate School of Urban Innovation: Y. Umemoto

PROFESSORS

Faculty of Business Administration (79-4 Tokiwadai, Hodogayaku, Yokohama 240-8501; tel. (45) 339-3654; fax (45) 339-3656; e-mail int.somu@nuc.ynu.ac.jp; internet www.business.ynu.ac.jp):

Cho, D., Business Admin.
Mogaki, H., International Personnel Management
Morita, H., Fiscal Studies, Finance Theory
Nakamura, H., Strategic Accounting, Capital Budgeting
Ohtsuka, E., Game Theory
Shirai, H., Management Information Systems, Business Modelling
Torii, A., Economic Policy
Yagi, H., Ecological Accounting
Yamakura, K., Management
Yamashita, S., Natural Economic Accounting
Yoshikawa, T., Cost Accounting, Management Accounting

Faculty of Economics (79-3 Tokiwadai, Hodogayaku, Yokohama 240-8501; tel. (45) 339-3510; fax (45) 339-3504; e-mail int.somu@nuc.ynu.ac.jp; internet www.econ.ynu.ac.jp):

Akiyama, T., Theoretical Economics
Fukagai, Y., History of Economic Thought, Economic Ethics
Hagiwara, S., US Economic Policy
Hasebe, Y., Input–Output Analysis
Kamikawa, T., International Finance, Money and Banking
Kanazawa, F., Public Finance, Local Finance
Kizaki, M., Modern Chinese Economy, Corporate Governance in China, Chinese Labour Affairs
Kobayashi, M., Statistical Science
Okado, M., Japanese Economic History
Omori, Y., Labour Economics
Tomiura, E., International Economics
Ui, T., Theoretical Economics
Yamazaki, K., Economic Policy

Faculty of Education and Human Sciences (79-2 Tokiwadai, Hodogayaku, Yokohama 240-8501; tel. (45) 339-3253; fax (45) 339-3264; e-mail edu.somu@nuc.ynu.ac.jp; internet www.edhs.ynu.ac.jp):

Arai, H., Pedagogy
Arai, M., Production Engineering, Processing Studies
Baba, Y., General Mathematics
Chomabayashi, T., Exercise Physiology
Ebihara, O., Sociology of Physical Education and Sport
Eto, T., Geology
Fujimori, T., Sculpture
Fukawa, G., Subject Pedagogy
Fukuda, S., Experimental Psychology
Harada, H., Soil Zoology
Hashimoto, Y., Science Education
Hayashibe, H., Developmental Psycholinguistics
Hori, M., Environmental Chemistry
Ichiyanagi, H., Japanese Modern Literature, Japanese Modern Culture
Imoto, S., German Literature, European Culture History
Inoue, K., Clinical Psychology
Ishida, J., Primary Mathematics Education
Kanai, Y., Ethics
Kanazawa, H., Japanese Linguistics
Kaneko, K., Eating Habits Studies
Kasahara, M., Cultural Anthropology
Kato, C., Japanese Modern History

KIKUCHI, T., Ecology, Environment
KIMURA, M., Sports Science
KITAGAWA, Y., Constitutional Law
KOBAYASHI, K., History of Thought
KOBAYASHI, N., Form, Structure
KOBAYASHI, Y., Movement Education Therapy
KOIZUMI, H., Teaching Methods
MAEDA, M., Geometry
MAJIMA, R., Palaeontology
MATSUISHI, T., Neuropsychiatric Studies
MIYAKE, A., Japanese Literature
MIYAZAKI, T., Philosphy, Ethics
MOCHIDA, Y., Ecology, Environment
MORIMOTO, S., Physiology and Applied Physiology, Exercise Physiology
MORIMOTO, S., Science Education
MOTEKI, K., Applied Musicology
MURATA, T., Modern Chinese History
MUROI, M., Aesthetics, Semiotics, Cultural Studies, Philosophy
NAKAGAWA, T., Education for the Hearing-impaired
NAKAMURA, E., Analytical Chemistry
NEGAMI, S., Topological Graph Theory
NISHIMURA, T., Consumer Policy
NISHIMURA, T., Geometry
NISHIWAKI, Y., Geographic Education
NUKATA, J., Cognitive Engineering
NUSHI, A., Educational Psychology
OCHIAI, M., Subject Pedagogy
OGAWA, M., Music Education
OKADA, M., Classical Chinese Literature
ONO, Y., Aesthetics, History of Art
OOISHI, A., Commutative Algebra
OSATO, T., Musicology
OSHIMA, A., Educational Technology
OTAKI, F., Piano Performance
SAKAI, Y., Computer Science
SANO, F., Outdoor Recreation
SASAKI, H., Pedagogy
SATO, Y., Form, Structure
SHIMOJO, H., Ethics
SHIROUZU, N., Modern Chinese Literature
SUGIMURA, H., Organic Chemistry
SUGIYAMA, T., Piano Performance
SUKAWA, H., Korean Economic History
SUZUKI, K., Weather, Oceanic Physics, Hydrology
SUZUKI, T., Home Economics Education, Family Studies
TAJIMA, F., Optical Measurement
TAKAGI, H., Adolescent Psychology
TAKAGI, M., Curriculum Studies
TAKAGI, N., Teaching Methodology
TAKAHASHI, K., Dance Education
TAKAHASHI, K., English Linguistics
TAKAHASHI, M., Educational Anthropology
TAKAYAMA, Y., Psychology of the Disabled
TAKUSARI, D., Aesthetics, History of Art
TANAKA, H., Environmental Physiology
TANEDA, Y., Colony Specificity
TANJI, Y., American Literature, Realism, Naturalism, Women's Studies
TANISHO, S., Biochemical Engineering
UMEMOTO, Y., History of French Theatre, Cinema Theory
WATABE, M., Sociology
YAMAMOTO, I., Experimental Condensed Matter Physics, Physics Education
YANAI, K., Philosophy
YOKOYAMA, N., Physical Education, Sports Science, Budo, Kendo

Faculty of Engineering (79-5 Tokiwadai, Hodogayaku, Yokohama 240-8501; tel. (45) 339-3804; fax (45) 339-3827; e-mail eng .somu@nuc.ynu.ac.jp; internet www.eng.ynu .ac.jp):

ADACHI, T., Electronic Devices, Electronic Equipment
AMEMIYA, N., Electric Power Engineering, Electronic Equipment Engineering
ANDO, K., Structural Ceramics
ARAI, H., Electromagnetics
ARAI, M., Ship Marine Engineering

ASAMI, M., Synthetic Chemistry
AZUSHIMA, A., Material Processing, Treatment
BABA, T., Applied Optics, Quantum Optical Engineering
FUKUTOMI, H., Structural/Functional Materials
HABUKA, H., Applied Physical Properties, Crystal Engineering
HANEJI, N., Electronic Device, Electronic Equipment
HIRAYAMA, T., Aeronautics
HIROSE, Y., Electronic Device, Electronic Equipment
IIDA, Y., Architectural History, Design
ISHIHARA, O., Plasma Science
ISHII, R., Digital Signal Processing
ITOH, K., Physical Chemistry
KAMEMOTO, K., Fluidics
KAMINOYAMA, M., Chemical Engineering
KAWAI, K., Metal Forming and Numerical Simulation
KAWAMURA, A., Power Electronics
KIMISHIMA, Y., Applied Solid-State Physics
KITADA, Y., Differential Topology
KITAYAMA, K., Architectural History, Design
KOBAYASHI, K., Earth Astrochemistry
KOBAYASHI, S., City Planning
KOHNO, R., Information Communication Technology
KOIZUMI, J., Bio-function, Bioprocessors
KOKUBUN, Y., Opto-electronics
KONNO, N., Mathematics
KUROKAWA, J., Fluid Engineering
MAEKAWA, T., Computer-aided Design
MATSUMOTO, K., Chemical Engineering, Material Properties, Transfer Operation, Unit Operation, Separation Engineering
MIURA, K., Metallic Physical Properties
MIZUGUCHI, J., Electronic Properties of Organic Semiconductors and Oxide Semiconductors
NAITO, A., Biophysics
NAKAMURA, F., Urban Transportation Planning
NISHINO, K., Thermal Engineering
OGINO, T., Surface Science and Nanotechnology of Semiconductors
OHARA, K., Theory of Architecture
OHNO, K., Mathematical Physics, Fundamental Theory of Physical Properties
OKUYAMA, K., Heat Transfer
ONO, T., Mathematical Physics, Fundamental Theory of Physical Properties
OTA, K., Energy
OYAMA, T., Power Systems Engineering
SAKAKIBARA, K., Physical Organic Chemistry
SANADA, K., Control Engineering
SASAKI, K., Elementary Particle Physics
SHIBATA, M., Elementary Particle Physics, Atomic Nucleus, Cosmic Ray, Space Physics
SHIBAYAMA, T., Civil Engineering
SHIRATORI, M., Machine Material, Material Mechanics
SUMI, Y., Naval Architecture and Ocean Engineering
SUZUKI, K., Naval Architecture and Ocean Engineering
SUZUKI, K., Physical Properties II
TAGAWA, Y., Building Construction/Material
TAKADA, H., Intelligent Mechanics, Mechanical Systems
TAKAGI, J., Production Engineering, Processing Studies
TAKAHASHI, A., Organic Polymer Chemistry, High Performance Polymers for Microelectronics
TAKANO, S., Mathematics
TAKEDA, J., Physical Properties II
TAKEMURA, Y., Magnetics
TAMANO, K., Geometry

TAMURA, A., Architectural Environment/ Equipment
TANAKA, H., Machine Element
TANAKA, M., Thin Film and Surface Interface Physical Properties
TANI, K., Rock Engineering
TASAI, A., Building Structure
TSUBAKI, T., Concrete Engineering
TSUBOI, T., Thermal Engineering
UEDA, K., Polymer/Textile Materials
UMEZAWA, O., Structural/Functional Materials
UTAKA, Y., Thermal Engineering
WATANABE, M., Carcinogenesis
WATANABE, M., Polymer Structure
YABUTA, T., Sensitivity Informatics, Soft Computing
YAGI, M., Physical Chemistry
YAKOU, T., Strength of Materials
YAMAMOTO, M., Architecture
YAMAZAKI, Y., Earthquake Engineering
YOKOYAMA, Y., Organic Industrial Materials
YOSHIDA, K., Architectural History, Design
YOSHIKAWA, N., Electronic Device, Electronic Equipment

Faculty of Environmental and Information Sciences (79-7 Tokiwadai, Hodogayaku, Yokohama 240-8501; tel. (45) 339-4422; fax (45) 339-4430; e-mail env-inf.somu@nuc.ynu .ac.jp; internet www.eis.ynu.ac.jp):

ARIMA, M., Petrology
ARISUKA, H., Media Informatics, Database
FUJIWARA, K., Ecology, Environment
GOTOH, T., Perception Information Processing, Intelligent Robotics
HARA, T., Catalysis by Metal Complexes
HIRANO, N., Functional Analysis
HIRATSUKA, K., Applied Molecular Cell Biology
INOUE, S., Synthetic Chemistry
INOUE, Y., Naval Architecture and Ocean Engineering
KAGEI, S., Fuzzy Control
KANEKO, N., Ecology
KONDO, M., Industrial Technology Policy
MASUNAGA, S., Environmental Dynamic Analysis
MATSUDA, H., Environmental Ecology
MATSUMOTO, T., Information Security
MEGURO, T., Inorganic Materials
MITSUI, I., Regional Industrial Policy
MIYAKE, A., Safety Engineering
MORI, T., Natural Language Processing
MORISHITA, S., Machine Mechanics, Control
NAGAO, T., Biological/Living Body Informatics
NAKAI, S., Environmental Health
OGAWA, T., Safety Engineering
OHNO, K., Landscape Ecology
OHTANI, H., Safety Engineering
OKUTANI, T., Inorganic Material, Physical Properties
SADOHARA, S., Social System Engineering, Safety Systems
SASAMOTO, H., Plant Physiology
SEKINE, K., Material Processing, Treatment
SHIDA, K., Mathematical Sociology
SHUSA, Y., Globalization of Firms
SUZUKI, A., Materials Science
TAKEDA, Y., Management Information Systems
TAMURA, N., Natural Language Processing
TERADA, T., Mathematics
UENO, S., Control Engineering
UESUGI, S., Molecular Biology
YAMADA, H., Structural Engineering
YAMADA, T., Computational Mechanics

Graduate School of Education (79-2 Tokiwadai, Hodogayaku, Yokohama 240-8501; tel. (45) 339-3253; fax (45) 339-3264; e-mail edu .somu@nuc.ynu.ac.jp; internet www.edhs .ynu.ac.jp):

INUZUKA, F., Guidance

International Graduate School of Social Sciences (79-4 Tokiwadai, Hodogayaku, Yokohama 240-8501; tel. (45) 339-3602; fax (45) 339-3661; e-mail int.somu@nuc.ynu.ac.jp; internet www.igss.ynu.ac.jp):

ABE, S., Marketing, Consumer Behaviour
ARAKI, I., International Law
ARIE, D., Economic Doctrine, Economic Thought
ASANO, Y., Finance
DOI, H., Economic Theory
FUJIMORI, T., Resolution Process in Interpersonal Conflicts
HAMAMOTO, M., Accounting
HARADA, K., Constitutional Law
HIGASHIDA, A., Economic Statistics
IGARASHI, A., International Accounting, International Auditing
IKEDA, T., Development Economics
IMAMURA, Y., Civil Law
INOWE, T., Finance, Macroeconomics
ISHIYAMA, Y., Economic History
IWASAKI, M., Tax Law
IZUMI, H., Accounting and Book-keeping Systems
KATO, M., Environmental Law
KAWABATA, Y., Public Law
KAWASHIMA, K., General Civil and Commercial Practice
KIMIZUKA, M., Public Law
KOBAYASHI, M., Linguistics
KODA, K., Macroeconomics
KOIKE, O., Politics
KURASAWA, M., Theoretical Economics
KURUSHIMA, T., Commercial Law
MATSUI, Y., Business Administration
MITO, H., Business Administration
MIZOGUCHI, S., Management Accounting
MORIKAWA, T., International Law
NAGAI, K., Mathematical Statistics
NAKAMURA, K., Regional and Local Political Economy
NAKAMURA, Y., English Studies
NAKAMURA, Y., General Theory of Economics
NEMOTO, Y., International Law
NOMURA, H., Civil Law
OKABE, J., Economic Statistics
OKADA, E., Business Administration
OKUMURA, T., Monetary Economics
OKUYAMA, K., Sociology of Law
OSAWA, Y., Commercial Law
SAINO, H., Criminal Law
SAITO, S., Accounting
SANBE, N., Administrative Law
SATO, M., Criminal Law
SHIBATA, H., International and Comparative Human Resource Management
SUGIHARA, M., Financial, Commercial and Civil Law
TAKAHASHI, J., Civil Law, Land Law, Sociology Law
TAKAHASHI, M., Fiscal Studies, Finance Theory
TANAKA, M., Business Administration
TANAKA, T., Criminal Law
TASHIRO, Y., Agricultural Policy
TOKUE, Y., Criminal and Procedure Law
UEMURA, H., Theoretical Economics
YAMAGUCHI, O., Pension Mathematics
YOO, H., Int. Law

ATTACHED RESEARCH INSTITUTES

Center for Future Medical Social Infrastructure Based on Information Communications Technology: 79-7 Tokiwadai, Hodogayaku, Yokohama; tel. and fax (45) 339-4490; e-mail mict@ynu.ac.jp; internet www.mict-ynu.ac.jp; Dir RYUJI KOHNO.

Center for Risk Management and Safety Sciences: 79-5 Tokiwadai, Hodogayaku, Yokohama 240-8501; tel. (45) 339-3776; fax (45) 339-4294; e-mail anshin@ynu.ac.jp;

internet www.anshin.ynu.ac.jp; Dir KAZUYOSHI SEKINE.

Cooperative Research and Development Center: 79-5 Tokiwadai, Hodogayaku, Yokohama 240-8501; tel. (45) 339-4381; fax (45) 339-4387; e-mail cordec@nuc.ynu.ac.jp; internet www.crd.ynu.ac.jp; Dir SHIN MORISHITA.

Education Center: 79-1 Tokiwadai, Hodogayaku, Yokohama 240-8501; tel. (45) 339-3135; fax (45) 339-3141; e-mail kyomu.gakumu@nuc.ynu.ac.jp; internet www.yec.ynu.ac.jp; Dir KUNIO SUZUKI.

Global–Local Education Research Center: 79-3 Tokiwadai, Hodogayaku, Yokohama 240-8501; tel. and fax (45) 339-3579; e-mail chiki-ct@ynu.ac.jp; internet www.crd.ynu.ac.jp/chiki-ct; Dir SHIGETAKA KOBAYASHI.

Health Service Center: 79-1 Tokiwadai, Hodogayaku, Yokohama 240-8501; tel. (45) 339-3153; fax (45) 339-3156; e-mail healths@nuc.ynu.ac.jp; internet www.hoken.ynu.ac.jp; Dir ETSUKO TANAKA.

Information Technology Service Center: 79-5 Tokiwadai, Hodogayaku, Yokohama 240-8501; tel. (45) 339-4390; fax (45) 339-4393; e-mail joho.kikaku@nuc.ynu.ac.jp; internet www.ipc.ynu.ac.jp; Dir EISAKU OTSUKA.

Instrumental Analysis Center: 79-5 Tokiwadai, Hodogayaku, Yokohama 240-8501; tel. (45) 339-4406; fax (45) 339-4406; e-mail iac@nuc.ynu.ac.jp; internet www.iac.ynu.ac.jp; Dir YASUSHI YOKOYAMA.

International Student Center: 79-1 Tokiwadai, Hodogayaku, Yokohama 240-8501; tel. (45) 339-3186; fax (45) 339-3189; e-mail ryugakusei.center@nuc.ynu.ac.jp; internet www.isc.ynu.ac.jp; Dir TOMOYA SHIBAYAMA.

Office of Industry and Community Liaison: 179-5 Tokiwadai, Hodogayaku, Yokohama 240-8501; tel. (45) 339-4449; fax (45) 339-4456; e-mail sangaku.sangaku@nuc.ynu.ac.jp; internet www.crd.ynu.ac.jp; Dir SHINSUKE WATANABE.

Radioisotope (RI) Center: 79-5 Tokiwadai, Hodogayaku, Yokohama 240-8501; tel. (45) 339-4410; fax (45) 339-4410; internet www.ric.ynu.ac.jp; Dir SHIGEMARU TANISHO.

Venture Business Laboratory: 79-5 Tokiwadai, Hodogayaku, Yokohama 240-8501; tel. (45) 339-4280; fax (45) 339-4280; e-mail ec-kanri@ynu.ac.jp; internet www.vbl.ynu.ac.jp; Dir AKIHIRO TAMURA.

Municipal Institutions

AOMORI UNIVERSITY OF HEALTH AND WELFARE

Mase 58-1 Hamadate, Aomori 030-8505
Telephone: (17) 765-2000
Fax: (17) 765-2188
E-mail: webmaster@auhw.ac.jp
Internet: www.auhw.ac.jp

Founded 1999

Pres.: SACHIE SHINDO

Faculty of Health Sciences, incl. divs of Human Sciences, Nursing, Social Welfare, Therapy.

DAIDO INSTITUTE OF TECHNOLOGY

10-3 Takiharu-cho, Minami-ku, Nagoya
Internet: www.daido-it.ac.jp

Founded 1961

Pres.: AKIRA SAWAOKA

Library of 170,000 vols
Number of teachers: 97
Number of students: 3,530

Schools of Informatics, Engineering, Liberal Arts and Sciences; Graduate School of Technology.

EDOGAWA UNIVERSITY

Komaki 474, Nagareyama-shi, Chiba-ken 270-0198
Telephone: (4) 7152-0661
Fax: (4) 7154-2490
E-mail: webmaster@edogawa-u.ac.jp
Internet: www.edogawa-u.ac.jp

Founded 1990

College of Sociology.

FUJI WOMEN'S UNIVERSITY

Kita 16-jo Nishi 2, Kita-ku, Sapporo-shi, Hokkaido 001-0016
Telephone: (11) 736-0311
Fax: (11) 709-8541
E-mail: somu@fujijoshi.ac.jp
Internet: www.fujijoshi.ac.jp

Founded 1961

Pres.: YOSHIKO NAGATA

Library of 300,000 vols
Number of teachers: 89
Number of students: 2,250

Faculties of Humanities, Life Sciences.

FUJITA HEALTH UNIVERSITY

1–98 Dengakugakubo, Kutsukake-cho, Toyoake, Aichi-ken 470-1192
Telephone: (562) 93-2504
Fax: (562) 93-4595

Founded 1964

Pres.: HIROSHI NAKANO

Library of 172,000 vols, 1,068 periodicals

Faculties of Medical Technology, Nursing, Radiological Technology, Rehabilitation.

FUKUI UNIVERSITY OF TECHNOLOGY

3-6-1 Gakuen, Fukui City, Fukui 910-8505
Telephone: (776) 29-2620
Fax: (776) 29-7891
E-mail: kouhou@fukui-ut.ac.jp
Internet: www.fukui-ut.ac.jp

Pres.: Prof. MASAHIRO JOHNO
Chancellor: Prof. KEN KANAI

Number of teachers: 160

Departments of Applied Nuclear Technology, Architecture and Civil Engineering, Electrical and Electronic Engineering, Environmental and Biotechnological Frontier Engineering, Management Information Science, Mechanical Engineering, Space Communication Engineering.

FUKUOKA INSTITUTE OF TECHNOLOGY

3-30-1 Wajiro-Higashi, Higashi-ku, Fukuoka 811-0295
Telephone: (92) 606-0607
Fax: (92) 606-7357
E-mail: www-staff@fit.ac.jp
Internet: www.fit.ac.jp

Pres.: KAORU YAMAFUJI

Faculties of Engineering, Information Engineering, Social and Environmental Studies.

FUKUSHIMA MEDICAL UNIVERSITY

1 Hikariga-oka, Fukushima City 960-1295
Telephone: (24) 547-1111
Fax: (24) 547-1995
E-mail: sshigeta@fmu.ac.jp
Internet: www.fmu.ac.jp

Founded 1950
Academic year: April to March
Pres.: SHIRO SHIGETA
Dir of Library: T. SUZUKI
Sec.: Y. YOSHIDA
Hospital Dir: S. NIWA

Library of 138,738 vols
Number of teachers: 330
Number of students: 820

Publications: *Fukushima Igaku Zasshi* (Fukushima Medical Journal, 4 a year), *Fukushima Journal of Medical Science* (2 a year)

Faculty of Medicine, Faculty of Nursing, Postgraduate Research Institute, Hospital

DEANS

Faculty of Medicine: HIDEO KOCHI
Faculty of Nursing: YOKO NAKAYAMA

GIFU PHARMACEUTICAL UNIVERSITY

5-6-1, Mitahora-higashi, 5-chome, Gifu 502-8585

Telephone: (58) 237-3931
Fax: (58) 237-5979
E-mail: iinuma@gifu-pu.ac.jp
Internet: www.gifu-pu.ac.jp

Founded 1932
Municipal Control
Academic year: April to March
Pres.: Prof. MASAYUKI KUZUYA
Chief Admin. Officer: TAKASHI SHINODA
Library Dir: Prof. HIROICHI NAGAI

Library of 59,000 vols
Number of teachers: 70
Number of students: 649

Publications: *Bulletin of Liberal Arts, Proceedings* (1 a year)

DEANS

Faculty of Manufacturing Pharmacy: Prof. TADASHI KATAOKA
Faculty of Pharmaceutical Science: Prof. KAZUYUKI HIRANO

PROFESSORS

FURUKAWA, S., Molecular Biology
GOTO, M., Pharmaceutical Analytical Chemistry
HARA, A., Biochemistry
HIRANO, K., Pharmaceutics
HIROTA, K., Medicinal Chemistry
INOUE, K., Pharmacognosy
KATAOKA, T., Pharmaceutical Chemistry
KAWASHIMA, Y., Pharmaceutical Engineering
KUZUYA, M., Pharmaceutical Physical Chemistry
MASAKI, Y., Pharmaceutical Synthetic Chemistry
MORI, H., Microbiology
NAGAI, H., Pharmacology
NAGASE, H., Hygienics

HACHINOHE INSTITUTE OF TECHNOLOGY

88-1 Ohbiraki Myo, Hachinohe, Aomori 031-8501

Telephone: (178) 25-3111
E-mail: www-admin@hi-tech.ac.jp
Internet: www.hi-tech.ac.jp

Founded 1972
Pres.: Dr SHOYA MASAMI

Library of 100,000 vols, 300 periodicals
Number of students: 5,000

Faculties of Architectural Engineering, Chemical Engineering on Biological Environments, Electronic Intelligence and Systems, Environmental and Civil Engineering, Mechanical Systems on Information Technology, System and Information Engineering, Liberal Arts and Technology.

HAKUOH UNIVERSITY

1117 Daigyoji, Oyama City, Tochigi Prefecture 323-8585

Telephone: (285) 22-1111
Fax: (285) 22-8989
E-mail: nyuushi@hakuoh.ac.jp
Internet: www.hakuoh.ac.jp

Pres.: MAYUMI MORIYAMA
Founded 1915
Number of students: 4,000
Library of 175,000 vols

Faculties of Business Management, Education and Law.

HAMAMATSU UNIVERSITY SCHOOL OF MEDICINE

1-20-1 Handayama Hamamatsu-shi Sizuoka, Hamamatsu City 431-3192

Telephone: (53) 435-2111
Fax: (53) 433-7290
Internet: www.hama-med.ac.jp

Founded 1974
Number of teachers: 273
Medical school.

HANNAN UNIVERSITY

5-4-3 Amami, Higashi, Matsubara, Osaka 580-8502

Telephone: (72) 332-1224
E-mail: webmaster@hannan-u.ac.jp
Internet: www.hannan-u.ac.jp

Founded 1965
Pres.: SHINICHI OTSUKI

Faculties of business, economics, international communication, management information.

HEALTH SCIENCES UNIVERSITY OF HOKKAIDO

1757 Kanazawa, Tobetsu-cho, Ishikari-gun, Hokkaido 061-0293

Telephone: (1332) 3-1211
Fax: (1332) 3-1669
E-mail: nice@hoku-iryo-u.ac.jp
Internet: www.hoku-iryo-u.ac.jp

Founded 1974
Library of 145,000 vols
Number of students: 2,400

HIMEJI INSTITUTE OF TECHNOLOGY

2167 Shosha, Himeji City, Hyogo 671-2201

Telephone: (792) 66-1661
Fax: (792) 66-8868
E-mail: www-adm@cnth.himeji-tech.ac.jp
Internet: www.himeji-tech.ac.jp

Founded 1944 as Hyogo Prefectural Special College of Technology, 1949 under present name
Academic year: April to March
President: TADAO HAKUSHI
Dean of Students: HIROSHI NAKAYAMA
Dir of Administration: TOSHIAKI SUZUKI
Library Dir: HIDEHIKO NAKANO

Library of 173,000 vols
Number of teachers: 354
Number of students: 3,222

Publication: *Reports of Himeji Institute of Technology* (1 a year)

DEANS

Department of General Education: YASUKAGE ODA

Faculty of Engineering: MOTOYOSHI HASEGAWA
Faculty of Science: SHIGERU TERABE
School of Humanities for Environmental Policy and Technology: JUNJI KIHARA

HOSHI UNIVERSITY

2-4-41 Ebara, Shinagawa, Tokyo 142-8501

Telephone: (3) 5498-5821
Fax: (3) 3787-0036
E-mail: www@hoshi.ac.jp
Internet: www.hoshi.ac.jp

Library of 85,000 vols, 716 periodicals
Number of students: 1,200

Faculty of Pharmaceutical Sciences.

IWATE PREFECTURAL UNIVERSITY

152-52 Takizawa-aza-sugo, Takizawa, Iwate 020-0193

Telephone: (19) 694-2012
Fax: (19) 694-2011
Internet: www.iwate-pu.ac.jp

Founded 1988
President: TANIGUCHI MAKOTO
Vice-President: (vacant)

DEANS

Faculty of Nursing: TSUBOYAMA MICHIKO
Faculty of Policy Studies: KOMARU MASAAKI
Faculty of Social Welfare: SATO TADASHI
Faculty of Software and Information Science: SUGAWARA MITSUMASA

KITAKYUSHU UNIVERSITY

4-2-1 Kitagata, Kokuraminami-ku, Kitakyushu-shi, Fukuoka 802-8577

Telephone: (93) 962-1837
E-mail: shomu@kitakyu-u.ac.jp
Internet: www.kitakyu-u.ac.jp

Founded 1946, university status 1950
Library of 379,000 vols
Number of students: 5,456

KOBE CITY UNIVERSITY OF FOREIGN STUDIES

9-1 Gakuen-higashi-machi, Nishi-ku, Kobe 6512187

Telephone: (78) 794-8121
E-mail: info@office.kobe-cufs.ac.jp
Internet: www.kobe-cufs.ac.jp

Founded 1946
Academic year: April to March
Pres.: EIICHI KIMURA
Registrar: MASAAKI OMORI
Librarian: SHIRO WADA

Library of 390,000 vols
Number of teachers: 90
Number of students: 2,300

KOBE UNIVERSITY OF COMMERCE

Gakuen-nishimachi, Nishi-ku, Kobe 651-2197

Telephone: (78) 794-6161
Fax: (78) 794-6166
E-mail: shomuka@kobuec.ac.jp
Internet: www.kobeuc.ac.jp/index_e.htm

Founded 1929
State control
Language of instruction: Japanese
Academic year: April to March
President: YASUO SAKAMOTO
Registrar: NOBUHIDE FUJIWARA
Librarian: KENTARO NOMURA

Library of 406,000 vols
Number of teachers: 103
Number of students: 2,050

KUMAMOTO PREFECTURAL UNIVERSITY

3-1-100 Tsukide, Kumamoto City 862-8502
Telephone: (96) 383-2929
Fax: (96) 384-6765
E-mail: www-admin@pu-kumamoto.ac.jp
Internet: www.pu-kumamoto.ac.jp
Founded 1947
Library of 300,000 vols
Faculties of Administration, Cultural Studies, Environmental and Symbiotic Sciences, Letters.

KYOTO PREFECTURAL UNIVERSITY OF MEDICINE

465 Kajii-cho, Kawaramachi, Hirokoji, Kamikyo-ku, Kyoto 602-8566
Telephone: (75) 251-5111
E-mail: kikaku01@koto.kpu-m.ac.jp
Internet: www.kpu-m.ac.jp
Founded 1873
President: IBATA YASUHIKO
Dean of Students: MARUNAKA YOSHINORI
Director of University Hospital: YAMAGISHI HISAKAZU
Director of Library: NISHIMURA TSUNEHIKO
Library of 218,000 vols
Number of teachers: 304
Number of students: 649 undergraduate, 193 postgraduate
Publication: *Kyoto Furitsu Ikadaigaku Zasshi* (Journal)

DEANS

College of Medical Technology: T. REIKO
Faculty of Culture and Education: M. SANO
Graduate School: F. SHINJI

KYOTO SANGYO UNIVERSITY

Motoyama, Kamigamo, Kita-ku, Kyoto City 603-8555
Telephone: (75) 705-1408
Fax: (75) 705-1409
E-mail: info-adm@star.kyoto-su.ac.jp
Internet: www.kyoto-su.ac.jp
Founded 1965
Pres.: TOYOH SAKAI
Number of teachers: 297
Number of students: 12,949 undergraduates, 301 graduates
Faculties of Business Administration, Cultural Studies, Economics, Engineering, Foreign Languages, Law, Science.

KYUSHU SANGYO UNIVERSITY

3-1 Matsukadai 2-chome, Higashi-ku, Fukuoka 813-8503
Telephone: (92) 673-5050
Fax: (92) 673-5599
Internet: www.ip.kyusan-u.ac.jp
Founded 1960
Chair.: YAMASHITA HIROHIKO
Pres.: SAGO TAKASHI
Library of 712,310 vols
Number of teachers: 330
Number of students: 15,200
Faculties of Commerce, Economics, Engineering, Fine Arts, Information Science, International Culture, Management.

NAGANO UNIVERSITY

Shimonogo 658-1, Ueda-shi, Nagano-ken 386-1298
Telephone: (268) 39-0001
Fax: (268) 39-0002
E-mail: kouhou@nagano.ac.jp
Internet: www.nagano.ac.jp

Founded 1966
Pres.: RIKIO SHIMADA
Library of 127,000 vols
Number of teachers: 120
Number of students: 1,656
Faculties of Social Science and Social Welfare.

NAGASAKI PREFECTURAL UNIVERSITY

123 Kawashimo-cho, Sasebo-shi, Nagasaki-ken 858-8580
Telephone: (956) 47-2191
Fax: (956) 47-6941
Internet: www.nagasakipu.ac.jp
Founded 1967
Depts of Distributive Science and Business Administration, Economics, Regional Policy; Graduate School of Economics.

NAGOYA CITY UNIVERSITY

1 Kawasumi, Mizuho-cho, Mizuho-ku, Nagoya
Telephone: (52) 841-6201
Fax: (52) 841-6201
E-mail: admin@cc.nagoya-cu.ac.jp
Internet: www.nagoya-cu.ac.jp
Founded 1950
Pres.: YOSHIRO WADA
Sec.-Gen.: S. ISOBE
Library Dir: S. SAITO
Library of 502,973 vols
Number of teachers: 536
Number of students: 3,500
Publications: *Nagoya Medical Journal* (in English, 4 a year), *NCU* (in Japanese), *Oikonomika* (in Japanese, 4 a year)

DEANS

Faculty of Economics: Y. NAITO
Faculty of Pharmaceutical Sciences: H. IKEZAWA
Medical School: M. SASAKI
School of Design and Architecture: T. YANAGISAWA
School of Humanities and Social Sciences: T. KIDO

OSAKA CITY UNIVERSITY

3-3-138, Sugimoto, Sumiyoshi-ku, Osaka-shi 558-8585
Telephone: (6) 6605-3411
Fax: (6) 6692-1295
E-mail: koho@ado.osaka-cu.ac.jp
Internet: www.osaka-cu.ac.jp
Founded 1949
Academic year: April to March
Pres.: Y. NISHIZAWA
Vice-Pres.: T. KIRIYAMA
Vice-Pres.: M. MIYANO
Vice-Chair.: T. KASHIWAGI
Dean of Bureau for Admissions and Education: K. TAMAI
Dean of Bureau for Students' Affairs: K. MIURA
Dir of Media Centre: H. HASHIMOTO
Library of 2,400,000 books, 9,500 periodicals
Number of teachers: 929
Number of students: 9,096
Publications: *Geosciences News Letter* (1 a year), *Journal of Geosciences, Osaka City University* (1 a year), *OCU Business News Letter* (1 a year), *OCU Prospectus* (every 2 years), *Osaka Journal of Mathematics* (4 a year)

DEANS

Graduate School and Faculty of Business: K. AOYAMA

Graduate School and Faculty of Economics: K. WAKIMURA
Graduate School and Faculty of Engineering: H. OOSHIMA
Graduate School and Faculty of Law: T. YASUTAKE
Graduate School and Faculty of Literature and Human Science: M. MURATA
Graduate School and Faculty of Human Life Science: S. TAJIMI
Graduate School and Faculty of Science: H. SAKURAGI
Graduate School for Creative Cities: S. NAKAMOTO
Graduate School of Medicine and Medical School: O. ISHIKO
Graduate School of Nursing: M. IMANAKA

OSAKA GAKUIN UNIVERSITY

2-36-1 Kishibe-Minami, Suita-shi, Osaka 564-8511
Telephone: (6) 6381-8434
Fax: (6) 6382-4363
E-mail: www-admin@uta.osaka-gu.ac.jp
Internet: www.osaka-gu.ac.jp
Pres.: YOSHIYASU SHIRAI
Library of 990,000 vols
Faculties of Business Administrative Sciences, Corporate Intelligence, Distribution and Communication Sciences, Economics, Foreign Languages, Informatics, International Studies, Law.

OSAKA PREFECTURE UNIVERSITY

1-1 Gakuen-cho, Sakai, Osaka 599-8531
Telephone: (72) 252-1161
Fax: (72) 254-9900
Internet: www.osakafu-u.ac.jp
Founded 1949 as Naniwa University; present name 1955
Prefectural control
Academic year: April to March
Pres.: TSUTOMU MINAMI
Admin.: TOSHIHIKO HONDA
Dir. of Library and Science Information Centre: YOJI HIMENO
Library of 1,072,033 vols
Number of teachers: 871
Number of students: 6,332
Publications: *British and American Language and Culture, DMSIS Research Report, Journal of Economics, Business and Law*

DEANS

College of Agriculture: MITSUNORI KIRIHATA
College of Economics: KATSUHIRO MIYAMOTO
College of Engineering: YOJI TAKEDA
College of Integrated Arts and Sciences: SIGEMITSU NAKANISI
College of Social Welfare: YOICHI DOI

SAPPORO MEDICAL UNIVERSITY

Nishi 17-chome, Minami 1-jo, Chuo-ku, Sapporo, Hokkaido 060
Telephone: (11) 611-2111
Fax: (11) 612-5861
E-mail: info@sapmed.ac.jp
Internet: www.sapmed.ac.jp
Founded 1945 as Hokkaido Prefectural School of Medicine; became Sapporo Medical College 1950; present name 1993
Academic year: April to March
Pres.: A. YACHI
Chief Admin. Officer: M. WATANABE
Librarian: S. URASAWA
Library of 214,000 vols
Number of teachers: 373
Number of students: 1,026

Publication: *Sapporo Igaku Zassi* (Sapporo Medical Journal, with English summaries, 6 a year)

DEANS

School of Health Sciences: T. SATO
School of Medicine: M. MORI

SHIMONOSEKI UNIVERSITY

2-1-1 Daigakucho, Shimonoseki City, Yamaguchi Prefecture 751-8510

Telephone: (832) 52-0288
Fax: (832) 52-8099
E-mail: www-admin@shimonoseki-cu.ac.jp
Internet: www.shimonoseki-cu.ac.jp
Founded 1962
Library of 171,200 vols
Number of students: 2,270

Schools of Economics and International Commerce.

TOKYO METROPOLITAN UNIVERSITY

Minami-Ohsawa 1-1, Hachioji-shi, Tokyo 192-0397

Telephone: (426) 77-1111
Fax: (426) 77-1221
Internet: www.metro-u.ac.jp
Founded 1949
Municipal control
Language of instruction: Japanese
Academic year: April to March (2 terms)
President: K. OGIUE
Director of Administrative Bureau: T. MORUOKA
Librarian: M. MAEDA
Library: see Libraries and Archives
Number of teachers: 646
Number of students: 6,540
Publications: *Bulletin* (1 a year), *Daigakuhiroba* (6 a year), *Gakuhou* (2 a year)

DEANS

Center for Urban Studies: TOSHIHIKO MOGI
Faculty of Economics: TOSHINAO NAKATSUKA
Faculty of Engineering: KOHEI SUZUKI
Faculty of Law: MASAHIDE MAEDA
Faculty of Science: HIDEYUKI SATO
Faculty of Social Sciences and Humanities: SATORU NAGUMO

PROFESSORS

Center for Urban Studies:

AKIYAMA, T., City Transportation Planning
HAGAI, M., Comparative Urban Public Administration
HAGIHARA, K., Urban and Regional Economics
HOSHI, T., Health Science
MATSUMOTO, Y., Social Network Theory
NAKABAYASHI, I., Urban Geography and City Planning
TAMAGAWA, H., Urban Space Analysis

Faculty of Economics:

ASANO, H., Marketing Science
ASANO, S., Econometrics
CHIBA, J., Financial Accounting
FUKAGAI, Y., History of Economic Thought
FUKUSHIMA, T., Public Economics, International Economics
HIGANO, M., Money and Banking
KANAYA, S., Fiscal and Monetary Policy
KUWATA, K., Management Strategy
MIYAKAWA, A., Marxian Economic Theory, History of Economic Thought
MURAKAMI, N., Chinese Enterprise Location
NAKAMURA, J., Labour Economics
NAKATSUKA, T., Business Administration, Operations Research
OMORI, Y., Econometrics
TODA, H., Econometrics

WAKITA, S., Japanese Labour Market
YAGO, K., French Economic History
YAMATO, T., Distribution Mechanism
YAMAZAKI, S., Distribution Policy

Faculty of Engineering:

ANDO, Y., River Engineering, Applied Hydrology
ASAKO, Y., Heat and Mass Transfer
CHIKAZAWA, M., Physical Chemistry of Solid Surfaces
FUKAO, S., Building Construction
FURUKAWA, Y., Precision Machining and Computer-Aided Manufacturing Systems
HOBO, T., Analytical Chemistry and Instrumental Analysis
IGOSHI, M., Computer-Aided Design and Manufacturing
IKUTA, S., Parallel Algorithms
INOUE, H., Physical Organic Photochemistry
ISHIKAWA, H., E-business Model and Database
ISHINO, H., Building Service Engineering
ITO, D., Superconductors and their Applications
IWASAKI, K., Computer Architecture
IWATATE, T., Geomechanics
IYODA, T., Molecular Functional Materials
KATAKURA, M., Traffic Engineering and Infrastructure Planning
KAWAI, T., Organic Chemistry
KAWATA, S., Control Engineering
KIMURA, G., Electrical Machinery and Power Electronics
KITSUTAKA, Y., Building Material Engineering
KIYA, T., Digital Signal Management
KOBAYASHI, K., Architectural Theory and Design
KOIZUMI, A., Sanitary Engineering
KOKUBU, K., Concrete Technology
MAEDA, K., Bridge and Structural Engineering
MASUDA, H., Electrical Chemistry
MISAWA, H., Strength of Materials
MORIYA, T., Applications of Ultrasonics
NAGAHAMA, K., Chemical Engineering, Phase Equilibrium and Related Properties
NAGAOKA, S., Functional Materials
NAGASAWA, S., Applications of Lasers and Remote Sensing
NAKAMURA, I., Robotics and Mechatronics
NISHIKAWA, T., Structural Engineering
NISHIMURA, K., Geomechanics
NISHIMURA, H., Plasticity and New Materials Processing
OKUMURA, T., Semiconductor Physics, Optoelectric Devices
OTA, M., Power Engineering
SAKAKI, T., Strength of Metals and Alloys
SEKIMOTO, H., Piezo-electrical Vibrations and their Applications
SUZUKI, K., Structural Dynamics
TAKAMIZAWA, K., City Planning
TAKI, M., Bioelectromagnetics, Noise Control Engineering
UENO, J., Architectural Planning
UMEGAKI, T., Ceramics, Inorganic Phosphate Chemistry
UMEYAMA, M., Water Environmental Engineering
WATANABE, K., Hydrodynamics, Hydraulic Machinery
WATANABE, T., Environment and Energy Saving
YAMADA, M., Chemical Sensing and Instrumentation
YAMAGISHI, T., Synthetic Organic Chemistry
YAMAZAKI, S., Structural Engineering
YOKOYAMA, R., Control and Optimization of Large-Scale Systems
YOSHIBA, M., High Temperature Material

Faculty of Law:

ASAKURA, M., Labour Law, Social Security Law
FUCHI, M., European Legal History
HITOMI, T., Decentralization and Local Autonomy
IKEDA, T., Civil Law, Law of Land Property
ISHIDA, A., Domestic Politics and International Politics
ISHII, M., Civil Law, Medical Law
ISHIKAWA, K., Constitutional Law
ISOBE, T., Administrative Law
KIMURA, M., Criminal Law
MAEDA, M., Criminal Law
MIYAMURA, H., History of Japanese Political Thought
MIZUBAYASHI, T., Japanese Legal History
MORIYAMA, S., East Asian Politics
MORITA, A., Outside Application of National Control
NAKAJIMA, H., Civil Procedure
NAWATA, Y., Philosophy of Law
NOGAMI, K., Political History of Western Countries
NOMURA, Y., Civil Law, Environmental Law
SHIBUYA, T., Commercial Law, Intellectual Property Law, Competition Law

Faculty of Science:

ABE, T., Physical Training
ACHIBA, Y., Laser Chemistry
AIHARA, Y., Ageing and Temperature Regulation
EBIHARA, M., Space Chemistry
FUKUSAWA, H., Classical Oceanography
GUEST, M., Geometry
HIROSE, T., Experimental High-Energy Physics
HISANAGA, S., Cell Biology
HORI, N., Environmental Geography
HUYAMA, Y., Genetics
IKEMOTO, I., Solid-State Chemistry
IMANAKA, K., Human Motor Behaviour, Perception and Motor Control
ISOBE, T., Biological Chemistry
ISOZAKI, H., Partial Differential Equations
IWATA, S., Glacial Geomorphology
IYODA, M., Organic Chemistry
IZAWA, T., Biochemistry and Physiology of Exercise
KACHI, N., Botanical Ecology
KAINOSHO, M., Biochemistry
KAMIGATA, N., Organic Chemistry
KAMISHIMA, Y., Topology
KATADA, M., Physical Inorganic Chemistry and Radiochemistry
KATO, T., Physical Chemistry
KIKUCHI, T., Topography
KOBAYASHI, N., Atomic and Molecular Physics (Experimental)
KOMANO, T., Molecular Genetics
KORANAGA, T., Micro-nano System
KOUGI, M., Neutron Scattering and Solid-State Physics
KUWASAWA, K., Neurobiology
MIKAMI, T., Climatology, Climate Change, Urban Climate
MINAKATA, H., High-energy Physics
MIYAHARA, T., Solid-State Spectroscopy
MIYAKE, K., Number Theory
MIZOGUCHI, K., Solid-State Physics and Magnetic Resonance
MOCHIZUKI, K., Partial Differential Equations
NAKAMURA, K., Algebraic Number Theory and Algorithms
OHASHI, T., X-ray Astronomy
OHNITA, Y., Differential Geometry and Lie Groups
OKA, M., Singularity Theory and Algebraic Geometry
OKABE, Y., Theoretical Condensed-Matter Physics
OKADA, M., Harmonious Analysis
OKUNO, K., Atomic Physics

PRICE, W. S., Biochemistry
SAITO, S., Elementary Particle Basic Theory
SAKAI, M., Analytic Functions
SATO, H., Electron Theory of Metals
SHIMADA, K., Bacteriology
SUGIURA, Y., Human Geography
SUZUKI, T., Atomic Nuclear Physics
TAKII, S., Microbial Ecology
TERAO, H., Singularities and Combinatorics
WADA, M., Photobiology
WAKABAYASHI, M., Systematic Botany
WATANABE, Y., Aquatic Ecology
YAMASAKI, H., Seismo-tectonics, Quaternary Geology
YAMASAKI, T., Systematic Zoology
YASUGI, S., Developmental Biology
YOMASHITA, M., Inorganic Chemistry

Faculty of Social Sciences and Humanities:
EBARA, Y., Theoretical Sociology
FUKUI, A., French Philosophy
FUKUMA, K., Modern English Poetry
FUKUMOTO, Y., German Linguistics
FUKUSHIMA, F., African Literature
HARA, K., European Culture
HIRAI, H., Modern Chinese Literature
ICHIHARA, S., Psychology of Perception
IDE, H., English Novels
INADA, A, Classical Literature
INUI, A., Secondary Education and Educational Practice
ISHIHARA, K., Family Studies, Social Research
ISHIKAWA, T., French Philosophy of the 17th Century
ISHINO, K., French Semantics
ITO, C., English Novels
JIN, K., Comparative Linguistics
JITSUKAWA, T., French Philosophy
KAI, H., Ethics
KANZAKI, S., Ancient Greek Philosophy
KATO, M., Modern English Poetry
KIMURA, M., Ancient Korean History
KISHI, Y., German Literature
KOBAYASHI, K., History of Japanese Language
KOBAYASHI, R., Social Studies and Administration
KOTANI, H., Indian History
KUROSAKI, I., Educational Administration
MANZAWA, M., Modern German Literature
MOGI, T., Educational Psychology
MORIOKA, K., Urban Sociology, Comparative Sociology
MURAYAMA, K., American Novels
NAGAI, T., Clinical Psychology
NAGUMO, S., Modern Chinese Literature
NAKAJIMA, H., Theoretical Linguistics
NAKANO, T., Modern French History
NARASAKI, H., Contemporary American Novel
NISHIKAWA, N., French Poetry of the 19th Century
OCHIAI, M., Chinese Dialectology
OGINO, T., Sociolinguistics
OHGUSHI, R., Adult Education
OKABE, H., Modern German Literature
OKABE, T., Social Welfare System
OKADA, E., History of Social Welfare
OKADA, M., Middle French Literature
OKADA, N., German Philosophy
OKAZAWA, S., Contemporary German Literature
OKUBO, Y., French Literature of the 16th Century
OKUMURA, S., Capitalism in Pre-Communist China
ONO, A., Archaeology
ORISHIMA, M., American Novels
OTSUKA, K., Social Anthropology
PEARSON, H. E., Applied Linguistics, TESOL
SATAKE, Y., Federal Chinese History
SATO, S., Chinese Philology

SEO, I., German Literature of the 20th Century
SOEDA, A., Social Methodology
SUDA, O., Developmental Study of Communication
SUZUKI, T., Contemporary Austrian Literature
TAKAHASHI, K., Political Sociology
TAKAYAMA, H., English Poetry of the 18th Century
TANJI, N., Philosophy of Science
UENO, Y., Shakespearian Studies
WATANABE, Y., Social Anthropology
YASUDA, T., Reading Process Research
YOSHIKAWA, K., French Literature of the 20th Century

WAKAYAMA MEDICAL UNIVERSITY

811-1 Kimiidera, Wakayama City 641-8509
Telephone: (73) 447-2300
E-mail: admin@wakayama-med.ac.jp
Internet: www.wakayama-med.ac.jp
Founded 1945
President: HIROYUKI YAMAMOTO
Library of 63,250 vols
Number of teachers: 260
Number of students: 399
Publications: *Wakayama Igaku* (in Japanese, 4 a year), *Wakayama Medical Reports* (in English, 4 a year).

YOKOHAMA CITY UNIVERSITY

22-2 Seto, Kanazawa-ku, Yokohama 236-0027
Telephone: (45) 787-2311
Fax: (45) 787-2316
E-mail: netadmin@yokohama-cu.ac.jp
Internet: www.yokohama-cu.ac.jp
Founded 1928
Municipal control
Academic year: April to March
Chancellor and Pres.: KEICHI OGAWA
Chief Admin. Officer: ROKUROU TAKAI
Library Dir: MASATAKA OZAKI
Library of 677,610 vols
Number of teachers: 640
Number of students: 5,480

Publications: *Yokohama Shiritu Daigaku Ronso* (Bulletin, 8 a year), *Yokohama Shiritu Daigaku Kiyo* (Journal, 1 a year), *Keizai-to-Boeki* (Industry and Trade, 2 a year), *Yokohama Medical Bulletin* (in English, 1 a year), *Yokohama Igaku* (Medical Journal, 6 a year), *Yokohama Mathematical Journal* (in English, 2 a year)

DEANS

Faculty of Economics and Business Administration: KAWAUCHI YOSHITADA
Faculty of Humanities and International Studies: FUNIO KANEKO
Faculty of Science: MAKI KUNISUKE
School of Medicine: OKUDA KENJI

Private Universities and Colleges

AICHI UNIVERSITY

1-1 Machihata-cho, Toyohashi-shi, Aichi-ken 441-8522
Telephone: (532) 47-4131
Fax: (532) 47-4144
E-mail: inted@aichi-u.ac.jp
Internet: www.aichi-u.ac.jp
Founded 1946
Academic year: April to March
President: NOBUTERU TAKEDA

Registrar: MASASHI WATANABE
Librarian: MITSUSHI TAMAKI
Library of 1,458,362 vols
Number of teachers: 714 (254 full-time, 460 part-time)
Number of students: 10,084

DEANS

Faculty of Business Administration: TATSUHISA MINAMI
Faculty of Economics: MOTOHIKO SATO
Faculty of International Communication: KENICHI TAMOTO
Faculty of Law: KOUJI SHINDO
Faculty of Letters: MASAYOSHI KATANO
Faculty of Modern Chinese Studies: SATOSHI IMAI
Graduate School of Business Administration: MITSUO FUJIMOTO
Graduate School of Chinese Studies: TSUYOSHI BABA
Graduate School of Economics: KOICHI MIYAIRI
Graduate School of Humanities: KAZUYOSHI SHIMIZU
Graduate School of International Communication: SHIN KOUNO
Graduate School of Law: KATSUYOSHI KATO
Junior College: TAKAO KUROYANAGI

AICHI GAKUIN UNIVERSITY

12 Araike, Iwasaki-cho, Nisshin-shi, Aichi-ken 470-0195
Telephone: (5617) 3-1111
Fax: (5617) 3-6769
E-mail: nyushi@dpc.agu.ac.jp
Internet: www.agu.ac.jp
Founded 1876
Private control
Language of instruction: Japanese
Academic year: April to March
Pres.: HIDETO OONO
Registrar: TAICHI HAYAKAWA
Librarian: KUNIHIRO TAKARADA
Library of 1,151,388 vols
Number of teachers: 506
Number of students: 13,273

Publications: *Transactions of the Institute for Cultural Studies* (1 a year), *Business Review of Aichi Gakuin University* (1 a year), *Aichi Gakuin Law Review* (4 a year), *Journal of the Research Institute of Zen* (1 a year), *The Journal of Aichi Gakuin University* (4 a year), *Foreign Languages and Literature* (1 a year), *Journal of Aichi Gakuin University Dental Society* (4 a year), *Regional Analysis* (2 a year)

DEANS

Faculty of Business and Commerce: MAKOTO OZAKI
Faculty of Dentistry: TOSHIHIDE NOGUCHI
Faculty of General Education: MASAMI INAGAKI
Faculty of Law: KEIICHI TAKAGI
Faculty of Letters: MITSURU ANDO
Faculty of Management: ICHIRO MUKAI
Faculty of Pharmacy: TAKUMA SASAKI
Faculty of Policy Studies: TSUDZUKI TAKAHIKO
Faculty of Psychological and Physical Science: YUZOU SATOU
Japanese Language Course for Foreign Students: KATSUSHI KONDO
Junior College: MASASHI MUKAI

UNIVERSITY OF AIZU

Aizu-Wakamatsu, Fukushima-ken 965-8580
Telephone: (242) 37-2500
Fax: (242) 37-2528
E-mail: daigakuin@u-aizu.ac.jp
Internet: www.u-aizu.ac.jp
Founded 1993

Public control
Languages of instruction: English, Japanese
Academic year: April to March

Pres.: SHIGEAKI TSUNOYAMA

Number of teachers: 112
Number of students: 1,283

DEANS

Computer Science and Engineering: RYUICHI
OKA

AOYAMA GAKUIN UNIVERSITY

4-4-25 Shibuya, Shibuya-ku, Tokyo 150-8366
Telephone: (3) 3409-8111
Fax: (3) 3409-0927
E-mail: iec-office@iec.aoyama.ac.jp
Internet: www.aoyama.ac.jp

Founded 1874
Academic year: April to March

Chancellor: M. FUKAMACHI
President: Dr M. HANDA
Vice-Pres: Dr M. NISHIZAWA, Dr M. TSUJI
Admin. Officer: T. MUNEKATA
Library Dir: Dr H. TAKAMORI

Library of 1,442,666 vols, 16,262 periodicals
Number of teachers: 1,422 (including 976
part-time)
Number of students: 19,372

Publications: *Aoyama Journal of Business* (4
a year), *Aoyama Journal of Economics* (4 a
year), *Aoyama Law Review* (4 a year),
Aoyama Journal of General Education,
Thought Currents in English Literature,
Educational Inquiry, *KIYO* (Journal of
Literature), *Aoyama Gobun* (Journal of
Japanese Literature), *Aoyama Shigaku*
(Journal of History), *Aoyama Business
Review*, *Aoyama Journal of International
Politics, Economics and Business*, *Etudes
Françaises*, *Aoyama International Com-
munication Studies*, *Aoyama Management
Review*

DEANS

College of Economics: Dr Y. YOSHIZOE
College of Law: Dr T. YAMAZAKI
College of Literature: H. ISHIZAKI
College of Science and Engineering: Dr K.
UOZUMI
Graduate School of International Manage-
ment: Dr F. ITOH
School of Business Administration: S. HASE-
GAWA
School of International Politics, Economics
and Business Administration: S. HAKA-
MADA

CHAIRS OF DEPARTMENTS

College of Economics (internet www.econ
.aoyama.ac.jp):
Department of Economics: N. HIRASAWA
Department of Economics (Evening Div-
ision): S. SUGIURA
College of Law (internet www.als.aoyama.ac
.jp):
Department of Law: T. DOBASHI
College of Literature (internet www.cl
.aoyama.ac.jp):
Department of Education: Y. SAKAI
Department of Education (Evening Div-
ision): Dr M. KITAMOTO
Department of English: M. AKIMOTO
Department of English (Evening Division):
Y. SAKUMA
Department of French: Dr T. TSUYUZAKI
Department of Japanese: Y. HIJIKATA
Department of History: Dr S. WATANABE
Department of Psychology: K. ENDO
College of Science and Engineering (internet
www.agnes.aoyama.ac.jp):
Department of Physics: Dr I. NISHIO

Department of Chemistry: Dr H. ITOH
Department of Mechanical Engineering:
Dr S. OHISHI
Department of Electrical Engineering and
Electronics: Dr A. SAWABE
Department of Industrial and Systems
Engineering: Dr M. KURODA
Departmet of Integrated Information
Technology: Dr S. NINOMIYA
School of Business Administration (internet
www.agub.aoyama.ac.jp):
Department of Business Administration:
Dr O. SATO
Department of Business Administration
(Evening Division): Dr N. IWATA
School of International Politics, Economics
and Business (internet www.sipeb.aoyama
.ac.jp):
Department of International Politics: Dr J.
TSUCHIYAMA
Department of International Economics:
K. SENBA

ASIA UNIVERSITY

5-24-10 Sakai, Musashino-shi, Tokyo 180-
8629
Telephone: (422) 36-3255
Fax: (422) 36-4869
E-mail: koryu@asia-u.ac.jp
Internet: www.asia-u.ac.jp/english

Founded 1941
Academic year: April to March

President: SHINICHI KOIBUCHI
Librarian: SEIJI NAKAMURA

Library of 548,000 vols
Number of teachers: 466 (174 full-time, 292
part-time)
Number of students: 8,029

DEANS

Asia University Junior College: S. USUI
Faculty of Business Administration: H.
OSHIMA
Faculty of Economics: T. KATO
Faculty of International Relations: H. OGAWA
Faculty of Law: H. NAKANO
Faculty of Liberal Arts: T. WATANABE
Graduate School of Business Administration:
K. KASAI
Graduate School of Economics: Y. TOZAWA
Graduate School of Law: T. MORIMOTO

AZABU UNIVERSITY

1-17-71 Fuchinobe, Sagamihara City, Kana-
gawa 229-8501
Telephone: (42) 754-7111
Fax: (42) 754-7661
Internet: www.azabu-u.ac.jp

Founded 1890
President: TSUNENORI NAKAMURA
Librarian: HIDEO FUJITANI

Library of 135,000 vols
Number of teachers: 182
Number of students: 2,300
Publication: *Bulletin*

DEANS

College of Environmental Health: TSUYOSHI
HIRATA
School of Veterinary Medicine: TOSHIO
MASAOKA

BUKKYO UNIVERSITY

96 Kitahananobo-cho, Murasakino, Kita-ku,
Kyoto 603-8301
Telephone: (75) 491-2141
Fax: (75) 495-5723
E-mail: mmc-info@bukkyo-u.ac.jp
Internet: www.bukkyo-u.ac.jp

Founded 1868
Private control
Academic year: April to March

Pres.: RYUZEN FUKUHARA
Vice-Pres.: E. NAKAMURA
Registrar: H. OHKITA
Librarian: Y. YAMADA

Library of 684,000 vols
Number of teachers: 164
Number of students: 6,457

Publications: *Journal of the Faculty of Letters* (1 a year), *Journal of the Faculty of
Education* (1 a year), *Journal of the Faculty of Sociology* (1 a year), *Bukkyo University Graduate School Review* (1 a year)

DEANS

Faculty of Letters: M. SHIMIZU
Faculty of Education: J. KAKUMOTO
Faculty of Sociology: M. HAMAOKA
Postgraduate Programmes in Literature: M.
SHIMIZU
Postgraduate Programmes in Education: J.
KAKUMOTO
Postgraduate Programmes in Sociology: M.
HAMAOKA
Independent Postgraduate Programmes in
Buddhism: S. ONODA
Training Programme for the Jodo Priest-
hood: T. TODO

CHIKUSHI JOGAKUEN UNIVERSITY

2-12-1 Ishizaka, Dazaifu City, Fukuoka Pre-
fecture 818-0192
Telephone: (92) 925-3511
Fax: (92) 924-4369
Internet: www.chikushi.ac.jp

Founded 1988

Depts of Asian Studies, Clinical Psychology,
English, English and Multimedia Studies,
Human Welfare, Japanese Language and
Literature.

CHUBU UNIVERSITY

1200 Matsumoto-cho, Kasugai-shi, Aichi-ken
487-8501
Telephone: (568) 51-1111
Fax: (568) 51-1141
E-mail: cucip@office.chubu.ac.jp
Internet: www.chubu.ac.jp

Founded 1964
Language of instruction: Japanese
Academic year: April to March

Chancellor: KAZUO YAMADA
President: ATSUO IIYOSHI

Library of 427,000 vols
Number of teachers: 491 (including 244 part-
time)
Number of students: 8,000 (including 200
postgraduate)

Publications: *Memoirs of the College of
Engineering* (1 a year), *Sogo Kogaku* (Journal of the Research Institute for Science
and Technology, 1 a year), *Journal of the
College of Business Administration and
Information Science* (2 a year), *Journal of
the College of International Studies* (2 a
year), *Journal of the Research Institute for
International Studies* (1 a year), *Journal of
the Research Institute for Industry and
Economics* (1 a year), *Journal of Information Science* (1 a year), *Journal of the
College of Humanities* (1 a year)

DEANS

College of Business Administration and
Information Science: Dr NOBUO KAMATA
College of Engineering: Dr MAKOTO WATA-
NABE
College of Humanities: YUKIO AKATSUKA

College of International Studies: Dr NOBU-HIRO NAGASHIMA

Graduate School of Business Administration and Information Science: Dr NOBUO KAMATA

Graduate School of Engineering: Dr MAKOTO WATANABE

Graduate School of International Studies: Dr NOBUHIRO NAGASHIMA

CHUO UNIVERSITY

742-1 Higashinakano, Hachioji-shi, Tokyo 192-0393

Telephone: (426) 74-2111
Fax: (426) 74-2214
E-mail: intlcent@tamajs.chuo-u.ac.jp
Internet: www.chuo-u.ac.jp

Founded 1885
Academic year: April to March (2 semesters)

Pres. and Chancellor: KOJI SUZUKI
Sec.-Gen.: SHUNSUKE HODOSHIMA
Dean of Students: HISAO FUKUCHI
Library Dir: KEN NAGASAKI
Library: see Libraries and Archives
Number of teachers: 2,009
Number of students: 29,573 (3,171 evening course), 1,833 graduates
Publications: various faculty bulletins, journals

DEANS

Correspondence Division, Faculty of Law: M. SUGAWARA
Faculty of Commerce: K. KITAMURA
Faculty of Economics: A. ICHII
Faculty of Law: K. NAGAI
Faculty of Literature: S. HAYASHI
Faculty of Policy Studies: M. KONO
Faculty of Science and Engineering: N. OKUBO
Graduate School of Commerce: M. TATEBE
Graduate School of Economics: H. TANAKA
Graduate School of Law: T. SHIIBASHI
Graduate School of Literature: S. MUTO
Graduate School of Policy Studies: T. MASU-JIMA
Graduate School of Science and Engineering: K. SUGIYAMA

DIRECTORS

Computer Center: T. SEKIGUCHI
Health Center: T. TSUKADA
Institute of Accounting Research: Y. WATABE
Institute of Business Research: T. ISHIZAKI
Institute of Comparative Law in Japan: T. KINOSHITA
Institute of Cultural Science: M. IRINODA
Institute of Economic Research: Y. KOGUCHI
Institute of Health and Physical Science: A. NISHITANI
Institute of Science and Engineering: M. IRI
Institute of Social Science: Y. KAWASAKI
International Center: H. HAYASHIDA

DAITO BUNKA UNIVERSITY

1-9-1 Takashimadaira, Itabashi-ku, Tokyo 175-8571

Telephone: (3) 5399-7323
Fax: (3) 5399-7823
E-mail: info@ic.daito.ac.jp
Internet: www.daito.ac.jp

Founded 1923
Private control
Academic year: April to March

Chair. of Board: T. TAKEUCHI
Pres.: M. WADA
Managing Dirs: K. SOEDA, S. TSUJINO
Dir of Admin. Office: S. TSUJINO
Dir of Academic Affairs: S. WATABE
Librarian: I. MIYOSHI
Library of 1,204,490 vols
Number of teachers: 1,070

Number of students: 13,315
Publications: *Daito Bunka Daigaku* (Bulletin), *Daito Bunka News* (10 a year)

DEANS

Faculty of Business Administration: Y. OKADA
Faculty of Economics: M. NAKAMURA
Faculty of Foreign Languages: K. NAKAMURA
Faculty of International Relations: H. MATSUI
Faculty of Law: H. TOKI
Faculty of Literature: J. SHIMOYAMA
Faculty of Social–Human Environmentology: Y. TAKAYAMA
Faculty of Sports and Health Science: J. OKADA

HEADS OF GRADUATE SCHOOLS

Asian Area Studies: K. OKADA
Business Administration: M. AMAGASA
Economics: Y. FUJIWARA
Foreign Languages: E. NISHIKAWA
Law: T. SONOHARA
Law School: T. HIRAGI
Literature: T. KAWACHI

JAPANESE LANGUAGE PROGRAMME FOR FOREIGN STUDENTS

Japanese Language Course: T. MIKAMI

DOHTO UNIVERSITY

149 Nakanoswawa, Kitahiroshima-shi, Hokkaido 061-1196

Telephone: (11) 372-3111
Fax: (11) 376-9706
E-mail: kokusai@dohto.ac.jp
Internet: www.dohto.ac.jp

Founded 1964

Chancellor: Dr JUN SAKURAI

Faculties of Fine Arts, Management, Social Welfare.

DOKKYO UNIVERSITY

1-1 Gakuen-cho, Soka-shi, Saitama-ken 340-0042

Telephone: (489) 46-1635
Fax: (489) 43-3160
E-mail: kouhou@stf.dokkyo.ac.jp
Internet: www.dokkyo.ac.jp

Founded 1964
Private control

Pres.: KO KAJIYAMA
Vice-Pres.: TAKAHIRO AZUMA
Vice-Pres.: TSUNEHISA YAMADA
Head Admin.: KAORU DOMON
Librarian: HEIZABURO SHIBATA

Library of 830,000 vols
Number of teachers: 646
Number of students: 8,892
Publications: *Dokkyo Law Journal, Dokkyo Law Review, Dokkyo Studies in Data Processing and Computer Science, Dokkyo Studies in Japanese Language Teaching, Dokkyo-Universität Germanistische Forschungsbeiträge, Dokkyo University Studies in English, Dokkyo University Studies in Foreign Language Teaching, Dokkyo University Studies of Economics, Études de Langue et Culture, Multidisciplinary Research for Regions, Studies on Environmental Symbiosis*

DEANS

Faculty of Economics: TADASHI INUI
Faculty of Foreign Languages: YOSHITAKA KAKINUMA
International Liberal Arts: KAZUHIKO IIJIMA
Faculty of Law: FUMIO FUKUNAGA
Graduate School of Economics: RUMI TATSUTA

Graduate School of Foreign Languages: TERUAKI EBANA
Graduate School of Law: TAKESHI KATADA

DOSHISHA UNIVERSITY

Karasuma Imadegawa, Kamigyo-ku, Kyoto 602-580

Telephone: (75) 251-3110
Fax: (75) 251-3075
E-mail: ji-shomu@mail.doshisha.ac.jp
Internet: www.doshisha.ac.jp

Founded 1875
Academic year: April to March

Chancellor: M. OYA
President: E. HATTA
Dean of Academic Affairs: N. TABATA
Dean of Student Affairs: A. MORITA
Administrative Officer: I. HARA
Library: Libraries with 715,027 vols
Number of teachers: 489 full-time
Number of students: 24,166

Publications: *Studies in Christianity, Studies in Humanities, Doshisha Studies in English, Social Science Review, Doshisha Law Review, Economic Review, Doshisha Business Review, Science and Engineering Review of Doshisha University, Doshisha American Studies, The Social Sciences, The Humanities, The Study of Christianity and Social Problems, Shuryu, Doshisha Literature, L.L.L., Studies in Cultural History, Annual of Philosophy, Philosophical Review, Journal of Education and Culture, Doshisha Psychological Review, Bigaku Geijutsugaku, Doshisha Kokungaku, Doshisha Review of Sociology, Doshisha Kogaku Kaiho, Doshisha Studies in Language and Culture, Doshisha Policy and Management Review, Doshisha Hokentaiiku, Doshisha Danso, Neesima Studies*

DEANS

Faculty of Commerce: T. UKAI
Faculty of Economics: T. NISHIMURA
Faculty of Engineering: M. SENDA
Faculty of Law: A. SEGAWA
Faculty of Letters: Y. KUROKI
Faculty of Theology: K. MORI
Graduate School of American Studies: T. KAMATA
Graduate School of Policy and Management: S. OTA

DIRECTORS

Center for American Studies: N. YAMAUCHI
Institute for Language and Culture: I. KOIKE
Institute for the Study of Humanities and Social Sciences: T. TAKITA
Science and Engineering Research Institute: O. YAMAGUCHI

DOSHISHA WOMEN'S COLLEGE OF LIBERAL ARTS

Kodo, Kyotanabe-shi, Kyoto-fu 610-0395

Telephone: (774) 65-8411
Fax: (774) 65-8461
E-mail: somu-t@dwc.doshisha.ac.jp
Internet: www.dwc.doshisha.ac.jp

Founded 1876
Academic year: April to March

Chancellor: M. OYA
Pres.: J. MORITA
Registrar: Y. HONMA
Librarian: Y. YODEN

Library of 445,983 vols
Number of teachers: 750
Number of students: 5,948

DEANS

Academic Affairs: Y. HONMA

Academic Research Promotion Center: K. MOROI
Accounting and Finance: S. TAKAMOTO
Admissions Center: N. YOSHIKAI
Career Support Center: N. MORISHITA
Contemporary Social Studies: T. KONO
General Affairs: K. KOSAKA
Human Life and Science: N. NISHIMURA
International Exchange Center: T. TAGUCHI
Liberal Arts: M. TERAKAWA
Library and information Services Center: Y. YODEN
Pharmaceutical Sciences: K. MORITA
Religious Affairs: J. KONDO
Student Affairs: Y. KOMOTO

FUKUOKA UNIVERSITY

8-19-1, Nanakuma, Jonan-ku, Fukuoka 814-0180

Telephone: (92) 871-6631
Fax: (92) 862-4431
E-mail: fupr@adm.fukuoka-u.ac.jp
Internet: www.fukuoka-u.ac.jp

Founded 1934
Private control
Academic year: April to March

Pres.: HIROYUKI YAMASHITA
Vice-Pres: KENROU KAWAIDA, KUNIHIDE MIHASHI, MASAHIRO KIKUCHI
Sec.-Gen.: K. SUETSUGU
Librarian: H. NAGATA

Library of 1,400,000 vols
Number of teachers: 928 full-time
Number of students: 22,319

Publication: *Bulletin*

DEANS
Faculty of Commerce: T. ETO
Faculty of Economics: T. TANAKA
Faculty of Engineering: H. YAMASHITA
Faculty of Humanities: S. MAMOTO
Faculty of Law: N. ASANO
Faculty of Pharmaceutical Sciences: H. SHIMENO
Faculty of Science: M. SAIGO
Faculty of Sports and Health Science: K. KANAMORI
School of Medicine: Y. IKEHARA

DIRECTORS
Animal Care Unit: S. KASHIMURA
Central Research Institute: Y. TOMINAGA
Computer Centre: K. SHUDO
Fukuoka University Chikushi Hospital: T. YAO
Fukuoka University Hospital: A. ARIYOSHI
Language Training Centre: K. TACHIBANA
Radioisotope Centre: S. TASAKI
Takamiya Evening School: M. MORI

GAKUSHUIN UNIVERSITY

1-5-1 Mejiro, Toshima-ku, Tokyo 171-8588
Telephone: (3) 3986-0221
Fax: (3) 5992-1005
E-mail: webmaster@gakushuin.ac.jp
Internet: www.gakushuin.ac.jp/univ
Founded 1949
Private control
Language of instruction: Japanese
Academic year: April to March

Chancellor: Y. HATANO
Pres.: N. FUKUI
Chief Admin. Officer: M. MIYAZAKI
Dean of Students: Y. KUSANO
Librarian: T. TAKANO

Library of 1,600,000 vols
Number of teachers: 281 full-time, 663 part-time
Number of students: 8,652 (8,066 undergraduate, 586 postgraduate)

Publications: *Gakushuin Daigaku Bungaku-Bu Kenkyu Nenpo* (Annual Collection of Essays and Studies, Faculty of Letters), *Gakushuin Daigaku Hogakkai Zasshi* (Gakushuin Review of Law and Politics, 2 a year), *Gakushuin Daigaku Keizai Ronshu* (Gakushuin Economic Papers, 4 a year), *Gakushuin Daigaku Kenkyusosho* (Gakushuin University Studies, 1 a year)

DEANS
Faculty of Economics: T. UEDA
Faculty of Law: M. KAMIYA
Faculty of Letters: T. KANDA
Faculty of Sciences: T. TAKAHASHI

CHAIRMEN
Graduate School of Economics: S. KAMBE
Graduate School of Humanities: T. KANDA
Graduate School of Law: T. TSUNEOKA
Graduate School of Management: T. SUZUKI
Graduate School of Politics: Y. NAKAI
Graduate School of Sciences: T. TAKAHASHI
Professional School of Law: Y. NOSAKA

PROFESSORS
Faculty of Economics:
  AOKI, Y., Consumer Behaviour
  ARAI, K., Stochastic Processes and Statistics
  ASABA, S., Business Economics and Strategic Management
  ENDO, H., Health Economics and Business Policy
  FUKUCHI, J., Statistics, Statistical Finance
  HOSONO, K., Macroeconomics
  IMANO, K., Human Resource Management
  ISHII, S., Economic History of Japan
  ITSUMI, Y., Public Finance
  IWATA, K., Japanese Economic Studies, Land and Housing Economics
  KAMBE, S., Microeconomic Theory and Game Theory
  KANEDA, N., Accounting
  KATSUO, Y., Financial Accounting
  KAWASHIMA, T., Special Economics and Econometrics
  KOYAMA, A., Business Finance and International Management
  MITSUI, K., Public Economics
  MIYAGAWA, T., Macroeconomics, Japanese Economy
  MORITA, M., Management Science and Strategic Management
  MUKUNOKI, H., International Economics
  NAMBU, T., Industrial Economics
  OKUMURA, H., Japanese Economic Studies, International Finance
  SHIROTA, Y., Computer Science
  SUGITA, Y., Marketing Science
  SUZUKI, T., Business History
  TANAKA, N., Systems and Simulation
  TATSUMI, K., Financial Markets and Investment
  UCHINO, T., Management and Organization Theory
  UEDA, T., Marketing
  WADA, T., Business Economics and Strategic Management
  WAKISAKA, A., Economics of Work and Pay
  WAKOH, J., Game Theory, Mathematical Economics
  YUZAWA, T., Business History

Faculty of Law:
  ENDO, K., Sociology
  FUKUMOTO, K., Politics
  HASEBE, Y., Law of Civil Procedure
  HASHIMOTO, Y., Labour and Employment Law
  HIRANO, H., Social Psychology
  IIDA, Y., Political History of Europe
  INOUE, T., History of Politics and Diplomacy in Japan
  ISOZAKI, N., Political Change in East Asia
  KAMIYA, M., Anglo-American Law

  KANZAKI, T., Conflict of Laws
  KATSUNAGI, T., Public Policy and Jurisprudence
  MAEDA, A., Commercial Law
  MIZUNO, K., Civil Law
  MORINAGA, T., History of Western Political Thought
  MURAMATSU, M., Public Administration
  MURANUSHI, M., International Politics
  NAKAI, Y., Comparative Politics
  NOMURA, T., Civil Law
  NONAKA, N., Principles of Political Science
  NOSAKA, Y., Constitutional Law
  OKA, T., Civil Law
  OKINO, M., Civil Law
  SAKAMOTO, K., Political Process of Japan
  SAKURAI, K., Administrative Law
  SASAKI, T., Political Theory
  SHIBAHARA, K., Criminal Law
  SHIZUMI, M., Criminal Law
  SUDO, N., Sociology
  SUNADA, I., American Government and Politics
  TAKAGI, H., Administrative Law
  TOMATSU, H., Constitutional Law
  TSUMURA, M., Law of Criminal Procedure
  TSUNEOKA, T., Administrative Law

Faculty of Letters:
  ABE, S., History of Japanese Language and Dialectology
  ARIKAWA, H., History of European Art
  CHUJOH, S., 19th-century French Novel
  FITZSIMMONS, A., Irish Literature, Modern British Poetry
  FUKUI, N., Contemporary European History
  HARADA, Y., French 17th-century Philosophy and Literature
  HASHIMOTO, M., Modern English Literature, Irish Literature
  HOSAKA, Y., Semantics, Syntax (German)
  HYODO, H., Japanese Medieval Literature, Culture of Japanese Performing Arts
  IENAGA, J., Medieval Japanese History
  INOUE, I., Modern Japanese History
  ITOH, K., Clinical Psychology, Supportive Psychotherapy
  IWASAKI, H., 20th-century French Novel
  KAMENAGA, Y., Medieval European History
  KAMIOKA, N., Contemporary American Novels
  KANDA, T., Medieval Japanese Literature
  KANEGAE, H., Ancient Japanese History
  KAWAGUCHI, Y., Educational Methodology
  KAWASAKI, Y., Psychotherapy, Transference
  KOBAYASHI, T., History of Japanese Art
  KOMATSU, E., Linguistics
  MAEDA, N., Modern Japanese Linguistics
  MANO, Y., British Novels
  MARÉ, T., French Literature
  MATSUSHIMA, S., English Romantic Poetry
  MIYASHITA, S., German Poetry
  MURANO, R., Cross-cultural Communication, Teaching Japanese as a Foreign Language
  NAGANUMA, Y., Volunteer Learning
  NAGASHIMA, Y., Linguistics (Semantics)
  NAGATA, Y., Social Psychology
  NAKAJIMA, H., English Linguistics
  NAKAMURA, I., History of Japanese Thought
  NAKANO, H., Elizabethan Drama
  NINOMIYA, R., 17th- and 18th-century French Literature
  NOMURA, R., 17th- and 18th-century French Literature
  OHNUKI, A., Cultural Studies
  OKAMOTO, J., German Linguistics, Cognitive Semantics, Linguistic Theory
  PEKAR, T., German Literature, Cultural Studies
  SAEKI, T., French Drama
  SAITOH, T., Educational History

SAKAI, K., Comparative Philosophy, Modern (18th- and 19th-century) Philosophy, Phenomenology

SAKONJI, S., Greek Philosophy, Neoplatonism, Renaissance Philosophy

SANO, M., History of Japanese Art

SASAKI, T., Ancient Japanese Linguistics

SHIMADA, M., Ancient Roman History

SHIMOKAWA, K., British Philosophy (Locke and Hume), Ethics and Political Philosophy

SHINKAWA, T., Medieval Thought and Buddhism in Japan

SHINODA, A., Comparative Psychology

SHINOHARA, S., Learning Theories

SHIOTANI, K., 18th- and 19th-century English Literature

SUGIYAMA, N., French Philosophy

SUWA, T., Cultural Geography

TAKADA, H., German Linguistics, History of the German Language, Historical Pragmatics

TAKAHASHI, H., History of European Art

TAKAMI, K., Linguistics (Syntax and Semantics)

TAKANO, T., Early Modern Japanese History

TAKETSUNA, S., Educational Psychology

TAKEUCHI, F., Modern Asian History

TANABE, C., American Literature

TOGAWA, S., Modern Japanese Literature

TOYAMA, M., Social Cognition, Causal Attribution

TSURUMA, K., Ancient Chinese History

UCHIDA, T., American Literature

WATANABE, M., History of German Linguistics, Sociolinguistics, Comparative Linguistics

YAHAGI, S., 19th-century American Literature

YAMAMOTO, M., Child Development, Developmental Disorder

YAMAMOTO, Y., Modern Japanese Literature

YOSHIDA, K., French Poetry and Poets

YOSHIKAWA, M., Clinical Psychology, Clinical Assessment

Faculty of Science (tel. (3) 3986-0221 ext. 6450; fax (3) 5992-1029; e-mail sci-off@gakushuin.ac.jp):

AKAO, K., Complex Manifolds

AKAOGI, M., Science of the Earth's Materials under High Pressure

AKIYAMA, T., Synthetic Organic Chemistry

ARAKAWA, I., Surface and Vacuum Science

FUJIWARA, D., Functional Analysis, Theory of Partial Differential Equations

HIRANO, T., Quantum Optics

IDA, D., Gravity and Relativistic Cosmology

IITAKA, S., Algebraic Geometry, Birational Geometry

ISHII, K., Vibrational Spectroscopy of Molecular Systems

KATASE, K., Differential Topology, Complex Dynamic Systems

KAWABATA, A., Theory of Solid-State Physics, Mesoscopic Physics

KAWASAKI, T., Topology and Geometry of Surfaces

KOTANI, M., Photochemistry and Photophysics of Organic Solids

MIZOGUCHI, T., Materials Science, Spin-polarized Electron Spectroscopy, Magnetism, Amorphous Materials

MIZUTANI, A., Numerical Analysis

MOCHIDA, K., Organometallic Chemistry of Group 14 Elements

MURAMATSU, Y., Geo- and Environmental Chemistry of Trace Elements and Isotopes

NAKAJIMA, S., Number Theory

NAKAMURA, H., Organic Synthesis

NAKANO, S., Number Theory

NISHIZAKA, T., Biophysics of Macromolecular Motion

TAKAHASHI, T., Electronic Properties of Small-dimensional Conductors, Organic Conductors and Superconductors

TASAKI, H., Theoretical Physics and Mathematical Physics

WATANABE, M., Physics of Crystal Growth

YAJIMA, K., Mathematical Physics, Partial Differential Equations

Center for Sports and Health Science (tel. (3) 3971-8989; fax (3) 5992-9306):

HANEDA, Y., Sports Biomechanics

HIRO, N., Sports Methodology

ONO, T., Exercise Physiology

SATO, Y., Applied Physiology, General Principle of Ball Game Strategy and Tactics

TAKAMARU, Y., Coaching Sciences

YAGI, Y., Sports Psychology

HAKODATE UNIVERSITY

5-1 Takaoka-cho, Hakodate 042-0955

Telephone: (138) 57-1181

Fax: (138) 57-0298

E-mail: post@hakodate-u.ac.jp

Internet: www.hakodate-u.ac.jp

Founded 1938

Pres.: HAKUSHI KAWAMURA

Number of students: 1,200

Faculty of Commerce.

HIROSHIMA JOGAKUIN UNIVERSITY

4-13-1, Ushita-higashi, Higashi-ku, Hiroshima 732-0063

Telephone: (82) 228-0386

Fax: (82) 227-4502

E-mail: kokusai@gaines.hju.ac.jp

Internet: www.hju.ac.jp

Founded 1886, as college 1949

Academic year: April to March

Pres.: HIROSHI IMADA

Vice-Pres.: SHIGEKI SATOH

Registrar: YUJI MAEWAKA

Chief Admin. Officer: SHIGENOBU HATAKEYAMA

Library of 200,000 vols

Number of teachers: 75

Number of students: 2,062

Publication: *Bulletin* (1 a year)

Departments of English Studies, Environmental Culture, Environmental Science, Graduate School of Language and Culture, Human and Cultural Studies, Human Life Science, Japanese Language and Literature.

HIROSHIMA UNIVERSITY OF ECONOMICS

5-37-1 Gion, Asaminami-ku, Hiroshima City 731-0192

Telephone: (82) 871-1002

Fax: (82) 871-1666

E-mail: int-sc@hue.ac.jp

Internet: www.hue.ac.jp

Founded 1967

Academic year: April to March

Chancellor: MASAO ISHIDA

President: TSUNEO ISHIDA

Chief Administrative Officer: SHIGEMITSU ARICHI

Librarian: HIROSHI SEIKE

Library of 281,050 vols

Number of teachers: 256 (150 full-time, 106 part-time)

Number of students: 5,000

DEANS

Faculty of Economics: TOSHIYUKI MIZOGUCHI

Graduate School of Economics: TOSHIYUKI MIZOGUCHI

HIROSHIMA SHUDO UNIVERSITY

1-1-1 Ozuka-higashi, Asaminami-ku, Hiroshima 731-3195

Telephone: (82) 830-1103

Fax: (82) 830-1303

Internet: www.shudo-u.ac.jp

President: MASANORI KODAMA

Library of 640,594 vols in Japanese and other languages; 4,999 periodicals, 655,112 other items

Number of teachers: 179

Number of students: 6,204

Publications: *Monographs of the Institute for Advanced Studies, Papers of the Research Society of Commerce and Economics, Studies in the Humanities and Sciences, Shudo Hogaku: Shudo Law Review, Journal of Human Environmental Studies, Journal of Economic Sciences*

Faculties of Commercial Sciences, Economic Sciences, Human Environmental Sciences, Humanities and Human Sciences and Law.

HOKKAI-GAKUEN UNIVERSITY

4-1-40, Asahi-machi, Toyohira-ku, Sapporo 062-8605

Telephone: (11) 841-1161

Fax: (11) 824-3141

Internet: www.hokkai-s-u.ac.jp

Founded 1952

Academic year: April to March

Chair.: MASAO MORIMOTO

Pres.: T. ASAKURA

Librarian: N. TSUNEMI

Library of 856,542 vols

Number of teachers: 243 full-time

Number of students: 9,084

Publications: *Keizai Ronshu* (Journal of Economics, 4 a year), *Hogaku Kenkyu* (Journal of the Faculty of Law, 4 a year), *Gakuen Ronshu* (Journal of Hokkai-Gakuen University, 4 a year), *Kogakubu Kenkyu Hokoku* (Bulletin of the Faculty of Engineering, 1 a year), *Jinbun Ronshu* (Studies in Culture, 3 a year), *Keiei Ronshu* (Journal of Business Administration, 4 a year)

DEANS

Faculty of Business Administration: A. FUKUNAGA

Faculty of Economics: M. KOBAYASHI

Faculty of Engineering: T. YAMANOI

Faculty of Humanities: C. OISHIO

Faculty of Law: N. MUKAIDA

CHAIRMEN

Graduate School of Business Administration: Y. HAYAKAWA

Graduate School of Economics: K. KODA

Graduate School of Engineering: T. KUWAHARA

Graduate School of Law: N. KATO

Graduate School of Literature: T. HAMA

Law School: O. MARUYAMA

ATTACHED INSTITUTES

Center for Academic Affairs: Dir H. MORISHITA.

Center for Development Policy Studies: f. 1957; Dir K. TAKAHARA; publ. *Kaihatsu Ronshu* (Journal of Policy Studies, 2 a year).

HOKURIKU UNIVERSITY

1-1 Taiyogaoka, Kanazawa City, Ishikawa Prefecture 920-1180

Telephone: (76) 229-1161

Fax: (76) 229-1393

E-mail: koho@hokuriku-u.ac.jp
Internet: www.hokuriku-u.ac.jp
Founded 1975
Academic year: April to March
Pres.: S. KAWASHIMA
Librarian: Y. KITANO
Library of 209,000 vols
Number of teachers: 144
Number of students: 3,000
Publications: *Hokuriku Daigaku Kiyo* (bulletin, 1 a year), *Hokuriku Hogaku* (journal of law and political science, 4 a year)

DEANS

Faculty of Future Learning: S. SONOYAMA
Faculty of Pharmaceutical Sciences: T. SAWA-NISHI
Graduate School of Pharmaceutical Research: T. SAWANISHI (Chair.)

HOSEI UNIVERSITY

2-17-1, Fujimi, Chiyoda-ku, Tokyo 102-8160
Telephone: (3) 3264-9662
Fax: (3) 3238-9873
Internet: www.hosei.ac.jp
Founded 1880
Private control
Language of instruction: Japanese
Academic year: April to March
Pres.: TOSHIO MASUDA
Vice-Pres: AKIRA HAMAMURA, YOSHIRO FUKUDA, JUN NAKAMURA, AKIRA TOKUYASU
Registrar: (vacant)
Library Dir: MITSUO NESAKI
Library of 1,620,000 vols
Number of teachers: 2,740 (746 full-time, 1,994 part-time)
Number of students: 36,302 , incl. graduate 2,268, correspondence education 6,375
Publications: *Daigakuin Kiyo* (Graduate School Bulletin, 2 a year), *Gendaifukushi Kenkyu* (Bulletin of the Faculty of Social Policy and Administration, 1 a year), *Hogaku-Shirin* (Law and Political Sciences Review, 4 a year), *Hosei Daigaku Bungakubu Kiyo* (Bulletin of Faculty of Letters, 1 a year), *Hosei Daigaku Kogakubu Kenkyu Shuho* (College of Engineering Bulletin, 1 a year), *Hosei Daigaku Kyariadezaingakubu Kiyo* (Bulletin of the Faculty of Lifelong Learning and Career Studies, 1 a year), *Ibunka* (Journal of Intercultural Communication, 1 a year), *Keiei Shirin* (Business Journal, 4 a year), *Keizai-Shirin* (Economic Review, 4 a year), *Ningen Kankyo Ronshu* (Journal of Humanity and the Environment, 2 a year), *Shakai Shirin* (Sociology and Social Sciences, 4 a year)

DEANS

Business School of Accountancy: KIKUYA MASATO
Business School of Innovation Management: KOSUKE OGAWA
Faculty of Bioscience and Applied Chemistry: TOSHIYUKI NAGATA
Faculty of Business Administration: MASAO YOKOUCHI
Faculty of Computer and Information Sciences: HIROSHI HANAIZUMI
Faculty of Economics: MICHIKI KIKUCHI
Faculty of Engineering: YASUHIRO YAMAMOTO
Faculty of Engineering and Design: YUTAKA TANAKA
Faculty of Global and Interdisciplinary Studies: MITSUTOSHI SOMURA
Faculty of Humanity and the Environment: KAZUO SEKIGUCHI
Faculty of Intercultural Communication: YASUSHI SUZUKI
Faculty of Law: YASUKO KONO

Faculty of Letters: TADASHI MIYAKAWA
Faculty of Lifelong Learning and Career Studies: KOICHIRO KOMIKAWA
Faculty of Science and Engineering: KIYOTAKA SAKINO
Faculty of Social Policy and Administration: IKUJI ISHIKAWA
Faculty of Social Sciences: MIZUHITO KANEHARA
Faculty of Sports and Health Studies: HARUO KARIYA
Graduate School Committee: YASUAKI KUMATA (Chair.)
Graduate School of Art and Technology: NORIO TAKEUCHI
Graduate School of Business Administration: YOSHIO OKUNISHI
Graduate School of Computer and Information Sciences: NOBUHIKO KOIKE
Graduate School of Economics: TOSHIYUKI OKUYAMA
Graduate School of Engineering: YASUHIRO YAMAMOTO
Graduate School of Environmental Management: RYO FUJIKURA
Graduate School of Humanities: TADASHI KANOU
Graduate School of Intercultural Communication: YOSHIAKI OSHIMA
Graduate School of Law: AKIMASA YANAGI
Graduate School of Policy Sciences: MASAHIDE MAJIMA
Graduate School of Politics: YOSHIHIKO NAWATA
Graduate School of Regional Policy Design: YOSHIYUKI OKAMOTO
Graduate School of Social Well-Being Studies: KENICHI BABA
Graduate School of Sociology: MAFUMI FUJITA
International Japan-Studies Institute: YUKO TANAKA
Law School: AKIMICHI IWAMA

ATTACHED INSTITUTES

Boissonade Institute of Modern Laws and Politics: 2-17-1 Fujimi, Chiyoda-ku, Tokyo 102-8160; f. 1977; Dir T. OHNO.
Computational Science Research Centre: 3-7-2 Kajino-cho, Koganei-shi, Tokyo 184-8584; f. 1969; Dir M. KUSAKABE.
Information Research Institute, California: 800 Airport Blvd, Suite 504, Burlingame, CA 94010, USA; f. 2000; Dir K. YANA.
Information Research Technology Centre: 2-17-1 Fujimi, Chiyoda-ku, Tokyo 102-8160; f. 2000; Dir G. SHIRAI.
Institute of Comparative Economic Studies: 4342 Aihara-machi, Machida-shi, Tokyo 194-0298; f. 1984; Dir K. ODAKA; publ. *Journal* (1 a year).
Institute of Nogaku Studies: 2-17-1 Fujimi, Chiyoda-ku, Tokyo 102-8160; f. 1952; Dir H. NISHINO; publ. *Catalogue Noh Drama Collections.*
Institute of Okinawan Studies: 2-17-1 Fujimi, Chiyoda-ku, Tokyo 102-8160; f. 1972; Dir T. YASUE; publ. *Bulletin.*
Japan Statistics Research Institute: 4342 Aihara-machi, Machida-shi, Tokyo 194-0298; f. 1946; Dir H. MORI; publ. *Bulletin* (1 a year).
Ohara Institute for Social Research: 4342 Aihara-machi, Machida-shi, Tokyo 194-0298; f. 1919; Dir S. HAYAKAWA; publ. *Labour Yearbook of Japan* (1 a year), *Report* (12 a year).
Research and Service Centre for Tama Community: 2-17-1 Fujimi, Chiyoda-ku, Tokyo 102-8160; Dir C. HIRABAYASHI; publ. *Newsletter* (4 a year).
Research Centre of Ion Beam Technology: 3-7-2 Kajino-cho, Koganei-shi, Tokyo 184-8584; f. 1979; Dir T. NAKAMURA.

Sports and Physical Education Research Centre: 2-17-1 Fujimi, Chiyoda-ku, Tokyo 102-8160; f. 1976; Dir K. GOMYO.

INTERNATIONAL CHRISTIAN UNIVERSITY

10-2, Osawa 3-chome, Mitaka-shi, Tokyo 181-8585
Telephone: (422) 33-3038
Fax: (422) 33-9887
E-mail: webmaster@icu.ac.jp
Internet: www.icu.ac.jp
Founded 1949
An ecumenical university, accepting students of high academic ability from all countries
Languages of instruction: Japanese, English
Academic year: April to March or September to June
Pres.: NORIHIKO SUZUKI
Vice-Pres. for Academic Affairs: KAZUAKI SAITO
Vice-Pres. for Financial Affairs: ICHIRO NISHIDA
Library Dir: YUKI NAGANO
Library: see Libraries and Archives
Number of teachers: 147 (full-time)
Number of students: 2,887
Publications: *Asian Cultural Studies, Educational Studies, Humanities—Christianity and Culture, Language Research Bulletin, Social Science*

DEANS

College of Liberal Arts: M. OKANO
Graduate School: S. KAWASHIMA
Student Affairs: A. AOI

ATTACHED INSTITUTES

Hachiro Yuasa Memorial Museum: f. 1982; collections of Japanese archaeology and folk art; Dir K. SAITO.
Institute of Asian Cultural Studies: f. 1971, replacing Committee f. 1958; Dir W. STEELE; publ. *Asian Cultural Studies* (1 a year).
Institute of Educational Research and Service: f. 1953; Dir J. MAHER; publ. *Educational Studies* (1 a year).
Institute for the Study of Christianity and Culture: f. 1963; Dir A. TANAKA; publ. *Humanities—Christianity and Culture* (1 a year).
Peace Research Institute: f. 1991; Dir J. WASILEWSKI.
Research Center for Japanese Language Education: f. 1991; Dir M. HIROSE.
Social Science Research Institute: f. 1953; Dir S. ISHIWATA; publ. *The Journal of Social Science* (2 a year).

ISHINOMAKI SENSHU UNIVERSITY

1 Shinmito, Minamisakai, Ishinomaki-shi, Miyagi 986-8580
Telephone: (225) 22-7711
Fax: (225) 22-7710
Internet: www.isenshu-u.ac.jp
Chair.: Dr MASAYOSHI DEUSHI
Pres.: RYOUJI KOBAYASHI
Library of 100,000 vols
Faculties of Business Administration and Science.

IWATE MEDICAL UNIVERSITY

19-1 Uchimaru, Morioka, Iwate 020-8505
Telephone: (19) 651-5111
Fax: (19) 624-1231
E-mail: webmaster@iwate-med.ac.jp
Internet: www.iwate-med.ac.jp

Founded 1928, University 1952
Private control
President: SHIGERU ONO
Librarian: TOKIO NAWA
Library of 249,221 vols
Number of teachers: 500
Number of students: 1,037

Publications: *Journal of the Iwate Medical Association* (6 a year), *Dental Journal* (4 a year)

DEANS

School of Dentistry: KIMIO SAKAMAKI
School of Liberal Arts and Sciences: KOKI KANNO
School of Medicine: CHUICHI ITO

JAPAN WOMEN'S UNIVERSITY

2-8-1 Mejirodai, Bunkyou-ku, Tokyo 112-8681

Telephone: (3) 3943-3131
Fax: (3) 5981-3353
E-mail: n-abroad@atlas.jwu.ac.jp
Internet: www.jwu.ac.jp

Founded 1901
Private control
Academic year: April to March

Pres.: YOSHIKO ARIKAWA
Vice-Pres.: IKUKO KOYABE
Vice-Pres.: TAKAMASA KOYAMA

Library of 806,842 vols
Number of teachers: 258
Number of students: 6,143

DEANS

Faculty of Human Sciences and Design: TAKASHIGE ISHIKAWA
Faculty of Humanities: YASUYUKI SHIMIZU
Faculty of Integrated Arts and Social Sciences: KIICHIRO IINAGA
Faculty of Science: RYOKO IMAICHI

JIKEI UNIVERSITY

3-25-8 Nishi-Shinbashi, Minato-ku, Tokyo 105-8461

Telephone: (3) 3433-1111
Fax: (3) 3435-1922
Internet: www.jikei.ac.jp

Founded 1881
Private control
Academic year: April to March

President: SATOSHI KURIHARA

Library of 227,036 vols
Number of teachers: 2,151
Number of students: 1,545

Publications: *Tokyo Jikeikai Medical Journal* (in Japanese, 6 a year), *Jikeikai Medical Journal* (in English, 4 a year), *Kyoiku Kenkyu Nenpo* (in Japanese, 1 a year), *Research Activities* (in English, 1 a year)

DEANS

School of Medicine and School of Nursing: S. KURIHARA

KANSAI UNIVERSITY

3-3-35 Yamate-cho, Suita-shi, Osaka 564-8680

Telephone: (6) 6368-1121
Fax: (6) 6330-3027
E-mail: www-adm@www.kansai-u.ac.jp
Internet: www.kansai-u.ac.jp

Founded 1886
Academic year: April to March

Pres.: TEIICHI KAWATA
Chair. of Board of Trustees: SEIICHIRO MORIMOTO
Dir of Educational Affairs Bureau: YASUHIRO KONISHI

Librarian: NOBORU TANAKA
Library: see Libraries and Archives
Number of teachers: 1,827
Number of students: 26,674

Publications: *Bungaku Ronshu* (Literary Essays, 3 a year), *Hogaku Ronshu* (Law Review, 4 a year), *Shakaigaku Kiyo* (Journal of Sociological Research, 2 a year), *Keizai Ronshu* (Economic Review, 6 a year), *Shogaku Ronshu* (Business Review, 5 a year), *Kogaku Kenkyu Hokoku* (Technology Reports, 1 a year), *Keizai-Seiji Kenkyusho Kenkyu Shoho* (Economic and Political Studies), *Tozaigakujutsu Kenkyusho Kiyo* (Bulletin of Institute of Oriental and Occidental Studies), *Kogaku to Gijutsu* (Engineering and Technology), *Hogaku Kenkyusho Kenkyu Shoho, Gien* (Industrial Technology), *Review of Law and Politics, Review of Economics, Review of Business and Commerce, Joho Kenkyu* (Informatics Research), *Senri eno Muchii* (Journal of Graduate School of Foreign Language Education and Research, 1 a year), *Hakubatsukan Kiyo* (1 a year), *Kokogakutsu Shiryoshitsu Kiyo* (1 a year), *Jinken Mondai Kenkyu Kiyo* (1 a year)

DEANS

Faculty of Commerce: Prof. HIROMI TSURUTA
Faculty of Economics: Prof. KANJI MORIOKA
Faculty of Engineering: Prof. TETSUAKO TSUCHIDO
Faculty of Informatics: Prof. TAKASHI KATO
Faculty of Law: Prof. KUMIHIRO OHNUMA
Faculty of Letters: Prof. KEIJI SHIBAI
Faculty of Sociology: Prof. ICHIRO MATSUHARA
Institute of Foreign Language Education and Research: Prof. TAICHI USAMI
School of Law: Prof. KEIICHI YAMANAKA

PROFESSORS

Faculty of Law
    Department of Jurisprudence:
FUKUTAKI, H., Commercial Law
GOTO, M., Civil Law
ICHIHARA, Y., History of Legal Thought
ICHIKAWA, K., Japanese Legal History
IKEDA, T., Administrative Law
IWASAKI, K., Insurance Law and Shipping Law
KAMEDA, K., Administrative Law II
KOCHU, N., Constitutional Law
KOIZUMI, Y., Constitutional Law
KOKUBU, T., Family Law and Succession Law
KURITA, K., Maritime Law
KURITA, T., Debtors' and Creditors' Rights
KUZUHARA, R., Criminal Law
NAGATA, S., Civil Law
OHNUMA, K., Labour Law
OHNUMA, K., Labour Law II
OKA, T., European Legal History
SASAMOTO, Y., Insurance Law
SATO, Y., Private International Law
SENTO, Y., Family Law and Succession Law
TSUKIOKA, T., Law of Real Property
YOSHIDA, E., Comparative Constitutional Law
YOSHIDA, N., Emancipation of Buraku

    Department of Politics:
MANABE, S., Diplomatic History
MORIMOTO, T., Political and Governmental Organization
OTSURU, C., International Politics
TERAJIMA, T., Political Philosophy
TOKURA, K., European Politics
WAKATA, K., Political Psychology
YAMAMOTO, K., Information Processing
YAMANO, H., Political History of Modern Japan

Faculty of Letters
Course of English Language and Literature:
AKIMOTO, H., American Literature
AOYAMA, T., Linguistics
HASEGAWA, A., English Linguistics
HOSHII, Y., Introductory Seminar
IRIKO, F., Study of American Literature
ISHIZAKA, K., Middle English
KAMIMURA, T., Modern British Novels
KIRWAN, J.
MAKIN, P. J., Modern British and American Poetry
SAKAMOTO, T., History of English Literature
SHIMAZAKI, M., British and American Prose
TANIGUCHI, Y., Modern American Literature
TSUTSUI, O., British and American Drama
    Course of Japanese Language and Literature:
ENDO, K., Japanese Linguistics
FUJITA, S., Japanese Literature (Edo Period)
KAMITANI, E., Japanese Linguistics
OHHAMA, M., Early Ancient Japanese Literature
SEKIYA, T., Textual Criticism of Noh Plays
TANAKA, N., Literature in the Heian Period
URANISHI, K., Modern and Contemporary Japanese Literature
YAMAMOTO, T., Early Modern Japanese Fiction
YAMAMOTO, T., Literature in the Heian Period
YOSHIDA, N., History of Modern Japanese Literature
    Course of Philosophy:
INOUE, K., Comparative Study of Eastern and Western Thought
KIOKA, N., Philosophy
NAKATANI, N., History of Art in the Far East
ODA, Y., History of Religions
SHINAGAWA, T., Ethics
YAMAMOTO, I., Philosophy
Course of French Language and Literature:
HIRATA, S., Modern French Literature
HONDA, T., French Linguistics
ITOH, M., French Philology
KASHIWAGI, O., French Literature
KAWAKAMI, M., Modern French Literature
NONAMI, T., French Literature
OKU, J., History of French Literature
Course of German Language and Literature:
HAMAMOTO, T., German Cultural Studies
KUDO, Y.
SHIBATA, T., German Literature
TAKEICHI, O., German Linguistics
USAMI, Y., Modern German Literature
WATANABE, Y., German Linguistics
YAKAME, T., German Literature
    Course of History and Geography:
ASAJI, K., European Medieval History
FUJITA, T., History of Early China
HASHIMOTO, S., Human Geography
ITOH, O., Human Geography
KOBA, M., Physical Geography
MATSUURA, A., History of Early Modern China
MORI, T.
NAKAMURA, H., History of Modern Russia
NISHIMOTO, M., History of Ancient Japan
NOMA, H., Human History
OHYA, W., History of Modern Japan
SHIBAI, K., History of Modern and Contemporary Europe
SHINTANI, H., History of West Asia
SUITA, H., History of Ancient Orient
TAKAHASHI, S., Human Geography
TAKAHASHI, T., History of Medieval Japan
YABUTA, Y., History of Early Modern Japan
YONEDA, F., Archaeology

Course of Chinese Language and Literature:

AZUMA, J., History of Chinese Philosophy
HAGINO, S., Modern and Contemporary Chinese Literature
INOUE, T., Early Modern Chinese Literature
KAWATA, T., History of Chinese Philosophy
KITAOKA, M., Modern Chinese Literature
KUSAKA, T., Chinese Linguistics
MORISE, T., Classical Chinese Poetry
NIKAIDO, Y., Chinese Popular Religion
TAKEUCHI, Y., Sociology of Education
TAO, D., History of Chinese Philosophy
UCHIDA, K., Chinese Linguistics

Course of Education:

AKAO, K., Adult Education Theory
FUJII, M., Psychology
HATASE, N., Clinical Psychology
MATSUMURA, N., Developmental Psychology
NAKATA, Y., Psychology
NOMURA, Y., Experimental Psychology
OKAMURA, T., Public Administration of Education
TAMADA, K., Pedagogy
TANAKA, T., Psychology
TANAKA, Y., Sociology of Education
YAMAMOTO, F., Pedagogy
YAMAZUMI, K., Educational Research

Inter-Departmental Course:

HAZAMA, K., Social Welfare
KURAHASHI, E., Library and Information Science
SAWAI, S.
SHIBATA, H., Information Processing
UEDA, Y., Liberation of Buraku

Course of Physical Arts:

AOKI, S., Health and Physical Education
BAN, Y., Health and Physical Education
KAWAMOTO, T., Health and Physical Education
KIMURA, S., Health and Physical Education
MIURA, T., Health and Physical Education
MIZOHATA, K., Health and Physical Education
OITA, K., Health and Physical Education
SHIRAFUJI, I., Health and Physical Education
TAKECHI, H., Health and Physical Education
TAMURA, N., Health and Physical Education
ZAKO, T., Health and Physical Education

Faculty of Economics:

AKIOKA, H., Microeconomics
HAMANO, K., Economic History of Japan
HASHIMOTO, K., Public Finance
HASHIMOTO, N., Econometrics
HASHIMOTO, S., History of Economic Theories
HAYASHI, H., Public Finance
HIROE, M., Monetary Policy
ICHIEN, M., Social Security
ICHIKAWA, K., Commercial Economics
ISHIDA, H., Economics of Modern China
IWAI, H., Economic Statistics
KASEDA, H., Economic History
KASHIHARA, M., Agricultural Economics
KASUGA, J., Principles of Economics
KITAGAWA, K., European Economic History
KOIKE, H., Introduction to Political Economy
KUSUNOKI, S., International Economics
LEE, Y., Social Economics
MATSUO, A., Mathematical Statistics
MATSUSHITA, K., Demography
MORIOKA, K., Introduction to Political Economy
MOTOKI, H., Macrodynamics
NAGAHISA, R., Principles of Economics
OTSUKA, T., Social Policy
SATO, M., Macroeconomics

TAKESHITA, K., Theory of Economic Systems
TANIDA, N., Information Processing
UEMURA, K., History of Social Thought
WAKAMORI, F., Political Economy
YASUKI, H., Industrial Organization
YOSHINAGA, K., Economic Statistics

Faculty of Commerce:

ABE, S., Public Sector Economics
ARAKI, T., Information Processing Practice
HABARA, K., Non-Life Insurance
HATORI, Y., International Relations
HIROSE, M., General Management
HIROTA, T., Corporate Strategy
IKEJIMA, M., Securities Markets
INOUE, S., Business History
ITO, K., Human Resources Management
IWASA, Y., Financial Intermediation and Institutions
KATO, Y., Distribution Theory
MATSUMOTO, Y., Monitoring Theory for Fair Disclosure
MATSUO, N., Financial Accounting
MIKAMI, H., Economics of Transport and Communication
MIZUNO, I., Management Accounting
MYOJIN, N., Book-keeping
NAGANUMA, H., History of Commerce
NAKAJIMA, M., Cost Accounting and Accounting History
NAKAMURA, M., Business Communication
OKU, K., Theory of International Trade
OKURA, Y., Tax Accounting
SASAKURA, A., International Accounting
SHIBA, K., Accounting Information Theory
SUYAMA, K., Marketing Management
TAKAHASHI, N., International Transport
TAKAYA, S.
TSURUTA, H., Public Finance
UE, K., Monetary Theory
YOKOTA, S., European and American Economy
YOSHIDA, T., Management of International Trade

Faculty of Sociology

Major in Sociology:

ISHIMOTO, K., Theory of Buraku Liberation
IWAMI, K., Understanding Modern Societies
KAKEBA, H., Sociology of Knowledge
KATAGIRI, S., Theoretical Sociology
KUMANO, T., Cultural Anthropology
MATSUHARA, I., Social Policy and Planning
NAGAI, Y., Urban Studies
SUGINO, A., Social Welfare Policy and Planning
YAMAMOTO, Y., Sociology of Knowledge
YAMATO, R., Sociology of Family

Major in Industrial Psychology:

AMEMIYA, T., Ergonomics
ENDO, Y., Social Cognition
HIGASHIMURA, T., Information Processing
IIDA, N., Psychiatry
KAWASAKI, T., Vocational Guidance
KURATO, Y., Clinical Psychology
SEKIGUCHI, R., Experimental Psychology
SHIMIZU, K., Psychometrics
TAKAGI, O., Interpersonal Psychology
TERASHIMA, S., Clinical Psychology
TSUCHIDA, S., Social Psychology

Major in Mass Communication:

FUJIOKA, S., Journalism
KIMURA, Y., Social Communication
KURODA, I., Sociology of Broadcasting Culture
MIZUNO, Y.
OGAWA, H., Media and Culture
SENO, G., Human Communication
TSUNEKI, T., Communication Behaviour
YOSHIOKA, I., Communication Theory

Major in Industrial Sociology:

ASADA, M., Policy for Economic Stabilization

FUNABA, T., Human Resource Studies
HASHIMOTO, K., Philosophy of Science
MORITA, M., Personnel Management
OH, Y., Industrial Information Theory
ONISHI, M., Labour–Management Relations
SAITOU, Y., Industrial Technology
TAKASE, T., Industrial Sociology
WAKABAYASHI, M., Business Administration
YANO, H., Economic Theory
YOSANO, A., Mathematical Sociology

Faculty of Informatics:

AOYAMA, C., Global Environmentology
ATSUJI, S., Organizational Decision Making
COOK, N. D., General Systems Theory
EZAWA, Y., Computer Science
FUKADA, Y., Image Processing and Pattern Recognition
FUKE, H., International Networks
FURUTA, H., Fuzzy Logic, Theory and Application
HAYASHI, I., Information Systems Management
HAYASHI, T., Computer Graphics
HIJIKATA, H., Mathematics
HIROKAME, M., Mathematics
HORI, M., File Structure
ITO, T., Computer Simulation
KAMEI, K., Management
KATO, M., Philosophy
KATO, T., Cognitive Science
KATO, T., Computer Crime
KITAJIMA, O., Business Behaviour
KITANI, S., Public Administration
KOMATSU, Y., Business Administration
KUBOTA, K., Audiovisual Media Production
KUBOTA, M., Communication
KUROKAMI, H., Multimedia Education
KUROKUZU, H., Accounting Information Systems
KUWABARA, T., Psychology
MIYASHITA, F., Computer Science
NAKAGAWA, Y., Data Structure and Algorithm
NOGUCHI, H., Business Information
OKAMOTO, T., Public Policy
SANO, M., Community Networks
SHIOMURA, T., Microeconomic Models
SHYI, S. C., Management Information Systems
SUGA, T., Computer-based Communication
TANAKA, S., Knowledge Information Processing
TSUJI, M., Software Architecture
UESHIMA, S., Principles of Database Management
UKAI, Y., Economic Policy
YAMAGUCHI, S., Cultural Studies of Information Society
YAMANA, T., Macroeconomic Models
YOSHIDA, N., Principles of Computer Electronics

Faculty of Engineering

Department of Mechanical Engineering:

ARAI, Y., Measurement Systems
ISHIHARA, I., Thermal Engineering
KITAJIMA, K., Manufacturing Processes
SHINGUABARA, S., Nanophysics and Nanofabrication Technology
SHINKE, N., Strength of Materials
TAGAWA, N., Micromechatronics
TAKUMA, M., Experiments on Mechanical Engineering

Department of Mechanical Systems Engineering:

BANDO, K., Computational Fluid Dynamics
FUJITA, T., Analytical Dynamics
HIGUCHI, M., Production Engineering
IWATSUBO, T., Measurement Systems
MORI, A., Machine Design and Engineering Tribology

OHBA, K., Fluids Engineering and Biomechanics
OZAWA, M., Engineering Thermodynamics
UCHIYAMA, H., Control Engineering

Department of Electrical Engineering and Computer Science:

HARA, T., Theory of Electricity and Magnetism
HORIBA, Y., System LSI
KUMAMOTO, A., Flexible and Intelligent Image Processing
MAEDA, Y., Control Theory and Neural Computation
OHNISHI, M., Study of Ion Beam Colliding Fusion Neutron Source
TAMURA, H., Applied Systems Science
YAMAMOTO, M., Computer Networking

Department of Electronics:

IIDA, Y., Microwave and Millimetre-Wave Engineering
KOJIMA, T., Optical and Electromagnetic Engineering
MUNEYASU, M., Image Processing
MURAMAKA, N., Computer Systems Engineering
NOMURA, Y., Information and Intelligent Systems
OKADA, H., Information Networks
OMURA, Y., Device Physics and Modelling
YOKOTA, K., Semiconductor Engineering

Department of Chemical Engineering:

MIYAKE, T., Catalyst Engineering
MIYAKE, Y., Separation Engineering
MUROYAMA, K., Chemical Reaction Engineering
ODA, H., Physical Chemistry
OKADA, Y., Nanoparticle Engineering
SHIBATA, J., Physical Chemistry
SUZUKI, T., Catalyst Engineering
YAMAMOTO, H., Experimental Chemical Engineering

Department of Applied Chemistry:

ARAKAWA, R., Analytical Chemistry
ISHII, Y., Organometallic Chemistry
ISHIKAWA, T., Electrochemistry and Electrochemical Devices
MATSUMOTO, A., Polymer Chemistry
OCHI, M., Polymer Engineering
OUCHI, T., Functional Polymers
TANEKA, K., Organic Supramolecular Chemistry

Department of Materials Science and Engineering:

AKAMATSU, K., Functional Materials
IKEDA, M., Environmental Conscious Materials Laboratory
KOBAYASHI, T., Processing of Molten Metals
KOMATSU, S., Strength of Materials
KOZUKA, H., Ceramic Engineering
MIYAKE, H., Foundry Engineering
OISHI, T., Physical Chemistry of Materials Processing
SUGIMOTO, T., Nonferrous Metallic Materials

Department of Systems Management Engineering:

AOYAGI, S., Automatic Control Theory
FUYUKI, M., Production Systems Engineering
HORII, K., Human Factors Engineering
MORI, K., Production Management
NAKAI, T., Operations Research
UEMURA, T., Visual Information Engineering

Department of Civil and Environmental Engineering:

DOGAKI, M., Structural Mechanics
ISHIGAKI, T., Hydraulic Engineering for Environment and Disaster Prevention
KAWAKAMI, S., Traffic Engineering
KUSUMI, H., Rock Mechanics and Geological Engineering

MIKAMI, I., Design of Civil Engineering Structures
SAKANO, M., Structural Engineering
TOYOFUKU, T., Construction Materials
WADA, Y., Sanitary Engineering

Department of Architecture:

ASANO, K., Structural Engineering
EGAWA, N., Architectural Environmental Design Laboratory
KAWAI, Y., Environmental Engineering
KAWAMICHI, R., Architectural Theory and Design
MARUMO, H., Urban Design
NAGAI, N., History of Architecture
NOGUCHI, T., Environmental Engineering
YAO, S., Structural Engineering

Department of Biotechnology:

HASEGAWA, Y., Genetic Engineering
OBATA, H., Microbial Technology
TSUCHIDO, T., Biocontrol Technology
UESATO, S., Pharmaceutical Technology
YAGI, H., Biochemical Engineering
YOSHIDA, M., Food Biotechnology

General Education in Natural Sciences:

AKI, S.
FUKUSHIMA, M., Probability Theory
ICHIHARA, K., Probability Theory
IKEUCHI, I., Intracellular Signals Transduction Mechanism of Neuronal Cells
KURISU, T., Game Theory
KURIYAMA, A., Mathematical Physics
KUSUDA, M., Functional Analysis
SAITO, T.
SEKI, M., Fluid Dynamics
SHIRAIWA, T., Chiral Molecular Chemistry
TAJITSU, Y.
TAMURA, H., Naturally Occurring Polymer Chemistry
TATSUMI, M., Applied Analytical Chemistry
URAGAMI, T., Functional Polymer Science
YAMAMURA, M., Quantum Many-body Physics
YAMAUCHI, O., Bio-inorganic Chemistry
YANAGAWA, T., Knot Group Theory

Institute of Foreign Language Education and Research:

FUKUI, N., Study of Japanese Culture and Ruth Benedict
GEN, YUKIKOI, Diachronic Study of Colloquial Chinese
GIBBS, A. S., Approach to Foreign Language Communication through Pragmatics, Stylistics and Discourse Analysis, Reading and Writing for Academic Purposes
HIRATA, W., Spanish and Latin American Literature
ISHIHARA, T., American Literature
JOHNSON, G. S., Presentation, Oral Interpretation
KAWAI, T., English Education, English Linguistics
KIKUCHI, A., Linguistics
KIKUCHI, U., Experimental Phonetics
KITAMURA, Y., Cognitive Science, Education Technology
KITE, Y., Sociolinguistics, Second Language Acquisition
KONDO, M., Russian Literature
KUMATANI, A., Korean Linguistics, Sociolinguistics
MOCHIZUKI, M., Applied Linguistics, Japanese Linguistics
NISHIKAWA, K., Chinese Linguistics
SAITO, E., English Education
SCHAUWECKER, D. F., Japanese–German Relationships
SHEN, G., Chinese Language Education
SUGITANI, M., German Language, Education and Intercultural Communication
TAKAHASHI, H., Sociolinguistics
TAKAHASHI, T., English Language Education

TAKEUCHI, O., Applied Linguistics, Educational Technology
USAMI, T., English Literature, English Education
WADA, Y., Medieval Manuscript Studies
YAMAMOTO, E., English Linguistics
YAMANE, S., English Phonetics
YASHIMA, T., Applied Linguistics, Intercultural Communication
YOSHIZAWA, K., Applied Linguistics

School of Law:

FUJITA, H., International Law
HAYAKAWA, T., Commercial Law
IMANISHI, Y., Civil Law
ISHII, K., Criminal Procedure
KAMEDA, K., Administrative Law
KAWAGUCHI, M., Labour Law
KIMURA, T., Civil Law
KINOSHITA, S., Constitutional Law
KITAGAWA, T., Law of International Transactions
KUBO, H., Civil Law
MURATA, H., Constitutional Law
MUROTA, G.
NOVO, M., Administrative Law
ODO, Y., Civil Law
SHIMADA, R., Civil Procedure
TAKESHITA, K., Philosophy of Law
TAKIGAWA, T., Economic Law, International Economic Law
TATSUMI, N., Intellectual Property Law
WAKAMATSU, Y., Civil Law
YAMANAKA, K., Criminal Law
YAMATO, M., Commercial Law

KEIO UNIVERSITY

2-15-45 Mita, Minato-ku, Tokyo 108-8345
Telephone: (3) 5427-1517
Fax: (3) 3769-1564
E-mail: www@info.keio.ac.jp
Internet: www.keio.ac.jp/index-en.html

Founded 1858
Private control
Academic year: April to March

Pres.: ATSUSHI SEIKE
Vice-Pres. for Education, Student Affairs, Facilities and Admin.: AKIRA HASEYAMA
Vice-Pres. for Research, Academic-Industry Collaboration, Information Technology: TOSHIAKI MAKABE
Vice-Pres. for Financial Affairs and Accounting, Management Reform: MASAHIKO SHIMIZU
Vice-Pres. for Gen. and Legal Affairs, Public Relations, Alumni Relations, Procurement, Strategic Planning, Crisis Management: MAKOTO IDA
Vice-Pres. for Human Resource Management, Community and Regional Affairs, Gender Equality: NAOKI WATANABE
Vice-Pres. for Keio Univ. Hospital: YOSHIAKI TOYAMA
Vice-Pres. for Int. Collaboration: NAOYUKI AGAWA
Vice-Pres. for Environment: TADASHI KASAHARA
Sec.-Gen.: MASAHIRO KOYA
Registrar: BUNJI KURIYA
Dirs of Libraries: YUKIO ITO (Hiyoshi Media Centre), YOSHIKAZU SUGIMOTO (Information and Media Center for Pharmaceutical Sciences), KAZUO SHIIKI (Information and Media Center for Science and Technology), SHINYA SUGIYAMA (Mita Media Centre), ATSUKO KOISHI (SFC Media Center), KEIICHI FUKUDA (Shinanomachi Media Center)

Library of 4,783,740 vols
Number of teachers: 2,177
Number of students: 33,827 (regular course), 9,266 (correspondence course)
Publications: *Keio Business Review* (1 a year), *Keio Communication Review* (1 a year), *Keio Economic Studies* (2 a year),

Keio Journal of Medicine (4 a year), *Okajima's Folia Anatomica Japonica* (4 a year), *Keio Economic Observatory* (irregular)

DEANS

Faculty of Business and Commerce: YOSHIO HIGUCHI
Faculty of Economics: MASAMICHI KOMURO
Faculty of Environment and Information Studies: JUN MURAI
Faculty of Law: RYOSEI KOKUBUN
Faculty of Letters: KEN SEKINE
School of Medicine: MAKOTO SUEMATSU
Faculty of Nursing and Medical Care: KIKUKO OTA
Faculty of Pharmacy: TADAHIKO MASHINO
Faculty of Policy Management: JIRO KOKURYO
Faculty of Science and Technology: TOJIRO AOYAMA

CHAIRPERSONS

Graduate School of Business Administration: KYOICHI IKEO
Graduate School of Business and Commerce: YOSHIO HIGUCHI
Graduate School of Economics: SHINSUKE NAKAMURA
Graduate School of Health Management: SHOHEI ONISHI
Graduate School of Human Relations: NOR-IYUKI SUGIURA
Graduate School of Law: RYOSEI KOKUBUN
Graduate School of Letters: AKIO USHIBA
Graduate School of Media and Governance: IKUYO KANEKO
Graduate School of Media Design: MASA INAKAGE
Graduate School of Medicine: HIDEYUKI OKANO
Graduate School of Pharmaceutical Sciences: TADASHI KASAHARA
Graduate School of Science and Technology: TOSHIAKI MAKABE
Graduate School of System Design and Management: YOSHIAKI OHKAMI
Law School: KANTARO TOYOIZUMI

DIRECTORS

Fukuzawa Memorial Center for Modern Japanese Studies: MASAMICHI KOMURO
Institute of Cultural and Linguistic Studies: SUMIO NAKAGAWA
Institute for Economic and Industry Studies (Sangyo Kenkyujo): HITOSHI HAYAMI
Institute for Media and Communications Research: YUTAKA OISHI
Institute of Physical Education: FUMIO UEDA
Keio Institute of East Asian Studies: YOSHI-HIDE SOEYA
Keio Research Center for Foreign Language: KAZUMI SAKAI
Sports Medicine Research Center: SHOHEI ONISHI

KINKI UNIVERSITY

Kowakae 3-4-1, Higashiosaka-shi, Osaka 577-8502

Telephone: (6) 6721-2332
Fax: (6) 6721-2353
E-mail: koho@msa.kindai.ac.jp
Internet: www.kindai.ac.jp

Founded 1925
Private control
Language of instruction: Japanese
Academic year: April to March

Pres.: HIROYUKI HATA
Head Administrator: HIROAKI SEKOH

Library of 1,200,000 vols
Number of teachers: 1,563
Number of students: 29,794

Publications: *Acta Medica Kinki University* (2 a year), *Annals of the Molecular Engineering Institute* (1 a year), *Bulletin of the Fisheries Laboratory of Kinki University* (irregular), *Bulletin of the Pharmaceutical Research and Technology Institute* (1 a year), *Bulletin of the School of Literature, Arts and Cultural Studies* (1 a year), *Ikoma Journal of Economics* (2 a year), *Journal of Business Administration and Marketing Strategy* (3 a year), *Journal of the Faculty of Science and Engineering at Kinki University* (1 a year), *Law Review of Kinki University* (4 a year), *Medical Journal of Kinki University* (2 a year), *Memoirs of the Faculty of Agriculture of Kinki University* (1 a year), *Memoirs of the Institute of Advanced Technology* (2 a year), *Memoirs of the School of Biology-Oriented Science and Technology* (1 a year), *Multimedia Education* (1 a year), *Research Journal of the Department of Teacher Education* (2 a year), *Research Reports of the Faculty of Engineering of Kinki University* (1 a year), *Science and Technology* (1 a year)

DEANS

School of Agriculture: KOICHIRO KOMAI
School of Biology-Oriented Science and Technology: KAZUO YAMAMOTO
School of Business Administration: HIROYASU OKITSU
School of Economics: KYOUZOU TAKECHI
School of Engineering: HIROSHI TSUBAKIHARA
School of Humanity-Oriented Science and Engineering: MASAYUKI ONO
School of Law: HIDEJIRO ISHIDA
School of Literature, Arts and Cultural Studies: YUTAKA ARAMAKI
School of Medicine: HARUMASA OYANAGI
School of Pharmaceutical Sciences: KAZUAKI KAKEHI
School of Science and Engineering: MEGUMU MUNAKATA

KOBE GAKUIN UNIVERSITY

518 Arise, Ikawadani-cho, Nishiku, Kobe 651-2180

Telephone: (78) 974-1551
Fax: (78) 974-5689
E-mail: kgu@j.kobegakuin.ac.jp
Internet: www.kobegakuin.ac.jp

Founded 1966
Academic year: April to March

Campuses at Nagata and Port Island

Pres.: YOSHIO OKADA
Dir-Gen. for Admin.: TTETSUAKI TAKENAKA
Librarian: HIROMI YOSHIDA

Library of 955,062 vols
Number of teachers: 284
Number of students: 10,172

Publications: *Kobe Gakuin Hogaku* (Law and Politics Review), *Kobe Gakuin Economic Papers*, *Memoirs of the Faculty of Pharmaceutical Sciences*, *Journal of Business Management*

DEANS

Faculty of Business Admin.: NOBUO TSUNO
Faculty of Economics: YOSHIO TANAKA
Faculty of Humanities and Sciences: HIRO-NORI MIZUMOTO
Faculty of Law: TOYOKI OKADA
Faculty of Nutrition: KIYOSHI GODA
Faculty of Pharmaceutical Sciences: HIROSHI OKAMOTO
Faculty of Rehabilitation: ISAO NARA
Graduate School of Economics: YOSHIO TANAKA
Graduate School of Food and Medicinal Sciences: KIYOSHI GODA

Graduate School of Humanities and Sciences: HIRONORI MIZUMOTO
Graduate School of Law: TOYOKI OKADA
Graduate School of Law Practices: KENJI SANEKATA
Graduate School of Nutrition: KIYOSHI GODA
Graduate School of Pharmaceutical Sciences: HIROSHI OKAMOTO

KOGAKUIN UNIVERSITY

1-24-2, Nishi-shinjuku, Shinjuku-ku, Tokyo 163-8677

Telephone: (3) 3342-1211
Fax: (3) 3342-5304
E-mail: kokusai@sc.kogakuin.ac.jp
Internet: www.kogakuin.ac.jp

Founded 1887, university status 1949
Language of instruction: Japanese
Academic year: April to March

Pres.: Prof. Dr. AKISATO MIZUNO
Vice-Pres.: Prof. Dr. YASUSHI NAGASAWA
Library Dir: Prof. Dr. KIYOSHI KATO

Library of 261,000 vols, 2,847 periodicals
Number of teachers: 684 incl. full-time: 221, part-time: 463, f.t.e.: 375
Number of students: 6,923 full-time 6,104 undergraduates, 621 masters students, 20 doctoral students, part-time 178, f.t.e.: 6,804)

Publications: *Kogakuin Daigaku Kenkyu Hokoku* (research reports, 2 a year), *Kogakuin Daigaku Kyotukatei Kenkyu Ronso* (research reports, 2 a year)

DEANS

Faculty of Engineering: Prof. JUNICHI ARAI
Faculty of Global Engineering: Prof. TAKASHI SAIKA
Faculty of Informatics: Prof. EIJIROH OHKI
Graduate School of Engineering: Prof. YASUSHI NOZAWA (Chair.)
School of Architecture: Prof. YASUSHI NAGA-SAWA

KOKUGAKUIN UNIVERSITY

4-10-28, Higashi, Shibuya-ku, Tokyo 150-8440

Telephone: (3) 5466-0111
Fax: (3) 5778-7061
E-mail: kokusai@kokugakuin.ac.jp
Internet: www.kokugakuin.ac.jp

Founded 1882
Academic year: April to March

President: Prof. MASAHIKO ASOYA
Secretary-General: SHOZO SANAGI
Librarian: T. SAWANOBORI

Library: see Libraries and Archives
Number of teachers: 790
Number of students: 10,319

Publications: *Kokugakuin Zasshi* (Journal of Kokugakuin University), *Kokugakuin Keizaigaku* (Kokugakuin University Economic Review), *Kokugakuin Hogaku* (Journal of the Faculty of Law and Politics), *Kokugakuin Daigaku Kiyo* (Transactions of Kokugakuin University), *Kokugakuin Daigaku Daigakuin Bungaku Kenkyuka Ronshu* (Journal of the Graduate School, Kokugakuin University), *Kokugakuin Daigaku Kenzaigaku Kenkyuka Kiyo* (Kokugakuin University Economic Studies), *Kokugakuin Hokenronso* (Journal of Law and Politics, Graduate School of Law), *Nihonbunka-Kenkyusho-Kiyo* (Transactions of the Institute for Japanese Culture and Classics)

DEANS

Faculty of Economics: HIRONORI KON'I
Faculty of Law: SEIICHI NAGAMORI
Faculty of Letters: SHUHEI AOKI
Faculty of Shinto Studies: SOJI OKADA

Graduate School: TSUYOSHI FUJIMOTO
Law School: KATSUMASA HIRABAYASHI

ATTACHED RESEARCH INSTITUTE

Institute for Japanese Culture and Classics: 4-10-28, Higashi, Shibuya-ku, Tokyo 150-8440.

KOKUSHIKAN UNIVERSITY

4-28-1 Setagaya, Setagaya-ku, Tokyo 154-8515

Telephone: (3) 5481-3112
Fax: (3) 3413-7420
E-mail: wwwadmin@kiss.kokushikan.ac.jp
Internet: www.kokushikan.ac.jp
Founded 1917
Private control
Academic year: April to March
Chairman: HARUO NISHIHARA
Pres.: HIDEO OSAWA
General Dir: ATSUSHI MATSUMOTO
Librarian: SHOICHI YAMAMOTO
Library of 630,638 vols
Number of teachers: 310
Number of students: 12,677

Publications: *Politics and Economics Review, Kokushikan Law Review,* various faculty journals and reviews

DEANS

Faculty of Engineering: KATSUHIKO WAKABAYASHI
Faculty of Law: NORIYOSHI WATANABE
Faculty of Letters: AKIRA ABE
Faculty of Political Science and Economics: HIROYUKI YAMAZAKI
Faculty of Political Science and Economics (Evening Session): RYOZO SHIROGANE
Faculty of Physical Education: KAZUYUKI NISHIYAMA
Junior College: HIROSHI TASHIRO
School of Asia 21: KAGEAKI KAJIWARA

KOMAZAWA UNIVERSITY

1-23-1 Komazawa, Setagaya-ku, Tokyo 154-8525

Telephone: (3) 3418-9011
Fax: (3) 3418-9017
E-mail: info-soumu@komazawa-u.ac.jp
Internet: www.komazawa-u.ac.jp
Academic year: April to March
Pres.: KIYOZUMI ISHII
Vice-Pres.: TADASHI SAITO
Registrar: KOUICHI ONO
Librarian: MITSUYOSHI OKUNO
Library of 1,163,495 vols
Number of teachers: 353
Number of students: 16,333

Publications: *Journal of the Faculty of Buddhism, Journal of Buddhist Studies, Komazawa Educational Review, Regional Views, Journal of the Faculty of Letters, Komazawa Japanese Literature, Studies in British and American Literature, Komazawa Geography, Journal of the Historical Association of Komazawa, Komazawa Journal of Sociology, Journal of the Faculty of Economics, The Economic Review of Komazawa University, Journal of the Faculty of Law of Komazawa University, Komazawa Law and Political Science Review, Komazawa Business Studies, Komazawa Business Review, Journal of the Faculty of Foreign Languages, The Review of Foreign Languages, Bunka* (Komazawa University Journal of Culture), *Journal of Health Sciences of Komazawa University, Journal of Radiological Sciences of Komazawa University, Komazawa Annual of Sociology, Komazawa University Journal of Health and Physical Education*

DEANS

Faculty of Buddhism: MASASHI NAGAI
Faculty of Business Administration: MITSUAKI TAKADA
Faculty of Economics: YOSHIHARU HYAKUTA
Faculty of Health Sciences: YUSUKE YAMAMOTO
Faculty of Law: NORIO KOBORI
Faculty of Letters: MASAKI KUBOTA

CHAIRMEN

Graduate Division of Arts and Sciences I: KANAZAWA ATSUSHI
Graduate Division of Arts and Sciences II: MASATOSHI KAWASAKI
Graduate Division of Business Administration: SHIGERU HATORI
Graduate Division of Commerce: NOBUTAKA SOGA
Graduate Division of Economics: TADAMITSU YASHIKI
Graduate Division of Health Sciences: KOUKI YOSHIKAWA
Graduate Division of Law: SHOHEI KANEKO
Graduate Division of Legal Research and Training: YUTAKA USUKI

KONAN UNIVERSITY

8-9-1 Okamoto, Higashinada-ku, Kobe 658-8501

Telephone: (78) 431-4341
Fax: (78) 435-2306
E-mail: d-jimu@adm.konan-u.ac.jp
Internet: www.konan-u.ac.jp
Founded 1918
President: Y. SUGIMURA
Library of 775,000 vols
Number of teachers: 240 full-time
Number of students: 9,578

Publications: *Journal of Konan University Faculty of Letters* (irregular), *Memoirs of Konan University* (science and engineering series, 2 a year), *Konan Economic Papers* (irregular), *Konan Hogaku* (Konan Law Review, irreg.), *Konan Business Review* (irregular), *Journal of the Institute for Language and Culture* (irregular)

DEANS

Faculty of Business Administration: Y. NAKATA
Faculty of Economics: H. KOBAYASHI
Faculty of Law: T. MAEDA
Faculty of Letters: T. HISATAKE
Faculty of Science and Engineering: T. SHIGEMATSU

KOSHIEN UNIVERSITY

Momijigaoka, Takarazuka, Hyogo 665-0006
Telephone: (797) 87-5111
Fax: (797) 87-5666
E-mail: nyuushi@koshien.ac.jp
Internet: www.koshien.ac.jp
Founded 1967
President: TOMIO KINOSHITA
Library of 106,942 vols
Number of teachers: 170
Number of students: 1,428

Colleges of Business Administration, Humanities, Information Sciences, Nutrition.

KURUME UNIVERSITY

67 Asahi-Machi, Kurume 830-0011
Telephone: (942) 35-3311
Fax: (942) 32-5191
E-mail: soumu@med.kurume-u.ac.jp
Internet: www.kurume-u.ac.jp
Founded 1928

Pres.: KYOZO KOKETSU
Dir of Admin. Office: KATSUMI YOSHIHISA
Library of 415,000 vols
Number of teachers: 534
Number of students: 5,808

Publications: *The Kurume Medical Journal* (4 a year), *The Journal of the Kurume Medical Association* (12 a year), *The Journal for Studies on Industrial Economics* (4 a year)

Faculties of Commerce, Economics, Law, Literature and Medicine.

KWANSEI GAKUIN UNIVERSITY

1-1-155 Uegahara, Nishinomiya, Hyogo 662-8501

Telephone: (798) 51-0952
Fax: (798) 51-0954
E-mail: ciec@kwansei.ac.jp
Internet: www.kwansei.ac.jp
Founded 1889
Academic year: April to March
Chancellor: MICHIYA HATA
President: KAZUO HIRAMATSU
Vice-Presidents: KOHEI ASANO, TOKUTOSHI INOUE, HIDEKI MINE
Library Director: TAKUTOSHI INOUE
Library: see Libraries and Archives
Number of teachers: 435 full-time
Number of students: 18,702

Publications: *Theological Studies, Humanities Review, Journal of the School of Sociology, Journal of Law and Politics, Journal of Economics, Journal of Business Administration, Law Review, Economic Review, Journal of Policy Studies, Review of Economics and Business Management, Studies in Computer Science, Language and Culture, Studies in Teacher Development, Social Sciences Review, Natural Sciences Review*

DEANS

School of Business Administration: AKIRA MIYAMA
School of Economics: SHIN NEGISHI
School of Humanities: ATSUHIDE SAKAKURA
School of Law and Politics: YOZO SAWADA
School of Policy Studies: TOYOO FUKUDA
School of Science: YAICHI SHINOHARA
School of Sociology: MICHIHITO TSUSHIMA
School of Theology: ETSURO KINOWAKI
Graduate School of Language, Communication and Culture: TAKAAKI KANZAKI
Institute of Business and Accounting: MARTIN COLLICK
Law School: TOORU KATO

KYOTO NOTRE DAME UNIVERSITY

1–2 Minami Nonogami-cho, Shimogamo, Sakyo-ku, Kyoto 606-0847

Telephone: (75) 781-1173
Fax: (75) 706-3707
E-mail: international@notredame.ac.jp
Internet: www.notredame.ac.jp

Founded 1961
Private control
Language of instruction: Japanese
Academic year: April to March
Pres.: M. YABUUCHI
Vice-Pres.: N. MAKINAI

Library of 200,000 vols
Number of teachers: 223 (70 full-time, 153 part-time)
Number of students: 1,792

DEANS

Dept of Cross-Cultural Studies: KATSUHIRO HORI

Dept of English Language and Literature: YASUTOMO ARAI

Faculty of Home Sciences and Welfare: YASUKO YONEDA
Faculty of Psychology: ETSUKO UEDA
Graduate School for Applied English and Intercultural Studies: IZUMI SUGAWA
Graduate School for Clinical Psychology: YOKO FUJIKAWA
Graduate School for Home Sciences and Welfare: HISAYUKI MURATA

KYOTO PHARMACEUTICAL UNIVERSITY

5, Misasagi-Nakauchi-cho, Yamashina-ku, Kyoto 607-8414
Telephone: (75) 595-4600
Fax: (75) 595-4750
E-mail: kpu-koho@mb.kyoto-phu.ac.jp
Internet: www.kyoto-phu.ac.jp
Founded 1884
Pres.: MASAZUMI IKEDA
Registrar: Dr NORIAKI FUNASAKI
Librarian: Dr TAKESI NISINO
Library of 91,260 vols
Number of teachers: 104
Number of students: 1,821

PROFESSORS

FUJIMOTO, S., Environmental Biochemistry
FUNASAKI, N., Physical Chemistry
HAMAZAKI, H., Health and Sports Sciences
HATAYAMA, T., Biochemistry
HIRAYAMA, T., Public Health
KAMBE, T., Mathematics
KIM, J., Cell Biology
KISO, Y., Medicinal Chemistry
KITAMURA, K., Analytical Chemistry
KOHNO, S., Pharmacology
KOIKE, C., Physics Laboratory
KONOSHIMA, T., Pharmaceutical Sciences and Natural Resources
MURANISHI, S., Pharmaceutics
NAKATA, T., Clinical Pharmacology
NISHINO, T., Microbiology
NODE, M., Pharmaceutical Manufacturing Chemistry
OHTA, S., Chemistry of Functional Molecules
OKABE, S., Applied Pharmacology
SAKURAI, H., Analytical and Bioinorganic Chemistry
SATO, T., Pathological Biochemistry
TAKADA, K., Pharmacokinetics
TAKEUCHI, K., Pharmacology and Experimental Therapeutics
TANIGUCHI, T., Neurobiology
UENISHI, J., Pharmaceutical Chemistry
YAMAMOTO, A., Biopharmaceutics
YOKOYAMA, T., Hospital Pharmacy
YOSHIKAWA, M., Pharmacognosy

MATSUYAMA UNIVERSITY

4–2 Bunkyo-cho, Matsuyama Ehime 790-8578
Telephone: (89) 925-7111
Fax: (89) 922-6064
E-mail: mu-koho@matsuyama-u.ac.jp
Internet: www.matsuyama-u.ac.jp
Founded 1923
Academic year: April to March
President: Prof. SATORU KANIMORI
Registrar: SANIMOTU OCHI
Library: see Libraries and Archives
Number of teachers: 308
Number of students: 5,730

Publications: Matsuyama Daigaku Ronshu (6 a year), Studies in Language and Literature (2 a year)

DEANS

Faculty of Business Administration: Prof. N. IDIIDA
Faculty of Economics: Prof. J. IRIE, Prof. Y. SEINO

Faculty of Humanities: Prof. T. KANAMURA
Faculty of Law: Prof. T. TAKEMIYA
Junior College: Prof. K. YAGI

MEIJI UNIVERSITY

1-1 Kanda-Surugadai, Chiyoda-ku, Tokyo 101-8301
Telephone: (3) 3296-4545
Fax: (3) 3296-4087
E-mail: koho@isc.meiji.ac.jp
Internet: www.meiji.ac.jp
Founded 1881
Private control
Academic year: April to March (2 semesters)
Pres.: Prof. HIROMI NAYA
Dir of Library: Prof. MASAHIKO YOSHIDA
Library of 2,350,000 vols
Number of teachers: 2,803 (1,002 full-time, 1,801 part-time)
Number of students: 32,713 (29,944 undergraduate, 2,769 postgraduate)

DEANS

Graduate School: TAKEHIKO YOSHIMURA
School of Agriculture: FUMITAKA HAYASE
School of Arts and Letters: YOSHIKATSU HAYASHI
School of Business Admin.: ETSUO ABE
School of Commerce: KATSUHIKO YOKOI
School of Global Japanese Studies: SEIICHI KANISE
School of Information and Communication: HARUMI HOSONO
School of Law: SHIGEYO TAKACHI
School of Political Science and Economics: KOSAKU DAIROKUNO
School of Science and Technology: ICHIRO MIKI

GRADUATE SCHOOL CHAIRMEN

Dept of Agriculture: KOSUKE NOBORIO
Dept of Arts and Letters: MASATO GODA
Dept of Advanced Mathematical Science: MASAYASU MIMURA
Dept of Business Administration: MASAYASU TAKAHASHI
Dept of Commerce: TOSHIHIRO SARUWATARI
Dept of Global Business: YUKIHIKO UEHARA
Dept of Governance Studies: HIROO ICHIKAWA
Dept of Humanities: SUSUMU YAMAIZUMI
Dept of Information and Communication: TAKEHIKO DAIKOKU
Dept of Law: KAZUHIRO MURAKAMI
Dept of Law School: TAKASHI KAWACHI
Dept of Political Science and Economics: OSAMU OGO
Dept of Professional Accountancy: NOBUHIKO SATO
Dept of Science and Technology: ICHIRO MIKI

MEIJI GAKUIN UNIVERSITY

1-2-37 Shirokanedai, Minato-ku, Tokyo 108-8636
Telephone: (3) 5421-5165
Fax: (3) 5421-5185
E-mail: koho@mguad.meijigakuin.ac.jp
Internet: www.meijigakuin.ac.jp
Founded 1877
Private control
Language of instruction: Japanese
Academic year: April to July, September to March
Chancellor: Prof. SATORU KUZE
Pres.: Prof. YOSHIKAZU WAKITA
Vice-Pres: Prof. MIKIKO YAMAZAKI, Prof. TOMOYOSHI KOIZUMI, Prof. TOSHIO HASHIMOTO
Admin. Officer: SHUJI SHIBASAKI
Librarian: Prof. KUNIO IWAYA
Library of 825,000 vols
Number of teachers: 256
Number of students: 13,639

Publications: Meiji Gakuin Review, English Language and Literature, Papers and Proceedings of Economics, Proceedings of Integrated Arts and Sciences, Law Review (3 a year), International and Regional Studies (2 a year), French Literature, Art Studies, Psychology, Sociology and Social Welfare Review (1 a year)

DEANS

Faculty of Economics: Prof. TAKESHI OSHIO
Faculty of General Education: Prof. YASUO IKEGAMI
Faculty of International Studies: Prof. NOZOMO AKIZUKI
Faculty of Law: Prof. MITSURU ABE
Faculty of Literature: Prof. RYUUICHI HIGUCHI
Faculty of Sociology and Social Work: Prof. KATSUYOSHI KAWAI
Graduate School of Economics: Prof. MASAAKI TAKAMATSU
Graduate School of International Studies: Prof. SHIGEMOCHI HIROSHIMA
Graduate School of Law: Prof. AKIRA OKI
Graduate School of Literature: Prof. MASAAKI TSUTSUI
Graduate School of Sociology and Social Work: Prof. KIYOSHI MATSUI

MEIJO UNIVERSITY

1-501 Shiogamaguchi, Tempaku-ku, Nagoya, Aichi 468-8502
Telephone: (52) 832-1151
Fax: (52) 833-9494
E-mail: kikaku@meijo-u.ac.jp
Internet: www.meijo-u.ac.jp
Founded 1949
Private control
Academic year: April to March
President: MASAKI AMINAKA
Administrative Officer: RYOICHI ARAI
Library Director: YUICHIROU OZAKI
Library of 735,994 vols, 7,047 periodicals
Number of teachers: 431 (full-time)
Number of students: 15,495

Publications: Meijo Hogaku, Meijo Ronsou, faculty bulletins and reports

DEANS

Faculty of Agriculture: NAOSUKE NII
Faculty of Business: HITOSHI IMAI
Faculty of Economics: UMEGAKI
Faculty of Education: KOUJI ITOU
Faculty of Law: YUZOU KIMURA
Faculty of Pharmacy: YOSHIO SUZUKI
Faculty of Science and Technology: TETSO HUJIMOTO
Faculty of Urban Science: TODASHI USHIJIMA
Junior College: SHINJI MORITA

MEISEI UNIVERSITY

2-1-1 Hodokubo, Hino-shi, Tokyo 191-8506
Campuses at Hino and Ome
Telephone: Hino: (42) 591-5111; Ome: (428) 25-5111
Fax: Hino: (42) 591-8181; Ome: (428) 25-5182
E-mail: office@flc.meisei-u.ac.jp
Internet: www.meisei-u.ac.jp
Founded 1964
Private control
Academic year: April to March
Pres.: JUN'ICHI UJIHARA
Vice-Pres: TAKEHIKO MARUYAMA, TETSUO OGAWA
Dirs of Student Affairs: TOSHIAKI UEDA, KAZUYOSHI YAMANAKA
Sec.-Gen.: KATSUNORI KANATANI
Library Dir: YOSHIAKI FIUNATSU
Library of 880,305 vols, 4,300 periodicals
Number of teachers: 243

Number of students: 8,651 (correspondence courses 8,152)

Publications: *Research Bulletin of Meisei University. Humanities and Social Sciences* (1 a year), *Research Bulletin of Meisei University. Physical Sciences and Engineering* (1 a year), *Bulletin of Meisei University. Department of Arts, Faculty of Japanese Culture* (1 a year), *Research Bulletin of Meisei University. Faculty of Informatics* (1 a year), *Annual Bulletin of the Graduate School of Humanities and Social Sciences, Meisei University*

DEANS

Faculty of Economics (Hino): Prof. YOSHIHIKO NISHINO

Faculty of Humanities (Hino): Prof. KOICHI TSUKADA

Faculty of Informatics (Ome): Prof. KANJI OTSUKA

Faculty of Japanese Culture (Ome): Prof. KENJI IKAWA

Faculty of Physical Sciences and Engineering (Hino): Prof. MUNEKAZU TAKANO

MEJIRO UNIVERSITY

4-31-1 Nakaochiai, Shinjuku-ku, Tokyo 161-8539

Telephone: (3) 5996-3121
Fax: (3) 5996-3238
E-mail: webmaster@mejiro.ac.jp
Internet: www.mejiro.ac.jp
Founded 1923
Pres.: KOKI SATO

DEANS

Faculty of Business Administration: (vacant)
Faculty of Human and Social Sciences: OSAMI HUKUSHIMA
Faculty of Humanities: KISAKU KUDO

MOMOYAMA GAKUIN UNIVERSITY
(St Andrew's University)

1-1 Manabino, Izumi, Osaka 594-1198

Telephone: (725) 54-3131
Fax: (725) 54-3215
E-mail: kokusai@andrew.ac.jp
Internet: www.andrew.ac.jp
Founded 1959
Languages of instruction: Japanese, English
Academic year: April to March
President: MICHIO MATSUURA
Vice-Presidents: AKIRA HASEGAWA, YOJI IWATSU, JIRO KIMURA
Library Director: NORIO KITAGAWA
Library of 646,000 vols
Number of teachers: 156
Number of students: 7,387

Publications: *Economic & Business Review, English Review, Human Sciences Review, Intercultural Studies, Journal of Christian Studies, Pan-Pacific Business Review, Research Institute Bulletin, St. Andrew's University Law Review, Sociological Review*

DEANS

Faculty of Business Administration: KICHIZO AKASHI
Faculty of Economics: NORIO TAKEHARA
Faculty of Law: NORIYUKI HONMA
Faculty of Letters: NATSUKI KUNIMATSU
Faculty of Sociology: YOSHIFUMI SHIMIZU

CHAIRS OF GRADUATE SCHOOLS

Graduate School of Business Administration: SHINSHI KATAOKA
Graduate School of Economics: MITSUHIKO IYODA
Graduate School of Letters: NOBUAKI TERAKI
Graduate School of Sociology: OSAMU UEDA

MIYAGI GAKUIN WOMEN'S COLLEGE

9-1-1 Aoba-ku, Sendai Miyagi 981-8557

Telephone: (22) 279-1311
Fax: (22) 279-7566
E-mail: www-admin@mgu.ac.jp
Internet: www.mgu.ac.jp
Founded 1886
Private control
Language of instruction: Japanese
Academic year: April to March
Chancellor: K. MATSUZAKI
President: M. ANBE
Librarian: T. ONODERA
Library of 320,000 vols
Number of teachers: 100
Number of students: 3,094

Publications: *Bulletin of English Department* (1 a year), *Christianity and Culture* (1 a year), *Japanese Literature Note* (1 a year), *Journal of Miyagi College for Women* (1 a year), *Annals of the Institute for Research in Humanities and Social Sciences* (1 a year)

DEANS

Department of Cultural Studies: W. TAKAHASHI
Department of Developmental and Clinical Studies: T. ADAOHI
Department of Domestic and Cultural Sciences: N. OKABO
Department of English Literature: K. ISOZAKI
Department of Food and Nutritional Science: H. HIRAMOTO
Department of Intercultural Studies: M. KUROTAKI
Department of Japanese Literature: M. HAKAZAWA
Department of Music: T. SUMIKAWA

NAGOYA UNIVERSITY OF COMMERCE AND BUSINESS

4-4 Sagamine, Komenoki-cho, Nisshin-shi, Aichi 470-0193

Telephone: (561) 73-2111
Fax: (561) 75-2430
Internet: www.nucba.ac.jp
Founded 1953
Private control
Language of instruction: Japanese
Academic year: April to February (2 terms)
Pres.: HIROSHI KURIMOTO
Dir: MASAHIDE KURIMOTO
Dir of Library: (vacant)
Library of 70,000 vols
Number of teachers: 160 (102 full-time, 58 part-time)
Number of students: 3,389

Publications: *Journal of Economics and Management* (2 a year), *Journal of Language, Culture and Communication* (2 a year), *Bulletin of the Yuichi Kurimoto Memorial Graduate School of Business Administration* (1 a year)

DEANS

Faculty of Accounting and Finance: Prof. AKIRA KOBASHI
Faculty of Business Administration: Prof. HIROKO KAKITANI
Faculty of Foreign Languages and Asian Studies: Prof. GEORGE WATT
Faculty of Management Information Science: Prof. NAMIO HONDA

NANZAN UNIVERSITY

18 Yamazato-cho, Showa-ku, Nagoya 466-8673

Telephone: (52) 832-3111
Fax: (52) 833-6985
E-mail: webmaster@nanzan-u.ac.jp

Internet: www.nanzan-u.ac.jp
Founded 1949
Private control
Language of instruction: Japanese
Academic year: April to March
Pres.: MICHAEL CALMANO
Vice-Pres.: K. AOKI, N. KINOSHITA, M. NORO
Chief of Gen. Affairs Section: S. SAWAGUCHI
Librarian: H. HOSOYA
Library of 745,014 vols, 16,655 periodicals, 7,425 audiovisual titles
Number of teachers: 805 (320 full-time, 485 part-time)
Number of students: 10,011

Publications: *Academia (Humanities and Natural Sciences)* (in Japanese and English, 2 a year), *Academia (Information Sciences and Engineering)* (in Japanese and English, 1 a year), *Academia (Literature and Language)* (in Japanese and English, 2 a year), *Academia (Social Sciences)* (in Japanese and English, 2 a year), *Nanzan Journal of Theological Studies* (in Japanese and English, 1 a year), *Nanzan Law Review* (in Japanese, 4 a year), *Nanzan Management Review* (in Japanese and English, 3 a year), *Nanzan Studies on Japanese Language and Culture* (in Japanese, 1 a year), *The Nanzan Journal of Economic Studies* (in Japanese and English, 3 a year)

DEANS

Faculty of Business Administration: Y. KAORU
Faculty of Economics: Y. ARAI
Faculty of Foreign Studies: H. FUJIMOTO
Faculty of Humanities: S. SAKAI
Faculty of Information Sciences and Engineering: A. SUZUKI
Faculty of Law: T. SOEDA
Faculty of Policy Studies: T. MATSUDO
General Education: Y. NAKA

ATTACHED INSTITUTES

Center for American Studies: 18 Yamazato-cho, Showa-ku, Nagoya; tel. (52) 832-3111; fax (52) 832-6825; e-mail center-as@ic.nanzan-u.ac.jp; internet www.ic.nanzan-u.ac.jp/america/index.html; study of American politics, economics, diplomacy, culture and society and US-Japan relations; library of 17,454 vols, 327 periodicals, 19 audiovisual items; Dir Prof. T. SUZUKI; publ. *Nanzan Review of American Studies* (in English, 1 a year).

Center for Asia–Pacific Studies: 18 Yamazato-cho, Showa-ku Nagoya; tel. (52) 832-3111; fax (52) 832-6825; e-mail cfes-cfas-all@nanzan-u.ac.jp; internet www.ic.nanzan-u.ac.jp/asiapacific; interdisciplinary study of the politics, int. relations, economics, society, history, culture, and literature of the Asia–Pacific region; library of 6,175 vols, 243 periodicals, 83 audiovisual items; Dir Prof. T. HAYASHI; publ. *Bulletin* (in Japanese, 1 a year).

Center for European Studies: 18 Yamazato-cho, Showa-ku, Nagoya; tel. (52) 832-3111; fax (52) 832-6825; e-mail cfes-cfas-all@nanzan-u.ac.jp; internet www.ic.nanzan-u.ac.jp/europe; interdisciplinary study of European politics, economics and society; library of 4,580 vols, 204 periodicals, 9 audiovisual items; Dir Prof. R. MANO; publ. *Bulletin* (in Japanese, 1 a year).

Center for Japanese Studies: 18 Yamazato-cho, Showa-ku, Nagoya; tel. (52) 832-3123; fax (52) 832-5490; e-mail cjs@ic.nanzan-u.ac.jp; internet www.nanzan-u.ac.jp/english/cjs; one-semester or one-year programme in language-related studies, area studies and practical courses in traditional arts; Dir Prof. N. KINOSHITA.

Center for Latin American Studies: 18 Yamazato-cho, Showa-ku, Nagoya; tel. (52) 832-3111; fax (52) 832-6825; e-mail centro-latino@ic.nanzan-u.ac.jp; internet www.ic.nanzan-u.ac.jp/latin/index.html; study of Latin America, particularly the humanities and social sciences (history, anthropology, education, economics, literature, philosophy, politics, archaeology and linguistics); library of 11,417 vols, 313 periodicals, 45 audiovisual items; Dir Prof. T. KATO; publ. *Perspectivas Latinoamericanas* (in Spanish, Portuguese and English, 1 a year).

Center for Linguistics: 18 Yamazato-cho, Showa-ku, Nagoya; tel. (52) 832-3111; fax (52) 832-5688; e-mail ling@ic.nanzan-u.ac.jp; internet www.nanzan-u.ac.jp/linguistics; research in comparative syntax and language acquisition: int. jt research projects with Cambridge, Siena, Connecticut, Hyderabad, and Tsing Hua; library of 5,000 vols; Dir Prof. M. SAITO; publ. *Nanzan Linguistics* (in English, 1 or 2 a year).

Center for Legal Practice-Education and Research: 18 Yamazato-cho, Showa-ku, Nagoya; tel. (52) 832-8197; fax (52) 832-8204; e-mail housou-jitsumu@nanzan-u.ac.jp; internet www.ic.nanzan-u.ac.jp/housou; research and practice of legal practical education; implement business studies and lectures about legal practice; Dir Prof. Y. KATO.

Center for Management Studies: 18 Yamazato-cho, Showa-ku, Nagoya; tel. (52) 832-3111; e-mail mcenter@ic.nanzan-u.ac.jp; specializing in the study of management issues; Dir Prof. H. GANKOJI.

Center for Research in Mathematical Sciences and Information Engineering: 27 Seirei-cho, Seto; tel. (561) 89-2081; fax (561) 89-2082; e-mail liaison-msie@nanzan-u.ac.jp; internet www.seto.nanzan-u.ac.jp/msie; research into information engineering and quantitative sciences; coordination of collaboration between industry and academia; Dir Prof. S. OSAKI; publ. *Academia (Information Sciences and Engineering)* (in Japanese and English, 1 a year).

Center for the Study of Human Relations: 18 Yamazato-cho, Showa-ku, Nagoya; tel. (52) 832-5002; fax (52) 832-3202; e-mail ninkan-c@nanzan-u.ac.jp; internet www.ic.nanzan-u.ac.jp/ninkan; Dir Prof. T. TSUMURA; publ. *The Nanzan Journal of Human Relations* (in Japanese, 1 a year).

Institute for Social Ethics: 18 Yamazato-cho, Showa-ku, Nagoya; tel. (52) 832-3111; fax (52) 832-3703; e-mail sharink@ic.nanzan-u.ac.jp; internet www.ic.nanzan-u.ac.jp/ise/index.html; research on the principles of social ethics and the ethical problems of contemporary society; library of 21,893 vols; Dir Prof. M. MARUYAMA; publ. *Society and Ethics* (in Japanese, 1 a year).

Nanzan Anthropological Institute: 18 Yamazato-cho, Showa-ku, Nagoya; tel. (52) 832-3111; fax (52) 833-6157; e-mail ai-nu@ic.nanzan-u.ac.jp; internet www.ic.nanzan-u.ac.jp/jinruiken/index.html; research in cultural anthropology, mainly in SE, E and S Asia; library of 10,950 vols, 673 periodicals, 22 audiovisual titles; Dir Prof. A. GOTO; publ. *Nanzan Studies in Cultural Anthropology* (in Japanese, irregular).

Nanzan Institute for Religion and Culture: 18 Yamazato-cho, Showa-ku, Nagoya; tel. (52) 832-3111; fax (52) 833-6157; e-mail nirc@ic.nanzan-u.ac.jp; internet nirc.nanzan-u.ac.jp/index.htm; research in the area of world religions with spec. reference to the religions of Asia and to the dialogue between religions; library of 20,772 vols, 570 periodicals, 104 audiovisual titles; Dir Prof. P. SWANSON; publ. *Nanzan Symposia* (in

Japanese, irregular), *Religious Studies Today* (in Japanese, irregular), *Bulletin* (in Japanese and English, 1 a year), *Japanese Journal of Religious Studies* (in English, 2 a year), *Asian Ethnology* (fmrly Asian Folklore Studies, in English, 2 a year), *Nanzan Library of Asian Religion and Culture* (in English, irregular), *Nanzan Studies in Asian Religions* (in English, irregular), *Nanzan Studies in Religion and Culture* (in English, irregular).

NIHON UNIVERSITY

8–24, Kudan-Minami 4-chome, Chiyoda-ku, Tokyo 102-8275
Telephone: (3) 5275-8116
Fax: (3) 5275-8315
E-mail: intldiv@adm.nihon-u.ac.jp
Internet: www.nihon-u.ac.jp

Founded as Nihon Law School 1889, University status 1903
Private control
Academic year: April to March

Chair. of Board: H. TANAKA
Pres.: T. SAKAI
Vice-Pres.: H. ONAGI
Vice-Pres.: M. MAKIMURA
Vice-Pres.: K. IDEMURA

Library of 5,894,567 vols
Number of teachers: 3,041 full-time
Number of students: 82,677

Publications: *Johokagaku Kenkyu* (information science studies), *Journal of Oral Science*, *Kaikeigaku Kenkyu* (accounting), *Kenkyu Kiyo* (humanities and social sciences), *Kenkyu Kiyo* (proceedings of the Institute of Natural Sciences), *Kenkyu Kiyo Nihon Daigaku Shigakubu (Ippan Kyouiku)* (transactions of the School of Dentistry (General Studies)), *Kokusai Kankei Gakubu Nenpo* (international relations), *Kokusai Kankei Kenkyu* (international relations), *Kokusai Chiiki Kenkyujo Shoho* (RRIAP proceedings of symposium), *Nichidai Igaku Zasshi* (journal of Nihon University Medical Association), *Nihon Daigaku Geijutsu Gakubu Kiyo Ronbunhen* (research in fine art at the College of Art), *Nihon Daigaku Geijutsu Gakubu Kiyo Sousakuhen* (artistic works of the College of Art), *Nihon Daigaku Kokusai Kankei Gakubu Seikatsu Kagaku Kenkyujo Hokoku*, *Nihon Daigaku Kou Gakubu Kiyo* (journal of the College of Engineering), *Nihon Daigaku Kyouiku Seido Kenkyujo Kiyo* (bulletin of the Educational Systems Research Institute), *Nihon Daigaku Igakubu Kiyo* (bulletin of the liberal arts and sciences), *Nihon Daigaku Seibutsushigenkagakubu Sogokenkyujo Kenkyugyosekishu* (proceedings of the General Research Institute, College of Bioresource Sciences), *Nihon Daigaku Seibutsushigenkagakubu ei Kenkyu* (proceedings of the Life Science Research Center, College of Bioresource Sciences), *Nihon Daigaku Seisanko Gakubu Kenkyu Houkoku* (journal of the College of Industrial Technology, in editions A and B), *Nihon Daigaku Seisankogaku Kenkyujo Shohou* (journal of the College of Industrial Technology), *Nihon Daigaku Seishin Bunka Kenkyujo Kiyo* (bulletin of the Culture Research Institute), *Nihon Daigaku Tsushinkyoikubu Kenkyu Kiyo* (bulletin of the Correspondence Division of Nihon University), *Nihon Daigaku Yakugakubu Kenkyu Kiyo* (bulletin of the College of Pharmacy), *Nihon Hogaku* (law), *Nihon University Comparative Law*, *Rikogaku Kenkyu Shoho* (journal of the Institute of Science and Technology), *PRIAP Circular*, *Sou-Ka-Ken Nyusu* (URC news), *Seikei*

Kenkyu (political science and economics), *Shogaku Kenkyu* (business and industry), *Nihon University Journal of Medicine*

DEANS
College of Art: Y. NODA
College of Bioresource Sciences: T. TOKUYAMA
College of Commerce: S. KATSUYAMA
College of Economics: H. ONAGI
College of Engineering: K. IDEMURA
College of Humanities and Sciences: N. KATO
College of Industrial Technology: S. ISHII
College of International Relations: S. SATO
College of Law: M. SUGIMOTO (acting)
College of Pharmacy: T. KUSAMA
College of Science and Technology: T. TAKIDO
Correspondence Division: H. TAKATSUNA
Junior College: T. SAKAI
School of Dentistry: K. OOTSUKA
School of Dentistry at Matsudo: M. MAKIMURA
School of Medicine: Y. KATAYAMA

NIPPON DENTAL UNIVERSITY

1-9-20 Fujimi, Chiyoda-ku, Tokyo 102-8159
Telephone: (3) 3261 8311
Fax: (3) 3264-8399
E-mail: web-master@tokyo.ndu.ac.jp
Internet: www.ndu.ac.jp

Founded 1907
Academic year: April to March

Pres.: SEN NAKAHARA
Deans: SEN NAKAHARA (Niigata Faculty), SHIGEO YOKODUKA (Tokyo Faculty)
Registrars: KENEI OHBA (Niigata), SHINICHI TAKIZAWA (Tokyo)
Librarians: KAN KOBAYASHI (Niigata Faculty), TAKEJI AYUKAWA (Tokyo Faculty)

Library of 96,822 vols (Tokyo Faculty), 89,217 vols (Niigata Faculty)
Number of teachers: 1,000
Number of students: 2,000

Publication: *Odontology* (6 a year)

PROFESSORS
Tokyo:

AIYAMA, S., Anatomy
AOBA, T., Pathology
FURUTA, Y., Anatomy
FURUYA, H., Anaesthesiology
ISHIKAWA, H., Orthodontics
KAMOI, K., Periodontology
KATSUUMI, I., Conservative Dentistry
KOBAYASHI, Y., Prosthodontics
MATSUMOTO, S., Physiology
NAKAHARA, S., Dentistry in Society
NIWA, M., Hygiene
OGIWARA, K., Paedodontics
SANADA, K., Biochemistry
SATO, T., Anatomy
SIRAKAWA, M., Oral Surgery
SUZUKI, T., Surgery
TANAKA, H., Conservative Dentistry
TSUTSUI, T., Pharmacology
UCHIDA, M., Oral and Maxillofacial Surgery
YOKOZUKA, S., Prosthodontics
YOSHIDA, T., Dental Materials Science
YOSIKAWA, M., Microbiology
YOSUE, T., Radiology

Niigata
1-8 Hamauracho, Niigata-shi, Niigata 951; tel. (25) 267-1500; fax (25) 267-1134

HASEGAWA, A., Periodontology
HATA, Y., Prosthodontics
HATATE, S., Prosthodontics
IGARASHI, F., Otorhinolaryngology
KAMEDA, A., Orthodontics
KANRI, T., Anaesthesiology
KATAGIRI, M., Oral Pathology
KATOH, Y., Conservative Dentistry

KAWASAKI, K., Conservative Dentistry
KIMURA, T., Dental Pharmacology
KOBAYASHI, K., Oral Anatomy
MATAGA, I., Oral Surgery
MATSUKI, H., Surgery
MORITA, O., Prosthodontics
MURAKAMI, T., Oral Physiology
NAKAHARA, S., Dentistry in Society
OGURA, H., Dental Materials Science
NISHIMURA, K., Oral Surgery
SAITO, K., Oral Microbiology
SHIBAZAKI, K., Internal Medicine
SHIMAMURA, H., Oral Biochemistry
SHIMOOKA, S., Paedodontics
SUETAKA, T., Oral Hygiene
TSUCHIKAWA, K., Oral Surgery
TSUCHIMOTO, M., Radiology

NIPPON SPORT SCIENCE UNIVERSITY

Tokyo Campus: 1-1 Fukasawa 7-chome, Setagaya-ku, Tokyo 158-8508

Telephone: (3) 5706-0900
Fax: (3) 5706-0912

Yokohama Campus: 1221-1 Kamoshida-cho, Aoba-ku, Yokohama 227-0033, Kanagawa Pref.

Telephone: (45) 963-7900
Fax: (45) 963-7903
E-mail: international@nittai.ac.jp
Internet: www.nittai.ac.jp

Founded 1891, present status 1949
Private
Language of instruction: Japanese
Academic year: April to March (2 semesters)
Pres.: Prof. Dr RYOSHO TANIGAMA
Vice-Pres. for Academic and Student Affairs: Prof. KOJI TAKIZAWA
Vice-Pres. for Management and Planning: Prof. SHIGEAKI ABE
Exec. Dir., Admin. Office: MASAHIRO FUJINO
Library of 435,000 vols, 6,367 periodicals
Number of teachers: 130
Number of students: 6,000

DEANS

Graduate School of Health and Sport Science: Prof. Dr TAKEO TAKAHASHI
Faculty of Sport Science: DAIZO HAKAMADA
Teaching Credential Course in PE: KEIJI HONMA
Women's Junior College of NSSU: HAJIME SAKAI

PROFESSORS

ABE, S., Physical Education (Graduate School)
AKIYAMA, A., Cultural Education (Graduate School)
ARAKI, T., Physical Education
ENDA, Y., Physical Education
FUJIMOTO, H., Physical Education
FUJITA, S., Cultural Education
FUJIWARA, S., Physical Education
FUNATO, K., Physical Education (Graduate School)
GUSHIKEN, K., Physical Education
HAKAMADA, D., Martial Arts
HIRANUMA, K., Health Science (Graduate School)
HONMA, K., Cultural Education
HOSOKAWA, S., Early Child Education
IGAWA, S., Health Science (Graduate School)
IRIE, K., Health Science (Graduate School)
ITO, N., Physical Education (Graduate School)
ITO, T., Health Science (Graduate School)
IWASA, K., Physical Education
KENMOTSU, E., Lifelong Sports and Recreation (Graduate School)
KIBAMOTO, H., Physical Education
KIMURA, N., Health Science (Graduate School)

KIYOTA, H., Health Science (Graduate School)
KOBAYAKAWA, Y., Health Science
KOIZUMI, N., Lifelong Sports and Recreation
KUBO, T., Physical Education
KURODA, M., Cultural Education
KUSUMOTO, Y., Cultural Education (Graduate School)
MATSUI, K., Physical Education (Graduate School)
MATSUMOTO, S., Physical Education (Graduate School)
MIYAKE, K., Martial Arts (Graduate School)
MORISHIMA, A., Cultural Education
MORITA, J., Physical Education
MURAKAMI, O., Physical Education (Graduate School)
MURAMOTO, K., Physical Education
NARITA, K., Cultural Education
NISHIDA, T., Physical Education
NISHIO, S., Lifelong Sports and Recreation (Graduate School)
OCHIAI, T., Cultural Education
ODE, K., Lifelong Sports and Recreation (Graduate School)
OGAWA, K., Physical Education
OKADA, A., Cultural Education
OKUIZUMI, K., Early Childhood Education
ONO, M., Health Science
OSAFUNE, T., Cultural Education
OSAKABE, H., Cultural Education
OUCI, T., Physical Education
SAIJO, O., Physical Education (Graduate School)
SAKAI, H., Early Childhood Education
SAKURAI, T., Health Science (Graduate School)
SEKIGUCHI, O., Physical Education
SEKINE, Y., Physical Education
SHIMZU, Y, Physical Education
SUGAWARA, I., Physical Education
TAKADA, R., Physical Education
TAKAHASHI, K., Health Science (Graduate School)
TAKAHASHI, T., Physical Education (Graduate School)
TAKIZAWA, K., Physical Education (Graduate School)
TANIGMA, R., Martial Arts
TOKIMOTO, K., Early Childhood Education
UEDA, Y., Lifelong Sports and Recreation
UENO, J., Health Science (Graduate School)
WATANABE, I., Physical Education
YAMADA, T., Health Science (Graduate School)
YAMAMOTO, I., Health Science
YASUHIRO, Y., Physical Education

OBIRIN UNIVERSITY

3758 Tokiwa-machi, Machida-shi, Tokyo 194-0294

Telephone: (42) 797-5419
Fax: (42) 797-0790
E-mail: cis@obirin.ac.jp
Internet: www.obirin.ac.jp

Founded 1966
President: TOYOSHI SATOW
Number of students: 7,000

Colleges of Business and Public Administration, Economics, Humanities, International Studies.

OSAKA MEDICAL COLLEGE

2–7 Daigakumachi, Takatsuki City, Osaka 569-8686

Telephone: (72) 683-1221
Fax: (72) 683-3723
E-mail: hp-info@poh.osaka-med.ac.jp
Internet: www.osaka-med.ac.jp

Founded 1927
Private control
Language of instruction: Japanese
Academic year: April to March

Chair.: TADAHIRO TANAKA
Pres.: MASAHISA SHIMADA
Sec.-Gen: (vacant)
Librarian: AKIRA SHIMIZU
Library of 221,160 vols
Number of teachers: 362
Number of students: 601

Publications: *Journal* (in Japanese, 1 a year), *Bulletin* (in English, 1 a year).

OSAKA SANGYO UNIVERSITY

3-1-1 Nakagaito, Daito-shi, Osaka 574-8530

Telephone: (72) 875-3001
Fax: (72) 875-6551
Internet: www.osaka-sandai.ac.jp

Founded 1965
Chair. of the Board of Trustees: SHIMEJI FURUTANI
Pres.: JUNICHIRO SEJIMA
Number of teachers: 250
Number of students: 15,634

Faculties of Business Management, Economics, Engineering, Human Environment; College of General Education; Graduate School.

OTEMON GAKUIN UNIVERSITY

1-15 Nishiai 2-chome, Ibaraki, Osaka 567-8502

Telephone: (72) 641-9631
Fax: (72) 643-5651
E-mail: kokusai@jimu.otemon.ac.jp
Internet: www.otemon.ac.jp

Founded 1966
Pres.: TAKASHI SUZUKI
Library of 450,000 vols

Faculties of economics, international liberal arts, management, psychology, sociology.

RIKKYO UNIVERSITY
(St Paul's University)

3-34-1 Nishi-Ikebukuro, Toshima-ku, Tokyo 171-8501

Telephone: 3985-2204
Fax: 3986-8784
E-mail: cis@grp.rikkyo.ne.jp
Internet: www.rikkyo.ne.jp

Founded 1874
Private control
Academic year: April to March
Chancellor: Rev. TOSHIHIKO HAYAMI
President: TERUO OSHIMI
Registrar: Prof. Y. HIKITA
Librarian: Prof. H. SENGOKU
Library of 1,540,558 vols
Number of teachers: 1,110
Number of students: 15,000

Publications: *Rikkyo* (4 a year), *Rikkyo Daigaku Toshokan Dayori* (library news), *Rikkyo Daigaku Shokuin Kiyo* (administrative staff research proceedings, 1 a year), *Kiristokyo Kyoiku Kenkyu* (Studies in Christian Education), *Rikkyo University Bulletin* (every 2 years), *Rikkyo Koho* (Rikkyo news bulletin, 6 a year), and numerous faculty journals

DEANS

Faculty of Arts: H. MAEDA
Faculty of Community and Human Services: M. SEKI
Faculty of Economics: N. OIKAWA
Faculty of General Curriculum Development: Y. SHOJI
Faculty of Law and Politics: T. AWAJI
Faculty of Science: T. MOTOBAYASHI
Faculty of Social Relations: N. SHIRAISHI
Faculty of Tourism: N. OKAMOTO

RISSHO UNIVERSITY

4-2-16 Osaki, Shinagawa-ku, Tokyo 141
Telephone: (3) 3492-5262
Fax: (3) 5487-3343
E-mail: kint@ris.ac.jp
Internet: www.ris.ac.jp

Founded 1872
Private control
Language of instruction: Japanese
Academic year: April to March

Chancellor: N. TANAKA
President: H. SAKAZUME
Vice-President: Z. KITAGAWA
Registrar: (vacant)
Chief Librarians: H. FUJITA (Osaki), Y. IKOMA (Kumagaya)
Number of teachers: 700 (217 full-time, 483 part-time)
Number of students: 11,900
Publications: *Bulletin* (1 a year), *Journal of Buddhist Studies*, *Journal of Nichiren Buddhism* (1 a year), *Quarterly Report of Economics*, etc

DEANS

Faculty of Buddhist Studies: K. MITOMO
Faculty of Business and Management: Y. KATO
Faculty of Economics: K. FUKUOKA
Faculty of Geo-Environmental Science: Y. YOSHIDA
Faculty of Law: S. IWAI
Faculty of Letters: S. TEGAWA
Faculty of Social Welfare: T. HOSHINO
Graduate School (Business Administration): T. OKUMURA
Graduate School (Economics): K. FUKUOKA
Graduate School (Law): T. SUZUKI
Graduate School (Literature): Y. TAKAGI

RITSUMEIKAN UNIVERSITY

56-1 Tojiin Kitamachi, Kita-ku, Kyoto 525-8577
Telephone: (75) 465-1111
E-mail: kokusai@st.ritsumei.ac.jp
Internet: www.ritsumei.ac.jp

Founded 1900
Private control
Academic year: April to March

President: TOYO OMI NAGATA
Vice-Presidents: SADAO KAWAMURA, KIMIO YAKUSHIJI
Dean (Academic Affairs): MITSURU SATO
Dean (Graduate Affairs): YOSHINOBU KUSA-KABE
Dean (Research Affairs): MAKOTO SATO
Dean (Student Affairs): KATSUO NAKAGAWA
Dean (Library): YOSHIHIRO TANIGUCHI
Library of 2,532,945 vols
Number of teachers: 1,312 full-time
Number of students: 35,604 full-time
Publications: *Ritsumeikan Business Review*, *Ritsumeikan Economic Review*, *Ristumeikan Journal of International Studies*, *Ritsumeikan Journal of International Relations and Area Studies*, *Ritsumeikan International Affairs*, *Ritsumeikan Shigaku*, *Memoirs of Research Institute of Humanities and Social Science*, *Journal of Ritsumeikan Geographical Society*, *Proceedings of the Philosophical Society of Ritsumeikan University*, *Ritsumeikan Law Review*, *Memoirs of the SR Center, Ritsumeikan University*, *Ritsumeikan Annual Review of International Studies* (in English), *Ritsumeikan Eibei Bungaku*, *Ritsumeikan Torena Haiho*, *Ritsumeikan Toyoshigaku*, *Core Ethics*, *Ritsumeikan Sangyo Shyakaironsyu*, *Memoirs of the Institute of Humanities, Human and Social Science*, *Ritsumeikan Seisaku Kagaku*, *Studies in Language and Culture*,

Ritsumeikan Bungaku, *Journal of Human Science*, *Art Research*, *Ritsumeikan Ronkyu Nihon Bungaku*, *Ritsumeikan Gakurin*, *Social Systems Studies*

DEANS

College and Graduate School of Business Administration: TERUYOSHI TANAKA
College and Graduate School of International Relations: HIROFUMI OGI
College and Graduate School of Policy Science: KIYOFUMI KAWAGUCHI
College and Graduate School of Science and Engineering: HIDEYUKI TAKAKURA
College and Graduate School of Social Sciences: KUNIHIRO TOSHIFUMI
College of Economics: JUNICHI HIRATA
College of Law: RYOICHI YOSHIMURA
College of Letters: KAZUAKI KIMURA
College of Information Science and Engineering: TAKEO IIDA
Graduate School for Core Ethics and Frontier Sciences: KOZO WATANABE
Graduate School of Economics: SHUJI MATSU-KAWA
Graduate School of Language Education and Information Science: JUNSAKU NAKAMURA
Graduate School of Science for Human Services: CHUICHIRO TAKAGAKI
Graduate School of Law: SHIRO AKAZAWA
Graduate School of Letters: HIROHIDE TAKEYAMA
Law School: MASATO ICHIKAWA

PROFESSORS

College and Graduate School of Business Administration:

ANDO, T., Technology Transfer
BAILEY, A., English
CHIYODA, K., Accounting
DOI, Y., Transportation
ENNO, B., Corporate Culture and Governance
FUJITA, T., Business Accounting
HARA, Y., International Corporations
HASHIMOTO, T., Business Administration History
HATTORI, Y., Modern Financial Markets
HIRAI, T., Environmental Accounting Theory
HYOUDO, T., Contemporary Science and Technology
IDA, T., English
IKEDA, S., Cultural Studies, Total Quality Management
IMADA, O., Production Management
ITO, T., Politics and Literature in the Weimar Republic
IWATA, N., Japanese Language Education and Linguistics
KINOSHITA, A., Distribution Procedures
KOEZUKA, H., Product Planning, Marketing Channels
KOKUBO, M., Industrial and Social Psychology
KOSAKA, K., Communicative and Cognitive Mechanisms
MATSUI, T., Medium Enterprises
MATSUMURA, K., Business Financial Management
MIURA, I., Japanese Retail Business
MIURA, M., Health Science
MIYOSAWA, T., Managerial Accounting
MUKAI, J., International Finance
MURAYAMA, T., International Investment
NAGASHIMA, O., Japanese Economy
NAKAMURA, M., Multinationals
NAKANISHI, I., Industrial Economics, Comparative Economic Studies
NAKATA, M., General Business Administration
NAMIE, I., Labour Problems
OKAMOTO, N., Physical Fitness
OKUMURA, Y., Business Strategies
SAITO, M., Business Administration

SASABE, A., History of Science and Engineering
SATO, N., Design Management
SCHLUNZE, R. D., International Management, Economic Geography
SHIOMI, K., Cross-cultural Communication
SUZUKI, Y., French
TAKEDA, M., Management Organization and Information Systems
TAKI, H., Corporations and Accounting
TAMAMURA, H., Privatization
TANAKA, A., Asian Enterprises
TANAKA, T., History of Business Thought
TANAKA, T., Statistics
TANEDA, Y., Managerial Accounting
WATANABE, T., Business Management
YAMAZAKI, S., Spanish
YAMAZAKI, T., Business Administration
YANAGASE, K., Public Finance, Public Economics, Development Policy
YOSHIDA, K., Mathematical Programming

College and Graduate School of Economics:

AGATSUMA, N., Economic Policy
ASADA, K., Public Finance, Money and Banking
FUJIOKA, A., Economic Analysis of Nuclear-based Military Expansion
FURUKAWA, A., Economic Policy
HAMADA, S., Corporate Law
HATANAKA, T., Early Modern Japanese History
HIRATA, J., Economic Statistics
INABA, K., Economic Statistics
IWATA, K., International Economics
IZAWA, H., Economic Theory
KAJIYAMA, N., Currency Exchange System and Economic Development
KAKIHARA, H., Economic Policy, Medicine
KAKUTA, S., Economic Theory
KANEMARU, Y., East Asian Economic History and Modern Chinese History
KASAI, T., International Economic Cooperation
MATSUBARA, T., Agricultural Economics
MATSUI, S., Political Economy, Economic Philosophy
MATSUKAWA, S., General Theory of Economics
MATSUMOTO, A., Political, Financial and Monetary Economics
MATSUNO, S., East Asian Economic Relations
NISHIGUCHI, K., Economic Theory of Developing Nations
NOZAWA, T., Phonology, Psycholinguistics
OHKAWA, M., Economic Theory, International Economics
OHKAWA, T., Industrial Organization
OKAO, K., History of Modern Sports
SAITO, T., Modern Chinese Literature
SAKAMOTO, K., Economic Policy
SATO, T., Social Policy
SATOU, Y., Sport Psychology
SHIMADA, Y., Area Environmental Systems
SHIMIZU, Y., Educational Technology, Intercultural Communication
TAKAGI, A., Contemporary Capitalism
TANAKA, H., Russian and Eastern European Economic Studies
TANAKA, Y., International Economics
TANIGAKI, K., International Trade Theory
TOMATSURI, T., Tourism
TSUJII, E., English
UCHIYAMA, A., Public Finance
WAKABAYASHI, H., Comparative Research of Policy Theories, Regional Policy
YAMADA, H., Econometrics
YAMAI, T., German Economics
YAMAMOTO, S., Actuarial Economics, Insurance, US–Japanese Comparative Economics and Portfolio Theory
YOKOYAMA, M., International Economics
YOSHIDA, C., International Economics
ZHENG, X., Urban and Regional Economics

College and Graduate School of Law:

AKAZAWA, S., Politics, History
ARAKAWA, S., Civil Law, Sociology of Law
DEGUCHI, M., Civil Procedure Law
HANATATE, F., Civil Law
HIRANO, H., Basic Science of Law
HISAOKA, Y., Criminal Law, Criminal Procedure Law
HONDA, M., German Criminal Law
HORI, M., Politics
IKUTA, K., Criminal Law, Criminal Procedure Law
ISHIHARA, H., English Literature
KATSUI, H., Civil Law
KOBORI, M., Modern British Politics
KOYAMA, Y., Civil Law
KURATA, M., Human Rights Theory, Constitutional Law
KUZUNO, H., Criminal Justice and Juvenile Justice
MIKI, Y., Taxation Law
MIYAI, M., International Economic Law
MIZUGUCHI, N., Public Administration, Regional Autonomy
MOTOYAMA, A., Family Law
MURAKAMI, H., Political Science
NAKAJIMA, S., Public Law
NAKAMURA, Y., French Modern Legal History, French Criminal Procedure
NAKATANI, Y., Politics
NISHIMURA, M., International Politics
NOGUCHI, M., English
OHGAKI, H., Financial Law
OHIRA, Y., Japanese Legal History
OKAWA, S., Civil Law
SATO, K., Social Law
SO, S., East Asian Law and Human Rights
SUTO, Y., Proportional Doctrines
TAKEHAMA, O., Insurance
TAKEHARU, S., German, German Literature
TANIMOTO, K., German Language and Literature
TOKUGAWA, S., Civil Law
UNOKI, Y., Chinese Language and Literature
YAKUSHIJI, K., International Law
YAMAMOTO, T., Social Security Law
YASUMOTO, N., Public Administrative Law
YOSHIDA, M., Labour Law
YOSHIMURA, R., Law of Damage
YOSHIOKA, K., Literary Theory

College and Graduate School of Letters:

AKAMA, R., Modern Drama, Literature and Ukiyoe
ASAO, K., Applied Linguistics
EGUCHI, N., Caribbean Studies
FOX, C. E., Modern Japanese Verse
FUJI, K., Experimental Analysis of Behaviour
FUJIMAKI, M., Human Geography, Urban Social Geography
HATTORI, K., Philosophy of Nature and Social Philosophy
HAYASHI, N., Study of True Human Education
HIEDA, Y., Comparative Literature
HIGASHIYAMA, A., Psychology of Sensation and Perception, Geometry of Visual Space
HIKOSAKA, Y., History of Japanese Dialects
HONDA, O., History of Agricultural Development
HONGO, M., National Law of Ancient Japan, Royal Authority and Religion
HOSHINO, Y., Human Memory and Learning, Cognitive Processes
HOSOI, K., Personality
IKEDA, Y., Modern Philosophy
IKUTA, M., Comparative Study of Large Asian Cities
ISE, T., Philosophy
ISHII, F., German Literature in the Pre-March Revolution Period
KASUGAI, T., Clinical Education

KATAHIRA, H., Land Use in the Semi-arid Regions of Australia, Landscape Reproduction
KATSURAJIMA, N., Japanese Early Modern History, Tokugawa Intellectual History
KAWAGUCHI, Y., The English Novel: Forster, Austen, Golding
KAWASHIMA, K., Study of Artisan Guilds and the Rural Traditional Handicraft Industry
KAWASHIMA, M., Life and Culture in Late Medieval Japan
KIDACHI, M., Archaeology
KIMURA, K., Modern Japanese Literature
KITAMURA, M., Political and Cultural Development in the Republic of China
KITANO, K., Film Studies
KITAO, H., Ethics and Philosophy
KO, J. Y., Korean Archaeology
KOBAYASHI, K., Poetry and Painting of William Blake
KUSAKABE, Y., Greek Philosophy, History of Ontology
MACLEAN, R., English and American Literature since the 18th Century
MARUYAMA, M., 20th-century American Literature
MASHIMO, A., Ancient Japanese Literature, Manyoshu and Oral Literature
MATSUDA, K., English Romantic Poets of the 18th and 19th Centuries
MATSUDA, T., Perception and Cognition
MATSUMOTO, H., Late 19th- to Early 20th-century Politics
MATSUMOTO, Y., Medieval Chinese History, Political System of the Tang Dynasty
MOCHIZUKI, A., Applied Behaviour Analysis, Behavioural Human Serviceology
MUKAI, T., Hegelian Philosophy, Culture and Ideology
MURASHIMA, Y., Educational Philosophy, Moral Education
NAGATA, T., Modern and Contemporary American History
NAKAGAWA, S., Modern Japanese Literature
NAKAGAWA, Y., American Literature, Women's Studies
NAKAGAWA, Y., Holistic Education, Women's Studies
NAKANISHI, K., Heian Literature
ODA, M., Cognitive Science, Concept and Imagery
ODAUCHI, T., Religious Movements and Heresy in Medieval Europe
OHTO, C., Greek and Hellenistic History
OKADA, H., Contemporary Chinese Literature
OUJI, T., Area Studies
OZEKI, M., Political Thought and History in Modern Japan, Cultural Theory
PEATY, D., English Language Education
SAITO, T., Research on Altered States of Consciousness
SANO, M., Generative-grammatical Analyses of Japanese and English
SATO, T., Educational and Social Psychology, Experimental Psychology
SHIMA, H., Studies in Tang Dynasty Thought
SHIMIZU, Y., Medieval Chinese Literature and Criticism
SHIMOKAWA, S., Life and Works of Stendhal
SUGIHASHI, T., History of the Warrior Government Formation
TADAI, T., Evidence-based Clinical Psychology and Psychiatry
TAKAGI, K., Developmental Psychology
TAKAHASHI, H., Contemporary German History
TAKAHASHI, M., Natural Environmental Changes and Relationship to Human Lifestyles
TAKASHIMA, K., 19th-century American Literature

TAKEYAMA, H., Italian Literature, Ethnography and Comparative Culture
TAKIMOTO, K., Modern Japanese Literature, Mori Ogai
TANI, T., Phenomenology and Contemporary Philosophy
TOBINO, K., Philosophical Study in Education and Human Relations
TSUCHIDA, N., Developmental Psychology
TSUKAMA, Y., Linguistics, Phonetics, Foreign Language Education
UEDA, H., Meiji Japanese Literature
UEDA, T., History of Contemporary Western Art, Art Criticism
UENO, R., Classical Chinese Literature
WADA, S., Archaeological Research of the Yayoi and Kofun Peirods
WELLS, K., American Poetry, Folklore and Folksong, Comparative Culture
YAGI, Y., Psychology of Self; Personality and Social Psychology
YAMAMOTO, M., Psychotherapy and Psychoanalysis
YANO, K., Archaeology
YANO, K., Human Geography
YONEYAMA, H., American History, Japanese American History
YOSHIDA, H., Learning Psychology
YOSHIKOSHI, A., Human Impact on the Hydrological Environment
YOSHIMURA, H., Chinese Tang Dynasty Literature
YUKAWA, E., Applied Linguistics and Bilingualism

College and Graduate School of International Relations:

ANDO, T., Western Political History
ANZAI, I., International Peace Theory
ASAHI, M., Contemporary Global Economics
HARA, T., South American Anthropology
HOSHINO, K., European Economics, Monetary Integration
INOUE, J., Cultural Sociology
ITAKI, M., Social Science Methodology
KA, G., Japanese and Chinese Comparative Studies
KANEKO, H., Contemporary German Poetry
KATO, T., Black African-American Literature
KATSURA, R., Asian and International Social Welfare, Family Welfare and Policy
KIMIJIMA, A., Peace Studies, Constitutional Law
KIYOMOTO, O., Contemporary South East Asian History
KOBAYASHI, M., Political Science
KOYAMA, M., International Relations
MATSUSHITA, K., Politics of Developing Countries
MINAMINO, Y., Comparative Politics, Political History, Irish Political History
MIYAKE, M., Linguistic Analysis
MUN, G. S., North East Asian History
NAGASU, M., Japanese Development Assistance, International Cooperation
NAKAGAWA, R., Asian Economics
NAKAMURA, Y., French Thought and Literature, Contemporary Japanese Literature
NAKATSUJI, K., Modern Political History
ODAIRA, K., International Cooperation Law, Francophone and EU Studies
OGI, H., Asian Studies, Chinese Education and Literature
OIKAWA, M., Contemporary American Theatre
OKUDA, H., International Finance
OZORA, H., Mass Media
SATO, M., Comparative Sociology, African Politics
SHAWBACK, M., Foreign Languages, General Studies
TAKAHASHI, N., Japanese Economy

TAKEUCHI, T., Comparative Analysis of Family Structure

TATSUZAWA, K., International Law Relations, Islamic Law, Space Law

WAKANA, M., American Literature

WASSERMAN, M., Theatrical Arts of the West and Japan

YAMADA, H., Japanese Language

YAMAMOTO, S., American Drama

College and Graduate School of Policy Science:

HIRAO, H., Use of Computers in English Education

HONDA, Y., Econometrics

HOSOI, K., Modern Management Theory

JIDOU, Y., History of Industrial Technology

KAWAGUCHI, K., Citizen Participation, Cooperatives and NPOs

KISHIMOTO, T., International Politics and Economics

MIKAMI, T., Artificial Intelligence, Memory and Decision-Making

MIKAMI, T., Administrative Law, Planning Law

MURAYAMA, H., Political Attitude and Political Behaviour

OBATA, N., Environmental Policy

SATOH, M., Policy Formation

SHIGEMORI, T., Political Theory

SHIRAKAWA, I., Economic Policy, International Economics

TAKADA, S., Urban and Regional Planning

TAKAO, K., Environmental Policies, Development Economics

TONEGAWA, K., System Simulation and Management Problems

YAMAMOTO, R., Obligation, Medical Malpractice and Consumer Law

YAMANE, H., Post-war German Literature

YASUE, N., EU and Other International Organizations

ZHOU, W., Environmental Policy, Energy Systems Engineering

College and Graduate School of Science and Engineering:

ABE, A., Technology Management

AKISHITA, S., Active Noise Control in Machinery, Robotics

AMANO, K., Environmental Systems Analysis

AMASAKI, S., Concrete Engineering

AMEYAMA, K., Physical Metallurgy, Microstructure Control, Electron Microscopy

AOYAMA, A., Life-Cycle Engineering

ARAI, M., Spectral Theory of Differential Operators

ARAKI, Y., Educational Technology

ARASE, M., Linguistics, English, Japanese, Substance-Dependence Research

ARIMOTO, S., Robotics, Mechatronics, Machine Intelligence

CHEN, E., Image-Processing, Radioactive Rays Image Measurement, Soft Computing

EGASHIRA, S., Solid Particle and Water Tow Phase Flows, Watercourse and Riverbed Variations

ENDO, A., Community Structure of Terrestrial Invertebrate Animals

FUJIEDA, I., Graphic Information Machinery

FUJIMURA, S., Riemannian Geometry

FUJINO, T., Electrical Engineering

FUKAGAWA, R., Geomechanics, Geomechatronics

FUKUI, M., System LSIs

FUKUMOTO, T., Soil Mechanics and Geotechnical Engineering

FUKUYAMA, H., Elementary Particles, High Energy Astrophysics

HARUNA, M., Urban and Regional Planning Systems

HAYAKAWA, K., Traffic-induced Ground Vibration Propagation and Reduction Measures

HIRAI, S., Robotic Manipulation

IIDA, T., Ergonomics

IKEDA, K., Nonlinear Physical Phenomena

IMAI, S., Atomic Layer CVD and Fabrication of Single Electron Devices

IMAMURA, N., Chemistry of Bio-active Compounds produced by Micro-organisms

ISAKA, T., Sports Biomechanics, Analysis of Human Movement

ISHII, A., Robot Vision, Sensors and Image Analysis

ISHII, H., Number Theory of Automorphic Forms

ISONO, Y., Computational Material Science

ITO, M., Strength and Design of Steel Structures

IWASHIMIZU, Y., Solid Mechanics, Ultrasonic Materials Evaluation

IZUNO, K., Earthquake Resistant Design of Structures

KAITO, C., Quantum Dots Formation

KASAHARA, K., Optical Communication Devices

KATO, M., Physical Chemistry

KAWABATA, T., Power Electronics

KAWAGUCHI, A., Preparation of Functional Polymer Materials Using Epitaxies, and Study of their Properties

KAWAMURA, S., Robotics

KIDO, Y., Investigation of Surface and Interface Structures

KIMATA, M., Engineering

KITAZAWA, T., Numerical Analysis of Electromagnetic Wave Problems

KOBAYASHI, H., Wind-tunnel Experiments and Analyses of Long Bridges Subject to Wind Load

KOJIMA, K., Material and Inorganic Chemistry, Optical Materials

KOJIMA, T., FEM Analysis of Hybrid Concrete Structures Using Discrete Elements

KOMATSU, Y., Online Parameter Estimations of the Induction Machine Utilizing Extension Slip Method

KONDO, K., Synthesis of Functional Polymers

KONISHI, S., Micronanomechatronics and Micromachines, Systems Engineering, Electronic Devices

KOYANAGI, S., Parallel Computation, Database Computer Engineering, Data Mining

KUBO, M., Applied Microbiology

KURATSUJI, H., Quantum Phenomenology

KUSAKA, T., Fracture Mechanics

MAEDA, H., Robot Intelligence for Action and Tasks

MAKIKAWA, M., Biomedical Engineering, Application of Human Motion for Engineering

MATSUDA, T., Separation Analysis, Electroanalysis, Environmental Analysis Chemistry

MATSUOKA, M., Nickel-hydride Batteries, Solar Cells Electrocatalysis, Titanium Dioxide Photocatalysis

MIKI, H., Semiconductor Materials, Solid-state Devices

MIYANO, T., Complex Systems Science, Artificial Intelligence

MIZOSHIRI, I., Medical Electronics and Biological Engineering

MORIMOTO, A., Ultrafast Photonics, Ultrafast Laser Technology, and Terahertz Optoelectronics

MORISAKI, H., Analysis of the Surface Characteristics of Microbial Cells, and the Interaction between Micro-organisms and Interfaces

MURAHASHI, M., Regional and Urban Structure Analyses and Development Techniques

NAKADA, T., Surface Properties

NAKAJIMA, H., Theoretical Analysis of the Interaction Structures of Multi-component Systems

NAKAJIMA, J., Waste Water Treatment Systems, Nitrogen and Phosphorus Removal

NAKAJIMA, K., Homogeneous Kähler Manifolds

NAKAMURA, N., Structure and Physical Properties of Normal Long Chain Compounds, Ionomers and Liquid Crystals

NAKANISHI, T., Measurement and Estimation of Automobile Traffic Flow

NAKAYA, Y., Human Interface, Artificial Intelligence, Recognition Engineering

NAMBA, H., Surfaces as New Materials, Surface Chemical Dynamics

NANISHI, Y., Semiconductor Optoelectronic Devices, Physical Properties of Quantum Structures, Plasma-excited Semiconductor Processes

NARUKI, I., Analysis and Geometry of Complex Manifolds

NISHIO, S., Surface Science

NISHIWAKI, K., Gas Flow, Turbulence, Heat Transfer and Combustion in Combustion Chambers

NUMAI, T., Optical Electronics

OGAMI, Y., Fluid Dynamics

OGASAWARA, H., Geophysics

OGAWA, H., Intelligence Information Science

OGAWA, S., Analysis of Moduli Spaces

OGURA, T., Si System Architecture

OIKAWA, K., Architectural and Urban Space Planning, Environmental Design

OKADA, M., Magnetic and Dielectric Materials, Semiconductor Lasers

ONO, B., Cellular and Molecular Study of the Biological Functions of the Budding Yeast

ONO, Y., Optical Periodic Microstructure

OSAKA, H., Operator Algebras

OZUTSUMI, K., Structural and Thermodynamic Studies of Metal Complexes in Solution

SAITO, S., Optical Communications

SAKAI, J., Optical Fibre Communications and Optical Information Processing

SAKAI, T., Statistical Research on Reliability Engineering

SAKANE, M., Strength Evaluation of Heat-resistant Materials at High Temperatures

SATOMI, J., Basic Physiological and Biochemical Study of Sports Training

SAWAMURA, S., High-pressure Physical Chemistry of Solutions

SHIMAKAWA, H., Social Systems, Computer Software, Information Systems

SHINODA, H., Environmental Studies

SHINYA, H., Functional Analysis

SHIRAISHI, H., Electro-analytical Chemistry

SUGIMOTO, S., Systems and Control Engineering

SUGINO, N., Teaching English as a Foreign Language

SUGIYAMA, S., Microsystem Technology

SUZUKI, K., MEMS for Information and Telecommunication

SUZUKI, K., Pharmaceutical Development, Molecular Biology

TACHIKI, T., Physiology, Biochemistry and the Breeding of Useful Micro-organisms

TAKAKURA, H., High-efficiency Solar Cell Research

TAKANO, N., Computational Mathematics

TAKAYAMA, S., Advanced Sensing Systems and Measurement Science

TAKAYAMA, Y., Computative Algebra

TAKENAKA, A., Properties of Elementary Particles and their Interactions

TAMAKI, J., Design of Functional Interface between Inorganic Materials for Gas-sensing Devices

TAMIAKI, H., Bio-organic Chemistry

TAMURA, H., Information Engineering, Virtual Reality

TANAKA, H., Computer Vision, Visual Communication, Intelligent Information Systems

TANAKA, K., Micro-electric Machine Systems

TANAKA, S., Computer Graphics Systems

TANAKA, T., Precision Processing

TANIGUCHI, Y., High-pressure Physical Chemistry of Liquids, Solutions and Biological Materials

TANIKAGA, R., Organic Synthesis Using Biocatalysts and Organic Sulphurous Reagents

TATEYAMA, K., Construction Engineering

TERAI, H., Research into Computer and LSI Design Automation Systems

THAWONMAS, R., Artificial Intelligence, Entertainment Computing

TOKI, K., Earthquake Engineering, Natural Disaster Science

TORIYAMA, T., Optical Applied Measurements

TSUDAGAWA, M., Analysis and Application of Space Filters

TSUKAGUCHI, H., Transport System Planning and Management

UKITA, H., Optomechatronics

WAKAYAMA, M., Food and Nutrition

WAKAYAMA, M., Food and Nutrition, Microorganisms

WATANABE, T., Control Engineering

XU, G., Pattern Recognition, Computer Science, Robotics

YAMADA, H., Development of Free-electron Laser

YAMADA, K., Water Demand Analyses and Predictions

YAMADA, O., Mathematical Analysis

YAMADA, T., Probability and Statistics

YAMADA, T., Telecommunication

YAMAMOTO, N., Biomechanics and Function of Living Systems

YAMASAKI, M., Urban Landscape Planning

YAMAUCHI, H., System VLSI Architecture and Implementation

YAMAZAKI, K., Parallel Computing, Computer Graphics, Case-based Reasoning

YOSHIDA, M., Ecology, Ethology

YOSHIHARA, Y., Formation Mechanisms of Harmful Combustion Products and Methods for their Reduction

YOSHIMURA, Y., Structural Phase Transition in Alkali Metal Cyanide

College and Graduate School of Social Sciences:

AKAI, S., Sociology

ARAKI, H., Human Development

ARUGA, I., Turn-Verein

FUKASAWA, A., French Labour and Social History

HIGASHI, J., Critical Applied Linguistics, Sociology of Education

HOGETSU, M., Sociology of Deviance and Sociological Theories

IIDA, T., Sociology

IKEUCHI, Y., American Playwrights

IKUTA, M., Welfare and Information Technology

INUI, K., Social Planning

ISHIKURA, Y., Welfare Sociology, Child and Clinical Psychiatry

JINBO, T., Alternative Media, Media Ethics and Journalism

KANAI, J., Sports Sociology

KIDA, A., Japanese Sociology

KOIZUMI, H., Advertising

KUNIHIRO, T., Political Sociology

KUSAFUKA, N., Physical Education

KUTSUNAI, K., French Literature

LIM, B., Urban Planning

MAEDA, N., Welfare Sociology and Comparative Research in Welfare

MATSUBA, M., German Capitalism

MATSUDA, H., History of Modern Social Thought

MINESHIMA, A., Welfare of the Disabled

MIYASHITA, S., History of Science and Technology

MONDEN, K., History of Science and Technology

MORINISHI, M., History of the Performing Arts

NAGASAWA, K., General Theory of Economics, Economical Statistics

NAKAFUMI, S., Chinese Language and Study of the Tale of the Heike

NAKAGAWA, K., Sociology

NAKAMA, Y., Art History

NAKAMURA, T., Cultural Anthropology

NODA, M., Judicial Welfare

OGAWA, E., Elderly Home Care

OKADA, M., Health Education and Social Work

OKUGAWA, O., Cross-cultural Communication

OZAWA, W., Cross-cultural Communication

SAKAMOTO, T., Sociology

SAKATA, K., Local Media Theory, Broadcast Media Theory

SAKURADANI, M., Sociology

SASAKI, K., Cultural Anthropology

SATO, Y., Sociology, Philosophy

SATOU, H., Sociology, Social Security

SHIBATA, H., Social Security

SHINODA, T., Theory of Political Economy

SUDO, Y., Modern Capitalism

SUZUKI, M., Social Consciousness

TAKAGAKI, C., Mass Communication

TAKAGI, M., Clinical Psychology

TAKAHASHI, M., Sociology

TAKEHAMA, A., Consumer Behaviour

TSUDA, M., Public Access

TSUDOME, M., Social Welfare

TSUJI, K., Disaster Behaviour

WADA, T., Labour Sociology

WEN, C., the Tale of the Heike, Chinese Language

YAMAMOTO, T., Welfare Budget and Administration

YAMASHITA, T., Leisure and Sports Sociology

YANAGISAWA, S., Sociology

YOSHIDA, M., Psycholinguistics

College of Information Science and Engineering:

ASANO, S., Bioscience and Bio-informatics

CHEN, Y. W., Media Technology

ENDO, H., Computer Science

FUJITA, N., Bioscience and Bio-informatics

FUKUMOTO, J., Natural Language Processing

FUSAOKA, A., Human and Computer Intelligence

HACHIMURA, K., Media Technology

HAGIWARA, H., Human and Computer Intelligence

HATTORI, F., Information and Communication Science

HAYANO, T., Proteomics, Molecular Biology, Biochemistry

HAYASHI, T., Media Technology

HIGUCHI, N., Media Technology

IIDA, T., Human and Computer Intelligence

IKEDA, H., Computer Science

INOUE, Y., Information Systems Engineering

KAMEI, K., Human and Computer Intelligence

KAWAI, M., Wireless and Network Systems

KAWAGOE, K., Information and Communication Science

KIKUCHI, M., Bioscience and Bio-informatics

KIKUCHI, T., Bioscience and Bio-informatics

KISHIMOTO, R., Information and Communication Science

KITAMOTO, S., Computer-Generated Animation

KOTSUKI, S., Genetic Informatics

KUNIEDA, Y., Computer Science

KUWABARA, K., Knowledge Processing, Communication Science

MAEDA, T., Electromagnetic Waves and Data Transmission

NAGANO, S., Systems Biology

NAKATANI, Y., Information and Communication Science

NISHIKAWA, I., Human and Computer Intelligence

NISHIO, N., Computer Science

NOZAWA, K., Educational Technology, Inter-cultural Communication

OGAWA, E., Knowledge Engineering

OHNISHI, A., Operating Systems

OKUBO, E., Computer Science

OSHIMA, T., Artificial Reality

OYANAGI, S., Computer Science

RINALDO, F. J., Artificial Intelligence, Expert Systems and Knowledge Information Processing

SHIMAKAWA, H., Computer Science

SHINODA, H., Human and Computer Intelligence

SHIRAI, Y., Robot Intelligence

SUGINO, N., Teaching English as a Foreign Language

SUZUKI, K., Bioscience and Bio-informatics

TAMURA, H., Media Technology

TANAKA, H., Human and Computer Intelligence

TANAKA, S., Media Technology

THAWONMAS, R., Intelligent Entertainment Computing

XU, G., Media Technology

YAMASHITA, Y., Media Technology

YOSHIKAWA, T., Mechatronics, Control Engineering and Robotics

Graduate School for Core Ethics and Frontier Sciences:

AKAMA, R., Japanese Literature

DUMOUCHEL, P., Economic Philosophy

ENDO, A., Symbiosis Theory

GOTO, R., Economic Philosophy

KAMBAYASHI, T., Aesthetics, Art

KOIZUMI, Y., Philosophy

MATSUBARA, Y., History of Science, Scientific Theory

NISHI, M., Comparative Literature

NISHIKAWA, N., French Language, Japanese History, European History

TATEIWA, S., Ethics

UEMURA, M., Television Gaming

WATANABE, K., Cultural Anthropology, African Studies, History of Anthropology

Graduate School of Sciences for Human Services:

AKIRA, H., Genetic Psychology

DAN, S., Family Medical Treatment Methods

FUJI, N., Clinical Psychology

HAYASHI, N., Education, Theory of Character Building

MOCHIZUKI, A., Experimental Action Analysis

MURAMOTO, K., Clinical Psychology, Trauma

NAKAGAWA, Y., Clinical Pedagogics

NAKAMURA, J., Intelligence Development, Life-Span Development, Counselling

NAKAMURA, T., Sociology, Social Welfare

NODA, M., Administration of Welfare Justice, Child Welfare

TADAI, T., Clinical Psychology, Psychiatry

TAKAGAKI, C., Clinical Psychology

TAKINO, I., Clinical Psychology

TOKUDA, K., Clinical Psychology

Graduate School of Language Education and Information Science:

AZUMA, S., Code-switching, Socio-linguistic Significance

LEE, N., Linguistics
KAWAMURA, K., English as a Foreign or Second Language
MATSUDA, K., English Literature
NAKAMURA, J., English Corpus Linguistics
NOZAWA, K., Teaching English as a Foreign Language
OHNO, Y., Japanese Pedagogics, Formal Language Studies
OKURA, M., Japanese Language Teaching Methodology
RATZLAFF, G., Second Language Pedagogy and Acquisition
SHIMIZU, Y., Teaching English as a Foreign Language
SUGIMORI, M., Applied Linguistics
TSUKUMA, Y., Linguistics, Phonetics
UMESAKI, A., English Education
YAMADA, H., Linguistics, Phonetics
YOSHIDA, S., Psychology Linguistics

Law School:

DANBAYASHI, K., Women and Law, Trial Procedure
FUJITA, M., Criminal Practice Law
HANATATE, F., Civil Law
HIRAI, T., Civil, Merchant and Medical Law
IBUSUKI, M., Legal Informatics, Criminal Procedure
ICHIKAWA, M., Constitutional Case Law
KATSUI, H., Civil Law
KITAMURA, K., Public Law
KOMATSU, Y., Bankruptcy Law, Consumer Law and Intellectual Property Law
KURONO, Y., Civil Law
MATSUI, Y., International Law
MATSUMIYA, T., Criminal Law
MATSUMOTO, K., Civil Liability, Limitation Act
MORISHITA, H., Criminal Law and Criminal Defence
NINOMIYA, S., Civil Law
OKAHARA, F., Civil Law
OKAMOTO, M., Real Estate Law
OKAWA, S., Civil Case Law, Criminal Case Law
OKUBO, S., Public Law
SAGAMI, Y., Civil Law
SAKAI, H., International Civil Procedure
SHINATANI, T., Corporate Law, Securities Regulation
TANAKA, T., Enterprise Law
UEDA, K., Criminology
WADA, S., Civil Law
WATANABE, S., International Private Law and Civil Procedure
YAMAGUCHI, K., Consumer Protection and International Trade
YAMAMOTO, T., International Conflict Management
YAMANA, T., Tax and Inheritance Tax Law
YASUMOTO, N., Administrative Law, Tax Law

RITSUMEIKAN ASIA PACIFIC UNIVERSITY

1-1 Jumonjibaru, Beppu-shi, Oita 874-8577
Telephone: (977) 78-1111
Fax: (977) 78-1123
Internet: www.apu.ac.jp
Founded 2000
Private control
Languages of instruction: English, Japanese
Academic year: September to July andApril to February

Pres.: Prof. SHUN KORENAGA
Vice-Pres.: Prof. MASAO HOMMA
Vice-Pres.: Prof. JUNICHI HIRATA
Vice-Pres.: Prof. SUSUMU YAMAGAMI
Vice-Pres.: Prof. A. MANI
Dean of Academic Affairs: Prof. JUNICHI HIRATA
Dean of Admissions: Prof. YUICHI KONDO
Dean of Student Affairs: Prof. CHAN HOE KIM

Library of 65,000 vols
Number of teachers: 120
Number of students: 6,040 (5,708 undergraduate, 254 postgraduate)
Publications: *Journal of Asia Pacific Studies* (3 a year), *Polyglossia* (2 a year)

DEANS

College of Asia Pacific Studies: JEREMY EADES
College of Int. Management: KENJI YOKOYAMA
Graduate School of Asia Pacific Studies: JEREMY EADES
Graduate School of Int. Management: KENJI YOKOYAMA

RYUKOKU UNIVERSITY

67 Tsukamoto-cho, Fukakusa, Fushimi-ku, Kyoto 612-8577
Telephone: (75) 642-1111
Fax: (75) 642-8867
E-mail: ric@rnoc.fks.ryukoku.ac.jp
Internet: www.ryukoku.ac.jp
Founded 1639
Private control
Academic year: April to March
Chancellor: KOSHO FUJIKAWA
Pres.: DOSHO WAKAHARA
Vice-Pres: TAKESHI HORIKAWA, YOSHIO KAWAMURA
Sec.-Gen.: CHIKO IWAGAMI
Librarian: JITSUZO SHIGETA

Library: see libraries and Archives
Number of teachers: 501
Number of students: 19,830
Publications: *Ryukoku Law Review* (4 a year), *Journal of Economic Studies* (4 a year), *Journal of Ryukoku University* (2 a year), *Ryukoku Journal of Humanities and Sciences* (2 a year), *Journal of Intercultural Communication* (1 a year)

DEANS

Faculty of Business Administration: RINPACHI MISHIMA
Faculty of Economics: HIROKUNI TERADA
Faculty of Intercultural Communication: MASANORI HIGA
Faculty of Law: KEIJI NAGARA
Faculty of Letters: EGUN MIKOGAMI
Faculty of Science of Technology: YOUICHI KOBUCHI
Faculty of Sociology: KAZUNORI KOGA
Japanese Culture and Language Programme: ITSUYO HIGASHINAKA
Junior College: DOSHO WAKAHARA

PROFESSORS

Faculty of Business Administration:

ABE, D., Theoretical Economics
FUJITA, N., Japanese Business History
HARA, M., International Accounting Theory
HAYASHI, A., Corporate Accounting
HAYASHI, K., Cost Accounting
HITOMI, K., Manufacturing Systems Engineering
HONDA, H., Corporate Finance Theory
INOUE, H., Business Management
INOUE, K., Finance Theory
KAMEI, M., International Business Management
KANEKO, A., Insurance Theory
KATAGIRI, M., Marketing Theory
KAWASHIMA, M., Marketing Theory
KITAZAWA, Y., Small Business Management
KOIKE, T., Information Processing Management
KONNO, T., Information Processing Management
MASAOKA, M., Managerial Accounting
MISHIMA, R., Business Administration Psychology

MORIYA, H., Merchandise Studies
NAKAYAMA, J., German Literature
NATSUME, K., International Business Strategy
NISHIHARA, J., Japanese Language Education
NISHIKAWA, K., Labour Management
NOMA, K., Marketing Research
OHGAI, T., International Business
OHNISHI, K., Information Industry
OHSUGI, M., International Finance Theory
ONO, K., Accounting
SATO, K., Marketing
SHIGEMOTO, N., Business Organization Theory
SHIMADA, H., Business Management
SHIMADA, M., English Linguistics
SUGIMURA, M., French Literature
TAKADA, S., Religion
TERASHIMA, K., Information Management
TOGAMI, M., Sociology
TOYOSHIMA, M., Engineering Management
YAMASHITA, A., Macroeconomics
YOKOYAMA, K., Regional Sociology
YOSHIHIRO, S., Primate Ecology
YUI, H., Industrial Engineering

Faculty of Economics:

AZUMA, T., Applied Physiology
HATA, N., Health Industry Economics
HIGUCHI, M., Middle Spanish Literature
IGUCHI, T., Industrial Organization
ISHIKAWA, R., Labour Economics
ITOH, T., Mathematics
KANEKO, H., Economic Theory
KAWAMURA, T., German Literature
KAWAMURA, Y., Development Sociology
LAKSHMAN, W. D., Economic Theory
MATSUOKA, K., Economic Policy
MATSUOKA, T., Theory of Modern Capitalism
MISAKI, S., Economic Theory
MIZUHARA, S., Economic Thought
NAKAMURA, H., Regional Economics
NISHIBORI, F., Theoretical Economics
OBAYASHI, M., African American Development
OISHI, M., English Language
OKACHI, K., International Economic Theory
OMAE, S., Social Policy
OTSUKI, M., German Economic History
SHIMUZU, K., American Literature
TAJIRI, E., Teaching Japanese
TAKADA, M., Public Finance
TAKENAKA, E., Labour Economics
TANAKA, Y., Economic Systems Theory
TERADA, H., Financial Theory
TSUBOUCHI, R., Sociology
YAMAMOTO, S., International Economics
YOSHIMURA, H., Indian Mahayanist Buddhist Thought
YUNO, T., International Finance

Faculty of Intercultural Communication:

AKAGI, H., Japanese Industrial Arts
FUKUDA, K., The United Nations and Japan
FURMANOVSKY, M., American History, TESOL
HABITO, R., Indian and Buddhist Philosophy
HAMANO, S., Human Rights Law, Western Political Thought
HIGA, M., Applied Linguistics
KIGLICS, I., Economics
KIMURA, B., Psychiatry
KOIZUMI, T., Comparative Study of Civilizations
KWON, O., Education
MACADAM, J., Comparative Culture
MATSUBARA, H., Western History
MATSUI, K., Energy Economics
MIYAKAWA, C., French Literature and Language
MURATA, S., Comparative Study of Educational Systems

NAGASAKI, N., Modern South Asian History
PANG, C., Japanese Language, Chinese Language
SAKAMOTO, S., Food Culture, Ethnobotany
SIMPSON, J., World Agriculture
SUDO, M., Comparative Study of Folklore
SUEHARA, T., Cultural Anthropology, Economic Anthropology
SUGIMURA, T., History of Middle Eastern Art
TOH, N., International Communications and Relations
TSURUTA, K., Comparative Literature
UEYAMA, D., Buddhist Studies

Faculty of Law:

FUJIWARA, H., Civil Law
FUKUSHIMA, I., Criminal Law
HAYASHI, T., Buddhism
HIGASHI, F., Physical Education
HIRANO, T., Political Processes
HIRANO, T., The Constitution; Religious Law
HONMA, Y., Civil Proceedings Act
ISHIDA, T., Political Theory
ISHII, K., Philosophy of Law
ISHIZUKA, S., Criminology
IWATA, N., Chinese Language
KATSURA, F., English Language and Literature
KAWABATA, M., African Politics
KAWASUMI, Y., Civil Law
KIM, D., International Human Rights Laws
KISAKA, J., Japanese Political History
KONDO, H., 18th-century English Novel
KUBOTA, M., Sports Sociology
MIKAMI, T., Administrative Law
MIZUNO, T., Tax Law
NAGARA, K., Administrative Law
NISHIO, S., Commercial Law
SAKAI, S., Current Middle East Politics
SAKAMOTO, M., Administration
SHIRAISHI, K., Public Administration
TAKAHASHI, S., Italian Fascism
TAKEHISA, S., Commercial Law
TAKITA, R., Commercial Politics
TANAKA, N., International Law
TODORIKI, K., Sports Sociology
TOMINO, K., Regional Autonomy
TSUJITA, J., Astrophysics
UEDA, K., Constitutional Law
WAKITA, S., Labour Law
YOROI, T., Labour Law

Faculty of Letters:

AKAMATSU, T., History of Japanese Buddhism
AKIMOTO, M., Japanese Language and Literature
ASADA, M., Japanese Tendai Sect
ASAI, N., Shin Buddhism
CHIN, K., Chinese Language and Literature
DOI, J., Modern Japanese Literature
ECHIZENYA, H., Modern Japanese Culture
FUJIMOTO, M., American Culture
FUKUSHIMA, H., Modern Japanese History
FUROMOTO, T., Anglo-Irish Literature
HAYASHIDA, Y., Eastern History
HIGASHINAKA, I., English Romantic Literature
HIRATA, A., Modern Japanese Thought
ICHIMURA, T., Psychology
INOUE, Y., English Language
ITOI, M., Japanese Language
IZUMOJI, O., Japanese Literature
KAGOTANI, M., Japanese History
KATSUBE, M., Japanese Archaeology
KIDA, T., Modern Chinese History
KITANO, A., Modern Japanese Literature
KODAMA, D., History of Indian Buddhism
KODAMA, S., History of Japanese Religion
KODANI, S., English Literature
KOJIMA, M., Intercultural Pedagogy
KUDARA, K., Buddhism
LAZARIN, M., Philosophy
MARUYAMA, T., Philosophy

MASUDA, R., English Literature
MIKOGAMI, E., Indian Philosophy
MIKOGAMI, E., Modern Western Philosophy
MITSUKAWA, T., Indian Buddhism
MIYAMA, Y., Japanese Literature of the Edo Period
MIYAMOTO, S., Modern English Novels
MIZOGUCHI, K., Philosophy
NAGAKAWA, H., American Literature
NAKAYAMA, S., Chinese Buddhism
NISHIYAMA, R., Mathematics
ODA, Y., Eastern History
OHMINE, A., Philosophy
OHTA, T., Shin Buddhism
OHTORI, K., Tanka Poetry in the Middle Ages
OKA, R., Thought of Shiran
OKAZAKI, K., Japanese Archaeology
SHIYOUBO, T., English Linguistics
TAKEDA, H., History of Indian Buddhism
TAKEDA, R., Buddhism
TANAKA, M., Educational Psychology
TANAKA, S., Psychology
TATSUGUCHI, M., Buddhist Theology
TOKUNAGA, D., Shin Buddhism
TOMITA, M., Educational Technology
TSUNEYOSHI, K., Methods and Curriculum of Education
TSUZUKI, A., East Asian History
UESUGI, T., Philosophy of Education
UMITANI, N., Philosophy of Education
UWAYOKOTE, M., Japanese History
WATANABE, K., History of Sports Philosophy
WATANABE, T., Chinese Buddhist Theory
YAMADA, Y., English Literature
YATA, R., History of Shin Buddhism

Faculty of Science and Technology:

ABE, H., Plasma Physics
ARIKI, Y., Pattern Recognition
DOHSHITA, S., Speech and Audio Media Processing
ENAMI, K., Materials Science and Engineering
FUJIMOTO, Y., Information Engineering
GOTOH, Y., Materials Science
HARADA, T., Catalytic Chemistry
HAYASHI, H., Polymer Science
HORIKAWA, T., Mechanical Engineering and Materials Science
IIDA, S., Solid State Physics
IKEDA, T., Applied Analysis and Computational Science
IWAMOTO, T., Robot Engineering
JIKU, F., Environmental Engineering
KAIYOH, H., Communications Engineering
KAMIJOH, E., Inorganic Functional Materials
KATOH, K., Multivariable Functions
KAWASHIMA, H., Mechanical Engineering
KOBAYASHI, K., Metallic Materials Chemistry
KOBUCHI, Y., Information Science
KOKUBU, H., Mathematics and Dynamic Systems
KONDOH, H., Germanic Literature and Languages
KUNIHIRO, T., Nuclear and Elementary Particle Physics
KUTSUNA, H., Mechanical Engineering
MATSUMOTO, W., Mathematics (Analysis)
MATSUSHITA, T., Coordination Chemistry
MIYASHITA, T., Mechanical Physics
MORITA, Y., Nonlinear Differential Equations
NAKAMURA, T., Computer Science
NAKANISHI, S., Mechanical Engineering
NISHIHARA, H., Superconductivity; Physics
OHJI, K., Mechanical Engineering
OHTSUKA, N., Materials Strength and Fracture Mechanics
OKADA, Y., Information Processing
OKAMOTO, Y., Anglo-Irish Literature
OZAWA, T., Information Technology
SAITOH, M., Optics

SOHMA, K., Buddhism
TAGUCHI, T., Health and Physical Education
TAKAHASHI, T., Science Education and Educational Technology
TAKAYANAGI, K., Astronomy
TSUBOI, Y., Mechatronics and Electronic Control
TSUTSUMI, K., Intelligent Robotic Systems
UDO, A., Systems Engineering
URABE, K., Ceramics
WADA, T., Inorganic Materials Chemistry
YOTSUTANI, S., Mathematics (Analysis)
YUKIMOTO, Y., Semiconductor Electronics

Faculty of Sociology:

FUKUZAKI, S., Health Science
FUNAHASHI, K., Community and Regional Studies
FUSHIMI, Y., Social Welfare Finance
HAYASE, K., Senior Citizens' Welfare
KAMEYAMA, Y., Sociology
KANBAYASHI, S., Social Technology for the Disabled
KASAHARA, S., Industrial Sociology
KISHIDA, H., Clinical Psychology
KODAMA, N., Sociology
KOGA, K., Religion
KOSHII, I., Social Psychology
KUCHIBA, M., Comparative Sociology
MATSUSHITA, K., Population Economics
MATSUTANI, N., Social Security Theory
MORI, Y., Social Welfare Institutions
MUKAI, T., Rural Sociology
MURAI, R., Welfare for the Disabled
NORIKUMO, S., Information Engineering
ODA, K., Social Welfare
OGASAWARA, M., Theoretical Sociology
OSHIDA, E., Mass Media Civilization
SASAKI, M., Social Work
SEKIGUCHI, S., Psychology
SHIMIZU, H., Everyday Life and Religion
SHIMIZU, K., Social Welfare
TAKEHARA, H., Principles of Education
TANAKA, S., Industrial Sociology
TANO, T., Health and Physical Education
TERAKAWA, Y., Religious Psychology
WATARI, H., English Philology

Junior College:

ASAEDA, Z., History of Japanese Buddhism
HAMAGAMI, Y., Child Welfare
IHARA, K., Nursing Technology
IIDA, K., International Social Welfare
IKUTA, M., Social Welfare for the Elderly
KATOH, H., History of Social Welfare Policy
KAWAZOE, T., Shin Buddhism
NAGAI, T., Developmental Psychology
OHNISHI, M., Community Health
TANIMOTO, M., Philosophy
TATSUDANI, A., History of Shin Buddhism
WAKAHARA, D., Pedagogy
YAMADA, M., Indian Buddhism
YAMADA, Y., Shin Buddhism
YOSHIDA, K., Discrimination Problems

ATTACHED RESEARCH INSTITUTES

Institute of Buddhist Cultural Studies: Shichijo Ohmiya, Shimogyo-ku, Kyoto 600; Dir KYOSHIN ASANO.

Joint Research Centre for Science and Technology: 1-5 Yokoya, Seta Ohe-cho, Otsu, Shiga 520-21; Dir KEISUKE KOBAYASHI.

Research Institute for the Social Sciences: 67 Tsukamoto-cho, Fukakusa, Fushimi-ku, Kyoto; Dir TAKESHI HIRANO.

Socio-cultural Research Institute: 1-5 Yokoya, Seta Ohe-cho, Otsu, Shiga 520-21; Dir KENICHI MATSUI.

UNIVERSITY OF THE SACRED HEART, TOKYO

Hiroo 4-chome 3-1, Shibuya-ku, Tokyo 150-8938

Telephone: (3) 3407-5811

Fax: (3) 5485-3884
E-mail: wwwadmin@u-sacred-heart.ac.jp
Internet: www.u-sacred-heart.ac.jp
Founded 1948
Private control
Academic year: April to March
Pres.: Prof. HEIJI TERANAKA
Vice-Pres. for Graduate Studies: YOSHIKO OKAZAKI
Vice-Pres. for Students: MITSUKO KANEKO
Vice-Pres. for Studies: KENSUKE SUGAWARA
Business Chief: KIMIO MURAMATSU
Registrar: YORIKO YOSHIDA
Librarian: Prof. HITOSHI OBARA
Library of 390,000 vols
Number of teachers: 68 full-time, 318 part-time
Number of students: 2,241
Publications: *Seishin Ronso* (Seishin Studies, 2 a year), *Religion and Civilization* (Bulletin of the Research Institute for the Study of Christian Culture, 1 a year).

SANNO INSTITUTE OF MANAGEMENT

6-39-15 Todoroki, Setagaya, Tokyo 158-8630
Telephone: (3) 3704-1111
Fax: (3) 3704-1608
Internet: www.sanno.ac.jp
Founded 1925
Consists of SANNO Graduate School (MBA Programme), SANNO University Isehara (4-year degree course in Management and Informatics, and distance education course), SANNO College Jiyugaoka (2-year degree course, and distance education course)
Academic year: April to March
Chair.: SHUNICHI UENO
Pres., Sanno University: MASAAKI HARADA
Exec. Dir: TOSHIKAZU TAMURA
Library of 345,000 vols
Number of teachers: 126
Number of students: 7,410 (excluding distance education course students)
Publications: *SANNO College Bulletin* (2 a year), *SANNO College Jiyugaoka Bulletin* (1 a year), *Journal of the Management Research Centre* (irregular)

DEANS

Business Administration: MICHIKO MORIWAKI
Graduate School: TOSHIKAZU TAMURA
School of Management and Information Science: MINAMI MIYAUCHI

SAPPORO GAKUIN UNIVERSITY

11-Banchi, Bunkyodai, Ebetsu, Hokkaido 069-8555
Telephone: (11) 386-8111
Fax: (11) 386-8113
E-mail: kouhou@ims.sgu.ac.jp
Internet: www.sgu.ac.jp
Founded 1946
Pres.: AKIKO FUSE
Faculties of Commerce, Economics, Humanities, Law, Social Information.

SAPPORO UNIVERSITY

3-7-3-1 Nishioka, Toyohira-ku, Sapporo 062-8520
Telephone: (11) 852-1181
E-mail: koho@sapporo-u.ac.jp
Internet: www.sapporo-u.ac.jp
Founded 1967
Private control
Academic year: April to March
Pres.: MASAYUKI KIMURA
Head Administrator: K. KUROSAWA
Librarian: N. TAKAMATSU

Library of 426,000 vols
Number of teachers: 162
Number of students: 6,700
Publications: *Sapporo Law Review* (2 a year), *Journal of Comparative Cultures* (2 a year), *Sapporo University Journal* (2 a year), *Industrial and Business Journal* (2 a year)

DEANS

Faculty of Business Administration: J. ARAKAWA
Faculty of Cultural Studies: M. YAMAGUCHI
Faculty of Economics: K. MOTODA
Faculty of Foreign Languages: M. KATO
Faculty of Law: H. TANAKA
Graduate School of Law: K. SAKAI
Women's Junior College: A. TODA

SEIJO UNIVERSITY

6-1-20 Seijo, Setagaya-ku, Tokyo 157-8511
Telephone: (3) 3482-6020
Fax: (3) 3482-6360
E-mail: info@seijo.ac.jp
Internet: www.seijo.ac.jp
Founded 1950
Private control
Academic year: April to March
Pres.: YUJI YUI
Admin. Sec.: M. SHIMANO
Librarian: H. FUKUMITSU
Library of 688,395 vols
Number of teachers: 584 (148 full-time, 436 part-time)
Number of students: 5,999

DEANS

Faculty of Arts and Literature: EIJI UENO
Faculty of Economics: YOSHIO ASAI
Faculty of Law: HIROYUKI KONNO
Faculty of Social Innovation: MITSUNOBU SHINOHARA
Junior College: MASUMI ISHINABE

SEIKEI UNIVERSITY

3-3-1 Kichijoji-Kitamachi, Musashino City, Tokyo 180-8633
Telephone: (422) 37-3531
Fax: (422) 37-3883
Internet: www.seikei.ac.jp
Founded 1949
Academic year: April to March
President: KEISUKE KURITA
Librarian: HARUO TANAKA
Library of 742,000 vols
Number of teachers: 183 full-time
Number of students: 8,840 (8,584 undergraduate, 256 postgraduate)
Publications: *Seikei Daigaku Ippankenkyu Hokoku* (Bulletin), *Seikei Daigaku Kogaku Hokoku* (Technology Report), *Journal of Asian and Pacific Studies*

DEANS

Faculty of Economics: C. KOMURA
Faculty of Engineering: Y. KAWADA
Faculty of Humanities: K. AONO
Faculty of Law: E. UEMURA

DIRECTORS

Center for Asian and Pacific Studies: T. TOMITA
Information Processing Center: A. NAKAZATO

SENSHU UNIVERSITY

8 Kandajimbo-cho 3-chome, Chiyoda-ku, Tokyo 101-8425
Telephone: (44) 911-1250
Fax: (44) 911-1243
E-mail: iaffairs@acc.senshu-u.ac.jp

Internet: www.senshu-u.ac.jp
Founded 1880
Academic year: April to March
Pres.: YOSHIHIRO HIDAKA
Librarian: T. OBA
Library of 1,110,000 vols
Number of teachers: 400 full-time
Number of students: 20,472

DEANS

School of Business Administration: K. UOTA
School of Commerce: K. ONISHI
School of Economics: S. SAKAI
School of Law: B. KOHATA
School of Literature: T. ARAKI
School of Network and Information: M. SAKAMOTO
Graduate School of Business Administration: N. TAKEMURA
Graduate School of Commerce: N. OGUCHI
Graduate School of Economics: M. YABUKI
Graduate School of Humanities: T. SUZUKI
Graduate School of Law: T. TAKAGAI
Professional School of Legal Affairs: Y. HIRAI

SETSUNAN UNIVERSITY

17-8 Ikedanakamachi, Neyagawa-shi, Osaka 572-8508
Telephone: (72) 839-9102
Fax: (72) 826-5100
Internet: www.setsunan.ac.jp
Founded 1975
Chair.: MASAO SAKAGUCHI
Pres.: MITSUNORI IMAI

DEANS

Faculty of Business Administration and Information: TATSUMI SHIMADA
Faculty of Engineering: YOSHIO NAMITA
Faculty of International Languages and Cultures: MITSUNORI IMAI
Faculty of Law: MASUYUKI MORIMOTO
Faculty of Pharmaceutical Sciences: NOBORU YATA

SHIKOKU UNIVERSITY

Ojin-cho, Tokushima-shi, Tokushima, 771-1192
Telephone: (88) 665-9911
Fax: (88) 665-8037
E-mail: oip@shikoku-u.ac.jp
Internet: www.shikoku-u.ac.jp
Founded 1966
Pres.: NOBORU FUKUOKA
Library of 317,470 vols
Number of teachers: 163
Number of students: 3,114
Faculty of Literature; Graduate School of Management and Information Science.

SOKA UNIVERSITY

1-236, Tangi-cho, Hachioji, Tokyo 192-8577
Telephone: (426) 91-8200
Fax: (426) 91-2039
E-mail: adm@j.soka.ac.jp
Internet: www.soka.ac.jp
Founded 1971
Private control
Academic year: April to March
Pres.: Prof. Dr MASAMI WAKAE
Vice-Pres: Prof. KATSUHIKO FUKUSHIMA, Prof. MASASUKE NIHEI
Librarian: Prof. EIICHI IMAGAWA
Library of 1,005,000 vols
Number of teachers: 295
Number of students: 7,842
Publication: *SUN* (Soka University News, 4 a year)

DEANS

Division of Correspondence Education: Prof. TADASHIGE TAKAMURA

Faculty of Business Administration: Prof. KAORU YAMANAKA

Faculty of Economics: Prof. Dr HIDETAKA HASEBE

Faculty of Education: Prof. RIKIO KIMATA

Faculty of Engineering: Prof. YOSHIMI TESHI-GAWARA

Faculty of Law: Prof. AKIRA KIRIGAYA

Faculty of Letters: Prof. YUTAKA ISHIGAMI

Graduate School of Economics: Prof. KINJI UEDA

Graduate School of Engineering: Prof. KOJIRO KOBAYASHI

Graduate School of Law: Prof. KAZUO KAWA-SAKI

Graduate School of Letters: Prof. KAZUNORI KUMAGAI

Institute of Japanese Language: Prof. KEIKO ISHIKAWA

DIRECTORS

Institute for the Comparative Study of Cultures: M. KITA

Institute of Asian Studies: E. IMAGAWA

Institute of Life Science: M. WAKAE

Institute of Systems Science: M. WAKAE

International Research Institute for the Advanced Study of Buddhism: H. KANNO

Peace Research Institute: T. TAKAMURA

SOPHIA UNIVERSITY
(Jôchi Daigaku)

Chiyoda-ku, Kioicho 7–1, Tokyo 102-8554

Telephone: (3) 3238-3111

Fax: (3) 3238-3885

Internet: www.sophia.ac.jp

Founded 1913

Private control (Society of Jesus)

Languages of instruction: Japanese, English

Academic year: April to March

Chancellor: TOSHIAKI KOSO

Pres.: YOSHIAKI ISHIZAWA

Vice-Pres.: J. HOLLERICH

Vice-Pres.: J. KOBAYASHI

Vice-Pres.: M. YAJIMA

Registrar: M. FUJIMURA

Library: see Libraries and Archives

Number of teachers: 505

Number of students: 11,963 (1,182 graduates, 10,509 undergraduates, 272 law school)

Publications: Monumenta Nipponica (in English, 4 a year), Sophia (in Japanese, 4 a year)

DEANS

Faculty of Comparative Culture: Y. OKADA

Faculty of Economics: K. YAMADA

Faculty of Foreign Studies: T. UENO

Faculty of Human Sciences: I. TOCHIMOTO

Faculty of Humanities: Y. OHASHI

Faculty of Law: N. TSUJI

Faculty of Science and Technology: T. HAYA-SHITA

Faculty of Theology: T. SAKUMA

DIRECTORS

European Institute: M. NAKAMURA

Iberoamerican Institute: M. NEVES

Institute for Global Concern: K. NAKANO

Institute for Studies of the Global Environment: H. KITO

Institute of American and Canadian Studies: K. OSHIO

Institute of Asian Cultures: T. TERADA

Institute of Christian Culture: T. SAKUMA

Institute of Comparative Culture: J. FARRER

Institute of Medieval Thought: N. SATO

Life Science Institute: K. KUMAKURA

Linguistic Institute for International Communication: K. YOSHIDA

TAKUSHOKU UNIVERSITY

3-4-14 Kohinata, Bunkyo-ku, Tokyo 112

Telephone: (3) 3947-2261

E-mail: web_int@ofc.takushoku-u.ac.jp

Internet: www.takushoku-u.ac.jp

Founded 1900

Campuses at Hachioji and Bunkyo

Chancellor: S. ODAMURA

Pres.: TOSHIO WATANABE

Chair. of Board of Directors: T. FUJITO

Librarian: S. KORI

Library of 440,000 vols

Number of teachers: 528

Number of students: 10,377

Publications: Hokoku (1 a year), Kaigai Jijo (Journal of World Affairs, 12 a year), Takushoku Daigaku Ronshu (6 a year)

DEANS

Faculty of Commerce: T. TAKAHASHI

Faculty of Engineering: M. SAKATA

Faculty of Foreign Languages: T. WADA

Faculty of Political Science and Economics: K. KOBAYASHI

Graduate School: T. OSAKAI

Hokkaido Takushoku Junior College: T. ISHIKAWA

Special Japanese Language Course for Foreign Students: M. ARAKI

Takushoku Junior College: T. GOTO

TAMAGAWA UNIVERSITY

6-1-1 Tamagawa Gakuen 6-chome, Machida, Tokyo 194-8610

Telephone: (427) 39-8111

Fax: (427) 39-1181

E-mail: webmaster@tamagawa.ac.jp

Internet: www.tamagawa.ac.jp

Founded 1929

Private control

Language of instruction: Japanese

Academic year: April to March

Pres.: YOSHIAKI OBARA

Registrar: TAKASHI URATA

Librarian: HARUA TODA

Library of 860,000 vols, 8,000 periodicals

Number of teachers: 787 (351 full-time, 436 part-time)

Number of students: 7,774

Publications: Mitsubachi Kagaku (4 a year), Shoho (1 a year), Zenjin Education (12 a year)

DEANS

Associate Degree Junior College for Women: TOMIO OZAWA

Department of Education by Correspondence: HIROSHI YONEYAMA

Faculty of Agriculture: TADAYUKI ISHIYAMA

Faculty of Arts and Education: HIROSHI YONEYAMA

Faculty of Engineering: HIDETAKE TANIBAYA-SHI

Graduate School for Agriculture: MITSUO MATSUKA

Graduate School for Education and Letters: YASUTADA TAKAHASHI

Graduate School for Engineering: TAKURO KOIKE

Junior College for Women: MICHIAKI NAGAI

TEZUKAYAMA UNIVERSITY

7-1-1 Tezukayama, Nara City 631-8501

Telephone: (742) 48-9122

Fax: (742) 48-9135

E-mail: webmaster@tezukayama-u.ac.jp

Internet: www.tezukayama-u.ac.jp

Founded 1941

Library of 280,000 vols

Number of teachers: 109

Number of students: 4,166

Faculties of Business Administration, Economics, Humanities, Law and Policy.

TOHOKU GAKUIN UNIVERSITY

1-3-1 Tsuchitoi, Aoba-ku, Sendai 980-8511

Telephone: (2) 264-6425

Fax: (2) 264-6515

E-mail: ico@tscc.tohoku-gakuin.ac.jp

Internet: www.tohoku-gakuin.ac.jp

Founded 1886

Private control

Language of instruction: Japanese

Academic year: April to March

Library of 1,200,000 vols

President: NOZOMU HOSHIMIYA

Vice-Presidents: YOSHITAKA SHIBATA, MAKOTO SAITO

Number of teachers: 511

Number of students: 12,518

Publications: Church and Theology (2 a year), Economics (3 a year), History and Geography (2 a year), Human, Jurisprudence (2 a year), Linguistic and Information Sciences (3 a year), Science and Engineering Report (2 a year), Tohoku Gakuin University Review English Language and Literature (2 a year)

DEANS

Faculty of Economics: YOSHINORI HARADA

Faculty of Engineering: GINRO ENDO

Faculty of Fitness and Administration: NOBU-MASA YAMAMOTO

Faculty of Law: RYUICHIRO TAKAGI

Faculty of Letters: KENICHI ENDO

Faculty of Liberal Arts: MASAHIRO SAKUMA

TOKAI UNIVERSITY EDUCATIONAL SYSTEM

2-28-4 Tomigaya, Shibuya-ku, Tokyo 151-8677

Telephone: (3) 3467-2211

Fax: (3) 3467-0197

E-mail: pr@yyg.u-tokai.ac.jp

Internet: www.pr.tokai.ac.jp

Founded 1942

Chairman and President: TATSURO MATSU-MAE

DIRECTORS

Okinawa Regional Research Centre: SOUNO-SUKE KATORI

Research Institute for Educational Development: SOUNOSUKE KATORI

Research Institute of Modern Civilization: TATSURO MATSUMAE

Research Institute of Science and Technology: SOUNOSUKE KATORI

Strategic Peace and International Affairs Research Institute: NORIO MATSUMAE

Tokai University European Centre (Denmark): MORITO TAKAHASHI

Tokai University Pacific Centre (Hawaii): KIYOSHI YAMADA

Tokai University Research and Information Centre: YOSHIAKI MATSUMAE

Tokai University Space Information Centre: HARUHISA SHIMODA

CONSTITUENT UNIVERSITIES

Hokkaido Tokai University

Telephone: (11) 571-5111
Fax: (11) 571-7879
E-mail: kikaku@ss.htokai.ac.jp
Internet: www.htokai.ac.jp

Sapporo Campus: 5-1-1-1 Minamisawa, Minami-ku, Sapporo, Hokkaido 005-8601; tel. (11) 571-5111; fax (11) 571-7879
Asahikawa Campus: 224 Chuwa, Kamui-cho, Asahikawa, Hokkaido 070-8601; tel. (166) 61-5111; fax (166) 62-8180

Founded 1977
Academic year: April to March
President: SHUNMEI MITSUZAWA
Librarian: EIICHI SATO
Library of 179,000 vols
Number of teachers: 112 full-time
Number of students: 2,515

DEANS

School of Art and Technology: JUN MIKAMI
School of International Cultural Relations: KOUJI KOBAYASHI
School of Engineering: MINORU KOUTAKI

CHAIRMEN

Graduate School of Arts: JUN MIKAMI
Graduate School of Science and Engineering: TETSUO SHIMONO

DIRECTORS

Research Institute for Higher Education Programmes: YASUNARI KURIHARA
Cultural Institute of Northern Region: TSUTOMU KOKAWA
Environmental Research Institute: HIROYUKI NISHIMURA

Kyushu Tokai University

Telephone: (96) 382-1141
Fax: (96) 381-7956
E-mail: kikaku@jsmail.js.ktokai-u.ac.jp
Internet: www.ktokai-u.ac.jp

Kumamoto Campus: 9-1-1 Toroku, Kumamoto-shi, Kumamoto 862-8652; tel. (96) 382-1141; fax (96) 381-7956
Aso Campus: Kawayou, Choyo-son, Aso-gun, Kumamoto 869-1404; tel. (9676) 7-0611; fax (9676) 7-2053

Founded 1973
Academic year: April to March
President: YOSHIAKI MATSUMAE
Librarian: TAKAAKI TSUKIJI
Library of 240,965 vols
Number of teachers: 138 full-time
Number of students: 3,437

DEANS

School of Agriculture: KIHACHIROU NOBUKUNI
School of Engineering: CHIKAE WATANABE
School of Information Science: SHOJI KAIDA

CHAIRMEN

Graduate School of Agriculture: KIHACHIROU NOBUKUNI
Graduate School of Engineering: CHIKAE WATANABE

DIRECTORS

Institute of Industrial Science and Technology: ICHIRO TAKAGI
Agricultural Research Institute: TAKAO TORIKATA

Tokai University

Telephone: (463) 58-1211
Fax: (463) 50-2052
E-mail: kikaku@tsc.u-tokai.ac.jp
Internet: www.u-tokai.ac.jp

Shonan Campus: 4-1-1 Kitakaname, Hiratsuka-shi, Kanagawa 259-1292; tel. (463) 58-1211; fax (463) 35-2458
Yoyogi Campus: 2-28-4 Tomigaya, Shibuya-ku, Tokyo 151-8677; tel. (3) 3467-2211
Shimizu Campus: 3-20-1 Orido, Shimizu-shi, Shizuoka 424-8610; tel. (543) 34-0411
Isehara Campus: Bouseidai, Isehara-shi, Kanagawa 259-1193; tel. (463) 93-1121
Numazu Campus: 317 Nishino, Numazu-shi, Shizuoka 410-0395; tel. (559) 68-1111
Kumamoto Campus: 9-1-1, Toroku, Kumamoto 862-8656; tel. (96) 382-1141
Aso Campus: Kawayo, Minami-Aso-mura, Aso-gun, Kumamoto 869-1404
Sapporo Campus: Minamisawa 5-jo 1-1-1, Minami-ku, Sapporo-shi, Hokkaido 005-8601; tel. (11) 571-5111
Asahikawa Campus: Chuwa 224, Kamii-cho, Asahikawa-shi, Hokkaido 070-8601

Founded 1946
Private control
Language of instruction: Japanese
Academic year: April to March
Chancellor: Prof. JIRO TAKANO
Librarian: TASUKU HAYAMI
Library of 2,647,482 vols
Number of teachers: 1,736 full-time
Number of students: 30,000
Publication: *Tokai Journal of Experimental and Clinical Medicine*

DEANS

Agriculture: TATSURO MURATA
Art and Technology: TAKUMI HAYASHI
Biological Science and Engineering: KENJI YANO
Business Studies: JINICHI OKUYAMA
Foreign Language Centre: RYOJI OKUDA (Exec. Dir)
Health Sciences: MICHIKO MIZOGUCHI
High Technology for Human Welfare: KIYOSHI NOZU
Humanities and Culture: RYUTARO KAJII
Industrial Engineering: TSUTOMU ICHIKAWA
Information and Telecommunicatoin Engineering: TOSHIO NAKASHITA
Information Sciences and Technology: TOSHIO NAKASHITA
International Cultural Relations: SATORU MABUCHI
Japanese Language Course for Foreign Students: HARUMI MURAKAMI (Head)
Law: KAZUHIRO YOSHIKAWA
Letters: MICHIKO SAITO (Dean)
Marine Science and Technology: NOBORU KATO
Medicine: YUTAKA IMAI
Physical Education: YASUHIRO YAMASHITA
Political Science and Economics: AKIRA KONAKAYAMA
Science: YASUYUKI MIURA
Tokai Institute of Global Education and Research: HIROHISA UCHIDA (Exec. Dir)
Tourism: RYOZO MATSUMOTO

CHAIRMEN

Graduate School of Arts: HARUMI KOSHIBA
Graduate School of Economics: OSAMU TAKENAKA
Graduate School of Engineering: HIROMASA TAKEUCHI
Graduate School of Health Sciences: KEIKO SHICHITA
Graduate School of High Technology for Human Welfare: MASAAKI SHINJI
Graduate School of Law: SHIGERU OTSUKA
Graduate School of Letters: NOBUYUKI WATASE
Graduate School of Marine Science and Technology: YOSHIMASA TOYOTA
Graduate School of Medicine: KIYOSHI KUROKAWA

Graduate School of Physical Education: NAOHISA MATSUNAGA
Graduate School of Political Science: YOSHITERU MAKITA
Graduate School of Science: JIRO TAKANO

TOKIWA UNIVERSITY

1-430-1 Miwa, Mito-shi, Ibaraki Prefecture 310-8585

Telephone: (29) 232-2511
Fax: (29) 231-6078
E-mail: kouhou@tokiwa.ac.jp
Internet: www.tokiwa.ac.jp

Founded 1983
Chair.: HIDEMICHI MOROSAWA
Pres.: ISATO TAKAGI

Colleges of Applied International Studies, Community Development, Human Science; Graduate School of Human Science.

TOKYO UNIVERSITY OF PHARMACY AND LIFE SCIENCES

1432-1 Horinouchi, Hachioji, Tokyo 192-03

Telephone: (426) 76-5111
Internet: www.toyaku.ac.jp

Founded 1880
Pres.: Dr T. YAMAKAWA
Librarian: Prof. A. OHTA
Library of 100,000 vols, 500 periodicals
Number of teachers: 200
Number of students: 2,200

Schools of Life Sciences and Pharmacy.

TOKYO DENKI DAIGAKU
(Tokyo Denki University)

2-2 Kanda-Nishiki-cho, Chiyoda-ku, Tokyo 101-8457

Telephone: (3) 5280-3555
Fax: (3) 5280-3623
E-mail: gakuchoshitsu@jim.ac.jp
Internet: www.dendai.ac.jp

Founded 1907
Academic year: April to March
President: Dr YOSHIHIRO TOMA
General Director of Multimedia Resource Centre and Library: Dr T. SAITO
Library of 321,481 vols, 2,975 periodicals
Number of teachers: 748 (355 full-time, 393 part-time)
Number of students: 11,563

DEANS

Graduate School of Engineering: J. IWAMOTO
Graduate School of Science and Engineering: M. TAKIZAWA
School of Engineering: T. IBAMOTO
School of Engineering (Evening Programme): S. MURAKAMI
School of the Information Environment: S. NAKAMURA
School of Science and Engineering: Y. KASHIMURA

DIRECTORS

Applied Superconductivity Research Laboratory: I. NEMOTO
Centre for Research Collaboration: H. TOMITA
Frontier Research and Development Centre: Y. UCHIKAWA
Research Institute for Construction Technology: M. TACHIBANA
Research Institute for Technology: H. INABA

TOKYO DENTAL COLLEGE

1-2-2 Masago, Mihama-ku, Chiba 261-8502

Telephone: (43) 270-3764
Fax: (43) 270-3765
E-mail: int@tdc.ac.jp
Internet: www.tdc.ac.jp
Founded 1890
Academic year: April to March
Dean: Prof. YUZURU KANEKO
Vice-Deans: Prof. MASASHI YAKUSHIJI
Library of 198,000 vols
Number of teachers: 306
Number of students: 983 (802 undergraduate, 181 postgraduate)
Publications: *Bulletin* (in English, 4 a year), *Shikwa Gakuho* (research journal, in Japanese, every 2 months).

TOKYO KEIZAI UNIVERSITY

1-7-34 Minami-cho, Kokubunji-shi, Tokyo 185-8502

Telephone: (42) 328-7711
Internet: www.tku.ac.jp
Founded 1900 as Okura Commerce School
Private control
Academic year: April to March
President: KATSUHIKO MURAKAMI
Chief Administrative Officer: TOURU SASAKI
Librarian: SHIGEKAZU KUKITA
Library of 640,000 vols
Number of teachers: 445
Number of students: 7,673
Publications: *Journal of Tokyo Keizai University* (6 a year), *Journal of Humanities and Natural Sciences* (2 a year), *Journal of Communication Studies* (2 a year), *Tokyo Kezai Law Review* (2 a year)

DEANS

Faculty of Business Administration: YOSHIAKI JINNAI
Faculty of Communication Studies: KAORU YAMAZAKI
Faculty of Contemporary Law: KAZUO SHIMADA
Faculty of Economics: MASAHIRO FUKUSHI
Graduate School of Business Administration: KENJI OMORI (Chair.)
Graduate School of Communication Studies: TERUO ARIYAMA (Chair.)
Graduate School of Contemporary Law: YOSHIO MIYAZAKI (Chair.)
Graduate School of Economics: HISASHI WATANABE (Chair.)

TOKYO UNIVERSITY OF AGRICULTURE

1-1-1 Sakuragaoka, Setagaya-ku, Tokyo 156-8502

Telephone: (3) 5477-2560
Fax: (3) 5477-2635
E-mail: tuacip@nodai.ac.jp
Internet: www.nodai.ac.jp
Founded 1891
Languages of instruction: Japanese, English
Academic year: April to March
President: Dr KANJU OHSAWA
Chief Administrative Officer: YUJI FURUYA
Library of 665,000 vols
Number of teachers: 357
Number of students: 13,000
Publication: *Journal of Agricultural Science* (1 a year)

DEANS

Faculty of Agriculture: Dr SHUJI OKAJIMA
Faculty of Applied Bioscience: Dr HARUKAZU SUZUKI
Faculty of Bio-Industry: Dr MICHINARI YOKOHAMA

Faculty of International Agriculture and Food Studies: Dr HISAMITSU TAKAHASHI
Faculty of Regional Environmental Science: Dr SHIGEYUKI MIYABAYASHI
Graduate School of Agriculture: Dr TOSHIYUKI MONMA
Graduate School of Bio-Industry: Dr TOHRU OHYAMA
Junior College: Dr HIROSHI TACHI

TOKYO UNIVERSITY OF SCIENCE

1-3 Kagurazaka, Shinjuku-ku, Tokyo 162-8601

Telephone: (3) 3260-4271
E-mail: intlexchg@admin.tus.ac.jp
Internet: www.tus.ac.jp
Founded 1881
Private control
Language of instruction: Japanese
Academic year: April to March
President: AKIRA FUJISHIMA
Librarian: MASAAKI UEKI
Library of 1,007,422 vols
Number of teachers: 732
Number of students: 20,755
Publication: *Science Forum* (12 a year)

DEANS

Faculty of Engineering Division I: SEIICHIRO HANGAI
Faculty of Engineering Division II: TOSHIAKI YACHI
Faculty of Industrial Science and Technology: YASUHIRO AKIRA
Faculty of Pharmaceutical Sciences: SEIICHI TANUMA
Faculty of Science Division I: YOSHIHIRO MARUYAMA
Faculty of Science Division II: AKIRA YOSHIOKA
Faculty of Science and Technology: YASUHIRO HIRAKAWA
School of Management: HITOTORA HIGASHIKUNI

ATTACHED INSTITUTES

Research Education Organization for Information Science and Technology: 1–3 Kagurazaka, Shinjuku-ku, Tokyo 162-8601; tel. (3) 3260-4271; Principal MASANORI OHYA.

Research Institute for Biological Sciences: 2641 Yamazaki, Noda-shi, Chiba 278-8510; tel. (4) 7124-1501; Principal TAKACHIKA AZUMA.

Research Institute for Science and Technology: 2641 Yamazaki, Noda-shi, Chiba 278-8510; tel. (4) 7124-1501; Principal YOSHIMASA NIHEI.

TOKYO WOMEN'S CHRISTIAN UNIVERSITY

2-6-1, Zempukuji, Suginami-ku, Tokyo 167-8585

Telephone: (3) 5382-6340
Fax: (3) 3395-1037
E-mail: iec@office.twcu.ac.jp
Internet: www.twcu.ac.jp
Founded 1918
Private control
Language of instruction: Japanese
Academic year: April to March
Pres.: AKIKO MINATO
Librarian: SHINSUKE MUROFUCHI
Library of 600,000 vols
Number of teachers: 142
Number of students: 4,208 , including 78 graduates
Publications: *Annals of Institute for Comparative Studies of Culture* (1 a year), *Essays and Studies in British and Ameri-

can Literature* (2 a year), *Historica* (1 a year), *Japanese Literature* (2 a year), *Science Reports* (1 a year), *Sociology and Economics* (1 a year)

DEANS

College of Arts and Sciences: SANAE INOUE
College of Culture and Communication: YUKO KOBAYASHI
Graduate School: HIROSHI IMAI

CHAIRMEN

Graduate School of Culture and Communication: RYOICHI SATO
Graduate School of Humanities: HIROSHI IMAI
Graduate School of Science: MASAHIKO SHINOHARA

TOKYO WOMEN'S MEDICAL UNIVERSITY

8-1 Kawada-cho, Shinjuku-ku, Tokyo 162-8666

Telephone: (3) 3353-8111
Fax: (3) 3353-6793
Internet: www.twmu.ac.jp
Founded 1900
Private control
Language of instruction: Japanese
Academic year: April to March
President: K. TAKAKURA
Registrar: H. YOSHIOKA
Librarian: M. KOBAYASHI
Library of 227,850 vols
Number of teachers: 2,178
Number of students: 961
Publication: *Journal of Tokyo Women's Medical University* (in English or Japanese, 12 a year).

TOYO UNIVERSITY

28-20 Hakusan 5-chome, Bunkyo-ku, Tokyo 112-8606

Telephone: (3) 3945-7557
Fax: (3) 3942-2489
E-mail: ipo@hakusrv.toyo.ac.jp
Internet: www.toyo.ac.jp
Founded 1887
Private control
Academic year: April to March
Pres.: TOMONORI MATSUO
Dir of Academic Affairs: MIKIO AKIYAMA
Librarian: TAKITARO MORIKAWA
Library of 1,101,256 vols
Number of teachers: 1,269 (523 full-time, 746 part-time)
Number of students: 29,819
Publications: faculty bulletins, journals, etc.

DEANS

Undergraduate School of Business Administration: YOUICHI KAKIZAKI
Undergraduate School of Economics: SHUNICHI KIGAWA
Undergraduate School of Engineering: MASAHIDE YONEYAMA
Undergraduate School of Law: HIDETOSHI KOBAYASHI
Undergraduate School of Life Sciences: AKIRA SAKURAI
Undergraduate School of Literature: TASHIAKI YAMADA
Undergraduate School of Regional Development Studies: HAJIME NAGAHAMA
Undergraduate School of Sociology: MAMORA FUNATSU
Graduate School of Business Administration: YASUHIRO OGURA
Graduate School of Economics: KIYOSHI ASUNO
Graduate School of Engineering: TOHRU IUCHI

Graduate School of Law: MASUO IMAGAMI

Graduate School of Life Sciences: AKIRA INOUE

Graduate School of Literature: KAZUO ARITA

Graduate School of Regional Development Studies: TOMONORI MARSUO

Graduate School of Sociology: KOJUN FURU-KAWA

TSUDA COLLEGE

2-1-1 Tsuda-machi, Kodaira-shi, Tokyo 187-8577

Telephone: (42) 342-5111
Fax: (42) 341-2444
E-mail: info-admin@tsuda.ac.jp
Internet: www.tsuda.ac.jp

Founded 1900
Academic year: April to March

Chair.: REIJIROU HATTORI

Library of 350,000 vols, 3,400 periodicals

Number of teachers: 83 full-time

Number of students: 2,830 (incl. 85 post-graduate)

Publications: *Journal of Tsuda College* (1 a year), *The Study of International Relations* (1 a year), *The Tsuda Review* (1 a year)

Faculty of liberal arts, departments of English language and literature, international and cultural studies, mathematics and computer science; postgraduate schools of international and cultural studies, literary studies, mathematics.

TSURU UNIVERSITY

3-8-1 Tahara, Tsuru, Yamanashi 402-8555

Telephone: (554) 43-4341
Fax: (554) 43-4347
E-mail: gakusei@tsuru.ac.jp
Internet: www.tsuru.ac.jp

Founded 1955

Number of teachers: 74 (full-time)

Number of students: 3,000

Teacher training college.

WASEDA UNIVERSITY

1-104 Totsukamachi, Shinjuku-ku, Tokyo 169-8050

Telephone: (3) 3203-4141
Fax: (3) 3203-7051
E-mail: intl-ac@list.waseda.jp
Internet: www.waseda.jp

Founded 1882
Private control
Academic year: April to February

Pres.: KATSUHIKO SHIRAI

Vice-Pres. for Fundraising Promotion (Head), Alumni Relations, Management Planning, and Research Promotion: KENJI HORIGUCHI

Vice-Pres. for Legal Affairs and Operational Audit: TERUAKI TAYAMA

Vice-Pres. for Academic Affairs (Head), Cultural Program, and Honjo Project: KENJIRO TSUCHIDA

Vice-Pres. for Personnel and Labour Affairs: SATOSHI SHIMIZU

Vice-Pres. for Int. Affairs (Head): KATSUICHI UCHIDA

Vice-Pres. for Public Relations, Affiliated Schools: TOMOKI WARAGAI

Vice-Pres. for Academic Affairs, Int. Affairs and Fundraising Promotion: MASATAKA OTA

Vice-Pres. for Campus Planning, Promotion of IT and Fundraising Promotion: AKIRA NISHITANI

Vice-Pres. for Research Promotion (Head) and Fundraising Promotion: YOSHIJI HOR-IKOSHI

Vice-Pres. for Student Affairs, Career Support and Affiliated Schools: EIICHIRO NOJIMA

Vice-Pres. for General Affairs, Affiliated Companies (Head), and Personnel of Admin. Staff: HIDEAKI TAUCHI

Vice-Pres. for Finance: EIICHIRO KOBAYASHI

Vice-Pres. for Sports Promotion: ISAO MUR-AOKA (Exec. Dir)

Vice-Pres. for Strategic Management Planning, Alumni Relations, Fundraising Promotion: SEIJI HONDA

Vice-Pres. for Devt of Univ.-Local Relations, Honjo Project, Strategic Management Planning, Holding Company and Cultivation of Human Resources (Admin. Staff): KUNIO TANIGUCHI

Vice-Pres. for Alumni Relations: EIKO KONO

Vice-Pres. for Research Promotion and Alumni Relations: YASUMASA UMESATO

Vice-Pres. for Alumni Relations and Alumni Asscn.: AKIHIDE FUKUDA

Dir of Library: NOBUYUKI KAMIYA

Library of 5,100,000 vols

Number of teachers: 6,560

Number of students: 53,522 (44,829 undergraduate, 8,693 postgraduate)

The Schools of Letters, Arts and Sciences I and II will be terminated when all existing students graduate; they are replaced from 2007 by the School of Culture, Media and Society and the School of Humanities and Social Sciences. The Schools of Science and Engineering will also be terminated when all existing students graduate; they are replaced from 2007 by the School of Fundamental Science and Engineering, the School of Creative Science and Engineering and the School of Advanced Science and Engineering.

DEANS

Graduate School of Accountancy: YOSHITAKA KOBAYASHI

Graduate School of Advanced Science and Engineering: ATSUSHI ISHIYAMA

Graduate School of Asia-Pacific Studies: MICHIO YAMAOKA

Graduate School of Commerce: MASATAKA OTA

Graduate School of Creative Science and Engineering: HIROSHI YAMAKAWA

Graduate School of Economics: RYO NAGATA

Graduate School of Education: TSUGIYOSHI YUKAWA

Graduate School of Environment and Energy Engineering: KATSUYA NAGATA

Graduate School of Finance, Accounting and Law: MEGUMI SUTO

Graduate School of Global Information and Telecommunication Studies: YOSHIYORI URANO

Graduate School of Human Sciences: HIR-OYUKI TORIGOE

Graduate School of Information Production, and Systems: KOTARO HIRASAWA

Graduate School of Japanese Applied Linguistics: HIROSHI KABAYA

Graduate School of Law: KOJI OHMI

Graduate School of Letters, Arts and Sciences: KOICHI OUCHI

Faculty of Science and Engineering: SHUJI HASHIMOTO (Sr Dean)

Graduate School of Fundamental Science and Engineering: SUNAO KAWAI

Graduate School of Political Science: SEISHI SATO

Graduate School of Social Sciences: YASUHIRO ONISHI

Graduate School of Sport Sciences: TETSUO FUKUNAGA

School of Advanced Science and Engineering: ATSUSHI ISHIYAMA

School of Commerce: NAOTO ONZO

School of Creative Science and Engineering: HIROSHI YAMAKAWA

School of Culture, Media and Society: SUMIO OBINATA

School of Education: TATSUYUKI KAMIO

School of Fundamental Science and Engineering: SUNAO KAWAI

School of Human Sciences: MIHO SAITO

School of Humanities and Social Sciences: SUMIO OBINATA

School of International Liberal Studies: PAUL SNOWDEN

School of Law: TATSUO UEMURA

School of Letters, Arts and Sciences I: TERUHISA TAJIMA

School of Letters, Arts and Sciences II: TERUHISA TAJIMA

School of Political Science and Economics: SHOZO IIJIMA

School of Science and Engineering: SHUJI HASHIMOTO

School of Social Science: HIDETOSHI TAGA

School of Sport Sciences: ISAO MURAOKA

The Okuma School of Public Management: KOICHIRO AGATA

Waseda Law School: KAORU KAMATA

Schools of Art and Music

Elizabeth University of Music: 4–15 Noboricho, Naka-ku, Hiroshima; tel. (82) 221-0918; fax (82) 221-0947; internet www.eum.ac.jp; f. 1952; library: 88,750 vols, 18,000 sound recordings; 47 full-time, 70 part-time teachers; 656 undergraduates, 53 postgraduates; Pres. HIDEAKI NAKAMURA; Dean of Academic Affairs K. NAGAI; publ. *Kenkyuu Kiyoo* (1 a year).

Kanazawa College of Art: 5-11-1, Kodatsuno, Kanazawa, Ishikawa 920-8656; tel. (76) 262-3531; fax (76) 262-6594; e-mail admin@kanazawa-bidai.ac.jp; internet www.kanazawa-bidai.ac.jp; f. 1946; depts of Fine Art, Design, Crafts; Graduate School; Research Institute of Art and Craft, f. 1972; 67 full-time staff, 200 part-time staff; 665 students; library: 72,000 vols; Pres. YOSHIAKI INUI.

Kunitachi College of Music: 5-5-1 Kashiwa-cho, Tachikawa-shi, Tokyo 190-8520; tel. (42) 536-0321; fax (42) 535-2313; internet www.kunitachi.ac.jp; f. 1950; library: 155,000 books, 120,000 vols of sheet music, 170,000 audio-visual items; 417 teachers; 2,439 students; Pres. NORIKO TAKANO; publs *Kenkyu Kiyo* (Memoirs, 1 a year), *Daigakuin Nempo* (publication of the postgraduate school, 1 a year), *Ongaku Kenkyujo Nempo* (publication of the research institute, 1 a year).

Kyoto City University of Arts: 13-6 Kutsukake-cho, Ohe, Nishikyo-ku, Kyoto 610-1197; tel. (75) 332-0701; fax (75) 332-0709; internet w3.kcua.ac.jp; Pres. Dr YASUNORI NISHIJIMA; 740 undergraduate students, 134 graduates; Faculties of Fine Arts and Music.

Musashino Academia Musicae: 1-13-1 Hazawa, Nerima-ku, Tokyo 176-8521; tel. (3) 3992-1121; fax (3) 3991-7599; internet www.musashino-music.ac.jp; f. 1929; 382 teachers; 2,269 students; library: 200,000 vols; Pres. NAOKATA FUKUI; Librarian HACHIRO CHIKURA; publ. *Review of Studies* (in Japanese, 1 a year).

Osaka College of Music: 1-1-8, Shonai-saiwaimaohi, Toyonaka City, Osaka 561-8555; tel. (6) 6334-2131; fax (6) 6333-0286; e-mail info@daion.ac.jp; internet www.daion.ac.jp; f. 1915; courses in composition, vocal music and instrumental music; library: 123,500 vols; 376 teachers; 1,171 students; Pres. NOBUO NISHIOKA.

Tama Art University: 3-15-34 Kaminoge, Setagaya-ku, Tokyo 158; tel. (3) 3702-1141; fax 03-702-2235; e-mail pro@tamabi.ac.jp; internet www.tamabi.ac.jp; f. 1935; undergraduate division established 1953; departments within the Faculty of Art and Design: ceramic, glass and metal works; environmental design; graphic design; information design; art science; painting; product and textile design; sculpture; 415 teachers; 4,718 students, incl. 3,491 undergraduates and 235 graduates; Pres. SHIRO TAKAHASHI.

Toho Gakuen School of Music: 41-1 1-chome, Wakaba-cho, Chofu-shi, Tokyo 182-8510; tel. (3) 3307-4101; fax (3) 3307-4354; internet www.tohomusic.ac.jp; f. 1961; 83 teachers; 1,400 students; library: 133,000 vols; Pres. T. TSUTSUMI.

Tokyo College of Music: 3-4-5, Minami-Ikebukuro, Toshima-ku, Tokyo 171-8540; tel. (3) 3982-3186; fax (3) 3982-2883; internet www.tokyo-ondai.ac.jp; f. 1907; 1,702 stu-

dents; library: 130,000 vols, 11,300 CDs; Pres. YOSHIO UNNO.

Ueno Gakuen University: Department of Music, Faculty of Music and Cultural Studies, 24-12 Higashi-Ueno 4-chome, Taito-ku, Tokyo 110-8642; tel. (3) 3842-1021; fax (3) 3843-7548; e-mail info@uenogakuen.ac.jp; internet www.uenogakuen.ac.jp; f. 1904; library: 175,000 vols; 184 teachers; 580 students; Pres. Prof. HIRO ISHIBASHI.

JORDAN

The Higher Education System

In 1920 Jordan (formerly Transjordan) became a League of Nations mandate under British administration. The mandate was terminated in 1946 and Jordan became an independent sovereign state. Wars with Israel in 1948 and 1967 led to an influx of Palestinian refugees; moreover, after the Six Day War (1967) Jerusalem and the West Bank fell wholly under Israeli control. Until 1967 the oldest institution of higher education in Jordan was Birzeit University in the West Bank, which was founded as a school in 1924, added post-secondary courses in 1953 and became a two-year junior college in 1961. However, after 1967 Birzeit University came under Israeli jurisdiction and since 1994 has been part of the Palestinian (National) Authority (PA). The oldest university is now the University of Jordan (founded 1962). The Ministry of Higher Education and Scientific Research and the Council of Higher Education are the bodies responsible for higher education, which consists of public and private universities. In addition, there are approximately 40 community colleges offering diploma-level post-secondary programmes of study. In 2009 there were 23 public and private universities with approximately 220,000 students enrolled. Enrollment in higher education was growing rapidly; the projected number of students entering university was 92,000 per year by 2013, up from 50,469 in 2005.

Universities admissions operate on the basis of the General Secondary Examination. Jordanian universities operate a US-style 'credit semester' system, under which students are required to accumulate a given number of credits each semester in order to graduate. The standard undergraduate Bachelors degree is a four-year programme of study and requires at least 132 credits. Degrees in professional fields of study, such as medicine, engineering and dentistry, may last from five to six years. In 2005 the Council of Higher Education introduced the University Achievement Examination, to be taken by all undergraduates in the final year of the Bachelors degree. The purpose of this examination is to develop a standard measure for evaluating students and courses at both public and private institutions on a subject by subject basis. Success in this examination leads to the award of the University Achievement Examination Qualification Certificate. There are three postgraduate degrees: the Higher Diploma, Masters and Doctor of Philosophy. The Higher Diploma is a one- to three-year course in a professional field of study. The Masters is often a two-year course requiring at least 33 credits. Finally, the Doctor of Philosophy lasts for three to five years, and is a combination of both coursework and original research. The full scope of postgraduate degrees is only available at public universities.

Post-secondary vocational and technical education is serviced in the main by community colleges. There are also accredited workplace-based training schemes. Courses at community colleges last two to three years, require at least 66 credits for completion and lead to the award of a Diploma. All public community colleges are affiliated to Al-Balqa' Applied University. In 1999 a law was passed establishing a five-tier framework for post-secondary non-university education, graded Semi-Skilled, Skilled, Craftsman, Technician and Professional.

As a part of the Ministry of Higher Education and Scientific Research, the Accreditation Council was responsible for quality assurance until June 2007 when it was dissolved and the Higher Education Accreditation Commission was set up in its place. The Commission Council consists of a president, a vice-president, two full-time members, and three part-time members. In 2006 Jordan signed the Catania Declaration to put into place a 'Euro-mediterranean Higher Education Area' which seeks to carry out the directives of the Barcelona Declaration of 1995, which later became the Bologna Process. In 2007 a number of priorities were highlighted to bring Jordan's higher education system into line with the European model.

The Higher Education Reform for Knowledge Economy, a project to improve the higher education system in Jordan through policy reforms, was approved in 2009. It was expected to be fully completed by December 2015.

Regulatory and Representative Bodies

GOVERNMENT

Council of Higher Education: Ministry of Higher Education and Scientific Research, POB 35262, Amman; tel. (6) 5347671; fax (6) 5337616; e-mail mohe@mohe.gov.jo; internet www.mohe.gov.jo; f. 1982; controls the devt of private higher education and ensures that minimum standards are maintained; Chair. THE MINISTER OF HIGHER EDUCATION AND SCIENTIFIC RESEARCH.

Ministry of Culture: POB 6140, Amman; tel. (6) 5696218; fax (6) 5696598; e-mail info@culture.gov.jo; internet www.culture.gov.jo; Minister NANCY BAKIR.

Ministry of Education: POB 1646, Amman 11118; tel. (6) 5607181; fax (6) 5666019; e-mail moe@moe.gov.jo; internet www.moe.gov.jo; Minister TAYSEER NUEIMI.

Ministry of Higher Education and Scientific Research: POB 35262, Amman; tel. (6) 5347671; fax (6) 5337616; e-mail mohe@mohe.gov.jo; internet www.mohe.gov.jo; Minister Dr OMAR SHDEIFAT.

ACCREDITATION

Higher Education Accreditation Commission: POB 138, Amman 11941; tel. (6) 5347671; fax (6) 5354562; e-mail a_hunaiti@mohe.gov.jo; f. 2007; Pres. ABDELRAHIM A. HUNAITI.

Learned Societies

GENERAL

Aal Al-bayt Foundation for Islamic Thought: POB 950361, Amman 11195; tel. (6) 4633642; fax (6) 4633887; e-mail aalal-bayt@rhc.jo; internet www.aalalbayt.org; f. 1980; research is divided into 2 main categories: long-term projects such as the issuing of the *Encyclopedia of Arab Islamic Civilization*, the *Comprehensive Catalogue of Arab Islamic MSS*, the *Annotated Bibliographies of Islamic Economy and Islamic Education* and the Great Tafsirs project; and medium-term projects dealing with contemporary Muslim life and thought; 130 mems from 42 countries; library of 26,146 vols, 562 periodicals; special collns: Hashemite and Jordanian Collns; Dir FARUK JARRAR; Librarian NOUZAT ABU LABAN.

UNESCO Office Amman: POB 2270, Amman 11181; Wadi Saqra St, Amman 11181; tel. (6) 5516559; fax (6) 5532183; e-mail amman@unesco.org; f. 1973; Dir MOHAMED DJELID.

BIBLIOGRAPHY, LIBRARY SCIENCE AND MUSEOLOGY

Jordan Library and Information Association: POB 6289, Amman; tel. (6) 4629412; fax (6) 4629412; internet www.jorla.org; f. 1963; 600 mems; Pres. FADIL KLAYB; Sec. YOUSRA ABU AJAMIEH; publs *Directory of the Libraries in Jordan*, *Directory of Periodicals in Jordan*, *Jordanian National Bibliography 1979–*, *Palestinian Bibliography*, *Palestinian-Jordanian Bibliography*, *Rissalat al-Maktaba* (The Message of the Library, 4 a year).

LANGUAGE AND LITERATURE

British Council: First Circle, Jebel Amman, POB 634, Amman 11118; tel. (6) 4603420; fax (6) 4656413; e-mail info@britishcouncil.org.jo; internet www.britishcouncil.org/jordan.htm; teaching centre; offers courses and examinations in English language and British culture and promotes cultural exchange with the UK; Dir TIM GORE.

Goethe Institut Jordanien: POB 1676, Amman 11118; 5 Abdel Mun'im Al Rifa'i St, Amman 11118; tel. (6) 4641993; fax (6)

4612383; e-mail info@amman.goethe.org; internet www.goethe.de/na/amm/enindex.htm; offers courses and exams in German language and culture and promotes cultural exchange with Germany; library of 3,000 vols; Dir Dr CHRISTIANE KRÄMER-HUS-HUS.

Instituto Cervantes: Mohammad Hafiz Ma'ath St 10, POB 815467, Amman 11180; tel. (6) 4610858; fax (6) 4624049; e-mail cenamm@cervantes.es; internet amman.cervantes.es; offers courses and examinations in Spanish language and culture and promotes cultural exchange with Spain and Spanish-speaking Latin and Central America; library of 14,000 vols; Dir MARÍA CARMEN ORDÓÑEZ CARVAJAL.

NATURAL SCIENCES
Biological Sciences

Royal Marine Conservation Society of Jordan: POB 831051, Amman 11183; tel. (6) 5676173; fax (6) 5676183; e-mail information@jreds.org; internet www.jreds.org; f. 1993; conservation and sustainable use of the marine environment through conservation programmes, advocacy, education, outreach and empowerment; 250 mems; Exec. Dir FADI F. SHARAIHA.

Research Institutes
AGRICULTURE, FISHERIES AND VETERINARY SCIENCE

National Center for Agricultural Research and Extension: POB 226, Amman; internet www.ncartt.gov.jo; f. 1958 as Dept of Agricultural and Scientific Research and Extension; 1985 became the National Center for Agricultural Research and Technology Transfer; present name 2007; covers all branches of agricultural research, information and extension; library of 18,500 vols; Dir SAID GHEZAWI.

HISTORY, GEOGRAPHY AND ARCHAEOLOGY

Council for British Research in the Levant: POB 519, Jubaiha, Amman 11941; tel. (6) 5341317; fax (6) 5337197; e-mail info@cbrl.org.uk; internet www.cbrl.org.uk; f. 1996 as the merger of the British Institute in Amman for Archaeology and History with the British School of Archaeology in Jerusalem; supports British post-doctoral research in social sciences and the contemporary Levant; provides some limited grant funding and a hostel, library and laboratory facilities to members; 296 individual mems, 27 institutional mems; library of 24,000 vols, divided between Amman and Jerusalem; Dir Dr ALEX BELLAM; publs *Levant* (1 a year), *Bulletin* (1 a year), *Levant Supplementary Series* (monograph series).

TECHNOLOGY

Royal Scientific Society: POB 1438, Al-Jubaiha 11941; tel. (6) 5344701; fax (6) 5344806; e-mail rssinfo@rss.gov.jo; internet www.rss.gov.jo; f. 1970; independent, non-profit industrial research and development centre; electronic services and training centre, computer systems, mechanical engineering, chemical industry, building research centre, economics, wind and solar energy research centre; 10 technical centres housing 38 specialized laboratories; library: see Libraries and Archives; Exec. Vice-Pres. Dr SEYFEDDIN MUAZ.

Libraries and Archives
Amman

Abdul Hameed Shoman Public Library: POB 940255, Amman 11194; tel. (6) 4633627; fax (6) 4633565; e-mail library@shoman.org; internet www.shoman.org; f. 1986; 120,000 vols, 1,200 periodicals; Librarian EMAD ABU-EID.

Greater Amman Public Library: POB 182181, Amman; tel. (6) 4627718; fax (6) 4649420; f. 1960; 257,179 vols in Arabic and English; 500,000 vols, 256 current periodicals; 31 brs for adults and children, Deposit Library for UNESCO (5,000 vols); Jordanian publications; Chief Officer MOHAMED AL-KFAWIN.

National Library: POB 6070, Amman 11118; 9 Haroun al-Rasheed St, Amman 11118; tel. (6) 5662845; fax (6) 5662865; e-mail nl@nl.gov.jo; internet www.nl.gov.jo; f. 1994; prepares and issues the nat. bibliography and union catalogue; responsible for copyrights and legal deposits; responsible for enforcing Jordanian copyright law; depository for nat., UNESCO and WIPO publs; 123,076 vols, 49,784 titles; Dir-Gen. MAMOUN THARWAT TALHOUNI.

El Hassan Library and Media Centre, Princess Sumaya University for Technology: POB 1438, Amman; tel. (6) 5359949; fax (6) 5347295; e-mail info@psut.edu.jo; internet www.psut.edu.jo; f. 2004; core collection includes energy, civil engineering, construction, industrial chemistry, mechanical engineering, computer science, economics, electronics; 72,000 vols, 106 periodical titles, 200 theses, 2,000 non-print media, 450 maps, 15,000 specifications; online service from Dialog, BRS, Infoline; Dir Dr NERMEEN SHUQOM.

University of Jordan Library: Univ. of Jordan, Amman; tel. (6) 5355000; fax (6) 5355570; e-mail library@ju.edu.jo; internet library.ju.edu.jo; f. 1962; 789,000 vols, 350 current Arabic periodicals, 19,977 online periodicals, mainly in English; 15 reading rooms; legal deposit for UN, WHO, FAO, World Bank, UNESCO, IMF, SIPRI, UNU, ILO, Institute for Peace Research documents; legal deposit for dissertations from all Arab universities; Dir Dr MOHAMMAD RAQAB; publs *Bibliographical list and indexes* (irregular), Directory for Theses Deposited at University Library (2 a year), *Library Guide* (1 a year).

Irbid

Irbid Public Library: POB 348, Irbid; f. 1957; 30,000 vols; Librarian ANWAR ISHAQ AL-NSHIWAT.

Museums and Art Galleries
Amman

Folklore Museum: POB 88, Amman; housed by the Department of Antiquities; f. 1972; colln of nat. traditional costumes; Curator Mrs SA'DIYA AL-TEL.

Jordan Archaeological Museum: POB 88, Amman; tel. (6) 46319768; fax (6) 46319768; e-mail doa@nic.net.jo; f. 1951; 13,000 objects, 36,000 coins; 20 staff; library of 3,560 vols; Curator AIDA NAGHAURY.

Museum of Popular Traditions: POB 88, Amman; f. 1971; local domestic history; brs in Petra, Madaba, Salt and Kerak; Curator IMAN QUDA.

Universities
AL-AHLIYYA AMMAN UNIVERSITY

Al-Ahliyya Amman Univ. POB, Amman 19328

Telephone: (5) 3500211
Fax: (6) 5336104
E-mail: info@ammanu.edu.jo
Internet: www.ammanu.edu.jo
Founded 1990
Private control
Language of instruction: Arabic
Language of instruction: English
Pres.: Prof. Dr MAHER SALIM

DEANS

Faculty of Administrative and Financial Science: Dr HUSSEIN EL-YASEEN
Faculty of Arts: Dr WAFA EL-KHADRA
Faculty of Engineering: Prof. Dr SADIQ HAMED
Faculty of Information Technology: Dr MUSTAFA YASEEN
Faculty of Law: Dr OMAR EL-BOURINI
Faculty of Nursing: Prof. Dr WASEELA PETRO
Faculties of Pharmacy and Medical Sciences: Dr MAHER SHORBAJI

AL-BALQA' APPLIED UNIVERSITY

POB 19117, Al-Salt, Al-Balqa' Governorate

Telephone and fax (5) 3491111
E-mail: davana@bau.edu.jo
Internet: www.bau.edu.jo
Founded 1997
State control
There are 14 affiliated univ. colleges and around 36 affiliated private, military and UN-operated colleges
Pres.: Prof. Dr OMAR ABDALKARIM RIMAWI
Vice-Pres.: Prof. ABDALLAH S. AL-ZOUBI
Vice-Pres.: Prof. NAIM M. ALJOUNI
Dean of Student Affairs: Dr HAMDAN AWAMLEH
Librarian: NIDAL AL-AHMAD
Library of 38,500 vols
Number of teachers: 1,460
Number of students: 45,000

DEANS

Faculty of Agricultural Technology: Dr YASIN ALZU'BI
Faculty of Engineering: Dr MAHER KHAKISH
Faculty of Graduate Studies and Scientific Research: Dr GHANDI ANFOKA
Faculty of Planning and Management: JIHAD ABU AL SONDOS
Faculty of Science and Information Technology: Dr IBRAHIM HAMARNEH

AL AL-BAYT UNIVERSITY

POB 130040, Mafraq 25113

Telephone: (2) 6297000
Fax: (2) 6297021
E-mail: programmer@aabu.edu.jo
Internet: www.aabu.edu.jo
Founded 1992
Public control
Languages of instruction: Arabic, English
Academic year: September to June
Pres.: Prof. NABIL T. SHAWAGFEH
Vice-Pres. for Admin. and Finance: Prof. JIHAD SHAHER AL-MAJALI
Registrar: QFTAN AL-MONANI
Library: 122,005 Arabic Books, 36,019 English books, 23,000 electronic books 43000
Number of teachers: 317
Number of students: 11,897
Publications: *Al-Manara* (Journal of Academic Research, 4 a year, in English and

Arabic), *Al-Zahra* (12 a year, in English and Arabic)

DEANS

Faculty of Arts and Humanities: Prof. MOHAMMAD AL DROBI
Faculty of Educational Sciences: Dr AWATIF ABU SHAOR
Faculty of Engineering: Dr ALI ABU KANEE-MAH
Faculty of Finance and Business Adminis-tration: Dr JAMAL AL-SHARAIRI
Faculty of Law: Dr EID AL-HUSSBAN
Faculty of Nursing: Dr OMAR RAWAJFEH
Faculty of Science: Dr EQAB RABIE
Faculty Sharia: Dr MOHAMMAD AL-ZUGHOL
Prince Hussein Bin Abdullah College for Information Technology: Dr ISMAIL ABAB-NEH

AL-HUSSEIN BIN TALAL UNIVERSITY

POB 20, Ma'an
Telephone: (3) 2179000
Fax: (3) 2179050
E-mail: ahu@go.com.jo
Internet: www.ahu.edu.jo
Founded 1999
State control
Pres.: ALI KHALAF AL-HROOT
Dean of Academic Research: Prof. KAMAL AYOUB MOMANI
Number of teachers: 58
Number of students: 1,948
Publication: *Al-Haq Ya'lu* (2 a year)

DEANS

College of Archaeology, Tourism and Hotel Management: Prof. HANI HAYAJNEH
College of Arts: Dr TAISIR KHALIL EL-ZAWAREH
College of Business Administration and Eco-nomics: (vacant)
College of Computer Engineering and Infor-mation Technology: Dr FARES FRAIJ
College of Education: Dr MONA ALI ABU DARWESH
College of Mining and Environmental Engin-eering: Dr MARWAN BATIHA
College of Science: Dr ALI MAHMUD ATEIWI

AL-ISRA PRIVATE UNIVERSITY

POB 22/33, Amman 11622
Telephone: (6) 4711710
Fax: (6) 4711505
E-mail: info@isra.edu.jo
Internet: www.isra.edu.jo
Founded 1991
Private control
Language of instruction: Arabic,
Language of instruction: English
Pres.: ABDUL BARI DURA
Vice-Pres.: NAYEF KHARMA
Dean of Research: GHANEM EL-HASAWI
Dean of Student Affairs: HOSNI AL-SHEYYIB

DEANS

Faculty of Administrative and Financial Sci-ences: MUSA ALMADHOON
Faculty of Engineering: AHMAD AL-FAHED NUSEIRAT
Faculty of Law: AHMED ABU SHANAB
Faculties of Pharmacy and Medical Sciences: MAZEN QATTO
Faculty of Science and Information Technol-ogy: AYMAN AL-NSOUR

AL-ZAYTOONAH UNIVERSITY

POB 130, Amman 11733
Telephone: (6) 4291511
Fax: (6) 4291432
E-mail: information@alzaytoonah.edu.jo
Internet: www.alzaytoonah.edu.jo

Founded 1993
Private control
Language of instruction: Arabic,
Language of instruction: English
Pres.: Prof. NASR SALEH
Number of teachers: 300
Number of students: 8,000

DEANS

Faculty of Arts: ISAM MAHMOOD ABU SALEEM
Faculty of Economics and Administrative Science: GHALIB AWAD RIFA'I
Faculty of Law: HUSSEIN ATTA HAMDAN
Faculties of Nursing: AHLAM YOUSSEF HAM-DAN
Faculty of Pharmacy: SAYYED ISMAIL MOHAM-MAD
Faculty of Science: ABDEL FATAH ARIF TAMIMI

APPLIED SCIENCE UNIVERSITY

POB 166, Amman 11931
Telephone: (6) 5609999
Fax: (6) 5232899
E-mail: info@aspu.edu.jo
Internet: www.aspu.edu.jo
Private control
Language of instruction: Arabic,
Language of instruction: English
Academic year: September to June
Chair.: ABDALLAH ABU KHADEJEH
Pres.: ZEYAD RAMADAN
Number of teachers: 319
Number of students: 8,000
Publication: *Jordanian Journal of Applied Sciences* (2 a year)

DEANS

Faculty of Allied Medical Sciences: SUHAILA ALKAYALI
Faculty of Art and Design: AHMAD MURSI
Faculty of Arts and Humanities: KAYED QUR'OUSH
Faculty of Economics and Administrative Sciences: MAHFOUZ JUDEH
Faculty of Engineering: YEHYA ABDELLATIF
Faculty of Information Technology: ABDAL-LAH ALASHQUR
Faculty of Law: TALIB MOUSA
Faculty of Nursing: SAMIHA JARRAH
Faculty of Pharmacy: SUHAIR SALEH

THE HASHEMITE UNIVERSITY

POB 330127, Zarqa 13115
Telephone: (5) 3903333
Fax: (5) 3826613
E-mail: huniv@hu.edu.jo
Internet: www.hu.edu.jo
Founded 1992
State control
Languages of instruction: Arabic, English
Academic year: August to June
Pres.: Prof. ROWAIDA AL-MAAITAH
Vice-Pres.: Prof. ABDUL RAHIM HAMDAN
Vice-Pres.: Prof. KAMAL BANI-HANI
Vice-Pres.: Prof. MOHAMMAD MISMAR
Dean of Student Affairs: Prof. MAJED AL-QUR'AN
Librarian: MOHAMMAD T. S. D. DARWISH
Library of 250,000 vols, 25,652 periodicals
Number of teachers: 510
Number of students: 19,116
Publications: *Jordan Journal of Biological Sciences*, *Jordan Journal of Earth and Environmental Sciences*, *Jordan Journal of Mechanical and Industrial Engineering*

DEANS

Faculty of Allied Health Sciences: Dr MANAR ATOUM
Faculty of Arts: Prof. MUSTAFA ABDEL RAHIM
Faculty for Childhood: Dr THEODORA DE BAZ

Faculty of Economics and Administrative Science: Dr SAMER AL-RJOUB
Faculty of Educational Sciences: Prof. MAH-MOUD ALWEHER
Faculty of Engineering: Dr HASAN TANTAWI
Faculty of Information Technology: Dr JAMAL AL-KARAKI
Faculty of Medicine: Prof. KAMAL BANI-HANI
Faculty of Natural Resources and Environ-ment: Prof. ISSA MAKHLOUF
Faculty of Nursing: Prof. NIJMEH AL-ATIYYAT
Faculty of Physical Education and Sports Sciences: Dr OMAR HINDAWI
Faculty of Research and Graduate Studies: Prof. SADI ABDUL-JAWAD
Faculty of Sciences: Prof. ALI ELKARMI

UNIVERSITY OF JORDAN

Amman 11942
Telephone: (6) 5355000
Fax: (6) 5355522
E-mail: admin@ju.edu.jo
Internet: www.ju.edu.jo
Founded 1962
State and autonomous control
Languages of instruction: Arabic, English
Academic year: September to August (two semesters and a summer session)
Pres.: KHALED AL-KARAKI
Dir of Registration and Admission: GHALEB AL-HOURANI
Dir of the Library: Dr HANI AL-AMAD
Number of teachers: 931
Number of students: 23,623
Publication: *Dirasat* (scientific research)

DEANS

Faculty of Agriculture: Prof. MOHAMMED ISAM YAMAMI
Faculty of Arts: Dr SALAMEH NAIMT
Faculty of Arts and Design: Dr ABDUL-HAMEED HAMAM
Faculty of Business: Prof. HANI AL-DMOUR
Faculty of Dentistry: Prof. LAMIS RAJAB
Faculty of Educational Sciences: Prof. MOHAMMAD NAZIH HAMDI
Faculty of Engineering and Technology: Prof. RAED M. SAMRA
Faculty of Foreign Languages: Prof. AHMAD MAJDOUBEH
Faculty of Graduate Studies: Prof. MUNA S. AL-HADIDI
Faculty of International Studies: Prof. ABDULLAH NAGRASH
Faculty of Law: Prof. GEORGE HAZBOUN
Faculty of Medicine: Dr SLAM SALEH DARAD-KEH
Faculty of Nursing: Dr INAAM KHALAF
Faculty of Pharmacy: Dr KHALED M. AIEDEH
Faculty of Physical Education: Prof. SUHA ADEEB DAOUD
Faculty of Rehabilitation Sciences: Prof. BASSAM AMMARI
Faculty of Science: Dr HALA KHYAMI-HORANI
Faculty of Shari'a (Islamic Studies): Prof. MOHAMMAD KHAZER AL-MAJALI
King Abdullah II Faculty for Information Technology: Dr FAWAZ AHMAD M. MASOUD AL-ZAGHOUL

JORDAN UNIVERSITY OF SCIENCE AND TECHNOLOGY (JUST)

POB 3030, Irbid 22110
Telephone: (2) 7201000
Fax: (2) 7095123
E-mail: just@just.edu.jo
Internet: www.just.edu.jo
Founded 1986
State control
Languages of instruction: Arabic, English
Academic year: September to September
Pres.: Prof. WAJIH M. OWAIS

Dean of Research: Prof. FAWZI BANAT
Dir of Public Relations: MUHANNAD MALKAWI
Registrar: FAISAL AL RIFAIE
Librarian: ISSA LELLO
Library of 90,000 vols
Number of teachers: 750
Number of students: 18,850 undergraduate and 1,559 graduate students

DEANS

College of Architecture and Design: Dr NATHEER ABU OBEID
Faculty of Agriculture: Prof. MUNIR J. RUSAN
Faculty of Applied Medical Sciences: Prof. LAILA NIMRI
Faculty of Computer Information Technology: Dr MOHAMMAD AL-ROUSAN
Faculty of Dentistry: Prof. ANWAH BATAINEH
Faculty of Engineering: Prof. KHALED A. MAYYAS
Faculty of Medicine: Prof. KAMAL E. BANI-HANI
Faculty of Nursing: Dr MUNTAHA GHARAIBEH
Faculty of Pharmacy: Dr KHOULOUD ALKHA-MIS
Faculty of Science and Arts: Prof. AHMED M. ELBETIEHA
Faculty of Veterinary Medicine: Prof. SAEB AL-SUKHON

MU'TAH UNIVERSITY

POB 7, Mu'tah, Al Karak 61710
Telephone: (3) 2372380
Fax: (3) 2375540Amman Liaison Office: POB 5076, Amman
Telephone: (6) 4617860
Fax: (6) 4654061
E-mail: hunaiti@hu.edu.jo
Internet: www.mutah.edu.jo
Founded 1981
State control
Languages of instruction: Arabic, English
Academic year: September to June
Pres.: Prof. Dr ABDEL RAHIM A. HUMAITI
Vice-Pres. for Academic Affairs: Prof. MOHAMMAD ABBADI
Vice-Pres. for Admin. Affairs: Prof. QUBLAN AL-MAJALI
Vice-Pres. for Humanities and Science: Prof. MOHANNAD AMIN ABBADI
Vice-Pres. for Military Affairs: ESMAEL E. AL-SHOBAKI
Dean for Academic Research: Prof. MOHAM-MAD AL-TARAWNEH
Dean for Graduate Studies: Prof. NIDAL HAWAMDEH
Dean for Student Affairs: Prof. AHMAD BAT-TAH
Dir of Cultural and Public Affairs: JAZA' MOHAMMAD AL-MASARWEH
Registrar: YASER KASASBEH
Librarian: Dr ABDEL WAHAB MOBIDEEN
Library of 534,753 vols
Number of teachers: 530
Number of students: 16,000
Publication: Mu'tah Journal for Research and Studies

DEANS

Faculty of Agriculture: Dr AMER MAMKAGH
Faculty of Arts: Prof. HUSSAM ALDEEN MUBAIDEEN
Faculty of Business Administration: Dr FAHAD S. KHATEEB
Faculty of Education: Prof. MOHAMMAD RABA-BAA
Faculty of Engineering: Prof. AYMAN AL-MAAYTEH
Faculty of Law: Dr NIZAM AL-MAJALI
Faculty of Medicine: Prof. ADEL ABU AL-HAIJA
Faculty of Nursing: Prof. SAMEER AL-TAWEEL
Faculty of Physical Education: Prof. MOUTA-SEM SHATNAWI

Faculty of Sciences: Prof. MAHDI LATAIFEH
Faculty of Shari'a: Prof. NAEL ABU ZAID
Faculty of Social Sciences: Prof. IBRAHIM AL-OROUD

PHILADELPHIA UNIVERSITY

POB 1, Amman 19392
Telephone: (2) 64799000
Fax: (2) 64799040
E-mail: info@philadelphia.edu.jo
Internet: www.philadelphia.edu.jo
Founded 1989
Private control
Languages of instruction: Arabic, English
Vice-Pres. for Academic Affairs: Prof. MOHAMMAD AWWAD
Vice-Pres. for Admin. and Financial Affairs: Prof. SALEH ABU OSBA
Dean of Academic Research and Graduate Studies: Prof. MAHMOUD KISHTA
Dean of Student Affairs: Dr MOUSTAFA AL-JALABNEH
Dir of Admissions and Registration: Dr KHALDOUN BATIHA
Number of teachers: 300
Number of students: 5,000

DEANS

Faculty of Admin. and Financial Sciences: Prof. KHALID AL-SARTAWI
Faculty of Arts: Dr MOHAMMAD OBAIDELLAH
Faculty of Engineering: Prof. KASIM AL-AUBAIDY
Faculty of Information Technology: Dr KHAL-DOUN BATIHA
Faculty of Law: Dr BASSAM AL-TRAWNEH
Faculty of Nursing: Dr FADIA HASNA
Faculty of Pharmacy: Dr JALAL AL-JAMAL
Faculty of Science: Dr RIYAD JABRI

PRINCESS SUMAYA UNIVERSITY FOR TECHNOLOGY

POB 1438, Al-Jubaiha 11941
Telephone: (6) 5359967
Fax: (6) 5347295
E-mail: info@psut.edu.jo
Internet: www.psut.edu.jo
Founded 1991
Private control
Pres.: Prof. HISHAM GHASSIB
Librarian: NERMEEN SHUQOM
Library of 68,000 vols
Number of teachers: 10
Number of students: 120

DEANS

King Abdullah II School For Electrical Engineering: Prof. BASSAM KAHHALEH
King Hussein School for Information Technology: Prof. YAHIA AL-HALABI

UNIVERSITY OF PETRA

POB 961343, Amman 11196
Telephone: (6) 5799555
Fax: (6) 5715570
E-mail: registrar@uop.edu.jo
Internet: www.uop.edu.jo
Founded 1991 as Jordan Univ. for Women
Languages of instruction: Arabic, English
Private control
Pres.: Prof. ADNAN BADRAN
Vice-Pres. for Academic Affairs and Dean of Research and Graduate Studies: Prof. NIZAR EL-RAYYES
Dean of Admissions and Registration: Dr NASER AL-JARNAL
Dean of Student Affairs: Dr MOUHAMAD EL-KASASBEH
Library of 91,411 vols, 65,387 titles, 52,000 e-books

Number of teachers: 266
Number of students: 6,000
Publications: Al-Basair (scientific journal, 2 a year), Awraq Jamie'ya (2 a year)

DEANS

Faculty of Administrative and Financial Services: Dr RAFIQ OMAR
Faculty of Architecture and Arts: Dr AHMAD ABDEL-JAWAD
Faculty of Arts and Sciences: Prof. MOHAM-MAD ISHAQ AL-ANANI
Faculty of Information Technology: Dr GAS-SAN ISSA
Faculty of Pharmacy and Medical Sciences: Prof. TAWFEEQ ARAFAT

YARMOUK UNIVERSITY

POB 566, Irbid 21163
Telephone: (2) 7211111
Fax: (2) 7211199
E-mail: yarmouk@yu.edu.jo
Internet: www.yu.edu.jo
Founded 1975
National and autonomous control
Languages of instruction: Arabic, English
Academic year: October to June
Pres.: Prof. Dr FAYEZ I. KHASAWNEH
Vice-Pres. for Academic Affairs: Prof. Dr HISHAM S. GHARAIBEH
Vice-Pres. for Admin. Affairs: Prof. Dr MOHAMMED S. SUBBARINI
Registrar: ZACHARIAH ABU-ALDAHAB
Librarian: Dr MOHAMMAD SARAYRAH
Library: Central Library of 300,000 vols, 800 current periodicals
Number of teachers: 687
Number of students: 21,205
Publications: Abhath al-Yarmouk (Yarmouk Research Journal), Yarmouk Numismatics (journal)

DEANS

Faculty of Archaeology and Anthropology: Prof. ZAIDON AL-MUHASIN
Faculty of Arts: Prof. FAHMI GHAZWI
Faculty of Economics and Administrative Sciences: Prof. WALEED HMEDAT
Faculty of Education: Prof. YOUSEF SAWAL-MEH
Hijjawi Faculty of Engineering Technology: Prof. FAROQ AL-OMARY
Faculty of Fine Arts: Prof. KHALID AL-HAMZEH
Faculty of Information Technology: Prof. SULEIMAN MUSTAFA
Faculty of Law: Dr AYMEN MASADEH
Faculty of Physical Education: Prof. Dr ALI AL-DEIRY
Faculty of Science: Prof. IBRAHIM ABU AL-JARAIESH
Faculty of Shari'a (Islamic Law): Dr MUHAM-MAD AL-OMARI

PROFESSORS

ABDUL-ALMAJED, M., Usul al-Din
ABDUL-HAFEZ, S., Biology
ABDULHAY, W., Political Science
ABDUL-RAHMAN, A., Arabic
ABO-ZEID, M., Electronic Engineering
ABU AL-JARAYESH, I., Physics
ABU HELOU, Y., Education
ABU-HILAL, A., Geology
ABU-RAHMAH, K., Arabic
ABU-SALEH, M., Statistics
ABUL-UDOUSS, Y., Arabic
ADWAN, Y., Public Administration
AL-ADWAN, S., Chemistry
AL-AHMADI, A., Usul al-Din
AL-ARAIBI, M., Fine Arts
AL-AWNEH, S., Education Psychology
AL-FAYOUMI, I., Arabic
AL-HAQ, F., Linguistics
AL-HASSAN, K., Chemistry

AL-HASSAN, S., English
AL-HIARY, H., Education
AL-JUBOORY, K., Epigraphy
AL-KATIB, R., Education
AL-KAYSI, M., Islamic Studies
AL-MUHEISEN, Z., Archaeology
AL-NOURI, Q., Anthropology
AL-QUDAH, M., Chemistry
AL-QURAISH, T., Semitic and Oriental Languages
AL-SAADI, W., Public Law
AL-SALEM, H., Physical Education
AL-SALIM, M., Business Administration
AL-SHEIKH, K., Arabic
AL-SHMAI, F., Private Law
AL-TELL, SH., Education
ARAJI, A., Public Administration
AREDAH, F., Sports Science
ASFAR, O., Engineering Science and Mechanics
ATHAMNEH, N., English
ATIYYAT, A., Chemistry
ATOUM, A., Education
AWAD, A., History
AYYOUB, N., Physics
BADER, Y., Linguistics
BAKKAR, Y., Arabic
BANI HANI, A., Economics
BARQAWI, K., Chemistry
BATAYNEH, M., History
DAIRY, A., Physical Education
DARABSEH, M., Arabic
DWAIRI, I., Geology
ESMADI, F., Chemistry
FAOURI, R., Public Administration
FARGHAL, M., English
FATAFTAH, Z., Chemistry
FORA, A., Mathematics
GHARAIBEH, H., Banking and Finance
GHARAIBEH, S., Geology
GHAWANMEH, Y., History
GHAZWI, F., Sociology
GHAZZAWI, M., Education
HADDAD, H., Arabic
HADDAD, M., Anthropology
HADDAD, N., Arabic
HAJ-HUSSEIN, A. T., Chemistry
HAMAD, A., Arabic
HAMAM, A., Music
HAMDAN, A., Linguistics
HAMMAD, KH., Economics
HIJAZI, M., Usul al-Din
HIJJEH, M., Mathematics
HMEDAT, W., Economics
HUNAITI, A., Biology
IDRES, A., Fiqh
JIBRIL, I., Chemistry
KAFAFI, Z., Archaeology
KHARBUTLI, M., English
KHASAWNEH, F., Biology
KHASAWNEH, I., Chemistry
KHATEEB, A., Education
KHAWALDEH, M., Education

KHRAIWISH, H., Arabic
KOFAHI, M., Physics
KURDI, Z., Physical Education
LAHAM, N., Physics
LAHHAM, J., Biology
MADAN, K., Statistics
MAHADIN, R., Linguistics
MAHMOUD, S., Physics
MAKKI, A., Electrical Power Engineering
MARI, T. A., Education
MASHAGBAH, F., English
MOMANI, Q., Arabic
MOMANI, R., Economics
MOMANI, R., Islamic Economy
MRYYAN, N., Economics
NAFI, A., Arabic
NAJJAR, M., Anthropology
NUSAIR, N., Public Administration
ODEH, A., Education
OGLAH, A., Biology
OLAIMAT, M., Education
OLWAN, M., Law
OMARI, M., Usul al-Din
OWEIS, W., Biology
QASSEM, W., Biomechanics
QUDAH, S., Arabic
QUTTOUS, B., Arabic
RABABAH, M., Arabic
RABBA'I, A., Arabic
RASHID, M., Chemistry
RAWI, Z., Statistics
RAYYAN, M., History
REFAI, M., Mathematics
REFAIE, S., Electronic Engineering
RHAYYEL, A., Mathematics
SABBAGH, Z., Business Administration
SADEDDIN, W., Geology
SADIQ, W., Fine Arts
SAFA, F., Arabic
SALEM, A., Physics
SALHIEH, M., History
SARI, S., Archaeology
SERYANI, M., Geography
SHARE'E, M., Economics
SHARI, A., Arabic
SHAYEB, F., Arabic
SHORFAT, M., Linguistics
SMADI, A., Education Psychology
STATIYYEH, S., Arabic
SUBBARINI, M., Education
SULEIMAN, I., Journalism
TALAFHA, H., Economics
TALIB, M., Chemistry
TASHTOUSH, H., Chemistry
THALJI, A., English
UGAILI, S., Computer Science
UGLAH, M., Fiqh and Islamic Studies
WARDAT, R., Linguistics
WAZARMAS, I., Physical Education
YOUNIS, M., Mathematics
YUSUF, N., Physics
ZAGHAL, A., Sociology
ZAGHAL, M., Chemistry

ZIADAT, A., Journalism
ZUBI, A., Arabic
ZUGHOUL, M., English

ZARQA PRIVATE UNIVERSITY

POB 2000, al Zarqa 13110

Telephone and fax (5) 3821100
E-mail: info@zpu.edu.jo
Internet: www.zpu.edu.jo

Founded 1994
Languages of instruction: Arabic, English
Private control

Pres.: Prof. ADNAN HASAN NAYFEH
Vice-Pres. and Dean of Scientific Research: Prof. SAADI M. S. ABDUL JAWAD
Dean of Student Affairs: Dr BASSAM A. AL-BTOOSH

DEANS

Faculty of Art: ABDALLAH AWAD AL KHABASS
Faculty of Economics and Administrative Sciences: MAHMOOD HUSSEIN WADI
Faculty of Educational Sciences: MOHAMMAD ABDEL KAREEM ABU SUL
Faculty of Law: MUNIR HAMID BAYATI
Faculty of Medical Sciences: MUSA TAWFIQ AQTAM
Faculty of Science: IMAD EL DIN MOHAMMAD SADIQ ABU AL RAB
Faculty of Shari'ah (Islamic Studies): ABDAL-LAH AWAD AL KHABASS

Colleges

Al-Husn Polytechnic: POB 50, Al-Husn; tel. (2) 7210397; f. 1981; 2-year diploma courses; library: 10,000 vols; 60 teachers; 800 students; Dean Dr HUSEIN SARHAN.

Amman University College for Applied Engineering: POB 15008, Marka, Amman; tel. (6) 4892345; f. 1975; two-year diploma course; four-year Bachelors of Applied Engineering; library: 17,000 vols; 91 teachers; 2,000 students; Dean MOHAMMAD A. K. ALIA.

Jordan Statistical Training Centre: POB 2015, Amman; tel. (6) 4842171; fax (6) 4833518; f. 1964 for the training of government employees and other applicants in statistical methods; library: c. 700 vols; Dir ABDULHADI ALAWIN.

National Institute of Training: POB 960383, Amman; tel. (6) 4664155; fax (6) 4680731; f. 1968 as the Jordanian Institute for Public Administration; present name and status 2001; administrative training, research and consultation; library: 5,386 vols; Dir-Gen. ABDULLAH ELAYYAN.

KAZAKHSTAN

The Higher Education System

The Kazakh (formerly Kyrgyz) Autonomous Soviet Socialist Republic was founded in 1920 and became a full Union Republic of the USSR in 1936. In 1991 Kazakhstan declared independence from the USSR, and was renamed the Republic of Kazakhstan. The oldest institutions of higher education date from the Soviet period, and include Almaty Abai State University (founded 1928), Western Kazakhstan State University (founded 1932; current name and status 2000) and Al-Farabi Kazakh National University (founded 1934; current name and status 1994). The Ministry of Education and Science oversees higher education, which is governed according to the Law on Higher Education (1993). The languages of instruction are Kazakh and Russian, although Kazakhs constitute the majority of students in higher education and ethnic Russians mostly choose to attend institutions outside Kazakhstan. Among institutions offering higher education are universities, academies, institutes, conservatories, higher schools and higher vocational schools. In 2003/04 there were 134 non-governmental higher education institutes with 297,900 students. In 2008/09 there were 108,000 students enrolled in professional-technical schools and 633,800 in higher education at 143 state-run higher schools, including universities.

Since 2004 admission to higher education has been on the basis of both the old Diploma of Completed Secondary Education and the new Unified National Testing Examination. The university awards system is moving away from the Soviet-era Specialist Diploma (undergraduate), Candidate of Sciences and Doctor of Sciences (both postgraduate) and towards the European-style Bachelors, Masters and Doctor of Philosophy (PhD) degrees. Although it is not a signatory to that agreement, Kazakhstan is, in effect, implementing the Bologna Process to establish a European Higher Education Area, the first phase of which is to adopt a credit-based system of comparable degrees with two main cycles (undergraduate and graduate). The undergraduate-level Specialist Diploma is still offered in most disciplines, notably professional fields of study, and lasts up to six years. Graduates with this degree may advance straight to doctoral-level studies. The Bachelors is a four-year degree; students pursue a general programme of studies in the first two years before majoring in one subject in the final two years. Graduates with a Bachelors may then study for a Masters degree, a two-year course of study (or one year following the Specialist Diploma). The Candidate of Sciences (Aspirantura) is a research-based degree lasting two to three years, following which the student must defend a thesis. Finally, the highest university-level degree is the Doctor of Sciences, a period of study with no fixed duration, which allows the student to pursue a career in academia or research.

Technical and vocational education at post-secondary level is offered by vocational schools, technical schools and colleges. The standard entry requirement is 11–12 years of completed education or the Diploma of Completed Secondary Education. Courses leading to the award of the Diploma of Completed Vocational Secondary Education last between six months to one year. There are also vocational colleges, which administer courses of two to three years leading to the award of the Specialized Secondary Education in a professional field of study.

The National Accreditation Centre at the Ministry of Education and Science is responsible for quality assurance and accreditation, which consists of a three-stage process: licensing, attestation and accreditation. First, an institution's legal status is affirmed by the award of an operational licence. Second, a process of attestation assesses the institution's compliance with minimum educational standards defined by the Ministry of Education and Science. Third, and finally, institutions that have met the appropriate standards of quality assurance receive accreditation, which is then dependent on future five-yearly attestation processes.

Regulatory Bodies

GOVERNMENT

Ministry of Culture: 010000 Astana, pr. Respubliki 24; tel. (7172) 33-32-82; e-mail prmin@mininfo.katelco.kz; internet www.sana.gov.kz; Minister MUXTAR A. QUL-MUX-AMMED.

Ministry of Education and Science: 010000 Astana, Beibitshilik 11; tel. (7172) 75-20-27; fax (7172) 75-28-71; e-mail pressa@edu.gov.kz; internet www.edu.gov.kz; Minister BAQITIAN T. JUMAĞULOV.

ACCREDITATION

National Accreditation Centre: Astana, Office 504, 19 Imanova St; tel. (7172) 78-71-63; e-mail nshakhanova@mail.ru; internet nac.edu.kz; Dir NURILYA SHAKHANOVA.

Learned Societies

GENERAL

National Academy of Sciences of Kazakhstan: 050021 Almaty, Shevchenko 28; tel. (7272) 69-55-93; fax (7272) 69-57-09; f. 1947; sections of biological and medical sciences, chemical engineering, earth sciences, humanities and social sciences, physical and mathematical sciences; attached research institutes: see Research Institutes; Pres. SERIKBEK DAUKEYEV; Sec.-Gen. MURAT MUKHAMEDZHANOV.

UNESCO Office Almaty: 480091 Almaty, ul. Tole Bi 67, 4th Fl., UN Bldg; tel. (7272) 58-26-46; fax (7272) 69-58-63; e-mail almaty@unesco.org; internet www.unesco.kz; designated Cluster Office for Kazakhstan, Kyrgyzstan and Tajikistan; Dir (vacant).

LANGUAGE AND LITERATURE

British Council: 050013 Almaty, Republic Sq. 13; tel. (7272) 72-01-11; fax (7272) 72-01-13; e-mail general@kz.britishcouncil.org; internet www.britishcouncil.kz; offers courses and examinations in English language and British culture and promotes cultural exchange with the UK; attached office in Astana; also responsible for British Council work in Kyrgyzstan; library of 10,000 vols; Dir JAMES KENNEDY.

Goethe-Institut: 050040 Almaty, Dschandosowa 2; tel. (7272) 47-27-04; fax (7272) 47-29-72; internet www.goethe.de/oe/alm/deindex.htm; offers courses and examinations in German language and culture and promotes cultural exchange with Germany; library of 5,000 vols; Dir RICHARD KÜNZEL.

Research Institutes

AGRICULTURE, FISHERIES AND VETERINARY SCIENCE

Akmola Agricultural Research Institute: 021231 Akmola obl., Zerendinsky raion, Selo Charlinka; tel. (71172) 2-41-86; fax (71172) 2-17-33; f. 1984; Dir BAKYTZHAN ZHANAIDAROVICH KHAMZIN.

Aral Scientific and Research Institute of Agroecology and Agriculture: 467918 Kyzylorda obl., Aralsk, Lenina 2A; fax (72422) 7-45-63; f. 1995; Dir TOREKHAN KARLKIKHANOVICH KARLIKHANOV.

Atyrau Scientific and Research Institute of Agriculture: 060002 Atyrau, Azattyk 1; tel. (71022) 2-90-46; fax (71022) 2-91-41; f. 1995; Dir GULSYM SISENGALIYEVA.

Barayev, A. I., Research Centre for Grain Farming: 021600 Akmola obl., Shortandy, Nauchnyi; tel. and fax (71631) 2-10-59; e-mail kanal@kepter.kz; f. 1956; library of 56,000 vols; Dir ZH. A. KASKARBAYEV.

Central Kazakhstan Scientific and Research Institute of Agriculture: 100435 Karaganda obl., Buchar Zhyrau raion, Selo Tsentralnoye; tel. (72138) 3-12-51; fax (72138) 3-18-48; f. 1937; Dir ELAMAN SHAKHANOVICH SHAKHANOV.

East Kazakhstan Scientific and Research Institute of Agriculture:

070512 Eastern Kazakhstanv obl., Glubo-kovsky raion, Pos. Opytnoye Pole, Ul. Nagornaya 3A; tel. (7272) 29-56-54; fax (7272) 29-56-65; Dir SAINELHAN ZHEKSEKENOVICH ZHEKSEKENOV.

Kazakh Research Technological Institute for Operation and Maintenance of Agricultural Machinery: 020100 Akmola obl., Akkol, Lenina 176; tel. (71638) 2-12-75; fax (71638) 2-06-43; e-mail kazniti@mail.kz; f. 1962; Dir A. P. SOLOMKIN.

Kazakh Scientific and Research Institute of Astrakhan Sheep Breeding: 160019 Shymkent, pr. Lenina 3; tel. (7252) 12-04-09; f. 1962; Dir ABDRAHMAN MOLDANA-SAROVICH OMBAEV.

Kazakh Scientific and Research Institute of Feedstuffs Production and Pasture: 050035 Almaty, ul. Dzhandosova 51; tel. (7272) 21-45-86; f. 1969; Dir KASYM ABUOVICH ASANOV.

Kazakh Scientific and Research Institute of Fruit Growing and Viticulture: 050035 Almaty, pr. Gagarina 238A; tel. (7272) 48-47-92; fax (7272) 48-10-50; f. 1978; Dir EDUARD DAULETOVICH MADENOV.

Kazakh Scientific and Research Institute of Grain and Processed Grain Products: 478000 Astana, ul. Ugolnaya 26; tel. (7172) 31-01-93; fax (7172) 31-01-96; f. 1953; Dir A. A. OSPANOV.

Kazakh Scientific and Research Institute of Mechanization and Electrification in Agriculture: 050005 Almaty, pr. Raimbeka 312; tel. (7272) 40-48-00; fax (7272) 77-52-61; f. 1978; Dir ASAN BEKENOVICH OSPANOV.

Kazakh Scientific and Research Institute of Poultry: 040933 Almaty obl., Karasaisky raion, Pos. 50 Let Kazakhskoi SSR, Ul. Maslieva 8; tel. (72771) 9-56-31; fax (72771) 9-56-45; f. 1966; Dir AIDAR KALDYBEKOVICH SABDENOV.

Kazakh Scientific and Research Institute of the Economics and Organization of the Agroindustrial Complex: 050057 Almaty, ul. Tsatpaeva 30B; tel. (7272) 43-64-11; f. 1934; Dir GANI ALIMOVICH KALIEV.

Kazakh Scientific and Research Institute of the Fishing Industry: 050016 Almaty, ul. Suyunbay 89A; fax (7272) 30-47-93; Dir SHOKAN ASHENOVICH ALPEYISOV.

Kazakh Scientific and Research Institute of the Food Industry: 050060 Almaty, pr. Gagarina 238A; tel. (7272) 48-28-90; fax (7272) 48-10-50; f. 1993; Dir DUISENBAY SAILAUBAYEVICH IZBASAROV.

Kazakh Scientific and Research Institute of Water Management: 0800003 Taraz, ul. Kogueldy 12; tel. (7262) 42-60-71; fax (7262) 42-55-40; e-mail iwre@nursat.kz; internet www.kaziwr.isd.kz; f. 1950; Dir Prof. SAGHIT RAHMATULLAEVICH IBATULLIN.

Kazakh Scientific, Research and Design Institute of the Meat and Milk Industry: 490035 Semipalatinsk, ul. Baitursunova 29; tel. (7222) 44-26-15; fax (7222) 44-09-90; e-mail nikimmp@ok.kz; f. 1958; Dir MEIRAM ARYNOVICH MYRZABAYEV.

Kazakh Veterinary Scientific and Research Institute: 480029 Almaty, pr. Raimbeka 223; tel. (7272) 32-17-55; fax (7272) 32-16-11; f. 1925; Dir ABYLAI RYSBAIULY SANSYZBAI.

Kostanai Scientific and Research Institute of Agriculture: 485000 Kostanai, 50 Let Oktobra 94; tel. (7142) 27-80-34; fax (7142) 54-24-72; f. 1984; Dir BERIKZHAN BALAPANULY KAIYPAI.

National Academic Centre of Agrarian Research: 480091 Almaty, 79 Abylai Khan; tel. (7272) 62-52-17; fax (7272) 62-38-31;

depts of economics and information in agriculture, crop science and plant breeding, farming, agrochemistry, water and forest production and agroecology, livestock production and veterinary science, mechanization of agricultural production, processing and storing agricultural produce.

Northern Kazakhstan Research Institute of Animal Breeding and Veterinary Science: 150700 Northen Kazakhstan obl., Bishkul raion, Bishkul, Ul. Institutskaya 1; tel. (71538) 2-13-44; fax (71538) 2-12-53; f. 1962; library of 41,000 vols; Dir KANAT. R. MYNZHASOV.

Pavlodar Scientific and Research Institute of Agriculture: 140909 Pavlodar obl., Pavlodar raion, Pos. Krasnoarmeika; tel. and fax (71845) 53003; e-mail nii07@inbox.ru; f. 1993; Gen. Dir BAKYT IRMULATOV.

Research and Technological Institute of Livestock Raising: 040918 Almaty obl., Kaskelensky raion, Tausamaly; tel. (7272) 34-16-45; f. 1974; library of 18,000 vols, 3,300 journals; Dir A. M. MELDEBEKOV.

Research Institute for Plant Protection: 040924 Almaty obl., Karasai raion, Selo Rakhat; fax (7272) 29-56-22; e-mail kazniizr@nursat.kz; f. 1958; library of 29,134 vols; Dir ABAI ORAZULY SAGITOV.

Kazakh Scientific and Research Institute of Forestry JSC KazAgroInnovation: 021704 Shchuchinsk, Kirov Str. 58; tel. (71636) 4-11-53; fax (71636) 4-11-53; e-mail kafri50@mail.ru; f. 1957; library of 160,000 vols; Dir-Gen. Prof. Dr BOLAT MAZHITOVICH MUKANOV.

Research Institute of Potato and Vegetable Growing: 040917 Almaty obl., Karasai raion, Pos. Kainar; tel. and fax (7272) 98-37-06; f. 1945; Dir TIMUR AITPAYEV.

Research Institute of Sheep Breeding: 040622 Almaty obl., Zhambulsky raion, Mynbayeva; tel. (72770) 6-41-20; f. 1933; sheep, goat, horse and camel breeding; library of 100,000 vols; Dir B. S. SEYIDALIYEV.

South Kazakhstan Scientific and Research Institute of Agriculture: 160813 Shymkent, Soviyetskaya 111; tel. (7252) 22-20-98; fax (7252) 55-16-30; f. 1988; Dir MUHTAR ZHANBYRBAYEVICH ZHANBYRBAYEV.

Taldykorgan Agricultural Research Institute: 040000 Almaty obl., Taldykorgan raion, Pos. Zarya; tel. (72822) 9-94-45; fax (72822) 7-12-34; f. 1992; Dir M. K. KOZHAHMETOV.

Tselinny Scientific and Research Institute of Mechanization and Electrification in Agriculture: 110011 Kostanai, pr. Abaya 34; fax (7142) 55-81-47; e-mail celin@mail.kz; Dir VLADIMIR LEONIDOVICH ASTAFEV.

Uspanov Institute of Soil Science: 050060 Almaty, Akademgorodok; fax (7272) 48-14-69; e-mail soil@nursat.kz; f. 1945; attached to Nat. Acad. of Sciences of Kazakhstan; Dir A. S. SAPAROV.

ECONOMICS, LAW AND POLITICS

Institute of Economics: 050010 Almaty, Kurmangazy 29; tel. (7272) 93-01-75; fax (7272) 62-78-19; e-mail ieconom@academset .kz; f. 1952; attached to Nat. Acad. of Sciences of Kazakhstan; Dir M. B. KENGHEGUZIN.

Institute of State and Law: 050000 Almaty, Kurmangazy 29; tel. (7272) 69-59-11; f. 1961; attached to Nat. Acad. of Sciences of Kazakhstan; Dir E. K. NURPEISOV.

HISTORY, GEOGRAPHY AND ARCHAEOLOGY

Institute of Geography: 050010 Almaty, ul. Kalinina 69A; tel. (7272) 61-81-29; f. 1983; attached to Nat. Acad. of Sciences of Kazakhstan; Dir N. K. MUKITANOV.

Margulan Institute of Archaeology: 050010 Almaty, pr. Dostvyk 44; tel. and fax (7272) 61-86-63; e-mail margulan@freenet .kz; f. 1991; attached to Nat. Acad. of Sciences of Kazakhstan; Dir A. K. MARGULANA.

Valikhanov, Ch. Ch., Institute of History and Ethnology: 050021 Almaty, ul. Shevchenko 28; tel. (7272) 62-92-37; f. 1945; attached to Nat. Acad. of Sciences of Kazakhstan; Dir M. K. KOZYBAYEV.

LANGUAGE AND LITERATURE

Auezov, M. O., Institute of Literature and Arts: 050010 Almaty, ul. Kurmangazy 29; tel. (7272) 72-74-11; fax (7272) 72-79-43; e-mail lit_art@academset.kz; internet litart .mindlab.kz; f. 1934; attached to Min. of Education and Science and Nat. Acad. of Sciences of Kazakhstan; Dir SEIT ASKAROVICH KASKABASOV; publ. *Keruen* (4 a year).

Baitursynov Institute of Linguistics: 050021 Almaty, ul. Kurmangazy 29; tel. (7272) 61-56-35; fax (7272) 72-80-59; e-mail tilbilimi@bk.ru; f. 1961; attached to Dept of Science of Min. of Education and Science; researches in Kazakh linguistics; library of 500,000 vols; Dir Dr SHERUBAI KURMANBAIULY; publ. *Linguistic*.

MEDICINE

Central Asian Plague Prevention Research Institute: 050034 Almaty, Kopalskaya ul. 14; tel. (7272) 35-75-48; Dir V. M. STEPANOV.

Dermatovenereological Research Institute of the Committee for Health: Ministry of Education and Science, 050002 Almaty, ul. Raimbeka 60; tel. (7272) 30-40-85; fax (7272) 50-23-77; f. 1931; library of 250,000 vols; Dir ZURA B. KESHILEVA.

Institute of Microbiology, Epidemiology and Infectious Diseases: 050002 Almaty, ul. Pastera 34; tel. (7272) 33-04-26; Dir I. K. SHURATOV.

Institute of Nutrition: 050008 Almaty, ul. Klochkova 66; tel. (7272) 42-92-03; fax (7272) 42-97-20; f. 1974; attached to Nat. Acad. of Sciences of Kazakhstan; Dir T. SH. SHARMANOV; publs *Voprosy pitaniya*, *Zdravookhranenie Kazakhstana* (8–10 a year).

Kazakhstan Paediatrics Research Institute: 050000 Almaty, Al-Farabi 146; tel. (7272) 48-81-21; fax (7272) 63-12-07; f. 1932; library of 36,000 vols; Dir A. K. MASKAKEYEV.

National Centre of Labour Hygiene and Occupational Diseases: 100012 Karaganda, 15 Mustafina; tel. and fax (7212) 56-52-63; fax (7212) 56-10-21; e-mail ncgtpz@ gmail.com; internet ncgtpz.kz; f. 1958 as Institute of Physiology and Occupational Diseases; present name 2002; attached to Min. of Health; Dir Dr ZHAMILYA BATTAKOVA; publ. *Occupational Hygiene and Medical Ecology* (4 a year).

National Centre for Tuberculosis Problems: 050000 Almaty, Bekhozhin ul. 5; tel. (7272) 91-86-57; fax (7272) 91-86-58; e-mail ncpt@itte.kz; f. 1932; library of 11,000 vols; Dir SH. ISMAILOV.

Research Institute of Clinical and Experimental Surgery: 050003 Almaty, ul. Mira 62; Dir M. A. ALIEV.

NATURAL SCIENCES

Biological Sciences

Aitkhozhin, M. A., Institute of Molecular Biology and Biochemistry: 050012 Almaty, ul. Dosmuhamedova 86; tel. (7272) 67-63-06; fax (7272) 67-19-47; f. 1983; attached to Nat. Acad. of Sciences of Kazakhstan; Dir Prof. N. A. Aitkhozhin (acting).

Institute of Botany: 050029 Almaty, Timiryazeva 36D; tel. (7272) 47-66-92; fax (7272) 47-90-42; f. 1995; attached to Nat. Acad. of Sciences of Kazakhstan; Dir S. A. Abiyev.

Institute of Experimental Biology: 050022 Almaty, pr. Abaya 38; tel. (7272) 67-23-03; attached to Min. of Education and Science; Dir A. M. Murzamadiev.

Institute of General Genetics and Cytology: 050040 Almaty; f. 1995; attached to Nat. Acad. of Sciences of Kazakhstan.

Institute of Human and Animal Physiology: 480032 Almaty, Akademgorodok; tel. (7272) 48-04-88; f. 1945; attached to Nat. Acad. of Sciences of Kazakhstan; Dir Kh. D. Duisembin.

Institute of Microbiology and Virology: 050010 Almaty, ul. Kirova 103; tel. (7272) 61-84-97; e-mail adm@imv.academ.alma-ata.su; f. 1956; attached to Nat. Acad. of Sciences of Kazakhstan; Dir A. N. Ilyaletdinov.

Institute of Zoology: 050034 Almaty, Akademgorodok; tel. (7272) 48-19-32; e-mail common@zoo/2.academ.alma-ata.su; f. 1943; attached to Nat. Acad. of Sciences of Kazakhstan; Dir T. N. Doszhanov.

Mathematical Sciences

Institute of Mathematics: 050010 Almaty, Pushkina 125; tel. (727) 272-70-95; fax (727) 272-33-99; e-mail dzhenali@math.kz; internet www.math.kz; f. 1965; attached to Nat. Acad. of Sciences of Kazakhstan; Dir Prof. M. T. Dzhenaliev; Scientific Sec. Sholpan Balgimbaeva.

Institute of Theoretical and Applied Mathematics: 050021 Almaty, ul. Pushkina 125; tel. (7272) 61-37-40; f. 1965; attached to Nat. Acad. of Sciences of Kazakhstan; Dir N. K. Bliev.

Physical Sciences

Akhmedsafin, U. M., Institute of Hydrogeology and Hydrophysics: 050010 Almaty, ul. Krasina 94; tel. (7272) 61-50-51; f. 1965; attached to Nat. Acad. of Sciences of Kazakhstan; Dir V. V. Veselov.

Bekturov Institute of Chemical Sciences: 050010 Almaty, Ualikhanov 106; tel. (7272) 91-23-89; fax (7272) 91-24-80; e-mail labsp@ics.scinet.kz; internet www.chemistry .kz; f. 1945; attached to Min. of Education and Science; library of 83,000 vols; Dir Prof. Dr E. E. Ergozhin; publ. *Chemical Journal of Kazakhstan* (4 a year).

Chemical-Metallurgical Institute: 100009 Karaganda, Ermekov 63; tel. and fax (7212) 43-31-61; e-mail hmi@mail.krg.kz; f. 1958; attached to Nat. Acad. of Sciences of Kazakhstan; Dir Dr Bolat Khassen.

Fesenkov Astrophysical Institute: 480068 Almaty, Kamenskoe plato; tel. (7272) 65-00-40; e-mail adm@afi.academ .alma-ata.su; f. 1950; attached to Nat. Acad. of Sciences of Kazakhstan; Dir B. T. Tashenov.

Geological Surveying Oil Research Institute: 060002 Atyrau, ul. Ordzhonikidze 43; tel. (71222) 3-33-86; Dir S. U. Utgaliyev.

Institute of Nuclear Physics: 050032 Almaty, Ibragimova 1; tel. (7272) 54-64-67; fax (7272) 54-65-17; internet inp1.sci.kz; f. 1957; attached to Nat. Acad. of Sciences of Kazakhstan; Dir K. K. Kadyrzhanov.

Institute of Organic Catalysis and Electro-chemistry: 050010 Almaty, D. Kunayev 142; tel. (7272) 61-58-08; fax (7272) 91-57-22; e-mail orgcat@nursat.kz; internet www .catalysis.nsk.su; f. 1969; attached to Nat. Acad. of Sciences of Kazakhstan; Dir M. Z. Zhurinov.

Institute of Organic Synthesis and Carbon Chemistry: 100000 Karaganda, ul. 40-let Kazakhstana; tel. (7272) 52-60-85; f. 1983; attached to Nat. Acad. of Sciences of Kazakhstan; Dir S. M. Moldakhmetov.

Institute of Petroleum Chemistry and Natural Salts: 060002 Atyrau, ul. Lenina 2; tel. (7122) 22-26-74; f. 1960; attached to Nat. Acad. of Sciences of Kazakhstan; Dir N. R. Bukeikhanov.

Institute of Physics and Technology: 050032 Alatau, Ibragimova 11; tel. (7272) 26-24-95; fax (7272) 26-25-11; e-mail mukashev@sci.kz; internet www.sci.kz; f. 1991; attached to Nat. Acad. of Sciences of Kazakhstan; depts of condensed matter physics, material science and nanotechnology, spectroscopic methods of research, high-energy physics and cosmic rays, information technology; Dir Dr B. N. Mukashev.

Institute of Phytochemistry: 100009 Karaganda, Ministry of Education and Science, ul. Gazalieva, 4; e-mail kms@phyto .karaganda.su; f. 1995; attached to Nat. Acad. of Sciences of Kazakhstan.

Institute of Seismology: 050060 Almaty, pr. Al-Farabi 75; tel. (7272) 48-21-34; fax (7272) 49-44-17; e-mail adm@seism.academ .alma-ata.su; f. 1976; attached to Nat. Acad. of Sciences of Kazakhstan; Dir A. K. Kurskeyev.

Institute of Space Research: 050034 Almaty, Akademgorodok; tel. (7272) 62-38-96; e-mail silakaziki@akma-ata.su; f. 1991; attached to Nat. Acad. of Sciences of Kazakhstan; Dir U. M. Sultangazin.

Institute of the Ionosphere: 050020 Almaty, Kamenskoe plato; tel. (7272) 54-80-74; fax (7272) 65-09-93; f. 1983; attached to Nat. Acad. of Sciences of Kazakhstan; Dir V. I. Drobzhev.

National Nuclear Centre: 071100 Kurchatov, Lenina 6; tel. (72251) 2-33-33; fax (72251) 2-38-58; internet www.nnc.kz; f. 1992; Dir S. T. Tukhvatulin.

Physical Technical Institute: 050032 Almaty, Alatau; tel. (7272) 69-05-66; fax (7272) 54-52-24; e-mail mukashev@sci.kz; internet www.sci.kz; f. 1991; attached to Nat. Acad. of Sciences of Kazakhstan; Dir Prof. B. N. Mukashev.

Satpaev, K. I., Institute of Geological Sciences: 050010 Almaty, ul. Kalinina 69A; tel. (7272) 61-56-08; e-mail adm@geol .academ.alma-ata.su; f. 1940; attached to Nat. Acad. of Sciences of Kazakhstan; Dir A. A. Abdullin.

PHILOSOPHY AND PSYCHOLOGY

Institute of Philosophy: 050021 Almaty, ul. Kurmangazy 29; tel. and fax (7272) 69-59-11; f. 1991; attached to Nat. Acad. of Sciences of Kazakhstan; Dir Prof. A. N. Nysanbayev.

RELIGION, SOCIOLOGY AND ANTHROPOLOGY

Institute of Orient Studies: 050010 Almaty, ul. Pushkina 111/113; tel. (7272) 61-53-71; f. 1996; attached to Nat. Acad. of Sciences of Kazakhstan; Dir K. T. Talipov.

TECHNOLOGY

Eastern Mining and Metallurgical Research Institute of Non-ferrous Metals: 070002 Ust-Kamenogorsk, Promyshlennaya 1; tel. (7232) 75-37-73; fax (7232) 75-37-71; e-mail vcmnauka@mail .east.telecom.kz; internet vcm.ukg.kz; f. 1950; attached to Min. of Industry and New Technologies; carries out research and semi-commercial scale tests; provides scientific and technical assistance in the introduction of technologies and equipment in the fields of polymetal ores mining and dressing, heavy non-ferrous metals metallurgy, applied and analytical chemistry, environment protection; library of 169,500 vols; Dir Dr Nikolay Ushakov.

Institute of Informatics and Control Problems: 050010 Almaty, Pushkina str. 125; tel. and fax (7272) 72-37-11; e-mail office@ipic.kz; internet www.ipic.kz; f. 1991; attached to Science Cttee of MES RK; Dir M. N. Kalimoldayev.

Institute of Metallurgy and Ore Enrichment: 050010 Almaty, ul. Shevchenko 29/33; tel. (7272) 91-57-81; fax (7272) 91-46-60; e-mail imo-almaty@nursat.kz; internet www .imo.nursat.kz; f. 1945; attached to Nat. Acad. of Sciences of Kazakhstan; Dir Prof. Dr Bagdaulet Kenzhaliev; publ. *Kompleksnoe Ispolzovanie Mineralnogo Siria* (6 a year).

Kunayev Institute of Mining: 050046 Almaty, Ave Abai 191; tel. (727) 376-53-00; fax (727) 376-52-97; e-mail igdkpms@mail.ru; internet www.igd.kz; f. 1944; attached to Nat. Centre for Integrated Minerals Recycling of the Republic of Kazakhstan; scientific and research activity in mining; devt of rational methods of design and management of production processes at mining companies; creation of effective and environmentally safe technologies and minerals mining equipment; postgraduate training of scientific personnel, training of mining specialists, scientific and technical popularization of latest achievements of science and equipment; editorial activity; int. cooperation; economic activity; library of 70,153 vols,incl. 21,724 periodicals; 255 teachers; Dir Prof. Dr Galiev Seitgali Joldasovich; publ. *Scientific and Technical Provision of Mining Production* (2 a year).

National Centre for Complex Processing of Mineral Raw Materials: 050036 Almaty, Dzhandosov 67; tel. (7272) 59-00-70; fax (7272) 59-00-75; internet www .innovation.kz; attached to Nat. Academy of Sciences of Kazakhstan; Dir A. Zharmenov.

Scientific and Technological Centre of Machinery Construction: 480064 Almaty, pr. Abaya 191; tel. (7272) 46-97-50; e-mail mntc@mail.ru; f. 1998; Dir S. U. Joldasbekov.

Libraries and Archives

Almaty

Al-Farabi Kazakh National University Central Library: 050010 Almaty, Timiryazeva ul. 42; tel. (7272) 47-27-61; fax (7272) 49-26-09; e-mail guljan_m@kazsu.kz; internet lib.kazsu.kz; f. 1934; 1.5m. vols; Dir E. D. Abulkayirova.

Central Scientific Library of the Ministry of Education & Science of the Republic of Kazakhstan: 050010 Almaty, ul. Shevchenko 28; tel. (7272) 72-83-41; fax (7272) 61-00-37; e-mail cnb@library.kz; internet www.library.kz; f. 1932; 5.5m. vols, 2,041 MSS; Dir Kulzhikhan Abugaliyeva; publ. *Kitapkhana Alemi* (Library World, 4 a year).

National Library of the Republic of Kazakhstan: 480013 Almaty, Abaya Ave 14; tel. (7272) 62-28-83; fax (7272) 69-28-83;

e-mail intrel@nlrk.kz; internet www.nlrk.kz; f. 1931; legal deposit library; 6m. vols; Dir-Gen. ORYNBASSAR ISSAKHOV.

Scientific and Technical Library of Kazakhstan: 050026 Almaty, S. Mukanov 223B; tel. and fax 727) 378-41-95; internet www.rntb.kz; f. 1960; 35.3m. vols (incl. patents); Dir-Gen. K. G. URMURZINA.

Karaganda

Karaganda State University Library: 100026 Karaganda, ul. Universitetskaya 28; tel. (7212) 74-53-00; fax (7212) 74-47-67; internet library.ksu.kz; 400,000 vols; Dir S. M. ZHERZHISOVA.

Museums and Art Galleries

Almaty

Central State Museum of Kazakhstan: 050059 Almaty, Samal-1 44; tel. (7272) 64-22-00; e-mail csmrk@hn.freenet.kz; internet www.unesco.kz/heritagenet/kz/hn-english/csmrk/engl/index_en.htm; history and natural history of Kazakhstan; Dir NURSAN ALIMBAY.

Kasteyev Kazakh State Art Museum: 050040 Almaty, ul. Satpayeva 30A; tel. (7272) 47-82-49; fax (7272) 47-86-69; e-mail kazart@nursat.kz; internet www.art.nursat.kz; f. 1976; Kazakh art, folk art, Soviet and European art; library of 23,000 vols; Dir BAYTURSUN E. UMORBEKOV.

Universities

AKTAU SH. YESENOV UNIVERSITY

466200 Aktau, Mikro raion 14

Telephone: (7292) 43-85-68

Fax: (7292) 33-42-21

State control

Rector: ASHIMZHAN S. AKHMETOV.

AKTOBE K. ZHUBANOV STATE UNIVERSITY

030014 Aktobe, Molgagulova 34

Telephone: (7132) 55-37-56

Fax: (7132) 57-78-43

E-mail: zhubanov@samgau.kz

State control.

AL-FARABI KAZAKH NATIONAL UNIVERSITY

050038 Almaty, Al-Farabi 71

Telephone: (7272) 47-14-88

Fax: (7272) 47-26-09

E-mail: anurmag@kazsu.kz

Internet: www.kazsu.kz

Founded 1934 (fmrly Kazakh S. M. Kirov State University), present name and status 1994

State control

Languages of instruction: Kazakh, Russian

Academic year: September to July (two semesters)

Rector: Prof. T. A. KOZHAMKULOV

Pro-Rectors: Dr G. K. AKHMETOVA, Prof. ZH. D. DADEBAYEV, Prof. A. I. KUPCHISHIN, Prof. Z. A. MANSUROV, Prof. N. O. OMASHEV, Dr S. T. SHALGYMBAYEV

Librarian: E. DZ. ABULKAIROVA

Library: see Libraries and Archives

Number of teachers: 1,618

Number of students: 14,500

Publication: *Vestnik KazGNU* (1 a year)

DEANS

Dept of Biology: Prof. R. I. BERSIMBAYEV

Dept of Chemistry: Prof. Z. A. ABILOB

Dept of Economics and Business: Prof. R. Y. YELEMESSOV

Dept of Geography: Dr K. M. BAIMYRZAYEV

Dept of History: Prof. ZH. K. TAIMAGAMBETOV

Dept of Int. Relations: Prof. Y. B. ZHATKAN-BAYEV

Dept of Journalism: Prof. B. O. ZHAKYP

Dept of Law: Prof. D. L. BAIDELDINOV

Dept of Literary and Language Studies: Prof. K. A. ABDEZULY

Dept of Mechanics and Mathematics: Prof. M. K. ORUNKHANOV

Dept of Oriental Studies: Prof. S. M. SYZDY-KOV

Dept of Philosophy and Political Science: Prof. G. Y. YESSIM

Dept of Physics: Prof. A. S. ASKAROVA

Preparatory Dept for Foreign Citizens: Dr G. Y. UTEBALIYEVA

ALMATY ABAI STATE UNIVERSITY

050010 Almaty, Dostyk 12

Telephone: (7272) 91-63-39

Fax: (7272) 91-30-50

E-mail: rector@bai.uni.sci.kz

Internet: www.abai.uni.sic.kz

Founded 1928

State control

Languages of instruction: Kazakh, Russian

Academic year: September to June

Rector: TOKMUKHAMED S. SADYKOV

Library: 1m. vols

Number of teachers: 730

Number of students: 8,877

DEANS

Arts and Graphics: BAIMURAT OSPANOV

Finance and Economics: MIRSEDA ALIM-BAYEVA

Geography and Ecology: AZIMKHAN SEITZHA-NOV

History: SAIYN BORBASOV

Int. Relations: EUGENI KUZNETSOV

Kazakh Philology: SAUL DAUTOVA

Law: KAMAL BURKHANOV

Physics and Mathematics: MAKTAGALI BEKTE-MISOV

Psychology and Pedagogy: ROMSEIT KOJAN-BAYEV

Russian Philology: MANAT MUSATAYEVA

ALMATY TECHNOLOGICAL UNIVERSITY

050012 Almaty, Tole-bi 100

Telephone: (7272) 68-83-35

Fax: (7272) 68-63-30

E-mail: atukz@mail.kz

Internet: www.atu.kz

Founded 1952

State control

Rector: K. S. KULAZHANOV

Faculties of cybernetics, economics, extra-mural studies, food science and technology.

ATYRAU H. DOSMUHAMEDOV STATE UNIVERSITY

465017 Atyrau, ul. Pushkina 12

Telephone: (7122) 23-30-44

Fax: (7122) 23-30-17

State control

Rector: ASHAT IMANGALIYEV.

DZHAMBUL UNIVERSITY

080003 Taraz, Dzhambul 16A

Telephone: (7262) 23-19-78

State control.

EAST KAZAKHSTAN STATE UNIVERSITY

070002 Ust-Kamenogorsk, 30 Gvardeiskoy Divisii 34B

Telephone: (7232) 540-411

Fax: (7232) 540-407

E-mail: rector@vkgu.kz

Internet: www.vkgu.kz

Founded 1952

State control

Languages of instruction: Kazakh, Russian

Academic year: September to June

Rector: BEIBIT MAMRAYEV

First Vice-Rector: GAINELGAZY ADILGAZINOV

Library of 992,710 vols

Number of teachers: 700

Number of students: 11,079

DIRECTORS

Adult Education: FARXAD KURMANOV

Continuing Education: MAJAK ZHAKSILIKOV

Economics and Finance: TOXTAR BOLGAUOV

Law: KUAT RAKHIMBERDINOV

History and International Relations: RIZABEK SARMULDINOV

Natural Sciences, Ecology: ANAR MYRZAGA-LIYEVA

Philology: SLYAMBEK ORAZALIN

Physics, Mathematics and Technology: BEI-SEN AKHMETZHANOV

GUMILEV, L. N., EURASIAN UNIVERSITY

010008 Astana, Tsiolkovsky 6

Telephone: (7172) 24-32-93

Fax: (7172) 24-30-90

E-mail: root@lceu.ricc.kz

Founded 1962 as teacher-training institute; became Akmola University 1992; present name 1996

State control

Languages of instruction: Kazakh, Russian

Academic year: September to June

Rector: Prof. Dr AMANGHELDY HUSSAYNOVICH HUSSAINOV

Pro-Rector for Coordination and Academic Programmes: MUKHTAR USSINOVICH ISMA-GAMBETOV

Pro-Rector for Financial Admin.: MUKHTAR MUKHAMEDIEVICH URAZALIN

Pro-Rector for Research and Int. Relations: Prof. Dr RAHMETULLA SHARAPIDENOVICH YERKASSOV

Pro-Rector for Social Activities: MINA EMA-NUILOVNA ROMANENKO

Senior Adminstrative Officer: Prof. AMAN-GHELDY ZHAKSYLIKOVICH ISMAILOV

Library: 1m. vols

DEANS

Faculty of Culture and Art: IRINA UMAN-GIREEVNA AUSHEVA

Faculty of Economics: Prof. SAYRAN KAB-DRAKHMANOVNA SURAGANOVA

Faculty of Engineering: Prof. Dr SERIK NURAKOV

Faculty of Engineering and Economics (extramural): Prof. VYACHESLAV VIKTORO-VICH TARASSOV

Faculty of Foreign Languages: SAULE BAZY-LOVNA ZAGATOVA

Faculty of History and Int. Relations: KADYR ABILZHANOVICH AKHMETOV

Faculty of Humanities (extramural): MARAT TOKENOVICH ZHOLBARISSOV

Faculty of Law: ZHUMAHAN ZHARKINBEKOVICH UTENOV

Faculty of Natural Sciences and Physical Education: Prof. AMANZHOL KUSSEPOVICH KUSSEPOV

Faculty of Oriental Studies: Prof. Dr SEYIT ASKAROVICH KASKABASOV

Faculty of Philology: GALINA ALEXANDROVNA CHERNETSKAYA

Faculty of Physics and Mathematics: YERLAN SERIKOVICH BAIGOZHIN

KARAGANDA E. A. BUKETOV STATE UNIVERSITY

100028 Karaganda, Universitetskaya ul. 28
Telephone: (7212) 77-03-89
Fax: (7212) 77-03-84
E-mail: office@ksu.kz
Internet: www.ksu.kz
Founded 1972
State control
Academic year: September to June
Rector: YERKIN KINAYATOVICH KUBEYEV
Number of teachers: 1,200
Number of students: 13,000
Publication: *Vestnik* (4 a year)
Faculties of biology, chemistry, economics, education, foreign languages, history, law, mathematics, philology, philosophy and psychology, physical culture and sport, physics, social sciences, vocational and continuing improvement.

KAZAKH HUMANITARIAN LAW UNIVERSITY

050008 Almaty, pr. Abaya 50A
Telephone: (7272) 42-52-25
Fax: (7272) 77-97-53
Founded 1994
State control
Languages of instruction: Kazakh, Russian
Academic year: September to June
Rector: MAKSUT NARIKBAYEV
Vice-Rector: BOLAT BEYEKENOV
Library of 100,237 vols
Number of teachers: 545
Number of students: 1,883
Publication: *State and Law* (3 a year)

DEANS

Commercial Law: SERGEY MARKIN
Criminal Law and Trial Investigation Law: RAMASAN NURTAYEV
Int. Law: IRINA KHAN
Judicial and State Prosecution Law: OMIRBAY KYSTAUBAY

KAZAKH K. I. SATBAYEV NATIONAL TECHNICAL UNIVERSITY

050013 Almaty, Satbayev 22
Telephone: (7272) 92-60-25
Fax: (7272) 92-60-26
E-mail: allnt@kazntu.sci.kz
Internet: www.ntu.kz
Founded 1934 as Kazakh Polytechnic Institute; present name and status 1996
State control
Languages of instruction: Kazakh, Russian
Academic year: September to July
Rector: Prof. ZHEXENBEK M. ADILOV ADILOV
Library of 2,000,147 vols
Number of teachers: 1,268
Number of students: 12,086
Publication: *KazNTU Herald* (scientific magazine).

KAZAKH STATE WOMEN'S PEDAGOGICAL INSTITUTE

480083 Almaty, Aiteke-bi 99
Telephone: (7272) 39-42-83
Founded 1944
State control
Languages of instruction: Kazakh, Russian
Academic year: September to July

Rector: SELIKBEK ISAYEV
Library of 860,000 vols
Number of teachers: 650
Number of students: 2,600
Faculties of economics, education, history, library science, modern languages, music education, natural sciences, philology, philosophy, primary education, sports, teacher training.

KAZAKH-TURKISH HODJA AHMET YESEVI INTERNATIONAL UNIVERSITY

487010 Turkistan, Maydan Yesim-Khan 2
Telephone: (7253) 34-11-44
Fax: (7253) 34-14-47
E-mail: webmaster@mktu.turkistan.kz
Internet: www.turkistan.kz
Founded 1991 jtly by Govts of Kazakhstan and Turkey
State control
Languages of instruction: Kazakh, Turkish, Russian, English
Academic year: September to July
Rector: MURAT ZHURINOV
Library of 480,000 vols
Number of teachers: 700
Number of students: 10,200
Publication: *Scientific Methodological Articles* (fortnightly)
Faculties of art, art studies, ecology, economics, history, history and philology, languages and literature, law, mathematics and econ., medicine, natural sciences, oriental studies.

KOKSHETAU SH. VALIHANOV UNIVERSITY

100001 Kokshetau, ul. Karla Marksa 76
Telephone: (7162) 25-55-84
Fax: (7162) 25-55-83
E-mail: universi@kokc.kz
Founded 1962
State control
Languages of instruction: Kazakh, Russian
Academic year: September to July
Rector: ABAI A. AITMUHAMBETOV
Library of 600,000 vols
Number of teachers: 450
Number of students: 4,900

DEANS

Faculty of Agriculture and Technology: ALEKSANDR PODDUBNY
Faculty of Chemistry and Biology: TOLEGEN SEILHANOV
Faculty of Economics: KOSYBAI AITKOZHIN
Faculty of Foreign Languages: NATALYA ZHUMANGULOVA
Faculty of History and Art: ZHARAS ERMEKBAYEV
Faculty of Philology: OLGA ANITSHENKO
Faculty of Physics and Mathematics: KADYRHAN MUSABAYEV

KOSTANAI A. BAITURSYNOV STATE UNIVERSITY

110000 Kostanai, ul. Baitursynova 47
Telephone: (7142) 54-25-94
Fax: (7142) 54-25-94
E-mail: ksu47@mail.kz
Internet: www.ksu.kst.kz
Founded 1939, present status 1992
State control
Rector: KHUSAIN KH. VALIYEV
Publications: *Bilim zharysy* (12 a year), *Zharsken-Kostanai* (6 a year), *Mezhvuzovskii nauchnyi zhurnal* (Intercollegiate Scientific Journal), *Vestnik Nauki* (Herald of Science, 4 a year)

Faculty of journalism; institutes of agriculture, economy and management, engineering and physics, humanities, law, mathematics and information technology, veterinary studies; college of Kazakh State University.

KYZYLORDA KORKYT ATA HUMANITARIAN UNIVERSITY

120000 Kyzylorda, Zheltoksan 40
State control.

KYZYLORDA KORKYT ATA STATE UNIVERSITY

467021 Kyzylorda, Aiteke-bi 29A
Telephone: (72422) 6-17-95
Fax: (72422) 6-17-25
E-mail: ksu@kyzstun.asdc.kz
Founded 1937
State control
Languages of instruction: Kazakh, Russian
Academic year: September to June
Rector: KYLYSHBAI A. BISSENOV
Library: 1.8m. items
Number of teachers: 460
Number of students: 8,000
Publications: *Syr Tulegu* (news), *Vestnik* (sciences, quarterly)
Faculties of correspondence and evening courses, economics and ecology, economics and engineering, history and law, natural sciences, philology and arts, physics and mathematics.

M. KOZEYBAYEV NORTH KAZAKHSTAN STATE UNIVERSITY

150000 Petropavlovsk, Pushkin St 86
Telephone: (152) 49-33-52
Fax: (152) 49-33-42
E-mail: mail@nkzu.kz
Internet: www.nkzu.kz
Founded 1937
State control
Languages of instruction: Kazakh, Russian
Academic year: September to August
Rector: ASHIMOV UNDASSYN BAIKENOVICH
Vice-Rector for Academic Work: GUSAKOV VIKTOR PETROVICH
Vice-Rector for Scientific Work and External Relations: TUKACHYOV ALEXANDER ANDREEVICH
Vice-Rector for Educational Work: TAIZHANOVA MUKARAM MURZATOVNA
Vice-Rector for House-Keeping Unit: KUSHUMBAEV AKBAY BAGYTKEREEVICH
Library: 1m. vols
Number of teachers: 440
Number of students: 10,000

DEANS

Faculty of Economics: A. S. ISMAGULOVA
Faculty of Energetic and Mechanical Engineering: KAIRAT T. KOSHEKOV
Faculty of History and Law: SABYR I. IBRAEV
Faculty of Information Technology: B. E. BATYROV
Faculty of Music: N. I. PYSTOVALOVA
Faculty of Natural Sciences: NIKOLAI N. SEMENOV
Faculty of Physical Education: VICTOR K. KULAYEV
Faculty of Transport-building Engineering: R. S. IMAMBAEVA
Institute of Language and Literature: ZH. S. TALASPAEVA
Qualification Development Institute: A. SH. YASHKINA

SEMEY STATE SHAKARIM UNIVERSITY

490035 Semipalatinsk, ul. Gleynky 20A

Telephone: (7222) 42-29-37
Fax: (7222) 35-95-49
E-mail: info@semgu.kz
Internet: www.semgu.kz

Founded 1995
State control
Languages of instruction: Kazakh, Russian
Academic year: September to June

Rector: YERLAN SYDYKOV
Vice-Rector: MIKHAIL PANIN

Library: 1m. vols
Number of teachers: 648
Number of students: 8,682

DEANS

Faculty of Economcs: SERIKTAY BAIMUKHANOV
Faculty of Engineering and Technology: SERIK TUMENOV
Faculty of Finance: BEGMAN KOZHEGELDIYEV
Faculty of Humanities: ALMAGUL MUKHAMEDKHANOVA
Faculty of Natural Sciences: BENUR MUSABALINA
Faculty of Philology: FARIDA ZHAKSYBAYEVA
Faculty of Veterinary Medicine and Agriculture: ZEINOLLA TOKAYEV

SOUTHERN KAZAKHSTAN AUZEV HUMANITIES UNIVERSITY

160018 Shymkent, Beibitshilik 3

Telephone: (72522) 44-99-88
E-mail: ukrgi-smh@nursat.kz
State control.

SOUTHERN KAZAKHSTAN MEDICAL ACADEMY

160000 Shymkent, Lenina 1
Founded 1944
State control.

STATE FINANCIAL INSTITUTE

071403 Semipalatinsk, ul. Shugajeva 159

Telephone: (7222) 63-59-20
Fax: (7222) 66-28-83

Founded 1995
State control

Rector: GENNADI N. GARMANIĆ.

TARAZ M. KH. DULATI STATE UNIVERSITY

080000 Jambul obl., Taraz, Tole

Telephone: (7262) 45-36-64
Fax: (7262) 43-24-02
E-mail: info@targu.kz
Internet: www.tarsu.kz

Founded 1998
State control

Rector: ASHIMZHAN S. AKHMETOV

Number of teachers: 500
Number of students: 6,326

ZHETYSU I. ZHANSUGUROV UNIVERSITY

040009 Taldykorgan, ul. I. Zhansugurova 187A

Telephone: (72722) 2-00-20
Fax: (72722) 1-22-61
E-mail: tk_jgu@mail.ru

Founded 1972
State control
Languages of instruction: Kazakh, Russian
Academic year: September to June

Rector: ESENGELDY MEDEUYOV
Pro-Rector: ASKHAT SARSENBAYEV

Number of teachers: 307
Number of students: 6,985

Faculties of business and commerce, computer education, finance, foreign languages, humanities, law, mathematics, pedagogy.

ZHEZKAZGAN O. A. BAIKONUROV UNIVERSITY

100600 Zhezkazgan, pr. Alashahana 1

Telephone: (7102) 73-63-24
Fax: (7102) 73-01-15
E-mail: univer@iftc.zhez.kz

Founded 1956
State control
Languages of instruction: Kazakh, Russian, English

Rector: ZHUMAGALI NAURYZBAI
Vice-Rector: KALI KISHAUOV

Library: 1.1m. vols
Number of teachers: 1,035
Number of students: 3,061

DIRECTORS

Institute of Economics and Law: GULNAR TEMIRBAYEVA
Institute of Mining Engineernig: MUHAMEDZHAN AUEZOV
Institute Natural Sciences: OMITRAI ZHALELOV
Institute of Philology and Arts: MURAT ABEUOV

Other Higher Educational Institutes

Aktobe State Medical Institute: 463022 Aktobe, ul. Lenina 52; tel. (7132) 54-39-04; library: 62,000 vols.

Almaty Institute of Power Engineering and Telecommunication: 050013 Almaty, ul. Baytursynova 126; tel. (7272) 92-57-40; fax (7272) 92-50-57; e-mail aipet@aipet.kz; internet www.aipet.kz; f. 1975; faculties of power engineering, radio engineering, thermal engineering; part-time courses and retraining; pre-institutional training; ENTEL College; br. in Ust Kamenogorsk; library: 465,000 vols; 284 teachers; 4,856 students; Rector GUMARBEK ZH. DAUKEYEV; publs *Collections of Scientific Works* (2 a year), *Collections of Postgraduate Works* (1 a year).

Almaty Kurmangazy State Conservatoire: 480091 Almaty, Ablaikhan pr. 90; tel. (7272) 62-76-40; courses in academic and folk singing, choral and symphonic conducting, composition, cultural management, musicology, orchestral and folk instruments, piano; library: 266,060 vols.

Almaty State Theatrical and Cinema Institute: 480091 Almaty, ul. Bogenbai Batyr 136; tel. (7272) 63-66-52; fax (7272) 50-62-84; f. 1992; acting and directing apprenticeship; 10 teachers; library: 400 vols.

Astana State Medical Academy: 473013 Astana, pr. Mira 51A; tel. (7172) 26-07-829; fax (7172) 26-39-18; e-mail akma@asdc.kz; f. 1964, present name and status 1997; faculties of medicine and biological sciences, medicine, paediatrics; library: 381,500 vols; 370 teachers; 2,100 students; Rector R. K. TULEBAYEV.

D. Serikbaev East Kazakhstan State Technical University: 69 H. K. O., 070004 Ust-Kamenogorsk; tel. (7232) 26-28-89; fax (7232) 26-74-09; e-mail ekstu@ektu.kz; internet www.ektu.kz; f. 1958; academic divisions: Centre of Humanities Education, Faculty with the Kazakh Language of Instruction, Institute of Building Technologies and Architecture, Institute of Economics and Management, Institute of Information Technologies, Institute of Mechanics and Technology, Institute of Mining and Metallurgical Engineering, Postgraduate and New Technologies Institute, Virtual Institute; Bachelors degrees, specialist diplomas, Masters degrees and Doctoral programmes; library: 859,800 vols; 660 teachers; 10,400 students; Rector GALYMKAIR MUTANOV; First Vice-Rector ZHENIS KULSEITOV; Vice-Rector for Science and Int. Cooperation Matters TULEGEN IPALAKOV; publs *Collections of Scientific Works* (1 a year), *Vestnik* (scientific journal, 4 a year), *Za znanie!* (To Knowledge!, 12 a year).

Karaganda Kazpotrebsoyuz University of Economics: 100009 Karaganda, ul. Akademicheskaya 9; tel. (7212) 44-16-22; fax (7212) 44-16-32; e-mail keu@city.krg.kz; internet www.keu.pmicro.kz; f. 1966; accountancy and audit, commodity management and analysis, computer systems, customs business, econ. and management, law, finance and credit, marketing and commerce, merchandizing, state and local govt, standardization and certification; brs in Aktobe, Astana, Kostanai, Pavlodar, Shymkent; library: 580,000 vols; 170 teachers; 5,000 students; Rector Prof. Dr ERKARA AIMAGAMBETOV.

Karaganda Metallurgical Institute: 101400 Temirtau, pr. Lenina 34; tel. (7213) 91-56-26; fax (7213) 91-62-80; e-mail karmeti@temirtau.kz; f. 1963; library: 288,000 vols; faculties of chemical eng., mechanical eng., metallurgy; 175 teachers; 2,500 students; Rector Prof. ABDRAKHMAN NAIZABEKOV.

Karaganda State Medical Academy: 100008 Karaganda, ul. Gogolya 40; tel. (7212) 51-34-79; fax (7212) 51-89-31; e-mail kgma@nursat.kz; internet www.ksma.kz; f. 1950, present name and status 1997; faculties of biology, dentistry, eastern medicine, medicine, paediatrics, pharmacy, postgraduate studies, public health; 520 teachers; 2,954 students; library: 400,000 vols, 186 periodicals; Rector I. KOOLMAGEMBETOV; publ. *Medicine and Ecology* (6 a year).

Karaganda State Technical University: 100027 Karaganda, Bulvar Mira 56; tel. (7212) 56-88-95; fax (7212) 56-88-95; e-mail ivc@kstu.kz; internet www.kstu.kz; f. 1953 as Karaganda Mining Institute; present name and status 1996; faculties of business management, civil engineering, economics and management, electromechanical engineering, geoecology, information technology, machine building, mining, transport and road engineering; library: 1.5m. books; 762 teachers; 8,166 students; Rector GENNADY G. PIVEN.

Kazakh Ablai Khan University of International Relations and World Languages: 050022 Almaty, Muratbaev 200; tel. (7272) 92-19-97; fax (7272) 92-19-91; e-mail kazumo@ablaikhan.kz; internet www.ablaikhan.kz; f. 1941; faculties of English, French, German; 668 teachers; 5,000 students; library: 630,000 vols; Rector SALIMA S. KUNANBAEVA; Vice-Rector for Scientific and Research Work KUSAYIN T. RYSSALDY; Vice-Rector for Social Work ZHUMAGUL A. ISMAGAMBETOVA; Vice-Rector for Study and Methodical Work SATIMA S. ZHUMAGULOVA; Vice-Rector for Study Dept NAGIMA A. SARSEMBAEVA; publ. scientific papers.

Kazakh Leading Academy of Architecture and Civil Engineering: 050043 Almaty, ul. Ryskulbeka 28; tel. (7272) 29-46-11; fax (7272) 20-59-79; e-mail kazgasa@itte.kz; internet www.kazgasa.kz; f. 1980;

State control; academic year September to July; undergraduate and postgraduate courses and scientific research, PhD programmes; faculties of architecture, civil engineering, environmental engineering, economics. and management in construction, social sciences; 309 teachers; 4,262 students; Pres. AMIRLAN KUSSAINOV; Rector GULZADA MUKTAPOVA; publ. *Messenger of KazGASA* (4 a year).

Kazakh S. D. Asfendijarov National Medical University: 050012 Almaty, ul. Tole-bi 88; tel. (7272) 92-78-85; fax (7272) 92-69-97; e-mail kaznmu@arna.kz; internet www.kaznmu.kz; f. 1931; present name and status 2001; faculties of dentistry, gen. medicine, health sciences, paediatrics, pharmacy, public health; library: 221,000 vols; 883 teachers; 5,349 students; Rector T. MUMINOV.

Kazakh S. Seifullin Agrarian University: 473032 Astana, pr. Pobedy 116; tel. (7172) 31-75-47; fax (7172) 32-22-94; e-mail agun@kepter.kz; internet www.agun.kz; f. 1957; library: 400,000 vols; 402 teachers; 2,043 students; Rector B. ALIMZHANOV.

Kazakh State University of Agriculture: 050010 Almaty, pr. Abaya 8; tel. (7272) 65-19-48; fax (7272) 62-44-09; e-mail info@kgau .almaty.kz; internet www.agriun.almaty.kz; f. 1996 by merger of Kazakh State Institute of Agriculture (f. 1929) and Alma-Ata Veterinary Institute (f. 1910); depts of agricultural biology, engineering, forestry and horticulture, microbiology, veterinary medicine; library: 800,000 vols; 670 teachers; 7,600 students; Rector K. A. SAGADIYEV.

Kazakh T. Ryskulov Economic University: 050035 Almaty, ul. Dzhandosova 55; tel. (7272) 20-28-45; fax (7272) 21-96-31; e-mail kazeu@pisem.net; internet www .kazeu.com; f. 1963; faculties of accounting and information technology, finance and credit, management and marketing, world economy and int. relations; banking and finance management research institute, Faculty development institute; market economy research institute; Kazakh economic, finance and int. trade univ.; 520 teachers; 5,177 students; Rector N. K. MAMYROV.

Kazakhstan Institute of Management, Economics and Strategic Research: 050100 Almaty, ul. Abaya 4; tel. (7272) 70-42-00; fax (7272) 70-43-38; internet www .kimep.kz; f. 1992; colleges of business, continuing education, social sciences; 184 teachers; 3,529 students; Pres. Dr CHAN YOUNG BANG.

Kustanai Agricultural Institute: 110000 Kustanai, pr. Sverdlova 28; tel. (7142) 25-12-23; fax (7142) 25-34-76; f. 1966; library: 341,000 vols; Dirs L. M. OVCHINIKOVA, V. S. PROKURATOVA.

Rudnyi Industrial Institute: 111500 Rudnyi, ul. 50 let Oktyabrya 38; tel. and fax (71431) 5-07-03; e-mail rii@krcc.kz; f. 1958; faculties of automation of production processes, construction, economics, mining; attached institute in Lisakovsk; 200 teachers; 4,250 students; Rector Prof. U. T. ABDRAKHIMOV.

Semipalatinsk State Medical Academy: 490019 Semipalatinsk, Abaya ul. 103; tel. (7222) 62-39-65; fax (7222) 66-34-01; f. 1953; library: 315,000 vols; 900 teachers; 2,500 students; Rector T. K. RAISSOV.

South Kazakhstan Technical University: 160018 Shymkent, Tauke-han 5; tel. (7252) 53-50-48; f. 1943; faculties of chemical technology, economics, mechanical technology; library: 524,000 vols; Rector T. SH. KALMENOV; publ. *Science and Education in South Kazakhstan*.

Taraz State Pedagogical University: 080000 Taraz, Zhambyl obl., ul. Tole-bi 62; tel. (7262) 45-13-94; fax (7262) 34-35-30; e-mail gylym_targpi@mail.ru; f. 1967; teacher training and research; Rector Prof. Dr MACHMETGALY N. SARYBEKOV.

Western Kazakhstan State University: 090000 Uralsk, ul. Krasnoarmejskaja 19; tel. and fax (7112) 51-26-32; e-mail zapkazgu@wkau.kz; internet www.wkau.kz; f. 1932, current name and status following merger of Western Kazakhstan Agrarian University, Western Kazakhstan Humanities University and Western Kazakhstan Dauletkerey Institute of Arts 2000; faculties of agribusiness and ecology, culture and library science, economics, finance and accountancy, fine arts, geography and natural sciences, history and human rights, musical arts, oil and gas, pedagogy, philology, physics and mathematics, polytechnic, sports and physical training, veterinary medicine and sanitation; library: 1.2m. vols; 899 teachers; 17,052 students; Rector B. K. DAMITOV.

KENYA

The Higher Education System

Until independence was achieved in 1963 Kenya was part of British East Africa. The oldest institutions of higher education were established during British colonial rule, such as Egerton University (founded 1939; current name and status 1987), the University of Nairobi (founded 1956; current name and status 1970) and Strathmore University (founded 1961; current name and status 1993). There are public and private universities, which are both accredited by the Commission for Higher Education. In 2007 an estimated 118,000 students were enrolled in universities. In both public and private universities the senior officer is the Chancellor, who in public universities is appointed by the President and in private universities is an appropriate or distinguished personage. University governance is handled by the Governing Council or Board of Trustees, and the chief executive is the Vice-Chancellor, who is also head of the University Senate, which is responsible for academic affairs, and financial and administrative management. Faculty Boards and Departments are the main units of academic administration. The Ministry of Higher Education, Science and Technology is the government ministry in charge of higher education, acting under the aegis of the Commission for Higher Education. Universities are funded by the state budget and by students' tuition fees.

Admission to university undergraduate degree programmes is on the basis of at least an average C+ score in the Kenya Certificate of Secondary Education. Admission to Diploma or Certificate programmes requires at least C− or D+, respectively. Students who have been awarded the Diploma or Certificate may be admitted to degree-level programmes.

Diplomas and Certificates are awarded after up to a year of intensive study at universities and polytechnics or through 'open' and distance-learning schemes. The standard undergraduate Bachelors degree lasts for four years, except in disciplines such as veterinary medicine (five years), architecture and medicine (both six years). Upon completion of the Bachelors degree, students may take either a one-year Postgraduate Diploma course or a one- to three-year Masters degree. The most advanced university-level degree programme is the Doctorate, which requires two years of study following award of the Masters.

Post-secondary vocational and technical education is available through a number of different institutions: craft training institutes, youth polytechnics, institutes of technology and polytechnics. Although there is not yet a uniform national framework for vocational qualifications, they are roughly separated into four levels: artisan, craftsman, technician and technologist. The Kenya Institute of Education and Kenya National Examinations Council are responsible for developing curricula and testing at these four levels. Qualifications offered include Higher Diploma, Higher Technician Diploma, Ordinary Diploma and Ordinary Technician Diploma.

In the late 2000s Kenya's higher education, science and technology sector was preparing for major legislative and institutional reforms aimed at promoting a knowledge-based economy to improve national prosperity and global competitiveness. Three new bills were being developed in 2009 to ensure quality, equity and reliability in the delivery of post-secondary education.

Regulatory and Representative Bodies

GOVERNMENT

Ministry of Higher Education, Science and Technology: Jogoo House 'B', Harambee Ave, POB 9553, 00200 Nairobi; tel. (20) 318581; e-mail info@scienceandtechnology.go.ke; internet www.scienceandtechnology.go.ke; Min. of Higher Education, Science and Technology Prof. HELEN JEPKEMOI SAMBILI (acting).

Ministry of Gender, Children and Social Development: NSSF Bldg, Block 'A', E Wing, 6th Fl., Bishop Rd, POB 16939, 00100 Nairobi; tel. (20) 2727980; fax (20) 2734417; e-mail information@gender.go.ke; internet www.gender.go.ke; Min. Dr NAOMI NAMSI SHABAN.

ACCREDITATION

Commission for Higher Education: POB 54999, 00200 Nairobi; Red Hill Rd, off Limuru Rd, Gigiri; tel. (20) 720500; fax (20) 2021172; e-mail che@kenyaweb.com; internet www.che.or.ke; f. 1985; plans for the establishment and devt of higher education and training; organizes resources for higher education and training; accredits and regularly inspects univs; co-ordinates and regulates admission to univs; 28 mems; library of 4,284 vols; Sec. and CEO Prof. EVERRETT M. STANDA.

Learned Societies

GENERAL

African Network of Scientific and Technological Institutions (ANSTI): UNESCO Nairobi Office, POB 30592, Nairobi; tel. (20) 622620; fax (20) 622750; e-mail info@ansti.org; internet www.ansti.org; f. 1980 under the auspices of UNESCO and UNDP, aided by Germany and based at the UNESCO Regional Bureau for Science and Technology (q.v.); aims to bring about collaboration between African engineering, scientific and technological institutions involved in postgraduate training, and to undertake research and development in areas of developmental significance in the region; mems: 85 institutions in 32 countries; Coordinator Prof. J. G. MASSAQUOI; publs African Journal of Science and Technology, Directory of ANSTI Institutions.

Kenya National Academy of Sciences: POB 39450, Nairobi; tel. (20) 311714; fax (20) 311715; e-mail secretariat@knascience.org; internet www.knascience.org; f. 1977; advancement of learning and research; 200 mems; Hon. Chair. Prof. JOSEPH O. MALO; Hon. Sec. Prof. FELIX M. LUTI; publs Kenya Journal of Science and Technology (2 a year), Newsletter, Post Magazine, Proceedings of Symposia.

National Council for Science and Technology: POB 30623, Nairobi; tel. (20) 336173; f. 1977; attached to Ministry of Higher Education, Science and Technology; semi-autonomous government agency; provides advisory services to the Government; 35 council mems; library of 3,000 vols,

collection of research reports; Sec. Prof. P. GACII; publ. NCST Newsletter.

UNESCO Nairobi Regional Bureau for Science and Technology for Sub-Saharan Africa and Cluster Office: POB 30592, Nairobi 00100 GPO; United Nations Offices, Gigiri, Block C, United Nations Ave, Gigiri, Nairobi; tel. (20) 622353; fax (20) 622750; e-mail nairobi@unesco.org; internet www.unesco-nairobi.org; f. 1965; regional office for 47 African countries; designated Cluster Office for Burundi, Kenya, Rwanda and Uganda; library of 10,000 vols, 400 periodicals; Dir PAUL VITTA; publ. African Journal of Science and Technology (2 a year).

AGRICULTURE, FISHERIES AND VETERINARY SCIENCE

Agricultural Society of Kenya: POB 30176, Nairobi; tel. (20) 566655; fax (20) 573838; e-mail chiefexecutive@ask.kenya.com; f. 1901; encourages and assists agriculture in Kenya; holds 12 shows a year and farming competitions; sponsors Young Farmers' Clubs of Kenya; 12,000 mems; Chair. TIMOTHY O. OMATO; Chief Exec. BATRAM M. MUTHOKA; publ. The Kenya Farmer (12 a year).

BIBLIOGRAPHY, LIBRARY SCIENCE AND MUSEOLOGY

Kenya Library Association: POB 46031, 00100 Nairobi; tel. (20) 736625237; fax (20) 811455; e-mail ekobachi@yahoo.com; internet www.kla.or.ke; f. 1956; organizes, unites and represents the professions concerned with information work in Kenya;

promotes professional integrity and governs the members of the asscn in all matters of professional practice; 200 mems; Chair. Prof. NYAMBOGA; Nat. Sec. HELLEN AMUNGA; Nat. Sec. ESTHER K. OBACHI; publs *Kelias News* (6 a year), *Maktaba—Official Journal* (2 a year).

ECONOMICS, LAW AND POLITICS

Law Society of Kenya: POB 72219-00200, Nairobi; Professional Centre, First Floor, Parliament Rd, Nairobi; tel. (20) 311337; fax (20) 223997; e-mail lsk@lsk.or.ke; internet www.lsk.or.ke; f. 1949; 4,000 mems; Sec. GEORGE KEGORO; publ. *The Advocate* (4 a year).

HISTORY, GEOGRAPHY AND ARCHAEOLOGY

Historical Association of Kenya: c/o Prof. B. A. Ogot, Moi University, POB 3900, Eldoret; f. 1966; Chair. Prof. BETHWELL A. OGOT; Sec. Dr KARIM K. JANMOHAMED; publs *Hadith Series* (1 a year), *Kenya Historical Review* (2 a year).

LANGUAGE AND LITERATURE

Alliance Française: Maison Française Monrovia, Loila St, POB 45475, 0100 Nairobi; tel. (20) 340054; fax (20) 315207; offers courses and examinations in French language and culture and promotes cultural exchange with France; attached teaching centre in Mombasa.

British Council: Upperhill Rd, POB 40751, 00100 Nairobi; tel. (20) 2836000; fax (20) 2836500; e-mail information@britishcouncil.or.ke; internet www.britishcouncil.org/kenya; teaching centre; offers courses and examinations in English language and British culture and promotes cultural exchange with the UK; Dir for Kenya and Regional Dir for East Africa PHILIP GOODWIN.

Goethe-Institut: Maendeleo House, POB 49468, 00100 Nairobi; tel. (20) 2224640; fax (20) 340770; e-mail info@nairobi.goethe.org; internet www.goethe.de/nairobi; offers courses and examinations in German language and culture and promotes cultural exchange with Germany; provides information on Germany's cultural, social and political life; library of 6,000 vols; Dir JOHANNES HOSSFELD.

MEDICINE

Kenya Medical Association: Chyulu Road, Upper Hill, POB 48502, Nairobi; tel. (20) 724617; f. 1962; 1,500 mems; Chair. Dr JAMES W. NYIKAL; Sec. Dr KAVOO KILONZO; publs *East African Medical Journal* (12 a year), *Medicus* (12 a year).

NATURAL SCIENCES

Biological Sciences

East African Wildlife Society: POB 20110, 00200 City Sq., Riara Rd, off Ngong Rd, Nairobi; tel. (20) 574145; fax (20) 570335; e-mail info@eawildlife.org; internet www.eawildlife.org; f. 1961; non-profit org.; safeguards and promotes the conservation and sustainable management of wildlife resources and their natural habitats in East Africa; 6,000 mems; Exec. Dir ALI AKBER KAKA; publs *African Journal of Ecology* (4 a year), *Swara* (4 a year), *Wildlife Info* (4 a year).

Nature Kenya, the East Africa Natural History Society: POB 44486, GPO, 00100 Nairobi; tel. (20) 3749957; fax (20) 3741049; e-mail office@naturekenya.org; internet www.naturekenya.org; f. 1909; 1,000 mems; library of 10,000 vols; Chair. Dr IAN GORDON; publs *Journal of East African Natural His-*

tory (2 a year), *Kenya Birds* (2 a year), *Nature East Africa (the EANHS Bulletin)* (2 a year).

Physical Sciences

Kenya Astronomical Society: POB 59224, Nairobi.

RELIGION, SOCIOLOGY AND ANTHROPOLOGY

Theosophical Society: 55A Third Parklands Ave, POB 45928, Nairobi; e-mail cprdunn@nbnet.co.ke; Gen. Sec. C. P. ROBERTSON-DUNN; publ. *The Theosophical Light* (2 a year).

TECHNOLOGY

Institution of Engineers of Kenya: 1st Fl., KRBC Annex, POB 41346, 00100 Nairobi; tel. (20) 729326; fax (20) 716922; e-mail iek@iekenya.org; internet www.iekenya.org; f. 1945, present name 1973; 2,100 mems; Hon. Sec. Eng. J M. WANYOIKE; publ. *Kenya Engineer* (6 a year).

Research Institutes

AGRICULTURE, FISHERIES AND VETERINARY SCIENCE

Coffee Research Foundation: CRF Coffee Research Station, POB 4, Ruiru; tel. (151) 54027; fax (151) 54133; f. 1949; research on coffee cultivation, agronomy and management, marketing and economics of production; Dir W. R. OPILE; publ. *Kenya Coffee Bulletin*.

Interafrican Bureau for Animal Resources: Maendeleo House, Monrovia St, POB 30786, Nairobi; tel. (20) 338544; fax (20) 220546; internet www.au-ibar.org; f. 1951; veterinary and livestock health and production covering all mem. states of the OAU; library of 5,000 vols; Dir Dr J. T. MUSIIME; publ. *Bulletin of Animal Health and Production in Africa* (4 a year).

Kenya Agricultural Research Institute: City Square, POB 57811, Nairobi; tel. (20) 4183720; fax (20) 4183344; e-mail .center@kari.org; internet www.kari.org; f. 1979; agricultural and veterinary sciences research; Dir Dr R. M. KIOME.

Attached Centre:

> **National Veterinary Research Centre (MUGUGA):** POB 32, Kikuyu; preparation and issue of biological products and research into animal health and animal diseases; Dir D. P. KARIUKI; publ. *Record of Research*.

Ministry of Livestock Development, Department of Veterinary Services: Private Bag Kangemi (00625), Nairobi; tel. (20) 632231; fax (20) 631273; f. 1903; control and diagnosis of animal diseases, advisory service to farmers, animal health policy formulation, veterinary research and investigation services, veterinary regulation services; library of 27,500 vols; Dir Dr WILLIAM TOROITICH K. GHONG'.

National Agricultural Research Laboratories: POB 14733, Nairobi; tel. and fax (20) 444144; f. 1908; soil science research, crop protection research; library of 4,000 vols; Dir Dr F. N. MUCHENA; publ. *Soil Survey Report*.

National Horticultural Research Centre: POB 220, Thika; tel. (67) 21283; fax (67) 21285; e-mail karithika@africaonline.co.ke; internet www.kari.org; f. 1955; research into crop protection, seed production, citriculture, viticulture, floriculture, temperate and tropical fruits, post-harvest physiology, vegetables; breeds for multiple

disease resistance to common bean diseases; Dir Dr C. N. WATURU.

Plant Breeding Station: Ministry of Agriculture, PO Njoro; tel. (51) 48150; fax (51) 47986; f. 1927; improvement of wheat, barley and oats; 20 professional staff; Officer-in-Charge Dr R. C. MCGINNIS.

Pyrethrum Board of Kenya: POB 420, Nakuru; tel. (51) 2211567; fax (51) 2210466; e-mail marketing@kenya-pyrethrum.com; internet www.kenya-pyrethrum.com; f. 1948; research and information on pyrethrum as a natural insecticide; Dir SAMUEL KIHIU; publ. *Pyrethrum Post* (2 a year).

Tea Research Foundation of Kenya: POB 820, 20200 Kericho; tel. (52) 20598; fax (52) 20575; e-mail lib-trfk@kenyaweb.com; internet www.tearesearch.or.ke; f. 1951; research and technology devt on the production and manufacture of tea, with spec. emphasis on agronomic, botanical, environmental and physical parameters; pests and diseases management; tea biochemistry and processing of tea, technology, knowledge and information transfer, training and advisory services; value addition, product diversification and market research; library of 12,000 vols; Dir Dr FRANCIS N. WACHIRA; publs *Tea Growers' Handbook*, *Tea Journal* (2 a year), *TRFK Quarterly Bulletin*.

HISTORY, GEOGRAPHY AND ARCHAEOLOGY

British Institute in Eastern Africa: POB 30710, GPO 0100 Nairobi; tel. (20) 4343190; fax (20) 4343365; e-mail office@biea.ac.uk; internet www.biea.ac.uk; f. 1960; library of 5,000 vols, 100 periodicals; research into the history and archaeology of Eastern Africa, for which occasional grants and studentships are offered; 350 mems; Dir Dr JUSTIN WILLIS; publ. *Azania* (1 a year).

MEDICINE

Alupe Leprosy and Other Skin Diseases Research Centre (The John Lowe Memorial): POB 3, Busia; tel. and fax (55) 22410; f. 1952; part of KEMRI; Dir Dr P. A. OREGE.

Institute for Medical Research and Training: National Public Health Laboratory Services, POB 20750, Nairobi; f. 1964 for research and medical training; see also College of Health Professions, Medical School, under Colleges.

Kenya Medical Research Institute (KEMRI): POB 54840-00200, Nairobi; tel. (20) 722541; fax (20) 720030; internet www.kemri.org; f. 1979; under the Min. of Public Health and Sanitation; research in biomedical sciences, cooperates with other instns in training programmes and research, cooperates with the relevant ministries, the Nat. Ccl for Science and Technology and the Medical Science Advisory Research Cttee; 11 centres: Centre for Biotechnology Development Research, Centre for Clinical Research, Centre for Geographic Medicine Research, Centre for Infections and Parasitic Diseases Research, Centre for Microbiology Research, Centre for Public Health Research, Centre for Respiratory Diseases Research, Centre for Traditional Medicines and Drugs Research, Centre for Vector Biology and Control Research, Centre for Virus Research, Eastern and Southern Africa Centre of International Parasite Control (ESACIPAC); coordinates the annual African Health Sciences Congress and is secretariat for African Forum for Health Sciences (AFHES); library of 3,000 vols, collection of scientific reprints, theses and dissertations; Dir Dr DAVY KOECH; publs *African Journal of Health Sciences* (4 a year), *AIDS Update* (6 a year), *KEMRI Abstracts*.

National Public Health Laboratory Services (Medical Department): POB 20750, Nairobi; tel. (20) 725601; fax (20) 729504; all branches of medicine; library; Dir Dr JACK NYAMONGO.

Respiratory Diseases Research Centre: POB 47855, Nairobi; tel. (20) 724262; fax (20) 720030; f. 1960; part of KEMRI; research on all aspects of respiratory diseases, with special reference to diagnostic and treatment procedures relevant to developing country situations and to the epidemiology of respiratory diseases; Dir Dr J. A. ODHIAMBO.

NATURAL SCIENCES

Biological Sciences

Institute of Primate Research: National Museums of Kenya, POB 24481, Nairobi; tel. (20) 882571; fax (20) 882546; e-mail directoripr@museums.or.ke; internet www.primateresearch.org; research in ecology and conservation, infectious diseases, primate medicine, reproductive biology and virology; Dir Dr THOMAS M. KARIUKI; publ. *IPR Report* (1 a year).

TECHNOLOGY

Kenya Industrial Research and Development Institute: Lusaka Rd, Dunga, POB 30650, Nairobi; tel. (20) 535966; fax (20) 555738; e-mail kirdi@arcc.or.ke; internet www.kirdi.go.ke; f. 1948; provides advice for established local industrial concerns and gives assistance in the establishment of new industries on the utilization of local materials; Dir Dr P. M. MUTURI.

Mines and Geological Department: Madini House, Machakos Rd, POB 30009, 00100 Nairobi; tel. (20) 541040; e-mail cmg@bidii.com; f. 1932; geological survey and research; mineral resources development; administers mineral and explosives laws; library of 32,000 vols, 10,000 periodicals; Commr L. K. BIWOTT; publs *Mineral Statistics Data*, bulletins, maps, reports, statistics.

National Fibre Research Centre, Kibos: POB 1490, Kisumu; Dir J. H. BRETTELL.

Libraries and Archives

Mombasa

British Council Library: Jubilee Insurance Bldg, Moi Ave, POB 90590, Mombasa; tel. (41) 2223076; fax (41) 2315349; 3,000 vols, 32 periodicals; Information Centre Man. MARY STEVENS.

Nairobi

Desai Memorial Library: POB 1253, Nairobi; f. 1942; public library and reading room; 31,800 vols; books in Swahili, English, Gujarati, Gurumukhi, Hindi and Urdu; reference, newspaper and periodical sections; 1,151 mems; Pres. A. M. SADARUDDIN; Sec. HARSHAD JOSHI.

High Court of Kenya Library: Law Courts, POB 30041, Nairobi; tel. (20) 221221; f. 1935; comprises High Court Library and Court of Appeal Library in Nairobi and 10 major br. libraries at Bungoma, Eldoret, Kakamega, Kisii, Kisumu, Machakos, Mombasa, Nakuru and Nyeri; 100,000 vols, 65 periodicals on practitioner's law, with special emphasis on Kenyan and English law; Head Librarian E. N. JUMA.

Ismail Rahimtulla Trust Library: POB 40333, Nairobi; tel. (20) 212660; f. 1953; 7,200 vols; Librarian P. GITAU.

Kenya Agricultural Research Institute Library: POB 57811, Nairobi; tel. (20) 4183301; fax (20) 4183344; e-mail resource .centre@kari.org; internet www.kari.org; f. 1928; extends current scientific awareness service to all agricultural research and academic centres and official depts within Kenya; 150,000 vols; Asst Dir Information and Documentation Services REGE RACHEL; Librarian PATRICK MAINA; publ. *East African Agricultural and Forestry Journal* (4 a year).

Kenya National Archives and Documentation Service: POB 49849, Moi Ave, 00100 Nairobi; tel. (20) 250576; fax (20) 316187; e-mail info@kenyarchives.go.ke; internet www.kenyarchives.go.ke; f. 1965; preservation and custody of public records; assists government offices in the maintenance of public records; over 1m. items, incl. reports, maps, films, microfilms, photographs, slides; archival materials accessible to national and international researchers; five records centres in Mombasa, Nairobi, Nakuru, Kisumu and Kakamega; 50,000 vols and periodicals, incl. 9,000 government monographs; 600 annual reports from government ministries and depts; Kenya Gazette, Laws of Kenya and parliamentary debates; 20,000 general and Africana vols; 700 theses and dissertations; 5,000 legal deposit collections; 1,600 periodicals and journals, incl. 30 current titles; the library prepares accession lists for all collections, and alphabetical lists for annual reports and periodicals, and publs indexes and guides to public records; databases accessible via website; Dir L. I. MWANGI.

Kenya National Library Services: POB 30573, Ngong Rd, Nairobi; tel. (20) 725550; fax (20) 721749; e-mail knls@nbnet.co.ke; internet www.knls.or.ke; f. 1967; 621,000 vols, 120 periodicals; public library services through Nat. Lending Library in Nairobi, 19 brs and 8 mobile units; Nat. Reference and Bibliographic Dept f. 1980; special collections: East Africana and Kenyana; Chair. Archbishop STEPHEN ONDIEKI; Dir S. K. NG'ANG'A; publs *Kenya National Bibliography* (1 a year), *Kenya Periodical Directory* (every 2 years).

McMillan Memorial Library: POB 40791, Banda St, Nairobi; tel. (20) 221844; f. 1931; two branch libraries at Kaloleni and Eastlands; comprises Nairobi City Library Services; collns of old photographs, microfilms of East Africa, serial publs; Africana colln of 20,000 vols; 400,000 vols; Chief Librarian A. O. ESILABA.

University of Nairobi Libraries: POB 30197, 00100 Nairobi; tel. (20) 318262; internet www.library.uonbi.ac.ke; f. 1959; 850,000 vols, 600 periodicals, 7,000 electronic journals; 11 brs; acts as legal nat. depository and UN deposit library; Librarian SALOME MUNAVU (acting).

Museums and Art Galleries

Nairobi

National Museums of Kenya: Museum Hill, POB 40658, 00100 Nairobi; tel. (20) 742131; fax (20) 741424; e-mail dgnmk@museums.or.ke; internet www.museums.or.ke; f. 1910 by the E African Natural History Soc.; all brs of natural sciences, prehistory, geology, education, ethnography; library: joint library with E African Natural History Soc., 30,000 vols; Dir Dr IDLE OMAR FARAH; Librarian A. H. K. OWANO; publs *Horizons*, *Journal of East Africa Natural History*, *Kenya Past and Present*.

Attached Museums:

Fort Jesus Museum: POB 82412, Mombasa; tel. (41) 312839; fax (41) 227797; e-mail nmkfortj@swiftmombasa.com; f. 1960; inside 16th-century Portuguese fortress overlooking Mombasa harbour; finds from various coastal Islamic sites, from Fort Jesus, and from a 17th-century Portuguese wreck illustrate the history of the Kenyan coast; library of 1,000 vols and numerous offprints; Curator ALI BAAKABE.

Kisumu Museum: POB 1779, Kisumu; tel. (57) 40804; e-mail kisumuse@africaonline.co.ke; Curator PETER NYAMENYA.

Kitale Museum: POB 1219-30200, Kitale; tel. (54)30996; e-mail jogega@museums.or .ke; internet www.museums.or.ke/kitale; f. 1926; natural and cultural museum; history and science, emphasis on education; library of 5,000 vols; Sr Curator JULIAS JUMA OGEGA.

Lamu Museum: POB 48, Lamu; tel. (42) 633073; e-mail lamuse@hotmail.com; internet www.museums.or.ke; Curator ATHMAN HUSSEIN.

Universities

AFRICA NAZARENE UNIVERSITY

POB 53067-00200, Nairobi

Telephone: (45) 24350
Fax: (45) 24352
E-mail: admit@anu.ac.ke
Internet: www.anu.ac.ke

Founded 1994
Private control; administered by Church of the Nazarene International
Academic year: September to August (3 trimesters)

Vice-Chancellor: Prof. LEAH MARENGU
Deputy Vice-Chancellor for Academic Affairs: Prof. MARY JONES

Number of teachers: 50
Number of students: 850

Departments of commerce, computer science and theology.

AFRICAN VIRTUAL UNIVERSITY

POB 25405–00603, Nairobi
Cape Office Park, Ring Rd, Kilimani, Nairobi

Telephone: (20) 2528333
Fax: (20) 3861460
E-mail: contact@avu.org
Internet: www.avu.org

Founded 1997
Languages of instruction: English, French

Ind. distance-learning institution sponsored by the World Bank, providing education in 18 African countries through a network of 33 Learning Centres

Rector: BAKARY DIALLO
Dir for Academic Programmes Management and Devt: Dr FRED BARASA.

CATHOLIC UNIVERSITY OF EASTERN AFRICA

POB 62157-00200, Nairobi

Telephone: (20) 891601
Fax: (20) 891261
E-mail: linkages@cuea.edu
Internet: www.cuea.edu

Founded 1984 as Catholic Higher Institute of Eastern Africa; present name and status 1992
Private control
Language of instruction: English
Academic year: August to July

Rector: Rev. Prof. JOHN C. MAVIIRI
Vice-Rector and Deputy Vice-Chancellor for Academic Affairs: Dr JUSTUS MBAE
Vice-Rector and Deputy Vice-Chancellor for Admin.: Rev. Prof. JUVENALIS BAITU
Dir of Academic Linkages: Rev. Dr PETER I. GICHURE
Library of 61,705 vols, 11,553 periodicals
Number of teachers: 362 (141 full-time, 120 visiting)
Number of students: 7,000
Publications: *African Christian Studies* (4 a year), *Eastern Africa Journal of Humanities and Science* (1 a year)

DEANS

Centre for Social Justice and Ethics: Dr ELIZABETH NDUKO
Faculty of Arts and Social Sciences: FREDERICK MVUMBI
Faculty of Commerce: ALOYS AYAKO
Faculty of Education: Dr AMANUEL TEKLEMARIAM
Faculty of Law: EMILIUS NDERITU
Faculty of Science: GENEVIEVE MWAYULI
Faculty of Theology: Rev. Prof. CLEMENT MAJAWA

DAYSTAR UNIVERSITY

Athi River Campus, POB 17, 90145 Athi-River
Telephone: (45) 6622601
Fax: (45) 6622420
E-mail: vc@daystar.ac.ke
Nairobi Campus, POB 44400-00100, Nairobi
Telephone: (20) 2723002
Fax: (20) 2728338
E-mail: vc@daystar.ac.ke
Mombasa Campus, POB 99483-80107, Kilindini, Mombasa
Telephone: (41) 2312777
E-mail: mombasa@daystar.ac.ke
Internet: www.daystar.ac.ke
Founded 1974
Private control
Non-profit, non-denominational Christian
Vice-Chancellor: Dr TIMOTHY WACHIRA
Deputy Vice-Chancellor for Academic Affairs: Prof. JAMES KOMBO
Deputy Vice-Chancellor for Finance, Admin. and Planning: Dr PHILIP KITUI
Deputy Vice-Chancellor for Institutional Advancement: Dr JON MASSO
Library of 73,600 vols, 365 audiovisual resources, 13,600 electronic journals, 40 print journals
Number of teachers: 230
Number of students: 3,937

DEANS

School of Arts and Humanities: PURITY KIAMBI
School of Business and Economics: MUTURI WACHIRA
School of Communication, Language and Performing Arts: Prof. FAITH NGURU
School of Human and Social Sciences: Dr ALICE MUNENE
School of Science, Engineering and Health: Dr PETER NGURE

UNIVERSITY OF EASTERN AFRICA, BARATON

POB 2500, Eldoret
Telephone: (53) 52625
Fax: (53) 52263
E-mail: dvc@ueab.ac.ke
Internet: www.ueab.ac.ke
Private control; Seventh-Day Adventist
Founded 1980

Chancellor: GEOFFREY MBWANA
Vice-Chancellor: Prof. R. TIMOTHY MCDONALD
Deputy Vice-Chancellor: Dr NATHANIEL WALEMBA
Dean of Students: BENSON NYAGWENCHA
Library of 50,000 vols
Number of teachers: 89
Number of students: 1,502 (1,286 full-time, 216 part-time)

DEANS

School of Business: SAMUEL OYIEKE
School of Education: Prof. DENFORD MUSVOSVI
School of Humanities and Social Sciences: Prof. WA-GITHUMO MWANGI
School of Science and Technology: Prof. ASAPH MARADUFU

EGERTON UNIVERSITY

POB 536, 20115 Egerton
Telephone: (51) 2217891
Fax: (51) 2217827
E-mail: info@egerton.ac.ke
Internet: www.egerton.ac.ke
Founded 1939; university status 1987
State control
Language of instruction: English
Academic year: August to May
Vice-Chancellor: Prof. J. K. TUITOEK
Deputy Vice-Chancellor for Academic Affairs: Prof. ROSE MWONYA
Deputy Vice-Chancellor for Administration and Finance: Prof. L. M. MUMERA
Deputy Vice-Chancellor for Research and Extension: Prof. JUDE M. MATHOOKO
Academic Registrar: Prof. S. M. NGARE
Registrar for Administration and Finance: Dr T. K. SEREM
Prin. of Chuka Constituent College: E. M. NJOKA
Prin. of Kisii Constituent College: Prof. JOHN AKAMA
Prin. of Laikipia Campus: Prof. F. K. LELO
Dean of Students: J. K. KIBET (acting)
Librarian: S. C. OTENYA
Library of 77,439 vols
Number of teachers: 570
Number of students: 10,149
Publications: *Agricultural Bulletin* (2 a year), *Egerton Journal of Humanities, Social Sciences and Education* (2 a year), *Egerton Journal of Science and Technology* (2 a year), '*Kumekucha*' (2 a year)

DEANS

Agriculture: I. K. KOSKEY
Arts and Social Sciences: Dr F. WAKO
College of Open and Distance Learning: Prof. J. CHANGEIYWO
Commerce (Kisii Campus): P. A. C. KAPSOOT
Education (Laikipia Campus): Dr M. MATEE
Education and Human Resources: Dr B. N. GITHUA
Engineering: P. K. KIMANI
Environmental Science and Natural Resources: Prof. F. K. LELO
Graduate School: Prof. B. K. KITUR (Dir)
Health Sciences: Dr D. K. NGOTHO
Humanities and Development Studies (Laikipia Campus): Dr F. A. YIEKE
School of Continuing Education: Prof. F. N. WEGULO (Dir)
School of Education: Dr F. S. BARASA (Dir)
Science: Dr M. K. ROTICH

JOMO KENYATTA UNIVERSITY OF AGRICULTURE AND TECHNOLOGY

POB 62000, City Sq., 0200 Nairobi
Telephone: (67) 52711
Fax: (67) 52030
E-mail: jkuat.main@gmail.com

Internet: www.jkuat.ac.kec
Founded 1981; university status 1994
State control
Language of instruction: English
Academic year: May to April
Chancellor: Prof. FRANCIS JOHN GICHAGA
Vice-Chancellor: Prof. NICK G. WANJOHI
Deputy Vice-Chancellor for Academic Affairs: Prof. MABEL IMBUGA
Deputy Vice-Chancellor for Administration, Planning and Development: Prof. FRANCIS M. NJERUH
Deputy Vice-Chancellor for Research, Production and Extension: Prof. ESTHER M. KAHANGI
Registrar for Academic Affairs: Dr SULEMAN AKECH
Registrar for Administration, Planning and Development: Prof. ISAAC INOTI
Registrar for Research, Production and Extension: P. D. MUCHAI MBUGUA
Dean for Students Welfare: Dr MARANGI MBOGHO
Librarian: LAWRENCE M. WANYAMA
Library of 85,302 vols
Number of teachers: 546
Number of students: 15,000
Publications: *Horizon DAT* (architecture, 1 a year), *Journal of Agriculture Science and Technology* (2 a year), *Journal of Civil Engineering* (1 a year)

DEANS

Civil, Environmental and Construction Engineering: Dr ALFRED MAYABI
Faculty of Agriculture: Dr KAMAU NGAMAU
Faculty of Engineering: Dr MARY NDUNG'U
Faculty of Science: Prof. R. O. ODHIAMBO
School of Architecture and Building Sciences: Dr CRISPINO C. OCHIENG
School for Human Resource Development: Dr ELEGWA MUKULU
School of Electrical, Electronics & Information Engineering: Dr JOHN NDERU
School of Mechanical, Manufacturing and Materials Engineering: Dr BERNARD IKUA

KENYA METHODIST UNIVERSITY

POB 267, Meru
Telephone: (164) 30301
Fax: (164) 30162
E-mail: info@kemu.ac.ke
Internet: www.kemu.ac.ke
Founded 1997
Private control
Chancellor: Dr Rev. STEPHEN KANYARU M'IMPWI
Vice-Chancellor: Prof. MUTUMA MUGAMBI
Registrar: Dr Rev. STEPHEN KANYARU M'IMPWI
Librarian: JOE C. NYAMULUI

CHAIRS OF FACULTIES

Agriculture and Natural Resources: Prof. KABURU M'RIBU
Applied Biology: Prof. ALICE N. MURITHI
Business Administration: Prof. BENJAMIN MAKUYU
Education and Counselling: JOHN GIKUNDA MARIENE
Maths and Computer Science: Prof. LUHAHI LAHI
Theology: Rev. PETER MUKUCCIA

KENYATTA UNIVERSITY

POB 43844, Thika Road, GPO 00100, Nairobi
Telephone: (20) 8710901
Fax: (20) 8711575
E-mail: registrar-acad@ku.ac.ke
Internet: www.ku.ac.ke
Founded 1972 as constituent college of Univ. of Nairobi, present status 1985

State control
Language of instruction: English
Academic year: September to July
Chancellor: ONESMUS MUTUNGI
Vice-Chancellor: Prof. OLIVE M. MUGENDA
Deputy Vice-Chancellor for Academic Affairs: Prof. JOHN OKUMU
Deputy Vice-Chancellor for Admin.: Prof. P. K. WAINAINA
Deputy Vice-Chancellor for Finance, Planning and Devt: Prof. D. M. MUGENDI
Registrar for Academic Affairs: Dr D. M. MUINDI
Registrar for Admin.: Dr G. S. MSE
Registrar for Finance, Planning and Devt: Dr N. M. KARAGU
Librarian: J. K. GAKOBO (acting)
Library of 352,361 vols, 108,000 print and electronic periodicals
Number of teachers: 785
Number of students: 32,256
Publications: African Journal of Educational Studies, Chemchemi, International Journal of the School of Humanities and Social Sciences, East African Journal of Life Sciences, East African Journal of Physical Sciences

DEANS

School of Agriculture and Enterprise Development: Prof. WACHEKE WANJOHI
School of Applied Human Sciences: Prof. KEREN MBURUGU
School of Business: Dr J. M. CHEGE
School of Economics: Dr TOM KIMANI
School of Education: Prof. J. OGENO
School of Engineering and Technology: Dr W. MUTHUMBI
School of Environmental Studies: Prof. S. G. NJUGUNA
School of Graduate Studies: Prof. J. WAUDO
School of Health Sciences: Dr B. M. OKELLO-AGINA
School of Hospitality and Tourism: Dr ALICE ONDIGI
School of Humanities and Social Sciences: Prof. OLUOCH OBURA
School of Law: Dr LINDA A. MUSUMBA
School of Pure and Applied Sciences: Dr E. W. KAIRU
School of Visual and Performing Arts: Dr BEATRICE DIGOLO

MASENO UNIVERSITY

Private Bag, Maseno
Telephone: (57) 351620
Fax: (57) 351221
E-mail: vc@maseno.ac.ke
Internet: www.maseno.ac.ke
Founded 2000 upon independence of Moi University's Maseno Univ. College
State control
3 Univ. campuses; constituent college: Bondo Univ. College
Chancellor: FLORIDA A. KARANI
Chair.: Prof. NIMROD BWIBO
Vice-Chancellor: Prof. FREDRICK N. ONYANGO
Deputy Vice-Chancellor for Academic Affairs: Prof. DOMINIC MAKAWITI
Deputy Vice-Chancellor for Admin. and Finance: Prof. MARY K. WALINGO
Deputy Vice-Chancellor for Planning and Extension Services: Prof. GEORGE MARK ONYANGO
Prin.: Prof. STEPHEN AGONG
Librarian: SYLVIA OGOLA
Library of 150,000 vols
Number of teachers: 320
Number of students: 5,250
Publications: Equator News (4 a year), General Information Booklet (1 a year), Graduation Bulletin (1 a year), Maseno Journal

of Education, Arts and Science (1 a year), Maseno University Calendar (every 5 years)

DEANS

Faculty of Arts and Social Sciences: Prof. CALEB OKUMU
Faculty of Education: Dr EDWARDS KOCHUNG'
Faculty of Science: Prof. AGURE JOHN OGONJI
School of Medicine: Prof. JOASH ALUOCH

DIRECTORS

Bondo University College: STEPHEN AGONG (Prin.)
City Campus: Dr KATHERINE MUHOMA
School of Development and Strategic Studies: Dr FREDRICK WANYAMA
School of Environment and Earth Sciences: Prof. JOSEPHINE NGAIRA
School of Graduate Studies: Prof. PHILIP OKINDA
School of Public Health and Community Development: Prof. WILSON ODERO

MOI UNIVERSITY

POB 3900, Eldoret 30100
Telephone: (53) 43620
Fax: (53) 43047
E-mail: vcmu@mu.ac.ke
Internet: www.mu.ac.ke
Founded 1984
State control
Language of instruction: English
Academic year: September to June
Chancellor: Prof. BETHWEL ALLAN OGOT
Vice-Chancellor: Prof. DAVID K. SOME
Deputy Vice-Chancellor for Planning and Development: Prof. S. GUDU
Deputy Vice-Chancellor for Research and Extension: Dr M. J. KAMAR
Chief Academic Officer: Prof. K. OLE KAREI
Chief Administrative Officer: Dr J. K. SANG
Principal of Chepkoilel Campus: Dr J. K. LONYANGAPUO
Finance Officer: BENSON MUIRURI
Librarian: TIRONG ARAP TANUI
Library of 200,000 vols, 50,000 periodicals
Number of teachers: 709
Number of students: 5,266

DEANS

School of Agriculture and Biotechnology: Dr REUBEN M. MUASYA
School of Arts and Social Sciences: Dr PETER O. NDEGE
School of Economics and Business Management: Prof. HENRY K. MARITIM
School of Education: Prof. RUTH N. OTUNGA
School of Engineering: Prof. ABEL N. MAYAKA
School of Environmental Sciences: Prof. WILSON K. YABANN
School of Human Resources Development: Dr MARY C. LUTTA-MUKKHEBI
School of Information Sciences: Prof. JOSEPH B. OJIAMBO
School of Law: Prof. JOHN K. CHEBII
School of Medicine: Dr FABIAN ESAMAI
School of Natural Resources Management: Prof. ERICK KOECH
School of Public Health: Prof. JOSEPH ROTICH
School of Science: Dr PETER K. TORONGEY

UNIVERSITY OF NAIROBI

POB 30197-00100, Nairobi
Telephone: (20) 318262
Fax: (20) 2246655
E-mail: postmaster@unics.gn.apc.org
Internet: www.uonbi.ac.ke
Founded 1956 as Royal Technical College of E Africa, present name 1970
State control
Language of instruction: English

Academic year: October to July
Chancellor: JOE B. WANJUI
Vice-Chancellor: Prof. GEORGE A. O. MAGOHA
Deputy Vice-Chancellor for Academic Affairs: Prof. JACOB T. KAIMENYI
Deputy Vice-Chancellor for Administration and Finance: Prof. PETER M. F. MBITHI
Registrar for Academic Affairs: BERNARD M. WAWERU (acting)
Registrar for Admin.: ONAYA ODECK N. P.
Registrar for Planning: WYCLIFFE J. ASILLA (acting)
Librarian: SALOME N. MUNAVU
Number of teachers: 1,662
Number of students: 45,548
Publication: Academic Calendar

PRINCIPALS

College of Agriculture and Veterinary Medicine: Prof. AGNES W. MWANG'OMBE
College of Architecture and Engineering: Prof. BERNARD N. K. NJOROGE
College of Biological and Physical Sciences: Prof. LUCY W. IRUNGU
College of Education and External Studies: Prof. HENRY W. MUTORO
College of Health Sciences: Prof. ISAAC O. KIBWAGE
College of Humanities and Social Sciences: Prof. ISAAC M. MBECHE

DEANS

Faculty of Agriculture: Prof. SHIBAIRO S. I.
Faculty of Arts: Prof. ENOS H. N. NJERU
Faculty of Veterinary Medicine: Prof. JOHN MUNENE NJENGA
School of Biological Sciences: Dr ELIJAH AKUNDA
School of Business: Prof. STEPHEN NZUVE
School of Continuing and Distance Education: Dr GUANTAI MBOROKI
School of Dental Sciences: Dr EVELYN G. WAGAIYU
School of Economics: FRANCIS M. MWEGA
School of Education: Dr GENEVIEVE WANJALA
School of Engineering: Dr PATTIS M. A. ODIRA (acting)
School of Law: BEN SIHANYA
School of Mathematics: JAMEN H. WERE
School of Medicine: Prof. ZIPPORAH W. NGUMI
School of Nursing Sciences: Dr GRACE M. OMONI
School of Pharmacy: Prof. GRACE N. THOITHI
School of Physical Sciences: Prof. PAUL M. SHIUNDU
School of the Arts and Design: WALTER H. ONYANGO
School of the Built Environment: HEZEKIAH GICHUNGE

PROFESSORS

Faculty of Agriculture (POB 29053, Nairobi; tel. (20) 631340; fax (20) 632121):

IMUNGI, J. K., Food Technology and Nutrition
KANYARI, P. W. N., Veterinary Pathology and Microbiology
KARUE, C. N., Range Management
LARMAT, NANCY K. KARANJA
MARIBEI, JAMES M., Clinical Studies
MBUGUA, SAMUEL K., Food Technology and Nutrition
MICHIEKA, R. W., Crop Protection
MITARU, B., Animal Production
MUKUNYA, D. M., Crop Protection
MWANGOMBE, A., Crop Protection
OGUTU, A., Agricultural Economics
WAITHAKA, K., Crop Science

Faculty of Architecture (tel. (20) 2724521):

ROSTOM, R. S., Geospatial and Space Technology
SYAGGA, P. M., Land Development

Faculty of Arts (tel. (20) 318362; e-mail arts@uonbi.ac.ke):

ABDULAZIZ, M. H., Linguistics and African Languages
CHESAINA, C., Literature
INDANGASI, H., Literature
KIMUYU, PETER K.
MUGAMBI, J. N. K., Religious Studies
MUREITHI, L. P., Economics
MURIUKI, G., History
MWABU, G. M., Economics
NYASANI, J., Philosophy
ODINGO, R. S., Geography
OJANY, F. F., Geography
OMONDI, L. N., Linguistics and African Languages
OYUGI, W. O., Political Science and Public Administration
WANYANDE, PETER, Political Science and Public Administration

Faculty of Veterinary Sciences (POB 29053, Nairobi; tel. (20) 631007; fax (20) 631007; e-mail deanfvm@uonbi.ac.ke):

AGUMBAH, G. J. O., Clinical Studies
GATHUMA, J. M., Public Health, Pharmacology and Toxicology
KIPTOON, J. C., Clinical Studies
MAINA, J. N., Veterinary Anatomy
MAITHO, T. E., Public Health, Pharmacology and Toxicology
MALOIY, G. M. O., Physiology
MITEMA, S. E. O., Public Health, Pharmacology and Toxicology
MUNYUA, W. K., Veterinary Pathology
MUTIGA, E. R., Clinical Studies
NYAGA, P. N., Veterinary Pathology
ODUOR-OKELLO, D., Veterinary Anatomy

School of Business (tel. (20) 2059163):

KIBERA, F. N., Business Administration

School of Dental Sciences (tel. (20) 2720322; fax (20) 723252):

GUTHUA, S. W., Oral Surgery
KAIMENYI, J. T., Periodontology and Community Dentistry
MAKAWITI, DOMINIC W., Biochemistry
MWANG'OMBE, JOSEPH K., Community Health
OPINYA, G. N., Paediatric Dentistry, Orthodontics

School of Education (POB 97, Kikuyu; tel. (66) 6750940; e-mail deanedu@uonbi.ac.ke):

KARANI, F. A., Educational Communication and Technology
MACHARIA, D., Education
OKOMBO, O., Linguistics and Literature
WANJALA, Linguistics and Literature

School of Engineering (tel. (20) 339061):

ADUOL, F. W. O., Surveying
GICHAGA, F. J., Civil Engineering
LUTI, F. M., Mechanical Engineering
OBUDHO, R. A., Urban and Regional Planning
OTIENO, A. V., Electrical and Electronics Engineering
SHARMA, T. C., Agricultural Engineering

School of Law (tel. (20) 3740366):

MUTUNGI, O. K., Commercial Law
OJWANG, J. B., Private Law

School of Medicine (tel. (20) 2726300; fax (20) 714048):

ATINGIA, J. E. U., Orthopaedic Surgery
BHATT, S. M., Medicine
BWIBO, N. O., Paediatrics
KIGONDU, C., Clinical Chemistry
KUNGU, A., Human Pathology
KYAMBI, J. M., Surgery
MALEK, A. K., Human Anatomy
MATTA, W. M., Human Anatomy
MEME, J. S., Paediatrics
NDELE, J., Pharmacology
NDETEI, D. M., Psychiatry
ODHIAMBO, P. A., Surgery

OJWANG, S. B. O., Obstetrics and Gynaecology
OLIECH, J. S., Surgery
OTIENO, L. S., Medicine
PAMBA, H. O., Medical Microbiology
SINEI, S. K., Obstetrics and Gynaecology
THAIRU, K., Physiology
WAMOLA, I. A., Medical Microbiology
WASUNA, A. E. U., Surgery

School of Pharmacy (tel. (20) 2726771):

GUANTAI, A.
KOKWARO, G. O., Pharmaceutics and Pharmacy Practice
MAITAI, C. K., Pharmacology and Pharmacognosy
MWANGI, J. W., Pharmacology and Pharmacognosy

School of Physical Sciences (tel. (20) 4443181; e-mail deanscience@uonbi.ac.ke):

GENGA, R., Physics
GITU, P. M., Chemistry
JUMBA, ISAAC, Chemistry
KAMAU, G. N., Chemistry
KHAMALA, C. P. M., Zoology
KOKWARO, J. O., Botany
MAVUTI, KENNETH M., Zoology
MIBEY, R. K., Botany
MIDIWO, J. O., Chemistry
MUKIAMA, T. K., Botany
MUNAVU, R. M., Chemistry
MWANGI, R. W., Zoology
NYAMBOK, I. O., Geology
ODADA, E., Geology
ODHIAMBO, J. W., Mathematics
OGALLO, L. T., Meteorology
OGANA, B. W., Mathematics
ONYANGO, F. N., Physics
OTIENO-MALO, J. B., Physics
PATEL, P. J., Physics
POKHRIYAL, G. P., Mathematics
WANDIGA, S. O., Chemistry

Institutes:

ALILA, P., Institute for Development Studies
OCHOLLA-AYAYO, A. B. C., Population Studies and Research Institute
OKIDI, C. O., Institute for Development Studies
RODRIGUES, A. J., School of Informatics and Computing
SUDA, C., Institute of African Studies
WANDIBBA, S. B. A., Institute of African Studies

STRATHMORE UNIVERSITY

POB 59857, City Sq., 00200 Nairobi

Telephone: (20) 606155
Fax: (20) 607498
E-mail: admissions@strathmore.edu
Internet: www.strathmore.edu

Founded 1961 as Strathmore College; present name c. 1993
Private control (non-profit)
Academic year: July to June

Vice-Chancellor: Prof. JOHN ODHIAMBO
University Sec.: Dr CHARLES SOTZ
Deputy Vice-Chancellor for Academic Affairs: Dr FLORENCE OLOO
Librarian: GEORGE GITAU

Library of 60,000 vols
Number of teachers: 167
Number of students: 2,476 full-time, 1,825 part-time

DEANS

Faculty of Commerce: DAVID WANG'OMBE
Faculty of Information Technology: Dr REUBEN MARWANGA
Faculty of Tourism and Hospitality: Dr JOSEPH WADAWI
Institute of Continuous Education: Dr RUTH KIRAKA

Institute of Humanities, Education and Development Studies: MARGARET ROCHE
School of Accountancy: GODFREY MADIGU
Strathmore Business School: Dr EDWARD MUNGAI

Colleges

Bukura Agricultural College: POB 23, Sigalagala-Butere Rd, Bukura; tel. (56) 20023; f. 1958; language of instruction: English; academic year October to October; depts: agricultural economics, agricultural education and extension, agricultural engineering, agronomy, basic sciences, home economics, horticulture; 240 students; Principal F. O. ANDITI.

Eldoret Polytechnic: POB 4461, Eldoret; tel. (53) 32661; fax (53) 33188; e-mail eldopoly@africaonline.co.ke; offers certificate and diploma courses in library and information studies; Principal CLEOPHAS LAGAT.

Kenya Conservatoire of Music: POB 41343, Nairobi; tel. (20) 222933; f. 1944; library of instrumental and vocal scores; Dir CAROL NGANGA.

Kenya Institute of Administration: POB 23030, Lower Kabete, Nairobi; tel. (20) 582311; fax (20) 582306; e-mail kia@africaonline.co.ke; f. 1961; residential training for the Kenya Public Service in public administration, project development and management, senior management seminars, research and consultancy, computer courses, effective management communication, management information systems, policy analysis, management of public enterprises, French courses, finance management, environmental management, performance improvement programmes, human resource management, customer care and ethics, disaster management, training for trainers; library: 47,067 vols, 30 current periodicals and a fully equipped audiovisual aids centre; 30 teachers; 280 students; Dir TITUS J. K. GATEERE; publs K. I. A. Occasional Papers (12 a year), Newsline (3 a year).

Kenya Medical Training College: POB 30195, Nairobi; tel. (20) 725711; fax (20) 722907; e-mail kmtc@nbnet.ke; f. 1924; library: 18,000 vols, 150 periodicals; 195 teachers; 2,000 students; Principal W. K. A. BOIT.

Kenya Polytechnic: POB 52428, Nairobi; f. 1961 with UNDP aid; depts of building, business studies, computing, electrical and electronic engineering, general studies, institutional management, library and archive studies, mathematics, mechanical, media services, printing, science, statistics; library: 40,000 vols, 150 periodicals; 300 teachers; 6,504 students; Principal P. O. OKAKA; Librarian S. K. NG'ANG'A.

Kenya School of Law: POB 30369, Nairobi; tel. (20) 890044; fax (20) 891722; e-mail lawschool@kenyaschooloflaw.com; f. 1963; library: 4,730 vols; 13 teachers; 400 students; Principal Prof. W. KULUNDU-BITONYE; Senior Principal Lecturer ANTHONY MUNENE; Librarian BENTA NARKISO.

Kiambu Institute of Science and Technology: POB 414, Kiambu; tel. (66) 22236; fax (66) 22319; f. 1973; library: 10,000 vols; depts of bakery technology, building, business education, computer studies, electrical engineering, electronics,; 61 teachers; 600 students; Principal SIMON IRUNGU.

Kisumu Polytechnic: POB 143, Kisumu; tel. (35) 40161; fax (35) 44417; f. 1997; courses offered in accounting and business administration, analytical chemistry, automotive engineering, building, computer studies, electrical engineering, electronics, food and beverage management, mechanical engineering, personnel management; 112 teachers; 2,000 students; Principal FRANCIS IMBO.

Mombasa Polytechnic: POB 90420, Mombasa; tel. (41) 492222; fax (41) 495632; e-mail msapoly@kenyaweb.com; internet www .mombasapoly.ac.ke; f. 1948; full-time, 'sand-wich', block-release and day-release courses; library: 20,000 vols; 200 teachers; 4,037 students; Principal C. T. AKUMU OWUOR; Registrar A. M. GEKONGE; Librarian R. KASINA.

Rift Valley Institute of Science and Technology: POB 7182, Nakuru; tel. (37) 211974; fax (37) 45656; f. 1972; library: 9,000

vols; 125 teachers; 1,200 students; Principal FRANCIS Z. K. MENJO.

Western University College of Science and Technology: POB 190, Kakamega; tel. (56) 20724; e-mail weco@africaonline.co.ke; f. 1977; library: 4,000 vols; 56 teachers; 500 students; Principal ALFRED F. O. MACHUKI; Librarian ROBERT KIMAKWA.

KIRIBATI

The Higher Education System

In 1979 the Gilbert Islands became an independent republic within the Commonwealth, under the name of Kiribati. Higher education consists mostly of a branch of the University of the South Pacific. In addition, there are the Kiribati Teachers College and the Tarawa Technical Institute, both operated by the Government. All these institutions are located on the Tarawa Atoll. Students from Kiribati also attend establishments of higher education in Australia, New Zealand and Canada. The Ministry of Education, Youth and Sport Development is responsible for tertiary education. The Ministry of Health and Medical Services runs a School of Nursing, also based on Tarawa. There were 198 students enrolled in teacher training and 1,303 in other vocational training in 2001.

Regulatory Body

GOVERNMENT

Ministry of Education, Youth and Sport Development: POB 263, Bikenibeu, Tarawa; tel. 28091; fax 28222; Minister JAMES TAOM.

Library

Bairiki

National Library and Archives: POB 6, Bairiki, Tarawa; tel. 21337; fax 28222; f. 1979 (fmrly Gilbert Islands Nat. Archives); lending section of 30,000 vols; reference library of 2,000 vols; 18,000 vols in small library units throughout Kiribati; Nat. Colln (housed in Archives) of 3,500 published items; archives records of 70,000 items; spec. collns incl. 600 rolls of microfilm and 4,000 microfiches; small philatelic, photograph, and sound recording collns; Librarian and Archivist KUNEI ETEKIERA.

Museum

Bairiki

National Museum: POB 75, Bairiki, Tarawa; in process of formation; items stored in Nat. Archives; Cultural Affairs Officer BWERE ERITAIA.

College

University of the South Pacific, Kiribati Extension Centre: POB 59, Bairiki, Tarawa; tel. 21085; fax 21419; e-mail mackenzie_u@usp.ac.fj; internet www.usp.ac.fj; f. 1973; an external campus of the University of the South Pacific; part-time undergraduate and diploma courses; library: 5,000 vols; 5 teachers; 300 students; Dir URIAM TIMITI (acting).

Attached Institute:

Atoll Research Activities: POB 206, Bikenibeu, Tarawa; marine science and biology; Programme Man. TEMAKEI TEBANO; publ. *Atoll Bulletin*.

DEMOCRATIC PEOPLE'S REPUBLIC OF KOREA

The Higher Education System

The Democratic People's Republic of Korea (North Korea) occupies the northern part of the Korean peninsula. In 1945 Korea was divided into military occupation zones, with Soviet forces in the North and US forces in the South. A provisional People's Committee, led by Kim Il Sung of the Korean Communist Party, was established in the North in 1946 and accorded government status. In 1948 the Democratic People's Republic of Korea was proclaimed. The oldest university is Kim Il Sung University, founded in 1946. A report submitted to UNESCO by the North Korean Government in 2000 stated that there were more than 300 universities and colleges with 1.89m. students and academics. In March 2001 the Ministry of Education announced plans for the establishment of a university of information science and technology in Pyongyang, in cooperation with a South Korean education foundation. The new university, named the Pyongyang University of Science and Technology (PUST), officially opened in September 2009 and 250 faculty members, mostly from South Korea, are expected to teach around 200 North Korean postgraduate students.

Regulatory Bodies

GOVERNMENT

Ministry of Culture: Pyongyang; Min. AN TONG CHUN.

Ministry of Education: Pyongyang; Minister KIM, YONG JIN.

Learned Societies

GENERAL

Academy of Sciences: Ryonmotdong, Jangsan St, Sosong District, Pyongyang; tel. (2) 51956; f. 1952; brs of biology (Pres. SON KYONG NAM), construction and building materials (Pres. KIM MAN HYONG), electronics and automation design (Pres. LI SON BONG), light industry (Pres. PYON SOK CHON), and brs in Pyongsong (Chair. HAN BYONG HUI) and Hamhung (Pres. RI HYO SON); attached research institutes: see Research Institutes; libraries: see Libraries and Archives; Pres. JANG CHOL; publs *Bulletin* (6 a year), journals for analysis (4 a year each), biology, mathematics, mechanical engineering, metals, physics, and for chemical engineering and chemistry, electronic and automatic engineering, mining, geography and geology (6 a year each).

Academy of Social Sciences: Central District, Pyongyang; f. 1952; attached research institutes: see Research Institutes; library: see Libraries and Archives; Pres. KIM SOK HYONG.

AGRICULTURE, FISHERIES AND VETERINARY SCIENCE

Academy of Agricultural Science: Ryongsong District, Pyongyang; f. 1948; attached to Acad. of Sciences; attached research institutes: see Research Institutes; Pres. KYE YONG SAM.

Academy of Fisheries: Namgangdong, Sung Ho District, Pyongyang; attached to Acad. of Sciences; f. 1969; 6 attached research institutes; Chair. SO GYONG HO.

Academy of Forestry: Samsindong, Taesong District, Pyongyang; f. 1948; attached to Acad. of Sciences; 5 attached research institutes; Pres. IM ROK JAE.

LANGUAGE AND LITERATURE

Goethe-Informationszentrum: Chollima Cultural House, 8-33 Jonggwang St, Central Area, Pyongyang; internet www.goethe.de/ seoul; library of 4,000 vols; promotes cultural exchange with Germany; Dir Dr UWE SCHMELTER (based in Seoul).

MEDICINE

Academy of Medical Sciences: Saemauldong, Pyongchon District, POB 305, Pyongyang; tel. (2) 46924; attached to Acad. of Sciences; attached research institutes: see Research Institutes; Pres. RI CHOL.

TECHNOLOGY

Academy of Light Industry Science: Kangan 1-dong, Songyo District, Pyongyang; f. 1954; 7 attached research institutes; Chair. LI JU UNG.

Academy of Railway Sciences: Namgyodong, Hyongjaesan District, Pyongyang; attached to Acad. of Sciences; 5 attached research institutes; Chair. MAENG YUN CHOL.

Research Institutes

AGRICULTURE, FISHERIES AND VETERINARY SCIENCE

Agricultural Chemical Research Institute: Ryongsong District, Pyongyang; attached to Acad. of Agricultural Science; Dir PAK JAE KUN.

Agricultural Irrigation Research Institute: Onchon County, South Pyongan Province; attached to Acad. of Agricultural Science; Dir HWANG CHANG HONG.

Agricultural Mechanization Research Institute: Sadong District, Pyongyang; attached to Acad. of Agricultural Science; Dir KANG SONG RYONG.

Crop Cultivation Research Institute: Ryongsong District, Pyongyang; attached to Acad. of Agricultural Science; Dir RYEM DOK SU.

Crop Science Research Institute: Sunchon City, South Pyongan Province; attached to Acad. of Agricultural Science; Dir PAK BYONG MUK.

Fruit Cultivation Research Institute: Sukchon County, South Pyongan Province; attached to Acad. of Agricultural Science; Dir JANG HY KUNG.

Poultry Science Research Institute: Hyongjaesan District, Pyongyang; attached to Acad. of Agricultural Science; Dir CHOI MAN SANG.

Reed Research Institute: Haeju City, South Hwanghae Province; attached to Acad. of Agricultural Science; Dir KIM IN SU.

Rice Research Institute: Ryongsong District, Pyongyang; attached to Acad. of Agricultural Science; Dir KIM SANG RYEN.

Sericulture Research Institute: Dongrim County, North Pyongan Province; attached to Acad. of Agricultural Science; Dir KIM SUN JONG.

Soil Science Research Institute: Ryongsong District, Pyongyang; attached to Acad. of Agricultural Science; Dir LI KUN HAENG.

Vegetable Science Research Institute: Sadong District, Pyongyang; attached to Acad. of Agricultural Science; Dir KIM HAK SON.

Veterinary Science Research Institute: Ryongsong District, Pyongyang; attached to Acad. of Agricultural Science; Dir PAK WON KUN.

Zoology Research Institute: Sariwon City, North Hwanghae Province; attached to Acad. of Agricultural Science; Dir KIM KYANG JUNG.

ARCHITECTURE AND TOWN PLANNING

Institute of Architecture and Building Engineering: c/o Academy of Sciences, Namgangdong, Sung Ho District, Pyongyang; Dir SIN DONG CHOL.

ECONOMICS, LAW AND POLITICS

Institute of International Affairs: c/o Academy of Social Sciences, Central District, Pyongyang; Dir KIM HYONG U.

Institute of Law: c/o Academy of Social Sciences, Central District, Pyongyang; Dir SIM HYONG IL.

Institute of Trade and Economics: c/o Academy of Social Sciences, Central District, Pyongyang; Dir (vacant).

HISTORY, GEOGRAPHY AND ARCHAEOLOGY

Institute of Archaeology: c/o Academy of Social Sciences, Central District, Pyongyang; Dir KIM MYONG NAM.

Institute of Geography: Ryonmotdong, Jangsan St, Sosong District, Pyongyang;

attached to Acad. of Sciences; Dir KIM JONG RAK.

Institute of History: c/o Academy of Social Sciences, Central District, Pyongyang; Dir CHON YONG RYUL.

LANGUAGE AND LITERATURE

Institute of Ethnic Classics: c/o Academy of Social Sciences, Central District, Pyongyang; Dir KIM SUNG PHIL.

Institute of Juche Literature: c/o Academy of Social Sciences, Central District, Pyongyang; Dir KIM HA MYONG.

Institute of Linguistics: c/o Academy of Social Sciences, Central District, Pyongyang; Dir JONG SUN GI.

MEDICINE

Industrial Medicine Institute: Sapodong, Sapo District, Hamhung City; tel. (850) 2810; attached to Acad. of Medical Sciences; Dir JO UN HO.

Research Institute for the Cultivation of Medicinal Herbs: Wonjudong, Sariwon City, North Hwanghae Province; attached to Acad. of Medical Sciences; Dir KIM KWANG SOP.

Research Institute of Antibiotics: Ryonpodong, Sunchon City, South Pyongan Province; attached to Acad. of Medical Sciences; Dir CHOE SUN JONG.

Research Institute of Biomedicine: Dongsandong, Rangnang District, Pyongyang; tel. (2) 23545; attached to Acad. of Medical Sciences; Dir PAK YUI SUN.

Research Institute of Child Nutrition: Dangsandong, Mangyongdae District, Pyongyang; tel. (2) 73430; attached to Acad. of Medical Sciences; Dir KIM YONG KWANG.

Research Institute of Endocrinology: Mirimdong, Sadong District, Pyongyang; tel. (2) 623828; attached to Acad. of Medical Sciences; Dir JANG HON CHOL.

Research Institute of Experimental Therapy: c/o Academy of Medical Sciences, Chonsongdong, Haesang District, Hamhung City, South Hamgyong Province; Dir NAM ON GIL.

Research Institute of Hygiene: Dangsandong, Mangyongdse District, Pyongyang; tel. (2) 44925; attached to Acad. of Medical Sciences; Dir JE HYONG DO.

Research Institute of Microbiology: Pyongsong City, South Pyongan Province; attached to Acad. of Medical Sciences; Dir KIM CHANG JIN.

Research Institute of Natural Drugs: Somundong, Donghumsan District, Hamhung City, South Hamgyong Province; tel. (850) 53905; attached to Acad. of Medical Sciences; Dir LI HWAI SU.

Research Institute of Oncology: Saemauldong, Pyongchon District, Pyongyang; tel. (2) 42208; attached to Acad. of Medical Sciences; Dir KIM CHUN WON.

Research Institute of Pharmacology: Daehungdong, Songyo District, Pyongyang; tel. 623868; attached to Acad. of Medical Sciences; Dir RYU GYONG HUI.

Research Institute of Psychoneurology: Uiju County, North Pyongan Province; attached to Acad. of Medical Sciences; Dir LI GYUN.

Research Institute of Radiological Medicine: Saemauldong, Pyongchon District, Pyongyang; tel. (2) 45347; attached to Acad. of Medical Sciences; Dir O SOK ROK.

Research Institute of Respiratory Ducts and Tuberculosis: c/o Academy of Medical Sciences, Chongsongdong, Haesang District, Hamhung City, South Hamgyong Province; Dir LI CHU WAN.

Research Institute of Surgery: c/o Academy of Medical Sciences, Chongsongdong, Haesang District, Hamhung City, South Hamgyong Province; Dir HAN BYONG GAP.

Research Institute of Synthetic Pharmacy: Sapodong, Sapo District, Hamhung City, South Hamgyong Province; attached to Acad. of Medical Sciences; Dir LI GI SOP.

NATURAL SCIENCES
General

Central Institute of Experimental Analysis: c/o Academy of Sciences, Kwahak-Idong, Unjong District, Pyongsong City, South Pyongan Province; tel. (2) 422-5044; f. 1983; attached to Acad. of Sciences; Dir RIM CHUN RYOB; publs *Bulletin, Punsok* (analysis, 4 a year).

Institute of Environmental Protection: Ryusongdong, Central District, Pyongyang; attached to Acad. of Sciences; Dir KIM YONG CHAN.

Biological Sciences

Institute of Botany: Kosandong, Daesong District, Pyongyang; attached to Acad. of Sciences; Dir GUAK JONG SONG.

Institute of Genetics: c/o Academy of Sciences, Ryonmotdong, Jangsan St, Sosong District, Pyongyang; Dir BAEK MUN CHAN.

Institute of Molecular Biology: c/o Academy of Sciences, Ryonmotdong, Jangsan St, Sosong District, Pyongyang; Dir KO GWANG UNG.

Institute of Plant Physiology: c/o Academy of Sciences, Ryonmotdong, Jangsan St, Sosong District, Pyongyang; Dir KIM SONG OK.

Institute of Zoology: Daesongdong, Daesong District, Pyongyang; attached to Acad. of Sciences; Dir BAEK JONG HWAN.

Mathematical Sciences

Institute of Mathematics: c/o Academy of Sciences, Doksandong, Pyongsong City, South Pyongan Province; Dir HO GON.

Physical Sciences

Institute of Analytical Chemistry: c/o Academy of Sciences, Chongsongdong, Hoesang District, Hamhung City, South Hamgyong Province; Dir RIM CHUN RYOP.

Institute of Ferrous Metals: Sae Goridong, Chollima District, Nampo City; attached to Acad. of Sciences; Dir LI BANG GUN.

Institute of Geology: c/o Academy of Sciences, Doksandong, Pyongsong City, South Pyongan Province; Dir KIM ZONG HUI.

Institute of Inorganic Chemistry: c/o Academy of Sciences, Chongsongdong, Hoesang District, Hamhung City, South Hamgyong Province; Dir CHU SUNG.

Institute of Macromolecular Chemistry: c/o Academy of Sciences, Chongsongdong, Hoesang District, Hamhung City, South Hamgyong Province; Dir LI JANG HYOK.

Institute of Non-Ferrous Metals: Jungdaedudong, Hangku District, Nampo City; attached to Acad. of Sciences; Dir KIM MYONG RIN.

Institute of Physical Chemistry: c/o Academy of Sciences, Chongsongdong, Hoesang District, Hamhung City, South Hamgyong Province; Dir KIM JUNG BAE.

Institute of Physics: c/o Academy of Sciences, Doksandong, Pyongsong City, South Pyongan Province; Dir RYO IN KWANG.

Institute of Pure Metals: Kumbitdong, Ryongsong District, Hamhung City, South Hamgyong Province; attached to Acad. of Sciences; Dir LI SANG BOM.

Pyongyang Astronomical Observatory: Daesongdong, Daesong District, Pyongyang; attached to Acad. of Sciences; Dir KIM YONG HYOK.

Research Centre for Atomic Energy: Mangyongdae District, Pyongyang; fax (2) 3814416; attached to General Dept of Atomic Energy; Pres. RIM PONG SIK.

PHILOSOPHY AND PSYCHOLOGY

Institute of Philosophy: c/o Academy of Social Sciences, Central District, Pyongyang; Dir KIM CHANG WON.

TECHNOLOGY

Institute of Chemical Engineering: c/o Academy of Sciences, Chongsongdong, Hoesang District, Hamhung City, South Hamgyong Province; Dir LI JAE OP.

Institute of Constructional Mechanization: c/o Academy of Sciences, Namgangdong, Sung Ho District, Pyongyang; Dir PAK RYANG SOP.

Institute of Electricity: c/o Academy of Sciences, Doksandong, Pyongsong City, South Pyongan Province; Dir CHOE WON GYONG.

Institute of Fuel: Dongsandong, Songrim City, North Hwanghe Province; attached to Acad. of Sciences; Dir KO YONG JIN.

Institute of Hydraulic Engineering: c/o Academy of Sciences, Namgangdong, Sung Ho District, Pyongyang; Dir KIM RYONG GYUN.

Institute of Industrial Biology: c/o Academy of Sciences, Doksandong, Pyongsong City, South Pyongan Province; Dir LI CHUN HO.

Institute of Mechanical Engineering: c/o Academy of Sciences, Doksandong, Pyongsong City, South Pyongan Province; Dir KIM UNG SAM.

Institute of Ore Dressing Engineering: c/o Academy of Sciences, Doksandong, Pyongsong City, South Pyongan Province; Dir LI WON SOK.

Institute of Organic Building Materials: c/o Academy of Sciences, Namgangdong, Sung Ho District, Pyongsong; Dir PAK CHANG SUN.

Institute of Paper Engineering: Songdori, Anju City, South Pyongan Province; attached to Acad. of Sciences; Dir RYU SAM JIP.

Institute of Silicate Engineering: Sijonggu, Taedong County, South Pyongan Province; attached to Acad. of Sciences; Dir KIM UNG SANG.

Institute of Thermal Engineering: c/o Academy of Sciences, Doksandong, Pyongsong City, South Pyongan Province; Dir HAN DONG SIK.

Institute of Tideland Construction: c/o Academy of Sciences, Namgangdong, Sung Ho District, Pyongyang; Dir CHO SOK.

Institute of Welding: Ponghwadong, Chollima District, Nampo City; attached to Acad. of Sciences; Dir CHAE HON MUK.

Research Centre of Electronics and Automation: c/o Academy of Sciences, Doksandong, Pyongsong City, South Pyongan Province; incorporates institutes of electronics, of computer science, of automation, of technical cybernetics, of electronic materials; Gen. Dir LI SON BONG.

Research Institute of Medical Instruments: Daesindong, Dongdaewon District,

Pyongyang; tel. (2) 623839; attached to Acad. of Medical Sciences; Dir Jo Myong Sam.

Libraries and Archives

Chongjin

Chongjin City Library: Chongjin; Librarian Kang Chae Gum.

Chongjin Historical Library: Chongjin; Curator Eu Jai Gyong.

North Hamgyong Provincial Library: Chongjin; Librarian Choi Myong Ok.

Haeju

South Hwanghae Provincial Library: Haeju; Librarian Choi Chi Do.

Hamhung

South Hamgyong Provincial Library: Hamhung; Librarian Kim Sook Jong.

Hesan

Ryanggang Provincial Library: Hesan; Librarian Kim Chol Woo.

Kaesong

Kaesong City Library: Kaesong; Librarian Han Il.

Kaesong Historical Library: Kaesong; Curator Choi Sae Yong.

Kangge

Chagang Provincial Library: Kangge; Librarian Song Aai Gun.

Pyongsong

South Pyongan Provincial Library: Pyongsong; Librarian Kim Duk Kwan.

Pyongyang

Academy of Sciences Library: POB 330, Kwahakdong 1, Unjong District, Pyongyang; tel. (2) 32353968; fax (2) 814580; f. 1952; 3.2m. vols; Dir Prof. Kim Hyon Ok; Chief Librarian Assoc. Prof. Hong Sang Su; publ. *Bulletin*.

Academy of Social Sciences Library: Central District, Pyongyang; Chief Librarian Kim Sae Song.

Grand People's Study House/State Central Library: POB 200, Pyongyang Central District; tel. (2) 3215614; fax (2) 3814427; f. 1982; in charge of nat. bibliography; also functions as correspondence univ.; 20m. vols; Dir Choe Hui Jong.

Pyongyang Scientific Library: Central District, POB 109, Pyongyang; tel. (2) 321-2314; f. 1978.

Sariwon

North Hwanghae Provincial Library: Sariwon; Librarian Kim Hyo Dal.

Shinuiju

North Pyongan Provincial Library: Shinuiju; Librarian Li Yong Sik.

Wonsan

Kangwon Provincial Library: Wonsan; Librarian Ji Gyu Hyok.

Museums and Art Galleries

Haeju

Haeju Historical Museum: Haeju, South Hwanghae Province.

Hamhung

Hamhung Historical Museum: Hamhung, South Hamgyong Province; Curator Kim Ik Myon.

Hyangsan County

Mt Myohyang-san Museum: Hyangsan County, North Pyongan Province; Curator Choi Hyong Min.

Pyongyang

Korean Art Gallery: Pyongyang; Curator Kim Sang Chol.

Korean Central Historical Museum: Central District, Pyongyang; prehistory to early 20th century; Curator Jang Jong Sin.

Korean Ethnographic Museum: Central District, Pyongyang; Curator Jon Moon Jin.

Korean Revolutionary Museum: Central District, Pyongyang; history from second half of 19th century to the present; Dir Hwang Sun Hui.

Memorial Museum of the War of Liberation: Moranbong District, Pyongyang; history from second half of the 19th century to the present; Dir Thae Pyong Ryol.

Shinchon County

Shinchon Museum: Shinchon County, South Hwanghae Province; Curator Pak In Chaik.

Shinuiju

Shinuiju Historical Museum: Shinuiju, North Pyongan Province; Curator Pak Yong Gwan.

Wonsan

Wonsan Historical Museum: Wonsan, Kangwon Province; Curator Jo Gang Baik.

Universities and Colleges

KIM IL SUNG UNIVERSITY

Daesong District, Pyongyang
Telephone: (2) 54946
Founded 1946
State control
Academic year: September to August

Faculties of atomic energy, biology, chemistry, computer science, economics, foreign literature, geography, geology, history, law, philosophy, physics and mathematics, religion

Pres.: Song Ja Rip
Vice-Pres: Choe Jand Ryong, Jo Chol, Kim Il Gwang, O Kil Bang, Paek Chol, Paek Jae Uk, Ri Jae Myon, Ri Song Chol, Ro Song Chan

Number of teachers: 2,000
Number of students: 12,000

Publications: natural science magazine, social science magazine.

ATTACHED RESEARCH INSTITUTES

Computer Science College: Dir Kim Yong Jun.

Doctoral Institute: Dir Han Yong Gu.

Literature College: Dir Un Jong Sop.

Kim Chaek University of Technology: Waesong District, Pyongyang; faculties of geology, mining, metallurgy, mechanical and electrical engineering, shipbuilding, electronics, nuclear technology; Pres. Hong So Hon.

Kim Hyong-Jik University of Education: Pyongyang; f. 1946; faculties of revolutionary history, pedagogy, history and geography, language and literature, foreign languages, mathematics, physics, biology, music, fine arts, physical education; 5-year degree course, short-term courses for teachers, correspondence and postgraduate courses; 2,500 students; Pres. Hong Il Chon.

Pyongyang University of Agriculture: Pyongyang; f. 1981; depts of fruit and vegetable cultivation, poultry, stockbreeding; Pres. Chon Si Gon.

Pyongyang University of Medicine: Woesong District, Pyongyang; colleges of higher and professional education (engineering, agriculture, fisheries, teacher training) situated in all the main towns; also Factory (Engineering) Colleges; Pres. Ri Won Gil.

REPUBLIC OF KOREA

The Higher Education System

The country's oldest institutions of higher education were founded during the final years of the Joseon dynasty (1392–1910), among them Yonsei and Paichai Universities (both founded 1885), Ewha Women's University (founded 1886), Korea University (founded 1905; formerly Posung College) and Dongguk University (founded 1906). Several were established during the early years of the Japanese occupation of the Korean peninsula (1910–45), including Jinju National University (founded 1910), Seoul Theological University (founded 1911), Chung-Ang University (founded 1918) and Miryang National University (founded 1923). Consequently, the Korean education system at all levels displayed strong Japanese influences. Following the Allied defeat of Japan in 1945, Korea was divided at latitude 38°N into military occupation zones, with Soviet forces in the north and US forces in the south. In 1948 the US-administered south became the independent Republic of Korea, while the Democratic People's Republic of Korea was proclaimed in the Soviet-administered north. A three-year war between north and south ended in 1953, and the two countries remain divided at the cease-fire line, separated by a UN-supervised demilitarized zone. Post-1945 education became influenced by the US system and from 1945 has been structured with six years of primary education, six years of secondary education and four years of higher education. A consequence of military control from the 1960s, and particularly during the 1980s, was that specialized and technical education became more respected than the general cultural knowledge traditionally held in high esteem. In recent years a high value has been placed upon scientific education, which resulted in South Korea becoming one of the world's most technologically advanced countries by the 1980s.

Higher education consists of seven types of institution: Junior Colleges, Colleges and Universities, Broadcast and Correspondence Universities, Industrial Universities, Universities of Education, Technical Colleges and miscellaneous colleges. Junior Colleges are distinguished from the other types of institution by the fact that they do not offer four-year undergraduate Bachelors degree programmes. Instead, they offer two- to three-year mainly technical and professionally oriented programmes. Junior Colleges are regulated by the Korean Council for College Education. The remaining six types of institution are grouped under the term Colleges and Universities, and are coordinated by the Korean Council for University Education. The acronym 'SKY' is used to denote the three most prestigious universities: Seoul National University, Korea University and Yonsei University. In 2007 there were 175 colleges and universities, with a student enrolment of 1,919,504. A further 296,576 students were enrolled in 1,042 graduate schools.

Since 1993 the US-style College Scholastic Aptitude Test has been the main basis for admission to higher education. Applicants are also assessed on their scholastic record and institutions may set their own entrance examination. The College Scholastic Aptitude Test is administered by the Institute of Curriculum and Evaluation. The main undergraduate degree is the four-year Bachelors (Haksa), although programmes in professional disciplines such as dentistry and medicine last up to six years. Degrees are awarded on the basis of the US-style 'credit semester' system, and students usually need to accrue 140 credits for award of the Bachelors, of which 35 must be in a designated 'major' subject. The postgraduate (or graduate), Masters (Suksa) and Doctorate (Paksa) degrees are offered primarily by university graduate schools. The Masters lasts two years and requires 24–36 credits, the Doctorate two years and 36 credits. Junior colleges, specialist vocational schools and technical schools are the leading institutions of vocational and technical education. Students usually work towards a vocational qualification and then sit the examination for the National Technical Certificate.

Regulatory and Representative Bodies

GOVERNMENT

Ministry of Culture, Sports and Tourism: 42 Sejong-no, Jongno-gu, Seoul 110-703; tel. (2) 3704-9114; fax (2) 3704-9154; e-mail webadmin@mcst.go.kr; internet www.mcst.go.kr; Minister YU, IN-CHON.

Ministry of Education, Science and Technology: 77-6, Sejong-no, Jongno-gu, Seoul 110-760; tel. (2) 2100-6060; fax (2) 2100-6133; internet www.mest.go.kr; Minister AHN, BYONG MAN.

ACCREDITATION

Korean Council for University Education (KCUE): KGIT Sangam Centre, 11 Fl., Mapo-gu, Sangam-dong 1601 , Seoul 121-270; tel. (2) 6393-5225; fax (2) 6393-5230; e-mail intl@kcue.or.kr; internet english.kcue.or.kr; f. 1982; 201 mems, incl. most four-year univs in Republic of Korea; Chair. LEE, BAE YONG; Sec.-Gen. Prof. PARK, CHONG YUL; publ. *Daehak Gyoyuk* (Higher Education, in Korean).

NATIONAL BODY

Korean Federation of Teachers' Associations: 142 Woomyeon-dong, Seocho-Ku, Seoul 137-715; tel. (2) 570-5500; fax (2) 576-1081; e-mail kfta2@kfta.or.kr; internet www.kfta.or.kr; f. 1947; Pres. LEE, WON-HEE; Dir JEONG, DONG-SEOB.

Learned Societies

GENERAL

Korea Foundation: 10-11F Diplomatic Centre Bldg, 2558 Nambusunhwanno, Seocho-gu, Seoul 137-863; 1F Joongang Ilbo Bldg, Sunhwa-dong 7, Jung-gu, Seoul 100-759; tel. (2) 2046-8500; fax (2) 3463-6076; e-mail kfcenter@kf.or.kr; internet www.kf.or.kr; f. 1991 (fmrly Int. Cultural Soc. of Korea); promotes mutual understanding and friendship between Korea and the rest of the world; 60 mems; library of 8,000 vols; Pres. YIM SUNG-JOON; publs *Koreana* (in English and Chinese, 4 a year), *Korea Focus* (in English, 6 a year).

National Academy of Sciences: San-94-4, Banpo 4-dong, Seocho-gu, Seoul 137-044; tel. (2) 534-0737; fax (2) 537-3183; internet www.nas.go.kr; f. 1954; 150 mems; library of 15,000 vols; Pres. KIM SANG-JOO; Vice-Pres. PARK YOUNG-SIK; publs *Development of Science Study in Korea* (in Korean, 1 a year), *Journal of NAS* (in Korean, 1 a year), *NAS Annual Bulletin* (in Korean), *NAS Bulletin* (in English, every 2 years), *Proceedings of the International Symposium* (in Korean, 1 a year).

Royal Asiatic Society, Korea Branch: CPO Box 255, Seoul; tel. (2) 763-9483; fax (2) 766-3796; f. 1900 to encourage interest in, and promote study and dissemination of knowledge about, the arts, history, literature and customs of Korea and the neighbouring countries; 1,600 mems; library of 1,000 vols; Gen. Man. SUE J. BAE; publ. *Transactions* (1 a year).

AGRICULTURE, FISHERIES AND VETERINARY SCIENCE

Korean Forestry Society: c/o Dept of Forest Resources, Seoul National University, Suwon, Kyonggido Seoul 441-744; tel. (331) 290-2330; f. 1960 to foster the study of all aspects of forestry, to promote cooperation among members; 800 mems; Pres. Prof. JONG HWA YOUN; Sec. Assoc. Prof. JOO SANG CHUNG; publ. *Journal* (4 a year).

BIBLIOGRAPHY, LIBRARY SCIENCE AND MUSEOLOGY

Korean Library Association: San 60-1, Banpo-dong, Seocho-gu, Seoul 137-702; tel. (2) 535-4868; fax (2) 535-5616; e-mail klanet@hitel.net; internet www.korla.or.kr; f. 1945; a social and academic instn comprising all the libraries and librarians in Korea;

1,115 institutional, 1,865 individual mems; Pres. KI-NAM SHIN; Exec. Dir KYUNG-KU LEE; publs *KLA Bulletin* (6 a year), *Statistics on Libraries in Korea* (1 a year).

Korean Museum Association: c/o National Museum of Korea, 168-6 Yongsan-dong, Yongsan-gu, Seoul 140-026; tel. (2) 795-0937; fax (2) 795-0939; e-mail webmaster@museum.or.kr; internet www.museum.or.kr; f. 1976; devt of museums through collaborative networking and of institutional museum policies for the benefits of the preservation of culture and education; Pres. KIDONG BAE.

Korean Research and Development Library Association: Room 0411, KIST Library, POB 131, Cheongryang, Seoul; tel. (82) 967-3692; fax (82) 2963-4013; f. 1979; Pres. KE HONG PARK; Sec. KEON TAK OH.

ECONOMICS, LAW AND POLITICS

Korean Association of Sinology: c/o Asiatic Research Centre, Korea University, Anam-dong, Seoul; f. 1955; 100 mems; Chair. JUN-YOP KIM; publ. *Journal of Chinese Studies*.

Korean Economic Association: 45, 4-ga, Namdae-mun-ro, Chung-gu, Seoul; tel. (2) 3210-2522; fax (2) 3210-2555; e-mail kea1952@kea.ne.kr; internet www.kea.ne.kr; f. 1952; theory, policy and history of economics and business administration; 2,800 mems; library of 3,000 vols; Pres. PYUNG-JOO KIM; Sec.-Gen. JOON-WOO NAHM; publ. *Korean Economic Review* (2 a year).

FINE AND PERFORMING ARTS

Music Association of Korea: Bldg 1-117, Dongsung-dong, Chongro-gu, Seoul 110-765; tel. (2) 744-8060; fax (2) 741-2378; e-mail music@mak.or.kr; internet www.mak.or.kr; f. 1961 to develop Korean nat. music and to promote and protect Korean musicians; organizes concerts, encourages musical composition and nationwide singing; is active in the int. musical exchange and in music education; awards the Prize of Musical Culture; 700 mems; small library; Pres. Dr KIM YONG-JIN.

HISTORY, GEOGRAPHY AND ARCHAEOLOGY

Korean Geographical Society: Dept of Geography, College of Social Sciences, Seoul National University, Seoul 151-746; tel. (2) 875-1463; fax (2) 876-2853; e-mail geography77@daum.net; internet www.kgeography.or.kr; f. 1945 to promote mutual cooperation in academic work and int. understanding; 772 individual mems, 69 institutional mems; Pres. LEE JEONG ROCK; Sec.-Gen. YONG-CHUL SHIN; publ. *Journal* (5 a year).

LANGUAGE AND LITERATURE

Alliance Française: 63-2 Hoehyun-dong 1-ga, Jung-gu, Seoul 100-873; tel. (2) 755-5702; fax (2) 774-4252; e-mail alliance@nuri.net; internet www.afcoree.co.kr; offers courses and examinations in French language and culture and promotes cultural exchange with France; attached teaching centres in Busan, Chonju, Daegu, Daejon, Gwangju, Jeonju; Dir MARC SARRAZIN.

British Council: 4th Fl., Hungkuk Life Insurance Bldg, 226 Shinmunro 1-ga, Jongro-gu, Seoul 110-786; tel. (2) 3702-0600; fax (2) 3702-0660; e-mail info@britishcouncil.or.kr; internet www.bckorea.or.kr; teaching centre; offers courses and examinations in English language and British culture and promotes cultural exchange with the UK; Dir ROLAND DAVIES.

Goethe-Institut: 339-1 Huam-dong, Yongsan-ku, Seoul 140-901; tel. (2) 754-9831; fax (2) 754-9834; e-mail info@seoul.goethe.org; internet www.goethe.de/os/seo/deindex.htm; offers courses and examinations in German language and culture and promotes cultural exchange with Germany; library of 12,000 vols; Dir JURGEN KEIL.

MEDICINE

Korean Medical Association:; tel. (2) 794-2474; fax (2) 793-9190; e-mail intl@kma.org; internet www.kma.org; f. 1908 to develop the medical sciences and medical education by encouraging research and investigation; 59,292 mems; library of 10,000 vols; Pres. KYUNG MAN HO; publs *Journal* (12 a year), *The KMA News* (2 a week).

PHILOSOPHY AND PSYCHOLOGY

Korean Psychological Association: Dept of Psychology, Seoul National University, Shinrim 2-dong, Kwanak-gu, Seoul; tel. 877-0101, ext. 2528; e-mail kpa0102@chol.com; internet www.koreanpsychology.or.kr; f. 1946; 420 mems; Pres. KIM MYUNG UN; Sec.-Gen. JUNGOH KIM; publs *Korean Journal of Psychology* (2 a year), *Korean Journal of Clinical Psychology* (2 a year), *Korean Journal of Social Psychology* (1 a year), *Korean Journal of Industrial Psychology* (1 a year), *Korean Journal of Developmental Psychology* (1 a year).

Research Institutes

GENERAL

Academy of Korean Studies: 110 Haogo-gae-gil, Bundang-gu, Seongnam-si, Gyeonggi-do, Seoul 463-791; tel. (31) 709-8111; fax (342) 709-1531; internet www.aks.ac.kr; f. 1978 to research and re-evaluate traditional Korean culture; library of 361,000 vols incl. 35,000 in Western languages; Pres. KIM JEONG-BAE; publ. *Chongsin Munhwa/Academy News* (3–4 a year).

AGRICULTURE, FISHERIES AND VETERINARY SCIENCE

Rural Development Administration: Suin-ro, 150 (250 Seodun-dong), Gwonseon-gu, Suwon Gyeonggi-do, Seoul 441-707; tel. (31) 299-2200; fax (31) 299-2469; e-mail rda@rda.go.kr; internet www.rda.go.kr; f. 1906 to carry out agricultural research and rural community devt; 11 subordinate research orgs, 9 provincial offices, 34 regional specialized crop stations; library of 190,000 vols; Administrator KIM JAE-SOO; publs *Agricultural Technology* (in Korean, 12 a year), *Annual Research Report* (Korean and English editions), *Research and Extension* (in Korean, 12 a year).

ECONOMICS, LAW AND POLITICS

Korea Development Institute: POB 113, Cheongnyang, Seoul 130-868; tel. (2) 958-4114; e-mail kdiweb@kdi.re.kr; internet www.kdi.re.kr; f. 1971 to help determine the basic direction of the nation's development by formulating long-term goals and strategies based on accurate economic analysis; to conduct policy-oriented research relating to individual sectors of the economy that will help the country to maintain high economic growth with price stability; to provide consultation on policy issues relating to short-term economic management and planning; library of 100,000 vols, 39,000 research reports, govt documents, also data bank; Pres. OH SEOK HYUN; publs *KDI Journal of*

Economic Policy (in Korean, 4 a year), *KDI Economic Outlook* (in Korean, 4 a year).

Korea Institute for Industrial Economics and Trade (KIET): 66 Hoegiro, Dongdaemun-gu, Seoul 130-742; tel. (2) 3299-3114; internet www.kiet.re.kr; f. 1976 as Korea Foundation for Middle East Studies; separated from Centre for Industrial and Technical Information and took present name 1991; advises govt on industrial, trade and commercial policies; analyses Korean industry, int. economies, new technology and promotion of trade; library of 45,000 vols, 1,500 periodicals; Pres. OH SANG-BONG; publ *KIET Real Economy* (fortnightly), *Journal of Industrial Competitiveness* (1 a year), *KIET Economic Outlook* (2 a year).

Korean Research Center: 228 Pyong-dong, Chongno-gu, Seoul; f. 1956; research in social sciences; maintaines library; Pres. MUNAM CHON; publs *Journal of Social Sciences and Humanities*, *Korean Studies Series*.

EDUCATION

Korean Educational Development Institute: 92–6 Umyeon-dong, Seocho-gu, Seoul 137-791; tel. (2) 3460-0216; fax (2) 3460-0156; e-mail international@kedi.re.kr; internet eng.kedi.re.kr; f. 1972; ind., govt-funded research and devt institute; undertakes research and devt activities on education; assists govt in formulation of educational policies and in long-term devt of education; library of 121,197 vols, 88 periodicals, 499,018 microfiches; Pres. TAE-WAN KIM; publs *KEDI Journal of Education Policy* (in English, 2 a year), *Research Abstracts* (in English, 1 a year), *Statistical Yearbook of Education* (in Korean and English, 1 a year).

National Institute for Training of Educational Administrators: c/o Ministry of Education, Science and Technology, 77-6 Sejong-ro, Jongno-gu, Seoul 110-760; tel. (2) 733-2741; fax (2) 733-0149; f. 1970; government institute; attached to Min. of Education, Science and Technology; library of 21,000 vols; Dir CHONG-TAEK CHANG.

NATURAL SCIENCES
Physical Sciences

Korea Meteorological Administration: 45 Gisangcheong-gil, Dongjak-gu, Seoul 156-720; tel. (2) 836-2385; fax (2) 836-2386; e-mail pb_int@kma.go.kr; internet web.kma.go.kr; under the control of the Min. of Education, Science and Technology; Administrator CHUN BYUNG-SEONG.

PHILOSOPHY AND PSYCHOLOGY

Korean Institute for Research in the Behavioural Sciences: 1606-3 Socho-Dong, Kangnam-gu, Seoul 137-071; tel. (2) 581-8611; f. 1968; basic and applied research in 5 areas: social, child, learning, organization, and psychological testing; 70 researchers; library of 5,000 vols; Dir SUNG JIN LEE; publs *Research Bulletin*, *Research Notes*, *Research Monograph*.

TECHNOLOGY

Electronics and Telecommunications Research Institute (ETRI): 138 Gajeongno, Yuseong-gu, Daejeon City, Seoul 305-700; tel. (42) 860-6114; e-mail sloh@etri.re.kr; internet www.etri.re.kr; f. 1976; undertakes research and devt in field of advanced information technology; library of 40,000 vols, 30,000 technical reports, and ETLARS databases; Pres. CHOI MUN-KEE; publs *Electronics and Telecommunications Trends* (4 a year), *ETRI Journal* (4 a year), *Patent Announcement* (26 a year), *Patent*

Information (12 a year), *Weekly Technology Trends* (52 a year).

Korea Atomic Energy Research Institute (KAERI): POB 105, Yu-seong, Daejeon, Seoul 305-600; tel. (42) 868-2000; fax (42) 862-8465; internet www.kaeri.re.kr; f. 1959; reactor-related research and devt and security and R&D of nuclear fuel, nuclear policy research, radiation application technology devt and research and treatment of nuclear radiation, nuclear personnel training and other aspects of nuclear energy; library of 61,000 vols, 700,000 technical reports and 950 periodicals; Pres. MYUNG SEUNG YANG; publs *Journal*, *KAERI Research Papers* (1 a year), *Won Woo* (6 a year).

Korea Institute of Energy Research: 102 Gajeong-ro, Yuseong-gu, Daejeon, Seoul 305-343; tel. (42) 860-3114; fax (42) 861-6224; e-mail webadmin@kier.re.kr; internet www.kier.re.kr; f. 1977 to conduct research on energy and technology; supported by Min. of Education, Science and Technology; 500 mems; library of 30,000 vols; Pres. HAN MOON-HEE; publs *Energy R&D*, *Technical Trends on NRSE*.

Korea Institute of Science and Technology (KIST): 39-1 Hawolkok-dong, Songbuk-ku, Seoul 136-791; tel. (2) 958-6114; fax (2) 958-5478; e-mail cglee@kist.re.kr; internet www.kist.re.kr; f. 1966; research in applied science, chemical engineering, polymer engineering, materials science and engineering, mechanical and control systems, electronics and information technology, environment and CFC alternatives technology, systems engineering, genetic engineering, science and technology policy; library of 50,000 vols, 15,000 technical reports; Pres. Dr HAHN HONG THOMAS; publ. *Collection of Abstracts* (in Korean and English, 1 a year).

Libraries and Archives

Busan

Banyeo Library: San 129-9, Banyeo 3-dong, Haeundae-gu, Busan; tel. (51) 749-5731; fax (51) 749-5739; internet www.banyeolib.or.kr.

Dong-Eui University Central Library: Kaya-dong, Pusanjin-ku, Busan, Seoul 614-714; tel. (51) 890-1155; fax (51) 890-1165; e-mail hjahn@deu.ac.kr; internet lib.deu.ac.kr; f. 1979; 810,000 vols; Library Dean Dr NAM SOO-HYUN.

Gang Seo Public Library: 2011-2 Daeju 2-dong, Ganseo-gu, Busan 618-807; tel. (51) 973-5274; fax (51) 973-5275; internet library.bsgangseo.go.kr.

Pusan National University Library: 30 Jangjeon-dong, Keumjeong-gu, Pusan 609-735; tel. (51) 510-1800; fax (51) 513-9787; f. 1946; 650,000 vols, 5,000 periodicals; Dir DONG-HYUN JUNG.

Daegu

Bukbu Library: 447-10 Chimsan 3-dong, Buk-gu, Daegu, Seoul 702-857; tel. (53) 350-0800; fax (53) 358-2535; internet www.bukbu-lib.daegu.kr; f. 1982.

Daebong Library: Daebong-dong, Jung-gu, Daegu; tel. (53) 422-0958; internet www.db.dblib.daegu.kr.

Dongbu Library: 664-19 Sinam 4-dong, Dong-gu, Daegu, Seoul 701-014; tel. (53) 603-6100; fax (53) 941-8076; internet www.dongbu-lib.daegu.kr.

Duryu Public Library: 154 Duryu 3-dong, Dalseo-gu, Daegu; tel. (53) 650-0200; internet www.duryu-lib.daegu.kr.

Jungang Library: 42 Dongin-dong 2-ga, Munhwa-gil, Jung-gu, Daegu, Seoul 700-422; tel. (53) 420-2700; fax (53) 420-2750; internet www.tglnet.or.kr; f. 1918 as Daegu Bu Library, renamed in 1995; Dir HONG-MAN KIM.

Kyungpook National University Library: 1370 Sankyuk-dong, Puk-ku, Taegu 702-701; tel. (53) 950-6510; fax (53) 950-6533; e-mail mspark@kyungpook.ac.kr; internet kudos.knu.ac.kr; f. 1952; 2.1m. vols; Dir SEO, JONG-MOON.

Nambu Metropolitan Library: San 192-4 Daemyeong 9-dong, Nam-gu, Daegu; tel. (53) 620-5511; fax (53) 623-2308; e-mail nbl@edunavi.kr; internet www.nbl.or.kr; f. 1995; Curator JOHOSIK.

Seobu Public Library: 1230-1 Pyeongni 3-dong, Seo-gu, Daegu; tel. (53) 560-8800; fax (53) 560-8819; internet www.seobu-lib.daegu.kr.

Suseong Library: 54 Art Gallery park-route (gil), Manchon 1 (il)-dong, Suseong-gu, Daegu, Seoul 706-707; tel. (53) 740-5532; internet www.hyomok-lib.daegu.kr; f. 1988. as Hyomok Library; present name in 2008.

Daejeon

Daejeon Student Education and Culture Centre: 701 Jung-gu, Daejeon, Seoul 301-807; tel. (42) 229-1490; internet www.djsecc.or.kr.

Daejeon University Library: Daejeon, Seoul 300-718; tel. (42) 280-2681; fax (42) 283-7174; internet libweb.dju.ac.kr.

Hanbat Library: Daejeon, Seoul 301-711; tel. (42) 580-4114; fax (42) 580-4204; e-mail hanbat@its.daejeon.kr; internet hanbat.metro.daejeon.kr; 568,028 vols.

National Archives of Korea: Govt Complex, Seonsaro, 139 (920 Dusan 2-Dong), Seo-gu, Daejeon 302-701; tel. (42) 481-6300; fax (42) 472-3906; f. 1969, relocated from Seoul in 1998; 336,275 vols, 1.2m. diagrams, 1.5m. cards, 181,311 rolls of microfilm, 740,463 audiovisual items; colln of records of the Yi dynasty.

Branches:

National Archives, Busan: 2-dong, Geoje-dong San 126, Girokgwan 1st Fl., Busan; tel. (51) 550-8025; fax (51) 504-6963.

National Archives, Seoul: Gwanghwa-mun Jeokseon-dong Platinum 201, 156-dong, Jongro-gu, Seoul; tel. 720-2721; fax 739-8944.

Gwangju

Chonnam University Library: Buk-gu, Yongbong to 77 Daechulbannap-sil, Gwangju, Seoul 500-757; tel. (62) 530-3571; fax (62) 530-3529; internet library.chonnam.ac.kr; f. 1953; 2m. vols, 680,000 books, 20,000 journals and periodicals.

Honam University Library: Gwangsan Seobongdong 59-1, Gwangju, Seoul 506-714; tel. (62) 940-5185; fax (62) 940-5183; e-mail bss@honam.ac.kr; internet library.honam.ac.kr; f. 1979.

Gyeonggi-do

Gamgol Library: 83-8 Sa-dong, Sangrok-gu, Ansan-si, Gyeonggi-do, Seoul 425-170.

Gwacheon Provincial Library of Gyeonggi: 12 Dosegwangil, Gwacheon, Gyeonggi-do; tel. (2) 3677-0371; e-mail webmaster@kwalib.or.kr; internet eng.kwalib.or.kr; f. 1984; 298,587 vols, 778 periodicals and magazines; Dir LEE WOON SUN.

Seoul

Chung-Ang University Library: 221 Huk-suk-dong, Dongjak-ku, Seoul; f. 1949; 442,667 vols; Dir TOO YOUNG LEE.

Dongguk University Library: 263-ga, Pil-dong, Seoul; internet lib.dongguk.edu; f. 1906; Buddhist and Oriental studies; 350,000 vols, 1,100 periodicals; Dir Dr JAE HO SHIN.

Ewha Woman's University Library: 11–1, Daehyun-dong, Sudaemun-gu, Seoul 120-750; tel. 3277-3124; fax 3277-2857; e-mail jnam@mm.ewha.ac.kr; internet lib.ewha.ac.kr; f. 1923; 1.7m. vols; Dir BONG HEE KIM.

Korea Foundation and Cultural Centre Library: Joogang Ilbo Bldg, 1st Fl., Sunhwa-dong 7, Jung-gu, Seoul 100-759; tel. (2) 2151-6500; fax (2) 2151-6590; e-mail kfcenter@kf.or.kr; internet library.kfcenter.or.kr; f. 2005.

Korea University Library: 1 Anam-dong, Sungbuk-gu, Seoul 136-701; tel. (2) 3290-1470; f. 1937; 400,132 vols; Dir SUNG GI JON.

Korean Braille Library: 510-23 Amsa-dong, Kang dong-ku, Seoul 134-052; tel. (2) 3426-7411; fax (2) 3426-7415; e-mail kbl@kbll.or.kr; internet www.infor.kbll.or.kr; f. 1969; Dir KEUN HAE YOUK.

National Assembly Library: 1 Yoido-dong, Seoul; tel. (2) 784-3565; fax (2) 788-4193; e-mail webw3@nanet.go.kr; internet www.nanet.go.kr; f. 1952; library service for members of the National Assembly, the Executive, the Judiciary, and for scholars and legislative research activities and int. book exchange with 360 institutions worldwide; 900,000 vols, 12,101 current periodicals, 700 newspapers; Librarian JONG PIL YOO; publs *Acquisitions List* (1 a year), *Index to Korean-Language Periodicals* (6 a year and 1 a year), *Index to Korean Laws and Statutes* (2 a year), *Index to National Assembly Debates* (irregular), *Issue Briefs* (irregular), *Legislative Information Analysis* (4 a year), *List of Theses for the Doctor's and Master's Degree in Korea* (1 a year), *National Assembly Library Review* (12 a year).

National Library of Korea: Banpo-ro 664, Seocho-gu, Seoul 137-702; tel. (2) 535-4142; fax (2) 590-0530; e-mail nlkpc@www.nl.go.kr; internet www.nl.go.kr; f. 1945; 3.9m. vols; legal deposit library for Korean publications, ISBN, ISSN nat. centre, KOLIS-NET (Korean Library Information System Network) centre, international exchange, research in library and information science, publishes nat. bibliographies, operates National Digital Library (www.dlibrary.go.kr) and training centre for librarians; Dir GI-YOUNG JEONG; publ. *Doseogwan* (4 a year).

Seoul National University Library: San 56-1, Shillim-dong, Kwanak-gu, Seoul 151-742; tel. (2) 880-5284; fax (2) 871-2972; internet library.snu.ac.kr; f. 1946; 2.1m. vols, 13,000 periodicals, incl. Agricultural Library (121,000 vols), Medical Library (123,000 vols), Law Library (65,000 vols), Business Library (11,000 vols), Social Sciences Library (20,000 vols), Dental Library (9,000 vols) and Kyujang-gak Archives (special collection on Choseon Dynasty, 152,000 vols); collns on the arts, sciences, law, education, music, medicine, engineering, economics and commerce; Dir CHONG SUH KIM; publs *Kyujang-gak* (1 a year), *Ko-munseo* (1 a year).

Transport Library: 168, 2-ka, Bongnae-dong, Seoul; f. 1920; 32,000 vols; Dir CHO WOO HYUN; Chief Librarian KIM DOO HO; publ. *Korean National Railroad Bulletin* (12 a year).

United Nations Depository Library: Korea University, 1 An-Am-dong, Sungbuk-gu, Seoul; tel. (2) 3290-1492; fax (2) 922-4633; f. 1957; 38,000 vols; Dir HWA-YOUNG KIM; Librarian MI-GYOUNG CHO.

Yonsei University Library: Yonsei University, 134 Sinchon-dong, Sudaemoon-gu,

Seoul; tel. (2) 361-3308; e-mail leehg@yonsei
.ac.kr; internet library.yonsei.ac.kr; f. 1915;
1.5m. vols, incl. Korean archives, 10,700
periodicals; Dir JONG CHUL HAN; publs *Dong
Bang Hak Chi* (Journal of Korean Studies),
Inmun Kwahak (Journal of Humanities),
International Journal of Korean Studies,
Journal of East and West Studies, *Kyo Yuk
Non Jib* (Journal of Education), *Yonsei Non-
Chong* (Journal of Graduate School), *Yonsei
Social Science Review*, *Abstracts of Faculty
Research Report*, *Yonsei Magazine*.

Museums and Art Galleries

Busan

Busan Museum: 48-1 Daeyeon 4-dong,
Namgu, Busan, Seoul 608-092; tel. (51) 610-
7111; fax (51) 610-7130; e-mail museum@
metro.busan.kr; internet museum.busan.kr;
f. 1978, renovated in 2002; collns from prehistoric period to the present.

Attached Museums:

Bokcheon Museum: 50 Bokcheon-dong
Dongnae-gu, Busan, Seoul 607-020; tel.
(51) 554-4263; fax (51) 554-4265; f. 1996;
displays artifacts excavated from the
tumulus group in Bokcheon-dong that
show the history of Busan from the prehistoric age to the Three Kingdoms Era.

Busan Modern History Museum:.

Dongsam-dong Shell Midden Museum:
750-1 Dongsam-dong, Yeongdo-gu Busan.

Busan Museum of Modern Art: 1413 Woo
2 dong, Haeundae-gu, Busan; tel. (51) 744-
2602; fax (51) 740-4280; internet www
.busanmoma.org; f. 1998; exhibitions, scholastic research, archive and presentation, int.
exchange, education, cultural events; Dir
CHO IL SANG.

Pusan National University Museum: San
30, Jangjeon-dong, Geumjeong-gu, Busan,
609-735; internet www.pnu-museum.org;
tel. (51) 510-1838; tel. (51) 581-2455; f.
1956; Korean archaeology with special collection of historical remains of Kyongsang-
Namdo province, arts, ethnology, etc.; Dir
Prof. GYEONGCHEOL SHIN; publ. *Research
Reports* (irregular).

Daegu

Daegu Bangjja Yugi Museum: 399 Dohak-
dong, Dong-gu, Daegu; tel. (53) 606-6171; fax
(53) 606-6179; internet artcenter.daegu.go
.kr/bangjja; f. 2000, opened in 2007; built to
preserve Bangjja Yugi (Korean Bronzewear)
considered a traditional cultural property;
major items of the Bangjja Yugi incl. musical
instruments, utensils and other items for
religious services, tableware and living
goods.

Daegu National Museum: San 41, Hwang-
geum-dong, Suseong-gu, Daegu; tel. (53) 768-
6051; fax (53) 768-6053; e-mail webadmin@
daegu.museum.go.kr; internet daegu
.museum.go.kr; f. 1994; 30,000 items, art and
archaeology; main collns on the material
culture of Daegu, and western and northern
parts of the Gyeongsangbuk-do province.

Daegu University Central Museum:
Daegu University Museum, 15 Naeri, Jillyang, Daegu, Gyeongbuk 712-714; tel. (53)
850-5621; fax (53) 850-5629; internet
museum.daegu.ac.kr; f. 1981; 19 cultural
property excavations, 33 cultural property
surfaces and 37 academic reports.

Daejeon

Daejeon Metropolitan Museum of Arts:
near 396 Mannyeon-dong, Seo-gu, Expo Park

Daejeon; tel. (42) 602-3225; fax (42) 602-
3299; e-mail mintae@daejeon.go.kr; internet
dmma.metro.daejeon.kr; f. 1998; features
modern art from both domestic and foreign
artists; outdoor sculpture park.

Daejeon Prehistoric Museum: Oeun-
dong, Yuseong-gu, Daejeon, Seoul 305-330;
tel. (42) 826-2814; fax (42) 826-2811; internet
museum.daejeon.go.kr; f. 2007; prehistory of
the Daejeon region, collns and artifacts.

Geological Museum: Daejeon, Seoul 305-
350; tel. (42) 868-3797; fax (42) 868-3424;
internet museum.kigam.re.kr; history of the
earth, fossils, evolution; rocks and geological
structures, minerals and human, environment and geology.

Ungno Lee Museum: 396 Mannyon-dong,
Seo-gu, Daejeon; tel. (42) 602-3270; fax (42)
602-3280; internet www.ungnolee-museum
.daejeon.kr; f. 2007, in memory of late
Korean painter Goam Ungno Lee.

**Yeojin Buddhist Art Gallery and
Museum:** 442-1 Tablib-dong, Yuseong-gu,
Daejeon, Seoul 450-702; tel. (42) 934-8466;
fax (42) 933-8477; internet www
.yeojingallery.co.kr.

Gwangju

Gwangju Museum of Art: 48 Bagmulgwan,
Ro Buk-gu, Gwangju, Seoul 500-170; tel. (62)
510-0113; fax (62) 510-0119; internet www
.artmuse.gjcity.net; f. 1992.

Gwangju National Museum: 114 Bak-
mulgwan-lo St, Maegok-dong, Buk-gu,
Gwangju, Seoul 500-150; tel. (62) 570-7014;
fax (62) 570-7015; e-mail webadmin@
gwangju.museum.go.kr; internet gwangju
.museum.go.kr; f. 1978; cultural heritage of
Gwangju.

Gyeonggi-do

Ansan Fishing Village Folk Museum: 717
Seongam-dong, Danwon-gu, Ansan-si,
Gyeonggi-do; tel. (32) 886-0126; preserves
and exhibits traditional folk customs and
fishing culture of Ansan fishing village.

Bucheon Museum of Bow: 8 Sports Complex, Chunui-dong, Wonmi-gu, Bucheon-si,
Gyeonggi-do; tel. (32) 614-2678; internet
www.bcmuseum.or.kr; f. 2004; preserving
traditional bow kukgung culture.

Chunghyeon Museum: 1085-16 Soha 2-
dong, Gwangmyeong-si, Gyeonggi-do 423-
828; tel. (2) 898-0505; fax (2) 898-2507;
e-mail manager@chunghyon.com; internet
www.chunghyeon.org; f. 2003; Dir HAM
GEUMJA.

Deung-Jan Museum: 258-9 Nyeoungwon,
Myonhun-myeon, Yongin-si, Gyeonggi-do
449-850; tel. (31) 334-0797; e-mail
deungjan@deungjan.or.kr; internet www
.deungjan.or.kr; f. 1997; colln of ethnic
antique lamps.

Gyeonggi Museum of Modern Art: Dong-
sangil 36, 667-1 Choji-Dong, Danweon-gu,
Ansan-si, Gyeonggi-do 425-866; tel. (31) 481-
7007; fax (31) 481-7045; e-mail minerva8@
hanmir.com; internet www.gma.or.kr; f.
2006; Dir KIN HONG-HEE.

Gyeonggi Provincial Museum: 85 Sang-
gal-dong, Giheung-gu, Yongin-si, Gyeonggi-
do, Seoul 446-905; tel. (31) 288-5300; fax (31)
288-5390; e-mail museum@kg21.net;
internet www.musenet.or.kr; f. 1996; spec.
exhibitions on culture of Gyeonggi province;
Dir KIM JAE-YEOL.

Haegang Ceramics Museum: 330-1
Suwang-li, Shintun-myeon, Icheon,
Gyeonggi-do; tel. (31) 634-2266; fax (31)
634-2267; internet www.haegang.org; f.
1990; Korean ceramics; offers ceramic production courses.

Ho-Am Art Museum: 204 Gasil-ri, Pogok-
eup, Cheoin-gu, Yongin-si, Gyeonggi-do 449-
811; tel. (31) 320-1801; fax (31) 320-1809;
e-mail juliana.park@samsung.com; internet
hoam.samsungfoundation.org; f. 1982; largest privately owned museum in South Korea;
colln of over 1,200 Korean works of art;
sculpture garden of works by French sculptor
Bourdelle.

Woljeon Museum of Art: 467-020, Expo-gil
48, Gwango-dong 378, Icheon-si, Gyeonggi-
do; tel. (31) 637-0033; e-mail iwoljeon@
iwoljeon.org; internet www.iwoljeon.org; f.
1991 in Seoul, moved to Icheon in 2007;
commemorates work of Korean painter Woljeon Chang Woo-Soung; 1,532 artworks.

Gyeongsangbuk-do

**Andongsoju and Traditional Food
Museum:** 280 Susang-dong, Andong,
Gyeongsangbuk-do; tel. (54) 858-4541;
internet www.andongsoju.net; f. 2000;
museum of traditional Andong distilled
liquor.

Gyeongju National Museum: 118
Iljeongno, Gyeongju, Gyeongsangbuk-do,
Seoul 780-150; tel. (54) 740-7500; internet
gyeongju.museum.go.kr; f. 1945; preserves
culture of the Silla Kingdom; Dir YOUNG-
HOON YI.

**Gyeongsangbuk-do Forest Science
Museum:** tel. (54) 855-8681; fax (54) 855-
8684; internet www.gbfsm.or.kr; preserves
historical material and data on forests and
conducts academic research; outdoor facilities divided by themes into hydroponics
zone, landscaping zone, wooded zone, clean
zone, ecological zone, botanical communities,
traditional culture practice zone (mountain
village culture), ornithological facility and
greenhouse zone.

Hahoe Mask Museum: 287 Hahoe-ri, Pung-
chun-myun, Andong Gyeongsangbuk-do; tel.
(571) 853-2288; fax (571) 853-0114; internet
www.tal.or.kr; hahoe masks and Korean
masks.

Silla Art and Science Museum: Gyeongju
Folk Hand Craft Village, Gyeongju, Gyeongsangbuk-do; tel. (54) 745-4998; fax (54) 746-
5134; internet www.sasm.or.kr; f. 1988; represents the scientific advancements and
achievement of the Silla period; incl. spec.
exhibits on the Sokkuram Grotto and Chom-
songdae observatories.

Jeollabuk-do

Gangam Calligraphy Museum: 197-2
Gyo-dong, Wansan-gu, Jeonju-si, Jeollabuk-
do; tel. (63) 285-7442; f. 1995; 1,000 works by
Korean calligraphers Jeong-hui Kim (1786–
1856), Sam-man Lee (1770–1845) and Yak-
yong Jeong (1762–1836).

Jeonju National Museum: 900 Hyoja-dong
2 Ga, Wansa-Gu, Jeonju, Jeollabuk-do, Seoul
560-859; tel. (63) 223-5651; fax (63) 223-5653;
internet jeonju.museum.go.kr; 24,000 artifacts; history and culture of Jeollabuk-do;
Buddhist art works, pottery, gold artifacts
and folk material; Dir HYUNG SIK YOO.

Jeollanam-do

Mokpo Natural History Museum: 9-28
Yonghae-dong, Mokpo-si, Jeollanam-do; tel.
(61) 274-3655; fax (61) 270-8298; internet
museum.mokpo.go.kr; f. 2004; natural history; 40,000 artifacts.

National Maritime Museum: 8 Yonghae-
dong, Mokpo, Jeollanam-do; tel. (61) 270-
2000; fax (61) 270-2080; internet www
.seamuse.go.kr; f. 1994; exhibits underwater
cultural heritage from the Korean waters
and maritime culture incl. nautical traditions and Korean traditional boats.

Seoul

Chiwoo Craft Museum: 610-11 Woomyun-dong, Seocho-gu, Seoul; internet www.chiwoocraftmuseum.org; f. 2002; modern crafts; Curator LEE IN BEOM.

National Museum of Contemporary Art: Deoksugung, 5-1 Jeong-dung, Jung-gu, Seoul 100-120; e-mail miaya@mct.go.kr; internet www.moca.go.kr; exhibitions; educational programmes for art professionals and school liaison; general programmes, programmes for children and youth.

National Museum of Korea: 135 Seobinggo-ro, Yongsan-gu, Seoul 140-026; tel. (2) 2077-9000; internet www.museum.go.kr; f. 1908; Korean archaeology, culture and folklore; 100,000 artefacts representing over 5,000 years of human endeavour on the Korean peninsula; education centre; library of 20,000 vols; brs in 8 other towns; Dir CHOE KWANG-SHIK; publs *Bakmulkwan Sinmun* (Museum News, 12 a year), *Misul Charyo* (Materials in Art, 2 a year), *Report of Researches of Antiquities*, *The International Journal of Korean Art and Archeology*.

National Science Museum: 2 Waryong-dong, Jongno-gu, Seoul 110-360; tel. (2) 3668-2200; fax (2) 3668-2246; internet www.ssm.go.kr; f. 1926; holds National Science Fair, exhibitions, science classrooms, film service, etc.; library of 2,000 vols on science and technology; Dir CHI-EUN KIM; publ. *Bulletin*.

Seoul National University Museum: 599 Gwanak-ro, Gwanak-gu, Seoul 151-742; tel. (2) 880-5333; fax (2) 874-3999; internet museum.snu.ac.kr; f. 1941; exhibition of Korean culture totalling 8,058 artefacts; library specializing in Korean archaeology, art history, anthropology and folklore; Dir Dr NAK-KYU PARK; publ. *Bulletin* (1 a year).

Yonsei University Museum: Shinchon-dong, Sudaemun-gu, Seoul; tel. (2) 123-3335; e-mail art@yonsei.ac.kr; internet museum.yonsei.ac.kr; f. 1965; research; pre-history, history, fine arts, ethnic customs, medicine, geology, etc.; Curator YOUNG CHEOL BAK; publs occasional papers, excavation reports.

Universities

PUBLIC UNIVERSITIES

ANDONG NATIONAL UNIVERSITY

388 Songcheon-dong, Andong-si, Gyeongsangbuk, Seoul 460-380

Telephone: (54) 820-5114
Fax: (54) 820-7115
Internet: www.andong.ac.kr

Founded 1979

Pres.: LEE HEE JAE
Registrar: KIM JONG-SIK
Librarian: KU SANG-MAN

Library of 55,000 vols
Number of teachers: 113
Number of students: 2,900

CHANGWON NATIONAL UNIVERSITY

9 Sarim-dong, Changwon, Gyeongnam, Seoul 641-773

Telephone: (55) 213-3000
Fax: (55) 283-2970
E-mail: admission@changwon.ac.kr
Internet: www.changwon.ac.kr

Founded 1969 as Masan Jr College of Education; became Changwon Nat. College 1984; present name 1991

Pres.: HO PARK SEONG.

CHONBUK NATIONAL UNIVERSITY

664-14 Deogjin-dong 1-ka, Chonju 561-756, Chonbuk

Telephone: 70-2114
Fax: 0652-70-2188
Internet: www.chonbuk.ac.kr

Founded 1947
State control
Academic year: March to February (two semesters)

President: Dr MYUNG SOO CHANG
Library Director: JIN KON OH

Library of 385,000 vols
Number of teachers: 800
Number of students: 24,000

Publications: *The Chonbuk University Newspaper*, *The Chonbuk University Herald* (52 a year), *Chonbuk National University Bulletin* (1 a year), annual bulletins of research institutes

VICE-PRESIDENTS

Academic Affairs: YEONG CHUL KIM
Student Affairs: EUNG KYO RYU
Research and Development: JEONG KEUN PARK
Graduate School: SUN YUNG CHO
Graduate School of Agricultural Development: SUNG YUN KANG
Graduate School of Business Administration: SUNG WOO HYUNG
Graduate School of Education: GWANG HYUN CHOI
Graduate School of Environmental Studies: JE BIN IM
Graduate School of Industrial Technology: SUK PYO HONG
Graduate School of Public Administration: YOUNG MIN HEO
College of Agriculture: JAI SIK HONG
College of Arts: KYE IL SONG
College of Commerce: YEONG HEE CHEONG
College of Dentistry: CHAN UN PARK
College of Education: SEUNG TAI PARK
College of Engineering: CHUL RO YU
College of Home Economics: KEUM SODU CHI
College of Humanities: YOUNG CHUEL KIM
College of Law: KYU SUK SUH
College of Natural Science: CHOON HO LEE
College of Social Science: JAE YOUNG KIM
College of Veterinary Medicine: JOO MOOK LEE
Medical School: NO SUK KI

DIRECTORS

American Studies Research Institute: JANG RYUNG KIM
Biosafety Research Institute: BYUNG MOO LIM
Cholla Cultural Research Centre: HEE KWON LEE
Electric and Electronic Circuit and Systems Research Institute: DONG YONG KIM
Humanities Research Institute: KANG JE KWAK
Information Industry Research Institute: OK BAE CHANG
Institute for Medical Science: HONG BAI EUN
Institute for Molecular Biology and Genetics: KWANG YEOP JANG
Institute of Advanced Materials Development: CHONG KYO KIM
Institute of Animal Research and Development: WON JIB SHIN
Institute of Basic Science: KWANG HO SO
Institute of Dental Science: EUN CHUNG JHEE
Institute of Local Government and Autonomy: CHEOL JONG RYU
Institute of Rural Development: DONG HO LEE
Institute of Science Education: SEUK BEUM KO
Institute of Social Education: DAE WOON CHANG

Laboratory of Electronics Industry and Development: SUNG JOONG KIM
Language Research Institute: KYU TAE CHO
Research Institute of Agricultural Development: SUN YOUNG CHOI
Research Institute of Communist Countries: WON HO YOON
Research Institute of Engineering Technology: HAK SHIN KIM
Research Institute of Industry and Economy: SEUNG KI PARK
Research Institute of Law: KYU SUK SUH
Research Institute of Semiconductors: HYUNG JAE LEE
Research Institute of Sports Science: SANG JONG LEE
Research Institute of Urban and Environmental Studies: EUNG KYO RYU
Social Science Research Institute: SOON GOO CHO

CHONNAM NATIONAL UNIVERSITY

300 Yongbong-dong, Buk-gu, Gwangju, Seoul 500-757

Telephone: (62) 530-1265
Fax: (62) 530-1269

Gwangju Campus: 77 Yongbong-ro, Buk-gu, Gwangju, Seoul 500-757

Telephone: (62) 530-5114
Fax: (62) 530-1139

Yeosu Campus: San 96-1 Doondeok-dong, Jeonnam, Seoul

Telephone: (61) 659-2114
Fax: (61) 659-3003
E-mail: cnupr@chonnam.ac.kr
Internet: www.chonnam.ac.kr

Founded 1952
State control
Language of instruction: Korean
Academic year: March to February (2 semesters)

Pres.: Dr KIM YOON SOO
Dean of Academic Affairs: Dr JONG MOK LEE
Dean of Planning and Research: Dr SUNG SOO PARK
Dean of Student Affairs: Dr JUNG MOOK YOON
Librarian: Dr YOON JUNG HAN

Library of 600,000 vols, 6,000 periodicals
Number of teachers: 2,435
Number of students: 24,000

Publications: *Chonnam Medical Journal*, *Chonnam Review of American Studies*, *Industrial Relations Research*, *Journal of Agricultural Science and Technology*, *Journal of Arts*, *Journal of Drug Development*, *Journal of Humanities Studies*, *Journal of Natural Science*, *Journal of Regional Development*, *Journal of Research Institute for Catalysis*, *Journal of Sciences for Better Living*, *Journal of Sports Science*, *Journal of Unification Studies*, *Language Teaching*, *Research on Honam Culture*, *Rural Development Review*, *Social Science Review*, *Technological Review*, *Yongbong Review*

DEANS

College of Agriculture: JAE HONG KIM
College of Arts: JONG IL KIM
College of Business Administration: SOUG SHIN CHOI
College of Dentistry: MONG SOOK VANG
College of Education: KEUN HO CHUNG
College of Engineering: KWAN SOO LEE
College of Home Economics: DUCK SOON HWANG
College of Law: SEONG KIE KIM
College of Medicine: YOUNG HONG PAIK
College of Natural Sciences: JAE KEUN KIM
College of Pharmacy: BYUNG HO CHUNG
College of Social Sciences: YOUNG KWAN CHOI

College of Veterinary Medicine: NAM YONG PARK
Graduate School: HA IL PARK
Graduate School of Business Administration: SOUG SHIN CHOI
Graduate School of Education: KEUN HO CHUNG
Graduate School of Industry: KWAN SOO LEE
Graduate School of Public Administration: SEONG KIE KIM

CHUNGBUK NATIONAL UNIVERSITY

410 Seongbong-ro, Heungdeok-gu, Cheongju, Chungbuk, Seoul 361-763

Telephone: (43) 261-3172
Internet: www.chungbuk.ac.kr

Founded 1951 as Agricultural College, univ. status 1970
Academic year: March to December (semesters)

Pres.: LIM DONG CHOL
Dir of Admin.: KEE UN CHUNG
Dean of Academic Affairs: YOUNG SOO JEONG
Dean of Planning and Research Affairs: SOON SEOP KWAK
Dean of Student Affairs: SUNG HOO HONG
Dir of Library: SOON KEY JUNG

Library of 520,000 vols
Number of teachers: 700
Number of students: 18,000

Publications: *Journal of Agricultural Science Research*, *Journal of Genetic Engineering Research*, *Journal of Humanities*, *Journal of Language and Literature*, *Journal of Pharmaceutical Science*, *Journal of Social Science*, *Journal of the Industrial Science and Technology Institute*, *Journal of the Institute of Construction Technology*, *Journal of the Research Institute for Computer and Information Communication*, *Jungwon Munhwa Nonchong*, *Juris Forum*, *Law Journal*, *Review of Industry and Management*

DEANS
College of Commerce and Business Administration: DO WON SUH
College of Education: SHEON JOO CHIN
College of Engineering: LEE JAE KI
College of Home Economics: KI NAM KIM
College of Humanities: JANG SUNG JOONG
College of Law: JUN HUR
College of Medicine: YOUNG JIN SONG
College of Natural Science: BYUNG CHOON LEE
College of Pharmacy: HAN KUN
College of Social Science: HEE KYUNG KANG
College of Veterinary Medicine: YOUNG WON YUN

CHUNGNAM NATIONAL UNIVERSITY

79 Daehangno, Yuseong-gu, Daejon, Seoul 305-764

Telephone: (42) 821-5013
Fax: (42) 823-1469
Internet: www.chungnam.ac.kr

Founded 1952
Academic year: March to June, September to December

Pres.: SONG, YONG-HO
Dean of Academic Affairs: CHUL KYU CHOI
Dean of Student Affairs: KUN MOOK CHOI
Registrar: MYUNG KYUN KIM
Librarian: JONG UP CHO

Number of teachers: 880
Number of students: 20,000

DEANS
College of Agriculture: JONG WOO KIM
College of Economics and Management: CHUL HWAN CHUN
College of Engineering: SOO YOUNG CHUNG

College of Fine Arts and Music: CHEOL NAM
College of Home Economics: YOUNG JIN CHUNG
College of Humanities: HAE KIL SUH
College of Law: KANG YONG LEE
College of Medicine: JIN SUN BAI
College of Natural Sciences: JONG SUK CHOI
College of Pharmacy: BYUNG ZUN AHN
College of Social Sciences: TONG HOON KIM
College of Veterinary Medicine: MOO HYUNG JUN
Graduate School: CHONG HOE PARK
Graduate School of Business Administration: KEAN SHIK LEE
Graduate School of Education: SANG CHUL KANG
Graduate School of Industry: GUNG SUCK NAM
Graduate School of Public Administration: JAE CHANG KA
Graduate School of Public Health: SAE JIN CHOI

GYEONGSANG NATIONAL UNIVERSITY

900 Gazwa-dong, Jinju, Seoul 660-701
Telephone: (55) 751-6229
Fax: (55) 751-6121
E-mail: belle@gshp.gsnu.ac.kr
Internet: www.gsnu.ac.kr
Founded 1948 as Gyeongnam Provincial Junior Agricultural College; became Gyeongnam Nat. College 1968 and Gyeongsang Nat. College 1972; present name 1979

Pres.: HA WOO-SONG

Number of teachers: 670
Number of students: 23,300 (21,100 undergraduate, 2,200 postgraduate)

Colleges of Humanities, Social Sciences, Natural Sciences, Business Administration, Engineering, Agriculture and Life Science, Law, Education, Veterinary Medicine, Medicine and Marine Science.

JEJU NATIONAL UNIVERSITY

Jejudaehakno 66, Jeju, Jeju-si 690-756
Telephone: (64) 754-2114
Fax: (64) 755-6130
E-mail: webmaster@jejunu.ac.kr
Internet: www.jejunu.ac.kr
Founded 1952 as Jeju Provincial Junior College; became Jeju Nat. College 1962; present name 1982
Academic year: March to February

Pres.: Dr CHOONG-SUK KOH

Number of teachers: 600
Number of students: 10,000

KANGWON NATIONAL UNIVERSITY

192-1 Hyoja-dong, Chuncheon-si, Gangwon-do, Seoul 200-701
Telephone: (33) 250-6114
Fax: (33) 250-9556
E-mail: intn@cc.kangwon.ac.kr
Internet: www.kangwon.ac.kr
Founded 1947

Pres.: KWON YONG JUNG
Registrar: LIM HYUNG-SIK
Librarian: PARK KYUNG-HO

Library of 206,000 vols
Number of teachers: 378
Number of students: 16,000

DEANS
College of Agriculture: LEE SANG-YOUNG
College of Business Administration: SHIM JONG-SEOP
College of Education: CHOI KEUN-SEONG
College of Engineering: PARK JE-SEON

College of Forestry: KIM SU-CHANG
College of Humanities and Social Science: PARK HAN-SEOL
College of Law: KIM JEUNG-HU
College of Natural Sciences: LEE CHONG-HYEOK

GANGNEUNG–WONJU NATIONAL UNIVERSITY

Gangneung Campus: 120 Gangneung Daehangno, Gangneung City, Gangwon-do, Seoul 210-702
Telephone: (33) 642-7001
Fax: (33) 643-7110

Wonju Campus: 901 Namwon-ro, Wonju City, Gangwon-do, Seoul 220-711
Telephone: (33) 760-8114
Fax: (33) 760-8059
E-mail: ciec@nukw.ac.kr
Internet: www.gwnu.ac.kr
Founded 1968 as Kangnung Educational College; became Kangnung Junior College 1977 and Kangnung Nat. College 1979; present name 1991
State control
Academic year: March to December (two semesters)

Colleges of Humanities, Social Sciences, Natural Sciences, Engineering, Life Sciences, Arts and Physical Education, Dentistry; 17 research institutes, museum, gallery

Pres.: Dr HAN SONG
Dean of Center for Int. Exchange and Cooperation: CHI SUNG-PA

Library of 250,000 vols, 9,044 periodicals
Number of teachers: 258 full-time, 370 part-time
Number of students: 7,321

KONGJU NATIONAL UNIVERSITY

182 Shinkwan-dong, Kongju, Chungnam
Telephone: (416) 850-8114
Fax: (416) 853-3517
Internet: www.kongju.ac.kr
Founded 1948 as Kongju Provincial Teachers' College; became Kongju National Teachers' College 1950; present name 1991

President: Dr SUCK-WON CHOI
Dean of Academic Affairs: HYUNG-TAE MOON
Director General: CHANG-YONG PARK

Library of 360,000 vols
Number of teachers: 602
Number of students: 13,560

DEANS
College of Education: BYUNG-MOO KIM
College of Engineering: KUM-BAE LEE
College of Humanities and Social Sciences: PIL-YOUNG LEE
College of Industrial Sciences: SEONG-MIN KIM
College of Sciences: YOUNG-KYUN WOO

KOREA ADVANCED INSTITUTE OF SCIENCE AND TECHNOLOGY (KAIST)

335 Gwahak-ro (373-1 Guseong-dong), Yuseong-gu, Daejeon, Seoul 305-701
Telephone: (42) 350-2114
Fax: (42) 350-2210
Internet: www.kaist.ac.kr
Founded 1981 by merger of Korea Advanced Institute of Science (KAIS) and Korea Institute of Science and Technology (KIST); KIST separated from KAIST 1989; Korea Institute of Technology (KIT) merged with KAIST 1989
State control
Academic year: March to February

Pres.: NAM PYO SUH

Number of teachers: 541
Number of students: 8,217
Colleges of Natural Science, Life Science and Bioengineering, Engineering, Information Science and Technology, Cultural Science, Business, and Interdisciplinary Studies.

KOREA MARITIME UNIVERSITY

1 Dongsam-dong, Yeongdo-gu, Busan, Seoul 606-791

Telephone: (51) 410-4114
E-mail: webmaster@hhu.ac.kr
Internet: www.hhu.ac.kr

Colleges of Engineering, International Studies, Maritime Sciences, Ocean Science and Technology

Pres.: OH KEO DON.

KOREA NATIONAL OPEN UNIVERSITY

169 Dongsung-dong, Chongro-ku, Seoul 110-791

Telephone: (2) 744-114
Fax: (2) 744-5882
E-mail: webmaster@knou.ac.kr
Internet: www.knou.ac.kr

Founded 1972
State control
Academic year: March to February
Pres.: CHANG SEE WOM
Registrar: KIM EUI-DONG
Library Dir: KIM SUNG-KIH

Library of 412,000 vols
Number of teachers: 112
Number of students: 199,000

Publications: *Distance Education*, *KNOU Journal*, *KNOU Weekly*

DEANS

College of Education: CHOI CHONG-SOOK
College of Liberal Arts: LEE YONG-HAK
College of Natural Science: KIM HYE-SEON
College of Social Science: KIM SOO-SIN
School of General Education: LEE YUNG-HO

ATTACHED RESEARCH INSTITUTES

Educational Media Development Centre: Dir KWAK DUK-HUN.

Institute of Distance Education: Dir HONG SOON-JEONG.

KOREA NATIONAL UNIVERSITY OF THE ARTS

120-3 Yesuk-gil, Seongbuk-gu, Seoul 136-716
Telephone: (2) 746-9042
E-mail: admissions@knua.ac.kr
Internet: www.knua.ac.kr

Founded 1993

Pres.: LEE GEON-YONG
Provost: KIM BONG-RYOL

Number of teachers: 730
Number of students: 2,600

Colleges of Dance, Drama, Film, Korean Traditional Arts, Music, Television and Multimedia, Visual Arts.

KUNSAN NATIONAL UNIVERSITY

1170 Daehangno, Gunsan, Seoul 573-701
Telephone: (63) 469-4134
Fax: (63) 469-4197
E-mail: inter@kunsan.ac.kr
Internet: www.kunsan.ac.kr

Founded 1979
Languages of instruction: Korean, English
Academic year: March to February
Pres.: Dr LEE HEE-YEON
Library of 280,000 vols

Number of teachers: 327
Number of students: 11,065

PROFESSORS

College of Arts, School of Fine Arts and Design:

CHO, Y. B., Department of Industrial Design
KIM, S. T., Department of Industrial Ceramic Arts
KIM, Y. O., Department of Music

College of Engineering, Faculty of Electronic and Information Engineering:

HEO, B. M., Department of Mechanical Design Engineering
KIM, S. G., Materials Science and Engineering
LEE, H. Y., Department of Chemical Engineering
LEE, J. I., Electronic and Information Engineering
LIM, B. Y., Department of Civil Engineering
MOON, C. H., Department of Architectural Engineering

College of Humanities, Faculty of Oriental Language and Literature:

CHO, S. H., Department of Korean Language and Literature
LEE, H. H., Department of History
LIM, K.-J., Department of Philosophy
MOON, C.-S., Department of Japanese Language and Literature
PAE, B. H., Department of German Literature and Language
PARK, B.-S., Department of Chinese Language and Literature
SEO, H. S., Department of English Language and Literature

College of Natural Sciences:

CHOI, H. S., Department of Chemistry
HANG, T. S., Department of Mathematics
KIM, A. S., Department of Clothing and Textiles
KIM, S. Y., Department of Food Science and Nutrition
LEE, K. S., Department of Biological Science
PARK, Y. S., Department of Informatics and Statistics
RYOU, O. S., Department of Human Ecology
YOON, C. S., Department of Physics

College of Ocean Science and Technology:

CHANG, S. H., Department of Food Science and Technology
CHUNG, E. Y., Department of Aquaculture and Biotechnology
JEONG, K. J., Department of Marine Engineering
KIM, Y. G., Department of Marine Life Science
LEE, K. R., Department of Marine Science and Production
SEO, S. W., Department of Ocean System Engineering
YIH, W. H., Department of Ocean Information Science

College of Social Sciences:

HWANG, H. M., International Trade
KIM, Y.-J., Public Administration
KWON, E. M., Business Administration and Accounting
LIM, H. J., Economics and Trade

KWANGJU UNIVERSITY

Kwangju, Seoul 503-703
Telephone: (80) 670-2600
Internet: kwangju.ac.kr

Founded 1981 as Kwangju Kyung Sang Jr College; became Kwangju Open College 1984; present name 1989

Pres.: Dr LEE JAE-WOON

Library of 230,000 vols

Colleges of Management, Commerce and Social Welfare, Humanities and Social Sciences, Engineering, Arts; Graduate School.

KYUNGPOOK NATIONAL UNIVERSITY

1370 Sankyuk-dong, Buk-gu, Daegu, Seoul 702-701

Telephone: (53) 950-6091
Fax: (53) 950-6093
E-mail: kunglobal@knu.ac.kr
Internet: www.knu.ac.kr

Founded 1946
State control
Academic year: March to February (two semesters)

Pres.: NOH DONGIL
Dean of Academic Affairs: Dr KIM KEE CHAN
Dean of General Affairs: Dr PARK SEUNG TAE
Dean of Planning and Research Support: Dr SOHN JAE KEUN
Dean of Student Affairs: LEE MIN HYUNG

Library: see Libraries
Number of teachers: 825
Number of students: 24,504

Publication: *Research Review* (1 a year)

DEANS

Graduate School: Dr KWON YON-UNG
College of Agriculture and Life Sciences: Dr CHOI JONG-UCK
College of Dentistry: Dr KYUNG HEE-MOON
College of Economics and Commerce: Dr SOHN BYEONG-HAE
College of Engineering: Dr LEE DONG-HO
College of Human Ecology: Dr YOO YOUNG-SUN
College of Humanities: Dr KIM KEE-CHAN
College of Law: Dr KANG TAE-SEONG
College of Medicine: Dr KWAK JOUNG-SIK
College of Music and Visual Arts: Dr KWON KI-DUCK
College of Natural Sciences: Dr MOON BYUNG-JO
College of Social Sciences: Dr KIM JAE-HONG
College of Veterinary Medicine: Dr LEE CHA-SOO
School of Electrical Engineering and Computer Science: Dr LEE YONG-HYUN

PROFESSORS

College of Agriculture and Life Sciences (#223 College of Agriculture and Life Sciences Building I, Kyungpook National University, Daegu Seoul 702-701; tel. (53) 950-5700; fax (53) 950-6701):

CHEONG, S.-T., Fruit Science, Plant Propagation
CHO, R.-K., Food Chemistry
CHOI, J., Soil Science
CHOI, J.-U., Food Preservation Engineering
CHOI, K., Forest Management and Economics
CHOI, K.-S., Animal Breeding
CHOI, K.-S., Economic Statistics
CHOI, S.-T., Floriculture, Protected Cultivation
CHOI, Y.-H., Food Engineering
CHUNG, J.-D., Plant Tissue Culture
CHUNG, M.-S., Tree Cultivation
CHUNG, S.-K., Food Analysis and Sanitation
CHUNG, S.-O., Irrigation and Drainage Engineering
EOM, T.-J, Woody Plant Biochemistry
HONG, S.-C., Forest Ecology

Hwang, Y.-H., Plant Genetics
Jang, I.-J., Agricultural Robot for Control Measurements
Jo, J.-K., Grass Physiology
Jung, S.-K., Landscape Construction
Kim, B.-S., Vegetable Cultivation, Pepper Cultivation
Kim, C.-S., Agricultural Policy
Kim, D.-S., Dairy Microbiology
Kim, D.-U., Plant Molecular Biology
Kim, J.-E., Environmental Chemistry
Kim, K.-U., Weed Science
Kim, S.-G., Agricultural Marketing
Kim, S.-K., Maize Breeding
Kim, T.-H., Agricultural Power Energy Conservation
Kim, Y.-S., Landscape Planning
Kwon, M.-N., Geotechnical and Foundation Engineering
Kwon, Y.-J., Systematic Entomology
Lee, H.-C., Agricultural Economic History
Lee, H.-T., Landscape Design
Lee, J.-T., Fungal Plant Pathology
Lee, J.-Y., Wood Chemistry
Lee, K.-C., Landscape Management
Lee, K.-M., Terramechanics, Greenhouse Controls
Lee, K.-W., Viral Plant Pathology
Lee, S.-C., Crop Production and Management
Lee, S.-G., Agricultural Buildings
Noh, S.-K., Insect Genetic Resources
Park, I.-H., Landscape Plants
Park, K.-K., Post-Harvest Process, Systems Mechanics
Park, S.-J., Wood Anatomy
Park, W.-C., Plant Nutrition
Park, Y.-G., Forest Genetics
Rhee, I.-J., Fibre Materials Science
Rhee, I.-K., Biochemistry
Ryu, J.-C., Agricultural Crops
Sohn, H.-R., Sericulture
Sohn, J.-K., Rice Cultivation
Son, D.-S., Forest Cultivation
Suh, S.-D., Hydrology, Land Engineering
Syn, Y.-B., Fruit Science, Plant Physiology
Uhm, J.-Y., Bacterial Plant Pathology
Yeo, Y.-K., Lipid Chemistry

College of Dentistry (#211 College of Dentistry, Kyungpook National University, Daegu Seoul 702-701; tel. (53) 420-6801; fax (53) 425-6025):

Bae, Y.-C., Oral Anatomy
Cho, S.-A., Prosthodontics
Choi, J.-K., Oral Medicine
Jo, K.-H., Prosthodontics
Kim, C.-S., Oral and Maxillofacial Surgery
Kim, K.-H., Dental Materials
Kim, Y.-J., Paediatric Dentistry
Kwon, O.-W., Orthodontics
Kyoung, H.-M., Orthodontics
Lee, S.-H., Oral and Maxillofacial Surgery
Nam, S.-H., Paediatric Dentistry
Song, S.-B., Preventive Dentistry and Public Health Dentistry
Sung, J.-H., Orthodontics

College of Economics and Commerce (#213 College of Economics and Commerce, Kyungpook National University, Daegu, Seoul 702-701; tel. (53) 950-5403; fax (53) 950-5405):

Bae, B.-H., Managerial Accounting
Chang, H.-S., Marketing
Chang, J.-S., Industrial Organization
Cho, S.-P., Financial Accounting
Choe, J.-M., Managerial Accounting
Choi, Y.-H., Korean Economy
Ha, I.-B., Macroeconomics
Han, D.-H., International Economics
Jung, C.-Y., Operations Management
Kang, H.-Y., Managerial Accounting
Kim, H.-K., Labour Economics
Kim, J.-J., Marketing
Kim, S.-H., Monetary Economics, International Economics

Kim, Y.-H., Economic Development, Korean Economic History
Kwon, C.-T., Financial Accounting
Kwon, S.-C., Financial Accounting
Kwon, S.-K., Financial Accounting
Lee, D.-M., Management Information Systems
Lee, H.-W., Operations Management
Lee, J.-D., Financial Management
Lee, J.-K., International Commercial Law
Lee, J.-W., Income Distribution, Comparative Economics
Lee, J.-W., Personnel and Organization Management
Lee, S.-D., Personnel and Organization Management
Lee, S.-H., Marketing
Lee, Y.-S., International Transportation and Logistics
Moon, S.-H., Operations Management
Nah, K.-S., Economic History
Park, C.-S., Financial Management
Park, J.-H., Macroeconomics
Shin, M.-S., Financial Management
Sohn, B.-H., International Economics

College of Engineering (#211 College of Engineering Building VI, Kyungpook National University, Daegu, Seoul 702-701; tel. (53) 950-5500; fax (53) 958-5054):

Ahn, K.-S., Digital Engineering
Bae, K.-S., Digital Signal Processing, Speech Signal Processing, Digital Communication
Bae, K.-S., Geochemical Engineering
Baek, Y.-S., Power Systems Analysis
Chien, S.-I., Vision
Cho, J.-H., Bioelectronics, Electronic Measurements
Cho, S.-H., Ceramics for Electronics
Cho, Y.-J., Computer Networks
Cho, Y.-K., Antenna and Propagation, Ultrasonics
Choi, H.-C., Wave Propagation
Choi, H.-M., Parallel Distributed Processing, Processors, Logic Design
Choi, M.-J., Architectural Planning and Design
Choi, S.-J., Water Supply and Waste Water Treatment Engineering
Choi, S.-Y., Semiconductor Engineering
Choi, T.-H., Robotics
Chung, I.-S., Mechanical Metallurgy
Ha, J.-M., Urban Design and City Planning
Ha, Y.-H., Image Processing and Computer Vision Digital Signal Processing
Han, K.-J., Computer Networks
Han, K.-Y., Water Resources Engineering
Heo, N.-H., Zeolite Chemistry, Physical Chemistry
Hong, J.-K., Speech Signal Processing
Hong, S.-M., Control Theory
Hwang, C.-S., Visual Communication
Jeon, G.-J., Intelligent Control, Systems Engineering
Ji, B.-C., Polymer and Fibre Physics
Joo, E.-K., Digital Communication
Kang, I.-K., Biopolymers
Kang, M.-M., Architectural Structure
Kim, C.-H., Applied Mechanics
Kim, C.-J., Architectural Design
Kim, C.-Y., Microwave Engineering
Kim, D.-G., Power Electronics
Kim, D.-H., Reaction Engineering
Kim, D.-R., Surface Science and Engineering
Kim, H.-G., Power Electronics
Kim, H.-J., Pattern Recognition
Kim, H.-S., Synthetic Organic Chemistry
Kim, J.-J., Structural Ceramics
Kim, N.-C., Digital Communications, Image Communications
Kim, N.-K., Dielectric Materials
Kim, S.-H., Computational Geometry
Kim, S.-H., Synthetic Functional Dyes

Kim, S.-J., Geometry, Numerical Analysis
Kim, S.-J., Optical Signal Processing, Circuits and Systems
Kim, S.-M., Automata Theory
Kim, S.-S., Tribology
Kim, T.-J., Inorganic and Organometallic Chemistry, Homogeneous Catalysis
Kim, W.-J., Architectural Construction
Kim, W.-S., Architectural Construction
Kim, W.-S., Polymer Synthesis
Kim, Y.-M., Computer Graphics, Image Processing
Kim, Y.-S., Geotechnical Engineering
Kwon, O.-J., Powder Metallurgy
Kwon, S.-B., Fluid Mechanics
Kwon, W.-H., Powder Electronics
Kwon, Y.-D., Structural Analysis
Kwon, Y.-H., Architectural Structure
Lee, B.-K., Powder Synthesis
Lee, C.-W., Combustion
Lee, D.-D., Semiconductor Engineering
Lee, D.-H., Polymerization Catalysis
Lee, J.-H., Semiconductor Technology
Lee, J.-T., Process Control
Lee, K.-I., Audio and Video Engineering, Electronic Measurements
Lee, K.-K., Non-linear Control Theory
Lee, M.-H., Instrumental Analysis, NMR Spectroscopy
Lee, S.-J., Natural Language
Lee, S.-R., Control and Automation
Lee, T.-J., Process and Property Thermodynamics
Lee, Y.-H., Semiconductor Engineering
Lee, Y.-M., Precision Machining
Lim, Y.-J., Dyeing Chemistry
Min, K.-E., Physical Properties of Solid Polymers
Min, K.-S., Water Quality Engineering
Moon, J.-D., Applied Electrostatics and High Voltage Applications
Oh, C.-S., Computation, Analysis and Design of Electrical Machinery
Oh, T.-J., Polymer and Fibre Chemistry
Park, B.-O., Composite Materials
Park, H.-B., Robust Control Theory
Park, J.-K., Biochemical Engineering and Transport Phenomena
Park, J.-S., Instrumentation, CAD, VLSI Design
Park, K.-C., Joining and Metal Forming
Park, K.-H., Robotics and Control
Park, L.-S., Physical Properties of Polymer Solutions
Park, M.-H., Structural Engineering
Park, S.-K., Microelectronics
Park, S.-T., Computer Networks, Databases
Riu, K.-J., Heat Transfer
Ryu, K.-W., Parallel Algorithms
Seo, B.-H., Automatic and Digital Control, Computer Applications
Seo, K.-H., Polymer Processing
Shim, S.-C., Petroleum Chemistry, Organic and Organometallic Chemistry
Shin, K.-Y., Semiconductor Engineering
Sohn, B.-K., Semiconductor Engineering
Sohn, J.-R., Catalytic Chemistry, Inorganic Material
Sohng, K.-I., Video Engineering, Multiple Valued Logic Systems
Song, D.-I., Polymer Rheology
Song, J.-W., Optical Communication
Suh, C.-M., Materials and Mechanics
Ye, B.-J., Casting, Solidification
Yoo, K.-Y., Parallel Processing
Yu, S.-D., Integrated Circuits

College of Human Ecology (#212 College of Human Ecology, Kyungpook National University, Daegu, Seoul 702-701; tel. (53) 950-6200; fax (53) 950-6205):

Choi, B.-G., Child Development
Choi, M.-S., Nutritional Biochemistry
Kang, M.-Y., Nutrition
Lee, H.-S., Nutrition

College of Humanities (#209 College of Humanities, Kyungpook National University, Daegu, Seoul 702-701; tel. (53) 950-5100; fax (53) 950-6101):

BANG, I., Oriental Philosophy
CHEON, K.-S., Korean Syntax
CHO, M.-H., British and American Drama
CHOI, S.-S., German Literature, Classical Literature
CHOY, C.-H., Korean History
CHUNG, I.-S., Chinese Linguistics
CHUNG, J.-S., English Linguistics, Syntax
EUN, J.-N., Modern Anglo-American Literature
HAN, S.-Z., German Literature
HONG, S.-M., Korean Linguistics
HWANG, W.-Z., Korean Literature
JANG, T.-W., Chinese Linguistics
JU, B.-D., Korean History
KIM, C.-D., Political and Economic Anthropology
KIM, C.-G., Western History
KIM, C.-S., British Poetry
KIM, C.-W., German Drama
KIM, D.-M., Oriental Philosophy
KIM, I.-L., Korean Classical Literature
KIM, K.-C., English Linguistics
KIM, K.-S., Korean Classical Literature
KIM, S.-W., Korean Chinese Literature
KIM, Y.-D., Western Philosophy
KIM, Y.-K., Western Philosophy
KWON, K.-H., Modern Korean Literature
KWON, T.-R., Chinese Linguistics
KWON, Y.-U., Korean History
LEE, C.-S., Chinese Literature
LEE, D.-H., German Literature
LEE, E.-Y., French Phonology
LEE, H.-J., Archaeology
LEE, H.-J., Chinese Literature
LEE, J.-H., Japanese Literature
LEE, K.-E., Russian Literature
LEE, K.-J., German Idealism
LEE, P.-S., French Syntax
LEE, S.-G., Korean Dialectology
LEE, W.-K., English Literature
PAEK, D.-H., Korean Philology
PARK, C.-B., English Literature
PARK, J.-G., French Literature
PARK, S.-W., German Linguistics
PARK, Y.-H., Korean Chinese Literature
SHIN, O.-H., Western Philosophy
SOHN, H.-S., English Linguistics
YI, B.-K., Bronze Age Archaeology, Museology
YI, K.-S., Chinese History
YOO, K.-S., Western History

College of Law (#305 College of Law, Kyungpook National University, Daegu, Seoul 702-701; tel. (53) 950-5456; fax (53) 950-5455):

CHANG, J.-H., Civil Law
KANG, T.-S., Civil Law
KIM, S.-T., Local Public Administration and Finance
KIM, Y.-S., Land Policy
LEE, Y.-J., Financial Administration
MOON, K.-S., Policy Sciences, Financial Management
PARK, J.-H., Urban Planning
PARK, J.-T., Commercial Law
RHEE, W.-W., Urban Administration

College of Medicine (#208 College of Medicine, Kyungpook National University, Daegu, Seoul 702-701; tel. (53) 420-6901; fax (53) 421-6585; internet med.knu.ac.kr):

BAEK, W.-Y., Intensive Care Therapy
BAIK, B.-S., Craniofacial Surgery
CHAE, J.-M., Forensic Pathology
CHAE, S.-C., Cardiology
CHANG, S.-I., Surgery, Paediatric Surgery
CHANG, S.-K., Transplantation, Tumours
CHO, D.-K., Nephrology
CHO, D.-Y., Molecular Genetics
CHO, H.-J., Neuroanatomy
CHO, T.-H., Oncology

CHO, Y.-L., Gynaecological Oncology
CHOI, Y.-H., Gastroenterology
CHUN, B.-Y., Health Care Administration and Health Policy
CHUN, S.-S., Reproductive Endocrinology and Infertility
CHUNG, B.-Y., Adult Nursing, Cancer Nursing
CHUNG, J.-M., Gastroenterology
CHUNG, S.-L., Dermatology, Leprosy
CHUNG, T.-H., Immunology
DOH, B.-N., Psychiatric and Mental Health Nursing
HAMM, I.-S., Cerebrovascular Disease, Neuro-Oncology
HONG, H.-S., Anatomy, Medical Genetics
HONG, J.-G., Pain Clinic
HWANG, S.-K., Paediatric Neurosurgery
IHN, J.-C., Joint Reconstructive Surgery
JUN, J.-B., Dermatology, Mycology, Dermatopathology
JUN, J.-E., Cardiology
JUN, S.-H., Surgery, Colorectal Surgery
JUNG, M.-S., Women's Health Nursing
JUNG, S.-K., Paediatric Urology, Traumatology
KANG, D.-J., Psychiatry, Psychopharmacology
KANG, D.-S., Thoracic Radiology
KIM, B.-W., Endocrinology, Metabolism
KIM, B.-W., Tumours
KIM, C.-Y., Cardiovascular Pharmacology
KIM, D.-W., Dermatology
KIM, H.-M., Paediatrics, Neonatology
KIM, I.-T., Vitreous Humour and Retina
KIM, J.-C., Cellular and Molecular Immunology
KIM, K.-T., Paediatric Cardiovascular Surgery
KIM, M.-Y., Paediatric Nursing
KIM, N.-S., Allergology, Rheumatology
KIM, P.-T., Hand Surgery
KIM, S.-L., Cerebrovascular Disease
KIM, S.-Y., Vitreous Humour and Retina
KIM, T.-H., Diagnostic Radiology
KIM, Y.-I., Surgery
KIM, Y.-J., Interventional Radiology
KIM, Y.-W., Vascular Surgery
KOO, J.-H., Paediatrics, Nephrology
KWAK, J.-S., Forensic Pathology
KWAK, Y.-S., Pharmacy
KWON, J.-Y., Paediatric Ophthalmology
LEE, J.-B., Family Medicine
LEE, J.-T., Cardiovascular Surgery
LEE, J.-Y., Occupational Neurology
LEE, K.-B., Nuclear Medicine
LEE, K.-S., Paediatrics, Haemato-Oncology and Genetics
LEE, M.-G., Neuropsychological Pharmacology
LEE, S.-B., Paediatrics, Cardiology
LEE, S.-H., Otology, Neuro-Otology
LEE, S.-K., Biostatistics and Nutritional Epidemiology
LEE, S.-N., Psychiatry, Psychotherapy
LEE, W.-J., Renal Physiology
LEE, W.-K., Clinical Microbiology
LEE, Y.-C., Virology
LEE, Y.-H., Surgery, Head and Neck Endocrine Surgery
PARK, B.-C., Paediatric and Spinal Surgery
PARK, I.-H., Oncology and Infection
PARK, I.-K., Radiation Oncology, Radiation Biology
PARK, I.-S., Gynaecological Oncology
PARK, J.-H., Fundamentals of Nursing
PARK, J.-S., Cardiovascular Physiology
PARK, J.-S., Head and Neck Oncology
PARK, J.-W., Vascular Pharmacology and Anaesthesia
PARK, J.-Y., Health Care Administration and Health Policy
PARK, S.-Y., Adult Nursing
PARK, W.-H., Cardiology
PARK, Y.-K., Andrology

PARK, Y.-M., Spinal Neuro-Oncology, Neurotrauma
RIM, H.-D., Psychiatry, Psychosomatics
SEOL, S.-Y., Molecular Epidemiology
SOHN, Y.-K., Neuropathology
SUH, C.-K., Neurology
SUH, I.-S., Pathology of the Gastrointestinal Tract
SUH, J.-S., Diagnostic Haematology
SUH, S.-R., Adult Nursing
YEO, M.-H., Epidemiology and Population Dynamics
YU, W.-S., Surgery, Surgical Oncology
YUN, Y.-K., Surgery, Hepatobiliary Surgery

College of Music and Visual Arts (#217 College of Music and Visual Arts, Kyungpook National University, Daegu, Seoul 702-701; tel. (53) 950-5650; fax (53) 950-5655):

BYUN, Y.-B., Sculpture
CHONG, H.-I., Kayagum (12-Stringed Zither)
CHUNG, H.-C., Composition
JUNG, W.-H., Piano
KANG, C.-S., Piano
KIM, G.-J., Voice (Soprano)
KIM, J.-W., Voice (Baritone)
KIM, K.-I., Piano
KIM, W.-S., Korean Painting
KU, Y.-K., Komungo (6-Stringed Zither)
KWON, K.-D., Visual Design
LEE, D.-C., Oil Painting
LEE, E.-S., Piano
LEE, K.-J., Kayagum (12-Stringed Zither)
LEE, W.-S., Visual Design
LIM, H.-S., Clarinet
OH, H.-C., Oil Painting
PARK, N.-H., Art History
SHIM, S.-H., Voice (Tenor)
YI, T.-B., Theory of Korean Music and Taegum (Korean Transverse Flute)
YOO, H., Korean Painting
YOON, J.-R., Cello
YUN, M.-G., Piri (Korean Oboe)

College of Natural Sciences (#201 College of Natural Sciences, Kyungpook National University, Daegu, Seoul 702-701; tel. (53) 950-5300; fax (53) 957-0431):

BAE, Z.-U., Analytical Chemistry
CHANG, T.-W., Structural Geology
CHO, K.-H., Statistical Inference
CHOI, J.-K., Probability, Stochastic Processes
CHOI, S.-D., Condensed Matter Theory
HA, J.-H., Microbial Genetics
HUH, T.-L., Molecular Genetics
JEE, J.-G., Physical Chemistry
JEONG, J.-H., Inorganic Chemistry
JIN, I.-N., Enzymology
JO, S.-G., High Energy Physics Theory
JUNG, I.-B., Analysis
KANG, H.-D., Experimental Nuclear Physics
KANG, S.-S., Biochemistry and Animal Physiology
KIM, E.-S., Algebra
KIM, H.-S., Analysis
KIM, I.-S., Biochemistry
KIM, J.-G., Microbial Genetics
KIM, K.-E., Precipitation Mechanism
KIM, S.-W., Computer Languages
KIM, S.-W., Petrology
KIM, Y.-H., Cellular Immunobiology
KOH, I.-S., Sedimentology, Sedimentary Petrology
KWAK, Y.-W., Organic Chemistry
LEE, E.-W., Surface and Thin Films Experiments
LEE, H.-H., Analysis
LEE, H.-L., Analytical Chemistry
LEE, H.-R., Condensed Matter Theory
LEE, I.-S., Statistical Inference, Theoretical Statistics
LEE, J.-K., Organic Chemistry
LEE, J.-Y., Virology

LEE, K.-M., Radiative Transfer, Upper Atmosphere
LEE, S.-H., Analysis
LEE, S.-K., Information Visualization
LEE, S.-Y., Thin Film and Electroluminescence Experiments
LEE, Y.-H., Biochemical Engineering
LEE, Y.-S., Cellular Biochemistry
MIN, K.-D., Atmospheric Energetics
MOON, B.-J., Biochemistry
PARK, B.-G., Reliability Analysis
PARK, C.-Y., Topology
PARK, H.-C., Animal Taxonomy
PARK, J.-H., Plant Systematics
PARK, J.-W., Biochemical Carcinogenesis
PARK, W., Molecular Biology
PARK, Y.-B., Biochemistry
PARK, Y.-C., Database Systems
PARK, Y.-C., Inorganic Chemistry
PARK, Y.-S., Algebra
PARK, Y.-T., Organic Chemistry
SEO, B.-B., Genetics
SOHN, J.-K., Bayesian Decision Theory, Statistical Computing
SOHN, K.-S., Condensed Matter Theory
SOHN, U.-I., Molecular Biology
SON, D.-C., Experimental High Energy Physics
SONG, J.-K., Mulitivariate Data Analysis
SONG, S.-D., Plant Physiology
SUH, Y.-J., Geometry

College of Social Sciences (#315 College of Social Sciences, Kyungpook National University, Daegu, Seoul 702-701; tel. (53) 950-5200; fax (53) 950-5205):

CHIN, S.-M., Industrial Sociology
CHO, H.-C., Counselling Psychology
CHOI, C.-M., Social Welfare Administration
CHOI, K.-S., Social Psychology
HAN, N.-J., Sociology of Family
JIN, Y.-S., Cognitive Psychology
KIM, J.-H., Ethics and Legal Studies in Mass Communication
KIM, W.-H., International Relations
KIM, Y.-H., Clinical Psychology
KIM, Y.-H., Social Policy
LEE, J.-H., Regional Geography
LEE, Y.-J., Information Science
NAM, K.-H., Bibliography
NOH, D.-I., Korean Politics
PARK, B.-S., Clinical Social Work
PARK, J.-S., Political Communication Theory
PARK, J.-W., Population Studies
PARK, K.-S., Broadcasting
PARK, S.-D., Social Security
PARK, Y.-C., Regional Development, Economic Geography
SHON, J.-P., Library Management
YOON, Y.-H., Comparative Politics

College of Veterinary Medicine (#205 College of Veterinary Medicine, Kyungpook National University, Daegu, Seoul 702-701; tel. (53) 950-5950; fax (53) 950-5955):

BYUN, M.-D., Veterinary Obstetrics
CHOI, W.-P., Veterinary Microbiology
JANG, I.-H., Veterinary Surgery, Veterinary Obstetrics
KIM, B.-H., Veterinary Microbiology
KIM, Y.-H., Veterinary Obstetrics
LEE, C.-S., Veterinary Pathology
LEE, J.-H., Veterinary Medicine
MOON, M.-H., Veterinary Parasitology
PARK, C.-K., Veterinary Microbiology
TAK, R.-B., Veterinary Public Health
YU, C.-J., Veterinary Physiology

Teachers' College:

AHN, B.-H., Space Physics
BAE, H.-D., Politics, Political Thought
BAE, J.-E., English Literature
CHAE, H.-W., Training
CHANG, D.-I., Medieval Korean History
CHUNG, D.-H., German Linguistics
CHUNG, H.-P., Philosophy of Education

CHUNG, H.-S., Cell Biology, Photosynthesis
CHUNG, S.-T., Sport Psychology
CHUNG, W.-W., Mineralogy
HONG, Y.-P., Politics, Political Thought
HWANG, B.-S., French Linguistics
HWANG, S.-G., Algebra
IM, J.-R., Korean Linguistics
JANG, H.-S., Nutrition
JANG, Y.-O., Home Management
JO, P.-G., Clothing
JO, W.-R., Geomorphology
JUN, B.-Q., English Linguistics
KANG, Y.-H., Astronomy
KI, U.-H., Geometry
KIM, B.-K., Counselling
KIM, H.-K., Economic Development
KIM, H.-S., Early Modern East Asian History
KIM, J.-J., Dance
KIM, J.-T., Korean Linguistics
KIM, J.-W., Contemporary Western History
KIM, K.-H., Measurement and Evaluation for Physical Education
KIM, M.-H., Educational Administration
KIM, M.-K., Korean Literature
KIM, M.-N., Philosophy of Education
KIM, S.-H., Educational Psychology
KIM, Y.-H., Geometry
KOH, J.-K., Particle Physics, Physics Education
LEE, A.-H., Educational Psychology
LEE, B.-H., Early Modern Korean History
LEE, J.-H., Korean Literature
LEE, J.-H., Politics, International Politics
LEE, J.-W., Population Geography, Geographical Education
LEE, M.-H., Biomechanics
LEE, M.-J., Educational Psychology
LEE, M.-K., Ancient Korean History
LEE, M.-S., Physical Chemistry
LEE, N.-G., Rural Sociology
LEE, O.-B., Social Education
LEE, S.-B., Statistics and Critical Phenomena
LEE, S.-C., Sports Nutrition
LEE, S.-T., Korean Linguistics
LEE, W.-B., Organic Chemistry
LEE, Y.-J., Petrology
LIM, J.-K., German Literature
MOON, S.-H., Western Philosophy
OH, C.-H., Optics, Quantum Electronics
OH, D.-S., History of Physical Education
OH, Y.-S., Public Economics
PAK, J.-S., Geometry
PARK, C.-Y., Educational Administration
PARK, D.-K., Plasma Physics
PARK, J.-Y., English Literature
PARK, K.-S., Teaching English as a Second Language
PARK, T.-H., Urban Geography
RIM, S.-H., Algebra
RYU, S.-E., German Drama
SEO, J.-M., Korean Literature
SHIN, K.-J., French Literature
SHIN, Y.-G., Teaching of Physical Education
SOHN, J.-K., Animal Physiology
SONG, B.-H., Microbiology, Molecular Biology
SONG, W.-C., Politics, Political Thought
YANG, H.-J., Animal Morphology, Ecology
YANG, J.-S., Climatology
YANG, S.-Y., Palaeobiology
YI, M.-S., French Linguistics
YOH, S.-D., Organic Chemistry
YOO, Y.-J., Analysis
YOON, I.-H., Micrometeorology
YOON, J.-L., Educational Psychology

MOKPO NATIONAL MARITIME UNIVERSITY

571-2 Jugkyo-dong, Mokpo, Chonnam 530-729

Telephone: (631) 240-7045

E-mail: ryujb@mmu.ac.kr
Internet: www.mmu.ac.kr

Founded 1950

President: Dr BYUNGJU OH

Number of teachers: 72
Number of students: 1,800

Divisions of Maritime Transportation Systems, Nautical Science, Navigation System Engineering, Maritime Safety Systems Engineering, Maritime Information Systems, International Logistics Systems, Maritime Policing.

MOKPO NATIONAL UNIVERSITY

61 Torim-ri, Chonggye-myon, Muan-gun, Chonnam 534-729

Telephone: (61) 450-2114
Fax: (61) 452-4793
Internet: www.mokpo.ac.kr

Founded 1946 as Mokpo Teacher-Training School; became Mokpo Teachers' College 1963, Mokpo Junior College 1978 and Mokpo National College 1979; present name and status 1990

President: WOONG-BAE KIM

Number of teachers: 334
Number of students: 9,986

Colleges of Humanities, Social Sciences, Natural Sciences, Engineering, Home Ecology, Business Administration.

NATIONAL FISHERIES UNIVERSITY OF BUSAN

599-1 Daeyun-dong, Nam-gu, Busan 608-737

Telephone: (51) 622-3951
Fax: (51) 625-9947

Founded 1941 as Busan Fisheries College, attained university status 1990

Pres.: SUN-DUCK CHANG
Dean of Academic Affairs: YONG RHIM YANG
Dean of Student Affairs: HYUN WOO CHUNG
Dean of Planning Research: YONG JOO KANG
Dean of General Affairs: SE WHA SONG
Librarian: JAI YUL KONG

Library of 130,000 vols
Number of teachers: 306
Number of students: 7,700

Publications: Bulletin, Natural Sciences (2 a year), The Theses Collection of the Faculty Members, Social Sciences (2 a year), Publication of Institute of Marine Sciences (1 a year)

DEANS

College of Business Administration: CHUNG YUL YU
College of Engineering: CHUNG KIL PARK
College of Fisheries Sciences: CHUL HYUN SOHN
College of Marine Sciences and Technology: YONG QUIN KANG
College of Natural Sciences: MAN DONG HUR
College of Social Sciences: CHARLES KIM

PUKYONG NATIONAL UNIVERSITY

559-1 Daeyon-dong, Nam-gu, Busan Seoul

Telephone: (51) 620-6114
Fax: (51) 620-1114
E-mail: web@pknu.ac.kr
Internet: www.pknu.ac.kr

Founded 1996 by the amalgamation of Nat. Fisheries Univ. of Pusan and Pusan Nat. Univ. of Technology

Pres.: PARK MAENG EON
Dean of Academic Affairs: NAM SONG-WOO
Dean of Student Affairs: HEUNG IL-PARK
Dean of Planning Office: JUNG HYUN-CHAN
Dean of Gen. Affairs: HWANG IN-CHUL
Dir of Library: PYO YONG-SOO

Number of teachers: 664
Number of students: 23,671 (23,336 under-graduates, 335 graduates)

DEANS

Faculty of Business Administration: HA JONG-WOOK
Faculty of Engineering: LEE HYUNG-GI
Faculty of Environmental and Marine Science and Technology: KIM DAE-CHOUL
Faculty of Fisheries Science: BYUN DAE-SEOK
Faculty of Humanities and Social Sciences: SEUNG RAE-LEE
Faculty of Natural Sciences: KIM SE-KWON

PUSAN NATIONAL UNIVERSITY

30 Jangjeon-dong, Kumjeong-ku, Pusan 609-735

Telephone: (51) 510-1293
Fax: (51) 512-9049
Internet: www.pusan.ac.kr

Founded 1946
Academic year: March to February

Pres.: INN-SE KIM
Dean of Academic Affairs: SANG-WOOK PARK
Dean of Planning and Research: JUNG-DUK LIM
Dean of Student Affairs: IN-BO SIM
Dir of General Affairs: SANG-WOO HAN
Dir of Library: DONG-HYUN JUNG

Library: see Libraries
Museum: see Museums
Number of teachers: 967
Number of students: 24,670
Publications: *University Academic Journal* (annual collection of theses), *College Academic Journal*

DEANS

College of Arts: EUL-MEE PARK
College of Business: BEUNG-GEUN MUN
College of Dentistry: LI-HEE YUN
College of Education: HONG-WOOK HUH
College of Engineering: MAN-HYUNG LEE
College of Human Ecology: YEONG-OK SONG
College of Humanities: JIN-NONG CHUNG
College of Law: BAE-WON KIM
College of Medicine: YONG-KI KIM
College of Natural Sciences: SANG-JOON LEE
College of Pharmacy: JEE-HYUNG JUNG
College of Social Sciences: HYUN-JUNG SHIN
Graduate School: JUNG-KEUN KIM
Graduate School of Education: HONG-WOOK HUH
Graduate School of Environment: MAN-HYUNG LEE
Graduate School of Industry: MAN-HYUNG LEE
Graduate School of Management: BEUNG-GEUN MUN
Graduate School of Public Administration: KI-HYUNG RYU

SEOUL NATIONAL UNIVERSITY

599 Gwanak-ro, Gwanak-gu, Seoul 151-742

Telephone: (2) 880-5114
Fax: (2) 885-5272
E-mail: webmaster@snu.ac.kr
Internet: www.snu.ac.kr

Founded 1946
State control
Academic year: March to February

Pres.: JANG-MOO LEE
Vice-Pres.: SHIN BOK KIM
Vice-Pres. and Dean of Graduate School: HASUCK KIM
Dean of Academic Affairs: MYUNG HWAN KIM
Dean of Planning and Devt: CHONG NAM CHU
Dean of Research Affairs: JIN-HO SEO
Dean of Student Affairs: CHAE-SEONG CHANG
Chief of Gen. Admin.: IN-CHEOL HWANG
Dir-Gen. of Library: NAM JIN HUH

Library: see Libraries and Archives
Number of teachers: 4,063
Number of students: 26,030
Publication: *University Gazette* (52 a year)

DEANS

College of Agriculture and Life Sciences: MOO HA LEE
College of Business Administration: TAE SIK AHN
College of Dentistry: PILL HOUN CHOUNG
College of Education: CHUNG-IL YUN
College of Engineering: TAI JIN KANG
College of Fine Arts: YOUNG GULL KWON
College of Human Ecology: IN KYEONG HWANG
College of Humanities: CHANG-KU BYUN
College of Law: JONG-SUP CHONG
College of Medicine: JUNG-GI IM
College of Music: TAI-BONG CHUNG
College of Natural Sciences: JONG SEOB LEE
College of Nursing: MI SOON SONG
College of Pharmacy: YOUNG-GER SUH
College of Social Sciences: HYUN-CHIN LIM
College of Veterinary Medicine: OH KYEONG KWEON
Graduate School: TAE SOO LEE
Graduate School of Business: TAE SIK AHN
Graduate School of Dentistry: PILL-HOON CHOUNG
Graduate School of Environmental Studies: KEE WON HWANG
Graduate School of Int. Studies: TAEHO BARK
Graduate School of Public Administration: JONGWON CHOI
Graduate School of Public Health: HAI WON CHUNG

SUNCHON NATIONAL UNIVERSITY

315 Maegok-dong, Sunchon, Chonnam 540-742

Telephone: (661) 750-3114
Fax: (661) 750-3117
E-mail: webmaster@sunchon.ac.kr
Internet: www.sunchon.ac.kr

Founded 1935
State control
Academic year: March to December

Pres.: Dr JAE-KI KIM
Deans: Dr WON-OG YANG (Academic Affairs), Dr JONG-CHUN CHOI (Student Affairs), Dr NAM-HOON CHO (University Planning and Research), DOO-HEE LEE (General Affairs)
Librarian: Dr JIN-IL DOO

Library of 211,000 books
Number of teachers: 340
Number of students: 12,560 (11,117 under-graduate, 1,443 postgraduate)

DEANS

College of Agriculture and Life Science: Dr DONG-HWAN OH
College of Education: Dr SANG-WOOK HAN
College of Engineering: Dr BONG-CHAN BAN
College of Humanities and Social Sciences: Dr JUNG-SUN SHIM
College of Natural Sciences: Dr MAN-CHAI JANG

SUWON UNIVERSITY

San 2-2 Wawoo-ri, Bongnam-myun, Hwa-sung-si, Gyeonggi-do 445-743

E-mail: info@suwon.mail.co.kr
Internet: www.suwon.ac.kr

Founded 1982

Chair.: IN-SOO LEE
Pres.: D. Y. YOON.

YOSU NATIONAL UNIVERSITY

96-1 Dundeok-dong, Yosu-shi, Chollanam-do 550-749

Telephone: (662) 659-2114
Fax: (662) 659-3003
Internet: www.yosu.ac.kr

Founded 1917 as Yosu Public Fisheries School; became Yosu Public Fisheries Middle School 1946, Yosu National Fisheries High School 1963, Yosu National Fisheries Junior College 1979, Yosu National Fisheries College 1987, Yosu National Fisheries University 1993; present name 1998

President: HA-JOON KIM
Number of teachers: 212
Number of students: 5,064

Colleges of Humanities and Social Science, Natural Science, Engineering, Fisheries and Ocean Science, Graduate School of Industry and Technology; Graduate School of Education.

PRIVATE UNIVERSITIES

AJOU UNIVERSITY

5 Woncheon-dong, Yeongtong-gu, Suwon, Seoul 443-749

Telephone: (2) 231-7121
Internet: www.ajou.ac.kr

Founded 1973

Pres.: SUH MOON HO
Registrar: JOON YOP KIM
Librarian: JAE SUK LEE

Library of 230,000 vols
Number of teachers: 750
Number of students: 10,954

Colleges of engineering, business administration, natural sciences, medicine, social sciences, humanities; graduate school.

CATHOLIC UNIVERSITY OF KOREA

Songeui Campus:, 505 Banpo-dong, Socho-gu, Seoul 137-701

Telephone: (2) 590-1081
Fax: (2) 590-1100

Songsim Campus:, 43-1 Yeokgok 2-dong, Wonmi-gu, Bucheon City, Gyeonggi-do 420-743

Telephone: (2) 2164-4000
Fax: (2) 2164-4778

Songsin Campus:, 90-1 Hyehwa-dong, Jon-gro-gu, Seoul 110-758

Telephone: (2) 740-9704
Fax: (2) 741-2801
E-mail: webmaster@catholic.ac.kr
Internet: www.cuk.ac.kr

Founded 1995 by merger of Catholic Univ. (f. c. 1984 from existing colleges) and Songsim Women's Univ. (f. 1957)

Pres.: Rev. PAHK JOHAN YEONG-SIK
Number of teachers: 914
Library of 160,000
Number of students: 8,075 (6,772 under-graduate, 1,303 postgraduate)
Publication: *Catholic Theology and Thoughts* (1 a year)

Songeui Campus: incl. Colleges of Medicine, and Nursing; Graduate Schools of Occupational Health, and Health Management. Songsin Campus: incl. College of Theology. Songsim Campus: incl. Colleges of Humanities, Social Sciences, Science and Technology, and Human Ecology.

CATHOLIC UNIVERSITY OF TAEGU-HYOSUNG

330 Kumnak 1-ri, Hayang-up, Kyongsan-shi, Kyongbuk, Seoul 712-702

Telephone: (53) 850-3001

Fax: (53) 850-3600

E-mail: presid@cuth.cataegu.ac.kr

Internet: www.cataegu.ac.kr

Founded 1995 as a result of merger of Hyosung Women's University and Taegu Catholic University

Private control

President: SOO-EUP KIM

Library of 410,000 vols

Number of teachers: 780

Number of students: 11,132

Publications: *Research Bulletin* (1 a year), *University Bulletin* (1 a year)

Colleges of Humanities, Theology, Foreign Studies, Natural Sciences, Engineering, Medicine, Social Sciences, Law and Politics, Economics and Commerce, Home Economics, Pharmacy, Education, Music, and Fine Arts.

CHEONGJU UNIVERSITY

36 Naedok-dong, Sangdang-ku, Cheongju 360-764

Telephone: (43) 229-8114

Fax: (43) 229-8110

Internet: www.cheongju.ac.kr

Founded 1946 as Cheongju Commercial College; became Cheongju College 1951; present name 1981

President: KIM YOON BAE.

CHOSUN UNIVERSITY

375 Seosuk-dong, Dong-gu, Gwangju, Seoul 501-759

Telephone: (62) 230-7114

Internet: www.chosun.ac.kr

Founded 1946

Private control

Language of instruction: Korean

Academic year: March to February

Pres.: JEON HO-JONG

Dean of Academic Affairs: CHAI-KYUN PARK

Dean of Finance: JEI-WON KOH

Dean of General Affairs: PYUNG-JOON PARK

Dean of Student Affairs: YANG-SOO SON

Librarian: KI-SANG KIM

Library of 597,032 vols

Number of teachers: 556

Number of students: 26,164

DEANS

College of Arts: YONG-HYUN KUK

College of Business Administration: BYUNG-KYU KIM

College of Dentistry: CHANG-KEUN YOON

College of Education: HONG-WON PARK

College of Engineering: WHAN-KYU PARK

College of Foreign Languages: YONG-HERN LEE

College of Humanities: JEONG-SEOK KANG

College of Industry: HEUNG-KYU JOO

College of Law and Political Science: CHANG-HYEON KOH

College of Medicine: YO-HAN JUNG

College of Natural Science: HAK-JIN JUNG

College of Pharmacy: YEONG-JONG YOO

College of Physical Education: DONG-YOON CHOE

Evening College: JEONG-JOO CHOE

Graduate School: JOON-CHAE PARK

Graduate School of Education: SEOK-CHEOL PARK

Graduate School of Industry: SEONG-HYU JO

CHUNG-ANG UNIVERSITY

221 Heukseok–dong, Dongjak-gu, Seoul 156-756

Telephone: (2) 820-6202

Fax: (2) 813-8069

E-mail: interedu@cau.ac.kr

Internet: www.cau.ac.kr

Founded 1918

Private control

Academic year: March to February (2 semesters)

Chair. and Chancellor: KIM HEE SU

Pres.: PARK BUM HONN

Vice-Pres.: SIK KIM DAE (Seoul Campus): SANG YOON LEE (Ansung Campus): HWANG YUN-WON

Provost of Medical Centre: CHANG KWUN HONG

Dirs of Library: TAE WOO NAM (Seoul Campus): YANG HYUN LEE (Ansung Campus)

Library: 1.2m. vols

Number of teachers: 2,127

Number of students: 22,071 (undergraduate), 4,563 (graduate)

Publications: *Chung-Ang Herald* (12 a year), *Chung-Ang Press* (52 a year), *College Journals* (1 a year), *Journal of Chung-Ang Pharmacy* (1 a year), *Journal of Economic Development* (1 a year), *Korean Education Index* (1 a year), *Korean Journal of Comparative Law* (1 a year), *Korean Studies Journal* (4 a year), *Theses Collection*

DEANS

College of Arts: SANG JUE SHIN

College of Construction Engineering: KI BONG KIM

College of Education: YOUNG DUCK CHOI

College of Engineering: SUNG SUN KIM

College of Foreign Languages: SUNG MOO YANG

College of Home Economics: YANG HEE KIM

College of Industrial Studies: KWANG RO YOON

College of Law: YOUNG SOL KWON

College of Liberal Arts: NAM JOON CHANG

College of Medicine: IM WON CHANG

College of Music: LEE SUK CHEH

College of Pharmacy: IN HOI HUH

College of Political Science and Economics: IN KIE KIM

College of Sciences: SUK YONG LEE

College of Social Sciences: CHI SOON JANG

Graduate School: JO SUP CHUNG

Graduate School of Construction Engineering: SUNG SUN KIM

Graduate School of Education: JAE WOO LEE

Graduate School of the Information Industry: YOUNG CHAN KIM

Graduate School of International Management: HUN CHU

Graduate School of Mass Communication: SANG CHUL LEE

Graduate School of Public Administration: SANG YOON REE

Graduate School of Social Development: KYONG SUH PARK

DIRECTORS

Australian Studies Institute: HYUNG SHIK KIM

Chung-Ang Music Institute: HAK WON YOON

Institute of Advertising and Public Relations: JUN IL RYEE

Institute of Arts: SEUNG KIL KOH

Institute of Basic Sciences: KYUNG HEE CHOI

Institute of Economic Research: YEN KYUN WANG

Institute of Environmental Science: SEI KWAN SOHN

Institute of Family Life: HYUN OK LEE

Institute of Food Resources: SOO SUNG LEE

Institute of Genetic Engineering: YUNG CHAI CHUNG

Institute of Humanities: JOONG SHIK HYUN

Institute of Industrial Construction Technology: YONG JU HWANG

Institute of Industrial Design: WON MO KWAK

Institute of Industrial Management: SEONG MU SUH

Institute of International Trade: JU SUP HAHN

Institute of International Women's Studies: JAE WOO LEE

Institute of Japanese Studies: KYUN IL KIM

Institute of Korean Education: SUNG YOON HONG

Institute of Korean Folklore: SEON POONG KIM

Institute of Legal Research: HYUK JU LEE

Institute of Management Research: DONG SUNG KWAK

Institute of Medical Science: DAE YONG UHM

Institute of North-East Asian Studies: JAE SUN CHOI

Institute of Overseas Korean Residents: SANG MAN LEE

Institute of Pharmaceutical Science: KI HO KIM

Institute of Production Engineering: SOO SAM KIM

Institute of Public Policy and Administration: SANG YOON RHEE

Institute of Social Sciences: HYUNG KOOK KIM

Institute of Sports Sciences Research: JIN YOO

Institute of Technology and Science: YOUNG CHAN KIM

Institute of Third World Studies: UJIN YI

DAEBUL UNIVERSITY

72 Samho-ri, Samho-myeun, Yangam-gun, Chonnam, Seoul 526-702

Telephone: (61) 469-1114

Fax: (61) 462-2510

E-mail: webmaster@mail.daebul.ac.kr

Internet: www.daebul.ac.kr

Founded 1994 as Daebul Institute of Technology and Science; present name 1996

Private control

Pres.: LEE GYEONG-SU.

DAEGU UNIVERSITY

Jillyang, Gyeongsan, Gyeongbuk, Seoul 712-714

Telephone: (53) 850-5681

Fax: (53) 850-5689

E-mail: oia@daegu.ac.kr

Internet: www.daegu.ac.kr

Private control

Languages of instruction: English, Korean

Academic year: March to February

Pres.: Dr DUCKRYUL HONG

Number of teachers: 1,682

Number of students: 30,885

DANKOOK UNIVERSITY

Jukjeon Campus: 126 Jukjeon-dong, Suji-gu, Yongin-si, Gyeonggi-do, Seoul 448-701

Cheonan Campus: San 29, Anseo-dong, Dongnam-gu, Cheonan-si,Chugnam, Seoul 330-714

Telephone: (31) 8005-2102

Internet: www.dankook.ac.kr

Founded 1947, univ. status 1967

Private control

Language of instruction: Korean

Academic year: March to February

Chancellor: CHANG CHOONG-SIK

Pres.: CHANG HOSUNG

Registrar: YONG-WOO LEE

Library of 140,000 vols

Number of teachers: 321
Number of students: 13,557

DEANS

College of Commerce and Economics: KIM
HAENG-XUH
College of Education: KIM SEUNG-KOOK
College of Engineering: KO MYUNG-WON
College of Law: KIM YOO-HYUK
College of Liberal Arts and Sciences: CHA
MOON-SUP

DONG-A UNIVERSITY

840 Hadan 2-dong, Saha-gu, Busan, Seoul
604-714

Telephone: (51) 200-6442
Fax: (51) 200-6445
E-mail: president@donga.ac.kr
Internet: www.donga.ac.kr

Founded 1946
Private control
Language of instruction: Korean
Academic year: March to February

Pres.: CHOI JAE-RONG
Vice-Pres.: CHO BYUNG-TAE
Head of Secretariat: LEE YEONG-GI
Dean of Academic Affairs: CHOI CHANG-OCK
Dean of Admin.: KIM LI-KYOO
Dean of Financial Affairs: HWANG YOON-SIK
Dean of Research: CHOI SOON-KYU
Dean of Student Affairs: LEE DAE-KYU
Dir of Library: HAHN KUN-BAE

Library of 582,134 vols
Number of students: 17,217

DEANS

College of Agriculture: CHUNG DAE-SOO
College of Arts: PARK SOO-CHUL
College of Business Administration: JUN TAE-
YOON
College of Engineering: PARK CHUN-KEUN
College of Human Ecology: KIM SEOK-HWAN
College of Humanities: CHUNG SANG-BAK
College of Law: JEONG MAN-HEE
College of Medicine: CHUNG DUCK-HWAN
College of Natural Sciences: UHM TAE-SEOP
College of Physical Education: PARK CHEOL-
HO
College of Social Sciences: SUL KWANG-SUK
Graduate School: RYOO WOONG-DAL
Graduate School of Business Administration:
KIM YONG-DAE
Graduate School of Education: TCHOI CHONG-
IL
Graduate School of Industry: HAN KUN-MO
Graduate School of Mass Communication:
KIM MIN-NAM

DIRECTORS

Agricultural Resources Research Institute:
KIM YOUNG-KIL
Basic Science Research Institute: KIM WAN-
SE
Business Management Research Institute:
KIM SEONG-HWAN
Environmental Problems Research Institute:
KIM JANG-HO
German Studies Institute: RHIE SANG-UG
Industrial Medicine Research Institute: KIM
JUNG-MAN
Industrial Technology Research Centre: JUN
TAE-OK
Institute for the Study of Law: KIM SANG-HO
Institute of Data Communication: HONG
CHANG-HI
Institute of Korean Resources Development:
CHUNG SUNG-GYO
Language Research Institute: HA CHI-GUN
Life Science Research Institute: CHOI YONG-
CHUN
MIS Research Institute: HAN KAY-SEOB
Ocean Resources Research Institute: KIM JIN-
HOO

Plastic Arts Research Institute: BACK SUNG-
DO
Population Research Centre: CHOI SOON
Research Institute for Clinical Medicine: KIM
JEONG-MAN
Research Institute for Genetic Engineering:
CHUNG CHUNG-HAN
Research Institute for Human Ecology: PARK
EUN-JOO
Research Institute for Humanities: CHUNG
YOUNG-DO
Research Institute of Sports Science: AN
YOUNG-PIL
Social Science Research Institute: KIM JAE-
GYONG
Sokdang Academic Research Institute of
Korean Culture: HYENG-JU KIM
Tourism and Leisure Research Institute:
AHN YUNG-MYUN

DONG-EUI UNIVERSITY

24 Kaya-dong, Pusanjin-ku, Busan 614-714

Telephone: (51) 890-1114
Fax: (51) 890-1234
E-mail: wwwadmin@www.dongeui.ac.kr
Internet: www.dongeui.ac.kr

Founded 1976 as Kyungdong Engineering
Technical College; became Dong-Eui Col-
lege 1979; present name 1983
Private control

Pres.: Dr KEUN-WU PAK

Library of 336,000 vols
Number of students: 3,704 (3,420 undergraduate, 284 postgraduate)

DONG YANG UNIVERSITY

1 Kyochon-dong, Punggi, Youngju, Kyungbuk, Seoul 750-711

Telephone: (572) 630-1114
Fax: (572) 636-8523
E-mail: wwwadmin@dyu.ac.kr
Internet: www.dyu.ac.kr

Founded 1994
Private control
Academic year: March to December

Pres.: Dr CHOI SUNG-HAE
Vice-Pres.: Dr PARK YOUNG-HWAN
Librarian: BYUN BOK-SOO

Library of 150,000 vols
Number of teachers: 80
Number of students: 3,100 (3,000 under-
graduate, 100 postgraduate)

Colleges of Science and Engineering, Human
and Social Science, Arts and Graduate
Schools of Information and Education.

DONGDUK WOMEN'S UNIVERSITY

23-1 Wolgok-dong, Sungbuk-ku, Seoul 136-
714

Telephone: (2) 940-4000
Fax: (2) 940-4182
E-mail: master@dongduk.ac.kr
Internet: www.dongduk.ac.kr

Founded 1950
Private control
Language of instruction: Korean
Academic year: March to February (2 semes-
ters)

Chancellor: WON-YOUNG CHO
Vice-Chancellor: YOUNG-YON YOON
Registrar: DO-SEOK CHANG
Librarian: YOON-SIK KIM

Library of 232,000 vols
Number of teachers: 154
Number of students: 6,155

Publications: Dongduk News Letter (2 a
year), Dongduk Women's Newspaper (52 a
year), Journal of Dongduk Women's University, Treatise (1 a year)

DEANS

College of Arts: SUN-BAEK JANG
College of Computer and Information Sci-
ences: YANG-HEE LEE
College of Design: DONG-JO KOO
College of Humanities: SANG-GI CHO
College of Natural Sciences: SANG-SOON LEE
College of Performing Arts: (vacant)
College of Pharmacy: IN-KOO CHUN
College of Social Sciences: SAE-YOUNG OH
General Studies and Teaching Profession
Division: HONG-TAE PARK

DONGGUK UNIVERSITY

26, Pil-dong, 3-ga Jung-gu, Seoul 100-715

Telephone: (2) 2260-3114
Fax: (2) 2277-1274
E-mail: iie@dongguk.edu
Internet: www.dongguk.ac.kr

Founded 1906, univ. status 1953
Private control

Chair.: OH IN-GAB
Pres.: Dr SONG SUK-KU
Librarian: Dr KIM BO HWAN

Library: see Libraries
Number of teachers: 500
Number of students: 16,050

Publications: Dongguk Journal, Dongguk
Post (12 a year), Dongguk Sasang (Dongguk Thought), Dongguk Shinmun (52 a
year), Pulgyo Hakpo (Journal of Buddhist
Studies), and 20 others

Colleges of Buddhism, liberal arts and sciences, law and political science, economics
and commerce, agriculture and forestry,
engineering, education, medical science;
graduate school, graduate school of public
administration, graduate school of business
administration, graduate school of education,
graduate school of information industry; colleges on Kyongju Campus

Research Institutes: Buddhist culture, comparative literature, statistical science, law
and political science, business management,
agriculture and forestry, overseas development, national security, computer science,
Middle Eastern and East European affairs,
Korean studies, Saemaul research, landscape
art, industrial technology, translation of
Buddhist scriptures.

DONGSEO UNIVERSITY

San 69-1, Churye-2-Dong, Sasang-gu, Busan,
Seoul 617-716

Telephone: (51) 320-2092
Fax: (51) 320-2094
E-mail: anna1974@dongseo.ac.kr
Internet: www.dongseo.ac.kr

Founded 1991 as Dongseo College of Technology; present name 1996

Pres.: Dr PARK DONG-SOON
Exec. Dir of Int. Cooperation Cttee: CHANG
JEKUK
Number of students: 7,000

DONGSHIN UNIVERSITY

252 Daeho-hong, Naju, Jeonnam, Seoul 520-
714

Telephone: (61) 330-3114
Fax: (61) 330-2909
Internet: www.dongshinu.ac.kr

Pres.: LEE KYUM-BUM

Library of 500,000
Number of students: 1,604

Colleges of arts, engineering, humanities and
social science, information and science, oriental medicine.

DAEJON UNIVERSITY

96-3 Yongun-dong, Tong-gu, Daejon, Seoul
300-716

Telephone: (42) 282-0231
Fax: (42) 283-8808
E-mail: contact@dju.ac.kr
Internet: www.dju.ac.kr.

DUKSUNG WOMEN'S UNIVERSITY

19 Geunhwagyo-gil, 419 Ssangmoon-dong,
Dobong-gu, Seoul 132-714

Telephone: (2) 901-8691
Fax: (2) 901-8690
E-mail: djsuk@duksung.ac.kr
Internet: www.duksung.ac.kr

Founded 1950
Private control
Language of instruction: Korean
Academic year: March to February

Pres.: CHI EUN HEE
Registrar: LIM SOOK-JA
Librarian: CHUNG YOUNG-HWAN

Library of 328,000 vols
Number of teachers: 310 (148 full-time, 162
part-time)
Number of students: 5,250

Publications: *Duksung Women's University
Journal, Duksung Women's University
Newsletter* (24 a year), *Duksung Women's
University Newsletter, Geunmack* (1 a
year)

DEANS

College of Fine Arts: KIM AIE-YUNG
College of Humanities: YOON JUNG-BOON
College of Natural Science: YOON SUK-IM
College of Pharmacy: JUNG KI-HWA
College of Social Sciences: KIM SUNG-CHUL

EWHA WOMEN'S UNIVERSITY

11-1 Daehyun-dong, Seodaemun-gu, Seoul
120-750

Telephone: (2) 3277-2114
Fax: (2) 393-5903
E-mail: master@ewha.ac.kr
Internet: www.ewha.ac.kr

Founded 1886
Languages of instruction: Korean, English
Academic year: March to December (two
semesters)

Chancellor: YOON HOO-JUNG
Pres.: Dr SHIN IN-RYUNG
Librarian: KIM BONG-HEE

Library: see Libraries
Number of teachers: 800
Number of students: 21,000 (graduates
6,000; undergraduates 15,000)

Publications: *Edae Hakbo* (in Korean, 52 a
year), *Ewha News* (in Korean, 12 a year),
Ewha Voice (in English, 12 a year)

DEANS

College of Arts and Design: Prof. KIM YOUNG-
KI
College of Business Administration: Dr SUH
YOON-SUK
College of Education: Dr JU YOUNG-JU
College of Engineering: Dr SHIN YEONG-SOO
College of Home Science and Management:
Dr PARK SEONG-YEON
College of Human Movement and Perform-
ance: Dr KIM KEE-WOONG
College of Law: Dr YANG MYEONG-CHO
College of Liberal Arts: Dr KIM HYUN-JA
College of Medicine: Dr CHUNG HWA-SOON
College of Music: Prof. LEE KYU-DO
College of Natural Sciences: Dr LEE NAM-SOO
College of Nursing: Dr BYUN YOUNG-SOON
College of Pharmacy: Dr KIM CHOON-MI
College of Social Sciences: Dr AHN HONG-SIK

Institute of Science and Technology: Dr KIM
WON
Graduate School: Dr CHANG PIL-WHA
Graduate School of Business Administration:
Dr SUH YOON-SUK
Graduate School of Clinical Health Sciences:
Dr KIM CHOON-MI
Graduate School of Design: Dr KIM YOUNG-KI
Graduate School of Education: Dr CHOI
WOUN-SIK
Graduate School of Information Science: Dr
AHN HONG-SIK
Graduate School of International Studies: Dr
YOO JANG-HEE
Graduate School of Policy Sciences: Dr AHN
HONG-SIK
Graduate School of Practical Music: Dr CHOI
YOO-RI
Graduate School of Social Welfare: Dr CHOI
WOUN-SIK
Graduate School of Theology: Dr YANG
MYUNG-SU
Graduate School of Translation and Inter-
pretation: Dr CHOI YOUNG

HALLYM UNIVERSITY

39 Hallymdaehak-gil, Chunchon, Kangwon-
do, Seoul 200-702

Telephone: (33) 248-1000
Fax: (33) 256-3333
E-mail: parkphil@hallym.ac.kr
Internet: www.hallym.ac.kr

Founded 1982
Private control
Academic year: March to December

Pres.: LEE YOUNG-SUN
Vice-Pres.: Dr HAN SIL
Dean for Academic Affairs: Dr CHOI SOO-
YOUNG
Dean for Gen. Affairs: SUNG NAK-SUNG
Dean for Planning and Coordination: Dr LEE
KI-WON
Dean for Student Affairs: Dr LEE CHOONG-IL
Library Dir: Dr BAK GEUN-GAB

Library of 373,000 books
Number of teachers: 591
Number of students: 10,119 (9,353 under-
graduate, 766 postgraduate)

Publication: *Hallym News* (26 a year)

DEANS

College of Humanities: Prof. OH CHUN-TAEK
College of Information and Electronics
Engineering: Prof. SONG CHANG-GEUN
College of Medicine: Prof. PARK HYOUNG-JIN
College of Natural Sciences: Prof. KIM RAK-
JOONG
College of Social Sciences: Prof. KIM YUNG-
MYUNG

HAN NAM UNIVERSITY

133 Ojeong-dong, Daedeok-gu, Daejon, Seoul
306-791

Telephone: (42) 629-7739
Fax: (42) 629-7779
E-mail: webmaster@hannam.ac.kr
Internet: www.hannam.ac.kr

Founded 1956
Academic year: March to December

Pres.: KIM HYUNG-TAE
Dir of Int. Relations Centre: Dr KYU TAE
JUNG

Library: Univ. possesses Central Library,
Central Museum, Natural History
Museum, Academic Information Centre
Number of teachers: 965
Number of students: 11,441

Colleges of liberal arts, education, natural
sciences, engineering, economics and business administration, law, social sciences.

HANKUK UNIVERSITY OF FOREIGN STUDIES

270 Imun-dong, Dongdaemun-gu, Seoul 130-
791

Telephone: (2) 2173-2063
Fax: (2) 2173-3387
E-mail: gyoh@hufs.ac.kr
Internet: www.hufs.ac.kr

Founded 1954
Private control

Pres.: PARK CHUL
Dean of Academic Affairs: Prof. PAK SUNG
RAE
Dean of Student Affairs: Prof. LEE CHANG
BOK
Chief Admin. Officer: SEOK JOO YOON
Librarian: Prof. CHO KYU CHUL

Library of 303,900 vols
Number of teachers: 292
Number of students: 12,838

Publications: *Argus* (English and other foreign languages, 12 a year), *Journal* (1 a
year), *Oe-Dae Hakbo* (in Korean, 52 a year)

DEANS

Academic and Student Affairs (Evening
Courses): Prof. WOO DUCK YONG
College of Education: Prof. OH HAN-JIN
College of Foreign Languages: Prof. CHOI
JONG SOO
College of Law and Political Science: Prof.
KIM DEOK
College of Liberal Arts and Sciences: Prof.
KIM JIK HYUN
College of Occidental Languages: Prof. LEE
YOUNG GUL
College of Oriental Languages: Prof. CHUNG
KI IOB
College of Social Sciences: Prof. PARK BYUNG
HO
College of Trade and Economics: Prof. LEE
HEE JOON
Graduate School: Prof. REW JOUNG YOLE
Graduate School of Education: Prof. RHIM JIN
KWON
Graduate School of International Trade:
Prof. LEE HEE JOON
Graduate School of Interpretation and
Translation: Prof. KIM I BAE
Graduate School of Management Informa-
tion Systems: Prof. JUNG JAE SEOK

DIRECTORS

Audio-Visual Education Institute: Prof. PARK
SOON-HAM
Chinese Studies Institute: Prof. CHOI KWAN-
JANG
Foreign Language Training and Research
Centre: Prof. KIM JAI MIN
Institute for Research in Languages and
Linguistics: Prof. REW SEONG JOON
Institute of African Studies: Prof. PARK WON
TAK
Institute of Foreign Language Studies: Prof.
KIM YOUNG JO
Institute of History: Prof. PAK SUNG RAE
Institute of Humanities: Prof. KANG SUNG WI
Institute of International Communication:
Prof. KIM JONG KI
Institute of Korean Regional Studies: Prof.
AHN BYONG MAN
Institute of Latin-American Studies: Prof.
MIN MAN SHIK
Institute of the Middle East: Prof. HONG
SOON NAM
Interpretation and Translation Centre: Prof.
KIM I-BAE
Research Institute for Economics and Busi-
ness Administration: Prof. MIN BYUNG
KWOON
Russian and East European Institute: Prof.
CHO KYU WHA
Student Guidance Centre: Prof. YOON JONG
GEON

HANSEO UNIVERSITY

360 Daegok-ri, Haemi-Myun, Seosan City, Chungcheongnam, Seoul 360-706
Telephone: (41) 660-1144
Fax: (41) 660-1149
E-mail: webmaster@hanseo.ac.kr
Internet: www.hanseo.ac.kr
Founded 1989
Number of students: 1,927
Pres.: HAM KEE-SUN

Colleges of aeronautical engineering, arts, engineering, graduate school, health science, liberal arts, science, social science.

HANSHIN UNIVERSITY

Hanshin, Seoul
Telephone: (31) 379-0103
Fax: (31) 372-6101
Internet: www.hs.ac.kr
Founded 1980
Number of students: 6,000
Pres.: YOON EUNG JIN

Colleges of humanities, information sciences, management and trade, social sciences, theology.

HANSUNG UNIVERSITY

389 Samseon-Dong 2-ga, Seongbuk-gu, Seoul
Telephone: (2) 760-4114
Fax: (2) 745-8943
E-mail: getsmile@hansung.ac.kr
Internet: www.hansung.ac.kr
Founded 1945
Pres.: CHUNG JOO-TAEK

Colleges of arts, engineering, humanities, liberal arts and science, social sciences.

HANYANG UNIVERSITY

17 Haengdang-dong, Seongdong-gu, Seoul 133-791
Telephone: (2) 2220-0114
E-mail: w3master@hanyang.ac.kr
Internet: www.hanyang.ac.kr
Founded 1939 as Hanyang Institute of Technology; present status 1959
Private control
Academic year: March to July, September to December
Pres.: Dr KIM CHONG YANG
Academic Dean: Dr SONG CHANG SEOP
Library of 350,000 vols
Number of teachers: 958
Number of students: 24,508
Publications: *Hanyang Nonmun Dzip*, *Journal of Economic Studies*, *Journal of Korean Studies*, *Journal of Student Guidance Research*, *Sino-Soviet Affairs*, and numerous others

Colleges of engineering (incl. architectural engineering), liberal arts and sciences (incl. journalism and cinema), commerce and economics, law and political science, music, physical education, education, medicine; evening engineering college; graduate school, graduate school of industrial management.

HONAM UNIVERSITY

Gwangsan Campus: 59-1 Seobong-Dong, Gwangsan-gu, Gwangju City, Seoul 506-714
Telephone: (62) 940-5114
Fax: (62) 940-5005
Ssangchom Campus: 148 Ssangchon-dong, Seo-Ku, Gwangju City, Seoul 502-791
Telephone: (62) 370-8114
Fax: (62) 370-8008

Internet: www.honam.ac.kr
Founded 1978
Chair.: Dr PARK KI-IN
Pres.: CHUNG BYOUNG-WAN
Library of 400,000 vols

Colleges of arts and physical education, business administration, engineering, internet and media, humanities, natural science, social sciences.

HONG-IK UNIVERSITY

Seoul Campus: 72-1 Sangsu-dong, Mapo-gu, Seoul 121-791
Jochiwon Campus: Jochiwon-eup, Yeongi-gun, Chungcheongnam-do 339-701
Telephone: (2) 320-1114
Fax: (2) 320-1122
E-mail: webm@wow.hongik.ac.kr
Internet: www.hongik.ac.kr
Founded 1946
Private control
Language of instruction: Korean
Academic year: March to June, September to December
Chair.: Dr LEE MYEON YOUNG
Pres.: KWON MYUNG KWANG
Vice-Pres: CHANG YOUNG TAE, LIM HAE CHULL
Vice-Pres. for Jochiwon Campus: LEE KI BOK
Dir of Univ. Library: KIM KUN HO
Library: 1m. vols
Number of teachers: 853 (463 full-time, 390 part-time)
Number of students: 16,679
Publications: *Hong-Ik University Journal* (1 a year), *Hong-Ik Economic Review* (1 a year), *Journal of Student Life* (1 a year), *Management Review* (1 a year), *Papers on the Study of Education* (1 a year)

DEANS

College of Architecture: KIM UK
College of Business Administration: KIM DONG HUN
College of Business Management (Jochiwon Campus): CHOI YEON
College of Design and Arts (Jochiwon Campus): PARK YON SUN
College of Education: KIM MIN JAE
College of Engineering: CHUNG JOON KI
College of Fine Arts: CHOI BYUNG HOON
College of Law: MIN KYOUNG-DO
College of Law and Economics: BAEK SEUNG GWAN
College of Liberal Arts: CHIN HYUNG JOON
College of Science and Technology (Jochiwon Campus): SHIN PAN SEOK
Graduate School: YOUNG TAE JANG
Graduate School of Advertising and Public Relations: CHANG DON RYUN
Graduate School of Architecture and Urban Design: CHUNG MYUNG WON
Graduate School of Business: LEE KWANG CHUL
Graduate School of Education: PARK SANG OK
Graduate School of Educational Management: PARK SANG OK
Graduate School of Film and Digital Media: KIM JONG DEOK
Graduate School of Fine Arts: KIM TAE HO
Graduate School of Industrial Arts: BYUN KUN HO
Graduate School of Industry (Jochiwon Campus): CHANG HO SUNG
International Design School for Advance Studies: KIM CHUL HO

HOSEO UNIVERSITY

Asan Campus: 165 Sechul-ri, Baebang-myun, Asan, Chungnam, Seoul 336-795
Cheonan Campus: 268, Anseo-dong, Cheonan, Chungnam, Seoul 330-713
Telephone: (41) 540-5017
Fax: (41) 540-5019
Internet: www.hoseo.ac.kr
Founded 1978
Private control
Pres.: KANG IL-KU
Library of 300,000 vols
Number of teachers: 520
Number of students: 12,000

INHA UNIVERSITY

253 Yonghyun-dong, Nam-gu, Inchon, Seoul 402-751
Telephone: (32) 860-7030
Fax: (32) 867-7222
E-mail: orir@inha.ac.kr
Internet: www.inha.ac.kr
Founded 1954
Private control
Academic year: March to February
Pres.: Dr LEE BON-SU
Vice-Pres.: Dr CHOI BYUNG-HA
Registrar: Dr KIM CHONG-BO
Librarian: Dr YUN MYUNG-KOO
Library of 350,000 vols
Number of teachers: 644
Number of students: 18,116
Publications: bulletins of the research institutes

DEANS

College of Business and Economics: Dr KIM KI-MYUNG
College of Education: Dr KIM CHANG-GEOL
College of Engineering: Dr KANG BYUNG-HEE
College of Home Economics: (vacant)
College of Humanities: Dr KIM WOO-JIN
College of Law and Political Science: Dr LEE YOUNG-HEE
College of Medicine: Dr KIM SEH-HWAN
College of Natural Sciences: Dr PARK DAE-YOON
Graduate School: Dr CHOI JI-HOON
Graduate School of Business Administration: Dr SHINN YONG-HWI
Graduate School of Education: Dr CHUNG KI-HO
Graduate School of Engineering: Dr KIM DONG-IL
Graduate School of Public Administration: Dr SHIN YOUNG-SANG

INJE UNIVERSITY

Kimhae Campus, 607 Obang-dong, Gimhae, Gyeongnam, Seoul 621-749
Telephone: (55) 334-7111
Fax: (55) 334-0712
E-mail: webmaste@inje.ac.kr
Internet: www.inje.ac.kr
Founded 1983
Chair.: PAIK NAK WHAN
Pres.: LEE KYEONGHO
Library of 500,000 vols

Colleges of Medicine, Biomedical Science and Engineering, Humanities and Social Sciences, Natural Sciences, Engineering, Design, Music.

JEONJU UNIVERSITY

1200 Hyoja-dong, Wansangu, Chonju Jeolla-bukdo, Seoul 520-759
Telephone: (652) 220-2122
Fax: (652) 220-2074
Internet: www.jeonju.ac.kr

Colleges of Christian Studies, Language and Culture, Law and Public Administration, Social Science, Economics and Information, Business Administration, Natural Science, Information Technology and Computer Science, Engineering, Architecture, Arts, Athletics and Visual Communication, Culture and Tourism, Teachers' College.

KANGNAM UNIVERSITY

111 Gugal-dong, Gihoung-gu, Yongin-si, Gyeonggi-do, Seoul 449-702

Telephone: (31) 280-3500
Fax: (31) 280-3428
E-mail: master@kangnam.ac.kr
Internet: www.kangnam.ac.kr

Founded 1946
Private control
Academic year: March to December

Chair.: YOON DO-HAN
Pres.: YOON SHINIL
Chief Librarian: KIM SEUNG-HWAN

Library of 240,000 vols
Number of teachers: 170
Number of students: 6,534 (6,433 undergraduate, 101 postgraduate)

DEANS

College of Art and Physical Education: Prof. YANG JAE-YONG
College of Humanities: Prof. JO SUNG-MO
College of Management and Economics: Prof. JAE-HA HWANG, Prof. HWANG JAE-HA
College of Science and Engineering: Prof. PARK KI-SUNG
College of Social Sciences: Prof. LEE CHANG-SUK
College of Social Welfare: Prof. KIM YOUNG-HO
College of Theology: Prof. LEE SOOK-JONG
Graduate School: NO SANG-HAK (Pres.)

PAICHAI UNIVERSITY

14 Yeon-ja, 1-gil, Seo-gu, Daejeon 302-735
Telephone: (42) 520-5114
E-mail: jd1234@mail.pcu.ac.kr
Internet: www.paichai.ac.kr

Founded 1885

Pres.: CHUNG SOON-HOON

Colleges of Humanities, Foreign Studies, Business Administration, Social Sciences, Tourism, Natural Sciences, Engineering, Arts.

KAYA UNIVERSITY

120 Jisan-ri, Koryong-kun, Kyungbuk 717-800
Telephone: (543) 954-1438
Fax: (543) 954-6094
E-mail: webmaster@kaya.ac.kr
Internet: www.kaya.ac.kr

Founded 1993
Private control
Languages of instruction: Korean, English
Academic year: March to December

President: Dr KYUNG-HEE LEE
Librarian: Prof. DONG-HAE LEE

Library: 2.8m. vols
Number of teachers: 103
Number of students: 4,120 (4,000 undergraduate, 120 postgraduate)

DEANS

Faculty of Social Sciences: Prof. CHANG-HUN OK
Department of Engineering: Prof. SANG-HEE PARK

KEIMYUNG UNIVERSITY

2800 Dalgubeoldaero, Dalseo-gu, Daegu 704-701

Telephone: (53) 580-6023
Fax: (53) 580-6025
E-mail: intl@kmu.ac.kr
Internet: www.kmu.ac.kr

Founded 1954
Private control
Academic year: March to February

Pres.: SYNN ILHI
Vice-Pres. for Academic Affairs: PAEK SEUNG KYUN
Vice-Pres. for Medical Affairs: KANG JIN-SUNG
Dean of Dongsan Library: PARK JOON-SHIK

Library: 1.2m. vols
Number of teachers: 1,284 (604 full-time, 680 part-time)
Number of students: 21,126

Publications: *Accounting Information Review, Asian Journal of Business and Entrepreneurship, Bulletin of the Institute for International Science, Business Management Review, Journal of Art and Culture, Journal of International Studies, Journal of Life Science Research, Journal of Nakdonggang Environmental Research Institute, Journal of Social Sciences, Journal of the Institute for Cross-Cultural Studies, Journal of the Institute for Japanese Studies, Journal of the Institute of Natural Sciences, Keimyung Journal of Nursing Science, Keimyung Law Review, Keimyung University Medical Journal, Proceedings of Mathematical Science*

DEANS

College of Education: SIM HO TACK
Faculty of Applied Sciences: MIN HYUNG-JIN
Faculty of Automotive Engineering: SHIN SUNG-HEON
Faculty of Basic Sciences: UHM JAE-KUK
Faculty of Business Administration: PARK MYUNG-HO
Faculty of Chemical and Materials Engineering: SYNN DONG-SU
Faculty of Commerce: OH SEI-CHANG
Faculty of Computer and Electronic Engineering: SON YOO-EK
Faculty of Environmental Studies: KIM IN-HWAN
Faculty of Fashion: JON KYONG-TAE
Faculty of Fine Arts: HUR YONG
Faculty of Humanities: JIN WON-SUK
Faculty of Human Life Sciences: JOO KWANG JEE
Faculty of International Studies: LI JONG-KWANG
Faculty of Language and Literature: KIM JONG SUN
Faculty of Law: CHOI SANG-HO
Faculty of Music: KIM JEONG GIL
Faculty of Nursing: KIM JEONG NAM
Faculty of Physical Education: KIM SANG HONG
Faculty of Police Sciences: CHOI EUNG RYUL
Faculty of Politics and Economics: CHO YONG SANG
Faculty of Social Sciences: KIM SE SHUL
Graduate School: PARK YOUNG CHOON
Graduate School of Arts: KIM JEONG GIL
Graduate School of Business Administration: KIM JIN TAK
Graduate School of Education: KIM KI-HAN
Graduate School of Industrial Design: HUR YONG
Graduate School of Industrial Technology: KIM HONG YOUNG
Graduate School of International Studies: OH SEI-CHANG
Graduate School of Medical Management: PARK YOUNG NAM
Graduate School of Pastoral Theology: CHONG JOONG-HO

Graduate School of Policy Development: CHOI BONG KI
Graduate School of the Sports Industry: KIM SANG-HONG
School of Medicine: PARK YOUNG NAM

KON-KUK UNIVERSITY

1 Hwayang-dong, Gwangjin-gu, Seoul 143-701

Telephone: (2) 450-3259
Fax: (2) 450-3257
Internet: www.konkuk.ac.kr

Founded 1946, university status 1959
Private control
Academic year: March to February

Chair.: KYUNG-HEE KIM
Pres.: KIL-SAENG CHUNG
Vice-Pres: YUNG-KYE KANG (Seoul Campus): MOON-JA UM (Chungju Campus)
Registrar: HYEON-LYONG KIM
Librarian: YUNG-KWON KIM

Library: 1.1m. vols
Number of teachers: 589 (full-time)
Number of students: 17,177

Publications: *English Newspaper* (12 a year), *Newspaper* (52 a year)

DEANS

College of Agriculture: CHONG-CHON KIM
College of Animal Husbandry: CHANG-WON KANG
College of Architecture: YONG-SIK KIM
College of Art: HO-CHANG RYU
College of Arts and Design: HYUNG-JAE MAENG
College of Arts and Home Economics: WON-JA LEE
College of Business Administration: THOMAS T. H. JOH
College of Commerce and Economics: JEONG-PYO CHOL
College of Education: II HWANG
College of Engineering: KWANG-SOO KIM
College of Humanities: SOON-BONG PACK
College of Information & Telecommunication: SUN-YOUNG HAN
College of Law: SEUNG-HO LEE
College of Liberal Arts: OH-HYUN CHO
College of Life Environment: SUK-HUN KYUNG
College of Medicine: TAE-KYU PACK
College of Natural Sciences: LEE-CHOI CHANG
College of Political Science: SUNG-BOK LEE
College of Sciences: JUNE-TAK RHEE
College of Social Sciences: YOUNG-BOON LEE
College of Veterinary Medicine: BYUNG-JOO KIM
Graduate School: JOO-YOUNG LEE
Graduate School of Agriculture and Animal Science: SUN-JOO KIM
Graduate School of Architecture: BYOUNG-KEUN KANG
Graduate School of Business Administration: DAE-HO KIM
Graduate School of Design: LEE-SANG EUN
Graduate School of Education: DONG-OK LEE
Graduate School of Engineering: JOONG-RIN SHIN
Graduate School of Information and Telecommunication: CHUN-HYON CHANG
Graduate School of Mass Communication: DAE-IN KANG
Graduate School of Medicine: KYUNG-YUNG LEE
Graduate School of Public Administration: EUN-JAE LEE
Graduate School of Real Estate Studies: CHO-JOO HYUN
Graduate School of Social Sciences: NAM-KYU PARK

KONYANG UNIVERSITY

26 Nae-dong, Nonsan, Chungnam, Seoul 320-711

Telephone: (41) 730-5114
Fax: (41) 733-2070
E-mail: webmaster@konyang.ac.kr
Internet: www.konyang.ac.kr
Founded 1991
Pres.: KIM HEE-SOO
Library of 250,000 .

KOOKMIN UNIVERSITY

Jeongneung-gil 77, 861-1 Chongnung-dong, Songbuk-ku, Seoul 136-702

Telephone: (2) 910-4115
Fax: (2) 910-4115
Internet: www.kookmin.ac.kr
Founded 1946
Pres.: LEE SUNG WOO
Dean of Academic Affairs: Prof. KIM YOUNG-JEON
Dean of Student Affairs: Prof. LEE JONG-EUN
Dean of Gen. Affairs: KIL YEONG-BAE
Dean of Planning and Devt Affairs: Prof. KANG SIN-DON
Library of 200,000 vols
Number of teachers: 370 (159 full-time, 211 part-time)
Number of students: 15,000
Publications: *Kookmin University Press* (52 a year), *Kookmin Tribune* (English, 12 a year), *Kookmin University Bulletin* (1 a year), *Theses* (1 a year), *Design Review, Economic and Business Administration Review, Education Review, Journal of Language and Literature, Journal of Sports Science Research, Journal of the Scientific Institute, Law and Political Review, Papers in Chinese Studies, Theses of Engineering, Theses of Korean Studies*

DEANS

College of Architecture and Design: Prof. KIM CHUL-SOO
College of Economics and Business Administration: NAH OH-YOUN
College of Education: SHIN JOONG-SHIK
College of Engineering: Prof. YOON TAI-YOON
College of Forestry: KO YUNG-ZU
College of Law and Political Science: LEE YONG-SUN
College of Liberal Arts: Prof. LEE JUNG-KEE
Graduate School: CHOI HWAN-YOL
Graduate School of Business Administration: CHOI HWAN-YOL
Graduate School of Education: CHOI HWAN-YOL
Graduate School of Public Administration: LEE YOUNG-SUN

KOREA UNIVERSITY

1 5-ga, Anam-dong, Sungbuk-gu, Seoul 136-701

Telephone: (2) 3290-1152
Fax: (2) 922-5820
Internet: www.korea.ac.kr
Founded 1905, as Posung College
Private control: financed by the Korea-Choongang Educational Foundation
Language of instruction: Korean
Academic year: March to February (two semesters)
Pres.: EUH YOON-DAE (acting)
Dean of Planning and Public Relations: PARK MANN-JANG
Dean of Academic Affairs: AHN CHANG-YIL
Dean of Students: KIM SONG-BOK
Dean of Gen. Affairs: YOUN SA-SOON
Dean of Construction and Facility Management: PAIK YOUNG-HYUN

Librarian: SHIN IL-CHUL
Library: see Libraries
Number of teachers: 1,408 (627 full-time, 781 part-time)
Number of students: 21,685
Publications: *Gyongyong Shinmoon* (Korean, 52 a year), *Kodai Moonwha* (Korean, 1 a year), *Kodai Shinmoon* (Korean, 52 a year), *Korea University Bulletin* (English, 1 a year), *Phoenix* (bilingual, 1 a year), *The Granite Tower* (English, 26 a year)

DEANS

College of Agriculture: KWACK BEYOUNG-HWA
College of Business Administration: LEE JANG RHO
College of Education: YOU IN-JONG
College of Engineering: HONG JONG-HWI
College of Law: BAE JONG-DAE
College of Liberal Arts: HAN PONG-HEUM
College of Medicine: PARK SUNG-YONG
College of Political Science and Economics: CHO YONG-BUM
College of Science: KIM SI-JOONG
Graduate School: LAU BONG-WHAN
Graduate School of Business Administration: KIM DONG-KI
Graduate School of Education: KIM SUNG-TAI
Graduate School of Food and Agriculture: YANG HAN-CHUL
College of Economics and Commerce (Jochiwon campus): KIM JUNG-BAI
College of Liberal Arts and Science (Jochiwon campus): KIM JUNG-BAI

KOSIN UNIVERSITY

149-1 Dongsam-dong, Yeongdo-gu, Busan, Seoul 606-701

Telephone: (51) 990-2114
Fax: (51) 911-2525
E-mail: logos@kosin.ac.kr
Internet: www.kosin.ac.kr
Founded 1946
Pres.: KIM SUNG-SOO
Library of 120,000 vols
Colleges of Arts, Computer Sciences, Health Sciences, Human Ecology, Humanities and Social Sciences, Medicine, Natural Sciences, Theology.

KWANDONG UNIVERSITY

522 Naegok-dong, Kangnung-si, Gangwon-do, Seoul 210-701

Telephone: (33) 641-1011
Fax: (33) 641-1010
Internet: www.kwandong.ac.kr
Founded 1959
Pres.: PARK HUI-JONG
Number of students: 8,000
Colleges of Arts, Education, Humanities, Law and Politics, Medicine, Science and Engineering.

KWANGWOON UNIVERSITY

447-1 Wolgye-dong, Nowon-gu, Seoul 139-701

Telephone: (2) 940-5114
Internet: www.kwangwoon.ac.kr
Pres.: PARK YOUNG-SHIK
Colleges of Electronics and Information, Engineering, Natural Sciences, Humanities and Social Sciences, Law, Business.

KYONGGI UNIVERSITY

San 94-6 Iui-dong, Yeongtong-gu, Suwon-si, Gyeonggi-do, Seoul 443-760

Telephone: (31) 249-8770
Fax: (31) 255-5915

E-mail: oia@kgu.ac.kr
Internet: www.kgu.ac.kr
Founded 1947
Private control
Colleges of arts, economics and business administration, engineering, humanities, int. studies, law, natural sciences, physical education, social sciences, tourism sciences; graduate schools of alternative medicine, architecture, art and design, business administration, construction, culture and arts, education, engineering and industry, politics and policy, public administration, social welfare, sports science, tourism and hospitality
Chair.: CHU CHEONG-SOO
Chancellor: Dr HO JOON CHOI
Library of 1,500,000 vols
Number of teachers: 800
Number of students: 16,000

KYUNG HEE UNIVERSITY

Seoul Campus: Hoegi-dong, Dongdaemun-gu, Seoul 130-701

Telephone: (2) 961-0031
Fax: (2) 962-4343
E-mail: cie@khu.ac.kr
Global Campus: Seocheon-Dong, Seoul 446-701

Telephone: (31) 201-3177
Fax: (31) 201-3179
E-mail: intlctr@khu.ac.kr
Internet: www.kyunghee.ac.kr
Founded 1949, renamed 1952
Private control
Academic year: March to December (two terms)
Founder-Chancellor: Dr CHOUE INWON
Pres.: KIM BYUNG-MOOK
Vice-Pres.: KIM BYUNG MOOK (Seoul Campus): PARK KYU HONG (Suwon Campus): PARK MYUNG KWAN (Devt)
Registrars: CHOO DONG JOON (Seoul Campus): CHO WON-KYUNG (Suwon Campus)
Librarians: KIM JAE HONG (Seoul Campus): KIM HAN WON (Suwon Campus)
Library of 1,200,000 vols, separate medical library of 15,000 vols
Number of teachers: 2,300
Number of students: 29,080
Publications: *University Life* (in English, 12 a year), *University Weekly* (in Korean), *Kohwang* (in Korean, 1 a year), *Peace Forum* (in English, every 2 years), research bulletins for each college

DEANS

Seoul Campus:

College of Dentistry: LEE SANG RAE
College of Human Ecology: PARK HYUN-SUH
College of Law: LEE SHIYOON
College of Liberal Arts and Sciences: CHUNG BOK-KEUN
College of Medicine: CHO YOUG HO
College of Music: HWANG SUN
College of Oriental Medicine: LEE HYUNG KOO
College of Pharmacy: RHO YOUNG SOO
College of Political Science and Economics: SUH SUNG-HAN
College of Tourism and Hotel Management: YOO KON-JO
Graduate School: SOHN KWANG SHIK
Graduate School of Business Administration: LEE KEUN SOO
Graduate School of East–West Medicine: RYU KI-WON
Graduate School of Education: PARK KEE-SAW
Graduate School of International Legal Affairs: YUN MYUNG-SUNG
Graduate School of Journalism and Mass Communication: LEE SUK-WOO

Graduate School of NGO: PARK KUN WOO
Graduate School of Peace Studies: SOHN JAE-SHIK
Graduate School of Physical Education: KOH KI CHAE
Graduate School of Public Administration: OH SEI DEUK
Graduate School of Tourism: YOO KONG-JO
Suwon Campus:
College of Engineering and Department of Electronics and Information Technology: JUN KYE SUK
College of Foreign Languages: HUH JONG
College of Industry and Department of Life Science: JO JAE SUN
College of Natural Sciences and Department of the Environment and Applied Chemistry: CHOUNG SUK JIN
College of Social Sciences and Department of Management and International Relations: PARK WON-KYU
College of Sports Science and Department of Physical Education: KIM JIN HO
Department of Art and Design: LEE HEON LOOK
Department of Civil and Architectural Engineering: ON YOUNG TAE
Department of Mechanical and Industrial Systems Engineering: PARK KYOUNG SUK
Graduate School of Information and Communication: CHIN YONG-OHK
Graduate School of Industry and Information Science: LEE KYE TAK
Graduate School of Pan-Pacific International Studies: KIM CHONGSOO

KYUNGIL UNIVERSITY

33 Puho-ri, Hayang-up, Kyungsan-si, Kyung-sangpuk-do, Seoul 712-701
Telephone: (53) 853-8001
Fax: (53) 853-8800
E-mail: webmaster@kiu.ac.kr
Internet: www.kyungil.ac.kr
Founded 1963 as Technical High School attached to Chunggu College; renamed Jr Technical College attached to Yeungnam Univ. 1967; separated from Yeungnam Univ. as Yeungnam Jr Technical College 1975; renamed Kyungpook Jr Technical College 1976; renamed Kyungpook Jr College of Technology 1978; became Kyungpook Open Univ. 1985; renamed Kyungpook Sanup Univ. 1988; became Kyungil Univ. 1997
Private control
Academic year: March to December
Pres.: LEE NAM-KYO
Dir for Gen. Affairs: KIM JONG-SEOK
Dir of the Office for Planning and Devt: LEE WEON-SIK
Chief Librarian: PARK HA-YONG
Number of teachers: 250
Number of students: 10,000

DEANS

College of Engineering: YOON MYUNG-JIN
College of Formative Arts: KIM JUNG-WON
College of Humanities and Social Sciences: ANH YOOL-CHONG
College of Information Technology: KIM LEE-KOK
Graduate School: KIM JIN-HO
Graduate School of Design: KIM JIN-HO
Graduate School of Industry: KIM JIN-HO
School of General Education: SUH BO-GUN

KYUNGNAM UNIVERSITY

449 Wolyoung-dong, Masan, Kyungnam, Seoul 631-701
Telephone: (55) 245-5000
Fax: (55) 246-6184
E-mail: aadm@kyungnam.ac.kr

Internet: www.kyungnam.ac.kr
Founded 1946
Private control
Pres.: Dr PARK JAE KYU
Registrar: Dr YANG JAE IN
Librarian: Dr YOUN DOCK JOUNG
Library of 537,887 vols
Number of teachers: 674
Number of students: 15,000

DEANS

College of Arts: Dr CHO JIN KI
College of Business Administration: Dr KOH HYUN WOOK
College of Education: Dr LEE SEOK ZOO
College of Engineering: Dr LEE SOO HEUM
College of Law and Political Science: Dr RA KYUNG SIK
College of Science: Dr LEE SUE DAE
Graduate School: Dr CHONG CHOONG KYUN

KYUNGSUNG UNIVERSITY

110-1 Daeyeon-dong, Nam-gu, Pusan 608-736
Telephone: (51) 620-4114
E-mail: www@www.ks.ac.kr
Internet: kyungsung.ac.kr
Founded 1955
Chair.: KIM DAE-SEONG
Pres.: KYUNG MOON-PARK
Library of 500,000 vols
Number of students: 12,000
Colleges of Liberal Arts, Law and Political Science, Commerce and Economics, Science, Engineering, Pharmacy, Arts, Theology, Multimedia; Graduate Schools of International Business, Multimedia, Social Welfare, Education, Clinical Pharmacology, Digital Design.

KYUNGWON UNIVERSITY

San 65 Bokjeong-dong, Sujeong-gu, Seongnam, Gyeonggi-do 461-701
Telephone: (31) 750-5901
E-mail: webmaster@kyungwon.ac.kr
Internet: www.kyungwon.ac.kr
Founded 1982
Chair.: MEN JEONG GWANG-MO
Pres.: LEE GIL-YA
Number of teachers: 165
Number of students: 8,609
Colleges of Humanities, Business and Economics, Law and Science, Engineering, Natural Science, Software, Arts, Music, Oriental Medicine, Human Ecology.

MOKWON UNIVERSITY

Doan-dong 800, Seo-ku, Taejon 302-729
Telephone: (42) 829-7114
Fax: (42) 825-5020
E-mail: webmaster@mokwon.ac.kr
Internet: www.mokwon.ac.kr
Founded 1954
Pres.: KEUN JOHN LYU
Library of 340,000 vols
Colleges of Theology, Humanities, Natural Sciences, Engineering, Social Sciences, Music, Fine Arts.

POHANG UNIVERSITY OF SCIENCE AND TECHNOLOGY

San 31, Hyoja-dong, Nam-gu, Pohang, Gyungbuk, Seoul 790-784
Telephone: (54) 279-0114
Fax: (54) 279-2099
E-mail: webmaster@postech.edu
Internet: www.postech.ac.kr

Founded 1986
Academic year: March to January
Pres.: Prof. SUNGGI BAIK
Vice-Pres.: Prof. IN-SIK NAM
Dean of Policy and Planning (Int. Affairs): Prof. YUSHIN HONG
Number of teachers: 243
Number of students: 3,097 (1,360 undergraduate, 1,737 postgraduate)

PUSAN UNIVERSITY OF FOREIGN STUDIES

55-1 Uan-dong, Nam-gu, Pusan 608-738
Telephone: (51) 640-3000
Fax: (51) 645-4525
E-mail: webmaster@www.pufs.ac.kr
Internet: www.pufs.ac.kr
Library of 320,000 vols
Colleges of Occidental Studies, Oriental Studies, Humanities and Social Sciences, Commerce and Business, Information and Sciences, Leisure Sports Studies.

SANGJI UNIVERSITY

660 Woosan-dong, Wonju, Kangwon-do
Telephone: (371) 730-0182
Fax: (371) 730-0128
E-mail: webmaster@mail.sangji.ac.kr
Internet: www.sangji.ac.kr
Founded 1962
Pres.: Dr SUNG-HOON KIM
Number of teachers: 473
Colleges of Humanities and Social Sciences, Life Science and Natural Resources, Oriental Medicine, Science and Engineering, Economics and Business Administration, Art and Sports.

SANGMYUNG UNIVERSITY

20 Samjidong 2nd St, Jongno-gu, Seoul 110-743
Telephone: (2) 2287-5196
Fax: (2) 2287-0017
E-mail: secint@smu.ac.kr
Internet: www.smu.ac.kr
Founded 1965
Private control
Academic year: March to September
Pres.: Prof. HYUNCHONG LEE
Vice-Pres. for Cheonan Campus: JAEKEUN LEE
Vice-Pres. for Seoul Campus: EHUNGGI BACK
Vice-Pres. for Planning and Coordination: KEEHEON GOO
Vice-Pres. for Industry and Academic Cooperation: KYOUNGYUL BAE
Library of 500,000 books, 4,000 vols of periodicals
Number of teachers: 330
Number of students: 14,064 (12,719 undergraduate, 1,345 postgraduate)

DEANS

College of Arts: SANGKYU PARK
College of Arts and Physical Education: Prof. INSOO YOO
College of Business: HEETAK KIM
College of Convergence: JINHWAN LEE
College of Design: HAESOOK KWON
College of Education: KWONBAE MOON
College of Engineering: BEUMJUN AHN
College of Humanities and Social Sciences: SEONGHO OH
College of Industry: DOOCHEOL KIM
College of Language and Literature: YEUNGSHIM WOO
College of Music: JOONMO DONG
College of Natural Sciences: MINSUN LEE
College of Software: HYUKSOO HAN

SEJONG UNIVERSITY

98 Kunja-dong, Kwangjin-gu, Seoul
Telephone: (2) 3408-3499
Fax: (2) 3408-3561
E-mail: semyaje@sejong.ac.kr
Internet: sejong.ac.kr
Founded 1947
President: Dr CHUL-SU KIM
Vice-Presidents: Dr SUK-MO KOO (Academic Affairs, and Provost), Dr HYUN-JU SHIN (International Programmes and Christian Ministry), YOUNG-HWAN CHOI (Research and Development)
Dean of Academic Affairs: Dr YONG-U SOK
Dean of Student Support: Dr EUI-JANG KO
Dean of Finance: KWANG-HO PARK
Dean of Admissions and Planning: Dr JA-MO KANG
Number of students: 7,337

DEANS

College of Business Administration: Dr SOO-SUP SONG
College of Engineering: Dr HOON-IL OH
College of Liberal Arts: Dr CHON-SUN IHM
College of Music, Fine Arts and Physical Education: Dr DUCK-BOON LEE
College of Natural Sciences: Dr SUNG-CHUNG AN
College of Social Sciences: Dr KI-SANG LEE
College of Tourism: Dr SO-YOON CHO
Graduate School: Dr YANG-JA YOO
Graduate School of Business: Dr B. J. YANG
Graduate School of Education: Dr HYUN-WOOK NAM
Graduate School of Information and Communication: Dr JOUNG-WON KIM
Graduate School of Mass Communication: DON-SHIK CHOO
Graduate School of Public Administration: Dr KYUNG-SHIK JOO
Graduate School of Tourism: Dr CHOL-YONG KIM

SEOKYEONG UNIVERSITY

16-1 Jungneung-dong, Sungbuk-ku, Seoul 136-704
Telephone: (2) 940-7114
Fax: (2) 919-0345
E-mail: webadmin@bukak.seokyeong.ac.kr
Internet: www.seokyeong.ac.kr
Founded 1947
Pres.: CHUL-SOO HAN
Colleges of Humanities, Social Sciences, Natural Science and Engineering, Arts.

SEOUL THEOLOGICAL UNIVERSITY

Kyungki-do, Buchon City
E-mail: admin@stui.net
Internet: www.stu.ac.kr
Founded 1911
President: JOSEPH JONG JIN CHOE
Departments of Theology, Christian Education, Social Welfare, Church Music, Mission English, Childcare, Education.

SEOUL WOMEN'S UNIVERSITY

126 Kongnung 2-dong, Nowon-gu, Seoul 139-144
Telephone: (2) 970-5114
Fax: (2) 978-7931
E-mail: webmaster@mail.swu.ac.kr
Internet: www.swu.ac.kr
Founded 1961
Private control
Academic year: March to February
President: Dr KWANG-JA LEE
Dean of Academic Affairs: Dr KI SUK PARK
Dean of Student Affairs: Dr JU HAN PARK

Dean of General Affairs: Dr HEI JUNG CHUN
Dean of Planning and Budget: Dr EON HO CHOI
Chief Librarian: Dr ON ZA PARK
Number of teachers: 136
Number of students: 5,911
Publications: *Journal of Art and Design* (1 a year), *Journal of Child Studies* (1 a year), *Journal of Student Guidance and Counselling* (1 a year), *Journal of Women's Studies* (1 a year), *Journal of the Graduate School Seoul Women's University* (1 a year), *Journal of the Institute of Humanities* (1 a year), *Journal of the Natural Science Institute* (1 a year), *Journal of the Social Science Research Institute* (1 a year), *Seoul Women's University News* (26 a year)

DEANS

College of Humanities: Prof. YOUNG CHUL LEE
College of Information and Communication: Dr MOON HEE KANG
College of Natural Sciences: Dr JONG SUK LEE
College of Social Sciences: Dr MOON HEE KANG
Division of Fine Arts: Prof. BOK HEE CHEON

SEOWON UNIVERSITY

231 Mochung-dong, Hongduk-ku, Cheongju 361-742
Telephone: (43) 299-8114
Fax: (43) 283-8822
Internet: www.seowon.ac.kr
Founded 1968
Number of teachers: 506
Number of students: 8,760
Colleges of Art, Education, Liberal Arts, Social Sciences, Natural Sciences.

SILLA UNIVERSITY

617-736 San 1-1 Gwaebop-dong, Sasang-gu, Busan
Telephone: (51) 999-5000
E-mail: webadm@silla.ac.kr
Internet: silla.ac.kr
Chair.: HAE-GON PARK
Pres.: BYUNG-HWA LEE
Colleges of Humanities and Social Sciences, Economics and Business Administration, Natural Sciences, Engineering, Information Technology Design, Education, Arts.

SOGANG UNIVERSITY

CPO 1142, Seoul 100-611
Telephone: (2) 705-8114
Fax: (2) 705-8119
E-mail: interrel@sogang.ac.kr
Internet: www.sogang.ac.kr
Founded 1960
Private control
Languages of instruction: Korean, English
Academic year: March to December (2 semesters)
Pres.: CHANG-SUP CHOI (acting)
Man. of Academic Affairs: MOON-SEOB YOUM
Man. of Student Affairs: MYEONG-HOON CHEON
Dir of Library: SEOG PARK
Number of teachers: 302
Number of students: 10,900
Publications: *Sogang Hakbo* (52 a year), *Sogang Herald* (12 a year)

DEANS

College of Engineering: YOUNG GOO LEE
College of Humanities: IN CHAI CHUNG
College of Natural Sciences: KWAE HI LEE

College of Social Science: KAP YUN LEE
General Education Division: HEE NAM CHOI
Graduate School: CHUL AN
Graduate School of Business: WOON YOUL CHOI
Graduate School of Economics: YOUNG GOO LEE
Graduate School of Education: JUNG TAEK KIM
Graduate School of Information and Technology: JUNG YUN SEO
Graduate School of International Studies: SE YOUNG AHN
Graduate School of Mass Communication: HAK SOO KIM
Graduate School of Media Communications: KAK YOON
Graduate School of Public Policy: KAP YUN LEE
Graduate School of Theology: TAE SU HA
School of Business Administration: JANG HO LEE
School of Economics: BOK UNG KIM

PROFESSORS

College of Engineering:

AN, C., Electronic Engineering
CHANG, I. S., Electronic Engineering
CHANG, J. H., Computer Science
CHOI, C. S., Chemical Engineering
CHOI, J.-W., Chemical Engineering
CHOI, M., Computer Science
HONG, D.-H., Electronic Engineering
HUR, N., Mechanical Engineering
HWANG, S. Y., Electronic Engineering
IHM, I., Computer Science
JANG, J. W., Electronic Engineering
JEE, Y., Electronic Engineering
JEON, D., Mechanical Engineering
JEONG, S., Mechanical Engineering
KIM, N., Mechanical Engineering
KIM, S. C., Computer Science
KOO, K. K., Chemical and Biomolecular Engineering
LEE, H. Y., Mechanical Engineering
LEE, J. W., Chemical Engineering
LEE, K. H., Electronic Engineering
LEE, K. S., Chemical Engineering
LEE, S. H., Electronic Engineering
LEE, T. S., Mechanical Engineering
NANG, J., Computer Science
OH, K. W., Computer Science
OH, S. Y., Chemical and Biomolecular Engineering
PARK, H. M., Chemical and Biomolecular Engineering
PARK, H. S., Chemical and Biomolecular Engineering
PARK, R. H., Electronic Engineering
PARK, S., Computer Science
RHEE, H. W., Chemical and Biomolecular Engineering
RIM, C. S., Computer Science
SEO, J., Computer Science
YOO, K.-P., Chemical and Biomolecular Engineering
YUN, S. W., Electronic Engineering

College of Humanities:

AN, S. J., English Language and Literature
BAIK, I. H., History
BAK, J. S., French Language and Literature
CHANG, S. N., German Language and Literature
CHANG, Y. H., English Language and Literature
CHO, B. H., History
CHO, S. W., English Language and Literature
CHOI, H.-M., French Language and Literature
CHUNG, D. H., History
CHUNG, I. C., Philosophy
JEONG, Y. I., Korean Language and Literature

KANG, Y. A., Philosophy
KEEL, H. S., Religious Studies
KIM, G., Chinese Culture
KIM, H. G., History
KIM, S. H., Religious Studies
KIM, S. N., Religious Studies
KIM, W. S., Philosophy
KIM, Y. H., History
KIM, Y. S., English Language and Literature
KWAK, C. G., Korean Language and Literature
LEE, J. D., German Language and Literature
LEE, J. W., History
LEE, S. B., English Language and Literature
LIM, S. W., History
PAK, C. T., Philosophy
SEONG, Y., Philosophy
SHIN, K., English Language and Literature
SHIN, S. W., English Language and Literature
SONG, H. S., Korean Language and Literature
SONG, W. Y., German Language and Literature
SPALATIN, C. A., Philosophy
SUH, C. M., Korean Language and Literature
SUNG, H. K., Korean Language and Literature
UM, J., Philosophy

College of Natural Sciences:

CHIN, C. S., Chemistry
CHO, K., Physics
CHO, S. H., Mathematics
CHUNG, D. M., Mathematics
CHUNG, S. Y., Mathematics
HONG, S. S., Mathematics
KANG, J., Chemistry
KIM, D. H., Chemistry
KIM, D. S., Mathematics
KIM, J., Mathematics
KIM, S. R., Life Science
KIM, W. S., Life Science
KIM, W. T., Physics
LEE, B. H., Physics
LEE, D., Chemistry
LEE, H., Chemistry
LEE, J. B., Mathematics
LEE, J. G., Mathematics
LEE, J. K., Life Science
LEE, W. K., Chemistry
PARK, G. S., Physics
PARK, S. A., Mathematics
PARK, S. H., Mathematics
PARK, Y. J., Physics
RHEE, B. K., Physics
SHIN, C. E., Mathematics
SHIN, W., Chemistry
SO, H., Chemistry
YANG, J. M., Life Science
YOON, K. B., Chemistry

College of Social Science:

CHANG, Y. H., Mass Communication
CHO, H., Sociology
CHO, O., Sociology
CHOI, C. S., Mass Communication
CHOI, O. C., Law
CHUNG, H.-J., Law
EOM, D. S., Law
HONG, S. B., Law
KANG, J. I., Political Science
KIM, H. S., Mass Communication
KIM, K. M., Sociology
KIM, Y. S., Political Science
LEE, K. Y., Political Science
OH, B. S., Law
PARK, H. S., Political Science
PARK, S. T., Sociology
SHIN, Y. H., Political Science
SONN, H. C., Political Science
SUH, K. M., Law
YOON, Y. D., Sociology

General Education Division:

CHO, G. H., General Education
CHOI, H. N., General Education
KIM, J.-W., General Education
KIM, O. S., General Education

Graduate School of International Studies:

AHN, S. Y.
CHO, Y. J.

Graduate School of Media Communications:

BYUN, D. H.
JUNG, M.-R.
KIM, C. H.
KIM, Y. Y.
LEE, S. W.
SHIN, H. C.
YOON, K.

Graduate School of Theology:

CHUNG, W. S.
MOON, J. Y.
SIM, J. H.

School of Business Administration:

CHEE, Y. H.
CHOI, J. H.
CHOI, S. J.
CHOI, W. Y.
CHUN, S. B.
HA, Y. W.
JON, J. S.
KANG, H. S.
KIM, S. K.
KOOK, C. P.
LEE, C.
LEE, D. S.
LEE, J. B.
LEE, J. H.
LEE, J. J.
LEE, K. L.
LEE, N. J.
LEE, W. Y.
LIM, C. U.
MIN, J. H.
PARK, K. K.
PARK, N. H.
PARK, Y. S.
RHO, B. H.
SUH, C. J.

School of Economics:

CHO, C. O.
GILL, I. S.
JEON, S. H.
KIM, B. U.
KIM, K. D.
KIM, K. H.
KIM, S. Y.
KWACK, T.
LEE, D. S.
LEE, H. K.
LEE, H. S.
LEE, Y. G.
NAHM, J. W.
NAM, S. I.
SONG, E. Y.
SUH, J. H.
WANG, G. H.

SOOKMYUNG WOMEN'S UNIVERSITY

53-12 Chungpa-dong 2-ka, Yongsan-gu, Seoul 140-742

Telephone: (2) 710-9114
Fax: (2) 718-2337
E-mail: kslee@sookmyung.ac.kr
Internet: www.sookmyung.ac.kr

Founded 1906
Private control
Language of instruction: Korean
Academic year: March to February

Pres.: KYUNG-SOOK LEE
Dean of Academic Affairs: EUN-GYUN MOK
Dean of Student Affairs: YOUNG-SOOK SUH
Dean of Administrative Affairs: CHUN-HAK OH
Dean of Planning: MOO-SEUCK CHO
Library Dir: HEE-JAE LEE

Library of 628,688 vols
Number of teachers: 370
Number of students: 13,315

Publications: *Sookdae Shinbo* (in Korean, 52 a year), *Bulletin* (in English and Korean, 1 a year), *Sookmyung Times* (in English, 12 a year), *Asian Women* (in English)

DEANS

College of Economics and Commerce: WON-BAE YOON
College of Fine Arts: HAK-SEONG KIM
College of Home Economics: SUN-JAE LEE
College of Liberal Arts: JUNG-SHIN HAN
College of Music: MAN-BANG YI
College of Natural Sciences: YOUNG-HEE HONG
College of Pharmacy: AN-KEUN KIM
College of Political Science and Law: SANG-KWANG LEE
Graduate School: JUNG-WOO LEE
Graduate Schools of Special Subjects: SOOK-HEE PARK

SOONGSIL UNIVERSITY

1-1 Sangdo 5-dong, Dongjak-ku, Seoul 156-743

Telephone: (2) 820-0111
Fax: (2) 814-7362
Internet: www.ssu.ac.kr
Founded 1897
Private control
Academic year: March to December

Chancellor: SUN-HEE KWAK
Pres.: YOON-BAE OUH
Vice-Pres. for International Affairs: HAE-SEOK OH
Vice-Pres. for Academic Affairs: BONG-CHUL SEO
Librarian: PYUNG-SYK RO

Library of 367,000 vols
Number of teachers: 586 (252 full-time, 334 part-time)
Number of students: 10,167

DEANS

College of Economics and Commerce: WON-WOO LEE
College of Engineering: MUN-HEON KIM
College of Humanities: HONG-ZIN KIM
College of Information Science: CHUL-HEE LEE
College of Law: SUNG-SOOK KIM
College of Natural Sciences: YOUNG-JA YUN
College of Social Sciences: KWANG-SEOB SHIN

DIRECTORS

Christian Institute of Social Studies: SAM-YEUL LEE
Institute for Adult and Continuing Education: KWANG-MYUNG KIM
Institute of Business and Economic Strategies: DAE-YONG JEONG
Institute of Humanities: HONG-ZIN KIM
Institute of Industrial Technology: YOUNG-PIL KWON
Institute of Korean Christian Culture Research: YOUNG-HAN KIM
Institute of Law: DOO-HWAN KIM
Institute of Natural Sciences: CHONG-IN YU
Institute of Social Science: SOO-EON MOON
Resource Recycling Research Centre: KAP-SOO DOH

SUNGKYUL CHRISTIAN UNIVERSITY

147-2 Anyang 8-dong, Manan-gu, Anyang, Kyungki-do 430-742

Telephone: (343) 467-8114
Internet: www.sungkyul.ac.kr

Founded 1962 as a seminary; present name 1992

Pres.: Dr KEE-HO SUNG
Library of 170,000 vols.

SUNGKYUNKWAN UNIVERSITY

Humanities and Social Sciences Campus: 53 Myongnyun-dong 3-ga, Chongo-gu, Seoul 110-745
Natural Sciences Campus: 300 Chunchun-dong, Changan-gu, Suwon, Kyonggi-do 440-746

Telephone: (2) 760-0114
Fax: (2) 744-2453
E-mail: webmaster@www.skku.ac.kr
Internet: www.skku.ac.kr

Founded 1398; university status 1953
Private control
Academic year: March to February
Chairman of the Board of Trustees: E-HOUCK KWON
Pres.: JUNG DON SEO
Vice-Pres.: CHAE-WOONG LEE (Humanities and Social Sciences Campus), YUN-HEUM PARK (Natural Sciences Campus)
Academic Affairs Officer: HYUK KIM
Librarian: PYUNG-U PARK

Library: 1.4m. vols
Number of teachers: 980
Number of students: 24,098

Publications: *Journal of Eastern Culture* (in Korean, 1 a year), *Journal of Humanities Sciences* (in Korean, 1 a year), *Journal of Human Life Sciences* (in Korean, 1 a year), *Journal of Korean Economics* (1 a year), *Journal of Modern China* (in Korean, 1 a year), *Journal of Social Sciences* (in Korean, 1 a year), *Learned Papers in Science and Technology* (in Korean, 2 a year), *Learned Papers in the Natural Sciences* (in Korean, 2 a year), *Sung Kyun Law Review* (in Korean, 2 a year), *Suson Learned Papers* (in Korean, 1 a year)

DEANS
College of Education: YOUNG-EUN CHIN
College of Law: KYU-SANG JUNG
School of Architecture, Landscape Architecture and Civil Engineering: SANG-HAE CHOI
School of Art: HAK-SUN LIM
School of Business Administration: YOUNG-KYU KIM
School of Chemical, Polymer and Textile Engineering: BOONG-SOO JEON
School of Confucian and Oriental Studies: YOUNG-JIN CHOI
School of Economics: SUNG-SOON LEE
School of Electrical and Computer Engineering: CHIL-GEE LEE
School of Humanities: HAN-GU LEE
School of Human Life Sciences: YANG-HEE LEE
School of Language and Literature: BONG-WON CHOI
School of Life Sciences and Technology: KYU-SEUNG LEE
School of Mechanical Engineering: HYUN-SOO KIM
School of Medicine: DAY-YONG UHM
School of Metallurgical and Materials Engineering: JOEN-GEON HAN
School of Natural Sciences: SANG-TAE LEE
School of Pharmacy: WON-HUN HAM
School of Social Sciences: CHANG-SOO CHUNG
School of Sports Science: EUNG-NAM AHM
School of Systems Management Engineering: HOO-GON CHOI

SUNGSHIN WOMEN'S UNIVERSITY

249-1 Dongseon-dong 3-ga, Seongbuk-do, Seoul 136-742

Telephone: (2) 920-7114
E-mail: www@cc.sungshin.ac.kr
Internet: www.sungshin.ac.kr

Founded 1936
Library of 500,000 vols
Number of students: 13,000
Colleges of arts, education, human ecology, humanities, music, natural sciences, social sciences.

UNIVERSITY OF ULSAN

POB 18, Ulsan, Seoul 680-049

Telephone: (52) 277-3101
Fax: (52) 277-3419
E-mail: webmaster@mail.ulsan.ac.kr
Internet: uou.ulsan.ac.kr

Founded 1970
Private control
Academic year: March to December
Chair.: MONG-JOON CHUNG
Pres.: CHUNG-KIL CHUNG
Head of Academic Information Centre: Prof. JEONG-SEOK HEO

Library of 700,000 books, 909 periodicals
Number of teachers: 723
Number of students: 11,659 (6,121 undergraduate, 5,538 postgraduate)

DEANS
College of Business Administration: HI-KYOON LEE
College of Design: SANG-HYE HAN
College of Engineering: DONG-KEE LEE
College of Fine Arts: PYUNG-HUI PARK
College of Human Ecology: HYE-KYUNG KIM
College of Humanities: CHUNG-HOO SUH
College of Industry and Management: KYU-CHO LEE
College of Medicine: WON-DONG KIM
College of Music: HYUN-KYUNG CHAE
College of Natural Sciences: TAE-SOO KIM
College of Social Sciences: YEON-JAE SHIN
Graduate School: KANG-MOON KOH
Graduate School of Business Administration: JOONG-HEON NAM
Graduate School of Education: MYEUNG-HAK YANG
Graduate School of Industrial Technology: SEONG-DEUK KIM I
Graduate School of Information and Communications Technology: KYUNG-SUP PARK
Graduate School of Regional Development: WOO-SUNG KIM

WON KWANG UNIVERSITY

344-2 Shinyong-dong, Iksan, Jeonbuk, Seoul 570-749

Telephone: (63) 850-5114
Fax: (63) 850-6666
Internet: www.wonkwang.ac.kr

Founded 1946
Private control
Academic year: March to August, September to February

Pres.: GAB-WOEN JEONG
Vice-Pres. for Academy: SONG CHON-EUN
Vice-Pres. for Medicine: CHON PAL-KHN
Dean of Academic Affairs: GO GUN-IL
Dean of Planning Office: CHOI SEONG-SIK
Dean of Student Affairs: KIM JONG-SU
Dean of Financial and General Affairs: OH HAE-GEUM
Dir of Library: LEE MAN-SANG

Number of teachers: 462
Number of students: 23,200

DEANS
College of Agriculture: LEE KAP-SANG
College of Dentistry: KIM SU-NAM
College of Education: SHIN YO-YOUNG
College of Engineering: CHUNG SA-HEE
College of Home Economics: MOON BUM-SOO
College of Law: KIM DAE-KYOO

College of Liberal Arts and Sciences: OHM JEONG-OAK
College of Management: PARK JAE-ROK
College of Oriental Medicine: MAENG UNG-JAEO
College of Pharmacy: OCK CHI-WAN
College of Social Sciences: KIM GUY-KON
College of Won Buddhism: KIM HONG-CHULO
Graduate School: YU GI-SU
Graduate School of Education: YU JAE-YEONG
Graduate School of Industry: YUN YANG-WOONG
School of Medicine: CHUNG YEUN-TAI

YEUNGNAM UNIVERSITY

Gyongsan 632, Taegu

Telephone: (53) 810-2114
Fax: (53) 810-2036
E-mail: webadmin@yu.ac.kr
Internet: www.yu.ac.kr

Founded 1967 by amalgamation of Taegu College and Chunggu College
Private control
Academic year: March to February (2 semesters)

Pres.: Dr LEW JOON
Dean of Academic Affairs: Dr PARK BONG MOK
Dean of Student Affairs: Dr KIM JUNG YUEP
Dean of Business Affairs: Dr PARK SUNG KYU
Dean of Planning and Development: Dr YOON BYUNG TAE
Dir of Library: Dr OH MYUNG-KUN

Library of 398,690 vols
Number of teachers: 549
Number of students: 22,506

Publications: *Library Guide*, *Student Guide* (1 a year), *Yeungdae Munha* (Yeungnam University Culture), *Yeungnam University Theses Collection*, and various faculty and institutional publs

DEANS
College of Agriculture and Animal Sciences: SYE YOUNG-SYEK
College of Commerce and Economics: RYU CHANG OU
College of Education: SONG BYUNG SOON
College of Engineering: LEE DONG IN
College of Fine Arts: HONG SUNG MOON
College of Home Economics: LEE KAP RANG
College of Law and Political Science: RHEE CHANGWOO
College of Liberal Arts: KIM TAIK-KYOO
College of Medicine: KIM WON JOON
College of Music: KIM SHIN WHAN
College of Pharmacy: SEO BYEONG CHEON
College of Science: KIM JONG DAE
Evening College: BYUN JAE-OCK
Graduate School: KIM HOGWON
Graduate School of Business Administration: KIM KIE-TAEK
Graduate School of Education: CHUNG SOON MOK
Graduate School of Environmental Studies: JIN KAP DUCK

PROFESSORS
College of Agriculture and Animal Sciences:
BYUN, J. K., Horticulture
CHOI, C., Food Technology and Science
CHUNG, H. D., Horticulture
CHUNG, Y. G., Food Science and Technology
JUNG, K. J., Animal Science
KIM, B. D., Community Development
KIM, J. K., Applied Microbiology
LEE, H. C., Animal Science
PARK, C. H., Agronomy
SON, J. Y., Animal Science
SYE, Y. S., Animal Science
YOON, W., Community Development

College of Commerce and Economics:

Bae, Y. S., Economics
Har, C. D., Business Policy
Kim, J. H., Foreign Trade
Kim, K.-T., Economics
Kim, T. W., Business Administration
Kwon, B. T., Economics
Lee, W.-D., Economics
Park, S.-K., Business Administration
Ryu, C. O., Foreign Trade
Sang, M. D., Business Administration
Shin, H. J., International Theory and Policy
Yi, Y. W., Economics
Yoon, I. H., Economics
Yu, H. K., Economics

College of Education:

Ahn, Y. T., Business Education
Baek, U. H., Developmental Psychology
Cho, D. B., Personality and Education
Chun, B. K., Audiovisual Method
Chung, S. M., History of Korean Education
Chung, Y. K., Linguistics
Kim, H., Evaluation
Kim, J. R., Physical Education
Kwon, J. W., Educational Psychology
Lee, J. H., Physical Education
Lee, K. T., English Language Education
Lee, S. B., Mathematics Education
Lim, M. S., Physical Education
Park, B. M., Philosophy of Education
Park, Y. B., Curriculum and Instruction
Song, B. S., Educational Psychology

College of Engineering:

Bae, J. H., Electrical Engineering
Byun, D. K., Civil Engineering
Chang, D. H., Textile Engineering
Cho, B., Chemical Engineering
Cho, H., Textile Engineering
Choi, S.-G., Electronic Engineering
Choi, S.-H., Mechanical Design
Chung, K.-H., Eletronic Engineering
Chung, W.-G., Textile Engineering
Ha, Z.-H., Mechanical Engineering
Joo, H., System Engineering
Kang, S. H., Chemical Engineering
Kim, D. O., Traffic Engineering
Kim, G.-C., Civil Engineering
Kim, H. S., Architectural Engineering
Kim, I.-J., Architectural Engineering
Kim, J. Y., Mechanical Engineering
Kim, K. S., Industrial Chemistry
Kim, S.-K., Textile Engineering
Lee, D. H., Control Engineering
Lee, D.-I., Electrical Engineering
Lee, J. H., Industrial Chemistry
Lee, K. S., Mechanical Engineering
Lee, M. H., Industrial Chemistry
Lee, M. Y., Electronic Communication
Lee, S. T., Civil Engineering
Lee, T.-S., Marine Engineering
Park, J. Y., Civil Engineering
Park, W.-K., Chemical Engineering
Park, Y. C., Industrial Chemistry
Ro, C. K., Electrical Engineering
Ro, H. J., Architectural Engineering
Sohn, Y. K., Computer Engineering
Song, J. S., Textile Engineering
Um, W.-T., Urban Engineering
Wu, M. J., Civil Engineering

College of Fine Arts:

Hong, S. M., Sculpture
Kim, Y. Z., Painting

College of Home Economics:

Cho, S. Y., Food and Nutrition
Han, J. S., Food Preparation
Kim, K. S., Food Science
Lee, J. O., Clothing Science
Lee, J. S., Home Management
Lee, K. R., Food and Nutrition
Park, J. R., Food Science

College of Law and Political Science:

Byun, J.-O., Constitutional and Administrative Law
Chang, T.-O., Public Administration
Cheung, W. J., International Law
Cho, C.-H., Civil Law
Choi, J.-C., Public Administration
Kim, J.-S., Public Administration
Kim, K.-D., Civil Law
Kwon, H. K., Political Science and Diplomacy
Lee, W. S., Political Science and Diplomacy
Paik, S. K., Public Administration
Park, S.-W., Criminal Law
Rhee, C.-W., Political Science and Diplomacy
Yoon, B. T., Public Administration

College of Liberal Arts:

Chae, S. H., Buddhist Philosophy
Chang, H. K., Psychology
Cho, K.-S., Korean Language and Literature
Chung, Y. W., Archaeology
Hu, J. W., Western Philosophy
Huh, C. Y., European History
Hwang, S.-M., English and Linguistics
Kewn, S.-H., English Drama
Kim, B. K., Western Philosophy
Kim, C. S., Korean Language and Literature
Kim, S. H., English Novels
Kim, S. J., Korean History
Kim, S. K., English Literature
Kim, S. M., English Poetry
Kim, T. K., Anthropology
Kim, W.-W., English Poetry
Kwon, Y. G., English Language and Literature
Lee, B. J., Asian History
Lee, B. L., Korean Language and Literature
Lee, C. H., Western Philosophy
Lee, J. W., Chinese Prose, Phonology
Lee, S.-D., English Poetry
Lee, S. K., Korean History
Lee, S.-T., English Literature
Lee, W. J., Philosophy
Lee, Y. K., Philosophy of History, Social Philosophy
Lim, B.-J., French Language
Mun, C.-B., English Philosophy
O, S. C., Korean History
Oh, M.-K., Sociology
Suh, I., American Literature
Suh, K. B., Chinese Poetry
Yoh, K. K., English Language
Youn, Y.-O., Korean Literature

College of Medicine:

Chung, J. H., Preventive Medicine
Chung, J. K., Microbiology
Chung, W. Y., Obstetrics and Gynaecology
Hah, Y. M., Dermatology
Hahn, D. K., Ophthalmology
Ham, D. S., Anatomy
Ihin, J. C., Orthopaedic Surgery
Kim, C. S., Internal Medicine
Kim, C. S., Pathology
Kim, S. H., General Surgery
Kim, W. J., Pharmacology
Kwun, K. B., General Surgery
Lee, S. K., Physiology
Lee, T. S., Pathology
Lee, Y. C., Anatomy
Park, C. S., Neurology
Song, K. W., Otorhinolaryngology

College of Music:

Kim, S. W., Vocal Music

College of Pharmacy:

Chang, U. K., Pharmacy
Chung, K. C., Pharmacy
Chung, S. R., Pharmacy
Do, J. C., Industrial Pharmacy
Han, B. S., Industrial Pharmacy

Huh, K., Pharmacy
Jin, K. D., Pharmacy
Kim, J. Y., Industrial Pharmacy
Lee, M. K., Industrial Pharmacy
Lee, S. W., Pharmacology
Seoh, B. C., Industrial Pharmacy

College of Science:

Chang, G. S., Physics
Chang, K., Mathematics
Cho, H. S., Physics
Cho, Y., Mathematics
Choe, O.-S., Physics
Doh, M. K., Inorganic Chemistry
Kang, S. G., Physics
Kim, D. S., Analytical Chemistry
Kim, J.-C., Mathematics
Kim, J. D., Organic Chemistry
Kim, M. M., Physics
Kim, Y. H., Physics
Pahk, G.-H., Mathematics
Park, B. K., Physical Chemistry
Park, H.-S., Mathematics
Park, W. H., Biology
Ro, H. K., Physics
Woo, J., Statistics

YONSEI UNIVERSITY

Room 217B Baekyang Hall, 262 Seongsanno, Seodaemun-gu, Seoul 120-749

Telephone: (2) 2123-3488
Fax: (2) 2123-8636
E-mail: oia@yonsei.ac.kr
Internet: www.yonsei.ac.kr

Founded 1885
Private control
Languages of instruction: Korean, English
Academic year: March to February (2 semesters)

Pres.: Han-joong Kim
Vice-Pres. for Academic Affairs: Kyung-duck Min
Vice-Pres. for External Affairs and Alumni: Han-joong Kim
Vice-Pres. for Medical Affairs: Jin-kyung Kang
Vice-Pres. for Wonju Campus: Dai-woon Lee
Dir of University Planning and Public Relations: In-ki Joo
Dean of Academic Affairs: Hi-soo Moon
Dean of Admissions: Yong-hak Kim
Dean of Student Affairs and Services: Tae-seung Paik
Dir of General Affairs: Hyuk-geun Choi
Dir of the Central Library: Young-soo Shin

Library: see Libraries and Archives
Number of teachers: 3,324
Number of students: 28,409

Publications: *Abstracts of Faculty Research Reports, Business Review, Engineering Review, Focus on Genetic Science, Global Economic Review, Infection Control Newsletter, Korean Journal of Nursing Questions, Journal of East and West Studies, Journal of Far Eastern Studies, Journal of Education Science, Journal of Engineering Research, Journal of Humanities, Journal of Korean Informatics, Journal of Korean Studies, Journal of Medical Technology, Journal of Nursing Science, Journal of the Radio Communication Research Centre, Journal of the Institute of Basic Science, Journal of the Natural Science Research Institute, Journal of the Research Institute of ASIC Design, Journal of the Research Institute of Information and Telecommunications, Journal of the Yonsei Institute for Cancer Research, Korean Journal of Health Science, New Energy and Environmental Systems, Social Science Review, Theological Forum, Theology and Modern Times, Tropical Medicine News, Yonsei Annals, Yonsei Biochemistry, Yonsei Chunchu, Yonsei Communication, Yonsei*

Economics Review, Yonsei Engineering Magazine, Yonsei Journal of Social Science, Yonsei Law Journal, Yonsei Law Review, Yonsei Health Science, Yonsei Journal of Clinical Orthodontics, Yonsei Journal of Dental Science, Yonsei Journal of Human Ecology, Yonsei Journal of Language and Literature, Yonsei Journal of Medical Education, Yonsei Journal of Medical History, Yonsei Journal of Public Administration, Yonsei Journal of Sport and Leisure Studies, Yonsei Journal of Women's Studies, Yonsei Medical Journal, Yonsei Non-Chong, Yonsei Nursing Journal, Yonsei Philosophy Review, Yonsei Review of Educational Research, Yonsei Review of Theology and Culture, Yonsei Social Welfare Review, Yonsei Unification Studies, Yonsei University Counselling Centre Research Review

DEANS

College of Business and Economics: SUNG-KUN HA
College of Dentistry: MOON KYU CHUNG
College of Engineering: DAE-HEE YOON
College of Government and Business: PYEONG-JUN YU
College of Health Sciences: SOO-HONG NOH
College of Human Ecology: YOUNG LEE
College of Humanities and Arts: (vacant)
College of Law: SANG-KI PARK
College of Liberal Arts: YOUNG MEE CHUNG
College of Life Science and Biotechnology: (vacant)
College of Medicine: NAM-SIK CHUNG
College of Music: MYUNG-JA CHO
College of Nursing: SO YA JA KIM
College of Science: YOUNG-MIN KIM
College of Science and Technology: (vacant)
College of Sciences in Education: INTACK OH
College of Social Sciences: WOO-SUH PARK
College of Theology: YANG-HO LEE
Graduate School: TAE-YOUNG LEE
Yonsei School of Business: SANG YONG PARK
Graduate School of Communication and Arts: YOUNG-SEOK KIM
Graduate School of Economics: SUNG-KUN HA
Graduate School of Education: SANG-WAN HAN
Graduate School of Engineering: JINHO LEE
Graduate School of Government and Business: KYUNG-SIHK AHN
Graduate School of Health and Environment: SOO-HONG NOH
Graduate School of Human Environmental Science: CHUNG-SOOK YOON
Graduate School of Information: KAP-YOUNG JEONG
Graduate School of International Studies: CHUNG MIN LEE
Graduate School of Journalism and Mass Communication: YANG-SOO CHOI
Yonsei Law School: HYUN YOON SHIN
Graduate School of Nursing: SO YA JA KIM
Graduate School of Public Administration: MYUNG-SOON SHIN
Graduate School of Public Health: P. H. OHRR HEECHOUL
Graduate School of Social Welfare: JAE-YOP KIM
United Graduate School of Theology: YANG-HO LEE
EastAsia Int. College: INSUNG LEE
Underwood Int. College: JUNG HOON LEE
University College: KYUNG-CHAN MIN
Wonju College of Medicine: SEONG-JOON KANG

PUBLIC UNIVERSITIES OF EDUCATION

CHEONGJU NATIONAL UNIVERSITY OF EDUCATION

135 Sugok-dong, Heung Duk-gu, Cheongju, Chungbuk 361-712
Telephone: (43) 279-0800
Fax: (43) 279-0797
Internet: www.chongju-e.ac.kr
Founded 1941
Pres.: YONG-WOO LIM
Library of 100,000 vols
Departments of Ethics Education, Korean Education, Social Studies, Mathematics, Science, Physical Education, Music, Fine Arts, Practical Arts; Graduate School of Education.

DAEGU NATIONAL UNIVERSITY OF EDUCATION

1797-6 Daemyung 2-dong, Namgu, Daegu, Seoul
Telephone: (53) 620-1114
Fax: (53) 651-5369
E-mail: abc@dnue.ac.kr
Internet: www.dnue.ac.kr
Founded 1950
Teacher-training univ.
Pres.: SOHN SEOKRAK
Number of teachers: 112
Number of students: 3,512 (2,775 undergraduates, 737 graduates)

KOREA NATIONAL UNIVERSITY OF EDUCATION

7 Darak-ri, Kangnae-myon, Chongwon-gun, Chungbuk, Seoul 363-791
Telephone: (43) 230-3114
Fax: (43) 233-2207
E-mail: internat@knuecc-sun.knue.ac.kr
Internet: www.knue.ac.kr
Founded 1984
Pres.: PARK BAE-HUN
Library of 300,000 vols
Number of teachers: 331
Number of students: 6,060

PUSAN NATIONAL UNIVERSITY OF EDUCATION

Pusan
Internet: www.pusan-e.ac.kr
Founded 1946 as Pusan Normal School; became Pusan Teachers' College 1955 and Pusan College of Education 1961; name reverted to Pusan Teachers' College 1963; present name 1993
President: Dr CHI-YUL OK.

SEOUL NATIONAL UNIVERSITY OF EDUCATION

Seocho-dong 1650, Seocho-gu, Seoul 137-742
E-mail: center@snue.ac.kr
Internet: www.snue.ac.kr
Founded 1945
Pres.: KWANG-YONG SONG.

PUBLIC UNIVERSITIES OF TECHNOLOGY

CHUNGJU NATIONAL UNIVERSITY

72 Daehak-ro, Chungju-si, Chungbuk 380-702
Telephone: (43) 841-5011
Fax: (43) 841-5017
Internet: www.chungju.ac.kr
Founded 1962 as Chungju Techincal Junior College, present status in 1999
Public Control
Pres.: Dr JANG BYUNG-JIB
Number of teachers: 295
Number of students: 8,200
Campuses in Chungju and Jeungpyeong

Colleges of Advanced Science and Technology, Engineering, Humanities, Social Sciences and Fine Arts, Health, Biology and Aeronautical Engineering; Graduate Schools of Business Administration, Public Administration and Foreign Languages, Industry; Division of Liberal Arts.

HANKYONG NATIONAL UNIVERSITY

67 Sukjong-dong, Ansung-City, Kyonggi-do, Seoul 456-749
Telephone: (31) 670-5114
Fax: (31) 673-2704
E-mail: master@hnu.hankyong.ac.kr
Internet: www.hankyong.ac.kr
Founded 1939
State control
Academic year: March to February
Pres.: Dr KIM SUNG-JIN
Dir of the Office for Academic Affairs: CHOE Il-SHIN
Dir of the Office of Gen. Affairs: LEE JONG-NAM
Dir of the Office of Strategy Dept: RYU HO-SANG
Dir of the Office of Student Affairs: AN JAE-HO
Library Dir: YOU SHI-GYUN
Library of 82,000 books, 175 periodicals
Number of teachers: 458
Number of students: 7,718 (7,558 undergraduate, 160 postgraduate)

DEANS

College of Agriculture and Life Science: KIM YOUNG-HO
College of Humanities and Social Sciences: HONG WAN-PYO
College of Science and Engineering: LEE HAK-YOUNG
Graduate School of Industry: RHEE SONG-KAP

JINJU NATIONAL UNIVERSITY

150 Chilamdong, Jinju, Kyongnam, Seoul 660-758
Telephone: (55) 751-3114
Fax: (55) 752-9554
Internet: www.chinju.ac.kr
Founded 1910
Pres.: JUNG HAE-JU
Colleges of Agriculture, Science and Engineering, Humanities and Social Services.

KUMOH NATIONAL UNIVERSITY OF TECHNOLOGY

Sanho-to 77 (Yangho-dong), Gumi, Gyeongbuk, Seoul 730-701
Telephone: (54) 478-7114
Fax: (54) 478-7100
Internet: www.kumoh.ac.kr
Founded 1979 as Kumoh Institute of Technology; became Kumoh Nat. Institute of Technology 1990; present name 1993
Pres.: Dr HWAN CHOI.

MIRYANG NATIONAL UNIVERSITY

1025-1 Naei-dong, Miryang, Kyungnam 627-702
Telephone: (527) 354-3181
Fax: (527) 355-3186
E-mail: sdlee@arang.miryang.ac.kr
Internet: www.miryang.ac.kr
Founded 1923 as a public school of agricultural sericulture
President: TAE-KIL CHOI

DEANS AND CHAIRMEN

Graduate School: YON-GYU PARK
School of Architecture: KANG-GEUN PARK

School of Computer, Information and Communication Engineering: SUN-JONG KIM
School of Food Science and Environmental Engineering: DONG-SEOP KIM
School of Materials Engineering: SU-CHAK RYU

SAMCHOK NATIONAL UNIVERSITY

253 Gyodong, Samchok, Kangwon-do, Seoul 245-080

Telephone: (397) 572-8611
Fax: (397) 572-8620
E-mail: webadmin@samchok.ac.kr
Internet: www.samchok.ac.kr

Founded 1939 as Samchok Public Vocational School; became Samchok Public Industrial School 1944, Samchok Public Industrial Middle School 1946 and Samchok Industrial High School 1950; present name 1991

Pres.: Dr TAE-YUN CHANG.

SANGJU NATIONAL UNIVERSITY

Sangju, Gyeongsangbuk-do
E-mail: jkang@sangju.ac.kr
Internet: www.sangju.ac.kr

Founded 1921
Public

Pres.: KIM JONG-HO

Number of teachers: 104
Number of students: 4,350

PRIVATE UNIVERSITIES OF TECHNOLOGY

CHODANG UNIVERSITY

419 Muan-goon, Muan-eup, Seonnam-ree, Jeonnam, Seoul 534-701

Telephone: (61) 450-1012
E-mail: president@chodang.ac.kr
Internet: www.chodang.ac.kr

Founded 1979
Private

Pres.: JIN-YOUNG NOH

Colleges of Arts and Physical Education, Humanities and Social Sciences, Science and Engineering; Graduate Divisions of Business and Public Admin., Computer and Information Engineering, Culinary Arts, Environmental Engineering, Information Design, Nursing Science, Ophthalmic Optics, Social Welfare, Social Physical Education.

HANKUK AVIATION UNIVERSITY

100, Hanggongdae gil, Hwajeon-dong, Gyeonggi-do Goyang City, Seoul 412-791

Telephone: (2) 300-0114
Fax: (2) 3158-5769
Internet: www.hangkong.ac.kr

Founded 1952 as National Aviation College; became Hankuk Aviation College 1968

Pres.: YUH JUNKU
Dean of Academic Affairs: LEE YEONG-HOOK
Dean of Student Affairs: KIM CHIL-YOUNG
Dean of Planning and Int. Affairs: BOO JOON-HONG
Dean of Research Affairs and Faculty Evaluation: HWANG SOO-CHAN

Library of 247,000 vols

DEANS

Graduate School: LEE YUN-HYUN
Graduate School of Aviation and Information Industry: HONG SOON-KIL
Graduate School of Business Administration: CHA GUN-HO

HANLYO UNIVERSITY

199-4 Deongrae-ri, Gwangyang-eup, Gwangyang-si, Jeollanam-do, Seoul 545-704

Telephone: (61) 761-6700
Fax: (61) 761-6709
E-mail: ipsimast@hanlyo.ac.kr
Internet: www.hanlyo.ac.kr

Founded 1993
Private.

HOWON UNIVERSITY

727 Wolha-ri, Impi, Kunsan, Chonbuk, Seoul 573-718

Telephone: (63) 450-7114
Fax: (63) 450-7777
Internet: www.howon.ac.kr

Founded 1977 as Kunsan Technical Advanced School; renamed Sohae Technical Jr College 1979; became Chonbuk Sanup Univ. 1988; present name 1998
Private control
Academic year: March to February

Pres.: KANG HEE-SUNG.

WOOSONG UNIVERSITY

17-2 Jayang-dong, Dong-gu, Daejeon 300-718

Telephone: (42) 630-9600
Fax: (42) 630-6629
E-mail: international@wsu.sc.kr
Internet: english.wsu.ac.kr

Founded 1954
Private

Chair.: KIM SUNG KYUNG
Pres.: JOHN E. ENDICOTT

Library of 275,063 vols, 3,152 reference books, 367 periodicals
Number of teachers: 212 full-time
Number of students: 7,037

Schools of Railroad and Transportation, Technomedia, Health and Welfare, Hotel and Culinary, Asia Management, SolBridge International School of Business.

MUNICIPAL UNIVERSITIES

UNIVERSITY OF INCHEON

319 Incheondae gil, Nam-gu, Incheon, Seoul

Telephone: (32) 770-8114
Fax: (32) 762-1548
E-mail: sysop@incheon.ac.kr
Internet: www.inchon.ac.kr

Pres.: AHN KYUNG SOO

Colleges of arts and physical education, economics and business administration, engineering, humanities, law, natural sciences, North-East Asian studies, social sciences.

UNIVERSITY OF SEOUL

90 Jeonnong-dong, Dongdaemun-gu, Seoul 130-743

Telephone: (2) 2210-2114
Fax: (2) 2243-2732
E-mail: w3adm@uos.ac.kr
Internet: www.uos.ac.kr

Founded 1918; Seoul City University until 1996
Maintained by Seoul Metropolitan Government
Language of instruction: Korean
Academic year: March to February

President: Dr SANG-BUM LEE
Provost of Academic Affairs: Dr HYUN-SOO MIN
Provost of General Administration: IN-SONG CHANG
Provost of Planning and Development: Dr EUI-YOUNG SON

Provost of Student Affairs: Dr KEUN-HEE CHOI
Director of Central Library: Dr YONG-GUN KIM

Library of 554,895 vols
Number of teachers: 302
Number of students: 14,867

Publication: *University Press* (26 a year)

DEANS

College of Economics and Business Administration: Dr JONG-DAE LEE
College of Engineering: Dr SUNG-IL CHO
College of Law and Public Administration: Dr YONG-CHAN PARK
College of Liberal Arts and Natural Sciences: Dr JUN-HO SONG
College of Urban Sciences: Dr HYUNG-SU HAN
Liberal Arts Division: Dr DONG-HA LEE
Graduate School: Dr JAE-BOK PARK
Graduate School of Business Administration: Dr JONG-DAE LEE
Graduate School of Engineering: Dr SUNG-IL CHO
Graduate School of Urban Administration: Dr HYUNG-SU HAN

DISTANCE LEARNING UNIVERSITIES (CYBER AND DIGITAL UNIVERSITIES)

BUSAN DIGITAL UNIVERSITY

167, Jurei-dong, Sasang-gu Bang Busan Seoul 617-701

Telephone: (51) 320-1919
Fax: (51) 320-1922
Internet: www.bdu.ac.kr

Founded 2002
Private

Divisions of Social Welfare, Society and Management, Hospitalities and Tourism. Digital Contents

Pres.: KIM MIN-SIK.

DAEGU CYBER UNIVERSITY

15 Naeri-ri, Jillyang-eup, Gyeongsan-si, Gyeongsangbuk-do, Seoul 712-714

Telephone: (53) 850-4000
Fax: (53) 850-4019
E-mail: idaegu@dcu.ac.kr
Internet: english.dcu.ac.kr

Founded 2001
Private

Pres.: LEE YOUNG SAE.

GUKJE DIGITAL UNIVERSITY

950-12 Ingye-dong, Paldal-gu, Suwon Gyeonggi-do, Seoul 442-832

Telephone: (31) 229-6200
Fax: (31) 267-0750
E-mail: admin@gdu.ac.kr
Internet: eng.gdu.ac.kr

Founded 2003
Private

Schools of Business Administration, Social Sciences, Lifelong Education, Physical and Health Arts

Pres.: PARK YOUNG-KYU
Vice-Pres.: LEE KYOUNG-WOO.

KOREA DIGITAL UNIVERSITY

1-21 Gye-dong, Jongno-gu, Seoul 110-800

Telephone: (2) 6361-1810
Internet: www.kdu.edu

Founded 2001

Pres.: KIM CHOONG SOON

Depts of applied culture, art studies, business administration, child english education, computer and information communication, continuing education, counselling psychology, information management and services, law, media design, media studies, practical foreign languages, real estate and economics, social welfare, taxation and accounting, youth studies.

KYUNG HEE CYBER UNIVERSITY

Seoul Campus: Hoegi-dong, Dongdaemun-gu, Seoul 130-701
Telephone: (2) 961-0031
Fax: (2) 962-4343
E-mail: cie@khu.ac.kr*Global Campus*: Seocheon-dong, Giheung-hu, Yongin-si, Gyeonggi-do, Seoul 446-701
Telephone: (31) 201-3177
Fax: (31) 201-3179
E-mail: intlctr@khu.ac.kr
Internet: www.kyunghee.edu
Founded 1949 as Shinheung Junior College, univ. status 1955, established online univ. 2000

Pres.: INWON CHOUE.

SEOUL CYBER UNIVERSITY

Mia 3-dong 193, Gangbuk-gu, Seoul 142-700
Telephone: (2) 944-5000
Fax: (2) 980-2222
E-mail: joynlife@iscu.ac.kr
Internet: www.iscu.ac.kr
Founded 2000
Pres.: Dr SUSIE KIM
Number of students: 8,000
Schools of business and international management, general education, human welfare, information technology and design, psychology and counselling, social science.

SEOUL DIGITAL UNIVERSITY

Jungdong Wonmi-gu, Bucheon, Gyeonggi-do, Seoul 420-020
Telephone: (2) 1544-0981
Fax: (2) 2128-300
E-mail: go@sdu.ac.kr
Internet: en.sdu.ac.kr
Pres.: PAEK J. CHO
Division of Liberal Arts and Social Science, IT and Cultural Arts.

WONKWANG DIGITAL UNIVERSITY

344-2 Sinyong-dong, Iksan-si, North Jeolla
Telephone: 1588-28554
Fax: (63) 843-2856
Internet: www.wdu.ac.kr
Founded 2001
Pres.: SUNG SI-JONG
Divisions of Wellbeing and Culture, Utility and Welfare.

Colleges
PUBLIC COLLEGES

Busan Women's College: 74 Yangjung-dong, Pusan Jin-ku, Pusan 614-734; tel. (51) 852-0081; fax (51) 867-4705; internet www.bwc.ac.kr; f. 1954; Divisions of Child Education, Tourism, Welfare and Health, Art, Business and Management, Applied Art.

Iksan National College: Seoul 570-752; tel. (63) 850-0500; e-mail w3master@iksan.ac.kr; internet www.iksan.ac.kr; f. 1922.

Korea National College of Rehabilitation and Welfare: 5-3 Jangan-dong, Pyongtaek-si, Gyeonggi-do; tel. (31) 610-4600; fax (31) 610-4930; internet www.hanrw.ac.kr; f. 2002.

Korea National Railroad College: 374-18 Wolam-dong, Uiwang-si, Gyeonggi-do; tel. (31) 461-4011; fax (31) 462-2944; internet english.krc.ac.kr; f. 1905; depts of introduction to liberal art, railroad electrical control, railroad facility engineering, railroad management information, railroad operation mechanism, railroad transportation management, railroad vehicle machine, railroad vehicle electricity; 27 teachers; 610 students.

National Medical Centre College of Nursing: Euljiro 6 St, 18-79 Jongno-gu, Seoul 100-196; tel. and fax (2) 2265-6339.

PRIVATE COLLEGES

Ansan College of Technology: 671 Choji-dong, Danwon-gu, Ansan Gyeonggi-do; tel. (31) 490-6191; e-mail sysop@act.ac.kr; internet eng.ansantc.ac.kr; f. 1979; Degree programmes in arts and sports, liberal arts and social sciences, natural sciences, technology; Pres. KANG SUNG NAK.

Agricultural Cooperative College: San 38-27, Goyang, Seoul 412-038; tel. (31) 960-4117; fax (31) 960-4119; e-mail hanaok@nonghyup.or.kr; internet www.nonghyup.or.kr; f. 1962; courses in agricultural technology, computer science, marketing and MBA.

Andong Institute of Information and Technology: Andong, Gyeongsangbuk-do, Seoul 760-833; tel. (54) 820-8053; fax (54) 820-8055; e-mail info@ait.ac.kr; internet www.ait.ac.kr; f. 1972; library: 18,500 vols.

Busan Gyeongsang College: 277-4 Yeonsan 8-dong, Yeonje-gu, Busan; tel. (51) 850-1000; fax (51) 862-7577; e-mail busybee@bsks.ac.kr; internet www.cwc.ac.kr; f. 1977; Depts of advertising and interior design, advertising and public relations, airline services, child studies, distribution and logistics, early childhood education, hotel and tourism English, hotel and tourism management, international trade by Air and Sea, management, real estate management, social welfare and medical health administration, tax accounting, tourism Japanese; Pres. LEE DAL-DUK.

Cheju Tourism College: Seoul 690-791; tel. (64) 740-8700; fax (64) 748-2829; internet www.cjtour.ac.kr; f. 1993; as Jeju Tourism Technical College, present name 1998; courses in tourism, sports and leisure studies, and casino and hotel management; Pres. KIM CHANG-HU.

Chungkang College of Cultural Industries: Icheon, Seoul 467-810; tel. (31) 639-5743; fax (31) 639-5749; e-mail mjkang@chungkang.ac.kr; internet www.chungkang.ac.kr; f. 1996; divs of Games and Animation, Industrial Design, Performing Arts, Information Communications, and Human Care; Pres. LEE SU-HYEONG.

Daedong College: 373-4 Bugok 2-dong, Keumjeong-gu, Busan, Seoul 609-715; tel. (51) 518-5444; fax (51) 514-5847; internet www.daedong.ac.k; f. 1971 as Daedong Nursing School, jnr college in 1979, full college

status 1998; programmes in Nursing, Cosmetology, Child Welfare, and Leisure Tourism Management; Pres. KIM KYUNGHEE.

Daegu Mirae College: Mirae-gil 13, Gyeongsan, Gyeongbuk, Seoul 712-716; tel. (53) 810-9200; fax (53) 813-3162; internet www.dmc.ac.kr; f. 1981; Depts of engineering, fine arts, humanities and society, natural sciences, physical education; Pres. YONG BUM-KWON.

Gangneung Yeongdong College: 1009 Hongje-dong, Gangneung, Kangwon-do, Seoul 210-792; tel. (33) 610-0114; fax (33) 644-8809; internet www.yeongdong.ac.kr; f. 1963; programmes in nursing and health, depts of social welfare, tourism; Pres. KIM MYUNG HYUN.

Inha Technical College: 253 Yonghyundong, Nam-ku, Incheon, Seoul 402-752; tel. (32) 870-2114; fax (32) 868-3408; internet english.inhatc.ac.kr; f. 1958; 6,500 students; Pres. PARK CHOON-BAE.

Kaywon School of Art and Design: 66 Kaywondaehangno (Naeson-dong), Uiwang, Gyeonggi-do, Seoul 437-712; tel. (31) 420-1700; e-mail choihs@kaywon.ac.kr; internet foreign.kaywon.ac.kr; f. 1979 as Institute Foundation Kaywon School, present status 1990; faculties of Design, Fine Arts and Information Technology; Pres. KANG YOUNG-JIN.

KDI School of Public Policy and Management: 87 Hoegiro Dondaemun, Seoul 130-868; tel. (2) 3299-1114; e-mail admissions@kdischool.ac.kr; internet kdischool.ac.kr; f. 1997; Masters degree programme, PhD programme, and non-degree programmes; Dean SANG-MOON HAHM.

Seoul Institute of the Arts: 640 Gojan 2-dong, Dwang-gu, Ansan, Gyeonggi-do; tel. (31) 412-7100; fax (31) 412-7149; e-mail mschoi@seoularts.ac.kr; internet www.seoularts.ac.kr; f. 1958; programmes in applied music, broadcasting, creative advertising, creative writing, dance, digital arts and humanities, film, interior design, Korean traditional music, photography, playwriting, theatre, visual design; Chair. LEE GI HUNG.

Taekyeung College: 24 Tanpuk-ri, Chainmyun, Kyungsan, Gyeongsangbuk-do, Seoul 712-851; tel. (53) 850-1361; fax (53) 850-1363; e-mail clsfae@tk.ac.kr; internet www.tk.ac.kr; f. 1993; offers 3-year programmes in early childhood education, entertainment and event management, film and broadcasting, nursing, theatre, visual optics; 2-year programmes in baking technology, beauty design and modelling, hotel culinary arts, police administration, real-estate management, security administration, social welfare, sports science, tourism and hotel management; Pres. YOO JIN-SUN.

Yeungnam College of Science and Technology: 274 Hyeonchung-ro, 1737 Daemyeong 7-dong, Nam-gu, Daegu, Seoul 705-703; tel. (53) 650-9114; fax (53) 624-7871; internet eng.ync.ac.kr; f. 1968; schools of civil engineering-architecture, cosmetics-chemistry, design, food-tourism, information technology, mechanical and automotive engineering technology, nursing healthpractical sociology; divs of electronics and information engineering, health science; Pres. LEE HO-SUNG.

KOSOVO

The Higher Education System

On 17 February 2008 the Serbian province of Kosovo unilaterally declared independence from the Republic of Serbia. By late June 2009 60 countries, including 19 European Union member states and the USA, had formally recognized the Republic of Kosovo. However, several countries, including the People's Republic of China and Russia, continued to withhold recognition. Russian opposition to independence for Kosovo prevented the approval of a resolution on the status of Kosovo by the UN Security Council.

Higher Education in Kosovo is regulated by the Ministry of Education, Science and Technology. Institutions licensed by the Ministry are permitted to operate; however, this does not equate to accreditation. That function is performed by the United Nations Mission in Kosovo (UNMIK). The Universiteti i Prishtinës (University of Prishtina) is the only public university. Private universities have been permitted to operate since 1999. Figures for 2007/08 show that there were 25,840 students enrolled at university level.

Individual universities have specific entrance requirements as well as admission examinations organized by each institution. The University of Prishtina began using the European Credit Transfer and Accumulation System (ECTS) in 2001/02 and the Ministry of Education, Science and Technology (MEST) is working with all higher education institutions to implement ECTS in all institutions. From 2001/02, the University of Prishtina adopted the system of three study cycles, which includes the three-year Bachelors, two-year Masters, and three-year PhD. Exceptions to this are the Faculty of Medicine, the Department of Albanian Language and Literature, and the newly established Faculty of Education. During 2004/05 the university enrolled the first students of the second cycle (Master of Arts or Science—two-year programme) in 45 departments across 11 Faculties. As a result of the 2003/04 higher education reforms a new Bologna-compliant three-cycle degree structure was introduced in Kosovo. Since 2006/07 the new programmes have been introduced gradually across all institutions.

At undergraduate level the qualifications are: Baccalaureus—the first cycle academic qualification leading to a Bachelors and requiring completion of 180–240 ECTS credits over a period of three to four years; Professional Baccalaureus—awarded with a professional title, requiring completion of 180–240 ECTS credits over a period of three to four years; Diplomirani (Graduation Diploma)—offered by universities after four to six or more years of full-time study following completion of secondary school; Diplomirani (Graduation Diploma)—awarded by higher schools after two to three years of full-time study; Proffesor—awarded after four years of full-time study following completion of the Secondary School Leaving Certificate; Doktor (Medical science)—awarded after six years of full-time study upon completion of 360 ECTS credits. At postgraduate level two types of qualification are offered: Masters—represents one year of postgraduate study (60 ECTS credits) after a four-year first cycle qualification or two years of postgraduate study (120 ECTS credits) after a three-year first cycle qualification, making a total of 300 ECTS credits in the first and second cycles; Magistar Umjetnosti/Znanosti (Master of Arts/Science)—awarded upon completion of two or more years of full-time study following a four-year Diplomirani; Specijalista—Specialist Diploma (professional or academic studies)—represents one year of full-time study following a Baccalaureus and to pass students must complete all examinations and a thesis; Doctor (Doctorate)—requires at least three years of full-time study and completion of 180 ECTS credits following a Masters degree; Doktor Znanosti (Doctor of Science)—can be completed in four or more years of full-time study following a Magistar.

The Kosovo Agency for Accreditation (KAA) was founded by the Ministry of Education, Science and Technology (MEST) in accordance with the Law on Higher Education (2003/14) in Kosovo, as an Agency which provides external evaluation and assists institutions to carry out self-evaluation. The KAA comprises three overseas and six Kosovo experts. This organization guarantees the quality of educational and scientific research work of public and private institutions of higher education.

Regulatory Bodies

GOVERNMENT

Ministry of Culture, Youth and Sports: 10000 Prishtina; tel. (38) 211-064; fax (38) 211-440; e-mail info@mkrs-ks.org; internet www.mkrs-ks.org; Minister VALTON BEQIRI.

Ministry of Education, Science and Technology: Rr. Musine Kokollari 18, Lagjja Dadania Blloku-III, 10000 Prishtina; tel. (38) 541-035; e-mail masht@ks-gov.net; internet www.masht-gov.net; Minister ENVER HOXHAJ; Permanent Sec. ADEM SALLAUKA.

Learned Societies

GENERAL

Akademia e Shkencave dhe e Arteve e Kosovës (Kosovo Academy of Sciences and Arts): Rr. Emin Duraku 1, 10000 Prishtina; tel. (38) 249-303; fax (38) 244-636; e-mail ashak_pr@hotmail.com; internet www.ashak.org; f. 1975; promotes research in science, culture and language; Pres. REXHEP ISMAJLI;

Vice-Pres. BESIM BOKSHI; Sec.-Gen. HIVZI ISLAMI.

Fondacionin e Kosovës për Shoqëri të Hapur (Kosovo Foundation for Open Society): Ulpiana, Imzot Nikëprelaj, Villa 13, 10000 Prishtina; tel. (38) 542-157; fax (38) 542-157; e-mail info@kfos.org; internet www.kfos.org; f. 1993, present status and name 1999; non-governmental org.; focuses on minority rights, civic participation, European integration, governance and education; Exec. Dir LUAN SHILAKU; Chair. BLERIM SHALA.

BIBLIOGRAPHY, LIBRARY SCIENCE AND MUSEOLOGY

Shoqata e Bibliotekarëve të Kosovës (Association of Libraries of Kosovo): Sheshi 'Hasan Prishtina', 10000 Prishtina; tel. (38) 212-419; f. 1971; protects the rights of library employees; creates better working conditions; raises professionalism and expands professional activity of the libraries.

ECONOMICS, LAW AND POLITICS

Riinvest Instituti për Hulumtime Zhvillimore (Institute for Development Research): AAB-Riinvest Univ., Bldg 2, K/4

Industrial Zone, 10000 Prishtina; tel. (38) 601-320; fax (38) 601-233; e-mail riinvest@riinvestinstitute.org; internet www.riinvestinstitute.org; f. 1995; non-profit, research organization; research and analysis of business sectors, policy-making and advocacy in business devt; Pres. MUHAMET MUSTAFA; Vice-Pres Dr MUHAMET SADIKU, SEJDI OSMANI.

Research Institutes

GENERAL

Instituti Kosovar për Kërkime dhe Zhvillime të Politikave (Kosovar Institute for Policy Research and Development): Rexhep Mala 5A, 2nd Fl., Prishtina; tel. (38) 227-778; e-mail info@kipred.net; internet www.kipred.net; f. 2002; independent research; policy-making; political analysis; discussion papers and publs; training of political parties and govt; Chair. MENTOR AGANI; Exec. Dir ILIR DEDA.

MEDICINE

Instituti Kombëtar i Shëndetësisë Publike te Kosoves (National Institute of Public

Health of Kosovo): Rr. Nëna Tereze, Rrethi i Spitalit, 10000 Prishtina; tel. (38) 550-585; e-mail info@niph-kosova.org; internet www .niph-kosova.org; f. 1925; prepares and implements nat. public health strategy; Dir Assoc. Prof. Dr NASER RAMADANI.

Libraries

Prishtina

Biblioteka 'Hivzi Sylejmani':tel. (38) 232-980; f. built in 1930, 1948 as Prishtina City Library.

Biblioteka Kombëtare dhe Universitare e Kosovës (National and University Library of Kosovo): Sheshi Nëna Tereza 5, 10000 Prishtina; internet www.biblioteka-ks.org; f. 1944; 600,000 vols; Dir Prof. Dr SALI BASHOTA.

Museums and Art Galleries

Prishtina

Galeria e Arteve e Kosovës (Kosovo Art Gallery): Rr. Agmin Ramadani 60, Prishtina; tel. (38) 227-833; e-mail gak@ipko.org; internet www.kosovaart.com; attached to Min. of Culture and Sports; exhibits 2-dimensional work of young local artists; workshops with children.

Muzeu i Kosovës (Kosovo Museum): Sheshi Adam Jashari; tel. (38) 249-964; f. built 1898, served as HQ for Yugoslav Nat. Army 1945–75; colln of prehistoric objects uncovered in Kosovo; exhibits incl. clay statue of sitting goddess from the late Neolithic period found in Tjerrtorja in 1955, also featured in Prishtina city emblem; archeological and ethnological artefacts, approx. 1,250 items moved to Belgrade for an exhibition are still to be returned.

Prishtina Ethnological Museum: Emin Gjik Complex, Rr. Zija 1, Prishtina; tel. (38) 211-394; f. 1957 as home to Emin Gjinolli's family, used as Natural museum until 1990, renovated with int. donations 2003, opened in present form 2006; attached to Muzeu i Kosovës (Kosovo Museum); displays the urban oda (saloon), folk dresses, folk instruments, Kosovo's heritage of filigree jewellery influenced by Sephardic Jews and practiced in Prizren and Gjakova, carpet work, locally produced weapons of the time and religious objects dating back to the Illyrian ancestors.

Universities

AMERICAN UNIVERSITY IN KOSOVO (AUK)

Nazim Gafurri 21, 10000 Prishtina
Telephone: (38) 518-542
Fax: (38) 518-458
E-mail: info@aukonline.org
Internet: www.aukonline.org
Private control
Language of instruction: English
Founded 2003

In partnership with the Rochester Institute of Technology, New York; offers undergraduate and graduate courses

Library of 900 books, magazines, daily newspapers, reference materials, classroom materials, electronic technology resources, videos and DVDs

Pres.: CHRISTOPHER HALL
Registrar: ARIANA HAXHIU-KADRIU
Librarian: HAZBIJE QERIQI
Dir of AUK Institute: BEKIM KASUMI
Academic Dir: PETER BOYD.

UNIVERSITETI AAB (AAB University)

Zona Industriale, 10000 Prishtina
Telephone: (38) 247-524
E-mail: info@universitetiaab.com
Internet: www.universitetiaab.com

Founded 2001 as Academy of Liberal Arts
Private control

Offers Bachelors and Masters courses in Economics, Law, Mass Communication, Sport; houses Research Centre for Juridical, Criminological and Security Studies, Research Centre for Economic Prognoses, Centre for Sport Research, Centre for Architecture and Arts, Centre for Culture and Language Research and Centre for Public Opinion Research

Rector: Dr UROS LIPUSCEK

Library: scientific and academic publs, electronic study material

DEANS

Faculty of Applied and Figurative Arts: Prof. Dr BUJAR DEMJAHA
Faculty of Criminological Sciences: Prof. Dr RAMO MASLESA
Faculty of Economics: Prof. Dr FETAH REÇICA
Faculty of Education: Prof. Dr ISMAIL HASANI
Faculty of Foreign Languages: Prof. Dr MASAR STAVILECI
Faculty of Law: Prof. Dr MERSIM MAKSUTI
Faculty of Mass Communication: Prof. Dr RRAHMAN PAÇARIZI
Faculty of Music Arts: Prof. Dr BAKI JASHARI
Faculty of Sport: Prof. Dr MEHDI JASHARI

UNIVERSITETI I PRISHTINËS (University of Prishtina)

Sheshi Nëna Tereze 5, 10000 Prishtina
Telephone: (38) 244-183
Fax: (38) 244-187
E-mail: info@uni-pr.edu
Internet: www.uni-pr.edu

Founded 1970
State control
Academic year: September to June
Rector: Prof. Dr MUJË RUGOVA
Vice-Rector for Int. Cooperation: Prof. Dr NASER MRASORI
Vice-Rector for Resources and Infrastructure: Prof. Dr ENVER KUTLLOVCI
Vice-Rector for Teaching and Scientific Research: Prof. Dr BAJRAM BERISHA

Library: see Libraries and Archives
Number of teachers: 756
Number of students: 14,000

Publications: *Acta Biologiae et Medicinae Experimentalis, Pregled Predavanja, Univerzitetska Misao*

DEANS

Faculty of Agriculture: Prof. SHUKRI FETAHU
Faculty of Arts: Prof. Dr HIVZI MUHARREMI
Faculty of Business: (vacant)
Faculty of Civil Engineering and Architecture: Prof. Dr MUSA STAVILECI
Faculty of Economics: Prof. Dr IBRAHIM KUKA
Faculty of Electrical Engineering and Computing: Dr LUAN AHMA
Faculty of Journalism: (vacant)
Faculty of Law: Prof. Dr BEQIR SADIKAJ
Faculty of Mechanical Engineering: Prof. Dr ISMAJL GOJANI

Faculty of Medicine: Prof. Dr BAJRAM NURAJ
Faculty of Mining and Metallurgy: Prof. Dr KADRI BERISHA
Faculty of Natural Sciences and Mathematics: Prof. Dr MUSTAFË BYTYÇI
Faculty of Philology: Prof. Dr NUHI REXHEPI
Faculty of Philosophy: Dr SELIM DACI
Faculty of Physical Education and Sport: Prof. Dr MUSTAFË ALIU
Faculty of Political Science: (vacant)
Faculty of Teacher Training: Prof. Dr SADIK RASHITI

UNIVERSITETI I PRIZRENIT (University of Prizren)

Tirana St, 20000 Prizren
Telephone: (29) 631-403
E-mail: info@uni-pz.org
Internet: www.uni-pz.org

Founded 2006
Private control

Faculties of Architecture, Computer Science, Economy, English Literature, Law, Political Science, Psychology

Library of 13,398 vols, 3,600 periodicals.

UNIVERSITETI I VIZIONIT EVROPIAN (European Vision University)

Rr. Wesley Clark, 30000 Pejë
Telephone: (39) 431-684
Fax: (39) 431-676
E-mail: info@evun.eu
Internet: www.evun.eu

Founded 2006
Private control
Languages of instruction: Albanian, English
Academic year: October to September
Rector: Prof. Dr EDMOND BEQIRI

Library of 150,000 vols
Number of teachers: 78
Number of students: 783

UNIVERSITETI MBRETËROR ILIRIA (Iliria Royal University)

Rr. Gamend Zajmi 75, 10000 Prishtina
Telephone: (38) 233-951
E-mail: info@uiliria.org
Internet: www.uiliria.org
Private control

Univ. under patronage of the royal family; offers Bachelors, Masters, doctoral courses.

UNIVERSITETI PËR BIZNES DHE TEKNOLOGJI (University of Business and Technology)

Lagjja Kalabria, 10000 Prishtina
Telephone: (38) 541-400
Fax: (38) 542-138
E-mail: info@ubt-uni.net
Internet: www.ubt-uni.net
Private control
Languages of instruction: English, Albanian, French, German

Bachelors and Masters courses in Architecture and Spatial Planning, Computer Science and Engineering, Law, Political Science and Economy, Management, Business and Economy, Public Health and Social Sciences; attached institutes: Institute for Enterprise Management and Engineering (IEME), Int. Languages and Intercultural Competence (ILIC), Institute for Int. Relations and European Studies (IIRES)

Pres.: Dr EDMOND HAJRIZI.

KUWAIT

The Higher Education System

Kuwait University (founded 1962) is the sole public university. In 2005/06 it had about 20,000 students enrolled out of an estimated total of 37,521 students in tertiary education. In 2009 there were also 12 private universities, including the American University of the Middle East, American University of Kuwait and the Arab Open University, which were accredited by the Private Universities Council of the Ministry of Higher Education. It is Government policy to provide free education for all Kuwaiti citizens from primary to tertiary level. Students wishing to undertake courses not offered by Kuwait University are offered scholarships to study abroad. In May 1996 the National Assembly approved a draft law to regulate students' behaviour, dress and activities, with regard to observance of the teachings of Shari'a (Islamic) law, and to eradicate coeducational classes at Kuwait University over a five-year period. A KD-1,000m. project to build a new university campus and to gather the institution's dispersed facilities on to one site was in the planning stages in early 2005.

Admission to university-level undergraduate courses is on the basis of the General Secondary Education Certificate (Shahadat-al-thanawia-al-a'ama). The Bachelors degree is arranged on a US-style 'credit semester' system and usually lasts four years, except for professional programmes such as engineering and medicine, which last five and seven years, respectively. Masters degrees at Kuwait University last up to two years and are available in most subjects.

The Public Authority for Applied Education and Training oversees technical and vocational education. The institutions that offer vocational education are the Vocational Training Institute, Industrial Training Institute, College of Technological Studies and Nursing Institute. There are also Colleges of Basic Education, Business Studies and Health Studies offering two- to four-year courses leading to the award of a professional Diploma.

Regulatory and Representative Bodies

GOVERNMENT

Ministry of Education: POB 7, 13001 Safat, Hilali St, Kuwait City; tel. 24836800; fax 22423676; e-mail webmaster@moe.edu.kw; internet www.moe.edu.kw; Minister AHMAD ABD AL-MOHSEN AL-MLAIFI.

Ministry of Higher Education: Safat; tel. 22401300; e-mail info_minister@mohe.edu.kw; internet www.mohe.edu.kw; Minister AHMAD ABD AL-MOHSEN AL-MLAIFI.

ACCREDITATION

Private Universities Council: POB 26166, 13122 Safat; tel. 22240591; fax 22455326; e-mail imad@puc.edu.kw; internet www.puc.edu.kw; f. 2001; affiliated to Higher Education Council; ensures conformity with all rules and stipulations for licensing private educational instns; Chair. MINISTER OF HIGHER EDUCATION; Sec.-Gen. IMAD ALATIQI.

NATIONAL BODY

Public Authority for Applied Education and Training: POB 23167, 13092 Safat; tel. 22564960; fax 22528915; e-mail bscg@paaet.edu.kw; internet www.paaet.edu.kw; f. 1982; autonomous body supervising technical and vocational training; the applied education sector comprises College of Basic Education, College of Business Studies, College of Technological Studies and College of Health Sciences; institutes in operation are Telecommunications and Navigation Institute, Electricity and Water Institute, Industrial Training Institute (brs in Shuwaikh and Subbah al-Salem), Nursing Institute, Constructional Training Institute and Vocational Training Institute.

Learned Societies

GENERAL

National Council for Culture, Arts and Letters: POB 23996, 13100 Safat; tel. 22469090; fax 22432331; internet www.kuwait-info.com/a_culture/culture_nccal.asp; f. 1973; guidance and support in all fields of culture; sponsors art exhibitions, drama, publishes books and periodicals; Sec.-Gen. ALI AL YOHA; publs Al-Thaqafa al-'Alamiyah, Alam al-Fikr, Alam Al-Ma'arifa, Ibda'at 'Alamiyah, Al-Fonon.

LANGUAGE AND LITERATURE

British Council: 2 Al Arabi St, Block 2, POB 345, 13004 Safat, Mansouria, Kuwait City; tel. 22520067; fax 22520069; e-mail info@kw.britishcouncil.org; internet www.britishcouncil.org/kuwait; teaching centre; offers courses and exams in English language and British culture and promotes cultural exchange with the UK; library of 9,000 vols; Dir, Teaching Centre Man. JOHN PARE (acting).

MEDICINE

Kuwait Medical Association: POB 1202, 13013 Safat; tel. 25312630; fax 25317972; e-mail kmj@kma.org.kw; internet www.kma.org.kw/kmj; f. 1967; library of 43 vols; Pres. Dr ALI ALMUKAIMI; Sec.-Gen. Dr MOHAMMED SHAMSAH; publ. Kuwait Medical Journal (4 a year).

Kuwait Medical Genetics Centre: tel. 24814328; fax 24842073; e-mail ihgck2008@gmail.com; internet www.kmgc.info; Chair. Dr SADIKA AL-AWADI.

Research Institutes

ECONOMICS, LAW AND POLITICS

Arab Planning Institute, Kuwait: POB 5834, 13059 Safat; tel. 24843130; fax 24842935; e-mail api@api.org.kw; internet www.arab-api.org; f. 1966 with assistance from the UN Devt Programme, and since 1972 financed by 15 Arab mem. states; trains personnel in economic and social devt planning; undertakes research and advisory work and organizes confs and seminars on problems affecting economic and social devt in the Arab world; library of 70,000 vols (28,000 Arabic, 42,000 English), 400 periodicals; Dir-Gen. Dr ALI ABDELGADIR ALI (acting); publs API working paper series (in Arabic and English, irregular), Development Bridge (in Arabic, 10 a year), Journal of Development and Economic Policies (in Arabic and English, 2 a year).

EDUCATION

Gulf Arab States Educational Research Centre: POB 12580, 71656 Shamia; tel. 24835203; fax 24830571; e-mail gaserc@kuwait.net; internet www.gaserc.edu.kw; f. 1978 as part of Arab Bureau of Education for the Gulf States; research on all educational topics; also provides training courses in developed curricula, educational statistics, educational evaluation, and educational research; Dir Prof. MARZOUG Y. AL-GHOUNIAM; Librarian MOHEI A. HAK; publ. Al-Hasaad Al-Terbawi (Arabic Text) (6 a year).

MEDICINE

Arabization Centre for Medical Sciences: POB 5225, 13053 Safat; tel. 25338610; fax 25338618; e-mail acmls@acmls.org; internet www.acmls.org; f. 1983; part of Council of Arab Ministers of Health—Arab League; aims: the Arabization of medical literature and translation into Arabic of medical sciences, development of a current bibliographic database, issuing of Arabic medical directories, training of manpower in the field of medical information and library science; library of 1,000 vols; Sec.-Gen. Dr ABDEL RAHMAN AL-AWADI; publs Arab Medical Doctors' Directory, Directory of Health Education and Research Organizations in Arab Countries, Directory of Hospitals and Clinics in Arab World.

Kuwait Institute for Medical Specialization: POB 1793, 13018 Safat; tel. 22418782; fax 22410028; e-mail info@kims.org.kw; internet www.kims.org.kw; attached to Ministry of Health; f. 1984; publ. Journal.

NATURAL SCIENCES

General

Kuwait Foundation for the Advancement of Science: POB 25263, 13113 Safat; tel. 22425898; fax 22415365; internet www.kfas.com; f. 1976; promotes scientific and technological advancement, provides financial aid for research projects, organizes symposia and conferences, develops Arabic-language publications; Dir ALI A. AL-SHAMLAN; publs *Al-Taqaddum al-Ilmi* (Scientific Advancement, 4 a year), *Majallat Al-Oloom* (12 a year).

Kuwait Institute for Scientific Research: POB 24885, 13109 Safat; tel. 24989360; fax 24989359; e-mail public_relations@safat.kisr.edu.kw; internet www.kisr.edu.kw; f. 1967; promotes and conducts scientific research in the fields of economics and applied systems, environmental studies, food resources, infrastructure services and urban devt, oil sector support and water resources; Dir-Gen. Dr NAJI MOHAMED AL-MUTAIRI; publ. *Science and Technology*.

Libraries and Archives

Kuwait City

Kuwait University Libraries: POB 23558, Kuwait City; e-mail jac.lib@kuniv.edu; internet library.kuniv.edu.kw; f. 1966; 233,733 vols, 2,445 periodicals, 1,298 electronic journals, 20,000 audiovisual items; Dir DHIYA' ALJASIM.

Safat

National Library of Kuwait: POB 26182, 13122 Safat; tel. 22415181; fax 22415195; e-mail acq@nlk.gov.kw; internet www.nlk .gov.kw; f. 1936; nat. and UN depository library; nat. ISBN agency; nat. bibliographic centre; special colln *Kuwaitiana*; over 300,000 vols in Arabic and English, 750 periodicals; Dir-Gen. IMAD ABULBANAT.

National Scientific and Technical Information Centre: Kuwait Institute for Scientific Research, POB 24885, 13109 Safat; tel. 4818713; fax 4836097.

Museums and Art Galleries

Safat

Department of Antiquities and Museums: POB 23996, 13100 Safat; tel. 22426521; fax 22404862; Dir Dr FAHED AL-WOHAIBI.

Museums Controlled by the Department:

Failaka Island Archaeological Museum:exhibits from excavations.

Failaka Island Ethnographic Museum:colln of material from Failaka Island, housed in the old residence of the island's Sheikh.

Kuwait National Museum: Arabian Gulf St, Kuwait City; f. 1957; antiquities from late Bronze Age to Hellenistic period found at Failaka Island; ethnographic material.

Educational Science Museum: Ministry of Education, POB 7, 13001 Safat; tel. 22421268; fax 22446078; f. 1972; lectures, exhibitions, film shows, etc.; sections on natural history, science, space, oil, health; planetarium, meteorology; library of 2,000 vols; Dir ADNAN AL-ALI.

Salmiya

Scientific Centre: POB 3504, 22036 Salmiya; tel. 1848888; fax 25710298; e-mail info@tsck.org.kw; internet www.tsck.org.kw; educational facility with architectural design reflecting Islamic art and culture; walls contain ceramic depictions of Kuwait's history; bldg comprises Aquarium, Discovery Place and IMAX Theatre.

Universities

AMERICAN UNIVERSITY OF KUWAIT

POB 3323, 13034 Safat
Telephone: 2224399
Fax: 25715860
E-mail: president@auk.edu.kw
Internet: www.auk.edu.kw

Founded 2003, accredited in 2006
Private control
Liberal arts, co-educational
Pres.: Dr TIM SULLIVAN
Exec. Dir: ERNEST E. COKLIN
Dean for Academic Affairs: Dr NIZAR HAMZEH
Dean for Student Affairs: Dr CAROL ROSS
Dir for Public Relations: AMAL AL-BINALI
Registrar: JILL ALLGIER
Librarian: AMNA AL-OMARE
Number of teachers: 125

ARAB OPEN UNIVERSITY

POB 32004, Al-Jabria
Telephone: 24767291
Fax: 24767286
E-mail: director@aou.edu.kw
Internet: www.aou.edu.kw

Founded 2003
Private control, in partnership with Open University, UK
Pres. and Chair.: HRH Prince TALAL BIN ABDULAZIZ
Dir: Prof. ISMAIL TAQI
Faculties of business administration, education, general studies, IT and computing, language studies.

AUSTRALIAN COLLEGE OF KUWAIT

POB 1411, 13015 Safat
Telephone: 25376111
Fax: 25376222
Internet: www.ack.edu.kw

Founded 2004
Private control
Pres.: ABDULLAH ABDUL MOHSEN AL SHARHAN
Depts of business studies and engineering.

GULF UNIVERSITY FOR SCIENCE AND TECHNOLOGY

POB 7207, 32093 Hawally
Telephone: 25307000
Fax: 25307030
E-mail: info@gust.edu.kw
Internet: www.gust.edu.kw

Founded 2002
Private control
Pres.: Dr ABDUL-RAHMAN SALEH AL-MUHAILAN
Dean of Student Affairs: Dr SABAH AL-QUADDOOMI
Librarian: SHOBHITA KOHLI
Library of 8,500 vols, 170 periodicals

DEANS

College of Arts and Sciences: Dr RAY WEISBORN
College of Business Administration: Prof. HUSSEIN AL-TALAFHA

PROFESSORS

AL-TALAFHA, H., Business Administration
ANKLI, R., Economics and Management
SAVAGE, A. J., Managemant and Marketing

KUWAIT UNIVERSITY

POB 5969, 13060 Safat
Telephone: 24845839
Fax: 24848648
E-mail: info@kuniv.edu

Internet: www.kuniv.edu.kw
Founded 1962, inaugurated 1966
State control
Language of instruction: Arabic, except in faculties of science, engineering and petroleum, allied health science and nursing, medicine and department of English
Academic year: September to June (2 semesters)
Chancellor: HE THE MINISTER OF HIGHER EDUCATION
Pres.: Prof. NADER AL-JALLAL
Vice-Pres. for Academic Affairs: Prof. HASSAN AL-ALAWI
Vice-Pres. for Planning and Evaluation: Dr MOUDI AL-HUMOUD
Vice-Pres. for Research and Graduate Studies: Dr ASSAD ISMAEL
Dean of Admissions and Registration: Dr ABDULLA AL-FUHAID
Sec.-Gen.: Dr AHMED AL-DEKHIL (acting)
Library Dir: Dr HUSEIN AL-ANSARI
Library: see Libraries and Archives
Number of teachers: 4,530
Number of students: 19,320
Publications: *Annals of the Faculty of Arts* (12 a year), *Arab Journal for the Humanities* (4 a year), *Arab Journal of Linguistics*, *Arab Journal of Management Sciences* (3 a year), *Educational Journal* (4 a year), *Islamic Studies Magazine* (3 a year), *Journal of Gulf and Arabian Peninsula* (4 a year), *Journal of Law* (4 a year), *Journal of Palestine Studies*, *Journal of Science* (2 a year), *Journal of the Social Sciences* (4 a year), *Medical Principles and Practice* (4 a year)

DEANS

College of Allied Health Sciences and Nursing: Dr HABIB ABUL
College of Arts: Dr SHAFIQA BASTAKI
College of Business Administration: Dr ADEL AL-HUSSAINAN
College of Dentistry: Dr JAWAD BEHBEHANI
College of Education: Dr RASHID ALI AL-SAHEL
College of Engineering and Petroleum: Prof. ABDUL-LATEEF AL-KHALEEFI
College of Graduate Studies: Dr ABDULLA AL-SHEIKH
College of Law: Dr FADEL NASRALLAH
College of Medicine: Dr JAWAD BEHBEHANI
College of Pharmacy: Dr LADISLAV NOVOTNY
College of Science: Prof. REDHA AL-HASAN
College of Shari'a and Islamic Studies: Dr MOHAMMED AL-TABTABAIE
College of Social Sciences: Dr ALI A. AL-TARRAH
Women's College: Dr AHMET YIGIT

KUWAIT–MAASTRICHT BUSINESS SCHOOL

Block 3, Kazima St, Dasma
Telephone: 22517091
Fax: 22545791
E-mail: info@kmbs.edu.kw
Internet: www.kmbs.edu.kw

Founded 2003
Private control
Pres.: KHALEEL AL-ABDULLAH
Dir: ROSEMARY LLOYD
Head of Academic Affairs: Prof. HERNAN RIQUELME

PROFESSORS

MAGALHAES, R., Information Systems and Organization
NIKOLIK, D. A., E-Business
RIQUELME, H., Entrepreneurship and Strategy
RWEGASIRA, K. S. P., Financial Management and Accounting

SYBRANDY, A., Marketing
TUNINGA, R. S. J., International Business and Marketing

Colleges

Box Hill College Kuwait: POB 29192, 13152 Safat; tel. 22471703; fax 22471701; e-mail info@bhck.edu.kw; internet www.bhck.edu.kw; private college for women; attached to Box Hill Institute TAFE, Melbourne, Australia; Pres. EISA AL-REFAI; Exec. Vice-Pres. for Admin. JOE ALBAYATI.

College of Basic Education: Female Campus, POB 34053, 73251 Adailiya; tel. 24816044; e-mail bscg@paaet.edu.kw; f. 1973; attached to Public Authority for Applied Education and Training; BA degree courses in education; depts of Arabic language, education, educational technology, home economics, library sciences, interior design, Islamic sciences, mathematics, music education, physical education, psychology, sciences, social studies, teaching of arts.

College of Business Studies: Male Campus, POB 43197, 32046 Hawalli; tel. 22633622; fax 22622439; e-mail bim@paaet.edu.kw female Campus, POB 44069, 32055 Hawalli; tel. 26169913; e-mail bif@paaet.edu.kw; f. 1975; attached to Public Authority for Applied Education and Training; depts of accountancy, administration and secretarial studies, economics, English language, insurance and banking, office training, typewriting.

College of Health Sciences: Female Campus, POB 14281, 72853 Shuwaikh; tel. 24837056; fax 24811920; e-mail chsh@paaet.edu.kw Male Campus, POB 33496, 73455 Rawda; tel. 22570115; fax 22527187; e-mail chsm@paaet.edu.kw; f. 1974; attached to Public Authority for Applied Education and Training; Assoc. Degree courses; depts of environmental health, food sciences and nutrition, medical records, natural sciences, nursing, oral and dental health, pharmaceutical and medical sciences.

College of Technological Studies: POB 42325, 70654 Shuwaikh; tel. 24816122; fax 24843143; internet www.paaet.edu.kw/cts; f. 1976; attached to Public Authority for Applied Education and Training; Assoc. Degree courses; depts of air conditioning and refrigeration, applied sciences, chemical engineering, civil engineering, electrical engineering, and power engineering, electronic engineering, motor vehicle and marine engineering, production engineering and welding; library: 6,510 vols, 180 periodicals; 322 teachers; 1,950 students; Dean Dr ADEL S. AL-JIMAZ.

Constructional Training Institute: POB 23167, 13092 Safat; tel. 4833186; fax 4838719; f. 2000; Public Authority for Applied Education and Training; attached to German Institute for Technical Cooperation; training programmes in building construction, civil engineering, interior finishing, mechanics.

Electricity and Water Institute: POB 15196, 35452 Daiyah; tel. 22570252; fax 2575293; Public Authority for Applied Education and Training; two-year courses aimed at fulfilling requirements of Ministry of Electricity and Water in electrical power stations, water distillation plants, water pumps, operation of reverse osmosis units, maintenance of electrical networks.

Industrial Training Institute: POB 1236, 44000 Subbah al-Salem; tel. 25520037; f. 1992; Public Authority for Applied Education and Training; three-year courses to Technician level.

Institute of Banking Studies: POB 1080, 13011 Safat; tel. 22458460; fax 22434705; internet www.kibs.edu.kw; f. 1970 as Banking Studies Center; present name and Specialized Institute status 1982; Dir RIDHA M. AL KHAYYAT; accredited certificates in Islamic banking and financial services, credit management, investment management.

Nursing Institute: Al-Sabah Hospital, POB 22195, 13098 Safat; tel. 24819036; f. 1962; Public Authority for Applied Education and Training; General Nursing Programme.

Vocational Training Institute: Sharq, POB 23167, 13092 Safat; tel. 22422116; Public Authority for Applied Education and Training; four-year courses in automotive electric, refrigeration and air conditioning maintenance, automotive mechanics, cabinet work and decoration, formwork and reinforced concrete, electrical installation, offset printing, welding and metal casting.

KYRGYZSTAN

The Higher Education System

Following the Russian revolution in 1917, Kyrgyzstan was established as an autonomous region within the Russian Soviet Federated Socialist Republic (RSFSR). In 1936 it was recognized as a full Union member of the Soviet Union and became the Kyrgyz Soviet Socialist Republic. The oldest institutions of higher education were founded during the early years of Soviet rule, among them Jalal-Abad State University (founded 1926), Kyrgyz National University 'Zhusup Balasagyn' (founded 1932; current name 1993) and Kyrgyz Agrarian Academy (founded 1933). In August 1991 Kyrgyzstan declared its independence from the Soviet Union. The Ministry of Education and Science is responsible for the administration of higher education, which in 2007/08 consisted of 49 public and private establishments, with total enrolment of 250,460 students. Higher education is governed according to the Law on Education (1992). Some institutions of a specialist or professional nature are administered by the appropriate Government ministry, and several universities are run on a cooperative basis between the Kyrgyz Government and governments of other countries, such as Kyrgyz–Russian Slavic University (founded 1992) and Kyrgyz–Turkish University 'Manas' (founded 1995). The State Licence and Attestation Inspection of Educational Institutions of the Ministry of Education is the accrediting agency for higher education.

Admission to higher education is on the basis of the Certificate of Completed Secondary Education and success in university entrance examinations (which have been administered since 2003 by the United States Agency for International Development). Kyrgyzstan operates a dual system of the old Soviet-style degrees alongside Bachelors and Masters degrees. The old-style Specialist Diploma is a five-year programme of study, followed by the Candidate of Science (two years) and Doctor of Science (research only) programmes. Alternatively, an undergraduate may study for four years for the Bachelors degree, followed by a two-year Masters degree, before progressing onto the Candidate of Science and Doctor of Science programmes.

In 2002 the Ministry of Education and Science established a quality assurance department and universities are now required to introduce measures for quality assurance.

The Education Development Strategy of the Kyrgyz Republic (2007–10) includes plans to bring the education system in line with the Bologna Declaration.

Regulatory Bodies

GOVERNMENT

Ministry of Culture and Information: 720040 Bishkek, Pushkina 78; tel. (312) 62-12-00; Minister SULTAN A. RAYEV.

Ministry of Education and Science: 720040 Bishkek, Tynystanova 257; tel. (312) 66-24-42; fax (312) 62-15-20; e-mail monk@monk.bishkek.gov.kg; internet edu.gov.kg; Minister KANAT SADYKOV.

ACCREDITATION

State Licence and Attestation Inspection of Educational Institutions of the Ministry of Education: Bishkek; tel. (312) 66-22-87; e-mail bakul@yandex.ru; Head BAKTYHBEK ISKAKOVICH ISMAILOV.

Learned Societies

GENERAL

National Academy of Sciences of the Kyrgyz Republic: 720071 Bishkek, Chuy pr. 265A; tel. (312) 61-00-93; fax (312) 24-36-07; e-mail interdep@aknet.kg; internet academ.aknet.kg; f. 1954; depts of Physical-Engineering, Mathematical and Mining-Geological Sciences, Chemical-Technological, Medical-Biological and Agricultural Sciences, Humanities; 133 mems (42 permanent, 58 corresp., 33 foreign); attached research institutes: see Research Institutes; library: see Libraries and Archives; Pres. J. JEYENBAYEV; Chief Sec. Academician A. ALDASHEV; publ. *Izvestiya* (bulletin).

BIBLIOGRAPHY, LIBRARY SCIENCE AND MUSEOLOGY

Library Association of Kyrgyzstan: 720044 Bishkek, pr. Tynchtyk 27; tel. (312) 48-41-34; fax (312) 48-40-35; Pres. T. SHAYMERGENOVA.

HISTORY, GEOGRAPHY AND ARCHAEOLOGY

Kyrgyz Geographical Society: 720081 Bishkek, bul. Erkindik 30; tel. (312) 26-47-21; Chair. S. U. UMURZAKOV.

LANGUAGE AND LITERATURE

Alliance Française: 720026 Bishkek, c/o French Consulate, ul. Razakov 49; tel. (312) 66-03-64; fax (312) 66-04-41; e-mail alliancefrancokirghiz@yahoo.fr; offers courses and examinations in French language and culture and promotes cultural exchange with France.

British Council: see entry in Kazakhstan chapter.

Research Institutes

AGRICULTURE, FISHERIES AND VETERINARY SCIENCE

Institute of Forest and Walnut Studies: 720015 Bishkek, Karagachovaya rosha 15; tel. and fax (312) 67-90-82; e-mail institute@lesic.elcat.kg; f. 1992; attached to Nat. Acad. of Sciences of the Kyrgyz Republic; research in forestry, forest soil science, entomology, phytopathology, forestry economy fields; Dir ESHALY TURDUKULOV.

ECONOMICS, LAW AND POLITICS

Centre for Economic Research: 720071 Bishkek, Chuy pr. 265A; tel. (312) 24-26-90; fax (312) 24-36-07; e-mail cer49@mail.ru; f. 1998; attached to Nat. Acad. of Sciences of the Kyrgyz Republic; Dir T. S. DYIKANBAYEVA.

Institute of Philosophy and Law: 720071 Bishkek, Chuy pr. 265A; tel. (312) 24-38-27; e-mail togusakov@mail.ru; f. 1958; attached to Nat. Acad. of Sciences of the Kyrgyz Republic; Dir O. A. TOGUSAKOV.

FINE AND PERFORMING ARTS

National Centre for 'Manas' Studies and Fine Arts: 720071 Bishkek, Chuy pr. 265A; tel. (312) 24-34-68; f. 1995; attached to Nat. Acad. of Sciences of the Kyrgyz Republic; Dir A. AKMATALIYEV.

HISTORY, GEOGRAPHY AND ARCHAEOLOGY

Institute of History: 720071 Bishkek, Chuy pr. 265A; tel. (312) 65-54-95; e-mail inst_history@hotmail.kg; f. 1954; attached to Nat. Acad. of Sciences of the Kyrgyz Republic; Dir J. JUNASHALIYEV.

LANGUAGE AND LITERATURE

Institute of Linguistics: 720071 Bishkek, Chuy pr. 265A; tel. (312) 24-34-95; f. 1924; attached to Nat. Acad. of Sciences of the Kyrgyz Republic; Dir T. AHMATOV.

MEDICINE

Institute of Medical Problems: 714000 Osh, Ozgon 52; tel. (3222) 2-84-44; f. 1994; attached to Nat. Acad. of Sciences of the Kyrgyz Republic; Dir R. TOYCHUYEV.

Kyrgyz Research Institute of Obstetrics and Paediatrics: 720040 Bishkek, Togolok Moldo 1; tel. (312) 22-67-19; fax (312) 26-42-75; e-mail oroz@uzakov.bishkek.su; f. 1961; library of 14,000 vols; Dir DUYSHA KUDAYAROV.

Research and Development Institute of Molecular Biology and Medicine: 720040 Bishkek, Togolok Moldo 3; e-mail cardio@elcat.kg; f. 2002; library of 5,000 vols; Dir A. ALDASHEV.

Scientific and Production Centre for Preventive Medicine: 720005 Bishkek, Baitik Baatyr 34; tel. (312) 54-45-78; fax (312) 54-45-73; e-mail npopm@mail.ru; f. 1938; researches into public health, and environment and health; library of 13,500 vols; Dir Prof. Dr OMOR T. KASYMOV.

NATURAL SCIENCES
Biological Sciences

Institute of Biology and Soil Studies: 720071 Bishkek, Chuy pr. 265; tel. (312) 65-56-87; f. 1994; attached to Nat. Acad. of Sciences of the Kyrgyz Republic; Dir S. KASIYEV.

Institute of Biotechnology: 720071 Bishkek, Chuy pr. 265; tel. (312) 65-55-07; fax (312) 64-19-55; e-mail acan@rambler.ru; f. 1964; attached to Nat. Acad. of Sciences of the Kyrgyz Republic; Dir Acad. ASANKADYR JUNUSHOV.

Mathematical Sciences

Institute of Mathematics: 720071 Bishkek, Chuy pr. 265; tel. (312) 24-35-61; fax (312) 24-36-07; e-mail mathnas@aknet.kg; internet www.math.aknet.kg; f. 1984; attached to Nat. Acad. of Sciences of the Kyrgyz Republic; fields of research: integro-differential equations, singular perturbations, reverse and ill-posed problems, computer proof of theorems, economical-mathematical methods; 55 mems; Dir MURZABEK I. IMANALIEV; Scientific Sec. MARYAM A. ASANKULOVA.

Physical Sciences

Institute of Geology: 720481 Bishkek, bul. Erkindik 30; tel. (312) 66-47-37; fax (312) 66-42-56; e-mail geol@aknet.kg; f. 1943; attached to Nat. Acad. of Sciences of the Kyrgyz Republic; Dir A. B. BAKIROV.

Institute of High-Altitude Physiology and Experimental Pathology of High Rocks: 720048 Bishkek, ul. Gorkogo 1/5; tel. (312) 23-93-52; f. 1954; attached to Nat. Acad. of Sciences of the Kyrgyz Republic; Dir A. SHANAZAROV.

Institute of Physics: 720071 Bishkek, Chuy pr. 265; tel. (312) 25-52-59; fax (312) 24-36-07; e-mail interdep@aknet.kg; internet academ.aknet.kg; f. 1984; attached to Nat. Acad. of Sciences of the Kyrgyz Republic; Dir Prof. Dr TOKTOSUN OROZOBAKOV.

Institute of Rocks, Physics and Mechanics: 720815 Bishkek, ul. Mederova 98; tel. (312) 54-11-15; fax (312) 54-11-17; e-mail ifmgp@totel.kg; internet www.ifmgp.to.kg; f. 1960; attached to Nat. Acad. of Sciences of the Kyrgyz Republic; library of 500,000 vols; Dir I. T. AITMATOV; publ. Proceedings (every 2 years).

Institute of Seismology: 720060 Bishkek, Asanbay 52/1; tel. (312) 46-29-42; fax (312) 46-29-04; e-mail kis@mail.elcat.kg; f. 1975; attached to Nat. Acad. of Sciences of the Kyrgyz Republic; Dir A. TURDULKULOV.

Institute of the Biosphere: 715600 Dzhalal-Abad, Uzbekistan 130; tel. (3722) 5-26-00; attached to Nat. Acad. of Sciences of the Kyrgyz Republic; Dir T. RAHMANOV.

RELIGION, SOCIOLOGY AND ANTHROPOLOGY

Centre for Dungan Studies: 720071 Bishkek, Chuy pr. 265A; tel. (312) 24-34-89; f. 1954; attached to Nat. Acad. of Sciences of the Kyrgyz Republic; Dir M. IMAZOV.

Centre for Social Research: 720071 Bishkek, Chuy pr. 265A; tel. (312) 24-37-35; attached to Nat. Acad. of Sciences of the Kyrgyz Republic; Dir N. OMURALIYEV.

Institute of Social Sciences: 714000 Osh, Mominova 11; tel. (3222) 2-92-44; f. 1994; attached to Nat. Acad. of Sciences of the Kyrgyz Republic; Dir E. SULAYMANOV.

TECHNOLOGY

Institute for the Complex Utilization of Natural Resources (ICUNR): 714000 Osh, Mominova 11; tel. (3222) 2-60-10; fax (3222) 2-03-42; e-mail ikipr@aknet.kg; f. 1988; attached to Nat. Acad. of Sciences of the Kyrgyz Republic; f. 1988; Dir Prof. JAPAR TEKENOVICH TEKENOV.

Institute of Automatics: 720071 Bishkek, Chuy pr. 265; tel. (312) 65-55-22; e-mail automatics@aknet.kg; f. 1960; attached to Nat. Acad. of Sciences of the Kyrgyz Republic; Dir T. OMOROV.

Institute of Chemistry and Chemical Technology: 720071 Bishkek, Chuy pr. 267; tel. (312) 39-19-48; fax (312) 39-19-86; e-mail icctkr@inbox.ru; f. 1994; attached to Nat. Acad. of Sciences of the Kyrgyz Republic; research on devt of technology of reworking of metallic ores, mineral and organic raw material; creation of new materials (high effective plant growth stimulators and protection means, organic and organo-mineral fertilizers on the base of acid amides, natural polymers, carbohydrates, amine acids, vitamins, nanomaterials); library of 65,000 vols; Dir B. MURZUBRAIMOV.

Institute of Machinery Research: 720055 Bishkek, ul. Skryabina 23; tel. (312) 54-11-13; fax (312) 42-27-85; e-mail impulse@elcat.kg; attached to Nat. Acad. of Sciences of the Kyrgyz Republic; Dir Prof. M. DZHUMATAEV; publ. Collected Scientific Articles of the Institute of Machinery Research (every 2 years).

Institute of New Technologies: 714000 Osh, Ermaka 301; tel. (3222) 2-45-32; f. 1993; attached to Nat. Acad. of Sciences of the Kyrgyz Republic; 3 laboratories; Dir JOROMAMAT ARZIEV.

Institute of Power Engineering and Microelectronics: 715600 Dzhalal-Abad, Toktogul 43; tel. (3722) 5-24-85; f. 1993; attached to Nat. Acad. of Sciences of the Kyrgyz Republic; Dir S. KYDYRALIYEV.

Institute of Water Problems and Hydropower: 720033 Bishkek, ul. Frunze 533; tel. (312) 32-37-27; fax (312) 32-39-28; e-mail iwp@istc.kg; internet www.caresd.net/iwp; f. 1992; attached to Nat. Acad. of Sciences of the Kyrgyz Republic; researches on water resources of Central Asia; 60 mems; Dir Acad. DUSHEN MAMATKANOV.

Libraries and Archives
Bishkek

Central Library of the National Academy of Sciences of the Kyrgyz Republic: 720071 Bishkek, Chuy pr. 265A; tel. (312) 64-26-93; e-mail tokonovatt@hotmail.kg; f. 1943; 985,000 vols; Dir IBRAIMOVA SHIRIN ZHAPAROVNA.

Kyrgyz State National University Library: 720024 Bishkek, ul. Frunze 547; tel. (312) 9-98-26; 931,500 vols; Dir M. A. ASANBAYEV.

National Library of the Kyrgyz Republic: 720040 Bishkek, ul. Abdrakhmanova 208; tel. (312) 30-46-75; fax (312) 30-46-88; e-mail library@nlkr.gov.kg; internet www.nlkr.gov.kg; f. 1934; 21,700 mems; 5.8m. vols; Dir JULDYZ BAKASHOVA.

Scientific and Technical Library of Kyrgyzstan: 720302 Bishkek, Chuy pr. 106; tel. (312) 6-23-66; f. 1967; 5,817,000 vols (not incl. patents); Dir S. I. MAKAROV.

Museums and Art Galleries
Bishkek

Botanical Garden: 720064 Bishkek, Akhunbayev 1A; tel. (312) 43-53-55; e-mail bigarden@mail.ru; internet bigarden.by.ru; f. 1938; attached to Nat. Acad. of Sciences of the Kyrgyz Republic; library of 15,000 vols; Dir I. SODOMBEKOV; publ. Introduktsiya i Akklimatizatsiya Rastenii v Kyrgyzstane (1 a year).

State Historical Museum of Kyrgyzstan: Bishkek, Krasnooktyabrskaya ul. 236; f. 1925; Dir N. M. SEITKAZIYEVA.

The Gapar Aitiev Kyrgyz State Museum of Fine Arts: 720000 Bishkek, Abdrahmanova St 196; tel. (312) 66-16-23; fax (312) 62-05-48; e-mail knmii@mail.ru; internet www.knmii.lg.kg; f. 1935; paintings, drawings, sculptures and works of decorative and applied art, based on Kyrgyz and world art; modern Kyrgyz culture; works of S. Chuikov; 18,000 items: fine arts-painting fund about 4 000 exhibits, black-and-white arts 9 600, sculptures 1 000, decorative and applied arts more than 3 000; Dir Prof. YURISTANBEK SHYGAEV.

Universities

ACADEMY OF MANAGEMENT UNDER THE PRESIDENT OF THE KYRGYZ REPUBLIC

720040 Bishkek, ul. Panfilova 237

Telephone: (312) 22-13-85
Fax: (312) 66-36-14
E-mail: reception@amp.aknet.kg
Internet: www.amp.aknet.kg

Founded 1992
State control
Languages of instruction: Russian, English
Academic year: September to June

Rector: ASKAR KUTANOV
Provost: GROGORI FREIUK
Dean: ANARBEK ADYJAPAROV

Library of 17,394 vols
Number of teachers: 90
Number of students: 678

BISHKEK HUMANITIES UNIVERSITY

720044 Bishkek, pr. Tynchtyk

Telephone: (312) 48-40-35
Fax: (312) 54-14-05
E-mail: rectorat@bgupub.freent.bishkek.su
Internet: www.bhu.kg

Founded 1979
State control

Rector: ISHENGUL BOLJUROVA
Librarian: ROSA TURDUKEEVA

Library of 300,000 vols
Number of teachers: 280
Number of students: 6,000

Faculties of Administration and Sociology, Ecology and Management, German Philology, Information, Social Work and Psychology, Kyrgyz and Russian Philology, Oriental Studies and International Relations, Turkish Relations.

I. ARABAEV KYRGYZ STATE UNIVERSITY

720026 Bishkek, Razakov St 51, Block 2

Telephone: (312) 66-03-47
Fax: (312) 66-05-88
E-mail: taku55@mail.ru
Internet: www.arabaevarunet.kg

Founded 1952
State control; attached to Min. of Education and Science of the Kyrgyz Republic
Languages of instruction: Kyrgyz, Russian, English, German, French, Chinese, Arabic, Japanese
Academic year: September to June

Rector: Prof. TOLOBEK ABYLOVICH ABDYRACH-MANOV

Vice-Rector for Academic Affairs: Doc. TUU-GANBAI ABDYRACMANOVICH KONURBAEV

Librarian: DAVLETYAROVA NURILYA AITBAEVNA

Library of 500,000 vols textbooks

Number of teachers: 1,200

Number of students: 15,000

Publication: *Vestnik*

DEANS AND DIRECTORS

Economics and Management Institute: FELIKS TURDUKULOV

Institute of Linguistics: Prof. SYRTBAI MUSAEV

Faculty of Oriental Studies and International Relations: ZAMIR ALYMKULOV

Humanities Institute: JUMAN BEGIMATOV

Institute of History and Socio-legal Education: GULNARA KURUMBAEVA

Institute of Innovation and Communication Technologies: K.ADYRBEK KALDYBAEV

Institute of In-service Teacher Training: GULDANA AKIEVA

Institute of Pedagogies: JOOMART BAISALOV

State Language and Culture Institute: AIGUL DUISHEMBIEVA

PROFESSORS

AKIEVA, G.

AKMATALIEV, A.

ALIEV, SH.

ARTYKBAEV, M.

ASANKANOV, A.

BAIGAZIEV, S.

BAISALOV, J.

BEKBOEV, A.

BEKBOLOTOVA, A.

BORUBAVA, A.

CHOROV, M.

DABAEV, K.

DYUSHALIAEV, K.

RAKHIMOVA, M.

SATYVAYLDIEV, A.

INTERNATIONAL UNIVERSITY OF KYRGYZSTAN

720001 Bishkek, Chui pr. 255

Telephone: (312) 31-04-71

Fax: (312) 61-37-18

E-mail: iuk@mail.elcat.kg

Internet: www.iuk.kg

Founded 1993

State control

Language of instruction: Russian

Academic year: September to June

Pres.: ASYLBEK A. AIDARALIEV

Librarian: GULMIRA T. ABDYRAKOVNA

Library of 45,000 vols

Number of teachers: 43

Number of students: 3,250

Publication: *Bulletin of the IUK*

DEANS

Faculty of Humanitarian, Natural and Scientific Branches of Science: KUBAN B. AMANALIEV

Faculty of Law, Business and Computer Technology: AINURA A. ADIEVA

College of Ecology and Biotechnology: ALMAZBEK SHANAZAROV

College of Economics and Business: SHAYLOOBEK MUSAKODJOYEV

College of Foreign Languages: ZINAIDA KARAYEVA (Dir)

Polytechnic College: AMAN TOHLUKOV (Dir)

Virtual Academy of IUK: TILEK A. ASANALIEV

ISSYK-KUL STATE UNIVERSITY 'K. TYNYSTANOV'

722200 Karakol, Abdrahmanova 103

Telephone: (3922) 5-01-23

Fax: (3922) 5-04-98

E-mail: indepiksu@gmail.com

Founded 1940

State control

Language of instruction: Russian

Rector: Dr KURMANBEK ABDYLDAEV

Number of teachers: 382

Number of students: 6,710

DEANS

Faculty of Art and Culture: TYNCHYLYK KULCHUNOV

Faculty of Environmental Sciences and Tourism: RAHAT KERMALIEV

Faculty of Foreign Languages: SAYFULLA ABDULLAEV

Faculty of History: JENISHBEK KERIMKULOV

Faculty of Mathematics and Computer Science: RYSPEK ISKAKOV

Faculty of Natural Sciences: GULMIRA SARIEVA

Faculty of Philology, Pedagogy and Journalism: MURAT SADYROV

Faculty of Physical-Technical Studies: DAMIR ABDYLDAEV

Institute of Economics and Management: SALAMAT JOLDOSHEV

JALAL-ABAD STATE UNIVERSITY

715600 Jalal-Abad, ul. Lenina 57

Telephone: (3722) 5-59-68

Fax: (3722) 5-03-33

E-mail: jasu@infotel.kg

Founded 1926

State control

Languages of instruction: Russian, Kyrgyz

Academic year: September to June

Rector: JAMGYRBEK BOKOSHOV

Vice-Rector: NURMAT JAILOOBAYEV

Library of 58,000 vols

Number of teachers: 600

Number of students: 16,000

DEANS

Faculty of Agriculture and Biology: TALCHA AMANKULOVA

Faculty of Economics: BEKMAMAT JOOSHBAYEV

Faculty of Engineering and Technology: EGEMBERDI UMETOV

Faculty of Foreign Languages: ASKAR MURZAKULOV

Faculty of Medicine: SHAIRBEK SULAIMANOV

Faculty of Philology: ANARA KADYROVA

Faculty of Technology: MANAS SOORONBAYEV

KYRGYZ NATIONAL UNIVERSITY 'ZHUSUP BALASAGYN'

720024 Bishkek, ul. Frunze 547

Telephone: (312) 32-31-26

Internet: www.university.kg

Founded 1925, as Kyrgyz State Pedagogical Univ.; became Kyrgyz State Univ. 1951; present name 1993

State control

Academic year: September to June

Rector: AALYBEK AKUNOV

First Vice-Rector: KENESHBEK ALYMBEKOV

Number of teachers: 1,819

Number of students: 22,000

KYRGYZ–RUSSIAN SLAVIC UNIVERSITY

720000 Bishkek, ul. Kievskaya 44

Telephone: (312) 28-28-59

Fax: (312) 28-28-59

E-mail: krsu@krsu.edu.kg

Internet: www.krsu.edu.kg

Founded 1992

State control

Rector: Prof. VLADIMIR I. NIFADEV

Pro-Rectors: Prof. IMIL A. AKKOZIEV (Academic), Prof. EDNAN O. KARABAEV (Foreign Relations), Prof. VALERI M. LELELKIN (Scientific)

Number of teachers: 234

Number of students: 2,200

DEANS

Faculty of Distance Education: Asst. Prof. YURI D. SURODIN

Faculty of Economics: Prof. VICKTOR K. GAIDAMAKO

Faculty of Humanities: Prof. ABDYKADYR O. ORUSBAEV

Faculty of International Relations: (vacant)

Faculty of Law: Asst. Prof. LEILA CH. SYDYKOVA

Faculty of Medicine: Prof. ANES G. ZARUFYAN

Faculty of Science and Technology: Asst. Prof. VLADIMIR A. YURIKOV

KYRGYZ STATE UNIVERSITY OF CONSTRUCTION, TRANSPORT AND ARCHITECTURE

720020 Bishkek, ul. Maldybayeva 34

Telephone: (312) 44-35-61

Fax: (312) 44-51-36

E-mail: ksucta@elcat.kg

Founded 1954

State control

Rector: JUMABEK TENTIYEV

Faculties of Humanities, Kyrgyz and Arabic, Military Studies.

KYRGYZ TECHNICAL UNIVERSITY 'I. RAZZAKOV'

720044 Bishkek, pr. Mira 66

Telephone: (312) 54-51-25

Fax: (312) 54-51-62

E-mail: ktu@transfer.kg

Internet: ktu.edu.kg

Founded 1954 as Frunze Polytechnic Institute; present name 2005

State control

Academic year: September to July

Rector: Prof. MURATALY DJAMANBAEV

Vice-Rector for Academic Affairs: Prof. BEKJAN TOROBEKOV

Vice-Rector for Economics and Finance: Prof. JALALADIN GALBAEV

Vice-Rector for Science and External Connections: Prof. TURATBEK DUISHENALIEV

Vice-Rector for Social Affairs and Devt of State Language: GULMIRA BELEKOVA

Library of 550,000 vols

Number of teachers: 900

Number of students: 16,000

Publications: *Herald* (2 a year), *Science and New Technologies* (4 a year)

Faculties of food and textile technologies, information technology, machine building and transport, power engineering; institute of business and management; centre of distance education.

ATTACHED RESEARCH INSTITUTES

Educational Scientific Technological Centre 'Vostok-Mir' for Textile and Light Industry: e-mail ias52@mail.ru; Dir Prof. AIYM IMANKULOVA.

Kyrgyz Research Institute of Mineral Raw Materials: tel. (312) 61-34-85; Dir Prof. OMURKUL KABAEV.

Scientific and Research Institute for Chemical and Technical Problems: tel. (312) 54-51-29; e-mail mb051@jandex.ru; Dir Prof. MINARA BATKIBEKOVA.

Scientific and Research Institute for Energy and Communications: tel. (312)

54-90-35; e-mail suerkul@mail.ru; Dir Prof.
SUERKUL KADYRKULOV.

**Scientific and Research Institute for
Physical and Technical Problems:** tel.
(312) 54-57-86; e-mail jenishtur@yahoo.com;
Dir Prof. JENISHBEK TURGUMBAEV.

KYRGYZ–TURKISH UNIVERSITY 'MANAS'

720000 Bishkek, ul. Manasa 56

Telephone: (312) 54-19-42

Fax: (312) 54-19-35

E-mail: webmaster@manas.kg

Internet: www.manas.kg

Founded 1995 by govts of Kyrgyzstan and
Turkey

State control

Languages of instruction: Kyrgyz, Turkish

Academic year: September to June

Rectors: Prof. Dr SEYFULLAH ÇEVIK (acting),
Prof. Dr KARYBEK MOLDOBAEV

Pro-Rector: Prof. Dr ANVAR MOKEEV

Library of 44,000 books

Number of teachers: 179

Number of students: 1,369

Publications: *Fen Bilimleri Dergisi* (Journal
of Science and Engineering, 2 a year),
Sosyal Bilimler Dergisi (Journal of Social
Sciences, 2 a year)

DEANS

Faculty of Arts and Sciences: Assoc. Prof.
SUAYIP KARAKAŞ

Faculty of Communication: Prof. Dr YÜKSEL
KAVAK

Faculty of Management: Assoc. Prof. SEYFUL-
LAH ÇEVIK

Faculty of Technology: Prof. Dr EROL ÖZTE-
KIN

Higher Modern Language School: Assoc.
Prof. ZAMIRA DERBIŞEVA

Higher Vocational School: Dr HALIL SEVAL

KYRGYZ–UZBEK UNIVERSITY

723500 Osh, ul. Aitiyeva 27

Telephone: (3222) 5-70-55

Fax: (3222) 2-54-73

E-mail: kuu@oshmail.kg

Founded 1994

State control

Languages of instruction: Russian, Kyrgyz,
Uzbek

Academic year: September to June

Rector: IDRIS ERGESHOV

Vice-Rector: TOPCHUBAI ERGESHOVICH

Dean of World Languages and Int. Relations:
Dr ARSTAN KULNAZAROV

Library of 108,272 vols

Number of teachers: 420

Number of students: 8,000

Publication: *Science, Education, Technic* (4 a
year).

NARYN STATE UNIVERSITY

722600 Naryn, ul. Sagynbay Orozbak Uulu
25

Telephone: (3522) 5-08-14

Fax: (3522) 5-08-14

E-mail: nsu@ktnet.kg

Founded 1996

State control

Languages of instruction: Kyrgyz, Russian

Rector: ALMAZ AKMATALIYEV

Vice-Rector: TASHTANBEK SIYAYEV

Number of teachers: 240

Number of students: 4,500

DEANS

Faculty of Agro-Technology: KUBANYEBBEK
DUISHEKEYEV

Faculty of Economics: DAMIRA OMURALIYEVA

Faculty of Humanities: YRYS JAKEYEVA

Faculty of Information Technologies: ALMAN-
BET AMANALIEYEV

Faculty of Law: SALIDIN KALDYBAYEV

Faculty of Philology: ALI TURDUGULOV

OSH STATE UNIVERSITY

723500 Osh, ul. Lenina 331

Telephone: (3222) 2-29-12

Fax: (3222) 5-75-58

E-mail: oshsu@mail.ru

Internet: www.oshsu.kg

Founded 1951 as Osh Pedagogical Institute;
present name and status 1992

State control

Academic year: September to July

Rector: Prof. Dr MUHTAR OROZBEKOV

First Vice-Rector: Prof. Dr TURDUMAMAT
KADYROV

Vice-Rector for Part-Time Education: Prof.
ABDIMALIK OMORALIEV

Vice-Rector for Science: Prof. TASYLKAN JUMA-
BAEVA

Number of teachers: 1,600

Number of students: 30,000

Publication: *Vestnik* (research, 4 a year)

DEANS

Faculty of Business and Management: ASA-
NOV AVAZBEK RAIMZHANOVICH

Faculty of Economy and Finance: KUPUEV
PIRMAT

Faculty of Education: ATTOKUROV ASAMIDIN

Faculty of Kyrgyz Philology: JAMGYRCHIEVA
GULINA TOLOBAEVNA

Faculty of Law and History: KULDYSHEVA
GULSARA KENJEEVNA

Faculty of International Relations and State
Services: SULAIMANOV JOOMART MYRZAE-
VICH

Faculty of Mathematics and Information
Technology: ABDUVALIEV ABDYGANY

Faculty of Medicine: JEENBAEV JOLBORS

Faculty of Natural Science: KOLANOV ORUN-
BEK

Faculty of Nature Use and Geography:
NIZAMIEV ABDURASHIT

Faculty of Pedagogy: AKMATOVA TANAVAR

Faculty of Physics and Technics: KENZHAEV
IDIRISBEK

Faculty of Russian Philology: ATTOKUROV
ASAMIDIN

Faculty of Theology: ALIEV ASYLBEK

Faculty of Uzbek Humanities and Education:
TURSUNOV RAVSHANBEK

Faculty of World Languages: ANARBAEV ARAP
ANARBAEVICH

Financial-Juridical College: ERKEBAEV TAZHI-
MAMAT

Medical College in Osh: BERKMAMATOV SHA-
MYRBEK TOKTOSUNOVICH

Medical College in Uzgen: STANBAEV OZGON-
BAI TILLEBAEVICH

OSH TECHNOLOGICAL UNIVERSITY

723500 Osh, ul. Isanova 81

Telephone: (3222) 5-40-87

Fax: (3222) 5-30-53

E-mail: provsdo@mail.ru

Internet: www.oshtu.kg

Founded 1993; previously Osh Higher College of Technology

State control

Rector: Prof. TOKTOMAMATOV ABDIBALI TOKTO-
MAMATOVICH

Vice-Rector: SOPUEV ADAHIMJAN SOPUEVICH

Library of 72,540

Number of teachers: 482

Number of students: 11,939

Faculties of construction engineering, cybernetics and information technology, ecology
and geology, energetics and new energy
technology, finance and economics, language
technology, law, social sciences, State
Administration and Business, technological
engineering, transport and service technology; basic and professional education; evening and correspondence education

Publication: *Izvestiya OshTU*.

TALAS STATE UNIVERSITY

722720 Talas, ul. Karla Marksa 25

Telephone: (3422) 5-20-15

Fax: (3422) 5-25-80

E-mail: tsu1exrel@hotmail.kg

Founded 1996

State control

Languages of instruction: Kyrgyz, Russian,
English

Academic year: September to June

Rector: TOROKBEK OMURBEKOV

Library of 101,000 vols

Number of teachers: 248

Number of students: 2,983

DEANS

Faculty of Ecology and Agronomy: AIBEK
UPENOV

Faculty of Economics and Law: ESENGUL
OMUSHEV

Faculty of Education: ERKIN ABDRAIMOV

Faculty of Modern Languages: MANAS KAL-
MANBETOV

Faculty of Technology: NURLAN ASYLBEKOV

TŠUJ UNIVERSITY

720023 Bishkek, Kievskaya 187

Telephone: (312) 24-77-95

Fax: (312) 24-78-84.

Other Higher Educational Institutes

**Bishkek Academy of Finance and Eco-
nomics:** 720010 Bishkek, bul. Molodoi Gvar-
dii 55; tel. (312) 65-04-86; fax (312) 65-02-17;
e-mail kubat@freenet.kg; internet bafe
.freenet.kg; f. 1994; 53 teachers; 567 students; Rector Prof. ABDRAKHMAN S. MAVLYA-
NOV.

Kyrgyz Agrarian Academy: 720005 Bishkek, ul. Mederova 68; tel. (312) 54-52-10; fax
(312) 54-05-45; e-mail kaa@imfiko.bishkek
.su; f. 1933; depts: agronomy, agricultural
engineering, veterinary science, agricultural
economics, zootechnics, irrigation and land
reclamation, agricultural business; library:
1,043,000 vols; 280 teachers; 4,547 students;
Pres. J. AKIMALIYEV.

Kyrgyz State Academy of Medicine:
720000 Bishkek, Akhunbaeva 92; tel. (312)
54-58-81; fax (312) 54-58-59; e-mail is@ksma
.elcat.kg; internet www.ksma.edu.kg; f. 1939;
faculties of general medicine, sanitation and
hygiene, paediatric medicine, stomatology,
pharmaceutics, and foreign and contract
students; 408 teachers; 2,646 students; Rector (vacant).

Kyrgyz State Institute of Fine Art:
720460 Bishkek, ul. Dzhantosheva 115; tel.
(312) 47-02-25; f. 1967; music, cultural studies, language and literature, theatre, ballet;
library: 4,500 vols; 186 teachers; 765 students; Rector A. ASAKEYEV.

LAOS

The Higher Education System

In 1946 the French Indo-China provinces of Luang Prabang, Vientiane and Champasak were united as the Kingdom of Laos, which became independent within the French Union in 1949 and achieved sovereignty in 1953. Sisavangvong University, the country's first university and named after the King, was founded in 1958. However, in 1975 the insurgent Neo Lao Haksat (Lao Patriotic Front) gained control of the country, abolished the monarchy and established the Lao People's Democratic Republic; Sisavangvong University was dissolved into separate colleges. In 1995 the National University of Laos was created from a merger of various institutions of higher education. In 2006/07 there were 30,600 students enrolled at three university-level institutions and 30,100 in other institutions of higher education. The Ministry of Education has overall responsibility for higher education.

Admission to higher education requires the main secondary school certificate (Baccalauréat), and the applicant is required to sit an entrance examination. The undergraduate degree is the Bachelors and the course lasts four years; however, some disciplines, notably pharmacy, dentistry, engineering (all five years) and medicine (six years) require longer. There are no postgraduate degrees.

Vocational and technical education is offered by three kinds of institution: Vocational Schools, specializing in accountancy, teaching and nursery teaching; Middle Technical Schools, for training middle-level technicians; and Higher Technical Schools of Institutes, providing training for higher-level technicians. Both the Middle and Higher Technical Schools offer Diploma courses.

A formal accreditation and quality assurance process has been set up by the Ministry of Education. A new institution called the Accreditation and Quality Assurance Centre is the first National Accreditation Board.

Regulatory Bodies

GOVERNMENT

Ministry of Education: 1 rue Xan Lan, BP 67, Vientiane; tel. (21) 216013; fax (21) 216006; e-mail esitc@moe.gov.la; internet www.moe.gov.la; Min. PHANKHAM VIPHAVANH.

Ministry of Information and Culture: Thanon Setthathirat, Ban Xiengnheun Tha, Muang Chanthaburi, Vientiane; tel. (21) 212406; fax (21) 212408; e-mail email@mic.gov.la; internet www.mic.gov.la; Min. Dr BOSENGKHAM VONGDARA.

Learned Society

RELIGION, SOCIOLOGY AND ANTHROPOLOGY

Lao Buddhist Fellowship Organization: POB 775, 01000 Vientiane; tel. and fax (21) 412193; f. 1976; manages, develops and educates the Buddhist sangha and ensures that its members observe the laws of the country; 8,796 monks, 13,376 novices, 450 nuns and 563 sanghali; Pres. Rev. VICHIT SINGHARAJ.

Libraries and Archives

Vientiane

Bibliothèque Nationale du Laos (National Library of Laos): POB 704, Ministry of Information and Culture, Vientiane; tel. (21) 212452; fax (21) 213029; e-mail bailane@laotel.com; internet bnlaos.org; f. 1956; compiles nat. bibliography; 300,000 vols, 120 periodicals, 250 maps, 6,000 MSS; spec. collns incl. palm-leaf MSS; Dir KONGDEUANE NETTAVONGS; publs *Khao Bailan* (3 a year), *Lao Literature Series* (1 a year), *Siengkhene* (3 a year), *Vannasinh* (3 a year).

National University of Laos Central Library: Dongdok Campus, POB 7322, Dongdok, Vientiane; tel. (21) 770068; fax (21) 770381; e-mail nuol@nuol.edu.la; internet www.nuol.edu.la; f. 1995; 26,165 vols; Dir CHANSY PHUANGSOUKETH; Pres. Assoc. Prof. SOUKKONGSENG SAIGNALEUTH.

Museums and Art Galleries

Luang Phrabang

Haw Kham Royal Palace Museum (National Museum): Luang Phrabang; tel. (71) 212122; e-mail sisavath64@yahoo.com; f. 1976 as National Museum; Man. SISAVATH NHILATCHAY.

Pakse

Champasak Provincial Museum: Nat. Highway, 13S, Champasak, Pakse; tel. (31) 212501; f. 1995; archaeological, historical, ethnological artefacts; Dir THONGTINH PHOMPAKDY; Deputy Dir OUTHAI SENERATH; Deputy Dir PHOMMA NOYKHOUNSAVANH.

Vientiane

Ho Phra keo: Setthathirat Rd, 01000 Vientiane; tel. (21) 212618; fax (21) 212619; f. 1565 by King Setthathirat, became national museum 1965; colln of consecrated art objects; bronze statues of the Buddha in various positions of meditation; Dir THONGKHOUN SENGDALA.

Lao National Museum: Samsenthai Rd, 01000 Vientiane; tel. (21) 212460; fax (21) 212408; f. 1985 as Lao Revolutionary Museum, present status 2000; colln of historical and revolutionary exhibits; Dir PENGSAVANH VONGCHANDEE; Deputy Dir BOUNHUANG SISENGPASETH; Deputy Dir PHETMALAYVANH KEOBOUNMA.

Pha That Luang: Saysettha District, 01000 Vientiane; tel. (21) 212618; fax (21) 212619; f. 1566 by King Setthathirat, restored 1930; exhibits incl. a hair from the Buddha; built on the ruins of a 11th–13th-century Khmer temple; Dir THONGKHOUN SENGDALA.

Wat Si Saket: Lane Xang Ave, 01000 Vientiane; tel. (21) 212618; fax (21) 212619; f. 1818 by King Anouvong; constructed in the early Bangkok style; temple and nat. museum; colln of miniature statues and images of Buddha; Dir THONGKHOUN SENGDALA.

University

NATIONAL UNIVERSITY OF LAOS

POB 7322, Dongdok, 01000 Vientiane
Telephone: (21) 770068
Fax: (21) 770381
E-mail: nuol@nuol.edu.la
Internet: www.nuol.edu.la

Founded 1995 by merger of 10 existing institutions of higher education and a centre of agriculture
State control
Language of instruction: Lao
Academic year: September to June
Pres.: Assoc. Prof. SOUKKONGSENG SAIGNALEUTH
Rector: Dr SOMKOT MANGNOMEK
Vice-Rector for Academic Affairs: SAYAMANG VONGSAK
Vice-Rector for Planning and International Cooperation: TUYEN DONGVAN
Vice-Rector for Student Affairs: LAMMAY PHIPHAKKHAVONG
Chief Administrative Officer and Director of Rectorate Cabinet: Dr KONGSY SENGMANY
Dir of Central Library: CHANSY PHUANGSOUKET

Library of 120,000 vols
Number of teachers: 1,986
Number of students: 26,673

Publication: *Mahavithagnalay Heang Xath Lao* (Activities in the National Univeristy of Laos, 4 a year)

DEANS

Faculty of Agriculture: THONGPHANH KOUSONSAVATH
Faculty of Economics and Management: KHAMLUSA NOUANSAVANH
Faculty of Education: KHAM-ANE SAYASONE
Faculty of Engineering and Architecture: BOUALINH SOYSOUVANH
Faculty of Forestry: SOUCKONGSENG SAYALEUT

Faculty of Humanities and Social Sciences: SOUPHAP KHOUANGVICHITH

Faculty of Law and Political Science: KHAMSONE SOULIYASENG

Faculty of Letters: Assoc. Prof. Dr PHETSAMONE KHOUNSAVATH

Faculty of Medical Science: Assoc. Prof. Dr SOMOK KINGSADA

Faculty of Philology: PHETSAMONE KHOUNSAVAT

Faculty of Sciences: Assoc. Prof. Dr SOMKIAT PHASY

Faculty of Social Sciences: PHOUT SIMMALAVONG

School of Foundation Studies: Assoc. Prof. PHOUMY DOUANGCHAN (Dir)

Colleges

Lao–American College: Phonkeng Rd, Ban Phonkeng, Xaysettha Dist., 01000 Vientiane; tel. (21) 900454; fax (21) 900453; e-mail lac@laopdr.com; internet www.lac.edu.la; f. 1993; Dir GINNY VAN OSTRAND.

Sangkha College: Muang Chanthaburi, 01000 Vientiane; tel. (21) 212141; f. 1929 as Pariyatti Dhamma School, present name 1996; attached to Ministry of Education; faculties of arts, education; Dir Rev. BOUAKHAM SARIBOUT.

Sengsavanh College: 124 Dongmieng Rd, Sisavath Neua, Chanthabuli Dist., 01000 Vientiane; tel. and fax (21) 223822; e-mail info@sengsavanh.net; internet www.sengsavanh.net; f. 1997 as language centre, present status 2000; Dir KHAMSENE SISAVONG.

LATVIA

The Higher Education System

Until Latvia first achieved independence in 1921, it was under Russian Tsarist and then Russian Bolshevik rule. The earliest surviving institutions of higher education were established during the period (1918–20) of de facto civil war involving the Latvian provisional Government, the Russian Bolsheviks, German volunteers and White Russians (Mensheviks). Institutions dating from this period include the University of Latvia, the Latvian Academy of Music, and the Transport and Telecommunication Institute (all founded in 1919). Institutions founded during the early independent period include Daugavpils University and the Latvian Academy of Arts (both founded in 1921). In June 1940 the USSR invaded and occupied Latvia, which then became a Soviet Socialist Republic until regaining independence in 1991. The higher education system is administered according to the Education Act (1991) and Law on Higher Education Institutions (1995). A legal distinction is made between 'academic' and 'professional' higher education: university-level institutions offer both academic and professional qualifications; however, non-university level institutions of higher education offer only professional qualifications. The Ministry of Education and Science is the government body responsible for higher education. Latvia participates in the Bologna Process to establish a European Higher Education Area, the first phase of which is to adopt a credit-based system of comparable degrees with two main cycles (undergraduate and graduate). In 2006/07 higher education was offered at 57 institutions, with a total enrolment of 129,503 students.

Admission to higher education is on the basis of relevant passes in the General Secondary Education Certificate, often based on criteria established by individual institutions. In 2000 Latvia ratified the Bologna Process, and a two-tier Bachelors (Bakalaurs) and Masters (Magistrs) degree system has been established for both the academic and professional streams of higher education (although old-style professional diplomas are still offered by non-university-level institutions). Degrees are awarded on a credits-accrued basis. The standard undergraduate Bachelors degree course lasts three to four years and students must acquire 120–160 credits. Only a four-year Bachelors programme is regarded as a complete degree; a three-year course is regarded as an intermediate qualification. Bachelors degree courses in professional fields may last longer, such as dentistry (five years) and medicine (six years), and are regarded as equivalent to the Masters. The Masters is either a one- to two-year degree course requiring 40–80 credits, taken after the Bachelors, or a five-year undergraduate and postgraduate combined professional degree requiring 200 credits for completion. The Doctorate (Doktors) is the highest university-level degree and involves three to four years of full-time study, culminating with public defence of a thesis.

Technical and vocational education is principally available at post-secondary vocational colleges. The main award is the First Level (Higher) Vocational Diploma, which requires two to three years of study. In 2006/07 there were 40,439 students enrolled in vocational schools.

In 2010 the Government proposed significant reforms to the national system of higher education, including the closure of some of the country's universities and research institutes and the merging of others.

Regulatory and Representative Bodies

GOVERNMENT

Ministry of Culture: K. Valdemara iela 11A, Rīga 1364; tel. 6733-0200; fax 6733-0292; e-mail pasts@km.gov.lv; internet www.km.gov.lv; Min. SARMĪTE ĒLERTE; Head of Bureau VITA CĪRULE.

Ministry of Education and Science: Vaļņu iela 2, Rīga 1050; tel. 6722-6209; fax 6722-3905; internet www.izm.gov.lv; Min. ROLANDS BROKS.

ACCREDITATION

Nodibinājums Augstākās izglītības kvalitātes novrtšanas centrs (Foundation Higher Education Quality Evaluation Centre): Vaļņu iela 2, Rīga 1050; tel. 6721-3870; fax 6721-2558; e-mail aiknc@aiknc.lv; internet www.aiknc.lv; f. 1994; NGO carrying out assessment and accreditation of specific higher education instns and study programmes following recommendations of the Rectors' Ccl and the EU's requirements; Chair. Dr JURIS DZELME.

Academic Information Centre: Valnu iela 2, 1050 Rīga; tel. 6722-5155; fax 6722-1006; e-mail baiba@aic.lv; internet www.aic.lv; f. 1994; rep. to European diploma recognition networks; ENIC/NARIC Information instn on recognition of professional qualifications in regulated professions Latvian National Observatory; Dir BAIBA RAIMINA.

NATIONAL BODIES

Augstākās izglītības padome (Higher Education Council): Meistaru iela 21, Rīga 1050; tel. 6722-3392; fax 6722-0423; e-mail aip@latnet.lv; internet www.aip.lv; ind. instn that plans the devt of higher education and higher education establishments; 12 mems; Vice-Chair. Prof. Dr JURIS EKMANIS.

Latvijas Rektoru padome (Latvian Rectors' Council): Raiņa blvd 19, Rīga 1586; tel. 6703-4338; fax 6703-4368; e-mail rp@lanet.lv; internet www.rektorupadome.lv; 32 mems; Pres. Prof. ARVIDS BARSEVSKIS; Sec.-Gen. Prof. ANDREJS RAUHVARGERS.

Learned Societies

GENERAL

Latvian Academy of Sciences: Akadēmijas laukums 1, Rīga 1050; tel. 6722-5361; fax 6782-1153; e-mail lza@ac.lza.lv; internet www.lza.lv; f. 1946; divs of chemical, biological and medical sciences (Chair. R. VALTERS), physical and technical sciences (Chair. J. JANSONS), social sciences and humanities (Chair. I. JANSONE), agriculture and forestry (Chair. A. TREIMANIS); attached research institutes: see Research Institutes; library: see Libraries and Archives; 367 mems (105 full, 54 hon., 116 corresp., 92 foreign); Pres. JURIS EKMANIS; Sec.-Gen. V. KAMPARS; publs *Automātika un Skaitlošanas Tehnika* (Automation and Computer Engineering), *Heterociklisko Savienojumu Ķīmija* (Chemistry of Heterocyclic Compounds), *Kompozītmateriālu Mehānika* (Mechanics of Composite Materials), *Latvijas Fizikas un Tehnisko Zinātnu Žurnāls* (Latvian Journal of Physical and Technical Sciences), *Latvijas Ķīmijas Žurnāls* (Latvian Chemical Journal), *Magnitnaya Gidrodinamika* (Magnetic Hydrodynamics), *Proceedings of the Latvian Academy of Sciences* (in 2 sections: humanitarian sciences, and natural, exact and applied sciences).

LANGUAGE AND LITERATURE

Alliance Française: Merkela iela 13, Rīga 1050; tel. 6714-0175; offers courses and examinations in French language and culture and promotes cultural exchange with France.

British Council: Blaumana iela 5a-2, Rīga 1011; tel. 6728-1730; fax 6750-4100; e-mail mail@britishcouncil.lv; internet www.britishcouncil.lv; offers courses and examinations in English language and British culture and promotes cultural exchange with the UK in arts, science and education; library; Dir AGITA KALVINA.

Goethe-Institut: Torna iela 1, via Klostera iela, Rīga 1050; tel. 6750-8194; fax 6732-3999; e-mail info@riga.goethe.org; internet www.goethe.de/ms/pra/deindex.htm; offers courses and examinations in German language and culture and promotes cultural exchange with Germany; library of 7,000 vols; Dir RUDOLF DE BAEY.

Research Institutes

ECONOMICS, LAW AND POLITICS

Institute of Economics: Akadēmijas laukums 1, Rīga 1050; tel. and fax 6782-1289; e-mail raimara@ac.lza.lv; internet www .economics.lv; f. 1997; attached to Latvian Acad. of Sciences; Dir RAITA KARNĪTE.

EDUCATION

Educator Training Support Centre: Brivibas iela 72, Rīga 1011; tel. 6731-2081; fax 6731-2082; f. 1995; responsible for implementing and supporting govt policy on teacher-training and the devt of teaching skills; attached to Min. of Education and Science; Dir Dr SARMIS MIKUDA; publ. *Skolotājs*.

HISTORY, GEOGRAPHY AND ARCHAEOLOGY

Institute of History of Latvia: Akadēmijas laukums 1, Rīga 1050; tel. 6522-3715; fax 6722-5044; e-mail lvi@lza.lv; internet www .lvi.lv; f. 1936; attached to Univ. of Latvia; library of 4,000 vols; Dir Dr GUNTIS ZEMITIS; publ. *Latvijas Vestures Institūta Žurnāls* (Journal, 4 a year).

LANGUAGE AND LITERATURE

Institute of Literature, Folklore and Art: Akadēmijas laukums 1, Rīga 1050; tel. 6721-2872; fax 6722-9017; e-mail litfom@lza .lv; f. 1992; attached to Univ. of Latvia; Dir BENEDIKTS KALNAČS; publ. *Letonica* (2 a year).

Latvian Language Institute: Akadēmijas laukums 1, Rīga 1050; tel. and fax 6722-7696; e-mail latv@ac.lza.lv; attached to Latvian Acad. of Sciences; Dir J. VALDMANIS; publ. *Linguistica Lettica* (2 a year).

MEDICINE

Institute of Experimental and Clinical Medicine, University of Latvia: O. Vaciesa iela 4, Rīga 1004; tel. 6761-2038; e-mail ekmi@lu.lv; internet www.lu.lv; f. 1946; physiology, oncology; Dir Dr PETERIS TRETJAKOVS.

NATURAL SCIENCES

Biological Sciences

August Kirchenstein Institute of Microbiology and Virology: Rīga Stradiņs Univ., Ratsupites str. 5, Rīga 1067; tel. 6742-6197; fax 6742-8306; e-mail rsu_mvi@latnet.lv; internet www.rsu.lv/ augusta-kirhensteina-mikrobiologijas-un--virusologijas-instituts; f. 1946, re-f. 1993; attached to Min. of Education and Science and Univ. of Latvia, Rīga Stradiņs Univ; Dir Dr MODRA MUROVSKA.

Institute of Biology: Miera iela 3, Salaspils 2169; tel. and fax 6794-4988; e-mail office@ email.lubi.edu.lv; internet www.lubi.edu.lv; f. 1951; attached to Univ. of Latvia; 12 laboratories and 1 research group; provides theoretical basis for sustainable devt of natural resources; library of 23,673 vols; Dir Dr VIESTURS MELECIS.

Latvian Institute of Organic Synthesis: Aizkraukles iela 21, Rīga 1006; tel. 6755-1822; fax 6755-0338; e-mail sinta@osi.lv; f. 1957; attached to Latvian Acad. of Sciences; Dir Prof. I. KALVINSH; publ. *Chemistry of Heterocyclic Compounds* (in Russian and English, 12 a year).

Latvian State Institute of Wood Chemistry: Dzērbenes str. 27, Rīga 1006; tel. 6755-3063; fax 6755-0635; e-mail koks@edi.lv; internet www.kki.lv; f. 1946; devt of technologies for obtaining materials and products from wood and wood biomass; science-based sustainable utilization of Latvia's wood resources for economic, social and environmental benefits; 60 academic staff; library of 10,000 vols; Scientific Dir Dr BRUNO ANDERSONS; Dir Dr AIVARS ZHURINSH; Scientific Sec. Dr ARNIS KOKOREVICS.

Physical Sciences

Institute of Astronomy of the University of Latvia: Raiņa bulv. 19, Rīga 1586; tel. 6703-4580; fax 6703-4582; internet www.astr .lu.lv; f. 1946; satellite laser ranging; low dispersion spectral and photometric studies of carbon stars; digitalization of wide field Schmidt camera astro plates covering time span from 1966 to 2005; updating of Catalog of Carbon stars (CGCS); optical system design and calculation; Dir Dr ILGMĀRS EGLĪTIS; Scientific Sec. KALVIS SALMINS; publ. *Zvaigžņotā Debess* (The Starry Sky, 4 a year).

Institute of Inorganic Chemistry: Miera iela 34, Rīgas rajons, Salaspils 2169; tel. 6794-4711; fax 6780-0779; e-mail nki@nki.lv; internet www.nki.lv; f. 1946; attached to Rīga Technical Univ. and Latvian Acad. of Sciences; Dir Dr Ing. JANIS GRABIS; publ. *Latvijas kīmijas žurnals* (Latvian Journal of Chemistry, 4 a year).

Institute of Physical Energetics: Aizkraukles iela 21, Rīga 1006; tel. 6755-2011; fax 6755-0839; e-mail fei@edi.lv; internet www .innovation.lv/fei; f. 1946; clean fossil energy technologies; electrical devices and machines; energy efficiency; energy–environmental policy studies; energy saving management; grids and electricity supply systems; regional energy sector analysis and optimization; renewable energy resources; researches into advanced materials and solid state physics problems; Dir Prof. J. EKMANIS; Vice-Dir Dr GUNTA SLIHTA; publ. *Latvian Journal of Physics and Technical Sciences* (6 a year, print and online).

Institute of Physics: Miera iela 32, Rīgas rajons, Salaspils 2169; tel. 6794-4700; fax 6790-1214; e-mail fizinst@sal.lv; internet www.ipul.lv; f. 1946; attached to Univ. of Latvia; engineering physics and liquid metal technologies; Dir Dr JĀNIS FREIBERGS.

Nuclear Research Centre: Miera iela 31, Salaspils 2169; tel. 6790-1210; fax 6790-1212; e-mail brzs@lanet.lv; attached to Latvian Acad. of Sciences; Dir A. LAPENAS.

PHILOSOPHY AND PSYCHOLOGY

Institute of Philosophy and Sociology: Akadēmijas laukums 1, Rīga 1940; tel. 6722-9208; fax 6721-0806; e-mail fsi@lza.lv; internet www.fsi.lv; f. 1981; attached to Univ. of Latvia; Dir MAIJA KŪLE; publs *Filozofia* (1 a year), *Religiski-filozofiski raksti* (religious-philosophical writings).

TECHNOLOGY

Institute of Electronics and Computer Science: Dzērbenes iela 14, Rīga 1006; tel. 6755-4500; fax 6755-5337; e-mail info@edi.lv; internet www.edi.lv; f. 1960; research and design in fields of electronics, signal processing and computerized systems; design and production of hardware/software systems and virtual instruments; library of 10,000 vols; Dir Dr MODRIS GREITANS; publ. *Avtomatika i vychislitelnaya technika* (6 a year).

Institute of Polymer Mechanics: Aizkraukles iela 23, Rīga 1006; tel. 6755-1145; fax 6782-0467; e-mail polmech@pmi.lv; f. 1963; attached to Univ. of Latvia; Dir J. JANSONS; publ. *Mechanics of Composite Materials* (6 a year).

Research Institute of Water and Land Management: Dobeles iela 43, Jelgava 3000; tel. 6302-5517; fax 6302-7180; e-mail janis.valters@apollo.lv; f. 1940; Dir Dr JANIS VALTERS.

Scientific Research Institute of Microdevices: Maskavas iela 240, Rīga 1063; tel. 6725-1619; fax 6725-1000; f. 1962; semi-conductor devices and integrated circuits; Dir ARNIS KUNDZINS.

Libraries and Archives

Rīga

Latvian Academic Library: Rūpniecības iela 10, Rīga 1235; tel. 6710-6206; fax 6710-6202; e-mail acadlib@lib.acadlib.lv; internet www.acadlib.lv; f. 1524; 3,100,000 vols, incunabula, MSS; spec. collns incl. Latvian literature; Dir VENTA KOCERE.

National Library of Latvia: Kr. Barona iela 14, Rīga 1423; tel. 6736-5250; fax 6728-0851; e-mail lnb@lnb.lv; internet www.lnb.lv; f. 1919; 4,478,424 vols; Dir ANDRIS VILKS; publs *Bibliotēku zinātnes aspekti* (irregular), *Latviešu Zinātne un Literatūra* (irregular).

Patent and Technology Library: Šķūņu 17, Rīga 1974; tel. (7) 6722-7310; fax (7) 6721-0767; e-mail patbib@patbib.gov.lv; internet www.patbib.gov.lv; f. 1949; part of Patent Office of the Republic of Latvia; 38.7m. patents; Dir AGNESE BUHOLTE.

The Library of the University of Latvia: 4 Kalpaka Blvd, Rīga 1820; tel. 6703-4432; e-mail info-bibl@lu.lv; internet www.lu.lv/ eng/library; f. 1862; 2m. vols; Dir Dr IVETA GUDAKOVSKA; Librarian UGIS SKELE.

Museums and Art Galleries

Bauska

Bauska Castle Museum: Pilskalns, Bauska 3901; tel. and fax 6392-3793; e-mail bauska .pils@e-apollo.lv; f. 1990; Bauska Castle history; Dir M. SKANIS.

Cēsis

Cēsis Museum of History and Art: Pils laukums 9, Cēsis 4100; tel. 6412-2615; f. 1925; history, ethnography; library of 8,000 vols; Dir A. VANADZIŅŠ.

Rīga

Latvian Museum of Natural History: K. Barona iela 4, Rīga 1050; tel. 6735-6023; fax 6735-6027; e-mail ldm@dabasmuzejs.gov.lv; internet www.dabasmuzejs.gov.lv; f. 1845; zoology, entomology, botany, mycology, palaeontology, geology, anthropology, environmental science, pedagogy and museology; library of 18,000 vols; Dir SKAIDRĪTE RUSKULE; publ. *Daba un Muzejs* (1 a year).

Latvian Open-Air Ethnographical Museum: Brīvības iela 440, Rīga 1056; tel. 6799-4510; fax 6799-4178; e-mail info@ brivdabas-muzejs.lv; internet www.muzejs .lv; f. 1924; wooden architecture since 17th century; archive of 70,000 units; Dir JURIS INDĀNS.

Museum of Foreign Art: Pils laukumā 3, Rīga 1050; tel. 6722-6467; fax 6722-8776; e-mail arzemju.mm@apollo.lv; internet www .amm.lv; f. 1773; library of 15,300 vols; Dir DAIGA UPENIECE.

Museum of the History of Rīga and Navigation: Palasta iela 4, Rīga 1050; tel. 6721-1358; fax 6721-0226; e-mail direkt@ rigamuz.lv; internet www.vip.latnet.lv/

museums/riga; f. 1773; library of 24,000 vols; Dir K. RADZIŅA.

National History Museum of Latvia: Pils laukumā 3, Rīga 1050; tel. 6722-3004; fax 6722-0586; e-mail museum@history-museum .lv; internet www.history-museum.lv; f. 1869; Dir A. RADIŅŠ.

Rainis Museum of the History of Literature and Arts: Pils laukums 1050; tel. and fax 6721-6425; e-mail pumpurs@acad .latnet.lv; f. 1925; Dir I. ZUKULIS.

State Museum of Art: K. Valdemāra iela 10A, Rīga 1010; tel. 6732-5051; fax 6735-7408; e-mail vmm@latnet.lv; internet www .vmm.lv; f. 1905; Dir MĀRA LĀCE.

Stradiņ Museum of the History of Medicine: Antonijas iela 1, Rīga 1360; tel. 722-29-14; fax 721-13-23; e-mail museum2@apollo .lv; internet www.mwm.lv; f. 1957; library of 39,851 vols, 16,368 rare books; Dir E. BERZINA; publ. *Acta medico-historica Rigensia*.

Salaspils

National Botanic Garden: Miera iela 1, Salaspils 2169; tel. and fax 6794-5460; e-mail sekretare@nbd.gov.lv; internet www.nbd.gov .lv; f. 1956; attached to Min. of the Environment and Regional Devt; library of 24,000 vols; Dir ANDREJS SVILANS; publs *Index Seminum* (1 a year), *The Baltic Botanical Gardens* (every 2 years).

Universities

DAUGAVPILS UNIVERSITY

Vienības ielā 13, Daugavpils 5400
Telephone: 6542-2180
E-mail: du@du.lv
Internet: du.lv/lv
Founded 1921
State control
Rector: Prof. ARVĪDS BARŠEVSKIS
Vice-Rector for Research: Assoc. Prof. ELITA JERMOLAJEVA
Vice-Rector for Studies: Doc. IRĒNA KAMINSKA
Library of 400,000 vols
Number of teachers: 260
Number of students: 4,700

DEANS

Dept of Sports Pedagogy: JĀNIS JAUJA (Head)
Faculty of Education and Management: ILGA SALĪTE
Faculty of Humanities: VALENTĪNA LIEPA
Faculty of Music and Arts: MĀRIS ČAČKA
Faculty of Natural Sciences and Mathematics: VALFRĪDS PAŠKEVIČS
Faculty of Social Sciences: VLADIMIRS MEŅŠIKOVS

LATVIA UNIVERSITY OF AGRICULTURE

Lielā iela 2, Jelgava 3001
Telephone: 6302-2584
Fax: 6302-7238
E-mail: rector@llu.lv
Internet: www.llu.lv
Founded 1939 as Jelgava Agricultural Acad.; present name and status 1991
State control
Languages of instruction: Latvian, English, German and Russian
Rector: JURIS SKUJĀNS
Vice-Rector for Research: PĒTERIS RIVŽA
Vice-Rector for Studies: ARNIS MUGURĒVIČS
Library of 509,173 vols
Number of teachers: 482
Number of students: 4,691

Publication: *Works* (1 a year).

RĪGA STRADIŅŠ UNIVERSITY

Dzirciema iela 16, Rīga 1007
Telephone: 6740-9232
Fax: 6747-1815
E-mail: rsu@rsu.lv
Internet: www.rsu.lv
Founded 1951 as Rīga Medical Institute; present name and status 2002
State control
Languages of instruction: Latvian, English
Academic year: September to June
Rector: JĀNIS VĒTRA
Vice-Rector for Science: IVETA OZOLANTA
Vice-Rector for Teaching: ILZE AKOTA
Library of 294,000 vols
Number of teachers: 355
Number of students: 4,846
Publications: *Dentistry* (1 a year), *Kirurģija* (Surgery, 2 a year), *Zinātniskie raksti* (medicine and pharmacy)
Faculties of communication studies, continuing education, European studies, medicine, nursing, pharmacy, public health, rehabilitation medicine, stomatology; division of doctoral studies and institute of law.

RĪGA TECHNICAL UNIVERSITY

Kaļķu iela 1, Rīga 1658
Telephone: 6708-9333
Fax: 6782-0094
Internet: www.rtu.lv
Founded 1990
Rector: Dr IVARS KNĒTS
Library of 2,000,000 vols
Number of teachers: 589
Number of students: 15,330
Publications: *Jaunais Inzenieris* (newspaper), *Scientific Proceedings of RTU* (4 a year)
Brs in Daugavpils, Liepaja and Ventspils.

DEANS

Faculty of Architecture and Urban Planning: Prof. Dr IVARS STRAUTMANIS
Faculty of Building and Civil Engineering: Dr Ing. JURIS SMIRNOVS
Faculty of Computer Science and Information Technology: Dr Ing. JANIS GRUNDSPENKIS
Faculty of Electronics and Telecommunications: Assoc. Prof. ILMARS SLAIDINS
Faculty of Engineering Economics: Prof. Dr KONSTANTĪNS DIDENKO
Faculty of Materials Science and Applied Chemistry: Prof. VALDIS KAMPAR
Faculty of Power and Electrical Engineering: Prof. JĀNIS GERHARDS
Faculty of Transport and Mechanical Engineering: Prof. GUNDARS LIBERTS

ATTACHED CENTRES

Institute of Humanities: Āzenes iela 16/20, Rīga 1048; e-mail huminst@bf.rtu.lv; internet www.bf.rtu.lv; Dir Dr ANITA LANKA.

Institute of Languages: Meža iela 1/1–409, Rīga 1048; e-mail valodu.instituts@rtu.lv; internet omega.rtu.lv/vi; Dir Dr LARISA IĻJINSKA.

Rīga Business School: Skolas iela 1, Rīga 1010; e-mail admin@rbs.lv; internet www.rbs .lv; Dir Dr JĀNIS GRĒVIŅŠ.

UNIVERSITY OF LATVIA

Raiņa bulvāris 19, Rīga 1586
Telephone: 6703-4444
Fax: 6722-5039
E-mail: lu@lu.lv

Internet: www.lu.lv
Founded 1919
Language of instruction: Latvian
Academic year: September to June
Rector: Prof. Dr MĀRCIS AUZIŅŠ
Vice-Rector: JURIS KRŪMIŅŠ
Vice-Rector: INDRIĶIS MUIŽNIEKS
Librarian: IVETA GUDAKOVSKA
Number of teachers: 1,023
Number of students: 17,257
Publications: *Acta Universitatis Latviensis* (10 a year), *Agora* (2 a year), *Ceļš* (theology, 1 a year), *History of Latvia* (4 a year), *Journal of Baltic Psychology* (1 a year), *Journal of the Latvian Institute of History* (4 a year), *Lettonics* (every 2 years), *Linguistica Lettica* (every 2 years), *Magnetohydrodynamics* (4 a year), *Mechanics of Composite Materials* (6 a year), *The Starry Sky* (4 a year)

DEANS

Faculty of Biology: Dr NILS ROSTOKS
Faculty of Computing: Prof. JURIS BORZOVS
Faculty of Chemistry: Assoc. Prof. JĀNIS SVIRKSTS
Faculty of Economics and Management: Assoc. Prof. MĀRIS PURGAILIS
Faculty of Education, Psychology and Art: Assoc. Prof. ANDRIS KANGRO
Faculty of Geography and Earth Sciences: Prof. OLGERTS NIKODEMUS
Faculty of History and Philosophy: Prof. GVIDO STRAUBE
Faculty of Law: Prof. KRISTĪNE STRADA-ROZENBERGA
Faculty of Medicine: Prof. INGRĪDA RUMBA-ROZENFELDE
Faculty of Humanities: Prof. ILZE RŪMNIECE
Faculty of Physics and Mathematics: Assoc. Prof. LEONĪDS BULIGINS
Faculty of Social Sciences: Prof. JURIS ROZENVALDS
Faculty of Theology: Dr RALFS KOKINS

ATTACHED RESEARCH INSTITUTES

August Kirhenshtein Institute of Microbiology and Virology: Dir Dr VAIRA SAULĪTE.

Biomedical Research and Study Centre: Dir Dr ZINAIDA SOMŠTEINE.

Institute of Accountancy: Dir Dr INTA BRUNA.

Institute of Aquatic Ecology: Dir Dr chem. JURIS AIGANS.

Institute of Astronomy: Dir Dr ARTURS BALKAVS-GRĪNHOFS.

Institute of Atomic Physics and Spectroscopy: Dir Dr hab. ph. JANIS SPIGULIS.

Institute of Biology: Dir Dr VIESTURS MELECIS.

Institute of Chemical Physics: Dir Dr chem. DONATS ERTS.

Institute of Educational Research: Dir Dr ANDRIS KANGRO.

Institute of Electronics and Computer Science: Dir Dr IVARS BILINSKIS.

Institute of Environmental Science and Management: Dir Dr RAIMONDS ERNŠTEINS.

Institute of Experimental and Clinical Medicine: Dir Dr RENATE LIGENE.

Institute of Finance: Dir Prof. Dr ELMĀRS ZELGALVIS.

Institute of Geodesy and Geoinformatics: Dir Dr JĀNIS BALODIS.

Institute of Geology: Dir Assoc. Prof. EDVINS LUKSHEVICHS.

Institute of History of Latvia: Dir Dr hist. JANIS BERZINŠ.

Institute of Human Rights: Alternate Dir GITA FELDHŪNE.

Institute of International Affairs: Dir Prof. Dr JURIS BOJĀRS.

Institute of Literature, Folklore and Art: Dir Dr BENEDIKTS KALNAČS.

Institute of Marketing and Quality Management: Dir Prof. Dr VALĒRIJS PRAUDE.

Institute of Mathematics: Dir Dr ANDREJS REINFELDS.

Institute of Mathematics and Computer Science: Dir Prof. Dr JĀNIS BĀRZDIŅŠ.

Institute of Microbiology and Biotechnology: Dir Prof. Dr ULDIS VIESTURS.

Institute of National Economy: Dir Dr ROBERTS ŠKAPARS.

Institute of Philosophy and Sociology: Dir Prof. Dr MAIJA KŪLE.

Institute of Physics: Dir Dr JĀNIS FREIBERGS.

Institute of Polymer Mechanics: Dir Dr JURIS JANSONS.

Institute of Postgraduate Education in Medicine: Dir Dr JUNIS ZEMMERIS.

Institute of Solid State Physics: Dir Dr ANDRIS ŠTERNBERGS.

Latvian Language Institute: Dir Dr ILGA JANSONE.

Other Higher Educational Institutions

Latvian Academy of Arts: Kalpaka bulvāris 13, Rīga 1867; tel. 6733-2202; fax 6722-8963; e-mail lma@latnet.lv; internet www.lma.lv; f. 1921; depts of art education, art history and theory, ceramics, environmental art, fashion design, glass, graphic arts, graphic design, industrial design, interior design, metal design, painting, sculpture, textiles; library: 32,000 vols; 100 teachers;

638 students; Rector Prof. JĀNIS ANDRIS OSIS; Dean of Students Assoc. Prof. UGIS AUZIŅŠ.

Latvian Academy of Music: Krishyana Barona iela 1, Rīga 1050; tel. 6722-8684; fax 6782-0271; e-mail academy@music.lv; internet www.lmuza.lv; f. 1919; choral conducting, composition, music education, musicology, orchestral instruments, piano, singing; library: 150,000 vols, 47,000 tape recordings, 36,000 records, 1,300 audio cassettes, 2,800 CDs, 1,000 video cassettes; 246 teachers; 426 students; Rector Prof. JURIS KARLSONS.

Transport and Telecommunication Institute: Lomonosova str. 1, Rīga 1019; tel. 6710-0650; fax 6710-0660; e-mail tsi@tsi.lv; internet www.tsi.lv; f. 1919, fmrly Rīga Aviation Univ., present status 1999; faculties of computer science and electronics, economics and transport, management; library: 15,000 vols; 140 teachers; 3,500 students; Rector EUGENE KOPYTOV.

LEBANON

The Higher Education System

The two oldest universities in Lebanon are private institutions founded by Christian denominations in the 19th century while Lebanon was still under Ottoman Turkish rule; they are the American University of Beirut (founded 1866; formerly Syrian Protestant College) and the Université Saint Joseph (founded 1875; Jesuit control). Following the dissolution of the Ottoman Empire after the First World War (1914–18), a Greater Lebanese state was created by the Allied powers, administered by France under a League of Nations mandate from 1920 until independence was declared in 1941. Institutions of higher education established in this period include the Lebanese American University (founded 1924 by the United Presbyterian Church, USA), the Near East School of Theology (founded 1932) and the Académie Libanaise des Beaux-Arts (founded 1937). The higher education system displays strong French and US influences, which vary from institution to institution reflecting whether they were set up by US missionaries or the French authorities. Furthermore, higher education is dominated by private institutions; only the Université Libanaise (founded 1951) is under state control. In 1998 Lebanon secured a loan of US $60m. from the World Bank, in order to restructure the country's system of technical and vocational education. Some 196,682 Lebanese students were enrolled in higher education in the 2007/08 academic year.

Admission to university undergraduate courses is on the basis of the secondary school qualification (Baccalauréat), and students may also be required to sit an entrance examination. Depending on the institution, the main undergraduate degree is known as the Licence, Bachelors, Maîtrise or Diploma, and is usually three to five years in duration. Medical students are awarded a professional degree called the Doctorat after seven years. A range of degrees is also available at the first stage of postgraduate study, including Masters, Maîtrise or Diplôme d'études Supérieures. The final stage of university-level degrees is the Doctorat d'état.

Institutions of higher education are accredited by the Ministry of Education and Higher Education and the Commission of Equivalences. The Université Libanaise is the only institution accredited solely by the Ministry, being the only public university in the country. Other institutions must be individually accredited by the Commission of Equivalences. Accreditation is given in the form of a government decree. Each decree has a number and a date (the Faculty of Arts at the University of Balamand is accredited according to edict 4885 from 4/6/1988). The American University of Beirut is a US institution that is accredited by the Middle States Association of Schools and Colleges. It is recognized by the Government of Lebanon but does not have its courses accredited in the same way as Lebanese private universities.

Regulatory Bodies

GOVERNMENT

Ministry of Culture: Immeuble Hatab, rue Madame Curie, Verdun, Beirut; tel. (1) 744250; fax (1) 756303; e-mail omarhala_48@hotmail.com; internet www .culture.gov.lb; Min. GABY LAYYOUN.

Ministry of Education and Higher Education: UNESCO Palace Quarter, Habib Abi Chahla Sq., Beirut; tel. (1) 789611; fax (1) 789606; e-mail info@higher-edu.gov.lb; internet www.higher-edu.gov.lb; f. 1992 as Directorate Gen. of Culture and Higher Education as part of Min. of Culture, present status 2002; Min. HASSAN DIAB.

Learned Societies

GENERAL

UNESCO Office Beirut and Regional Bureau for Education in the Arab States: POB 5244, Beirut; located at: Cité Sportive Blvd, Beirut; tel. (1) 850013; fax (1) 824854; e-mail beirut@unesco.org; internet www.unesco.org.lb; designated Cluster Office for Iraq, Jordan, Lebanon, Syria and Palestinian Autonomous Territories; Regional Bureau for Education in the Arab States; Dir RAMZI SALAMÉ.

BIBLIOGRAPHY, LIBRARY SCIENCE AND MUSEOLOGY

Lebanese Library Association: POB 113/5367, Beirut; or c/o American University of Beirut, University Library/Serials Dept, Beirut; tel. (1) 350000; fax (1) 744703; f. 1960; 218 mems; Pres. FAWZ ABDALLAH; Sec. RUDAYNAH SHOUJAH.

ECONOMICS, LAW AND POLITICS

Association Libanaise des Sciences Juridiques: Faculté de Droit et des Sciences politiques, Université Saint Joseph, BP 17-5208, Beirut; tel. (1) 421000; fax (1) 421045; f. 1963; represents Lebanon in the Int. Asscn of Legal Science; study of legal problems in Lebanon, conferences, etc.; 40 mems; Pres. PIERRE GANNAGÉ; Sec.-Gen. NABIL MAAMARY; publ. *Proche-Orient* (judicial studies).

LANGUAGE AND LITERATURE

British Council: Sadat/Sidani St, Azar Bldg, Ras Beirut; tel. (1) 740123; fax (1) 739461; e-mail general.enquiries@lb .britishcouncil.org; internet www .britishcouncil.org/lebanon; teaching centre; offers courses and exams in English language and British culture and promotes cultural exchange with the UK; Dir Dr KEN CHURCHILL; Teaching Centre Man. ANDREW MACKENZIE.

Goethe-Institut: Damascus Rd, Berythech Bldg, 7th Floor, Beirut; tel. (1) 422291; fax (1) 422294; e-mail info@beirut.goethe.org; internet www.goethe.de/beirut; offers courses and exams in German language and culture and promotes cultural exchange with Germany; library of 9,000 vols; Dir FAREED C. MAJARI.

Instituto Cervantes: Centre Ville, 287 A/B Maarad St, BP 11-1202, Beirut; tel. (1) 970253; fax (1) 970291; e-mail cenbei@ cervantes.es; internet beirut.cervantes.es; offers courses and exams in Spanish language and culture and promotes cultural exchange with Spain and Spanish-speaking Latin and Central America; library of 5,000 vols; Dir ANDRÉS PÉREZ SÁNCHEZ-MORATE.

Research Institutes

GENERAL

Institut Français du Proche-Orient: c/o Abou Roumaneh, 11, rue Chukri Al-Assali (à côté de l'ambassade du Japon), 344 Damas, Syria; tel. (1) 420291; fax (1) 420295; e-mail contact@ifporient.org; internet www .ifporient.org; f. 2003; study of Middle East in all its aspects: economy, history, human geography, physical geography, sociology, towns; library of 125,000 vols; Dir FRANÇOIS BURGAT.

Orient-Institut der Deutschen Morgenländischen Gesellschaft Beirut (Orient Institute of the German Institute of Oriental Studies, Beirut): POB 11-2988, Riad el-Solh 1107 2120, Beirut; tel. (1) 359424; fax (1) 359176; e-mail dir@oidmg.org; internet www .oidmg.org; f. 1961 by the Deutsche Morgenländische Gesellschaft (DMG); since 2002 part of DIGA (German Institutes for Humanities Abroad); activities in the field of Oriental research (Islamic, Arabic, Persian, Turcological, Semitic), philology, and contemporary history, incl. field research, history of the eastern Churches; cooperation with univs in the Middle East and Germany; library of 133,000 vols; Dir Prof. Dr MANFRED KROPP; publs *Beiruter Blätter* (every 2 years), *Bibliotheca Islamica—Beiruter Texte und Studien*.

ECONOMICS, LAW AND POLITICS

Centre for Arab Unity Studies: Beit Al-Nahda Bldg, Basra Str., Hamra Hamra, POB 113-6001, Beirut 2034 2407; tel. (1) 750084; fax (1) 750088; e-mail info@caus.org.lb; internet www.caus.org.lb; f. 1975; an ind., non-political centre for scientific research on all aspects of Arab soc. and Arab unity, particularly in the fields of economics, politics, sociology and education; activities are governed and implemented by 3 bodies: Board of Trustees, Exec. Cttee and Gen. Secretariat; library of 18,000 vols, 1,657 periodicals; Dir-Gen. Dr YOUSSEF CHOUEIRY; publ. *Al-Mustaqbal Al-Arabi* (The Arab Future, 12 a year).

Lebanese Center for Policy Studies: POB 55-215, Vanlian Center, 8th Fl., Mkalles, Beirut; tel. (1) 486429; fax (1) 490375; e-mail info@lcps-lebanon.org; internet www .lcps-lebanon.org; f. 1989; research into political, social and economic development; library facilities; Dir Dr OUSSAMA SAFA.

HISTORY, GEOGRAPHY AND ARCHAEOLOGY

Institut Français d'Archéologie du Proche Orient: rue de Damas, POB 11-1424, Beirut; tel. (1) 615844; fax (1) 615866; e-mail ifapo@lb.refer.org; f. 1946; Dir JEAN-LOUIS HUOT; library of 45,000 vols; brs in Syria and Jordan; publs *Bibliothèque Archéologique et Historique*, *Revue d'Art et d'Archéologie*, *Syria*.

Libraries and Archives

Beirut

American University of Beirut Libraries: POB 11/0236, Riad El-Solh 1107 2020, Beirut; tel. (1) 340460 ext. 2600; fax (1) 744703; e-mail library@aub.edu.lb; internet www.aub.edu.lb/libraries; f. 1866; 587,778 vols, 1,398 MSS, 923 periodicals, 1,139,346 audiovisual items, 1,902 maps; Librarian Dr LOKMAN MEHO.

Beirut Arab University Library: POB 11-5020, Beirut; tel. (1) 300110; fax (1) 818402; f. 1960; important collections on Lebanese, Arabic and Islamic studies; 110,000 vols and 1,500 periodicals; Chief Librarian SAID TAYARA.

Bibliothèque Nationale du Liban: Immeuble Hatab, 6th Fl., rue Madame Curie, Beirut; tel. (1) 756321; fax (1) 756319; e-mail info@bnlb.org; internet www.bnlb.org; f. 1921; library closed and collections put in storage 1979, due to civil war; restoration and reconstruction of the library began 2003; 150,000 vols, 2,500 MSS.

Bibliothèque Orientale: rue de l'Université St Joseph, POB 166 775, Achrafieh, Beirut 1100-2150; tel. (1) 421810; fax (1) 421081; e-mail bo@usj.edu.lb; internet www .usj.edu.lb; f. 1875; attached to Centre Pouzet d'Étude des Civilisations Anciennes et Médiévales; 286,000 vols, 2,000 periodicals, 3,500 MSS, 50,000 photographs, 2,000 maps; Dir MAY SEMAAN SEIGNEURIE; publ. *Mélanges de L'Université Saint-Joseph* (1 a year).

Bibliothèques de l'Université St Joseph: BP 175 208, Beirut; faculties of law, economics, politics, administration: 100,000 vols, 550 periodicals; medical sciences (POB 115076): 12,000 vols, 125 periodicals; engineering (POB 1514): 10,000 vols, 115 periodicals; arts: 65,000 vols, 300 periodicals.

Attached Library:

Bibliothèque de la Faculté des Lettres et des Sciences Humaines: rue de Damas, BP 17-5208, Beirut 1104 2020; tel. (1) 421000 ext. 5105; fax (1) 421055; e-mail flsh.biblio@usj.edu.lb; f. 1977; 118,000 vols; Librarian LEILA BOU NADER ELIAN.

Near East School of Theology Library: POB 13-5780, Chouran, Beirut 1102 2070; tel. (1) 354194; fax (1) 347129; e-mail library@theonest.edu.lb; internet www.pcusa .org/pcusa/wmd/globaled/institutes/nest.htm; f. 1932; 40,000 vols; colln of MSS, colln of The

American Press; 135 religious periodicals (of which 80 are current); Librarian RITA KHARRAT; Librarian MARTINE; publ. *Theological Review* (2 a year).

Daroon-Harissa

Library of the Syrian Patriarchal Seminary: Seminary of Charfet, Daroon-Harissa; tel. (9) 260750; f. 1786; 55,000 vols, 2,100 MSS; Rector Fr ANTOINE NASSIF; publ. *Trait d'Union* (1 a year).

Khonchara

Library of the St John Monastery: Khonchara; f. 1696; Basilian Shweiriet Order; 12,000 vols, 372 MSS; the Order preserves the first printing press in the Middle East with Arabic and Greek letters (first book 1734); Abbot-General Rt Rev. Mgr ATHANASE HAGE.

Saïda

Library of the Monastery of Saint-Saviour: Saïda; tel. 7975064; fax 7975066; e-mail makarioshaidamous@gmail.com; f. 1711; Basilian Missionary Order of Saint-Saviour; 28,500 vols and 2,550 MSS; Librarian MAKARIOS HAIDAMOUS; Librarian FAYEZ FREIJAT; publs *An-Nahlat* (4 a year), *Nafhat Al-Moukhalles* (4 a year).

Museums and Art Galleries

Beirut

American University Museum: Ras, Beirut; tel. (1) 340549; fax (1) 363235; e-mail museum@aub.edu.lb; internet www.aub.edu .lb/museum_archeo; f. 1868; Neolithic flint implements; bronze tools and implements from the Early Bronze Age to the Byzantine period; pottery and other artefacts from the Bronze and Iron Ages, and Classical, Hellenistic, Roman and Byzantine periods; Arabic pottery from the 8th to the 16th century; Phoenician glassware; Egyptian artefacts from the Neolithic to the Dynastic period; pottery from the Neolithic period of Mesopotamia and cylinder seals and cuneiform tablets from Sumer and Akkad; numismatics of the countries in the eastern basin of the Mediterranean; Dir Dr LEILA BADRE; publ. *Berytus* (1 a year).

Daheshite Museum and Library: POB 202, Beirut; contains watercolours, gouaches, original paintings, engravings, sculptures in marble, bronze, ivory and wood carvings; library of 30,000 vols (20,000 Arabic, 10,000 English and French), on arts, philosophy, history, literature, religions, etc.; Dir Dr A. S. M. DAHESH.

Musée des Beaux-Arts: POB 3939, Beirut; Dir Dr DAHESH.

Musée National (National Museum of Lebanon): rue de Damas, Beirut; f. 1920; exhibits: royal jewellery, arms and statues of the Phoenician epoch; sarcophagus of King Ahiram (13th century BC), with first known alphabetical inscriptions; the collection of Dr G. Ford of 25 sarcophagi of the Greek and Hellenistic epoch; large collection of terracotta statuettes of the Hellenistic period; Roman and Byzantine mosaics; Arabic woods and ceramics; Dir-Gen. Dr CAMILE ASMAR; publ. *Bulletin*.

Sursock Museum: Sursock St, Ashrafieh, Beirut.

Besharre

Musée Khalil Gibran: Besharre; dedicated to the life and works of the author.

Universities

AL-IMAM AL-OUZAI UNIVERSITY

POB 14-5355, Beirut 2802-1105
Telephone: (1) 704454
Fax: (1) 704449
E-mail: islamic-studies@ouzai.org
Internet: www.ouzai.org
Founded 1979
Private control
Language of instruction: Arabic
Academic year: October to June
Chairman: TOUFIC EL-HOURI
Library Administrator: SAMIR OMARI
Library of 115,000 vols
Number of teachers: 120
Number of students: 4,450

DEANS

Imam Ouzai College of Islamic Studies: Prof. Dr KAMEL MOUSA
Islamic College of Business Administration: Prof. Dr MOHAMED ISKANDARANI

DIRECTORS

Documentation Centre for Bibliographic Information on Islam and the Muslim World: Dr BASSAM ABDEL HAMID
Documentation Centre on World Countries and Major Cities: Dr IBRAHIM ASSAL
Documentation Centre on World Leading Banks: HODA AL-KHARSA
Islamic Institute for the Supervision of Food Products: Dr IBRAHIM ADHAM

AMERICAN UNIVERSITY OF BEIRUT

Bliss St, Beirut
Telephone: (1) 350000
Fax: (1) 351706
Internet: www.aub.edu.lb
Founded 1866
Private control
Language of instruction: English
Academic year: October to June
Pres.: JOHN WATERBURY
Vice-Pres for Academics: MAKHLUF HADDADIN
Vice-Pres for Admin.: GEORGES TOMEY
Vice-Pres for Regional External Programmes: GEORGE NAJJAR
Provost: PETER HEATH
Registrar: SALIM KANAAN (acting)
Librarian: HELEN BIKHAZI
Number of teachers: 420
Number of students: 5,000

Publications: *Al-Abhath* (Arab Studies, in English and Arabic, 1 a year), *Berytus Archaeological Studies* (in English, 1 a year), *Research Report* (2 a year)

DEANS

Faculty of Agricultural and Food Sciences: NUHAD DAGHIR
Faculty of Arts and Sciences: KHALIL BITAR
Faculty of Engineering and Architecture: IBRAHIM HAJJ
Faculty of Health Sciences: HUDA ZURAYK
Faculty of Medicine and Medical Center: NADIM CORTAS
Student Affairs: DEAN KEULIN

BEIRUT ARAB UNIVERSITY

POB 11-5020, Riad El-Solh 1107 2809, Beirut
Telephone: (1) 300110
Fax: (1) 818402
E-mail: bau@bau.edu.lb
Internet: www.bau.edu.lb
Founded 1960 by the El-Ber Wa El-Ehsan Asscn, academically associated with the Univ. of Alexandria, Egypt
Private control

Languages of instruction: Arabic, English, French

Academic year: September to June

Pres.: Prof. Dr AMR AL ADAWI

Sec.-Gen.: ISSAM HOURY

Dir for Student Affairs: MOHAMED HAMOUD

Dir for Information Systems: Prof. WALID SHATILA

Chief Librarian: SAEED TAYARA

Library of 125,000 vols

Number of teachers: 784

Number of students: 12,194

Publications: *Architecture and Planning Journal* (1 a year), *Human Sciences Journal* (2 a year), *Journal of Commercial Research and Studies* (2 a year), *Revue des Études Juridiques* (2 a year)

DEANS

Faculty of Architecture: Prof. Dr RAMADAN ABDEL MAKSOUD

Faculty of Arts: Prof. Dr OLGA MATTAR MOHAMED GHAZI

Faculty of Commerce: Prof. Dr SAID ABDEL AZIZ OSMAN

Faculty of Dentistry: Prof. Dr MOSTAFA FAKHRI KHALIL

Faculty of Engineering: Prof. Dr IBRAHIM ABDEL-SALAM AWAD

Faculty of Health Sciences: Prof. Dr HIND MITWALLI

Faculty of Law: Prof. Dr HAFIZA EL-HADDAD

Faculty of Medicine: Prof. Dr MOUNIR MOHAMED ZEERBAN

Faculty of Pharmacy: Prof. Dr FAWZI ALI YAZIBI

Faculty of Science: Prof. Dr SAMY HAMED CHAABAN

PROFESSORS

Faculty of Architecture:

ABDEL MAKSOUD, R., Building Science and Technology

HAMDI, E. F., Environmental Design

Faculty of Arts:

ABDUL RAHMAN, A. M., Sociology

EBRAHEEM, E. A., Geography

FAHMI, N. A., English Language and Literature

GHAZI, O. M. M., General and Applied Linguistics

Faculty of Commerce:

OSMAN, S. A., Public Economics

Faculty of Dentistry:

AMER, W. A.-A., Oral Medicine, Periodontics and Diagnosis

EL-MULHALLAWI, A. S., Oral and Maxillofacial Surgery

KHALIL, M. F., Dental Biomaterials

MOSTAFA, A. M. M., Conservative Dentistry, Operative Dentistry

SEGAAN, G. I., Prosthodontics

Faculty of Engineering:

AWAD, I. A., Computer Engineering and Systems

BAGHDADI, K. H., River Engineering

ELGHAMMAL, M. A., Electrical Systems

EL-GHAZOULY, H. G., Surveying and Geodesy

EL-SHERBINY, M. M., Electrical and Computer Engineering

FARROUKH, O. O., Electro-magnetics and Optics

FATAH EL-BAB, F. A. I., Stability and Analysis of Space Structures

GHABASHI, M. A-L., Theoretical Physics and Materials Science

HASAB, M. A. H., Design of Thermal Systems

KHALIL, M. F., Fluid Mechanics

MOSTAFA, M. A. F., Mechanical Vibrations

RAJAB, M. M. E., Microelectronics

RASHED, A. M. H., Power Systems Analysis

SOROUR, M. K., Thermal Engineering

Faculty of Law:

ABD AL-WAHHAB, M. A., Public Law

AL-HADDAD, H. S. A., Private International Law

DWIDAR, M. H. I., Economy Planning

EL-MAGZOUB, M. M., Public International Law

KHALIL, A. A. S., Procedure Law

Faculty of Medicine:

ABOU AL-OLA, M. M., Histology: Histochemistry and Electron Microscopy

AHMED, S. I., Internal Medicine—Gastrointestinal

EL-BAHEI, N. M., Clinical Pharmacology

EL-GEBALY, F. F., Embryology and Genetics

EL-SAWWA, E. A.-K., Anatomy: Embryology and Genetics

KHEDR, M. M. S., Clinical Pharmacology

MADWAR, A., Histology: Histochemistry and Electron Microscopy

MASHALI, N. A.-R., Gynaecological Pathology and Haematopathology

SALEH, M. N.-D. A., Anatomy: Genetics of Development

ZEERBAN, M. M., Cardiothoracic Surgery

Faculty of Pharmacy:

BORAI, N. A., Pharmaceutics

EL-KHODAIRY, K. A.-H., Microencapsulation and Drug Delivery Systems

EL-LAKANY, A. M., Chemistry of Natural Products

EL-YAZBI, F. A., Pharmaceutical Analysis and Drug Quality Control

MOHYEEDIN, M. M., Neurohumoral Transmission in Pharmacology

OSHBA, N. H. M., Synthetic Medicinal Chemistry

Faculty of Science:

ABD EL-JAWAD, N. M. A., Enzymology

ALI, A. M. A. M., Nuclear Physics

BADAWI, N. S. A., Cell Biology

DUKAINESH, S. I. A., Invertebrate Ecology

FALTAS, M. S., Fluid Dynamics

HAMAD, H. H. A., Fluid Dynamics

IBRAHIM, H. I., Solid State Physics

KOREK, M., Molecular Physics

MANSOUR, S. M. S., Organic Chemistry

SHAALAN, S. H., Phycology

LEBANESE AMERICAN UNIVERSITY

Beirut Campus, POB 13-5053, Chouran, Beirut 1102 2801

Telephone: (1) 786456

Fax: (1) 867098

Byblos Campus, POB 36, Byblos

Telephone: (9) 547254

Fax: (9) 944851

Internet: www.lau.edu.lb

Founded 1924 by the United Presbyterian Church, USA

Private control

Language of instruction: English

Academic year: October to September

Pres.: Dr JOSEPH G. JABBRA

Vice-Pres. for Academic Affairs: Dr ABDALLAH SFIER

Vice-Pres. for Advancement and Devt: ROBERT STODDARD

Vice-Pres. for Finance: EMILE LAMAH

Vice-Pres. for Student Enrolment and Management: Dr ELISE SALEM

Vice-Pres. (Gen. Counsel and Spec. Advisor to the Pres.): Dr CEDAR MANSOUR

Registrars: VATCHE PAPAZIAN (Beirut Campus): FOUAD SALIBI (Byblos Campus)

Librarians: CINDERELLA HABRE (Beirut Campus): JOSEPH HAJJ (Byblos Campus)

Libraries with combined total of 392,670 vols, 2,447 periodicals, 38,500 eBooks, 80 databases

Number of teachers: 517 (170 full-time, 347 part-time)

Number of students: 6,300

Publications: *Al-Raida magazine* (4 a year), *Alumni Bulletin* (4 a year), *LAU magazine* (4 a year)

DEANS

School of Arts and Sciences (Beirut Campus): Dr SAMIRA AGHACY

School of Arts and Sciences (Byblos Campus): Dr FOUAD HASHWA

School of Business (Beirut Campus): Dr TAREK MIKDASHI

School of Business (Byblos Campus): Dr WASSIM SHAHINE

School of Engineering and Architecture: Dr GEORGES NASR (acting)

School of Medicine: Dr KAMAL BADR

School of Pharmacy: Dr FARID SADIK

Student Affairs: Dr TAREK NAAWAS (Beirut Campus): Dr MARS SEMAAN (Byblos Campus)

NOTRE DAME UNIVERSITY LOUAIZE

POB 72, Zouk Mikael, Zouk Mosbeh, Kesrwan

Telephone: (9) 218950

Fax: (9) 218771

E-mail: webm@ndu.edu.lb

Internet: www.ndu.edu.lb

Founded 1987 by the Maronite Order of the Holy Virgin Mary

Private control

Academic year: October to September

President: Rev. BOUTROS TARABAY

Vice-Pres. for Academic Affairs: Dr GEORGE M. EID

Vice-Pres. for Sponsored Research and Development: Dr AMEEN A. RIHANI

Dir of Administration: Fr ROGER CHUKRI

Dir of Admissions: ELHAM HASHEM

Dir of Finance: Fr SAMIR GHSOUB

Dir of Public Relations and Presidential Counsellor: SUHEIL MATAR

Dir of Student Affairs: Fr BOULOS WEHBEH

Registrar: LEA EID

Dir of Libraries: LESLIE A. HAGE

Number of teachers: 233

Number of students: 4,263

Publications: *PALMA Journal* (2 a year), *Spirit* (4 a year)

DEANS

Faculty of Architecture, Art and Design: Dr SHAHWAN KHOURY (acting)

Faculty of Business Administration and Economics: Dr ELIE YACHOUI

Faculty of Engineering: Dr SHAHWAN KHOURY

Faculty of Humanities: Dr BOULOS SARRU

Faculty of Natural and Applied Sciences: Dr JEAN FARES

Faculty of Political Science, Public Affairs and Diplomacy: Dr MICHEL NEHME

DIRECTORS

Division of Continuing Education: FAWZI BAROUD

North Lebanon Campus: SALIM KARAM

Shouf Campus: Dr ASSAAD EID

UNIVERSITÉ ANTONINE

BP 40016, Hadath Baabda

Telephone: (5) 924076

Fax: (5) 924075

E-mail: contact@upa.edu.lb

Internet: www.upa.edu.lb

Founded 1996

Private control

Academic year: October to July
Number of teachers: 120
Number of students: 850

Publications: *Al-Antouniyah* (1 a year), *Our Liturgic Life* (2 series: research, 2 a year; celebrations, 4 a year)

Faculties of biblical studies, computer studies, ecumenical and religious studies, multimedia and telecommunications engineering, nursing and theology, pastoral studies; higher institute of music; institute of physical education and sport; university technical institute of laboratory science and dental prosthetics.

UNIVERSITY OF BALAMAND

POB 100, Tripoli
Balamand-Koura
Telephone: (6) 930250
Fax: (6) 930278
E-mail: pr@balamand.edu.lb
Internet: www.balamand.edu.lb

Founded 1988
Private control
Languages of instruction: Arabic, English, French
Academic year: October to June
Pres.: ELIE A. SALEM
Vice-Pres. for Devt and Public Affairs: MICHEL NAJJAR
Vice-Pres. for Health and Community Relations: NADIM KARAM
Vice-Pres. for Medical Affairs in the USA: TALI' BASHOUR
Vice-Pres. for Planning and Educational Relations: GEORGES N. NAHAS
Dean of Admissions and Registration: WALID MOUBAYED
Dean of Student Affairs: ANTOINE GERJESS
Librarian: SAMEERA BASHIR

Library of 70,000 vols
Number of teachers: 667 (incl. full-time and part-time)
Number of students: 4,200
Publications: *Al-Inaa* (irregular), *Al-Marquab* (1 a year), *Chronos* (2 a year), *Hawliyat* (Theology, 1 a year), *Revue Médicale Libanaise* (4 a year)

DEANS

Faculty of Arts and Social Sciences: GEORGE BAHR
Faculty of Business Administration: KARIM NASR (acting)
Faculty of Engineering: JIHAD ATTIEH (acting)
Faculty of Health Sciences: NADIM KARAM
Faculty of Medicine: CAMILLE NASSAR
Faculty of Sciences: MICHEL NAJJAR
Lebanese Acad. of Fine Arts: ANDRE BEKHAZI
St George Faculty of Postgraduate Medical Education: CAMILLE NASSAR
St John of Damascus Institute of Theology: Bishop KHATTAS HAZIM

UNIVERSITÉ LIBANAISE

place du Musée, Beirut
Telephone: (1) 612830
Fax: (1) 612572
E-mail: sgul@ul.edu.lb
Internet: www.ul.edu.lb
Founded 1951
State control
Languages of instruction: Arabic, French, English
Academic year: October to June
Rector: Dr ZOHEIR CHOKR
Sec.-Gen.: MOHAMAD EL BABA
Head of Administrative Services: RITA WEHBEH
Librarian: DINA SUCCAR

Library of 750,000 vols, 27,932 electronic journals, 55,722 electronic books
Number of teachers: 4,404
Number of students: 72,500
Publications: *Art and Architecture* (1 a year), *Dirassat* (1 a year), *Hannoun* (1 a year), *Pedagogic Research* (1 a year), *Social Sciences* (1 a year), *Tourism and Hospitality* (1 a year)

DEANS

Doctoral School of Literature, Humanities and Social Sciences: Dr IBRAHIM MOHSEN
Doctorate School of Science and Technology: Dr ZEINAB SAAD
Faculty of Agronomy: Dr TAYSSIR HAMIEH
Faculty of Dentistry: Dr MOUNIR DOUMIT
Faculty of Economics and Business Administration: Dr KAMEEL HABIB
Faculty of Engineering: Dr MOHAMED ZOAETER
Faculty of Information and Documentation: Dr GEORGE KHATOURA
Faculty of Law, Political and Administrative Sciences: Dr FELOMEN NASER
Faculty of Literature and Humanities: Dr ZOHEIR CHOKR
Faculty of Medical Sciences: Dr PIERRE YARD
Faculty of Pedagogy: Dr MAZEN EL KHATIB
Faculty of Pharmacy: Dr MARIE TOUEINY
Faculty of Public Health: Dr NINA SAADALLAH
Faculty of Sciences: Dr ALI MNEIMNEH
Faculty of Tourism and Hospitality Management: Dr KAMAL HAMMAD
Institute of Fine Arts: Dr MAAMOUN CHAABAN
Institute of Social Sciences: Dr FREDRICK MAATOUK
University Institute of Technology: Dr ALI ISMAIL

UNIVERSITÉ SAINT-ESPRIT DE KASLIK

POB 446, Jounieh
Telephone: (9) 934444
Fax: (9) 642333
E-mail: rectorat@usek.edu.lb
Internet: www.usek.edu.lb
Founded 1950
Private control (Lebanese Maronite Order of Monks)
Languages of instruction: French, English, Arabic
Academic year: October to July
Chancellor: Abbé ÉLIAS KHALIFE
Rector: Père ANTOINE AL AHMAR
First Vice-Rector: Abbé PAUL NAAMAN
Vice-Rector for Admin.: Père ANTOINE AL-AHMAR
Vice-Rector for External Relations and Research: Père GEORGES HOBEIKA
Sec.-Gen.: Père PIERRE BOU ZEIDAN
Librarian: Père JOSEPH MOUKARZEL

Library of 250,000 vols
Number of teachers: 620
Number of students: 5,180
Publications: *Actes de Colloques tenus à l'Université Saint-Esprit de Kaslik*, *Annales de Philosophie et des Sciences Humaines* (1 a year), *Annales de Recherches Scientifiques* (1 a year), *Bibliothèque de l'Université Saint-Esprit de Kaslik*, *Bulletin de l'Université Saint-Esprit de Kaslik* (2 a year), *Cahiers Annuels* (1 a year), *Parole de l'Orient* (1 a year), *Revue de la Faculté des Beaux Arts* (1 a year), *Revue Juridique* (1 a year)

DEANS

Faculty of Agricultural Sciences: Fr JOSEPH WAKIM
Faculty of Business Administration and Commercial Sciences: Fr KARAM RIZK
Faculty of Fine Arts: ALEXIS MOUZARKEL

Faculty of Law: Dr JOSEPH CHAOUL
Faculty of Literature: Dr ANTOINE NOUJAIM
Faculty of Medicine: Fr GÉDÉON MOHASSEB
Faculty of Music: Fr LOUIS HAJJE
Faculty of Philosophy and Human Sciences: Fr JEAN AKIKI
Faculty of Sciences and Computer Engineering: Fr ANTOINE AL-AHMAR
Pontifical Faculty of Theology: Fr THOMAS MOUHANNA

DIRECTORS

Institute of History: Dr ANTOINE NOUJAIM
Institute of Liturgy: Fr AYOUB CHAHWAN
Institute of Nursing: Dr JEAN-CLAUDE LAHOUD
Institute of Sacred Art: Fr ABDO BADWI
Department of Architecture: ALEXIS MOUZARKEL
Department of Graphic Design: ELIE KHOURY
Department of Interior Design: PIERRE HAGE BOUTROS
Department of Visual and Scenic Arts: PAUL ZGHEIB

UNIVERSITÉ SAINT JOSEPH

rue de Damas, BP 17-5208, Mar Mikhaël, Beirut 1104 2020
Telephone: (1) 421000
Fax: (1) 421001
E-mail: rectorat@usj.edu.lb
Internet: www.usj.edu.lb
Founded 1875
Private control (Jesuit)
Languages of instruction: French, Arabic, English
Academic year: September to June (2 semesters)
Rector: Rev. Fr RENÉ CHAMUSSY
Vice-Rector for Academic Affairs: HENRI AWIT
Vice-Rector for Admin.: WAJDI NAJEM
Vice-Rector for Devt: Dr KHALIL KARAM
Vice-Rector for Int. Relations: Dr ANTOINE HOKAYEM
Vice-Rector for Research: GEORGES AOUN
Sec.-Gen.: FOUAD MAROUN

Library: see Libraries and Archives
Number of teachers: 1,709
Number of students: 12,299
Publications: *ACES—Actualités Cliniques et Scientifiques* (dental medicine, 2 a year), *Annales de Géographie—Géosphères* (1 a year), *Annales d'Histoire—Tempora* (1 a year), *Annales de la Faculté de Droit* (irregular), *Annales de Lettres Françaises—Acanthe* (1 a year), *Annales de l'Institut de Langues et de Traduction—Al-Kimiya* (1 a year), *Annales de l'Institut de Lettres Orientales* (1 a year), *Annales de Philosophie—Iris* (1 a year), *Annales de Psychologie et des Sciences de l'Education—Psy-écho* (1 a year), *Annales de Sociologie et d'Anthropologie* (1 a year), *Bulletin Annuel de la Faculté de Médecine* (1 a year), *Bulletin intérieur de l'Institut libanais d'éducateurs* (1 a year), *Chroniques du CEMAM* (modern Arab world, 1 a year), *Chroniques Politiques* (1 a year), *Chroniques Sociales* (irregular), *Conférences de l'ALDEC* (1 a year), *Enseignement Continu Post-universitaire* (medicine, 1 a year), *Études de droit libanais* (irregular), *Hommes et Sociétés du Proche-Orient* (1 a year), *Journées d'Études Post-universitaires* (midwifery, 1 a year), *L'Orient des Dieux* (1 a year), *Mélanges de l'Université Saint-Joseph* (1 a year), *Proche Orient Chrétien* (2 a year), *Proche Orient, Études Économiques* (irregular), *Proche Orient, Études en Management* (irregular), *Proche Orient, Études Juridiques* (irregular), *Publications techniques et scientifiques de l'École supérieure d'ingénieurs de Beyrouth*

(irregular), *Regards* (theatre, audiovisual studies and cinema, 1 a year), *Revue de l'Institut Libanais d'Éducateurs* (1 a year), *Travaux et Jours* (2 a year)

DEANS AND DIRECTORS

Centre of Banking Studies: FADWA MANSOUR
Faculty of Arts and Human Sciences: JAR-JOURA HARDANE
Faculty of Business Admin.: TONI GIBEILY
Faculty of Dentistry: Dr NADA NAAMAN
Faculty of Economics: IRMA MAJDALANI
Faculty of Education Sciences: NADA MOGHAI-ZEL NASR
Faculty of Engineering: FADI GEARA
Faculty of Law and Political Science: FAYEZ HAGE-CHAHINE
Faculty of Medicine: Dr FERNAND DAGHER
Faculty of Nursing: CLAIRE ZABLIT
Faculty of Pharmacy: DOLLA SARKIS
Faculty of Religious Studies: Rev. Fr SALIM DACCACHE
Faculty of Sciences: TOUFIC RIZK
Higher Institute of Insurance Sciences: NADI JAZZAR
Higher Institute of Religious Studies: Rev. Fr. EDGARD EL HAIBY
Higher Institute of Speech Therapy: CAMILLE MOITEL MESSARA
Institute of Business Admin.: PHILIPPE FAT-TAL
Institute of Health and Social Protection Management: WALID KHOURY
Institute of Islamic-Christian Studies: Rev. Fr AZIZ HALLAK
Institute of Languages and Translation: HENRI AWAISS
Institute of Oriental Arts: Rev. Fr SALIM DACCACHE
Institute of Physiotherapy: NISRINE ABDEL-NOUR LATTOUF
Institute of Political Science: FADIA KIWAN

Institute of Psychomotricity: CARLA ABI ZEID DAOU
Institute of Theatrical, Audiovisual and Cinema Studies: PAUL MATTAR
Lebanese Institute for Educators: DUNIA AL MUKKADAM
Lebanese School of Social Work: MARYSE TANNOUS JOMAA
National Institute of Communication and Information: HADY SAWAYA
Open University: HENRI AWIT
School of Agro-Industrial Engineers: FADI GEARA
School of Laboratory Technicians in Medical Analysis: MARIE-CHRISTINE BAZ HOMSI
School of Mediterranean Agricultural Engineers: FADI GEARA
School of Midwifery: YOLLA ATALLAH
School of Translators and Interpreters of Beirut: HENRI AWAISS

Colleges

Académie Libanaise des Beaux-Arts: POB 55251, Sin-El-Fil, Beirut; tel. (1) 480056; f. 1937; schools of architecture, decorative arts, plastic arts, publicity,; library: 4,300 vols; 180 teachers; 600 students; Chair. Mgr GEORGES KHODR; Dir-Gen. GEORGES HADDAD.

Haigazian University: POB 11-1748, Beirut; tel. (1) 349230; fax (1) 350926; e-mail rartinian@haigazian.edu.lb; internet www .haigazian.edu.lb; f. 1955; Private control; academic year: October to June; BA and BSc in Arabic studies, Armenian studies, biology, business administration, chemistry, Christian education, computer science, education, English literature, history, hospitality management, mathematics, medical laboratory

technology, physics, political science, psychology; MA programmes in educational administration and supervision, general psychology and clinical psychology; MBA; library: libraries (Armenian, Arabic and English) of 66,000 vols; 63 teachers (23 full-time, 40 part-time); 743 students; Pres. Rev. PAUL HAIDOSTIAN; Librarian ZEVART TANIELIAN; publs *Armenological Review* (1 a year), *Business News* (4 a year), *Haigazian Focus* (1 a year), *Haigazian Herald* (4 a year), *In Spirit* (2 a year)

DEANS

Faculty of Arts and Sciences: ARDA EKMEKJI
Faculty of Business and Economics: FADI ASRAWI

Middle East University: POB 90481, Jdeidet El Matn 1202-2040; tel. (1) 685800; fax (1) 684800; e-mail meu@meu.edu.lb; internet www.meu.edu.lb; f. 1939; private control; language of instruction: English; academic year October to June; offers degrees in business administration, computer science, education (elementary and secondary), religion; MBA; also diploma courses; library: 20,000 vols; 29 teachers (13 full-time, 16 part-time); 200 students; Pres. S. MYKLEBUST; Registrar S. ISSA.

Near East School of Theology: POB 13-5780, Beirut 1102 2070; tel. (1) 354194; fax (1) 347129; e-mail nest.adm@inco.com.lb; internet www.pcusa.org/pcusa/wmd/globaled/institutes/nest.htm; f. 1932; Protestant ecumenical institution of higher learning; offers theological education and pastoral training to qualified candidates for church ministries, as well as to lay candidates regardless of church affiliation, sex, race or nationality; library: 40,000 vols; 7 teachers; 36 students; Pres. Dr MARY MIKHAEL; publ. *Theological Review*.

LESOTHO

The Higher Education System

The Roman Catholic Hierarchy of South Africa founded Pius XII College in 1945, while Lesotho was part of the British protectorate of Basutoland. Pius XII College became known as the University of Basutoland, Bechuanaland and Swaziland in 1963, and after the Kingdom of Lesotho was declared an independent state in 1966 it was renamed the University of Botswana, Lesotho and Swaziland. In 1975 the University of Botswana, Lesotho and Swaziland was divided into separate national universities, and the branch at Roma, Lesotho, was reconstituted as the National University of Lesotho. Higher education is funded by the central Government, which accounts for about 90% of the National University of Lesotho's income. Some 3,266 students were enrolled at the National University of Lesotho, at Roma, in 2002. A total of 4,195 students were enrolled at tertiary-level institutions in 2002/03.

Governance of the National University of Lesotho consists of the Council (appointed by the Head of State), Senate, Congregation, Student Union, non-academic staff and external members. The Head of State is the Chancellor of the University, and the Vice-Chancellor, Pro-Vice Chancellor, Registrar, Bursar and Librarian are the primary management staff, responsible for the day-to-day affairs of the university. Overall responsibility for policy lies with the Council, and the Senate oversees all academic affairs. Deans of Faculty and Directors of Institutes are the heads of academic units.

Admission to the National University of Lesotho is on the basis of the Cambridge Overseas School Certificate in the first or the second division. A Diploma is awarded in theology and agriculture after two years, otherwise the undergraduate Bachelors degree last four years, divided into two two-year cycles. Award of the Bachelors of Law requires a further two years of study. The postgraduate Masters degree lasts two years and is awarded in arts, science and education. Doctoral degree programmes are available in agriculture, education and the humanities, and last for two years after the award of the Masters.

Technical and vocational education consists of a College Certificate or Diploma. Courses are offered by a number of different institutions, including home economics and craft schools, trade schools, Lesotho Agricultural College and Lerotholi Polytechnic.

Regulatory Bodies

GOVERNMENT

Ministry of Education and Training: POB 47, Maseru 100; tel. 22313045; fax 22310562; e-mail semakalem@education.gov.ls; internet www.education.gov.ls; Minister Dr 'Mamphono Khaketla.

Ministry of Tourism, Environment and Culture: POB 52, Maseru 100; tel. 22313034; fax 22310194; e-mail pmasita.mohale@mtec.gov.ls; internet www.mtec.gov.ls; Min. Mannete Ramaili.

Learned Societies

BIBLIOGRAPHY, LIBRARY SCIENCE AND MUSEOLOGY

Lesotho Library Association: Private Bag A26, Maseru; tel. 22213420; fax 22340000; f. 1978; 60 individual mems, 22 institutions; Chair. S. M. Mohai; Sec. N. Taole; publ. *Journal* (1 a year).

LANGUAGE AND LITERATURE

Alliance Française: cnr Pioner Rd and Kingsway, Private Bag A106, Maseru 100; tel. 22325722; fax 22310475; e-mail maseru@alliance.org.za; internet www.alliancefrancaise.co.za/lesotho; offers courses and exams in French language and culture, and promotes cultural exchange with France.

Research Institutes

AGRICULTURE, FISHERIES AND VETERINARY SCIENCE

Department of Agricultural Research: POB 829, Maseru 100; tel. 22312395; research station at Maseru and field experimental stations.

NATURAL SCIENCES

Physical Sciences

Geological Survey Department: Dept of Mines and Geology, POB 750, Maseru 100; tel. 22323750; fax 22310498; Dir Matsepo C. Ramaisa.

Libraries and Archives

Maseru

Lesotho National Archives: POB 52, Maseru 100; tel. 22312047; fax 22310194; f. 1958; undertakes research and preservation of nat. documents since 1869; Sr Archivist M. Qhobosheane.

Lesotho National Library Service: POB 985, Maseru 100; tel. 22323100; fax 22310194; f. 1976; 30,000 vols; Sr Librarian M. Mabathoana (acting).

University

NATIONAL UNIVERSITY OF LESOTHO

PO Roma 180
Telephone: 22340601
Fax: 22340000
E-mail: registrar@nul.ls
Internet: www.nul.ls
Founded 1945 as Pius XII College, became campus of University of Botswana, Lesotho and Swaziland 1966; present name 1975
Language of instruction: English
Academic year: August to May
Chancellor: HM King Letsie III
Vice-Chancellor: Dr T. H. Mothibe
Pro-Vice-Chancellor: Dr N. L. Mahao
Registrar: J. M. Hlalele
Librarian: A. M. Lebotsa
Library of 205,150 vols, 500 periodicals
Number of teachers: 171
Number of students: 3,266
Publications: *Announcer*, *Lesotho Law Journal*, *Light in the Night*, *Mohlomi Journal* (History), *Mophatlatsi*, *NUL News*, *NUL Research Journal*

DEANS

Faculty of Agriculture: Prof. P. M. Sutton
Faculty of Education: Dr E. M. Maruping
Faculty of Health Science: Prof. P. O. Odonkor
Faculty of Humanities: Rev. J. Khutlang
Faculty of Law: O. M. Owori
Faculty of Postgraduate Studies: (vacant)
Faculty of Science and Technology: Prof. K. Gopinathan
Faculty of Social Sciences: Prof. S. G. Hoohlo

DIRECTORS

Institute of Education: S. T. Motlomelo
Institute of Extra-Mural Studies: Prof. D. Braimoh, Prof. Y. D. Bwatwa, Dr A. M. Setsabi
Institute of Labour Studies: S. Santho (acting)
Institute of Southern African Studies: Dr M. Mochebelele

PROFESSORS

Faculty of Agriculture:
  Braide, F. G.
  Ebenene, A. C.
  Okelw-Uma, I.
  Sutton, P. M.
Faculty of Education:
  Mats'ela, Z. A., Language and Social Education
Faculty of Law:
  Kumar, U., Private Law
Faculty of Postgraduate Studies:
  Balogun, T. A.
Faculty of Science and Technology:
  Gopinathan, K. K., Physics
  Malu, O.
Faculty of Social Sciences:
  Ejigou, A., Statistics
Institute of Southern African Studies:
  Prasad, G.

College

Lesotho Agricultural College: POB 139, Maseru; tel. 22322484; fax 22400022; f. 1955; State control; language of instruction: English; academic year August to May (2 semesters); library: 60,000 vols; Prin. Dr S. L. Ralits'oele.

LIBERIA

The Higher Education System

From 1821 onwards emancipated slaves from the southern states of the USA were resettled along the West Guinean coast, and in 1847 the independent, sovereign state of Liberia was declared, with a Constitution based on that of the USA. Liberia College, the first institution of higher education, was founded in 1862 and became a university in 1951. In 1889 Cuttington University College was founded by the Episcopal Church in the USA, by whom it is still maintained in conjunction with the Episcopal Church in Liberia. Other institutions of higher education include the William V. S. Tubman College of Technology (founded 1970; formerly Harper Technical College) and the Booker Washington Institute (founded 1929). There are also junior colleges offering two-year degree programmes. In the academic year 1999/2000 there were 44,107 students enrolled in university-level institutions and 15,631 students enrolled in post-secondary and vocational education.

Universities must be chartered by the Ministry of Education, but higher education in Liberia is decentralized in that each institution is autonomous and governed by a Board of Trustees. The Minister of Education is the government representative on each Board of Trustees, which is advised by an Administrative Council, comprising all academic and administrative staff, two elected faculty members and two elected student representatives. The Council also advises the President of the University and coordinates the day-to-day running of the institution. The State provides funding to both public and private institutions and also offers financial aid to students, which covers one-half of the cost of tuition and study materials.

Applicants must hold the Senior High School certificates to gain admission to higher education and are also required to sit entrance examinations in English and mathematics. Students at junior colleges study for the two-year Associate degree, and university undergraduates take a four-year Bachelors degree. The Bachelors of Law degree is awarded after five years and medical degrees after seven years. Postgraduate degrees, such as the Masters, are available on a limited basis.

In addition to junior colleges, post-secondary technical and vocational education is offered by technical colleges.

In 2007 the Government consulted with the American Association of State Colleges and Universities for help and advice in rebuilding Liberia's post-secondary education system, which had been severely affected by 14 years of civil war.

Regulatory Bodies

GOVERNMENT

Ministry of Education: E. G. N. King Plaza, Broad St, POB 10-1545, 1000 Monrovia 10; tel. 226216; internet www.moe.gov.lr; Min. OTHELLO GONGAR.

Ministry of Information, Culture and Tourism: Capitol Hill, POB 10-9021, 1000 Monrovia 10; tel. 226269; internet www.micat.gov.lr; Min. CLETUS SIEH.

Learned Societies

LANGUAGE AND LITERATURE

Alliance Française: 28 Payne Ave, POB 10, 3016 Sinkor 14th/15th Sts, 1000 Monrovia 10; tel. and fax 226888; e-mail alliancefr_monrovia@yahoo.com; offers courses and exams in French language and culture, and promotes cultural exchange with France.

Society of Liberian Authors: POB 2468, Monrovia; f. 1959; aims to encourage general interest in writing and encourage literature in local vernacular; publ. *Kaafa* (2 a year).

TECHNOLOGY

Geological, Mining and Metallurgical Society of Liberia: POB 902, Monrovia; f. 1964; 78 mems; Pres. CLETUS S. WOTORSON; Sec. Dr MEDIE-HEMIE NEUFVILLE; publ. *Bulletin* (2 a year).

Liberia Arts and Crafts Association: POB 885, Monrovia; f. 1964; 14 mems; aims to encourage artists and craftsmen through exhibitions, sales, workshops; Pres. R. VANJAH RICHARDS.

Research Institutes

AGRICULTURE, FISHERIES AND VETERINARY SCIENCE

Central Agricultural Research Institute: Mailbag 3929, Suakoko, Bong County; tel. 223443; f. 1946; under Min. of Agriculture; programmes in four key areas: infrastructure and manpower development, crop improvement and urban agriculture, livestock and fisheries improvement, natural resource management and value addition; library of 8,700 vols; Dir-Gen. Dr J. QWELIBO SUBAH; publ. *CARI News*.

MEDICINE

Liberian Institute for Biomedical Research: POB 10-1012, 1000 Monrovia 10; f. 1952, renamed 1975; administrative centre for biomedical research; conducts research and attracts research projects; Dir Dr ALOYSIUS P. HANSON.

NATURAL SCIENCES

Biological Sciences

Nimba Research Laboratory: c/o Lamco J. V. Operating Co, Grassland, Nimba, Robertsfield; POB 69, Monrovia; f. 1962; under supervision of Nimba Research Committee of International Union for Conservation of Nature and Natural Resources, in conjunction with UNESCO; biological and ecological exploration and conservation in the Mount Nimba region; library of 100 vols and access to LAMCO library, Yekepa; Chair. KAI CURRY-LINDAHL.

Libraries and Archives

Monrovia

Government Public Library: Ashmun St, Monrovia; f. 1959; 15,000 vols.

Liberian Information Service Library: POB 9021, Monrovia; reference.

University of Liberia Libraries: University of Liberia, POB 9020, Monrovia; tel. 222448; f. 1862; general library and separate law library; 107,384 vols, 2,118 periodicals; Dir ANNABEL U. TINGBA (acting).

Museums and Art Galleries

Cape Mount

Tubman Centre of African Cultures: Cape Mount; local art, history and ethnology.

Monrovia

Africana Museum: Cuttington Univ. College, c/o Episcopal Church Office, POB 277, Monrovia; f. 1960; items from Liberia and neighbouring countries; traditional arts and crafts, ethnographical material; depository for archaeological collns; serves as a teaching colln for the college and as a research facility for visiting scholars; Dir Dr ADETOKUNBO K. BORISHADE.

National Museum: Broad and Buchanan Sts, POB 3223, Monrovia; f. 1962; Liberian history, art and ethnography; Dir BURDIE UREY-WEEKS.

University

UNIVERSITY OF LIBERIA

POB 9020, Monrovia
Telephone: 224670
Fax: 226418
Founded as Liberia College 1862, univ. status 1951
State control
Language of instruction: English
Academic year: March to December (2 semesters)

Pres.: Dr BEN ROBERTS

Vice-Pres. for Academic Affairs: Dr FREDER-
ICK S. GREGBE
Vice-Pres. for Administration: Dr WINGROVE
C. DWAMINA (acting)
Dean of Admissions: MOORE T. WORRELL
Libraries: see Libraries and Archives
Number of teachers: 260
Number of students: 3,400
Publications: *Liberian Law Journal, This
Week on Campus, University of Liberia
Catalogue and Announcements, University
of Liberia Journal, Varsity Pilot*

DEANS

A. M. Douglas College of Medicine: Dr TAIWO
DARAMOLA
College of Agriculture and Forestry: Dr
BISMARCK REEVES
College of Business and Public Administra-
tion: Prof. WILLIE BELLEH, Jr
College of Science and Technology: Prof.
FREDERICK D. HUNDER (acting)
College of Social Sciences and Humanities
(Liberia College): Dr BEN A. ROBERTS
Louis Arthur Grimes School of Law: Cllr
LUVENIA ASH-THOMPSON

Student Affairs: HARRISON MLE-SIE WOART
William V. S. Tubman Teachers' College: Dr
JOSHUA D. CLEON

COORDINATORS OF SCHOOLS

Graduate School of Education Administra-
tion: Dr HENRY KWEKWE
Graduate School of Regional Planning: Dr
JAMES N. KOLLIE, Sr
School of Pharmacy: Dr ARTHUR S. LEWIS

Colleges

Booker Washington Institute: POB 273,
Kakata; tel. 331048; f. 1929; state control; 52
teachers; 750 students; agricultural and
industrial courses; secondary high school
courses; basic computer literacy; Principal
MULBAH JACKOLLIE.

Cuttington University College: c/o Episcopal Church Building, POB 10-277, 1000
Monrovia 10; tel. 227413; fax 226059; e-mail
cuttingtonuniversity@yahoo.com; internet
cuttington.org; f. 1889; maintained by int.
donors, incl. Episcopal Church in the USA,
Episcopal Church of Liberia; applied for
subsidies from the Liberian Government;
language of instruction: English; academic
year September to June; library stock subjected to looting during civil war (1990–
1996), 250 periodicals; 110 teachers; 1,545
undergraduate students, 225 graduate students; Pres. Dr HENRIQUE F. TOKPA; Vice-
Pres. for Academic Affairs Dr JAMES E.
MOCK; Vice-Pres. for Administration Dr
CHARLES K. MULBAH; Dean of Students
HILARY W. COLLINS; Registrar and Dean of
Admissions BENGALY M. KAMARA; Librarian
FORKPA H. KEMAH.

**William V. S. Tubman College of Tech-
nology:** POB 3570, Monrovia; f. 1970; state
control; language of instruction: English;
academic year: March to December; 21
teachers; 200 students; 3-year associate
degree course in engineering technology;
Pres. Dr THEOPHILUS N. SONPON; Dean Dr
SOLOMON S. B. RUSSELL.

LIBYA

The Higher Education System

All current institutions of higher education have been founded since Libya became an independent kingdom in 1951. (Following a military coup in 1969, it became known as the Libyan Arab Republic, and since 1986 it has been known as the Great Socialist People's Libyan Arab Jamhariya.) The oldest university is the University of Garyounis, which was founded in 1955 as the Faculty of Arts and Education, Benghazi, became the University of Benghazi in 1973 and adopted its current name in 1976. Both the University of Garyounis and Al-Fateh University (founded in 1957; formerly Faculty of Science, Tripoli) were part of the former federal University of Libya until 1973. In 2002/03 there were an estimated 375,028 students in recognized institutions of higher education. The Secretariat for Education and Research is the responsible body for higher education, which is financed from the state budget. However, due to the expansion in student numbers and growing pressure on Government funding, greater autonomy has been granted to local public administrations in allowing the establishment of new, mostly private, universities.

A People's Committee, headed by a Dean (who acts as the Secretary), is the management body of each University. The main academic units are the Faculty and the Department. Faculties are also governed by a People's Committee, the Secretary of which represents the Faculty on the University People's Committee. Heads of Department are members of the Faculty People's Committee. Students sit on University and Faculty People's Committees.

Admission to higher education is on the basis of the Secondary Education Certificate, with different pass marks depending on the type of institution or degree applied for. Most undergraduate Bachelors degrees from universities require four years of study, but architecture, engineering (both five years) and medicine (six years) require longer. There are also technical and vocational institutions, which offer four- to five-year Bachelors degree courses in the sciences, technology and engineering. The main postgraduate degrees are the Masters and Doctorate. The Masters is a two-year programme of study following award of the Bachelors, and study for the Doctorate also lasts two years, culminating in public defence of a thesis.

Technical and vocational training at post-secondary level is offered by technical institutes.

The Centre for Quality Assurance and Accreditation for Higher Education Institutions, part of the Ministry of Education and Research, is the body responsible for the quality assurance and accreditation of all higher education providers.

Since its re-engagement with the international community, following the renunciation of weapons of mass destruction, Libya has worked to reform its higher education system and in 2007 produced a five-year strategic plan.

Regulatory Body

GOVERNMENT

General People's Committee: Tripoli; Sec. for Education and Research ABD AL-KABIR AL-FAKHRI.

ACCREDITATION

Centre for Quality Assurance and Accreditation for Higher Education and Training Institutions: Ben Ashur St, 80767 Tripoli; tel. (21) 3617328; fax (21) 3619604; e-mail elkabir@qaa.ly; internet www.qaa.ly; f. 2006; dept in the Min. of Education and Research; accredits all basic, vocational and higher education providers in Libya; evaluation of qualification from overseas for Libyan and non-Libyan; Dir Prof. MOHAMMED ELKABIR.

Learned Societies

LANGUAGE AND LITERATURE

British Council: POB 6797, Tripoli; Casablanca St, Hey El Wihda El Arabia, Siyahia, Tripoli; tel. (21) 4843164; fax (21) 4840178; e-mail info.libya@ly.britishcouncil.org; internet www.britishcouncil.org/libya; offers courses and exams in English language and British culture and promotes cultural exchange with the UK; Dir CARL REUTER.

Union of Libyan Authors, Writers and Artists: POB 1017, Tripoli; f. 1980; all fields of culture, education and art; 800 mems; library of 4,000 vols; Pres. AMIN MAZEN.

Research Institutes

GENERAL

National Academy for Scientific Research: POB 12312, Tripoli; tel. (21) 3339101; fax (21) 3341019; f. 1981 to conduct, finance and support scientific studies and research in all branches of knowledge; 330 mems; library of 19,000 vols; Dir-Gen. Dr TAHER H. JEHEMI; publs Al-Fikr Al-Arabi, Al-Fikr Al-Istratiji Al-Arabi, Al-Ilm Wa Atteknolojia.

National Scientific Research and Study Centre: POB 84662 Shara Azawia, Tripoli; tel. (21) 3602783; fax (21) 3602788; e-mail ncrss@ncrss.com; internet www.ncrss.com; f. 1995; centres of scientific research and studies; library and documentation; publishing and information; documentation and information; publ. Al Jadeed (4 a year).

Tajoura Nuclear Research Center: POB 30878, Tajoura; tel. (21) 3614130; fax (21) 3614142; e-mail admin@tnrc.org; internet www.tnrc.org; f. 1995; research in basic and applied science, nuclear energy, renewable sources of energy, desalination of water; publ. Al Nawah.

HISTORY, GEOGRAPHY AND ARCHAEOLOGY

Libyan Studies Centre: POB 5070, Sidi Munaider, Tripoli; tel. (21) 3333996; fax (21) 3331616; e-mail libyanjihad@libsc.org.ly; internet www.libsc.org.ly; f. 1978; historical studies and documentation; 140 mems; library of 100,000 vols, 700 periodicals, 3,000 MSS, 60,000 photographs; Dir Dr MOHAMED T. JERARY; publs Al-Insaf (1 a year), Al-Kunnasha (The Scrap Book, 2 a year), As-Shahid (The Martyr, 1 a year), Al-Wathaiq wa Al-Makhtutat (1 a year), Index of Libyan Periodicals (1 a year), Majallat Al-Buhuth At-Tarikhia (2 a year).

Libraries and Archives

Benghazi

National Library of Libya: POB 9127, Benghazi; tel. (61) 9096379; fax (61) 9096380; e-mail nat-lib-libya@hotmail.com; internet www.nllnet.net; f. 1973; Gen. Sec. MOHAMMAD A. ESHOWEIHDI.

University of Garyounis Library: POB 1308, Benghazi; tel. (61) 87633; f. 1955; 294,844 vols; 2,170 periodicals; 7 depts, including 2,360 MSS, 70,000 documents, 10,000 microfilms and rare books; Chief Librarian AHMED GALLAL; publs available for exchange.

Tripoli

Agricultural Research Centre Library: POB 2480, Tripoli; tel. (21) 3616865; fax (21) 3614993; e-mail taherazzabi@mailcity.com; f. 1973; 6,000 vols, 220 periodicals; Librarian LAMIS AL-GABSI.

Government Library: 14 Shar'a Al-Jazair, Tripoli; f. 1917; 35,500 vols; Librarian BASHIR AL-BADRI.

National Archives: Castello, Tripoli; tel. (21) 40166; internet www.nllnet.net; f. 1928; controlled by Department of Antiquities, General People's Committee for Education, Tripoli; extensive colln of documents relating to the history of Libya, mostly in Turkish from the Ottoman period; 5 libraries, 55,000 vols; Curator ABDULAALI OWN; publ. Libya Antiqua.

Museums and Art Galleries

Shahat

Department of Antiquities, Shahat (Cyrene): responsible for archaeological sites from Shahat west to the frontiers of Tocra, east to Msa'd; Controller BRAYEK ATTIYA.

Tripoli

Department of Antiquities: Assarai Al-Hamra, Tripoli; responsible for all museums and archaeological sites in Libya; Pres. Dr ABDULLAH SHAIBOUB.

Museums controlled by the Department:

Apollonia Museum: Marsa Soussa.

Archaeological, Natural History, Epigraphy, Prehistory and Ethnography Museums: Assarai Al-Hamra, Tripoli.

Benghazi Museum: Benghazi; mausoleum of Omar El Mukhtar.

Cyrene Museum: Cyrene (Shahat).

Gaigab Museum: Gaigab (near Cyrene).

Germa Museum: Germa (Fezean).

Islamic Museum: Tripoli.

Leptis Magna Museum: Leptis Magna.

Ptolemais Museum: Tolmeitha.

Sabratha Museum of Antiquities: Sabratha.

Tauchira Museum: Tokra.

Zanzur Museum: Zanzur (Tripoli).

Universities

AL-ARAB MEDICAL UNIVERSITY

POB 18251, Benghazi
Telephone: (61) 225007
Fax: (61) 222195
Founded 1984
State control
Languages of instruction: Arabic, English
Academic year: September to May
Pres.: Dr AMER RAHIL
Registrar: ABU-BAKER AMMARI
Librarian: MOHAMMED EL-SAID
Library of 30,000 vols, 600 periodicals
Number of teachers: 256
Number of students: 1,615
Publication: *Garyounis Medical Journal* (2 a year)

DEANS

Faculty of Dentistry: Dr ABDULLA OMAR DOURDA
Faculty of Medicine: Dr ABDUL HADI MOUSSA
Faculty of Pharmacy: Dr ABDUSALAM A. AL-MAYHOUB

AL-FATEH UNIVERSITY

POB 3601381, Tripoli
Telephone: (22) 605441
Fax: (22) 605460
E-mail: n.bazina@alfateh.edu.ly
Internet: www.alfateh.edu.ly
Founded 1957
State control
Language of instruction: Arabic
Academic year: September to June
Pres.: Dr MOHAMED L. FARHAT
Vice-Pres.: Dr NAJAH S. ELGABSI
Sec.-Gen.: Dr YOUNIS ALAGILI
Gen. Registrar: Dr AWEDAT GANDOUR
Librarian: Dr MOHAMED ABDUL JALEEL
Number of teachers: 3,200
Number of students: 75,000

Publications: *Bulletin of the Faculty of Education, Bulletin of the Faculty of Engineering, Bulletin of the Faculty of Law, Libyan Journal of Agriculture, Libyan Journal of Sciences*

DEANS

Faculty of Agriculture: Dr AMER ELMIGRI
Faculty of Economics and Political Science: Dr HAFAD SHAILI
Faculty of Education: Dr TOHAMI TARHOUNI
Faculty of Engineering: Dr ABDULHAMID ASHOUR
Faculty of Fine Arts: Dr HAMID
Faculty of Law: Dr OMAR HUSSIN
Faculty of Physical Education: Dr SADDIK EL KABOLI
Faculty of Science: Dr OMAR ELHAJI
Faculty of Veterinary Medicine: Dr SALAH ZWAI (acting)

AL-FATEH UNIVERSITY FOR MEDICAL SCIENCES

POB 13040, Tripoli
Telephone: (21) 4625060
Fax: (21) 4625883
E-mail: info@aums.edu.ly
Internet: www.aums.edu.ly
Founded 1986
State control
Languages of instruction: Arabic, English
Faculties of dentistry, medical technology, medicine and pharmacy.

BRIGHT STAR UNIVERSITY OF TECHNOLOGY

POB 58158, Ajdabia
Telephone: (64) 23012
Fax: (64) 61870
Founded 1981
State control
Language of instruction: Arabic
Academic year: October to June
Chancellor: Eng. ALI SALEH ELFAZZANI
Registrar: Eng. MANSOOR MASOOD FARAJ
Chief of Admin.: Eng. ABD ELSALAM ELZAROUG
Librarian: IBRAHIM MOHAMED AMIR
Number of teachers: 67
Number of students: 1,160

DERNA UNIVERSITY

Derna
Founded 1995
State control
Languages of instruction: Arabic, English
Faculties of accountancy and economics, fine arts and architecture, law, medical technology and social sciences.

UNIVERSITY OF GARYOUNIS

POB 1308, Benghazi
Telephone: (61) 2220147
Fax: (61) 2230315
Internet: www.garyounis.edu
Founded 1955 as the Faculty of Arts and Education, Benghazi; became University of Benghazi 1973; present name 1976
State control
Language of instruction: Arabic
Chancellor: Dr MUHAMID A. ALMAHDAWI
Registrar: MAHMUD M. FAKHRI
Library: see Libraries and Archives
Number of teachers: 1,300
Number of students: 35,230
Publications: various faculty bulletins.

DEANS

Faculty of Arts and Education: Dr FATHI AL-HARIM
Faculty of Economics: Dr ABDELGADIR AMIR
Faculty of Engineering: Dr BELAID EIKWARI
Faculty of Law: Dr SULMAN AL-GURISH
Faculty of Science: Dr MUHAMID EL-AWIME

NASIR UNIVERSITY

POB 48222, Al-Khums Tripoli
Telephone: (325) 660080
Fax: (325) 660048
Founded 1986
State control
Academic year: September to July
Faculties of arts, economics and political science, education and science, engineering, law, science.

OMAR AL-MUKHTAR UNIVERSITY

POB 991, Al-Bayda
Telephone: (84) 6310719
Fax: (84) 632233
E-mail: info@omulibya.org
Founded 1985
State control
Pres.: ABDALLA A. M. ZAIED
Faculties of agriculture, engineering, literature and education, science and veterinary medicine.

OPEN UNIVERSITY

POB 13375, Tripoli
Telephone: (21) 4874000
Fax: (21) 4874000
E-mail: info@libopenuniv-edu.org
Internet: www.libopenuniv-edu.org
Founded 1987
State control
Language of instruction: Arabic
Academic year: September to July
Pres.: IBRAHIM ABU-FARWA
Number of teachers: 52
Number of students: 8,410
Faculties of accountancy, administration, arabic, economics, education and psychology, geography, history, Islamic studies, law, political science, sociology and social work; dept of continuing education.

SEBHA UNIVERSITY

POB 18758, Sebha
Telephone: (71) 626012
Fax: (71) 627019
E-mail: info@sebhau.edu.ly
Internet: www.sebhau.edu.ly
Founded 1983 from the Faculty of Education of Al-Fateh University
State control
Languages of instruction: Arabic, English
Academic year: October to August
Chancellor: Dr MOHAMED MUFTAH SALEH
Vice-Chancellor: SALEM ABDULLAH SAID
Registrar: MISBAH AL-GHAWIL
Librarian: ZIDAN AL-BREIKY
Number of teachers: 646
Number of students: 9,403
Publications: *Al-Shifa* (medicine, 1 a year), *Physical Education Magazine* (2 a year)

DEANS

Faculty of Agriculture: Dr MOHAMMAD ABDUL KARIM
Faculty of Arts and Education: HAMED MASH-MOOR
Faculty of Dentistry: Dr HASAN AL-BUSAIFY
Faculty of Economics and Accountancy: Dr BASHIR ABU-QILA

Faculty of Engineering and Technology: MOHAMMAD ARAHOOMA
Faculty of Medicine: Dr OMAR IBRAHIM AL-SHAIBANI
Faculty of Physical Education: ABDUL RAHMAN AL-ANSARI
Faculty of Science: Dr MOHAMMAD BASHIR HASAN

SEVENTH OF APRIL UNIVERSITY

POB 16418, Al-Zawia
Telephone: (23) 24035
Fax: (23) 24030
E-mail: 7april_univ@mail.lttnet.net
Founded 1988
State control
Pres.: Prof. SHABAN T. AL ASWAD
Languages of instruction: Arabic, English
Faculties of education, engineering, physical education (women only), science.

SEVENTH OF OCTOBER UNIVERSITY

POB 2478, Misurata
Telephone: (51) 2627201
Fax: (51) 2627350
Internet: www.7ou.edu.ly
Founded 2004
State control
Number of teachers: 961
Number of students: 20,000

Faculties of agriculture, arts, education, engineering, information technology, law, medical technology, medicine, nursing, pharmacy, science; MSc in information technology

in partnership with Nottingham Trent University, UK.

UNIVERSITY OF SIRT

POB 674, Sirt
Telephone: (54) 5260363
Fax: (54) 5262152
E-mail: info@su.edu.ly
Internet: www.su.edu.ly
Founded 1989
State control
Faculties of agriculture, arts, dentistry, economics, education, engineering, law, medical, medicine, nursing, science, technology
Pres.: Dr MOHAMMED A. A. ABDULLA.

Colleges

African Centre for Applied Research and Training in Social Development (ACARTSOD): POB 80606, Tripoli; tel. (21) 4835103; fax (21) 4835066; e-mail fituri_acartsod@hotmail.com; f. 1977 as an intergovernmental institution under the auspices of the UN Economic Comm. for Africa and the OAU; aims to promote and coordinate applied research and training in the field of social development at regional and sub-regional levels, organizes seminars, etc.; Deputy Exec. Dir Dr AHMED SAID FITURI; publ. *African Social Challenges* (1 a year).

Faculty of Islamic Call: POB 71771 Tripoli; tel. (21) 4801472; fax (21) 4800059;

e-mail mu_dyab@yahoo.com; internet www.islamic-call.org/web_fic.html; f. 1974; private control, World Islamic Call Society; 300 students; 4-year courses in Koranic and Arabic studies.

Higher Institute of Industry: Misurata; internet www.hii.edu.ly; f. 1988; state control; Higher National Diplomas, Bachelors of Technology, Masters of Technology; Dean Dr MAJDI A. ASHIBANI.

Higher Institute of Mechanical and Electrical Engineering: POB 61160, Hoon; tel. (57) 602841; fax (57) 602842; e-mail aisa_jadi@yahoo.com; f. 1976; BSc-level studies; library: 22,000 vols, 100 periodicals; 48 teachers; 336 students; Dean AISA S. JADI.

Higher Institute of Technology: POB 68, Brack; tel. (71) 45300; fax (71) 27600; f. 1976; first degree courses in general sciences, medical technology, food technology and environmental sciences; library: 10,000 vols; 60 teachers; 500 students; Dean Dr ABDUSSALAM M. ALMETHNANI.

Islamic Arts and Crafts School: Shar'a 1 September, Tripoli; tel. (21) 3334315.

National Institute of Administration: POB 3651, Tripoli; tel. (21) 4623420; fax (21) 4623423; f. 1953; offers higher diploma in administration and accounting; library: 10,000 vols; 30 teachers; publ. *National Magazine of Administration.*

Posts and Telecommunications Institute: POB 2428, Tripoli; f. 1963; library: 510 vols; Dir K. MARABUTACI.

LIECHTENSTEIN

The Higher Education System

The Principality's first university was not founded until 1992 when the former Liechtensteinische Ingenieurschule (founded 1961; formerly Abendtechnikum Vaduz) achieved university status; it is now known as Hochschule Liechtenstein (Liechtenstein University of Applied Sciences) and is a state-run institution. A private university, Universität für Humanwissenschaften (University of Human Sciences), was founded in Triesen in 2000 and there is also a publicly funded music school in Vaduz. Many Liechtensteiners continue their studies at universities in Austria and Switzerland. In 2004/2005 there were 527 students in higher education in Liechtenstein and 931 attending institutions abroad.

The Hochschule Liechtenstein fully implemented the Bologna Process in 2003. A law approved in 2005 regulates the compulsory use of ECTS (European Credit Transfer and Accumulation System) with both Masters and Bachelors degrees; it also stipulates that Diploma Supplements should be issued in both German and English. Since the education sector of Liechtenstein is quite small, there is no national qualification framework. Liechtenstein is affiliated to the European Network for Quality Assurance in Higher Education and is committed to the quality standards targeted by that organization.

Admission to higher education depends upon completion of secondary education and award of the Matura. The undergraduate degree is the Bachelors, a three-year programme of study. Following the Bachelors, postgraduate students may be awarded the Nachdiplom (a short-course degree), Magister Philosophiae (requiring five years of study) and finally Doctor of Philosophy.

Vocational and technical training consists of either workplace-orientated apprenticeship schemes or four-year professional courses in civil engineering, mechanical engineering, economics or architecture at Hochschule Liechtenstein.

Regulatory and Representative Bodies

GOVERNMENT

Regierungsgebäude (Government Offices): Postfach 684, 9490 Vaduz; tel. 236-61-11; fax 236-60-22; e-mail office@liechtenstein.li; internet www.liechtenstein.li; Min. of Education, of Home Affairs and of Sport HUGO QUADERER; Min. of Foreign Affairs, of Justice and of Cultural Affairs Dr AURELIA FRICK.

ACCREDITATION

ENIC/NARIC Liechtenstein: Schulamt, Europark, Austr. 79, POB 684, 9490 Vaduz; tel. 236-67-58; fax 236-67-71; e-mail helmut.konrad@sa.llv.li; internet www.sa.llv.li; Head of Upper Secondary and Higher Education Division HELMUT KONRAD.

NATIONAL BODY

Schulamt (Education Office): Austr. 79, Postfach 684, 9490 Vaduz; tel. 236-67-70; fax 236-67-71; e-mail info@sa.llv.li; internet www.sa.llv.li; undertakes the devt of education in kindergartens, schools and colleges; drafts and refines curricula; supervises and manages teaching staff; administers educational programmes; Chief Officer GUIDO WOLFINGER.

Learned Societies

HISTORY, GEOGRAPHY AND ARCHAEOLOGY

Historischer Verein für das Fürstentum Liechtenstein (Historical Society for the Principality of Liechtenstein): Plankner Str. 39, 9494 Schaan; tel. 392-17-47; fax 392-17-05; e-mail info@historischerverein.li; internet www.historischerverein.li; f. 1901; 850 mems; library of 3,000 vols; Pres. Lic. phil. EVA PEPIĆ-HELFERICH; publ. *Jahrbuch*.

NATURAL SCIENCES

General

Liechtensteinische Gesellschaft für Umweltschutz (Liechtenstein Society for Environmental Protection): Im Bretscha 22, 9494 Schaan; tel. 232-52-62; fax 237-40-31; e-mail info@lgu.li; internet www.lgu.li; f. 1973; 750 mems; Pres. RAINER KÜHNIS; Man. Dir MORITZ RHEINBERGER; publs *LGU-Liewoseiten* (irregular), *Mitteilungen* (4 a year).

Research Institute

ECONOMICS, LAW AND POLITICS

Liechtenstein-Institut: Auf dem Kirchhügel, St Luziweg 2, 9487 Gamprin-Bendern; tel. 373-30-22; fax 373-54-22; e-mail admin@liechtenstein-institut.li; internet www.liechtenstein-institut.li; f. 1986; research on topics related to Liechtenstein in the fields of law, political science, history, economics and social science; library of 8,000 vols; Pres. Dr Iur. GUIDO MEIER; Dir Dr WILFRIED MARXER.

Libraries and Archives

Vaduz

Liechtensteinische Landesbibliothek National Library of Liechtenstein (National Library of Liechtenstein): Gerberweg 5, Postfach 385, 9490 Vaduz; tel. 236-63-63; fax 233-14-19; e-mail info@landesbibliothek.li; internet www.landesbibliothek.li; f. 1961; public, academic and nat. library; 250,000 vols; Nat. Librarian BARBARA VOGT.

Liechtensteinisches Landesarchiv (National Archives of Liechtenstein): Peter-Kaiser-Pl. 2, POB 684, 9490 Vaduz; tel. 236-63-40; fax 236-63-59; e-mail info@la.llv.li; internet www.la.llv.li; f. 1961; nat. archives; reference library of 7,000 linear metres of documents; Dir Lic. Phil. PAUL VOGT; Deputy Archivist Mag. Phil. RUPERT TIEFENTHALER; publ. *Veröffentlichungen des Liechtensteinischen Landesarchivs*.

Museums and Art Galleries

Vaduz

Kunstmuseum Liechtenstein: Städtle 32, POB 370, 9490 Vaduz; tel. 235-03-00; fax 235-03-29; e-mail mail@kunstmuseum.li; internet www.kunstmuseum.li; f. 2000; museum of modern and contemporary art; nat. colln; Dir Dr FRIEDEMANN MALSCH; Curator CHRISTIANE MEYER-STOLL.

Liechtensteinisches Landesmuseum (Liechtenstein National Museum): Städtle 43, Postfach 1216, 9490 Vaduz; tel. 239-68-20; fax 239-68-37; e-mail landesmuseum@llm.llv.li; internet www.landesmuseum.li; f. 1954; incl. items from collns of the Prince, the State and the Liechtenstein Historical Soc.; Pres. EVA PEPIĆ.

Postmuseum des Fürstentums Liechtenstein: Städtle 37, 9490 Vaduz; tel. 239-68-46; internet www.llm.li/d/postmuseum.asp; f. 1930; Liechtenstein stamps, historical postal documents, postal machinery; Dir NORBERT HASLER.

Universities

HOCHSCHULE LIECHTENSTEIN (Liechtenstein University of Applied Sciences)

Fürst-Franz-Josef-Str., 9490 Vaduz

Telephone: 265-11-11
Fax: 265-11-12
E-mail: info@hochschule.li
Internet: www.hochschule.li

Founded 1961 as Abendtechnikum Vaduz; renamed Liechtensteinische Ingenieurschule 1985; university status 1992; renamed Fachhochschule Liechtenstein 1997; present name 2005
State control
Languages of instruction: German, English
Rector: KLAUS NÄSCHER
Vice-Rector: Prof. Dipl. Ing. HANSJÖRG HILTI
Librarian: ELISABETH EMMA WEILER
Number of students: 1,000

Publication: *Denkfabrik* (magazine, 2 a year)

DEANS

Institute of Architecture and Planning: Prof. Dipl. Ing. HANSJÖRG HILTI
Institute of Business Information Systems: Prof. Dr JAN VOM BROCKE
Institute of Entrepreneurship: Prof. Dr URS BALDEGGER
Institute of Financial Services: Prof. Dr MARTIN WENZ

PROFESSORS

BALDEGGER, U., Entrepreneurship
EISINGER, A., Urban Construction and Development
HILTI, H., Design and Woodwork
KÄFERSTEIN, J., Design and Construction
MEISTER, U., Design and Construction
MENICHETTI, M. J., Business Economics
WEINMANN, S, Information Technology for Business
WENZ, M., Business Management and International and Liechtenstein Tax Law
WINNING, H.-H., Urban Construction, Planning and Transport

INTERNATIONAL AKADEMIE FÜR PHILOSOPHIE IM FÜRSTENTUM LIECHTENSTEIN
(International Philosophy Academy in the Principality of Liechtenstein)

Im Schwibboga 7 B–C, 9487 Bendern
Telephone: 265-43-43
Fax: 265-43-01
E-mail: admin@iap.li
Internet: www.iap.li
Private control
Rector: JOSEF SEIFERT
Gen. Sec.: HUBERTUS DESSLOCH
Chief Librarian: MECHTHILD WEISS-RAICHLE
Library of 14,000 vols

PROFESSORS

MCCORMICK, P. POREBSKI, C. SEIFERT, J.

UFL PRIVATE UNIVERSITÄT IM FÜRSTENTUM LIECHTENSTEIN
(Private University of the Principality of Liechtenstein)

Dorfstr. 24, 9495 Triesen
Telephone: 392-40-10
Fax: 392-40-11
E-mail: info@ufl.li
Internet: www.ufl.li
Founded 2000
Private control
Rector: Prof. Dr KARL M. SUDI
Dir of Studies: Prof. Dr PATRICIA SCHIESS

DEANS

Faculty of Law: (vacant)
Faculty of Medical Science: Prof. Dr HEINZ DREXEL

College

Liechtensteinische Musikschule: St Florinsgasse 1, Postfach 435, 9490 Vaduz; tel. 235-03-30; fax 235-03-31; e-mail info@musikschule.li; internet www.musikschule.li; f. 1963; 100 teachers; 2,600 students; library: 12,000 vols, special colln of works of composer Josef Gabriel Rheinberger; int. masterclasses June to September; Dir KLAUS BECK.

LITHUANIA

The Higher Education System

The oldest existing institution of higher education in Lithuania is Vilniaus Universitetas (Vilnius University), founded in 1579 when Lithuania was united in a Commonwealth with Poland. The next oldest institution is Vilniaus Dailes Akademija (Vilnius Academy of Fine Arts), founded in 1793. In 1795 Lithuania was annexed by the Russian Empire and remained under Russian (and later, Bolshevik) rule until 1920, when the USSR recognized Lithuanian independence. In 1922 Lithuania was declared a parliamentary democracy under the terms of its first Constitution. Several university-level institutions date from this year, among them Kauno Medicinos Universitetas (Kaunas Medical University), Kauno Technologijos Universitetas (Kaunas University of Technology) and Vytauto Didžiojo Universitetas (Vytautas Magnus University). According to the 'Secret Protocols' to the 1939 Treaty of Non-Aggression signed by the USSR and Nazi Germany, Lithuania was to come under German influence. However, the subsequent Nazi-Soviet Treaty on Friendship and Existing Borders granted the USSR control of Lithuania. In 1940 the Lithuanian Government was forced to resign and a Soviet Socialist Republic was established. In 1990 Lithuania was the first Soviet republic to declare independence, although this was not recognized by the USSR State Council until 1991. In February of that year the Supreme Council of the Republic of Lithuania adopted the Law on Science and Studies, which established the guidelines of higher education reform, with the intention of bringing Lithuania's research and higher education system closer to that of Western Europe. Following the introduction of the Law on Education in 2000, Lithuania participates in the Bologna Process to establish a European Higher Education Area, the first phase of which is to adopt a credit-based system of comparable degrees with two main cycles (undergraduate and graduate). From 2003 a uniform tuition fee was introduced for students in higher education, although there were exemptions for the highest achievers. In 2007/08 there were 22 universities and 28 colleges. In that year total enrolment in higher education was an estimated 204,432. External evaluation of university studies is carried out by the Centre for Quality Assessment in Higher Education, which was founded in 1995.

The main requirement for admission to university is the Certificate of Maturity (Brandos Atestatas), the main secondary school qualification. Institutions receiving more applications than places available set competitive entrance examinations. Lithuania has established a two-tier Bachelors (Bakalauras) and Masters (Magistras) degree system in accordance with the principles of the Bologna Process. The Bachelors is a four-year programme of study and students are required to accrue 160 credits for award of the degree. Following the Bachelors is the Masters, the first postgraduate-level degree. This is a programme of study lasting one-and-a-half to two years, and may be awarded in conjunction with a professional title. The Doctorate (Daktaras) follows the Masters and requires up to four years of study, covering classroom-based instruction and original thesis research. A 2006 amendment to the Law on Higher Education enabled colleges to award a Professional Bachelor degree (profesinis bakalauras) from 2007 onwards. Since 2007 college graduates wishing to continue Masters studies in universities do not have to complete university Bachelors programmes.

Technical and vocational education at post-secondary level is available at junior colleges and vocational schools (Aukstesnioji mokykla). Qualifications offered include the Higher Education Diploma (Aukštojo Mokslo Diplomas) and College Diploma (Aukštesniojo Mokslo Diplomas).

In 2007 the Ministry of Education and Science launched a reform of scientific research in higher education institutes with the Law on Science and Studies. In 2009 a new law was approved outlining how a number of research institutes would be incorporated into certain universities and other reform measures on funding.

Regulatory and Representative Bodies

GOVERNMENT

Ministry of Culture: J. Basanavičiaus 5, 01118 Vilnius; tel. (5) 261-9486; fax (5) 262-3120; e-mail culture@muza.lt; internet www.muza.lt; Min. ARŪNAS GELŪNAS.

Ministry of Education and Science: A. Volano 2/7, 01516 Vilnius; tel. (5) 219-1190; fax (5) 261-2077; e-mail smmin@smm.lt; internet www.smm.lt; Min. GINTARAS STEPONAVIČIUS.

ACCREDITATION

ENIC/NARIC Lithuania: Suvalku g. 1, 03106 Vilnius; tel. (5) 210-4777; fax (5) 213-2553; e-mail enicnaric@skvc.lt; internet www.skvc.lt; Deputy Dir AURELIJA VALEIKIENE.

NATIONAL BODIES

Lietuvos kolegijų direktorių konferencija (Lithuanian College Directors' Conference): Antakalnio g. 54, 10303 Vilnius; tel. (5) 234-3516; fax (5) 234-3769; e-mail a.aleknaviciene@vsdk.lt; internet www.kolegijos.lt; Pres. NIJOLĖ KIKUTIENĖ; Exec. Dir ANA ALEKNAVIČIENĖ.

Lietuvos mokslo taryba (Research Council of Lithuania): Gedimino ave 3, 01103 Vilnius; tel. (5) 212-4933; fax (5) 261-8535; e-mail lmt@ktl.mii.lt; internet www.lmt.lt; f. 1991; promotes the devt of higher education and research; funds research projects; advises the Seimas (Parliament) and the Govt in these areas; initiates and evaluates legislative proposals in the field of science; 29 mems; Chair. Prof. Dr Habil EUGENIJUS BUTKUS; Dir AUSRA VILUTIENE.

Lietuvos Respublikos Valstybinis Patentų Biuras (State Patent Bureau of the Republic of Lithuania): Kalvarijų g. 3, 09310 Vilnius; tel. (5) 278-0290; fax (5) 275-0723; e-mail info@vpb.gov.lt; internet www.vpb.lt; Dir RIMVYDAS NAUJOKAS.

Lietuvos Universitetų Rektorių Konferencija (Lithuanian University Rectors' Conference): Tilto str. 16, 01101 Vilnius; tel. and fax (5) 212-0629; e-mail lurkbiuras@gmail.com; internet www.lurk.lt; Pres. Prof. Dr ROMUALDAS GINEVIČIUS; Gen. Sec. Prof. KĘSTUTIS KRIŠČIŪNAS.

Mokslo, Inovacijų ir Technologijų Agentūra (Agency for Science, Innovation and Technology): A. Goštauto 12–219, 01108 Vilnius; tel. (5) 264-4708; fax (5) 231-2292; e-mail tpa@tpa.lt; internet www.tpa.lt; f. 1999 as Eureka Information Center, renamed as Agency for International Science and Technology Development Programmes 2002, present name 2010; Dir BIRUTĖ BUKAUSKAITĖ (acting).

Nacionalinis egzaminų centras (National Examination Centre): M. Katkaus g. 44, Vilnius; tel. (5) 275-6180; fax (5) 275-2268; e-mail centras@nec.lt; internet www.egzaminai.lt; f. 1996; organizes and carries out examination of candidates' knowledge and skills; Dir DANUTĖ ŠUKIENĖ.

Studijų kokybės vertinimo centras (Centre for Quality Assessment in Higher Education—CQAHE): A. Goštauto g. 12, 01108 Vilnius; tel. (5) 210-4772; fax (5) 213-2553; e-mail skvc@skvc.lt; internet www.skvc.lt; f. 1995; Dir ARTŪRAS GREBLIAUSKAS.

Valstybinis Studijų Fondas (State Studies Foundation): A. Goštauto g. 12–407, 01108 Vilnius; tel. (5) 263-9152; fax (5) 263-9153; e-mail fondas@vsf.lt; internet www.vsf.lt; f. 1993 as Lithuanian State Science and Studies Foundation, present name and status 2010; Dir Dr SIGITAS RENČYS.

Learned Societies

GENERAL

Lithuanian Academy of Sciences: 3 Gedimino pr., 01103 Vilnius; tel. (5) 261-3651; fax

Research Institutes

GENERAL

Inovacinis Specialiųjų Konstrukcijų ir Statinių Mokslo Institutas 'Kompozitas' (Innovatory Scientific Institute of Special Structures 'Kompozitas'): Saulėtekio al.11, SRL-II, Room 29, 10223 Vilnius; tel. (5) 274-5227; fax (5) 237-0569; e-mail kmi@vgtu.lt; internet www.isksmi.st.vgtu.lt; f. 1992; attached to Vilniaus Gedimino Technikos Universitetas; construction process of scientific technical expertise; innovative actions; engineering and consultancy work; building, engineering, construction , technology and lifting machinery construction surveys; Dir Prof. Dr Habil AUDRONIS KAZIMIERAS KVE-DARAS.

Institute of Open Source Research: Naugarduko g. 41, 03227 Vilnius; tel. (5) 274-4765; e-mail info@aki.lt; attached to Vilniaus Gedimino Technikos Universitetas.

International Studies Centre: Saulėtekio al.11, 10223 Vilnius; tel. (5) 274-50-26; fax (5) 274-4897; e-mail tsc@vgtu.lt; attached to Vilniaus Gedimino Technikos Universitetas; Dir BIRUTĖ TAMULAITIENĖ.

AGRICULTURE, FISHERIES AND VETERINARY SCIENCE

Institute of Agriculture: Instituto al. 1, LT- 58344 Akademija, Kėdainių Dist.; tel. (4) 737-271; fax (4) 737-096; e-mail lzi@lzi.lt; internet www.lzi.lt; f. 1956, present status 2009; attached to Lietuvos Agrarinių ir Miškų Mokslų Centras; carries out collects and disseminates scientific knowledge for the devt of agricultural and rural areas, plant generic resources, seed production to conduct soil agrochemical research; in cooperation with higher education institutions trains scientists and assists these institutions in training specialists, promoting sustainable devt and research work in the fields of agrochemistry, agroecology, apiculture, biotechnology, breeding, crop management, and rural devt in conformity with the research directions approved by the Govt; Dir Prof. Dr. Habil. ZENONAS DABKEVIČIUS; Deputy Dir for Science Dr ŽYDRĖ KADŽIULIENĖ; Scientific Sec. VITA TILVIKIENĖ; publ. *Zemdirbyste-Agriculture* (4 a year).

Institute of Forestry: Liepų g. 1, 53101 Girionys, Kauno Dist.; tel. (3) 754-7221; fax (3) 754-7446; e-mail miskinst@mi.lt; internet www.mi.lt; f. 1950, present status 2009; attached to Lietuvos Agrarinių ir Miškų Mokslų Centras; conducts fundamental and applied forest research to obtain new knowledge for social, ecological and economical devt; disseminates scientific and technical information about forest and environment; Dir Prof. Dr Habil. REMIGIJUS OZOLINČIUS; Deputy Dir Dr MARIUS ALEINIKOVAS; Scientific Sec. Dr DIANA MIZARAITE; publs *Baltic Forestry* (2 a year), *Miskininkyste* (2 to 4 a year).

Institute of Horticulture: Kauno g. 30, 54333 Babtai Kauno Dist.; tel. (3) 755-5395; fax (3) 755-5176; e-mail miskinst@lsdi.lt; internet www.lsdi.lt; f. 1938 as Horticulture Test Station, present name 1990, present status 2009; attached to Lietuvos Agrarinių ir Miškų Mokslų Centras; develops scientific investigations and technology of modern horticulture, and ecological and integrated vegetable-growing to guarantee the security of food quality, competitive ability and production quality; develops or introduces modern horticulture and vegetable-growing; conducts scientific investigations for storage and processing of fruit and vegetables; Dir ČESLOVAS BOBINAS; Deputy Dir for Science AUDRIUS SASNAUSKAS; Deputy Dir for Admin.

Lietuvos Agrarinių ir Miškų Mokslų Centras (Lithuanian Research Centre for Agriculture and Forestry):tel. (3) 473-7057; e-mail lammc@lammc.lt; internet www .lammc.lt; f. 2009; focuses on energy crops and their devt; 3 research institutes; library of 60,000 vols; Dir Prof. Dr Habil ZENONAS DABKEVIČIUS; Sec. ELENA PURAUSKIENĖ.

ARCHITECTURE AND TOWN PLANNING

Architektūros mokslo institutas (Institute of Architecture): Pylimo g. 26/1, AR-I, room 1.5, 01132 Vilnius; tel. and fax (5) 274-5214; e-mail archinst@ar.vgtu.lt; internet www.ami.ar.vgtu.lt; f. 1999; attached to Vilniaus Gedimino Technikos Universitetas; Dir Prof. JONAS ANUŠKEVIČIUS.

ECONOMICS, LAW AND POLITICS

Institute of Economics: Goštauto g. 12, 01108 Vilnius; tel. (5) 262-3502; fax (5) 212-7506; e-mail ei@ktl.mii.lt; f. 1941; attached to Lithuanian Acad. of Sciences; research in mathematical modelling; devt of Lithuanian economy; integration into EU; history of economic thought; library of 5,000 vols; Dir Prof. EDUARDAS VILKAS.

Institute for Social Research: Saltoniškių 58, 08105 Vilnius; tel. (5) 275-8667; fax (5) 275-4896; e-mail sti@ktl.mii.lt; internet www .sti.lt; f. 1977; Dir Prof. ARVYDAS VIRGILIJUS MATULIONIS; publs *Humanistika, Logos, Philosophy and Sociology* (4 a year).

FINE AND PERFORMING ARTS

Institute of Culture and Arts: Tilto 4, 01101 Vilnius; tel. (5) 262-6091; fax (5) 261-0989; Dir Prof. Dr A. MATULIONIS; Scientific Sec. Dr A. ŠIMĖNIENĖ; publ. *The Art Studies* (2 a year).

HISTORY, GEOGRAPHY AND ARCHAEOLOGY

Geodezijos Institutas (Research Institute of Geodesy): Saulėtekio al. 11, 10223 Vilnius; tel. and fax (5) 274-4705; e-mail gi@vgtu.lt; internet www.gi.ap.vgtu.lt; f. 1992; attached to Vilniaus Gedimino Technikos Universitetas; researches on gravity field, magnetic field, on geodetic coordinate systems; establishment of GPS precision networks, Lithuanian nat. gravity network, Lithuanian nat. geodetic vertical network; investigates geoid of Lithuanian territory, permanent GPS stations network devt, geodynamic processes, aero photogrammetric methods; development of information system for geodetic reference, preparation of aero navigation data in WGS 84 coordinate system; researches and improves surveying instruments and calibration methods; Dir Assoc. Dr EIMUNTAS KAZIMIERAS PARŠELIŪNAS.

Institute of Geology and Geography: T. Ševčenkos g. 13, 03223 Vilnius; tel. (5) 210-4690; fax (5) 210-4695; e-mail info@geo.lt; internet www.geo.lt; f. 1941, present status 2002; attached to Gamtos Tyrimų Centras; researches structure, composition and evolution of the Earth's crust, and its surface and subsurface resources; structure, state and dynamics of climate, hydrosphere and geological environment; analysis and prediction of processes for conservation, sustainable devt and geotechnologies; geosystems in the Baltic Sea and the coastal zone and prediction of their future devt; analysis, cartographic modelling and prediction of landscape and human geographic processes for territorial planning; Dir Dr MIGLĖ STAN-ČIKAITĖ; publs *Annales Geographicae* (Geografijos metraštis, Geographical Yearbook, 1

---

(5) 261-8464; e-mail prezidiumas@lma.lt; internet www.lma.lt; f. 1941; divs of agricultural and forestry sciences (Chair. Prof. ALBINAS KUSTA), biological, medical and geosciences (Chair. Prof. VYTAUTAS BASYS), humanities and social sciences (Chair. Prof. ALEKSANDRAS VASILIAUSKAS), mathematical, physical and chemical sciences (Chair. Prof. FELIKSAS IVANAUSKAS), technical sciences (Chair. Prof. VYTAUTAS OSTAŠEVIČIUS); 194 mems (40 full, 60 corresp., 50 expert, 44 foreign); library: see Libraries and Archives; Pres. VALDEMARAS RAZUMAS; Sec.-Gen. Prof. DOMAS KAUNAS; publs *Acta medica Lituanica* (3 or 4 a year), *Arts Studies* (5 a year), *Journal of Agricultural Sciences* (4 a year), *Journal of Biology* (4 a year), *Journal of Chemistry* (4 a year), *Journal of Ecology* (3 or 4 a year), *Journal of Geography* (4 a year), *Journal of Geology* (4 a year), *Journal of Philosophy and Sociology* (3 or 4 a year), *Journal of Power Engineering* (4 a year), *Lithuanian Science* (5 or 6 a year), *Lituanistica* (3 or 4 a year), *Science and Technology* (12 a year).

BIBLIOGRAPHY, LIBRARY SCIENCE AND MUSEOLOGY

Association of Lithuanian Serials: Saulėtekio al. 11, 10223 Vilnius; tel. (5) 274-5038; fax (5) 237-0602; e-mail info@moksloperiodika.lt; internet www.serials.lt; an ind. asscn of Lithuanian instns, agencies, cos, orgs and persons related to serials publishing; serves and represents the interests and needs of its mems; 9 mems; Pres. Prof. Dr RAIMUNDAS KIRVAITIS.

Lithuanian Research Libraries Consortium: Gedimino pr. 51, 01504 Vilnius; tel. (5) 249-7023; fax (5) 249-6129; e-mail lmba@lnb .lt; internet www.lmba.lt; f. 2001; promotes devt of virtual libraries; prepares and implements advanced technology and innovative projects in the libraries; subscribes to electronic databases for the consortium mems and other libraries; 48 mems; Pres. EMILIJA BANIONYTĖ.

LANGUAGE AND LITERATURE

Alliance Française: Mykolo Romerio Universitetas, Ateities g. 20-118, 08303 Vilnius; tel. (5) 271-4672; fax (5) 271-4522; offers courses and exams in French language and culture and promotes cultural exchange with France.

British Council: Jogailos 4, 01116 Vilnius; tel. (5) 264-4890; fax (5) 264-4893; e-mail mail@britishcouncil.lt; internet www .britishcouncil.org/lithuania; f. 1992; offers courses and exams in English language and British culture and promotes cultural exchange with the UK; library of 5,201 vols; Dir LINA BALENAITE; Information Centre Man. RIMA KLUSOVSKIENE.

Goethe-Institut: Tilto g. 3-6, 01101 Vilnius; tel. (5) 231-4433; fax (5) 231-4432; e-mail info@vilnius.goethe.org; internet www .goethe.de/ne/vil/deindex.htm; offers courses and exams in German language and culture and promotes cultural exchange with Germany; Dir IRMTRAUT HUBATSCH.

PEN Centre of Lithuania: K. Sirvydo 6, 01101 Vilnius; tel. (6) 169-5138; fax (5) 212-6556; e-mail almantsam@yahoo.com; f. 1989; promotes friendship and cooperation among writers internationally; campaigns for freedom of expression, human rights and democratic causes; 34 mems; Pres. Assoc. Prof. Dr ALMANTAS SAMALAVICIUS; Sec. LAIMANTAS JONUSYS.

a year), *Baltica* (1 a year), *Geografija* (Geography), *Geologija* (Geology, 4 a year).

Institute of Lithuanian History: Kražių g. 5, 01108 Vilnius; tel. (5) 261-4436; fax (5) 261-4433; e-mail istorija@istorija.lt; internet www.istorija.lt; f. 1941; promotes study of archaeology, ethnology (and social anthropology), heraldry, sigillography, numismatics, palaeography and genealogy; library of 142,000 vols; Dir Dr RIMANTAS MIKNYS; Vice-Dir Dr ZITA MEDIŠAUSKIENĖ; publs *Archaeologija Baltica* (Lithuanian Archaeology), *Lietuvos archeologija* (Lithuanian Archaeology), *Lithuanian Ethnology, Lithuanian Historical Studies, Lithuanian Metrica, Lituanistica, Urban Past, Yearbook of Lithuanian History.*

Teritorijų Planavimo Institutas (Research Institute of Territorial Planning): Saulėtekio al. 11, 10223 Vilnius; tel. (5) 274-5072; fax (5) 274-4731; e-mail marbur@vgtu .lt; internet www.tpi.vgtu.lt; f. 1992; attached to Vilniaus Gedimino Technikos Universitetas; prepares planning documents; advises planning issues; develops residential projects, urban digital plans, storing information in databases; prepares landscape architectural projects; Dir Prof. Dr MARIJA BURINSKIENĖ; publs *Baltic Journal of Road and Bridge Engineering, Technological and Economic Development of Economy.*

LANGUAGE AND LITERATURE

Institute of Lithuanian Language: P. Vileisio 5, 10308 Vilnius 55; tel. (5) 234-6472; fax (5) 234-7200; e-mail lki@lki.lt; internet www.lki.lt; f. 1939; library: Archives of Lithuanian Dialects; Dir Asst Prof. JOLANTA ZABARSKAITĖ; Vice-Dir ARTŪRAS JUDZENTIS; publs *Acta Linguistica Lithuanica* (2 a year), *Archivum Lithuanicum* (1 a year), *Culture of Language* (1 a year), *Terminology* (1 a year).

Institute of Lithuanian Literature and Folklore: Antakalnio 6, 10308 Vilnius; tel. (5) 262-1943; fax (5) 261-6254; e-mail direk@ llti.lt; internet www.llti.lt; f. 1939; library of 240,000 vols and other printed matter; Dir MINDAUGAS KVIETKAUSKAS; publs *Colloquia* (2 a year), *Senoji Lietuvos literatura* (Old Lithuanian Literature, 2 a year), *Tautosakos darbai* (Folklore Studies, 2 a year).

MEDICINE

Institute of Hygiene: Didžioji 22, 01128 Vilnius; tel. (5) 262-4583; fax (5) 262-4663; e-mail institutas@hi.lt; internet www.hi.lt; f. 1808; library of 8,000 vols; Dir Prof. Habil Dr JULIUS KALIBATAS; publ. *Public Health* (4 a year).

Institute of Oncology, Vilnius University: Santariškių St. 1, 08660 Vilnius; tel. (5) 278-6700; fax (5) 272-0164; e-mail administracija@loc.lt; internet www.loc.lt; f. 1990; Dir Prof. Dr K. P. VALUCKAS.

State Research Institute Centre for Innovative Medicine: Žygimantų g. 9, 01102 Vilnius; tel. (5) 262-8636; fax (5) 212-3073; e-mail algirdas.venalis@ekmi.vu.lt; internet www.imcentras.lt; f. 2010; rheumatology, regenerative medicine, immunology, immunotechnology, molecular biology; Dir Prof. Dr Habil ALGIRDAS VENALIS.

NATURAL SCIENCES

Biological Sciences

Aplinkos Apsaugos Institutas (Research Institute of Environment Protection): Saulėtekio al. 11, SRK-II, Room 309, 10223 Vilnius; tel. (5) 274-4723; e-mail aai@vgtu .lt; internet www.aai.ap.vgtu.lt; f. 2002; attached to Vilniaus Gedimino Technikos Universitetas; environmental investigations,

evaluation, education and training; devt of new technologies; organizes scientific meetings, seminars, workshops; Dir Prof. Dr Habil PRANAS BALTRĖNAS.

Gamtos Tyrimų Centras (Nature Research Centre): Akademijos g. 2, 08412 Vilnius; tel. (5) 272-9257; fax (5) 272-9352; e-mail ekoi@ ekoi.lt; internet www.gamtostyrimai.lt; 3 research institutes; Dir Dr Habil MEČISLOVAS ŽALAKEVIČIUS; Deputy Dir for Science and Higher Education Dr Habil LINAS BALČIAUSKAS.

Institute of Biochemistry: Mokslininkų 12, 08662 Vilnius; tel. (5) 272-9144; fax (5) 272-9196; e-mail biochemija@bchi.lt; internet www.bchi.lt; f. 1967; Dir Prof. Dr Habil VALDAS LAURINAVICIUS.

Institute of Botany: Žaliųjų ežerų 49, 08406 Vilnius; tel. (5) 271-1618; fax (5) 272-9950; e-mail botanika@botanika.lt; internet www.botanika.lt; f. 1959, present status 1992; attached to Gamtos Tyrimų Centras; identifies and generalizes botanical diversity of Lithuania; researches on the control possibilities of genetic and physiological processes determining growth and productivity; identifies and generalizes species level; confers PhD in the field of biomedical sciences and degree of Habilitated Doctor of biomedical sciences; Dir Dr DANGUOLĖ RAKLEVIČIENĖ; Science Sec. Dr AURIKA RIČKIENĖ; publ. *Botanica Lithuanica* (4 a year).

Nature Research Centre: Akademijos g. 2, 08412 Vilnius; tel. (5) 272-9257; fax (5) 272-9352; e-mail sekretoriatas@gamtostyrimai.lt; internet www.gamtostyrimai.lt; f. 2009 by merger of Institute of Ecology, Institute of Botany, and Institute of Geology and Geography; attached to Vilnius Univ.; researches preservation, restoration and sustainable use of natural and biological resources; library of 90,000 vols; Dir Dr MEČISLOVAS ŽALAKEVIČIUS; publs *Acta Zoologica Lituanica* (English, 4 a year), *Baltica* (English, 2 a year), *Botanica Lithuanica* (English, 4 a year).

Mathematical Sciences

Institute of Mathematics and Informatics: Akademijos g. 4, 08663 Vilnius; tel. (5) 210-9300; fax (5) 272-9209; e-mail mathematica@ktl.mii.lt; internet www.mii.lt; f. 1956; Dir Prof. Dr Habil GINTAUTAS DZEMYDA; publs *Informatica, Informatics in Education, Lithuanian Mathematical Journal* (4 a year), *Mathematical Modelling and Analysis, Nonlinear Analysis: Modelling and Control.*

Physical Sciences

Institute of Chemistry: A. Goštauto 9, 01108 Vilnius; tel. (5) 261-2663; fax (5) 261-7018; e-mail chemins@ktl.mii.lt; internet www.chi.lt; f. 1945; Dir Prof. Dr Habil EIMUTIS JUZELIŪNAS.

Institute of Physics: Savanorių pr. 231, 02300 Vilnius; tel. (5) 266-1640; fax (5) 260-2317; e-mail fi@fi.lt; internet www.fi.lt; f. 1977; environmental physics and chemistry, in atmosphere and hydrosphere, investigations of atmospheric pollution regularities, background and anthropogenic pollution monitoring; molecular biophysics and chemical physics, incl. dynamic processes in proteins, polymers and organized molecular structures; nuclear physics, devt and application of nuclear spectroscopy methods, environmental radioactivity research; nonlinear optics and spectroscopy, devt and applications of lasers, investigations of mega system evolution; Dir Prof. Dr VIDMANTAS REMEIKIS.

Institute of Theoretical Physics and Astronomy of Vilnius University: A. Goštauto g. 12, 01108 Vilnius; tel. (5) 262-

0947; fax (5) 212-5361; e-mail atom@itpa.lt; internet www.itpa.lt; f. 1990; attached to Lithuanian Acad. of Sciences and Vilnius University; library of 250,000 vols; investigations of atoms, subatomic particles, molecules, their structures and plasma spectroscopy, their application in nanophysics and astrophysics; Dir and Head of Astronomical Observatory Dr Habil GRAŽINA TAUTVAIŠIENĖ; publs *Baltic Astronomy* (4 a year), *Lietuvos dangus* (Sky of Lithuania; in Lithuanian, 1 a year), *Lithuanian Journal of Physics* (4 a year).

TECHNOLOGY

Institute of Biotechnology: A. V. Graičiūno st 8, 02241 Vilnius; tel. (5) 260-2112; fax (5) 260-2116; e-mail giedre@ibt.lt; internet www.ibt.lt; f. 1975; state research institute and biotechnology centre active in multidisciplinary studies of restriction, modification enzymes, research and devt of recombinant biomedical proteins; 7 laboratories specializing in protein–DNA interactions, biological DNA modification, prokaryote gene engineering, eukaryote gene engineering, immunology, biothermodynamics and drug design and bioinformatics; Dir Dr Habil A. PAULIUKONIS.

Internetinių ir Intelektualiųjų Technologijų Institutas (Research Institute of Internet and Intelligent Technologies): Saulėtekio al. 11, 10223 Vilnius; tel. (5) 274-5002; e-mail edmundas.zavadskas@vgtu.lt; internet www.vgtu.lt/padaliniai/institutai/ iiti; attached to Vilniaus Gedimino Technikos Universitetas; develops web-based intelligent systems, intelligent tutoring systems, computer learning systems, audio and visual aids, e-books for distance learning; analysis of electronic city systems; knowledge management; electronic commerce, e-business; smart technologies; biometric technologies.

Lithuanian Energy Institute: Breslaujos g. 3, 44403 Kaunas; tel. (3) 740-1805; fax (3) 735-1271; e-mail rastine@mail.lei.lt; internet www.lei.lt; f. 1956; library of 80,000 vols; Dir Prof. Dr Habil EUGENIJUS UŠPURAS; publs *Energetika* (Power Engineering, 4 a year), *Environmental Research, Engineering and Management* (4 a year), *Lietuvos Energetika* (Energy in Lithuania, 1 a year).

Road Research Institute: Saulėtekio al. 11, 10223 Vilnius; tel. (5) 274-4712; fax (5) 237-0661; e-mail kti@vgtu.lt; attached to Vilniaus Gedimino Technikos Universitetas; Dir Dr VAITKUS AUDRIUS.

Scientific Institute of Thermal Insulation: Linkmenų g. 28, 08217 Vilnius; tel. (5) 275-0001; e-mail termo@aiva.lt; attached to Vilniaus Gedimino Technikos Universitetas; Dir Dr Habil ANTANAS LAUKAITIS.

Semiconductor Physics Institute: A. Goštauto g. 11, 01108 Vilnius; tel. (5) 261-9759; fax (5) 262-7123; e-mail spiadm@pfi.lt; internet www.pfi.lt; f. 1967; Dir Prof. Dr Habil STEPONAS ASMONTAS.

Suvirinimo ir Medžiagotyros Problemų Institutas (Research Institute of Welding And Materials Science): J. Basanavičiaus g. 28, MR-I, Room 127, 10225 Vilnius; tel. (5) 274-5053; fax (5) 274-4740; e-mail suvirinimo-institutas@vgtu.lt; internet www .smpi.me.vgtu.lt; f. 1994; attached to Vilniaus Gedimino Technikos Universitetas; develops welding technologies, modern materials, dangerous welding design reliability, durability and ageing; Dir DANUTĖ ŠČEKATUROVIENĖ.

Transporto Institutas (Transport Research Institute): Plytinės g. 27, 10105 Vilnius; tel. (5) 274-5070; fax (5) 237-0555; e-mail tmi@vgtu.lt; internet www.tmi.vgtu

.lt; f. 1998; attached to Vilniaus Gedimino Technikos Universitetas; forecasts transport system devt; methodology and strategy of transport infrastructure devt and modernization; develops intermodal transport; researches on innovative transport technologies; interaction, harmonization of transport networks and transportation technologies; structural changes of transport system; modelling of transport processes; modernization, devt of different transport modes; drafts regulations for transport system activities and harmonization; Dir Prof. Dr Habil ADOLFAS BAUBLYS.

Libraries and Archives
Vilnius

Library of the Lithuanian Academy of Sciences: Žygimantu 1/8, 01102 Vilnius; tel. (5) 262-9537; fax (5) 262-1324; e-mail biblioteka@mab.lt; internet www.mab.lt; f. 1941; 3,733,000 vols, incl. 250,610 MSS; Dir Dr JUOZAS MARCINKEVIČIUS.

Lithuanian Technical Library: Šv. Ignoto 6, 01120 Vilnius; tel. (5) 261-8718; fax (5) 261-0379; e-mail info@tb.lt; internet www.tb.lt; f. 1957; patent information centre; publishes official bulletins and patent documents of the State Patent Bureau; 45,844,124 vols, incl. 329,389 books, 743,392 periodicals and 44,003,108 patent documents; Dir KAZYS MACKEVIČIUS.

Martynas Mažvydas National Library of Lithuania: Gedimino pr. 51, 01109 Vilnius; tel. (5) 262-9023; fax (5) 262-7129; e-mail biblio@lnb.lrs.lt; internet www.lnb.lt; f. 1919; incorporated National Printing Archive 1992; 7m. vols in total, incl. 4m. books, periodicals, and reference publications, 70,000 MSS, 103,000 microforms, 63,000 audiovisual items, 30,000 old and rare books; National Printing Archive consists of 2,174,574 items, including books, maps and periodicals since the 16th century, as well as books printed in Lithuania since the 16th century in Latin, Polish and Russian; Rare Book and Manuscript department contains 70,000 items, including 30,000 books from the 15th to the 18th century (including works by early Church reformers, Martin Luther and Philip Melanchton, and the humanist Erasmus), private archives of prominent Lithuanians since the 19th century, 149 parchments (including privileges of the Grand Dukes of Lithuania and the Kings of Poland), as well as autographs, legal documents and photographs since the 15th century; 200,000 items in Music Department, including 100,000 items of printed music since the 16th century, 500 rare music scores and 55,000 audiovisual items; Dir VYTAUTAS GUDAITIS; publ. *Tarp Knygų* (12 a year).

Vilnius University Library: Universiteto g. 3, 01122 Vilnius; tel. (5) 268-7101; fax (5) 268-7104; e-mail mb@mb.vu.lt; internet www.mb.vu.lt; f. 1570; 5,349,881 vols, 251,320 MSS, 87,928 graphic art items, 437,367 UN publs; Dir IRENA KRIVIENĖ.

Museums and Art Galleries
Kaunas

Kaunas Botanical Garden: Ž. E. Žilibero 6, 46324 Kaunas; tel. (3) 739-0033; fax (3) 739-0133; e-mail bs@bs.vdu.lt; internet www.vdu.lt/botanika/bot_garden.htm; f. 1923; attached to Vytautas Magnus University; 62 hectares; research into botany, ecology and the natural environment; library of 10,000 vols; Dir Dr REMIGIJUS DAUBAZAS.

M. K. Čiurlionis National Museum of Art: Vlado Putvinskio 55, 44248 Kaunas; tel. (3) 722-9475; fax (3) 722-2606; e-mail mkc@takas.lt; internet www.ciurlionis.lt; f. 1921; Lithuanian and European art, folk art, oriental and ancient Egyptian art, numismatics; named after Lithuanian artist M. K. Čiurlionis (1875–1911); library of 30,000 vols; Dir OSVALDAS DAUGELIS; Deputy Dir DAINA KAMARAUSKIENĖ.

Vytautas the Great War Museum: K. Donelaičio 64, 44248 Kaunas; tel. (3) 742-2146; fax (3) 742-0765; e-mail v.d.karomuziejus@takas.lt; f. 1921; archaeological finds, weapons, fire-arms, ammunition, army uniforms, objects and documents relating to the transatlantic flight of the 'Lituanica'; colln of ethnographic photographs by Balys Buracas (1897–1972); Dir JUOZAPAS JUREVIČIUS.

Trakai

Trakai Historical Museum: Kęstučio 4, 21104 Trakai; tel. (5) 285-8241; e-mail trakai.museum@is.lt; f. 1948; 16th- and 17th-century tiles, coins, pottery, bone chessmen and other artefacts discovered during excavations at Trakai Castle; also ethnographic and applied art collections; Dir VIRGILIJUS POVILIŪNAS.

Vilnius

Lithuanian Art Museum: Didžioji 4, 01128 Vilnius; tel. (5) 262-8030; fax (5) 212-6006; e-mail muziejus@ldm.lt; internet www.ldm.lt; f. 1933; library of 25,166 vols; Lithuanian and foreign works of fine and applied art; br. museums, incl. Clock Museum, Foreign Art Gallery, Juodkrant Exhibition Hall, Klaipėda Picture Gallery, Museum of Applied Art, Palanga Amber Museum, Pranas Gudynas Restoration Centre of Museum Treasures, Vilnius Picture Gallery; Dir ROMUALDAS BUDRYS; publ. *Issues of the Museum* (1 a year).

National Museum of Lithuania: Arsenalo 1, 01100 Vilnius; tel. (5) 262-7774; fax (5) 261-1023; e-mail muziejus@lnm.lt; internet www.lnm.lt; f. 1855; archaeology, ethnography, history, iconography numismatics; library of 55,000 vols; Dir BIRUTĖ KULNYTĖ; publs *Archaeology*, *Ethnography* (1 a year), *Museum* (1 a year), *Numismatics* (1 a year).

Universities

KAUNO MEDICINOS UNIVERSITETAS
(Kaunas Medical University)

A. Mickevičiaus str. 9, 44307 Kaunas

Telephone: (3) 732-7201

Fax: (3) 722-0733

E-mail: rektoratas@kmu.lt

Internet: www.kmu.lt

Founded 1922 as Faculty of Medicine of Kaunas Univ.; Kaunas Medical Institute 1950; Kaunas Medical Acad. 1989; univ. status 1998

State control

Rector: Prof. REMIGIJUS ŽALIŪNAS

Vice-Rector for Research: Prof. VAIVA LESAUS-KAITĖ

Vice-Rector for Studies: Prof. RENALDAS JUR-KEVIČIUS

Vice-Rector for University Clinics: Prof. JUOZAS PUNDZIUS

Library of 650,000 vols (53% in Russian, 28% in Lithuanian, 19% in English, German, French and Polish)

Number of teachers: 450 (incl. researchers)

Number of students: 5,250

DEANS

Faculty of Medicine: Prof. ALGIMANTAS TAME-LIS

Faculty of Nursing: Prof. JŪRATĖ MACIJAUS-KIENĖ

Faculty of Odontology: Prof. RIČARDAS KUBI-LIUS

Faculty of Pharmacy: Prof. VITALIS BRIEDIS

Faculty of Public Health: Prof. RAMUNĖ KALĖDIENĖ

KAUNO TECHNOLOGIJOS UNIVERSITETAS
(Kaunas University of Technology)

K. Donelaičio 73, 44029 Kaunas

Telephone: (3) 7 30-0011

Fax: (3) 732-4144

E-mail: rastine@ktu.lt

Internet: www.ktu.lt

Founded 1922

State control

Academic year: September to June

Rector: Prof. RAIMUNDAS ŠIAUČIŪNAS

Vice-Rector for Infrastructure: Prof. SIGITAS STANYS

Vice-Rector for Research: Prof. RYMANTAS KAZYS

Vice-Rector for Strategic Devt: Prof. GINTAU-TAS ŽINTELIS

Vice-Rector for Studies: Prof. PRANAS ŽILIU-KAS

Head of Admin: Prof. ALGIMANTAS NAVICKAS

Librarian: GENOVAITE DUOBINIENĖ

Library of 1,314,245 vols

Number of teachers: 988

Number of students: 14,366

Publications: *Chemical Technology* (4 a year), *Economics and Management* (1 a year), *Electronics and Electrical Engineering* (8 a year), *Engineering Economics* (5 a year), *Environmental Research, Engineering and Management* (4 a year), *Humanistica* (2 a year), *Information Technology and Control* (4 a year), *Language Teaching and Learning in the Context of Social Changes* (2 a year), *Materials Science* (4 a year), *Measurements* (4 a year), *Mechanics* (6 a year), *Public Politics and Administration* (4 a year), *Social Sciences* (4 a year), *Studies about Languages* (2 a year), *Ultrasound* (4 a year)

DEANS

Faculty of Chemical Technology: Prof. ZIG-MUNTAS JONAS BERESNEVIČIUS

Faculty of Civil Engineering and Architecture: Dr ŽYMANTAS RUDZIONIS

Faculty of Design and Technology: Dr VIRGI-NIJA JANKAUSKAITE

Faculty of Economics and Management: Prof. Dr GRAZINA STARTIENE

Faculty of Electrical Engineering and Control Systems: Prof. JONAS DAUNORAS

Faculty of Fundamental Sciences: Dr VYTAU-TAS JANILIONIS

Faculty of Humanities: Prof. GIEDRIUS KUPREVIČIUS

Faculty of Informatics: Prof. EDUARDAS BARE-IŠA

Faculty of Mechanical Engineering: Prof. ALGIMANTAS FEDARAVIČIUS

Faculty of Social Sciences: Dr VIKTORIJA BARŠAUSKIENE

Faculty of Telecommunications and Electronics: Dr ALGIMANTAS VALINEVICIUS

International Studies Centre: Dr ARVYDAS PALEVICIUS

Panevėžys Institute: Prof. ŽILVINAS BAZARAS

KLAIPĖDOS UNIVERSITETAS
(Klapėda University)

H. Manto 84, 92294 Klaipėda
Telephone: (4) 639-8900
Fax: (4) 639-8902
E-mail: vladas.zulkus@ku.lt
Internet: www.ku.lt

Founded 1991
State control
Academic year: September to June

Rector: Prof. Dr Habil VLADAS ŽULKUS
Vice-Rector for Academic Affairs: Prof. Dr VAIDUTIS LAURĖNAS
Vice-Rector for Administration: Doc. Dr ADOLFAS BRĖSKIS
Vice-Rector for International Relations: Prof. Dr VILIJA TARGAMADZĖ
Vice-Rector for Research and Art: Prof. Dr Habil BENEDIKTAS TILICKIS
Library Dir: JANINA PUPELIENĖ

Library of 458,275 books, 30,453 periodicals
Number of teachers: 431 full-time
Number of students: 7,666 (7,578 undergraduate, 88 postgraduate)

Publications: *Acta Historica Universitatis Klavpeolencis* (1 a year), *Archiviem Lituanuciem* (1 a year), *Jura ir aplinka* (Sea and Environment, 4 a year), *Sociologija: miutis ir veolumas* (Sociology: Thought and Action, 2 a year), *Tiltai* (Bridges, 4 a year)

DEANS

Faculty of Arts: Prof. VYTAUTAS TETENSKAS
Faculty of Education: Doc. ANTANAS LUKOŠEVIČIUS
Faculty of Health Sciences: Prof. Dr Habil ALGIMANTAS KIRKUTIS
Faculty of Humanities: Doc. ALEKSANDRAS ŽALYS
Faculty of Marine Engineering: Prof. Dr VYTENIS ALBERTAS ZABUKAS
Faculty of Science and Mathematics: Doc. PETRAS GRECEVIČIUS
Faculty of Social Sciences: Doc. ANTANAS BUČINSKAS

LIETUVOS ŽEMĖS ŪKIO UNIVERSITETAS
(Lithuanian University of Agriculture)

Akademija, Studentu 11, 53361 Kaunas
Telephone: (3) 775-2300
Fax: (3) 739-7500
E-mail: laa@lzuu.lt
Internet: www.lzuu.lt

Founded 1924
State control
Languages of instruction: Lithuanian, English, Russian
Academic year: September to June

Rector: Prof. Dr ANTANAS MAZILIAUSKAS
Vice-Rector: Prof. Dr JONAS ČAPLIKAS
Vice-Rector: Assoc. Prof. Dr VIDMANTAS BUTKUS
Vice-Rector: Assoc. Prof. Dr LAIMA TAPARAUSKIENE
Vice-Rector:
Dir of Library: AUŠRA RAGUCKAITĖ

Library of 672,888 vols, 224 periodicals, 20,000 scientific journals
Number of teachers: 390
Number of students: 6,150

Publications: *Agricultural Engineering, Agricultural Sciences, Agriculture, Agronomy Research, Baltic Forestry, Economics and Rural Development, Environmental Research Engineering and Management, Horticulture and Vegetable Science, Management Theory and Studies for Rural Business and Infrastructure Development, The Quality of Higher Education, Veterinary and Zootechnic, Water Management*

DEANS

Faculty of Agricultural Engineering: Assoc. Prof. Dr ROLANDAS DOMEIKA
Faculty of Agronomy: Assoc. Prof. Dr VIKTORAS PRANCKIETIS
Faculty of Economics and Management: Prof. Dr NERINGA STONČIUVIENĖ
Faculty of Forestry and Ecology: Assoc. Prof. Dr ĖDMUNDAS BARTKEVIČIUS
Faculty of Water and Land Management: Assoc. Prof. Dr VIDMANTAS GURKLYS

ATTACHED RESEARCH INSTITUTES

Institute of the Environment: Dir Assoc. Prof. Dr VIDA RUTKOVIENĖ.
Institute of Information Technologies: Dir Assoc. Prof. Dr ALEKSANDRAS SAVILIONIS.
Institute of Rural Culture: Dir Assoc. Prof. Dr SVETLANA STATKEVIĖIENĖ.
Research Institute of Agricultural Engineering: Instituto 20, Raudondvaris, 54132 Kauno; tel. (37) 44-96-43; fax (37) 54-93-66; e-mail institutas@mei.lt; internet www.mei.lt; Dir Dr GVIDAS RUTKAUSKAS.
Water Management Institute of Lithuanian University of Agriculture: Parko 6, 58102 Vilainiai Kėdainiai; tel. (34) 76-81-00; fax (34) 76-81-05; e-mail sigitas@water.omnitel.net; internet www.waterland.lt; Dir Dr ANTANAS SIGITAS ŠILEIKA.

MYKOLO ROMERIO UNIVERSITETAS
(Mykolas Romeris University)

Ateities 20, 08303 Vilnius
Telephone: (5) 271-4647
Fax: (5) 267-0000
E-mail: roffice@mruni.lt
Internet: www.mruni.lt

Founded 1990 as Law University of Lithuania; present name 2000
State control

Rector: Prof. Dr ALVYDAS PUMPUTIS
University Secretary: ANTANAS KERAS
Librarian: ALMONE JAKUBCIONIENE

Library of 156,042 vols, 188 periodicals
Number of students: 16,000

DEANS

Faculty of Economics and Management: Assoc. Prof. Dr VITALIJA RUDZKIENE
Faculty of Law: Prof. Dr JUOZAS ZILYS
Faculty of Public Administration: Dr TADAS SUDNICKAS
Faculty of Social Policy: Assoc. Prof. Dr LETA DROMANTIENE
Faculty of Strategic Management and Policy: Prof. Dr Habil VYGANDAS K. PAULIKAS
Kaunas Faculty of Police: ANTANAS BUTAVIČIUS

ATTACHED RESEARCH INSTITUTE

Centre for Research: Deputy Dir SAULĖ MAČIUKAITĖ-ŽVINIENĖ.

ŠIAULIŲ UNIVERSITETAS
(Šiauliai University)

Vilniaus g. 88, 76285 Šiauliai
Telephone: (4) 159-5800
Fax: (4) 159-5809
E-mail: all@cr.su.lt
Internet: www.su.lt

Founded 1997 by merger of Šiauliai Pedagogical Institute and Šiauliai Polytechnical Faculty of Kaunas University of Technology
State control

Rector: Prof. habil. dr VINCAS LAURUTIS
Librarian: LORETA BURBAITĖ

Library of 400,000 vols, 550 periodicals
Number of teachers: 840
Number of students: 10,000

Publications: *Jaunujų mokslininkų darbai* (Young Researchers' Works; 3 a year), *Kūrybos erdvės* (Spaces of Creation; 2 a year), *Special Education*

DEANS

Faculty of Arts: Assoc. Prof. Dr LEONAS PAULAUSKAS
Faculty of Education: Assoc. Prof. Dr AUŠRINĖ GUMULIAUSKIENĖ
Faculty of Humanities: Prof. GENOVAITĖ KAČIUŠKIENE
Faculty of Physics and Mathematics: Assoc. Prof. Dr ALFREDAS LANKAUSKAS
Faculty of Social Sciences: Assoc. Prof. Dr TEODORAS TAMOŠIŪNAS
Faculty of Special Education: Assoc. Prof. Dr JUOZAS PUMPUTIS
Faculty of Technology: Prof. Dr VIDAS LAURUŠKA

VILNIAUS GEDIMINO TECHNIKOS UNIVERSITETAS
(Vilnius Gediminas Technical University)

Saulėtekio alėja 11, 10223 Vilnius
Telephone: (5) 274-5030
Fax: (5) 270-0112
E-mail: rastine@vgtu.lt
Internet: www.vgtu.lt

Founded 1956
State control
Languages of instruction: Lithuanian, English
Academic year: September to June

Chancellor: Assoc. Prof. Dr ARŪNAS KOMKA
Rector: Prof. Dr Habil ROMUALDAS GINEVIČIUS
Prin. Vice-Rector: Prof. Dr Habil EDMUNDAS KAZIMIERAS ZAVADSKAS
Vice-Rector for Research: Prof. Dr Habil RAIMUNDAS KIRVAITIS
Vice-Rector for Strategic Devt: Assoc. Prof. Dr LIUDVIKAS RIMKUS
Vice-Rector for Studies: Assoc. Prof. Dr ALFONSAS DANIŪNAS
Librarian: RIMUTĖ ABRAMČIKIENĖ

Library of 583,445 vols, 120,415 titles
Number of teachers: 900
Number of students: 14,000

Publications: *Aviation* (4 a year), *Business: Theory and Practice* (4 a year), *Coactivity* (4 a year), *Engineering Structures and Technologies* (4 a year), *Evolution of Science and Technology* (2 a year), *Geodesy and Cartography* (4 a year), *International Journal of Strategic Property Management* (4 a year), *Journal of Business Economics and Management* (4 a year), *Journal of Civil Engineering and Management* (4 a year), *Journal of Environmental Engineering and Landscape Management* (4 a year), *Limes* (2 a year), *Mathematical Modelling and Analysis* (4 a year), *Science—Future of Lithuania* (6 a year), *Technological and Economic Development of Economy* (4 a year), *The Baltic Journal of Road and Bridge Engineering* (4 a year), *Town Planning and Architecture* (4 a year), *Transport* (4 a year)

DEANS

Antanas Gustaitis' Aviation Institute: Prof. Dr Habil JONAS STANKŪNAS
Faculty of Architecture: Prof. Dr RIMANTAS BUIVYDAS
Faculty of Business Management: Prof. Dr Habil ALEKSANDRAS VYTAUTAS RUTKAUSKAS
Faculty of Civil Engineering: Prof. Dr POVILAS VAINIŪNAS
Faculty of Electronics: Prof. Dr Habil ROMA RINKEVIČIENĖ
Faculty of Environmental Engineering: Prof. Dr DONATAS ČYGAS

Faculty of Fundamental Sciences: Prof. Dr Habil ANTANAS ČENYS
Faculty of Mechanics: Prof. Dr Habil ALGIRDAS VACLOVAS VALIULIS
Faculty of Transport Engineering: Assoc. Prof. Dr VILIUS BARTULIS
Institute of Humanities: Prof. Dr Habil POVILAS TAMOŠAUSKAS

PROFESSORS

Antanas Gustaitis' Aviation Institute (Rodūnios Kelias 30, AV-I, Room 28, 02187 Vilnius; tel. (5) 274-4809; fax (5) 232-9321; e-mail avinst@vgtu.lt):

PILECKAS, E.
STANKŪNAS, J.
ŽILIUKAS, A.

Faculty of Architecture (Pylimo g. 26/1, 03227 Vilnius; tel. (5) 274-5212; fax (5) 274-5213; e-mail archdek@vgtu.lt):

ANUŠKEVIČIUS, J.
BUIVYDAS, R.
ČAIKAUSKAS, G
ČEREŠKEVIČIUS, S.
DAUNORA, Z. J.
DIČIUS, V.
DINEIKA, V.
JUREVIČIENĖ, J.
PALEKAS, R.
ŠEIBOKAS, J.
STAUSKIS, V. J.
VYŠNIŪNAS, A.
ZIBERKAS, L. P.

Faculty of Business Management (Saulėtekio al. 11, SRC, Room 614, 10223 Vilnius; tel. (5) 274-4888; fax (5) 274-4892; e-mail management@vgtu.lt):

BIVAINIS, J.
CHLIVICKAS, E.
DUBAUSKAS, G.
GINEVIČIUS, R.
MELNIKAS, B.
MITKUS, S.
PALIULIS, N.
RAKAUSKIENĖ, O. G.
RUTKAUSKAS, A. V.
STAŠKEVIČIUS, J.
TVARONAVIČIENĖ, M.

Faculty of Civil Engineering (Saulėtekio al. 11, SRC, Room 422, 10223 Vilnius; tel. (5) 274-5239; fax (5) 274-5016; e-mail stfdek@vgtu.lt):

ANDRUŠKEVIČIUS, A.
ATKOČIŪNAS, J.
CYRAS, P.
GAILIUS, A.
JUOZULYNAS, J.
KAKLAUSKAS, A.
KAKLAUSKAS, G.
KALANTA, S.
KARKAUSKAS, R.
KVEDARAS, A.
LAUKAITIS, A.
MAČIULAITIS, R.
MARČIUKAITIS, J.
NORKUS, A.
PARASONIS, J.
RASLANAS, S.
ŠAPALAS, A.
USTINOVIČIUS, L.
VADLŪGA, R.
VAIDOGAS, E.
VAINIŪNAS, P.
VALIVONIS, J.
ZAVADSKAS, E.
TURSKIS, Z.

Faculty of Electronics (Naugarduko g. 41, 03227 Vilnius; tel. (5) 274-4753; fax (5) 274-4770; e-mail dekanatas@el.vgtu.lt):

BALEVIČIUS, S.
BAŠKYS, A.
DAMBRAUSKAS, A.
GALDIKAS, A.

JANKAUSKAS, Z.
KAJACKAS, A.
KIRVAITIS, R.
KVEDARAS, V.
MARCINKEVIČIUS, A.
MARTAVIČIUS, R.
NAVAKAUSKAS, D.
NAVICKAS, R.
NICKELSON, L.
NOVICKIJ, J.
PAULIKAS, Š.
POŠKA, A.
RINKEVIČIENĖ, R.
SKUDUTIS, J.
ŠMILGEVIČIUS, A.
ŠTARAS, S.
URBANAVIČIUS, V.

Faculty of Environmental Engineering (Saulėtekio al. 11, SRK-II, Room 502, 10223 Vilnius; tel. (5) 274-4727; fax (5) 274-4731; e-mail info@ap.vgtu.lt):

BALTRĖNAS, P.
BURINSKIENĖ, M.
BUTKUS, D.
ČESNULEVIČIUS, A.
ČESNA, B.
ČYGAS, D.
GINIOTIS, V.
JAKOVLEVAS-MATECKIS, K.
JANKAUSKAS, V.
JUODIS, E.
LAURINAVIČIUS, A.
LUKIANAS, A.
MARTINAITIS, V.
MATUZEVIČIUS, A.
PARŠELIŪNAS, E.
PETKEVIČIUS, K.
PETROŠKEVIČIUS, P.
ŠAKALAUSKAS, K.
ŠAULYS, V.
SKEIVALAS, J.
VAIKASAS, S.
VAITIEKŪNAS, P.
VASAREVIČIUS, S.
ZAKAREVIČIUS, A.

Faculty of Fundamental Sciences (Saulėtekio al. 11, SRL-I, Room 416, 10223 Vilnius; tel. (5) 274-4843; fax (5) 274-4844; e-mail fmf@vgtu.lt):

ADOMĖNAS, P.
BAUŠYS, R.
BELEVIČIUS, R.
BUSILAS, A.
ČENYS, A.
ČIEGIS, R.
ČIŽAS, A.
DZEMYDA, G.
GEDVILAITĖ, A.
GIRGŽDYS, A.
JUKNA, A.
KAČIANAUSKAS, R.
KAZRAGIS, A.
KERIENĖ, J.
KIRJACKIS, E.
KLEIZA, J.
KLIUKAS, R.
KRENEVIČIUS, A.
KRYLOVAS, A.
KUBILIUS, K.
KULVIETIS, G.
KULYS, J.
LAURINAVIČIUS, V.
LEONAVIČIUS, M.
LIPEIKA, A.
MIŠKINIS, P.
MOCKUS, J.
NAVAKAUSKIENĖ, R.
PODVEZKO, V.
PRAGARAUSKAS, H.
RADAVIČIUS, M.
RUDZKIS, R.
RUTKAUSKAS, S.
ŠABLINSKAS, V.
ŠAKALAUSKAS, L.
ŠATKOVSKIS, E.

SAULIS, L.
STYRO, D.
SUNKLODAS, J.
SUŽIEDĖLIS, A.
VASILECAS, O.
ŽILINSKAS, J.
ŽURAUSKIENĖ, N.

Faculty of Mechanics (J. Basanavičiaus g 28, MR-IV, Room 114, 03224 Vilnius; tel. (5) 274-4745; fax (5) 274-5043; e-mail mechanik@vgtu.lt):

AUGUSTAITIS, V.
KASPARAITIS, A.
MARCINKEVIČIUS, A. H.
MARIŪNAS, M.
MASKELIŪNAS, R.
SIDARAVIČIUS, D. J.
TURLA, V.
VALIULIS, A.
VASILIONKAITIS, V.
VEKTERIS, V.

Faculty of Transport Engineering (J. Basanavičiaus g. 28, MR-V, Room 10, 03224 Vilnius; tel. (5) 274-4797; fax (5) 274-4800; e-mail tif@vgtu.lt):

BAUBLYS, A.
BAUBLYS, J.
BOGDEVIČIUS, M.
BUTKEVIČIUS, J.
BUTKUS, A.
JARAŠŪNIENĖ, A.
LINGAITIS, L.
PALŠAITIS, R.
PIKŪNAS, A.
SIVILEVIČIUS, H.
SPRUOGIS, B.
ŽVIRBLIS, A.

Institute of Humanities (Saulėtekio alėja 28, SS, Room S1, 10223 Vilnius; tel. (5) 237-0636; fax (5) 269-8695; e-mail hinst@vgtu.lt):

GRINCEVIČIENĖ, V.
KAČERAUSKAS, T.
PRUSKUS, V.
TAMOŠAUSKAS, P.

VILNIAUS PEDAGOGINIS UNIVERSITETAS
(Vilnius Pedagogical University)

Studentų g. 39, 08106 Vilnius

Telephone and fax (5) 279-0281
E-mail: studsk@vpu.lt
Internet: www.vpu.lt

Founded 1935 as National Pedagogical Institute in Klaipeda; moved to Vilnius 1939; present name and status 1992

State control

Rector: Acad. Prof. Dr Habil ALGIRDAS GAIŽUTIS

Librarian: EMILIJA BANIONYTE

Number of teachers: 420
Number of students: 12,400

DEANS

Faculty of Foreign Languages: Dr ALGIMANTAS MARTINKĖNAS
Faculty of History: Prof. Dr LIBERTAS KLIMKA
Faculty of Lithuanian Philology: DALIA PŪRIENĖ
Faculty of Mathematics and Informatics: Assoc. Prof. Dr DALIA KUMPONIENĖ
Faculty of Natural Sciences: Assoc. Prof. Dr BRONISLOVAS ŠALKUS
Faculty of Pedagogy and Psychology: Dr RITA MAKARSKAITĖ-PETKEVIČIENĖ
Faculty of Physics and Technology: Dr KAZIMIERAS SADAUSKAS
Faculty of Slavonic Philology: Dr GINTAUTAS KUNDROTAS

VILNIAUS UNIVERSITETAS
(Vilnius University)

Universiteto g. 3, 01513 Vilnius
Telephone: (5) 268-7010
Fax: (5) 268-7009
E-mail: infor@cr.vu.lt
Internet: www.vu.lt

Founded 1579
State control
Language of instruction: Lithuanian
Academic year: September to July

Rector: Prof. BENEDIKTAS JUODKA
Pro-Rectors: Prof. JUOZAS RIMANTAS LAZUTKA, Dr RIMANTAS VAITKUS, Dr JUOZAS GALGINAITIS, Prof. JŪRAS BANYS, Dr ALEKSAS PIKTURNA
Director of the Library: Prof. AUDRONĖ GLOSIENĖ
Library: see Libraries and Archives
Number of teachers: 1,388
Number of students: 22,060

Publications: *Acta Orientalia Vilnensia* (1 a year), *Acta Paedagogica Vilnensia* (2 a year), *Archaeologica Lituana* (1 a year), *Baltic Astronomy*, *Book Science* (2 a year), *Economics* (4 a year), *Informatica* (4 a year), *Informatics in Education* (2 a year), *Information Sciences* (4 a year), *Journal of Baltic Linguistics (Baltistica)* (3 a year), *Journal of Political Sciences* (4 a year), *Law* (4 a year), *Linguistics* (2 a year), *Literature* (4 a year), *Lithuanian Foreign Policy Review*, *Lithuanian Mathematical Journal*, *Lithuanian Political Science Yearbook* (1 a year), *Nonlinear Analysis: Modelling and Control* (4 a year), *Olympiads in Informatics*, *Organizations and Markets in Emerging Economies* (2 a year), *Problems* (2 a year), *Psychology* (2 a year), *Respectus Philologicus* (1–2 a year), *Sociology, Thought and Action* (2 a year), *STEP: Social Theory, Empirics, Policy and Practice* (2 a year), *Studies of Lithuanian History* (2 a year), *Transformation in Business and Economics* (1 a year), *Translations Studies* (2 a year)

DEANS

Faculty of Chemistry: Prof. AIVARAS KAREIVA
Faculty of Communication: Prof. DOMAS KAUNAS
Faculty of Economics: Dr BIRUTĖ GALINIENĖ
Faculty of History: Prof. ZENONAS BUTKUS
Faculty of Humanities in Kaunas: Dr STASYS ALBINAS GIRDZIJAUSKAS
Faculty of Law: Prof. VYTAUTAS NEKROŠIUS
Faculty of Mathematics and Informatics: Prof. FELIKSAS IVANAUSKAS
Faculty of Medicine: Prof. ZITA KUČINSKIENĖ
Faculty of Natural Sciences: Prof. KĘSTUTIS KILKUS
Faculty of Philology: Dr ANTANAS SMETONA
Faculty of Philosophy: Dr KĘSTUTIS DUBNIKAS
Faculty of Physics: Prof. JŪRAS BANYS
Institute of Applied Research: Prof. ARTŪRAS ŽUKAUSKAS
Institute of Biochemistry: Prof. VALDAS STANISLOVAS LAURINAVIČIUS
Institute of Biotechnology: Prof. KĘSTUTIS SASNAUSKAS
Institute of Foreign Languages: Dr NIJOLĖ BRAŽĖNIENĖ
Institute of Int. Relations and Political Science: Prof. RAMŪNAS VILPIŠAUSKAS
Institute of Mathematics and Informatics: Prof. GINTAUTAS DZEMYDA
Institute of Theoretical Physics and Astronomy: Prof. GRAŽINA TAUTVAIŠIENĖ

PROFESSORS

Faculty of Chemistry (Naugarduko g. 24, 03225 Vilnius; tel. (5) 233-09-87; fax (5) 233-09-87; e-mail chf@chf.vu.lt; internet www.chf.vu.lt):

ABRUTIS, A., Inorganic Chemistry
ARMALIS, S., Analytical Chemistry
BALTRŪNAS, G., Electrochemistry
BARKAUSKAS, J., Inorganic Chemistry
DAUJOTIS, V., Surface and Boundary-layer Chemistry
KAREIVA, A., Inorganic Chemistry
KAZLAUSKAS, R., Analytical Chemistry
MAKUŠKA, R., Polymer Chemistry
PADARAUSKAS, A., Analytical Chemistry
RAMANAVIČIUS, A., Biochemistry, Immunology
TAUTKUS, S., Analytical Chemistry
TUMKEVIČIUS, S., Organic Chemistry
VAINILAVIČIUS, P., Organic Chemistry

Faculty of Communication (Saulėtekio alėja 9, 10222 Vilnius; tel. (5) 236-61-00; fax (5) 236-61-04; e-mail kf@kf.vu.lt; internet www.kf.vu.lt):

KAUNAS, D., Book History, Book Science

Faculty of Economics (Saulėtekio alėja 9, 10222 Vilnius; tel. (5) 236-61-20; fax (5) 236-61-27; e-mail ef@ef.vu.lt; internet www.ef.vu.lt):

BERŽINSKAS, G., Quality Management
GYLYS, P., Economics Theory
LAKIS, V., Audit
MACKEVIČIUS, J., Accounting and Audit
MARČINSKAS, A., Management
MARTIŠIUS, S., Econometrics
PRANULIS, V., Marketing
RUŽEVIČIUS, J., Quality Management
SIMANAUSKAS, L., Economic Informatics
VENGRAUSKAS, P. V., Research in field of Cooperative Trade
ŽEBRAUSKAS, A., Chemical Technology

Faculty of History (Universiteto g. 7, 01122 Vilnius; tel. (5) 268-72-80; fax (5) 268-72-82; e-mail if@if.vu.lt; internet www.if.vu.lt):

BUMBLAUSKAS, A., Theory of History and History of Culture
BUTKUS, Z., Contemporary History since 1914
GUDAVIČIUS, E., Medieval History
LUCHTANAS, A., Archaeology
MICHELBERTAS, M., Archaeology, Numismatics
VALIKONYTĖ, J., Medieval History

Faculty of Humanities in Kaunas (Muitinės g. 8, 44280 Kaunas; tel. (37) 42-25-23; fax (37) 42-32-22; e-mail dekanas@vukhf.lt; internet www.vukhf.lt):

ČIEGIS, R., Economics
GRONSKAS, V., Economics
POLIAKOVAS, O., Diachronic Balto-Slavic Linguistics

Faculty of Law (Saulėtekio alėja 9, 10222 Vilnius; tel. (5) 236-61-60; fax (5) 236-61-63; e-mail tf@tf.vu.lt; internet www.tf.vu.lt):

MARCIJONAS, A., Environmental Law
NEKROŠIUS, V., Civil Proceedings, Roman Law
ŠILEKIS, E., Constitutional Law
VANSEVIČIUS, S., History of Lithuanian State and Law

Faculty of Mathematics and Informatics (Naugarduko g. 24, 03225 Vilnius; tel. (5) 233-60-28; fax (5) 215-15-85; e-mail maf@maf.vu.lt; internet www.mif.vu.lt):

BAGDONAVIČIUS, V., Probability Theory and Mathematical Statistics
BIKELIS, A., Probability Theory and Mathematical Statistics
BLOZNELIS, M., Probability Theory
ČEKANAVIČIUS, V., Probability Theory and Mathematical Statistics
IVANAUSKAS, F., Numerical Analysis
KUBILIUS, J., Probabilistic Number Theory, History of Mathematics
LAURINČIKAS, A., Probabilistic Number Theory
LEIPUS, R., Probability Theory and Mathematical Statistics

MACKEVIČIUS, V., Theory of Probability
MANSTAVIČIUS, E., Probabilistic Number Theory
PAULAUSKAS, V., Theory of Probability
RAČKAUSKAS, A., Theory of Probability

Faculty of Medicine (M. K. Čiurlionio g. 21, 03101 Vilnius; tel. (5) 239-87-00; fax (5) 239-87-05; e-mail mf@mf.vu.lt; internet www.mf.vu.lt):

AMBROZAITIS, A., Infectious Diseases
BALČIŪNIENĖ, I., Cardiology
BARKAUSKAS, E. V., Vascular Surgery
BAUBINAS, A., Environmental Hygiene, Paediatric Hygiene
BUBNYS, A., Surgery
ČESNYS, G., Anatomy, Anthropology
DAINYS, B., Transplantation, Urology, Nephrology
DEMBINSKAS, A., Psychiatry
DUBAKIENĖ, R., Allergology
IRNIUS, A., Gastroenterology
IVAŠKEVIČIUS, J., Anaesthesiology, Intensive Care
JANILIONIS, R., Pulmonology
KALIBATIENĖ, D., Gastroenterology, Therapy, Nursing
KALTENIS, P., Paediatrics, Paediatric Nephrology
KUČINSKAS, V., Human Genetics
KUČINSKIENĖ, Z. A., Medical Biochemistry
LAUCEVIČIUS, A., Cardiology
NOREIKA, L. A., Surgery
PARNARAUSKIENĖ, R., Neurology, Neurophysiology
PLIUŠKYS, J. A., Internal Medicine
PORVANECKAS, N., Traumatology-Orthopaedics
PRONCKUS, A., Surgery
RAMANAUSKAS, J., Pharmacology
RAUGALĖ, A., Paediatrics
SIAURUSAITIS, B. J., Paediatric Surgery
SIRVYDIS, V., Cardiac Surgery
STRUPAS, K., Surgery
TRIPONIS, V. J., Vascular Surgery
USONIS, V., Paediatric Infectology
UŽDAVINYS, G., Cardiac Surgery
VAIČEKONIS, V., Pulmonology
VALANTINAS, J., Hepatology
VALIULIS, A., Paediatric Pulmonology
VENALIS, A., Rheumatology
VITKUS, K., Reconstructive Surgery
ŽVIRONAITĖ, V., Cardiology

Faculty of Natural Sciences (M. K. Čiurlionio g. 21/27, 03101 Vilnius; tel. (5) 239-82-00; fax (53) 239-82-04; e-mail gf@gf.vu.lt; internet www.gf.vu.lt):

BUKANTIS, A., Climatology
ČESNULEVIČIUS, A., Geomorphology
ČITAVIČIUS, D. J., Molecular Genetics of Microorganisms
DUNDULIS, K. J., Engineering Geology
GAIGALAS, A. J., Lithology
JANKAUSKAS, T. R., Palaeontology and Stratigraphy
JUODKA, B., Molecular Biology
JURGAITIS, A., Lithology and Mineral Deposits
KABAILIENĖ, M., Palaeontology and Stratigraphy
KAVALIAUSKAS, P., Land Management
KILKUS, K., Hydrology
KIRVELIENĖ, V., Cell Biochemistry
LAZUTKA, J. R., Human Cytogenetics
MOKRIK, R., Palaeohydrogeology, Hydrochemistry, Groundwater Formation
NAUJALIS, J. R., Botany
PODĖNAS, S., Entomology
RAKAUSKAS, R., Entomology
RANČELIS, V. P., Genetics
SLAPŠYTĖ, G., Animal Genetics
TRIMONIS, A. E., Oceanography
VALENTA, V. J., Biology
ŽAROMSKIS, R. P., Oceanology

Faculty of Philology (Universiteto g. 5, 01122 Vilnius; tel. (5) 268-72-02; fax (5) 268-72-08; e-mail flf@flf.vu.lt; internet www.flf.vu.lt):

GIRDENIS, A. S., General Linguistics, Baltic Linguistics
JAKAITIENĖ, E. M., Lexicology, Semantics
KOSTIN, E., Russian Literature
KOŽENAUSKIENĖ, R., Stylistics
LASSAN, E., Syntax, Cognitive Linguistics
NASTOPKA, K. V., Literary Theory, Lithuanian Literature
NORKAITIENĖ, I. N., History of German Language, German Philology, Semantics, Semiotics
PAKERIENĖ-DAUJOTYTĖ, V., History and Philosophy of Literature
PAULAUSKIENĖ, A., Grammar
ROSINAS, A., Comparative Linguistics, History of Baltic Languages
STUNDŽIA, B., Phonetics, Phonology
TEMČINAS, S., Old Church Texts, Balto-Slavic Linguistics
ULČINAITĖ, E., Neo-Latin Literature
USONIENĖ, A., English Linguistics, Semantics, Syntax

Faculty of Philosophy (Universiteto g. 9/1, 01513 Vilnius; tel. (5) 266-76-06; fax (5) 266-76-00; e-mail fsf@fsf.vu.lt; internet www.fsf.vu.lt):

BAGDONAS, A., Developmental Psychology
DOBRYNINAS, A., Philosophy of Social Sciences, Criminology
GAILIENĖ, D., Differential and Individual Psychology
KALENDA, C., Ethics
KOČIŪNAS, R. A., Clinical Psychology
NORKUS, Z., History of Philosophy
PLEČKAITIS, R., History of Philosophy
PŠIBILSKIS, V., Political Science
ŠAULAUSKAS, M. P., Contemporary Philosophy, Theories of Social Change, Postmodern Theories
ŠLIOGERIS, M. A., Metaphysics
VAITKEVIČIUS, P. H., Applied and Experimental Psychology
VALICKAS, G., Social Psychology

Faculty of Physics (Saulėtekio alėja 9, 10222 Vilnius; tel. (5) 236-60-00; fax (5) 236-60-03; e-mail ff@ff.vu.lt; internet www.ff.vu.lt):

ARLAUSKAS, K., Solid State Physics, Noncrystalline Materials
BALEVIČIUS, V., Theoretical Physics, Optics, Spectroscopy
BANDZAITIS, A., Atomic Physics
BANYS, J., Solid State Physics, Ferroelectrics
DIKČIUS, G., Optics, Spectroscopy
GADONAS, R. E., Optics
GARŠKA, E., Acoustics
GAVRIUŠINAS, V., Semiconductor Physics
GRIGAS, J., Ferroelectrics and Phase Transitions
IVAŠKA, V., Electromagnetism
JARAŠIUNAS, K., Semiconductor Physics
JURŠĖNAS, S. A., Semiconductor Physics
JUŠKA, G., Solid State Physics, Noncrystalline Materials
KAŽUKAUSKAS, V., Semiconductor Physics
KIMTYS, L., Magnetic Resonance, Relaxation, Spectroscopy
MONTRIMAS, E., Semiconductor Physics, Electronics Structure
ORLIUKAS, A. F., Solid State Ionics
PALENSKIS, V., Superconductor Physics
PISKARSKAS, A., Optics
ROTOMSKIS, R., Biophysics
SAKALAUSKAS, S., Electronics and Physical Instrumentation
SIRUTKAITIS, V., Optics
SMILGEVIČIUS, V., Optics
STABINIS, A. P., Optics
STORASTA, J., Semiconductor Physics
TAMULAITIS, G., Semiconductor Physics
VAITKUS, J. V., Semiconductor Physics

VALKŪNAS, L., Clinical Physics, Biophysics
ŽILINSKAS, P. J., Metrology, Physical Instrumentation
ŽUKAUSKAS, A., Semiconductor Physics

Sports Centre (Saulėtekio alėja 2, 10222 Vilnius; tel. (5) 269-87-20; fax (5) 269-88-56; e-mail sveikata.sportas@kkc.vu.lt):

JANKAUSKAS, J. P., Sports Education
SAPLINSKAS, J., Physiology

ATTACHED RESEARCH INSTITUTES

Algirdas Greimas Centre for Semiotics: Universiteto g. 5, Vilnius; tel. (5) 268-71-61; e-mail greimocentras@cr.vu.lt; internet www.gc.vu.lt; Head Dr DALIA SATKAUSKYTĖ.

Centre for Environmental Studies: Head Dr STASYS SINKEVIČIUS.

Centre for Gender Studies: Head Dr DALIA MARCINKEVIČIENĖ.

Centre for Oriental Studies: Head AUDRIUS BEINORIUS.

Centre for Religious Studies and Research: Head Dr Habil RITA ŠERPYTYTĖ.

Institute of Foreign Languages: Dir Dr NIJOLĖ BRAŽĖNIENĖ.

Institute of International Relations and Political Science: Dirs Prof. RAIMUNDAS LOPATA, Prof. J. ČIČINSKAS.

Institute of Materials Science and Applied Research: Dir Prof. ARTŪRAS ŽUKAUSKAS.

International Centre of Knowledge Economy and Knowledge Management: Dir Prof. RENALDAS GUDAUSKAS.

Stateless Cultures Centre: Head Dr GRIGORIJUS POTAŠENKO.

VYTAUTO DIDŽIOJO UNIVERSITETAS
(Vytautas Magnus University)

K. Donelaicio g. 58, 44248 Kaunas
Telephone: (37) 22-2739
Fax: (37) 20-3858
E-mail: info@adm.vdu.lt
Internet: www.vdu.lt
Founded 1922, closed 1950, re-opened 1989
Public control
Languages of instruction: Lithuanian, English
Academic year: September to June
State-funded
Rector: Prof. ZIGMAS LYDEKA
Vice-Rector for Devt: Assoc. Prof. NATALIJA MAŽEIKIENĖ
Vice-Rector for Public Communication: Prof. AUKSĖ BALČYTIENĖ
Vice-Rector for Research: Prof. JUOZAS AUGUTIS
Vice-Rector for Studies: Assoc. Prof. KĘSTUTIS ŠIDLAUSKAS
Univ. Sec.: Prof. A. BALČYTIENĖ
Chair. of the Senate: Prof. ZIGMANTAS KIAUPA
Chair. of the Ccl: Hon. Dr VALDAS ADAMKUS
Librarian: LINA BLOVEŠČIŪNIENĖ
Library of 262,797 vols, 185 periodicals
Number of teachers: 550
Number of students: 9,000

Publications: *Applied Economics: Systematic Research, Art History & Criticism, Baltic Journal of Law & Politics, Culture and Society: Journal of Social Research, Groups and Environments, Humanities in New Europe, International Journal of Psychology: A Biopsychosocial Approach, Journal of Religious Science, Lithuanian Migration and Diaspora Studies, Management of Organizations: Systematic Research, Media Transformations, Scripta Horti Botanici Universitatis Vytauti Magni, SOTER, The Quality of Higher Education, Vocational Training: Research and Realities, Works and Days*

DEANS

Faculty of Arts: Assoc. Prof. INA PUKELYTĖ
Faculty of Catholic Theology: Assoc. Prof. BENAS ULEVIČIUS
Faculty of Economics and Management: Prof. PRANAS ŽUKAUSKAS
Faculty of Humanities: Prof. INETA DABAŠINSKIENĖ
Faculty of Informatics: Assoc. Prof. DAIVA VITKUTĖ-ADŽGAUSKIENĖ
Faculty of Law: JULIJA KIRŠIENĖ
Faculty of Natural Sciences: Prof. ALGIMANTAS PAULAUSKAS
Faculty of Political Sciences and Diplomacy: Prof. ŠARŪNAS LIEKIS
Faculty of Social Sciences: Prof. JONAS RUŠKUS
Faculty of Social Welfare: Assoc. Prof. J. VAIČENONIS
Music Academy: Assoc. Prof. SAULIUS GERULIS

PROFESSORS

Faculty of Arts:

LEVANDAUSKAS, V.
STAUSKAS, V.
VAŠKELIS, B.

Faculty of Catholic Theology:

MOTUZAS, A.
NARBEKOVAS, A.
PUZARAS, P.
ŽEMAITIS, K.

Faculty of Economics and Management:

CEPINSKIS, J.
KVEDARAVIČIUS, P.
ZAKAREVIČIUS, P.
ZUKAUSKAS, P.

Faculty of Humanities:

ALEKSANDRAVIČIUS, E.
APANAVIČIUS, R.
DONSKIS, L.
GAMZIUKAITE-MAŽIULIENĖ, R.
GENZELIS, B.
GUDAITIS, L. F.
KARALIŪNAS, S.
KERBELYTĖ, B.
KIAUPA, Z.
MARCINKEVICIENE, R.
SKRUPSKELYTE, V.

Faculty of Informatics:

AUGUTIS, J.
KAMINSKAS, V.
SAPAGOVAS, M.
SKUČAS, I.

Faculty of Natural Sciences:

GRAŽULEVIČIENĖ, R.
JUKNYS, R.
KAMUNTAVIČIUS, G.
MARUSKA, A,
MILDAŽIENE, V.
PRANEVIČIUS, L.
STRAVINSKIENE, V.

Faculty of Political Sciences and Diplomacy:

PRAZAUSKAS, A.

Faculty of Social Sciences:

GOŠTAUTAS, A.
LAUŽACKAS, R.
PUKELIS, K.
TERRESEVIČIENE, M.
VAŠTOKAS, R.

Other Higher Educational Institutes

Generolo Jono Žemaičio Lietuvos Karo Akademija (General Jono Žemaičio Military

Academy of Lithuania): Šilo g. 5A, 10322 Vilnius; tel. (5) 210-3688; fax (5) 212-7318; e-mail info@lka.lt; internet www.lka.lt; f. 1994; State control; depts of applied sciences, engineering management, foreign languages, humanities, management, political science; military depts of tactics, combat support and physical training; Centre of Science; Military History Centre; Strategic Research Centre; library: 132,000 vols and periodicals; 424 cadets; Dir Col ALGIMANTAS VYŠNIAUSKAS; publ. *The Military Archives*.

International School of Management: E. Ozeskienes 18, 44254 Kaunas; tel. (37) 30-2402; fax (37) 20-5676; e-mail ism@ism.lt; internet www.ism.lt; f. 1999; Private control; library: 7,518 vols; 60 teachers; 900 students (600 undergraduate, 300 postgraduate); Pres. VIRGINIJUS KUNDROTAS; publ. *Business Training Centre News* (12 a year).

Lietuvos Kūno Kultūros Akademija (Lithuanian Academy of Physical Education): Sporto 6, 44221 Kaunas; tel. (3) 730-2621; internet www.lkka.lt; f. 1945 as Lithuanian National Institute of Physical Education; State control; faculties of sports biomedicine, sports education and sports technologies, tourism; Rector ALBERTAS SKURVYDAS; publ. *Education. Physical Training. Sport*.

Lietuvos Muzikos ir Teatro Akademija (Lithuanian Academy of Music and Theatre): Gedimino pr. 42, 01110 Vilnius; tel. (5) 261-2691; fax (5) 212-6982; e-mail rektoratas@lma.lt; internet www.lma.lt; f. 1933; study programmes: accordion, arts management, camera, choir conducting, composition, drama (theory, history, acting and directing), ethnomusicology, film and sound directing, folk instruments, musical education, musicology, music performance (piano, singing, orchestral instruments, symphony orchestra and opera-conducting), television; library: libraries with 213,000 vols, record libraries with 29,000 records; 274 teachers; 1,167 students; Rector Prof. Dr EDUARDAS GABNYS; publ. *Menotyra* (Science of Art, 1 a year).

Lietuvos Veterinarijos Akademija (Lithuanian Veterinary Academy): Tilžės g. 18, 47181 Kaunas; tel. (3) 736-2383; fax (3) 736-2417; e-mail reklva@lva.lt; internet www.lva.lt; f. 1936; faculties: animal husbandry, veterinary medicine, technology; library: 231,486 vols; 120 teachers; 1,369 students; Rector HENRIKAS ŠILINSKAS; publ. *Veterinary Science and Zootechnics* (1 a year).

Vilniaus Dailes Akademija (Vilnius Academy of Fine Arts): Maironio 6, 01124 Vilnius; tel. (5) 210-5430; fax (5) 210-5463; e-mail vda@vda.lt; internet www.vda.lt; f. 1793; depts: architecture, art theory and history, ceramics, design, fashion design, industrial art, interior and furnishing, monumental and decorative arts, painting, printmaking, sculpture, textiles; library; museum; 280 teachers; 1,700 students; Rector Prof. ADOMAS BUTRIMAS.

LUXEMBOURG

The Higher Education System

In 1867 the London Congress declared Luxembourg to be an independent, sovereign state, although it remained under Dutch hegemony until 1890. The oldest existing institution of higher education is the Conservatoire de Musique de la Ville de Luxembourg (founded 1906), but the first university-level institution, the Université du Luxembourg, was not established until 2003. Prior to the foundation of the Université du Luxembourg, an Act of 1969 permitted the recognition of qualifications awarded by overseas universities in Luxembourg; one such institution is Sacred Heart University in Luxembourg (founded 1991; attached to Sacred Heart University, CT, USA). Under the Law of 11 January 1995, a new higher education qualification, the Diplôme d'ingénieur industriel, was introduced.

The Université du Luxembourg participates in the Bologna Process to establish a European Higher Education Area, the first phase of which is to adopt a credit-based system of comparable degrees with two main cycles (undergraduate and postgraduate). The Bachelors is the primary undergraduate degree and requires three years of study; the first postgraduate degree is the Masters, and lasts two years; and the Doctorate is the highest university degree, lasting three years. Students at all levels are required to spend a period studying abroad. There are several non-university institutions offering a variety of two- to four-year diploma courses. In 2005/06 some 9,227 students were enrolled at university-level institutions, including 6,063 who were studying abroad.

Technical and vocational education takes the form of adult and continuing programmes, and is offered by a range of institutions and agencies, including Centres of Continuing Vocational Training, the Ministry of National Education and Vocational Training, Chambers of Commerce and Trades, the Communes and Private Associations. In 2002 a new centre was established by the then Ministry of Education, Vocational Training and Sport and the Ministry of Health to cater for the demand for vocational training in the health sector.

Regulatory and Representative Bodies

GOVERNMENT

Ministry of Culture, Higher Education and Research: 20 montée de la Pétrusse, 2912 Luxembourg; tel. 24786619; fax 402724; e-mail info@mcesr.public.lu; internet www.mcesr.public.lu; Min. of Culture OCTAVIE MODERT; Min. of Higher Education and Research FRANÇOIS BILTGEN.

Ministry of National Education and Vocational Training: 29 rue Aldringen, 1118 Luxembourg; tel. 24785100; fax 24785113; e-mail info@men.public.lu; internet www.men.public.lu; Min. MADY DELVAUX-STEHRES.

ACCREDITATION

ENIC/NARIC Luxembourg: Min. of Culture, Higher Education and Research, 18–20 montée de la Pétrusse, 2912 Luxembourg; tel. 4785139; fax 26296037; e-mail jean.tagliaferri@mcesr.etat.lu; internet www.cedies.public.lu; Contact Prof. JEAN TAGLIAFERRI.

Learned Societies

GENERAL

Institut Grand-Ducal: 2A rue Kalchesbruck, 1852 Luxembourg; tel. 24788640; fax 26094788; e-mail sekretariat@igd-leo.lu; internet www.igd-leo.lu; incl. 6 sections: (a) History (Pres. PAUL SPANG), (b) Medicine (Pres. HENRI METZ), (c) Natural Sciences (Pres. PIERRE SECK), (d) Linguistics, Ethnology and Place Names (Pres. HENRI KLEES), (e) Arts and Literature (Pres. PIERRE SCHUMACHER), (f) Moral and Political Sciences (Sec. GASTON REINESCH).

LANGUAGE AND LITERATURE

Institut Pierre Werner: Bâtiment Robert Bruch, 2e étage, 28 rue Münster, 2162 Luxembourg; tel. 490443; fax 490643; e-mail info@ipw.lu; internet www.ipw.lu; f. 2003 jtly by the Centre Culturel Français, Goethe-Institut (Germany) and Ministère de la Culture Luxembourgeois; named after fmr Luxembourgeois Prime Minister; promotes cultural diversity and exchange in Europe; Dir MARIO HIRSCH.

MEDICINE

Collège Médical: 7–9 ave Victor Hugo, 1750 Luxembourg; tel. 24785514; fax 475679; e-mail info@collegemedical.lu; internet www.collegemedical.lu; f. 1818; governmental consultative body; 12 mems; Pres. Dr PIT BUCHLER; Sec. ROGER HEFTRICH.

NATURAL SCIENCES

Biological Sciences

Société des Naturalistes Luxembourgeois: POB 327, 2013 Luxembourg; e-mail info@snl.lu; internet www.snl.lu; f. 1890; promotes nature conservation and studies natural environment of Luxembourg and modifications of animal and plant communities caused by environmental changes; working groups: botany, mycology, and entomology; organizes conferences and guided excursions; promotes nature conservation; 410 mems; Pres. Dr CHRISTIAN RIES; Sec. YVES KRIPPEL; Treas. Dr GUY COLLING; publ. Bulletin Soc. Nat. luxemb. (1 a year).

Research Institutes

ECONOMICS, LAW AND POLITICS

Institut National de la Statistique et des Études Économiques: BP 304, Luxembourg 2013; 13 rue Erasme, 1463 Luxembourg; tel. 24784219; e-mail info@statec.etat.lu; internet www.statec.public.lu; f. 1962; attached to Min. of the Economy and External Trade; library of 9,000 vols, 500 periodicals; Dir Dr SERGE ALLEGREZZA; publs Annuaire Statistique du Luxembourg (1 a year), Bulletin du STATEC (10 a year), Cahiers Économiques (irregular), Conjoncture Flash (12 a year), Economie et Statistiques (irregular), Indicateurs Rapides (15 series), Kaléidoscope (irregular), Luxembourg en Chiffres (1 a year), Note de Conjoncture (3 a year), Regards (irregular).

EDUCATION

Commission Grand-Ducale d'Instruction: 29 rue Aldringen, 2926 Luxembourg; tel. 4785254; fax 4785188; f. 1843; Pres. FRANCIS JEITZ; Sec. PAUL KLEIN.

MEDICINE

Centre de Recherche Public de la Santé: 1 A–B, rue Thomas Edison, 1445 Strassen; tel. 26970880; fax 26970719; e-mail aurelia.derischebourg@crp-sante.lu; internet www.crp-sante.lu; f. 1988; applied, clinical and public health research; Pres. FRANK GANSEN; CEO JEAN-CLAUDE SCHMIT.

TECHNOLOGY

Centre de Recherche Public Henri Tudor: 29 ave John F. Kennedy, 1855 Luxembourg-Kirchberg; tel. 4259911; fax 425991777; e-mail info@tudor.lu; internet www.tudor.lu; f. 1988; applied science; Pres. GEORGES BOURSCHEID; Dir Dr MARC LEMMER; publ. Les Cahiers de l'Innovation (irregular).

Libraries and Archives

Esch-sur-Alzette

Bibliothèque de la Ville: 26 rue Emile Mayrisch, 4240 Esch-sur-Alzette; tel. 547383; fax 552037; e-mail bibliotheque@villeesch.lu; internet www.esch.lu; f. 1919; English, French, German, Italian and Portuguese literature; popular science books; non-fiction books, spec. colln: Luxemburgensia; 65,000 vols; Chief Librarian HENRI LUTGEN.

Luxembourg

Archives Nationales: Plateau du Saint Esprit, BP 6, 2010 Luxembourg; tel. 24786660; fax 474692; e-mail archives.nationales@an.etat.lu; internet www.anlux.lu; f. 19th century; 40,000 vols; Dir JOSÉE KIRPS.

Bibliothèque Nationale: 37 blvd F. D. Roosevelt, 2450 Luxembourg; tel. 2297551; fax 475672; e-mail info@bnl.etat.lu; internet www.bnl.lu; f. 1798, reorganized 1897, 1945, 1958, 1973, 1988 and 2010; nat. and research library open to the gen. public; 1.4m. items; Dir Dr MONIQUE KIEFFER.

Mersch

Centre National de Littérature: 2 rue Emmanuel Servais, 7565 Mersch; tel. 3269551; fax 327090; e-mail info@cnl.public .lu; internet www.literaturarchiv.lu; f. 1986; spec. colln of works published in Luxembourg: Luxembourgish literatures, edits literary reference books, reedits Luxembourgish texts, evaluates archives; 40,000 vols, 500 periodicals, author archives, posters, audiovisual items, spec. collns; Dir GERMAINE GOETZINGER; Librarian CHARLOTTE ZIGER; publ. *Bibliographie courante de la littérature luxembourgeoise* (1 a year).

Museum

Luxembourg

Musée National d'Histoire et d'Art: Marché-aux-Poissons, 2345 Luxembourg; tel. 4793301; fax 479330271; e-mail musee@ mnha.etat.lu; internet www.mnha.public.lu; f. 1845; archaeology, fine arts, industrial and popular arts, weaponry, history of Luxembourg; library of 25,000 vols; archive of photographs dating from 1865; Dir MICHEL POLFER; publ. *L'Annuaire* (1 a year).

University

UNIVERSITÉ DU LUXEMBOURG

Limpertsberg Campus: 162A ave de la Faïencerie, 1511 Luxembourg

Kirchberg Campus: 6 rue Richard Coudenhove-Kalergi, 1359 Luxembourg

Walferdange Campus: route de Diekirch, 7220 Walferdange

Telephone: 4666445000

Fax: 466644508

Internet: www.uni.lu

Founded 1969, present name and status 2003

State control

Languages of instruction: French, German, English

Academic year: October to June

Rector: ROLF TARRACH

Vice-Rector for Academic Affairs: Prof. Dr LUCIEN KERGER

Vice-Rector for Int. Relations and Special Projects: Prof. Dr FRANCK LEPRÉVOST

Vice-Rector for Research: Prof. Dr LUCIËNNE BLESSING

Dir for Admin.: Prof. Dr ERIC TSCHIRHART

Library Dir: MARIE-PIERRE PAUSCH

Library of 220,000 vols, 900 periodicals

Number of teachers: 350 (mostly part-time)

Number of students: 1,600

Publications: *Avis de la CNE, Cahiers d'Economie, Cahiers d'Histoire, Cahiers de Pédagogie, Cahiers de Philosophie— série A, Cahiers de Philosophie—série B, Cahiers de Physique, Cahiers ISIS, Editions Spéciales, English Studies, Etudes Classiques, Etudes de Biologie, Etudes de Géographie, Etudes de Philosophie, Etudes Romanes, Germanistik, Les Droits de l'Homme, Travaux de Linguistique, Travaux de Mathématiques*

DEANS

Faculty of Language and Literature, Humanities, Arts and Education: Prof. Dr MICHEL MARGUE

Faculty of Law, Economics and Finance: Prof. Dr ANDRÉ PRÜM (acting)

Faculty of Science, Technology and Communication: Prof. Dr PAUL HEUSCHLING

Colleges

Conservatoire de Musique d'Esch-sur-Alzette: BP 310, 4004 Esch-sur-Alzette; 50 rue d'Audun, 4218 Esch-sur-Alzette; tel. 549725; fax 549731; e-mail contact@ conservatoire-esch.lu; internet www.esch.lu/ culture/conservatoire; f. 1926 as Ecole Municipale de Musique; present status 1969; 60 teachers; 1,000 students; Prin. Prof. FRED HARLES; publ. *Annuaire* (1 a year).

Conservatoire de Musique de la Ville de Luxembourg: 33 rue Charles Martel, 2134 Luxembourg; tel. 47965555; e-mail cml@vdl .lu; internet www.cml.lu; f. 1906; 136 teachers; 2,600 students; Dir FERNAND JUNG; publ. *Compte rendu* (1 a year).

Institut Universitaire International de Luxembourg: Château de Munsbach, 31 rue du Parc, 5374 Luxembourg; tel. 26159212; fax 26159228; internet www.iuil .lu; f. 1974; Dir POL WAGNER.

Lycée Technique pour Professions Educatives et Sociales: rue de Bettembourg, 3378 Livange; tel. 5235251; fax 523526; e-mail secretariat@ltpes.lu; internet www .iees.lu; f. 2005; library: 24,000 vols; 800 students; Dir HENRY R. WELSCHBILLIG.

Sacred Heart University in Luxembourg: 7 rue Alcide de Gasperi, 2981 Luxembourg; tel. 227613; fax 227623; e-mail arech@shu.lu; internet www.shu.lu; f. 1991; attached to Sacred Heart Univ., Connecticut, USA; US-accredited MBA programme; 80 students; Dir Dr PETRA GARNJOST.

FORMER YUGOSLAV REPUBLIC OF MACEDONIA

The Higher Education System

After the First World War (1914–18) Vardar Macedonia, the area now known as the Former Yugoslav Republic of Macedonia (FYRM), became part of the new Kingdom of Serbs, Croats and Slovenes (formally named Yugoslavia in 1929). Following the Second World War (1939–45) Macedonia became part of the new communist-led Federative People's Republic of Yugoslavia. In 1991 the Macedonian Sobranie (Assembly) declared the republic of Macedonia to be a sovereign territory. Macedonian secession was effectively acknowledged by the Federal Republic of Yugoslavia in 1992. Univerzitet 'Sv. Kiril I Metodij' (University of Skopje—founded 1949) is the oldest of the eight universities in Macedonia; the others are Univerzitet 'Sv. Kliment Ohridski' Bitola (St Kliment Ohridski University of Bitola—founded 1979) and Universiteti I Ejl (South-East European University—founded 2001). The last of these was established following new legislation in 2000 which permitted the use of Albanian and other languages in private tertiary institutions, and in 2004, under further amendments to legislation on higher education, it became the third state-funded university. In 2003/04 some 46,637 students were enrolled at the universities at Skopje and at Bitola.

The Republic of Macedonia became a member of the Bologna Process in 2003. However, it started to change the higher education system much earlier (in 2000) when the Ministry of Education and Science passed the new Law on Higher Education. The Law required universities to start introducing the European Credit Transfer System (ECTS) and design study and subject programmes according to the principles of the Bologna Process. The European Credit Transfer System (ECTS) has been implemented across all higher education providers in the country at the first and second cycle.

Admission to higher education is on the basis of the Secondary Leaving Diploma and entrance examinations. Higher education is divided between colleges and universities/ university faculties. Colleges specialize in two- to three-year diploma courses leading to a professional title. Universities and university faculties offer four- to six-year diploma and degree programmes. The first postgraduate degree is the Masters (Magister) and is a two-year research degree culminating in public defence of a thesis. The final university-level degree is the Doctor of Science (Doktor na nauiki).

The Board for Accreditation of Higher Education (Odbor za Akreditacija vo Vissokoto Obrazovanie) is the national body responsible for all higher education institutions. Staff are externally evaluated by the Higher Education Evaluation Agency (Agencija za evaluacija na visokoto obrazovanie). This is a legally independent organization established by the Higher Education Accreditation Board.

Regulatory and Representative Bodies

GOVERNMENT

Ministry of Culture: ul. Gjuro Gjakovik 61, 1000 Skopje; tel. (2) 324-0600; fax (2) 324-0561; e-mail info@kultura.gov.mk; internet www.kultura.gov.mk; Minister ELIZABETH KANCESKA-MILEVSKA.

Ministry of Education and Science: Mito Hadzivasilev Jasmin bb, 1000 Skopje; tel. (2) 311-7896; fax (2) 311-8414; e-mail contact@mon.gov.mk; internet www.mon.gov.mk; Minister NIKOLA TODOROV.

ACCREDITATION

ENIC/NARIC Macedonia: Information Centre, Ministry of Education and Science, Mito Hadzivasilev Jasmin bb, 1000 Skopje; tel. (2) 311-7896; fax (2) 311-8414; e-mail nadezda.uzelac@mofk.gov.mk; internet www.mon.gov.mk; Head, Information Centre NADEZDA UZELAC.

Learned Societies

GENERAL

Makedonska Akademija na Naukite i Umetnostite (Macedonian Academy of Sciences and Arts): Blvr Krste Misirkov 2, POB 428, 1000 Skopje; tel. (2) 323-5400; fax (2) 323-5500; e-mail manu@manu.edu.mk; internet www.manu.edu.mk; f. 1967; sections of arts (Sec. VLADA UROŠEVIĆ), biological and medical sciences (Sec. RISTO LOZANOVSKI), linguistics and literary sciences (Sec. KATA UULAVKOVA), mathematical and technical sciences (Sec. GLIGOR KANEVČE), social sciences (Sec. IVAN KATARDŽIEV); 72 mems (43 ordinary, 29 foreign); library of 145,000 vols, incl. 52,000 monographs, 1,500 journals and magazines; Pres. GEORGI STARDELOV; Vice-Pres VLADO KAMBOVSKI, BOJAN SOPTRAJANOV; Sec. LJUPČO KOCAREV; publs *Letopis* (1 a year), *Prilozi na Oddelenieto za biološki i medicinski nauki* (Contributions of the Dept of Biological and Medical Sciences, 2 a year), *Prilozi na Oddelenieto za lingvistika i literaturna nauka* (Contributions of the Dept of Linguistics and Literary Sciences, 2 a year), *Prilozi na Oddelenieto za matematičko-tehnički nauki* (Contributions of the Dept of Mathematical and Technical Sciences, 2 a year), *Prilozi na Oddelenieto za opštestveni nauki* (Contributions of the Dept of Social Sciences, 2 a year).

Makedonsko Naucno Drustvo-Bitola (Macedonian Scientific Society-Bitola): POB 145, 7000 Bitola; tel. (47) 222-683; e-mail mnd-bitola@t-home.mk; internet www.mnd-bitola.mk; f. 1960, as Association for Science and Art (ASA); scientific meetings, symposia, research; sections of arts, history and geography, linguistics and literature, medical, natural and mathematical sciences, social sciences and law, technical and applied sciences; has 7 depts; 300 mems, 25 assocs; Pres. Prof. Dr BORIS ANGELKOV; Vice-Pres. Prof. Dr VIOLETA MANEVSKA; Sec. ELISABETH CASITOVSKA; publs *Prilozi* (Contributions, 2 a year), *Scientific Thought*.

AGRICULTURE, FISHERIES AND VETERINARY SCIENCE

Sojuz na Društvata na Veterinarnite Lekari i Tehničari na Makedonija (Union of Associations of Veterinary Surgeons and Technicians of Macedonia): Veterinaren institut c/o Faculty of Veterinary Medicine, Lazar Pop-Trajkov 5, POB 95, 1000 Skopje; tel. (2) 324-0700; fax (2) 311-4619; f. 1950; attached to Sts Cyril and Methodius Univ.; 450 mems; Pres. SILJAN ZAHARIEVSKI; Sec. ADŽIEVSKI BLAŽE; publ. *Makedonski veterinaren pregled* (Macedonian Veterinary Review).

Sojuz na Inženeri i Tehničari po Sumarstvo i Industrija za Prerabotka na Drvo na Makedonija (Union of Forestry Engineers and Technicians of Macedonia): Šumarski institut, Engelsova 2, 1000 Skopje; f. 1952; 500 mems; Pres. Dipl. Ing. ŽIVKO MINČEV; Sec. Dipl. Ing. MILE STAMENKOV; publ. *Sumarski pregled* (Forester's review).

Združenie na Zemjodelski Inženeri na Makedonija (Association of Agricultural Engineers of Macedonia): Zemjodelski fakultet, POB 297, 1000 Skopje; tel. (2) 311-5277; fax (2) 323-8218; f. 1994; 3,000 mems; Sec Prof. DRAGOSLAV KOCEVSKI; publ. *Macedonian Agriculture Review* (1 a year).

BIBLIOGRAPHY, LIBRARY SCIENCE AND MUSEOLOGY

Bibliotekarsko Zdruzenie na Makedonija (Macedonian Library Association): c/o Narodna i univerzitetska biblioteka 'St Kliment Ohridski', Blvr Goce Delčev 6, 1000 Skopje; tel. (2) 7026-2120; e-mail bzm@bzm.org.m; internet www.bzm.org.mk; f. 1949; oversees functioning of libraries; organizes seminars; 500 mems; Pres. NIKOLCE VELJANOVSKI; Sec. ROZITA PETRINSKA; publ. *Bibliotekarstvo* (2 a year).

Društvo na Muzejskite Rabotnici na Makedonija (Museum Society of Macedonia): Muzej na grad Skopje, Mito Hadži-Vasilev-Jasmin bb, 1000 Skopje; f. 1951;

100 mems; Pres. KUZMAN GEORGIEVSKI; Sec. GALENA KUCULOVSKA.

Sojuz na društvata na arhivskite rabotnici na Makedonija (Union of Societies of Archivists of Macedonia): Gligor Prličev 3, POB 496, 1000 Skopje; tel. (2) 323-7211; fax (2) 323-4461; f. 1954; 340 mems; publ. *Makedonski arhivist* (1 a year).

ECONOMICS, LAW AND POLITICS

Društvo za Filozofija, Sociologija i Politikologija na Makedonija (Society for Philosophy, Sociology and Politics of Macedonia): Institut za sociološki i političko-pravni istražuvanja, Blvr Partizanski odredi bb, 1000 Skopje; f. 1960; 170 mems; Pres. Dr DRAGAN TAŠKOVSKI; Sec. SVETA SKARIĆ; publ. *Zbornik* (Collected Papers).

Sojuz na Ekonomistite na Makedonija (Union of Economists of Macedonia): Ekonomiski Fakultet, K. Misirkov bb, 1000 Skopje; tel. (2) 322-4311; fax (2) 322-4973; f. 1950; 3,000 mems; Pres. Prof. Dr TAKI FITI; Sec. ACO SPASOVSKI; publ. *Stopanski pregled* (Economic review).

Sojuz na Združenijata na Pravnicite na Makedonija (Union of Associations of Jurists of Macedonia): Ustaven sud na Makedonija, XII udarna brigada 2, 1000 Skopje; f. 1946; 4,000 mems; Pres. BORO DOGANDŽISKI; Sec. PETAR GOLUBOVSKI; publ. *Pravna misla* (Legal opinion).

FINE AND PERFORMING ARTS

Društvo na Istoričarite na Umetnosta od Makedonija (Society of Art Historians of Macedonia): Arheološki muzej na Makedonija, Curčiska bb, 1000 Skopje; f. 1970; 130 mems; Pres. MILANKA BOŠKOVSKA; Sec. MATE BOŠKOVSKI; publ. *Likovna umetnost* (Plastic Arts).

Društvo na Likovnite Umetnici na Makedonija (Association of Artists of Macedonia): Makedonija str. 12, POB 438, 1000 Skopje; tel. and fax (2) 321-1533; e-mail dlum .makedonija@hotmail.co.uk; internet www .dlum.org.mk; f. 1944; 450 mems; Pres. TANJA BALAC; Sec. BRANISLAV MIRČEVSKI.

Sojuz na Kompozitorite na Makedonija (Composers Association of Macedonia): Maksim Gorki 18, 1000 Skopje; tel. and fax (2) 311-9824; e-mail socom@socom.com.mk; internet www.socom.com.mk; f. 1950; preserves the tradition of folk music; collects and processes folk music material; 49 mems; Pres. MARKO KOLOVSKI; Gen-Sec. LAZAR MOJSOVSKI; publ. *Informer*.

HISTORY, GEOGRAPHY AND ARCHAEOLOGY

Geografsko Društvo na R. Makedonija (Geographical Society of Macedonia): Geografski institut pri Prirodnomatematički fakultet, POB 146, 1000 Skopje; f. 1949; 600 mems; Pres. Prof. VASIL GRAMATNIKOVSKI; Sec.-Asst NIKOLA PANOV; publs *Geografski razgledi* (Geographical surveys), *Geografski vidik* (Geographical outlook).

Makedonsko Arheološko Naučno Društvo (Macedonian Archaeological Research Society): Curčiska bb, 1000 Skopje; tel. (2) 311-6044; fax (2) 311-6439; e-mail contact@mand.org.mk; internet www.mand .org.mk; f. 1972 as Archaeological Society of the Republic of Macedonia; symposia, lectures, publs; 150 mems; Chair. MARINA ONCHEVSKA TODOROVSKA; Pres. IRENA KOLISTRKOSKA NASTEVA; Sec. SILVANA BLAZEVSKA; publ. *Macedoniae acta archaeologica*.

Sojuz na Istoricarite na Republika Makedonija (Association of the Historians of Republic of Macedonia): Institut za nacionalna istorija, ul. Grigor Prličev br.3, POB 591, 1000 Skopje; tel. (2) 311-4078; fax (2) 311-5831; e-mail kotlarn@yahoo.com; f. 1952; 120 mems; Pres. Dr NATASHA KOTLAR-TRAJKOVA; Sec. TEON DZINGO; Treas. DRAGAN ZAJKOVSKI; publ. *Spisanie Istorija* (History).

LANGUAGE AND LITERATURE

Alliance Française: N. U. U. B. 'Sv. Kliment Ohridski', Leninova 39, 7000 Bitola; tel. and fax (47) 232-363; e-mail afbitola@ yahoo.fr; f. 2001; library of 400 vols; offers courses and examinations in French language and culture and promotes cultural exchange with France; Dir MARIE-CLEMENCE VATELOT.

British Council: Blvr Goce Delcev 6, POB 562, 1000 Skopje; tel. (2) 313-5035; fax (2) 313-5036; e-mail info@britishcouncil.org.mk; internet www.britishcouncil.org/macedonia; f. 1996; offers courses and examinations in English language and British culture and promotes cultural exchange with the UK; library of 6,000 vols; Dir ANDREW HADLEY.

Društvo na Literaturnite Preveduvači na Makedonija (Society of Literary Translators of Macedonia): POB 3, 1000 Skopje; f. 1955; 102 mems; Pres. Prof. Dr BOŽIDAR NASTEV; Sec. TAŠKO SIRILOV.

Društvo na Pisatelite na Makedonija (Writers' Association of Macedonia): Maksim Gorki 18, 1000 Skopje; tel. and fax (2) 322-8039; f. 1947; 269 mems; Pres. JOVAN PAVLOVSKI; Sec. PASKAL GILOVSKI; Sec. SVETLANA HRISTOVA-JOCIĆ.

Sojuz na Društvata za Makedonski Jazik i Literatura (Union of Associations for Macedonian Language and Literature): Filološki fakultet, Blvr Krste Misirkov bb, 1000 Skopje; f. 1954; 700 mems; Pres. ELENA BENDEVSKA; Sec. LJUPČO MITREVSKI; publ. *Literaturen zbor* (Literary word).

Združenie na Folkloristite na Makedonija (Association of Folklorists of Macedonia): Institut za folklor, Ruzveltova 3, 1000 Skopje; tel. (2) 323-3876; f. 1952; 60 mems; Pres. GORGI SMOKVARSKI; Sec. ERMIS LAFAZANOVSKY; publ. *Narodno Stvaralaštvo* (1 or 2 a year).

MEDICINE

Farmaceutsko Društvo na Makedonija (Pharmacological Society of Macedonia): Ivo Ribar Lola MI/6, 1000 Skopje; Pres. LAZAR TOLOV; Sec. GALABA SRBINOVSKA; publ. *Bilten* (Bulletin).

Makedonsko Lekarsko Društvo (Macedonian Medical Association): Dame Gruev 3, 1000 Skopje; tel. (2) 316-2577; e-mail mld@ unet.com.mk; internet www.mld.org.mk; f. 1945; promotes medical and related sciences; conserves and promotes the dignity and reputation of the medical profession and protects the interests of doctors; 4,490 mems; Pres. Prof. JOVAN TOFOSKI; publ. *Makedonski medicindki pregled* (Macedonian Medical Review).

NATURAL SCIENCES

General

Makedonskoto Ekološko Društvo (Macedonian Ecological Society): Blvr Kuzman Josifovski Pitu, 28/III-7, 1000 Skopje; tel. (2) 240-2773; fax (2) 240-2774; e-mail contact@mes.org.mk; internet www.mes.org .mk; f. 1972; devt of ecology, promotion of environmental science and protection of environment and nature; Chair. Dr LJUPČO MELOVSKI; publ. *Ekologija i zaštita na životnata sredina* (Ecology and Environmental Protection, every 4 years).

Mathematical Sciences

Sojuz na Matematičari na Makedonija (Society of Mathematicians of Macedonia): Blvr Aleksandar Makedonski bb, POB 10, 1000 Skopje; tel. (2) 311-6053; fax (2) 322-8141; e-mail vesname@iunona.pmf.ukim.edu .mk; internet www.smm.org.mk; f. 1950; Chief Officers Prof. Dr BORKO ILIEVSKI, Prof. Dr NIKOLA PANDESKI; publ. *Matematički Bilten* (Mathematical Bulletin).

Physical Sciences

Društvo na Fizičarite na Republika Makedonija (Society of Physicists of Republic of Macedonia): Arhimedova 5, POB 162, 1000 Skopje; tel. (2) 324-9857; fax (2) 322-8141; e-mail nenad@iunona.pmf.ukim.edu .mk; internet dfrm.pmf.ukim.edu.mk; f. 1949; promotes research in physics, natural sciences and protection of environment; 139 mems; Pres. Prof. Dr NENAD NOVKOVSKI; Sec. Assoc. Prof. Dr DANICA KRSTOVSKA; Treas. LAMBE BARANDOVSKI; publs *Bilten* (1 a year), *Impuls* (jt publ. with Institute of Physics, Faculty of Natural Sciences, 2 a year), *Macedonian Physics Teacher*.

Makedonsko Geološko Društvo (Macedonian Geological Society): Geološki zavod, POB 28, 1000 Skopje; tel. (2) 323-0873; f. 1954; 300 mems; library of 20,000 vols; Pres. NIKOLA TUDŽAROV; Sec. ROZA PETROVSKA.

TECHNOLOGY

Sojuz na Inženeri i Tehničari na Makedonija (Society of Engineers and Technicians of Macedonia): Nikola Vapcarov bb, 1000 Skopje; f. 1945; 27,000 mems; Pres. Prof. Dr Ing. DIME LAZAROV; Sec. BORO RAVNJANSKI.

Research Institutes
GENERAL

Institutot za Životna Sredina i Zdravje (Institute for Environment and Health): Ilindenska nn, Campus Bldg 201.01/1, 1200 Tetovo; tel. (44) 356-114; fax (44) 356-001; e-mail ieh@seeu.edu.mk; internet ieh.seeu .edu.mk; f. 2005; attached to SEE Univ.; programmes in education, research, building partnerships and environmental awareness; 30 research students, 5 external research assocs.

AGRICULTURE, FISHERIES AND VETERINARY SCIENCE

Institut za Južni Zemjodelski Kulturi (Institute of Southern Crops): Goce Delčev bb, 2400 Strumica; tel. and fax (34) 345-096; e-mail admin@isc.ukim.edu.mk; f. 1956; attached to Dept of Plant Protection, Sts Cyril and Methodius Univ.; Dir Dr SAŠA MITREV; publ. *Zbornik* (Collected Papers).

Institut za Ovoštarstvo (Institute of Pomology): Prvomajska 5, 1000 Skopje; tel. (2) 323-0557; f. 1953; attached to Sts Cyril and Methodius Univ.; fruit research; library of 3,670 vols; Dir Dr IVAN KUZMANOVSKI.

Institut za Tutun Prilep (Scientific Tobacco Institute Prilep): Kičevsko Džade, 7500 Prilep; tel. (48) 412-760; fax (48) 412-763; e-mail tobacco_institute_prilep@yahoo .com; internet www.tip.edu.mk; f. 1924; attached to St Kliment Ohridski Univ. Bitola; scientific research investigations, education, application and production activities in tobacco breeding; tobacco museum and meteorological station; depts of agrotechnics, chemistry of tobacco, tobacco smoke, residues from pesticides and biochemistry; economic planning and programming; genetics, selection and seed control; technology, fermentation and fabrication; library of 4,211 books, 125 titles of scientific and research publications; Pres. Dr JORDAN TRAJKOSKI; Vice-Pres. Dr VERA DIMESKA; Dir Prof. Dr KIRIL FILIPOSKI; publ. *Tutun* (Tobacco, 6 a year).

Univerzitet Sv.Kiril i Metodij Institut za Stočarstvo (University "St. Ciril and Methodius" Institute of Animal Science): Bul. Ilinden br. 92, A 1000 Skopje; tel. (2) 306 5120; fax (2) 306 2358; e-mail institut za stocarstvo@live.com; f. 1952; attached to Sts Cyril and Methodius Univ.; Gen. Man. Dr VASIL KOSTOV; Sec. ALEN SALIU.

Zavod za Unapreduvanje na Lozarstvoto i Vinarstvoto na Makedonija (Institute for the Advancement of Viticulture of Macedonia): Naselba Butel 1, 1000 Skopje; f. 1952; Dir Dr DIME PEMOVSKI; publ. *Lozarstvo i vinarstvo* (Viticulture).

Zavod za Unapreduvanje na Stočarstvoto na Makedonija (Institute for the Advancement of Animal Husbandry of Macedonia): Avtokomanda, 1000 Skopje; f. 1952; Dir Prof. Dr BLAGOJ VASKOV.

Zemjodelski institut (Institute of Agriculture): Blvr Aleksandar Makedonski bb, 1000 Skopje; tel. (2) 3230-910; fax (2) 3114-283; e-mail d.mukaetov@zeminst.edu.mk; attached to Sts Cyril and Methodius Univ.; Dir Dr DUSKO MUKAETOV; Sec. VIKTORIJA KALAJDZISKA.

ECONOMICS, LAW AND POLITICS

Ekonomski Institut -Skopje Univerzitet Sv.Kiril i Metodij (Institute of Economics-Skopje at the Sts Cyril and Methodius University of Skopje):e-mail sretanka@ek-inst .ukim.edu.mk Prolet 1, POB 250, 1000 Skopje; tel. (2) 311-5076; fax (2) 322-6350; e-mail eis@ek-inst.ukim.edu.mk; internet www.ek-inst.ukim.edu.mk; f. 1952; attached to Sts Cyril and Methodius Univ.; scientific research and educational instn; offers postgraduate studies in agrobusiness, entrepreneurship, financial management, int. economics, int. management; library of 15,947 vols, 13,743 books, 327 internal projects and 204 periodicals; Dir Prof. Dr BILJANA ANGELOVA; Librarian SRETANKA GJORGJIEVSKA; publ. *Economic Development-Journal of the Institute of Economics* (3 a year).

HISTORY, GEOGRAPHY AND ARCHAEOLOGY

Institut za Nacionalna Istorija (Institute of National History): ul. Gligor Prličev br. 3, 1000 Skopje; tel. (2) 311-4078; fax (2) 311-5831; e-mail inimak@on.net.mk; internet www.makedonika.org/ini; f. 1948; attached to Sts Cyril and Methodius Univ.; history of the Macedonian and Balkan peoples and ethnic communities; 56 mems; library of 27,350 vols, 37,500 periodicals, 1,300 vols of newspapers; Dir Prof. Dr NOVICA VELJANOVSKI; Sec. TATIANA DOJCINOVSKA; publ. *Glasnik* (Journal).

LANGUAGE AND LITERATURE

Institut za Folklor 'Marko Cepenkov' (Institute of Folklore 'Marko Cepenkov'): Ruzveltova 3, POB 319, 1000 Skopje; tel. (2) 338-0176; fax (2) 338-0177; e-mail ifmarkocepenkov@mt.net.mk; internet www .ifmc.ukim.mk; f. 1950 as Folklore Institute of the Republic, present status 1979; attached to Sts Cyril and Methodius Univ.; study of the spiritual and material culture of the Macedonian people: people's literature, ethnology, vernacular architecture, textile ornaments, traditional arts and crafts and skills; Dir Dr SEVIM PILICKOVA; Sec. TODOR ANDREEV; publ. *Makedonski folklor* (2 a year).

Institut za Makedonska Literatura (Institute of Macedonian Literature): Gligor Prlicev 5, 1000 Skopje; tel. and fax (2) 322-0309; e-mail maclit@iml.ukim.edu.mk; internet iml.ukim.edu.mk; f. 1998; attached to Sts Cyril and Methodius Univ.; continuous and systematic research, adherence and interpretation of literature and its tradition in Macedonia; training of young personnel for scientific work; depts of contributing scientific activities—bibliography, documentation, library and informatics, medieval Macedonian literature, Macedonian folk literature, Macedonian literature of the 19th century, Macedonian literature of the 20th century, Macedonian–Balkan literary-historical relations, literatures of the nationalities in Macedonia, theory of literature and comparative literature; Dir LORETA GEORGIEVSKA-JAKOVLEVA; Sec. SARITA TRAJANOVA; Treas. VESELA KRALJEVA; publs *Spectrum* (scientific magazine), *Literary Context* (scientific publ. for comparative literature).

Institut za Makedonski Jazik 'Krste Misirkov' (Krste Misirkov Institute of Macedonian Language): Grigor Prličev 5, 1000 Skopje; tel. (2) 311-4733; fax (2) 322-2225; f. 1953; attached to Sts Cyril and Methodius Univ.; depts of contemporary Macedonian, dialectology, history of the Macedonian language, Macedonian lexicology and lexicography, onomastics; Dir Dr LILJANA MAKARIJOSKA; Sec. TODE BLAZEVSKI; publs *Makedonistika* (Macedonian Studies), *Makedonski jazik* (The Macedonian Language), *Stari tekstovi* (Ancient Texts).

Research Centre for Areal Linguistics: bul. Krste Misirkov 2, 1000 Skopje; tel. (2) 323-5400; fax (2) 323-5500; e-mail ical@manu .edu.mk; internet www.manu.edu.mk; f. 2000; attached to Macedonian Acad. of Arts and Sciences; researches the role of spatial factors in the devt and function of language; archives rare books and MSS; organizes meetings and lectures; library of 10,000 vols, spec. colln of rare books, 40 CDs, 2,000 minutes of audio material; Dir Prof. ZUZANNA TOPOLINSKA; Deputy Dir Prof. MARJAN MARKOVIC.

NATURAL SCIENCES

Institut za Zemjotresno Inženerstvo i Inženerska Seizmologija (Institute of Earthquake Engineering and Engineering Seismology): 73, Salvador Aljende str., POB 101, 1000 Skopje; tel. (2) 3107-701; fax (2) 3112-163; e-mail garevski@pluto.iziis.ukim .edu.mk; internet www.iziis.edu.mk; f. 1965; attached to Sts Cyril and Methodius Univ.; supervises post-earthquake reconstruction, revitalization and devt of Skopje; depts of building structures and materials, dynamic testing laboratory and informatics, engineering structures, geotechnics and special structures and informatics, natural and technological hazards ecology, risk disaster management and strategic planning; Dir MIHAIL GAREVSKI; Deputy Dir GOLUBKA NECEVSKA-CVETANOVSKA.

RELIGION, SOCIOLOGY AND ANTHROPOLOGY

Institut za Sociološki i Političko-pravni Istražuvanja (Institute of Sociological, Political and Juridical Research): Blvr Partizanski odredi bb, 1000 Skopje; tel. (2) 3061-119; fax (2) 3061-282; e-mail jakjor@isppi .ukim.edu.mk; internet www.isppi.ukim.edu .mk; f. 1965; attached to Sts Cyril and Methodius Univ.; study of sociological, political and juridical phenomena; research; collaboration with instns and orgs engaged in research in sociology, political science and law; depts of information and documentation, political science, sociology; centres for ethnic relations, management and human resource devt, public policy and public admin., criminology, crime prevention and law enforcement policy, communication, media, and culture, human rights and nat. security, strategic studies; Dir JORDE JAKIMOVSKI.

TECHNOLOGY

Geološki Zavod (Geology Institute): POB 28, 1000 Skopje; f. 1944; geological mapping, exploration of mineral deposits, drilling, mining, grouting; 700 mems; library of 10,000 vols; Gen Dir DRAGAN ANGELESKY; publ. *Trudovi* (Transactions).

Research Centre for Energy, Informatics and Materials: Krste Misirkov 2, 1000 Skopje; tel. (2) 323-5400; fax (2) 323-5423; e-mail jpj@manu.edu.mk; internet www .manu.edu.mk/icei; f. 1986; attached to Macedonian Acad. of Sciences and Arts; initiates and coordinates nat. research programmes; conducts research; divs of energy, environment, materials and neuroinformatics; Dir Acad. JORDAN POP-JORDANOV.

Zavod za Ispituvanje na Materijali i Razvoj na novi Tehnologii (Institution for Research of Materials and Development of New Technologies): Rade Koncar 16, 1000 Skopje; tel. (2) 311-6610; fax (2) 321-1996; e-mail zimad@mt.net.mk; internet www.zim .com.mk; f. 1956, present status 2007; attached to Sts Cyril and Methodius Univ.; comprises 3 instns: Institute of Materials, Institute for Transport and Environment and Institute to Develop New Technologies; scientific research; publishing scientific achievements; Dir BORCE TANEVSKI.

Hidro Energo In'enering Skopje R. Makedonija (Hydro Energo Engineering DOO Skopje—Republic of Macedonia): Blvr Jane Sandanski 76, 1000 Skopje; tel. and fax (2) 245-4333; e-mail hei@hei.com.mk; internet www.hei.com.mk; f. 2008; design and devt of investment and technical documentation from the fields of hydro-technical engineering, hydro-energetics, hydro-informatics and geotechnical engineering; library of 1,800 vols; Dir Ing. METODI BOEV; Man. Dr Ing. KAEVSKI IVANCO; publ. *Vodostopanski problemi* (Water Development Problems, every 5 years).

Libraries and Archives

Bitola

Nacionalna Ustanova Univerzitetska Biblioteka 'Kliment Ohridski' (National Institution University Library 'St Kliment Ohridski'): Leninova 39, 7000 Bitola; tel. (47) 220-208; fax (47) 220-515; e-mail @nuub .mk; internet www.nuub.mk; f. 1945; 500,000 vols; Dir NAUME GORGIEVSKI; publ. *Library Trend* (1 a year).

Skopje

Biblioteka 'Braka Miladinovci' (City Library 'Braka Miladinovci'): Partizanski odredi 22, 1000 Skopje; tel. (2) 323-2544; fax (2) 312-7016; e-mail direktor@gbiblsk.edu .mk; internet www.gbiblsk.edu.mk; f. 1945 as City Library, present name 1963; 800,000 vols; 27 brs; Pres. PETRE M. ANDREEVSKI; Dir FILIP PETROVSKI (acting).

Državen Arhiv na Republika Makedonija (State Archives of the Republic of Macedonia): Gligor Prličev 3, 1000 Skopje; tel. (2) 311-5783; fax (2) 316-5944; e-mail arhiv@unet.com.mk; internet www.arhiv.gov .mk; f. 1951; 70m. documents; 9 regional depts: Skopje, Bitola, Prilep, Tetovo, Shtip, Strumica, Kumanovo, Ohrid and Veles; Dir Dr ZORAN TODOROVSKI; publ. *Makedonski archivist*.

Attached Departments:

Oddelenie Bitola (Department of Bitola): Blvr 1 Maj 55, 7000 Bitola; tel. (47) 241-740; f. 1954 as municipal archive, present status 1990; conservation, colln and printing of archive materials; 3,823 books, 163 magazines and 155 newspapers; Dir JOVAN KOCHANKOVSKY.

Oddelenie Kumanovo (Department of Kumanovo): Goce Delchev Str. 25, 1300 Kumanovo; tel. and fax (31) 420-464; f. 1954; 543 archive groups and 8 archival collns; documents on economics, sociology, culture and politics.

Oddelenie Ohrid (Department of Ohrid): Nikola Karev Str. 6, 6000 Ohrid; tel. and fax (46) 252-104; f. 1955, since 1990 as dept of Ohrid of the State Archives of the Republic of Macedonia; 3,000 vols; spec. collns: Old Church Slavonic MSS (14th–19th centuries), early Greek and Arabic books; 598 record groups and 17 archival collns; Dir DIMITAR SMILESKI.

Oddelenie Prilep (Department of Prilep): Aleksandar Makedonski Str. 134, 7500 Prilep; tel. (48) 424-192; fax (48) 424-334; f. 1955; jurisdiction over municipalities of Prilep, Dolneni, Krivogashtani, Krushevo, Zhitoshe, Makedonski Brod and Plasnica; 540 archive groups and 7 archival collns.

Oddelenie Skopje (Department of Skopje): Moskovska 1, 1000 Skopje; tel. and fax (2) 307-6461; f. 1952; 3,000 vols, 1.5 km of archive records, 333,152 units of published information, 675 record groups and 10 archival collns, 30,000 photographs from 1928 to 1983; Dir Dr MILOŠ KONSTANTINOV; publ. *Dokumenti i materiali za istorijata na Skopje* (irregular).

Oddelenie Stip (Department of Stip): Sane Georgiev Str. 35, 2000 Stip; tel. and fax (32) 391-337; f. 1956; jurisdiction over municipalities of Stip, Karbinci, Sveti Nikole, Lozovo, Probishtip, Kochani, Chreshinovo-Obleshevo, Zrnovci, Vinica, Delchevo, Makedonska Kamenica, Radovish and Konche; working with 275 archive owners; 523 record groups and 22 archival collns.

Oddelenie Strumica (Department of Strumica): 27 Mart Str. 2, 2400 Strumica; tel. and fax (34) 322-083; internet www .arhiv.gov.mk; f. 1956; jurisdiction over municipalities of Strumica, Berovo, Novo Selo, Pehchevo, Vasilevo and Bosilovo; working with 225 archive owners; 453 record groups and 8 archival collns.

Oddelenie Tetovo (Department of Tetovo): Cvetan Dimov Str. 1, 1220 Tetovo; tel. and fax (44) 332-209; f. 1961 as Historical Archives of the Municipalities of Tetovo and Gostivar; jurisdiction over municipalities of Gostivar, Tetovo, Brvenica, Bogovinje, Zhelino, Yegunovce, Tearce, Vrapchtishte, Mavrovi Anovi-Rostushe; working with 183 archive owners; 701 record groups and archival collns; colln of documents in Old Turkish from the Casa of Tetovo (1705–1924).

Oddelenie Veles (Department of Veles): Naum Naumovski, Borche Str., 1400 Veles; tel. and fax (43) 234-784; f. 1954 as Archiv na Veles (Archives of Veles); jurisdiction over municipalities of Veles, Chashka, Gradsko, Rosoman, Negotino, Kavadarci, Demir Kapiya, Valandovo, Gevgeliya, Bogdanci and Doyran; working with 267 archive owners; 538 record groups and 8 archival collns.

Nacionalna i univerzitetska biblioteka 'Sv. Kliment Ohridski' (National and University Library 'St Kliment Ohridski'): Blvr Goce Delčev 6, POB 566, 1000 Skopje; tel. (2) 311-5177; fax (2) 322-6846; e-mail kliment@ nubsk.edu.mk; internet www.nubsk.edu.mk; f. 1944; state copyright, central and deposit library; nat. centre for ISSN (international standard serial number) and nat. agency for ISBN (international standard book number), int. agency for ISMN (int. Standard music number), centre for int. landing of library materials, ECRIS – scholars and scientific workers in European CRIS database; 3m. vols, spec. collns: Slav MSS, incunabula and rare books, oriental, music, cartography, doctoral theses, fine art; Dir MILE BOSHESKI; publ. *Makedonska bibliografija* (in 3 series, each 4 a year).

Museums and Art Galleries

Bitola

NU Zavod i Muzej Bitola (NI Institute and Museum Bitola): ul. Kliment Ohridski bb, 7000 Bitola; tel. (47) 233-187; fax (47) 229-525; e-mail muzej@muzejbt.org.mk; internet www.muzejbt.org.mk; f. 1948 as The Museum of the town of Bitola, as the Art Gallery of Bitola 1958, given status nat. instn of culture 2003; archaeology, art, ethnology, history; library of 10,000 vols; Dir IVAN JOLEVSKI.

Kratovo

Centar za Karpesta umetnost, Kratovo (Centre of Rock Art, Kratovo): Planinska 1, 1360 Kratovo; tel. and fax (31) 481-572; e-mail lcfrockart@yahoo.com; internet www .rock-art.mk; f. 2004; protects rock engravings; exhibits artefacts and rock engravings; organizes scientific excursions, expeditions and lectures; field research; collns of engravings, 500 images, 12 documentaries, objects made from stones, bones, wood and pottery; handmade crafts; Pres. STEVCE DONEVSKI.

Ohrid

National Workshop for Handmade Paper 'St. Kliment Ohridski': Samoilova 60, 6000 Ohrid; tel. (46) 253-610; internet www.ohridpaper.com.mk; f. 2002; paper produced in original Chinese tradition of 2nd century BC; presents procedure of making paper, with knowledge of the history of paper and method of first printing on Gutenberg press (15th century).

Skopje

Muzej na Grad Skopje (Museum of Skopje): Mito Hadživasilev Jasmin bb, 1000 Skopje; tel. and fax (2) 311-5367; f. 1949; 21,950 exhibits incl. 12,000 archaeological, 2,965 historical, 5,010 ethnographic and 2,965 history of art exhibits and 182 photographs; Dir JOVAN SHURBANOVSKI; Sr Curator MILOS BILBIJA.

Muzej na Makedonija (Museum of Macedonia): ul. Curčiska bb, 1000 Skopje; tel. (2) 311-6044; fax (2) 311-6439; e-mail musmk@ mt.net.mk; internet www.musmk.org.mk; f. 1924; anthropology, archaeology, art history and conservation, history, ethnology; exhibits folk costumes, jewellery, traditional architecture, textiles, crafts, economy, customs and traditional musical instruments, fresco replicas, icons from 14th–19th centuries; library of 19,000 vols; Dir MARY ANICIN PEJOSKA; Programme Dir PERO JOSIFOVSKI; publs *Numizmatičar* (1 a year), *Zbornik* (Collected Papers, 1 a year).

Nacionalna Ustanova Muzej na Sovremena Umetnost vo Skopje (National Institution Museum of Contemporary Art Skopje): Samoilova bb, POB 482, 1000 Skopje; tel. (2) 311-7734; fax (2) 311-0123; e-mail msu-info@ msuskopje.org.mk; internet www.msuskopje .org.mk; f. 1964, present bldg 1970; depts of collections and exhibitions, education and conservation and restoration, research and documentation; organizes exhibitions and events of Macedonian and foreign art, discussions with artists, panels, film and video presentations and lectures; library of 20,000 titles (research and documentation dept); Dir ELIZA SULEVSKA; publs *Large Glass Magazine*, publs catalogues and monographs and spec. editions of *Psyce*, *Playtime*, *Macedonian Critic* and *Dossier MoCA Skopje*.

Prirodonaučen muzej na Makedonija (Macedonian Museum of Natural History): Blvr Ilinden 86, 1000 Skopje; tel. (2) 311-7669; fax (2) 311-6453; e-mail macmusnh@ unet.com.mk; f. 1926; collects, studies and exhibits natural resources of Macedonia; 4,000 original exhibits on display in glass showcases and dioramas; displays fossils that date back 8m.–10m. years; library of 44,000 vols; Dir Dr SVETOZAR PETKOVSKI; Curator GUTE MLADENOOVSKI; publs *Acta*, *Fauna na Makedonija*, *Fragmenta Balcanica*.

Umetnička Galerija (Art Gallery): Kruševska 1A, POB 278, 1000 Skopje; tel. (2) 323-3904; f. 1948; modern art; Dir VIKTORIJA VASEVA-DIMESKA.

Universities

DRŽAVNIOT UNIVERZITET VO TETOVO
(State University of Tetova)

Rruga e Ilindenit pn, 1200 Tetova

Telephone: (44) 356-500
Fax: (44) 334-222
E-mail: international@unite.edu.mk
Internet: www.unite.edu.mk

Founded 1994, officially recognized as State Univ. 2004
State control
Languages of instruction: Albanian, English, Macedonian

Rector: Prof. Dr AGRON REKA

Faculties of applied sciences, arts, business administration, economics, food technology, law, mathematics and natural sciences, medical sciences, philology, philosophy, physical education.

FON UNIVERZITET
(FON University)

Str. Vojvodina bb, 1000 Skopje

Telephone: (2) 244-5555
Fax: (2) 244-5550
E-mail: info@fon.edu.mk
Internet: www.fon.edu.mk

Founded 2003 as Faculty of Social Studies FON
Private control

Chancellor: Prof. Dr ALEKSANDAR NIKOLOVSKI
Vice-Chancellor for Science and Technology: Prof. Dr SIME ARSENOVSKI
Vice-Chancellor for Science and Technology: Prof. Dr BAJRAM POLOZANI
Vice-Chancellor for Studies: Prof. Dr RISTO MALCESKI
Pres.: FIJAT CANOSKI
Gen.-Sec.: BILJANA KAROVSKA-ANDONOVSKA

DEANS

Faculty of Applied European Languages: Prof. Dr ALEKSA POPOSKI

Faculty of Design and Multimedia: Assoc. Prof. ALEKSANDAR NOSPAL

Faculty for Detectives and Security: Prof. Dr ALEKSANDAR DONCEV

Faculty of Economics: Prof. Dr MIRKO TRIPUNOSKI

Faculty of Information and Communication Technology: Prof. Dr OLIVER ILIEV

Faculty of Law: Prof. Dr GJORGI TONOVSKI

Faculty of Politics and International Relations: Prof. Dr NANO RUZIN

Faculty of Sport and Sport Management: Prof. Dr VANGEL SIMEV

MEGUNARODEN BALKANSKI UNIVERZITET
(International Balkan University)

Samoilova 10, 1000 Skopje

Telephone: (2) 321-4831

Fax: (2) 321-4832

E-mail: info@ibu.edu.mk

Internet: www.ibu.edu.mk

Founded 2006

Private control

Rector: Prof. Dr HÜNER SENCAN

Vice-Rector: Prof. Dr MEHMET ZELKA, Prof. Dr ABDURAUF PRUTHI

Library of 3,000 (2,000 English, 1,000 Turkish) reference books

Faculties of communication, economics and administrative sciences, languages and fine arts, technical sciences.

UNIVERSITETI I EJL
(South East European University)

Ilindenska bb, 1200 Tetovo

Telephone: (44) 356-000

Fax: (44) 356-001

E-mail: t.selimi@seeu.edu.mk

Internet: www.seeu.edu.mk

Founded 2001

State control

Languages of instruction: Albanian, English

Academic year: August to June

Rector: Dr ALAJDIN ABAZI

Pro-Rector for Academic Issues: Prof. Dr ZAMIR DIKA

Pro-Rector for Finance Planning and Development: Prof. Dr ABDYLMENAF BEXHETI

Pro-Rector for Research and Quality Assurance: Prof. Dr MURTEZAN ISMAILI

Sec.-Gen: XHEVAIR MEMEDI

Library of 26,000 books, 11,350 titles

Number of teachers: 300

Number of students: 7,000

DEANS

Faculty of Business Administration: Prof. Dr IZET ZEQIRI

Faculty of Contemporary Sciences and Technologies: Dr BEKIM FETAJI (acting)

Faculty of Languages, Cultures and Communication: Prof. Dr VEBI BEXHETI

Faculty of Law: Prof. Dr ISMAIL ZENNELI

Faculty of Public Administration: Prof. Dr ETEM AZIRI

Faculty of Teacher Training: Dr TEUTA ARIFI

UNIVERZITET 'SV. KIRIL I METODIJ' VO SKOPJE
(Sts Cyril and Methodius University in Skopje)

Blvr Krste Misirkov bb, 1000 Skopje

Telephone: (2) 329-3293

Fax: (2) 329-3202

E-mail: ukim@ukim.edu.mk

Internet: www.ukim.edu.mk

Founded 1949

State control

Language of instruction: Macedonian

Academic year: September to May

Rector: Prof. Dr VELIMIR STOJKOVSKI

Vice-Rector for Finance, Investments and Devt: Prof. Dr PECE NEDANOVSKI

Vice-Rector for Int. Cooperation: Prof. Dr MOME SPASOVSKI

Vice-Rector for Teaching: Prof. Dr ELENA DUMOVA-JOVANOSKA

Vice-Rector for Science: Prof. Dr KOLE VASILEVSKI

Sec.-Gen.: ILIJA PIPERKOSKI

Number of teachers: 2,700

Number of students: 50,000

Publications: *Univerzitetski bilten, Univerzitetski vesnik i Studentski zbor*

DEANS

Faculty of Agricultural Sciences and Food: Prof. DRAGI DIMITRIEVSKI

Faculty of Architecture: Prof. Dr TIHOMIR STOJKOV

Faculty of Civil Engineering: Prof. Dr PETER CVETANOVSKI

Faculty of Dentistry: Prof. Dr ALEKSANDAR GRCEV

Faculty of Dramatic Arts: Prof. KIRIL RISTOSKI

Faculty of Economics: Prof. Dr LJUBOMIR KEKENOVSKI

Faculty of Education (Skopje): Prof. Dr NIKOLA PETROV

Faculty of Education (Stip): Prof. SPASKO SIMONOVSKI

Faculty of Electrical Engineering and Information Technologies: Prof. Dr MILE STANKOVSKI

Faculty of Fine Arts: Prof. DIMITAR MALIDANOV

Faculty of Forestry: Prof. Dr BRANKO RABADZISKI

Faculty of Law: Prof. Dr BORCE DAVITKOVSKI

Faculty of Mechanical Engineering: Prof. Dr ATANAS KOCOV

Faculty of Medicine: Prof. Dr NIKOLA JANKULOVSKI (acting)

Faculty of Mining and Geology: Prof. Dr TODOR DELIPETROV

Faculty of Music: Prof. Dr EVUSKA ELEZOVIC-TRPKOVA

Faculty of Natural and Mathematical Sciences: Prof. Dr DONE GERSHANOVSKI

Faculty of Pedagogy: Prof. Dr VLADO TIMOVSKI

Faculty of Pharmacy: Prof. Dr ALEKSANDAR DIMOVSKI

Faculty of Philology: Prof. Dr MAKSIM KARANFILOVSKI

Faculty of Philosophy: Prof. Dr GORAN AJDINSKI

Faculty of Physical Education: Prof. Dr GINO STREZOVSKI

Faculty of Technology and Metallurgy: Prof. Dr ALEKSANDAR DIMITROV

Faculty of Veterinary Medicine: Prof. Dr DINE MITROV

PROFESSORS

Faculty of Agricultural Sciences and Food (Blvr Aleksandar Makedonski bb, 1000 Skopje; tel. (2) 311-5277; fax (2) 313-4310; e-mail d.dimitrievski@fznh.ukim.edu.mk; internet www.fznh.ukim.edu.mk):

ANCEV, E.

AZDERSKI, J.

BELIČOVSKI, S.

BELKOVSKI, N.

BOZINOVIK, Z.

CUKALIEV, O.

DZABIRSKI, V.

EGUMENOVSKI, P.

GICEV, A.

GORGEVSKI, G.

GOŠEVSKI, D.

HADŽI PECOVA, S.

HRISTOV, P.

ILIK-POPOVA, S.

IVANOVSKI, P.

JANKULOVSKI, D.

MARINKOVIK, L.

MARTINOVSKI, G.

MIHAJLOVSKI, M.

MITRIKESKI, J.

NAUMOVSKI, M.

PEJKOVSKI, C.

PEŠEVSKI, M.

POSTOLOVSKI, M.

SIVAKOV, L.

STOJKOVSKI, C.

TANEVSKI, D.

USALESKI, V.

VASILEVSKI, G.

VIDOJA, T.

ZIBEROSKI, J.

ŽIVKO, D.

Faculty of Electrical Engineering and Information Technologies (Karpos II bb, 1000 Skopje; tel. (2) 306-2224; fax (2) 306-4262; e-mail dekan@feit.ukim.edu.mk; internet www.feit.ukim.edu.mk):

ACKOVSKI, R.

ARSENOV, A.

ARSOV, D.

ARSOV, G.

ARSOV, L.

BOGDANOVA, S.

CEKREDZI, N.

CUNDEV, M.

DAVCEV, D.

FILIPOSKI, V.

FUSTIC, V.

GAVRILOVSKA, L.

GAVROVSKI, C.

GEORGIEVA, V.

GLAMOCANIN, V.

GRCEV, L.

HANDZISKI, B.

JANEV, L.

KAMILOVSKI, M.

KARADZINOV, L.

KOCAREV, L.

KOCEV, K.

KOLEMISEVSKA-GUGULOVSKA, T.

KUJUMDZIEVA-NIKOLOSKA, M.

LAZOV, P.

LOSKOVSKA, S.

MIHAJLOV, S.

MIRCEVSKI, S.

NIKOLOVSKI, L.

PANOVSKI, L.

PIPEREVSKI, B.

POPOVSKI, B.

TALESKI, R.

TENTOV, A.

ULCAR STAVROVA, T.

ZLATANOVSKI, M.

Faculty of Forestry (Blvr Aleksandar Makedonski bb, 1000 Skopje; tel. (2) 316-5777; fax (2) 316-4560; e-mail sumarski@sf.ukim.edu.mk; internet www.sf.ukim.edu.mk):

DIMESKA, J.

DINA KOLEVSKI, D.

EFREMOVSKI, V.

MALETIKJ, V.

MANE, T.

NACEVSKA, M.

NACHESKI, S.

NIKOLOV, V.

RABADZHISKI, B.

RISTEVSKA, P.

RIZOVSKA ATANASOVSKI, J.

ROSE, A.

SIMAKOSKI, N.

TRAJKOV, P.

TRPOSKI, Z.

VASILEVSKI, K.

Faculty of Law (Blvr Krste Petkov Misirkov bb, 1000 Skopje; tel. (2) 311-7244; fax (2) 322-7549; e-mail dekan@pf.ukim.edu.mk; internet www.pf.ukim.edu.mk):

BAJALDZIEV, D.
BELICANEC, T.
DAVITKOVSKI, B.
FRCKOSKI, L.
GAVROSKA, P.
GEORGIEVSKI, S.
GRADISKI-LAZAREVSKA, E.
IVANOV, G.
JANEVSKI, A.
KALAMATIEV, T.
KAMBOVSKI, V.
KANDIKJAN, V.
KANEVCEV, M.
KLIMOVSKI, S.
MALESKI, D.
MANOLEVA-MITROVSKA, D.
MICAJKOV, M.
MUKOSKA-CINGO, V.
PENDOVSKA, V.
PETRUSEVSKA, T.
POLENAK-AKIMOVSKA, M.
POPOVSKA, B.
SILJANOVSKA-DAVKOVA, G.
STAROVA, G.
TODOROVA, S.
TUPURKOVSKI, V.
ZIVKOVSKA, R.

Faculty of Physical Education (ul. Zeleznicka bb, 1000 Skopje; tel. (2) 311-3654; fax (2) 311-9755; e-mail kontakt@ffk.ukim.edu.mk; internet www.ffk.ukim.edu.mk):

DZHAMBAZOVSKI, A.
IVANOV, D.
JOVANOVSKI, J.
NASTEVSKA, V.
NAUMOVSKI, A.
PETROVSKI, V.
RADIC, Z.
STREZOVSKI, G.
TUFEKCHIEVSKI, A.

UNIVERZITET 'SV. KLIMENT OHRIDSKI' BITOLA
(St Kliment Ohridski University of Bitola)

Blvr 1 Maj bb, 7000 Bitola
Telephone: (47) 223-788
Fax: (47) 223-594
E-mail: rektorat@uklo.edu.mk
Internet: www.uklo.edu.mk
Founded 1979
State control
Language of instruction: Macedonian
Rector: Prof. Dr ZLATKO ZHOGLEV
Vice-Rector for Academic Affairs: SASHO ATANASOSKI
Vice-Rector for Student Affairs: PERE ASLIMOSKI
Vice-Rector for Financial Issues and Devt: LUPCO TRPEZANOVSKI
Sec.-Gen.: OFELIJA HRISTOVKSA

Library of 160,000 vols, 500 periodicals, 1,000 microforms

Number of teachers: 337
Number of students: 11,644
Publication: *Scientific Review* (1 a year)

DEANS

Faculty of Administration and Management of Information Systems: Prof. Dr VIOLETA MANEVSKA

Faculty of Economics: Prof. Dr GORDANA TRAJKOSKA

Faculty of Education: Prof. Dr JOVE DIMITRI TALEVSKI

Faculty of Law: Prof. Dr ILIJA TODOROVSKI

Faculty of Technical Sciences: Dr. VESNA MIKAROVSKA

PROFESSORS

Faculty of Administration and Management of Information Systems (Partizanska bb (Kompleks Kasarni), 7000 Bitola; tel. (47) 259-921; fax (47) 259-917; internet famis.edu .mk):

PANOVSKA-BOSKOSKA V.

Faculty of Economics (Gorče Petrov bb, 7500 Prilep; tel. (48) 427-020; fax (48) 426-927; internet www.eccfp.edu.mk):

ATANASOSKI, S.
BASESCU-GJORGJIESKA, M.
DIMKOV, D.
GEORGIEVSKI, M.
ILIESKA, C.
JANESKA, M.
KOKAROSKI, D.
LASHKOSKA, V.
PECHIJARESKI, L.
RISTESKA, A.
ROCHESKA, S.
SOKOLOSKI, B.
SOTIROSKI, K.
STOJANOSKI, L.
TALESKA, S.
TRAJKOSKA, G.

Faculty of Education (ul. Vasko Karangelevski bb, 7000 Bitola; tel. (47) 253-652; fax (47) 203-385; e-mail contact@pfbt.uklo.edu .mk; internet www.pfbt.uklo.edu.mk):

ASLIMOVSKI, P.
GRUEVSKI, T.
KOLONDZHOVSKI, B.
METHODS, P.
RISTOVSKI, D.
SMILEVSKI, C.
STOILKOVA-KAVKALESKA, M.

Faculty of Law (ul. Prilepska bb, Bitola; tel. and fax (47) 221-115; e-mail pfk@uklo.edu .mk; internet www.pfk.uklo.edu.mk):

TODOROVSKI, E.

Faculty of Technical Sciences (I. L. Ribar bb, 7000 Bitola; tel. (47) 207-702; fax (47) 203-370; e-mail info.tfb@uklo.edu.mk; internet www.tfb.edu.mk):

ANDREEVSKA, A.
BOMBOL, C.
DESKOVSKI, S.
DONEVSKI, B.
EMS, I.
GERAMITCIOSKI, T.
JOLEVSKI, T.
KANEVCE, G.
KANEVCE, L.
KRSTANOSKI, N.
MIJAKOVSKI, E.
MIKAROVSKA, V.
PANOVSKI, S.
PAVLOV, V.
POPNIKOLOVA-RADEVSKA, M.
POPOVSKI, D.
POPOVSKI, K.
STOJANOVSKA, L.
TALEVSKI, J.
TRAJKOVSKI, D.
TROMBEV, G.
ZLATKOVSKI, S.

UNIVERZITET 'GOCE DELČEV' ŠTIP
(Goce Delcev University of Stip)

Krste Misirkov bb, POB 201, 2000 Stip
Telephone: (32) 550-000
Fax: (32) 390-700
E-mail: contact@ugd.edu.mk
Internet: www.ugd.edu.mk
Founded 2007
State control
Rector: Prof. Dr SASA MITREV
Vice Rector for Finance, Investments and Development: BORIS KRSTEV
Vice Rector for Science: BLAZO BOEV
Sec.-Gen.: RISTO KOSTURANOV
Library of 1,000 titles
Number of students: 5,000

Faculties of agriculture, computer science and information technology, economics, education, geosciences and technology, law, mechanical engineering and electrical engineering, medicine, mines, music, philology, technology, tourism and business logistics.

UNIVERZITET ZA TURIZAM I MENADŽMENT SKOPJE
(Skopje University of Tourism and Management)

ul. Partizanski Odredi br. 99, 1000 Skopje
Telephone: (2) 309-3209
Fax: (2) 309-3213
Internet: www.utms.edu.mk
Private control
Chancellor: Prof. Dr ACE MILENKOVSKI

Faculties of economy, entrepreneurial business, international marketing and management, management of human resources, public relations, sport tourism, tourism.

MADAGASCAR

The Higher Education System

In 1896 Madagascar came under French colonial rule and in 1958 it became an autonomous state (as the Malagasy Republic) within the French Community; full independence was achieved in 1960. The Université d'Antananarivo (founded 1961) is the oldest current institution of higher education; it was formed from a merger of pre-existing colleges. It was reorganized in 1976 as a decentralized institution and the six centres acquired the status of independent universities in 1988. The Ministry of National Education and Scientific Research has overall responsibility for higher education, which consists of universities, technical institutes and teacher training colleges. In 2005/06 there were six universities and 14 private institutions of higher education and in 2006/07 58,300 students were enrolled in tertiary education. The degree system (see below) is based upon the French cyclical model.

The Rector or President is the head of the University, governing in conjunction with Councils for administrative and academic affairs. The Administrative Council oversees the institutional budget, stipulates rules and regulations and ensures good governance. The Academic Council is responsible for matters of teaching and research.

The secondary school Baccalauréat is required for admission to university. The university degree system consists of three cycles. The first cycle lasts for two years after which a student receives one of two diplomas, either Diplôme Universitaire d'Etudes Littéraires or Diplôme Universitaire d'Etudes Scientifiques. Engineering students are awarded either the Diplôme Universitaire de Technicien Supérieur en Informatique or the Diplôme Universitaire d'Etudes Technologiques before studying for another two to three years for the Diplôme d'Ingénieur. Law students are awarded the Capacité en Droit after two years, and can then take the four-year Licence. The Doctorat de Médecine is a seven-year programme. The second cycle is a period of specialization of either one year, resulting in award of the Licence (undergraduate degree), or two years, resulting in award of the Maîtrise (postgraduate degree). Following the Maîtrise, the third cycle is a two-year period of study leading to the award of the Diplôme d'Etudes Supérieures, followed by research and thesis for the degree of Doctorat de Troisième Cycle.

The main post-secondary qualification for technical and vocational education is the Brevet de Technicien, awarded after three years' study at technical institutes.

Regulatory and Representative Bodies

GOVERNMENT

Ministry of National Education and Scientific Research: BP 247, Anosy, Antananarivo 101; tel. (20) 22-243-08; fax (20) 22-238-97; e-mail mlraharimalala@yahoo.fr; internet 196.192.32.105/menrs; Minister ANDRIAMPARANY BENJAMIN RADAVIDSON.

Ministry of Sports, Culture and Leisure: Ambohijatovo, pl. Goulette, BP 681, Antananarivo 101; tel. (20) 22-277-80; fax (20) 22-342-75; e-mail mjs_101@yahoo.fr; internet www.mjs.gov.mg; Minister PATRICK RAMIARAMANANA.

NATIONAL BODY

Maison de la Communication des Universités (Universities' Communication Centre): Immeuble Ex-Super bazar Analakely, 28 rue Andrianampoinimerina, Antananarivo; tel. (20) 22-636-19; e-mail contact@mcumadagascar.org; internet enduma.africa-web.org; f. 1993; acts as an intermediary between the univs and public life; 12 mems; Pres. of Admin. Council ARMAND RASOAMIARAMANANA; Gen. Dir MICHEL NORBERT REJELA.

Learned Societies

GENERAL

Académie Nationale Malgache: BP 6217, Tsimbazaza, Antananarivo; f. 1902; studies in human and natural sciences; four sections: language, literature and arts, moral and political sciences, basic sciences, applied sciences; 140 mems, 60 foreign mems in each section; library of 100,000 vols; Pres. Dr C. RABENORO; publs *Bulletin de l'Académie* (1 a year), *Bulletin d'Information et de Liaison*, *Mémoires*.

BIBLIOGRAPHY, LIBRARY SCIENCE AND MUSEOLOGY

Association des Bibliothécaires, Documentalistes, Archivistes et Muséographes de Madagascar: Bibliothèque Nationale, BP 257, Antananarivo; tel. (20) 22-258-72; f. 1976; promotion, development, preservation and conservation of national collections; Pres CHRISTIANE ANDRIAMIRADO; Secs SAMOELA ANDRIANKOTONIRINA, FRANÇOISE RAMANANDRAISOA; publ. *Haren-tsaina* (2 a year).

LANGUAGE AND LITERATURE

Alliance Française: Ambavamamba 101, BP 916 Antananarivo; tel. (20) 22-232-63; fax (20) 22-225-04; e-mail webmaster@alliancefr.mg; internet www.alliancefr.mg; offers courses and exams in French language and culture and promotes cultural exchange with France; attached teaching centres in Ambanja, Ambatondrazaka, Ambilobe, Ambositra, Ambovombe, Andapa, Antalaha, Antananarivo, Antsahabe, Antsalova, Antsirabé, Antsiranana, Antsohihy, Fandriana, Farafangana, Fianarantsoa, Fort Dauphin, Mahajanga, Maintirano, Manakara, Mananjary, Moramanga, Morombe, Morondava, Nosy Be, Sainte Marie, Sambava, Toamasina, Tolagnaro, Toliara, Tsiroanomandidy, and Vohemar; Dir of Operations HERVÉ LE PORZ.

British Council: see chapter on Mauritius.

Research Institutes

GENERAL

Institut de Recherche pour le Développement (IRD): BP 434, Antananarivo 101; tel. (20) 22-330-98; fax (20) 22-369-82; e-mail irdmada@ird.mg; internet www.ird.mg; research into economics, statistics, fisheries, environment, health, deforestation, biodiversity and water; library of 200 vols; Dir CHRISTIAN FELLER; (see main entry under France).

AGRICULTURE, FISHERIES AND VETERINARY SCIENCE

Centre National de Recherche Appliquée au Développement Rural (CENRADERU): BP 1690, Antananarivo; f. 1994; research into agriculture, forestry and fisheries, zoology, veterinary studies and rural economy; publ. *Rapport d'activité* (1 a year).

Attached Institute:

CENRADERU—IRCT: BP 227, Mahajanga; research on cotton and other fibres; main research station at Toliary; regional station at Tanandava; sisal research at Mandrare.

Centre Technique Forestier Tropical: BP 745, Antananarivo; f. 1961; silviculture, genetics, soil conservation; Dir J. P. BOUILLET; (see main entry under France).

Département de Recherches Agronomiques de la République Malgache: Centre National de la Recherche Appliquée au Développement Rural (FOFIFA), BP 1444 Ambatobe, Antananarivo 101; tel. (20) 225-2707; e-mail rag@fofifa.mg; internet www.fofifa.mg; stations at Alaotra, Antalaha, Ambanja, Ambovombe, Ivoloina, Mahajanga, Fianarantsoa, Ilaka Est, Kianjavato, Kianjasoa, Tanandava; Dept Chief LÉA RANDRIAMBOLANORO.

Institut d'Elevage et de Médecine Vétérinaire des Pays Tropicaux: Antananarivo; central laboratory, research stations at Kianjasoa and Miadana; (see main entry under France).

Institut de Recherches Agronomiques Tropicales (IRAT): 4 rue Rapiera, Anjohy, BP 853, Antananarivo; tel. (20) 22-271-82; attached to Centre de Co-operation Internationale en Recherche Agronomique pour le Développement (CIRAD).

HISTORY, GEOGRAPHY AND ARCHAEOLOGY

Institut Géographique et Hydrographique National: Rue Dama-Ntsoha, Ambanidia, BP 323, Antananarivo 101; tel. (20) 22-229-35; fax (20) 22-252-64; e-mail ftm@moov.mg; internet www.ftm.mg; f. 1945; Dir ANDRIANJAFIMBELO RAZAFINAKANGA.

NATURAL SCIENCES

Biological Sciences

Institut Pasteur: BP 1274, Antananarivo 101; tel. (20) 22-412-72; fax (20) 22-415-34; e-mail ipm@pasteur.mg; internet www.pasteur.mg; f. 1898; biological research; library of 6,200 vols; Dir Dr MAUCLÈRE; publ. *Archives* (2 a year).

Physical Sciences

Institute and Observatory of Geophysics at Antananarivo: University of Antananarivo (Rectorate), Antananarivo 101; tel. and fax (20) 22-253-53; f. 1889, affiliated to the Univ. 1967; study of seismology, geomagnetism, applied geophysics, exploration geophysics, time service, meteorological and astronomical observation; library of 3,000 vols, 800 periodicals; Dir J. B. RATSIMBAZAFY; publs *Bulletin Magnetique* (13 a year), *Bulletin Météorologique* (12 a year), *Bulletin Sismique* (1 a year), *Mada–Geo* (4 a year).

Service Géologique: BP 322, Antananarivo 101; tel. (20) 22-400-48; fax (20) 22-418-73; internet www.cite.mg/mine; f. 1926; library of 3,000 vols; Dir A. RANANDARIVELO; publs *Annales géologiques, Atlas des fossiles caractéristiques de Madagascar, Documentation du Service Géologique, Travaux du Bureau Géologique*.

TECHNOLOGY

Bureau de Recherches Géologiques et Minières (BRGM): BP 458, Antananarivo; Dir G. BOURNAT; (see main entry under France).

Libraries and Archives

Antananarivo

Archives Nationales: BP 3384, Antananarivo; tel. and fax (20) 22-235-34; e-mail rijandriamihamina@malagasy.com; f. 1958; historical library of 30,000 vols; Dir SAHONDRA ANDRIAMIHAMINA.

Bibliothèque Municipale: Ave du 18 juin, Antananarivo; f. 1961; 22,600 vols.

Bibliothèque Nationale: Anosy, BP 257, Antananarivo; tel. (20) 22-258-72; fax (20) 22-294-48; f. 1961; 236,800 books, 2,660 periodicals, 2,912 MSS, 2,600 maps; special collections: history, literature, the arts, applied sciences, information on Madagascar; Dir L. RALAISAHOLIMANANA; publ. *Bibliographie Nationale de Madagascar* (1 a year).

Bibliothèque Universitaire d'Antananarivo: Campus Universitaire Ambohitsaina, BP 908, Antananarivo 101; tel. (20) 22-612-28; fax (20) 22-612-29; e-mail bu@univ-antananarivo.mg; internet www.bu.univ-antananarivo.mg; f. 1960; spec. MSS colln: Madagascar and Indian Ocean; 310,451 vols; Dir JEAN-MARIE ANDRIANIAINA; publ. *Bibliographie Annuelle de Madagascar* (madarevues.recherches.gov.mg).

Médiathèque du Centre Culturel 'Albert Camus': 14 ave de l'Indépendance, BP 488, Antananarivo 101; tel. (20) 22-236-47; fax (20) 22-213-38; e-mail mediatheque@ccac.mg; internet www.ccac.mg; f. 1964; 32,140 vols, 35 periodicals, 418 CD-ROMs, 2704 CDs, 4451 video cassettes and DVDs; 5,527 mems;

Dir ALAIN MONTEIL; Librarian CHRISTIANE LAROCCA.

Antsirabé

Bibliothèque Municipale: Antsirabé; tel. 44-484-57; f. 1952; 2,700 vols; Librarian ALBERT DENIS RAKOTO.

Museums and Art Galleries

Antananarivo

Institut de Civilisations/Musée d'Art et d'Archéologie Université d'Antananarivo: Isoraka, 17 rue Dr Villette, BP 564, Antananarivo 101; tel. 2422165; e-mail vohitra@refer.mg; f. 1970; attached to Institut de Civilisations; art, archaeology and social sciences; library of 2,000 vols; Dir Dr RADIMILAHY CHANTAL; publs *Taloha* (1 a year), *Travaux et Documents* (irregular).

Musée Historique et Ethnographique: Palais Andafiavaratra, Rue Pasteur Ravelojaona, Antananarivo; tel. (20) 22-200-91; f. 1897; history and arts; Curator JEAN CLAUDE ANDRIANIMANANA.

Universities

UNIVERSITÉ D'ANTANANARIVO

Campus Universitaire Ambohitsaina, BP 566, 101 Antananarivo

Telephone: (20) 22-326-39

Fax: (20) 22-279-26

Internet: www.univ-antananarivo.mg

Founded 1961

Public control

Language of instruction: French

Academic year: March to November

Rector: ABEL ANDRIANTSIMAHAVANDY

Vice-Rector: BAKOLINIRINA ANDRIAMIHAJA

Vice-Rector: JEAN-JULES HARIJAONA

Vice-Rector: Dr JEAN ERIC RAKOTOARISOA

Library: see Libraries and Archives

Number of teachers: 739

Number of students: 27,000

DEANS

Agriculture: JEAN RASOARAHONA

Higher Normal School: JEAN CLAUDE OMER ANDRIANARIMANANA

Polytechnic: PHILIPPE ANDRIANARY

Sciences: Dr BRUNO ANDRIANANTENAINA

UNIVERSITÉ DE FIANARANTSOA

BP 1264, 301 Fianarantsoa

Telephone: (20) 75-508-02

Fax: (20) 75-506-19

E-mail: ufianara@syfed.refer.mg

Internet: www.misa.mg/univ

Founded 1988

State control

Language of instruction: French

Academic year: November to July

Rector: MARIE DIEUDONNÉ MICHEL RAZAFINDRANDRIATSIMANIRY

Administrative and Financial Dir: DOMINIQUE RAZAFIMANAMPY

Dir of Studies and Research: RIVO RAKOTOZAFY

Librarian: BRUNO JEAN ROMUALD RANDRIAMORA

Number of teachers: 63

Number of students: 1,836

DEANS

Faculty of Law: PATRICE GOUSSOT

Faculty of Sciences: TSILAVO MANDRESY RAZAFINDRAZAKA

École Nationale d'Informatique: JOSVAH PAUL RAZFIMANDIMBY

École Normale Supérieure: ROGER RATOVONJANAHARY

Institut des Sciences et Techniques de l'Environnement: PASCAL RATALATA

UNIVERSITÉ DE MAHAJANGA

BP 652, 401 Mahajanga

Telephone: (20) 62-908-34

Fax: (20) 62-233-12

Founded 1977

State control

Language of instruction: French

Academic year: March to October

Rector: Prof. ANTOINE ZAFERA RABESA

Registrar: DIANA VOAHANGINIRINA RAHARINIAINA

Librarian: JUSTINE RAZANAMANITRA

Library of 8,054 vols

Number of teachers: 83 full-time

Number of students: 2,129

Publication: *JSPM* (2 a year)

DEANS

Faculty of Dentistry and Stomatology: HENRI MARTIAL RANDRIANARIMANANA

Faculty of Medicine: LISY RAVOLAMANANA

Faculty of Natural Sciences: JOHNSON CHRISTIAN MILADERA

UNIVERSITÉ NORD MADAGASCAR

BP 0, 201 Antsiranana

Telephone: (20) 82-29-409

Fax: (20) 82-29-409

E-mail: unm@dts.mg

Founded 1976

State control

Academic year: January to September

President: CÉCILE MARIE ANGE MANOROHANTA-DOMINIQUE

Administrative Director: ALY AHMAD

Librarian: VIRGINIE MILISON

Number of teachers: 97 (64 permanent, 33 temporary)

Number of students: 826

DEANS

Faculty of Arts and Humanities: (vacant)

Faculty of Science: JEAN VICTOR RANDRIANOHAVY

DIRECTORS

Ecole Normale Supérieure pour l'Enseignement Technique: ANDRÉ TOTOHASIN

Ecole Supérieur Polytechnique: MAX ANDRIANANTENAINA

UNIVERSITÉ DE TOAMASINA

BP 591, Toamasina

Telephone: (20) 53-322-44

Fax: (20) 53-335-66

Internet: www.univ-toamasina.mg

Founded 1977 as Centre Universitaire Régional de Toamasina, present status 1988

State control

Language of instruction: French

Rector: ROGER RAJAONARIVELO

Secretary-General: ANDRÉ BIAS RAMILAMANANA

Librarian: ELIANE JOSÉPHINE RENÉ

Number of teachers: 54

Number of students: 3,391

DEANS

School of Arts and Research: ABRAHAM LATSAKA

School of Economics and Management: SETH ARSÈNE RATOVOSON

UNIVERSITÉ DE TOLIARA

BP 185, Maninday, Toliara 601

Telephone: (20) 94-410-33

Fax: (20) 94-443-07

E-mail: presidence@univ-toliara.mg

Internet: www.univ-toliara.mg

Founded 1977 as Regional Centre of Université de Madagascar; independent university status 1988

State Control

Languages of instruction: French, Malagasy

Academic year: November to July

Rector: M. THEODORET

Library of 8,000 vols

DEANS

Faculty of Arts and Humanities: MARC JOSEPH RAZAFINDRAKOTO

Faculty of Science: HERY ANTENAINA RAZAFIMANDIBY

Ecole Normale Supérieure: JEAN RAKOTOARIVELO

Colleges

Collège Rural d'Ambatobe: BP 1629, Antananarivo; Dir M. ROGER RAJOELISOLO.

Institut National des Sciences Comptables et de l'Administration d'Entreprises: Maison des Produits, 67 Ha, BP 946, Antananarivo 101; tel. (20) 22-660-65; fax (20) 22-308-95; e-mail drinscae@simicro.mg; f. 1986; 4-year courses and in-service training in accountancy, management and banking; library: 17,230 vols, 24 periodicals; 24 teachers; 1,051 students (325 full-time, 726 in-service); Dir-Gen. VICTOR HARISON.

Institut National des Sciences et Techniques Nucléaires: BP 4279, Antananarivo 01; tel. (20) 22-611-81; fax (20) 22-355-83; e-mail instn@dts.mg; internet www.geocities .com/mada_instn; f. 1976 as laboratory; institute status 1992; depts of Dosimetry and Radiation Protection, X-Ray Fluorescence Techniques and Environment, Nuclear Techniques and Analysis, Theoretical Physics, Instrumentation and Maintenance, Computer Science and Renewable Energies; Dir RAOELINA ANDRIAMBOLOLONA; publ. *Journal des Sciences et Techniques Nucléaires*.

Institut National des Télécommunications et des Postes: Antanetibe, 101 Antananarivo; f. 1968; 200 students.

MALAWI

The Higher Education System

The former British protectorate of Nyasaland gained independence, as Malawi, in 1964 and became a republic in 1966. Higher education consists of two state universities, the University of Malawi (founded 1964) and the Mzuzu University (founded 1999).

The University of Malawi has a federal structure, consisting of five colleges, each headed by a Principal, assisted by a Vice-Principal, Registrar and Deans of Faculty. The Head of State is the Chancellor of the University, and the Vice-Chancellor is the senior governing officer, overseeing the day-to-day running of the institution. The Chancellor is guided by the University Council, the University policy-making body. Although there are no concrete plans at present, in due course the University may devolve with the five constituent colleges becoming universities in their own right. There were 6,458 students in further and higher education in 2006/07. Some students attend institutions in the United Kingdom and the USA. The Ministry of Educa-

tion and Vocational Training is responsible for providing higher education.

Admission to university is mainly on the basis of the Malawi School Certificate of Education, but O-Levels and the Cambridge Overseas Higher School Certificate are also accepted. The colleges of the University of Malawi offer three-year Diploma courses, and the main undergraduate degree is the Bachelors, which lasts either four years for the Bachelors (General) or five to six years for the Bachelors (Honours). On completion of the Bachelors postgraduates can study for one to two years for the Masters. The final university-level degree is the PhD, lasting three to five years.

The National Apprenticeships Scheme is the principal form of post-secondary technical and vocational education. Programmes last for four years and are offered in a number of professional fields. The main qualifications are the Craft Certificate and Trade Test Certificate.

Regulatory Body

GOVERNMENT

Ministry of Education and Vocational Training: Private Bag 328, Capital City, Lilongwe 3; tel. (1) 789422; fax (1) 788064; e-mail secretaryforeducation@sdnp.org.mw; internet www.malawi.gov.mw; Minister ANNA KACHIKHO.

Learned Societies

GENERAL

Society of Malawi: POB 125, Blantyre; tel. (1) 872617; e-mail info@societyofmalawi.org; internet www.societyofmalawi.org; f. 1946; study and records of history and natural sciences; 250 mems; library of 3,000 vols, 2,000 periodicals, 5,000 photographs; Chair. CARL BRUESSOW; Hon. Sec. MIKE BAMFORD; publ. *Journal* (2 a year).

BIBLIOGRAPHY, LIBRARY SCIENCE AND MUSEOLOGY

Malawi Library Association: POB 429, Zomba; tel. (1) 524265; fax (1) 525225; e-mail fkachala@sobomw.com; f. 1976; trains library assistants, provides professional advice, holds seminars and workshops; 340 mems; Pres. GEOFFREY F. SALANJE; Sec.-Gen. FRANCIS F. C. KACHALA; publs *MALA Bulletin* (1 a year), *MALA Trends* (every 2 years), *MALA Update*.

LANGUAGE AND LITERATURE

British Council: Plot no. 13/20 City Centre, POB 30222, Lilongwe 3; tel. (1) 773244; fax (1) 772945; e-mail info@britishcouncil.org.mw; internet www.britishcouncil.org/malawi; offers courses and exams in English language and British culture and promotes cultural exchange with the UK; library of 5,991 vols; Dir MARC JESSEL.

MEDICINE

Medical Association of Malawi: Private Bag 360, Chichiri, Blantyre 3; tel. (1) 630333; fax (1) 631353; f. 1967; 265 mems; 100 assoc.

mems; Chair. Dr B. MWALE; Sec. Dr E. MTITIMILA; publ. *Malawi Medical Journal*.

Research Institutes

AGRICULTURE, FISHERIES AND VETERINARY SCIENCE

Agricultural Research and Extension Trust: PMB 9, Lilongwe; tel. (1) 761148; fax (1) 761615; e-mail iphiri@aret.org.mw; f. 1995; attached to Tobacco Asscn of Malawi; applied research on improvement of burley, flue-cured and fire-cured tobacco in Malawi; Dir Dr IBRAHIM PHIRI; publs *Coresta Bulletin* (4 a year), *Tobacco Science*.

Baka Agricultural Research Station: POB 97, Karonga; f. 1974; attached to Min. of Agriculture; applied research on the general agronomy of the Karonga and Chitipa regions.

Bvumbwe Agricultural Research Station: POB 5748, Limbe; tel. (1) 662206; f. 1940; attached to Min. of Agriculture; conducts applied research into tree and horticultural crops, especially tung, macadamia, cashew, vegetables, spices, coffee, mushrooms, roots and tubers, and the general agronomy of the Southern uplands; Head N. NSANJAMA.

Central Veterinary Laboratory: POB 527, Lilongwe; tel. (1) 766341; fax (1) 766010; e-mail dahi.cvl@malawi.net; f. 1974; attached to Min. of Agriculture; research into endemic diseases.

Chitala Agricultural Research Station: Private Bag 13, Salima; e-mail agric-research@sdnp.org.mw; f. 1978; attached to Min. of Agriculture; part of Lakeshore Rural Development Programme; conducts research on cereals, cotton, groundnuts, mango, roots and tubers, livestock; Station Man. L. R. NTUANA.

Chitedze Agricultural Research Station: POB 158, Lilongwe; tel. (1) 773252; fax (1) 773184; e-mail icrisat-malawi@cgiar.com; f. 1948; attached to Min. of Agriculture; conducts applied research into cereals, grain legumes, oil seeds, pasture and the general agronomy of the Central Region and into

livestock improvement, especially of local Zebu cattle; library of 10,000 vols, 300 periodicals; Head Dr P. SIBALE.

Fisheries Research Station: POB 27, Monkey Bay; tel. (1) 587360; fax (1) 587249; f. 1954; attached to Min. of Agriculture and Food Security; research into fisheries of Lake Malawi; social economic surveys; Chief Fisheries Research Officer Dr M. C. BANDRA; publs *Fisheries Bulletin* (12 a year), *Survey Reports* (4 a year), *Technical Reports* (12 a year).

Forest Research Institute of Malawi: POB 270, Zomba; attached to Min. of Forestry and Natural Resources; research into silviculture, tree breeding, pathology, entomology, soils, mycorrhizae and wood products.

Kasinthula Agricultural Research Station: POB 28, Chikwawa; tel. (1) 423207; e-mail agric-research@sdnp.org.mw; f. 1976; attached to Min. of Agriculture; irrigation research; Officer in Charge JULIAN W. MCHOWA.

Lifuwu Agricultural Research Station: POB 102, Salima; tel. (0) 9145004; fax (0) 1707374; e-mail lifuwu@malawi.net; 50 mems; f. 1973; attached to Dept of Agricultural Research Services; rice research; Asst Dir. T. R. MZENGEZA.

Lunyangwa Agricultural Research Station: POB 59, Mzuzu; tel. (1) 332633; f. 1968; attached to Min. of Agriculture; conducts applied research into the general agronomy of the Northern Region, specializing in rice, coffee, tea, cassava, pasture work, and tropical fruits at its Mkondezi sub station; Head Dr A. LOWOLE.

Makoka Agricultural Research Station: Private Bag 3, Thondwe; tel. (881) 198635; e-mail entomology@broadbandmw.com; f. 1967; research into cotton, cassava, sweet potato, maize, groundnuts, soya beans, pigeon peas, cowpeas, sunflowers, sorghum and rice; agroforestry species and domestication of wild fruits; library of 1,600 vols; Head KETULO SALIPIRA; Deputy Head ROSE MKANDAWIRE; publs *Makoka Agricultural Research Station*, *Malawi Journal of Agricultural Sciences*, *Report*.

Mbawa Agricultural Research Station: POB 8, Embangweni; tel. (1) 342362; fax (1) 332687; e-mail agric-research@sdnp.org.mw; internet www.agricresearch.gov.mw; f. 1936; attached to Dept of Agricultural Research Services, Min. of Agriculture; applied research into livestock, cereals, grain legumes and technology transfer initiatives; publs *Quarterly Report, Station Guide* (1 a year).

Mikolongwe Livestock Improvement Centre: POB 5193, Limbe; f. 1955; attached to Min. of Agriculture; seeks to improve productive capacity of local Zebu cattle and fat-tailed sheep; the station also contains the Poultry Improvement Unit and the Veterinary Staff training school.

Mwimba Tobacco Research Station: POB 224, Kasungu; f. 1979; attached to Min. of Agriculture; applied research on improvement and production of flue-cured and oriental tobacco in Malawi.

Tea Research Foundation (Central Africa): POB 51, Mulanje; tel. (1) 467277; fax (1) 467209; e-mail trfca@africa-online.net; f. 1966; conducts research on the genetic improvement of tea and associated agronomic research and training for the tea industry in southern Africa; Dir Dr A. S. KUMWENDA.

NATURAL SCIENCES

Physical Sciences

Geological Survey of Malawi: POB 27, Zomba; tel. (1) 524166; fax (1) 524716; e-mail geomalawi@chirunga.sdnp.org.mw; f. 1921; attached to Ministry of Mines, Natural Resources and Environmental Affairs; geological mapping and surveys; mineral investigation, engineering, geology, geophysics, drilling, seismology; library of 5,000 vols; Dir C. E. KAPHWIYO; publ. *Bulletin.*

Libraries and Archives

Lilongwe

Malawi National Library Service: POB 30314, Lilongwe 3; tel. (1) 773700; fax (1) 771616; e-mail gnyali@nlsmw.org; f. 1968; provides public library services; publishes children's books; 1,000,000 vols; Nat. Librarian G. L. NYALI; publ. *Accessions Bulletin.*

Zomba

National Archives of Malawi: Mkulichi Rd, POB 62, Zomba; tel. and fax (1) 525240; e-mail archives@sdnp.org.mw; internet chambo.sdnp.org.mw/ruleoflaw/archives; f. 1947 as br. of Central African Archives, became Nat. Archives of Malawi 1964; public archives, records management, historical MSS, legal deposit library, films, tapes, microfilms, gramophone records, philatelic colln, maps, and plans; nat. ISBN agency; 30,000 vols, 240 periodicals; Dir PAUL LIHOMA; Librarian STANLEY S. GONDWE; publ. *Malawi National Bibliography* (1 a year).

University of Malawi Libraries: POB 280, Zomba; tel. (1) 524222; fax (1) 525239; e-mail dbvphiri@chanco.unima.mw; f. 1965; 450,000 vols; Librarian D. B. VUWA PHIRI.

Museums

Blantyre

Museums of Malawi: POB 30360, Chichiri, Blantyre 3; tel. (1) 672438; fax (1) 676615; e-mail museums@malawi.net; f. 1959; Dir of Museums Dr M. E. D. NHLANE.

Universities

UNIVERSITY OF MALAWI

POB 278, Zomba
Telephone: (1) 524282
Fax: (1) 524760
E-mail: uniregistrar@usdnp.org.mw
Internet: www.unima.mw

Founded 1964
Language of instruction: English
State control
Academic year: June to September
Number of teachers: 710
Number of students: 5,400

Chancellor: THE PRESIDENT OF MALAWI
Vice-Chancellor: Dr E. FABIANO
Registrar: BEN WOKOMAATANI MALUNGA
Librarian: F. G. HOUSE (acting)

Publications: *Journal of Humanities, Journal of Social Science, Malawi Journal of Science and Technology, Research Report to Senate.*

CONSTITUENT INSTITUTES

Bunda College of Agriculture: POB 219, Lilongwe; tel. (1) 277226; fax (1) 277364; library of 50,000 vols; 131 teachers; 681 students; Principal Prof. M. B. KWAPATE; Registrar M. CHIMOYO

DEANS

Faculty of Agriculture: Dr M. MTITILODGE
Faculty of Development Studies: Dr S. KHAILA
Faculty of Environmental Science: Dr G. MATIYA
Postgraduate Studies: Dr A. A. KALIMBIRA

PROFESSORS

KAMWANJA, L. A., Animal Science
KWAPATA, M. B., Forestry and Horticulture
MTIMUNI, J. P., Animal Science
PHOYA, R. K. D., Animal Science
SAKA, V. W., Crop Science
MUMBA, P. P. E., Basic Sciences
NG'ONG'OLA, D. H., Agriculture and Applied Economics
MSUKU, W. A. B., Crop Science
EDRISS, A. K., Agriculture and Applied Economics
KANYAMA-PHIRI, G.Y., Crop Sciences

Chancellor College: POB 280, Zomba; tel. (1) 524222; fax (1) 524046; library of 300,000 vols; 250 teachers; 1,812 students; Principal Prof. C KUMLONGERA; Registrar U JEDEGWA

DEANS

Faculty of Education: Dr MERCY KATZUMI-KUZINDO
Faculty of Humanities: Prof. B. WEDI KUMANGA
Faculty of Law: Dr P. G. KANYONGOLO
Faculty of Science: Dr L. KAZEMBTA
Faculty of Social Science: Dr L. MALEKANO
Postgraduate Studies: Prof. K. PHIRI

PROFESSORS

CHIRWA, W. C., History
Prof. MTENJE, A., African Languages
KALUWA, B. M., Economics
KISHINDO, P. A. K., Sociology
PHIRI, K. M., History
SAKA, J. D. K., Chemistry
ULEDI-KAMANGA, B. J., English
Prof. MOTO, F. B., African Languages
Prof. DZIMBIN, L. B., Political Science

College of Medicine: PB 360, Chichiri, Blantyre 3; tel. (1) 671911; fax (1) 674700; e-mail registrar@admin.medicol.mw; library of 18,000 vols; 87 teachers; 169 students; Principal Prof. ROBIN BROADHEAD; Registrar C. TRIGU-LEMANI

DEANS

Faculty of Medicine: Prof. J. E. CHISI
Postgraduate Studies: Prof. E. BERGSTEIN

PROFESSORS

Prof. BORYSTEIN, E. S., Surgery
BROADHEAD, R. L., Paediatrics
KOMOLAFE, O. O., Microbiology
LIOMBA, G. N., Pathology
MADUAGWU, E. N., Biochemistry
MOLYNEUX, M. E., Paediatrics
MSAMATI, B. C., Anatomy
MUKIIBI, J. M., Haematology
ZIJLSTRA, E. E., Medicine

Kamuzu College of Nursing: PB 1, Lilongwe; tel. (1) 751622; fax (1) 756424; library of 24,000 ; 66 teachers; 300 students; Principal Dr ADDRESS MALUTA; Registrar MARY WASIN

DEANS

Faculty of Nursing: E. B. CHILEMBA
Postgraduate Studies: C. KAPONDA

Malawi Polytechnic: PB 303, Chichiri, Blantyre 3; tel. (1) 670411; fax (1) 670578; library of 38,745 vols; 176 teachers; 2,549 students; Principal Y. A. ALIDE (acting); Registrar A. KUMWENDA

DEANS

Faculty of Applied Sciences: A. MADHLOPA
Faculty of Commerce: B. T. NJOBVU
Faculty of Education and Media Studies: G. MANGANDA
Faculty of Engineering: N. T. BEN
Postgraduate Studies: F. GOMILE CLU-DYAONGA

MZUZU UNIVERSITY

Private Bag 201, Luwinga, Mzuzu 2
Telephone: (1) 320575
Fax: (1) 320568
E-mail: registrar@mzuni.ac.mw
Founded 1999
State control

Chancellor: THE PRES. OF MALAWI
Vice-Chancellor: Prof. LANDSON MHANGO
Deputy Vice-Chancellor: Prof. ORTON MSISKA
Registrar: REGINALD MUSHANI
Librarian: Prof. JOSEPH UTA

Library of 27,000 vols, 250 periodicals
Number of teachers: 132
Number of students: 1,350

DEANS

Faculty of Education: GOLDEN MSILIMBA
Faculty of Environmental Sciences: JARRET MHANGO
Faculty of Information Science and Communication: Prof. JOSEPH J. UTA
Faculty of Health Sciences: Prof. YOHANE NYASULU
Faculty of Tourism and Hospitality Management: BRIGHT M.C. NYIRENDA

MALAYSIA

The Higher Education System

The country's oldest existing institution of higher education is Universiti Teknologi Malaysia (Malayasia University of Technology), Johor, which was founded in 1904 (current name and status 1972) when Johor was still an independent Malay state (it came under British control in 1914). The next oldest institution is Universiti Pendidikan Sultan Idris (Sultan Idris Education University—founded 1922). Malaya was granted independence, within the Commonwealth, in 1957 and Malaysia was established in 1963, through the union of the independent Federation of Malaya (renamed the States of Malaya), Singapore, and the former British colonies of Sarawak and Sabah. Subsequently, Singapore left the federation and the States of Malaya were styled Peninsular Malaysia. In October 1994 the Government introduced a bill that would allow foreign universities to establish branch campuses in Malaysia. From the end of that year the Government permitted the use of English as a medium of instruction in science and engineering subjects at tertiary level. In 1998 the Government's incorporation of higher education gave greater powers of autonomy to the universities, which are governed by an executive body (Board of Governors) and academic council (Senate). At the seventh ASEAN summit meeting in November 2001 it was decided that the town of Bandar Nusajaya in Johor would be the location for the first ASEAN university. It would be Malaysia's second international university. In 2004/05 there were 696,760 students enrolled in tertiary education. In 2008 there were 20 government-funded universities and 33 private universities.

The main criteria for admission to higher education are the Malaysia Higher Certificate of Education and Matriculation Certificate. Applications are made through the central Unit Pusat Universiti (Central University Unit). The undergraduate Bachelors degree course lasts three to four years, though some disciplines require longer periods of study, such as medicine and dentistry (which require five years). Following the Bachelors, the Masters is the first postgraduate degree, requiring one to two years' further study; finally, after award of the Masters, study for a PhD lasts a minimum of two years.

Post-secondary vocational and technical education is available at specialist schools.

The Malaysian Qualification Agency (MQA) was established under the Malaysian Qualifications Agency Act 2007 by the merger of the previous National Accreditation Board (LAN) and the Quality Assurance Division of the Ministry of Higher Education. The merger was approved in December 2005 and the MQA was launched in November 2007. Before the merger, LAN (founded in 1998) acted as a statutory body under the Ministry of Education of Malaysia to ensure the standard and quality of certificates, diplomas and degree courses run by the private higher education institutions. There are two processes involved in the current MQA accreditation system: Provisional Accreditation—this initial process will help higher education providers to achieve accreditation by enhancing the standards and quality set in the provisional accreditation evaluation; and Accreditation—this is a formal recognition that the certificates, diplomas and degrees awarded by higher education institutions are in accordance with the standards set.

Regulatory and Representative Bodies

GOVERNMENT

Ministry of Education: Kompleks Kerajaan Persekutuan, Parcel E, Pusat Pentadbiran Kerajaan Persekutuan, 62604 Putrajaya; tel. (3) 88846000; fax (3) 88895235; e-mail webmaster@moe.gov.my; internet www.moe.gov.my; Minister Datuk HISHAMMUDDIN TUN HUSSEIN.

Ministry of Higher Education: Blok E3, Parcel E, Pusat Perbadanan Kerajaan Persekutuan, 62505 Putrajaya; tel. (3) 88835000; fax (3) 88893921; e-mail menteri@mohe.gov.my; internet www.mohe.gov.my; Minister Dato' Seri MOHAMED KHALED BIN NORDIN.

Ministry of Unity, Arts, Culture and Heritage: 16th Floor, TH Perdana Tower, Maju Junction, 1001 Jalan Sultan Ismail, 50694 Kuala Lumpur; tel. (3) 26127600; fax (3) 26935114; e-mail info@heritage.gov.my; internet www.heritage.gov.my; Minister Datuk MOHD SHAFIE BIN HAJI APDAL.

ACCREDITATION

Malaysian Qualifications Agency: Tingkat 14B, Menara PKNS-PJ, 17, Jalan Yong Shook Lin, Petaling Jaya, Selangor Darul Ehsan, 46050 Malaysia; tel. (3) 79687002; fax (3) 79569496; e-mail akreditasi@mqa.gov.my; internet www.mqa.gov.my; f. 2007 by merger of National Accreditation Board (LAN) and the Quality Assurance Division; attached to Min. of Higher Education; responsible for quality assurance of higher education for both private and public sectors to maintain Malaysian qualification standards; facilitates articulation and recognition of qualifications; Chair Dr MOHAMED SALLEH MOHAMED YASIN; Deputy Chair Prof. Dr MOHAMAD ZAWAWI ISMAIL.

NATIONAL BODY

Malaysian Association of Private Colleges and Universities: c/o International Medical University, 126 Jalan 19/155B, Bukit Jalil, 57000 Kuala Lumpur; tel. (3) 86569980; fax (3) 86569981; e-mail info@mapcu.com.my; internet www.mapcu.com.my; f. 1997; promotes and coordinates the devt of private higher education in Malaysia; 70 mems (45 ordinary mems, 15 assoc. mems and 10 br. mems); Pres. Dr PARMJIT SINGH; Sec.-Gen. Y.Bhg. Dato' PETER NG.

Learned Societies

ARCHITECTURE AND TOWN PLANNING

Malaysian Institute of Architects: 4–6 Jalan Tangsi, POB 10855, 50726 Kuala Lumpur; tel. (3) 2693-4182; fax (3) 2692-8782; e-mail info@pam.org.my; f. 1967; 3,005 mems; library of 1,000 vols; Pres. Ar Dr TAN LOKE MUN; publs *Berita Akitek* (12 a year), *Majalah Akitek* (Architecture Malaysia, 6 a year), *PAM Directory* (1 a year), *Panduan Akitek* (1 a year).

BIBLIOGRAPHY, LIBRARY SCIENCE AND MUSEOLOGY

Librarians' Association of Malaysia: POB 12545, 50782 Kuala Lumpur; Perpustakaan Negara Malaysia, 232 Jalan Tun Razak, 50572 Kuala Lumpur; tel. and fax (3) 26947390; e-mail pustakawan55@gmail.com; internet www.ppm55.org.my; f. 1955; 600 mems; Pres. ZAWIYAH BABA; Sec. NAFISAH AHMAD; publ. *Jurnal PPM* (1 a year).

HISTORY, GEOGRAPHY AND ARCHAEOLOGY

Malaysian Historical Society: 958 Jl. Hose, 50460 Kuala Lumpur; tel. (3) 2481469; fax (3) 2487281; f. 1953; activities include restoration and preservation of historical sites; 200 indiv. and institutional mems; Pres. Dato' MUSA HITAM; publs *Malaysia Dari Segi Sejarah* (1 a year), *Malaysia in History*.

LANGUAGE AND LITERATURE

Alliance Française de Kuala Lumpur: 15 Lorong Gurney, 54100 Kuala Lumpur; tel. (3) 26947880; fax (3) 26930502; e-mail info@alliancefrancaise.org.my; internet www.alliancefrancaise.org.my; f. 1961; offers courses and exams in French language and culture and promotes cultural exchange with France; 3 centres in Kuala Lumpur and Alliance Française de Penang in Georgestown; 2,300 mems; library of 5,500 vols; Dir BRUNO PLASSE.

British Council: POB 10539, 50916 Kuala Lumpur; Ground Fl., West Block, Wisma Selangor Dredging, 142C Jalan Ampang, 50450 Kuala Lumpur; tel. (3) 27237900; fax (3) 27136599; internet www.britishcouncil.org.my; teaching centre; offers courses and exams in English language and British culture and promotes cultural exchange with the UK; attached offices in Kota Kinabalu,

Kuching, Penang (teaching centre) and Subang Jaya (teaching centre); library of 14,000 vols, 100 periodicals; Dir GERRY LISTON; Dir, English Language STEVE BATES.

Dewan Bahasa dan Pustaka (National Language and Literary Agency): POB 10803, 50926 Kuala Lumpur; tel. (3) 21481011; fax (3) 21489245; internet www.dbp.gov.my; f. 1956; develops and enriches the Malay language; develops literary talent; standardizes spelling and pronunciation and devises technical terms, etc. in Malay; prints or assists in the production of publs in Malay and the translation of books into Malay; 1,171 mems; library: see Libraries and Archives; Dir-Gen. Dato' Hj. TERMUZI HJ. ABDUL AZIZ; publs *Dewan Bahasa* (12 a year), *Dewan Budaya* (12 a year), *Dewan Sastera* (12 a year), *Pelita Bahasa* (12 a year).

Goethe-Institut: 1, Jalan Langgak Golf, 55000 Kuala Lumpur; tel. (3) 21422011; fax (3) 21422282; internet www.goethe.de/so/kua/deindex.htm; offers courses and exams in German language and culture and promotes cultural exchange with Germany; Dir Dr VOLKER WOLF.

Tamil Language Society: c/o Department of Indian Studies, University of Malaya, Kuala Lumpur; f. 1957; 350 mems; aims at the promotion and propagation of the Tamil language and Indian culture; Pres. M. JAYAKUMAR; Hon. Sec. L. KRISHNAN; publ. *Tamil Oli* (in Tamil, English and Malay, 1 a year).

MEDICINE

Academy of Family Physicians of Malaysia: Room 6, 5th Floor, MMA House, 124 Jalan Pahang, 53000 Kuala Lumpur; tel. (3) 40417735; fax (3) 40425206; e-mail afpm@po.jaring.my; f. 1973; 800 mems; Pres. Dr M. K. RAJAKUMAR; Chair. (vacant); publ. *The Family Physician* (3 a year).

Malaysian Medical Association: 4th Floor, MMA House, 124 Jl. Pahang, 53000 Kuala Lumpur; tel. (3) 40411375; fax (3) 40418187; e-mail info@mma.org.my; internet www.mma.org.my; f. 1959; 10,000 mems; Pres. Dr DAVID QUEK KWANG LENG; Man. RISSA SOETAMA; publ. *Medical Journal of Malaysia* (4 a year).

NATURAL SCIENCES

General

Malaysian Scientific Association: Room 1, 2nd Floor, Bangunan Sultan Salahuddin Adbul Aziz Shah, 16 Jalan Utara, POB 48, 46700 Petaling Jaya; tel. (3) 79578930; fax (3) 79541644; e-mail malsci@tm.net.my; f. 1955; 388 mems, engaged in scientific and technological works; Pres. Dr SOON TING KUEH; Hon. Sec. Dr ZURAINEE MOHD NOR.

Biological Sciences

Malaysian Nature Society: POB 10750, 60724 Kuala Lumpur; tel. (3) 22879422; fax (3) 22878773; e-mail natsoc@po.jaring.my; internet www.mns.org.my; f. 1940; an independent society to promote the study, appreciation and conservation of nature; 5,000 mems; library: small library; Pres. Dato' Dr SALLEH MOHD NOR; Exec. Dir Dr LOH CHI LEONG; publs *The Malayan Nature Journal* (4 a year), *Malaysian Naturalist* (4 a year).

Malaysian Society for Biochemistry and Molecular Biology: d/a Pusat Pengajian Biosains dan Bioteknologi Fakulti Sains dan Teknologi, Universiti Kebangasaan Malaysia, 43600 Selangor; f. 1973; lectures, workshops and seminars, annual conference; 120 mems; Pres. Prof. PERUMAL RAMASAMY; Sec. Dr SHEILA NATHAN; publs *Malaysian Journal of Biochemistry and Molecular Biology*, *Proceedings of Annual Conference*.

Malaysian Zoological Society: 68000 Ampang Selangor, Darul Ehsan; tel. (603) 4083422; fax (603) 4075375; e-mail zoonegara@tm.net.my; f. 1961; Pres. Tan Sri Dato' V. M. HUTSON; Sec.-Treas. YUEN TANG.

RELIGION, SOCIOLOGY AND ANTHROPOLOGY

Royal Asiatic Society, Malaysian Branch: 130M Jl. Thamby Abdullah, off Jl. Tun Sambanthan, Brickfields, 50470 Kuala Lumpur; tel. (3) 22748345; fax (3) 22743458; e-mail mbras@tm.net.my; internet www.mbras.org.my; f. 1877; 935 mems; history, literature, sociology, anthropology; Pres. Datuk ABDULLAH BIN ALI; Sec. Datuk BURHANUDDIN BIN AHMAD TAJUDIN; publ. *Journal* (2 a year).

Research Institutes

AGRICULTURE, FISHERIES AND VETERINARY SCIENCE

Department of Agriculture: Ministry of Agriculture, Wisma Tani, Jl. Mahameru, 50624 Kuala Lumpur; f. 1905; undertakes all aspects of research and extension for improvement of crops; pest forecasting and surveillance; establishing Agricultural Information System; library of 15,000 vols; Dir ABU BAKAR BIN MAHMUD; publs *Malaysian Agricultural Journal, Statistical Digest.*

Forest Research Institute Malaysia (FRIM): Kepong, 52109, Selangor Darul Ehsan, Kuala Lumpur; tel. (3) 62797000; fax (3) 62731314; internet www.frim.gov.my; f. 1929; consists of 485.2 ha of experimental plantations, 5 arboreta, a nursery, a museum, a herbarium of 300,000 sheets of tree species, a wood colln of nearly 10,000 specimens, and a library (see Libraries and Archives); 9 substations consisting of 2,988 ha; Rattan Information Centre est. 1982; Dir-Gen. Dato' Dr ABDUL LATIF MOHMOD; publs *Bamboo Bulletin, Conservation Malaysia Bulletin, FRIM in Focus, FRIM Technical Information, Journal of Tropical Forest Products, Journal of Tropical Forest Science, Malayan Forest Records, Research Pamphlets, Research Programme, RIC Bulletin, Siri Alam & Rimba, Timber Technology Bulletin, Tree Flora of Sabah and Sarawak, Urban Forestry Bulletin.*

Freshwater Fisheries Research Centre: Batu Berendam, 75350 Malacca; tel. (6) 8172485; fax (6) 3175705; e-mail pppat@po.jaring.my; f. 1957; attached to Dept of Fisheries, Malaysia; research on freshwater fisheries and aquaculture; special emphasis on indigenous carp, study of fishes in lakes and reservoirs, breeding of indigenous freshwater fish; air-breathing fish, cichlid (Tilapia), aquarium fish, and aquatic plants; library of 3,800 vols; Chief Officer HAMBAL HANAFI.

Malaysian Agricultural Research and Development Institute (MARDI): POB 12301, GPO, 50774 Kuala Lumpur; tel. (3) 89437111; fax (3) 89483664; e-mail enquiry@mardi.gov.my; internet www.mardi.my; f. 1969; an autonomous organization that conducts scientific, technical, economic and sociological research in Malaysia with respect to the production, utilization and processing of all crops (except rubber and oil palm) and livestock; library of 50,000 vols; Dir-Gen. Dr SAHARAN BIN ANANG; Librarian KHADIJAH IBRAHIM; publs *Agromedia* (4 a year), *Journal of Tropical Agriculture and Food Sciences* (2 a year).

Malaysian Rubber Board: POB 10150, 50450 Kuala Lumpur; tel. (3) 92062000; fax

(3) 21634492; e-mail general@lgm.gov.my; f. 1998; consists of a directorate, 5 depts and 34 units, 2 research centres namely Tun Abdul Razak Research Centre in Hertford, England and RRIM in Sungai Buloh, Selangor, Malaysia; engaged in rubber research and devt; technical advisory service and information on all aspects of rubber production; library: see Libraries and Archives; Dir-Gen. Dr SALMIAH AHMAD; publs *Journal of Rubber Research* (4 a year), *Malaysian Rubber Technology Development* (4 a year).

ECONOMICS, LAW AND POLITICS

Asian and Pacific Development Centre: Pesiaran Duta, POB 12224, 50770 Kuala Lumpur; tel. (3) 6511088; fax (3) 6510316; internet www.apdc.com.my/apdc; f. 1980; promotes and undertakes research and training, acts as a clearing house for information on development, offers consultancy services; current programme: to overcome poverty, to assist development instns to manage national development and change, to increase the policy-making capacity of Asian-Pacific countries, to increase the capacity of the region to adjust to the changing world environment; 19 full mem. govts, 1 assoc. mem., 1 contributing non-mem.; library of 43,200 vols; Dir Dr MOHD NOOR HJ HARUN; publs *Asia-Pacific Development Monitor* (2 a year), *Issues in Gender and Development.*

MEDICINE

Institute for Medical Research (IMR): Jl. Pahang, 50588 Kuala Lumpur; tel. (3) 2986033; f. 1901; attached to Min. of Health; researches into biomedical and social aspects of tropical diseases, provides specialized diagnostic, consultative and information services, trains medical and paramedical staff, also WHO Centre for Research and Training in Tropical Diseases for the Western Pacific Region, and SEAMEO-TROPMED National Centre, WHO Collaborating Centre for Taxonomy and Immunology of Filariasis and Screening and Clinical Trials of Drugs against Brugian Filariasis, and WHO Collaborating Centre for Ecology, Taxonomy and Control of Vectors of Malaria, Filariasis and Dengue; 598 staff; library of 20,000 vols; Dir Dr M. S. LYE (acting); publs *Bulletin of the Institute for Medical Research* (irregular), *IMR Handbook, International Medical Journal, Quarterly Bulletin, Study of the Institute for Medical Research* (irregular).

NATURAL SCIENCES

Physical Sciences

Minerals and Geoscience Department Malaysia: Locked Bag 2042, 88999 Kota Kinabalu, Sabah; tel. (88) 260311; fax (88) 240150; e-mail jmgsbh@jmg.gov.my; internet www.jmg.gov.my; f. 1949; geological mapping, minerals research, engineering geology, hydrogeology, geophysics, mineralogy and petrology, laboratory analysis; library of 3,500 vols; Dir N. K. ANG; publs *Malaysian Mineral Yearbook*, industrial mineral production statistics and directory of producers in Malaysia.

Minerals and Geoscience Malaysia, Ipoh Department: Scrivenor Rd, Ipoh, Perak; f. 1903; 792 mems; basic geological information on E and W Malaysia with spec. emphasis on mineral resources; library of 18,720 vols (E Malaysia), 34,000 vols (W Malaysia); Dir-Gen. E. H. YIN; publs regional memoirs, reports and bulletins (E Malaysia), map reports and proceedings (W Malaysia), economic bulletins (W Malaysia), *Geochemical Report.*

Minerals and Geoscience Malaysia, Sarawak Department: POB 560, 93712 Kuching, Sarawak; tel. (82) 244666; fax (82) 415390; e-mail jmgswk@jmg.gov.my; f. 1949; geological mapping, mineral investigations, engineering geology, hydrogeology; library of 18,000 vols; Dir Dato' Hj. YUNUS BIN ABD. RAZAK; publ. bulletins, geological papers, technical papers, maps, memoirs, reports.

TECHNOLOGY

Malaysian Institute of Microelectronic Systems (MIMOS): MIMOS Berhad, Technology Park Malaysia, 57000 Kuala Lumpur; tel. (3) 89965000; fax (3) 89960527; internet www.mimos.my; f. 1985; research and development in microelectronics, information technology and related areas; provides advisory and technical services to the govt and the private sector; encourages and supports the creation of new industries based on high technology and modern microelectronics; collaborates with other bodies in the fields; library of 6,200 vols, 202 periodicals; Dir-Gen. Dr TENGKU MOHD AZZMAN SHARIFFADEEN; publs *MIMOS IT Paper* (2 a year), *MIMOS Teknologi Buletin* (4 a year), *MOS-MEDIA* (4 a year).

Standards and Industrial Research Institute of Malaysia (SIRIM): POB 35, 40700 Shah Alam, Selangor; tel. (3) 5591630; fax (3) 5508095; f. 1975 by merger of National Institute of Scientific and Industrial Research and the Standards Institution of Malaysia; facilitates industrial development through research into existing and future problems relating to engineering and production of processed and fabricated industrial products; provides a range of technical services which include quality assurance, metrology, industry testing, technology modification and improvement, technology transfer, consultancy, industrial information and extension services; undertakes applied research and prototype production to adapt or modify known processes and technologies; finds new uses for locally available raw materials and by-products, and develops new products and processes based on indigenous raw materials; undertakes the drafting and publication of Malaysian standards and standards testing; library of 13,000 vols, 165,000 standards and specifications, 400 periodicals; Controller Dr AHMAD TAJUDDIN ALI; publs *Berita SIRIM* (SIRIM News, 4 a year), *Malaysian Standards*.

Libraries and Archives

Alor Setar

Kedah State Public Library Corporation: Jalan Kolam Air, 05100 Alor Setar, Kedah Darul Aman; tel. (4) 7333592; fax (4) 7336232; e-mail pengarah@kdhlib.gov.my; internet www.kdhlib.gov.my; f. 1974; incl. Alor Setar Public Library, eight br. libraries, six mobile libraries and 88 village libraries; 675,677 vols; Dir Dr ZAHIDI BIN DATO' HAJI ZAINOL RASHID.

Ipoh

Tun Razak Library: Jl. Panglima Bukit Gantang Wahab, 30000 Ipoh, Perak Darul Ridzuan; tel. (5) 508073; f. 1931; special collns on Malaysia and Singapore; UNESCO depository; special language section; 245,816 vols in English, Chinese, Malay and Tamil; Asst Librarian NOOR AFITZA HJ. PAWAN CHIK; publ. *Malaysiana Collection*.

Jitra

Perpustakaan, Universiti Utara Malaysia: Sintok, 06010 Jitra, Kedah; tel. (4) 9241740; fax (4) 9241959; f. 1984; 183,000 vols, 6,000 periodicals; Chief Librarian PUAN JAMILAH MOHAMED.

Johor Baharu

Perpustakaan Sultan Ismail: Jl. Dato Onn, Johor Baharu; f. 1964; administered by the Town Council; 40,600 vols in Chinese, English, Malay and Tamil; Librarian (vacant).

Perpustakaan Sultanah Zanariah, Universiti Teknologi Malaysia: 81310 Utm Skudai, Johor Bahru; tel. (7) 5576160; fax (7) 5572555; internet www.psz.utm.my; f. 1972; 344,000 vols, 9,300 periodicals; audiovisual collection; Chief Librarian ROSNA TAIB; publs *Berita Perpustakaan Sultanah Zanariah* (2 a month), *Buletin MAKIN*.

Kota Baharu

Kelantan Public Library Corporation: Jl. Mahmood, 15200 Kota Baharu, Kelantan; tel. (9) 7444522; fax (9) 7487736; f. 1938, present name 1974; 261,000 vols; special collection: Kelantan Collection; State Librarian NIK ARIFF BIN NIK MANSOR.

Kota Kinabalu

Sabah State Library/Perpustakaan Negeri Sabah: 88572 Kota Kinabalu, Sabah; tel. (88) 54333; fax (88) 233167; f. 1951; now a state department within the Ministry of Social Services (Sabah); public reference and lending library of 841,914 vols, mainly in Malay, English and Chinese; special local history collection on Borneo; comprises 20 brs (in addition to main library), 10 mobile libraries for rural areas and 26 village libraries; Dir ADELINE LEONG.

Kuala Lumpur

Kuala Lumpur Public Library: Sam Mansion, Jl. Tuba, Kuala Lumpur; f. 1966; 45,000 vols; Librarian SOONG WAN YOONG.

Library, Forest Research Institute Malaysia: Kepong, 52109 Selangor; tel. (3) 62797497; fax (3) 62804624; e-mail zaki@frim.gov.my; internet www.frim.gov.my; f. 1929; 62,000 vols on forestry and related subjects, incl. medicinal plants, biodiversity, the environment; colln consists of books, scientific and technical reports, reprints, standards, conference papers, theses, newspaper clippings, gazettes, maps; services incl. SDI, Rattan Information Centre, current awareness services, literature searches, OPAC, etc.; Library Head MOHAMAD ZAKI HAJI MOHD ISA; publs *FRIM in Focus* (4 a year), *FRIM Reports* (irregular), *FRIM Research Pamphlet* (irregular), *FRIM Technical Information* (irregular), *Journal of Tropical Forest Science* (4 a year), *Timber Technology Bulletin* (irregular).

Malaysian Rubber Board Library: Jl. Ampang, POB 10150, 50908 Kuala Lumpur; tel. 4567033; fax (3) 4573512; e-mail rabiah@lgm.gov.my; f. 1925; 150,000 vols, mainly science and technology, particular emphasis on subjects relating to rubber research; Librarian RABIAH BT MOHD. YUSOF; publs *Bibliographies*, *List of Forthcoming Conferences*, *List of Journal Holdings*, *List of RRIM Translations*, *Recent Additions to the Library*, etc.

Ministry of Agriculture Library: Wisma Tani, Jl. Sultan Salahuddin, 50624 Kuala Lumpur; tel. (3) 88701786; fax (3) 88895239; internet www.moa.gov.my; f. 1906; 80,000 vols; publ. *Bulletin* (irregular).

National Archives of Malaysia: Jl. Duta, 50568 Kuala Lumpur; tel. (3) 6510688; fax (3) 6515679; e-mail query@arkib.gov.my; internet www.arkib.gov.my; f. 1957; public records, archives, audiovisual records, private and business records; Prime Minister's archives; 10,471 vols; Dir-Gen. Dato' HABIBAH ZON; publs *Hari ini Dlm. Sejarah* (Today in History, 4 a year), *National Archives of Malaysia*.

National Library of Malaysia: 232 Jalan Tun Razak, 50572 Kuala Lumpur; tel. (3) 2943488; fax (3) 2927899; f. 1966; nat. bibliographic centre, nat. depository, nat. centre for Malay MSS, nat. centre for ISBN and ISSN; depository for UN publs; 1,413,348 vols; Dir-Gen. CIK SHAHAR BANUN JAAFAR; publs *Jurnal Filologi Melayu* (1 a year), *Selitan Perpustakaen* (2 a year).

Pusat Dokumentasi Melayu (Dewan Bahasa dan Pustaka) (Malay Documentation Centre, Institute of Language and Literature): POB 10803, 50926 Kuala Lumpur; tel. (3) 21481030; fax (3) 21429903; e-mail aizan@dbp.gov.my; internet www.dbp.gov.my; f. 1956; directory of Malaysian writers; bibliography of modern Malaysian literature; 141,105 vols, 80 periodicals, 5,107 audiovisual items; Head AIZAN MOHD ALI; publs *Mutiara Pustaka* (1 a year), *Subject Bibliography* (Bulletin, irregular).

University of Malaya Library: Pantai Valley, 50603 Kuala Lumpur; tel. (3) 7575887; fax (3) 7573661; f. 1957; 1,239,749 vols, 8,040 periodicals; spec. collns incl. medical, law, Malay language and culture, E Asia studies and Tamil studies; Chief Librarian Assoc. Prof. Dr NOR EDZAN CHE NASIR; publ. *Kekal Abadi* (2 a year).

Kuching

Sarawak State Library: Jl. P. Ramlee, 93572 Kuching; tel. (82) 242911; fax (82) 246552; f. 1950; administered by the Ministry of Environment; 1,232,780 vols in Malay, English, Iban and Chinese; State Librarian JOHNNY K. S. KUEH.

Melaka

Malacca Public Library Corporation: 242-1 Jalan Bukit Baru, 75150 Melaka; tel. (6) 2824859; fax (6) 2824798; e-mail admin@perpustam.edu.my; internet www.perpustam.edu.my; f. 1977; 526,375 vols; Librarian RIZA FEISAL BIN SHEIK SAID.

Penang

Penang Public Library Corporation: 2nd Floor, Dewan Sri Pinang, 10200 Penang; tel. (4) 2622255; fax (4) 2628820; f. 1817; reorganized 1973; 415,000 vols; Chair. Y. B. Dr TOH KIN WOON; Dir ENCIK ONG CHAI LIN; publ. *Buletin Mutiara* (4 a year).

Perpustakaan Universiti Sains Malaysia: Minden, 11800 Penang; tel. (4) 6577888; fax (4) 6571526; e-mail chieflib@usm.my; internet www.lib.usm.my; f. 1969; 809,000 vols (main library 644,000 vols, 5,500 periodicals; medical library 87,000 vols, 1,370 periodicals; engineering library 78,000 vols, 487 periodicals), media 122,916 items, 9,969 reels microfilm, 105,809 sheets microfiche; Chief Librarian Hon. Datin MASRAH HAJI ABIDIN; publ. *MIDAS Bulletin* (6 a year).

Serdang

Perpustakaan Sultan Abdul Samad (Sultan Abdul Samad Library): 43400 UPM Serdang, Selangor Darul Ehsan; tel. (3) 89468601; fax (3) 89483745; e-mail lib@lib.upm.edu.my; internet www.lib.upm.edu.my; f. 1971 by merger of College of Agriculture, Malaya and the Faculty of Agriculture, Universiti Putra Malaysia; renamed Universiti Putra Malaysia Library in 1997; present name 2002; attached to Unversiti Putra Malaysia; brs in Faculty of Medicine and Health Sciences, Faculty of Veterinary Medicine, Faculty of Engineering and the UPM Campus Bintulu in Sarawak; 601,663 vols and bound periodicals; colln of maps, sound recordings, microforms, video tapes and slides; subscribes to 3,000 print journals and 60 online databases providing access to 56,000 full-text online journals; Chief Librarian AMIR HUSSAIN MOHAMMAD ISHAK (acting); Deputy Chief Librarians HAFIZAH HASSAN, ROSMALA ABDUL RAHIM.

Shah Alam

Selangor Public Library Corporation: c/o Perpustakaan Raja Tun Uda, Persiaran Bandaraya, 40572 Shah Alam, Selangor; tel. (3) 55197667; fax (3) 55196045; e-mail jothi@ppas.org.my; internet www.ppas.org.my; f. 1971; 1,435,803 vols; main library; 8 brs, 4 township libraries;55 village libraries and 13 mobile units; Dir SHAHANEEM HANOUM; publ. *Accession List* (12 a year).

Tun Abdul Razak Library: MARA Institute of Technology, 40450 Shah Alam, Selangor; tel. (3) 5564041; fax (3) 5503648; f. 1957; two main libraries and 10 brs; 898,000 vols; Chief Librarian RAHMAH MUHAMAD.

Museums and Art Galleries

Kota Kinabalu

Sabah Museum: Jl. Muzium, 83000 Kota Kinabalu, Sabah; tel. (88) 538228; fax (88) 240230; e-mail muzium.sabah@sabah.gov .my; internet www.mzm.sabah.gov.my; f. 1886 in Sandakan; anthropological, archaeological, natural history and historical, ethnobotanical and ethnological collections; Islamic Civilization Museum, Agop Batu Tulug Museum, Kinabatangan, Sandakan Heritage museum, Sandakan Agnes Keith House, Sandakan Memorial Tun Abdul Razak, Tambunan Datu Paduka Mat Salleh Memorial, Kinarut Panoramic Mansion House, Tenom Murut Culture Museum, Semporna Bukit Tengkorak; Lahad Datu Mansuli archaeological site, Tambunan Mat Sator Monument, Tenom Ulu Tomani Lamuyu Rock Carving, Penampang Pogunon Burial Ancient Site, Keningau Heritage Museum, Tenom Antoros Antenom Monument; library of 7,000 vols; Dir Datuk JOSEPH POUNIS GUNTAVID; publs *Buletin Muzium* (1 a year), *Journal* (1 a year).

Kuala Lumpur

Islamic Arts Museum Malaysia: Jalan Lembah Perdana, 50480 Kuala Lumpur; tel. (3) 22742020; fax (3) 22740529; e-mail info@iamm.org.my; internet www.iamm.org.my; f. 1998; art and culture of Islam from the 7th century to the present; incl. 12 permanent galleries; Architecture, Qu'rans and Manuscript, India, China, Malay World, Textiles, Jewellery, Arms and Armour, Coins and Seals, Metalwork, Ceramics and Glasses, and Living with Wood; 2 spec. galleries; Dir SYED MOHAMAD ALBUKHARY.

National Museum of Malaysia/Muzium Negara: Jl. Damansara, 50566 Kuala Lumpur; tel. (3) 22826255; fax (3) 22827294; e-mail info@jma.gov.my; internet www.jma .gov.my; f. 1963; houses collections of ethnographical, archaeological and zoological materials; comprehensive reference library on Malaysia and many Asian subjects, reference collections of archaeology, zoology and ethnography are also preserved in the Perak Museum, Taiping; Dir-Gen. Dr ADI HAJI TAHA; publ. *Federation Museums Journal* (1 a year).

Kuching

Sarawak Museum: Jl. Tun Abang Haji Openg, 93566 Kuching, Sarawak; tel. (82) 258388; fax (82) 246680; f. 1886; ethnographic, archaeological, natural history and historical collections; reference library; state archives; Dir SANIB SAID; publ. *Sarawak Museum Journal*.

Penang

Penang Museum and Art Gallery: Farquhar St, Penang; tel. (4) 2613144; f. 1963; Chair., Penang State Museum Board NAZIR ARIFF; Curator Encik KHOO BOO CHIA.

Taiping

Perak Museum: Taiping, Perak; f. 1883; antiquities, Perak archives, ethnography, zoology and a library; Dir-Gen. SHAHRUM BIN YUB.

Universities

INTERNATIONAL ISLAMIC UNIVERSITY MALAYSIA

Jalan Gombak, 53100 Kuala Lumpur
Telephone: (3) 20564000
Fax: (3) 20564053
E-mail: pro@iiu.edu.my
Internet: www.iiu.edu.my
Founded 1983
Ministry of Education control
Languages of instruction: Arabic, English
Open to Muslims and non-Muslims from Malaysia and abroad
Constitutional Head: HRH THE SULTAN OF PAHANG
Pres.: Y.B. Tan Sri Dato' SERI SANUSI BIN JUNID
Rector: Prof. Dr MOHD. KAMAL HASSAN
Deputy Rector for Academic Affairs: Assoc. Prof. Dato' Haji JAMIL HAJI OSMAN
Deputy Rector for Planning and Development: Prof. Dr ISMAWI HAJI ZEN
Deputy Rector for Student Affairs and Discipline: Assoc. Prof. Dr SIDEK BABA
Chief Librarian: Assoc. Prof. SYED SALIM AGHA BIN SYED AZAMTHULLA

Library of 356,700 vols
Number of teachers: 1,166
Number of students: 16,649

Publications: *At-Tajdid* (in Arabic, 2 a year), *Gombak Review* (in English, 2 a year), *IIUM* (in English, 2 a year), *IIUM Journal of Economics and Management* (in English, 2 a year), *IIUM Law Journal* (in English, 2 a year), *Intellectual Discourse* (in English, 2 a year)

DEANS OF KULLIYYAH

Ahmad Ibrahim Kulliyyah of Laws: Assoc Prof. Dr NIK AHMAD KAMAL NIK MAHMOD
Kulliyyah of Architecture and Environmental Design: Assoc. Prof. Dr CHE MUSA CHE OMAR
Kulliyyah of Economics and Management Sciences: Assoc. Prof. Dr MOHD. AZMI OMAR
Kulliyyah of Education: Assoc. Prof. Dr MOHD. SAHARI NORDIN
Kulliyyah of Engineering: Assoc. Prof. Dr AHMAD FARIS ISMAIL
Kulliyyah of Information and Communications Technology: Dr MOHD. ADAM SUHAIMI
Kulliyyah of Islamic Revealed Knowledge and Human Sciences: Prof. Dr MOHAMED ARIS HAJI OSMAN
Kulliyyah of Medicine: Prof. Dato' Dr MD. TAHIR AZHAR
Kulliyyah of Pharmacy: Prof. Dr TARIQ ABDUL RAZAK

Kulliyyah of Science: Assoc. Prof. Dr TORLA HAJI HASSAN

ATTACHED INSTITUTE

International Institute of Islamic Thought and Civilization (ISTAC): 205A Jl. Damansara, Bukit Damansara, 50480 Kuala Lumpur; tel. (3) 2544444; fax (3) 2548343; f. 1991; financed by Ministry of Education; postgraduate research and teaching in fields of Islamic thought and civilization; library of 149,686 vols; Dir Prof. Dr SYED MUHAMMAD NAQUIB AL-ATTAS.

UNIVERSITI KEBANGSAAN MALAYSIA (National University of Malaysia)

43600 UKM Bangi, Selangor
Telephone: (3) 89214187
Fax: (3) 89254890
E-mail: kbha@pkrisc.cc.ukm.my
Internet: www.ukm.my
Founded 1970
State control
Languages of instruction: Malay, English, Arabic
Academic year: May to April
Chancellor: Tuanku JAAFAR IBNI AL-MARHUM ABDUL RAHMAN
Vice-Chancellor: Prof. Dato' Dr MOHD SALLEH MOHD. YASIN
Deputy Vice-Chancellors: Prof. Dr SUKIMAN SARMANI (Academic and International Affairs), Prof. Dato' Dr MOHD WAHID SAMSUDIN (Students and Alumni Affairs)
Registrar: Hj MOHAMED MUSTAFA MOHTAR
Bursar: Hj MOHD ABDUL RASHID MOHD FADZIL
Chief Librarian: PUTRI SANIAH MEGAT ABDUL RAHMAN

Library of 945,000 vols, 4,000 journals
Number of teachers: 1,781
Number of students: 24,487

Publications: *Jurnal Sari, Jurnal Islamiyyat, Jurnal Jebat, Jurnal Pendidikan, Jurnal Pengurusan, Jurnal Psikologi Malaysia, Jurnal Kejuruteraan* (2 a year), *Jurnal Ekonomi Malaysia, Jurnal Perubatan UKM, Jurnal Akademika, Sains Malaysiana* (4 a year), *Jurnal Undang-Undang and Masyarakat, Buletin Pusat Pengajian Umum, Journal of Language Teaching, Linguistics and Literature*

DEANS

Faculty of Allied Health Sciences: Prof. Dr MOHD AZMAN ABU BAKAR
Faculty of Dentistry: Prof. Dato' Dr Hj. MOHD ARIFFIN HJ. MOHAMED
Faculty of Economics and Business: Prof. Dr NOOR AZLAN GHAZALI
Faculty of Education: Assoc. Prof. Dr LILIA HALIM
Faculty of Engineering: Prof. Ir. Dr HASSAN BASRI
Faculty of Islamic Studies: Prof. Dr ZAKARIA SETAPA
Faculty of Law: Assoc. Prof. KAMAL HALILI HASSAN
Faculty of Medicine: Prof. Dr LOKMAN SAIM
Faculty of Social Sciences and Humanities: Prof. Dr YUSUF ISMAIL
Faculty of Science and Information Technology: Prof. Dr AZIZ DERAMAN
Faculty of Science and Technology: Prof. Dr ABDUL JALIL ABDUL KADER
Centre for General Studies: Prof. Dr ABDUL LATIF SAMIAN
Institute for Environment and Development (LESTARI): Prof. Dr IBRAHIM KOOMOO
Institute of Malay World and Civilization (ATMA): Prof. Dato' Dr SHAMSUL AMRI BAHARUDDIN

Institute of Malaysian and International Studies (IKMAS): Prof. Dr ROGAYAH HJ. MAT ZIN

Institute of Medical Molecular Biology (UMBI): Prof. Dr A. RAHMAN A. JAMAL

Institute of Microengineering and Nanoelectronics (IMEN): Prof. Dr BURHANUDDIN YEOP MAJLIS

Institute of Occidental Studies (IKON): Prof. Dato' Dr SHAMSUL AMRI BAHARUDDIN

Institute of Space (ANGKASA): Prof. Dr BAHARUDDIN YATIM

National Institute for Genomics and Molecular Biology—Malaysia: Prof. Dr NOR MUHAMMAD MAHADI

PROFESSORS

ABDUL HAMID, Z., Genetics and Plant Biotechnology
ABDUL KADER, A. J., Microbial Physiology
ABDUL KADIR, K., Endocrinology and Metabolism
ABDUL RAHMAN, R., Environmental Engineering
ABDUL RASHID, A. H., Anatomy
ABDULLAH, A., Food Science and Nutrition
ABDULLAH, I., Structural Geology and Tectonics
ABDULLAH, M., Statistics
ABDULLAH, P., Analytical and Environmental Chemistry
ABU BAKAR, M. A., Lipid Biochemistry
ABU TALIB, I., Material Physics
AHMAD, I., Virology
AHMAD, Z., Political Science
ALI, A., Industrial Planning and Strategies
ALI, O., Community Health
ALI JAMAL, A. R., Paediatric Haematology
ALI RAHIM, S., Development Communications
AZMAN ALI, RAYMOND, Neurology, Epilepsy and Stroke Medicine
BABA, I., Inorganic Chemistry
BABJI, A. S., Food Science
BAHARUDDIN, S. A., Anthropology and Sociology
BASRI, H., Civil and Environmental Engineering
BIDIN, A. A., Taxonomy of Lower Plants
BOO NEM YUN, Neonatology
CHOO, O. L., Child Neurology and Development Paediatrics
DAUD, W. R. W., Drying, Separation and Fuel Cell Technology
DIN, L., Organic Chemistry
EMBI, M. N., Protein Biochemistry
GEORGE, E., Haematology
HADI, A. S., Urbanization, Industrialization and Migration
HAMDAN, A. R., Artificial Intelligence
HASAN, M. N. H., Zoology
HASAN, Z. A. A., Parasitology
HASSAN, H. R., Psychiatry
HASSAN, S. Z. S., Anthropology of Religion, Gender Studies
ISKANDAR, T. M., Internal Control and Auditing
ISMAIL, M. Y., Minority and Sub-culture Studies
ISMAIL, N. M. N., Obstetrics and Gynaecology
IZHAM CHEONG, Medicine
JAHI, J. M., Physical Geography
JAMAL, F., Clinical Bacteriology
JASIN, B., Micropalaeontology
KADRI, A., Zoology
KAMIS, A., Animal Physiology, Comparative Endocrinology
KENG, C. S., Haematology
KOMOO, I., Engineering Geology and Conservation Geology
KONG, C. T. N., Nephrology
KRISHNASWAMY, S., Psychiatry
LAZAN, H., Plant Physiology and Biochemistry
LIEW, C. G., Family Medicine
LIM, A., Clinical Microbiology and Antimicrobial Chemotherapy

LONG, J., Education
MAHADI, N. M., Environmental Microbiology
MAJLIS, B. Y., Integrated Circuit Technology
MAJZUB, R. M., Pre-school and Adolescent Education and Development
MANSOR, M., Cytogenetics, Cytology
MAT SALLEH, M., Solid State Physics
MEAH, F. A., Surgery
MEERAH, T. S. M., Science Education
MD. HASHIM MERICAN, Z. M., Neuromuscular Pharmacology
MISIRAN, K., Anaesthesiology
MOHAMAD, A. L., Plant Systematics
MOHAMAD, H., Petrology and Geochemistry
MOHAMED, M. A., Oral Health
MOHAMED, R., Bacterial Serology
MOHAMED YASIN, M. S., Medical Mycology
MOHAMMED ZAIN, S. BIN, Mathematics
MOHD NOOR, N., Plant Tissue Culture
MOHD SALLEH, K., Science and Society
NGAH, W. Z. W., Medical Biochemistry
NIK ABD. RAHMAN, N. H. S., Archaeology
NOOR, M. I., Nutrition
NOR, G. M., Oral Surgery
OTHMAN, A. H., Coordination Chemistry
OTHMAN, B. H. R., Marine Biology
OTHMAN, M., Signals Processing
OTHMAN, M. Y. H., Energy Physics
PIHIE, A. H. L., Clinical Biochemistry
SAHID, I., Weed and Environmental Science
SAID, I. M., Organic Chemistry
SAIM, L., Otology and Neuro-otology
SALLEH, A. R., Algebraic Topology, Ethnomathematics
SALLEH, RAMLI MD, Malay Syntax and Translation
SALLEH, S. H. H., Traditional Malay Literature
SAMSUDIN, A. R., Geophysics
SAMSUDIN, M. W., Organic Chemistry
SARMANI, S., Radiochemistry
SHAH, F. H., Molecular Biology
SHAMSUDIN, A. H., Mechanical Engineering
SIWAR, C., Rural Economics
SULAIMAN, N. A., Bioscience and Clinical Pharmacology
SULAIMAN, S., Vector Control, Vectorecology
SYED HUSSAIN, S. N. A., Histopathology, Cytopathology
TAHIR, U. M. M., Modern Malay Literature, Literary Criticism
TAMIN, N. M., Eco-engineering Restoration
TAP, A. O. M., Pure Mathematics
TEH, W. H. W., Rural Culture and Society
TENGKU SEMBOK, T. M., Information Retrieval
YAHAYA, MUHAMMAD, Physics
YAMIN, B. M., Chemistry
YATIM, B., Applied Physics
YONG, O., Investment
YUSOFF, K., Cardiology
YUSUF, M. HL., Social Psychology
ZAMAN, H. B., Information Technology Policy and Strategic Studies

UNIVERSITI MALAYA
(University of Malaya)

50603 Kuala Lumpur
Telephone: (3) 79677022
Fax: (3) 79560027
E-mail: icr@um.edu.my
Internet: www.um.edu.my
Founded 1962
State control
Languages of instruction: Malay, English
Academic year: May to April (2 semesters)
Chancellor: His Royal Highness Sultan AZLAN MUHIBBUDDIN SHAH IBNI ALMARHUM SULTAN YUSSUF IZZUDDIN SHAH GHAFARUL-LAHU-LAH
Pro-Chancellors: His Royal Highness Raja Dr NAZRIN SHAH IBNI SULTAN AZLAN MUHIB-BUDDIN SHAH, Toh Puan Datuk Hajjah Dr

AISHAH ONG, Tan Sri Dato' Seri SITI NORMA YAAKOB
Vice-Chancellor: Dr GHAUTH JASMON
Deputy Vice-Chancellor for Academic and Int. Affairs: Prof. Dr HAMZAH HJ. ABDUL RAHMAN
Deputy Vice-Chancellor for Devt: Prof. Datuk Dr KHAW LAKE TEE
Deputy Vice-Chancellor for Research and Innovation: Prof. Dato' Dr MOHD JAMIL MAA
Deputy Vice-Chancellor for Student Affairs and Alumni: Assoc. Prof. Datuk Dr AZARAE HJ. IDRIS
Registrar: NORILAH SALAM
Librarian: Assoc. Prof. Dr NOR EDZAN HJ. CHE NASIR

Number of teachers: 2,613
Number of students: 25,474

Publications: *Berita UM* (newsletter, 24 a year), *Budiman* (4 a year), *University of Malaya Gazette* (1 a year)

DEANS

Faculty of Arts and Social Sciences: Prof. Dr MOHAMMAD REDZUAN OTHMAN
Faculty of Built Environment: Assoc. Prof. Dr Sr NOOR ROSLY HANIF
Faculty of Business and Accountancy: Assoc. Prof. Dr M. FAZILAH ABD SAMAD
Faculty of Computer Science and Information Technology: Prof. Dr WAN AHMAD TAJUDDIN WAN ABDULLAH (acting)
Faculty of Dentistry: Prof. Dr ISHAK ABDUL RAZAK
Faculty of Economics and Administration: Prof. RAJAH RASIAH
Faculty of Education: Prof. SAEDAH SIRAJ
Faculty of Engineering: Assoc. Prof. Dr MOHD HAMDI ABD SHUKOR
Faculty of Languages and Linguistics: Prof. ZURAIDAH MD DON
Faculty of Law: Prof. Dr CHOONG YEOW CHOY
Faculty of Medicine: Prof. Dr IKRAM SHAH ISMAIL
Faculty of Science: Prof. Dr MOHD SOFIAN BIN AZIRUN
Asia-Europe Institute: Prof. Datuk Dr ROZIAH OMAR (Exec. Dir)
Institute of China Studies: Assoc. Prof. Dr YEOH KOK KHENG
Institute of Graduate Studies: Prof. Dr NORHANOM ABDUL WAHAB
Institute of Principalship Studies: Prof. Dr SHAHRIL @ CHARIL MARZUKI (Dir)
Int. Institute of Public Policy and Management: Dr KHADIJAH MD KHALID (Dir)
Institute of Research Management and Monitoring: Prof. Dr NOORSAADAH ABD. RAHMAN (Dir)
Academy of Islamic Studies: Prof. Dr AHMAD HIDAYAT BUANG (Dir)
Academy of Malay Studies: Assoc. Prof. Datuk ZAINAL ABIDIN BORHAN (Dir)
Academic Devt Centre: Prof. Dr RAJA MAZ-NAH RAJA HUSSAIN (Dir)
Centre for Civilisational Dialogue: Prof. Datin Dr AZIZAN BAHARUDDIN (Dir)
University of Malaya Centre of Continuing Education: Prof. Datuk Dr MANSOR MD ISA (Dir)
Cultural Centre: Assoc. Prof. Dr MOHD NASIR BIN HASHIM (Dir)
Centre for Foundation Studies in Science: Assoc. Prof. Dr AZILAH ABDUL RAHMAN (Dir)
Sports Centre: Dr ABDUL HALIM MOKHTAR (Dir)

PROFESSORS

Faculty of Arts and Social Sciences:
ABDULLAH ZAKAVIA, G., History
ALI, S. H., Sociology
AZIZAH, K., Anthropology and Sociology
CHENG, G. N., Chinese Studies

FATIMAH HASNAH, D., Anthropology and Sociology
LEE, B. T., Geography
LIM, C. S., English Studies
MOHD FAUZI, Y., Anthropology and Sociology
MOHD YUSOFF, H., History
NATHAN, K. S.
RAMLAH, A., History
RANJIT SINGH, D. S., History
SHAHARIL, T. R., Southeast Asia Studies
VOON, P. K., Land Use Studies
ZAINAL, K., Anthropology and Sociology

Faculty of Business and Accounting:
MANSOR, M. I., Financial Management
SIEH, M. L., Business Administration

Faculty of Computer Science and Information Technology:
MASHKURI, Y., Computer Science

Faculty of Dentistry:
HASHIM, Y., Oral Pathology and Oral Medicine
ISHAK, A. R., Preventive Dentistry
LIAN, C. B., Oral Surgery
LING, B. C., Prosthetics
LUI, J. L., Conservative Dentistry
RAHIMAH, A. K., Community Dentistry
SIAR, C. H., Periodontology
TOH, C. G., Conservative Dentistry
ZUBAIDAH ABD, R., Oral Biology

Faculty of Economics and Administration:
FIRDAUS, A., Administration and Political Science
JAHARA, Y., Development Studies
JAMILAH, M. A., Development Studies
JOMO, K. S., Applied Economics
KOK, K. L., Applied Economics
LEE, K. H., Analytical Economics
NAGARAJ, S., Applied Statistics
NAIDU, G., Applied Economics
TAN, P. C., Applied Statistics

Faculty of Education:
CHEW, S. B., Sociology of Education
CHIAM, H. K., Social Psychology of Education
GAUDART, H. M., Language Education
ISHAK, H., Pedagogy and Educational Psychology
NIK AZIS, N. P., Mathematics and Science Education
RAHIMAH HJ., A., Educational Development
RAMIAH, A. L., Educational Development
SAFIAH, O., Language Education
SURADI, S., Pedagogy and Educational Psychology
YONG, M. S. LEONARD, Pedagogy and Educational Psychology

Faculty of Engineering:
ABDUL GHANI, K., Computer-aided Design and Manufacturing
EZRIN, A., Built Environment
FAISAL, A., Civil and Environmental Engineering
GOH, S. Y., Mechanical and Material Engineering
KHALID, M. N., Electrical and Telecommunications Engineering
LU, S. K. S., Electrical Engineering
MASITAH, H., Chemical Engineering
MOHD ALI, H., Chemical Engineering
MOHD ZAKI, A. M., Mechanical and Material Engineering
RAMACHANDRAN, K. B., Biochemical Engineering
WAN ABU BAKAR, W. A., Mechanical Engineering
WOODS, P. C., Built Environment

Faculty of Law:
BALAN, P., Company Law and Civil Procedure
HARI, C., Jurisprudence and Legal Philosophy

KHAW, L. T., Law of Intellectual Property and Land Law
MIMI KAMARIAH, A. M., Family Law and Criminal Procedures
SOTHI RACHAGAN, N. S., Environmental and Consumer Law
SURYA, P. S., International Law

Faculty of Medicine:
ALJAFRI, A. M., Surgery
ANUAR ZAINI, M. Z., Medicine
ASMA, O., Paediatrics
CHANDRA, S. N., Parasitology
CHUA, C. T., Medicine
DELLIKAN, A. E., Anaesthesiology
DEVA, M. P., Psychological Medicine
EL-SABBAN, FAROUK M. F., Physiology
GOH, K. L., Medicine
KHAIRULL, A. A., Parasitology
KULENTHRAN, A., Obstetrics and Gynaecology
LAM, S. K., Medical Microbiology
LANG, C. C., Medicine
LIM, C. T., Paediatrics
LIM, Y. C., Surgery
LIN, H. P., Paediatrics
LOOI, L. M., Pathology
MENAKA, N., Pathology
NGEOW, Y. F., Medical Microbiology
ONG, S. Y. G., Anaesthesiology
PARAMSOTHY, M., Medicine
PERUMAL, R., Biochemistry
PRASAD, U., Oto-rhino-laryngology
PUTHUCHEARY, S. D., Medical Microbiology
RAMAN, A., Physiology
RAMANUJAM, T. M., Surgery
ROKIAH, I., Medicine
RUBY, H., Physiology
SENGUPTA, S., Orthopaedic Surgery
SIVANESARATNAM, V., Obstetrics and Gynaecology
SUBRAMANIAM, K., Anatomy
TAN, C. T., Medicine
TAN, N. H., Biochemistry
TEOH, S. T., Social and Preventive Medicine
YAP, S. F., Pathology
YEOH, P. N., Pharmacy

Faculty of Science:
ANSARY, A., Microbiology and Bacteriology
HAMID, A. H. A., Natural Product Chemistry
HARITH, A., Physics
KOH, C. L., Genetics
LIM, M. H., Multilinear Algebra
LOW, K. S., Lasers and Optoelectronics
MAK, C., Plant Breeding
MOHAMED, A. M., Taxonomy and Ecology
MUHAMAD RASAT, M., Molecular Electronics
MUHAMAD, Z., Botany
MUKHERJEE, T. K., Genetics
NAIR, H., Plant Physiology
OSMAN, B., Philosophy of Science
RAHIM, S., Semiconductor Physics
RAJ, J. K., Engineering Geology
RAMLI, A., Zoology
WONG, C. S., Plasma Physics
YEAP, E. B., Geology

Academy of Islamic Studies:
ABDULLAH ALWI, H., Syariah and Economics
MAHFODZ, M., Syariah and Law
MAHMOOD ZUHDI, A. M., Fiqh and Usul

Academy of Malay Studies:
ABU HASSAN, M. S., Malay Literature
ASMAH, O., Malay Linguistics
HASHIM, M., Linguistics
NORAZIT, S., Economic Anthropology
RAHMAH, B., Malay Culture and Arts
WAN ABDUL KADIR, W. Y., Popular Culture Studies
YAACOB, H., Development Studies and Change

UNIVERSITI MALAYSIA SABAH

Tingkat 9, Gaya Centre, Jalan Tun Fuad Stephens, Locked Bag 2073, 88999 Kota Kinabalu, Sabah
Telephone: (88) 320789
Fax: (88) 320223
E-mail: pejcslor@ums.edu.my
Internet: www.ums.edu.my
Founded 1994
Academic year: June to March
Vice-Chancellor: Prof. Datuk Seri Panglima Dr ABU HASSAN OTHMAN
Deputy Vice-Chancellors: Prof. Dr MOHD ZAHEDI DAUD (Academic), Prof. Datuk Dr KAMARUZZAMAN AMPON (Research and Development), Prof. Datuk Dr MOHD NOH DALIMIN (Student Affairs)
Registrar: HELA LADIN bin MOHD DAHALAN
Librarian: CHE SALMAH MEHAMOOD

Number of teachers: 476
Number of students: 8,300

Publications: *Borneo Science* (2 a year), *Kinabalu* (1 a year), *Manu* (1 a year)

DEANS

School of Arts Studies: Assoc. Prof. Haji INON SHAHARUDDIN ABD. RAHMAN
School of Business and Economics: Assoc. Prof. SYED AZIZI SYED WAFA
School of Business and Finance, Labuan: Assoc. Prof. Dr ZAINAL ABIDIN SAID
School of Education and Social Development: Prof. Dr SHUKERY MOHAMED
School of Engineering and Information Technology: Assoc. Prof. Dr SAZALI YAACOB
School of Food Science and Nutrition: Assoc. Prof. Dr MOHD ISMAIL ABDULLAH
School of Informatic Sciences, Labuan: AWANG ASRI AWANG IBRAHIM (acting)
School of International Forestry: Assoc. Prof. Dr AMINUDDIN MOHAMED
School of Psychology and Social Work: Prof. Dato' Dr ABDUL HALIM OTHMAN
School of Science and Technology: Assoc Prof. Dr AMRAN AHMED
School of Social Sciences: Assoc. Prof. HASSAN bin MAT NOR
Centre for Postgraduate Studies: Prof. Dr ZAINODIN HJ. JUBOK
Centre for the Promotion of Knowledge and Language Learning: Prof. Dr AHMAT ADAM

UNIVERSITI MALAYSIA SARAWAK (UNIMAS)

Jalan Dato' Mohd Musa, 94300 Kota Samarahan, Sarawak
Telephone: (82) 671000
Fax: (82) 672411
Internet: www.unimas.my
Chairman: Tan Sri Datuk Amar Haji BUJANG MOHD NOR
Chancellor: Tun Yang Terutama Tun Datuk PATINGGI ABANG HAJI MUHAMMAD SALAHUDDIN
Pro-Chancellor: Yang Amat Berhormat Pehin Sri Dr Haji ABDUL TAIB MAHMUD
Vice-Chancellor: Prof. Dr ABDUL RASHID ABDULLAH
Deputy Vice-Chancellors: Prof. Haji SULAIMAN HANAPI (Student Affairs and Alumni), Prof. Dr MOHD AZIB SALLEH (Academic and Internationalization)
Registrar: Prof. Dr HAMSAWI SANI
Library of 108,000 vols, 10,000 journals
Number of teachers: 464
Number of students: 5,675 (5,112 undergraduate, 563 postgraduate)

DEANS

Faculty of Applied and Creative Arts: Assoc. Prof. MOHD FADZIL ABDUL RAHMAN

Faculty of Cognitive Science and Human Development: Prof. Dr Datin NAPSIAH MAHFOZ

Faculty of Computer Science and Information Technology: Assoc. Prof. NARAYANAN KULATHURAMAIYER

Faculty of Economy and Business: Assoc. Prof. Dr SHAZALI ABU MANSOR

Faculty of Engineering: Prof. Dr KHAIRUDDIN AB HAMID

Faculty of Medicine and Health Sciences: Prof. Dr SYAED HASSAN AL MASHOOR

Faculty of Resource Science and Technology: Assoc. Prof. Dr SABDIN MOHD LONG

Faculty of Social Sciences: Assoc. Prof. Dr MUTALIP ABDULLAH

PROFESSORS

ABDULLAH, M. S., Medicine and Health Sciences

AB HAMID, K., Engineering

ABU MANSOR, S., Engineering

AL MASHOOR, S. H., Medicine and Health Sciences

BOHARI, H., Medicine and Health Sciences

GUDUM, H., Medicine and Health Sciences

HADI, Y., Resource Science and Technology

HARUN, W. S. W., Resource Science and Technology

LONG, P. K., Medicine and Health Sciences

MAHFOZ, N., Cognitive Science and Human Development

MALIK, A. S., Medicine and Health Sciences

NGIDANG, D., Social Sciences

SAID, S., Engineering

SINGH, B., Medicine and Health Sciences

THAMBYRAJAH, V., Medicine and Health Sciences

MALAYSIA UNIVERSITY OF SCIENCE AND TECHNOLOGY (MUST)

GL 33 (Ground Fl.), Block C, Kelana Sq., 17 Jl. SS 7/26, 47301, Kelana Jaya, Petaling Jaya, Selangor Darul Ehsan

Telephone: (3) 78801777

Fax: (3) 78801762

E-mail: admin@must.edu.my

Internet: www.must.edu.my

Private control

Academic year: September to June

Postgraduate research univ.

Pres.: Dr OMAR ABDUL RAHMAN

Provost: Dr MOHD NIZAM ISA

Vice-Pres. for Finance and Business Affairs: BADLY SHAH BIN ARIFF SHAH

Registrar and Head of Admin.: STEPHEN JOHN LEE

Chief Librarian: JOHARI AFFANDI OMAR

DEANS

Biotechnology: Assoc. Prof. Dr LIM SAW HOON

Construction Engineering and Management: Assoc. Prof. Dr CHAN TOONG KHUAN

Energy and Environment: Asst Prof. Dr SCOTT KENNEDY

Information Technology: Assoc. Prof. Dr NOR ADNAN YAHYA

Materials Science and Engineering: Prof. Dr ZANULDIN AHMAD

Systems Engineering and Management: Asst Prof. Dr ASGARI BEHROOZ

Transportation and Logistics: Assoc. Prof. Dr LEONG CHOON HENG

MULTIMEDIA UNIVERSITY

Jalan Multimedia, 63100 Cyberjaya, Selangor

Telephone: (3) 83125018

Fax: (3) 83125022

E-mail: mkt@mmu.edu.my

Internet: www.mmu.edu.my

Chancellor: Yang Amat Berbahagia Dato' Seri Dr SITI HASMAH BINTI HAJI MOHD ALI

President: Prof. Dr GHAUTH JASMON

DEANS

Faculty of Business and Law (Melaka Campus): Dr HISHAMUDDIN BIN ISMAIL

Faculty of Creative Multimedia (Cyberjaya Campus): Assoc. Prof. Dr ABU HASSAN ISMAIL

Faculty of Engineering (Cyberjaya Campus): Prof. CHUAH HEAN TEIK

Faculty of Engineering and Technology (Melaka Campus): Dr PETER VON BREVERN

Faculty of Information Science and Technology (Melaka Campus): Assoc. Prof. Dr ENG KIONG WONG

Faculty of Information Technology (Cyberjaya Campus): Prof. LEE POH AUN

Faculty of Management (Cyberjaya Campus): Assoc. Prof. Dr MOHD ISMAIL SAYYED AHMAD

UNIVERSITI PENDIDIKAN SULTAN IDRIS
(Sultan Idris Education University)

35900 Tanjong Malim, Perak Darul Ridzuan

Telephone: (5) 4506332

Fax: (5) 4582776

E-mail: admin@upsi.edu.my

Internet: www.upsi.edu.my

Founded 1922

Chancellor: HRH RAJA PERMAISURI PERAK DARUL RIDZUAN TUANKU BAINUN

Vice-Chancellor: Y. Bhg. Prof. Dato' AMINAH AYOB

Deputy Vice-Chancellor for Academic and Int. Affairs: Prof. Dr ZAKARIA KASA

Deputy Vice-Chancellor for Student Affairs and Alumni: Y. Bhg. Prof. Dr SHAHARUDIN ABDUL AZIZ

Deputy Vice-Chancellor for Research and Innovation: Y. Bhg. Prof. Dr MOHD. MUSTAMAM ABD. KARIM

Registrar: Y. Bhg. Dato' RUSLEY BIN TAIB

Chief Bursary: HAJJAH KHADIJAH HAMDAN

Chief Librarian: CIK ZAHARIAH BINTI MOHAMED SHAHAROON

DEANS

Faculty of Art and Music: Dr MOHD. HASSAN ABDULLAH

Faculty of Business and Economics: Dr NORLIA MAT NORWANI

Faculty of Cognitive Science and Human Development: Assoc. Prof. Dr ABDUL LATIF HJ. GAPOR

Faculty of Information and Communication Technology: Prof. Dr MOHAMAD IBRAHIM

Faculty of Languages: Dr ABDUL GHANI ABU

Faculty of Science and Technology: Assoc. Prof. Dr MUSTAFFA AHMAD

Faculty of Social Sciences and Humanities: IBRAHIM HASHIM

Faculty of Sports Sciences: Dr MOHD. SANI MADON

Institute of Graduate Studies: Prof. Dr OMAR ABDULL KAREEM

UNIVERSITI PUTRA MALAYSIA
(Putra University, Malaysia)

43400 Serdang, Selangor Darul Ehsan

Telephone: (3) 89486101

Fax: (3) 89483244

E-mail: cans@admin.upm.edu.my

Internet: www.upm.edu.my

Founded 1971

State control

Languages of instruction: Malay, English

Academic year: May to November (two semesters)

Chancellor: THE GOVERNOR OF PENANG

Vice-Chancellor: Prof. Dato' Dr MOHD ZOHADIE BARDAIE

Deputy Vice-Chancellor for Academic Affairs: Prof. Dr MUHAMAD AWANG

Deputy Vice-Chancellor for Devt: Assoc. Prof. Dr MAKHDZIR MARDAN

Deputy Vice-Chancellor for Student Affairs: Assoc. Prof. Dr Haji IDRIS ABDOL

Registrar: KAMALUL ARIFFIN MUSA

Librarian: KAMARIAH BT ABDUL HAMID

Number of teachers: 1,074

Number of students: 33,566

Publication: *Tribun Putra* (12 a year)

DEANS

Faculty of Agriculture: Prof. Dr MOHD. YUSOF HUSSEIN

Faculty of Computer Science and Information Technology: Dr ABD. AZIM BIN ABD. GHANI

Faculty of Design and Architecture: Assoc. Prof. Dr MUSTAFA KAMAL

Faculty of Economics and Management: Prof. Dr NIK MUSTAFA RAJA ABDULLAH

Faculty of Educational Studies: Assoc. Prof. KAMARIAH BT ABU BAKAR

Faculty of Engineering: Prof. Dr Ir. RADIN UMAR RADIN SOHADI

Faculty of Food Science and Biotechnology: Prof. Dr GULAM RUSUL BIN RAHMAT ALI

Faculty of Forestry: Prof. Dato' Dr NIK MUHAMAD NIK MAJID

Faculty of Human Ecology: Prof. Dr ABDULLAH AL-HADI HJ. MUHAMED

Faculty of Medicine and Health Sciences: Assoc. Prof. Dr JAMMAL AHMAD ESSA

Faculty of Modern Languages and Communication: Prof. Dr SHAIK MOHD NOOR ALAM SHAIK MOHD HUSSEIN

Faculty of Science and Environmental Studies: Prof. Dr WAN ZIN WAN YUNUS

Faculty of Veterinary Medicine: Prof. Dato' Dr SHEIK OMAR ABDUL RAHMAN

School of Graduate Studies: Prof. Dr AINI IDERIS

External Programme Centre: Assoc. Prof. Dr ABDUL AZIZ SAHAREE (Dir)

Graduate School of Management: Assoc. Prof. ZAINAL ABIDIN KIDAM

Institute for Distance Education and Learning: Assoc. Prof. AZAHARI ISMAIL (Dir)

Islamic Centre: Assoc. Prof. Dr Haji MUHD. FAUZI BIN MOHAMAD (Dir)

UNIVERSITI SAINS MALAYSIA
(University of Science, Malaysia)

Minden, 11800 Penang

Telephone: (4) 6533888

Fax: (4) 6565401

E-mail: pro@notes.usm.my

Internet: www.usm.my

Founded 1969

Federal control

Languages of instruction: Malay, English

Academic year: September to August

Chancellor: HRH TUANKU SYED SIRAJUDDIN IBNI AL-MARHUM TUANKU SYED PUTRA JAMALULLAIL

Pro-Chancellor: Hon. Tan Sri RAZALI ISMAIL

Pro-Chancellor: Hon. Tan Sri Dato' Dr JEGATHESAN MANIKAVASAGAM

Vice-Chancellor: Hon. Prof. Dato' DZULKIFLI ABDUL RAZAK

Deputy Vice-Chancellor: Hon. Dato' Prof. OMAR OSMAN

Deputy Vice-Chancellor: Prof. AHAMD SHUKRI MUSTAPA KAMAL

Deputy Vice-Chancellor: Prof. ASMA ISMAIL

Registrar: JAMAHYAH BASIRON

Library: see Libraries and Archives

Number of teachers: 1,938

Number of students: 26,837 (18,295 undergraduate, 8,542 postgraduate)

Publications: *Frontiers* (3 a year), *Graduate Infolink* (3 a year), *Kejuruteran* (3 a year), *Mediskop* (3 a year), *Perantara* (3 a year)

DEANS

Biomedical and Health Sciences Platform: Prof. SYED MOHSIN SYED SAHIL JAMALUL-LAIL

Clinical Sciences Research Platform: Prof. Dr NOR HAYATI OTHMAN

Engineering and Technology Research Platform: Prof. ZAINAL ARIFFIN MOHD ISHAK

Fundamental Sciences Research Platform: Prof. ABDUL LATIF AHMAD

Information and Communication Technology Research Platform: Assoc. Prof. BAHARI BELATON

Institute of Postgraduate Studies: Prof. ROSHADA HASHIM

Life Sciences Research Platform: Prof. MOHD. NAZALAN MOHD. NAJIMUDIN

School of Aerospace Engineering: Hon. Prof. HASNAH HJ. HARON

School of Arts: Assoc. Prof. A. RAHMAN HJ. MOHAMED

School of Biological Sciences: Prof. ABU HASSAN AHMAD

School of Chemical Engineering: Prof. AZLINA HARUN KAMARUDDIN

School of Chemical Sciences: Prof. WAN AHMAD KAMIL MAHMOOD

School of Civil Engineering: Prof. HAMIDI ABDUL AZIZ

School of Communication: Assoc. Prof. ADNAN HUSSEIN

School of Computer Sciences: Prof. ROSNI ABDULLAH MUSTAFA

School of Dental Sciences: Dr ADAM HUSEIN

School of Distance Education: OMAR MAJID

School of Education Studies: Assoc. Prof. ANNA CHRISTINA ABDULLAH

School of Electrical and Electronic Engineering: Prof. MOHD ZAID ABDULLAH

School of Health Sciences: Prof. AHMAD ZAKARIA

School of Housing, Building and Planning: Prof. Ir. MAHYUDDIN RAMLI

School of Humanities: Hon. Prof. Dr ABU TALIB AHMAD

School of Industrial Technology: Prof. ROZMAN HJ. DIN

School of Languages, Literacy and Translation: Prof. AMBIGAPATHY PANDIAN

School of Management: Hon. Dato' Assoc. Prof. ISHAK ISMAIL

School of Materials and Mineral Resources Engineering: Prof. AHMAD FAUZI MOHD. NOOR

School of Mathematical Sciences: Assoc. Prof. AHMAD IZANI MD ISMAIL

School of Mechanical Engineering: Assoc. Prof. ZAIDI MOHD. RIPIN

School of Medical Sciences: Prof. Dr ABDUL AZIZ BABA

School of Pharmaceutical Sciences: Prof. SYED AZHAR SYED SULAIMAN

School of Physics: Prof. ZAINURIAH HASSAN

School of Social Sciences: Assoc. Prof. ISMAIL BABA

Social Transformation Research Platform: Prof. BADARUDDIN MOHAMED

PROFESSORS

ABDUL AZIZ, B., Medical Oncology, Haematology and Palliative Medicine

ABDUL AZIZ, T., Radiation Biophysics, Medical Physics

ABDUL GHANI, S., Urban and Regional Planning

ABDUL RASHID, A. R., Clinical Pharmacology and Therapeutics

ABDUL WAHAB, A. R., Vector Ecology

AB RANI, S., Maxillofacial Surgery, Tissue Banking, Bone Banking

ABU HASSAN, A., Mosquito and Urban Pest Control, Aquatic Insects, Insect Ecology

ABU TALIB, A., South-east Asian History

AHMAD PAUZI, M. Y., Physiology

AHMAD SHUKRI, M. K., Radiation Biophysics, Medical Physics

AHMAD YUSOFF, H., Mechanical Computer-Aided Engineering, CAD-CAM

AISHAH, A. L., Pharmacology

AMBIGAPATHY, P., English as a Second Language and Sociolinguistics

AMINAH, A., Science Education

AMIR HUSSIN, B., Economics

ASMA, I., Medical Microbiology, Molecular Biology of Infectious Diseases, Rapid Diagnosis of Infectious Diseases esp. Typhoid and Paratyphoid Fevers

BAHARUDDIN, S., Plant Pathology

BAHRUDDIN, S., Chemical Resistance Measurements

BOEY, P. L., Palm Oil Chemistry and Technology

CHAN, K. L., Pharmaceutical Chemistry

CHAN, N. W., Water Resources, Hydrology and Flood Hazard Management, Climatology

CHONG, C. S., Biophysics

DAING MOHD NASIR, D. I., Accounting, Business Administration

DZULKIFLI, A. R., Pharmacology

FARID, G., Digital and Data Communication

FUN, H. K., Solid State Physics

GOON, W. K., Environmental Studies, Mangrove Ecosystem, Tropical Rain Forest

HANAFI, I., Plastic Composite and Rubber

HARBINDAR JEET SINGH, G. S., Calcium Metabolism

HASSAN, S., Applied Mathematics

IBRAHIM, C. O., Biotechnology

IBRAHIM, W., Transport Planning

ILYAS, M., Geophysics

ITAM, S., Medical Parasitology and Entomology

JAFRI MALIN, A., Neurosurgery

JAMIL, I., Polymers

JEYARATNAM, K., Policy Studies

JUNAIDAH, O., Scattering of Electromagnetic Waves

KAMARULAZIZI, I., Semiconductor Energy Studies, Clean Room Fabrication Technology

KOH, H. L., Environmental and Ecosystem Modelling EIA Simulation

LEE, C. Y., Geophysics Exploration, Applied Geophysics

LIM, K. O., Biophysics

LIM, P. E., Waste Water Treatment

LOH, K. W., Economics

MAFAUZY, M., Endocrinology, Effect of Natural Products on Diabetes

MAHYUDDIN, R., Building Technology

MASHHOR, M., Botany

MASHUDI, K., Linguistics

MD SALLEH, Y., Literature

MOHAMAD AZEMI, M. N., Food Technology

MOHAMAD, S., Literature

MOHAMED, S., Marketing

MOHAMED GHOUSE, N., Theatre and Dance

MOHAMED ISA, A. M., Biodegradable Plastics, Biotechnology

MOHAMED OMAR, K., Environmental Technology

MOHAMED RAZALI, S., Social Psychiatry and Rehabilitation

MOHAMED SHUKRI, S., Planning and Development Management

MOHAMMAD MAHFOOZ, A. A., Management

MORSHIDI, S., Urban Planning and Development

MUHAMAD, J., Management Science, Statistics, Operations Management

MUHAMMAD IDIRIS, S., Analytical Chemistry

MUSTAFFA, E., Medicine

NAVARATNAM, V., Clinical Pharmacology

NOR HAYATI, O., Surgical Pathology with special interest in Gynaepathology, Dermatopathology and Oncopathology

NORZAMI, M. N., Immunology

OMAR, S., Inorganic Chemistry

ONG, B. H., Computer-aided Geometric Design

OSMAN, M., Marketing

PLOTNIKOV IOURI, P., Flight Dynamics and Control Systems, Applied Optimal Control

POH, B. L., Organic Chemistry

QUAH, S. H., Applied Mathematics

RADZALI, O., Materials and Bioceramics Engineering

RAHMAT, A., Clinical Pharmacy and Toxicology

RAMLI, M., Persuasive Communication

ROGAYAH, J., Curricular Development and Problem-based Learning

ROSHADA, H., Biomedical Analysis

ROSHIHAN, M. A., Quality Control

ROZHAN, M. I., Solid State Physics

ROZMAN, D., Chemistry of Wood

RUSLAN, R., Geographic Information Systems

RUSLI, N., Public Health, Islamic Occupational and Health Medicine, AIDS Prevention and Counselling, Islamic Perspectives in Medicine and Health, Occupational Health and Safety

SARINGAT, B., Quality Control Tablets, Capsules, Herbal Formulations

SEETHARAMU, K. N., Heat Transfer, Computational Fluid Dynamics, Stress Analysis

SHARIF MAHSUFI, M., Pharmacokinetics, Drug Metabolism

SITI ZURAINA, A. M., Anthropology and Sociology

SUBASH, B., Chemical Reaction Engineering, Zeolite Catalysis, Environmental Catalysis, Process Design and Development

SUKOR, K., Poverty-focused Micro-credit Programme

SURESH, N., Economics

SYED IDRIS, S. H., Communications, Radar Systems, Microwave, Antenna and Propagation

SYED MOHSIN, S. S. J., Pharmacology

TENG, C. S., Chemical Engineering

TEOH, S. G., Inorganic and Organo-metallic Chemistry

WAN ABDUL MANAN, W. M., Nutrition, Public Health and Quality of Life

WAN MOHAMAD, W. B., Endocrinology, Impaired Glucose Tolerance Test

WAN ROSLI, W. D., Paper Technology

YUEN, K. H., Pharmaceutical Technology

ZABIDI AZHAR, H., Paediatric Neurology

ZAHARIN, Y., Computational Linguistics and Algebraic Geometry

ZAINAL ABIDIN, A., Electroplating, Waste Water Treatment

ZAINAL ARIFIN, A., Materials, Ceramics

ZAINAL ARIFIN, M. I., Polymer Technology

ZAINUL FADZIRUDDIN, Z., Molecular Biology

ZAKARIA, M. A., Colloid Surface and Cement Sciences

ZHARI, I., Pharmaceuticals

ZUBIR, D., Pollution

ZULFIGAR, Y., Coral and Marine Biology

ZULMI, W., Hand and Reconstructive Surgery

UNIVERSITI TEKNOLOGI MALAYSIA (University of Technology Malaysia)

Skudai, 81310 Johor

Telephone: (7) 5530222

Fax: (7) 5561722

E-mail: pendaftar@utm.my

Internet: www.utm.my

Founded 1904; university status 1972

State control

Languages of instruction: English, Malay

Academic year: June to March

Vice-Chancellor and Pres.: Dato' Prof. Ir. Dr ZAINI BIN UJANG

Deputy Vice-Chancellor for Academic and International Affairs: Prof. Dr Ir. MOHD. AZRAAI BIN KASSIM

Deputy Vice-Chancellor for Research and Innovation: Prof. Dr MARZUKI BIN KHALID

Deputy Vice-Chancellor for Student Affairs and Alumni: Prof. Datuk Dr. MOHD. TAJUDIN BIN HJ. NINGGAL

Registrar: WAN MOHD ZAWAWI BIN WAN ABD. RAHMAN

Librarian: KAMARIAH BINTI NOR MOHD DESA

Library: see Libraries and Archives

Number of teachers: 1,633

Number of students: 31,529

Publication: *Journal of Technology* (in 6 series, each 2 a year)

DEANS

Faculty of Bioscience and Bioengineering: Prof. Dr ROSLI BIN MD. ILLIAS

Faculty of Built Environment: Assoc. Prof. Dr AHMAD NAZRI BIN MUHAMAD LUDIN

Faculty of Chemical Engineering: Prof. Dr ZAINUDDIN BIN ABDUL MANAN

Faculty of Civil Engineering: Assoc. Prof. Dr Ir. SHAHRIN BIN MOHAMMAD

Faculty of Computer Science and Information Systems: Prof. Dr ABDUL HANAN BIN ABDULLAH

Faculty of Education: Assoc. Prof. Dr MOHAMAD BIN BILAL ALI

Faculty of Electrical Engineering: Prof. Ir. Dr ABDUL HALIM BIN MOHD. YATIM

Faculty of Geoinformation and Real Estate: Prof. Dr ALIAS BIN ABD. RAHMAN

Faculty of Health Science and Biomedical Engineering: Prof. Dr JASMY BIN YUNUS

Faculty of Islamic Civilisation: Assoc. Prof. AZMI SHAH BIN SURATMAN

Faculty of Management and Human Resources Development: Assoc. Prof. Dr AMRAN BIN MD. RASLI

Faculty of Mechanical Engineering: Prof. Dr ROSLAN BIN ABDUL RAHMAN

Faculty of Petroleum and Renewable Energy Engineering: Prof. Dr ARIFFIN BIN SAMSURI

Faculty of Science: Prof. Dr MADZLAN BIN AZIZ

Malaysian-Japan International Institute of Technology: Prof. Ir. MEGAT JOHARI BIN MEGAT MOHD. NOR

School of Graduate Studies: Prof. Dr ROSE ALINDA BINTI ALIAS

UTM Advanced Informatics School: Prof. Dr SHAMSUL BIN SHAHIBUDIN

UTM International Business School: Assoc. Prof. Dr MOHD. HASSAN BIN MOHD. OSMAN

UTM Perdana School of Science, Technology and Innovation Policy: Prof. ZAMRI BIN MOHAMED

UTM Razak School of Engineering and Advanced Technology: Prof. Dr AWALUDDIN BIN MOHAMED SHAHAROUN

UTM School of Professional and Continuing Education: Assoc. Prof. Dr KHAIRUL ANUAR ABDULLAH

UNIVERSITI TEKNOLOGI MARA

40450 Shah Alam, Selangor, Darul Ehsan

Telephone: (3) 55442000

Fax: (3) 55442223

E-mail: webadmin@www.uitm.edu.my

Internet: www.uitm.edu.my

Founded 1956 as Dewan Latihan RIDA, became Maktab MARA 1965 and Institut Teknologi MARA 1967, present name 1999

Academic year: May to April

Vice-Chancellor: Dato' Seri Prof. Dr IBRAHIM ABU SHAH

Number of teachers: 4,200

Number of students: 100,000

Publications: *Accountancy Newsletter, Info UiTM, International Research Journal*

DEANS

Centre for Graduate Studies: Datin ZUBAIDAH ALSREE

Faculty of Accountancy: Prof. Dr Hj. IBRAHIM KAMAL ABDUL RAHMAN

Faculty of Administration and Law: Prof. Madya RAMLA BINTI MOHD NOH

Faculty of Applied Science: Prof. Madya Dr AHMAD SAZALI HAMZAH

Faculty of Architecture, Planning and Surveying: Prof. Madya Dr MOHAMED YUSOFF ABBAS

Faculty of Art and Design: Prof. Madya Dr BAHARUDIN UJANG

Faculty of Business and Management: Prof. Madya Dr JAMIL HAMALI

Faculty of Chemical Engineering: Prof. Madya Dr SHARIFAH AISHAH AYED A. KADIR

Faculty of Civil Engineering: Prof. Madya Ir Dr Hj. MOHD YUSOF ABD RAHMAN

Faculty of Communication and Media Studies: Prof. Madya ALIAS MD SALLEH

Faculty of Education: Prof. Dr HAZADIAH MOHD DAHAN

Faculty of Electrical Engineering: Prof. Madya Dr YUSOF MD SALLEH

Faculty of Health Science: Prof. Dr ABD RAHIM MD NOOR

Faculty of Hotel and Tourism Management: EN ABDUL AZIZ ABDUL MAJID

Faculty of Information Science: Prof. Madya Dr LAILI HJ HASHIM

Faculty of Information Technology and Quantitative Science: Prof. Madya AZIZI NGAH TASIR

Faculty of Mechanical Engineering: Prof. Madya Dr SHANRANI ANUAR

Faculty of Medicine: Y. Bhg Dato' Prof. Dr KHALID YUSOF

Faculty of Office Management and Technology: Prof. Madya Dr HALIMATON HJ. KHALID

Faculty of Performing Arts: Prof. Madya Md RUSHDIE KUBON MD SHARIFF

Faculty of Pharmacy: Prof. Dr ABU BAKAR ABD MAJEED (acting)

Faculty of Sports Science and Recreation: Prof. Madya Dr Muhd KAMIL IBRAHIM

UNIVERSITI TEKNOLOGI PETRONAS

31750 Bandar Seri Iskandar, Tronoh, Perak Darul Ridzuan

Telephone: (5) 3688000

Fax: (5) 3654075

E-mail: utp@petronas.com.my

Internet: www.utp.edu.my

Founded 1995 as Institute of Technology Petronas; present name 1997.

UNIVERSITI TENAGA NASIONAL

km 7 Jalan IKRAM-UNITEN, Kajang-Puchong, 43009 Kajang, Selangor

Telephone: (3) 89212113

Fax: (3) 89287106

E-mail: rusmala@uniten.edu.my

Internet: www.uniten.edu.my

Founded 1976 as Institut Latihan Sultan Ahmad Shah; re-named Tenaga Nasional Berhad 1990 and Institut Kerjuruteraan Teknologi Tenaga Nasional 1994; present name 1997

Private control

Languages of instruction: English, Malay

Academic year: July to June

Vice-Chancellor: Prof. Ir Dr MASHKURI YAACOB

Deputy Vice-Chancellor for Academics: Prof. Ir Dr IBRAHIM HUSSEIN

Deputy Vice-Chancellor for Student Affairs, Alumni and Management: Dr MOHAMED NASSER MOHAMED NOOR

Deputy Vice-Chancellor for KSHAS: Assoc. Prof. Dr SHAARI MD NOR

Int. Relations Office: RUSMALA MOHD DAUD

Librarian: SAZALI SULAIMAN

Library of 80,000 vols

Number of teachers: 418

Number of students: 8,614 (6,240 undergraduate, 260 postgraduate)

Publications: *Electronic Journal of Computer Science and Information Technology* (2 a year), *Journal of Business Management* (2 a year), *Journal of Energy & Environment* (2 a year)

DEANS

College of Business Management: Dr Hj. SHAARI MOHD NOR

College of Engineering: Dr IBRAHIM HUSSEIN

College of Information Technology: Dr ZAINUDDIN HASSAN (Deputy Dean)

Institute of Liberal Studies: Prof. Datin Dr Hj. KOBKUA SUWANNATHAT-PIAN

Bandar Muadzam Shah Branch Campus: Prof. Dr ZULKIFLI ABDUL HAMID (Provost)

UNIVERSITI UTARA MALAYSIA
(Northern University of Malaysia)

06010 UUM Sintok, Kedah Darul Aman

Telephone: (4) 9284000

Fax: (4) 9283016

Internet: www.uum.edu.my

Founded 1984

State control

Languages of instruction: Malay, English

Academic year: September to August (2 semesters)

Chancellor: HRH THE SULTAN OF KEDAH

Pro-Chancellor: Yang Berbahagia Tan Sri Dato' Seri Dr ABDUL HAMID PAWANTEH

Pro-Chancellor: Yang Amat Berbahagia Tun Dato' Sri Dr AHMAD FAIRUZ DATO' SHEIKH ABDUL HALIM

Vice-Chancellor: Yang Berbahagia Prof. Dato' Dr MOHAMED MUSTAFA ISHAK

Deputy Vice-Chancellor for Academic and International Affairs: Prof. Dr ROSNA AWANG HASHIM

Deputy Vice-Chancellor for Research and Innovation: Prof. Dr ABDUL RAZAK SALEH

Deputy Vice-Chancellor for Student Affairs and Alumni Relations: Datuk Dr AHMAD FAIZ HAMID

Bursar: AMRON MAN

Registrar: MOHAMAD AKHIR HAJI YUSUF

Chief Librarian: SALLEH HUDIN MUSTAFFA

Library of 1,136,803 vols

Number of teachers: 1,321

Number of students: 34,424

Publications: *International Journal of Management Studies* (2 a year), *International Journal of Banking and Finance* (2 a year), *Journal of Technology and Operations Management* (1 a year), *Journal of Information and Communication Technology* (1 a year), *Journal of International Studies* (1 a year), *Journal of Law, Government and Social Science* (1 a year), *Journal of Legal Studies* (1 a year), *Jurnal Pembangunan Sosial* (Journal of Social Development, 1 a year), *Malaysian Management Journal* (2 a year), *Malaysian Journal of Learning and Instruction* (1 a year), *Malaysian Journal of Language and Communication* (1 a year)

DEANS

Awang Had Salleh Graduate School of Arts and Sciences: Assoc. Prof. Dr ABDUL MALEK ABDUL KARIM

Ghazali Shafie Graduate School of Government: Assoc. Prof. Dr AHMAD MARTADHA MOHAMED

Othman Yeop Abdullah Graduate School of Business: Prof. Dr NOOR AZIZI ISMAIL

UUM College of Arts and Sciences: Assoc. Prof. AZMI SHAARI

UUM College of Business Studies: Assoc. Prof. Dr NASRUDDIN ZAINUDIN

PROFESSORS
ABAS, Z.
ABD KARIM, MOHD. Z.
ABDUL AZIZ, A. R.
ABDULLAH, C. S.
AHMAD, N. H.
CHIK, A. R.
HIAU ABDULLAH, N. A.
KU MAHAMUD, KU R.
LEBAI DIN, A. K.
MAHMOOD, R.
MOHAMAD, M. H.
OMAR, Z.
YAAKUB, A. R.
YUSOFF, R. Z.

Colleges

Cooperative College of Malaysia: 103 Jl. Templer, 46700 Petaling Jaya, Selangor; tel. (3) 7574911; fax (3) 7570434; e-mail mkm@mkm.edu.my; f. 1956; provides in-service and pre-service training; Diploma and Certificate courses in cooperative management; specialized courses in business management, accounting, computer studies, cooperative management; library: 30,000 vols; 2,905 students; Dir ARMI HJ. ZAINUDIN.

Institut Bahasa Melayu Malaysia (Malaysian Institute of the Malay Language): Lembah Pantai, 59990 Kuala Lumpur; tel. (3) 22822389; fax (3) 22826076; internet www2.moe.gov.my/ibmm; f. 1958; 81 teachers; 778 students; offers a 3-year pre-service diploma course, a 14-week in-service course in the teaching of the Malay language by trained teachers; students are selected by the Ministry of Education; also offers short courses of Malay language as a foreign and second language; Principal ENCIK SALLEH BIN MOHD. HUSEIN.

KDU College: Jl. SS 22/41, 47400 Petaling Jaya, Selangor; tel. (3) 77288123; fax (3) 77277096; e-mail best@kdu.edu.my; internet www.kdu.edu.my; f. 1983 as Kolej Damansara Utama; library: 25,300 vols; 250 teachers; 6,000 students; pre-university and foundation courses, diploma courses in business administration, computer science, engineering, hotels and tourism; degrees in business, accounting and finance, economics; CEO Dr YAP CHEE SING; Registrar TAN JING KUAN.

Politeknik Kuching, Sarawak: Km. 22, Jl. Matang, Locked Bag 3094, 93050 Kuching, Sarawak; tel. (82) 428796; fax (82) 428023; f. 1989; library: 10,000 vols; diploma and certificate courses in civil, electrical and mechanical engineering and commerce/business, apprentice training in oil, gas and petroleum technology in cooperation with Petronas; 130 teachers; 1,200 students; Prin. AYOB BIN HJ. JOHARI (acting).

Tunku Abdul Rahman College: POB 10979, 50932 Kuala Lumpur; tel. (3) 4214977; fax (3) 4226336; f. 1969; library: 122,715 vols; 290 teachers; 8,123 students; Principal Dr LIM KHAIK LEANG; Registrar CHEE AH KIOW.

Ungku Omar Polytechnic: Dairy Rd, 31400 Ipoh, Perak; tel. (5) 5457656; fax (5) 5471162; f. 1969 with UNESCO aid; library: 33,300 vols, 60 periodicals; 549 teachers; 6,451 students; Prin. Mej. Ir HAJI MOHAMED ZAKARIA B. MOHD NOOR; Admin. Officer ROFBIAH BT KAMARUDDIN; Librarian NOR AINON B. ZAKARIA.

Yayasan Pengurusun Malaysia (Malaysian Institute of Management): 227 Jl. Ampang, 50450 Kuala Lumpur; tel. (3) 2425255; fax (3) 2643168; f. 1966; MBA, BA, diploma and certificate courses; Pres. Raja Tun MOHAR BIN RAJA BADIOZAMAN; CEO Dr TARCISIUS CHIN; publs *Malaysian Management Review* (2 a year), *Management Newsletter* (4 a year).

MALDIVES

The Higher Education System

The Maldives became fully independent, outside the Commonwealth, on 26 July 1965. The first institution of higher education, the Maldives College of Higher Education, was founded in 1998. All higher, technical and vocational qualifications in the Maldives are awarded by this institution. The first Bachelors degree programme was launched in 2000 and in 2001 the Ministry of Education established the Maldives National Qualifications Framework. The Maldives Accreditation Board is responsible for quality assurance and accreditation of higher education programmes of study. In 2007 4,388 students were enrolled at the Maldives College of Higher Education.

Bachelors degrees are three-year programmes of study. The only postgraduate award is the Graduate Certificate. Technical and vocational education consists of Certificate and Diploma courses run by the Maldives College of Higher Education.

Regulatory and Representative Bodies

GOVERNMENT

Ministry of Education: Ghaazee Bldg, 2nd Floor, Ameer Ahmed Magu, Malé 20-05; tel. 3323262; fax 3321201; e-mail e_sec@ thauleem.net; internet www.moe.gov.mv; Minister ZAHIYA ZAREER.

Ministry of Higher Education, Employment and Social Security: Haveeree Hingun, Malé 20-125; tel. 3317172; fax 3331578; e-mail admin@employment.gov.mv; internet www.employment.gov.mv; Minister ABDULLA YAMEEN.

ACCREDITATION

Maldives Accreditation Board: H. Velaanaage, Malé; tel. 3344077; fax 3344079; e-mail amuhsin@mqa.gov.mv; internet www .mqa.gov.mv; f. 2000; attached to Min. of Education; 12 mems; CEO Dr ABDUL MUHSIN MOHAMED.

Research Institutes

GENERAL

Institute of Islamic Studies: Malé; tel. 3322718; fax 3313953; e-mail rasheed .moosa@thauleem.net; f. 1980; attached to Min. of Education; aims to provide educational opportunities for the country's young people, to encourage the spread of the Arabic language, to provide training and refresher courses for imams, lawyers, judges, and teachers of the Koran and Islamic studies, to promote study of the Koran, to upgrade the Islamic curriculum in accordance with the needs of the country, to publish and translate books on all aspects of Islam; library of 19,000 vols; Dir-Gen. IBRAHIM RASHEED MOOSA; publ. *Al-Manhaj* (1 a year).

National Centre for Linguistic and Historical Research: Sosun Magu, Malé 20-05, Henveiru; tel. 3323206; fax 3326796; e-mail nclhr@dhivehinet.net.mv; internet www .qaumiyyath.gov.mv; f. 1982; research on history, culture and language of the Republic of Maldives; restoration and preservation of the nation's heritage; preservation and promotion of the Dhivehi language; Dir IBRAHIM ZUHOOR; publs *Dhivehinge Tharika* (2 a year), *Faiythoora* (12 a year).

Libraries and Archives

Malé

Islamic Library: Islamic Centre, Medhuziyaaraiy Magu, Malé 20-02; tel. 3323623; f. 1985; Islamic Studies and literature; 4,500 vols; Dir Imam AHMED SHATHIR.

National Library: 59 Majeedi Magu, Galolhu, Malé 20158; tel. 3323943; fax 3313712; e-mail info@nlm.gov.mv; internet www.nlm.gov.mv; f. 1945, as the State Library of Maldives, renamed Majeedi Library 1948, present name 1982; attached to Min. of Tourism, Arts and Culture; nat. library colln; public library facilities; recreation and research support; preserves nat. literature; 62,520 vols, spec. collns in Dhivehi, English, Arabic, Urdu; Dir-Gen. IBRAHIM SHIYAM; Chief Librarian FATHMATH SHIHAM; publs *Bibliography of Dhivehi Publications*, *Bibliography of English Publications*, *Mathifushuge Mauloomaathu* (information on Maldivian family trees).

Museum

Malé

National Museum: National Centre for Linguistic and Historical Research, Malé 20-05; tel. 3322254; fax 3326796; e-mail nclhr@dhivehinet.net.mv; internet www .geocities.com/bnaseem/welcome.htm; f. 1952; conservation and display of historical items; Senior Curator ALI WAHEED.

College

Maldives College of Higher Education: Nikagas Magu, Machchangolhi, Malé; tel. 3345155; fax 3315411; internet www.mche .edu.mv; f. 1998; academic year January to November (2 terms); campuses at Hithadhoo (2), Kulthudhuffushi and Thinadhoo; Faculties of education, engineering technology, health sciences, hospitality and tourism studies, management and computing, Shari'a and law; centres of maritime studies, open learning; Vice-Rector for Admin. HUSSAIN HALEEM.

MALI

The Higher Education System

Mali, the former French colony of Soudan, became an independent state in 1960, following the secession of Senegal from the Federation of Mali, founded in 1959. Tertiary education facilities include the national Université de Bamako (founded 1996) and several colleges of higher education. Many students also receive higher education abroad, mainly in France and Senegal. In 2004/05 there were 32,600 students enrolled at the Université de Bamako.

The Ministry of Higher Education and Scientific Research controls higher education, but the state-run Université de Bamako is financially autonomous. The University Council is the policy-making body of the Université and the Rector acts as chief executive. The main academic divisions are the Colleges, Schools and Institutes.

The secondary school Baccalauréat is the main requirement for admission to higher education. The first (undergraduate) stage of higher education lasts four years in most fields and leads to the award of a Diplôme; some disciplines such as medicine and pharmacy last five to six years. Students at the Ecoles are awarded specialist Diplômes, depending on the field of study. The second (postgraduate) level of higher education is the two-year Diplôme d'Etudes Approfondies, which is only offered by the Institut Supérieur pour la Formation et la Recherche Appliquée, and the three-year Doctorat Malien research degree, awarded after submission of a thesis.

Post-secondary technical and vocational education consists of programmes of study and professional training leading to the award of Brevet de Technicien, Diplôme de Technicien Supériur and Diplôme des Sciences Appliquées.

Regulatory Bodies

GOVERNMENT

Ministry of Culture: Quartier du Fleuve, Bamako; tel. 223-26-44; fax 490-03-46; e-mail info@culture.gov.ml; internet www .maliculture.net; Minister MOHAMMED EL MOCTAR.

Ministry of Higher Education and Scientific Research: BP 71, Bamako; tel. 222-57-80; fax 222-21-26; e-mail info@education .gov.ml; internet www.education.gov.ml; Minister AMADOU TOURÉ.

Learned Society

GENERAL

UNESCO Office Bamako: Badalabougou Est, BP E 1763 Bamako; tel. 223-34-92; fax 223-34-94; e-mail bamako@unesco.org; designated Cluster Office for Burkina Faso, Mali and Niger; Dir AHMED OULD DEIDA.

Research Institutes

GENERAL

Centre National de la Recherche Scientifique et Technologique: BP 3052, Bamako; tel. 222-90-85; f. 1986; coordinates all research activity in Mali; 57 research instns, 443 staff; Dir-Gen. Dr MAMADOU DIALLO IAM; publs *Revue Malienne de Science et de Technologie* (1 a year), *Vie de la Recherche* (4 a year).

Institut de Recherche pour le Développement (IRD): BP 2528, Bamako; tel. 221-05-01; fax 221-64-44; e-mail granjon@sahel .ird.ml; environmental and social sciences for development; library of 4,000 books and journals; Dir JOSEPH BRUNET-JAILLY; (see main entry under France); publ. *Actualités de la Recherche au Mali* (6 a year).

AGRICULTURE, FISHERIES AND VETERINARY SCIENCE

Centre National de Recherches Fruitières: BP 30, Bamako; f. 1962; controls experimental plantations, phytopathological laboratory, technological laboratory and pilot schemes; Dir P. JEANTEUR.

Centre National de Recherches Zootechniques: BP 262, Bamako; f. 1927; experimental farm with sections on genetics (bovine, swine, poultry), nutrition and biochemistry, pasture, veterinary medicine; library of 1,000 vols; Dir Dr FERNAND TRAORE.

Centres de Recherche Rizicole: 2 rice research centres at Kankan and Ibetemi.

Institut de Recherches Agronomiques Tropicales et des Cultures Vivrières (IRAT): BP 438, Bamako; f. 1962; controls stations at Bamako, Koulikoro, Kogoni par Nioro, Ibetemi (Mopti), and sub-stations at Kita and Koporokenie-Pe; general agronomy, land amelioration, cultivation techniques, fertilization needs, plant breeding (sorghum, pennisetum, short and floating rices, maize, wheat, groundnuts and formerly sugar cane); Dir M. THIBOUT; (see main entry under France).

Institut du Sahel: BP 1530, Bamako; tel. 222-21-48; fax 222-59-80; e-mail administration@insah.org; internet www .insah.org; f. 1976; a specialized institution of the Comité de Lutte contre la Sécheresse dans le Sahel (CILSS); aims to combat effects of drought and achieve food security in the Sahel (consisting of Burkina Faso, Cape Verde, The Gambia, Guinea-Bissau, Mali, Mauritania, Niger, Senegal, Chad) through the promotion and coordination of research, circulating scientific and technical information; library of 12,000 vols, 240 periodicals; Dir Gen. MOUSTAPHA AMADOU; publs *Actes, Etudes & Travaux, Etudes et Recherches, Recherche et Développement.*

Office du Niger: BP 106, Ségou; tel. 232-02-92; fax 232-01-41; f. 1932, taken over by Mali govt 1958; research stations at Bougomi and Sahel (cotton), Kayo (rice), Soninkoura (fruit); Dir-Gen. NANCOMA KEITA.

MEDICINE

Institut Marchoux: BP 251, Bamako; tel. 222-51-31; fax 222-95-44; f. 1935; part of *Organisation de Co-ordination et de Coopération pour la Lutte contre les Grandes Endémies*; medical research, teaching, treatment and epidemiology, specializing in leprosy; Dir SOMITA KEITA.

Institut d'Ophtalmologie Tropicale de l'Afrique de l'Ouest Francophone: BP 248, Bamako; tel. 222-27-22; fax 222-51-86; e-mail iota@malinet.ml; f. 1953; research in tropical eye diseases and prevention of blindness, training courses for technicians and doctors specializing in ophthalmology; Dir Prof. ABDOULAYE DIALLO.

NATURAL SCIENCES

Physical Sciences

Direction Nationale de la Météorologie: BP 237, Bamako; tel. and fax 229-21-01; e-mail dnm@afribone.net.ml; library of 1,265 vols; Dir K. KONARE; publs *Bulletin Agrométéorologique, Bulletin Climatologique* (12 a year).

TECHNOLOGY

Société Nationale de Recherches et d'Exploitation des Ressources Minières de Mali (SONAREM), Service de Documentation: BP 2, Kati; tel. 222-41-84; fax 222-21-60; f. 1961; geology, mining (gold mining in Kalana, phosphates in Bourem), hydrogeology; 5 staff; library of 5,000 vols; Dir DAOUDA DIAKITE.

Libraries and Archives

Bamako

Bibliothèque Nationale du Mali: BP 159, Ave Kassé Keïta, Bamako; tel. 222-49-63; f. 1913; 60,000 vols, 2,000 current periodicals; Dir MAMADOU KONOBA KEÏTA.

Attached Institution:

Archives Nationales du Mali: Koulouba, Bamako; tel. 222-58-44; f. 1913; Archivist LAMINE CAMARA.

Centre Culturel Français: Blvd de l'Indépendance, BP 1547, Bamako; tel. 222-40-19; fax 222-58-28; e-mail ccfmedia@afribone.net .ml; internet www.ccfbamako.org; f. 1962; public library of 27,000 vols; Dir NICOLE SEURAT.

Timbuktu

Centre d'Etudes, de Documentation et de Recherches Historiques 'Ahmed Baba' (CEDRAB): BP 14, Timbuktu; tel. and fax 292-10-81; f. 1970; to preserve the historical heritage of the region; collects and conserves Arabic MSS; 15,000 archives; Dir MOHAMED GALLAH DICKO.

Museum

Bamako

Musée National du Mali: BP 159, Bamako; tel. 222-34-86; fax 223-19-09; e-mail musee@malinet.ml; library of 1,900 vols; Dir Dr SAMUEL SIDIBE.

University

UNIVERSITÉ DE BAMAKO

BP 2528, Rue Baba Diarra Porte 113, Bamako

Telephone: 222-19-33

Fax: 222-19-32

E-mail: u-bamako@ml.refer.org

Internet: www.ml.refer.org/u-bamako

Founded 1996, as Université de Mali; present name 2006

State control

Language of instruction: French

Academic year: October to June

Rector: Prof. AMADOU BALLO

Number of teachers: 706

Number of students: 64,059

Publication: *Recherches Africaines*

DEANS

Faculty of Economics and Management: ABDOULAYE SANOGO

Faculty of Law and Politics: CHEICK HAMALLA FOFANA

Faculty of Letters, Languages, Arts and Humanities: SALIF BERTHE

Faculty of Medicine, Pharmacy and Dentistry: ANATOLE TOUNKARA

Faculty of Science and Technology: HAMIDOU DOUCOURE

School of Engineering: MOUSSA KANTE (Dir)

School of Teacher Training: BOUBA DIARRA (Dir)

Colleges

Ecole des Hautes Etudes Pratiques: BP 242, Bamako; tel. 222-21-47; f. 1974, present name 1979; diploma courses in accountancy, business studies; 35 teachers; 471 students; Dir-Gen. SIDI MOHAMED TOURE.

Ecole Nationale d'Ingénieurs: BP 242, Bamako; tel. 222-21-47; Dir MAMADOU DIAKITE.

Ecole Normale Supérieure: BP 241, Bamako; tel. 222-21-89; f. 1962; 150 teachers; 1,754 students; Dir SÉKOU B. TRAORÉ; publ. *Cahiers de l'ENSup.*

Faculté de Médecine, de Pharmacie et d'Odonto-Stomatologie: BP 1805, Bamako; tel. 222-52-77; fax 222-96-58; f. 1969 (formerly Ecole Nationale de Médecine et de Pharmacie); library: 6,800 vols, 289 periodicals; 100 teachers; 1,800 students; Dir Prof. ISSA TRAORE; publ. *Mali Médical.*

Faculté des Sciences Juridiques et Economiques: 1185 Ave de la Liberté (Route de Koulouba), BP 276, Bamako; tel. 222-27-19; fax 223-18-95; e-mail sacko@ena.ena.ml; f. 1958 (formerly École Nationale d'Administration); Dean DUSMANE O. SIDIBE; publ. *Cahier du CERES.*

Institut de Productivité et de Gestion Prévisionnelle: BP 1300, Bamako; tel. 222-55-11; f. 1971; library: 3,000 vols; in-service training, business advice; 15 staff; Dir-Gen. SIDIKI TRAORE.

Institut Polytechnique Rural de Katibougou: BP 6, Koulikoro; tel. 226-20-12; f. 1965; teaching and research in agronomy, agricultural economics, stockbreeding, forestry, veterinary science, rural technology; 300 teachers; 12,000 students; Dir-Gen. OUSMANE BELCO TOURE.

MALTA

The Higher Education System

In 1592 the Jesuit Order founded the Collegium Melitense and in 1769 it was elevated to university status by Grandmaster Manoel Pinto de Fonseca; it is now known as the University of Malta (L-Università ta' Malta). From 1814 to 1964 Malta was a Crown Colony of the United Kingdom, before becoming an independent sovereign state, within the Commonwealth, in 1964. Malta became a republic in 1974. Education is governed by the Education Act (1988), which is the responsibility of the Education Division of the Ministry of Education, Employment and Family. Education is free at all levels. The Council and the Senate are the supreme governing bodies of the University, which is an autonomous institution funded by the Government. In 2006/07 there were 9,416 students enrolled at the University. Malta participates in the Bologna Process to establish a European Higher Education Area, the first phase of which is to adopt a credit-based system of comparable degrees with two main cycles (undergraduate and graduate).

Admission to the University is on the basis of the Matriculation Certificate Examination. The University operates a US-style 'credit semester' system, under which students have to accrue a minimum number of credits each semester in order to earn a degree. A full-time year of study is usually equivalent to 60 credits. Non-degree university studies last one to two years and result in award of either a Certificate or Diploma. The undergraduate Bachelors degree is classified as either 'Ordinary' or 'Honours': the former requires three years of study, and the latter at least three, usually four. Dual subject Honours degrees require a minimum of four years, and degrees in professional fields of study may last longer, such as medicine (five years) and law (six years). The first postgraduate-level degree at the University is the Masters, which is open to anyone with a Bachelors (Honours) degree of at least second-class classification. A Masters lasts one to two years and may be either a 'research' or a 'taught' degree. Finally the second postgraduate and highest university-level degree is the Doctor of Philosophy, awarded after three to six years of original research and submission of a thesis.

In late 2009 the Ministry of Education, Employment and Family announced that it was preparing draft legislation on further and higher education to regulate fully private provision by creating the structures to license, accredit and quality-assure further and higher education.

Regulatory and Representative Bodies

GOVERNMENT

Ministry of Education, Employment and the Family: Palazzo Ferreria 310, Republic Str., Valletta VLT 1110; tel. 23886114; fax 25903121; e-mail bryan.magro@gov.mt; internet www.education.gov.mt; Min. for Education, Employment and the Family JAMES CALLEJA; Permanent Sec. PAUL ZAHRA (acting).

ACCREDITATION

ENIC/NARIC Malta: Malta Qualification Recognition Information Centre (Malta QRIC), 16–18 Tower Promenade, St Lucia SLC 1019; tel. 27540051; fax 21801411; e-mail qric.malta@gov.mt; internet www.mqc.gov.mt; Dir Dr JAMES CALLEJA.

Kunsill Malti għall Kwalifiki (Malta Qualifications Council): 16–18 Tower Promenade, St Lucia SLC 1019; tel. and fax 27540051; fax 21808758; e-mail mgc@gov.mt; internet www.mqc.gov.mt; f. 2005; Chair. JOSEPH ABELA FITZPATRICK.

Learned Societies

AGRICULTURE, FISHERIES AND VETERINARY SCIENCE

Agrarian Society: Palazzo de la Salle, 219 Triq ir-Repubblika Valletta VLT 1116; tel. 21244339; fax 21246074; agraria@searchmalta.com; f. 1844; 200 mems; Pres. JOSEPH BORG.

ARCHITECTURE AND TOWN PLANNING

Kamra tal-Periti Malta (Chamber of Architects and Civil Engineers): The Professional Centre, Triq Tas-Sliema, Gzira GZR 1633; tel. and fax 21314265; e-mail info@ktpmalta.com; internet www.ktpmalta.com; f. 1920; mem. of Malta Fed. of Professional Asscns, Architects Council of Europe and Union Internationale des Architectes; 600 mems; Pres. VINCENT CASSAR; Hon. Sec. SIMONE VELLA LENICKER; publ. *The Architect* (4 a year).

BIBLIOGRAPHY, LIBRARY SCIENCE AND MUSEOLOGY

Malta Library and Information Association (MaLIA): c/o Univ. of Malta Library, Msida MSD 2080; tel. 22012262; fax 25997205; e-mail info@malia-malta.org; internet www.malia-malta.org; f. 1969; professional asscn to safeguard the interests of library and information workers; promotes legislation concerning libraries; holds training courses in library and information science; one of the founding mems of the Commonwealth Library Asscn; 100 mems; Chair. LAURENCE ZERAFA; Deputy Chair. ROBERT MIZZI; Sec. CALUDIO LAFERLA.

ECONOMICS, LAW AND POLITICS

Malta Society of Arts, Manufactures and Commerce: Palazzo de la Salle, 219 Triq ir-Republika, Valletta VLT 1116; tel. 21244339; fax 21246074; e-mail info@artsmalta.org; internet www.artsmalta.org; f. 1852; Pres. JOSEPH J. MIFSUD; Hon. Sec. STEPHEN SANT'ANGELO.

FINE AND PERFORMING ARTS

Malta Cultural Institute: 'La Paloma', 16 Triq Sant'Enriku, Sliema SLM 1321; tel. 21338923; e-mail maltacultinst@yahoo.com; internet maltaculturalinstitute.yolasite.com; f. 1949; concerts, ballet, book presentations, painting and sculpture and ceramic exhibitions; 200 mems; Dir and Concert Coordinator MARIE THERESE VASSALLO; Sec. and Legal Advisor VANESSA MAGRO.

LANGUAGE AND LITERATURE

British Council: Exchange Bldgs, Triq ir-Republika, Valletta VLT 1117; tel. 23232403; fax 23232402; e-mail mt.information@britishcouncil.org; internet www.britishcouncil.org/malta; f. 1937; offers courses and examinations in English language and British culture and promotes cultural exchange with the United Kingdom; Dir Dr PETRA BIANCHI.

NATURAL SCIENCES

Biological Sciences

Malta Ecological Foundation (ECO): Dar ECO, 10B Triq Sant' Andrija, Valletta VLT 1341; tel. 21641486; fax 21338780; e-mail eco@ecomalta.org; internet www.ecomalta.org; f. 1992; 4,018 mems; library of 5,100 vols; Dir DUNSTAN HAMILTON; publ. *Stakeholder*.

Research Institutes

LANGUAGE AND LITERATURE

Institute of Linguistics: University of Malta, Msida, MSD 2080; tel. 23403081; internet www.um.edu.mt/linguistics; f. 1988; attached to University of Malta; aims to teach as well as promote and coordinate research in both general and applied linguistics, furthering research involving the description of particular languages, not least Maltese, fostering the study of the various sub-fields of linguistics, and promoting interdisciplinary research; Dir Dr MARTIN R. ZAMMIT.

TECHNOLOGY

Institute for Sustainable Development: University of Malta, Msida, MSD 2080; tel. 23402147; fax 23402565; internet www.um.edu.mt/isd; f. 2009; attached to University of Malta; aims to promote sustainability through interdisciplinary research, focusing on the deployment of information technology to support decision-making and strategy, while encouraging science and technology commercialization to enhance infrastructures, productivity and entrepreneurship; Dir Dr MARIA ATTARD.

Libraries and Archives

Gozo

Gozo Public Library: Triq Vajringa, Victoria, Gozo VCT 105; tel. 21556200; fax 21560599; e-mail gozo.libraries@gov.mt; internet www.libraries.gov.mt/gpl; f. 1853, merged with the Royal Malta (now Nat.) Library 1948; nat. and reference library; copyright deposit library; 35,000 vols; Librarian GEORGE V. BORG.

Msida

University of Malta Library: Msida MSD 2080; tel. 23402316; e-mail dls@um.edu.mt; internet www.um.edu.mt/library; f. 1954 at the Old Univ. bldgs in Valletta; present location 1967; 1,000,000 vols, 1,500 print and 23,000 electronic journals; Dir KEVIN J. ELLUL.

Valletta

National Library of Malta: Valletta CMR 02; tel. 21243297; fax 21235992; e-mail customercare.nlm@gov.mt; internet www .libraries.gov.mt/nlm; f. 1555; incorporates the archives of the Order of St John of Jerusalem; colln of 1,600 historical MSS; 60 incunabula; Dir PHILIP BORG; publ. *Bibljografija Nazzjonali Malta/Malta National Bibliography* (1 a year).

Museums and Art Galleries

Gozo

Archaeology Museum of Gozo: Triq Bieb i-Imdina, The Citadel, Victoria, Gozo VCT 104; tel. 21556144; fax 21559008; f. 1960 as Gozo Museum; present name 1986; illustrates the cultural history of Gozo from the prehistoric era to the early modern period.

Valletta

National Museum of Archaeology: Auberge de Provence, Triq ir-Republika, Valletta VLT 1117; tel. 21221623; fax 21241975; internet www.maltavoyager.com/ moa; array of artefacts dating back to the Neolithic period, covering the period 5200 BC to 2500 BC; library of 2,300 vols.

National Museum of Fine Arts: South St, Valletta VLT 11; tel. 21225769; fax 21239915; f. 1974; colln ranges from early Renaissance period to 20th century; exhibits incl. paintings by Guido Reni, Valentin de Boulogne, Jusepe Ribera, Albert Bierstadt and William Turner.

Sovrintendenza Tal-Patrimonju Kulturali (Superintendence of Cultural Heritage): 173 St Christopher St, Valletta VLT 2000; tel. 23950000; fax 23950555; e-mail heritage .superintendence@gov.mt; internet www .culturalheritage.gov.mt; f. 2002 to replace Museums Dept (f. 1903); govt agency; fulfils duties of the state in ensuring the protection and accessibility of Malta's cultural heritage; responsible for all scientific investigation regarding cultural assets such as the conducting of field work and archaeological excavation, and for the full record keeping and management of documentation resulting from such interventions; evaluates art objects, objects of cultural value and collns of such items; advises and coordinates with the Malta Environment and Planning Authority on issues regarding land use and devt to safeguard cultural heritage when considering applications for planning permission; monitors and controls import and export of goods that are of cultural significance, whether the movement is temporary (for example, for exhibition or restoration purposes) or permanent; issues permits needed for such movements; has a number of direct commitments with regional and int. instns relating to the conservation and promotion of Malta's cultural heritage on int. basis; liaises with UNESCO, the Council of Europe and the European Union; participates in European and Euro-Med programmes; responsible for policy, standards, and guidelines related to cultural heritage and regulates heritage management plans; advises govt on heritage matters; Superintendent ANTHONY PACE.

University

UNIVERSITY OF MALTA

Msida, MSD 2080

Telephone: 23402340
Fax: 23402342
E-mail: comms@um.edu.mt
Internet: www.um.edu.mt

Founded 1592 as Collegium Melitense; elevated to univ. status 1769

Language of instruction: English
Academic year: October to July

Chancellor: Prof. D. J. ATTARD
Pro-Chancellor: B. MIZZI
Rector: Prof. JUANITO CAMILLERI
Pro-Rector for Academic Affairs: Prof. ALFRED J. VELLA
Pro-Rector for Research and Innovation: Prof. RICHARD MUSCAT
Pro-Rector for Student and Institutional Affairs: Prof. MARY ANNE LAURI
Registrar: VERONICA GRECH
Dir of Finance: MARK DEBONO
Dir of Library Services: KEVIN ELLUL

Library of 810,000 vols, 1,500 periodicals in print, 24,000 online periodicals
Number of teachers: 1,333
Number of students: 10,637

Publications: *Journal of Anglo-Italian Studies*, *Journal of Baroque Studies*, *Journal of Education*, *Journal of Maltese Studies*, *Journal of Mediterranean Studies*, *Malta Medical Journal*, *Mediterranean Human Rights Journal*, *Mediterranean Journal of Educational Studies*

DEANS

Faculty for the Built Environment: Prof. A. TORPIANO
Faculty of Arts: Prof. D. FENECH
Faculty of Dental Surgery: Dr NIKOLAI ATTARD
Faculty of Economics, Management and Accountancy: Dr S. GAUCI
Faculty of Education: Prof. V. SOLLARS
Faculty of Engineering: Prof. JOHN BETTS
Faculty of Information and Communication Technology: Dr E .A. CACHIA
Faculty of Health Sciences: Prof. A. XUEREB
Faculty of Laws: Prof. KEVIN AQILINA
Faculty of Media and Knowledge Sciences: Prof. S. CHIRCOP
Faculty of Medicine and Surgery: Prof. G. LAFERLA
Faculty of Science: Prof. C. V. SAMMUT
Faculty of Theology: Rev. Prof. E. AGIUS

College

Malta College of Arts, Science and Technology (MCAST): Triq Kordin, Paola PLA 9032; tel. 23987100; fax 23987316; e-mail information@mcast.edu.nt; internet www .mcast.edu.mt; f. 2001; Bachelors, diploma and certificate courses; Principal and CEO Prof. MAURICE GRECH; Dir EMANUEL ATTARD.

MARSHALL ISLANDS

The Higher Education System

The Republic of the Marshall Islands lies within the area of the Pacific Ocean known as Micronesia. In 1947 the UN authorized the USA to administer the Islands within a Trust Territory of the Pacific Islands. The 1986 Compact of Free Association between the Marshall Islands and the USA was renewed in May 2003. The College of the Marshall Islands (which became independent from the College of Micronesia in 1993) is based on Majuro and had an estimated 919 students enrolled in 2002/03. In 1993 the University of the South Pacific opened an extension centre on Majuro. The Fisheries and Nautical Training Centre offers vocational courses for Marshallese seeking employment in the fishing industry or on passenger liners, cargo ships and tankers. The Ministry of Education is responsible for providing higher education.

Regulatory Body

GOVERNMENT

Ministry of Education: POB 3, Majuro 96960; tel. 625-5262; fax 625-3861; e-mail rmimoe@rmimoe.net; internet www.rmimoe.net; Minister NIDEL LORAK.

Learned Societies

NATURAL SCIENCES

Biological Sciences

Marshall Islands Conservation Society: POB 649, Majuro 96960; e-mail info@coralatolls.org; internet www.coralatolls.org; f. to help Marshallese to manage and protect their atoll environments and to use their resources sustainably; promotes community-based fisheries management, protection for endangered species (humphead wrasse, giant groupers, turtles and sharks); organizes community awareness workshops, conservation practitioner and fisheries observer training; monitors live reef food fish trade and aquarium trade exports.

Research Institutes

AGRICULTURE, FISHERIES AND VETERINARY SCIENCE

Marshall Islands Marine Resources Authority (MIMRA): POB 860, Majuro 96960; tel. 625-8262; fax 625-5447; e-mail mimra@ntamar.com; internet www.mimra.com; research and devt to generate awareness and promote involvement of the local population in sustainable management of coastal resources, incl. outer island fish market, community based fisheries management projects; grant aid projects in partnership with Japanese govt.

HISTORY, GEOGRAPHY AND ARCHAEOLOGY

Historic Preservation Office: POB 1454, Majuro 96960; tel. and fax 625-4476; e-mail rmihpo@ntamar.com; internet members.tripod.com/~alelemuseum/hpo.html; f. 1991 by the Historic Preservation Act of 1991 (amended in 1992) to preserve Marshallese culture; operates with advice and assistance from Advisory Council on Historic Preservation; conducts archaeological survey and inventory, outer island surveys, underwater surveys, oral history and ethnography; maintains RMI Register of Historic Places; attached to Cultural Affairs Div., Min. of Internal Affairs; Historic Preservation Officer FREDERICK DEBRUM; Chief Archaeologist RICHARD WILLIAMSON.

Nuclear Institute: Oscar deBrum Memorial Hall, Majuro; f. 1997; promotes research on and public understanding of history of nuclear weapons and their effects on culture and diplomacy, incl. US nuclear testing programme in the Marshall Islands; partnership with Nuclear Studies Institute of the American Univ. (Washington, DC, q.v.) incl. exchange programme for students and faculty; attached to College of the Marshall Islands; Dir MARY SILK.

Museum

Majuro

Alele Museum, Library and National Archives: POB 629, Majuro 96960; tel. 625-3372; fax 625-3226; e-mail alele@ntamar.com; internet members.tripod.com/~alelemuseum/; f. 1981; Joachim deBrum Colln of over 2,500 glass-plate negatives showing Marshallese life and landscapes during 1880–1930; Bogan Colln of Marshallese crafts from 1940s; recordings of traditional oral literature, video documentaries on cultural and community themes; organizes annual cultural festival (*Lutok Kobban Alele*); incorporates Nat. Archives, 2,500 microfilms covering Trust Territory of the Pacific Islands, Marshall Islands High Court Proceedings, Congress and *Nitijela* legislation, journal colln, Joachim deBrum Memorial Trust Corpn colln, birth and death certificates; library: incl. Pacific Colln of published and unpublished material specific to the Marshall Islands and Oceania; Curator TERRY MOTE.

University

UNIVERSITY OF THE SOUTH PACIFIC, MARSHALL ISLANDS CAMPUS

POB 3537, Majuro 96960
Telephone: 625-7279
Fax: 625-7282
E-mail: uspmaj@ntamar.com
Internet: www.usp.ac.fj/index.php?id=marshall_centre
Founded 1993
Dir: Dr IRENE TAAFAKI
Sec.: LYDIA TIBON
Number of teachers: 10

Colleges

College of the Marshall Islands: POB 1258, Majuro 96960; e-mail webmaster@cmi.edu; internet www.cmi.edu; f. 1989 as College of Micronesia-Majuro, a constituent body of the Community College of Micronesia; accredited and adopted present name 1991; became independent institution 1993; campuses at Arrak (Marshall Islands Science Station) and at Gugeegue on Kwajalein Atoll; Pres. WILSON G. HESS; library: 15,000 vols, 140 periodicals, CD-ROMs, video cassettes, DVDs, maps, microfilm; spec. collns incl. Micronesian Colln (articles, books, proceedings and reports on the area), Marshall Islands Colln (local flora and fauna, historical and cultural materials); 42 teachers; 903 students.

Fisheries and Nautical Training Centre: POB 860 Majuro 96960; tel. 625-7449; fax 625-6221; e-mail mimra@ntamar.com; offers vocational courses for Marshallese seeking employment in the fishing industry or on passenger liners, cargo ships and tankers; attached to Marshall Islands Marine Resources Authority; Instructor WILLIAM SOKOMI.

MAURITANIA

The Higher Education System

Mauritania, formerly part of French West Africa, achieved full independence on 28 November 1960 (having become a self-governing member of the French Community two years earlier). The earliest institution of higher education was the Institut National des Hautes Etudes Islamiques (founded 1961). Université de Nouakchott, the only university-level institution, was founded in 1981. In 2005/06 there were 10,157 students enrolled in the four higher education institutions. The Ministry of National Education is the responsible government body for higher education, which is free (barring a nominal registration fee).

Université de Nouakchott is governed by the University Assembly, the membership of which is made up from the staff, students and government officials. The University Assembly is headed by the university President or Rector. The Vice-Chancellor is in charge of administration, and the senior academic officers are the Deans, Vice-Deans and General Secretary.

The secondary school Baccalauréat is the main requirement for admission to tertiary education. The university degree system is based on the old-style French model and consists of two cycles. The first cycle lasts for two years and results in award of the Diplôme d'Etudes Universitaires Générales. An exception to this is the Ecole Nationale d'Administration, which awards a Diplôme after five years of study. The second cycle is two years in duration and culminates with the award of the Maîtrise. There are no postgraduate-level degrees; students usually complete their higher education abroad.

The Centre Supérieur d'Enseignement Technique is the leading institution of technical and vocational education, and specializes in mechanical and electrical engineering.

Regulatory Bodies

GOVERNMENT

Ministry of Culture, Youth and Sports: BP 223, Nouakchott; tel. 525-11-30; Minister MOHAMED VALL OULD CHEIKH.

Ministry of National Education: BP 387, Nouakchott; tel. 525-12-37; fax 525-12-22; Minister NEGGHOUHA MINT MOHAMED VALL.

Learned Societies

BIBLIOGRAPHY, LIBRARY SCIENCE AND MUSEOLOGY

Association Mauritanienne des Bibliothécaires, Archivistes et Documentalistes: c/o Bibliothèque Nationale, BP 20, Nouakchott; f. 1979; Pres. O. DIOUWARA; Sec. SID'AHMED FALL.

LANGUAGE AND LITERATURE

Alliance Française: BP 5022, Nouakchott; tel. and fax 525-31-48; e-mail afm@mauritel.mr; offers courses and exams in French language and culture and promotes cultural exchange with France; attached teaching centres in Atar, Kaedi and Nouadhibou.

Research Institutes

GENERAL

Institut Mauritanien de Recherche Scientifique: BP 196, Nouakchott; Dir Prof. MOHAMED LEMINE OULD HAMMADI.

AGRICULTURE, FISHERIES AND VETERINARY SCIENCE

Institut Supérieur des Sciences et Techniques Halieutiques: Nouadhibou-Cansado; tel. 554-90-47; fax 554-90-28; f. 1983; part of Economic Community of West Africa; research and training in the fisheries industry; Dir-Gen. D. SOGUI.

TECHNOLOGY

Direction des Mines et de la Géologie: Ministère des Mines et de l'Industrie, BP 199, Nouakchott; tel. 225-30-83; fax 225-69-37; e-mail mmi@mauritania.mr; f. 1968; 17 mems; library of 3,000 vols; Dir WANE IBRAHIMA LAMINE.

Libraries and Archives

Boutilimit

Arab Library: Boutilimit; library of the late Grand Marabout, Abd Allah Ould Chelkh Sidya.

Chinguetti

Arab Library: Chinguetti; several private religious libraries, with a total of 3,229 vols, including pre-Islamic MSS; Librarian MOHAMED ABDALLAHI OULD FALL.

Kaédi

Arab Library: Kaédi; ancient religious texts.

Nouakchott

Archives Nationales: BP 77, Nouakchott; tel. 225-23-17; fax 225-26-36; f. 1955; 3,000 vols, 1,000 periodicals; documentation centre; Dir NAGI OULD MOHAMED MAHMOUD; publ. *Chaab* (daily).

Bibliothèque Nationale: BP 20, Nouakchott; f. 1965; deposit library; documentation centre for W Africa; 10,000 vols, 4,000 old MSS; 8 mems; Head Librarian OUMAR DIOUAWARA; Historian Prof. MOKTAR OULD HAMIDOU.

Centre de Documentation Pédagogique: BP 171, Nouakchott; f. 1962; 1,000 vols; 58 periodicals; educational and general works; Librarian MOHAMMED SAID.

Oualata

Arab Library: Oualata.

Tidjikja

Arab Library: Tidjikja; Librarian AHMEDOU OULD MOHAMED MAHMOUD.

University

UNIVERSITÉ DE NOUAKCHOTT

BP 798, Nouakchott
Telephone: 525-13-82
Fax: 525-39-97
E-mail: webmaster@univ-nkc.mr
Internet: www.univ-nkc.mr
Founded 1981
State control
Languages of instruction: Arabic, French, English
Academic year: October to June
Rector: MOHAMED EL HACEN OULD LEBATT
Librarian: ISSA OULD MOHAMED AHMED
Library of 20,059 vols
Number of teachers: 254
Number of students: 10,000
Publications: *Annales de la Faculté des Lettres et Sciences Humaines* (1 a year), *Revue d'Études Juridiques et Économiques* (1 a year)

DEANS

Faculty of Law and Economics: SIDI MOHAMED ABDELLAHI
Faculty of Letters and Human Sciences: DIALLO IBRAHIMA MOUSSA
Faculty of Science and Technology: AHMEDOH OULD HAOUBA

Colleges

Ecole Nationale d'Administration: BP 252, Nouakchott; tel. 525-32-22; fax 525-75-17; f. 1966; library: 8,000 vols; a documentation and research centre for the study of administration and politics in Mauritania; first degree courses; 33 teachers; 266 students; Librarian YARBA FALL; Dir CHEIK MOHAMED SALEM OULD MOHAMED LEMINE; publs *Annales, Futurs Cadres* (3 a year).

Institut National des Hautes Etudes Islamiques: Boutilimit; f. 1961; 300 students.

Institut Supérieur Scientifique: BP 5026, Nouakchott; tel. 525-11-68; fax 525-39-97; f. 1986; mathematics, physics, chemistry, biology, geology, computer studies, natural resources, ecology; library: 30,000 vols; Dir AHMEDOU OULD HAMED.

MAURITIUS

The Higher Education System

Mauritius became independent, within the Commonwealth, in 1968. In 1992 the Republic of Mauritius was proclaimed. The University of Mauritius (founded 1965) is the oldest existing institution of higher education in Mauritius. In 2006/07, 7,531 students were enrolled at the University (34.3% of whom were part-time students); in addition, many students receive further education abroad. In 2007, 9,573 students were enrolled in technical and vocational institutions. Government funding accounts for an estimated 85% of the University's running costs; the rest is made up from students' tuition fees, consultancy work and commercial rent.

The Council is the University policy-making body with control of administration and finance, and the Senate is the highest academic body. The Court is a body that meets annually to discuss general plans. The five Faculty Boards coordinate all teaching and research, administer examinations and evaluate programmes of study, and act on the instructions of the Vice-Chancellor and Senate. The Mahatma Gandhi Institute also offers Bachelors degree courses.

Two GCE A-Levels are the minimum requirement for admission to higher education, although for one- to three-year Certificate and Diploma courses the minimum requirement is the Cambridge Overseas School Certificate. Undergraduate Bachelors degree courses at the University last three to four years, depending on the subject, but students wishing to study for professional degrees in dentistry or medicine must attend institutions outside the country. Following the Bachelors, the first postgraduate degree is the Masters, which lasts two to three years. The Masters of Philosophy is a research-based degree available in a number of subject areas. Finally, the Doctor of Philosophy is the highest university-level degree and is a research-based period of study lasting at least three years.

Post-secondary vocational and technical qualifications include several Brevets and Diplomas.

The Tertiary Education Commission is aiming to promote, plan, develop and coordinate post-secondary education in Mauritius and implement a regulatory framework to achieve an international-quality education system. It is also responsible for allocating government funds to the tertiary education institutions under its purview and ensuring accountability and optimum use of resources.

Regulatory and Representative Bodies

GOVERNMENT

Ministry of Arts and Culture: Renganaden Seeneevassen Bldg, 7th Floor, cnr Pope Hennessy and Maillard Sts, Port Louis; tel. 212-9993; fax 208-0315; e-mail minoac@intnet.mu; internet culture.gov.mu; Minister MAHENDRA GOWRESSOO; Permanent Sec. NAYEN KOOMAR BALLAH.

Ministry of Education and Human Resources: IVTB House, Pont Fer, Phoenix; tel. 601-5200; fax 698-2550; e-mail moeps@mail.gov.mu; internet ministry-education.gov.mu; Minister DHARAMBEER GOKHOOL.

NATIONAL BODY

Tertiary Education Commission: Réduit; tel. 467-8800; fax 467-6579; e-mail mohadeb@tec.mu; internet www.tec.mu; f. 1988; allocates funds to tertiary education instns from govt and other sources; oversees quality of educational provision in these instns; accredits tertiary-level programmes offered by the private sector; 9 mems; Chair. Prof. DONALD AH-CHUEN; Exec. Dir Dr PRAVEEN MOHADEB (acting).

Learned Societies

GENERAL

Royal Society of Arts and Sciences of Mauritius: c/o Mauritius Sugar Industry Research Institute, Réduit; tel. 454-1061; fax 454-1971; e-mail rsas@msiri.mu; f. 1829; Royal title 1847; 210 mems; Pres. Dr ASHA DOOKUN-SAUMTALLY; Hon. Sec. ROSEMAY NG KEE KWONG; publ. *Proceedings* (irregular).

AGRICULTURE, FISHERIES AND VETERINARY SCIENCE

Société de Technologie Agricole et Sucrière de Maurice: Mauritius Sugar Industry Research Institute, Réduit; tel. 454-1061; fax 454-1971; e-mail rngcheong@msiri.intnet.mu; f. 1910; 390 mems; Pres. Dr K. F. NG KEE KWONG; Hon. Sec. Dr R. NG CHEONG; publ. *Revue Agricole et Sucrière de l'Ile Maurice*.

HISTORY, GEOGRAPHY AND ARCHAEOLOGY

Société de l'Histoire de l'Ile Maurice: rue de Froberville, Curepipe Rd, BP 150, Port Louis; f. 1938; 810 ordinary mems; Hon. Sec. G. RAMET; publs *Bulletin*, *Dictionary of Mauritian Biography*.

LANGUAGE AND LITERATURE

Alliance Française: 1, rue Victor Hugo, Bell Village, Port Louis; tel. 212-2949; fax 212-2812; e-mail afim@intnet.mu; internet www.afmccf.com; offers courses and examinations in French language and culture and promotes cultural exchange with France; six attached teaching centres in Port Louis.

British Council: Royal Rd, POB 111, Rose Hill, Mauritius; tel. 454-9550; fax 454-9553; e-mail general.enquiries@mu.britishcouncil.org; internet www.britishcouncil.org/mauritius; offers courses and examinations in English language and British culture and promotes cultural exchange with the UK; also responsible for British Council work in Madagascar and the Seychelles; Dir ROSALIND BURFORD.

Research Institutes

AGRICULTURE, FISHERIES AND VETERINARY SCIENCE

Mauritius Sugar Industry Research Institute: 1 Moka Rd, Réduit; tel. 454-1061; fax 454-1971; e-mail contact@msiri.intnet.mu; internet www.msiri.mu; f. 1953; research on cane breeding, agronomy, soils, diseases, pests, weeds, botany, mechanization, biotechnology, sugar manufacture, by-products, also on food crops cultivated in association with sugar-cane and between cane cycles; library: see Libraries and Archives; Dir Dr KWET FONG NG KEE KWONG; publs *Flore de Mascareignes* (irregular), *Occasional Papers* (irregular), *Occasional Reports & Monographs* (irregular).

NATURAL SCIENCES

Biological Sciences

Research Centre for Mauritius Flora and Fauna: c/o Mauritius Institute, POB 54, Port Louis; tel. 212-0639; fax 212-5717; attached to Mauritius Institute.

Libraries and Archives

Coromandel

National Archives: Devt Bank of Mauritius Complex, Coromandel; tel. 233-4211; fax 233-4299; e-mail arc@mail.gov.mu; f. 1815; the Conservation Unit is responsible for the repair of damaged records, incl. Photographic Section, Microfilm Section, Bindery, Oral History Unit and Paper Restoration Unit; 500,000 vols; records of the French (1721–1810) and British (1810–1968) Administrations consisting of MSS and printed matters, notarial papers, Land Court registers, maps and plans; open to the public; Chief Archives Officer PIERRE ROLAND CHUNG SAM WAN; Archivist DIANA ISOBELLE BABLEE.

Curepipe

Carnegie Library: Queen Elizabeth II Ave, Curepipe; tel. 674-2287; fax 676-5054; f. 1920; spec. colln on Indian Ocean islands; 90,000 vols; Senior Librarian T. K. HURRYNAG-RAMNAUTH.

Port Louis

City Library: City Hall, POB 422, Port Louis; tel. 212-0831 ext. 163; fax 212-4258; internet mpl.intnet.mu/library.htm; f. 1851; 110,000 vols; important collections on Mauritius and archives of Port Louis Municipal Council; music scores; depository for WHO publications; Head Librarian BENJAMIN SILARSAH; publs *Subject Bibliography on Mauritius* (1 a year), *Subject Index to Local Newspapers* (2 a year).

Mauritius Institute Public Library: POB 54, Port Louis; tel. 212-0639; fax 212-5717; f. 1902; legal deposit library and depository library for UNESCO; 60,000 vols, including an extensive collection of books, articles and reports on Mauritius; Head Librarian S. ANKIAH.

Réduit

Mauritius Sugar Industry Research Institute (MSIRI) Library: Réduit; tel. 454-1061; fax 454-1971; e-mail library@msiri.mu; internet www.msiri.mu; f. 1953; rep. colln on all aspects of sugar cane cultivation and sugar manufacture, and expanding colln on food crops; wide coverage of technical periodical literature; colln of prints and drawings and early publs on sugar cane; in-house databases and int. colln of CD-ROM databases and full texts; 31,790 vols; Man. of Scientific Information and Publs Dept ROSEMAY NG KEE KWONG.

University of Mauritius Library: Réduit; tel. 454-1041; fax 464-0905; e-mail uomlibrary@uom.ac.mu; internet www.uom.ac.mu; f. 1965; important collns in fields of admin., social sciences, agriculture, science and technology, law, textile engineering, medical research and Mauritiana; partial depository for UN and World Bank publs; 175,000 vols (140,000 books, 35,000 bound vols of periodicals); Chief Librarian ISHWARDUTH DASSYNE.

Museums and Art Galleries

Mahebourg

Historical Museum: Mahebourg; tel. 631-9329; f. 1950; a branch of the Mauritius Institute; comprises collection of old maps, engravings, watercolours and naval relics of local interest, exhibited in an 18th-century French house; Dir R. GAJEELEE.

Port Louis

Port Louis Museum: Mauritius Institute, Port Louis; tel. 212-2815; fax 212-5717; e-mail mimuse@intnet.mu; f. 1880; comprises a Natural History Museum, collections of fauna, flora and geology of Mauritius and of the other islands of the Mascarene region; Dir S. ABDOOLRAHAMAN.

Réduit

Mauritius Herbarium: c/o Mauritius Sugar Industry Research Institute, Réduit; tel. 454-1061; fax 454-1971; e-mail cbaider@msiri.intnet.mu; internet www.msiri.mu; f. 1960; public herbarium for education and research about native flora; specializes in flora of Mascarene Islands; Herbarium Officer Dr CLAUDIA BAIDER; Librarian ROSEMARY NG KEE KWONG; publ. *Flore des Mascareignes* (irregular).

Universities

UNIVERSITY OF MAURITIUS

Réduit

Telephone: 454-1041
Fax: 454-9642
E-mail: website@uom.ac.mu
Internet: www.uom.ac.mu

Founded 1965
Languages of instruction: English, French
partly State funded
Academic year: August to July

Chancellor: Sir RAMESH JEEWOOLALL
Pro-Chancellor: Prof. S. JUGESSUR
Vice-Chancellor: Prof. I. FAGOONEE
Pro-Vice-Chancellor for Research, Consultancy and Innovation: Prof. SOONIL RUGHOOPUTH
Pro-Vice-Chancellor for Teaching and Learning: Prof. B. AMEENATH GURIB-FAKIM
Registrar: S. REKHA ISSUR-GOORAH
Chief Librarian: I. DASSYNE (acting)

Library: see Libraries and Archives
Number of teachers: 510 (248 full-time, 262 part-time)
Number of students: 8,474

Publications: *Calendar* (1 a year), *Research Journal* (1 a year), *Vice-Chancellor's Report*

DEANS

Faculty of Agriculture: Assoc. Prof. Dr D. PUCHOOA (acting)
Faculty of Engineering: Prof. Dr R. MOHEE
Faculty of Law and Management: Assoc. Prof. T. D. JUWAHEER
Faculty of Science: Prof. H. T. Y. LI KAM WAH
Faculty of Social Studies and Humanities: Assoc. Prof. Dr S. K. SOBHEE

PROFESSORS

BAHORUN, T. (Applied Biochemistry)
BHURUTH, M. (Computational Mathematics)
BUNWAREE, S. S. (Gender and Development Studies)
JHURRY, D. (Chemistry)
MOHEE, R., Chemical and Environmental Engineering
RAMJEAWON, T. (Environmental Engineering)
RUGHOOPUTH, H. C. S., Electrical and Electronic Engineering
SOBHEE, S. K. (Applied Economics and Development Studies)
SOYJAUDAH, K. M. S. (Communication Engineering)
SUBRATTY, A. H. (Biochemistry)

UNIVERSITY OF TECHNOLOGY, MAURITIUS

La Tour Koenig, Pointe-aux-Sables

Telephone: 234-7624
Fax: 234-1660
E-mail: registrar@umail.utm.ac.mu
Internet: www.utm.ac.mu

Founded 2000 by Act of Parliament
Language of instruction: English
Academic year: August to June
State control

Dir-Gen.: DHARMANAND GUPT FOKEER
Registrar: Dr SANJIV KUMAR BABOOA
Librarian: SAVITA BHOOABUL

Library of 20,500 vols
Number of teachers: 341 (40 full-time, 301 part-time)
Number of students: 3,938 (3,279 full-time, 659 part-time)

HEADS OF SCHOOLS

School of Business, Management and Finance: Dr H. CHITTOO
School of Innovative Technologies and Engineering: Dr N. MOHAMUDALLY
School of Sustainable Development and Tourism: Dr R. DURBARRY

Colleges

Mahatma Gandhi Institute: Moka; tel. 403-2000; fax 433-2235; e-mail vkoonjal@intnet.mu; internet mgi.intnet.mu; f. 1970; serves as a centre for the study of Indian culture and traditions, and the promotion of education and culture; courses in Indian music and dance, fine arts, Indian languages, Mandarin and Indian philosophy; research in Indian and immigration studies, culture and civilization, Bhojpuri, folklore and oral traditions and Mauritian history, geography and literature; spec. collns: Gandhi, Mauritius, archives relating to Indian immigration to Mauritius 1842–1912; library: 100,000 vols; 218 secondary teachers, 76 in tertiary sector; 2,336 students; Chair. L. NUCKCHADY; Dir-Gen. S. NIRSIMLOO GAYAN (acting); Registrar Dr V. D. KOONJAL; publs *Journal of Mauritian Studies* (2 a year, in English), *Rimjhim* (4 a year, in Hindi), *Vasant* (4 a year, in Hindi).

Mauritius College of the Air: Réduit; tel. 403-8200; fax 464-8854; e-mail mca@mca.ac.mu; internet www.mca.ac.mu; f. 1972; runs distance education programmes; provides the national broadcasting organization with programmes for schools; produces audiovisual material for use by children and adults in formal and non-formal education; acquires pre-recorded media-based educational material from overseas and makes it available to schools in Mauritius; library: 9,500 vols; 62 part-time tutors; 1,780 students; Dir MEENA SEETULSINGH.

Robert Antoine Sugar Industry Training Centre: Royal Rd, Réduit; tel. 454-7024; fax 454-7026; e-mail rasitc@intnet.mu; internet pages.intnet.mu/rasitc; f. 1980; courses in sugar cane agronomy, cane sugar manufacture and chemical control in sugar factories, mechanization of field operations, power generation for sugar factories, management skills, supervisory skills, leadership development, communications; courses in English and French at various levels; 100 part-time specialists; 800 part-time students; Dir Dr LINDA MAMET.

MEXICO

The Higher Education System

From the 1520s until independence in 1821 Mexico was under Spanish rule. The oldest current institutions of higher education date from this period, among them Universidad Nacional Autónoma de México (founded 1551), Universidad de Guanajuato (founded 1732; current name 1945), Universidad Autónoma de Campeche (founded 1756) and Universidad de Guadalajara (founded 1792). The Secretaría de Educación Pública (SEP) is the government ministry responsible for the administration of education at all levels, but following legislation enacted in 1992 granting greater autonomy to the Federal States, there has been an increase in the number of privately run institutions of higher education. In early 2006 the Congreso de la Unión (Parliament) passed legislation requiring all public and private institutions of higher education that offered degree programmes to be accredited; before this there were no national standards for accreditation or quality assurance. In 2007/08 there were an estimated 5,549 institutes of higher education, attended by 2,528,700 students in 2006/07, including postgraduates. Institutions of higher education are classified as Universities, Technological Universities or Institutes, Polytechnics or Teachers' Colleges.

To gain admission to a first degree programme, an applicant must possess the certificate for completion of secondary school, the Bachillerato, and sit an entrance examination. The Technological Universities have introduced a specialist two-year course (Técnico Superior Universitario), which can either be used to transfer to the four-year Licenciado (see below) or as a complete qualification in its own right. The Licenciado is offered at undergraduate level by all institutions of higher education and usually lasts four years, although degrees awarded in conjunction with a professional title may last longer. The first postgraduate degree is the Maestría, which is a one- or three-year research-based course of study. Finally, the Doctorado is a two- to three-year period of research and represents the highest level of university qualifications.

Post-secondary awards for vocational and technical education include the Salida Lateral or Carrera Corta (two to three years) leading to a Diploma or Titulo Técnico.

A bill passed in 2006 by the Mexican Senate required all degrees offered by Mexican universities to undergo external evaluation. Institutions awarding degrees that do not meet the required national standards will have their licenses suspended.

Regulatory and Representative Bodies

GOVERNMENT

Secretariat of State for Public Education: Dinamarca 84, 5°, Col. Juárez, 06600 México, DF; tel. (55) 5510-2557; fax (55) 5329-6873; e-mail educa@sep.gob.mx; internet www.sep.gob.mx; Sec. of Public Education JOSEFINA VÁZQUEZ MOTA; Permanent Sec. Lic. JULIO CASTELLANOS RAMÍREZ.

ACCREDITATION

Consejo para la Acreditación de la Educación Superior (COPAES) (Higher Education Accreditation Council): Av. San Jerónimo 120, Col. Jardines del Pedregal, Del. Álvaro Obregón, 04500 México, DF; tel. (55) 5616-5210; e-mail acreditacion@copaes.org; internet www.copaes.org.mx; f. 2000; non-profit NGO contributing towards the quality assurance of academic programmes in public and private instns by recognizing official accrediting orgs that in turn accredit undergraduate degree programmes in many study areas; Gen. Dir Dr JAVIER DE LA GARZA AGUILAR.

NATIONAL BODIES

Asociación Nacional de Universidades e Instituciones de Educación Superior (ANUIES) (National Association of Universities and Institutions of Higher Education): Tenayuca 200, Col. Santa Cruz Atoyac, 03310 México, DF; tel. (55) 5420-4900; e-mail rlc@anuies.mx; internet www.anuies.mx; f. 1950; coordinates and represents instns of higher education, studies academic and admin. problems of the nat. higher education system; promotes exchange of personnel, information and services between the affiliated instns; 145 affiliated univs, centres and colleges; library of 11,500 vols; Exec. Sec.-Gen. Dr RAFAEL LÓPEZ CASTAÑARES;

publs *Confluencia* (12 a year), *Revista de la Educación Superior* (4 a year).

Centro de Cooperación Regional para la Educación de Adultos en América Latina y el Caribe (CREFAL)/Centre for Regional Cooperation for Adult Education in Latin America and the Caribbean: Avda Lázaro Cárdenas 525, Col. Revolución, 61609 Pátzcuaro, Michoacán; tel. (434) 342-8200; fax (434) 342-8151; e-mail crefal@crefal.edu.mx; internet www.crefal.edu.mx; f. 1951 by UNESCO and OAS, now administered by a Board of Dirs from mem. countries; regional technical assistance, specialist training in literary and adult education, research; library of 80,416 vols; library: CEDEAL/CREFAL Adult Education documentation centre for Latin America: database of 17,347 entries; Dir HUMBERTO SALAZAR HERRERA; publs *Decisio—saberes para la Acción en Educación de Adultos* (3 a year), *Revista Interamericana de Educación de Adultos* (3 a year).

Dirección General de Relaciones Educativas, Científicas y Culturales (Board of Educational, Scientific and Cultural Relations): Secretaría de Educación Pública, Argentina 28, Centro Histórico, 06029 México, DF; tel. (55) 3601-1000; f. 1960; comprises Sections of Technical Assistance, Int. Relations in the fields of Education, Science and Culture and Exchange; serves as co-ordinating agency between the UN, UNESCO, the OAS and the Mexican Govt; Dir Dr ENRIQUE G. LEÓN LÓPEZ.

Federación de Instituciones Mexicanas Particulares de Educación Superior (Federation of Mexican Higher Education Institutions): Río Guadalquivir 50, 4° piso, Col. Cuauhtémoc, 06500 México, DF; tel. (55) 5514-5514; fax (55) 5207-0581; e-mail vcampuza@fimpes.org.mx; internet www.fimpes.org.mx; f. 1981; comprises 114 higher education instns incl. the principal private univs; works to improve communication and collaboration between its mems and the other educational instns in the country; promotes

high academic standards; Exec. Sec. Lic. VICTOR CAMPUZANO TARDITI.

Learned Societies

GENERAL

Colegio Nacional (National College): Luis González Obregón 23, Centro Histórico, 06020 México, DF; tel. (55) 5789-4330; fax (55) 5702-1779; e-mail colnal@mx.inter.net; internet www.colegionacional.org.mx; f. 1943; disseminates nat. culture; 38 mems; library of 35,000 vols, 10,000 periodicals; Sec./Administrator Lic. FAUSTO VEGA Y GÓMEZ; publ. *Memoria* (1 a year).

UNESCO Office Mexico: Pte Masaryk no. 526, 3er piso, Colonia Polanco, 11560 México, DF; tel. (55) 3601-1650; fax (55) 3601-1652; e-mail mexico@unesco.org; internet www.unesco-mexico.org; f. 1967; Dir Dr KATHERINE GRIGSBY.

AGRICULTURE, FISHERIES AND VETERINARY SCIENCE

Sociedad Agronómica Mexicana (Mexican Agricultural Society): Mariano Azuela 121, 2° piso, Del. Cuauhtémoc, 06400 México, DF; f. 1921.

Sociedad Forestal Mexicana (Mexican Forestry Society): Calle de Jesús Terán 11, México 1, DF; f. 1921; 225 mems; Exec. Pres. Ing. RIGOBERTO VÁSQUEZ DE LA PARRA; Sec.-Gen. Lic. ADOLFO AGUILAR Y QUEVEDO; publ. *México Forestal* (6 a year).

ARCHITECTURE AND TOWN PLANNING

Asociación de Ingenieros y Arquitectos de México (Association of Mexican Engineers and Architects): Av. Constituyentes 800 (Oficina AIAM), Col. Belén de las Flores, México, DF; f. 1868; 560 mems; library of 7,565 vols; Pres. Ing. FEDERICO DOVALI RAMOS; Sec. Ing. JOSÉ ACOSTA SÁNCHEZ;

publ. *Revista Mexicana de Ingeniería y Arquitectura* (4 a year).

BIBLIOGRAPHY, LIBRARY SCIENCE AND MUSEOLOGY

Asociación Mexicana de Bibliotecarios, AC (Mexican Library Association): Apdo 12-792, Administración de Correos 12, 03001 México, DF; Angel Urraza 817-A, Col. Del Valle, 03100 México, DF; tel. (55) 5575-3396; fax (55) 5575-1135; e-mail correo@ambac.org .mx; internet www.ambac.org.mx; f. 1924; 1,061 mems; Pres. FELIPE BECERRIL TORRES; Sec. ELÍAS CID RAMÍREZ; publs *Memorias de las Jornadas Mexicanas de Biblioteconomía* (1 a year), *Noticiero de la AMBAC* (4 a year), *Revista Liber*.

Dirección General de Bibliotecas (Main Directorate of Libraries): Universidad Nacional Autónoma de México, Ciudad Universitaria, Apdo 70–392, 04510 México, DF; tel. (55) 5622-3960; fax (55) 5622-4938; e-mail sinfo@dgb.unam.mx; internet dgb.unam.mx; f. 1966; documentation service, current awareness and SDI services, computerized bibliographical searches; digital library of 6,000 periodical titles with full text; 140 specialized databases; library of 3,485 vols; special collection of 230 titles of abstracting and indexing periodicals; 2,500 Latin American periodicals; Dir Dra SILVIA GONZÁLEZ MARÍN; publs *Biblioteca Universitaria* (electronic, irregular), *CLASE* (quarterly index of Latin American citation in social sciences and humanities), *PERIODICA* (quarterly index of Latin American science and technology journals).

ECONOMICS, LAW AND POLITICS

Barra Mexicana—Colegio de Abogados (Mexican Bar Association—College of Advocates): Varsovia No. 1, Colonia Juárez, 06600 México, DF; tel. (55) 5208-3115; fax (55) 5208-3117; e-mail labarra@bma.org.mx; internet www.bma.org.mx; f. 1922; 1,732 mems; library of 5,260 vols; Pres. Lic. FABIÁN AGUINACO BRAVO; Sec. Lic. CARLOS PASTRANA Y ÁNGELES; publs *El Foro* (2 a year), *La Barra* (6 a year).

Instituto Nacional de Estadística, Geografía (National Institute of Statistics and Geography): Avda Héroe de Nacozari sur 2301, Fracc. Jardines del Parque, Puerta 10 basamento, Departamento de Comunicación Social, 20276 Aguascalientes, AGS; tel. (449) 910-53-00; fax (449) 462-4133; e-mail comunicacionsocial@inegi.org.mx; internet www.inegi.gob.mx; f. 1983; integrates and develops the Nat. System of Statistics and the Geographic Information System; undertakes the Nat. Census; library of 15,000 vols; Pres. Dr EDUARDO SOJO GARZA ALDAPE; publs *Agenda Estadística de los Estados Unidos Mexicanos* (1 a year), *Anuario de Estadísticas por Entidad Federativa* (1 a year), *Anuario Estadístico del Comercio Exterior* (electronic, 1 a year), *Anuario Estadístico del Estado* (separate vol. for each state of Mexico), *Anuario Estadístico de los Estados Unidos Mexicanos* (electronic, 1 a year), *Boletín de los Sistemas Nacionales Estadístico y de Información Geográfica* (electronic, 1 a year), *Cuaderno Estadístico de la Zona Metropolitana de la Ciudad de México* (electronic, 1 a year), *El Sector Alimentario en México* (1 a year), *Encuesta Nacional de Ocupación y Empleo* (electronic, 1 a year), *La Industria Automotriz en México* (1 a year), *La Industria Maquiladora de Exportación*, *La Industria Química en México* (1 a year), *La Industria Siderúrgica en México* (1 a year), *La Industria Textil y del Vestido en México* (1 a year), *La Minería en México* (1 a year), *México en el Mundo* (every 2 years).

EDUCATION

Centro Nacional de Documentación e Información Pedagógica y Museo Pedagógico Nacional (National Centre for Educational Documentation and Information and National Educational Museum): Calle Presidente Masaryk 526, México 5, DF; f. 1971; library of 10,000 vols; Dir Prof. MARIANO CRUZ PÉREZ; publs *Documentación e Información* (12 a year), *Lista de Canje* (2 a year), *Sep-Forjadores* (12 a year).

FINE AND PERFORMING ARTS

Asociación Musical Manuel M. Ponce, AC (Manuel M. Ponce Musical Association): Espíritu Santo 75, Col. Coyoacán. 0400, México DF; tel. and fax (55) 5554-4028; e-mail tere_castrillon@terra.com.mx; f. 1949; promotes annual concert seasons of traditional, modern and contemporary Mexican and foreign music; library of musical scores, tapes, records and books; Hon. Pres. LUIS HERRERA DE LA FUENTE; Pres. MARIA TERESA CASTRILLÓN; Vice-Pres. RAMÓN ROMO; Musical Dir MARIA TERESA CASTRILLÓN; Sec. MANUEL ZACARÍAS.

Ateneo Veracruzano (Veracruz Athenaeum): Edif. Lonja Mercantil, Independencia 924, Vera Cruz; f. 1933; 68 mems (18 corresp.); Pres. C.P.T. FRANCISCO BROISSIN A.; Sec. Prof. ANTONIO SALAZAR PÁEZ; publ. *Boletín* (12 a year).

Instituto Nacional de Bellas Artes y Literature (National Institute of Fine Arts and Literature): Paseo de la Reforma y Campo Marte s/n, Col. Chapultepec Polanco, 11560 México, DF; tel. (55) 5521-9251; internet www.cnca.gob.mx/cnca/buena/inba/intro.html; f. 1947; consists of depts of music, visual arts, opera, literature, dance, theatrical production, architecture, artistic education and admin.; responsible for cultural insts throughout Mexico; Dir GERARDO ESTRADA; publs *Boletín de Literatura* (6 a year), *Revista de Educación Artística* (4 a year), *Revista Hetereofonía* (3 a year), *Revista Pauta* (6 a year).

Affiliated institution:

Centro Nacional de Conservación y Registro del Patrimonio Artístico Mueble (National Centre for Conservation and Registry of Movable Art Heritage): San Ildefonso 60, Col. Centro, Del. Cuauhtémoc, México DF; tel. (55) 5702-2323; fax (55) 5702-2143; f. 1958; restoration of works of art; Dir LUCIA GARCIA NORIEGA Y NIETO.

HISTORY, GEOGRAPHY AND ARCHAEOLOGY

Academia Mexicana de la Historia (Mexican Academy of History): Plaza Carlos Pacheco 21, Col. Centro, Cuauhtémoc, 06070 México, DF; tel. (55) 5518-2708; fax (55) 5521-9653; e-mail informes@acadmexhistoria.org.mx; internet www .acadmexhistoria.org.mx; f. 1919; 30 mems; correspondent of Real Academia, Madrid; library of 10,000 vols; Dir Dr MIGUEL LEÓN-PORTILLA; Sec. Dr GISELA VON WOBESER; publ. *Memorias* (2 a year).

Academia Nacional de Historia y Geografía (National Academy of History and Geography): Londres 60, Col. Juárez, Del. Cuauhtémoc, 06600 México 6, DF; tel. (55) 5533-4149; f. 1925; 179 mems; Dir Dr JESÚS FERRER GAMBOA; publ. *Revista*.

Departamento de Antropología e Historia de Nayarit (Department of Anthropology and History in Nayarit): Avda México 91, Tepic, Nayarit; f. 1946; Dir EVERARDO PEÑA NAVARRO; Sec. MARÍA A. GONZÁLEZ A.

Sociedad Mexicana de Geografía y Estadística (Mexican Society of Geography and Statistics): Calle de Justo Sierra 19, Apdo 10739, Del. Cuauhtémoc, 06020 México, DF; tel. (55) 5542-7341; fax (55) 5522-2055; e-mail ismge@prodigy.net.mx; f. 1833; 1,204 active mems, 640 corresponding mems; library of 450,000 vols; Pres. Lic. JULIO ZAMORA BÁTIZ; Sec.-Gen. LEOPOLDO CHAGOYA MORGAN; publs *Boletín* (3 a year), and special works.

Sociedad Mexicana de Historia de la Ciencia y la Tecnología (Mexican Society for History of Science and Technology): Edif. de las Sociedades Científicas, Avda Cipreses s/n, Col. San Andrés Totoltepec, 14400 México, DF; tel. (55) 5849-6830; fax (55) 5849-6831; e-mail info@smhct.org; internet www.smhct.org; f. 1964; Pres. Dr JUAN JOSÉ SALDAÑA; publs *Anales*, *Memorias*, *Quipu*.

LANGUAGE AND LITERATURE

Academia Mexicana de la Lengua (Mexican Academy of Letters): Liverpool 76, Col. Juárez, 06600 México, DF; tel. (55) 5208-2526; fax (55) 5208-2416; e-mail academia@ academia.org.mx; internet www.academia .org.mx; f. 1875; corresp. of the Real Academia Española (Madrid); 178 mems; Dir JOSÉ G. MORENO DE ALBA; Sec. MANUEL ALCALÁ ANAYA.

Alliance Française–Alianza Francesa México: Socrates 156, Esq. Homero Col. Los Morales Polanco Del Miguel Hidalgo, 11560 México, DF; tel. (55) 1084-4190; fax (55) 5395-5182; internet www .alianzafrancesa.org.mx; f. 1884; offers courses and examinations in French language and culture and promotes cultural exchange with France; attached teaching centres in 36 other cities; Pres. AGUSTÍN LEGORRETA CHAUVET; Gen. Dir YVES CORBEL.

British Council: Lope de Vega 316, Col. Chapultepec Morales, 11570 México, DF; tel. (55) 5263-1900; fax (55) 5263-1940; e-mail bcmexico@britishcouncil.org.mx; internet www.britishcouncil.org.mx; f. 1943; teaching centre; offers courses and exams in English language and British culture and promotes cultural exchange with the UK; Dir CLIVE BRUTON.

Goethe-Institut: Liverpool 89, Col. Juárez, 06600, México, DF; tel. (55) 5207-0487; fax (55) 5533-1057; e-mail cursos@mexiko.goethe .org; internet www.goethe.de/hn/mex/ deindex.htm; f. 1966; offers courses and exams in German language and culture and promotes cultural exchange with Germany; attached centre in Guadalajara; library of 13,000 vols, 35 periodicals; Dir FOLCO NÄTHER.

PEN Club de México (PEN Club of Mexico): Heriberto Frías 1452-407, Col. del Valle, 03100 México, DF; tel. (55) 5564-5078; e-mail presidencia@penmexico.org.mx; internet www.penmexico.org.mx; f. 1924; 62 mems; Pres. MARÍA ELENA RUIZ CRUZ; Sec. JAIME RAMÍREZ GARRIDO; publ. *Directory of Writers* (1 a year).

MEDICINE

Academia Mexicana de Cirugía (Mexican Academy of Surgery): Avda Cuauhtémoc 330, Bloque B 3o piso, Col. Doctores, 06725 México DF; tel. (55) 5761-2581; e-mail amc06@prodigy.net.mx; internet www.amc .org.mx; f. 1933; Pres. FERNANDO BERNAL SAHAGÚN; Sec. FRANCISCO JAVIER OCHOA CARRILLO; publ. *Revista* (12 a year).

Academia Mexicana de Dermatología (Mexican Academy of Dermatology): Georgia 114, Despacho 503, Col. Nápoles. Del. Benito

Juárez, 03810 México, DF; tel. (55) 5682-2545; fax (55) 5682-8963; e-mail academiadermatologia@prodigy.net.mx; internet www.amd.org.mx; f. 1952; Dir Dr GILBERTO ADAME MIRANDA; Sec. Dra GABRIELA FRIAS ANCONA.

Academia Nacional de Medicina de México (Mexican National Academy of Medicine): Apdo 7–813, Avda Cuauhtémoc 330, Bloque B planta baja, Col. Doctores, 06725 México, DF; tel. (55) 5519-8679; e-mail contacto@anmm.org.mx; internet www .anmm.org.mx; f. 1865; 14 sections; 340 mems; library of 20,000 vols; Pres. Dr MISAEL URIBE ESQUIVEL; Gen. Sec. Dra TERESA COR-ONA VÁZQUEZ; publ. *Gaceta Médica de México*.

Asociación de Médicas Mexicanas, AC (Mexican Association of Women Doctors): Bruselas 10 Int. 403, Col. Juárez, 06600 México, DF; tel. (55) 5591-0159; fax (55) 5546-8202; f. 1925; 3,000 mems; represents members' interests as doctors, citizens and women; Pres. Dra IRENE TALAMAS V.; publ. *Revista*.

Asociación Mexicana de Facultades y Escuelas de Medicina (Mexican Association of Faculties and Schools of Medicine): López Cotilla 754, Col. del Valle, 03100 México, DF; tel. (55) 5682-9482; fax (55) 5687-9323; e-mail amfem@prodigy.net.mx; internet www.amfem.edu.mx; f. 1957; mems 30 medical schools; Pres. Dr HUMBERTO A. VERAS GODOY; Admin. Sec. Lic. YVONNE E. FISCHER HESS.

Consejo Mexicano de Dermatología, AC (Mexican Dermatological Council): Instituto Dermatológico de Jalisco, Guadalajara; tel. (33) 3660-1515 ext. 200; f. 1974; 349 mems; qualifies specialists as part of Nat. Academy of Medicine Comm. of Postgraduate Studies; Gen. Sec. Prof. ERNESTO MACOTELA RUÍZ; publ. *Roster*.

Federación Mexicana de Ginecología y Obstetricia (Mexican Federation of Gynaecology and Obstetrics): Nueva York 38, Col. Nápoles, 03810 México, DF; tel. (55) 5669-0211; fax (55) 5682-0160; e-mail secretario@ femego.org.mx; internet www.femego.org .mx; f. 1961; 4,600 mems; Pres. Dr JESÚS LEAL DEL ROSAL; Sec. Dr FERNANDO GAVIÑO GAVIÑO; publ. *Ginecología y Obstetricia de México*.

Sociedad Mexicana de Cardiología (Mexican Cardiological Society): Juan Badiano 1, Sección XVI Tlalpan, 14080 México, DF; tel. (55) 5655-7694; fax (55) 5573-2111; e-mail info@smcardiologia.org.mx; internet www .smcardiologia.org.mx; f. 1935; 1,250 mems; Pres. Dr JORGE GASPAR; Sec. Dr ERICK ALEXÁNDERSON; publs *Arch.Cardio.Méx.*, *Revista Mexicana de Enfermería Cardiológica* (3 a year).

Sociedad Mexicana de Nutrición y Endocrinología, AC (Mexican Society for Nutrition and Endocrinology): Ohio 27, Col. El Rosedal, Del. Coyoacán, 04330 México, DF; tel. (55) 5636-2216; internet www .endocrinologia.com.mx; f. 1960; 660 mems; Pres. Dr ALFONSO VILLASEÑOR RUÍZ; Sec. Dr RAÚL GUTIÉRREZ GUTIÉRREZ; publ. *Revista de Endocrinología y Nutrición*.

Sociedad Mexicana de Parasitología, AC (Mexican Parasitological Society): Casa Tlalpan, Avenida Cipreses S/N, km 23.5 de la Antigua Carretera México-Cuernavaca, Col. San Andrés Totoltepec, 14400 México, DF; tel. (55) 5747-3348; fax (55) 5747-3398; e-mail mineko@cinvestav.mx; internet www .facmed.unam.mx/smp; f. 1960; 51 mems (20 active; 31 hon.) from 14 countries; organizes congresses and symposia; Pres. Dr MINEKO SHIBAYAMA; Sec. Dr ROSAMARIA BERNAL.

Sociedad Mexicana de Pediatría (Mexican Paediatrics Society): Tehuantepec 86-503, Col. Roma Sur, Del. Cuauhtémoc, 06760 México, DF; tel. (55) 5564-8371; e-mail smp1930@socmexped.org.mx; internet www .socmexped.org.mx; f. 1930; 1,200 mems; Pres. Dr XAVIER DE JESÚS NOVALES CASTRO; Gen. Sec. Dr MARIO GONZÁLEZ VITE; publ. *Revista Mexicana de Pediatría* (6 a year).

Sociedad Mexicana de Salud Pública (Mexican Public Health Society): Herschel 109, Col. Anzures, Del. Miguel Hidalgo, 11590 México, DF; tel. (55) 5203-4291; fax (55) 5203-4229; e-mail smsp@prodigy.net.mx; internet www.smsp.org.mx; f. 1944; 6,000 mems; small library; Exec. Dir HUMBERTO MUÑOZ GRANDÉ; publ. *Higiene* (3 a year).

NATURAL SCIENCES
General

Academia Mexicana de Ciencias (Mexican Academy of Sciences): Calle Cipreses s/n, km 23.5 de la Carretera federal México-Cuernavaca, San Andrés Totoltepec, Tlalpan, 14400 México, DF; tel. (55) 5849-4905; fax (55) 5849-5112; e-mail academia@amc.unam .mx; internet www.amc.unam.mx; f. 1959; research in fields of exact, natural and social sciences, humanities and engineering; training and acknowledging the scientific work of researchers; encourages communication and collaboration between the various orgs responsible for research in Mexico; strengthening int. presence; consultancy services and performance evaluations for Fed. and local govt, legislative and judicial branches and other orgs in civil soc.; facilitates decision making based on scientific and technical evidence; library of 1,000 vols; 2,156 mems; Exec. Coordinator RENATA VILLALBA; Admin. Sec. ROCÍO MÉNDEZ-PADILLA; Technical Sec. CLAUDIA JIMÉNEZ; publ. *Ciencia* (4 a year).

Ateneo Nacional de Ciencias y Artes de México (National Athenaeum of Sciences and Arts): Bucareli 12, México, DF; f. 1920 as Ateneo Estudiantil de Ciencias y Artes, then Ateneo de Ciencias y Artes de México 1926, present name 1934; comprises sections of architecture, astronomy and mathematics, biology, broadcasting, cinematography, criminology and penal law, engineering, eugenics, geography, history, hygiene, law (civil, industrial, and international), literature, medicine, military studies, music, pedagogics, political economy, natural science, statistics; 7 corresp. centres: Monterrey, Mérida, Veracruz, Chiapas, Tijuana, Oaxaca, Tlaxcala; over 1,000 mems, including hon. and corresponding; library of 10,000 vols; Hon. Pres. Dr ALFONSO PRUNEDA; Pres. EMILIO PORTES GIL; Vice-Pres LUIS GARRIDO, Arq. EDMUNDO ZAMUDIO; Sec.-Gen. JOSÉ L. COSSIO; publs *Boletín*, pamphlets.

Biological Sciences

Asociación Mexicana de Microbiología, AC (Mexican Microbiological Association): Centro de Ciencias Genómicas, Avda Universidad s/n, Col. Chamilpa, Cuernavaca, Mor.; e-mail informes@microbiologia.org.mx; internet www.microbiologia.org.mx; f. 1949; Pres. Dra ESPERANZA MARTÍNEZ-ROMERO; Sec. BRENDA VALDERRAMA; publ. *Revista Latinoamericana de Microbiología*.

Sociedad Botánica de México, AC (Mexican Botanical Society): Centro de Investigaciones en Ecosistemas, Universidad Nacional Autónoma de México, Campus Morelia, Antigua Carretera a Pátzcuaro 8701, Col. San José de La Huerta, 58190 Morelia, Mich.; e-mail sbm@socbot.org.mx; internet www .socbot.org.mx; f. 1941; promotes the study, teaching and technology of botany; organizes the National Botanic Congress every 3 years;

1,000 mems; library of 850 vols, 350 periodicals; Pres. Dr MIGUEL MARTÍNEZ RAMOS; Exec. Sec. Dr JORGE ARTURO MEAVE DEL CASTILLO; publs *Boletín* (2 a year), *Macpalxochitl* (newsletter, 12 a year).

Sociedad Mexicana de Biología (Mexican Biological Society): Avda de Brasil, México 1, DF; f. 1921; Pres. FERNANDO OCARANZ; publ. *Revista Mexicana de Biología*.

Sociedad Mexicana de Entomología (Mexican Entomological Society): Apdo 63, 91000 Jalapa, Veracruz; internet www .iztacala.unam.mx/sme; f. 1952; 650 mems; Pres. CÁNDIDO LUNA LEÓN; publs *Boletín* (irregular), *Folia Entomológica Mexicana* (3 a year).

Sociedad Mexicana de Fitogenética (Mexican Society of Plant Genetics): Apdo 21, 56230 Chapingo, Edo de México; tel. (55) 5954-2200; fax (55) 5954-6652; e-mail revfitotecniamex@hotmail.com; internet www.somefi.org; f. 1965; 1,000 mems; Pres. Dr BULMARO COUTIÑO ESTRADA; Sec. Dr SALVADOR MONTES HERNÁNDEZ; publs *Revista Fitotecnia Mexicana*, *Revista Germen*.

Sociedad Mexicana de Fitopatología, AC (Mexican Society of Phytopathology): Apdo postal 85, 56230 Chapingo, Edo de México; e-mail sandoval@colpos.mx; internet www .colpos.mx/ifit/smf/somefit.htm; f. 1958; 400 mems; holds one national meeting per year; Pres. Dr GUSTAVO MORA AGUILERA; Sec. Dr SERGIO SANDOVAL; publs *El Vector*, *Revista Mexicana de Fitopatología* (2 a year).

Sociedad Mexicana de Historia Natural (Mexican Natural History Society): Avda Dr Vertiz 724, Col. Vertiz Narvarte, 03020 México, DF; tel. (55) 5519-4505; fax (55) 5538-4505; internet smhn.org.tripod.com; f. 1868, refounded 1936; 400 mems; library of 5,000 vols; Pres. Dr RAUL GIO ARGAEZ; publ. *Revista*.

Sociedad Mexicana de Micología (Mexican Society of Mycology): Apdo 41, 67700 Linares, Nuevo León; tel. (55) 5541-1333; e-mail smdm@tap-ecosur.edu.mx; internet www.smdm.org.mx; f. 1965; 400 mems; library of 12,000 vols; Pres. Dr FORTUNATO GARZA OCAÑAS; Sec. Dr RICARDO VALENZUELA GARZA (acting); publ. *Revista Mexicana de Micología* (1 a year).

Mathematical Sciences

Centro de Investigación en Computación (Computing Research Centre): Avda Juan de Dios Batiz s/n, Casi esq. Miguel Othón de Mendizabal, Unidad Profesional Adolfo López Mateos, Col. Nueva Industrial Vallejo, Del. Gustavo A. Madero, 07738 México City; tel. (55) 5729-6000 ext. 56604; fax (55) 5586-2936; e-mail webmaster@cic .ipn.mx; internet www.cic.ipn.mx; f. 1996; 250 mems; library of 14,000 vols; Dir Dr OSCAR CAMACHO NIETO; publs *Computación y Sistemas* (4 a year), *Research on Computing Science* (6 a year).

Sociedad Matemática Mexicana (Mexican Mathematical Society): Apdo 70-450, Coyoacán, 04510 México, DF; tel. (55) 5622-4481; fax (55) 5622-4479; internet www.smm .org.mx; f. 1943; 1,100 mems, 20 institutional mems; promotes mathematics, sponsors National Congresses and Regional Assemblies of mathematicians, and The National Mathematical Olympics; Pres. Dr EMILIO LLUIS-PUEBLA; Sec. Dr PABLO PADILLA-LONGORIA; publs *Aportaciones Matemáticas*, *Boletín de la SMM* (2 a year), *Carta informativa* (4 a year), *Miscelánea Matemática* (2 a year).

Physical Sciences

Asociación Mexicana de Geólogos Petroleros (Mexican Association of Petroleum Geologists): Torres Bodet 176, 06400 México,

DF; internet www.amgp.org; f. 1949; 600 mems; Pres. J. ANTONIO ESCALERA ALCOCER; Sec. JOSÉ GPE. GALICIA BARRIOS; publ. *Boletín* (4 a year).

Sociedad Astronómica de México, AC (Mexican Astronomical Society): Apdo M 9647, Jardín Felipe Xicoténcatl, Colonia Alamos, 03400 México, DF; tel. (55) 5519-4730; e-mail sociedadastronomica@gmail .com; internet www.sociedadastronomica.org .mx; f. 1902; library of 5,000 vols; 500 mems; Pres. MARTE TREJO SANDOVAL; Sec.-Gen. JORGE RUBÍ GARZA; publ. *El Universo* (4 a year).

Sociedad Geológica Mexicana, AC (Mexican Geological Society): Torres Bodet 176, Del. Cuauhtémoc, 06400 México, DF; tel. (55) 5541-0879; e-mail publigl@geologia.igeolcu .unam.mx; internet www.geociencias.unam .mx/sgm.html; f. 1904; 1,000 mems; library of 4,500 vols; Pres. Ing. BERNARDO MARTELL ANDRADE; Vice-Pres. Ing. HERIBERTO PALACIOS; Sec. Ing. LUIS VELÁZQUEZ AGUIRRE; publs *Boletín* (3 a year), *Revista Mexicana de Ciencias Geológicas* (jtly, 3 a year).

Sociedad Química de México (Mexican Chemical Society): Barranca del Muerto 26, Esquina Hércules, Col. Crédito Constructor, Del. Benito Juárez, 03940 México, DF; tel. (55) 5662-6837; fax (55) 5662-6823; e-mail soquimex@prodigy.net.mx; internet www .sqm.org.mx; f. 1956; 2,300 mems; Pres. ANDRÉS CERDA ONOFRE; Sec. (vacant); publ. *Revista de la SQM* (4 a year).

PHILOSOPHY AND PSYCHOLOGY

Sociedad Mexicana de Estudios Psico-Pedagógicos (Mexican Society for Psycho-Pedagogical Studies): Nayarit 86, México, DF.

RELIGION, SOCIOLOGY AND ANTHROPOLOGY

Sociedad Mexicana de Antropología (Mexican Anthropological Society): Apdo 100, C. A. P. Polanco, 11550 México, DF; tel. (55) 5622-9570; fax (55) 5622-9651; e-mail somedean@yahoo.com.mx; internet morgan.iia.unam.mx/usr/sma/index.html; f. 1937; 480 mems; Sec. Dr LEONARDO LÓPEZ LUJÁN; publ. *Revista Mexicana de Estudios Antropológicos* (1 a year).

TECHNOLOGY

Sociedad Mexicana de Ingeniería Sísmica, AC (Mexican Society of Seismic Engineering): Camino de Santa Teresa 187, Col. Parques del Pedregal, Tlalpan, 14020 México, DF; tel. (55) 5606-1314; fax (55) 5606-1314; e-mail smis@smis.org.mx; internet www.smis.org.mx; f. 1962; library of 82 vols; 350 mems; Pres. JORGE AGUIRRE; Operation Man. FERNANDO HEREDIA ZAVONI; publ. *Revista de Ingeniería Sísmica* (2 a year).

Research Institutes

GENERAL

Institut de Recherche pour le Développement (IRD) (Development Research Institute): Cicerón 609, Col. Los Morales, 11530 México, DF; tel. (55) 5280-7688; fax (55) 5282-0800; e-mail mexique@ird.fr; internet www.mx.ird.fr; Rep. PASCAL LABAZÉE; (see main entry under France).

AGRICULTURE, FISHERIES AND VETERINARY SCIENCE

Campo Agrícola Experimental Río Bravo (Río Bravo Agricultural Research Station): Apdo 172, Río Bravo, Tamps; f. 1965; research into regional problems and diversification; Dir Ing. Agr. MANUEL CARNERO HERNÁNDEZ.

Instituto Nacional de Investigaciones Forestales, Agrícolas y Pecuarias (National Institute of Forestry, Agriculture and Livestock Research): Serapio Rendón 83, Col. San Rafael, Del. Cuauhtémoc, 06470 México, DF; tel. (55) 5484-1900; e-mail contactenos@inifap.gob.mx; internet www .inifap.gob.mx; f. 1985 through the integration of Instituto Nacional de Investigaciones Agrícolas, Instituto Nacional de Investigaciones Pecuarias and Instituto Nacional de Investigaciones Forestales; conducts research in all aspects of agricultural development and production; agronomy library, livestock library and forestry library; Gen. Dir Dr PEDRO BRAJCICH GALLEGOS; publs *Agricultura Técnica en México* (2 a year), *Ciencia Forestal* (2 a year).

BIBLIOGRAPHY, LIBRARY SCIENCE AND MUSEOLOGY

Instituto de Investigaciones Bibliográficas (Institute of Bibliographical Research): c/o Biblioteca Nacional de México and Hemeroteca Nacional de México, Centro Cultural Universitario, Ciudad Universitaria, Del. Coyoacán, 04510 México, DF; tel. (55) 5622-6827; fax (55) 5665-0951; e-mail webmast@biblional.bibliog.unam.mx; internet biblional.bibliog.unam.mx; f. 1899, present name 1967; compiles the national bibliographies and books on bibliographical subjects; Dir VICENTE QUIRARTE CASTAÑEDA; publs *Boletín* (2 a year), *Nueva Gaceta Bibliográfica* (4 a year).

ECONOMICS, LAW AND POLITICS

Centro de Estudios Demográficos, Urbanos y Ambientales (Centre for Demographic, Urban and Environmental Studies): Camino al Ajusco 20, 14200 México, DF; tel. (55) 5449-3000; fax (55) 5645-0464; e-mail direccion.ceddu@colmex.mx; internet www.colmex.mx/centros/ceddu; f. 1964; library of 500,000 vols; Dir Dr JOSÉ LUIS LEZAMA DE LA TORRE; publ. *Revista de Estudios Demográficos y Urbanos* (3 a year).

Centro de Estudios Económicos (Centre for Economic Studies): Camino al Ajusco 20, Pedregal de Santa Teresa, Apdo 20671, 10740 México, DF; tel. (55) 5449-3000; fax (55) 5645-0464; e-mail webmaster@colmex .mx; internet www.colmex.mx; f. 1981; research areas include microeconomics, macroeconomics, economic development, statistics, game theory, environmental economics, industrial organization, international economics, public finance; masters and doctorate programmes; library of 8,000 vols; Dir JAIME SEMPERE CAMPELLO; publ. *Estudios Económicos* (2 a year).

Centro de Estudios Internacionales (Centre for International Studies): Camino al Ajusco 20, Col. Pedregal de Sta. Teresa, 10740 México, DF; tel. (55) 5449-3000 ext. 3110; fax (55) 5645-0464; e-mail psoto@ colmex.mx; internet www.colmex.mx/ centros/cei; f. 1960; research areas include international relations, politics, federal and local public administration, Mexico's political system and foreign policy, and regional studies of North America, Europe and Latin America; undergraduate programmes in Politics and Public Administration, and International Relations; Dir GUSTAVO VEGA; publ. *Foro Internacional* (4 a year).

Centro de Relaciones Internacionales: Ciudad Universitaria, FCPS, UNAM, 04510 México, DF; tel. (55) 5622-9412; fax (55) 5622-9413; attached to the Faculty of Political and Social Sciences of the Universidad Nacional Autónoma de México; f. 1970; coordinates and promotes research in all aspects of international relations and Mexico's foreign policy, as well as the training of researchers in different fields: disciplinary construction problems, cooperation and international law, developing nations, actual problems in world society, Africa, Asia, peace research; 30 full mems; library of 6,000 vols, 35 spec. collns, 16,000 journals, etc; Dir Lic. ROBERTO PEÑA GUERRERO; publs *Boletín Informativo del CRI*, *Cuadernos*, *Relaciones Internacionales* (4 a year).

Instituto Mexicano del Desarrollo, AC: M. Escobedo 510, 8° piso, México 5, DF; tel. (55) 5531-0823; research on socio-economic development and planning; 470 staff; Dir-Gen. Lic. ERNESTO SANCHEZ AGUILAR.

EDUCATION

Centro de Estudios Educativos, AC (Centre for Educational Studies): Avda Revolución 1291, Col. Tlacopac–San Angel, Del. Alvaro Obregón, 01040 México, DF; tel. (55) 5593-5719; fax (55) 5651-6374; e-mail cee@ cee.edu.mx; internet www.cee.edu.mx; f. 1963; scientific research into the problems of education in Mexico and Latin America; library of 33,288 vols, 11,100 journals, 539 serial titles; Dir-Gen. FERNANDO MEJIA BOTERO; publ. *Revista Latinoamericana de Estudios Educativos* (4 a year).

HISTORY, GEOGRAPHY AND ARCHAEOLOGY

Centro de Estudios de Asia y África (Centre for Asian and African Studies): Camino al Ajusco 20, Pedregal de Santa Teresa, 10740 México, DF; tel. (55) 5449-3000; fax (55) 5645-0464; e-mail direccion .ceaa@colmex.mx; internet ceaa.colmex.mx/ sitioceaa; f. 1964; studies of and research on Africa, China, Korea, Japan, S Asia, SE Asia, Middle East and N Africa; Masters and doctorate programmes; library of 30,000 vols, 130 periodicals; Dir BENJAMÍN PRECIADO SOLÍS; publs *Anuario Asia Pacífico* (1 a year), *Cuadernos de Trabajo*, *Estudios de Asia y África* (3 a year).

Centro de Estudios Históricos (Centre for Historical Studies): Coordinación Académica, Centro de Estudios Históricos, Camino al Ajusco 20, 10740 México, DF; tel. (55) 5449-3000 ext. 3132; fax (55) 5645-0464; e-mail coord.acad.ceh@colmex.mx; internet www .colmex.mx/centros/ceh; f. 1941; history of Mexico and Latin America; Dir Dr GUILLERMO PALACIOS; publ. *Historia Mexicana* (4 a year).

Instituto Nacional de Estudios Históricos de las Revoluciones de México (INEHRM) (National Institute for Historical Studies of the Mexican Revolutions): Francisco I. Madero 1, Colonia San Ángel, 01000 México, DF; tel. (55) 5616-3808; e-mail contactoinehrm@segob.gob.mx; internet www.inehrm.gob.mx; f. 1953; library of 43,000 vols; Man. Lic. JOSE MANUEL VILLALPANDO.

LANGUAGE AND LITERATURE

Centro de Estudios Lingüísticos y Literarios (Centre for Linguistic and Literary Studies): Coordinación Académica, Centro de Estudios Lingüísticos y Literarios, Camino al Ajusco 20, 10740 México, DF; tel. (55) 5449-3018; fax (55) 5255-5645; e-mail coord.acad .cell@colmex.mx; internet www.colmex.mx/ centros; f. 1947; Spanish linguistics and literature (PhD degrees), Indian languages, translation; Dir Dr LUZ ELENA GUTIÉRREZ DE VELASCO; Academic Coordinator Dr MARÍA

ÁGUEDA MÉNDEZ HERRERA; publ. *Nueva Revista de Filología Hispánica* (2 a year).

MEDICINE

Instituto Nacional de Cardiología 'Ignacio Chávez' (National Cardiological Institute): Juan Badiano 1, Col. Sección XVI, Del. Tlalpan, 14080 México, DF; tel. (55) 5573-2911; fax (55) 5573-0994; e-mail webmaster@cardiologia.org.mx; internet www.cardiologia.org.mx; f. 1944; 390 medical mems; library of 8,465 vols, 569 periodicals; Dir Dr FAUSE ATTIÉ CURY; Sub-Dirs L. C. CUAUHTÉMOC SOTO CASTILLO (Administrative Division), Dr MARCO ANTONIO MARTÍNEZ RÍOS (Medical Attendance), Dr JOSÉ FERNANDO GUADALAJARA BOO (Medical Education Division), Dr PEDRO ANTONIO REYES LÓPEZ (Research Division); Library Dir MARIO FLAVIO FUENTES INIESTRA; publ. *Archivos de Cardiología de México* (6 nos, 1 vol per year).

Instituto Nacional de Diagnóstico y Referencia Epidemiológicos (National Institute of Epidemiological Diagnosis and Reference): Calle de Carpio 470, Santo Tomás, Miguel Hidalgo, 11340 México, DF; tel. (55) 5341-4389; fax (55) 5341-3264; e-mail indre@cenids.ssa.gob.mx; f. 1938; performs epidemiological laboratory reference services nationwide; carries out technological development and research in laboratory for support of epidemiological surveillance; trains and supervises laboratory personnel and performs quality control procedures for the National Laboratory Network; library of 3,930 vols, 603 journals. MEDLINE terminal; Dir Dr ANA FLISSER.

Instituto Nacional de Higiene de la S.S.A. (National Institute of Hygiene): Gerencia General de Biológicas y Reactivos, Czda Mariano Escobedo 20, Col. Popotla, Del. Miguel Hidalgo, 11400 México, DF; tel. (55) 5527-7368; fax (55) 5527-6693; f. 1895; 300 mems; library of 10,000 vols; Dir (vacant).

Instituto Nacional de Neurología y Neurocirugía (National Institute of Neurology and Neurosurgery): Insurgentes Sur 3877, Col. La Fama, Deleg. Tlalpan, 14269 México, DF; tel. (55) 5606-3822; fax (55) 5606-3245; internet www.innn.edu.mx; f. 1964; library of 2,700 vols, 270 periodicals; Dir-Gen. Dr JULIO SOTELO MORALES; publ. *Archivos de Neurociencias* (review, 4 a year).

Instituto Nacional de Salud Pública (National Institute of Public Health): Avda Univ. 655, Col. Santa María Ahuacatitlán, 62100 Cuernavaca, Morelos; e-mail contacto@insp.mx; internet www.insp.mx; f. 1987; incl. School of Public Health in Mexico (f. 1922) and research centres on public health, health systems: infectious diseases, malaria, and nutrition and health; masters and doctorate programmes; library of 35,000 vols; Dir-Gen. Dr MARIO HENRY RODRIGUEZ LÓPEZ; publ. *Salud Pública de México* (6 a year).

NATURAL SCIENCES
General

Centro de Investigación y de Estudios Avanzados del Instituto Politécnico Nacional (Centre for Research and Advanced Studies, National Polytechnic Institute): Apdo 14-258, 07360 México, DF; Av. Instituto Politécnico Nacional 2508, Col. San Pedro Zacatanco, 07360 México, DF; tel. (55) 5747-3800; fax (55) 5747-3814; e-mail azurita@cinvestav.mx; internet www.cinvestav.mx; f. 1961; postgraduate research and training centre in sciences; integrates the work of the depts of biochemistry, physics, applied physics, physiology, biophysics and neurosciences, electrical engineering, mathematics, genetics and molecular biology, cellular biology, marine resources, experimental pathology, chemistry, biotechnology and bioengineering, biotechnology and biochemistry, pharmacology, bioelectronics, educational mathematics, toxicology, metallurgical engineering, computer science, mechatronics, solid-state electronics, automatic control, molecular biomedicine, communications, ceramic engineering, genetic engineering, materials, engineering drawing, human ecology and educational research; library of 256,000 vols, 3,200 spec. collns; Dir Gen. Dr RENE ASOMOZA PALACIO; publs *Avance y Perspectiva* (4 a year), *Morfismos* (2 a year).

Consejo Nacional de Ciencia y Tecnología (CONACYT) (National Council for Science and Technology): Avda Insurgentes Sur 1582, Col. Crédito Constructor, Del. Benito Juárez, 03940 México, DF; tel. (55) 5322-7700; e-mail snicst@conacyt.mx; internet www.conacyt.mx; f. 1970; co-ordinates scientific research and development and formulates policy; Dir JUAN CARLOS ROMERO HICKS; publ. *Ciencia y Desarrollo* (12 a year).

Instituto Mexicano de Recursos Naturales Renovables, AC (Institute for the Conservation of Natural Resources): Dr Vertiz 724, Narvarte, 03020 México, DF; tel. (55) 5519-4505; fax (55) 5519-1633; e-mail imernar@laneta.apc.org; internet www.imernar.org; f. 1952; library of 7,000 vols and 200 regular periodicals; Dir (vacant).

Biological Sciences

Instituto de Ecología, AC (Institute of Ecology): Apdo Postal 63, Carretera Antigua a Coatepec No. 351, El Haya, 91070 Xalapa, Veracruz; tel. (228) 842-1800; fax (228) 818-7809; internet www.ecologia.edu.mx; f. 1975; plant and animal ecology and taxonomy, biogeography, dynamics and structure of ecosystems, conservation and management of natural resources, environmental biotechnology, wood technology, coastal management, entomology, flora and fauna inventory; postgraduate programmes in ecology and natural resources management, in wildlife management; library of 24,000 vols, 4,000 current periodicals incl. maps and databases; Dir-Gen. Dr MARTIN R. ALUJA SCHUNEMAN-HOFER; publs *Acta Botánica Mexicana* (4 a year), *Acta Zoológica Mexicana* (4 a year), *Flora del Bajío y de Regiones Adyacentes*, *Flora de Veracruz*, *Madera y Bosques* (2 a year).

Instituto Nacional de la Pesca (National Fishery Institute): Pitágoras 1320, Col. Santa Cruz Atoyac, Del. Benito Juárez, 03310 México, DF; tel. (55) 5605-2424; e-mail correoweb@inp.sagarpa.gob.mx; internet www.inp.sagarpa.gob.mx; f. 1962; research in marine biology; library of 3,000 vols; Dir Dr GUILLERMO ALBERTO COMPEÁN JIMÉNEZ.

Instituto Tecnológico del Mar (Institute of Marine Technology): km 12 Carretera Veracruz-Córdoba, Apdo Postal 68, 94290 Boca del Río, Ver.; tel. (229) 986-0189; fax (229) 986-1894; internet www.itmar1.edu.mx; f. 1975, renamed 1981; 150 mems; library of 4,500 vols; Dir ALMILCAR SUÁREZ ALLEN.

Mathematical Sciences

Instituto de Matemáticas (Institute of Mathematics): Area de la Investigación Científica, Circuito Exterior, Ciudad Universitaria, Coyoacán, 04510 México, DF; tel. (55) 5622-4523; fax (55) 5550-1342; e-mail rosi@matem.unam.mx; internet www.matem.unam.mx; f. 1942; research in mathematics; 59 mems; library of 20,000 vols; Dir Dr JAVIER BRACHO CARPIZO; publs *Anales* (1 a year), *Aportaciones Matemáticas* (irregular), *Monografías* (irregular), *Publicaciones Preliminares*.

Physical Sciences

Instituto de Astronomía (Institute of Astronomy): Apdo postal 70–264, 04510 México, DF; tel. (55) 5622-3906; fax (55) 5616-0653; e-mail direc@astroscu.unam.mx; internet www.astroscu.unam.mx; f. 1878; an Institute of the Universidad Nacional Autónoma de México; research in astronomy and astrophysics; library of 7,000 vols, 1,550 journals; Dir Dr JOSÉ FRANCO; publs *Anuario del Observatorio Astronómico Nacional* (1 a year), *Revista Mexicana de Astronomía y Astrofísica* (2 a year).

Instituto Nacional de Astrofísica, Optica y Electrónica (National Institute of Astrophysics, Optics and Electronics): Luis Enrique Erro 1, Apdos 216 y 51, 72000 Tonantzintla, Pue.; tel. (222) 266-3100; fax (222) 247-2231; e-mail astrofi@inaoep.mx; internet www.inaoep.mx; f. 1971 formerly Observatorio Nacional de Astrofísica, f. 1942; 22 research mems; library of 7,000 vols, 144 periodicals; Gen. Dir Dr ALFONSO SERRANO PÉREZ-GROVAS; Gen. Academic Sec. Dr MANUEL G. CORONA GALINDO; publ. *Boletín del Instituto de Tonantzintla*.

Instituto Nacional de Investigaciones Nucleares (National Institute of Nuclear Research): km 36.5, Carretera México-Toluca, 52045, Ocoyoacac, Edo. de México; tel. (55) 5329-7200; fax (55) 5329-7299; internet www.inin.mx; f. 1979 (previously part of Instituto Nacional de Energía Nuclear, f. 1955); planning, research and development of atomic technology, including non-military use of atomic energy; library of 41,500 vols (incl. theses), 75,000 periodicals, 7,300 consulting works, 6,000 pamphlets, 1,000 official publs, 125 video cassettes, 835,000 reports on microfiche and 25,000 in printed form; Gen. Dir JOSÉ RAÚL ORTÍZ MAGAÑA; Technical Sec. Dr JULIÁN SÁNCHEZ GUTIERREZ; publ. *Contacto Nuclear* (4 a year).

Servicio Meteorológico Nacional (National Meteorological Dept): Avda Observatorio 192, Col. Observatorio, Del. M. Hidalgo, 11860 México, DF; tel. (55) 2636-4600; fax (55) 5271-0878; internet smn.cna.gob.mx; f. 1915; library of 80,000 vols, 90,180 pamphlets; Dir Dr MICHEL ROSENGAUS MOSHINSKY.

RELIGION, SOCIOLOGY AND ANTHROPOLOGY

Centro Co-ordinador y Difusor de Estudios Latinoamericanos (Coordinating and Information Centre for Latin American Studies): Piso 8, Torre II de Humanidades, Ciudad Universitaria, 04510 México, DF; tel. (55) 5623-0211; e-mail moce@servidor.unam.mx; internet www.ccydel.unam.mx; f. 1978; attached to Universidad Nacional Autónoma de México; study of Latin America and the Caribbean in all disciplines (history, literature, philosophy, etc.); library of 11,898 monographs, 8,700 magazines, 3,000 pamphlets, 160 theses and 150 records; Dir Dra ESTELA MORALES CAMPOS; publs *Archipiélago, Revista Cultural de Nuestra América* (4 a year), *Latinoamérica, Revista de Estudios Latinoamericanos*.

Centro de Estudios Sociológicos (Centre for Sociological Studies): Camino al Ajusco 20, 10740 México, DF; tel. (55) 5449-3000; fax (55) 5645-0464; e-mail direccion.ces@colmex.mx; internet www.colmex.mx; f. 1973; research areas include sociological theory, economic sociology and the sociology of work, social movements and civil organizations, class and family, political parties, elections and politics, education, labour markets, migration and emigration, reproductive health, religion, culture; doctorate programme in Social Science; Dir ROBERTO BLANCARTE PIMENTEL; publ. *Estudios Sociológicos*.

Comisión Nacional para el Desarrollo de los Pueblos Indígenas (National Commission for the Development of Indian Peoples): Avda México-Coyoacán 343, Col. Xoco, Del. Benito Juárez 03330 México, DF; tel. (55) 9183-2100; e-mail dirgral@cdi.gob.mx; internet www.cdi.gob.mx; f. 1948; forms links with indigenous communities of Mexico; organs incl. 23 co-ordinating centres in the interior, radio stations transmitting in 31 indigenous languages, 29 regional documentation and information centres; library: specialized library of 25,000 vols; Dir-Gen. XÓCHITL GÁLVEZ RUIZ; publs *Colección Historia de los Pueblos Indígenas de México*, *México Indígena*.

Instituto Indigenista Interamericano (Inter-American Indian Institute): Avda de las Fuentes 106, Col. Jardines de Pedregal, Del. Álvaro Obregón, 01900 México, DF; tel. (55) 5595-8410; e-mail ininin@prodigy.net .mx; internet www.indigenista.org; f. 1940; supplies technical assistance to member governments for the Indian population of the continent; library of 40,000 vols; Dir GUILLERMO ESPINOSA VELASCO; publ. *América Indígena* (4 a year).

Instituto Nacional de Antropología e Historia (National Institute of Anthropology and History): Córdoba 45, Col. Roma, 06700 México, DF; tel. (55) 5533-2015; fax (55) 5525-2213; internet www.inah.gob.mx; f. 1939; govt organization for research, conservation and promotion of Mexican cultural heritage, especially archaeological and historical sites; controls 105 museums, incl. Museo Nacional de Antropología, Museo Nacional de Historia, Museo Nacional del Virreinato, Museo Nacional de las Intervenciones, Museo Nacional de las Culturas, Museo del Templo Mayor and Galería de Historia; manages Escuela Nacional de Antropología e Historia, Escuela Nacional de Conservación, Restauración y Museografía, National Anthropology and History Library, National Photographic Archives and Phonographic Archive; Dir-Gen. SERGIO RAÚL ARROYO GARCÍA; publs *Alquimia* (conservation and photographic archives, 3 a year), *Arqueología* (archaeology, 2 a year), *Boletín* (anthropology, ethnology, history and archaeology, 4 a year), *Dimensión Antropológica* (anthropology, linguistics and ethnology, 3 a year), *Historias* (history and related subjects, 3 a year), *Museos de México y del Mundo* (museology, 2 a year, in English and Spanish).

TECHNOLOGY

Instituto de Investigaciones Eléctricas (Institute of Electrical Research): Calle Reforma No. 113, Col. Palmira, 62490 Cuernavaca, Mor.; tel. (777) 362-3811; fax (777) 318-9854; e-mail difusion@iie.org.mx; internet www.iie.org.mx; f. 1975; promotes and undertakes research and experimental devt in the electrical industry; consulting service; library of 61,284 vols; Exec. Dir Ing. JULIÁN ADAME MIRANDA; publs *Boletín IIE*, *Referencias IIE*.

Instituto Mexicano de Investigaciones Tecnológicas (IMIT, AC): Calz. Legaria 694, Col. Irrigación, Del. Miguel Hidalgo, 11500 Mexico DF; tel. (55) 5557-1022; fax (55) 5395-4147; f. 1950; applied research on natural resources and development of industrial processes; pre-investment studies,

reports process and conceptual engineering; library: specialized library in chemical technology of 12,000 vols, 250 periodicals; Dir Dr MARTÍNEZ FRÍAS.

Instituto Mexicano del Petróleo (Mexican Petroleum Institute): Eje Central Norte L. Cárdenas 152, Col. San Bartolo Atepehuecan, Apdo 14–805, 07730 México, DF; tel. (55) 9175-7944; fax (55) 9175-7934; e-mail sabugalp@imp.mx; internet www.imp.mx; f. 1965; research on petroleum products and equipment, petroleum and petrochemical industries, economic studies, exploration, refining; training and specialist courses; 3,600 mems; library of 46,000 vols; Gen. Dir Dr HÉBER CINCO LEY; publ. *Electronic Journal* (daily).

Libraries and Archives

Chapingo

Biblioteca Central–Universidad Autónoma Chapingo (Central Library–Chapingo Autonomous University): km 38.5 Carretera México-Texcoco, 56230 Texcoco, Edo de México; tel. and fax (595) 952-1501; e-mail ramsestexcoco@yahoo.com; internet www .ceres.chapingo.mx; Public control; language of instruction: Spanish; f. 1854, present name 1974; interlibrary loans, digital library, reproduction; 200,000 vols, 4,000 periodicals, 11,000 maps; specializes in agricultural and forestry sciences; Dir Lic. RAMÓN SUÁREZ ESPINOSA; publs *Ingeniería Agrícola y Biosistemas*, *Revista de Chapingo* (in 3 series, irregular), *Revista de Geografía Agrícola* (in 3 series, irregular), *Revista Textual*.

Guadalajara

Coordinación de Bibliotecas, Universidad de Guadalajara (University of Guadalajara Library Services): Avda Juárez 976, Edif. Cultural y Administrativo, piso 7, 44100 Guadalajara, Jalisco; tel. (33) 3134-2277; fax (33) 3134-2205; e-mail sergiolr@ redudg.udg.mx; internet www.rebiudg.udg .mx; f. 1861, present name 1994; depository for UNESCO publs; 1,995,164 vols, 15,261 periodicals (1,761 print, 13,500 electronic); Man. Dir SERGIO LÓPEZ RUELAS.

Mexico City

Archivo General de la Nación (National Archives): Avda Eduardo Molina y Albañiles s/n, Col. Penitenciaría Ampliación, Deleg. Venustiano Carranza, 15350 México, DF; tel. (55) 5133-9900; fax (55) 5789-5296; e-mail argena@segob.gob.mx; internet www .agn.gob.mx; f. 1795; documents relating to the vice-regal administration of New Spain, the Inquisition, independence 1821–40, the 19th century, the Mexican Revolution 1910, and the years up to 1976 (50 km of documents); 49,000 books; 1,050 prehispanic paintings; newspaper collection of 1,272,000 copies; microfilm service and library; Dir-Gen. Mtro JORGE RUIZ DUEÑAS; publ. *Boletín* (4 a year).

Biblioteca Central de la Universidad Nacional Autónoma de México (Central Library of the National Autonomous University of Mexico): Ciudad Universitaria, 04510 México, DF; tel. (55) 5622-1603; fax (55) 5616-0664; e-mail web-bc@dgb.unam.mx; internet bc.unam.mx; f. 1924; 350,000 vols, 2,883 periodicals, 265,000 theses; Dir-Gen. of Libraries Dra SILVIA GONZÁLEZ MARÍN; Sub-Dir of the Central Library Lic. ADRIANA HERNÁNDEZ SÁNCHEZ.

Biblioteca de Derecho y Legislación de la Secretaría de Hacienda (Law Library, Finance Ministry): Correo Mayor 31, México, DF; f. 1925, present form 1928; 13,000 vols;

specialized library relating to ancient and existing federal laws, tax laws from 1831, foreign and international laws; Librarian SOFÍA SILVA.

Biblioteca de Historia de la Secretaría de Hacienda (Historical Library, Finance Ministry): Palacio Nacional, 06066 México, DF; f. 1939 with the collections of the old library of the Finance Ministry and those of Genaro Estrada acquired by the Government; 8,750 vols, 14,000 pamphlets relating to Mexico.

Biblioteca de la Secretaría de Comunicaciones y Transportes (Library of the Ministry of Communications and Transport): Tacuba y Xicotecatl, México, DF; f. 1891; 10,000 vols; Dir RENATO MOLINE ENRÍQUEZ.

Biblioteca de la Secretaría de Gobernación (Library of the Ministry of the Interior): Bucareli 99, 06699 México, DF; f. 1917; 45,000 vols.

Biblioteca del Honorable Congreso de la Unión (Congress Library): Biblioteca Unidad Centro Histórico, Edif. de la ex-Iglesia de Santa Clara, Tacuba 29, 06000 México, DF; tel. (55) 5510-3866; fax (55) 5512-1085; internet www.cddhcu.gob.mx/bibcong; f. 1936; 110,000 vols, 95 periodicals; Dir ENRIQUE MOLINA LEÓN.

Attached Institution:

Sistema Integral de Información y Documentación (SIID) (Integral System of Information and Documentation): Palacio Legislativo de San Lázaro, Avda Congreso de la Unión s/n, 15969 México, DF; tel. (55) 5628-1318; fax (55) 5522-1463; e-mail siid@info.cddhcu.gob.mx; internet www.cddhcu.gob.mx/bibcongr/integra/siid .htm; f. 1991; collns of the old libraries of the Chamber of Deputies and the Chamber of Senators; 60,000 vols, 489 periodicals; Dir Lic. D. M. LIAHUT BALDOMAR.

Biblioteca del Instituto Nacional de Salud Pública (National Institute of Public Health Library): Insp-Biblioteca, Avda Universidad 655, Cerrada los Pinos y Caminera, Col. Santa Maria Ahuacatitlán, 62100 Cuernavaca, Mor.; tel. (777) 3-29-30-65; fax (777) 101-29-10; e-mail atalani@insp.mx; internet www.insp.mx; f. 1922; spec. collns in public health medical admin., hygiene, preventative medicine, epidemiology, statistics, mental hygiene, nutrition, rehabilitation, occupational safety, industrial hygiene and water, air, noise and waste pollution engineering, behavioural sciences; spec. colln in health economics 'Julio Frenk Mora', historical documentary colln in public health from 1826; 45,000 vols, 800 periodicals; Librarian Lic. NATALIA LÓPEZ LÓPEZ; publs *Salud Pública de México* (6 a year), *VIVA SALUD Gaceta Informátiva del Instituto Nacional de Salud Pública* (11 a year).

Biblioteca 'José Ma. Lafragua' ('José Ma. Lafragua' Library): Ex Colegio de la Santa Cruz de Tlatelolco, Plaza de las Tres Culturas, Avda R. Flores Magón 1, Col. Guerrero, 06995 México, DF; tel. (55) 5063-3000, ext. 4102; e-mail sgaytan@sre.gob.mx; internet www.gob.mx/wb/egobierno/ egob_biblioteca_jose_ma_lafragua; f. 19th century; 35,000 vols; specializes in international relations and social sciences; Dir Dra MERCEDES DE VEGA ARMIJO.

Biblioteca 'Miguel Lerdo de Tejada' de la Secretaría de Hacienda y Crédito Público (General Library, Finance Ministry): Avda República de El Salvador 49, Centro Histórico, México, DF; tel. (55) 9158-9837; fax (55) 5709-5144; e-mail publica_web@hacienda.gob.mx; internet www.shcp.gob.mx/servs/dgpcap/bmlt; f. 1928; 250,000 vols; Dir ROMÁN BELTRÁN MARTÍNEZ.

Biblioteca Nacional de Antropología e Historia 'Dr Eusebio Dávalos Hurtado' (National Library of Anthropology and History): Avda Paseo de la Reforma y Calzada Gandhi, 1er Piso, Col. Polanco, 11560 México, DF; tel. (55) 5553-6865; fax (55) 5286-1743; e-mail subtec.bnah@inah.gob.mx; internet www.bnah.inah.gob.mx; f. 1888 as Library of the Instituto Nacional de Antropología e Historia de México (see Research Institutes); 550,000 vols, 8,000 periodicals; Dir CÉSAR MOHENO; publs *Alquimía* (4 a year), *Arqueología* (4 a year), *Arqueología Mexicana* (6 a year), *Dimensión Antropológica* (3 a year), *Historias* (2 a year).

Biblioteca Nacional de México (National Library): Centro Cultural Universitario, C.U., Delegación Coyoacán, 04510 México, DF; tel. (55) 5622-6800; fax (55) 5665-0951; e-mail gasca@biblional.bibliog.unam.mx; internet www.bibliog.unam.mx/bib/biblioteca.html; f. 1867; run by Bibliographic Research Institute of the National University of Mexico; 1,250,000 vols, and other items relating to the political, social, artistic, literary and historical development of Mexico; Library Coordinator Mtra. ROSA MARÍA GASCA NUÑEZ.

Biblioteca Vasconcelos (Vasconcelos Library): Eje 1 Norte esq Aldama, Buenavista, México, DF; tel. (55) 1253-9100 ext. 8102; internet www.bibliotecavasconcelos.gob.mx; f. 1946; 500,000 vols, spec. collns, hall for the blind and visually impaired; Dir JORGE VON ZIEGLER; publ. *Biblioteca de México* (6 a year).

Centro de Documentación de la Oficialía Mayor de la Secretaría de Economía: Alfonso Reyes 30 PB, Col. Hipódromo Condesa, Del. Alvaro Obregón, 06140 México DF; tel. 5729-9100 ext. 17071; e-mail blopezl@economia.gob.mx; internet www.economia.gob.mx/?p=2575; f. 1918; international business, business guides, statistics on foreign investment, legislation; trade statistics; 42,250 vols; Librarian Lic. BERENISSE LÓPEZ LÓPEZ.

Hemeroteca Nacional de México (National Library of Periodicals): Centro Cultural Universitario, C.U., Delegación Coyoacán, 04510 México, DF; tel. (55) 5622-6818; fax (55) 5665-0951; e-mail curielg@biblional.bibliog.unam.mx; internet www.bibliog.unam.mx/hem/hemeroteca.html; f. 1912; run by Bibliographic Research Institute of the National University of Mexico; 250,000 vols; newspapers and periodicals; Mexican Gazette of 18th century; Coordinator Mtra GUADALUPE CURIEL DEFOSSÉ.

Instituto Nacional de Bellas Artes y Literatura (Educación e Investigación Artísticas) (National Institute of Fine Arts and Literature (Art Education and Research)): Paseo de la Reforma y Campo Marte s/n, Col. Chapultepec Polanco, 11560 México, DF; tel. (55) 5521-9251; fax (55) 5280-5364; internet www.cnca.gob.mx/cnca/buena/inba; f. 1947; incorporates several centres, each of which inherited specialist material from the former Biblioteca Ibero-Americana y de Bellas Artes.

Incorporated Centres:

Centro de Documentación y Biblioteca (Documentation Centre and Library): Eje Lázaro Cárdenas 2, 3er Piso (Torre Latinoamericana), Col. Centro, 06007 México, DF; f. 1984; specializes in Mexican literature; 3,500 vols; database LIME-INBA of the Mexican literature contained in the principal libraries of Mexico City; Dir Lic. JORGE PEREZ-GROVAS.

Centro Nacional de Investigación de Información y Documentación de la

Danza José Limón (José Limón National Centre for Research, Information and Dance Documentation): Campos Eliseos 480, Col. Polanco, 11560 México, DF.

Centro Nacional de Investigación e Información Teatral Rodolfo Usigli (Rodolfo Usigli National Centre for Research and Theatre Information): Chihuahua 216, Esquina Monterrey, Col. Roma, 06760 México, DF.

Centro Nacional de Investigación y Documentación de las Artes Plásticas (National Centre for Research and Documentation on the Plastic Arts): Calle Nueva York 224, Col. Nápoles, 03810 México, DF.

Centro Nacional de Investigación y Documentación Musical Carlos Chávez (Carlos Chávez National Centre for Research and Music Documentation): Liverpool 16, Col. Juárez, 06600 México, DF.

Monterrey

Biblioteca del Instituto Tecnológico y de Estudios Superiores de Monterrey (Library of the Monterrey Institute of Technology and Higher Studies): Avda Eugenio Garza Sada 2501 Sur, Sucursal de Correos 'J', Col. Tecnológico, 64849 Monterrey (Nuevo León); tel. (81) 8328-4096; fax (81) 8328-4067; e-mail miguel_arreola@itesm.mx; internet biblioteca.mty.itesm.mx; f. 1943; c. 200 library instructional workshops annually; nat. and int. interlibrary loan (to USA and Europe); organizes int. book fair, confs., academic congresses; 418,244 vols, digital library with 111 databases, 6,482 audiovisuals; Dir Ing. MIGUEL ARREOLA; publs *Calidad Ambiental* (4 a year), *Integratec* (6 a year), *Revista de Humanidades* (2 a year), *Transferencia* (4 a year).

Puebla

Biblioteca de la Universidad de las Américas (Library of the Universidad de las Américas): POB 100, Santa Catarina Mártir, San Andrés, 72820 Cholula, Pue.; tel. (222) 229-2257; fax (222) 229-2078; e-mail bibinfo@mail.udlap.mx; internet ciria.udlap.mx/bibliotecas; f. 1940; humanities, science and technology; 400,000 vols, 2,200 periodicals; special collection; M. Covarrubias archives, R. Barlow archives, Herrera Carrillo archives, Porfirio Díaz archives; Dir Mtro ARTURO ARRIETA.

Toluca

Biblioteca Pública Central del Estado de México (Main Public Library of México State): Centro Cultural Mexiquense, 50000 Toluca (Estado de México); f. 1827; 40,012 vols, 128 periodicals; Dir MARÍA CRISTINA PÉREZ GÓMEZ.

Tuxtla Gutiérrez

Biblioteca Pública del Estado de Chiapas (Public Library of Chiapas State): Blvd Angel Albino Corzo Km 1087, Tuxtla Gutiérrez, Chiapas; tel. (961) 3-06-64; f. 1910; 45,000 vols; Dir JOSÉ LUIS CASTRO.

Zacatecas

Bibliotecas Públicas de Zacatecas (Zacatecas Public Libraries): Plaza Independencia 1, 98000 Zacatecas; internet www.angelfire.com/nh/luishugo; f. 1832; consists of the following libraries: Biblioteca Central Estatal 'Mauricio Magdaleno', Biblioteca de Colecciones Especiales 'Elias Amador'; Dir (vacant).

Museums and Art Galleries

Campeche

Museo Regional de Campeche (Campeche Regional Museum): Calle 59 entre 16 y 14, Campeche, Camp.; f. 1985; archaeology and history; Dir Arq. JOSÉ E. ORTÍZ LAN.

Guadalajara

Casa Taller José Clemente Orozco (House and Studio of José Clemente Orozco): Calle Aurelio Aceves 27, Col. Arcos Vallarta, 44120 Guadalajara, Jalisco; tel. (33) 3818-2800 ext. 31063; fax (33) 3818-2800 ext. 31014; e-mail museocabanas_lpb@yahoo.com.mx; internet vive.guadalajara.gob.mx/puntos/puntose.asp?which=221; f. 1951; paintings and sketches by the artist; Dir MARGARITA V. DE OROZCO.

Museo del Estado de Jalisco (Jalisco State Museum): Liceo 60, Centro Histórico, 44100 Guadalajara, Jalisco; tel. (33) 3613-2703; fax (33) 3614-5257; f. 1918; collections of early Mexican objects; folk art and costumes; archaeological discoveries; anthropological, archaeological and historical research; library of 6,000 vols; Dir CARLOS R. BELTRÁN BRISEÑO.

Museo Regional de Guadalajara (Guadalajara Regional Museum): Liceo 60, Zona Centro, 44100 Guadalajara, Jalisco; tel. (33) 3613-2705; fax (33) 3614-5257; internet vive.guadalajara.gob.mx/puntos/puntose.asp?which=221; f. 1918; special collections of pre-Spanish and Colonial period art and paintings; archaeological and palaeontological collections; Dir Lic. CRISTINA SÁNCHEZ DEL REAL.

Guanajuato

Museo de Historia Natural Alfredo Dugès Universidad de Guanajuato (Natural History Museum Alfredo Dugès Guanajuato University): Planta baja, Lascuráin de Retana 5, zona centro, 36000 Guanajuato, Guan.; tel. (473) 732-0006 ext. 1005; fax (473) 732-0006 ext. 1004; e-mail duges@quijote.ugto.mx; internet www.daip.ugto.mx/sitiodaip/estructura; f. 1870; colln Natural History, incl. natural history colln of Alfredo Dugès with rare specimens.; Curator GLORIA E. MAGAÑA-COTA.

Madero

Museo de la Cultura Huasteca (Museum of Huastec Culture): POB 12, 89050 Madero, Tamaulipas; located at: Blvd A. López Mateos s/n, Tampico, Tamaulipas; tel. and fax (833) 210-2217; f. 1960; attached to the Instituto Nacional de Antropología e Historia; library of 1,750 vols, 95 discs; Dir C. P. MA. ALEJANDRINA ELÍAS ORTIZ.

Mérida

Museo Regional de Antropología (Regional Museum of Anthropology): Palacio Canton, Calle 43 por Paseo de Montejo, Mérida, Yucatán; tel. (999) 923-0557; fax (999) 9230557; e-mail palacio.canton@inah.gob.mx; f. 1959; attached to the Instituto Nacional de Antropología e Historia; collns of pre-Hispanic Mayan and Olmec culture, precious stones, ceramics, jade, objects in copper and gold; Dir ABRAHAM GUERRERO; Curator PETER SCHMIEDT.

Mexico City

Laboratorio Arte Alameda (Alameda Laboratory of Arts): Dr Mora 7, Col. Centro Histórico, 06050 México, DF; tel. (55) 5510-2793; fax (55) 5512-2079; e-mail info.artealameda@gmail.com; internet www.artealameda.inba.gob.mx; f. 1962 as Pinacoteca Virreinal de San Diego, present name and collns 2000; attached to Instituto Nacional de Bellas Artes; collns of new media and electronic art; museum of Mexican colonial arts; library of 5,000 vols; Dir TANIA AEDO; Curator KARLA JASSO.

Museo de Arte Alvar y Carmen T. de Carrillo Gil (Alvar and Carmen T. de Carrillo Gil Museum of Art): Avda Revolución 1608, Col. San Angel, Del. Alvaro Obregón, 01000 México, DF; tel. (55) 5550-3983; fax (55) 5550-4232; internet www.macg .inba.gob.mx; f. 1974; contemporary Mexican art; library of 3,500 vols; Dir CARLOS ASHIDA; publ. *Gazeta del Museo* (12 a year).

Museo de Arte Contemporáneo Rufino Tamayo (Rufino Tamayo Museum of Contemporary Art): Paseo de la Reforma y Gandhi s/n, Bosque de Chapultepec, Del. Miguel Hidalgo, 11580 México, DF; tel. (55) 5286-5839; fax (55) 5286-6539; f. 1981; permanent collection of contemporary art, permanent exhibition of Rufino Tamayo's work; temporary exhibits of international artists; library specializing in Rufino Tamayo, contemporary art and artists; Dir CRISTINA GÁLVEZ GUZZY.

Museo de Arte Moderno (Museum of Modern Art): Bosque de Chapultepec, Paseo de la Reforma y Gandhi, 11560 México, DF; tel. (55) 5211-2934; fax (55) 5553-6211; e-mail info@mam.org.mx; internet www .mam.org.mx; f. 1964; Mexican colln of modern and contemporary art and temporary exhibitions of modern Mexican and foreign art; organizes Symposiums, temporary exhibitions, conversations with artists, confs, cultural activities, books presentations, workshops; Dir OSVALDO SÁNCHEZ; publ. *Critical Gazette*.

Museo de Historia Natural de la Ciudad de México (Natural History Museum of the City of Mexico): 2° Sección del Bosque de Chapultepec, Apdo Postal 18–845, Del. Miguel Hidalgo, 11800 México, DF; tel. (55) 5515-6304; fax (55) 5515-2222; e-mail mhn@ df.gob.mx; internet www.sma.df.gob.mx/ mhn; f. 1964; exhibitions on the universe, the earth, the origin of life, plant and animal taxonomy, evolution and adaptation of species, biology, man and bio-geographical areas; contains replicas of prehistoric creatures; library of 6,000 vols; Dir Biol. NEMESIO CHÁVEZ ARREDONDO.

Museo del Palacio de Bellas Artes (Museum of the Palace of Fine Arts): Avda Juárez y Eje Central 'Lázaro Cardenas', Centro Histórico, Del. Cuauhtémoc, 06050 México, DF; tel. (55) 5512-2593; fax (55) 5510-1388; e-mail difusion@ museobellasartes.artte.com; internet www .cnca.gob.mx/palacio/museo.htm; f. 1934; attached to the Instituto Nacional de Bellas Artes; permanent exhibition 'Los Grandes Muralistas'; Dir Arq. AGUSTÍN ARTEAGA.

Museo Estudio Diego Rivera (Museum of Diego Rivera's Studio): Calle Diego Rivera s/ n esq. Avda Altavista, Col. San Angel Inn, 01060 México, DF; tel. (55) 5550-1518; fax (55) 5550-1004; internet www.cnca.gob.mx/ cnca/buena/inba/subbellas/museos/rivera .html; f. 1986; permanent exhibition 'Estudio Taller de Diego Rivera'.

Museo Nacional de Antropología (National Museum of Anthropology): Avda Paseo de la Reforma y Calzada Gandhi s/n, Col. Chapultepec Polanco, Delegación Miguel Hidalgo, 11560 México, DF; tel. (55) 5553-6266; fax (55) 5286-1791; e-mail atencion .mna@inah.gob.mx; internet www.mna.inah .gob.mx; f. 1940; attached to the Instituto Nacional de Antropología e Historia; anthropological, ethnological, and archaeological subjects relating to Mexico; 6,000 exhibits;

library of 300,000 vols; Dir Arqlgo. FELIPE SOLÍS OLGUÍN; publs *Cuadernos, Guides*.

Museo Nacional de Arquitectura (National Museum of Architecture): Palacio de Bellas Artes, Avda Juárez 4, Centro Histórico, Del. Cuauhtémoc, 06050 México, DF; tel. (55) 5510-2475; fax (55) 5510-2853; internet www.inba.gob.mx; f. 1984; important examples of Mexican architecture through the ages; photographic archive; original plans by Adamo Boari, Federico Mariscal, Juan O'Gorman, Carlos Obregón Santacilia, Mario Pani, Enrique del Moral, José Villagrán, Juan Segura, Francisco Centeno and Francisco J. Serrano; original drawings of the Palacio de Bellas Artes; Dir XAVIER GUZMÁN.

Museo Nacional de Arte (National Museum of Art): Tacuba 8, Centro Histórico, Del. Cuauhtémoc, 06010 México, DF; tel. (55) 5130-3400; fax (55) 5130-3401; e-mail munal@munal.com.mx; internet www.munal .com.mx; f. 1982; permanent exhibitions of Mexican art from 16th century to 1950; library of 39,000 vols; Dir ROXANA VELÁSQUEZ; publ. *Revista Memoria*.

Museo Nacional de Artes e Industrias Populares del Instituto Nacional Indigenista (National Museum of Traditional Arts and Crafts, National Institute of Indigenous People): Avda Juárez 44, 06050 México, DF; internet www.cuauhtemoc.df .gob.mx/turismo/museos/corpus.html; f. 1951; examples of traditional Mexican art of all periods, conservation and encouragement of traditional handicrafts; Dir MARÍA TERESA POMAR.

Museo Nacional de Historia (National Historical Museum): Reforma y Gandhi, 1A Sección del Bosque de Chapultepec, Delegación Miguel Hidalgo, 11580 México, DF; tel. (55) 5241-3100; fax (55) 5241-3132; e-mail difusion.mnh@inah.gob.mx; internet www .mnh.inah.gob.mx; f. 1944; attached to the Instituto Nacional de Antropología e Historia; history of Mexico since the 16th century; historical paintings, flags, weapons, documents, jewellery, textiles, ceramics, furniture, clothing and other objects of social and cultural history; Dir Lic. LUCIANO CEDILLO ÁLVAREZ.

Museo Nacional de la Estampa: Avda Hidalgo 39, Plaza de la Santa Vercruz, Col. Centro, Delg. Cuauhtémoc, 06050 México, DF; tel. (55) 5521-2244; fax (55) 5521-2244; engraving, graphic arts; permanent exhibition 'Proceso Histórico de la Estampa en México'.

Museo Nacional de las Culturas (National Museum of Cultures): Calle de Moneda 13, Col. Centro Histórico, 06060 México, DF; tel. (55) 5542-0165; fax (55) 5542-0422; e-mail direccion.cmuseo@inah .gob.mx; internet www.inah.gob.mx/muse1/ html/muse13.html; attached to the Instituto Nacional de Antropología e Historia; f. 1965; collections of archaeology and ethnology from all over the world; public lectures, special courses for teachers, training in plastic arts; library of 11,862 vols; Dir Antrop. MOISÉS LEONEL DURÁN SOLÍS.

Museo Nacional de las Intervenciones (National Museum of the Interventions in Mexico): General Anaya y 20 de agosto, Del. Coyoacán, 04100 México, DF; tel. (55) 5604-0699; fax (55) 5604-0981; internet www.cnca .gob.mx/cnca/inah/museos/munaint.html; f. 1981; government-owned museum attached to the Instituto Nacional de Antropología e Historia; exhibitions show history of foreign interventions and Mexican independence; library of 800 vols; Dir Lic. MONICA CUEVAS Y LARA.

Museo Nacional de San Carlos (San Carlos Museum): Puente de Alvarado 50, Col. Tabacalera, 06030 México, DF; tel. (55) 5566-8085; fax (55) 5535-1256; e-mail mnsancarlos@mail.com; internet www .bellasartes.gob.mx/inba/templateinba; f. 1968; attached to Instituto Nacional de Bellas Artes; colln of 14th–19th century European panels, paintings, sculpture, drawings and prints; housed within the Palace of the Counts of Buenavista designed by Manuel Tolsá; library of 2,633 vols; Dir MARÍA FERNANDA MATOS MOCTEZUMA; publ. *Bulletin* (3 a year).

Monterrey

Museo Regional de Nuevo León (Regional Museum of Nuevo León): Rafael José Verger s/n, Col. Obispado, 64010 Monterrey, Nuevo León; tel. (81) 8333-9588; fax (81) 8346-0404; internet dti.inah.gob.mx; f. 1956; regional and Mexican history, archaeology and painting; Dir Arq. JAVIER SÁNCHEZ GARCÍA.

Morelia

Museo Regional Michoacano (Michoacan Museum): Calle de Allende 305 esq. con Abasolo, Centro, 58000 Morelia, Michoacán; tel. (443) 312-0407; internet dti.inah.gob.mx; f. 1886; archaeological, ecological, ethnographical and prehistoric collections of the district; library of 10,000 vols; Dir Arq. PAUL DELGADO LAMAS; publ. *Anales*.

Oaxaca

Museo de las Culturas de Oaxaca (Museum of the Cultures of Oaxaca): Apdo 68000, 'Ex-Convento de Santo Domingo de Guzmán', Macedonio Alcalá y Adolfo Gurrión s/n, Oaxaca, Oax.; tel. (951) 5162991; internet www.inah.gob.mx/muse2/htme/ mure2001.html; f. 1933; anthropology, archaeology, ethnography and religious art; contains the famous archaeological treasures found in Tomb No. 7, Monte Albán, jewellery; Dir ENRIQUE FRANCO CALVO.

Patzcuaro

Museo Regional de Artes Populares (Regional Museum of Arts and Crafts): Enseñanza y Alcantarilla s/n, Pátzcuaro, Michoacán; f. 1935; ancient and modern ethnographical exhibits relating to the Tarascan Indians of Michoacán; colonial and contemporary native art; Dir RAFAELA LUFT DÁVALOS.

Puebla

Museo de Arte 'José Luis Bello y González' ('José Luis Bello y González' Museum of Art): 5 de Mayo 408, Puebla, Pue.; f. 1938, opened to the public 1944; contains: ivories, porcelain, wrought iron, furniture, clocks, watches, musical instruments, etc., Mexican, Chinese and European paintings, sculptures, pottery, vestments, tapestries, ceramics, miniatures, etc.

Museo Regional de Santa Mónica (Santa Monica Regional Museum): Avda Poniente 103, Puebla, Pue.; f. 1940; religious art; comprises the collections of various disbanded convents and now housed in that of Santa Mónica.

Museo Regional del Estado de Puebla (Puebla State Regional Museum): Casa del Alfeñique, Calle Oriente 4, Norte 416, 72000 Puebla, Pue.; f. 1931; notable historical collections; Dir JUAN ARMENTA CAMACHO.

Querétaro

Museo Regional de Querétaro (Querétaro Historical Museum): Calle Corregidora Sur 3, 76000 Querétaro, Qro; tel. (442) 20-2031; internet www.queretaro-mexico.com.mx/

coneculta/regional.html; f. 1936; local history and art; Dir MANUEL OROPEZA SEGURA.

Tepotzotlán

Museo Nacional del Virreinato (National Museum of the Vice-Royalty): Plaza Hidalgo 99, 54600 Tepotzotlán, Estado de México; tel. (55) 5876-0245; fax (55) 5876-0332; e-mail virreinato.museo@inah.gob.mx; internet www.munavi.inah.gob.mx; f. 1964; attached to the Instituto Nacional de Antropología e Historia; collections on the art and culture of the Colonial period; housed in 17th- and 18th-century buildings, formerly belonging to the Jesuits; library of 4,000 vols from the 16th to the 19th century; Dir MIGUEL EMIGDIO FERNÁNDEZ FÉLIX.

Toluca

Museo de las Bellas Artes (Museum of Fine Arts): Calle de Santos Degollado 102, Toluca Edo. de México; internet www.turista.com.mx/edomexico; paintings, sculptures, Mexican colonial art; Dir Prof. JOSÉ M. CABALLERO-BARNARD.

Tuxtla Gutiérrez

Museo Regional de Chiapas (Chiapas Regional Museum): Calzada de los Hombres Ilustres s/n, Parque Madero, 29000 Tuxtla Gutiérrez, Chiapas; tel. (961) 622-0459; fax (961) 623-4554; f. 1939; archaeological and historical collections; Dir ROBERTO RAMOS MAZO.

Tzintzuntzan

Museo Etnográfico y Arqueológico (Ethnographical and Archaeological Museum): 58440 Tzintzuntzan, Michoacán; f. 1944; ethnographical and archaeological collections relating to the Tzinztuntzan and Tarascan zones of Lake Pátzcuaro.

Xalapa

Museo de Antropología de Xalapa, Universidad Veracruzana (Xalapa Museum of Anthropology, Veracruzana University): Avda Xalapa s/n, 91010 Xalapa, Veracruz; tel. (228) 815-0920; fax (228) 815-4952; e-mail museo@uv.mx; internet www.uv.mx/max; f. 1959; spe. regional archaeological collns of the Olmec, Totonac and Huastec cultures of ancient Mexico; Dir Dra SARA LADRÓN DE GUEVARA.

Universities

BENEMÉRITA UNIVERSIDAD AUTÓNOMA DE PUEBLA

4 Sur No 104, 72000 Puebla, Pue.
Telephone: (222) 229-5500
Fax: (222) 211-0821
E-mail: ciari@siu.buap.mx
Internet: www.buap.mx
Founded 1937
State control
Academic year: August to May
Rector: Dr ENRIQUE DOGER GUERRERO
Sec.-Gen.: Lic. GUILLERMO NARES RODRÍGUEZ
Librarian: Mtro ENRIQUE HUITZIL MUÑOZ
Number of teachers: 3,608
Number of students: 42,055

DIRECTORS

Hospital: Dr ADALBERTO BAIGHTS
Institute of Physics: Dr RUTILO NICOLÁS SILVA GONZÁLEZ
Institute of Physiology: Dr JOSÉ RAMÓN EGUIBAR CUENCA
Institutes of Sciences: Dra MARÍA LILIA CEDILLO RAMÍREZ

Institute of Social Sciences and Humanities: Mtro ROBERTO M. VÉLEZ PLIEGO
School of Agricultural Engineering: Ing. ROSALBA SOLÍS GÓMEZ
School of Architecture: Arq. JOSÉ ANTONIO RUÍZ TENORIO
School of Arts: Mtro DAVID CORNISH BECERRA
School of Biology: Biol. GONZALO YANES GÓMEZ
School of Chemical Engineering: Mtro IGNACIO ROJAS
School of Chemical Sciences: M.C. JOSÉ JAVIER SOSA RIVADENEIRA
School of Civil and Technological Engineering: Mtro NICOLÁS FUEYO MACDONALD
School of Communication: Lic. EDUARDO GARZÓN VALDÉS
School of Computing: Dr GUILLERMO DE ITA LUNA
School of Economics: Mtro DANTE MÉNDEZ JIMÉNEZ
School of Electronics: M.C. JAIME CID MONJARAZ
School of Languages: Mtro ANTONIO VERA GARCÍA DE LEÓN
School of Law and Social Sciences: Lic. EMILIANO PEREA PELAEZ
School of Medicine: Dr MANUEL MORALES CAMACHO
School of Nursing and Obstetrics: Lic. en Enf. MARÍA MARGARITA CAMPOS VÁZQUEZ
School of Philosophy and Letters: Dr ROBERTO HERNÁNDEZ ORAMAS
School of Physical Culture: Mtra MARÍA VÉLEZ MORA
School of Physics and Mathematics: Dra SORAYA GÓMEZ Y ESTRADA
School of Psychology: Psic. J. FERNANDO TURRENT RODRÍGUEZ
School of Public Administration: Mtra SARA AMALIA VÉLEZ MEJÍA
School of Public Accountancy: M.A. MARÍA DE LOURDES MEDINA HERNÁNDEZ
School of Stomatology: M.C. LUIS ANTONIO GONZÁLEZ SALAZAR
School of Veterinary Medicine and Animal Husbandry: Dr FRANCISCO JAVIER FRANCO GUERRA

UNIVERSIDAD ANÁHUAC

Apdo 10-844, 11000 México, DF
Avda Universidad Anáhuac s/n, Lomas Anáhuac, 52760 Huixquilucan, Estado de México
Telephone: (55) 5627-0210
Fax: (55) 5589-9796
E-mail: anahuac@anahuac.mx
Internet: www.anahuac.mx
Founded 1963
Private control
Academic year: August to June (two terms)
Rector: Lic. RAYMUND COSGRAVE
Sec.-Gen.: Arq. JOSÉ MATEOS
Gen. Academic Dir: Dr CRISTIAN NAZER
Librarian: Mtro DANIEL MATTES
Library of 163,500 vols
Number of teachers: 1,100
Number of students: 7,000
Publications: *Carta Económica—Boletín Instituto Desarrollo Empresarial Anáhuac (IDEA)* (6 a year), *Generación Anáhuac* (6 a year), *Iuris Tantum* (1 a year), *Medicina y Etica* (4 a year)

DEANS

Faculty of Bioethics: Dr JOSÉ KUTHY PORTER
Faculty of Education: Mtra LUZ DEL CARMEN DÁVALOS
Faculty of Engineering: Dr ALEJANDRO MONTANO
School of Actuarial Sciences: Act. OLIVA SÁNCHEZ

School of Architecture: Arq. FERNANDO PAZ Y PUENTE
School of Communication Sciences: Dr CARLOS GÓMEZ PALACIO
School of Economics and Business: Dr RAMÓN LECUONA
School of Industrial and Graphic Design: Lic. LEONOR AMOZURRUTIA
School of Law: Dr JOSÉ ANTONIO NÚÑEZ
School of Medicine: Dr TOMÁS BARRIENTOS
School of Psychology: Mtro JOSÉ MARÍA LÓPEZ
School of Tourism Administration: Prof. LOUIS PASCAL

UNIVERSIDAD AUTÓNOMA AGRARIA 'ANTONIO NARRO'

Buenavista, 25315 Saltillo, Coah.
Telephone: (844) 411-0275
Fax: (844) 411-0207
E-mail: docencia@uaaan.mx
Internet: www.uaaan.mx
Founded 1923, university status 1975
Academic year: January to December
Rector: Ing. EDUARDO FUENTES RODRÍGUEZ
Vice-Rector: M. V. Z. JOSÉ L. BERLANGA FLORES
Registrar: Ing. GUSTAVO OLIVARES SALAZAR
Librarian: LUZ ELENA PEREZ MATA (acting)
Number of teachers: 430
Number of students: 2,583

COORDINATORS OF FACULTIES

Agronomy: Dr MARCO ANTONIO BUSTAMANTE G.
Animal Science: Dr EDUARDO AIZPURU GARCIA
Engineering: M. C. LUIS M. LASSO MENDOZA
Social and Economics Science: Ing. FRANCISCO MARTINEZ GOMEZ

UNIVERSIDAD AUTÓNOMA 'BENITO JUÁREZ' DE OAXACA

Avda Universidad s/n, Ex-Hacienda de 5 Señores, 68120 Oaxaca, Oax.
Telephone: (951) 511-0688
Internet: www.uabjo.mx
Founded 1827, university status 1955
Private control
Academic year: September to July
Rector: Mtro. Arq. RAFAEL TORRES VALDEZ
Gen.–Sec.: Dr EDUARDO L. PEREZ CAMPOS
Librarian: Lic. DONAJI MENDOZA LUNA
Library of 77,237 vols
Number of teachers: 980
Number of students: 15,000
Publication: *Planeación*

DEANS

Faculty of Commerce and Administration: L.A.E. SEVERINO ROJAS LÁZARO
Language Centre: Prof. ERIC O'CONNEL
School of Architecture: Arq. JORGE VARGAS GUZMÁN
School of Chemistry: Dr ARTURO SANTAELLA V.
School of Fine Arts: Lic. EVELIO BAUTISTA TORRES
School of Law and Social Sciences: Lic. ABEL GARCÍA RAMÍREZ
School of Medicine: Dr ALFONSO SANTOS ORTÍZ
School of Nursing and Obstetrics: Enf. NOEMI CÓRDOVA VARGAS
School of Odontology: C.D. AUSTREBERTO MARTÍNEZ MOLINA
School of Veterinary Studies: M.V.Z. CARLOS A. DE J. LEÓN LEDEZMA

UNIVERSIDAD AUTÓNOMA CHAPINGO

km 38.5 Carretera México-Veracruz, Texcoco, Edo de México

Telephone: (595) 952-1500
Fax: (595) 952-1565
Internet: www.chapingo.mx

Founded 1854 as Escuela Nacional de Agricultura; named changed 1978
Government control
Academic year: August to June

Rector: Dr José Sergio Barrales Dominguez
Dir-Gen. for Academic Affairs: Dr Javier Ruiz Ledesma
Dir-Gen. for Admin.: José Solis Ramírez
Dir-Gen. for Research: Dr Enrique Serrano Gálvez
Librarian: Rosa María Ojeda Trejo
Library: see Libraries and Archives
Number of teachers: 1,200
Number of students: 6,800 (6,500 undergraduates, 300 graduates)
Publications: *Revista Chapingo* (6 a year), *Revista de Geografía Agrícola* (6 a year), *Textual* (social sciences, 2 a year)

DEANS

Agricultural Mechanical Engineering: Martín Soto Escobar
Agricultural Parasitology: Francisco Ponce Gonzalez
Agroecology: Dr Laksmi Reddiar Krishnmurthy
Agroindustrial Engineering: Dr Luis Ramiro García Chavez
Dry Area Science: Santiago Ramon Mendoza Moreno
Earth Science: Dr David Cristóbal Acevedo
Economic and Administrative Science: Jaime Ruvalcaba Limon
Forestry: Angel Leyva Ovalle
Irrigation: Rene Martinez Elizondo
Phytotechnics: Dr Mario Perez Grajales
Rural Sociology: Jesus Carlos Morett Sanchez
Zootechnology: Meliton Cordoba Alvarez

UNIVERSIDAD AUTÓNOMA DE AGUASCALIENTES

Avda Universidad 940, Ciudad Universitaria, 20100 Aguascalientes, Ags

Telephone: (449) 910-7400
Fax: (449) 910-7409
Internet: www.uaa.mx

Founded 1973
State control
Language of instruction: Spanish
Academic year: August to June (two semesters)

Rector: Dr. Antonio Avila Storer
Sec.-Gen.: Mtro. Jasé Ramiro Alemán López
Librarian: C.P. Irma de Leon de Muñoz
Library of 152,150 vols
Number of teachers: 1,461
Number of students: 11,501

Publications: *Caleidoscopio* (2 a year), *Correo Universitario*, *Evaluación* (1 a year), *Gaceta Universitaria* (12 a year), *Investigación y Ciencia* (2 a year), *Scientiae Naturae* (2 a year)

DEANS

Centre for Agricultural Sciences: I.B.Q. Nara Aurora Guerrero García
Centre for Arts and Humanities: Mtro José Alfredo Ortiz Garza
Centre for Basic Sciences: Ing Angel Díaz Palos
Centre for Biomedical Sciences: Dra Ruby S. Libreros Agudelo
Centre for Design and Construction Sciences: Ing. Jorge Pio Monsivais Santoyo

Centre for Economics and Administration: C.P. Ricardo González Alvarez
Centre for Secondary Education: Lic. Ernestina León Rodríguez

UNIVERSIDAD AUTÓNOMA DE BAJA CALIFORNIA

Apdo Postal 459, Avda Alvaro Obregón y Julian Carrillo s/n, 21100 Mexicali, Baja California

Telephone: (686) 554-2200
Fax: (686) 554-2200
Internet: www.uabc.mx

Founded 1957
Language of instruction: Spanish
Academic year: August to June

Rector: C.P. Víctor Everardo Beltrán Corona
Vice-Rector: M.C. René Andrade Peterson
Sec.-Gen.: M.C. Juan José Sevilla García
Librarian: Lic. Alma Lorena Camarena Flores
Number of teachers: 3,099
Number of students: 21,548

Publications: *Caláfia, Ciencias Marinas, Cuaderno de Taller Literario, Cuadernos de Ciencias Sociales, Divulgare, Estudios Fronterizos, Paradigmas, Revista de Investigación Educativa, Revistas Universitarias, Semillero, Yubai*

PRINCIPALS

Ensenada Campus:

Faculty of Marine Sciences: Dr Roberto Millán Núñez
Faculty of Sciences: M.C. Ernesto Campos González
School of Accountancy and Administration: Lic. Saúl Méndez Hernández
School of Engineering: M.C. José de Jesús Zamarripa Topete

Mexicali Campus:

Faculty of Architecture: Arq. Aarón G. Bernal Rodríguez
Faculty of Humanities: M.C. Angel Manuel Ortiz Marín
Faculty of Law: Lic. Ma. Aurora Lacavex Berumen
Faculty of Odontology: C.D. Manuel Oscar Lara Betancourt
School of Accountancy and Administration: C.P. Placido Valenciana Moreno
School of Engineering: Ing. César Raúl Reyes Mazón
School of Languages: Lic. Kora Evangelina Basich Peralta
School of Medicine: Med. Sergio Romo Barraza
School of Nursing: Lic. Andrea Verdugo Batiz
School of Pedagogy: Prof. Jesús Aceves Gutiérrez
School of Social Sciences: Lic. Miguel Angel Rendón Martínez

Tecate Campus:

School of Engineering: Quim. Sergio Vale Sánchez (Dir)

Tijuana Campus:

Faculty of Accountancy and Administration: C.P. Luis Meza Aristigue
Faculty of Chemistry: M.C. Ma. Eugenia Pérez Morales
Faculty of Economics: Dra Sonia Yolanda Lugo Morones
Faculty of Law: Lic. José de Jesús Díaz de la Torre
Faculty of Medicine: Dra Adriana Carolina Vargas Ojeda
Faculty of Odontology: Dr Miguel Angel Cadena Alcántar
School of Humanities: Lic. Jorge Gustavo Mendoza González

School of Tourism: Lic. Onésimo Cuamea Velázquez

DIRECTORS OF RESEARCH INSTITUTES

Agricultural Sciences Institute (Mexicali Campus): Dr Miguel Cervantes Ramírez
Agriculture and Stockbreeding Research Institute: Ing. Víctor Manuel Vega Kuri
Educative Development and Research Institute: Mtro Eduardo Backhoff Escudero
Engineering Institute (Mexicali Campus): Dr Benjamín Valdez Salas
History Research Centre (Tijuana Campus): Dra Catalina Velázquez Morales
Oceanology Research Institute (Ensenada Campus): Dr José A. Zertuche González
Social Research Institute (Mexicali Campus): Dr Pablo Jesús González Reyes
Veterinary Science Research Institute (Mexicali Campus): Dr Eduardo Sánchez López

UNIVERSIDAD AUTÓNOMA DE BAJA CALIFORNIA SUR
(Autonomous University of Baja California Sur)

Carretera al Sur km 5.5, 23080 La Paz, BCS

Telephone: (612) 128-8800
Fax: (612) 128-0880
E-mail: webmaster@uabcs.mx
Internet: www.uabcs.mx

Founded 1975
State control
Language of instruction: Spanish

Rector: Lic. Juan Rodrigo Guerrero Rivas
Secretary-General: Publio Octavio Romero Martínez
Director of Planning and Programming: Dr Arturo Hernández Prado
Head Librarian: Lic. José Alfredo Verdugo Sánchez

ACADEMIC AREA COORDINATORS

Agricultural Sciences: José Guadalupe Loya Ramírez
Marine Sciences: Jorge García Pámanes
Social Sciences and Humanities: Ma. Luisa Cabral Bowling

UNIVERSIDAD AUTÓNOMA DE CAMPECHE

Av. Agustín Melgar s/n entre Calle 20 y Juan de la Barrera, Col. Buenavista, 24030 Campeche, Camp.

Telephone: (981) 811-9800
E-mail: webmaster@etzna.uacam.mx
Internet: www.uacam.mx

Founded 1756, refounded 1965
State control
Academic year: September to June

Rector: Licda. Adriana del Pilar Ortiz Lanz
Sec.-Gen.: Lic. Joaquín Uc Valencia
Librarian: Lic. Araceli May Canul

Number of teachers: 443
Number of students: 4,760

Publications: *Panorama* (6 a year), *Pinceladas* (6 a year)

DIRECTORS OF FACULTIES AND SCHOOLS

'Dr Nazario Víctor Montejo Godoy' Preparatory School: Lic. Alma Lorena Guzman García
Faculty of Chemical and Biological Sciences: Mtra Angelica Soto Martínez
Faculty of Engineering: Ing. Domingo Berman Ordaz
Faculty of Humanities: Lic. José Manuel Alcocer Bernés
Faculty of Law: Lic. Jorge Rodríguez Vargas
Faculty of Social Sciences: Dr Gerardo Mixcoatl Tinoco

Higher School of Nursing: Lic. MARÍA CANDE-
LARIA AGUILAR BRICEÑO
'Lic. Ermilo Sandoval Campos' Preparatory
School: Lic. VÍCTOR ORTIZ PASOS
School of Accounting and Administration: M.
en C. ENNA SANDOVAL CASTELLANOS
School of Dentistry: C. D. LUIS HERRERA
LÓPEZ
School of Medicine: Dr CARLOS EDUARDO
GARCÍA SOLIS

UNIVERSIDAD AUTÓNOMA DE CHIAPAS

Blvd Belisario Domínguez km 1081, Edificio
de Rectoría, Colina Universitaria s/n,
29020 Tuxtla Gutiérrez, Chiapas

Telephone: (961) 617-8000
Internet: www.unach.mx

Founded 1975
Private control
Academic year: September to July (two
semesters)

Rector: Dr ÁNGEL RENÉ ESTRADA ARÉVALO
Sec.-Gen.: LUIS MANUEL MARTÍNEZ ESTRADA
Academic Sec.: Ing. ROBERTO CRUZ DE LEÓN
Librarian: Lic. DOLORES SERRANO CANCINO

Number of teachers: 906
Number of students: 12,052

Publication: *Gaceta Universitaria*

DIRECTORS

Campus I (Tuxtla Gutiérrez):

Faculty of Accounting and Administration:
C.P. CESAR MAZA GONZÁLEZ
Faculty of Architecture: Arq. RICARDO GUIL-
LÉN CASTAÑEDA
School of Civil Engineering: Ing. ROBERTON Y
CRUZ DIAZ

Campus II (Tuxtla Gutiérrez):

Faculty of Human Medicine: Dr JOSÉ LUIS
AQUINO HERNÁNDEZ
School of Veterinary Medicine and Zootech-
nics: MVZ. ALBERTO YAMAZAKI MAZA

Campus III (San Cristóbal de las Casas):

Faculty of Law: Lic. ALFONSO RAMÍREZ MAR-
TÍNEZ
Faculty of Social Sciences: JORGE ALBERTO
LÓPEZ AREVALO

Campus IV (Tapachula):

Faculty of Accounting: C.P. JORGE FERNANDO
ORDAZ RUÍZ
Faculty of Administration Sciences: KENY
ORDAZ ESCOBAR
Faculty of Agriculture: Ing. ALFONSO PÉREZ
ROMERO
School of Chemical Sciences: JOSÉ RAMÓN
PUIG COTA

Campus V (Villaflores):

School of Agronomy: Dr ALFREDO MEDINA
MELÉNDEZ

Campus VI (Tuxtla Gutiérrez):

Faculty of Humanities: CARLOS RINCÓN
RAMÍREZ

UNIVERSIDAD AUTÓNOMA DE CHIHUAHUA

Av. Escorza 900, Zona Centro, 31000 Chihuahua, Chih.

Telephone: (614) 439-1500
Fax: (614) 439-1529
E-mail: webmaster@uach.mx
Internet: www.uach.mx

Founded 1954
Language of instruction: Spanish
Academic year: August to June

Rector: Dr JESÚS ENRIQUE GRAJEDA HERRERA
Sec.-Gen.: Dr JESÚS XAVIER VENEGAS HOL-
GUÍN

Admin. Dir: C.P. y L.A.E. GABRIELA RICO
CABRERA
Librarian: C.P. FERNANDO SALOMÓN BEYER
Library: various faculty journals
Number of teachers: 1,428
Number of students: 12,429

DIRECTORS

Faculty of Accountancy and Administration:
C.P. y M.A. FRANCISCO JAVIER LUJÁN DE LA
GARZA
Faculty of Agricultural Engineering: M.C.
ALMA PATRICIA HERNÁNDEZ RODRÍGUEZ
Faculty of Agriculture and Forestry: M.S.
ARTURO JAVIER OBANDO RODRÍGUEZ
Faculty of Chemical Sciences: Ing. MANUEL
RUÍZ ESPARZA MEDINA
Faculty of Engineering: Ing. ARTURO LEAL
BEJARANO
Faculty of Law: Lic. MARIO TREVISO SALAZAR
Faculty of Medicine: Dr CARLOS ENRIQUE
MORALES ORTEGA
Faculty of Philosophy and Literature: Lic.
ISELA YOLANDA DE PABLO PORRAS
Faculty of Physical Education and Sport
Science: L.E.F. PRIMO ALBERTO GONZÁLEZ
ARZATE
Faculty of Political and Social Sciences: Lic.
SAMUEL GARCÍA SOTO
Faculty of Stockbreeding: Dr GUILLERMO
VILLALOBOS VILLALOBOS
Institute of Fine Arts: Lic. RUBEN TINAJERO
MEDINA
School of Dentistry: Dr JESÚS DUARTE MAYA-
GOITIA
School of International Economics: Lic. MAN-
UEL PARGA MUÑOZ
School of Nursing and Nutrition Science:
M.E.M.I. ROSA MARÍA DOZAL MOLINA

UNIVERSIDAD AUTÓNOMA DE CIUDAD JUÁREZ

Calle Henri Dunant 4016, Zona Pronaf,
Ciudad Juárez, Chihuahua

Telephone: (656) 688-2100
E-mail: daramire@uacj.mx
Internet: www.uacj.mx

Founded 1973
State control
Language of instruction: Spanish
Academic year: August to June

Rector: Lic. JORGE QUINTANA SILVEYRA
Gen.-Sec.: M.C. DAVID RAMÍREZ PEREA
Chief Admin. Officer: Lic. RICARDO DUARTE
JÁQUEZ
Dean of Academic Affairs: Quim. HÉCTOR
REYES LEAL
Director of Research and Graduate Studies:
Dra MARTHA PATRICIA BARRAZA DE ANDA

Number of teachers: 710
Number of students: 12,200

Publications: *Entorno*, *Nóesis*

DEANS

College of Architecture, Design and Art: Arq.
ARTURO MARTÍNEZ LASSO
College of Biomedical Sciences: Dr FELIPE
FORNELLI
College of Engineering and Technology: Dr
RAMÓN PARRA
College of Social Sciences and Administra-
tion: Lic. LUIS A. MAYORGA

UNIVERSIDAD AUTÓNOMA DE COAHUILA

Blvd V. Carranza esq. González Lobo, Col.
República Oriente, 25280 Saltillo, Coah.

Telephone: (844) 438-1600
Fax: (844) 438-1600
Internet: www.uadec.mx

Founded 1867, refounded 1957
State control

Language of instruction: Spanish
Academic year: August to June (two terms)

Rector: Lic. MARIO OCHOA RIVERA
Sec.-Gen.: L.Ab.L. ALBERTO L. SALAZAR
RODRÍGUEZ
Librarian: ANTONIO MALACARA

Number of teachers: 900
Number of students: 13,923

UNIVERSIDAD AUTÓNOMA DE GUADALAJARA

Apdo Postal 1-440, 44100 Guadalajara,
Jalisco
Avda Patria No. 1201, Lomas del Valle, 3a
Sección, Guadalajara, Jalisco

Telephone: (33) 3638-8463
E-mail: uag@uag.mx
Internet: www.uag.mx

Founded 1935
Private control
Language of instruction: Spanish
Academic year: August to May

Rector: Lic. ANTONIO LEAÑO ALVAREZ DEL
CASTILLO
Vice-Rector: Ing. JUAN JOSÉ LEAÑO ALVAREZ
DEL CASTILLO
Chief Admin. Officer: Lic. RUBÉN QUIROZ V.
Chief Academic Officer: Dr NÉSTOR VELASCO
P.
Librarian: Lic. ALBERTO OLIVARES DUARTE
Library of 178,000 vols, 3,760 maps, 3,400
periodicals
Number of teachers: 1,622
Number of students: 14,102

Publications: *Academia* (6 a year), *Actas de
la Facultad de Medicina* (2 a year),
Docencia (3 a year), *Item Histórico* (12 a
year)

DEANS

College of Architecture and Design: Arq.
RAÚL MENDOZA R.
College of Business: C.P. JAVIER GONZÁLEZ C.
College of Engineering: Ing. RAFAEL JAIME A.
College of Health Sciences: Dr NÉSTOR
VELASCO P.
College of Humanities and Social Sciences:
Lic. ISMAEL ZAMORA TOVAR
College of Law: Lic. HUMBERTO LÓPEZ DELGA-
DILLO
College of Sciences: Ing. JAIME HERNÁNDEZ O.
Continuing Education: Dr JOSÉ MORALES G.
(Dir)
Postgraduate Studies: Dr MAURICIO ALCOCER
RUTHLING (Dir)
Research Administration: Dr RODOLFO CASIL-
LAS V. (Dir)
Universidad en la Comunidad (UNICO, Jun-
ior College): Lic. PEDRO RODRÍGUEZ L. (Dir)

DIRECTORS

College of Architecture and Design (Avda
Patria 1201, Lomas del Valle, 45110 Guadalajara, Jalisco; tel. (33) 6610-1010 ext. 32669;
fax (33) 6610-1610; e-mail rmendoz@cu.gdl
.uag.mx; internet www.uag.edu):

    School of Architecture: Arq. RAÚL MENDOZA
    R.
    School of Graphic Design: Lic. CARLOS
    HERRERA P.
    School of Industrial Design: Arq. ALFREDO
    AMBRIZ T.
    School of Landscape and Interior Design:
    Lic. SUSANA MAYTORENA

College of Business (Avda Patria 1201,
Lomas del Valle, 45110 Guadalajara, Jalisco;
tel. (33) 6610-0412; fax (33) 6610-0412;
e-mail jgcastil@uagunix.gdl.uag.mx):

    School of Business Administration: Lic.
    MA. ELENA MONROY L.
    School of Economics: Lic. JOSÉ LUIS SÁN-
    CHEZ DE LA F.

School of International Business: Lic. ATALA SOSA H.

School of Public Accountancy: C.P. JOSÉ ARZATE V.

School of Tourism: Lic. CELINA GALLEGOS S.

College of Engineering (Avda Patria 1202, Lomas del Valle, 45110 Guadalajara, Jalisco; tel. (33) 6610-1010 ext. 32216; fax (33) 6610-1010 ext. 32211; e-mail rjaime@uagunix.gdl .uag.mx):

School of Civil Engineering: Ing. MIGUEL ANGEL PARRA MENA

School of Computer Engineering: Ing. RAFAEL JAIME ALEJO

School of Electronic Engineering: Ing. RAMÓN VÁZQUEZ E.

School of Information Management and Computer Systems: Ing. GONZALO OSUNA

School of Mechanical and Electrical Engineering: Ing. MANUEL URIARTE RAZO

College of Health Sciences (Avda Patria 1201, Lomas del Valle, 45110 Guadalajara, Jalisco; tel. (33) 6610-1010 ext. 32737; fax (33) 6610-0244; e-mail nperez@med.gdl.uag .mx):

School of Dentistry: Dr RAFAEL CHACÓN V.

School of Medicine: Dr. RICARDO LEÓN B.

School of Nursing: Enf. GLORIA DE LA CERDA

College of Humanities and Social Sciences (Avda Patria 1202, Lomas del Valle, 45110 Guadalajara, Jalisco; tel. (33) 6610-1010 ext. 32237; fax (33) 6610-1610; e-mail izamora@ uagunix.gdl.uag.mx; internet www.uag.edu):

International Language Centre: Lic. MA. ESTHER DE LA CUESTA D.

School of Anthropology, Philosophy and Letters: Lic. CRISTINA RUÍZ DE HERNÁNDEZ

School of Communication Sciences: Lic. VÍCTOR ESCALANTE VERA

School of International Relations: Prof. FERNANDO TORRES DE LA T.

School of Linguistics: Lic. MARÍA ESTHER DE LA CUESTA DÍAZ

School of Pedagogy: Lic. ISMAEL ZAMORA T.

School of Psychology: Lic. GABRIEL MORALES HERNÁNDEZ

College of Law (Avda Patria 1201, Lomas del Valle, 45110 Guadalajara, Jalisco; tel. (33) 6610-1010 ext. 32739; fax (33) 6610-1610 ext. 32276; e-mail hdelgadi@uagunix.gdl.uag .mx):

School of Law: Lic. HUMBERTO LÓPEZ D.

School of Social Work: Lic. ELSA ESPINOZA T.

College of Sciences (Avda Patria 1202, Lomas del Valle, 45110 Guadalajara, Jalisco; tel. (33) 6610-1010 ext. 32813; fax (33) 6610-1010 ext. 32219; e-mail jhernan@uagunix.gdl.uag .mx):

School of Chemical Sciences: Ing. ANTONIO PEIMBERT V.

School of Mathematics: Ing. EDUARDO OJEDA P.

School of Natural Sciences and Agriculture: Biol. JORGE FLORES M.

UNIVERSIDAD AUTÓNOMA DE GUERRERO

Av. Javier Méndez Aponte 1, 03900 Chilpancingo, Guerrero

Telephone: (747) 471-9310

Internet: www.uagro.mx

Founded 1869

Private control

Language of instruction: Spanish

Academic year: August to June

Rector: Ing. Agron. RAMÓN REYES CARRETO

Gen. Sec.: M. C. CATALINO MACEDO VENCES

Librarian: Lic. ROBERT ALEXANDER ENDEAN GAMBOA

Number of teachers: 1,600

Number of students: 49,000

Publications: *Gaceta Popular*, *Otatal*, *Revista de la UAG*

DIRECTORS

Higher School of Agriculture: Q.B. GILBERTO BIBIANO MORENO

Higher School of Tourism: Lic. ARMANDO BELLO RODRÍGUEZ

Regional School of Earth Sciences: Geol. GERMÁN URBAN LAMADRID

School of Architecture and Town Planning: Arq. CLAUDIO RIOS TORRES

School of Chemical-Biological Sciences: Q. B. P. MARCO ANTONIO LEYVA VÁZQUEZ

School of Commerce and Administration: C.P. SALVADOR OLIVAR CAMPOS

School of Engineering: Ing. RODOLFO VÁZQUEZ ZEFERINO

School of Economics: M. C. S. ANGEL CRESPO ACEVEDO

School of Law: Lic. ALEJANDRO BERNABE GONZÁLEZ

School of Marine Ecology: Biol. ARMANDO YOKOYAMA KANO

School of Medicine: Dr ASCENCIO VILLEGAS ARRIZON

School of Philosophy: Lic. FAUSTO AVILA JUÁREZ

School of Social Sciences: Lic. ANGEL ASCENCIO ROMERO

School of Veterinary Medicine and Animal Husbandry: M. V. Z. SALVADOR SÁNCHEZ PADILLA

UNIVERSIDAD AUTÓNOMA DE NAYARIT

Ciudad de la Cultura 'Amado Nervo', 63155 Tepic, Nayarit

Telephone: (311) 211-8800

Internet: www.uan.mx

Founded 1930 as Instituto de Ciencias y Letras de Nayarit, refounded as university 1969

Rector: M.C. OMAR WICAB GUTIÉRREZ

Gen.-Sec.: M.C. ADRIÁN NAVARRETE MÉNDEZ

Number of teachers: 230

Number of students: 2,400

Schools of agriculture, chemical engineering, commerce and administration, dentistry, economics, law, medicine, nursing, veterinary medicine, zoology.

UNIVERSIDAD AUTÓNOMA DE NUEVO LEÓN

Ciudad Universitaria, 66451 San Nicolás de los Garza, Nuevo León

Telephone: (81) 8329-4000

E-mail: webmaster@uanl.mx

Internet: www.uanl.mx

Founded 1933

Academic year: August to July

Rector: Ing. JOSÉ ANTONIO GONZÁLEZ TREVIÑO

General Sec.: Dr JESÚS ANCER-RODRÍGUEZ

Academic Sec.: Dr UBALDO ORTIZ-MÉNDEZ

Library of 1,500,000 vols

Number of teachers: 5,671

Number of students: 122,501

DEANS

Faculty of Agronomy: Dr JUAN F. VILLARREAL ARREDONDO

Faculty of Architecture: Arq. GUILLERMO ROBERTO WAH ROBLES

Faculty of Biological Sciences: M.C. JUAN M. ADAME RODRÍGUEZ

Faculty of Chemical Sciences: Ing. JOSÉ MANUEL MARTÍNEZ DELGADO

Faculty of Civil Engineering: Ing. FRANCISCO GÁMEZ TREVIÑO

Faculty of Communication Sciences: Lic. JUAN MARIO GÁMEZ CRUZ

Faculty of Earth Sciences: Dr COSME POLA SIMUTA

Faculty of Economics: Lic. JORGE MELÉNDEZ BARRÓN

Faculty of Forestry Sciences: Dr ALFONSO MARTÍNEZ MUÑOZ

Faculty of Law and Social Sciences: Lic. ALEJANDRO IZAGUIRRE GONZÁLEZ

Faculty of Mechanical and Electrical Engineering: Ing. CÁSTULO E. VELA VILLARREAL

Faculty of Medicine: Dr JESÚS Z. VILLARREAL PÉREZ

Faculty of Music: Lic. JUAN LUIS RODRÍGUEZ TRUJILLO

Faculty of Nursing: Lic. MARÍA GPE. MARTÍNEZ DE DÁVILA

Faculty of Odontology: Dr ROBERTO CARRILLO GONZÁLEZ

Faculty of Philosophy and the Arts: Lic. RICARDO C. VILLARREAL ARRAMBIDE

Faculty of Physical and Mathematical Sciences: Ing. JOSÉ OSCAR RECIO CANTÚ

Faculty of Political Science and Public Administration: Lic. RICARDO A. FUENTES CAVAZOS

Faculty of Psychology: Lic. GUILLERMO HERNÁNDEZ MARTÍNEZ

Faculty of Public Accounting and Administration: C.P. RAMIRO SOBERÓN PÉREZ

Faculty of Public Health: Lic. ELIZABETH SOLÍS DE SÁNCHEZ

Faculty of Social Work: Lic. MA. IRENE CANTÚ REYNA

Faculty of Sports Administration: Lic. RENÉ SALGADO MÉNDEZ

Faculty of Veterinary Medicine and Zootechnics: Dr JOSÉ ANTONIO SALINAS MELÉNDEZ

Faculty of the Visual Arts: Arq. MARIO ARMENDARIZ VELÁZQUEZ

UNIVERSIDAD AUTÓNOMA DE QUERÉTARO

Centro Universitario, Av. Hidalgo s/n, Col. Las Campanas, 76010 Santiago de Querétaro, Qro

Telephone: (442) 192-1200

Fax: (442) 216-4917

E-mail: webmaster@uaq.mx

Internet: www.uaq.mx

Founded 1951

State control

Language of instruction: Spanish

Academic year: July to June

Rector: M. en A. RAÚL ITURRALDE OLVERA

Academic Sec.: Dr GUILLERMO CABRERA LÓPEZ

Administrative Sec.: Dr JOSÉ AMBROSIO OCHOA OLVERA

Librarian: ARTURO HERNÁNDEZ SIERRA

Number of teachers: 1,428

Number of students: 18,000

Publications: *Autonomía*, *Revista Auriga*, *Revista Bellas Artes*, *Revista de Egresados de Contabilidad*, *Revista de Informática*, *Revista de Investigación*, *Revista de Medicina*, *Revista de Sociología*, *Revista Extensión Universitaria*

DEANS

Faculty of Chemistry: J. MERCED ESPARZA AGUILAR

Faculty of Engineering: JESÚS HERNÁNDEZ ESPINO

Faculty of Humanities: GABRIEL CORRAL BASURTO

Faculty of Law: ARSENIO DURAN BECERRA

Faculty of Psychology: ANDRES VELÁZQUEZ ORTEGA

Preparatory Faculty: DOLORES CABRERA MUÑOZ

School of Computer Science: LUIS F. SAAVEDRA URIBE

School of Fine Arts: José Roberto González García
School of Journalism: Luis Roberto Amieba Perez
School of Languages: Aurora Ivette Silva Rodriguez
School of Medicine: Dr Salvador Guerrero Servin
School of Nursing: Alejandrina Franco Esguerra
School of Social Enterprise Management: Felipe Samayoa
School of Sociology: Carlos Dorantes Gonzalez
School of Veterinary Science and Zoology: M.V.Z. Guillermo de la Isla Herrera

UNIVERSIDAD AUTÓNOMA DE SAN LUIS POTOSÍ

Alvaro Obregón 64 Antiguo, Centro Histórico, 78000 San Luis Potosí

Telephone: (444) 826-1381
Fax: (444) 812-3343
Internet: www.uaslp.mx

Founded 1826 as Instituto Científico y Literario
Federal control
Language of instruction: Spanish
Academic year: August to June

Rector: Lic. Mario García Valdez
Gen.-Sec.: Arq. Manuel F. Villar Rubio
Particular Sec.: Lic. María del Pilar Delgadillo Silva
Admin. Sec.: Ricardo Segovia Medina
Finance Dir: José E. Hernández Garza
Libraries System Dir: Dr Luis Del Castillo Mora

Library of 3,000,000 vols in 28 libraries
Number of teachers: 2,290
Number of students: 19,400

Publications: *Alfa y Omega* (2 a year), *Convergencia* (2 a year), *Escenario* (2 a year), *Hábitat* (1 a year), *Horizonte Administrativo* (3 a year), *La Rueda* (2 a year), *Lex Universitatis* (3 a year), *Revista del Instituto de Investigaciones Jurídicas* (2 a year), *Universitarios Potosinos* (2 a year)

DEANS

Accountancy and Administration: Juan Manuel Buenrostro Morán
Agronomy: M. C. Miguel Angel Tiscareño Iracheta
Chemistry: Dr Jorge F. Toro Vázquez
Communications: Lic. Jorge Arturo Mirabal Martínez
Economics: Lic. David Vega Niño
Engineering: Ing. Arnoldo González Ortíz
Habitat: Arq. Alejandro Galván Arellano
Law: Lic. Ricardo Sanchez Marquez
Library Science: Lic. Rosa María Martínez Rider
Medicine: Dr Jesus Eduardo Noyola Bernal
Nursing: Mtra. Magdalena Miranda
Psychology: Lic. Victor Manuel Arreguín Rocha
Science: M. C. Benito Pineda Reyes
Stomatology: Dr Mario Arevalo Mendoza

UNIVERSIDAD AUTÓNOMA DE SINALOA

Calle Gral. Angel Flores Pte. s/n, Colonia Centro, 80000 Culiacán Rosales, Sin.

Telephone: (667) 7125441
Fax: (667) 7169848
E-mail: rector@uas.uasnet.mx
Internet: www.uasnet.mx

Founded 1873
State control
Languages of instruction: Spanish, English
Academic year: August to June

Chancellor: Dr Víctor Antonio Corrales Burgueño
Vice-Chancellor for Academic Affairs: Dr Ismael García Castro
Gen. Dir of External Affairs and Int. Relations: Lic. Luis Gilberto Castro Pietsch

Library of 73,143 vols
Number of teachers: 7,846
Number of students: 116,531

Publication: *Buelna* (52 a year).

UNIVERSIDAD AUTÓNOMA DE TAMAULIPAS

Matamoros 8 y 9, Col. Centro, 87000 Victoria, Tamaulipas

Telephone: (834) 318-1800
Internet: www.uat.mx

Founded 1955
Private control
Language of instruction: Spanish
Academic year: August to June

Rector: Ing. Humberto Filizola Haces
Sec.-Gen.: M.V.Z. Fernando Arizpe García
Academic Sec.: C.P. Uriel Davila Herrera
Admin. Sec.: Ing. Miguel Cantu Caballero
Dir of Planning and Institutional Devt: Dr. Marco Aurelio Navarro

Number of teachers: 2,848 (912 full-time, 1,936 part-time)
Number of students: 36,000

Publications: *Biotam* (2 a year), *Sociotam* (2 a year)

DIRECTORS

Mante Campus:
Faculty of Agriculture: Ing. Alejandro Hernández

Matamoros Campus:
Faculty of Human Medicine: Dr Juan Carlos Cantó
Faculty of Nursing: Mtra Antonia Hernández

Nuevo Laredo Campus:
Faculty of Commerce and Administration: Lic Ramiro Garza
Faculty of Nursing: Lic Rosalinda Medina

Reynosa Campus:
Faculty of Agro-industrial Sciences: Ing. Jose Suárez Fernández
Faculty of Chemical Sciences: L.Q.I. Rene Fuentes

Tampico Campus:
Faculty of Architecture: Arq. Juan José Cuevas
Faculty of Commerce and Administration: C.P. José Luis Lizardi
Faculty of Dentistry: Dr Delfino Alviso
Faculty of Engineering: Ing. Moises Barcenas
Faculty of Law and Social Sciences: Lic. Salvador Esteve
Faculty of Medicine: Dr Atenogenes Saldivar
Faculty of Nursing and Obstetrics: Mtra Paulina Aguilera
Higher School of Music: Mtro Edgar Zaragoza

Victoria Campus:
Faculty of Agriculture: Ing. Mario Lara
Faculty of Commerce and Administration: Mtro Hugo Valladares
Faculty of Education: Lic. Valentín Avila
Faculty of Law and Social Sciences: Lic. J. Lavin
Faculty of Social Work: Lic. Gonzalo Hernández
Faculty of Veterinary Medicine: M.V.Z. Sergio Garza
School of Nursing: Lic Cinthya Ibarra

UNIVERSIDAD AUTÓNOMA DE TLAXCALA

Avda Universidad 1, 90000 Tlaxcala, Tlax.

Telephone and fax (246) 462-1167
E-mail: rectoria@cci.uatx.mx
Internet: www.uatx.mx

Founded 1976
Academic year: July to June

Depts of biomedical sciences, education, humanities, social sciences; Research centres: animal physiology and behaviour, animal reproduction, biological sciences and biotechnology, genetics and environment, regional development

Rector: J.A. René Grada Yautentzi
Admin. Dir: Doroteo Nava
Librarian: Osvaldo Ramírez Ortiz

Number of teachers: 700
Number of students: 10,000

UNIVERSIDAD AUTÓNOMA DE YUCATÁN

Calle 60 491–A por 57 Centro, 97000 Mérida, Yucatán

Telephone: (999) 930-0900
Internet: www.uady.mx

Founded 1922
Independent
Academic year: September to July

Rector: Alfredo Javier Dájer Abimerhi
Dir-Gen. for Academic Development: José Williams

Library: 20 libraries with 227,022 vols, 7,401 periodical titles
Number of teachers: 1,158 (640 full-time)
Number of students: 15,823

Publication: *Revista*

DIRECTORS

Faculty of Accountancy and Administration: Jorge Humberto Basulto Triay
Faculty of Anthropology: Dr Genny Negroe
Faculty of Architecture: Arq. Ginés Laucirica
Faculty of Chemical Engineering: Carlos Estrada Pinto
Faculty of Chemistry: José Antonio Manzanilla Cano
Faculty of Dentistry: José Luis Villamil
Faculty of Economics: Dr Alberto Quintal Pañomo
Faculty of Education: Gladys Julieta Guerrero
Faculty of Engineering: Ing. José Loria
Faculty of Law: Abog. José Luis Vargas Aguilar
Faculty of Mathematics: Luci del Carmen Torres Sánchez
Faculty of Medicine: Guillermo Storey Montalvo
Faculty of Nursing: Lic. Lizbeth Padrón Aké
Faculty of Psychology: Mtro Efraín Duarte Briceño
Faculty of Veterinary Studies: Marco A. Torres
Preparatory School 1: Juan Manuel Méndez Arcila
Preparatory School 2: Luz Elizabeth Pérez Esquivel

UNIVERSIDAD AUTÓNOMA DE ZACATECAS

Jardin Juárez 147, Centro Histórico, 98000 Zacatecas, Zac.

Telephone: (492) 922-9109
E-mail: sii@uaz.edu.mx
Internet: www.ciu.reduaz.mx

Founded 1832
State control

Rector: Francisco Flores Sandoval

Sec.-Gen: DELFINO GARCÍA HERNÁNDEZ
Admin. Sec.: SALVADOR SANTILLÁN HERNÁNDEZ
Academic Sec.: FRANCISCO VALERIO QUINTERO
Librarian: JUAN IGNACIO PIÑA MARQUINA

Library of 35,265 vols
Number of teachers: 1,100
Number of students: 14,800

Publications: *Azogue, Cuadernos de investigación, Diálogo, Gaceta universitaria*

DIRECTORS

School of Accounting and Administration: JESÚS LIMONES HERNÁNDEZ
School of Agronomy: Ing. PEDRO ZESATI DEL VILLAR
School of Animal Breeding and Veterinary Medicine: ANTONIO MEJÍA HARO
School of Chemistry: JUANA MARÍA VALADEZ CASTREJÓN
School of Dentistry: Dr RAÚL BERMEO PADILLA
School of Economics: Lic. RODOLFO GARCÍA ZAMORA
School of Education: SERGIO ESPINOSA PROA
School of Engineering: Ing. JUAN FRANCISCO ROCHÍN SALINAS
School of Humanities: Lic. VEREMUNDO CARRILLO TRUJILLO
School of Law: Lic. VIRGILIO RIVERA DELGADILLO
School of Mathematics: Lic. JUAN ANTONIO PÉREZ
School of Medicine: Dr GERARDO DE JESÚS FÉLIX DOMÍNGUEZ
School of Mines and Metallurgy: Ing. RUBEN DE JESÚS DEL POZO MENDOZA
School of Music: Lic. ESAUL ARTEAGA DOMÍNGUEZ
School of Nursing: MA ISABEL MEDINA HERNÁNDEZ
School of Physics: Lic. HUMBERTO VIDALES ROQUE
School of Psychology: Lic. RICARDO BERMEO PADILLA
School of Social Sciences: PEDRO GÓMEZ SÁNCHEZ

UNIVERSIDAD AUTÓNOMA DEL CARMEN

Calle 56 #4 por Avenida Concordia, 24180 Ciudad del Carmen, Camp.

Telephone: (938) 381-1018 ext. 1007
Fax: (938) 381-1018 ext. 1328
Internet: www.unacar.mx

Founded 1967

Faculties of commerce and administration, law, chemistry, education

Rector: C. SERGIO AUGUSTO LÓPEZ PEÑA
Sec.-Gen.: Lic. RAFAEL HUGO GARCÍA MORENO
Chief Admin. Officer: Lic. HILDA LÓPEZ LÓPEZ
Librarian: C. OLGA SÁNCHEZ PÉREZ

Number of teachers: 340
Number of students: 4,484

Publications: *Senda Universitaria, Voz Universitaria.*

UNIVERSIDAD AUTÓNOMA DEL ESTADO DE HIDALGO

Carr. Pachuca-Actopan km 4.5, Edificio B, 4to. nivel Universidad Virtual, 48900 Pachuca, Hidalgo

Telephone: (771) 717-2000
Internet: www.uaeh.edu.mx

Founded 1869 as the Instituto Científico y Literario, present status 1961
Academic year: September to June

Rector: C.D. LUIS GIL BORJA
Sec.: M. en A.H. HUMBERTO AUGUSTO VERAS GODOY
Registrar: L.A.E. JORGE DEL CASTILLO TOVAR
Librarian: Lic. EVARISTO LUVIAN TORRES

Number of teachers: 700
Number of students: 9,000

Publications: *Boletín Informativo, Informe Anual de Rectoría, Revista Técnica de Información*

COURSE COORDINATORS

Education: Quim. F.B. SILVIA PARGA MATEOS
Professional Studies: Lic. YOLANDA MEJÍA VELASCO
Science and Technology: Ing. CARLOS HERRERA ORDOÑEZ
Special Studies: Lic. FRANCISCO MURILLO BUTRON

DIRECTORS OF SCHOOLS AND INSTITUTES

Institute of Accountancy and Administration: C.P. HORACIO SOLIS LEYVA
Institute of Exact Sciences: Ing. JOSÉ CALDERÓN HERNÁNDEZ
Institute of Social Sciences: Lic. ALEJANDRO STRAFFON ARTEAGA
Preparatory School I: Ing. ERNESTO HERNÁNDEZ OCAÑA
Preparatory School II: Lic. LAURO PEREA MONTIEL
Preparatory School III: Lic. JUAN MANUEL CAMACHO BERTRAN
School of Medicine: Dr LUIS CORZO MONTAÑO
School of Nursing: Enf. LUZ MARÍA FLORES RAMÍREZ
School of Odontology: Dr MIGUEL ANGEL ANTON DE LA C.
School of Social Work: T.S. IMELDA MONROY DEL ANGEL

UNIVERSIDAD AUTÓNOMA DEL ESTADO DE MÉXICO

Avda Instituto Literario 100 Oriente, Col. Centro Municipio, 50000 Toluca, Méx.

Telephone: (722) 226-23-00
E-mail: rectoria@uaemex.mx
Internet: www.uaemex.mx

Founded 1956
State control
Language of instruction: Spanish
Academic year: September to August

Rector: Dr en A. P. JOSÉ MARTÍNEZ VILCHIS
Academic Sec.: M. en S.P. EZEQUIEL JAIMES FIGUEROA
Admin. Sec.: M.A.E. PEDRO LIZOLA MARGOLIS
Librarian: M. en E.L. RUPERTO RETANA RAMIREZ

Library of 292,000 vols
Number of teachers: 3,045
Number of students: 36,642

DIRECTORS

School of Accountancy and Administration: M.A.E. IGNACIO MERCADO
School of Agricultural Sciences: Ing. ARTURO MAYA GOMEZ
School of Anthropology: M. en E.L. RODRIGO MARCIAL JIMENEZ
School of Art and Architecture: M. en Pl. JESUS AGUILUZ LEON
School of Behavioural Sciences: Lic. en Psic. TERESA PONCE DAVALOS
School of Chemistry: M. en C. JUAN CARLOS SANCHEZ MEZA
School of Dentistry: C.D. FRANCISCO MONTIEL CONZUELO
School of Economics: M. en E. RICARDO RODRIGUEZ MARCIAL
School of Engineering: M. en I. ANGEL ALBITER RODRIGUEZ
School of Geography: L. en G. VICENTE PEÑA MANJARREZ
School of Humanities: L. en E.L. GERARDO MEZA GARCIA
School of Law: M. en D. JOAQUIN BERNAL SANCHEZ

School of Medicine: M.C. GABRIEL GERARDO HUITRON BRAVO
School of Nursing: L. en Enf. LUZ MARIA FRANCO BERNAL
School of Political Sciences and Public Administration: M. en C.P. JOSE MARTINEZ VILCHIS
School of Sciences: Biol. PEDRO DEL AGUILA JUAREZ
School of Tourism: L. en T. MARICRUZ MORENO ZAGAL
School of Urban and Regional Planning: M. en Pl. ALBERTO VILLAR CALVO
School of Veterinary Medicine: M. en C.E. EDUARDO GASCA PLIEGO

UNIVERSIDAD AUTÓNOMA DEL ESTADO DE MORELOS

Avda Universidad 1001, Col. Chamilpa, 62210 Cuernavaca, Morelos

Telephone: (777) 329-7083
Fax: (777) 329-7083
E-mail: dicodi@uaem.mx
Internet: www.uaem.mx

Founded 1953
State control
Language of instruction: Spanish
Academic year: September to July

Rector: RENÉ SANTOVEÑA ARREDONDO
Sec.-Gen.: Lic. MANUEL PRIETO GÓMEZ
Academic Sec.: ELISEO GUAJARDO RAMOS
Librarian: Arq. JORGE SALAZAR DÍAZ

Number of teachers: 1,473
Number of students: 17,500

DEANS AND DIRECTORS

Faculty of Accountancy, Administration and Informatics: REY MARTÍNEZ MENDOZA
Faculty of Agriculture: Lic. ARTURO TAPIA DELGADO
Faculty of Architecture: Arq. EFRÉN ROMERO BENÍTEZ
Faculty of Arts: Dr JESÚS NIETO SOTELO
Faculty of Biological Sciences: ALFONSO VIVEROS MIRAMONTES
Faculty of Chemical and Industrial Sciences: MODESTO MÉNDEZ RDRÍGUEZ
Faculty of Human Communication: Lic. LILIANA ARCE FLORES
Faculty of Human Sciences: Dra ANGÉLICA TORNERO SALINAS
Faculty of Law and Social Sciences: Lic. JORGE ARTURO GARCÍA RUBÍ
Faculty of Medicine: Dr MIGUEL ÁNGEL CASTAÑEDA CRUZ
Faculty of Pharmacy: Dr ALEJANDRO NIETO RODRÍGUEZ
Faculty of Psychology: Dr FERNANDO BILBAO MARCOS
Faculty of Sciences: Dr VERÓNICA NARVÁEZ PADILLA
Institute of the Eastern Region: Lic. JOSÉ PATRICIO DURÁN CAMPOAMOR
Institute of the Southern Region: Lic. AURORA CEDILLO MARTÍNEZ
Language Centre: Prof. J. REYES AGUIRRE PALACIOS
School of Educational Sciences: ANTONIO ARANA PINEDA
School of Laboratory Technicians: MARÍA ISABEL NERI FIGUEROA
School of Nursing: ALEJANDRA RIVERA GUTIÉRREZ
Spanish School for Foreign Learners: WILFRIDO ÁVILA GARCÍA

There are also 9 Preparatory Schools

UNIVERSIDAD AUTÓNOMA DEL NORESTE

Blvd Enrique Reyna y Américas Unidas s/n, 25100 Saltillo, Coahuila

Telephone: (844) 438-4000

Fax: (844) 438-4009
Internet: www.uane.edu.mx

Founded 1974
Private control
Academic year: January to December (2 terms)

Rector: HIGINIO GONZÁLEZ CALDERÓN
Vice-Rector for Academic Affairs: Lic. MARÍA DEL CARMEN RUÍZ ESPARZA
Vice-Rector for Admin. Affairs: C.P. GABRIEL DURÁN MALTOS
Librarian: Lic. NELLY BERMÚDEZ ARRAZATE

Number of teachers: 708
Number of students: 5,000

Courses in business administration, accountancy, architecture, computer studies, education and psychology, graphic design, industrial and systems engineering, law, political science, tourism.

UNIVERSIDAD AUTÓNOMA INDÍGENA DE MÉXICO

Juárez 39, Mochicahui, 81890 El Fuerte, Sinaloa

Telephone: (698) 892-0008
Fax: (698) 892-0042
E-mail: uaim@uaim.edu.mx
Internet: www.uaim.edu.mx

Founded 2001

President: Lic. JOAQUÍN VEGA ACUÑA
Rector: JESÚS ÁNGEL OCHOA ZAZUETA
Sec.-Gen.: MANUEL DE JESÚS VALDEZ ACOSTA
Director-General for Academic Affairs: ERNESTO GUERRA GARCÍA
Director-General for Admin.: CARLOS ERNESTO VILLA PANQUIÁN
Director-General for Institutional Development: JOSÉ HUMBERTO GALAVIZ ARMENTA
Librarian: ERNESTO GAXIOLA ENCINAS

DIRECTORS

Los Mochis Campus: Lic. ROSARIO ROCHÍN NAPUS
Mochicahui Campus: Lic. JUAN ANTONIO DELGADO MORALES
Sinaloa de Leyva Campus: (vacant)

UNIVERSIDAD AUTÓNOMA METROPOLITANA

Rectoría General, Prolongación Canal de Miramontes 3855, Col. Ex-Hacienda San Juan de Dios, Delegación Tlalpan, 14387 México, DF

Telephone: (55) 5723-5644
Fax: (55) 5576-6888
E-mail: riebeling@tonatiuh.uam.mx
Internet: www.uam.mx

Founded 1973
State control
Language of instruction: Spanish
Academic year: September to July

Rector-Gen.: JULIO RUBIO OCA
Sec.-Gen.: MAGDALENA FRESAN OROZCO
Librarian: KAMILA KNAP ROUBAL

Number of teachers: 3,700
Number of students: 45,000

Publications: *Alegatos* (3 a year), *Argumentos* (3 a year), *Casa del Tiempo* (12 a year), *Contactos* (6 a year), *Diseño UAM* (3 a year), *Economía, El Cotidiano* (6 a year), *Pauta, Reencuentro* (irregular), *Revista A* (2 a year), *Revista Iztapalapa* (2 a year), *Semanario de la UAM* (52 a year), *Teoría y Práctica Sociológica, Topodrilo* (6 a year), *Universidad Futura* (irregular).

CONSTITUENT CAMPUSES

Azcapotzalco Campus

Avda San Pablo 180, Col. Reynosa-Tamaulipas, Del. Azcapotzalco, 02000 México, DF

Telephone: (55) 5485-9510
Internet: www.azc.uam.mx

Rector: EDMUNDO JACOBO MOLINA
Secretary: JORDY MICHELI THIRIÓN
Librarian: FERNANDO VELÁZQUEZ MERLO

DIRECTORS

Basic Sciences and Engineering: ANA MARISELA MAUBERT FRANCO
Design, Arts and Sciences: JORGE SÁNCHEZ DE ANTUÑANO BARRANCO
Social Sciences and Humanities: MONICA DE LA GARZA MALO

Iztapalapa Campus

San Rafael Atlixco 186, Col. Vicentina, Del. Iztapalapa, 09340 México, DF

Telephone: (55) 5612-4665
Internet: www.iztapalapa.uam.mx

Rector: JOSÉ LUIS GÁZQUEZ MATEOS
Secretary: ANTONIO AGUILAR AGUILAR
Librarian: ALFONSO ROMERO SÁNCHEZ

DIRECTORS

Basic Sciences and Engineering: LUIS MIER Y TERÁN CASANUEVA
Biological and Health Sciences: JOSÉ LUIS ARREDONDO FIGUEROA
Social Sciences and Humanities: JOSÉ GREGORIO VIDAL BONIFÁZ

Xochimilco Campus

Calzada del Hueso 1100, Col. Villa Quietud, Del. Coyoacán, 04960 México, DF

Telephone: (55) 5594-6656
Internet: cueyatl.uam.mx

Rector: JAIME KRAVZOV JINICH
Secretary: MARINA ALTAGRACIA MARTÍNEZ
Librarian: MARGARITA LUGO HUBP

DIRECTORS

Art and Design: EMILIO PRADILLA COBOS
Biological and Health Sciences: NORBERTO MANJARRÉZ ALVAREZ
Social Sciences and Humanities: GUILLERMO VILLASEÑOR GARCÍA

UNIVERSIDAD COMUNITARIA DE SAN LUIS POTOSÍ

Arista 1000, Barrio del Tequis, San Luis Potosí, SLP

Telephone: (444) 815-3190
E-mail: salsilca@terra.com.mx

Founded 2002
State control

Rector: Prof. SALVADOR SILVA CARRILLO

Main subject areas: administrative information technology, anthropology, community health, economic development, indigenous law

DIRECTORS

Tamazunchale Campus: Lic. RAFAEL MURGÍA FRANCISCO
Tamuín Campus: MARTHA INÉS FLORES PACHECO
Tonkanhuitz Campus: Ing. ALFREDO GURROLA GRAVE

UNIVERSIDAD DE CIENCIAS Y ARTES DE CHIAPAS (UNICACH) (Chiapas State University of Arts and Sciences)

1A Avda Sur Poniente 1460, Zona Centro, 29000 Tuxtla Gutiérrez, Chiapas

Telephone: (961) 617-0400
Fax: (961) 147-6242
E-mail: secgral@unicach.edu.mx
Internet: www.unicach.edu.mx

Founded 1893, as Industrial School of Chiapas; current name and status 1995
State control
Language of instruction: Spanish

Rector: Ing. ROBERTO DOMÍNGUEZ CASTELLANOS
Gen. Sec.: Mtro. JOSÉ FRANCISCO NIGENDA PÉREZ
Dir of Information: Ing. MARINO PEREZ MARTINEZ

DIRECTORS

Centre for Human Development: Lic. MARINA IDALIA GUIZAR CORDOVA
School of Biology: Mtra ADELINA SCHLIE GUZMAN
School of Music: Lic. LUIS FELIPE MARTÍNEZ GORDILLO
School of Nutrition: Lic. VIDALMA DEL ROSARIO BEZARES SARMIENTO
School of Odontology: C.D. JUAN JOSÉ ORTEGA ALEJANDRE
School of Psychology: Lic. GERMAN ALEJANDRO GARCIA LARA
School of Topography: Ing. LISANDRO MARTÍNEZ POZO
University Centre for Information and Documentation: Ing. ARQUIMEDES R. LÓPEZ ROBLERO

UNIVERSIDAD DE COLIMA

Avda Universidad 333, Colonia Las Víboras, 28040 Colima, Col.

Telephone: (312) 316-1000
E-mail: rector@ucol.mx
Internet: www.ucol.mx

Founded 1940 as Universidad Popular de Colima, reorganized 1962
State control
Language of instruction: Spanish
Academic year: August to July

Rector: M.C. MIGUEL ÁNGEL AGUAYO LÓPEZ
Gen.-Sec.: Dr RAMÓN ARTURO CEDILLO NAKAY
Librarian: Dra EVANGELINA SERRANO

Number of teachers: 1,204
Number of students: 19,000

Publication: *Estudios Sobre las Culturas Contemporáneas*

DEANS

Faculty of Accountancy and Administration: M.A. JOSÉ ALFREDO CANO ANGUIANO
Faculty of Accountancy and Administration 1: C.P. TOBIAS ALVAREZ LUNA
Faculty of Accountancy and Administration 2: JOSÉ MARTÍN TORRES RÍOS
Faculty of Architecture: Arq. JULIO DE JESÚS MENDOZA JIMÉNEZ
Faculty of Arts and Communications: Lic. LUIS MIGUEL BUENO SÁNCHEZ
Faculty of Biological Sciences and Agronomy: Mtro. ARNOLDO MUCHEL ROSALES
Faculty of Chemical Science: M.C. SANTIAGO E. VELASCO VILLALPANDO
Faculty of Civil Engineering: M.C. GERARDO CERRATO OSEGUERA
Faculty of Economics: Dr ERNESTO RANGEL DELGADO
Faculty of Education: Mtra CARMEN ALICIA SANTOS ANDRADE
Faculty of Educational Science: Prof. JOSÉ FRANCISCO BALLESTEROS SILVA

Faculty of Electromechanical Engineering: M.C. ANDRÉS G. FUENTES COVARRUBIAS
Faculty of Law: Lic. MARIO DE LA MADRID ANDRADE
Faculty of Marine Science: O.Q. ADRÍAN TINTOS GÓMEZ
Faculty of Medicine: Dr RAMÓN A. CEDILLO NAKAY
Faculty of Nursing: Licda ANA MARÍA CHAVEZ ACEVEDO
Faculty of Social and Political Sciences: Lic. FERNANDO H. ALCARAZ INIGUEZ
Faculty of Social Studies: Licda MARISA MESINA POLANCO
Faculty of Telematics: M.C. RAUL AQUINO SANTOS
Faculty of Veterinary Studies and Zoology: Dr ENRIQUE SILVA PENA
School of Languages: Licda GRISELDA P. CEBALLOS LLERENAS

UNIVERSIDAD DE GUADALAJARA

Avda Juárez 975, Sector Juárez, 44100 Guadalajara, Jal.
Telephone: (33) 3825-8888
Fax: (33) 3626-0668
E-mail: webudg@cencar.udg.mx
Internet: www.udg.mx
Founded 1792, restructured 1925
State control
Academic year: March to February
Rector: Lic. JOSÉ TRINIDAD PADILLA LÓPEZ
Sec.-Gen.: Mtro CARLOS BRISEÑO TORRES
Chief Admin. Officer: Mtro GUSTAVO ALFONSO CÁRDENAS CUTIÑO
Librarian: Mtro SERGIO LÓPES RUELAS
Library: see Libraries and Archives
Number of teachers: 11,784
Number of students: 180,776

Publications: *Gaceta, Jures, Revista Universidad de Guadalajara* (4 a year).

UNIVERSITY CENTRES

Art, Architecture and Design: Rector Arq. CARLOS CORREA CESEÑA.

Biological Sciences and Farming: Rector M. en C. SALVADOR MENA MUNGUIA.

Del Norte: Executive Coordinator Dr CÁNDIDO GONZÁLEZ PÉREZ.

Economic and Administrative Sciences: Rector Mtro IXCOATL TONATIUH BRAVO PADILLA.

El Sur: Rector Lic. JESÚS ALBERTO ESPINOZA ARIAS.

Exact and Engineering Sciences: Rector Mtro HECTOR ENRIQUE SALGADO RODRÍGUEZ.

Health Sciences: Rector Dr RAÚL VARGAS LÓPEZ.

La Cienega: Rector Mtro PEDRO JAVIER GUERRERO MEDINA.

La Costa: Rector M. en C. JEFFRY STEVEN FERNÁNDEZ RODRÍGUEZ.

La Costa Sur: Rector Dr JUAN JOSÉ PALACIOS LARA.

Los Altos: Rector Dr HÉCTOR ARMANDO MACÍAS MARTÍNEZ.

Los Valles: Executive Coordinator Dr MIGUEL ANGEL NAVARRO NAVARRO.

Social Sciences and Humanities: Rector Dr JUAN MANUEL DURÁN JUÁREZ.

UNIVERSIDAD DE GUANAJUATO

Lascuráin de Retana 5, 36000 Guanajuato, Gto.
Telephone: (473) 732-0006
Fax: (473) 735-1902
E-mail: info@quijote.ugto.mx
Internet: www.ugto.mx

Founded 1732 as Colegio de la Purísima Concepción; changed in 1928 to Colegio del Estado; present name 1945
State control
Academic year: August to June
Rector: Dr ARTURO LARA LÓPEZ
Sec.: Dra MARÍA GUADALUPE MARTÍNEZ CADENA
Librarian: Mtra ROSALÍA DEL CARMEN MACÍAS RODRÍGUEZ
Library of 372,963 vols
Number of teachers: 2,900 (808 full-time, 2,092 part-time)
Number of students: 24,406

Publications: *Acta Universitaria* (6 a year), *Azogue* (2 a year), *Centro, Textos de la Historia Guanajuatense* (1 a year), *Colmena Universitaria* (2 a year), *Comunidad Universitaria* (2 a year), *Gaceta Naturaleza* (2 a year), *Investigaciones Jurídicas* (2 a year), *Regiones* (2 a year), *Tarea Universitaria* (6 a year), *Voces, Laboratorio de Historia Oral* (2 a year)

DIRECTORS

Faculty of Accountancy and Administration: Mtro PORFIRIO TAMAYO CONTRERAS
Faculty of Administrative Sciences: C.P. EMIGDIO ARCHUNDIA FERNÁNDEZ
Faculty of Architecture: Arq. J. JESÚS OCTAVIO HERNÁNDEZ DÍAZ
Faculty of Chemical Sciences: Dr ALBERTO FLORENTINO AGUILERA ALVARADO
Faculty of Civil Engineering: Ing. CARLOS ARNOLD OJEDA
Faculty of Electronics, Mechanical and Electronic Engineering: OSCAR G. IBARRA MANZANO
Faculty of Geophysics and Hydraulic Engineering: Ing. JUAN MANUEL TOVAR ALCANTAR
Faculty of Industrial Relations: L.R.I. DOMINGO HERRERA BRIBIESCA
Faculty of Law: Lic. JUAN RENÉ SEGURA RICAÑO
Faculty of Mathematics: Dr IGNACIO BARRADAS BRIBIESCA
Faculty of Medicine: Dr FRANCISCO JAVIER GUERRERO MARTÍNEZ
Faculty of Mining, Metallurgy and Geology: Ing. RENÉ ECHEGOYEN GUZMÁN
Faculty of Nursing and Midwifery (Celaya): M.A.E. ROSALINA DÍAZ GUERRERO
Faculty of Nursing and Midwifery (Guanajuato): L.E. LETICIA SOTO FRANCO
Faculty of Nursing and Midwifery (Irapuato): Mtra LETICIA CAMPOS ZERMEÑO
Faculty of Nursing and Midwifery (León): ROSA MA. RICO VENEGAS
Faculty of Philosophy, History and Letters: GENARO ANGEL MARTELL AVILA
Faculty of Psychology: M.C. LETICIA CHACÓN GUTIÉRREZ

UNIVERSIDAD DE LA CIUDAD DE MÉXICO

Fray Servando Teresa de Mier 99, Centro, 06080 Cuauhtémoc, México, DF
Telephone: (55) 5134-9804
E-mail: rectoria_ucm@df.gob.mx
Internet: www.ucm.df.gob.mx
Founded 2001
State control
Rector: Ing. MANUEL PÉREZ ROCHA
Director for Academic Affairs: FLORINDA RIQUER FERNÁNDEZ
Director for Admin.: PATRICIA FUENTES RANGEL
Director for University Development: Lic. OSCAR GONZÁLEZ
Librarian: Lic. BLANCA ESTELA VELÁZQUEZ MORALES

Publications: *Mano Vuelta, Noticiario*

Campuses in Iztapalapa, Del Valle and San Lorenzo Tezonco.

ATTACHED RESEARCH INSTITUTES

Centro de Estudios sobre La Ciudad: Fray Servando Teresa de Mier 92, Cubículos 9 y 10, Tercer piso Col. Centro, 06080 Cuauhtémoc, México, DF; tel. (55) 5134-9804; e-mail centroestudiosucm@yahoo.com.mx; Dirs SILVIA BOLOS JACOB, ANA HELENA TREVIÑO CARRILLO.

UNIVERSIDAD DE LA SALLE BAJÍO

Ave Universidad 602, Col. Lomas del Campestre, 37000 Léon, Gto.
Telephone: (477) 710-8500
E-mail: informes@delasalle.edu.mx
Internet: www.delasalle.edu.mx
Founded 1968
Private control
Academic year: August to December, February to June
Rector: Lic. ANDRÉS GOVELA GUTIÉRREZ
Vice-Rector: Lic. FELIPE AURELIO PELCASTRE ARENAS
Registrar: Lic. LUIS ERNESTO RÍOS PÉREZ
Librarian: Lic. ISIDRO CONDE GONZÁLEZ
Library of 108,529 vols
Number of teachers: 1,231
Number of students: 12,923

Publications: *Cuadernos* (2 a year), *Entornos* (6 a year), *Espíritu Lasallista* (12 a year), *Magazine Lasalle* (6 a year)

DIRECTORS OF FACULTIES

Accountancy Administration and International Marketing: Lic. JOSÉ JULIO CARPIO MENDOZA
Agronomy: Ing. MARIO ALBERTO ROMERO PÉREZ
Architecture: Arq. DAVID CABRERA RUIZ
Civil, Industrial and Mechanical Engineering: Ing. MAURICIO SALVATORI MORALES
Communication Sciences and Marketing: Lic. ALFREDO LING ALTAMIRANO
Computer and Electronic Engineering: Ing. ARTURO SUÁSTEGUI RODRÍGUEZ
Dentistry: Dr MARY JEAN MCGRATH BERNAL
Design: Lic. ADRIAN GUERRERO CASTRO
Education and Human Development: Mtra SOCORRO DURÁN GONZÁLEZ
Graduate School of Administration: Lic. GUSTAVO A. HERNÁNDEZ MORENO
Graduate School of Architecture: M. A. GREGORIO G. DE LA ROSA FALCON
Graduate School of Dentistry: Dr ENRIQUE NIEMBRO CAMPUZANO
Graduate School of Education: Lic. MANUEL CASTRO VILLICAÑA
Graduate School of Electronics and Computational Engineering: Ing. JAIME PALACIOS CASTAÑÓN
Law: Lic. MARIELA DEL CARMEN HUERTA GUERRERO
Preparatory School: Dr SALVADOR MUÑOZ SOLIS
Telecommunications Engineering: Ing. JAIME PALACIOS CASTAÑÓN
Tourism and Hotel Studies: Dr RAFAEL GUIZAR MONTÚFAR
Veterinary Studies: EDUARDO HERNÁNDEZ GONZÁLEZ DEL CASTILLO

CAMPUSES

Américas Campus: ; 864 students; Dir Lic. FERNANDO MONROY VIVAS.

Juan Alonso de Torres Campus: ; 1,290 students; Dir Lic. JOSÉ AMONARIO ASIÁN DÍAZ DE LEÓN.

Salamanca Campus: ; 1,321 students; Dir Mtra ESTEBAN MARTÍNEZ HERNÁNDEZ.

San Francisco del Rincón Campus: ; 1,021 students; Dir Ing. MARTHA ELENA BERMÚDEZ FUNES.

UNIVERSIDAD DE LA SIERRA

Carretera Moctezuma-Cumpas km 2.5, 84561 Moctezuma, Sonora

Telephone and fax (634) 342-9600

E-mail: rectoria@universidaddelasierra.edu .mx

Internet: www.universidaddelasierra.edu .mx

Founded 2002

State control

Academic year: August to June

Prin.: Ing. GUADALUPE RODRÍGUEZ VALEN-ZUELA

Sec. for Academic Affairs: Lic. JULIÁN MOR-ENO BARCELÓ

Librarian: CESAR IVAN MARTÍNEZ ARMENTA

Librarian: Lic. IMELDA MONTAÑO AGUILAR

Library of 4,536 vols.

UNIVERSIDAD DE LAS AMÉRICAS – PUEBLA

Sta Catarina Mártir, Apdo Postal 100, 72820 Cholula, Puebla

Telephone: (222) 229-2000

Fax: (222) 229-2009

Internet: www.udlap.mx

Founded 1940 as Mexico City College; became Universidad de las Américas in 1963

Private control

Languages of instruction: Spanish, English

Academic year: August to May

Pres.: Dra NORA LUSTIG TENENBAUM

Academic Vice-Pres.: Dr EDUARDO LASTRA Y PÉREZ SALAZAR

Vice-Pres. for Admin. and Finance: Mtro JOSÉ MANUEL BLANCO ASPURU

Registrar: Mtra MARTHA FERNÁNDEZ DE LARA

Librarian: Dr ALFREDO SÁNCHEZ HULTRÓN SANTOS

Library: see Libraries

Number of teachers: 325 full-time

Number of students: 8,300

Publications: *La Catarina, UDLA Informa*

DEANS

Faculty of Administration: Dr FRANCISCO GUERRA VÁZQUEZ

Faculty of Arts and Humanities: Dra LUISA VILAR PAYÁ

Faculty of Business: Dr ROBERTO SOLANO

Faculty of Engineering: Dr JUAN MANUEL RAMÍREZ

Faculty of Social Sciences: Dr ISIDRO MOR-ALES MORENO

Research and Graduate Studies: Dr GERARDO AYALA SAN MARTÍN

UNIVERSIDAD DE MONTEMORELOS

Apdo 16-5, Montemorelos, 67530 Nuevo León

Telephone: (826) 263-0900

Fax: (826) 263-6185

E-mail: umontemorelos@edu.mx

Internet: um.edu.mx

Founded 1973

Private control

Language of instruction: Spanish

Academic year: August to May

Pres.: Dr ISMAEL CASTILLO OSUNA

Vice-Pres for Academic Affairs: RAQUEL KOR-NIEJCZUK

Vice-Pres. for Admin. Affairs: RUBEN MEZA

Vice-Pres. for Finance: BENJAMIN LAZARO

Vice-Pres. for Student Affairs: ABRAHAM MURILLO

Dir of Admissions and Records: EKEL COLLINS

Librarian: ADÁN SURIANO

Number of teachers: 175

Number of students: 2,350

Publications: *Logos* (1 a year), *Memorias del Centro de Investigaciones Educativas* (1 a year), *Perspectivas Teológicas* (1 a year), *Revista Internacional de Estudios en Educación* (2 a year)

DEANS

School of Administrative Sciences: ARIEL QUINTEROS

School of Arts and Communications: EUNICE AGUILAR

School of Biomedical Sciences: ALEJANDRO GIL

School of Education: JULIAEMY DE FLORES

School of Engineering and Technology: JORGE MANRIQUE

School of Health Sciences: ZENO CHARLES MICHEL

School of Music: NORKA DE CASTILLO

School of Theology: OMAR VELÁZQUEZ

UNIVERSIDAD DE MONTERREY

Avda Ignacio Morones Prieto 4500 Pte, 66238 San Pedro Garza García, Nuevo León

Telephone: (81) 8125-1000

Fax: (81) 8215-1023

Internet: www.udem.edu.mx

Founded 1969

Private control

Languages of instruction: Spanish, English

Academic year: January to December

President: Dr ANTONIO J. DIECK ASSAD

Vice-Pres. for Admin.: Lic. RICARDO SADA VILLARREAL

Vice-Pres. for Integral Education: Lic. ISA-BELLA NAVARRO GRUETER

Vice-Pres. for Institutional Devt: Ing. AGUS-TÍN LANDA GARCÍA-TÉLLEZ

Vice-Pres. for Undergraduate and Graduate Programmes: Dr FERNANDO MATA CAR-RASCO

Registrar and Dean of Admissions: Ing. LUCÍA M. TREVIÑO VILLARREAL

Librarian: SAUL HIRAM SOUTO FUENTES

Library of 409,796 units

Number of teachers: 704

Number of students: 9,000

DEANS

School of Architecture and Design: JOEL HERRERA NORMAN

School of Business: Dr CARLOS E. BASURTO MEZA

School of Engineering and Technology: Dr JOSÉ BENITO FLORES JUÁREZ

School of Humanities and Education: Dr VÍCTOR A. ZÚNIGA GONZÁLEZ

School of Law: Dr ARTURO AZUARA FLORES

School of Medicine: Dr EDUARDO GARCÍA LUNA

HEADS OF ACADEMIC DIVISIONS

Graduate Studies: Dr ARNAUD CHEVALLIER DELABASLE

School of Architecture, Design and Engin-eering: Ing. JOSÉ ALFREDO GALVÁN GALVÁN

School of Business: Dr MARIO ALANIS GARZA

School of Health Sciences: Dr EDUARDO GARCÍALUNA MARTÍNEZ

School of Humanistic Studies and Education: Dr VÍCTOR AURELIO ZÚNIGA GONZÁLEZ

School of Law and Social Sciences: Lic. JORGE MANUEL AGUIRRE HERNÁNDEZ

UNIVERSIDAD DE OCCIDENTE

Gabriel Leyva No.169 Sur, Col. Centro, Apartado Postal 936, 81200 Los Mochis, Sin.

Telephone: (668) 816-1000

Internet: www.udo.mx

Founded 1978

Academic year: September to August

Chancellor: Dr FRANCISCO CUAUHTEMOC FRIAS CASTRO

Rector: RUBEN ELIAS GIL LEYVA

Sec.-Gen.: M. S. P. JOSE GUILLERMO ALVAREZ GUERRERO

Chief Admin. Officer: Lic. FERNANDO ORPI-NELA LIZARRAGA

Librarian: DELPHA DELLA ROCCA KING

Number of teachers: 414

Number of students: 4,344

Publications: *Ciencia Jurídica, Los Mochis, Un Sueño del Paraíso.*

CAMPUSES

Campus Culiacan: Blvd Madero 34 pte, Culiacan; tel. (667) 540-495; Dir Lic. GIL-BERTO HIGUERA BERNAL.

Campus Guamuchil: Jose Maria Vigil y Blvd Lazaro Cardenas, Guamuchil, Sinaloa; tel. (673) 2-03-83; Dir Lic. BENITO GOMEZ URBALEJO.

Campus Guasave: Corregidora y Zaragoza, Guasave; tel. (667) 872-0065; Dir Lic. JESUS TEODORO RAMIREZ JACOBO.

Campus Los Mochis: Carretera Internacio-nal y Blvd Macario Gaxiola, Los Mochis; tel. (668) 816-1000; Dir CILA MARIA HERNANDEZ ROJO.

Campus Mazatlan: Avda del Mar 1200, Mazatlan; Dir Lic. LUIS O. MONTOYA HIGUERA.

UNIVERSIDAD DE QUINTANA ROO
(University of Quintana Roo)

Blvd Bahía s/n esquina Ignacio Comonfort, Col. del Bosque, 77019 Chetumal, Q. Roo

Telephone: (983) 835-0300

Fax: (983) 832-9656

E-mail: lchan@uqroo.mx

Internet: www.uqroo.mx

State control

Language of instruction: Spanish

Rector: EFRAÍN VILLANUEVA ARCOS

Director of Administration and Finance: FELIPE CRIOLLO RIVERO

Director of Planning: CARLOS BRACAMONTES Y SOSA

Secretary-General: FRANCISCO MORIENTES DE ORCA GARRO

Head Librarian: ELÍAS LEÓN ISLAS

Library of 30,479 vols

Publication: *Revista* (scientific journal, 2 a year)

ACADEMIC DIRECTORS

Economic, Management and Social Sciences: FERNANDO CABRERA CASTELLANOS

Engineering and Sciences: MEDINA LEYVA LUIS FELIPE

Humanities and International Studies: ANTO-NIO HIGUERA BONFIL

UNIVERSIDAD DE SONORA

Blvd. Luis Encinas y Rosales s/n, Col. Centro, 83000 Hermosillo, Sonora

Telephone: (662) 259-2136

Fax: (662) 259-2135

E-mail: webmaster@informatica.uson.mx

Internet: www.uson.mx

Founded Charter granted 1938; opened and officially inaugurated 1942

Private control

Language of instruction: Spanish

Academic year: September to June

Rector: Dr PEDRO ORTEGA ROMERO

Sec.-Gen.: Ing. MANUEL BALCÁZAR MEZA

Librarian: Lic. ANA LILYA MOYA

Library of 45,000 vols

Number of teachers: 1,025
Number of students: 18,000

Publications: *Gaceta Universitaria* (12 a year), *Poemarios* (6 a year), *Revista de Economía* (2 a year), *Revista de Física* (2 a year), *Revista de la Universidad* (4 a year), *Sonora Agropecuario* (6 a year)

COORDINATORS

Department of Biochemistry: HECTOR ESCÁRCEGA
Department of Geology: Ing. EFRÉN PÉREZ SEGURA
Department of Humanities: JOSÉ SAPIEN DURÁN
Department of Mathematics: EDUARDO TELLECHEA ARMENTA
Department of Physics: ANTONIO JAUREGUI D.
School of Accountancy and Administration: C.P. RAMÓN CÁRDENAS VALDÉS
School of Advanced Studies: Ing. IGNACIO AYALA ZAZUETA
School of Agriculture and Animal Husbandry: Ing. MARIO GUZMÁN
School of Chemical Sciences: Ing. OSVALDO LANDAVAZO
School of Economics: Lic. RODOLFO DÍAZ CASTAÑEDA
School of Engineering: Ing. MIGUEL A. MORENO N.
School of Law and Social Sciences: Lic. MIGUEL CÁRDENAS
School of Nursing: Prof. ELVIRA COTA
School of Psychology and Communication Sciences: Lic. DANIEL C. GUTIÉRREZ C.
School of Social Work: T.S. AMELIA I. DE BLANCO

CAMPUS DIRECTORS

Unidad Norte: Ing. RODOLFO GUZMÁN
Unidad Santana: Ing. MARIO TARAZÓN H.
Unidad Sur: Lic. JOSÉ A. VALENZUELA

UNIVERSIDAD DEL CARIBE

Lote 1, Manzana 1, Region 78, Esq. con Tabachines, 77528 Cancún, Quintana Roo
Telephone and fax (998) 881-4400
E-mail: rectoria@unicaribe.edu.mx
Internet: www.unicaribe.edu.mx
Founded 2000
State control
Languages of instruction: English, Spanish
Academic year: August to May
Pres.: EDUARDO PATRÓN AZUETA
Rector: ARTURO ESCAIP MANZUR
Registrar: YUNUEN ARREGUIN VILLANUEVA
Academic Sec.: PEDRO MONCADA JIMÉNEZ
Admin. Sec.: PEDRO ANTONIO MORENO SÁNCHEZ
Librarian: LORENA CAREAGA VILIESID
Library of 17,000 vols
Number of teachers: 600
Number of students: 2,500

UNIVERSIDAD DEL EJÉRCITO Y FUERZA AÉREA
(University of the Army and Air Force)

Calzada México Tacuba s/n, Popotla, Delegación Miguel Hidalgo, México, DF
Telephone: (55) 5396-9106
Internet: www.sedena.gob.mx/educacion/index.html
Founded 1975
Rector: JUAN HERNÁNDEZ ÁVALOS.

CONSTITUENT MILITARY SCHOOLS

Escuela Médico Militar
(Military Medical School)

Cerrada de Palomas esq. con Periférico s/n, Lomas de San Isidro, Delegación Miguel Hidalgo, CP 11200, México, DF
Telephone: (55) 5540-7726
Internet: www.sedena.gob.mx/educacion/planteles/emm/index.html
Founded 1881
Dir: Gen. de Brigada Dr RODOLFO LERMA SHIUMOTO.

Escuela Militar de Aviación
(Military School of Aviation)

Colegio del Aire, Base Aérea Militar No. 5, Zapopan, Jalisco
Telephone: (33) 3624-1470
Internet: www.sedena.gob.mx/educacion/planteles/ema/index.htm
Founded 1915
Dir: Col PEDRO VALENCIA SAUCEDO.

Escuela Militar de Clases de Transmisiones
(Military School of Signals Classes)

Campo Militar No. 15-A, General Ramón Corona en la Mojonera, Zapopan, Jalisco
Telephone: (33) 3832-0462
Internet: www.sedena.gob.mx/educacion/planteles/emct/index.htm
Founded 1953
Dir: Col SAÚL CONTRERAS OJEDA.

Escuela Militar de Enfermeras
(Military School of Nurses)

Calle Idelfonso Vázquez e Industria Militar, Jardines Poniente del Hospital Central Militar, Lomas de Sotelo, México, DF
Telephone: (55) 5580-6913
Internet: www.sedena.gob.mx/educacion/planteles/eme/index.html
Founded 1938
Dir: Lt-Col IRMA RÍOS SANDOVAL.

Escuela Militar de Especialistas de Fuerza Aérea
(Military School of Air Force Specialists)

Colegio del Aire, Base Aérea Militar No. 5, Zapopan, Jalisco
Telephone: (33) 3624-1470
Internet: www.sedena.gob.mx/educacion/planteles/emefa/index.htm
Founded 1934
Dir: Col RAMIRO MARMOLEJO GUZMÁN.

Escuela Militar de Graduados de Sanidad
(Graduate Military School of Public Health)

Cerrada de Palomas s/n, Lomas de San Isidro, CP 11620, México, DF
Telephone: (55) 5520-2079
Internet: www.sedena.gob.mx/educacion/planteles/emgs/index.htm
Founded 1970
Dir: Gen. de Brigada Dr LUIS GONZÁLEZ Y GUTIÉRREZ.

Escuela Militar de Ingenieros
(Military School of Engineers)

Calzada México Tacuba s/n, Popotla, Delegación Miguel Hidalgo, México, DF
Telephone: (55) 5396-3596
Internet: www.sedena.gob.mx/educacion/planteles/emi/index.htm
Founded 1822

Dir: Gen. Brig. I. C. GILBERTO GARCIA CAMPANTE.

Escuela Militar de Mantenimiento y Abastecimiento
(Military School of Supply and Maintenance)

Colegio del Aire, Base Aérea Militar No. 5, Zapopan, Jalisco
Telephone: (33) 3624-1470
Internet: www.sedena.gob.mx/educacion/planteles/emma/index.htm
Founded 1942
Dir: Col JESÚS ULLOA GONZÁLEZ.

Escuela Militar de Materiales de Guerra
(Military School of War Materials)

Campo Militar 1-F, Santa Fe, DF
Telephone: (55) 5570-2549
Internet: www.sedena.gob.mx/educacion/planteles/emmg/index.htm
Founded 1946
Dir: Col FELIPE VARGAS TAPIA.

Escuela Militar de Odontología
(Military School of Dentistry)

Calle Batalla de Celaya e Idelfonso Vázquez s/n, Lomas de Sotelo, México, DF
Telephone: (55) 5520-2591
Internet: www.sedena.gob.mx/educacion/planteles/emo/index.html
Founded 1976
Dir: Gen. Brig. C. D. MIGUEL ANGEL GUTIÉRREZ PÉREZ.

Escuela Militar de Oficiales de Sanidad
(Military School of Public Health Officers)

Calle General Francisco Murguía s/n, Unidad Habitacional Militar, Lomas de Sotelo, México, DF
Telephone: (55) 5557-6807
Internet: www.sedena.gob.mx/educacion/planteles/emos/index.htm
Founded 1927
Dir: Col Dr ROBERTO CASTILLO MARÍN.

Escuela Militar de Transmisiones
(Military School of Signals)

Campo Militar No. 1-H, Los Leones Tacuba, México, DF
Telephone: (55) 5387-8943
Internet: www.sedena.gob.mx/educacion/planteles/emt/index.htm
Founded 1925
Dir: Gen. de Brigada LEOVIGILDO MUÑOZ HERNÁNDEZ.

Escuela Militar de Tropas Especialistas de Fuerza Aérea
(Military School of Specialist Air Force Troops)

Campo Militar No. 37-D, Santa Lucia, México, DF
Telephone: (55) 5557-6070
Internet: www.sedena.gob.mx/educacion/planteles/emtefa/index.htm
Founded 1981
Dir: Gen. JAVIER POSADAS MEJÍA.

Heroico Colegio Militar
(Heroic Military College)

Carretera México-Cuernavaca Km 22, San Pedro Mártir, Tlalpan, México, DF
Telephone: (55) 5676-5044
Internet: www.sedena.gob.mx/educacion/planteles/hcm/index.html
Founded 1818

Dir: Gen. de Brigada D. E. M. Carlos García Priani.

UNIVERSIDAD DEL GOLFO

Obregón 203 Pte, Zona Centro, 89000 Tampico, Tamaulipas
Telephone: (833) 212-9222
Fax: (833) 212-9725
E-mail: publicidad@univgolfo.edu.mx
Internet: www.unigolfo.edu.mx
Founded 1972
Private control
Languages of instruction: English, German, Spanish
Academic year: September to July
Rector: Dr Heriberto Florencia Menéndez
Vice-Rector: Lic. Hilario Zuñiga Menchaca
Chief Admin. Officer: Lic. Francisco Genaro Zuñiga Izaguirre
Librarian: Lic. Gabriel Palencia Cruz
Library of 25,000 vols
Number of teachers: 148 (25 full-time, 123 part-time)
Number of students: 4,800

DIRECTORS

European Faculty for Foreign Students: Dr Heriberto Florencia Menéndez
Faculty of Accounting and Admin.: Lic. Alma Juliana Sain-Andre Gutierrez
Faculty of Economics and Computing: Ing. Marco Antonio Cañedo Obeso
Faculty of Law: Lic. Victor Manuel Gonzalez Mendez
Postgraduate Studies: Lic. Elizabeth Barron Balleza

UNIVERSIDAD DEL MAR, PUERTO ÁNGEL
(University of the Sea, Puerto Ángel)

Ciudad Universitaria, 70902 Puerto Ángel, Distrito de San Pedro Pochutla, Oax.
Telephone: (958) 584-3078
E-mail: msv@huatulco.umar.mx
Internet: www.umar.mx
Founded 1992
State control
Language of instruction: Spanish
Rector: Dr Modesto Seara Vazquez
Vice-Rector for Academic Affairs: Biol. Mario Fuente Carrasco
Vice-Rector for Admin.: C.P. Andrés Hernández Santiago
Vice-Rector for Relations and Research: Lic. Martha Isabel Pérez Hernández
Head of Postgraduate Studies: Dra Beatriz Avalos Sartorio
Head Librarian: Lic. Ursula Navarro Alvarado
Publication: Ciencia y Mar

HEADS OF STUDIES

Huatulco campus:
International Relations: Mtra Alicia Fuentes Roldan
Tourism Administration: Lic. Olinca Paez Dominguez
Puerto Ángel campus:
Aquaculture: M.C. José Arturo Martínez Vega
Environment: M.C. Héctor López Arjona
Marine Biology: M.C. Antonio López Serrano
Maritime Studies: M.C. Carlos Gabriel Arguelles Redondo
Oceanology: Dr Roberto Esteban Martínez López
Puerto Escondido campus:
Biology: (vacant)
Forestry: (vacant)
Zootechnology: (vacant)

UNIVERSIDAD DEL VALLE DE MÉXICO

Mérida 33, Col. Roma, Del. Cuauhtémoc, 06700 México, DF
Telephone: (55) 5533-6915
E-mail: jnajera@uvmnet.edu
Internet: www.uvmnet.edu
Founded 1960
Private control
Languages of instruction: Spanish, English, French
Academic year: August to June
Rector: Dr César Morales Hernández
Vice-Rector for Academic Affairs: Lic. Sergio Linares
Head of Admin.: Lic. Jesús Carranza
Registrar: Lic. Edith Terán
Librarian: Lic. Salvador Cipres
Number of teachers: 8,000
Number of students: 100,000
Publications: *Academias* (12 a year), *Adelante* (12 a year), *Lince* (12 a year)

DEANS OF CAMPUSES

Chapultepec: Lic. Elizabeth Manning
Guadalupe Insurgentes: Lic. Martha Anides
Lago Guadalupe: Lic. Gabriela Mota
Lomas Verdes: Lic. Patricia Puente
Querétaro: Lic. Silvia Rivera
Roma: Lic. Guadalupe Zuñiga
San Angel: Lic. Griselda Vega Tato
San Miguel de Allende: Dr Francisco Martínez
San Rafael: Lic. María de la Luz Díaz Miranda
Tlalpan: Lic. Luis Silva Guerrero
Xochimilco: Lic. Salvador Silva

UNIVERSIDAD ESTATAL DE ESTUDIOS PEDAGÓGICOS

Fresnillo y Cañitas 310, Ex-ejido, Zacatecas, 21090 Mexicali, Baja California
Telephone and fax (686) 555-4959
State control
Teacher training
Dir: Prof. Alfonso Sepúlveda Ornelas.

UNIVERSIDAD ESTATAL DEL VALLE DE ECATEPEC

Avda Central s/n, Esq. Leona Vicario, Valle de Anáhuac, 66120 Ecatepec, México, DF
Telephone: (55) 710-4560
Fax: (55) 710-2688
E-mail: israelrios413@hotmail.com
Founded 2001
State control
Rector: Ismael Sáenz Villa.

UNIVERSIDAD FEMENINA DE MÉXICO

Avda Constituyentes 151, 11850 México, DF
Telephone: (55) 5515-1311
Founded 1943
Private control
Language of instruction: Spanish
Academic year: September to June
Rector: Dra Elizabeth Baquedano
Sec.-Gen.: Lic. Luis Silva Guerrero
Registrar: Lic. Pablo Torres Morán
Librarian: Srta Agueda Canedo Gutiérrez
Library of 12,000 vols
Number of teachers: 243
Number of students: 1,300
Publications: *Catálogo General Anual*, *Periódico Bimestral*

DEANS

School of Clinical Laboratories: Q.B.P. Víctor Manuel Sánchez Hidalgo, Dr José Aguilar Castillo (daytime courses)
School of Education: Lic. Luz Beatriz Unna de Torres
School of History of Art: Elizabeth Baquedano
School of Interior Decoration: Arq. Carlos Cantú Bolland
School of International Relations: Lic. Emilia Witte Montes de Oca
School of Interpreting and Translating: Lic. Maureen Anne Ivens McCullagh
School of Law: Lic. Antonio Adolfo López García
School of Museology: Lic. Roberto Alarcón
School of Pedagogy: Lic. María Elena Navarrete Toledo
School of Pharmacobiological Chemistry: Q.F.B. Enrique Calderón García
School of Psychology: Lic. Luz Antonieta Polanco de Garzón
School of Social Work: Profa T.S. María del Socorro Susana Campos García
School of Tourist Business Administration: Lic. Armando González Flores

UNIVERSIDAD IBEROAMERICANA

Prolongación Paseo de la Reforma 880, Col. Lomas de Santa Fe, 01219 México, DF
Telephone: (55) 5950-4000
Fax: (55) 5267-4005
Internet: www.uia.mx
Founded 1943, university status 1954
Private control
Language of instruction: Spanish
Academic year: August to July
Rector: Dr José Morales Orozco
Vice-Rector for Academic Affairs: Dr Javier Prado Galán
Librarian: Ing. Pilar Verdejo
Library of 204,000 vols, 1,395 periodicals
Number of teachers: 1,668 (279 full-time, 1,389 part-time)
Number of students: 10,508 (9,770 undergraduate, 738 postgraduate)
Publications: *Boletín Bibliográfico* (12 a year), *Boletín Bolsa de Trabajo* (12 a year), *Didac* (2 a year), *El Ladrillo* (52 a year), *Gallo* (5 a year), *Historia y Grafía* (3 a year), *Jurídica* (1 a year), *Poesía y Poética* (3 a year), *Prometeo* (3 a year), *Revista de Filosofía* (4 a year), *Revista del Departamento de Psicología* (3 a year), *Umbral XXI* (4 a year)

DIRECTORS OF DEPARTMENTS

Architecture, Urban Planning and Design: Arq. Jorge Ballina
Art: Lic. Aída Sierra
Basic Sciences: Mtro Arturo Fregoso
Business Administration and Accounting: Mtro Javier Cervantes
Communication: Mtro José Carreño
Economics: Dr Gerardo Jacobs
Engineering: Ing. Santiago Martínez
Health: Dr Felipe Vadillo
History: Dra Valentina Torres-Septién
Human Development: Lic. Jorge Martínez
International Studies: Lic. Agustín Gutiérrez
Law: Lic. Loretta Ortiz
Literature: Mtra Silvia Ruíz
Philosophy: Lic. Francisco Galán
Political and Social Sciences: Dra Carmen Bueno
Psychology: Dr Pedro Alvarez
Religious Sciences: Dr Carlos Soltero

REGIONAL CAMPUSES

Universidad Iberoamericana—León

Libramiento Norte km 3, Apdo Postal 26, 37000 León, Guanajuato

Telephone: (477) 11-38-60

Fax: (477) 11-54-77

Founded 1978

Private control

Language of instruction: Spanish

Academic year: August to July

Rector: Ing. CARLOS ALBERTO SEBASTIÁN SERRA MARTÍNEZ

Director-General for Academic Affairs: Biol. ARTURO MORA ALVA

Director-General for University Educational Services: Lic. DAVID MARTÍNEZ MENDIZÁBAL

Registrar: Quím. MARIO ALBERTO ARREDONDO MORALES

Librarian: Ing. AMADOR CENDEJAS MELGOZA

Library of 41,000 vols, 691 periodicals

Number of teachers: 86 (48 full-time, 38 part-time)

Number of students: 2,319 (1,864 undergraduate, 455 postgraduate)

Publication: *Presencia Universitaria* (12 a year)

Universidad Iberoamericana—Puebla

Blvd del Niño Poblano 2901, U. Territorial Atlixcayotl, 72430 Puebla, Puebla

Telephone: (222) 229-0700

E-mail: webmaster@uiagc.pue.uia.mx

Internet: www.pue.uia.mx

Founded 1983

Private control

Academic year: August to July

Rector: Arq. CARLOS VELASCO ARZAC

Dir-Gen. for Academic Affairs: Mtro JAVIER SÁNCHEZ DÍAZ DE RIVERA

Dir-Gen. for Univ. Educational Services: Mtro RAMIRO BERNAL CUEVAS

Registrar: Lic. FRANCISCO JAVIER GARCÍA GARCÍA

Librarian: Lic. LUISA GONZÁLEZ GARDEA

Library of 66,000 vols, 480 periodicals

Number of teachers: 132 (126 full-time, 6 part-time)

Number of students: 5,139 (4,181 undergraduate, 958 postgraduate)

Publications: *Comunidad* (3 a year), *Magistralis* (every 2 years).

Universidad Iberoamericana—Tijuana

Apdo 185, 22200 Tijuana, Baja California

Located at: Avda Centro Universitario 2501, Playas de Tijuana, 22200 Tijuana, Baja California

Telephone: (664) 630-1577

Fax: (664) 630-1591

Internet: www.tij.uia.mx

Founded 1982

Language of instruction: Spanish

Academic year: August to July

Rector: Mtro HUMBERTO BARQUERA GÓMEZ

Director-General for Academic Affairs: Dr ALBERTO ODRIOZOLA

Director-General: Lic. ARIEL GARCÍA

Registrar: Lic. ISABEL HUERTA

Library of 29,000 vols, 465 periodicals

Number of teachers: 328

Number of students: 1,221 (823 undergraduate, 398 postgraduate)

Universidad Iberoamericana—Torreón

Calz. Iberoamericana No. 2255, C.P. 27010, Sucursal Torreón, Coahuila

Telephone: (871) 729-1010

Fax: (871) 729-1080

Internet: www.lag.uia.mx

Founded 1982

Private control

Academic year: August to July

Rector: Ing. HECTOR ACUÑA NOGUEIRA

Director-General for Academic Affairs: Ing. GABRIEL MONTERRUBIO ALVAREZ

Director-General for University Educational Services: Mtro FELIPE ESPINOZA TORRES

Registrar: C.P. CLAUDIA RODRÍGUEZ TORRES

Librarian: Lic. MARTHA I. MCANALLY SALAS

Library of 23,000 vols, 307 periodicals

Number of teachers: 387

Number of students: 2,299 (2,125 undergraduate, 174 graduate)

Publications: *Acequias* (4 a year), *Notilaguna* (12 a year).

UNIVERSIDAD INTERCONTINENTAL

Insurgentes Sur 4303, Col. Santa Úrsula Xitla, 14420 México, DF

Telephone: (55) 5487-1300

Internet: www.uic.edu.mx

Founded 1976

Private control

Language of instruction: Spanish

Academic year: August to July

Rector: JUAN JOSÉ CORONA LÓPEZ

Gen. Sec.: JOSÉ-LUIS VEGA ARCE

Admin. Officer: C.P. JOSÉ LUIS LEON ZAMUDIO

Head Librarian: MIGUEL ÁNGEL LEÓN FABELA

Number of teachers: 773

Number of students: 4,500

Publications: *Boletín Jurídico*, *Extensiones*, *Intersticios*, *Psicología y Educación Turismo*, *Traduic*, *Voces*.

UNIVERSIDAD JUÁREZ AUTÓNOMA DE TABASCO

Avda Universidad s/n, Zona de la Cultura, 86040 Villahermosa, Tabasco

Telephone: (993) 314-0698

Internet: www.ujat.mx

Founded 1958

State control

Academic year: September to August

Rector: M.A. Candita VICTORIA GIL JIMÉNEZ

Academic Sec.: M.P.E.S. MARÍA ISABEL ZAPATA VÁSQUEZ

Administrative Sec.: Dr JOSÉ MANUEL PIÑA GUTIÉRREZ

Sec. of the Rectorate: Dra VIRGINIA ARCEO GIORGANA

Librarian: Lic. TOMASA BARRUETA GARCÍA

Library of 174,608 vols

Number of teachers: 1,050

Number of students: 20,470

Publications: *Gaceta Juchiman*, *Perspectivas Docentes*, *Revista de la División de Ciencias Sociales y Humanidades*, *Revista de la Unidad Chontalpa*, *Revista de la Universidad*, *Revista Hitos de la División de Ciencias Economico-Administrativas / Centro*, *Revista Temas Biomédicos*, *Revista Zenzontle de la División de Educación y Artes*, *Universidad y Ciencias*

DIRECTORS

Chontalpa Unit: Ing. JUAN LUIS RAMIREZ MARROQUIN (Dir-Gen.)

Division of Agricultural Sciences: M. V. Z. VICTOR DE JESUS PEREZPRIEGO COBIAN

Division of Arts and Education: Lic. EFRAIN PÉREZ CRUZ

Division of Basic Sciences: Fis. CARLOS GONZÁLEZ ARIAS

Division of Biological Sciences: M. C. ANDRÉS ARTURO GRANADOS BERBER

Division of Economic and Administrative Sciences: C.P. OLGA YERI GONZÁLEZ LÓPEZ (Centre Unit)

Division of Engineering and Technology: Ing. ARTURO ARIAS RODAS

Division of Health Sciences: Dr ESMELIN TRINIDAD VÁZQUEZ

Division of Humanities and Social Sciences: Lic. FREDDY PRIEGO PRIEGO

UNIVERSIDAD JUÁREZ DEL ESTADO DE DURANGO

Constitución 404 sur, Zona Centro, 34000 Durango, Dgo

Telephone: (618) 811-4275

Internet: www.ujed.mx

Founded as a Civil College 1856, became University 1957

Private control

Language of instruction: Spanish

Academic year: January to December (2 terms)

Rector: C.P. RUBÉN CALDERÓN LUJÁN

Sec.-Gen.: C.P. JUAN FRANCISCO SALAZAR BENÍTEZ

Chief Admin. Officer: T.S. ADRIANA AVELAR VILLEGAS

Librarian: A.B. JOSÉ LINO HERNÁNDEZ CAMPOS

Number of teachers: 1,116

Number of students: 20,160

DEANS

Faculty of Accountancy and Administration: C.P. MARÍA MAGDALENA MEDINA CÓRDOBA M.A.

Faculty of Law: Lic. VICENTE GUERRERO ITURBE

Faculty of Medicine: Dr JORGE RUIZ LEÓN

Faculty of Veterinary Medicine and Zootechnics: M.V.Z. RAÚL RANGEL ROMERO

School of Applied Mathematics: Ing. UBALDO ARENAS JUÁREZ

School of Chemical Sciences: Ing. ENRIQUE TORRES CABRAL

School of Dentistry: C.D. MIGUEL ROJAS REGALADO

School of Forestry: Ing. ALFONSO HERRERA AYÓN

School of Music: Prof. ABRAHAM E. VIGGERS ARREOLA

School of Nursing and Obstetrics: Lic. MARÍA ELENA VALDEZ DE REYES

School of Painting, Sculpture and Crafts: Prof. FRANCISCO MONTOYA DE LA CRUZ

School of Social Work: T.S. MARÍA ANTONIA HERNÁNDEZ ESCAREÑO

Gómez Palacio Campus:

School of Agriculture and Stockbreeding: Ing. JESÚS JOSÉ QUIÑONES VERA

School of Biology: BIOL. M.C. RAÚL DÍAZ MORENO

School of Civil Engineering: Ing. EVERARDO F. DELGADO SOLIS

School of Food Science and Technology: Ing. GERARDO FRANCISCO ALDANA RUIZ

School of Medicine: Dr LUIS DE VILLA VÁZQUEZ

UNIVERSIDAD LA SALLE

Benjamin Franklin 47, Col. Hipódromo Condesa, 06140 México, DF

Telephone: (55) 5278-9501

Fax: (55) 5516-2537

Internet: www.ulsa.edu.mx

Founded 1962

Private control

Language of instruction: Spanish

Academic year: August to June

Rector: MARTÍN ROCHA PEDRAJO

Vice-Rector for Academics: Ing. EDMUNDO BARRERA MONSIVÁIS

Vice-Rector for Formation and Campus Life: JOSÉ ANTONIO VARGAS AGUILAR

Registrar: RAUL HAUSER LUNA

Librarian: MARÍA ASUNCIÓN MENDOZA BECERRA

Library of 160,000 vols
Number of teachers: 996
Number of students: 8,937

Publications: *Boletín Agora de la Facultad de Derecho, Boletín de Biblioteca, Colección Jurídica Posiciones de la Facultad de Derecho, Diez Días, Gaceta ULSA, Humanitas, La Luciérnaga (Preparatoria), Logos, Reflexiones Universitarias, Revista Académica de la Facultad de Derecho, Revista Dirección, Revista Médica La Salle, Serie Cultura de la Facultad de Derecho, Siempre Unidos, Vera Humanitas*

DIRECTORS

Faculty of Business: ADOLFO CERVANTES RUIZ
Faculty of Chemical Sciences: JOSÉ ELÍAS GARCÍA ZAHOUL
Faculty of Engineering: EDUARDO GÓMEZ RAMÍREZ
Faculty of Law: JORGE NADER KURI
Faculty of Medicine: Dr PEDRO ARGÜELLES DOMENZAIN
Faculty of Humanities and Social Sciences: JOSÉ IGNACIO RIVERO CALDERÓN
Graduate and Research Studies: MARÍA TERESA ESTRADA
School of Architecture , Design and Communication: JORGE ITURBE BERMEJO
School of Education: CARLOS DAVID DOMÍNGUEZ TROLLE
School of Philosophy: JOSÉ ANTONIO DACAL ALONSO
School of Preparatory Studies: MARCO AURELIO ANTONIO GONZÁLEZ CERVANTES
School of Religious Sciences: Dr JORGE BONILLA SORT DE SANTZ

UNIVERSIDAD MICHOACANA DE SAN NICOLÁS DE HIDALGO

Edif. 'TR', Ciudad Universitaria s/n, Col. Felicitas del Río, 58030 Morelia, Mich.

Telephone: (443) 322-3500
Internet: www.umich.mx

Founded 1539, University in 1917
State control
Language of instruction: Spanish
Academic year: September to June

Rector: Lic. DANIEL TRUJILLO MESINA
Gen. Sec.: Dr SALVADOR JARA GUERRERO
Admin. Sec.: L.A.E. DOMINGO BAUTISTA FARIAS
Dir of Library: Lic. ADALBERTO ABREGO GUTIERREZ

Library of 150,000 vols
Number of teachers: 2,158
Number of students: 31,769

Publications: *Boletín de Rectoría, Cuadernos de Centro de Investigación de la Cultura Puehépecha, Cuadernos de Derecho, Polemos.*

UNIVERSIDAD MOTOLINIA AC

Cda. de Ameyalco 227, Col. Del Valle, 03100 México, DF

Telephone: (55) 5543-6679
E-mail: informes@motolinia.com.mx
Internet: www.motolinia.com.mx

Founded 1918
Private control
Language of instruction: Spanish
Academic year: August to July

Schools of chemistry and law; there is also a campus at Pedregal

Prin.: LUZ MARÍA PORTILLO ARROYO
Chief Admin. Officer: MARÍA DEL REFUGIO HERRERA FLORES
Librarian: JUANA MARÍA CAMARGO MUÑOZ.

UNIVERSIDAD NACIONAL AUTÓNOMA DE MÉXICO

Ciudad Universitaria, Del. Coyoacán, 04510 México, DF

Telephone: (55) 5622-0958
Fax: (55) 5616-0245
E-mail: lal@hp.fciencias.unam.mx
Internet: www.unam.mx

Founded 1551
Language of instruction: Spanish
Academic year: August to May

Rector: Dr JOSÉ NARRO ROBLES
Gen. Sec.: Dr SERGIO M. ALCOCER MARTÍNEZ DE CASTRO
Administrative Sec.: Mtro JUAN JOSÉ PÉREZ CASTAÑEDA
Sec. for Institutional Devt: Dra ROSAURA RUIZ GUTIÉRREZ
Sec. for Community Services: M.C. RAMIRO JESÚS SANDOVAL
Humanities Coordinator: Dra ESTELA MORALES CAMPOS
Scientific Research Coordinator: Dr CARLOS ARÁMBURO DE LA HOZ
Cultural Dissemination Coordinator: Mtro SEALTIEL ALATRISTE
Planning Coordinator: Lic. ENRIQUE DEL VAL BLANCO
Innovation Coordinator: Dr JAIME MARTUSCELLI QUINTANA
Gen. Dir for Social Communication: ENRIQUE BALP DÍAZ
Librarian: Dra SILVIA GONZÁLEZ MARÍN

Library: in addition to the National Library and Central Library (see under Libraries and Archives), there are 142 specialized libraries

Number of teachers: 35,057
Number of students: 314,557

Publications: *Acta Poética* (1 a year), *Acta Sociológica* (3 a year), *Anales de Antropología* (1 a year), *Anales del Instituto de Biología: Serie Botánica* (2 a year), *Anales del Instituto de Biología: Serie Zoología* (2 a year), *Anales del Instituto de Investigaciones Estéticas* (2 a year), *Anuario Jurídico* (1 a year), *Anuario de la Historia del Derecho Mexicano* (1 a year), *Anuario de Letras* (1 a year), *Anuario de Letras Modernas* (1 a year), *Antropología Física Latinoamericana* (1 a year), *Antropológicas* (3 a year), *Archivos Hispanoamericanas de Sexología* (2 a year), *Atmósfera* (4 a year), *Bibliografía Filosófica Mexicana* (1 a year), *Bibliografía Latinoamericana* (2 a year), *Biblioteca Universitaria* (2 a year), *Bien. Boletín de Investigación, Educación y sus Nexos* (3 a year), *Bien. Revista Especializada en Ciencias Sociales y la Educación* (2 a year), *Boletín de la Escuela Nacional de Música* (12 a year), *Boletín del Instituto de Investigaciones Bibliográficas* (2 a year), *Boletín Mexicano de Derecho Comparado* (3 a year), *Carrizos* (4 a year), *Chicomóztoc: Boletín del Seminario de Estudios para la Descolonización de México* (1 a year), *Ciencias* (4 a year), *Clase: Citas Latinoamericanas en Ciencias Sociales y Humanidades* (4 a year), *¿Cómo ves?* (12 a year), *Contaduría y Administración* (4 a year), *Crítica Jurídica* (2 a year), *Crítica: Revista Hispanoamericana de Filosofía* (3 a year), *Cuadernos Americanos* (6 a year), *Demos: Carta Demográfica sobre México* (1 a year), *Desde el Sur: Humanismo y Ciencia* (4 a year), *Dianoia: Anuario de Filosofía* (1 a year), *Diógenes* (4 a year), *Discurso: Cuadernos de Teoría y Análisis* (2 a year), *Economía Informa* (12 a year), *Educación Química* (4 a year), *Emprendedores* (6 a year), *Estudios de Antropología Biológica* (every 2 years), *Estudios de Cultura Maya* (every 2 years), *Estudios de Cultura Náhuatl* (every 2 years), *Estudios de Cultura Otopame* (every 2 years), *Estudios de Historia Moderna y Contemporánea de México* (1 a year), *Estudios de Historia Novohispana* (1 a year), *Estudios de Lingüística Aplicada* (2 a year), *Estudios Latinoamericanos* (2 a year), *Estudios Políticos* (3 a year), *Experiencia Literaria* (irregular), *Ingeniería, Investigación y Tecnología* (4 a year), *Investigación Bibliotecológica* (2 a year), *Investigación Económica* (4 a year), *Investigaciones Geográficas* (2 a year), *La Experiencia Literaria* (irregular), *Latinoamérica: Anuario de Estudios Latinoamericanos* (irregular), *Los Universitarios* (6 a year), *Mathesis* (4 a year), *Medievalia* (2 a year), *Momento Económico—Información y Análisis de la Conjuntura Económica* (6 a year), *Nova Tellus: Anuario del Centro de Estudios Clásicos* (2 a year), *Nuevo Consultorio Fiscal–Laboral y Contable-Financiero* (26 a year), *Omnia* (4 a year), *Perfiles Educativos* (4 a year), *Periódica: Índice de Revistas Latinoamericanas en Ciencias* (4 a year), *Pluralitas* (electronic, 12 a year), *Poligrafías—Revista de Literatura Comparada* (1 a year), *Problemas del Desarrollo: Revista Latinoamericana de Economía* (4 a year), *Punto de Partida* (6 a year), *Relaciones Internacionales* (3 a year), *Revista CIHMECH* (1 a year), *Revista de Derecho Privado* (3 a year), *Revista de la Facultad de Medicina* (6 a year), *Revista de Zoología* (3 a year), *Revista Mexicana de Astronomía y Astrofísica* (2 a year), *Revista Mexicana de Ciencias Geológicas* (2 a year), *Revista Mexicana de Ciencias Políticas y Sociales* (4 a year), *Revista Mexicana de Sociología* (4 a year), *Revista Veterinaria—México* (4 a year), *Sinopsis* (1 a year), *Tempus* (irregular), *Theoría: Revista del Colegio de Filosofía* (3 a year), *Tip. Revista Especializada en Ciencias Químicas Biológicas* (2 a year), *Tip. Tópicos de Investigación y Posgrado* (3 a year), *Trabajo Social* (4 a year), *UNAM Hoy* (6 a year), *Universidad de México* (12 a year), *Vertientes—Revista Especializada en Ciencias de la Salud* (2 a year), *Voices of México* (4 a year)

DIRECTORS OF FACULTIES AND SCHOOLS

Faculty of Accounting and Administration: Dr JUAN ALBERTO ADAM SLADE
Faculty of Architecture: Arq. JORGE TAMÉS Y BATTA
Faculty of Chemistry: Dr EDUARDO BÁRZANA GARCÍA
Faculty of Dentistry: Mtro JAVIER DE LA FUENTE HERNÁNDEZ
Faculty of Economics: Dr LEONARDO LOMELÍ VANEGAS
Faculty of Engineering: Mtro JOSÉ GONZALO GUERRERO ZEPEDA
Faculty of Law: Dr RUPERTO PATIÑO MANFFER
Faculty of Medicine: Dr ENRIQUE GRAUE WIECHERS
Faculty of Philosophy and Letters: Dr GLORIA VILLEGAS MORENO
Faculty of Political and Social Sciences: Dr FERNANDO CASTAÑEDA SABIDO
Faculty of Psychology: Dr JAVIER NIETO GUTIÉRREZ
Faculty of Sciences: Dr RAMÓN PERALTA Y FABI
Faculty of Veterinary Medicine and Animal Husbandry: Dr FRANCISCO JOSÉ TRIGO TAVERA

National Schools:

College of Sciences and Humanities: Lic. LUCÍA LAURA MUÑOZ CORONA (Gen. Dir)
National School of Music: Lic. FRANCISCO JOSÉ VIESCA TREVIÑO
National School of Nursing and Obstetrics: Lic. Enf. SEVERINO RUBIO DOMÍNGUEZ

National School of Plastic Arts: Dr José Daniel Manzano Águila

National School of Social Work: Mtra Graciela Casas Torres

Preparatory National School: Lic. María de Lourdes Sánchez Obregón (Gen. Dir)

Multidisciplinary Units of Professional Studies:

Faculty of Advanced Studies Acatlán: Dr J. Alejandro Salcedo Aquino

Faculty of Advanced Studies Aragón: Arq. Lilia Turcott González

Faculty of Advanced Studies Cuautitlán: Dr Juan Antonio Montaraz y Crespo

Faculty of Advanced Studies Iztacala: Dr Sergio Cházaro Olvera

Faculty of Advanced Studies Zaragoza: C.D. Alfredo Salvador Sánchez Figueroa

UNIVERSIDAD PANAMERICANA

Augusto Rodin 498, Col. Insurgentes Mixcoac, Del. Benito Juárez, 03920 México, DF

Telephone: (55) 5482-1600

Internet: www.mixcoac.upmx.mx

Founded 1966

Private control

Academic year: August to June

Rector: Dr Ramón Ibarra

Vice-Rectors: Jesús Magaña Bravo, Lic. Sergio Raimond-Kedilhac Navarro

Admin. Dir: Dr Víctor Manuel Pizá

Librarian: Elisa Riva Palacio

Library of 45,000 vols

Number of teachers: 450

Number of students: 5,000

Publications: *Ars Juris* (2 a year), *Boletín* (12 a year), *Revista Istmo* (6 a year), *Tópicos Journal of Philosophy* (2 a year)

Preparatory and first degree courses

DIRECTORS

School of Accounting: Claudio M. Rivas

School of Administration: Ing. Amadeo Vázquez

School of Economics: Lic. Flavia Rodríguez

School of Education: Dra Carmen Ramso

School of Engineering: Ing. Pedro Creuheras

School of Law: Dr Roberto Ibáñez Mariel

School of Philosophy: Dr Rocio Mier y Terán

AFFILIATED INSTITUTIONS

Instituto de Capacitación de Mandos Intermedios (Mid–Management Institute): Mar Mediterráneo 183, Col. Popotla, 11400 México, DF; tel. (55) 5399-7272; f. 1966; 170 teachers; 2,400 students; library of 1,200 vols; business administration to supervisor and head of dept level; Dir Conrado Antonio Larios.

Instituto de Desarrollo para Operarios: Norte 182, No. 477, Col. Peñón de los Baños, 15520 México, DF; tel. (55) 5760-3464; f. 1968; 45 teachers; 550 students; library of 500 vols; courses for worker-management; Dir Enrique Sierra.

Instituto Panamericano de Alta Dirección de Empresa (Pan-American Institute of Higher Business Studies): Floresta 20, Col. Clavería, 02080 México, DF; tel. (55) 5527-0260f. 1967; library of 8,000 vols; 40 teachers; 1,900 students; Dir Sergio Raimond-Kedilhac Navarro.

Instituto Panamericano de Ciencias de la Educación (Pan-American Institute of Education): Augusto Rodin 498, Col. Mixcoac, 03920 México, DF; Dir Dra Marcela Chavarría.

UNIVERSIDAD PANAMERICANA DE NUEVO LAREDO

Ave Morelos 2311, Col. Juárez, Nuevo Laredo, Tam.

Telephone: (867) 715-2731

Fax: (867) 715-2562

E-mail: universipanameri@netscape.net

Internet: www.unipanam.edu.mx

Founded 1980

Private control

Academic year: September to July

Rector: Lic. Francisco Balderas García

Sec.-Gen.: C.P. Victor M. Castillo Avendaño

Dir of Academic Affairs: Profa Guadalupe Jasso Juárez

Dir of Services: Profa Ma. Monica Balderas Alcocer

Dir of Preparatory Division: Prof. Carlos Camacho Mancillas

Dir of Undergraduate Division: Profa Norma Gallegos Calderón

Dir of Postgraduate Division: Dr José de Jesús Leal Mahmuud

Librarian: Lic. Abelardo Gloria Hinojosa

Number of teachers: 105

Number of students: 1,800 (1,200 undergraduate, 600 postgraduate)

DEANS

Faculty of Education: Prof. Carlos Camacho Mancillas

Faculty of Law, Public Finance and Administration: Lic. Fernando Ríos Rodríguez

Faculty of Masters Degree Courses: Profa Ma. Balderas Alcocer

Faculty of Medicine: Dr Wenceslao Lozano Rendón

Faculty of Primary School Education: Profa Juana María Cerda Torres

Faculty of Psychology: Lic. Virginia Zapata Rodríguez

Faculty of Secondary School Education: Profa Norma Gallegos Calderón

Faculty of Veterinary and Zoological Sciences: MVZ Alejandro Gurrola Granados

UNIVERSIDAD PEDAGÓGICA DE DURANGO

Avda 16 de Septiembre 132, Col Silvestre Dorador, 3407 Durango, Durango

Telephone: (618) 812-9509

Fax: (618) 812-9509

E-mail: upndgo@gauss.logicnet.com.mx

Founded 1997

State control

Dir: Prof. Bernardo del Real Sarmiento.

UNIVERSIDAD PEDAGÓGICA NACIONAL
(National Pedagogic University)

Carretera al Ajusco No. 24 Col. Héroes de Padierna Delegación, Tlalpan, 14200 México, DF

Telephone: (55) 5645-6213

Fax: (55) 5645-5340

E-mail: rectoria@upn.mx

Internet: www.upn.mx

State control

Language of instruction: Spanish

Rector: Marcela Santillán Nieto

Director of Planning: Abraham Sánchez Contreras

Director of Studies: Elsa Mendiola Sanz

Director of Library and Academic Support Services: Fernando Velázquez Merlo

Number of teachers: 3,989

Number of students: 69,300

Major subject areas: methods of teaching: education administration, pedagogy, educational psychology, educational sociology,

indigenous education; part-time teaching: pre-school, primary and adult education; distance-learning: teaching French.

UNIVERSIDAD PEDAGÓGICA VERACRUZANA

Calle Museo 133, Unidad Magisterial, 91010 Xalapa, Veracruz

Telephone: (228) 814-1594

Fax: (228) 814-0036

E-mail: sec.academica@secupv.org

Internet: www.secupv.org

Founded 1980

State control

Rector: Dr Marco Wilfredo Salas Martínez

Academic Sec.: Reynaldo Castillo Aguilar.

UNIVERSIDAD POLITÉCNICA DE SAN LUIS POTOSÍ

Iturbide 140, Centro, 78000 San Luis Potosí, SLP

Telephone: (444) 814-4714

Fax: (444) 812-6519

Founded 2001

Rector: Juan Antonio Martínez Martínez.

UNIVERSIDAD POLITÉCNICA DE ZACATECAS

Carretera Zacatecas-Guadalupe Km 4, Dependencias Federales, 98600 Guadalupe, Zacatecas

Telephone: (492) 923-6966

Fax: (492) 923-9666

E-mail: demsys@zac.sep.gob.mx

Founded 2002

State control

Rector: José Guadalupe Estrada.

UNIVERSIDAD POPULAR AUTÓNOMA DEL ESTADO DE PUEBLA

21 Sur 1103, Col. Santiago, 72160 Puebla, Pue.

Telephone: (222) 229-9400

Fax: (222) 232-5251

Internet: web.upaep.mx

Founded 1973

Private control

Academic year: August to July

Rector: Dr Alfredo Miranda López

General-Secretary: Ing. Vicente Pacheco Ceballos

Registrar: Lic. María de los Angeles Rondero Chew

Public Relations Officer: Arq. José M. Argüelles Reyes Nieva

Librarian: Lic. Leobardo Reyes Jiménez

Number of teachers: 652

Number of students: 5,084

Publication: *Vertebracíon* (6 a year).

UNIVERSIDAD POPULAR DE LA CHONTALPA
(People's University of Chontalpa)

Galeana s/n Esq. Morelos, Centro, 86500 Cárdenas, Tabasco

Telephone: (937) 372-5743

Fax: (937) 372-5743

E-mail: informacion@upchontalpa.edu.mx

Internet: www.upchontalpa.edu.mx

Founded 1998

State control

Main subject areas: agricultural engineering, business and international finance, civil engineering, electrical and mechanical engineering, petrochemical engineering, political science and public administration, psychology and pharmaceutical chemistry, zootechnical engineering

Rector: Ing. RAMÓN ALEJANDRO FIGUEROA CANTORAL
Sec. for Academic Affairs: Dr ARQUÍMEDES ORAMAS VARGAS
Sec. for University Extension and Social Services: MANUEL AYSA JIMÉNEZ
Sec. for Administration and Finance: ELVIS SEGURA CÓRDOVA

Publications: *Expresión Universitaria, Gaceta Enlace Universitario, Revista Tecnociencia Universitaria*.

UNIVERSIDAD REGIOMONTANA

Villagrán 238 Sur, Centro, 64000 Monterrey, N.L.

Telephone: (81) 8220-4620
Fax: (81) 8344-3470
E-mail: webmaster@mail.ur.mx
Internet: www.ur.mx

Founded 1969
Private control
Language of instruction: Spanish
Academic year: September to August

Rector: Dr PABLO A. LONGORIA TREVIÑO
Admin. Dir: Ing. GUILLERMO CHARLES LOBO
Registrar: Ing. GERARDO GONZÁLEZ
Librarian: Ing. JORGE MERCADO SALAS

Library of 42,952 vols
Number of teachers: 450
Number of students: 4,500

Publications: *Espresión* (52 a year), *Veritas* (1 a year)

DEANS

Faculty of Economic and Administrative Sciences: Dr CARLOS OLIVARES LEAL
Faculty of Engineering and Architecture: Dr RODOLFO SALINAS HERNÁNDEZ
Faculty of Humanities and Social Sciences: Lic. DORA ANTINORI CARLETTI
Preparatory Division: Lic. NICOLÁS PALACIOS LOZANO

UNIVERSIDAD TECNOLÓGICA DE LA MIXTECA
(Mixteca Technological University)

Carretera a Acatlima km 2.5, 69000 Huajuápan de León, Oax.

Telephone: (919) 532-0214
E-mail: msv@mixteco.utm.mx
Internet: www.utm.mx

Founded 1990
State control
Language of instruction: Spanish

Rector: Dr MODESTO SEARA VÁZQUEZ
Vice-Rector for Academic Affairs: Ing. GERARDO GARCÍA HERNÁNDEZ
Vice-Rector for Admin.: C.P. JAVIER JOSÉ RUIZ SANTIAGO
Vice-Rector for University Relations and Research: Lic. SERGIO GUERRERO VERDEJO
Librarian: Lic. MANUEL BARRAGÁN ROJAS

HEADS OF STUDIES

Applied Mathematics: Mtro JUAN CARLOS MENDOZA SANTOS
Computer Engineering: Ing. FRANCISCO ESPINOSA MACEDA
Design: D.I. ROBERTO ESQUIVEL JAIME
Electrical Engineering: ENRIQUE GUZMÁN RAMÍREZ
Food Science: Q.F.B. JUANA RAMÍREZ ANDRADE
Industrial Engineering: Dr DANIEL ERASTE SANTOS REGES
Management Sciences: Lic. MARÍA GUADALUPE NORIEGA GÓMEZ

UNIVERSIDAD VERACRUZANA

Zona Universitaria, Lomas del Estadio s/n, 91090 Jalapa, Ver.

Telephone: (228) 842-17-63
Fax: (228) 817-63-70
E-mail: rarias@uv.mx
Internet: www.uv.mx

Founded 1944
Academic year: September to August

Rector: Dr RAÚL ARIAS LOVILLO
Vice-Rector (Coatzacoalcos-Minatitlán Campus): ENRIQUE RAMÍREZ NAZARIEGA
Vice-Rector (Orizaba-Córdoba Campus): Arq. ROBERTO OLAVARRIETA MARENCO
Vice-Rector (Poza Rica-Tuxpan Campus): Dra CLARA CELINA MEDINA SAGAHÓN
Vice-Rector (Veracruz Campus): EMILIO ZILLI DEBERNARDI
Academic Sec.: Mtra MARIA DEL PILAR VELASCO MUÑOZ LEDO
Dean of Planning and Institutional Research: Mtra LAURA ELENA MARTÍNEZ MÁRQUEZ
Librarian: Lic. DIANA GONZÁLEZ ORTEGA

Number of teachers: 5,064
Number of students: 44,903

Publications: *La Ciencia y el Hombre, La Palabra y el Hombre*

HEADS OF DIVISIONS

Agricultural and Biological Sciences: Mtro ERNESTO RODRÍGUEZ LUNA
Arts: Mtro ENRIQUE SALMERÓN CÓRDOBA
Economics: Dr MARIO MIGUEL OJEDA RAMÍREZ
Health Sciences: Dr RAMÓN FLORES LOZANO
Humanities: Dr Ma MAGDALENA HERNÁNDEZ ALARCÓN
Technology: Mtro WALTER LUIS SAIZ GONZÁLEZ

DIRECTORS

Coatzacoalcos-Minatitlán Campus:

Faculty of Accounting and Business Management: JAVIER ARENAS WAGNER
Faculty of Agricultural Production Systems Engineering: Ing. ALBERTO HERNÁNDEZ QUIROZ
Faculty of Chemistry (Coatzacoalcos): ERUVIEL FLANDÉS ALEMÁN
Faculty of Dentistry: Dr JAVIER GASTÓN PÉREZ ORTIZ
Faculty of Engineering: Ing. CIRO CASTILLO PÉREZ
Faculty of Medicine: Dr FRANCISCO ORTIZ GUERRERO
Faculty of Nursing: MORAIMA KATZ
Faculty of Social Work: Lic. LUCINDA MIRANDA CHIÑAS

Orizaba-Córdoba Campus:

Faculty of Accountancy and Business Management: IDELFONSO VÍCTOR MUÑOZ ROSAS
Faculty of Architecture: Arq. ABEL COLORADO SAINZ
Faculty of Biological and Agricultural Sciences: ANTONIO PÉREZ PACHECO
Faculty of Chemical Sciences: SOFÍA CANALES CHÁVEZ
Faculty of Dentistry: GUILLERMO MERAZ ZÚÑIGA
Faculty of Mechanical and Electrical Engineering: Ing. GUILLERMO CABALLERO LEÓN
Faculty of Medicine: Dr JORGE E. LÓPEZ GONZÁLEZ
Faculty of Nursing: Enf. INÉS HUERTA VÁSQUEZ

Poza Rica-Tuxpan Campus:

Faculty of Accountancy: Mtro MARIO SOTO DEL ANGEL
Faculty of Architecture: Arq. LUIS MANUEL VILLEGAS SALGADO
Faculty of Biology, Agriculture and Animal Husbandry: Biol. JOSÉ LUIS ALANIS MÉNDEZ
Faculty of Chemical Sciences: Ing. SERGIO NATAN GONZÁLEZ ROCHA

Faculty of Civil Engineering: Ing. ALEJANDRO CÓRDOVA CEBALLOS
Faculty of Dentistry: JAVIER AGUIRRE BACEROT
Faculty of Education: Lic. ADORACIÓN BARRALES VILLEGAS
Faculty of Electronic Engineering and Communications: SILVERIO PÉREZ CÁCERES
Faculty of Mechanical and Electrical Engineering: Ing. JOSÉ LUIS JUÁREZ SUÁREZ
Faculty of Medicine: Dr JORGE C. VILLEGAS PATIÑO
Faculty of Nursing: JUANA PERALTA SANTIAGO
Faculty of Psychology: Mtro FRANCISCO BERMÚDEZ JIMÉNEZ
Faculty of Social Work: Lic. VIRGINIA CALLEJAS MATEOS

Veracruz Campus:

Faculty of Accounting: CELIA DEL PILAR GARRIDO VARGAS
Faculty of Business Management: LILIANA IVONNE BETANCOURT TRAVENDHAN
Faculty of Clinical Chemistry: MA. DEL REFUGIO SALAS ORTEGA
Faculty of Communications Science: Lic. JOSÉ LUIS CERDÁN DÍAZ
Faculty of Dentistry: Dra EMMA HERNÁNDEZ FIGUEROA
Faculty of Education: Mtra LETICIA SÁNCHEZ TETUMA
Faculty of Engineering: Ing. JOSÉ A. TELLO ALLENDE
Faculty of Medicine: Dr FRANCISCO MANUEL SANTIAGO SILVA
Faculty of Nursing: SOFÍA DELFÍN BADUY
Faculty of Nutrition: Lic. MA. DE LOURDES MALPICA CARLÍN
Faculty of Physical Education, Sports and Recreation: Mtro SERGIO HERNÁNDEZ LÓPEZ
Faculty of Psychology: Psic. MA. EUGENIA PADILLA FARÍAS
Faculty of Veterinary Medicine and Zootechnics: CARLOS LAMONTHE ZAVALETA

Xalapa Campus:

Faculty of Accounting and Business Management: LUIS RICARDO OLIVARES MENDOZA
Faculty of Administrative and Social Sciences: ADELAIDA RODRÍGUEZ ARCOS
Faculty of Agriculture: Ing. GABRIEL MAY MORA
Faculty of Anthropology: Mtro FRANCISCO JAVIER KURI CAMACHO
Faculty of Architecture: Arq. MIGUEL ÁNGEL CORTÉS ZAHAR
Faculty of Biology: Biol. SOLEDAD ROCHA FLORES
Faculty of Chemical Biological Pharmacy: Dr RAFAEL DÍAZ SOBAC
Faculty of Chemical Engineering: Mtro MIGUEL ÁNGEL FRAGOSO LÓPEZ
Faculty of Civil Engineering: Ing. ARURO ORTIZ CEDANO
Faculty of Clinical Chemistry: SANDRA LUZ GONZÁLEZ HERRERA
Faculty of Dance: Mtra NATALIA JUAN GIL
Faculty of Dentistry: MARINA FERNÁNDEZ CONTI
Faculty of Economics: Dr REY ACOSTA BARRADAS
Faculty of Education: Mtra ROCÍO L. GONZÁLEZ GUERRERO
Faculty of Electronic Instrumentation: Mtro ANGEL BARRIENTOS SANTIAGO
Faculty of Fine Arts: Mtro HÉCTOR VINICIO REYES CONTRERAS
Faculty of History: Mtro HÉCTOR MÁRTINEZ DOMÍNGUEZ
Faculty of Languages: Mtra ROSALBA HESS MORENO
Faculty of Law: Lic. MANLIO FABIO CASARÍN NAVARRETE
Faculty of Mathematics: Dr JOSÉ RIGOBERTO GABRIEL ARGÜELLES
Faculty of Mechanical and Electrical Engineering: Mtro RAFAEL LOZANO GONZÁLEZ

Faculty of Medicine: Dr RAFAEL CANO ORTEGA
Faculty of Music: Mtra PATRICIA CASTILLO DÍAZ
Faculty of Nursing: CRISTINA SAAVEDRA VÉLEZ
Faculty of Nutrition: CONCEPCIÓN SÁNCHEZ ROVELO
Faculty of Philosophy: Mtro ALBERTO C. RUIZ QUIROZ
Faculty of Physics: Dr CÉSAR RENÉ DE LA CRUZ LASO
Faculty of Psychology: Mtro AGUSTÍN AGUIRRE PITALÚA
Faculty of Sociology: Mtro LUIS MAGAÑA CUELLAR
Faculty of Spanish Language and Literature: Lic. NIDIA VINCENT ORTEGA
Faculty of Statistics and Computing: ALMA ROSA GARCÍA GAONA
Faculty of Theatre: Mtra ELKA FEDIUK WALCZEWSKA

Technical Universities

INSTITUTO POLITÉCNICO NACIONAL

Unidad Profesional 'Adolfo López Mateos', Zacatenco, Del. Gustavo A. Madero, 07738 México, DF

Telephone: (55) 5729-6300
E-mail: contacto@ipn.gob.mx
Internet: www.ipn.mx

Founded 1936
State control
Language of instruction: Spanish
Academic year: September to July

Gen. Dir: Dr JOSÉ ENRIQUE VILLA RIVERA
Sec.-Gen.: Ing. ALFREDO LÓPEZ HERNÁNDEZ
Administrative Dir: Ing. HÉCTOR URIEL MAYAGOITIA PRADO
Librarian: Lic. CESAR SANTÓME FIGUEROA

Number of teachers: 12,356
Number of students: 107,200

Publications: *Gaceta Politécnica*, *Acta Politécnica*, *Acta Médica*, *Anales de la Escuela Nacional de Ciencias Biológicas*, *Economía Política*

DIRECTORS

Centre for Research and Development in Digital Technology (in Tijuana): Dr JOSÉ MÁRIA MONTOYA FLORES
Higher School of Chemical Engineering and Mining Industries: Ing. TIMOTEO PASTRANA APONTE
Higher School of Commerce and Administration: C.P. JOSÉ DE JESÚS VÁZQUEZ BONILLA
Higher School of Economics: Lic. MIGUEL ANGEL CORREA JASSO
Higher School of Engineering and Architecture: Ing. SALVADOR PADILLA ALONSO
Higher School of Mechanical and Electrical Engineering: Ing. ARTURO ZEPEDA SALINAS
Higher School of Medicine: Dr JUAN ORDORICA VARGAS
Higher School of Physics and Mathematics: M. en C. OLGA LETICIA HERNÁNDEZ CHÁVEZ
Higher School of Textile Engineering: Ing. CASSIN FRANCISCO ALE GUERRERO
Higher School of Tourism: Lic. VÍCTOR CHALE GÓNGORA
Interdisciplinary Centre for Health Sciences: Lic. Nut. ADRIÁN GUILLERMO QUINTERO GUTIÉRREZ
Interdisciplinary Centre for Marine Sciences: M. en C. JULIAN RENÉ TORRES VILLEGAS
Interdisciplinary Professional Unit of Engineering and Social and Administrative Sciences: Ing. ERNESTO ANGELES MEJÍA
Interdisciplinary Project for the Environment and Integrated Development: Dr JUAN MANUEL NAVARRO PINEDA

Interdisciplinary Research Centre for Regional Development (Durango Centre): Dr JÓSE ANGEL L. ORTEGA HERRERA
Interdisciplinary Research Centre for Regional Development (Michoacán): M. en C. VÍCTOR MANUEL LÓPEZ LÓPEZ
Interdisciplinary Research Centre for Regional Development (Oaxaca Centre): Ing. FERNANDO ELI ORTÍZ HERNÁNDEZ
National School of Biological Sciences: Dra THELMA LILIA VILLEGAS GARRIDO
National School of Medicine and Homeopathy: Dr JAIME ERNESTO SÁNCHEZ GONZÁLEZ
Project for Technological and Scientific Social Studies: M. en C. LUIS FERNANDO CASTILLO GARCÍA

INSTITUTO TECNOLÓGICO Y DE ESTUDIOS SUPERIORES DE MONTERREY

Avda Eugenio Garza Sada 2501 Sur, Col. Tecnológico, 64849 Monterrey, Nuevo León

Telephone: (81) 8358-2000
Fax: (81) 8358-1400
Internet: www.itesm.mx

Founded 1943
Private control
Languages of instruction: Spanish, English
Academic year: August to May

Rector: Dr RAFAEL RANGEL SOSTMANN
Rector for Monterrey Campus: Dr ALBERTO BUSTANI
Rector for Mexico City Campus: Ing. JUAN DURÁN
Rector for Central Zone: Dr ROBERTO RUEDA
Rector for N, S and W Zones: C. P. DAVID NOEL RAMÍREZ
Registrar: Lic. ALEJANDRA GARCÍA
Librarian: Ing. MIGUEL ARREOLA

Library: 2.6m. vols, 53,000 periodicals
Number of teachers: 8,694
Number of students: 96,649

DEANS

EGADE Business School: Dr ROBERT GROSSE
Graduate School of Public Administration and Public Policy (EGAP): Dr BERNARDO GONZÁLEZ
School of Architecture, Art and Design: Arq. JAMES MAYEUX
School of Biotechnology and Health: Dr MARTÍN HERNÁNDEZ
School of Business, Social Sciences and Humanities: Dr HUMBERTO CANTÚ
School of Engineering and Information Technology: Dr JAIME BONILLA

The Institute comprises 32 campuses in addition to the main one in Monterrey

Colleges

CETYS UNIVERSIDAD – CENTRO DE ENSEÑANZA TÉCNICA Y SUPERIOR

Calzada CETYS s/n, Col. Rivera, 21259 Mexicali, Baja California

Telephone: (686) 567-3701
Fax: (686) 565-0241
E-mail: info@cetys.mx
Internet: www.cetys.mx

Founded 1961
Academic year: September to June

Courses in fields of engineering (industrial, mechanical, manufacturing, electronics, computers, digital graphic design), computer sciences, corporate information systems, international business, management, finance, accountancy, behavioural sciences, international and corporate law, continuous education, executive development programmes

Rector: Ing. ENRIQUE CARLOS BLANCAS DE LA CRUZ
Vice-Rector for Academic Affairs: Dr FERNANDO LEÓN GARCÍA
Dir-Gen. of Mexicali Campus: Ing. SERGIO REBOLLAR McDONOUGH
Dir-Gen. of Tijuana Campus: Lic. MIGUEL ANGEL SALAS MARRÓN
Dir-Gen. of Ensenada Campus: Ing. FRANCISCO VILLALBA ROSARIO

Library: Libraries with 57,000 vols
Number of teachers: 487
Number of students: 3,700

COLEGIO DE LA FRONTERA SUR

Apdo Postal 63, 29290 San Cristóbal de las Casas, Chiapas
Carretera Panamericana y Periférico Sur s/n, Barrio Ma. Auziliadora, 29290 San Cristóbal de las Casas, Chiapas

Telephone: (967) 674-9000
E-mail: contacto@ecosur.mx
Internet: www.ecosur.mx

Founded 1994

Gen.-Dir: Dra ESPERANZA TUÑON PABLOS

Divs of alternative means of production, of agroecological technology, of health and population, of the conservation and exploitation of biodiversity.

COLEGIO DE MÉXICO

Apdo 20671, 01000 México
Located at: Camino al Ajusco 20, Pedregal de Santa Teresa, 10740 México, DF

Telephone: (55) 5449-3000
Fax: (55) 5645-0464
E-mail: webmaster@colmex.mx
Internet: www.colmex.mx

Founded 1940
Academic year: September to July

President: Dr JAVIER GARCIADIEGO DANTÁN
Secretary-General: MANUEL ORDORICA MELLADO
Academic Coordinator: JEAN FRANÇOIS PRUD'HOMME
Library Director: MICAELA CHÁVEZ VILLA

Library of 780,000 vols
Number of teachers: 305 (incl. researchers)
Number of students: 313

Publications: *Estudios de Asia y África* (3 a year), *Estudios Demográficos y Urbanos* (3 a year), *Estudios Económicos* (2 a year), *Estudios Sociológicos* (3 a year), *Foro Internacional* (4 a year), *Historia Mexicana* (4 a year), *Nueva Revista de Filología Hispánica* (2 a year)

DIRECTORS

Centre for Asian and African Studies: JUAN JOSÉ RAMÍREZ BONILLA
Centre for Demographic, Urban and Environmental Studies: JOSÉ LUIS LEZAMA
Centre for Economic Studies: JAIME SEMPERE CAMPELLO
Centre for Historical Studies: GUILLERMO PALACIOS Y OLIVARES
Centre for International Studies: GUSTAVO VEGA
Centre for Linguistics and Literary Studies: AURELIO GONZÁLEZ PÉREZ
Centre for Sociological Studies: ROBERTO BLANCARTE PIMENTEL

ESCUELA NACIONAL DE ANTROPOLOGÍA E HISTORIA (National School of Anthropology and History)

Periférico Sur y Zapote s/n, Col. Isidro Fabela, C.P. 14030, México, DF
Telephone: (55) 5606-8946

Fax: (55) 5606-0197
E-mail: enahdir@yahoo.com
Internet: www.enah.inah.gob.mx
Founded 1938
Academic year: January to December
Dir: Francisco Ortiz Pedraza
Librarian: María de Lourdes Méndez Campos

Library of 37,575 vols
Number of teachers: 395
Number of students: 2,296

Publications: *Folleto de Información Básica y Cuadernos de Trabajo* (irregular), *Revista Cuicuilco* (4 a year)

Faculties of physical anthropology, social anthropology, archaeology, ethno-history, linguistics and history.

ESCUELA NACIONAL DE BIBLIOTECONOMÍA Y ARCHIVONOMÍA
(National School of Librarianship and Archives)

Calz. Ticoman 645, Col. Santa Ma. Ticoman, CP 07330 México, DF
Telephone: (55) 3752-7475
Fax: (55) 2752-7575
Founded 1945
Director: Mtro Nahum Perez Paz
Library of 5,000 vols
Number of teachers: 72
Number of students: 420

Publication: *Bibliotecas y Archivos.*

ESCUELA NACIONAL DE CONSERVACIÓN, RESTAURACIÓN Y MUSEOGRAFÍA 'MANUEL DEL CASTILLO NEGRETE'
(Manuel del Castillo Negrete National School of Conservation, Restoration and Museography)

Ex-Convento de Churubusco, Xicoténcatl y Gral Anaya, 04120 México, DF
Telephone: (55) 5604-5188
Fax: (55) 5604-5163
E-mail: inahmex@telecomm.net.mx
Internet: www.telecomm.net.mx/encrym
Founded 1968
Academic year: September to July
Director: M. A. Mercedes Gomez-Urquiza
Deputy Director: Daniel Camacho Uribe
Head of Academic Extension: Gina Saldaña Lozano
Library of 15,000 vols
Number of teachers: 116
Number of students: 126

INSTITUTO TECNOLÓGICO AUTÓNOMO DE MÉXICO

Campus Río Hondo: Río Hondo 1, Col. Tizapán San Ángel, Del. Alvaro Obregón, 01000 México, DF
Campus Santa Teresa: Cetro de Investigación y Estudios de Posgrado (CIEP), Avda Camino Santa Teresa 930, Col. Héroes de Padierna, Del. Magdalena Contreras, 10700 México, DF
Telephone: (55) 5628-4000
Fax: (55) 5628-4102
E-mail: itam@itam.mx
Internet: www.itam.mx
Founded 1946
Academic year: January to December
President: Alberto Bailleres
Rector: Arturo Fernández Pérez
Library of 106,000 vols, 1,202 periodicals
Number of students: 3,500

Publication: *Revista Estudios* (4 a year)

Courses in business administration, economics, accounting, mathematics, law, computer sciences, public policy, literature, history, statistics and social sciences.

INSTITUTO TECNOLÓGICO DE BOCA DEL RIO

km 12 Carretera Veracruz–Córdoba, Apartado Postal 68, 94290 Boca del Río, Ver.
Telephone: (229) 986-0189
Fax: (229) 986-1894
E-mail: dir_ibtocadelrio@dgest.gob.mx
Internet: www.itbocadelrio.edu.mx
Founded 1957
Dependent on the Dirección General de Enseñanzas Tecnológicas (Min. of Education)
Language of instruction: Spanish
Academic year: August to June
Dir: Jorge Luis Hernandez Mortera
Library of 550 vols
Number of teachers: 150
Number of students: 1,420

INSTITUTO TECNOLÓGICO DE CELAYA

Avda Tecnológico y A. García Cubas s/n, Apdo Postal 57, 38010 Celaya, Gto
Telephone: (461) 611-7575
Fax: (461) 611-7979
E-mail: lince@itc.mx
Internet: www.itc.mx
Founded 1958
Director: Dr Juan Sillero Pérez
Academic Vice-Director: M.C. Samuel Domínguez Tamayo
Administrative Vice-Director: M.C. Ruben Martínez Balderas
Librarian: Lic. Teodoro Villalobos Salinas
Library of 16,600 vols
Number of students: 2,623

Publications: *Apertura*, *Pistas Educativas*

Courses in industrial engineering, mechanics, chemistry and biochemistry, production and business administration, computer systems, electronics.

INSTITUTO TECNOLÓGICO DE CHIHUAHUA

Ave. Tecnológico No 2909, 31310 Chihuahua, Chih.
Telephone: (614) 201-2000
Fax: (614) 413-5187
Internet: www.itch.edu.mx
Founded 1948
Dir: Ing. Leonel Gildardo Loya Pacheco
Admin. Vice-Dir: Ing. Juan de Dios Ruiz
Academic Vice-Dir: Ing. Antonio Treviño Ruiz
Library of 29,000 vols
Number of teachers: 350
Number of students: 4,400

Publication: *Electro* (1 a year)

Degree courses in industrial, electrical, mechanical, chemical, electronic and materials engineering; postgraduate courses in electronics; degree and postgraduate courses in administration.

INSTITUTO TECNOLÓGICO DE CIUDAD JUÁREZ

Avda Tecnológico 1340, 32500 Ciudad Juárez, Chih.
Telephone: (656) 688-2500
Fax: (656) 688-2501
E-mail: webmaster@itcj.edu.mx
Internet: www.itcj.edu.mx
Founded 1964

Director: Roberto Arana Moran
Vice-Directors: Humberto C. Morales Moreno (Administrative), Alfredo Estrada García (Academic), Salvador Sánchez Cruz (Academic Support)
Library of 13,300 vols
Number of teachers: 268
Number of students: 4,468

INSTITUTO TECNOLÓGICO DE CIUDAD MADERO

Avda 1° de Mayo esq. Sor Juana Inés de la Cruz s/n, Col. Los Mangos, 89440 Ciudad Madero, Tamaulipas
Telephone: (833) 357-4820
Fax: (833) 357-4820 ext. 1002
E-mail: wmaster@itcm.edu.mx
Internet: www.itcm.edu.mx/itcm06/html
Founded 1954
Dir: Ing. Juan Manuel Turrubiate Martínez
Library of 17,781 vols
Number of students: 5,000

INSTITUTO TECNOLÓGICO DE DURANGO

Blvd F. Pescador 1830 Ote. Durango, 34080 Durango
Telephone: (618) 818-5706
Fax: (618) 818-4813
E-mail: director@itdgo.mx.mx
Internet: www.anuies.mx/servicios/d_estrategicos/afiliadas/92.html
Founded 1948
Dependent on the Dirección General de Institutos Tecnológicos Regionales, SEP
Director: Ing. Tomás Palomino Solórzano
Librarian: Jesús Lau
Library of 19,000 vols
Number of teachers: 267
Number of students: 2,677

First degree courses in industrial engineering in electronics, electricity, biochemistry, mechanics, information science, chemistry and civil engineering; Masters in industrial planning, biochemistry, civil engineering.

INSTITUTO TECNOLÓGICO DE MÉRIDA

Avda Tecnológico km 5, Apdo Postal 9–11, 97118 Mérida, Yucatán
Telephone and fax (999) 944-8171
E-mail: itm@uxmal.itmerida.mx
Internet: www.itmerida.mx
Founded 1961
Academic year: August to June
Dir: Ing. Gelasio Luna Conzuelo
Vice-Dir for Admin.: Ing. William Ramírez Romero
Vice-Dir for Academic Affairs: Ing. Isidro Calderón Acosta
Vice-Dir for Planning: Ing. Herbert Loría Sunza
Librarian: Ing. Norina Lizarraga Cetina
Library of 20,000 vols
Number of teachers: 369
Number of students: 4,146

Publications: *La Quincena* (26 a year), *Revista del Centro de Graduados e Investigación* (4 a year).

INSTITUTO TECNOLÓGICO DE MORELIA

Avda Tecnológico 1500, Col. Lomas de Santiaguito, 58120 Morelia, Michoacán
Telephone: (443) 312-1570
Fax: (443) 312-1570 ext. 211
E-mail: direccion@itmorelia.edu.mx
Internet: www.itmorelia.edu.mx

Founded 1965
Director: Ing. IGNACIO LÓPEZ VALDOVINOS
Library of 15,000 vols
Number of students: 3,500
Courses in industrial engineering and iron and steel industry.

INSTITUTO TECNOLÓGICO DE OAXACA

Avda Ing. Victor Bravo Ahuja 125 esq. Calz. Tecnológico, 68030 Oaxaca de Juárez, Oax.
Telephone: (951) 501-5016
Internet: www.itox.mx
Founded 1968
Director: Ing. SERGIO ISIDRO LÓPEZ PÉREZ
Number of teachers: 280
Number of students: 3,000
Publication: *Itrosíntesis*
Courses in mechanical, electrical, chemical and civil engineering, business management and industrial planning.

INSTITUTO TECNOLÓGICO DE ORIZABA

Avda Oriente 9 no. 852, Col. Emiliano Zapata, 94320 Orizaba, Ver.
Telephone: (272) 724-4096
Fax: (272) 725-1728
E-mail: centrodeinformacion@itorizaba.edu.mx
Internet: ssfe.itorizaba.edu.mx/joomla
Founded 1957
Courses in chemical, industrial mechanical, electrical and electronic engineering, and computer science
Dir: Ing. JUAN RENE CABALLERO GONZÁLEZ
Administrative Asst Dir: Ing. BLAS REYES T.
Asst Dir for Planning: Ing. ROSENDO MARTÍNEZ
Academic Asst Dir: Ing. KIKEY GONZÁLEZ F.
Number of teachers: 308
Number of students: 2,994

INSTITUTO TECNOLÓGICO DE QUERÉTARO

Avda Tecnológico s/n esq. Escobedo, Col. Centro, 76000 Querétaro, Qro
Telephone: (442) 227-4400
Fax: (442) 216-9931
E-mail: webmaster@itq.edu.mx
Internet: www.itq.edu.mx
Founded 1967

Courses in industrial and mechanical engineering, architecture, systems engineering, electrical and electronic engineering and industrial administration
Dir: Ing. OSCAR ARMANDO LÓPEZ GONZÁLEZ
Academic Vice-Dir: Ing. JORGE MARIO ELIAS MARTÍNEZ
Vice-Dir for Planning and Extension: Ing. FERNANDO QUIROZ GATICA
Library of 28,000 vols
Number of teachers: 314
Number of students: 3,596

INSTITUTO TECNOLÓGICO DE SALTILLO

V. Carranza 2400, Col. Tecnológico, 25280 Saltillo, Coahuila
Telephone and fax (844) 438-9500
E-mail: webm@its.mx
Internet: www.its.mx
Founded 1951
Courses in industrial, metallurgical and computer science engineering and technology
Dir: M.C. JESÚS CONTRERAS GARCÍA
Library: c. 15,100 vols
Number of students: 3,000
Publications: *Boletín de Fundación*, *Boletín de Microenseñanza*, *Boletín de Seguridad Industrial*, faculty bulletins.

INSTITUTO TECNOLÓGICO DE SONORA

5 de Febrero 818 Sur, Col. Centro, 85000 Ciudad Obregón, Son.
Telephone: (644) 410-0900
E-mail: agutierrez@itson.mx
Internet: www.itson.mx
Founded 1955 as Preparatory school, became University in 1973
Courses in biotechnological, electrical, electronic, systems and industrial, civil, chemical and agricultural engineering, chemistry, business administration, accounting, management information systems, education, psychology, veterinary medicine, natural resources and water resources management
Rector: Mtro. GONZALO RODRÍGUEZ VILLANUEVA
Vice-Rector for Academic Affairs: Lic. JAVIER VALES GARCÍA
Vice-Rector for Administrative Affairs: Lic. JORGE OROZCO PARRA
Library of 87,000 vols

Number of teachers: 914
Number of students: 16,355
Publications: *ITSON-DIEP* (research reports, 2 a year), *Revista de la Sociedad Académica* (2 a year).

INSTITUTO TECNOLÓGICO Y DE ESTUDIOS SUPERIORES DE OCCIDENTE, AC

Periférico Sur Manuel Gómez Morín 8585, 45604 Tlaquepaque, Jal.
Telephone: (33) 3669-3434
Fax: (33) 3669-3435
E-mail: rectoria@iteso.mx
Internet: www.iteso.mx
Founded 1957
Academic year: January to December
Undergraduate courses in architecture, business administration, communications, environmental engineering, finance, international business, international relations, management of information systems, mechanical engineering, philosophy, public accountancy, civil, industrial and electronic engineering, chemical processing and administration, computer systems, design, psychology, industrial relations, educational sciences, law, marketing. Postgraduate courses in business management, education, engineering, communications, human development, industrial electronics, applied information systems, global marketing, politics, public management
Rector: Dr JUAN LUIS OROZCO HERNÁNDEZ
Library of 113,000 vols
Number of teachers: 945
Number of students: 6,796
Publications: *Huella* (3 a year), *Renglones* (Review 3 a year), *Sinectica* (2 a year).

School of Music

Conservatorio Nacional de Música (National Conservatoire): Avda Presidente Mazaryk 582, Col. Polanco, México, DF; tel. (55) 5280-6347; e-mail cnm@correo.inba.gob.mx; internet www.conservatorianos.com.mx; f. 1866; library: 48,900 vols; 170 teachers; Dir Maestro LEOPOLDO TELLEZ; publs *Gaceta de la Biblioteca*, *Heterofonía*.

FEDERATED STATES OF MICRONESIA

The Higher Education System

The Federated States of Micronesia comprise the four named and autonomous states, namely Chuuk, Pohnpei, Yap and Kosrae. It is a small, developing nation made up of 87 islands and islets spread over four major island groups in 2.5m. sq. km of the Western Pacific. Its citizens speak 17 different languages and dialects. Higher education is provided by one institution: the College of Micronesia. The Department of Education is the government ministry responsible for overseeing the education sector. Education is governed by Act PL 7-97, which was approved by Congress in 1992. In 2005/06 there were approximately 2,283 students studying at college level.

Regulatory Body

GOVERNMENT

Department of Education: POB PS-87, Palikir, Pohnpei, 96941; tel. 320-2643; fax 320-5500; Sec. CASIANO SHONIBER.

Learned Societies

NATURAL SCIENCES

Chuuk Conservation Society: Chuuk; f. 2005 to protect and preserve local natural resources in order to sustain community livelihoods; Chair JOE KONNO; Sec. MARY ROSE NAKAYAMA.

Conservation Society of Pohnpei: POB 2461, Kolonia, Pohnpei 96941; tel. 320-5409; fax 320-5063; e-mail csp@mail.fm; internet www.serehd.org; f. 1998; aims to increase community involvement in the conservation and management of Pohnpei's natural resources, to build local capacity through public and private partnerships, to develop alternatives to unsustainable practices and to promote laws and policies that support these objectives; current programmes: marine, terrestrial and educational awareness; Exec. Dir PATTERSON SHED.

Kosrae Conservation and Safety Organization: POB 539, Tofol, Kosrae 96944; tel. 370-3391; fax 370-3000; e-mail kcso@mail.fm; promotes conservation of the natural environment and awareness creation; Chair. MADISON NENA; Exec. Dir ANDY GEORGE.

Micronesia Conservation Trust: POB 2177, Kolonia, Pohnpei 96941; tel. 320-5670; fax 320-8903; e-mail mct@mail.fm; internet mctconservation.org; f. 2002; provides long-term, sustained funding to community-based orgs and other NGOs through a grants programme; supports biodiversity conservation and related sustainable devt; Exec. Dir WILLIAM KOSTKA; Deputy Exec. Dir LISA RANAHAN ANDON.

Yap Institute of Natural Science: POB 215, Colonia, Yap 96943; tel. 350-4630; e-mail mfalanruw@mail.fm; promotes sustainable use of local resources; Dir Dr MARJORIE C. FALANRUW.

Libraries and Archives

Kolonia

College of Micronesia Learning Resources Center: POB 159, Kolonia, Pohnpei 96941; tel. 320-2480; e-mail comfsmlib@comfsm.fm; internet www.comfsm.fm/library; comprises general library, serials section, US Govt documents library; Micronesia-Pacific Research Center; depository for the Secretariat of the Pacific Community materials and a partial depository for UN documents; Nat. Archives contains materials from the Navy and Trust Territory eras; 34,000 vols; Dir SUE CALDWELL.

Pohnpei Public Library: POB 284, Kolonia, Pohnpei 96941; tel. 320-2423; fax 320-2693; e-mail ppl@mail.fm; f. 1987; 30,000 vols; 1 mobile library; Head Librarian LESTER EZEKIAS.

Palikir

Congress Library: POB PS3, Palikir, Pohnpei 96941; tel. 320-2324; fax 320-5122; e-mail liwi@mail.fm; f. 1978; library of the legislative br. of nat. Govt; 15,000 vols, 30 periodicals; Librarian MARIETA J. PAIDEN.

Museums and Galleries

Kolonia

Lidorkini Museum: Kolonia, Pohnpei 96941; tel. 320-5299; artefacts from the Nan Madol site, pounding stones, handicrafts, items from the Japanese occupation of the islands (1914–44); Curator HENTER LAWRENCE.

Tofol

Kosrae State Museum: Tofol, Kosrae; artefacts, photographs of Kosrae history and culture.

College

College of Micronesia: National Campus, POB 159, Kolonia, Pohnpei 96941; tel. 320-2480; fax 320-2479; e-mail national@comfsm.fm; internet www.comfsm.fm; f. 1963; offers assoc. of arts and assoc. of science degrees; other campuses located in Chuuk State, Kosrae State, Pohnpei State and Yap State; its Fisheries and Maritime Institute is located on Yap; library: see Libraries and Archives; 798 students; Pres. SPENSIN JAMES.

MOLDOVA

The Higher Education System

The oldest institution of higher education is the Academia de Mizică, Teatru și Arte Plastice (Academy of Music, Theatre and Fine Arts of Republic of Moldova—founded 1919), which was established when the former Russian territory of Bessarabia was part of Romania. Other institutions dating from the period of Romanian control include Universitatea Agrară de Stat din Moldova (Moldovan State Agrarian University—founded 1933) and Universitatea Pedagogică de Stat 'Ion Creangă' (Ion Creangă Pedagogical State University—founded 1940). However, the USSR refused to recognize Romania's claims to the territory, and in October 1924 formed a Moldovan Autonomous Soviet Socialist Republic (ASSR) on the eastern side of the Dniester, in the Ukrainian Soviet Socialist Republic (SSR). The current institution of Universitatea de Stat din Tiraspol (Tiraspol State University), was founded in the Moldovan ASSR in 1930 (it was re-located to the capital Chișinău in 1992). In June 1940 Romania was forced to cede Bessarabia and northern Bucovina to the USSR, under the terms of the Treaty of Non-Aggression (the 'Molotov-Ribbentrop Pact'), concluded with Nazi Germany in August 1939. Northern Bucovina, southern Bessarabia and the Kotovsk-Balța region of the Moldovan ASSR were incorporated into the Ukrainian SSR. The remaining parts of the Moldovan ASSR and of Bessarabia were merged to form the Moldovan SSR, which formally joined the USSR on 2 August 1940 and remained under Soviet rule until independence was declared in 1991. Following independence the self-styled 'Transnistrian Moldovan Republic' (formerly 'Transnistrian Moldovan SSR') was declared on the eastern side of the Dniester. The Law on Education of 1995 classified higher education as either long-term study programmes offered by universities, academies, and institutes or short-term study programmes offered by vocational colleges. In 2000 Moldova adopted the European Credit Transfer System in public universities and from 2005 the ECTS was introduced in all higher education institutions. Moldova has been a full member of the Bologna process since 2005. In 2007/08 122,939 students were enrolled in universities and 31,307 in colleges of higher education.

Admission to higher education is determined by fixed quotas (numerus clausus/numerus fixus) drawn up by the Government. Consequently, students are usually required to sit a competitive entrance examination as well as holding the Diplomă de Bacalaureat, the main secondary school-leavers' certificate. Undergraduate degrees are divided into short- and long-term programmes of study. The Diploma of Short-Term Higher Education (Diplomă de Studii Superioare de Scurtă Durată) is the primary programme of short-term study and lasts two to three years. These are the only kinds of degrees offered by vocational colleges. The Diplomă de Licență is a long-term programme of study lasting four to six years and culminates with the defence of a thesis. Students who do not defend their thesis are awarded the Diploma of University Higher Studies (Diplomă de Studii Superioare Universitare). The first postgraduate-level degree is the Diplomă de Magistru, awarded upon completion of one to two years of research following the Diplomă de Licență. There are two doctoral degrees, Doctor of Sciences (Doctor în Stiinte) and Doctor Abilitat. The Doctor în Stiinte is awarded after three years of research and successful defence of a thesis. Doctor Abilitat is a post-doctoral degree, awarded after two years following the Doctor în Stiinte.

Post-secondary technical and vocational education is available mainly through colleges and is regarded as short-term higher education.

The National Council for Accreditation and Attestation is the body responsible for the accreditation of institutions in the field of science and the attestation of scientific and scientific-pedagogical personnel of higher qualification. It gives out certificates of accreditation on the basis of which scientific institutes are financed from the state budget. It also approves the programmes of examinations for doctoral students and competitors, confers the scientific degrees, scientific and scientific-pedagogical ranks and gives out the diplomas of scientific degrees and certificates of scientific and scientific-pedagogical ranks.

Regulatory and Representative Bodies

GOVERNMENT

Ministry of Culture and Tourism: 2033 Chișinău, Piața Marii Adunări Naționale 1, Of. 326; tel. (22) 22-76-20; fax (22) 23-23-88; e-mail culture@turism.md; internet www.turism.md; Minister ARTUR COZMA.

Ministry of Education and Youth: 2033 Chișinău, Piața Marii Adunări Naționale 1; tel. (22) 23-33-48; fax (22) 23-35-15; e-mail consilier@edu.md; internet www.edu.md; Minister LARISA SAVGA.

ACCREDITATION

Consiliul Național pentru Acreditare și Atestare (CNAA) (National Council for Accreditation and Attestation): 2004 Chișinău, Stefan cel Mare bd 180; tel. and fax (22) 29-62-71; e-mail cnaa@cnaa.md; internet www.cnaa.md; f. 2004; 17 mems; Pres. Acad. Dr hab. VALERIU CANTER; Vice-Pres. Acad. Dr hab. SIMION TOMA; Vice-Pres. Acad. Dr hab. VEACESLAV PERJU; Scientific Sec. Dr GHEORGHE GLADCHI.

Department of Higher Education Institution Accreditation: 2033 Chișinău, Piața Marii Adunări Naționale 1; tel. (22) 21-03-79; fax (22) 23-32-83; e-mail mrotaru@inbox.ru; Dir MICHAEL EFIMOVICH ROTARU.

ENIC/NARIC Moldova: Information and Qualification Recognition Office, International Relations and European Integration Department, Ministry of Education and Youth, Piața Marii Adunări Naționale 1, 2033 Chișinău; tel. (22) 27-75-69; fax (22) 23-37-85; e-mail recognition@edu.md; internet www.edu.md; Head ISAC RODICA.

Learned Societies

GENERAL

Academy of Sciences of Moldova: 2001 Chișinău, bd. Ștefan cel Mare și Sfint 1; tel. (22) 27-14-78; fax (22) 54-28-23; e-mail consiliu@asm.md; internet www.asm.md; f. 1946; sections of agricultural sciences (Academician-Co-ordinator SIMION TOMA), biological, chemical and ecological sciences (Academician-Co-ordinator ION TODERAS), economical and mathematical sciences (Academician-Co-ordinator GHEORGE MIS-

COI), humanities and arts (Academician-Co-ordinator ALEXANDRU ROSCA), medical sciences (Academician-Co-ordinator GHEORGHE GHIDIRIM), physical and engineering sciences (Academician-Co-ordinator VALERIUS CANTER); 112 mems (48 full, 64 corresp.); attached research institutes: see Research Institutes; library: see Libraries and Archives; Pres. GHEORGHE DUCA; General Scientific Sec. BORIS GAINA; publs Buletinul (Biological and Chemical and Agricultural Sciences, 4 a year, Mathematics, 3 a year), Computer Science Journal of Moldova (4 a year), Economy and Sociology (4 a year), Elektronnaya Obrabotka Materialov (Electronic Processing of Materials, 6 a year), Moldavian Journal of Physical Sciences (4 a year), Revista de Filozofie și Drept (Journal of Philosophy and Law, 6 a year), Revista de Istorie a Moldovei (Moldovan Historical Journal, 4 a year), Revista de Lingvistică și Știință Literară (Journal of Linguistics and Study of Literature, 6 a year).

HISTORY, GEOGRAPHY AND ARCHAEOLOGY

Geographical Society of Moldova: 2028 Chișinău, str. Academiei 1; tel. (22) 73-96-18;

e-mail geography_md@yahoo.com; Head of Laboratory Dr NICOLAE BOBOC.

LANGUAGE AND LITERATURE

Alliance Française: 2012 Chişinău, str. Sfatul Tarii 18; tel. (22) 23-45-10; fax (22) 23-47-81; e-mail alfr@alfr.md; internet www .alfr.md; f. 1993; offers courses and exams in French language and culture and promotes cultural exchange with France and French-speaking countries; has a media library; Dir EMMANUEL SKOULIOS; Deputy Dir ADRIAN CIBOTARU.

Goethe-Institut: see entry in Romania chapter.

PEN Centre of Moldova: 2012 Chişinău, bd. Ştefan cel Mare şi Sfînt 134, PO 12, POB 231; tel. (22) 23-24-79; e-mail contrafort@ moldnet.md; f. 1991; 25 mems; Pres. VITALIE CIOBANU.

NATURAL SCIENCES

Biological Sciences

Entomological Society of Moldova: 2028 Chişinău, str. Academiei 1; tel. (22) 73-98-96; Chair B. V. VEREŞCIAGHIN.

Microbiological Society of Moldova: 2028 Chişinău, str. Academiei 1; tel. (22) 73-98-78; e-mail acadrudic@yahoo.com; Chair. Prof. VALERY RUDIC.

Ornithological Society of Moldova: 2028 Chişinău, str. Academiei 1; tel. (22) 73-75-09; Chair. (vacant).

Society of Botanists of Moldova: 2002 Chişinău, str. Pădurii 18; tel. (22) 52-38-96; Chair. A. G. NEGRU.

Society of Geneticists of Moldova: 2049 Chişinău, str. Mirceşti 44; tel. (22) 43-23-08; Chair. V. D. SIMINEL.

Society of Hydrobiologists and Ichthyologists: 2028 Chişinău, str. Academiei 1; tel. (22) 57-75-30; fax (22) 73-12-55; e-mail izoolasm@mail.md; f. 1968; 36 mems; Chair. Prof. ION TODERAŞ.

Society of Plant Physiology and Biochemistry of Moldova: 2002 Chişinău, str. Pădurii 26/1; tel. (22) 56-79-59; fax (22) 55-00-26; e-mail sbiochim@bio.asm.md; f. 1988; 40 mems; Pres. Prof. SIMION I. TOMA.

Teriological Society of Moldova: 2028 Chişinău, str. Academiei 1 (Room 220); tel. (22) 72-55-66; fax (22) 73-12-55; e-mail amunteanu@as.md; 19 mems; Chair. Dr ANDREI MUNTEANU.

Physical Sciences

Physical Society of Moldova: 2928 Chişinău, str. Academiei 5; tel. and fax (22) 73-90-60; e-mail kantser@lises.asm.md; Chair. Acad. Prof. VALERIU KANTSER.

RELIGION, SOCIOLOGY AND ANTHROPOLOGY

Moldovan Sociological Association: 3121 Balti, str. Puşkin 38; tel. (231) 2-44-79; Chair. N. V. ŢURCANU.

Research Institutes

AGRICULTURE, FISHERIES AND VETERINARY SCIENCE

National Institute for Viticulture and Vinification: 2070 Chişinău, s. Codru, str. Vierul 59; tel. (22) 28-54-31; e-mail invv@ moldova.md; internet www.agriculture.md/ ispha; f. 1909; prepares nat. strategies for the devt of viticulture; creates new types of grapes, resistant to diseases and frost; elaboration of modern technologies for producing cuttings without viruses; devt of storage

methods and use of grapes with nutritive and therapeutic purposes; creation of new wines, champagnes and liqueurs; design and sale of machines and equipment for viticulture.

Research Institute for Maize and Sorghum: 4834 Criuleni, s. Paşcani; tel. and fax (22) 24-10-07; e-mail porumbeni@agriculture .md; internet www.agriculture.md/ porumbeni; f. 1973; research into the improvement of seed strains, seed production and cultivation of maize, sorghum, vegetables, medicinal and aromatic plants; Dir Dr MICU VASILE.

Scientific and Practical Institute of Biotechnologies in Animal Husbandry and Veterinary Medicine: 6525 Anenii Noii, v. Maximovca; tel. (22) 35-93-50; fax (22) 35-93-51; e-mail shumanskii@mail.ru; f. 1958; devt of scientific base and preservation of genetic fund of agricultural animals; devt of technologies of breeding, reproduction, and exploitation of animals; devt of technologies for production and storage of animal feeds; devt of new procedures for prevention and treatment of animal diseases; library of 19,000 vols; Dir Dr hab. ANDREI SHUMANSKII; publ. *Scientific Transactions* (1 a year).

Tobacco Research Institute: Chişinău, s. Gratieşti, str. Prieteniei 1; tel. (22) 46-06-86; fax (22) 46-04-87; e-mail tutunix@agriculture .md; internet www.agriculture.md/tutun; f. 1968; Dir Dr TUDOR ZAGORNEANU.

ECONOMICS, LAW AND POLITICS

Centre for the Study of Marketing Problems: 2001 Chişinău, bd. Ştefan cel Mare şi Sfînt; tel. and fax (22) 26-23-91; attached to Acad. of Sciences of Moldova; Dir P. V. COJUCARI.

Institute of Economic Research: 2001 Chişinău, bd. Ştefan cel Mare şi Sfînt 1; tel. (22) 26-24-01; attached to Acad. of Sciences of Moldova; Dir V. CIOBANU.

FINE AND PERFORMING ARTS

Institute of the History and Theory of Art: 2001 Chişinău, bd. Ştefan cel Mare şi Sfînt 1; tel. (22) 26-06-02; fax (22) 22-33-48; f. 1991; attached to Acad. of Sciences of Moldova; fine art, architecture, music, performing arts; Dir LEONID M. CEMORTAN; publ. *Arta* (2 series: fine arts and architecture, 1 a year, music and the performing arts, 1 a year).

HISTORY, GEOGRAPHY AND ARCHAEOLOGY

Institute of Archaeology and Ancient History: 2712 Chişinău, str. Mitropolitul Banulescu-Bodoni 35; tel. and fax (22) 22-22-42; attached to Acad. of Sciences of Moldova; Dir VALENTIN DERGACEV.

Institute of Ecology and Geography: 2028 Chişinău, str. Academiei 1; tel. and fax (22) 73-98-38; e-mail ieg@asm.md; internet ieg.asm.md; f. 1992; attached to Acad. of Sciences of Moldova; scientific and applied research in the fields of geography and ecology; Dir Acad. TATIANA S. CONSTANTINOVA; publs *Buletinul Academiei de Stiinte a Moldovei. Stiintele vietii, Mediul Ambiant*.

Institute of History: 2012 Chişinău, str. 31 August 1989 82; tel. (22) 23-33-10; e-mail iist_asm@mtc.md; f. 1958; attached to Acad. of Sciences of Moldova; Dir DEMIR DRAGNEV.

LANGUAGE AND LITERATURE

Institute of Linguistics: 2012 Chişinău, str. 31 August 1989 82; tel. (22) 23-33-05; fax (22) 23-77-52; e-mail lingva@moldova.md; f. 1991; attached to Acad. of Sciences of Moldova; library of 10,000 vols; Dir Acad.

SILVIU BEREJAN; publ. *Revistă de Lingvistică şi Ştiinţă Literară* (6 a year).

Institute of Literature and Folklore: 2001 Chişinău, bd. Ştefan cel Mare şi Sfînt; tel. (22) 27-27-19; e-mail ilfasm@yahoo.it; f. 1991; attached to Acad. of Sciences of Moldova; Dir Acad. HARALAMBIE CORBU; publ. *Revistă de Lingvistică şi Ştiinţă Literară* (6 a year).

MEDICINE

National Centre of Preventive Medicine: 2025 Chişinău, str. Gh. Asachi 67A; tel. (22) 72-96-47; fax (22) 72-97-25; Dir-Gen. MIHAI MAGDEI.

NATURAL SCIENCES

Biological Sciences

Botanical Garden Institute of the Academy of Sciences of Moldova: 2002 Chişinău, str. Pădurii 18; tel. (22) 52-38-98; fax (22) 52-04-43; e-mail gradinabotanica@ moldnet.md; internet www.gradinabotanica .asm.md; f. 1950; attached to Acad. of Sciences of Moldova; more than 10,000 species of plants; library of 43,000 items; Dir Dr ALEXANDRU TELEUTA; publ. *Revista Botanica*.

Centre for Pathology and Pathobiology: 2004 Chişinău, str. 31 August 1989 151; tel. (22) 22-75-19; attached to Acad. of Sciences of Moldova; Dir. Acad. VASILE ANESTIADE.

Institute of Genetics and Plant Physiology: 2002 Chişinău, str. Pădurii 20; tel. (22) 77-04-47; fax (22) 55-61-80; e-mail dobynda@mail.md; f. 2005 by merger of the Institute of Genetics, the Institute of Plant Physiology, the aromatic and medicinal plant branch of the Research Institute for Maize and Sorghum, and the Centre of Plant Genetic Resources; attached to Acad. of Sciences of Moldova; Dir ANATOL JACOTĂ.

Institute of Microbiology and Biotechnology: 2028 Chişinău, str. Academiei 1; tel. (22) 72-55-24; fax (22) 72-57-54; e-mail microbiologie@mail.md; internet www.asm .md; f. 1992; attached to Acad. of Sciences of Moldova; Dir Acad. VALERIU RUDIC; publ. *Bulletin* (2 a year).

Institute of Physiology and Sanocreatology: 2028 Chişinău, str. Academiei 1; tel. (22) 72-51-55; attached to Acad. of Sciences of Moldova; specializes in study of the pancreas; Dir Acad. TEODOR FURDUI.

Institute of Zoology: 2028 Chişinău, str. Academiei 1; tel. (22) 73-98-09; fax (22) 73-12-55; e-mail izoolasm@mail.md; attached to Acad. of Sciences of Moldova; Dir ION TODERAŞ.

Research Institute for Plant Protection and Agricultural Ecology (Institutul de Protecţie a Plantelor şi Agricultură Ecologică): 2060 Chişinău, str. Padurii, 26/1; tel. (22) 77-04-66; fax (22) 77-96-41; e-mail volosciuc@netscape.net; internet agriculture .md/icpp/index.shtml; attached to Acad. of Sciences of Moldova; Dir LEONID VOLOSCIUC.

Mathematical Sciences

Institute of Mathematics and Computer Science: 2028 Chişinău, str. Academiei 5; tel. (22) 72-59-82; fax (22) 73-80-27; e-mail imam@math.md; internet www.math.md; f. 1964; attached to Acad. of Sciences of Moldova; Dir Dr hab. COJOCARU SVETLANA; Scientific Sec. Dr NAVAL ELVIRA; publs *Buletinul Academiei de Ştiinţe a Republicii Moldova: Matematica* (3 a year), *Computer Science Journal of Moldova* (3 a year), *Quasigroups and Related Systems* (2 a year).

Physical Sciences

Center of Experimental Seismology, Central Station: 2028 Chişinău, str. Academiei 3; tel. (22) 73-71-79; attached to Acad. of Sciences of Moldova; forms the central unit of the Institute of Geophysics and Geology's seismic network; operates in conjunction with four local stations and four strong-motion recorders; Dir I. ILIEŞ.

Institute of Applied Physics: 2028 Chişinău, str. Academiei 5; tel. (22) 73-81-50; fax (22) 73-81-49; e-mail director@phys.asm.md; internet www.phys.asm.md; f. 1964; attached to Acad. of Sciences of Moldova; Dir Prof. L. KULYUK; publs *Moldavian Journal of Physical Sciences* (4 a year), *Surface Engineering and Applied Electrochemistry* (6 a year).

Institute of Chemistry: 2028 Chişinău, str. Academiei 3; tel. (22) 72-54-90; fax (22) 73-99-54; e-mail ichem@asm.md; f. 1959; attached to Acad. of Sciences of Moldova; Dir Dr hab. TUDOR LUPASCU.

Institute of Geology and Seismology: 2028 Chişinău, str. Academiei 3; tel. (22) 73-90-27; fax (22) 73-97-29; e-mail cancelaria@igs.asm.md; internet www.igs.asm.md; f. 1967, present name 2006; attached to Acad. of Sciences of Moldova; scientific research; Dir Prof. Dr VASILE ALCAZ; Scientific Sec. IGOR NICOARA; publ. *Buletinul Institutului de Geologie si Seismologie al Academiei de Stiinte a Moldovei.*

RELIGION, SOCIOLOGY AND ANTHROPOLOGY

Institute of Ethnography and Folklore: 2001 Chişinău, bd. Ştefan cel Mare şi Sfint 1; tel. (22) 26-45-14; f. 1991; attached to Acad. of Sciences of Moldova; Dir N. A. DEMCENCO; publ. *Revista de Etnologie* (1 a year).

Institute of National Minorities Studies: 2001 Chişinău, bd. Ştefan cel Mare şi Sfint 1; tel. (22) 26-44-91; attached to Acad. of Sciences of Moldova; Dir C. F. POPOVICI.

Institute of Philosophy, Sociology and Political Sciences: 2001 Chişinău, bd. Ştefan cel Mare şi Sfint 1; tel. (22) 27-05-37; fax (22) 27-14-69; e-mail ifilos@cc.acad.md; internet www.asm.md; attached to Acad. of Sciences of Moldova; f. 2006; philosophy; sociology; political sciences; mythology; history of religion; social-demographic researches on families; 54 mems; Dir Dr ION RUSANDU; publs *Iconomie şi Sociologie* (Economy and Sociology), *Revistă de Filosofie şi Drept* (Philosophy and Law).

TECHNOLOGY

Institute of Power Engineering: 2028 Chişinău, str. Academiei 5; tel. (22) 72-70-40; fax (22) 73-53-86; e-mail mkiorsak@cc.asm.md; f. 1964; attached to Acad. of Sciences of Moldova; Dir Dr MIHAI V. CHIORSAC.

Libraries and Archives
Bălţi

Bălţi Municipal Library: 3121 Bălţi, str. A. Puşkin 34; tel. (231) 2-34-59; f. 1880; Dir INGA COJOCARU.

Chişinău

Central Scientific Library 'Andrei Lupan' of the Academy of Sciences of Moldova: 2028 Chişinău, Str. Academiei 5A; tel. (22) 72-74-01; fax (22) 73-98-29; e-mail library@asm.md; internet www.amlib.asm.md; f. 1947; 1,406,887 vols; Dir AURELIA HANGANU.

Centre for Scientific Information in the Social Sciences: 2001 Chişinău, bd. Ştefan cel Mare şi Sfint 1; tel. (22) 23-23-39;

attached to Acad. of Sciences of Moldova; Dir V. I. MOCREAC.

Moldova State University Library: 2009 Chişinău, str. A. Mateevici 60; tel. (22) 57-75-05; e-mail library@usm.md; internet www.usm.md/bcu; f. 1946; 1,810,000 vols; Dir ECATERINA ZASMENCO.

National Library of the Republic of Moldova: 2012 Chişinău, str. 31 August 1989 78A; tel. and fax (22) 22-14-75; e-mail bnrm@bnrm.md; internet www.bnrm.md; f. 1832; national library and principal depository of Moldova; national centre for inter-library loans; national centre for library automation and information; national centre for library science; 2,507,055 vols, 834 periodicals; Dir A. A. RĂU.

Scientific and Technical Library of Moldova: Chişinău, str. Creanga 45; tel. (22) 62-87-42; fax (22) 62-34-47; f. 1968; 560,000 vols, 11,000,000 patents, 750,000 standards; Dir P. T. RACU.

Tighina

Tighina County Public Library: Tighina; e-mail bpjt@fromru.com; internet ournet.md/~bpjt; f. 1943; 3 brs; 106,787 vols; Dir LARISA CAMENSCIC.

Museums
Chişinău

National Museum of Archaeology and History of Moldova: str. 31 August nr. 121A, Chişinău 2012; tel. (22) 244325; fax (22) 244326; e-mail museum@starnet.md; internet www.nationalmuseum.md; f. 1983; museum pedagogy, scientific exhibitions; Gen. Dir Dr hab. EUGEN SAVA.

National Museum of Fine Arts of Moldova: Chişinău, str. 31 August 1989 115; tel. (22) 24-17-30; f. 1944; Dir VASILE NEGRUŢĂ.

Universities

UNIVERSITATEA AGRARĂ DE STAT DIN MOLDOVA
(Moldovan State Agrarian University)

2049 Chişinău, str. Mirceşti 44
Telephone: (22) 31-22-58
Fax: (22) 31-22-76
E-mail: cimpoies@uasm.md
Internet: www.uasm.md
Founded 1933
State control
Languages of instruction: Romanian, English, Russian
Rector: Prof. Dr GHEORGHE P. CIMPOES
Library of 789,000 vols
Number of teachers: 400
Number of students: 6,400 (3,700 on campus, 2,700 distance)

DEANS

Faculty of Accountancy: Assoc. Prof. Dr VERONICA PRISACARU
Faculty of Agricultural Engineering and Transport: Assoc. Prof. Dr GRIGORE MARIAN
Faculty of Agronomy: Assoc. Prof. Dr MIHAI RURAC
Faculty of Animal Husbandry and Biotechnology: Prof. Dr NICOLAE EREMIA
Faculty of Economics: Assoc. Prof. Dr PETRU TOMITA
Faculty of Horticulture: Prof. Dr VALERIAN BALAN
Faculty of Land Surveying and Law: Prof. Dr TEODOR MORARU

Faculty of Veterinary Medicine: Assoc. Prof. Dr GHEORGHE DONICA

UNIVERSITATEA COOPERATIST COMERCIALĂ DIN MOLDOVEI
(Cooperative Trade University of Moldova)

2027 Chişinău, bd. Gagarin 8
Telephone: (22) 27-07-84
Fax: (22) 54-12-10
E-mail: webmaster@uccm.md
Internet: www.uccm.md
Founded 1993
State control
Languages of instruction: French, German, Russian, Spanish, Ukranian
Rector: Dr TUDOR MALECA
Pro-Rector: LARISA ŞAVGA
Library of 92,000 vols
Number of teachers: 200
Number of students: 1,200

DEANS

Faculty of Accountancy and Business Informatics: Dr SERGIU OPREA
Faculty of Management and Economics: Dr ELENA GRAUR
Faculty of Marketing and the Science of Commodities: Dr FEODOSIE PITUŞCAN
Faculty of Part-Time Studies: Dr SVETLANA MUŞTUC

UNIVERSITATEA DE STAT DIN BĂLŢI 'ALECU RUSSO'
(Alecu Russo Balti State University)

3121 Balti, 38 Puskin str.
Telephone: (231) 2-30-66
Fax: (231) 2-30-39
E-mail: rectorat@usb.md
Internet: www.usb.md
Founded 1945
State control
Languages of instruction: English, French, German, Romanian, Russian, Spanish, Ukrainian
Academic year: September to June
Rector: Prof. Dr Hab. GHEORGHE POPA
First Vice-Rector for Didactic Activity: Dr ALEXANDRU BALANICI
Vice-Rector for Scientific Activity: Dr MARIA ŞLEAHTIŢCHI
Vice-Rector for International Relations and European Integration: Dr VALENTINA PRIŢCAN
Vice-Rector for Part-Time Studies and Continuous Formation: Dr GHEORGHE NEAGU
Head of Univ. Scientific Library: ELENA HARCONIŢĂ
Library of 1,200,000 vols
Number of teachers: 315
Number of students: 7,210
Publications: *Art and Artistic Education*, *Biannual Journal of Applied Linguistics*, *Bulletin of Administration* (12 a year), *Scientific Papers* (every 2 years), *Speech and Context*, *University Yearbook* (every 5 years)

DEANS

Faculty of Economics: Dr ALA TRUSEVICI
Faculty of Foreign Languages and Literatures: Dr ELENA DRAGAN
Faculty of Law: Dr VEACESLAV PINZARI
Faculty of Music and Musical Pedagogy: Dr MARGARITA TETELEA
Faculty of Natural Science and Agro-Ecology: Dr STANISLAV STADNIC
Faculty of Pedagogy, Psychology and Social Work: Dr GALINA PETCU
Faculty of Philology: Dr NICOLAE LEAHU
Faculty of Technics, Physics, Mathematics and Informatics: Dr PAVEL TOPALA

UNIVERSITATEA DE STAT 'BOGDAN PETRICEICU HASDEU' DIN CAHUL
('Bogdan Petriceicu Hasdeu' State University of Cahul)

3901 Cahul, str. Piaţa Independenţei 1

Telephone: (299) 2-24-81

Founded 1999

Rector: Dr ION ŞIŞCANU.

UNIVERSITATEA DE STAT DIN COMRAT
(Comrat State University)

3900 Comrat, str. A. Galaţan 17

Telephone: (298) 2-43-45

Fax: (298) 2-40-91

E-mail: kdu@moldnet.md

Founded 1991

State control

Languages of instruction: Romanian, Bulgarian, Russian

Rector: Dr STEFANN VARBAN

Library of 50,200 vols

Number of teachers: 190

Number of students: 1,780

Faculties of agricultural technology, economics and national culture.

UNIVERSITATEA DE STAT DE MEDICINĂ ŞI FARMACIE 'NICOLAE TESTEMIŢANU' DIN REPUBLICA MOLDOVA
('Nicolae Testemiţanu' State Medical and Pharmaceutical University)

2004 Chişinău, bd. Ştefan cel Mare şi Sfint 165

Telephone: (22) 24-34-08

Fax: (22) 24-23-44

E-mail: rector@usmf.md

Internet: www.usmf.md

Founded 1945

State control

Languages of instruction: English, French, Romanian, Russian

Rector: Prof. Dr ION ABABII

Vice-Rector for Education and Social Issues: Dr EMIL CEBAN

Vice-Rector for Int. Relations: Dr VALERIU TEODOR CHICU

Vice-Rector for Quality Assurance and Integration in Education: Prof. Dr OLGA CERNETCHI

Vice-Rector for Scientific Activity: Prof. Dr VIOREL PRISACARI

Librarian: LIUBOVI KARNAEVA

Library of 950,369 vols, 511 periodicals

Number of teachers: 1,062

Number of students: 5,059

Publication: *Curieurul medical* (6 a year)

DEANS

Faculty of Dentistry: Prof. Dr ION LUPAN

Faculty of Medicine I: Prof. Dr GHEORGHE PLĂCINTĂ

Faculty of Medicine II: Prof. Dr MIHAIL GAVRILIUC

Faculty of Pharmacy: Dr NICOLAE CIOBANU

Faculty of Postgraduate Continuous Education: Prof. Dr EUGEN BENDELIC

Faculty of Postgraduate Residency and Fellowship Training: Prof. Dr VALERIU REVENCO

UNIVERSITATEA DE STAT DIN MOLDOVA
(Moldova State University)

2009 Chişinău, str. A. Mateevici 60

Telephone: (22) 57-74-01

Fax: (22) 24-42-48

E-mail: rector@usm.md

Internet: www.usm.md

Founded 1946

Private control

Languages of instruction: Romanian, Russian

Academic year: September to June

Rector: Prof. GHEORGHE CIOCANU

Vice-Rector: Prof. MIHAIL REVENCO

Vice-Rector: Assoc. Prof. OTILIA DANDARA

Vice-Rector: Assoc. Prof. TUDOR ARNAUT

Registrar: Assoc. Prof. TUDOR LUCHIAN

Librarian: ECATERINA ZASMENCO

Library: see Libraries and Archives

Number of teachers: 1,200

Number of students: 17,000

Publications: *Revista Nationala de Drept (National Journal of Law)* (12 a year), *Scientific Annals* (1 a year), *Universitatea* (12 a year)

DEANS

Faculty of Biology and Soil Science: MIHAIL LESANU

Faculty of Chemistry and Chemical Technology: VIORICA GLADCHI

Faculty of Economic Sciences: IGOR ENICOV

Faculty of Foreign Languages and Literature: LUDMILA ŽBANT

Faculty of History and Philosophy: IGOR SAROV

Faculty of International Relations, Political and Admin. Sciences: VASILE CUJBĂ

Faculty of Journalism and Communication: MIHAIL GUZUN

Faculty of Law: GHEORGHE AVORNIC

Faculty of Mathematics and Computer Science: ANDREI PERJAN

Faculty of Philology: CLAUDIA CEMARTAN

Faculty of Physics: PETRU GAŞIN

Faculty of Psychology and Educational Sciences: VLADIMIR GUTU

Faculty of Sociology and Social Work: MARIA BULGARU

UNIVERSITATEA DE STAT DIN TIRASPOL
(Tiraspol State University)

2069 Chişinău, str. Ghenadie Iablocichin 5

Telephone: (22) 75-49-24

Fax: (22) 75-49-24

E-mail: scs_ust@moldova.cc

Founded 1930; moved from Tiraspol to present location in 1992, due to civil unrest

State control

Languages of instruction: Romanian, Russian

Rector: Prof. LAURENTIU CALMUTCHI

Vice-Rector: Prof. IGOR POSTOLACHI

Number of students: 3,140

Publication: *Light* (12 a year)

DEANS

Faculty of Biology and Chemistry: BORIS NEDBALIUC

Faculty of Geography: ION MIRONOV

Faculty of Pedagogy: VASILE PANICO

Faculty of Philology: LUDMILA SOLOVIOV

Faculty of Physics and Mathematics: BORIS KOROLEVSKI

UNIVERSITATEA PEDAGOGICĂ DE STAT 'ION CREANGĂ'
(Chişinău 'Ion Creangă' Pedagogical State University)

2069 Chişinău, str. I. Creangă 1

Telephone and fax (22) 74-54-14

E-mail: creangaups@yahoo.com

Internet: www.upsc.md

Founded 1940

State control

Languages of instruction: Bulgarian, French, German, Italian, Russian, Spanish

Rector: Dr NICOLAE CHICUŞ

Number of teachers: 388

Number of students: 5,125 , (3,214 full-time, 1,911 part-time)

Publication: *Annual Scientific Edition Psychology. Special Pedagogy. Social Assistance Metaliteratura*

DEANS

Faculty of Computer Studies and Informational Technologies in Education: Dr PORT SERGIU

Faculty of Fine Arts: Dr VATAVU ALEXANDRU

Faculty of Foreign Languages and Literatures: Dr GOGU TAMARA

Faculty of History and Ethno-Pedagogy: Dr TVERDOHLEB AUREL

Faculty of Pedagogy: Dr SADOVEI LARISA

Faculty of Philology: Dr TOPOR GABRIELA

Faculty of Psychology and Special Psycho-Pedagogy: Dr PERJAN CAROLINA

Faculty of Teacher Training: Dr COJOCARU VASILE

UNIVERSITATEA TEHNICĂ A MOLDOVEI
(Technical University of Moldova)

2004 Chişinău, bd. Ştefan cel Mare şi Sfint 168

Telephone: (22) 23-78-61

Fax: (22) 23-22-52

E-mail: extrel@adm.utm.md

Internet: www.utm.md

Founded 1964

State control

Languages of instruction: Romanian, Russian

Academic year: September to June

Rector: Acad. Prof. ION BOSTAN

First Vice-Rector for Education: Prof. Dr PETRU TODOS

Vice-Rector for Administration and Capital Construction: PAVEL SPÂNU

Vice-Rector for Continuing Education and International Relations: Assoc. Prof. Dr VALENTIN AMARIEI

Vice-Rector for Part-Time Studies and Distance Education: Assoc. Prof. Dr TIMOFEI ANDROS

Vice-Rector for Research: Prof. Dr hab. VALERIAN DOROGAN

Vice-Rector for Studies and Relations with Colleges: Prof. Dr DUMITRU UNGUREANU

Dean of Students: Dr CONSTANTIN STRATAN

Library of 1,080,000 vols

Number of teachers: 750

Number of students: 17,000

Publications: *Meridian Inginersc* (4 a year), *Mesager* (newspaper, 12 a year)

DEANS

Faculty of Computers, Informatics and Microelectronics: Assoc. Prof. Dr ION BALMUS

Faculty of Economic Engineering and Business: Prof. Dr NICOLAE TURCANU

Faculty of Engineering and Management in Machine-Building: Assoc. Prof. Dr ALEXEI TOCA

Faculty of Engineering and Management in Mechanics: Assoc. Prof. Dr VASILE CARTOFEANU

Faculty of Power Engineering: Prof. Dr ION STRATAN

Faculty of Radioelectronics and Telecommunications: Assoc. Prof. Dr SERGIU ANDRONIC

Faculty of Surveying, Geodesy and Civil Engineering: Assoc. Prof. Dr VICTOR TOPOREŢ

Faculty of Technology and Management in the Food Industry: Assoc. Prof. Dr GRIGORE MUSTEATA

Faculty of the Textile Industry: Assoc. Prof. Dr CONSTANTIN SPINU

Faculty of Urban Planning and Architecture: Assoc. Prof. Dr NISTOR GROZAVU

Other Higher Educational Institutions

Academia de Mizică, Teatru şi Arte Plastice (Academy of Music, Theatre and Fine Arts of Republic of Moldova): 2014 Chişinău, str. A. Mateevici 87; tel. and fax (22) 22-19-49; e-mail usam@moldovacc.md; internet www.amtap.mdl.net; f. 1919; 1,500 students; Rector Dr AURELIAN DANILĂ.

Academia de Studii Economice (Academy of Economic Studies): 2005 Chişinău, str. Mitropolit Bănulescu-Bodoni 61; tel. (22) 22-41-28; fax (22) 22-19-68; e-mail r_gb@ase.md; internet www.ase.md; f. 1991; library: 317,000 vols; faculties of accountancy, business and administration, economics and law, finance, information technology and statistics and international economic relations; Rector Prof. Dr Hab. GRIGORII BELOSTECINIC.

Institutul Naţional de Educaţie Fizică şi Sport (National Institute of Physical Education and Sport): 2024 Chişinău, str. A. Doga 28/2; tel. (22) 49-40-81; fax (22) 49-76-71; e-mail inefs@mdl.net; faculties of part-time studies, pedagogy, sports and teacher development; Rector VEACESLAV MANOLACHE.

Institutul de Relaţii Internaţionale din Moldova (International Relations Institute of Moldova): 2009 Chişinău, str. Gh. Caşu 28/2; tel. (22) 73-59-43; fax (22) 73-59-42; e-mail infoirim@mail.ru; f. 2003; Rector CONSTANTIN MARIN.

MONACO

The Higher Education System

In 1861 Monaco became an independent state under the protection of France. There is only one public institution of higher education, the Académie de Musique et de Théâtre Foundation Prince Rainier III de Monaco (founded 1933), and one private higher educational institution, the International University of Monaco (founded 1986), a business school where instruction is conducted in English. The latter is recognized by the Department of National Education, Youth and Sports in Monaco and quality-assured by the Comité d'Evaluation et de Surveillance; it is the only higher education provider with this type of recognition in Monaco. Most Monégasque students undertake higher education in France. Post-secondary technical and vocational education is provided by the Sections de Technicien Supérieur. Programmes of study last for two years and lead to the award of the Higher Technician Certificate (Brevet de Technicien Supérieur).

Regulatory and Representative Bodies

GOVERNMENT

Directorate of National Education, Youth and Sports: ave de l'Annonciade, 98000 Monaco; tel. 98-98-83-05; fax 98-98-85-74; e-mail denjs@gouv.mc; internet www .education.gouv.mc; attached to Department of the Interior; Dir CATHERINE CHALA.

ACCREDITATION

ENIC/NARIC Monaco: Centre d'Information de l'Éducation Nationale, 18 ave des Castelans, 98000 Monaco; tel. 98-98-87-74; fax 98-98-41-74; e-mail cien@monaco.mc; internet www.education.gouv.mc; Coordinator CÉCILE KAPPLER.

Learned Societies

HISTORY, GEOGRAPHY AND ARCHAEOLOGY

Association Monégasque de Préhistoire: Musée d'Anthropologie, 56 bis blvd du Jardin Exotique, 98000 Monte Carlo; tel. 98-98-80-06; fax 98-98-02-46; e-mail suzanne_simone@ libello.com; internet www .monaco-prehistoire.com; f. 1984; 50 mems; Pres. Dr SUZANNE SIMONE.

LANGUAGE AND LITERATURE

Alliance Française: Maison de France, 42 rue Grimaldi, BP 300, 98006 Monte Carlo; tel. 93-50-08-24; offers courses and exams in French language and culture and promotes cultural exchange with France.

Research Institute

NATURAL SCIENCES

General

Centre Scientifique de Monaco: Villa les Pins, bloc C, 7 rue Honoré Labande, 98000 Monte Carlo; tel. 98-98-86-60; fax 92-16-79-81; e-mail centre@centrescientifique.mc; internet www.centrescientifique.mc; f. 1960; pure and applied research in the fields of oceanography, marine biology and the protection and regeneration of the marine environment; laboratories in Musée Océanographique de Monaco (q.v.); Pres. of Admin. Council Prof. PATRICK RAMPAL; Sec.-Gen. CORINNE GAZIELLO; publ. *Bulletin* (in French and in English, 1 a year).

Libraries and Archives

Monte Carlo

Archives du Palais Princier de Monaco: BP 518, 98015 Monaco Cedex; tel. 93-25-18-31; internet www.palais.mc; private archives of the Princes of Monaco; Curator RÉGIS LÉCUYER; publ. *Annals Monegasque* (1 a year).

Bibliothèque Louis Notari: 8 rue Louis Notari, 98000 Monaco; tel. 93-15-29-40; fax 93-15-29-41; f. 1909; 310,000 vols, 18,000 phonograms, 4,000 video cassettes; Librarian HERVÉ BARRAL; publ. *Bibliographie de Monaco* (database).

Princess Grace Irish Library: 9 rue Princesse Marie de Lorraine, 98000 Monaco; tel. 93-50-12-25; fax 93-50-66-65; e-mail pglib@monaco.mc; internet www.monaco.mc/ pglib; f. 1984; functions under the aegis of the Fondation Princesse Grace; Irish and Celtic studies library; more than 8,000 vols, 2,000 sheet items of Irish music and folk songs, 250 theses, 250 video cassettes and DVDs; reproduction of the Book of Kells; paintings, prints, sculptures; young readers' colln; English language activities for local school students; theatre, writing and poetry workshops; Administrator JUDITH A. GANTLEY; Sec. GÉRALDINE LANCE.

Museums and Art Galleries

Monte Carlo

Musée d'Anthropologie Préhistorique de Monaco: 56 bis blvd du Jardin Exotique, 98000 Monte Carlo; tel. 98-98-80-06; fax 93-30-02-46; e-mail map@map-mc.com; internet www.map-mc.com; f. 1902; prehistory, Quaternary geology; library of 3,000 vols, 200 periodicals; Dir and Curator PATRICK SIMON; publ. *Bulletin* (1 a year).

Musée Naval de Monaco: Terrasses de Fontvieille, Niveau 2, 98000 Monte Carlo; tel. 92-05-28-48; fax 93-50-55-91; e-mail claude_pallanca@libello.com; internet www .musee-naval.mc; more than 250 marine objects and models of famous ships, incl. several pieces from private colln of Prince Rainier III; Dir CLAUDE PALLANCA.

Musée Océanographique de Monaco: ave Saint-Martin, 98000 Monte Carlo; tel. 93-15-36-00; fax 93-50-52-97; e-mail musee@oceano .mc; internet www.oceano.org; f. 1910 by Prince Albert I of Monaco; part of Institut Océanographique, Paris; museum of natural history and art collns; aquarium contains more than 6,000 fishes of 400 species, 200 species of invertebrates and 100 species of corals; mother-of-pearl holy art shells; library of 10,000 vols, 1,200 theses, 1,000 periodicals, 1,000 maps and charts; Dir ROBERT CALCAGNO; Dir of Heritage and Curator PATRICK PIGUET; publs *Anales* (1 a year), *Bulletin* (irregular), *Mémoires* (irregular).

Nouveau Musée National de Monaco Villa Sauber/Villa Paloma: Villa des Pins, bloc B, 8 rue Honoré Labande, 98000 Monaco; tel. 98-98-19-62; fax 93-50-94-38; e-mail contact@nmnm.mc; internet www .nmnm.mc; f. 1972; Galéa colln: automatons, miniature furniture, antique dolls, nativity scenes; Dir MARIE-CLAUDE BEAUD.

University

INTERNATIONAL UNIVERSITY OF MONACO (IUM)

2 ave Albert III, 98000 Monte Carlo

Telephone: 97-98-69-86

Internet: www.monaco.edu/ international-university-monaco.cfm

Founded 1986

Private control

Language of instruction: English

Bachelors, Masters and MBA courses in business administration, finance, international business; also offers courses in Paris, France, and London, UK

Prin.: Dr SANDRINE RICARD
Vice-Prin.: Dr ANTONELLA PATRAS
Registrar and Bursar: DAVID CRANMAN
Head of Library and Research Services: SUSAN WANGECI EKLÖW

Number of teachers: 61

College

Académie de Musique et de Théâtre Foundation Prince Rainier III de Monaco: 1 blvd Albert 1er, 98000 Monaco; tel. 93-15-28-91; f. 1933; 56 professors; 650 students; Dir MICHEL CROSSET.

MONGOLIA

The Higher Education System

Mongolia was formerly the Manchu province of Outer Mongolia. In 1911, following the republican revolution in China, Mongolian princes declared the province's independence. Russia (and, later, the USSR) competed with China for control of Mongolia and in November 1924 the Mongolian People's Republic was proclaimed. The oldest institutions of higher education date from this year, among them the Academy of Management, Higher School of Finance and Economics and Higher School of Trade and Industry. The oldest multi-faculty university-level institution is the National University of Mongolia (founded 1942). Higher education consists of universities, higher schools and colleges. In 2008/09 there were 48 state-owned universities and colleges with 106,600 students, and 101 private universities and colleges with 54,100 students. Many Mongolian students continue their academic careers at universities and technical schools in Russia, Germany, the United Kingdom and the USA. Higher education is the responsibility of the Ministry of Education, Culture and Science, while the Consortium of Mongolian Universities and Colleges (founded 1995) is a non-governmental body representing 14 public and private universities.

Admission to higher education is on the basis of the Certificate of Secondary Education, students' academic records and relevant entrance examinations according to the programme of study applied for. The first stage of undergraduate study is the Diploma of Higher Education, which is awarded after two to three years. The second stage of undergraduate higher education is the Bachelors degree, which lasts four years (including time spent on the Diploma), and for which students are required to accumulate 120 'credit hours' for successful completion of the degree. After the Bachelors has been awarded students are eligible to study for the Masters, which usually lasts a year and requires 30 credit hours. Finally, the Doctorate is the highest university-level degree, and requires a minimum of 60 credit hours.

The Certificate of Vocational Education is the main qualification for technical and vocational education, which is widely available at junior, senior and post-secondary levels.

Regulatory and Representative Bodies

GOVERNMENT

Ministry of Education, Culture and Science: Government Bldg 3, Baga Toiruu 44, Sükhbaatar District, Ulan Bator; tel. (11) 322480; fax (11) 323158; internet www.mecs.pmis.gov.mn; Minister NORDOVYN BOLOR-MAA.

ACCREDITATION

Mongolian National Council for Education Accreditation: Government Bldg 10, Barilgachdyn talbai-2 38, Ulan Bator; tel. and fax (11) 324507; e-mail accmon@mongolnet.mn; internet www.accmon.mn; f. 1998; Contact SARUUL BAT-ULZII.

NATIONAL BODY

Consortium of Mongolian Universities and Colleges: Box 672, POB 46, Ulan Bator; tel. (11) 318154; fax (11) 324121; e-mail cmuc@mtu.edu.mn; internet www.cmuc.edu.mn; f. 1995; represents the common interests of public and private univs and colleges; supports scientific co-operation between the academic community and industry; promotes int. scientific co-operation; organizes biennial conferences on higher education reform; 18 mem. instns; Pres. Prof. Dr BADARCH DENDEV; publ. *Tavan Ukhaan* (12 a year).

Learned Societies

GENERAL

Mongolian Academy of Sciences: Sükhbaataryn talbai 3, Ulan Bator; tel. and fax (11) 321638; f. 1921; Depts of agriculture (Dir N. ALTANSÜKH), geology and geography (Dir, vacant), medicine and biology (Dir P. NYAMDAVAA), chemistry, mathematics, physics and technology (Dir D. KHAISAMBUU), social sciences (Dir KH. NAMSRAI); attached research institutes: see Research Institutes; Pres. BAATARYN CHADRAA; Scientific Sec. DÜGERIN REGDEL; publs *Proceedings of the Mongolian Academy of Sciences* (4 a year), *Studia Archaeologica, Studia Ethnographica, Studia Folclorica, Studia Historica, Studia Mongolica, Studia Museologica*.

AGRICULTURE, FISHERIES AND VETERINARY SCIENCE

Academy of Agricultural Sciences: Ulan Bator; f. 1998; Pres. N. ALTANSÜKH.

Association of Private Veterinary Surgeons: Ulan Bator; Pres. GOTOVYN BATTULGA.

BIBLIOGRAPHY, LIBRARY SCIENCE AND MUSEOLOGY

Academy of Information Sciences: Ulan Bator; f. 2004; Vice-Pres. CH. DALAI.

ECONOMICS, LAW AND POLITICS

Academy of State and Law: Ulan Bator; f. 2003; Pres. T. SENGEDORJ.

FINE AND PERFORMING ARTS

Academy of Cinematic Art: Ulan Bator; f. 2003; Pres. T. GANDI.

LANGUAGE AND LITERATURE

Association of Mongolian Writers: Ulan Bator; Exec. Dir KHAIDAVYN CHILAAJAV.

MEDICINE

Academy of Health Management: Ulan Bator; Pres. N. UDVAL.

Academy of Medical Sciences: Ulan Bator; f. 2005; Pres. PAGVAJAVYN NYAMDAVAA.

Society of Mongolian Surgeons: Ulan Bator; Pres. B. GOOSH.

NATURAL SCIENCES

General

Academy of Natural Sciences: Ulan Bator; f. 1998; Pres. JAMTSYN GARIDKHÜÜ; Learned Sec. T. ERDENEJAV.

RELIGION, SOCIOLOGY AND ANTHROPOLOGY

Academy of Anthropology: Ulan Bator; f. 1998; Pres. L. DASHNYAM.

Academy of Astrology: Mongolian Youth Association Bldg, Baga Toiruu, Sükhbaatar district, Ulan Bator; tel. and fax (11) 322982.

Academy of Nomadic Culture and Civilization: 'Ikh Zasag' University Bldg, 4th khoroo, B.Dorjiin St, Bayanzurkh dist., Ulan Bator; tel. (70) 157770; fax (70) 155736; e-mail ikhzasag@ikhzasag.edu.mn; internet www.ikhzasag.edu.mn; f. 2002; research and scientific works in Mongolian studies; 80 mems; Pres. NAMSRAIN NYAM-OSOR; publ. *Ikh Zasag* (2 a year).

Genghis Khan World Academy: Bldg 6, 2nd sub-district, Bayanzürkh district, Ulan Bator (POB 21/174); fax (11) 315846; internet www.chinggesacademy.mn.

Mongolian Muslims' Society: Ulan Bator; tel. (99) 110789; fax (70) 124666; e-mail mail@mongolianislam.mn; internet www.mongolianislam.mn; f. 1990; Pres. KADYRYN SAIRAAN; Exec. Dir BAATARBEK KAHDES.

TECHNOLOGY

Association of Academies of Science and Technology: Ulan Bator; f. 1998; Pres. L. DASHNYAM.

Mongolian Civil Engineers' Association: Baruun Dörvön Zam, Ikh Toiruu 1, Ulan Bator (POB 44/7); tel. (11) 328097; fax (11) 325580; e-mail midiid@magicnet.mn.

Mongolian National Mining Association: Ulan Bator; f. 2003; Dir N. ALGAA.

Mongolian National Water Association: Ulan Bator; f. 2000; Pres. S. CHULUUNKHUYAG.

National Academy of Engineering: Ulan Bator; f. 1998; Pres. P. OCHIRBAT.

Science and Technology Foundation: Ulan Bator; Dir KH. TSOOKHÜÜ.

Research Institutes

AGRICULTURE, FISHERIES AND VETERINARY SCIENCE

Agricultural Economics Research Institute: c/o Academy of Sciences, Sükhbaataryn talbai 3, Ulan Bator; attached to Mongolian Acad. of Sciences; Dir YU. ADYAA.

Agricultural Research Institute: Khovd; tel. (43) 3720; f. 1994; library of 10,000 vols; Dir P. BAATARBILEG.

Institute of Pasture and Fodder: Darkhan; Dir D. TSEDEV.

Institute of Veterinary Research: Zaisan, Ulan Bator; tel. (11) 341553; f. 1960; attached to Mongolian Agricultural Univ.; library of 4,000 vols; Dir B. BYAMBAA; publ. *Proceedings of the Institute of Veterinary Research and Training.*

Research Institute of Animal Husbandry 'J. Sambuu': Zaisan, Ulan Bator; tel. (11) 341572; e-mail riah@magicnet.mn; f. 1961; attached to Mongolian Acad. of Sciences; library of 800 vols; Dir DONDOVYN ALTANGEREL; publ. *Proceedings* (in Mongolian, with English summary).

Research Institute of Pastoral Animal Husbandry in the Gobi Region: Bulgan district, Ömnögobi province; f. 1959; attached to Mongolian Acad. of Sciences; camel and goat husbandry; Dir N. BIICHEE.

Research Institute of Plant Protection: c/o Academy of Sciences, Sükhbaataryn talbai 3, Ulan Bator; attached to Mongolian Acad. of Sciences; Dir D. TSEDEV.

Research Institute of Vegetable Growing and Land Cultivation Training: Darkhan-Uul province; tel. and fax (37) 24132; attached to Mongolian Agricultural Univ.; 138 teachers; 1,050 students.

ARCHITECTURE AND TOWN PLANNING

Building Institute: c/o Academy of Sciences, Sükhbaataryn talbai 3, Ulan Bator; attached to Mongolian Acad. of Sciences; Dir D. LKHANAG.

Construction and Architecture Research, Experimental, Production and Business Corporation: c/o Academy of Sciences, Sükhbaataryn talbai 3, Ulan Bator; tel. (11) 341437; Exec. Dir D. KHAISAMBUU.

Institute of Agricultural Architecture: Ulan Bator; Dir O. JADAMBA.

Institute of Architecture and Town Planning: c/o Academy of Sciences, Sükhbaataryn talbai 3, Ulan Bator; attached to Mongolian Acad. of Sciences; Dir (vacant).

Research Institute of Soils and Foundations Engineering: c/o Academy of Sciences, Sükhbaataryn talbai 3, Ulan Bator; attached to Mongolian Acad. of Sciences; Dir Dr A. ANAND.

ECONOMICS, LAW AND POLITICS

Centre for North-East Asian Studies: Mongolian Technical University Bldg (2nd Fl.), Ulan Bator (POB 51/4); tel. (11) 458317; fax (11) 458317; f. 1990; attached to Mongolian Acad. of Sciences; library of 2,000 vols; Dir Prof. CH. DALAI; publ. *North-East Asian Studies* (2 a year).

Institute of Economics: Ulan Bator; tel. (11) 320802; fax (11) 322216; f. 1962; attached to National University of Mongolia; fmrly attached to Mongolian Acad. of Sciences; library of 2,000 vols; Dir P. LUVSANDORJ.

Institute of International Studies: Room 806, Soyolyn töv örgöö, Sükhbaataryn talbai, Ulan Bator; tel. and fax (11) 322613;

attached to Mongolian Acad. of Sciences; Dir LUVSANGIIN KHAISANDAI; Scientific Sec. D. SHÜRKHÜÜ.

Institute of Management Development: Ulan Bator; Dir D. TSERENDORJ.

Institute of Market Studies: Chamber of Commerce and Industry, Ulan Bator; Dir S. DEMBEREL.

Institute of Mongol Studies: c/o Academy of Sciences, Sükhbaataryn talbai 3, Ulan Bator 11; attached to Mongolian Acad. of Sciences; Dir SH. BIRA.

Institute of National Development: Ulan Bator; attached to Mongolian Acad. of Sciences and the Presidential Secretariat; Dir RADNAASÜMBERELIIN RENCHINBAZAR; Scientific Sec. L. TSEDENDAMBA.

Institute of Oriental and International Studies: c/o Academy of Sciences, Sükhbaataryn talbai 3, Ulan Bator; attached to Mongolian Acad. of Sciences; Dir A. OCHIR.

Institute of Strategic Studies: Partizany gudamj, Ulan Bator (POB 870); tel. (11) 328188; fax (11) 324055; attached to Min. of Defence; Dir Maj.-Gen. CHOYJAMTSYN ULAANKHÜÜ; Vice-Dir MASHBAT OTGONBAYAR.

Mongolian Development Research Centre: Room 50, Baga Toiruu 13, Chingeltei district, Ulan Bator (POB 20A/63); tel. and fax (11) 315686; internet www.mdrc.mn.

'Prognoz' Institute of Socio-Political Studies: Ulan Bator; attached to Mongolian People's Revolutionary Party; Dir O. ERDENECHIMEG.

Research Institute for Land Policy: Chingünjavyn gudamj 2, Ulan Bator; tel. (11) 60506; f. 1975; library of 1,100 vols; Dir Dr G. PÜREVSÜREN.

Research Institute of Economic Studies: Ulan Bator; f. 1991; microeconomics; Dir Prof. T. DORJ.

FINE AND PERFORMING ARTS

Research Institute of Culture and Arts: c/o Academy of Sciences, Sükhbaataryn talbai 3, Ulan Bator 11; attached to Mongolian Acad. of Sciences; Dir S. TSERENDORJ.

HISTORY, GEOGRAPHY AND ARCHAEOLOGY

Institute of Archaeology: c/o Academy of Sciences, Sükhbaataryn talbai 3, Ulan Bator; attached to Mongolian Acad. of Sciences; Dir D. TSEVEENDORJ; Scientific Sec. B. TSOGTBAATAR.

Institute of Geography: c/o Academy of Sciences, Sükhbaataryn talbai 3, Ulan Bator; tel. (11) 350472; attached to Mongolian Acad. of Sciences; Dir Dr S. DORJGOTOV.

Institute of History: Jukovyn gudamj 77, Bayanzürkh district, Ulan Bator; tel. and fax (11) 458305; internet www.mas.ac.mn; attached to Mongolian Acad. of Sciences; archaeology, ethnography, Mongolian history; Dir D. DASHDAVAA.

LANGUAGE AND LITERATURE

Folk Literature Research Institute: Ulan Bator; Dir B. KATUU.

Institute of Mongolian Language and Literature: c/o Academy of Sciences, Sükhbaataryn talbai 3, Ulan Bator; tel. and fax (11) 451762; e-mail language@lang.mas.ac.mn; internet www.language.mas.ac.mn; f. 1921, present name and status 1961; attached to Mongolian Acad. of Sciences; organizes research and training to improve the language orthographical knowledge of the public; Dir TUMURTOGOO DOMII; publs *Folklore Studies* (1 a year), *Language and*

Literature Studies (1 a year), *Mongolian Studies* (1 a year).

MEDICINE

Institute of Hygiene, Epidemiology and Microbiology: c/o Academy of Sciences, Sükhbaataryn talbai 3, Ulan Bator 13; tel. and fax (1) 45-26-77; internet www.mas.ac.mn; attached to Mongolian Acad. of Sciences; Dir J. KUPUL.

Institute of Public Health: Enkh taivny gudamj 17, Ulan Bator; tel. (11) 458645; fax (11) 458645; Dir L. NARANTUYAA.

Institute of Traditional Medicine: c/o Academy of Sciences, Sükhbaataryn talbai 3, Ulan Bator; attached to Mongolian Acad. of Sciences; Dir D. DAGVATSEREN.

Medical Research Institute: c/o Academy of Sciences, Sükhbaataryn talbai 3, Ulan Bator; attached to Mongolian Acad. of Sciences; Dir YO. BODIKHÜÜ.

National Centre for Communicable Diseases: Bayanzürkh district, Ulan Bator; tel. and fax (11) 458699; f. 2001; Dir TOGOOGIIN ALTANTSETSEG.

National Forensic Research Centre: Ulan Bator; Dir CH. ALTANKHISHIG.

National Institute of Medicine: c/o Academy of Sciences, Sükhbaataryn talbai 3, Ulan Bator; attached to Mongolian Acad. of Sciences; Learned Sec. B. TSERENDASH.

Research and Production Centre of Biotechnology: Ulan Bator; attached to Min. of Health and Inst. of Public Health; Dir J. OYUUNBILEG.

Research and Production Institute of Biological Preparations and Blood: Ulan Bator; Dir A. DANDII.

State Research Centre for Maternal and Child Health: Amarsanaagiin gudamj, Bayangol district, Ulan Bator; tel. (11) 362633; fax (11) 302316; f. 1930; attached to Mongolian Acad. of Sciences; Dir G. CHOIJAMTS; publ. *Mother and Child* (2 a year).

NATURAL SCIENCES

General

Institute of Scientific and Technical Development: Ulan Bator; Dir D. NYAMAA.

Biological Sciences

Institute of Biology: Ulan Bator; tel. (11) 458851; f. 1965; attached to Mongolian Acad. of Sciences; Dir TS. JANCHIV.

Institute of Botany: Jukovyn gudamj 77, Ulan Bator; tel. (11) 451837; fax (11) 323158; e-mail ibot@mongol.net; attached to Mongolian Acad. of Sciences; Learned Sec. D. MAGSAR.

Institute of Geoecology: c/o Academy of Sciences, Sükhbaataryn talbai 3, Ulan Bator; tel. (11) 321862; attached to Mongolian Acad. of Sciences; Dir J. TSOGTBAATAR.

Palaeontology Centre: Enkh Taivny gudamj 63, Ulan Bator; fax (11) 458935; e-mail barsgeodin@magicnet.mn; attached to Mongolian Acad. of Sciences; Dir R. BARSBOLD.

Mathematical Sciences

Institute of Mathematics: Ulan Bator; attached to National University of Mongolia; fmrly attached to Mongolian Acad. of Sciences; Dir A. MEKEI.

Physical Sciences

Astronomical Observatory: Khürel-Togoot, Ulan Bator (POB 788); tel. (11) 52929; f. 1961; attached to Mongolian Acad. of Sciences; library of 1,500 vols; Dir G. NOONOI.

Centre of Seismology and Geomagnetism: c/o Academy of Sciences, Sükhbaataryn talbai 3, Ulan Bator; attached to Mongolian Acad. of Sciences; Dir U. SÜKHBAATAR.

Institute of Chemistry and Chemical Technology: Züün Dörvön Zam, Bayanzürkh district, Ulan Bator; tel. (11) 453133; attached to Mongolian Acad. of Sciences; Dir B. PÜREVSÜREN.

Institute of Geology and Mineral Enrichment: Peace Ave 63, POB 118, Ulan Bator; tel. (11) 457858; fax (11) 457858; f. 1966; attached to Mongolian Acad. of Sciences; library of 1,000 vols; Dir O. TÖMÖRTOGOO; publ. *Khaiguulchin* (4 a year).

Institute of Meteorology and Hydrology: Khudaldaany gudamj 5, Ulan Bator; tel. and fax (11) 326614; e-mail meteoins@magicnet.mn; f. 1966; library of 13,000 vols; Dir D. AZZAYAA; publ. *Environment*.

Institute of Physics and Technology: Enkh Taivny gudamj 54B, Ulan Bator; tel. (11) 458397; fax (11) 458397; f. 1961; attached to Mongolian Acad. of Sciences; library of 50,000 vols; Dir Ts. BAATAR.

Research Centre for Astronomy and Geophysics: c/o Academy of Sciences, Sükhbaataryn talbai 3, Ulan Bator; tel. (11) 458849; attached to Mongolian Acad. of Sciences; Dir B. BEKHTÖR.

RELIGION, SOCIOLOGY AND ANTHROPOLOGY

Institute of Astrology: Ulan Bator; Dir SH. JARGALSAIKHAN.

Institute of Buddhist Studies: Ulan Bator; Dir G. LUVSANTSEREN.

Institute of Philosophy, Sociology and Law: Jukovyn gudamj 77, Ulan Bator; tel. (11) 453752; f. 1972; attached to Mongolian Acad. of Sciences; Dir G. CHULUUNBAATAR.

Social Sciences Institute: Ulan Bator; attached to National University of Mongolia (fmrly attached to Mongolian Acad. of Sciences); Dir O. MÖNKHBAT.

TECHNOLOGY

Agricultural Technology Science, Technology and Production Corporation: Ulan Bator; tel. (11) 341155; attached to Mongolian Academy of Sciences.

Communications Research and Production Corporation: c/o Academy of Sciences, Sükhbaataryn talbai 3, Ulan Bator; attached to Mongolian Acad. of Sciences; Dir D. LKHAGVAA.

Electronic Equipment and Machine Studies Science, Technology and Production Corporation: Ulan Bator; tel. (11) 328025; attached to Mongolian Acad. of Sciences.

Experimental and Research Centre for Leather: c/o Academy of Sciences, Sükhbaataryn talbai 3, Ulan Bator; attached to Mongolian Acad. of Sciences; Dir D. GANBOLD.

Experimental and Research Centre for Wool: c/o Academy of Sciences, Sükhbaataryn talbai 3, Ulan Bator; attached to Mongolian Acad. of Sciences; Dir G. YONDONSAMBUU.

Forestry and Wood Processing Industry Institute: c/o Academy of Sciences, Sükhbaataryn talbai 3, Ulan Bator; attached to Mongolian Acad. of Sciences; Dir SAINBAYAR.

Geodesic and Geological Engineering Institute: Ulan Bator; Dir Ts. TSERENBAT.

Heat Technology and Industrial Ecology Institute: Ikh Surguuliin gudamj 2A, Sükhbaatar district, Ulan Bator; tel. 324959;

attached to Mongolian Acad. of Sciences; Dir S. BATMÖNKH.

Informatics Institute: c/o Academy of Sciences, Sükhbaataryn talbai 3, Ulan Bator; tel. (11) 458090; attached to Mongolian Acad. of Sciences; Dir MAIDARJAVYN GANZORIG.

Information Technology Science, Technology and Production Corporation: Ulan Bator; tel. (11) 327133; attached to Mongolian Acad. of Sciences.

Light Industry Scientific, Technological and Production Corporation (ARMONO): Chingisiin örgön chölöö, Ulan Bator; tel. and fax (11) 342536; e-mail armonocor@mongol.net; internet www.aeromongolia.co.kr; f. 1997; research into leather and timber industrial products; attached to Mongolian Acad. of Sciences.

Military Science Research Institute: Ministry of Defence, Ulan Bator; Dir SH. PALAMDORJ.

Mining Institute: c/o Academy of Sciences, Sükhbaataryn talbai 3, Ulan Bator; attached to Mongolian Acad. of Sciences; Dir S. MANGAL.

Natural Freezing and Food Technology Institute: c/o Academy of Sciences, Sükhbaataryn talbai 3, Ulan Bator; attached to Mongolian Acad. of Sciences; Dir N. LONJID.

Petrochemical Technology Research Centre: Ulan Bator; tel. (11) 24779.

Power Institute: c/o Academy of Sciences, Sükhbaataryn talbai 3, Ulan Bator; attached to Mongolian Acad. of Sciences; Dir D. BUMAYUUSH.

Renewable Energy Science, Technology and Production Corporation: Chingisiin örgön chölöö, Khan-Uul district, Ulan Bator (POB 35/479); tel. and fax (11) 342377; attached to Mongolian Acad. of Sciences; Dir B. CHADRAA.

Roads Research and Production Corporation: c/o Academy of Sciences, Sükhbaataryn talbai 3, Ulan Bator; attached to Mongolian Acad. of Sciences; Dir B. KHUNDGAA.

Standardization and Metrology National Centre: Enkh Taivny gudamj 46A, Ulan Bator (POB 51/48); tel. (11) 458349; fax (11) 458032; f. 1953; attached to Min. of Industry and Trade; library of 130,000 vols; Dir NYAMJAVYN JANCHIVDORJ; publ. *Standards and Metrology* (12 a year).

Traditional Medicine Science, Technology and Production Corporation: Ulan Bator; tel. (11) 343103; attached to Mongolian Acad. of Sciences.

Transport Research and Production Corporation: c/o Academy of Sciences, Sükhbaataryn talbai 3, Ulan Bator; attached to Mongolian Acad. of Sciences; Dir L. TÜDEV.

Water Policy Research Institute: Baruunselbe 13, Ulan Bator 211238; tel. (11) 325487; fax (11) 321862; f. 1965; library of 3,500 vols; Dir N. CHULUUNKHUYAG.

Libraries and Archives
Ulan Bator

Gandan Library: Gandantegchinlen Buddhist Monastery, Ulan Bator; tel. (11) 360023; f. 1838; Buddhist theology and philosophy, xylographs, secular works of science and literature.

National Archives of Mongolia: Ulan Bator 210646; tel. (11) 324533; fax (11) 324533; f. 1996; history, art, literature, science, technology, film, sound recordings; Dir-Gen. DEMBERELIIN ÖLZIIBAATAR; publ. *Archives News* (2 a year).

Natsagdorj Central Public Library: 2nd sub-dist., Sükhbaatar dist., Ulan Bator; tel. (11) 70115705; fax (11) 70115703; e-mail info@pl.ub.gov.mn; internet pl.ub.gov.mn; f. 1980, centralized 1986; 4 br. libraries; 400,000 vols; Dir GANULZII U.; Deputy Dir ALTANTSETSEG CHOI.

State Central Library: Söüliin gudamj, Sükhbaatar district, Ulan Bator; tel. and fax (11) 323100; f. 1921; 4m. vols, incl. rare and ancient editions; Dir GOTOVYN AKIM.

Museums and Art Galleries
Arkhangai

Ethnographical Museum: Arkhangai; located in the Zayain Gegeenii Süm (temple founded in 1536).

Bayan-Ölgii

Town Museum: Bayan-Ölgii; Kazakh culture, especially costume and artefacts.

Dornogobi

Danzan Ravjaa Museum: Dornogobi; commemorates the life and works of the 19th-century writer and lama, Danzan Ravjaa.

Khentii

Ethnographical Museum: Khentii; located in the home of the former Tsetseg Khan.

Ulan Bator

Botanical Garden: Ulan Bator; attached to Mongolian Acad. of Sciences; Dir G. OCHIRBAT.

Memorial Museum of Victims of Political Persecution: Genden St 1, Ulan Bator; tel. (70) 110915; e-mail info@memorialmuseum.info; internet www.memorialmuseum.info; f. 1996; located in home of executed PM Genden; commemorates in documents and photographs the victims of the 1930s Stalinist purges; Dir BEKHBAT SODNOM.

Mongolian National Gallery of Modern Art: Ulan Bator; tel. (11) 327177; fax (11) 313191; e-mail mnartgallery@mongolnet.mn; internet www.ulaanbaatar.net/artgallery; f. 1991; Dir D. ENKHTSETSEG.

Museum of Asian Art: Juulchny gudamj, Ulan Bator; private collection of religious art and artefacts in precious metals; Dir A. ALTANGEREL.

Museum of Military History: Enkh Taivny örgön chölöö, Ulan Bator; tel. (11) 454292; Dir Col P. BYAMBASÜREN.

Museum of Mongolian Costume: Enkh Taivny örgön chölöö, Ulan Bator; f. 2005; folk costume, felt tents and artefacts since the Genghis Khan period.

Museum of Mongolian Traditional Medicine: Next to Bogd Khan's Winter Palace (Museum of Religious History), Ulan Bator; f. 2005; Dir D. TSERENSODNOM.

Museum of Religious History: Chingis Khaany örgön chölöö, Ulan Bator; tel. (11) 324788; housed in Choyjin Lamyn Khüree, a former lamasery, and Bogd Khan's Winter Palace; Dir G. TÖVSAIKHAN.

National Museum of Mongolian History: Juulchmii gudamj 1, Ulan Bator 46, (POB 46/332); tel. (11) 326802; fax (11) 326802; e-mail nmm@mongolnet.mn; internet www.nationalmuseum.mn; f. 1924 as Mongolian National Museum; present name 1990 by merger of State Central Museum and Museum of the Revolution; 46,000 historical and ethnographical objects from prehistory to present day; Dir Dr J. SARUULBUYAN; publ. *Museologia* (1 a year).

Natsagdorj Museum: Chingis Khaany örgön chölöö, Ulan Bator; tel. (11) 327879; life and works of the author and poet Dashdorjiin Natsagdorj.

Natural History Museum: Khuvisgalchdyn örgön chölöö, Ulan Bator; tel. (11) 321716; natural history, Gobi desert dinosaur eggs and skeletons; Dir P. ERDENEBAT.

Theatre Museum: Cultural Palace, Sükhbaatar Square, Ulan Bator; tel. (11) 326820.

Ulan Bator Museum: Enkh Taivny örgön chölöö, Ulan Bator; located in old Russian house; history of Ulan Bator.

Wildlife Museum: Öndör Gegeen Zanabazaryn gudamj, Ulan Bator; tel. (11) 360248; fax (11) 360067.

Zanabazar Fine Arts Museum: Barilgachdyn talbai, Ulan Bator; sculptures by Mongolia's first Buddhist leader and *tankas* (religious paintings); Dir D. GUNGAA.

Zhukov, G. K., House Museum: Enkh Taivny örgön chölöö, 15th sub-district, Ulan Bator; tel. (11) 453781; career of Soviet Marshal Zhukov.

Universities

'CHOI LUVSANJAV' UNIVERSITY OF LANGUAGE AND CIVILIZATION

11th microraion, 7th sub-district, Sükhbaatar district, Ulan Bator (POB 13/550)

Telephone: (11) 353524
Fax: (11) 353524
Founded 1993
Vice-President: SOYOMBO LUVSANJAV
Number of teachers: 40 (22 full-time, 18 part-time)
Number of students: 380
Library of 10,000 vols

Mongolian and Chinese studies; training of English- and Japanese-speaking teachers and interpreters.

GENGHIS KHAN 'IKH ZASAG' UNIVERSITY

4 khoroo, B.Dorjiin st, Bayanzurkh District, Ulaanbaatar (POB 349), 13381

Telephone: (976) 70155736
Fax: (11) 455736
E-mail: ikhzasag@ikhzasag.edu.mn
Internet: www.ikhzasag.edu.mn
Private control; attached to Nat. Ccl on Higher Educational Accreditation
Languages of instruction: English, Mongolian
Academic year: September to July
Number of teachers: 250
Number of students: 7,000
Pres.: NAMSRAIN NYAM-OSOR
Vice-Pres.: JAMBAL TSETSEGMAA
Vice Pres. for Justice and Home Affairs: SUREN DAMCHAASUREN
Vice Pres. for Marketing: NYAM-OSOR UCHRAL

Publications: *Ikh Zasag* (newspaper, 2 a year), *Ikh Zasag* (journal, jtly with Acad. of Nomadic Civilization and Culture, 2 a year).

MONGOLIAN AGRICULTURAL UNIVERSITY

Zaisan, Ulan Bator

Telephone: (11) 341592
Fax: (11) 341770
E-mail: haaint@magicnet.mn
Internet: www.msua.edu.mn

Founded 1942 as veterinary dept of Mongolian State University; became Institute of Agriculture 1958; university status 1991; present name 1996
State control
Director: Dr J. GANBOLD
Rector: B. BYAMBAA
Pro-Rector: L. NYAMBAT
Library of 200,000 vols
Number of teachers: 300
Number of students: 6,700

DEANS

Faculty of Agricultural Economics: A. BAKEI
Faculty of Agricultural Engineering and Product Technology: L. LUVSANSHARAV
Faculty of Agronomy: BEGZIIN DORJ
Faculty of Animal Husbandry: (vacant)
Faculty of Basic Education: H. KHÜRELTOGOO
Faculty of Veterinary Medicine: B. LUVSANSHARAV

MONGOLIAN STATE EDUCATION UNIVERSITY

Baga toiruu 14, Sükhbaatar district, Ulan Bator

Telephone: (11) 326010
Fax: (11) 322705
E-mail: togmid@mspu.edu.mn
Internet: www.mspu.edu.mn
Founded 1951
State control
Academic year: September to June
Rector: Prof. B. JADAMBAA
Vice-Rector for International Relations and Information: Prof. B. JADAMBAA
Vice-Rector for Research: Prof. D. TÖMÖRTOGOO
Vice-Rector for Teaching: Prof. Ts. BATSUURI
Head of Academic Affairs: Prof. D. PÜREVDORJ
Head of Graduate Studies: Prof. N. JADAMBAA
Library of 300,000 vols
Number of teachers: 330
Number of students: 5,261
Publication: *Teacher Education* (2 a year)

DIRECTORS

School of Art and Technology: Prof. G. BATDORJ
School of Computer Science and Information Technology: Prof. L. CHOIJOOVAANCHIG
School of Education Studies: Prof. Ts. SUMYAA
School of Foreign Languages: Prof. Z. GULIRAANZ
School of History and Social Sciences: Prof. D. NARANTSETSEG
School of Mathematics and Statistics: Prof. Ts. BATKHÜÜ
School of Mongolian Studies: Prof. Ts. ÖNÖRBAYAN
School of Natural Sciences: Prof. M. ÜINDEN
School of Physical Education: Prof. S. JAMTS
School of Physics and Technology: Prof. R. BAZARSÜREN
School of Pre-School Education: Prof. J. BATDELGER
School of Teacher Training: Prof. S. BATKHUYAG

MONGOLIAN STATE UNIVERSITY OF ARTS AND CULTURE

Baga Toiruu 22, Chingeltei Dist., Ulan Bator, 210646

Telephone: (11) 329137
Fax: (11) 325205
E-mail: avrora2002@yahoo.com
Internet: www.msuac.edu.com
Founded 1990
State control
Academic year: September to June

Rector: ERDENETSOGT SONINTOGOS
Vice-Rector for Academic Affairs: GUNCHIN ALTANGEREL
Vice-Rector for Research: CHULUUN ALTANTSETSEG
Registrar: ALTANGERELIIN GANBAATAR
Librarian: BANZRAGCH TUNGALAG
Number of teachers: 237
Number of students: 3,117

DEANS

School of Culture: DASH BAT-ERDENE
School of Culture and Civilisation: GURRINCHIN SUKHBAT
School of Fine Arts: LKHAGVAA BUMANDORJ
School of Music Arts: ADILBISH DASHPELJEE
School of Radio and Television: DORJ OYUNGEREL
School of Stage and Screen Arts: NAMSRAI SUVD

MONGOLIAN UNIVERSITY OF SCIENCE AND TECHNOLOGY

Baga Toiruu 34, Sükhbaatar district, Ulan Bator (POB 46/520)

Telephone: (11) 325109
Fax: (11) 324121
E-mail: info@must.edu.mn
Internet: www.must.edu.mn
Founded 1969
State control
Academic year: September to July
Rector: D. DASHJAMTS (acting)
Vice-Rector for Academic Affairs: Z. TSERENDORJ
Vice-Rector for Finance and Development: L. BOLDBAATAR
Vice-Rector for Research and Technology: D. DASHJAMTS
Chief Admin. Officer: O. NASANBAT
Librarian: G. PÜREV
Library of 170,000 vols
Number of teachers: 781
Number of students: 17,000

Publications: *MUST News* (in Mongolian, 12 a year), *Science and Technology* (in Mongolian, 4 a year), *Scientific Transactions* (in Mongolian, 4 a year)

DIRECTORS

School of Civil Engineering: Z. BINDERYAA
School of Computer Science and Management: S. BAIGALTUGS
School of Food and Biotechnology: D. NANSALMAA
School of Foreign Languages: T. BATBAYAR
School of Geology: D. CHULUUN
School of Humanities: A. ENKHBAATAR
School of Industrial Technology and Design: B. DAVAASÜREN
School of Materials Technology: P. MÖNKHBAATAR
School of Mathematics: J. BAASANDORJ
School of Mechanical Engineering: G. BATKHÜREL
School of Mining Engineering: B. PÜREVTOGTOKH
School of Power Engineering: H. ENKHJARGAL
School of Technology in Darkhan: S. TSEVEL
School of Technology in Erdenet: S. DAVAANYAM
School of Technology in Övörhangai Province: J. JANTSANDORJ
School of Technology in Sükhbaatar Province: MAJIGIIN KHÜRLEE
School of Telecommunications and Information Technology: B. DAMDINSÜREN
Graduate Study Centre: H. BUYANNEMEKH

NATIONAL UNIVERSITY OF MONGOLIA

Ikh Surguuliin gudamj 1, Sükhbaatar district, Ulan Bator (POB 46A/523)

Telephone: (11) 320892
Fax: (11) 320668
E-mail: numelect@magicnet.mn
Internet: www.num.edu.mn

Founded 1942
State control
Academic year: September to June

President: TSERENSODNOMYN GANTSOG
Vice-Pres. for Academic: SÜRENGIIN DAVAA
Vice-Pres. for Research: R. SAMYAA

Library of 350,000 vols
Number of teachers: 500
Number of students: 6,500

Publication: *Proceedings*.

FACULTIES AND TRAINING AND RESEARCH INSTITUTES

Faculty of Biology: incl. depts of biochemistry and microbiology, biophysics, botany, ecology, forestry, genetics, zoology; Dir R. SAMYAA.

Faculty of Chemistry: incl. depts of chemistry and technology of new materials, ferrous-metal and rare-element chemistry, general chemistry (Analytical and Physical Chemistry), organic chemistry (Coal and Petrochemistry); Dean D. DORJ.

Faculty of Earth Sciences: Dean CH. GONCHIGSUMLAA.

School of Economic Studies: incl. depts of accountancy, credit and finance, demography, economic data processing, foreign languages, management, marketing, mathematics, statistics, theory of economics; Dir CH. HASHCHULUUN.

School of Foreign Languages and Cultures: English, Chinese, Czech, French, German, Japanese, Korean, Polish, Russian.

School of Foreign Service: training of diplomats.

School of Information Technology.

School of International Relations: postgraduate studies in foreign relations; Dir J. BOR.

School of Law: incl. depts of civil law, constitutional law, criminal process law, International law, State Administration; Dir S. NARANGEREL.

School of Mathematics and Computer Science: incl. depts of algebra, applied mathematics and methods of teaching mathematics, computer programming; geometry, mathematical analysis, probability theory and mathematical statistics; Dean JAMTSYN BAATAR.

School of Mongolian Language and Culture: incl. depts of linguistics, literature, journalism, Mongolian Language; Dir D. BADAMDORJ.

School of Physics and Electronics: incl. depts of electronics, geophysics, hydrology, meteorology, optics, nuclear physics, radiophysics, solid-state physics, theoretical physics; Dean CHÜLTEMIIN BAYARKHÜÜ.

School of Social Sciences: incl. depts of culture and art, history, philosophy, politics, sociology; Dean SH. SODNOM.

Graduate School: Dean A. MEKEI.

Office of International Affairs: Dean S. ALTANTSETSEG.

Office of Undergraduate Studies: Dean N. BATCHIMEG.

'ORKHON' UNIVERSITY

Chinggis Khaany örgön chölöö, Khan-Uul district, Ulan Bator (POB 36/176)

Telephone: (11) 342696
Fax: (11) 341276
E-mail: info@orkhon.edu.mn
Internet: www.orkhon.edu.mn

Founded 1992
Private control

Director: Prof. Dr NYAMAAGIIN KHAJIDSÜREN

Library of 25,000 vols
Number of teachers: 70
Number of students: 1,000

BA degree courses in languages (English, French, German, Japanese, Korean, Russian) and law; MA degree courses in linguistics.

ULAANBAATAR UNIVERSITY

Bayanzürkh district, Ulan Bator (POB 44/658)

Telephone: (11) 450179
Fax: (11) 311080
E-mail: ubuniv@mongol.net
Internet: www.ulaanbaatar.edu.mn

Founded 1993 as Higher Technical School; received charter 1996
State control
Academic year: September to July

Rector: YONG SUNG JE
Vice-Rector: D. BOLD
Scientific Sec.: T. NAMJIL

Number of teachers: 78
Number of students: 800

Publication: *Proceedings of the Ulaanbaatar University* (1 a year)

Faculties of language and literature, social sciences and technology.

UNIVERSITY OF HEALTH SCIENCES

POB 48/111, Ulaanbaatar 210648
Zorig St 3, Sükhbaatar Dist., Ulaanbatar 210648

Telephone: (11) 328670
Fax: (11) 321249
E-mail: int_rel@hsum.edu.mn
Internet: www.hsum-ac.mn

Founded 1942
State control
Academic year: September to July

Pres.: Prof. Dr TS. LKHAGVASÜREN
Vice Pres. for Research and Int. Relations: Prof. Dr N. SUMBERZUL
Vice Pres. for Clinical Affairs: Prof. Dr KH. ALTAISAIKHAN
Vice Pres. for Academic Affairs: Prof. Dr D. AMARSAIKHAN
Centre for Medical Education: Dr D. OTGON-BAYAR
Centre for Student Affairs: Dr A. GURBADAM
Graduate Training Centre: Dr G. ARIUNTUUL
Postgraduate Training Institute: Dr D. ZORIG
Librarian: N. TSAGAACH

Library of 300,000 vols, 100,000 periodicals
Number of teachers: 536
Number of students: 10,096

Publication: *Mongolian Journal of Health Sciences*

DEANS

Darkhan Medical College: Prof. Dr M. NYAM-SUREN
Dornogobi Medical College: Prof. Dr B. NYAMKHUU
Gobi-Altai Medical College: Prof. Dr KH. OROSOO
School of Biomedicine: Prof. Dr G. BATBAATAR
School of Dentistry: B. AMARSAIKHAN
School of Medicine: Prof. Dr D. GONCHIGSU-REN
School of Nursing: Prof. Dr D. TSERENDAGVA
School of Pharmacy: Prof. Dr D. ENKHJARGAL
School of Public Health: O. CHIMEDSUREN
School of Traditional Medicine: Prof. S. OLD-OKH

UNIVERSITY OF THE HUMANITIES

POB 53, Ulan Bator 210646
Sükhbaatar district, Small Ring Rd, Ulan Bator 46

Telephone: (11) 322702
Fax: (11) 322702
E-mail: uh@humanities.mn
Internet: www.humanities.mn

Founded 1979 as Higher School of Russian Language Teachers; present name and status 2000
State control

Dir: Prof. BEGZIIN CHULUUNDORJ

Schools of foreign languages, social sciences; Depts of culture and American and British studies, foreign languages, human resource management, journalism, literature.

Higher Schools

Academy of Management: Chingisiin örgön chölöö 7, Khan-Uul district, Ulan Bator; tel. and fax (11) 343037; e-mail td@aom.edu.mn; f. 1924; govt agency; depts of computer science, economics; English language, management, public administration; 52 teachers; 739 students; Rector TOGOOCHIN LKHAGVAA; publs *Management* (in Mongolian, 4 a year), *Public Administration* (in Mongolian, 4 a year).

Darkhan Higher School: 4th sub-district, Darkhan district, Darkhan-Uul Province (Darkhan POB 520); tel. and fax (372) 35652; internet www.darkhandeed.mn; f. 1997; accounting, Chinese, English, hotel and restaurant management, Japanese, Korean, tourism; library: 25,000 vols; 90 teachers; 1,000 students.

Defence Academy: 16th sub-district, Bayanzükh district, Ulan Bator; tel. (11) 458673; Law, Accounting, State Administration, Operation of Motor Vehicles, Tracked Vehicles And Bridge-Building Machinery, Electronics, Communications, Military Science, Military History; Dir Col N. JALBAJAV.

Higher School of Arts and Crafts: Ulan Bator.

Higher School of Culture: Erkh Chölöönii talbai, Chingeltei district, Ulan Bator (POB 46/982); tel. (11) 326759; fax (11) 329328; e-mail cclib@mongol.net; internet www.moncollege.150m.com; training of librarians, cultural managers, museum workers and archivists, printers, and music, song and dance teachers; Dir G. BAATAR.

Higher School of European Languages: located at: Ikh Surguuliin gudamj 9, Sükhbaatar district, Ulan Bator (POB 46/982); tel. (11) 320993; f. 1993; English, French, Russian and German interpreting; 52 teachers (11 full-time, 41 part-time); 632 students; Rector T. PELJID.

Higher School of Finance and Economics: Enkh Taivny gudamj 12A, Bayanzürkh district, Ulan Bator 49; tel. and fax (11) 458378; internet www.ife.edu.mn; f. 1924; 65 teachers; 1,200 students; depts of accounting and audit, banking and finance, business and management, Economics and Econometrics, information technology, international studies; Dir JAMYANDORJIIN BATKHUYAG.

Higher School of Information Technology: Ulan Bator; Dir G. TSOGBADRAKH.

Higher School of International Economics and Business: 20th sub-district, Bayangol district, Ulan Bator; tel. (11) 681525; fax (11) 452067; e-mail iieb_elselt@yahoo.com; internet www.iieb.edu.mn; banking and accounting, business management, international economics, taxation and audit.

Higher School of International Studies: Ikh Surguuliin gudamj 2A, Sükhbataar district, Ulan Bator, (POB 46/205); tel. (11) 329860; fax (11) 329450; Dir NARANDULAM.

Higher School of Labour: Erkh Chölöönii talbai (bldg behing the Tengis cinema), Chingeltei district, Ulan Bator; tel. (11) 318176; fax (11) 312629; e-mail mli_999@ yahoo.com; attached to Mongolian Confederation of Trade Unions; accountancy and social work, business, finance, labour economics and management.

Higher School of Legal Studies: Ulan Bator; tel. (11) 529798; Dir L. DASHNYAM.

Higher School of Literature: Ulan Bator; Dir SHIRSEDIIN TSEND-AYUUSH.

Higher School of Mongolian Language and Literature: Chingisiin örgön chölöö 29, 3rd sub-district, Khan-Uul district, Ulan Bator; tel. (11) 342210; fax (11) 342210; trains teachers and interpreters in French, German and Japanese; English-language journalism.

Higher School of Oriental Literature: Ulan Bator; Dir S. BATMÖNKH.

Higher School of Oriental Philosophy and Anthropology: 17th sub-district, Bayangol district, Ulan Bator; tel. and fax (11) 361461; e-mail ophsi@mongolnet.mn; Dir NANSALYN SARANTUYAA.

Higher School of Religion: Ulan Bator; tel. (11) 457454; Dir SH. SONINBAYAR.

Higher School of Social Studies: 2nd sub-district, Bayanzürkh district, Ulan Bator (POB 23/277); tel. and fax (11) 460356; e-mail uuds@magicnet.mn; f. 1993; library: 12,000 vols; Dir TS. ENKHEE.

Higher School of Technology: Darkhan, Darkhan-Uul province; tel. (372) 23368; fax (372) 23760; e-mail technol@mongol.net; fmr polytechnic and technical college; electrical and heating engineering, geology, mining and ore concentration, power supply management.

Higher School of Trade and Industry: Oyuutny gudamj 14, Enkh Taivny örgön chölöö, Ulan Bator, (POB 48/404); tel. (11) 325724; fax (11) 326748; e-mail icbm@ magicnet.mn; f. 1924; accountancy, business management, international trade, marketing; library: two libraries, with 22,000 vols;

60 teachers; 1,200 students; Rector S. BUD-NYAM; publ. *Mercury* (3 a year).

'Khalkha Juram' Higher School of Law: Tulga Co. Bldg, Ikh Toiruu 20, Sükhbaatar district, Ulan Bator, (POB 51/128); tel. and fax (11) 350480; Dir T. DOOKHÜÜ.

Khan-Uul Higher School: located at: Tulga Co. Bldg, Ikh Toiruu 20, Sükhbaatar district, Ulan Bator (POB 46/419); tel. (11) 351032; e-mail khan-uul@mongol.net; internet www .khan-uul.mn; f. 1994; applied mathematics, business economics, computer programming, computer technology; 25 teachers; 280 students; Dir TSERENGIIN DEMBEREL.

'Mongol' Higher School: Ulan Bator; Dir NAMJAAGIIN DASHZEVEG.

Mongolian Business Institute: Enkh Taivny örgön chölöö, Bayangol district, Ulan Bator, (POB 24/715); tel. (11) 361589; e-mail mbi_191@mol.mn; internet www.mbi .edu.mn; f. 1991; degree courses in economics, finance, management, marketing; 40 teachers; 500 students; Dir Dr B. ERDENESÜREN.

Mongolian National Higher School: Enigma Centre, 11th sub-district, Bayangol district, Ulan Bator; tel. (11) 300900; fax (11) 300799; e-mail mni@mongolnet.mn; f. 1998; economics, economics of tourism, financial and business management, hotel and restaurant management, international trade, law, marketing; Dir TÖMÖRBAATARYN KHERÜÜGA.

'Monos' Higher School of Medicine: Songolongiin toiruu 5, 20th sub-district, Songinokhairkhan district, Ulan Bator; tel. (11) 633235; medicine and pharmacy.

'Otgontenger' University: Jukovyn örgön chölöö, Bayangzürkh district, Ulan Bator, (POB 51/35); tel. (11) 454560; e-mail oy_oyun@magicnet.mn; internet www .otgontenger.edu.mn; f. 1991; training of Russian- and English-language teachers and interpreters, Japanese-, German-, French-, Chinese- and Korean-language business and tourism managers, and Japanese-language international tour guides, training in English-language journalism; 48 teachers; 650 students; Founder and Chair. DULAMSÜRENGIIN OYUUNKHOROL; Rector D. NARANCHIMEG.

'Otoch Maramba' Higher School of Medicine: 2nd sub-district, Bayanzürkh district, Ulan Bator (POB 49/235); tel. (11) 457489; fax (11) 358489; f. 1991; study of traditional medicine; 6 teachers; 68 students; Dir TSERENSODNOM.

Private Higher School of Oriental Philosophy and History: Enkh Taivny gudamj 35 Ulan Bator (POB 44/283); tel. (11) 322628;

fax (11) 320210; f. 1992; library: 5,000 vols; 150 students; Dir R. NANSAL.

Radio and Television Higher School: Mongolian Radio and Television Bldg, Khuvisgalyn zam 3, Ulan Bator 11; tel. (11) 369223; training of radio and television journalists and producers, television camera operators and engineers.

Railway College: Enkh Taivny örgön chölöö 44, Bayangol district, Ulan Bator (POB 35/76); tel. (11) 322723; fax (11) 322797; e-mail mtzcoll@mongolnet.mn; automation and telecommunications, construction, management, maintenance, railway transport organization, rolling-stock maintenance, passenger services; trains staff for Mongolian railways, the country's largest employer; Dir B. SERÜÜD.

'Shikhikhutug' Higher School of Law: Ikh Surguuliin gudamj 1, 6th sub-district, Ulan Bator (POB 46/1033); tel. and fax (11) 323392; e-mail shihihutug@mongol.net; Dir D. OYUUNTSETSEG.

'Shonkhor' Higher School of Physical Culture: Baga Toiruu 55, 8th sub-district, Sükhbaatar district, Ulan Bator (POB 960); tel. and fax (11) 319858; Dir KH. BAYANMÖNKH.

'Tenger' Socio-Economic Higher School: Chinggissin örgön chölöö, 2nd sub-district, Khan-Uul district, Ulan Bator; tel. (11) 342651; accounting, anthropology, business economics, social sciences, social work, state administration, tourism, trade economics; Chinese language jtly with Shandong University, China.

'Zanabazar' Buddhist University: Ulan Bator; attached to Gandantegchinlen monastery; Dir SH. SONINBAYAR.

Colleges

College of Agriculture: Darkhan; hydrology, land improvement, meteorology.

'O. Tleikhan' Building College: Baruun Dörvön Zam, Enkh Taivny örgön chölöö 35, Ulan Bator (POB 24/643); tel. (11) 322723; fax (11) 322797; e-mail cwc@magicnet.mn; civil engineering, computer operations, electrical engineering, machine and vehicle repair, utilities; Dir B. CHIMIDDORJ.

Ulan Bator College: Construction College Bldg, West side of rd to Gandan monastery, Baruun Dörvön Zam, Bayangol district, Ulan Bator; depts of business management and computer programming, Korean-language teacher-training and interpreting; 10 teachers; 140 students; Rector YUM SUN JE.

MONTENEGRO

The Higher Education System

Following the dissolution of the Socialist Federal Republic of Yugoslavia in 1992, Montenegro became part of the Federal Republic of Yugoslavia, which was renamed the State Union of Serbia and Montenegro in 2003. In 2006 Montenegro declared independence from the State Union of Serbia and Montenegro. The Univerzitet Crne Gore Podgorica (University of Montenegro, Podgorica—founded 1974) is the main institution of higher education and was established while Montenegro was part of the Socialist Federal Republic of Yugoslavia. In 2006 the Univerzitet Mediteran (Mediterranean University), a private university, was founded. The newly established Ministry of Education and Science has assumed responsibility for higher education, which is still strongly based on the former Yugoslav system. In 2002 the New University Law introduced a range of reforms, including adoption of the European Credit Transfer System and increased autonomy for institutions of higher education. Consequently, Montenegro also participates in the Bologna Process to establish a European Higher Education Area, the first phase of which is to adopt a credit-based system of comparable degrees with two main cycles (undergraduate and graduate). In 2005/06 there were 21 institutions of higher education, including faculties, art academies and private institutions, with 12,903 students.

Under the old system, admission to higher education was based on completion of general secondary education or four-year vocational certificate programmes and award of the Secondary School Leaving Diploma. Universities also set their own entrance examinations. Quotas for admissions were set by the Government. The new undergraduate Bachelors degree (four years) replaces the old-style awards of Diplom Višeg Obrazovanje (two to three years) and Diplom Visokog Obrazovanja (four to six years). The Masters degree (Magistarska Diploma) is a one-year programme of study following the Bachelors. Finally, the Doctorate (Doktorat Nauka) is the highest university-level degree and is awarded after a period of research culminating with defence of a thesis.

The Montenegro Council of Higher Education (MCHE), set up in 2003, is responsible for accreditation of higher educational institutions.

Regulatory and Representative Bodies

GOVERNMENT

Ministry of Culture, Sports and Media: Vuk Karadžića 3, 81000 Podgorica; tel. (20) 231-561; fax (20) 231-540; e-mail kabinet@min-kulture.mn.yu; internet www.ministarstvokulture.gov.me; Min. BRANISLAV MIĆUNOVIĆ.

Ministry of Education and Science: Vaka Đurovića bb, 81000 Podgorica; tel. (20) 410-100; fax (20) 410-101; e-mail mpin@gov.me; internet www.mpin.gov.me; Min. SLAVOLJUB STIJEPOVIC.

ACCREDITATION

ENIC/NARIC Montenegro: ENIC Centre Montenegro, Rimski trg bb, 81000 Podgorica; tel. and fax (20) 265-014; fax (20) 265-014.

Montenegro Council of Higher Education: c/o Vaka Đurovića bb, 81000 Podgorica; f. 2003; responsible for assuring high quality higher education; advises Govt and assists the instns in improving and sustaining quality; evaluation and accreditation of instns and study programmes.

Learned Societies

GENERAL

Crnogorska akademija nauka i umjetnosti (CANU) (Montenegrin Academy of Sciences and Arts): Rista Stijovića 5, 81000 Podgorica; tel. (20) 655-450; fax (20) 655-451; e-mail canu@canu.ac.me; internet www.canu.org.me; f. 1971, as Society of Sciences and Arts of Montenegro, present name and status 1976; depts of arts, natural sciences, social sciences; 70 mems (32 full and 10 assoc. mems in the working body of the Academy, 28 foreign mems); library of 80,000 vols; Pres. MOMIR ĐUROVIĆ; Vice Pres. MIJAT ŠUKOVIĆ; Sec.-Gen. RANISLAV BULATOVIĆ; publs *Bibliografije* (Bibliographies), *Glasnik* (Review), *Godišnjak CANU* (1 a year), *Istorijski izvori* (Historical Issues), *Naučni skupovi* (Symposia), *Posebna izdanja* (Special Editions), *Posebni radovi* (Special Works), *Zbornici radova* (Works).

EDUCATION

Pedagogical Centre of Montenegro: Bulvr Lenjina 25/V, 81000 Podgorica; tel. and fax (20) 248-668; internet www.pccg.co.me; f. 2000; deals with professional, advanced teacher training; edits professional literature and textbooks; organizes nat. and int. professional meetings, seminars, conferences; helps continual process of innovating and improving the educational system; works in cooperation with Open Soc. Institute Montenegro, Open Soc. Institute NY (USA), Min. of Education of Montenegro, Univ. of Montenegro, Int. Step by Step Asscn, Centre for Interactive Pedagogy Belgrade, Parents Asscn, Pedagogical Centre, British Council Office; Dir SASA MILIC.

LANGUAGE AND LITERATURE

Montenegrin PEN Centre: St Gipos 1/3 postanski fah 117, Cetinje; tel. (20) 241-733; fax (20) 241-733; e-mail sreten@cg.yu; f. 1990; promotes democratic values, friendship, cooperation and use of the Montenegrin language; defends freedom of expression; 53 mems; Pres. SRETEN PEROVIC; publ. *Doclea*.

Research Institutes

BIBLIOGRAPHY, LIBRARY SCIENCE AND MUSEOLOGY

Republički zavod za zaštitu spomenika kulture (Republic Institute for the Protection of Cultural Monuments of Montenegro): Bajova 150, 81250 Cetinje; tel. (41) 231-039; fax (41) 231-753; e-mail rzzsk@t-com.me; f. 1948 as Institute for Protection and Scientific Research of Cultural Monuments and Natural Rarities; attached to Min. of Culture, Sports and Media; research, registration, conservation and protection of cultural property in Montenegro; library of 2,500 vols; Dir DJORDJIJE VUSUROVIC; publ. *Starine Crne Gore* (1 a year).

HISTORY, GEOGRAPHY AND ARCHAEOLOGY

Istorijski institut Crne Gore (Historical Institute of Montenegro): Blvr Revolucije 5, 81000 Podgorica; tel. (20) 241-624; fax (20) 241-336; e-mail iicg@ac.me; internet www.iicg.ac.me; f. 1948; attached to Univ. of Montenegro; educates experts; organizes professional devt of researchers; conducts research and publishing; Dir Dr RADOSLAV RASPOPOVIC; publ. *Istorijski zapisi* (4 a year).

LANGUAGE AND LITERATURE

Institute of Foreign Languages: Jovana Tomaševića 37, 81000 Podgorica; tel. (20) 245-453; fax (20) 243-516; e-mail isj@ac.me; internet www.ucg.ac.me; f. 1978; attached to University of Montenegro; courses in English, Russian, Italian, French and German; promotes research in linguistics, literature and interdisciplinary fields (literary linguistics, sociolinguistics, psycholinguistics); Dir Dr IGOR LAKIC.

NATURAL SCIENCES

Hidrometeorološki zavod Crne Gore (Hydrometeorological Institute): Hydrometeorological Service of Montenegro, IV proleterske 19, 81000 Podgorica; tel. (20) 655-183; fax (20) 655-197; internet www.meteo.co.me; f. 1947; meteorological, hydrological, water quality and air quality stations; activities incl. automatic measuring of land temperature, agroclimatic research, agrometeorological service, quality control of surface and underground waters and air; scientific programmes, studies and projects related to environmental field; hydrographic, topographic surveys; data colln from hydrography, navigation, geology and geophysics; Dir LUKA MITROVIC.

Institut za biologiju mora (Institute of Marine Biology): Dobrota 66, POB 69, 85330 Kotor; tel. (32) 334-569; fax (32) 334-570;

e-mail acojo@ac.me; internet www.ibmk.org; f. 1961; attached to University of Montenegro; scientific investigation, exploitation, control and protection of the sea; Dir Dr ALEKSANDAR JOKSIMOVIC; Sec. EMILIJA NIKCEVIC; Sec. Gen. RADOVAN KRIVOKAPIC; publ. *Studia Marina* (2 or 3 a year).

Institute of Biotechnology: Cetinjski put bb, 81000 Podgorica; tel. (20) 268-437; fax (20) 268-432; e-mail bti@ac.me; internet www.ucg.ac.me; f. 1937 as Centre for Subtropical cultures in Bar; attached to University of Montenegro; agriculture, veterinary medicine and forestry; Dir Dr LJUBOMIR PEJOVIĆ.

Libraries and Archives

Cetinje

Biblioteka Narodnog muzeja Crne Gore (Library of the National Museum of Montenegro): Novice Cerovica bb., 81250 Cetinje; tel. and fax (41) 230-310; e-mail nmcg@t-com.me; internet www.mnmuseum.org; f. 1926; 20,000 vols; Exec. Dept Prof. KRSTO MIJANOVIĆ.

Centralna narodna biblioteka Crne Gore (Central National Library of Montenegro): Blvr crnogorskih junaka br. 163, 81250 Cetinje; tel. (41) 231-143; fax (41) 231-020; e-mail info@cnbct.vbcg.me; internet www.cnb.me; f. 1592, present name 1964, present bldg 1980; 2,000,000 vols; spec. colln of MSS, maps, picture postcards, photographs, records, exhibition catalogues; nat. copyright and deposit library; inter-library loan; Dir DJUROVIC JELENA; publ. *Bibliografski vjesnik* (3 a year).

Državni arhiv Crne Gore (Public Records Office of Montenegro): Novice Cerovica 2, 81250 Cetinje; tel. (41) 231-045; fax (41) 232-670; f. 1951, inherited documents of the State Archive of Montenegro (f. 1895); explores and publishes archival heritage; official state documents of Montenegro since 1878; 3,760 m of documents; oldest document dates from 1539; Dir STEVAN RADUNOVIĆ; publ. *Arhivski zapisi* (Archive Records).

Herceg Novi

Herceg Novi Library: Herceg Stephan Sq. 6, Herceg Novi; tel. (31) 321-900; collns of Dušan Petkovic (5,000 books); Veljka Radojevic (1,500); Doklestic, Daljev, Lucic, Subotic; heritage colln; 30,000 vols.

Podgorica

Biblioteka istorijskog instituta Crne Gore (Library of the Historical Institute of Montenegro): Blvr revolucije 3, 81000 Podgorica; tel. (20) 241-336; fax (20) 241-624; e-mail ii@ac.me; internet www.ucg.ac.me; f. 1948; 38,000 vols.

Museums and Art Galleries

Cetinje

Narodni muzej Crne Gore (National Museum of Montenegro): Novice Cerovica bb, 81250 Cetinje; tel. and fax (41) 230-310; e-mail nmcg@t-com.me; internet www.mnmuseum.org; f. 1896; consists of five depts: Art Museum, Ethnographic Museum, Historical Museum, King Nikola's Palace and Njegoš's Museum Biljarda; contains archaeological sources, written and printed documents, war relics, furniture, ethnographic subject matter of present-day Montenegro; art works from medieval period to late 20th century; library of 30,000 vols; Dir Prof. PAVLE PEJOVIĆ; publs *Glasnik Cetinjskih Muzeja, Messenger.*

Herceg Novi

Josip Bepo Benković: Marka Vojnovića 4, Herceg Novi; tel. (31) 324-051; f. 1966; permanent exhibition of 200 paintings, sculptures and graphics; workshop for preservation and restoration; ateliers for painters and sculptors.

Zavicajni muzej Herceg-Novi (The Regional Museum of Herceg-Novi): Ulica Mirka Komnenovica 9, 85340 Herceg Novi; tel. (31) 322-485; e-mail muzej@cg.yu; internet www.rastko.org.yu/rastko-bo/muzej; f. 1949 as Nat. Museum of Herceg Novi, present bldg 2001; colln from Neolithic period to beginning of the Christian era; 30 icons; objects of traditional culture of the region, incl. tools for cattle breeding, agriculture, oil growing; nat. costumes, music instruments and household furniture; 100 Mediterranean and subtropical plants over 1,000 sq. m; Dir DJORDJE CAPIN; Curator VIKTOR VARGA; publs *Muzejske Sveske* (irregular), *Posebna Izdanja.*

Kotor

Pomorski muzej (Maritime Museum): Boka Marine Sq. 391, Kotor; tel. (32)304-720; fax (32) 325-883; internet museummaritimum.com; f. 1880 by Marina Bay Fraternity, present bldg 1984; models of ships, documents, paintings, weapons, Turkish guns, navigation instruments and compasses, folk costumes, jewellery, ornamental items and antique furniture; library of 16,000 vols; Dir JOVAN MARTINOVIĆ; publ. *Godišnjak Pomorskog Muzeja u Kotoru* (Yearbook).

Podgorica

Centar za arheološka istraživanja Crne Gore (Centre for Archaeological Research of Montenegro): Gojko Radonjic 33A, 20000 Podgorica; tel. (20) 620-018; fax (20) 620-018; e-mail czaicg@t-com.me; f. 1961, fmrly Archaeological Colln of Montenegro, present name 1997; colln, arrangement, maintenance, study and presentation of archaeological excavation sites in Montenegro.

Muzej grada Podgorice (Museum of the City of Podgorica): Marka Miljahova 4, 81000 Podgorica; tel. (20) 242-543; e-mail pgmuzeo@t-com.me; f. 1950; 4 areas of study: archaeological, ethnographic, historical and cultural-historical; colln of displays from the classical period to the present; Roman fibula, Illyrian jewellery, old coins, metal objects and bones related to the settlements and influences of different civilizations and cultures in the area.

Prirodnjački muzej Crne Gore (Natural History Museum of Montenegro): Trg Vojvode Bećir Bega Osmanagića 16, 20000 Podgorica; tel. (20) 633-184; fax (20) 623-933; e-mail zastitaprirode@t-com.me; f. 1961; research; exhibits on the fauna and palaeontology of Montenegro; museum collns; publ. *Natura Montenegrina.*

Universities

UNIVERZITET CRNE GORE, PODGORICA
(University of Montenegro, Podgorica)

Cetinjska br.2, 81000 Podgorica

Telephone: (20) 414-255
Fax: (20) 414-230
E-mail: rektor@ac.me

Internet: www.ucg.ac.me

Founded 1974, present name 1992
State control
Academic year: September to June

Rector: Prof. Dr PREDRAG MIRANOVIĆ
Vice-Rector for Teaching: Prof. Dr ANDJELKO LOJPUR
Vice-Rector for International Cooperation: Prof. Dr MIRA VUKCEVIC
Provost: Prof. ZDRAVKO USKOKOVIC
Provost: Prof. NATASA DJUROVIC
Sec.-Gen.: JELENA PAJKOVIĆ
Dir of Library: BOSILJKA CICMIL

Library of 1,030 vols, 9992 library units of monographs (including a collection of 665 doctoral dissertations and Masters theses published at the University of Montenegro)
Number of teachers: 1,273
Number of students: 11,000

Publication: *Bilten* (4 a year)

DEANS

Faculty of Architecture: Prof. Dr GORAN RADOVIĆ
Faculty of Biotechnology: Prof. Dr NATALIJA PEROVIĆ
Faculty of Civil Engineering: Dr DUSKO LUCIC
Faculty of Drama (Cetinje): SINIŠA JELUŠIĆ
Faculty of Economics: Prof. Dr MILORAD JOVOVIĆ
Faculty of Electrical Engineering: Prof. Dr SRDJAN STANKOVIC,
Fine Arts (Cetinje): NENAD ŠOŠKIĆ
Faculty of Law: Prof. Dr RANKO MUJOVIĆ
Maritime Studies (Kotor): Prof. Dr MILORAD RASKOVIC
Faculty of Mechanical Engineering: Prof. Dr GORAN ĆULAFIĆ
Faculty of Medicine: Prof. Dr BOGDAN AŠANIN
Faculty of Metallurgy and Chemical Technology: Prof. Dr KEMAL DELIJIĆ
Faculty of Natural Sciences: Prof. Dr PREDRAG STANISIC
Faculty of Political Sciences: Prof. Dr SRĐAN DARMANOVIĆ
Faculty of Philosophy: Prof. Dr BLAGOJE CEROVIC
Faculty of Sport and Physical Education: Doc. Dr DUŠKO BJELICA
College of Physiotherapy: Prof. Dr SOFIJA ŽITNIK-SIVAČKI
Faculty of Tourism and Hotel: Doc. Dr TATJANA STANOVČIĆ
Independent Study Programme for Education of Teachers in Albanian language: Prof. DAVID KALAJ (acting)
Independent Study Programme Geodesy: Prof. MITAR CVOROVIĆ (acting)
Independent Study Programme Pharmacy: Prof. REFIK ZEJNILOVIĆ
Institute of Foreign Languages: Doc. Dr IGOR LAKIĆ
Music Acad.: Prof. Dr VLADIMIR BOČKARJOV

UNIVERZITET MEDITERAN
(Mediterranean University)

Vaka Đurovića bb, 81000 Podgorica

Telephone: (20) 409-200
Fax: (20) 409-232
E-mail: office@unimediteran.net
Internet: www.unimediteran.net
Private control
Academic year: September to July (2 Semesters)

Rector: Prof. Dr STEVAN POPOVIĆ
Vice Rector for Int. Cooperation: Dr JANKO RADULOVIĆ
Sec.-Gen.: DRAGICA ANDJELIC

DEANS

Business School: Doc. Dr DRAGOLJUB JANKO-VIC

Faculty of Foreign Languages: Prof. Dr ZELJKO DJURIC

Faculty of Information Technology: Doc. Dr RAMO ŠENDELJ

Faculty of Law: Doc. Dr MLADEN VUKCEVIC

Faculty of Tourism and Management: Doc. Dr SANJA VLAHOVIC

Faculty of Visual Arts: Prof. Dr NENAD VUKOVIC

Colleges

Montenegro Business School: ul. Kralja Nikole 114, 81000 Podgorica; tel. and fax (20) 602-545; e-mail ssluzba.mbs@unimediteran .net; internet www.fps.unimediteran.net; f. 2005; offers courses in financial management, marketing; 654 students; Dean DRA-GOLJUB JANKOVIĆ; Sec. VESNA MIJATOVIĆ.

Montenegro Tourism School: c/o Univer-zitet Mediteran, Vaka Đurovića bb, 81000 Podgorica; e-mail fakultetht_bar@t-com.me; internet www.ftht.unimediteran.net; f. 2004; offers gen. Masters and Doctoral studies; courses in management, marketing, information technology in tourism and hotel management; sustainable devt; strategic management; contemporary trends and devts in tourism; Dean Doc. Dr SANJA VLAHOVIC; Vice-Dean of Finance and Development Doc. Dr DARKO LACMANOVIĆ; Sec. SNEŽANA PETROVIĆ.

MOROCCO

The Higher Education System

Université Quaraouyine Fès (founded 859), an institution for Koranic, Islamic and Arabic studies, is among the oldest universities in continuous existence in the world. From 1912 until 1958 Morocco was a French protectorate and, consequently, the higher education system displays strong French influences. The Université Mohammed V Agdal (founded 1957) is the oldest multi-disciplinary institution of secular studies. In 1997/98 there were 68 state university-level institutions and in 2006/07 there were some 369,142 students in further and higher education.

The Ministry of National Education, Higher Education, Staff Training and Scientific Research is the supreme authority of higher education, which is free to Moroccan students. The senior officers of universities, such as Presidents and Deans of Faculty, are state appointees, and are responsible for running universities in conjunction with University Councils, Faculty Councils and Faculty Scientific Councils. The main types of institutions of higher education are universities, higher schools (grandes écoles), teacher-training institutes and other specialist institutes.

Admission to higher education is often on the basis of the secondary school awards, Diplôme du Baccalauréat and Diplôme du Baccalauréat Technique, but additional two-year courses (classes préparatoires aux grandes écoles) are required for entry to the grandes écoles. Most university degrees fall into one of three cycles, with some exceptions; these include degrees for disciplines that require longer periods of undergraduate study than the standard four years, such as engineering (five years), veterinary medicine and agronomy (six years) and medicine (seven years). The first cycle of higher education consists of certificates and diplomas awarded after two years of a broad-based programme of study in one of four subject groups (arts and humanities, science and economics, applied sciences, engineering and agriculture) appropriate to the intended area of specialization. Students in the arts and humanities are awarded the Certificat Universitaire d'études Littéraires; students in science and economics receive the Certificat Universitaire d'études Scientifiques; students in applied sciences are awarded Diplôme d'études Universitaires Générales or Diplôme d'études Universitaires de Technologie; while students in engineering and agriculture undertake a two-year preparatory programme of study. The second cycle of higher education is a period of specialist training and culminates in the award of either the Licence or the Maîtrise. Students who have the Certificat Universitaire d'études Littéraires or Certificat Universitaire d'études Scientifiques undertake a further two years of study for the Licence, while holders of the Diplôme d'études Universitaires Générales or Diplôme d'études Universitaires de Technologie are awarded the Maîtrise after the same period. Professional titles are awarded in some disciplines, like engineering (Diplôme d'Ingénieur d'état), veterinary medicine (Docteur Vétérinaire) and medicine (Doctorat en Médecine). The third cycle of higher education awards consists mainly of three degrees, Diplôme d'études Supérieures Approfondies, Diplôme d'études Supérieures Spécialisées and Doctorat d'État. Holders of the Licence are eligible for admission to the Diplôme d'études Supérieures Approndies, a two-year programme of study and research, culminating in submission of a dissertation, that allows admission to doctoral-level studies. The Diplôme d'études Supérieures Spécialisées is also a two-year course, open to holders of either the Licence or Maîtrise, but does not qualify the student for doctoral-level studies. The Doctorat d'État is the highest university-level degree and comprises three to five years of research. Outside the university system, the grandes écoles offer specialist degrees such as Diplôme de Technicien Supérieur and Diplôme d'Ingénieur d'État.

Students with Diplôme du Baccalauréat and the Diplôme du Baccalauréat Technique may attend post-secondary vocational and technical education and study for the Brevet de Technicien Supérieur, which requires successful completion of a two-year programme of study.

In 2004 a number of faculties at Morocco's universities underwent reforms to bring them into line with European universities. As part of the new degree structure new curriculums and a system of transferable credits were introduced, allowing students to take courses from different departments and different institutions or to leave university and continue their studies later. Under the new structure the studies were reorganized into three years of first-cycle studies (Licence), two years of second-cycle studies (Masters) and three years of doctoral studies (Doctorat).

The national accreditation body for tertiary education is the National Accreditation and Evaluation Committee (Commission Nationale d'Accreditation et d'Évaluation).

Regulatory Bodies

GOVERNMENT

Ministry of Culture: 1 rue Ghandi, Rabat; tel. 37-20-94-94; fax 37-20-94-01; e-mail webmaster@minculture.gov.ma; internet www.minculture.gov.ma; Min. BENSALEM HIMMICH.

Ministry of National Education, Higher Education, Staff Training and Scientific Research: Bab Rouah, Rabat; tel. 37-77-48-39; fax 37-77-90-01; e-mail divcom@men.gov.ma; internet www.men.gov.ma; Minister AHMED AKHCHICHINE.

Learned Societies

GENERAL

Académie du Royaume du Maroc: Charia Mohammed VI, Km 11, BP 5062, 10100 Rabat,; tel. (5) 37-75-51-99; fax (5) 37-75-51-01; e-mail arm@alacademia.org.ma; f. 1980; promotes devt of research and reflection in principal fields of intellectual activity, publishes books on Moroccan and Islamic heritage; library of 20,000 vols; 60 mems; Permanent Sec. Dr ABDELLATIF BERBICH; publs *Academia* (1 a year), *Colloquiums* (2 a year), *Proceedings of Sessions* (2 a year).

UNESCO Office Rabat: BP 1777 RP, 10106 Rabat; 35 ave du 16 Novembre, Agdal, 10000 Rabat; tel. 37-67-03-72; fax 37-67-03-75; e-mail rabat@unesco.org; f. 1991; designated Cluster Office for Algeria, Libya, Mauritania, Morocco and Tunisia; Dir ROSAMARIA DURAND.

AGRICULTURE, FISHERIES AND VETERINARY SCIENCE

Société d'Horticulture et d'Acclimatation du Maroc: BP 13.854, 20001 Casablanca; f. 1914; 260 mems; Pres. JOSETTE DUPLAT; Sec. RENÉ TRIPOTIN.

ECONOMICS, LAW AND POLITICS

Société d'Etudes Economiques, Sociales et Statistiques du Maroc: BP 535, Chellah, 10002 Rabat; f. 1933; 20 mems; Dir NACER EL FASSI; publ. *Signes du Présent* (4 a year).

FINE AND PERFORMING ARTS

Association des Amateurs de la Musique Andalouse: c/o 133 blvd Ziraoui, 20000 Casablanca; f. 1956 to preserve and catalogue traditional Moroccan (Andalusian) music; maintains a School of Andalusian music at Casablanca, directed and subsidized by the Ministry of Culture; Dir Hadj DRISS BENJELLOUN.

HISTORY, GEOGRAPHY AND ARCHAEOLOGY

Association Nationale de Géographie Marocaine: Faculté des Lettres et des Sciences Humaines, Université Mohammed V Adgal, 10100 Rabat; tel. 37-77-18-93; fax 37-77-20-68; f. 1916; Sec.-Gen. TAOUFIK AGOUMI;

publ. *Revue de Géographie du Maroc* (2 a year).

LANGUAGE AND LITERATURE

Alliance Française: 22 ave de la Marche Verte, 24000 El Jadida; tel. 23-34-21-06; fax 23-35-31-82; e-mail afm.eljadida@iam.net .ma; internet www.ambafrance-ma.org/ institut/afm-eljadida; offers courses and examinations in French language and culture and promotes cultural exchange with France; attached teaching centre in Essaouira.

British Council: 11, rue Allal Ben Abdellah, BP 427, Rabat; tel. (5) 37-21-81-30; fax (5) 37-76-08-50; e-mail info@britishcouncil .org.ma; internet www.britishcouncil.org/ morocco; teaching centre; offers courses and examinations in English language and British culture and promotes cultural exchange with the UK; attached teaching centre in Casablanca; library of 8,000 vols, 20 periodicals; Dir MARTIN ROSE; Teaching Centre Man. MARK BUCCIANTI.

Goethe-Institut: 7 rue Sana'a, 10001 Rabat; tel. 537-70-65-44; fax 537-70-82-66 11, Place du 16 Novembre, 20000 Casablanca; tel. 522-20-04-45; fax 522-48-37-32; e-mail progr@ rabat.goethe.org; internet www.goethe.de/ rabat; offers courses and examinations in German language and promotes cultural exchange; library of 20,000 vols; Dir WOLF-GANG MEISSNER.

Instituto Cervantes: 5 Zankat Madnine, 10000 Rabat; tel. 37-70-87-38; fax 37-70-02-79; e-mail cenrabat@cervantes.org.ma; internet rabat.cervantes.es; offers courses and examinations in Spanish language and culture and promotes cultural exchange with Spain and Spanish-speaking Latin and Central America; attached centres in Casablanca, Fez, Tangier and Tétouan; library; Dir XABIER MARKIEGI CANDINA.

Research Institutes
GENERAL

Centre National pour la Recherche Scientifique et Technique: 52 Charii Omar Ibn Khattab, BP 8027, 10102 Agdal-Rabat; tel. 37-77-28-03; fax 37-77-12-88; e-mail cnr@cnr.ac.ma; internet www.cnr.ac .ma; f. 1976; attached to Min. of Nat. Education, Higher Education, Staff Training and Scientific Research; research fields include food and agriculture, communication, environment, natural resources, astronomy, geophysics, biotechnology, geology, computer science, mathematics, social sciences, int. business, environmental science, energy and maintenance; library of 3,500 vols, 70 periodicals; Dir SAID BELCADI (acting); Sec.-Gen. (vacant); publ. *Lettre d'Information* (1 a year).

AGRICULTURE, FISHERIES AND VETERINARY SCIENCE

Institut National de la Recherche Agronomique: BP 6512 RI, Rabat; tel. 37-77-55-30; fax 37-77-40-03; internet www.inra.org .ma; f. 1930; research in agronomy; library of 40,000 vols, 300 periodicals; Dir A. ARIFI; publs *Al Awamia* (4 a year), *Les Cahiers de la Recherche Agronomique* (irregular).

Institut National de Recherche Halieutique: 2 rue de Tiznit, Casablanca; tel. 22-22-88-70; fax 22-26-88-57; f. 1947; applied fisheries oceanography, marine biology, evaluation of resources, aquaculture, environmental studies, fishing gear technology, fish processing technology, fisheries management; library of 1,050 vols, 70 periodicals; Dir

MOHAMED SEDRATI; publs *Bulletin, Notes d'Information, Travaux et Documents.*

Mission Pédologique: Min. of Agriculture and Fisheries, BP 432, Rabat; pedology; Dir J. L. GEOFFROY.

ECONOMICS, LAW AND POLITICS

Centre d'Etudes, de Documentation et d'Informations Economiques et Sociales (CEDIES–Informations): Angle ave des Forces Armées Royales et angle rue Mohamed Errachid, 20100 Casablanca; tel. 22-25-26-96; fax 22-25-38-39; Pres. ABDERRA-HIM LAHJOUJI; publ. *CEDIES Informations.*

La Fondation du Roi Abdul Aziz pour les Etudes Islamiques et les Sciences Humaines: BP 12585, 20052 Casablanca; located at: blvd de la Corniche, Ain Diab, Anfa, 20050 Casablanca; tel. 22-39-10-27; fax 22-39-10-31; e-mail secretariat@fondation .org.ma; internet www.fondation.org.ma; f. 1985; promotes the study of social sciences and humanities in the Maghreb, by means of documentation and cultural activities; library of 310,000 vols, 1,289 periodicals; Dir PRINCE ABDULLAH IBN-ABD-AL-AZIZ-AL-SA'UD; publ. *Lettre d'Information* (2 a year).

HISTORY, GEOGRAPHY AND ARCHAEOLOGY

Comité National de Géographie du Maroc: Institut Universitaire de la Recherche Scientifique, BP 2122 Riad, Rabat; f. 1959; Pres. THE MIN. OF NAT. EDUCATION, HIGHER EDUCATION, STAFF TRAINING AND SCIENTIFIC RESEARCH; Sec.-Gen. A. LAOUINA; publ. *Atlas du Maroc.*

LANGUAGE AND LITERATURE

Instituto Muley El Hassan: PB 84, Tétouan; research on Hispano-Muslim works; library of 5,500 vols; Dirs MOHAMMED BEN TAUÍT, MARIANO ARRIBAS PALAU.

MEDICINE

Direction de l'Epidémiologie et de Lutte Contre les Maladies: 71 ave Ibn Sina, Agdal, Rabat; tel. 37-67-12-71; fax 37-67-12-98; e-mail delm@sante.gov.ma; internet www .sante.gov.ma/departements/delm/index--delm.htm; f. 1990; applied research in epidemiology and environmental health; Dir Dr NOUREDDINE CHAOUKI; publ. *Bulletin Epidémiologique* (3 a year).

Institut National d'Hygiène: POB 769, Rabat Agdal; tel. 37-77-19-02; fax 37-77-20-67; e-mail relaouad@sante.gov.ma; internet www.sante.gov.ma/inh; f. 1930; depts of microbiology, parasitology, physics and chemistry, toxicology, serology, immunology, molecular biology, genetics, entomology; Nat. Poison Control Centre; 266 mems; library: Toxicological Documentation Centre of 400 vols; library of 3,000 vols; Dir Prof. RAJAE EL AOUAD.

Institut Pasteur du Maroc: 1 pl. Louis Pasteur, 20100 Casablanca; tel. 22-43-44-50; fax 22-26-09-57; e-mail pasteur@pasteur.ma; internet www.pasteur.ma; f. 1911; research into infectious diseases, bacteriology, parasitology and virology, biochemistry and genetics, food and environmental safety; promotion of public health; Dir Prof. MOHAM-MED HASSAR.

NATURAL SCIENCES
Physical Sciences

Direction de la Géologie: c/o Ministry of Energy, Mining, Water, and Environment, BP 6208, Rabat-Instituts; tel. 37-68-88-57; fax 37-68-88-63; e-mail dsi@mem.gov.ma; f. 1921; Nat. Geological Survey; library of 25,000 vols; Pres ABDELHAQ SMIDI; publs

Mines, Géologie et Energie, Notes et Mémoires du Service Géologique du Maroc.

TECHNOLOGY

Bureau de Recherches et de Participations Minières (BRPM): 5 Charia Moulay Hassan, BP 99, Rabat; tel. 37-76-30-35; fax 37-76-24-10; f. 1928; state agency to develop mining research and industry; Gen. Man. ASSOU LHA TOUTE.

Laboratoire Public d'Essais et d'Etudes: 25 rue d'Azilal, Casablanca; tel. 22-30-04-50; fax 22-30-15-50; f. 1947; hydraulics, environment, roads, study of soil, materials and methods of construction; library of 7,000 vols; Dir-Gen. MOHAMED JELLALI; publs *LPEE-Magazine* (4 a year), *Revue Marocaine de Génie Civil* (4 a year).

Libraries and Archives
Casablanca

Bibliothèque de la Communauté Urbaine de Casablanca: 142 ave des Forces Armées Royales, Casablanca; tel. 22-31-41-70; f. 1917; law, political economy, sciences, philosophy, history, literature, the arts, geography, medicine, sport, travel, fiction; 91,307 vols in Arab section, 267,149 vols in foreign section; 137 periodicals, several foreign daily newspapers; Dir HAJ MOHAMED BOUZID.

Fez

Bibliothèque de l'Université Quaraouyine Fès: Place des Seffarines, Fez; 22,071 vols, 5,157 MSS, 38 archives.

Marrakesh

Bibliothèque Ben Youssef: ave 11 Janvier, Hay Mohamadi Daoudiat, Marrakesh; 21,223 vols, 586 periodicals, 1,840 MSS; Dir SEDDIK BELLARBI.

Rabat

Bibliothèque de l'Institut Scientifique: ave Ibn Battota, BP 703, Agdal, 10106 Rabat; tel. 37-77-45-48; fax 37-77-45-40; f. 1920; zoology, botany, geomorphology, cartography, ecology, earth sciences, geophysics, remote detection; 15,700 vols, 1,728 periodicals; Librarian ABDELLATIF BAYED; publs *Bulletin de l'Institute Scientifique, Travaux de l'Institut Scientifique.*

Bibliothèque Générale et Archives: BP 1003, ave Ibn Battouta, Rabat; tel. 37-77-18-90; fax 37-77-60-62; f. 1920; 600,000 vols, 31,000 MSS and 2,000 linear metres of archives; Dir AHMED TOUFIQ; publ. *Bibliographie Nationale* (2 a year).

Centre National de Documentation:; tel. 37-77-49-44; fax 37-77-31-34; internet www .abhatoo.net.ma; f. 1966; documentation on the economic, social, scientific and technical development of Morocco; library depository of World Bank publications; regional reps in Fès, Tangier, Casablanca, Agadir, Marrakesh, Meknès, Oujda; mem. of FID and IFLA; 9,000 vols, 120,000 microfiches, 350 periodicals; Dir ADNANE BENCHAKROUN; publ. *KATAB* (bibliography).

Tangier

Biblioteca Juan Goytisolo: 99 ave Sidi Mohamed Ben Abdellah, 90000 Tangier; tel. 39-93-23-99; fax 39-94-76-03; e-mail bibtan@ cervantes.es; internet tanger.cervantes.es/es/ biblioteca_espanol/biblioteca_espanol.htm; f. 1941; attached to Instituto Cervantes; main collection in the Spanish language; antique Spanish publications from 18th and 19th centuries; periodical library includes Spanish, Arab and African titles; Spanish sheet music from early 20th century; photographic archive from former Spanish tourist office in Tangier; 90,000 vols; Librarian SÍLVIA MONTERO GÓMEZ; publ. *Miscelanea de la Biblioteca Española*.

Tétouan

Bibliothèque Générale et Archives: 32 ave Mohammed V, BP 692, Tétouan; tel. 39-96-32-58; fax 39-96-10-04; e-mail bgatetou@imam.net.ma; internet www.minculture.gov.ma; f. 1939; research and public library; 50,000 books, 3,500 periodicals, 2,400 MSS, 23,000 historical archive items, 1,200,000 admin. archive items, 45,000 photographs, 1,429 numismatic items; Dir Dr M. ZOUAK.

Museums and Art Galleries

Chefchaouen

Musée Ethnographique de Chefchaouen: Kasbah Outa Hammam, Chefchaouen; tel. 39-98-67-61; f. 1985; musical instruments, arms, embroidery, carved boxes, local pottery.

Essaouira

Musée Sidi Mohamed ben Abdellah: Derb Laalouj, Essaouira; tel. 24-47-23-00; f. 1981; musical instruments, jewellery, arms, carved wooden objects.

Fez

Musée d'Armes du Borj-Nord: Borj-Nord, Fez; tel. 35-64-52-41; built as a military fort in the 16th century, converted into a museum in 1963; collection of 1,100 military artefacts; Curator MOHAMED ZAIM.

Musée Batha: Ksar el Batha, Fez; tel. 35-63-41-16; built as a royal residence in 19th century; converted into a museum in 1915; colln incl. sculpted wood and plaster objects, cast iron, local blue ceramics, embroidery, coins, carpets, jewellery, astrological instruments; Curator HNIA CHIKHAOUI.

Larache

Musée Archéologique: Larache; tel. 39-51-20-92; f. 1973; remains found primarily at the Lixus archaeological site, from the Phoenician, Carthaginian, Mauritanian, Roman and Islamic ages.

Marrakesh

Musée Dar Si Saïd: Derb el Bahia, Riad El Zaitoun El Jadid, Marrakesh; tel. 24-44-24-64; internet www.minculture.gov.ma/fr/musee%20dar%20si%20said.htm; f. as a royal residence in 19th century, converted into a museum in 1932; artefacts from the Marrakesh region and southern Morocco, incl. wooden objects, jewellery, pottery and ceramics, arms, carpets and woven materials; archaeological remains; Dir HASSAN BEL ARBI.

Meknès

Musée Dar El Jamaï: Pl. El Hedime, Meknès; tel. 35-53-08-63; f. 1920; handicraft items from the region, incl. embroidery, wood carvings, leatherwork, carved chests, carpets, ceramics, ancient jewellery, wrought ironwork, copper and brass objects, painted woodwork, traditional costumes and ancient Korans; Chief Curator HASSAN CHERRADI.

Moulay Driss Zerhoun

Site Archéologique de Volubilis: Conservation du Site de Volubilis, Moulay Driss Zerhoun, Meknès; tel. and fax 35-54-41-03; e-mail volubilisarcheosite@yahoo.fr; f. 1950; archaeological site; library of 250 vols; Archaeologist YOUSSEF BOKBOT.

Rabat

Musée Archéologique: 23 rue Al-Brihi, Rabat; tel. 37-70-19-19; fax 37-75-08-84; f. 1931; history of Morocco from prehistory until the Islamic era; collns incl. stone tools, primitive furniture, Roman divinities, bronze and marble statues, early Islamic ceramics; Curator ABDELWAHED BEN-NCER.

Musée Ethnographique des Oudaïa: Kasba des Oudaïa, Rabat; tel. 37-72-64-61; f. 1915; clothing from various regions of Morocco, jewellery, astronomical tools, carpets, pottery, musical instruments; Curator HOUCEINE EL KASRI.

Musée de la Kasbah: 23 rue el Brihi, Rabat; archaeology and folklore; Curator MOHAMMED HABIBI.

Safi

Musée National de la Céramique: Kachla, Safi; tel. 24-46-38-95; f. 1990; originally a military fort; Curator NOUREDDINE ESSAFSAFI.

Tangier

Musée d'Art Contemporain: 52 ave d'Angleterre, Tangier; tel. 39-94-99-72; f. 1990; constructed as British consulate; modern Moroccan art.

Tangier American Legation Institute for Moroccan Studies (TALIM): 8 Zankat America, Tangier; tel. 39-93-53-17; fax 39-93-59-60; e-mail director.talim@gmail.com; internet www.legation.org; f. 1976; operated by the Tangier American Legation Museum Soc., Inc.; permanent colln paintings since 16th century, etchings, aquatints, prints and maps of Morocco; also documentation and artefacts concerning Moroccan-American relations; sponsors short-term exhibitions of contemporary artists; library: research library of 8,000 vols on North Africa and Morocco in Arabic, English, French, Portuguese, Spanish; Dir GERALD LOFTUS.

Tétouan

Musée Archéologique: 2 rue Ben Hussain, Tétouan; tel. 39-96-73-03; f. 1939; prehistoric and pre-Islamic archaeological remains from northern Morocco; mosaics and coins.

Musée des Arts Traditionnels: Tétouan; Curator AMRANI AHMED.

Musée Ethnographique: BP 41 Tétouan; Zankat Skala, 65 Bab El Okla, 93000 Tétouan; tel. 39-97-05-05; f. 1928; originally a fortress; carved wooden objects, copperware, pottery, embroidery.

Universities

UNIVERSITÉ ABDELMALEK ESSAÂDI TÉTOUAN

BP 211, Route de l'Aéroport, Tétouan

Telephone: 39-99-51-34

Fax: 39-97-91-51

Internet: www.uae.ma

Founded 1989

State control

Languages of instruction: Arabic, French

Campus in Tangier; Faculties of arts and humanities, economics and social sciences, law, science and technology; schools of commerce and management, and translation

Rector: MUSTAPHA BENNOUNA

Number of teachers: 632

Number of students: 17,150

Publication: *Tourjouman* (Journal of the School of Translation).

UNIVERSITÉ AL AKHAWAYN IFRANE

BP 104, ave Hassan II, 53000 Ifrane

Telephone: 35-86-20-00

Fax: 35-56-71-50

E-mail: devcom@alakhawayn.ma

Internet: www.alakhawayn.ma

Founded 1995

Private control

Language of instruction: English

Academic year: September to July

Pres.ident: Prof. RACHID BENMOKHTAR BENABDELLAH

Vice-Pres.ident for Academic Affairs: Prof. ABDELLATIF BENCHERIFA

Vice-Pres.ident for Finance and Admin.istration: ABDELILAH KAMAL

Exec.utive Director for Development and Communication: RACHID SLIMI

Dean of Student Affairs: Dr CHARIF BELFEKIH

Library of 65,000 books, 400 periodicals

Number of teachers: 90

Number of students: 1,012 (899 undergraduate, 113 postgraduate)

DEANS

School of Business Administration: Dr AHMED DRIOUCHI

School of Humanities and Social Sciences: Dr MOHAMED DAHBI (acting)

School of Science and Engineering: Dr AMINE BENSAID

DIRECTORS

Center for Academic Development and Study Skills: CATHERINE OWENS

Center of Environmental Issues and Regional Development: Dr BACHIR RAISSOUNI

Executive Education Center: NADIA SANDI

Hillary Rodham Clinton Women's Empowerment Center: LEÏLA BOUASRIA

Institute of Economic Analysis and Prospective Studies: RACHID SLIMI

Language Center: MONCEF LAHLOU

UNIVERSITÉ CADI AYYAD MARRAKECH

Blvd Prince Moulay Abdellah, POB 511, Marrakesh

Telephone: (524) 43-48-13

Fax: (524) 43-44-94

E-mail: presidence@ucam.ac.ma

Internet: www.ucam.ac.ma

Founded 1978

State control

Languages of instruction: Arabic, French, English

Academic year: September to July

Rector: Prof. MOHAMED MARZAK

Vice-Pres.: Prof. BOUMEDIEN TANOUTI

Vice-Pres.: Prof. MOHAMED LARBI SIDMOU

Sec.-Gen.: RACHID HILAL

Number of teachers: 1,868

Number of students: 33,359

Publications: *Revue de la Faculté de Droit*, *Revue de la Faculté des Lettres*, *Revue de la Faculté des Sciences*, *Manarat Al Jamiaa*

DEANS

Faculty of Law, Economics and Social Sciences: MRANI ZANTAR M'HAMMED

Faculty of Letters and Humanities: TEBBAA OUIDAD

Faculty of Medicine and Pharmacy: ALAOUI YAZIDI

Faculty of Sciences (Semlalia): Prof. LOUIDIKI AHMED

Faculty of Science and Technics: ABBOUSSALAH MOHAMED

Higher School of Technology (Essaouira): BELAID BOUGADIR

Higher School of Technology (Safi): MOHAMED EL ARBI EL ACHHAB

National School of Applied Sciences: AIT OUAHMAN ABDELLAH

National School of Applied Sciences (Safi): AHMED DERJA

National School of Business and Administration: RIGAR SIDI MOHAMED

Poly-disciplinary Faculty: EL HASSANE BOU-MAGGARD

University Centre (Kalaat Sraghna): HAMMADI BOUSLOUSS

UNIVERSITÉ CHOUAÏB DOUKKALI EL JADIDA

BP 299, 2 bis, ave Mohamed ben Larbi Alaoui, Koudiate ben Driss, 24000 El Jadida

Telephone: 23-34-44-47
Fax: 23-34-44-49
Internet: www.ucd.ac.ma
Founded 1989
State control
Languages of instruction: Arabic, English, French
Faculties of arts and humanities, science
Rector: ABDELHAMID AHMADY
Library of 14,460 vols
Number of teachers: 440
Number of students: 8,100
Publications: *Magazine de la Faculté des Lettres Parallèles*, *Revue de la Faculté des Lettres*.

UNIVERSITÉ HASSAN I SETTAT

BP 539, 50 rue Ibn Al Haithem, 26000 Settat
Telephone: 23-72-12-75
Fax: 23-72-12-74
Internet: www.uh1.ac.ma
State control
Rector: MOHAMED RAHJ
Number of teachers: 204
Number of students: 6,679

Faculties of economics and social sciences, law, science and technology; School of commerce and management.

UNIVERSITÉ HASSAN II — CASABLANCA

BP 9167, 19 rue Tarik Bnou Ziad, Mers Sultan, Casablanca
Telephone: 522-43-30-30
Fax: 522-27-61-50
Internet: www.uh2c.ac.ma
Founded 1975
Languages of instruction: Arabic, French
Academic year: September to July
Pres.: MOHAMMED BARKAOUI
Vice-Pres. for Academic Affairs: IDRISS MANSOURI
Vice-Pres. for Research and Cooperation: JAAFAR KHALID NACIRI
Sec-Gen.: ABDELHADI MOSLIH
Librarian: (vacant)
Number of teachers: 1,027
Number of students: 26,000
Publication: faculty reviews, newsletter

DEANS

Faculty of Arts and Human Sciences: SAID BENNANI

Faculty of Dentistry: AMAL OUAZZANI ECHCHAHDI

Faculty of Law: ESSALMI IDRISSI

Faculty of Medicine and Pharmacy: LHOUSSAINE LOUARDI

Faculty of Sciences: OUZZANI

National Higher School of Electronics and Mechanics: JANAH SAADI (Dir)

Teacher-Training College: OUBAHAMMO (Dir)

Technology High School: SARSOURI (Dir)

UNIVERSITÉ HASSAN II MOHAMMEDIA

BP 150, 279 Cité Yassmina, Mohammedia
Telephone: 23-31-46-35
Fax: 23-31-46-34
Internet: www.uh2m.ac.ma
Founded 1992
State control
Rector: RAHMA BOURQIA

DEANS

Faculty of Arts and Humanities, Ben Msik Campus: ABDELHAK HAMAM

Faculty of Arts and Humanities, Mohammedia Campus: ABDELJAWAD SEKKAT

Faculty of Economics, Law and Social Science, Mohammedia Campus: MOHAMED DASSER

Faculty of Science, Ben Msik Campus: MOHAMMED BERRADA

Faculty of Science and Technology, Mohammedia Campus: MOHAMED RAFIQ

UNIVERSITÉ IBN TOFAIL KÉNITRA

BP 242, 104 rue Ahmed Boughaba, Bir rami Est, 14000 Kénitra
Telephone: 37-32-28-09
Fax: 37-37-40-52
E-mail: ruitk@iam.net.ma
Internet: www.univ-ibntofail.ac.ma
Founded 1989
State control
Pres.: MOHAMMED ESSOUARI
Sec.-Gen.: ABDALLAH EL MALIKI
Library of 42,007 vols
Number of teachers: 405
Number of students: 11,884

DEANS

Faculty of Arts and Humanities: ABDELFETTAH BENKADDOUR

Faculty of Science: ALI BOUKHARI

UNIVERSITÉ IBNOU ZOHR AGADIR

BP 3215, Agadir
Founded 1989
Rector: MUSTAPHA DKHISSI
Number of students: 9,724

Faculties of letters and humanities, sciences.

UNIVERSITÉ MOHAMMED I OUJDA

BP 524, 60000 Oujda
Telephone: 36-74-47-83
Fax: 36-74-47-79
Internet: www.univ-oujda.ac.ma
Founded 1978
State control
Languages of instruction: Arabic, French
Academic year: October to June
Rector: EL-MADANI BELKHADIR
Secretary-General: ABDERRAHMAN HOUTECH
Librarian: ZOUBIDA CHAHI
Number of teachers: 593
Number of students: 19,872
Publications: *Al Mayadine*, *Cahiers du CEMM*, *Revue de la Faculté des Lettres*

DEANS

Faculty of Law and Economics: EL-LARBI M'RABET

Faculty of Letters and Human Sciences: MOHAMMED LAAMIRI

Faculty of Science: BENAÏSSA N'CIRI

Institute of Technology: MOHAMMED BARBOUCHA (Dir)

UNIVERSITÉ MOHAMMED V AGDAL

BP 554, Ave des Nations Unies, Agdal, Rabat
Telephone: 37-27-27-50
Fax: 37-67-14-01

E-mail: presidence@um5a.ac.ma
Internet: www.um5a.ac.ma
Founded 1957
State control
Languages of instruction: Arabic, French
Academic year: September to July
Pres.: WAIL BENJELLOUN
Sec.-Gen.: MOHAMMED HOUMINE
Librarian: ILHAM YACOUBI
Number of teachers: 992
Number of students: 19,498

Publications: *Annales du Centre des Études Stratégiques*, *Bulletin de l'Institut Scientifique*, *Bulletin Magnétique*, *Bulletin Séismologique*, *Documents de l'Institut Scientifique*, *Hespéris Tamuda* (1 a year, in English, French and Spanish), *Langues et Littératures* (1 a year, in European languages), *Revue de la Faculté des Lettres et des Sciences Humaines* (1 a year, in Arabic), *Revue des Sciences de la Terre*, *Revue Marocaine de l'Automatique, de l'Informatique et du Traitement du Signal*, *Revue Marocaine Juridique, Politique et Economique*, *Travaux de l'Institut Scientific*

DEANS

Faculty of Law and Economics: LAHCEN OULHAJ

Faculty of Letters and Human Sciences: ABDERRAHIM BENHADDA

Faculty of Sciences: WAIL BENJELLOUN

Higher School of Technology (Salé): MOHAMMED RHACHI

Mohammadia School of Engineering: DRISS BOUAMI

Institute of Hispano-Lusophone Studies: FATIHA BENLABAH

Scientific Institute: AHMED EL HASSANI

UNIVERSITÉ MOHAMMED V SOUISSI RABAT

BP 8007, N.U. Agdal, Rabat
ave Med Benabdellah Regragui, Madinat al-Irfane, Rabat
Telephone: 37-68-11-60
Fax: 37-68-11-63
E-mail: presidence@um5s.ac.ma
Internet: www.um5s.ac.ma
Founded 1993
Languages of instruction: Arabic, English, French, French, English
Academic year: September to July
Pres.: Prof. RADOUANE MRABET
Vice Pres. for Academic Affairs: Prof. HASSAN ABOUABDELMAJID
Vice Pres. ifor Research and Cooperation: Prof. RACHID BEZAD
Sec.-Gen.
Number of teachers: 1,200
Number of students: 19,000
Publications: *Al Irfane* (information bulletin, 3 a year), *Reflexions* (science, 4 a year)

DEANS

ENSET (Electrical and Mechanical Engineering): LARBI BELARBI

Faculty of Dentistry: SANA RIDA

Faculty of Education: ABDESSALAM OUAZANI

Faculty of Law: KHALID BERJAOUI

Faculty of Law, Salé: EL HOUSSINE SNOUSSI

Faculty of Medicine and Pharmacy: NAJIA HAJJAJ

National Higher School of Informatics and Systems Analysis: ILHAM BERRADA (Dir)

Research Institute of Arabisation (IERA): MOHAMMED BENMOUSSA

Research Institute for Africa (IEA): YAHYA ABOUALFARAH

Research Institute of Science (IURS): AMINA AOUCHAR

UNIVERSITÉ MOULAY ISMAIL MEKNÈS

BP 298, Marjane I, Meknès
Telephone: (5) 35-46-73-06
Fax: (5) 35-46-73-05
Founded 1982; univ. status 1989
State control
Pres.: MOHAMMED ZAHIR BEN ABDELLAH
Number of teachers: 722
Number of students: 25,137
Publications: *Maksanat* (Journal of the Faculty of Arts and Human Sciences), *Minbar Al Mamiaa* (1 a year), *Zetouna* (Journal of the Faculty of Law, Economics and Social Studies)

DEANS

Faculty of Arts and Human Sciences: ABDELLAH MALKI
Faculty of Law, Economics and Social Studies: MOHAMED BENJELOUN
Faculty of Sciences: MOHAMED KEROUAD
Faculty of Sciences and Technology: ABDELLAH EL MANSSOUR
Polydisciplinary Faculty: MOHAMMED EDDOUKSSE

UNIVERSITÉ QUARAOUYINE FÈS

Dhar Mahraz, BP 2509, Fez
Telephone: 35-64-10-06
Fax: 35-64-10-13
Founded AD 859, enlarged in 11th century, reorganized 1963
State control
Language of instruction: Arabic
Academic year: September to July
Rector: Prof. ABDELOUAHHAB TAZI SAOUD
Secretary-General: MOHAMMED BENNANI ZOUBIR
Number of teachers: 115
Number of students: 6,000.

CONSTITUENT INSTITUTES

Faculty of Arabic Studies: ave Allal Al-Fassi, BP 1483, Marrakesh; Dean Prof. HASSAN JELLAB.
Faculty of Sharia: BP 52, Agadir; Dean Prof. MOHAMMED ATTAHIRI.
Faculty of Sharia (Law): BP 60, Saïs, Fez; Dean Prof. MOHAMMED YESSEF.
Faculty of Theology: blvd Abdelkhalek Torres, BP 95, Tétouan; Dean Prof. DRISS KHALIFA.

UNIVERSITÉ SIDI MOHAMED BEN ABDELLAH FÈS

BP 2626, ave des Almohades, 30000 Fez,
Telephone: 35-60-96-60
Fax: 35-60-96-50
Founded 1975
State control
Languages of instruction: Arabic, French
Academic year: September to July
Pres.: ESSERRHINI FARISSI
Vice-Pres. for Academic Affairs: MOHAMED AÏT EL MEKKI
Vice-Pres. for Scientific Research and Cooperation: MOULHIME EL BEKKALI
Sec.-Gen.: ABDELKADER MAROUANE
Library of 225,000 vols
Number of teachers: 1,274
Number of students: 56,762

DEANS

Faculty of Law, Economics and Social Sciences (Agdal): ABDELAZIZ SQUALLI
Faculty of Letters and Human Sciences (Agdal): ABDELILLAH BENMLIH

Faculty of Letters and Human Sciences (Saiss): IBRAHIM AKDIM
Faculty of Medicine and Pharmacy (Saiss): MOULAY HASSAN FARIH
Faculty of Science (Agdal): MOHAMMED OUAZZANI JAMIL
Faculty of Science and Technology (Saiss): MOHCINE ZOUAK
High School of Technology (Saiss): ABDELLATI SAFOUANE
Higher Normal School (Saiss): ABDENABI RAJWANI
National Institute of Medicinal and Aromatic Plants (Taounate): ABDESLAM KHENCHOUFI
National School of Applied Sciences (Saiss): MOSTAFA MRABTI
National School of Business and Management (Saiss): MILOUD EL HAFIDI
Polydisciplinary Faculty of Taza: AHMED TALOUIZTE

Colleges

Conservatoire de Casablanca: Complexe Culturel Benmsik, Casablanca; tel. 22-37-21-89; 120 students; Dir MOHAMED LACHHAB.

Conservatoire de Fès: rue Mustapha Lamaani, Dar Adaîl, Fez; tel. 35-62-39-93; f. 1960; 366 students; Dir MOHAMED BRIOUEL.

Conservatoire de Marrakech: Arçat al Hamed Bab Doukkala, 40000 Marrakech; tel. 24-38-70-66; f. 1948; teaches Western classical and modern music and classical Moroccan and Arab music; 320 students; Dir MOHAMED MAHASSIN.

Conservatoire National de Musique et de Danse, Rabat: 33 rue Tensift-Agdal, Rabat; tel. 37-77-37-94; trains students in Western and Arabic music and classical dance; the Conservatoire has an orchestra for modern Arab music, an orchestra for Andalusian and Moroccan music, two youth orchestras and a big-band orchestra; 1,685 students; Dir MOHAMMED EL BAHJA.

Ecole Hassania des Travaux Publics: km 7, route d'El Jadida, BP 8108, Oasis, Casablanca; tel. 22-23-07-06; fax 22-23-07-17; e-mail ehtpdg@menara.ma; internet www.ehtp.ac.ma; f. 1971; civil engineering, industrial engineering and telecommunication systems, meteorology, sciences of geographical information, computer engineering; MBA, Masters programmes, specialized courses, seminars; 7 research and study centres; library: 15,000 vols; 73 full-time teachers, 180 visiting teachers; 480 students; Dir ABDESLAM MESSOUDI.

Ecole des Métiers d'Art (School of Native Arts and Crafts): Bab Okla, BP 89, Tétouan; f. 1921; textiles, carpets, rugs, ceramics, engraving, plaster inlays, woodwork, precious metal work, leather and Arabic woodcarving; 350 mems; Dir ABDELLAH FEKHAR.

Ecole Nationale d'Administration: BP 165, 2 ave de la Victoire, Rabat; tel. 37-73-14-50; fax 37-73-09-29; f. 1948; library: 18,000 vols; 36 teachers; 646 students; Dir AMINE MZOURI; publ. *Administration et Société* (3 a year).

Ecole Nationale d'Architecture: BP 6372, Chariaa Allal El Fassi, Rabat; tel. 37-77-52-29; fax 37-77-52-76; e-mail e.n.a@smartnet.net.ma; f. 1980 under the Ministry of Territorial Administration, Water Resources and the Environment; courses in architecture, regional town planning and housing; 60 teachers; 400 students; Dir ABDERRAHMANE CHORFI.

Ecole Nationale des Beaux-Arts: ave Mohamed V, Cité Scolaire BP 89, Tétouan; f. 1946; drawing, painting, sculpture, decorative arts; Dir MOHAMMED M. SERGHINI.

Ecole Nationale Forestière d'Ingénieurs: BP 511, Salé; tel. 37-78-97-04; fax 37-78-71-49; f. 1968; library: 5,000 vols; 20 teachers; 160 students; Dir MY Y. ALAOUI.

Ecole Nationale de l'Industrie Minérale: rue Hadj Ahmed Cherkaoui, BP 753, Agdal, Rabat; tel. 37-68-02-28; fax 37-77-10-55; e-mail info@enim.ac.ma; internet www.enim.ac.ma; f. 1972; specializes in geology, material sciences, mining sciences, chemical process engineering, electro-mechanical engineering, energy sciences, computer science, industrial maintenance, production systems, energy systems; library: 11,000 vols; 86 teachers; 420 students; Dir OMAR DEBBAJ; publ. *Liaison Bulletin* (12 a year).

Ecole des Sciences de l'Information: BP 6204, Rabat-Instituts; tel. 37-77-49-04; fax 37-77-02-32; e-mail esi@esi.ac.ma; internet www.esi.ac.ma; f. 1974; 4-year undergraduate courses and 2-year postgraduate courses for archivists, librarians, documentalists; language of instruction: English; library: 18,000 vols, 50 current periodicals, 415 audiovisual documents; also UNESCO publications, research papers, courses, syllabuses, etc.; 64 teachers; 512 students; Dir MOHAMED BENJELLOUN.

Ecole Supérieure de l'Agro-Alimentaire (Higher School of Food Science): 22 rue Catelet, Belvédère, Casablanca; tel. 22-24-54-05; fax 22-24-53-99; e-mail supagro@casanet.net.ma; f. 1997; 90 teachers; 70 students; Dir ABDELRHAFOUR TANTAOUI ELARAKI.

Institut Agronomique et Vétérinaire Hassan II: BP 6202, Madinat El-Irfane-Instituts, Rabat; tel. 37-77-17-58; fax 37-77-81-35; e-mail dg@iav.ac.ma; internet www.iav.ac.ma; f. 1966; library: 45,000 documents, 1,200 periodicals; 327 teachers; 1,606 students; Dir Prof. FOUAD GUESSOUS; Sec.-Gen. Prof. MOSTAFA AGBANI; publs *Actes de l'Institut Agronomique et Vétérinaire Hassan II* (4 a year, in English and French), *AgroVet Magazine* (4 a year, in French), *IAVinfo* (6 a year).

Institut National des Sciences de l'Archéologie et du Patrimoine: ave Kennedy, route des Zaers, 10000 Rabat-Souissi; tel. 37-75-09-61; fax 37-75-08-84; e-mail archeo@iam.net.ma; f. 1986; departments of anthropology, archaeology and cultural heritage, heritage studies, Islamic studies and archaeology and prehistory; 60 teachers; 50 students; Dir JOUDIA HASSAR-BENSLIMANE; publ. *Bulletin d'Archéologie Marocaine* (1 a year).

Institut National de Statistique et d'Economie Appliquée: BP 6217, Rabat; tel. 37-77-09-15; fax 37-77-94-57; f. 1961; library: 15,000 vols; 398 students; Dir ABDELAZIZ EL GHAZALI; publ. *Revue* (1 a year).

Institut Supérieur d'Art Dramatique et d'Animation Culturelle: Charia Al Mansour Eddahbi, BP 1355, Rabat; tel. 37-72-17-02; fax 37-70-34-23; internet www.minculture.gov.ma/fr/isadac.htm; f. 1985; provides practical and academic training in all areas of the dramatic arts; Dir AHMED MASSAIA.

Instituto Español de Enseñanza Secundaria 'Severo Ochoa' (Spanish Institute in Tangier): Plaza El Koweit 1, Tangier; tel. 39-93-63-38; fax 39-93-60-22; e-mail luisbadosa@hotmail.com; internet arce.cnice.mecd.es/instituto.severo.ochoa; f. 1949; Dir LUIS BADOSA ORTUÑO; library: 8,000 vols; 38 teachers; 360 students; publs *Revista Babel* (1 a year, in several languages), *Revista Kasbah* (1 a year, in Spanish).

MOZAMBIQUE

The Higher Education System

From the 19th century until independence in 1975 Mozambique was a Portuguese colony. The oldest current institutions of higher education were founded during the period of Portuguese rule, most prominently the state-run Universidade Eduardo Mondlane (founded 1962; current name 1976). The other leading state institution is the Universidade Pedagógica (founded 1986); a third public university, the Universidade Lúrio, was founded in 2007. The main private institutions include the Catholic University and Higher Polytechnic Institute. The Ministry of Education and Culture is the agency responsible for state provision of higher education, which is publicly funded.

Students must be awarded the Certificado de Habilitações Literarias upon completion of secondary education and sit an entrance examination in order to be admitted to higher education. Currently, only undergraduate degrees are available. The Bacharelato is awarded after the first cycle of higher education, which lasts three years and is available in most subject areas. Depending on 'good' or 'very good' grades, students may be admitted to a Licenciatura programme of study, which lasts two years following the Bacharelato. Students of architecture, medicine and veterinary medicine study for the Licenciatura. Since 1976, students have been required to spend as many years in state employment (usually teaching) as the length of the course, their degree being awarded once their public service has been completed.

Technical and vocational education is offered by technical schools and institutes controlled by the Secretary of State for Technical and Professional Education. In 2005 there were 41 technical institutes with 21,752 students. In 2002 there were 18 teacher training institutes with 9,314 students. Completion of medium-level technical and vocational education results in award of either the Engenheiro Técnico (technician engineer) or Técnico Medio (middle level technician).

Regulatory Body

GOVERNMENT

Ministry of Education and Culture: Av. 24 de Julho 167, CP 34, Maputo; tel. 21492006; fax 21492196; internet www.mec.gov.mz; Minister AIRES BONIFÁCIO ALI.

Learned Societies

GENERAL

UNESCO Office Maputo: CP 1397, Maputo; Av. Frederick Engels 515, Maputo; tel. 21494450; fax 21493431; e-mail maputo@unesco.org; Dir BENOÎT SOUSSOU.

LANGUAGE AND LITERATURE

British Council: Rua John Issa 226, POB 4178, Maputo; tel. 21226776; fax 21421577; e-mail general.enquiries@britishcouncil.org.mz; internet www.britishcouncil.org/mozambique; offers courses and exams in English language and British culture and promotes cultural exchange with the UK; Dir SIMON INGRAM-HILL.

Research Institutes

AGRICULTURE, FISHERIES AND VETERINARY SCIENCE

Instituto de Algodão de Moçambique (Mozambique Institute for Cotton): Av. Eduardo Mondlane 2221 (1° andar), CP 806, Maputo; tel. 21431015; fax 21430679; e-mail iampab@zebra.uem.mz; f. 1991; depts of analysis and classing fibre, finance and administration, supporting the cotton associative sector, studies and projects; library of 2,500 vols, 260 journals and reviews; Dir NORBERTO MAHALAMBE; Deputy Dir GABRIEL PAPOSSECO; publs *Relatório Anual de Actividades* (1 a year), *Relatório Trimestral* (4 a year).

Instituto Nacional de Investigação Agronómica: CP 3658, Maputo 4; tel. 21460190; fax 21460074; f. 1965; Dir Dr CALISTO BIAS; publ. *Comunicacões/INIA*.

MEDICINE

Instituto Nacional de Saúde (National Health Institute): Av. Eduardo Mondlane 296, CP 264, Maputo; fax 21423726; f. 1980; study, research and training in ecology, epidemiology, immunology, malaria, microbiology, parasitology, trypanosomiasis; traditional medicine; documentation and information depts; 32 staff; library of 6,500 vols; Dir Dr RUI GAMA VAZ; publ. *Revista Médica de Moçambique*.

NATURAL SCIENCES

Physical Sciences

Direcção Nacional de Geologia: CP 217, Maputo; tel. 21427121; fax 21420796; e-mail geologia@zebra.uem.mz; f. 1928; regional geology, geological mapping and mineral exploration; library of 30,000 vols, maps, technical material, etc; Dir ELIAS XAVIER DAUDI; publs *Bibliografia Geológico-Mineira de Moçambique* (1 a year), *Boletim Geológico de Moçambique* (1 a year), *Boletim Informativo da DNG* (1 a year), *Notícias Explicativas da Geológico de Moçambique* (irregular), *Relatório Anual* (1 a year).

Instituto Nacional de Meteorologia: CP 256, Maputo; tel. and fax (21) 491150; e-mail mozmet@inam.gov.mz; internet www.inam.gov.mz; f. 1907; library of 750 vols; Nat. Dir MOISES VICENTE BENESSENE; publs *Anuário de Observações* (in 2 vols: I *Observações Meteorológicas de Superficie*, II *Observações Meteorológicas de Altitude*), *Boletim Meteorológico para a Agricultura* (every 10 days), *Informações de Carácter Astronómico* (1 a year).

Libraries and Archives

Maputo

Arquivo Histórico de Moçambique: Av. Filipe Samuel Magaia 717, CP 2033, Maputo; tel. (1) 431296; fax (1) 423428; e-mail rafaluga@hotmail.com; internet www.ahm.uem.mz; f. 1934; attached to Universidade Eduardo Mondlane; 25,000 vols, 11,600 periodicals; spec. collns: written reports of admin. or governmental offices and business; cartography; iconography; oral history; Dir Prof. Dr JOEL DAS NEVES TEMBE; publs *Arquivo*, *Documentos* (series), *Estudos* (series), *Instrumentos de Pesquisa* (series).

Biblioteca Nacional de Moçambique (National Library of Mozambique): Av. 25 de Setembro 1384, CP 141, Maputo; tel. 21425676; f. 1961; 110,000 vols; Dir ANTÓNIO M. B. COSTA E SILVA.

Centro Nacional de Documentação e Informação de Moçambique: CP 4116, Maputo; tel. and fax 21311246; e-mail cedimo@cedimo.gov.mz; internet www.cedimo.gov.mz; f. 1977; part of Council of Ministers Secretariat; 12,000 vols; Dir ARLANZA EDUARDO SABINO DIAS; publ. *Documento Informativo*.

Direcção Nacional de Geologia, Centro de Documentação: CP 217, Maputo; tel. 21420797; fax 21429216; e-mail geologia@zebra.uem.mz; f. 1928; documentation centre for geology and mineral exploration; 10 spec. collns; Dir ELIAS XAVIER DAUDI; publs *Bibliografia Geológico-Mineira* (1 a year), *Boletim Geológico* (1 a year), *Boletim Informativo* (4 a year), *Notícias Explicativas da Geologia de Moçambique* (irregular), *Relatório Anual da DNG* (1 a year).

Museum

Maputo

Museu de História Natural: Praça da Travessia do Zambeze, CP 1780, Maputo; tel. 21491145; fax 21490879; e-mail mnhi@zebra.uem.mz; internet www.museu.org.mz; f. 1911; natural history museum and ethnographic gallery; attached to Universidade Eduardo Mondlane; Dir AUGUSTO J. PEREIRA CABRAL.

Universities

UNIVERSIDADE EDUARDO MONDLANE

CP 257, Maputo
Telephone: 21427851

Fax: 21326426
Internet: www.uem.mz
Founded 1962
State control
Language of instruction: Portuguese
Academic year: February to December

Rector: Prof. Dr BRAZÃO MAZULA
Vice-Rector for Academic Affairs: (vacant)
Vice-Rector for Admin. and Resources: (vacant)
Dir of Documentation Services: POLICARPO MATIQUITE

Number of teachers: 1,069
Number of students: 9,712

DEANS

Faculty of Agriculture: Prof. Dr ANDRADE F. EGAS
Faculty of Architecture: Prof. JOSÉ FORJAZ
Faculty of Arts and Social Science: Prof. Dr ARMINDO NGUNGA
Faculty of Economics: Dr FERNANDO LICHUCHA (acting)

Faculty of Education: Prof. Dr MOUZINHO MÁRIO (acting)
Faculty of Engineering: Prof. Dr GABRIEL AMOS
Faculty of Law: Dr TAÍBO MUCOBORA (acting)
Faculty of Medicine: Prof. Dr EMILIA NOORMAHOMED
Faculty of Science: Dr FRANCISCO VIEIRA
Faculty of Veterinary Science: Dr LUÍS NEVES

UNIVERSIDADE LÚRIO

Av. Eduardo Mondlane 39, CP 364, Nampula
Internet: www.unilurio.ac.mz
Founded 2007
State control
Language of instruction: Portuguese
Library of 2,500 vols, 273 periodical titles
Number of students: 600

Faculty of health sciences—Nampula: courses in dentistry, pharmacology and medicine, nutrition and optometry; Faculty of engineering and natural sciences—Pemba

(Cabo Delgado); Faculty of agrarian sciences—Lichinga (Niassa); Faculty of architecture

Rector: Prof. Dr JORGE FERRÃO.

UNIVERSIDADE PEDAGÓGICA

Com. Augusto Cardoso 135, Maputo
Telephone: 21420860
Fax: 21422113
E-mail: grupsede@zebra.uem.mz
Founded 1986
State control
Language of instruction: Portuguese
Academic year: August to June

Rector: CARLOS MACHILI

Number of teachers: 215
Number of students: 1,400

Faculties of languages, natural sciences and mathematics, pedagogy, physical education and sports and social sciences.

The Higher Education System

In the 19th century Burma (now Myanmar) was annexed to British India and remained under British rule until independence was achieved in 1948 (with a period under Japanese occupation in 1942–45). The oldest current institutions of higher education date from the 1920s, among them University of Yangon (founded 1920), University of Forestry (founded 1923), Yangon Technological University and Yezin Agricultural University (both founded 1924). The Ministry of Education has overall responsibility for higher education, with the exception of specialized institutions attached to other ministries. In 2001/02 there were an estimated 587,300 students at 958 institutions of tertiary education.

Admission to higher education is on the basis of results in the secondary school Matriculation and, in some instances, an entrance examination. Bachelors degrees are classified as either 'Pass' or 'Honours' depending on the length of study: four years for Bachelors (Pass) and five years for Bachelors (Honours). Bachelors degrees in professional fields of study (engineering, forestry, medicine) take upwards of six years. Postgraduate degrees include the ordinary Masters and Masters of Research.

Admission to post-secondary technical and vocational education is also on the basis of secondary school Matriculation and entrance examination. State-run technical institutes specialize in three-year training programmes leading to the award of the Diploma.

Regulatory Bodies

GOVERNMENT

Ministry of Culture: Bldg 35, Nay Pyi Taw, Mandalay; tel. (67) 408023; fax (1) 283794; internet www.myanmar.com/ministry/culture; Minister Major Gen. KHIN AUNG MYINT.

Ministry of Education: Bldg 13, Nay Pyi Taw, Pyinmana, Mandalay; tel. (67) 407131; f. 1950; Minister Dr CHAN NYEIN.

Learned Societies

LANGUAGE AND LITERATURE

British Council: 78 Kanna Rd, POB 638, Yangon; tel. (1) 254658; fax (1) 245345; e-mail enquiries@mm.britishcouncil.org; internet www.britishcouncil.org/burma; offers courses and exams in English language and British culture; promotes cultural exchange with the UK; teaching centre; library of 30,000 books, video cassettes, DVDs and magazines; Dir Dr MARCUS MILTON; Teaching Centre Man. MICHAEL GORDON.

Research Institutes

AGRICULTURE, FISHERIES AND VETERINARY SCIENCE

Forest Research Institute: Yezin, Pyinmana, Nay Pyi Taw, Mandalay; tel. (67) 416521; fax (67) 416524; e-mail friyezin@myanmar.com.mm; f. 1978; library of 9,207 vols; herbarium with limited colln of bamboo and rattan specimens; Dir OHN WINN; Asst Dir DAW Y. Y. KYI.

MEDICINE

Department of Medical Research (Lower Myanmar): 5 Ziwaka Rd, Dagon PO, Yangon, 11191; tel. (1) 375457; fax (1) 251514; internet www.moh.gov.mm; f. 1963, fmrly Burma Medical Research Institute; 24 divs and 7 clinical research units: animal services, bacteriology, biochemistry, computer diagnostics and vaccine research, epidemiology, experimental medicine, finance and budget, health systems research, clinical research, immunology, instrumentation, library, medical entomology, medical research statistics, nuclear medicine, nutrition, parasitology, pathology, pharmacology, physiology, publications, radioisotope and virology; clinical research units: malaria (DSGH), malaria (2MH), cerebral and complicated malaria (DMR), snakebites, traditional medicine, HIV/AIDS, research unit (IM II), oncology; WHO Collaborating Centre for Research and Training on Malaria; Dir-Gen. Dr MYO KHIN; publs *DMR Bulletin, Myanmar Health Sciences Research Journal.*

National Health Laboratories: Yangon; f. 1968 by amalgamating the Harcourt Butler Institute of Public Health, the Pasteur Institute, Office of the Chemical Examiner and Office of the Public Analyst; composed of five divs: Admin., Public Health, Chemical, Food and Drugs and Clinical; Dir Dr MEHM SOE MYINT.

RELIGION, SOCIOLOGY AND ANTHROPOLOGY

Department of Religious Affairs: Kabaaye Pagoda compound, Yangon; internet www.mora.gov.mm; f. as a government supported centre for research and studies in Buddhist and allied subjects; reorganized 1972 as dept under the Min. of Religious Affairs; library of 17,000 vols, 7,000 periodicals, 7,650 palm-leaf MSS, etc.; Dir Gen. U ANT MAUNG.

TECHNOLOGY

Department of Atomic Energy: Central Research Organization, 6 Kaba Aye Pagoda Rd, Yangon; f. 1955 as Union of Myanmar Atomic Energy, current name 1997; attached to Min. of Science and Technology; environmental radiation monitoring, nuclear instrumentation; Chair. U ANG KOE.

Myanmar Scientific and Technological Research Department: No 6 Kanbe, Pagoda Rd, Yankin PO, Yangon; tel. (1) 663024; fax (1) 668033; e-mail most7@myanmar.com.mm; internet www.most.gov.mm; a dept of the Min. of Science and Technology; composed of the Analysis Dept, Metallurgy Research Dept, Physics and Engineering Research Dept, Technical Information Centre, Fine Instruments Dept and Workshop, Applied Chemistry Research Dept, Ceramics Research Dept, Standards and Specifications Dept, Polymer Research Dept, Pharmaceutical Research Dept, Food Technology Research Dept; research in applied sciences; corresp. mem. of the International Organization for Standardization (ISO); library of 17,000 vols, 1,200 periodicals; Dir Gen. Col TIN HTUT.

Libraries and Archives

Ayeryarwaddy

Bassein Degree College Library: Bassein, Ayeyarwaddy; f. 1958; 27,560 vols; Librarian NYAN HTUN.

State Library: Bassein, Ayeyarwaddy; f. 1963; 1,453 vols.

Kachin

Myitkyina Degree College Library: Myitkyina, Kachin; Librarian (vacant).

Magway

Magway University Library: Magway; tel. (62) 21522; f. 1958; 50,000 vols; Dir KHIN MYINT MYINT.

Mandalay

State Library: Mandalay; f. 1955; 7,004 vols.

University of Mandalay Library: University Estate, Mandalay; 146,000 vols; Librarian U NYAN TUN.

University of Medicine Library: Seiktaramahi Quarters, Mandalay; f. 1964; 28,362 vols, 47 periodicals; Librarian KAUNG NYUNT.

University of Veterinary Science Library: Yezin, Pyinmana, Mandalay; tel. (67) 22449; fax (67) 642927; e-mail drhsuvs@myanmar.com.mm; f. 1964; 4,500 vols; Librarian HTAY HTAY KHIN.

Yezin Agricultural University Library: Yezin, Pyinmana, Mandalay; tel. (67) 416516; fax (67) 416517; f. 1924, autonomous 1964; 26,000 vols, 130 periodicals; Chief Librarian WYNN LEI LEI THAN.

Mon

Mawlamyine University Library: Mawlamyine, Mon; f. 2004; 106,920 books and periodicals; Librarian U THEIN LWIN; Rector U SAN TINT.

State Library: Mawlamyine, Mon; f. 1955; 13,265 vols; 1,262 MSS.

Rakhine

State Library: Kyaukpyu, Rakhine; f. 1955; 8,651 vols.

Shan

Taunggyi Degree College Library: Taunggyi, Shan; Librarian (vacant).

Yangon

Central Biomedical Library: Department of Medical Research (Lower Myanmar), 5 Ziwaka Rd, Dagon PO, Yangon, 11191; tel. (1) 251508; fax (1) 251504; e-mail dmrlower@baganmail.net.mm; f. 1963, fmrly Burma Medical Research Institute Library; 27,000 vols, 250 periodicals on health and biomedical sciences; Chief Librarian DAW NYUNT NYUNT SWE.

Institute of Education Library: University Estate, Yangon; f. 1964; 36,166 vols; Librarian DAW GILDA TWE.

Myanmar Education Research Bureau: 426 Pyay Rd, University PO, Yangon, 11041; tel. (1) 531468; fax (1) 525049; f. 1966; dept of the Min. of Education; educational materials resource centre promoting and supporting research activities; 56,000 vols; Chair. U MYINT HAN; publ. *The World of Education* (4 a year).

National Archives Department: 114, Pyidaungsu Yeiktha Rd, Dagon Township, Yangon; fax (1) 254011; e-mail nad@mptmail.net.mm; internet www.mnped.gov.mm/nationalchives.asp; f. 1972; attached to Min. of National Planning and Economic Development; preserves national records and archives; retrieves records and archives that had migrated to a foreign land or are in the possession of any other organization or individual; 50,000 books and 15,000 microfilms, microfiches, tapes and photographs.

National Library: 85 Thirimingala Ave, Yankin, Yangon; tel. (1) 272058; f. 1952, incorporating the Bernard Free Library, present name 1967, present location 2008; 158,800 vols, 12,321 MSS, 411,426 periodicals; Chief Librarian SAN WIN.

Sarpay Beikman Public Library: 529 Merchant St, Yangon; f. 1956; 74,404 vols (56,729 Burmese, 17,675 English); Librarian NU NU.

Universities' Central Library: University PO, Yangon; f. 1929; central library for all higher education institutes; specializes in Burmese books, palm-leaf MSS (over 11,000), and books on Burma and Asia; 350,000 vols; Chief Librarian THAW KAUNG.

University of Computer Studies Library: Yangon Hlaing Campus, Myanmar Thaming College PO, Yangon, 11052; tel. (1) 664709; fax (1) 665686; e-mail ucsy1@most.gov.mm; internet www.ucsy.edu.mm; provides up-to-date computer books for students for their reference courses; Library Asst Daw YU YU TIN.

University of Medicine I Library: 245 Myoma Kyaung St, Lanmadaw Township, Yangon, 11131; tel. (1) 395560; fax (1) 251037; e-mail khinmmtun07@googlemail.com; internet www.um1ygn.edu.mm; f. 1929; 40,000 vols; Librarian KHIN MAW MAW TUN.

University of Medicine 2 Library: N Okkalapa, Yangon, 11031; tel. (1) 699064; fax (1) 690265; e-mail thelibrary@iomnoka.com.mm; internet www.um2ygn.edu.mm; f. 1964; fmrly Institute of Medicine II Library; participates in HELLIS; access to UN and WHO databases online (HINARI, AGORA, and OARE); 31,000 vols; Librarian U THI TAR.

University of Yangon Library: Yangon, 11041; tel. (1) 530376; fax (1) 664889; f. 1927; 200,000 vols; Head Librarian KHIN HNIN OO.

WHO Library: 12A Traders Hotel, 223 Sule Pogoda Rd, Kyauktada Township, Yangon, 11182; provision of WHO information material and global health literature.

Workers' College Library: Yangon; f. 1964; 19,500 vols; Librarian KHIN THIN KYU.

Yangon Institute of Economics Library: University Estate, POB 473, Yangon, 11041; tel. (1) 535847; fax (1) 545750; e-mail ucl@dhelm-edu.gov.mm; f. 1964; 87,000 vols; Librarian DAW KHIN KYU.

Yangon Institute of Technology Library: Insein PO, Gyogone, Yangon, 11011; tel. (1) 665678; e-mail yit.yangon@pemail.net; internet welcome.to/yit; f. 1964; caters to the needs of postgraduate students and academic staff; 48,000 vols, 560 periodicals; Librarian U TIN MAUNG LWIN.

Museums and Art Galleries

Mandalay

Bagan Archaeological Museum: opposite Gawdawpalin Temple, Bagan, Upper Myanmar, Mandalay; f. 1904, new bldg opened 1975, new Bagan Archaeological Museum opened 1998; site museum for ancient capital from 11th to 14th century; lithic inscriptions, Buddha's images, statuary and artefacts; administered by Dept of Archaeology; Curator U KYAW NYEIN.

Mandalay Cultural Museum: 80th Rd and 24th Rd, Aung Myay Tha San Township, Mandalay; tel. (1) 239859; fax (1) 212367; e-mail dcicoci@mptmail.net.mm.

State Museum: Cnr of 24th and 80th Sts, Mandalay; f. 1955; over 1,500 exhibits; Br. museum in fmr Mandalay Palace grounds; Curator U SOE THEIN.

Mon

Mon State Museum: Dawei Tada Rd, Mawlamyine, Mon; f. 1955; over 750 exhibits; Curator U MIN KHIN MAUNG.

Rakhine

Mrauk U Archaeological Museum: Rakhine; displays artefacts from the Vesali, Launggret and Mrauk U periods, bronze Buddha icons of Rakhine, stone inscriptions in Sanskrit, Rakhine and Arabic, votive tablets, Krishna Vishnu, Bodhisattvas, dvarapala, stone htis, lintels coins, musical instruments and ceramic wares.

Rakhine State Cultural Museum: 70 Main Rd and Yetwin Rd, Sittwe, Rakhine; f. 1996; displays traditional dresses, traditional looms and arts of Rakhine people, models of stone inscriptions, musical instruments, coins, images and paintings of Buddha.

Rakhine State Museum: Chin Pyan Rd, Kyaung-gyi Quarter, Sitture, Rakhine; f. 1955; over 500 exhibits (silver coins, costumes, etc.); also site museum at Mrauk U, ancient capital; Curator DAW NU MYA ZAN.

Shan

Shan State Museum: Min Lan, Thittaw Quarter, Taunggyi, Shan; f. 1957; over 600 exhibits; Curator U SAN MYA.

Yangon

Bogyoke Aung San Museum: 15 Bogyoke Aung San Lane, Bahan Township, Yangon; tel. (1) 250600; f. 1962; 571 exhibits related to the life and work of General Aung San.

Gems Museum: No 66, Kaba Aye Pagoda Rd, Mayangon, Yangon; tel. (1) 660365; fax (1) 665092; original clay votive tablets; cultural artefacts from the Bagan period; items from the Pinya, Innwa, Taungoo and Nyaung Yan periods.

National Museum: No 66/74, Pyay Rd, Dagon Township, Yangon; tel. (1) 282563; fax (1) 282608; f. 1952; displays ancient artefacts, works of art and historic memorabilia; exhibits on the evolution the Myanmar script and alphabet, the Lion Throne Room and Yatanabon period pieces.

National Museum of Art and Archaeology: 26/42 Pansodan, Yangon; f. 1952; 1,652 antiquities; 354 paintings; replica of King Mindon's Mandalay Palace; Dir Gen. Dr YE TUT; Chief Curator U KYAW WIN.

Yangon Drugs Elimination Museum: Cnr of Kyundaw Rd and Hanthawady Rd, Kamayut Township, Yangon; internet www.myanmar-narcotic.net/heroin/drug_museum/museum.html; f. 2001; records and showcases national efforts to combat narcotics drugs trade in the country.

Universities

COMPUTER UNIVERSITY

Taungoo, Bago

Telephone: (54) 27173

Fax: (54) 27008

Internet: www.ucsy.edu.mm/taungoocu/index.php

Founded 2000, fmrly the Government Computer College, university status 2007; attached to Min. of Science and Technology.

DAGON UNIVERSITY

North Dagon Township, Yangon

Telephone: (1) 584550

Language of instruction: Myanmar

Academic year: July to March; attached to Min. of Education

Faculties of arts and humanities, mathematics and computer science, natural sciences.

HMAWBI TECHNOLOGICAL UNIVERSITY

Hmawbi Township, Yangon

Telephone: (1) 620072

Fax: (1) 620454

Internet: www.most.gov.mm/hmawbitu

Founded 1989 as Technical High School, later Government Institute of Technology, university status 2007; attached to Min. of Science and Technology

Public

Rector: Dr AYE MYINT.

INTERNATIONAL THERAVĀDA BUDDHIST MISSIONARY UNIVERSITY

Dhammapāla Hill, Mayanggone PO, Yangon

Telephone: (1) 650713

Fax: (1) 650700

Internet: www.itbmu.org.mm

Founded 1998; attached to Min. of Religious Affairs

Public

Rector: Dr Sayadaw BHADDANTA NANDA

Library of 25,670 books, the *International Encyclopedia on Buddhism* 75 vols, *Encyclopedia of Religions and Ethics*.

MAGWE UNIVERSITY

University Campus, Magwe, Magway

Telephone: (63) 21030

Founded 1958; attached to Min. of Education

Number of teachers: 130

Number of students: 3,550

MANDALAY TECHNOLOGICAL UNIVERSITY

Patheingyi, M. T. U., PO, Mandalay

Telephone: (2) 57006

E-mail: admin@mtu.edu.mm

Internet: www.most.gov.mm/mtu

Founded 1991; attached to Min. of Science and Technology

Bachelors, Masters and doctoral courses; Depts of architecture, chemical engineering, civil engineering, electrical power engineering, electronics engineering, mechanical engineering

Number of teachers: 144

Number of students: 2,418

Pro-Rector: Prof. Dr AUNG KYAW MYAT.

MAWLAMYINE UNIVERSITY

Taung Waing Rd, Mawlamyine, Mon

Telephone: (32) 21180

Founded 1953, university status 1986; attached to Min. of Education

Languages of instruction: Myanmar, English

State control

Academic year: November to September

Rector: HLA TUN AUNG

Pro-Rector: HLA PE

Librarian: THEIN LWIN

Number of teachers: 300

Number of students: 8,100

Library of 106,000 books and periodicals

PROFESSORS

Chemistry: Prof. MAUNG MAUNG HTAY

Geography: Prof. THAN MYA

Geology: Prof. NYAN THIN

Physics: Prof. SEIN HTOON

AFFILIATED COLLEGES

Bago College: Prin. HLA MYINT.

Dawei College: Prin. THIN HLAING.

Hpa-an College: Prin. LAWRENCE THAW.

MONYWA UNIVERSITY

Monywa, Sagaing

Founded 1996; attached to Min. of Education

Faculties of arts and humanities, mathematics and computer science, natural sciences

Rector: MAUNG HTOO.

MYANMAR AEROSPACE ENGINEERING UNIVERSITY

Meiktila, Mandalay

Internet: www.most.gov.mm/maeu

Founded 2002; attached to Min. of Science and Technology

Public

Five-year Bachelor of Engineering programme; one-year postgraduate diploma in aerospace engineering for male students only

Rector: NYI HLA NGE

Number of students: 455

MYANMAR MARITIME UNIVERSITY

Thilawar, Thanhlyin, Yangon, 11293

E-mail: myanmarivarsity@mmu.gov.mm

Internet: www.mot.gov.mm/mmu/index.html

Founded 2004; attached to Min. of Transport

Public

Depts of naval architecture and ocean engineering, marine engineering, port and harbours engineering, river and coastal engineering, marine electrical systems and electronics, nautical science, shipping management, port management

Rector: CHARLES THAN

Number of students: 1,741

PATHEIN UNIVERSITY

Pathein, Ayeyarwaddy

Founded 1996; attached to Min. of Education

Faculties of arts and humanities, mathematics and computer science, natural sciences.

PYAY TECHNOLOGICAL UNIVERSITY

Pyay, Bago

Telephone: (53) 25806

Fax: (53) 25805

Internet: www.most.gov.mm/ptu

Founded 1999; attached to Min. of Science and Technology

Offers Dipl. in Engineering, Bachelor of Technology, BEng, MEng programmes

Rector: AUNG KYAW MYAT.

SITTWE UNIVERSITY

Sittwe, Rakhine

Telephone: (1) 246704

E-mail: hivdig@indp.org

Founded 1996; attached to Min. of Education

Faculties of arts and humanities, mathematics and computer science, natural sciences

Rector: SEIN MOE MOE.

TAUNGGYI UNIVERSITY

Taunggyi, Shan, 06011

Telephone: (81) 21160

Founded 1961; attached to Min. of Education

Faculties of arts and humanities, mathematics and computer science, natural sciences

Number of teachers: 125

Number of students: 3,500

Rector: Dr MAUNG KYAW.

TAUNGOO TECHNOLOGICAL UNIVERSITY

Taungoo Township, Bago

Telephone: (54) 23734

Fax: (54) 23734

Internet: www.most.gov.mm/taungootu

Founded 1982 as Technical High School, university status 2007; attached to Min. of Science and Technology

Offers BEng, Bachelor of Technology, Dipl. Civil Engineering, Dipl. Electronic Engineering, Dipl. Electrical Power Engineering, Dipl. Mechanical Engineering, Dipl. Mechatronic Engineering, Dipl. Architecture Engineering, Dipl. Chemical Engineering, Dipl. Information Technology Engineering, Dipl. Bio-technology.

THANLYIN TECHNOLOGICAL UNIVERSITY

Thanlyin, Yangon

Telephone: (56) 25058

E-mail: dr.akmyat@gmail.com

Internet: www.most.gov.mm/thanlyintu

Founded 1993 as Industrial Training Centre, Govt Technological Institute 1995, univ. status 2007; attached to Min. of Science and Technology

Public

Academic year: December to September

Offers four-year Bachelor of Technology, five-year BEng and BArch and two-year MEng programmes

Rector: Prof. Dr AUNG KYAW MYAT

Number of teachers: 173

Number of students: 10,080

UNIVERSITY OF COMMUNITY HEALTH

Magway

Telephone: (9563) 23413

Fax: (9563) 23415

E-mail: prof.ssma@gmail.com

Founded 1951 as Health Assistant Training School, university status 1995; attached to Min. of Health

State Control

Language of instruction: English

Rector: Prof. Dr SAN SAN MYINT AUNG

Chief Admin. Officer: Prof. Dr MYO THAN

Registrar: DAW KYI KYI MIN

Librarian: U WAI MAUNG

Library of 4,997 vols, 1,000 periodicals

Number of teachers: 72

Number of students: 735

DEANS

Department of Biomedical Science: Dr SOE MIN NAING

Department of Botany: U THEIN ZAN

Department of Chemistry: Dr CHO LWIN OO

Department of Community Health: Dr AYE AYE OO

Department of Educational Science: Dr THAN SOE LIN

Department of English: DAW NANG KHAM SET

Department of Environmental Health: Dr MYA THANDAR

Department of Field Training: Prof. Dr MYO THAN

Department of Health Education: Dr MYAT OHNMAR WIN

Department of Physics: DAW MU MU THET

Department of Zoology: DAW SU SU THAN

Myanmar Subject: DAW AYE AYE MYINT

UNIVERSITY OF COMPUTER STUDIES

Hlaing Campus, Thaming College PO, Yangon, 11052

Telephone: (1) 664709

Fax: (1) 665686

Hlawgar Campus, No 4 Rd, ShwePyiThar Township, Yangon

Telephone: (1) 610633

Fax: (1) 610622

E-mail: ucsy1@most.gov.mm

Internet: www.ucsy.edu.mm

Founded 1971 as Universities Computer Centre, autonomous Institute of Computer Science and Technology 1988, present name and status 1998; attached to Min. of Science and Technology

Public

Language of instruction: English

Academic year: July to March

Rector: Dr NI LAR THEIN

Pro-Rector: Dr KYAW THEIN

Registrar: U KYIN HTWE

Librarian: DAW KHIN MAR AYE

Library of 11,000 vols

Number of teachers: 20

Number of students: 100

UNIVERSITY OF CULTURE, MANDALAY

Shwesayan Pagoda Rd, Patheingyi, Mandalay

Founded 2001; attached to Min. of Culture

Public

Language of instruction: English

Programmes in music, dramatic arts, painting and sculpture

Rector: NGWE TUN.

UNIVERSITY OF CULTURE, YANGON

No 26 Quarter, Aung Zeta Rd, South Dagon Myothit Township, Yangon, 11431

Telephone: (1) 590250

Fax: (1) 590250

Founded 1993; attached to Min. of Culture

Language of instruction: English

Academic year: November to September

Depts of fine arts, dance, music, drama, painting and sculpture

Rector: TIN SOE

Number of teachers: 135

Number of students: 733

UNIVERSITY OF DENTAL MEDICINE, YANGON

Thanthumar Rd, Thingankyun POB, Yangon, 11071

Telephone: (1) 571270
Fax: (1) 571269

Founded 1964, Institute of Dental Medicine 1974, present status 1998; attached to Min. of Health

Language of instruction: English
Academic year: November to September
Public control

Rector: PAING SOE

Publication: *Myanmar Dental Journal* (1 a year).

UNIVERSITY OF DISTANCE EDUCATION

Kamayut Yangon, 11041

Founded 1992; attached to Min. of Education
Public

32 Campuses across Myanmar

Rector: Dr TIN MAY TUN
Number of students: 560,000

UNIVERSITY OF EAST YANGON

Thanlyin, Yangon, 11292; attached to Min. of Education

Offers three-year and four-year courses in BA, BSc and Bachelor of Law
Public

Rector: KYAW YE TUN
Number of students: 11,000

UNIVERSITY OF FOREIGN LANGUAGES, YANGON

119-131 University Ave, Kamayut, Yangon, 11041

Telephone: (1) 513193
Fax: (1) 513194
E-mail: rectorufly@mptmail.net.mm

Founded 1964 as the Institute of Foreign Languages, current name and status 1996; attached to Min. of Education

Language courses in Chinese, English, French, German, Japanese, Korean, Russian and Thai; Myanmar language courses for foreign students

Rector: Dr MYO MYINT
Librarian: DAW HLA HLA MYINT

Library of 26,000 vols
Number of teachers: 100
Number of students: 3,000

UNIVERSITY OF FORESTRY, YEZIN

Yezin, Pyinmana, Mandalay

Telephone: (67) 21436
E-mail: teaknet@mtpt400.stems.com

Founded 1923, present status 1992; attached to Min. of Forestry
Public

Offers a five-year BSc degree programme in forestry

Rector: AUNG THAN

Library of 10,000 vols
Number of teachers: 45
Number of students: 300

UNIVERSITY OF MANDALAY

University Estate, Mandalay

Telephone: (2) 21211

Founded 1925 as a college of the University of Rangoon, independent university status 1958; attached to Min. of Education
Language of instruction: Myanmar
Academic year: July to March

9 Affiliated colleges

Rector: Dr MYA AYE
Pro-Rector: U LU NI
Registrars: U WIN MYINT (Student Affairs and Hostels), DAW SEIN SEIN (Examination and Convocation)
Librarian: U NYAN TUN

Library of 175,000 vols
Number of teachers: 860
Number of students: 22,700

UNIVERSITY OF MEDICAL TECHNOLOGY

Patheingyi, Mandalay

Founded 2000; attached to Min. of Health
Public

Offers a four-year Bachelor of Medical Technology degree programme in medical laboratory technology, physiotherapy, radiography and medical imaging technology

Rector: SOE TUN.

UNIVERSITY OF MEDICINE I

No 245 Myoma Kyaung St, Lanmadaw POB, Yangon, 11131

Telephone: (1) 251136
Fax: (1) 243910
E-mail: rct.imy@mptmail.net.mm
Internet: www.um1ygn.edu.mm

Founded 1927 as first Dept of Medicine at Yangon Univ., Institute of Medicine 1964, present status 1973; attached to Min. of Health
State control

Offers a six-year MBBS course

Rector: Prof. PE THET KHIN

Number of teachers: 685
Number of students: 3,500

UNIVERSITY OF MEDICINE II

North Okkalapa, Yangon

Telephone: (1) 45507

Founded 1963 as Medical College 2 affiliated to Yangon Univ., Institute of Medicine 2 1964, present status 1973
Languages of instruction: Myanmar, English
Academic year: November to July
Min. of Health

Rector: THA HLA SHWE

Library of 24,000 vols
Number of teachers: 320
Number of students: 1,500

Publication: *Medical Education Report* (4 a year).

UNIVERSITY OF MEDICINE, MAGWAY

Magway

Telephone: (9) 56323701
Fax: (9) 56325309
E-mail: r4-dms@moh.gov.mm
Internet: www.ummg.edu.mm

Founded 2001
Min. of Health
Languages of instruction: Burmese, English
Academic year: January to November

Library of 5,713 vols
Number of teachers: 270
Number of students: 2,387

Rector: Prof. Dr WIN MYAT AYE

DEANS

Clinical subjects: ZAW LIN AUNG
Pre-clinical subjects I: THAN THAN AYE
Pre-clinical subjects II: KHIN THIDA

UNIVERSITY OF MEDICINE, MANDALAY

Between 73 and 74 Sts, 30-31 St, Chanayethazan, Mandalay

Telephone: (1) 236634
Fax: (1) 236639
E-mail: ret.ummdy@dms.gov.mm

Founded 1954 as Branch Medical Faculty of Yangon Univ., Faculty of Medicine, Mandalay 1958, Institute of Medicine, Mandalay 1964, present status 1968
Min. of Health

Dir: Prof. THAN WIN

Library of 39,319 vols, 9,104 clinical and public health journals
Number of teachers: 727

UNIVERSITY OF PARAMEDICAL SCIENCE, YANGON

Insein, Yangon, 11011

Founded 1993, fmrly the Institute of Paramedical Sciences; attached to Min. of Health
Public

Offers a four-year Bachelor of Paramedical Science degree programme

Rector: SAW KYAW AUNG.

UNIVERSITY OF PHARMACY, YANGON

North Okkalapa, Yangon, 11031

Founded 1992; attached to Min. of Health
Public

Offers Bachelor of Pharmacy and Master of Pharmacy degree programmes

Rector: Dr AUNG MON.

UNIVERSITY OF VETERINARY SCIENCE, YEZIN

Yezin, Pyinmanar Tsp., Mandalay

Telephone: (1) 22447
Fax: (1) 642927
E-mail: tintinmyaing@mail4u.com.mm
Internet: www.myanmar.gov.mm/ministry/live&fish/university.htm

Founded 1957 as part of University of Yangon, Institute of Animal Husbandry and Veterinary Science, present status 1999; attached to Min. of Livestock and Fisheries

Languages of instruction: Myanmar, English

Faculties of animal husbandry, veterinary science; offers Bachelor of Veterinary Science, Master of Veterinary Science, MPhil and MSc programmes

Rector: Dr MYINT THEIN
Librarian: HTAY HTAY SAN

Library of 13,204 vols, 53 periodicals
Number of teachers: 65
Number of students: 620

UNIVERSITY OF YANGON

University Ave Rd, Kamayut, Yangon, 11041

Telephone: (1) 537250

Founded 1878 as Univ. College affiliated to Univ. of Calcutta, Univ. of Yangon (f. 1920) by merger of Univ. College and Judson College; attached to Min. of Education
Academic year: July to March
Language of instruction: Myanmar

Campuses in Hlaing Region, Kyimyindine Region, Botataung Region; 3 affiliated degree-granting colleges in Pathein, Sittwe and Yangon, and 2 colleges in Hinthada and Pyay

Rector: Dr TIN TUN
Registrar: NYUNT NYUNT WIN

Number of teachers: 2,060
Number of students: 47,131

WEST YANGON TECHNOLOGICAL UNIVERSITY

Hlaing Tha Yar Township, Yangon

Telephone: (1) 655266
Fax: (1) 642959
Internet: www.most.gov.mm/wytu

Founded 2005; attached to Min. of Science and Technology

Depts of civil engineering, electronic and communication engineering, electrical power engineering, mechanical engineering, chemical engineering, mechatronic engineering, information technology, petroleum engineering, metallurgy engineering, textile engineering, architecture engineering, mining engineering, engineering physics, engineering mathematics, engineering English, Myanmar
Public

Rector: Dr WIN.

YADANABON UNIVERSITY

Amarapura, Mandalay

Telephone: (2) 53894
Fax: (2) 53895

Founded 2000 as Yadanabon College, university status 2003; attached to Min. of Education
Public

Bachelors and Masters programmes in Burmese, English, geography, history, philosophy, psychology, botany, chemistry, mathematics, physics and zoology

Rector: WIN MAUNG
Number of students: 22,000

YANGON TECHNOLOGICAL UNIVERSITY

Gyogon, Insein, Yangon, 11011

Telephone: (1) 651717
Fax: (1) 642564
Internet: www.most.gov.mm/ytu

Founded 1924, independent status 1961; attached to Min. of Science and Technology
Public

Academic year: October to July

Six-year first degree courses, one-year postgraduate diploma and two- and three-year postgraduate degree courses

Rector: Dr MYA MYA OO
Number of teachers: 204
Number of students: 8,000

YEZIN AGRICULTURAL UNIVERSITY

Yezin, Pyinmana, Mandalay

Telephone: (67) 416516
Fax: (67) 416517
E-mail: rector-yau@cybertech.net.mm

Founded 1924, independent status 1964; present name 1998; attached to Min. of Agriculture

Depts of agronomy, agriculture botany, agriculture chemistry, entomology, horticulture, agriculture, economics, animal science, agriculture engineering, Myanmar, English, physics and mathematics

Rectors: Dr MYINT THAUNG
Pro-Rector for Academic Affairs: Dr CHO CHO MYINT
Pro-Rector for Admin.: HLA TUN
Registrars: TIN WAN, AUNG SAN
Number of teachers: 121
Number of students: 1,200

University-Level Institutions

Central Institute of Civil Service: Near Phaunggyi Village, Hlegu Township, Yangon; tel. (1) 629501; fax (1) 629507; e-mail rector@cics-phaunggyi.gov.mm; internet www.csstb.gov.mm; f. 1965 as Central People's Training School, upgraded as Central Institute of Civil Service 1977; attached to Min. of Home Affairs; Rector Col WIN MAUNG.

Defence Services Technological Academy: Pyin Oo Lwin, Mandalay; tel. (55) 532851; f. 1993; attached to Min. of Defence; offers five-year BEng degree programmes; Rector Brig. Gen. WIN MYINT.

Institute of Education: Pyay Rd, University PO, Kamayut Township, Yangon, 11041; tel. (1) 504772; fax (1) 504773; e-mail rectoryjoe@mptmail.net.mm; f. 1931, present status since 1964; attached to Min. of Education; languages of instruction: Myanmar, English; academic year June to March; a teachers training college; offers Bachelors and Masters and doctorate programmes in education; 126 teachers; 2,535 students; publ. *Magazine* (1 a year); Pro-Rector KHIN ZAW.

Institute of Marine Technology: Bayint Naung Rd, Kamayut Township, Yangon, 11041; tel. (1) 536166; fax (1) 513448; e-mail principal.imt@mptmail.net.mm; internet www.mot.gov.mm/imt; f. 1972; attached to Min. of Transport; offers courses in both nautical and engineering fields; Prin. WIN THEIN.

Mandalay Institute of Nursing: 62nd-63rd Sts, Chanmyathazi, Mandalay; f. 1998; attached to Min. of Health; offers a four-year Bachelors degree in nursing; Rector KHIN NYUNT THAN.

Yangon Institute of Economics: University Estate, Kamayut Township, Yangon, 11041; tel. (1) 664684; f. 1964; attached to Min. of Education; city campus in Kamayut and satellite campuses in Hlaing and Ywathagi; library: 87,000 vols; 243 teachers; 7,000 students; academic year November to September; Rector Dr KAN ZAW.

Yangon Institute of Nursing: 677-709 Bogyoke Aung San Rd, Lanmadaw, Yangon, 11131; f. 1986, as Nurse Training Center, university status 1991; attached to Min. of Health; offers a four-year Bachelors degree programme in nursing; Rector Dr WIN MAY.

Yangon Institute of Technology: Insein PO, Gyogon, Yangon, 11011; tel. (1) 665678; fax (1) 663357; e-mail yit.yangon@pemail.net; internet welcome.to/yit; f. 1924, independent status 1964; languages of instruction: Myanmar, English; academic year October to July; Depts of civil engineering, mechanical engineering, electrical engineering, electronic engineering, chemical engineering, textile engineering, mining engineering, petroleum engineering, metallurgical engineering, aeronautical engineering, architecture; library: 48,000 vols, 560 journals; 250 teachers; 4,500 students.

Colleges

Defence Services Academy: Pyin Oo Lwin, Mandalay; f. 1954; attached to Min. of Defence; an independent degree college under the Min. of Defence; degree courses for cadets training for service as regular commissioned officers in the Burma Army, Navy and Air Force; 300 faculty; 6,500 students

(5,000 undergraduates, 1,500 postgraduates); Rector Col ZAW WIN; Prin. Major Gen. ZAYAR AUNG.

Lacquerware Technological College: Maha Bawdi St, Bagan, Mandalay; f. 1924 as Government Lacquerware Training School, present status 2003; attached to Min. of Cooperatives; f. by the Cottage Industries Dept, Min. of Cooperatives; offers training in lacquerware production.

Magway Degree College: University Campus, Magway; tel. (63) 21030; attached to Min. of Education; 129 teachers; 3,555 students; Prin. U SEIN WIN.

Meiktila Institute of Economics: Meiktila, Mandalay; f. 2006; attached to Min. of Education; programmes in commerce, economics and statistics; Rector Dr HSAN LWIN.

Myitkyina Degree College: University Campus, Myitkyina, Kachin; tel. (101) 21053; attached to Min. of Education; 90 teachers; 1,752 students; Prin. U SUM HLOT NAW.

Nationalities Youth Resource Development Degree College: c/o Ministry for Progress of Border Areas and National Races and Devt Affairs, Office No 42, Nay Pyi Daw, Mandalay; e-mail edutd@mptmail.net.mm; 2 campuses: affiliated to Yangon and Mandalay Universities.

Pathein Degree College: University Campus, Pathein, Ayeyarwaddy; tel. (42) 21135; attached to Min. of Education; 178 teachers; 5,158 students; Prin. Dr MAUNG KYAW.

Sittwe Degree College: University Campus, Sittwe, Rakhine; tel. (43) 21236; attached to Min. of Education; 97 teachers; 1,730 students; Prin. U KWAW MYA THEIN.

State School of Fine Arts: Ministry of Culture, Dept of Fine Arts, 66 Rd, Between 20th and 22nd St, Nan Shae (In front of the Mandalay Nan Taw), Mandalay; tel. (85) 40296; f. 1953; attached to Min. of Culture; Prin. KAN NYUNT.

State School of Fine Arts: No 131, Kanbawza Yeiktha, Kaba Aye Pagoda Rd, Bahan PO, Yangon; tel. (1) 52176; f. 1952; courses in commercial art, drawing, fine art, sculpture, wood-carving; Prin. U SOE TINT; Dir MYAT THU YA.

State School of Music and Drama: East Moat Rd, Mandalay; tel. (2) 21176; f. 1953; offers courses in dancing, singing, Burmese harp and orchestra, xylophone, piano, oboe, stringed instruments and stave notation; Prin. KAN NYUNT; Dir MYAT THU YA.

State School of Music and Drama: No 135, Kanbawza Yeiktha, Kaba Aye Pagoda Rd, Bahan PO, Yangon; tel. (1) 544151; f. 1952; offers courses in dancing, singing, Burmese harp and orchestra, piano, oboe, xylophone, stringed instruments, stave notation and Burmese verse; Prin. U AUNG THWIN; Dir MYAT THU YA.

Taunggyi State College: Taunggyi, Shan, 06011; tel. (81) 21160; 125 teachers; 3,456 students; Prin. U SAW HLINE.

Workers' College: 273/279 Konthe Lan, Botahtaung PO, Yangon, 11161; tel. (1) 292825; f. 1964 as the University for the Aged, renamed 1974; 47 teachers; 5,650 students; Prin. U SAN MAUNG.

Zomi Theological College: Falam, Chin, 03031; tel. (70) 40081; fax (70) 40243; e-mail ztc1953@gmail.com; internet www.ztccollege.com; f. 1959; attached to Myanmar Baptist Convention; undergraduate and graduate degrees in divinity, theology and religious education; library: 13,754 vols; Prin. DO SIAN THANG; Librarian HRANG PENG LING.

World Who's Who
EUROPA BIOGRAPHICAL REFERENCE
www.worldwhoswho.com

30-day **FREE** trials available for libraries and institutions

EUROPA BIOGRAPHICAL REFERENCE ONLINE

An essential online biographical reference tool, the *World Who's Who* brings together hard-to-find details for over 60,000 of the world's most eminent personalities.

Key Features:

- quick and easy access to current biographical details for the most prominent and influential individuals
- comprehensive world-wide coverage
- thousands of click through web links and email addresses
- tracks and provides current details on entrants' changing career moves and contact information
- unique section provides information on the world's royal families
- continually updated to ensure information is as current as possible
- advanced search functions enabling users to search by name, nationality, place and date of birth and by profession.

"Highly recommended for those in need of international biographical listings." – *Reference Reviews*

World Who's Who
EUROPA BIOGRAPHICAL REFERENCE ●●●●

SEARCH
ADVANCED SEARCH

R Routledge
Taylor & Francis Group

HOME   BROWSE   INTERNATIONAL DIALLING CODES   ABBREVIATIONS   HELP

Welcome to World Who's Who

The comprehensive, newly-expanded **World Who's Who** brings together current and hard-to-find biographical information on almost 60,000 of the most gifted, famous and influential men and women in all fields.

Using a full range of sophisticated search and browse functions in **World Who's Who**, researchers can quickly find the current career, contact and other biographical details that they need on their most eminent contemporaries. Heads of state, key ministers, politicians, diplomats and religious leaders, the famous and successful in business, finance, technology, film, music, literature, fashion, sport and a host of other professions have been carefully selected by the Europa Biographical Reference team of editors. **World Who's Who** is regularly updated.

For more information please contact us at:

UK/Rest of World customers: reference.online@tandf.co.uk
North/South American customers: e-reference@taylorandfrancis.com

Athens authentication now available for UK Higher and Further Education institutions. Please contact reference.online@tandf.co.uk for more details.

Also available online

Europa World Plus - Europa World and the Regional Surveys of the World

Europa World of Learning - the international guide to the academic world

Routledge Reference Resources - now available in Religion and in Politics and International Relations

Quotation
Free Trial
Facts and figures
Series Titles
Free demo
Feedback
Credits
Licence Agreement

Logout

Updates
BONGO ONDIMBA, Ali resigns as Minister of National Defence of Gabon. 14 August 2009
ALVA, Margaret appointed Governor of Uttarakhand, India. 6 August 2009
More..

Obituaries
KIM, Dae-jung South Korean politician. Died 18 August 2009
CAMPBELL, Alistair Te Ariki New Zealand poet, dramatist and novelist. Died 16 August 2009
More..

Royal Families

30-DAY FREE TRIALS AVAILABLE   30-DAY FREE TRIALS AVAILABLE   30-DAY FREE TRIALS AVAILABLE

Alternatively, to register for your free 30-day trial or for more information please contact your sales representative:

UK and Rest of World customers:
Tel: +44 (0)20 701 76062
Fax: +44 (0)20 701 76699
Email: **online.sales@tandf.co.uk**

US, Canadian and South American customers:
Tel: 1-888-318-2367
Fax: 212-244-1563
Email: **e-reference@taylorandfrancis.com**

 Taylor & Francis
Taylor & Francis Group

Taylor & Francis Group

US, Canadian and South American customers:
Tel: 1-888-318-2367
Fax: 212-244-1563
Email: e-reference@taylorandfrancis.com

UK and Rest of World customers:
Tel: +44 (0)20 701 76062
Fax: +44 (0)20 701 76699
Email: online.sales@tandf.co.uk

Alternatively, to register for your free 30-day trial or for more information please contact your sales representative:

30-DAY FREE TRIALS AVAILABLE   30-DAY FREE TRIALS AVAILABLE   30-DAY FREE TRIALS AVAILABLE

EUROPA WORLD

Select a country then press GO

Welcome to Europa World

Europa World is the online version of the Europa World Year Book, the indispensable source of information on world-wide affairs.

First published in 1926, the year book is renowned as one of the world's leading reference works, covering political and economic information in over 250 countries and territories, from Afghanistan to Zimbabwe. This invaluable resource is now available in a dynamic online format.

PRODUCT NEWS

Europa World Plus has been designated a CHOICE Outstanding Academic Title

Subscribers may now download archival content from the Europa World Year Book.

Routledge Online - Politics, Religion and Music now available.

Armed Conflict Database in association with The International Institute for Strategic Studies.

For further information please visit www.reference.routledge.com and www.iiss.org/acd.

Recent Elections

Iraq, 7 March 2010
Togo, 4 March 2010
Tajikistan, 28 February and 14 March 2010
Costa Rica, 7 February 2010
Ukraine, 17 January and 7 February 2010
Sri Lanka, 26 January 2010
Saint Christopher and Nevis, 25 January 2010

Recent Events

15 APRIL 2010 Kyrgyzstan

Officials of the transitional administration led by Roza Otunbayeva, which had assumed power.

13 MARCH 2010 Taiwan

Wang Ching-feng resigned as Minister of Justice, having refused to approve the enforcement of the

Featured Country

Iraq

The Republic of Iraq lies in western Asia. In 1921 Amir Faisal Ibn Hussain, a member of the Hashimi dynasty of Arabia, was proclaimed King of Iraq. The monarchy was overthrown in 1958 and replaced by a left-wing nationalist regime. In 1963 members — (more)

HOME ADVANCED SEARCH COUNTRIES ORGANIZATIONS HELP

SEARCH

Routledge

LOGOUT
COMPARATIVE STATISTICS
INTERNATIONAL ORGANIZATIONS
PRICING ENQUIRY
- FEEDBACK FORM
- SITE LICENCE
- ABOUT EUROPA WORLD PLUS
- REVIEWS
- CREDITS
- CONTACT US
OTHER PRODUCTS

A CHOICE Outstanding Resource

Key Features:

- impartial coverage of issues of regional importance from acknowledged experts
- a vast range of up-to-date economic, political and statistical data
- book and periodical bibliographies – direct you to further research
- extensive directory of research institutes specializing in the region
- ability to search by content type across regions
- thousands of click-through web links to external sites.

EUROPA WORLD AND THE EUROPA REGIONAL SURVEYS OF THE WORLD ONLINE

An interactive online library for all the countries and territories of each of the world regions

Europa World enables you to subscribe to The Europa World Year Book online together with as many of the nine Europa Regional Surveys of the World as you choose, in one simple annual subscription. The Europa Regional Surveys of the World complement and expand upon the information in The Europa World Year Book with in-depth, expert analysis at regional, sub-regional and country level.

30-day FREE trials available for libraries and institutions

EUROPA WORLD

www.europaworld.com